LITERARY MARKET PLACE™

LMP 2018

Literary Market Place™
78th Edition

Publisher
Thomas H. Hogan

Vice President, Content
Dick Kaser

Senior Director, ITI Reference Group
Owen O'Donnell

Managing Editor
Karen Hallard

Assistant Editor
Karen DiDario

Tampa Operations:

Manager, Tampa Editorial Operations
Debra James

Project Coordinator, Tampa Editorial
Carolyn Victor

Graphics & Production:

Production Manager
Tiffany Chamenko

Production
Dana Stevenson
Jackie Crawford

LITERARY MARKET PLACE™

LMP 2018

THE DIRECTORY OF THE AMERICAN BOOK PUBLISHING INDUSTRY WITH INDUSTRY INDEXES

Volume

1

Published by

Information Today, Inc.
143 Old Marlton Pike
Medford, NJ 08055-8750
Phone: (609) 654-6266
Fax: (609) 654-4309
E-mail (Orders): custserv@infotoday.com
Web site: www.infotoday.com

ISSN 0000-1155
ISBN 978-1-57387-540-0 (set)
Library of Congress Catalog Card Number 41-51571

Information Today, Inc.
143 Old Marlton Pike
Medford, NJ 08055-8750
Phone: 800-300-9868 (Customer Service)
800-409-4929 (Editorial)
Fax: 609-654-4309
E-mail (orders): custserv@infotoday.com
Web Site: www.infotoday.com

Printed in the United States of America

US $429.50
ISBN 13: 978-1-57387-540-0
42950>
9 781573 875400

CONTENTS

VOLUME 1

VOLUME 2

SERVICES & SUPPLIERS

INDEXES

Preface

The 2018 edition marks the 78th annual publication of *Literary Market Place*™—the leading directory of the American and Canadian book publishing industry. Covering publishers and literary agents to manufacturers and shipping services, *LMP* is the most comprehensive directory of its kind. Completely revised, *LMP* 2018 contains over 8,600 entries. Of these listings 2,437 are publishers—including Canadian houses and small presses. Together with its companion publication, *International Literary Market Place*™, these directories cover the global book publishing industry.

Organization & Content

Volume 1 covers core publishing industry information: Book Publishers; Editorial Services and Agents; Associations, Events, Courses and Awards; and Books and Magazines for the Trade.

Volume 2 contains information on service providers and suppliers to the publishing industry. Advertising, Marketing and Publicity; Book Manufacturing; Sales and Distribution; and Services and Suppliers can be found in this volume.

Entries generally contain name, address, telephone and other telecommunications data, key personnel, company reportage, branch offices, brief statistics and descriptive annotations. Where applicable, Standard Address Numbers (SANs) have been included. SANs are unique numbers assigned to the addresses of publishers, wholesalers and booksellers. Publishers' entries also contain their assigned ISBN prefixes. Both the SAN and ISBN systems are administered by R.R. Bowker LLC, 630 Central Avenue, New Providence, NJ 07974.

Indexes

In addition to the numerous section-specific indexes appearing throughout, each volume of *LMP* contains four indexes that reference listings appearing in that volume. The Industry Indexes cover two distinct areas of data: a Company Index that includes the name, address, communications information and page reference for company listings and a separate Personnel Index that includes the main personnel associated with each entry as well as the page reference. Other indexes include the Index to Sections for quickly finding specific categories of information and the Index to Advertisers.

A Note to Authors

Prospective authors seeking a publisher should be aware that there are publishers who, as a condition for publishing and marketing an individual's work, may require a significant sum of money be paid to the publisher. This practice is known by a number of terms including author subsidized publishing, author investment, and co-operative publishing. Before entering an agreement involving such a payment, the author is advised to make a careful investigation to determine the standing of the publisher's imprint in the industry.

Similarly, authors seeking literary representation are advised that some agents request a nominal reading fee that may be applied to the agent's commission upon representation. Other agencies may charge substantially higher fees which may not be applicable to a future commission and which are not refundable. The recommended course is to first send a query letter with an outline, sample chapter, and a self-addressed stamped envelope (SASE). Should an agent express interest in handling the manuscript, full details of fees and commissions should be obtained in writing before the complete manuscript is sent. Should an agency require significant advance payment from an author, the author is cautioned to make a careful investigation to determine the agency's standing in the industry before entering an agreement. The author should always retain a copy of the manuscript in his or her possession.

Occasionally, the editors of *LMP* will receive complaints against publishers or agents listed in the work. If, after investigation and review, the editors determine that the complaints are significant and justified, we may exclude the company or individual in question. However, the absence of a listing in *LMP* for any particular publisher or agent should not be construed as a judgment on the legitimacy or integrity of that organization or individual.

Compilation

LMP is updated throughout the year via a number of methods. A request for updated information is sent to current entrants to corroborate and update the information contained on our database. All updates received are edited for the next product release. Those entrants who do not respond to our request are verified through telephone interviews. Entrants who cannot be verified or who fall short of entry criteria are dropped from the current edition.

Information for new listings is gathered in a similar method. Possible new listings are identified through ongoing research, or when a listing request is received either from the organization itself or from a third party. If sufficient information is not initially gathered to create a listing, a data collection form is provided to the organization to submit essential listing information.

Updated information or suggestions for new listings can be submitted by mail to:

Literary Market Place
Information Today, Inc.
121 Chanlon Rd, Suite G-20
New Providence, NJ 07974-2195

An updating method using the Internet is also available for *LMP* listings:

Visit the *Literary Market Place* web site to update an *LMP* listing. **Literarymarketplace.com** allows you the opportunity to provide new information for a listing by clicking on the "Update or Correct Your Entry" option. The Feedback option on the home page of the web site can be used to suggest new entries as well.

Related Services

Literary Market Place, along with its companion volume *International Literary Market Place*, is available through the Internet at **www.literarymarketplace.com**. Designed to give users simple, logical access to the information they require, the site offers users the choice of searching for data alphabetically, geographically, by type, or by subject. Continuously updated by Information Today's team of editors, this is a truly enhanced version of the *LMP* and *ILMP* databases, incorporating features that make "must-have" information easily available.

Arrangements for placing advertisements in *LMP* can be coordinated through Lauri Rimler by telephone at 800-409-4929 (press 1) or 908-219-0088, or by e-mail at lwrimler@infotoday.com.

Your feedback is important to us. We strongly encourage you to contact us with suggestions or comments on the print edition of *LMP*, or its web site. Our editorial office can be reached by telephone at 800-409-4929 (press 3) or 908-219-0277, or by e-mail at khallard@infotoday.com.

The editors would like to thank those entrants who took the time to respond to our requests for current information.

Abbreviations & Acronyms

The following is a list of acronyms & abbreviations used throughout *LMP*.

AAP - Association of American Publishers
AAR - Association of Authors' Representatives
AB - Alberta
ABA - American Booksellers Association
Acct(s) - Account(s)
Acctg - Accounting
Acq(s) - Acquisition(s)
Ad - Advertising
Admin - Administrative, Administration
Aff - Affairs
AK - Alaska
AL - Alabama
ALA - American Library Association
ALTA - American Literary Translators Association
APA - American Photographic Artists
appt - appointment
Apt - Apartment
AR - Arkansas
ASMP - American Society of Media Photographers
ASPP - American Society of Picture Professionals
Assoc(s) - Associate(s)
Asst(s) - Assistant(s)
ATA - American Translators Association
AV - Audiovisual
Ave - Avenue
AZ - Arizona

B&W - Black & White
BC - British Columbia
Bd - Board
bio - biography
BISAC - Book Industry Standards & Communications
BISG - Book Industry Study Group
Bldg - Building
Blvd - Boulevard
BMI - Book Manufacturers' Institute
Br - Branch
Busn - Business

CA - California
CEO - Chief Executive Officer
CFO - Chief Financial Officer
Chmn - Chairman
Chpn - Chairperson
CIO - Chief Information Officer
Circ - Circulation
CN - Canada
CO - Colorado
Co(s) - Company(-ies)
Co-edns - Co-editions
Coll(s) - College(s)
Comm - Committee
Commun(s) - Communication(s)
Comp - Compiler
Compt - Comptroller
Cont - Controller
Contrib - Contributing
COO - Chief Operating Officer
Coord(s) - Coordinator(s)
Corp - Corporate, Corporation
Coun - Counsel
CT - Connecticut
Ct - Court
CTO - Chief Technical / Technology Officer
Ctr - Center
Curr - Current
Cust - Customer
CZ - Canal Zone

DC - District of Columbia
DE - Delaware
Dept - Department
Devt - Development
Dir(s) - Director(s)
Dist - Distributed, Distribution, Distributor
Div - Division
Dom - Domestic
Dr - Drive

ed - edition
Ed(s) - Editor(s)
Edit - Editorial
Educ - Education, Educational
El-hi - Elementary-High School
Elem - Elementary
Ency - Encyclopedia
Eng - English
Engg - Engineering
Engr - Engineer
Equip - Equipment
ESL - English as a Second Language
Est - Established
EVP - Executive Vice President
exc - except
Exec(s) - Executive(s)
Expwy - Expressway
ext - extension

Fed - Federal
Fin - Finance, Financial
fl - floor
FL - Florida
Freq - Frequency
Fwy - Freeway

GA - Georgia
Gen - General
Govt - Government
GU - Guam

HD - High-definition
HI - Hawaii
HR - Human Resources
HS - High School
Hwy - Highway

IA - Iowa
ID - Idaho
IL - Illinois
Illus - Illustrator
IN - Indiana
indiv(s) - individual(s)
Indus - Industrial, Industry
Info - Information
Instl - Institutional
Instn(s) - Institution(s)
Instrl - Instructional
Intl - International
ISBN - International Standard Book Number
ISSN - International Standard Serial Number
IT - Information Technology

Jt - Joint
Jr - Junior
Juv - Juvenile

K - Kindergarten
KS - Kansas
KY - Kentucky

LA - Louisiana
Lang(s) - Language(s)
Lib(s) - Library(-ies)
Libn(s) - Librarian(s)
Lit - Literature

MA - Massachusetts
MB - Manitoba
MD - Maryland
Mdse - Merchandise
Mdsg - Merchandising
ME - Maine
Med - Medical
Memb(s) - Member(s)
Metro - Metropolitan
Mfg - Manufacturing
Mgmt - Management
Mgr(s) - Manager(s)
MI - Michigan
Mkt(s) - Market(s)
Mktg - Marketing
MLA - Modern Language Association
MN - Minnesota
Mng - Managing
MO - Missouri
mo - month
MS - Mississippi
ms(s) - manuscript(s)
MT - Montana

Natl - National
NB - New Brunswick
NC - North Carolina

ND - North Dakota
NE - Nebraska
NH - New Hampshire
NJ - New Jersey
NL - Newfoundland and Labrador
NM - New Mexico
No - Number
NS - Nova Scotia
NT - Northwest Territories
NU - Nunavut
NV - Nevada
NY - New York

Off(s) - Office(s)
Offr - Officer
OH - Ohio
OK - Oklahoma
ON - Ontario
Oper(s) - Operation(s)
OR - Oregon

PA - Pennsylvania
Pbk(s) - Paperback(s)
PE - Prince Edward Island
Perms - Permissions
Photo - Photograph
Photog - Photographer, Photography
Pkwy - Parkway
pp - pages
PPA - Professional Photographers of America
PR - Public Relations
PR - Puerto Rico
Pres - President
Proc - Processing
Prod(s) - Product(s)
Prodn - Production
Prodr - Producer
Prof - Professional
Prog(s) - Program(s)
Proj(s) - Project(s)
Promo(s) - Promotion(s)
Prop - Proprietor
Pub Aff - Public Affairs
Publg - Publishing
Publr - Publisher
Pubn(s) - Publication(s)
Purch - Purchasing

QC - Quebec

R&D - Research & Development
Rd - Road
Ref - Reference
Reg - Region
Regl - Regional
Rel - Relations
Rep(s) - Representative(s)
Res - Research
RI - Rhode Island
Rm - Room
Rte - Route
Rts - Rights

SAN - Standard Address Number
SASE - Self-Addressed Stamped Envelope
SATW - Society of American Travel Writers
SC - South Carolina
Sci - Science
SD - South Dakota
Secy - Secretary
Serv(s) - Service(s)
SK - Saskatchewan
SLA - Special Libraries Association
Soc - Social, Sociology
Spec - Special
Sq - Square
Sr - Senior
St - Saint, Street
Sta - Station
Ste - Sainte
Subn(s) - Subscription(s)
Subs - Subsidiary
Supv - Supervisor
SVP - Senior Vice President
Synd - Syndicated, Syndication

Tech - Technical
Technol - Technology
Tel - Telephone
Terr - Terrace
TN - Tennessee
Tpke - Turnpike
Treas - Treasurer
TX - Texas

UK - United Kingdom
Univ - University
unsol - unsolicited
UT - Utah

V - Vice
VA - Virginia
VChmn - Vice Chairman
VI - Virgin Islands
vol(s) - volume(s)
VP - Vice President
VT - Vermont

WA - Washington
WI - Wisconsin
WV - West Virginia
WY - Wyoming

yr - year
YT - Yukon Territory

Book Publishers

U.S. Publishers

Listed in alphabetical order are those U.S. publishers that have reported to *LMP* that they produce an average of three or more books annually. Publishers that have appeared in a previous edition of *LMP*, but whose output currently does not meet our defined rate of activity, will be reinstated when their annual production reaches the required level. It should be noted that this rule of publishing activity does not apply to publishers of dictionaries, encyclopedias, atlases or Braille books or to university presses.

The definition of a book excludes charts, pamphlets, folding maps, sheet music and material with stapled bindings. Publishers that make their titles available only in electronic or audio format are included if they meet the stated criteria. In the case of packages, the book must be of equal or greater importance than the accompanying piece. With few exceptions, new publishers are not listed prior to having published at least three titles within a year.

§ before the company name indicates publishers involved in electronic publishing.

The following indexes can be found immediately after the publishers' listings:

U.S. Publishers–Geographic Index
U.S. Publishers–Type of Publications Index
U.S. Publishers–Subject Index

See **Imprints, Subsidiaries & Distributors** for additional information on the companies listed herein. This section should also be checked for apparently active companies that are no longer listed in the U.S. Publishers section. In many cases, they have been acquired as an imprint or subsidiary of a larger entity and no longer have a discrete listing.

A Cappella Books, see Chicago Review Press

§A-R Editions Inc
1600 Aspen Commons, Suite 100, Middleton, WI 53562
Tel: 608-836-9000 *Toll Free Tel:* 800-736-0070 (North America book orders only) *Fax:* 608-831-8200
E-mail: info@areditions.com; orders@areditions.com
Web Site: www.areditions.com
Key Personnel
Pres & CEO: Patrick Wall *Tel:* 608-203-2575 *E-mail:* patrick.wall@areditions.com
Dir, Spec Projs: James Zychowicz *Tel:* 608-203-2580 *E-mail:* james.zychowicz@areditions.com
Founded: 1962
Scholarly critical editions of music for performance & study; computer music & digital audio professional books, electronics & Internet technology, online music anthology (www.armusicanthology.com) & co-published series with MLA: Index & Bibliography, Basic Manual & Technical Reports Series.
ISBN Prefix(es): 978-0-89579
Number of titles published annually: 25 Print
Total Titles: 500 Print
Imprints: Greenway Music Press
Distributor for AIM (American Institute of Musicology)

A 2 Z Press LLC
445 Cortez Ave, Deleon Springs, FL 32130
Mailing Address: PO Box 582, Deleon Springs, FL 32130
Tel: 386-681-7402
Web Site: www.a2zpress.com; www.terriesizemorestoryteller.com
Key Personnel
CEO: Terrie Sizemore
E-mail: terriesizemorestoryteller@gmail.com
Asst: Gale Kovach
Proofreader/Asst: Holly Westfall
Founded: 2016
Small publishing press that has the vision to receive submissions from writers who have quality titles that meet our submission guidelines but have been rejected by other publishing houses.
ISBN Prefix(es): 978-0-9976407
Number of titles published annually: 12 Print; 12 Online; 12 E-Book
Total Titles: 3 Print; 1 E-Book
Distribution Center: Ingram

§AAAI Press
Imprint of Association for the Advancement of Artificial Intelligence
2275 E Bayshore Rd, Suite 160, Palo Alto, CA 94303
Tel: 650-328-3123 *Fax:* 650-321-4457
E-mail: publications17@aaai.org
Web Site: www.aaaipress.org; www.aaai.org
Key Personnel
Exec Dir: Carol Hamilton
Pubns Dir: David M Hamilton
Ed: Anthony G Cohn
Founded: 1989
Publishing books on all aspects of artificial intelligence.
ISBN Prefix(es): 978-0-929280; 978-1-57735
Number of titles published annually: 30 Print; 4 CD-ROM; 2 Online
Total Titles: 500 Print; 30 CD-ROM; 2 Online

AACC International
3340 Pilot Knob Rd, St Paul, MN 55121
Tel: 651-454-7250 *Fax:* 651-454-0766
E-mail: aacc@scisoc.org
Web Site: www.aaccnet.org
Key Personnel
Mktg Coord: Dawn Wuest *E-mail:* dwuest@scisoc.org
Dir, Pubns: Greg Grahek *E-mail:* ggrahek@scisoc.org
Founded: 1920
Source for cereal science information.
ISBN Prefix(es): 978-1-891127; 978-0-9624407
Number of titles published annually: 5 Print; 1 CD-ROM
Total Titles: 100 Print; 1 CD-ROM; 1 Online; 1 E-Book
Imprints: Eagan Press
See separate listing for:
Eagan Press

AACC Press, see AACC International

AAPC Publishing, see Autism Asperger Publishing Co

§AAPG (American Association of Petroleum Geologists)
1444 S Boulder Ave, Tulsa, OK 74119
Mailing Address: PO Box 979, Tulsa, OK 74101-0979
Tel: 918-584-2555 *Toll Free Tel:* 800-364-AAPG (364-2274) *Fax:* 918-580-2665
E-mail: info@aapg.org
Web Site: www.aapg.org
Key Personnel
Mng Ed, Tech Pubns: Beverly Molyneux *Tel:* 918-560-2670 *E-mail:* molyneux@aapg.org
Founded: 1917
Peer-reviewed geological science tomes.
ISBN Prefix(es): 978-0-89181; 978-1-58861
Number of titles published annually: 10 Print; 10 CD-ROM
Total Titles: 100 Print; 80 CD-ROM
Distributed by Affiliated East-West Press Private Ltd; Canadian Society of Petroleum Geologists; Geological Society of London
Distributor for Geological Society of London
Shipping Address: 125 W 15 St, Tulsa, OK 74119

AAVIM, see American Association for Vocational Instructional Materials

Abaris Books
Division of Opal Publishing Corp
70 New Canaan Ave, Norwalk, CT 06850
Tel: 203-838-8402 *Fax:* 203-857-0730
E-mail: abaris@abarisbooks.com
Web Site: abarisbooks.com
Key Personnel
Publr: Anthony S Kaufmann
Mng Ed: J C West *Tel:* 203-838-8625
Founded: 1973
Art, art history, art reference, philosophy & metaphysics.
ISBN Prefix(es): 978-0-913870; 978-0-89835
Number of titles published annually: 7 Print
Total Titles: 185 Print

§Abbeville Press
Imprint of Abbeville Publishing Group
116 W 23 St, 5th fl, New York, NY 10011
Tel: 212-366-5585 *Toll Free Tel:* 800-ART-BOOK (278-2665); 800-343-4499 (orders) *Fax:* 646-375-2359 *Toll Free Fax:* 800-351-5073 (orders)
E-mail: abbeville@abbeville.com; sales@abbeville.com; marketing@abbeville.com; rights@abbeville.com
Web Site: www.abbeville.com
Key Personnel
Sr Ed: Will Lach
Cust Serv Mgr: Nadine Winns
Rts & Perms: David Fabricant
Founded: 1977
Fine arts publisher.
ISBN Prefix(es): 978-0-89659; 978-1-55859; 978-0-7892
Number of titles published annually: 25 Print

Abbeville Publishing Group
137 Varick St, Suite 504, New York, NY 10013-1105
SAN: 211-4755
Tel: 212-366-5585 *Toll Free Tel:* 800-ART-BOOK (278-2665) *Fax:* 212-366-6966
E-mail: abbeville@abbeville.com; marketing@abbeville.com; sales@abbeville.com; rights@abbeville.com
Web Site: www.abbeville.com
Key Personnel
Pres & Publr: Robert E Abrams
Dir, Fin Analysis: John Olivieri
Warehouse Dir: Arthur Goldberg
Cust Serv Mgr: Nadine Winns *E-mail:* nwinns@abbeville.com
Rts & Perms: David Fabricant
Founded: 1977
Publishers of high-quality, fine art books, nonfiction illustrated books, children's books, limited editions, prints, gift line.
ISBN Prefix(es): 978-0-89659; 978-1-55859; 978-0-89660; 978-0-7892
Number of titles published annually: 40 Print
Total Titles: 700 Print
Imprints: Abbeville Kids; Abbeville Press; Artabras; Modern Masters
Foreign Rep(s): Book Promotions (Nicky Stubbs) (South Africa); Gilles Fauveau (Japan, Korea); Jaime Gregorio (Philippines); Sharad Mohan (Bangladesh, India, Maldives, Nepal, Pakistan, Sri Lanka); Peribo Pty Ltd (Eddie Coffey) (Australia); Perseus Books Group UK (Europe, Ireland, UK); June Poonpanich (Cambodia, Indonesia, Laos, Thailand, Vietnam); Publishers Group Canada (Canada); Steimatzky (2005) Ltd (Diane Levy) (Israel); Wei Zhao (China, Hong Kong, Taiwan)
Foreign Rights: Bookbank, SA (Latin America, Mexico, Spain); Motovun Tokyo (Japan); Ultreya srl (Italy)
Orders to: Publishers Group Worldwide, 250 W 57 St, 15th fl, New York, NY 10107 *Tel:* 212-581-7839 *E-mail:* intlorders@pgw.com
Warehouse: Client Distribution Services, 193 Edwards Dr, Jackson, TN 38301 *Toll Free Tel:* 800-343-4499 *Toll Free Fax:* 800-351-5073
See separate listing for:
Abbeville Press

§ABC-CLIO
130 Cremona Dr, Santa Barbara, CA 93117
Tel: 805-968-1911 *Toll Free Tel:* 800-368-6868 *Fax:* 805-685-9685 *Toll Free Fax:* 866-270-3856
E-mail: customerservice@abc-clio.com
Web Site: www.abc-clio.com
Key Personnel
CEO: Ronald Boehm
Pres: Becky Snyder
Founded: 1955
A privately held corporation which has for many years enjoyed an international reputation for high quality & innovation. As an educational reference publisher, the company has received critical acclaim for its computer assisted abstracting & indexing services, world renowned book program & cutting-edge online products.
ISBN Prefix(es): 978-0-87436; 978-1-57607
Number of titles published annually: 300 Print; 300 Online; 300 E-Book
Total Titles: 20,000 Print; 15,000 Online; 15,000 E-Book
Imprints: Greenwood Publishing Group; Libraries Unlimited; Linworth Publishing; Praeger
See separate listing for:
Libraries Unlimited

ABDO Publishing Group
Subsidiary of Abdo Consulting Group Inc (ACGI)
8000 W 78 St, Suite 310, Edina, MN 55439
Mailing Address: PO Box 398166, Minneapolis, MN 55439-8166
Tel: 952-831-2120 *Toll Free Tel:* 800-800-1312 *Toll Free Fax:* 800-862-3480
E-mail: customerservice@abdopublishing.com
Web Site: abdopublishing.com
Key Personnel
Pres & Dir: Jill Hansen
Publr & Natl Sales Mgr: Jim Abdo
VP, Sales & Mktg: Paul Skaj *Tel:* 952-698-2403 *E-mail:* pskaj@abdopublishing.com
Mng Dir: Jennie Forsberg
Dir, Mktg: Dan Verdick *Tel:* 952-698-2404 *E-mail:* dverdick@abdopublishing.com
Mktg & Communs Mgr: BreAnn Rumsch *Tel:* 952-698-2413 *E-mail:* brumsch@abdopublishing.com
Ed-in-Chief: Paul Abdo *E-mail:* pabdo@abdopublishing.com
Founded: 1985
Children's books for the library market.
ISBN Prefix(es): 978-1-56239; 978-1-57765
Number of titles published annually: 350 Print; 350 Online
Total Titles: 3,000 Print; 2,000 Online; 500 E-Book
Imprints: A&D Xtreme (grades 3-9); Abdo & Daughters Publishing (grades 5-9); Abdo Kids (grades PreK-2 beginning readers); Big Buddy Books (grades 2-5 larger trim size); Buddy Books (grades 2-5); Calico (grades 2-8 chapter books); Chapter Books; Checkerboard Library (grades 3-6); Core Library (grades 3-6); Essential Library (grades 6-12); Graphic Planet (grades 2-10 graphic novels); Looking Glass Library (grades PreK-6 picture books); Magic Readers (grades K-3 leveled readers); Sandcastle (grades PreK-3); Short Tales (grades 1-6 adapted stories); SportsZone (grades 2-12); Spotlight (grades PreK-8 popular fiction); Super Sandcastle (grades K-4)
Distributed by Rockbottom Book Co
Warehouse: 1920 Lookout Dr, North Mankato, MN 56003

Aberdeen Bay
3848 Dominion Mill Dr, Alexandria, VA 22304
Tel: 703-473-1392
Web Site: aberdeenbay.azurewebsites.net
Founded: 2007
Traditional publisher with focus on mainstream fiction, memoirs & motivational books.
ISBN Prefix(es): 978-0-9814725; 978-1-60830
Number of titles published annually: 20 Print; 1 Online
Total Titles: 60 Print; 1 Online

§Abingdon Press
Imprint of The United Methodist Publishing House
201 Eighth Ave S, Nashville, TN 37203-3919
SAN: 201-0046
Mailing Address: PO Box 801, Nashville, TN 37202-0801
Tel: 615-749-6000 (academic books) *Toll Free Tel:* 800-251-3320 *Fax:* 615-749-6056 (academic books) *Toll Free Fax:* 800-836-7802 (orders)
E-mail: orders@abingdonpress.com
Web Site: www.abingdonpress.com
Key Personnel
Pres & Publr: Neil M Alexander
Exec Dir, Mktg: Tamara Crabtree
Assoc Publr, Christian Fiction: Pamela Clements
Assoc Publr & Ed-in-Chief: Mary Catherine Dean
Sr Acqs Ed: Ramona Richards
Regl Sales Mgr: Bryan C Williams *Tel:* 615-749-6295 *E-mail:* bwilliams@abingdonpress.com
Mature Years Ed: Marvin Cropsey
Founded: 1789
Religion/ecumenical Christianity; general interest, children's, family, church professional, academic, reference, lay spiritual; United Methodist history, doctrine, polity.
ISBN Prefix(es): 978-0-687; 978-1-4267; 978-1-63088; 978-1-5018
Number of titles published annually: 175 Print
Total Titles: 270 Print; 10 CD-ROM; 3 Online
Imprints: Upper Room Books
Distributor for Church Publishing Inc; Judson Press; Upper Room Books
Foreign Rep(s): Ausburg Fortress Canada (Canada); Canaanland Distributors Sdn Bhd (Malaysia); Christian Connexion Methodist Publishing House (South Africa); Cross Communications Co (Hong Kong); KCBS Inc (Korea); Lion Hudson PLC (UK); MediaCom Education Inc (Australia); Rainbow Book Agencies (Australia); SKS Books (Singapore)
Orders to: Ingram Publisher Services, One Ingram Blvd, La Vergne, TN 37086 *Tel:* 615-793-5000 *Web Site:* www.ingrampublisherservices.com
Warehouse: 341 Great Circle Dr, Nashville, TN 37228-1703
Distribution Center: Ingram Publisher Services, One Ingram Blvd, La Vergne, TN 37086 *Tel:* 615-793-5000 *Web Site:* www.ingrampublisherservices.com

Harry N Abrams Inc
Subsidiary of La Martiniere Groupe
195 Broadway, 9th fl, New York, NY 10007
SAN: 200-2434
Tel: 212-206-7715 *Toll Free Tel:* 800-345-1359 *Fax:* 212-519-1210
E-mail: abrams@abramsbooks.com
Web Site: www.abramsbooks.com
Key Personnel
Pres & CEO: Michael Jacobs
SVP & Chief Mktg Offr: Steve Tager
SVP & Publr, Children's Books: Andrew Smith
VP & CFO: Thomas Moloney

VP, Publg Opers: Anet Sirna-Bruder
VP, Publr, Abrams Plus: Jess Brallier
VP, Publr, Adult Trade: Michael Sand
VP, Dir, Children's Mktg & Publicity: Melanie Chang
VP, Ed-in-Chief, Adult Trade: Eric Himmel
VP, Sales & Intl Sales: Mary Wowk
Assoc Publr, Abrams Plus, Digital Publg: Lindy Humphreys
Assoc Publr, Adult Trade: Shawna Mullen
Assoc Publr, Children's Books: Jody Mosley
Exec Dir, Adult Trade Publicity: Jennifer Brunn
Exec Dir, Trade Sales: Elisa Gonzalez
Contracts Dir: Peggy Garry
Creative Dir, Adult Trade: John Gall
Creative Dir, Children's Books & ComicArts: Chad Beckerman
Dir, Franchise Mktg, Children's Books: Elizabeth Fithian
Dir, Intl Rts & Subs: Yulia Borodyanskaya
Dir, Mng Edit, Adult Trade: Mary O'Mara
Dir, Museum Sales/Dist: Marti Malovany
Dir, Online Mktg Opers: Chris Blank
Dir, Spec Mkts: Monica Shah
Edit Dir, Abrams Image & Exec Ed, Adult Trade: Rebecca Kaplan
Edit Dir, Calendars: Miriam Tribble
Edit Dir, Children's Books: Tamar Brazis
Edit Dir, ComicArts: Charles Kochman
Edit Dir, Noterie: Karrie Witkin
Assoc Art Dir, Children's Books & ComicArts: Pam Notarantonio
Assoc Dir, Children's Mktg & Publicity: Hallie Patterson
Assoc Mktg Dir, Adult Trade: Paul Colarusso
Exec Ed, Abrams Press: Jamison Stoltz
Exec Ed, Adult Trade: David Cashion; Holly Dolce
Exec Ed, Children's Books: Traci Todd
Sr Mng Ed, Children's Books: Amy Vreeland
Sr Ed, Adult Trade: Laura Dozier; Eric Klopfer
Sr Ed, Children's Books: Anne Heltzel
Ed-at-Large, Children's Books: Howard Reeves
Sr Subs Rts Mgr: Karin Schulze
Mgr, Corp Events & Exec Asst to CEO: Merle Brown
Founded: 1949
Art & architecture, photography, natural sciences, performing arts & children's books, gifts, calendars & stationary.
ISBN Prefix(es): 978-0-8109
Number of titles published annually: 300 Print
Total Titles: 2,600 Print
Imprints: Abrams Appleseed; Abrams Books; Abrams Books for Young Readers; Abrams ComicArts; Abrams Image; Abrams Noterie; Abrams Press; Amulet Books
Distributed by Abrams & Chronicle Books (Great Britain); Editions Alain
Distributor for Booth-Clibborn Editions; Editions Alain Ducasse; 5 Continents Editions; Getty Publications; Museum of Modern Art Children's Books; SelfMadeHero; Tate Publishing; V&A Publishing; The Vendome Press
Foreign Rep(s): Canadian Manda Group
Orders to: Hachette Book Group (North America) *Toll Free Tel:* 800-759-0190 *Toll Free Fax:* 800-286-9471; Littlehampton Book Services Ltd, Faraday Close, Durrington, Worthing, West Sussex BN13 3RB, United Kingdom (UK, Africa, Asia, Europe & Middle East) *Tel:* (019) 0382-8500; (014) 7655-1080 (orders only) *Fax:* (019) 7654-1060; (014) 7654-1061 (orders only) *Web Site:* www.pubeasy.com
Distribution Center: Littlehampton Book Services Ltd, Faraday Close, Durrington, Worthing, West Sussex BN13 3RB, United Kingdom (UK, Africa, Asia, Europe & Middle East) *Tel:* (019) 0382-8500; (014) 7655-1080 (orders only) *Fax:* (019) 7654-1060; (014) 7654-1061 (orders only) *Web Site:* www.pubeasy.com
Membership(s): AAP
See separate listing for:
Stewart, Tabori & Chang

§Abrams Learning Trends
Subsidiary of Learning Trends LLC
16310 Bratton Lane, Suite 250, Austin, TX 78728-2403
Toll Free Tel: 800-227-9120 *Toll Free Fax:* 800-737-3322
E-mail: customerservice@abramslearningtrends.com (orders, cust serv); contactus@abramslearningtrends.com
Web Site: www.abramslearningtrends.com (orders, cust serv)
Key Personnel
CEO & Pres: Roy Mayers
VP & Cont: Peter Dunn
EVP & Publr: Erin Kinard
EVP & Gen Mgr: William Thomas
EVP, Sales: Gunnar Voltz
VP, Sales: Bruce Warren
Founded: 2008
PreK-5 educational materials.
ISBN Prefix(es): 978-0-7665; 978-0-7664
Number of titles published annually: 100 Print; 6 CD-ROM; 15 Audio
Total Titles: 1,000 Print; 36 CD-ROM; 36 Audio
Imprints: The Letter People®
Distributor for General Education Services (New Zealand)

§Academic Press
Imprint of Elsevier BV
50 Hampshire St, 5th fl, Cambridge, MA 02139
Tel: 781-663-5200 *Fax:* 937-247-0808
Web Site: store.elsevier.com/Academic-Press
Founded: 1942
Scientific, technical & professional information in multiple media formats.
ISBN Prefix(es): 978-0-12
Number of titles published annually: 375 Print; 8 E-Book
Total Titles: 4,700 Print; 14 CD-ROM; 175 E-Book

Academica Press
1727 Massachusetts Ave NW, Suite 507, Washington, DC 20036
Tel: 978-829-2577
E-mail: editorial@academicapress.com
Web Site: www.academicapress.com
Key Personnel
Publr & Dir: Dr Paul du Quenoy
Founded: 2002
Publish scholarly research, monographs & collections in humanities, social sciences, education & law.
ISBN Prefix(es): 978-1-933146; 978-1-930901
Number of titles published annually: 40 Print
Total Titles: 250 Print; 50 Online
Imprints: Maunsel & Co Publishers (Dublin); W B Sheridan (law books)
Foreign Rep(s): Eurospan Group (London) (Europe, Middle East, UK)
Orders to: PSSC, 46 Development Rd, Fitchburg, MA 01420, Contact: Erika Wilson *Tel:* 978-345-2121 *E-mail:* ewilson@pssc.com
Returns: Books International Inc, 22883 Quicksilver Dr, Dulles, VA 20166 *Tel:* 703-661-1500 *Fax:* 703-661-1501 *E-mail:* todd@booksintl.com
Shipping Address: PSSC, 46 Development Rd, Fitchburg, MA 01420, Contact: Erika Wilson *Tel:* 978-345-2121 *E-mail:* ewilson@pssc.com
Warehouse: PSSC, 46 Development Rd, Fitchburg, MA 01420, Contact: Erika Wilson *Tel:* 978-345-2121 *E-mail:* ewilson@pssc.com
Distribution Center: PSSC, 46 Development Rd, Fitchburg, MA 01420, Contact: Erika Wilson *Tel:* 978-345-2121 *E-mail:* ewilson@pssc.com
Membership(s): American Conference on Irish Studies

Academy Chicago
Imprint of Chicago Review Press
814 N Franklin St, Chicago, IL 60610
Tel: 312-337-0747 *Toll Free Tel:* 800-888-4741 (orders) *Fax:* 312-337-5110
E-mail: frontdesk@chicagoreviewpress.com
Web Site: www.chicagoreviewpress.com
Key Personnel
Acqs Ed: Cynthia Sherry *E-mail:* csherry@chicagoreviewpress.com
Founded: 1975
Fiction, nonfiction, history, mysteries, women's studies; emphasis on neglected classics & books for women.
ISBN Prefix(es): 978-0-915864; 978-0-89733
Number of titles published annually: 12 Print
Total Titles: 367 Print
Distribution Center: Independent Publishers Group, 814 N Franklin St, Chicago, IL 60610 *Tel:* 312-337-0747 *Toll Free Tel:* 800-888-4741 (orders) *Fax:* 312-337-5985

The Academy of Northwest Writers & Publishers, see Lost Horse Press

Academy of Nutrition & Dietetics
120 S Riverside Plaza, Suite 2000, Chicago, IL 60606-6995
Tel: 312-899-0040 (ext 5000) *Toll Free Tel:* 800-877-1600
E-mail: sales@eatright.org
Web Site: www.eatright.org
Key Personnel
Publr: Cathy Iammartino
Acqs & Devt Mgr: Laura Pelehach
Prodn Ed: Carissa Vardanian
Founded: 1917
Information on food, nutrition & fitness for dieticians & other allied health professionals.
ISBN Prefix(es): 978-0-88091; 978-0-9837255 (Eat Right Press)
Number of titles published annually: 12 Print; 4 Online
Total Titles: 70 Print
Branch Office(s)
1120 Connecticut Ave NW, Suite 480, Washington, DC 20036 *Tel:* 202-775-8277 *Toll Free Tel:* 800-877-0877
Distributed by Small Press United (Eat Right Press)

§Accuity
Division of Reed Business Information Ltd
4709 W Golf Rd, Skokie, IL 60076
Tel: 847-676-9600 *Toll Free Tel:* 800-321-3373 *Fax:* 847-933-8101
E-mail: custserv@accuity.com; sales@accuity.com
Web Site: www.accuity.com
Key Personnel
Pres & CEO: Hugh Jones
EVP: Brent Newman
Sr Dir, HR: Patty Pickett
Founded: 1876
Leading worldwide provider of information on depository financial institutions throughout the world; specialize in Internet references/directories; software; databases.
ISBN Prefix(es): 978-1-56310
Number of titles published annually: 30 Print; 1 CD-ROM; 2 E-Book
Total Titles: 30 Print; 4 CD-ROM; 3 E-Book
Foreign Office(s): Level 10, 10 Help St, Chatswood, NSW 2067, Australia *Tel:* (02) 8006 0584 *E-mail:* asiasales@accuity.com
999 Jin Zhong Rd, 4F, Tower C, Shanghai 200335, China *Tel:* (021) 5155 1222 *Fax:* (021) 5155 0509 *E-mail:* asiasales@accuity.com
Rm 1204-6, Tai Tung Bldg, 8 Fleming Rd, Wanchai, Hong Kong *Tel:* 2280 9570 *Fax:* 2813 6357 *E-mail:* asiasales@accuity.com
1-9-15 Higashi-Azabu, Minato-ku, Tokyo 106-0044, Japan *Tel:* (03) 5561 5363 *Fax:* (065) 6544 1171 *E-mail:* asiasales@accuity.com

Killiney Rd, No 08-01, Winsland House 1, Singapore 239519, Singapore (asi-asales@accuity.com) *Tel:* 6780 4814 *Fax:* 6544 1171

Proctor House, 110 High Hilborn, London WC1V 6EU, United Kingdom *Tel:* (020) 7653 3800 *Fax:* (020) 7653 3828

Acres USA
Division of Acres USA Inc
501 Eighth Ave, Greenley, CO 80631
Mailing Address: PO Box 1690, Greeley, CO 80632-1690
Tel: 512-892-4400 *Toll Free Tel:* 800-355-5313
E-mail: orders@acresusa.com; editor@acresusa.com; info@acresusa.com
Web Site: www.acresusa.com
Founded: 1970
Books & a monthly periodical on organic & sustainable agriculture.
ISBN Prefix(es): 978-0-911311; 978-1-60173
Number of titles published annually: 6 Print; 10 Audio
Total Titles: 100 Print; 100 Audio

ACTA Publications
4848 N Clark St, Chicago, IL 60640
Tel: 773-271-1030 *Toll Free Tel:* 800-397-2282 *Fax:* 773-271-7399 *Toll Free Fax:* 800-397-0079
E-mail: info@actapublications.com
Web Site: www.actapublications.com
Key Personnel
Co-Owner: John Dewan
Pres & Publr: Gregory Pierce
Founded: 1957
Books, audio & video tapes for the Christian market & baseball statistics market.
ISBN Prefix(es): 978-0-87946; 978-0-914070; 978-0-915388
Number of titles published annually: 15 Print; 2 Audio
Total Titles: 150 Print; 20 Audio
Imprints: Corbey Books; In Extenso Press
Distributor for Grief Watch; Veritas
Foreign Rep(s): John Garratt Publishing (Australia); Veritas (Ireland, UK)
Membership(s): Association of Catholic Publishers Inc

ACU Press
Affiliate of Abilene Christian University
1648 Campus Ct, Abilene, TX 79601
SAN: 207-1681
Tel: 325-674-2720 *Toll Free Tel:* 877-816-4455
Web Site: www.acupressbooks.com; www.leafwoodpublishers.com
Key Personnel
Dir, Opers: Duane Anderson
Founded: 1984
Religion & ethics.
ISBN Prefix(es): 978-0-915547; 978-0-89112
Number of titles published annually: 35 Print; 30 E-Book
Total Titles: 480 Print; 170 E-Book
Imprints: Leafwood Publishers (Christian trade imprint)

Adams & Ambrose Publishing
PO Box 259684, Madison, WI 53725-9684
SAN: 655-5624
Tel: 608-977-1825
E-mail: info@adamsambrose.com
Key Personnel
Mktg Dir & Intl Rts: Joyce Harrington *E-mail:* jharrington@adamsambrose.com
Sr Ed: Jill Robinson Wren *E-mail:* jrwren@adamsambrose.com
Edit: Roger B Oakes *E-mail:* rboakes@adamsambrose.com
Founded: 1983
Publication of nonfiction books. Specialize in academic, professional & how-to books.
ISBN Prefix(es): 978-0-916951
Number of titles published annually: 6 Print
Total Titles: 6 Print
Returns: c/o United Parcel Service, 8350 Murphy Dr, Middleton, WI 53562 (hold for pick up)

§Adams Media
Imprint of Simon & Schuster
57 Littlefield St, Avon, MA 02322
Tel: 508-427-7100
Web Site: www.simonandschuster.com
Key Personnel
VP & Publr: Karen Cooper
Mktg & Publicity Dir: Beth Gissinger-Rivera
Ed-in-Chief: Brendan O'Neill
Dir of Mng Edit: Meredith O'Hayre
Mng Ed: Lisa Laing
Exec Ed: Tara Gelsomino
Assoc Publr: Stephanie McKenna
Mgr, Publg: Katherine Corcoran-Lytle
Sr Ed: Jacqueline Musser; Laura Daly; Brett Palana-Shanahan
Ed: Rebecca Tarr Thomas; Eileen Mullan; Ragnar Carlson
Assoc Ed: Julia Jacques; Alexander Hatch; Peter Archer
Edit Asst: Khelsea Purvis
Mgr, Publicity: Bethany Carland-Adams
Creative Dir & Design Mgr: Frank Rivera
Natl Sales Dir: Karen Patterson
Founded: 1980
General nonfiction, including business, self-help, inspiration, careers, teen nonfiction, women's issues, cooking, parenting, reference, relationships, weddings, pets.
ISBN Prefix(es): 978-0-937860; 978-1-55850; 978-1-58062; 978-1-59337; 978-1-59869; 978-1-60550; 978-1-4405; 978-1-5072
Number of titles published annually: 200 Print
Total Titles: 1,200 Print; 20 CD-ROM
Imprints: Adams Business (busn); Crimson Romance (romance); Everything (series)
Foreign Rights: Bardon-Chinese Media Agency (China, Hong Kong, Taiwan); Graal Literary Agency (Poland); Imprima Korea Agency (Korea); Japan Uni Agency (Japan); Alexander Korzhenevski Agency (Russia); Michael Meller Literary Agency GmbH (Germany); H Katia Schumer Literary Agency (Brazil); Silkroad Publishers Agency (Jane Vejjajiva) (Thailand); Julio F Yanez, Agencia Literaria S L (Spain)

ADASI Publishing Co
13 Riverdale Ave, Dover, NH 03820-4698
Tel: 603-866-9426
E-mail: info@adasi.com
Web Site: www.adasi.com
Key Personnel
Mktg Dir: Parvaneh Ghavami
Founded: 1996
ADASI is a consulting, technology transfer, decision science & education company. Physics, math & history of those subjects.
ISBN Prefix(es): 978-0-9641295
Number of titles published annually: 6 Print
Total Titles: 12 Print
Distributor for Wall & Thompson

ADD WareHouse, see Specialty Press Inc

Addicus Books Inc
PO Box 45327, Omaha, NE 68145
Tel: 402-330-7493 *Fax:* 402-330-1707
E-mail: info@addicusbooks.com; addicusbks@aol.com
Web Site: www.addicusbooks.com
Key Personnel
Publr: Rod Colvin *E-mail:* rod@addicusbooks.com
Assoc Publr: Jack Kusler *E-mail:* jackaddicusbks@aol.com
Founded: 1994
Independent press, publishing high-quality trade paperbacks. Submissions by mail only, no phone inquiries.
ISBN Prefix(es): 978-1-886039; 978-1-936374; 978-1-938803; 978-1-940495
Number of titles published annually: 9 Print; 10 E-Book
Total Titles: 200 Print; 200 Online; 185 E-Book
Billing Address: IPG Books, 814 Franklin St, Chicago, IL 60610 *Tel:* 312-337-0747 *Toll Free Tel:* 800-888-4741 *Fax:* 312-337-5985 *Web Site:* ipgbook.com
Returns: IPG Warehouse, 600 N Pulaski, Chicago, IL 60624, Contact: Tom Greene
Warehouse: IPG Warehouse, 600 N Pulaski, Chicago, IL 60624, Contact: Tom Greene
Distribution Center: IPG Books, 814 Franklin St, Chicago, IL 60610 *Tel:* 312-337-0747 *Toll Free Tel:* 800-888-4741 *Fax:* 312-337-5985 *Web Site:* ipgbook.com
Membership(s): AAP; The Imaging Alliance; Independent Book Publishers Association; National Association of Independent Publishers

Adirondack Mountain Club (ADK)
814 Goggins Rd, Lake George, NY 12845-4117
SAN: 204-7691
Tel: 518-668-4447 *Toll Free Tel:* 800-395-8080 *Fax:* 518-668-3746
E-mail: info@adk.org
Web Site: www.adk.org
Key Personnel
Pres: John Gilewicz
VP: Robert Manning
Exec Dir: Neil Woodworth *Tel:* 518-449-3870 *Fax:* 518-669-0128
Founded: 1922
Wall calendar; trade, hiking, canoeing, skiing & climbing guidebooks & maps for New York State; natural history field guides; cultural & literary works on the Adirondacks, members journals, *Adirondac*.
ISBN Prefix(es): 978-0-935272; 978-1-931951; 978-0-9896073
Number of titles published annually: 4 Print
Total Titles: 39 Print

Adler Publishing Inc
46937 Monarch Dr, Parker, CO 80138
Tel: 303-660-2158 *Toll Free Tel:* 800-660-5107 (sales & orders)
E-mail: customerservice@adlerpublishing.com; orders@4wdbooks.com
Web Site: www.adlerpublishing.com
Key Personnel
Publr: Peter Massey
Mktg Dir: Jeanne Massey
Founded: 1999
ISBN Prefix(es): 978-0-930657; 978-0-9665675; 978-1-930193
Number of titles published annually: 5 Print
Total Titles: 70 Print
Imprints: Outdoor Books & Maps

Advance Publishing Inc
6950 Fulton St, Houston, TX 77022
SAN: 263-9572
Tel: 713-695-0600 *Toll Free Tel:* 800-917-9630 *Fax:* 713-695-8585
E-mail: info@advancepublishing.com
Web Site: www.advancepublishing.com
Key Personnel
VP: John Sommer *E-mail:* johnsommer@advancepublishing.com
Founded: 1984
Publish children's picture books, junior biographies & general nonfiction, technical books & current events.
ISBN Prefix(es): 978-1-57537; 978-0-9610810

Number of titles published annually: 20 Print
Total Titles: 150 Print; 72 CD-ROM; 75 Online
Imprints: Another Great Achiever Series (biographies of men & women of inspiring accomplishment); Number Success (online video practical mathematics program for adult & children); Phonics Adventure (motivational phonics literature-based children's reading program); Quest for Success (short stories for upper elementary & reluctant middle & high school readers); Reading Success (adult intensive phonics literature-based reading program); Sommer-Time Story Classics Series (inspirational picture books with a fun & modern take on timeless folktales & fables); Sommer-Time Story Series (character-building books for children)
Membership(s): The Children's Book Council; Independent Book Publishers Association

Adventure House
914 Laredo Rd, Silver Spring, MD 20901
Tel: 301-754-1589
Web Site: www.adventurehouse.com
Key Personnel
Publr & Ed: John P Gunnison *E-mail:* gunnison@adventurehouse.com
Founded: 1985
Special reprints; fiction from the pulp fiction era.
ISBN Prefix(es): 978-1-886937; 978-1-59798
Number of titles published annually: 60 Print
Total Titles: 300 Print

AdventureKEEN
2204 First Ave S, Suite 102, Birmingham, AL 35233
SAN: 212-7199
Tel: 763-689-9800 *Toll Free Tel:* 800-678-7006 *Fax:* 763-689-9039 *Toll Free Fax:* 877-374-9016
E-mail: info@adventurewithkeen.com
Web Site: adventurewithkeen.com
Key Personnel
Owner & Publr: Robert W Sehlinger
COO: Molly Merkle
Pres: Richard Hunt
Dir, Mktg & PR: Liliane Opsomer *E-mail:* liliane@adventurewithkeen.com
Sales Mgr: Meredith Hutchins
Founded: 1988
General trade & regional.
ISBN Prefix(es): 978-0-934860; 978-1-885061; 978-1-59193
Number of titles published annually: 30 Print
Total Titles: 435 Print; 12 CD-ROM
Imprints: Adventure Publications; Clerisy Press; Menasha Ridge Press; Nature Study Guides; Unofficial Guides; Wilderness Press
Distributor for Blacklock Nature Photography; Kollath-Stensaas; Nodin Press; Pocket Guides Publishing
Distribution Center: Ingram Content Group LLC, One Ingram Blvd, La Vergne, TN 37086 *Tel:* 615-793-5000
See separate listing for:
Clerisy Press
Menasha Ridge Press Inc

§Adventures Unlimited Press (AUP)
One Adventure Place, Kempton, IL 60946
Mailing Address: PO Box 74, Kempton, IL 60946-0074
Tel: 815-253-6390 *Fax:* 815-253-6300
E-mail: auphq@frontiernet.net; info@adventuresunlimitedpress.com
Web Site: www.adventuresunlimitedpress.com
Key Personnel
Pres & Intl Rts Contact: David H Childress
Mng Dir: Jennifer Bolm
Founded: 1983
Eclectic variety of books on mysteries of the past, alternative technologies & conspiracy theories.
ISBN Prefix(es): 978-0-932813; 978-1-931882; 978-1-935487; 978-1-939149
Number of titles published annually: 11 Print
Total Titles: 215 Print
Distributor for Eagle Wing Books; EDFU Books; Yelsraek Publishing
Foreign Rep(s): Brumby Books (Australia); Speaking Tree (UK)
Foreign Rights: Il Caduceo (Italy)

Aegean Publishing Co
PO Box 6790, Santa Barbara, CA 93160
Tel: 805-964-6669 *Fax:* 805-683-4798
E-mail: info@aegeanpublishing.com
Web Site: aegeanpublishing.com
Key Personnel
Gen Mgr: Mary Morgan
Founded: 1993
Book publisher.
ISBN Prefix(es): 978-0-9636178
Number of titles published annually: 3 Print
Total Titles: 4 Print
Foreign Rights: Japan UNI Agency Inc (Japan)
Membership(s): Independent Book Publishers Association

The AEI Press
Division of American Enterprise Institute
1789 Massachusetts Ave NW, Washington, DC 20036
SAN: 202-4527
Tel: 202-862-5800 *Fax:* 202-862-7177
Web Site: www.aei.org
Key Personnel
Co-Chmn of the Bd: Tully M Friedman
Pres: Arthur Brooks
Founded: 1943
Public policy economics, foreign affairs & defense, government & politics, law; research on education, energy, government regulation & tax policy.
ISBN Prefix(es): 978-0-8447
Number of titles published annually: 15 Print
Total Titles: 300 Print
Distributed by MIT (selected titles)
Foreign Rep(s): Eurospan
Orders to: c/o National Book Network, 4501 Forbes Blvd, Suite 200, Lantham, MD 20706 *Toll Free Tel:* 800-462-6420 *Toll Free Fax:* 800-338-4550 *E-mail:* custserv@nbnbooks.com

§AFB Press
Imprint of American Foundation for the Blind
1401 S Clark St, Suite 730, Arlington, VA 22202
Tel: 304-710-3043 *Toll Free Tel:* 800-232-3044 (orders) *Fax:* 917-210-3979 (orders)
E-mail: afbpress@afb.net
Web Site: www.afb.org
Key Personnel
Dir, AFB Press & Prof Devt: George Abbott
Rts & Admin Dir: Jenese Griffiths
Mgr, Fulfillment & Cust Serv: Heather Spence *Tel:* 304-710-3027 *E-mail:* hspence@afb.net
Founded: 1921
Text & professional books in the fields of visual impairment & blindness.
ISBN Prefix(es): 978-0-89128; 978-1-68413
Number of titles published annually: 4 Print; 4 Online
Total Titles: 100 Print; 70 Online
Branch Office(s)
AFB Atlanta, 739 W Peachtree St NW, Suite 250, Atlanta, GA 30308 *Tel:* 404-525-2303 *Fax:* 646-478-9260 *E-mail:* literacy@afb.net
AFB Center on Vision Loss, 11030 Ables Lane, Dallas, TX 75229 *Tel:* 214-352-7222 *Fax:* 646-478-9260 *E-mail:* dallas@afb.net
AFB Huntington, 1000 Fifth Ave, Suite 350, Huntington, WV 25701 *Tel:* 304-523-8651 *Fax:* 646-478-9260
Membership(s): AAP

Africa World Press Inc
541 W Ingham Ave, Suite B, Trenton, NJ 08638
Tel: 609-695-3200 *Fax:* 609-695-6466
E-mail: customerservice@africaworldpressbooks.com
Web Site: www.africaworldpressbooks.com
Key Personnel
Owner: Kassahun Checole
Founded: 1983
Research on Latin America, the Caribbean, Africa, Afrocentric children's books.
ISBN Prefix(es): 978-0-86543; 978-1-59221
Number of titles published annually: 100 Print
Total Titles: 1,400 Print; 10 Online; 10 E-Book
Foreign Office(s): East Africa, PO Box 48, Asmara, Eritrea *Tel:* (01) 120707 *Fax:* (01) 123369
Foreign Rights: Turnaround Publisher Services Ltd (Europe, London)

§African American Images
PO Box 1799, Chicago Heights, IL 60412
Tel: 708-672-4909 (cust serv) *Fax:* 708-672-0466
E-mail: customersvc@africanamericanimages.com
Web Site: www.africanamericanimages.com
Key Personnel
Pres & Intl Rts: Dr Jawanza Kunjufu, PhD
Founded: 1983
Publish & distribute books of an Africentric nature that promote self-esteem, collective values, liberation & skill development.
ISBN Prefix(es): 978-0-913543; 978-0-9749000; 978-1-934155
Number of titles published annually: 8 Print
Total Titles: 130 Print; 2 CD-ROM

Africana Homestead Legacy Publishers Inc
926 Haddonfield Rd, Suite E, No 329, Cherry Hill, NJ 08002
SAN: 941-4811
Tel: 856-673-0363 *Fax:* 856-486-1135
E-mail: customer-service@ahlpub.com; sales@ahlpub.com; editors@ahlpub.com
Web Site: www.ahlpub.com
Key Personnel
Pres & Publr: Carolyn C Williams *E-mail:* publisher@ahlpub.com
Dir, Prodn & Design: Brian Lancaster *E-mail:* blancaster@ahlpub.com
Founded: 1996
Small independent book publisher of scholarly nonfiction, literary fiction, autobiography & memoirs focused on the experience of black people in the US & worldwide.
ISBN Prefix(es): 978-0-9653308; 978-0-9770904; 978-0-9799537; 978-0-9818939; 978-0-9825842; 978-0-9831151; 978-1-937622
Number of titles published annually: 4 Print; 2 E-Book
Imprints: AHLP Books; AHLP Communications; Nefu Books; Oyinde Publishing
Membership(s): Independent Book Publishers Association

§Ageless Press
3759 Collins St, Sarasota, FL 34232
SAN: 297-830X
Tel: 941-365-1367 *Fax:* 941-365-1367
E-mail: irishope@comcast.net
Key Personnel
Owner: Hope Day
Ed: Iris Forrest
Founded: 1992
Publish short stories by various authors.
ISBN Prefix(es): 978-0-9635177
Number of titles published annually: 6 Print
Total Titles: 3 Print; 1 Online

AGU, see American Geophysical Union (AGU)

Ahsahta Press
Boise State University, Mail Stop 1525, 1910 University Dr, Boise, ID 83725-1525
Tel: 208-426-3134
E-mail: ahsahta@boisestate.edu
Web Site: ahsahtapress.org
Key Personnel
Dir & Ed: Prof Janet Holmes *E-mail:* jholmes@boisestate.edu
Founded: 1974
Trade paperback books. Specialize in American poetry. Accept editorial submissions through our submissions manager.
ISBN Prefix(es): 978-0-916272; 978-1-934103
Number of titles published annually: 8 Print
Total Titles: 135 Print
Orders to: Small Press Distribution, 1341 Seventh St, Berkeley, CA 94710-1409, Contact: Nicole Trigg *Tel:* 510-524-1668 *Toll Free Tel:* 800-869-7553 *Fax:* 510-524-0852 *E-mail:* spd@spdbooks.org *Web Site:* www.spdbooks.org
Membership(s): Community of Literary Magazines & Presses

§AICPA Professional Publications
Subsidiary of American Institute of Certified Public Accountants
220 Leigh Farm Rd, Durham, NC 27707
SAN: 202-4578
Tel: 919-402-4500 *Toll Free Tel:* 888-777-7077 (memb serv ctr) *Fax:* 919-402-4505
Toll Free Fax: 800-362-5066 (memb serv ctr)
E-mail: acquisitions@aicpa.org; service@aicpa.org
Web Site: www.aicpa.org
Key Personnel
Pres & CEO: Barry C Melancon
E-mail: bmelancon@aicpa.org
Founded: 1959
Technical guidance for accountants & auditors, books on practice management & specialized topics, research & practice development tools, magazines, newsletters, online & downloadable products.
ISBN Prefix(es): 978-0-87051; 978-1-937350; 978-1-937351; 978-1-937352; 978-1-940235; 978-1-941651
Number of titles published annually: 150 Print; 10 CD-ROM; 20 Online; 100 E-Book
Total Titles: 600 Print; 20 CD-ROM; 50 Online; 200 E-Book
Branch Office(s)
1455 Pennsylvania Ave NW, Washington, DC 20004-1081 *Tel:* 202-737-6600 *Fax:* 202-638-4512
Princeton South Corporate Ctr, Suite 200, 100 Princeton S, Ewing, NJ 08628 *Tel:* 609-671-2902 *Fax:* 609-671-2922
1211 Avenue of the Americas, New York, NY 10036-8775 *Tel:* 212-596-6200 *Fax:* 212-596-6213
Distributed by CCH; Practitioners Publishing Co; Thomson Reuters
Distributor for Wiley
Membership(s): Association for Talent Development; EBSCO; ISO

AIP Publishing, see American Institute of Physics

AK Press Distribution
Subsidiary of AK Press Inc
370 Ryan Ave, Unit 100, Chico, CA 95973
Tel: 510-208-1700 *Fax:* 510-208-1701
E-mail: info@akpress.org
Web Site: www.akpress.org
Key Personnel
Ed: Zach Blue; Charles Weigl
Founded: 1990
Specialize in publishing & distribution of radical & small press nonfiction.
ISBN Prefix(es): 978-1-873176; 978-1-902593; 978-1-904859
Number of titles published annually: 20 Print
Total Titles: 500 Print
Distributor for Arbeiter Ring; Autonomedia; Crimethinc; Freedom Press; Charles H Kerr; Kersplebedelo

Akashic Books
232 Third St, Suite A-115, Brooklyn, NY 11215
Tel: 718-643-9193 *Fax:* 718-643-9195
E-mail: info@akashicbooks.com
Web Site: www.akashicbooks.com
Key Personnel
Publr & Ed-in-Chief: Johnny Temple
Edit Dir: Ibrahim Ahmad
Dir, Publicity & Soc Media: Susannah Lawrence
Mng Ed: Johanna Ingalls
Prodn Mgr, Ebook Developer & Assoc Ed: Aaron Petrovich
Founded: 1997
Specialize in urban literary fiction & political nonfiction.
ISBN Prefix(es): 978-1-888451; 978-0-9719206; 978-1-933354; 978-1-936070; 978-1-61775
Number of titles published annually: 30 Print
Total Titles: 300 Print
Imprints: RDV Books
Orders to: Consortium Book Sales & Distribution, The Keg House, Suite 101, 34 13 Ave NE, Minneapolis, MN 55413 *Tel:* 612-746-2600 *Toll Free Tel:* 800-283-3572 (cust serv) *E-mail:* orders@cbsd.com *Web Site:* www.cbsd.com
Returns: Consortium Book Sales & Distribution, The Keg House, Suite 101, 34 13 Ave NE, Minneapolis, MN 55413 *Tel:* 612-746-2600 *Toll Free Tel:* 800-283-3572 (cust serv) *E-mail:* orders@cbsd.com *Web Site:* www.cbsd.com
Warehouse: Consortium Book Sales & Distribution, c/o Perseus, 210 American Dr, Jackson, TN 38301 *Toll Free Tel:* 800-283-3572 *Toll Free Fax:* 800-351-5073 *E-mail:* orders@cbsd.com *Web Site:* www.cbsd.com
Distribution Center: Consortium Book Sales & Distribution, The Keg House, Suite 101, 34 13 Ave NE, Minneapolis, MN 55413 *Tel:* 612-746-2600 *Toll Free Tel:* 800-283-3572 (cust serv) *E-mail:* orders@cbsd.com *Web Site:* www.cbsd.com

ALA, see The American Library Association (ALA)

§ALA Neal-Schuman
Imprint of The American Library Association (ALA)
50 E Huron St, Chicago, IL 60611
Toll Free Tel: 800-545-2433 *Fax:* 312-280-5275
E-mail: editionsmarketing@ala.org
Web Site: www.alastore.ala.org
Key Personnel
Mktg Coord: Rob Christopher *Tel:* 312-280-5052
E-mail: rchristopher@ala.org
Founded: 1976
How-to manuals, technology, library & information science texts.
ISBN Prefix(es): 978-0-918212; 978-1-55570
Number of titles published annually: 32 Print; 5 CD-ROM
Total Titles: 320 Print; 25 CD-ROM
Membership(s): Ontario Library Association

Aladdin, see Simon & Schuster Children's Publishing

Alaska Native Language Center
Division of University of Alaska Fairbanks
PO Box 757680, Fairbanks, AK 99775-7680
SAN: 692-9796
Fax: 907-474-6586
E-mail: uaf-anlc@alaska.edu (orders)
Web Site: www.uaf.edu/anlc
Key Personnel
Dir: Lawrence D Kaplan *Tel:* 907-474-6582
E-mail: ldkaplan@alaska.edu
Ed: Leon Unruh *Tel:* 907-474-6577
E-mail: ldunruh@alaska.edu
Founded: 1972
Publish books in & about Alaska's 20 indigenous languages, including dictionaries, grammars & collections of folktales & oral history, language maps.
ISBN Prefix(es): 978-1-55500; 978-0-933769
Number of titles published annually: 3 Print
Total Titles: 200 Print; 3 Audio

Albert Whitman & Co
250 S Northwest Hwy, Suite 320, Park Ridge, IL 60068
SAN: 201-2049
Tel: 847-232-2800 *Toll Free Tel:* 800-255-7675
Fax: 847-581-0039
E-mail: mail@albertwhitman.com
Web Site: www.albertwhitman.com
Key Personnel
Pres & Co-Owner: John Quattrocchi
VP & Co-Owner: Pat McPartland
Busn Dir: Joe Campbell
Creative Dir: Jordan Kost
Assoc Mktg Mgr: Laurel Symonds
Ed: Eliza Swift
Assoc Ed: Andrea Hall
Founded: 1919
Juveniles, language arts, fiction & nonfiction.
ISBN Prefix(es): 978-0-8075
Number of titles published annually: 50 Print
Total Titles: 800 Print
Distributed by Open Road
Distribution Center: Independent Publishers Group (IPG), 814 N Franklin St, Chicago, IL 60610 *Toll Free Tel:* 800-808-4741 *E-mail:* orders@ipgbook.com *Web Site:* www.ipgbook.com

The Alexander Graham Bell Association for the Deaf & Hard of Hearing
3417 Volta Place NW, Washington, DC 20007
SAN: 203-6924
Tel: 202-337-5220 *Toll Free Tel:* 866-337-5220 (orders) *Fax:* 202-337-8314
E-mail: info@agbell.org; publications@agbell.org
Web Site: www.agbell.org
Key Personnel
CEO: Emilio Alonso-Mendoza
E-mail: ealonsomendoza@agbell.org
Chief Devt Offr: Lisa Chutjian
E-mail: lchutjian@agbell.org
Chief Strategy Offr: Gayla Guignard
E-mail: gguignard@agbell.org
Dir, Communs: Chris Gensch *E-mail:* cgensch@agbell.org
Mgr, Association Rel: Gary Yates *Tel:* 202-204-4683 *E-mail:* gyates@agbell.org
Founded: 1890
Resource, support network & advocate for listening, learning, talking & living independently with hearing loss. Through publications, outreach, training, scholarships & financial aid, AG Bell promotes the use of spoken language & hearing technology. Headquarted in Washington, DC with chapters located in the US & CN & a network of international affiliates. AG Bell's global presence provides its members & the public with the support they need close to home. With over a century of service, AG Bell supports it's mission, advocating independence through listening & talking.
ISBN Prefix(es): 978-0-88200
Number of titles published annually: 9 Print
Total Titles: 70 Print

Alexander Street, a ProQuest Company
3212 Duke St, Alexandria, VA 22314
SAN: 858-5512
Tel: 703-212-8520 *Toll Free Tel:* 800-889-5937
Fax: 703-940-6584
E-mail: sales@alexanderstreet.com; marketing@alexanderstreet.com; info@alexanderstreet.com
Web Site: alexanderstreet.com
Key Personnel
COO: Andrea Eastman-Mullins
E-mail: aeastmanmullins@astreetpress.com
Pres: Stephen Rhind-Tutt *E-mail:* rhindtutt@alexanderstreet.com
VP, Busn Devt: Greg Urquhart
E-mail: gurquhart@alexanderstreet.com
VP, Licensing: Will Whalen *E-mail:* whalen@alexanderstreet.com
VP, Sales: Eileen Lawrence *E-mail:* lawrence@alexanderstreet.com
Dir: Nathalie Duval *E-mail:* nduval@astreetpress.com
Founded: 2000
Publish large-scale digital collections of works in the humanities & social sciences.
ISBN Prefix(es): 978-1-4631; 978-1-5016; 978-1-5034
Number of titles published annually: 30 Print; 6 Online; 2,000 E-Book; 4 Audio
Total Titles: 34 Online; 10,000 E-Book; 6 Audio
Imprints: Filmakers Library; Insight Media; Microtraining Associates
Foreign Office(s): 2123 Pudong Ave, Rm 805, Shanghai 200135, China *Tel:* (021) 386875
Business & Technology Ctr, Unit G04, Bessemer Dr, Stevenage SG1 2DX, United Kingdom *Tel:* (01438) 310193
Membership(s): ALA

§Alfred Music Publishing
PO Box 10003, Van Nuys, CA 91410
Tel: 818-891-5999 (dealer sales, intl); 818-891-2452 (cust serv) *Toll Free Tel:* 800-292-6122 (dealer sales, US & CN) *Fax:* 818-893-5560 (dealer sales); 818-830-6252 (cust serv)
Toll Free Fax: 800-632-1928 (dealer sales)
E-mail: customerservice@alfred.com; sales@alfred.com
Web Site: www.alfred.com
Key Personnel
CEO: Ron Manus
CFO: Steven Raft
Chief Mktg Offr: Andrew Surmani
Pres: Morty Manus
Founded: 1922
Publisher of music education; music books & software, performance & instructional.
ISBN Prefix(es): 978-0-88284; 978-0-87487; 978-0-7390; 978-1-58951; 978-1-4574; 978-1-4706
Number of titles published annually: 500 Print; 4 CD-ROM
Total Titles: 18,000 Print; 20 CD-ROM
Imprints: Belwin; Highland/Etling; Kalmus; Music Inc; Warner/Chappell Music Inc
Foreign Office(s): Bankstown M5 Business Park, Units 3 & 4, 17 Willfox St, Condell Park, NSW 2200, Australia *Tel:* 8707 3600 *Toll Free Tel:* 800-257-161 *E-mail:* promo@alfredpu.com.au
Lutzerathstr 127, 51107 Cologne, Germany
Tel: 221 93 35 3913 *Fax:* 221 93 35 3916
E-mail: info@alfredverlag.de *Web Site:* www.alfredverlag.de
20 Sin Ming Lane, 5th fl, 05-54 Midview City 573968, Singapore, SE Asia Mktg Mgr: Larry Bong *Tel:* 6659 8919 *Fax:* 6659 8908
E-mail: enquiries@alfred.com.sg
Burnt Mill, Elizabeth Way, Harlow, Essex CM20 2HX, United Kingdom *Tel:* (01279) 828960
Fax: (01279) 828961 *E-mail:* music@alfred.uk.com
Distributor for Daisy Rock Girl Guitars; Dover Publications; Drum Channel; Faber Music; MakeMusic Inc; Penguin; WEA
Foreign Rep(s): Dave Bolden (Australia, New Zealand); Larry Bong (Asia); Gerry Mooney (UK); Thomas Petzold (Europe)
Membership(s): MPA - The Association of Magazine Media

Algonquin Books
Division of Workman Publishing Co Inc
400 Silver Cedar Ct, Suite 300, Chapel Hill, NC 27514-1585
SAN: 282-7506
Mailing Address: PO Box 2225, Chapel Hill, NC 27515-2225
Tel: 919-967-0108 *Fax:* 919-933-0272
E-mail: inquiry@algonquin.com
Web Site: www.workman.com/algonquin
Key Personnel
Publr: Elisabeth Scharlatt
Assoc Publr: Craig Popelars *E-mail:* craig@algonquin.com
Assoc Publr, Children's: Eileen Lawrence
Publr, Young Adult & Middle Grade: Elise Howard
Exec Dir, Publicity: Michael McKenzie
Art & Creative Dir: Anne Winslow *Tel:* 919-967-0108 ext 29
Edit Dir: Betsy Gleick
Mktg Mgr: Lauren Moseley
Online Mktg Mgr: Debra Linn
Mng Ed & ISBN Contact: Brunson Hoole
Tel: 919-967-0108 ext 22 *E-mail:* brunson@algonquin.com
Ed: Chuck Adams
Ed, Algonquin Young Readers: Krestyna Lypen
Publicity Mgr: Jackie Burke
Publicist: Brooke Csuka
Intl Rts: Kendra Poster *Tel:* 212-614-7506
Founded: 1982
Trade books, fiction & nonfiction.
ISBN Prefix(es): 978-0-912697; 978-0-945575; 978-1-56512
Number of titles published annually: 38 Print
Imprints: Algonquin Young Readers
Sales Office(s): Workman Publishing Co Inc, 225 Varick St, New York, NY 10014-4381
Tel: 212-254-5900 *Fax:* 212-254-8098
Distributed by Workman Publishing Co Inc
Distributor for Fearless Critic Media; Greenwich Workshop Press; HighBridge Audio
Foreign Rep(s): Thomas Allen & Son Ltd (Canada)
Foreign Rights: Big Apple Agency Inc (China, Taiwan); Copenhagen Literary Agency ApS (Scandinavia); Graal Literary Agency (Poland); The Deborah Harris Agency (Israel); The Italian Literary Agency srl (Italy); Japan UNI Agency Inc (Japan); JLM Literary Agency (Greece); Katai & Bolza Literary Agency (Hungary); Korea Copyright Center Inc (KCC) (Korea); Kristin Olson Literary Agency SRO (Czech Republic); Plima Literary Agency (Bulgaria, Croatia, Macedonia, Serbia, Slovenia); Sebes & Bisseling Literary Agency (Netherlands); Julio F Yanez Agencia Literaria SL (Portugal, Spain)
Billing Address: Workman Publishing Co Inc, 225 Varick St, New York, NY 10014-4381
Tel: 212-254-5900 *Fax:* 212-254-8098
Orders to: Workman Publishing Co Inc, 225 Varick St, New York, NY 10014-4381
Tel: 212-254-5900 *Toll Free Tel:* 800-722-7202
Fax: 212-254-8098
Returns: Workman Publishing Co Inc, c/o RR Donnelly, 677 Brighton Beach Rd, Menasha, WI 54952-2998
Warehouse: Workman Publishing Co Inc, c/o RR Donnelly, 677 Brighton Beach Rd, Menasha, WI 54952-2998

Algora Publishing
1732 First Ave, No 20330, New York, NY 10128
Tel: 212-678-0232 *Fax:* 212-666-3682
E-mail: editors@algora.com
Web Site: www.algora.com
Key Personnel
Publr: Claudiu A Secara
Ed: Martin De Mers
Author Rel: Andrea Secara
Founded: 1992
Books on subjects of history, international affairs, current issues, political economy, philosophy, etc in the tradition of independent progressive thinking.
ISBN Prefix(es): 978-0-87586; 978-0-9646073; 978-1-892941; 978-1-62894
Number of titles published annually: 25 Print; 25 E-Book
Total Titles: 400 Print; 400 E-Book
Imprints: Agathon Press
Membership(s): AAP; Independent Book Publishers Association

Alice James Books
Division of Alice James Poetry Cooperative Inc
114 Prescott St, Farmington, ME 04938
SAN: 201-1158
Tel: 207-778-7071 *Fax:* 207-778-7766
E-mail: info@alicejamesbooks.org
Web Site: alicejamesbooks.org
Key Personnel
Exec Dir: Carey Salerno
Mng Ed: Alyssa Neptune
Edit Asst: Alicia Hynes
Bookkeeper: Debra Norton
Founded: 1973
ISBN Prefix(es): 978-0-914086; 978-1-882295; 978-1-938584
Number of titles published annually: 6 Print
Total Titles: 115 Print; 3 Audio
Distribution Center: Consortium Book Sales & Distribution, The Keg House, Suite 101, 34 13 Ave NE, Minneapolis, MN 55413 *Tel:* 612-746-2600 *Toll Free Tel:* 800-283-3572 (cust serv) *Fax:* 612-746-2606 *E-mail:* info@cbsd.com *Web Site:* www.cbsd.com

All About Kids Publishing
PO Box 159, Gilroy, CA 95021
Tel: 408-337-1152
E-mail: info@allaboutkidspub.com
Web Site: www.allaboutkidspub.com
Key Personnel
Publr: Mike G Guevara
Ed: Linda L Guevara *E-mail:* lguevara@allaboutkidspub.com
Founded: 2000
Strives to set the standards in children's book publishing by creating innovative books of the highest quality with beautiful art work for children of all walks of life. See submission guidelines on web site.
ISBN Prefix(es): 978-0-9700863; 978-0-9710278; 978-0-9744446
Number of titles published annually: 6 Print
Total Titles: 20 Print
Membership(s): Independent Book Publishers Association

§All Things That Matter Press
79 Jones Rd, Somerville, ME 04348
E-mail: allthingsthatmatterpress@gmail.com
Web Site: www.allthingsthatmatterpress.com
Key Personnel
CEO: Debra Harris
Founded: 2008
ISBN Prefix(es): 978-0-9966634
Number of titles published annually: 15 Print; 15 E-Book; 10 Audio
Total Titles: 225 Print; 225 E-Book; 68 Audio

§Allium Press of Chicago
1530 Elgin Ave, Forest Park, IL 60130
SAN: 858-3331
Tel: 708-689-9323
E-mail: info@alliumpress.com
Web Site: www.alliumpress.com

Key Personnel
Publr: Emily Victorson
Founded: 2009
Small independent press publishing fiction with a Chicago connection. Publish literary fiction, historical fiction, mysteries, thrillers & young adult fiction.
ISBN Prefix(es): 978-0-9840676; 978-0-9831938; 978-0-9890535; 978-0-9967558
Number of titles published annually: 5 Print; 5 E-Book
Total Titles: 15 Print; 15 E-Book
Membership(s): Historical Novel Society; Independent Book Publishers Association; Sisters in Crime; Society of Midland Authors

Alloy Entertainment LLC
Member of Warner Bros Entertainment Group
1325 Avenue of the Americas, 29th fl, New York, NY 10019
E-mail: collaborative@alloyentertainment.com
Key Personnel
Pres: Leslie Morgenstein
EVP: Josh Bank
SVP, Edit: Sara Shandler
VP, Book Devt: Joelle Hobeika
Ed: Hayley Wagreich
Founded: 1987
Hardcover, trade, mass market juvenile & young adult fiction & nonfiction; adult trade fiction & mass market fiction.
ISBN Prefix(es): 978-0-9850261; 978-1-939106
Number of titles published annually: 50 Print
Distributed by Avon Books; HarperCollins; Hyperion; Little, Brown & Co; Penguin Group USA, A Penguin Random House Company; Penguin Random House Inc; Scholastic Books; Simon & Schuster
Foreign Rep(s): Rights People (UK)

§Allworth Press
Imprint of Skyhorse Publishing Inc
307 W 36 St, 11th fl, New York, NY 10018
Tel: 212-643-6816 *Fax:* 212-643-6819
Web Site: www.allworth.com
Key Personnel
Founder & Publr: Tad Crawford
E-mail: crawford@allworth.com
Founded: 1989
Business & self-help books for artists, crafters, designers, photographers, authors & film & performing artists; books about business & law for the general public.
ISBN Prefix(es): 978-0-927629; 978-0-9607118; 978-1-880559; 978-1-58115; 978-1-62153
Number of titles published annually: 20 Print; 20 E-Book
Total Titles: 400 Print; 400 E-Book
Sales Office(s): Perseus Book Distribution, 1400 Broadway, New York, NY 10018
Foreign Rights: Jean V Naggar Literary Agency (worldwide)
Distribution Center: Perseus Book Distribution, 1400 Broadway, New York, NY 10018

AllWrite Advertising & Publishing
241 Peachtree St NE, Suite 400, Atlanta, GA 30303
Mailing Address: PO Box 1071, Atlanta, GA 30301
Tel: 404-221-0703 *Fax:* 770-284-8986
E-mail: questions@allwritepublishing.com; support@allwritepublishing.com (orders & returns)
Web Site: allwritepublishing.com
Key Personnel
Pres & Publr: Annette R Johnson *Tel:* 770-284-8956 *E-mail:* annette@allwritepublishing.com
Founded: 2003
A conventional small press. Books that we do not decide to publish are given thorough feedback.
ISBN Prefix(es): 978-0-9744935
Number of titles published annually: 5 Print
Membership(s): Independent Book Publishing Professionals Group; Writers Guild of America, East

§Alpha Books
Subsidiary of DK Publishing
6081 E 82 St, 4th fl, Indianapolis, IN 46250
Tel: 212-366-2000
E-mail: ecommerce@us.penguingroup.com
Web Site: www.dk.com; www.idiotguides.com
Key Personnel
Publr: Michael Sanders
Founded: 2003
Publisher of *Idiot's Guides*®.
ISBN Prefix(es): 978-1-61564
Number of titles published annually: 88 Print
Total Titles: 580 Print

Alpha II LLC
7480 Halcyon Pointe Dr, Suite 204, Montgomery, AL 36117
Tel: 334-260-8150 *Toll Free Tel:* 800-825-7421 *Toll Free Fax:* 800-305-8030
E-mail: sales@alphaii.com
Web Site: www.alphaii.com
Key Personnel
CEO: Jan Powell
VP, Pubns: Nikki V Siler *E-mail:* nikki.siler@alphaii.com
Founded: 2014
Health information/medical coding books & revenue cycle management software.
ISBN Prefix(es): 978-1-56781
Number of titles published annually: 8 Print

Alpine Publications Inc
PO Box 188, Crawford, CO 81415
Tel: 970-921-5005 *Toll Free Tel:* 800-777-7257
E-mail: alpinepublishing@aol.com; customerservice@alpinepub.com
Web Site: www.alpinepub.com
Key Personnel
Publr: Betty McKinney
Founded: 1975
Dog & horse nonfiction titles.
ISBN Prefix(es): 978-0-931866; 978-0-87714; 978-1-57779
Number of titles published annually: 6 Print; 2 E-Book
Total Titles: 70 Print; 3 E-Book
Advertising Agency: Artline
Membership(s): ABA

AltaMira Press
Imprint of Rowman & Littlefield Publishing Group
4501 Forbes Blvd, Suite 200, Lanham, MD 20706
Tel: 301-459-3366 *Toll Free Tel:* 800-462-6420 (cust serv) *Fax:* 301-429-5748
E-mail: custserv@rowman.com
Web Site: www.altamirapress.com
Key Personnel
Exec Ed: Charles Harmon *Tel:* 212-529-3888 ext 305 *E-mail:* charmon@rowman.com
Founded: 1995
Academic & professional materials, anthropology, museum & cultural studies, religion, archeology, history & humanities.
New titles to be released under the Rowman & Littlefield imprint.
ISBN Prefix(es): 978-0-8039; 978-0-7619 (shared with Sage Publications); 978-0-930390; 978-0-910050; 978-0-942063; 978-0-7425 (shared with Rowman & Littlefield); 978-0-8039 (shared with Sage Publications); 978-1-4422 (shared with Rowman & Littlefield)
Number of titles published annually: 75 Print; 1 CD-ROM
Total Titles: 500 Print; 3 CD-ROM
Distributor for American Association for State & Local History
Foreign Rep(s): National Book Network International (Europe, UK)
Shipping Address: National Book Network, 15200 NBN Way, PO Box 191, Blue Ridge Summit, PA 17214 *Toll Free Tel:* 800-462-6420 *Toll Free Fax:* 800-338-4550 *E-mail:* customercare@rowman.com
Distribution Center: National Book Network/University Press of America, 15200 NBN Way, PO Box 191, Blue Ridge Summit, PA 17214 *Toll Free Tel:* 800-462-6420 *Toll Free Fax:* 800-338-4550 *E-mail:* customercare@rowman.com
Membership(s): AAP

Althos Publishing, see DiscoverNet Publishing

§AMACOM Books
Division of American Management Association (AMA)
1601 Broadway, New York, NY 10019-7420
SAN: 201-1670
Tel: 212-586-8100 *Toll Free Tel:* 800-250-5308 (cust serv) *Fax:* 212-903-8083; 518-891-2372 (orders)
E-mail: pubs_cust_serv@amanet.org
Web Site: www.amacombooks.org
Key Personnel
Pres & Publr: Nancy Roberson
VP, Mktg: Rosemary Kane Carlough *E-mail:* rcarlough@amanet.org
Dir, Publicity: Irene Majuk *Tel:* 212-903-8087 *E-mail:* imajuk@amanet.org
Dir, Subs Rts & Intl Sales: Therese Mausser *Tel:* 212-903-8084 *E-mail:* tmausser@amanet.org
Dir, Trade Sales & Mktg: Jenny Wesselmann Schwartz *Tel:* 212-903-8448 *E-mail:* jwesselmann@amanet.org
Exec Ed: Ellen Kadin *E-mail:* ekadin@amanet.org
Sr Ed: Timothy H Burgard *E-mail:* tburgard@amanet.org
Founded: 1972
Publish books on business management, career growth, current events, technology & personal finance. AMACOM books help readers enhance their personal & professional growth & reach into the future to understand emerging trends & cutting-edge thinking.
ISBN Prefix(es): 978-0-8144; 978-0-7612
Number of titles published annually: 60 Print; 30 E-Book
Total Titles: 500 Print; 150 E-Book; 54 Audio
Foreign Rep(s): McGraw-Hill Education (Africa, Asia, Australia, Eastern Europe, Europe, Middle East, New Zealand, South Africa, UK); Publishers Group Canada (Canada)
Returns: 600 AMA Way, Saranac Lake, NY 12983
Warehouse: 600 AMA Way, Saranac Lake, NY 12983 *E-mail:* pubservice@amanet.org

Amadeus Press/Hal Leonard Performing Arts Publishing Group
Division of Hal Leonard Performing Arts Publishing Group
33 Plymouth St, Suite 302, Montclair, NJ 07042
Tel: 973-337-5034 *Toll Free Tel:* 800-524-4425
E-mail: info@halleonardbooks.com
Web Site: www.amadeuspress.com; www.halleonardbooks.com
Key Personnel
Group Publr: John Cerullo *Tel:* 973-337-5034 ext 210
Founded: 1987
Full service trade publisher that produces books, book/CDs & DVDs about classical music & opera.
ISBN Prefix(es): 978-1-57467
Number of titles published annually: 40 Print; 30 E-Book

Total Titles: 1,200 Print; 1,000 E-Book
Foreign Rep(s): Publishers Group UK (Europe, UK)

§Amakella Publishing
PO Box 9445, Arlington, VA 22219
Tel: 202-239-8381
E-mail: info@amakella.com
Web Site: www.amakella.com
Independent publisher interested in publishing books in areas such as social sciences, international development, environmental conservation & current affairs.
ISBN Prefix(es): 978-1-63387
Number of titles published annually: 3 Print; 3 E-Book
Total Titles: 3 Print; 3 E-Book
Membership(s): Independent Book Publishers Association

Frank Amato Publications Inc
4040 SE Wister St, Milwaukie, OR 97222
Mailing Address: PO Box 82112, Portland, OR 97282
Tel: 503-653-8108 *Toll Free Tel:* 800-541-9498 *Fax:* 503-653-2766
E-mail: customerservice@amatobooks.com; info@amatobooks.com
Web Site: www.amatobooks.com
Key Personnel
Publr: Frank W Amato
Co-Publr & Ed: Nick S Amato *E-mail:* n.amato@comcast.net
Co-Publr: Tony F Amato *E-mail:* tony@amatobooks.com
Ad & Inquiries: Dave Eng *E-mail:* deng@amatobooks.com
Founded: 1967
Fishing books & magazines, some outdoor sport titles & cookbooks.
ISBN Prefix(es): 978-0-936608; 978-1-878175; 978-1-57188
Number of titles published annually: 30 Print
Total Titles: 800 Print
Distributor for Haugen Enterprises (cooking & hunting titles)
Membership(s): Pacific Northwest Booksellers Association

§Ambassador International
Division of Emerald House Inc
411 University Ridge, Suite B14, Greenville, SC 29601
Tel: 864-751-4844
E-mail: info@emeraldhouse.com; publisher@emeraldhouse.com (ms submissions); sales@emeraldhouse.com (orders/order inquiries)
Web Site: ambassador-international.com; www.facebook.com/AmbassadorIntl; twitter.com/ambassadorintl
Key Personnel
CEO & Pres: Dr Samuel Lowry
COO: Timothy Lowry *E-mail:* tlowry@emeraldhouse.com
Creative Dir: Hannah Nichols
Publicist: Alison Storm
Digital Prodr: Anna Riebe
Ed: Brenda Covert
Founded: 1980 (UK, 1996 US)
Christian publisher. Works with authors to create quality Christian literature of several genres - fiction, devotional & children's books. The company's vision has always been to create products that strengthen believers in their Christian walk & direct the lost to the way of salvation. New titles each year in both print & ebook format. Offices in the US & Northern Ireland, distribution partnerships on four continents & books in the hands of readers around the world.
This publisher has indicated that 90% of their product line is author subsidized.
ISBN Prefix(es): 978-1-889893; 978-1-932307; 978-1-620202
Number of titles published annually: 50 Print; 50 E-Book
Total Titles: 250 E-Book
Foreign Office(s): Ambassador Books & Media, The Mount, 2 Woodstock Link, Belfast BT6 8DD, United Kingdom *Tel:* (028) 9073 0184 *Fax:* (028) 9073 0199 *Web Site:* www.ambassadormedia.co.uk
Distribution Center: Baker & Taylor, 2550 W Tyvola Rd, Suite 300, Charlotte, NC 28217 (US dist) *Tel:* 704-998-3100 *Toll Free Tel:* 800-775-1800 *Web Site:* www.baker-taylor.com
Ingram/Spring Arbor, One Ingram Blvd, La Vergne, TN 37086 (US dist) *Tel:* 615-793-5000 *Web Site:* www.ingramcontent.com

Amber Lotus Publishing
PO Box 11329, Portland, OR 97211
SAN: 247-6819
Tel: 503-284-6400 *Toll Free Tel:* 800-326-2375 (orders only) *Fax:* 503-284-6417
E-mail: info@amberlotus.com
Web Site: www.amberlotus.com
Key Personnel
Co-Owner & Pres: Lawson Day
Co-Owner & Creative Dir: Leslie Gignilliat-Day
VP, Sales: Tim Campbell
Prodn Mgr: Aleta Florentin
Mktg: Dianne Foster
Opers: Ethan Disbrow
Founded: 1988
Calendars, greeting cards, journals & books.
ISBN Prefix(es): 978-1-885394; 978-1-56937; 978-1-60237
Number of titles published annually: 65 Print

AMC Books, see Appalachian Mountain Club Books

America West Publishers
Subsidiary of Global Insights Inc
5872 Government Way, Unit 1-10, Dalton Gardens, ID 83814
Mailing Address: PO Box 599, Hayden, ID 83835
Tel: 208-762-0633 *Toll Free Tel:* 800-729-4131
Web Site: www.nohoax.com
Key Personnel
Pres: George Green *E-mail:* geo@nohoax.com
Founded: 1986
New science, UFOs, healing, metaphysics, spiritual, political & economic.
ISBN Prefix(es): 978-0-922356
Number of titles published annually: 5 Print; 1 CD-ROM
Total Titles: 100 Print; 20 CD-ROM; 5 Audio

American Academy of Environmental Engineers & Scientists™
147 Old Solomons Island Rd, Suite 303, Annapolis, MD 21401
Tel: 410-266-3311 *Fax:* 410-266-7653
E-mail: info@aaees.org
Web Site: www.aaees.org
Key Personnel
Exec Dir: Burk Kalweit *E-mail:* bkalweit@aaees.org
Prodn Mgr: Yolanda Moulden *E-mail:* ymoulden@aaees.org
Exec Asst: Joyce Dowen *E-mail:* jdowen@aaees.org
Founded: 1955
Journals & textbooks for the environmental engineering & science professions.
ISBN Prefix(es): 978-1-883767
Number of titles published annually: 5 Print
Total Titles: 49 Print
Distributor for The ABS Group; CRC Press; McGraw-Hill; Pearson Education; Prentice Hall; John Wiley & Sons Inc

§American Academy of Orthopaedic Surgeons (AAOS)
9400 W Higgins Rd, Rosemont, IL 60018-4976
SAN: 228-2097
Tel: 847-823-7186 *Toll Free Tel:* 800-346-2267
E-mail: custserv@aaos.org
Web Site: www.aaos.org
Key Personnel
Dir, Dept of Pubns: Han Koelsch
Pubns Mgr: Joan Golembiewski *Tel:* 847-384-4144 *Fax:* 847-268-9644 *E-mail:* golembiewski@aaos.org
Founded: 1933
Scientific & technical books, including annual updates on orthopaedic procedures; home study programs & examinations; symposium volumes; monographs on scientific, clinical, practice management & socioeconomic topics in orthopaedics; clinical review journal.
ISBN Prefix(es): 978-0-89203
Number of titles published annually: 15 Print; 12 CD-ROM; 2 Online; 1 Audio
Total Titles: 100 Print; 38 CD-ROM; 5 Online; 5 Audio
Branch Office(s)
317 Massachusetts Ave NE, 1st fl, Washington, DC 20002 *Tel:* 202-546-4430 *Fax:* 202-546-5051
Distributed by Jones & Bartlett Publishers
Foreign Rep(s): Eurospan (Europe, Middle East); Nankodo Co Inc (Japan)
Warehouse: Dearborn Distribution Center, 940 Enterprise St, Aurora, IL 60504 *Toll Free Fax:* 800-823-8025 *E-mail:* custserv@aaos.org

American Academy of Pediatrics
141 NW Point Blvd, Elk Grove Village, IL 60007-1098
Tel: 847-434-4000 *Toll Free Tel:* 888-227-1770 *Fax:* 847-434-8000
E-mail: pubs@aap.org
Web Site: www.aap.org
Key Personnel
Pres: Dr James Perrin
Dir, Prod Devt Div: Mark Grimes *Tel:* 847-434-7822 *E-mail:* mgrimes@aap.org
Dir, Sales: Mark Voigt
Founded: 1930
Patient educational material, medical textbooks, professional textbook, patient education & practice management materials; pediatrics; family & emergency medicine.
ISBN Prefix(es): 978-0-910761; 978-0-87493; 978-0-915473; 978-0-87553; 978-0-553; 978-0-89707; 978-1-56055; 978-1-58110
Number of titles published annually: 40 Print; 5 CD-ROM; 10 Online; 120 E-Book
Total Titles: 400 Print; 10 CD-ROM; 10 Online; 120 E-Book
Branch Office(s)
601 13 St NW, Suite 400-N, Washington, DC 20005 *Tel:* 202-347-8600 *Fax:* 202-393-6137
Foreign Rights: John Scott & Co

The American Alpine Club Press
Division of The American Alpine Club
710 Tenth St, Suite 100, Golden, CO 80401
Tel: 303-384-0110 *Fax:* 303-384-0111
E-mail: info@americanalpineclub.org
Web Site: americanalpineclub.org
Key Personnel
Exec Ed: Dougald MacDonald *E-mail:* dmacdonald@americanalpineclub.org
Founded: 1902
Mountaineering: general, regional guides, safety, medical & scientific, annual journals & historical.
ISBN Prefix(es): 978-0-930410
Number of titles published annually: 3 Print; 2 E-Book
Total Titles: 57 Print
Distributed by Mountaineers Books

Foreign Rep(s): Mountaineers Books (worldwide)
Foreign Rights: Mountaineers Books (worldwide)

§American Anthropological Association (AAA)
2300 Clarendon Blvd, Suite 1301, Arlington, VA 22201
Tel: 703-528-1902 *Fax:* 703-528-3546
E-mail: pubs@americananthro.org
Web Site: www.americananthro.org
Key Personnel
Dir, Publg: Janine Chiappa McKenna *Tel:* 703-528-1902 ext 1174 *E-mail:* jmckenna@americananthro.org
Asst to Dir, Publg: Chelsea Horton *Tel:* 703-528-1902 ext 1181 *E-mail:* chorton@americananthro.org
Mng Ed: Natalie Konopinski *Tel:* 703-528-1902 ext 1184 *E-mail:* nkonopinski@americananthro.org
Founded: 1902
Publish scholarly journals.
ISBN Prefix(es): 978-0-913167; 978-1-931303; 978-0-9799094; 978-0-9826767; 978-0-9836822
Number of titles published annually: 100 Print
Total Titles: 27 Print
Distributed by Wiley-Blackwell
Membership(s): AAP; World Council of Anthropological Associations

§American Association for Vocational Instructional Materials
220 Smithonia Rd, Winterville, GA 30683
Tel: 706-742-5355 *Fax:* 706-742-7005
E-mail: sales@aavim.com
Web Site: www.aavim.com
Key Personnel
Dir: Gary Farmer
Founded: 1949
Consortium formed for development, publishing & distribution of instructional materials for vocational education.
ISBN Prefix(es): 978-0-89606
Number of titles published annually: 4 Print
Total Titles: 182 Print; 10 CD-ROM
Distributor for Southeastern Cooperative Wildlife Disease Study

§American Association of Blood Banks
North Tower, 4550 Montgomery Ave, Suite 700, Bethesda, MD 20814
Tel: 301-907-6977 *Toll Free Tel:* 866-222-2498 (sales) *Fax:* 301-907-6895
E-mail: aabb@aabb.org; sales@aabb.org (ordering); publications1@aabb.org (catalog)
Web Site: www.aabb.org
Key Personnel
Dir, Pubns: Laurie Munk *Tel:* 301-215-6595 *E-mail:* laurie@aabb.org
Mgr, Pubns: Jennifer Boyer *Tel:* 301-215-6596 *E-mail:* jboyer@aabb.org
Founded: 1947
Texts in blood banking standards, transfusion medicine, transplantation & cellular therapy.
ISBN Prefix(es): 978-0-915355
Number of titles published annually: 20 Print; 14 Audio
Total Titles: 73 Print; 42 Online; 60 Audio
Returns: BrightKey Inc, Attn: AABB Returns, 1780 Crossroads Dr, Odenton, MD 21113

American Association of Cereal Chemists, see AACC International

American Association of Collegiate Registrars & Admissions Officers (AACRAO)
One Dupont Circle NW, Suite 520, Washington, DC 20036
Tel: 202-293-9161 *Fax:* 202-872-8857
Web Site: www.aacrao.org
Key Personnel
Exec Dir: Michael Reilly *E-mail:* reillym@aacrao.org
Dir, Opers, Membership & Pubns: Martha Henebry *Tel:* 202-263-0285 *E-mail:* henebrym@aacrao.org
Founded: 1910
Periodicals, monograph series, higher education-general, international, technology & higher education.
ISBN Prefix(es): 978-0-929851; 978-0-910054
Number of titles published annually: 4 Print; 4 E-Book
Total Titles: 118 Print; 11 E-Book
Distribution Center: AACRAO Distribution Center, PO Box 231, Annapolis Junction, MD 20701 *Tel:* 301-263-0292 *Fax:* 240-396-5986 *E-mail:* pubs@aacrao.org *Web Site:* www.aacrao.org/bookstore

American Bar Association
321 N Clark St, Chicago, IL 60654
Tel: 312-988-5000 *Toll Free Tel:* 800-285-2221 (orders) *Fax:* 312-988-6281
E-mail: orders@abanet.org
Web Site: www.americanbar.org
Key Personnel
Dir, Publg: Donna Gollmer
Founded: 1878
Books, magazines, journals, newsletters & AV materials.
ISBN Prefix(es): 978-1-57073; 978-1-59031; 978-1-60442
Number of titles published annually: 170 Print; 25 CD-ROM; 100 Online; 100 E-Book
Total Titles: 1,000 Print; 150 CD-ROM; 250 Online; 250 E-Book
Branch Office(s)
1050 Connecticut Ave NW, Suite 400, Washington, DC 20036 *Tel:* 202-662-1000
Warehouse: Thomson Reuters, 610 Opperman Dr, Eagan, MN 55123 *Tel:* 651-687-7000
Distribution Center: National Book Network, 4501 Forbes Blvd, Suite 200, Lanham, MD 20706
Membership(s): Independent Book Publishers Association

§American Bible Society
101 N Independence Mall E, 8th fl, Philadelphia, PA 19106-2112
SAN: 203-5189
Tel: 215-309-0900 *Toll Free Tel:* 800-322-4253 (cust serv); 888-596-6296
E-mail: info@americanbible.org
Web Site: www.americanbible.org
Key Personnel
Mng Dir, Opers: John Greco
Founded: 1816
Publisher, producer & distributor of Bibles, books, audio, video & software products emphasizing Christian, inspirational & family values.
ISBN Prefix(es): 978-1-58516
Number of titles published annually: 20 Print
Total Titles: 800 Print
Warehouse: PO Box 2854, Tulsa, OK 74101-9921 *Toll Free Fax:* 866-570-1777

§American Carriage House Publishing
400 Idaho Maryland Rd, Grass Valley, CA 95945
Tel: 530-432-8860 *Toll Free Tel:* 866-986-2665
E-mail: editor@carriagehousepublishing.com
Web Site: www.americancarriagehousepublishing.com
Founded: 2003
Focused on providing traditional & family values in a new fresh approach.
ISBN Prefix(es): 978-0-970
Number of titles published annually: 8 Print; 20 CD-ROM; 8 Online; 14 E-Book; 68 Audio
Total Titles: 16 E-Book; 240 Audio
Distributed by Faith Works Books
Distribution Center: Baker & Taylor
Ingram Book Group
Quality Books Inc
Membership(s): The Association of Publishers for Special Sales; Independent Book Publishers Association

American Catholic Press (ACP)
16565 S State St, South Holland, IL 60473
SAN: 162-4989
Tel: 708-331-5485 *Fax:* 708-331-5484
E-mail: acp@acpress.org
Web Site: www.acpress.org
Key Personnel
Exec Dir: Rev Michael Gilligan, PhD
Devt Dir: Peter Ruhl
Subscriber Serv Dir: Michael Yukich
Founded: 1967
Christian liturgy, especially in the Roman Catholic Church including music resources for churches. No poetry or fiction.
ISBN Prefix(es): 978-0-915866
Number of titles published annually: 5 Print; 1 Audio
Total Titles: 25 Print; 1 CD-ROM; 4 Audio

§The American Ceramic Society
600 N Cleveland Ave, Suite 210, Westerville, OH 43082
Tel: 240-646-7054 *Toll Free Tel:* 866-721-3322 *Fax:* 240-396-5637
E-mail: customerservice@ceramics.org
Web Site: ceramics.org
Key Personnel
Exec Dir: Charles Spahr *E-mail:* cspahr@ceramics.org
Dir, Communs & Mktg: Eileen De Guire *E-mail:* edeguire@ceramics.org
Dir, Membership, Meetings & Tech Pubns: Mark Mecklenborg *Tel:* 240-646-7054 ext 5829 *E-mail:* mmecklenborg@ceramics.org
Founded: 1898
Dedicated to the advancement of ceramics, serving more than 8,000 members & subscribers. Members include engineers, scientists, researchers & others in the ceramics & materials industry. Provides the latest technical, scientific & educational information.
ISBN Prefix(es): 978-0-944904; 978-1-57498; 978-0-916094
Number of titles published annually: 25 Print
Total Titles: 250 Print; 8 CD-ROM

The American Chemical Society
1155 16 St NW, Washington, DC 20036
SAN: 201-2626
Tel: 202-872-4600 *Toll Free Tel:* 800-227-5558 (US) *Fax:* 202-872-6067
E-mail: help@acs.org
Web Site: www.acs.org
Key Personnel
Asst Dir: Joseph Graham *E-mail:* j_graham@acs.org
Founded: 1876
Serials, proceedings, reprint collections, monographs & other professional & reference books; specializes in food chemistry, environmental sciences & green chemistry, analytical, inorganic, medicinal, organic & physical chemistries, biochemistry, polymer & materials science & nanotechnology.
ISBN Prefix(es): 978-0-8412
Number of titles published annually: 31 Print
Total Titles: 500 Print; 1 CD-ROM
Distributed by Oxford University Press
Distributor for Royal Society of Chemistry
Foreign Rep(s): Maruzen Co Ltd (Japan); Sonya Nickson (UK); Andrew Pitts (UK)
Membership(s): AAP

American College
270 S Bryn Mawr Ave, Bryn Mawr, PA 19010
SAN: 240-5822
Tel: 610-526-1000 *Toll Free Tel:* 888-263-7265 *Fax:* 610-526-1310
Web Site: www.theamericancollege.edu
Key Personnel
Pres: Bob Johnson
Chief Academic Offr: Michael Finke
Founded: 1927
An independent, accredited nonprofit educational institution offering financial services texts & course guides online & life insurance for students in financial services programs at colleges & universities including American College programs: CLU, ChFC, CLF, LUTCF, RHU, REBC, CASL & CFP certification curriculum & MSFS degree for professionals in the financial services industry. Subject specialties: business, finance, insurance & securities.
ISBN Prefix(es): 978-0-943590; 978-1-57996; 978-1-932819
Number of titles published annually: 42 Print; 60 Online; 11 Audio
Total Titles: 42 Print; 15 CD-ROM; 60 Online; 11 Audio

American College of Surgeons
633 N Saint Clair St, Chicago, IL 60611-3211
Tel: 312-202-5000 *Fax:* 312-202-5001
E-mail: postmaster@facs.org
Web Site: www.facs.org
Key Personnel
Gen Pubns Mgr: Katie McCauley *E-mail:* kmccauley@facs.org
Founded: 1913
Publishes reference books & manuals. Specialize in surgery, trauma, cancer & professional liability. Also publishes the *Journal of the American College of Surgeons* (monthly) & the *Bulletin of the American College of Surgeons* (monthly).
ISBN Prefix(es): 978-0-9620370
Number of titles published annually: 5 Print; 10 Online
Total Titles: 20 Print; 2 CD-ROM
Distributed by Cine-Med Inc; Scientific American Medicine

American Correctional Association
206 N Washington St, Suite 200, Alexandria, VA 22314
Tel: 703-224-0000 *Toll Free Tel:* 800-222-5646 *Fax:* 703-224-0179
E-mail: publications@aca.org
Web Site: www.aca.org
Key Personnel
Dir, Communs & Pubns: Mina Grace *Tel:* 703-224-0193 *E-mail:* MinaG@aca.org
Founded: 1870
Corrections professionals.
ISBN Prefix(es): 978-1-56991
Number of titles published annually: 6 Print
Total Titles: 200 Print

American Council on Education
One Dupont Circle NW, Washington, DC 20036
Tel: 202-939-9300; 202-939-9452 (publg dept); 301-632-6757 (orders)
E-mail: pubs@acenet.edu
Web Site: www.acenet.edu
Key Personnel
Pres: Molly Corbett Broad
Dir, Pubns: Felicia Carr
Founded: 1917
Books, directories & handbooks in higher education, monographs.
ISBN Prefix(es): 978-0-8268; 978-0-89774
Number of titles published annually: 70 Print
Total Titles: 200 Print
Distributed by Rowman & Littlefield

American Counseling Association
6101 Stevenson Ave, Suite 600, Alexandria, VA 22304
Tel: 703-823-9800 (ext 222, book orders) *Toll Free Tel:* 800-347-6647 (ext 222, book orders) *Fax:* 703-823-0252 *Toll Free Fax:* 800-473-2329
E-mail: membership@counseling.org (book orders)
Web Site: www.counseling.org
Key Personnel
Assoc Publr: Carolyn C Baker *Tel:* 703-823-9800 ext 356 *Fax:* 703-823-4786 *E-mail:* cbaker@counseling.org
Digital & Print Devt Ed, Rts & Perms: Nancy Driver *Tel:* 703-823-9800 ext 253 *Fax:* 703-823-4786 *E-mail:* ndriver@counseling.org
Founded: 1952
More than 55,000 members from the school counseling, mental health & human development professions at all educational levels. Publishes 10 scholarly journals, a magazine & approximately 8-10 new professional book titles a year for members & nonmembers.
ISBN Prefix(es): 978-1-55620
Number of titles published annually: 10 Print; 10 E-Book
Total Titles: 100 Print; 50 E-Book
Imprints: ACA

§American Diabetes Association
1701 N Beauregard St, Alexandria, VA 22311
Toll Free Tel: 800-342-2383
E-mail: booksinfo@diabetes.org
Web Site: www.diabetes.org
Key Personnel
VP of Content & Creative Solutions: Kelly Rawlings
Dir, Book Publg: Abe Ogden
Sr Mgr, Acqs: Victor Van Beuren
Mgr, Book Editing: Lauren Wilson
Mgr, Mktg: Katherine Curran
Founded: 1945
Books, handouts & collateral materials pertaining to diabetes for patients & health-care professionals.
ISBN Prefix(es): 978-1-58040; 978-0-94544
Number of titles published annually: 20 Print; 15 E-Book
Total Titles: 180 Print; 80 E-Book
Distribution Center: Publishers Group West (PGW), 1700 Fourth St, Berkeley, CA 94710 *Toll Free Tel:* 800-788-3123 (cust serv) SAN: 202-8522

American Federation of Arts
305 E 47 St, 10th fl, New York, NY 10017
Tel: 212-988-7700 *Toll Free Tel:* 800-232-0270 *Fax:* 212-861-2487
E-mail: pubinfo@amfedarts.org
Web Site: www.amfedarts.org
Key Personnel
Mgr, Pubns: Audrey Walen *Tel:* 212-988-7700 ext 255 *E-mail:* awalen@amfedarts.org
Mgr, Communs: Natalie Espinosa *Tel:* 212-988-7700 ext 205 *E-mail:* nespinosa@amfedarts.org
Founded: 1909
Publisher of exhibition catalogues (books) that accompany art exhibitions organized by the AFA.
ISBN Prefix(es): 978-0-917418; 978-1-885444
Number of titles published annually: 4 Print
Total Titles: 47 Print
Distributed by Harry N Abrams Inc; Delmonico/Prestel; Distributed Art Publishers; D Giles Ltd; Hudson Hills Press Inc; Scala Publishers; Skira Rizzoli Publishers; University of Washington Press; Yale University Press

American Federation of Astrologers Inc
6535 S Rural Rd, Tempe, AZ 85283-3746
Tel: 480-838-1751 *Toll Free Tel:* 888-301-7630 *Fax:* 480-838-8293
Web Site: www.astrologers.com
Key Personnel
Exec Dir: Kris Brandt Riske
Founded: 1938
Astrology book publisher & membership organization.
ISBN Prefix(es): 978-0-86690
Number of titles published annually: 25 Print
Total Titles: 250 Print

American Fisheries Society
425 Barlow Place, Suite 110, Bethesda, MD 20814-2144
Tel: 301-897-8616; 703-661-1570 (book orders) *Fax:* 301-897-8096; 703-996-1010 (book orders)
E-mail: main@fisheries.org
Web Site: www.fisheries.org
Key Personnel
Dir, Pubns: Aaron Lerner *Tel:* 301-897-8616 ext 231 *E-mail:* alerner@fisheries.org
Off & Admin Mgr: Denise Spencer *Tel:* 301-897-8616 ext 212 *E-mail:* dspencer@fisheries.org
Founded: 1870
Fisheries science, aquaculture & management materials, aquatic ecology, fisheries law, fisheries history, conservation biology & publishing.
ISBN Prefix(es): 978-0-913235; 978-1-888569; 978-1-934874
Number of titles published annually: 10 Print; 5 Online
Total Titles: 180 Print
Advertising Agency: Media West Inc, 230 Kings Hwy E, Suite 316, Haddonfield, NJ 08033 (Fisheries Magazine only), Contact: Steve West *Tel:* 856-432-1501 *Fax:* 856-494-1455 *E-mail:* steve@afs-fisheries.com

American Foundation for the Blind Press, see AFB Press

American Geophysical Union (AGU)
2000 Florida Ave NW, Washington, DC 20009
SAN: 202-4489
Tel: 202-462-6900 *Toll Free Tel:* 800-966-2481 (North America) *Fax:* 202-328-0566
E-mail: service@agu.org (cust serv); earthspacescience@agu.org
Web Site: www.agu.org
Key Personnel
SVP, Pubns: Brooks Hanson *E-mail:* bhanson@agu.org
Dir, Pubns: Jenny Lunn *E-mail:* jlunn@agu.org; Jeanette Panning *E-mail:* jpanning@agu.org
Founded: 1919
International scientific society with more than 50,000 members in over 135 countries. For over 80 years, AGU researchers, teachers & science administrators have dedicated themselves to advancing the understanding of earth & its environment in space. AGU now stands as a leader in the increasingly interdisciplinary global endeavor that encompasses the geophysical sciences.
ISBN Prefix(es): 978-0-87590
Number of titles published annually: 15 Print; 20 Online
Total Titles: 500 Print
Membership(s): AAP; Society for Scholarly Publishing

§American Geosciences Institute (AGI)
4220 King St, Alexandria, VA 22302-1502
Tel: 703-379-2480 (ext 246) *Fax:* 703-379-7563
E-mail: pubs@agiweb.org
Web Site: www.agiweb.org
Key Personnel
Exec Dir: P Patrick Leahy, PhD *Tel:* 703-379-2480 ext 202 *E-mail:* pleahy@agiweb.org
Fin & Admin Dir: Walter R Sisson *Tel:* 703-379-2480 ext 209 *E-mail:* wsisson@agiweb.org
Info Servs Dir: Sharon Tahirkheli *Tel:* 703-379-2480 ext 231 *E-mail:* snt@agiweb.org

Mktg Dir: John P Rasanen *Tel:* 703-379-2480 ext 224 *E-mail:* jr@agiweb.org
Technol & Communs Dir: Christopher Keane *Tel:* 703-379-2480 ext 219 *E-mail:* cmk@agiweb.org
Founded: 1948
Geoscience reference books.
ISBN Prefix(es): 978-0-922152; 978-0-913312; 978-1-941878
Number of titles published annually: 5 Print; 3 E-Book
Total Titles: 60 Print; 10 CD-ROM; 2 Online; 5 E-Book
Distributed by W H Freeman; It's About Time Inc; Prentice Hall
Orders to: AGI Book Center *Web Site:* www.agiweb.org/pubs

American Girl Publishing
Subsidiary of Mattel
8400 Fairway Place, Middleton, WI 53562
Mailing Address: PO Box 620497, Middleton, WI 53562-0497
Tel: 608-836-4848; 608-831-5210 (outside US & CN) *Toll Free Tel:* 800-233-0264; 800-360-1861; 800-845-0005 (US & CN) *Fax:* 608-836-1999
Web Site: www.americangirl.com
Key Personnel
Pres: Jean McKenzie
Founded: 1986
Children's fiction & nonfiction.
ISBN Prefix(es): 978-0-937295; 978-1-56247; 978-1-58485
Number of titles published annually: 40 Print; 1 CD-ROM; 6 Audio
Total Titles: 350 Print; 3 CD-ROM; 18 Audio
Imprints: A G Fiction™; American Girl Library®; The American Girls Collection®
Membership(s): The Children's Book Council

§American Historical Association (AHA)
400 "A" St SE, Washington, DC 20003
Tel: 202-544-2422 *Fax:* 202-544-8307
E-mail: aha@historians.org; awards@historians.org
Web Site: www.historians.org
Key Personnel
Exec Dir: Jim Grossman
Founded: 1884
The umbrella organization for the history profession.
ISBN Prefix(es): 978-0-87229
Number of titles published annually: 15 Print; 3 Online
Total Titles: 100 Print

American Industrial Hygiene Association - AIHA
3141 Fairview Park Dr, Suite 777, Falls Church, VA 22042
Tel: 703-849-8888 *Fax:* 703-207-3561
E-mail: infonet@aiha.org
Web Site: www.aiha.org
Key Personnel
Sr Mgr, Memb & Cust Rel: Wanda Barbour *Tel:* 703-846-0782 *E-mail:* wbarbour@aiha.org
Mgr, Prod Devt: Katie Robert *Tel:* 703-846-0738 *E-mail:* krobert@aiha.org
Founded: 1939
Serves the needs of occupational & environmental health professionals practicing industrial hygiene in industry, government, labor, academic institutions & independent organizations.
ISBN Prefix(es): 978-1-931504
Number of titles published annually: 15 Print; 15 E-Book
Total Titles: 150 Print

§American Institute for Economic Research (AIER)
250 Division St, Great Barrington, MA 01230
Mailing Address: PO Box 1000, Great Barrington, MA 01230-1000
Tel: 413-528-1216 *Toll Free Tel:* 888-528-1216 (orders)
E-mail: info@aier.org
Web Site: www.aier.org
Key Personnel
Pres & CEO: Edward Stringham
COO: John Sylbert
Libn: Suzanne Hermann *Tel:* 413-528-1216 ext 3116
Founded: 1933
Conducts independent, scientific, economic research to educate individuals, thereby advancing their personal interests & those of the nation.
ISBN Prefix(es): 978-0-913610
Number of titles published annually: 3 Print; 8 Online; 4 E-Book
Total Titles: 50 Print; 46 Online; 4 E-Book

American Institute of Aeronautics & Astronautics (AIAA)
1801 Alexander Bell Dr, Suite 500, Reston, VA 20191-4344
Tel: 703-264-7500 *Toll Free Tel:* 800-639-AIAA (639-2422) *Fax:* 703-264-7551
E-mail: custserv@aiaa.org
Web Site: www.aiaa.org
Key Personnel
Exec Dir: Dr Sandra Magnus *Tel:* 703-264-7512 *E-mail:* sandym@aiaa.org
Dir, Cust Serv: Aida Davis *E-mail:* aidad@aiaa.org
Ed-in-Chief, Aerospace America: Ben Iannotta *Tel:* 703-284-7528 *E-mail:* beni@aiaa.org
Mgr, Edit & Prodn: Craig Byl *Tel:* 703-264-7590 *E-mail:* craigb@aiaa.org
Founded: 1963
Professional technical books; archival journals & technical meeting papers in the science & technology of aerospace engineering & systems, print CD-ROMs & online delivery.
ISBN Prefix(es): 978-0-915928; 978-0-930403; 978-1-56347; 978-1-60086; 978-1-62410
Number of titles published annually: 20 Print
Total Titles: 600 Print
Foreign Rep(s): ACCUCOMS BV (Europe); ACCUCOMS India (India); ACCUCOMS MENA (Eyad Mohammad) (Middle East, North Africa); Publishers Communication Group (Rebekah Matthews) (North America, South America); Transatlantic Publishers Group (Europe)
Distribution Center: AIAA Publications Customer Service, PO Box 960, Herndon, VA 20172-0960 *Tel:* 703-661-1595 *Toll Free Tel:* 800-682-2422 *Fax:* 703-661-1501 *E-mail:* aiaamail@presswarehouse.com

American Institute of Certified Public Accountants, see AICPA Professional Publications

§American Institute of Chemical Engineers (AIChE)
120 Wall St, 23rd fl, New York, NY 10005-4020
Tel: 203-702-7660 *Toll Free Tel:* 800-242-4363 *Fax:* 203-775-5177
E-mail: customerservice@aiche.org
Web Site: www.aiche.org
Key Personnel
Pres: Otis Shelton
Exec Dir: June C Wispelwey *Tel:* 646-495-1310 *E-mail:* junew@aiche.org
Dir, Meeting & Conference Programming: Kristine Chin *Tel:* 646-495-1366 *E-mail:* krisc@aiche.org
Pubns Dir: Stephen R Smith *Tel:* 646-495-1360 *E-mail:* steps@aiche.org
Founded: 1908
Chemical engineering books & journals, technical manuals, symposia proceedings, directories, software, CD-ROM.
ISBN Prefix(es): 978-0-8169
Number of titles published annually: 15 Print; 4 CD-ROM
Total Titles: 300 Print; 4 CD-ROM
Distributed by Dechema (selected titles)
Distributor for ASM International (selected titles); Dechema (selected titles); Engineering Foundation; IchemE (selected titles)
Foreign Rep(s): Ric Bessford (Europe, UK); Patrick Connolly (Belgium, France, Switzerland)
Distribution Center: Institution of Chemical Engineers, Davis Bldg, 165-189 Railway Terr, Rugby CV21 3HQ, United Kingdom

American Institute of Physics
One Physics Ellipse, College Park, MD 20740-3843
Tel: 516-576-2200; 301-209-3165 (orders) *Fax:* 301-209-0882 (orders)
E-mail: aipinfo@aip.org
Web Site: www.aip.org
Key Personnel
CEO: John Haynes *Tel:* 516-576-2253 *E-mail:* jhaynes@aip.org
Founded: 1931
Publisher of conference proceedings, professional journals, magazines & books.
ISBN Prefix(es): 978-0-88318; 978-1-56396; 978-0-7354
Number of titles published annually: 13 Print; 8 CD-ROM; 3 Online
Total Titles: 700 Print; 200 Online
Distributed by Springer-Verlag
Membership(s): AAP

§American Law Institute
4025 Chestnut St, Philadelphia, PA 19104-3099
SAN: 204-756X
Tel: 215-243-1600 *Toll Free Tel:* 800-253-6397 *Fax:* 215-243-1664
Web Site: www.ali.org
Key Personnel
Deputy Dir: Stephanie Middleton
Founded: 1923
Professional & scholarly legal books & treatises.
ISBN Prefix(es): 978-0-8318
Number of titles published annually: 10 Print

§American Law Institute Continuing Legal Education (ALI CLE)
Affiliate of American Law Institute
4025 Chestnut St, Philadelphia, PA 19104
Tel: 215-243-1600 *Toll Free Tel:* 800-CLE-NEWS (253-6397) *Fax:* 215-243-1664; 215-243-1608
Web Site: www.ali-cle.org
Key Personnel
Deputy Dir, ALI: Stephanie Middleton
Founded: 1947 (as ALI-ABA; reconstituted as ALI CLE in 2012)
Publish law books & legal periodicals.
ISBN Prefix(es): 978-0-8318
Number of titles published annually: 2 Print; 2 Online

§The American Library Association (ALA)
50 E Huron St, Chicago, IL 60611
Tel: 312-944-6780 *Toll Free Tel:* 800-545-2433 *Fax:* 312-280-5275
E-mail: editionsmarketing@ala.org
Web Site: www.alastore.ala.org
Key Personnel
Assoc Exec Dir, Publg: Mary Mackay
Sr Ed, Lib Technol: Patrick Hogan *Tel:* 800-545-2433 ext 3240 *E-mail:* phogan@ala.org
Acqs Ed, Prof Devt & Librarianship: Jamie Santoro *Tel:* 800-545-2433 ext 5107 *E-mail:* jsantoro@ala.org

Acqs Ed, Textbooks: Rachel Chance *Tel:* 800-545-2433 ext 1548 *E-mail:* rchance@ala.org
Mktg Dir: Jill Davis *Tel:* 800-545-2433 ext 5418 *E-mail:* jdavis@ala.org
Mktg Coord: Rob Christopher *Tel:* 800-545-2433 ext 5052 *E mail:* rchristopher@ala.org
Rts & Perms: Mary Jo Bolduc *Tel:* 312-280-5416 *E-mail:* mbolduc@ala.org
Founded: 1876
Publisher of titles for librarians & educators; library & information science, professional books.
ISBN Prefix(es): 978-0-8389; 978-1-937589
Number of titles published annually: 36 Print; 1 CD-ROM; 1 Online
Total Titles: 400 Print; 2 CD-ROM; 1 Online
Imprints: ALA Neal-Schuman
Foreign Rep(s): Eurospan (Africa, Europe, Israel, UK)
Foreign Rights: Canadian Library Association (Canada); Inbooks (James Bennett) (Australia)
Orders to: ALA, PO Box 932501, Atlanta, GA 31193-2501 *Toll Free Tel:* 866-SHOP-ALA (746-7252) *Fax:* 770-280-4155 *E-mail:* ala-orders@pbd.com
Returns: ALA Distribution Center, 905 Carlow Dr, Unit B, Bolingbrook, IL 60490
See separate listing for:
ALA Neal-Schuman
Association of College & Research Libraries (ACRL)

American Map Corp
Member of Kappa Map Group
36-36 33 St, 4th fl, Long Island City, NY 11106
SAN: 202-4624
Tel: 718-784-0055 *Toll Free Tel:* 888-774-7979 *Fax:* 718-784-0640 (admin); 718-784-1216 (sales & orders)
E-mail: info@kappamapgroup.com
Web Site: www.kappamapgroup.com
Founded: 1923
Maps & atlases; charts.
ISBN Prefix(es): 978-0-8416
Number of titles published annually: 30 Print
Total Titles: 1 CD-ROM
Imprints: Cleartype American Map Corp; Colorprint American Map Corp
Subsidiaries: ADC the Map People; Arrow Maps Inc; Creative Sales Corp; Hagstrom Map Co Inc; Hammond World Atlas Corp; Trakker Maps Inc
Distributed by Arrow Maps Inc; Creative Sales Corp
Distributor for De Lorme Atlas; Kappa Map Group; RV Guides; Stubs Magazine
Advertising Agency: ATL/SD, 46-35 54 Rd, Maspeth, NY 11378, Contact: Sara Ascalon *Tel:* 718-784-0555 *Fax:* 718-784-0640 *E-mail:* sascalon@americanmap.com
See separate listing for:
Hagstrom Map

American Mathematical Society
201 Charles St, Providence, RI 02904-2294
SAN: 201-1654
Tel: 401-455-4000 *Toll Free Tel:* 800-321-4267 *Fax:* 401-331-3842; 401-455-4046 (cust serv)
E-mail: ams@ams.org; cust-serv@ams.org
Web Site: www.ams.org
Key Personnel
Exec Dir: Dr Donald E McClure
Publr: Dr Sergei Gelfand
Assoc Exec Dir: Dr Robert M Harrington
Assoc Exec Dir, Washington, DC: Samuel M Rankin, III
Founded: 1888
Membership society & publisher of mathematics.
ISBN Prefix(es): 978-0-8218; 978-0-8284; 978-1-4704
Number of titles published annually: 100 Print
Total Titles: 3,400 Print; 2 CD-ROM; 28 Online
Imprints: Chelsea Publishing Co Inc
Branch Office(s)
1527 18 St NW, Washington, DC 20036-1358 (govt rel & sci policy) *Tel:* 202-588-1100 *Fax:* 202-588-1853 *E-mail:* amsdc@ams.org
Mathematical Reviews®, 416 Fourth St, Ann Arbor, MI 48103-4820 (edit) *Tel:* 734-996-5250 *Fax:* 734-996-2916 *E-mail:* mathrev@ams.org
Secretary of the AMS - Society Governance, Dept of Computer Science, North Carolina State University, Box 8206, Raleigh, NC 27695-8206 *Tel:* 919-515-7863 *Fax:* 919-515-7896 *E-mail:* secretary@ams.org
Distributor for Annales de la faculte des sciences de Toulouse mathematiques; Bar-Ilan University; Brown University; European Mathematical Society; Hindustan Book Agency; Independent University of Moscow; International Press; Mathematica Josephina; Mathematical Society of Japan; Narosa Publishing House; Ramanujan Mathematical Society; Science Press New York & Science Press Beijing; Societe Mathematique de France; Tata Institute of Fundamental Research; Theta Foundation of Bucharest; University Press; Vieweg Verlag Publications
Foreign Rep(s): Eurospan Australia (Australia, New Zealand, Oceania); Eurospan Group (Africa, Europe, Middle East, Southeast Asia); Hindustan Book Agency (India); IBH Book & Magazines Distributors Pvt Ltd (India); Maruzen Co Ltd (Japan); Neutrino Inc (Japan); Segment Book Distributors (India)
Returns: Pawtucket Warehouse, 35 Monticello Place, Pawtucket, RI 02861
Warehouse: Pawtucket Warehouse, 35 Monticello Place, Pawtucket, RI 02861, Contact: Donald Proulx *Tel:* 401-729-4184 *Fax:* 401-728-3564 *E-mail:* dap@ams.org
Distribution Center: Pawtucket Warehouse, 35 Monticello Place, Pawtucket, RI 02861, Contact: Donald Proulx *Tel:* 401-729-4184 *Fax:* 401-728-3564 *E-mail:* dap@ams.org

American Medical Association
AMA Plaza, 330 N Wabash, Suite 39300, Chicago, IL 60611-5885
Tel: 312-464-5000 *Toll Free Tel:* 800-621-8335 *Fax:* 312-464-4184
Web Site: www.ama-assn.org
Key Personnel
CEO & EVP: James L Madara, MD
SVP & Publr, Periodic Pubns: Thomas J Easley *Tel:* 312-464-5000 ext 5740
SVP & Ed-in-Chief, Scientific Pubns: Howard C Bauchner, MD
VP/Exec Mng Ed, Edit Opers: Annette Flanagin
VP & Exec Dir, Scientific Pubns: Phil B Fontanarosa, MD
VP/Deputy Ed, Edit Graphics: Ronna Henry, MD
Founded: 1847
Medical profession.
ISBN Prefix(es): 978-0-89970; 978-1-57947; 978-1-60359; 978-1-62202
Number of titles published annually: 30 Print
Total Titles: 150 Print
Advertising Agency: GSP Marketing Services Inc
Warehouse: Catalog Resources Inc, 100 Enterprise Dr, Dover, DE 19901
Membership(s): AAP

American Numismatic Society
75 Varick St, 11th fl, New York, NY 10013
Tel: 212-571-4470 *Fax:* 212-571-4479
E-mail: ans@numismatics.org; orders@numismatics.org
Web Site: www.numismatics.org
Key Personnel
Exec Dir: Ute Wartenberg Kagan
Ad Ed, ANS Magazine: Joanne Isaac *Tel:* 212-571-4470 ext 112 *E-mail:* isaac@numismatics.org
Founded: 1858
Scholarly materials.
ISBN Prefix(es): 978-0-89722
Number of titles published annually: 5 Print
Total Titles: 100 Print

The American Occupational Therapy Association Inc (AOTA)
4720 Montgomery Lane, Suite 200, Bethesda, MD 20814-3449
Mailing Address: PO Box 31220, Bethesda, MD 20814
Tel: 301-652-6611 *Toll Free Tel:* 800-377-8555 (TDD); 877-404-AOTA (404-2682, orders) *Fax:* 301-652-7711; 770-238-0414 (orders)
E-mail: aotacustomerservice@pbd.com
Web Site: www.aota.org; store.aota.org
Key Personnel
Dir: Chris Davis *Tel:* 301-652-6611 ext 2653 *E-mail:* cdavis@aota.org
Founded: 1918
Single titles, newsletters, journals & magazines.
ISBN Prefix(es): 978-0-910317; 978-1-56900
Number of titles published annually: 25 Print
Total Titles: 150 Print
Orders to: PO Box 347036, Pittsburgh, PA 15251-4036

American Oil Chemists' Society, see AOCS Press

American Philosophical Society
104 S Fifth St, Philadelphia, PA 19106
SAN: 206-9016
Tel: 215-440-3425 *Fax:* 215-440-3450
E-mail: orders@dianepublishing.net
Web Site: www.amphilsoc.org
Key Personnel
Pres: Clyde F Barker
Exec Offr: Keith Thomson
Ed: Mary McDonald *E-mail:* mmcdonald@amphilsoc.org
Founded: 1743
Nonprofit educational institution for promotion of useful knowledge in humanities & sciences.
ISBN Prefix(es): 978-0-87169; 978-1-60618
Number of titles published annually: 13 Print
Total Titles: 1,100 Print
Imprints: Lightning Rod Press; Memoirs; Proceedings; Transactions
Distributed by Diane Publishing Co
Billing Address: Diane Publishing Co, APS Fulfillment, 330 Pusey Ave, Unit 3 (rear), Collingdale, PA 19023 *Tel:* 610-461-6200 *Toll Free Tel:* 800-782-3833 *Fax:* 610-461-6130 *E-mail:* orders@dianepublishing.net
Orders to: Diane Publishing Co, APS Fulfillment, 330 Pusey Ave, Unit 3 (rear), Collingdale, PA 19023 *Tel:* 610-461-6200 *Toll Free Tel:* 800-782-3833 *Fax:* 610-461-6130 *E-mail:* orders@dianepublishing.net
Warehouse: Diane Publishing Co, Contact: Herman Baron *Tel:* 610-461-6200 *Toll Free Tel:* 800-782-3833

American Press
60 State St, Suite 700, Boston, MA 02109
SAN: 210-7007
Tel: 617-247-0022
E-mail: americanpress@flash.net
Web Site: www.americanpresspublishers.com
Key Personnel
Publr: R K Fox
Ed: Marci Taylor
Founded: 1911
College textbooks, study guides, lab manuals & handbooks.
ISBN Prefix(es): 978-0-89641
Number of titles published annually: 20 Print
Total Titles: 300 Print

§American Printing House for the Blind Inc
1839 Frankfort Ave, Louisville, KY 40206
SAN: 203-5235

Mailing Address: PO Box 6085, Louisville, KY 40206-0085
Tel: 502-895-2405 *Toll Free Tel:* 800-223-1839 (cust serv) *Fax:* 502-899-2274
E-mail: info@aph.org
Web Site: www.aph.org; shop.aph.org
Key Personnel
Pres: Craig Meador *E-mail:* cmeador@aph.org
VP, Pub Aff: Gary Mudd *E-mail:* gmudd@aph.org
PR Mgr: Rebecca Snider *Tel:* 502-899-2357 *E-mail:* rsnider@aph.org
Founded: 1858
Literature & aids for people who are visually impaired: braille text books, magazines & other items, large-type textbooks, talking books & magazines, educational & miscellaneous aids, talking PC hardware & software. Publisher of braille & reprints in braille.
ISBN Prefix(es): 978-1-61648
Number of titles published annually: 4,500 Print
Total Titles: 6,300 Print

American Products Publishing Co
Division of American Products Corp
8260 SW Nimbus Ave, Beaverton, OR 97008
Tel: 503-672-7502 *Toll Free Tel:* 800-668-8181 *Fax:* 503-672-7104
E-mail: info@american-products.com
Web Site: www.american-products.com
Key Personnel
Pres: Robert Shangle
VP: Barbara Shangle *E-mail:* barbara@american-products.com
Sales Mgr: David Mulder
Publisher of scenic books & wall calendars for the individual US states, American historic documents, books & prints.
ISBN Prefix(es): 978-1-58583; 978-1-884958; 978-1-55988
Number of titles published annually: 16 Print; 72 Online
Total Titles: 72 Print; 72 Online
Membership(s): ABA

§American Psychiatric Association Publishing
Division of American Psychiatric Association (APA)
1000 Wilson Blvd, Suite 1825, Arlington, VA 22209
SAN: 293-2288
Tel: 703-907-7322 *Toll Free Tel:* 800-368-5777 *Fax:* 703-907-1091
E-mail: appi@psych.org
Web Site: www.appi.org; www.psychiatryonline.org
Key Personnel
Publr: Rebecca D Rinehart *E-mail:* rrinehart@psych.org
Dir, Sales & Mktg: Patrick Hansard *E-mail:* phansard@psych.org
Edit Dir: John McDuffie *Tel:* 703-907-7871 *E-mail:* jmcduffie@psych.org
Edit Dir, American Journal of Psychiatry: Michael Roy
Ed-in-Chief, Books: Laura Weiss Roberts, MD
Mng Ed, Books: Greg Kuny
Opers Mgr: Debra Eubanks
Founded: 1981
Professional, reference & general trade books, college textbooks; behavioral & social sciences, psychiatry, medicine.
ISBN Prefix(es): 978-0-88048; 978-0-89042; 978-0-87318; 978-1-58562; 978-1-61537
Number of titles published annually: 30 Print; 40 Online; 30 E-Book
Total Titles: 750 Print; 3 CD-ROM; 300 Online; 350 E-Book; 1 Audio
Distributor for American Psychiatric Association (APA); Group for the Advancement of Psychiatry
Foreign Rep(s): CBS Publishers (India); Cranbury International (Latin America); Eurospan (Central Asia, China, East Asia, Singapore, South Korea); Footprint Books Pty Ltd (Australia, New Zealand); International Publishers Representatives (Africa, Middle East); Login Canada (Canada); Nankodo (Japan); NBN International (Europe, UK); Oxford University Press (Southern Africa)
Foreign Rights: John Scott Agency
Warehouse: Ware-Pak, 2427 Bond St, University Park, IL 60484-3170
Membership(s): AAP; American Association of University Presses

American Psychological Association
750 First St NE, Washington, DC 20002-4242
Tel: 202-336-5510 *Toll Free Tel:* 800-374-2721 *Fax:* 202-336-5502
E-mail: order@apa.org
Web Site: www.apa.org/books
Key Personnel
Exec Publr: Jasper Simons
Publr, APA Books: Brenda Carter
Sr Dir, Prod Mgmt: Aaron Wood
Founded: 1892
Publish scholarly & professional works including books, journals & related materials; the PsycINFO® database & products derived from that database; the *APA Monitor*, a monthly magazine & a variety of other products including brochures & reports.
ISBN Prefix(es): 978-0-912704; 978-1-55798; 978-0-945354; 978-0-9792125; 978-1-59147; 978-1-4338
Number of titles published annually: 65 Print
Total Titles: 700 Print
Imprints: APA Books®
Warehouse: APA Order Dept, PO Box 92984, Washington, DC 20090-2984

American Public Works Association (APWA)
2345 Grand Blvd, Suite 700, Kansas City, MO 64108-2625
Tel: 816-472-6100 *Toll Free Tel:* 800-848-APWA (848-2792) *Fax:* 816-472-1610
Web Site: www.apwa.net
Key Personnel
Pubns Mgr: Connie Hartline *Tel:* 816-595-5258 *E-mail:* chartline@apwa.net
Ed, APWA Reporter: Kevin Clark *Tel:* 816-595-5230 *E-mail:* kclark@apwa.net
Founded: 1894
Public work related publications. Also publishes *APWA Reporter* magazine.
ISBN Prefix(es): 978-0-917084; 978-1-60675
Number of titles published annually: 12 Print
Total Titles: 12 Print
Branch Office(s)
1275 "K" St NW, Suite 750, Washington, DC 20005 *Tel:* 202-408-9541 *Fax:* 202-408-9542

American Quilter's Society
5801 Kentucky Dam Rd, Paducah, KY 42003-9323
Mailing Address: PO Box 3290, Paducah, KY 42002-3290
Tel: 270-898-7903 *Toll Free Tel:* 800-626-5420 (orders) *Fax:* 270-898-1173
E-mail: orders@americanquilter.com
Web Site: www.americanquilter.com
Key Personnel
Co-Founder & Pres: Meredith Schroeder
Mktg Dir: Katherine Rupp
Founded: 1983
Publish books & magazines, distributes books & operates quilting shows.
ISBN Prefix(es): 978-0-89145; 978-1-57432; 978-1-60460
Number of titles published annually: 20 Print; 10 CD-ROM; 4 E-Book
Total Titles: 300 Print; 20 CD-ROM; 7 E-Book
Imprints: AQS

American Society for Nondestructive Testing
1711 Arlingate Lane, Columbus, OH 43228-0518
Mailing Address: PO Box 28518, Columbus, OH 43228-0518
Tel: 614-274-6003 *Toll Free Tel:* 800-222-2768 *Fax:* 614-274-6899
Web Site: www.asnt.org
Key Personnel
Sr Mgr, Pubns: Tim Jones *Tel:* 614-274-6003 ext 204 *E-mail:* tjones@asnt.org
Founded: 1941
Nonprofit association producing educational materials for members & nonmembers engaged in nondestructive testing.
ISBN Prefix(es): 978-0-931403; 978-1-57117
Number of titles published annually: 12 Print; 6 CD-ROM
Total Titles: 250 Print; 6 CD-ROM
Distributed by American Ceramic Society (ACerS); American Society for Mechanical Engineers (ASME); American Society for Metals (ASM); The American Welding Society (AWS); ASTM; Edison Welding Institute; Mean Free Path

§American Society for Quality (ASQ)
600 N Plankinton Ave, Milwaukee, WI 53203
Mailing Address: PO Box 3005, Milwaukee, WI 53201-3005
Tel: 414-272-8575 *Toll Free Tel:* 800-248-1946 (US & CN); 800-514-1564 (Mexico) *Fax:* 414-272-1734
E-mail: help@asq.org
Web Site: www.asq.org
Key Personnel
Proj Ed: Paul O'Mara
Founded: 1983
Publisher of technical books: quality, statistical process control, ISO9000, six sigma, QS9000, ISO14000, statistics, reliability, auditing, sampling, standards' supplier quality & quality costs. Also management topics: total quality management, human resources & teamwork, health care, government, education & benchmarking, quality tools.
ISBN Prefix(es): 978-0-87389
Number of titles published annually: 25 Print; 5 E-Book
Total Titles: 300 Print; 5 CD-ROM; 15 E-Book
Distributed by GOAL/QPC; IEEE Computer Society Press; McGraw-Hill Professional Publishing; Productivity Press
Distribution Center: PBD Worldwide Inc, 905 Carlow Dr, Unit B, Bolingbrook, IL 60490

§American Society of Agricultural & Biological Engineers (ASABE)
2950 Niles Rd, St Joseph, MI 49085-9659
Tel: 269-429-0300 *Toll Free Tel:* 800-371-2723 *Fax:* 269-429-3852
E-mail: hq@asabe.org
Web Site: www.asabe.org
Key Personnel
Exec Dir: Darrin Drollinger *Tel:* 269-932-7007 *E-mail:* drollinger@asabe.org
Dir, Pubns: Joe Walker *Tel:* 269-932-7026 *E-mail:* walker@asabe.org
Book & Journal Ed: Peg McCann *Tel:* 269-932-7019 *E-mail:* mccann@asabe.org
Journal Ed: Glenn Laing *Tel:* 269-932-7014 *E-mail:* laing@asabe.org; Melissa Miller *Tel:* 269-932-7017 *E-mail:* miller@asabe.org
Pubns Asst: Sandy Rutter *Tel:* 269-932-7004 *E-mail:* rutter@asabe.org
Founded: 1907
Agricultural, biological & food systems, books & journals.
ISBN Prefix(es): 978-0-916150; 978-0-929355; 978-1-892769
Number of titles published annually: 4 Print
Total Titles: 150 Print; 1 CD-ROM; 2 Online

American Society of Agronomy
5585 Guilford Rd, Madison, WI 53711-5801
Tel: 608-273-8080 *Fax:* 608-273-2021
E-mail: headquarters@sciencesocieties.org
Web Site: www.agronomy.org
Key Personnel
CEO: Ellen Bergfeld *Tel:* 608-268-4979
E-mail: ebergfeld@sciencesocieties.org
Dir, Pubns: Mark Mandelbaum *Tel:* 608-268-4974
E-mail: mmandelbaum@sciencesocieties.org
Founded: 1907
Technical books for professionals in agronomy; crop science, soil science, environmental sciences & related fields.
ISBN Prefix(es): 978-0-89118
Number of titles published annually: 12 Print
Total Titles: 90 Print

§American Society of Civil Engineers (ASCE)
1801 Alexander Bell Dr, Reston, VA 20191-4400
SAN: 204-7594
Tel: 703-295-6300 *Toll Free Tel:* 800-548-2723
Fax: 703-295-6278
E-mail: ascelibrary@asce.org
Web Site: www.asce.org
Key Personnel
Mng Dir, Pubns: Bruce Gossett *Tel:* 703-295-6311 *E-mail:* bgossett@asce.org
Dir, Busn Opers: Gina Lindquist
E-mail: glindquist@asce.org
Dir, Journals: Angela Cochran *Tel:* 703-295-6242
E-mail: acochran@asce.org
Dir, Mktg: William Nara *E-mail:* wnara@asce.org
Dir, Prodn: Matt Boyle *Tel:* 703-295-6241
E-mail: mboyle@asce.org
Dir, Publg Technol: Charlotte McNaughton
E-mail: cmcnaughton@asce.org
Founded: 1852
Books, technical journals, information products on civil engineering & related fields; online & print.
ISBN Prefix(es): 978-0-87262; 978-0-7844
Number of titles published annually: 60 Print; 25 E-Book
Total Titles: 1,400 Print; 425 E-Book
Imprints: ASCE Press
Foreign Rep(s): Aditya Books (P) Ltd (India); Allied Book Co (Pakistan); Apex Knowledge Sdn Bhd (Brunei, Malaysia); Areesh Education & Trading Sdn Bhd (Brunei, Malaysia); Booknet Co Ltd (Cambodia, Laos, Myanmar, Thailand, Vietnam); Capital Books Pvt Ltd Delhi (India); ChoiceTEXTS (Asia) Pte Ltd (Philip Ang) (Indonesia, Singapore); Eurospan Group (Africa, Continental Europe, Middle East, UK); IBH Books & Magazines Distributors Ltd (India); ICaves Ltd (China, Hong Kong, Macau); IDC Asia (iGroup Korea) (D J Kim) (Korea); MegaTEXTS Phil Inc (Philippines); Multi-Line Books (Pakistan); Shankar's Book Agency Pvt Ltd (India); Taiwan Publishers Marketing Services Ltd (Taiwan)

American Society of Electroneurodiagnostic Technologists Inc, see ASET - The Neurodiagnostic Society

§American Society of Health-System Pharmacists (ASHP)
4500 East-West Hwy, Suite 900, Bethesda, MD 20814
Tel: 301-657-3000; 301-664-8700
Toll Free Tel: 866-279-0681 (orders) *Fax:* 301-657-1251 (orders)
E-mail: custserv@ashp.org
Web Site: www.ashp.org
Key Personnel
Mktg Mgr: Rachel Gellman
Founded: 1943
Medical scholarly books.
ISBN Prefix(es): 978-0-930530; 978-1-879907; 978-1-58528
Number of titles published annually: 20 Print
Total Titles: 115 Print
Foreign Rep(s): APAC (Asia); L Horvath (Eastern Europe); LPR (Middle East); LR International (Brazil); R Seshadri (India)
Advertising Agency: Cunningham Associates, 180 Old Tappan Rd, Old Tappan, NJ 07675, Contact: Jim Pattis *Tel:* 201-767-4170
E-mail: jpattis@cunnasso.com

§American Society of Mechanical Engineers (ASME)
2 Park Ave, New York, NY 10016-5990
SAN: 201-1379
Tel: 212-591-7000 *Toll Free Tel:* 800-843-2763 (cust serv-US, CN & Mexico) *Fax:* 212-591-7674; 973-882-8113 (cust serv); 973-882-1717 (orders & inquiries)
E-mail: infocentral@asme.org
Web Site: www.asme.org
Key Personnel
Exec Dir: Thomas G Loughlin
E-mail: execdirector@asme.org
Mng Dir, Mktg & Online Servs: Peter Hess
Mng Dir, Publg: Philip DiVietro *Tel:* 212-591-7696 *Fax:* 212-591-7292 *E-mail:* divietrop@asme.org
Dir, Media Sales & Publg Devt: Nick Ferrari
E-mail: ferrarin@asme.org
Ad Promo Mgr: Anthony Asiaghi *Tel:* 212-591-7345 *Fax:* 212-591-7841 *E-mail:* asiaghia@asme.org
Mgr, Corp Devt: Paul Francis *Tel:* 973-244-2304
E-mail: francisp@asme.org
Mktg & Quality Assurance: John Yelavich
E-mail: yelavichj@asme.org
Founded: 1880
Publisher of codes & standards, journals, conference proceedings, professional references, *Mechanical Engineering* magazine, technical papers & reports.
ISBN Prefix(es): 978-0-7918
Number of titles published annually: 185 Print
Total Titles: 1,500 Print
Imprints: ASME Press
Branch Office(s)
1828 "L" St NW, Suite 810, Washington, DC 20036-5104 *Tel:* 202-785-3756 *Fax:* 202-429-9417 *E-mail:* grdept@asme.org
Warehouse: 150 Clove Rd, Little Falls, NJ 07424-2100 *Tel:* 973-882-1170

American Society of Plant Taxonomists
University of Wyoming, Dept of Botany 3165, 1000 E University Ave, Laramie, WY 82071
SAN: 282-969X
Tel: 307-766-2556 *Fax:* 307-766-2851
E-mail: aspt@uwyo.edu
Web Site: www.aspt.net
Key Personnel
Contact: Linda Brown
Founded: 1980
Botanical monographs.
ISBN Prefix(es): 978-0-912861
Number of titles published annually: 3 Print
Total Titles: 102 Print

American Technical Publishers Inc
10100 Orland Pkwy, Suite 200, Orland Park, IL 60467-5756
SAN: 206-8141
Toll Free Tel: 800-323-3471 *Fax:* 708-957-1101
E-mail: service@atplearning.com; order@atplearning.com
Web Site: www.atplearning.com
Key Personnel
Pres: Robert D Deisinger *E-mail:* robert.deisinger@atplearning.com
SVP: J David Holloway *E-mail:* david.holloway@atplearning.com
Ed-in-Chief: Jonathan F Gosse *E-mail:* jonathan.gosse@atplearning.com
Founded: 1898
Technical, industrial & vocational textbooks, reference books & related materials.
ISBN Prefix(es): 978-0-8269
Number of titles published annually: 8 Print; 2 CD-ROM; 25 Online; 3 E-Book
Total Titles: 200 Print; 10 CD-ROM; 25 Online; 3 E-Book
Distributor for Craftsman Book Co
Orders to: Nelson Publishing, 1120 Birchmount Rd, Toronto, ON M1K 5G4, Canada (CN school orders) *Tel:* 416-752-9448 *Toll Free Tel:* 800-268-2222
Returns: 1155 W 175 St, Homewood, IL 60430, Contact: Gail Prohaska *E-mail:* gail.prohaska@atplearning.com

American Traveler Press, see Golden West Cookbooks

§American Water Works Association (AWWA)
6666 W Quincy Ave, Denver, CO 80235
Tel: 303-794-7711 *Toll Free Tel:* 800-926-7337
Fax: 303-347-0804
E-mail: service@awwa.org (cust serv)
Web Site: www.awwa.org
Key Personnel
Deputy CEO: Paula I MacIlwaine *Tel:* 303-347-6135 *Fax:* 303-795-1440
Dir of Pubns: Zsolt Silberer
Founded: 1881
Water works technology & management.
ISBN Prefix(es): 978-0-89867; 978-1-58321; 978-1-61300; 978-1-62576
Number of titles published annually: 50 Print
Total Titles: 500 Print; 12 CD-ROM; 2 Online
Imprints: AWWA
Distributor for CRC Press; McGraw-Hill; John Wiley & Sons
Foreign Rep(s): Australian Water Association (Australia); Canadian Water & Wastewater Association (Canada)
Membership(s): Association Media & Publishing; Publishers Association of the West

§Amherst Media Inc
PO Box 538, Buffalo, NY 14213
Tel: 716-874-4450
E-mail: marketing@amherstmedia.com
Web Site: www.amherstmedia.com
Key Personnel
Owner, Pres & Publr: Craig Alesse
Assoc Publr: Kathryn Kingsbury Neaverth
E-mail: kneaverth@amherstmedia.com
Founded: 1979
Publisher of photography books & more.
ISBN Prefix(es): 978-0-936262; 978-1-58428
Number of titles published annually: 36 Print; 24 E-Book
Total Titles: 500 Print; 500 E-Book
Foreign Rep(s): Peribo Pty Ltd (Australia, New Zealand); Publishers Group West (PGW) (worldwide exc Australia, Ireland, New Zealand & UK); Turnaround Publisher Services (Ireland, UK)
Foreign Rights: Publishers Group West (PGW) (worldwide)
Distribution Center: Publishers Group West (PGW), 1700 Fourth St, Berkeley, CA 94710 *Tel:* 510-809-3700 *Fax:* 510-809-3777
E-mail: info@pgw.com *Web Site:* www.pgw.com
Peribo Pty Ltd, 58 Beaumont Rd, Mount Kuring-gai NSW 2080, Australia *Tel:* (02) 9457 0011 *Fax:* (02) 9457 0022 *E-mail:* info@peribo.com.au *Web Site:* www.peribo.com.au
Turnaround Publisher Services, Unit 3, Olympia Trading Estate, Coburg Rd, Wood Green, London N22 6TZ, United Kingdom *Tel:* (020) 8829 3002 *E-mail:* customercare@turnaround-uk.com *Web Site:* www.turnaround-uk.com

Amicus
PO Box 1329, Mankato, MN 56002
Tel: 507-388-9357 *Fax:* 507-388-1779
E-mail: info@amicuspublishing.us; orders@amicuspublishing.us
Web Site: www.amicuspublishing.us
Key Personnel
Publr: Rebecca Glaser *E-mail:* rglaser@amicuspublishing.us
Dir, Opers: Cathy Stuve *E-mail:* cstuve@amicuspublishing.us
Sales Mgr: Dave Schlichte
Founded: 2010
Promotes the wonder, diversity & challenges of the modern world. From our line for grades K-2 to career advice & healthy living for middle school & everything in between, you'll find library-bound books that not only inform but also move readers past passive reading into critical thinking & deeper understanding.
ISBN Prefix(es): 978-1-60753
Number of titles published annually: 150 Print
Total Titles: 450 Print
Imprints: Amicus Ink
Distribution Center: Saunders Book Co, PO Box 308, Collingwood, ON L9Y 3Z7, Canada (CN only) *Tel:* 705-445-4777 *Toll Free Tel:* 800-461-9120 *Fax:* 705-445-9569 *Toll Free Fax:* 800-561-1763 *E-mail:* info@saundersbooks.ca

AMMO Books LLC
5022 N Eagle Rock Blvd, Los Angeles, CA 90041
Mailing Address: PO Box 412402, Los Angeles, CA 90041
Tel: 323-223-AMMO (223-2666) *Fax:* 323-978-4200
E-mail: weborders@ammobooks.com; orders@ammobooks.com
Web Site: ammobooks.com
Key Personnel
Co-Founder & Pres: Paul Norton *E-mail:* paul@ammobooks.com
Publr: Steve Crist
Founded: 2006
Provocative, one-of-a-kind titles that highlight the best of the visual arts & pop culture.
ISBN Prefix(es): 978-0-9786076; 978-1-934429; 978-1-62326
Number of titles published annually: 50 Print

§Ampersand Inc/Professional Publishing Services
515 Madison St, New Orleans, LA 70116
Tel: 312-280-8905 *Fax:* 312-944-1582
E-mail: info@ampersandworks.com
Web Site: www.ampersandworks.com
Key Personnel
Pres & Publr: Suzanne Talbot Isaacs *E-mail:* suzie@ampersandworks.com
Founded: 1995 (began publishing in 2005)
Private publisher. Work is highly customized, tailored to the author's specific objectives & developed by professionals with over 30 years of publishing experience. Able to publish from ms to finished book in a matter of weeks, on time & on budget. Also supports marketing efforts, warehouse & distributes authors' books.
This publisher has indicated that 90% of their product line is author subsidized.
ISBN Prefix(es): 978-1-4507; 978-0-9818126; 978-0-9761235; 978-0-873671; 978-1-4675; 978-0-9962525
Number of titles published annually: 10 Print; 5 E-Book
Total Titles: 53 Print; 19 E-Book
Branch Office(s)
203 Finland Place, New Orleans, LA 70131
Foreign Rights: Laurie Blum Guest
Membership(s): Association of Independent Authors; The Association of Publishers for Special Sales; Independent Book Publishers Association; Society of Children's Book Writers & Illustrators

Anaphora Literary Press
1898 Athens St, Brownsville, TX 78520
Tel: 470-289-6395
Web Site: anaphoraliterary.com
Key Personnel
Dir: Dr Anna Faktorovich *E-mail:* director@anaphoraliterary.com
Founded: 2009
Publisher of paperback, hardcover & ebook originals in poetry, short stories, novels & nonfiction critical, academic & business. Anaphora has released books by best-selling/award-winning novelists like Bob Van Laerhoven, academic books by Ivy League professors & works by innovative new writers. 50/50% split of royalties. Only e-mailed submissions with the ms, bio, summary & marketing plan will be accepted. Anaphora helps with marketing by designing releases & exhibiting titles at conventions like ALA/SIBA.
ISBN Prefix(es): 978-1-937536; 978-1-68114
Number of titles published annually: 50 Print; 6 Online; 50 E-Book
Total Titles: 200 Print; 26 Online; 170 E-Book
Distribution Center: Coutts Information Services Ltd, 3 Ingram Blvd, La Vergne, TN 37086 SAN: 169-5401
Lightning Source, 1246 Heil Quaker Blvd, La Vergne, TN 37086
Membership(s): Community of Literary Magazines & Presses; Independent Book Publishers Association; Independent Book Publishing Professionals Group; MLA

Anchor Books
Imprint of Knopf Doubleday Publishing Group
c/o Penguin Random House Inc, 1745 Broadway, New York, NY 10019
Tel: 212-572-2420
E-mail: vintageanchorpublicity@randomhouse.com
Web Site: knopfdoubleday.com/imprint/anchor
Key Personnel
EVP & Publr: Anne Messitte
SVP & Edit Dir: Luann Walther
VP & Assoc Publr: Beth Lamb
VP & Exec Dir, Publicity & Soc Media: Russell Perreault
VP & Exec Ed: Edward Kastenmeier
Design Dir: Claudia Martinez
Dir, Ad & Promo: Irena Vukov-Kendes
Dir, Digital Mktg: Paige Smith
Dir, Digital Publg & Busn Devt: Laura Crisp
Dir, Publicity: Kate Runde
Mng Ed: Barbara Richard
Sr Ed: Lexy Bloom
Ed: Margaux Weisman
Publicity Mgr: Angie Venezia
Founded: 1953
ISBN Prefix(es): 978-0-385; 978-0-7679; 978-0-307; 978-1-4000
Number of titles published annually: 175 Print; 190 E-Book
Total Titles: 2,650 Print; 1,750 E-Book
Foreign Rights: Anthea Agency (Katalina Sabeva) (Bulgaria); Bardon-Chinese Media Agency (Xu Weiguang) (China); Bardon-Chinese Media Agency (Yu Shiuan Chen & David Tsai) (Taiwan); The English Agency (Hamish Macaskill & Junzo Sawa) (Japan); Graal Literary Agency (Maria Strarz-Kanska) (Poland); The Deborah Harris Agency (Ilana Kurshan) (Israel); JLM Literary Agency (Nelly Moukakou) (Greece); Katai & Bolza Literary (Peter Bolza) (Croatia, Hungary, Serbia); Simona Kessler Agency (Simona Kessler) (Romania); Korea Copyright Center (MiSook Hong) (Korea); Licht & Burr Literary Agency (Trine Licht) (Scandinavia); La Nouvelle Agence (Vanessa Kling) (France); Kristin Olson Literary Agency (Kristin Olson) (Czech Republic); Agenzia Letteraria Santachiara (Roberto Santachiara) (Italy); Sebes & Bisseling Literary Agency (Holland)

Anchor Group Publishing
PO Box 551, Flushing, MI 48433
E-mail: anchorgrouppublishing@gmail.com
Web Site: anchorgrouppublishing.com
Key Personnel
Owner & CEO: Stacey Rourke
Founded: 2012
Independently owned, traditional publisher of quality literary works meant to engage & inspire readers.
ISBN Prefix(es): 978-0-9852663; 978-0-9855385; 978-0-9886334; 978-0-9882707; 978-0-9888476; 978-0-9891753; 978-0-9897073; 978-0-9915174
Number of titles published annually: 15 Print; 15 Online; 15 E-Book
Total Titles: 30 Print; 30 Online; 30 E-Book
Membership(s): Independent Book Publishers Association

Ancient Faith Publishing
Division of Ancient Faith Ministries
2747 Bond St, University Park, IL 60484
Mailing Address: PO Box 748, Chesterton, IN 46304
Tel: 219-728-2216 *Toll Free Tel:* 800-967-7377 *Toll Free Fax:* 866-599-5208
E-mail: info@ancientfaith.com; orders@ancientfaith.com
Web Site: www.ancientfaith.com/publishing
Key Personnel
CEO: John Maddex *E-mail:* jmaddex@ancientfaith.com
Edit Dir: Katherine Hyde *E-mail:* khyde@ancientfaith.com
Mktg Dir: Matthew Dorning *E-mail:* mdorning@consiliarmedia.com
Prodn Mgr: Carla Zell *E-mail:* czell@ancientfaith.com
Founded: 1978
Books, booklets, brochures, greeting cards, icons, liturgical & quarterly magazines.
ISBN Prefix(es): 978-0-9622713; 978-0-888212; 978-0-9822770; 978-1-936270
Number of titles published annually: 12 Print
Total Titles: 120 Print
Distributed by Light & Life; St Vladimir's
Distributor for Light & Life
Foreign Rights: Rainbow Books (Australia)

Sara Anderson Children's Books
PO Box 47182, Seattle, WA 98146
Tel: 206-285-1520
Web Site: www.saranderson.com
Key Personnel
Founder & CEO: Sara Anderson *E-mail:* sara@saranderson.com
Founded: 2008
Specialize in colorful, innovatively designed early-concept books for babies & toddlers, picture books & a line of bilingual (Spanish-English) children's books.
ISBN Prefix(es): 978-0-9702784; 978-0-9911933; 978-1-943459
Number of titles published annually: 5 Print
Total Titles: 18 Print

§Andrews McMeel Publishing LLC
Division of Andrews McMeel Universal
1130 Walnut St, Kansas City, MO 64106-2109
Toll Free Tel: 800-851-8923; 800-943-9839 (cust serv) *Toll Free Fax:* 800-943-9831 (orders)
Web Site: www.andrewsmcmeel.com
Key Personnel
Chmn, Andrews McMeel Universal: John P McMeel

VChmn, Andrews McMeel Universal: Hugh Andrews
Pres, Book Div: Kirsty Melville
VP & Creative Dir, Calendars & Greeting Cards: Michael Nonbello
VP, Mktg, Book Div: Kathy Hilliard
Ed: Allison Adler
Founded: 1973
Publish calendars & humor.
ISBN Prefix(es): 978-0-8362; 978-88-7407; 978-1-4494
Number of titles published annually: 300 Print
Imprints: Accord Publishing; Udig (ebooks)
Distributor for Gooseberry Patch (North America); Signatures Network; Sporting News; Universe Publishing Calendars; Vegan Heritage Press
Foreign Rights: Big Apple Agency Inc (China, Taiwan); The Book Publishers' Association of Israel, International Promotion & Literary Rights Department (Israel); DS Druck und Verlag (Eastern Europe); Europa Press (Scandinavia); Gamma Medya Agency (Turkey); The Italian Literary Agency srl (Italy); Japan UNI Agency Inc (Japan); JLM Literary Agents (Greece); Korea Copyright Center Inc (KCC) (Korea); Andrew Nurnberg Associates Ltd (Bulgaria); Abner Stein Agency (Australia, UK); Tuttle-Mori Agency Inc (Thailand); VVV Agency (France); Julio F Yanez Agencia Literaria SL (Brazil, Latin America, Portugal, Spain)
Orders to: c/o Simon & Schuster Inc, 100 Front St, Riverside, NJ 08075 *Toll Free Tel:* 800-943-9839 (US orders); 800-268-3216 (CN orders)
Returns: Simon & Schuster, c/o Jacobson Logistics, 4406 Industrial Park Rd, Bldg 7, Camp Hill, PA 17011; c/o Georgetown Terminal Warehouses, 34 B Armstrong Ave, Georgetown, ON L7G 4R9, Canada
Distribution Center: Simon & Schuster, Inc, 100 Front St, Riverside, NJ 08075 *Toll Free Tel:* 800-943-9839 (US orders); 800-268-3216 (CN orders)
Vearsa, 79 Madison Ave, New York, NY 10016 (digital dist) *Tel:* 646-568-7797 *E-mail:* info@vearsa.com *Web Site:* www.vearsa.com

Andrews University Press
Division of Andrews University
Sutherland House, 8360 W Campus Circle Dr, Berrien Springs, MI 49104-1700
SAN: 241-0958
Tel: 269-471-6134 *Toll Free Tel:* 800-467-6369 (Visa, MC & American Express orders only) *Fax:* 269-471-6224
E-mail: aupo@andrews.edu; aup@andrews.edu; aupress@andrews.edu
Web Site: www.universitypress.andrews.edu
Key Personnel
Dir: Ronald Knott *E-mail:* knott@andrews.edu
Edit & Mktg Coord: Scottie Baker *Tel:* 269-471-6133 *E-mail:* aup@andrews.edu
Ed: Deborah L Everhart *E-mail:* aupress@andrews.edu
Selected areas of theology, education, philosophy, science, faith & learning.
ISBN Prefix(es): 978-0-943872; 978-1-883925; 978-1-936337; 978-1-940980
Number of titles published annually: 7 Print
Total Titles: 100 Print; 1 CD-ROM; 1 Online

Angel City Press
2118 Wilshire Blvd, Suite 880, Santa Monica, CA 90403
Tel: 310-395-9982 *Toll Free Tel:* 800-949-8039 *Fax:* 310-395-3353
E-mail: info@angelcitypress.com
Web Site: www.angelcitypress.com
Key Personnel
Publr & CEO: Paddy Calistro
Publr & Treas: Scott McAuley
Founded: 1993
Publish books on California & Southern California social & cultural history.
ISBN Prefix(es): 978-1-883318; 978-1-62640
Number of titles published annually: 8 Print
Total Titles: 100 Print
Foreign Rep(s): Turnaround Publishing Services (London)

§Angelus Press
2915 Forest Ave, Kansas City, MO 64109
Mailing Address: PO Box 217, St Marys, KS 66536
Tel: 816-753-3150 *Toll Free Tel:* 800-966-7337 *Fax:* 816-753-3557
E-mail: support@angeluspress.org
Web Site: www.angeluspress.org
Key Personnel
Ed: James Vogel
Founded: 1978
Monthly journal of Catholic Tradition; traditional Roman Catholic books.
ISBN Prefix(es): 978-0-935952; 978-1-892331; 978-1-937843
Number of titles published annually: 10 Print
Total Titles: 100 Print
Imprints: Sarto House
Branch Office(s)
907 E Jesuit Lane, St Marys, KS 66536 *E-mail:* accounts@angeluspress.org
Distributed by Catholic Treasures; Fatima Crusader

Anhinga Press
PO Box 3665, Tallahassee, FL 32315
Tel: 850-577-0745
E-mail: info@anhinga.org
Web Site: www.anhingapress.org; www.facebook.com/anhingapress
Key Personnel
Dir: Kristine Snodgrass *E-mail:* kristine.snodgrass@gmail.com
Founded: 1972
ISBN Prefix(es): 978-0-938078; 978-1-934695
Number of titles published annually: 8 Print
Total Titles: 70 Print
Distribution Center: SPD/Small Press Distribution Inc, 1341 Seventh St, Berkeley, CA 94710-1409 *Tel:* 510-524-1668 *Toll Free Tel:* 800-869-7553 *E-mail:* spd@spdbooks.org *Web Site:* www.spdbooks.org

Animal Media Group LLC
Subsidiary of Animal Inc
100 First Ave, Suite 1100, Pittsburgh, PA 15222-1519
Tel: 412-566-5656 *Fax:* 412-566-5656
E-mail: info@animalmediagroup.com
Web Site: www.animalmediagroup.com
Key Personnel
Dir, Publg: Howard Shapiro
Founded: 2012
ISBN Prefix(es): 978-0-9912550
Number of titles published annually: 4 Print; 4 Online; 4 E-Book
Total Titles: 12 Print; 10 Online; 4 E-Book
Distribution Center: Consortium Book Sales & Distribution, The Keg House, 34 13 Ave, Suite 101, Minneapolis, MN 55413-1007

Annual Reviews
4139 El Camino Way, Palo Alto, CA 94306
SAN: 201-1816
Mailing Address: PO Box 10139, Palo Alto, CA 94303-0139
Tel: 650-493-4400 *Toll Free Tel:* 800-523-8635 *Fax:* 650-424-0910; 650-855-9815
E-mail: service@annualreviews.org
Web Site: www.annualreviews.org
Key Personnel
CFO: Steve Castro *E-mail:* scastro@annualreviews.org
Pres & Ed-in-Chief: Richard Gallagher
Dir, HR: Lisa Wucher *E-mail:* lwucher@annualreviews.org
Dir, Prodn: Jennifer Jongsma *E-mail:* jjongsma@annualreviews.org
Dir, Technol: Paul Calvi *E-mail:* pcalvi@annualreviews.org
Mktg Mgr: Jenni Rankin *E-mail:* jrankin@annualreviews.org
Founded: 1932
Scientific review literature, in print & online, in the biomedical, life, physical & social sciences.
ISBN Prefix(es): 978-0-8243
Number of titles published annually: 20 Print; 50 Online
Total Titles: 50 Online
Foreign Rep(s): Gazelle Book Services Ltd (Africa, Continental Europe, Ireland, Middle East, UK); SARAS Books (Bangladesh, India, Pakistan, Sri Lanka)
Returns: 526 N Earl Ave, PO Box 5685, Lafayette, IN 47903 (return authorization required)
Membership(s): ALA; International Federation of Library Associations & Institutions; Medical Library Association; National Federation of Advanced Information Services; SLA; Society for Scholarly Publishing; STM

§ANR Publications University of California
Division of Agriculture & Natural Resources, University of California
1301 S 46 St, Bldg 478 - MC 3580, Richmond, CA 94804
Mailing Address: 2801 Second St, Davis, CA 95618
Tel: 510-665-2195 (cust serv) *Toll Free Tel:* 800-994-8849 *Fax:* 510-665-3427
E-mail: anrcatalog@ucdavis.edu
Web Site: anrcatalog.ucanr.edu
Key Personnel
Pubns Mgr: Ann Senuta *Tel:* 530-750-1224 *E-mail:* aesenuta@ucanr.edu
Mktg Dir & Foreign Rts: Cynthia Kintigh *Tel:* 530-750-1217 *E-mail:* cckintigh@ucanr.edu
Fulfillment Mgr & Cust Serv: Jon Mercy *Tel:* 510-665-2161 *E-mail:* jrmercy@ucanr.edu
Peer reviewed publications on agriculture, gardening, integrated pest management, nutrition, childhood obesity & natural resources.
ISBN Prefix(es): 978-0-931876; 978-1-879906; 978-1-60107
Number of titles published annually: 16 Print; 2 CD-ROM; 30 Online; 5 E-Book
Total Titles: 850 Print; 15 CD-ROM; 500 Online; 5 E-Book
Membership(s): Publishers Association of the West

Antique Collectors' Club Ltd
Division of Antique Collectors Club Ltd (England)
6 W 18 St, Suite 4B, New York, NY 10011
Tel: 212-645-1111 *Toll Free Tel:* 800-252-5231 *Fax:* 212-989-3205
E-mail: ussales@accpublishinggroup.com
Web Site: www.accdistribution.com
Key Personnel
Div Dir & Intl Rts: John Boncottie
Founded: 1966
Books on fine & decorative arts, gardening, architecture & antiques, multicultural.
ISBN Prefix(es): 978-1-85149; 978-0-907462; 978-0-902028
Number of titles published annually: 300 Print
Total Titles: 1,500 Print
Imprints: ACC Editions; Garden Art Press
Divisions: ACC Distribution
Foreign Office(s): Sandy Lane, Old Martlesham, Woodbridge, Suffolk 1P12 4SD, United Kingdom *Tel:* (01394) 389950 *Fax:* (01394) 389999 *E-mail:* sales@antique-acc.com *Web Site:* www.antiquecollectorsclub.com

Foreign Rep(s): Jenny Gosling (Belgium, London, Luxembourg, Netherlands); Lilian Koe (Malaysia); Clive & Moira Malins (Northeast England, Scotland); Michael Morris (Middle East, Near East); Penny Padovani (Italy, Portugal, Spain); David Pearson (France); Ian Pringle (Brunei, Indonesia, Singapore, Thailand); Ed Summerson (China, Hong Kong, Philippines, South Korea, Taiwan); Ralph & Sheila Sumners (Japan); Robert Towers (Ireland, Northern Ireland)

Antique Trader
Imprint of Krause Publications Inc
c/o Krause Publications, 700 E State St, Iola, WI 54990-0001
Tel: 715-445-2214 *Toll Free Tel:* 888-457-2873 *Fax:* 715-445-4087
Web Site: www.krausebooks.com
Founded: 1952
Collectibles, books, magazines, trades & crafts.
ISBN Prefix(es): 978-0-930625; 978-1-58221; 978-1-4402
Number of titles published annually: 20 Print
Total Titles: 200 Print

Antrim House
21 Goodrich Rd, Simsbury, CT 06070-1804
Tel: 860-217-0023
E-mail: eds@antrimhousebooks.com
Web Site: www.antrimhousebooks.com
Key Personnel
Publr & Ed: Robert Rennie McQuilkin
Founded: 1990
Publish cloth bound editions, perfect bound paperbacks & saddle stitched chapbooks by poets & memoirists. Also a limited number of art books. On occasion, issue CDs by these poets.
This publisher has indicated that 100% of their product line is author subsidized.
ISBN Prefix(es): 978-0-9662783; 978-0-9792226; 978-0-9770633; 978-0-9762091; 978-0-9798451; 978-0-9817883; 978-0-9823970; 978-0-9843418; 978-1-936482
Number of titles published annually: 17 Print; 1 Audio
Total Titles: 140 Print; 3 E-Book; 3 Audio

AOCS Press
Division of American Oil Chemists' Society
2710 S Boulder Dr, Urbana, IL 61802-6996
Mailing Address: PO Box 17190, Urbana, IL 61803-7190
Tel: 217-693-4838 *Fax:* 217-351-8091
E-mail: general@aocs.org
Web Site: www.aocs.org
Key Personnel
CEO: Patrick Donnelly *Fax:* 217-693-4881 *E-mail:* patrick.donnelly@aocs.org
Founded: 1909
Journals & monographs.
ISBN Prefix(es): 978-0-935315; 978-1-893997; 978-0-9818936
Number of titles published annually: 5 Print; 5 CD-ROM
Total Titles: 100 Print; 21 CD-ROM; 2 Audio

AOTA Press, see The American Occupational Therapy Association Inc (AOTA)

APA Planners Press
Imprint of American Planning Association
205 N Michigan Ave, Suite 1200, Chicago, IL 60601
Tel: 312-431-9100 *Fax:* 312-786-6700
E-mail: customerservice@planning.org
Web Site: www.planning.org
Key Personnel
Sr Ed: Julie von Bergen *E-mail:* jvonbergen@planning.org
Founded: 1978
Books on planning.
ISBN Prefix(es): 978-0-918286; 978-1-884829; 978-1-932364
Number of titles published annually: 5 Print
Total Titles: 120 Print; 15 E-Book
Warehouse: Ware-Pak, 2427 Bond St, University Park, IL 60484 *Tel:* 708-534-2600 *Fax:* 708-524-7803

Aperture Books
Division of Aperture Foundation Inc
547 W 27 St, 4th fl, New York, NY 10001
SAN: 201-1832
Tel: 212-505-5555 *Toll Free Tel:* 800-929-2323 *Fax:* 212-979-7759
E-mail: info@aperture.org
Web Site: www.aperture.org
Key Personnel
Publr: Lesley Martin
Exec Dir: Chris Boot
Dir, Sales & Mktg: Kellie McLaughlin
Sales Dir, Books: Richard Gregg
Intl Rts Contact: Amelia Lang
Founded: 1952
Quarterly magazine; books on photography as fine art, history of photography, photojournalism, environment.
ISBN Prefix(es): 978-0-89381
Number of titles published annually: 25 Print
Total Titles: 250 Print
Imprints: Aperture Monographs; Masters of Photography; Writers & Artists on Photography Series
Distributed by Farrar, Straus & Giroux Inc
Foreign Rep(s): General Publishing (Canada); Robert Hale Ltd (UK); InterArt (France); Nilsson & Lamm (Belgium, Netherlands); Onslow Books Ltd (Western Europe); Penny Padovani (Greece, Italy, Portugal, Spain); Southern Publisher (New Zealand); Tower (Australia); Roger Ward (East Asia)
Shipping Address: Farrar, Straus & Giroux, c/o MPS, 16365 James Madison Hwy, Gordonsville, VA 22942
Distribution Center: Ingram Publisher Services, One Ingram Blvd, La Vergne, TN 37086 *Toll Free Tel:* 866-400-5351

The Apex Press
Imprint of Rowman & Littlefield Publishers Inc
4501 Forbes Blvd, Suite 200, Lanham, MD 20706
SAN: 281-8752
Tel: 301-459-3366 *Toll Free Tel:* 800-462-6420 (orders) *Toll Free Fax:* 800-388-4450
E-mail: customercare@rowman.com
Web Site: rowman.com/page/apex
Key Personnel
VP, Mktg & Sales: Linda May
Founded: 1990
Specialize in books on education, economics, social & political issues, human rights, corporate power.
ISBN Prefix(es): 978-0-945257; 978-0-938960 (CITE); 978-1-891843
Number of titles published annually: 8 Print
Total Titles: 100 Print

The Apocryphile Press
1700 Shattuck Ave, Suite 81, Berkeley, CA 94709
Tel: 510-290-4349
E-mail: apocryphile@me.com
Web Site: www.apocryphilepress.com
Key Personnel
Publr & Ed: John R Mabry
Assoc Ed: Michael Asteriou
Founded: 1994
Publishes edgy spirituality, liberal religious fiction & mystical poetry.
ISBN Prefix(es): 978-1-933993; 978-0-9747623; 978-0-9764025; 978-0-9771461; 978-1-937002; 978-1-940671
Number of titles published annually: 12 Print
Total Titles: 200 Print

Apogee Press
2308 Sixth St, Berkeley, CA 94710
E-mail: editors.apogee@gmail.com
Web Site: www.apogeepress.com
Key Personnel
Ed: Alice Jones; Edward Smallfield *Tel:* 510-845-8800
Founded: 1998
Publishes innovative poetry with an emphasis on West Coast writers.
ISBN Prefix(es): 978-0-9669937; 978-0-9744687; 978-0-9787667; 978-0-9851007
Number of titles published annually: 3 Print
Total Titles: 38 Print; 2 E-Book
Orders to: Small Press Distribution, 1341 Seventh St, Berkeley, CA 94710-1409, Deputy Dir: Laura Moriarty *Toll Free Tel:* 800-869-7553 *Fax:* 510-524-1563 *E-mail:* spd@spdbooks.org *Web Site:* www.spdbooks.org
Returns: Small Press Distribution, 1341 Seventh St, Berkeley, CA 94710-1409, Deputy Dir: Laura Moriarty *Toll Free Tel:* 800-869-7553 *Fax:* 510-524-1563 *E-mail:* spd@spdbooks.org *Web Site:* www.spdbooks.org
Shipping Address: Small Press Distribution, 1341 Seventh St, Berkeley, CA 94710-1409, Deputy Dir: Laura Moriarty *Toll Free Tel:* 800-869-7553 *E-mail:* spd@spdbooks.org *Web Site:* www.spdbooks.org
Warehouse: Small Press Distribution, 1341 Seventh St, Berkeley, CA 94710-1409 *Toll Free Tel:* 800-869-7553 *E-mail:* spd@spdbooks.org *Web Site:* www.spdbooks.org
Distribution Center: Small Press Distribution, 1341 Seventh St, Berkeley, CA 94710-1409, Deputy Dir: Laura Moriarty *Toll Free Tel:* 800-869-7553 *Fax:* 510-524-1563 *E-mail:* spd@spdbooks.org *Web Site:* www.spdbooks.org
Membership(s): Community of Literary Magazines & Presses

Apollo Managed Care Inc
1100 Town & Country Rd, Suite 1250, Orange, CA 92868
Toll Free Tel: 888-276-5563
E-mail: info@apollomanagedcare.com
Web Site: www.apollomanagedcare.com
Key Personnel
Chief Med Offr: Dr Margaret Bischel *E-mail:* mbischel@cox.net
Founded: 1987
Publish comprehensive evidence-based healthcare review criteria & clinical guidelines.
ISBN Prefix(es): 978-1-893826; 978-1-939209
Number of titles published annually: 35 Print; 1 CD-ROM; 5 Online
Total Titles: 40 Print; 1 CD-ROM; 40 Online

APPA: The Association of Higher Education Facilities Officers
1643 Prince St, Alexandria, VA 22314-2818
Tel: 703-684-1446 *Fax:* 703-549-2772
Web Site: www.appa.org
Key Personnel
Dir, Knowledge Mgmt: Steve Glazner *E-mail:* steve@appa.org
Pubn Mgr: Anita Dosik *E-mail:* anita@appa.org
Founded: 1914
All titles seek to enhance the development of leadership & professional management applicable to the planning, design, construction & operation of higher education facilities.
ISBN Prefix(es): 978-0-913359; 978-1-890956
Number of titles published annually: 5 Print
Total Titles: 60 Print
Branch Office(s)
APPA Publications, PO Box 1201, Alexandria, VA 22313-1201
Distribution Center: 13119 Pelfrey Lane, Fairfax, VA 22033

Appalachian Mountain Club Books
Division of Appalachian Mountain Club
5 Joy St, Boston, MA 02108
SAN: 203-4808
Tel: 617-523-0655 *Toll Free Tel:* 800-262-4455 (orders) *Fax:* 617-523-0722
E-mail: amcbooks@outdoors.org
Web Site: www.outdoors.org
Key Personnel
VP, Communs & Mktg: Kevin Breunig
Founded: 1897
Guidebooks, maps, outdoor recreation & conservation, mountain history, nature & travel for Northeast US.
ISBN Prefix(es): 978-0-910146; 978-1-878239; 978-1-929173; 978-1-934028; 978-1-62842
Number of titles published annually: 20 Print
Total Titles: 110 Print
Imprints: AMC Discover Series; AMC Nature Walks Series; AMC Quiet Water Guides; AMC River Guides; AMC Trail Guides
Foreign Rep(s): Canadian Manda Group (Canada); Windsor Books Ltd (Europe)
Distribution Center: National Book Network (NBN), 15200 NBN Way, Blue Ridge Summit, PA 17214 *Tel:* 717-794-3800 *Toll Free Tel:* 800-462-6420 *Fax:* 717-794-3828 *Toll Free Fax:* 800-338-4550 *E-mail:* customercare@nbnbooks.com *Web Site:* www.nbnbooks.com

Appalachian Trail Conservancy
799 Washington St, Harpers Ferry, WV 25425
Mailing Address: PO Box 807, Harpers Ferry, WV 25425-0807
Tel: 304-535-6331 *Toll Free Tel:* 888-287-8673 (orders only) *Fax:* 304-535-2667
E-mail: publisher@appalachiantrail.org
Web Site: www.appalachiantrail.org; www.atctrailstore.org
Key Personnel
Publr: Brian B King *Tel:* 304-885-0823 *E-mail:* bking@appalachiantrail.org
Founded: 1925
Books & maps related to the Appalachian Trail.
ISBN Prefix(es): 978-0-917953; 978-1-889386; 978-1-944958
Number of titles published annually: 5 Print
Total Titles: 46 Print
Sales Office(s): 179 E Burr Blvd, Unit N, Kearneysville, WV 25430
Billing Address: PO Box 807, Harpers Ferry, WV 25425-0807
Distribution Center: 179 E Burr Blvd, Unit N, Kearneysville, WV 25430 *Tel:* 304-724-8386 *Toll Free Tel:* 888-287-8673 *E-mail:* sales@appalachiantrail.org *Web Site:* www.atctrailstore.org

Applause Theatre & Cinema Books
Imprint of Hal Leonard Performing Arts Publishing Group
33 Plymouth St, Suite 302, Montclair, NJ 07042
Tel: 973-337-5034 *Toll Free Tel:* 800-637-2852 *Fax:* 973-337-5227
E-mail: info@applausepub.com
Web Site: www.applausepub.com
Key Personnel
Assoc Ed: Carol Flannery *E-mail:* cflannery@halleonard.com
Founded: 1983
Plays, theatre books, cinema books, entertainment, television; including DVDs.
ISBN Prefix(es): 978-0-936839; 978-1-55783
Number of titles published annually: 25 Print; 15 E-Book
Total Titles: 1,000 Print; 500 E-Book
Sales Office(s): 7777 W Bluemound Rd, Milwaukee, WI 53213
Distributed by Hal Leonard LLC
Distributor for The Working Arts Library; Glenn Young Books
Foreign Rep(s): GPS (Africa, Asia, Central America, Europe, India, Latin America, Mexico, Pacific Rim, Russia & former USSR, South America); Publishers Group UK (UK); Woodslane (Australia, New Zealand)
Foreign Rights: Robert Lecker Agency Inc (worldwide)
Billing Address: 1210 Innovation Dr, Winona, MN 55987
Orders to: 7777 W Bluemound Rd, Milwaukee, WI 53213 *Toll Free Tel:* 800-554-0626
Returns: 1210 Innovation Dr, Winona, MN 55987
Warehouse: 1210 Innovation Dr, Winona, MN 55987 *Tel:* 507-454-2920 *Fax:* 507-454-8334

Appletree Press Inc
151 Good Counsel Dr, Suite 125, Mankato, MN 56001
Tel: 507-345-4848 *Fax:* 507-345-3002
E-mail: eatwell@hickorytech.net
Web Site: www.appletreepress.com; www.letscookhealthymeals.com
Key Personnel
CEO & Publr: Linda Hachfeld *E-mail:* lindah@hickorytech.net
Founded: 1989
Independent health & nutrition publisher of cookbooks, food diaries, journaling tools & nutrition reference books. Focus on heart health, diabetes management, weight management, arthritis, vegetarian cooking, how-to cookbooks for & by people with intellectual & developmental disabilities.
ISBN Prefix(es): 978-1-891011; 978-0-962047
Number of titles published annually: 3 Print
Total Titles: 20 Print
Imprints: HealthCheques (self-monitoring tools, heart health journal & nutrient guides for weight & diabetes management); On My Own (pictorial cookbooks for individuals with special needs, intellectual & developmental disabilities)
Membership(s): Academy of Nutrition and Dietetics; Independent Book Publishers Association; Midwest Independent Publishing Association; Women Executives in Business; Women of Words

Applewood Books Inc
One River Rd, Carlisle, MA 01741
SAN: 210-3419
Mailing Address: PO Box 365, Bedford, MA 01730
Tel: 781-271-0055 *Toll Free Tel:* 800-277-5312 (orders) *Fax:* 781-271-0056
E-mail: bookorder@awb.com; customercare@awb.com
Web Site: www.awb.com
Key Personnel
Pres & ISBN Contact: Phil Zuckerman *E-mail:* philz@awb.com
VP, Opers: Sue Cabezas *E-mail:* suec@awb.com
Founded: 1976
Americana reprints.
ISBN Prefix(es): 978-0-918222; 978-1-55709; 978-1-889833; 978-1-933212; 978-1-4290; 978-0-9819430; 978-1-60889; 978-0-9844156; 978-0-9836416; 978-1-938700; 978-0-9882885; 978-1-5162
Number of titles published annually: 500 Print
Total Titles: 2,500 Print
Imprints: Commonwealth Editions; Grab a Pencil Press
Orders to: PO Box 27, Carlisle, MA 01741
Warehouse: Ingram Publishers Services, 1280 Ingram Dr, Chambersburg, PA 17201
See separate listing for:
Commonwealth Editions

Appraisal Institute
200 W Madison, Suite 1500, Chicago, IL 60606
Tel: 312-335-4100 *Toll Free Tel:* 888-756-4624 *Fax:* 312-335-4400
Web Site: www.appraisalinstitute.org
Key Personnel
Sr Mgr, Pubns: Tep Shea-Joyce *E-mail:* tshea-joyce@appraisalinstitute.org
Founded: 1932
Professional real estate appraisal books, monographs, periodicals & videos.
ISBN Prefix(es): 978-0-911780; 978-0-922154
Number of titles published annually: 6 Print
Total Titles: 60 Print
Branch Office(s)
122 "C" St NW, Suite 360, Washington, DC 20001 *Tel:* 202-298-6449
Distributed by Dearborn Trade
Foreign Rep(s): Royal Institution of Chartered Surveyors (Africa, Caribbean, Commonwealth, Ethiopia, Europe, Far East)

Apress Media LLC
Subsidiary of Springer Science+Business Media LLC
233 Spring St, New York, NY 10013
Tel: 212-460-1500
E-mail: editorial@apress.com
Web Site: www.apress.com
Key Personnel
Mng Dir: Welmoed Spahr *E-mail:* Welmoed.Spahr@springer.com
Technical publisher devoted to meeting the needs of IT professionals, software developers & programmers with books in print & electronic format.
ISBN Prefix(es): 978-1-893115; 978-1-59059; 978-1-4302
Total Titles: 1,000 Print

§APS PRESS
Imprint of The American Phytopathological Society (APS)
3340 Pilot Knob Rd, St Paul, MN 55121
Tel: 651-454-7250 *Toll Free Tel:* 800-328-7560 *Fax:* 651-454-0766
E-mail: aps@scisoc.org
Web Site: www.shopapspress.org
Key Personnel
EVP: Amy Hope *E-mail:* ahope@scisoc.org
Pubns Mktg Dir: Greg Grahek *Tel:* 651-454-7250 ext 141 *E-mail:* ggrahek@scisoc.org
Pubns Mktg Coord: Dawn Wuest *E-mail:* dwuest@scisoc.org
Founded: 1908
Publishers of key reference books, field guides, laboratory manuals & other scientific titles related to plant health.
ISBN Prefix(es): 978-0-89054
Number of titles published annually: 10 Print; 2 CD-ROM; 4 Online
Total Titles: 300 Print; 40 CD-ROM; 2 Online

Aqua Quest Publications Inc
486 Bayville Rd, Locust Valley, NY 11560-1209
Tel: 516-759-0476
E-mail: info@aquaquest.com
Web Site: www.aquaquest.com
Key Personnel
Pres: Anthony A Bliss, Jr *E-mail:* tbliss@aquaquest.com
Founded: 1989
Publishes & distributes books on scuba diving, dive travel destinations, underwater photo/video, marine life, technical diving, marine related children's books, shipwrecks & dive related fiction.
ISBN Prefix(es): 978-0-9623389; 978-1-881652; 978-0-9752290
Number of titles published annually: 3 Print
Total Titles: 30 Print; 4 E-Book
Imprints: Watersport Books

§Arbordale Publishing
612 Johnnie Dodds Blvd, Suite A2, Mount Pleasant, SC 29464
SAN: 256-6109

Tel: 843-971-6722 *Toll Free Tel:* 877-243-3457 *Fax:* 843-216-3804
E-mail: customerservice@arbordalepublishing.com; info@arbordalepublishing.com
Web Site: www.arbordalepublishing.com
Key Personnel
Publr: Mr Lee German *E-mail:* leegerman@arbordalepublishing.com
Ed: Donna German *E-mail:* donna@arbordalepublishing.com
PR: Heather Williams *E-mail:* heather@arbordalepublishing.com
Bookstore & Gift Shop Sales: Jordan Fredrickson *E-mail:* jordan@arbordalepublishing.com
School & Lib Sales: Emily Gooch *E-mail:* emily@arbordalepublishing.com
Off Mgr: Elma Haley *E-mail:* elma@arbordalepublishing.com
Founded: 2005
Company on a mission to create picture books that will excite children's imagination, are artistically spectacular & have educational value. Most of our stories are fictional but relate to a nonfictional theme of science, nature or animals. Each book is seriously vetted for scientific accuracy before publication. We reserve 3-5 pages in the back of each book to add our "Creative Minds" section, loaded with fun facts, crafts & games to supplement the educational thread of the book. Ebooks with auto read, auto flip & selectable English & Spanish text in audio.
ISBN Prefix(es): 978-0-9777423; 978-1-60718; 978-1-62855; 978-1-934358; 978-0-9764943; 978-0-9768823
Number of titles published annually: 36 Print; 36 Online; 36 E-Book; 36 Audio
Total Titles: 228 Print; 228 Online; 228 E-Book; 228 Audio
Foreign Rep(s): Fitzhenry & Whiteside (Canada); Ediciones Enlace de PR (Puerto Rico)
Foreign Rights: Sylvia Hayes Literary Agency
Distribution Center: The Reading Warehouse, PO Box 41328, North Charleston, SC 29423 *E-mail:* customerservice@thereadingwarehouse.com *Web Site:* www.thereadingwarehouse.com
Bound to Stay Bound, 1880 W Morton Ave, Jacksonville, IL 62650 *Toll Free Tel:* 800-637-6586 *Toll Free Fax:* 800-747-2872 *E-mail:* btsb@btsb.com *Web Site:* www.btsb.com
Perma-Bound, 617 E Vandalia Rd, Jacksonville, IL 62650 *Tel:* 217-243-5451 *Toll Free Tel:* 800-637-9581 *Fax:* 217-243-7505 *Toll Free Fax:* 800-551-1169 *E-mail:* books@perma-bound.com *Web Site:* www.perma-bound.com
Follett School Solutions Inc, 1340 Ridgeview Dr, McHenry, IL 60050 *Tel:* 815-759-1700 *Toll Free Tel:* 888-511-5114 (cust serv) *Fax:* 815-459-9831 *Toll Free Fax:* 800-852-5458 *E-mail:* info@follettlearning.com *Web Site:* www.follettlearning.com SAN: 169-1902
Mackin Educational Resources, 3505 County Rd 42 W, Burnsville, MN 55306 *Tel:* 952-895-9540 *Toll Free Tel:* 800-245-9540 *Fax:* 952-894-8806 *Toll Free Fax:* 800-369-5490 *E-mail:* customerservice@mackin.com *Web Site:* www.mackin.com
Baker & Taylor, 2550 W Tyvola Rd, Suite 300, Charlotte, NC 28217 *Toll Free Tel:* 800-775-1800 *Fax:* 704-998-3100 *E-mail:* btinfo@baker-taylor.com *Web Site:* www.btol.com
Brodart, 500 Arch St, Williamsport, PA 17701 *Tel:* 570-326-2461 *Toll Free Tel:* 800-233-8487 *Fax:* 570-326-1479 *E-mail:* support@brodart.com *Web Site:* www.brodart.com
Davidson Titles, PO Box 3538, Jackson, TN 38303-3538 *Toll Free Tel:* 800-433-3903 *Toll Free Fax:* 800-787-7935 *E-mail:* info@davidsontitles.com *Web Site:* www.davidsontitles.com
Ingram, One Ingram Blvd, La Vergne, TN 37086 *Tel:* 615-793-5000 *Toll Free Tel:* 800-937-8200 *E-mail:* customer.service@ingrambook.com *Web Site:* www.ingrambook.com
Penworthy, 219 N Milwaukee St, Milwaukee, WI 53202 *Tel:* 414-287-4600 *Toll Free Tel:* 800-262-2665 *Fax:* 414-287-4602 *E-mail:* info@penworthy.com *Web Site:* www.penworthy.com
Membership(s): ABA; ABC; BookSense Publisher Partner; The Children's Book Council; Florida Authors & Publishers Association Inc; Independent Book Publishers Association; International Literacy Association; MSA; NAIPR; National Association for Bilingual Education; National Association of Book Entrepreneurs; Northern California Independent Booksellers Association; Southern Independent Booksellers Alliance

Arbutus Press
2364 Pinehurst Trail, Traverse City, MI 49696
Tel: 231-946-7240
E-mail: info@arbutuspress.com
Web Site: www.arbutuspress.com
Key Personnel
Publr: Susan Bays
Founded: 1998
Midwest regional history & travel related.
ISBN Prefix(es): 978-0-9665316; 978-0-9766104; 978-1-933926
Number of titles published annually: 12 Print
Total Titles: 90 Print; 25 E-Book; 3 Audio
Membership(s): Great Lakes Independent Booksellers Association; Independent Book Publishers Association

Arcade Publishing Inc
Imprint of Skyhorse Publishing Inc
307 W 36 St, 11th fl, New York, NY 10018
Tel: 212-643-6816 *Fax:* 212-643-6819
E-mail: info@skyhorsepublishing.com (subs & foreign rts)
Web Site: www.arcadepub.com
Key Personnel
Pres & Publr: Tony Lyons
VP: Bill Wolfsthal *E-mail:* bwolfsthal@skyhorsepublishing.com
Founded: 1988
Trade fiction & nonfiction; adult & juvenile.
ISBN Prefix(es): 978-1-61145; 978-1-62872
Number of titles published annually: 100 Print; 100 E-Book
Total Titles: 700 Print
Foreign Rights: Biagi Literary Management
Distribution Center: Perseus Book Distribution/Ingram Content Group, 1400 Broadway, New York, NY 10018 *E-mail:* orderentry@perseusbooks.com

Arcadia Publishing Inc
420 Wando Park Blvd, Mount Pleasant, SC 29464
SAN: 255-268X
Tel: 843-853-2070 *Toll Free Tel:* 888-313-2665 (orders only) *Fax:* 843-853-0044
E-mail: sales@arcadiapublishing.com
Web Site: www.arcadiapublishing.com
Key Personnel
Cont: Kristen Crawford
Dir, Mktg & Corp Communs: Kelly Bowen
Sales Dir: Kate Everingham *E-mail:* keveringham@arcadiapublishing.com
Founded: 1992
Local history & vintage images.
ISBN Prefix(es): 978-0-7385; 978-1-4396; 978-1-4671
Number of titles published annually: 900 Print
Total Titles: 12,000 Print; 6,000 E-Book
Imprints: History Press; Legendary Locals
Distributor for Cool Springs Press; Voyageur Press
Warehouse: Arcadia Distribution Center, Receiving Dock, Mount Pleasant, SC 29464 SAN: 255-2698
Distribution Center: Baker & Taylor Global Publishers Services (GPS)

Arcana Publishing, see Lotus Press

ARE Press
Division of The Association for Research & Enlightenment Inc (ARE)
215 67 St, Virginia Beach, VA 23451
Tel: 757-428-3588 *Toll Free Tel:* 800-333-4499 *Fax:* 757-491-0689
Web Site: www.edgarcayce.org
Key Personnel
Mktg Dir: Jennie Taylor Martin *Tel:* 757-457-7249 *E-mail:* jennie@edgarcayce.org
Prodn, Rts & Trade Sales Dir: Cassie McQuagge *Tel:* 757-457-7239 *E-mail:* cassie@edgarcayce.org
Founded: 1931
Holistic health & spiritual development, based on Edgar Cayce material.
ISBN Prefix(es): 978-0-87604
Number of titles published annually: 8 Print; 8 E-Book
Total Titles: 160 Print; 1 CD-ROM; 64 E-Book
Imprints: 4th Dimension Press

Ariadne Press
270 Goins Ct, Riverside, CA 92507
Tel: 951-684-9202 *Fax:* 951-779-0449
E-mail: ariadnepress@aol.com
Web Site: www.ariadnebooks.com
Key Personnel
Partner: Jorun Johns
Founded: 1988
Studies in Austrian literature, culture & thought.
ISBN Prefix(es): 978-0-929497; 978-1-57241
Number of titles published annually: 12 Print
Total Titles: 205 Print
Foreign Rep(s): Gazelle Book Services Ltd (UK); Schaden (Austria)
Foreign Rights: Gazelle Book Services Ltd (UK)

§Ariel Press
Subsidiary of Light
2317 Quail Cove Dr, Jasper, GA 30143
Mailing Address: PO Box 251, Marble Hill, GA 30148
Tel: 770-894-4226
E-mail: lig201@lightariel.com
Web Site: www.lightariel.com
Key Personnel
Pres & Publr: Carl Japikse
Art Dir: Nancy Maxwell
Founded: 1976
Nonfiction hardcover & paperbound books; essays & subscription series on personal growth, creativity, holistic health & psychic phenomena; esoteric fiction; reprints.
ISBN Prefix(es): 978-0-89804
Number of titles published annually: 11 Print; 10 E-Book
Total Titles: 200 Print; 25 E-Book
Imprints: Enthea Press; Kudzu House
Distributor for Enthea Press; Kudzu House

§Ariel Starr Productions Inc
PO Box 575, Woodstock, NY 12498
Tel: 201-784-9148
E-mail: arielstarrprod@aol.com
Web Site: arielstarrprod.wix.com/arielstarr
Key Personnel
Pres: Cynthia Soroka-Dunn
Founded: 1991
Publish any new & innovative projects.
ISBN Prefix(es): 978-1-889122
Number of titles published annually: 3 Print; 4 E-Book; 2 Audio
Total Titles: 20 Print; 1 Audio

The Arion Press
Division of Lyra Corp
The Presidio, 1802 Hays St, San Francisco, CA 94129

SAN: 203-1361
Tel: 415-668-2542 *Fax:* 415-668-2550
E-mail: arionpress@arionpress.com
Web Site: www.arionpress.com
Key Personnel
Publr: Andrew Hoyem
Dir, Mktg & Sales: Chris Dunlap
Founded: 1974
Fine, limited edition illustrated books of fiction, literature & poetry.
ISBN Prefix(es): 978-0-910457
Number of titles published annually: 3 Print
Total Titles: 110 Print
Divisions: M & H Type

Arkham House Publishers Inc
PO Box 546, Sauk City, WI 53583
SAN: 206-9741
Tel: 608-643-4500 *Fax:* 608-643-5043
E-mail: sales@arkhamhouse.com
Web Site: www.arkhamhouse.com
Key Personnel
Pres: Danielle Hackett
VP: Damon Derleth
Founded: 1939
Fantasy fiction, horror, macabre, science fiction.
ISBN Prefix(es): 978-0-87054
Number of titles published annually: 3 Print
Total Titles: 54 Print; 54 Online; 54 E-Book
Imprints: Mycroft & Moran

Aro Book Publishing Co
130 S 800 W, Salt Lake City, UT 84104-1120
Tel: 801-637-9115 *Fax:* 801-419-0125
E-mail: arobook@yahoo.com
Web Site: www.arobookpublishing.com
Key Personnel
Pres: Bob Reese
Founded: 1973
K-4 beginning to read.
ISBN Prefix(es): 978-0-89868
Number of titles published annually: 30 Print
Total Titles: 35 Print; 65 Online; 35 E-Book

Jason Aronson Inc
Imprint of Rowman & Littlefield Publishing Group
4501 Forbes Blvd, Suite 200, Lanham, MD 20706
SAN: 201-0127
Tel: 301-459-3366 *Toll Free Tel:* 800-462-6420 (orders) *Fax:* 301-429-5748
Web Site: www.rowman.com
Key Personnel
Mktg Dir: Dave Horvath
Rts & Perms: Patricia Zline *Tel:* 301-459-3366 ext 5420 *E-mail:* pzline@rowman.com
Acqs Ed: Molly White *E-mail:* mwhite@rowman.com
Founded: 1965
Professional books in psychotherapy, psychoanalysis & psychology.
ISBN Prefix(es): 978-0-87668; 978-1-56821; 978-0-7657; 978-1-4425
Number of titles published annually: 25 Print; 25 E-Book
Total Titles: 1,700 Print
Foreign Rep(s): Academic Marketing Services Pty Ltd (Botswana, Namibia, South Africa, Zimbabwe); APD Singapore Pte Ltd (Brunei, Cambodia, Indonesia, Laos, Malaysia, Singapore, Thailand, Vietnam); Asia Publishers Service Ltd (China, Hong Kong, Korea, Philippines, Taiwan); Avicenna Partnership Ltd (Afghanistan, Algeria, Armenia, Bahrain, Cyprus, Egypt, Iran, Iraq, Jordan, Kuwait, Lebanon, Libya, Morocco, Oman, Palestine, Qatar, Saudi Arabia, Sudan, Syria, Tunisia, United Arab Emirates, Yemen); Cranbury International LLC (Caribbean, Central America, Mexico, Pakistan, Puerto Rico, South America); Durnell Marketing Ltd (Austria, Baltic States, Belgium, Czech Republic, Denmark, Finland, France, Germany, Greece, Hungary, Iceland, Italy, Malta, Netherlands, Norway, Poland, Portugal, Slovakia, Slovenia, Spain, Sweden, Switzerland); NBN International; Overleaf (Bangladesh, Bhutan, India, Nepal, Sri Lanka); United Publishers Service Ltd (Japan, South Korea)

Art Image Publications
Division of GB Publishing Inc
PO Box 160, Derby Line, VT 05830
Toll Free Tel: 800-361-2598 *Toll Free Fax:* 800-559-2598
E-mail: info@artimagepublications.com; customer.service@artimagepublications.com
Web Site: www.artimagepublications.com
Key Personnel
Pres: Yvan Boulerice
Secy: Francoise Desjardins
Founded: 1980
ISBN Prefix(es): 978-1-896876; 978-1-55292
Number of titles published annually: 12 Print
Total Titles: 52 Print

The Art Institute of Chicago
111 S Michigan Ave, Chicago, IL 60603-6404
SAN: 204-479X
Tel: 312-443-3600; 312-443-3540 (pubns) *Fax:* 312-443-1334 (pubns)
Web Site: www.artic.edu; www.artinstituteshop.org
Key Personnel
Pres & Dir: James Rondeau *Tel:* 312-443-3632
Exec Dir, Pubns: Gregory Nosan *Tel:* 312-443-4964 *E-mail:* gnosan@artic.edu
Dir, Prodn: Joseph Mohan *Tel:* 312-443-4955 *E-mail:* jmohan@artic.edu
Asst Dir, Prodn: Lauren Makholm *Tel:* 312-443-3539 *E-mail:* lmakholm@artic.edu
Ed: Amy Peltz *Tel:* 312-443-4963 *E-mail:* apeltz@artic.edu; Maia M Rigas *Tel:* 312-443-4774 *E-mail:* mrigas@artic.edu
Photo Ed: Katie Levi *Tel:* 312-443-4974 *E-mail:* klevi@artic.edu
Asst Ed: Sara Carminati *Tel:* 312-857-7612 *E-mail:* scarmi@artic.edu
Fin & Admin Coord: Jessica Applebee *Tel:* 312-443-4962 *E-mail:* japplebee@artic.edu
Prodn Coord: Rachel Edsill *Tel:* 312-443-1334 *E-mail:* redsill@artic.edu
Digital Catalog Designer: Beata Hosea *Tel:* 312-443-3727 *E-mail:* bhosea@artic.edu
Founded: 1879
Exhibition catalogues, popular & scholarly art books on the museum's permanent collection: African art & Indian art of the Americas; American art; Ancient & Byzantine art; architecture & design; Asian art; contemporary art; European painting, sculpture & decorative arts; photography; prints & drawings; textiles.
ISBN Prefix(es): 978-0-86559
Number of titles published annually: 10 Print; 1 Online
Total Titles: 60 Print; 10 Online; 1 E-Book
Distributed by Yale University Press

Art of Living, PrimaMedia Inc
1250 Bethlehem Pike, Suite 241, Hatfield, PA 19440
SAN: 299-8858
Tel: 215-660-5045
E-mail: primamedia4@yahoo.com
Key Personnel
Ed: Gia Carispat *E-mail:* primamedia12@yahoo.com
Billing: Joan Campo *E-mail:* primamedia40@gmail.com
Orders & Cust Serv: Sue Thomson
Orders & Returns: Sue Timmons Thomas
Contact: Katherine Rafter *E-mail:* primamedia9@yahoo.com
Founded: 2005
Boutique publishing company. Publisher of the award-winning book series *The Basic Art of Italian Cooking & The Basic Art*. Can place orders by telephone or e-mail, but prefer e-mail.
ISBN Prefix(es): 978-1-928911
Number of titles published annually: 20 Print; 10 E-Book
Total Titles: 25 Print; 35 Online; 35 E-Book
Foreign Rep(s): Rebecca Ferrone (Australia, Canada, Europe)
Distribution Center: Amazon.com
Follett School Solutions Inc, 1340 Ridgeview Dr, McHenry, IL 60050 *Tel:* 815-759-1700 *Toll Free Tel:* 888-511-5114 (cust serv) *Fax:* 815-759-9831 *Toll Free Fax:* 800-852-5458 *E-mail:* info@follettlearning.com *Web Site:* www.follettlearning.com SAN: 169-1902

ArtAge Publications
PO Box 19955, Portland, OR 97280
Tel: 503-246-3000 *Toll Free Tel:* 800-858-4998
Web Site: www.seniortheatre.com
Key Personnel
Pres: Bonnie L Vorenberg *E-mail:* bonniev@seniortheatre.com
Founded: 1997
The Senior Theatre Resource Center has the largest collection of plays, books & information for older performers. We help older performers fulfill their theatrical dreams.
ISBN Prefix(es): 978-0-9669412
Number of titles published annually: 45 Print; 45 Online; 27 E-Book; 5 Audio
Total Titles: 400 Print; 300 Online; 275 E-Book; 11 Audio
Distributor for Heinemann; Hal Leonard
Returns: 7845 SW Capitol Hwy, Suite 12, Portland, OR 97219

Arte Publico Press
Affiliate of University of Houston
University of Houston, Bldg 19, Rm 100, 4902 Gulf Fwy, Houston, TX 77204-2004
Tel: 713-743-2998 (sales) *Toll Free Tel:* 800-633-2783 *Fax:* 713-743-2847 (sales)
E-mail: appinfo@uh.edu; bkorders@uh.edu
Web Site: artepublicopress.com
Key Personnel
Publr: Nicolas Kanellos
Founded: 1979
Books by American Hispanic authors.
ISBN Prefix(es): 978-0-934770; 978-1-55885
Number of titles published annually: 30 Print
Total Titles: 400 Print
Imprints: Pinata Books
Subsidiaries: The Americas Review
Distributor for Bilingual Review Press; Latin American Review Press
Foreign Rights: Raquel de la Concha (Spain); Agencia Literaria Virginia Lopez-Ballesteros (Spain)
Membership(s): AAP

§Artech House Inc
Subsidiary of Horizon House Publications Inc
685 Canton St, Norwood, MA 02062
SAN: 201-1441
Tel: 781-769-9750 *Toll Free Tel:* 800-225-9977 *Fax:* 781-769-6334
E-mail: artech@artechhouse.com
Web Site: www.artechhouse.com
Key Personnel
COO: Christopher R Ernst *E-mail:* cernst@artechhouse.com
Pres & Publr: William M Bazzy *E-mail:* wmbazzy@artechhouse.com
Edit & Prodn Dir: Darrell Judd
Dir, Sales, Mktg & Busn Devt: Kevin Danahy *E-mail:* kdanahy@artechhouse.com
Exec Ed: Judi Stone

Acq Ed: David Michelson *E-mail:* dmichelson@artechhouse.com
Founded: 1970
Technical & engineering.
ISBN Prefix(es): 978-0-89006; 978-1-58053; 978-1-59693; 978-1-60807; 978-1-60783; 978-1-63081
Number of titles published annually: 35 Print; 35 E-Book
Total Titles: 1,500 Print; 600 E-Book
Foreign Office(s): 16 Sussex St, London SW1V 4RW, United Kingdom, Sales & Mktg Mgr: Alison Hope *Tel:* (020) 7596 8750 *Fax:* (020) 7630 0166 *E-mail:* artech-uk@artechhouse.com
Foreign Rep(s): Akateeminen (Finland); Anglo-American Book Co (Italy); Asian Books Pvt Ltd (India, Pakistan); C V Toko Buku Topen (Indonesia); Clarke Associates Ltd (Pacific Basin); Computer Press (Sweden); D A Book Pty Ltd (Australia, New Zealand); Dai-Iti Publications Trading Co Ltd (Japan); Diaz de Santos (Spain); Dietmar Dreier (Germany); DK Book House Co Ltd (Thailand); Freihofer AG (Switzerland); Kumi Trading Co Ltd (South Korea); Librairie Lavoisier (France); Login Canada (Canada); Julio Logrado de Figueiredo Lda (Portugal); The Modern Book Co (UK); Pak Book Corp (Pakistan); Polyteknisk (Denmark); Sejong (Korea); Ta Tong Book Co Ltd (Taiwan); Tapir (Norway); Tecmedd (Brazil); UBS Library Services (Singapore); United Publishers Services Ltd (Japan, South Korea); L Wouters (Belgium)
Foreign Rights: ABE Marketing (Poland); BSB Distribution (Germany); Fleet Publications (Chile); Foyles (UK); Hoepli (Italy); Kuwkab (Mideast); Livraria Canuto (Brazil); Papsotiriou (Greece)
Returns: NBN International, Airport Busn Ctr, 10 Thornbury Rd, Plymouth PL6 7PP, United Kingdom; Publishers Storage & Shipping Corp (US only), 231 Industrial Park, 46 Development Rd, Fitchburg, MA 01420 *Tel:* 978-345-2121 *Fax:* 978-348-1233
Warehouse: Publishers Storage & Shipping Corp (US only), 231 Industrial Park, 46 Development Rd, Fitchburg, MA 01420 *Tel:* 978-345-2121 *Fax:* 978-348-1233

Artisan Books
Division of Workman Publishing Co Inc
225 Varick St, New York, NY 10014-4381
Tel: 212-254-5900 *Toll Free Tel:* 800-722-7202 *Fax:* 212-677-6692
E-mail: artisaninfo@artisanbooks.com
Web Site: www.workman.com/artisanbooks
Key Personnel
Publr: Lia Ronnen
Assoc Publr: Allison McGeehon
Creative Dir: Michelle Ishay-Cohen
Prodn Dir: Nancy Murray
Mng Ed: Zachary Greenwald
Sr Ed: Shoshana Gutmajer
Ed: Bridget Monroe Itkin
Sr Publicist & Assoc Mktg Mgr: Theresa Collier
Founded: 1993
Illustrated books & calendars to the trade.
ISBN Prefix(es): 978-1-885183; 978-1-57965
Number of titles published annually: 15 Print
Distributor for Greenwich Workshop Press
Foreign Rep(s): Thomas Allen & Son Ltd (Canada); Bookreps New Zealand (New Zealand); Hardie Grant Books (Australia); Melia Publishing Services (UK)
Foreign Rights: Big Apple Agency Inc (China, Taiwan); Graal Literary Agency (Poland); The Deborah Harris Agency (Israel); The Italian Literary Agency srl (Italy); Japan UNI Agency Inc (Japan); JLM Literary Agency (Greece); Katai & Bolza Literary Agents (Hungary); Korea Copyright Center Inc (KCC) (Korea); Kristin Olson Literary Agency SRO (Czech Republic); Plima Literary Agency (Bulgaria, Croatia, Macedonia, Serbia, Slovenia); Sebes & Bisseling Literary Agency (Netherlands); Julio F Yanez Agencia Literaria SL (Latin America, Portugal, Spain)
Shipping Address: RR Donnelley, 1077 Prospect Lane, Kaukauna, WI 54130

§Artisan Bookworks
921 S Third Ave, No 8, Sequim, WA 98382
Mailing Address: PO Box 1972, Sequim, WA 98382
Tel: 425-954-5277
E-mail: books@artisanbookworks.com
Web Site: www.artisanbookworks.com
Key Personnel
Publr: Kelly Lenihan
Founded: 2012
Artisan Bookworks mission is to discover, nurture, publish & promote emerging writers. Author-subsidized publishing services include book layout (print & digital), copy-editing, proofreading & cover design for children's books, picture books & general fiction. Some nonfiction & memoirs will be considered.
This publisher has indicated that 75% of their product line is author subsidized.
ISBN Prefix(es): 978-0-9898692; 978-0-9911747; 978-0-9979578
Number of titles published annually: 10 Print; 10 E-Book
Shipping Address: Ingram Books Direct Distribution Services, 1246 Heil Quaker Blvd, La Vergne, TN 37086
Membership(s): The Association of Publishers for Special Sales; Book Publishers of the Northwest; Pacific Northwest Booksellers Association

ArtWrite Productions
1555 Gardena Ave NE, Minneapolis, MN 55432-5848
Tel: 612-803-0436
E-mail: artwriteprod@gmail.com
Web Site: artwriteproductions.com; adaptedclassics.com
Key Personnel
Owner: Jerome Tiller
Founded: 2003
Publishes books using humorous storytelling to enhance lessons in natural & social sciences & gallery-worthy illustrations to adapt stories by the world's greatest authors.
ISBN Prefix(es): 978-1-939846; 978-0-9777693
Number of titles published annually: 3 Print; 3 E-Book
Total Titles: 6 Print; 6 E-Book
Imprints: Adapted Classics
Distribution Center: Follett School Solutions, 1340 Ridgeview Dr, McHenry, IL 60050, Contact: Liz Michmershuizen *Tel:* 708-884-5000 *Fax:* 815-578-3951 *E-mail:* lmichmershuizen@follett.com
Membership(s): Independent Book Publishers Association; Midwest Independent Publishing Association; Society of Children's Book Writers & Illustrators

ASBO International, see Association of School Business Officials International

§ASCD
1703 N Beauregard St, Alexandria, VA 22311-1714
SAN: 201-1352
Tel: 703-578-9600 *Toll Free Tel:* 800-933-2723 *Fax:* 703-575-5400
E-mail: member@ascd.org
Web Site: www.ascd.org
Key Personnel
Publr: Stefani Roth
Dir, Book Editing & Prodn: Julie Houtz *Tel:* 703-575-5706 *E-mail:* jhoutz@ascd.org
Dir, Acqs: Genny Ostertag *Tel:* 703-575-5469 *E-mail:* gostertag@ascd.org
Founded: 1943
Professional books for educators.
ISBN Prefix(es): 978-0-87120; 978-1-4166
Number of titles published annually: 50 Print; 35 E-Book
Total Titles: 480 Print; 460 E-Book
Orders to: PO Box 17035, Baltimore, MD 21297-8431

Ascend Books LLC
12710 Pflumm Rd, Suite 200, Olathe, KS 66062
SAN: 856-3454
Tel: 913-948-5500
Web Site: www.ascendbooks.com
Key Personnel
CEO & Publr: Robert Snodgrass *E-mail:* bsnodgrass@ascendbooks.com
Mng Ed: Aaron Cedeno *E-mail:* acedeno@ascendbooks.com
Pubn Sales Mgr: Christine Drummond *Tel:* 913-948-7635 *Fax:* 913-948-7770 *E-mail:* cdrummond@ascendbooks.com
Founded: 2009
Publisher of books on sports & entertainment topics. Some children's books.
ISBN Prefix(es): 978-0-9830619
Number of titles published annually: 12 Print; 10 E-Book
Total Titles: 52 Print; 35 E-Book
Distribution Center: Baker & Taylor, 1120 Rte 22 E, PO Box 6885, Bridgewater, NJ 08807, Small Press Buyer: Robin Bright *Tel:* 908-541-7425 *Toll Free Tel:* 800-541-7425 *Fax:* 908-541-7862 *E-mail:* robin.bright@baker-taylor.com
Ingram Book Co, One Ingram Blvd, La Vergne, TN 37086, Contact: Kitti McConnell *Tel:* 615-213-5335 *Toll Free Tel:* 800-937-8200 *E-mail:* kitti.mcconnell@ingramcontent.com *Web Site:* www.ingrambook.com
Membership(s): Independent Book Publishers Association

Ascension Press
PO Box 1990, West Chester, PA 19380
Tel: 610-696-7795; 484-875-4550 (admin) *Toll Free Tel:* 800-376-0520 (sales & cust serv)
Web Site: ascensionpress.com
Key Personnel
Pres: Matthew Pinto
Dir, Mktg: Chris Michalski *E-mail:* cmichalski@ascensionpress.com
Dir, Sales: Deb Varnado *E-mail:* dvarnado@ascensionpress.com
Exec Prodr: Steve Motyl *E-mail:* smotyl@ascensionpress.com
Exec Ed: Mike Flickinger *E-mail:* mflickinger@ascensionpress.com
Assoc Ed: Lora Brecker *E-mail:* lbrecker@ascensionpress.com
Religious educational publishers.
ISBN Prefix(es): 978-1-932645; 978-0-9742238; 978-0-9659228; 978-0-9744451; 978-1-932631; 978-1-932927; 978-1-934217; 978-1-935940
Number of titles published annually: 15 Print
Total Titles: 250 Print; 200 Online; 40 Audio
Sales Office(s): 4001 W Greentree Rd, Milwaukee, WI 53209 *Toll Free Tel:* 800-376-0520
Orders to: 4001 W Greentree Rd, Milwaukee, WI 53209 *Toll Free Tel:* 800-376-0520
Returns: 4001 W Greentree Rd, Milwaukee, WI 53209 *Toll Free Tel:* 800-376-0520
Warehouse: 4001 W Greentree Rd, Milwaukee, WI 53209 *Toll Free Tel:* 800-376-0520
Distribution Center: 4001 W Greentree Rd, Milwaukee, WI 53209 *Toll Free Tel:* 800-376-0520

ASCP Press
Subsidiary of American Society for Clinical Pathology

33 W Monroe St, Suite 1600, Chicago, IL 60603
SAN: 207-9429
Tel: 312-541-4999 *Toll Free Tel:* 800-267-2727
Fax: 312-541-4998
Web Site: www.ascp.org
Key Personnel
Publr: Joshua R Weikersheimer *Tel:* 312-541-4866 *E-mail:* joshua.weikersheimer@ascp.org
Founded: 1959
Books, multimedia, slide sets, atlases, audiovisual seminars, videotapes, manuals, interactive software & videodiscs for lab professionals. Subjects include continuing education.
ISBN Prefix(es): 978-0-89189
Number of titles published annually: 21 Print; 10 Online
Total Titles: 238 Print; 112 Online

ASCSA Publications
6-8 Charlton St, Princeton, NJ 08540-5232
Tel: 609-683-0800 *Fax:* 609-924-0578
Web Site: www.ascsa.edu.gr/publications
Founded: 1881
Publishing office for the American School of Classical Studies at Athens, an advanced research & teaching institution focused on the history & culture of Greece & the wider Greek world.
ISBN Prefix(es): 978-0-87661 (print titles); 978-1-62139 (e-book titles)
Number of titles published annually: 12 Print; 5 E-Book
Total Titles: 300 Print; 1 Online; 25 E-Book
Imprints: American School of Classical Studies at Athens; Gennadeion Monographs; Hesperia
Billing Address: Casemate | academic, 1950 Lawrence Rd, Havertown, PA 19083 *Tel:* 610-853-9131 *Fax:* 610-853-9146 *E-mail:* info@casemateacademic.com *Web Site:* www.oxbowbooks.com/dbbc
Orders to: Casemate | academic, 1950 Lawrence Rd, Havertown, PA 19083 *Tel:* 610-853-9131 *Fax:* 610-853-9149 *E-mail:* info@casemateacademic.com *Web Site:* www.oxbowbooks.com/dbbc
Returns: Casemate | academic, 1950 Lawrence Rd, Havertown, PA 19083 *Tel:* 610-853-9131 *Fax:* 610-853-9146 *E-mail:* info@casemateacademic.com *Web Site:* www.oxbowbooks.com/dbbc
Shipping Address: Casemate | academic, 1950 Lawrence Rd, Havertown, PA 19083 *Tel:* 610-853-9131 *Fax:* 610-853-9146 *E-mail:* info@casemateacademic.com *Web Site:* www.oxbowbooks.com/dbbc
Warehouse: Casemate | academic, 1950 Lawrence Rd, Havertown, PA 19083 *Tel:* 610-853-9131 *Fax:* 610-853-9146 *E-mail:* info@casemateacademic.com *Web Site:* www.oxbowbooks.com/dbbc
Distribution Center: Casemate | academic, 1950 Lawrence Rd, Havertown, PA 19083 *Tel:* 610-853-9131 *Fax:* 610-853-9146 *E-mail:* info@casemateacademic.com *Web Site:* www.oxbowbooks.com/dbbc
Membership(s): AAP Professional & Scholarly Publishing Division; American Association of University Presses; Society for Scholarly Publishing

ASET - The Neurodiagnostic Society
402 E Bannister Rd, Suite A, Kansas City, KS 64131-3019
Tel: 816-931-1120 *Fax:* 816-931-1145
E-mail: info@aset.org
Web Site: www.aset.org
Key Personnel
Exec Dir: Arlen Reimnitz *Tel:* 816-931-1120 ext 101 *E-mail:* arlen@aset.org
Mktg & Communs Mgr: Sarah Dolezilek
Tel: 816-931-1120 ext 106 *E-mail:* sarah@aset.org
Founded: 1959
Books on EEG, evoked potentials, nerve conduction studies, long-term monitoring for epilepsy, intraoperative neuromonitoring & polysomnography/sleep technology.
ISBN Prefix(es): 978-1-57797
Number of titles published annually: 8 Print
Total Titles: 55 Print; 59 CD-ROM

Ash Tree Publishing
PO Box 64, Woodstock, NY 12498
Tel: 845-246-8081 *Fax:* 845-246-8081
Web Site: www.ashtreepublishing.com
Key Personnel
Founder & Owner: Susun Weed
E-mail: wisewoman@herbshealing.com
Orders: Michael Dattorre
Founded: 1985
ISBN Prefix(es): 978-1-888123; 978-0-9614620
Number of titles published annually: 3 Print; 2 Audio
Total Titles: 14 Print; 3 Audio
Distributed by Brumby Sunstate; Dempsey Your Distributor; New Leaf; Nutri-Books

Ashland Creek Press
2305 Ashland St, Suite C417, Ashland, OR 97520
Tel: 760-300-3620
E-mail: editors@ashlandcreekpress.com
Web Site: www.ashlandcreekpress.com
Key Personnel
Founder & Ed: Midge Raymond *E-mail:* midge@ashlandcreekpress.com; John Yunker
E-mail: john@ashlandcreekpress.com
Founded: 2011
Small, independent publisher of books with a worldview. Our mission is to publish a range of books that foster an appreciation for worlds outside our own, for nature & the animal kingdom & for the ways in which we all connect.
ISBN Prefix(es): 978-0-9796475; 978-1-61822
Number of titles published annually: 5 Print; 5 E-Book
Total Titles: 25 Print; 25 E-Book
Imprints: Ashland Creek Press; Byte Level Books
Membership(s): Independent Book Publishers Association

ASIS International
1625 Prince St, Alexandria, VA 22314
Tel: 703-519-6200 *Fax:* 703-519-6299
E-mail: asis@asisonline.org
Web Site: www.asisonline.org
Key Personnel
Educ Publg Mgr: Evangeline A Pappas
E-mail: evangeline.pappas@asisonline.org
Founded: 1955
Organization for security professionals, with more than 33,000 members worldwide. Dedicated to increasing the effectiveness & productivity of security professionals by developing educational programs & certification reference materials that address broad security interests, such as the annual seminar & exhibits, as well as specific security topics. Also advocates the role & value of the security management profession to business, the media, government entities & the public.
ISBN Prefix(es): 978-1-887056
Number of titles published annually: 3 Print; 2 CD-ROM
Total Titles: 35 Print; 2 CD-ROM

Aslan Publishing
Division of Renaissance Book Services Corp
857 Post Rd, Suite 302, Fairfield, CT 06824
SAN: 242-6129
Tel: 203-372-0300; 203-374-6224 *Fax:* 203-374-4766
E-mail: information@aslanpublishing.com
Web Site: www.aslanpublishing.com
Key Personnel
Pres & Lib Sales Dir: Harold Levine
E-mail: harold@aslanpublishing.com
Founded: 1984
Publish nonfiction books on personal growth, psychology & inspiration, parenting & education, health & cooking.
ISBN Prefix(es): 978-0-944031
Number of titles published annually: 3 Print
Total Titles: 32 Print

§ASM International
9639 Kinsman Rd, Materials Park, OH 44073-0002
SAN: 204-7586
Tel: 440-338-5151 *Toll Free Tel:* 800-336-5152; 800-368-9800 (Europe) *Fax:* 440-338-4634
E-mail: memberservicecenter@asminternational.org
Web Site: www.asminternational.org
Key Personnel
Mgr, Prodn: Madrid Tramble *Tel:* 440-338-5151 ext 5241
Founded: 1913
Technical & reference books.
ISBN Prefix(es): 978-0-87170
Number of titles published annually: 10 Print; 1 CD-ROM; 35 Online
Total Titles: 210 Print; 1,000 Online

§ASM Press
Division of American Society for Microbiology
1752 "N" St NW, Washington, DC 20036-2904
Tel: 202-737-3600 *Fax:* 202-942-9342
E-mail: books@asmusa.org
Web Site: www.asmscience.org
Key Personnel
Dir: Christine Charlip *E-mail:* ccharlip@asmusa.org
Edit & Rts Coord: Lindsay Williams
E-mail: lwilliams@asmusa.org
Founded: 1899
Microbiology, cell biology, medicine, books, journals, proceedings & abstracts.
ISBN Prefix(es): 978-1-55581
Number of titles published annually: 14 Print; 15 Online
Total Titles: 250 Print; 25 Online
Foreign Rep(s): Cranbury International LLC (Latin America); Information & Culture Korea (ICK) (South Korea); Donald MacIvor & Associates (Canada); Taylor & Francis Group (UK)
Foreign Rights: Aditya Books Pvt Ltd (Bangladesh, India, Nepal, Pakistan, Sri Lanka); Apex Knowledge Sdn Bhd (Brunei, Malaysia); Booknet Co Ltd (Cambodia, Laos, Myanmar, Thailand, Vietnam); iCaves Ltd (China, Hong Kong, Macau); IG Knowledge Services Ltd (Taiwan); MegaTEXTS Phil Inc (Philippines); United Publishers Services Ltd (Japan); John Wiley & Sons Ltd (Africa, Europe, Middle East); Woodslane (Australia, Fiji, New Zealand, Papua New Guinea, Solomon Islands)
Orders to: PO Box 605, Herndon, VA 20172
Tel: 703-661-1593 *Fax:* 703-661-1501
E-mail: asmmail@presswarehouse.com
Returns: PO Box 605, Herndon, VA 20172
Tel: 703-661-1593 *Fax:* 703-661-1501
E-mail: asmmail@presswarehouse.com
Warehouse: 22883 Quicksilver Dr, Dulles, VA 20166 *Toll Free Tel:* 800-546-2416

§Aspatore Books
Division of Thomson Reuters
610 Opperman Dr, Eagan, MN 55123
Tel: 651-687-7000 *Toll Free Tel:* 866-ASPATORE (277-2867); 888-728-7677; 800-328-4880
E-mail: customerservice@thomsonreuters.com
Web Site: legalsolutions.thomsonreuters.com; www.aspatore.com
Founded: 1999

Publish only the biggest names in the business world, including C-Level leaders (CEO, CTO, CFO, COO, CMO, Partner) from over half the world's 500 largest companies & other leading executives. By focusing on publishing only C-Level executives, we provide professionals of all levels with proven business intelligence from industry insiders, rather than relying on the knowledge of unknown authors & analysts.
ISBN Prefix(es): 978-0-314; 978-1-58762; 978-1-59622
Number of titles published annually: 150 Print
Total Titles: 500 Print
Imprints: Aspatore Thought Leadership; Bigwig Briefs; Executive Reports; Inside the Minds; Line by Line

Aspen Publishers Inc, see Wolters Kluwer Law & Business

Associated University Presses
10 Schalks Crossing Rd, Suite 501-330, Plainsboro, NJ 08536
Tel: 609-269-8094 *Fax:* 609-269-8096
E-mail: aup440@aol.com
Founded: 1968
Book publisher & licensor of intellectual property rights.
ISBN Prefix(es): 978-0-8453
Number of titles published annually: 3 Print; 3 E-Book
Total Titles: 3,000 E-Book
Distributor for Susquehanna University Press

§Association for Computing Machinery
2 Penn Plaza, Suite 701, New York, NY 10121-0701
SAN: 267-7784
Mailing Address: PO Box 30777, New York, NY 10087-0777
Tel: 212-869-7440 *Toll Free Tel:* 800-342-6626 *Fax:* 212-944-1318 (memb servs)
E-mail: acmhelp@acm.org
Web Site: www.acm.org
Key Personnel
Publg Dir: Scott Delman *E-mail:* scott.delman@hq.acm.org
Founded: 1947
Computer science.
ISBN Prefix(es): 978-0-89791; 978-1-58113; 978-1-59593; 978-1-60558; 978-1-4503
Number of titles published annually: 150 Print
Total Titles: 500 Print
Foreign Office(s): FIT Bldg 1-118, Tsinghua University, Beijing 100084, China *Tel:* (010) 62783549 *E-mail:* acmchina@tsinghua.edu.cn
Membership(s): AAP

Association for Information Science & Technology (ASIS&T)
8555 16 St, Suite 850, Silver Spring, MD 20910
Tel: 301-495-0900 *Fax:* 301-495-0810
E-mail: asist@asist.org
Web Site: www.asist.org
Key Personnel
Exec Dir: Lydia Middleton
Founded: 1937
Provides high-quality conference programs & publications for information systems developers, online professionals, information resource managers, librarians, records managers, academics & others who "bridge the gap".
ISBN Prefix(es): 978-0-87715
Number of titles published annually: 12 Print; 1 CD-ROM; 1 Online
Total Titles: 12 Print; 1 CD-ROM; 1 Online
Distributed by Information Today, Inc; John Wiley & Sons Inc

Association for Talent Development (ATD) Press
1640 King St, Box 1443, Alexandria, VA 22313-1443
SAN: 224-8972
Tel: 703-683-8100 *Toll Free Tel:* 800-628-2783 *Fax:* 703-299-8723; 703-683-1523 (cust care)
E-mail: customercare@td.org
Web Site: www.astd.org; www.td.org
Key Personnel
Pres & CEO: Tony Bingham
Dir, Pubns & Edit: Kristine Luecker *E-mail:* kluecker@td.org
Mktg Mgr, Pubns: Deborah Orgel Hudson *E-mail:* dhudson@td.org
Founded: 1944
Internationally renowned source of insightful & practical information for professionals & general readers on workplace learning & performance topics, including training basics, evaluation & return-on investment, instructional systems development, e-learning, leadership & career development.
ISBN Prefix(es): 978-1-56286; 978-1-60728
Number of titles published annually: 25 Print; 4 CD-ROM
Total Titles: 200 Print
Distributed by Cengage Learning Asia Pte Ltd (Asia); Eurospan Group (Europe, Middle East & the former Soviet Bloc); Knowledge Resources (South Africa); National Book Network (NBN) (US, CN, Australia & New Zealand)
Membership(s): AAP; Association Media & Publishing

Association of College & Research Libraries (ACRL)
Division of The American Library Association (ALA)
50 E Huron St, Chicago, IL 60611
Tel: 312-280-2523 *Toll Free Tel:* 800-545-2433 (ext 2523) *Fax:* 312-280-2520
E-mail: acrl@ala.org
Web Site: www.ala.org/acrl
Key Personnel
Exec Dir: Mary Ellen K Davis *Tel:* 312-280-3248 *E-mail:* mdavis@ala.org
Founded: 1938
Higher education association for librarians. Representing more than 11,000 academic & research librarians & interested individuals, ACRL develops programs, products & services to help academic & research librarians learn, innovate & lead within the academic community. ACRL is the largest division of the American Library Association (ALA).
ISBN Prefix(es): 978-0-8389
Number of titles published annually: 15 Print; 15 E-Book
Total Titles: 125 Print; 70 E-Book
Foreign Rep(s): Baker & Taylor International; Booknet Co Ltd (Cambodia, Laos, Thailand); Cranbury International (Caribbean, Latin America, Mexico, Puerto Rico); Eurospan (Africa, Europe, Israel, UK); iGroup (Asia-Pacific); Ontario Library Association (Canada); PMS Publishers Services Pte Ltd (Singapore)
Orders to: American Library Association, PO Box 17219, Atlanta, GA 30368-7219 *Toll Free Tel:* 866-746-7252 *Fax:* 312-280-5860 *E-mail:* alastore@ala.org *Web Site:* www.alastore.ala.org
Returns: American Library Association, Attn: Receiving Dept, 3280 Summit Ridge Pkwy, Duluth, GA 30096-1616
Membership(s): ALA; Association for Information Science & Technology; Association of Research Libraries; MLA

Association of Research Libraries
21 Dupont Circle NW, Suite 800, Washington, DC 20036
Tel: 202-296-2296 *Fax:* 202-872-0884
E-mail: arlhq@arl.org
Web Site: www.arl.org
Key Personnel
Pubns Prog Offr: Lee Anne George *E-mail:* leeanne@arl.org
Founded: 1932
Serial, occasional paper series & special topics of interest.
ISBN Prefix(es): 978-0-918006; 978-1-59407
Number of titles published annually: 8 Print; 14 Online; 8 E-Book
Total Titles: 600 Print; 100 Online; 74 E-Book
Distribution Center: ARL Publications Distribution Center, PO Box 531, Annapolis Junction, MD 20701-0531 *Tel:* 301-362-8196 *Fax:* 240-396-2479 *E-mail:* arl@brightkey.net
Membership(s): AAP

Association of School Business Officials International
11401 N Shore Dr, Reston, VA 20190
Tel: 703-478-0405 *Toll Free Tel:* 866-682-2729 *Fax:* 703-708-7060
E-mail: asboreq@asbointl.org; asbosba@asbointl.org
Web Site: www.asbointl.org
Founded: 1910
Professional books co-published with Rowman & Littlefield Education.
ISBN Prefix(es): 978-0-910170; 978-0-810847; 978-1-1578860
Number of titles published annually: 8 Print
Total Titles: 40 Print

Asta Publications LLC
275 W Clarkstown Rd, New City, NY 10956
Tel: 678-814-1320 *Toll Free Tel:* 800-482-4190 *Fax:* 678-814-1370
E-mail: info@astapublications.com
Web Site: www.astapublications.com
Key Personnel
CEO: Assuanta Howard *E-mail:* ahoward@astapublications.com
Founded: 2004
Delivering first-class book publishing services for corporations, entrepreneurs & individuals who understand the power of being a published author.
This publisher has indicated that 30% of their product line is author subsidized.
ISBN Prefix(es): 978-0-9777060; 978-1-934947
Number of titles published annually: 200 Print; 200 Online; 200 E-Book
Total Titles: 500 Print; 500 Online; 500 E-Book
Membership(s): The Association of Publishers for Special Sales; The Imaging Alliance

§ASTM International
100 Barr Harbor Dr, West Conshohocken, PA 19428-2959
Mailing Address: PO Box C-700, West Conshohocken, PA 19428
Tel: 610-832-9500; 610-832-9585 (intl) *Toll Free Tel:* 877-909-2786 (sales & cust support) *Fax:* 610-832-9555
E-mail: service@astm.org
Web Site: www.astm.org
Key Personnel
Pres: James A Thomas *Tel:* 610-832-9598 *Fax:* 610-832-9599 *E-mail:* jthomas@astm.org
VP, Pubns & Mktg: John Pace *Tel:* 610-832-9632 *E-mail:* jpace@astm.org
Mgr, Sales & Mktg: George Zajdel *Tel:* 610-832-9614 *E-mail:* gzajdel@astm.org
Founded: 1898
Standards, technical publications, data series manuals & journals on engineering, science, materials testing, safety, quality control.
ISBN Prefix(es): 978-0-8031
Number of titles published annually: 176 Print; 125 CD-ROM
Total Titles: 1,500 Print; 125 CD-ROM; 80 Online

Astragal Press
Imprint of Finney Company Inc
5995 149 St W, Suite 105, Apple Valley, MN 55124
Tel: 952-469-6699 *Toll Free Tel:* 866-543-3045 *Fax:* 952-469-1968 *Toll Free Fax:* 800 330 6232
E-mail: info@finneyco.com
Web Site: www.astragalpress.com
Key Personnel
Pres: Alan Krysan *E-mail:* akrysan@finneyco.com
Founded: 1983
Early tools, trades & technology.
ISBN Prefix(es): 978-0-9618088; 978-1-879335; 978-1-931626
Number of titles published annually: 5 Print
Total Titles: 89 Print; 89 Online

The Astronomical Society of the Pacific
390 Ashton Ave, San Francisco, CA 94112
Tel: 415-337-1100 *Toll Free Tel:* 800-335-2624 *Fax:* 415-337-5205
Web Site: www.astrosociety.org
Key Personnel
Exec Dir: Dr Linda Shore *Tel:* 415-715-1411 *E-mail:* lshore@astrosociety.org
Founded: 1889
Books, booklets, tapes, slide sets, software & other educational materials about astronomy; conference proceedings. Publisher of *Mercury Magazine*. PASP (Publications of the Astronomical Society of the Pacific) Journal.
ISBN Prefix(es): 978-0-937707; 978-1-886733; 978-1-58381
Number of titles published annually: 20 Print; 1 CD-ROM; 20 E-Book; 1 Audio
Total Titles: 360 Print; 1 CD-ROM; 60 E-Book; 1 Audio

ATD Press, see Association for Talent Development (ATD) Press

Atheneum Books for Young Readers, see Simon & Schuster Children's Publishing

Athletic Guide Publishing
PO Box 1050, Flagler Beach, FL 32136
Tel: 386-439-2050 *Toll Free Tel:* 800-255-1050
E-mail: flaglernet@gmail.com
Web Site: www.athleticguidepublishing.com
Key Personnel
Ed: Tom Keegan
Founded: 1990
Publishes college & prep school sports guides for all NCAA sports.
ISBN Prefix(es): 978-1-880941; 978-1-60179
Number of titles published annually: 35 Print
Total Titles: 120 Print
Imprints: American Sports Publishing; Old Kings Road Press
Membership(s): Independent Book Publishers Association

Atlantic Law Book Co
Division of Peter Kelsey Publishing Inc
22 Grassmere Ave, West Hartford, CT 06110-1215
Tel: 860-231-9300 *Toll Free Tel:* 800-259-5534 *Fax:* 860-231-9242
E-mail: atlanticlawbooks@aol.com
Web Site: www.atlanticlawbooks.com
Key Personnel
VP: Richard Epstein
Founded: 1945
Law books for Connecticut legal practice. Marketed in Connecticut & other states & used by practitioners & judges in this state. The books are all written by law professors, lawyers or judges who are recognized experts in their respective fields. The material is updated regularly, usually by annual pocket supplements.
This publisher has indicated that 100% of their product line is author subsidized.
ISBN Prefix(es): 978-1-878698
Number of titles published annually: 12 Print; 2 CD-ROM
Total Titles: 12 Print; 2 CD-ROM

§Atlantic Publishing Group Inc
1405 SW Sixth Ave, Ocala, FL 34471
Tel: 352-622-1825 *Toll Free Tel:* 800-814-1132 *Fax:* 352-622-1875
E-mail: sales@atlantic-pub.com
Web Site: www.atlantic-pub.com
Key Personnel
Pres: Douglas R Brown
VP: Sherri L Brown
Founded: 1982
Provides millions of readers information to jump-start their careers, start businesses, manage employees, invest, plan for retirement, learn technologies, build relationships & live rewarding, fulfilling lives.
ISBN Prefix(es): 978-0-910627; 978-1-60138; 978-1-62023
Number of titles published annually: 100 Print; 25 CD-ROM
Total Titles: 500 Print; 150 CD-ROM
Returns: 315 E Washington St, Starke, FL 32091
Distribution Center: 315 E Washington St, Starke, FL 32091
Membership(s): AAP; ABA; American Publishers Association; The Association of Publishers for Special Sales; Florida Authors & Publishers Association Inc; Independent Book Publishers Association; Young Adult Library Services Association

§Atlas Publishing
25185 Madison Ave, Suite A, Murrieta, CA 92562
Tel: 858-222-3747
E-mail: permissions@atlaspublishing.biz
Web Site: www.atlaspublishing.biz
Key Personnel
Mng Ed: Brent D Tharp *E-mail:* brent@atlaspublishing.biz
Founded: 2011
Traditional publisher of children's & nonfiction titles. Author services also available for books not printed under our imprint. Please note that the only fiction titles that we print under our imprint are children's books. We can provide editing services for all genres, but publish only children's books & nonfiction titles. Writers interested in submitting materials may do so directly, but initial submissions should be limited to query letters, sell sheets, & synopses. Please do not submit full mss or attachments at the initial query stage as they will not be reviewed.
ISBN Prefix(es): 978-0-9969679; 978-1-945033
Number of titles published annually: 4 Print; 3 E-Book
Total Titles: 10 Print; 10 E-Book
Distribution Center: Ingram
Membership(s): Editorial Freelancers Association; Independent Book Publishers Association

Atria Books
Imprint of Atria Publishing Group
1230 Avenue of the Americas, New York, NY 10020
Tel: 212-698-7000 *Fax:* 212-698-7007
Web Site: www.simonandschuster.com
Key Personnel
Pres & Publr, Atria Publishing Group: Judith Curr *Tel:* 212-698-1260 *E-mail:* judith.curr@simonandschuster.com
SVP & Ed-in-Chief, Emily Bestler Books: Emily Bestler *Tel:* 212-698-7685 *E-mail:* emily.bestler@simonandschuster.com
VP & Ed-in-Chief: Peter Borland *Tel:* 212-698-7569 *E-mail:* peter.borland@simonandschuster.com
VP & Exec Ed: Johanna Castillo *Tel:* 212-698-7339 *E-mail:* johanna.castillo@simonandschuster.com
VP & Dir, Subs Rts: Lisa Keim *Tel:* 212-698-7397 *E-mail:* lisa.keim@simonandschuster.com
VP, Dir of Publicity: Paul Olsewski *Tel:* 212-698-7089 *E-mail:* paul.olsewski@simonandschuster.com
VP, Publr, 37 Ink: Dawn Davis *Tel:* 212-698-2246 *E-mail:* dawn.davis@simonandschuster.com
Exec Ed: Sarah Pelz *Tel:* 212-698-7172 *E-mail:* sarah.pelz@simonandschuster.com
Sr Dir, Art & Design: Albert Tang *Tel:* 212-698-7255 *E-mail:* albert.tang@simonandschuster.com
Sr Ed: Mr Rakesh Satyal *E-mail:* rakesh.satyal@simonandschuster.com; Sarah Cantin *Tel:* 212-698-7057 *E-mail:* sarah.cantin@simonandschuster.com; Jhanteigh Kupihea *Tel:* 212-698-1102 *E-mail:* jhanteigh.kupihea@simonandschuster.com
Ed: Todd Hunter *Tel:* 212-698-7696 *E-mail:* todd.hunter@simonandschuster.com; Daniella Wexler *Tel:* 212-698-2822 *E-mail:* daniella.wexler@simonandschuster.com
Founded: 2002
ISBN Prefix(es): 978-0-671; 978-0-7434; 978-0-7432
Imprints: Atria Trade Paperback; Emily Bestler Books; Beyond Words; Enliven; Keywords Press; Marble Arch; Skybound Books; Strebor Books; 37 Ink; Washington Square Press
Foreign Rights: Akcali Copyright Agency (Turkey); Antonella Antonelli Agenzia (Italy); Bardon-Chinese Media Agency (China, Thailand); The Book Publishers' Association of Israel, International Promotion & Literary Rights Department (Israel); Japan UNI Agency Inc (Japan); JLM Literary Agency (Greece); MOHRBOOKS AG, Literary Agency (Germany); La Nouvelle Agency; Andrew Nurnberg Associates Ltd (Bulgaria, Croatia, Estonia, Hungary, Latvia, Lithuania, Montenegro, Poland, Romania, Russia, Serbia, Slovakia, Slovenia); Sane Toregard Agency (Denmark, Finland, Norway, Sweden); Sebes & Bisseling Literary Agency; Tuttle-Mori Agency Inc (Thailand); Eric Yang Agency

Atwood Publishing
PO Box 3185, Madison, WI 53704
Tel: 608-242-7101 *Toll Free Tel:* 888-242-7101 *Fax:* 608-242-7102
E-mail: customerservice@atwoodpublishing.com
Web Site: www.atwoodpublishing.com
Key Personnel
Publr: Linda Babler *E-mail:* lindab@atwoodpublishing.com
Founded: 1997
Book publishing for higher education market: teaching improvement, distance, education, student affairs, semiotics & administration.
ISBN Prefix(es): 978-1-891859
Number of titles published annually: 6 Print
Total Titles: 60 Print; 2 CD-ROM; 8 E-Book
Returns: 2095 Winnebago St, Suite B, Madison, WI 53704

§Augsburg Fortress Publishers, Publishing House of the Evangelical Lutheran Church in America
510 Marquette Ave S, Minneapolis, MN 55402
SAN: 169-4081
Mailing Address: PO Box 1209, Minneapolis, MN 55440-1209
Tel: 612-330-3300 *Toll Free Tel:* 800-426-0115 (ext 639, subns); 800-328-4648 (orders)
Fax: 612-330-3455

E-mail: info@augsburgfortress.org; copyright@augsburgfortress.org (reprint permission requests); customercare@augsburgfortress.org
Web Site: www.augsburgfortress.org
Key Personnel
Pres & CEO: Beth A Lewis *E-mail:* ceo@1517.media
CFO: John Rahja *E-mail:* rahjaj@1517.media
SVP & Publr: Tim Blevins *Tel:* 612-330-3300 ext 400 *E-mail:* blevinst@1517.media
VP & Publr, Fortress Press: Will Bergkamp *E-mail:* bergkampw@1517.media
VP & Publr, Sparkhouse: Tim Paulson *E-mail:* paulsont@1517.media
VP, HR: Sandy Amundson *E-mail:* amundsons@1517.media
Publr, Worship & Music: Martin Seltz *E-mail:* seltzm@1517.media
Perms, Pubns: Michael Moore *E-mail:* moorem@1517.media
Founded: 1855
ISBN Prefix(es): 978-0-8066; 978-0-8006
Number of titles published annually: 100 Print
Total Titles: 4,600 Print; 1,700 E-Book; 3,500 Audio
Imprints: Augsburg Books; Fortress Press; Sparkhouse
Sales Office(s): PO Box 1209, Minneapolis, MN 55440-1209
Foreign Rep(s): Asian Trading Corp (India); Australian Church Resources (Australia); Canaanland Distributors Sdn Bhd (Malaysia); Cross Communications Ltd (Hong Kong); Durnell Marketing (Israel); John Garratt Publishing (Australia); Glad Sounds Sdn Bhd (Malaysia); KCBS Inc (Korea); Kyo Bun Kwan Inc (Japan); Logos Publishers Ltd (Hong Kong); MediaCom Education (Australia); N-Online Co Ltd (Japan); NBN International (Europe, UK); Pustaka Sufes Sdn Bhd (Malaysia); SKS Books Warehouse (Singapore); Soul Distributors Ltd (New Zealand); Taosheng Publishing House (Hong Kong); Tecman Management Services (Singapore)
Foreign Rights: Rowman & Littlefield Publishing Group (worldwide exc Korea)
Billing Address: PO Box 1209, Minneapolis, MN 55440-1209
Orders to: PBD Worldwide, c/o AF Distribution, 905 Carlow Dr, Unit B, Bolingbrook, IL 60490
Warehouse: PBD Worldwide, c/o AF Distribution, 905 Carlow Dr, Unit B, Bolingbrook, IL 60490
Distribution Center: PBD Worldwide, c/o AF Distribution, 905 Carlow Dr, Unit B, Bolingbrook, IL 60490

August House Inc
3500 Piedmont Rd NE, Suite 310, Atlanta, GA 30305
Tel: 404-442-4420 *Toll Free Tel:* 800-284-8784 *Fax:* 404-442-4435
E-mail: ahinfo@augusthouse.com
Web Site: www.augusthouse.com
Key Personnel
CEO: Steve Floyd *E-mail:* steve@augusthouse.com
EVP & Creative Dir: Graham Anthony *E-mail:* graham@augusthouse.com
Dir, Devt: Rob Cleveland *E-mail:* rob@augusthouse.com
Founded: 1979
Folklore, multicultural folktales & storytelling.
ISBN Prefix(es): 978-0-87483
Number of titles published annually: 15 Print; 30 Online; 15 E-Book
Total Titles: 350 Print; 300 Online; 15 E-Book; 71 Audio
Imprints: August House Audio; August House Little Folk; August House Story Cove
Foreign Rights: The Fielding Agency (Whitney Lee)

Aum Publications
86-10 Parsons Blvd, Jamaica, NY 11432-3314
SAN: 201-128X
Tel: 347-744-3199
Key Personnel
Pres: Carl Brown
Founded: 1973
Trade paperbacks; literature, Eastern philosophy, theology, occult, poetry, meditation; only books on or by Sri Chinmoy.
ISBN Prefix(es): 978-0-88497
Number of titles published annually: 5 Print
Total Titles: 53 Print; 2 CD-ROM
Distribution Center: Heart-Light Distributors, PO Box 85464, Seattle, WA 98145 *Toll Free Tel:* 800-739-2885 *Fax:* 206-523-5637

AuthorHouse
Division of Author Solutions LLC
1663 Liberty Dr, Bloomington, IN 47403
Tel: 812-339-6000 (outside US) *Toll Free Tel:* 888-519-5121
E-mail: authorsupport@authorhouse.com
Web Site: www.authorhouse.com
Key Personnel
CEO: Andrew Phillips
COO: Kevin G Gregory
CIO: Randy Davis
SVP, Mktg: Keith Ogorek
SVP, Prodn Servs & Output Opers: Bill Becher
SVP, Worldwide Sales: Don Seitz
VP, Mktg: Tracey Rosengrave
VP, Sales & Mktg: Bruce Bunner
Founded: 1997
The leading provider of indie book publishing, marketing & bookselling services for authors around the globe. Committed to providing the highest level of customer service. Assign each author personal publishing & marketing consultants who provide guidance throughout the process.
This publisher has indicated that 100% of their product line is author subsidized.
ISBN Prefix(es): 978-1-58500; 978-0-9675669; 978-1-58721; 978-1-58820; 978-0-7596; 978-1-4033; 978-1-4107; 978-1-4140; 978-1-4184; 978-1-4208
Number of titles published annually: 7,500 Print
Total Titles: 80,000 Print
Foreign Office(s): AuthorHouse UK, 500 Avebury Blvd, Milton Keynes MK9 2BE, United Kingdom *Toll Free Tel:* 800-197-4150 *Toll Free Fax:* 800-197-4151
Distribution Center: Baker & Taylor Inc, 2550 W Tyvola Rd, Suite 300, Charlotte, NC 28217
Ingram Book Group, One Ingram Blvd, La Vergne, TN 37086-1986
Membership(s): ABA; Canadian Booksellers Association

§Authorlink Press
Imprint of Authorlink®
103 Guadalupe Dr, Irving, TX 75039-3334
Tel: 972-402-0101
E-mail: admin@authorlink.com
Web Site: www.authorlink.com
Key Personnel
Founder, CEO & Ed-in-Chief: Doris Booth *E-mail:* dbooth@authorlink.com
Founded: 1996
E-book publishing services to approximately 150-200 authors each year, from design & production to conversion & consulting on distribution. Also acts as a traditional publisher specializing in true crime, books about the craft of writing, books on women's issues & some self-help. All print titles are on demand. Award-winning rights market-place where editors & agents buy & sell unpublished & published mss & screenplays. Provide the serious writer with exposure to the broadest range of publishing professionals. Plus industry news & information for publishers, literary agents, writers & readers.
This publisher has indicated that 60% of their product line is author subsidized.
ISBN Prefix(es): 978-1-928704
Number of titles published annually: 10 Print; 150 E-Book
Total Titles: 10 Print; 150 E-Book
Orders to: Lightning Source, 1246 Heil Quaker Blvd, La Vergne, TN 37086 *Tel:* 615-213-5815 *Fax:* 615-213-4426 *E-mail:* inquiry@lightningsource.com *Web Site:* www.lightningsource.com
Distribution Center: Lightning Source, 1246 Heil Quaker Blvd, La Vergne, TN 37086 *Tel:* 615-213-5815 *Fax:* 615-213-4426 *E-mail:* inquiry@lightningsource.com *Web Site:* www.lightningsource.com
Membership(s): Independent Book Publishers Association

Autism Asperger Publishing Co
11209 Strang Line Rd, Lenexa, KS 66215
Tel: 913-897-1004 *Toll Free Tel:* 877-277-8254 *Fax:* 913-681-9473
E-mail: info@aapcpublishing.net
Web Site: www.aapcpublishing.net
Key Personnel
Pres: Keith Myles *Tel:* 913-232-4500 *E-mail:* keith.myles@aapcpublishing.net
Dir, Opers: James Jones *Tel:* 913-232-4501 *E-mail:* james.jones@aapcpublishing.net
Gen Mgr: Serdar Marun *Tel:* 913-232-4505 *E-mail:* serdar.marun@aapcpublishing.net
Specialize in books & multimedia on autism spectrum disorders (ASD) & related exceptionalities for individuals on the spectrum, their parents, families, peers, educators & other professionals.
ISBN Prefix(es): 978-0-9672514; 978-1-931282; 978-1-937473; 978-1-934575
Number of titles published annually: 24 Print
Branch Office(s)
122 "C" St NW, Suite 360, Washington, DC 20001 *Tel:* 202-298-6449

Autumn House Press
5530 Penn Ave, Pittsburgh, PA 15206
Tel: 412-362-2665
E-mail: info@autumnhouse.org
Web Site: www.autumnhouse.org
Key Personnel
Ed-in-Chief: Christine Stroud *E-mail:* cstroud@autumnhouse.org
Mng Ed: Ryan Kaune *E-mail:* rkaune@autumnhouse.org
Asst Ed: Alison Taverna *E-mail:* ataverna@autumnhouse.org
Founded: 1998
Nonprofit corporation with the mission of publishing poetry, fiction & nonfiction. Submissions should be through one of the annual contests. Guidelines are posted on the web site.
Publish the online journal *Coal Hill Review.*
ISBN Prefix(es): 978-0-9669419; 978-1-932870
Number of titles published annually: 10 Print; 1 Online; 10 E-Book
Total Titles: 100 Print; 12 Online; 50 E-Book
Distribution Center: University Press of New England (UPNE), One Court St, Suite 250, Lebanon, NH 03766 *Tel:* 603-448-1533 *Toll Free Tel:* 800-421-1561 *E-mail:* university.press@dartmouth.edu *Web Site:* www.upne.com

Ave Maria Press
PO Box 428, Notre Dame, IN 46556
SAN: 201-1255
Tel: 574-287-2831 *Toll Free Tel:* 800-282-1865 *Fax:* 574-239-2904 *Toll Free Fax:* 800-282-5681
E-mail: avemariapress.1@nd.edu
Web Site: www.avemariapress.com
Key Personnel
CEO & Publr: Thomas Grady *Tel:* 574-287-2831 ext 212 *E-mail:* tgrady@nd.edu

VP & Creative Dir: Kristen Bonelli *Tel:* 574-287-2831 ext 240 *E-mail:* hornyak.3@nd.edu
VP & Dir, Sales & Mktg: Karey Circosta *Tel:* 574-287-2831 ext 219 *E-mail:* kcircosta@nd.edu
Exec Ed: Jon M Sweeney
Sales Mgr: Kay Luther *Tel:* 574-287-2831 ext 232 *E-mail:* k.luther.8@nd.edu
Acqs Ed: Heidi Hess Saxton
Founded: 1865
Adult paperback books of religious interest; prayer books & religious education materials, programs & textbooks.
ISBN Prefix(es): 978-0-87793 (Ave Maria Press); 978-0-939516 (Forest of Peace); 978-0-87061 (Christian Classics); 978-1-893732 (Sorin Books); 978-1-59471 (Ave Maria Press); 978-1-933495 (Sorin Books)
Number of titles published annually: 40 Print
Total Titles: 550 Print
Imprints: Ave Maria Press; Christian Classics; Forest of Peace; Sorin Books
Foreign Rep(s): Alban Books Ltd (UK); John Garratt Publishing (Australia); Joseph's Inspirational (Canada); Pleroma Christian Supplies (New Zealand)
Returns: 1865 Moreau Dr, Notre Dame, IN 46556

§Avention Inc
300 Baker Ave, Concord, MA 01742
Tel: 978-318-4300 *Toll Free Tel:* 866-354-6936 *Fax:* 978-318-4690
E-mail: sales@avention.com
Web Site: www.avention.com
Key Personnel
CEO: Steve Pogorzelski
CTO: Hank Weghorst
Database of approximately 50,000 US technicians, manufacturers, developers & services.
ISBN Prefix(es): 978-1-57114
Number of titles published annually: 5 Online
Total Titles: 5 CD-ROM; 5 Online
Branch Office(s)
6801 N Capital of Texas Hwy, Bldg 2, Suite 150, Austin, TX 78731 *Tel:* 512-614-5447
Foreign Office(s): Citigroup Ctr, Level 39, 2 Park St, Sydney, NSW 2000, Australia *Tel:* (02) 9004 7868 *Fax:* (02) 9004 7070
Global Business Park, MG Rd, Gurgaon 122 002, India *Tel:* (0124) 4934700
208-A Telok Ayer St, Singapore 068642, Singapore *Tel:* 6221 7920 *Fax:* 6221 7929
55 Old Broad St, 3rd fl, London EC2M 1RX, United Kingdom *Tel:* (020) 7382 8800 *Fax:* (020) 7382 8801

Avery
Imprint of Penguin Group USA, A Penguin Random House Company
375 Hudson St, New York, NY 10014
SAN: 282-5074
Tel: 212-366-2000 *Fax:* 212-366-2643
Web Site: www.penguin.com; www.penguinrandomhouse.com
Key Personnel
VP & Publr: Megan Newman
VP & Publr, Pam Krauss Books & Ed-at-Large, Avery: Pam Krauss
Exec Ed: Lucia Watson
Ed-in-Chief: Caroline Sutton
Publicity & Mktg Dir: Lindsay Gordon
Assoc Dir, Publicity: Anne Kosmoski
Asst Dir, Publicity: Casey Maloney
Assoc Publicist: Ally Bruschi
Founded: 1976 (acquired by The Penguin Group in the fall of 1999)
The imprint is dedicated to publishing books on health & nutrition with a complimentary, natural, or alternative focus.
ISBN Prefix(es): 978-0-89529; 978-1-58333
Number of titles published annually: 35 Print
Total Titles: 247 Print
Imprints: Pam Krauss Books

Avery Color Studios
511 "D" Ave, Gwinn, MI 49841
Tel: 906-346-3908 *Toll Free Tel:* 800-722-9925 *Fax:* 906-346-3015
E-mail: averycolor@averycolorstudios.com
Web Site: www.averycolorstudios.com
Key Personnel
Pres: Wells Chapin
Busn Mgr: Amy Chapin
Founded: 1956
Regional publisher specializing in nautical books.
ISBN Prefix(es): 978-0-932212; 978-1-892384
Number of titles published annually: 4 Print
Total Titles: 46 Print

AVKO Educational Research Foundation Inc
3084 Willard Rd, Birch Run, MI 48415-9404
Tel: 810-686-9283 (orders & billing) *Fax:* 810-686-1101
E-mail: info@avko.org (gen inquiry)
Web Site: www.avko.org; www.avko.blogspot.org
Key Personnel
Res Dir: Don McCabe *Tel:* 810-686-9283 ext 203 *E-mail:* donmccabe@aol.com
Opers Mgr: Robert McCabe *Tel:* 810-686-9283 ext 202 *E-mail:* brian@avko.org
Accts Receivable & Accts Payable: Sue Johnson *Tel:* 810-686-9283 ext 201 *E-mail:* avkosueat@aol.com
Founded: 1974
Nonprofit organization devoted to providing free & low-cost materials for teaching language arts, keyboarding & reference. Our materials work great for dyslexics, homeschoolers & school teachers.
ISBN Prefix(es): 978-1-56400
Total Titles: 49 Print; 6 CD-ROM; 60 E-Book

AVKO Foundation, see AVKO Educational Research Foundation Inc

Avotaynu Inc
794 Edgewood Ave, New Haven, CT 06515
Tel: 475-202-6575 *Toll Free Tel:* 800-AVOTAYNU (286-8296)
E-mail: info@avotaynu.com
Web Site: www.avotaynu.com
Key Personnel
Publr: Gary Mokotoff *E-mail:* garymokotoff@avotaynu.com
Founded: 1984
Publisher of information & products of interest to persons researching their Jewish family history. This includes the journal & books.
ISBN Prefix(es): 978-0-9626373; 978-1-886223; 978-0-9836975
Number of titles published annually: 3 Print
Total Titles: 75 Print

§Awe-Struck Publishing
Imprint of Mundania Press LLC
6457 Glenway Ave, Suite 109, Cincinnati, OH 45211-5222
Toll Free Tel: 888-402-6657 *Toll Free Fax:* 888-460-4752
E-mail: inquiry@mundania.com; orders@mundania.com; submissions@awe-struck.net; books@mundania.com
Web Site: www.awe-struck.net; www.mundania.com
Founded: 1998
Full service, royalty paying publisher of electronic books in the following formats: HTML, Rocket, Palm, Visor, Pocket PC, Franklin, eBookman, Hiebook, PDF, MS Reader.
Subsidiary, Earthlink Press, publishes trade paperbacks; fiction (romance & science fiction) for disabled readers (Ennoble Line).
ISBN Prefix(es): 978-1-928670; 978-1-58749
Number of titles published annually: 12 Print; 42 Online; 42 E-Book
Total Titles: 104 Print; 200 Online; 200 E-Book
Subsidiaries: Earthling Press (trade quality print editions); HeatWave Romance (erotic romance/erotica)
Orders to: Celeritas Unlimited LLC, 6457 Glenway Ave, No 109, Cincinaati, OH 45211-5222 (wholesale & volume discounts) *Toll Free Tel:* 888-232-0808 *Toll Free Fax:* 888-460-4752
Membership(s): Independent Book Publishers Association

AZ Books LLC
320 Fifth Ave, New York, NY 10001
Toll Free Tel: 888-945-7723 *Toll Free Fax:* 888-945-7724
Web Site: www.azbooksusa.com
Key Personnel
VP: Robert Tod *Tel:* 888-945-7723 ext 10 *E-mail:* robert@azbooksusa.com
Natl Accts Mgr: Tom Jourdane *Tel:* 801-641-3184 *E-mail:* tom@azbooksusa.com
Edit: Kate Kmit *E-mail:* kate.kmit@az-books.com
Sales: Anastasia Lobynko *E-mail:* anastasia.lobynko@az-books.com
ISBN Prefix(es): 978-0-938045
Number of titles published annually: 20 Print

Azro Press
1704 Llano St B, PMB 342, Santa Fe, NM 87505
Tel: 505-989-3272 *Fax:* 505-989-3832
E-mail: books@azropress.com
Web Site: www.azropress.com
Key Personnel
Pres: Gae Eisenhardt
Founded: 1997
Publish illustrated children's books with a Southwestern flavor.
ISBN Prefix(es): 978-1-929115
Number of titles published annually: 3 Print
Total Titles: 20 Print
Imprints: Green Knees

Babalu Inc
PO Box 23026, Santa Barbara, CA 93121
Toll Free Tel: 877-522-2258
E-mail: morefun@babaluinc.com
Web Site: www.babaluinc.com
Key Personnel
Pres: Blair Everett
Off Mgr: Kylie Castro
Founded: 2006
Children's books, toys & advent calendars.
ISBN Prefix(es): 978-1-56021
Number of titles published annually: 10 Print
Total Titles: 60 Print
Membership(s): ABA; Museum Store Association

Baby Tattoo Books
6045 Longridge Ave, Van Nuys, CA 91401
Tel: 818-416-5314
E-mail: info@babytattoo.com
Web Site: www.babytattoo.com
Key Personnel
Pres & Publr: Robert Self *E-mail:* bob@babytattoo.com
Founded: 2003
Publisher of art books by contemporary artists.
ISBN Prefix(es): 978-0-9729388; 978-0-9778949; 978-0-9793307; 978-0-9845210; 978-1-61404
Number of titles published annually: 4 Print
Total Titles: 30 Print
Orders to: SCB Distributors Inc, 15608 S New Century Dr, Gardena, CA 90248 *Toll Free Tel:* 800-729-6423
Returns: SCB Distributors Inc, 15608 S New Century Dr, Gardena, CA 90248 *Toll Free Tel:* 800-729-6423
Shipping Address: SCB Distributors Inc, 15608 S New Century Dr, Gardena, CA 90248 *Toll Free Tel:* 800-729-6423

Warehouse: SCB Distributors Inc, 15608 S New Century Dr, Gardena, CA 90248 *Toll Free Tel:* 800-729-6423
Distribution Center: SCB Distributors Inc, 15608 S New Century Dr, Gardena, CA 90248 *Toll Free Tel:* 800-729-6423

Back to Eden Books, see Lotus Press

Backbeat Books
Imprint of Hal Leonard Performing Arts Publishing Group
33 Plymouth St, Suite 302, Montclair, NJ 07042
Tel: 973-337-5034 *Toll Free Tel:* 800-637-2852 (Music Dispatch) *Fax:* 973-337-5227
Web Site: www.backbeatbooks.com
Key Personnel
Sr Ed: Bernadette Malavarca
Founded: 1991
Books about popular music & musical instruments.
ISBN Prefix(es): 978-0-87930
Number of titles published annually: 30 Print; 20 E-Book
Total Titles: 400 Print; 300 E-Book
Foreign Rep(s): GPS (Europe, India, Latin America, Mexico, Middle East, Pacific Rim, Russia & former USSR, South America); Publishers Group UK (UK); Woodslane (Australia, New Zealand)
Distribution Center: Hal Leonard Performing Arts Publishing Group, 1210 Innovation Dr, Winona, MN 55987

The Backwaters Press
1124 Pacific St, Suite 8392, Omaha, NE 68108
Tel: 402-451-4052
E-mail: thebackwaterspress@gmail.com
Web Site: www.thebackwaterspress.org
Key Personnel
Ed: James Cihlar
Founded: 1997
Nonprofit 501(c)(3) literary press.
ISBN Prefix(es): 978-0-9677149; 978-0-9726187; 978-0-9765231; 978-0-9785782; 978-0-9793934; 978-0-9816936; 978-1-935218
Number of titles published annually: 5 Print
Total Titles: 95 Print
Membership(s): Association of Writers and Writing Programs; Community of Literary Magazines & Presses

Baen Publishing Enterprises
PO Box 1188, Wake Forest, NC 27588
Tel: 919-570-1640 *Fax:* 919-570-1644
E-mail: info@baen.com
Web Site: www.baen.com
Key Personnel
Publr: Toni Weisskopf *E-mail:* toni@baen.com
Founded: 1984
Only science fiction & fantasy.
ISBN Prefix(es): 978-0-671; 978-0-7434; 978-1-4165
Number of titles published annually: 70 Print; 50 Online; 48 E-Book
Total Titles: 700 Print; 250 Online; 200 E-Book
Distributed by Simon & Schuster
Foreign Rep(s): EYA (South Korea); Lora Fountain (France); Grayhawk Agency (China, Taiwan); Alex Korzhenevshi (Russia); Kristin Olson (Czech Republic); PNLA (Italy); Thomas Schlueck GmbH (Germany); Tuttle-Mori Agency Inc (Japan)

§Bagwyn Books
Imprint of Arizona Center for Medieval & Renaissance Studies (ACMRS)
Lattie F Coor Hall, 4th fl, Rms 4426-4442, 975 S Myrtle Ave, Tempe, AZ 85281
Mailing Address: ACMRS/ASU, PO Box 874402, Tempe, AZ 85287-4402
Tel: 480-965-5900 *Fax:* 480-965-1681
E-mail: bagwynbooks@acmrs.org
Web Site: acmrs.org/publications/bagwyn
Key Personnel
Mng Ed: Roy Rukkila *Tel:* 480-727-6503 *E-mail:* roy.rukkila@acmrs.org
Founded: 2011
Publisher of historical fiction & fantasy from young adult to adult.
ISBN Prefix(es): 978-0-86698
Number of titles published annually: 4 Print; 7 E-Book
Total Titles: 27 Print
Orders to: Chicago Distribution Center, 11030 S Langley Ave, Chicago, IL 60628 *Tel:* 773-702-7000 *Toll Free Tel:* 800-621-2736 *Fax:* 773-702-7212 *Toll Free Fax:* 800-621-8476 *E-mail:* orders@press.uchicago.edu
Returns: Chicago Distribution Center, 11030 S Langley Ave, Chicago, IL 60628 *Tel:* 773-702-7000 *Toll Free Tel:* 800-621-2736 *Fax:* 773-702-7212 *Toll Free Fax:* 800-621-8476 *E-mail:* orders@press.uchicago.edu
Shipping Address: Chicago Distribution Center, 11030 S Langley Ave, Chicago, IL 60628 *Tel:* 773-702-7000 *Toll Free Tel:* 800-621-2736 *Fax:* 773-702-7212 *Toll Free Fax:* 800-621-8476 *E-mail:* orders@press.uchicago.edu
Warehouse: Chicago Distribution Center, 11030 S Langley Ave, Chicago, IL 60628 *Tel:* 773-702-7000 *Toll Free Tel:* 800-621-2736 *Fax:* 773-702-7212 *Toll Free Fax:* 800-621-8476 *E-mail:* orders@press.uchicago.edu
Distribution Center: Chicago Distribution Center, 11030 S Langley Ave, Chicago, IL 60628 *Tel:* 773-702-7000 *Toll Free Tel:* 800-621-2736 *Fax:* 773-702-7212 *Toll Free Fax:* 800-621-8476 *E-mail:* orders@press.uchicago.edu

Baha'i Publishing
Subsidiary of The National Spiritual Assembly of the Baha'is of the United States
401 Greenleaf Ave, Wilmette, IL 60091
Tel: 847-425-7950 *Toll Free Tel:* 800-999-9019 (orders) *Fax:* 847-425-7951
E-mail: bds@usbnc.org
Web Site: books.bahai.us; www.bahaibookstore.com
Key Personnel
Gen Mgr & Rts & Perms: Tim Moore
Founded: 1902
Religion (Baha'i).
ISBN Prefix(es): 978-0-87743; 978-1-931847
Number of titles published annually: 15 Print
Total Titles: 2,000 Print; 250 Audio
Shipping Address: Perseus Distribution, 905 Carlow Dr, Unit B, Bolingbrook, IL 60490

§Baker Books
Division of Baker Publishing Group
PO Box 6287, Grand Rapids, MI 49516-6287
SAN: 299-1500
Tel: 616-676-9185 *Toll Free Tel:* 800-877-2665; 800-679-1957 *Fax:* 616-676-9573 *Toll Free Fax:* 800-398-3111
Web Site: www.bakerpublishinggroup.com
Key Personnel
CEO & Chmn: Richard Baker
Pres: Dwight Baker
EVP, Academic Publg: Jim Kinney
EVP, Sales & Mktg: Dave Lewis
EVP, Trade Publg: Jennifer Leep
Sr Art Dir: Cheryl Van Andel
Dir, Rts & Contracts: Marilyn Gordon
Dist Mgr: Jack Boers
Prodn Mgr: Bob Bol
Founded: 1939
Religion (Protestant).
ISBN Prefix(es): 978-0-8010
Number of titles published annually: 75 Print; 1 CD-ROM; 1 Audio
Total Titles: 1,000 Print
Imprints: Hamewith; Hourglass
Foreign Rep(s): Christian Art (South Africa); Family Reading Publications (Australia); R Mitchell (Canada); Soul Distributors (New Zealand)
Shipping Address: 6030 E Fulton Rd, Ada, MI 49301

Balance Sports Publishing LLC
195 Lucero Way, Portola Valley, CA 94028
SAN: 857-3298
Tel: 650-561-9586 *Fax:* 650-391-9850
E-mail: info@balancesportspublishing.com
Web Site: www.balancesportspublishing.com
Key Personnel
Founder & Publr: Jim Lobdell *E-mail:* jlobdell@balancesportspublishing.com
Founder & Dir, Busn Opers: Colleen Anderson *E-mail:* canderson@balancesportspublishing.com
Founder & Dir, Prod Devt: Steve Seely *E-mail:* sseely@balancesportspublishing.com
Founded: 2008
Publishes high-quality youth sports books for youth sports coaches, parents, athletes & organization leaders. Our mission is to create titles that ensure every child has a positive youth sports experience & that every coach is inspired to help youngsters achieve their goals in sports while developing important life skills & character traits.
ISBN Prefix(es): 978-0-9821317
Number of titles published annually: 3 Print
Total Titles: 12 Print
Returns: 3623 Munster St, Suite B, Hayward, CA 94545, Contact: Bill Armor *Tel:* 510-732-6521 *Fax:* 510-732-6523 *E-mail:* orders@balancesportspublishing.com
Shipping Address: 3623 Munster St, Suite B, Hayward, CA 94545, Contact: Bill Armor *Tel:* 510-732-6521 *Fax:* 510-732-6523
Warehouse: 3623 Munster St, Suite B, Hayward, CA 94545, Contact: Bill Armor *Tel:* 510-732-6521 *Fax:* 510-732-6523
Distribution Center: 3623 Munster St, Suite B, Hayward, CA 94545, Contact: Bill Armor *Tel:* 510-732-6521 *Fax:* 510-732-6523
Membership(s): Independent Book Publishers Association

Ball Publishing, see Chicago Review Press

Ball-Stick-Bird Publications Inc
PO Box 429, Williamstown, MA 01267-0429
SAN: 222-5565
Tel: 413-664-0002 *Fax:* 413-664-0002
E-mail: info@ballstickbird.com
Key Personnel
Pres & Rts & Perms: Dr Renee Fuller, PhD
Founded: 1975
Children's reading series.
ISBN Prefix(es): 978-0-917740
Number of titles published annually: 13 Print
Total Titles: 13 Print; 13 Online

Ballinger Publishing
314 N Spring St, Suite A, Pensacola, FL 32501
Mailing Address: PO Box 12665, Pensacola, FL 32591-2665
Tel: 850-433-1166 *Fax:* 850-435-9174
E-mail: info@ballingerpublishing.com
Web Site: www.ballingerpublishing.com
Key Personnel
Owner & Publr: Malcolm Ballinger *Tel:* 850-433-1166 ext 27 *E-mail:* malcolm@ballingerpublishing.com
Owner: Glenys Ballinger *Tel:* 850-433-1166 ext 22 *E-mail:* glenys@ballingerpublishing.com
Exec Ed: Kelly Oden *Tel:* 850-433-1166 ext 23 *E-mail:* kelly@ballingerpublishing.com
Founded: 2001
Publishers of local & regional magazines.
This publisher has indicated that 100% of their product line is author subsidized.

ISBN Prefix(es): 978-0-9791103
Number of titles published annually: 80 Print

Bancroft Press
3209 Bancroft Rd, Baltimore, MD 21215
Mailing Address: PO Box 65360, Baltimore, MD 21209-9945
Tel: 410-358-0658 *Fax:* 410-764-1967
Web Site: www.bancroftpress.com
Key Personnel
Publr & Design Dir: Andrew Bortz
E-mail: abortz@bancroftpress.com
Ed, Fiction & Nonfiction: Bruce L Bortz
E-mail: bruceb@bancroftpress.com
Founded: 1995
General interest trade book publisher; has received special recognition & ranks among the nation's top 100 independent presses. Worldwide rights & distribution.
ISBN Prefix(es): 978-1-890862
Number of titles published annually: 5 Print; 1 Audio
Total Titles: 60 Print; 1 Audio
Foreign Rights: Barbara Newman
Distribution Center: Bookmasters, 30 Amberwood Pkwy, Ashland, OH 44805

Bandanna Books
1212 Punta Gorda St, No 13, Santa Barbara, CA 93103
SAN: 238-7956
E-mail: bandanna@cox.net
Web Site: www.bandannabooks.com; www.mudbornpress.us; www.betabooks.us; www.shakespeareplaybook.com; www.bookdoc.us; catandbirdiebooks.com
Key Personnel
Publr: Sasha "Birdie" Newborn *E-mail:* birdie.newborn@gmail.com
Founded: 1981 (Outgrowth of Mudborn Press)
College market in literature, poetry, history, translations. Also BetaBooks imprint for DIY authors.
ISBN Prefix(es): 978-0-942208; 978-0-930012; 978-1-944371
Number of titles published annually: 12 Print
Total Titles: 110 Print; 35 E-Book; 5 Audio
Imprints: Beta Books (pre-publishing option of mini-editions for DIY authors & modern poetry); Dictionary Series (series of little dictionaries: Italian for Opera Lovers, French for Food Lovers, Yiddish, You Say? Nu?, Doctorese for the imPatient); Gender Genre (classic transgender literature, 8 variants for third-person singular unknown or hypothetical); Mudborn Press (reprints, poetry, bilingual-Portuguese, Nahuatl, Latvian); Shakespeare Playbooks (series of playbooks designed for directors to envision a play & to keep track of production details); Supplement Editions (texts with supplementary background materials for teachers)

B&H Publishing Group
Imprint of LifeWay Christian Resources
One LifeWay Plaza, Nashville, TN 37234
SAN: 201-937X
Tel: 615-251-2520 *Fax:* 615-251-5004
Web Site: www.bhpublishinggroup.com
Key Personnel
Pres & Publr, LifeWay Christian Resources: Thom S Rainer
VP, Intl Sales: Craig Featherstone
VP, Mktg: Dave Schroeder
Founded: 1934
Religious trade publisher of nonfiction (Christian living, inspirational, devotional, contemporary issues); fiction; children's books; Bibles; Biblical reference; Biblical commentaries.
ISBN Prefix(es): 978-0-8054
Number of titles published annually: 95 Print
Total Titles: 700 Print; 5 Audio
Foreign Rep(s): David C Cook Distribution Canada (Canada)
Foreign Rights: Riggins International Rights Services (worldwide exc USA)

Banner of Truth
63 E Louther St, Carlisle, PA 17013
Mailing Address: PO Box 621, Carlisle, PA 17013-0621
Tel: 717-249-5747 *Toll Free Tel:* 800-263-8085 (orders) *Fax:* 717-249-0604
E-mail: info@banneroftruth.org
Web Site: www.banneroftruth.co.uk; www.banneroftruth.org
Key Personnel
Mgr: Patrick Daly
Founded: 1957
Not-for-profit Evangelical Christian publisher.
ISBN Prefix(es): 978-0-85151
Number of titles published annually: 15 Print
Total Titles: 802 Print
Foreign Office(s): The Banner of Truth Trust, The Grey House, 3 Murrayfield Rd, Edinburgh EH12 6EL, United Kingdom *Tel:* (0131) 337 7310 *Fax:* (0131) 346 7484 *E-mail:* info@banneroftruth.co.uk
Membership(s): CBA: The Association for Christian Retail; Evangelical Christian Publishers Association

Baptist Spanish Publishing House, see Casa Bautista de Publicaciones

Barbour Publishing Inc
1810 Barbour Dr, Uhrichsville, OH 44683
Tel: 740-922-6045 *Fax:* 740-922-5948
E-mail: info@barbourbooks.com
Web Site: www.barbourbooks.com
Key Personnel
Pres & CEO: Tim H Martins *E-mail:* tmartins@barbourbooks.com
VP, Edit: Kelly McIntosh *E-mail:* kmcintosh@barbourbooks.com
VP, Sales & Mktg: William Westfall
E-mail: bwestfall@barbourbooks.com
Founded: 1981
Christian books, Bibles, fiction, gift books, devotional journals, reference.
ISBN Prefix(es): 978-1-57748; 978-0-916441; 978-1-55748; 978-1-58660; 978-1-59310; 978-1-59789; 978-1-60260; 978-1-61626; 978-1-63058; 978-1-63409; 978-1-62416
Number of titles published annually: 244 Print
Total Titles: 793 Print
Imprints: Barbour Books; Shiloh Kidz; Shiloh Run Press
Foreign Rights: Christian Art Wholesale (South Africa); R G Mitchell; Nova Distributors (Canada, UK)

Barcelona Publishers
27602 Bogen Rd, New Braunfels, TX 78132-3873
Tel: 830-980-6422
E-mail: barcelonapublishers@gvtc.com; barcelonapublishers@ware-pak.com (orders)
Web Site: www.barcelonapublishers.com
Key Personnel
Prop: Kenneth E Bruscia
Founded: 1991
Music therapy books & materials.
ISBN Prefix(es): 978-0-9624080; 978-1-891278; 978-1-937440
Number of titles published annually: 3 Print
Total Titles: 72 Print

Barefoot Books
2067 Massachusetts Ave, 5th fl, Cambridge, MA 02140
Tel: 617-576-0660 *Toll Free Tel:* 866-215-1756 (cust serv); 866-417-2369 (orders) *Fax:* 617-576-0049
E-mail: help@barefootbooks.com
Web Site: www.barefootbooks.com
Key Personnel
CEO: Nancy Traversy *E-mail:* nancy.traversy@barefootbooks.com
Group Opers Dir: Karen Janson *E-mail:* karen.janson@barefootbooks.com
Ed-in-Chief (UK off): Tessa Strickland
E-mail: tessa.strickland@barefootbooks.co.uk
Founded: 1993
Publishes high quality picture books for children of all ages specializing in the work of authors & artists from many cultures, wrapping paper, artists prints & cards.
ISBN Prefix(es): 978-1-898000; 978-1-901223; 978-1-902283; 978-1-84148; 978-1-84686; 978-1-905236
Number of titles published annually: 30 Print; 12 Audio
Total Titles: 300 Print
Foreign Office(s): 294 Banbury Rd, Summertown, Oxford OX2 7ED, United Kingdom, Contact: Liz Sampson *Tel:* (01865) 311100
Returns: RR Donnelley Packaging & Fulfillment, 655 Brighton Beach Rd, Menasha, WI 54952
Warehouse: RR Donnelley Packaging & Fulfillment, 655 Brighton Beach Rd, Menasha, WI 54952
Membership(s): ALA; The Children's Book Council

Barnhardt & Ashe Publishing Inc
444 Brickell Ave, Suite 51, PMB 432, Miami, FL 33131
Toll Free Tel: 800-283-6360 (orders)
E-mail: barnhardtashe@aol.com
Web Site: barnhardtashepublishing.com
Founded: 2001
ISBN Prefix(es): 978-0-9715402; 978-0-9801744
Number of titles published annually: 10 Print
Total Titles: 9 Print
Membership(s): AAP

Barranca Press
1450 Couse St, No 10, Taos, NM 87571
Tel: 575-613-1026
E-mail: editor@barrancapress.com
Web Site: www.barrancapress.com
Key Personnel
Ed: Lisa Noudehou *E-mail:* lisa@barrancapress.com
Founded: 2012
Booklist includes photojournalism, novels, literary collections, children's books & memoirs. Unsol mss accepted March-Aug annually. E-mail submissions preferred.
ISBN Prefix(es): 978-1-939604
Number of titles published annually: 3 Print
Total Titles: 12 Print
Membership(s): Independent Book Publishers Association; New Mexico Book Co-op

Barricade Books Inc
2037 LeMoine Ave, Fort Lee, NJ 07024
Tel: 201-944-7600
E-mail: customerservice@barricadebooks.com
Web Site: www.barricadebooks.com
Key Personnel
Pres: Carole Stuart *E-mail:* cstuart@barricadebooks.com
Prodn Mgr: Carmela Cohen
Founded: 1992
ISBN Prefix(es): 978-1-56980; 978-0-156980
Number of titles published annually: 6 Print; 100 E-Book; 50 Audio
Total Titles: 100 Print; 200 E-Book; 50 Audio
Imprints: Barricade Books
Foreign Rights: Waterside (Europe exc UK)
Returns: National Book Network, 4501 Forbes Blvd, Suite 200, Lanham, MD 20706 *Tel:* 301-459-3366 *Toll Free Tel:* 800-462-6420 *Fax:* 301-429-5746

Warehouse: National Book Network, 4501 Forbes Blvd, Suite 200, Lanham, MD 20706 *Tel:* 301-459-3366 *Toll Free Tel:* 800-462-6420 *Fax:* 301-429-5746
Distribution Center: National Book Network, 4501 Forbes Blvd, Suite 200, Lanham, MD 20706 *Tel:* 301-459-3366 *Toll Free Tel:* 800-462-6420 *Fax:* 301-429-5746
Membership(s): AAP

Barringer Publishing
Division of Schlesinger Advertising & Marketing
3259 Sundance Circle, Naples, FL 34109
Tel: 239-514-7364
E-mail: schlesadv@gmail.com
Web Site: www.barringerpublishing.com
Key Personnel
Owner: Jeff Schlesinger *E-mail:* js@barringerpublishing.com
Founded: 2009
Full service: cover & book design, editing, printing, marketing, advertising & public relations, web sites, graphics, displays & illustrations.
ISBN Prefix(es): 978-0-9825109
Number of titles published annually: 15 Print
Total Titles: 120 Print
Membership(s): Independent Book Publishers Association

Barron's Educational Series Inc
250 Wireless Blvd, Hauppauge, NY 11788
SAN: 201-453X
Tel: 631-434-3311 *Toll Free Tel:* 800-645-3476 *Fax:* 631-434-3723
E-mail: barrons@barronseduc.com
Web Site: www.barronseduc.com
Key Personnel
Chmn & CEO: Manuel H Barron
Pres & Publr: Ellen Sibley
VP, Sales & Mktg: Alex Holtz
Sr Mktg Dir: Lonny R Stein
Intl & Spec Sales Dir: Jackie Raab
Dir, Rts & Digital Content: Patricia Doyle
Sales Dir, Academic & E-Trade Mkt: Frederick Glasser
Natl Sales Mgr: Jeff Goldman
Acqs Mgr: Wayne Barr
Founded: 1941
El-hi & college education; guidance & test review.
ISBN Prefix(es): 978-0-8120; 978-0-7641
Number of titles published annually: 300 Print
Total Titles: 3,000 Print; 125 Audio
Foreign Rep(s): Book Marketing Services Inc (Canada)
Foreign Rights: Anthea Literary Agency (Bulgaria); Big Apple Agency Inc (China); Contacts/The Rights Agency (Canada); DRT International (Korea); Lora Fountain & Associates Literary Agency (France); International Editors' Co (Latin America, Portugal, Spain); Nurcihan Kesim Literary Agency Inc (Turkey); David Matlock Agency (Russia); Montreal Contacts/The Rights Agency (Canada (French-speaking)); OA Literary Agency (Greece); Tuttle-Mori Agency Inc (Japan)
Advertising Agency: Friedman, Harris & Partners

Barrytown/Station Hill Press
120 Station Hill Rd, Barrytown, NY 12507
SAN: 214-1485
Tel: 845-758-5293
E-mail: publishers@stationhill.org
Web Site: www.stationhill.org
Key Personnel
Dir: Sam Truitt
Pubns & Ed: George Quasha
Founded: 1977
General trade books, quality paperbacks & fine editions; poetry, fiction & discourse; visual arts; studies in literature & psychology, classics, translations, theater, creative nonfiction, health/New Age.
ISBN Prefix(es): 978-0-930794; 978-0-88268
Number of titles published annually: 6 Print
Total Titles: 300 Print
Foreign Rep(s): Lora Fountain (France); Gara Media (Germany); Japanville (Japan); Kerrigan (Spain); Living Weary (Italy)
Distribution Center: Midpoint Trade Books, 1263 Southwest Blvd, Kansas City, KS 66103 *Tel:* 913-362-7400 *Fax:* 913-362-7401 *E-mail:* info@midpointtradebooks.com *Web Site:* www.midpointtradebooks.com

Bartleby Press
Subsidiary of Jackson Westgate Publishing Group
8926 Baltimore St, No 858, Savage, MD 20763
SAN: 241-2098
Tel: 301-589-5831 *Toll Free Tel:* 800-953-9929
E-mail: inquiries@bartlebythepublisher.com
Web Site: www.bartlebythepublisher.com
Key Personnel
Publr: Jeremy Kay *E-mail:* publisher@bartlebythepublisher.com
Proj Ed: Greg Giroux
Founded: 1981
ISBN Prefix(es): 978-0-910155; 978-0-9625963; 978-0-935437
Number of titles published annually: 4 Print; 8 E-Book
Total Titles: 52 Print; 22 E-Book
Imprints: Elstreet Educational; Eshel Books; PS&E Publications
Distribution Center: Casemate | IPM, 1950 Lawrence Rd, Havertown, PA 19083, Contact: Christine Wolf *Tel:* 610-853-9131 *Fax:* 610-853-9146 *E-mail:* casemate@casematepublishers.com *Web Site:* www.casemateipm.com
Membership(s): Independent Book Publishers Association

Basic Health Publications
Imprint of Turner Publishing Co
4507 Charlotte Ave, Suite 100, Nashville, TN 37209
Tel: 615-255-2665
Key Personnel
Mktg: Caroline Herd
Founded: 2001
ISBN Prefix(es): 978-1-59120
Number of titles published annually: 15 Print; 15 Online; 15 E-Book
Total Titles: 250 Print; 250 Online; 250 E-Book
Imprints: Basic Health Guides; User's Guides
Foreign Rights: Athena Productions Inc (worldwide)
Distribution Center: Ingram Content Group, One Ingram Blvd, La Vergne, TN 37086 *Tel:* 615-793-5000 *Web Site:* www.ingramcontent.com

Bay Tree Publishing LLC
1400 Pinnacle Ct, Suite 406, Point Richmond, CA 94801
Tel: 510-236-1475 *Toll Free Fax:* 866-552-7329
Web Site: www.baytreepublish.com
Key Personnel
Publr: David Cole *E-mail:* dcole@baytreepublish.com
Founded: 2002
ISBN Prefix(es): 978-0-9801758; 978-0-9720021; 978-0-9819577
Number of titles published annually: 4 Print; 5 E-Book
Total Titles: 20 Print; 8 E-Book
Foreign Rep(s): National Book Network (Les Petriw) (Australia, Canada, New Zealand, UK)
Orders to: National Book Network (NBN), 15200 NBN Way, Blue Ridge Summit, PA 17214 *Toll Free Tel:* 800-462-6420
Returns: National Book Network (NBN), 15200 NBN Way, Blue Ridge Summit, PA 17214
Shipping Address: National Book Network (NBN), 15200 NBN Way, Blue Ridge Summit, PA 17214
Warehouse: National Book Network (NBN), 15200 NBN Way, Blue Ridge Summit, PA 17214
Distribution Center: National Book Network (NBN), 15200 NBN Way, Blue Ridge Summit, PA 17214
Membership(s): Bay Area Independent Publishers Association; Independent Book Publishers Association

Baylor University Press
Baylor University, One Bear Place, Waco, TX 76798-7363
SAN: 685-317X
Mailing Address: PO Box 97363, Waco, TX 76798-7363
Tel: 254-710-3164 *Fax:* 254-710-3440
Web Site: www.baylorpress.com
Key Personnel
Dir: Dr Carey C Newman
E-mail: carey_newman@baylor.edu
Prodn Mgr: Diane E Smith *E-mail:* diane_smith@baylor.edu
Founded: 1955
Scholarly books & monographs.
ISBN Prefix(es): 978-0-918954; 978-1-932792
Number of titles published annually: 30 Print
Total Titles: 110 Print
Distribution Center: Johns Hopkins University Press Fulfillment Service, PO Box 50370, Baltimore, MD 21211-4370, Contact: Melinda Kelly *Tel:* 410-516-6956 *Fax:* 410-516-6998 *E-mail:* mrk@press.jhu.edu
Membership(s): American Political Science Association; Society of Bible Literature

Beach Lane Books, see Simon & Schuster Children's Publishing

Beach Lloyd Publishers LLC
40 Cabot Dr, Wayne, PA 19087-5619
SAN: 255-4992
Tel: 610-407-9107 *Fax:* 775-254-0633
E-mail: beachlloyd@erols.com
Web Site: www.beachlloyd.com
Key Personnel
Owner & Mgr: Joanne S Silver
Founded: 2002
Distribution Center: Baker & Taylor.
ISBN Prefix(es): 978-0-9743158; 978-0-9792778
Number of titles published annually: 3 Print; 1 Audio
Total Titles: 18 Print
Distributed by Tralco (CN)
Distributor for Le Chambon-sur-Lignon; CIDEB (Italy); Fondation pour la Memoire de la Shoah (Paris); Kar-Ben Publishing; Kiron Editions du Felin (Paris); JP Lattes (Paris); Le Manuscrit (Paris); Oxford University Press (NYC)
Membership(s): American Association of Teachers of French

Beacon Hill Press of Kansas City
Subsidiary of Nazarene Publishing House
PO Box 419527, Kansas City, MO 64141
SAN: 202-9022
Tel: 816-931-1900 *Toll Free Tel:* 800-877-0700 (cust serv) *Fax:* 816-753-4071
Web Site: www.nph.com
Key Personnel
Dir: Bonnie Perry
Head, Mktg: Bruce Nuffer
Mgr, Rts & Perms: Janet Stapleton
Founded: 1912
Religion (Nazarene), ministry resources, Christian care & spiritual growth.
ISBN Prefix(es): 978-0-83412
Number of titles published annually: 30 Print

Total Titles: 700 Print
Imprints: Lillenas Publishing Co (church music); Nazarene Publishing House

Beacon Press
24 Farnsworth St, Boston, MA 02210-1409
SAN: 201-4483
Tel: 617-742-2110 *Fax:* 617-723-3097; 617-742-2290
Web Site: www.beacon.org
Key Personnel
CFO: Cliff Manko
Dir: Helene Atwan
Assoc Publr: Tom Hallock
Dir, Communs: Pamela MacColl
Dir, Sales & Mktg: Sanj Kharbanda
Edit Dir: Gayatri Patnaik
Prodn Dir: Marcy Barnes
Prodn Mgr: Beth Collins
Reprint & Digital Prodn Mgr: Daniel Barks
Exec Ed: Amy Caldwell
Sr Ed: Joanna Green
Publicity Mgr: Caitlin Meyer
Publicist: Nicholas DiSabatino
Founded: 1854
General nonfiction, religion & theology, current affairs, anthropology, women's studies, history, gay & lesbian studies, African-American studies, Latino studies, education, hardcover, paperback, ebook & audio.
ISBN Prefix(es): 978-0-8070
Number of titles published annually: 60 Print; 35 E-Book
Total Titles: 800 Print; 350 E-Book; 5 Audio
Imprints: Concord Library; The King Legacy (writings of Dr Martin Luther King Jr)
Foreign Rep(s): New South Books (Australia, New Zealand); Publishers Group UK (UK)
Foreign Rights: Akcali Copyright Agency (Mustafa Urgen) (Turkey); Eliane Benisti Literary Agency (Noemie Rollet) (France); Chinese Connection Agency (Mei Yao) (China); The Deborah Harris Agency (Rene Rossner) (Israel); International Editors' Co (Isabel Monteagudo) (Portugal, Spain); Agenzia Internazionale Literaria (Stefania Fietta) (Italy); Maxima Creative Agency (Santo Manurung) (Indonesia); Prava i prevodi (Milena Lukic) (Eastern Europe exc Estonia, Latvia, Lithuania & Russia, Greece); Agencia Riff (Roberto Matos) (Brazil); Sebes & Bisseling Literary Agency (Netherlands, Scandinavia); Synopsis Literary Agency (Olga Zasetskaya) (Russia); Tuttle-Mori Agency Inc (Shoko Kobayashi & Youthapong Charoenpan) (Japan); Eric Yang Agency (Jackie Yang) (Korea)
Returns: Penguin Random House Returns Dept, 1019 N State Rd 47, Crawfordsville, IN 47933
Warehouse: Penguin Random House Publisher Services (PRHPS), 400 Hahn Rd, Westminster, MD 21157 *Toll Free Tel:* 800-733-3000 *Toll Free Fax:* 800-659-2436 *E-mail:* customerservice@penguinrandomhouse.com
Distribution Center: Penguin Random House Publisher Services (PRHPS), 400 Hahn Rd, Westminster, MD 21157 *Toll Free Tel:* 800-733-3000 *Toll Free Fax:* 800-659-2436 *E-mail:* customerservice@penguinrandomhouse.com
Membership(s): American Association of University Presses; New England Independent Booksellers Association

Bear & Co Inc
Imprint of Inner Traditions International Ltd
One Park St, Rochester, VT 05767
Mailing Address: PO Box 388, Rochester, VT 05767-0388
Tel: 802-767-3174 *Toll Free Tel:* 800-932-3277 *Fax:* 802-767-3726
E-mail: customerservice@InnerTraditions.com
Web Site: InnerTraditions.com
Key Personnel
Pres: Ehud C Sperling *E-mail:* prez@InnerTraditions.com
VP, Opers: Diane Shepard *E-mail:* dianes@InnerTraditions.com
Dir, Content & Consumer Sales: Rob Meadows *E-mail:* robm@InnerTraditions.com
Dir, Sales & Mktg: John Hays *E-mail:* johnh@InnerTraditions.com
Ed-in-Chief: Jeanie Levitan *E-mail:* jeaniel@InnerTraditions.com
Acqs Ed: Jon Graham *E-mail:* jong@InnerTraditions.com
Print Mgr: Jon Desautels *E-mail:* jond@InnerTraditions.com
Foreign Rts & Perms: Maria Loftus *E-mail:* marial@InnerTraditions.com
Publicity: Manzanita Carpenter *E-mail:* manzanitac@InnerTraditions.com
Sales & Mktg: Andrea Raymond *E-mail:* andyr@InnerTraditions.com
Spec Sales: Jessica Arsenault *E-mail:* jessa@InnerTraditions.com
Founded: 1980
Mysticism, philosophy, spirituality & medieval studies, contemporary prophecy, earth sciences, indigenous wisdom, new thought, alternative healing.
ISBN Prefix(es): 978-1-879181; 978-0-939680; 978-1-59143
Number of titles published annually: 19 Print
Total Titles: 330 Print
Foreign Rights: Akcali Copyright Agency (Turkey); Big Apple Agency Inc (China, Taiwan); Blackbird Literary Agency (Netherlands); The Book Publishers' Association of Israel, International Promotion & Literary Rights Department (Israel); Graal Literary Agency (Poland); International Editors' Co SA (Argentina, Spain); The Italian Literary Agency (Italy); Simona Kessler International Copyright Agency Ltd (Romania); Alexander Korzhenevski Agency (Russia); Zvonimir Majdak (Croatia); Ilidio Matos Agency (Portugal); Montreal-Contacts/The Rights Agency (Canada); Andrew Nurnberg Associates (Baltic States, Bulgaria, Czech Republic, Hungary); Read n Right Agency (Greece); Schindler's Literary Agency (Brazil); Thomas Schlueck GmbH (Germany); Agence Schweiger (France); Tuttle-Mori Agency Inc (Indonesia, Japan, Thailand); Eric Yang Agency (Korea)
Orders to: Inner Traditions International - Bear & Co, c/o Simon & Schuster, 100 Front St, Riverside, NJ 08075 *Toll Free Tel:* 800-223-2336 *Toll Free Fax:* 800-943-9831 *E-mail:* purchaseorders@simonandschuster.com
Returns: Simon & Schuster, c/o Jacobson Logistics, 4406 Industrial Park Rd, Bldg 7, Camp Hill, PA 17011 (truckload shipments must call for an appointment: 800-967-3914 ext 5318)
Warehouse: Inner Traditions International - Bear & Co, c/o Simon & Schuster, 100 Front St, Riverside, NJ 08075 *Toll Free Tel:* 800-943-9831 *E-mail:* purchaseorders@simonandschuster.com

§BearManor Media
PO Box 71426, Albany, GA 31708
Tel: 580-252-3547
E-mail: orders@benohmart.com; books@benohmart.com
Web Site: www.bearmanormedia.com
Key Personnel
Pres & Owner: Ben Ohmart
ISBN Prefix(es): 978-0-9714570; 978-1-59393; 978-1-62933
Number of titles published annually: 70 Print; 1 CD-ROM; 90 E-Book; 20 Audio
Total Titles: 1,100 Print; 2 CD-ROM; 1,100 Online; 900 E-Book; 60 Audio
Imprints: BearManor Bare (adult film biographies); BearManor Fiction (fiction about or by Hollywood stars)
Membership(s): Independent Book Publishers Association

Bearport Publishing Co Inc
45 W 21 St, Suite 3B, New York, NY 10010
Tel: 212-337-8577 *Toll Free Tel:* 877-337-8577 *Fax:* 212-337-8557 *Toll Free Fax:* 866-337-8557
E-mail: service@bearportpublishing.com; info@bearportpublishing.com
Web Site: www.bearportpublishing.com
Key Personnel
Pres & Publr: Kenn Goin
VP, Design & Prodn: Spencer Brinker
Sr Ed: Joyce Tavolacci
Natl Sales Mgr: Linda McGee
Founded: 2003
Curriculum-aligned, high-interest nonfiction for the library market.
ISBN Prefix(es): 978-1-59716; 978-1-936087; 978-1-61772
Number of titles published annually: 68 Print; 440 E-Book
Total Titles: 570 Print
Returns: Corporate Grapics, 2025 Lookout Dr, North Mankato, MN 56002 *Toll Free Tel:* 800-851-8767 *Fax:* 507-389-3399 *E-mail:* marketing@cgintl.com
Shipping Address: Corporate Grapics, 2025 Lookout Dr, North Mankato, MN 56002 *Toll Free Tel:* 800-851-8767 *Fax:* 507-389-3399
Warehouse: Corporate Grapics, 2025 Lookout Dr, North Mankato, MN 56002 *Toll Free Tel:* 800-851-8767 *Fax:* 507-389-3399
Membership(s): ALA; The Children's Book Council

Beaver's Pond Press Inc
7108 Ohms Lane, Edina, MN 55439
Tel: 952-829-8818
E-mail: info@beaverspondpress.com
Web Site: www.beaverspondpress.com
Key Personnel
CEO & Publr: Tom Kerber *Tel:* 952-641-5250 *E-mail:* tom@beaverspondpress.com
Publg Dir: Lily Coyle *Tel:* 952-641-5254 *E-mail:* lily@beaverspondpress.com
Mktg Mgr: Heather Kerber *Tel:* 952-641-5251 *E-mail:* heather@beaverspondpress.com
Founded: 1998
Mission is to mentor authors to publish the best book possible through strategic marketing & creative collaboration, with quality, commitment & connection as the 3 guiding principles.
ISBN Prefix(es): 978-1-59298
Number of titles published annually: 60 Print; 50 E-Book
Total Titles: 250 Print; 100 E-Book
Branch Office(s)
Book House Fulfillment, 5120 Cedar Lake Rd S, Minneapolis, MN 55416 *Web Site:* www.bookhousefulfillment.com
Membership(s): Independent Book Publishers Association; Midwest Independent Booksellers Association; Midwest Independent Publishing Association

Bedford, Freeman & Worth Publishing Group, LLC, see Macmillan Learning

Bedford/St Martin's
Imprint of Macmillan Learning
75 Arlington St, Boston, MA 02116
Tel: 617-399-4000 *Toll Free Tel:* 800-779-7440 *Fax:* 617-426-8582
Web Site: www.bedfordstmartins.com
Key Personnel
Edit Dir, Eng: Karen Henry
Founded: 1981

Humanities publisher specializing in English composition, literature, history, communication & college success.
ISBN Prefix(es): 978-0-312; 978-1-457
Number of titles published annually: 200 Print; 50 E-Book
Branch Office(s)
One New York Plaza, New York, NY 10003
Tel: 212-375-7000 *Toll Free Tel:* 800-223-1715
Warehouse: MPS Distribution Center, 16365 James Madison Hwy (US Rte 15), Gordonsville, VA 22942 *Toll Free Tel:* 888-330-8477 *Fax:* 540-672-7540 (cust serv) *Toll Free Fax:* 800-672-2054 (orders)
Membership(s): AAP

Beekman Books Inc
300 Old All Angels Hill Rd, Wappingers Falls, NY 12590
Tel: 845-297-2690 *Fax:* 845-297-1002
E-mail: beekmanbooks@yahoo.com
Web Site: www.beekmanbooks.com
Key Personnel
Pres: Michael Arthur
Founded: 1972
New titles, reprints & imported titles from England, Wales, India & Russia in all subject areas, particularly music, holistic healing, homeopathic medicine, business, medical & computer books.
ISBN Prefix(es): 978-0-8464
Number of titles published annually: 3 Print
Total Titles: 3,026 Print
Distributor for C W Daniel; Gomer Press; Music Sales Corp; Kogan Page

Begell House Inc Publishers
50 North St, Danbury, CT 06810
Tel: 203-456-6161 *Fax:* 203-456-6167
E-mail: orders@begellhouse.com
Web Site: www.begellhouse.com
Key Personnel
VP & COO: Vicky Lipowski *E-mail:* vicky@begellhouse.com
Pres: Yelena Shafeyeva *E-mail:* elena@begellhouse.com
Mktg Dir: Peter White *E-mail:* peterw@begellhouse.com
Founded: 1992
Science books & journals.
ISBN Prefix(es): 978-1-56700
Number of titles published annually: 43 Print; 43 Online
Total Titles: 200 Print; 105 E-Book
Subsidiaries: Begell-Atom LLC
Membership(s): AAP

Behrman House Inc
11 Edison Place, Springfield, NJ 07081
SAN: 201-4459
Tel: 973-379-7200 *Toll Free Tel:* 800-221-2755 *Fax:* 973-379-7280
E-mail: customersupport@behrmanhouse.com
Web Site: www.behrmanhouse.com
Key Personnel
CEO & Pres: David Behrman
VP & Dir: Terry Kaye
Exec Ed: Dena Neusner
Founded: 1921
Synagogue school textbooks & trade books (Jewish).
ISBN Prefix(es): 978-0-87441
Number of titles published annually: 212 Print
Total Titles: 500 Print; 3 CD-ROM
Distributor for Rossel Books

Frederic C Beil Publisher Inc
609 Whitaker St, Savannah, GA 31401
Tel: 912-233-2446
E-mail: editor@beil.com; order@beil.com
Web Site: www.beil.com
Key Personnel
Pres & Publr: Frederic C Beil
Founded: 1982
Biography, history & fiction.
ISBN Prefix(es): 978-0-913720; 978-1-929490
Number of titles published annually: 6 Print
Total Titles: 186 Print
Imprints: Hypermedia Inc; The Sandstone Press
Foreign Rep(s): Gazelle Book Services Ltd (Europe, UK)

Bell Springs Publishing
PO Box 1240, Willits, CA 95490-1240
SAN: 209-3138
Tel: 707-272-3472
E-mail: publisher@bellsprings.com
Web Site: bellsprings.com; aboutpinball.com
Key Personnel
Publr: Sam Leandro *E-mail:* sam@bellsprings.com
Ed: Bernard Kamoroff *E-mail:* bk@bellsprings.com
Founded: 1976
Books, small business, pinball machines.
ISBN Prefix(es): 978-0-917510
Number of titles published annually: 10 Print
Total Titles: 20 Print
Shipping Address: 106 State St, Willits, CA 95490

Bella Books
PO Box 10543, Tallahassee, FL 32302
Tel: 850-576-2370 *Toll Free Tel:* 800-729-4992 *Fax:* 850-576-3498
E-mail: info@bellabooks.com; orders@bellabooks.com; ebooks@bellabooks.com
Web Site: www.bellabooks.com
Key Personnel
CEO & Publr: Linda Hill *E-mail:* linda@bellabooks.com
Founded: 1991
Publish books for, by & about women; fiction & nonfiction.
ISBN Prefix(es): 978-0-9628938; 978-1-883061
Number of titles published annually: 10 Print
Total Titles: 35 Print
Imprints: Spinsters Ink
Distributed by Turnaround (London)
See separate listing for:
Spinsters Ink

BelleBooks
PO Box 300921, Memphis, TN 38130
Tel: 901-344-9024 *Fax:* 901-344-9068
E-mail: bellebooks@bellebooks.com
Web Site: www.bellebooks.com
Key Personnel
CEO & Pres: Debra Dixon
Dir, Mktg: Deborah Smith
Edit Dir, ImaJinn: Brenda Chin
Opers Mgr: Pamela Ireland
Founded: 1999
ISBN Prefix(es): 978-0-9768760
Number of titles published annually: 100 Print
Total Titles: 500 Print
Imprints: Bell Bridge Books; ImaJinn Books
Editorial Office(s): 1092 Ridgeway Rd, Dahlonega, GA
See separate listing for:
ImaJinn Books

Bellerophon Books
PO Box 21307, Santa Barbara, CA 93121-1307
SAN: 202-392X
Tel: 805-965-7034 *Toll Free Tel:* 800-253-9943 *Fax:* 805-965-8286
E-mail: sales.bellerophon@gmail.com
Web Site: www.bellerophonbooks.com
Key Personnel
Pres: Ellen Knill
Founded: 1969
Children's art & history.
ISBN Prefix(es): 978-0-88388
Number of titles published annually: 6 Print
Total Titles: 142 Print
Returns: 331 N "G" St, Lompoc, CA 93436

§Belltown Media
PO Box 980985, Houston, TX 77098
Tel: 713-344-1956 *Fax:* 713-583-7956
E-mail: subs@linuxjournal.com
Web Site: www.belltownmedia.com
Key Personnel
Publr: Carlie Fairchild *E-mail:* publisher@linuxjournal.com; Mark Irgang *E-mail:* mark@linuxjournal.com
Founded: 1968
Publish Linux Journal, a computer magazine.
ISBN Prefix(es): 978-0-916151; 978-1-57831
Number of titles published annually: 4 Print
Total Titles: 29 Print; 1 CD-ROM; 1 Online; 12 E-Book
Imprints: Linux Journal Press

Ben Yehuda Press
122 Ayers Ct, No 1B, Teaneck, NJ 07666
Tel: 201-836-0180 *Fax:* 201-917-1278
E-mail: orders@benyehudapress.com; yudel@benyehudapress.com
Web Site: www.benyehudapress.com
Key Personnel
Owner & Edit Dir: Larry Yudelson *E-mail:* larry@benyehudapress.com
Sr Ed: Eve Yudelson *E-mail:* eve@benyehudapress.com
Founded: 2005
Pluralistic Jewish publisher. We accept agented & unagented material. Prefer to see queries of a short synopsis (less than a page), the table of contents & the first 5 chapters if by mail or the complete ms by electronic submission.
ISBN Prefix(es): 978-0-9769862; 978-0-9789980
Number of titles published annually: 6 Print
Total Titles: 28 Print; 3 Online; 3 E-Book
Membership(s): Independent Book Publishers Association

§BenBella Books Inc
10300 N Central Expwy, Suite 400, Dallas, TX 75231
Tel: 214-750-3600 *Fax:* 214-750-3645
E-mail: feedback@benbellabooks.com
Web Site: www.benbellabooks.com; www.smartpopbooks.com
Key Personnel
Publr: Glenn Yeffeth *Tel:* 214-750-3628 *E-mail:* glenn@benbellabooks.com
Admin Dir: Aida Herrera *Tel:* 214-361-7901 *E-mail:* aida@benbellabooks.com
Mktg Dir: Jennifer Canzoneri *Tel:* 214-750-3600 ext 104 *E-mail:* jennifer@benbellabooks.com
Ed-in-Chief, General Nonfiction: Debbie Harmsen *E-mail:* debbie@benbellabooks.com
Ed-in-Chief, Smart Pop: Leah Wilson *E-mail:* leah@benbellabooks.com
Founded: 2001
The best of health & nutrition, pop culture & smart nonfiction.
ISBN Prefix(es): 978-1-932100; 978-1-933771
Number of titles published annually: 30 Print
Total Titles: 150 Print
Imprints: Smart Pop
Orders to: Perseus Distribution, Cust Serv, 1049 Flex Dr, Jackson, TN 38301 *Toll Free Tel:* 800-343-4499 *Toll Free Fax:* 800-351-5073 *E-mail:* orderentry@perseusbooks.com
Returns: Perseus Distribution, Returns Dept, 193 Edwards Dr, Jackson, TN 38301 *Tel:* 731-423-1973 *Fax:* 731-422-4044
Shipping Address: 193 Edwards Dr, Jackson, TN 38301 *Toll Free Tel:* 800-343-4499 *Toll Free Fax:* 800-351-5073
Warehouse: Perseus Distribution, 193 Edwards Dr, Jackson, TN 38301 *Toll Free Tel:* 800-343-4499 *Toll Free Fax:* 800-351-5073

Distribution Center: Perseus Distribution, 193 Edwards Dr, Jackson, TN 38301 *Toll Free Tel:* 800-343-4499 *Toll Free Fax:* 800-351-5073
Membership(s): Independent Book Publishers Association

Matthew Bender & Co Inc, see LexisNexis® Matthew Bender®

R James Bender Publishing
PO Box 23456, San Jose, CA 95153-3456
Tel: 408-225-5777 *Fax:* 408-225-4739
Web Site: www.bender-publishing.com
Key Personnel
Prop & Dir: Roger J Bender *E-mail:* rbender@bender-publishing.com
Founded: 1967
Military books & magazines.
ISBN Prefix(es): 978-0-912138
Number of titles published annually: 6 Print
Total Titles: 35 Print

John Benjamins Publishing Co
763 N 24 St, Philadelphia, PA 19130
SAN: 219-7677
Tel: 207-725-7250 *Toll Free Tel:* 800-562-5666 (orders) *Fax:* 207-725-7252
E-mail: service@benjamins.com
Web Site: www.benjamins.com
Key Personnel
Consultant: Paul Peranteau *E-mail:* paul@benjamins.com
Founded: 1981
Linguistics, language studies, ESL, terminology & art; translation studies; literacy; scientific study of consciousness & communication.
ISBN Prefix(es): 978-1-55619; 978-0-915027; 978-90-272; 978-1-58811
Number of titles published annually: 165 Print; 1 CD-ROM; 2 Online; 165 E-Book
Total Titles: 4,500 Print; 10 CD-ROM; 4 Online; 4,500 E-Book
Imprints: B R Gruener Publishing Co
Subsidiaries: John Benjamins North America Inc
Foreign Office(s): Box 36224, 1020 ME Amsterdam, Netherlands
Orders to: John Benjamins, PO Box 960, Herndon, VA 20172 *E-mail:* benjamins@presswarehouse.com
Returns: Books International, 22883 Quicksilver Dr, Dulles, VA 20166
Shipping Address: Books International, 22883 Quicksilver Dr, Dulles, VA 20166, Contact: Todd Riggelman *E-mail:* benjamins@presswarehouse.com
Warehouse: Books International, 22883 Quicksilver Dr, Dulles, VA 20166 *Fax:* 703-661-1501
Distribution Center: Books International, 22883 Quicksilver Dr, Dulles, VA 20166

§Bentley Publishers
Division of Robert Bentley Inc
1734 Massachusetts Ave, Cambridge, MA 02138-1804
SAN: 213-9839
Tel: 617-547-4170 *Toll Free Tel:* 800-423-4595 *Fax:* 617-876-9235
E-mail: sales@bentleypublishers.com
Web Site: www.bentleypublishers.com
Key Personnel
Chmn & Pres: Michael Bentley
Dir, Publg: Janet Barnes
Sr Ed: Charlie Burke
Founded: 1949
Technical automotive reference, automotive repair manuals, automotive history, automotive performance driving & motorsports.
ISBN Prefix(es): 978-0-8376
Number of titles published annually: 35 Print
Total Titles: 400 Print; 30 CD-ROM; 30 Online

BePuzzled
Division of University Games
2030 Harrison St, San Francisco, CA 94110
Tel: 415-503-1600 *Toll Free Tel:* 800-347-4818 *Fax:* 415-503-0085
E-mail: info@ugames.com
Web Site: www.ugames.com
Key Personnel
Pres: Bob Moog
Sr Prods Mgr: Connie Gee
Puzzles with a plus-ages from preschool to adult.
ISBN Prefix(es): 978-1-57528; 978-1-57561
Number of titles published annually: 15 Print
Total Titles: 50 Print

Berghahn Books
20 Jay St, Suite 512, Brooklyn, NY 11201
Tel: 212-233-6004 *Fax:* 212-233-6007
E-mail: info@berghahnbooks.com; salesus@berghahnbooks.com; editorial@journals.berghahnbooks.com
Web Site: www.berghahnbooks.com
Key Personnel
Publr & Ed-in-Chief: Dr Marion Berghahn *E-mail:* publisher@berghahnbooks.com
Mng & Journals Edit Dir: Vivian Berghahn
Sr Ed, History & Film: Chris Chappell
Prodn Mgr: Melissa Spinelli
Sales & Mktg Mgr: Jeremy Wang-Iverson
US Sales Mgr: Paul Harrington
Founded: 1994
Scholarly books & journals in humanities & social sciences.
ISBN Prefix(es): 978-1-57181; 978-1-84545
Number of titles published annually: 150 Print; 1,000 E-Book
Total Titles: 1,600 Print; 1,500 E-Book
Divisions: Berghahn Books Ltd (UK)
Foreign Office(s): 3 Newtec Place, Magdalen Rd, Oxford OX4 1RE, United Kingdom *Tel:* (01865) 250011 *Fax:* (01865) 250056
Foreign Rep(s): The African Moon Press (Chris Reinders) (South Africa); Avicenna (Middle East exc Israel); Co Info Pty Ltd (Australia, New Zealand); Cranbury International LLC (Ethan Atkin) (Caribbean, Central America, Latin America); Laszlo Horvarth (Central Europe, Eastern Europe); Iberian Book Services (Peter Prout) (Portugal, Spain); K L Books Distributor (K L Lee) (Malaysia, Southeast Asia); Flavio Marcello (Italy); Missing Link (Germany); Probook (Israel); Sara Books Pvt Ltd (Ravindra Saxena) (India); Ian Taylor Associates Ltd (China); David Towle International (David Towle) (Scandinavia); Unifacmanu Trading Co Ltd (Celine Li) (Taiwan); UPS (Japan)
Foreign Rights: Afroditi Forti (worldwide)
Billing Address: Books International Inc, PO Box 605, Herndon, VA 20172 *Tel:* 703-661-1500 *Toll Free Tel:* 800-540-8663 *Fax:* 703-661-1501
Orders to: Books International Inc, PO Box 605, Herndon, VA 20172 *Tel:* 703-661-1500 *Toll Free Tel:* 800-540-8663 *Fax:* 703-661-1501
Returns: Books International Inc, 22883 Quicksilver Dr, Sterling, VA 20166 *Tel:* 703-661-1500 *Toll Free Tel:* 800-540-8663 *Fax:* 703-661-1501
Warehouse: Books International Inc, PO Box 605, Herndon, VA 20172 *Tel:* 703-661-1500 *Toll Free Tel:* 800-540-8663 *Fax:* 703-661-1501

Berkeley Slavic Specialties
PO Box 3034, Oakland, CA 94609-0034
SAN: 212-7245
Tel: 510-653-8048 *Fax:* 510-653-6313
E-mail: 71034.456@compuserve.com
Web Site: www.berkslav.com
Key Personnel
Owner: Gareth K Perkins
Founded: 1971
Slavic culture, literature, language & history.
ISBN Prefix(es): 978-0-933884; 978-1-57201; 978-0-936041
Number of titles published annually: 3 Print
Total Titles: 120 Print
Imprints: Scythian Books
Subsidiaries: Barbary Coast Books

Berkley Publishing Group
Division of Penguin Group USA, A Penguin Random House Company
375 Hudson St, New York, NY 10014
SAN: 282-5074
Tel: 212-366-2000 *Fax:* 212-366-2385
Web Site: www.penguin.com
Key Personnel
SVP & Publr, Putnam Dutton Berkley: Leslie Gelbman
VP & Deputy Publr: Christine Ball
VP & Assoc Publr: Jeanne-Marie Hudson
VP & Ed-in-Chief: Claire Zion
VP & Edit Dir: Tom Colgan; Cindy Hwang
VP & Sr Exec Ed: Natalee Rosenstein
VP & Art Dir: Judy Murello
VP & Dir, Prodn: Patricia King
VP & Exec Dir, Publicity: Craig Burke
Sr Art Dir: Anthony Ramondo
Dir, Contracts: Robin Simon
Publicity Dir: Heather Connor
Assoc Publicity Dir: Diana Franco
Assoc Mktg Dir: Jin Yu
Exec Mng Ed: Lara Robbins
Exec Ed: Amanda Bergeron; Anne Sowards
Assoc Ed: Katherine Pelz
Founded: 1954
ISBN Prefix(es): 978-0-425; 978-0-515
Number of titles published annually: 700 Print
Imprints: Ace Books; Berkley Books; Caliber; Diamond Books; HPBooks; Jove; Perigee; Prentice Hall Press; Prime Crime; Riverhead Books (Paperback); Roc; Sensation; Signet
Advertising Agency: Spier NY

Berkshire Publishing Group LLC
PO Box 177, Great Barrington, MA 01230
E-mail: info@berkshirepublishing.com
Web Site: www.berkshirepublishing.com
Key Personnel
CEO: Karen Christensen
Founded: 2005
Specialize in international relations, cross-cultural communication, global business & economic information, environmental sustainability.
ISBN Prefix(es): 978-1-933782
Number of titles published annually: 7 Print; 6 E-Book

Bernan
Imprint of Rowman & Littlefield Publishing Group
4501 Forbes Blvd, Suite 200, Lanham, MD 20706
Mailing Address: PO Box 191, Blue Ridge Summit, PA 17214-0191
Tel: 301-459-7666 (cust serv & orders) *Fax:* 301-459-6988
E-mail: customercare@bernan.com
Web Site: www.bernan.com
Key Personnel
Mktg Mgr: Veronica Dove *Tel:* 301-459-2255 ext 5716 *E-mail:* vdove@bernan.com
Founded: 1952
Publishes original government-related reference works & provides a wide range of services to help librarians build their government information collections.
ISBN Prefix(es): 978-1-59888
Number of titles published annually: 45 Print
Total Titles: 336 Print
Distribution Center: National Book Network, 15200 NBN Way, Blue Ridge Summit, PA 17214 *Tel:* 301-459-7666 *Toll Free Tel:* 800-865-3457 *Fax:* 301-459-6988 *Toll Free Fax:* 800-865-3450

§Berrett-Koehler Publishers Inc
1333 Broadway, Suite 1000, Oakland, CA 94612
Tel: 510-817-2277 *Fax:* 510-817-2278
E-mail: bkpub@bkpub.com
Web Site: www.bkconnection.com
Key Personnel
Pres & Publr: Steven Piersanti
VP, Edit & Digital: David Marshall
VP, Intl Sales & Busn Devt: Johanna Vondeling
VP, Sales & Mktg: Kristen Frantz
Mng Dir, Edit: Jeevan Sivasubramaniam
Edit Dir: Neal Maillet
Dir, Subs Rts: Maria Jesus Aguilo
Sr Mgr, Digital Communs: Katie Sheehan
Sr Sales Mgr: Michael Crowley
Online Mktg & Intl Sales Mgr: Zoe Mackey
Assoc Ed: Anna Leinberger
Founded: 1992
Publications on business, work, stewardship, leadership, management, career development, human resources, entrepreneurship & global sustainability for the trade, scholarly, text & professional reference markets.
ISBN Prefix(es): 978-1-881052; 978-1-57675; 978-1-62656
Number of titles published annually: 40 Print
Total Titles: 320 Print
Foreign Rep(s): Eurospan Group (Australia, New Zealand, Oceania); HarperCollins Publishers India (Bangladesh, Bhutan, India, Maldives, Nepal, Pakistan, Sri Lanka); McGraw-Hill Education (Africa, Europe, Middle East, UK); McGraw-Hill Education Asia (East Asia, South Asia, Southeast Asia); Raincoast Books (Canada)
Warehouse: AIDC, 82 Winter Sport Lane, Williston, VT 05495 *Toll Free Tel:* 800-929-2929 *Toll Free Fax:* 800-864-7626
Distribution Center: Ingram Publisher Services, One Ingram Blvd, La Vergne, TN 37086 *Toll Free Tel:* 800-509-4887 *Toll Free Fax:* 800-838-1149

§Bess Press
3565 Harding Ave, Honolulu, HI 96816
Tel: 808-734-7159 *Fax:* 808-732-3627
E-mail: customerservice@besspress.com
Web Site: www.besspress.com
Key Personnel
Owner & Publr: Benjamin E Bess *Tel:* 808-734-7159 ext 123
Exec Dir: David DeLuca *Tel:* 808-734-7159 ext 124 *E-mail:* deluca@besspress.com
Cust Sales Mgr: Helene Honda *Tel:* 808-734-7159 ext 110
Founded: 1979
Books about the Pacific Islands, with a special emphasis on Hawaii. Includes elementary & secondary level textbooks in Hawaiian & Pacific Island history, geography & environment, Hawaiian & Pacific bilingual language materials, popular regional trade paperbacks, cookbooks, anthologies, humor, Christmas, guides, how-to & children's books on Hawaii & Oceania.
ISBN Prefix(es): 978-0-935848; 978-1-880188; 978-1-57306
Number of titles published annually: 17 Print
Total Titles: 285 Print; 12 Audio
Distributed by The Islander Group (TIG) (Hawaii wholesaler/book dist)

A M Best Co
One Ambest Rd, Oldwick, NJ 08858
Tel: 908-439-2200 (ext 5311, sales); 908-439-2200 *Fax:* 908-439-3385
E-mail: customer_service@ambest.com; sales@ambest.com
Web Site: www.ambest.com
Founded: 1899
Insurance industry statistics & supporting material, rate & provide financial information about insurance companies.
ISBN Prefix(es): 978-0-89408
Number of titles published annually: 3 Print
Total Titles: 17 Print
Foreign Office(s): A M Best Asia-Pacific, Central Plaza, Suite 4004, 18 Harbour Rd, Hong Kong, Hong Kong *Tel:* 2827 3400 *Fax:* 2824 1833
A M Best American Latina SA de CV, Paseo de la Reforma 412, Piso 23, Col Juarez, Mexico, DF, Mexico *Tel:* (0155) 5208-1264
A M Best MENA South & Central Asia, Off 102, Tower 2, Currency House, DIFC, PO Box 506617, Dubai, United Arab Emirates *Tel:* (04) 375 2780 *Fax:* (04) 431 3485
A M Best Europe, 12 Arthur St, 6th fl, London EC4R 9AB, United Kingdom *Tel:* (020) 7626 6264

Bethany House Publishers
Division of Baker Publishing Group
11400 Hampshire Ave S, Bloomington, MN 55438
SAN: 201-4416
Tel: 952-829-2500 *Toll Free Tel:* 800-877-2665 (orders) *Fax:* 952-829-2568 *Toll Free Fax:* 800-398-3111 (orders)
Web Site: www.bethanyhouse.com; www.bakerpublishinggroup.com
Key Personnel
EVP & Dir: Jim Parrish
VP, Edit: David Horton *Fax:* 952-829-2568
VP, Mktg: Steve Oates
Natl Sales Mgr: Rob Teigen
Pres, Baker Publishing Group: Dwight Baker
EVP, Sales & Mktg, Baker Publishing Group: Dave Lewis
Founded: 1956
Religion (Evangelical).
ISBN Prefix(es): 978-0-87123; 978-1-55661; 978-0-7642; 978-0-76428
Number of titles published annually: 90 Print; 90 E-Book
Total Titles: 500 Print
Foreign Rep(s): Challenge Bookshops Enterprises of Ghana (Nigeria); Christian Literature Center (Hong Kong); Christian Literature Crusade (Japan); David C Cook (Canada); Filadelfiaforlaget A-S (Norway, Sweden); Glad Sounds (Malaysia); International Boekencentrum Pelgrim (Netherlands); Nova Distribution (UK); Omega Distributors Ltd (New Zealand); Salvation Book Center (Malaysia); Scripture Union (Singapore); Word of Life Press (Japan, Korea)
Foreign Rights: Winfried Bluth (Europe)

Bethlehem Books
Affiliate of Bethlehem Community
10194 Garfield St S, Bathgate, ND 58216
Toll Free Tel: 800-757-6831 *Fax:* 701-265-3716
E-mail: contact@bethlehembooks.com
Web Site: www.bethlehembooks.com
Key Personnel
Pres: Jim Rasmussen
Gen Mgr & Publr: Jack Sharpe *E-mail:* jsharpe@bethlehembooks.com
Founded: 1993
Children's & youth books.
ISBN Prefix(es): 978-1-883937; 978-1-932350
Number of titles published annually: 8 Print; 10 E-Book; 1 Audio
Total Titles: 49 Print; 2 Audio
Distributed by Ignatius Press
Foreign Rights: Canadian Home Education Resources (Canada); St Andrews Books (Canada); Saint Benedicts Book Centre (Australia); Sunrise Marian Distributors (Canada)

Betterway Books
Imprint of F+W Media Inc
10151 Carver Rd, Suite 200, Blue Ash, OH 45242
Tel: 513-531-2690 *Toll Free Tel:* 800-666-0963 *Fax:* 513-891-7185 *Toll Free Fax:* 888-590-4082
Web Site: www.fwmedia.com
Key Personnel
SVP & Gen Mgr: Ray Chelstowski *Tel:* 646-779-0369 *E-mail:* ray.chelstowski@fwmedia.com
Founded: 1981
Instructional & self-help books for creative people in the areas of home maintenance, repair, woodworking, home-based business, sports & recreation, theater, arts, genealogy & gardening.
ISBN Prefix(es): 978-0-932620; 978-1-55870
Number of titles published annually: 10 Print
Total Titles: 130 Print
Imprints: Family Tree Books; Horticulture Books; Numismatics Books; Popular Woodworking Books; Sports Collectors Digest
Returns: F+W Media Inc, c/o Aero Fulfillment Services, 6023 Union Centre Blvd, West Chester, OH 45014
Shipping Address: F+W Media Inc, c/o Aero Fulfillment Services, 6023 Union Centre Blvd, West Chester, OH 45014

§Bhaktivedanta Book Trust (BBT)
9701 Venice Blvd, Suite 3, Los Angeles, CA 90034
Mailing Address: PO Box 341445, Los Angeles, CA 90034
Tel: 310-837-5283 *Toll Free Tel:* 800-927-4152 *Fax:* 310-837-1056
E-mail: store@krishna.com
Web Site: www.krishna.com
Key Personnel
Mktg & Dist Mgr: Stuart Kadetz *E-mail:* sura108@gmail.com
Founded: 1972
Books of Vedic culture & philosophy, vegetarianism, reincarnation & karma.
ISBN Prefix(es): 978-0-89213; 978-91-7149; 978-0-912776
Number of titles published annually: 3 Print; 2 CD-ROM
Total Titles: 96 Print; 1 CD-ROM; 2 E-Book; 84 Audio
Warehouse: 13569 Larwin Circle, Santa Fe Springs, CA 90670-5032, Contact: Efren Gonzalez *Tel:* 562-229-1234 *Fax:* 562-229-1080

BHB, see BrickHouse Books Inc

Bibliotheca Persica Press
450 Riverside Dr, Suite 4, New York, NY 10027
Tel: 212-851-9150 *Fax:* 212-749-9524
E-mail: ey4@columbia.edu
Web Site: www.iranicaonline.org
Key Personnel
Publr: Prof Ehsan Yarshater
Multidisciplinary humanities/Iranian studies.
ISBN Prefix(es): 978-0-933273
Number of titles published annually: 3 Print
Total Titles: 40 Print
Sales Office(s): Eisenbrauns Inc, PO Box 275, Winona Lake, IN 46590-0275 *Tel:* 574-269-2011 *Toll Free Tel:* 800-736-7921 (US only) *E-mail:* orders@eisenbrauns.com *Web Site:* www.eisenbrauns.com
Billing Address: Eisenbrauns Inc, PO Box 275, Winona Lake, IN 46590-0275 *Tel:* 574-269-2011 *Toll Free Fax:* 800-736-7921 (US only) *E-mail:* orders@eisenbrauns.com *Web Site:* www.eisenbrauns.com
Returns: Eisenbrauns Inc, PO Box 275, Winona Lake, IN 46590-0275 *Tel:* 574-269-2011 *Toll Free Fax:* 800-736-7921 (US only) *E-mail:* orders@eisenbrauns.com *Web Site:* www.eisenbrauns.com
Shipping Address: Eisenbrauns Inc, PO Box 275, Winona Lake, IN 46590-0275

Distribution Center: Eisenbrauns Inc, PO Box 275, Winona Lake, IN 46590-0275 *Tel:* 574-269-2011 *Toll Free Fax:* 800-736-7921 (US only) *E-mail:* orders@eisenbrauns.com *Web Site:* www.eisenbrauns.com

Bick Publishing House
75 Mungertown Rd, Madison, CT 06443
Tel: 203-245-0341 *Fax:* 203-208-5253
E-mail: bickpubhse@aol.com
Web Site: www.bickpubhouse.com
Key Personnel
Pres & Owner: Hannah Carlson Jurewicz
Edit Dir: Dale Carlson
Founded: 1993
Adult & young adult professional information for general audience & teens on health & recovery, adult & teenage psychology, meditation, neuroscience, general science, special needs & wildlife rehabilitation.
ISBN Prefix(es): 978-1-884158
Number of titles published annually: 4 Print
Total Titles: 36 Print
Foreign Rep(s): Bob Erdmann (worldwide)
Foreign Rights: Bob Erdmann (worldwide)
Distribution Center: Bookmasters, 30 Amberwood Pkwy, Ashland, OH 44805, Acct Exec: Regina Hamner *Toll Free Tel:* 800-BOOKLOG (266-5564) *E-mail:* rhamner@bookmasters.com *Web Site:* www.bookmasters.com
Membership(s): Independent Book Publishers Association

Big Guy Books Inc
1042 N El Camino Real, Suite B-231, Encinitas, CA 92024
SAN: 253-0392
Tel: 760-652-5360 *Toll Free Tel:* 800-536-3030 (booksellers' cust serv) *Fax:* 760-652-5362
E-mail: info@bigguybooks.com
Web Site: www.bigguybooks.com
Key Personnel
Pres: Robert Gould *E-mail:* robert@bigguybooks.com
Founded: 2000
Publishes high quality adventure stories for children. Combine cutting-edge graphics & old fashioned values to increase literacy as well as confidence & self-respect in young readers.
ISBN Prefix(es): 978-1-929945
Number of titles published annually: 3 Print
Distributed by Arcturus Publishing Ltd (United Kingdom); Bookwise International (Australia); Independent Publishers Group (handles all trade dist in the US); Scholastic New Zealand (New Zealand); Iwasaki Shoten (Japanese translation)
Membership(s): ABA; ALA; Independent Book Publishers Association

Bilingual Press/Editorial Bilingue
Arizona State Univ, Hispanic Research Ctr, Tempe, AZ 85287-2702
SAN: 208-5526
Mailing Address: PO Box 875303, Tempe, AZ 85287-5303
Tel: 480-965-3867 *Toll Free Tel:* 866-965-3867 *Fax:* 480-965-0315
E-mail: brp@asu.edu
Web Site: www.asu.edu/brp
Key Personnel
Publr: Gary D Keller *Tel:* 480-965-3990 *E-mail:* gary.keller@asu.edu
Exec Ed, Bilingual: Karen Van Hooft *Tel:* 480-727-0712 *E-mail:* karen.vanhooft@asu.edu
Founded: 1973
Publisher & distributor of US Hispanic creative literature, literary criticism & scholarship.
ISBN Prefix(es): 978-0-916950; 978-0-927534; 978-1-931010
Number of titles published annually: 6 Print
Total Titles: 200 Print; 2 CD-ROM
Shipping Address: Administration Bldg, A Wing, Rm 207, Tempe, AZ 85281

Biographical Publishing Co
95 Sycamore Dr, Prospect, CT 06712-1011
Tel: 203-758-3661 *Fax:* 253-793-2618
E-mail: biopub@aol.com
Web Site: www.biopub.us
Key Personnel
Ed: John R Guevin
Founded: 1991
Pre-print, printing & marketing services.
ISBN Prefix(es): 978-0-9637240; 978-1-929882
Number of titles published annually: 15 Print; 10 E-Book
Total Titles: 85 Print; 98 Online; 30 E-Book
Distributor for Eagles Landing Publishing; Spyglass Books LLC
Distribution Center: Pathway Book Service, PO Box 89, Gilsum, NH 03448, Serv Contact: Julie Ballough *Tel:* 603-357-0236 *Toll Free Tel:* 800-345-6665 *Fax:* 603-357-2073 *E-mail:* julie.ballough@pathwaybook.com *Web Site:* www.pathwaybook.com

BioTechniques Books
Division of Informa Business Information
52 Vanderbilt Ave, 11th fl, New York, NY 10017
Tel: 212-520-2777 *Fax:* 212-520-2705
Web Site: www.biotechniques.com
Key Personnel
Ed-in-Chief: Nathan S Blow, PhD *Tel:* 646-651-9084 *E-mail:* nathan.blow@informausa.com
Mktg Mgr: Damon Mastandrea *E-mail:* damon.mastandrea@informausa.com
Mgr, Prodn: Genevieve McCarthy *Tel:* 212-520-2752 *E-mail:* genevieve.mccarthy@informausa.com
Mng Ed: Amy Volpert *Tel:* 212-520-2719 *E-mail:* amy.volpert@informausa.com
Founded: 1996
Research monographs, laboratory manuals & reference books in biotechnology, medicine & the life sciences.
ISBN Prefix(es): 978-1-881299
Number of titles published annually: 12 Print
Total Titles: 29 Print

Birch Brook Press
PO Box 81, Delhi, NY 13753-0081
Tel: 607-746-7453 (book sales & prodn) *Fax:* 607-746-7453
E-mail: birchbrook@copper.net
Web Site: www.birchbrookpress.info
Key Personnel
Publr & Ed: Tom Tolnay
Art Dir: Leigh Eckmair *E-mail:* birchbrook@copper.net
Sales Mgr: Tim Grain
Assoc Ed: Barbara de la Cuesta
Founded: 1982
Popular culture & literary books, some of which are printed letterpress on fine stock as well as offset trade editions. Also have begun publishing hybrid print books consisting of letterpress covers & offset printed text. Books about books, fly fishing, the outdoors, baseball, fine poetry & theme-oriented anthologies of short fiction. Limited editions club for signed/numbered letterpress editions.
No new mss accepted at this time.
ISBN Prefix(es): 978-0-913559; 978-0-978997
Number of titles published annually: 3 Print; 1 E-Book
Total Titles: 100 Print; 4 E-Book
Imprints: Brief Books (miniature handcrafted books); Persephone Press (chapbooks, handcrafted, for outside organizations)
Subsidiaries: Birch Brook Impressions (designs, typesets & prints letterpress editions for outside publishers & organizations)
Distributor for Carpenter Gothic Press; Natural Heritage Press; Persephone Press
Foreign Rep(s): Gazelle Book Services Ltd (Europe, UK); Japan UNI Agency (Japan); Multicultural Books (Canada)
Foreign Rights: Chinese Connection (Hong Kong, Mainland China, Taiwan)
Returns: 2309 County Hwy 16, Delhi, NY 13753 (returns accepted eight months after purchase if in clean saleable condition for credit on new purchases), Billing & Returns Contact: Joyce Tolnay
Warehouse: 2309 County Hwy 16, Delhi, NY 13753
Membership(s): Academy of American Poets; Independent Book Publishers Association

Bird Dog Publishing, see Bottom Dog Press

§George T Bisel Co Inc
710 S Washington Sq, Philadelphia, PA 19106-3519
Tel: 215-922-5760 *Toll Free Tel:* 800-247-3526 *Fax:* 215-922-2235
E-mail: gbisel@bisel.com
Web Site: www.bisel.com
Key Personnel
Pres: Franklin Jon Zuch *E-mail:* fjzuch@bisel.com
VP: James L Betz *E-mail:* jbetz@bisel.com
Ed-in-Chief: Tony Di Gioia *E-mail:* tonyd@bisel.com
Ed: Frank Coyne *E-mail:* fcoyne@bisel.com
Founded: 1876
Pennsylvania, New Jersey, Florida law practice subjects.
ISBN Prefix(es): 978-1-887024
Number of titles published annually: 8 Print
Total Titles: 75 Print; 10 CD-ROM; 1 Audio

§Bisk Education
9417 Princess Palm Ave, Suite 400, Tampa, FL 33619
Tel: 813-621-6200 *Toll Free Tel:* 800-280-9718 (cust serv)
E-mail: customerservice@bisk.com
Web Site: www.bisk.com
Key Personnel
Founder & Chmn: Nathan M Bisk
CEO: Andrew Titen
CFO: William Geary, III
Pres: Michael D Bisk
EVP & COO: Joseph Smith
Chief Strategy Offr & VP, Devt: George Straschnov
VP & Chief HR Offr: Philip Kenney
VP & Corp Coun: Alison L Bisk
VP, New Busn: Blair Stobaugh
Gen Coun: Ravi Seepersad
Mktg Mgr: Kathy McDonald
Founded: 1971
One of the leading providers of online, interactive continuing professional education, including continuing education for accountants, attorneys, physicians & nurses, CPA Exam preparation materials & web-based certificate, associate's, bachelor's & master's degree programs from nationally known, regionally accredited universities, including Villanova University, Regis University, the University of South Florida, Saint Leo University & Jacksonville University.
ISBN Prefix(es): 978-1-57961
Number of titles published annually: 50 Print
Total Titles: 500 Print; 50 CD-ROM; 150 Online; 9 E-Book; 90 Audio
Distributed by Bisk Publishing Co

§Bitingduck Press LLC
1262 Sunnyoaks Circle, Altadena, CA 91001
Tel: 626-679-2494; 626-507-8033
E-mail: notifications@bitingduckpress.com
Web Site: bitingduckpress.com

Key Personnel
Ed-in-Chief: Jay Nadeau *E-mail:* jay@bitingduckpress.com
Creative Dir: Dena Eaton *E-mail:* dena@bitingduckpress.com
Technol Dir: Chris Lindensmith *E-mail:* chris@bitingduckpress.com
Ed: Susan Foster
Acqs Ed: Marie Nadeau *E-mail:* marie@bitingduckpress.com
Mktg/Contracts: Gretchen Lindensmith
Founded: 2012
Quality electronic publishing for a digital world.
ISBN Prefix(es): 978-1-938463
Number of titles published annually: 8 Print; 20 E-Book
Total Titles: 50 Print; 140 E-Book
Imprints: Boson Books
Distribution Center: Small Press Distribution, 1341 Seventh St, Berkeley, CA 94710, Opers Dir: Brent Cunningham *Toll Free Tel:* 800-869-7553 *Fax:* 510-524-0852 *E-mail:* spd@spdbooks.org *Web Site:* www.spdbooks.org
Ingram Book Group, One Ingram Blvd, La Vergne, TN *Tel:* 615-793-5000
Membership(s): The Authors Guild; Independent Book Publishing Professionals Group
See separate listing for:
Boson Books

§BJU Press
Unit of BJU Education Group
1430 Wade Hampton Blvd, Greenville, SC 29609-5046
SAN: 223-7512
Tel: 864-770-1317; 864-546-4600
Toll Free Tel: 800-845-5731
E-mail: bjupinfo@bju.edu
Web Site: www.bjupress.com
Key Personnel
Chief Pubn Offr, BJUEG: Bill Apelian
Founded: 1974
El-hi textbooks & trade media.
ISBN Prefix(es): 978-0-89084; 978-1-57924; 978-1-59166
Number of titles published annually: 24 Print
Total Titles: 2,500 Print
Imprints: JourneyForth Books; ShowForth Videos; SoundForth Music
Divisions: JourneyForth Books; ShowForth Videos; SoundForth Music
Warehouse: 134 White Oak, Greenville, SC 29607-1218
Membership(s): CBA

BkMk Press - University of Missouri-Kansas City
University House, 5101 Rockhill Rd, Kansas City, MO 64110-2499
Tel: 816-235-2558 *Fax:* 816-235-2611
E-mail: bkmk@umkc.edu
Web Site: www.umkc.edu/bkmk
Key Personnel
Exec Ed: Robert Stewart *Tel:* 816-235-2610 *E-mail:* stewartr@umkc.edu
Mng Ed: Ben Furnish *E-mail:* furnishb@umkc.edu
Assoc Ed: Michelle Boisseau *Tel:* 816-235-2561 *E-mail:* boisseau@umkc.edu
Founded: 1971
Fine literature & essays.
ISBN Prefix(es): 978-0-933532; 978-1-886157
Number of titles published annually: 8 Print
Total Titles: 130 Print
Distribution Center: SPD (Small Press Distribution), 1341 Seventh St, Berkeley, CA 94710 (recent titles) *Toll Free Tel:* 800-869-7553
Membership(s): AAP; Association of Writers and Writing Programs; Community of Literary Magazines & Presses

Black Classic Press
3921 Vero Rd, Suite F, Baltimore, MD 21203-3414
SAN: 219-5836
Mailing Address: PO Box 13414, Baltimore, MD 21203-3414
Tel: 410-242-6954 *Toll Free Tel:* 800-476-8870 *Fax:* 410-242-6959
E-mail: email@blackclassicbooks.com; blackclassicpress@yahoo.com
Web Site: www.blackclassicbooks.com; www.bcpdigital.com
Key Personnel
Pres: W Paul Coates
Publr: Natalie Stokes-Peters
Digital Print Consultant: Damani Coates
Founded: 1978
Publishing obscure & significant works by & about people of African descent.
ISBN Prefix(es): 978-0-933121; 978-1-57478
Number of titles published annually: 20 Print
Total Titles: 100 Print
Imprints: Inprint Editions
Distributed by Publishers Group West (PGW)
Membership(s): Independent Book Publishers Association

Black Dome Press Corp
649 Delaware Ave, Delmar, NY 12054
Tel: 518-439-6512 *Fax:* 518-439-1309
E-mail: blackdomep@aol.com
Web Site: www.blackdomepress.com
Key Personnel
Owner: Steve Hoare
Founded: 1990
Regional small press publishing New York State history & guide books.
ISBN Prefix(es): 978-1-883789; 978-0-9628523
Number of titles published annually: 5 Print
Total Titles: 80 Print

Black Heron Press
PO Box 13396, Mill Creek, WA 98082-1396
Tel: 425-355-4929 *Fax:* 425-355-4929
Web Site: blackheronpress.com
Key Personnel
Publr & Lib Sales Dir: Jerry Gold *E-mail:* jgoldberon@aol.com
Founded: 1984
Literary fiction & nonfiction pertaining to independent publishing & the writing craft; literature, science fiction (not dungeons & dragons).
ISBN Prefix(es): 978-0-930773; 978-1-936364
Number of titles published annually: 4 Print
Total Titles: 80 Print
Foreign Rep(s): Eulama International Literary Agency (Pina von Prellwitz) (worldwide)
Foreign Rights: Eulama International Literary Agency (Pina von Prellwitz) (France, Italy, Latin America, Portugal, Spain); International Titles (Loris Essary)
Warehouse: 620 112 St SE, Suite 355, Everett, WA 98208
Distribution Center: Midpoint Trade Books, 27 W 20 St, Suite 1102, New York, NY 10011 *Tel:* 212-727-0190 *Fax:* 212-727-0195

§Black Mountain Press
PO Box 9907, Asheville, NC 28815
Tel: 828-273-3332
Web Site: www.theblackmountainpress.com
Key Personnel
Publr: Jack Moe *E-mail:* jackmoe@theblackmountainpress.com
Sr Ed: Carlos Steward *E-mail:* carlos@theblackmountainpress.com
Ed: Joline Mechanic *E-mail:* jolene99@bellsouth.net
Founded: 1994
Literary press for emerging & established creative writers, with or without literary agents. Specialize in literary novels, short story collections, poetry & creative nonfiction.
ISBN Prefix(es): 978-0-9700165; 978-1-940605
Number of titles published annually: 12 Print; 10 E-Book
Total Titles: 25 Print; 10 E-Book

Black Rabbit Books
515 N Riverfront Dr, Suite 200, Mankato, MN 56001
Mailing Address: PO Box 3263, Mankato, MN 56002-3263
Tel: 507-388-1609 *Fax:* 507-388-1364
E-mail: info@blackrabbitbooks.com; orders@blackrabbitbooks.com
Web Site: www.blackrabbitbooks.com
Key Personnel
Natl Mktg Mgr: Ann Schwab
Assoc Publr: Jonathan Strickland
Founded: 2006
Founded on the principle that quality books produce quality readers. Our list of K-12 books has a wide variety of topics, innovative approaches & multiple reading levels to serve all facets of the school library market.
ISBN Prefix(es): 978-1-84234; 978-1-84193; 978-1-59920; 978-1-58340; 978-1-59771; 978-1-59566; 978-1-59604; 978-1-93288; 978-8-86098; 978-1-93383; 978-1-93279; 978-1-84837
Number of titles published annually: 375 Print
Total Titles: 2,000 Print
Imprints: Arcturus Publishing; Brown Bear Books; New Forest Press; Sea-to-Sea Publishing; Smart Apple Media; Stargazer Books; Zak Books
Foreign Rep(s): Saunders Book Co (Canada)
Distribution Center: Saunders Book Co, PO Box 308, Collingwood, AB L9Y 3Z7, Canada *Tel:* 705-445-4777 *Toll Free Tel:* 800-461-9120 *Fax:* 705-445-9569 *Toll Free Fax:* 800-561-1763 *E-mail:* info@saundersbooks.ca

The Blackburn Press
PO Box 287, Caldwell, NJ 07006-0287
Tel: 973-228-7077 *Fax:* 973-228-7276
Web Site: www.blackburnpress.com
Key Personnel
Edit Dir & Publr: Frances Reed *E-mail:* freed@blackburnpress.com
Gen Mgr: Maryanne Kenny *E-mail:* mkenny@blackburnpress.com
Mktg & Cust Serv: Barbara R Chmiel *E-mail:* bchmiel@blackburnpress.com
Founded: 1999
Book titles, largely reprints, of classics in science & technology. Worldwide distributors.
ISBN Prefix(es): 978-1-930665; 978-1-932846
Number of titles published annually: 20 Print
Total Titles: 100 Print
Distribution Center: Baker & Taylor, 2550 W Tyvola Rd, Charlotte, NC *Toll Free Tel:* 800-775-1800 *Toll Free Fax:* 800-998-3316 *E-mail:* btinfo@baker-taylor.com *Web Site:* www.baker-tayor.com
Barnes & Noble, One Barnes & Noble Way, Monroe, NJ 08831 *Tel:* 732-656-7400
NACSCORP, 528 E Lorain St, Oberlin, OH 44074-1298, Dir, Merchandise Mktg: Joan Keehan *Tel:* 440-775-7777 *Toll Free Tel:* 800-321-3883 (orders) *E-mail:* service@nascorp.com *Web Site:* www.nascorp.com
Ingram, One Ingram Blvd, La Vergne, TN *Tel:* 615-793-5000 *Toll Free Tel:* 800-937-8200 *E-mail:* customer.service@ingrambook.com *Web Site:* www.ingrambook.com
Amazon.com, 440 Terry Ave N, Seattle, WA *E-mail:* amazonpublishing-pr@amazon.com *Web Site:* www.amazon.com
Adlibris.com, Box 3367, 103 59 Stockholm, Sweden
Mallory International Ltd, Aylesbeare Common Business Park, Exmouth Rd, Aylesbeare, Devon

EX5 2DG, United Kingdom, Contact: Julian Hardinge *Tel:* (01395) 239199 *Fax:* (01395) 239168 *E-mail:* julian@malloryint.co.uk *Web Site:* www.malloryint.co.uk
Blackwell, Unipart House, Garsington Rd, Cowley, Oxford 0X4 2PG, United Kingdom *Tel:* (01865) 382 524 *Fax:* (01865) 382 790 *E-mail:* sales@blackwell.co.uk *Web Site:* bookshop.blackwell.co.uk
Gardners Books, One Whittle Dr, Eastbourne, East Sussex, United Kingdom *Tel:* (01323) 521777 *Fax:* (01323) 521666 *E-mail:* custcare@gardners.com *Web Site:* www.gardners.com
Paperback Shop, Horcott Industrial Estate, Unit 22, Horcott Rd, Fairford, Glos GL7 4BX, United Kingdom *Tel:* (01285) 712 917
Coutts & Co, 440 Stand, London WC2R 0QS, United Kingdom *Tel:* (020) 7753 1000 *Web Site:* www.coutts.com
Book Depository, PO Box 91, St Peter Port GY1 3EG, United Kingdom, Contact: Steve Potter *E-mail:* steve@bookdepository.co.uk
Aphrohead, 277-A Wennington Rd, Southport, Merseyside PR9 7TW, United Kingdom, Mng Dir: Paul Anderson *E-mail:* enquiries@aphrohead.com *Web Site:* aphrohead.com
Bertrams, Wakefield House, Pipers Way, Swindon, Wilts SN3 1RF, United Kingdom *Tel:* (0871) 803 6666 *Web Site:* www.bertrams.com

John F Blair Publisher
1406 Plaza Dr, Winston-Salem, NC 27103
SAN: 201-4319
Tel: 336-768-1374 *Toll Free Tel:* 800-222-9796 *Fax:* 336-768-9194
Web Site: www.blairpub.com
Key Personnel
Pres & Spec Projs Dir: Carolyn Sakowski *E-mail:* sakowski@blairpub.com
Founded: 1954
General trade.
ISBN Prefix(es): 978-0-910244; 978-0-89587
Number of titles published annually: 18 Print; 18 E-Book
Total Titles: 300 Print; 200 E-Book; 3 Audio
Distributor for Bandit Books; Bright Mountain Books; Carolina Wren Press; Down Home Press; Eno Publishers; Hub City Press; Looking Glass Books; Lookout Books; NewSouth Books; Niche Publishing; Pennywell Press; Upper Ohio Valley Books

§Bloch Publishing Co
10030 E W Pappy Rd, PMB 0015, Jacksonville, FL 32259
Tel: 904-880-7302 *Fax:* 904-880-7307
E-mail: info@blochpub.com
Web Site: www.blochpub.com
Key Personnel
Pres: Mitchell Bloch
Founded: 1854
Judaica.
ISBN Prefix(es): 978-0-8197
Number of titles published annually: 8 Print
Total Titles: 100 Print
Distributor for Biblio; Menorah; Scarf Press; Sephardic House; Soncino

Blood Moon Productions Ltd
75 Saint Marks Place, Staten Island, NY 10301-1606
Tel: 718-556-9410
E-mail: editors@bloodmoonproductions.com
Web Site: bloodmoonproductions.com
Key Personnel
Pres & Publr: Danforth Prince *E-mail:* danforthprince@bloodmoonproductions.com
Founded: 2004
A New York-based publishing enterprise dedicated to researching, salvaging & indexing the oral histories of America's entertainment industry.
ISBN Prefix(es): 978-0-9748118; 978-0-9786465; 978-1-936003
Number of titles published annually: 4 Print; 4 E-Book
Total Titles: 50 Print; 50 E-Book
Imprints: The Georgia Literary Association (earlier titles)
Distribution Center: National Book Network, 4501 Forbes Blvd, Suite 200, Lanham, MD 20706 (North America, Australia, New Zealand & UK) *Tel:* 301-459-3366 *Toll Free Tel:* 800-462-6420 *Fax:* 301-429-5746 *Toll Free Fax:* 800-338-4550 *E-mail:* customercare@nbnbooks.com *Web Site:* www.nbnbooks.com
Membership(s): ABA; Independent Book Publishers Association; NAIBA; Southern Independent Booksellers Alliance

Bloomberg BNA Books
Formerly BNA Books
Division of Bloomberg BNA
1801 S Bell St, Arlington, VA 22202
SAN: 201-4262
Tel: 732-476-6397 *Toll Free Tel:* 800-960-1220 *Fax:* 732-346-1624
E-mail: books@bna.com
Web Site: www.bna.com/bnabooks
Key Personnel
CEO: Greg McCaffery
Pres: Scott Mozarsky
Publr: Margret S Hullinger *Tel:* 703-341-5742 *E-mail:* mhullinger@bna.com
Acqs Mgr: Robert Anderson *Tel:* 703-341-5765 *E-mail:* randerson@bna.com
Founded: 1929
Employment law: labor law, labor relations, employee benefits, labor arbitration, intellectual property law; tax law: estate & insurance company tax; health law: legal practice & reference.
ISBN Prefix(es): 978-0-87179; 978-1-57018
Number of titles published annually: 60 Print
Total Titles: 160 Print; 120 Online
Orders to: 2500 Main St, Unit 12, Sayreville, NJ 08872
Returns: 2500 Main St, Unit 12, Sayreville, NJ 08872
Warehouse: 2500 Main St, Unit 12, Sayreville, NJ 08872

Bloom's Literary Criticism
Imprint of Infobase Learning
132 W 31 St, 17th fl, New York, NY 10001
Toll Free Tel: 800-322-8755 *Toll Free Fax:* 800-678-3633
E-mail: custserv@factsonfile.com
Web Site: www.infobasepublishing.com
Key Personnel
Chmn, Infobase Learning: Mark McDonnell
CFO, Infobase Learning: Jim Housley
Edit Dir, Infobase Learning: Laurie Likoff
Dir, Licensing & Busn Devt, Infobase Learning: Ben Jacobs *Tel:* 212-896-4268 *E-mail:* bjacobs@factsonfile.com
Dir, Mktg, Infobase Learning: Zina Scarpulla
Dir, Opers, Infobase Learning: Mark Zielinski
Offers hundreds of volumes of literary criticism edited by Harold Bloom, focusing on the writers & works most often studied in high schools & universities.
ISBN Prefix(es): 978-0-7910; 978-1-4381
Number of titles published annually: 67 Print; 67 E-Book
Total Titles: 453 Print; 525 E-Book
Returns: Maple Logistics Solutions, Lebanon Distribution Ctr, 704 Legionaire Dr, Fredericksburg, PA 17026
Warehouse: Maple Logistics Solutions, Lebanon Distribution Ctr, 704 Legionaire Dr, Fredericksburg, PA 17026
Distribution Center: Maple Logistics Solutions, Lebanon Distribution Ctr, 704 Legionaire Dr, Fredericksburg, PA 17026

Bloomsbury Academic
1385 Broadway, 5th fl, New York, NY 10018
SAN: 213-8220
Tel: 212-419-5300
Web Site: www.bloomsbury.com/us/academic
Key Personnel
Mng Dir: Jonathan Glasspool
Mng Dir, Digital Resources Div: Kathryn Earle
Mktg Mgr: Joe Kreuser *E-mail:* joseph@bloomsbury.com
Mktg Assoc: Laura Ewen *E-mail:* laura.ewen@bloomsbury.com
Conference & Events Coord: Jessica Tackett
Founded: 1999 (result of a merger between The Continuum Publishing Company of NY & the academic & religious publishing programs of Cassell plc in London)
Hardcover & paperbacks; scholary & professional & general interest; music, film, literature, media studies, the arts & popular culture; philosophy, religion, biblical studies, theology & spirituality, history, politics & contemporary issues, education; women's studies & reference.
ISBN Prefix(es): 978-0-304; 978-0-7201; 978-0-8264; 978-1-56338; 978-0-7136; 978-0-86012; 978-0-225; 978-0-264; 978-0-7185; 978-0-86187; 978-1-85567; 978-0-7220; 978-0-567; 978-0-485; 978-1-84127; 978-1-85805; 978-1-84371; 978-0-8044; 978-0-223
Number of titles published annually: 1,200 Print
Total Titles: 6,000 Print
Distributor for Paragon House; Spring Publications
Foreign Rights: Allen & Unwin Pty Ltd (Australia); APD (Brunei, Indonesia, Malaysia, Singapore, Thailand, Vietnam); APS Ltd (China, Hong Kong, Philippines, South Korea, Taiwan); Robert Barnett (USA); BCR University Bookstore (Jamaica); Bounty Press Ltd (Nigeria); Codasat Canada Ltd (Canada); Continuum (Africa exc North & South Africa, Caribbean, Germany, Israel, Netherlands, North America); Cranbury International LLC (Central America, Mexico, South America); Durnell Marketing Ltd (Europe); Horizon Books (Botswana, Lesotho, Namibia, South Africa, Swaziland); IPS (Middle East exc Israel, North Africa); Richard Lyle (London); Maya Publishers Pvt Ltd (Bangladesh, India, Sri Lanka); Richard McNeace (USA); Natoli Stefan & Oliva Literary Agency (Italy); Novalis (Canada); Nick Pepper (Northern England, Scotland); Publishers Consultants & Representatives (Pakistan); Jonathan Rhodes (England, Midlands); Andrew Toal (England); United Publishers Services Ltd (Japan)

Bloomsbury Publishing Inc
1385 Broadway, 5th fl, New York, NY 10018
Tel: 212-419-5300
E-mail: marketingusa@bloomsbury.com; adultpublicityusa@bloomsbury.com; askacademic@bloomsbury.com
Web Site: www.bloomsbury.com
Key Personnel
VP, Mktg & Sales: Christina Gilbert
Sr Dir, Publicity & Communs: Marie Coolman
Publg Dir, Bloomsbury Children's Books USA & Bloomsbury USA: Cindy Loh
Assoc Publr & Edit Dir: Nancy Miller
Publicity Dir, Bloomsbury Children's Books: Lizzy Mason
Assoc Publicity Dir, Bloomsbury USA: Summer Smith
Mng Dir, Digital Resources Div: Kathryn Earle

Dir, Adoption Sales, Bloomsbury Academic & Professional: Melanie Sankel
Dir, Mktg Design & Opers: Alona Fryman
Dir, Trade & Digital Mktg: Laura Keefe
Dir, Children's Trade & Digital Mktg: Erica Barmash
Global Sales & Mktg Dir, Bloomsbury Digital Resources: Lenny Allen
Sales Dir, Latin America, Caribbean & Canada: Nick Parker
Mktg Mgr, Adult Trade Div: Megan Ernst
Mktg Mgr for School & Lib, Children's Trade Group: Linette Kim
US Trade Sales Opers Mgr: Doug White
Head, Academic Mktg (Americas): Abigail Naqvi
Edit Dir, Children's: Bethany Buck
Edit Dir, Fiction: Liese Mayer
Exec Mng Ed, Bloomsbury Children's Books: Melissa Kavonic
Exec Ed, Bloomsbury Children's Books: Mary Kate Castellani
Sr Ed, Bloomsbury Children's Books: Sarah Shumway
Sr Ed, Bloomsbury USA: Lea Beresford
Sr Ed Nonfiction, Adult Trade Div: Ben Hyman
Ed: Rachel Mannheimer
Ed, Children's: Allison Moore
Prodn Ed: Sara Kitchen
Assoc Ed, Bloomsbury Children's Books: Hali Baumstein; Laura Whitaker; Brett Wright
Asst Prodn Ed, Bloomsbury Children's Books: Nick Sweeney
Sr Publicist: Anthony LaSasso
Publicist, Adult Trade Dept: Lauren Hill
Publicist, Children's: Courtney Griffin
Inventory Mgr, Bloomsbury USA: Donna Gautier
Mktg Mgr, Children's: Emily Ritter
Founded: 1998
No unsol mss.
ISBN Prefix(es): 978-1-58234; 978-1-61963; 978-1-62040; 978-1-63286; 978-1-68119; 978-1-59691; 978-1-59990; 978-1-60819
Number of titles published annually: 100 Print
Imprints: Bloomsbury; Bloomsbury Press (nonfiction); Bloomsbury USA (adult); Osprey Publishing
Distributed by Macmillan
Orders to: MPS Distribution Center, 16365 James Madison Hwy, Gordonsville, VA 22942-8501 *Toll Free Tel:* 888-330-8477 *Toll Free Fax:* 800-672-2054
Returns: MPS Returns Center, 14301 Litchfield Rd, Orange, VA 22960
Distribution Center: MPS Distribution Center, 16365 James Madison Hwy, Gordonsville, VA 22942-8501 *Toll Free Tel:* 888-330-8477 *Toll Free Fax:* 800-672-2054

Blue Apple Books
515 Valley St, Suite 170, Maplewood, NJ 07040
Tel: 973-763-8191 *Toll Free Tel:* 800-283-3572 (orders) *Fax:* 973-763-5944
E-mail: info@blueapplebooks.com
Web Site: blueapplebooks.com
Key Personnel
Publr: Harriet M Ziefert
Assoc Publr: Elliot Kreloff
Dir, Opers: Kip Jacobson
Founded: 2003
Publisher of innovative children's books. No unsol mss accepted at this time.
ISBN Prefix(es): 978-1-59354; 978-1-934706
Number of titles published annually: 60 Print
Total Titles: 300 Print
Distribution Center: Consortium, The Keg House, 34 13 Ave NE, Suite 101, Minneapolis, MN 55413-1007 *Tel:* 612-746-2600 *Fax:* 612-746-2606 *E-mail:* info@cbsd.com *Web Site:* www.cbsd.com

Blue Book Publications Inc
8009 34 Ave S, Suite 250, Minneapolis, MN 55425
Tel: 952-854-5229 *Toll Free Tel:* 800-877-4867 *Fax:* 952-853-1486
E-mail: support@bluebookinc.com
Web Site: www.bluebookofgunvalues.com; www.bluebookofguitarvalues.com
Key Personnel
Publr & Author: S P Fjestad *Tel:* 952-853-1486 ext 13 *E-mail:* stevef@bluebookinc.com
Sales Mgr: Tom Toupin *Tel:* 952-253-2932 *E-mail:* tomt@bluebookinc.com
Founded: 1989
Industry leader in up-to-date & accurate values & information for firearms, airguns, modern black powder replicas, amplifiers & fretted instruments. Publisher of reference books, consumer pricing guides, encyclopedias & coffee table books. Online information provider/appraisals.
ISBN Prefix(es): 978-1-936120
Number of titles published annually: 20 Print; 8 Online; 2 E-Book
Total Titles: 36 Print; 8 Online; 2 E-Book
Membership(s): ABA; Midwest Independent Booksellers Association; Outdoor Writers Association of America

Blue Crane Books Inc
36 Hazel St, Watertown, MA 02472
Tel: 617-926-8989
Key Personnel
Pres: Alvart Badalian
Secy: Mr Aramais Andonian
Founded: 1991
Publish adult trade fiction & nonfiction, history, political & social sciences, culture & art. Special line of adult & children's books in Armenian & English translations of Armenian originals. No unsol mss.
ISBN Prefix(es): 978-0-9628715; 978-1-886434
Number of titles published annually: 3 Print
Total Titles: 20 Print

Blue Mountain Arts Inc
2905 Wilderness Place, Suite 100, Boulder, CO 80301
Mailing Address: PO Box 4549, Boulder, CO 80306-4549 SAN: 299-9609
Tel: 303-449-0536 *Toll Free Tel:* 800-525-0642 *Fax:* 303-417-6472 *Toll Free Fax:* 800-545-8573
E-mail: info@sps.com
Web Site: www.sps.com
Key Personnel
Pres: James Gurney
Sales Admin: Vicki Cornelius
Founded: 1971
Publisher of trade books: inspirational, poetry, juvenile, young adult & gift books & sidelines.
ISBN Prefix(es): 978-0-88396; 978-1-58786; 978-1-59842
Number of titles published annually: 20 Print; 20 Online
Total Titles: 120 Print; 120 Online
Imprints: Artes Monte Azul; Blue Mountain Press®; Orphiflamme Press™; Rabbit's Foot Press™
Editorial Office(s): PO Box 1007, Boulder, CO 80301, Contact: P Wayant
Returns: 6455 Spine Rd, Boulder, CO 80301
Shipping Address: 6455 Spine Rd, Boulder, CO 80301, Contact: Wayne Ivers
Membership(s): ABA; CBA; National Association of College Stores

Blue Note Books, see Blue Note Publications Inc

Blue Note Publications Inc
Tel: 321-799-2583 *Toll Free Tel:* 800-624-0401 (orders) *Fax:* 321-799-1942
E-mail: bluenotepress@gmail.com
Web Site: www.bluenotebooks.com
Key Personnel
Pres: Paul Maluccio
Founded: 1988
Small press book publishing, production, printing, distribution, marketing.
ISBN Prefix(es): 978-1-878398; 978-0-9963066
Number of titles published annually: 25 Print; 20 Online; 15 E-Book
Total Titles: 180 Print; 2 CD-ROM; 80 Online; 40 E-Book
Imprints: Blue Note; Blue Note Books
Membership(s): Independent Book Publishers Association

§Blue Poppy Press
Division of Blue Poppy Enterprises Inc
1990 57 Ct, Unit A, Boulder, CO 80301
Tel: 303-447-8372 *Toll Free Tel:* 800-487-9296 *Fax:* 303-245-8362
E-mail: info@bluepoppy.com
Web Site: www.bluepoppy.com
Key Personnel
Gen Mgr: Bruce Staff *E-mail:* bruce@bluepoppy.com
Founded: 1982
Books on acupuncture & Chinese medicine.
ISBN Prefix(es): 978-0-936185; 978-1-891845
Number of titles published annually: 10 Print; 3 E-Book
Total Titles: 12 Print; 100 E-Book
Distributed by China Books; New Leaf Books; Partner's Book Distributing Inc; Partner's/West Book Distributing Inc; Redwing Book Co; Satas

BlueBridge
Imprint of United Tribes Media Inc
PO Box 601, Katonah, NY 10536
Tel: 914-301-5901
Web Site: www.bluebridgebooks.com
Key Personnel
Founder & Publr: Jan-Erik Guerth *E-mail:* janguerth@aol.com
Founded: 2004
Independent publisher of international nonfiction based near New York City. Subjects include culture, history, biography, nature & science, inspiration & self-help.
ISBN Prefix(es): 978-1-933346; 978-0-9742405; 978-1-62919
Number of titles published annually: 4 Print
Total Titles: 40 Print
Distribution Center: Legato/Publishers Group West, 1700 Fourth St W, Berkeley, CA 94710 *Web Site:* www.legatopublishersgroup.com

Bluestocking Press
3045 Sacramento St, No 1014, Placerville, CA 95667-1014
SAN: 667-2981
Mailing Address: PO Box 1014, Placerville, CA 95667-1014
Tel: 530-622-8586 *Toll Free Tel:* 800-959-8586 *Fax:* 530-642-9222
E-mail: customerservice@bluestockingpress.com; orders@bluestockingpress.com
Web Site: www.bluestockingpress.com
Key Personnel
Owner & Pres: Jane A Williams *E-mail:* jane@bluestockingpress.com
Founded: 1987
Other subjects offered: free market economics, business, finance, justice, ancient Rome, World Wars, Mideast War. Sell on nonreturnable basis (except for books received damaged) to the reseller market.
ISBN Prefix(es): 978-0-942617
Number of titles published annually: 21 Print
Total Titles: 23 Print
Sales Office(s): PO Box 1014, Placerville, CA 95667-1014, Contact: Ann Marie *E-mail:* annmarie@bluestockingpress.com

Billing Address: PO Box 1014, Placerville, CA 95667-1014, Accts Payable: Jane Williams *E-mail:* jane@bluestockingpress.com
Orders to: PO Box 1014, Placerville, CA 95667-1014, Contact: Ann Marie *E-mail:* annmarie@bluestockingpress.com

BNA Books, see Bloomberg BNA Books

BNi Building News
990 Park Center Dr, Suite E, Vista, CA 92081-8352
Tel: 760-734-1113 *Toll Free Tel:* 888-BNI-BOOK (264-2665)
Web Site: www.bnibooks.com
Key Personnel
Dir, Sales: Bill Grote
Gen Mgr: John Moore
Founded: 1946
Construction & engineering.
ISBN Prefix(es): 978-1-55701; 978-1-878088
Number of titles published annually: 100 Print
Total Titles: 120 Print

BOA Editions Ltd
250 N Goodman St, Suite 306, Rochester, NY 14607
Tel: 585-546-3410 *Fax:* 585-546-3913
E-mail: contact@boaeditions.org
Web Site: www.boaeditions.org
Key Personnel
Publr: Peter Conners *E-mail:* conners@boaeditions.org
Devt Dir & Off Mgr: Melissa Hall *E-mail:* hall@boaeditions.org
Dir, Mktg & Prodn: Jenna Fisher
Founded: 1976
Publication of books of poetry, poetry in translation & fiction.
ISBN Prefix(es): 978-0-918526; 978-1-880238; 978-1-929918; 978-1-934414
Number of titles published annually: 10 Print
Total Titles: 205 Print
Orders to: Consortium Book Sales & Distribution, The Keg House, Suite 101, 34 13 Ave NE, Minneapolis, MN 55413-1007 *Tel:* 612-746-2600 *Toll Free Tel:* 800-283-3572 (cust serv) *Fax:* 612-746-2606 *Web Site:* www.cbsd.com
Shipping Address: Perseus Distribution, 193 Edwards Dr, Jackson, TN 38301 *Toll Free Tel:* 800-343-4499 *Toll Free Fax:* 800-351-5073 *Web Site:* www.perseusdistribution.com
Warehouse: Perseus Distribution, 1094 Flex Dr, Jackson, TN 38301 *Toll Free Tel:* 800-343-4499 *Toll Free Fax:* 800-351-5073 *Web Site:* www.perseusdistribution.com
Distribution Center: Consortium Book Sales & Distribution, The Keg House, Suite 101, 34 13 Ave NE, Minneapolis, MN 55413-1007 *Tel:* 612-746-2600 *Toll Free Tel:* 800-283-3572 (cust serv) *Fax:* 612-746-2606 *Web Site:* www.cbsd.com

§BoardSource
750 Ninth St NW, Suite 650, Washington, DC 20001-4793
Tel: 202-349-2500 *Toll Free Tel:* 877-892-6273 *Fax:* 202-349-2599
E-mail: members@boardsource.org
Web Site: www.boardsource.org
Key Personnel
CEO & Pres: Anne Lawson
Founded: 1988
Premier resource for practical information, tools & best practices, training & leadership development for board members of nonprofit organizations. Enables organizations to fulfill their missions by helping build effective nonprofit boards, offering credible support in solving tough problems.
ISBN Prefix(es): 978-0-925299; 978-1-58686
Number of titles published annually: 6 Print; 3 CD-ROM; 2 E-Book
Total Titles: 100 Print; 6 E-Book
Distributed by American Society of Association Executives

§Bolchazy-Carducci Publishers Inc
1570 Baskin Rd, Mundelein, IL 60060
SAN: 219-7685
Tel: 847-526-4344 *Toll Free Tel:* 800-392-6453 *Fax:* 847-526-2867
E-mail: info@bolchazy.com; orders@bolchazy.com
Web Site: www.bolchazy.com
Key Personnel
Owner & Pres: Dr Marie Carducci Bolchazy, PhD *E-mail:* marie@bolchazy.com
VP: Allan Bolchazy *E-mail:* abolchazy@bolchazy.com
Founded: 1978
Scholarly books, textbooks, CD-ROM Latin series, Latin music CDs & Slovak publications.
ISBN Prefix(es): 978-0-86516
Number of titles published annually: 15 Print; 3 CD-ROM; 5 Online; 10 E-Book; 5 Audio
Total Titles: 450 Print; 29 CD-ROM; 5 Online; 20 E-Book; 20 Audio
Advertising Agency: De Chant Hughes
Returns: 1576 Baskin Rd, Mundelein, IL 60060, Returns Coord: Betty Brendal *Tel:* 847-388-7144 *Fax:* 847-367-7684 *E-mail:* returns@bolchazy.com
Warehouse: 1576 Baskin Rd, Mundelein, IL 60060
Distribution Center: 1576 Baskin Rd, Mundelein, IL 60060 *Tel:* 847-388-7144 *Fax:* 847-367-7684

§Bold Strokes Books Inc
PO Box 249, Valley Falls, NY 12185
Tel: 518-677-5127 *Fax:* 518-677-5291
E-mail: bsb@boldstrokesbooks.com
Web Site: www.boldstrokesbooks.com
Key Personnel
Pres: Len Barot *E-mail:* publisher@boldstrokesbooks.com
Founded: 2004
Independent publishing company publishing works of gay, lesbian & feminist themed fiction in all genres, including general, genre & young adult fiction. Readership is international & all titles are released in print & multi-format ebook version. Employs conventional distribution channels to bring products to the customers.
ISBN Prefix(es): 978-1-9331100; 978-1-60282; 978-1-62639
Number of titles published annually: 110 Print; 110 Online; 110 E-Book; 25 Audio
Total Titles: 850 Print; 950 Online; 950 E-Book; 75 Audio
Orders to: Bella Distribution, 1041 Aenon Church Rd, Tallahassee, FL 32304
Returns: Bella Distribution, 1041 Aenon Church Rd, Tallahassee, FL 32304
Shipping Address: Bella Distribution, 1041 Aenon Church Rd, Tallahassee, FL 32304
Warehouse: Bella Distribution, 1041 Aenon Church Rd, Tallahassee, FL 32304
Distribution Center: Bella Distribution, 1041 Aenon Church Rd, Tallahassee, FL 32304, Contact: Becky Arbogast *Toll Free Tel:* 800-533-1973 *Fax:* 850-576-3498 *E-mail:* info@belladistribution.com
Membership(s): Independent Book Publishers Association; Mystery Writers of America; Romance Writers of America; Science Fiction & Fantasy Writers of America

Bonasa Press
PO Box 340, Crosby, ND 58730
Tel: 701-965-3974
E-mail: new@bonasapress.com (inquiries)
Web Site: www.bonasapress.com
Key Personnel
Publr & Ed: John D Taylor *E-mail:* jdt@bonasapress.com
Sales & Mktg: Nancy E Whiting *E-mail:* new@bonasapress.com
Founded: 2002
ISBN Prefix(es): 978-0-9725594; 978-0-9772778
Number of titles published annually: 4 Print
Total Titles: 14 Print
Membership(s): Outdoor Writers Association of America; Pennsylvania Outdoors Writers Association

§Bondfire Books
7680 Goddard St, Suite 220, Colorado Springs, CO 80920
Tel: 719-260-7080
Web Site: www.bondfirebooks.com
Key Personnel
Founder: Rick Christian
ISBN Prefix(es): 978-1-939952
Number of titles published annually: 25 Print

Book Marketing Works LLC
50 Lovely St (Rte 177), Avon, CT 06001
Mailing Address: PO Box 715, Avon, CT 06001-0715
Tel: 860-675-1344
Web Site: www.bookmarketingworks.com
Key Personnel
Pres: Brian Jud *E-mail:* brianjud@bookmarketingworks.com
Founded: 1990
ISBN Prefix(es): 978-1-928782
Number of titles published annually: 10 Print
Total Titles: 26 Print
Imprints: Strong Books
Subsidiaries: Book Marketing Works

Book Peddlers
18330 Minnetonka Blvd, Deephaven, MN 55391
Tel: 952-544-1154 *Fax:* 206-339-6913
E-mail: bookpeddlers@aol.com
Web Site: www.bookpeddlers.com
Key Personnel
Owner & Publr: Diane Schwarze *E-mail:* diane@bookpeddlers.com
Founded: 1985
Nonfiction hardcover & CDs; gift-giving occasion books.
ISBN Prefix(es): 978-0-916773; 978-1-931863
Number of titles published annually: 1 Print; 2 E-Book
Total Titles: 20 Print; 3 CD-ROM; 15 E-Book
Orders to: Publishers Group West (PGW), 1094 Flex Dr, Jackson, TN 38301 *Toll Free Tel:* 800-788-3123 *Toll Free Fax:* 800-351-5073 *E-mail:* orderentry@perseusbooks.com
Distribution Center: Publishers Group West (PGW)/Perseus, 1700 Fourth St, Berkeley, CA 94710

Book Publishing Co
415 Farm Rd, Summertown, TN 38483
Mailing Address: PO Box 99, Summertown, TN 38483-0099
Tel: 931-964-3571 *Fax:* 931-964-3518
E-mail: info@bookpubco.com
Web Site: www.bookpubco.com
Key Personnel
Pres: Robert Holzapfel
Ed: Cynthia Holzapfel
Mktg: Anna Pope *E-mail:* annap@bookpubco.com
Founded: 1974
Community-owned independent press committed to promoting books that educate, inspire & empower. Books on vegan & vegetarian cooking & nutrition, raw food lifestyle, natural health care & Native American culture.

ISBN Prefix(es): 978-0-913990; 978-1-57067; 978-1-55312
Number of titles published annually: 10 Print
Total Titles: 250 Print; 2 Audio
Imprints: Books Alive; Botanica Press; Healthy Living; Native Voices; Norwalk Press; 7th Generation
Distributor for Cherokee Publications; Crazy Crow; CRCS Publications; Critical Path; Gentle World; Hippocrates Publications; Magni Co; Sproutman Publications
Foreign Rep(s): Brumby Books (Australia); Faradawn (South Africa); Publishers Group UK (England)

Book Sales
Division of Quarto Publishing Group USA Inc
142 W 36 St, 4th fl, New York, NY 10018
SAN: 299-4062
Tel: 212-779-4972; 212-779-4971 *Fax:* 212-779-6058
E-mail: booksales@quarto.com; customerservice@quarto.com
Web Site: www.quartoknows.com
Key Personnel
VP, Mktg & Acqs: Frank Oppel *Tel:* 212-779-4974 *E-mail:* frank.oppel@quarto.com
Sales Dir: Steven Wilson *Tel:* 212-779-4973 *E-mail:* steve.wilson@quarto.com
Spec Sales: Amanda Martinez *Tel:* 212-779-1816 *E-mail:* amanda.martinez@quarto.com
Exec Asst: Jennifer Yee *E-mail:* jennifer.yee@quarto.com
Founded: 1952
Publisher & supplier of books to wholesalers, mail order companies & retail stores for over 60 years. In addition to books published, we are one of the largest purchasers of other publishers' remainder +/or overstock titles for resale at significantly reduced prices. Categories include novels, cookbooks, history, juvenile, Civil War, militaria, fine art, art instruction, how-to craft books, natural history, gardening & more.
ISBN Prefix(es): 978-0-89009; 978-1-55521; 978-0-7858
Number of titles published annually: 300 Print
Total Titles: 2,500 Print
Imprints: Blue & Gray; Castle Books; Chartwell Books; Crestline; Poplar Books
Billing Address: Quarto Publishing Group USA Inc, 401 Second Ave N, Suite 310, Minneapolis, MN 55401 *Tel:* 612-344-8100 *Toll Free Tel:* 800-328-0590 *Fax:* 612-344-8691
Orders to: Hachette Book Group, 53 State St, Boston, MA 02109 *Toll Free Tel:* 800-759-0190
Returns: Hachette Book Group, 322 S Enterprise Blvd, Lebanon, IN 46052 (accepted only with pre-approval prior to return)
Warehouse: 121 N Enterprise Blvd, Lebanon, IN 46052
Membership(s): ABA

The Book Tree
3316 Adams Ave, Suite A, San Diego, CA 92116
Mailing Address: PO Box 16476, San Diego, CA 92176
Tel: 619-280-1263 *Toll Free Tel:* 800-700-8733 (orders) *Fax:* 619-280-1285
E-mail: orders@thebooktree.com; titles@thebooktree.com; info@thebooktree.com
Web Site: thebooktree.com
Key Personnel
Owner: Paul Willey
Founded: 1992
Metaphysical, spiritual & controversial books; do not accept, respond to or return unsol mss.
ISBN Prefix(es): 978-1-885395; 978-1-58509
Number of titles published annually: 10 Print
Total Titles: 300 Print
Membership(s): Independent Book Publishers Association

Bookhaven Press LLC
302 Scenic Ct, Moon Township, PA 15108
SAN: 668-7075
Tel: 412-494-6926
E-mail: info@bookhavenpress.com; orders@bookhavenpress.com
Web Site: bookhavenpress.com
Key Personnel
Pres & Publr: Dennis V Damp *E-mail:* ddamp@aol.com
Assoc Publr: Victor Richards *E-mail:* vrichards@bookhavenpress.com
Publicist: Kate Bandos *Tel:* 800-304-3269 *E-mail:* kate@ksbpromotions.com
Off Mgr: Mary McGraw
Founded: 1985
Independent publishing house dedicated to producing award-winning business, career & finance books & companion web sites. *The Book of U.S. Government Jobs* was awarded "Best Career Title" by the Benjamin Franklin Awards Committee. Our 4th edition of *Health Care Job Explosion* was nominated for Best Books 2006 (Business-Career) title by USA Book News. Bookhaven's titles have been reviewed & recommended by Library Journal, Booklist, the New York Times & Washington Post, Career Opportunities News & over 100 magazines, newspapers & journals. We also publish environmental compliance books & comprehensive web sites for our titles.
ISBN Prefix(es): 978-0-943641
Number of titles published annually: 2 Print; 2 E-Book
Total Titles: 5 Print; 3 E-Book
Membership(s): Independent Book Publishers Association

§BookLogix
1264 Old Alpharetta Rd, Alpharetta, GA 30005
SAN: 860-0376
Tel: 470-239-8547 *Toll Free Fax:* 888-564-7890
E-mail: sales@booklogix.com
Web Site: www.booklogix.com
Key Personnel
Pres & CEO: Ahmad Meradji *E-mail:* ahmad@booklogix.com
COO: Akash Mangru *E-mail:* kash@booklogix.com
Founded: 2009
This publisher has indicated that 80% of their product line is author subsidized.
ISBN Prefix(es): 978-1-61005
Number of titles published annually: 60 Print; 100 E-Book
Total Titles: 800 Print; 300 E-Book
Distribution Center: Baker & Taylor, 2550 W Tyvola Rd, Suite 300, Charlotte, NC 28217 *Tel:* 704-998-3100 *Toll Free Tel:* 800-775-1800 *Web Site:* www.btol.com

Books In Motion
Division of Classic Ventures Ltd
9922 E Montgomery, Suite 31, Spokane Valley, WA 99206
Tel: 509-922-1646 *Toll Free Tel:* 800-752-3199 *Fax:* 509-922-1445
E-mail: info@booksinmotion.com
Web Site: www.booksinmotion.com
Key Personnel
Pres: Gary Challender
Founded: 1980
Produce fiction books on CD & MP3. Does not accept unsol mss. Criteria is exceptionally high for acceptance. There is no cost to the authors. Currently seeking subsidiary audio rights on previously print published titles.
ISBN Prefix(es): 978-1-55686; 978-1-58116; 978-1-59607; 978-1-60548
Number of titles published annually: 24 Print; 60 Audio
Total Titles: 2,000 Audio

Books on Tape®
Imprint of Penguin Random House Audio Publishing
1745 Broadway, New York, NY 10019
Toll Free Tel: 800-733-3000 (cust serv) *Toll Free Fax:* 800-940-7046
Web Site: www.booksontape.com
Key Personnel
VP, Lib & Academic Sales: Skip Dye
SVP & Publr, Random House Audio: Amanda D'Acierno
Edit Dir, Listening Library®: Rebecca Waugh
Mktg Dir: Cheryl Herman
Ed, Listening Library®: Emily Parliman
Asst Acqs Ed, Listening Library®: Megan Mills
Coord, Digital Opers, Listening Library®: Renee Watson
Founded: 1975
For over 30 years Books on Tape® has offered the best in unabridged audiobooks. Our best selling & award-winning titles are produced in NY & LA studios & read by the finest narrators in the industry. Select from over 3,000 titles available, durable library packaging & delivered with a complement of services tailored to meet special needs of librarians & educators. Flexible standing order plans, featuring the freedom to choose your titles & free lifetime replacement guarantees. Books on Tape® is proud to exclusively have Listening Library®, the premier audio book publisher of children's & young adult literature, as its children's imprint.
Number of titles published annually: 300 Audio
Total Titles: 3,000 Audio
Imprints: Listening Library®
Divisions: Listening Library®
Distributor for Listening Library®
Orders to: Penguin Random House Publisher Services (PRHPS), Library & School Services, 400 Hahn Rd, Westminster, MD 21157
Returns: Penguin Random House Inc, 1019 N SR 47, Crawfordville, NJ 47933
Membership(s): AASL; ALA; ALSC; California Library Association; National Council of Teachers of English; Public Library Association; Young Adult Library Services Association

Boom! Studios
5670 Wilshire Blvd, Suite 450, Los Angeles, CA 90036
Web Site: www.boom-studios.com
Key Personnel
Founder & CEO: Ross Richie
Pres, Publg & Mktg: Filip Sablik
VP, Licensing & Mdsg: Lance Kreiter
Ed-in-Chief: Matt Gagnon
Founded: 2005
ISBN Prefix(es): 978-1-934506; 978-1-60886; 978-1-61398; 978-1-932386; 978-1-936393; 978-1-68159; 978-1-939867
Distributed by Simon & Schuster Sales & Marketing

§Boson Books
Imprint of Bitingduck Press LLC
1262 Sunnyoaks Circle, Altadena, CA 91001
Tel: 626-507-8033; 626-395-2405
Web Site: www.bosonbooks.com; bitingduckpress.com
Key Personnel
Ed-in-Chief: Jay Nadeau *E-mail:* jay@bitingduckpress.com
Publr & Ed: Chris Lindensmith *E-mail:* chris@bitingduckpress.com
Founded: 1994
Publish ebooks & selected print books. First commercial general ebook publisher.
ISBN Prefix(es): 978-1-886420; 978-0-917990; 978-1-932482
Number of titles published annually: 8 Print; 13 E-Book

Total Titles: 25 Print; 350 E-Book
Distribution Center: Small Press Distribution (SPD), 1341 Seventh St, Berkeley, CA 94710-1409 *Tel:* 510-524-1668 *Toll Free Tel:* 800-869-7553 *Fax:* 510-524-0852 *Web Site:* www.spdbooks.org
Membership(s): The Authors Guild

Bottom Dog Press
813 Seneca Ave, Huron, OH 44839
SAN: 689-5492
Mailing Address: PO Box 425, Huron, OH 44839-0425
Tel: 419-433-3573 *Fax:* 419-616-3966
Web Site: smithdocs.net
Key Personnel
Dir & Publr: Larry Smith *E-mail:* lsmithdog@smithdocs.net
Assoc Ed: Susanna Sharp Schwacke; Laura Smith
Founded: 1985
ISBN Prefix(es): 978-0-933087; 978-1-933964
Number of titles published annually: 6 Print; 6 E-Book; 2 Audio
Total Titles: 185 Print; 2 CD-ROM; 16 E-Book; 4 Audio
Imprints: Bird Dog Publishing
Distributor for The Firelands Writing Center (Heartlands Magazine)
Distribution Center: Small Press Distribution, 1341 Seventh St, Berkeley, CA 94710-1409 *Tel:* 510-524-1668 *Toll Free Tel:* 800-869-7553 *Fax:* 510-524-0852 *E-mail:* spd@spdbooks.org *Web Site:* www.spdbooks.org
Baker & Taylor, 501 Gladiolus St, Momence, IL 60954
Membership(s): Community of Literary Magazines & Presses

R R Bowker LLC
Subsidiary of ProQuest LLC
789 E Eisenhower Pkwy, Ann Arbor, MI 48106
SAN: 214-1191
Tel: 908-286-1090 *Toll Free Tel:* 888-269-5372 (edit & cust serv, press 2 for returns) *Fax:* 908-219-0098; (020) 7832 1710 (UK for intl) *Toll Free Fax:* 877-337-7015 (US & CN)
E-mail: orders@proquest.com (dom orders); isbn-san@bowker.com
Web Site: www.bowker.com
Founded: 1872
Leading provider of bibliographic information & management solutions designed to help publishers, booksellers & libraries better serve their customers. Creators of products & services that make books easier for people to discover, evaluate, order & experience. The company also generates research & resources for publishers, helping them understand & meet the interests of readers worldwide. Bowker, an affiliated business of ProQuest & the official ISBN Agency for Australia, US & US territories, is headquartered in New Providence, NJ with additional operations in England & Australia.
ISBN Prefix(es): 978-0-8352
Number of titles published annually: 13 Print; 8 Online
Total Titles: 29 Print; 8 Online
Editorial Office(s): 630 Central Ave, New Providence, NJ 07974
Foreign Office(s): Thorpe-Bowker, Level One, 607 St Kilda Rd, Melbourne, Victoria 3004, Australia, Mng Dir: Gary Pengelly *Tel:* (03) 8517 8345 *Fax:* (03) 8517-8399 *E-mail:* yoursay@thorpe.com.au *Web Site:* www.thorpe.com.au
Bowker, an affiliate of ProQuest, 3 Dorset Rise, 5th floor, London EC4Y 8EN, United Kingdom, Mng Dir: Doug McMillan *Tel:* (020) 7832 1700 *E-mail:* sales@bowker.co.uk
Membership(s): AAP; ALA; BISG; Canadian Booksellers Association; Evangelical Christian Publishers Association; National Association of College Stores

Boydell & Brewer Inc
Affiliate of Boydell & Brewer Ltd (UK)
668 Mount Hope Ave, Rochester, NY 14620-2731
Tel: 585-275-0419 *Fax:* 585-271-8778
E-mail: boydell@boydellusa.net
Web Site: www.boydellandbrewer.com
Key Personnel
Mng Dir: Sue Smith *Tel:* 585-273-2817 *E-mail:* smith@boydellusa.net
Edit Dir: Sonia Kane *Tel:* 585-273-5778
Sales & Mktg Mgr: Sue Miller *Tel:* 585-273-5787
Accts Asst: Olga Reshota *Tel:* 585-273-5777
Founded: 1989
Publisher of scholarly books.
ISBN Prefix(es): 978-0-85115; 978-0-85991; 978-0-86193; 978-0-7293; 978-0-900411; 978-1-85566; 978-1-878822; 978-1-58046; 978-1-57113; 978-1-900639
Number of titles published annually: 200 Print
Total Titles: 3,100 Print
Imprints: Camden House; Companion Guides; James Curry Ltd; Early English Text Society; Plumbago Books; Royal Historical Society; Scholarly Digital Editions; Scottish Text Society; Suffolk Records Society; Tamesis Books; Toccata Press; University of Rochester Press; Victory History of the Counties of England; York Medieval Press
Foreign Office(s): Boydell & Brewer Ltd, Bridge Farm Business Park, Top St, Martlesham, Suffolk 1P12 4RB, United Kingdom, Mng Ed: Peter Clifford *Tel:* (01394) 610600 *Fax:* (01394) 610316 *E-mail:* editorial@boydell.co.uk
Orders to: Boydell & Brewer Ltd, Bridge Farm Business Park, Top St, Martlesham, Suffolk 1P12 4RB, United Kingdom *Tel:* (01394) 610600 *Fax:* (01394) 610316 *E-mail:* editorial@boydell.co.uk
Returns: c/o PSSCMA, 46 Development Rd, Fitchburg, MA 01420-6019
Warehouse: c/o PSSCMA, 46 Development Rd, Fitchburg, MA 01420-6019 *Tel:* 978-345-2121 *Fax:* 978-348-1233
College Farm, Forward Green, Stawmarket, Suffolk IP14 SEH, United Kingdom

Boyds Mills Press
Division of Highlights for Children Inc
815 Church St, Honesdale, PA 18431
Tel: 570-253-1164 *Toll Free Tel:* 800-490-5111 *Fax:* 570-253-0179
E-mail: contact@boydsmillspress.com
Web Site: www.boydsmillspress.com
Key Personnel
VP: Mary-Alice Moore
VP, Sales & Mktg: Jack Perry
Edit Dir, Book Publg: Elizabeth Van Doren *Tel:* 570-251-4570 *Fax:* 570-253-3110 *E-mail:* liz.vandoren@highlights.com
Dir, Book Mktg: Michael Eisenberg
Dir, Retail Specialty & Gift Sales: Janine Webb
Author & Promos Mgr: Kerry Mcmanus
Natl Accts Mgr: Mr Kreig Krumpe *Fax:* 614-324-7943 *E-mail:* kreig.krumpe@boydsmillspress.com
Mng Ed: Sarah Lozo
Sr Ed, WordSong & Boyds: Rebecca Davis
Founded: 1990
Books for children of all ages.
ISBN Prefix(es): 978-1-56397; 978-1-878093; 978-1-59078
Number of titles published annually: 60 Print
Total Titles: 500 Print
Imprints: Calkins Creek (history); WordSong (poetry)
Distribution Center: INscribe Digital, 55 Francisco St, Suite 710, San Francisco, CA 94133 *Tel:* 415-489-7000 *Fax:* 415-489-7049 *Web Site:* www.inscribedigital.com

Boynton/Cook Publishers
Imprint of Heinemann
361 Hanover St, Portsmouth, NH 03801-3912
SAN: 210-5829
Mailing Address: PO Box 6926, Portsmouth, NH 03802-6926
Tel: 603-431-7894 *Toll Free Tel:* 800-225-5800 *Fax:* 603-431-2214 *Toll Free Fax:* 877-231-6980
E-mail: custserv@heinemann.com
Web Site: www.heinemann.com/boyntoncook
Key Personnel
SVP & Publr, Heinemann: Vicki Boyd *E-mail:* vicki.boyd@heinemann.com
Founded: 1981
College composition & rhetoric textbooks.
ISBN Prefix(es): 978-0-86709
Number of titles published annually: 25 Print
Total Titles: 250 Print
Distributed by Pearson Australia-Schools Division; Pearson Education Canada; Pearson New Zealand-Schools Division
Orders to: PO Box 6926, Portsmouth, NH 03802-6926
Warehouse: 465 S Lincoln Dr, Troy, MO 63376

Boys Town Press
Division of Boys Town
13603 Flanagan Blvd, 2nd fl, Boys Town, NE 68010
Tel: 402-498-1320 *Toll Free Tel:* 800-282-6657 *Fax:* 402-498-1310
E-mail: btpress@boystown.org
Web Site: www.boystownpress.org
Key Personnel
Dir: Jeff Tierney *E-mail:* jeff.tierney@boystown.org
Sales & Mktg Mgr: Patricia Martens *Tel:* 531-355-1334 *E-mail:* patricia.martens@boystown.org
Founded: 1992
Youth care & education books, parenting books, children's books, videos & audio, sign language products, inspirational titles.
ISBN Prefix(es): 978-0-938510; 978-1-889322; 978-1-934490; 978-1-944882
Number of titles published annually: 15 Print; 3 E-Book
Total Titles: 110 Print; 2 CD-ROM; 45 E-Book; 7 Audio
Distributed by Deep Books Ltd (Europe & UK); Footprint Books (Australia & New Zealand); University of Toronto Press (Canada)
Foreign Rights: Amer-Asia Books (Evelyn Lee) (China, Japan, Korea, Taiwan)
Returns: 250 Monsky Dr, Boys Town, NE 68010
Warehouse: 250 Monsky Dr, Boys Town, NE 68010
Distribution Center: Follett School Solutions Inc, 1340 Ridgeview Dr, McHenry, IL 60050 *Tel:* 815-759-1700 *Toll Free Tel:* 888-511-5114 (cust serv) *Fax:* 815-759-9831 *Toll Free Fax:* 800-852-5458 *E-mail:* info@follettlearning.com *Web Site:* www.follettlearning.com SAN: 169-1902
Baker & Taylor, 2550 W Tyvola Rd, Suite 300, Charlotte, NC 28217 *Tel:* 815-802-2479 *Toll Free Fax:* 800-411-8433 *Web Site:* www.baker-taylor.com
Ingram Book Co, One Ingram Blvd, La Vergne, TN 37086-3650
Membership(s): Independent Book Publishers Association

§Bradford Publishing Co
1743 Wazee St, Denver, CO 80202

Tel: 303-292-2590 *Toll Free Tel:* 800-446-2831 *Fax:* 303-298-5014
E-mail: marketing@bradfordpublishing.com; customerservice@bradfordpublishing.com
Web Site: www.bradfordpublishing.com
Key Personnel
Owner & Pres: Candace Boyle *E-mail:* candace@bradfordpublishing.com
Founded: 1881
Specialize in Colorado legal forms & law books.
ISBN Prefix(es): 978-1-883726
Number of titles published annually: 10 Print
Total Titles: 45 Print
Membership(s): Independent Book Publishers Association; Publishers Association of the West

Branden Books
Subsidiary of Branden Publishing Co
PO Box 812094, Wellesley, MA 02482-0013
SAN: 201-4106
Tel: 781-235-3347
E-mail: branden@brandenbooks.com
Web Site: www.brandenbooks.com
Key Personnel
Pres: Margaret Starrett
VP: Robert Caso
Ed & Treas: Adolph Caso
Founded: 1909
Publisher of fiction & nonfiction books. Distribution center in Ypsilanti, MI.
ISBN Prefix(es): 978-0-8283
Number of titles published annually: 15 Print; 4 CD-ROM; 300 E-Book
Total Titles: 400 Print; 4 CD-ROM; 410 Online; 300 E-Book
Imprints: Art Treasures; Brandon Books Cinematic Novels (cinematicnovels.com); Brashear Music Co; Four Seas; Bruce Humphries; International Pocket Library; Popular Technology
Distributor for Dante University of America Press Inc
Foreign Rep(s): Baker & Taylor (worldwide); Gazelle Book Services Ltd (England); Ingram (worldwide)
Advertising Agency: ADS-IPL
Returns: Publishers Storage & Shipping Corp, 660 S Mansfield, Ypsilanti, MI 48197

Brandylane Publishers Inc
5 S First St, Richmond, VA 23219
Tel: 804-644-3090 *Fax:* 804-644-3092
Web Site: brandylanepublishers.com
Key Personnel
Publr: Robert H Pruett *E-mail:* rhpruett@brandylanepublishers.com
Sr Ed: Mary A Tobey
Founded: 1985
Publisher & packager of books. Work with previously unpublished writers.
This publisher has indicated that 20% of their product line is author subsidized.
ISBN Prefix(es): 978-1-883911
Number of titles published annually: 15 Print; 15 Online; 15 E-Book
Total Titles: 60 Print; 40 Online; 7 E-Book
Imprints: Belle Isle Books
Billing Address: PO Box 274, Kilmarnock, VA 22482 *Tel:* 804-435-6900
Membership(s): Independent Book Publishers Association

George Braziller Inc
277 Broadway, Suite 708, New York, NY 10007
SAN: 201-9310
Tel: 212-260-9256 *Fax:* 212-267-3165
E-mail: editorial@georgebraziller.com
Web Site: www.georgebraziller.com
Key Personnel
Pres & Ed: Michael Braziller *E-mail:* mbraziller@georgebraziller.com
Founded: 1955
Publishers of fine illustrated art books.
ISBN Prefix(es): 978-0-8076
Number of titles published annually: 12 Print
Total Titles: 300 Print
Distributed by Antique Collectors' Club Ltd; W W Norton & Company Inc
Foreign Rep(s): Antique Collectors' Club Ltd (Australia, England, Europe, India, New Zealand)
Orders to: W W Norton & Company Inc, 500 Fifth Ave, New York, NY 10110-0017 *Toll Free Tel:* 800-233-4830 *Toll Free Fax:* 800-458-6515

Breakaway Books
PO Box 24, Halcottsville, NY 12438-0024
Tel: 607-326-4805
E-mail: breakawaybooks@gmail.com
Web Site: www.breakawaybooks.com
Key Personnel
Publr: Garth Battista
Founded: 1994
Sports literature & books.
ISBN Prefix(es): 978-1-891369; 978-1-55821; 978-1-62124
Number of titles published annually: 10 Print
Total Titles: 100 Print; 1 E-Book
Distribution Center: Consortium, 34 13 Ave NE, Suite 101, Minneapolis, MN 55413-1007 *Toll Free Tel:* 800-283-3572 *Toll Free Fax:* 800-351-5073 *Web Site:* www.cbsd.com

Breakthrough Publications Inc
3 Iroquois St, Barn, Emmaus, PA 18049
Toll Free Tel: 800-824-5001 (ext 12) *Fax:* 610-928-4064
E-mail: dot@booksonhorses.com; ruth@booksonhorses.com
Web Site: www.booksonhorses.com
Key Personnel
Pres & Publr: Peter E Ognibene *Tel:* 914-928-4061 ext 12 *E-mail:* peter@workkplace.com
Founded: 1980
Career & equestrian.
ISBN Prefix(es): 978-0-914327
Number of titles published annually: 30 Print
Total Titles: 50 Print
Imprints: Breakthrough Publications

Nicholas Brealey Publishing
Imprint of John Murray (Publishers) Ltd (UK)
53 State St, 9th fl, Boston, MA 02109
Tel: 617-523-3801
E-mail: info@nicholasbrealey.com; sales-us@nicholasbrealey.com
Web Site: www.nicholasbrealey.com
Key Personnel
Dir, Prodn: Michelle Morgan
Sales Mgr: Melissa Carl
Founded: 1992
Professional/trade business book (hardcover & original paperback) publisher. Additional subjects include: international business & culture, training & human resources.
ISBN Prefix(es): 978-0-89106 (Davies-Black); 978-1-85788; 978-1-90483; 978-1-93193 (Intercultural Press); 978-1-87786 (Intercultural Press); 978-0-93366 (Intercultural Press)
Number of titles published annually: 50 Print
Total Titles: 330 Print
Divisions: Intercultural Press Inc
Distributed by Hachette Book Group
Membership(s): AAP
See separate listing for:
Intercultural Press Inc

Brentwood Christian Press
4000 Beallwood Ave, Columbus, GA 31904
Mailing Address: PO Box 4773, Columbus, GA 31914-4773
Toll Free Tel: 800-334-8861
E-mail: brentwood@aol.com
Web Site: www.brentwoodbooks.com
Key Personnel
Owner: U D Roberts
Founded: 1982
Custom self-publishing of Christian books.
This publisher has indicated that 100% of their product line is author subsidized.
ISBN Prefix(es): 978-1-55630
Number of titles published annually: 220 Print
Total Titles: 3,744 Print

Brethren Press
Division of Church of the Brethren
1451 Dundee Ave, Elgin, IL 60120
SAN: 201-9329
Tel: 847-742-5100 *Toll Free Tel:* 800-323-8039 *Toll Free Fax:* 800-667-8188
E-mail: brethrenpress@brethren.org
Web Site: www.brethrenpress.com
Key Personnel
Publr: Wendy McFadden *Tel:* 847-742-5100 ext 307 *E-mail:* wmcfadden@brethren.org
Dir, Mktg & Sales: Jeff Lennard *Tel:* 847-742-5100 ext 321 *E-mail:* jlennard@brethren.org
Founded: 1897
Trade books, church school curriculum, tracts & pamphlets & various media resources. Specialize in Bible study, theology, church history, practical discipleship, personal lifestyle issues, social concerns, peace & justice, devotional life & personal growth.
ISBN Prefix(es): 978-0-87178
Number of titles published annually: 6 Print
Total Titles: 100 Print
Imprints: faithQuest
Membership(s): Protestant Church-Owned Publishers Association

Brewers Publications
Division of Brewers Association
1372 Spruce St, Boulder, CO 80302
Mailing Address: PO Box 1679, Boulder, CO 80306
Tel: 303-447-0816 *Toll Free Tel:* 888-822-6273 (CN & US) *Fax:* 303-447-2825
E-mail: info@brewersassociation.org
Web Site: www.brewersassociation.org
Key Personnel
Publr: Kristi Switzer *Tel:* 720-473-7660 *E-mail:* kristi@brewersassociation.org
Founded: 1986
Not-for-profit educational publishing house & the foremost publisher of books on the art, science, history & culture of brewing for professional & amateur brewers & serious beer enthusiasts. Must know at least 10 brewers to query.
ISBN Prefix(es): 978-0-937381
Number of titles published annually: 2 Print; 28 E-Book
Total Titles: 50 Print
Foreign Rep(s): Sylvia Hayse (worldwide exc North America)
Foreign Rights: Sylvia Haase (worldwide exc North America)
Shipping Address: National Book Network, 15200 NBN Way, Blue Ridge Summit, PA 17214 *Toll Free Tel:* 800-462-6420 *Toll Free Fax:* 800-338-4550 *E-mail:* custserv@nbnbooks.com
Warehouse: National Book Network, 15200 NBN Way, Blue Ridge Summit, PA 17214 *Tel:* 717-794-3800 *Toll Free Tel:* 800-462-6420 *Toll Free Fax:* 800-338-4550 *E-mail:* custserv@nbnbooks.com

§Brick Mantel Books
Imprint of Pen & Publish Inc
4735 S State Rd 446, Bloomington, IN 47401
Tel: 314-827-6567; 812-837-9226
E-mail: info@brickmantelbooks.com
Web Site: brickmantelbooks.com
Key Personnel
Publr: Jennifer Geist *E-mail:* jennifer@brickmantelbooks.com

Co-Founder & Pres: Paul Burt *E-mail:* paul@penandpublish.com
Co-Founder: Dee Burt *E-mail:* dee@penandpublish.com
Founded: 2015
Publish innovative works of literary excellence by new & established writers. We value literature as an art & publish literary fiction & thought-provoking poetry that leave a lasting impression. We want to help readers gain a stronger sense of the world & humanity through literature.
ISBN Prefix(es): 978-1-941799
Number of titles published annually: 3 Print; 3 E-Book
Total Titles: 3 Print; 3 E-Book
Membership(s): Independent Book Publishers Association

Brick Tower Press
Subsidiary of J T Colby & Co Inc
Manhanset House, PO Box 342, Shelter Island Heights, NY 11965-0342
Tel: 212-427-7139
E-mail: bricktower@aol.com
Web Site: www.bricktowerpress.com
Key Personnel
Publr: John T Colby, Jr
Founded: 1993
ISBN Prefix(es): 978-1-883283; 978-0-9531737; 978-1-899694
Number of titles published annually: 20 Print; 10 E-Book
Total Titles: 150 Print; 50 E-Book
Foreign Rep(s): Gazelle Book Services Ltd (Europe, UK); Ingram Content (Australia, Canada, New Zealand)
Foreign Rights: Creative Management Partners (Canada, USA); Bob Diforio (worldwide)
Warehouse: Ingram Digital, 1246 Heil Quaker Blvd, La Vergne, TN 37086 *Toll Free Tel:* 800-509-4156 *E-mail:* inquiry@lightningsource.com
Distribution Center: Ingram Digital, 1246 Heil Quaker Blvd, La Vergne, TN 37086 *Toll Free Tel:* 800-509-4156 *E-mail:* inquiry@lightningsource.com

BrickHouse Books Inc
306 Suffolk Rd, Baltimore, MD 21218
Fax: 410-235-7690
Web Site: brickhousebooks.wordpress.com
Key Personnel
Publr & Ed-in-Chief: Clarinda Harriss *E-mail:* charriss@towson.edu
Founded: 1970
Poetry; mixed genres by gay & lesbian (Stonewall only); artistic prose, experimental, memoirs, plays.
ISBN Prefix(es): 978-1-938144
Number of titles published annually: 6 Print
Total Titles: 240 Print
Imprints: Chestnut Hills Press; New Poets Series; Side Street; Stonewall
Foreign Rep(s): Salmon Publishing (Ireland)
Distribution Center: Itasca Books, 5120 Cedar Lake Rd, Minneapolis, MN 55416, Dist Mgr: Mark Jung *Tel:* 952-345-4488 ext 118 *Toll Free Tel:* 800-901-3480 ext 118 *Fax:* 952-920-0541 *E-mail:* orders@itascabooks.com *Web Site:* www.itascabooks.com
Membership(s): AAP; Academy of American Poets

Bridge-Logos
1426W Newberry Rd, No 409, Newberry, FL 32669-2765
Toll Free Tel: 800-320-4108
Web Site: www.bridgelogos.com
Key Personnel
Pres & CEO: Suzi Wooldridge
Founded: 1969
Bibles, Christian classics, spirit-filled life, Christian books, parenting, family, Eschatological, evangelism, revival, children's bibles.
ISBN Prefix(es): 978-0-88270; 978-0-61036
Number of titles published annually: 20 Print
Total Titles: 216 Print
Imprints: Bridge; Haven; Logos; Open Scroll; Synergy
Foreign Office(s): The Coach House Annexe, Wellington Lane, Cheltenham, Glos GL50 4JF, United Kingdom *Tel:* (01242) 300860
Distributor for Warboys LLC
Foreign Rep(s): Winfried Bluth (Germany)
Foreign Rights: Winfried Bluth (Germany)
Orders to: Anchor Distributors, 1030 Hunt Valley Circle, New Kensington, PA 15058 *Tel:* 724-334-7000 *Toll Free Tel:* 800-444-4484 *Fax:* 724-334-1200 *Toll Free Fax:* 800-765-1960 *E-mail:* anchor.customerservice@anchordistributors.com *Web Site:* www.anchordistributors.com
Returns: Anchor Distributors, 1030 Hunt Valley Circle, New Kensington, PA 15058 *Tel:* 724-334-7000 *Toll Free Tel:* 800-444-4484 *Fax:* 724-334-1200 *Toll Free Fax:* 800-765-1960 *E-mail:* anchor.customerservice@anchordistributors.com *Web Site:* www.anchordistributors.com
Shipping Address: Anchor Distributors, 1030 Hunt Valley Circle, New Kensington, PA 15058 *Tel:* 724-334-7000 *Toll Free Tel:* 800-444-4484 *Fax:* 724-334-1200 *Toll Free Fax:* 800-765-1960 *E-mail:* anchor.customerservice@anchordistributors.com *Web Site:* www.anchordistributors.com
Distribution Center: Anchor Distributors, 1030 Hunt Valley Circle, New Kensington, PA 15058 *Tel:* 724-334-7000 *Toll Free Tel:* 800-444-4484 *Fax:* 724-334-1200 *Toll Free Fax:* 800-765-1960 *E-mail:* anchor.customerservice@anchordistributors.com *Web Site:* www.anchordistributors.com

Bridge Publications Inc
5600 E Olympic Blvd, Commerce, CA 90022
SAN: 208-3884
Tel: 323-888-6200 *Toll Free Tel:* 800-722-1733 *Fax:* 323-888-6202
E-mail: info@bridgepub.com
Web Site: www.bridgepub.com
Key Personnel
Pres: Blake Silber
EVP: Ann Arnow *E-mail:* annarnow@bridgepub.com
Trade Sales Mgr: Don Arnow *E-mail:* darnow@bridgepub.com
Founded: 1981
US & international nonfiction publisher of L Ron Hubbard's Dianetics & Scientology materials.
ISBN Prefix(es): 978-0-88404; 978-1-57318; 978-1-4031
Number of titles published annually: 3,200 Print; 400 CD-ROM; 52 Online; 5 Audio
Total Titles: 32,400 Print; 3,500 CD-ROM; 257 Online; 288 Audio
Imprints: BPI Records; Bridge Audio; Theta Books
Branch Office(s)
Bridge Publications Canada, 696 Yonge St, Toronto, ON M4Y 2A7, Canada, Contact: Emily Harris *Tel:* 416-964-8927 *Fax:* 416-964-3201
Foreign Office(s): Era Dinamica Editores SA de CV, Pablo U Cello, No 16, Colonia de los Deportes, 03710 Mexico, DF, Mexico, Contact: Irma Macias *Tel:* (0155) 5984487 *Fax:* (0155) 5984624
Foreign Rep(s): New Era Publications International (Copenhagen, Europe, Russia & former USSR)
Distribution Center: Amazon.com (house acct)
Baker & Taylor, 2550 Tyvola Rd, Suite 300, Charlotte, NC 28217 (house acct) *Tel:* 815-802-2479 *Fax:* 815-411-8433 *Web Site:* www.baker-taylor.com
Follett School Solutions Inc, 1340 Ridgeview Dr, McHenry, IL 60050 *Tel:* 815-759-1700 *Toll Free Tel:* 888-511-5114 (cust serv) *Fax:* 815-759-9831 *Toll Free Fax:* 800-852-5458 *E-mail:* info@follettlearning.com *Web Site:* www.follettlearning.com

Brigantine Media
211 North Ave, St Johnsbury, VT 05819
Tel: 802-751-8802 *Fax:* 802-751-8804
Web Site: brigantinemedia.com
Key Personnel
Acqs Ed: Neil Raphel *E-mail:* neil@brigantinemedia.com
Edit Chief: Janis Raye
Founded: 1990
ISBN Prefix(es): 978-0-9826644
Number of titles published annually: 12 Print; 2 Online; 12 E-Book
Total Titles: 50 Print; 2 Online; 40 E-Book
Imprints: Compass (educational materials for teachers); Voyage (fiction, primarily from VT & regional authors)

Bright Connections Media, A World Book Encyclopedia Company
Imprint of World Book Inc
180 N LaSalle St, Suite 900, Chicago, IL 60601
Tel: 312-729-5800
Web Site: www.brightconnectionsmedia.com
Key Personnel
Pres: Jim O'Rourke *E-mail:* jim.orourke@worldbook.com
VP, Edit: Paul Kobasa *E-mail:* paul.kobasa@worldbook.com
VP, Mktg: Jean Lin *E-mail:* jean.lin@worldbook.com
Founded: 2012
Nonfiction & playful educational material for young children through young adults.
ISBN Prefix(es): 978-1-62267
Number of titles published annually: 8 Print
Total Titles: 20 Print

§Brill Inc
Subsidiary of Koninklijke Brill NV
2 Liberty Sq, 11th fl, Boston, MA 02109
Tel: 617-263-2323 *Toll Free Tel:* 800-962-4406 *Fax:* 617-263-2324
E-mail: cs@brillusa.com
Web Site: www.brill.com
Key Personnel
Pres, Sales & Mktg: Steve Dane
Off Mgr: Rose Luongo
Founded: 1683
Publishes high-level, specialized, academic titles.
ISBN Prefix(es): 978-90-04
Number of titles published annually: 600 Print
Total Titles: 6,000 Print
Orders to: *Toll Free Tel:* 800-337-9255
Returns: Books International Inc, c/o Brill Academic Publishers Inc, 22883 Quicksilver Dr, Sterling, VA 20166
Warehouse: PO Box 605, Herndon, VA 20172 *Tel:* 703-661-1500 *Toll Free Tel:* 800-337-9255 *Fax:* 703-661-1501
Distribution Center: Books International Inc, 22883 Quicksilver Dr, Sterling, VA 20166 *Tel:* 703-661-1500

Brilliance Audio
Subsidiary of Amazon.com
1704 Eaton Dr, Grand Haven, MI 49417
Tel: 616-846-5256 *Toll Free Tel:* 800-648-2312 (orders only) *Fax:* 616-846-0630
E-mail: customerservice@brillianceaudio.com
Web Site: www.brillianceaudio.com
Key Personnel
VP & Assoc Publr: Gary Krebs

Mng Dir: Mark Pereira *E-mail:* mpereira@brillianceaudio.com
Creative Dir: Kathlyn Miller *Tel:* 616-846-5256 ext 709
Fin Dir: Brad Dahl *Tel:* 616-846-5256 ext 750 *E-mail:* bdahl@brillianceaudio.com
Sales Dir: Steve Woessner *Tel:* 616-846-5256 ext 705 *E-mail:* swoessner@brillianceaudio.com
Acqs Ed: Sheryl Zajechowski *Tel:* 616-846-5256 ext 726 *E-mail:* szajechowski@brillianceaudio.com
Ed, Adult Nonfiction: Joe McNeely *Tel:* 616-846-5256 ext 755 *E-mail:* jmcneely@brillianceaudio.com
Ed, Waterfall Press: Tammy Faxel
Acqs, Grand Harbor Press: Amy Hofford
Founded: 1984
Country's leading independent audiobook publisher.
ISBN Prefix(es): 978-0-930435; 978-1-56100; 978-1-56740; 978-1-58788; 978-1-59086; 978-1-59355; 978-1-59600; 978-1-59710; 978-1-59737; 978-1-4233; 978-1-4418; 978-1-61106; 978-1-4558
Number of titles published annually: 700 Audio
Total Titles: 6,500 Audio
Imprints: Grand Harbor Press; Waterfall Press
Membership(s): Audio Publishers Association

Bristol Park Books
252 W 38 St, Suite 206, New York, NY 10018
Tel: 212-842-0700 *Fax:* 212-842-1771
E-mail: info@bristolparkbooks.com
Web Site: bristolparkbooks.com
Key Personnel
VP: Richard Alexander
Promotional hardcover reprints.
ISBN Prefix(es): 978-0-88365; 978-0-88486; 978-1-57866
Number of titles published annually: 50 Print
Total Titles: 100 Print
Orders to: National Book Network, 4501 Forbes Blvd, Suite 200, Lantham, MD 20706 *Tel:* 301-459-3366 *Web Site:* nbnbooks.com
Distribution Center: National Book Network, 4501 Forbes Blvd, Suite 200, Lantham, MD 20706 *Tel:* 301-459-3366 *Web Site:* nbnbooks.com

Broden Books LLC
3824 Sunset Dr, Spring Park, MN 55384
SAN: 920-0614
Tel: 952-471-1066
E-mail: media@brodenbooks.com
Web Site: www.brodenbooks.com
Key Personnel
CEO & Pres: Kathy La Pointe
Founded: 1999
Early childhood literacy resources for parents, schools & libraries. We are engaged in ongoing research into issues impacting literacy in the US. Our resources are sold worldwide through online & retail stores.
ISBN Prefix(es): 978-0-9832023
Number of titles published annually: 3 Print
Total Titles: 3 Print
Imprints: REAL Phonics™

§Brookes Publishing Co Inc
PO Box 10624, Baltimore, MD 21285-0624
SAN: 212-730X
Tel: 410-337-9580 (outside US & CN) *Toll Free Tel:* 800-638-3775 (US & CN) *Fax:* 410-337-8539
E-mail: custserv@brookespublishing.com
Web Site: www.brookespublishing.com
Key Personnel
Chmn of the Bd: Paul H Brookes
Pres: Jeffrey D Brookes *E-mail:* jbrookes@brookespublishing.com
EVP: Melissa A Behm *E-mail:* mbehm@brookespublishing.com
VP & Publr: George S Stamathis *E-mail:* gstamathis@brookespublishing.com
Edit Dir: Heather Shrestha *E-mail:* hshrestha@brookespublishing.com
Dir, HR & Opers: Erika Kinney *E-mail:* ekinney@brookespublishing.com
Dir, Mktg: Jessica Reighard *E-mail:* jreighard@brookespublishing.com
Sr Subs Rts & Contracts Mgr: Heather Lengyel *Tel:* 410-205-0466 *E-mail:* hlengyel@brookespublishing.com
Founded: 1978
Publishes professional books, textbooks, assessments, curricula & web-based products in the areas of: early childhood, early intervention, social-emotional development, literacy, learning disabilities, autism, behavior, special education, developmental disabilities, communication & language.
ISBN Prefix(es): 978-0-933716; 978-1-55766; 978-1-59857; 978-1-68125
Number of titles published annually: 65 Print; 5 CD-ROM; 5 Online; 50 E-Book
Total Titles: 600 Print; 20 CD-ROM; 10 Online; 50 E-Book
Subsidiaries: Health Professions Press (specialist publisher focused on the broad range of issues in gerontology, long-term care & health administration)
Foreign Rep(s): Cranbury International LLC (Caribbean, Latin America); CRW Marketing Services for Publishers Inc (Guam, Northern Mariana Islands, Palau, Philippines); Eurospan Group (Africa, Europe, Middle East, UK); Footprint Books Pty Ltd (Australia, Fiji, New Zealand, Papua New Guinea); Tahir Lodhi Publishers' Representatives (Pakistan); Sara Books Pvt Ltd (Bangladesh, India, Sri Lanka); STM Publishers Services Pte Ltd (China, Hong Kong, Macau, Malaysia, Myanmar, Singapore, Thailand, Vietnam); Unifacmanu Trading Co Ltd (Taiwan)
Returns: Maple Logistics Solutions, 60 Grumbacher Rd, I-83 Industrial Park, York, PA 17406
Warehouse: Maple Logistics Solutions, PO Box 15100, York, PA 17405 *Web Site:* www.maplelogisticssolutions.com
Membership(s): AAP PreK-12 Learning Group
See separate listing for:
Health Professions Press

§The Brookings Institution Press
Division of Brookings Institution
1775 Massachusetts Ave NW, Washington, DC 20036-2188
SAN: 201-9396
Tel: 202-536-3600 *Toll Free Tel:* 800-537-5487 *Fax:* 202-536-3623
E-mail: permissions@brookings.edu
Web Site: www.brookings.edu
Key Personnel
Pres: Strobe Talbott
Dir: Valentina Kalk
Edit Dir: Bill Finan
Mng Ed: Janet Walker *E-mail:* jwalker@brookings.edu
Dist Mgr: Laura Baida
Publicity & Mktg Mgr: Carrie Engel
Sales Mgr: Yelba Quinn
Libn: Cyrus Behroozi
Founded: 1916
Economics, foreign policy & government affairs.
ISBN Prefix(es): 978-0-8157
Number of titles published annually: 45 Print; 50 E-Book
Total Titles: 1,205 Print; 1 CD-ROM; 1,031 E-Book
Foreign Rep(s): APD Singapore Pte Ltd (Brunei, Indonesia, Korea, Malaysia, Singapore, Thailand, Vietnam); Eurospan Group (Africa, China, Europe, Hong Kong, Middle East, Taiwan, UK); Far Eastern Booksellers (Mr Nobuyuki Namekawa) (Japan); MHM Ltd (Japan); NewSouth Books (Australia, New Zealand); Perseus Books Group (Estefania Garcia-Correa) (Caribbean, Latin America); Publishers Group Canada (Canada); Viva Books Pvt Ltd (Bangladesh, India, Nepal, Pakistan, Sri Lanka)
Foreign Rights: Agency Literaria Internazionale (Italy); Big Apple Agency (China); Tuttle-Mori Agency Inc (Japan)
Distribution Center: Perseus Academic, c/o Perseus Book Group, 250 W 57 St, 15th fl, New York, NY 10107 (US & CN) *E-mail:* client.info@perseusbooks.com
Membership(s): AAP; American Association of University Presses

Brookline Books
8 Trumbull Rd, Suite B-001, Northampton, MA 01060
Tel: 603-669-7032 (orders) *Toll Free Tel:* 800-666-2665 (orders) *Fax:* 413-584-6184
E-mail: brbooks@yahoo.com
Founded: 1985
Education, special needs, readings, general trade.
ISBN Prefix(es): 978-0-914797; 978-1-57129
Number of titles published annually: 5 Print
Total Titles: 125 Print

Brooklyn Publishers LLC
PO Box 248, Cedar Rapids, IA 52406
Tel: 319-368-8012 *Toll Free Tel:* 888-473-8521 *Fax:* 319-368-8011
E-mail: customerservice@brookpub.com; editor@brookpub.com
Web Site: www.brookpub.com
Key Personnel
Sr Ed: David Burton
ISBN Prefix(es): 978-1-930961; 978-1-931000; 978-1-931805; 978-1-932404; 978-1-60003
Number of titles published annually: 100 Print
Total Titles: 600 Print

Brown Books Publishing Group
16250 Knoll Trail, Suite 205, Dallas, TX 75248
Tel: 972-381-0009 *Fax:* 972-248-4336
E-mail: publishing@brownbooks.com
Web Site: www.brownbooks.com
Key Personnel
CEO & Publr: Milli Brown
PR: Kathy Williams
Founded: 1994
Full service independent publisher. Committed to producing high quality books of all genres for authors who choose to retain the rights to their intellectual property.
This publisher has indicated that 85% of their product line is author subsidized.
ISBN Prefix(es): 978-1-933285; 978-1-934812
Number of titles published annually: 150 Print
Total Titles: 1,000 Print
Divisions: Brown Books Agency; Brown Books Kids; Christian Press; Personal Profiles
Warehouse: Cenveo, 3210 Miller Park Dr S, Suite 100, Garland, TX 75041 *Tel:* 972-271-0591
Distribution Center: Quality Books, 1003 W Pines Rd, Oregon, IL 61061
Follett School Solutions Inc, 1340 Ridgeview Dr, McHenry, IL 60050 SAN: 169-1902
Baker & Taylor Inc, 2550 W Tyvola Rd, Suite 300, Charlotte, NC 28217
Ingram, One Ingram Blvd, La Vergne, TN 37086
Membership(s): Independent Book Publishers Association

Karen Brown's Guides Inc
16 E Third Ave, Suite 9, San Mateo, CA 94401
Mailing Address: PO Box 70, San Mateo, CA 94401-0070
Tel: 650-342-9117 *Fax:* 650-342-9153
Web Site: www.karenbrown.com

Key Personnel
Pres: Karen Brown Herbert *E-mail:* karen@karenbrown.com
Founded: 1977
General.
ISBN Prefix(es): 978-0-930328; 978-1-928901; 978-1-933810; 978-1-63371
Number of titles published annually: 17 Print
Total Titles: 17 Print
Foreign Rep(s): National Book Network (Australia, Europe, New Zealand)
Distribution Center: National Book Network, 4501 Forbes Blvd, Suite 200, Lanham, MD 20706, Pres: Jed Lyons *Toll Free Tel:* 800-462-6420 *Toll Free Fax:* 800-338-4550 *Web Site:* www.nbnbooks.com

Bucknell University Press
6 Taylor Hall, Bucknell University, Lewisburg, PA 17837
Tel: 570-577-3674
E-mail: universitypress@bucknell.edu
Web Site: www.bucknell.edu/universitypress
Key Personnel
Dir: Greg Clingham *Tel:* 570-577-1552 *E-mail:* clingham@bucknell.edu
Edit Assoc: Pam Dailey *Tel:* 570-577-3674 *E-mail:* pad024@bucknell.edu
Founded: 1968
ISBN Prefix(es): 978-0-8387
Number of titles published annually: 35 Print
Total Titles: 700 Print
Distributed by Rowman & Littlefield

BuilderBooks.com
Division of National Association of Home Builders (NAHB)
1201 15 St NW, Washington, DC 20005
SAN: 207-7035
Tel: 202-822-0200 *Toll Free Tel:* 800-223-2665 *Fax:* 202-266-8096 (edit)
E-mail: builderbooks@nahb.com
Web Site: www.builderbooks.com
Key Personnel
SVP & Mktg Offr: Lakisha Campbell *E-mail:* lcampbell@nahb.com
Mng Dir, Mktg: Patricia Potts
Mktg Mgr, NAHB: Jacqueline Barnes
Founded: 1943
Publish books about home construction & design, remodeling, land development, housing & construction management, sales & marketing of new homes, safety & seniors housing.
ISBN Prefix(es): 978-0-86718
Number of titles published annually: 7 Print
Total Titles: 150 Print
Distributor for National Association of Home Builders (NAHB)
Orders to: c/o Returns, National Association of Home Builders, 905 Carlow Dr, Unit B, Bolingbrook, IL 60490

Bull Publishing Co
PO Box 1377, Boulder, CO 80306
SAN: 208-5712
Tel: 303-545-6350 *Toll Free Tel:* 800-676-2855 *Fax:* 303-545-6354
E-mail: bullpublishing@msn.com
Web Site: www.bullpub.com
Key Personnel
CFO: Emily Sewell
Pres & Publr: James Bull
Dir, Mktg: Claire Cameron
Founded: 1974
Self-care, nutrition & health care, physical fitness, weight loss, mental health, parenting & child care, psychology, self-help.
ISBN Prefix(es): 978-0-915950; 978-0-923521; 978-1-933503
Number of titles published annually: 6 Print; 1 Audio
Total Titles: 70 Print; 6 Audio

Foreign Rep(s): Gazelle Book Services Ltd (UK & the continent)
Warehouse: A & A Quality Shipping Services, 3623 Munster Ave, Unit B, Hayward, CA 94545
Distribution Center: Independent Publishers Group, 814 N Franklin St, Chicago, IL 60610 *Toll Free Tel:* 800-888-4741 *Web Site:* www.ipgbook.com

The Bureau for At-Risk Youth, see Prevention Products & Services Inc dba The Bureau for At-Risk Youth

§Bureau of Economic Geology, University of Texas at Austin
Division of University of Texas at Austin
10100 Burnet Rd, Bldg 130, Austin, TX 78758
Mailing Address: University Sta, Box X, Austin, TX 78713-8924
Tel: 512-471-1534 *Fax:* 512-471-0140
E-mail: pubsales@beg.utexas.edu
Web Site: www.beg.utexas.edu
Key Personnel
Dir: Scott W Tinker
Mgr, Pubn Sales: Amanda Masterson *E-mail:* amanda.masterson@beg.utexas.edu
Founded: 1909
Scientific & technical books in geosciences.
Number of titles published annually: 6 Print; 1 CD-ROM
Total Titles: 1,700 Print; 8 CD-ROM; 1,500 E-Book
Distributor for Gulf Coast Association of Geological Societies; Gulf Coast Section; Texas Memorial Museum (selected titles)
Orders to: University Sta, Box X, Austin, TX 78713-8924 *Tel:* 512-471-7144 *Web Site:* begstore/beg.utexas.edu

Burford Books
101 E State St, No 301, Ithaca, NY 14850
Tel: 607-319-4373 *Fax:* 607-319-4373 *Toll Free Fax:* 866-212-7750
E-mail: info@burfordbooks.com
Web Site: www.burfordbooks.com
Key Personnel
Pres: Peter Burford
Founded: 1997
Publisher of books on the outdoors, sports, food & wine, fitness, nature, travel, fishing, military, Finger Lakes area.
ISBN Prefix(es): 978-1-58080
Number of titles published annually: 6 Print; 6 E-Book
Total Titles: 115 Print; 34 E-Book
Foreign Rep(s): Gazelle Book Services Ltd (UK)
Distribution Center: National Book Network, 15200 NBN Way, Blue Ridge Summit, PA 17214 *Tel:* 717-794-3800
Membership(s): Independent Publishers Association

Burns Archive Press
Imprint of Burns Archive Photographic Distributors Ltd
140 E 38 St, New York, NY 10016
Tel: 212-889-1938 *Fax:* 212-481-9113
E-mail: info@burnsarchive.com
Web Site: www.burnsarchive.com
Key Personnel
CEO & Pres: Stanley B Burns, MD *E-mail:* burns@inch.com
Founded: 1979
Renowned for images of the darker side of life: death, disease, crime, racism, revolution & war. Provides a unique source of historic visual documentation containing over 700,000 vintage photographs. The Archive houses world-class holdings of African-American imagery & Judaica, as well as the foremost collection of early medical photography. More than a century of iconographic & historic photographs from the 1840s through the 1950s are available as stock photography. In addition, The Archive provides consultation, prepares exhibitions & publishes books on photographic history.
ISBN Prefix(es): 978-0-9612958; 978-0-9748688; 978-0-9748688; 978-0-9764495; 978-0-9764495; 978-1-934421; 978-1-936002
Number of titles published annually: 4 Print
Total Titles: 35 Print
Membership(s): American Book Producers Association

§Business & Legal Resources Inc
100 Winners Circle, Suite 300, Brentwood, TN 37027
Tel: 860-510-0100 *Toll Free Tel:* 800-727-5257
E-mail: service@blr.com
Web Site: www.blr.com
Key Personnel
Founder: Robert L Brady
CEO: Dan Oswald
Sr Mng Ed: Catherine Moreton Gray
Sr Ed: Celeste Blackburn
Founded: 1977
Business newsletters, books, booklets, films & CD-ROMs. Specialize in safety, human resource & environmental training & compliance.
ISBN Prefix(es): 978-1-55645
Number of titles published annually: 100 Print
Total Titles: 380 Print; 113 CD-ROM; 4 Online; 4 E-Book
Membership(s): NEPA

Business Expert Press
Subsidiary of IGroup
222 E 46 St, New York, NY 10017-2906
Tel: 630-207-5927
E-mail: charlene.kronstadt@businessexpertpress.com
Web Site: www.businessexpertpress.com
Key Personnel
EVP: Stewart Mattson *E-mail:* stewart.mattson@businessexpertpress.com
Exec Dir, Global Sales & Mktg: Sean Kaneski *Tel:* 218-820-3756 *E-mail:* sean.kaneski@businessexpertpress.com
Founded: 2008
Providing MBA level students with applied, concise textbooks that can be used in & out of the classroom.
ISBN Prefix(es): 978-1-60649
Number of titles published annually: 100 Print; 100 Online; 100 E-Book
Total Titles: 300 Print; 300 Online; 300 E-Book

§Business Research Services Inc
4641 Montgomery Ave, Suite 208, Bethesda, MD 20814
SAN: 691-8522
Tel: 301-229-5561 *Toll Free Tel:* 800-845-8420 *Toll Free Fax:* 877-516-0818
E-mail: brspubs@sba8a.com
Web Site: www.sba8a.com; www.setasidealert.com
Key Personnel
Pres & Publr: Thomas D Johnson *E-mail:* tjohnson@setasidealert.com
Founded: 1984
Directories/lists of minority & women's businesses; small business newsletters & contract opportunities services.
ISBN Prefix(es): 978-0-933527
Number of titles published annually: 4 Print; 4 CD-ROM; 1 Online; 1 E-Book
Total Titles: 7 Print; 4 CD-ROM; 1 Online; 1 E-Book
Distributed by Basch; Book House; Coutts; Gale Research Inc; Midwest Library Service
Distributor for Riley & Johnson

Butte Publications Inc
PO Box 1328, Hillsboro, OR 97123-1328
SAN: 299-8866

Toll Free Tel: 866-312-8883 *Toll Free Fax:* 866-412-8883 (orders only)
E-mail: service@buttepublications.com
Web Site: www.buttepublications.com
Key Personnel
Pres & Publr: Matthew H Brink
E-mail: mbrink@buttepublications.com
Founded: 1992
Resources serving the deaf community.
ISBN Prefix(es): 978-1-884362; 978-1-939349
Number of titles published annually: 1 Print
Total Titles: 12 Print; 1 E-Book

By Design Press, see Quite Specific Media Group Ltd

Bywater Books
PO Box 3671, Ann Arbor, MI 48106-3671
Tel: 734-662-8815
Web Site: bywaterbooks.com
Key Personnel
Owner & Ed-in-Chief: Kelly Smith
Owner: Marianne K Martin
E-mail: mkmbywater@aol.com
Publr: Salem West
Dir, Creative Servs: Ann McMan
Founded: 1992
Publish top quality lesbian fiction. Our Bloody Brits imprint publishes the finest mainstream British mysteries in the US.
ISBN Prefix(es): 978-1-932859
Number of titles published annually: 10 Print
Total Titles: 42 Print
Imprints: Amble Press; Bloody Brits Press

Caissa Editions
Affiliate of Dale A Brandreth Books
PO Box 151, Yorklyn, DE 19736-0151
Tel: 302-239-4608
Web Site: www.chessbookstore.com
Key Personnel
Owner & Pres: Dale Brandreth
E-mail: dbrandreth3@comcast.net
Founded: 1971
Publisher of books that are primarily on chess.
ISBN Prefix(es): 978-0-939433
Number of titles published annually: 3 Print
Total Titles: 23 Print

§Cambridge Educational
Imprint of Infobase Learning
132 W 31 St, 17th fl, New York, NY 10001
Toll Free Tel: 800-322-8755 *Fax:* 609-671-0266 *Toll Free Fax:* 800-329-6687
E-mail: custserve@infobaselearning.com
Web Site: www.infobasepublishing.com
Key Personnel
Pres, Infobase Learning: Mark McDonnell
Founded: 1980
Produce & distribute educational materials & CD-ROMs. Specialize in crime & legal studies, family & consumer science, health & guidance, social studies & vocational/technical education & career education. Cambridge Educational is a trademark of Films Media Group.
ISBN Prefix(es): 978-0-927368; 978-1-56450
Number of titles published annually: 5 Print; 20 CD-ROM
Total Titles: 35 Print; 150 CD-ROM

§Cambridge University Press
Division of University of Cambridge
1 Liberty Plaza, 20th fl, New York, NY 10006
SAN: 200-206X
Tel: 212-924-3900; 212-337-5000 *Fax:* 212-691-3239
E-mail: newyork@cambridge.org
Web Site: www.cambridge.org/us
Key Personnel
SVP, Academic Publg, Americas: Brigitte Shull
Mng Dir, Americas & Global Mng Dir, Eng Lang Teaching: Michael Peluse
HR Dir: Nick Correa
Press Dist Dir: Ian R Bradie
Publg Dir, Humanities & Soc Sci: Dr Beatrice Rehl *E-mail:* brehl@cambridge.org
Journals Mktg Mgr: Susan Soule
Mktg Mgr, Humanities, Law & Psychology: Michael Duncan
Mktg Communs Mgr: Carine Mitchell
Journals Ed: Mark Zadrozny
Sr Ed, Engg: Peter Gordon
Sr Ed, Law: Dr John Berger
Sr Ed, Soc Sci: Lewis Bateman; Robert Dreesen
Sr Commissioning Ed: Marigold Acland
E-mail: macland@cambridge.org
Ed, Math & Computer Sci: Lauren Cowles
Founded: 1534
Scholarly & trade books, college textbooks & journals.
ISBN Prefix(es): 978-0-521
Number of titles published annually: 2,400 Print
Total Titles: 45,000 Print; 160 Online
Foreign Office(s): The Edinburgh Bldg, Shaftesbury Rd, Cambridge CB2 8BS, United Kingdom *Tel:* (01223) 358331
Warehouse: One Ingram Blvd, La Vergne, TN 17202
Membership(s): AAP; Association of American University Presses; BISG

Camino Books Inc
PO Box 59026, Philadelphia, PA 19102-9026
Tel: 215-413-1917 *Fax:* 215-413-3255
E-mail: camino@caminobooks.com
Web Site: www.caminobooks.com
Key Personnel
Pres & Publr: Edward J Jutkowitz
E-mail: ejutkowitz@caminobooks.com
Founded: 1987
Regional trade books for the Mid-Atlantic states.
ISBN Prefix(es): 978-0-940159; 978-1-933822; 978-1-68098
Number of titles published annually: 10 Print; 10 E-Book
Total Titles: 100 Print; 65 E-Book
Warehouse: Whitehurst & Clark Book Fulfillment Inc, 1200 County Rd, Rte 523, Flemington, NJ 08822 *Tel:* 908-782-2323

Campfield & Campfield Publishing LLC
6521 Cutler St, Philadelphia, PA 19126
Toll Free Tel: 888-518-2440 *Fax:* 215-224-6696
E-mail: info@campfieldspublishing.com
Web Site: www.campfieldspublishing.com
Key Personnel
Publr: Charlene M Campfield
Founded: 2009
Publisher of Christ-centered children's & young adult books.
ISBN Prefix(es): 978-0-9817025
Number of titles published annually: 4 Print; 4 Online
Total Titles: 10 Print; 10 Online; 1 E-Book

Candied Plums
Imprint of Paper Republic LLC
7548 Ravenna Ave NE, Seattle, WA 98115
Mailing Address: 2301 N 65 St, Seattle, WA 98103
E-mail: candiedplums@gmail.com
Web Site: www.candiedplums.com
Key Personnel
Publr: Richard Lee *E-mail:* richard.candiedplums@gmail.com
Publg Consultant: Roxanne Feldman
E-mail: roxannefeldman@gmail.com
Edit Coord: Lisa Lee *E-mail:* lisa.candiedplums@gmail.com
Ed: Nancy Zhang *E-mail:* nancy.candiedplums@gmail.com
Founded: 2016
ISBN Prefix(es): 978-1-945295
Number of titles published annually: 20 Print
Total Titles: 20 Print
Orders to: Pathway Book Service, 34 Production Ave, Keene, NH 03431, Contact: Julie Ballou *Toll Free Tel:* 800-345-6665 *Fax:* 603-965-2181 *E-mail:* julie.ballou@pathwaybook.com
Returns: Pathway Book Service, 34 Production Ave, Keene, NH 03431, Contact: Julie Ballou *Toll Free Tel:* 800-345-6665 *Fax:* 603-965-2181 *E-mail:* julie.ballou@pathwaybook.com
Warehouse: Global Union International Inc, 16801 Gale Ave, Unit C, City of Industry, CA 91745, Contact: Allen Wang *Tel:* 626-965-8878 *Fax:* 626-965-8877 *E-mail:* allenwang@globalunionintl.com
Distribution Center: Pathway Book Service, 34 Production Ave, Keene, NH 03431, Contact: Julie Ballou *Toll Free Tel:* 800-345-6665 *Fax:* 603-965-2181 *E-mail:* julie.ballou@pathwaybook.com

§Candlewick Press
Subsidiary of Walker Books Ltd (London)
99 Dover St, Somerville, MA 02144-2825
Tel: 617-661-3330 *Fax:* 617-661-0565
E-mail: bigbear@candlewick.com; salesinfo@candlewick.com
Web Site: www.candlewick.com
Key Personnel
Pres & Publr: Karen Lotz
EVP, Exec Edit Dir & Assoc Publr: Liz Bicknell
SVP & Group Sales Dir: John Mendelson
SVP, Commercial Opers: Susan Batcheller
SVP, Fin: Hilary Berkman
VP, Contracts, Rts & Royalties: Becky S Hemperly
VP, Publicity & Exec Dir, Mktg Campaigns: Jennifer Roberts
Assoc Publr & Creative Dir: Chris Paul
Exec Dir, Educ Sales & Mktg: Kathleen Rourke
Dir, Edit Opers & Edit Dir: Mary Lee Donovan
Group Edit Dir, Candlewick Entertainment & Walker Entertainment: Joan Powers
Dir, Mass Mkt Sales: Laura Pennock
Publicity & Mktg Campaigns Dir: Tracy Miracle
Publicity, Brands & Consumer Outreach Dir: Laura Rivas
Sr Exec Ed: Sarah Ketchersid
Exec Ed: Hilary Van Dusen
Mgr, Lib Mktg & Outreach: Andie Krawczyk
Founded: 1992
ISBN Prefix(es): 978-1-56402; 978-0-7636
Number of titles published annually: 300 Print
Total Titles: 2,250 Print; 230 E-Book
Imprints: Big Picture Press; Candlewick Entertainment; Candlewick Studio; Nosy Crow; Templar Books
Foreign Rights: Walker Books Australia; Walker Books London
Returns: Penguin Random House LLC, 1019 N State Rd 47, Crawfordsville, IN 47933; Penguin Random House Canada, 6971 Columbus Rd, Mississauga, ON L5T 1K1, Canada
Distribution Center: Penguin Random House Publisher Services (PRHPS), 400 Hahn Rd, Westminster, MD 21157 *Toll Free Tel:* 800-733-3000 *Toll Free Fax:* 800-659-2436 *E-mail:* customerservice@randomhouse.com
Penguin Random House Canada, 75 Sherbourne St, 5th fl, Toronto, ON M5A 2P9, Canada *Toll Free Tel:* 888-523-9292 *Toll Free Fax:* 888-562-9924
Membership(s): The Children's Book Council

C&T Publishing Inc
1651 Challenge Dr, Concord, CA 94520-5206
Tel: 925-677-0377 *Toll Free Tel:* 800-284-1114 *Fax:* 925-677-0373
E-mail: support@ctpub.com
Web Site: www.ctpub.com
Key Personnel
CEO: Todd Hensley

CFO: Tony Hensley
Edit Dir: Gailen Runge
Dir, Sales & Mktg: Sandy Balin
E-mail: sandyb@ctpub.com
Publr: Amy Marson
Founded: 1983
Specialize in fiber & paper craft books & products.
ISBN Prefix(es): 978-0-914881; 978-1-57120
Number of titles published annually: 60 Print; 2 CD-ROM
Total Titles: 300 Print; 5 CD-ROM; 10 Online
Distributed by Watson-Guptill Publications
Membership(s): Craft Hobby Association; Independent Book Publishers Association

Canon Law Society of America
Hecker Ctr, Suite 111, 3025 Fourth St NE, Washington, DC 20017-1102
SAN: 237-6296
Tel: 202-832-2350 *Fax:* 202-832-2331
E-mail: coordinator@clsa.org; info@clsa.org
Web Site: www.clsa.org
Key Personnel
Exec Coord: Rev Roger H Keeler
E-mail: rhkeeler@clsa.org
Founded: 1939
Books on canon law & marriage.
ISBN Prefix(es): 978-0-943616
Number of titles published annually: 3 Print
Total Titles: 58 Print

Cantos Para Todos
(Songs for Everyone)
4749 Hillcrest St, Bel Aire, KS 67220
Tel: 316-239 6477
E-mail: cantos@cantos.org
Web Site: www.cantos.org
Key Personnel
Publr: Roy Howard *E-mail:* 2rhoward@att.net
Founded: 1989
Materials with multiworlds in mind. Multimedia, multicultural, multilingual materials for schools & homes.
This publisher has indicated that 100% of their product line is author subsidized.
ISBN Prefix(es): 978-0-9768650
Number of titles published annually: 4 Print; 10 CD-ROM; 12 Online; 5 E-Book
Total Titles: 50 Print; 75 CD-ROM; 60 Online; 5 E-Book

Capital Enquiry Inc
1034 Emerald Bay Rd, No 435, South Lake Tahoe, CA 96150
Tel: 916-442-1434 *Toll Free Tel:* 800-922-7486
Fax: 916-244-2704
E-mail: info@capenq.com
Web Site: www.govbuddy.com
Key Personnel
Owner & Mktg Dir: Bruce Campbell
Founded: 1973
Legislative directories, information, interactive maps (CA) zip code directory, mobile apps & *US Congress Directory*.
ISBN Prefix(es): 978-0-917982
Number of titles published annually: 7 Print
Total Titles: 15 Print
Distributor for Center for Investigative Reporting

CAPPA, see University of Texas at Arlington College of Architecture, Planning & Public Affairs

Capstone Publishers™
1710 Roe Crest Dr, North Mankato, MN 56003
Toll Free Tel: 800-747-4992 (cust serv)
Toll Free Fax: 888-262-0705
Web Site: www.capstonepress.com
Key Personnel
Owner: Robert Coughlan
CEO: G Thomas Ahern
COO & CFO: William R Rouse
Chief Content Offr: Ashley Andersen-Zantop
Pres: Matthew A Keller
Edit Dir: Nick Healy
Book Trade Sales Mgr: Larry Dorfman
Founded: 1991
Provides new & struggling readers with a strong foundation on which to build reading success. Our broad range of nonfiction titles for grades PreK-8 easily blends a world of books with the world children experience every day.
ISBN Prefix(es): 978-1-56065; 978-0-7368
Number of titles published annually: 250 Print
Total Titles: 2,100 Print
Imprints: Capstone Press; Capstone Young Readers; Compass Point Books; Heinemann Raintree; Picture Window Books; Stone Arch Books
Divisions: Heinemann Raintree
Branch Office(s)
5050 Lincoln Dr, Suite 200, Edina, MN 55436
Billing Address: 3680 Momentum Place, Chicago, IL 60689-5336
Distribution Center: 1905 Lookout Dr, North Mankato, MN 56003

Captain Fiddle Music & Publications
94 Wiswall Rd, Lee, NH 03861
Tel: 603-659-2658
E-mail: cfiddle@tiac.net
Web Site: captainfiddle.com
Key Personnel
Owner: Ryan J Thomson
Founded: 1985
ISBN Prefix(es): 978-0-931877
Number of titles published annually: 3 Print
Total Titles: 24 Print

§Cardiotext Publishing
3405 W 44 St, Minneapolis, MN 55410
SAN: 852-2251
Tel: 612-925-2053 *Fax:* 612-922-7556
E-mail: info@cardiotextpublishing.com
Web Site: www.cardiotextpublishing.com
Key Personnel
Pres: Mike Crouchet *Tel:* 612-746-3699
E-mail: mike.crouchet@cardiotext.com
Founded: 2007
Independent print & digital publisher specializing in the field of cardiovascular medicine.
ISBN Prefix(es): 978-1-935395; 978-1-942909; 978-0-979016
Number of titles published annually: 10 Print; 10 Online; 10 E-Book
Total Titles: 35 Print; 35 Online; 35 E-Book
Foreign Rights: John Scott & Co (worldwide exc North America)
Distribution Center: NBN International, 10 Thornbury Rd, Plymouth PL6 7PP, United Kingdom *Tel:* (01752) 202 301 *Fax:* (01752) 202 333 *E-mail:* orders@nbninternational.com *Web Site:* distribution.nbni.co.uk

Cardoza Publishing
808 S Main St, Las Vegas, NV 89101
Tel: 702-870-7200 *Toll Free Tel:* 800-577-WINS (577-9467) *Fax:* 702-822-6500
E-mail: info@cardozabooks.com
Web Site: www.cardozabooks.com
Key Personnel
Publr & Author: Avery Cardoza
Founded: 1981
An independent publisher specializing in gaming, gambling, poker, backgammon & chess titles.
ISBN Prefix(es): 978-1-58042
Number of titles published annually: 15 Print
Total Titles: 200 Print
Distributor for Simon & Schuster
Orders to: Simon & Schuster, 100 Front St, Riverside, NJ 08075, Order Processing Dept *Toll Free Tel:* 800-223-2336 *Toll Free Fax:* 800-943-9831 *E-mail:* order_desk@distican.com

The Career Press Inc
12 Parish Dr, Wayne, NJ 07470
Tel: 201-848-0310 *Toll Free Tel:* 800-CAREER-1 (227-3371) *Fax:* 201-848-1727
E-mail: sales@careerpress.com
Web Site: www.careerpress.com
Key Personnel
Pres: Ronald W Fry
Edit Dir: Gina Schenck *E-mail:* gschenck@careerpress.com
Dir, Sales & Publicity: Laurie Kelly-Pye
E-mail: lkellypye@careerpress.com
Sr Acqs Ed: Michael Pye *E-mail:* mpye@careerpress.com
Acqs Ed: Adam Schwartz *E-mail:* aschwartz@careerpress.com
Founded: 1985
Reference books, careers, business & financial how-to, educational, New Age, weddings & motivational.
ISBN Prefix(es): 978-1-56414; 978-1-60163; 978-1-63265
Number of titles published annually: 75 Print
Total Titles: 400 Print
Imprints: New Page Books (www.newpagebooks.com)
Foreign Rep(s): Artemis Agency (Michelle Lin) (Taiwan); Brumby Sunstate (Australia, New Zealand); Deep Books Ltd (Europe, UK); Hornblower Group (Canada); McGraw-Hill Education (Asia); Pansing Distribution Pte Ltd (Malaysia, Singapore); Phambili Agencies (South Africa); The White Partnership (Andrew White) (Hong Kong, Indonesia, Japan, Korea, Philippines, Taiwan, Thailand)
Foreign Rights: Amo Agency (Korea); CA-Link International LLC (China); Graal Literary Agency (Zbigniew Kanski) (Poland); Grayhawk Agency (Michelle Lin) (Taiwan); Letter Soup Rights Agency (Allison Olson) (worldwide); Tuttle-Mori Agency (Manami Tamaoki) (Japan); Yu Ri Jang Literary Agency (Christine Yi) (Korea)
Returns: Books International, 22883 Quicksilver Dr, Dulles, VA 20166 *Tel:* 703-661-1516
Distribution Center: University of Toronto Press, 5201 Dufferin St, North York, ON M3H 5T8, Canada *Tel:* 416-667-7791 *Toll Free Tel:* 800-565-9523 *Fax:* 416-667-7823 *E-mail:* utpbooks@utpress.utoronto.ca *Web Site:* utoronto.ca

§Caribe Betania Editores
Division of Grupo Nelson Inc
PO Box 141000, Nashville, TN 37214-1000
Tel: 615-902-1893 *Fax:* 615-883-9376
Web Site: www.caribebetania.com
Key Personnel
Mktg: Jake Salomon
Founded: 1949
Publisher of Spanish books & Bibles.
ISBN Prefix(es): 978-0-88113; 978-0-89922
Number of titles published annually: 100 Print
Total Titles: 480 Print

Carlisle Press - Walnut Creek
2673 Township Rd 421, Sugarcreek, OH 44681
Tel: 330-852-1900 *Toll Free Tel:* 800-852-4482
Fax: 330-852-3285
Key Personnel
Publr: Marvin Wengerd
Founded: 1992
Amish books & cookbooks, *Keeper's at Home* Magazine.
ISBN Prefix(es): 978-1-890050; 978-0-9642548; 978-1-933753
Number of titles published annually: 6 Print
Total Titles: 60 Print

Carnegie Mellon University Press
5032 Forbes Ave, Pittsburgh, PA 15289-1021
SAN: 211-2329
Tel: 412-268-2861 *Fax:* 412-268-8706
E-mail: carnegiemellonuniversitypress@gmail.com
Web Site: www.cmu.edu/universitypress
Key Personnel
Dir: Gerald Costanzo
Sr Ed: Cynthia Lamb
Prodn Mgr: Connie Amoroso *E-mail:* camoroso@andrew.cmu.edu
Founded: 1974
ISBN Prefix(es): 978-0-915604; 978-0-88748
Number of titles published annually: 15 Print
Total Titles: 280 Print
Billing Address: University Press of New England, One Court St, Suite 250, Lebanon, NH 03766 (order dept) *Toll Free Tel:* 800-421-1561 *Fax:* 603-448-9429
Orders to: University Press of New England, One Court St, Suite 250, Lebanon, NH 03766 (order dept) *Toll Free Tel:* 800-421-1561 *Fax:* 603-448-9429 *Web Site:* www.upne.com/distributed/dist_cmu.html
Returns: University Press of New England, c/o Maple Logistics Solutions, 704 Legionaire Dr, Fredericksburg, PA 17026 *Tel:* 603-448-1533 ext 503 *Fax:* 603-448-9429
Warehouse: University Press of New England, c/o Maple Logistics Solutions, 704 Legionaire Dr, Fredericksburg, PA 17026, Cust Serv Supv: Barbara Benson *Tel:* 603-448-1533 ext 255 *Toll Free Tel:* 800-421-1561 *Fax:* 603-448-9429 *E-mail:* university.press@dartmouth.edu *Web Site:* www.upne.com

Carolina Academic Press
700 Kent St, Durham, NC 27701
SAN: 210-7848
Tel: 919-489-7486 *Toll Free Tel:* 800-489-7486 *Fax:* 919-493-5668
E-mail: cap@cap-press.com
Web Site: www.cap-press.com; www.caplaw.com
Key Personnel
Publr: Keith R Sipe *Tel:* 919-489-7486 ext 120 *E-mail:* ksipe@cap-press.com
Assoc Publr, List Devt: Scott Sipe *Tel:* 919-489-7486 ext 129 *E-mail:* css@cap-press.com
Mng Ed: Ryland Bowman *Tel:* 919-489-7486 ext 133 *E-mail:* rbowman@cap-press.com
Sr Ed: Linda M Lacy *Tel:* 919-489-7486 ext 128 *E-mail:* linda@cap-press.com
Founded: 1974
Scholarly books & journals; anthropology, archaeology, criminal justice, economics, government, political science, history, reference, law, social science, african studies.
ISBN Prefix(es): 978-0-89089; 978-1-59460; 978-1-61163
Number of titles published annually: 150 Print; 150 E-Book
Total Titles: 1,100 Print; 350 E-Book
Returns: 101 Tobacco Rd, Oxford, NC 27565
Warehouse: 101 Tobacco Rd, Oxford, NC 27565

Carolrhoda Books
Imprint of Lerner Publishing Group Inc
241 First Ave N, Minneapolis, MN 55401
SAN: 201-9671
Tel: 612-332-3344 *Toll Free Tel:* 800-328-4929 *Fax:* 612-332-7615 *Toll Free Fax:* 800-332-1132
E-mail: info@lernerbooks.com; custserve@lernerbooks.com
Web Site: www.lernerbooks.com; www.facebook.com/lernerbooks
Key Personnel
Chmn: Harry J Lerner
CFO & EVP: Margaret Thomas
Pres & Publr: Adam Lerner
Assoc Trade Publr: Alix Reid
EVP, Sales: David Wexler
VP, Ed-in-Chief: Patricia M Stockland
Dir of Rts, Spec Sales & Intl Dist: Maria Kjoller
Group Mktg Dir: Jill Braithwaite
School & Lib Mktg Dir: Lois Wallentine
Dir, HR: Cyndi Radant
Founded: 1969
Juveniles: picture books & young adult fiction.
Number of titles published annually: 20 Print
Total Titles: 70 Print; 334 E-Book
Foreign Rep(s): INT Press Distribution (Australia); Monarch Books of Canada (Trade) (Canada); Phambili (Southern Africa); Publishers Marketing Services (Malaysia, Singapore); Saunders Book Co (Education) (Canada); South Pacific Books (New Zealand)
Foreign Rights: Japan Foreign Rights Centre (Japan); Korea Copyright Center (Korea); Michelle Lapautre Agence Junior (France); Literarische Agentur Silke Weniger (Germany)
Warehouse: Lerner Publishing Group, 1251 Washington Ave N, Minneapolis, MN 55401, Mgr: Ken Rued

Carolrhoda Lab™
Imprint of Lerner Publishing Group Inc
241 First Ave N, Minneapolis, MN 55401
Tel: 612-332-3344 *Toll Free Tel:* 800-328-4929 *Fax:* 612-332-7615 *Toll Free Fax:* 800-332-1132 (US)
E-mail: info@lernerbooks.com; custserve@lernerbooks.com
Web Site: www.lernerbooks.com; www.facebook.com/lernerbooks
Key Personnel
Chmn: Harry J Lerner
CFO & EVP: Margaret Thomas
Pres & Publr: Adam Lerner
Assoc Trade Publr: Alix Reid
EVP, Sales: David Wexler
VP, Ed-in-Chief: Patricia M Stockland
Dir of Rts, Spec Sales & Intl Dist: Maria Kjoller
Group Mktg Dir: Jill Braithwaite
School & Lib Mktg Dir: Lois Wallentine
Dir, HR: Cyndi Radant
Founded: 2010
Dedicated to distinctive, provocative, boundary-pushing fiction for teens & their sympathizers.
Number of titles published annually: 10 Print
Total Titles: 95 E-Book
Foreign Rep(s): INT Books Distribution (Australia); Monarch Books of Canada (Canada); Phambili Agency (Southern Africa); Publishers Marketing Services (Malaysia, Singapore); Saunders Book Co/Education (Canada); South Pacific Books (New Zealand)
Foreign Rights: Japan Foreign-Rights Centre (Japan); Korea Copyright Center (Korea); Agence Michelle Lapautre (France); Silke Weniger (Germany)
Shipping Address: Lerner Publishing Group Inc, 1251 Washington Ave N, Minneapolis, MN 55401, Mgr: Ken Rued *Fax:* 612-204-9208
Warehouse: Lerner Publishing Group Inc, 1251 Washington Ave N, Minneapolis, MN 55401, Mgr: Ken Rued *Fax:* 612-204-9208

Carroll Publishing
4701 Sangamore Rd, Suite S-155, Bethesda, MD 20816
SAN: 237-6334
Tel: 301-263-9800 *Toll Free Tel:* 800-336-4240 *Fax:* 301-263-9801
E-mail: info@carrollpub.com; customersvc@carrollpub.com
Web Site: www.carrollpublishing.com
Key Personnel
VP, Fin & Admin: Shirley Paris *Tel:* 301-263-9800 ext 107 *E-mail:* smparis@carrollpub.com
Founded: 1973
Number of titles published annually: 21 Print; 4 Online
Total Titles: 21 Print; 4 Online
Membership(s): National Directory Publishing Association

Carson-Dellosa Publishing LLC
PO Box 35665, Greensboro, NC 27425-5665
Tel: 336-632-0084 *Toll Free Tel:* 800-321-0943 *Fax:* 336-632-0087 *Toll Free Fax:* 800-535-2669
E-mail: custsvc@carsondellosa.com
Web Site: www.carsondellosa.com
Key Personnel
CEO: Al Greco
Founded: 1976
Publishes supplementary educational materials, including activity books, resource guides, classroom materials & reproducibles, toddler-grade 8. Topics include reading, language arts, mathematics, science, the arts, social studies, English language learners, early childhood learning, Christian books & crafts.
ISBN Prefix(es): 978-0-513; 978-0-7424; 978-1-56822; 978-0-88012; 978-0-88724; 978-1-59441; 978-1-60022; 978-1-60418
Number of titles published annually: 80 Print; 10 E-Book
Total Titles: 700 Print
Imprints: DJ Inkers; Rainbow Bridge Publishing; Kelley Wingate Publications
Branch Office(s)
8720 Orion Place, Suite 200, Columbus, OH 43240, Cust Serv Mgr: Alba Jaimes *Toll Free Tel:* 800-228-6898
Distributor for Key Education; Mark Twain Media

CarTech Inc
39966 Grand Ave, North Branch, MN 55056
Tel: 651-277-1200 *Toll Free Tel:* 800-551-4754 *Fax:* 651-277-1203
E-mail: info@cartechbooks.com
Web Site: www.cartechbooks.com
Key Personnel
Owner & Publr: David Arnold
Mktg & Sales Mgr: Molly Koecher *E-mail:* mollyk@cartechbooks.com
Founded: 1993
Automotive books.
ISBN Prefix(es): 978-1-884089; 978-1-932494; 978-1-61325
Number of titles published annually: 25 Print
Total Titles: 100 Print
Imprints: S-A Design Books
Distributor for Brooklands Books Ltd; Wolfgang Publications
Foreign Rights: Publishers Group UK (PGUK) (Australia, England)
Returns: RR Donnelley, 677 Brighton Beach Rd, Menasha, WI 54952 *Tel:* 920-751-7621
Warehouse: RR Donnelley, N9234 Lake Park Rd, Appleton, WI 54915 *Tel:* 920-969-6434

Casa Bautista de Publicaciones
Affiliate of Southern Baptist Convention
7000 Alabama Ave, El Paso, TX 79904
Tel: 915-566-9656 *Toll Free Tel:* 800-755-5958 (cust serv & orders) *Fax:* 915-562-6502; 915-565-9008 (orders)
E-mail: orders@editorialmh.org
Web Site: www.editorialmh.org
Key Personnel
Gen Dir: Raquel Contreras
Mktg & Sales Dir: Pedro Slachta
Secy: Norma C Armengol *Tel:* 915-566-9656 ext 288 *E-mail:* narmengol@editorialmh.org
Founded: 1905
Religious publications in Spanish. Foreign distributors also located in all Latin.
ISBN Prefix(es): 978-0-311
Number of titles published annually: 16 Print
Total Titles: 895 Print; 895 E-Book; 40 Audio
Imprints: CBP/EMH
Distributed by LifeWay Christian Resources

§Cascade Pass Inc
4223 Glencoe Ave, Suite C-105, Marina del Rey, CA 90292-8801
Tel: 310-305-0210 *Toll Free Tel:* 888-837-0704 *Fax:* 310-305-7850
Web Site: www.cascadepass.com
Key Personnel
Owner & Pres: David Katz *E-mail:* dkatz@cascadepass.com
Proj Mgr: Judith Cohen *E-mail:* jlc@cascadepass.com
Founded: 1989
Science career books for children, environmental & sports.
ISBN Prefix(es): 978-1-880599
Number of titles published annually: 3 Print
Total Titles: 84 Print; 18 CD-ROM; 2 E-Book

Casemate | publishers
Division of Casemate Group
1950 Lawrence Rd, Havertown, PA 19083
Tel: 610-853-9131 *Fax:* 610-853-9146
E-mail: casemate@casematepublishers.com
Web Site: www.casematepublishers.com
Key Personnel
Pres/CEO, Casemate Group: David Farnsworth
VP: Sarah Farnsworth
US Group Publicity Dir: Samuel M Caggiula
Founded: 2001
Publisher & distributor of military history, defense & travel books.
ISBN Prefix(es): 978-0-9711709; 978-1-932033; 978-1-935149; 978-1-61200
Number of titles published annually: 30 Print; 30 E-Book; 5 Audio
Total Titles: 175 Print; 175 E-Book
Distributor for AF Editions; AVF Modeller; Air Sea Media; Air War Publications; Airfile Publications; Amber Books (UK); Amberley (UK); Andrea Press; Aviaeology; Big Sky Publishing; Birlinn (UK); Casemate (USA); Chipotle Publishing; Claymore Press; Clear Vue Publishing; Colourpoint; Compendium (UK); Compendium Films; D-Day Publishing (Belgium); Fighting High Publishing; Fonthill Media; Formac (Canada); Foundry; Front Street Press (USA); Frontline Books; Greenhill Books; Grub Street Publishing (UK); Harpia Publishing; Heimdal; Helion & Co (UK); Helion & Co/CG Books; Editions Charles Herissey (France); Histoire & Collections (France); Historical Indexes (USA); History Facts; Kagero; De Krijger (Belgium); Lombardy Studios; Lorimer; LRT Editions; Military History Press; MMP-Books (UK/Poland); Model Çentrum Progres; Moselle River; Panzerwrecks; PeKo Publishing; PelikaanPers; Pen & Sword (UK); Pen & Sword Digital; Philedition; Pool of London Press; Pritzker Military Museum & Library; Riebel-Roque; RN Publishing (USA); S I Publicaties BV; Sabrestorm Publishing; Savas Beatie (USA); Savas Publishing; Scarab Miniatures; Seaforth Publishing; Tattered Flag; 30 Degrees South Publishers; WAG Books; Warlord Games
Foreign Rep(s): Casemate UK (UK & Commonwealth)
Returns: c/o Casemate, 22883 Quicksilver Dr, Dulles, VA 20166
Shipping Address: c/o Casemate, 22883 Quicksilver Dr, Dulles, VA 20166
Membership(s): The Imaging Alliance

Castle Connolly Medical Ltd
42 W 24 St, 2nd fl, New York, NY 10010
Tel: 212-367-8400 *Fax:* 212-367-0964
Web Site: www.castleconnolly.com
Key Personnel
Founder & Chmn: John K Castle
Founder, Pres & CEO: John J Connolly, EdD
VP, Chief Strategy & Opers Offr: William Liss-Levinson, PhD *E-mail:* bliss-levinson@castleconnolly.com
VP, Chief Med & Res Offr: Dr Jean Morgan
Mgr, Client Rel & Res Opers: Nicki Hughes *Tel:* 212-367-8400 ext 138 *E-mail:* nhughes@castleconnolly.com
Founded: 1991
Publishing company whose mission is to help consumers find the best healthcare with its "Top Doctors" guides.
ISBN Prefix(es): 978-1-883769; 978-1-935036; 978-0-984
Number of titles published annually: 3 Print
Total Titles: 10 Print
Membership(s): The Association of Publishers for Special Sales

§Catholic Book Publishing Corp
77 West End Rd, Totowa, NJ 07512
Tel: 973-890-2400 *Toll Free Tel:* 877-228-2665 *Fax:* 973-890-2410
E-mail: info@catholicbookpublishing.com
Web Site: www.catholicbookpublishing.com
Founded: 1911
For over 90 years, the leading publisher of quality Catholic resources—including Bibles, Missals, Prayer books, liturgical books, spirituality books, Spanish titles & children's books. The company's trademark St. Joseph Editions are distinctive for their large, easy-to-read typefaces; magnificent, full-color illustrations; & helpful & plentiful guides, summaries, notes, indices & photographs. Imprint Resurrection Press is noted for spirituality & personal growth titles. Imprint World Catholic Press complements the company's rich tradition of Bible publishing.
ISBN Prefix(es): 978-0-89942; 978-1-878718 (Resurrection Press); 978-0-529 (World Catholic Press); 978-1-933066 (Resurrection Press)
Number of titles published annually: 25 Print
Total Titles: 750 Print; 9 Audio
Imprints: Resurrection Press; World Catholic Press

The Catholic Health Association of the United States
4455 Woodson Rd, St Louis, MO 63134-3797
SAN: 201-968X
Tel: 314-427-2500 *Fax:* 314-427-0029
E-mail: servicecenter@chausa.org
Web Site: www.chausa.org
Key Personnel
VP, Communs & Mktg: Edward J Giganti *E-mail:* egiganti@chausa.org
Founded: 1915
Catholic health care resources, Catholic ministry, health, labor, medicine & nursing.
ISBN Prefix(es): 978-0-87125
Number of titles published annually: 3 Print; 1 CD-ROM; 2 Audio
Total Titles: 58 Print; 1 CD-ROM; 4 Audio
Branch Office(s)
1875 Eye St NW, Suite 1000, Washington, DC 20006 *Tel:* 202-296-3993 *Fax:* 202-296-3997

The Catholic University of America Press
240 Leahy Hall, 620 Michigan Ave NE, Washington, DC 20064
SAN: 203-6290
Tel: 202-319-5052 *Toll Free Tel:* 800-537-5487 (orders only) *Fax:* 202-319-4985
E-mail: cua-press@cua.edu
Web Site: cuapress.cua.edu
Key Personnel
Dir & Ed-in-Chief: Trevor C Lipscombe *E-mail:* lipscombe@cua.edu
Mng Ed: Theresa Walker *E-mail:* walkert@cua.edu
Acqs Ed, Philosophy & Theology: John B Martino *E-mail:* martinoj@cua.edu
Sales & Mktg Mgr: Brian Roach *E-mail:* roach@cua.edu
Founded: 1939
ISBN Prefix(es): 978-0-8132
Number of titles published annually: 38 Print; 25 Online; 25 E-Book
Total Titles: 580 Print; 300 Online; 300 E-Book
Distributor for American Maritain Association; Institute for the Psychological Sciences Press (IPS); Sapientia Press
Foreign Rep(s): Eurospan University Press Group (Africa, Asia, Australia, Europe, Middle East, New Zealand, UK); Scholarly Book Services (Canada)
Orders to: Hopkins Fulfillment Services, PO Box 50370, Baltimore, MD 21211-4370 *Toll Free Tel:* 800-537-5487 *Fax:* 410-516-6998 *E-mail:* hfscustserv@mail.press.jhu.edu
Returns: Hopkins Fulfillment Services, c/o Maple Logistics Solutions, Lebanon Distribution Ctr, PO Box 1287, Lebanon, PA 17042-1287
Warehouse: Maple Logistics Solutions, Lebanon Distribution Ctr, 704 Legionaire Dr, Fredricksburg, PA 17042
Membership(s): Association of American University Presses

Cato Institute
1000 Massachusetts Ave NW, Washington, DC 20001-5403
Tel: 202-842-0200 *Toll Free Tel:* 800-767-1241 *Fax:* 202-842-3490
E-mail: catostore@cato.org
Web Site: www.cato.org
Key Personnel
Founder: Edward H Crane
Pres: Peter Goettler
Pubns Dir: David Lampo
Founded: 1977
Non-partisan, public-policy think tank.
ISBN Prefix(es): 978-0-932790; 978-1-882577; 978-1-930865; 978-1-933995
Number of titles published annually: 15 Print
Total Titles: 150 Print
Foreign Rights: Rights & Distribution Inc (worldwide)
Distribution Center: National Book Network, 15200 NBN Way, Blue Ridge Summit, PA 17214, VP, Opers: Mike Cornell *Tel:* 717-794-3800 *Toll Free Tel:* 800-462-6420 *Fax:* 717-794-3828 *Web Site:* www.nbnbooks.com

Frank W Cawood & Associates Inc, see FC&A Publishing

Caxton Press
Division of The Caxton Printers Ltd
312 Main St, Caldwell, ID 83605-3299
SAN: 201-9698
Tel: 208-459-7421 *Toll Free Tel:* 800-657-6465 *Fax:* 208-459-7450
E-mail: publish@caxtonpress.com
Web Site: www.caxtonpress.com
Key Personnel
Pres & Publr: Scott Gipson *E-mail:* sgipson@caxtonpress.com
Publg Asst/Web Site: Amanda Halverson *E-mail:* ahalverson@caxtonprinters.com
Founded: 1925
Founded by J H Gipson, Caxton Press is still owned & managed by the Gipson family.
ISBN Prefix(es): 978-0-87004
Number of titles published annually: 8 Print
Total Titles: 165 Print
Distributor for Hambleton Publishing; Historic Idaho Series; Photosmith Books; Snake Country Publishing; University of Idaho Asian American Comparative Collection; University of Idaho Press
Membership(s): AAP

§CCH, a Wolters Kluwer business
Subsidiary of Wolters Kluwer
2700 Lake Cook Rd, Riverwoods, IL 60015
SAN: 202-3504

Tel: 847-267-7000
Web Site: www.cch.com
Key Personnel
Pres & CEO: Teresa Mackintosh
Dir, Communs: Leslie Bonacum *Tel:* 847-267-7153 *E-mail:* mediahelp@cch.com
Founded: 1913
Current US international tax law, business, human resources, securities & health care law, tax, small business, home office human resources & health care.
ISBN Prefix(es): 978-0-8080
Number of titles published annually: 100 Print
Total Titles: 400 Print
Subsidiaries: CCH Peterson; CCH Riverwoods; CCH St Petersburg; CCH Tax Compliance; CCH Washington DC; LIS (Legal Information Services); Washington Service Bureau
Foreign Office(s): Wolters Kluwer nv, Zuidpoolsingel 2, PO Box 1030, 2400 BA Alphen aan den Rijn, Netherlands *Tel:* (0172) 641 400 *Fax:* (0172) 474 889 *E-mail:* info@wolterskluwer.com *Web Site:* www.wolterskluwer.com
Billing Address: PO Box 4307, Carol Stream, IL 60197-4307
Returns: 7201 McKinney Circle, Frederick, MD 21704-8356
Warehouse: 4025 Peterson Ave, Chicago, IL 60646-6085

CCL - Americas, see Center for Creative Leadership LLC

CDL Press
PO Box 34454, Bethesda, MD 20827
Tel: 301-762-2066 *Fax:* 253-484-5542
E-mail: cdlpress@erols.com
Web Site: www.cdlpress.com
Key Personnel
Pres: Mark E Cohen
Founded: 1981
ISBN Prefix(es): 978-1-883053
Number of titles published annually: 6 Print
Total Titles: 63 Print
Imprints: University Press of Maryland
Returns: 11903 Reynolds Ave, Potomac, MD 20827

Cedar Fort Inc
2373 W 700 S, Springville, UT 84663
Tel: 801-489-4084 *Toll Free Tel:* 800-SKY-BOOK (759-2665) *Fax:* 801-489-1097 *Toll Free Fax:* 800-388-3727
Web Site: cedarfort.com
Key Personnel
Owner & Chmn: Bryce Mortimer *E-mail:* brycemortimer@cedarfort.com
VP: Katriena Eden *E-mail:* kat@cedarfort.com
Founded: 1986
Christian (primarily Latter-Day Saints), inspirational, motivational, LDS fiction & doctrinal.
ISBN Prefix(es): 978-1-55517
Number of titles published annually: 120 Print; 50 E-Book; 5 Audio
Total Titles: 500 Print
Imprints: Bonneville Books; CFI; Front Table Books; Hobble Creek Press; Horizon Publishers; Pioneer Press; Plain Sight Publishing; Sweetwater Books

§Cedar Grove Books
Subsidiary of Inkbaby Intermedia
2215 High Point Dr, Carrollton, TX 75007
SAN: 255-3732
Tel: 415-364-8292 *Fax:* 415-276-9858
E-mail: queries@cedargrovebooks.com
Web Site: www.cedargrovebooks.com
Key Personnel
Publr & Mktg Dir: Rochon Perry *E-mail:* rperry@cedargrovebooks.com
Acqs Dir: Nancy A Paniagua *E-mail:* nancya.paniagua@cedargrovebooks.com
Edit Dir: J Cameron McClain *E-mail:* j.cameron.mcclain.stories@gmail.com
Dir, Soc Media: Rebecca Sims-Nichols *E-mail:* bexlnichols@gmail.com
Dir, Latino Books: Sam Cannon *E-mail:* samscannon@cedargrovebooks.com
Founded: 2010
Publish multicultural books with protagonists that overcome adversity by staying true to themselves.
ISBN Prefix(es): 978-0-9835077
Number of titles published annually: 12 Print; 2 CD-ROM; 9 Online; 12 E-Book
Total Titles: 8 Print; 1 CD-ROM; 9 Online; 8 E-Book
Imprints: The Blaxis (multicultural comics directory); CGN (graphic novels); Griot Enterprises (graphic novels); L'il Acorns (children's books); Make Prophetz (academic art & essay books); Sapling (young adult books)
Editorial Office(s): Cedar Grove Publishing, 236 W Portal St, Suite 18, San Francisco, CA 94127
Distribution Center: Small Press United, c/o Independent Publishers Group, 814 N Franklin St, Chicago, IL 60610 *Web Site:* www.smallpressunited.com
Membership(s): Independent Book Publishers Association

Cedar Tree Books
PO Box 4256, Wilmington, DE 19807
Tel: 302-998-4171 *Fax:* 302-998-4185
E-mail: books@ctpress.com
Web Site: www.cedartreebooks.com
Founded: 1925
This publisher has indicated that 30% of their product line is author subsidized.
ISBN Prefix(es): 978-1-892142
Number of titles published annually: 8 Print
Total Titles: 53 Print

CEF Press
Subsidiary of Child Evangelism Fellowship Inc
17482 State Hwy M, Warrenton, MO 63383-0348
Mailing Address: PO Box 348, Warrenton, MO 63383-0348
Tel: 636-456-4321 *Toll Free Tel:* 800-748-7710 (cust serv); 800-300-4033 (USA ministries) *Fax:* 636-456-2078 (cust serv)
E-mail: custserv@cefonline.com
Web Site: www.cefonline.com
Founded: 1937
Christian education curriculum.
ISBN Prefix(es): 978-1-55976
Number of titles published annually: 30 Print
Total Titles: 300 Print
Foreign Rep(s): CEFMARK (Australia)

Celebra
Imprint of Penguin Group USA, A Penguin Random House Company
375 Hudson St, New York, NY 10014
Tel: 212-366-2000
E-mail: ecommerce@us.penguingroup.com
Web Site: www.penguin.com
Key Personnel
Publr: Ray Garcia
Assoc Publr & Exec Mng Ed: Steve Meltzer
ISBN Prefix(es): 978-0-451; 978-1-101
Number of titles published annually: 10 Print

Celebrity Profiles Publishing
Division of Edison & Kellogg
PO Box 344, Stony Brook, NY 11790
Tel: 631-862-8555 *Fax:* 631-862-0139
E-mail: celebpro4@aol.com
Web Site: www.richardgrudens.com; richardgrudensblog.blogspot.com
Key Personnel
Pres: James Snyder
Author: Richard Grudens
Founded: 1995
ISBN Prefix(es): 978-0-9763877
Number of titles published annually: 3 Print
Total Titles: 15 Print; 2 Audio
Membership(s): Independent Book Publishers Association

§Cengage Learning
20 Channel Center St, Boston, MA 02210
Tel: 617-289-7700 *Toll Free Tel:* 800-354-9706 *Fax:* 617-289-7844 *Toll Free Fax:* 800-487-8488
E-mail: esales@cengage.com
Web Site: www.cengage.com
Key Personnel
CEO: Michael Hansen
CFO: John Leahy
CTO: George Moore
Chief Acctg Offr & SVP, Fin Planning & Analysis: Bob Gibney
Chief Mktg Offr: Sandi Kirshner
Chief People Offr & Gen Coun: Ken Carson
Chief Prod Offr: Jim Donohue
Chief Sales & Mktg Offr: Kevin Stone
Pres, Intl: Alexander Broich
EVP & Chief Strategy Offr: Fernando Bleichmar
SVP & Treas: Richard Veith
SVP, Brand Strategy: Daniel Sieger
SVP, Corp Aff: Josef Blumenfeld
SVP, Corp Devt & M&A: Torsten Geers
SVP, Pub Aff: Susan Aspey
SVP, Tax: Frank Vari
Sr Dir, Corp Communs: Lindsay Stanley
Sr Educ Advisor: George Miller
Cengage Learning delivers highly-customized learning solutions for colleges, universities, instructors, students, libraries, government agencies, corporations & professionals around the world. These solutions are delivered through specialized content, applications & services that foster academic excellence & professional development, as well as provide measurable learning outcomes to its customers.
Number of titles published annually: 150 Print
Subsidiaries: Gale (www.gale.com); Heinle (www.heinle.com); Thorndike Press; Wadsworth (www.wadsworth.com)
Billing Address: Cengage Learning Distribution Center, 10650 Toebben Dr, Independence, KY 41051 *Tel:* 859-525-2230 *Fax:* 859-282-5700
Orders to: Cengage Learning Distribution Center, 10650 Toebben Dr, Independence, KY 41051 *Tel:* 859-525-2230 *Fax:* 859-282-5700
Returns: Cengage Learning Distribution Center, 10650 Toebben Dr, Independence, KY 41051 *Tel:* 859-525-2230 *Fax:* 859-282-5700
Warehouse: Cengage Learning Distribution Center, 10650 Toebben Dr, Independence, KY 41051 *Tel:* 859-525-2230 *Fax:* 859-282-5700
Distribution Center: Cengage Learning Distribution Center, 10650 Toebben Dr, Independence, KY 41051 *Tel:* 859-525-2230 *Fax:* 859-282-5700
Membership(s): AAP
See separate listing for:
Charles River Media
Gale
Milady
National Geographic Learning

Center for Creative Leadership LLC
Affiliate of Smith Richardson Foundation
One Leadership Place, Greensboro, NC 27410-9427
Mailing Address: PO Box 26300, Greensboro, NC 27438-6300
Tel: 336-545-2810; 336-288-7210 *Fax:* 336-282-3284
E-mail: info@ccl.org
Web Site: www.ccl.org/publications

Key Personnel
Pres & CEO: John R Ryan
EVP & CFO: Bradley E Shumaker
EVP & Mng Dir, CCL-EMEA: David G Altman
Founded: 1970
Books on leadership & leadership development.
ISBN Prefix(es): 978-0-912879; 978-0-9638301; 978-1-882197
Number of titles published annually: 10 Print
Total Titles: 123 Print
Foreign Office(s): CCL-Europe, Rue Neerveld 101-103 Neerveldstr, 1200 Brussels, Belgium *Tel:* (02) 679 0910 *Fax:* (02) 673 6306 *E-mail:* ccl.emea@ccl.org
CCL-Asia, The Rutherford, Lobby B, No 03-07/08, 89 Science Park Dr 1, Singapore 118261, Singapore *Tel:* 6854 6000 *Fax:* 6854 6001 *E-mail:* ccl.apac@ccl.org
Distributed by Jossey-Bass; John Wiley & Sons Inc
Distributor for Free Press; Harvard Business School Press; Jossey-Bass; Lominger Inc; John Wiley & Sons Inc

Center for East Asian Studies (CEAS)
Subsidiary of Western Washington University
Western Washington University, 516 High St, Bellingham, WA 98225
Tel: 360-650-3339 *Fax:* 360-650-6110
E-mail: easpress@wwu.edu
Web Site: www.wwu.edu/eas
Key Personnel
Dir: Prof Massimiliano Tomasi *E-mail:* massimiliano.tomasi@wwu.edu
Mng Ed: Dr Scott Pearce *Tel:* 360-650-3897 *E-mail:* pearce@cc.wwu.edu
Founded: 1971
East Asia & Iran; Asia mainly monographs.
ISBN Prefix(es): 978-0-914584
Number of titles published annually: 3 Print
Total Titles: 30 Print

§Center for Futures Education Inc
345 Erie St, Grove City, PA 16127
Mailing Address: PO Box 309, Grove City, PA 16127
Tel: 724-458-5860 *Fax:* 724-458-5962
E-mail: info@thectr.com
Web Site: www.thectr.com
Key Personnel
Treas: Lyn M Sennholz *E-mail:* lyn@thectr.com
Founded: 1981
Print & online books on commodity futures & securities.
ISBN Prefix(es): 978-0-915513
Number of titles published annually: 12 Print
Total Titles: 50 Print; 15 E-Book

The Center for Learning
Division of Social Studies School Service
10200 Jefferson Blvd, Culver City, CA 90232
Mailing Address: PO Box 802, Culver City, CA 90232
Tel: 310-839-2436 *Toll Free Tel:* 800-421-4246 *Fax:* 310-839-2249 *Toll Free Fax:* 800-944-5432
E-mail: customerservice@centerforlearning.org
Web Site: www.centerforlearning.org
Key Personnel
HR Mgr: Stephanae Benson
Founded: 1965
Founded to publish values based curriculum materials. All materials are written by master teachers who integrate academic objectives & ethical values. Nonprofit educational publisher of value based curriculum units with reproducible handouts for teachers of English/Language Arts, social studies, novel/dramas, biographies & religion. Specialize in advanced placement, genres; American, British & World novels & literature; skills, supplementary topics, writing; economics, social & global issues, US government & history, world history; Catholic teaching, ministry, retreats, adult faith resources, marriage & parenting, divorce & blended families, abstinence education & chastity; publish lesson plans for elementary & secondary grades.
ISBN Prefix(es): 978-1-56077
Number of titles published annually: 20 Print
Total Titles: 600 Print

Center for the Collaborative Classroom
1250 53 St, Suite 3, Emeryville, CA 94608
Tel: 510-533-0213 *Toll Free Tel:* 800-666-7270 *Fax:* 510-464-3670
E-mail: info@collaborativeclassroom.org; clientsupport@collaborativeclassroom.org
Web Site: www.collaborativeclassroom.org
Key Personnel
Founder: Eric Schaps
SVP & CFO: Brent Welling *E-mail:* bwelling@collaborativeclassroom.org
Pres: Victor C Young *E-mail:* vyoung@collaborativeclassroom.org
VP, Dissemination: Kelly Stuart *E-mail:* kstuart@collaborativeclassroom.org
VP, IT: Mr Nazar Yousif *E-mail:* ynazar@collaborativeclassroom.org
VP, Prog Devt: Lana Costantini MFA
VP, Publg Servs: Lisa Kent Bandini *E-mail:* lbandini@collaborativeclassroom.org
Dir, Admin: Barbara Radcliffe
Founded: 1980
Books, teacher study packages, literature guides, in school & after school curricula in character education, reading & mathematics.
ISBN Prefix(es): 978-1-885603; 978-1-57621; 978-0-439
Number of titles published annually: 15 Print
Total Titles: 450 Print

Center for Women Policy Studies
4620 N Park Ave, Suite 302W, Chevy Chase, MD 20815
Tel: 301-986-0795
E-mail: cwps@centerwomenpolicy.org
Web Site: www.centerwomenpolicy.org
Key Personnel
Pres: Leslie R Wolfe, PhD *E-mail:* lwolfe@centerwomenpolicy.org
VP: Jennifer Tucker *E-mail:* jtucker@centerwomenpolicy.com
Founded: 1972
Violence against women, education, economic opportunity, work & family policy, workplace diversity, women's health policy, women & AIDS, human trafficking of women & girls.
ISBN Prefix(es): 978-1-877966
Number of titles published annually: 12 Print
Total Titles: 65 Print

Center Street, see Hachette Nashville

Centering Corp
7230 Maple St, Omaha, NE 68134
SAN: 298-1815
Tel: 402-553-1200 *Toll Free Tel:* 866-218-0101 *Fax:* 402-553-0507
E-mail: orders@centering.org
Web Site: www.centering.org
Key Personnel
Founder & Pres: Joy Johnson; Dr Marvin Johnson
Exec Dir: Janet Roberts *E-mail:* centeringcorp@aol.com
Busn Dir: Marc Roberts
Dir, Devt: Ben Schroeder
Founded: 1977
Bereavement support; specializes in divorce, grief & loss. Nonprofit organization.
ISBN Prefix(es): 978-1-56123
Number of titles published annually: 10 Print
Total Titles: 150 Print

Centerstream Publishing LLC
PO Box 17878, Anaheim Hills, CA 92817-7878
SAN: 683-8022
Tel: 714-779-9390
E-mail: centerstrm@aol.com
Web Site: www.centerstream-usa.com
Key Personnel
Owner: Ron Middlebrook
Founded: 1971
Music history, bios, music instruction books, videos & DVDs: all instruments.
ISBN Prefix(es): 978-0-931759; 978-1-57467
Number of titles published annually: 20 Print; 10 CD-ROM
Total Titles: 250 Print; 30 CD-ROM
Subsidiaries: Centerbrook Publishing
Distributed by Booklines Hawaii; Hal Leonard Corp
Membership(s): Independent Book Publishers Association

Central Conference of American Rabbis/CCAR Press
355 Lexington Ave, 18th fl, New York, NY 10017
Tel: 212-972-3636
E-mail: info@ccarnet.org
Web Site: www.ccarpress.org
Key Personnel
Chief Exec: Steven A Fox *Tel:* 212-972-3636 ext 238 *E-mail:* sfox@ccarnet.org
Publr & Dir, Press: Hara Person *Tel:* 212-972-3636 ext 222 *E-mail:* hperson@ccarnet.org
Exec Ed: Beth Lieberman
Founded: 1889
Books on liturgy & Jewish practices from a liberal point of view.
ISBN Prefix(es): 978-0-88123; 978-0-916694
Number of titles published annually: 5 Print
Total Titles: 57 Print
Shipping Address: Mercedes Distribution Center, Brooklyn Navy Yard, Bldg 3, Brooklyn, NY 11205
Warehouse: Mercedes Distribution Center, Brooklyn Navy Yard, Bldg 3, Brooklyn, NY 11205

Central European University Press
224 W 57 St, New York, NY 10019
Web Site: www.ceupress.com
Key Personnel
Sales Mgr, US & CN: Abel Meszaros *E-mail:* meszarosa@ceu.hu
Founded: 1993
Focuses on publications relating to the humanities & social sciences. Publishes high-quality mss, interpreting the past & present history, society, culture & economy of the countries of Central & Eastern Europe, the former Soviet Union & its neighbors. In the last couple of years, the Press has expanded its list to include books in the fields of higher education policy, gender studies, media studies & art history.
ISBN Prefix(es): 978-1-85866; 978-1-61055
Number of titles published annually: 20 Print
Total Titles: 400 Print; 150 E-Book
Editorial Office(s): Oktober 6, u 14, Budapest 1051, Hungary, Dir & Ed: Krisztina Kos *Tel:* (01) 327-3844 *Fax:* (01) 327-3183 *E-mail:* kosk@ceu.hu
Foreign Office(s): Oktober 6, u 14, Budapest 1051, Hungary, Dir & Ed: Krisztina Kos *Tel:* (01) 327-3844 *Fax:* (01) 327-3183 *E-mail:* kosk@ceu.hu
Distributed by University of Toronto Press (Canada)
Distributor for Apostrofa Publishers; Baltos Lankos; Helena History Press; International Debate Education Association; Open Society Institute
Foreign Rep(s): East West Export Books (Asia, Australia, Hawaii, New Zealand); Kubon & Sagner GmbH (Germany); NBN International

(UK, Western Europe); OPP (UK); Yushodo Co Ltd (Japan)
Orders to: Books International Inc, PO Box 605, Herndon, VA 20172 *Tel:* 703-661-1500 *Fax:* 703-661-1501 *E-mail:* meszarosa@ceu.hu *Web Site:* www.booksintl.com
Returns: Books International Inc, 22883 Quicksilver Dr, Dulles, VA 20166 *Tel:* 703-661-1500 *Fax:* 703-661-1501
Shipping Address: Books International Inc, PO Box 605, Herndon, VA 20172 *Tel:* 703-661-1500 *Fax:* 703-661-1501
Warehouse: Books International Inc, 22883 Quicksilver Dr, Dulles, VA 20166 *Tel:* 703-661-1500 *Fax:* 703-661-1501
Membership(s): Association of European University Presses

Central Recovery Press (CRP)
Unit of Central Recovery Treatment
3321 N Buffalo Dr, Suite 275, Las Vegas, NV 89129
Tel: 702-868-5830 *Fax:* 702-868-5831
E-mail: info@centralrecovery.com
Web Site: centralrecoverypress.com
Key Personnel
Exec Ed: Nancy Schenck *E-mail:* nschenck@centralrecovery.com
Mng Ed: Valerie Killeen *E-mail:* vkilleen@centralrecovery.com
Sales & Mktg Mgr: Patrick Hughes *E-mail:* phughes@centralrecovery.com
Spec Sales Mgr: John Davis
A progressive publishing company that sheds new light on an age-old problem: addiction. We hope to break the stigma of addiction by publishing quality books that holistically address the nature of this devastating disease. Offer a diverse selection of titles focused on recovery, addiction treatment & behavioral health topics. Our mission is to positively impact recovering individuals: their families, friends & allies, the behavioral health care field & the general public by creating, publishing & distributing a broad variety of unique & fresh publications that embrace best practices in addiction recovery & behavioral health care.
ISBN Prefix(es): 978-0-9799869
Number of titles published annually: 12 Print; 6 E-Book
Total Titles: 20 Print; 20 E-Book

The Century Foundation Press
Division of The Century Foundation
One Whitehall St, 15th fl, New York, NY 10004
Tel: 212-452-7700 *Fax:* 212-535-7534
E-mail: info@tcf.org
Web Site: www.tcf.org
Key Personnel
Pres: Mark Zuckerman
Edit Dir: Jason Renker *Tel:* 212-452-7715 *E-mail:* renker@tcf.org
Chief Admin Offr: Philip Li *E-mail:* li@tcf.org
Mgr, Pub Aff & Spec Events: Lucy Muirhead *E-mail:* lucy@tcf.org
Founded: 1984
Reports of task forces, papers & books covering international & domestic policy issues.
ISBN Prefix(es): 978-0-87078
Number of titles published annually: 3 Print
Total Titles: 185 Print
Branch Office(s)
1333 "H" St NW, 10th fl, Washington, DC 20005 *Tel:* 202-387-0400 *Fax:* 202-483-9430
Distribution Center: The Brookings Institution, 1775 Massachusetts Ave NW, Washington, DC 20036 *Tel:* 410-516-6956 *Toll Free Tel:* 800-537-5487

§Chain Store Guide (CSG)
10117 Princess Palm Ave, Suite 375, Tampa, FL 33610
Tel: 813-627-6957 *Toll Free Tel:* 800-927-9292 (orders) *Fax:* 813-627-6888
E-mail: info@csgis.com
Web Site: www.csgis.com
Key Personnel
VP: Carmen Vasquez-Perez
Dir, Prodn: Scott Mitchell
Mkt Res Ed: Lauren McCollum
Founded: 1934
Directories of retail & wholesale companies.
ISBN Prefix(es): 978-0-86730
Number of titles published annually: 8 Print
Total Titles: 21 Print; 21 Online

Chalice Press
Division of Christian Board of Publications
483 E Lockwood Ave, Suite 100, St Louis, MO 63119
SAN: 201-4408
Tel: 314-231-8500 *Toll Free Tel:* 800-366-3383 *Fax:* 314-231-8524; 770-280-4039 (orders)
E-mail: customerservice@chalicepress.com
Web Site: www.chalicepress.com
Key Personnel
Pres & Publr: Brad Lyons *E-mail:* blyons@chalicepress.com
VP, Opers & Assoc Publr: Lynne Letchworth *E-mail:* lletchworth@chalicepress.com
Sales & Mktg Dir: Deborah Arca *E-mail:* darca@chalicepress.com
Founded: 1911
Religion (Protestant) & hymnals.
ISBN Prefix(es): 978-0-8272
Number of titles published annually: 15 Print
Total Titles: 400 Print
Distributed by Cokesbury
Orders to: PO Box 933119, Atlanta, GA 31193-3119
Returns: 3280 Summit Ridge Pkwy, Suite 100, Duluth, GA 30096 *Fax:* 770-280-4039
Warehouse: 3280 Summit Ridge Pkwy, Suite 100, Duluth, GA 30096 *Fax:* 770-280-4039
Distribution Center: Bookmasters, 30 Amberwood Pkwy, Ashland, OH 44805
Sperlings Church Supply, 85 Bathurst Dr, Waterloo, ON N2V 1Z4, Canada *Toll Free Tel:* 888-838-6626 *Fax:* 519-725-0668
Rainbow Book Agencies, 303 Arthur St, Fairfield, Victoria 3078, Australia *Tel:* 9481-6611 *Fax:* 9481-2371 *E-mail:* rba@rainbowbooks.com.au

§Channel Photographics
980 Lincoln Ave, Suite 200-B, San Rafael, CA 94901
Tel: 415-456-2934 *Fax:* 415-456-4124
Web Site: www.channelphotographics.com
Key Personnel
Co-Publr: Adrianne Casey *E-mail:* adrianne@channelphotographics.com
Publr: Steven Goff *E-mail:* steven@channelphotographics.com
This publisher has indicated that 50% of their product line is author subsidized.
ISBN Prefix(es): 978-0-9819942; 978-0-9744029; 978-0-9766708; 978-0-9773399; 978-0-9826137; 978-0-9832983
Number of titles published annually: 10 Print
Total Titles: 50 Print
Branch Office(s)
244 Fifth Ave, Suite 2464, New York, NY 10001 *Tel:* 212-627-1400 *Toll Free Fax:* 866-729-2725
16510 203 Place NE, Woodinville, WA 98077 *Tel:* 425-354-3690; 206-390-9617 (cell) *Fax:* 425-354-3664
Foreign Office(s): 8 Commercial Tower, 30/F, Unit 06-07, 8 Sun Yip St, Chai Wan, Hong Kong
Via Meucci 24, 37036 San Martino Buon Albergo, Verona VR, Italy *Tel:* (045) 994855 *Fax:* (045) 994746

Chaosium Inc
3450 Wooddale Ct, Ann Arbor, MI 48104
SAN: 692-6460
Tel: 734-972-9551
E-mail: customerservice@chaosium.com
Web Site: www.chaosium.com
Key Personnel
Pres: Rick Meints *E-mail:* rick@chaosium.com
Founded: 1975
Publisher of horror anthologies & role playing games.
ISBN Prefix(es): 978-0-933635; 978-1-56882
Number of titles published annually: 15 Print; 12 E-Book
Total Titles: 241 Print; 60 E-Book
Orders to: 719 E Murray St, Rockport, TX 78382, Contact: Dustin Wright *Tel:* 361-727-9458 *E-mail:* dustin@chaosium.com
Warehouse: Bang Fulfillment Service, 217 Etak Dr, Brainerd, MN 56401

Character Publishing
PO Box 322, Pass Christian, MS 39571
Founded: 2010
Specialize in books that nurture a particular character trait(s) in children, listed in a gold seal on the book cover to simplify book selection. Mss accepted Jan 1-March 15 only.
ISBN Prefix(es): 978-0-9839355; 978-0-9890797
Number of titles published annually: 10 Print; 6 E-Book
Total Titles: 6 Print
Distribution Center: Amazon.com *Tel:* 206-266-7180 *E-mail:* amazon-pr@amazon.com *Web Site:* www.amazon.com
Baker & Taylor, 2550 W Tyvola Rd, Suite 300, Charlotte, NC 28217 *Toll Free Tel:* 800-775-1800 *E-mail:* btinfo@baker-taylor.com *Web Site:* www.btol.com
Barnes & Noble, 76 Ninth Ave, New York, NY 10011 *Toll Free Tel:* 800-843-2665 *E-mail:* info@bn.com *Web Site:* www.barnesandnoble.com
Ingram, One Ingram Blvd, La Vergne, TN 37086, Contact: Stephen Merritt *Toll Free Tel:* 800-937-8222 ext 28309 *E-mail:* stephen.merritt@ingramcontent.com *Web Site:* www.ingrambook.com
NACSCORP, 528 E Lorain St, Oberlin, OH 44074-1298 *Toll Free Tel:* 800-321-3883 *E-mail:* service@nacscorp.com *Web Site:* www.nacscorp.com
Membership(s): The Association of Publishers for Special Sales; Independent Book Publishers Association

Charisma Media
600 Rinehart Rd, Lake Mary, FL 32746
Tel: 407-333-0600 (all imprints) *Toll Free Tel:* 800-283-8494 (Charisma Media, Siloam Press, Creation House); 800-665-1468 *Fax:* 407-333-7100 (all imprints)
E-mail: charisma@charismamedia.com
Web Site: www.charismamedia.com
Key Personnel
Owner & Pres: Stephen Strang
Founded: 1975
Christianity.
ISBN Prefix(es): 978-0-88419
Number of titles published annually: 200 Print
Total Titles: 500 Print; 2 Audio
Imprints: Casa Creation (international publishing group); Creation House (co-publishing group); Siloam Press (health publishing group)
Membership(s): CBA: The Association for Christian Retail; Evangelical Christian Publishers Association

CharismaLife Publishers
600 Rinehart Rd, Lake Mary, FL 32746
Tel: 407-333-0600 *Toll Free Tel:* 800-451-4598 *Fax:* 407-333-7100

E-mail: charismalife@charismamedia.com
Web Site: www.charismamedia.com
Key Personnel
Owner & Pres: Stephen Strang *E-mail:* steve.strang@strang.com
Founded: 1990
Christian education materials such as: Sunday school curriculum, children's church programs, youth resources, training conferences.
ISBN Prefix(es): 978-1-57405
Number of titles published annually: 20 Print
Total Titles: 40 Print
Distributor for CharismaLife

§The Charles Press, Publishers
Subsidiary of The Oxbridge Corp
230 N 21 St, Suite 312, Philadelphia, PA 19103
Tel: 215-561-2786 *Fax:* 215-600-1248
E-mail: mail@charlespresspub.com
Web Site: www.charlespresspub.com
Key Personnel
Publr: Lauren Meltzer *E-mail:* lauren@charlespresspub.com
Founded: 1983
Independent publishing house that specializes in health & healthcare books for the academic, professional & trade markets.
ISBN Prefix(es): 978-0-914783
Number of titles published annually: 10 Print; 1 CD-ROM; 2 E-Book
Total Titles: 125 Print; 6 CD-ROM; 2 E-Book
Returns: c/o Self-Service Storage, 2000 Hamilton St, No 2884, Philadelphia, PA 19130 (permission must be requested in advance of returns)

Charles River Media
Imprint of Cengage Learning
20 Channel Center St, Boston, MA 02210
Toll Free Tel: 800-354-9706 *Toll Free Fax:* 800-487-8488
E-mail: crminfo@cengage.com
Web Site: www.cengage.com; www.delmarlearning.com/charlesriver
Founded: 1994
Publishing computer books for web development, music technology, game development, graphic design & digital video.
ISBN Prefix(es): 978-1-886801; 978-1-58450
Number of titles published annually: 50 Print; 2 CD-ROM; 150 Online; 100 E-Book
Total Titles: 200 Print; 5 CD-ROM; 150 Online; 100 E-Book
Foreign Rep(s): IPR (Middle East); Login Canada (Canada); Thomson Learning (Asia); Transatlantic (Europe); Woodslane (Australia)
Foreign Rights: David Pallai

Charles Scribner's Sons®
Imprint of Gale
27500 Drake Rd, Farmington Hills, MI 48331-3535
Toll Free Tel: 800-877-4253 *Toll Free Fax:* 800-414-5043
E-mail: gale.galeord@cengage.com
Web Site: www.gale.com/scribners
Founded: 1846
Publishes reference books in fields of history, science & literature for audiences ranging from high school students to professional researchers.
ISBN Prefix(es): 978-0-684
Number of titles published annually: 4 E-Book

Charlesbridge Publishing Inc
85 Main St, Watertown, MA 02472
Tel: 617-926-0329 *Toll Free Tel:* 800-225-3214 *Fax:* 617-926-5720 *Toll Free Fax:* 800-926-5775
E-mail: books@charlesbridge.com
Web Site: www.charlesbridge.com
Key Personnel
Pres & CEO: Brent Farmer *E-mail:* bfarmer@charlesbridge.com
EVP & Publisher: Mary Ann Sabia *E-mail:* masabia@charlesbridge.com
VP, Prodn: Brian Walker *E-mail:* bwalker@charlesbridge.com
Assoc Publr & Edit Dir: Yolanda Scott *E-mail:* yolanda@charlesbridge.com
Art Dir: Susan Sherman *E-mail:* ssherman@charlesbridge.com
Founded: 1980
Children's illustrated picture books, board books, early readers, chapter books, middle grade fiction & nonfiction. Adult general trade, cookbooks, puzzle/game, humor & supplemental educational materials K-8.
ISBN Prefix(es): 978-0-88106; 978-1-57091; 978-1-56566; 978-0-934738; 978-1-890674; 978-1-879085; 978-1-58089; 978-1-936140 (Imagine)
Number of titles published annually: 60 Print; 50 E-Book
Total Titles: 725 Print; 500 E-Book
Imprints: Imagine Publishing
Distributor for EarlyLight Books
Orders to: Penguin Random House Publisher Services (PRHPS), 400 Hahn Rd, Westminster, MD 21157 *Toll Free Tel:* 800-733-3000
Returns: Penguin Random House Inc, 1019 N State Rd 47, Crawfordsville, IN 47933
Distribution Center: Penguin Random House Publisher Services (PRHPS), 400 Hahn Rd, Westminster, MD 21157 *E-mail:* distribution@randomhouse.com
Membership(s): ABA; ALA; Association of Booksellers for Children; Bookbuilders of Boston; The Children's Book Council; Education Market Association; International Literacy Association; MSA; NCBA; NEBA; TLA

§Chelsea Green Publishing Co
85 N Main St, Suite 120, White River Junction, VT 05001
SAN: 669-7631
Tel: 802-295-6300 *Toll Free Tel:* 800-639-4099 (cust serv, consumer & trade orders) *Fax:* 802-295-6444
Web Site: www.chelseagreen.com
Key Personnel
Pres & Publr: Margo Baldwin *E-mail:* mbaldwin@chelseagreen.com
Busn & Dist Dir: Sandi Eaton *E-mail:* seaton@chelseagreen.com
Communs Dir: Shay Totten *E-mail:* stotten@chelseagreen.com
Prodn Dir: Patricia Stone *E-mail:* pstone@chelseagreen.com
Sr Ed & Subs Rts Mgr: Brianne Goodspeed *E-mail:* bgoodspeed@chelseagreen.com
Sr Ed: Fern Marshall Bradley *E-mail:* fbradley@chelseagreen.com; Joni Praded *E-mail:* jpraded@chelseagreen.com; Ben Watson *E-mail:* bwatson@chelseagreen.com
Assoc Ed: Michael Metivier *E-mail:* mmetivier@chelseagreen.com
Author Events Mgr: Jenna Stewart *E-mail:* jstewart@chelseagreen.com
Spec & Corp Sales Mgr: Darrell Koerner *E-mail:* dkoerner@chelseagreen.com
Trade Sales Mgr: Michael Weaver *E-mail:* mweaver@chelseagreen.com
Asst Trade Sales Mgr: Kate Weiss
Founded: 1984
Books for sustainable living including: environment, building, nature, outdoors, sustainability, organic gardening, home, renewable energy, homesteading, politics & current events.
ISBN Prefix(es): 978-0-930031; 978-1-890132; 978-1-933392; 978-1-60358
Number of titles published annually: 35 Print; 35 E-Book
Total Titles: 300 Print; 250 E-Book
Distributor for AATEC Publications; American Council for an Energy Efficient Economy (ACEEE); Anomaly Press; Avalon House; Boye Knives Press; Cal-Earth; Earth Pledge; Eco Logic Books; Ecological Design Institute; Ecological Design Press; Empowerment Institute; Filaree Productions; Flower Press; Foundation for Deep Ecology; Fox Maple Press; Green Books; Green Building Press; Green Man Publishing; Groundworks; Hand Print Press; Holmgren Design Services; Jenkins Publishing; Knossus Project; Left To Write Press; Madison Area Community Supported Agriculture Coalition; Marion Institute; marketumbrella.org; Metamorphic Press; Moneta Publications; Ottographics; Peregrinzilla; Permanent Publications; Daniela Piazza Editore; Polyface; Rainsource Press; Raven Press; Anita Roddick Publications; Rural Science Institute; Seed Savers; Service Employees International Union; Slow Food Editore; Solar Design Association; Stonefield Publishing; Sun Plans Inc; Sustainability Press; Trailblazer Press; Trust for Public Land; Yes Books
Foreign Rep(s): Codasat: Hargreaves, Fuller, Paton (Canada)
Warehouse: c/o Claremont Ctr, 425 Washington St, No 185, Claremont, NH 03743, Warehouse Mgr: Dianna Hart *Tel:* 802-295-6300 ext 124 *E-mail:* persephone@emlot.com

Chelsea House Publishers
Imprint of Infobase Learning
132 W 31 St, 17th fl, New York, NY 10001
SAN: 169-7331
Tel: 212-967-8800 *Toll Free Tel:* 800-322-8755 *Fax:* 917-339-0325 *Toll Free Fax:* 800-678-3633
E-mail: custserv@factsonfile.com
Web Site: www.infobasepublishing.com; www.infobaselearning.com
Key Personnel
Chmn: Mark McDonnell
CFO: Jim Housley
Dir, Publicity: Laurie Katz
Dir, Opers & Sales: Mark Zielinski
Dir, Mktg: Zina Scarpulla
Edit Dir: Laurie Likoff
Dir, Licensing & Intl Sales: Ben Jacobs
Founded: 1966
Offers timely & engaging young adult sets & series ebooks spanning a wide variety of subject areas. Chelsea Clubhouse, its elementary imprint, presents easy-to-read, full-color books for young readers in grades 2-6.
ISBN Prefix(es): 978-0-87754; 978-0-7910; 978-1-55546; 978-1-60413; 978-1-4381; 978-1-61753
Number of titles published annually: 230 E-Book
Total Titles: 1,866 Print; 1,680 E-Book
Imprints: Chelsea Clubhouse
Returns: Chelsea House Publishers Returns Dept, c/o Maple Press Distribution Ctr, 704 Legionaire Dr, Fredericksburg, PA 17026
Warehouse: Maple Logistics Solutions, Lebanon Distribution Ctr, 704 Legionaire Dr, Fredericksburg, PA 17026
Distribution Center: Maple Logistics Solutions, Lebanon Distribution Ctr, 704 Legionaire Dr, Fredericksburg, PA 17026
Membership(s): AAP; ALA

§Cheng & Tsui Co Inc
25 West St, 2nd fl, Boston, MA 02111-1213
Tel: 617-988-2401 *Toll Free Tel:* 800-554-1963 *Fax:* 617-426-3669; 617-556-8964
E-mail: service@cheng-tsui.com; orders@cheng-tsui.com
Web Site: www.cheng-tsui.com
Key Personnel
Pres: Jill Cheng
Founded: 1979

Publisher, importer & exporter of Asian books in English. Publish & distribute Asia related books & Chinese, Japanese & Korean language learning textbooks.
ISBN Prefix(es): 978-0-917056; 978-0-88727
Number of titles published annually: 30 Print
Total Titles: 640 Print; 75 CD-ROM; 4 Online; 4 E-Book
Distributor for Action Language Learning; aha! Chinese; Bider Technology; Cengage Learning Australia; China International Book Trading Co (Beijing, selected titles only); China Soft; China Sprout; Crabtree Publishing; Curriculum Corp; Facets Video; Ilchokak Publishers; Italian School of East Asian Studies; JPT America Inc; Oxford University Press; Pan Asian Publications; Panmun Academic Services; Panpac Education; Paradigm Busters; Pearson Australia; Royal Asiatic Society (Korea Branch); SMC Publishing; Sogang University Institute; Stone Bridge Press; SUP Publishing Logistics; Tuttle Publishing; US International Publishing; White Rabbit Press; Yale University Press; Zeitgeist Films
Warehouse: Publishers Storage & Shipping Corp, 46 Development Rd, Fitchburg, MA 01420 *Tel:* 978-345-2121 ext 223 *Fax:* 978-348-1233 *Web Site:* www.pssc.com

Cherry Hill Publishing LLC
24344 Del Amo Rd, Ramona, CA 92065
SAN: 255-0075
Tel: 858-829-5550 *Toll Free Tel:* 800-407-1072 *Fax:* 760-203-1200
E-mail: operations@cherryhillpublishing.com; sales@cherryhillpublishing.com
Web Site: www.cherryhillpublishing.com
Key Personnel
Pres: Rick Roane *E-mail:* rick@cherryhillpublishing.com
Returns: Sharon Roane *Tel:* 858-735-5397 *E-mail:* sharon@cherryhillpublishing.com
Founded: 2002
Publisher of audiobook titles.
ISBN Prefix(es): 978-0-9843759; 978-0-9723298; 978-0-9830086; 978-1-937028; 978-1-62079
Number of titles published annually: 5 CD-ROM; 20 Online; 5 E-Book; 15 Audio
Total Titles: 1 Print; 10 CD-ROM; 150 Online; 40 E-Book; 90 Audio
Distribution Center: Baker & Taylor, 2550 W Tyvola Rd, Suite 300, Charlotte, NC 28217 *Toll Free Tel:* 800-775-1800 *Fax:* 704-998-3100 *Web Site:* www.btol.com
Midwest Tape, 6950 Hall St, Holland, OH 43528 *Toll Free Tel:* 800-875-2785 *Toll Free Fax:* 800-444-6645 *E-mail:* info@midwesttapes.com *Web Site:* www.midwesttapes.com
Membership(s): Audio Publishers Association

Chestnut Hills Press, see BrickHouse Books Inc

Chicago Review Press
814 N Franklin St, Chicago, IL 60610
Tel: 312-337-0747 *Toll Free Tel:* 800-888-4741 *Fax:* 312-337-5110
E-mail: frontdesk@chicagoreviewpress.com
Web Site: www.chicagoreviewpress.com
Key Personnel
CEO: Joe Matthews
Publr: Cynthia Sherry
Mng Ed: Allison Felus
Mktg Mgr: Mary Kravenas
Sr Ed: Jerome Pohlen; Lisa Reardon; Yuval Taylor
Founded: 1973
ISBN Prefix(es): 978-1-56976; 978-1-55652; 978-1-88305 (Ball Publishing)
Number of titles published annually: 65 Print; 65 E-Book
Total Titles: 1,000 Print; 1,000 E-Book
Imprints: A Cappella Books; Academy Chicago Publishers; Ball Publishing; Lawrence Hill Books; Parenting Press; Zephyr Press
Divisions: Independent Publishers Group
Foreign Rights: The Susan Schulman Agency (worldwide)
Distribution Center: Independent Publishers Group *Fax:* 312-337-5985 *E-mail:* frontdesk@ipgbook.com *Web Site:* www.ipgbook.com
See separate listing for:
Academy Chicago
Parenting Press Inc

Child Welfare League of America (CWLA)
1726 "M" St, Suite 500, Washington, DC 20036
SAN: 201-9876
Tel: 202-688-4200 *Fax:* 202-833-1689
E-mail: cwla@cwla.org
Web Site: www.cwla.org/publications
Key Personnel
Dir, Mktg: Karen Dunn *E-mail:* kdunn@cwla.org
Founded: 1920
Provide relevant & timely publications that enable CWLA members & the child welfare field at large to improve services to children & their families.
ISBN Prefix(es): 978-0-87868; 978-1-58760
Number of titles published annually: 9 Print
Total Titles: 167 Print
Imprints: CWLA Press
Billing Address: CWLA, PO Box 345, Mount Morris, IL 61054-9834
Orders to: CWLA, PO Box 345, Mount Morris, IL 61054-9834 *Tel:* 770-280-4164 *Toll Free Tel:* 800-407-6273 *E-mail:* order@cwla.org
Returns: PBD Inc, c/o CWLA, 420 Eagleview Blvd, Exton, PA 19341
Shipping Address: PBD Inc, c/o CWLA, 420 Eagleview Blvd, Exton, PA 19341
Warehouse: PBD Inc, c/o CWLA, 420 Eagleview Blvd, Exton, PA 19341
Distribution Center: PBD Inc, c/o CWLA, 420 Eagleview Blvd, Exton, PA 19341

Children's Book Press
Imprint of Lee & Low Books
95 Madison Ave, Suite 1205, New York, NY 10016
Tel: 212-779-4400 *Fax:* 212-683-1894
E-mail: general@leeandlow.com; orders@leeandlow.com; sales@leeandlow.com
Web Site: www.leeandlow.com
Key Personnel
Pres: Craig Low
Opers & Client Servs Mgr: John Man
Founded: 1975
Multicultural & bilingual picture books for children. Central American, African-American, Asian-American, Hispanic-American, Native American tales, folklore, contemporary fiction & nonfiction.
ISBN Prefix(es): 978-0-89239
Number of titles published annually: 6 Print
Total Titles: 30 Print
Distribution Center: Ingram Books, One Ingram Blvd, La Vergne, TN 37086 *Tel:* 615-793-5000 *Toll Free Tel:* 800-932-8200 *E-mail:* customerservice@ingrambook.com *Web Site:* www.ingrambook.com

Child's Play®
Affiliate of Child's Play (International) Ltd
250 Minot Ave, Auburn, ME 04210
Tel: 207-784-7252 *Toll Free Tel:* 800-639-6404 *Fax:* 207-784-7358 *Toll Free Fax:* 800-854-6989
E-mail: chpmaine@aol.com; cplay@earthlink.net
Web Site: www.childs-play.com
Key Personnel
VP, Sales & Mktg: Joseph Gardner *Tel:* 973-761-4555 *Fax:* 973-761-1555 *E-mail:* joe@childsplayusa.com
Gen Mgr: Laurie Reynolds *E-mail:* laurie@childsplayusa.com
Founded: 1972
Children's books, games, toys & AV materials.
ISBN Prefix(es): 978-0-85953; 978-1-904550; 978-1-84643
Number of titles published annually: 30 Print
Total Titles: 450 Print; 8 Audio

§The Child's World Inc
1980 Lookout Dr, North Mankato, MN 56003-1705
Tel: 507-385-1044 *Toll Free Tel:* 800-599-READ (599-7323) *Toll Free Fax:* 888-320-2329
E-mail: sales@childsworld.com
Web Site: childsworld.com
Key Personnel
Pres: Mike Peterson
Off Mgr: Amy Dols
Founded: 1968
K-8 library books for childhood education; social studies.
ISBN Prefix(es): 978-0-89565; 978-0-913778; 978-1-56766; 978-1-59296; 978-1-60253; 978-1-60954; 978-1-60973; 978-1-61473; 978-1-62323; 978-1-62687; 978-1-63143; 978-1-63407; 978-1-5038
Number of titles published annually: 200 Print; 100 E-Book
Total Titles: 850 Print; 1,018 E-Book
Imprints: Tradition Books
Distributor for Tradition Books

§China Books
Division of Sinomedia International Group
360 Swift Ave, Suite 48, South San Francisco, CA 94080
SAN: 169-0167
Tel: 650-872-7076 *Toll Free Tel:* 800-818-2017 (US only) *Fax:* 650-872-7808
E-mail: info@chinabooks.com
Web Site: www.chinabooks.com
Key Personnel
Gen Mgr: Xin Wang
Sales Mgr: Kelly Feng *Tel:* 650-872-7076 ext 310 *E-mail:* kelly@chinabooks.com
Sr Mng Ed: Chris Robyn *E-mail:* chris@sinomediausa.com
Founded: 1960
Fiction, trade, nonfiction, dictionaries, encyclopedias, maps, atlases, periodicals, sidelines, foreign language, secondary textbooks, juvenile & young adult, subscription & mail order, hardcover & paperback trade books; government, language arts, travel.
ISBN Prefix(es): 978-0-8351
Number of titles published annually: 10 Print
Total Titles: 750 Print
Distributor for AsiaPac; CIBTC; Commercial Press; Foreign Languages Press; Joint Publishers; New World Press; Panda Books; Peace Books; Red Mansions Publishing

Chosen Books
Division of Baker Publishing Group
11400 Hampshire Ave S, Bloomington, MN 55438-2852
Tel: 616-676-9185 *Toll Free Tel:* 800-877-2665 (orders only) *Fax:* 616-676-9573 *Toll Free Fax:* 800-398-3111 (orders only)
Web Site: www.chosenbooks.com
Key Personnel
Pres, Baker Publishing Group: Dwight Baker
Edit Dir: Jane Campbell *E-mail:* jcampbell@chosenbooks.com
Founded: 1971
Christian.
ISBN Prefix(es): 978-0-8007
Number of titles published annually: 30 Print
Total Titles: 700 Print
Foreign Rep(s): Christian Art (South Africa); David C Cook Distribution (Canada); Fam-

ily Reading Publications (Australia); Marston Book Services Ltd (Europe, UK); Soul Distributors Ltd (New Zealand)

§Christian Liberty Press
502 W Euclid Ave, Arlington Heights, IL 60004-5402
Tel: 847-259-4444 *Toll Free Tel:* 800-832-2741 (cust serv) *Fax:* 847-259-2941
E-mail: custserv@christianlibertypress.com
Web Site: www.shopchristianliberty.com
Key Personnel
Dir: Lars Johnson *E-mail:* larsj@christianlibertypress.com
Founded: 1984
Publisher of Christian education materials.
ISBN Prefix(es): 978-1-930092; 978-1-930367; 978-1-932971; 978-1-935796; 978-1-62982
Number of titles published annually: 6 Print; 3 CD-ROM; 4 Audio
Total Titles: 150 Print; 8 CD-ROM; 38 Audio
Distribution Center: STL Distribution, 100 Biblica Way, Elizabethton, TN 37643 *Toll Free Tel:* 800-289-2772 *Toll Free Fax:* 800-759-2779
Membership(s): CBA: The Association for Christian Retail

Christian Light Publications Inc
1051 Mount Clinton Pike, Harrisonburg, VA 22802
Mailing Address: PO Box 1212, Harrisonburg, VA 22803-1212
Tel: 540-434-1003 *Toll Free Tel:* 800-776-0478 *Fax:* 540-433-8896
E-mail: info@clp.org; orders@clp.org
Web Site: www.clp.org
Key Personnel
Gen Mgr: Andrew Criler
Secy, Bd of Dirs: Merna B Shank *E-mail:* mernas@clp.org
Founded: 1969
Books, booklets, tracts, Sunday school, vacation Bible school & Christian day school curriculum.
ISBN Prefix(es): 978-0-87813
Number of titles published annually: 17 Print
Total Titles: 160 Print

Christian Schools International
3350 E Paris Ave SE, Grand Rapids, MI 49512-3054
SAN: 204-1804
Tel: 616-957-1070 *Toll Free Tel:* 800-635-8288 *Fax:* 616-957-5022
E-mail: info@csionline.org
Web Site: www.csionline.org
Key Personnel
CEO & Pres: David Koetje *Tel:* 616-957-1070 ext 254 *E-mail:* dkoetje@csionline.org
VP, Corp Devt & Innovation: Darryl Shelton *Tel:* 616-957-1070 ext 257 *E-mail:* dshelton@csionline.org
VP, Mktg: Jane Mulder *Tel:* 616-957-1070 ext 235 *E-mail:* jmulder@csionline.org
Founded: 1920
Classroom curriculum resources for students & teachers.
ISBN Prefix(es): 978-0-87463; 978-1-935876
Number of titles published annually: 18 Print; 2 CD-ROM
Total Titles: 172 Print; 11 CD-ROM
Imprints: CSI Publications

§The Christian Science Publishing Society
Division of The First Church of Christ, Scientist
210 Massachusetts Ave, Boston, MA 02115
Tel: 617-450-2000 *Toll Free Tel:* 800-288-7090 *Fax:* 617-450-7334
E-mail: contact@csps.com
Web Site: christianscience.com
Key Personnel
Mgr: Michael Zanoni
Founded: 1879
Books on healing, health & spirituality; major title: *Science & Health with Key to the Scriptures* by Mary Baker Eddy, available in 16 languages & English braille.
ISBN Prefix(es): 978-0-87952
Number of titles published annually: 17 Print
Total Titles: 17 Print

Chronicle Books LLC
680 Second St, San Francisco, CA 94107
SAN: 202-165X
Tel: 415-537-4200 *Toll Free Tel:* 800-759-0190 (cust serv) *Fax:* 415-537-4460 *Toll Free Fax:* 800-858-7787 (orders); 800-286-9471 (cust serv)
E-mail: frontdesk@chroniclebooks.com
Web Site: www.chroniclebooks.com
Key Personnel
Chmn & CEO: Nion McEvoy
Pres: Tyrrell Mahoney
VP, Opers & Fin: Tom Fernald
Publr: Christine Carswell
Exec Dir, Dom Sales: Rachel Geiger
Exec Dir, HR: Todd Presley
Exec Dir, Mktg & Publicity: Liza Algar
Exec Dir, Opers: John Carlson
Exec Dir, Prodn: Shona Burns
Exec Dir, Sales: Jane Manning Hyatt
Exec Edit Dir, Entertainment: Sarah Malarkey
Exec Publg Design Dir: Sara Schneider
Publg Dir, Children's: Ginee Seo
Publg Dir, Formats: Christina Amini
Edit Dir, Children's: Kelli Chipponeri
Sr Dir, Prodn: Lindsay Sablosky
Design Dir: Kristen Hewitt
Design Dir, Mktg Communs: Liz Rico
Dir, Independent Spec Sales: Lisa Bach
Dir, Natl Specialty, Mass Mkt, Premium & Licensing Sales: Lynda Zuber Sassi
Dir, Opers: Jeff Wiebe
Dir, Trade Sales: Eugenia Pakalik
Intl Sales & Subs Rts Dir: Johan Almqvist
Intl Sales Dir: Kristin Norell
IT Dir: Mike Conway
Mktg Dir, Adult Trade: Albee Dalbotten; Christina Loff
Mktg Dir, Children's: Laura Antonacci
Prodn Dir, Books & Sustainable Mfg: Beth Steiner
Prodn Dir, Formats: Erin Thacker
Assoc Dir, Online Mktg: Ali Presley
Sr Sales Mgr, Spec Mkts: Julia Carvalho
Natl Accts Mgr: Melissa Grecco; Genny McAuley
Natl Sales Mgr: Tim Wright
Natl Sales Mgr, Spec Mkts: Erynn Im-Sato
Sr Client Acct Mgr: Liz Marotte
Sr Mgr, Mktg & Publicity-Children's Books Div: Sally Kim
Sr Proj & Busn Process Mgr: Elke Olson
Sr Sales Mgr: Anna-Lisa Sandstrum
Sr Web Mgr: Viniita Moran
Compliance Mgr: Eliz Fink
Contracts Mgr: Yesenia Herrera
Dist Client Acct Mgr: Graham Barry; Mercury Ellis; Amy Kosar; Christina Mott
Foreign Rts Mgr: Jenifer Savasta
HR Mgr: Scott Haney
Inventory Planning Mgr: Mary O'Hara
Food & Drink Mktg & Publicity Mgr: Amy Cleary
Mktg & Publicity Mgr, Lifestyle: Alexandra Brown; Stephanie Wong
Mktg Mgr, Children's: Jaime Wong
Mktg Mgr, Entertainment & Art: Sandy Smith
Mgr, Prodn & Creative Systems: Tim Wudurski
Prodn Mgr, Children's: Wendy Thorpe
Oracle Tech Mgr: Hari Ram
Sales Mgr, Spec Mkts: Samantha Steele
Subs Rts Mgr: Joya Anthony
Assoc Dist Client Acct Mgr: Jodi Hammerworld
Assoc Mgr, Opers: Tracy Turpen
Assoc Mktg Mgr, Children's: Hannah Moushabeck
Mktg & Publicity Assoc Mgr, Art, Stationery & Formats: Sarah Lin Go
Prodn Developer: Freesia Blizard
Prodn Developer, Food & Lifestyle: Madeleine Moe
Assoc Prodn Developer, Children's: Ashley Despain
Assoc Sales Mgr, Independent Specialty: Vanessa Navarrete
Assoc Sales Mgr, Spec Mkts: Erin Dunigan
Assoc Sales Mgr, Specialty Mkts: Miriam Keil
Asst Sales Mgr: Morgan Amer; Ian Delaney
Events Coord: Casie Kolbeck
Opers Coord: Francesca Kelly
Prodn Coord, Reprints: Terri Lancaster
Sales Coord, Natl Specialty: Chelsea Masquelier
Sales Coord, Spec Mkts: Noelle Simkins
Sales Materials Coord: Katie Lindsey
Trade Show Coord: Eden Sugay
Trade Sales Rep, New England: Emily Cervone
Mng Ed, Food & Lifestyle: Marie Oishi
Mng Ed, Lifestyle Group: Sara Golski
Asst Mng Ed, Children's: Elizabeth Smith
Exec Ed, Food & Lifestyle: Sarah Billingsley
Sr Ed, Children's: Naomi Kirsten; Melissa Manlove
Sr Ed, Food & Lifestyle: Camaren Subhiyah
Sr Ed, Entertainment: Becca Hunt
Sr Ed, Entertainment & Lifestyle: Kim Romero
Ed, Children's Group: Ariel Richardson
Proj Ed, Food & Lifestyle: Rachel Hiles
Assoc Ed: Courtney Drew; Caitlin Kirkpatrick; Elizabeth Yarborough
Assoc Ed, Children's Group: Taylor Norman
Asst Ed: Zaneta Jung; Mirabelle Korn
Asst Ed, Entertainment: Julia Patrick
Asst Ed, Food & Lifestyle: Deanne Katz
Lead Designer: Brooke Johnson
Lead Designer, Children's Books: Amelia Mack
Sr Children's Book Designer: Ryan Hayes
Sr Indus Designer: Ben Laramie
Sr Prodn Developer: Yolanda Cazares
Sr Publicist: Diane Levinson
Sr Publicist, Children's Publg: Lara Starr
Sr Publicist, Entertainment: April Whitney
Contracts Mgr: Katherine McKim
Contracts & Perms Assoc: Madeline Carruthers
Design Studio Mgr: Victoria Chao; Meghan Nowell
Sr Designer: Allison Weiner
Sr Designer, Digital Mktg: Laura Bagnato
Sr Prodn Designer, Tech Lead: Steve Kim
Children's Book Designer: Tara Creehan; Alice Seiler
Designer: Kayla Ferriera; Anne Kenady; Lizzie Vaughn
Designer, Mktg Communs: Alina Buevich
Indus Designer: Lauren Grand Lubell
Jr Designer, Mktg Communs: Janice Echevarria; Lisa Ferkel
Jr Prodn Designer, Digital Lead: Kevin Armstrong
Jr Prodn Designer: Janine Sato
Dist Dept Coord: Iris Mori
Subs Rts & Custom Publg Coord: Ellise Yu
Visual Content Coord: Irene Kim; Michelle Park
Sr Busn Analyst: Molly Krauss
Sr Fin Analyst: Barrett Hooper
Jr Fin Analyst: Stephanie Blake
Metadata Specialist: Phuong Mai
Founded: 1967
General nonfiction & fiction, cloth & paperbound: fine arts, gift, nature, outdoors, nationwide regional guidebooks, stationery, calendars & ancillary products.
ISBN Prefix(es): 978-0-87701; 978-0-8118; 978-0-938491; 978-1-4521
Number of titles published annually: 300 Print
Total Titles: 1,500 Print
Distributor for Amicus Ink; Blue Apple Books; Handprint Books; Hardie Grant Books; Laurence King Publishing; Moleskine; Prince-

ton Architectural Press; Quadrille Publishing; SmartLab; SmartsCo
Foreign Rep(s): A-Z Africa Service (Anita Zih) (Eastern Africa, West Africa); Abrams & Chronicle Books (Europe, UK); Ampersand Inc (British Columbia, CN, Ontario, CN); Melanie Boesen (Denmark, Faroe Islands, Finland, Greenland, Iceland, Norway, Sweden); Bookreps NZ Ltd (New Zealand); Michelle Curreri & Sonja Merz (Asia exc China & Japan, India); Everest Int'l Publishing (Wei Zhao) (China); John Fitzpatrick (Ireland); Tiffany Georges (France); Hachette UK Ltd (Matthew Cowdery) (Algeria, Bahrain, Egypt, Iran, Iraq, Israel, Jordan, Kuwait, Lebanon, Libya, Morocco, Oman, Palestine, Saudi Arabia, Sudan, Syria, Tunisia, United Arab Emirates, Yemen); Hardie Grant Books (Australia); Hornblower Group Inc (Atlantic Canada, New Brunswick, CN, Nova Scotia, CN, Prince Edward Island, CN, Quebec, CN); JCC Enterprises Inc (Jerry C Carrillo) (Bermuda, Caribbean, Latin America); Cristian & Adriana Juncu (Eastern Europe, Russia); Padovani Books (Penny Padovani) (Italy, Portugal); Padovani Books (Isabella Curtis) (Greece); Padovani Books (Jenny Padovani Frias) (Spain); Publishers Group UK (Melanie Boesen) (Denmark, Faroe Islands, Finland, Greenland, Iceland, Norway, Sweden); Publishers Group UK (John Fitzpatrick) (Ireland); Publishers Group UK (Deborah Dyson) (Midlands, Northern England, Northern Wales, Scotland, Southern England, Southern Wales); Publishers Services (Gabriele Kern) (Austria, Germany, Switzerland); Raincoast Books (Canada); Real Books (South Africa); 62Damrak (Francine Siemer-Ankersmit) (Netherlands)
Foreign Rights: Bettina Nibbe (Germany); Nordin Agency (Netherlands, Scandinavia); Frederique Porretta (France); Tao Media (China)
See separate listing for:
Handprint Books Inc

Cider Mill Press Book Publishers LLC
12 Spring St, Kennebunkport, ME 04046
Mailing Address: PO Box 454, Kennebunkport, ME 04046
Tel: 207-967-8232 *Fax:* 207-967-8233
Web Site: www.cidermillpress.com
Key Personnel
Founder & Publr: John F Whalen, Jr *E-mail:* johnwhalen@cidermillpress.com
Founded: 2005
Publish creative, innovative, inspiring & visually stunning books & gift books.
ISBN Prefix(es): 978-1-933662; 978-1-60433; 978-1-941868
Number of titles published annually: 50 Print; 4 Audio
Total Titles: 135 Print
Imprints: Applesauce Press; Cider Mill Press
Distributed by Simon & Schuster
Foreign Rights: Print Co Verlagsgesellschaft (Gabriella Scolik) (Europe)
Membership(s): ABA

Cinco Puntos Press
701 Texas Ave, El Paso, TX 79901
Tel: 915-838-1625 *Toll Free Tel:* 800-566-9072 *Fax:* 915-838-1635
E-mail: info@cincopuntos.com
Web Site: www.cincopuntos.com
Key Personnel
Co-Publr, Sr Ed & Pres: Lee Byrd *E-mail:* leebyrd@cincopuntos.com
Mktg Dir & CFO: John Byrd
Co-Publr & VP: Bobby Byrd *E-mail:* bbyrd@cincopuntos.com
Founded: 1985
Books of the Southwest US & bilingual children's literature.
ISBN Prefix(es): 978-0-938317
Number of titles published annually: 23 Print
Total Titles: 130 Print; 9 Audio
Foreign Rep(s): Publishers Group Canada (Canada)
Distribution Center: Consortium Book Sales & Distribution, The Keg House, Suite 101, 34 13 Ave NE, Minneapolis, MN 55413-1007, VP, Sales: Jim Nichols *Tel:* 612-746-2600 *Toll Free Tel:* 800-283-3572 (cust serv) *Fax:* 612-746-2606 *E-mail:* info@cbsd.com *Web Site:* www.cbsd.com SAN: 631-760X

§Circlet Press Inc
39 Hurlbut St, Cambridge, MA 02138
Toll Free Tel: 800-729-6423
E-mail: circletintern@gmail.com
Web Site: www.circlet.com
Key Personnel
Founder & Publr: Cecilia Tan *E-mail:* ctan.circletpress@gmail.com
Publicist: Ava Perry
Founded: 1992
Anthologies of erotic science fiction/fantasy, paranormal romance, alternative sexuality & fiction with transgender themes.
ISBN Prefix(es): 978-0-9633970; 978-1-885865
Number of titles published annually: 10 Print; 2 Online; 25 E-Book; 5 Audio
Total Titles: 100 Print; 2 Online; 50 E-Book; 5 Audio
Imprints: Circumflex (nonfiction & how-to on sexuality); Luster Editions (alternative sexuality fiction & erotica); The Ultra Violet Library (gay & lesbian; science fiction not erotic)
Distributed by SCB Distributors
Foreign Rep(s): Bulldog Books (Australia); Turnaround Ltd (Europe, UK)
Foreign Rights: Lawrence Schimel (all other territories)

Cistercian Publications
Imprint of Liturgical Press
Saint John's Abbey, PO Box 7500, Collegeville, MN 56321
SAN: 202-1668
Tel: 320-363-2213 *Toll Free Tel:* 800-436-8431 *Fax:* 320-363-3299 *Toll Free Fax:* 800-445-5899
E-mail: sales@litpress.org
Web Site: www.cistercianpublications.org
Key Personnel
Dir: Peter Dwyer
Founded: 1969
Religion (Roman Catholic) & history.
ISBN Prefix(es): 978-0-87907
Number of titles published annually: 15 Print
Total Titles: 212 Print
Distributed by Liturgical Press
Returns: Warepak LLC, 2427 Bond St, University Park, IL 60484 *Tel:* 708-534-2600 *Fax:* 708-534-7803 *Web Site:* www.ware-pak.com
Shipping Address: Warepak LLC, 2427 Bond St, University Park, IL 60484 *Tel:* 708-534-2600 *Fax:* 708-534-7803 *Web Site:* www.ware-pak.com

Citadel Press, see Kensington Publishing Corp

City Lights Publishers
261 Columbus Ave, San Francisco, CA 94133
SAN: 202-1684
Tel: 415-362-8193 *Fax:* 415-362-4921
E-mail: staff@citylights.com
Web Site: www.citylights.com
Key Personnel
Exec Dir & Publr: Elaine Katzenberger
PR & Mktg Dir: Stacey Lewis
Sr Ed & Subs Rts Dir: Robert Sharrard *E-mail:* sharrard@citylights.com
Open Media Series Founder & Ed: Greg Ruggiero
Publicity & Mktg Assoc: Chris Carosi
Founded: 1955
Publisher of progressive political nonfiction, innovative literature & poetry.
ISBN Prefix(es): 978-0-87286
Number of titles published annually: 15 Print
Total Titles: 200 Print
Foreign Rights: Agencia Literaria Carmen Balcells SA (Spain); The Italian Literary Agency srl (Italy)
Distribution Center: Consortium Book Sales & Distribution, The Keg House, Suite 101, 34 13 Ave NE, Minneapolis, MN 55413-1007 *Tel:* 612-746-2600 *Toll Free Tel:* 800-283-3572 (cust serv) *Fax:* 612-351-5073 *E-mail:* orderentry@perseusbooks.com *Web Site:* www.cbsd.com

Clarion Books
Imprint of Houghton Mifflin Harcourt
3 Park Ave, New York, NY 10016
Tel: 212-420-5800 *Toll Free Tel:* 800-225-3362 (orders) *Fax:* 212-420-5855 *Toll Free Fax:* 800-634-7568 (orders)
Web Site: www.hmhco.com
Key Personnel
VP & Publr: Dinah Stevenson
VP & Assoc Publr: Anne Hoppe
Art Dir: Christine Kettner
Subs Rts Mgr: Candace Finn
Sr Ed: Jennifer Greene; Lynne Polvino
Founded: 1965
Picture, chapter, middle grade & young adult books, fiction & nonfiction.
ISBN Prefix(es): 978-0-547; 978-0-544; 978-1-328
Number of titles published annually: 40 Print
Distributed by Houghton Mifflin Harcourt

Clarity Press Inc
2625 Piedmont Rd NE, Suite 56, Atlanta, GA 30324
SAN: 688-9530
Toll Free Tel: 877-613-1495 (edit) *Toll Free Fax:* 877-613-7868
E-mail: claritypress@usa.net (foreign rts & perms)
Web Site: www.claritypress.com
Key Personnel
Edit Dir: Diana G Collier
Busn Mgr: Annette Gordon *E-mail:* businessmanager@claritypress.com
Founded: 1984
Scholarly works on contemporary justice & human rights issues.
ISBN Prefix(es): 978-0-932863
Number of titles published annually: 8 Print; 8 E-Book
Total Titles: 52 Print; 32 E-Book
Imprints: Clear Day Books (print-on-demand, rare books)
Foreign Rep(s): CIEL Book Distributors (Lebanon, Middle East); Marston Books (UK & the continent)
Foreign Rights: Luigi Celentano (Latin America, Spain); Chengdu Rightol Media (China)
Distribution Center: SCB Distributors, 15608 S New Century Dr, Gardena, CA 90248, Contact: Victor Duran *Tel:* 310-532-9400 *Toll Free Tel:* 800-729-6423 *Fax:* 310-532-7001 *E-mail:* victor@scbdistributors.com *Web Site:* www.scbdistributors.com
CIEL Book Co, Akef El Khoury Bldg, Dbayeh Hwy, Beirut, Lebanon (Middle East & North Africa) *Tel:* (04) 522149 ext 222 *Fax:* (04) 522144 *Web Site:* www.ciel.me
Marston Book Services Ltd, 160 Milton Park, Abingdon, Oxon OX14 4SD, United Kingdom (includes Europe) *Tel:* (01235) 465576 *Fax:* (01235) 465555 *E-mail:* trade.orders@marston.co.uk
Membership(s): AAP; Society for Scholarly Publishing

Classical Academic Press
2151 Market St, Camp Hill, PA 17011
Tel: 717-730-0711 *Fax:* 717-730-0721
E-mail: office@classicalsubjects.com
Web Site: classicalacademicpress.com
Key Personnel
Publr: Christopher Perrin
Founded: 2001
K-12 educational textbooks & media. Focus on classical education.
ISBN Prefix(es): 978-1-60051
Number of titles published annually: 12 Print; 2 Online; 12 E-Book; 3 Audio
Total Titles: 150 Print; 1 Online; 12 E-Book; 10 Audio
Imprints: Plum Tree Books
Foreign Rep(s): Baker & Taylor (New Zealand, UK)
Shipping Address: Baker & Taylor, 2550 W Tyvola Rd, Charlotte, NC 28217 *Tel:* 704-998-3100
Membership(s): Independent Book Publishers Association
See separate listing for:
Plum Tree Books

Clear Light Publishers
823 Don Diego Ave, Santa Fe, NM 87505
Tel: 505-989-9590 *Toll Free Tel:* 800-253-2747 (orders) *Fax:* 505-989-9519
E-mail: market@clearlightbooks.com
Web Site: www.clearlightbooks.com
Key Personnel
Publr: Harmon Houghton
Founded: 1981
ISBN Prefix(es): 978-0-940666; 978-1-57416
Number of titles published annually: 18 Print
Total Titles: 200 Print
Foreign Rights: Harmon Houghton Clear Light Books
Membership(s): ABA; ALA; Mountains & Plains Booksellers Association; New Mexico Book Association

§Clearfield Co Inc
Subsidiary of Genealogical Publishing Co
3600 Clipper Mill Rd, Suite 260, Baltimore, MD 21211
Tel: 410-837-8271 *Toll Free Tel:* 800-296-6687 (orders & cust serv) *Fax:* 410-752-8492
E-mail: sales@genealogical.com
Web Site: www.genealogical.com
Key Personnel
Mktg Dir: Joe Garonzik *E-mail:* jgaronzi@genealogical.com
Founded: 1989
Leading publisher of genealogy how-to books, reference books & CD-ROM publications in the US.
ISBN Prefix(es): 978-0-8063
Number of titles published annually: 40 Print; 4 CD-ROM
Total Titles: 2,000 Print; 90 CD-ROM
Membership(s): ABA; American Name Society; National Genealogical Society

Cleis Press
Imprint of Start Publishing LLC
2246 Sixth St, Berkeley, CA 94710
Tel: 510-845-8000 *Toll Free Tel:* 800-780-2279 (US) *Fax:* 510-845-8001
E-mail: orders@cleispress.com
Web Site: www.cleispress.com; www.vivaeditions.com
Key Personnel
Publr: Karen Thomas *Tel:* 212-431-5455
Founded: 1980
Outriders. Outwriters. Outliers. Cleis Press publishes works in the areas of fiction & LGBT studies, as well as romance, erotica, how-to sex guides, human rights, memoirs & women's studies. Viva Editions are books that inform, entertain & enlighten. Books contain inspiration, self-help, women's issues, lifestyle, health, parenting, reference, gift & relationship advice.
ISBN Prefix(es): 978-0-939416; 978-1-57344
Number of titles published annually: 60 Print; 60 E-Book; 150 Audio
Total Titles: 600 Print; 400 E-Book
Imprints: Midnight Editions; Viva Editions
Foreign Rep(s): PGW - New South (Australia); Turnaround (Europe, UK)
Foreign Rights: Linda Biagi (worldwide)
Distribution Center: Red Wheel/Weiser, 65 Parker St, Suite 7, Newburyport, MA 01950 *Toll Free Tel:* 800-423-7087 *E-mail:* orders@rwwbooks.com *Web Site:* redwheelweiser.com

Clerisy Press
Imprint of AdventureKEEN
306 Greenup St, Covington, KY 41011
Tel: 859-815-7200 *Toll Free Tel:* 888-604-4537 *Fax:* 859-291-9111
E-mail: info@clerisypress.com
Web Site: www.clerisypress.com
Key Personnel
Pres, AdventureKEEN: Richard Hunt *Tel:* 859-815-7204 *E-mail:* richard@clerisypress.com
Founded: 2006
Trade & custom publisher.
ISBN Prefix(es): 978-1-57860
Number of titles published annually: 10 Print; 10 E-Book
Total Titles: 100 Print; 100 E-Book
Billing Address: 2204 First Ave S, Suite 102, Birmingham, AL 35233, Contact: Lisa Myers *Tel:* 205-443-7992 *Fax:* 205-326-1012 *E-mail:* lisa@adventurewithkeen.com
Distribution Center: Publishers Group West (PGW), 1700 Fourth St, Berkeley, CA 94710
Membership(s): ABA; Great Lakes Independent Booksellers Association

§Clinical Laboratory & Standards Institute (CLSI)
950 W Valley Rd, Suite 2500, Wayne, PA 19087
Tel: 610-688-0100 *Toll Free Tel:* 877-447-1888 (orders) *Fax:* 610-688-0700
E-mail: customerservice@clsi.org
Web Site: www.clsi.org
Key Personnel
EVP: Glenn Fine
Sr Dir, Standards & Quality: Jennifer Adams *E-mail:* jadams@clsi.org
Dir, Mktg: Patrick McGinn *E-mail:* pmcginn@clsi.org
Dir, Memb Servs: Katie Barnett *E-mail:* kbarnett@clsi.org
Edit Mgr: Megan Tertel *E-mail:* mtertel@clsi.org
Founded: 1968
Voluntary consensus standards & guidelines for medical testing & in vitro diagnostic products & healthcare services.
ISBN Prefix(es): 978-1-56238
Number of titles published annually: 30 Print
Total Titles: 200 Print

Close Up Publishing
Division of Close Up Foundation
1330 Braddock Place, Suite 400, Alexandria, VA 22314
Tel: 703-706-3300 *Toll Free Tel:* 800-CLOSE-UP (256-7387) *Fax:* 703-706-3564
E-mail: info@closeup.org
Web Site: www.closeup.org
Key Personnel
Pres & CEO: Timothy S Davis, Esq
Sr Dir, Academic Outreach & Publg: Joe Geraghty
Founded: 1971
Publish supplemental texts, videos, teachers' guides & simulation activities for secondary school & college social studies, political science, government, economics, international relations & history courses & for general readership.
ISBN Prefix(es): 978-0-932765; 978-1-930810
Number of titles published annually: 1 Print; 12 Online; 3 Audio
Total Titles: 56 Print; 20 Online; 19 Audio

Closson Press
257 Delilah St, Apollo, PA 15613-1933
Tel: 724-337-4482 *Fax:* 724-337-9484
E-mail: clossonpress@comcast.net
Web Site: www.clossonpress.com
Key Personnel
Founder & Owner: Bob Closson; Marietta Closson
Founded: 1976
Printer & publisher of history, family history & genealogy books.
ISBN Prefix(es): 978-0-933227; 978-1-55856
Number of titles published annually: 40 Print
Total Titles: 800 Print
Distributed by Janaway Publishing; Masthof Press
Distributor for Hearthside Books; Darvin Martin CDs; Retrospect Publishing
Foreign Rep(s): Brian Mitchell (Ireland); Cornelia Schrader (France, Germany)

CMF Press, see Country Music Foundation Press

§CN Times Books
Imprint of CN Times Inc
501 Fifth Ave, Suite 1708, New York, NY 10017
Tel: 212-867-8666
Web Site: cntimesbooks.com
Key Personnel
Pres & Publr: George Zhu
VP & Assoc Publr: Paul Harrington
Mng Ed, Print & Digital Prodn: Heather McAdams
Sales & Mktg Mgr: Paul Myatovich
Ed: Karen Holt
Founded: 2013
ISBN Prefix(es): 978-1-62774
Number of titles published annually: 21 Print
Total Titles: 55 Print; 7 E-Book
Distributor for Bashu Publishing; Foreign Language Press; Intercontinental Press; Phoenix Publishing
Orders to: Ingram Publisher Serivces (IPS), One Ingram Blvd, La Vergne, TN 37086 *Toll Free Tel:* 855-802-8317 *Toll Free Fax:* 800-838-1149 *E-mail:* ips@ingramcontent.com *Web Site:* ipage.ingramcontent.com
Returns: Ingram Publisher Services, 1210 Ingram Dr, Chambersburg, PA 17202
Distribution Center: Ingram Publisher Serivces (IPS), One Ingram Blvd, La Vergne, TN 37086 *Toll Free Tel:* 855-802-8317 *Toll Free Fax:* 800-838-1149 *E-mail:* ips@ingramcontent.com *Web Site:* ipage.ingramcontent.com
Membership(s): ABA

Coaches Choice
514 Airport Way, Monterey, CA 93940
Mailing Address: PO Box 1828, Monterey, CA 93942-1828
Toll Free Tel: 888-229-5745 *Fax:* 831-372-6075
E-mail: info@coacheschoice.com
Web Site: www.coacheschoice.com
Key Personnel
Pres: James Peterson
Edit Mgr: Kristi Huelsing *E-mail:* kristih@coacheschoice.com
Founded: 1999
Instructional books & DVDs for coaches (football, basketball, baseball, softball, volleyball, soccer, track & field, etc); health, fitness & sports medicine professionals & camp professionals.
ISBN Prefix(es): 978-1-57167; 978-1-58518; 978-1-60679
Number of titles published annually: 40 Print

§Coachlight Press LLC
1704 Craig's Store Rd, Afton, VA 22920-2017
SAN: 254-2579
Tel: 434-823-1692
E-mail: sales@coachlightpress.com
Web Site: www.coachlightpress.com
Key Personnel
Mng Memb: Kim Murphy
Founded: 2001
ISBN Prefix(es): 978-0-9716790; 978-1-936785
Number of titles published annually: 1 Print; 2 E-Book
Total Titles: 9 Print; 8 E-Book
Membership(s): Independent Book Publishers Association

Codhill Press
One Arden Lane, New Paltz, NY 12561
E-mail: codhillpress@aol.com
Web Site: www.codhill.com
Key Personnel
Ed: David Appelbaum *E-mail:* appelbad@gmail.com
Founded: 1998
Literary small press.
ISBN Prefix(es): 978-1-930337
Number of titles published annually: 12 Print; 2 Online; 2 E-Book
Total Titles: 100 Print; 6 Online; 6 E-Book
Distributed by SUNY Press
Orders to: SUNY Press, PO Box 960, Herndon, VA 20172 *Tel:* 703-661-1575 *Toll Free Tel:* 877-204-6073 *Fax:* 703-996-1010 *Toll Free Fax:* 877-204-6074
Warehouse: Books International, 22883 Quicksilver Dr, Dulles, VA 20166 *Tel:* 703-661-1500
Membership(s): Community of Literary Magazines & Presses

Coffee House Press
79 13 Ave NE, Suite 110, Minneapolis, MN 55413
SAN: 206-3883
Tel: 612-338-0125 *Fax:* 612-338-4004
E-mail: info@coffeehousepress.org
Web Site: coffeehousepress.org
Key Personnel
Publr: Christopher Fischbach *E-mail:* fish@coffeehousepress.org
Mng Dir: Caroline Casey *E-mail:* caroline@coffeehousepress.org
Devt Mgr: Julie Strand *E-mail:* julie@coffeehousepress.org
Publicist: Amelia Foster *E-mail:* amelia@coffeehousepress.org; Mandy Medley
Publg Asst: Nica Carrillo *E-mail:* nica@coffeehousepress.org
Founded: 1984
Fine editions & trade books; contemporary poetry, short fiction, novels, literary essays & memoirs.
ISBN Prefix(es): 978-0-918273; 978-1-56689
Number of titles published annually: 14 Print
Total Titles: 250 Print
Distribution Center: Consortium Book Sales & Distribution, The Keg House, 34 13 Ave NE, Minneapolis, MN 55413 *Tel:* 612-746-2600 *Toll Free Tel:* 800-283-3572 *Fax:* 612-746-2606 *E-mail:* orderentry@perseusbooks.com

Cognizant Communication Corp
18 Peekskill Hollow Rd, Putnam Valley, NY 10579-0037
Mailing Address: PO Box 37, Putnam Valley, NY 10579-0037
Tel: 845-603-6440; 845-603-6441 (warehouse & orders) *Fax:* 845-603-6442
E-mail: inquiries@cognizantcommunication.com; sales@cognizantcommunication.com
Web Site: www.cognizantcommunication.com
Key Personnel
Chmn & Publr: Robert N Miranda
Pres: Lori Miranda
Founded: 1992
STM & social science books & journals. Subjects include: tourism research & leisure studies, medical research, engineering & psychology.
ISBN Prefix(es): 978-1-882345; 978-0-971587
Number of titles published annually: 11 Print; 23 Online
Total Titles: 53 Print; 1 CD-ROM; 1 Audio
Imprints: Innovation & Tourisms (INTO); Miranda Press Trade Division; Tourism Dynamic

Cokesbury, see Abingdon Press

§Cold Spring Harbor Laboratory Press
Division of Cold Spring Harbor Laboratory
500 Sunnyside Blvd, Woodbury, NY 11797-2924
SAN: 203-6185
Tel: 516-422-4100 *Toll Free Tel:* 800-843-4388 *Fax:* 516-422-4097; 516-422-4092 (submissions)
E-mail: cshpress@cshl.edu
Web Site: www.cshlpress.com
Key Personnel
Exec Dir: John Inglis *Tel:* 516-422-4005 *E-mail:* inglis@cshl.edu
Dir, Edit Devt: Jan Argentine *E-mail:* argentin@cshl.edu
Dir, Prod Devt & Mktg: Wayne Manos *E-mail:* manos@cshl.edu
Sr Mktg Mgr: Stephanie Novara *E-mail:* novara@cshl.edu
Mktg Mgr: Robert Redmond *Tel:* 516-422-4101 *E-mail:* rredmond@cshl.edu
Opers Mgr: Nancy Hodson *E-mail:* hodson@cshl.edu
Prodn Mgr: Linda Sussman *E-mail:* sussman@cshl.edu; Denise Weiss *E-mail:* weiss@cshl.edu
Head, Ad & Sponsorship Sales: Marcie Siconolfi *Tel:* 516-422-4010 *E-mail:* siconolf@cshl.edu
Founded: 1933
Scholarly & scientific books, journals & electronic media.
ISBN Prefix(es): 978-0-87969
Number of titles published annually: 20 Print
Total Titles: 220 Print; 1 CD-ROM; 15 E-Book; 2 Audio
Foreign Rep(s): Academic Books (Austria, Europe, Germany, Switzerland); Maruzen Co Ltd (Japan); NBN International (Europe exc Austria, Germany & Switzerland, UK); Viva Books Pvt Ltd (Indian subcontinent)
Distribution Center: Oxford University Press, 2001 Evans Rd, Cary, NC 27513

College & University Professional Association for Human Resources (CUPA-HR)
1811 Commons Point Dr, Knoxville, TN 37932
Tel: 865-637-7673 *Toll Free Tel:* 877-CUPA-HR4 (287-2474) *Fax:* 865-637-7674
E-mail: communications@cupahr.org
Web Site: www.cupahr.org/publications
Key Personnel
Dir, Communs & Mktg: Gayle Kiser *Tel:* 865-637-7673 ext 111 *E-mail:* gkiser@cupahr.org
Content Mgr, Communs & Mktg: Missy Kline *Tel:* 865-637-7673 ext 118 *E-mail:* mkline@cupahr.org
Founded: 1946
Serves more than 11,000 higher education human resource professionals at nearly 1,700 colleges & universities.
ISBN Prefix(es): 978-0-910402; 978-1-878240; 978-0-9725802
Number of titles published annually: 6 Print
Total Titles: 46 Print

§The College Board
250 Vesey St, New York, NY 10281
SAN: 269-0829
Tel: 212-713-8000
Web Site: www.collegeboard.com
Key Personnel
Pres & CEO: David Coleman
COO: Jeremy Singer
Founded: 1900
Educational & trade books in the fields of college admission, continuing education, guidance, curriculum, financial aid, educational research, college-level & advanced placement examinations & school reform.
ISBN Prefix(es): 978-0-87447
Number of titles published annually: 7 Print
Total Titles: 100 Print; 7 CD-ROM; 4 E-Book; 1 Audio
Branch Office(s)
1919 "M" St NW, Suite 300, Washington, DC 20036 *Tel:* 202-741-4700
11955 Democracy Dr, Reston, VA 20190-5662 *Tel:* 571-485-3000 *Fax:* 571-485-3099
Distributed by Macmillan

College Publishing
12309 Lynwood Dr, Glen Allen, VA 23059
Tel: 804-364-8410 *Toll Free Tel:* 800-827-0723 *Fax:* 804-364-8408
E-mail: collegepub@mindspring.com
Web Site: www.collegepublishing.us
Key Personnel
Publr: Stephen R Mosberg
Founded: 2001
Publish college textbooks in engineering, literature, linguistics & scholarly journals in engineering.
ISBN Prefix(es): 978-0-9679121; 978-1-932780
Number of titles published annually: 10 Print; 2 Online; 2 E-Book
Total Titles: 30 Print; 10 Online; 10 E-Book
Orders to: c/o Port City Fulfillment Services, 35 Ash Dr, Kimball, MI 48074 *Fax:* 810-388-9502
Returns: c/o Port City Fulfillment Services, 35 Ash Dr, Kimball, MI 48074

The Colonial Williamsburg Foundation
PO Box 1776, Williamsburg, VA 23187-1776
SAN: 203-297X
Tel: 757-229-1000 *Toll Free Tel:* 800-HISTORY (447-8679)
E-mail: geninfo@cwf.org
Web Site: www.colonialwilliamsburg.org
Key Personnel
Pres & CEO: Mitchell Reiss
Dir & Mng Ed, Pubns & Rts/Perms: Paul Aron *Tel:* 757-220-7341 *E-mail:* paron@cwf.org
Founded: 1930
Trade & scholarly nonfiction, children's, young adult, juveniles & regional books specializing in aspects of 18th century history in Virginia's colonial capital.
ISBN Prefix(es): 978-0-87935; 978-0-910412
Number of titles published annually: 5 Print
Total Titles: 115 Print; 28 Audio
Imprints: Colonial Williamsburg
Distributed by Harry N Abrams Inc; John F Blair Publisher; Clarkson Potter Publishers; Lexington Books; National Geographic; Ohio University Press; Quite Specific Media Group Ltd; Rodale; Rowman & Littlefield; Scholastic Inc; Stackpole Books; Texas Tech University Press; The University of Virginia Press; University Press of New England; Yale University Press
Shipping Address: c/o Coastal Forms & Data Products, 141 Enterprise Dr, Newport News, VA 23603 *Tel:* 757-873-8806 *Toll Free Tel:* 800-241-4067 *Fax:* 757-873-7619
Distribution Center: 201 Fifth Ave, Williamsburg, VA 23185

§Columbia Books & Information Services (CBIS)
4340 East-West Hwy, Suite 300, Bethesda, MD 20814
Tel: 202-464-1662 *Fax:* 301-664-9600
E-mail: info@columbiabooks.com

Web Site: www.columbiabooks.com; www.lobbyists.info; www.associationexecs.com
Key Personnel
Pres: Brittany Carter *E-mail:* bcarter@columbiabooks.com
Dir, Edit & Data Servs: Duncan Bell
Dir, Fin: Anna Magallanes
Dir, Opers: Renee Cannady
Dir, Sales & Mktg: Jamie Herring *Tel:* 240-235-0271
Founded: 1965
Publish print directories, reference books, newsletters & reports. Do not accept mss.
ISBN Prefix(es): 978-0-910416; 978-1-880873; 978-0-9715487; 978-0-9747322; 978-1-938939
Number of titles published annually: 10 Print; 2 Online; 1 E-Book
Total Titles: 10 Print; 2 Online; 1 E-Book

§Columbia University Press
61 W 62 St, New York, NY 10023
SAN: 212-2472
Tel: 212-459-0600 *Toll Free Tel:* 800-944-8648 *Fax:* 212-459-3678
E-mail: cup_book@columbia.edu (orders & cust serv)
Web Site: cup.columbia.edu
Key Personnel
CFO: Robert Abrams
Assoc Provost & Dir: Jennifer Crewe
Dir, Editing, Design & Prodn: Marielle Poss
Dir, Sales & Opers: Brad Hebel
Edit Dir: Eric Schwartz
Promos Dir: Meredith Howard
Publr, Fin & Economics: Myles Thompson
Publr, Life Sciences: Patrick Fitzgerald
Publr, Philosophy & Religion: Wendy Lochner
Sr Ed: Philip Leventhal
Ed, Economics & US History: Bridget Flannery-McCoy
Ed, Global History & Politics: Caelyn Cobb
Founded: 1893
Books of scholarly value, including nonfiction, general interest, scientific & technical books, textbooks in special fields at the university level & reference books.
ISBN Prefix(es): 978-0-231
Number of titles published annually: 500 Print; 120 E-Book
Total Titles: 7 CD-ROM; 4 Online; 350 E-Book
Imprints: Columbia Business School Publishing (business, finance & economics titles); Wallflower Press (film titles)
Distributor for Agenda Publishing; American Institute of Buddhist Studies; Austrian Film Museum Books; Auteur Publishing; Barbara Budrich Publishers; Chinese University Press; Columbia Books on Architecture & the City; Columbia University Press (Hitchcock Annual); Maria Curie-Sklodowska University Press; Harrington Park Press (frontlist titles); Hong Kong University Press; ibidem Press (English lang titles exc China & India); Jagiellonian University Press; Peterson Institute for International Economics; Slovenian Cinematheque; Social Science Research Council; Transcript Verlag; Tulika Books; University of Tokyo Press; Woodrow Wilson Center Press
Foreign Rep(s): Apex Knowledge Sdn Bhd (Simon Tay) (Brunei, Malaysia); Aromix Books Co Ltd (Nick Woon & Jane Lam) (Hong Kong); Avicenna Partnership Ltd (Claire de Gruchy) (Algeria, Cyprus, Jordan, Malta, Morocco, Palestine, Tunisia, Turkey); Avicenna Partnership Ltd (Bill Kennedy) (Bahrain, Egypt, Iran, Iraq, Kuwait, Lebanon, Libya, Oman, Qatar, Saudi Arabia, Syria, United Arab Emirates); Dominique Bartshukoff (Austria, Croatia, Czech Republic, Eastern Europe, Germany, Greece, Holland, Portugal, Russia, Slovenia, Spain); Book Marketing Services (S Janakiraman) (India); Booknet Co Ltd (Suphaluck Sattabuz) (Thailand); Everest International Publishing Services (Wei Zhao) (China); Footprints Books (Australia, New Zealand); Information & Culture Korea (Se-Yung Jun) (Korea); Peter Jacques (Belgium, Denmark, Finland, France, Italy, Norway, Poland, Sweden, Switzerland); MegaTEXTS Phil Inc (Jean Lim) (Philippines); MHM Limited (Mark Gresham) (Japan); B K Norton Ltd (Chiafeng Peng) (Singapore, Taiwan); Rockbook (Akiko Iwamoto & Gilles Fauveau) (Japan); The University Press Group Ltd (Lois Edwards) (Europe, UK); Kelvin van Hasselt Publishing Services (Africa); Wiley Distribution Services Ltd (Africa, Europe, Middle East, South Africa, South Asia, UK); World Press (Saleem A Malik) (Pakistan)
Foreign Rights: Akcali Copyright Agency (Mustafa Urgen) (Turkey); L'Autre Agence (Corinne Marotte) (France); Bardon-Chinese Media Agency (Simplified-Ivan Zhang) (China); Bardon-Chinese Media Agency (Complex-Luisa Yeh) (China); Bestun Korea (Ms Yumi Chun) (Korea); Dar Cherlin (Amelie Cherlin) (Arab Middle East); Agencia Literaria Raquel de la Concha (Spain); The English Agency (Tsutomu Yawata) (Japan); Paul & Peter Fritz AG (Germany); Graal Literary Agency (Lukasz Wrobel) (Poland); Danny Hong Agency (Danny Hong) (Korea); Andrew Nurnberg Associates International (Complex-Whitney Hsu & Jackie Huang) (China); Reiser Literary Agency (Roberto Gilodi) (Italy); Karin Schindler Agency (Suely Pedro dos Santos) (Brazil, Portugal); Tuttle-Mori Agency Inc (Fumika Ogihara) (Japan); Eric Yang Agency (Jackie Yang) (Korea)
Advertising Agency: Columbia Advertising Group
Orders to: Perseus Distribution, 210 American Dr, Jackson, TN 38301 *Tel:* 731-988-4440 *Toll Free Tel:* 800-343-4499 *Toll Free Fax:* 800-351-5073 *E-mail:* orderentry@perseusbooks.com
Membership(s): AAP; American Association of University Presses

§Comex Systems Inc
101 Pleasant Hill Rd, Chester, NJ 07930
Tel: 908-881-6301 *Toll Free Tel:* 800-543-6959 *Fax:* 908-879-0070
E-mail: mail@comexsystems.com
Web Site: www.comexsystems.com
Key Personnel
VP: Doug Prybylowski *E-mail:* dpryb@comexsystems.com
Founded: 1973
Publish test preparation & other educational books.
ISBN Prefix(es): 978-1-56030
Number of titles published annually: 5 Print; 10 CD-ROM; 5 E-Book
Total Titles: 30 Print; 50 CD-ROM; 5 E-Book

Common Courage Press
One Red Barn Rd, Monroe, ME 04951
Mailing Address: PO Box 702, Monroe, ME 04951-0702
Tel: 207-525-0900 *Toll Free Tel:* 800-497-3207 *Fax:* 207-525-3068
Web Site: www.commoncouragepress.com
Key Personnel
Publr: Greg Bates *E-mail:* gbates@commoncouragepress.com
Founded: 1991
Books on race, feminism, gender issues, class, media, economics, ecology & foreign policy to help readers in the struggle for social justice. Accepting no new submissions.
ISBN Prefix(es): 978-0-9628838; 978-1-56751
Number of titles published annually: 20 Print
Total Titles: 90 Print
Distributor for Odonian Press; Real Story Series
Foreign Rights: James Bier (worldwide exc USA)
Distribution Center: LPC Group, 1436 W Randolph St, Chicago, IL 60607 *Toll Free Tel:* 800-243-0138 *Toll Free Fax:* 800-334-3892

Commonwealth Editions
Imprint of Applewood Books Inc
One River Rd, Carlisle, MA 01741
Tel: 781-271-0055 *Toll Free Tel:* 800-277-5312 *Fax:* 781-271-0056
E-mail: customercare@awb.com
Web Site: www.awb.com
Key Personnel
Pres & Publr: Phil Zuckerman *E-mail:* philz@awb.com
Founded: 1988
Publisher of nonfiction books about New England & its historic places.
ISBN Prefix(es): 978-1-889833; 978-1-933212
Number of titles published annually: 12 Print
Total Titles: 125 Print
Membership(s): NEBA

Concordia Publishing House
Subsidiary of The Luthern Church, Missouri Synod
3558 S Jefferson Ave, St Louis, MO 63118-3968
SAN: 202-1781
Tel: 314-268-1000; 314-268-1268 (bookshop) *Toll Free Tel:* 800-325-3040 (cust serv) *Toll Free Fax:* 800-490-9889 (cust serv)
E-mail: order@cph.org
Web Site: www.cph.org
Key Personnel
Pres & CEO: Dr Bruce G Kintz *Tel:* 314-268-1190 *E-mail:* bruce.kintz@cph.org
VP & Corp Coun: Jonathan D Schultz *E-mail:* jonathan.schultz@cph.org
Publr & Exec Dir: Rev Paul T McCain *E-mail:* paul.mccain@cph.org
Exec Dir, Innovation Technologies: Steve Harris *E-mail:* steve.harris@cph.org
Exec Dir, Mktg & E-Commerce: Mr Loren Pawlitz *E-mail:* loren.pawlitz@cph.org
Exec Dir, Prodn Control & Quality Systems: Karen Capps *E-mail:* karen.capps@cph.org
Dir, Facilities: Tony Shimkus *E-mail:* tony.shimkus@cph.org
Dir, Fin: Collin Bivens *E-mail:* collin.bivens@cph.org
Dir, Graphic Design: Tim Agnew *E-mail:* tim.agnew@cph.org
Dir, HR: Dana Neuhaus *E-mail:* dana.neuhaus@cph.org
Dir, Opers: Bob Rothmeyer *E-mail:* bob.rothmeyer@cph.org
Dir, Sales: Paul Brunette *E-mail:* paul.brunette@cph.org
Founded: 1869
Theological works, sacred & family, devotional music, curriculum, computer software, bulletins, envelopes.
ISBN Prefix(es): 978-0-570; 978-0-7586
Number of titles published annually: 150 Print; 2 CD-ROM
Total Titles: 1,000 Print; 10 CD-ROM
Divisions: Concordia Academic Press; Editorial Concordia; Family Films
Membership(s): CBA: The Association for Christian Retail; Evangelical Christian Publishers Association; Protestant Church-Owned Publishers Association

The Conference Board Inc
845 Third Ave, New York, NY 10022-6600
SAN: 202-179X
Tel: 212-759-0900; 212-339-0345 (cust serv) *Fax:* 212-980-7014; 212-836-9740 (cust serv)
E-mail: customer.service@conferenceboard.org; membership@conferenceboard.org
Web Site: www.conference-board.org; www.linkedin.com/company/the-conference-board

Key Personnel
CEO: Jon Spector
SVP: Janet Etsch
Exec Dir, Knowledge Content & Quality: Chuck Mitchell
Exec Dir, Governance Ctr: Douglas Chia
Founded: 1916
Periodic studies in management practices, economics & public affairs.
ISBN Prefix(es): 978-0-8237
Number of titles published annually: 25 Print; 25 Online
Branch Office(s)
1530 Wilson Blvd, Suite 400, Arlington, VA 22209
The Conference Board of Canada, 255 Smyth Rd, Ottawa, ON, Canada (affiliate), Pres & CEO: Daniel Muzyka *Tel:* 613-526-3280 *Toll Free Tel:* 866-711-2262 *Fax:* 613-526-4857 *E-mail:* contactcboc@conferenceboard.ca *Web Site:* www.conferenceboard.ca
Foreign Office(s): Chaussee de La Hulpe 130, 6th fl, 1170 Brussels, Belgium, VP & Mng Dir: Rainer Schultheis *Tel:* (02) 675 5405 *E-mail:* brussels@conferenceboard.org
7-2-72 Qijiayuan, 9 Jianwai St, Beijing 100600, China, VP & Mng Dir: David Hoffman *Tel:* (010) 8532 4688 *E-mail:* david.hoffman@conferenceboard.org
Room 1213, 12/F, Tai Yau Bldg, 181 Johnston Rd, Wanchai, Hong Kong, Exec Dir, Asia Pacific Region: Nick Sutcliffe *Tel:* 2804 1000 *E-mail:* service.ap@conferenceboard.org
22-81 The Central, 8 Eu Tong Sen St, Singapore 059818, Singapore, Exec Dir, Asia Pacific Region: Nick Sutcliffe *Tel:* 6325 3121 *E-mail:* service.ap@conferenceboard.org

§The Connecticut Law Tribune
Division of ALM Media LLC
201 Ann Uccello St, 4th fl, Hartford, CT 06103
Tel: 860-527-7900 *Toll Free Tel:* 877-256-2472
Web Site: www.ctlawtribune.com/book-center; www.lawcatalog.com
Key Personnel
Busn Mgr: Heather Granger *Tel:* 860-757-6612 *E-mail:* hgranger@alm.com
Founded: 1974
Publisher of books, newspapers & other materials for the legal community & the public.
ISBN Prefix(es): 978-0-910051; 978-1-62881; 978-1-57625
Number of titles published annually: 5 Print
Total Titles: 40 Print; 1 E-Book

Consumer Press
13326 SW 28 St, Suite 102, Fort Lauderdale, FL 33330-1102
SAN: 297-7888
Tel: 954-370-9153 *Fax:* 954-472-1008
E-mail: info@consumerpress.com
Web Site: www.consumerpress.com
Key Personnel
Pres: Diana Gonzalez
Edit Dir: Joseph J Pappas
Publicity Dir: Linda Muzzarelli
Founded: 1989
Consumer-oriented self-help & how-to titles. Specialize in nutrition, health & homeowner issues.
ISBN Prefix(es): 978-0-9628336; 978-1-891264; 978-0-9637641
Number of titles published annually: 9 Print
Total Titles: 12 Print
Imprints: Women's Publications
Membership(s): Independent Book Publishers Association

Consumertronics
Affiliate of Top Secret Consumertronics Global (TSC-Global)
PO Box 23097, Albuquerque, NM 87192
Tel: 505-321-1034
E-mail: wizguru@consumertronics.net
Web Site: www.consumertronics.net
Key Personnel
Pres & CEO: John J Williams
VP: Laurencia Williams
Founded: 1971
Technical books, manuals & software.
ISBN Prefix(es): 978-0-934274
Number of titles published annually: 60 Print; 60 CD-ROM
Total Titles: 150 Print

Contemporary Publishing Co of Raleigh Inc
5849 Lease Lane, Raleigh, NC 27617
Tel: 919-851-8221 *Fax:* 919-851-6666
E-mail: questions@contemporarypublishing.com
Web Site: www.contemporarypublishing.com
Key Personnel
Publr: Charles E Grantham *E-mail:* chuck246cp@aol.com
Lib Sales Dir & Prodn Mgr: Erika Kessler *E-mail:* erikacpc@aol.com
Mktg Dir: Sherri Powell
Founded: 1977
Laboratory textbooks for college.
ISBN Prefix(es): 978-0-89892
Number of titles published annually: 10 Print
Total Titles: 120 Print; 1 CD-ROM

Continental AfrikaPublishers
Division of Afrikamawu Miracle Mission, AMI Inc
182 Stribling Circle, Spartanburg, SC 29301
Tel: 864-576-7992 *Fax:* 864-576-7992
E-mail: afrikalion@aol.com; profafrikadzatadeku@facebook.com; profafrikadzatadeku@yahoo.com; afrikapharaoh@gmail.com
Web Site: www.afrikacentricity.com
Key Personnel
Publr: Prof Afrikadzata Deku, PhD
Founded: 1990
Afrikacentric books, booklets & video documentaries, calendars, films on Continental Afrikan studies, Afrika Centricity, Pan-Continental Afrikanism, Continental Afrikan Government MIRACLE Project of the Century-its what, why, how & when.
ISBN Prefix(es): 978-1-56454
Number of titles published annually: 20 Print; 260 Online; 500 E-Book; 20 Audio
Total Titles: 260 Print; 260 Online; 638 E-Book; 20 Audio
Foreign Office(s): PO Box 209, Dansoman-Accra, Ghana, Chmn: Afrikanenyo Deku
Foreign Rep(s): Continental/Diaspora Afrikan (worldwide)

David C Cook
4050 Lee Vance View, Colorado Springs, CO 80918
Tel: 719-536-0100 *Toll Free Tel:* 800-708-5550; 800-323-7543 (orders & cust serv) *Toll Free Fax:* 800-430-0726 (cust serv)
Web Site: www.davidccook.com
Key Personnel
CEO: Cris Doornbos
COO: Scott Miller
CIO: Sean Everhart
Chief Advancement Offr: Tim MacDonald
Chief Global Offr: Gary Hopwood
Exec Publr: Verne Kenney
Pres, Integrity Music: C Ryan Dunham
EVP, Global Dist: Greg Tombs
VP & Publr, Learning Resources Group: Dr Michelle Anthony
VP, Mktg & Sales, Learning Resources Strategic Ministry Unit: Chriscynethia Floyd
VP, Sales: Marilyn Largent
VP, Strategic Partnerships: Dave Thornton
Publr, Children's Resources: Catherine DeVries
Publr, Standard Lesson Commentary, Bible-in-Life Curriculum & Adult Trade Book Resources: Matthew Lockhart
Publr, Traditional Children's Resources: Lindsay Black
Sr Dir, Mktg: Tim Close
Founded: 1875
Publish & distribute leadership & discipleship resources.
ISBN Prefix(es): 978-0-912692; 978-0-89191; 978-1-55513; 978-1-56476; 978-0-89693; 978-0-7814; 978-0-88207; 978-1-4347
Number of titles published annually: 50 Print
Total Titles: 2,500 Print
Divisions: Integrity Music (music publg & recording)
Returns: 850 N Grove, Elgin, IL 60120

Copley Custom Textbooks
Imprint of XanEdu Publishing Inc
530 Great Rd, Acton, MA 01720
Tel: 978-263-9090 *Toll Free Tel:* 800-562-2147 *Fax:* 978-263-9190
E-mail: textbookorders@xanedu.com; publish@copleycustom.com
Web Site: www.xanedu.com
Key Personnel
CEO: John DeBoer
Founded: 1984
Custom publishing for the higher education market.
ISBN Prefix(es): 978-0-87411; 978-1-58152; 978-1-58390; 978-1-50669
Number of titles published annually: 85 Print; 5 CD-ROM; 10 E-Book
Total Titles: 400 Print
Imprints: Copley Editions; Copley Publishing Group

§Copper Canyon Press
Fort Worden State Park, Bldg 313, Port Townsend, WA 98368
SAN: 206-488X
Mailing Address: PO Box 271, Port Townsend, WA 98368
Tel: 360-385-4925 *Toll Free Tel:* 877-501-1393 (orders) *Fax:* 360-385-4985
E-mail: poetry@coppercanyonpress.org
Web Site: www.coppercanyonpress.org
Key Personnel
Co-Publr: Joseph Bednarik *E-mail:* joseph@coppercanyonpress.org; George Knotek *E-mail:* george@coppercanyonpress.org
Dir, Publicity: Kelly Forsythe *E-mail:* kelly@coppercanyonpress.org
Exec Ed: Michael Wiegers *E-mail:* michael@coppercanyonpress.org
Mng Ed: Tonaya Craft *E-mail:* tonaya@coppercanyonpress.org
Experimental Progs Mgr: Victoria Poling *E-mail:* victoria@coppercanyonpress.org
Fin Mgr: Randy Sturgis *E-mail:* randy@coppercanyonpress.org
Community Engagement Coord/Assoc Ed: Elaina Ellis *E-mail:* elaina@coppercanyonpress.org
Warehouse Mgr: Christopher Overman *E-mail:* christopher@coppercanyonpress.org
Fin/Opers: Margaret Kirk *E-mail:* margaret@coppercanyonpress.org
Founded: 1972
Hardcover & paperback trade books of poetry.
ISBN Prefix(es): 978-0-914742; 978-1-55659; 978-1-61932
Number of titles published annually: 32 Print
Total Titles: 400 Print
Branch Office(s)
216 First Ave, Suite 480, Seattle, WA 98104
Distributor for American Poetry Review/Honickman
Distribution Center: Consortium Book Sales & Distribution, The Keg House, Suite 101, 34 13 Ave NE, Minneapolis, MN 55413-1007

Tel: 612-746-2600 *Toll Free Tel:* 800-283-3572 (cust serv) *Fax:* 612-746-2606 *E-mail:* info@cbsd.com *Web Site:* www.cbsd.com

§Copywriter's Council of America™ (CCA)
Division of The Linick Group Inc
CCA Bldg, 7 Putter Lane, Middle Island, NY 11953-1920
Mailing Address: PO Box 102, Middle Island, NY 11953-0102
Tel: 631-924-3888; 631-775-6075 *Fax:* 631-924-8555
E-mail: cca4dmcopy@gmail.com
Web Site: www.andrewlinickdirectmarketing.com/Copywriters-Council.html; www.newworldpressbooks.com
Key Personnel
Chmn, Consulting Group: Andrew S Linick, PhD *E-mail:* andrew@asklinick.com
EVP: Roger Dextor
Lib Sales Dir: John Kelty
Founded: 1974
Article reprints, monographs; educational, professional & trade, fiction, nonfiction publications in direct response advertising, direct marketing, mail order, sales promotion, measurable response public relations, telemarketing, business-to-business marketing, desktop publishing, Internet marketing, e-commerce, ebooks, consulting & management. Confidential reports, newsletters, little known business secrets library of super money makers you can use tomorrow. Also 300 ebooks & e-reports available for licensing. Free 15 minute phone consultation for LMP readers - code LMP.
This publisher has indicated that 50% of their product line is author subsidized.
ISBN Prefix(es): 978-0-917098 (New World Press)
Number of titles published annually: 36 Print; 25 E-Book
Total Titles: 350 Print; 50 E-Book
Imprints: CCA; National Association of Photo Sellers; New World Press; Publishers Trade Secrets Library
Distributor for Compu-Tek; National Association of Photo Sellers; PictureProfits® Tool Kit; World Dating Consultants™
Advertising Agency: LK Advertising Agency, 7 Putter Lane, Middle Island, NY 11953, EVP: Roger Dextor *Tel:* 631-924-3888 *Web Site:* www.AndrewLinickDirectMarketing.com/LK-Advertising.html
Membership(s): ABA; American Association of Journalists & Authors; American Association of Magazine Photographers; American Book Producers Association; American Business Women's Association; American Marketing Association; American Medical Publishers Association; American Medical Writers Association; American Publishers Association; American Society of Magazine Editors; Association of Advertising & Marketing Professionals; Association of Directory Publishers; Data & Marketing Association; Direct Marketing Club of New York; International Food, Wine and Travel Writers Association

Cornell Maritime Press Inc
Imprint of Schiffer Publishing Ltd
4880 Lower Valley Rd, Atglen, PA 19310
SAN: 203-5901
Tel: 610-593-1777 *Fax:* 610-593-2002
E-mail: info@schifferbooks.com
Web Site: www.cmptp.com
Key Personnel
Pres: Pete Schiffer
EVP: Nancy Schiffer
Founded: 1938
Professional, technical books in maritime arts & sciences; boats & boat building; related hobbies & crafts.
ISBN Prefix(es): 978-0-87033
Number of titles published annually: 15 Print
Total Titles: 300 Print
Imprints: Tidewater Publishers
Distributor for Chesapeake Bay Maritime Museum; Independent Seaport Museum; Literary House Press; Maryland Historical Trust Press; Maryland Sea Grant Program
Membership(s): ABA; Mid-Atlantic Publishers Association

Cornell University Press
Division of Cornell University
Sage House, 512 E State St, Ithaca, NY 14850
SAN: 202-1862
Tel: 607-277-2338 *Fax:* 607-277-2374
E-mail: cupressinfo@cornell.edu; cupress-sales@cornell.edu
Web Site: www.cornellpress.cornell.edu
Key Personnel
CFO & Asst Dir: Roger A Hubbs *Tel:* 607-882-2209 *E-mail:* rah9@cornell.edu
Dir: Dean J Smith *Tel:* 607-882-2226 *E-mail:* djs486@cornell.edu
Ed-in-Chief: Peter Potter *Tel:* 607-882-2254 *E-mail:* pjp33@cornell.edu
Edit Dir, ILR Press: Ms Frances Benson *Tel:* 607-882-2255 *E-mail:* fgb2@cornell.edu
Dir, Mktg: Mr Mahinder S Kingra *Tel:* 607-882-2239 *E-mail:* msk55@cornell.edu
Exec Ed: Roger Haydon *Tel:* 607-882-2236 *E-mail:* rmh11@cornell.edu
Sr Ed: James Lance *E-mail:* jml554@cornell.edu; Michael J McGandy *Tel:* 607-882-2250 *E-mail:* mjm475@cornell.edu
Assoc Ed, Comstock Publishing: Kitty Lu *Tel:* 607-882-2247 *E-mail:* khl8@cornell.edu
Asst Dir & Mng Ed: Priscilla Hurdle *Tel:* 607-277-2338 ext 244 *E-mail:* plh9@cornell.edu
Design & Prod Mgr: Karen Kerr *Tel:* 607-882-2238 *E-mail:* kg99@cornell.edu
Sales Mgr: Nathan D Gemignani *Tel:* 607-882-2234 *E-mail:* ndg5@cornell.edu
Subs Rts Mgr: Tonya Cook *Tel:* 607-882-2252 *E-mail:* tcc6@cornell.edu
Asst to the Dir: Michael A Morris *Tel:* 607-882-2256 *E-mail:* mam278@cornell.edu
Founded: 1869 (reconstituted in 1930)
General nonfiction, scholarly books & monographs; hardcover & paperbacks.
ISBN Prefix(es): 978-0-8014; 978-0-87546; 978-1-5017
Number of titles published annually: 120 Print
Total Titles: 2,200 Print
Imprints: Comstock Publishing Associates; ILR Press
Distributor for Cornell Southeast Asia Program (SEAP) Publications; Leuven University Press
Foreign Rep(s): East-West Export Books (Royden Muranaka) (Asia); Footprint Books Pty Ltd (Australia, Fiji, New Zealand, Papua New Guinea); KW Publishers Pvt Ltd (Kalpana Shukla) (Afghanistan, Bangladesh, Bhutan, India, Maldives, Myanmar, Nepal, Pakistan, Sri Lanka, Thailand); Ewa Ledochowicz (Eastern Europe); Lexa Publishers' Representatives (Mical Moser) (Canada); Uwe Luedemann (Austria, Germany, Italy, Liechtenstein, Portugal, Spain, Switzerland); US PubRep Inc (Craig Falk) (Latin America)
Foreign Rights: Eulama (Dr Pina von Prellwitz) (Italy); Graal Literary Agency (Poland); Maya Publishers (Mr Surit Mitra) (India); La Nouvelle Agence (Vanessa King) (France); RDC Agencia Literaria (Beatriz Coll & Lukasz Wrobel) (Albania, Bulgaria, Croatia, Czech Republic, Estonia, Hungary, Latvia, Lithuania, Montenegro, Portugal, Romania, Serbia, Slovakia, Spain)
Distribution Center: Longleaf Services Inc, 116 S Boundary St, Chapel Hill, NC 27514-3808 *Toll Free Tel:* 800-848-6224 *Toll Free Fax:* 800-272-6817 *E-mail:* customerservice@longleafservices.org
Codasat Canada, 1153 56 St, Delta, BC V4L 2P8, Canada *Tel:* 604-228-9952 *E-mail:* info@codasat.com *Web Site:* www.codasat.com
Footprint Books Pty Ltd, 1/6a Prosperity Parade, Warriewood, NSW 2102, Australia *Tel:* (02) 9997 3973; 1300 260 090 (toll free) *Fax:* (02) 9997 3185
NBN International, 10 Thornbury Rd, Plymouth PL6 7PP, United Kingdom *Tel:* (01752) 202301 *Fax:* (01752) 202333 *E-mail:* orders@nbninternational.com
Membership(s): AAP; Association of American University Presses

Cornerstone Book Publishers
PO Box 24652, New Orleans, LA 70184
E-mail: info@cornerstonepublishers.com
Web Site: www.cornerstonepublishers.com
Key Personnel
Owner: Michael R Poll
Founded: 1995
Masonic, Scottish Rite, Rosicrucian, metaphysical, Louisiana themed & classic outdoor & bushcraft books.
ISBN Prefix(es): 978-1-887560
Number of titles published annually: 6 Print; 10 E-Book
Total Titles: 33 Print; 65 E-Book
Foreign Rep(s): Ingram (UK)

Cortina Institute of Languages
Division of Cortina Learning International Inc (CLI)
9 Hollyhock Rd, Wilton, CT 06897
Tel: 203-762-2510 *Toll Free Tel:* 800-245-2145
Web Site: www.cortina-languages.com
Key Personnel
Pres: Magdalen B Livesey *Tel:* 203-762-2510 ext 109 *E-mail:* m.livesey@cortinalearning.com
Gen Mgr: George Bollas *Tel:* 203-762-2510 ext 105 *E-mail:* g.bollas@cortinalearning.com
Founded: 1958
Learning foreign languages for English speakers; ESL.
ISBN Prefix(es): 978-0-8489
Number of titles published annually: 6 Print
Total Titles: 277 Print

Cortina Learning International Inc
9 Hollyhock Rd, Wilton, CT 06897
Tel: 203-762-2510 *Toll Free Tel:* 800-245-2145 *Fax:* 203-762-2514
Web Site: www.cortinalearning.com
Key Personnel
Pres: Magdalen B Livesey *Tel:* 203-762-2510 ext 109 *E-mail:* m.livesey@cortinalearning.com
Gen Mgr: George Bollas *Tel:* 203-762-2510 ext 105 *E-mail:* g.bollas@cortinalearning.com
Founded: 1882
Foreign languages, ESL, art instruction, writing instruction, fiction & nonfiction.
ISBN Prefix(es): 978-0-8327; 978-0-8489
Number of titles published annually: 5 Print
Total Titles: 50 Print
Divisions: Cortina Institute of Languages; Famous Artists School; Famous Writers School
See separate listing for:
Cortina Institute of Languages

§Corwin, a Sage Co
2455 Teller Rd, Thousand Oaks, CA 91320
Tel: 805-499-9734 *Toll Free Tel:* 800-233-9936 *Fax:* 805-499-5323 *Toll Free Fax:* 800-417-2466
E-mail: info@corwin.com; order@corwin.com
Web Site: www.corwin.com
Key Personnel
Pres: Mike Soules
VP, Mktg & Channel Devt: Elena Nikitina
VP, Publg & Prof Learning: Lisa Shaw
Dir, Prof Learning: Kristin Anderson
Sr Licensing Mgr & Foreign Rts Agent: Anna Termine *E-mail:* anna.termine@sagepub.com

Founded: 1990
Offers practical, research-based books, journals & multimedia resources specifically developed for principals, administrators, teachers, staff developers, curriculum developers, special & gifted educators & other PreK-12 education professionals.
ISBN Prefix(es): 978-0-7619; 978-0-8039; 978-1-4129; 978-1-8904; 978-1-57517; 978-1-5697; 978-1-879179
Number of titles published annually: 120 Print
Total Titles: 1,900 Print
Distributor for SAGE UK Resources for Educators
Foreign Rep(s): SAGE India (India); SAGE London (Europe, UK); SAGE Singapore (Asia-Pacific)

§Cosimo Inc
Old Chelsea Sta, PO Box 416, New York, NY 10011-0416
Tel: 212-989-3616 *Fax:* 212-989-3662
E-mail: info@cosimobooks.com
Web Site: www.cosimobooks.com
Founded: 2005
Specialty publisher for independent authors, not-for-profit organizations & innovative businesses, dedicated to publishing books that inspire, inform & engage readers around the world. We offer authors & organizations full publishing support, while using the newest technologies to present their works in the most timely & effective way.
ISBN Prefix(es): 978-1-931044 (Paraview print on demand titles); 978-1-4165 (Paraview Pocket Books); 978-1-59605; 978-1-60206; 978-1-60520; 978-1-61640
Number of titles published annually: 12 Print; 12 E-Book
Total Titles: 45 Print
Imprints: Cosimo Books; Cosimo Classics; Cosimo Reports; Paraview Pocket Books; Paraview Special Editions
Divisions: Paraview Press

Costume + Fashion Press, see Quite Specific Media Group Ltd

Cotsen Institute of Archaeology Press
Division of University of California, Los Angeles
308 Charles E Young Dr N, Fowler A163, Box 951510, Los Angeles, CA 90095
Tel: 310-206-9384 *Fax:* 310-206-4723
E-mail: cioapress@ioa.ucla.edu
Web Site: www.ioa.ucla.edu
Key Personnel
Dir, Institute: Willeke Wendrich
Dir, Pubns: Randi Danforth
Founded: 1974
Books, monographs & occasional papers in the field of archaeology.
ISBN Prefix(es): 978-0-917956; 978-1-938770; 978-1-931745
Number of titles published annually: 5 Print; 5 E-Book
Total Titles: 100 Print; 50 E-Book
Distribution Center: University of New Mexico Press, 1312 Basehart Rd SE, Albuquerque, NM 87106-4363, Cust Serv: Stewart Marshall *Tel:* 505-275-9506 *Toll Free Tel:* 800-249-7737 (ordering) *Fax:* 505-272-7778 *Toll Free Fax:* 800-622-8667 *E-mail:* unmpress@unm.edu *Web Site:* www.unmpress.com

Cottonwood Press
University of Kansas, Kansas Union, Rm 400, 1301 Jayhawk Blvd, Lawrence, KS 66045
Tel: 785-864-4520
Web Site: www.englishcw.ku.edu/cottonwood
Key Personnel
Ed: Tom Lorenz *Tel:* 785-864-2516 *E-mail:* tlorenz@ku.edu
Poetry Ed: Phil Wedge *E-mail:* pwedge@ku.edu
Founded: 1965
Poetry & fiction.
ISBN Prefix(es): 978-1-878434
Number of titles published annually: 4 Print
Total Titles: 15 Print
Membership(s): Community of Literary Magazines & Presses

§Council for Exceptional Children (CEC)
2900 Crystal Dr, Suite 100, Arlington, VA 22202
Toll Free Tel: 888-232-7733; 866-915-5000 (TTY)
E-mail: service@cec.sped.org
Web Site: www.cec.sped.org
Key Personnel
Exec Dir: Alexander T Graham *Tel:* 703-264-9415 *E-mail:* agraham@cec.sped.org
Mgr, Prof Pubns: Lorraine Sobson *Tel:* 703-264-9466 *E-mail:* lorraines@cec.sped.org
Founded: 1922
Mail order books & other products to improve the educational success of individuals with disabilities +/or gifts & talents.
ISBN Prefix(es): 978-0-86586
Number of titles published annually: 6 Print
Total Titles: 75 Print
Branch Office(s)
CEC Publications, PO Box 79026, Baltimore, MD 21279-0026
Distributed by ASCD; National Professional Resources (selected titles)
Distributor for Brookes (selected titles); Corwin (selected titles); Free Spirit (selected titles); Guilford (selected titles); National Professional Resources (selected titles)
Distribution Center: Amazon
Baker & Taylor
Barnes & Noble

Council for Research in Values & Philosophy (RVP)
The Catholic University of America, Gibbons Hall, Rm B-12, 620 Michigan Ave NE, Washington, DC 20064
Mailing Address: PO Box 261, Cardinal Sta, Washington, DC 20064-0261
Tel: 202-319-6089 *Fax:* 202-319-6089
E-mail: cua-rvp@cua.edu
Web Site: www.crvp.org
Key Personnel
Pres: George F McLean *E-mail:* mclean@cua.edu
Dir, Opers & Treas: Hu Yeping *E-mail:* huy@cua.edu
Founded: 1982
Works on philosophy, values, education, civil society, culture.
ISBN Prefix(es): 978-1-56518
Number of titles published annually: 12 Print; 12 Online
Total Titles: 220 Print; 215 Online
Imprints: The Council for Research in Values & Philosophy
Orders to: Oblate School of Theology (OST), 285 Oblate Dr, San Antonio, TX 78216

Council Oak Books LLC
2822 Van Ness Ave, San Francisco, CA 94109
SAN: 689-5522
Tel: 415-931-7700 *Toll Free Tel:* 888-275-2596
E-mail: marketing@counciloakbooks.com
Web Site: www.counciloakbooks.com
Founded: 1984
Publisher of nonfiction titles that point the way to a richer life & a better world. Areas of special interest include world religions, Native American, Americana (especially Route 66), animals & nature.
ISBN Prefix(es): 978-0-933031; 978-1-57178; 978-1-885171 (Wildcat Canyon Press)
Number of titles published annually: 10 Print
Total Titles: 300 Print
Imprints: Wildcat Canyon Press (women's relationships)
Distribution Center: Independent Publishers Group (IPG), 814 N Franklin St, Chicago, IL 60610 *Tel:* 312-337-0747 *Toll Free Tel:* 800-888-4741 *E-mail:* orders@ipgbook.com

Council of State Governments
2760 Research Park Dr, Lexington, KY 40511
Mailing Address: PO Box 11910, Lexington, KY 40578-1910
Tel: 859-244-8000 *Toll Free Tel:* 800-800-1910 *Fax:* 859-244-8001
E-mail: sales@csg.org
Web Site: www.csg.org; www.csgstore.org
Key Personnel
Exec Dir & CEO: David Adkins *E-mail:* dadkins@csg.org
Founded: 1933
Nonprofit association representing state government officials in all three branches. Publish reference guides, books, directories, journals, newsletters & conference proceedings & hold major regional & special topical conferences. Will contract or do grant-funded topic research. Specialize in corrections & public safety.
ISBN Prefix(es): 978-0-87292
Number of titles published annually: 10 Print
Total Titles: 72 Print
Branch Office(s)
1107 Ninth St, Suite 730, Sacramento, CA 95814, Exec Dir: Edgar E Ruiz *Tel:* 916-553-4423 *Fax:* 916-446-5760 *E-mail:* csgw@csg.org *Web Site:* www.csgwest.org
444 N Capitol St NW, Suite 401, Washington, DC 20001 *Tel:* 202-624-5460 *Fax:* 202-624-5452 *Web Site:* www.csgdc.org
PO Box 98129, Atlanta, GA 30359, Dir: Colleen Cousineau *Tel:* 404-633-1866 *Fax:* 404-633-4896 *E-mail:* slc@csg.org *Web Site:* www.slcatlanta.org
701 E 22 St, Suite 110, Lombard, IL 60148, Dir: Michael H McCabe *Tel:* 630-925-1922 *E-mail:* csgm@csg.org *Web Site:* www.csgmidwest.org
22 Cortlandt St, 22nd fl, New York, NY 10007, Dir: Wendell Hannaford *Tel:* 212-482-2320 *Fax:* 212-482-2344 *E-mail:* info@csg-erc.org *Web Site:* www.csg-erc.org

Council on Foreign Relations Press
Division of Council on Foreign Relations
The Harold Pratt House, 58 E 68 St, New York, NY 10065
SAN: 201-7784
Tel: 212-434-9400 *Fax:* 212-434-9800
E-mail: publications@cfr.org
Web Site: www.cfr.org
Key Personnel
Edit Dir: Patricia Dorff *Tel:* 212-434-9514 *Fax:* 212-434-9807 *E-mail:* pdorff@cfr.org
Founded: 1922
Scholarly books on foreign policy, international economics, international affairs.
ISBN Prefix(es): 978-0-87609
Number of titles published annually: 10 Print
Total Titles: 228 Print
Branch Office(s)
1777 "F" St NW, Washington, DC 20006 *Tel:* 202-509-8400 *Fax:* 202-509-8490
Distributed by Brookings Institution Press
Membership(s): AAP

Council on Social Work Education (CSWE), see CSWE Press

Counterpath Press
613 22 St, Denver, CO 80205
E-mail: counterpath@counterpathpress.org; editors@counterpathpress.org
Web Site: www.counterpathpress.org
Key Personnel
Assoc Dir & Co-Founder: Julie Carr

Dir: Tim Roberts
Assoc Ed: Will Skinker
Founded: 2006
Independent, nonprofit, literary publisher of poetry, fiction, drama, cross-genre work, literary & cultural theory & criticism, translations, reprints & high-quality Internet material.
ISBN Prefix(es): 978-1-933996
Number of titles published annually: 6 Print
Total Titles: 15 Print
Distribution Center: Small Press Distribution, 1341 Seventh St, Berkeley, CA 94710-1409, Deputy Dir: Laura Moriarty *Tel:* 510-524-1668 *Fax:* 510-524-0852 *E-mail:* laura@spdbooks.org *Web Site:* www.spdbooks.org
Membership(s): Community of Literary Magazines & Presses

Counterpoint Press LLC
1919 Fifth St, Berkeley, CA 94710
Tel: 510-704-0230 *Fax:* 510-704-0268
E-mail: info@counterpointpress.com
Web Site: counterpointpress.com; www.sierraclub.org/books; softskull.com
Key Personnel
Publr: Andy Hunter
Assoc Publr: Jennifer Abel Kovitz
Assoc Publr & Dir, Publicity: Megan Fishmann
VP & Edit Dir: Jack Shoemaker
Creative Dir & Art Dir: Nicole Caputo
Exec Ed: Dan Smetanka
Soc Media Ed, Catapult/Counterpoint/Soft Skull: Dustin Kurtz
Ed-at-Large: Charlie Winton
Busn Mgr: Kelli Adams
Events Coord, Catapult/Counterpoint/Soft Skull: Sarah Baline
Founded: 2007 (through acquisition of Counterpoint, Shoemaker & Hoard, & Soft Skull Press)
Publish literary work with an emphasis on fiction, natural history, philosophy & contemporary thought, history, art, poetry, narrative & nonfiction.
ISBN Prefix(es): 978-1-887178; 978-1-58243; 978-1-61902 (Counterpoint); 978-1-933368 (Soft Skull); 978-1-57805 (Sierra Club Books); 978-0-9796636 (Soft Skull); 978-1-932360 (Soft Skull); 978-1-887128 (Soft Skull)
Number of titles published annually: 60 Print
Total Titles: 60 Print
Imprints: Catapult; Counterpoint; Sierra Club Books; Soft Skull Press
Foreign Rep(s): Bookwise International (Australia, New Zealand); Publishers Group Canada (Canada); Publishers Group Worldwide (worldwide exc Australia, Canada, Ireland, New Zealand, UK & USA); Turnaround Publisher Service (Ireland, UK)
Foreign Rights: AnatoliaLit Agency (Amy Marie Spangler) (Turkey); Big Apple Agency (Wendy King) (China); Big Apple Agency (Chris Lin) (Taiwan); Katai Bolza Agency (Peter Bolza) (Hungary); Ersilia Literary Agency (Evangelia Avloniti) (Greece); The Foreign Office (Teresa Vilarrubla) (Brazil, Portugal, South America, Spain); Graal Literary Agency (Parcin Biegaj) (Poland); Deborah Harris Agency (Ilana Kurshan) (Israel); Mohrbooks AG Literary Agency (Annelie Geissler) (Germany); Piergiorgio Nicolazzini Literary Agency (Maura Solinas) (Italy); La Nouvelle Agence (Anne Maizeret, Michele Kanonidis & Vanessa Kling) (France); Prava i prevodi (Milena Kaplarevic) (Eastern Europe); Sebes & Bisseling Literary Agency (Jeanine Langenberg & Paul Sebes) (Netherlands); Abner Stein Agency (Anna Carmichael) (UK)
Distribution Center: Publishers Group West, 1700 Fourth St, Berkeley, CA 94710 *Toll Free Tel:* 800-788-3123 *Fax:* 510-528-3444 *Web Site:* www.pgw.com

Country Music Foundation Press
Division of Country Music Hall of Fame® & Museum
222 Fifth Ave S, Nashville, TN 37203
Tel: 615-416-2001 *Fax:* 615-255-2245
E-mail: info@countrymusichalloffame.com
Web Site: www.countrymusichalloffame.com
Key Personnel
Writer/Ed: Michael McCall
Founded: 1967
Publish books & calendars. Also author books for trade publications & co-publish with Vanderbilt University Press.
ISBN Prefix(es): 978-0-8265; 978-0-915608
Number of titles published annually: 3 Print
Total Titles: 40 Print
Distributed by Chronicle; Oxford University Press Inc; Providence Publishing; Universe; Vanderbilt University Press

§The Countryman Press
Division of W W Norton & Company Inc
c/o W W Norton & Company Inc, 500 Fifth Ave, New York, NY 10110
SAN: 206-4901
Tel: 212-354-5500 *Fax:* 212-869-0856
E-mail: countrymanpress@wwnorton.com
Web Site: www.countrymanpress.com
Key Personnel
Chmn & Pres, W W Norton: W Drake McFeely
Publicity & Mktg Mgr: Devorah Backman
Founded: 1973
ISBN Prefix(es): 978-0-936399; 978-1-58157; 978-0-914378; 978-0-88150; 978-0-942440
Number of titles published annually: 70 Print
Total Titles: 350 Print
Distributed by W W Norton & Company Inc; Penguin Books (CN only)
Foreign Rep(s): W W Norton & Co Inc
Foreign Rights: Casanovas & Lynch (Portugal, Spain)
Advertising Agency: Bennett Book Advertising
Warehouse: National Book Co Inc, 800 Keystone Industrial Park, Scranton, PA 18512-4601

§Covenant Communications Inc
920 E State Rd, Suite F, American Fork, UT 84003-0416
Mailing Address: PO Box 416, American Fork, UT 84003-0416
Tel: 801-756-1041
E-mail: info@covenant-lds.com
Web Site: www.covenant-lds.com
Key Personnel
VP, Mktg: Robby Nichols *Tel:* 801-756-1041 ext 106 *E-mail:* robbyn@covenant-lds.com
Mng Ed, Multimedia & Electronic Publg: Phil Reschke *Tel:* 801-756-1041 ext 114
Sales Mgr: Tammy Kolkman *Tel:* 801-756-1041 ext 122
Founded: 1958
Publish for the LDS (Mormon) market.
ISBN Prefix(es): 978-1-55503; 978-1-57734; 978-1-59156; 978-1-59811; 978-1-60681; 978-1-62108; 978-1-68047
Number of titles published annually: 60 Print; 60 E-Book; 50 Audio
Total Titles: 300 Print; 500 E-Book; 450 Audio

Coyote Press
Affiliate of Archaeological Consulting
PO Box 3377, Salinas, CA 93912-3377
Tel: 831-422-4912 *Fax:* 831-422-4913
E-mail: orders@coyotepress.com
Web Site: www.coyotepress.com
Key Personnel
Owner & Ed: Gary Breschini, PhD
Founded: 1980
Archaeology, history, pre-history, ethnography, linguistics, rock art & Native American studies of Western North America.
ISBN Prefix(es): 978-1-55567; 978-1-4044
Number of titles published annually: 50 Print
Total Titles: 3,000 Print

CQ Press
Imprint of SAGE Publications
2300 "N" St NW, Suite 800, Washington, DC 20037
Tel: 202-729-1900 *Toll Free Tel:* 866-4CQ-PRESS (427-7737) *Fax:* 202-729-1923 *Toll Free Fax:* 800-380-3810
E-mail: customerservice@cqpress.com; librarysales@cqpress.com
Web Site: www.cqpress.com
Founded: 1959
Publisher of books, directories, subscriptions & web products on American politics, federal & state government, American institutions, campaigns & elections, current events & world affairs.
ISBN Prefix(es): 978-0-87187; 978-1-56802; 978-0-9625531; 978-1-56692; 978-0-7401; 978-1-933116; 978-1-60426; 978-0-9823537; 978-1-60871
Number of titles published annually: 50 Print
Total Titles: 300 Print; 4 CD-ROM; 1 Online; 3 E-Book
Foreign Rep(s): SAGE Publications (Amanda Fox); SAGE Publications (Sarah Broomhead); SAGE Publications Asia-Pacific Pte Ltd (Rosalia da Garcia)

§Crabtree Publishing Co
350 Fifth Ave, 59th fl, PMB 59051, New York, NY 10118
Tel: 212-496-5040 *Toll Free Tel:* 800-387-7650 *Toll Free Fax:* 800-355-7166
E-mail: custserv@crabtreebooks.com
Web Site: www.crabtreebooks.com
Key Personnel
Pres: Peter A Crabtree *Tel:* 212-496-5040 ext 225 *E-mail:* peter_c@crabtreebooks.com
Publr: Ms Bobbie Kalman *E-mail:* bobbiek@crabtreebooks.com
VP, Edit: Kathy Middleton *Tel:* 212-496-5040 ext 226 *E-mail:* kathy_m@crabtreebooks.com
VP, Mktg: Julie Alguire *Tel:* 212-496-5040 ext 235 *E-mail:* julie_a@crabtreebooks.com
VP, Opers: Craig Culliford *Tel:* 212-496-5040 ext 236 *E-mail:* craig_c@crabtreebooks.com
Dir, Art & New Media: Robert MacGregor *Tel:* 212-496-5040 ext 231 *E-mail:* rob_m@crabtreebooks.com
Sales Dir: Andrea Crabtree *Tel:* 212-496-5040 ext 265 *E-mail:* andrea_c@crabtreebooks.com
Cust Serv Mgr: Linda Wade *Tel:* 212-496-5040 ext 223 *E-mail:* linda_w@crabtreebooks.com
Warehouse Mgr: Karl Kasper *Tel:* 212-496-5040 ext 237 *E-mail:* warehouse@crabtreebooks.com
Founded: 1978
Publisher of children's nonfiction & fiction; library binding & paperback for school & trade.
ISBN Prefix(es): 978-0-86505; 978-0-7787; 978-1-4271
Number of titles published annually: 300 Print; 150 E-Book
Total Titles: 4,612 Print; 1,665 E-Book; 105 Audio
Subsidiaries: Crabtree Publishing Co Ltd (CN)
Distributor for Bayard; Maren Green
Foreign Rep(s): Everybody's Books (Namibia, South Africa); INT Press (Australia); Roundhouse Group (European Union, UK); South Pacific Books (New Zealand)
Warehouse: 2321 Kenmore Ave, Buffalo, NY 14207
Membership(s): ABA; ALA; American Alliance of Museums; Educational Book & Media Association; Museum Store Association; NAIPR; National Science Teachers Association

§Craftsman Book Co
6058 Corte Del Cedro, Carlsbad, CA 92011

SAN: 159-7000
Tel: 760-438-7828 *Toll Free Tel:* 800-829-8123
Fax: 760-438-0398
Web Site: www.craftsman-book.com
Key Personnel
Chmn & Intl Rts: Gary Moselle *E-mail:* gary@costbook.com
Publr, Data Licensing: Ben Moselle *Tel:* 760-438-7828 ext 122 *E-mail:* ben@costbook.com
Dir, Lib Sales & Mgr, Sales & Ad: Jennifer Johnson *Tel:* 760-438-7828 ext 105 *E-mail:* johnson@costbook.com
Edit Mgr & Rts & Perms: Laurence Jacobs *Tel:* 760-438-7828 ext 108 *E-mail:* jacobs@costbook.com
Founded: 1952
Estimating software, trade & professional, state-specific contract-writing software, subscription, mail order & download, reference; construction industry.
ISBN Prefix(es): 978-0-934041; 978-0-910460; 978-1-57218
Number of titles published annually: 10 Print; 9 CD-ROM; 150 Online; 5 E-Book
Total Titles: 150 Print; 9 CD-ROM; 150 Online; 8 E-Book
Distributed by The Aberdeen Group; BNI Publications; Builders Book Inc
Distributor for BNI Publications; Builders Book Inc; Building News Inc; Home Builders Press
Foreign Rep(s): Gauge Publications (Canada)
Distribution Center: Quality Books Inc, 103 W Pines Rd, Oregon, IL 61061-9680 *Tel:* 815-732-4450 *Toll Free Tel:* 800-323-4241 *Fax:* 815-732-4499 *E-mail:* info@quality-books.com *Web Site:* www.quality-books.com

§CRC Press
Imprint of Taylor & Francis Group, an Informa Business
6000 Broken Sound Pkwy NW, Suite 300, Boca Raton, FL 33487
Tel: 561-994-0555 *Toll Free Tel:* 800-272-7737 (orders) *Toll Free Fax:* 800-643-9428 (sales); 800-374-3401 (orders)
E-mail: orders@crcpress.com; orders@taylorandfrancis.com
Web Site: www.crcpress.com
Key Personnel
Pres: Emmett Dages
SVP, Publg & Online Prods: John Lavender *Tel:* 561-998-2579 *E-mail:* john.lavender@taylorandfrancis.com
SVP, Sales: Dennis Weiss *Tel:* 561-998-2510 *Fax:* 561-998-2580 *E-mail:* dennis.weiss@taylorandfrancis.com
VP, Mktg: Stacey Mironov *E-mail:* stacey.mironov@taylorandfrancis.com
Founded: 1913
Premier publisher of science, technology & medical reference books, textbooks & online content.
ISBN Prefix(es): 978-0-8493; 978-0-935184; 978-1-57491; 978-0-87762; 978-1-56676; 978-0-87819; 978-1-58488; 978-1-58716; 978-1-4200; 978-1-4398; 978-1-4665; 978-1-4822; 978-1-4987
Number of titles published annually: 900 Print
Total Titles: 14,000 Print
Imprints: Productivity Press
Warehouse: Taylor & Francis, 7625 Empire Dr, Florence, KY 41042
See separate listing for:
Productivity Press

§The Creative Co
PO Box 227, Mankato, MN 56002
Tel: 507-388-6273 *Toll Free Tel:* 800-445-6209 *Fax:* 507-388-2746
E-mail: info@thecreativecompany.us; orders@thecreativecompany.us
Web Site: www.thecreativecompany.us
Key Personnel
Owner & Publr: Tom Peterson *Tel:* 507-388-6273 ext 225
VP, Retail Sales, Creative Editions & Creative Pbks: Anna Erikson
Founded: 1932
Gift books.
ISBN Prefix(es): 978-0-87191; 978-0-88682; 978-0-89812; 978-1-56660; 978-1-56846; 978-1-60818; 978-1-62832; 978-1-58341
Number of titles published annually: 110 Print
Total Titles: 3,500 Print
Imprints: Creative Editions; Creative Education; Creative Paperbacks
Foreign Rep(s): JCC Enterprises Inc (Jerry C Carrillo) (Canada); Raincoast Books (Canada)
Warehouse: 2140 Howard Dr W, North Mankato, MN 56003

Creative Homeowner
Imprint of Fox Chapel Publishing Co Inc
1970 Broad St, East Petersburg, PA 17520
Tel: 717-560-4703 *Toll Free Tel:* 800-475-9112 *Fax:* 717-560-4702 *Toll Free Fax:* 888-369-2885
E-mail: customerservice@foxchapelpublishing.com; sales@foxchapelpublishing.com
Web Site: www.foxchapelpublishing.com/home-and-garden/creative-homeowner
Founded: 1978
Quality trade paperbacks for kitchen & bath design & decor, gardening, landscaping, outdoor hobbies & home improvement.
ISBN Prefix(es): 978-0-932944; 978-1-880029; 978-1-58011
Number of titles published annually: 20 Print
Total Titles: 220 Print

§Cricket Cottage Publishing LLC
Unit of Justice & Chaos Entertainment LLC
1500 Beville Rd, Suite 606-346, Daytona Beach, FL 32114
Tel: 585-687-7291
E-mail: cricketcottage@att.net
Web Site: thecricketpublishing.com
Key Personnel
Partner: Michael Murray
Contact: Josh Jones *E-mail:* j@thecricketpublishing.com
Founded: 2012
Micro-publisher combining the best of traditional & modern publishing. Strictly royalty-based, giving authors a new chance & making use of social media to help promote the company & its books. Basic editing/proofing, book formatting & cover design. Online distribution for paperback & ebook versions.
Number of titles published annually: 15 Print; 12 Online; 15 E-Book
Total Titles: 28 Print; 24 Online; 24 E-Book

Crickhollow Books
Imprint of Great Lakes Literary LLC
3147 S Pennsylvania Ave, Milwaukee, WI 53207
Tel: 414-294-4319
E-mail: info@crickhollowbooks.com
Web Site: www.crickhollowbooks.com
Key Personnel
Edit Dir: Philip Martin
Founded: 1993
Publish books on regional heritage, with a focus on books for children, fiction & chapter books with a regional slant.
ISBN Prefix(es): 978-1-883953
Number of titles published annually: 3 Print
Total Titles: 12 Print
Membership(s): Independent Book Publishers Association

§Cross-Cultural Communications
Division of Cross-Cultural Literary Editions Inc
239 Wynsum Ave, Merrick, NY 11566-4725
SAN: 208-6122
Tel: 516-868-5635 *Fax:* 516-379-1901
E-mail: info@cross-culturalcommunications.com; cccbarkan@optonline.net; cccpoetry@aol.com
Web Site: www.cross-culturalcommunications.com
Key Personnel
Publr & Ed-in-Chief: Stanley H Barkan
Art Ed: Bebe Barkan
Asst Ed: Mia Barkan Clarke
Founded: 1971
Traditionally neglected languages & cultures in bilingual format, primarily poetry, some fiction, drama, music & art. Cross-cultural review series of world literature & art in sound, print & motion.
ISBN Prefix(es): 978-0-89304
Number of titles published annually: 20 Print; 1 CD-ROM; 100 Online; 1 Audio
Total Titles: 450 Print; 3 CD-ROM; 400 Online; 16 Audio
Imprints: ARC (Magazine & Press) (Israel); Cross-Cultural Prototypes; Expressive Editions; Fact Publishers (Ukraine); Midrashic Editions; Nightingale Editions; Ostrich Editions; The Seventh Quarry (Wales, Seventh Quarry Chapbook Series); The Seventh Quarry Press
Subsidiaries: Bulgarian-American Cultural Society ALEKO (Chicago/Sofia, Bulgaria); Varlik (Turkey)
Branch Office(s)
3131 Mott Ave, Far Rockaway, NY 11691, Contact: Roy Cravzow *Tel:* 718-327-4714
HC 67, Box 1206, Big Sur, CA 93920-9629, Contact: Patricia Holt *Tel:* 831-667-2433 *E-mail:* surph8@yahoo.com
Foreign Office(s): Antigruppo Siciliano, Via Mogia 8, 90138 Palermo, Sicily PA, Italy, Contact: Nicolo D'Alessandro *Tel:* (091) 322030 *E-mail:* nicolodalessandro@virgilio.it
Distributed by Ad Infinitum Books; Hochelaga (Canada)
Distributor for Ad Infinitum Press; Arba Sicula (Magazine, US); Center of Emigrants from Serbia (Serbia); Decalogue Books (US); The Feral Press (US); Greenfield Review Press (US); Hochelaga (Canada); Immagine&Poesia (Italy); Legas Publishers (CN); Lips (Magazine & Press) (US); Pholiota Press Inc (England); The Seventh Quarry Press (Wales); Shabdaguchha (Magazine & Press) (Bangladesh & US); Sicilia Parra (Magazine, US); Word & Quill Press (US)
Foreign Rep(s): Hassanal Abdullah (Bangladesh, USA); Karen Alkalay-Gut (Israel); Max Babi (India); Vahe Baladouni (Armenia, USA); Raymond Beauchemin (Canada); August Bover (Spain); Bohdan Boychuk (Ukraine); Gaetano Cipolla (Italy, USA); Nicolo D'Alessandro (Italy); Kristine Doll (Spain, USA); Christopher Fauske (Norway, USA); Isaac Goldemberg (Peru, USA); Theofil Halama (Czech Republic, USA); Luisa A Igloria (Philippines, USA); Vladimir Kandelaki (Georgia); Dovid Katz (UK); Naoshi Koriyama (Japan); Dariusz Thomasz Lebioda (Poland); Vladimir Levchev (Bulgaria, USA); Bijana D Obradovic (Montenegro, Serbia, USA); Ritva Poom (Estonia, Finland, USA); Kyung-Nyun "Kay" Kim Richards (South Korea, USA); Stephen A Sadow (Argentina, USA); Marco Scalabrino (Italy); Stoyan "Tchouki" Tchoukanov (Bulgaria); Peter Thabit Jones (UK); Tino Villanueva (Mexico, USA); Claire Nicolas White (Netherlands, USA); Sara Wolosker (Brazil)
Membership(s): ALTA

Crossquarter Publishing Group
PO Box 23749, Santa Fe, NM 87502
Tel: 505-690-3923 *Fax:* 214-975-9715
E-mail: sales@crossquarter.com; info@crossquarter.com
Web Site: www.crossquarter.com

Key Personnel
Exec Dir: Therese Francis
Founded: 1986
Small book press with some sidelines. Publishes books, ebooks & information packages. No longer accept fiction queries.
ISBN Prefix(es): 978-1-890109
Number of titles published annually: 25 Print; 3 E-Book
Total Titles: 57 Print; 2 E-Book
Imprints: Crossquarter Breeze; CrossTIME; Fenris Brothers; Herb & Spice; Xemplar
Membership(s): The Association of Publishers for Special Sales; Independent Book Publishers Association

§The Crossroad Publishing Co
831 Chestnut Ridge Rd, Chestnut Ridge, NY 10977
SAN: 287-0118
Tel: 845-517-0180 *Toll Free Tel:* 800-888-4741 (orders) *Fax:* 845-517-0181
E-mail: office@crossroadpublishing.com
Web Site: www.CrossroadPublishing.com
Key Personnel
CEO & Publr: Dr Gwendolin Herder
Off Admin: Stephanie Marchese
Founded: 1980
Independent book publisher in religion, spirituality, theology, personal growth, leadership & parenting.
ISBN Prefix(es): 978-0-8245
Number of titles published annually: 30 Print; 1 CD-ROM; 1 Online; 20 E-Book; 1 Audio
Total Titles: 550 Print; 1 CD-ROM; 1 Online; 20 E-Book; 4 Audio
Imprints: Crossroad (trade secular & religious); Herder & Herder (Catholic parish & academic)
Foreign Rep(s): John Garratt (Australia); Novalis (Canada)
Billing Address: Independent Publishers Group, 814 N Franklin St, Chicago, IL 60610 *E-mail:* orders@ipgbook.com *Web Site:* www.ipgbook.com
Membership(s): Association of Catholic Publishers Inc

Crossway
Division of Good News Publishers
1300 Crescent St, Wheaton, IL 60187
SAN: 211-7991
Tel: 630-682-4300 *Toll Free Tel:* 800-635-7993 (orders); 800-543-1659 (cust serv) *Fax:* 630-682-4785
E-mail: info@crossway.org
Web Site: www.crossway.org
Key Personnel
Pres: Lane T Dennis
EVP, Bible Publg: Dane Ortlund
EVP, Book Publg: Justin Taylor
EVP, Busn Opers: Anthony Gosling
EVP, Creative: Josh Dennis
SVP, Fin: Paul Thomas
SVP, Ministry & Licensing: Randy Jahns
Edit Admin, Perms & ISBN Contact: Jill Carter *E-mail:* jcarter@crossway.org
Intl Rts: Aaron Camp
Founded: 1969
Books with an evangelical Christian perspective aimed at the religious market.
ISBN Prefix(es): 978-0-89107; 978-1-58134; 978-1-4335
Number of titles published annually: 80 Print
Total Titles: 354 Print; 9 Audio

§Crown House Publishing Co LLC
Division of Crown House Publishing Ltd (UK Co)
81 Brook Hills Circle, White Plains, NY 10605
SAN: 013-9270
Tel: 914-946-3517 *Toll Free Tel:* 877-925-1213 (cust serv) *Fax:* 914-946-1160
E-mail: info@chpus.com
Web Site: www.crownhousepublishing.com
Key Personnel
Pres: Mark Tracten *E-mail:* mtracten@chpus.com
Founded: 1996
Publisher of quality books in psychology & education.
ISBN Prefix(es): 978-1-89983; 978-1-90442; 978-1-84590; 978-0-98235
Number of titles published annually: 30 Print; 1 CD-ROM; 6 Audio
Total Titles: 330 Print; 2 CD-ROM; 30 Audio
Distributor for Developing Press Co; Human Alchemy Publications; Institute Press; Transforming Press
Foreign Rep(s): Footprint Books Pty Ltd (Australia, New Zealand)
Foreign Rights: Anglo-American Book Co Ltd (Europe, UK)
Billing Address: PO Box 2223, Williston, VT 05495
Orders to: PO Box 2223, Williston, VT 05495, Contact: Matt Drake *Fax:* 802-864-7626 *E-mail:* mdrake@aidcvt.com
Returns: 82 Wintersport Lane, Williston, VT 05496, Contact: Matt Drake *E-mail:* mdrake@aidcvt.com
Shipping Address: PO Box 2223, Williston, VT 05495, Contact: Laurie Kenyon *Tel:* 802-862-0095 ext 113 *Fax:* 802-864-7626
Warehouse: PO Box 2223, Williston, VT 05495
Distribution Center: 82 Wintersport Lane, Williston, VT 05496, Contact: Laurie Kenyon *Fax:* 802-864-7626 *E-mail:* lkenyon@aidcvt.com

Crown Publishing Group
Division of Penguin Random House LLC
1745 Broadway, New York, NY 10019
Tel: 212-782-9000 *Toll Free Tel:* 888-264-1745 *Fax:* 212-940-7408
E-mail: crownosm@penguinrandomhouse.com
Web Site: crownpublishing.com
Founded: 1933
Leading publisher of bestselling fiction & critically acclaimed narrative nonfiction in categories that include biography & memoirs, history, science, politics & current events.
ISBN Prefix(es): 978-0-553; 978-0-609; 978-0-307; 978-0-8129; 978-1-4000; 978-0-8041; 978-0-517
Number of titles published annually: 400 Print
Imprints: Amphoto Books; Broadway Books; Clarkson Potter; Convergent Books; Crown Archetype; Crown Business; Crown Forum; Crown Publishers; Currency; Tim Duggan Books; Harmony Books; Hogarth; Image Books; Multnomah; Ten Speed Press; Three Rivers Press; WaterBrook; Watson-Guptill
See separate listing for:
Clarkson Potter Publishers
Ten Speed Press
WaterBrook
Watson-Guptill Publications

Crumb Elbow Publishing
PO Box 294, Rhododendron, OR 97049-0294
Tel: 503-622-4798
Key Personnel
Publr: Michael P Jones
Founded: 1979
Send an SASE for all mss, no exceptions.
ISBN Prefix(es): 978-0-89904
Number of titles published annually: 20 Print; 5 Audio
Total Titles: 500 Print
Imprints: Bear Meadows Research Group; Cascade Expeditions; Cascade Geographic Society; Ecosystem Research Group; Elbow Books; The Final Edition; Horse Latitudes Press; Lady Fern Press; Meadow Creek Press; Oregon Fever Books; Oregon River Watch; Read'n Run Books; Research Centrex; Sealife Research Alliance; Silhouette Imprints; Timberline Productions; Trillium Mountain Productions; Tyee Press; Wildlife Research Group; Wild Mountain Press; Windflower Press

§Crystal Clarity Publishers
14618 Tyler Foote Rd, Nevada City, CA 95959
Tel: 530-478-7600 *Toll Free Tel:* 800-424-1055 *Fax:* 530-478-7610
E-mail: clarity@crystalclarity.com
Web Site: www.crystalclarity.com
Key Personnel
Pres & Publr: Richard Salva *Tel:* 530-478-7600 ext 7606
Sales Mgr: Avital Miller *Tel:* 530-478-7600 ext 7605 *E-mail:* sales@crystalclarity.com
Founded: 1968
Self-help, psychology, philosophy, religion, business, books, tapes, videos, sidelines, metaphysical, health/healing.
ISBN Prefix(es): 978-0-916124; 978-1-878265; 978-1-56589
Number of titles published annually: 6 Print
Total Titles: 104 Print; 15 Audio
Imprints: Clarity Sound & Light
Foreign Rep(s): Brumby Books (Australia); Deep Books Ltd (England, Europe); National Book Network (Canada, New Zealand); New Horizons (South Africa)
Foreign Rights: Alexandra McGilloway

Crystal Productions
5320 Carpinteria Ave, Suite K, Carpinteria, CA 93013-2107
Tel: 847-657-8144 *Toll Free Tel:* 800-255-8629 *Fax:* 847-657-8149 *Toll Free Fax:* 800-657-8149
E-mail: custserv@crystalproductions.com
Web Site: www.crystalproductions.com
Key Personnel
Pres: Amy L Woodworth *E-mail:* alwcp@aol.com
Founded: 1973
Art education resources including interactive digital software, digital downloads, DVDs, posters, prints, books & more for PreK, elementary, middle, secondary & college.
ISBN Prefix(es): 978-0-924509; 978-1-56290
Number of titles published annually: 2 Print; 1 CD-ROM

Crystal Publishers Inc
3460 Lost Hills Dr, Las Vegas, NV 89122
Tel: 702-434-3037 *Fax:* 702-434-3037
Web Site: www.crystalpub.com
Key Personnel
Pres: Frank Leanza *E-mail:* leanzaent@centurylink.net
Exec Dir: Inge Allen
Founded: 1985
Music books for schools & professionals.
ISBN Prefix(es): 978-0-934687
Number of titles published annually: 15 Print
Total Titles: 45 Print

CSHL Press, see Cold Spring Harbor Laboratory Press

The CSIS Press
Division of Center for Strategic & International Studies
1616 Rhode Island Ave NW, Washington, DC 20036
Tel: 202-887-0200 *Fax:* 202-775-3199
E-mail: books@csis.org
Web Site: www.csis.org
Key Personnel
Pres & CEO: John J Hamre
Dir: James R Dunton *Tel:* 202-775-3160 *E-mail:* jdunton@csis.org
Founded: 1962
Public policy research organization.
ISBN Prefix(es): 978-0-89206

Number of titles published annually: 65 Print; 65 Online; 25 E-Book
Total Titles: 250 Print; 100 Online; 200 E-Book
Distributed by Rowman & Littlefield
Membership(s): AAP

§CSLI Publications
Stanford University, Cordura Hall, 220 Panama St, Stanford, CA 94305-4115
Tel: 650-723-1839 *Fax:* 650-725-2166
E-mail: pubs@csli.stanford.edu
Web Site: cslipublications.stanford.edu
Key Personnel
Dir: Dikran Karagueuzian *Tel:* 650-723-1712 *E-mail:* dikran@csli.stanford.edu
Founded: 1985
Subjects include computer science, computational linguistics, linguistics & philosophy.
ISBN Prefix(es): 978-0-937073; 978-1-881526; 978-1-57586; 978-0-226
Number of titles published annually: 10 Print
Total Titles: 339 Print; 7 Online
Distributed by University of Chicago Press
Advertising Agency: University of Chicago Press, 1427 E 60 St, Chicago, IL 60637-2954 *Tel:* 773-568-1550 *Toll Free Tel:* 800-621-2736 *Fax:* 773-660-2235 *Toll Free Fax:* 800-621-8471

CSWE Press
Division of Council on Social Work Education
1701 Duke St, Suite 200, Alexandria, VA 22314-3457
Tel: 703-683-8080 *Fax:* 703-683-8493
E-mail: publications@cswe.org; info@cswe.org
Web Site: www.cswe.org
Key Personnel
Pres & CEO: Darla Spence Coffey, PhD
Pubns Mgr: Elizabeth Simon *Tel:* 703-519-2076 *E-mail:* esimon@cswe.org
Founded: 1952
Professional books.
ISBN Prefix(es): 978-0-87293
Number of titles published annually: 6 Print
Total Titles: 75 Print
Membership(s): Copyright Clearance Center

Cumberland House
Imprint of Sourcebooks Inc
1935 Brookdale Rd, Suite 139, Naperville, IL 60563
Tel: 630-961-3900 *Toll Free Tel:* 800-43-BRIGHT (432-7444) *Fax:* 630-961-2168
E-mail: info@sourcebooks.com
Web Site: www.sourcebooks.com
Key Personnel
CEO & Publr, Sourcebooks: Dominique Raccah
Founded: 1996
Nonfiction books & current subjects include cooking, regional topics, humor & lifestyle books.
ISBN Prefix(es): 978-1-888952; 978-1-58182
Number of titles published annually: 60 Print
Total Titles: 240 Print
Membership(s): ABA; Independent Book Publishers Association; Southern Independent Booksellers Alliance

Cummings & Hathaway Publishers
395 Atlantic Ave, East Rockaway, NY 11518
Tel: 516-593-3607 *Fax:* 516-593-1401
Key Personnel
Pres: William Burke
Founded: 1980
Publish paperback books only.
ISBN Prefix(es): 978-1-57981; 978-0-943025
Number of titles published annually: 5 Print
Total Titles: 48 Print

CUNY Journalism Press
Division of CUNY Graduate School of Journalism
219 W 40 St, New York, NY 10018
Tel: 646-758-7824 *Fax:* 646-758-7809
Web Site: www.journalism.cuny.edu; press.journalism.cuny.edu
Founded: 2012
Publish serious books about journalism & the news media - history, theory, criticism, craft, memoirs & more.
ISBN Prefix(es): 978-1-939293
Number of titles published annually: 6 Print
Total Titles: 6 E-Book
Distributed by OR Books

§Cup of Tea Books
Imprint of PageSpring Publishing
PO Box 21133, Columbus, OH 43221
Tel: 614-264-5588
E-mail: sales@pagespringpublishing.com
Web Site: www.cupofteabooks.com
Key Personnel
Publr & Ed: Rebecca Seum
Founded: 2012
Independent publisher. Specialize in quality women's fiction.
ISBN Prefix(es): 978-1-939403
Number of titles published annually: 2 Print; 2 E-Book
Total Titles: 9 Print; 8 E-Book

Cycle Publishing LLC
1282 Seventh Ave, San Francisco, CA 94122-2526
Tel: 415-665-8214 *Fax:* 415-753-8572
Web Site: www.cyclepublishing.com
Key Personnel
Principal & Publr: Rob van der Plas *E-mail:* rvdp@vanderplas.net
Founded: 1997
Books on sports, fitness, home building & home buying; emphasis on cycling.
ISBN Prefix(es): 978-1-892495
Number of titles published annually: 3 Print
Total Titles: 30 Print
Imprints: Cycle Publishing; Van der Plas Publications
Foreign Rights: Bicycling (Australia); Fahrradbuch.de (Austria, Germany); Orca Book Services (UK)
Warehouse: PCFS, 35 Ash Dr, Kimball, MI 48074
Membership(s): The Association of Publishers for Special Sales; Independent Book Publishers Association

Cyclotour Guide Books
160 Harvard St, Rochester, NY 14607-3174
Tel: 585-244-6157
E-mail: cyclotour@cyclotour.com
Web Site: www.cyclotour.com
Key Personnel
Publr & Author: Harvey Botzman
Founded: 1993
Books, bicycling related, bicycle (cycling), travel guides.
Publisher is a member of the League of American Bicyclists, New York Bicycling Coalition & New York State Travel Industry Association (NYSTIA).
ISBN Prefix(es): 978-1-889602
Number of titles published annually: 4 Print
Total Titles: 5 Print

Cypress House
Imprint of Comp-Type Inc
155 Cypress St, Fort Bragg, CA 95437
Tel: 707-964-9520 *Toll Free Tel:* 800-773-7782 *Fax:* 707-964-7531
E-mail: cypresshouse@cypresshouse.com
Web Site: www.cypresshouse.com
Key Personnel
Pres: Cynthia Frank *E-mail:* cynthia@cypresshouse.com
Mng Ed: Joe Shaw *E-mail:* joeshaw@cypresshouse.com
ISBN Prefix(es): 978-1-879384
Number of titles published annually: 10 Print
Total Titles: 1 Audio
Imprints: Lost Coast Press; QED Press
Membership(s): ABA; Independent Book Publishers Association; Northern California Independent Booksellers Association; Pacific Northwest Booksellers Association

Dalkey Archive Press
University of Houston-Victoria, 3402 N Ben Wilson, Victoria, TX 77901
E-mail: contact@dalkeyarchive.com
Web Site: www.dalkeyarchive.com
Key Personnel
Dir: John O'Brien
Assoc Dir: Jake Snyder
Founded: 1984
Literary fiction, translations & criticism. We keep works of literary value in print.
ISBN Prefix(es): 978-0-916583; 978-1-56478; 978-1-62897; 978-1-943150
Number of titles published annually: 60 Print
Total Titles: 710 Print
Foreign Rep(s): Canadian Manda Group (Canada); John Toomey (Europe, UK & Commonwealth)
Distribution Center: Ingram Publisher Services, One Ingram Blvd, La Vergne, TN 37086 (worldwide exc Europe) *Toll Free Tel:* 866-400-5351 (orders)
Central Books Ltd, One Heath Park Industrial Estate, Freshwater Rd, Dagenham RM8 1RX, United Kingdom (Europe), Contact: Bill Norris *Tel:* (020) 8525 8800 *Fax:* (020) 8599 2694 *E-mail:* bill@centralbooks.com *Web Site:* www.centralbooks.com

Damron Co
PO Box 422458, San Francisco, CA 94142-2458
Tel: 415-255-0404 *Toll Free Tel:* 800-462-6654 *Fax:* 415-703-9049
E-mail: info@damron.com
Web Site: www.damron.com
Key Personnel
Mng Ed: Erika O'Connor *E-mail:* erika@damron.com
Founded: 1964
Annual travel guides.
ISBN Prefix(es): 978-0-929435
Number of titles published annually: 5 Print
Total Titles: 5 Print; 1 Online
Distribution Center: SCB Distributors, 15608 S New Century Dr, Gardena, CA 90248 *Tel:* 310-532-9400 *Toll Free Tel:* 800-729-6423 *Fax:* 310-532-7001 *E-mail:* scb@scbdistributors.com

Dancing Dakini Press
77 Morning Sun Dr, Sedona, AZ 86336
Tel: 928-852-0129
E-mail: editor@dancingdakinipress.com
Web Site: www.dancingdakinipress.com
Key Personnel
CEO: Robin Weeks *Tel:* 505-699-6044 *E-mail:* robin@dancingdakinipress.com
CFO: Ben Long *Tel:* 503-415-0229 *E-mail:* ben@benllong.com
Founded: 2012
Small publisher creating well-crafted books to inspire compassionate awareness, skillful means, authentic lives & a deep respect for all.
ISBN Prefix(es): 978-0-9836333
Number of titles published annually: 3 Print; 2 E-Book
Total Titles: 7 Print; 5 E-Book
Orders to: New Leaf Distribution Co, 401 Thornton Rd, Lithia Springs, GA 30122-1557, Contact: Lenora Whitmire *Tel:* 770-948-7845 *Fax:* 770-944-2313 *E-mail:* domestic@newleaf-dist.com

Returns: New Leaf Distribution Co, 401 Thornton Rd, Lithia Springs, GA 30122-1557, Contact: Lenora Whitmire *Tel:* 770-948-7845 *Fax:* 770-944-2313 *E-mail:* lwhitmire@newleaf-dist.com
Shipping Address: New Leaf Distribution Co, 401 Thornton Rd, Lithia Springs, GA 30122-1557 *Tel:* 770-948-7845 *Fax:* 770-944-2313
Warehouse: New Leaf Distribution Co, 401 Thornton Rd, Lithia Springs, GA 30122-1557 *Tel:* 770-948-7845 *Fax:* 770-944-2313
Distribution Center: New Leaf Distribution Co, 401 Thornton Rd, Lithia Springs, GA 30122-1557, Contact: Lenora Whitmire *Tel:* 770-948-7845 *Fax:* 770-944-2313 *E-mail:* lwhitmire@newleaf-dist.com

Dancing Lemur Press LLC
PO Box 383, Pikeville, NC 27863-0383
E-mail: inquiries@dancinglemurpressllc.com
Web Site: www.dancinglemurpressllc.com
Founded: 2008
We strive to publish works that uplift & inspire, encouraging the reader to explore & discover while remaining morally grounded. At the heart of our science fiction, mystery, new adult/young adult & fantasy lies positive relationship dynamics, optimistic attitudes & non-salacious material. Our nonfiction offers insightful information, uplifting ideas & real-life opportunities. Our goal is to provide hope for the reader's dreams & aspirations.
ISBN Prefix(es): 978-0-9816210; 978-0-9827139; 978-1-939844
Number of titles published annually: 5 Print; 6 E-Book
Total Titles: 20 Print; 22 E-Book
Imprints: Freedom Fox Press
Distribution Center: Ingram Content Group, One Ingram Blvd, La Vergne, TN 37086 (US) *Tel:* 615-793-5000 *Web Site:* www.ingramcontent.com

John Daniel & Co
Division of Daniel & Daniel Publishers Inc
PO Box 2790, McKinleyville, CA 95519-2790
SAN: 215-1995
Tel: 707-839-3495 *Toll Free Tel:* 800-662-8351 *Fax:* 707-839-3242
E-mail: dandd@danielpublishing.com
Web Site: www.danielpublishing.com
Key Personnel
Owner & Publr: John Daniel *E-mail:* john@danielpublishing.com
Owner & Sales Mgr: Susan Daniel *E-mail:* susan@danielpublishing.com
Founded: 1985
ISBN Prefix(es): 978-1-56474
Number of titles published annually: 5 Print
Total Titles: 200 Print
Branch Office(s)
2611 Kelly Ave, McKinleyville, CA 95519
Distributor for Fithian Press; Perseverance Press
Returns: 2611 Kelly Ave, McKinleyville, CA 95519
Distribution Center: SCB Distributors, 15608 S New Century Dr, Gardena, CA 90248, Contact: Aaron Silverman *Toll Free Tel:* 800-729-6423
Membership(s): Independent Book Publishers Association

§Dante University Press
PO Box 812158, Wellesley, MA 02482-0014
SAN: 220-150X
Tel: 781-235-3634
Web Site: www.danteuniversity.org/books
Founded: 1980
Italian Americana.
ISBN Prefix(es): 978-0-937832
Number of titles published annually: 7 Print
Distributed by Branden Publishing Co
Foreign Rep(s): Baker & Taylor (worldwide)
Foreign Rights: Gazelle Book Services Ltd (England)

Dark Horse Comics
Affiliate of Dark Horse Entertainment
10956 SE Main St, Milwaukie, OR 97222
Tel: 503-652-8815 *Fax:* 503-654-9440
E-mail: dhcomics@darkhorse.com
Web Site: www.darkhorse.com
Key Personnel
Founder & Pres: Michael Richardson
Head, Berger Books: Karen Berger
Online Mktg Mgr: Matt Parkinson
Founded: 1986
Primary area is graphic novels; pop culture; limited edition hardcovers & comics.
ISBN Prefix(es): 978-1-56971
Number of titles published annually: 200 Print
Total Titles: 600 Print
Imprints: Berger Books; Dark Horse Books
Distributed by LPC Group Inc
Foreign Rights: Anita Nelson
Distribution Center: Penguin Random House Publisher Services (PRHPS), 1745 Broadway, New York, NY 10019 *E-mail:* distribution@penguinrandomhouse.com

§The Dartnell Corporation
Subsidiary of Eli Research Inc
2222 Sedwick Dr, Durham, NC 27713
Toll Free Tel: 800-223-8720; 800-472-0148 (cust serv) *Toll Free Fax:* 800-508-2592
E-mail: customerservice@dartnellcorp.com
Web Site: www.dartnellcorp.com
Founded: 1916
Business information, training, motivation.
ISBN Prefix(es): 978-0-85013
Number of titles published annually: 20 Print
Total Titles: 150 Print

The Darwin Press Inc
PO Box 2202, Princeton, NJ 08543
SAN: 201-2987
Tel: 609-737-1349 *Fax:* 609-737-0929
E-mail: books@darwinpress.com
Web Site: www.darwinpress.com
Key Personnel
Publr & Mng Dir: Ed Breisacher
Founded: 1970
Natural & behavioral sciences; Near Eastern studies; technical, scientific, reference.
ISBN Prefix(es): 978-0-87850
Number of titles published annually: 5 Print
Total Titles: 70 Print
Imprints: Darwin® Books
Foreign Rep(s): Gazelle Book Services Ltd (Europe)

Data & Marketing Association (DMA)
Formerly Direct Marketing Association (DMA)
1333 Broadway, Suite 301, New York, NY 10018
SAN: 692-6487
Tel: 212-768-7277 *Fax:* 212-302-6714
E-mail: memberservices@the-dma.org
Web Site: thedma.org
Key Personnel
CEO: Thomas J Benton
Sr Dir, Memb Communs & Sr Ed: Susan Taplinger *Tel:* 212-790-1589
Dir, Educ & Prof Devt: Michelle Tiletnick
Founded: 1917
Directories, consumer guides, industry resource guides, statistical compilations, newsletter & council publications, quarterly magazine & electronic newsletter.
ISBN Prefix(es): 978-0-933641; 978-1-931361; 978-0-9817604; 978-0-9833791
Number of titles published annually: 5 Print
Total Titles: 5 Print
Branch Office(s)
1615 "L" St NW, Suite 1100, Washington, DC 20036 *Tel:* 202-955-5030 *Fax:* 202-955-0085

§Data Trace Publishing Co (DTP)
110 West Rd, Suite 227, Towson, MD 21204-2316
Mailing Address: PO Box 1239, Brooklandville, MD 21022-1239
Tel: 410-494-4994 *Toll Free Tel:* 800-342-0454 (orders only) *Fax:* 410-494-0515
E-mail: info@datatrace.com; salesandmarketing@datatrace.com; editorial@datatrace.com; info@datatrace.com
Web Site: www.datatrace.com
Key Personnel
VP, Edit & Client Servs: Kimberly Collignon
Dir, Mktg: Holly Ballard
Ad Mgr: Frank Tufariello
Founded: 1987
Full service specialty publisher with interest in science, technical, law & medicine.
ISBN Prefix(es): 978-0-9637468; 978-1-57400
Number of titles published annually: 20 Print; 25 E-Book
Total Titles: 125 Print; 15 CD-ROM; 30 Online; 15 E-Book
Foreign Rep(s): Eurospan (worldwide exc Canada & USA)

Daughters of St Paul, see Pauline Books & Media

May Davenport Publishers
26313 Purissima Rd, Los Altos Hills, CA 94022
Tel: 650-947-6499
E-mail: mdbooks@earthlink.net
Web Site: www.maydavenportpublishers.org
Key Personnel
Ed & Publr: May Davenport
Founded: 1975
Publish & distribute books for children/young adults (grades K-12). Books are written by teachers, writers, social workers, mental clinicians & counselors. We sell books by direct mail. Remainders are donated to schools in depressed areas who ask for free copies for their students to take home. The company originally created *Comic Tales* to read-aloud happy stories for children to color the illustrations. Titles include *Comic Tales Anthology No 1*, *Pogo Sticks* by Andrea Ross plus two others, *Comic Tales No 2* by five authors, *The Runaway Game* by Kevin Casey, *A Time to Fantasize* by May Davenport, *Windriders* by Blake F Grant & *Comic Tales No 3* by 31 authors.
ISBN Prefix(es): 978-0-9603118; 978-0-943864; 978-0-9794140
Number of titles published annually: 3 Print; 8 Online
Total Titles: 32 Print; 32 Online
Imprints: Md Books

Davies-Black Publishing
53 State St, Boston, MA 02109
Tel: 617-523-3801 *Fax:* 617-523-3708
E-mail: info@nicholasbrealey.com
Web Site: www.nicholasbrealey.com
Key Personnel
Head: Janet Crockett
Dir, Prodn: Jennifer Delaney
Sales Mgr: Melissa Carl
Founded: 1995
Book publishing in leadership & management, organization development, human resources & career management.
ISBN Prefix(es): 978-0-89106
Number of titles published annually: 12 Print
Total Titles: 120 Print
Foreign Rep(s): Bacchus Books CC (South Africa); Cengage Learning Asia (Asia-Pacific);

Cengage Learning India (India); Eurospan Group (Europe, Middle East, North Africa, UK); NBN Canada (Canada); NBN/Central Book Services (Australia, New Zealand)
Orders to: National Book Network, 15200 NBN Way, Blue Ridge Summit, PA 17214 *Toll Free Tel:* 800-462-6420
Warehouse: 1150 Hamilton Ct, Menlo Park, CA 94025
Distribution Center: National Book Network, 15200 NBN Way, Blue Ridge Summit, PA 17214 *Toll Free Tel:* 800-462-6420
Membership(s): BISG; Independent Book Publishers Association

The Davies Group Publishers
PO Box 440140, Aurora, CO 80044-0140
Tel: 303-750-8374 *Fax:* 303-337-0952
E-mail: info@thedaviesgrouppublishers.com; daviesgroup@msn.com (orders)
Web Site: www.thedaviesgrouppublishers.com
Key Personnel
Ed: Victor E Taylor
Founded: 1991
Scholarly publisher; philosophy, humanities & social sciences.
ISBN Prefix(es): 978-1-888570; 978-0-9630076; 978-1-934542; 978-1-935790; 978-1-943047
Number of titles published annually: 3 Print; 10 E-Book
Total Titles: 85 Print; 85 E-Book
Imprints: Noesis Press; PenMark Press

§Davies Publishing Inc
32 S Raymond Ave, Suites 4 & 5, Pasadena, CA 91105-1961
SAN: 217-3255
Tel: 626-792-3046 *Toll Free Tel:* 877-792-0005 *Fax:* 626-792-5308
E-mail: info@daviespublishing.com
Web Site: daviespublishing.com
Key Personnel
Pres & Publr: Michael Davies *E-mail:* mikedavies@daviespublishing.com
Edit Dir: Christina Moose *E-mail:* chrismoose@daviespublishing.com
Corp Secy & Opers Mgr: Janet Heard *E-mail:* janetheard@daviespublishing.com
Prodn Mgr: Charlene Locke *E-mail:* charlenelocke@daviespublishing.com
Digital Media Specialist: Dan Liota *E-mail:* danliota@daviespublishing.com
Founded: 1981
Ultrasound education & test preparation: books, software, DVDs, mock examinations & flashcards.
ISBN Prefix(es): 978-0-941022
Number of titles published annually: 8 Print; 2 CD-ROM
Total Titles: 48 Print; 6 CD-ROM
Membership(s): AAP; Independent Book Publishers Association

§F A Davis Co
1915 Arch St, Philadelphia, PA 19103
SAN: 200-2078
Tel: 215-568-2270; 215-440-3001 *Toll Free Tel:* 800-523-4049 *Fax:* 215-568-5065; 215-440-3016
E-mail: info@fadavis.com; orders@fadavis.com
Web Site: www.fadavis.com
Key Personnel
Chmn of the Bd: Robert H Craven, Sr
Pres: Robert H Craven, Jr
SVP: Judith Illov Neely
VP & CFO: Robert B Schenck
Exec Dir, Sales: Neil K Kelly
Dir, HR: Crystal Spraggins
Publr: Joanne DaCunha; Lisa Deitch; Robert Martone
Ed-in-Chief, Nursing: Jean Rodenberger
Founded: 1879
Publisher of nursing, medical & health profession texts, podcasts & clinical simulations.
ISBN Prefix(es): 978-0-8036
Number of titles published annually: 75 Print; 1 Online; 65 E-Book; 5 Audio
Total Titles: 399 Print; 150 E-Book; 10 Audio
Distribution Center: 404 N Second St, Philadelphia, PA 19123, Gen Mgr: John Lancaster *Tel:* 215-440-3001 *Toll Free Tel:* 800-323-3555 (orders, cust serv, returns) *Fax:* 215-440-3016

§DAW Books Inc
Imprint of Penguin Group USA, A Penguin Random House Company
375 Hudson St, New York, NY 10014
SAN: 282-5074
Tel: 212-366-2096 *Fax:* 212-366-2090
E-mail: daw@penguinrandomhouse.com
Web Site: www.dawbooks.com; www.penguin.com; www.penguinrandomhouse.com
Key Personnel
Publr: Sheila E Gilbert; Elizabeth R Wollheim
Submission Ed: Peter Stampfel *E-mail:* submissions@us.penguingroup.com
Founded: 1971
Science fiction; fantasy; paperbound originals & reprints; hardcover editions, trade paperbacks & ebooks.
ISBN Prefix(es): 978-0-8099; 978-0-88677; 978-0-7564
Number of titles published annually: 60 Print; 60 E-Book
Total Titles: 325 Print
Imprints: DAW/Fantasy; DAW/Fiction; DAW/Science Fiction
Distributed by Penguin Group USA, A Penguin Random House Company

The Dawn Horse Press
Division of Avataric Pan-Communion of Adidam
10336 Loch Lomond Rd, No 305, Middletown, CA 95461
Tel: 707-928-6590 *Toll Free Tel:* 877-770-0772 *Fax:* 707-928-6590
E-mail: dhp@adidam.org
Web Site: www.dawnhorsepress.com
Key Personnel
Publr: Neil Panico *E-mail:* npanico@adidam.org
Founded: 1972
Produces & markets books, CDs & AV materials on every aspect of authentic spiritual life & human development based upon the wisdom & teaching of Avatar Adi Da Samraj.
ISBN Prefix(es): 978-0-913922; 978-0-918801; 978-0-918801; 978-1-57097; 978-0-929929
Number of titles published annually: 8 Print; 8 CD-ROM; 12 Online; 4 Audio
Total Titles: 49 Print; 19 CD-ROM; 65 Online; 1 E-Book; 33 Audio
Shipping Address: 12312 Hwy 175, Cobb Mountain, CA 95426, Contact: Patrick Forristal
Distribution Center: New Leaf Distributing Co, 401 Thorton Rd, Lithia Springs, GA 30122-1557 *Tel:* 770-948-7845 *Fax:* 770-944-2313 *E-mail:* newleaf@newleaf-dist.com *Web Site:* www.newleaf-dist.com
Membership(s): Independent Book Publishers Association

Dawn Publications Inc
12402 Bitney Springs Rd, Nevada City, CA 95959
Tel: 530-274-7775 *Toll Free Tel:* 800-545-7475 *Fax:* 530-274-7778
E-mail: nature@dawnpub.com; orders@dawnpub.com
Web Site: www.dawnpub.com
Key Personnel
Publr & Ed: Glenn Hovemann *E-mail:* glenn@dawnpub.com
Art Dir & Publr: Muffy Weaver *E-mail:* muffy@dawnpub.com
Mktg Dir: Bruce Malnor *E-mail:* bruce@dawnpub.com
Founded: 1979
Nature awareness nonfiction picture books for children, teachers, naturalists & parents; character value education; natural science.
ISBN Prefix(es): 978-0-916124; 978-1-883220; 978-1-58469
Number of titles published annually: 6 Print; 6 E-Book
Total Titles: 95 Print; 75 E-Book
Foreign Rep(s): Deep Books Ltd (UK); Fitzhenry & Whiteside (Canada); SULA Book Distributors (South Africa)
Membership(s): ABA; APPL; Independent Book Publishers Association; Publishers Association of the West

DawnSignPress
6130 Nancy Ridge Dr, San Diego, CA 92121-3223
Tel: 858-625-0600 *Toll Free Tel:* 800-549-5350 *Fax:* 858-625-2336
E-mail: contactus@dawnsign.com
Web Site: www.dawnsign.com
Key Personnel
Founder & Pres: Joe Dannis
Mktg & Lib Sales Dir: Becky Ryan
Founded: 1979
Specialty publisher of instructional sign language & educational deaf studies materials for both children & adults.
ISBN Prefix(es): 978-0-915035; 978-1-58121
Number of titles published annually: 5 Print
Total Titles: 65 Print; 1 CD-ROM
Distributed by Gryphon House
Distributor for Gallaudet University Press; MIT Press; Penguin Random House Inc
Foreign Rights: Gloval Interprint (Hong Kong)

Day Owl Press Corp
201 W Ocean Ave, Unit 3574, Lantana, FL 33465
Mailing Address: PO Box 3574, Lantana, FL 33465
Toll Free Tel: 888-806-6981 *Toll Free Fax:* 866-854-4375
E-mail: info@dayowl.net
Web Site: www.dayowl.net
Key Personnel
Pres: Carolyn Clay
Founded: 2011
Independent publisher of offbeat unusual new works. Interested in books that are new, funny, intelligent, prophetical, unconventional, controversial, cutting edge, innovative, radical, Christian, revolutionary +/or otherwise atypical.
ISBN Prefix(es): 978-1-940401
Number of titles published annually: 30 Print; 30 Online; 30 E-Book; 5 Audio
Total Titles: 37 Print; 37 Online; 37 E-Book; 5 Audio
Membership(s): Independent Book Publishers Association

dbS Productions
PO Box 94, Charlottesville, VA 22902
Tel: 434-293-5502 *Toll Free Tel:* 800-745-1581 *Fax:* 434-293-5502
E-mail: info@dbs-sar.com
Web Site: www.dbs-sar.com
Key Personnel
CEO & Sr Scientist: Robert J Koester *E-mail:* robert@dbs-sar.com
Founded: 1989
Search & rescue.
ISBN Prefix(es): 978-1-879471
Number of titles published annually: 5 Print; 1 CD-ROM
Total Titles: 15 Print; 2 CD-ROM
Distributed by CMC

DC Entertainment
Division of Warner Bros Entertainment Co
2900 Alameda, Burbank, CA 91505
Toll Free Tel: 800-887-6789
E-mail: dccomics@cambeywest.com
Web Site: www.dcentertainment.com; www.dccomics.com; www.madmag.com
Key Personnel
Chief Creative Offr: Geoff Johns
Pres: Diane Nelson
EVP, Busn & Mktg Strategy, Direct to Consumer & Global Franchise Mgmt: Amit Desai
Co-Publr: Dan Didio; Jim Lee
Ed, Vertigo: Ellie Pyle
Founded: 1935
Innovative comics publishing in periodical & book formats. In addition to the world's most popular superheroes, Superman, Batman & Wonder Woman, DC publishes cutting edge fantasy, horror, mystery, adventure, humor, nonfiction & general interest titles & maintains a 500+ title backlist in print. *MAD* Books is based on the classic magazine featuring Alfred E Neuman, Spy vs Spy & other icons. DC/MAD properties are also licensed for various publishing formats, as well as media, promotions & consumer products. DC Comics does not accept unsol mss. For more information, visit our web site at www.dcentertainment.com.
ISBN Prefix(es): 978-0-930289; 978-1-56389; 978-1-4012
Number of titles published annually: 240 Print
Total Titles: 2,778 Print
Imprints: DC Comics; DC Nation; MAD Books; Vertigo
Distribution Center: Penguin Random House Publisher Services (PRHPS), 1745 Broadway, New York, NY 10019 *E-mail:* distribution@randomhouse.com

§Walter De Gruyter Inc
Division of Walter de Gruyter GmbH & Co KG
125 Pearl St, 3rd fl, Boston, MA 02110
Tel: 857-284-7073 *Fax:* 857-284-7358
E-mail: service@degruyter.com
Web Site: www.degruyter.com
Key Personnel
VP, De Gruyter Americas: Paul Manning
Founded: 1749
Scholarly & scientific books, journals, paperbacks & hardcover reprints.
ISBN Prefix(es): 978-0-311; 978-0-89925; 978-3-11; 978-1-56445; 978-1-934078; 978-1-61451; 978-1-5015
Number of titles published annually: 200 Print; 5 CD-ROM
Total Titles: 8,500 Print; 20 CD-ROM; 15 Online; 10 E-Book
Foreign Office(s): Walter de Gruyter GmbH & Co KG, Genthinerstr 13, 10785 Berlin, Germany *Tel:* (030) 260 05 0 *Fax:* (030) 260 05 251 *E-mail:* info@degruyter.com
Foreign Rep(s): Allied Publishers (India, Nepal, Sri Lanka); Book Club International (Bangladesh); Combined Representatives Worldwide Inc (Philippines); D A Books & Journals (Australia, New Zealand); Verlags und Kommissionsbuchhandlung Dr Franz Hain (Austria); Kumi Trading (South Korea); Kweilin Bookstore (Taiwan); Maruzen Co Ltd (Japan); Pak Book Corp (Pakistan); Parry's Book Center (Sendjrjan Berhad) (Brunei, Malaysia, Singapore); Swinden Book Co Ltd (Hong Kong)
Orders to: TriLiteral, 100 Maple Ridge Dr, Cumberland, RI 02864 *Tel:* 401-531-2800 *Toll Free Tel:* 800-405-1619 *Fax:* 401-531-2801 *Toll Free Fax:* 800-406-9145 *E-mail:* orders@triliteral.org

§Deep River Books LLC
PO Box 310, Sisters, OR 97759
Tel: 541-549-1139
E-mail: info@deepriverbooks.com
Web Site: deepriverbooks.com
Key Personnel
Publr: Bill Carmichael; Nancie Carmichael
Founded: 2001
Publisher of Christian/inspirational books.
This publisher has indicated that 70% of their product line is author subsidized.
ISBN Prefix(es): 978-1-940269; 978-1-63269
Number of titles published annually: 40 Print; 40 E-Book
Total Titles: 500 Print; 300 E-Book
Imprints: Deep River Books; Fish Pond; Trusted Books; WaterLife Books
Orders to: Bookmasters, 30 Amberwood Pkwy, Ashland, OH 44805 *Tel:* 419-281-5100 *Toll Free Tel:* 800-537-6727 *Fax:* 419-281-0200 *Web Site:* www.bookmasters.com
Returns: Bookmasters, 30 Amberwood Pkwy, Ashland, OH 44805 *Tel:* 419-281-5100 *Toll Free Tel:* 800-537-6727 *Fax:* 419-281-0200 *Web Site:* www.bookmasters.com
Distribution Center: Bookmasters, 30 Amberwood Pkwy, Ashland, OH 44805 *Tel:* 419-281-5100 *Toll Free Tel:* 800-537-6727 *Fax:* 419-281-0200 *Web Site:* www.bookmasters.com
Membership(s): Evangelical Christian Publishers Association

Delphinium Books
PO Box 703, Harrison, NY 10528
Tel: 917-301-7496 (e-mail first)
E-mail: contactform@delphiniumbooks.com
Web Site: www.delphiniumbooks.com
Founded: 1986
ISBN Prefix(es): 978-1-883285
Number of titles published annually: 5 Print; 5 E-Book; 5 Audio
Total Titles: 45 Print; 30 E-Book; 7 Audio
Distributed by HarperCollins
Foreign Rights: David Marshall (worldwide exc Canada)

§Demos Medical Publishing
Division of Springer Publishing Co
11 W 42 St, 15th fl, New York, NY 10036
Tel: 212-683-0072
E-mail: info@demosmedpub.com; orderdept@demosmedical.com; editorial@demosmedical.com
Web Site: www.demosmedical.com
Key Personnel
Publr: Beth Barry *E-mail:* bbarry@demosmedical.com
Spec Sales & Foreign Rts: Reina Santana
Founded: 1985
Publish medical & nursing text & patient education titles in trade paperback.
ISBN Prefix(es): 978-1-888799; 978-0-939957; 978-1-932603; 978-1-933864; 978-1-934559; 978-1-935281; 978-1-936287; 978-1-936303; 978-1-61705; 978-1-62070
Number of titles published annually: 40 Print; 2 CD-ROM
Total Titles: 150 Print; 2 CD-ROM; 100 E-Book
Imprints: Demos Health
Foreign Rep(s): Cranbury International LLC (Caribbean, Latin America); Eurospan Group (Africa, Brunei, Cambodia, China, Europe, Hong Kong, Indonesia, Korea, Malaysia, Middle East, Philippines, Singapore, Taiwan, Thailand, UK, Vietnam); Footprint Books Pty Ltd (Australia, Fiji, New Zealand); Taylor & Francis Books Pvt Ltd (Ritesh Kumar) (India, South Asia)
Membership(s): AAP

§Deseret Book Co
Subsidiary of Deseret Management Corp
57 W South Temple, Salt Lake City, UT 84101-1511
SAN: 201-3185
Mailing Address: PO Box 30178, Salt Lake City, UT 84130
Tel: 801-517-3369 *Toll Free Tel:* 800-453-4532 (orders); 888-846-7302 (orders) *Fax:* 801-517-3126
E-mail: service@deseretbook.com
Web Site: www.deseretbook.com
Key Personnel
CEO & Pres: Sheri L Dew
Publr: Lisa Mangum *E-mail:* lmangum@deseretbook.com
Founded: 1886
Juveniles & young adults, trade paperbacks; fiction, general nonfiction, religion (Mormon).
ISBN Prefix(es): 978-0-87747; 978-1-59038; 978-1-57345; 978-0-87579; 978-1-60908; 978-1-60641; 978-1-60907; 978-1-62972; 978-1-62973
Number of titles published annually: 150 Print
Total Titles: 1,100 Print; 1 CD-ROM; 120 Audio
Imprints: Deseret Book; Ensign Peak; Shadow Mountain
Shipping Address: 2240 W 1500 S, Salt Lake City, UT 84104 *Tel:* 801-517-3285 *Fax:* 801-972-4823

§DEStech Publications Inc
439 N Duke St, Lancaster, PA 17602-4967
Tel: 717-290-1660 *Toll Free Tel:* 877-500-4337 *Fax:* 717-509-6100
E-mail: info@destechpub.com
Web Site: www.destechpub.com
Key Personnel
Pres: Anthony Deraco *E-mail:* aderaco@destechpub.com
Edit Dir: Dr Joseph Eckenrode *E-mail:* jeckenrode@destechpub.com
Prodn Dir: Stephen Spangler *E-mail:* sspangler@destechpub.com
Mktg Mgr: Michael T Hauck *E mail:* mhauck@destechpub.com
Founded: 2001
Science, technical & medical publisher; proceedings publishing.
ISBN Prefix(es): 978-1-605950
Number of titles published annually: 12 Print; 5 CD-ROM; 2 Online; 5 E-Book
Total Titles: 135 Print; 10 E-Book
Foreign Rep(s): Areesh Education & Trading Sdn Bhd (Malaysia); CRW Marketing Services for Publishers Inc (American Samoa, Guam, Philippines, Virgin Islands); DKG Info Systems (China, Hong Kong, Indonesia, Japan, Malaysia, Singapore, South Korea, Taiwan, Thailand); LSR Libros Servicios y Representaciones (Caribbean, Central America, Mexico, South America); Publisher's Representatives (Pakistan); Shankars Book Agency Pvt Ltd (India); Transatlantic Publishers Group Ltd (Europe, Middle East, North Africa, UK)

§Destiny Image Inc
Subsidiary of Nori Media Group
167 Walnut Bottom Rd, Shippensburg, PA 17257-0310
SAN: 253-4339
Mailing Address: PO Box 310, Shippensburg, PA 17257-0310
Tel: 717-532-3040 *Toll Free Tel:* 800-722-6774 (orders only) *Fax:* 717-532-9291
Web Site: www.destinyimage.com
Key Personnel
Pres & CEO: Don Nori
Founded: 1983
Publisher of Christian books.
ISBN Prefix(es): 978-0-914903; 978-1-56043; 978-0-938612; 978-0-7684
Number of titles published annually: 60 Print
Total Titles: 1,500 Print

Foreign Rep(s): Koorong (Australia)
Membership(s): ABA; CBA: The Association for Christian Retail; Evangelical Christian Publishers Association

Development Concepts Inc, see Impact Publications/Development Concepts Inc

DeVorss & Co
553 Constitution Ave, Camarillo, CA 93012-8510
SAN: 168-9886
Mailing Address: PO Box 1389, Camarillo, CA 93011-1389
Tel: 805-322-9010 *Toll Free Tel:* 800-843-5743 *Fax:* 805-322-9011
E-mail: service@devorss.com
Web Site: www.devorss.com
Key Personnel
Pres: Gary R Peattie *Tel:* 805-322-9010 ext 14 *E-mail:* gpeattie@devorss.com
Off & Cust Serv Mgr: Debbie Krovitz *E-mail:* dkrovitz@devorss.com
Buyer: Sonia Dominguez *E-mail:* sdominguez@devorss.com
Founded: 1929
Publisher & distributor of metaphysical, spiritual, inspirational, self-help, body/mind/spirit & new thought books & sidelines since 1929.
ISBN Prefix(es): 978-0-87516
Number of titles published annually: 10 Print
Total Titles: 270 Print; 85 E-Book; 4 Audio
Distributor for Acropolis Books (Joel S Goldsmith titles); Touch for Health; White Eagle Publishing Trust (England)
Foreign Rep(s): Brumby Books (Australia); Deep Books (UK); Dempsey Canada (Canada); New Horizons (South Africa)
Billing Address: PO Box 1389, Camarillo, CA 93011-1389

§Dewey Publications Inc
1840 Wilson Blvd, Suite 203, Arlington, VA 22201
SAN: 694-1451
Tel: 703-524-1355 *Fax:* 703-524-1463
E-mail: deweypublications@gmail.com
Web Site: www.deweypub.com
Key Personnel
Owner & Author: Peter Broida
Busn Mgr: Karen Troutman
Founded: 1984
ISBN Prefix(es): 978-1-878810; 978-1-932612
Number of titles published annually: 8 Print; 4 CD-ROM; 8 E-Book
Total Titles: 36 Print; 8 CD-ROM; 36 E-Book; 5 Audio

Dharma Publishing
35788 Hauser Bridge Rd, Cazadero, CA 95421
SAN: 201-2723
Tel: 707-847-3717 *Toll Free Tel:* 800-873-4276 *Fax:* 707-847-3380
E-mail: contact@dharmapublishing.com; customerservice@dharmapublishing.com
Web Site: www.dharmapublishing.com
Key Personnel
Mng Dir: Arnaud Maitland
Sales Dir: Rima Tamar *Tel:* 707-847-3717 ext 210 *E-mail:* rimat@dharmapublishing.com
Founded: 1971
Asian art, Eastern philosophy & psychology, Tibetan meditation & yoga, scholarly, history, biography, cosmology, juveniles, Asian culture.
ISBN Prefix(es): 978-0-913546; 978-0-89800
Number of titles published annually: 10 Print; 6 E-Book; 36 Audio
Total Titles: 120 Print; 12 E-Book; 48 Audio
Sales Office(s): 2210 Harold Way, Berkeley, CA 94704 *Tel:* 510-809-1540
Foreign Rep(s): Ka-Nying (India, Nepal); Nyingma Centrum Nederland (Netherlands); Nyingma Do Brazil (Brazil); Nyingma Gemeinschaft (Germany); Windhorse (Australia); Wisdom Publications (UK)
Membership(s): AAP

Dial Books for Young Readers
Imprint of Penguin Group USA, A Penguin Random House Company
345 Hudson St, New York, NY 10014
SAN: 282-5074
Tel: 212-366-2000 *Toll Free Tel:* 800-733-3000 (orders) *Fax:* 212-414-3396
Web Site: www.penguin.com
Key Personnel
Pres & Publr, Dial: Lauri Hornik
VP & Publr, Kathy Dawson Books: Kathy Dawson
Assoc Publr & Exec Mng Ed: Steve Meltzer
Edit Dir, Dial: Namrata Tripathi
Sr Ed: Katherine Harrison; Lucia Monfried
Ed: Jessica Garrison
Founded: 1961
ISBN Prefix(es): 978-0-8037
Number of titles published annually: 70 Print
Total Titles: 383 Print

Diane Publishing Co
330 Pusey Ave, Suite 3 (rear), Collingdale, PA 19023-0617
Mailing Address: PO Box 617, Darby, PA 19023-0617
Tel: 610-461-6200 *Toll Free Tel:* 800-782-3833 *Fax:* 610-461-6130
Web Site: www.dianepublishing.net
Key Personnel
Pres & Publr: Herman Baron
VP, Edit: Dorothy Perkins
Mgr, Opers & Technol: Curtis Fisher *E-mail:* cfisher@dianepublishing.net
Founded: 1987
Publishes & repackages over 45,000 books, documents & reports in law enforcement, intelligence, security, military, education, biotechnology, medicine & health & high-technology. Most titles were originally prepared by US government agencies. Also distributes 9,000 nonfiction remainder books.
ISBN Prefix(es): 978-0-941375; 978-1-56806; 978-0-7881; 978-0-7567; 978-1-4223; 978-1-4289; 978-1-4379; 978-1-4578
Number of titles published annually: 200 Print
Total Titles: 30,000 Print; 10,000 E-Book
Distributor for Academy of Natural Sciences; American Philosophical Society; American Swedish Historical Museum; Augustinian Press; Chemical Heritage Foundation; Christ Church-Philadelphia; Friends of University of Princeton; Geneological Society of Pennsylvania; Library Company of Philadelphia; University of Pennsylvania Libraries

Direct Marketing Association (DMA), see Data & Marketing Association (DMA)

DiscoverNet Publishing
Division of DiscoverNet
2474 Walnut St, Suite 105, Cary, NC 27518
Tel: 919-301-0109 *Fax:* 919-557-2261
E-mail: info@discovernet.com
Web Site: www.discovernet.com
Founded: 2002
ISBN Prefix(es): 978-0-9728053; 978-0-9742787; 978-0-9746943; 978-1-932813
Number of titles published annually: 50 Print; 45 Online; 45 E-Book
Total Titles: 140 Print; 130 Online; 130 E-Book

§Discovery House Publishers
Division of Our Daily Bread Ministries
3000 Kraft Ave SE, Grand Rapids, MI 49512
Mailing Address: PO Box 3566, Grand Rapids, MI 49501-3566
Tel: 616-942-2803 *Toll Free Tel:* 800-653-8333 (cust serv)
E-mail: support@dhp.org
Web Site: www.dhp.org
Key Personnel
Publr: Carol Holquist
Mng Ed: Judy Markham
Founded: 1987
Religious trade books; audio CDs (recorded music); DVDs.
ISBN Prefix(es): 978-0-929239; 978-1-57293
Number of titles published annually: 12 Print; 1 Audio
Total Titles: 3 CD-ROM; 150 Online; 1 Audio
Membership(s): CBA: The Association for Christian Retail; Evangelical Christian Publishers Association

Disney-Hyperion Books
Imprint of Disney Book Group
1101 Flower St, Glendale, CA 91201
Web Site: books.disney.com
Key Personnel
Dir, Ed-in-Chief & Assoc Publr: Emily Meehan
Ed-at-Large: Stephanie Owens Lurie
Exec Ed: Tracey Kevin; Rotem Moscovich
Mng Ed: Sara Liebling
Sr Ed: Kieran Viola; Laura Schreiber
Assoc Ed: Julie Rosenberg
Asst Ed: Hannah Allaman
Publg Coord: Liz Usuriello
Lead Designer: Marci Senders
Sr Mgr, Design: Joann Hill
Sr Designer: Maria Elias; Tyler Nevins
Designer: Phil Caminiti
Founded: 1991
Publish high quality picture books, young adult fiction & nonfiction.
ISBN Prefix(es): 978-0-7868
Number of titles published annually: 250 Print
Total Titles: 2,200 Print
Imprints: Michael di Capua Books; Jump at the Sun; Rick Riordan Presents; Volo
Foreign Rep(s): Little, Brown Canada Ltd; Little, Brown International
Foreign Rights: ACER Agencia Literaria (Spain); Big Apple Agency Inc (China); BMSR Agencia Literaria (Brazil); The English Agency (Japan) Ltd (Japan); Harris/Elon Agency (Israel); The Italian Literary Agency SRL (Italy); Jacqueline Miller (France); Sebes & Bisseling (Netherlands)
Membership(s): The Children's Book Council
See separate listing for:
Jump at the Sun

Disney Press
Division of The Walt Disney Co
1101 Flower St, Glendale, CA 91201
Web Site: books.disney.com
Key Personnel
Edit Dir: Wendy Lefkon
Dir, Subs Rts: Molly Kong
Exec Ed: Nachie Marsham
Sr Ed: Brooke Dworkin
Founded: 1990
Publish fiction & fantasy.
ISBN Prefix(es): 978-1-56282; 978-0-7868
Number of titles published annually: 55 Print
Total Titles: 1,000 Print
Distributed by Hachette Book Group (USA)
Foreign Rep(s): Little, Brown Canada Ltd; Little, Brown International
Foreign Rights: ACER Agencia Literaria (Spain); Big Apple Agency Inc (China); BMSR Agencia Literaria (Brazil); The English Agency Ltd (Japan); Harris/Elon Agency (Israel); A M Heath & Co Ltd (England); Monica Heyum Agency (Denmark, Finland, Iceland, Norway, Sweden); The Italian Literary Agency SRL (Italy); Michele Lapautre (France); Sebes & Bisseling (Netherlands)
Warehouse: 53 State St, Boston, MA 02109

Disney Publishing Worldwide
Subsidiary of The Walt Disney Co
1101 Flower St, Glendale, CA 91201
Web Site: books.disney.com
Key Personnel
Pres, Disney Consumer Prods: James Pitaro
EVP: Andrew Sugerman
VP & Publr, DBG Global: Mary Ann Naples
SVP Fin, IT & Global Opers: Raj Murari
VP, Digital Media: Yves Saada
VP, Publg Opers: Terry Downes
Publicity Dir: Seale Ballenger
Publicity Mgr: Mary Ann Zissimos
Mng Ed: Sara Liebling
Founded: 1930
Publisher of children's books, comics & magazines.
ISBN Prefix(es): 978-1-56115
Number of titles published annually: 275 Print
Total Titles: 1,000 Print
Imprints: Disney Editions; Disney-Hyperion; Disney Lucasfilm Press; Disney Press; Freeform; Hyperion Books for Children; Jump at the Sun; Kingswell; Marvel
Divisions: Disney Children's Book Group
Branch Office(s)
500 S Buena Vista St, Burbank, CA 91521
Tel: 914-288-4100
Foreign Rights: Sebes & Bisseling (Netherlands)

Dissertation.com
Imprint of Universal-Publishers Inc
23331 Water Circle, Boca Raton, FL 33486-8540
SAN: 299-3635
Tel: 561-750-4344 *Toll Free Tel:* 800-636-8329 *Fax:* 561-750-6797
Web Site: www.dissertation.com
Key Personnel
Publr & CEO: Dr Jeffrey Young
Artistic & Edit Dir: Shereen Siddiqui
Prodn Ed: Christie Mayer
Founded: 1997
Academic books.
ISBN Prefix(es): 978-1-58112; 978-0-9658564; 978-1-59942; 978-1-61233; 978-1-62734
Number of titles published annually: 50 Print; 50 Online; 50 E-Book
Total Titles: 300 Print; 300 Online; 300 E-Book
Distributed by Bertrams UK

Diversion Books
443 Park Ave S, Suite 1008, New York, NY 10016
Tel: 212-961-6390
E-mail: info@diversionbooks.com
Web Site: www.diversionbooks.com
Key Personnel
Co-Founder: Charles Platkin
Co-Founder & CEO: Scott Waxman
Publr: Jaime Levine
Sr Acqs Ed: Laura Duane
Sr Ed: Keith Wallman
Acqs Ed, EverAfter Romance: Caroline Acebo
Ed: Lia Ottaviano
Publicist: Christine Saunders
Founded: 2010
An innovative indie publisher, combining decades of traditional experience with new, digital strategies. In publishing a mix of original titles & giving old titles a digital life, our high royalties, quick turnaround & tailored marketing plans are helping us to create a space between legacy publishing & the uneven field of self-publishing. We are taking advantage of the abundance of opportunities that new models of distribution & purchasing provide, while executing our core publishing capabilities, ultimately connecting great books with avid readers.
ISBN Prefix(es): 978-0-9845151; 978-0-9829050; 978-0-9838395; 978-0-9839885; 978-0-9833371; 978-1-938120
Number of titles published annually: 50 Print; 350 E-Book
Total Titles: 50 Print; 1,000 E-Book
Distributor for Zubaan Books
Foreign Rights: Craig Literary (Jessica Craig) (worldwide)
Distribution Center: Ingram Publisher Services, One Ingram Blvd, La Vergne, TN 37086 *Toll Free Tel:* 866-400-5351 (orders)
Membership(s): AAP; Independent Book Publishers Association; International Thriller Writers Inc; Media Women's Association

DK Publishing
Division of Penguin Group USA, A Penguin Random House Company
345 Hudson St, 2nd fl, New York, NY 10014
Tel: 646-674-4000 *Toll Free Tel:* 877-342-5357 (cust serv); 800-733-3000
Web Site: www.dk.com; www.penguin.com
Key Personnel
VP, Dir, Fin & Opers: Simon Fraser
VP, Mktg & Publicity: Rachel Kempster
VP, Sales, Mktg & Publicity: Mary Marotta
VP, Publg: Brandi Larsen
VP, Sales: Tom Korman
Global Publr: Alex Allan
Edit Dir, Children's: Nancy Ellwood
Dir, Opers: Sheila Phelan
Assoc Dir, Publicity: Julia O'Halloran
Mktg Mgr, Licensing & Children's: Kell Wilson
Asst Mktg Mgr: Kathleen Quinlan
Assoc Sales Mgr, Digital, Premium & Custom: Ana Giovinazzo
Sales Coord, Online & Digital Sales: Kathi Gadow
Founded: 1974 (in UK)
Illustrated reference books on a wide range of topics for adults & children, including travel, health, history, sports, pets, atlases, dictionaries, music, art, decorating, astrology, sex & cooking.
ISBN Prefix(es): 978-1-879431; 978-1-56458; 978-0-7894; 978-0-7566
Number of titles published annually: 392 Print
Total Titles: 1,850 Print
Imprints: Prima Games
Subsidiaries: Alpha Books
Foreign Rep(s): Dorling Kindersley Ltd (UK)
Advertising Agency: Spier NY
Membership(s): ABA; ALA; The Children's Book Council; International Association of Culinary Professionals; International Literacy Association; National Council of Teachers of English; National Science Teachers Association
See separate listing for:
Alpha Books
Prima Games

Caitlyn Dlouhy Books, see Simon & Schuster Children's Publishing

Do It Now Foundation
PO Box 27568, Tempe, AZ 85285-7568
Tel: 480-736-0599 *Fax:* 480-736-0771
E-mail: e-mail@doitnow.org; orders@doitnow.org
Web Site: www.doitnow.org
Key Personnel
Exec & Creative Dir: Jim Parker
Founded: 1968
Drugs, alcohol & health.
ISBN Prefix(es): 978-0-89230
Number of titles published annually: 50 Print
Total Titles: 150 Print

§Dogwise Publishing
Division of Direct Book Service Inc
403 S Mission St, Wenatchee, WA 98801
SAN: 132-9545
Tel: 509-663-9115 *Toll Free Tel:* 800-776-2665
E-mail: mail@dogwise.com
Web Site: www.dogwise.com
Key Personnel
Owner & Publr: Charlene Woodward
Owner: Larry Woodward
Founded: 2000
Publish how-to books on dog care, training, behavior, health & competition.
ISBN Prefix(es): 978-1-929242; 978-1-61781
Number of titles published annually: 10 Print
Total Titles: 90 Print; 260 E-Book
Membership(s): Book Publishers of the Northwest; Dogwise Association of America; Independent Book Publishers Association

Tom Doherty Associates, LLC
Subsidiary of Macmillan
175 Fifth Ave, 14th fl, New York, NY 10010
Tel: 646-307-5511 *Toll Free Tel:* 800-455-0340
Web Site: www.tor-forge.com
Key Personnel
Pres & Publr: Thomas Doherty *E-mail:* thomas.doherty@tor.com
Publr, Tor Teen, Starscape, Tor Classics: Kathleen Doherty *E-mail:* kathleen.doherty@tor.com
VP & Publr, Forge Books: Linda Quinton *E-mail:* linda.quinton@tor.com
VP, Mktg & Publicity: Lucille Rettino
Assoc Publr, Tor Books: Patrick Nielsen Hayden *E-mail:* patrick.hayden@tor.com; Devi Pillai *E-mail:* devi.pillai@tor.com
Exec Dir, Mktg: Phyllis Azar *E-mail:* phyllis.azar@tor.com
Art Dir, Mass Market/Forge Books: Seth Lerner *E-mail:* seth.lerner@tor.com
Creative Dir, Assoc Publr Tor.com: Irene Gallo *E-mail:* irene.gallo@tor.com
Publicity Dir: Patty Garcia *E-mail:* patty.garcia@tor.com
Assoc Publicist, Tor/Forge: Desirae Friesen *E-mail:* desirae.friesen@tor.com
Exec Ed: Diana Gill *E-mail:* diana.gill@tor.com; Bob Gleason *E-mail:* bob.gleason@tor.com; Beth Meacham *E-mail:* beth.meacham@tor.com
Mgr, Admin: Robert Davis *E-mail:* robert.davis@tor.com
Founded: 1980
Mass market & trade paperbacks; trade hardcover: fiction, horror, science fiction, fantasy, mystery, suspense, techno-thrillers, western fiction, American historicals, nonfiction, paranormal romance, true crime & biography.
ISBN Prefix(es): 978-0-8125; 978-0-7653
Number of titles published annually: 425 Print
Total Titles: 2,224 Print
Imprints: Aerie Books; Forge Books; Orb Books; Starscape; Tor; Tor Classics; Tor Teen
Distributed by Macmillan
Foreign Rights: St Martin's Press
Advertising Agency: Slocum Advertising Agency
Distribution Center: MPS Distribution Center, 16365 James Madison Hwy, Gordonsville, VA 22942-8501 *Toll Free Tel:* 888-330-8477 *Fax:* 540-672-7540 (cust serv) *Toll Free Fax:* 800-672-2054 (orders) *E-mail:* firstinitial.lastname@mpsvirginia.com

The Donning Company Publishers
Subsidiary of Walsworth
184 Business Park Dr, Suite 206, Virginia Beach, VA 23462
SAN: 211-6316
Tel: 757-497-1789 *Toll Free Tel:* 800-296-8572 *Fax:* 757-497-2542
Web Site: www.donning.com
Key Personnel
Gen Mgr: Lex Cavanah *Tel:* 800-369-2646 ext 4320 *E-mail:* lex.cavanah@walsworth.com
Prodn Mgr: Nathan Stufflebean *Tel:* 660-376-6543 *E-mail:* nathan.stufflebean@donning.com
Founded: 1974
Specialty book publisher of limited-edition commemorative volumes, pictorial histories & contemporary portraits.
ISBN Prefix(es): 978-0-915442; 978-0-89865

Number of titles published annually: 80 Print
Imprints: Portraits of America
Branch Office(s)
306 N Kansas Ave, Marceline, MO 64658, Mktg Specialist: Nathan Stufflebean *Tel:* 660-376-3543 ext 3377 *Toll Free Tel:* 800-369-2646 ext 3377 *Fax:* 660-258-7798 *E-mail:* nathan.stufflebean@donning.com
Foreign Rights: Writers House Inc

Doodle and Peck Publishing
413 Cedarburg Ct, Yukon, OK 73099
Mailing Address: PO Box 852105, Yukon, OK 73085
Tel: 405-354-7422
E-mail: contact@doodleandpeck.com
Web Site: www.doodleandpeck.com
Key Personnel
Publr & Ed: Marla F Jones *E-mail:* iluvrocksmj@yahoo.com
Founded: 2015
Family-friendly publisher that pairs talented authors & illustrators in creating books that otherwise might not have been published.
ISBN Prefix(es): 978-0-9966205; 978-0-9972351
Number of titles published annually: 7 Print
Total Titles: 11 Print

Dordt College Press
Affiliate of Dordt College
498 Fourth Ave NE, Sioux Center, IA 51250-1606
Tel: 712-722-6420 *Toll Free Tel:* 800-343-6738 *Fax:* 712-722-6035
E-mail: dordtpress@dordt.edu; bookstore@dordt.edu
Web Site: www.dordt.edu/about-dordt/publications/dordt-press-catalog
Key Personnel
Mng Ed: John H Kok *Tel:* 712-722-2254 *E-mail:* jkok@dordt.edu
Founded: 1978
Publishes primarily academic books & monographs, plus a quarterly journal.
ISBN Prefix(es): 978-0-932914; 978-1-940567
Number of titles published annually: 6 Print
Total Titles: 45 Print

Dorland Health
Division of DecisionHealth LLC
4 Choke Cherry Rd, 2nd fl, Rockville, MD 20850
Tel: 301-354-2000 *Toll Free Tel:* 855-225-5341 *Fax:* 301-287-2535
E-mail: customer@decisionhealth.com
Web Site: www.dorlandhealth.com
Key Personnel
VP: Carol Brault *Tel:* 301-287-2470 *E-mail:* cbrault@decisionhealth.com
Mng Ed: Richard Scott *Tel:* 301-287-2582 *E-mail:* rscott@decisionhealth.com
Founded: 1950
Directories, market research, databases & mailing lists.
ISBN Prefix(es): 978-1-880874; 978-0-9624105; 978-1-933985; 978-0-9770821
Number of titles published annually: 6 Print; 1 CD-ROM; 4 Online
Total Titles: 6 Print; 1 CD-ROM; 4 Online

Dorrance Publishing Co Inc
585 Alpha Dr, Suite 103, Pittsburgh, PA 15238
Toll Free Tel: 800-695-9599; 800-788-7654 (gen cust orders) *Fax:* 412-288-1786
E-mail: dorrinfo@dorrancepublishing.com; redleadbookorders@dorrancepublishing.com; bookorders@rosedogbooks.com
Web Site: www.dorrancepublishing.com
Key Personnel
Mng Dir: David Zeolla
Founded: 1920
Full service author services company.
This publisher has indicated that 100% of their product line is author subsidized.
ISBN Prefix(es): 978-0-8059; 978-1-4349; 978-1-4809
Number of titles published annually: 360 Print; 360 Online; 360 E-Book; 10 Audio
Total Titles: 2,500 Print; 2,500 Online; 2,200 E-Book; 5 Audio
Imprints: Red Lead Press; Rose Dog Books

Doubleday/Nan A Talese
Imprint of Knopf Doubleday Publishing Group
c/o Penguin Random House Inc, 1745 Broadway, New York, NY 10019
Tel: 212-751-2600 *Fax:* 212-572-2662
E-mail: ddaypub@randomhouse.com
Web Site: knopfdoubleday.com
Key Personnel
Chmn & Ed-in-Chief, Knopf Doubleday Publishing Group: Sonny Mehta
Pres: Anthony Chirico
SVP, Publr & Ed-in-Chief: William Thomas
SVP, Publr, Pres & Edit Dir, Nan A Talese Books: Nan A Talese
EVP, Dir Publg: Suzanne Herz
VP & Exec Dir, Mktg: John Pitts
VP & Creative Mktg Dir: Judy Jacoby
VP & Dir, Busn Opers: Justine LeCates
SVP & Dir, Intl & Dom Rts: Sean Yule
Mgr, Foreign Rts: Suzanne Smith
Asst Dir, Publicity: Michael Goldsmith
Assoc Publicist: Mark Lee
Group Sales Dir: Janet Cooke
Imprint Sales Dir: James Kimball
VP & Dir, Prodn/Design: Andrew W Hughes
VP & Dir, Interior Design & Desktop Publg: Peter Andersen
Dir, Art Jacket: John Fontana
VP & Mng Ed: Katherine Hourigan
Asst Mktg Dir: Lauren Weber
Exec Ed: Gerry Howard; Jason Kaufman
Sr Ed: Kristine Puopolo; Jennifer Jackson; Yaniv Soha
Ed: Ronit Feldman
Assoc Ed: Dan Meyer
Mktg Mgr: Sarah Engelmann
Founded: 1897
Penguin Random House Inc & its publishing entities are not accepting unsol submissions, proposals, mss or submission queries via e-mail at this time.
ISBN Prefix(es): 978-0-385; 978-0-7679
Number of titles published annually: 100 Print
Total Titles: 2,500 Print
Foreign Rights: ALS-Agenzia Letteraria Santachiara (Roberto Santachiara) (Italy); Anthea Agency (Katalina Sabeva) (Bulgaria); Bardon-Chinese Media Agency (Xu-Weiguang) (China); Bardon-Chinese Media Agency (Yu-Shiuan Chen) (Taiwan); The English Agency (Junzo Sawa) (Japan); Graal Literary Agency (Maria Strarz-Kanska) (Poland); The Deborah Harris Agency (Ilana Kurshan) (Israel); JLM Literary Agency (Nelly Moukakos) (Greece); Katai & Bolza Literary (Peter Bolza) (Croatia, Hungary); KCC (MiSook Hong) (Korea); Simona Kessler International (Simona Kessler) (Romania); Licht & Burr Literary Agency (Trine Licht) (Scandinavia); La Nouvelle Agence (Vanessa Kling) (France); Kristin Olson Literary Agency (Kristin Olson) (Czech Republic); Sebes & Bisseling Literary Agency (Paul Sebes) (Netherlands)

§Dover Publications Inc
31 E Second St, Mineola, NY 11501-3852
Tel: 516-294-7000 *Toll Free Tel:* 800-223-3130 (orders) *Fax:* 516-742-6953
E-mail: rights@doverpublications.com; service@doverpublications.com
Web Site: store.doverdirect.com; www.doverpublications.com
Key Personnel
Pres: Frank Fontana
VP, Mktg: Ken Katzman *E-mail:* kkatzman@doverpublications.com
Asst to Pres & Sr Reprint Ed: John Grafton
Acqs Ed: Jeff Golick
Founded: 1941
Trade, scientific, paperbound books; posters, language, literature & stationery items.
ISBN Prefix(es): 978-0-486; 978-1-60660
Number of titles published annually: 670 Print; 8 CD-ROM
Total Titles: 8,000 Print; 36 CD-ROM; 22 Audio
Foreign Rep(s): David & Charles (UK)
Shipping Address: 11 E Second St, Mineola, NY 11501

Down East Books
Imprint of The Globe Pequot Press
680 Commercial St (US Rte 1), Rockport, ME 04856
Mailing Address: c/o Down East Enterprise, PO Box 679, Camden, ME 04843
Tel: 207-594-9544 *Toll Free Tel:* 800-685-7962 (US orders, cust serv); 800-766-1670
E-mail: support@downeast.com
Web Site: secure.downeast.com/books/maine/books.html
Key Personnel
Pres, Publr & CEO: Bob Fernald *E-mail:* bfernald@downeast.com
Founded: 1954
Tied directly to *Down East, The Magazine of Maine*, the book publishing mission is to bring Maine's excess of literary & artistic talent to the book marketplace.
ISBN Prefix(es): 978-0-924357; 978-0-89272
Number of titles published annually: 25 Print; 16 E-Book
Total Titles: 350 Print; 50 E-Book
Sales Office(s): National Book Network, 15200 NBN Way, Blue Ridge Summit, PA 17214 *Toll Free Tel:* 800-462-6420
Distributor for Nimbus Publishing Ltd (selected titles, CN sales only)
Distribution Center: National Book Network, 15200 NBN Way, Blue Ridge Summit, PA 17214 *Tel:* 717-794-3800 *Toll Free Tel:* 800-462-6420 *Fax:* 717-794-3828 *Toll Free Fax:* 800-338-4550 *E-mail:* customercare@nbnbooks.com

Down The Shore Publishing Corp
106 Stafford Forge Rd, West Creek, NJ 08092
SAN: 661-082X
Mailing Address: PO Box 100, West Creek, NJ 08092
Tel: 609-812-5076 *Fax:* 609-812-5098
E-mail: dtsbooks@comcast.net; info@down-the-shore.com
Web Site: www.down-the-shore.com
Key Personnel
Founder & Pres: Raymond G Fisk
Founded: 1984
Regional books, history; calendars; videos; note cards.
ISBN Prefix(es): 978-0-9615208; 978-0-945582; 978-1-59322
Number of titles published annually: 6 Print
Total Titles: 95 Print
Imprints: Bufflehead Books; Cormorant Books; Cormorant Calendars; Terrapin Greetings
Membership(s): Independent Book Publishers Association

§Dragon Door Publications
5 E Country Rd B, Suite 3, Little Canada, MN 55117
Tel: 651-487-2180 *Toll Free Tel:* 800-899-5111 (orders & cust serv)
E-mail: support@dragondoor.com
Web Site: www.dragondoor.com

Key Personnel
Publr & Ed-in-Chief: John Du Cane
ISBN Prefix(es): 978-0-938045
Number of titles published annually: 5 Print
Total Titles: 111 Print; 35 E-Book

§Dragonfairy Press
Imprint of Dragonfairy Press LLC
2107 N Decatur Rd, Suite 211, Decatur, GA 30033
Tel: 404-955-8150
E-mail: info@dragonfairypress.com
Web Site: www.dragonfairypress.com
Key Personnel
Exec Ed: Alicia Wright
Sr Ed: Kenya Wright
Founded: 2012
Independent publisher of adult & young adult speculative fiction, including fantasy, science fiction, urban fantasy, paranormal romance, supernatural horror, dystopia & other subgenres.
ISBN Prefix(es): 978-0-9850230; 978-1-939452
Number of titles published annually: 8 Print; 8 E-Book
Total Titles: 10 Print; 8 E-Book
Distribution Center: Small Press United, Independent Publishers Group, 814 N Franklin St, Chicago, IL 60610 *Tel:* 312-337-0747 *Fax:* 312-337-5985 *E-mail:* frontdesk@ipgbook.com
Membership(s): Independent Book Publishers Association

Drama Publishers, see Quite Specific Media Group Ltd

Dramatic Publishing Co
311 Washington St, Woodstock, IL 60098-3308
SAN: 201-5676
Tel: 815-338-7170 *Toll Free Tel:* 800-448-7469 *Fax:* 815-338-8981 *Toll Free Fax:* 800-334-5302
E-mail: plays@dramaticpublishing.com; customerservice@dpcplays.com
Web Site: www.dramaticpublishing.com
Key Personnel
Pres: Christopher Sergel, III
VP: Gayle Sergel; Susan Sergel
Dir: Kent Brown
Founded: 1885
Acting editions of plays & musicals & licensing productions of same.
ISBN Prefix(es): 978-0-87129; 978-1-58342; 978-1-61959
Number of titles published annually: 55 Print
Total Titles: 2,000 Print
Foreign Rep(s): DALRO Pty Ltd (Southern Africa); Origin Theatrical Pty Ltd (Australia); The Play Bureau NZ Ltd (New Zealand)

Dramatists Play Service Inc
440 Park Ave S, New York, NY 10016
Tel: 212-683-8960 *Fax:* 212-213-1539
E-mail: postmaster@dramatists.com; orders@dramatists.com; publications@dramatists.com
Web Site: www.dramatists.com
Key Personnel
Pres: Peter Hagan *E-mail:* hagan@dramatists.com
VP: Mary Harden
Edit Dir: Haleh Roshan Stilwell *E-mail:* stilwell@dramatists.com
Edit Assoc: Ben Keiper *E-mail:* keiper@dramatists.com
Edit Asst: Leah Barker *E-mail:* barker@dramatists.com
Founded: 1936
Publisher & licensor of plays & musicals.
ISBN Prefix(es): 978-0-8222
Number of titles published annually: 60 Print
Total Titles: 4,000 Print
Foreign Rights: DALRO (South Africa); Hal Leonard Australia Pty Ltd (Australia, New Zealand); Josef Weinberger (UK)

Dreaming Robot Press
Imprint of Studio Weaver
1214 San Francisco Ave, Las Vegas, NM 87701
Tel: 505-264-3830
E-mail: books@dreamingrobotpress.com
Web Site: dreamingrobotpress.com
Founded: 2013
Quality middle grade & young adult science fiction & fantasy novels.
ISBN Prefix(es): 978-1-940924
Number of titles published annually: 2 Print; 20 E-Book
Total Titles: 7 Print; 3 E-Book
Membership(s): Independent Book Publishers Association

Dreamscape Media LLC
Division of Midwest Tapes
6940 Hall St, Holland, OH 43528
Tel: 419-867-6965 *Toll Free Tel:* 877-983-7326
E-mail: info@dreamscapeab.com
Web Site: www.dreamscapeab.com
Key Personnel
Publr: Tammy Faxel *Tel:* 312-757-4759 *E-mail:* tfaxel@dreamscapeab.com
Edit Dir: Michael Olah *E-mail:* molah@dreamscapeab.com
Founded: 2010
Audio & video media publisher.
ISBN Prefix(es): 978-0-9745563; 978-0-9747118; 978-0-9760996; 978-0-9761981; 978-0-9771510; 978-0-9772338; 978-0-9774680; 978-0-9776262; 978-0-9777098; 978-1-933938; 978-1-61120; 978-1-62406; 978-1-62923; 978-1-63379
Number of titles published annually: 50 E-Book; 250 Audio
Total Titles: 600 E-Book; 1,500 Audio
Editorial Office(s): 150 N Wacker Dr, Suite 2250, Chicago, IL 60606
Distributor for Berrett-Koehler Publishers; Gildan Media; HarperCollins; Ideal Audiobooks; Penguin Random House Inc; Radio Archives
Foreign Rep(s): CVS Midwest Tape (Canada)
Membership(s): Audio Publishers Association

Dufour Editions Inc
PO Box 7, Chester Springs, PA 19425
SAN: 201-341X
Tel: 610-458-5005 *Fax:* 610-458-7103
E-mail: info@dufoureditions.com
Web Site: www.dufoureditions.com
Key Personnel
Pres & Publr: Christopher May
Ed, Sales Dir: Duncan May
Publicity & Prodn Dir: Miranda Elliott
Founded: 1949
Literary fiction, general nonfiction, literature, poetry, philosophy, history, drama & criticism, Irish.
ISBN Prefix(es): 978-0-8023
Number of titles published annually: 400 Print
Total Titles: 6,000 Print
Imprints: Dufour Editions' Distributed Presses
Distributor for Angel Books; Arcadia Books Ltd (London) (including BlackAmber, Bliss Books, Eurocrime & The Maia Press Ltd); Attic Press (including Atrium); Between the Lines; Blackstaff Press Ltd; Bloodaxe Books Ltd; Boatwhistle Books; Brandon Books; Clo Iar-Chonnachta; Collins Press; Columba Press; Currach Press; Eland Books/Sickle Moon Books; Flyleaf Press; Gill; Goblinshead; The Liffey Press; Lilliput Press Ltd; Little Toller Books; Y Lolfa (including Alcemi); Mercier; Messenger Publications; New Island Books; Norvik Press; O'Brien Press; Orpen Press; Persephone Books; Portnoy Publishing; Route; Salmon Poetry; Sandstone Press; Smokestack Books; Colin Smythe Ltd; Stinging Fly Press; University College Dublin Press; Vagabond Voices; Veritas; The Waywiser Press; Wordwell Books
Warehouse: 124 Byers Rd, Chester Springs, PA 19425

Duke University Press
905 W Main St, Suite 18B, Durham, NC 27701
SAN: 201-3436
Mailing Address: PO Box 90660, Durham, NC 27708-0660
Tel: 919-688-5134 *Toll Free Tel:* 888-651-0122 (US) *Fax:* 919-688-2615 *Toll Free Fax:* 888-651-0124
E-mail: orders@dukeupress.edu
Web Site: www.dukeupress.edu
Key Personnel
Edit Dir: Ken Wissoker *Tel:* 919-687-3648 *E-mail:* kwiss@dukeupress.edu
Dir, Mktg & Sales: Cason Lynley *E-mail:* cason.lynley@dukeupress.edu
Journals Acqs Ed: Erich Staib *Tel:* 919-687-3664 *E-mail:* erich.staib@dukeupress.edu
Books Metadata & Digital Systems Mgr: H Lee Willoughby-Harris
Sales Mgr: Jennifer Schaper
Assoc Mktg & Sales Mgr: Michael McCullough *Tel:* 919-687-3600 *E-mail:* mmccullough@dukeupress.edu
Founded: 1921
Scholarly, trade & textbooks.
ISBN Prefix(es): 978-0-8223
Number of titles published annually: 120 Print
Total Titles: 1,300 Print
Distributor for Forest History Society
Foreign Rep(s): Combined Academic Publishers Ltd (Africa, Asia, Australia, Europe, Middle East, New Zealand, UK); Lexa Publishers Representatives (Canada)
Warehouse: 120 Golden Dr, Durham, NC 27705, Dist Mgr: Don Griffin *Tel:* 919-384-0733 *Fax:* 919-384-9564 *E-mail:* don.griffin@dukeupress.edu

Dumbarton Oaks
1703 32 St NW, Washington, DC 20007
Tel: 202-339-6400 *Fax:* 202-339-6401; 202-298-8407
E-mail: doaksbooks@doaks.org
Web Site: www.doaks.org
Key Personnel
Dir, Pubns: Kathy Sparkes
Mng Ed, Art & Archaeology: Sara Taylor
Edit Asst: Meredith Baber
ISBN Prefix(es): 978-0-88402
Number of titles published annually: 8 Print
Total Titles: 260 Print
Distributed by Harvard University Press

§Dun & Bradstreet
103 JFK Pkwy, Short Hills, NJ 07078
Tel: 973-921-5500 *Toll Free Tel:* 800-526-0651; 800-234-3867 (cust serv)
E-mail: custserv@dnb.com
Web Site: www.dnb.com
Key Personnel
CEO & Dir: Bob Carrigan
Pres & COO: Josh Peirez
Chief Content & Technol Offr: Curtis Brown
Chief Mktg Offr: Rishi Dave
Chief Sales Offr: Mark Geneste
Business & business reference; US & international coverage, country information.
ISBN Prefix(es): 978-1-56203
Total Titles: 31 Print; 20 CD-ROM
Subsidiaries: Hoover's Inc
See separate listing for:
Hoover's Inc

Duquesne University Press
600 Forbes Ave, Pittsburgh, PA 15282
Tel: 412-396-6610 *Fax:* 412-396-5984
E-mail: dupress@duq.edu
Web Site: www.dupress.duq.edu
Key Personnel
Dir: Susan Wadsworth-Booth
E-mail: wadsworth@duq.edu
Mktg & Busn Mgr: Lori R Crosby
E-mail: crosbyl@duq.edu
Mng Ed: Kathleen Meyer *E-mail:* meyerk@duq.edu
Founded: 1927
Nonfiction: literary studies, ethics, philosophy, religion, philology, psychology, communication.
ISBN Prefix(es): 978-0-8207
Number of titles published annually: 10 Print
Total Titles: 120 Print
Foreign Rep(s): Gazelle Book Services Ltd (European Union)
Warehouse: CUP Services, 750 Cascadilla St, Ithaca, NY 14851-6525 *Toll Free Tel:* 800-666-2211 *Toll Free Fax:* 800-688-2877
E-mail: orderbook@cupserv.org
Membership(s): Association of American University Presses; Society for Scholarly Publishing

§Dustbooks
Affiliate of Associated Writing Programs
PO Box 100, Paradise, CA 95967-0100
SAN: 204-1871
Tel: 530-877-6110 *Fax:* 530-877-0222
E-mail: publisher@dustbooks.com; info@dustbooks.com
Web Site: www.dustbooks.com
Key Personnel
Publr: Kathleen Glanville
Founded: 1964
Full service publishing company founded by Len Fulton.
ISBN Prefix(es): 978-0-913218; 978-0-916685; 978-1-935742
Number of titles published annually: 3 CD-ROM
Total Titles: 4 CD-ROM; 4 Online
Distributor for American Dust Publications

Dutton
Division of Penguin Group USA, A Penguin Random House Company
375 Hudson St, New York, NY 10014
SAN: 282-5074
Tel: 212-366-2000 *Fax:* 212-366-2262
Web Site: www.penguin.com
Key Personnel
Publr: Ivan Held
SVP & Publr, Dutton, Putnam & Berkley: Christine Ball
VP & Publr, Dutton Children's: Julie Strauss-Gabel
VP & Assoc Publr, Pbks: Benjamin Lee
VP & Ed-in-Chief: John Parsley
Exec Dir, Mktg: Carrie Swetonic
Dir, Publicity: Jamie Knapp
Exec Mng Ed: Susan Schwartz
Exec Ed: Brent Howard; Stephen Morrow; Jill Schwartzman
Sr Ed: Jessica Renheim
Mktg Mgr, Putnam/Dutton: Katie Parry
Publicity Mgr: Liza Cassity
Sr Publicist: Emily Brock
Mktg Coord: Leila Siddiqui
ISBN Prefix(es): 978-0-525; 978-0-917657; 978-1-55611
Number of titles published annually: 12 Print
Total Titles: 130 Print
Advertising Agency: Spier NY

Dutton Children's Books
Imprint of Penguin Group USA, A Penguin Random House Company
345 Hudson St, New York, NY 10014
SAN: 282-5074
Tel: 212-366-2000
Web Site: www.penguin.com
Key Personnel
Pres & Publr, Dutton Children's: Julie Strauss-Gabel
Exec Ed: Andrew Karre
Assoc Publg Mgr: Melissa Faulner
Founded: 1852 (as Dutton)
Number of titles published annually: 12 Print
Total Titles: 355 Print
Imprints: Dutton

Eagan Press
Imprint of AACC International
3340 Pilot Knob Rd, St Paul, MN 55121
Tel: 651-454-7250 *Toll Free Tel:* 800-328-7560 *Fax:* 651-454-0766
E-mail: aacc@scisoc.org
Web Site: www.aaccnet.org
Key Personnel
EVP: Amy Hope *Tel:* 651-994-3827
E-mail: ahope@scisoc.org
Dir, Pubns: Greg Grahek *Tel:* 651-994-3841
E-mail: ggrahek@scisoc.org
Founded: 1995
Food science publishing.
ISBN Prefix(es): 978-1-891127
Number of titles published annually: 5 Print; 15 E-Book
Total Titles: 200 Print; 25 E-Book

Eagle's View Publishing
Subsidiary of Westwind Inc
6756 North Fork Rd, Liberty, UT 84310
SAN: 240-6330
Tel: 801-393-4555; 801-745-0905 (edit) *Fax:* 801-745-0903 (edit); 801-393-4647
E-mail: sales@eaglefeathertrading.com
Web Site: www.eaglefeathertrading.com
Key Personnel
Pres & Publr: Monte Smith
Sales Mgr: Sue Smith *Tel:* 801-393-3991
Ed & Publicity: Denise Knight
Founded: 1982
Books on Indian arts, crafts & culture, mountain men & the early frontier, beading, historical clothing patterns, jewelry & how-to craft books in these areas.
ISBN Prefix(es): 978-0-943604
Number of titles published annually: 3 Print
Total Titles: 50 Print
Orders to: 168 W 12 St, Ogden, UT 84404
Returns: 168 W 12 St, Ogden, UT 84404
Warehouse: 168 W 12 St, Ogden, UT 84404

Eakin Press
Imprint of Wild Horse Media Group
PO Box 331779, Fort Worth, TX 76163
Tel: 817-344-7036 *Toll Free Tel:* 888-982-8270 *Fax:* 817-344-7036
Web Site: www.eakinpress.com
Key Personnel
CEO: Billy Huckaby
COO: Ronna Huckaby
Founded: 1979
ISBN Prefix(es): 978-0-89015; 978-1-57168
Number of titles published annually: 25 Print
Total Titles: 1,000 Print; 220 E-Book; 1 Audio
Membership(s): Independent Publishers Association

East Asian Legal Studies Program (EALSP)
Division of University of Maryland School of Law
500 W Baltimore St, Suite 411, Baltimore, MD 21201-1786
Tel: 410-706-3870 *Fax:* 410-706-1516
E-mail: eastasia@law.umaryland.edu
Web Site: www.law.umaryland.edu/programs/international/eastasia
Key Personnel
Dir: Dr Michael Van Altine
Assoc Dir: Chih-Yu T Wu
Founded: 1977
East Asian legal studies, political, economic & legal.
ISBN Prefix(es): 978-0-942182; 978-0-925153; 978-1-932330
Number of titles published annually: 4 Print
Total Titles: 218 Print

East West Discovery Press
PO Box 3585, Manhattan Beach, CA 90266
Tel: 310-545-3730 *Fax:* 310-545-3731
E-mail: info@eastwestdiscovery.com
Web Site: www.eastwestdiscovery.com
Key Personnel
Publr & Ed: Icy Smith
Dir: Michael Smith
Founded: 2000
Independent publisher & distributor of multicultural & bilingual books in 50+ languages.
ISBN Prefix(es): 978-0-9701654; 978-0-9669437; 978-0-9799339; 978-0-9821675; 978-0-9856237; 978-0-9913454; 978-0-9832278; 978-0-9973947
Number of titles published annually: 5 Print
Total Titles: 60 Print
Membership(s): APALA; The Children's Book Council; Independent Book Publishers Association

EastBridge
70 New Canaan Ave, Norwalk, CT 06850
Tel: 203-855-9125 *Fax:* 203-857-0730
E-mail: asia@eastbridgebooks.org; ask@eastbridgebooks.org
Web Site: www.eastbridgebooks.org
Key Personnel
Founding Dir & Mng Ed: J C West
E-mail: west@eastbridgebooks.org
Dir & Sr Ed: Anthony S Kaufmann *E-mail:* ask@eastbridgebooks.org
Ed, D'Asia Vu Reprint Lib: Chuck Hayford
Ed, The Missionary Enterprise in Asia: Kathleen Lodwick
Founded: 1997
Not-for-profit publisher in Asian studies.
ISBN Prefix(es): 978-1-891936; 978-1-59988
Number of titles published annually: 20 Print
Total Titles: 75 Print
Imprints: D'Asia Vu Reprint Library (reprints of important classical works); The Missionary Enterprise in Asia (memoirs, autobiographies & biographies of missionaries in Asia); Signature Books (Asian literature, history & analysis); Voices of Asia (current books on Asia authoritatively translated from the original language)
Distributor for China Institute; John Helde; International Christian University Foundation; Nippon Foundation; Yosifumi Taguchi
Foreign Rep(s): Royal Asiatic Society, Korea Branch (Korea)
Membership(s): Association for Asian Studies

Eastland Press
1240 Activity Dr, Suite D, Vista, CA 92081
Mailing Address: PO Box 99749, Seattle, WA 98139
Tel: 206-217-0204 (edit); 760-598-9695 (orders) *Toll Free Tel:* 800-453-3278 (orders) *Fax:* 760-598-6083 (orders) *Toll Free Fax:* 800-241-3329 (orders)
E-mail: info@eastlandpress.com; orders@eastlandpress.com (credit card orders only)
Web Site: www.eastlandpress.com
Key Personnel
Mng Ed & Lib Sales Dir: John O'Connor
Author & Med Ed: Dan Bensky
Prodn Mgr: Patricia O'Connor
Founded: 1981
Chinese medicine, osteopathic & structural medicine, yoga. Use Seattle, WA address for

submitting a ms or inquiring about a publication. Use Vista, CA address for ordering books.
ISBN Prefix(es): 978-0-939616
Number of titles published annually: 5 Print; 1 CD-ROM
Total Titles: 55 Print
Distributor for Journal of Chinese Medicine Publications
Membership(s): Publishers Association of the West

Easy Money Press
Subsidiary of Wolford & Associates
5419 87 St, Lubbock, TX 79424
Tel: 806-543-5215
E-mail: easymoneypress@yahoo.com
Key Personnel
Creative Dir: Henry Wolford *E-mail:* hcwolford@yahoo.com
Mktg Dir: Sheri Kephart
Prodn Dir: P J Max
Founded: 1996
ISBN Prefix(es): 978-0-9654563; 978-1-929714
Number of titles published annually: 1 Print; 3 E-Book
Total Titles: 24 Print; 16 E-Book
Imprints: Big Tree Books; EMP; Haase House

Eaton Publishing, see BioTechniques Books

Eclectic Book Press
11 Larchdell Way, Mountain Lakes, NJ 07046
Mailing Address: PO Box 63, Mountain Lakes, NJ 07046
Tel: 862-251-2296
E-mail: info@eclecticbookpress.com
Web Site: eclecticbookpress.com
Key Personnel
Publr & Creative Dir: Lilian Rosenstreich *E-mail:* lili@eclecticbookspress.com
Publr & Busn Mgr: Mitchel Weiss *Tel:* 570-878-7960 *E-mail:* mitchel@eclecticbookpress.com
Founded: 2016
Publish a variety of children's books with a focus on redesign & reissue of vintage books.
ISBN Prefix(es): 978-0-9988527
Number of titles published annually: 6 Print
Total Titles: 3 Print
Distribution Center: Ingram Spark, 14 Ingram Blvd, La Vergne, TN 37086 *Toll Free Tel:* 855-997-7275 *E-mail:* ingramsparksupport@ingramcontent.com

Ecopress
Imprint of Finney Company Inc
5995 149 St W, Suite 105, Apple Valley, MN 55124
Tel: 952-469-6699 *Toll Free Tel:* 800-846-7027 *Fax:* 952-469-1968 *Toll Free Fax:* 800-330-6232
E-mail: info@finneyco.com
Web Site: www.ecopress.com
Key Personnel
Pres: Alan E Krysan
Founded: 1996
Produces books & art that enhance environmental awareness, offering high quality titles covering subjects such as rivers, hiking, plant & environmental guides.
ISBN Prefix(es): 978-1-89327; 978-0-96397
Number of titles published annually: 2 Print
Total Titles: 10 Print

ECS, see The Electrochemical Society (ECS)

ECS Publishing Corp
1727 Larkin Williams Rd, Fenton, MO 63026
Tel: 636-305-0100 *Toll Free Tel:* 800-647-2117
Web Site: ecspublishing.com; www.facebook.com/ecspublishing
Key Personnel
Pres: Mark Lawson
Mgr, Publg Rts & Mktg: Abi Enockson
Founded: 1993
Music publishing (sheet music).
ISBN Prefix(es): 978-0-911318
Number of titles published annually: 125 Print
Total Titles: 10,200 Print
Imprints: ARSIS Audio; Galaxy Music Corp; Highgate Press; Ione Press; E C Schirmer Music Co
Distributor for Randol Bass Music; Dunstan House; Edition Delrieu; Gaudia Music & Arts; Stainer & Bell Ltd; Vireo Press
Orders to: Canticle Distributing, 1727 Larkin Williams Rd, St Louis, MO 63026-2024 *Tel:* 636-305-0100 *Toll Free Tel:* 800-647-2117 (US only) *Fax:* 636-305-0121 *E-mail:* morningstar@morningstarmusic.com
Distribution Center: Canticle Distributing, 1727 Larkin Williams Rd, St Louis, MO 63026-2024 *Tel:* 636-305-0100 *Toll Free Tel:* 800-647-2117 (US only) *Fax:* 636-305-0121 *E-mail:* morningstar@morningstarmusic.com
Membership(s): Music Publishers Association; National Music Publishers' Association

EDC Publishing
Division of Educational Development Corp
10302 E 55 Place, Tulsa, OK 74146-6515
Mailing Address: PO Box 470663, Tulsa, OK 74147-0663
Tel: 918-622-4522 *Toll Free Tel:* 800-475-4522 *Fax:* 918-665-7919 *Toll Free Fax:* 800-743-5660
E-mail: edc@edcpub.com
Web Site: www.edcpub.com
Key Personnel
CEO & Pres: Randall White *E-mail:* rwhite@edcpub.com
VP, Publg & Natl Sales Mgr: Jeanie M Crone *E-mail:* jeanie.crone@edcpub.com
VP, Info Systems: Craig M White
Cont & Corp Secy: Marilyn R Pinney
Founded: 1978
Children's books (fiction & nonfiction) & kid kits.
ISBN Prefix(es): 978-0-88110; 978-0-7460; 978-0-86020; 978-0-7945; 978-1-58086; 978-1-60130
Number of titles published annually: 200 Print
Total Titles: 1,800 Print; 22 CD-ROM
Imprints: Usborne Books
Distributor for Usborne Publishing Ltd

Edda USA
Division of Edda Publishing Ltd (Iceland)
373 Park Ave S, 6th fl, New York, NY 10016
Tel: 646-755-9210
Web Site: eddausa.com
Key Personnel
CEO: Jon Axel Olafsson *E-mail:* jax@eddausa.com
Ed-in-Chief: Tinna Proppe *E-mail:* tinna@eddausa.com
Art Dir: Johann G Olafsson *E-mail:* gassi@eddausa.com
Founded: 2013
ISBN Prefix(es): 978-1-940787
Number of titles published annually: 10 Print
Distribution Center: Midpoint Trade Books Inc, 27 W 20 St, Suite 1102, New York, NY 10011, Natl Accts Mgr: Bill Huhn *Tel:* 847-985-3700 *Fax:* 212-727-0195 *E-mail:* wchesquire@aol.com *Web Site:* www.midpointtrade.com

Edgewise Press Inc
24 Fifth Ave, Suite 224, New York, NY 10011
Tel: 212-982-4818 *Fax:* 212-982-1364
E-mail: epinc@mindspring.com
Web Site: www.edgewisepress.org
Key Personnel
CEO: Howard Johnson, Jr
Ed: Joy L Glass; Richard Milazzo
Founded: 1995
Publisher of serious art & literary books.
ISBN Prefix(es): 978-0-9646466; 978-1-893207
Number of titles published annually: 3 Print
Total Titles: 29 Print
Distributor for Editions d'Afrique du Nord; Libri Canali Bassi; Paolo Torti degli Alberti

ediciones Lerner
Imprint of Lerner Publishing Group Inc
241 First Ave N, Minneapolis, MN 55401
Tel: 612-332-3344 *Toll Free Tel:* 800-328-4929 *Fax:* 612-332-7615 *Toll Free Fax:* 800-332-1132
E-mail: info@lernerbooks.com; custserve@lernerbooks.com
Web Site: www.lernerbooks.com; www.facebook.com/lernerbooks
Key Personnel
Chmn: Harry J Lerner
CFO & EVP: Margaret Thomas
Pres & Publr: Adam Lerner
EVP, Sales: David Wexler
VP, Ed-in-Chief: Patricia M Stockland
Dir of Rts, Spec Sales & Intl Dist: Maria Kjoller
Group Mktg Dir: Jill Braithwaite
School & Lib Mktg Dir: Lois Wallentine
Dir, HR: Cyndi Radant
Publishes fiction & nonfiction books for PreK-4 in Spanish.
ISBN Prefix(es): 978-0-8225; 978-0-7613
Total Titles: 150 Print; 100 E-Book
Warehouse: Lerner Publishing Group, 1251 Washington Ave N, Minneapolis, MN 55401, Mgr: Ken Rued

Editions Orphee Inc
1240 Clubview Blvd N, Columbus, OH 43235-1226
Tel: 614-846-9517 *Fax:* 614-846-9794
E-mail: sales@editionsorphee.com
Web Site: www.editionsorphee.com
Key Personnel
Pres: Mr Matanya Orphee *E-mail:* m.orphee@orphee.com
Classical sheet music, books on music.
ISBN Prefix(es): 978-0-936186; 978-1-882612
Number of titles published annually: 12 Print
Total Titles: 20 Print
Distributed by Theodore Presser Co
Foreign Rep(s): Chanterelle Verlag (Germany)

Editorial Bautista Independiente
Division of Baptist Mid-Missions
3417 Kenilworth Blvd, Sebring, FL 33870-4469
Tel: 863-382-6350 *Toll Free Tel:* 800-398-7187 (US) *Fax:* 863-382-8650
E-mail: info@ebi-bmm.org; ebiweb@ebi-bmm.org
Web Site: www.ebi-bmm.org
Key Personnel
Gen Dir & Busn Mgr: Bruce Burkholder
Founded: 1950
Sunday school materials, extension materials, Bible study-all in Spanish.
ISBN Prefix(es): 978-1-879892
Number of titles published annually: 5 Print
Total Titles: 200 Print
Distributor for Casa Bautista; CLIE; Portavoz

Editorial de la Universidad de Puerto Rico, see University of Puerto Rico Press

Editorial Portavoz
Division of Kregel Publications
2450 Oak Industrial Dr NE, Grand Rapids, MI 49505
SAN: 298-9115

Toll Free Tel: 877-733-2607 (ext 206) *Fax:* 616-493-1790
E-mail: portavoz@portavoz.com
Web Site: www.portavoz.com
Key Personnel
Pres: James R Kregel *E-mail:* president@kregel.com
Publr: Tito Mantilla
Founded: 1970
Christian products.
ISBN Prefix(es): 978-0-8254
Number of titles published annually: 30 Print
Total Titles: 600 Print
Membership(s): CBA: The Association for Christian Retail; Evangelical Christian Publishers Association; SEPA

Educational Directories Inc (EDI)
1025 W Wise Rd, Suite 101, Schaumburg, IL 60193
Mailing Address: PO Box 68097, Schaumburg, IL 60168-0097
Tel: 847-891-1250 *Toll Free Tel:* 800-357-6183 *Fax:* 847-891-0945
E-mail: info@ediusa.com
Web Site: www.ediusa.com
Key Personnel
Publr: Douglas Moody
Founded: 1904
Reference publications in education.
ISBN Prefix(es): 978-0-910536; 978-0-9821099; 978-0-9771602; 978-0-9883500
Number of titles published annually: 3 Print
Total Titles: 3 Print; 1 CD-ROM

Educational Impressions Inc
785 Franklin Ave, Franklin Lakes, NJ 07417
Tel: 201-644-0908 *Toll Free Tel:* 800-451-7450 *Fax:* 201-644-0907
Web Site: www.edimpressions.com; www.awpeller.com
Key Personnel
Pres: Allan W Peller *E-mail:* awpeller@optonline.net
Dir, Sales & Mktg: Neil Peller
Founded: 1983
Supplemental textbooks, literature guides.
ISBN Prefix(es): 978-0-910857; 978-1-56644
Number of titles published annually: 30 Print
Total Titles: 450 Print
Distributed by Newbridge Communications Inc; Scholastic Inc; Scholastic-Tab Publications

Educational Insights
Subsidiary of Learning Resources
152 W Walnut St, Suite 201, Gardena, CA 90248
SAN: 282-762X
Toll Free Tel: 800-995-4436 *Toll Free Fax:* 888-892-8731
E-mail: cs@educationalinsights.com
Web Site: www.educationalinsights.com
Key Personnel
Gen Mgr: Lisa Guili *Tel:* 847-968-3719
Press & Media: Courtney Wachs *Tel:* 847-968-3722
Founded: 1962
El-hi instructional materials; teacher's aids, teaching machines & games.
ISBN Prefix(es): 978-1-56767; 978-0-88679
Number of titles published annually: 4 Print; 2 Audio
Total Titles: 92 Print
Distribution Center: Learning Resources, 380 N Fairway Dr, Vernon Hills, IL 60061

Educator's International Press Inc (EIP)
84 Hardenburgh Ave, Haworth, NJ 07641
Tel: 518-334-0276 *Fax:* 703-661-1547
E-mail: info@edint.com
Web Site: edint.presswarehouse.com
Key Personnel
Pres: William Clockel
Founded: 1997
Educational foundations, teacher research, curriculum, special education.
ISBN Prefix(es): 978-0-9658339; 978-1-891928
Number of titles published annually: 4 Print; 4 E-Book
Total Titles: 40 Print; 4 E-Book

Educators Progress Service Inc
214 Center St, Randolph, WI 53956
SAN: 201-3649
Tel: 920-326-3126 *Toll Free Tel:* 888-951-4469 *Fax:* 920-326-3127
E-mail: epsinc@centurytel.net
Key Personnel
Pres: Kathy Nehmer
Founded: 1934
Educator guides to free materials in various subject areas; video.
ISBN Prefix(es): 978-0-87708
Number of titles published annually: 16 Print
Total Titles: 16 Print

Edupress Inc
Division of Demco Inc
4810 Forest Run Rd, Madison, WI 53704
Toll Free Tel: 800-835-7978 *Toll Free Fax:* 800-558-9332
E-mail: edupressdealers@edupress.com
Web Site: www.edupress.com
Founded: 1956
Publisher of teacher resource materials.
ISBN Prefix(es): 978-1-56472
Number of titles published annually: 20 Print
Total Titles: 220 Print

Wm B Eerdmans Publishing Co
2140 Oak Industrial Dr NE, Grand Rapids, MI 49505
SAN: 220-0058
Tel: 616-459-4591 *Toll Free Tel:* 800-253-7521 *Fax:* 616-459-6540
E-mail: customerservice@eerdmans.com; sales@eerdmans.com
Web Site: www.eerdmans.com
Key Personnel
Chmn of the Bd: William B Eerdmans, Jr
Pres & Publr: Anita Eerdmans
VP & Treas: Claire VanderKam
VP & Ed-in-Chief: James Ernest
VP, Content & Technol: Klaas Wolterstorff
Mktg Dir: Rachel Bomberger *E-mail:* rbomberger@eerdmans.com
Dir, Sales: Bob Hetico *E-mail:* bhetico@eerdmans.com
Sr Proj Mgr: Linda Bieze
Cust Serv & Order Entry Mgr: Karen Shippy *E-mail:* kshippy@eerdmans.com
Logistics Mgr & EDI Specialist: Duane Watson
Prodn Mgr: Jen Rose *E-mail:* jrose@eerdmans.com
Subs Rts Mgr: Tom DeVries *E-mail:* tdevries@eerdmans.com
Ad Coord: Vicky Fanning *E-mail:* vfanning@eerdmans.com
Sales & Exhibits Coord: Ingrid Wolf *E-mail:* iwolf@eerdmans.com
Sr Acqs Ed: Michael Thomson
Sr Acqs Ed, Gen Trade: Lil Copan
Mng Ed, EBYR: Kathleen Merz
Asst Mng Ed, EBYR: Katherine Gibson *E-mail:* kgibson@eerdmans.com
Publicist, Academic & Ministry Books: Laura Bardolph Hubers *E-mail:* lbhubers@eerdmans.com
Publicist, Trade & Children's Books: Rachel Brewer *E-mail:* rbrewer@eerdmans.com
Exec Asst: Amy R Kent *E-mail:* akent@eerdmans.com
Founded: 1911
Scholarly religious & religious reference, religion & social concerns, children's books.
ISBN Prefix(es): 978-0-8028; 978-1-4674
Number of titles published annually: 130 Print
Total Titles: 1,200 Print
Imprints: Eerdmans Books for Young Readers
Foreign Rep(s): Acts TCCN Bookshop (Nigeria); Alban Books Ltd (Europe, UK); Asian Trading Corp (India); Bethesda Book Centre (East Asia, Singapore); Challenge Enterprises of Ghana (Ghana); Christian Art Distributors (South Africa); Christian Book Discounters (South Africa); Co Info Pty Ltd (Australia); Cru Asia Ltd (East Asia, Singapore); Culturasia (East Asia, Singapore); Evangelical Outreach (Philippines); Foundation Distributing Inc (Canada); John Garratt Publishing (Australia); KCBS (Korea); Kyo Bun Kwan Inc (Japan); Manna Christian Stores (New Zealand); Momentum Christian Literature (Indonesia); OM Books Foundation (India); OMF Literature (Philippines); Pustaka Sufes Sdn Bhd (Malaysia); SKS Books Warehouse (East Asia, Singapore); Tien Dao Publishing House (Hong Kong)

§Eifrig Publishing LLC
PO Box 66, Lemont, PA 16851
Toll Free Tel: 888-340-6543
E-mail: info@eifrigpublishing.com
Web Site: www.eifrigpublishing.com
Key Personnel
Founder & Ed-in-Chief: Penny Smith Eifrig
Founded: 2006
Primarily children's titles with social, ecological, community & self-esteem emphasis.
ISBN Prefix(es): 978-1-63233
Number of titles published annually: 12 Print; 1 CD-ROM; 12 Online; 12 E-Book; 1 Audio
Total Titles: 85 Print; 3 CD-ROM; 85 E-Book; 5 Audio
Imprints: Eifrig Publishing; Getting Smart; Mt Nittany Press; YACK!
Foreign Office(s): Knobelsdorffstr 44, 14059 Berlin, Germany *Tel:* (030) 8310 3259
Foreign Rep(s): Sylvia Hayse Literary Agency (worldwide)
Foreign Rights: Sylvia Hayse Literary Agency (worldwide)
Membership(s): Independent Book Publishers Association

Eisenbrauns
PO Box 275, Winona Lake, IN 46590-0275
SAN: 200-7835
Tel: 574-269-2011 *Fax:* 574-269-6788
E-mail: customer_service@eisenbrauns.com; publisher@eisenbrauns.com
Web Site: www.eisenbrauns.com
Key Personnel
Pres & Publr: James E Eisenbraun *E-mail:* jeisenbraun@eisenbrauns.com
Ed: Amy Becker
Founded: 1975
Educational books, books on the Ancient Near East.
ISBN Prefix(es): 978-0-931464; 978-1-57506
Number of titles published annually: 40 Print; 40 E-Book
Total Titles: 615 Print; 10 CD-ROM; 432 E-Book

§Elderberry Press Inc
1393 Old Homestead Dr, Oakland, OR 97462-9690
Tel: 541-459-6043
Web Site: www.elderberrypress.com
Key Personnel
Co-Owner & Exec Ed: Valerie St John *E-mail:* editor@elderberrypress.com
Co-Owner: Asia St John
Founded: 1997
Works closely with authors, from first reading of their ms to publishing & long after to ensure their book finds up to 50,000 or more readers.
ISBN Prefix(es): 978-0-9658407; 978-1-930859; 978-1-932762; 978-1-934956

Number of titles published annually: 12 Print; 12 Online; 12 E-Book
Total Titles: 300 Print; 120 Online; 100 E-Book; 1 Audio
Imprints: Poison Vine Books; Red Anvil Press
Distributor for Poison Vine Books; Red Anvil Press
Foreign Rep(s): Ingram Book Co (worldwide)
Membership(s): Independent Book Publishers Association

§The Electrochemical Society (ECS)
65 S Main St, Bldg D, Pennington, NJ 08534-2839
Tel: 609-737-1902 *Fax:* 609-737-2743
E-mail: publications@electrochem.org; customerservice@electrochem.org
Web Site: www.electrochem.org
Key Personnel
Deputy Exec Dir & Chief Content Offr: Mary E Yess *Tel:* 609-737-1902 ext 119 *E-mail:* mary.yess@electrochem.org
Exec Dir & CEO: Roque J Calvo *Tel:* 609-737-1902 ext 101 *E-mail:* roque.calvo@electrochem.org
Dir, Mktg & Digital Engagement: Rob Gerth *Tel:* 609-737-1902 ext 114 *E-mail:* rob.gerth@electrochem.org
Dir, Pubns: James Ryan *Tel:* 609-737-1902 ext 107 *E-mail:* james.ryan@electrochem.org
Dir, Pubns Prodn: Annie Goedkoop *Tel:* 609-737-1902 ext 118 *E-mail:* ann.goedkoop@electrochem.org
Edit Mgr: Paul B Cooper *E-mail:* paul.cooper@electrochem.org
Pubns Specialist: Andrea L Guenzel *E-mail:* andrea.guenzel@electrochem.org; Beth Schademann *E-mail:* beth.schademann@electrochem.org
Founded: 1902
Technical journals, members magazine, proceedings volumes, monographs, ECS Digital Library.
ISBN Prefix(es): 978-1-56677; 978-1-60768; 978-1-62332
Number of titles published annually: 30 Print; 1 CD-ROM; 4 Online
Total Titles: 300 Print; 1 CD-ROM; 4 Online
Distributed by American Institute of Physics (AIP) (journals); John Wiley & Sons (monographs)

Edward Elgar Publishing Inc
The William Pratt House, 9 Dewey Ct, Northampton, MA 01060-3815
SAN: 299-4615
Tel: 413-584-5551 *Toll Free Tel:* 800-390-3149 (orders) *Fax:* 413-584-9933
E-mail: elgarinfo@e-elgar.com; elgarsales@e-elgar.com; elgarsubmissions@e-elgar.com (edit)
Web Site: www.e-elgar.com; www.elgaronline.com (ebooks & journals)
Key Personnel
Sales & Mktg Mgr: Katy Wight *E-mail:* kwight@e-elgar.com
Exec Ed: Alan Sturmer *E-mail:* asturmer@e-elgar.com
Founded: 1986
Leading international publisher of academic books, ebooks & journals in economics, finance, business & management, law, environment, public & social policy.
ISBN Prefix(es): 978-1-85898; 978-1-85278; 978-1-84064; 978-1-84376; 978-1-84542; 978-1-84720; 978-1-84844; 978-1-78536; 978-1-78471; 978-1-78347; 978-1-78100; 978-1-78254; 978-1-84980
Number of titles published annually: 350 Print; 300 E-Book
Total Titles: 5,600 Print; 3,000 E-Book
Foreign Office(s): Edward Elgar Publishing Ltd, the Lypiatts, 15 Lansdown Rd, Cheltenham, Glos GL50 2JA, United Kingdom, Mng Dir: Tim Williams *Tel:* (01242) 226934 *Fax:* (01242) 262111 *E-mail:* info@e-elgar.co.uk *Web Site:* www.e-elgar.co.uk
Warehouse: Books International Inc, 22883 Quicksilver Dr, Dulles, VA 20166, Cust Serv: Todd Riggleman *Tel:* 703-661-1596 *Toll Free Tel:* 800-390-3149 *Fax:* 703-996-1010 *E-mail:* elgar.orders@presswarehouse.com

Elite Books
Division of Author's Publishing Cooperative (APC)
PO Box 442, Fulton, CA 95439
Tel: 707-525-9292 *Toll Free Fax:* 800-330-9798
E-mail: support@eftuniverse.com
Web Site: www.elitebooksonline.com
Key Personnel
Ed: Stephanie Marohn *E-mail:* stephanie@stephaniemarohn.com
ISBN Prefix(es): 978-0-9720028; 978-0-9710888; 978-1-60070
Number of titles published annually: 5 Print
Total Titles: 40 Print
Distribution Center: Midpoint Trade, 27 W 20 St, Suite 1102, New York, NY 10010, Contact: Gail Kump *Tel:* 212-727-0190 *E-mail:* midpointny1@aol.com *Web Site:* www.midpointtrade.com
Membership(s): Independent Book Publishers Association

Elsevier Engineering Information (Ei)
Subsidiary of Elsevier Inc
230 Park Ave, 8th fl, New York, NY 10169-0123
Tel: 212-989-5800 *Fax:* 212-633-3990
E-mail: eicustomersupport@elsevier.com
Web Site: www.ei.org
Key Personnel
Dir, Scopus & EV Content Mgmt: Judy Salk
Founded: 1884
Provides online information, knowledge & support to engineering researchers. Flagship platform is Engineering Village & the primary database is Compendex.
ISBN Prefix(es): 978-0-87394
Number of titles published annually: 8 Online
Total Titles: 8 Online

Elsevier, Health Sciences Division
Division of RELX Group PLC
1600 John F Kennedy Blvd, Suite 1800, Philadelphia, PA 19103-2899
Tel: 215-239-3900 *Toll Free Tel:* 800-523-1649 *Fax:* 215-239-3990
Web Site: www.us.elsevierhealth.com
Key Personnel
CFO, Health Sci Div: Bob Munro
SVP, US Global Medicine: Linda Belfus
Founded: 1906
ISBN Prefix(es): 978-0-7506; 978-0-443; 978-0-444; 978-0-932883; 978-1-56053; 978-0-8016; 978-0-8151; 978-0-7216; 978-0-7020; 978-0-7234; 978-0-323; 978-0-7236; 978-1-4160; 978-1-55664; 978-0-920513; 978-1-898507; 978-1-932141; 978-1-4377; 978-1-4557
Number of titles published annually: 2,000 Print
Imprints: ASVP; B C Decker; Gower; Jems; Mosby; PSG; Saunders; Wolfe; Year Book
Branch Office(s)
3251 Riverport Lane, Maryland Heights, MO 63043 *Tel:* 314-872-8370 *Toll Free Tel:* 800-325-4177 *Fax:* 314-447-8033 SAN: 200-2280
360 Park Ave S, New York, NY 10010 *Tel:* 212-989-5800 *Fax:* 212-633-3990
Foreign Office(s): Tower 1, Level 12, 475 Victoria Ave, Chatswood, NSW 2067, Australia *Tel:* (02) 9422 8500 *Fax:* (02) 9422 8501
Beilstein Informationssysteme, Theodor-Heuss-Allee 108, 60486 Frankfurt, Germany *Tel:* (069) 5050 4242 *Fax:* (069) 5050 4245
2F Higashi Azabu, One Chome Bldg, 1-9-15 Higashi Azabu, Minato-ku 106-0044, Japan *Tel:* (03) 5561 5033 *Fax:* (03) 5561 5047
3 Killiney Rd 08-01, Winsland House I, Singapore 239519, Singapore *Tel:* (06) 349 0200 *Fax:* (06) 733 1510
The Blvd, Langford Lane, Kidlington, Oxford OX5 1GB, United Kingdom *Tel:* (01865) 843000 *Fax:* (01865) 843010
Distributor for G W Medical Publisher
Foreign Rights: John Scott & Co (Jake Scott)
Shipping Address: PO Box 437, Linn, MO 65051-0437
Distribution Center: 1799 Hwy 50 E, Linn, MO 65051 *Tel:* 573-897-3694 *Fax:* 573-897-4387

§Elsevier Inc
Subsidiary of RELX Group PLC
50 Hampshire St, 5th fl, Cambridge, MA 02139
Toll Free Tel: 866-607-1414 *Fax:* 617-661-7061
E-mail: usbkinfo@elsevier.com
Web Site: www.elsevier.com
Key Personnel
VP, Sales: Charles Withington
Founded: 1880
Books for professionals, researchers & students in the sciences, technology, engineering, business & media. Also research monographs, major reference works & serials.
Number of titles published annually: 2,500 Print; 400 E-Book
Total Titles: 40,000 Print
Foreign Office(s): Linacre House, Jordan Hill, Oxford OX2 8DP, United Kingdom, Contact: Duncan Enright *Tel:* (01865) 314563
Foreign Rep(s): Elsevier (UK) (Europe)
Foreign Rights: Elsevier; Linacre House (Europe)
Membership(s): AAP
See separate listing for:
Elsevier Engineering Information (Ei)
Morgan Kaufmann

Elva Resa Publishing
8362 Tamarack Village, Suite 119-106, St Paul, MN 55125
Tel: 651-357-8770 *Fax:* 501-641-0777
E-mail: staff@elvaresa.com
Web Site: www.elvaresa.com; www.militaryfamilybooks.com
Founded: 1997
Books for & about military families.
ISBN Prefix(es): 978-1-934617; 978-0-9657483
Number of titles published annually: 4 Print
Total Titles: 22 Print
Imprints: Alma Little (children's books); Elva Resa (books for & about military families); Juloya (inspirational works that help people celebrate life)
Membership(s): Independent Book Publishers Association; Midwest Independent Publishing Association

§EMC Publishing LLC
Division of New Mountain Learning LLC
875 Montreal Way, St Paul, MN 55102
SAN: 201-3800
Tel: 651-290-2800 (corp) *Toll Free Tel:* 800-328-1452 *Toll Free Fax:* 800-328-4564
E-mail: educate@emcp.com
Web Site: www.emcp.com
Key Personnel
EVP & COO: Joy Hoppe
VP, Info Technol: Chuck Bratton
VP, Sales: Joe Modzelewski
VP, Sales, Coll Div: Todd Larsen
Dir, Mktg: Peter Hodges
Gen Mgr: Michael Demakos
Cust Serv Mgr: Cheryl Monson
Founded: 1954
Paper & hardbound textbooks, audio, video, online Internet, CD-ROM, software microcomputer instructional materials in world language,

business education, literature & language arts, social studies, medical, computer technology.
ISBN Prefix(es): 978-0-8219; 978-1-56118; 978-0-7638; 978-0-88436; 978-0-912022
Number of titles published annually: 100 Print; 75 CD-ROM; 20 Online; 100 E-Book; 80 Audio
Total Titles: 3,700 Print; 300 CD-ROM; 75 Online; 3,500 E-Book; 1,035 Audio
Divisions: JIST Publishing; Paradigm Publishing Inc
Distributor for Sybex Inc
Foreign Rep(s): Wolfgang Kraft (worldwide)
Foreign Rights: Wolfgang Kraft (worldwide)
See separate listing for:
JIST Publishing

Emerald Books
Affiliate of YWAM Publishing
PO Box 55787, Seattle, WA 98155
Tel: 425-771-1153 *Toll Free Tel:* 800-922-2143 *Fax:* 425-775-2383
E-mail: books@ywampublishing.com
Web Site: www.ywampublishing.com
Key Personnel
Publr & Intl Rts: Warren Walsh
Mktg Dir: Wenke Warren
Ed: Ryan Davis
Founded: 1992
Christian theme.
ISBN Prefix(es): 978-1-883002; 978-1-932096; 978-1-62486
Number of titles published annually: 15 Print
Total Titles: 364 Print
Distributed by YWAM Publishing
Shipping Address: 7825 230 St SW, Edmonds, WA 98026 *Web Site:* ywampublishing.com

Emmaus Road Publishing Inc
Division of St Paul Center for Biblical Theology
1468 Parkview Circle, Steubenville, OH 43952
Tel: 740-283-2880 (outside US)
Toll Free Tel: 800-398-5470 (orders) *Fax:* 740-283-4011 (orders)
E-mail: questions@emmausroad.org
Web Site: www.emmausroad.org
Key Personnel
VP, Opers: Nate Roberts
Publr: Andrew Jones
Order Processing: Michelle Olenick
E-mail: molenick@emmausroad.org
Founded: 1998
Bible studies, biblically based apologetics & other materials faithful to the teaching of the Catholic church. Restocking fee of 20% for returns.
ISBN Prefix(es): 978-0-9663223; 978-1-931018; 978-1-937155; 978-1-941447; 978-1-940329; 978-1-63446
Number of titles published annually: 12 Print; 12 E-Book
Total Titles: 80 Print; 1 CD-ROM; 50 E-Book; 10 Audio

Empire Press Media/Avant-Guide
Unit of Empire Press Media Inc
244 Fifth Ave, Suite 2053, New York, NY 10001-7604
Tel: 917-512-3881 *Fax:* 212-202-7757
E-mail: info@avantguide.com; communications@avantguide.com; editor@avantguide.com
Web Site: www.avantguide.com
Key Personnel
Dir: Scott Walker
Founded: 1999
Publisher of nonfiction books on pop culture, travel, business & marketing, as well as handbooks for keynote speakers & trends titles by the global trends expert Daniel Levine.
ISBN Prefix(es): 978-1-891603
Number of titles published annually: 50 Print; 50 E-Book
Total Titles: 224 Print; 400 E-Book
Imprints: Avant-Guide; Empire; Keynote Speakers Today
Foreign Rep(s): Hi Marketing (Europe, UK)
Foreign Rights: PGW (Canada)
Distribution Center: Publishers Group West

Empire Publishing Service
Division of The Empire (media group)
PO Box 1344, Studio City, CA 91614-0344
Tel: 818-784-8918
E-mail: empirepubsvc@att.net
Key Personnel
Dir, Opers: Chris Cordero
Busn Dir: David Cole
Founded: 1960
Publisher & distributor of entertainment books, plays & musicals, specialty books & printed music.
ISBN Prefix(es): 978-1-58690; 978-0-934468
Number of titles published annually: 25 Print
Total Titles: 4,365 Print
Imprints: Arsis Press (music); Classics With a Twist; Gaslight Publications; Paul Mould Publishing; Phantom Books & Music; Sisra Music Publishing; Spotlight Books; Jack Spratt Choral Music
Subsidiaries: Best Books International
Distributor for Arsis Press; Arte Publico Press; Ian Henry Publications; ISH Group (worldwide exc Australia); Paul Mould Publishing

Enchanted Lion Books
351 Van Brunt St, Ground fl-Gallery, Brooklyn, NY 11231
Tel: 646-785-9272
E-mail: enchantedlion@gmail.com
Web Site: www.enchantedlionbooks.com
Key Personnel
Publr: Claudia Bedrick
Founded: 2002
Publish illustrated nonfiction picture books for children in the categories of art, biography & history, science & nature, folktales & mythology.
ISBN Prefix(es): 978-1-59270
Number of titles published annually: 16 Print
Total Titles: 100 Print
Distributed by Consortium; Farrar, Straus & Giroux, LLC
Orders to: Perseus Distribution Services, 1094 Flex Dr, Jackson, TN 38301-5070 *Toll Free Tel:* 800-283-3572 *Toll Free Fax:* 800-351-5073 *E-mail:* orderentry@perseusbooks.com
Returns: Perseus Distribution Services, 193 Edwards Dr, Jackson, TN 38301-5070 *Toll Free Tel:* 800-343-4499
Distribution Center: Consortium Book Sales & Distribution, The Keg House, 34 13 Ave NE, Minneapolis, MN 55413-1007 *Tel:* 612-746-2600 *Fax:* 612-746-2606 *E-mail:* info@cbsd.com

Encounter Books
900 Broadway, Suite 601, New York, NY 10003
Tel: 212-871-6310 *Toll Free Tel:* 800-786-3839 *Fax:* 212-871-6311
E-mail: publicity@encounterbooks.com
Web Site: www.encounterbooks.com
Key Personnel
Pres & Publr: Roger Kimball *E-mail:* kimball@encounterbooks.com
Exec Dir, Opers: Nola Tully *E-mail:* ntully@encounterbooks.com
Dir, Mktg: Sam Schneider
Dir, Prodn: Heather Ohle *E-mail:* ohle@encounterbooks.com
Publicity Dir: Lauren Miklos *E-mail:* lmiklos@encounterbooks.com
Founded: 1998
Serious nonfiction books about history, culture, current events, religion, politics, social criticism & public policy.
ISBN Prefix(es): 978-1-893554; 978-1-59403
Number of titles published annually: 30 Print; 30 E-Book
Total Titles: 400 Print; 250 E-Book
Orders to: Perseus Distribution, 1094 Flex Dr, Jackson, TN 38301 (US, CN & Australia) *Toll Free Tel:* 800-343-4499 *Toll Free Fax:* 800-351-5073 *Web Site:* www.perseusdistribution.com
Returns: PSSC-Returns, 660 S Mansfield, Ypsilanti, MI 48197
Distribution Center: Perseus Distribution, 1094 Flex Dr, Jackson, TN 38301 (US, CN & Australia) *Toll Free Tel:* 800-343-4499 *Toll Free Fax:* 800-351-5073 *Web Site:* www.perseusdistribution.com
Membership(s): ABA; ALA; Independent Book Publishers Association

§Encyclopaedia Britannica Inc
325 N La Salle St, Chicago, IL 60654
Tel: 312-347-7159 (all other countries)
Toll Free Tel: 800-323-1229 (US & CN)
Fax: 312-294-2104
E-mail: contact@eb.com
Web Site: www.eb.com; www.britannica.com
Key Personnel
Pres: Jorge Cauz
Gen Coun: Douglas Eveleigh
SVP, Corp Devt: Michael Ross
SVP, Intl Opers: Leah Mansoor
Founded: 1768
Reference works, print & online for consumers & institutions.
ISBN Prefix(es): 978-0-87827; 978-0-8347; 978-0-85229; 978-1-61535; 978-0-9823824; 978-1-62513; 978-1-59339; 978-1-60835; 978-0-9823823; 978-0-9823819; 978-0-7826; 978-0-9823820; 978-0-9823821; 978-0-9823822
Subsidiaries: Merriam-Webster Inc
Foreign Office(s): Encyclopaedia Britannica Australia Ltd, Level 1, 90 Mount St, North Sydney, NSW 2060, Australia (Australia & Asia Pacific) *Tel:* (02) 9923 5600 *Fax:* (02) 9929 3753 *E-mail:* sales@britannica.com.au *Web Site:* www.britannica.com.au
Encyclopaedia Britannica India Pvt Ltd, 140, Zamrudpur Shopping Complex, N-Block Rd, Greater Kailash-I, New Dehli 110048, India (Bahrain, Kuwait, Oman, Qatar, Saudi Arabia, United Arab Emirates, Yemen) *Tel:* (011) 4653-6450 *Fax:* (011) 2924-5116 *E-mail:* marketing@ebindia.com *Web Site:* www.britannicaindia.com
Britannica.com Israel Ltd, 16 Tozeret Ha'aretz St., Tel Aviv 67891, Israel *Tel:* (03) 607 0400 *Fax:* (03) 607 0401 *Web Site:* www.britannicaindia.co.il
Britannica Japan Co Ltd, Da Vinci Nishi-Gotanda 2-F, 8-3-16 Nishi-Gotanda, Shinagawa-ku, Tokyo 141-0031, Japan *Tel:* (03) 5436 1388 *Fax:* (03) 5436 1380 *E-mail:* info@britannica.co.jp *Web Site:* www.britannica.co.jp
Encyclopaedia Britannica (UK) Ltd, Unity Wharf, 2nd fl, Mill St, London SE1 2BH, United Kingdom (Africa, Europe, Middle East) *Tel:* (020) 7500 7800 *Fax:* (020) 7500 7878 *E-mail:* enquiries@britannica.co.uk *Web Site:* www.britannica.co.uk
See separate listing for:
Merriam-Webster Inc

Energy Information Administration (EIA)
Imprint of US Government Publishing Office
1000 Independence Ave SW, Washington, DC 20585
Tel: 202-586-8800 *Fax:* 202-586-0727
E-mail: infoctr@eia.doe.gov
Web Site: www.eia.doe.gov

Key Personnel
Dir: Gina Pearson *Tel:* 202-586-6537 *Fax:* 202-586-0114 *E-mail:* gina.pearson@eia.gov
Founded: 1977
Periodicals, analytical reports, energy statistics.
ISBN Prefix(es): 978-0-16; 978-0-18
Number of titles published annually: 37 Print
Distributed by EPO; NTIS

Energy Psychology Press
Division of Energy Psychology Group
1490 Mark West Springs Rd, Santa Rosa, CA 95404
Mailing Address: 3340 Fulton Rd, No 442, Fulton, CA 95439
Tel: 707-525-9292 *Toll Free Fax:* 800-330-9798
E-mail: support@eftuniverse.com
Web Site: www.energypsychologypress.com; www.elitebooksonline.com
Key Personnel
Publr: Dawson Church
Ed-in-Chief: Stephanie Marohn *E-mail:* stephanie@eftuniverse.com
Prodn Coord: Heather Montgomery *E-mail:* heather@eftuniverse.com
ISBN Prefix(es): 978-1-60415
Number of titles published annually: 5 Print
Total Titles: 40 Print
Distribution Center: Hay House, 2750 Progress St, Vista, CA 92081, Contact: Joe Koburn *Tel:* 760-419-1715 *E-mail:* jcoburn@hayhouse.com *Web Site:* www.hayhouse.com
Membership(s): Independent Book Publishers Association

§Enfield Publishing & Distribution Co
234 May St, Enfield, NH 03748
Mailing Address: PO Box 699, Enfield, NH 03748
Tel: 603-632-7377 *Fax:* 603-632-5611
E-mail: info@enfieldbooks.com
Web Site: www.enfieldbooks.com
Key Personnel
Mng Dir: Linda Jones
Founded: 1996
Distribute foreign publishers, regional publishers & educational titles.
ISBN Prefix(es): 978-0-9656184; 978-1-893598
Number of titles published annually: 5 Print
Total Titles: 11 Print
Membership(s): Independent Publishers of New England

§Enslow Publishing LLC
101 W 23 St, Suite 240, New York, NY 10011
Tel: 908-771-9400 *Toll Free Tel:* 800-398-2504 *Fax:* 908-771-0925 *Toll Free Fax:* 877-980-4454
E-mail: customerservice@enslow.com
Web Site: www.enslow.com
Key Personnel
Pres: Mark Enslow
VP & Publr: Brian D Enslow
Founded: 1976
Educational nonfiction books for children & young adults.
ISBN Prefix(es): 978-0-89490; 978-0-7760; 978-1-59845; 978-1-4644; 978-1-4645; 978-1-4646; 978-1-62285; 978-1-62293; 978-1-62324; 978-1-62400
Number of titles published annually: 200 Print; 200 E-Book
Total Titles: 2,400 Print
Imprints: Enslow (middle & high school books); Enslow Elementary (PreK-5); MyReportLinks.com Books (Internet supported books)
Foreign Rep(s): CrossCan Educational Services Inc (Canada); EduCan Media (Canada); Everybody's Books (Warren Halford) (South Africa); Read Pacific (New Zealand)
Membership(s): AASL; ALA; Educational Book & Media Association; TLA

Entangled Publishing
2614 S Timberline Rd, Suite 109, Fort Collins, CO 80525
Toll Free Tel: 877-677-9451
E-mail: publisher@entangledpublishing.com
Web Site: www.entangledpublishing.com
Key Personnel
Publr & Edit Dir, Covet: Liz Pelletier
Exec Publicity Dir: Melissa Bourbon Ramirez
Edit Dir, Brazen & Scorched: Brenda Chin
ISBN Prefix(es): 978-1-937044; 978-1-62266; 978-1-62061
Number of titles published annually: 48 Print; 312 E-Book
Imprints: Bliss (everyday heroes, sweet romance); Brazen (where romance begins in the bedroom); Covet (put a little para in your normal); Embrace (new adult romance); Entangled Edge (digital first romance); Entangled Select (adult single title romance); Entangled Teen (young adult romance); Ignite (intrigue, passion, heart-stopping suspense); Indulgence (powerful heroes, passionate romance); Lovestruck (romantic comedy & fun, flirty romance); Scandalous (daring love, timeless romance)
Distributed by Macmillan

EntertainmentPro, see Quite Specific Media Group Ltd

Entomological Society of America
3 Park Place, Suite 307, Annapolis, MD 21401-3722
Tel: 301-731-4535 *Fax:* 301-731-4538
E-mail: esa@entsoc.org
Web Site: www.entsoc.org
Key Personnel
Exec Dir: David Gammel *E-mail:* dgammel@entsoc.org
Dir, Communs: Lisa Junker *Tel:* 301-731-4535 ext 3020 *E-mail:* ljunker@entsoc.org
Dir, Strategic Initiatives: Christopher Stelzig *E-mail:* cstelzig@entsoc.org
Founded: 1889
Professional scientific society for entomologists. Publish research journals on all areas of entomology.
ISBN Prefix(es): 978-0-938522; 978-0-9776209; 978-0-9966674
Number of titles published annually: 9 Print; 1 CD-ROM; 5 Online
Total Titles: 57 Print; 1 CD-ROM; 5 Online
Distributed by Oxford University Press

§Environmental Law Institute
1730 "M" St NW, Suite 700, Washington, DC 20036
Tel: 202-939-3800 *Toll Free Tel:* 800-433-5120 *Fax:* 202-939-3868
E-mail: law@eli.org
Web Site: www.eli.org
Key Personnel
Chmn: Edward Strohbehn
Pres & VP, Pubns: Scott Schang *E-mail:* schang@eli.org
Ed, The Environmental Forum: Stephen Dujack *E-mail:* dujack@eli.org
Founded: 1969
Environmental studies, references, online database services, monographs, policy studies.
ISBN Prefix(es): 978-0-911937; 978-1-58576
Number of titles published annually: 6 Print; 30 Online
Total Titles: 53 Print; 1 CD-ROM; 200 Online
Distributed by Island Press

Epicenter Press Inc
6524 NE 181 St, Suite 2, Kenmore, WA 98028
Tel: 425-485-6822 (edit, mktg, busn off) *Fax:* 425-481-8253
E-mail: info@epicenterpress.com
Web Site: www.epicenterpress.com
Key Personnel
COO: J Stephen Lay *E-mail:* slay@epicenterpress.com
Dir, Sales & Mktg: Phil Garrett *E-mail:* phil@epicenterpress.com
Acqs Ed: Lael Morgan *E-mail:* lael@epicenterpress.com
Managerial Asst: Aubrey Anderson *E-mail:* aubrey@epicenterpress.com
Founded: 1988
Regional nonfiction trade publisher. Specialize in titles about Alaska & the Pacific Northwest. Trade distributor of titles by other publishers. Packager, print-broker & book publishing consultant.
ISBN Prefix(es): 978-0-945397; 978-0-9708493; 978-0-9724944; 978-0-9800825; 978-1-935347
Number of titles published annually: 8 Print; 10 E-Book
Total Titles: 100 Print
Divisions: Aftershocks Media (book packager, contract publishing services, consulting, book distribution)
Distributor for Appell Publishing; Camel Press; Coastal Publishing; Coffeetown Press; Copper Raven Press; Delano Publishing; Documentary Media; Far North Press; Five Star Misadventures; Gold Fever Press; Joyful Productions; McRoy & Blackburn, Publishers; Meditation Press; Old Seattle Press; Patos Island Press; Raising Lucy Studios LLC; Raleigh Press; Reach for the Sky Publishing; RLO Media Productions; Saltry Press; Sprucehaven Publishing; Westridge Art; Winternights Publishing; Yamhill Press
Foreign Rights: Wales Literary Agency (worldwide)
Membership(s): Book Publishers of the Northwest; Independent Book Publishers Association

EPS/School Specialty Literacy & Intervention
Division of School Specialty Inc
625 Mount Auburn St, 3rd fl, Cambridge, MA 02138-3039
SAN: 201-8225
Mailing Address: PO Box 9031, Cambridge, MA 02139-9031
Toll Free Tel: 800-225-5750 *Toll Free Fax:* 888-440-2665
E-mail: customerservice.eps@schoolspecialty.com
Web Site: eps.schoolspecialty.com
Key Personnel
VP & Publr: Charles Heinle
VP, Fin: Dave Ciommo
Founded: 1952
Technology & print educational materials for grades K-12, with particular emphasis on language arts, remedial reading skills, materials for the child with specific language disability, workbooks - elementary; workbooks - secondary, learning differences.
ISBN Prefix(es): 978-0-8388; 978-1-4293
Number of titles published annually: 25 Print
Total Titles: 800 Print
Imprints: Modern Learning Press
Branch Office(s)
555 Legget Dr, Suite 900, Tower B, Ottawa, ON K2K 2X3, Canada
Returns: 80 Northwest Blvd, Nashua, NH 03063

Ericson Books
1614 Redbud St, Nacogdoches, TX 75965-2936
Tel: 936-564-3625 *Fax:* 936-552-8999
Key Personnel
Owner & Publr: Carolyn Reeves Ericson
Exec Asst: Kimberly Whitmore
Founded: 1975
Genealogical & East Texas history.
ISBN Prefix(es): 978-0-911317
Number of titles published annually: 5 Print
Total Titles: 95 Print

Distributed by Mountain Press; Byron Sistler
Distributor for Clearfield; Dietz Press; Southern Historical Press

§Etruscan Press
Wilkes University, 84 W South St, Wilkes-Barre, PA 18766
Tel: 570-408-4546 *Fax:* 570-408-3333
E-mail: books@etruscanpress.org
Web Site: www.etruscanpress.org
Key Personnel
Exec Dir: Dr Philip Brady
Exec Ed: Dr Robert Mooney
Mng Ed: Bill Schneider *E-mail:* bill@etruscanpress.org
Founded: 2001
Housed at Wilkes University & partnering with Youngstown State University, Etruscan is a nonprofit literary press working to produce & promote books that nurture the dialogue among genres, cultures & voices. We publish books of poems, novels, short stories, creative nonfiction, criticism, translation & anthologies.
ISBN Prefix(es): 978-0-9832944; 978-0-9797450; 978-0-9833294; 978-0-9897532; 978-0-9886922; 978-0-9903221
Number of titles published annually: 6 Print
Total Titles: 75 Print
Distribution Center: Consortium Book Sales & Distribution, The Keg House, 34 13 Ave NE, Suite 101, Minneapolis, MN 55413-1007 *Toll Free Tel:* 800-283-3572 *Web Site:* www.cbsd.com
Membership(s): Community of Literary Magazines & Presses; Independent Book Publishers Association

Europa Editions
214 W 29 St, Suite 1003, New York, NY 10001
Tel: 212-868-6844 *Fax:* 212-868-6845
E-mail: info@europaeditions.com
Web Site: www.europaeditions.com
Key Personnel
Publr & Co-Founder: Sandro Ferri
Publr, Pres & Co-Founder: Sandra Ozzola Ferri
Ed-in-Chief: Michael Reynolds
Publr-at-Large: Kent Carroll
Sr Publicist: Rachael Small
Sales & Mktg Mgr: Christian Westermann
Founded: 2005
Publisher of international literary fiction in translation, domestic literary fiction, crime & narrative nonfiction.
ISBN Prefix(es): 978-1-933372; 978-1-60945
Number of titles published annually: 35 Print
Total Titles: 300 Print
Imprints: Europa World Noir; Tonga Books
Foreign Office(s): via Camozzi. 1, 00195 Rome RM, Italy, Mng Ed: Simona Olivito *Tel:* (06) 3722829 *Fax:* (06) 37351096
Distributed by Penguin Random House Inc; Penguin Random House Canada
Distribution Center: Penguin Group USA, A Penguin Random House Company, 405 Murray Hill Pkwy, East Rutherford, NJ 07073-2136 *Toll Free Tel:* 800-526-0275 *Toll Free Fax:* 800-227-9604 *E-mail:* orders@us.penguingroup.com
Turnaround Publisher Services Ltd, Unit 3, Olympia Trading Estate, Coburg Rd, Wood Green, London N22 6TZ, United Kingdom (UK & Ireland) *Tel:* (020) 8829 3000 *E-mail:* orders@turnaround-uk.com *Web Site:* www.turnaround-uk.com

§Evan-Moor Educational Publishers
18 Lower Ragsdale Dr, Monterey, CA 93940-5746
Tel: 831-649-5901 *Toll Free Tel:* 800-777-4362 (orders) *Fax:* 831-649-6256 *Toll Free Fax:* 800-777-4332 (orders)
E-mail: sales@evan-moor.com; marketing@evan-moor.com
Web Site: www.evan-moor.com
Key Personnel
Founder & CEO: William Evans *E-mail:* bill@evan-moor.com
Chief Mktg Offr: Trisha Thomas
VP, Sales: Glenn Aument
Exec Ed: Lisa Vitarisi Mathews
Dir, Fin: David Miller
Founded: 1979
Supplemental educational materials in print & digital formats for parents & teachers of children ages 3-14. Subjects include reading, math, writing, science, social studies, arts & crafts & literature.
ISBN Prefix(es): 978-1-55799; 978-1-62938; 978-1-61367; 978-1-61366; 978-1-59673; 978-1-4409; 978-1-60792; 978-1-61368; 978-1-61365; 978-1-60793; 978-1-935353; 978-1-60823; 978-1-60963
Number of titles published annually: 25 Print; 60 Online; 25 E-Book
Total Titles: 450 Print; 450 Online; 450 E-Book
Membership(s): AAP PreK-12 Learning Group; ABA; ALA; Education Market Association

M Evans & Company
Imprint of Rowman & Littlefield Publishing Group
c/o Rowman & Littlefield Publishing Group, 4501 Forbes Blvd, Suite 200, Lanham, MD 20706
Tel: 301-459-3366 *Fax:* 301-429-5748
Web Site: rowman.com
Key Personnel
Ed: Rick Rinehart *E-mail:* rrinehart@rowman.com
Founded: 1963
Health, medical & business books.
ISBN Prefix(es): 978-0-87131; 978-1-59077
Number of titles published annually: 30 Print
Total Titles: 250 Print
Foreign Rights: Rights Unlimited
Shipping Address: National Book Network, 15200 NBN Way, Blue Ridge Summit, PA 17214 *Tel:* 717-794-3800 *Toll Free Tel:* 800-462-6420 *Fax:* 717-794-4801 *Toll Free Fax:* 800-338-4550
Distribution Center: National Book Network, 4720 Boston Way, Lanham, MD 20706

Evergreen Pacific Publishing Ltd
4204 Russell Rd, Suite M, Mukilteo, WA 98275-5424
Tel: 425-493-1451 *Fax:* 425-493-1453
E-mail: sales@evergreenpacific.com
Web Site: www.evergreenpacific.com
Key Personnel
Pres: Paul Hamstra
Founded: 1996
Books, charts & guides for water related recreations.
ISBN Prefix(es): 978-0-945265; 978-0-9609036; 978-1-934707
Number of titles published annually: 4 Print
Total Titles: 25 Print
Imprints: Evergreen Pacific Publishing

Everything Goes Media LLC
PO Box 1524, Milwaukee, WI 53201
Tel: 312-226-8400
E-mail: info@everythinggoesmedia.com
Web Site: www.everythinggoesmedia.com
Key Personnel
Owner & Publr: Sharon Woodhouse *E-mail:* sharon@everythinggoesmedia.com
Founded: 1994
"The book is the medium." Traditional publisher with unconventional approaches.
ISBN Prefix(es): 978-1-893121
Number of titles published annually: 5 Print; 4 E-Book
Total Titles: 40 Print; 4 E-Book
Imprints: Everything Goes Media (nonfiction-lifestyle, hobby, gift & business); Lake Claremont Press (nonfiction-Chicago guidebooks & histories); S Woodhouse Books (nonfiction-ideas, history, trends & current events)
Divisions: Conspire Creative
See separate listing for:
Lake Claremont Press

Excalibur Publications
PO Box 89667, Tucson, AZ 85752-9667
Tel: 520-575-9057
E-mail: excaliburpublications@centurylink.net
Key Personnel
Ed-in-Chief: Alan M Petrillo
Founded: 1990
ISBN Prefix(es): 978-1-880677
Number of titles published annually: 3 Print; 2 E-Book
Total Titles: 16 Print; 4 E-Book
Distribution Center: Barnes & Noble, One Barnes & Noble Way, Suite B, Monroe, NJ 08831
Baker & Taylor, 2550 W Tyvola Rd, Suite 300, Charlotte, NC 28217
Amazon.com, 1200 12 Ave S, Suite 1200, Seattle, WA 98144-2734

Excelsior Editions
Imprint of State University of New York Press
10 N Pearl St, 4th fl, Albany, NY 12207
SAN: 760-7261
Tel: 518-944-2800 *Toll Free Tel:* 866-430-7869 *Fax:* 518-320-1592
E-mail: info@sunypress.edu
Web Site: www.sunypress.edu
Key Personnel
Co-Dir: James Peltz *Tel:* 518-944-2815 *E-mail:* james.peltz@sunypress.edu
Assoc Dir & Dir, Sales & Busn Devt: Daniel Flynn *Tel:* 518-944-2823 *E-mail:* daniel.flynn@sunypress.edu
Founded: 2008
Publish regional & trade books.
ISBN Prefix(es): 978-0-7914; 978-1-929373 (Hudson Valley region); 978-1-4384; 978-0-9722977 (Uncrowned Queens)
Number of titles published annually: 25 Print; 15 Audio
Total Titles: 230 Print; 155 E-Book; 1 Audio
Distributor for Albany Institute of History & Art; Uncrowned Queens
Foreign Rep(s): Lexa Publishers' Representatives (Elise & Mical Moser) (Canada); MHM Limited (Japan); NBN International (UK & the continent); US PubRep Inc (Craig Falk) (Caribbean, Central America, Mexico, Puerto Rico, South America)
Orders to: SUNY Press, PO Box 960, Herndon, VA 20172-0960, Cust Serv *Tel:* 703-661-1575 *Toll Free Tel:* 877-204-6073 *Fax:* 703-996-1010 *Toll Free Fax:* 877-204-6074 *E-mail:* suny@presswarehouse.com
Returns: SUNY Press, Returns Dept, 22883 Quicksilver Dr, Dulles, VA 20166, Cust Serv *Tel:* 703-661-1575 *Toll Free Tel:* 877-204-6073 *Fax:* 703-996-1010 *Toll Free Fax:* 877-204-6074 *E-mail:* suny@presswarehouse.com
Shipping Address: SUNY Press, 22835 Quicksilver Dr, Dulles, VA 20166, Cust Serv *Tel:* 703-661-1575 *Toll Free Tel:* 877-204-6073 *Fax:* 703-996-1010 *Toll Free Fax:* 877-204-6074 *E-mail:* suny@presswarehouse.com
Warehouse: SUNY Press, PO Box 960, Herndon, VA 20172-0960, Cust Serv *Tel:* 703-661-1575 *Toll Free Tel:* 877-204-6073 *Fax:* 703-996-1010 *Toll Free Fax:* 877-204-6074 *E-mail:* suny@presswarehouse.com

The Experiment
220 E 23 St, Suite 301, New York, NY 10010-4674

Tel: 212-889-1659
E-mail: info@theexperimentpublishing.com
Web Site: www.theexperimentpublishing.com
Key Personnel
COO & CFO: Peter Burri
Pres & Publr: Matthew Lore
Art Dir: Sarah Smith
Publicity & Mktg Dir: Jennifer Hergenroeder
Digital Publg Mgr: Karen Giangreco
Publg Mgr: Pamela Schechter
Contracts & Rts Assoc: Ana Ban
Mng Ed: Jeanne Tao
Sr Ed: Joan Strasbaugh
Ed: Nick Cizek; Jennifer Kurdyla
Asst Ed: Batya Rosenblum
Ed-at-Large: Anna Bliss
Founded: 2008
ISBN Prefix(es): 978-1-61519
Number of titles published annually: 40 Print; 40 E-Book
Total Titles: 150 Print; 150 E-Book
Sales Office(s): Workman Publishing, 225 Varick St, New York, NY 10014-4381 SAN: 631-760X
Distributed by Workman Publishing
Foreign Rep(s): Maribeth Casey (worldwide exc Australia, Brazil, New Zealand & UK); Gregory Messina (Australia, New Zealand, UK & Commonwealth); Agencia Riff (Brazil)
Orders to: Workman Publishing, 225 Varick St, New York, NY 10014-4381 *Toll Free Tel:* 800-722-7202 *E-mail:* orders@workman.com SAN: 631-760X
Returns: Workman Publishing Co Inc, c/o RR Donnelley, 677 Brighton Beach Rd, Menasha, WI 54952
Membership(s): AAP

Eye in the Ear Children's Audio
5 Crescent St, Portland, ME 04102
Toll Free Tel: 855-99-STORY (997-8679) *Fax:* 207-699-1380 (attn: Laurence Kelly)
E-mail: info@eyeintheear.com
Web Site: www.eyeintheear.com
Key Personnel
Owner: Frances Kelly
Pres: Laurence A Kelly *E-mail:* lk@maine.rr.com
Founded: 1985
Production & distribution of quality classic children's audio stories. Titles available from Amazon.com, Chinaberry & TEI Landmark Audio.
ISBN Prefix(es): 978-0-944168
Number of titles published annually: 3 Audio
Total Titles: 31 Online; 31 Audio
Editorial Office(s): c/o MBC, 415 Congress St, Portland, ME 04101
Returns: Fleetwood MultiMedia, 20 Wheeler St, St Lynn, MA 01910, Contact: Wayne Terminello *Toll Free Tel:* 800-353-1830 *Fax:* 781-599-2440 *E-mail:* wayne@fltwood.com
Shipping Address: Fleetwood MultiMedia, 20 Wheeler St, St Lynn, MA 01910, Contact: Wayne Terminello *Toll Free Tel:* 800-353-1830 *Fax:* 781-599-2440 *E-mail:* wayne@fltwood.com
Warehouse: Fleetwood MultiMedia, 20 Wheeler St, St Lynn, MA 01910, Contact: Wayne Terminello *Toll Free Tel:* 800-353-1830 *Fax:* 781-599-2440 *E-mail:* wayne@fltwood.com
Distribution Center: Christian Book Distributors, 1400 Summit St, Peabody, MA 01960 *Toll Free Tel:* 800-247-4784 *E-mail:* customer.service@christianbook.com
Fleetwood MultiMedia, 20 Wheeler St, St Lynn, MA 01910, Contact: Wayne Terminello *Toll Free Tel:* 800-353-1830 *Fax:* 781-599-2440 *E-mail:* wayne@fltwood.com

Facts Cures & Answers, see FC&A Publishing

§Facts On File
Imprint of Infobase Learning
132 W 31 St, 17th fl, New York, NY 10001
SAN: 201-4696
Tel: 212-967-8800 *Toll Free Tel:* 800-322-8755 *Toll Free Fax:* 800-678-3633
E-mail: custserv@factsonfile.com
Web Site: infobasepublishing.com
Key Personnel
Pres & CEO: Mark McDonnell
CFO: Jim Housley
Dir, Book & Ebook Sales: Justyna Pawluk *E-mail:* jpawluk@infobaselearning.com
Edit Dir, Print: Laurie Likoff
Dir, Licensing & Busn Devt: Ben Jacobs *E-mail:* bjacobs@infobaselearning.com
Dir, Mktg: Zina Scarpulla
Dir, Publicity: Laurie Katz *E-mail:* lkatz@infobaselearning.com
Dir, Sales: Mark Zielinski
Founded: 1941
Award-winning publisher of authoritative curriculum-related print & online reference materials for schools & libraries.
ISBN Prefix(es): 978-0-8160; 978-0-87196; 978-1-60057; 978-1-60413; 978-1-4381; 978-1-57852; 978-1-61753
Number of titles published annually: 135 Print; 28 Online; 135 E-Book
Total Titles: 940 Print; 37 Online; 934 E-Book
Returns: Maple Logistics Solutions, Lebanon Distribution Center, 704 Legionaire Dr, Fredericksburg, PA 17026
Warehouse: Maple Logistics Solutions, Lebanon Distribution Center, 704 Legionaire Dr, Fredericksburg, PA 17026
Distribution Center: Maple Logistics Solutions, Lebanon Distribution Center, 704 Legionaire Dr, Fredericksburg, PA 17026

Fair Winds Press
Imprint of Quarto Publishing Group USA
100 Cummings Ctr, Suite 406-L, Beverly, MA 01915
Tel: 978-282-9590 *Fax:* 978-282-7765
E-mail: sales@quarto.com
Web Site: www.quartoknows.com
Key Personnel
VP & Group Publr: Winnie Prentiss *E-mail:* winnie.prentiss@quarto.com
Founded: 2001
Offer nonfiction books in a range of practical categories, including nutrition & cookery, fitness, parenting, beauty, treating sickness, mental health & using new medicine.
ISBN Prefix(es): 978-1-59233
Number of titles published annually: 50 Print
Total Titles: 200 Print

Fairchild Books
Division of Bloomsbury Publishing PLC
1385 Broadway, 5th fl, New York, NY 10018
SAN: 201-470X
Tel: 212-419-5300 *Toll Free Tel:* 800-932-4724; 888-330-8477 (orders) *Fax:* 212-704-5975
Web Site: bloomsbury.com/us/academic/fairchildbooks
Key Personnel
Dir, Sales & Sr Devt Ed: Joe Miranda *E-mail:* joseph.miranda@bloomsbury.com
Sr Acct Mgr: Allison Jones *E-mail:* allison.jones@bloomsbury.com
Sr Prodn Ed: Claire Henry
Founded: 1910
Interior design, fashion, merchandising, marketing, management, retailing, careers market, research art foundation, clothing, textiles.
Membership(s): International Textiles Apparel Association (ITAA); Interior Design Educators Council (IDEC).
ISBN Prefix(es): 978-0-87005; 978-1-56367; 978-1-60901
Number of titles published annually: 40 Print; 30 CD-ROM
Total Titles: 375 Print; 60 CD-ROM
Orders to: MPS Distribution Center, 16365 James Madison Hwy, Gordonsville, VA 22942-8501
Returns: MPS Distribution Center, 16365 James Madison Hwy, Gordonsville, VA 22942-8501
Warehouse: MPS Distribution Center, 16365 James Madison Hwy, Gordonsville, VA 22942-8501
Distribution Center: MPS Distribution Center, 16365 James Madison Hwy, Gordonsville, VA 22942-8501

Fairleigh Dickinson University Press
Affiliate of Rowman & Littlefield
M-GH2-01, 285 Madison Ave, Madison, NJ 07940
Tel: 973-443-8564 *Fax:* 974-443-8364
E-mail: fdupress@fdu.edu
Web Site: www.fdupress.org
Key Personnel
Dir: Harry Keyishian *E-mail:* harry_keyishian@fdu.edu
Founded: 1967
Publish books in the humanities & social sciences, with special strengths in history & literature.
ISBN Prefix(es): 978-0-8386; 978-1-61147
Number of titles published annually: 30 Print; 30 E-Book
Total Titles: 1,500 Print; 280 E-Book
Distributed by Rowman & Littlefield
Foreign Rep(s): Eurospan (Europe, UK); Scholarly Book Services (Canada); United Publishers Services (Japan)

The Fairmont Press Inc
700 Indian Trail, Lilburn, GA 30047
SAN: 207-5946
Tel: 770-925-9388 *Fax:* 770-381-9865
Web Site: www.fairmontpress.com
Key Personnel
VP: Linda Hutchings *E-mail:* linda@fairmontpress.com
Book Prodn Mgr: Beth Pearce *E-mail:* beth@aeecenter.org
Founded: 1973
Professional & reference books on energy, safety, environment, how-to & facility management.
ISBN Prefix(es): 978-0-915586; 978-0-88173
Number of titles published annually: 12 Print; 1 CD-ROM; 12 E-Book
Total Titles: 425 Print; 8 CD-ROM; 125 E-Book
Distributed by CRC Press; Taylor & Francis
Foreign Rep(s): CRC Press

§Faith Alive Christian Resources
Imprint of Christian Reformed Church in North America
1700 28 St SE, Grand Rapids, MI 49508-1407
Tel: 616-224-0728 *Toll Free Tel:* 800-333-8300 *Toll Free Fax:* 888-642-8606
E-mail: info@faithaliveresources.org; sales@faithaliveresources.org; orders@faithaliveresources.org
Web Site: www.faithaliveresources.org
Key Personnel
Dir: Mark Rice *Tel:* 616-224-0795 *E-mail:* mrice@crcna.org
Mng Ed: Ruth Vanderhart *E-mail:* rvanderhart@crcna.org
Founded: 1928
Publish materials for Sunday school & other children's ministries, youth ministry, adults & small groups, prayer & evangelism, church leadership, worship & disability ministry. Also publish the monthly magazine *The Banner* & the quarterly journal *Reformed Worship*.
ISBN Prefix(es): 978-0-933140; 978-0-930265; 978-1-56212; 978-1-59255; 978-1-62025
Number of titles published annually: 50 Print
Total Titles: 307 Print
Imprints: Faith Alive; Friendship Bible Studies; Libros Desafio; World Literature Ministries

Distribution Center: 3475 Mainway, PO Box 5070, CTN LCD-1, Burlington, ON L7R 3Y8, Canada
RCA Resources, 2 Sydney Ave, Mount Evelyn, Victoria 3796, Australia *Tel:* (03) 9736 2412 *Fax:* (03) 9736 2654 *E-mail:* resources@crca.org.au

Faith & Fellowship Publishing
Subsidiary of Church of the Lutheran Brethren
1020 W Alcott Ave, Fergus Falls, MN 56537
Tel: 218-736-7357 *Toll Free Tel:* 800-332-9232
E-mail: clb@clba.org
Web Site: www.clba.org
Key Personnel
Dir: Tim Mathieson
Religious books, newsletters.
ISBN Prefix(es): 978-0-943167
Number of titles published annually: 8 Print
Total Titles: 59 Print

§Faith Library Publications
Subsidiary of RHEMA Bible Church
PO Box 50126, Tulsa, OK 74150-0126
Tel: 918-258-1588 (ext 2218) *Toll Free Tel:* 888-258-0999 (orders) *Fax:* 918-872-7710 (orders)
E-mail: flp@rhema.org
Web Site: www.rhema.org/store
Key Personnel
Dept Head, Kenneth Hagin Ministries: Brian Cumberland
Founded: 1963
ISBN Prefix(es): 978-0-89276; 978-1-60616
Number of titles published annually: 4 Print; 15 CD-ROM
Total Titles: 185 Print; 93 CD-ROM; 50 E-Book
Distributed by Appalachian; Harrison House; Spring Arbor; Whitaker

§Faithlife Corp
1313 Commercial St, Bellingham, WA 98225
Tel: 360-527-1700 *Toll Free Tel:* 800-875-6467 *Fax:* 360-527-1707
E-mail: sales@faithlife.com; customerservice@faithlife.com
Web Site: faithlife.com
Founded: 1992
Electronic & ebook publisher & technology provider.
ISBN Prefix(es): 978-1-57799
Number of titles published annually: 30 CD-ROM; 200 E-Book
Total Titles: 200 CD-ROM; 4,000 E-Book
Membership(s): CBA; Evangelical Christian Publishers Association; Society of Bible Literature

FaithWalk Publishing
Imprint of CSS Publishing Co Inc
5450 N Dixie Hwy, Lima, OH 45807
Tel: 419-227-1818 *Toll Free Tel:* 800-537-1030 (orders: non-bookstore mkts) *Fax:* 419-224-9184
E-mail: orders@csspub.com
Web Site: www.faithwalkpub.com
Key Personnel
Pres: David Runk *Tel:* 419-516-4205 *E-mail:* david@csspub.com
Prodn Mgr: Karyl Corson *E-mail:* kcorson@csspub.com
Acctg: Patti Furr *E-mail:* pfurr@csspub.com
Founded: 2002
ISBN Prefix(es): 978-0-9724196; 978-1-932902
Number of titles published annually: 10 Print
Total Titles: 31 Print
Membership(s): Independent Book Publishers Association

FaithWords, see Hachette Nashville

§Familius
1254 Commerce Way, Sanger, CA 93657
Tel: 559-876-2170 *Fax:* 559-876-2180
E-mail: orders@familius.com
Web Site: www.familius.com
Key Personnel
Founder & CEO: Christopher Robbins
Founder & Acqs: Michele Robbins
Mng Ed: Brooke Jorden *E-mail:* brooke@familius.com
Founded: 2012
ISBN Prefix(es): 978-1-938301; 978-1-939629; 978-1-942672
Number of titles published annually: 60 Print; 50 E-Book; 40 Audio
Total Titles: 170 Print; 120 E-Book; 100 Audio
Foreign Rep(s): Baker & Taylor (worldwide exc Australia, Canada, New Zealand, UK & USA)
Foreign Rights: Letter Soup Rights Agency (worldwide exc USA)
Membership(s): Independent Book Publishers Association

F+W Media Inc
10151 Carver Rd, Suite 200, Blue Ash, OH 45242
Tel: 513-531-2690 *Toll Free Tel:* 800-289-0963 (trade accts); 800-258-0929 (cust serv)
E-mail: contact_us@fwmedia.com
Web Site: www.fwcommunity.com
Key Personnel
CEO: Tom Beusse
Chief Digital Offr: Chad Phelps
CFO/COO: Jim Ogle
SVP, Opers: Phil Graham *E-mail:* phil.graham@fwcommunity.com
VP, Content, Lifestyle & Crafts: Karen Cooper
Sales Dir: Joanne Widmer *E-mail:* joanne.widmer@fwcommunity.com
Sales Dir, Adams Media: Karen Patterson
Edit Dir, Krause Publications: Paul Kennedy
Group Publr/Community Leader, Automotive/Outdoors: Jamie Wilkinson
Spec Sales Mgr, Adams Media: Lauren Rouleau
Digital Marketer: Bethany Carland-Adams
Exec Ed, Crimson Romance: Tara Gelsomino
Ed-in-Chief, Merit Press Books: Jacquelyn Mitchard
Founded: 1913
ISBN Prefix(es): 978-0-930625; 978-0-87349; 978-0-87341; 978-0-87069; 978-0-89689; 978-1-58221; 978-0-8019; 978-1-63250
Number of titles published annually: 200 Print
Total Titles: 860 Print
Imprints: Antique Trader Books; Crimson Romance (digital/POD); David & Charles; HOW Books; Interweave; Krause Publications; Merit Press Books (young adult); North Light Books; Prologue Books; Warman's; Writer's Digest Books
Branch Office(s)
10901 W 120 Ave, Suite 350, Broomfield, CO 80021 *Tel:* 303-442-0427
4868 Innovation Dr, Fort Collins, CO 80525
490 Boston Post Rd, Suite 15A, Sudbury, MA 01776 *Tel:* 978-203-5444
1140 Broadway, 14th fl, New York, NY 10001 *Tel:* 212-447-1400
Foreign Office(s): Brunel House, Forde Close, Newton, Abbot, Devon TQ12 4PU, United Kingdom *Tel:* (01626) 323200
Foreign Rep(s): David Bateman Ltd (New Zealand); Canadian Manda Group (Canada); Capricorn Link (Australia); China Publishers Services Ltd (Edwin Chu) (China); F+W International (Europe, UK); IPR (Middle East); JCC Enterprises Inc (Jerry Cruz Carrilo Ortiz) (Caribbean, Latin America); Penguin Books India (South Asia); Real Books (South Africa); Trinity Books (South Africa); The White Partnership (Andrew White) (East Asia, Southeast)
Returns: Aero Fulfillment Services, 6023 Union Centre Blvd, Fairfield, OH 45014; Fraser Direct, 100 Armstrong Ave, Georgetown, ON L7G 5S4, Canada *Tel:* 905-877-4411 *Toll Free Tel:* 800-840-5220 *Fax:* 905-877-4410
Distribution Center: Perseus Distribution, 250 W 57 St, 15th fl, New York, NY 10107 (North American print sales & worldwide digital)
See separate listing for:
Betterway Books
Interweave Press LLC
Krause Publications Inc
Writer's Digest

§Farcountry Press
2750 Broadwater Ave, Helena, MT 59602-9202
Mailing Address: PO Box 5630, Helena, MT 59604-5630
Tel: 406-422-1263 *Toll Free Tel:* 800-821-3874 (sales off) *Fax:* 406-443-5480
E-mail: books@farcountrypress.com; sales@farcountrypress.com
Web Site: www.farcountrypress.com
Key Personnel
Publr: Linda Netschert *E-mail:* linda.netschert@farcountrypress.com
Pubns Dir: Kathy Springmeyer *E-mail:* kathy@farcountrypress.com
Founded: 1980
Softcover & hardcover color photography books showcasing the nation's cities, states, national parks & wildlife. Also publish nonfiction children's series, guidebooks, cookbooks & regional history titles nationwide.
ISBN Prefix(es): 978-0-93814; 978-1-56037; 978-1-59152 (Sweetgrass Books)
Number of titles published annually: 25 Print
Membership(s): APPL; The Association of Publishers for Special Sales; Independent Book Publishers Association; Publishers Association of the West

Farrar, Straus & Giroux Books for Young Readers
Imprint of Macmillan Children's Publishing Group
175 Fifth Ave, 7th fl, New York, NY 10010
Tel: 212-741-6900 *Toll Free Tel:* 888-330-8477 (orders) *Fax:* 212-633-9385
Web Site: us.macmillan.com/mackids; www.mackidsbooks.com
Key Personnel
VP & Edit Dir: Joy Peskin *Tel:* 646-307-5187 *E-mail:* joy.peskin@macmillan.com
Exec Ed: Wesley Adams *Tel:* 646-307-5673 *E-mail:* wesley.adams@fsgbooks.com; Janine O'Malley *Tel:* 646-307-5598 *E-mail:* janine.omalley@fsgbooks.com
Founded: 1953
Preschool through young adult fiction & nonfiction, hardcover & paperback.
ISBN Prefix(es): 978-0-374
Number of titles published annually: 80 Print
Total Titles: 700 Print
Imprints: Frances Foster Books
Membership(s): The Children's Book Council

Farrar, Straus & Giroux, LLC
Subsidiary of Macmillan
18 W 18 St, New York, NY 10011
SAN: 206-782X
Tel: 212-741-6900
E-mail: fsg.publicity@fsgbooks.com
Web Site: us.macmillan.com/fsg.aspx
Key Personnel
Pres & Publr: Jonathan Galassi
EVP & Deputy Publr: Andrew Mandel *Tel:* 212-206-5354
SVP & Dir, Mktg & Publicity: Jeff Seroy *Tel:* 212-206-5323
SVP & Sales Dir: Spenser Lee
VP & Cont, Rts & Perms: Erika Seidman
VP, Dir of Digital & Pbk Publg, Publr, MCD/FSG & FSG Originals: Sean McDonald

VP & Dir, Publicity: Sarita Varma *Tel:* 212-206-5327 *E-mail:* svarma@fsgbooks.com
VP & Ed-in-Chief: Eric Chinski
Publr, Sarah Crichton Books: Sarah Crichton
Ad Dir: Victoria Genna
Creative Dir: Rodrigo Corral
Design Dir: Abby Kagan
Mktg Dir, Digital Strategy & Technol: Daniel Del Valle
Dir, Scientific American: Amanda Moon
Exec Ed: Jenna Johnson; Ileene Smith
Exec Ed, MCD/FSG: Daphne Durham
Exec Mng Ed: Debra Helfand
Sr Ed: Emily Bell; Alex Star
Ed: Jeremy Davies
Assoc Ed: Laird Gallagher; John Knight
Asst Ed: Julia Ringo
Ed-at-Large: Lorin Stein
Founded: 1946
General fiction, nonfiction, poetry & juveniles.
ISBN Prefix(es): 978-0-374
Number of titles published annually: 150 Print
Total Titles: 1,400 Print
Imprints: Farrar, Straus & Giroux Books for Young Readers; Hill & Wang; MCD/FSG; North Point Press; Scientific American
Distributor for Drawn & Quarterly; Gray Wolf Books
Foreign Rep(s): Pan Macmillan Ltd (UK); Raincoast Books (Canada)
Foreign Rights: ANA Baltic (Tatjana Zoldnere) (Estonia, Latvia, Lithuania); AnatoliatLit Agency (Amy Spangler & Eda Caca) (Turkey); Anthea Agency (Katalina Sabeva) (Bulgaria); L'Autre Agence (Corinne Marotte & Marie Lannurien) (France); Bardon-Chinese Media (David Tsai) (China, Taiwan); Anoukh Foerg Agency (Germany); Deborah Harris Agency (Geula Geurts) (Israel); International Copyright Agency (Simon Kessler & Marina Adriana) (Romania); The Italian Literary Agency srl (Claire Sabatie-Garat) (Italy); Anna Jarota Agency (Dominika Bojanowska) (Poland); Katai & Bolza (Peter Bolza) (Hungary); KCC (Kyung Kang) (Korea); MB Agencia Literaria (Monica Martin & Ines Planells) (Latin America, Spain); Kristin Olson Literarni Agentura (Czech Republic); Plima Literary Agency (Vuk Perisic) (Albania, Croatia, Serbia, Slovenia); Read 'n Right Agency (Nike Davarinou) (Greece); Riff Agency (Laura & Joao Paulo Riff) (Brazil); Sebes & Bisseling Literary Agency (Paul Sebes) (Netherlands); Synopsis Literary Agency (Olga Zasetskaya) (Russia); Tuttle-Mori Agency Inc (Asako Kawachi) (Japan)
Advertising Agency: Verso Advertising
Warehouse: MPS Distribution Center, 16365 James Madison Hwy, Gordonsville, VA 22942 *Toll Free Tel:* 888-330-8477
Membership(s): The Children's Book Council
See separate listing for:
Hill & Wang
North Point Press

§Father & Son Publishing Inc
4909 N Monroe St, Tallahassee, FL 32303-7015
Tel: 850-562-2612 *Toll Free Tel:* 800-741-2712 (orders only) *Fax:* 850-562-0916
Web Site: www.fatherson.com
Key Personnel
Pres: Lance Coalson *E-mail:* lance@fatherson.com
Founded: 1982
Publishers of nonfiction, historical fiction, cookbooks, giftbooks & children's books.
ISBN Prefix(es): 978-0-942407; 978-1-935802
Number of titles published annually: 12 Print; 3 Audio
Total Titles: 212 Print; 15 Audio
Distributor for BADM Books
Membership(s): ABA; Florida Authors & Publishers Association Inc; National Association of Independent Publishers

Favorable Impressions
Affiliate of The Lincoln Library (now part of the FactCite family of databases)
51910 Shoreview Dr, Shelby Township, MI 48316
Tel: 248-635-2957
Web Site: www.favimp.com
Key Personnel
Owner & SVP, Mktg & Opers: Dan R Harris *E-mail:* danh@favimp.com
Pres, Publr & Ed: Laurie Lanzen Harris *E-mail:* laurieh@favimp.com
Founded: 1995
Reference & nonfiction books, ebooks & databases for elementary school libraries & public libraries.
ISBN Prefix(es): 978-1-931360
Number of titles published annually: 5 Print
Total Titles: 40 Print; 40 Online; 40 E-Book

FC&A Publishing
103 Clover Green, Peachtree City, GA 30269
Tel: 770-487-6307 *Toll Free Tel:* 800-226-8024 *Fax:* 770-631-4357
E-mail: customer_service@fca.com
Web Site: www.fca.com
Key Personnel
CFO: Tim Anders
Creative Dir: Anne Kaufmann *Tel:* 770-487-6307 ext 2151 *E-mail:* anne_kaufmann@fca.com
Founded: 1969
ISBN Prefix(es): 978-0-915099; 978-1-890957; 978-1-932470; 978-1-935574
Number of titles published annually: 3 Print; 3 Online
Total Titles: 36 Print; 30 Online

§Federal Bar Association
1220 N Filmore St, Suite 444, Arlington, VA 22201
Tel: 571-481-9100 *Fax:* 571-481-9090
E-mail: fba@fedbar.org
Web Site: www.fedbar.org
Key Personnel
Exec Dir: Karen Silberman *E-mail:* ksilberman@fedbar.org
Deputy Exec Dir: Stacy King *E-mail:* sking@fedbar.org
Founded: 1920
Publish course materials, newsletters & *The Federal Lawyer* magazine.
ISBN Prefix(es): 978-1-56986
Number of titles published annually: 15 Print; 1 CD-ROM
Total Titles: 350 Print; 1 CD-ROM; 2 Audio

Federal Street Press
Division of Merriam-Webster Inc
25-13 Old Kings Hwy N, No 277, Darien, CT 06820
Tel: 203-852-1280 *Toll Free Tel:* 877-886-2830 *Fax:* 203-852-1389
E-mail: info@federalstreetpress.com; sales@federalstreetpress.com; customerservice@federalstreetpress.com; orders@federalstreetpress.com
Web Site: federalstreetpress.com
Key Personnel
Mng Dir: Virginia Guilfoyle *E-mail:* vguilfoyle@federalstreetpress.com
Founded: 1998
Offers up-to-date, quality, value-priced language reference titles created in cooperation with the editors of Merriam-Webster Inc.
ISBN Prefix(es): 978-1-892859; 978-1-59695
Number of titles published annually: 5 Print
Total Titles: 45 Print

Philipp Feldheim Inc, see Feldheim Publishers

Feldheim Publishers
208 Airport Executive Park, Nanuet, NY 10954
SAN: 207-0545
Tel: 845-356-2282 *Toll Free Tel:* 800-237-7149 (orders) *Fax:* 845-425-1908
E-mail: sales@feldheim.com
Web Site: www.feldheim.com
Key Personnel
Pres: Yitzchak Feldheim
Mng Dir: Elia Hollander
Sales Mgr: Moshe Grossman
Founded: 1939
Translations from Hebrew of Jewish classical works & works of contemporary authors in the field of Orthodox Jewish thought & contemporary Jewish literature for ages three & up.
ISBN Prefix(es): 978-0-87306; 978-1-58330; 978-1-59826; 978-1-68025
Number of titles published annually: 100 Print
Total Titles: 800 Print
Imprints: Feldheim Publishers USA
Foreign Office(s): Yaakov Feldheim Publishers Ltd, Box 43163, 91431 Jerusalem, Israel
Distributor for Hamadia Publishing; Jerusalem Publications

The Feminist Press at The City University of New York
365 Fifth Ave, Suite 5406, New York, NY 10016
SAN: 213-6813
Tel: 212-817-7915 *Fax:* 212-817-1593
E-mail: info@feministpress.org
Web Site: www.feministpress.org
Key Personnel
Exec Dir & Publr: Jamia Wilson
Mng Ed: Julia Berner-Tobin *E-mail:* jberner-tobin@gc.cuny.edu
Ed: Clarissa Wong
External Rel Mgr: Lucia Brown *E-mail:* lbrown@gc.cuny.edu
Prodn & Design Mgr: Drew Stevens *E-mail:* dstevens@gc.cuny.edu
Publicity Mgr: Kait Heacock *E-mail:* kheacock@gc.cuny.edu
Devt: Yamberlie Tavarez *E-mail:* ytavarez@gc.cuny.edu
Publicity: Kait Heacock *E-mail:* kheacock@gc.cuny.edu
Sales & Inventory: Jisu Kim *E-mail:* jkim@gc.cuny.edu
Edit Asst: Lauren Hook *E-mail:* lhook@gc.cuny.edu
Founded: 1970
Popular culture, African studies, Asian American studies, international studies, history of feminism, women's studies, working class studies, current issues & women's literature from the Middle East, Africa, Asia & Latin America & US women writers.
ISBN Prefix(es): 978-0-912670; 978-0-935312; 978-1-55861
Number of titles published annually: 18 Print; 10 E-Book
Total Titles: 400 Print; 50 E-Book
Foreign Rights: AnatoliaLit Agency (Amy Spangler) (Turkey); Japan Uni Agency (Miko Yamanouchi) (Japan); Natoli, Stefan & Oliva (Roberta Oliva) (Italy); VBMLitag (Luciana Villas-Boas) (Brazil); Literary Agent Silke Weniger (Germany)
Distribution Center: Baker & Taylor International, 652 E Main St, PO Box 6920, Bridgewater, NJ 08807-0920 (Worldwide exc Africa, Asia, Canada, Continental Europe, Middle East, UK & US) *Tel:* 908-218-0400 *Fax:* 908-707-4387 *E-mail:* btinfo@btol.com *Web Site:* btol.com/international.cfm
Consortium Book Sales & Distribution, c/o Perseus Distribution Services, 1094 Flex Dr, Jackson, TN 38301-5070 (US & CN) *Toll Free Tel:* 800-283-3572 *Toll Free Fax:* 800-351-5073 *E-mail:* info@cbsd.com *Web Site:* www.cbsd.com SAN: 631-760X

Turnaround Publisher Services Ltd, Unit 3, Olympia Trading Estate, Coburg Rd, Wood Green, London, United Kingdom (UK, Africa, Asia, Continental Europe & Middle East) *Tel:* (020) 8829 3000 *Fax:* (020) 8881 5088 *E-mail:* orders@turnaround-uk.com *Web Site:* www.turnaround-uk.com
Membership(s): AAP; Community of Literary Magazines & Presses; National Council for Research on Women

Fence Books
University at Albany, Science Library 320, 1400 Washington Ave, Albany, NY 12222
Tel: 518-591-8162
E-mail: fence.fencebooks@gmail.com
Web Site: www.fenceportal.org
Key Personnel
Publr & Ed: Rebecca Wolff *E-mail:* rebeccafence@gmail.com
Mng Ed: Jess Puglisi *E-mail:* jessp.fence@gmail.com
Founded: 2001
ISBN Prefix(es): 978-1-934200; 978-0-9771064; 978-0-9713189; 978-0-9663324; 978-0-9740909; 978-0-9864373
Number of titles published annually: 6 Print
Total Titles: 60 Print
Distribution Center: Small Press Distribution, 1341 Seventh St, Berkeley, CA 94710-1409 *Tel:* 510-524-1668 *Toll Free Tel:* 800-869-7553 *E-mail:* spd@spdbooks.org *Web Site:* www.spdbooks.org
Consortium Book Sales & Distribution, The Keg House, 34 13 Ave NE, Suite 101, Minneapolis, MN 55413 *Tel:* 612-746-2600 *Fax:* 612-746-2606 *E-mail:* info@cbsd.com *Web Site:* www.cbsd.com

Feral House
1240 W Sims Way, Suite 124, Port Townsend, WA 98368
Tel: 323-666-3311 *Fax:* 323-297-4331
E-mail: info@feralhouse.com
Web Site: feralhouse.com
Key Personnel
Pres & Publr: Adam Parfrey
Founded: 1989
Pop culture, alternative, art, nonfiction, religion, sociology & social sciences.
ISBN Prefix(es): 978-0-922915; 978-1-932595
Number of titles published annually: 10 Print
Total Titles: 66 Print
Imprints: Process Media
Distribution Center: Consortium Book Sales & Distribution, The Keg House, 34 13 Ave NE, Suite 101, Minneapolis, MN 55413-1007 *Tel:* 612-746-2600 *Toll Free Tel:* 800-283-3572 (cust serv) *Fax:* 612-746-2606 *Web Site:* www.cbsd.com
Turnaround Publisher Services, Olympia Trading Estate, Unit 3, Coburg Rd, London N22 6TZ, United Kingdom *Tel:* (020) 8829-3000 *Fax:* (020) 8881-5088 *E-mail:* orders@turnaround-uk.com

§Ferguson Publishing
Imprint of Infobase Learning
132 W 31 St, 17th fl, New York, NY 10001
Tel: 212-967-8800 *Toll Free Tel:* 800-322-8755 *Fax:* 917-339-0323 *Toll Free Fax:* 800-678-3633
E-mail: custserv@factsonfile.com
Web Site: infobasepublishing.com
Key Personnel
CEO & Pres: Mark McDonnell
CFO: Jim Housley
Edit Dir: Laurie Likoff
Dir, Book & Ebook Sales: Justyna Pawluk *E-mail:* jpawluk@infobaselearning.com
Dir, Licensing & Busn Devt: Ben Jacobs *E-mail:* bjacobs@infobaselearning.com
Dir, Mktg: Zina Scarpulla
Dir, Opers: Mark Zielinski
Dir, Publicity: Laurie Katz *E-mail:* lkatz@infobaselearning.com
With its acclaimed career guidance & reference materials, Ferguson Publishing is known among librarians & guidance counselors as the premier publisher in the career education field.
ISBN Prefix(es): 978-0-8160; 978-0-87196; 978-0-89434; 978-1-60413; 978-1-4381
Number of titles published annually: 74 Print; 74 E-Book
Total Titles: 333 Print; 363 E-Book

Howard Fertig, Publisher
80 E 11 St, New York, NY 10003
SAN: 201-4777
Tel: 212-982-7922 *Fax:* 212-982-1099
E-mail: enquiries@hfertigbooks.com; orders@hfertigbooks.com
Web Site: www.hfertigbooks.com
Key Personnel
Pres & Ed-in-Chief: Howard Fertig
Founded: 1966
Scholarly reprints & originals in European history, literature & social sciences.
ISBN Prefix(es): 978-0-86527
Number of titles published annually: 12 Print
Total Titles: 160 Print

Fiction Collective Two Inc (FC2)
Imprint of University of Alabama Press
c/o Dept of English, Languages & Communincations Bldg, 255 S Central Campus Dr, Rm 3500, Salt Lake City, UT 84112-0494
Tel: 773-702-7000
E-mail: fc2.cmu@gmail.com
Web Site: www.fc2.org/prizes.html
Key Personnel
Chair, Bd of Dirs: Lance Olsen
Founded: 1973
Publish formally innovative fiction.
ISBN Prefix(es): 978-1-57366
Number of titles published annually: 6 Print
Total Titles: 200 Print
Distributed by University of Alabama Press
Orders to: University of Alabama Press, PO Box 870380, Tuskaloosa, AL 35487-0380 *Tel:* 773-702-7000 *Fax:* 773-702-7212 *Toll Free Fax:* 800-621-8476
Returns: University of Alabama Press, Chicago Distribution Center, 11030 S Langley Ave, Chicago, IL 60628 *Tel:* 773-702-7000 *Toll Free Tel:* 800-621-2736 *Fax:* 773-702-7212 *Toll Free Fax:* 800-621-8476
Membership(s): Community of Literary Magazines & Presses

Fifth Estate Publishing
2795 County Hwy 57, Blounstville, AL 35031
SAN: 852-6419
Toll Free Tel: 855-299-2160
E-mail: fifth-estate@hotmail.com
Web Site: fifthestatepub.com
Founded: 2003
Publisher & distributor.
ISBN Prefix(es): 978-0-9746336; 978-0-9760992; 978-0-9768233; 978-1-933580; 978-1-936533
Number of titles published annually: 6 Print; 6 Online; 6 E-Book
Total Titles: 136 Print; 136 Online; 75 E-Book

Film-Video Publications/One on One Book Publishing, see One On One Book Publishing/Film-Video Publications

Filter Press LLC
PO Box 95, Palmer Lake, CO 80133
SAN: 201-484X
Tel: 719-481-2420 *Toll Free Tel:* 888-570-2663 *Fax:* 719-481-2420
E-mail: info@filterpressbooks.com; orders@filterpressbooks.com
Web Site: filterpressbooks.com
Key Personnel
Pres: Doris Baker *E-mail:* doris@filterpressbooks.com
Founded: 1957
Publisher of books on the American West, Western expansion, children's historical fiction, Colorado history & biography.
ISBN Prefix(es): 978-0-910584; 978-0-86541
Number of titles published annually: 5 Print; 1 Audio
Total Titles: 75 Print; 11 E-Book; 2 Audio
Returns: 19980 Top O'Moor W, Monument, CO 80132
Shipping Address: 19980 Top O'Moor W, Monument, CO 80132
Membership(s): Colorado Association of Libraries; Colorado Independent Publishers Association; Women Writing the West

Financial Executives Research Foundation Inc (FERF)
Affiliate of Financial Executives International (FEI)
West Tower, 7th fl, 1250 Headquarters Plaza, Morristown, NJ 07960-6837
Tel: 973-765-1000 *Fax:* 973-765-1023
Web Site: www.financialexecutives.org
Key Personnel
CEO: William Sinnett
Dir, Fin Servs & Devt: Lorna Raagas *Tel:* 973-765-1033 *E-mail:* lraagas@financialexecutives.org
Sr Mgr, Devt: Kit Hall
Sr Mgr, Res: Leena Roselli
Mgr, Res: Tom Thompson
Founded: 1944
Executive reports & full-length monographs of research related to financial topics. All publications available on PDF.
This publisher has indicated that 50% of their product line is author subsidized.
ISBN Prefix(es): 978-0-910586; 978-1-885065; 978-1-61509; 978-1-933130
Number of titles published annually: 20 Print; 20 Online
Total Titles: 120 Print; 120 Online

Financial Times Press
Imprint of Pearson Education Ltd
800 E 96 St, Indianapolis, IN 46240
Web Site: www.informit.com/ftpress
Publisher of business, management, investment & finance books for general consumers, professionals & students.
ISBN Prefix(es): 978-0-13
Number of titles published annually: 165 Print
Total Titles: 1,200 Print
Imprints: FT Press
Foreign Office(s): 128 Long Acre, London WC2E 9AN, United Kingdom *Tel:* (020) 7447 2000 *Fax:* (020) 7240 5771

Finding My Way Books
3512 SW Huntoon St, Topeka, KS 66604
Tel: 785-273-6239
E-mail: info@findingmywaybooks.com; findingmywaybooks@gmail.com
Web Site: www.findingmywaybooks.net
Key Personnel
Author & Publr: Jo Meserve Mach
Author: Vera Lynne Stroup-Rentier, PhD
Photog, Author & Designer: Mary Birdsell
Founded: 2014
Finding My Way Books honors children & adults with special needs or disabilities by sharing their stories. It supports educational inclusion through publications that are easy to read, with large print & easy to understand, with photographs. All books include tools for educators to promote learning & inclusion.

This publisher has indicated that 50% of their product line is author subsidized.
ISBN Prefix(es): 978-0-9903543; 978-0-9964449; 978-0-9863792; 978-0-9968357; 978-1-944764; 978-1-947541
Number of titles published annually: 10 Print; 5 E-Book
Total Titles: 21 Print; 6 E-Book
Membership(s): The Children's Book Council; Independent Book Publishers Association; Society of Children's Book Writers & Illustrators

Fine Creative Media, Inc
322 Eighth Ave, 15th fl, New York, NY 10001
Tel: 212-595-3500 *Fax:* 212-595-3779
Key Personnel
Founder & CEO, MJF Books, Barnes & Noble Classics, Mediander.com: Michael J Fine *E-mail:* mjf@mjfbooks.com
Dir of Prodn: Benjamin Lee
Dir of Fin & Acctg: Ian Teixeira
Dir of Admin & HR: Steven Fine
Dir of Acqs, MJF Books: Roz Siegel
Acqs Ed, MJF Books: Jo Fagan; Antony Fine; Kaethe Fine
Dir of Mktg: Keren Unrad
Reprint Mgr: Colin Warnock
Bookkeeper: Cindy Lew
Founded: 1991
Publish hardcover & paperback reprints of fiction & nonfiction as MJF Books; develop & produce Barnes & Noble Classics.
ISBN Prefix(es): 978-1-56731 (MJF Books); 978-1-59308 (Barnes & Noble Classics); 978-1-60671 (MJF Books)
Number of titles published annually: 80 Print
Total Titles: 1,500 Print
Imprints: Barnes & Noble Classics (produced & published in conjunction with Barnes & Noble Inc); MJF Books

FineEdge.com LLC
14004 Biz Point Lane, Anacortes, WA 98221
Tel: 360-299-8500 *Fax:* 360-299-0535
E-mail: pub@fineedge.com; orders@fineedge.com
Web Site: www.fineedge.com
Key Personnel
Publr: Mark Bunzel *E-mail:* mark@fineedge.com
Founded: 1986
Publishing, wholesaling, outdoor guidebooks & maps; specializing in nautical books & mountain biking publications.
ISBN Prefix(es): 978-0-938665; 978-1-932310
Number of titles published annually: 3 Print
Total Titles: 50 Print; 2 Online
Imprints: Mountain Biking Press
Distributed by Heritage House; Sunbelt Publications Inc
Membership(s): Independent Book Publishers Association

Finney Company Inc
5995 149 St W, Suite 105, Apple Valley, MN 55124
Tel: 952-469-6699 *Toll Free Tel:* 800-846-7027 *Fax:* 952-469-1968 *Toll Free Fax:* 800-330-6232
E-mail: info@finneyco.com
Web Site: www.finneyco.com
Key Personnel
Pres: Alan E Krysan
Founded: 1946
Publish books with educational value; children's books, trade, travel guides & educational reference/textbooks.
ISBN Prefix(es): 978-0-9618088; 978-1-879335; 978-0-944280; 978-0-913163; 978-0-912486; 978-0-8134; 978-1-883477; 978-0-9627860; 978-0-9617767; 978-1-880654; 978-0-89317; 978-0-933855; 978-1-931626; 978-0-9616847; 978-0-911781; 978-0-9639705; 978-1-893272; 978-1-879535; 978-0-8200; 978-1-885258; 978-1-888025; 978-0-9662589
Number of titles published annually: 15 Print
Total Titles: 400 Print
Imprints: Anacus Press; Astragal Press; Bancroft-Sage Publishing, Ecopress; Great Outdoors Publishing Co; Lone Oak Press; Pogo Press; SkipJack Press; Windward Publishing
Divisions: Chester Book Co; Hobar Publications; The New Careers Center (Live Oak Publications is an imprint of The New Careers Center)
Distributor for Drache Publications; Joyce Shellhart
Membership(s): Education Market Association
See separate listing for:
Astragal Press
Ecopress
Hobar Publications
Windward Publishing

Fire Engineering Books & Videos
Division of PennWell Books
1421 S Sheridan Rd, Tulsa, OK 74112
Tel: 918-831-9421 *Toll Free Tel:* 800-752-9764 *Fax:* 918-832-0319
E-mail: sales@pennwell.com
Web Site: www.pennwellbooks.com
Key Personnel
Dir: Matt Dresher *E-mail:* mattd@pennwell.com
Mktg Mgr: Sarah De Vos *Tel:* 918-831-9574 *E-mail:* sarahd@pennwell.com
Founded: 1877
Fire science, suppression & protection, petroleum, electric power, water, hazardous materials books & videos.
ISBN Prefix(es): 978-1-57340; 978-0-912212; 978-0-87814
Number of titles published annually: 10 Print; 5 CD-ROM
Total Titles: 120 Print; 10 CD-ROM
Distributed by David Publishing; Fire Protection Publications
Distributor for Brady; Idea Bank; IFSTA; Mosby

§Firefall Editions
4905 Tunlaw St, Alexandria, VA 22312
Tel: 510-549-2461
E-mail: literary@att.net
Web Site: www.firefallmedia.com
Key Personnel
Mng Dir: Robinson Joyce
Mktg Dir: Kathryn DeLappe *E-mail:* prize@att.net
Founded: 1996
Specialize in fiction, photography, art, autobiographies, textbooks, audiobooks & documentary films.
ISBN Prefix(es): 978-0-915090; 978-1-939434
Number of titles published annually: 7 Print; 2 E-Book; 7 Audio
Total Titles: 93 Print; 9 E-Book; 29 Audio
Foreign Office(s): Firefallmedia, 17 Shore Rd, Drummore, by Stranraer, Dumfries & Galloway DG9 9PU, United Kingdom
Distribution Center: Brodart, 500 Arch St, Williamsport, PA 17701

First Avenue Editions
Imprint of Lerner Publishing Group Inc
241 First Ave N, Minneapolis, MN 55401
Tel: 612-332-3344 *Toll Free Tel:* 800-328-4929 *Fax:* 612-332-7615 *Toll Free Fax:* 800-332-1132
E-mail: info@lernerbooks.com; custserve@lernerbooks.com
Web Site: www.lernerbooks.com; www.facebook.com/lernerbooks
Key Personnel
Chmn: Harry J Lerner
CFO & EVP: Margaret Thomas
Pres & Publr: Adam Lerner
EVP, Sales: David Wexler
VP, Ed-in-Chief: Patricia M Stockland
Dir of Rts, Spec Sales & Intl Dist: Maria Kjoller
Group Mktg Dir: Jill Braithwaite
School & Lib Mktg Dir: Lois Wallentine
Dir, HR: Cyndi Radant
Social studies, picture storybooks, art, multicultural issues, activity books & beginning readers.
Total Titles: 240 Print; 65 E-Book
Foreign Rep(s): INT Press Distribution (Australia); Monarch Books of Canada (Trade) (Canada); Phambili (Southern Africa); Publishers Marketing Services (Malaysia, Singapore); Saunders Book Co (Education) (Canada); South Pacific Books (New Zealand)
Foreign Rights: Japan Foreign-Rights Centre (Japan); Korea Copyright Center (Korea); Michelle Lapautre Agence Junior (France); Literarische Agentur Silke Weniger (Germany)
Warehouse: 1251 Washington Ave N, Minneapolis, MN 55401, Mgr: Ken Rued

Five Star Publications Inc, see Story Monsters LLC

FJH Music Co Inc
2525 Davie Rd, Suite 360, Fort Lauderdale, FL 33317-7424
Tel: 954-382-6061 *Toll Free Tel:* 800-262-8744 *Fax:* 954-382-3073
E-mail: custserv@fjhmusic.com; sales@fjhmusic.com
Web Site: www.fjhmusic.com
Key Personnel
CEO & Pres: Frank J Hackinson
VP: Kevin Hackinson; Kyle Hackinson *E-mail:* kyleh@fjhmusic.com
Founded: 1988
Educational music publications.
ISBN Prefix(es): 978-0-929666; 978-1-56939
Number of titles published annually: 100 Print

Flashlight Press
527 Empire Blvd, Brooklyn, NY 11225
Tel: 718-288-8300 *Fax:* 718-972-6307
Web Site: www.flashlightpress.com
Key Personnel
Publr: Harry Mauer *E-mail:* publisher@flashlightpress.com
Ed: Shari Dash Greenspan *E-mail:* editor@flashlightpress.com
Founded: 2004
Children's picture books that explore & illuminate. E-mail submissions only. See guidelines on web site.
ISBN Prefix(es): 978-0-9729225; 978-0-9799746; 978-1-993612; 978-1-94727
Number of titles published annually: 3 Print
Total Titles: 24 Print
Returns: Independent Publishers Group (IPG), c/o Returns Dept, 814 N Franklin St, Chicago, IL 60610 *Tel:* 312-337-0747 *Toll Free Tel:* 800-888-4741 *Fax:* 312-337-5985 *E-mail:* frontdesk@ipgbook.com *Web Site:* www.ipgbook.com
Distribution Center: Independent Publishers Group (IPG), 814 N Franklin St, Chicago, IL 60610 *Tel:* 312-337-0747 *Toll Free Tel:* 800-888-4741 *Fax:* 312-337-5985 *E-mail:* frontdesk@ipgbook.com *Web Site:* www.ipgbook.com

§FleetSeek
6190 Powers Ferry Rd, Suite 320, Atlanta, GA 30339
Tel: 540-899-9872 *Toll Free Tel:* 888-ONLY-TTS (665-9887) *Fax:* 540-899-1948
E-mail: fleetseek@fleetseek.com
Web Site: www.fleetseek.com
Founded: 1980
Directories online relating to data in the trucking industry.

ISBN Prefix(es): 978-1-880701
Number of titles published annually: 4 Online
Total Titles: 1 CD-ROM; 4 Online

§Fleur Publishing Inc
4 Embarcadero Ctr, 14th fl, San Francisco, CA 94111
Tel: 415-766-3512 *Fax:* 415-789-4525
Web Site: fleurpublishing.com
Founded: 2015
Boutique publisher of books related to social justice issues.
ISBN Prefix(es): 978-1-946167
Number of titles published annually: 8 Print; 6 E-Book; 3 Audio
Total Titles: 5 Print; 4 E-Book; 3 Audio

Florida Academic Press
Division of FAP Books Inc
PO Box 357425, Gainesville, FL 32635
SAN: 299-3643
Tel: 352-332-5104
E-mail: fapress@gmail.com
Web Site: www.florida-academic-press.com
Key Personnel
Exec Ed: Prof Sam Decalo
Founded: 1997
Please submit only complete ms, hard copy, with SASE +/or postage for return if needed. No general query letters. 4-6 week assessment time if not interested; 5-10 weeks if interested. Best, fastest responses are by e-mail. If a contract is cut, ms must be returned to us as ready to print electronic PDF files. We can refer you to several moderately-priced graphic designers for this if needed.
ISBN Prefix(es): 978-1-890357
Number of titles published annually: 10 Print; 8 E-Book
Total Titles: 48 Print; 20 E-Book
Imprints: New Voices (primarily fiction)
Distributor for Publisher's Stone Publications

Flying Pen Press LLC
1416 S Newport St, Denver, CO 80224
Tel: 303-375-0499 *Fax:* 303-375-0499
Web Site: www.flyingpenpress.com
Key Personnel
Publr: David A Rozansky
Founded: 2007
Publisher of fiction & nonfiction.
ISBN Prefix(es): 978-0-9795889
Number of titles published annually: 5 Print; 5 E-Book
Total Titles: 12 Print; 1 E-Book
Imprints: Carpe Diem Professional Calendars; Flying Pen Press Colorado; Flying Pen Press Park Trek; Flying Pen Press Rocky Mountain West; Flying Pen Press Science Fiction; Flying Pen Press Southwest; Flying Pen Press Travel Guides; Flying Piggybank Press; The Press for Humanitarian Causes; Traveling Pen Press
Distribution Center: Lightning Source Inc, 1246 Heil Quaker Blvd, La Vergne, TN 37086

§Focus
Imprint of Hackett Publishing Co Inc
PO Box 44937, Indianapolis, IN 46244-0937
Tel: 317-635-9250 *Fax:* 317-635-9292
E-mail: customer@hackettpublishing.com; editorial@hackettpublishing.com
Web Site: focusbookstore.com
Key Personnel
Pres, Publr & CEO: Deborah Wilkes
Edit Dir: Brian Rak
Rts Mgr & Edit Asst: Christina Kowalewski
Founded: 1985
Classical & modern languages.
ISBN Prefix(es): 978-0-941051; 978-1-58510
Number of titles published annually: 12 Print; 1 CD-ROM; 3 E-Book; 2 Audio
Total Titles: 200 Print; 5 CD-ROM; 1 E-Book; 2 Audio
Editorial Office(s): PO Box 390007, Cambridge, MA 02139-0001 *Tel:* 617-497-6303 *Fax:* 617-661-8703
Distributor for Domus Latina Publishing
Foreign Rep(s): Accademia Vivarium Novum (Lingua Latina titles) (Continental Europe exc Portugal & Spain); Cultura Clasica SL (Lingua Latina titles) (Portugal, Spain); Gazelle Book Services Ltd (Europe, UK); NewSouth Books (Australia, New Zealand)
Returns: 3333 Massachusetts Ave, Indianapolis, IN 46218
Shipping Address: 3333 Massachusetts Ave, Indianapolis, IN 46218

Focus on the Family
8605 Explorer Dr, Colorado Springs, CO 80920-1051
Tel: 719-531-5181 *Toll Free Tel:* 800-A-FAMILY (232-6459) *Fax:* 719-531-3424
Web Site: www.focusonthefamily.com; www.facebook.com/focusonthefamily
Key Personnel
VP, Communs: Paul Batura
Founded: 1986
Case bound & soft cover books (adult & children) dealing with family relationships & emphasizing the importance of values & Christian principles in people's lives.
ISBN Prefix(es): 978-0-929608; 978-1-56179; 978-1-58997; 978-1-60482; 978-1-62405; 978-1-62471
Number of titles published annually: 25 Print
Total Titles: 300 Print; 25 CD-ROM; 60 Audio
Imprints: Adventures in Odyssey; Heritage Builders; Life on the Edge; Radio Theatre; Ribbits; That the World May Know
Distributed by Baker Books; Moody Press; Tyndale House Publishers; Zondervan

Fodor's Travel Publications
Division of Internet Brands Inc
1745 Broadway, 15th fl, New York, NY 10019
SAN: 204-1073
Toll Free Tel: 800-733-3000
E-mail: publicity@fodors.com; editors@fodors.com
Web Site: www.fodors.com
Key Personnel
SVP & Publr: Amanda D'Acierno
VP & Assoc Publr: Siobhan O'Hare
Edit Dir: Linda Cabasin
Dir, Prod Mgmt, Fodors.com: Roxanne Chen
Dir, Publicity: Katherine Fleming
Sr Map Ed: Rebbecca Baer
Sr Content Mgmt Strategist: Cate Starmer
Founded: 1936
Travel guides, foreign & domestic.
ISBN Prefix(es): 978-0-679; 978-0-307; 978-0-676; 978-1-4000
Number of titles published annually: 100 Print
Total Titles: 800 Print; 800 E-Book
Imprints: Compass American Guides; Fodor's
Distribution Center: Ingram Publisher Services, One Ingram Blvd, La Vergne, TN 37086

Fons Vitae
49 Mockingbird Valley Dr, Louisville, KY 40207-1366
Tel: 502-897-3641 *Fax:* 502-893-7373
E-mail: fonsvitaeky@aol.com
Web Site: www.fonsvitae.com
Key Personnel
Dir: Gray Henry *E-mail:* grayh101@aol.com
Proj Dir: Elena Lloyd-Sidle
Busn Mgr: Lucy Langman
Mktg & Multimedia: Paul T Carney
Founded: 1997
Fons Vitae is both an academic charity with 501(c)(3) charitable status & a peer-reviewed publishing house which ensures the highest scholarly standards for its publications. Authentic text, impeccably translated & exquisitely produced, make these volumes useful for both the university classroom & for those interested in the eternal verities with no compromise to a recent soft focus on spirituality.
ISBN Prefix(es): 978-1-887752
Number of titles published annually: 10 Print; 5 CD-ROM
Total Titles: 130 Print; 5 CD-ROM
Distributor for African American Islamic Institute; Anqa Press (UK); Aperture (NY); Archetype (UK); Broadstone Books; Dar Nun; Golganooza Press (UK); Islamic Texts Society (UK); Matheson Trust; Parabola; Paragon; Parvardigar Press; Pir Press (NY); Qiblah Books; Quilliam Press (UK); Sandala Productions; Sophia Perennis; Sri Lanka Institute of Traditional Studies; Thesaurus Islamicus Foundation; Tradigital; White Thread Press (US); Wisdom Foundation; World Wisdom (US); Zaytuna Institute Press (US)
Foreign Rep(s): American University in Cairo Press (AUC) (Middle East)
Distribution Center: Independent Publishers Group (IPG), 814 N Franklin St, Chicago 60610, IL *Tel:* 312-337-0747 *Toll Free Tel:* 800-888-4741 *Fax:* 312-337-5985 *E-mail:* frontdesk@ipgbook.com *Web Site:* www.ipgbook.com

Fordham University Press
Joseph A Martino Hall, 45 Columbus Ave, New York, NY 10023
SAN: 201-6516
Fax: 347-842-3083
Web Site: www.fordhampress.com
Key Personnel
Dir: Fredric Nachbaur *E-mail:* fnachbaur@fordham.edu
Edit Dir: Richard Morrison *E-mail:* rmorrison@fordham.edu
Mktg Dir: Kathleen O'Brien-Nicholson *Tel:* 718-817-4782 *E-mail:* bkaobrien@fordham.edu
Busn Mgr: Margaret Noonan *E-mail:* mnoonan@fordham.edu
Prodn & Design Mgr: Ann-Christine Racette *E-mail:* aracette@fordham.edu
Asst Busn Mgr: Marie Hall *E-mail:* mhall21@fordham.edu
Asst Mktg Mgr: Katie Sweeney *E-mail:* kasweeney@fordham.edu
Mng Ed: Eric Newman *Tel:* 718-817-4786 *E-mail:* ernewman@fordham.edu
Edit Assoc & Asst to Dir: Will Cerbone *E-mail:* wcerbone@fordham.edu
Acqs Ed: Tom Lay *E-mail:* tlay@fordham.edu
Founded: 1907
Scholarly books & journals, New York regional books, general trade books & videos.
ISBN Prefix(es): 978-0-8232
Number of titles published annually: 42 Print
Total Titles: 450 Print
Imprints: Empire State Editions
Distributed by Oxford University Press (US & CN)
Distributor for Creighton University Press; Institute for Advanced Study in the Theatre Arts (IASTA); Little Room Press; The Reconstructionist Press; Rockhurst University Press; St Bede's Publications; University of San Francisco Press
Foreign Rep(s): Combined Academic Publishers Ltd (Africa, Europe, India, Middle East, UK); Cranbury International LLC (Ethan Atkin) (Latin America); East-West Export Books (EWEB) c/o University of Hawaii Press (Royden Muranaka) (Asia, The Pacific)
Returns: Maple Logistics Solutions, Lebanon Distribution Ctr, 704 Legionaire Dr, Fredricksburg, PA 17026

Distribution Center: Ingram Publisher Services, One Ingram Blvd, La Vergne, TN 37086 *Toll Free Tel:* 866-400-5351 *E-mail:* ips@ingramcontent.com *Web Site:* www.ingramcontent.com SAN: 631-8630
Membership(s): AAP; Association of American University Presses; Association of Jesuit University Presses

Fortress Press, see Augsburg Fortress Publishers, Publishing House of the Evangelical Lutheran Church in America

§Forum Publishing Co
383 E Main St, Centerport, NY 11721
Tel: 631-754-5000 *Toll Free Tel:* 800-635-7654 *Fax:* 631-754-0630
E-mail: forumpublishing@aol.com
Web Site: www.forum123.com
Key Personnel
CEO & Publr: Martin Stevens
Founded: 1981
Business magazines & books.
ISBN Prefix(es): 978-0-9626141
Number of titles published annually: 5 Print
Total Titles: 15 Print; 6 CD-ROM

Forward Movement
Affiliate of The Episcopal Church
412 Sycamore St, Cincinnati, OH 45202-4110
Tel: 513-721-6659 *Toll Free Tel:* 800-543-1813 *Fax:* 513-721-0729 (orders)
E-mail: orders@forwardmovement.org (orders & cust serv)
Web Site: www.forwardmovement.org
Key Personnel
Deputy Dir & Mng Ed: Richelle Thompson *E-mail:* rthompson@forwardmovement.org
Dir, Busn Opers: D Jane Paraskevopoulos *E-mail:* jparaskevo@forwardmovement.org
Mktg Mgr: Heidi Weaver-Smith *E-mail:* hweaver@forwardmovement.org
Founded: 1935
Inspires disciples & empowers evangelists around the globe through offerings that encourage spiritual growth in individuals & congregations.
ISBN Prefix(es): 978-0-88028
Number of titles published annually: 12 Print
Total Titles: 60 Print; 1 Audio
Imprints: FMP
Distributor for Anglican Book Centre
Warehouse: 10001 Alliance Rd, Cincinnati, OH 45242

Walter Foster Publishing Inc
Imprint of Quarto Publishing Group USA
6 Orchard Rd, Suite 100, Lake Forest, CA 92630
SAN: 249-051X
Tel: 949-380-7510 *Toll Free Tel:* 800-426-0099; 800-759-0190 (orders) *Fax:* 949-380-7575
E-mail: walterfoster@quartous.com
Web Site: www.quartous.com
Key Personnel
VP: Anne Landa
VP, Sales, Arts/Crafts: Dan Widner
Mktg Mgr: Angela Corpus
Founded: 1922
Instructional art books, specialty art & creative products.
ISBN Prefix(es): 978-0-929261; 978-1-56010
Number of titles published annually: 30 Print
Total Titles: 350 Print
Foreign Rep(s): Apple Press

§The Foundation Center
32 Old Slip, 24th fl, New York, NY 10005-3500
SAN: 207-5687
Tel: 212-620-4230 *Toll Free Tel:* 800-424-9836 *Fax:* 212-807-3677
E-mail: customerservice@foundationcenter.org
Web Site: foundationcenter.org
Key Personnel
Pres: Bradford K Smith *Tel:* 212-807-3602 *E-mail:* bks@foundationcenter.org
Dir, Busn Devt, Mktg & Communs: Elizabeth Bradley *Tel:* 212-807-3619 *E-mail:* eab@foundationcenter.org
Founded: 1956
Reference books on US foundations, corporations & their grant-making activities & books about philanthropy & nonprofit management.
ISBN Prefix(es): 978-0-87954; 978-1-931923; 978-1-59542
Number of titles published annually: 12 Print; 3 Online
Total Titles: 292 Print; 3 Online; 25 E-Book
Branch Office(s)
312 Sutter St, Suite 606, San Francisco, CA 94108-4314 *Tel:* 415-397-0902
1627 "K" St NW, 3rd fl, Washington, DC 20006-1708 *Tel:* 202-331-1400
133 Peachtree St NE, Lobby Suite 350, Atlanta, GA 30303-1804 *Tel:* 404-880-0094
1422 Euclid Ave, Suite 1600, Cleveland, OH 44115-2001 *Tel:* 216-861-1933

Foundation Press
Imprint of West Academic Publishing
c/o West Academic Publishing, 444 Cedar St, Suite 700, St Paul, MN 55101
Toll Free Tel: 877-888-1330
E-mail: customerservice@westacademic.com
Web Site: www.westacademic.com
Key Personnel
VP & Publr: Pamela Siege Chandler *E-mail:* pamela.siege@westacademic.com
Acct Mgr: Peter Hinsch *Tel:* 651-202-4780 *E-mail:* peter.hinsch@westacademic.org
Founded: 1931
Law, business, political science, criminal justice, curriculum books, graduate & undergraduate, primarily in law.
ISBN Prefix(es): 978-0-88277; 978-1-56662; 978-1-58778; 978-1-59941
Number of titles published annually: 120 Print
Total Titles: 500 Print

Foundation Publications
900 S Euclid St, La Habra, CA 90631
Mailing Address: PO Box 2935, La Habra, CA 90632-2935
Tel: 714-879-2286 *Toll Free Tel:* 800-257-6272 *Fax:* 714-535-2164
E-mail: info@foundationpublications.com
Web Site: www.foundationpublications.com
Key Personnel
EVP: Pike Lambeth *E-mail:* pike@foundationpublications.com
Founded: 1971
Publish New American Standard Bible, La Biblia de Las Americas & Nueva Biblia Latinoamericana de Hoy.
ISBN Prefix(es): 978-0-910618; 978-1-58135; 978-1-885217
Number of titles published annually: 5 Print
Total Titles: 8 Print; 1 CD-ROM
Distribution Center: Anchor Distributors, 1030 Hunt Valley Circle, New Kensington, PA 15068 *Toll Free Fax:* 800-444-4484
STL Distribution, 212 Industrial Dr, Bristol, TN 37620 *Toll Free Tel:* 800-289-2772
Membership(s): Evangelical Christian Publishers Association; SEPA

Fowler Museum at UCLA
PO Box 951549, Los Angeles, CA 90095-1549
Tel: 310-825-4361 *Fax:* 310-206-7007
E-mail: fowlerws@arts.ucla.edu
Web Site: www.fowler.ucla.edu
Key Personnel
Mng Ed & Intl Rts Contact: Lynne Kostman *Tel:* 310-794-9582 *E-mail:* lkostman@arts.ucla.edu
Founded: 1963
Active publisher of African, Southeast Asian & Latin American arts publications.
ISBN Prefix(es): 978-0-930741; 978-0-9748729
Number of titles published annually: 5 Print
Total Titles: 134 Print
Distributed by University of Washington Press
Shipping Address: 308 Charles E Young Dr N, Los Angeles, CA 90095

Fox Chapel Publishing Co Inc
1970 Broad St, East Petersburg, PA 17520
Tel: 717-560-4703 *Toll Free Tel:* 800-457-9112 *Fax:* 717-560-4702
E-mail: customerservice@foxchapelpublishing.com
Web Site: www.foxchapelpublishing.com
Key Personnel
CFO: Kerry Eltman
Pres: Alan Giagnocavo *E-mail:* alan@foxchapelpublishing.com
Dir, Edit: Peg Couch *E-mail:* peg@foxchapelpublishing.com
Dir, Prod Devt & Edit Opers, Companion House Press: Christopher Reggio
Prodn: Troy Thorne
Intl Rts: Jane Patukas *E-mail:* patukas@foxchapelpublishing.com
Founded: 1991
Publisher of illustrated nonfiction books, magazines, patterns & videos for craft, hobby & do-it-yourself enthusiasts. Fox Chapel Publishing inspires & informs readers who enjoy woodworking, needlework, pyrography, home & garden, cooking, outdoor recreation, coloring, Zentangle®, kids crafts & more. Fox Chapel publishes 2 magazines, *Woodcarving Illustrated & Scroll Saw, Woodworking & Crafts.*
ISBN Prefix(es): 978-1-56523
Number of titles published annually: 120 Print
Total Titles: 1,200 Print
Imprints: Companion House Press; Creative Homeowner; Design Originals; Heliconia Press; IMM Lifestyle Books
Distributor for Reader's Digest; Taunton Sterling Dover
Distribution Center: Ingram Publisher Services
Membership(s): Craft Hobby Association; Publishers Association of the West
See separate listing for:
Creative Homeowner

FPMI Solutions Inc
689 Discovery Dr, Suite 300, Huntsville, AL 35806
Toll Free Tel: 888-644-3764
E-mail: info@fpmi.com
Web Site: www.fpmisolutions.com; www.fpmi.com
Key Personnel
CEO: R Mark McLindon
COO: Dustin B DeFee
VP, Capture: Dawn B Winters
Founded: 1985
Government publications.
ISBN Prefix(es): 978-0-936295; 978-1-930542
Number of titles published annually: 4 Print
Total Titles: 20 Print
Branch Office(s)
66 Canal Center Plaza, Suite 305, Alexandria, VA 22314 *Tel:* 703-690-7000 *Fax:* 703-690-7009

§Franciscan Media
28 W Liberty St, Cincinnati, OH 45202
SAN: 204-6237
Tel: 513-241-5615 *Toll Free Tel:* 800-488-0488 *Fax:* 513-241-0399
E-mail: books@americancatholic.org
Web Site: www.americancatholic.org; www.franciscanmedia.org
Key Personnel
Pres: Rev Jeff Scheeler, OFM

CEO & Publr: Rev Dan Kroger, OFM
Tel: 513-241-5615 ext 127 *E-mail:* dank@americancatholic.org
Dir, Design & Prodn: Jeanne Kortekamp
Tel: 513-241-5615 ext 113 *E-mail:* jeannek@americancatholic.org
Mng Ed: Katie Carroll *Tel:* 513-241-5615 ext 141
E-mail: katiec@americancatholic.org
Founded: 1970
Religion (Catholic); inspirational resources for parishes, schools & individuals; books, videos, audiobooks, ebooks, weekly & Sunday homily programs; monthly subscription newsletters, monthly magazine; American Catholic (web site).
ISBN Prefix(es): 978-0-912228; 978-0-86716; 978-1-61636; 978-1-63253; 978-1-63254
Number of titles published annually: 30 Print; 35 E-Book; 25 Audio
Total Titles: 550 Print; 100 E-Book; 200 Audio
Imprints: Fisher Productions; Franciscan Communications; Ikonographics; Servant Books
Distributor for Franciscan Communications (books & videos); Ikonographics (videos)
Foreign Rep(s): Pleroma Christian Supplies (New Zealand); Rainbow/Word of Life (Australia); Redemptorist Publications Book Service (UK)
Membership(s): Association of Catholic Publishers Inc; Canadian Booksellers Association; Catholic Press Association; Society of Professional Journalists

§Franklin, Beedle & Associates Inc
2154 NE Broadway, Suite 100, Portland, OR 97232
Tel: 503-284-6348 *Toll Free Tel:* 800-322-2665
Fax: 503-625-4434
Web Site: www.fbeedle.com
Key Personnel
Ed: Tom Sumner *E-mail:* tsumner@fbeedle.com
Founded: 1985
College textbooks in computer science, information systems & computers in education, educational software, computer engineering, computer information systems, information technology.
ISBN Prefix(es): 978-0-938661; 978-1-887902; 978-1-59028
Number of titles published annually: 10 Print; 5 E-Book
Total Titles: 50 Print; 5 E-Book
Imprints: William, James & Co (humanities publr); Xpat Fiction
Distributor for Arcus; Battlebridge; Blue Sky Gallery; Photolucida Book; Ringing Bell Press; Tayo Press; Wordstock
Foreign Rep(s): Transatlantic Publishers (Europe, Middle East, UK)
Membership(s): Association for Computing Machinery

Frederick Fell Publishers Inc
2131 Hollywood Blvd, Suite 305, Hollywood, FL 33020
SAN: 208-2365
Tel: 954-925-5242
E-mail: fellpub@aol.com (admin only)
Web Site: www.fellpub.com
Key Personnel
Pres & Publr: Donald L Lessne
E-mail: donlessne@aol.com
Ed-in-Chief: Barbara Newman
E-mail: felleditor@aol.com
Founded: 1943
An award-winning publisher of general trade books. Series published include the Know-It-All Guides, Top 100 series, Heroes & Heroines series & So You Want To Be series.
ISBN Prefix(es): 978-0-88391
Number of titles published annually: 24 Print; 50 E-Book
Total Titles: 150 Print; 150 E-Book
Foreign Rep(s): Gazelle Book Services Ltd (UK & the continent); Jarir Bookstore (Tony Herold) (Saudi Arabia); Parrot Reads Publishers (Indian subcontinent); USBD Distribution (Singapore)
Foreign Rights: Akcali Copyright Agency (Turkey); Agencia Literaria Carmen Balcells SA (Latin America exc Brazil, Portugal, Spain); Lorella Belli Literary Agency (UK); Big Apple Agency (Maggie Han) (China); Big Apple Agency (Taiwan); Book Publishers Association of Israel (Beverley Levit) (Israel); Graal Literary Agency (Marcin Biegaj) (Poland); Imprima Korea Agency (Korea); International Copyright Agency Ltd (Simona Kessler) (Romania); Christiane Janssen (Germany); Japan UNI Agency Inc (Japan); Jarir Bookstore (Tony Herold) (Saudi Arabia); LEX Copyright Office (Norbert Uzseka) (Hungary); Maxima Creative Agency (Santo Manurung) (Indonesia); Nova Littera S L (Konstantin Paltchikov) (Russia); Andrew Nurnberg Associates Ltd (Tatjana Zoldnere) (Latvia, Lithuania, Ukraine); Andrew Nurnberg Associates Prague (Petra Tobiskova) (Czech Republic); Andrew Nurnberg Associates Sofia (Anna Droumeva) (Bulgaria); OA Literary Agency (Greece); Plima Literary Agency (Mila Perisic) (Croatia, Serbia, Slovenia); Schindler's Literary Agency (Brazil); Tuttle-Mori Agency (Thailand); Tuttle-Mori Agency Inc (Japan)
Distribution Center: Midpoint Trade Books, 27 W 20 St, New York, NY 10011, Pres: Eric Kampmann *Tel:* 212-727-0190 *Fax:* 212-727-0195 *Web Site:* www.midpointtrade.com
Gazelle Book Services Ltd, White Cross Mills, Hightown, Lancaster, Lancs LA1 4XS, United Kingdom *Tel:* (01524) 528500 *Fax:* (01524) 528510 *E-mail:* sales@gazellebookservices.co.uk *Web Site:* www.gazellebookservices.co.uk

§Free Spirit Publishing Inc
217 Fifth Ave N, Suite 200, Minneapolis, MN 55401-1299
Tel: 612-338-2068 *Toll Free Tel:* 800-735-7323
Fax: 612-337-5050 *Toll Free Fax:* 866-419-5199
E-mail: help4kids@freespirit.com
Web Site: www.freespirit.com
Key Personnel
Pres & Publr: Judy Galbraith
Intl Rts Mgr: Lindsey LaBore
Founded: 1983
Offer books & learning materials for parents, educators, children & teens. Topics include: self-esteem, stress management, school success, creativity, relationships with friends & family, social action, special needs (i.e. children with LD/learning differences, gifted & talented & at-risk youth), bullying & conflict resolution.
ISBN Prefix(es): 978-0-915793; 978-1-57542; 978-0-9665988
Number of titles published annually: 25 Print; 1 CD-ROM
Total Titles: 170 Print; 2 CD-ROM; 3 Audio
Foreign Rep(s): Educational Distributors (New Zealand); Georgetown Publications (Canada); Incentive Plus (UK)

§W H Freeman
Imprint of Macmillan Learning
41 Madison Ave, New York, NY 10010
Tel: 212-576-9400 *Fax:* 212-689-2383
Web Site: www.macmillanlearning.com
Founded: 1946
Science & mathematics texts for the higher education market & high school advanced courses.
ISBN Prefix(es): 978-1-57259; 978-1-4292; 978-0-7167; 978-0-9747077; 978-1-936221
Number of titles published annually: 25 Print; 20 Online; 20 E-Book
Total Titles: 500 Print
Foreign Rep(s): Macmillan Education East Asia (China, Hong Kong, Indonesia, Korea, Malaysia, Philippines, Singapore, Taiwan, Thailand, Vietnam); Palgrave Macmillan Australia (Australia, New Zealand); Palgrave Macmillan Ltd (Africa, Caribbean, Europe, India, Japan, Latin America, Middle East, Pakistan, UK)
Warehouse: MPS Distribution Center, 16365 James Madison Hwy, Gordonsville, VA 22942 *Toll Free Tel:* 888-330-8477 *Fax:* 540-672-7540 (cust serv) *Toll Free Fax:* 800-672-2054 (orders)

Samuel French Inc
235 Park Ave S, 5th fl, New York, NY 10003
Tel: 212-206-8990 *Toll Free Tel:* 866-598-8449
Fax: 212-206-1429
E-mail: info@samuelfrench.com; publications@samuelfrench.com
Web Site: www.samuelfrench.com
Key Personnel
Pres: Nate Collins *E-mail:* ncollins@samuelfrench.com
VP & Dir, Opers: Kenneth Dingledine
E-mail: kdingledine@samuelfrench.com
Literary Dir: Amy Rose Marsh *E-mail:* amarsh@samuelfrench.com
Pubns Mgr: David Geer *E-mail:* dgeer@samuelfrench.com
Founded: 1830
Plays.
ISBN Prefix(es): 978-0-573
Number of titles published annually: 130 Print
Total Titles: 5,000 Print
Branch Office(s)
Samuel French Bookshop, 7623 Sunset Blvd, Hollywood, CA 90046
Foreign Office(s): Samuel French Ltd, 52 Fitzroy St, London W1T 5JR, United Kingdom, Opers Dir: David Webster *Tel:* (020) 7387 9373 *Fax:* (020) 7387 2161 *E-mail:* theatre@samuelfrench-london.co.uk *Web Site:* www.samuelfrench-london.co.uk
Distributed by Baker's Plays; Samuel French Ltd (UK)
Distributor for Baker's Plays; Samuel French Ltd (UK)
Foreign Rights: DALRO Pty Ltd (Botswana, Lesotho, Namibia, South Africa, Swaziland); Drama League of Ireland (Ireland); Origin Theatrical (Australia); Play Bureau (NZ) Ltd (New Zealand)

Fresh Air Books
Imprint of Upper Room Books
1908 Grand Ave, Nashville, TN 37212
Tel: 615-340-7200 *Toll Free Tel:* 800-972-0433 (orders)
Web Site: books.upperroom.org
Key Personnel
Asst Ed & Admin Coord: Joanna Bradley
Tel: 615-340-7256 *E-mail:* jbradley@umcdiscipleship.org
Founded: 2009
Nonprofit publisher of religious materials.
ISBN Prefix(es): 978-1-935205
Number of titles published annually: 1 Print; 2 E-Book
Total Titles: 14 Print; 10 E-Book
Returns: PBD Worldwide Fulfillment Services, Discipleship Resources, Upper Rm, Return Door 16, 1650 Bluegrass Lakes Pkwy, Alpharetta, GA 30004 *Tel:* 770-442-8633 *Fax:* 770-442-9742
Warehouse: PBD Worldwide Fulfillment Services, 1650 Bluegrass Lakes Pkwy, Alpharetta, GA 30004 *Tel:* 770-442-8633 *Fax:* 770-442-9742
Distribution Center: PBD Worldwide Fulfillment Services, 1650 Bluegrass Lakes Pkwy, Alpharetta, GA 30004 *Tel:* 770-442-8633 *Fax:* 770-442-9742

Friends United Press
Subsidiary of Friends United Meeting
101 Quaker Hill Dr, Richmond, IN 47374
SAN: 201-5803
Tel: 765-962-7573 *Fax:* 765-966-1293
E-mail: friendspress@fum.org; orders@fum.org
Web Site: shop.fum.org
Key Personnel
Communs Ed: Annie Glen *E-mail:* annieg@fum.org
Founded: 1969
Paperbound books; religion.
ISBN Prefix(es): 978-0-913408; 978-0-944350
Number of titles published annually: 3 Print; 3 Online
Total Titles: 85 Print; 67 Online
Membership(s): The Associated Church Press; Independent Book Publishers Association; Protestant Church-Owned Publishers Association; Quakers Uniting in Publications

Fulcrum Publishing Inc
4690 Table Mountain Dr, Suite 100, Golden, CO 80403
SAN: 200-2825
Tel: 303-277-1623 *Toll Free Tel:* 800-992-2908 *Fax:* 303-279-7111 *Toll Free Fax:* 800-726-7112
E-mail: info@fulcrumbooks.com; orders@fulcrumbooks.com
Web Site: www.fulcrumbooks.com
Key Personnel
Publr: Sam Scinta
Dir, Sales & Mktg: Melanie Roth *Tel:* 800-922-2908 ext 213 *E-mail:* melanie@fulcrumbooks.com
Ed-in-Chief: Rebecca McEwen
Founded: 1984
Nonfiction trade: Western culture & history, Native American culture & history, environment & nature, popular culture, lifestyle, outdoor recreation, public policy & gardening.
ISBN Prefix(es): 978-1-55591; 978-1-56373; 978-0-912347; 978-1-936218; 978-1-938486
Number of titles published annually: 15 Print; 15 E-Book
Total Titles: 600 Print; 250 E-Book
Imprints: Speaker's Corner (public policy series)
Distribution Center: Consortium Book Sales & Distribution, The Keg House, 34 13 Ave NE, Suite 101, Minneapolis, MN 55413-1007, Contact: Jim Nichols *Tel:* 612-746-2600 *Toll Free Tel:* 800-283-3572 *Fax:* 612-746-2606 *Toll Free Fax:* 800-351-5073 *E-mail:* info@cbsd.com *Web Site:* www.cbsd.com
Membership(s): AAP; ABA; Midwest Independent Booksellers Association; Mountains & Plains Independent Booksellers Association; Pacific Northwest Booksellers Association

FurnitureCore
1389 Peachtree St NE, Suite 310, Atlanta, GA 30309
Tel: 404-961-3734 *Toll Free Tel:* 800-826-8868 *Fax:* 404-961-3749
E-mail: info@furniturecore.com
Web Site: www.furniturecore.com
Key Personnel
Owner & Pres: Bob George
Founded: 1985 (acquired in 2008)
Specialize in business, industry & statistical reports.
ISBN Prefix(es): 978-0-921577; 978-1-894330; 978-1-894960
Number of titles published annually: 12 Print; 10 Online
Total Titles: 56 Print; 30 Online
Distributor for AMA Research; Business & Research Associates

§Future Horizons Inc
721 W Abram St, Arlington, TX 76013
Tel: 817-277-0727 *Toll Free Tel:* 800-489-0727 *Fax:* 817-277-2270
E-mail: info@fhautism.com
Web Site: www.fhautism.com
Key Personnel
Pres: R Wayne Gilpin
Founded: 1996
Resources on Autism/Asperger's Syndrome, including books, CDs, DVDs, magazines & conferences.
ISBN Prefix(es): 978-1-885477; 978-1-932565; 978-1-935274
Number of titles published annually: 6 Print
Total Titles: 20 Print

Gagosian Gallery
980 Madison Ave, New York, NY 10075
Tel: 212-744-2313 *Fax:* 212-772-7962
E-mail: newyork@gagosian.com
Web Site: www.gagosian.com
Key Personnel
Publg Dir: Alison McDonald
Founded: 1989
Publish fine editions & illustrated books on contemporary & modern art.
ISBN Prefix(es): 978-1-880154
Number of titles published annually: 30 Print
Total Titles: 40 Print
Branch Office(s)
456 N Camden Dr, Beverly Hills, CA 90210 *Tel:* 310-271-9400 *Fax:* 310-271-9420 *E-mail:* losangeles@gagosian.com

§Galaxy Press
7051 Hollywood Blvd, Suite 200, Hollywood, CA 90028
SAN: 254-6906
Tel: 323-466-7815 *Toll Free Tel:* 877-8GALAXY (842-5299)
E-mail: info@galaxypress.com; customers@galaxypress.com
Web Site: www.galaxypress.com
Key Personnel
Pres: John Goodwin *Tel:* 323-466-7812 *E-mail:* jgoodwin@galaxypress.com
SVP, Intl Sales/Rts: Claude Sandoz *E-mail:* claude@asirights.com
SVP, US Sales & Rts: Kim Catalano *Tel:* 323-466-7815 ext 145 *E-mail:* kcatalano@galaxypress.com
VP, US Trade Sales: Juliet Wills *E-mail:* jwills@galaxypress.com
Consumer Sales: Sarah Toth *E-mail:* sarahc@galaxypress.com
Founded: 2002
Publisher of the fiction works of L Ron Hubbard.
ISBN Prefix(es): 978-1-59212
Number of titles published annually: 13 Print; 14 E-Book; 14 Audio
Total Titles: 60 Print; 50 E-Book; 40 Audio
Imprints: Galaxy Audio
Returns: 6121 Malburg Way, Vernon, CA 90058 *Tel:* 323-588-8777
Warehouse: 6121 Malburg Way, Vernon, CA 90058 *Tel:* 323-588-8777
Distribution Center: 6121 Malburg Way, Vernon, CA 90058 *Tel:* 323-588-8777

Galde Press Inc
PO Box 460, Lakeville, MN 55044
Tel: 952-891-5991 *Toll Free Tel:* 800-777-3454
Web Site: www.galdepress.com
Key Personnel
Founder & Pres: Phyllis Galde *E-mail:* phyllis@galdepress.com
Founded: 1991
Independent publisher of books on a variety of subjects with over 100 titles in print.
ISBN Prefix(es): 978-1-880090; 978-1-931942
Number of titles published annually: 11 Print
Total Titles: 108 Print

§Gale
Unit of Cengage Learning
27500 Drake Rd, Farmington Hills, MI 48331-3535
SAN: 213-4373
Tel: 248-699-4253 *Toll Free Tel:* 800-877-4253 *Toll Free Fax:* 800-414-5043 (orders)
E-mail: gale.customercare@cengage.com
Web Site: www.gale.com
Key Personnel
SVP, Mng Dir, Intl: Terry Robinson
SVP & Gen Mgr: Paul Gazzolo
SVP, North American Sales: Brian McDonough
VP, Mktg & Communs: Harmony Faust
Founded: 1954
Gale, part of Cengage Learning, serves the world's information & education needs through its vast & dynamic content pools, which are used by students & consumers in their libraries, schools & on the Internet. It is best known for the accuracy, breadth & convenience of its data, addressing all types of information needs – from homework help to health questions to business profiles – in a variety of formats.
ISBN Prefix(es): 978-0-8103; 978-0-7876
Number of titles published annually: 50 Print
Total Titles: 4,099 Print
Imprints: Charles Scribner's Sons®; Christian Large Print; Five Star™; Large Print Press™; Macmillan Reference USA™; Primary Source Media™; St James Press®; Schirmer Reference™; Scholarly Resources Inc; The TAFT Group®; Thorndike Press®; U X L™; Wheeler Publishing™
Distribution Center: 10650 Toebben Dr, Independence, KY 41051 *Tel:* 859-525-2230
See separate listing for:
Charles Scribner's Sons®
Macmillan Reference USA™
St James Press®
Thorndike Press

§Galen Press Ltd
PO Box 64400-WB, Tucson, AZ 85728-4400
Tel: 520-577-8363 *Fax:* 520-529-6459
E-mail: sales@galenpress.com
Web Site: www.galenpress.com
Key Personnel
Owner, CFO & Publr: Mary Lou Iserson
VP, Mktg & Spec Sales: Mary Lou Sherk *E-mail:* ml@galenpress.com
Ed: Jennifer G Gilbert *E-mail:* jennifer@galenpress.com
Founded: 1993
Publish non-clinical health related books in medical education, death & dying & bioethics.
ISBN Prefix(es): 978-1-883620
Number of titles published annually: 2 Print; 1 CD-ROM; 3 E-Book
Total Titles: 32 Print; 1 CD-ROM; 6 E-Book
Membership(s): The Association of Publishers for Special Sales

§Gallaudet University Press
800 Florida Ave NE, Washington, DC 20002-3695
SAN: 205-261X
Tel: 202-651-5488 *Fax:* 202-651-5489
E-mail: gupress@gallaudet.edu
Web Site: gupress.gallaudet.edu
Key Personnel
Exec Dir: Gary Aller
Edit Dir: Ivey P Wallace
Founded: 1980
Reference books, scholarly, educational & general interest books on deaf studies, deaf culture & issues, sign language textbooks.
ISBN Prefix(es): 978-0-913580; 978-0-930323; 978-1-56368; 978-1-944838
Number of titles published annually: 16 Print
Total Titles: 250 Print; 4 CD-ROM
Imprints: Clerc Books; Kendall Green
Distributor for Signum Verlag

Warehouse: Chicago Distribution Center, 11030 S Langley Ave, Chicago, IL 60628, Contact: Karen Hyzy *Tel:* 773-702-7000 *Toll Free Tel:* 800-621-2736 *Fax:* 773-702-7212 *Toll Free Fax:* 800-621-8476 *E-mail:* orders@press.uchicago.edu
Membership(s): American Association of University Presses

Gallery Books
Imprint of Gallery Publishing Group
1230 Avenue of the Americas, New York, NY 10020
Toll Free Tel: 800-456-6798 *Fax:* 212-698-7284
E-mail: consumer.customerservice@simonandschuster.com
Web Site: www.simonsays.com
Key Personnel
SVP & Publr, Gallery Books Group: Jennifer Bergstrom
Assoc Publr, Gallery Books Group: Jennifer Long
VP & Publr, North Star Way: Michele Martin
VP & Sr Ed, Gallery Books & VP & Edit Dir, Threshold Editions: Mitchell Ivers
VP & Dir, Publicity, Gallery Books, Pocket Books & Threshold Editions: Jennifer Robinson
VP & Dir, Rts, Gallery Books & Pocket Books: Paul O'Halloran
Exec Ed, Gallery Books & Pocket Books, Edit Dir, Pocket Star: Lauren McKenna
Exec Ed, Gallery Books/Scout Press: Allison Callahan
Exec Ed, Gallery Books: Jeremie Ruby-Strauss
Sr Ed, Gallery Books: Jackie Cantor
Sr Ed, Gallery Books, Pocket Books & Gallery 13: Edward Schlesinger; Adam Wilson
Ed, Gallery Books & Pocket Books: Kate Dresser
Ed, Gallery Books & Threshold Editions: Natasha Simons
Ed, North Star Way: Diana Ventimiglia
Dir, Publicity, Gallery Books, Pocket Books & Threshold Editions: Jean Anne Rose
Sr Art Dir, Gallery Books, Pocket Books & Threshold Editions: Lisa Litwack
Dir, Rts, Threshold Editions: Marie Florio
Dir, Mktg, Gallery Books, Pocket Books & Threshold Editions: Elizabeth Psaltis
Dir, Brand Devt, North Star Way: Cindy Ratzlaff
Assoc Dir, Mktg, Gallery Books, Pocket Books & Threshold Editions: Abby Zidle
Sr Online Mktg Mgr: Diana Velasquez
Subs Rts Assoc, Gallery Books: Elizabeth Lotto
Founded: 1939
Trade paperbacks & hardcovers; mass market, reprints & originals.
ISBN Prefix(es): 978-0-671; 978-0-7434; 978-1-4165
Imprints: Downtown Press; G-unit; Gallery 13; Jeter Publishing; Karen Hunter Publishing; MTV Books; North Star Way; Pocket Books Trade Paperback; Pocket Star; Scout Press; Star Trek®; Threshold Editions; VH-1; World Wrestling Entertainment
Foreign Rights: Antonella Antonelli Agenzia (Italy); Arts & Licensing International (Mainland China, Taiwan); Book Publishers Association of Israel (Israel); Japan UNI Agency (Japan); JLM Literary Agency (Greece); Nurcihan Kesim Literary Agency Inc (Turkey); Mohrbooks Literary Agency (Germany); La Nouvelle Agence (France); Andrew Nurnberg Associates (Bulgaria, Croatia, Czech Republic, Estonia, Hungary, Latvia, Lithuania, Montenegro, Poland, Romania, Russia, Serbia, Slovakia, Slovenia); Sane Toregard Agency (Denmark, Finland, Iceland, Norway, Sweden); Sebes & Bisseling Literary Agency (Netherlands); Tuttle-Mori Agency Inc (Thailand); Eric Yang Agency (Korea)

Gallery 13, see Gallery Books

§Gallopade International Inc
611 Hwy 74 S, Suite 2000, Peachtree City, GA 30269
SAN: 213-8441
Mailing Address: PO Box 2779, Peachtree City, GA 30269
Tel: 770-631-4222 *Toll Free Tel:* 800-536-2GET (536-2438) *Fax:* 770-631-4810 *Toll Free Fax:* 800-871-2979
E-mail: customerservice@gallopade.com
Web Site: www.gallopade.com
Key Personnel
Owner & CEO: Carole Marsh *E-mail:* carole@gallopade.com
Pres & Intl Rts: Michele Yother *E-mail:* michele@gallopade.com
VP: Michael Longmeyer *E-mail:* michael@gallopade.com
Founded: 1979
"State stuff" for all 50 states including activity books, games, maps, posters, stickies, etc. Subjects include travel, regional, school travel supply, home school, juvenile mysteries, human sex education, multicultural, preschool through adult.
ISBN Prefix(es): 978-0-935326; 978-1-55609; 978-0-7933; 978-0-635
Number of titles published annually: 500 Print; 50 CD-ROM; 200 Online; 200 E-Book
Total Titles: 15,000 Print; 200 CD-ROM; 10,050 Online; 10,050 E-Book; 13 Audio
Imprints: American Milestones; Black Heritage: Celebrating Culture; The Day That Was Different; Here & Now; Heroes & Helpers; Carole Marsh Books; Carole Marsh Mysteries; New Traditions; 1000 Readers; Smart Sex Stuff for Kids; State Experience; State Stuff
Subsidiaries: Six House; The World's Largest Publishing Co
Membership(s): Education Market Association

Gareth Stevens Publishing
Imprint of The Rosen Publishing Group Inc
111 E 14 St, Suite 349, New York, NY 10003
Mailing Address: PO Box 29088, New York, NY 10087-9088
Toll Free Tel: 800-542-2595 *Toll Free Fax:* 877-542-2596 (cust serv)
E-mail: customerservice@gspub.com
Web Site: garethstevens.com
Founded: 1983
ISBN Prefix(es): 978-0-918831; 978-1-55532; 978-0-8368; 978-1-4339
Number of titles published annually: 400 Print
Total Titles: 1,500 Print
Returns: Maple Logistics Solutions, York Distribution Ctr, 60 Grumbacher Rd, York, PA 17406

§Garland Science Publishing
Imprint of Taylor & Francis Group, an Informa Business
711 Third Ave, 8th fl, New York, NY 10017
Tel: 212-216-7800; 212-281-4487 *Fax:* 212-947-3027
E-mail: science@garland.com
Web Site: www.garlandscience.com
Key Personnel
Pres, Taylor & Francis US: Emmett Dages
VP, Sales, Taylor & Francis US: Dennis Weiss
VP, Garland Science: Denise Schanck *E-mail:* denise.schanck@taylorandfrancis.com
Founded: 1969
Textbooks & professional books in biology & chemistry.
ISBN Prefix(es): 978-0-8153; 978-1-5603
Number of titles published annually: 10 Print; 4 CD-ROM; 30 E-Book
Total Titles: 50 Print; 4 CD-ROM; 30 E-Book
Branch Office(s)
4133 Whitney Ave, Hamden, CT 06578 *Tel:* 203-281-4487 *Toll Free Tel:* 800-627-6273 *Fax:* 203-230-1186
Warehouse: Taylor & Francis/Garland, 7625 Empire Dr, Florence, KY 41042 *Toll Free Tel:* 800-634-7064 *Toll Free Fax:* 800-248-4724

§Gatekeeper Press
3971 Hoover Rd, Suite 77, Columbus, OH 43123-2839
Toll Free Tel: 866-535-0913 *Fax:* 216-803-0350
E-mail: info@gatekeeperpress.com
Web Site: www.gatekeeperpress.com
Key Personnel
Pres: Robert Price *Tel:* 866-535-0913 ext 713 *Fax:* 216-803-0350 *E-mail:* rprice@gatekeeperpress.com
Founded: 2015
Full service publishing house that partners with authors & publishers to produce & distribute high quality books in digital & print formats. Authors earn 100% of their royalties. Distribution networks reach readers worldwide. Provide services for all subjects & types of books, including ebook conversion & distribution, book cover design, paperback publishing & distribution, editing & proofreading.
This publisher has indicated that 100% of their product line is author subsidized.
ISBN Prefix(es): 978-1-61984
Number of titles published annually: 50 Print; 500 E-Book
Membership(s): Independent Book Publishers Association

§Gateways Books & Tapes
Division of Institute for the Development of the Harmonious Human Being Inc
PO Box 370, Nevada City, CA 95959
SAN: 211-3635
Tel: 530-271-2239 *Toll Free Tel:* 800-869-0658 *Fax:* 530-272-0184
E-mail: info@gatewaysbooksandtapes.com
Web Site: www.gatewaysbooksandtapes.com; www.retrosf.com (Retro Science Fiction imprint)
Key Personnel
Sr Ed & Intl Rts: Iven Lourie *E-mail:* ilourie@oro.net
Founded: 1971
Trade & fine art book publisher. Categories include psychology, spirituality, metaphysics, Judaica, science fiction & limited editions.
ISBN Prefix(es): 978-0-89556
Number of titles published annually: 6 Print; 4 CD-ROM; 4 Audio
Total Titles: 35 Print; 8 CD-ROM; 300 Audio
Imprints: Artemis Books (2 titles); Consciousness Classics; Gateways Fine Art Series; Retro Science Fiction
Distributor for Cloister Recordings (audio & video tapes)

Gault Millau Inc/Gayot Publications
4311 Wilshire Blvd, Suite 405, Los Angeles, CA 90010
Tel: 323-965-3529 *Fax:* 323-936-2883
E-mail: info@gayot.com
Web Site: www.gayot.com
Key Personnel
Pres: Andre Gayot
Publr & Ed-in-Chief: Alain Gayot
Founded: 1986
Publish travel guides to world destinations with a rating system to the best hotels, restaurants & shops.
ISBN Prefix(es): 978-1-881066
Number of titles published annually: 12 Print
Total Titles: 16 Print; 5 E-Book
Imprints: Gault Millau; GAYOT
Subsidiaries: Tastes Newsletter
Divisions: The Food Paper
Distributed by Publishers Group West

Gauthier Publications Inc
PO Box 806241, St Clair Shores, MI 48080
SAN: 857-2119
Tel: 313-458-7141 *Fax:* 586-279-1515
E-mail: info@gauthierpublications.com
Web Site: www.gauthierpublications.com
Key Personnel
CEO: Daniel J Gauthier *E-mail:* daniel@gauthierpublications.com
Creative Dir: Elizabeth Gauthier *E-mail:* elizabeth@gauthierpublications.com
Founded: 2008
Devoted to printing high quality literary work. Our mission is simple, to introduce reading early & help promote a lifetime love for the written word by putting out captivating & unique titles that are tailored to their audience. We are proud to say all of our books are printed & bound in the US & our Hungry Goat Press line is made with 100% post consumer recycled paper because we think a good book means more than an exciting plot-line. Distribution also by Amazon.
ISBN Prefix(es): 978-0-9820812; 978-0-9833593
Number of titles published annually: 15 Print
Total Titles: 35 Print
Imprints: DragonFish Comics (graphic novels); Frog Legs Ink (children's books); Hungry Goat Press (young adult books)
Distribution Center: Follett School Solutions Inc, 1340 Ridgeview Dr, McHenry, IL 60050 *Tel:* 815-759-1700 *Toll Free Tel:* 888-511-5114 (cust serv) *Fax:* 815-759-9831 *Toll Free Fax:* 800-852-5458 *E-mail:* info@follettlearning.com *Web Site:* www.follettlearning.com SAN: 169-1902
Diamond, 1966 Greenspring Dr, Suite 300, Timonium, MD 21093 *Toll Free Tel:* 800-452-6642
Membership(s): ABA

Gefen Books
c/o Storch, 255 Central Ave, B-206, Lawrence, NY 11559
Tel. 516-593-1234 *Toll Free Tel:* 800-477-5257 *Fax:* 516-295-2739
E-mail: gefenny@gefenpublishing.com; info@gefenpublishing.com
Web Site: www.gefenpublishing.com
Key Personnel
Contact: Maury Storch
Founded: 1981
General interest, mainly books from Israel. Specialize in Judaic interest, Israel, art, Holocaust & Jewish history. Can supply any books published in Israel +/or in the Hebrew language.
ISBN Prefix(es): 978-0-86343
Number of titles published annually: 25 Print
Total Titles: 425 Print; 400 Online; 400 E-Book
Subsidiaries: IsraBook
Divisions: Medical Publishing (Gefen)
Foreign Office(s): Gefen Publishing House Ltd, 6 Hatzvi St, 94386 Jerusalem, Israel *Tel:* (02) 538-0247 *Fax:* (02) 538-8423
Distributor for Bar Ilan; Magnes Press
Shipping Address: 11 Edison Place, Springfield, NJ 07081
Warehouse: 11 Edison Place, Springfield, NJ 07081

Gem Guides Book Co
1275 W Ninth St, Upland, CA 91786
Tel: 626-855-1611 *Toll Free Tel:* 800-824-5118 (orders) *Fax:* 626-855-1610
E-mail: info@gemguidesbooks.com
Web Site: www.gemguidesbooks.com
Key Personnel
Opers Mgr: Matt Warner
Chief Ed: Nancy Fox
Off Mgr: Nannette Becerra
Sales: Michael Moran
Founded: 1965
Publisher & distributor of regional & specialty trade books; rocks, minerals, crystals, Old West, western & southwestern region & local interests.
ISBN Prefix(es): 978-0-935182; 978-1-889786
Number of titles published annually: 7 Print
Total Titles: 80 Print
Imprints: Gembooks
Distributed by Nevada Publications
Distributor for Borden Publishing; Brynmorgen Press; Clear Creek Publishing; Earth Love Publishing; Editions du Signe; GemStone Press; Golden West Books; Grand Canyon Association; Heaven & Earth Press; Hexagon Press; International Jewelry Publications; George R Jezek Photography; Cy Johnson & Son; KC Publications Inc; Many Moons Press; Naturegraph; Nevada Publications; Out of This World Press; Pinyon Publishing; Primer Publications; Ram Publishing; Recreation Sales; Shortfuse Press; Sierra Press; Delos Toole; Trees Co; Tri-Star Boze Books; Weseanne Publications
Membership(s): ABA; Independent Book Publishers Association; Northern California Independent Booksellers Association

GemStone Press
Imprint of Turner Publishing Co
4507 Charlotte Ave, Suite 100, Nashville, TN 37209
SAN: 134-5621
Tel: 615-255-BOOK (255-2665) *Fax:* 615-255-5081
E-mail: marketing@turnerpublishing.com
Web Site: gemstonepress.com; www.turnerpublishing.com
Key Personnel
Pres & Publr, Turner Publishing Co: Todd Bottorff
Founded: 1987
Books on buying, enjoying, identifying & selling jewelry & gems for the consumer, collector, hobbyist, investor & jewelry trade.
ISBN Prefix(es): 978-0-943763
Number of titles published annually: 5 Print; 1 E-Book
Total Titles: 15 Print

§Genealogical Publishing Co
Subsidiary of Genealogical.com
3600 Clipper Mill Rd, Suite 260, Baltimore, MD 21211
Tel: 410-837-8271 *Toll Free Tel:* 800-296-6687 *Fax:* 410-752-8492 *Toll Free Fax:* 800-599-9561
E-mail: info@genealogical.com; web@genealogical.com
Web Site: www.genealogical.com
Key Personnel
VP & Ed-in-Chief: Michael Tepper *E-mail:* mtepper@genealogical.com
Mktg Dir: Joe Garonzik *E-mail:* jgaronzi@genealogical.com
Data Processing Mgr: Roger Sherr *E-mail:* rsherr@genealogical.com
Founded: 1959
Genealogy, local history, immigration history & source records. Products are nonreturnable, unless mis-shipped or damaged in shipment.
ISBN Prefix(es): 978-0-8063
Number of titles published annually: 50 Print; 2 CD-ROM
Total Titles: 352 Print; 84 CD-ROM
Subsidiaries: Clearfield Co Inc
See separate listing for:
Clearfield Co Inc

§Genesis Press Inc
PO Box 101, Columbus, MS 39701
Toll Free Tel: 888-463-4461 (orders only)
E-mail: customerservice@genesis-press.com
Web Site: www.genesis-press.com
Key Personnel
Pres & Co-Founder: Wilbur O Colom
Off Mgr: Diane Blair
Founded: 1993
Privately owned African-American book publisher.
ISBN Prefix(es): 978-1-885478; 978-1-58571
Number of titles published annually: 26 Print
Total Titles: 160 Print
Imprints: Black Coral; Indigo; Indigo Love Spectrum; Indigo Vibe; Mount Blue; Obsidian; Sage
Membership(s): AAP

Geological Society of America (GSA)
3300 Penrose Place, Boulder, CO 80301-1806
SAN: 201-5978
Mailing Address: PO Box 9140, Boulder, CO 80301-9140
Tel: 303-357-1000 *Fax:* 303-357-1070
E-mail: pubs@geosociety.org (prodn); editing@geosociety.org (edit)
Web Site: www.geosociety.org
Key Personnel
Exec Dir: John W Hess *Tel:* 303-357-1011 *E-mail:* jhess@geosociety.org
Ad Mgr: Ann H Crawford *Tel:* 303-357-1053 *E-mail:* acrawford@geosociety.org
Founded: 1888
General earth sciences, cover such areas as geology, economic geology, engineering geology, geochemistry, geomorphology, marine geology, mineralogy, paleontology, petrology, seismology, solid earth geophysics, structural geology, tectonics & environmental geology.
ISBN Prefix(es): 978-0-8137
Number of titles published annually: 9 Print
Total Titles: 200 Print
Branch Office(s)
1200 New York Ave NW, Suite 400, Washington, DC 20005, Dir, Geoscience Policy: Kasey White *Tel:* 202-669-0466 *E-mail:* kwhite@geosociety.org
Foreign Rep(s): Geological Society of London (UK)

§GeoLytics Inc
3322 Rte 22, Suite 806, Branchburg, NJ 08876
Mailing Address: PO Box 5336, East Brunswick, NJ 08876
Tel: 908-707-1505 *Toll Free Tel:* 800-577-6717 *Fax:* 908-707-1595
E-mail: support@geolytics.com; questions@geolytics.com
Web Site: www.geolytics.com
Key Personnel
Mktg Dir: Katia Segre Cohen
Founded: 1996
Provider of census, demographic & geographic data for academic & business researchers.
ISBN Prefix(es): 978-1-892445
Number of titles published annually: 7 CD-ROM; 7 Online
Total Titles: 55 CD-ROM; 55 Online

Georgetown University Press
3240 Prospect St NW, Suite 250, Washington, DC 20007
Tel: 202-687-5889 (busn) *Fax:* 202-687-6340 (edit)
E-mail: gupress@georgetown.edu
Web Site: press.georgetown.edu
Key Personnel
Interim Dir: Hope J LeGro *Tel:* 202-687-4704 *E-mail:* hjs6@georgetown.edu
Mktg & Sales Dir: Jessica Pellien *Tel:* 202-687-9856 *E-mail:* jhp73@georgetown.edu
Asst Dir of Press & Busn Mgr: Ioan Suciu *Tel:* 202-687-5641 *E-mail:* suciui@georgetown.edu
Sr Acqs Ed & Intl Aff, Public Policy & Public Mgmt: Donald Jacobs *Tel:* 202-687-5218 *E-mail:* dpj5@georgetown.edu

Edit Designer & Prodn Mgr: Glenn Saltzman *Tel:* 202-687-6251 *E-mail:* gls43@georgetown.edu
Founded: 1964
Bioethics; international affairs & human rights; languages & linguistics; political science, public policy & public management; religion & ethics.
ISBN Prefix(es): 978-0-87840; 978-1-58901
Number of titles published annually: 40 Print; 2 Audio
Total Titles: 500 Print; 9 Audio
Foreign Rep(s): Apex Knowledge Sdn Bhd (Simon Tay) (Brunei, Malaysia); Avicenna Partnership Ltd (Middle East); Booknet Co Ltd (Ms Suphaluck Sattabuz) (Cambodia, Laos, Myanmar, Thailand, Vietnam); ChoiceTEXTS (Asia) Pte Ltd (Philip Ang) (Indonesia, Singapore); Footprint Books (Australia, New Zealand); iCaves Ltd (Eddy Lam) (China, Hong Kong, Macau); iGroup (Asia Pacific) Ltd (Estela Suyat) (Philippines); iGroup Korea (IDC Asia) (Mr DJ Kim) (Korea); KW Publishers Pvt Ltd (India); Taiwan Publisher Marketing Service Ltd (George Liu) (Taiwan); United Publishers Services Ltd (Mark Gresham) (Japan)
Orders to: Hopkins Fulfillment Services, PO Box 50370, Baltimore, MD 21211-4370 *Tel:* 410-516-6956 *Toll Free Tel:* 800-537-5487 *Fax:* 410-516-6998 *E-mail:* hfscustserv@press.jhu.edu; NBN International Business Center, 10 Thornbury Rd, Plymouth PL6 7PP, United Kingdom (Africa, Europe, Middle East & UK) *Tel:* (01752) 202301 *Fax:* (01752) 202333 *E-mail:* orders@nbninternational.com *Web Site:* distribution.nbni.co.uk
Returns: Hopkins Fulfillment Services, c/o Maple Logistics Solutions, Lebanon Distribution Ctr, 704 Legionaire Dr, Fredericksburg, PA 17026
Warehouse: Maple Logistics Solutions, Lebanon Distribution Ctr, 704 Legionaire Dr, Fredericksburg, PA 17026
Distribution Center: Scholarly Book Services, 289 Bridgeland Ave, Unit 105, Toronto, ON M6A 1Z6, Canada *Toll Free Tel:* 800-847-9736 *Toll Free Fax:* 800-220-9895 *E-mail:* orders@sbookscan.com *Web Site:* www.sbookscan.com

§Gestalt Journal Press
PO Box 278, Gouldsboro, ME 04607-0278
Tel: 207-404-9954 *Fax:* 207-510-4889
E-mail: press@gestalt.org
Web Site: gestalt.org
Founded: 1975
Mental health, gestalt therapy specifically.
ISBN Prefix(es): 978-0-939266
Number of titles published annually: 5 Print; 11 E-Book
Total Titles: 41 Print; 5 E-Book; 6 Audio

§Getty Publications
1200 Getty Center Dr, Suite 500, Los Angeles, CA 90049-1682
SAN: 208-2276
Tel: 310-440-7365 *Toll Free Tel:* 800-223-3431 (orders) *Fax:* 310-440-7758
E-mail: pubsinfo@getty.edu
Web Site: www.getty.edu/publications
Key Personnel
Publr: Kara Kirk *Tel:* 310-440-6066 *E-mail:* kkirk@getty.edu
Ed-in-Chief: Karen Levine *Tel:* 310-440-6525 *E-mail:* klevine@getty.edu
Gen Mgr: Carolyn Simmons *Tel:* 310-440-7130 *E-mail:* csimmons@getty.edu
Rts Mgr: Leslie Rollins *Tel:* 310-440-7102 *E-mail:* lrollins@getty.edu
Sales & Mktg Mgr: Maureen Winter *Tel:* 310-440-6117 *E-mail:* mwinter@getty.edu
Founded: 1982
Produces a wide variety of books in the fields of art, photography, archaeology, architecture, conservation & the humanities for both general & specialized audiences. These award-winning publications complement & often result from the work of the J Paul Getty Museum, the Getty Conservation Institute & the Getty Research Institute. Publications include illustrated exhibition catalogues, illustrated works on single artists & art history, works on cultural history, scholarly monographs, critical editions of translated works, comprehensive studies of the Getty's collections, educational books to interest children of all ages in art & gift books.
ISBN Prefix(es): 978-0-89236; 978-1-60606
Number of titles published annually: 50 Print; 2 Online; 3 E-Book
Total Titles: 500 Print; 5 Online; 5 E-Book
Distributed by University of Chicago Press (US only)
Foreign Rep(s): Canadian Manda Group (Canada); EWEB (Asia, Pacific Rim); Orca Book Services (Europe, UK); Roundhouse Group (Europe, UK)
Distribution Center: Chicago Distribution Center, 11030 S Langley Ave, Chicago, IL 60628 *Tel:* 773-702-7000 *Toll Free Tel:* 800-621-2736 *Fax:* 773-702-7212 *Toll Free Fax:* 800-621-8476 *E-mail:* custserv@press.uchicago.edu *Web Site:* www.press.uchicago.edu
Membership(s): AAP; Association of American University Presses; CAA; International Association of Museum Publishers

GIA Publications Inc
7404 S Mason Ave, Chicago, IL 60638
Tel: 708-496-3800 *Toll Free Tel:* 800-GIA-1358 (442-1358) *Fax:* 708-496-3828
E-mail: custserv@giamusic.com
Web Site: www.giamusic.com
Key Personnel
COO & Pres: Alec Harris *E-mail:* alech@giamusic.com
Founded: 1941
Publish sacred choral music, hymnals, books, recordings & music education materials.
ISBN Prefix(es): 978-0-941050; 978-1-57999
Number of titles published annually: 200 Print
Total Titles: 6,000 Print; 250 Audio

§Gibbs Smith Publisher
1877 E Gentile St, Layton, UT 84041
Mailing Address: PO Box 667, Layton, UT 84041-0667 SAN: 201-9906
Tel: 801-544-9800 *Toll Free Tel:* 800-748-5439; 800-835-4993 (orders) *Fax:* 801-544-5582 *Toll Free Fax:* 800-213-3023 (orders only)
E-mail: info@gibbs-smith.com; tradeorders@gibbs-smith.com
Web Site: www.gibbs-smith.com
Key Personnel
CEO: Brad Farmer *E-mail:* brad.farmer@gibbs-smith.com
Gen Mgr, Trade Sales: Dan Moench *Tel:* 801-544-9800 ext 156 *E-mail:* dan.moench@gibbs-smith.com
Founded: 1969
ISBN Prefix(es): 978-0-87905; 978-1-58685
Number of titles published annually: 80 Print; 50 Online; 80 E-Book
Total Titles: 350 Print; 200 Online; 350 E-Book
Imprints: Ancient City Press; Wyrick & Co
Foreign Rep(s): Jonathan Ball & Nicky Stubbs (South Africa); Gilles Fauveau (Japan, Korea); Jaime Gregorio (Philippines); Penguin Books India Pvt Ltd (Sharad Mohan) (Bangladesh, India, Maldives, Nepal, Pakistan, Sri Lanka); Peribo (Australia, New Zealand); Perseus Books Group UK (Europe exc UK); Perseus International (Suk Lee) (Malaysia, Singapore); Perseus International (Edison Garcia) (Caribbean, Latin America, Middle East, North Africa); June Poonpanich (Cambodia, Indonesia, Laos, Thailand, Vietnam); Publishers Group UK (UK); Raincoast Books (Canada); Wei Zhao (China, Hong Kong, Taiwan)
Returns: 570 N Sportsplex Dr, Kaysville, UT 84037
Shipping Address: 570 N Sportsplex Dr, Kaysville, UT 84037
Membership(s): AAP

Gifted Education Press
10201 Yuma Ct, Manassas, VA 20109
Mailing Address: PO Box 1586, Manassas, VA 20109-1586
Tel: 703-369-5017
Web Site: www.giftededpress.com
Key Personnel
Publr & Dir: Maurice D Fisher *E-mail:* mfisher345@comcast.net
Founded: 1981
Books, quarterly newsletter, *Gifted Education News-Page* published 6 times a year, teaching guides & supplemental materials for students. Education of gifted children.
ISBN Prefix(es): 978-0-910609
Number of titles published annually: 10 Print
Total Titles: 80 Print

Gingko Press Inc
1321 Fifth St, Berkeley, CA 94710
Tel: 510-898-1195 *Fax:* 510-898-1196
E-mail: books@gingkopress.com
Web Site: www.gingkopress.com
Key Personnel
Chmn & CEO: Mo Cohen *E-mail:* mo@gingkopress.com
VP & Publr: David Lopes *E-mail:* david@gingkopress.com
VP, Sales & Mktg: Rick Markell *E-mail:* rick@gingkopress.com
Founded: 1991
Publisher & distributor.
ISBN Prefix(es): 978-1-58423; 978-1-934471
Number of titles published annually: 100 Print; 1 E-Book
Total Titles: 450 Print; 2 E-Book
Imprints: Rebel Arts
Foreign Office(s): Gingko Press Verlags GmbH, Schulterblatt 58, 20357 Hamburg, Germany, Contact: Anika Heusermann *Tel:* (040) 29 14 25 *Fax:* (040) 29 10 55 *E-mail:* gingkopress@t-online.de
Distributor for All Rights Reserved Ltd; Archimap; Art Power; Basheer; Choi's Gallery; CYPI; Gingko Press; Rebel Arts; Sandu Publications; Sendpoints Books Co Ltd; Upper Playground; Victionary; Wax Facts Press; Zero+ Publishing

Gival Press
Imprint of Gival Press LLC
5200 N First St, Arlington, VA 22203
Mailing Address: PO Box 3812, Arlington, VA 22203 SAN: 852-9787
Tel: 703-351-0079 *Fax:* 703-351-0079 (call first)
E-mail: givalpress@yahoo.com
Web Site: www.givalpress.com
Key Personnel
Publr & Ed: Robert L Giron
Founded: 1998
Small, independent literary press.
ISBN Prefix(es): 978-1-928589
Number of titles published annually: 3 Print; 3 E-Book
Total Titles: 70 Print; 35 E-Book
Distribution Center: Follett Higher Education Group, 3 Westbrook Corporate Ctr, Suite 200, Westchester, IL 60154 *Tel:* 708-884-0000 *Toll Free Tel:* 800-FOLLETT (365-5388) *Web Site:* www.follett.com/higher-ed
Membership(s): The Association of Publishers for Special Sales; Community of Literary Magazines & Presses; Independent Book Publishers Association; Publishing Triangle

§Glenbridge Publishing Ltd
19923 E Long Ave, Centennial, CO 80016-1969
SAN: 243-5403
Tel: 720-870-8381 *Toll Free Tel:* 800-986-4135 (orders) *Fax:* 720-230-1209
E-mail: glenbridge10@gmail.com
Web Site: www.glenbridgepublishing.com
Key Personnel
Pres & Intl Rts: Mary B Keene
VP & Ed: James A Keene
Founded: 1986
Publish nonfiction, hardcover originals, reprints & paperback originals.
ISBN Prefix(es): 978-0-944435
Number of titles published annually: 5 Print; 5 CD-ROM
Total Titles: 62 Print; 62 CD-ROM

§Peter Glenn Publications
Division of Blount Communications Corp
306 NE Second St, 2nd fl, Delray Beach, FL 33483
Tel: 561-404-4290 *Fax:* 561-892-5786
Web Site: pgdirect.com
Key Personnel
CEO & Publr: Gregory James Blount *E-mail:* gregjames@pgdirect.com
Dir: L Chip Brill; Umberto Guido, III
Ed: Todd Heustess
Founded: 1956
Directories for the world of advertising, TV & film publicity; directories & how-to books for performing arts, fashion & modeling industry.
ISBN Prefix(es): 978-0-87314
Number of titles published annually: 9 Print
Total Titles: 9 Print; 6 E-Book

Glimmer Train Press Inc
PO Box 80430, Portland, OR 97280-1430
Tel: 503-221-0836 *Fax:* 503-221-0837
E-mail: editors@glimmertrain.org
Web Site: www.glimmertrain.org
Key Personnel
Co-Ed: Susan Burmeister-Brown *E-mail:* susan@glimmertrain.org; Linda Swanson-Davies *E-mail:* linda@glimmertrain.org
Founded: 1990
In addition to books, also publishes triannual short story journal *Glimmer Train.*
ISBN Prefix(es): 978-1-880966; 978-1-59553
Number of titles published annually: 3 Print
Total Titles: 81 Print
Membership(s): Community of Literary Magazines & Presses

Glitterati Inc
630 Ninth Ave, Suite 603, New York, NY 10036
Tel: 212-362-9119 *Fax:* 646-607-4433
E-mail: info@glitteratiincorporated.com
Web Site: glitteratiincorporated.com
Key Personnel
CEO & Pres: Martha Hallett *E-mail:* mhallett@glitteratiincorporated.com
Assoc Publr: Brandon Schultz *E-mail:* bschultz@glitteratiincorporated.com
Publicity & Promos Dir: Sara Rosen *E-mail:* srosen@glitteratiincorporated.com
Mng Ed: Kiara Cobb *E-mail:* kcobb@glitteratiincorporated.com
Ed: Kristin Kulsavage
Assoc Publicity Dir: Gayatri Mullapudi *E-mail:* gmullapudi@glitteratiincorporated.com
Sales & Projs Mgr: Conor Romack
Publg Asst: Sarah Schreiber *E-mail:* sschreiber@glitteratiincorporated.com
Independent producer & publisher of distinctive illustrated books, ancillary gift products & electronic media for domestic & international markets.
ISBN Prefix(es): 978-0-9721152; 978-0-9765851; 978 0 9777531; 978 0 9793384; 978-0-9801557; 978-0-9822669; 978-0-9823412; 978-0-9823799; 978-0-9832702; 978-0-9851696; 978-0-9881745; 978-0-9891704; 978-0-9913419; 978-0-9905320; 978-0-9862500; 978-0-9962930; 978-1-943876; 978-0-9903808
Number of titles published annually: 9 Print
Total Titles: 58 Print; 1 Audio
Foreign Office(s): One Rona Rd, London NW3 2HY, United Kingdom, Edit: Chris Fagg *Tel:* (020) 7267 8339 *E-mail:* cfagg@glitteratiincorporated.com
Distribution Center: Baker & Taylor Global Publishers Services (GPS)

Global Authors Publications (GAP)
38 Bluegrass, Middleberg, FL 32068
Tel: 904-425-1608
E-mail: gapbook@yahoo.com
Web Site: www.globalauthorspublications.com
Key Personnel
Co-Owner & Publr: Kathleen Walls
Co-Owner: Tammy C McMullen
Founded: 2003
Offer complete subsidy publishing services & consider any genre except pornography or textbooks. Books must be at least 48 pages & not more than 700. We have set a literary standard with all the books we have published already & we do not plan to change our reputation. We won't publish everything that is offered us. Provide an affordable alternative to traditional publishing.
This publisher has indicated that 100% of their product line is author subsidized.
ISBN Prefix(es): 978-0-97
Number of titles published annually: 6 Print
Total Titles: 30 Print

§Global Publishing, Sales & Distribution
980 Lincoln Ave, Suite 200 B, San Rafael, CA 94901
Tel: 415-456-2934 *Fax:* 415-456-4124
Web Site: www.globalpsd.com
Key Personnel
Publr: Adrianne Casey *E-mail:* adrianne@globalpsd.com; Steven Goff *E-mail:* steven@globalpsd.com
ISBN Prefix(es): 978-0-9819942
Number of titles published annually: 50 Print; 50 CD-ROM; 100 Online
Total Titles: 50 Print; 50 CD-ROM; 100 Online
Branch Office(s)
244 Fifth Ave, Suite 2464, New York, NY 10001 *Tel:* 212-627-1400 *Toll Free Fax:* 866-729-2725
16510 203 Place NE, Woodinville, WA 98077 *Tel:* 425-354-3690 *Fax:* 425-354-3664
Foreign Office(s): 8 Commercial Tower, 30/F, Unit 06-07, 8 Sun Yip St, Chai Wan, Hong Kong *Tel:* 3576 3239 *Fax:* 3184 0728
Via Meucci 24, 37036 San Martino Buon Albergo, Verona, Italy *Tel:* (045) 994855 *Fax:* (045) 994746

Global Training Center Inc
550 S Mesa Hills Dr, Suite E4, El Paso, TX 79912
Mailing Address: PO Box 221977, El Paso, TX 79913
Tel: 915-534-7900 *Toll Free Tel:* 800-860-5030 *Fax:* 915-534-7903
E-mail: contact@globaltrainingcenter.com
Web Site: www.globaltrainingcenter.com
Key Personnel
Pres: Elsa Solorzano
Founded: 1992
Training seminar/workshops covering International Documentation, NAFTA, Importing, etc.
ISBN Prefix(es): 978-1-891249
Number of titles published annually: 23 Print
Total Titles: 23 Print

The Globe Pequot Press
Division of Rowman & Littlefield Publishing Group
246 Goose Lane, Guilford, CT 06437
SAN: 201-9892
Tel: 203-458-4500 *Toll Free Tel:* 800-243-0495 (orders only); 888-249-7586 (cust serv) *Fax:* 203-458-4601 *Toll Free Fax:* 800-820-2329 (orders & cust serv)
E-mail: editorial@globepequot.com; info@rowman.com; orders@rowman.com
Web Site: rowman.com
Key Personnel
Publr: Jim Childs
Edit Dir: Erin Turner *Tel:* 406-442-6597 *E-mail:* eturner@rowman.com
Exec Ed, Falcon: Ursula Cary
Mgr, Dist Busn: Andrea Jacobs *Tel:* 203-458-4552 *E-mail:* ajacobs@rowman.com
Founded: 1947
Travel guidebooks, regional books, sports, how-to, outdoor recreation, personal finance, self-help, sports, cooking, entertaining, military history, fishing, hunting, gift books.
ISBN Prefix(es): 978-0-937959; 978-1-56044; 978-1-57380; 978-1-57540; 978-1-882997; 978-0-87842; 978-0-87106; 978-0-7627; 978-0-89933; 978-0-934641; 978-1-56440; 978-0-912367; 978-0-933469; 978-0-934802; 978-0-934318; 978-1-57034; 978-1-58592; 978-1-901970 (Sawday)
Number of titles published annually: 500 Print; 500 E-Book
Total Titles: 2,800 Print; 1,000 E-Book
Imprints: Cheap Bastards; Down East Books; Falcon®; Globe Pequot; Gooseberry Patch; GPP® Travel; The Lyons Press; Taylor Trade; TwoDot®; Western Horseman
Distributor for Appalachian Mountain Club Books; Boone & Crockett Club; Thomas Cook Publishing; D&B Publishing; Day Hike Books Inc; Everyman Chess; Explorer Publishing; Globetrotter; Good Sam's; Jonglez Publishing; Montana Historical Society Press; New Holland Publishers (UK) Ltd; Oval Books (UK); Alastair Sawday Publishing (co-publr); Stoecklein Publishing; 30 Words; Trailblazer Publications; Western Horseman Books
Foreign Rep(s): Faradawn (South Africa); Pansing (Singapore); Les Petriw (Canada); Woodslane NZ Ltd (New Zealand); Woodslane Pty Ltd (Australia)
Returns: National Book Network (NBN), 15200 NBN Way, Blue Ridge Summit, PA 17214
Warehouse: National Book Network (NBN), 15200 NBN Way, Blue Ridge Summit, PA 17214
Distribution Center: National Book Network (NBN), 15200 NBN Way, Blue Ridge Summit, PA 17214
Membership(s): AAP; ABA; BISG; New England Independent Booksellers Association
See separate listing for:
Down East Books
The Lyons Press

David R Godine Publisher Inc
15 Court Sq, Suite 320, Boston, MA 02108-4715
SAN: 213-4381
Tel: 617-451-9600 *Fax:* 617-350-0250
E-mail: info@godine.com
Web Site: www.godine.com
Key Personnel
Pres & Publr: David R Godine
Assoc Publr: Sue Berger Ramin
Black Sparrow Publr: Chelsea Bingham
Prodn Mgr: Heather Tamarkin *E-mail:* htamarkin@godine.com
Founded: 1970
Fiction & nonfiction, history, biography, typography, art & photography, poetry, horticulture, Americana, cooking, regional, mysteries, juveniles.

ISBN Prefix(es): 978-0-87923; 978-1-56792; 978-0-87685; 978-1-57423
Number of titles published annually: 40 Print
Total Titles: 500 Print
Imprints: Black Sparrow; Imago Mundi; Nonpareil Books; Verba Mundi
Sales Office(s): 426 Nutting Rd, PO Box 450, Jaffrey, NH 03452
Foreign Rep(s): Big Apple Agency Inc (Kelly Chang) (Taiwan); Sandra Bruna Agency (Spain); The English Agency (Hamish Macaskill) (Japan); Paul & Peter Fritz Agency (Peter Fritz) (Switzerland); Graal Literary Agency (Magda Koceba) (Poland); Korea Copyright Center (Jae-Yeon Ryu) (Korea); Michelle Lapautre Agence (Michelle Lapautre) (France); Natoli Stefan & Oliva Agenzia (Roberta Oliva) (Italy); Agencia Literara SUN (Crina Chitan) (Romania)
Foreign Rights: Sandra Bruna Agency (Spain); The English Agency (Japan); Paul & Peter Fritz (Germany); Korea Copyright Center (Korea); Catherine Lapautre (France); Michelle Lapautre (France); Natoli, Stefan & Oliva (Italy)
Orders to: 426 Nutting Rd, PO Box 450, Jaffrey, NH 03452 *Toll Free Tel:* 800-344-4771 *Toll Free Fax:* 800-226-0934 *E-mail:* order@godine.com
Returns: 426 Nutting Rd, PO Box 450, Jaffrey, NH 03452 *Toll Free Tel:* 800-344-4771 *Toll Free Fax:* 800-226-0934
Warehouse: 426 Nutting Rd, PO Box 450, Jaffrey, NH 03452 *Tel:* 603-532-4100 *Toll Free Tel:* 800-344-4771 *Fax:* 603-532-5940 *Toll Free Fax:* 800-226-0934 *E-mail:* order@godine.com
Membership(s): AAP

Golden West Cookbooks
Division of American Traveler Press
5738 N Central Ave, Phoenix, AZ 85012-1316
Tel: 602-234-1574 *Toll Free Tel:* 800-521-9221 *Fax:* 602-234-3062
E-mail: info@americantravelerpress.com
Web Site: www.americantravelerpress.com
Key Personnel
Gen Mgr: Bill Fessler
Founded: 1973
Cookbooks & nonfiction books on the Southwest & the Rocky Mountains.
ISBN Prefix(es): 978-0-914846; 978-1-885590
Number of titles published annually: 5 Print
Total Titles: 150 Print
Membership(s): Publishers Association of the West

Gollehon Press Inc
3655 Glenn Dr SE, Grand Rapids, MI 49546
Tel: 616-949-3515 *Fax:* 616-949-8674
E-mail: sales@gollehonbooks.com; editorial@gollehonbooks.com
Web Site: www.gollehonbooks.com
Key Personnel
Pres: John T Gollehon *E-mail:* john@gollehonbooks.com
Publr: Kathy Gollehon *E-mail:* kathy@gollehonbooks.com
Ed: Becky Anderson
Sales Mgr: Jerome K Smith
Founded: 1983
Books related to Christian religions, young adult, seniors, health, how-to, reference, collectibles & current affairs. No unsol mss. Brief book proposals are reviewed. Simultaneous submissions are encouraged.
ISBN Prefix(es): 978-0-914839
Number of titles published annually: 10 Print
Total Titles: 97 Print
Imprints: Gollehon Books; GPC/Gollehon
Warehouse: Offset/Gollehon Distribution Center, 10 Passan Dr, Bldg 10, Laflin, PA 18702

Goodheart-Willcox Publisher
18604 W Creek Dr, Tinley Park, IL 60477-6243
SAN: 203-4387
Tel: 708-687-5000 *Toll Free Tel:* 800-323-0440 *Fax:* 708-468-8692 *Toll Free Fax:* 888-409-3900
E-mail: custserv@g-w.com; orders@g-w.com
Web Site: www.g-w.com
Key Personnel
CEO & Pres: John F Flanagan
VP, Admin & Treas: Robert Kelly
VP, Sales & Mktg: Todd Scheffers
Ad Coord: Zak Semens *Tel:* 708-623-1826 *E-mail:* zsemens@g-w.com
Founded: 1921
Industrial technical; family & consumer sciences & career textbooks.
ISBN Prefix(es): 978-0-87006; 978-1-56637; 978-1-59070; 978-1-60525
Number of titles published annually: 50 Print
Total Titles: 150 Print; 100 CD-ROM; 150 Online
Foreign Rep(s): Baker & Taylor International (Europe); Oxford University Press (Canada)

Goose River Press
3400 Friendship Rd, Waldoboro, ME 04572-6337
Tel: 207-832-6665
E-mail: gooseriverpress@roadrunner.com
Web Site: gooseriverpress.com
Key Personnel
Owner & Ed: Deborah J Benner
Acct Exec: Meredith K Sanders *E-mail:* mksanders@roadrunner.com
Founded: 1999
Traditional publisher, but also offers self-publishing services to the authors of books that do not meet literary quality or who would prefer to self-publish.
This publisher has indicated that 25% of their product line is author subsidized.
ISBN Prefix(es): 978-1-930648; 978-1-59713
Number of titles published annually: 15 Print; 10 E-Book
Total Titles: 100 Print; 30 E-Book
Distribution Center: Ingram Content Group, 1246 Heil Quaker Blvd, La Vergne, TN 37086, Contact: Jim Patterson *Tel:* 615-213-4475 *Fax:* 615-213-4725 *E-mail:* jim.patterson@lightningsource.com
Membership(s): Maine Writers & Publishers Alliance

Goosebottom Books
Imprint of Goosebottom Books LLC
543 Trinidad Lane, Foster City, CA 94404
SAN: 859-8029
Tel: 650-556-3782 *Toll Free Fax:* 888-407-5286
E-mail: info@goosebottombooks.com
Web Site: goosebottombooks.com
Key Personnel
Publr: Shirin Yim Bridges *E-mail:* shirin.bridges@goosebottombooks.com
Founded: 2010
A small press dedicated to stealth education through fun nonfiction.
ISBN Prefix(es): 978-0-9845098 (Real Princesses series); 978-0-9834256 (Dastardly Dames series); 978-1-937463 (all others)
Number of titles published annually: 6 Print; 6 Online; 6 E-Book
Total Titles: 19 Print; 19 Online; 19 E-Book
Foreign Rights: Perseus (worldwide)
Orders to: Publishers Group West (PGW), 1700 Fourth St, Berkeley, CA 94710 *Toll Free Tel:* 800-788-3123 *Toll Free Fax:* 800-351-5073 *E-mail:* orderentry@perseusbooks.com *Web Site:* www.pgw.com
Distribution Center: Publishers Group West (PGW), 1700 Fourth St, Berkeley, CA 94710 *Toll Free Tel:* 800-788-3123 *Toll Free Fax:* 800-351-5073 *E-mail:* orderentry@perseusbooks.com *Web Site:* pgw.com
Membership(s): The Children's Book Council

Gorgias Press LLC
PO Box 6939, Piscataway, NJ 08854-6939
Tel: 732-885-8900 *Fax:* 732-885-8908
E-mail: helpdesk@gorgiaspress.com
Web Site: www.gorgiaspress.com
Key Personnel
Co-Founder & Pres: George Anton Kiraz, PhD
Co-Founder & VP: Christine Kiraz, PhD
Acqs Ed: Melonie Schmierer-Lee, PhD
Founded: 2001
Academic publishers of specialty books; provides for author/small publisher's digitization & publishing services needs.
ISBN Prefix(es): 978-1-59333; 978-0-9713097; 978-0-9715986; 978-1-931956; 978-1-60724
Number of titles published annually: 70 Print
Total Titles: 320 Print
Distributor for Yeshiva University Museum Press
Membership(s): Independent Book Publishers Association

Gospel Publishing House (GPH)
Division of General Council of the Assemblies of God
1445 Boonville Ave, Springfield, MO 65802
SAN: 206-8826
Tel: 417-862-2781; 417-831-8000 (outside US) *Toll Free Tel:* 800-641-4310 *Fax:* 417-863-1874; 417-862-5881 *Toll Free Fax:* 800-328-0294
E-mail: custsrvreps@ag.org
Web Site: www.gospelpublishing.com
Key Personnel
VP: Steve Blount
Founded: 1914
Religion (Assemblies of God); sign language textbooks & curricular materials.
ISBN Prefix(es): 978-0-88243
Number of titles published annually: 6 Print
Total Titles: 250 Print
Imprints: Gospel Publishing House; Influence Resources; Logion Press; My Healthy Church; Radiant Life Curriculum; Salubris Resources; Vital Resources
Distribution Center: Bookmasters, 30 Amberwood Pkwy, Ashland, OH 44805 *Tel:* 419-281-5100 *Fax:* 419-281-0200 *E-mail:* info@bookmasters.com *Web Site:* www.bookmasters.com

The Graduate Group/Booksellers
86 Norwood Rd, West Hartford, CT 06117-2236
Mailing Address: PO Box 370351, West Hartford, CT 06137-0351
Tel: 860-233-2330
E-mail: graduategroup@hotmail.com
Web Site: www.graduategroup.com
Key Personnel
Partner: Mara Whitman
Lib Sales Dir: Robert Whitman *Tel:* 860-232-3100
Founded: 1964
Publish career oriented reference books & self-help books for libraries, career & placement offices in the US & abroad, law enforcement, career series, exam preparation.
ISBN Prefix(es): 978-0-938609
Number of titles published annually: 20 Print; 1 Online
Total Titles: 100 Print; 2 Online

§Grand & Archer Publishing
611 S Palm Canyon Dr, Suite 7451, Palm Springs, CA 92264
Tel: 323-493-2785
E-mail: grandandarcher@gmail.com
Key Personnel
Owner & CEO: Will Tom Shoaff
Chief Content Offr: Max Visconti
Founded: 2016
Boutique publishing agency.
ISBN Prefix(es): 978-1-929730

Number of titles published annually: 3 Print; 5 E-Book; 3 Audio
Total Titles: 3 Print
Shipping Address: Pathway Book Service, 34 Production Ave, Keene, NH 03431, Contact: Julie Ballou *Tel:* 603-357-0225 *Toll Free Tel:* 800-345-6665 *Fax:* 603-357-2073 *E-mail:* julie.ballou@pathwaybook.com SAN: 110-6430
Warehouse: Pathway Book Service, 34 Production Ave, Keene, NH 03431, Contact: Julie Ballou *Tel:* 603-357-0225 *Toll Free Tel:* 800-345-6665 *Fax:* 603-357-2073 *E-mail:* julie.ballou@pathwaybook.com SAN: 110-6430
Distribution Center: Pathway Book Service, 34 Production Ave, Keene, NH 03431, Contact: Julie Ballou *Tel:* 603-357-0225 *Toll Free Tel:* 800-345-6665 *Fax:* 603-357-2073 *E-mail:* julie.ballou@pathwaybook.com SAN: 110-6430
Membership(s): Independent Book Publishers Association

Grand Central Publishing
Division of Hachette Book Group
1290 Avenue of the Americas, New York, NY 10019
Tel: 212-364-1100
Web Site: www.hachettebookgroup.com
Key Personnel
SVP & Publr: Ben Sevier
Edit, Grand Central Publishing/VP & Publr, Twelve: Sean Desmond
VP, Digital & Pbk Publr: Beth de Guzman
VP, Assoc Publr & Mktg Dir, Grand Central Publishing & Twelve: Brian McLendon
VP, Edit Dir, Grand Central Life & Style: Karen Murgolo
Exec Ed, Ed-in-Chief, Forever & Forever Yours: Amy Pierpont
VP, Exec Dir, Publicity, Grand Central: Matthew Ballast
VP, Creative Dir: Anne Twomey
VP, Subs Rts: Nancy Wiese
Sr Dir, HBG Multicultural Publicity: Linda Duggins
Sr Publicity Dir: Jimmy Franco
Publicity & Mktg Dir, Forever & Forever Yours: Jodi Rosoff
Publicity Dir, Twelve: Paul Samuelson
Assoc Dir, Publicity (best-selling fiction brand authors): Andy Dodds
Assoc Dir, Publicity, Grand Central Life & Style: Nick Small
Assoc Dir, Publicity (bestselling fiction & non-fiction authors): Caitlin Mulrooney–Lyski
Founded: 1961
Hardcover, trade paperback & mass market paperback, reprint & original, fiction & nonfiction, audiobooks. Unsol/unagented mss not accepted.
ISBN Prefix(es): 978-0-445; 978-0-446; 978-0-89296
Number of titles published annually: 360 Print
Total Titles: 3,392 Print
Imprints: Forever; Forever Yours; Grand Central Life & Style (includes goop press); Twelve; Vision
Foreign Rights: Antonella Antonelli Agenzia (Italy); Bardon Far Eastern Agents (Taiwan); Graal Literary Agency (Poland); Imprima Korea Agency (Korea); Katai & Bolza Literary Agents (Hungary); Simona Kessler International Copyright Agency Ltd (Romania); La Nouvelle Agence (France); Andrew Nurnberg Associates Ltd (Baltic States, Bulgaria, Mainland China, Russia); OA Literary Agency (Greece); Kristin Olson Literary Agency SRO (Czech Republic, Slovakia); Pikarski Agency (Israel); Prava i prevodi (Croatia, Slovenia); RDC Agencia Literaria (Brazil, Latin America, Spain); Sane Toregard Agency (Denmark, Finland, Iceland, Norway, Sweden); Thomas Schlueck GmbH (Germany)
Advertising Agency: Publishers Advertising
Shipping Address: Hachette Book Group Distribution Center, 121 N Enterprise Blvd, Lebanon, IN 46052 *Tel:* 765-483-9900 *Fax:* 765-483-0706
Membership(s): AAP; BISG

Donald M Grant Publisher Inc
PO Box 187, Hampton Falls, NH 03844-0187
Tel: 603-778-7191 *Fax:* 603-778-7191
E-mail: office@grantbooks.com
Web Site: secure.grantbooks.com
Key Personnel
Pres: Robert K Wiener *E-mail:* robert@grantbooks.com
Founded: 1964
Horror, science fiction, art & fantasy illustrated books.
ISBN Prefix(es): 978-0-937986; 978-1-880418
Number of titles published annually: 6 Print
Total Titles: 50 Print
Distributor for Archival; Oswald Train

Graphic Arts Books
Unit of Ingram Content Group Inc
7820 NE Holman St, Suite B-9, Portland, OR 97218
Mailing Address: PO Box 56118, Portland, OR 97236-6618
Tel: 503-254-5591 *Fax:* 503-254-5609
E-mail: info-ga@graphicartsbooks.com
Web Site: www.graphicartsbooks.com
Key Personnel
Mktg Mgr: Angela Zbornik *Tel:* 970-375-7765 *E-mail:* angela.zbornik@graphicartsbooks.com
Ed: Kathy Howard
Creative Servs Specialist: Vicki Knapton *E-mail:* vicki.knapton@graphicartsbooks.com
Founded: 1967
ISBN Prefix(es): 978-1-55868; 978-0-88240; 978-0-8108; 978-1-94182; 978-0-78108
Number of titles published annually: 35 Print; 30 E-Book
Total Titles: 300 Print; 125 E-Book
Imprints: Alaska Northwest Books®; WestWinds Press®
Distribution Center: Ingram Publisher Services, One Ingram Blvd, La Vergne, TN 37086 *Toll Free Tel:* 866-400-5351 *Toll Free Fax:* 800-838-1149
Membership(s): Publishers Association of the West

Graphic Universe™
Imprint of Lerner Publishing Group Inc
241 First Ave N, Minneapolis, MN 55401
Tel: 612-332-3344 *Toll Free Tel:* 800-328-4929 *Fax:* 612-332-7615 *Toll Free Fax:* 800-332-1132
E-mail: info@lernerbooks.com; custserve@lernerbooks.com
Web Site: www.lernerbooks.com; www.facebook.com/lernerbooks
Key Personnel
Chmn: Harry J Lerner
CFO & EVP: Margaret Thomas
Pres & Publr: Adam Lerner
EVP, Sales: David Wexler
VP, Ed-in-Chief: Patricia M Stockland
Dir of Rts, Spec Sales & Intl Dist: Maria Kjoller
Group Mktg Dir: Jill Braithwaite
School & Lib Mktg Dir: Lois Wallentine
Dir, HR: Cyndi Radant
Founded: 2006
Publish graphic novel fiction & nonfiction books for children & young adults.
Total Titles: 150 Print; 520 E-Book
Foreign Rep(s): INT Press Distribution (Australia); Phambili (Southern Africa); Publishers Marketing Service (Brunei, Malaysia, Singapore); South Pacific Books (New Zealand)
Foreign Rights: Sandra Bruna Agencia Literaria (Spain); Japan Foreign-Rights Centre (JFC) (Japan); Korea Copyright Center Inc (KCC) (Korea); Agence Michelle Lapautre (France)
Warehouse: Lerner Publishing Group, 1251 Washington Ave N, Minneapolis, MN 55401, Mgr: Ken Rued

Gray & Company Publishers
1588 E 40 St, Suite 3A, Cleveland, OH 44103
Tel: 216-431-2665 *Toll Free Tel:* 800-915-3609
E-mail: sales@grayco.com; editorial@grayco.com; support@grayco.com; publicity@grayco.com
Web Site: www.grayco.com
Key Personnel
Pres: David Gray
Mktg: Chris Andrikanich *E-mail:* promotions@grayco.com
Founded: 1991
Books about Cleveland, Northeast Ohio & Ohio.
ISBN Prefix(es): 978-1-886228; 978-0-9631738; 978-1-59851; 978-1-938441
Number of titles published annually: 8 Print
Total Titles: 85 Print

Graywolf Press
250 Third Ave N, Suite 600, Minneapolis, MN 55401
Tel: 651-641-0077 *Fax:* 651-641-0036
E-mail: wolves@graywolfpress.org (no ms queries, sample chapters or proposals)
Web Site: www.graywolfpress.org
Key Personnel
Dir & Publr: Fiona McCrae
Assoc Dir: Katie Dublinski
Mng Dir: Leslie Johnson
Dir, Mktg & Engagement: Marisa Atkinson
Exec Ed: Jeffrey Shotts
Assoc Ed: Steve Woodward
Contrib Ed: Brigid Hughes
Sales & Mktg Mgr: Casey O'Neil
Publicist: Caroline Nitz
Founded: 1974
Graywolf Press publishes 21st century American & international literature in the form of poetry, fiction & nonfiction. Due to the volume of submissions & the size of their list, Graywolf Press no longer accepts unsol queries, book proposals or mss.
ISBN Prefix(es): 978-1-55597
Number of titles published annually: 30 Print
Total Titles: 200 Print; 30 E-Book
Foreign Rights: Agence Michelle Lapautre (France); Michael Meller Literary Agency GmbH (Germany)
Billing Address: MPS Distribution Center, 16365 James Madison Hwy, Gordonsville, VA 22942
Orders to: MPS Distribution Center, 16365 James Madison Hwy, Gordonsville, VA 22942
Warehouse: MPS Distribution Center, 16365 James Madison Hwy, Gordonsville, VA 22942
Distribution Center: MPS Distribution Center, 16365 James Madison Hwy, Gordonsville, VA 22942 *Tel:* 212-206-5311 *Toll Free Tel:* 888-330-8477 *Fax:* 540-672-7703

Great Potential Press Inc
Division of Anodyne Inc
1650 N Kolb Rd, Suite 200, Tucson, AZ 85715
Tel: 520-777-6161 *Fax:* 520-777-6217
Web Site: www.greatpotentialpress.com
Key Personnel
Pres & Publr: James T Webb
VP, Acq Ed, Devt Ed: Janet Gore *E-mail:* janet@greatpotentialpress.com
Founded: 1982
Educational guide books & books for parents & adults relating to social/emotional needs & other characteristics of gifted children & adults.
ISBN Prefix(es): 978-0-910707
Number of titles published annually: 5 Print
Total Titles: 58 Print; 4 CD-ROM; 1 Audio
Imprints: Gifted Psychology Press

Foreign Rights: Amer-Asia Books Inc (Evelyn K Lee) (Asia)
Distribution Center: Ingram Book Co, One Ingram Blvd, La Vergne, TN 37086
Membership(s): Arizona Book Publishing Association; Independent Book Publishers Association

Great Quotations Inc
1410 Brook Dr, Downers Grove, IL 60515
Tel: 630-985-2628 *Toll Free Tel:* 800-830-3020 *Fax:* 630-985-2610
E-mail: info@greatquotationsinc.com
Web Site: www.greatquotationsinc.com
Key Personnel
Pres: Ringo Suek
Founded: 1984
Motivation, inspiration & humor titles, also gifts.
ISBN Prefix(es): 978-1-56245; 978-0-931089
Number of titles published annually: 30 Print
Total Titles: 500 Print
Imprints: G Q Publishing

Green Dragon Books
2875 S Ocean Blvd, Suite 200, Palm Beach, FL 33480
Tel: 561-533-6231 *Toll Free Tel:* 800-874-8844 *Fax:* 561-533-6233 *Toll Free Fax:* 888-874-8844
E-mail: info@greendragonbooks.com
Web Site: greendragonbooks.com
Key Personnel
Chmn & Publr: Gary Wilson *E-mail:* garyw@greendragonbooks.com
Founded: 1969
Publications include Learning Center guides, early learning activity guides, children's picture books, general trade books, Legacies memoir series & SleuthHound mystery series.
ISBN Prefix(es): 978-1-62386; 978-0-89334
Number of titles published annually: 12 Print; 12 Online; 12 E-Book
Total Titles: 400 Print; 400 Online; 400 E-Book
Foreign Rights: Montreal-Contacts/The Rights Agency (worldwide)
Distribution Center: Baker & Taylor
Ingram Book Co
New Leaf Distributing Co, 401 Thornton Rd, Lithia Springs, GA 30122-1557 *Tel:* 704-948-7845 *Fax:* 704-944-2313 *Web Site:* www.newleaf-dist.com
Membership(s): ABA; American Marketing Association; ASCD; Data & Marketing Association; Independent Book Publishers Association; National Education Association; National Press Club; Southern Independent Booksellers Alliance; Toastmasters International

Green Integer
6210 Wilshire Blvd, Suite 211, Los Angeles, CA 90048
SAN: 216-3063
Tel: 323-857-1115 *Fax:* 323-857-0143
Web Site: www.greeninteger.com
Key Personnel
Publr: Douglas Messerli *E-mail:* douglas.messerli@gmail.com
Founded: 1978
Contemporary fiction, criticism, drama & poetry.
ISBN Prefix(es): 978-0-940650; 978-1-55713
Number of titles published annually: 15 Print
Total Titles: 300 Print
Imprints: New American Fiction Series; New American Poetry Series; Sun & Moon Classics
Foreign Rights: Eliane Benesti Literary Agency (France); Bookbank SA (Spain); Copenhagen Literary Agency ApS (Scandinavia); Paul & Peter Fritz AG Literary Agency (Germany, Switzerland); Japan UNI Agency Inc (Japan); Natoli, Stefan & Oliva Literary Agency (Italy); Rogan Pikarski Literary Agency (Israel)
Distribution Center: Consortium Book Sales & Distribution, The Keg House, 34 13 Ave NE, Minneapolis, MN 55413-1007 *Tel:* 651-746-2600 *Toll Free Tel:* 800-283-3572 (cust serv) *Fax:* 612-746-2606 *E-mail:* info@cbsd.com *Web Site:* www.cbsd.com

Greenhaven Press®
Imprint of The Rosen Publishing Group Inc
29 E 21 St, New York, NY 10010
Toll Free Tel: 800-237-9932 *Toll Free Fax:* 888-436-4643
Web Site: www.rosenpublishing.com
Founded: 1970
High school, college & secondary nonfiction social studies & debate books for classrooms & libraries: social studies reference series; library & paper bound books in area studies, criminal justice, the environment, health, Literary Companion & American History series & AT Issues series.
ISBN Prefix(es): 978-0-89908; 978-1-56510; 978-0-7377
Number of titles published annually: 200 Print
Total Titles: 3,500 Print

Greenleaf Book Group LLC
3 Park Place, 4005 Banister Lane, Suite B, Austin, TX 78704
Mailing Address: PO Box 91869, Austin, TX 78709
Tel: 512-891-6100 *Fax:* 512-891-6150
E-mail: contact@greenleafbookgroup.com
Web Site: www.greenleafbookgroup.com
Key Personnel
Founder: Clint Greenleaf
CEO: Tanya Hall
COO & Gen Coun: Bryan Goodwin
CFO: Brian Viktorin
Art Dir: Neil Gonzalez
Dir, Consulting: Justin Branch
Dir, Dist: Steve Elizalde
Dir, Mktg & Branding: Corrin Foster
Dir, Prodn: Carrie Jones
Mgr, Busn Devt: Emilie Lyons *E-mail:* elyons@greenleafbookgroup.com
Sr Ed: Nathan True
Founded: 1997
Publisher & distributor specializing in the development of independent authors & the growth of small presses. Our publishing model was designed to support independent authors & allow writers to retain the rights to their work & still compete with major publishing houses. We also distribute select titles from small & independent publishers to major trade outlets, including bookstores, libraries & airport retailers. We serve the small & independent publishing community by offering industry guidance, business development, production, distribution & marketing services.
ISBN Prefix(es): 978-0-9665319; 978-1-929774; 978-0-9790842; 978-1-60832; 978-1-61486; 978-1-62634
Number of titles published annually: 100 Print
Total Titles: 350 Print
Imprints: An Inc Original; Greenleaf Book Group Press; River Grove Books
Returns: Archway, 20770 Westwood Dr, Strongsville, OH 44149
Membership(s): AAP; ALA; American Society of Journalists & Authors; BookSense Publisher Partner; Independent Book Publishers Association; National Speakers Association

Greenleaf Book Group Press, see Greenleaf Book Group LLC

§Greenwood Research Books & Software
Division of Greenwood Research
PO Box 12102, Wichita, KS 67277-2102
Tel: 316-272-2937
Web Site: greenray4ever.com (ordering)
Key Personnel
Lib Sales Dir & Gen Mgr: James A Green *E-mail:* jimgreenhimself@gmail.com
Founded: 1990 (in Clearwater, FL, relocated 1991)
Science & engineering emphasis: Medical Image Processing.
ISBN Prefix(es): 978-1-890121
Number of titles published annually: 6 Print
Total Titles: 15 Print
Distribution Center: Midwest Library Service, 11443 St Charles Rock Rd, Bridgeton, MO 63044-2789 *Tel:* 314-739-3100 *Toll Free Tel:* 800-325-8833 *Fax:* 314-739-1326 *Toll Free Fax:* 800-962-1009 *E-mail:* mail@midwestls.com *Web Site:* midwestls.com
Membership(s): Independent Book Publishers Association

§Grey House Publishing Inc™
4919 Rte 22, Amenia, NY 12501
Mailing Address: PO Box 56, Amenia, NY 12501-0056
Tel: 518-789-8700 *Toll Free Tel:* 800-562-2139 *Fax:* 518-789-0556
E-mail: books@greyhouse.com; customerservice@greyhouse.com
Web Site: www.greyhouse.com
Key Personnel
Pres: Richard Gottlieb *E-mail:* rhg@greyhouse.com
VP, Mktg: Jessica Moody *Tel:* 518-789-8700 ext 101 *E-mail:* jmoody@greyhouse.com
Publr: Leslie Mackenzie *E-mail:* lmackenzie@greyhouse.com
Edit Dir: Laura Mars *E-mail:* lmars@greyhouse.com
Founded: 1981
Directories, reference books & encyclopedias in history, business, economics, health & demographic areas.
ISBN Prefix(es): 978-1-930956; 978-1-891482; 978-0-939300; 978-1-59237; 978-1-61925
Number of titles published annually: 55 Print
Imprints: R R Bowker's Books in Print Series; Grey House; Financial Ratings Series; Salem Press; H W Wilson
Divisions: Grey House Publishing Canada
Returns: 5979 N Elm Ave, Suite 113, Millerton, NY 12546
Warehouse: 5979 N Elm Ave, Suite 113, Millerton, NY 12546
Membership(s): ALA
See separate listing for:
Salem Press Inc

Grosset & Dunlap
Imprint of Penguin Group USA, A Penguin Random House Company
345 Hudson St, New York, NY 10014
Tel: 212-366-2000
Web Site: www.penguinrandomhouse.com
Key Personnel
Pres & Publr, Grosset & Dunlap/Price Stern Sloan: Francesco Sedita
Ed-in-Chief, Early Readers & Assoc Publr, Warne: Bonnie Bader
Ed-in-Chief, Series & Licenses: Sarah Fabiny
VP & Ed-at-Large: Jane O'Connor
Exec Ed: Rob Valois
Exec Dir, Licensing Acqs & Media: Lori Burke
Art Dir: Giuseppe Castellano
Founded: 1898
ISBN Prefix(es): 978-0-448; 978-1-58184
Number of titles published annually: 133 Print
Total Titles: 1,098 Print
Imprints: PSS; Somerville House USA

Group Publishing Inc
1515 Cascade Ave, Loveland, CO 80538
Tel: 970-669-3836 *Toll Free Tel:* 800-447-1070
E-mail: puorgbus@group.com (submissions)

Web Site: www.group.com
Key Personnel
Founder & Chmn: Thom Schultz
Founded: 1974
Books, magazines, vacation bible school, curriculum.
ISBN Prefix(es): 978-1-55945; 978-0-7644; 978-1-4707
Number of titles published annually: 40 Print
Total Titles: 300 Print; 20 CD-ROM; 30 E-Book
Imprints: Group Cares; Lifetree™; Simply Youth Ministry
Foreign Rights: Canaanland (Malaysia); CLC Wholesale (UK); Group Canada (Canada); KCBS Inc (Korea); Koorung Books Pty Ltd (Australia); Manna Christian Stores (New Zealand); SKS (Singapore); Word Bookstores (Australia)
Returns: 1615 Cascade Ave, Loveland, CO 80538
Membership(s): CBA; Evangelical Christian Publishers Association

Grove Atlantic Inc
154 W 14 St, 12th fl, New York, NY 10011
SAN: 201-4890
Tel: 212-614-7850 *Toll Free Tel:* 800-521-0178 *Fax:* 212-614-7886
E-mail: info@groveatlantic.com; sales@groveatlantic.com; publicity@groveatlantic.com; rights@groveatlantic.com
Web Site: www.groveatlantic.com
Key Personnel
CEO & Publr: Morgan Entrekin *E-mail:* mentrekin@groveatlantic.com
VP & Edit Dir: Elisabeth Schmitz *E-mail:* eschmitz@groveatlantic.com
Art Dir: Gretchen Mergenthaler
Dir, Publicity: Deb Seager *E-mail:* dseager@groveatlantic.com
Dir, Subs Rts & Ed: Amy Hundley *E-mail:* ahundley@groveatlantic.com
Exec Ed: George Gibson
Sr Ed: Corinna Barsan; Peter Blackstock
Ed: Katie Raissian
Assoc Ed: Allison Malecha
Asst Ed: Nicole Nyhan; Zachary Pace
Sr Publicity Mgr: John Mark Boling
Publicity Mgr: Justina Batchelor
Sales & Mktg Assoc & Academic Mktg Mgr: Becca Putman
Founded: 1917
General fiction & nonfiction, hardcover & paperbound.
ISBN Prefix(es): 978-0-8021; 978-1-55584; 978-0-87113; 978-1-61185
Number of titles published annually: 120 Print; 30 E-Book
Total Titles: 1,200 Print; 250 E-Book
Imprints: Atlantic Books Ltd; Atlantic Monthly Press; Black Cat; Grove Press; The Mysterious Press
Foreign Rep(s): Book Promotions (Nicky Stubbs) (South Africa); Gilles Fauveau (Japan, Korea); Jaime Gregorio (Philippines); Sharad Mohan (Bangladesh, India, Maldives, Nepal, Pakistan, Sri Lanka); NewSouth Books (Australia, New Zealand); Perseus Books Group UK (Europe, Ireland, UK); Perseus Distribution (Edison Garcia) (Latin America); Perseus International (Suk Lee) (Middle East); June Poonpanich (Cambodia, Indonesia, Laos, Thailand, Vietnam); Wei Zhao (China, Hong Kong, Taiwan)
Foreign Rights: AnatoliaLit Agency (Amy Spangler) (Turkey); Eliane Benisti Agency (Eliane Benisti) (France); Casanovas & Lynch Agencia Literaria (Maria Lynch) (Latin America, Portugal, Spain); Ersilia Literary Agency (Evangelia Avloniti) (Greece); Graal Literary Agency (Filip Wojciechowski) (Poland); International Copyright Agency (Simona Kessler) (Romania); The Italian Literary Agency srl (Claire Sabatie Garat) (Italy); Japan Uni Agency Inc (Miko Yamanouchi) (Japan); Katai & Bolza (Peter Bolza) (Hungary); Korea Copyright Center (Ms Kyung Kang) (Korea); Andrew Nurnberg Associates (Tatjana Zoldnere) (Estonia, Latvia, Lithuania); Andrew Nurnberg Associates, Beijing Representative Office (Jackie Huang) (China); Andrew Nurnberg Associates, Taiwan Representative Office (Whitney Hsu) (Taiwan); Kristin Olson Literary Agency (Kristin Olson) (Czech Republic); Plima Literary Agency (Vuk Perisic) (Bulgaria, Croatia, Serbia, Slovenia); The Riff Agency (Laura Riff & Joao Paulo Riff) (Brazil); Elisabeth Ruge Agentur GmbH (Elisabeth Ruge) (Germany); Synopsis Literary Agency (Natalia Sanina) (Russia); Ulf Toregard Agency (Ulf Toregard) (Netherlands, Scandinavia); Tuttle-Mori Agency Inc (Ken Mori) (Japan)
Orders to: Publishers Group Worldwide, 250 W 57 St, 15th fl, New York, NY 10107 *Tel:* 212-581-7839; Perseus Distribution, 210 American Dr, Jackson, TN 38301; Publishers Group Canada, 559 College St, Suite 402, Toronto, ON M6G 1A9, Canada *Tel:* 416-934-9900 *Toll Free Tel:* 800-747-8147 *Fax:* 416-934-1410 *E-mail:* info@pgcbooks.ca; Grantham Book Services, Trent Rd, Grantham NG31 7XQ, United Kingdom *Tel:* (0147) 654 1080 *Fax:* (0147) 654 1061 *E-mail:* orders@gbs.tbs-ltd.co.uk
Returns: Publishers Group West, Returns Dept, 40 Carl Kirkland Dr, Jackson, TN 38301; Raincoast Books, 2440 Viking Way, Richmond, BC V6V 1N2, Canada *Toll Free Tel:* 800-663-5714 *Toll Free Fax:* 800-565-3770 *E-mail:* customerservice@raincoast.com
Distribution Center: Perseus Distribution, 210 American Dr, Jackson, TN 38301
Membership(s): AAP

Gryphon Editions
PO Box 241823, Omaha, NE 68124
Tel: 402-298-5385 (intl) *Toll Free Tel:* 888-655-0134 (US & CN)
E-mail: customerservice@gryphoneditions.com
Web Site: www.gryphoneditions.com
Founded: 1977
Reprints: medicine, law, political philosophy, science; fine editions.
Number of titles published annually: 25 Print
Total Titles: 750 Print
Distribution Center: Bindtech Distribution, 428 Harding Industrial Blvd, Nashville, TN 37211

Gryphon House Inc
Subsidiary of Kaplan Early Learning Co
6848 Leon's Way, Lewisville, NC 27023
Mailing Address: PO Box 10, Lewisville, NC 27023
Toll Free Tel: 800-638-0928 *Toll Free Fax:* 877-638-7576
E-mail: info@ghbooks.com
Web Site: www.gryphonhouse.com
Key Personnel
Gen Mgr: Jennifer Lewis *E-mail:* jennifer@ghbooks.com
Mktg Mgr: Anna Wilmoth *E-mail:* anna@ghbooks.com
Sales: Amy Acocella *E-mail:* amy@ghbooks.com
Founded: 1971
Publishes & distributes books for teachers & parents of young children.
ISBN Prefix(es): 978-0-87659
Number of titles published annually: 12 Print; 12 E-Book
Total Titles: 275 Print; 80 E-Book
Distributor for Aha Communications; Book Peddlers; Deya Brashears; Bright Ring Publishing; Building Blocks; Center for the Child Care Workforce; Chatterbox Press; Chicago Review Press; Children's Resources International; Circle Time Publishers; Sydney Gurewitz Clemens; Conari Press; Council Oak Books, Dawn Sign Press; Delmar Publishers Inc; Early Educator's Press; Educators for Social Responsibility; Family Center of Nova University; Jean Feldman; Floris Books; Hawthorne Press; Hunter House Publishers; Kaplan Press; Miss Jackie Inc; Monjeu Press; National Center Early Childhood Workforce; New England AEYC; New Horizons; Nova Southeastern University; Pademelon Press; Partner Press; Pollyanna Productions; Robins Lane Press; School Renaissance; Southern Early Childhood Association; Steam Press; Syracuse University Press; Teaching Strategies; Telshare Publishing
Foreign Rep(s): Monarch Books (Canada); Pademelon Press (Australia)

Guideposts Book & Inspirational Media
16 E 34 St, 12th fl, New York, NY 10016
Tel: 212-251-8100 *Toll Free Tel:* 800-431-2344 (cust serv) *Fax:* 212-684-0689
E-mail: gpsprod@cdsfulfillment.com
Web Site: guideposts.org
Key Personnel
CEO & Pres: John F Temple
Founded: 1945
Inspirational books & videos.
ISBN Prefix(es): 978-0-9661766
Number of titles published annually: 30 Print

§The Guilford Press
370 Seventh Ave, Suite 1200, New York, NY 10001-1020
SAN: 212-9442
Tel: 212-431-9800 *Toll Free Tel:* 800-365-7006 *Fax:* 212-966-6708
E-mail: info@guilford.com
Web Site: www.guilford.com
Key Personnel
Pres & Gen Mgr: Robert Matloff *E-mail:* bob.matloff@guilford.com
Lib Sales Dir & Sales Mgr: Anne Patota *Tel:* 212-431-9800 ext 217 *E-mail:* anne.patota@guilford.com
Mktg Dir: Marian Robinson *E-mail:* marian.robinson@guilford.com
Ed-in-Chief: Seymour Weingarten *E-mail:* seymour.weingarten@guilford.com
Mng Ed: Judith Grauman *E-mail:* judith.grauman@guilford.com
Acct Mgr: Estefeni Estremera *Tel:* 212-431-9800 ext 258 *E-mail:* estefeni.estremera@guilford.com
Busn Mgr: David Mitchell *E-mail:* david.mitchell@guilford.com
Credit Mgr: Vernita Hurston *Tel:* 212-431-9800 ext 230 *E-mail:* vernita.hurston@guilford.com
Fulfillment Mgr: William McEvoy *E-mail:* william.mcevoy@guilford.com
Prodn Mgr: Katya Edwards *E-mail:* katya.edwards@guilford.com
Intl Rts, Perms & ISBN Contact: Kathy Kuehl *E-mail:* kathy.kuehl@guilford.com
Founded: 1973
Professional & reference books, videos, journals & software in psychology, psychiatry & the behavioral sciences, neuroscience, research methods, education & literacy & geography.
ISBN Prefix(es): 978-0-89862; 978-1-57230; 978-1-59385; 978-1-60623; 978-1-60918; 978-1-4625
Number of titles published annually: 90 Print; 90 E-Book
Total Titles: 1,350 Print; 2 CD-ROM; 850 E-Book
Foreign Rep(s): Avicenna Partnership (Middle East); Cranbury International LLC (Caribbean, Central America, Mexico, South America); Disvan Enterprises (India); Footprint Books (Australia, New Zealand); Juta (South Africa); MHM Ltd (Japan); Taylor & Francis Asia Pacific (Asia, China); Taylor & Francis Informa UK (Europe, UK); Unifacmanu (Taiwan)

Returns: Maple Logistics Solutions, York Distribution Ctr, 60 Grumbacher Rd, York, PA 17406
Warehouse: Maple Logistics Solutions, York Distribution Ctr, 60 Grumbacher Rd, York, PA 17406

Guilford Publications Inc, see The Guilford Press

§Gulf Publishing Co
2 Greenway Plaza, Suite 1020, Houston, TX 77046
Mailing Address: PO Box 2608, Houston, TX 77252
Tel: 713-529-4301 *Fax:* 713-520-4433
E-mail: store@gulfpub.com; customerservice@gulfpub.com
Web Site: www.gulfpub.com
Key Personnel
CEO & Pres: John T Royall
Publr, Hydrocarbon Processing: Bret Ronk
Publr, World Oil Magazine: Ron Higgins
Founded: 1916
Communications company dedicated to the petrochemical industry & related industries.
ISBN Prefix(es): 978-1-933762; 978-0-9765113
Number of titles published annually: 10 Print; 3 CD-ROM
Total Titles: 20 Print; 30 CD-ROM
Distributor for Elsevier; Pennwell; Simon & Schuster; Editions Technip; Wiley

Hachai Publishing
527 Empire Blvd, Brooklyn, NY 11225
SAN: 251-3749
Tel: 718-633-0100 *Fax:* 718-633-0103
E-mail: info@hachai.com
Web Site: www.hachai.com
Key Personnel
Pres: Yerachmiel Binyominson
Publr & Sales: Yossi Leverton *E-mail:* yossi@hachai.com
Ed: Dina Rosenfeld *E-mail:* dlr@hachai.com
Founded: 1988
Full color children's Judaica books.
ISBN Prefix(es): 978-0-922613; 978-1-929628
Number of titles published annually: 5 Print
Total Titles: 100 Print
Distributor for Attara; Kerem; Living Lessons
Membership(s): Association of Jewish Libraries; Independent Book Publishers Association

Hachette Audio
Division of Hachette Book Group
1290 Avenue of the Americas, New York, NY 10019
Tel: 212-364-1100
Web Site: www.hachetteaudio.com
Key Personnel
SVP, Content Devt & Publr, Hachette Audio & Large Print: Anthony Goff
Assoc Publr, Opers & Digital Audio: Kim Sayle
Sr Exec Dir, Content Devt: Tina McIntyre
Exec Dir, Prodn: Michele McGonigle
Exec Dir, Audio Mktg & Publicity: Megan Fitzpatrick
Number of titles published annually: 470 Audio
Total Titles: 4,421 Audio

Hachette Book Group
Division of Hachette Livre
1290 Avenue of the Americas, New York, NY 10019
Tel: 212-364-1100 *Toll Free Tel:* 800-759-0190 (cust serv) *Fax:* 212-364-0933 (intl orders) *Toll Free Fax:* 800-286-9471 (cust serv)
Web Site: www.hachettebookgroup.com
Key Personnel
CEO: Michael Pietsch
EVP & COO: Joe Mangan
EVP, Busn Aff & Gen Coun: Carol Ross
EVP, HBG & Publr, Little, Brown Books for Young Readers: Megan Tingley
SVP & Communs Dir: Sophie Cottrell
SVP & Dir, Mktg Strategy: Heather Fain
SVP & CFO: Stephen Mubarek
SVP, Group Sales Dir: Christopher Murphy
SVP, HR: Andrea Weinzimer
SVP & Publr, Grand Central Publishing: Ben Sevier
SVP, HBG & Publr, Little, Brown and Company: Reagan Arthur
SVP, HBG & Publr, Orbit: Tim Holman
SVP, HBG & Publr, Perseus Books: Susan Weinberg
SVP, HBG & Publr, Nashville Div: Rolf Zettersten
SVP, Content Devt & Publr, Hachette Audio: Anthony Goff
SVP, Intl, Canada, Spec Mkts: Jean Griffin
VP, Publr, Hachette Books: Mauro DiPreta
VP, Hachette Client Services: Todd McGarity
VP, Exec Mng Ed, Hachette: Rena Kornbluh
VP, Contracts: Andrea Shallcross
VP, Subs Rts: Nancy Wiese
Founded: 2006 (when Time Warner Book Group was purchased by Hachette Livre)
Hachette Book Group is a leading trade publisher based in New York & a division of Hachette Livre (a Lagardere company), the third largest trade & educational publisher in the world. HBG is made up of 8 publishing groups: Little, Brown and Company; Little, Brown Books for Young Readers; Grand Central Publishing; Perseus Books; Orbit; Hachette Books; Hachette Nashville; Hachette Audio.
ISBN Prefix(es): 978-1-56282; 978-0-7868; 978-0-316; 978-1-4013
Divisions: Grand Central Publishing; Hachette Audio; Hachette Books; Hachette Nashville; Little, Brown and Company; Little, Brown Books for Young Readers; Orbit; Perseus Books
Distributor for Harry N Abrams Inc; Nicholas Brealey Publishing; Chronicle Books; Disney Book Group; Gildan Media; Hachette UK; Houghton Mifflin Harcourt; Kids Can Press; Marvel Worldwide Inc; Moleskine; Octopus Books; Peterson's; Phaidon Press; Phoenix International Publications (PiKids); Quarto Publishing Group; Quercus Books; Time Inc Books; Yen Press
Orders to: Order Dept, 53 State St, Boston, MA 02109 (US orders) *Toll Free Tel:* 800-759-0190 *Toll Free Fax:* 800-286-9471
Returns: Returns Dept, 322 S Enterprise Blvd, Lebanon, IN 46052
Shipping Address: Hachette Book Group Distribution Center, 121 N Enterprise Blvd, Lebanon, IN 46052 *Tel:* 765-483-9900 *Fax:* 765-483-0706
See separate listing for:
Grand Central Publishing
Hachette Audio
Hachette Books
Hachette Nashville
Little, Brown and Company
Little, Brown Books for Young Readers
Orbit
Perseus Books

Hachette Books
Division of Hachette Book Group
1290 Avenue of the Americas, New York, NY 10019
Tel: 212-364-1100
Web Site: www.hachettebookgroup.com
Key Personnel
VP & Publr: Mauro DiPreta
Publr, Black Dog & Leventhal: J P Leventhal
Assoc Publr & Exec Dir of Publicity, Hachette Books & Black Dog & Leventhal: Michelle Aielli
Exec Ed: Michelle Howry
Sr Ed: Krishan Trotman
Sr Ed (acquires primarily non-fiction books): Paul Whitlatch
Sr Ed (acquires primarily illustrated non-fiction books for Black Dog & Leventhal): Lisa Tenaglia
Sr Ed (acquires illustrated nonfiction & educ workbooks for children for Black Dog & Leventhal): Dinah Dunn
Asst Ed: Lauren Hummel; David Lamb
Edit Dir, Black Dog & Leventhal: Becky Koh
Publicity Dir: Joanna Pinsker
Publicist, Black Dog & Leventhal: Kara Thornton
Mktg Dir, Black Dog & Leventhal: Betsy Hulsebosch
Mktg Assoc: Odette Fleming
Art Dir, Hachette Books & Black Dog & Leventhal: Amanda Kain
Designer, Hachette Books & Black Dog & Leventhal: Carlos Esparaza
ISBN Prefix(es): 978-1-884822 (Black Dog & Leventhal); 978-1-57912 (Black Dog & Leventhal); 978-1-56282; 978-0-7868; 978-0-316; 978-0-316 (Black Dog & Leventhal); 978-1-4013; 978-1-60376 (Black Dog & Leventhal); 978-1-63191 (Black Dog & Leventhal)
Number of titles published annually: 79 Print
Total Titles: 1,292 Print
Imprints: Black Dog & Leventhal
Orders to: Hachette Book Group, Order Dept, 53 State St, Boston, MA 02109 (US orders) *Toll Free Tel:* 800-759-0190 *Toll Free Fax:* 800-286-9471
Returns: Hachette Book Group, Returns Dept, 122 S Enterprise Blvd, Lebanon, IN 46052

Hachette Nashville
Division of Hachette Book Group
12 Cadillac Dr, Suite 480, Brentwood, TN 37027
Tel: 615-221-0996 *Fax:* 615-221-0962
Web Site: www.hachettebookgroup.com
Key Personnel
SVP & Publr, Nashville Div: Rolf Zettersten
VP, Mktg & Publicity: Patsy Jones
VP, Sales, Retail Analytics & Client Servs: Billy Clark
VP, Christian Booksellers Assn Sales: Gary Davidson
Exec Ed, Center Street: Kate Hartson
Sr Ed: Keren Baltzer; Adrienne Ingrum
Sr Ed, Fiction, FaithWords & Center Street: Christina Boys
Mktg Dir: Rudy Kish
Assoc Mktg Dir: Katie Connors
Channel Dir, Clients & Nashville: Gina Wynn
Digital Content Dir: Michele McKee
Art Dir: Jody Waldrup
Fin Dir: Deirdre Baule
Founded: 2001
Publish books for the growing inspirational market. No unsol mss.
ISBN Prefix(es): 978-0-446
Number of titles published annually: 95 Print
Total Titles: 556 Print
Imprints: Center Street; FaithWords
Orders to: Hachette Book Group, 53 State St, Boston, MA 02109 *Toll Free Tel:* 800-759-0190 *Toll Free Fax:* 800-286-9471
Membership(s): CBA; Evangelical Christian Publishers Association

Hackett Publishing Co Inc
3333 Massachusetts Ave, Indianapolis, IN 46218
SAN: 201-6044
Mailing Address: PO Box 390007, Cambridge, MA 02139
Tel: 317-635-9250 (orders & cust serv); 617-497-6303 (edit off & sales) *Fax:* 317-635-9292; 617-661-8703 (edit off) *Toll Free Fax:* 800-783-9213
E-mail: customer@hackettpublishing.com; editorial@hackettpublishing.com
Web Site: www.hackettpublishing.com

Key Personnel
Pres, Publr & CEO: Deborah Wilkes
VP, Mktg Dir & Dir, Opers: John Pershing
Tel: 617-234-0371 *Fax:* 617-661-8703
E-mail: johnp@hackettpublishing.com
Secy & Treas: Cheri Brown
Promos Mgr: Mr Ryan Picazio *Tel:* 617-497-6307
E-mail: ryanp@hackettpublishing.com
Founded: 1972
College textbooks & scholarly books; emphasis on philosophy, political theory, political science, classics, history & literature.
ISBN Prefix(es): 978-0-915144; 978-0-915145; 978-0-87220; 978-1-60384
Number of titles published annually: 30 Print; 30 E-Book
Total Titles: 840 Print; 300 E-Book
Imprints: Focus
Distributor for Bryn Mawr Commentaries
Foreign Rep(s): Gazelle Book Services Ltd (Europe, UK); UNIREPS (Australia, New Zealand)
Foreign Rights: Eulama
See separate listing for:
Focus

§Hagstrom Map
Subsidiary of American Map Corp
1800 Lovering Ave, Wilmington, DE 19806
Toll Free Tel: 800-432-MAPS (432-6277)
Toll Free Fax: 888-210-9654
Founded: 1916
Three million maps, atlases, guides.
ISBN Prefix(es): 978-0-88097; 978-0-910684; 978-1-59245
Total Titles: 1 CD-ROM
Distributor for ADC The Map People; American Map Corp; Arrow Maps Inc; Creative Sales Corp; De Lorme Atlas; Hammond World Atlas Corp; RV International Maps & Atlases; Stubs Guides; Trakker Maps Inc

§Haights Cross Communications®
136 Madison Ave, 8th fl, New York, NY 10016
Tel: 212-209-0500
E-mail: info@haightscross.com
Web Site: www.haightscross.com
Key Personnel
CEO & Pres: Rick Noble
CFO: Scott August
SVP, Fin & Planning & Treas: Melissa L Linsky
Founded: 1997
Educational & professional publishing group that creates books, instructional materials, audio products, periodicals, software & online services, serving the following markets: K-12 supplemental education, public & school library publishing, audiobooks & medical publishing.
Number of titles published annually: 856 Print; 10 CD-ROM; 50 Online; 10 E-Book; 787 Audio
Total Titles: 6,200 Print; 20 CD-ROM; 50 Online; 10 E-Book; 5,808 Audio
Divisions: Triumph Learning
Membership(s): AAP; ALA; Audio Publishers Association; International Literacy Association; Specialized Information Publishers Association
See separate listing for:
Triumph Learning LLC

§Hal Leonard Books
Imprint of Hal Leonard Performing Arts Publishing Group
33 Plymouth St, Suite 302, Montclair, NJ 07042
Toll Free Tel: 800-637-2852
E-mail: info@halleonardbooks.com; custserv@halleonardbooks.com
Web Site: www.halleonardbooks.com
Key Personnel
Group Publr: John Cerullo *E-mail:* jcerullo@halleonard.com
Founded: 1984
Publisher of books & online AV content on the music business, marketing, songwriting, audio technology, instrument history & more.
ISBN Prefix(es): 978-1-4234
Number of titles published annually: 30 Print; 30 E-Book; 10 Audio
Total Titles: 1,000 Print; 50 Online; 900 E-Book; 50 Audio
Imprints: Amadeus Press (classical music & opera); Applause Theatre & Cinema Books; Backbeat Books (music trade books); Limelight Editions (instruction, ref & how-to titles)
Sales Office(s): 7777 W Bluemound Rd, Milwaukee, WI 53213, Contact: Doug Lady *Tel:* 414-774-3630
Foreign Rep(s): GPS (Asia, Central America, China, Europe, India, Indonesia, Japan, Korea, Latin America, Mexico, Mideast, Pacific Rim, Russia & former USSR, South America); Publishers Group UK (UK); Woodslane (Australia, New Zealand)
Returns: Hal Leonard, 1210 Innovation Dr, Winona, MN 55987, Contact: Kim Jereczek
E-mail: kjereczek@halleonard.com
Warehouse: Hal Leonard, 1210 Innovation Dr, Winona, MN 55987, Contact: Tony Prodzinski
E-mail: tprodzinski@halleonard.com

§Hal Leonard Corp
7777 W Bluemound Rd, Milwaukee, WI 53213
Mailing Address: PO Box 13819, Milwaukee, WI 53213-0819
Tel: 414-774-3630 *Fax:* 414-774-3259
E-mail: halinfo@halleonard.com; info@halleonard.com
Web Site: www.halleonard.com
Key Personnel
Chmn & CEO: Keith Mardak
Pres: Larry Morton
Sr Sales & Mktg Mgr, Book Trade & Ebooks: Mike Hansen
Sr Key Accts Mgr: David Cywinski
Founded: 1947
The world's largest music print publisher, with an incomparable selection of sheet music, songbooks, music related books, self-instruction books, CD packs & videos, music reference & special interest titles, music biographies, children's music products; CD-ROMs, DVDs, performance videos & more. Additional offices in Minnesota, New York, Nashville, Australia, Belgium, France, Germany, Holland, Italy, Switzerland & the UK.
ISBN Prefix(es): 978-1-57467; 978-0-88188; 978-0-7935; 978-0-87910; 978-0-87930; 978-0-634; 978-1-4234; 978-0-9607350; 978-1-56516; 978-1-61713; 978-1-61774; 978-1-61780; 978-1-4584; 978-1-4768; 978-1-4803; 978-0-931340; 978-1-4950
Number of titles published annually: 2,000 Print
Total Titles: 200,000 Print; 15 CD-ROM
Imprints: Berklee Press; Centerstream Publications; Cherry Lane Music Co; Ashley Mark Publishing Co; Musicians Institute Press; G Shirmer; Vintage Guitar
Divisions: Hal Leonard Performing Arts Publishing Group
Distributor for Ableton; Acoustica; AirTurn; Amadeus Press; Antares; Apogee; Applause Books; Aquarius; Arrangers Publishing; Art String Publishing; Ashley Music; Avid; Axe Heaven; Backbeat Books; Berklee Press; Leonard Bernstein; Blue Microphones; Fred Bock Music Company; Boosey & Hawkes; CD Sheet Music; Cakewalk; Centerstream Publications; Cherry Lane Music Co; ChordBuddy; Curnow Music; De Haske Publications; Dots & Lines Inc; Editions Durand; EM Books; EMI Christian; Editions Max Eschig; Faber Music Ltd; Family Communications; Fleamarket Music; Griffin Technology; Guitar World; Hamilton Stands; Hartke; G Henle Verlag; Homespun Tapes; Hudson Music; IK Multimedia; Lauren Keiser Music; Lorie Lane; Line 6; M-Audio; Ashley Mark Publishing Co; Edward B Marks Music; Meredith Music; Mighty Bright; Modern Drummer Publications; Music Minus One; Music Sales America; Musicians Institute Press; Noteflight; Peermusic Classical; PreSonus; Professional Music Institute; Propellerhead; PWM Editions; QSC; Ricordi; Lee Roberts Publications; Rock House; Rubank Publications; St Nicolas Music Inc; Editions Salabert; Samson Audio; G Schirmer Inc (Associated Music Publishers); Schott Music; Shawnee Press; Sibelius; Sikorski; Sony; Steinberg; Sterling Publishing; String Letter Publishing; Tara Publications; Tycoon Percussion; Vintage Guitar; Voyageur Press; XLN Audio; Waltons Irish Music; Willis Music; Yamaha
Foreign Rep(s): Publishers Group UK (Europe, UK)
Foreign Rights: Robert Lecker Agency Inc
Returns: 1210 Innovation Dr, Winona, MN 55987
Shipping Address: 1210 Innovation Dr, Winona, MN 55987 *Tel:* 507-454-2920 *Fax:* 507-454-4042
Warehouse: 960 E Mark St, Winona, MN 55987
Distribution Center: 1210 Innovation Dr, Winona, MN 55987

Hal Leonard Performing Arts Publishing Group, see Amadeus Press/Hal Leonard Performing Arts Publishing Group

Hamilton Books
Imprint of Rowman & Littlefield Publishing Group
4501 Forbes Blvd, Suite 200, Lanham, MD 20706
Tel: 301-459-3366 *Toll Free Tel:* 800-462-6420 (cust serv) *Fax:* 301-429-5748
Toll Free Fax: 800-388-4550 (cust serv)
Key Personnel
VP & Publr: Julie Kirsch *E-mail:* jkirsch@rowman.com
Acqs Ed: Holly Buchanan *E-mail:* hbuchanan@rowman.com
Founded: 2002
Provides authors of serious nonfiction titles, including corporate leaders, politicians, scholars, war veterans & family historians, the opportunity to sign with a top-quality publisher without the typical hassles & extreme selectivity enforced by other publishers.
ISBN Prefix(es): 978-0-7618
Number of titles published annually: 40 Print; 40 E-Book
Total Titles: 250 Print; 125 E-Book
Membership(s): AAP

§Hamilton Stone Editions
PO Box 43, Maplewood, NJ 07040
Tel: 973-378-8361
E-mail: hstone@hamiltonstone.org
Web Site: www.hamiltonstone.org
Key Personnel
Edit Dir: Meredith Sue Willis
E-mail: meredithsuewillis@gmail.com
Artistic Dir: Lynda Schor *E-mail:* lynda.schor@gmail.com
Dir: Halvard Johnson *E-mail:* halvard@gmail.com; Edith Konecky *E-mail:* erkonecky@verizon.net; Nathan Leslie *E-mail:* nleslie@nvcc.edu; Carole Rosenthal
E-mail: crlrosenthal@gmail.com
Founded: 2003
Independent press for independent literary writing. Dedicated to vivid writing that probes the hidden realities of the everyday, valuing most highly the kind of writing that displays a multifaced vision. Interested in keeping new books in print & bringing forgotten, excellent old books back into print.
ISBN Prefix(es): 978-0-9654043; 978-0-9714873

Number of titles published annually: 4 Print; 4 E-Book
Total Titles: 39 Print; 115 E-Book
Imprints: Irene Weinberger Books (literary books in ebook & trade paperback format, often in collaboration with other presses)
Shipping Address: 311 Prospect St, South Orange, NJ 07079

Hampton Press Inc
307 Seventh Ave, Suite 506, New York, NY 10001
Tel: 646-638-3800 *Toll Free Tel:* 800-894-8955 *Fax:* 646-638-3802
E-mail: hamptonpr1@aol.com
Web Site: www.hamptonpress.com
Key Personnel
Pres: Barbara Bernstein
Founded: 1992
ISBN Prefix(es): 978-1-881303; 978-1-57273; 978-1-61289
Number of titles published annually: 20 Print
Total Titles: 775 Print
Foreign Rep(s): Eurospan Group (Asia, Australia, Europe, Far East, Latin America, UK)

Hampton Roads Publishing Co
Imprint of Red Wheel/Weiser/Conari
65 Parker St, Suite 7, Newburyport, MA 01950-4600
Tel: 978-465-0504 *Toll Free Tel:* 800-423-7087 (orders) *Fax:* 978-465-0243 *Toll Free Fax:* 877-337-3309
E-mail: orders@rwwbooks.com
Web Site: redwheelweiser.com
Key Personnel
Dir, Mktg & Digital Content: Bonni Hamilton *E-mail:* bhamilton@rwwbooks.com
Mktg Assoc: Eryn Carter *E-mail:* ecarter@rwwbooks.com
Founded: 1989
Trade publishing. Specialize in metaphysics, self-help, integrative medicine, visionary fiction & paranormal phenomena.
ISBN Prefix(es): 978-1-878901; 978-1-57174; 978-1-61283
Number of titles published annually: 30 Print
Total Titles: 350 Print; 2 Audio
Distributed by Red Wheel/Weiser/Conari
Foreign Rep(s): Brumby Sunstate (Australia); Deep Books Ltd (Europe, UK); Georgetown Publications (Canada); Publishers International Marketing (Asia, Middle East)
Foreign Rights: Biagi Rights Management (Linda Biagi) (worldwide)

§Hancock House Publishers
4550 Birch Bay Lynden Rd, Suite 104, Blaine, WA 98230-9436
Tel: 604-538-1114 *Toll Free Tel:* 800-938-1114 *Fax:* 604-538-2262 *Toll Free Fax:* 800-983-2262
E-mail: sales@hancockhouse.com
Web Site: www.hancockhouse.com
Key Personnel
Publr & Intl Rts: David Hancock
Founded: 1975
Specialize in natural history (world), regional northwest history & Native art.
ISBN Prefix(es): 978-0-88839
Number of titles published annually: 15 Print
Total Titles: 300 Print
Branch Office(s)
19313 Zero Ave, Surrey, BC V3Z 9R9, Canada

Handprint Books Inc
Imprint of Chronicle Books LLC
413 Sixth Ave, Brooklyn, NY 11215-3310
Tel: 718-768-3696 *Toll Free Tel:* 800-722-6657 (orders) *Fax:* 718-369-0844 *Toll Free Fax:* 800-858-7787 (orders)
E-mail: info@handprintbooks.com
Web Site: www.handprintbooks.com
Key Personnel
Pres & Publr: Christopher Franceschelli *E-mail:* cmf@handprintbooks.com
Founded: 2000
Publisher of high-quality books for children.
ISBN Prefix(es): 978-1-929766; 978-1-59354
Number of titles published annually: 12 Print
Distributed by Chronicle Books
Returns: Chronicle Books, c/o Genco Fulfillment, 1585 Linda Way, Door 1, Sparks, NV 89431

Hanging Loose Press
231 Wyckoff St, Brooklyn, NY 11217
SAN: 206-4960
Tel: 347-529-4738 *Fax:* 347-227-8215
E-mail: print225@aol.com
Web Site: www.hangingloosepress.com
Key Personnel
Ed & Intl Rts: Robert Hershon
Ed: Dick Lourie; Mark Pawlak
Founded: 1966
Poetry & short fiction.
ISBN Prefix(es): 978-0-914610; 978-1-882413; 978-1-931236
Number of titles published annually: 8 Print
Total Titles: 225 Print
Membership(s): Community of Literary Magazines & Presses

Hannacroix Creek Books Inc
1127 High Ridge Rd, No 110-B, Stamford, CT 06905-1203
SAN: 299-9560
Tel: 203-968-8098
Web Site: www.hannacroixcreekbooks.com
Key Personnel
CEO & Pres: Dr Jan Yager
Founded: 1996
Trade publisher of quality & innovative fiction & nonfiction books & journals that entertain, educate & inform.
ISBN Prefix(es): 978-1-889262; 978-1-938998
Number of titles published annually: 7 Print; 10 E-Book
Total Titles: 38 Print; 18 E-Book
Foreign Rep(s): International Editors' Co (Flavia Sala) (Brazil)
Foreign Rights: Guiliana Bernardi Literary Agent (Italy); DS Rights (Eastern Europe); Antonia Kerrigan Literary Agency (Spain); Eric Yang Agency (Korea)
Membership(s): AAP; Independent Book Publishers Association; Women's Media Group

§Hanser Publications LLC
Subsidiary of Carl Hanser Verlag GmbH & Co KG
6915 Valley Ave, Cincinnati, OH 45244-3029
Toll Free Tel: 800-950-8977; 877-751-5052 (orders) *Fax:* 513-527-8801
E-mail: info@hanserpublications.com
Web Site: www.hanserpublications.com
Key Personnel
Mktg Mgr: Valerie Lauer *Tel:* 513-527-8896 *Fax:* 513-534-7803 *E-mail:* valerie.lauer@hanserpublications.com
Founded: 1993
Technical & reference books & related products in manufacturing, metalworking & products finishing. Hanser Publishers: technical, engineering & science reference books, monographs, textbooks & journals in plastics technology, polymer & materials science.
ISBN Prefix(es): 978-1-56990
Number of titles published annually: 17 Print
Total Titles: 312 Print; 250 Online
Foreign Office(s): Carl Hanser Verlag, Kolbergerstr 22, 81679 Munich, Germany *Tel:* (089) 99 93 00 *Fax:* (089) 98 48 09
Distributor for Hanser Publishers
Foreign Rep(s): Alkem Co (S) Pte Ltd (Mr Adrian Tan) (Singapore); Allied Publishers Pvt Ltd (Mr R N Purwar) (India); Applied Market Information Ltd (Phil Cotterell) (Ireland, UK); Book Editions Pte Ltd (Brunei, Indonesia, Malaysia, Philippines, Singapore, Thailand, Vietnam); Booknet Co Ltd (Muntima Warangkanakooln) (Thailand); Bookshop Lux Libris (Andrej Pucnik) (Slovenia); Com.books Ltd (Eliad Sofi) (Israel); Faravaran Publication Distributor Co (Iran); Carl Hanser Verlag GmbH & Co KG (Germany); Inspirees International (China); Levant Distributors Sarl (Lebanon, Syria); Male centrum sro (Slovakia); MeBS (Maurizio Modugno) (Italy); Mirza Book Agency (Qasim Mahmood Mirza) (Pakistan); Nova Agora (Sandra Aguilera) (Portugal, Spain); Progressive International Agencies (Pvt) Ltd (Pakistan); Prospero's Konyvei Budapest KFT (Hungary); Publishers Consultants & Representatives (Tahir M Lodhi) (Pakistan); UBSD Distribution Sdn Bhd (Malaysia); Unifacmanu Trading Co Ltd (Ariel Lai) (Taiwan); Yuha Associates Sdn Bhd (Malaysia)
Warehouse: Ware-Pak LLC, 2427 Bond St, University Park, IL 60484 *Tel:* 708-587-4124 *Fax:* 708-534-7803 *E-mail:* hanser@ware-pak.com
Distribution Center: Ware-Pak LLC, 2427 Bond St, University Park, IL 60484 *Tel:* 708-587-4124 *Fax:* 708-534-7803 *E-mail:* hanser@ware-pak.com

§Hard Shell Word Factory
Imprint of Mundania Press LLC
6457 Glenway Ave, No 109, Cincinnati, OH 45211
Toll Free Tel: 888-232-0808 *Toll Free Fax:* 888-460-4752
E-mail: inquiry@mundania.com
Web Site: www.mundania.com
Founded: 1998
Royalty publisher of fiction & nonfiction books, ebooks & trade paperback.
ISBN Prefix(es): 978-1-58200; 978-0-7599
Number of titles published annually: 100 Print; 200 E-Book
Total Titles: 2,000 Print; 4,000 E-Book
Imprints: HSWF
Membership(s): Electronically Published Internet Connection; Independent Book Publishers Association

Harlequin Enterprises Ltd
Division of HarperCollins
233 Broadway, Suite 1001, New York, NY 10279
SAN: 200-2450
Tel: 212-553-4200 *Fax:* 212-227-8969
E-mail: customerservice@harlequin.com
Web Site: www.harlequin.com
Key Personnel
Edit Dir: Margaret Marbury
Edit Dir, TK: Peter Joseph
Sr Exec Ed: Glenda Howard
Exec Ed, Love Inspired: Tina James
Sr Mng Ed: Kathleen Reed
Mng Edit Coord, NY/Toronto: Beth Attwood
Asst Mng Ed: Kristin Errico
Sr Acqs Ed, MIRA: Kathy Sagan
Sr Ed: Gail Chasan; Patience Bloom; Ann Leslie Tuttle; Denise Zaza
Sr Ed, Carina Press: Kerri Buckley
Ed: Rebecca Hunt
Ed, Hanover Square Press: John Glynn
Ed, Harlequin Teen: Annie Stone
Ed, MIRA Books: Liz Stein
Assoc Ed, Harlequin Teen: Lauren Smulski
Assoc Ed, HQN & LUNA: Kate Dresser
Asst Ed: Carly Silver
Asst Ed, Desire & Romantic Suspense: Allison Carroll
Asst Ed/Edit Asst, Harlequin Historical & Love Inspired Suspense: Dina Davis

Asst Ed, Love Inspired: Emily Krupin
Ed-at-Large: Leslie Wainger
Publicity Dir: Shara Alexander
Sr Publicity Mgr, Fiction: Meredith Barnes
Publicity Mgr, Fiction: Emer Flounders
Asst Publicity Mgr, Harlequin Teen: Jennifer Abbots
Assoc Publicist: Sarah Hermalyn; Lauren Jackson; Jessica Rosenberg
Founded: 1980
Adult contemporary, historical romance novels & women's fiction.
ISBN Prefix(es): 978-0-373
Number of titles published annually: 1,400 Print
Imprints: Carina Press; Hanover Square Press; Harlequin; Harlequin Teen; HQ; HQN Books; Kimani; Luna Books; MIRA; Park Row Books; Red Dress Ink; Silhouette; Steeple Hill
Distributed by Simon & Schuster
Distribution Center: 3010 Walden Ave, Depew, NY 14043
Membership(s): AAP; Association of Canadian Publishers; BISG

HarperCollins Children's Books
Division of HarperCollins Publishers
195 Broadway, New York, NY 10007
SAN: 200-2086
Tel: 212-207-7000
Web Site: www.harpercollins.com/childrens
Key Personnel
Pres & Publr: Suzanne Murphy
SVP, Assoc Publr & Ed-in-Chief: Kate Jackson *E-mail:* Kate.Jackson@HarperCollins.com
SVP, Children's Sales: Andrea Pappenheimer *E-mail:* Andrea.Pappenheimer@HarperCollins.com
VP & Publg Dir: Rich Thomas
VP, Fin: Randy Rosema *E-mail:* Randy.Rosema@HarperCollins.com
Edit Dir: Rosemary Brosnan; Nancy Inteli
Dir, Integrated Mktg: Lauren Flower
Dir, Intellectual Property Devt: Dan Ehrenhaft
Assoc Art Dir, Ad Promo Design: Maggie Searcy
Sr Exec Ed, Katherine Tegen Books: Claudia Gabel
Exec Ed: Alexandra Cooper; Kristen Pettit
Exec Ed, Katherine Tegen Books: Anica Rissi
Sr Ed: Alyson Day; Sarah Landis; Karen Chaplin
Sr Ed, Katherine Tegen Books: Melissa Miller
Ed: Jocelyn Davies; Andrew Harwell
Dir, Publicity: Caroline Sun
Publicity Mgr: Olivia Russo
Publicity Mgr, School & Lib Team: Laura Kaplan
Picture books, juvenile fiction & nonfiction, young adult novels.
ISBN Prefix(es): 978-0-06; 978-0-688; 978-0-380; 978-0-694; 978-0-690
Imprints: Amistad; Balzer + Bray; Greenwillow Books; HarperAudio; HarperCollins e-books; HarperFestival; Rayo; Katherine Tegen Books; TOKYOPOP; Walden Pond Press
Membership(s): The Children's Book Council

HarperCollins General Books Group
Division of HarperCollins Publishers
195 Broadway, New York, NY 10007
SAN: 200-2086
Tel: 212-207-7000
Web Site: www.harpercollins.com
Key Personnel
Chief Mktg Offr: Angela Tribelli
Pres & Publr: Michael Morrison
Pres & Publr, Ecco: Daniel Halpern
SVP & Deputy Publr, Harper Group/Publr, Harper Perennial & Harper Paperbacks: Doug Jones
SVP & Publr, Dey Street Books & Deputy Publr, Morrow/Voyager/Avon: Lynn Grady
SVP & Publr, Elixir: Claudia Boutote
SVP & Publr, Harper: Jonathan Burnham
SVP & Publr, William Morrow/Eos/Avon/Harper Paperbacks: Liate Stehlik
SVP & Exec Ed, Harper Wave: Karen Rinaldi
SVP, Fin & Publg: Len Marshall *E-mail:* Len.Marshall@HarperCollins.com
SVP, Morrow/Avon: Carrie Feron
SVP, Publicity: Tina Andreadis
VP: Gideon Weil
VP & Publr, Harper Business: Hollis Heimbouch
VP & Publr, Harper Design: Marta Schooler
VP & Assoc Publr, HarperOne: Laina Adler
VP & Edit Dir, Broadside Books: Eric Nelson
VP & Edit Dir Nonfiction, William Morrow: Geoff Shandler
VP & Exec Ed: Jonathan Jao
VP & Exec Ed, William Morrow: Dan Mallory
VP & Art Dir, William Morrow: Jeanne Reina
VP & Dir, Sales: Andy LeCount
VP, Deputy Gen Coun: Beth Silfin
VP, Exec Ed & Spec Advisor to the Publr: Sara Nelson
VP, Mktg: Carrie Bloxson; Leah Wasielewski
VP, Prodn & Creative Opers: Tracey Menzies
VP, Spec Events & Creative Strategies: Shelby Meizlik
Publr, Amistad & Exec Ed, Ecco: Dawn Davis
Publr, HarperOne: Mark Tauber
Assoc Publr, Avon, Impulse & Witness: Shawn Nicholls
Assoc Publr, Dey Street Books: Benjamin Steinberg
Assoc Publr, Ecco: Miriam Parker
Assoc Publr, Harper Perennial & Harper Paperbacks: Amy Baker
Exec Dir, Digital Prod Devt: Adrianna Dufay
Sr Group Publicity Dir: Kelly Rudolph
Sr Dir, Audience Devt & Insight: Jim Hanas
Sr Dir, Mktg Digital Prod Devt, Harper Wave & Harper Business: Brian Perrin
Sr Dir, Publicity, Harper Wave: Yelena Gitlin Nesbit
Sr Dir, Publicity & Brand Devt, Avon/Voyager: Pamela Spengler-Jaffee
Sr Publicity Dir, HarperOne: Melinda Mullin; Suzanne Wickham
Sr Mktg Dir, William Morrow: Tavia Kowalchuk
Edit Dir, Amistad: Tracy Sherrod
Edit Dir, Dey Street Books: Carrie Thornton
Edit Dir, Ecco: Megan Lynch
Edit Dir, Harper Wave: Julie Will
Edit Dir, Harper Voyager: David Pomerico
Edit Dir, William Morrow/Avon: Erika Tsang
Dir, Prodn Edit, Harper, Harper Business & Collins Reference: John Jusino
Dir, Brand Devt, William Morrow: Kathryn Gordon
Dir, Fulfillment Opers: Joe Macavage
Dir, Publicity: Brianne Halverson
Publicity Dir, Ecco: Sonya Cheuse
Publicity Dir, Harper: Tracy Locke
Publicity Dir, HarperOne: Darcy Cohan
Publicity Dir, HarperCollins 360: Victoria Commella
Publicity Dir, William Morrow & Dey Street: Heidi Richter
Mktg Dir, Dey Street Books: Kendra Newton
Mktg Dir, Ecco: Meghan Deans
Mktg Dir, William Morrow: Molly Birckhead; Kaitlin Harri
Assoc Art Dir, Ecco: Sara Wood
Assoc Dir, Mktg: Brianne Halverson; Katie O'Callaghan
Assoc Dir, Online Mktg: Blaise Base
Assoc Dir, Publicity, Ecco: Ashley Garland
Assoc Dir, Publicity, HarperCollins One: Julie Burton
Assoc Dir, Publicity, William Morrow: Anwesha Basu; Maureen Cole
Assoc Dir, Publicity, Morrow/Avon: Danielle Bartlett
Sr Publicity Mgr, Ecco: Martin Wilson
Publicity Mgr, William Morrow: Kate Gales Schafer
Assoc Publicist, Ecco: Stephanie Mendoza
Sr Mktg Mgr: Penny Makras; Stephanie Selah
Sr Mgr, Digital Mktg: Dana Trombley
Mktg Mgr, William Morrow: Paul Lamb
Exec Ed: Luke Dempsey; Emily Griffin
Exec Ed, Creative Devt: Matt Harper
Exec Ed, Ecco: Denise Oswald; Zack Wagman
Exec Ed, Dey Street Books: Mark Chait; Julia Cheiffetz
Exec Ed, HarperOne: Roger Freet; Julia Pastore
Exec Ed, William Morrow: Peter Hubbard; Cassie Jones; Rachel Kahan; Adam Korn; Katherine Nintzel
Exec Ed, William Morrow/Avon: May Chen
Sr Ed: Amy Bendell
Sr Ed, Dey Street Books: Jessica Sindler
Sr Ed, HarperElixir: Libby Edelson
Sr Ed, HarperOne: Miles Doyle; Genoveva Llosa; Jeanette Perez
Sr Ed, William Morrow: Emma Brodie; Emily Krump
Sr Ed, William Morrow/Avon: Tessa Woodward
Ed, Dey Street Books: Matthew Daddona
Ed, Harper Business: Stephanie Hitchcock
Ed, Harper Design: Cristina Garces
Ed, Harper Voyager & William Morrow: Priyanka Krishnan
Ed, Harper Wave: Sarah Murphy
Ed, HarperOne: Hilary Lawson
Ed, William Morrow: Jessica Williams
Ed, William Morrow/Avon: Nicole Fischer
Assoc Ed: Sofia Groopman; Jillian Verrillo
Assoc Ed, Ecco: Emma Janaskie
Assoc Ed, Harper: Erin Wicks
Assoc Ed, William Morrow: Nick Amphlett
Asst Ed: Bridget Read
Asst Ed, Ecco: Emma Dries
Asst Ed, Harper Wave: Sarah Haugen
ISBN Prefix(es): 978-0-06
Imprints: Amistad; Avon; Avon Impulse (digital only); Avon Inspire; Avon Red; Bourbon Street Books; Broadside Books; Custom House; Dey Street Books; Ecco; Harper; Harper Business; Harper Design; Harper Luxe (large print); Harper Paperbacks; Harper Perennial; Harper Voyager; Harper Wave; HarperAudio; HarperBibles; HarperCollins; HarperCollins e-Books; HarperCollins 360; HarperElixir; HarperOne; Infinitum Nihil; Dennis Lehane Books; William Morrow; William Morrow Cookbooks; William Morrow Paperbacks; Newmarket Press for It Books; Witness Impulse

§HarperCollins Publishers
Subsidiary of News Corporation
195 Broadway, New York, NY 10007
SAN: 200-2086
Tel: 212-207-7000 *Fax:* 212-207-7145
Web Site: www.harpercollins.com
Key Personnel
CEO: Brian Murray *E-mail:* Brian.Murray@HarperCollins.com
CFO: Janet Gervasio *E-mail:* Janet.Gervasio@HarperCollins.com
Chief Digital Offr & EVP, Intl: Chantal Restivo-Alessi
CIO: Rick Schwartz *E-mail:* Rick.Schwartz@HarperCollins.com
SVP, Dist Opers: Joe Franceschelli
SVP, Dom & Foreign Rts, Gen Books: Juliette Shapland
SVP, Fin & Strategic New Busn Devt: Rob Zaffiris
SVP, HR: Diane Bailey
SVP, Intl Sales: David Wolfson
SVP, Mkt Insight & Sales Opers: Frank Albanese
EVP, Opers & Technol: Larry Nevins
VP, Global Insight: Catherine Makk
VP, Corp Communs: Erin Crum
VP, Assoc Gen Coun: Kyran Cassidy
VP, Prodn & Creative Opers: Tracey Menzies
Gen Coun Worldwide: Bill Adams
Affiliate Publr, HarperCollins 360: Jean Marie Kelly
Pres, Sales: Josh Marwell *E-mail:* Josh.Marwell@HarperCollins.com
Sr Dir, Audience Devt & Insight: Jim Hanas

Sr Dir, Intl Sales & Mktg: Samantha Hagerbaumer
Dir, Publicity: Kate D'Esmond; Rachel Elinsky
Assoc Dir, Mktg: Stephanie Cooper
Sr Mgr, Consumer Insight: Allison Jarvela
Asst Mgr, Corp Communs: Katie Levine
Sr Pricing Analyst: Ruchir Pandya
Founded: 1817
HarperCollins is one of the leading English-language publishers in the world & is a subsidiary of News Corp (NYSE: NWS, NWS.A; ASX: NCP, NCPDP). Headquartered in New York, the company has publishing groups in the US, Canada, Australasia & the UK. Its publishing groups (US) include the HarperCollins General Books Group, HarperCollins Children's Books Group, Zondervan; outside the US: HarperCollins Australia, HarperCollins Canada, HarperCollins India, HarperCollins New Zealand & HarperCollins UK.
ISBN Prefix(es): 978-0-06; 978-0-688; 978-0-380; 978-0-694
Number of titles published annually: 1,700 Print
Imprints: Beech Tree Books; Dey Street Books; HarperCollins; Hearst Books; Lothrop, Lee & Shepard Books; Morrow Junior Books; Mulberry Books; Quill Trade Paperbacks
Distributed by Cynthia Publishing Co; Ingram Publisher Services/Spring Arbor (Christian market)
Distributor for Perseus (Addison Wesley Trade); Basic Books; Civitas; Counterpoint; Delphinium Books; GT Publishing; Public Affairs; TV Books
Foreign Rep(s): Publishers International Marketing Services
Foreign Rights: Kezban Akcali Agency (Turkey); Antonella Antonelli Agenzia (Italy); Bardon Far Eastern Agents (China, Taiwan); Eliane Benisti Literary Agency (France); Mercedes Casanovas (Spain); Lynn Franklin (Russia); June Hall Literary Agency; Licht & Licht Agency (Denmark, Finland, Norway, Sweden); Rogan Pikarski Literary Agency (Israel); Gerd Plessl Agency (Czech Republic, Greece, Hungary, Montenegro, Poland, Serbia); Tuttle-Mori Agency Inc (Japan)
Advertising Agency: Franklin Spier Inc
Membership(s): AAP; BISG
See separate listing for:
HarperCollins Children's Books
HarperCollins General Books Group

Harper's Magazine Foundation
666 Broadway, 11th fl, New York, NY 10012
Tel: 212-420-5720 *Toll Free Tel:* 800-444-4653 *Fax:* 212-228-5889
E-mail: harpers@harpers.org
Web Site: www.harpers.org
Key Personnel
VP & Gen Mgr: Lynn Carlson *E-mail:* lynn@harpers.org
Ed: James Marcus
Ed-at-Large: Ellen Rosenbush
Founded: 1850
General trade.
ISBN Prefix(es): 978-1-879957
Number of titles published annually: 12 Print
Total Titles: 40 Print

§Harrison House Publishers
7498 E 46 Place, Tulsa, OK 74145
SAN: 208-676X
Mailing Address: PO Box 35035, Tulsa, OK 74153-1035
Tel: 918-523-5700 *Toll Free Tel:* 800-888-4126 *Toll Free Fax:* 800-830-5688
Web Site: www.harrisonhouse.com
Founded: 1975
Charismatic/Christian publishing house.
ISBN Prefix(es): 978-1-57794; 978-0-89274
Number of titles published annually: 50 Print
Total Titles: 400 Online

Hartman Publishing Inc
1313 Iron Ave SW, Albuquerque, NM 87102
Tel: 505-291-1274 *Toll Free Tel:* 800-999-9534 *Fax:* 505-291-1284 *Toll Free Fax:* 800-474-6106
E-mail: orders@hartmanonline.com; help@hartmanonline.com
Web Site: www.hartmanonline.com
Key Personnel
Publr: Mark Hartman
Mng Ed: Susan Alvare Hedman
Founded: 1994
Publish a variety of in-service training materials & textbooks for certified nursing assistants & home health aides. Subjects include Alzheimer's disease, infection control, body mechanics, abuse & neglect, AIDS/HIV & communication skills.
ISBN Prefix(es): 978-1-888343
Number of titles published annually: 12 Print; 1 CD-ROM; 1 Audio
Total Titles: 40 Print; 1 CD-ROM; 1 Audio
Membership(s): New Mexico Book Association

Harvard Art Museums
32 Quincy St, Cambridge, MA 02138
Tel: 617-495-1440; 617-496-6529 (edit) *Fax:* 617-495-9985
Web Site: www.harvardartmuseums.org
Key Personnel
Dir, Communs: Daron Manoogian
Mng Ed: Micah Buis
Ed: Cheryl Pappas
Asst Ed: Sarah Kuschner
Founded: 1901
Art history.
ISBN Prefix(es): 978-0-916724; 978-1-891771
Number of titles published annually: 5 Print
Total Titles: 70 Print
Distributed by Yale University Press

Harvard Business Review Press
Division of Harvard Business Publishing
300 N Beacon St, Watertown, MA 02472
SAN: 202-277X
Tel: 617-783-7400 *Fax:* 617-783-7489
E-mail: custserv@hbsp.harvard.edu
Web Site: www.harvardbusiness.org
Key Personnel
Publr: Sarah McConville
Assoc Publr: Keith Pfeffer
Ed-in-Chief: Adi Ignatius
Exec Ed: Jeff Kehoe
Assoc Ed: Ania Wieckowski
Publicity Mgr: Julie De Voll
Founded: 1984
Trade & professional books for the business management & academic audiences in the areas of strategy, leadership, innovation, organizational behavior/human resource management, finance management, marketing, production & operations management. *Harvard Business Review*, reference books & Internet.
ISBN Prefix(es): 978-0-87584; 978-1-57851; 978-1-4221; 978-1-59139
Number of titles published annually: 70 Print
Total Titles: 700 Print
Imprints: Harvard Business Reference
Distributed by Client Distribution Services
Foreign Rep(s): McGraw-Hill Education (Africa, Asia, Australia, Canada, Europe, Middle East, New Zealand); United Publishers Services Ltd (Japan)
Distribution Center: Perseus Distribution, 250 W 57 St, 15th fl, New York, NY 10107 *Tel:* 212-340-8100 *Fax:* 212-340-8105

The Harvard Common Press
Imprint of Quarto Publishing Group USA Inc
100 Cummings Ctr, Suite 265-D, Beverly, MA 01915
Tel: 978-282-9590 *Fax:* 978-282-7765
Web Site: www.quartoknows.com/harvard-common-press
Key Personnel
VP & Group Publr: Winnie Prentiss *E-mail:* winnie.prentiss@quarto.com
Edit Dir: Dan Rosenberg *E-mail:* dan.rosenberg@quarto.com
Founded: 1976
General nonfiction: cookbooks, health, self-help, child care & parenting.
ISBN Prefix(es): 978-0-916782; 978-0-87645; 978-1-55832
Number of titles published annually: 24 Print
Total Titles: 150 Print

§Harvard Education Publishing Group
Division of Harvard Graduate School of Education
8 Story St, 1st fl, Cambridge, MA 02138
Tel: 617-495-3432 *Toll Free Tel:* 800-513-0763 (subns); 888-437-1437 (orders) *Fax:* 617-496-3584; 978-348-1233 (orders)
E-mail: hepg@harvard.edu
Web Site: www.hepg.org
Key Personnel
Dir: Douglas Clayton *E-mail:* douglas_clayton@gse.harvard.edu
Asst Dir/Ed-in-Chief: Caroline Chauncey *E-mail:* caroline_chauncey@gse.harvard.edu
Dir, Sales & Mktg: Christina DeYoung *E-mail:* christina_deyoung@gse.harvard.edu
Edit & Prodn Dir: Chris Leonesio *E-mail:* christopher_leonesio@gse.harvard.edu
Publisher of books & journals on education practice, research & policy.
ISBN Prefix(es): 978-1-891792; 978-1-883433; 978-0-916690; 978-1-934742; 978-1-61250; 978-1-68253
Number of titles published annually: 25 Print; 12 E-Book
Total Titles: 200 Print; 65 E-Book
Imprints: Harvard Education Letter; Harvard Education Press; Harvard Educational Review
Foreign Rep(s): Eurospan Group (worldwide exc Canada & USA)
Orders to: 46 Development Rd, Fitchburg, MA 021420 *E-mail:* orders@pssc.com
Returns: 46 Development Rd, Fitchburg, MA 01420

Harvard Square Editions
2152 Beachwood Terr, Hollywood, CA 90068
Tel: 323-203-0233
E-mail: submissions@harvardsquareeditions.org
Web Site: harvardsquareeditions.org
Key Personnel
Ed-in-Chief: David Landau
Outreach Dir: Simone Weingarten *E-mail:* sw@harvardsquareeditions.org
Founded: 2000
Run by Harvard alumni, Harvard Square Editions publishes authors of literary fiction with an environmental or social conscience. HSE books have won National Book Foundation, Nautilus & other awards. Its mission is to publish fiction that transcends national boundaries, especially mss that are international, political, literary, diverse, multi-cultural, science fiction, climate fiction, fantasy, utopia & dystopia. We appreciate aesthetic value & constructive social & political content, especially mss related to climate change, deforestation & conservation, but have a low tolerance for profanity & graphic violence.
ISBN Prefix(es): 978-0-9833216; 978-0-9895960; 978-1-941861
Number of titles published annually: 12 Print; 14 E-Book
Total Titles: 50 Print; 55 E-Book
Distribution Center: Ingram Content Group, One Ingram Blvd, La Vergne, TN 37086 *Tel:* 615-793-5000 *Web Site:* www.ingramcontent.com

Gardners Books, One Whittle Dr, Eastbourne, East Sussex BN23 6QH, United Kingdom *Tel:* (01323) 521555 *Web Site:* www.gardners.com

Harvard Ukrainian Research Institute
Subsidiary of Harvard University
34 Kirkland St, Cambridge, MA 02138
SAN: 208-967X
Tel: 617-495-4053 *Fax:* 617-495-8097
E-mail: huri@fas.harvard.edu
Web Site: www.huri.harvard.edu
Key Personnel
Mgr, Pubns: Marika Whaley *E-mail:* mwhaley@fas.harvard.edu
Founded: 1973
ISBN Prefix(es): 978-0-916458; 978-1-932650
Number of titles published annually: 5 Print; 3 Online
Total Titles: 100 Print; 6 Online
Distributed by Harvard University Press

Harvard University Press
79 Garden St, Cambridge, MA 02138-1499
SAN: 200-2043
Tel: 617-495-2600; 401-531-2800 (intl orders) *Toll Free Tel:* 800-405-1619 (orders) *Fax:* 617-495-5898 (general); 617-496-4677 (edit & rts); 401-531-2801 (intl orders) *Toll Free Fax:* 800-406-9145 (orders)
E-mail: contact_hup@harvard.edu
Web Site: www.hup.harvard.edu
Key Personnel
CFO: Dan Wackrow *E-mail:* dan_wackrow@harvard.edu
Dir: George Andreou
Promo & Ad Dir: Sheila Barrett *E-mail:* sheila_barrett@harvard.edu
Dir, Design & Prodn: Tim Jones *E-mail:* tim_jones@harvard.edu
Dir, Intellectual Property: Stephanie Vyce *E-mail:* stephanie_vyce@harvard.edu
Asst Dir/Ed-in-Chief: Susan Wallace Boehmer *E-mail:* susan_boehmer@harvard.edu
Asst Dir, Sales & Mktg: Susan Donnelly *E-mail:* susan_donnelly@harvard.edu
Exec Ed-at-Large: Thomas LeBien *E-mail:* thomas_lebien@harvard.edu; Sharmila Sen *E-mail:* sharmila_sen@harvard.edu
Exec Ed-at-Large, Global: Ian Malcolm *E-mail:* imalcolm@harvardup.co.uk
Exec Ed-at-Large, History: Kathleen McDermott *E-mail:* kathleen_mcdermott@harvard.edu
Sr Exec Ed, History & Contemporary Aff: Joyce Seltzer *E-mail:* joyce_seltzer@harvard.edu
Exec Ed, Humanities: Lindsay Waters *E-mail:* lindsay_waters@harvard.edu
Exec Ed, Life Sciences: Janice Audet
Exec Ed, Physical Sciences & Technol: Jeff Dean
Gen Ed, Human Behavior, Educ & the Humanities: Andrew Kinney *E-mail:* andrew_kinney@harvard.edu
Sales Mgr & Digital Content Mgr: Vanessa Vinarub *E-mail:* vanessa_vinarub@harvard.edu
Founded: 1913
General scholarly, humanities, social sciences, life/physical sciences.
ISBN Prefix(es): 978-0-674
Number of titles published annually: 200 Print
Total Titles: 8,000 Print
Imprints: Belknap Press
Foreign Office(s): Vernon House, 23 Sicilian Ave, London WC1A 2QS, United Kingdom, Exec Ed-at-Large, Global: Ian Malcolm *Tel:* (020) 3463 2350 *Fax:* (020) 7831 9261 *E-mail:* imalcolm@harvardup.co.uk
Distributor for Harvard Center for Middle Eastern Studies; Harvard Center for Population Studies; Harvard Center for the Study of World Religions; Harvard College Library (including Houghton Library Judaica division); Harvard Department of Sanskrit & Indian Studies; Harvard Department of the Classics; Harvard Ukrainian Research Institute; Harvard University Asia Center; Harvard University David Rockefeller Center for Latin American Studies; Harvard-Yenching Institute; Peabody Museum of Archaeology & Ethnology
Foreign Rep(s): Academic Book Promotions (Benelux); Aromix Books (Hong Kong); Avicenna Ltd (Bill Kennedy) (Bahrain, Egypt, Iran, Iraq, Kuwait, Lebanon, Libya, Oman, Qatar, Saudi Arabia, Sudan, Syria, United Arab Emirates, Yemen); Avicenna Ltd (Claire de Gruchy) (Algeria, Cyprus, Jordan, Malta, Morocco, Palestine, Tunisia, Turkey); Amos Bampisaki (Burundi, Rwanda, Sudan, Tanzania, Uganda); John Eklund (Canada exc British Columbia, Midwestern States); Everest International Publishing Services (Wei Zhao) (China); Harvard Business Review Press (Bangladesh, Bhutan, India, Maldives, Nepal, Pakistan, Sri Lanka); Harvard University Press London (Greece, Ireland, Israel, UK); Havilah Procurement & Library Services (Ghana, Nigeria); IMA (Tony Moggach) (Cameroon, Ethiopia, The Gambia, Ghana, Kenya, Malawi, Mauritius, Nigeria, Rwanda, Tanzania, Uganda, Zambia); InBooks/James Bennett Pty Ltd (Australia, New Zealand); Information & Culture, Korea (South Korea); Ewa Ledochiwicz (Albania, Bosnia and Herzegovina, Croatia, Czech Republic, Estonia, Hungary, Kazakhstan, Latvia, Lithuania, Poland, Romania, Russia, Serbia, Slovakia, Slovenia); Uwe Ludemann (Austria, France, Germany, Italy, Portugal, Spain, Switzerland); Patricia Nelson (British Columbia, CN, Southwest, Western USA); B K Norton (Taiwan); Palgrave (Cory Voigt) (Southern Africa); Rockbook Inc (Japan); Joan Wamae (Kenya); Yuha Associates (Malaysia); Zimpfer Global Services (Caribbean, Central America)
Foreign Rights: Akcali Agency (Turkey); L'Autre Agence (France); Bardon-Chinese Media Agency (China, Hong Kong, Taiwan); Bookman Literary Agency (Denmark, Finland, Iceland, Norway, Sweden); Dar Cherlin (Arab Middle East); The English Agency (Japan); Graal Literary Agency (Bulgaria, Macedonia, Poland, Romania, Serbia, Slovakia); The Deborah Harris Agency (Israel); International Editors' Co (Central America, Latin America, South America, Spain); Alexander Korzhenevski Agency (Russia); Liepman Agency AG (Germany, Switzerland); Ilidio Matos Agencia (Portugal); OA Literary Agency (Greece); Oxford Literary & Rights Agency (Croatia, Czech Republic, Ukraine); Seibel Publishing Services (Brazil); Suzanna Zevi Agenzia Letteraria (Italy)
Shipping Address: Triliteral LLC, 100 Maple Ridge Dr, Cumberland, RI 02864-1769
Membership(s): AAP; American Association of University Presses; BISG

Harvest Hill Press
PO Box 55, Salisbury Cove, ME 04672-0055
Tel: 207-288-8900
E-mail: shop@harvesthillpress.com
Web Site: www.harvesthillpress.com
Founded: 1994
Cookbooks & printed kitchen stationery for gift, children's & book markets.
ISBN Prefix(es): 978-1-886862
Number of titles published annually: 3 Print
Total Titles: 40 Print
Imprints: Coastal New England Publications
Distributed by University Press of New England
Membership(s): Independent Book Publishers Association

Harvest House Publishers Inc
990 Owen Loop N, Eugene, OR 97402-9173
SAN: 207-4745
Tel: 541-343-0123 *Toll Free Tel:* 888-501-6991 *Fax:* 541-342-6410
E-mail: admin@harvesthousepublishers.com
Web Site: harvesthousepublishers.com
Key Personnel
Pres: Bob Hawkins, Jr
Sr Ed & Ms Coord: Nick Harrison
Intl Rts: Sharon Shook
Founded: 1974
Evangelical Christian books; no unsol mss.
ISBN Prefix(es): 978-0-89081; 978-1-56507; 978-0-7369
Number of titles published annually: 160 Print; 6 Audio
Total Titles: 1,100 Print; 6 Audio
Membership(s): BISG

§Hatherleigh Press Ltd
62545 State Hwy 10, Hobart, NY 13788
E-mail: info@hatherleighpress.com; publicity@hatherleighpress.com
Web Site: www.hatherleighpress.com
Key Personnel
CEO & Pres: Andrew Flach
Assoc Publr: Ryan Tumambing
Mng Ed: Anna Krusinski
Founded: 1995
Motto: "Improve your life. Change your world." Expert content in health, wellness, fitness, exercise, nutrition, inspiration, healthy living & sustainability. Print & ebooks, audio, digital & filmed entertainment.
ISBN Prefix(es): 978-1-886330; 978-1-57826
Number of titles published annually: 30 Print; 30 E-Book
Total Titles: 300 Print; 100 E-Book; 4 Audio
Imprints: GetFitNow.com Books; Healthy Living Books
Distributed by Penguin Random House Inc
Foreign Rep(s): Nigel Yorweth (worldwide)
Distribution Center: Penguin Random House Publisher Services (PRHPS) *Toll Free Tel:* 800-733-3000; 888-523-9292 (CN sales) *Toll Free Fax:* 800-659-2436; 888-562-9924 (CN sales) *E-mail:* csorders@randomhouse.com

§Hay House Inc
2776 Loker Ave W, Carlsbad, CA 92010
Mailing Address: PO Box 5100, Carlsbad, CA 92018-5100
Tel: 760-431-7695 (ext 2, intl) *Toll Free Tel:* 800-654-5126 (ext 2, US) *Toll Free Fax:* 800-650-5115
E-mail: info@hayhouse.com; editorial@hayhouse.com
Web Site: www.hayhouse.com
Key Personnel
Founder & Chmn: Louise Hay
Pres & CEO: Reid Tracy
COO: Margarete Nielsen
Founded: 1984
Self-help/New Age, health, philosophy, spiritual growth & awareness, mental & environmental harmony books; also self-healing; biography, producers & distributors of recordings & video pertaining to health of mind, body & spirit. Accept agented submissions only; SASE required.
ISBN Prefix(es): 978-0-937611; 978-1-56170; 978-1-4019
Number of titles published annually: 50 Print; 50 Audio
Total Titles: 1,000 Print; 1,000 Audio
Divisions: Balboa Press
Branch Office(s)
665 Broadway, Suite 1200, New York, NY 10012 *Tel:* 646-484-4950 *Fax:* 646-484-4956
Foreign Office(s): Hayhouse Australia Pty Ltd, 18/36 Ralph St, Alexandria, NSW 2015, Australia *Tel:* (02) 9669 4299 *Fax:* (02) 9669 4144 *Web Site:* www.hayhouse.com.au
Hayhouse Publishers India, Muskaan Complex, Plot No 3, B-2, Vasant Kunj, New Delhi 110

070, India *Tel:* (011) 4176 1620 *Fax:* (011) 4176 1630 *Web Site:* www.hayhouse.co.in
Hayhouse SA Pty Ltd, PO Box 990, Witkoppen 2068, South Africa *Tel:* (011) 326 3449 *Web Site:* www.hayhouse.co.za
Hayhouse UK Ltd, 33 Notting Hill Gate, London W11 3JQ, United Kingdom *Tel:* (020) 3675 2460 *Fax:* (020) 3675 2451 *Web Site:* www.hayhouse.co.uk
Returns: 2750 Progress St, Vista, CA 92081 *Toll Free Tel:* 800-654-5126
Warehouse: 2750 Progress St, Suite B, Vista, CA 92081 *Fax:* 760-431-6948
Distribution Center: Raincoast Books, 2440 Viking Way, Richmond, BC V6V 1N2, Canada *Toll Free Tel:* 800-663-5714 *Toll Free Fax:* 800-565-3770 *E-mail:* customerservice@raincoast.com

Haynes Manuals Inc
Division of The Haynes Publishing Group
859 Lawrence Dr, Newbury Park, CA 91320-2232
Tel: 805-498-6703 *Toll Free Tel:* 800-4-HAYNES (442-9637) *Fax:* 805-498-2867
E-mail: cstn@haynes.com
Web Site: www.haynes.com
Key Personnel
Chmn: J Haynes
Pres: Eric Oakley
Mktg Dir: George Brueggeman
Founded: 1960
Publisher & importer of books on domestic & foreign autos & motorcycles & historical & technical motoring.
ISBN Prefix(es): 978-0-946609; 978-1-56392
Number of titles published annually: 13 Print
Total Titles: 690 Print
Distributed by Motorbooks International
Distributor for G T Foulis; Haynes Owners Workshop Manuals; Oxford Illustrated Press
Warehouse: Eastern Warehouse, 1299 Bridgestone Pkwy, La Vergne, TN 37086 *Fax:* 615-793-5325

§Hazelden Publishing
Division of Hazelden Foundation
15251 Pleasant Valley Rd, Center City, MN 55012-0011
SAN: 125-1953
Mailing Address: PO Box 176, Center City, MN 55012-0176
Tel: 651-213-4200 *Toll Free Tel:* 800-257-7810 *Fax:* 651-213-4590
E-mail: info@hazelden.org
Web Site: www.hazelden.org
Key Personnel
SVP & COO, Publg: Joel Jaksah
Exec Dir: Kristine Van Hoof-Haines
Founded: 1954
Adult trade hardcover & paperbacks; curriculum, workbooks, giftbooks, video & audio; self-help, addiction & recovery, personal & spiritual growth; computer based products, wellness products, young adult nonfiction.
ISBN Prefix(es): 978-0-89486; 978-1-56838; 978-0-89638; 978-0-942421; 978-0-935908; 978-1-56246; 978-0-934125
Number of titles published annually: 12 Print
Total Titles: 500 Print; 500 E-Book; 10 Audio
Imprints: Hazelden/Johnson Institute; Hazelden/Keep Coming Back; Hazelden-Pittman Archives Press
Distributed by Health Communications Inc (trade); Simon & Schuster
Distributor for Obsessive Anonymous
Foreign Rep(s): Eurospan (Europe, Ireland, UK); RecoverOz (Australia, New Zealand)

§HCPro Inc
75 Sylvan St, Suite A-101, Danvers, MA 01923
Toll Free Tel: 800-650-6787 *Toll Free Fax:* 800-785-9212
E-mail: customerservice@hcpro.com
Web Site: www.hcpro.com
Founded: 1986
Specialize in healthcare administration & management.
ISBN Prefix(es): 978-1-885829; 978-1-55645
Number of titles published annually: 110 Print; 4 CD-ROM; 30 Online; 5 E-Book; 60 Audio
Total Titles: 125 Print; 5 CD-ROM; 40 Online; 25 E-Book; 75 Audio
Imprints: Opus Communications
Subsidiaries: The Greeley Co
Orders to: 100 Hoods Lane, Marblehead, MA 01945
Warehouse: 100 Hoods Lane, Marblehead, MA 01945
Distribution Center: 100 Hoods Lane, Marblehead, MA 01945
Membership(s): NEPA

Health Administration Press
Division of Foundation of the American College of Healthcare Executives
One N Franklin St, Suite 1700, Chicago, IL 60606-3491
SAN: 207-0464
Tel: 312-424-2800 *Fax:* 312-424-0014
E-mail: hap1@ache.org
Web Site: www.ache.org/publications (orders)
Key Personnel
Pres: Deborah J Bowen
SVP: Maureen Glass *Tel:* 312-424-9450 *E-mail:* mglass@ache.org
Assoc Dir & Mktg Mgr: Michael Cunningham *Tel:* 312-424-9470 *E-mail:* mcunningham@ache.org
Acqs Ed: Janet Davis *Tel:* 312-424-9460 *E-mail:* jdavis@ache.org
Founded: 1972
Health administration, health care, law & medicine, medical care organization.
ISBN Prefix(es): 978-0-910701; 978-1-56793
Number of titles published annually: 20 Print
Total Titles: 200 Print; 1 E-Book
Imprints: American College of Healthcare Executives Management Series; AUPHA Press/Health Administration Press; Executive Essentials; Gateway to Healthcare Management
Branch Office(s)
PO Box 75145, Baltimore, MD 21275, Contact: Melissa Lawson *Tel:* 301-362-6905 *Fax:* 301-206-9789
Foreign Rep(s): ELEA doo (Europe); iGroup (Asia); Login Bros (Canada)
Billing Address: 9050 Junction Dr, Annapolis Junction, MD 20701
Orders to: 9050 Junction Dr, Annapolis Junction, MD 20701 *Tel:* 301-362-6905 *Fax:* 240-396-5907 *E-mail:* hap@brightkey.net
Returns: 9050 Junction Dr, Annapolis Junction, MD 20701
Shipping Address: 9050 Junction Dr, Annapolis Junction, MD 20701 *Tel:* 301-362 6905 *E-mail:* hap@brightkey.net
Warehouse: 9050 Junction Dr, Annapolis Junction, MD 20701, Contact: Melissa Lawson *Tel:* 301-362-6905 *Fax:* 301-206-9789
Distribution Center: 9050 Junction Dr, Annapolis Junction, MD 20701

§Health Communications Inc
3201 SW 15 St, Deerfield Beach, FL 33442
SAN: 212-100X
Tel: 954-360-0909 *Toll Free Tel:* 800-851-9100; 800-441-5569 (cust serv & orders) *Fax:* 954-360-0034 *Toll Free Fax:* 800-424-7652 (cust serv & orders)
E-mail: customerservice2@hcibooks.com
Web Site: www.hcibooks.com
Key Personnel
CEO: Christian Blonshine *E-mail:* christian.blonshine@hcibooks.com
CFO: Craig Jarvie *E-mail:* craig.jarvie@hcibooks.com
Pres & Publr: Peter Vegso
Art Dir: Larissa Henoch
Edit Dir: Allison Janse Collins; Candace Johnson
Dir, PR: Kim Weiss *E-mail:* kim.weiss@hcibooks.com
Dir, Trade Sales, Intl Sales & Dist: Lori Golden *E-mail:* lori.golden@hcibooks.com
Founded: 1977
Publisher of nonfiction paperbacks & hardcover books on self-help, personal growth, diet, fitness, inspiration, health, parenting, women's issues, teens, religion, psychology, addiction & recovery.
ISBN Prefix(es): 978-0-932194; 978-1-55874; 978-0-7573; 978-0-9910732
Number of titles published annually: 50 Print; 50 E-Book
Total Titles: 500 Print; 500 E-Book; 18 Audio
Imprints: HCI Books; HCI Teens
Divisions: HCI Printing & Publishing
See separate listing for:
Simcha Press

§Health Forum Inc
Subsidiary of American Hospital Association
155 N Wacker Dr, Suite 400, Chicago, IL 60606
SAN: 216-5872
Tel: 312-893-6800 *Toll Free Tel:* 800-242-2626 *Fax:* 312-422-4500
E-mail: hfcustsvc@healthforum.com
Web Site: www.ahaonlinestore.com; www.healthforum.com
Key Personnel
Sr Ed: Rick Hill *Tel:* 312-893-6863 *E-mail:* rhill@aha.org
Founded: 1986
Publisher of professional books & textbooks for health care professionals. Specialize in books that help hospital executives & department heads manage their business better & achieve improved patient satisfaction. Also provide ICD-10-CM/PCS & data information from the AHA Central Office & the American Hospital Association annual survey of hospitals.
ISBN Prefix(es): 978-1-55648; 978-0-87258
Number of titles published annually: 10 Print; 2 CD-ROM; 2 E-Book
Total Titles: 30 Print; 2 CD-ROM; 3 E-Book
Imprints: AHA (American Hospital Association)
Billing Address: AHA Services Inc, Contact: Francine Adcock *Tel:* 312-422-3238 *Fax:* 312-422-4597 *E-mail:* fadcock@aha.org
Orders to: AHA Services Inc, PO Box 933283, Atlanta, GA 31193-3283 *Toll Free Fax:* 866-516-5817 *E-mail:* aha-orders@pbd.com
Returns: AHA Services Inc, Cust Returns, 3280 Summit Ridge Pkwy, Duluth, GA 30096
Warehouse: AHA Services Inc, 3280 Summit Ridge Pkwy, Duluth, GA 30096 (AHA order servs) *Toll Free Fax:* 866-516-5817 *E-mail:* aha-orders@pbd.com
Distribution Center: Rittenhouse Book Distributors, 511 Feheley Dr, King of Prussia, PA 19406, Contact: Nicole Gallo *Toll Free Tel:* 800-345-6425 *Fax:* 610-277-0390 *E-mail:* n.gallo@rittenhouse.com *Web Site:* www.rittenhouse.com
Majors Education Solutions, 500 E Corporate Dr, Suite 600, Lewisville, TX 75057, Contact: Martha Yeahquo *Tel:* 972-353-1100 *Toll Free Tel:* 800-633-1851 *Fax:* 972-353-1300 *E-mail:* customerservice@majors.com *Web Site:* www.majors.com
Membership(s): American Hospital Association; Independent Book Publishers Association

§Health Professions Press
Division of Paul H Brookes Publishing Co Inc
409 Washington Ave, Suite 500, Towson, MD 21204
SAN: 297-7338

Mailing Address: PO Box 10624, Baltimore, MD 21285-0624
Tel: 410-337-9585 *Toll Free Tel:* 888-337-8808 *Fax:* 410-337-8539
E-mail: custserv@healthpropress.com
Web Site: www.healthpropress.com
Key Personnel
Pres: Melissa A Behm *E-mail:* mbehm@healthpropress.com
Dir, Pubns: Mary H Magnus *E-mail:* mmagnus@healthpropress.com
Mktg Coord: Kaitlin Konecke
Founded: 1989
Hardcover, paperback & digital professional resources & textbooks in aging, Alzheimer's disease, long-term care & health administration.
ISBN Prefix(es): 978-1-878812; 978-1-932529; 978-1-938870
Number of titles published annually: 10 Print; 2 CD-ROM
Total Titles: 100 Print; 10 CD-ROM
Distributed by The Eurospan Group (Africa, Europe & Middle East); Footprint Books Pty Ltd (Australia, Fiji, New Zealand & Papua New Guinea); Login Canada (Canada); Unifacmanu Trading Co Ltd (Taiwan)
Foreign Rep(s): CRW Marketing Services for Publishers Inc (Guam, Northern Mariana Islands, Philippines); Tahir Lodhi Publishers' Representatives (Pakistan); Sara Books Pvt Ltd (Bangladesh, India, Sri Lanka); STM Publishers Services Pte Ltd (China, Hong Kong, Macau, Malaysia, Myanmar, Singapore, Thailand, Vietnam)
Warehouse: Maple Logistics Solutions, 60 Grumbacher Rd I-83 Industrial Park, PO Box 15100, York, PA 17406
Membership(s): Independent Book Publishers Association

Health Research Books
62 Seventh St, Pomeroy, WA 99347
Mailing Address: PO Box 850, Pomeroy, WA 99347
Tel: 509-843-2385 *Toll Free Tel:* 888-844-2386 *Fax:* 509-843-2387
E-mail: publish@pomeroy-wa.com
Web Site: www.healthresearchbooks.com
Key Personnel
Owner: Nikki Jones *E-mail:* nikkijones@pomeroy-wa.com
Founded: 1952
Publish reprints of rare, hard to find, out of print books. Subjects include mysticism, Egyptology, divination, UFOs, hypnotism, mental & spiritual healing, acupuncture, metaphysical, palmistry & many, many more.
ISBN Prefix(es): 978-0-7873
Number of titles published annually: 300 Print
Total Titles: 2,000 Print

Healthy Learning, see Coaches Choice

§HeartMath LLC
14700 W Park Ave, Boulder Creek, CA 95006
Tel: 831-338-8700 *Toll Free Tel:* 800-450-9111 *Fax:* 831-338-9861
E-mail: info@heartmath.com; inquiry@heartmath.com
Web Site: www.heartmath.com
Key Personnel
Global Dir: Bruce Cryer
EVP, Strategic Devt: Howard Martin
SVP, Sales & Mktg: Catherine Calarco
VP, Fin/COO: Chris Jacob
Dir, PR: Gabriella Boehmer *E-mail:* gboehmer@hearthmath.com
Founded: 1998
Publishers of The HeartMath System.
ISBN Prefix(es): 978-1-879052; 978-0-9700286
Number of titles published annually: 16 Print
Total Titles: 2 CD-ROM; 7 Audio

Hearts 'n Tummies Cookbook Co
Division of Quixote Press
3544 Blakslee St, Wever, IA 52658
Tel: 319-372-7480 *Toll Free Tel:* 800-571-2665 *Fax:* 319-372-7485
E-mail: quixotepress@gmail.com; heartsntummies@gmail.com
Web Site: www.heartsntummies.com
Key Personnel
Pres & Intl Rts: Bruce Carlson
Founded: 1982
Cookbooks.
ISBN Prefix(es): 978-1-878488; 978-1-57166
Number of titles published annually: 28 Print
Total Titles: 400 Print

Hebrew Union College Press
Division of Hebrew Union College
3101 Clifton Ave, Cincinnati, OH 45220
Tel: 513-221-1875 *Fax:* 513-221-0321
Web Site: press.huc.edu
Key Personnel
Co-Dir: David H Aaron *Tel:* 513-487-3265 *E-mail:* daaron@huc.edu; Jason Kalman *Tel:* 513-221-1875 ext 3248 *E-mail:* jkalman@huc.edu
Edit Dir: David Ellenson *Tel:* 800-424-1336 ext 2201 *E-mail:* dellenson@huc.edu; Sharon Gillerman *Tel:* 213-765-2152 *E-mail:* sgillerman@huc.edu; Alyssa Gray *Tel:* 212-824-2284 *E-mail:* agray@huc.edu; Richard Saranson *Tel:* 513-221-1875 ext 3245 *E-mail:* rsaranson@huc.edu
Proj Mgr: Angela Roskop Erisman *Tel:* 513-487-3035 ext 3335 *E-mail:* aerisman@huc.edu
Mng Ed: Sonja Rethy
Founded: 1921
Scholarly Jewish books.
ISBN Prefix(es): 978-0-87820
Number of titles published annually: 11 Print
Total Titles: 100 Print
Distributed by Wayne State University Press

Heian
Imprint of Stone Bridge Press Inc
1393 Solono Ave, Albany, CA 94706
Tel: 510-524-8732 *Toll Free Fax:* 888-411-8527
E-mail: sbp@stonebridge.com
Web Site: www.stonebridge.com
Key Personnel
Founder & Publr: Peter Goodman
Founded: 1973 (acquired by Stone Bridge Press in 2009)
General trade, juvenile; languages, dictionaries & literature, Oriental culture, customs, philosophy & religion; classic Japanese art calendars & books.
ISBN Prefix(es): 978-0-89346
Number of titles published annually: 8 Print
Total Titles: 40 Print

Heimburger House Publishing Co
7236 W Madison St, Forest Park, IL 60130
Tel: 708-366-1973 *Fax:* 708-366-1973
E-mail: info@heimburgerhouse.com
Web Site: www.heimburgerhouse.com
Key Personnel
Publr: Donald J Heimburger
Founded: 1962
Publish books & magazines on railroad & other transportation subjects; list includes more than 300 book titles.
ISBN Prefix(es): 978-0-911581
Number of titles published annually: 3 Print
Total Titles: 75 Print
Distributor for Child's Play International; Evergreen Press; Firefly Books Ltd; Fordham University Press; Globe Pequot Press; HarperCollins; Johns Hopkins University Press; Houghton Mifflin Harcourt; Iconografix; Indiana University Press; Kalmbach Publishing; Krause Publications; Motorbooks International; National Book Network; New York University Press; W W Norton & Company Inc; Penguin Putnam Inc; Pictorial Histories Publishing Co; Steam Passages Publishing; Sterling Publishing; Sugar Cane Press; Syracuse University Press; Thunder Bay Press; University of Minnesota Press; John Wiley & Sons

§William S Hein & Co Inc
2350 N Forest Rd, Getzville, NY 14068
Tel: 716-882-2600 *Toll Free Tel:* 800-828-7571 *Fax:* 716-883-8100
E-mail: mail@wshein.com; marketing@wshein.com
Web Site: www.wshein.com
Key Personnel
Chmn of the Bd: William S Hein, Jr *E-mail:* whein@wshein.com
Pres: Kevin M Marmion *Tel:* 716-882-2600 ext 115 *E-mail:* kmarmion@wshein.com
SVP: Daniel Rosati *E-mail:* drosati@wshein.com
Mktg Dir: Tim Hooge *E-mail:* thooge@wshein.com
Founded: 1961
Publish & reprint law & related materials, hard copy, micro, CDs & online products.
ISBN Prefix(es): 978-0-8377; 978-0-89941; 978-1-57588
Number of titles published annually: 30 Print; 2 CD-ROM; 1 Online
Total Titles: 5,000 Print; 5 CD-ROM; 2 Online
Distributor for Ashgate; Aspen; Butterworths; Sweet & Maxwell; John Wiley & Sons Inc
Membership(s): American Association of Law Libraries; Canadian Association of Law Libraries; Library Binding Institute

§Heinemann
Division of Houghton Mifflin Harcourt
361 Hanover St, Portsmouth, NH 03801-3912
SAN: 210-5829
Mailing Address: PO Box 6926, Portsmouth, NH 03802-6926
Tel: 603-431-7894 *Toll Free Tel:* 800-225-5800 (US) *Fax:* 603-431-2214 *Toll Free Fax:* 877-231-6980 (US)
E-mail: custserv@heinemann.com
Web Site: www.heinemann.com
Key Personnel
Pres: Vicki Boyd *E-mail:* vicki.boyd@heinemann.com
Founded: 1978
Education - professional books for teachers K-college. Literacy, math, social studies, drama, art & English teaching. Hardcover & paperbound. Trade - drama, world literature, education, African studies. Hardcover & paperbound class.
ISBN Prefix(es): 978-0-86709; 978-0-434; 978-0-325; 978-1-59469; 978-0-435
Number of titles published annually: 115 Print
Total Titles: 1,500 Print
Distributed by Pearson (Canada, Australia & New Zealand)
See separate listing for:
Boynton/Cook Publishers

§Hellgate Press
Imprint of L & R Publishing
PO Box 3531, Ashland, OR 97520
Tel: 541-973-5154 *Toll Free Tel:* 800-795-4059
E-mail: sales@hellgatepress.com
Web Site: www.hellgatepress.com
Key Personnel
Owner: Harley B Patrick *E-mail:* harley@hellgatepress.com
Founded: 1997
Military history, adventure travel, veteran memoirs, historical & adventure fiction.
ISBN Prefix(es): 978-1-55571
Number of titles published annually: 15 Print
Total Titles: 80 Print

Shipping Address: Midpoint Trade Books, 27 W 20 St, New York, NY 10011 *Tel:* 212-727-0190 *Fax:* 212-727-0195 *Web Site:* www.midpointtrade.com

§Helm Book Publishing
3437 Huntington Place Dr, Sarasota, FL 34237
SAN: 254-7562
Tel: 727-623-5014
Web Site: www.helmbookpublishing.com
Key Personnel
CEO: Dianne Helm *E-mail:* dianne@helmbookpublishing.com
Founded: 1994
Specialize in new & emerging authors in fiction/nonfiction genres.
This publisher has indicated that 50% of their product line is author subsidized.
ISBN Prefix(es): 978-0-9723011; 978-0-9760919; 978-0-9769193; 978-0-0930109; 978-0-9850488; 978-0-9841397; 978-0-9820605; 978-0-9801780; 978-0-9792328; 978-0-9778205
Number of titles published annually: 8 Print; 1 CD-ROM; 15 E-Book
Total Titles: 120 Print; 1 CD-ROM; 75 E-Book
Membership(s): ABA

Hendrickson Publishers Inc
PO Box 3473, Peabody, MA 01961-3473
Tel: 978-532-6546 *Toll Free Tel:* 800-358-3111 *Fax:* 978-573-8111
E-mail: orders@hendrickson.com
Web Site: www.hendrickson.com
Key Personnel
Sales: Bobby Koduvalil *E-mail:* bkoduvalil@hendrickson.com
Contract & Licensing/Digital Publg/Systems Mgr: Kris Orlando
Founded: 1978
Religious reference, language, history & theology.
ISBN Prefix(es): 978-0-913573; 978-0-943575; 978-0-917006; 978-1-56563
Number of titles published annually: 40 Print; 3 CD-ROM
Total Titles: 450 Print
Foreign Rep(s): Alban Books Ltd (Europe, UK)
Foreign Rights: KCBS (Korea)
Orders to: David C Cook Distribution Canada, 55 Woodslee Ave, PO Box 98, Paris, ON N3L 3E5, Canada (CN) *Toll Free Tel:* 800-263-2664 *Toll Free Fax:* 800-461-8575 *E-mail:* custserv@davidccook.ca *Web Site:* www.davidccook.ca; Alban Books Ltd, 14 Belford Rd, Edinburgh, Scotland EH4 3BL, United Kingdom *Tel:* (0131) 226 2217 *Fax:* (0131) 225 5999 *E-mail:* sales@albanbooks.com *Web Site:* www.albanbooks.com

Her Own Words LLC
PO Box 5264, Madison, WI 53705-0264
Tel: 608-271-7083 *Fax:* 608-271-0209
Web Site: www.herownwords.com; www.nontraditionalcareers.com
Key Personnel
Mgr: Jocelyn Riley *E-mail:* jocelynriley@herownwords.com
Founded: 1986
Women's history, literature, arts & women in non-traditional careers.
ISBN Prefix(es): 978-1-60118
Number of titles published annually: 3 Print; 3 Audio
Total Titles: 36 Print; 36 Audio
Imprints: Women In Nontraditional Careers

Herald Press
Imprint of MennoMedia
1251 Virginia Ave, Harrisonburg, VA 22802-2434
SAN: 202-2915
Toll Free Tel: 800-245-7894 (orders) *Toll Free Fax:* 877-271-0760
E-mail: info@MennoMedia.org
Web Site: www.heraldpress.com; store.mennomedia.org
Key Personnel
Exec Dir, MennoMedia: Russ Eanes *E-mail:* russe@mennomedia.org
Edit Dir: Amy Gingerich *E-mail:* amyg@mennomedia.org
Congregational Mktg & Sales Mgr, US: Josh Byler *E-mail:* joshb@mennomedia.org
Founded: 1908
General Christian trade books, family, devotional, cookbooks, juveniles, adult fiction, Bible study, theology, peace & social concerns, missions, Amish & Mennonite history & culture, songbooks.
ISBN Prefix(es): 978-0-8361
Number of titles published annually: 20 Print
Total Titles: 500 Print
Branch Office(s)
718 N Main St, Newton, KS 67114 *Tel:* 316-281-4412 *Toll Free Tel:* 800-245-7894 ext 220 *Fax:* 316-283-0454
Membership(s): CBA: The Association for Christian Retail; Evangelical Christian Publishers Association

Herald Publishing House
Division of Community of Christ
1001 W Walnut St, Independence, MO 64051
SAN: 202-2907
Mailing Address: PO Box 390, Independence, MO 64051-0390
Tel: 816-521-3015 *Toll Free Tel:* 800-767-8181 *Fax:* 816-521-3066
E-mail: sales@heraldhouse.org
Web Site: www.heraldhouse.org
Key Personnel
Fiscal Servs Specialist: Suzan Hudson
Founded: 1860
ISBN Prefix(es): 978-0-8309
Number of titles published annually: 12 Print
Total Titles: 360 Print
Imprints: Independence Press

Heritage Books Inc
5810 Ruatan St, Berwyn Heights, MD 20740
Toll Free Tel: 800-876-6103 *Toll Free Fax:* 800-876-6103
E-mail: orders@heritagebooks.com; submissions@heritagebooks.com
Web Site: www.heritagebooks.com
Key Personnel
Pres & CEO: Craig R Scott *E-mail:* crscott@heritagebooks.com
Founded: 1978
Books on local history, genealogy & Americana.
ISBN Prefix(es): 978-0-917890; 978-1-55613; 978-0-7884; 978-1-58549; 978-0-940907; 978-1-888265
Number of titles published annually: 200 Print; 5 CD-ROM; 200 E-Book
Total Titles: 5,300 Print; 1,200 CD-ROM; 2,000 E-Book
Imprints: Eagle Editions; Fireside Fiction; Heritage Books; Willow Bend Books
Distributor for Fairfax Genealogical Society; National Genealogical Society; Virginia Genealogical Society

§The Heritage Foundation
214 Massachusetts Ave NE, Washington, DC 20002-4999
Tel: 202-546-4400 *Toll Free Tel:* 800-544-4843 *Fax:* 202-546-8328
E-mail: info@heritage.org
Web Site: www.heritage.org
Key Personnel
Pres: Jim DeMint
Creative Dir: Melissa Bluey
Founded: 1973
Domestic policy, foreign policy & defense.
ISBN Prefix(es): 978-0-89195
Number of titles published annually: 10 Print; 2 CD-ROM
Total Titles: 19 Print; 2 CD-ROM; 8 E-Book

Heuer Publishing LLC
PO Box 248, Cedar Rapids, IA 52406
Tel: 319-368-8008 *Toll Free Tel:* 800-950-7529 *Fax:* 319-368-8011
E-mail: editor@heuerpub.com; customerservice@heuerpub.com
Web Site: www.hitplays.com
Key Personnel
Publr: Steven S Michalicek
Ed: Ms Geri Albrecht
Founded: 1928
Publishes plays, musicals, operas/operettas & guides (choreography, costume, production/staging) for amateur & professional markets including junior & senior high schools, college/university & community theatres. Focus includes comedy, drama, fantasy, mystery & holiday with special interest focus in multicultural, historic, classic literature, Shakespearian theatre, interactive, teen issues & biographies. Pays by percentage royalty or outright purchase.
ISBN Prefix(es): 978-1-61588
Number of titles published annually: 25 Print
Total Titles: 150 Print

Hewitt Homeschooling Resources
Division of Hewitt Research Foundation
3140 Evergreen Way, Washougal, WA 98671
Mailing Address: PO Box 9, Washougal, WA 98671
Tel: 360-835-8708 *Toll Free Tel:* 800-348-1750 *Fax:* 360-835-8697
E-mail: sales@hewitthomeschooling.com
Web Site: hewitthomeschooling.com
Key Personnel
Pres: April Purtell
Founded: 1964
Homeschooling, curriculum.
ISBN Prefix(es): 978-0-913717; 978-1-57896
Number of titles published annually: 6 Print
Total Titles: 150 Print

Heyday Books
1633 University Ave, Berkeley, CA 94703
SAN: 207-2351
Mailing Address: PO Box 9145, Berkeley, CA 94709-0145
Tel: 510-549-3564 *Fax:* 510-549-1889
E-mail: heyday@heydaybooks.com; orders@heydaybooks.com
Web Site: heydaybooks.com
Key Personnel
Publr & Exec Dir: Steve Wasserman
Edit Dir: Gayle Wattawa
Exec Ed: Narda Zacchino
Founded: 1974
Nonprofit company that specializes in California Indians, California history & literature, regional conservation & ecology; women of California; literary anthologies; Asian-American; art & photography.
ISBN Prefix(es): 978-0-930588; 978-1-890771; 978-0-9666691; 978-1-59714
Number of titles published annually: 25 Print
Total Titles: 110 Print
Imprints: Sierra College Press
Returns: Heyday Books, c/o Fulfillco, 2801 Merced St, San Leandro, CA 94577
Warehouse: Heyday Books, c/o Fulfillco, 2801 Merced St, San Leandro, CA 94577

Hi Willow Research & Publishing
123 E Second Ave, Suite 1106, Salt Lake City, UT 84103
Tel: 801-755-1122
E-mail: lmcsourcesales@gmail.com
Web Site: www.lmcsource.com; www.davidvl.org

Key Personnel
Owner: David V Loertscher
Founded: 1978
Books for schools & libraries.
ISBN Prefix(es): 978-0-931510; 978-1-933170
Number of titles published annually: 8 Print
Total Titles: 35 Print

Higginson Book Co
10 Colonial Rd, Salem, MA 01970
Mailing Address: PO Box 778, Salem, MA 01970
Tel: 978-745-7170 *Fax:* 978-745-8025
Web Site: www.higginsonbooks.com
Key Personnel
Mgr: Robert Murphy *E-mail:* robert.murphy1945@yahoo.com
Founded: 1969
Publish reprints of rare & out of print genealogies, local history & Civil War regimentals.
ISBN Prefix(es): 978-0-8328; 978-0-7404
Number of titles published annually: 200 Print
Total Titles: 15,000 Print

High Plains Press
PO Box 123, Glendo, WY 82213
Tel: 307-735-4370 *Toll Free Tel:* 800-552-7819 *Fax:* 307-735-4590
E-mail: editor@highplainspress.com
Web Site: highplainspress.com
Key Personnel
Publr & Primary Ed: Nancy Curtis
Founded: 1984
Books about Wyoming & the American West.
ISBN Prefix(es): 978-0-931271
Number of titles published annually: 3 Print; 3 E-Book
Total Titles: 70 Print; 15 E-Book; 1 Audio
Membership(s): Independent Book Publishers Association; Publishers Association of the West

High Tide Press
Subsidiary of The Trinity Foundation
301 Veterans Pkwy, New Lenox, IL 60451
Web Site: cherryhillhightide.com/high-tide-press/
Key Personnel
Dir: Anne C Ward *Tel:* 800-235-6009 *E-mail:* award@hightidepress.com
Founded: 1995
Full service publisher of hardcover & paperback books & one quarterly magazine for the book trade & professional niche markets. Specialize in the fields of developmental & intellectual disabilities, behavioral health, nonprofit management, social enterprise, leadership. The High Tide Monograph Series imprint focuses on high quality management practices in behavioral health & developmental disability services while the Midewin Series focuses on the prevention of abuse & neglect of persons with disabilities.
ISBN Prefix(es): 978-0-9653744; 978-1-892696
Number of titles published annually: 12 Print; 4 Online; 4 E-Book
Total Titles: 46 Print; 1 E-Book
Imprints: High Tide Monograph Series; Midewin Series
Orders to: Cherry Hill Bookstore, 1805 Ferro Dr, New Lenox, IL 60451 (part of Trinity Foundation), Cust Serv: Terra Radetski *Tel:* 815-723-0898 *Toll Free Tel:* 800-235-6009 *Fax:* 815-723-2760 *E-mail:* terra@cherryhillbooks.com *Web Site:* www.cherryhillbooks.com
Membership(s): Independent Book Publishers Association

Highlights for Children
1800 Watermark Dr, Columbus, OH 43215
Mailing Address: PO Box 269, Columbus, OH 43216-0269
Tel: 614-486-0631 *Toll Free Tel:* 800-962-3661 (Highlights Club cust serv); 800-255-9517 (Highlights Magazine cust serv)
Web Site: www.highlights.com; www.facebook.com/HighlightsforChildren
Key Personnel
CEO: Kent S Johnson
VP, Book Edit: Liz Van Doren
VP, Print & Ebook Sales: Jack W Perry
VP, Publg Strategy & Prod Devt: Mary-Alice Moore
Assoc Publr & Dir, Book Mktg, Highlights Retail Group: Michael Eisenberg
Dir, Retail Specialty & Gift Sales, Highlights Press & Boyds Mills Press: Janine Webb
Prodn Dir: Sue Cole
Ed-in-Chief (PA Off): Christine French Cully
Mng Ed, Highlights Retail Group: Amy Nathanson Heaslip
Sr Ed: Mary Colgan
Mgr, Retail Planning & Allocation: Ed White
Retail Mktg Mgr, Highlights Press: Monica Jankauskas
Founded: 1946
ISBN Prefix(es): 978-0-87534
Number of titles published annually: 150 Print
Imprints: Highlights Press
Editorial Office(s): 803 Church St, Honesdale, PA 18431 *Tel:* 570-253-1080 *Fax:* 570-251-7847
Distribution Center: Penguin Random House Publisher Services, 1745 Broadway, New York, NY 10019 *E-mail:* distribution@randomhouse.com

Hill & Wang
Division of Farrar, Straus & Giroux, LLC
18 W 18 St, New York, NY 10011
SAN: 201-9299
Tel: 212-741-6900 *Fax:* 212-633-9385
E-mail: fsg.publicity@fsgbooks.com; fsg.editorial@fsgbooks.com; sales@fsgbooks.com
Web Site: us.macmillan.com/hillandwang.aspx
Key Personnel
SVP, Mktg & Publicity, FSG: Jeff Seroy
VP & Contracts Dir, FSG: Erika Seidman
VP, Publicity: Sarita Varma
Dir, Ad & Promo, FSG: Victoria Genna
Founded: 1956
General nonfiction, history & drama.
ISBN Prefix(es): 978-0-8090
Number of titles published annually: 10 Print
Foreign Rights: ANA Baltic (Tatjana Zoldnere) (Estonia, Latvia, Lithuania); AnatoliaLit Agency (Amy Spangler & Eda Caca) (Turkey); Anthea Agency (Katalina Sabeva) (Bulgaria); L'Autre Agency (Corinne Marotte & Marie Lannurien) (France); Bardon-Chinese Media (David Tsai) (China, Taiwan); Anoukh Foerg Agency (Germany); Deborah Harris Agency (Geula Geurts) (Israel); International Copyright Agency (Simon Kessler & Marina Adriana) (Romania); The Italian Literary Agency srl (Claire Sabatie-Garat) (Italy); Anna Jarota Agency (Dominika Bojanowska) (Poland); Katai & Bolza (Peter Bolza) (Hungary); KCC (Kyung Kang) (Korea); MB Agencia Literaria (Monica Martin & Ines Planells) (Latin America, Spain); Kristin Olson Literarni Agentura (Czech Republic); Plima Literary Agency (Vuk Perisic) (Albania, Croatia, Serbia, Slovenia); Read 'n Right Agency (Nike Davarinou) (Greece); Riff Agency (Laura & Joao Paulo Riff) (Brazil); Sebes & Bisseling Literary Agency (Paul Sebes) (Netherlands); Synopsis Literary Agency (Olga Zasetskaya) (Russia); Tuttle-Mori Agency Inc (Asako Kawachi) (Japan)
Warehouse: MPS Distribution Center, 16365 James Madison Hwy, Gordonsville, VA 22942 *Toll Free Tel:* 888-330-8477

Lawrence Hill Books, see Chicago Review Press

Hillsdale College Press
Division of Hillsdale College
33 E College St, Hillsdale, MI 49242
Tel: 517-437-7341 *Toll Free Tel:* 800-437-2268 *Fax:* 517-607-2658
E-mail: news@hillsdale.edu
Web Site: www.hillsdale.edu
Key Personnel
Ed & VP, External Aff: Douglas A Jeffrey *Tel:* 517-607-2319
Founded: 1974
Single author books & collected essays of historical, political & economic interest.
ISBN Prefix(es): 978-0-916308

Hillsdale Educational Publishers Inc
39 North St, Hillsdale, MI 49242
SAN: 159-8759
Tel: 517-437-3179 *Fax:* 517-437-0531
E-mail: davestory@aol.com
Web Site: www.hillsdalepublishers.com; michbooks.com
Key Personnel
Pres & Author: David B McConnell
Founded: 1965
Publish & distribute regional titles for schools & libraries.
ISBN Prefix(es): 978-0-910726; 978-1-931466
Number of titles published annually: 4 Print; 1 CD-ROM; 1 Audio
Total Titles: 18 Print; 1 CD-ROM; 1 Audio

§Hilton Publishing
1630 45 St, Suite 103, Munster, IN 46321
Tel: 219-922-4868 *Fax:* 219-924-6811
E-mail: info@hiltonpub.com; orders@hiltonpub.com
Web Site: www.hiltonpub.com
Key Personnel
Dir, Mktg & Publg: Megan Lippert *E-mail:* mlippert@hiltonpub.com
Mktg Proj Mgr: Martha Jimenez
Founded: 1996
Publish books in health & wellness, minority health, religion (health-related). Consistent themes of publications include living with & preventing various disease states, illustrating & promoting components of healthy living, embracing & illuminating cultural diversity related to health & well-being & fostering health in the Christian community. Books are peer reviewed by experts in the appropriate fields to insure we have included the most current, accurate & relevant information. We publish informative & educational books for the general public as well as books aimed at the medical community.
ISBN Prefix(es): 978-0-9654553; 978-0-9675258; 978-0-9716067; 978-0-9743144; 978-0-9764443; 978-0-9773160; 978-0-9777779; 978-0-9800649; 978-0-9815381; 978-0-9841447; 978-0-9847566
Number of titles published annually: 12 Print; 3 CD-ROM; 12 Online; 7 E-Book; 3 Audio
Total Titles: 50 Print; 3 CD-ROM; 50 Online; 7 E-Book; 3 Audio
Foreign Rep(s): Gabriel Wilmoth (Canada, Germany, USA)
Foreign Rights: Nigel Yorwerth (worldwide)
Membership(s): Indiana Minority Supplier Development Council; National Minority Supplier Development Council; North Carolina Ministry Supplier Development Council

Himalayan Institute Press
Division of Himalayan International Institute of Yoga Science & Philosophy
952 Bethany Tpke, Honesdale, PA 18431
Tel: 570-253-5551 *Toll Free Tel:* 800-822-4547
E-mail: info@himalayaninstitute.org
Web Site: www.himalayaninstitute.org
Key Personnel
Chmn & Spiritual Head: Pandit Rajmani Tigunait, PhD

Dir: Stephen Moulton
Founded: 1971
Publish CDs, DVDs & books on yoga, meditation, holistic health, philosophy, psychology & stress management.
ISBN Prefix(es): 978-0-89389
Number of titles published annually: 4 Print; 3 E-Book; 2 Audio
Total Titles: 60 Print; 10 Audio
Foreign Rights: Hagenbach & Bender GmbH (worldwide)

§Hippocrene Books Inc
171 Madison Ave, New York, NY 10016
Tel: 212-685-4373 *Fax:* 212-779-9338
E-mail: info@hippocrenebooks.com; orderdept@hippocrenebooks.com (orders)
Web Site: www.hippocrenebooks.com
Key Personnel
Publr & Edit Dir: Priti Chitnis Gress *E-mail:* pgress@hippocrenebooks.com
Fin Offr: Awilda Alvarez *E-mail:* aalvarez@hippocrenebooks.com
Publicity Mgr & Ed: Colette Laroya *Tel:* 212-685-4371 *E-mail:* claroya@hippocrenebooks.com
Sales Acct Mgr: Melissa Santana *E-mail:* msantana@hippocrenebooks.com
Founded: 1971
Foreign language dictionaries & self-study guides in over 120 languages; international cookbooks, history & travel.
ISBN Prefix(es): 978-0-87052; 978-0-7818
Number of titles published annually: 25 Print
Total Titles: 500 Print; 150 E-Book
Foreign Rights: A B E Marketing (Poland); Bookery Pty Ltd (Australia); Gazelle Book Services Ltd (England); Publishers Group Canada (Canada)
Shipping Address: Whitehurst & Clark Book Services, 1200 County Rd, Rte 523, Flemington, NJ 08822
Warehouse: Whitehurst & Clark Book Services, 1200 County Rd, Rte 523, Flemington, NJ 08822
Membership(s): Independent Book Publishers Association

The Historic New Orleans Collection
533 Royal St, New Orleans, LA 70130
Tel: 504-523-4662 *Fax:* 504-598-7108
E-mail: wrc@hnoc.org
Web Site: www.hnoc.org
Key Personnel
Exec Dir: Priscilla Lawrence *Tel:* 504-598-7127 *E-mail:* priscill@hnoc.org
Dir, Pubns & Mktg: Dr Jessica Dorman *Tel:* 504-598-7174 *E-mail:* jessicad@hnoc.org
Founded: 1966
Publications related to Louisiana history & to the holdings of The Historic New Orleans Collection; preservation manuals for family papers, photographs, etc.
ISBN Prefix(es): 978-0-917860
Number of titles published annually: 3 Print
Total Titles: 54 Print

§History Publishing Co LLC
PO Box 700, Palisades, NY 10964
SAN: 850-5942
Tel: 845-359-1765 *Fax:* 845-818-3730 (sales)
E-mail: info@historypublishingco.com
Web Site: www.historypublishingco.com
Key Personnel
Owner & Publr: Don Bracken *E-mail:* djb@historypublishingco.com
Sr Ed: Alexis Starke *E-mail:* alex@historypublishingco.com
Founded: 2007
Trade book publisher. HPC imprint for early & recent history. Chronology books for history from a third party perspective, *Today's Books* for current issues. Introduced 2 new imprints in 2017 one for historical fiction & one for issues dealing with contemporary issues.
ISBN Prefix(es): 978-19339-09; 978-19407-73
Number of titles published annually: 12 Print; 75 Online; 100 E-Book
Total Titles: 75 Print; 75 Online; 100 E-Book
Imprints: Chronology Books; History Publishing Company (early & recent history); Today's Books; Today's Titles
Warehouse: Whitehurst & Clark, 1200 County Rte 523, Flemington, NJ 08822 *Tel:* 908-782-2323 *Fax:* 908-237-2407 *Web Site:* www.wcbks.com
Distribution Center: INscribe Digital, 444 Spear St, Suite 213, San Francisco, CA 94105
Membership(s): AAP; Independent Book Publishers Association

W D Hoard & Sons Co
28 W Milwaukee Ave, Fort Atkinson, WI 53538
Mailing Address: PO Box 801, Fort Atkinson, WI 53538-0801
Tel: 920-563-5551 *Fax:* 920-563-7298
E-mail: hdbooks@hoards.com; editors@hoards.com
Web Site: www.hoards.com; www.hoardprinting.com
Key Personnel
Book Ed: Maggie Seiler
Founded: 1870
Dairy oriented & some agricultural, regional publications, catalogs & specialty projects.
ISBN Prefix(es): 978-0-932147
Number of titles published annually: 5 Print
Total Titles: 22 Print
Imprints: Hoard's Dairyman Magazine

Hobar Publications
Division of Finney Company Inc
5995 149 St W, Suite 105, Apple Valley, MN 55124
Tel: 952-469-6699 *Toll Free Tel:* 800-846-7027 *Fax:* 952-469-1968 *Toll Free Fax:* 800-330-6232
E-mail: info@finneyco.com
Web Site: www.finney-hobar.com
Key Personnel
Pres: Alan E Krysan
Founded: 1964
Produces educational materials for grades 7-12 in the areas of agriculture, career exploration & guidance & technical education.
ISBN Prefix(es): 978-0-913163; 978-0-9616847
Number of titles published annually: 4 Print
Total Titles: 45 Print
Imprints: Agronomy Publications; K A Publishing
Divisions: National Farm Book Co
Distributor for Drache Publications
Membership(s): National Association of Agriculture Educators

§Hobbes End Publishing LLC
Subsidiary of Hobbes End Entertainment LLC
PO Box 193, Aubrey, TX 76227
Web Site: hobbesendpublishing.com
Founded: 2005
Specialize in adult fiction, children's fiction, fantasy, science fiction & horror.
ISBN Prefix(es): 978-0-9763510; 978-0-9859110
Number of titles published annually: 3 Print
Total Titles: 22 Print

Hobblebush Books
17-A Old Milford Rd, Brookline, NH 03033
Tel: 603-672-4317 *Fax:* 603-672-4317
E-mail: hobblebush@charter.net; info@hobblebush.com
Web Site: www.hobblebush.com
Key Personnel
Owner & Pres: Mr Sidney Hall, Jr
Mktg Dir: Kirsty Walker
Founded: 1993
Independent publisher of both literary & non-literary titles.
ISBN Prefix(es): 978-0-9636413; 978-0-9760896; 978-0-9801672; 978-1-939449
Number of titles published annually: 3 Print; 3 E-Book
Total Titles: 37 Print; 3 E-Book
Orders to: Small Press Distributors, 1341 Seventh St, Berkeley, CA 94710-1409 (bookstores & libs) *Toll Free Tel:* 800-869-7553 *Fax:* 510-524-0852 *Web Site:* www.spdbooks.org; Baker & Taylor, 2550 W Tyvola Rd, Suite 300, Charlotte, NC 28217 (trade) *Tel:* 704-998-3100 *Toll Free Tel:* 800-775-1800 *E-mail:* btinfo@btol.com *Web Site:* www.btol.com
Distribution Center: Small Press Distributors, 1341 Seventh St, Berkeley, CA 94710-1409 (bookstores & libs) *Toll Free Tel:* 800-869-7553 *Fax:* 510-524-0852 *Web Site:* www.spdbooks.org
Quality Books Inc, 1003 W Pines Rd, Oregon, IL 61061 *Toll Free Tel:* 800-323-4241 *Fax:* 815-732-4499 *Web Site:* www.quality-books.com
Baker & Taylor, 2550 W Tyvola Rd, Suite 300, Charlotte, NC 28217 (trade) *Tel:* 704-998-3100 *Toll Free Tel:* 800-775-1800 *Web Site:* www.btol.com
Membership(s): Community of Literary Magazines & Presses; Independent Publishers of New England; New Hampshire Writers Project

§Hogrefe Publishing Corp
Subsidiary of Hogrefe Verlag GmbH & Co Kg
7 Bulfinch Place, Suite 202, Boston, MA 02114
SAN: 293-2792
Toll Free Tel: 866-823-4726 *Fax:* 617-354-6875
E-mail: publishing@hogrefe.com; customerservice@hogrefe-publishing.com
Web Site: us.hogrefe.com
Key Personnel
Publg Mgr: Robert Dimbleby *E-mail:* robert.dimbleby@hogrefe.com
Founded: 1978
Books, journals & online resources in the fields of psychiatry, psychology, psychotherapy, medicine.
ISBN Prefix(es): 978-0-88937; 978-0-920887; 978-1-61676 (ebooks); 978-1-61334 (EPUB)
Number of titles published annually: 15 Print
Foreign Office(s): Hogrefe Verlag GmbH & Co Kg, Merkelstr 3, 37085 Goettingen, Germany *Tel:* (0551) 999 50-0 *Fax:* (0551) 999 50
Distributor for Verlag Hans Huber Hogrefe AG (Switzerland); Hogrefe Verlag (Germany)
Orders to: Bookmasters, 30 Amberwood Pkwy, Ashland, OH 44805, Dist Servs Mgr: Cheryl Householder *Tel:* 419-281-1802 *Toll Free Tel:* 800-228-3749 *Fax:* 419-281-6883
Returns: Bookmasters, 30 Amberwood Pkwy, Ashland, OH 44805, Dist Servs Mgr: Cheryl Householder *Tel:* 419-281-1802 *Toll Free Tel:* 800-228-3749 *Fax:* 419-281-6883
Distribution Center: Bookmasters, 30 Amberwood Pkwy, Ashland, OH 44805, Dist Servs Mgr: Cheryl Householder *Tel:* 419-281-1802 *Toll Free Tel:* 800-228-3749 *Fax:* 419-281-6883
Membership(s): AAP; STM

Hohm Press
Subsidiary of HSM LLC
PO Box 4410, Chino Valley, AZ 86323
Tel: 928-636-3331 *Toll Free Tel:* 800-381-2700 *Fax:* 928-636-7519
E-mail: hppublisher@cableone.net; hohmpresseditor@gmail.com
Web Site: www.hohmpress.com
Key Personnel
Gen Mgr & Publr: Dasya Anthony Zuccarello
Mng Ed: Regina Sara Ryan
Prodn Mgr: Joe Bala Zuccarello
Founded: 1975

Independent publisher of books on spirituality & consciousness studies.
ISBN Prefix(es): 978-0-934252; 978-1-890772
Number of titles published annually: 8 Print; 8 E-Book
Total Titles: 180 Print; 30 E-Book; 6 Audio
Imprints: Kalindi Press (books on natural health & nutrition, children's & family health)
Foreign Rep(s): Gazelle Book Services Ltd (Europe)
Foreign Rights: Hagenbach & Bender GmbH (Deanna Leah) (worldwide exc USA)
Shipping Address: 860 Staley Lane, Chino Valley, AZ 86323
Warehouse: 860 Staley Lane, Chino Valley, AZ 86323
Distribution Center: SCB Distributors, 15608 S New Century Dr, Gardena, CA 90248 (US & CN) *Toll Free Tel:* 800-729-6423 *Web Site:* www.scbdistributors.com

Holiday House Inc
425 Madison Ave, New York, NY 10017
SAN: 202-3008
Tel: 212-688-0085 *Fax:* 212-421-6134
E-mail: info@holidayhouse.com
Web Site: www.holidayhouse.com
Key Personnel
EVP & Gen Mgr: Derek Stordahl
VP & Ed-in-Chief: Mary Cash *E-mail:* mcash@holidayhouse.com
VP, Mktg: Terry Borzumato-Greenberg *E-mail:* tborzumato@holidayhouse.com
VP, Rts, Perms & Digital Publg: Julia Gallagher *E-mail:* jgallagher@holidayhouse.com
VP & Publr, Neal Porter Books: Neal Porter
Publr, Margaret Ferguson Books: Margaret Ferguson
Dir, Art & Design: Claire Counihan *E-mail:* ccounihan@holidayhouse.com
VP & Dir of Prodn: Lisa Lee-Pitts *E-mail:* llee@holidayhouse.com
Dir of Opers: Lisa Morales-Pitts *E-mail:* lisamorales@holidayhouse.com
Exec Ed: Grace Maccarone *E-mail:* gmaccarone@holidayhouse.com
Consulting Ed: Julie Amper *E-mail:* jamper@holidayhouse.com
Assoc Ed: Kelly Loughman *E-mail:* kloughman@holidayhouse.com
Asst Ed: Sally Morgridge *E-mail:* smorgridge@holidayhouse.com
Mktg Assoc: Sabrina Aballe *E-mail:* saballe@holidayhouse.com
Cust Serv: Kathryn Hoban *E-mail:* khoban@holidayhouse.com
Founded: 1935
Juvenile & young adult books.
ISBN Prefix(es): 978-0-8234
Number of titles published annually: 90 Print
Total Titles: 800 Print; 300 E-Book
Imprints: Margaret Ferguson Books; Neal Porter Books
Foreign Rep(s): Thomas Allen & Son Ltd (Canada)
Foreign Rights: Big Apple Agency Inc (China, Taiwan); Caroline Hill-Trevor (Europe exc Germany, Israel, Scandinavia, Spanish, Turkey, UK Commonwealth); Korea Copyright Center (Korea); Tuttle-Mori (Indonesia, Japan, Thailand, Vietnam); Silke Weniger (Austria, Germany)
Shipping Address: Maple Logistics Solutions, Mount Joy Distribution Ctr, 1000 Strickler Rd, Mount Joy, PA 17552 *Tel:* 717-653-5483
Distribution Center: Penguin Random House Publisher Services, 1745 Broadway, New York, NY 10019
Membership(s): The Children's Book Council

Hollym International Corp
18 Donald Place, Elizabeth, NJ 07208
SAN: 211-0172
Tel: 908-353-1655 *Fax:* 908-353-0255
E-mail: contact@hollym.com
Web Site: www.hollym.com
Key Personnel
Pres: Gene S Rhie
Founded: 1977
Publish & distribute books in English on Korea related topics.
ISBN Prefix(es): 978-0-930878; 978-1-56591
Number of titles published annually: 10 Print
Total Titles: 155 Print
Foreign Office(s): Hollym Corp, 13-13 Gwancheol-dong, Jongno-gu, 110-111 Seoul, South Korea, Contact: Kim-Man Ham *Tel:* (02) 735-7551 *Fax:* (02) 730-5149 *E-mail:* info@hollym.co.kr *Web Site:* www.hollym.co.kr

Hollywood Film Archive
8391 Beverly Blvd, Los Angeles, CA 90048
Tel: 323-655-4968
Web Site: hfarchive.com
Key Personnel
Dir: D Richard Baer
Dir, Admin: Howard Schiller
Founded: 1972
Publication, sales & distribution of comprehensive movie, video & TV reference books.
ISBN Prefix(es): 978-0-913616
Number of titles published annually: 3 Print
Total Titles: 50 Print
Advertising Agency: Tartan Advertising

Holmes Publishing Group LLC
PO Box 2370, Sequim, WA 98382
Tel: 360-681-2900
E-mail: holmespub@fastmail.fm
Web Site: www.jdholmes.com
Key Personnel
CEO & Pres: J D Holmes *E-mail:* jdholmes@fastmail.fm
Founded: 1971
Specialize in antiquarian, secondhand & rare books, as well as esoteric publications.
ISBN Prefix(es): 978-1-55818; 978-0-916411
Number of titles published annually: 16 Print
Total Titles: 389 Print
Imprints: Alchemical Press; Alexandrian Press; Contra/Thought; Holmes Publishing Group; Near Eastern Press; Sure Fire Press
Distributor for Capall-Bann (UK); Edda Publishing (Sweden); Fulgur Ltd (UK); Jerusalem Press (UK); Starfire Publishing (UK); Theion Publishing (Germany); Three Hands Press (US); Xoanon Publishing (US)
Distribution Center: New Leaf Distributing Co, 401 Thornton Rd, Lithia Springs, GA 30122-1557 *Tel:* 770-948-7845 *Fax:* 770-944-2313 *Web Site:* www.newleaf-dist.com

Henry Holt and Company, LLC
Division of Macmillan
175 Fifth Ave, New York, NY 10010
SAN: 200-2108
Tel: 646-307-5151 *Toll Free Tel:* 888-330-8477 (orders) *Fax:* 646-307-5285
E-mail: firstname.lastname@hholt.com
Web Site: www.henryholt.com
Key Personnel
Pres & Publr: Stephen Rubin
Deputy Publr, VP, Sales & Mktg: Maggie Richards
VP, Dir of Publicity: Patricia Eisemann
Publr, Godwin Books: Laura Godwin
Publr, Metropolitan Books: Sara Bershtel
Creative Dir: Richard Pracher
Dir, Mktg: Jessica Wiener
Dir, Perms & Copyright: Mimi Ross
Exec Mng Ed, Adult Trade: Kenn Russell
Ed-in-Chief, NY: Gillian Blake
Exec Ed: Serena Jones
Edit Dir, Holt Children's: Christian Trimmer
Sr Ed: Libby Burton; Caroline Zancan
Sr Ed, Metropolitan Books: Riva Hocherman
Ed: Tiffany Liao
Deputy Dir, Publicity: Carolyn O'Keefe
Sr Publicity Mgr: Leslie Brandon
Publicist-at-Large: Marian Brown; Tracy Locke
Founded: 1866
ISBN Prefix(es): 978-0-8050 (Holt)
Number of titles published annually: 56 Print
Total Titles: 3,000 Print
Imprints: Andy Cohen Books; Godwin Books; Henry Holt; Henry Holt Books for Younger Readers; Holt Paperbacks; John Macrae Books; Metropolitan Books; Christy Ottaviano Books; Times Books
Foreign Rep(s): Raincoast (Canada)
Foreign Rights: A/S Bookman Literary Agency (Denmark, Finland, Iceland, Norway, Sweden); AnatoliaLit Agency (Turkey); Anthea Agency (Bulgaria); Author Rights Agency Ltd (Russia); Bardon-Chinese Media Agency (Mainland China, Taiwan); Eliane Benisti Literary Agency (France); Copenhagen Literary Agency ApS (Scandinavia); The English Agency (Japan) Ltd (Japan); Farrar, Straus and Giroux (USA); Graal Literary Agency (Maria Strarz-Kanska) (Poland); The Deborah Harris Agency (Israel); Internationaal Literatuur Bureau BV (Netherlands); International Copyright Agency Ltd (Simona Kessler) (Romania); The Italian Literary Agency srl (Italy); Katai & Bolza Literary Agents (Hungary); Korea Copyright Center Inc (KCC) (Korea); Liepman Agency (Eva Koralnik & Ronit Zafran) (Germany); Literarni Aventura sro (Czech Republic, Slovakia); MB Agencia Literaria (Portugal, Spain); Plima Literary Agency (Croatia, Serbia, Slovenia); RIFF (Brazil)
Advertising Agency: Verso Advertising, 50 W 17 St, New York, NY 10010 *Tel:* 212-292-2990 *Web Site:* www.versoadvertising.com
Warehouse: MPS, 16365 James Madison Hwy, Gordonsville, VA 22942 *Tel:* 540-672-7698 SAN: 631-5011
Membership(s): AAP

Holy Cow! Press
PO Box 3170, Mount Royal Sta, Duluth, MN 55803
Tel: 218-724-1653
E-mail: holycow@holycowpress.org
Web Site: www.holycowpress.org
Key Personnel
Publr & Ed: Jim Perlman
Founded: 1977
ISBN Prefix(es): 978-0-930100; 978-0-9779458
Number of titles published annually: 4 Print; 3 E-Book
Total Titles: 120 Print; 8 E-Book
Distribution Center: Consortium Book Sales & Distribution, The Keg House, 34 13 Ave NE, Suite 101, Minneapolis, MN 55413-1007 *Tel:* 612-746-2600 *Toll Free Tel:* 800-283-3572 (cust serv) *Fax:* 612-746-2606 *E-mail:* info@cbsd.com *Web Site:* www.cbsd.com SAN: 200-6049

Holy Cross Orthodox Press
Division of Hellenic College Holy Cross
50 Goddard Ave, Brookline, MA 02445
Tel: 617-731-3500; 617-850-1200 *Fax:* 617-850-1460
E-mail: info@hchc.edu
Web Site: www.hchc.edu
Key Personnel
Dir: Dr Anton Vrame
Prodn Mgr: Sarah Parro
Founded: 1974
Books on Orthodox Christian religion.
This publisher has indicated that 25% of their product line is author subsidized.
ISBN Prefix(es): 978-0-917651; 978-1-885652; 978-0-916586; 978-1-935317
Number of titles published annually: 10 Print
Total Titles: 120 Print

§Homa & Sekey Books
140 E Ridgewood Ave, Paramus, NJ 07652
Tel: 201-261-8810 *Toll Free Tel:* 800-870-HOMA (870-4662 orders) *Fax:* 201-261-8890
E-mail: info@homabooks.com
Web Site: www.homabooks.com
Key Personnel
Publr: Shawn Ye
Founded: 1997
Publisher & distributor of books on Asia.
ISBN Prefix(es): 978-1-931907; 978-0-966542
Number of titles published annually: 15 Print
Distributor for China Encyclopedia Publishing House; China Intercontinental Press; China Zhejiang Publishing United Group
Foreign Rights: Eric Yang Agency (Korea)
Membership(s): Independent Book Publishers Association

Homestead Publishing
Affiliate of Book Design Ltd
Box 193, Moose, WY 83012-0193
Tel: 307-733-6248 *Fax:* 307-733-6248
E-mail: orders@homesteadpublishing.net
Web Site: www.homesteadpublishing.net
Key Personnel
Publr: Carl Schreier *Tel:* 415-621-5039
Contact: Diane Henderson
Founded: 1980
Publisher of guide books.
ISBN Prefix(es): 978-0-943972
Number of titles published annually: 12 Print; 2,000 Online; 6 E-Book
Total Titles: 268 Print; 4,500 Online; 16 E-Book
Branch Office(s)
1068 14 St, San Francisco, CA 94114 *Tel:* 415-621-5039 *Fax:* 415-621-5039
Returns: 4030 W Lake Creek Dr, Wilson, WY 83014
Warehouse: 4030 W Lake Creek Dr, Wilson, WY 83014

Hoover Institution Press
Subsidiary of Hoover Institution on War, Revolution & Peace
Stanford University, 434 Galvez Mall, Stanford, CA 94305-6003
SAN: 202-3024
Tel: 650-725-7146; 650-723-3373 *Toll Free Tel:* 800-935-2882 *Fax:* 650-723-8626
E-mail: hooverpress@stanford.edu
Web Site: www.hooverpress.org; www.hoover.org
Key Personnel
Book Prodn Mgr: Marshall Blanchard *Tel:* 650-725-3460
Founded: 1962
Studies on domestic & international policy, studies of nationalities in Central & Eastern Europe, history & political science; bibliographies & surveys of Hoover Institution's resources.
ISBN Prefix(es): 978-0-8179
Number of titles published annually: 20 Print
Total Titles: 675 Print; 75 Online
Foreign Rep(s): East-West Export Books (Asia, Hawaii, The Pacific); Eurospan (Europe)
Orders to: Independent Publishers Group (IPG), 814 N Franklin St, Chicago, IL 60610 *Tel:* 312-337-0747 *Toll Free Tel:* 800-888-4741 *Fax:* 312-337-5985 *E-mail:* orders@ipgbook.com *Web Site:* www.ipgbook.com
Returns: Independent Publishers Group (IPG), 814 N Franklin St, Chicago, IL 60610 *Tel:* 312-337-0747 *Toll Free Tel:* 800-888-4741 *Fax:* 312-337-5985 *E-mail:* orders@ipgbook.com *Web Site:* www.ipgbook.com
Distribution Center: Independent Publishers Group (IPG), 814 N Franklin St, Chicago, IL 60610 *Tel:* 312-337-0747 *Toll Free Tel:* 800-888-4741 *Fax:* 312-337-5985 *E-mail:* orders@ipgbook.com *Web Site:* www.ipgbook.com

Hoover's Inc
Subsidiary of Dun & Bradstreet
7700 W Parmer Lane, Bldg A, Austin, TX 78729
Tel: 512-374-4500 *Toll Free Tel:* 844-201-0407; 888-234-4567 (sales) *Fax:* 512-374-4501
Web Site: www.hoovers.com
Founded: 1990
Business reference books & online services.
ISBN Prefix(es): 978-1-878753; 978-1-57311; 978-1-59274
Number of titles published annually: 7 Print
Total Titles: 7 Print; 3 Online
Imprints: Hoover's Business Press; Hoover's Handbooks
Foreign Office(s): William Snyder Publishing Associates, 5 Five Mile Dr, Oxford OX2 8HT, United Kingdom
Foreign Rep(s): William Snyder Publishing Associates (England)

Hope Publishing Co
380 S Main Place, Carol Stream, IL 60188
Tel: 630-665-3200 *Toll Free Tel:* 800-323-1049 *Fax:* 630-665-2552
E-mail: hope@hopepublishing.com
Web Site: www.hopepublishing.com
Key Personnel
Pres: John Shorney *E-mail:* john@hopepublishing.com
VP: Scott A Shorney *E-mail:* scott@hopepublishing.com; Steve Shorney *E-mail:* steve@hopepublishing.com
Founded: 1892
Choir music, hymnals, instrumental music books & hand bell music.
ISBN Prefix(es): 978-0-916642
Number of titles published annually: 50 Print
Divisions: Agape; Providence Press; Somerset Press; Tabernacle Publishing
Advertising Agency: Lamplighter Agency

§Hope Street Publishing
PO Box 2705, Philadelphia, PA 19120
E-mail: contact@hopestreetpublishing.com
Web Site: www.hopestreetpublishing.com
Key Personnel
Founder & CEO: Vanna B
Founded: 2012
Committed to achieving literary excellence while providing moving, thought-provoking & entertaining publications.
ISBN Prefix(es): 978-0-9853515; 978-0-9888822
Number of titles published annually: 2 Print; 3 E-Book
Total Titles: 4 Print; 6 E-Book

Horizon Publishers & Distributors Inc
191 N 650 E, Bountiful, UT 84010-3628
Tel: 801-292-7102
E-mail: ldshorizonpublishers1@gmail.com
Web Site: www.ldshorizonpublishers.com
Key Personnel
Owner & CEO: Duane S Crowther; Jean D Crowther
Founded: 1971
Christian (primarily Latter-day Saints), inspirational, health foods, self-sufficient living, music, marriage & family, children's activities, needlework, nonfiction, biography paperbacks & hardbound.
ISBN Prefix(es): 978-0-88290
Number of titles published annually: 15 Print
Total Titles: 521 Print; 35 CD-ROM; 40 Audio
Distributed by Cedar Fort Inc

Hospital & Healthcare Compensation Service
Subsidiary of John R Zabka Associates Inc
3 Post Rd, Suite 3, Oakland, NJ 07436
Mailing Address: PO Box 376, Oakland, NJ 07436-0376
Tel: 201-405-0075 *Fax:* 201-405-2110
E-mail: allinfo@hhcsinc.com
Web Site: www.hhcsinc.com
Key Personnel
Dir, Reports: Rosanne Zabka *Tel:* 201-405-0075 ext 11 *E-mail:* rzabka@hhcsinc.com
Client Servs: Tracy Schilling *Tel:* 201-405-0075 ext 13 *E-mail:* tschilling@hhcsinc.com
Founded: 1971
Publisher of salary & benefits reports for hospital, nursing home, assisted living, CCRC, home care, hospice & rehabilitation employees.
ISBN Prefix(es): 978-0-939326; 978-1-934847
Number of titles published annually: 11 Print; 11 CD-ROM
Total Titles: 10 Print; 11 CD-ROM

Host Publications
3408 West Ave, Austin, TX 78705
Mailing Address: 3507 N Lamar Blvd, PO Box 302920, Austin, TX 78703
Tel: 512-236-1290 *Fax:* 512-236-1208
Web Site: www.hostpublications.com
Key Personnel
Pres: Joe W Bratcher, III *E-mail:* jbratcher@hostpublications.com
Dir, Fulfillment: Susan Lesak *E-mail:* slesak@hostpublications.com
Founded: 1987
ISBN Prefix(es): 978-0-924047
Number of titles published annually: 6 Print
Total Titles: 50 Print
Distribution Center: Small Press Distribution, 1341 Seventh St, Berkeley, CA 94710-1409, Opers Dir: Dr Brent Cunningham *Tel:* 510-524-1668 ext 308 *Toll Free Tel:* 800-869-7553 *E-mail:* spd@spdbooks.org *Web Site:* www.spdbooks.org
Membership(s): Independent Book Publishers Association

§Houghton Mifflin Harcourt
125 High St, Boston, MA 02110
SAN: 200-2388
Tel: 617-351-5000 *Toll Free Tel:* 855-969-4642; 800-225-5425 (K-12 educ materials); 800-323-9540 (assessment materials); 877-219-1537 (SkillsTutor); 888-242-6747 (Innovation in Educ Group); 800-225-3362 (Trade & Ref Div) *Toll Free Fax:* 800-269-5232
E-mail: myhmhco@hmhco.com
Web Site: www.hmhco.com
Key Personnel
Pres & CEO: John (Jack) J Lynch, Jr
CFO: Joseph P Abbott, Jr
Chief Platform Architect & EVP, Engg: Martin Davy
EVP & Gen Coun: William Bayers
Pres, Trade Publishing: Ellen Archer
EVP, Global Strategic Alliances: Timothy L Cannon
EVP & CTO: Brook Colangelo
EVP, Prof Servs: Rose Else-Mitchell
EVP & Chief, Consumer Brands & Strategy: CJ Kettler
EVP, Intervention Solutions: Margery Mayer
EVP, HR & Chief People Offr: Bridgett Paradise
EVP, Global Sales: Lee Ramsayer
SVP, Corp Aff: Bianca Olson
SVP, Consumer Digital Prods & Platforms: Leigh Zarelli Lewis
SVP & Gen Mgr, Specialized Curriculum Group: Scott Bowker
SVP, Prog Devt & Acq: Caroline Fraser
Exec Dir, Mass Mkt & Specialty Retail Channels: Colleen Murphy
Dir, Field Sales: Jen Reynolds
Dir, Mktg: Hannah Harlow
Assoc Dir, Publicity: Megan Wilson
Sr Mktg Mgr: Katrina Kruse
Dist Client Mgr & Natl Accts: Morgan Gould
Mktg & Soc Media Mgr: Elizabeth Anderson
Mktg Mgr: Liz Anderson
Specialty Retail Sales Mgr: Emily Logan
Publicist: Stephanie Buschardt
Publicity Assoc: Leila Meglio

Founded: 1832
With education products & services used by more than 50 million students in more than 150 countries, Houghton Mifflin Harcourt is a global education & learning company. The world's largest provider of materials for PreK-12 learning, HMH is leading the way with innovative solutions & approaches to the challenges facing education today. Through curricula excellence coupled with technology innovations & professional services, HMH collaborates with school districts, administrators, teachers, parents & students, providing interactive, results-driven learning solutions. Its Educational Consulting Services group works to increase student achievement in underperforming schools by developing, implementing & supporting education transformation through sustained district partnerships. With origins dating back to 1832, the company also publishes an extensive line of reference works & award-winning literature for adults & young readers.
ISBN Prefix(es): 978-0-395; 978-0-618; 978-0-547; 978-0-544; 978-0-9709455; 978-0-9747343; 978-1-933196; 978-1-935588
Divisions: Houghton Mifflin Harcourt K-12 Publishers; Houghton Mifflin Harcourt Trade & Reference Division; The Learning Company; SkillsTutor
Branch Office(s)
2180 S McDowell Blvd, Suite B, Petaluma, CA 94954 *Tel:* 707-769-2222
One Harbor Dr, Sausalito, CA 94965 *Tel:* 415-332-4181
5680 Greenwood Plaza Blvd, Suite 550, Greenwood Village, CO 80111 *Tel:* 303-504-9312
9400 Southpark Ctr Loop, Orlando, FL 32819 *Tel:* 407-345-2000
7584 Presidents Way, Orlando, FL 32809 *Tel:* 407-345-2000
909 Davis St, Suite 300, Evanston, IL 60201 *Toll Free Tel:* 800-225-5425
1900 S Batavia Ave, Geneva, IL 60134-3399 *Tel:* 630-232-2550
One Pierce Place, Suite 900W, Itasca, IL 60143 *Toll Free Tel:* 800-767-8420
761 District Dr, Itasca, IL 60143
255 38 Ave, Suite L, St Charles, IL 60174 *Tel:* 630-659-1200
2700 N Richardt Ave, Indianapolis, IN 46219 *Tel:* 317-359-5585
465 S Lincoln Dr, Troy, MO 63379 *Tel:* 636-528-8110
361 Hanover St, Portsmouth, NH 03801 *Tel:* 630-467-7000
3 Park Ave, New York, NY 10016 *Tel:* 212-420-5800
132 W 31 St, New York, NY 10001
1587 Rte 146, Rexford, NY 12148 *Tel:* 518-399-2776
2270 Spring Lake Rd, Suite 600, Farmers Branch, TX 75234 *Toll Free Tel:* 800-225-5425
2700 La Frontera Blvd, Round Rock, TX 78681 *Tel:* 512-721-7000
4200 Blvd St Laurent, Suite 1203, Montreal, QC H2W 2R2, Canada *Tel:* 514-598-0444
B7 Calle Tabonuco, Suite 1410, Guaynabo 00968-3003, Puerto Rico *Tel:* 787-520-9599; 787-520-9585
Foreign Office(s): 59 Zhongguancun St, Rm 1004, Haidian District, Beijing 100872, China *Tel:* (010) 62602236
152-16- Pearse St, Dublin 2, Ireland *Tel:* (01) 240 5900
67 Ubi Rd, No 05-08 Oxley Bizhub, Singapore 408730, Singapore *Tel:* 6635 6825
No 501 KGIT SangAm Ctr, 1601, SangAm-dong, Mapo-gu, Seoul 123-913, South Korea *Tel:* (02) 6393 5790; (02) 6393 5792
Distributor for The Old Farmer's Almanac
Membership(s): AAP; AAP PreK-12 Learning Group; ABA; ALA; American Bar Association; Association of Booksellers for Children; Association of Catholic Publishers Inc; Association of Test Publishers; The Children's Book Council; Dictionary Society of North America; National Catholic Education Association; Society of Printers; Software & Information Industry Association
See separate listing for:
Clarion Books
Heinemann
Houghton Mifflin Harcourt Assessments
Houghton Mifflin Harcourt K-12 Publishers
Houghton Mifflin Harcourt Trade & Reference Division
Math Solutions®

Houghton Mifflin Harcourt Assessments
Subsidiary of Houghton Mifflin Harcourt Publishing Co
900 Pierce Place, Suite 900, Itasca, IL 60143
SAN: 213-554X
Tel: 630-467-7000 *Toll Free Tel:* 800-323-9540 *Fax:* 630-467-7192 (cust serv)
E-mail: rpc_customer_service@hmhpub.com (cust serv)
Web Site: www.riversidepublishing.com
Key Personnel
VP, Sales & Mktg: Tim Cooper
VP, Sales Opers: Mort Cohen
Founded: 1852 (as Riverside Press)
Develops & sells print & digital assessment tools for the education & clinical markets.
ISBN Prefix(es): 978-0-8292
Number of titles published annually: 20 Print
Imprints: Wintergreen/Orchard House Inc
Foreign Rep(s): ACER (Australia); Artsberg (Hong Kong); Camera-Mundi (Puerto Rico); Nelson Canada (Canada); NFER-Nelson (UK); NZCER (New Zealand); Psicologiay Material-Tecnico (Spain); Taskmaster (UK)

Houghton Mifflin Harcourt K-12 Publishers
Division of Houghton Mifflin Harcourt
125 High St, Boston, MA 02110
SAN: 200-2388
Tel: 617-351-5000 *Toll Free Tel:* 800-225-5425 (cust serv)
Web Site: www.hmhco.com/classroom; www.hmhco.com
Key Personnel
Dir, School & Lib Mktg: Lisa Di Sarro
Digital Mktg & Publicity Specialist: Roshan Nozari
K-12 textbooks, educational materials & services.
Imprints: Rigby; Saxon
Sales Office(s): 637 Cypress Hills Dr, Encinitas, CA 92024, SVP, West Area Sales: John Sipe *Tel:* 858-535-3901
8400 E Prentice Ave, Denver, CO 80232-2550
5555 Triangle Pkwy, Suite 150, Norcross, GA 30092, VP & Regl Mgr: Deborah Sanders *Tel:* 404-449-5881
1900 S Batavia Ave, Geneva, IL 60134 *Tel:* 630-232-2550
307 Fellowship Rd, Suite 104, Mount Laurel, NJ 08054 *Tel:* 609-452-0200
13400 Midway Rd, Dallas, TX 75244, VP & Regl Mgr: Mary Lytle *Tel:* 972-980-1100

§Houghton Mifflin Harcourt Trade & Reference Division
Division of Houghton Mifflin Harcourt
125 High St, Boston, MA 02110
SAN: 200-2388
Tel: 617-351-5000 *Toll Free Tel:* 800-225-3362
Web Site: www.hmhco.com
Key Personnel
Pres & CEO: John (Jack) J Lynch, Jr
Pres, Trade Publg Group: Ellen Archer
SVP & Publr: Bruce Nichols
SVP & Publr, Children's Books: Catherine Onder
SVP, Content & Prod Innovation: Cheryl Cramer Toto
SVP, Edit Opers & Design: Becky Saikia-Wilson
SVP, Prodn & Creative Servs: Sandy Grebenar
SVP, Sales: Maire Gorman
VP & Assoc Publr: Ken Carpenter
VP, Mktg: Adriana Rizzo
VP, Prodn: Jill Lazer
VP & Exec Dir, Publicity: Lori Glazer
VP & Creative Dir: Michaela Sullivan
VP & Dir, Subs Rts: Deborah Engel
VP & Dir, Electronic Devt: David Jost
VP & Ed-in-Chief: Deb Brody
VP & Ed-in-Chief, Children's: Mary Wilcox
Exec Dir, Audience Devt & Engagement: Rachel Fershleiser
Exec Dir, Children's Publicity: Karen Walsh
Exec Dir, Prodn: Donna McCarthy
Natl Accts Dir: Josh Harwood
Dir, Culinary Mktg: Brad Parsons
Dir, School Supply & Ref Sales: Cheryl Dickemper
Edit Dir, Fiction: Helen Atsma
Mktg Dir, Children's: Ann Dye
Assoc Dir, Publicity: Taryn Roeder
Sr Exec Ed: Susan Canavan; Rux Martin; Margaret Raymo; Deanne Urmy; Rick Wolff
Sr Exec Ed, Books for Young Readers: Jeannette Larson
Sr Exec Ed, Children's: Kate O'Sullivan
Exec Mng Ed, Children's: Ann-Marie Pucillo
Exec Ed: Lauren Wein
Exec Ed, CliffsNotes: Greg Tubach
Exec Ed, Franchise Publg, Houghton Mifflin Harcourt Children's: Elizabeth Bennett
Mng Ed: Mary Huot
Mng Ed, Cookbooks: Marina Padakis
Mng Ed, Digital Cookbooks: Rebecca Springer
Sr Ed: Alex Littlefield
Ed: Nicole Angeloro; Naomi Gibbs
Ed, Culinary/Lifestyle: Stephanie Fletcher
Assoc Ed: Tim Mudie
Assoc Ed, Children's: Adah Nuchi
Ed-at-Large, Clarion Books: Dinah Stevenson
Sr Mktg Mgr: Katrina Krause
Sr Mktg Mgr, Gen Interest: Ayesha Mirza
Sr Mgr, Subs Rts: Candace Finn
Sr Designer: Patrick Barry; Whitney Leader-Picone; Brian Moore
Sr Publicist: Michelle Bonanno
Sr Publicity Assoc: Simmi Aujla
Sr Publicity Mgr, Children's: Tara Shanahan; Rachel Wasdyke
Culinary Publicity Mgr: Brittany Edwards
Digital Prod Mgr: Taylor Foley
Sales Mgr, Specialty Retail & Intl: Olivia Wilson
Soc Media Mgr, Children's: Meredith Wilson
Sr Prodn Coord: Kim Kiefer
Lead Sales Coord, Natl Accts: Jackie Sassa
Digital Mktg & Publicity Specialist: Tara Sonin
Mktg Specialist, Children's: Amanda Acevedo; Alia Almeida
Edit Assoc: Laney Everson; Pilar Garcia-Brown
Edit Assoc, Children's: Amy Cherrix; Anna Dobbin; Lily Kessinger; Christine Krones; Anna Meier; Allison Vroegop
General literature, fiction, nonfiction, biography, autobiography, history, poetry & juvenile publications, dictionary, reference books, cookbooks & guidebooks.
ISBN Prefix(es): 978-0-89919; 978-0-395; 978-1-85697; 978-0-7534; 978-0-618; 978-1-88152
Number of titles published annually: 400 Print; 1 CD-ROM; 1 Online; 14 Audio
Total Titles: 3,300 Print; 2 CD-ROM; 2 Online; 110 Audio
Imprints: American Heritage Dictionary; Betty Crocker®; Clarion Books; CliffNotes™; Eamon Dolan Books; Graphia; Harcourt Children's; HMH Franchise; Houghton Mifflin Books for Children; Houghton Mifflin Harcourt; Mariner Books; Rux Martin Books; New Harvest; Sandpiper
Editorial Office(s): 215 Park Ave S, New York, NY 10003 *Tel:* 212-420-5800
Distributed by Hachette Book Group
Distributor for Larausse; Old Farmers Almanac

Orders to: Houghton Mifflin Harcourt Trade Customer Service, 181 Ballardvale St, PO Box 705, Wilmington, MA 01887 *Toll Free Tel:* 800-225-3362 *Toll Free Fax:* 800-634-7568
Returns: Houghton Mifflin Harcourt Publishing Company, Trade Returns Department, 2700 N Richard Ave, Indianapolis, IN 46219
Distribution Center: Raincoast Books, 2440 Viking Way, Richmond, BC V6V 1N2, Canada *Tel:* 604-448-7100 *Fax:* 604-270-7161 *E-mail:* customerservice@raincoast.com

House of Collectibles
Imprint of Penguin Random House Inc
1745 Broadway, New York, NY 10019
Tel: 212-782-9000
Web Site: www.penguinrandomhouse.com
Publisher that collectors, dealers & investors around the world turn to for detailed reference information & current market values on all antiques & collectibles, whether they want to know the history of Gustav Stickley furniture, buy a Chinese vase, sell their grandmother's depression glass or evaluate the worth of their Star Wars memorabilia. The House of Collectibles books are compiled by experts, renowned for accuracy & completeness & profusely illustrated, many with full color. Accept unsol proposals & mss from authors who are experts in the antiques & collectibles areas, also accept mss & proposals from agents.
ISBN Prefix(es): 978-0-307; 978-0-676; 978-1-4000; 978-0-87637
Total Titles: 4 Print

House to House Publications
Division of DOVE International
11 Toll Gate Rd, Lititz, PA 17543
Tel: 717-627-1996 *Toll Free Tel:* 800-848-5892 *Fax:* 717-627-4004
E-mail: h2hp@dcfi.org
Web Site: www.h2hp.com
Key Personnel
Pubns Ed: Lou Anne Good
Founded: 1997
Provide resources for the body of Christ worldwide.
ISBN Prefix(es): 978-1-886973
Number of titles published annually: 4 Print; 15 E-Book; 1 Audio
Total Titles: 50 Print; 5 Audio
Imprints: Partnership Publications

Housing Assistance Council
1025 Vermont Ave NW, Suite 606, Washington, DC 20005
Tel: 202-842-8600 *Fax:* 202-347-3441
E-mail: hac@ruralhome.org
Web Site: www.ruralhome.org
Key Personnel
Sr Policy Analyst: Leslie R Strauss *E-mail:* leslie@ruralhome.org
Founded: 1971
Provides technical housing services, loans, program & policy assistance, training, research & information. Specialize in research reports, technical manuals & information pieces, all exclusively about low-income rural housing in the US.
ISBN Prefix(es): 978-1-58064
Number of titles published annually: 15 Print; 15 Online
Total Titles: 80 Print; 50 Online
Branch Office(s)
717 "K" St, Suite 404, Sacramento, CA 95814 *Tel:* 916-706-1836 *Fax:* 916-706-1849 *E-mail:* western@ruralhome.org
600 W Peachtree St NW, Suite 1500, Atlanta, GA 30308 *Tel:* 404-892-4824 *Fax:* 404-892-1204 *E-mail:* southeast@ruralhome.org
10100 NW Ambassador Dr, Suite 310, Kansas City, MO 64153-1362 *Tel:* 816-880-0400 *Fax:* 816-880-0500 *E-mail:* midwest@ruralhome.org
7510 Montgomery NE, Suite 205, Albuquerque, NM 87109 *Tel:* 505-883-1003 *Fax:* 505-883-1005 *E-mail:* southwest@ruralhome.org

Howard Books
Imprint of Atria Publishing Group
c/o Simon & Schuster, Inc, 1230 Avenue of the Americas, New York, NY 10020
E-mail: howardbooks@simonandschuster.com (info)
Web Site: simonandschusterpublishing.com/howard-books/
Key Personnel
Sr Ed: Beth Adams *Tel:* 212-698-7329 *E-mail:* beth.adams@simonandschuster.com; Philis Boultinghouse *E-mail:* philis.boultinghouse@simonandschuster.com
VP, Dir, Subs Rts (dom): Lisa Keim
Founded: 1969
Inspirational books.
ISBN Prefix(es): 978-1-4165; 978-1-58229; 978-1-4391
Number of titles published annually: 50 Print
Foreign Rights: Akcali Copyright Agency (Turkey); Antonella Antonelli Agenzia; Book Publishers' Association of Israel, International Promotion & Literary Rights Dept (Israel); International Editors' Company (Latin America, Portugal, Spain); Japan UNI Agency Inc (Japan); JLM Literary Agency (Greece); Korea Copyright Center Inc (KCC) (Korea); Mohrbooks AG, Literary Agency; La Nouvelle Agence; Andrew Nurnberg Associates Ltd (Bulgaria, China, Croatia, Czech Republic, Estonia, Hungary, Latvia, Lithuania, Montenegro, Poland, Romania, Russia, Serbia, Slovakia, Slovenia, Taiwan); Sane Toregard Agency (Denmark, Finland, Norway, Sweden); Schindler's Literary Agency (Brazil); Sebes & Bisseling Literary Agency (Netherlands); Tuttle-Mori Agency Inc (Thailand)
Membership(s): CBA: The Association for Christian Retail; Evangelical Christian Publishers Association

HPBooks
Imprint of Penguin Group USA, A Penguin Random House Company
375 Hudson St, New York, NY 10014
Tel: 212-366-2000
E-mail: online@penguinputnam.com
Web Site: www.penguinputnam.com; www.penguin.com
Key Personnel
VP, Publr: John Duff
Sales Rep: Hal Holding
Founded: 1964
Automotive book publisher. High performance, restoration & racing how-to books for automotive enthusiasts. Cover domestic & foreign vehicles. Also publishes cookbooks.
ISBN Prefix(es): 978-0-89586; 978-0-912656; 978-1-55788
Total Titles: 104 Print; 72 E-Book
Advertising Agency: Spier NY

§HRD Press
22 Amherst Rd, Amherst, MA 01002-9709
SAN: 201-9213
Tel: 413-253-3488 *Toll Free Tel:* 800-822-2801 *Fax:* 413-253-3490
E-mail: info@hrdpress.com; customerservice@hrdpress.com
Web Site: www.hrdpress.com
Key Personnel
Publr: Robert W Carkhuff
Cust Rel Mgr: Donna Long
Founded: 1972
Textbooks & off-the-shelf workshops on human resource development, management & training. Packaged training materials & assessments.
ISBN Prefix(es): 978-0-914234; 978-0-87425
Number of titles published annually: 25 Print
Total Titles: 600 Print; 20 E-Book
Distributed by Training & Development Materials of Canada (Canada)
Foreign Rep(s): Eurospan Ltd (Europe); HRD Central (Australia); Human Capital Partners (Nigeria); Management Learning Resources (UK); Multimedia HRD Pvt Ltd (India); Trainco (South Africa); Training & Development Materials of Canada (Canada)
Returns: c/o ViaTech Publishing Solutions Inc, 8857 Alexander Rd, Batavia, NY 14020

Hudson Institute
1015 15 St NW, 6th fl, Washington, DC 20005
Tel: 202-974-2400 *Fax:* 202-974-2410
E-mail: info@hudson.org
Web Site: www.hudson.org
Key Personnel
Pres & CEO: Kenneth R Weinstein
COO: John P Walters
SVP: Lewis Libby
Sr Fellow & Dir, Pub Aff & Spec Projs: David Tell
Founded: 1961
Books, monographs, briefing papers, newsletters.
ISBN Prefix(es): 978-1-55813
Number of titles published annually: 10 Print
Total Titles: 60 Print

§Human Kinetics Inc
1607 N Market St, Champaign, IL 61820
Mailing Address: PO Box 5076, Champaign, IL 61825-5076 SAN: 211-7088
Tel: 217-351-5076 *Toll Free Tel:* 800-747-4457 *Fax:* 217-351-1549 (orders/cust serv)
E-mail: info@hkusa.com
Web Site: www.humankinetics.com
Key Personnel
Founder & Pres: Rainer Martens
CEO: Brian Holding
CFO & Opers Dir: Tina Daniel
EVP: Julie S Martens
VP & Coach Educ Dir: Ted Miller
VP, Consumer Div: Jason Muzinic
VP, Higher Educ Div: Steve Ruhlig *E-mail:* stever@hkusa.com
VP, Prod Devt: Holly Gilly
Intl Devt Dir: Barry Johnson
Intl Sales & Translation Rts Mgr: Drew Tyler
Founded: 1974
Scholarly books, college textbooks, continuing education courses & trade books in physical education, sports medicine & science, coaching, sport technique & fitness, courses, CDs & DVDs.
ISBN Prefix(es): 978-0-931250; 978-0-87322; 978-0-88011; 978-0-918438; 978-0-7360; 978-0-912781; 978-1-4504
Number of titles published annually: 200 Print
Total Titles: 1,693 Print; 174 CD-ROM; 387 Online
Branch Office(s)
Human Kinetics Canada, 475 Devonshire Rd, Unit 100, Windsor, ON N8Y 2L5, Canada *Tel:* 519-971-9500 *Toll Free Tel:* 800-465-7301 (CN) *Fax:* 519-971-9797 *E-mail:* info@hkcanada.com
Foreign Office(s): Human Kinetics Australia, 57 A Price Ave, Lower Mitcham, SA 5062, Australia *Tel:* (08) 8372-0999 *Fax:* (08) 8372 0998 *E-mail:* info@hkaustralia.com
Human Kinetics New Zealand Pty Ltd, PO Box 80, Mitcham, SA 5062, Australia *Tel:* (08) 8372-0999; 0800 222 062 *Fax:* 0800 222 064 *E-mail:* info@hknewzealand.com
Human Kinetics UK, Europe & Middle East, 107 Bradford Rd, Stanningley, Leeds LS28 6AT, United Kingdom *Tel:* (0113) 255 5665

Fax: (0113) 255 5885 *E-mail:* hk@hkeurope.com
Foreign Rep(s): Aditya Books (India); Africa Connection, Old School House (Angola, Benin, Cameroon, Cape Verde, Cote d'Ivoire (Ivory Coast), Gabon, The Gambia, Ghana, Liberia, Mali, Mozambique, Niger, Sao Tome and Principe, Senegal, Uganda, Zambia, Zimbabwe); Alkem Co (Bangladesh, Brunei, Indonesia, Laos, Malaysia, Philippines, Singapore, Thailand); Asian Books (Sri Lanka); Atlantic Publishers & Distributors (India); Bookport (Trade) (Croatia, Gibraltar, Greece, Italy, Malta, Montenegro, Portugal, Serbia, Slovenia, Spain); CBS Publishers & Distributors (India); Charran Publishing House (Trinidad and Tobago); Comprajato (Brazil); Cranbury International LLC (Caribbean, Latin America); CRW Marketing Services for Publishers Inc (Philippines, Saipan); Dasansogo Co Ltd (Korea); Disvan Enterprises (India); Eureka Press (Japan); Laszlo Horvath (Austria, Czech Republic, Hungary, Macedonia, Montenegro, Poland, Romania, Russia, Slovakia); Icon Books (Malaysia, Singapore, Vietnam); IPR (Middle East, North Africa); Kemper Conseil (Belgium, France, Germany, Switzerland); Kinemed Technologies (Chile); KinesWorld (China, Hong Kong); Libreria Medica (Colombia); Flavio Marcello (Academic) (Italy, Portugal, Spain); Research Periodicals & Book Services (Tanzania); Saras Books (India); Unifacmanu Trading Co Ltd (Taiwan)

§Human Rights Watch
350 Fifth Ave, 34th fl, New York, NY 10118-3299
Tel: 212-290-4700 *Fax:* 212-736-1300
E-mail: hrwnyc@hrw.org
Web Site: www.hrw.org
Key Personnel
Communs Dir: Emma Daly *Tel:* 212-216-1835
Founded: 1978
Nonprofit human rights organization publishing books & newsletters on human rights practices in more than 80 countries worldwide; documents arbitrary imprisonment, censorship, disappearances, due process of law, murder, prison conditions, torture, violations of laws of war & other abuses of internationally recognized human rights.
ISBN Prefix(es): 978-0-938579; 978-0-929692; 978-1-56432
Number of titles published annually: 67 Print
Total Titles: 1,000 Print; 60 E-Book
Imprints: Human Rights Watch Books

§Humanix Books LLC
Division of Newsmax Media
8 W 40 St, 20th fl, New York, NY 10804
Toll Free Tel: 855-371-7810
E-mail: info@humanixbooks.com
Web Site: www.humanixbooks.com
Key Personnel
Publr: Mary Glenn *E-mail:* maryg@humanixbooks.com
Founded: 2012
Trade paperbacks, hardcover & ebooks in the following areas: finance, investing, health, wellness, lifestyle, business, leadership, management, politics, current events, success, motivation, history & military.
ISBN Prefix(es): 978-1-63006
Number of titles published annually: 8 Print; 8 Online; 8 E-Book
Total Titles: 15 Print; 15 Online; 15 E-Book; 1 Audio
Orders to: Perseus Distribution *Toll Free Tel:* 800-343-4499 *E-mail:* orderentry@perseusbooks.com
Distribution Center: Perseus Distribution *Toll Free Tel:* 800-343-4499 *E-mail:* orderentry@perseusbooks.com
Membership(s): AAP

§Hunter Publishing Inc
222 Clematis St, West Palm Beach, FL 33401
SAN: 695-3425
Tel: 561-835-2022
Web Site: guidestotheworld.com
Key Personnel
Founder & Pres: Michael Hunter *E-mail:* michael@hunterpublishing.com
Founded: 1985
Books for travelers.
ISBN Prefix(es): 978-0-935161; 978-1-55650; 978-0-85039; 978-0-681; 978-0-929756; 978-0-85285; 978-3-259; 978-3-88989; 978-1-85691; 978-2-89464; 978-1-84306; 978-1-58843
Number of titles published annually: 40 E-Book; 33 Audio
Total Titles: 650 E-Book; 250 Audio
Imprints: Adventure Guides; Alive Guides

Huntington Press Publishing
3665 Procyon St, Las Vegas, NV 89103-1907
Tel: 702-252-0655 *Toll Free Tel:* 800-244-2224 *Fax:* 702-252-0675
E-mail: sales@huntingtonpress.com
Web Site: www.huntingtonpress.com
Key Personnel
Publr: Anthony Curtis *E-mail:* publisher@huntingtonpress.com
Founded: 1983
Books relating to gambling & Las Vegas.
ISBN Prefix(es): 978-0-929712; 978-1-935396; 978-1-944877
Number of titles published annually: 8 Print
Total Titles: 134 Print; 200 Online; 66 E-Book
Imprints: Vegas Lit
Distribution Center: Publishers Group West, 210 American Dr, Jackson, TN 38301 *Web Site:* www.pgw.com

Hutton Publishing
140D Heritage Village, Southbury, CT 06488
Tel: 203-405-6227
E-mail: huttonbooks@hotmail.com
Web Site: www.huttonpublishing.com
Key Personnel
Ed-in-Chief: Caroline DuBois Hutton
Founded: 2004
Digital publishing for Kindle, Nook, etc; print-on-demand. All books receive personal attention & are professionally designed & listed for distribution in the Ingram catalog, available through Amazon, B&N Online & local bookstores. Promotion notes available for all Huttonelectronicpublishing.com authors. All royalties are split 50-50, author & publisher. Some books paid 100% by authors, others, by special arrangement with the publisher, at varying percentages subsidized by the publisher. Please inquire by e-mail for further information. Prize-winning illustrators available as needed.
This publisher has indicated that 100% of their product line is author subsidized.
ISBN Prefix(es): 978-0-9742894; 978-0-9785171
Number of titles published annually: 10 Print; 10 E-Book
Total Titles: 40 Print; 20 E-Book
Distribution Center: Lightning Source Inc, 1246 Heil Quaker Blvd, La Vergne, TN 37086

I-5 Publishing LLC
3 Burroughs, Irvine, CA 92618
Tel: 949-855-8822 *Toll Free Tel:* 888-738-2665 *Fax:* 949-458-3856
Web Site: www.i5publishing.com
Key Personnel
Founder & Pres: Mark Harris
Founder: David Fry
Mng Ed: April Balotro
Sales Mgr: Kim Huey-Steiner
Founded: 2013
Number of titles published annually: 18 Print

Ibex Publishers
PO Box 30087, Bethesda, MD 20824
SAN: 696-866X
Tel: 301-718-8188 *Toll Free Tel:* 888-718-8188 *Fax:* 301-907-8707
E-mail: info@ibexpub.com
Web Site: ibexpub.com
Key Personnel
Publr: Mr Farhad Shirzad *E-mail:* fs@ibex.net
Founded: 1979
English & Persian language books about Iran.
ISBN Prefix(es): 978-0-936347; 978-1-58814
Number of titles published annually: 15 Print
Total Titles: 450 Print; 3 CD-ROM; 5 Audio
Imprints: IBEX Press; Iranbooks Press
Distributor for Farhang Moaser

IBFD North America Inc (International Bureau of Fiscal Documentation)
Division of IBFD Foundation
8300 Boone Blvd, Suite 380, Vienna, VA 22182
Tel: 703-442-7757
E-mail: info@ibfd.org
Web Site: www.ibfd.org
Key Personnel
Mgr, Americas: Steven Stroschein *E-mail:* s.stroschein@ibfd.org
Founded: 1938
International taxation & investment & tax law.
Number of titles published annually: 30 Print
Total Titles: 30 Print; 1 CD-ROM; 42 Online
Foreign Office(s): Reitlandpark 301, 1019 DW Amsterdam, Netherlands (headquarters) *Tel:* (020) 554 0100

ICMA, see International City/County Management Association (ICMA)

Idyll Arbor Inc
39129 264 Ave SE, Enumclaw, WA 98022
Tel: 360-825-7797 *Fax:* 360-825-5670
E-mail: sales@idyllarbor.com
Web Site: www.idyllarbor.com
Key Personnel
Pres & Intl Rts: Tom Blaschko *E-mail:* tom@idyllarbor.com
Founded: 1984
Publish health care books, information for recreational therapists & activity directors & books on social issues. The Issues Press imprint covers important social issues such as addictions & health care for returning military personnel. Titles published under the Pine Winds Press imprint relate to discussions of the life force, including spiritual reality, Bigfoot, fairies & other strange phenomena.
ISBN Prefix(es): 978-1-882883; 978-0-937663; 978-1-930461; 978-1-61158
Number of titles published annually: 8 Print; 8 E-Book
Total Titles: 100 Print; 50 E-Book; 1 Audio
Imprints: Issues Press; Pine Winds Press
Foreign Rights: Columbine Communications (worldwide exc Canada & USA)
Membership(s): Book Publishers of the Northwest; Independent Book Publishers Association; Pacific Northwest Booksellers Association

§IEEE Computer Society
2001 "L" St NW, Suite 700, Washington, DC 20036-4928
SAN: 264-620X
Tel: 202-371-0101 *Toll Free Tel:* 800-272-6657 (memb info) *Fax:* 202-728-9614
E-mail: help@computer.org
Web Site: www.computer.org

Key Personnel
Exec Dir: Angela R Burgess *E-mail:* aburgess@computer.org
Dir, Sales & Mktg: Chris Jensen *E-mail:* cjensen@computer.org
Founded: 1980
Tutorials, reports, reprint collections, conference proceedings, textbooks & CD-ROMs.
ISBN Prefix(es): 978-0-8186; 978-0-7695
Number of titles published annually: 155 Print
Total Titles: 1,000 Print; 5 CD-ROM
Branch Office(s)
10662 Los Vaqueros Circle, Los Alamitos, CA 90720-1314 *Tel:* 714-821-8380 *Fax:* 714-821-4010
Foreign Office(s): KFK Bldg, 2-14-14 Minami-Aoyama, Minato-ku, Tokyo 107-0062, Japan *Tel:* (03) 3408 3118 *Fax:* (03) 3408 3553 *E-mail:* tokyo.ofc@computer.org

§IEEE Press
Division of Institute of Electrical & Electronics Engineers Inc (IEEE)
445 Hoes Lane, Piscataway, NJ 08854
Tel: 732-981-0060 *Fax:* 732-867-9946
E-mail: pressbooks@ieee.org (proposals & info)
Web Site: www.ieee.org/press
Key Personnel
Mng Ed: Vaishali Damle *Tel:* 732-465-6655 *E-mail:* v.damle@ieee.org
Founded: 1971
Professional books & texts in electrical & computer engineering, computer science, electrotechnology, general engineering, applied mathematics. Tutorials in technical subjects.
ISBN Prefix(es): 978-0-87942; 978-0-7803; 978-0-471
Number of titles published annually: 40 Print
Total Titles: 900 Print; 800 E-Book
Imprints: Wiley-IEEE Press
Distributed by John Wiley & Sons Inc
Foreign Rep(s): John Wiley & Sons Inc
Foreign Rights: John Wiley & Sons Inc
Membership(s): AAP

IET USA Inc
379 Thornall St, Edison, NJ 08837
Tel: 732-321-5575 *Fax:* 732-321-5702
E-mail: ietusa@theiet.org
Web Site: www.theiet.org
Key Personnel
VP & Gen Mgr: Michael Ornstein
Founded: 1871
Professional books, journals, magazines & conference proceedings in many areas of electrical & electronic engineering, including telecommunications, computing, power, control, radar, circuits, materials & more.
ISBN Prefix(es): 978-0-85296; 978-0-906048; 978-0-86341
Number of titles published annually: 30 Print
Total Titles: 500 Print; 300 E-Book
Imprints: IEE; Inspec; Peter Peregrinus Ltd
Foreign Office(s): The IET, Suite G, 10F, China Merchants Tower, No 118 Jianguo Rd, Chaoyang District, Beijing 100022, China *Tel:* (010) 6566 7697 *E-mail:* china@theiet.org *Web Site:* www.theiet.org/cn
IET Hong Kong, 4405-06 Cosco Tower, 183 Queen's Rd Central, Hong Kong, Hong Kong *Tel:* 2521 2140 *Fax:* 2778 1711 *E-mail:* adminap@theiet.org
IET India, Unit No 405 & 406, 4th fl, West Wing, Raheja Towers, MG Rd, Bangalore 560 001, India *Tel:* (080) 4089 2222 *E-mail:* india@theiet.in *Web Site:* theiet.in
The Institution of Engineering & Technology, Michael Faraday House, 6 Hills Way, Stevenage, Herts SG1 2AY, United Kingdom (journal & magazine sales), Contact: Neil Dennis *Tel:* (01438) 313 311 *E-mail:* postmaster@theiet.org
Foreign Rep(s): Cranbury International LLC (Latin America, Mexico, South America)
Orders to: c/o Books International Inc, PO Box 605, Herndon, VA 20172 *Tel:* 703-661-1573 *Toll Free Tel:* 800-230-7286 (US & CN) *Fax:* 703-661-1501 *E-mail:* ieemail@presswarehouse.com
Distribution Center: c/o Books International Inc, PO Box 605, Herndon, VA 20172 *Tel:* 703-661-1500 *Fax:* 703-661-1501
Membership(s): Association of Learned & Professional Society Publishers; STM

IFPRI, see International Food Policy Research Institute

§Ignatius Press
Division of Guadalupe Associates Inc
1348 Tenth Ave, San Francisco, CA 94122-2304
SAN: 214-3887
Toll Free Tel: 800-651-1531 (orders); 888-615-3186 (cust serv)
E-mail: info@ignatius.com
Web Site: www.ignatius.com
Key Personnel
Pres: Mark Brumley *E-mail:* mark@ignatius.com
Art Dir: Roxanne Lum
Mktg Dir: Anthony J Ryan
Ed: Fr Joseph Fessio SJ
Prodn Ed: Carolyn Lemon
Mktg Mgr: Eva Mutean *E-mail:* eva@ignatius.com
Foreign Rts: Penelope Boldrick
Founded: 1978
ISBN Prefix(es): 978-0-89870; 978-1-58617; 978-1-62164; 978-1-68149
Number of titles published annually: 60 Print
Total Titles: 750 Print; 55 Audio
Distributor for Bethlehem Books; Veritas
Foreign Rep(s): Ancoh Enterprises (Nigeria); B Broughton Co Ltd (Canada); Freedom Publishing (Australia, New Zealand); Gracewing Publishing (Europe, UK); John XXIII Fellowship Co-op Ltd (Australia, New Zealand); St Andrew's Church Supply (Canada); Sunrise Marian Distribution (Canada); Veritas Publications (Ireland)

§IHS Jane's
Subsidiary of IHS Markit
110 N Royal St, Suite 200, Alexandria, VA 22314-1651
SAN: 286-357X
Tel: 703-683-3700 *Toll Free Tel:* 800-824-0768 (sales) *Fax:* 703-836-0297 *Toll Free Fax:* 800-836-0297
E-mail: customercare@ihsmarkit.com
Web Site: www.ihs.com; ihsmarkit.com
Key Personnel
Supv Cust Care: Mike Wiman
Founded: 1897
Hard copy, online services, magazines, CD-ROM, electronic databases on defense aerospace, transportation & terrorism subjects.
ISBN Prefix(es): 978-0-7106; 978-0-354; 978-0-356
Number of titles published annually: 50 Print
Total Titles: 180 Print
Warehouse: ITP Distribution Center, 7625 Empire Dr, Florence, KY 41042

IHS Press
222 W 21 St, Suite F-122, Norfolk, VA 23517
Toll Free Tel: 877-447-7737 *Toll Free Fax:* 877-447-7737
E-mail: info@ihspress.com; tradesales@ihspress.com (wholesale sales); order@ihspress.com
Web Site: www.ihspress.com
Founded: 2001
ISBN Prefix(es): 978-0-9714894; 978-0-9718286; 978-1-932528; 978-1-60570
Number of titles published annually: 12 Print; 12 E-Book
Total Titles: 42 Print; 42 E-Book
Distribution Center: Intrepid Group, 1331 Red Cedar Circle, Fort Collins, CO 80524

§Illinois State Museum Society
Affiliate of Illinois State Museum
502 S Spring St, Springfield, IL 62706-5000
Tel: 217-782-7386 *Fax:* 217-782-1254
E-mail: editor@museum.state.il.us
Web Site: www.museum.state.il.us
Key Personnel
Museum Dir: Bonnie Styles *Tel:* 217-782-7011 *E-mail:* bwstyles@museum.state.il.us
Museum Ed: Andy Hanson *Tel:* 217-782-6700 *E-mail:* ahanson@museum.state.il.us
Founded: 1877
Softcover texts, quarterly magazines, quarterly newsletters, quarterly calendars of events & activities brochures, educational posters & CD-ROM.
ISBN Prefix(es): 978-0-89792
Number of titles published annually: 5 Print
Total Titles: 1 CD-ROM

§Illuminating Engineering Society of North America (IES)
120 Wall St, 17th fl, New York, NY 10005-4001
Tel: 212-248-5000 *Fax:* 212-248-5017; 212-248-5018
E-mail: ies@ies.org
Web Site: www.ies.org
Key Personnel
Mktg Mgr: Clayton Gordon *Tel:* 212-248-5000 ext 110 *E-mail:* cgordon@ies.org
Founded: 1906
ISBN Prefix(es): 978-0-87995
Number of titles published annually: 10 Print; 1 E-Book
Total Titles: 90 Print; 2 E-Book
Distributor for Taylor & Francis; Techstreet

Imagination Publishing Group
PO Box 1304, Dunedin, FL 34697
Toll Free Tel: 888-701-6481 *Fax:* 727-361-0584
E-mail: info@imaginationpublishinggroup.com
Web Site: www.imaginationpublishinggroup.com
Key Personnel
Pres: Alan Wayne
Asst: Miranda Jade
Founded: 2008
Publisher of fine quality printed products & educational apps for mobile devices.
ISBN Prefix(es): 978-0-9800
Number of titles published annually: 5 Print; 2 Audio
Total Titles: 3 Print; 1 Audio
Membership(s): ABA; Association of Booksellers for Children; Florida Association for Media in Education; Florida Association for Partners in Education; Florida Authors & Publishers Association Inc; Society of Children's Book Writers & Illustrators; Southern Independent Booksellers for Children

§Imago Press
3710 E Edison St, Tucson, AZ 85716
Tel: 520-444-2265
Web Site: www.oasisjournal.org
Key Personnel
Publr: Leila Joiner *E-mail:* ljoiner@dakotacom.net
Founded: 2002
Provide a place for older authors to present their work to appreciative audiences. Our flagship offering is the *OASIS Journal*, an annual anthology of short fiction, short nonfiction & poetry by writers over fifty, which originated with the OASIS Institute, a national nonprofit organization that promotes ongoing education for seniors.

ISBN Prefix(es): 978-0-9725303; 978-0-9799341; 978-1-935437; 978-0-9981791
Number of titles published annually: 2 Print; 2 E-Book
Total Titles: 54 Print; 24 E-Book
Imprints: As Sabr; Pennywyse Press
Membership(s): Independent Book Publishers Association

§ImaJinn Books
Imprint of BelleBooks
PO Box 74274, Phoenix, AZ 85087-4274
Tel: 623-236-3361 *Toll Free Tel:* 877-625-3592 (US & CN)
E-mail: orders@imajinnbooks.com; editors@imajinnbooks.com
Web Site: www.imajinnbooks.com
Founded: 1998
Specialize in publishing & selling paranormal romance, urban fantasy, regency romance & erotica.
ISBN Prefix(es): 978-1-893896; 978-0-9759653; 978-1-933417; 978-1-61026
Number of titles published annually: 24 Print
Total Titles: 100 Print
Imprints: Forever Regency (regency line); Silk & Magic (erotica line)
Membership(s): The Association of Publishers for Special Sales; Independent Book Publishers Association

Immedium
Imprint of Immedium Inc
535 Rockdale Dr, San Francisco, CA 94127
Mailing Address: PO Box 31846, San Francisco, CA 94131
Tel: 415-452-8546 *Fax:* 360-937-6272
E-mail: orders@immedium.com; sales@immedium.com
Web Site: www.immedium.com
Key Personnel
Publr: Oliver Chin *E-mail:* o.chin@comcast.net
Ed: Don Menn
Acqs Ed: Amy Ma
Graphic Design: Elaine Chu
Founded: 2005
Publish wonderfully illustrated children's picture books, Asian American topics & contemporary arts & culture.
ISBN Prefix(es): 978-1-59702
Number of titles published annually: 4 Print; 4 Online; 4 E-Book
Total Titles: 45 Print; 40 Online; 40 E-Book
Foreign Rights: HarperCollins UK (UK & Commonwealth)
Orders to: Consortium Book Sales & Distribution, 1045 Westgate Dr, Suite 90, St Paul, MN 55114-1065 *Tel:* 651-621-9035 *Toll Free Tel:* 800-283-3572 (cust serv) *Fax:* 651-221-0124 *E-mail:* info@cbsd.com *Web Site:* www.cbsd.com
Returns: Consortium Book Sales & Distribution, 1045 Westgate Dr, Suite 90, St Paul, MN 55114-1065 *Tel:* 651-621-9035 *Toll Free Tel:* 800-283-3572 (cust serv) *Fax:* 651-221-0124 *E-mail:* info@cbsd.com *Web Site:* www.cbsd.com
Shipping Address: Consortium Book Sales & Distribution, 1045 Westgate Dr, Suite 90, St Paul, MN 55114-1065 *Tel:* 651-621-9035 *Toll Free Tel:* 800-283-3572 (cust serv) *Fax:* 651-221-0124 *E-mail:* info@cbsd.com *Web Site:* www.cbsd.com
Warehouse: Consortium Book Sales & Distribution, 1045 Westgate Dr, Suite 90, St Paul, MN 55114-1065 *Tel:* 651-621-9035 *Toll Free Tel:* 800-283-3572 (cust serv) *Fax:* 651-221-0124 *E-mail:* info@cbsd.com *Web Site:* www.cbsd.com
Distribution Center: Consortium Book Sales & Distribution, 1045 Westgate Dr, Suite 90, St Paul, MN 55114-1065 *Tel:* 561-621-9035 *Toll Free Tel:* 800-283-3572 (cust serv) *Fax:* 651-221-0124 *E-mail:* info@cbsd.com *Web Site:* www.cbsd.com

§Impact Publications/Development Concepts Inc
9104 Manassas Dr, Suite N, Manassas Park, VA 20111-5211
Tel: 703-361-7300 *Toll Free Tel:* 800-361-1055 (cust serv) *Fax:* 703-335-9486
E-mail: query@impactpublications.com
Web Site: www.impactpublications.com; www.veteransworld.com
Key Personnel
Pres: Ronald Krannich, PhD
Founded: 1982
Career & travel publications.
ISBN Prefix(es): 978-1-57023; 978-0-942710
Number of titles published annually: 18 Print
Total Titles: 167 Print
Distributed by National Book Network

In the Garden Publishing
Division of What Would Love Do Intl
7525 Paragon Rd, No 752252, Dayton, OH 45459
Mailing Address: PO Box 752252, Dayton, OH 45475 SAN: 920-3389
Tel: 937-317-0859
E-mail: editor@inthegardenpublishing.com
Web Site: www.inthegardenpublishing.com
Key Personnel
Publr: Christine Horner *E-mail:* admin@inthegardenpublishing.com
Founded: 2012
Discover your inner guru. Conscious community & brilliant minds unite. Together, what can we create?
ISBN Prefix(es): 978-0-9855314; 978-0-9888333
Number of titles published annually: 5 Print; 5 Online; 5 E-Book
Total Titles: 9 Print; 15 Online; 8 E-Book
Imprints: Yugen Press (fiction)

§Incentive Publications by World Book
180 N LaSalle St, Suite 900, Chicago, IL 60101
Toll Free Tel: 800-967-5325; 800-975-3250; 888-482-9764 (trade dept) *Toll Free Fax:* 888-922-3766
E-mail: tradeorders@worldbook.com
Web Site: www.incentivepublications.com
Key Personnel
Trade Opers Specialist: Kyle Schultz
Founded: 1968 (acquired by World Book 2013)
Preschool through high school supplementary educational materials for students, parents & teachers.
ISBN Prefix(es): 978-0-913916; 978-0-86530
Number of titles published annually: 25 Print
Total Titles: 425 Print; 1 CD-ROM

§Independent Information Publications
Division of Computing!
3357 21 St, San Francisco, CA 94110
Tel: 415-643-8600
E-mail: sharisteiner@gmail.com
Web Site: www.movedoc.com
Founded: 1982
ISBN Prefix(es): 978-0-913733
Number of titles published annually: 4 Print; 1 CD-ROM; 6 Online; 2 E-Book
Total Titles: 5 Print; 1 CD-ROM; 4 Online; 2 E-Book
Imprints: IIP Consumers Series
Branch Office(s)
IIP, 500 Kentucky Ave, Savannah, GA 31404, Contact: Cima Star *Tel:* 912-233-8873
Shipping Address: Pathway Book Service, PO Box 89, Gilsum, NH 03448 *Tel:* 603-357-0236 *E-mail:* pbs@pathwaybook.com *Web Site:* www.pathwaybook.com
Distribution Center: Pathway Book Service, PO Box 89, Gilsum, NH 03448 *Tel:* 603-357-0236 *E-mail:* pbs@pathwaybook.com *Web Site:* www.pathwaybook.com
Membership(s): Bay Area Independent Publishers Association; Independent Book Publishers Association

§Independent Institute
100 Swan Way, Suite 200, Oakland, CA 94621-1428
Tel: 510-632-1366 *Toll Free Tel:* 800-927-8733 *Fax:* 510-568-6040
E-mail: orders@independent.org
Web Site: www.independent.org
Key Personnel
Founder & CEO: David J Theroux *Tel:* 510-632-1366 ext 104 *E-mail:* dtheroux@independent.org
VP & COO: Martin Buerger *Tel:* 510-568-6048 *E-mail:* mbuerger@independent.org
Acqs Dir: Roy M Carlisle *Tel:* 510-568-6049 *E-mail:* rcarlisle@independent.org
Communs Dir: Kim Cloidt *Tel:* 510-568-4092 *E-mail:* kcloidt@independent.org
Res Dir: William Shughart, II *E-mail:* william.shughart@usu.edu
Founded: 1986
Nonprofit research & publication. Branch office in Washington, DC.
ISBN Prefix(es): 978-0-945999; 978-1-59813
Number of titles published annually: 6 Print; 1 CD-ROM; 2 Online; 6 E-Book; 1 Audio
Total Titles: 98 Print; 50 E-Book
Distribution Center: Independent Publishers Group, 814 N Franklin St, Chicago, IL 60610 *Toll Free Tel:* 800-888-4741 *Web Site:* www.ipgbook.com
Membership(s): AAP; Independent Book Publishers Association; Independent Publishers Group

Indiana Historical Society Press (IHS Press)
450 W Ohio St, Indianapolis, IN 46202-3269
SAN: 201-5234
Tel: 317-232-1882; 317-234-0026 (orders); 317-234-2716 (edit) *Toll Free Tel:* 800-447-1830 (orders) *Fax:* 317-234-0562 (orders); 317-233-0857 (edit)
E-mail: ihspress@indianahistory.org; orders@indianahistory.org (orders)
Web Site: www.indianahistory.org; shop.indianahistory.org (orders)
Key Personnel
CEO & Pres: John Herbst *E-mail:* jherbst@indianahistory.org
Natl Sales Coord: Becke Bolinger *Tel:* 317-234-3683 *E-mail:* bbolinger@indianahistory.org
Sr Ed: Ray Boomhower *E-mail:* rboomhower@indianahistory.og
Founded: 1886
Books, journals & newsletters on Indiana history, including an illustrated history magazine & a family history magazine. Also offers videos, recordings, prints, note cards & other gift items.
ISBN Prefix(es): 978-0-87195
Number of titles published annually: 4 Print; 1 Online; 4 E-Book
Total Titles: 90 Print; 1 Online; 3 Audio

Indiana University African Studies Program
Indiana University, 221 Woodburn Hall, Bloomington, IN 47405
Tel: 812-855-8284 *Fax:* 812-855-6734
E-mail: afrist@indiana.edu
Web Site: www.indiana.edu/~afrist
Key Personnel
Dir: Samuel Obeng *E-mail:* sobeng@indiana.edu
Assoc Dir: Maria Grosz-Ngate *Tel:* 812-855-5081 *E-mail:* mgrosz@indiana.edu
Founded: 1965
Monograph & working papers, humanities, interdisciplinary study of Africa.
ISBN Prefix(es): 978-0-941934

Number of titles published annually: 50 Print
Total Titles: 52 Print

§Indiana University Press
Herman B Wells Library 350, 1320 E Tenth St, Bloomington, IN 47405-3907
SAN: 202-5647
Tel: 812-855-8817 *Toll Free Tel:* 800-842-6796 (orders only) *Fax:* 812-855-7931; 812-855-8507
E-mail: iupress@indiana.edu; iuporder@indiana.edu (orders)
Web Site: www.iupress.indiana.edu
Key Personnel
Dir: Gary Dunham
Assoc Dir: Dave Hulsey *Tel:* 812-855-6553 *E-mail:* hulseyd@indiana.edu
Dir, Acqs: Dee Mortensen *Tel:* 812-855-0268 *E-mail:* mortense@indiana.edu
Dir, Opers & Electronic Publg: Michael Regoli *Tel:* 812-855-3830 *E-mail:* regoli@indiana.edu
Technol Dir: Ted Boardman *Tel:* 812-855-6468 *E-mail:* tboardma@indiana.edu
Acq Ed: Jennika Baines *Tel:* 812-855-2756 *E-mail:* bainesj@indiana.edu; Janice Frisch *Tel:* 812-856-5810 *E-mail:* frishj@indiana.edu; Ashley Runyon *Tel:* 812-855-5262 *E-mail:* asrunyon@indiana.edu
Mgr, Accts Receivable: Kimberly B Childers *Tel:* 812-855-4134 *E-mail:* kchilder@indiana.edu
Mktg Mgr: Julie Davis *Tel:* 812-855-3113 *E-mail:* julmsmit@indiana.edu; Michelle Sybert *Tel:* 812-855-5031 *E-mail:* msybert@indiana.edu
Mktg Mgr, Journals: Jacklyn Lord *Tel:* 812-855-4522 *E-mail:* jvfarris@indiana.edu
Rts & Perms Mgr: Stephen Williams *Tel:* 812-855-6314 *E-mail:* smw9@indiana.edu
Acctg Assoc: Brent Starr *Tel:* 812-855-5366 *E-mail:* brstarr@indiana.edu
Founded: 1950
Trade & scholarly nonfiction; film & media studies, literature & music, African studies, backlist, classical studies, contemporary issues, cultural studies, folklore, international studies, Jewish studies, journals, Middle East studies, paleontology, philanthropy, politics/political science, railroads & transportation, Russian studies.
ISBN Prefix(es): 978-0-253
Number of titles published annually: 150 Print; 2 CD-ROM; 145 E-Book; 5 Audio
Total Titles: 3,672 Print; 8 CD-ROM; 1,548 E-Book
Imprints: Quarry Books (regional imprint for Midwest)
Foreign Rights: Agencia Literaria Carmen Balcells SA (Maribel Luque) (Spain); Bookman Literary Agency (Ib H Lauritzen) (Denmark); The English Agency (Tsutomu Yawata) (Japan); The Deborah Harris Agency (Efrat Lev) (Israel); The Italian Literary Agency srl (Maria Stefania Fietta) (Italy); Liepman AG (Marc Koralnik) (Germany); La Nouvelle Agence (Anne Maizeret) (France); O A Literary Agency (Michael Avramides) (Greece)
Orders to: Ingram Publisher Services, 1210 Ingram Dr, Chambersburg, PA 17202 *Tel:* 717-262-4860 *Toll Free Tel:* 800-648-3013 *E-mail:* pubsupport@ingramcontent.com *Web Site:* ipage.ingramcontent.com
Shipping Address: Ingram Publisher Services, 1210 Ingram Dr, Chambersburg, PA 17202 *Tel:* 717-262-4860 *Toll Free Tel:* 800-648-3013 *E-mail:* pubsupport@ingramcontent.com *Web Site:* ipage.ingramcontent.com
Distribution Center: Ingram Publisher Services, 1210 Ingram Dr, Chambersburg, PA 17202 *Tel:* 717-262-4860 *Toll Free Tel:* 800-648-3013 *E-mail:* pubsupport@ingramcontent.com *Web Site:* ipage.ingramcontent.com

§Industrial Press Inc
32 Haviland St, Suite 3, Norwalk, CT 06854
SAN: 202-6945
Tel: 203-956-5593 ext 0 (cust serv) *Toll Free Tel:* 888-528-7852 ext 0 (cust serv) *Fax:* 203-354-9391 (cust serv)
E-mail: info@industrialpress.com (cust serv)
Web Site: new.industrialpress.com
Key Personnel
Owner & Pres: Alex Luchars *E-mail:* aluchars@industrialpress.com
Edit Dir: Judy Bass *E-mail:* jbass@industrialpress.com
Cont: Peter Burri *E-mail:* pburri@industrialpress.com
Art Dir & Prodn Mgr: Janet Romano *E-mail:* jromano@industrialpress.com
Mng Ed: Laura Brengelman *E-mail:* lbrengelman@industrialpress.com
Founded: 1883
Scientific & technical handbooks, professional & reference books for engineering, technology, manufacturing & education.
ISBN Prefix(es): 978-0-8311
Number of titles published annually: 28 Print; 5 CD-ROM; 28 E-Book
Total Titles: 320 Print; 30 CD-ROM; 120 E-Book
Foreign Rep(s): Academic Marketing Services (Botswana, Lesotho, Namibia, South Africa, Swaziland); China Publishing Services Ltd (China); Co Info Pty Ltd (Australia, Fiji, New Zealand, Papua New Guinea); Cranbury International LLC (Central America, Mexico, Puerto Rico, South America, West Indies); Disvan Enterprises (India); Nelson Education Ltd (Canada); Transatlantic Publishers Group Ltd (Europe, Middle East); The White Partnership (Indonesia, Malaysia, Philippines, Singapore, South Korea, Sri Lanka, Thailand)
Membership(s): AAP

Information Age Publishing Inc
PO Box 79049, Charlotte, NC 28271-7047
Tel: 704-752-9125 *Fax:* 704-752-9113
E-mail: infoage@infoagepub.com
Web Site: www.infoagepub.com
Key Personnel
Pres & Publr: George F Johnson *E-mail:* george@infoagepub.com
Founded: 1999
Social science publisher of academic & scholarly book series & journals. Specialties include black studies, educational technology & leadership titles.
Information Age is a no returns publisher.
ISBN Prefix(es): 978-1-930608; 978-1-931576; 978-1-59311; 978-1-60752; 978-1-61735; 978-1-62396; 978-1-68123
Number of titles published annually: 240 Print; 120 E-Book
Total Titles: 3,500 Print; 1,500 E-Book
Foreign Rep(s): Co Info Pty Ltd (Australia); Cranbury International LLC (Caribbean, Puerto Rico, South America); The Eurospan Group (Europe); Mohamed Feroz (Indonesia); Jeffrey Lim (Indochina, Philippines, Vietnam); Login Canada (Canada); Maruzen Co Ltd (Japan); Mercury Retail Pty Ltd (Australia); Sara Books Pvt Ltd (India); Taylor & Francis Asia Pacific (China, Hong Kong, Korea, Singapore, Taiwan, Thailand); Taylor & Francis Publishing Services (Brunei, Malaysia)
Foreign Rights: International Publishers Representatives (IPR) (worldwide)

§Information Gatekeepers Inc (IGI)
Division of IGI Group Inc
1340 Soldiers Field Rd, Suite 2, Boston, MA 02135
Mailing Address: PO Box 35880, Brighton, MA 02135
Tel: 617-782-5033 *Fax:* 617-507-8338
E-mail: info@igigroup.com
Web Site: www.igigroup.com
Key Personnel
Chief Analyst & Ed-in-Chief: Hui Pan, PhD *E-mail:* hpan@igigroup.com
Mng Ed: Bev Wilson *E-mail:* editor@igigroup.com
Founded: 1977
Fiber optics, optical networks, wireless, ATM, XDSL & telecommunications, trade shows, conferences, newsletters, market studies & consulting.
ISBN Prefix(es): 978-0-918435; 978-1-56851
Number of titles published annually: 35 Print
Total Titles: 542 Print
Foreign Rep(s): Chiltern Magazine Services (England); Chongno Book Center Co Ltd (Korea); Global Information Inc (Japan); Investment Publications Information Service (Australia); Overseas Information Services (Korea)
Membership(s): IEEE; The Optical Society; Plastic Optical Fiber Trade Organization

§Information Today, Inc
143 Old Marlton Pike, Medford, NJ 08055-8750
Tel: 609-654-6266 *Toll Free Tel:* 800-300-9868 (cust serv) *Fax:* 609-654-4309
E-mail: custserv@infotoday.com
Web Site: www.infotoday.com
Key Personnel
Pres & CEO: Thomas H Hogan, Sr
VP, Admin: John Yersak
VP, Content: Richard T Kaser *E-mail:* kaser@infotoday.com
VP, Mktg & Busn Devt: Thomas Hogan, Jr
VP, IT: Bill Spence *E-mail:* spence@infotoday.com
Dir of Sales, Lib & Info Div: Lauri Rimler *E-mail:* lwrimler@infotoday.com
Prodn Mgr: Tiffany Chamenko *E-mail:* tchamenko@infotoday.com
Mktg & Exhibits Mgr: Robert Colding *E-mail:* rcolding@infotoday.com
Founded: 1980
Publisher specializing in: Books, directories, newspapers, journals, newsletters, conferences & information services for users & producers of digital information content & technologies, including professionals in the library, publishing, online information, K-12 education, business research & IT, knowledge management, customer relationship management, speech technology & streaming media industries. ITI's reference division is the publisher of *LMP, ILMP, American Book Trade Directory, Library and Book Trade Almanac* & other professional reference titles.
ISBN Prefix(es): 978-0-938734; 978-0-904933; 978-1-57387; 978-0-910965
Number of titles published annually: 28 Print; 15 E-Book
Total Titles: 460 Print; 230 E-Book
Imprints: ASI Books (books for indexing professionals from the American Society for Indexing); ASIS&T Monograph Series (scholarly monographs from the American Society for Information Science & Technology); CyberAge Books (books for tech-savvy consumers & business information users; nationally distributed to the book trade by IPG); Information Today Books (practical books for library & information professionals)
Membership(s): ALA; American Society for Indexing; Association for Independent Information Professionals; Association for Information

Science & Technology; Independent Book Publishers Association; Independent Publishers Group; Mystery Writers of America; NAIBA; SLA

Infosources Publishing
140 Norma Rd, Teaneck, NJ 07666
Tel: 201-836-7072
Web Site: www.infosourcespub.com
Key Personnel
Publr & Ed: Arlene L Eis
Founded: 1981
Legal reference books, newsletters, online databases. Publisher of *The Informed Librarian Online.*
ISBN Prefix(es): 978-0-939486; 978-0-9842928; 978-0-9842214
Number of titles published annually: 3 Print; 1 Online
Total Titles: 6 Print

Ink Smith Publishing
710 S Myrtle Ave, Suite 209, Monrovia, CA 91016
Tel: 626-415-7179
E-mail: contact@ink-smith.com
Web Site: ink-smith.com
Key Personnel
Owner: Ashley Howie
Founded: 2012
ISBN Prefix(es): 978-1-939156
Number of titles published annually: 24 Print; 24 Online; 24 E-Book
Imprints: Native Ink Press
Membership(s): Independent Book Publishers Association

Inkwater Press
Imprint of Firstbooks.com Inc
6750 SW Franklin St, Suite A, Portland, OR 97223
Tel: 503-968-6777 *Fax:* 503-968-6779
E-mail: orders@inkwaterbooks.com
Web Site: www.inkwater.com
Key Personnel
Pres: Jeremy Solomon *E-mail:* jeremy@inkwater.com
Founded: 2002
Publishing services to individuals & corporations as well as author subsidized publishing.
This publisher has indicated that 95% of their product line is author subsidized.
ISBN Prefix(es): 978-0-9719414; 978-1-59299; 978-1-62901
Number of titles published annually: 70 Print; 70 E-Book
Total Titles: 485 Print; 270 E-Book; 2 Audio
Imprints: Franklin Street Books

Inner Traditions International Ltd
One Park St, Rochester, VT 05767
Mailing Address: PO Box 388, Rochester, VT 05767
Tel: 802-767-3174 *Toll Free Tel:* 800-246-8648 *Fax:* 802-767-3726
E-mail: customerservice@InnerTraditions.com
Web Site: www.InnerTraditions.com
Key Personnel
Pres: Ehud C Sperling *E-mail:* prez@InnerTraditions.com
VP, Opers: Diane Shepard *E-mail:* dianes@InnerTraditions.com
Dir, Sales & Mktg: John Hays *E-mail:* johnh@InnerTraditions.com
Ed-in-Chief: Jeanie Levitan *E-mail:* jeaniel@InnerTraditions.com
Acqs Ed: Jon Graham *E-mail:* jong@InnerTraditions.com
Print Mgr: Jon Desautels *E-mail:* jond@InnerTraditions.com
Foreign Rts & Perms: Maria Loftus *E-mail:* marial@InnerTraditions.com
Publicity: Manzanita Carpenter *E-mail:* manzanitac@InnerTraditions.com
Sales & Mktg: Andrea Raymond *E-mail:* andyr@InnerTraditions.com
Spec Sales: Jessica Arsenault *E-mail:* jessa@InnerTraditions.com
Founded: 1975
Nonfiction cloth & quality trade paperbacks; audio cassettes & CDs (ethnic music & meditation aids).
ISBN Prefix(es): 978-0-89281; 978-1-59477; 978-1-62055
Number of titles published annually: 66 Print; 66 E-Book
Total Titles: 1,629 Print; 1,105 E-Book; 15 Audio
Imprints: Bear & Co Inc; Bear Cub Books; Bindu Books; Destiny Books; Destiny Recordings; Healing Arts Press; Inner Traditions; Inner Traditions en espanol; Inner Traditions India; Park Street Press
Foreign Rights: Akcali Copyright Agency (Turkey); Big Apple Agency Inc (China, Taiwan); Blackbird Literary Agency (Netherlands); The Book Publishers' Association of Israel, International Promotion & Literary Rights Dept (Israel); Graal Literary Agency (Poland); Ilidio Matos Agency (Portugal); International Editors' Co SA (Argentina, Spain); The Italian Literary Agency (Italy); Simona Kessler International Copyright Agency Ltd (Romania); Alexander Korzhenevski Agency (Russia); Zvonimir Majdak (Croatia); Montreal Contacts/The Rights Agency (Canada); Andrew Nurnberg Associates (Baltic States, Bulgaria, Czech Republic, Hungary); Read n Right Agency (Greece); Schindler's Literary Agency (Brazil); Thomas Schlueck GmbH (Germany); Agence Schweiger (France); Tuttle-Mori Agency Inc (Indonesia, Japan, Thailand); Eric Yang Agency (Korea)
Orders to: Inner Traditions International - Bear & Co, c/o Simon & Schuster, 100 Front St, Riverside, NJ 08075 *Toll Free Tel:* 800-223-2336 *Toll Free Fax:* 800-943-9831 *E-mail:* purchaseorders@simonandschuster.com
Returns: Simon & Schuster, c/o Jacobson Logistics, 4406 Industrial Park Rd, Bldg 7, Camp Hill, PA 17011 (truckload shipments must call for an appointment: 800-967-3914 ext 5318)
Warehouse: Inner Traditions International - Bear & Co, c/o Simon & Schuster, 100 Front St, Riverside, NJ 08075 *Toll Free Tel:* 800-943-9831 *E-mail:* purchaseorders@simonandschuster.com
See separate listing for:
Bear & Co Inc

The Innovation Press
1001 Fourth Ave, Suite 3200, Seattle, WA 98154
Tel: 360-870-9988
E-mail: info@theinnovationpress.com
Web Site: www.theinnovationpress.com
Key Personnel
Publr: Asia Citro *E-mail:* acitro@theinnovationpress.com
Founded: 2015
Publish quirky, creative books (often with a STEM-focus) for kids PreK-grade 6.
ISBN Prefix(es): 978-1-943147
Number of titles published annually: 5 Print; 5 E-Book
Total Titles: 6 Print; 5 E-Book
Foreign Rights: Kaplan/DeFiore Rights (Linda Kaplan) (worldwide)
Orders to: PGW Distribution, 210 American Dr, Jackson, TN 38301, Contact: Lony Haley-Nelson *Toll Free Tel:* 800-788-3123 *Toll Free Fax:* 800-351-5073 *E-mail:* orderentry@perseusbooks.com
Returns: Perseus Distribution, 193 Edwards Dr, Jackson, TN 38301 *Toll Free Tel:* 800-788-3123 *Toll Free Fax:* 800-351-5073
Warehouse: PGW Distribution, 210 American Dr, Jackson, TN 38301 *Toll Free Tel:* 800-788-3123 *Toll Free Fax:* 800-351-5073
Distribution Center: Publishers Group West (PGW)/Ingram, 1700 Fourth St, Berkeley, CA 94710 *Tel:* 510-809-3700 *Fax:* 510-809-3777 *E-mail:* info@pgw.com *Web Site:* www.pgw.com
Membership(s): ABA; The Children's Book Council; Pacific Northwest Booksellers Association; Publishers Association of the West

innovativeKids®
Division of Innovative USA® Inc
50 Washington St, Suite 201, Norwalk, CT 06854
Tel: 203-838-6400
E-mail: info@innovativekids.com
Web Site: www.innovativekids.com
Key Personnel
CEO: Michael S Levins *E-mail:* mlevins@innovativekids.com
Pres & Publr: Shari Kaufman *Tel:* 203-838-6400 ext 4305 *E-mail:* skaufman@innovativekids.com
Founded: 1989
Publishing interactive, tactile books for preschool through elementary school age children - unusual formats that foster the growth of essential learning skills.
ISBN Prefix(es): 978-1-58476; 978-1-60169
Number of titles published annually: 50 Print
Total Titles: 150 Print
Membership(s): ABA; American Book Producers Association; American Specialty Toy Retailing Association; Education Market Association; Independent Book Publishers Association; Toy International Association

Insight Editions
800 "A" St, San Rafael, CA 94901
Tel: 415-526-1370 *Toll Free Tel:* 800-809-3792 *Toll Free Fax:* 866-509-0515
E-mail: info@insighteditions.com
Web Site: www.insighteditions.com
Key Personnel
Pres & Publr: Raoul Goff
Head, Sales & Mktg: Terry Newell
Dir, Mktg: Joan Lee
PR Dir: Darcy Cohan
Sales Dir: Julie Hamilton
Sales Mgr: Jacqui Goff *E-mail:* j.goff@insighteditions.com; Jennifer Metzger
Sr Ed: Mark Irwin; Vanessa Lopez
Sr Ed, Children's: Jordan Hamessley
Sr Prodn Ed: Lauren LePera
Asst Design Mgr: Alison Corn
Publicist: Lauren Kretzschmar
Contracts Admin: Charr Treadway
Proj Coord: Colton Long
Copy Ed & Proofreader: Tessa Murphy
Foreign Rts Sales: Katrin Hagerty
Founded: 2000
Renowned for creating beautiful, innovative books that excel in the marketplace. Insight Editions brings the vision & style of high-end illustrated books to the realm of the arts & entertainment.
ISBN Prefix(es): 978-1-933784
Number of titles published annually: 75 Print
Total Titles: 300 Print
Distributed by Simon & Schuster
See separate listing for:
Mandala Earth

Institute of Continuing Legal Education
1020 Greene St, Ann Arbor, MI 48109-1444
Tel: 734-764-0533 *Toll Free Tel:* 877-229-4350 *Fax:* 734-763-2412 *Toll Free Fax:* 877-229-4351
E-mail: icle@umich.edu
Web Site: www.icle.org
Key Personnel
Dir: David R Watson

Educ Dir: Jeffrey E Kirkey
Founded: 1959
Michigan law books in print & online.
ISBN Prefix(es): 978-0-615
Number of titles published annually: 33 Print
Total Titles: 58 Print; 55 Online
Imprints: ICLE

§Institute of Environmental Sciences & Technology - IEST
2340 S Arlington Heights Rd, Suite 620, Arlington Heights, IL 60005-4510
Tel: 847-981-0100 *Fax:* 847-981-4130
E-mail: information@iest.org
Web Site: www.iest.org
Key Personnel
Exec Dir: Roberta Burrows *Tel:* 847-981-0100 ext 6015 *E-mail:* executive@iest.org
Tech Prog Mgr: Jennifer Sklena *Tel:* 847-981-0100 ext 6011 *E-mail:* iestservices@iest.org
Database & Acctg Coord: Mara Douvris *Tel:* 847-981-0100 ext 6109 *E-mail:* accounting@iest.org
Mktg & Membership Coord: Grant Polachek *Tel:* 847-981-0100 ext 6012 *E-mail:* gpolachek@iest.org
Educ & Meetings Mgr: Heather Wooden *Tel:* 847-981-0100 ext 6014 *E-mail:* education@iest.org
Membership & Admin Asst: Susan Stamatkin *Tel:* 847-981-0100 ext 6015 *E-mail:* customerservice@iest.org
Founded: 1953
A multidisciplinary, international society whose members are recognized worldwide for their contributions to the environmental sciences in the area of contamination control & cleanrooms; environmental testing; or nanotechnology facilities.
ISBN Prefix(es): 978-0-915414; 978-1-877862; 978-0-9747313; 978-0-9787868; 978-0-9841330; 978-1-937280
Number of titles published annually: 3 Print; 1 CD-ROM; 3 Online
Total Titles: 75 Print; 26 CD-ROM; 48 Online

Institute of Governmental Studies
Subsidiary of University of California, Berkeley
109 Moses Hall, No 2370, Berkeley, CA 94720-2370
Tel: 510-642-1428 *Fax:* 510-642-3020; 510-642-5537 (orders)
E-mail: igspress@berkeley.edu
Web Site: www.igs.berkeley.edu
Key Personnel
Dir, Pubns: Ethan Rarick *E-mail:* erarick@berkeley.edu
Pubns Ed: Maria Wolf *E-mail:* mariaw@berkeley.edu
Public policy issues.
ISBN Prefix(es): 978-0-87772
Number of titles published annually: 6 Print
Total Titles: 54 Print

§Institute of Jesuit Sources (IJS)
Boston College, Institute for Advanced Jesuit Studies, 140 Commonwealth Ave, Chestnut, MA 02467
Tel: 617-552-2568 *Fax:* 617-552-2575
E-mail: jesuitsources@bc.edu
Web Site: jesuitsources.bc.edu
Key Personnel
Dir: Fr John W Padberg *Tel:* 314-633-4400
Founded: 1961
Books on history & spirituality of the society of Jesus (Jesuits) translated from non-English sources & originally in English.
ISBN Prefix(es): 978-0-912422; 978-1-880810
Number of titles published annually: 8 Print
Total Titles: 103 Print; 1 CD-ROM

§Institute of Mathematical Geography
Division of Arlinghaus Enterprises LLC
1964 Boulder Dr, Ann Arbor, MI 48104
Tel: 734-975-0246
E-mail: image@imagenet.org
Web Site: www.imagenet.org
Key Personnel
Founding Dir: Sandra Lach Arlinghaus
Founded: 1986
Publish scholarly books & college textbooks, electronic journals & books.
ISBN Prefix(es): 978-1-877751
Number of titles published annually: 3 Print
Total Titles: 39 Print; 13 E-Book

Institute of Police Technology & Management
Division of University of North Florida
12000 Alumni Dr, Jacksonville, FL 32224-2678
Tel: 904-620-4786 *Fax:* 904-620-2453
E-mail: info@iptm.org
Web Site: www.iptm.org
Key Personnel
Dir: Cameron Pucci *E-mail:* cpucci@unf.edu
Founded: 1980
In-service training for law enforcement, civilian personnel; marketing of publications, templates & videos. Specialize in traffic crash investigation & reconstruction; law enforcement management & supervision; criminal investigation; forensic technology; DUI & drug law enforcement; radar/laser speed enforcement; gangs & other specialized subjects.
ISBN Prefix(es): 978-1-884566
Number of titles published annually: 7 Print; 2 CD-ROM
Total Titles: 65 Print; 6 CD-ROM
Foreign Rep(s): Paul Feenan (Australia, South Pacific)
Foreign Rights: Pacific Traffic Education Centre (Canada)

The Institutes™
720 Providence Rd, Suite 100, Malvern, PA 19355-3433
Tel: 610-644-2100 *Toll Free Tel:* 800-644-2101 *Fax:* 610-640-9576
E-mail: customerservice@theinstitutes.org
Web Site: www.theinstitutes.org
Key Personnel
Pres & CEO: Peter Miller
Property-casualty continuing insurance education.
ISBN Prefix(es): 978-0-89463; 978-0-89462
Number of titles published annually: 12 Print
Total Titles: 120 Print

The Institution of Engineering & Technology, see IET USA Inc

Inter-American Development Bank
Division of Multilateral Development Bank
1300 New York Ave NW, Washington, DC 20577
Tel: 202-623-1000 *Fax:* 202-623-3096
E-mail: pic@iadb.org
Web Site: www.iadb.org/pub
Key Personnel
Pres: Luis Alberto Moreno
EVP: Julie T Katzman
Founded: 1959
Economic development in Latin America & the Caribbean.
ISBN Prefix(es): 978-0-940602; 978-1-886938; 978-1-931003; 978-1-59782
Number of titles published annually: 30 Print
Total Titles: 160 Print
Distributed by Johns Hopkins University Press

§Inter-University Consortium for Political & Social Research (ICPSR)
Affiliate of University of Michigan Institute for Social Research
330 Packard St, Ann Arbor, MI 48104
Mailing Address: PO Box 1248, Ann Arbor, MI 48106-1248
Tel: 734-647-5000 *Fax:* 734-647-8200
E-mail: netmail@icpsr.umich.edu
Web Site: www.icpsr.umich.edu
Key Personnel
Dir: George Alter *Tel:* 734-615-7652 *E-mail:* altergc@umich.edu
Asst Dir: Mary Vardigan *Tel:* 734-615-7908 *E-mail:* vardigan@umich.edu
Founded: 1962
Provides access to social science data collections & documentation. Additional subjects include: demography & aging/gerontology.
ISBN Prefix(es): 978-0-89138
Number of titles published annually: 300 Online
Total Titles: 7,500 Online

Intercultural Development Research Association (IDRA)
5815 Callaghan Rd, Suite 101, San Antonio, TX 78228
Tel: 210-444-1710 *Fax:* 210-444-1714
E-mail: contact@idra.org
Web Site: www.idra.org
Key Personnel
CEO & Pres: Dr Maria "Cuca" Robledo Montecel, PhD
Communs Mgr: Christie Goodman
Founded: 1973
Independent & private, nonprofit organization dedicated to creating schools that work for all children; works with people to create & apply cutting-edge educational policies & practices that value & empower all children, families & communities. Conducts research & development activities, creates, implements & administers innovative education programs & provides teacher, administrator, parent training & technical assistance.
ISBN Prefix(es): 978-1-878550; 978-1-935737
Number of titles published annually: 10 Print
Total Titles: 50 Print

Intercultural Press Inc
Division of Nicholas Brealey Publishing
53 State St, Boston, MA 02109
Tel: 617-523-3801 *Toll Free Tel:* 888-273-2539 *Fax:* 617-523-3708
E-mail: info@interculturalpress.com
Web Site: nicholasbrealey.com
Key Personnel
Head: Janet Crockett
Dir, Prodn: Jennifer Delaney
Sales Mgr: Melissa Carl
Founded: 1980
Books, training & educational materials on international, cross-cultural & diversity subjects, including reference books, bibliographies, manuals, handbooks, nonfiction.
ISBN Prefix(es): 978-0-933662; 978-1-877864; 978-1-931930; 978-0-9842471
Number of titles published annually: 12 Print
Total Titles: 150 Print
Distribution Center: National Book Network, 15200 NBN Way, Blue Ridge Summit, PA 17214 *Toll Free Tel:* 800-462-6420

Interlink Publishing Group Inc
46 Crosby St, Northampton, MA 01060
SAN: 664-8908
Tel: 413-582-7054 *Toll Free Tel:* 800-238-LINK (238-5465) *Fax:* 413-582-7057
E-mail: info@interlinkbooks.com
Web Site: www.interlinkbooks.com
Key Personnel
Publr & Edit Dir: Michel Moushabeck *Tel:* 413-582-7054 ext 204 *E-mail:* michel@interlinkbooks.com
Lib Sales Dir: Brenda Eaton
Publicity Dir: Moira Megargee
Founded: 1987

World travel, world literature, world history/politics/current affairs, ethnic cooking & illustrated children's books.
ISBN Prefix(es): 978-0-940793; 978-1-56656
Number of titles published annually: 55 Print; 40 E-Book
Total Titles: 996 Print; 500 E-Book
Imprints: Clockroot Books; Codagen Guides USA; Crocodile Books; Interlink Books; Olive Branch Press
Distributor for Black & White Publishing (UK); Camerapix Publishers International; Georgina Campbell Guides (Ireland); Macmillan Caribbean (UK); Quartet Books (UK); Rucksack Readers (UK); Serif Publishing Ltd (UK); Sheldrake Press (UK); Signal Books (UK); Waverley Books (UK); Neil Wilson Publishing (UK)
Foreign Rep(s): Codasat Canada Ltd (Canada); Electra Media Group (Southeast Asia); Network Book Distribution Ltd (Europe, UK); Palgrave Macmillan (Australia, New Zealand); Peter Ward Book Exports (Middle East)
Distribution Center: Publishers Group West (digital dist servs via Constellation)

International Book Centre Inc
2391 Auburn Rd, Shelby Township, MI 48317
SAN: 208-7022
Mailing Address: PO Box 295, Troy, MI 48099
Tel: 586-254-7230 *Fax:* 586-254-7230
E-mail: ibc@ibcbooks.com
Web Site: www.ibcbooks.com
Key Personnel
Owner: Doris Mukalla
Founded: 1974
Publisher of foreign language books. Specialize in the language & culture of the Middle East.
ISBN Prefix(es): 978-0-86685
Number of titles published annually: 2 Print; 2 Audio
Total Titles: 28 Print; 5 Audio
Distributor for Compass Publications; Library du Liban (Lebanon); New Readers Press; Oxford University Press; Pro Lingua Associates; Stacey International Ltd (London); University of Michigan

§International City/County Management Association (ICMA)
777 N Capitol St NE, Suite 500, Washington, DC 20002-4201
Tel: 202-289-4262 *Toll Free Tel:* 800-745-8780 *Fax:* 202-962-3500
E-mail: customerservices@icma.org
Web Site: icma.org
Key Personnel
Exec Dir: Robert J O'Neill, Jr *E-mail:* roneill@icma.org
Dir, Pubns: Ann Mahoney *Tel:* 202-962-3643
Founded: 1914
Local government leadership & management organization that provides member support; publications, data & information; peer & results-oriented assistance; training & professional development to more than 8,200 city, town & county experts throughout the world.
ISBN Prefix(es): 978-0-87326
Number of titles published annually: 10 Print; 2 CD-ROM; 25 Online
Total Titles: 200 Print; 7 CD-ROM; 85 Online
Warehouse: PBD, 1650 Bluegrass Lakes Pkwy, Alpharetta, GA 30004 *Tel:* 770-442-8633
Distribution Center: PBD, 1650 Bluegrass Lakes Pkwy, Alpharetta, GA 30004 *Tel:* 770-442-8633

International Code Council Inc
3060 Saturn St, Suite 100, Brea, CA 92821
Tel: 562-699-0541 *Toll Free Tel:* 888-422-7233 *Fax:* 562-908-5524, 562-699-8031
E-mail: es@icc-es.org; order@icc-es.org
Web Site: www.iccsafe.org
Key Personnel
EVP, Busn Devt: Mark Johnson *Tel:* 562-699-0541 ext 3248 *E-mail:* mjohnson@icc-es.org
Founded: 1922
Publisher of construction codes & regulations used in US & abroad.
ISBN Prefix(es): 978-1-58001; 978-1-884590; 978-1-892395; 978-1-60983
Number of titles published annually: 60 Print; 10 CD-ROM
Total Titles: 300 Print; 20 CD-ROM

International Council of Shopping Centers (ICSC)
1221 Avenue of the Americas, 41st fl, New York, NY 10020-1099
Tel: 646-728-3800 *Fax:* 732-694-1755
E-mail: icsc@icsc.org
Web Site: www.icsc.org
Key Personnel
Dir, Pubns: Patricia Montagni *Tel:* 646-728-3494 *Fax:* 732-694-1767 *E-mail:* pmontagni@icsc.org
Founded: 1957
Books & ebooks.
ISBN Prefix(es): 978-0-927547; 978-0-913598; 978-1-58268
Number of titles published annually: 15 Print; 5 E-Book
Total Titles: 100 Print; 5 E-Book
Branch Office(s)
120 Eglinton Ave E, Suite 605, Toronto, ON M4P 1E2, Canada *Tel:* 416-486-4511 *Fax:* 416-486-3280 *E-mail:* bcarter@icsc.org
Foreign Office(s): 31-08, China World Off 1, No 1 Jian Guo Men Wai Ave, Beijing 100004, China *Tel:* (010) 65055103 ext 105 *Fax:* (010) 52214646 *E-mail:* xli@icsc.org
Homero 203, piso 9-97B, Polanco, 11570 Mexico, DF, Mexico *Tel:* (0155) 3300 5346 *Fax:* (0155) 5536 7673 *E-mail:* latam@icsc.org
138 Cecil St, Cecil Ct No 08-02, Singapore 069538, Singapore *Tel:* 6532 3722 *Fax:* 6532 7355 *E-mail:* info@icsc.org.sg
29 Queen Anne's Gate, London SW1H 9BU, United Kingdom *Tel:* (020) 7976 3102 *Fax:* (020) 7976 3101 *E-mail:* info.europe@icsc.org
Warehouse: BrightKey, 9050 Junction Dr, Annapolis Junction, MD 20701 *Tel:* 301-362-6900
Distribution Center: BrightKey, 9050 Junction Dr, Annapolis Junction, MD 20701 *Tel:* 301-362-6900

International Food Policy Research Institute
Member of Consultative Group on International Agricultural Research (CGIAR)
2033 "K" St NW, Washington, DC 20006-1002
Tel: 202-862-5600 *Fax:* 202-467-4439
E-mail: ifpri@cgiar.org
Web Site: www.ifpri.org
Key Personnel
Dir Gen: Shenggen Fan
Communs Dir: Klaus von Grebmer *E-mail:* k.vongrebmer@cgiar.org
Founded: 1975
Research reports, occasional papers & newsletter series, books, briefs, abstracts.
ISBN Prefix(es): 978-0-89629
Number of titles published annually: 270 Print; 2 CD-ROM; 270 Online
Total Titles: 3,980 Print; 21 CD-ROM; 3,634 Online
Distributed by Johns Hopkins University Press

International Foundation of Employee Benefit Plans
18700 W Bluemound Rd, Brookfield, WI 53045
Mailing Address: PO Box 69, Brookfield, WI 53008-0069
Tel: 262-786-6700 *Toll Free Tel:* 888-334-3327 *Fax:* 262-786-8780
E-mail: editor@ifebp.org
Web Site: www.ifebp.org
Key Personnel
Sr Dir, Info Servs & Pubns: Kelli Kolsrud *E-mail:* kellik@ifebp.org
Assoc Dir, Book Pubns: Pat Bonner *E-mail:* patb@ifebp.org
Founded: 1954
ISBN Prefix(es): 978-0-89154
Number of titles published annually: 2 Print; 2 E-Book
Total Titles: 30 Print; 15 CD-ROM; 30 E-Book
Membership(s): Association Media & Publishing; Independent Book Publishers Association

The International Institute of Islamic Thought
500 Grove St, Suite 200, Herndon, VA 20170
Tel: 703-471-1133 *Fax:* 703-471-3922
E-mail: iiit@iiit.org
Web Site: www.iiit.org
Key Personnel
Pres: Abusolayman Abdulhamid
Dir, Pubns: Dr Jamal Barzinji
Founded: 1981
Books, audiobooks & videos.
ISBN Prefix(es): 978-0-912463; 978-1-56564
Number of titles published annually: 40 Print
Total Titles: 500 Print

§International Linguistics Corp
12220 Blue Ridge Blvd, Suite G, Kansas City, MO 64030
Tel: 816-765-8855 *Toll Free Tel:* 800-237-1830 (orders) *Fax:* 816-765-2855
E-mail: learnables@sbcglobal.net
Web Site: www.learnables.com
Key Personnel
Gen Mgr: Jennifer Elliott
Founded: 1976
Foreign & English language materials, language teaching materials.
ISBN Prefix(es): 978-0-939990; 978-1-887371; 978-0-9814540
Number of titles published annually: 3 Print; 3 CD-ROM; 1 Online; 3 Audio
Total Titles: 52 Print; 10 CD-ROM; 1 Online; 50 Audio

International Literacy Association (ILA)
800 Barksdale Rd, Newark, DE 19711-3204
Mailing Address: PO Box 8139, Newark, DE 19714-8139
Tel: 302-731-1600 *Toll Free Tel:* 800-336-7323 (US & CN) *Fax:* 302-731-1057
E-mail: customerservice@reading.org
Web Site: www.literacyworldwide.org; www.reading.org
Key Personnel
Exec Dir: Marcie Craig Post *E-mail:* mpost@reading.org
Founded: 1956
Books & journals related to reading instruction & literary education.
ISBN Prefix(es): 978-0-87207
Number of titles published annually: 10 Print; 5 E-Book
Total Titles: 150 Print; 15 E-Book
Branch Office(s)
444 N Capitol St NW, Suite 640, Washington, DC 20001 *Tel:* 202-624-8800 *Fax:* 202-624-8826
Foreign Rights: Academics Plus (Andrea Permel) (UK); Eurospan Group (Catherine Lawn) (Trinidad and Tobago)

§International Monetary Fund (IMF), Editorial & Publications Division
700 19 St NW, HQ1-7-124, Washington, DC 20431
SAN: 203-8188

Tel: 202-623-7430 *Fax:* 202-623-7201
E-mail: publications@imf.org
Web Site: bookstore.imf.org; elibrary.imf.org (online collection)
Key Personnel
Publr: Jeffrey Hayden
Assoc Publr: Linda Griffin Kean
Founded: 1946
Publishes a wide variety of books, periodicals, multimedia & digital products covering global economics, international finance, monetary policy, statistics, exchange rates & general macroeconomic issues.
ISBN Prefix(es): 978-0-939934; 978-1-55775; 978-1-58906; 978-1-61635
Number of titles published annually: 120 Print; 12 CD-ROM; 120 Online; 200 E-Book
Total Titles: 1,200 Print
Orders to: IMF Publications, PO Box 92780, Washington, DC 20090
Membership(s): AAP; Association of American University Presses; Association of Learned & Professional Society Publishers; CrossRef

§International Press of Boston Inc
387 Somerville Ave, Somerville, MA 02143
Mailing Address: PO Box 502, Somerville, MA 02143
Tel: 617-623-3016 *Fax:* 617-623-3101
E-mail: ipb-info@intlpress.com; ipb-orders@intlpress.com
Web Site: www.intlpress.com
Key Personnel
Gen Mgr: Brian Bianchini *Tel:* 617-623-3855 *E-mail:* ipb-mgmt@intlpress.com
Founded: 1992
Publish books, monographs, conference proceedings in advanced mathematics.
ISBN Prefix(es): 978-1-57146
Number of titles published annually: 10 Print
Total Titles: 100 Print; 3 CD-ROM
Distributed by AMS

International Publishers Co Inc
235 W 23 St, New York, NY 10011
SAN: 202-5655
Tel: 212-366-9816 *Fax:* 212-366-9820
E-mail: service@intpubnyc.com
Web Site: www.intpubnyc.com
Key Personnel
Pres & Ed: Betty Smith
Founded: 1924
Short discount titles & Marxist classics. Trade in cloth & paperback, general nonfiction, social sciences, classic & contemporary Marxism-Leninism, literature, poetry & biography, labor, women's studies.
ISBN Prefix(es): 978-0-7178
Number of titles published annually: 4 Print
Total Titles: 160 Print
Imprints: New World Paperbacks
Foreign Rep(s): Global Book Marketing (London, UK)
Returns: Whitehurst & Clark, 1200 County Rd 523, Flemington, NJ 08822
Warehouse: Whitehurst & Clark, 1200 County Rd, Rte 523, Flemington, NJ 08822, Contact: Brad Searles *Tel:* 908-782-2323 *Fax:* 908-237-2407
Membership(s): ABA; The Association of Publishers for Special Sales; Independent Book Publishers Association; National Association of College Stores

International Research Center for Energy & Economic Development
850 Willowbrook Rd, Boulder, CO 80302
Tel: 303-442-4014 *Fax:* 303-442-5042
E-mail: info@iceed.org
Web Site: www.iceed.org
Key Personnel
Dir: Dorothea H El Mallakh
Lib Sales Dir: Helen El Mallakh
Founded: 1974
Monographs & hardcover; public policy; journal.
ISBN Prefix(es): 978-0-918714
Number of titles published annually: 4 Print
Total Titles: 86 Print
Warehouse: William S Hein & Co Inc, 1285 Main St, Buffalo, NY 14209 (for back orders of earlier volumes)

§International Risk Management Institute Inc
12222 Merit Dr, Suite 1600, Dallas, TX 75251-2266
Tel: 972-960-7693 *Fax:* 972-371-5120
E-mail: info27@irmi.com
Web Site: www.irmi.com
Key Personnel
CFO: Ron Allen
Pres: Jack Gibson
Founded: 1978
Publish both print & online books on commercial & personal lines of insurance.
ISBN Prefix(es): 978-1-886813; 978-0-938358; 978-1-933686
Number of titles published annually: 20 Print; 36 Online
Total Titles: 34 Print

International Society for Technology in Education
1530 Wilson Blvd, Suite 730, Arlington, VA 22209
Tel: 503-342-2848 (intl) *Toll Free Tel:* 800-336-5191 (US & CN)
E-mail: iste@iste.org
Web Site: www.iste.org; www.isteconference.org
Key Personnel
CEO: Richard Culatta
Chief Mktg Offr: Tracee Aliotti
Chief Membership Offr: Jessica Medaille
Founded: 1979
Work with experienced educators to develop & produce practical resources for classroom teachers, teacher educators & technology leaders. Home of the National Educational Technology Standards (NETS), ISTE is the trusted source for educational technology books & courseware.
ISBN Prefix(es): 978-1-56484
Number of titles published annually: 12 Print
Total Titles: 60 Print
Branch Office(s)
621 SW Morrison St, Suite 800, Portland, OR 97205 *Fax:* 503-882-0813

§International Society of Automation (ISA)
67 T W Alexander Dr, Research Triangle Park, NC 27709-0185
Mailing Address: PO Box 12277, Research Triangle Park, NC 27709-2277
Tel: 919-549-8411 *Fax:* 919-549-8288
E-mail: info@isa.org
Web Site: www.isa.org
Key Personnel
Exec Dir: Patrick Gouhin
Dir, Publg, Mktg & Sales: Tim Feldman
Founded: 1945
Technical books, references, journals, video-based training programs, directories, software, standards, proceedings, CD-ROM, electronic references.
ISBN Prefix(es): 978-1-55617; 978-1-939660; 978-0-87664; 978-0-9791330; 978-1-936007; 978-1-941546; 978-0-9792343; 978-1-934394; 978-1-937560
Number of titles published annually: 20 Print
Total Titles: 139 Print; 10 CD-ROM; 20 E-Book
Foreign Rep(s): Eurospan (Europe)

§International Wealth Success Inc
PO Box 186, Merrick, NY 11566-0186
Tel: 516-766-5850 *Toll Free Tel:* 800-323-0548 *Fax:* 516-766-5919
E-mail: admin@iwsmoney.com
Web Site: www.iwsmoney.com
Key Personnel
Pres & Ed: Tyler G Hicks *E-mail:* tyghicks@aol.com
Founded: 1966
Publish a variety of business & financial titles in the fields of small business, real estate, mail order, import-export & financing.
ISBN Prefix(es): 978-0-934311; 978-0-914306; 978-1-56150
Number of titles published annually: 6 Print; 6 CD-ROM; 4 Online; 70 E-Book; 4 Audio
Total Titles: 120 Print; 120 CD-ROM; 70 Online; 100 E-Book; 12 Audio

InterVarsity Press
Division of InterVarsity Christian Fellowship/USA
430 Plaza Dr, Westmont, IL 60559-1234
SAN: 202-7089
Mailing Address: PO Box 1400, Downers Grove, IL 60515
Tel: 630-734-4000 *Toll Free Tel:* 800-843-9487 *Fax:* 630-734-4200
E-mail: email@ivpress.com
Web Site: www.ivpress.com
Key Personnel
Publr: Jeff Crosby *Tel:* 630-734-4017 *E-mail:* jcrosby@ivpress.com
Assoc Publr, Edit: Cindy Bunch *Tel:* 630-734-4078 *E-mail:* cbunch@ivpress.com
Assoc Publr & Academic Edit Dir: Daniel Reid *Tel:* 360-379-2599 *E-mail:* dreid@ivpress.com
Art Dir: Cindy Kiple *Tel:* 630-734-4024 *E-mail:* ckiple@ivpress.com
Interim Dir, Fin & Acctg: David Page *Tel:* 630-734-4004 *E-mail:* dpage@ivpress.com
Dir, Mktg: Helen Lee *Tel:* 630-734-4038 *E-mail:* hlee@ivpress.com
Dir, Opers & Fulfillment: Anne Gerth *Tel:* 630-734-4027 *E-mail:* agerth@ivpress.com
Dir, Sales: Justin Paul Lawrence *Tel:* 630-734-4124 *E-mail:* jplawrence@ivpress.com
Sr Rts & Contracts Mgr: Ellen Hsu *Tel:* 630-734-4034 *E-mail:* ehsu@ivpress.com
Founded: 1947
Religion (interdenominational); textbooks.
ISBN Prefix(es): 978-0-87784; 978-0-8308
Number of titles published annually: 130 Print; 130 E-Book; 10 Audio
Total Titles: 2,000 Print; 1,200 E-Book; 50 Audio
Imprints: IVP Academic (publishing to facilitate broader conversations in the academy & the church); IVP Books (thoughtful books on church, culture & mission); IVP Connect (resources for Bible study & small groups); IVP Crescendo (women applying their vision & gifts to the good of the whole church); IVP Praxis (bringing together theory & practice for the advancement of ministry); LifeGuide Bible Studies (guides on books of the Bible & key Biblical topics)
Branch Office(s)
Port Townsend, WA 98368
Membership(s): Evangelical Christian Publishers Association

Interweave Press LLC
Imprint of F+W Media Inc
201 E Fourth St, Loveland, CO 80537
Toll Free Tel: 800-272-2193; 800-289-0963 *Fax:* 970-613-4656 *Toll Free Fax:* 888-590-4082
Web Site: www.interweave.com
Key Personnel
Founder & Creative Dir: Linda Ligon
Mng Ed: Rebecca Campbell
Sr Ed: Erica Smith
Founded: 1975

ISBN Prefix(es): 978-0-934026; 978-1-883010; 978-1-931499; 978-0-9796073; 978-1-4402; 978-1-63250; 978-1-59668; 978-1-62033
Number of titles published annually: 45 Print
Total Titles: 350 Print
Distributed by Keith Ainsworth Pty Ltd (Australia); David Bateman Ltd (New Zealand); Search Press (UK)
Membership(s): Publishers Association of the West

§The Intrepid Traveler
152 Staltonstall Pkwy (rear entrance), East Haven, CT 06512
Mailing Address: PO Box 531, Branford, CT 06405-0531
Tel: 203-469-0214
E-mail: admin@intrepidtraveler.com
Web Site: www.intrepidtraveler.com
Key Personnel
Publr: Kelly Monaghan
Assoc Publr: Sally Scanlon *E-mail:* sscanlon@intrepidtraveler.com
Founded: 1990
Publish travel how-to & guidebooks titles.
ISBN Prefix(es): 978-0-9627892; 978-1-887140; 978-1-937011
Number of titles published annually: 4 Print; 4 E-Book
Total Titles: 14 Print; 8 E-Book
Distribution Center: National Book Network Inc (NBN), 15200 NBN Way, Blue Ridge Summit, PA 17214 *Tel:* 717-794-3800 *Toll Free Tel:* 800-462-6420 *Fax:* 717-794-3828 *Toll Free Fax:* 800-338-4550 *E-mail:* customercare@nbnbooks.com *Web Site:* www.nbnbooks.com
Membership(s): Independent Book Publishers Association

Iris Press
Imprint of The Iris Publishing Group Inc
969 Oak Ridge Tpke, No 328, Oak Ridge, TN 37830
Web Site: www.irisbooks.com
Key Personnel
Publr: Robert Cumming *E-mail:* rcumming@irisbooks.com
Ed & Designer: Beto Cumming *E-mail:* bcumming@irisbooks.com
Audio Pubns: Willie Cumming *E-mail:* wcumming@irisbooks.com
Founded: 1975
Publisher of print editions of high quality poetry & literary prose.
ISBN Prefix(es): 978-0-916078; 978-1-60454
Number of titles published annually: 10 Print
Total Titles: 180 Print

Iron Gate Publishing
PO Box 999, Niwot, CO 80544
Tel: 303-530-2551 *Fax:* 303-530-5273
E-mail: editor@irongate.com
Web Site: www.irongate.com
Key Personnel
Publr & Ed: Dina C Carson *E-mail:* editor@irongate.com
Founded: 1990
Genealogy, local history Colorado, self-publishing, reference.
ISBN Prefix(es): 978-1-879579; 978-0-9724975; 978-1-68224
Number of titles published annually: 15 Print; 25 E-Book
Total Titles: 70 Print; 25 E-Book
Membership(s): The Association of Publishers for Special Sales; Colorado Independent Publishers Association; Independent Book Publishers Association; Publishers Association of the West

ISI Books
Imprint of Intercollegiate Studies Institute Inc
3901 Centerville Rd, Wilmington, DE 19807-1938
Tel: 302-652-4600 *Toll Free Tel:* 800-526-7022 *Fax:* 302-652-1760
E-mail: info@isi.org; isibooks@isi.org
Web Site: www.isibooks.org
Key Personnel
Pres: Charley Copeland
VP & Ed-in-Chief: Jed Donahue *E-mail:* jdonahue@isi.org
Founded: 1993
Publisher of serious but accessible nonfiction titles. ISI also publishes the esteemed quarterly journal *Modern Age* (founded in 1957 by Russell Kirk).
ISBN Prefix(es): 978-1-882926; 978-1-932236
Number of titles published annually: 4 Print; 4 E-Book
Total Titles: 50 Print; 100 E-Book

Island Press
2000 "M" St NW, Suite 650, Washington, DC 20036
SAN: 212-5129
Tel: 202-232-7933 *Toll Free Tel:* 800-828-1302 *Fax:* 202-234-1328
E-mail: info@islandpress.org
Web Site: www.islandpress.org
Key Personnel
Pres: David Miller
VP, Sales & Mktg: Julie Marshall
Exec Ed: Heather Boyer
Founded: 1984
Books about the environment for professionals, students & general readers, autobiography-scientific; land use planning; environmental economics; nature essays; "green" architecture.
ISBN Prefix(es): 978-0-933280; 978-1-55963; 978-1-59726; 978-1-61091
Number of titles published annually: 40 Print; 40 E-Book
Total Titles: 1,000 Print; 800 E-Book
Imprints: Shearwater Books
Distributor for IUCN; Techne Press
Shipping Address: University of Chicago Distribution Center, 11030 S Langley Ave, Chicago, IL 60628 *Tel:* 773-702-7000 *Toll Free Tel:* 800-621-2736 *Fax:* 773-702-7212 *Toll Free Fax:* 800-621-8476 *E-mail:* custserv@press.uchicago.edu
Membership(s): American Association of University Presses; BISG

ISTE, see International Society for Technology in Education

§Italica Press
595 Main St, Suite 605, New York, NY 10044
SAN: 695-1805
Tel: 917-371-0563
E-mail: inquiries@italicapress.com
Web Site: www.italicapress.com
Key Personnel
Pres & Publr, Electronic Publg: Eileen Gardiner *E-mail:* egardiner@italicapress.com
Secy & Publr, Electronic Publg: Ronald G Musto *E-mail:* rgmusto@italicapress.com
Founded: 1985
English translations of Latin & Italian works from the Middle Ages to the present.
ISBN Prefix(es): 978-0-934977; 978-1-59910
Number of titles published annually: 7 Print; 20 E-Book
Total Titles: 200 Print; 60 E-Book
Imprints: Pierrepont Street Press

iUniverse
Division of Author Solutions LLC
1663 Liberty Dr, Bloomington, IN 47403
Toll Free Tel: 800-AUTHORS (288-4677) *Fax:* 812-355-4085
Web Site: www.iuniverse.com
Key Personnel
Exec Chmn: Daniel Shum
SVP, Mktg: Keith Ogorek
SVP, Prodn Servs: Bill Becher
SVP, Worldwide Sales: Craig Lupinatci
Founded: 1999
iUniverse is the industry's leading book marketing, editorial services & supported self-publishing company. The iUniverse management team has extensive editorial & managerial experience with traditional publishers such as Random House, Wiley, Macmillan, Chronicle Books & Addison-Wesley. iUniverse maintains a strategic alliance with Chapters Indigo in Canada & titles accepted into the iUniverse Rising Star program are featured in a special collection on www.barnesandnoble.com.
This publisher has indicated that 100% of their product line is author subsidized.
ISBN Prefix(es): 978-0-9665514; 978-1-58348; 978-0-9668591; 978-1-893652; 978-0-595
Number of titles published annually: 2,500 Print
Total Titles: 40,000 Print
Distribution Center: Baker & Taylor Inc
Ingram Book Group

Jade Rabbit, see Quite Specific Media Group Ltd

§Jain Publishing Co
PO Box 3523, Fremont, CA 94539
SAN: 213-6503
Tel: 510-659-8272 *Fax:* 510-659-0501
E-mail: mail@jainpub.com
Web Site: www.jainpub.com
Key Personnel
Pres & Publr: Mukesh Jain
Founded: 1989
A humanities & social sciences publisher that publishes academic & scholarly references, as well as books for the general reader in both print & electronic formats.
ISBN Prefix(es): 978-0-89581; 978-0-87573
Number of titles published annually: 10 Print; 1 CD-ROM; 2 Online; 2 E-Book
Total Titles: 200 Print; 1 CD-ROM; 2 Online; 4 E-Book
Imprints: Asian Humanities Press

JayJo Books LLC
Subsidiary of The Guidance Group
One Huntington Quadrangle, Suite 1N03, Melville, NY 11747
Tel: 516-496-4863 *Toll Free Tel:* 800-999-6884 *Fax:* 516-496-4050 *Toll Free Fax:* 800-262-1886
E-mail: jayjobooks@guidance-group.com
Web Site: www.guidance-group.com; www.jayjo.com
Key Personnel
Publr: Ed Werz
Ed: Danielle Sensale
Founded: 1992
Educational books to help parents, teachers & children cope with chronic illness, special needs & health education.
ISBN Prefix(es): 978-0-9639449; 978-1-891383
Number of titles published annually: 4 Print
Total Titles: 26 Print

Jeter Publishing, see Gallery Books

Jewish Lights
Imprint of Turner Publishing Co
4507 Charlotte Ave, Suite 100, Nashville, TN 37209
SAN: 134-5621
Tel: 615-255-BOOK (255-2665) *Fax:* 615-255-5081
E-mail: marketing@turnerpublishing.com
Web Site: jewishlights.com; www.turnerpublishing.com

Key Personnel
Pres & Publr, Turner Publishing Co: Todd Bottorff
Founded: 1990
General trade adult & children's books on spirituality, theology, philosophy, mysticism, women's studies, recovery/self-help/healing & history for people of all faiths & backgrounds.
ISBN Prefix(es): 978-1-879045; 978-1-58023
Number of titles published annually: 5 Print; 5 E-Book
Total Titles: 500 Print; 450 E-Book

Jewish Publication Society
2100 Arch St, Philadelphia, PA 19103
SAN: 201-0240
Tel: 215-832-0600 *Toll Free Tel:* 800-234-3151
Fax: 215-568-2017
Web Site: www.jps.org
Key Personnel
Dir & Acqs Ed: Barry L Schwartz
E-mail: bschwartz@jps.org
Mng Ed: Joy Weinberg *Tel:* 215-832-0605
E-mail: jweinberg@jps.org
Off Mgr: Trisha Lubrant *Tel:* 215-832-0612
E-mail: tlubrant@jps.org
Founded: 1888
Books of Jewish interest.
ISBN Prefix(es): 978-0-8276
Number of titles published annually: 8 Print; 8 E-Book
Total Titles: 250 Print
Distributed by University of Nebraska Press
Foreign Rep(s): Eurospan (Europe, Latin America, Middle East, UK & Commonwealth); Scholarly Book Service (Canada)
Membership(s): Association of American University Presses

§Jhpiego
Affiliate of The Johns Hopkins University
1615 Thames St, Baltimore, MD 21231-3492
Tel: 410-537-1800 *Fax:* 410-537-1473
E-mail: info@jhpiego.net
Web Site: www.jhpiego.org
Key Personnel
Pres & CEO: Leslie D Mancuso, PhD
COO: Edwin J Judd
CIO: Glenn R Strachan
VP, External Aff & Communs: Melody McCoy
Founded: 1973
Reproductive health, medical texts, family planning, maternal health, HIV/AIDS & cervical cancer prevention & treatment, infection prevention.
ISBN Prefix(es): 978-0-929817; 978-1-943408
Number of titles published annually: 20 Print
Total Titles: 80 Print; 4 CD-ROM

JHU Press, see The Johns Hopkins University Press

§JIST Publishing
Division of EMC Publishing LLC
875 Montreal Way, St Paul, MN 55102
SAN: 240-2351
Toll Free Tel: 800-328-1452 *Toll Free Fax:* 800-328-4564
E-mail: educate@emcp.com
Web Site: jist.emcp.com
Key Personnel
Sr Acct Mgr: Bob Grilliot
Founded: 1981
Job search (resumes, cover letters, interviewing), career planning, job retention, occupational reference, assessment, self-help, career exploration, occupational information, character education, life skills, CD-ROMs & reference books, videos & software.
ISBN Prefix(es): 978-0-942784; 978-1-56370; 978-1-57112; 978-1-930780; 978-1-55864; 978-1-59357; 978-1-63332
Number of titles published annually: 50 Print; 2 CD-ROM; 20 E-Book; 1 Audio
Total Titles: 350 Print; 6 CD-ROM; 60 E-Book; 1 Audio
Imprints: JIST Career Solutions
Membership(s): Independent Book Publishers Association

The JOC Group Inc
Division of IHS Markit
2 Penn Plaza E, Newark, NJ 07105
Tel: 973-776-8660
Web Site: www.joc.com
Key Personnel
Sr Dir, Edit Content: Peter Tirschwell
E-mail: ptirschwell@joc.com
Exec Ed: Chris Brooks *E-mail:* cbrooks@joc.com
Exec Ed, JOC.com: Mark Szakonyi
E-mail: mszakonyi@joc.com
Founded: 2000
Provider of proprietary data, news, business intelligence & analytical content supporting commercial maritime, rail, trucking, warehousing & logistics industries worldwide.
ISBN Prefix(es): 978-0-9649630; 978-1-891131
Number of titles published annually: 40 Online
Total Titles: 24 Print; 40 Online

John Deere Publishing
Division of Deere & Co
5440 Corporate Park Dr, Davenport, IA 52807
Toll Free Tel: 800-522-7448 (orders) *Fax:* 563-355-3690
E-mail: johndeerepublishing@johndeere.com
Web Site: www.johndeere.com/publications
Founded: 1967
ISBN Prefix(es): 978-0-86691
Number of titles published annually: 8 Print
Total Titles: 27 Print
Warehouse: Quad City Consolidation, 2900 Research Pkwy, Davenport, IA 52806

§The Johns Hopkins University Press
Affiliate of The Johns Hopkins University
2715 N Charles St, Baltimore, MD 21218-4363
SAN: 202-7348
Tel: 410-516-6900; 410-516-6987 (journal orders outside US & CN) *Toll Free Tel:* 800-537-5487 (book orders & cust serv); 800-548-1784 (journal orders) *Fax:* 410-516-6968; 410-516-3866 (journal orders)
E-mail: hfscustserv@press.jhu.edu (cust serv); jrnlcirc@press.jhu.edu (journal orders)
Web Site: www.press.jhu.edu; muse.jhu.edu
Key Personnel
Dir: Barbara Kline Pope
Edit Dir: Greg Britton *E-mail:* gb@press.jhu.edu
Dir, Fin & Admin: Erik Smist *E-mail:* eas@press.jhu.edu
Dir, Mktg & Online Book Publg: Becky Brasington Clark *E-mail:* rbc@press.jhu.edu
Sales Dir: Kerry Cahill *E-mail:* kpc@press.jhu.edu
Journals Publr: William M Breichner
E-mail: wmb@press.jhu.edu
Exec Ed: Vincent J Burke *E-mail:* vjb@press.jhu.edu; Jacqueline C Wehmueller *E-mail:* jcw@press.jhu.edu
Mng Ed: Juliana M McCarthy *E-mail:* jmm@press.jhu.edu
Sr Acqs Ed: Elizabeth Sherburn Demers
E-mail: ed@press.jhu.edu; Matthew McAdam
E-mail: mxm@press.jhu.edu
Acqs Ed: Robin W Coleman *E-mail:* rwc@press.jhu.edu
Devt & Publicity Offr: Jack Holmes
E-mail: jmh@press.jhu.edu
Design & Prodn Mgr: John Cronin *E-mail:* jgc@press.jhu.edu
Fulfillment Opers Mgr: Davida Breier
E-mail: dgb@press.jhu.edu
Journals Mktg Mgr: Lisa Klose *E-mail:* llk@press.jhu.edu
Journals Prodn Mgr: Carol Hamblen
E-mail: crh@press.jhu.edu
Journals Subn Mgr: Robert White Goodman
E-mail: aha@press.jhu.edu
Publicity Mgr, Books Div: Gene Taft
Rts Mgr: Kelly Rogers *E-mail:* klr@press.jhu.edu
Mktg & Sales Coord: Catherine Bergeron
E-mail: cab@press.jhu.edu
Founded: 1878
Scholarly books, nonfiction of general interest, paperbacks, scholarly journals.
ISBN Prefix(es): 978-0-8018; 978-1-4214
Number of titles published annually: 175 Print
Total Titles: 4,200 Print; 5 Online; 3,200 E-Book
Sales Office(s): Terry & Read LLC, 2031 N Craig St, Altadena, CA 91001, Contact: Alan Read *Fax:* 626-356-4630 *E-mail:* alanread@earthlink.net
Terry & Read LLC, 247 Fourth St, Loft 402, Oakland, CA, Contact: David Terry *Tel:* 510-813-9854 *Fax:* 510-465-7668 *E-mail:* dmterry@aol.com
Miller Trade Book Marketing, 363 W Erie St, Suite 7-E, Chicago, IL 60654, Contact: Bruce Miller *Tel:* 312-423-7880 *Fax:* 312-276-8109 *E-mail:* orders@millertrade.com
Book Traveler, Box 193, 1289 N Fordham Blvd, Chapel Hill, NC 27514, Contact: Roger Sauls *Tel:* 919-490-5656 *Fax:* 919-490-0297 *E-mail:* roger_165@msn.com
Terry & Read LLC, 19216 SE 46 Place, Issaquah, WA 98027, Contact: Ted H Terry *Tel:* 425-747-3411 *Fax:* 425-747-0366 *E-mail:* colterryassoc@aol.com
Distributor for Baylor University Press; The Brookings Institution Press; Catholic University of America Press; Center for Talented Youth; Georgetown University Press; Howard University Press; Johns Hopkins Aids Service; Maryland Historical Society; Resources for the Future; University of Massachusetts Press; University of Pennsylvania Museum; University of Pennsylvania Press; University of Washington Press; The University Press of Kentucky; Urban Institute Press; The Woodrow Wilson Center Press; World Resources Institute
Foreign Rep(s): Apex Knowledge Sdn Bhd (Simon Tay) (Brunei, Malaysia); Aromix Books Co Ltd (Nick Woon) (Hong Kong); Avicenna Partnership Ltd (Bill Kennedy) (Bahrain, Egypt, Iran, Iraq, Kazakhstan, Kuwait, Kyrgyzstan, Lebanon, Oman, Qatar, Saudi Arabia, Sudan, Syria, Tajikistan, Turkmenistan, United Arab Emirates, Uzbekistan, Yemen); Avicenna Partnership Ltd (Claire de Gruchy) (Algeria, Cyprus, Greece, Israel, Jordan, Libya, Malta, Morocco, Palestine, Tunisia, Turkey); CRW Books (Tony Sagun) (Philippines); Everest International Publishing Services (Wei Zhao) (China); Footprint Books Pty Ltd (Kate O'Reilly) (Australia, Fiji, New Zealand, Papua New Guinea); ICK-Information & Culture Korea (Mr Se-Yung Jun) (Korea); Ewa Ledochowicz (Eastern Europe); Lexa Publishers' Representatives (Mical Moser) (Canada); Uwe Luedemann (Austria, France, Germany, Italy, Portugal, Spain, Switzerland); Mirjam Mayenburg (Benelux); B K Norton (Ms Meihua Sun) (Taiwan); Provider of Contents & Information (Mr P C Tham) (Singapore); Rockbook Inc (Japan); Christopher Stamp (Denmark, Iceland, Scandinavia); Robert Towers (Ireland, Northern Ireland); Kevin van Hasselt (Africa, Caribbean); The White Partnership (Andrew White) (Hong Kong, India, Indonesia, Malaysia, Thailand); John Wiley & Sons Ltd (Africa, Continental Europe, Middle East, South Asia, UK); World Press (Saleem Malik) (Pakistan); Yale Representation Ltd (Andrew Jarmain) (UK); YUHA Associates (Ahmed Zaharr Kamaruddin) (Brunei, Malaysia)

Foreign Rights: The Chinese Connection Agency (China); Du Ran Kim Agency (Korea); The English Agency (Japan); Graal Literary Agency (Poland); The Deborah Harris Agency (Israel); International Editors' Co (Spain); The Italian Literary Agency srl (Italy); Japan Uni Agency (Japan); The Kalem Literary Agency (Turkey); La Nouvelle Agence (France); Tuttle-Mori Agency Inc (Japan)
Advertising Agency: Welch, Mirabile & Co Inc
Orders to: PO Box 19966, Baltimore, MD 21211-0966
Returns: Hopkins Fulfillment Services, c/o Maple Logistics Solutions, Lebanon Distribution Ctr, PO Box 1287, Lebanon, PA 17042
Warehouse: Maple Logistics Solutions, Lebanon Distribution Ctr, 704 Legionaire Dr, Fredricksburg, PA 17026
Membership(s): AAP; BISG

§Jones & Bartlett Learning LLC
Division of Ascend Learning
5 Wall St, Burlington, MA 01803
Tel: 978-443-5000 *Toll Free Tel:* 800-832-0034 *Fax:* 978-443-8000
E-mail: info@jblearning.com
Web Site: www.jblearning.com
Key Personnel
CEO: Ty Field
Pres: James Homer
Founded: 1983
Academic & professional publisher.
ISBN Prefix(es): 978-0-86720; 978-0-7637; 978-1-4496; 978-1-284
Number of titles published annually: 300 Print
Total Titles: 2,500 Print; 100 CD-ROM
Foreign Office(s): Jones & Bartlett Learning International, The Exchange, Express Park, Bristol Rd, Bridgwater, Somerset TA6 4RR, United Kingdom *Tel:* (01278) 427800 *Fax:* (01278) 421077
Foreign Rep(s): Academic Marketing Services Ltd (Michael Brightmore) (South Africa); Advanced Marketing Associates (Kevin Fong) (Malaysia, Singapore); BNC Publishers Services Inc (Nanette Beramo) (Guam, Philippines); Cengage Learning Asia Pte Ltd (Cambodia, Hong Kong, Indonesia, Laos, Vietnam); Merry Chang (Taiwan); Cranbury International LLC (Caribbean, South America); Elsevier Australia (Australia, Fiji, New Zealand); Benjamin Ho (China, Thailand); Impact Korea (ChongHo Ra) (South Korea); IPR (International Publishers Representatives) (Middle East); Jones & Bartlett India Pvt Ltd (Vinod Vasishtha) (Bangladesh, India, Sri Lanka); The White Partnership (Andrew White) (Japan); World Press (Saleem Malik) (Pakistan)
Returns: 905 Carlow Dr, Unit 5, Bolingbrook, IL 60490
Warehouse: 905 Carlow Dr, Unit 5, Bolingbrook, IL 60490

Jones McClure Publishing
3131 Eastside St, Suite 300, Houston, TX 77098
Mailing Address: PO Box 3348, Houston, TX 77253-3348
Tel: 713-335-8200 *Toll Free Tel:* 800-626-6667 *Fax:* 713-335-8201
E-mail: comments@jonesmcclure.com
Web Site: www.jonesmcclure.com
Key Personnel
Pres: Baird Craft
Founded: 1992
Provides a comprehensive desk reference to the trial lawyer, through codes, commentaries & form covering several areas of Texas law & federal litigation, written in an easy to follow, plain English format.
ISBN Prefix(es): 978-1-884554; 978-1-59839
Number of titles published annually: 26 Print
Total Titles: 26 Print; 3 CD-ROM

§Joshua Tree Publishing
3 Golf Ctr, Suite 201, Hoffman Estates, IL 60169
Tel: 312-893-7525
E-mail: info@joshuatreepublishing.com
Web Site: www.joshuatreepublishing.com; www.centaurbooks.com (imprint); www.chiralhouse.com (imprint)
Key Personnel
Pres & Publr: John Paul Owles *E-mail:* jpo@joshuatreepublishing.com
Founded: 1977
Believe in authors & dedicated to making the dream of being a published author a reality. Specialize in works that uplift the human spirit, inspire people to reach for higher goals & touch the hearts of readers.
ISBN Prefix(es): 978-0-9710954; 978-0-9778311; 978-0-9768677; 978-0-9845904; 978-0-9823703; 978-0-9829803; 978-1-941049
Number of titles published annually: 18 Print; 18 E-Book
Total Titles: 70 Print; 50 E-Book
Imprints: Centaur Books; Chiral House; Heroides Publishing
Membership(s): Book Publicists of Southern California; Independent Book Publishers Association

Journal of Roman Archaeology LLC
95 Peleg Rd, Portsmouth, RI 02871
Tel: 401-683-1955 *Fax:* 401-683-1975
E-mail: jra@journalofromanarch.com
Web Site: www.journalofromanarch.com
Key Personnel
Publr & Gen Ed: John H Humphrey
Founded: 1988
Annual journal & supplementary series.
ISBN Prefix(es): 978-1-887829; 978-0-9913730
Number of titles published annually: 6 Print
Total Titles: 96 Print

§Joy Publishing Co
Division of California Clock Co
PO Box 9901, Fountain Valley, CA 92708
SAN: 663-3544
Tel: 714-545-4321 *Toll Free Tel:* 800-454-8228 (orders) *Fax:* 714-708-2099
Web Site: www.joypublishing.com; kit-cat.com
Key Personnel
Pres: Woody Young *E-mail:* woody@joypublishing.com
Founded: 1986
Publish spiritual books.
ISBN Prefix(es): 978-0-939513
Number of titles published annually: 10 Print; 1 E-Book
Total Titles: 70 Print; 3 CD-ROM; 3 Online; 1 E-Book; 3 Audio
Shipping Address: 16060 Abajo Circle, Fountain Valley, CA 92708

§Joyce Media Inc
3413 Soledad Canyon Rd, Acton, CA 93510-1974
Mailing Address: PO Box 57, Acton, CA 93510-0057
Tel: 661-269-1169 *Fax:* 661-269-2139
E-mail: help@joycemediainc.com
Web Site: www.joycemediainc.com
Key Personnel
Founder & Pres: John Joyce
Founded: 1968
General interest publications; specialize in sign language & newspapers.
ISBN Prefix(es): 978-0-913072
Number of titles published annually: 3 CD-ROM
Total Titles: 11 Print; 35 CD-ROM; 2 E-Book; 2 Audio

Judaica Press Inc
123 Ditmas Ave, Brooklyn, NY 11218
SAN: 204-9856
Tel: 718-972-6200 *Toll Free Tel:* 800-972-6201 *Fax:* 718-972-6204
E-mail: info@judaicapress.com; orders@judaicapress.com
Web Site: www.judaicapress.com
Key Personnel
Pres: Gloria Goldman
Mng Ed: Norman Shapiro *E-mail:* nshapiro@judaicapress.com
Founded: 1963
Classic & contemporary Jewish literature in Hebrew & English.
ISBN Prefix(es): 978-0-910818; 978-1-880582; 978-1-932443; 978-1-60763
Number of titles published annually: 25 Print; 6 E-Book
Total Titles: 400 Print; 12 E-Book
Imprints: Zahava Publications
Foreign Rep(s): Lehmanns (Europe, UK); Shanky's (Israel)

Judson Press
Division of American Baptist Churches in the USA
588 N Gulph Rd, King of Prussia, PA 19406
Mailing Address: PO Box 851, Valley Forge, PA 19482-0851 SAN: 201-0348
Toll Free Tel: 800-458-3766 *Fax:* 610-768-2107
Web Site: www.judsonpress.com
Key Personnel
Publr: Laura Alden *E-mail:* laura.alden@abhms.org
Mktg Dir: Linda Johnson-LeBlanc *Tel:* 610-768-2458 *E-mail:* linda.johnson-leblanc@abhms.org
Busn Mgr: Alma Hazboun
Ed: Rebecca Irwin-Diehl *Tel:* 610-768-2109 *E-mail:* rebecca.irwin-diehl@abhms.org
Founded: 1824
Religion (Baptist & nondenominational Christian), African American, women & multicultural; cloth & paperback.
ISBN Prefix(es): 978-0-8170
Number of titles published annually: 12 Print; 2 Audio
Total Titles: 350 Print; 1 CD-ROM; 2 Audio

Jump!
5357 Penn Ave, Minneapolis, MN 55419
Toll Free Tel: 888-799-1860 *Toll Free Fax:* 800-675-6679
E-mail: customercare@jumplibrary.com
Web Site: www.jumplibrary.com
Key Personnel
Pres: Gabe Kaufman *E-mail:* gabe@jumplibrary.com
Sales & Mktg Mgr: Laura Villano *E-mail:* laura@jumplibrary.com
Founded: 2012
Publish children's nonfiction with a focus on high-interest subjects for beginning & emergent readers. Books combine vibrant colors with captivating photography & corresponding text to draw readers into the subject & encourage reading success.
ISBN Prefix(es): 978-1-62031; 978-1-62496
Number of titles published annually: 100 Print; 100 E-Book; 30 Audio
Total Titles: 325 Print; 325 E-Book
Imprints: Bullfrog Books; Pogo
Distributed by myON, a division of Capstone
Foreign Rep(s): Saunders Book Co (Canada)
Returns: 2150 Howard Dr W, North Mankato, MN 56003
Shipping Address: 2150 Howard Dr W, North Mankato, MN 56003
Warehouse: 2150 Howard Dr W, North Mankato, MN 56003
Distribution Center: 2150 Howard Dr W, North Mankato, MN 56003
Membership(s): ALA; Educational Book & Media Association; TLA

Jump at the Sun
Imprint of Disney-Hyperion Books
125 West End Ave, 3rd fl, New York, NY 10023
Web Site: books.disney.com
Founded: 1998
Books celebrating the African-American experience & culture.
ISBN Prefix(es): 978-0-7868
Number of titles published annually: 2 Print; 2 E-Book
Total Titles: 100 Print; 100 E-Book

Jungle Wagon Press
5116 Didier Ave, Rockford, IL 61101
SAN: 920-6426
Tel: 815-988-9048
E-mail: junglewagonpress@gmail.com
Web Site: www.junglewagonpress.com
Key Personnel
Owner: Angela Malavolti
Founded: 2011
Provides publishing services including editing, professional illustrations, design, ISBN, copyright, printing & marketing. Specialize in high quality children's picture books, often with an educational element.
This publisher has indicated that 80% of their product line is author subsidized.
ISBN Prefix(es): 978-0-9834092; 978-0-9904271
Number of titles published annually: 3 Print
Total Titles: 5 Print

§Just World Books LLC
PO Box 5484, Charlottesville, VA 22905
Toll Free Tel: 888-506-3769
E-mail: sales@justworldbooks.com
Web Site: justworldbooks.com
Key Personnel
Owner: Helena Cobban
Assoc Publr: Kim MacVaugh
Founded: 2010
ISBN Prefix(es): 978-0-9845056; 978-1-935982
Number of titles published annually: 8 Print
Total Titles: 31 Print; 22 E-Book
Distribution Center: Independent Publishers Group (IPG), 814 N Franklin St, Chicago, IL 60610 *Toll Free Tel:* 800-888-4741

§Kabbalah Publishing
Division of Kabbalah Centre International
1100 S Robertson Blvd, Los Angeles, CA 90035
Tel: 310-601-1039 *Fax:* 310-657-7957
E-mail: customerservice@kabbalahpublishing.com; kcla@kabbalah.com
Web Site: publishing.kabbalah.com; www.kabbalah.com
Founded: 2002
Dedicated to bringing the world's oldest & deepest treasury of spiritual wisdom.
ISBN Prefix(es): 978-1-57189; 978-0-943688; 978-0-924457
Number of titles published annually: 15 Print; 2 CD-ROM; 2 Online; 2 E-Book; 2 Audio
Total Titles: 35 Print; 3 CD-ROM; 2 Online; 4 E-Book; 4 Audio
Foreign Rights: Kabbalah Agency (worldwide)
Distribution Center: Publishers Group West, 1700 Fourth St, Berkeley, CA 94710 *Tel:* 510-809-3700 *Fax:* 510-809-3777

Kaeden Corp
PO Box 16190, Rocky River, OH 44116-0190
Tel: 440-617-1400 *Toll Free Tel:* 800-890-7323 *Fax:* 440-617-1403
E-mail: info@kaeden.com
Web Site: www.kaeden.com
Key Personnel
Pres: Craig Urmston *E-mail:* curmston@kaeden.com
Founded: 1986
Books for emergent, early & fluent readers, grades K-3, reading recovery & guided reading programs.
ISBN Prefix(es): 978-1-879835; 978-1-57874; 978-1-61181; 978-1-61181
Number of titles published annually: 16 Print
Total Titles: 300 Print; 7 CD-ROM; 72 E-Book; 7 Audio
Imprints: Kaeden Books
Membership(s): AAP; American Educational Publishers; International Literacy Association; National Council of Teachers of English; Reading Recovery Council of North America

Kalmbach Publishing Co
21027 Crossroads Circle, Waukesha, WI 53186
Mailing Address: PO Box 1612, Waukesha, WI 53187-1612
Tel: 262-796-8776 *Toll Free Tel:* 800-533-6644 (cust serv & orders); 800-558-1544 *Fax:* 262-798-6592
E-mail: customerservice@kalmbach.com
Web Site: www.kalmbach.com
Key Personnel
SVP, Sales & Mktg: Dan Lance *E-mail:* dlance@kalmbach.com
Edit Dir: Diane M Bacha *E-mail:* dbacha@kalmbach.com
Books Ed-in-Chief: Diane Wheeler *E-mail:* dwheeler@kalmbach.com
Founded: 1934
Special interest books, calendars & magazines in the astronomy, jewelry making, crafts, hobby & collectibles market.
ISBN Prefix(es): 978-0-89024; 978-0-913135; 978-0-89778; 978-0-8238; 978-0-87116; 978-0-933168; 978-1-62700
Number of titles published annually: 35 Print
Total Titles: 135 Print
Imprints: Greenberg Books; Kalmbach Books
Distributed by Publishers Group West (PGW)

§Kamehameha Publishing
Division of Kamehameha Schools
567 S King St, Suite 118, Honolulu, HI 96813
Tel: 808-534-8205 *Fax:* 808-541-5305
E-mail: publishing@ksbe.edu
Web Site: kamehamehapublishing.org
Key Personnel
Dir: Ron Cox
Founded: 1933
Book, journal & poster publishing in the areas of Hawaiian history, studies, language & culture.
ISBN Prefix(es): 978-0-87336
Number of titles published annually: 12 Print
Total Titles: 100 Print
Imprints: Kamehameha Schools Press
Distributed by Islander Group
Membership(s): The Association of Publishers for Special Sales; Hawaii Book Publishers Association; Independent Book Publishers Association

Kane Miller Books
Division of Educational Development Corp
4901 Morena Blvd, Suite 213, San Diego, CA 92117
SAN: 295-8945
E-mail: submissions@kanemiller.com; info@kanemiller.com
Web Site: www.kanemiller.com
Key Personnel
Publr: Kira Lynn
Edit/Mktg: Lynn Kelley
Mktg/Soc Media: Kayla VernonClark
Founded: 1984
Juvenile board, novelty & picture books & middle grade fiction from around the world.
ISBN Prefix(es): 978-0-916291; 978-1-929132; 978-1-933605; 978-1-61067
Number of titles published annually: 100 Print
Total Titles: 328 Print
Warehouse: Educational Development Corp, 5402 S 122 E Ave, Tulsa, OK 74146
Distribution Center: Publishers Group Canada, 300-76 Stafford St, Toronto, ON M6J 2S1, Canada *Tel:* 416-934-9900 *E-mail:* info@pgcbooks.ca *Web Site:* www.pgcbooks.ca
Membership(s): ABA; ALA; Association of Booksellers for Children; United States Board on Books for Young People

Kane Press Inc
225 E 46 St, Suite 4D, New York, NY 10017-2924
Tel: 212-935-0246
Web Site: www.kanepress.com
Key Personnel
Publr: Joanne E Kane *E-mail:* jkane@kanepress.com
Sr Ed: Juliana Hanford
Edit Asst: Nadia DiMattia
Founded: 1996
Publishes books for children ages 3 to 11, including picture books & first chapter books.
ISBN Prefix(es): 978-1-57565
Number of titles published annually: 12 Print; 12 E-Book; 15 Audio
Total Titles: 190 Print; 175 E-Book; 41 Audio
Orders to: Lerner Publisher Services, 1251 Washington Ave N, Minneapolis, MN 55401-1036 *Tel:* 612-332-3344 *Toll Free Tel:* 800-328-4929 *Fax:* 612-215-6230 *E-mail:* custserve@lernerpublisherservices.com *Web Site:* lernerpublisherservices.com
Returns: Lerner Publisher Services, 1251 Washington Ave N, Minneapolis, MN 55401-1036 *Tel:* 612-332-3344 *Toll Free Tel:* 800-328-4929 *Fax:* 612-215-6230 *E-mail:* custserve@lernerpublisherservices.com *Web Site:* lernerpublisherservices.com
Shipping Address: Lerner Publisher Services, 1251 Washington Ave N, Minneapolis, MN 55401-1036 *Tel:* 612-332-3344 *Toll Free Tel:* 800-328-4929 *Fax:* 612-215-6230 *E-mail:* custserve@lernerpublisherservices.com *Web Site:* lernerpublisherservices.com
Warehouse: Lerner Publisher Services, 1251 Washington Ave N, Minneapolis, MN 55401-1036 *Tel:* 612-332-3344 *Toll Free Tel:* 800-328-4929 *Fax:* 612-215-6230 *E-mail:* custserve@lernerpublisherservices.com *Web Site:* lernerpublisherservices.com
Distribution Center: Lerner Publisher Services, 1251 Washington Ave N, Minneapolis, MN 55401-1036 *Tel:* 612-332-3344 *Toll Free Tel:* 800-328-4929 *Fax:* 612-215-6230 *E-mail:* custserve@lernerpublisherservices.com *Web Site:* lernerpublisherservices.com
Membership(s): The Children's Book Council; Educational Book & Media Association; International Literacy Association; NAIPR; National Council for the Social Studies; National Council of Teachers of Mathematics; National Science Teachers Association

Kapp Books LLC
3602 Rocky Meadow Ct, Fairfax, VA 22033
Tel: 703-261-9171 *Fax:* 703-621-7162
E-mail: info@kappbooks.com
Web Site: www.kappbooks.com
Key Personnel
Mng Dir: Parveen Ahuja
Founded: 2006
ISBN Prefix(es): 978-1-60346
Number of titles published annually: 100 Print
Total Titles: 350 Print; 10 CD-ROM
Membership(s): Independent Book Publishers Association

Kar-Ben Publishing
Division of Lerner Publishing Group Inc
241 First Ave N, Minneapolis, MN 55401

Tel: 612-332-3344 *Toll Free Tel:* 800-4-KARBEN (452-7236) *Fax:* 612-332-7615 *Toll Free Fax:* 800-332-1132
Web Site: www.karben.com
Key Personnel
Chmn: Harry J Lerner
Pres: Adam Lerner
Publr: Joni Sussman *E-mail:* jsussman@karben.com
Dir of Rts, Spec Sales & Intl Dist: Maria Kjoller
Founded: 1974
Jewish-themed picture books, calendars; preschool & primary, holiday books, folktales, bible stories.
ISBN Prefix(es): 978-1-58013
Number of titles published annually: 20 Print
Total Titles: 240 Print; 195 E-Book
Foreign Rep(s): Bravo (UK); Mazeltov Books (Australia)
Warehouse: Lerner Publishing Group, 1251 Washington Ave N, Minneapolis, MN 55401, Mgr: Ken Rued

Kazi Publications Inc
3023 W Belmont Ave, Chicago, IL 60618
Tel: 773-267-7001 *Fax:* 773-267-7002
E-mail: info@kazi.org
Web Site: www.kazi.org
Key Personnel
Pres: Liaquat Ali
Mktg Dir: Mary Bakhtiar
Founded: 1972
Nonprofit organization; print, publish & distribute; Islamic books in Arabic, English & Urdu.
ISBN Prefix(es): 978-0-935782; 978-1-56744; 978-0-933511; 978-1-871031; 978-1-930637
Number of titles published annually: 30 Print; 6 E-Book
Total Titles: 401 Print; 150 E-Book
Imprints: ABC International Group Inc; Abjad Books; Great Books of the Islamic World; Library of Islam

§J J Keller & Associates, Inc
3003 Breezewood Lane, Neenah, WI 54957
Mailing Address: PO Box 368, Neenah, WI 54957-0368
Tel: 920-722-2848 *Toll Free Tel:* 877-564-2333 *Toll Free Fax:* 800-727-7516
E-mail: contactus@jjkeller.com; customerservice@jjkeller.com
Web Site: www.jjkeller.com
Key Personnel
Chmn: Robert L Keller
VChmn & Treas: Jim Keller
Pres & CEO: Marne Keller-Krikava
EVP & COO: Rustin R Keller
CFO: Dana S Gilman
Dir, Creative & Promos: Tom Hines
Corp Mktg Communs Specialist: Mary Borsecnik
Founded: 1953
Publish regulatory compliance, "best practices" & training products dealing with occupational safety, job safety, environment & industry & motor-carrier (trucking) operations. On demand, print, CD-ROM, intranet & Internet formats.
ISBN Prefix(es): 978-1-57943; 978-0-934674; 978-1-877798; 978-1-59042; 978-0-9789130; 978-1-60287; 978-1-61099; 978-1-68008
Number of titles published annually: 4 Print; 12 E-Book
Total Titles: 300 Print; 100 CD-ROM
Branch Office(s)
7273 State Rd 76, Neenah, WI 54956-9614
Sales Office(s): 1315 Gillingham Rd, Neenah, WI 54956-4503
600 S Nicolet Rd, Appleton, WI 54914-8285
700 N Lynndale Dr, Appleton, WI 54914-3019
Distributed by AMACOM Books
Distributor for Chilton Book Co; International Air Transport Association; National Archives & Records Administration; National Institute of Occupational Safety & Health; Office of the Federal Register; Research & Special Programs Administration of the US Department of Transportation; John Wiley & Sons Inc

Kelsey Street Press
2824 Kelsey St, Berkeley, CA 94705
E-mail: info@kelseyst.com
Web Site: www.kelseyst.com
Key Personnel
Founding Ed: Patricia Dienstfrey; Rena Rosenwasser
Ed & Publr: Ramsay Breslin
Founded: 1974
Nonprofit press, publish experimental poetry & short fiction by women & collaborations between poets & artists.
ISBN Prefix(es): 978-0-932716
Number of titles published annually: 3 Print
Total Titles: 45 Print
Orders to: Small Press Distribution, 1341 Seventh St, Berkeley, CA 94710 (contact Small Press Distribution for large orders) *Tel:* 510-524-1668 *Toll Free Tel:* 800-869-7553 *E-mail:* orders@spdbooks.org *Web Site:* www.spdbooks.org
Membership(s): Community of Literary Magazines & Presses

Kendall Hunt Publishing Co
4050 Westmark Dr, Dubuque, IA 52002-2624
SAN: 203-9184
Mailing Address: PO Box 1840, Dubuque, IA 52004-1840
Tel: 563-589-1000 *Toll Free Tel:* 800-228-0810 (orders) *Fax:* 563-589-1046 *Toll Free Fax:* 800-772-9165
E-mail: orders@kendallhunt.com
Web Site: www.kendallhunt.com
Key Personnel
Chmn & CEO: Mark C Falb
Pres & COO: Chad M Chandlee
VP, Opers: Tim Beitzel
VP, Higher Educ Div: David Tart
VP, K-12 Div: Charles Cook
Founded: 1969
Higher education custom publishing, K-12 math & science.
ISBN Prefix(es): 978-0-8403; 978-0-7872; 978-0-7575; 978-1-4652
Number of titles published annually: 1,500 Print; 200 Online
Total Titles: 6,500 Print; 10 CD-ROM; 5,500 Online; 6,500 E-Book
Membership(s): National Council of Supervisors of Mathematics; National Council of Teachers of Mathematics; National Science Teachers Association

Kennedy Information Inc
Division of Bloomberg BNA
24 Railroad St, Keene, NH 03431
Tel: 603-924-0900 *Toll Free Tel:* 800-531-0140 *Fax:* 603-357-8112
E-mail: customerservice@kennedyinfo.com
Web Site: www.kennedyinfo.com
Key Personnel
COO: Daniel Houder *E-mail:* dhouder@kennedyinfo.com
Founded: 1970
Newsletters, special reports, books, directories of management consultants, executive recruiters & outplacement consultants.
ISBN Prefix(es): 978-0-916654; 978-1-885922; 978-1-58673; 978-1-932079; 978-1-934717
Number of titles published annually: 15 Print; 1 CD-ROM; 3 Online
Total Titles: 50 Print; 1 CD-ROM

Kensington Publishing Corp
119 W 40 St, New York, NY 10018
SAN: 207-9860
Tel: 212-407-1500 *Toll Free Tel:* 800-221-2647 *Fax:* 212-935-0699
Web Site: www.kensingtonbooks.com
Key Personnel
Chmn, Pres & CEO: Steven Zacharius *E-mail:* szacharius@kensingtonbooks.com
CFO: Michael Rosamilia
Publr: Lynn Cully
Edit Dir: Audrey La Fehr; Wendy McCurdy
Edit Dir, Brava Books: Alicia Condon
Mng Dir, Lyrical Press: Renee Rocco
Ed-in-Chief, Citadel Press: Michaela Hamilton
Ed-in-Chief, Kensington: John Scognamiglio
Exec Ed: Tara Gavin; Selena James
Exec Ed, Citadel: Denise Silvestro
Sr Ed: Gary Goldstein; Esi Sogah
Ed: Martin Biro
Assoc Ed: Peter Senftleben
Creative Dir: Janice Rossi
Dir, Publicity & PR: Karen Auerbach
Dir, Sales: Chris Grimm
Dir, Soc Media & Digital Sales: Alex Nicolajsen
Dir, Subs Rts: Jackie Dinas
Info Technol Dir: Jonathan Cohen
Prodn Dir: Joyce Kaplan
Assoc Dir, Communs: Vida Engstrand
Assoc Dir, Sales: Darla Freeman
Gen Mgr: Adam Zacharius
Communs & Mktg Mgr, Dafina & Women's Fiction: Mala Bhattacharjee
Communs & Mktg Mgr, Lyrical Press: Michelle Forde
Communs & Mktg Mgr, Mystery & Thrillers: Morgan Elwell
Communs Mgr, Fiction & Lead Suspense: Lulu Martinez
Assoc Communs Mgr, Thrillers & Dafina: Claire Hill
Gen Coun: Barbara Bennett
Inventory Mgr: Guy Chapman
Sr Designer: Barbara Brown
Founded: 1974
Mass market paperback originals including thillers & men's adventure.
ISBN Prefix(es): 978-0-89083; 978-0-8217
Number of titles published annually: 500 Print
Total Titles: 9,000 Print
Imprints: Aphrodisia; Brava; Caress (digital contemporary romance); Citadel; Dafina; Holloway House; Kensington Books; Kensington Hardcover; Kensington Mass-Market; Kensington Trade Paperback; KTeen; Liaison (digital romantic suspense); Lyrical Press; Lyrical Shine (contemporary romance); Lyrical Underground (thriller, mystery, suspense & horror); Pinnacle Books; Rebel Base Books; John Scognamiglio Books; Lyle Stuart Books; Urban Books; Urban Christian; Urban Renaissance; Zebra Books; Zebra Shout
Distributed by Penguin Group USA, A Penguin Random House Company
Distributor for Urban Books
Foreign Rights: Akcali Copyright Agency (Oz gur Emir) (Turkey); ANA Sofia (Anna Droumeva, Mira Droumeva, Kamelia Emilova) (Bulgaria); Big Apple Agency (Chris Lin) (Taiwan); Big Apple Agency Inc (Lily Chen) (China); The Book Publishers' Association of Israel, International Promotion & Literary Rights Dept (Beverly Levit) (Israel); Bookcase Literary Agency (Meira Dias & Flavia Viotti) (Brazil); Donzelli, Fietta Agency Srls (Stephania Fietta) (Italy); The English Agency Ltd (Corinne Shioji) (Japan); Graal Literary Agency (Ursula Jedrach) (Poland); Imprima Korea Agency (Terry Kim) (Korea); International Literatuur Bureau (ILB) (Linda Kohn) (Netherlands); The Italian Literary Agency srl (Italy); Kensington Publishing (Susanna Gruninger) (South America, Spain); Maxima Creative Agency (Santo Manurung) (Indonesia); La Nouvelle Agence (Vanessa King) (France); Andrew Nurnberg Associates (Tatjana Zoldnere) (Baltic States); Andrew Nurnberg Associates (Judit Hermann)

(Croatia, Hungary); Andrew Nurnberg Literary Agency (Ludmilla Sushkova) (Russia); Kristin Olson Literary Agency SRO (Czech Republic, Slovakia); ONK Agency Ltd (Turkey); Read n Right Agency (Nike Davarinou) (Greece); Lennart Sane Agency AB (Philip Sane) (Scandinavia); Schindler's Literary Agency (Brazil); Thomas Schlueck GmbH (Julia Amueller) (Germany); Shin Won Agency Co (Tae-Eun Kim) (Korea); Silkroad Publishers Agency (Jane Vejjajiva) (Thailand); Dori Simmonds Agency (British Commonwealth); Tuttle-Mori Agency Inc (Misa Morikawa) (Japan, Thailand)
Warehouse: Penguin Group USA, A Penguin Random House Company, Pittston, PA
Distribution Center: Penguin Random House Publisher Services, 400 Hahn Rd, Westminster, MD 21157 *Toll Free Tel:* 800-733-3000 *Toll Free Fax:* 800-659-2436 *E-mail:* customerservice@randomhouse.com

Kent State University Press
1118 University Library Bldg, 1125 Risman Dr, Kent, OH 44242
SAN: 201-0437
Mailing Address: PO Box 5190, Kent, OH 44242-0001
Tel: 330-672-7913 *Fax:* 330-672-3104
E-mail: ksupress@kent.edu
Web Site: www.kentstateuniversitypress.com
Key Personnel
Dir & Rts & Perms: Susan Cash *Tel:* 330-672-8097 *E-mail:* scash@kent.edu
Journals Mgr: Carol Heller *Tel:* 330-672-8090 *E-mail:* cheller1@kent.edu
Mktg Mgr: Susan L Cash *Tel:* 330-672-8097 *E-mail:* scash@kent.edu
Acquiring Ed: Will Underwood *Tel:* 330-672-8094 *E-mail:* wunderwo@kent.edu
Founded: 1965
Scholarly nonfiction, with emphasis on Civil War, military history, literary studies, archaeology, biography & Midwest regional.
ISBN Prefix(es): 978-0-87338; 978-1-60635
Number of titles published annually: 30 Print; 35 E-Book; 5 Audio
Total Titles: 850 Print; 1,250 E-Book; 20 Audio
Imprints: Black Squirrel Books
Foreign Rep(s): East-West Export Books (Asia, Australia, The Pacific); Eurospan Ltd (Africa, Europe, Middle East, UK); Scholarly Book Services (Canada)
Orders to: Bookmasters, 30 Amberwood Pkwy, Ashland, OH 44805, Contact: Elaine Lattanzi *Tel:* 419-281-1802 *Toll Free Tel:* 800-247-6553 *Fax:* 419-281-6883
Returns: Bookmasters, 30 Amberwood Pkwy, Ashland, OH 44805, Contact: Elaine Lattanzi *Tel:* 419-281-1802 *Toll Free Tel:* 800-247-6553 *Fax:* 419-281-6883
Warehouse: Bookmasters, 30 Amberwood Pkwy, Ashland, OH 44805, Contact: Elaine Lattanzi *Tel:* 419-281-1802 *Toll Free Tel:* 800-247-6553 *Fax:* 419-281-6883
Distribution Center: Bookmasters, 30 Amberwood Pkwy, Ashland, OH 44805, Contact: Elaine Lattanzi *Tel:* 419-281-1802 *Toll Free Tel:* 800-247-6553 *Fax:* 419-281-6883
Membership(s): ABA; American Association of University Presses

Kessinger Publishing LLC
PO Box 1404, Whitefish, MT 59937
Web Site: www.kessinger.net
Key Personnel
Pres: Roger A Kessinger
Founded: 1988
On demand publisher. Specialize in rare, scarce & out of print books.
ISBN Prefix(es): 978-0-922802; 978-1-56459; 978-0-7661; 978-1-4191; 978-1-161; 978-0-548; 978-1-104; 978-1-120; 978-1-160; 978-1-162; 978-1-163; 978-1-164; 978-1-165; 978-1-166; 978-1-167; 978-1-168; 978-1-169; 978-1-4179; 978-1-4253; 978-1-4254; 978-1-4286; 978-1-4304; 978-1-4325; 978-1-4326; 978-1-4367; 978-1-4370; 978-1-4373; 978-1-4365; 978-1-4368; 978-1-4371; 978-1-4374; 978-1-4366; 978-1-4369; 978-1-4372
Number of titles published annually: 5,000 Print; 5,000 E-Book
Imprints: Kessinger Publishing®

Kidsbooks LLC
3535 W Peterson Ave, Chicago, IL 60659
SAN: 666-3729
Tel: 773-509-0707 *Fax:* 773-509-0404
E-mail: sales@kidsbooks.com; customerservice@kidsbooks.com
Web Site: www.kidsbooks.com
Key Personnel
CEO & Foreign Rts Agent: Dan Blau
Founded: 1987
Promotional book publishers of children, juvenile & hardcover, Search & Find®, board books, cloth books & other novelty books.
ISBN Prefix(es): 978-0-942025; 978-1-56156; 978-1-58865; 978-1-62885
Number of titles published annually: 100 Print
Total Titles: 3,000 Print
Imprints: Fun For All; KidsBooks; Learning Challenge

Jessica Kingsley Publishers Inc
400 Market St, Suite 400, Philadelphia, PA 19106
SAN: 256-2391
Tel: 215-922-1161 *Toll Free Tel:* 866-416-1078 (cust serv) *Fax:* 215-922-1474
E-mail: orders@jkp.com; hello.usa@jkp.com
Web Site: www.jkp.com
Key Personnel
Chmn: Jessica Kingsley
VP, Sales & Mktg: David Corey
Spec Sales Mgr: Colin McGee
Mktg Assoc: Katelynn Bartleson
Sales & Mktg Assoc: Stephanie DeMuzio
Founded: 1987 (US office opened 2004)
Publish books for the consumer on autism spectrum disorders & related developmental disorders; books for professionals in expressive arts therapies: art, music, drama & dance & social work; books on Tai Chi & Quigong.
ISBN Prefix(es): 978-1-85302; 978-1-84310; 978-1-84819; 978-1-874579; 978-1-900990; 978-0-902817; 978-1-904787; 978-1-905818; 978-1-84642; 978-1-84905; 978-1-84985; 978-0-85701; 978-0-85700; 978-1-78450
Number of titles published annually: 250 Print
Total Titles: 1,800 Print
Imprints: Singing Dragon
Foreign Office(s): 73 Collier St, London N1 9BE, United Kingdom, Contact: Mark Scott *Tel:* (020) 7833 2307 *E-mail:* hello@jkp.com
Foreign Rep(s): Avicenna Partnership Ltd (Bill Kennedy) (Bahrain, Egypt, Iran, Iraq, Kuwait, Lebanon, Libya, Oman, Qatar, Saudi Arabia, Sudan, United Arab Emirates, Yemen); Avicenna Partnership Ltd (Claire de Gruchy) (Algeria, Jordan, Morocco, Palestine, Tunisia, Turkey); Brookside Publishing Services (Ireland); Compass Academic (UK); Durnell Marketing Ltd (Europe); Footprint Books Pty Ltd (Australia, New Zealand); Taylor & Francis Asia Pacific (Brunei, China, Hong Kong, Indonesia, Japan, Macau, Malaysia, Philippines, Singapore, Taiwan, Thailand, Vietnam); UBC Press (Canada); United Publishers Services Ltd (Japan)
Distribution Center: Books International, PO Box 960, Herndon, VA 20172 *Toll Free Tel:* 866-416-1078 *Fax:* 703-611-1501 *E-mail:* jkpmail@presswarehouse.com

Kinship Books
305 Cedar Heights Rd, Rhinebeck, NY 12572
Tel: 845-876-4592 (orders)
E-mail: kinship@hvc.rr.com
Web Site: www.kinshipny.com
Key Personnel
Owner: Susan Kelly Fitzgerald
Founded: 1967
Books of genealogical source information, histories, directory & journals.
ISBN Prefix(es): 978-1-56012
Number of titles published annually: 5 Print
Total Titles: 330 Print

Kirk House Publishers
PO Box 390759, Minneapolis, MN 55439
Tel: 952-835-1828 *Toll Free Tel:* 888-696-1828 *Fax:* 952-835-2613
E-mail: publisher@kirkhouse.com
Web Site: www.kirkhouse.com
Key Personnel
Publr: Karen Walhof
Founded: 1994
ISBN Prefix(es): 978-1-886513; 978-1-932688; 978-1-933794; 978-1-942304
Number of titles published annually: 15 Print; 3 E-Book
Total Titles: 300 Print; 15 E-Book; 4 Audio
Imprints: Quill House Publishers
Membership(s): Independent Book Publishers Association; Midwest Independent Publishing Association

§Kirkbride Bible Co Inc
1102 Deloss St, Indianapolis, IN 46203
Mailing Address: PO Box 606, Indianapolis, IN 46206-0606
Tel: 317-633-1900 *Toll Free Tel:* 800-428-4385 *Fax:* 317-633-1444
E-mail: sales@kirkbride.com; info@kirkbride.com
Web Site: www.kirkbride.com
Key Personnel
Pres: Michael Gage
Founded: 1915
Bible publisher, also children's Bible.
ISBN Prefix(es): 978-0-88707; 978-0-934854
Number of titles published annually: 5 Print
Total Titles: 7 Print; 3 CD-ROM
Advertising Agency: Canal Advertising

Kiva Publishing Inc
10 Bella Loma, Santa Fe, NM 87506
Tel: 909-896-0518
E-mail: kivapub@aol.com
Web Site: www.kivapub.com
Key Personnel
Publr: Stephen W Hill
Founded: 1993
Publish Native American & Southwest regional books & cards.
ISBN Prefix(es): 978-1-885772
Number of titles published annually: 3 Print
Total Titles: 40 Print
Membership(s): The Association of Publishers for Special Sales; Independent Book Publishers Association; New Mexico Publishers Association; Publishers Association of the West

Klutz
Division of Scholastic Corp
568 Broadway, Suite 503, New York, NY 10012
Tel: 212-343-6360 *Fax:* 212-343-6366
E-mail: sales@klutz.com
Web Site: store.scholastic.com
Key Personnel
SVP & Gen Mgr: Stacy Lellos
Founded: 1977
Premium brand of book-based activity kits, committed to inspiring creativity in every kid with a unique combination of crystal clear instructions, custom tools & materials & a hearty helping of humor.
ISBN Prefix(es): 978-0-932592; 978-1-57054; 978-1-878257; 978-1-59174; 978-0-545

Number of titles published annually: 14 Print
Total Titles: 90 Print
Foreign Rep(s): Scholastic Asia (Selina Lee) (Asia); Scholastic Australia Ltd (Australia); Scholastic Canada Ltd (Canada); Scholastic Ltd (UK); Scholastic New Zealand Ltd (New Zealand)
Orders to: 2931 E McCarty St, Jefferson City, MO 65101 *Toll Free Tel:* 888-724-1872 *Toll Free Fax:* 877-724-1872 *E-mail:* orders@klutz.com
Membership(s): American Specialty Toy Retailing Association

Kluwer Law International (KLI), see Wolters Kluwer Law & Business

§Wolters Kluwer Law & Business
Subsidiary of Wolters Kluwer
76 Ninth Ave, 7th fl, New York, NY 10011-5201
SAN: 203-4999
Tel: 212-771-0600; 301-698-7100 (cust serv outside US) *Toll Free Tel:* 800-234-1660 (cust serv)
E-mail: customer.service@wolterskluwer.com; sales@kluwerlaw.com
Web Site: www.wklawbusiness.com
Key Personnel
VP, Opers & IT: Gustavo Dobles
Founded: 1959
Publisher of legal, business & health care titles for professionals. Publishes more than 500 journals, newsletters, electronic products & loose-leaf manuals & has more than 1,000 active professional & textbook titles.
ISBN Prefix(es): 978-0-89443; 978-0-912862; 978-0-8342; 978-1-56706; 978-0-87189; 978-0-8080; 978-0-444; 978-1-56542; 978-1-878375; 978-0-9625969; 978-1-56759; 978-0-7355; 978-0-7896; 978-0-87457; 978-0-87622; 978-0-916592; 978-1-4548
Number of titles published annually: 100 Print; 16 CD-ROM; 55 Online
Total Titles: 1,500 Print; 107 CD-ROM; 55 Online; 1 Audio
Foreign Rep(s): David Bartolone
Distribution Center: 7201 McKinney Circle, Frederick, MD 21704 *Tel:* 301-698-7100 *Fax:* 301-695-7931

Allen A Knoll Publishers
200 W Victoria St, Santa Barbara, CA 93101-3627
SAN: 299-0539
Tel: 805-564-3377 *Toll Free Tel:* 800-777-7623 *Fax:* 805-966-6657
E-mail: bookinfo@knollpublishers.com
Web Site: www.knollpublishers.com
Key Personnel
Lib Sales & Mktg Dir: Abby Schott
Shipping & Receiving Mgr: Lisa Carroll
Accts: Elizabeth Hanning-Yu *E-mail:* elizabeth@knollpublishers.com
Founded: 1991
Books for intelligent people who read for fun. No unsol mss.
ISBN Prefix(es): 978-0-9627297; 978-1-888310
Number of titles published annually: 5 Print
Total Titles: 50 Print
Membership(s): Independent Publishers Association

Alfred A Knopf/Everyman's Library
Imprint of Knopf Doubleday Publishing Group
c/o Penguin Random House Inc, 1745 Broadway, New York, NY 10019
Tel: 212-751-2600 *Toll Free Tel:* 800-638-6460 *Fax:* 212-572-2593
Web Site: www.knopfdoubleday.com
Key Personnel
Chmn: Sonny Mehta
Pres: Anthony Chirico
EVP & Publr, Everyman's Library: Anne Messitte
EVP & Exec Dir, Publicity, Promo & Media Rel: Paul Bogaards
SVP & Assoc Publr: Christine Gillespie
SVP & Edit Dir, Everyman's Library: LuAnn Walther
VP & Dir, Art Jacket: Carol Carson
VP & Dir, Busn Opers: Justine LeCates
VP & Dir, Creative Mktg: Anne-Lise Spitzer
VP & Dir, Interior Design & Desktop Publg: Peter Andersen
VP & Dir, Prodn/Design: Andrew W Hughes
VP & Dir, Promo & Serial Rts: Gabrielle Brooks
VP & Dir, Publicity: Nicholas Latimer
VP & Edit Dir: Robin Desser
VP & Exec Ed: Jordan Pavlin
VP & Mng Ed: Katherine Hourigan
VP & Sr Ed: Victoria Wilson; Jonathan Segal
VP & Ed-at-Large: Gary Fisketjon
Sr Ed: Ann Close; Jennifer Jackson; Andrew Miller
Sr Ed, Poetry: Deborah Garrison
Ed: Diana Coglianese
Ed-at-Large: Carole Baron
Dir, Ad: Stephanie Kloss
Dir, Dom Rts: Sean Yule
Dir, Foreign Rts: Suzanne Smith
Dir, Mktg, Everyman's Library: Roz Parr
Group Sales Dir: Janet Cooke
Imprint Sales Dir: James Kimball
Dir, Publicity: Erinn Hartman
Deputy Dir, Publicity & Promo: Kathryn Zuckerman
Assoc Dir, Publicity: Josie Kals; Jessica Purcell
Publicity Mgr: Jordan Rodman
Publicist: Anna Dobben; Erica Hinsley; Elizabeth Lindsay; Brittany Morrongiello; Katie Schoder; Helen Tobin
Assoc Publicist: Erinn McGrath
Asst, Publicity: Madeline Caldwell
Mktg Mgr: Sara Eagle
Asst Mktg Mgr: Danielle Plafsky
Founded: 1915
Penguin Random House Inc & its publishing entities are not accepting unsol submissions, proposals, mss, or submission queries via e-mail at this time.
ISBN Prefix(es): 978-0-679; 978-0-7679; 978-1-4000; 978-0-394
Foreign Rights: ALS-Agenzia Letteraria Santachiara (Roberto Santachiara) (Italy); Anthea Agency (Katalina Sabeva) (Bulgaria); Bardon-Chinese Media Agency (Xu Weiguang) (China); Bardon-Chinese Media Agency (Yu-Shiuan Chen) (Taiwan); The English Agency (Junzo Sawa) (Japan); Graal Literary Agency (Maria Strarz-Kanska) (Poland); The Deborah Harris Agency (Ilana Kurshan) (Israel); JLM Literary Agency (Nelly Moukakos) (Greece); Katai & Bolza Literary (Peter Bolza) (Croatia, Hungary); KCC (MiSook Hong) (Korea); Simona Kessler International (Simona Kessler) (Romania); Licht & Burr Literary Agency (Trine Licht) (Scandinavia); La Nouvelle Agence (Vanessa Kling) (France); Kristin Olson Literary Agency (Kristin Olson) (Czech Republic); Sebes & Bisseling Literary Agency (Paul Sebes) (Netherlands)

Kodansha USA Inc
Subsidiary of Kodansha Ltd (Japan)
451 Park Ave S, 7th fl, New York, NY 10016
SAN: 201-0526
Tel: 917-322-6200 *Fax:* 212-935-6929
E-mail: info@kodansha-usa.com
Web Site: www.kodanshausa.com
Key Personnel
CEO: Takashi Sakuda
Founded: 2008
Publishes hardcover & paperback books in English on Japanese cultures, history, art, architecture, design, craft, gardening, literature, martial arts, language, cookbooks, travel & memoirs.
ISBN Prefix(es): 978-0-87011; 978-1-56836; 978-1-935429; 978-1-61262; 978-1-63236
Number of titles published annually: 4 Print
Total Titles: 270 Print
Imprints: Kodansha America; Kodansha Globe; Kodansha International
Distributed by Oxford University Press
Distributor for Japan Publications Inc; Japan Publications Trading Co Inc
Foreign Rep(s): Amin Al-Abini (Middle East); Bill Bailey Publishers' Representatives (Austria, Benelux, Bosnia and Herzegovina, Croatia, Cyprus, Estonia, France, Germany, Gibraltar, Greece, Hungary, Iceland, Italy, Latvia, Lithuania, Macedonia, Malta, Montenegro, Portugal, Scandinavia, Serbia, Slovenia, Spain, Switzerland, Turkey); DIP Inc (Japan); Fitzhenry & Whiteside (Canada); Intext Book Co (Australia, New Zealand); Japan Publications Trading Co Ltd (Japan); Kinokuniya Book Stores of Singapore Pte Ltd (Indonesia, Malaysia, Singapore, Taiwan, Thailand, United Arab Emirates); Kodansha Europe Ltd (Africa, Central America, Europe, Middle East, Near East, South America); Stephan Phillips (Pty) Ltd (Botswana, Lesotho, Mozambique, Namibia, South Africa, Swaziland, Zimbabwe); Publishers Group UK (Ireland, UK)
Warehouse: Oxford University Press, 2001 Evans Rd, Cary, NC 27513 *Toll Free Tel:* 800-451-7556 *Fax:* 919-677-1303

§Kogan Page Publishers
1518 Walnut St, Suite 900, Philadelphia, PA 19102
Tel: 215-928-9112 *Fax:* 215-928-9113
E-mail: info@koganpage.com
Web Site: www.koganpageusa.com
Key Personnel
Dir: Keith Ashfield
Founded: 1967
Publish books & e-versions of them.
ISBN Prefix(es): 978-0-7494
Number of titles published annually: 120 Print; 20 Online; 40 E-Book
Total Titles: 400 Print; 40 Online; 300 E-Book
Foreign Office(s): Kogan Page Ltd, 120 Pentonville Rd, London N1 9JN, United Kingdom *Tel:* (020) 7278 0433 *Web Site:* www.koganpage.com
Foreign Rep(s): Kogan Page Ltd (London) (worldwide exc USA)
Foreign Rights: Kogan Page Ltd (London) (worldwide exc USA)
Billing Address: Ingram Publisher Services, One Ingram Blvd, La Vergne, TN 37086
Orders to: Ingram Publisher Services, One Ingram Blvd, La Vergne, TN 37086 *Toll Free Tel:* 800-961-2026 *Toll Free Fax:* 800-838-1149 *E-mail:* customer.service@ingrampublisherservices.com
Returns: Ingram Publisher Services, 1210 Ingram Dr, Chambersburg, PA 17201
Distribution Center: Ingram Publisher Services, One Ingram Blvd, La Vergne, TN 37086

§Koho Pono LLC
15024 SE Pinegrove Loop, Clackamas, OR 97015
Tel: 503-723-7392 *Toll Free Tel:* 800-937-8000 (orders) *Toll Free Fax:* 800-876-0186 (orders)
E-mail: info@kohopono.com; orders@ingrambook.com
Web Site: kohopono.com
Key Personnel
Publr: Scott Burr *Tel:* 408-689-0888; Dayna Hubenthal
Founded: 2010
Multimedia publishing company that is passionate about growth & improvement for all aspects of life: business, career, relationships & personal. Specialize in innovation, awareness, process

improvement, change management & strengthening relationships for business & individuals. Support the evolution of consciousness, self-exploration & the pursuit of increasing relevance in life.
ISBN Prefix(es): 978-0-984554
Number of titles published annually: 3 Print; 3 Online; 3 E-Book; 3 Audio
Total Titles: 6 Print; 6 Online; 2 E-Book; 3 Audio
Shipping Address: Lightning Source Inc, 1246 Heil Quaker Blvd, La Vergne, TN 37086, Contact: Amy Waugh *Tel:* 615-213-5815 *Fax:* 615-213-4725 *E-mail:* inquiry@lightningsource.com
Warehouse: Lightning Source Inc, 1246 Heil Quaker Blvd, La Vergne, TN 37086, Contact: Amy Waugh *Tel:* 615-213-5815 *Fax:* 615-213-4725 *E-mail:* inquiry@lightningsource.com
Distribution Center: Ingram Book Co, One Ingram Blvd, La Vergne, TN 37086 *Tel:* 615-793-5000 *Toll Free Tel:* 800-937-8200 *E-mail:* customer.service@ingrambook.com
Lightning Source Inc, 1246 Heil Quaker Blvd, La Vergne, TN 37086, Contact: Amy Waugh *Tel:* 615-213-5815 *Fax:* 615-213-4725 *E-mail:* inquiry@lightningsource.com

Konecky & Konecky LLC
72 Ayers Point Rd, Old Saybrook, CT 06475
Tel: 860-388-0878 *Fax:* 860-388-0273
Web Site: www.koneckyandkonecky.com
Key Personnel
Publr: Sean Konecky *Tel:* 860-391-3165 *E-mail:* seankon@comcast.net
Founded: 1982
Hardcover art books & Civil War history, military history, biography, religion & spirituality.
ISBN Prefix(es): 978-1-56852; 978-0-914427
Number of titles published annually: 10 Print
Total Titles: 250 Print
Imprints: Konecky & Konecky (K&K); Tabard Press
Distributor for Octavo Editions

HJ Kramer Inc
Division of New World Library
PO Box 1082, Tiburon, CA 94920
Tel: 415-884-2100 (ext 10) *Toll Free Tel:* 800-972-6657 *Fax:* 415-435-5364
E-mail: hjkramer@jps.net
Web Site: www.hjkramer.com; www.newworldlibrary.com
Key Personnel
Pres: Linda Kramer
Intl Rts: Suezen Stone *Tel:* 415-499-1622 *Fax:* 415-499-1654 *E-mail:* Suezenstone@msn.com
Mktg & Publicity: Monique Muhlenkamp *E-mail:* monique@newworldlibrary.com
Founded: 1984
Personal growth, self-help, spiritual growth, trade paperbacks & hardcovers. Any correspondence regarding mss must be accompanied by an appropriately sized SASE.
ISBN Prefix(es): 978-0-915811; 978-1-932073
Number of titles published annually: 3 Print; 3 E-Book
Total Titles: 70 Print
Foreign Rep(s): Akasha Books Ltd (New Zealand); Brumby Books (Australia); Publishers Group Canada (Canada); Publishers Group UK (UK); Real Books (South Africa)
Orders to: Publisher Group West, 1700 Fourth St, Berkeley, CA 94710 *Toll Free Tel:* 800-788-3123 *Fax:* 510-528-3444

Krause Publications Inc
Subsidiary of F+W Media Inc
700 E State St, Iola, WI 54990
SAN: 202-6554
Tel: 715-445-2214 *Toll Free Tel:* 800-258-0929 (cust serv); 888-457-2873 (orders) *Fax:* 715-445-4087
E-mail: bookorders@krause.com
Web Site: www.krausebooks.com
Key Personnel
Founder: Chester L Krause
CFO: Jim Ogle
Pres: Sara Domville
Dir, E-Commerce: Corinne Zielke
Founded: 1952
ISBN Prefix(es): 978-0-930625; 978-0-87349; 978-0-87341; 978-0-87069; 978-0-89689; 978-1-58221; 978-0-8019; 978-1-63250; 978-0-934466
Number of titles published annually: 150 Print
Total Titles: 1,000 Print
Imprints: Antique Trader Books; Books Americana; DBI Books; Gun Digest® Books; Warman's
Distributor for Country Bumpkin; David & Charles; Colin Gower; Quarto Books
Foreign Rep(s): David Bateman Ltd (New Zealand); Canadian Manda Group (Canada); Capricorn Link (Australia); David & Charles (Europe, UK); Real Books (Southern Africa); Marta Schooler (Asia, Latin America, Middle East)
Returns: F+W Consumer Books, c/o Aero Fulfillment Services, 6023 Union Centre Blvd, Fairfield, OH 45014
See separate listing for:
Antique Trader

Kregel Publications
Division of Kregel Inc
2450 Oak Industrial Dr NE, Grand Rapids, MI 49505
SAN: 298-9115
Tel: 616-451-4775 *Toll Free Tel:* 800-733-2607 *Fax:* 616-451-9330
E-mail: kregelbooks@kregel.com
Web Site: www.kregel.com
Key Personnel
Pres: James R Kregel *E-mail:* president@kregel.com
VP, Publg: Jerold W Kregel
Exec Dir, Sales & Mktg: David Hill *Tel:* 616-451-4775 ext 235 *E-mail:* dave@kregel.com
Publr & Rts & Perms: Dennis Hillman
Founded: 1949
Evangelical Christian publications including devotionals, Bible study & reference.
ISBN Prefix(es): 978-0-8254
Number of titles published annually: 75 Print
Total Titles: 1,500 Print
Imprints: Editorial Portavoz; Kregel Academic & Professional; Kregel Classics; Kregel Kidzone; Kregel Publications
Distributor for Candle Books; Monarch Books
Foreign Rep(s): Christian Art Wholesale (South Africa); Christian Literature Crusade (Japan); David C Cook (Canada); Omega Distribution (New Zealand); STL Distribution (UK); Word of Life Press (Korea)
Membership(s): Evangelical Christian Publishers Association
See separate listing for:
Editorial Portavoz

Krieger Publishing Co
1725 Krieger Lane, Malabar, FL 32950
SAN: 202-6562
Tel: 321-724-9542 *Fax:* 321-951-3671
E-mail: info@krieger-publishing.com
Web Site: www.krieger-publishing.com
Key Personnel
Pres: Donald E Krieger
Cust Serv: Dianne Struckman
Founded: 1969
A scientific-technical publisher serving the college textbook market. Reprints & new titles: technical, science, psychology, geology, humanities, ecology, history, social sciences, engineering, mathematics, chemistry, adult educational, herpetology, space science.
ISBN Prefix(es): 978-0-88275; 978-0-89464; 978-0-89874; 978-1-57524
Number of titles published annually: 5 Print
Total Titles: 800 Print
Imprints: Anvil Series; Exploring Community History Series; Orbit Series; Professional Practices; Public History
Foreign Rep(s): Eurospan (Middle East, UK)
Advertising Agency: Krieger Enterprises Inc

KTAV Publishing House Inc
888 Newark Ave, Jersey City, NJ 07306
Tel: 201-963-9524 *Fax:* 201-963-0102
E-mail: orders@ktav.com
Web Site: www.ktav.com
Key Personnel
Pres: Moshe Heller
Founded: 1924
Books of Jewish interest; juvenile, textbooks; scholarly Judaica & interfaith issues.
ISBN Prefix(es): 978-0-87068; 978-0-88125; 978-1-60280
Number of titles published annually: 20 Print
Total Titles: 840 Print
Distributor for Yeshiva University Press

Kumarian Press
Division of Lynne Rienner Publishers Inc
1800 30 St, Suite 314, Boulder, CO 80301
Tel: 303-444-6684 *Fax:* 303-444-0824
E-mail: questions@rienner.com
Web Site: www.rienner.com
Key Personnel
CEO: Lynne Rienner
Founded: 1977
Academic, professional books, college textbooks in social sciences: international development, international relations, political science, political economy, economics, globalization, women & gender studies, conflict resolution, environment, sustainability, civil society & NGOs.
ISBN Prefix(es): 978-0-931816; 978-1-56549; 978-1-887208
Number of titles published annually: 18 Print; 10 E-Book
Total Titles: 300 Print; 100 E-Book
Foreign Rep(s): China Publishers Marketing (China, Hong Kong, Taiwan); Coinfo (Australia); Cranbury International LLC (Latin America); Eurospan (Europe, UK); Everest Media International Services (Nepal); KL Books Distributor (Malaysia); Maruzen Co Ltd (Japan); PMS Publishers Services (Malaysia); Viva Books (India)
Membership(s): AAP

Kumon Publishing North America
300 Frank Burr Blvd, Suite 6, Teaneck, NJ 07666
Tel: 201-836-2105 *Fax:* 201-836-1559
E-mail: books@kumon.com
Web Site: www.kumonbooks.com
Key Personnel
SVP: Brian Klingborg
Founded: 2004
Publisher of children's educational books & toys.
ISBN Prefix(es): 978-4-7743; 978-1-933241
Number of titles published annually: 30 Print
Total Titles: 160 Print

George Kurian Reference Books
3689 Campbell Ct, Yorktown Heights, NY 10598
Tel: 914-962-3287 *Fax:* 914-962-3287
Key Personnel
Pres & Ed: George Thomas Kurian *E-mail:* gtkurian@aol.com
Founded: 1972
Reference books for libraries, schools, colleges.
ISBN Prefix(es): 978-0-914746
Number of titles published annually: 7 Print
Total Titles: 102 Print
Imprints: Foreign Affairs Information Service
Foreign Rights: Gazelle Book Services Ltd (UK)

L & R Publishing, see Hellgate Press

Lake Claremont Press
Imprint of Everything Goes Media LLC
PO Box 711, Chicago, IL 60690
Mailing Address: PO Box 1524, Milwaukee, WI 53201
Tel: 312-226-8400 *Fax:* 312-226-8420
Web Site: www.lakeclaremont.com
Key Personnel
Owner & Publr: Sharon Woodhouse *E-mail:* sharon@lakeclaremont.com
Founded: 1994
Histories & guidebooks on the Chicago area by local authors with a passion & organizations with a mission.
ISBN Prefix(es): 978-1-893121; 978-0-9642426
Number of titles published annually: 3 Print; 6 E-Book
Total Titles: 50 Print

Lake Superior Port Cities Inc
310 E Superior St, Suite 125, Duluth, MN 55802
Mailing Address: PO Box 16417, Duluth, MN 55816-0417
Tel: 218-722-5002 *Toll Free Tel:* 888-BIG-LAKE (244-5253) *Fax:* 218-722-4096
E-mail: reader@lakesuperior.com
Web Site: www.lakesuperior.com
Key Personnel
Pres & Publr: Cynthia Hayden *E-mail:* cmh@lakesuperior.com
Publr: Paul L Hayden *E-mail:* plh@lakesuperior.com
Ed: Konnie Le May *E-mail:* kon@lakesuperior.com
Founded: 1979
Began as regional magazine publisher & expanded services to include books, travel guides, calendars, maps & merchandise.
ISBN Prefix(es): 978-0-942235
Number of titles published annually: 2 Print
Total Titles: 32 Print
Membership(s): Content Delivery & Storage Association; Midwest Independent Booksellers Association; Midwest Independent Publishing Association; Minnesota Magazine & Publications Association

LAMA Books
2381 Sleepy Hollow Ave, Hayward, CA 94545-3429
Tel: 510-785-1091 *Toll Free Tel:* 888-452-6244 *Fax:* 510-785-1099
Web Site: www.lamabooks.com
Key Personnel
Pres, Sales & Mktg Dir: Steve Meyer *E-mail:* steve@lamabooks.com
Founded: 1970
Develop & publish books for heating, ventilating & air conditioning (HVAC) field; occupational trades, reading development, teacher preparation; directories-occupational programs in California community colleges.
ISBN Prefix(es): 978-0-88069
Number of titles published annually: 5 Print
Total Titles: 50 Print

Lanahan Publishers Inc
324 Hawthorne Rd, Baltimore, MD 21210-2303
Tel: 410-366-2434 *Toll Free Tel:* 866-345-1949 *Fax:* 410-366-8798
E-mail: lanahan@aol.com
Web Site: www.lanahanpublishers.com
Key Personnel
Pres: Donald W Fusting
Founded: 1995
College textbook publisher.
ISBN Prefix(es): 978-0-9652687; 978-1-930398
Number of titles published annually: 4 Print
Total Titles: 20 Print

Landauer Corp
3100 101 St, Suite A, Urbandale, IA 50322
Tel: 515-287-2144 *Toll Free Tel:* 800-557-2144 *Fax:* 515-276-5102
E-mail: info@landauercorp.com
Web Site: www.landauercorp.com
Key Personnel
Pres & Publr: Jeramy Landauer
Founded: 1991
Publishing & licensing for the home arts working with leading designers & artists.
ISBN Prefix(es): 978-1-890621; 978-0-9646870; 978-0-9793711; 978-0-9770166; 978-1-935726; 978-0-9825586; 978-0-9818040
Number of titles published annually: 12 Print
Total Titles: 114 Print
Foreign Rep(s): A Great Notion (Canada); Alba Patchwork (Spain); N Jefferson (Canada); Quilt Source (Canada); John Reed Book Distribution (Australia); RJR Fabrics (Europe); Roundhouse Group (England); Stallion Press (Singapore); Virka (Iceland)
Membership(s): ABA; Independent Book Publishers Association

§Peter Lang Publishing Inc
Subsidiary of Peter Lang AG (Switzerland)
29 Broadway, 18th fl, New York, NY 10006-3223
SAN: 241-5534
Tel: 212-647-7706 *Toll Free Tel:* 800-770-5264 (cust serv) *Fax:* 212-647-7707
Web Site: www.peterlang.com
Key Personnel
SVP & Publg Dir: Dr Farideh Koohi-Kamali *E-mail:* farideh.koohi@plang.com
Sales & Mktg Dir: Patricia Mulrane Clayton *E-mail:* pattym@plang.com
Founded: 1982
Scholarly monographs & textbooks in the humanities, social sciences, media studies, Festschriften & conference proceedings.
ISBN Prefix(es): 978-0-8204; 978-1-4331; 978-1-4539 (ebooks)
Number of titles published annually: 240 Print
Total Titles: 2,500 Print
Foreign Office(s): Peter Lang GmbH, Eschborner Landstr 42-50, 60489 Frankfurt am Main, Germany *Tel:* (069) 78 07 05 0 *Fax:* (069) 78 07 05 50
Peter Lang AG, Hochfeldstr 32, 3012 Bern, Switzerland *Tel:* (031) 306 1717 *Fax:* (031) 306 1727
Foreign Rep(s): Peter Lang Verlag GmbH (Germany)

LangMarc Publishing
7500 Shadowridge Run, No 28, Austin, TX 78749
Tel: 512-394-0989 *Toll Free Tel:* 800-864-1648 (orders) *Fax:* 512-394-0829
E-mail: langmarc@booksails.com
Web Site: www.langmarc.com
Key Personnel
Pres & Lib Sales Dir: Lois Qualben
Founded: 1991
Publisher of inspirational titles.
ISBN Prefix(es): 978-1-880292
Number of titles published annually: 3 Print; 20 E-Book
Total Titles: 75 Print
Imprints: Harbor Lights
Orders to: PO Box 90488, Austin, TX 78709-0488 SAN: 297-519X

Lantern Books
Division of Booklight Inc
128 Second Place, Garden Suite, Brooklyn, NY 11231
Tel: 212-414-2275
E-mail: editorial@lanternbooks.com; info@lanternmedia.net
Web Site: lanternbooks.presswarehouse.com/Home/home.aspx
Key Personnel
Pres: Gene Gollogly *E-mail:* gene@lanternbooks.com
Mng Dir: Kara Davis *E-mail:* kara@lanternbooks.com
Dir, Publg: Martin Rowe
ISBN Prefix(es): 978-1-59056; 978-1-930051
Number of titles published annually: 15 Print
Total Titles: 150 Print
Foreign Rep(s): Ceres Books (New Zealand); Deep Books (Europe, UK)
Foreign Rights: Findhorn Press (Sabine Weeke)
Billing Address: Steiner Books, Quicksilver Dr, Sterling, VA 20166 *E-mail:* anthroposophicmail@presswarehouse.com
Orders to: PO Box 960, Herndon, VA 20172-0960 *Tel:* 703-661-1594 *Toll Free Tel:* 800-856-8664 *Fax:* 703-661-1501 *E-mail:* anthroposophicmail@presswarehouse.com
Returns: Steiner Books, Quicksilver Dr, Sterling, VA 20166 *E-mail:* anthroposophicmail@presswarehouse.com
Shipping Address: Steiner Books, Quicksilver Dr, Sterling, VA 20166 *Tel:* 703-661-1500 *E-mail:* anthroposophicmail@presswarehouse.com
Warehouse: Steiner Books, Quicksilver Dr, Sterling, VA 20166 *Tel:* 703-661-1500 *E-mail:* anthroposophicmail@presswarehouse.com
Distribution Center: Steiner Books, Quicksilver Dr, Sterling, VA 20166 *Tel:* 703-661-1500 *E-mail:* anthroposophicmail@presswarehouse.com
Membership(s): ABA

Laredo Publishing Co Inc
465 Westview Ave, Englewood, NJ 07631
Tel: 201-408-4048
E-mail: info@laredopublishing.com
Web Site: www.laredopublishing.com
Key Personnel
Pres: Sam Laredo *E-mail:* laredo@laredopublishing.com
VP & Exec Ed: Raquel Benatar *E-mail:* raquel@laredopublishing.com
Founded: 1991
ISBN Prefix(es): 978-1-56492
Number of titles published annually: 25 Print
Total Titles: 150 Print
Imprints: Renaissance House
See separate listing for:
Renaissance House

Lark Crafts
Imprint of Sterling Publishing Co Inc
1166 Avenue of the Americas, 17th fl, New York, NY 10036
Tel: 212-532-7160
E-mail: larkeditorial@sterlingpublishing.com; customerservice@sterlingpublishing.com
Web Site: larkcrafts.com; www.facebook.com/LarkCrafts; www.sterlingpublishing.com
Key Personnel
Asst Ed: Elysia Liang
Founded: 1979
How-to books in crafts & photography.
ISBN Prefix(es): 978-0-937274; 978-1-887374; 978-1-57990; 978-1-60059; 978-1-4547
Number of titles published annually: 120 Print
Total Titles: 400 Print
Foreign Rights: Sterling Publishing Co Inc
Shipping Address: Sterling Publishing Co Inc, 40 Saw Mill Pond Rd, Edison, NJ 08837 *Toll Free Tel:* 800-367-9692 *Toll Free Fax:* 800-542-7567

Larson Publications
4936 State Rte 414, Burdett, NY 14818

Tel: 607-546-9342 *Toll Free Tel:* 800-828-2197 *Fax:* 607-546-9344
E-mail: custserv@larsonpublications.com
Web Site: www.larsonpublications.com
Key Personnel
Mktg Dir & Publr: Amy Opperman Cash *E-mail:* amy@larsonpublications.com
Founded: 1982
Resources for spiritual independence & social relevance.
ISBN Prefix(es): 978-0-943914; 978-1-936012
Number of titles published annually: 6 Print; 1 CD-ROM; 1 Online; 5 E-Book
Total Titles: 90 Print; 1 CD-ROM; 25 E-Book; 3 Audio
Foreign Rep(s): Gazelle Book Services Ltd (Europe, UK); Bokforlaget Robert Larson (Scandinavia)
Foreign Rights: Literaryventuresfund (Mary Bisbee-Beek)
Distribution Center: New Leaf Distributing Co, 401 Thornton Rd, Lithia Springs, GA 30122-1557 *Tel:* 770-948-7845 *Toll Free Tel:* 800-326-2665 *Fax:* 770-944-2313 *E-mail:* newleaf@newleaf-dist.com *Web Site:* www.newleaf-dist.com
National Book Network, 15200 NBN Way, Blue Ridge Summit, PA 17214 *Toll Free Tel:* 800-462-6420 *Toll Free Fax:* 800-338-4550 *E-mail:* custserv@nbnbooks.com *Web Site:* www.nbnbooks.com

§Lasaria Creative Publishing
4094 Majestic Lane, Suite 352, Fairfax, VA 22033
E-mail: info@lasariacreative.com
Web Site: www.lasariacreative.com
Key Personnel
Publg Analyst: Adam Lee *E-mail:* adamlee@lasariacreative.com
Founded: 2008
Author-owned independent publishing company looking for nonfiction, general fiction, short stories & juvenile fiction books. We encourage first time authors & are willing to help get your work into mainstream distribution channels. Also offer editing services for new authors.
ISBN Prefix(es): 978-0-9818367; 978-0-9836671
Number of titles published annually: 10 Print; 10 Online; 10 E-Book
Total Titles: 14 Print; 12 Online; 12 E-Book

Latin American Literary Review Press
PO Box 7530, Pittsburgh, PA 15213
Tel: 412-824-7903
E-mail: lalrp.editor@gmail.com
Web Site: www.lalrp.org
Key Personnel
Founding Ed & Pres: Dr Yvette E Miller
Founded: 1980
Publish Latin American literature in English translation. Publish *Latin American Literary Review*, a semiannual journal of scholarly essays & book reviews on the literatures of Spanish America & Brazil, which also distributes Spanish books on social sciences, history & art.
ISBN Prefix(es): 978-0-935480; 978-1-891270
Number of titles published annually: 3 Print
Total Titles: 146 Print
Orders to: Independent Publishers Group, 814 N Franklin St, Chicago, IL 60610 *Toll Free Tel:* 800-888-4741 *E-mail:* orders@ipgbook.com *Web Site:* www.ipgbook.com
Membership(s): Community of Literary Magazines & Presses

Laughing Elephant
3645 Interlake N, Seattle, WA 98103
Tel: 206-447-9229 *Toll Free Tel:* 800-354-0400 *Fax:* 206-447-9189
E-mail: support@laughingelephant.com
Web Site: www.laughingelephant.com
Key Personnel
Pres & Publr: Harold Darling
Ed-in-Chief: Abigail Darling
Ed & Spec Sales & Licensing: Christina Darling
Founded: 1986
Publish books, cards & printed gifts with an emphasis on imagery, especially from antique children's books, self-generating content.
ISBN Prefix(es): 978-1-883211; 978-0-9621131; 978-1-59583
Number of titles published annually: 8 Print
Total Titles: 80 Print
Imprints: Darling & Co; Green Tiger Press

§Law School Admission Council
662 Penn St, Newtown, PA 18940
Mailing Address: PO Box 40, Newtown, PA 18940
Tel: 215-968-1101
E-mail: lsacaccounts@lsac.org
Web Site: www.lsac.org
Key Personnel
Dir, Communs: Wendy Margolis *Tel:* 215-968-1219 *E-mail:* wmargolis@lsac.org
Founded: 1947
Standardized testing, legal education & law school admission activities, law school admission test preparation.
ISBN Prefix(es): 978-0-9846360
Number of titles published annually: 4 Print; 2 Online; 3 E-Book
Total Titles: 30 Print; 2 Online; 8 E-Book
Sales Office(s): Ingram Publisher Services, One Ingram Blvd, La Vergne, TN 37086 *Toll Free Tel:* 866-400-5351 *Toll Free Fax:* 800-838-1149 *E-mail:* customer.service@ingrampublisherservices.com *Web Site:* ipage.ingramcontent.com SAN: 631-8630
Orders to: Ingram Publisher Services, One Ingram Blvd, La Vergne, TN 37086 *Toll Free Tel:* 866-400-5351 *Toll Free Fax:* 800-838-1149 *E-mail:* customer.service@ingrampublisherservices.com *Web Site:* ipage.ingramcontent.com SAN: 631-8630
Distribution Center: Ingram Publisher Services, One Ingram Blvd, La Vergne, TN 37086 *Toll Free Tel:* 866-400-5351 *Toll Free Fax:* 800-838-1149 *E-mail:* customer.service@ingrampublisherservices.com *Web Site:* ipage.ingramcontent.com SAN: 631-8630

Law Tribune Books, see The Connecticut Law Tribune

The Lawbook Exchange Ltd
33 Terminal Ave, Clark, NJ 07066-1321
Tel: 732-382-1800 *Toll Free Tel:* 800-422-6686 *Fax:* 732-382-1887
E-mail: law@lawbookexchange.com
Web Site: www.lawbookexchange.com
Key Personnel
Pres: Greg Talbot
Mng Ed, Pubns: Valerie Horowitz
Founded: 1981
Publisher of books on legal history. Also reprints of legal classics.
ISBN Prefix(es): 978-1-886363; 978-1-58477; 978-0-9630106
Number of titles published annually: 100 Print
Total Titles: 1,100 Print
Membership(s): Antiquarian Booksellers Association of America; International League of Antiquarian Booksellers

Merloyd Lawrence Inc
102 Chestnut St, Boston, MA 02108
SAN: 658-4012
Tel: 617-523-5895 *Fax:* 617-263-2749
Key Personnel
Pres & Ed: Merloyd Ludington Lawrence
Founded: 1982
Number of titles published annually: 5 Print; 4 E-Book
Total Titles: 80 Print; 42 E-Book

§Lawyers & Judges Publishing Co Inc
917 N Swan Rd, Suite 300, Tucson, AZ 85711
Mailing Address: PO Box 30040, Tucson, AZ 85751-0040
Tel: 520-323-1500 *Toll Free Tel:* 800-209-7109 *Fax:* 520-323-0055 *Toll Free Fax:* 800-330-8795
E-mail: sales@lawyersandjudges.com
Web Site: www.lawyersandjudges.com
Key Personnel
Pres & Publr: Steve Weintraub *E-mail:* steve@lawyersandjudges.com
Founded: 1963
Professional, text & reference materials in law, accident reconstruction, legal economics & taxation, forensics, medicine.
ISBN Prefix(es): 978-0-88450; 978-0-913875; 978-1-930056
Number of titles published annually: 25 Print; 8 CD-ROM
Total Titles: 103 Print; 16 CD-ROM

Leadership Directories
1407 Broadway, Suite 318, New York, NY 10018
Tel: 212-627-4140 *Toll Free Tel:* 800-627-0311 *Fax:* 212-645-0931
E-mail: info@leadershipdirectories.com
Web Site: www.leadershipdirectories.com
Key Personnel
CEO: Gretchen Teichgraeber *E-mail:* gteichgraeber@leadershipdirectories.com
CIO: Brian F Hanley *E-mail:* bhanley@leadershipdirectories.com
SVP, Prods & Content: Sue Healy *E-mail:* shealy@leadershipdirectories.com
SVP, Sales & Mktg: Tom Silver *E-mail:* tsilver@leadershipdirectories.com
VP, Admin & Treas: Jim Gee *E-mail:* jgee@leadershipdirectories.com
Sr Relationship Mgr: Jim Marcus *Tel:* 212-433-1408 *E-mail:* jmarcus@leadershipdirectories.com
Founded: 1969
Provider of premium contact solutions, covering the public & private sectors. Leadership Directories maintains a database of biographical & contact information on over 700,000 leaders & executives from more than 100,000 organizations. Content is available online, as datafeeds & pre-selected lists, or in print.
Number of titles published annually: 14 Print
Total Titles: 14 Print; 11 Online
Imprints: Yellow Books
Branch Office(s)
1667 "K" St NW, Suite 801, Washington, DC 20006, VP: Imogene Akins Hutchinson *Tel:* 202-347-7757 *Fax:* 202-628-3430 *E-mail:* iatkins@leadershipdirectories.com

Leadership Ministries Worldwide/OBR
3755 Pilot Point, Chattanooga, TN 37416
Mailing Address: PO Box 21310, Chattanooga, TN 37424-0310
Tel: 423-855-2181 *Toll Free Tel:* 800-987-8790 *Fax:* 423-855-8616
E-mail: info@outlinebible.org
Web Site: www.outlinebible.org
Key Personnel
Pres: Dave Worland
Commentaries.
ISBN Prefix(es): 978-1-57407; 978-0-945863
Number of titles published annually: 12 Print
Total Titles: 275 Print
Membership(s): Evangelical Christian Publishers Association

Leaf Storm Press
PO Box 4670, Santa Fe, NM 87502-4670
Tel: 505-216-6155
E-mail: leafstormpress@gmail.com
Web Site: leafstormpress.com
Key Personnel
Publr: Andy Dudzik *E-mail:* publisher@leafstormpress.com
Founded: 2014
ISBN Prefix(es): 978-0-9914105; 978-0-9970207
Number of titles published annually: 8 Print; 8 E-Book; 4 Audio
Total Titles: 8 Print; 6 E-Book
Distribution Center: Legato Publishers Group, 814 William St, River Forest, IL 60305
Tel: 630-947-2217 *Toll Free Tel:* 800-788-3123 *Toll Free Fax:* 800-351-5073
E-mail: orderentry@perseusbooks.com *Web Site:* www.pgw.com
Membership(s): AAP; ABA; Independent Book Publishers Association

Learnables Foreign Language Courses, see International Linguistics Corp

§THE Learning Connection®
4100 Silverstar Rd, Suite D, Orlando, FL 32808
Toll Free Tel: 800-218-8489 *Fax:* 407-292-2123
E-mail: tlc@tlconnection.com
Web Site: www.tlconnection.com
Key Personnel
Gen Mgr: Ryan Handberg *E-mail:* ryan@tlconnection.com
Founded: 1991
Thematic Literacy Centers & teacher's guides for early childhood & middle school; parent involvement & family literacy; bilingual, math, science, multicultural, manipulatives, technology.
ISBN Prefix(es): 978-1-56831
Number of titles published annually: 15 Print; 15 CD-ROM; 5 Audio
Total Titles: 1,000 Print; 15 CD-ROM; 50 Audio
Imprints: Computer Connections; PAKS-Parents & Kids
Branch Office(s)
300 E 93 St, Suite 29C, New York, NY 10128, VP, NJ Accts: Timothy Sasman
Membership(s): International Literacy Association

Learning Links Inc
PO Box 326, Cranbury, NJ 08512
SAN: 175-081X
Tel: 516-437-9071 *Toll Free Tel:* 888-960-2508 *Fax:* 516-437-5392
E-mail: info@learninglinks.com
Web Site: www.learninglinks.com
Key Personnel
Pres: Rikki Kessler
Founded: 1976
Publish study guides for novels for school use, grades 1-12. Distribute paperback books, audios, videos, craft kits & book-related toys.
ISBN Prefix(es): 978-0-88122; 978-1-56982; 978-0-7675
Number of titles published annually: 25 Print
Total Titles: 850 Print
Imprints: Novel-Ties Study Guides
Divisions: Swan Books
Distributor for Harcourt; HarperCollins; Houghton Mifflin Harcourt Publishing Company; Little, Brown & Company; Penguin Group USA, A Penguin Random House Company; Penguin Random House Inc; Scholastic; Simon & Schuster
Membership(s): International Literacy Association

LearningExpress LLC
80 Broad St, 4th fl, New York, NY 10004
Toll Free Tel: 800-295-9556 (ext 2)
E-mail: marketing@learningexpressllc.com (cust serv)
Web Site: www.learningexpressllc.com
Key Personnel
CEO & Pres: Barry Lippman
COO & Gen Mgr: Kheil McIntyre
E-mail: webkmcintyre@learningexpressllc.com
CTO: Tammy Cunningham
E-mail: webtcunningham@learningexpressllc.com
SVP, Content: Ilsa Halpern, PhD
E-mail: ihalpern@learningexpressllc.com
VP, Busn Devt: Helen Sileno
Dir, Cust Serv: Shana Ashwood-Viala
Dir, Mktg: Janine Y Swenson *E-mail:* jswenson@learningexpressllc.com
Founded: 1995
Publishes print & online test-preparation resources, skill building tools, study guides & career guidance materials for the trade, library, school & consumer markets.
ISBN Prefix(es): 978-1-57685; 978-1-61103
Number of titles published annually: 40 Print; 4 CD-ROM; 30 Online; 40 E-Book
Total Titles: 200 Print; 12 CD-ROM; 300 Online; 150 E-Book
Imprints: LearningExpress
Sales Office(s): National Book Network, 4501 Forbes Blvd, Suite 200, Lanham, MD 20706
Distributed by National Book Network
Orders to: National Book Network, 15200 NBN Way, Blue Ridge Summit, PA 17214 *Tel:* 717-794-3800 *Toll Free Tel:* 800-462-6420 *Toll Free Fax:* 800-338-4550 *E-mail:* customercare@nbnbooks.com
Returns: National Book Network, 15200 NBN Way, Blue Ridge Summit, PA 17214 *Tel:* 717-794-3800 *Toll Free Tel:* 800-462-6420 *Toll Free Fax:* 800-338-4550 *E-mail:* customercare@nbnbooks.com
Warehouse: National Book Network, 15200 NBN Way, Blue Ridge Summit, PA 17214

Lectorum Publications Inc
205 Chubb Ave, Lyndhurst, NJ 07071
Toll Free Tel: 800-345-5946 *Fax:* 201-559-2201
Toll Free Fax: 877-532-8676
E-mail: lectorum@lectorum.com
Web Site: www.lectorum.com
Key Personnel
Pres & CEO: Alex Correa *E-mail:* acorrea@lectorum.com
Opers Mgr: Fernando Febus *E-mail:* ffebus@lectorum.com
Lib & Trade Sales Mgr: Laura Bejarano
E-mail: lbejarano@lectorum.com
Educ Sales: Hilda Viskovic *E-mail:* hviskovic@lectorum.com
Founded: 1960
Distribute children & adult books in Spanish, with over 25,000 titles from more than 500 domestic & foreign publishers. Serves schools & libraries, as well as the trade & various specialized markets, with children's books in Spanish, including works originally written in Spanish, translations from other languages & the Spanish language editions of many popular children's books.
ISBN Prefix(es): 978-1-880507; 978-1-930332; 978 0 9625162; 978-1-933032; 978-1-941802; 978-1-63245
Number of titles published annually: 10 Print

Lederer Books
Division of Messianic Jewish Publishers
6120 Day Long Lane, Clarksville, MD 21029
Tel: 410-531-6644 *Toll Free Tel:* 800-410-7367 (orders) *Fax:* 410-531-9440
E-mail: lederer@messianicjewish.net; customerservice@messianicjewish.net
Web Site: www.messianicjewish.net
Key Personnel
Pres: Barry Rubin *E-mail:* president@messianicjewish.net
Founded: 1949
Publish & distribute Messianic Jewish books, bibles & other resources.
ISBN Prefix(es): 978-1-880226; 978-1-936716
Number of titles published annually: 6 Print
Total Titles: 100 Print
Distributor for Chosen People Ministries; First Fruits of Zion; Jewish New Testament Publications
Foreign Rep(s): Winfried Bluth (Europe)
Foreign Rights: Winfried Bluth (Europe)
Membership(s): CBA: The Association for Christian Retail; Evangelical Christian Publishers Association

Lee & Low Books Inc
95 Madison Ave, New York, NY 10016
Tel: 212-779-4400 *Toll Free Tel:* 888-320-3190 (ext 28, orders only) *Fax:* 212-683-1894 (orders only); 212-532-6035
E-mail: general@leeandlow.com
Web Site: www.leeandlow.com
Key Personnel
Pres: Craig Low *E-mail:* clow@leeandlow.com
Publr: Jason Low *E-mail:* jlow@leeandlow.com
Edit Dir: Cheryl Klein
Ed-at-Large: Louise May
Founded: 1991
Publisher of high quality multicultural children's books. We provide for the school, library & bookstore market.
ISBN Prefix(es): 978-1-880000; 978-1-885008; 978-1-58430; 978-1-60060; 978-0-89239; 978-1-62014
Number of titles published annually: 15 Print; 15 E-Book
Total Titles: 650 Print; 50 E-Book; 50 Audio
Imprints: Bebop Books; Children's Book Press; Shen's Books; Tu Books
See separate listing for:
Children's Book Press
Shen's Books

Legacy Press, see Rainbow Publishers

Lehigh University Press
Affiliate of Rowman & Littlefield Publishing Group (RLPG)
B-040 Christmas-Saucon Hall, 14 E Packer Ave, Bethlehem, PA 18015
Tel: 610-758-3933 *Fax:* 610-758-6331
E-mail: inlup@lehigh.edu
Web Site: inpress.sites.lehigh.edu
Founded: 1985
18th century American studies, East Asian studies, literary theory & criticism, history & technology, science, sociology, biography & the arts. Submissions welcome on any topic that is intellectually substantive.
ISBN Prefix(es): 978-1-61146
Number of titles published annually: 10 Print
Total Titles: 149 Print
Distributed by Rowman & Littlefield

§Leilah Publications
510 E University Dr, No 3413, Tempe, AZ 85281
Tel: 847-275-1657
E-mail: leilah@leilahpublications.com
Web Site: facebook.com/leilahpublications
Key Personnel
CEO: Joshua Seraphim
Creative Consultant: Amany El-Ameera Daghesty
Founded: 2006
Brings a global vision of art & writing for the 21st century, publishing & investing in avante-garde artists, lyricists, writers, actors, actresses & poets.
ISBN Prefix(es): 978-0-9829992; 978-0-9963338
Number of titles published annually: 3 Print; 3 Online; 3 E-Book; 1 Audio
Total Titles: 16 Print; 16 Online; 3 E-Book; 1 Audio
Subsidiaries: Brigids Books

Warehouse: Ingram/Lightning Source, 1246 Neil Quaker Blvd, La Vergne, TN 37086
Distribution Center: Ingram/Lightning Source, 1246 Neil Quaker Blvd, La Vergne, TN 37086
Membership(s): American Academy of Religion

§Leisure Arts Inc
Division of Liberty Media
104 Champs Blvd, Suite 100, Maumelle, AR 72113
SAN: 666-9565
Tel: 501-868-8800 *Toll Free Tel:* 800-643-8030
E-mail: customer_service@leisurearts.com
Web Site: www.leisurearts.com
Key Personnel
VP, Retail Sales: Martha Adams
Founded: 1971
Hard & soft cover books featuring instructions for needlework, crafts, cooking & gardening.
ISBN Prefix(es): 978-0-942237; 978-1-57486; 978-1-60140; 978-1-60900; 978-1-4647
Number of titles published annually: 200 Print
Total Titles: 2,000 Print

§The Lentz Leadership Institute LLC
Imprint of The Refractive Thinker Press
7124 Glyndon Trail NW, Albuquerque, NM 87114
SAN: 857-7994
Tel: 702-719-9214
E-mail: orders@lentzleadership.com
Web Site: www.lentzleadership.com; www.refractivethinker.com
Key Personnel
The Academic Entrepreneur: Dr Cheryl Lentz *E-mail:* drcheryllentz@gmail.com
Founded: 2008
Publishes scholarly materials as part of The Anthology Series: The Refractive Thinker Series, to include the educational seminar series for public speaking. Individual books & individual doctoral or graduate level publications by participating authors are also published. Offer APA doctoral & graduate editing services.
This publisher has indicated that 85% of their product line is author subsidized.
ISBN Prefix(es): 978-0-9823036; 978-0-9828740; 978-0-9840054
Number of titles published annually: 14 Print; 2 Online; 97 E-Book; 1 Audio
Total Titles: 16 Print; 14 Online; 132 E-Book; 2 Audio
Imprints: Pensiero Press
Distribution Center: Ingram/Lightning Source Inc, 1246 Heil Quaker Blvd, La Vergne, TN 37086 *Tel:* 615-213-5815 *Fax:* 615-213-4725 *E-mail:* inquiry@lightningsource.com *Web Site:* www.lightningsource.com
Membership(s): The Association of Publishers for Special Sales; Independent Book Publishers Association

Lerner Publications
Imprint of Lerner Publishing Group Inc
241 First Ave N, Minneapolis, MN 55401
SAN: 201-0828
Tel: 612-332-3344 *Toll Free Tel:* 800-328-4929 *Fax:* 612-332-7615 *Toll Free Fax:* 800-332-1132
E-mail: info@lernerbooks.com; custserve@lernerbooks.com
Web Site: www.lernerbooks.com; www.facebook.com/lernerbooks
Key Personnel
Chmn: Harry J Lerner
CFO & EVP: Margaret Thomas
Pres & Publr: Adam Lerner
EVP, Sales: David Wexler
VP, Ed-in-Chief: Andy Cummings
Edit Dir: Ashley Kuehl
Group Mktg Dir: Jill Braithwaite
Dir, HR: Cyndi Radant
Dir of Rts, Spec Sales & Intl Dist: Maria Kjoller
School & Lib Mktg Dir: Lois Wallentine
Founded: 1959
Juveniles: science, history, sports, fiction, art, geography, aviation, environment, ethnic, multicultural issues & activity books.
Number of titles published annually: 225 Print; 225 E-Book
Total Titles: 1,680 Print; 920 E-Book
Foreign Rep(s): INT Press Distribution (Australia); Monarch Books of Canada (Trade) (Canada); Phambili (Southern Africa); Publishers Marketing Service (Malaysia, Singapore); Saunders Book Co (Education) (Canada); South Pacific Books (New Zealand)
Foreign Rights: Japan Foreign-Rights Centre (Japan); Korea Copyright Center (KCC) (Korea); Michelle Lapautre Agence Junior (France); Literarische Agentur Silke Weniger (Germany)
Warehouse: Lerner Publishing Group, 1251 Washington Ave N, Minneapolis, MN 55401, Mgr: Ken Rued

Lerner Publishing Group Inc
Division of Lerner Universal Corp
241 First Ave N, Minneapolis, MN 55401
SAN: 201-0828
Tel: 612-332-3344 *Toll Free Tel:* 800-328-4929 *Fax:* 612-332-7615 *Toll Free Fax:* 800-332-1132
E-mail: info@lernerbooks.com; custserve@lernerbooks.com
Web Site: www.lernerbooks.com; www.facebook.com/lernerbooks
Key Personnel
Chmn: Harry J Lerner
CFO & EVP: Margaret Thomas
Pres & Publr: Adam Lerner
EVP, Sales: David Wexler
VP & Ed-in-Chief: Andy Cummings
Group Mktg Dir: Jill Braithwaite
Dir, HR: Cyndi Radant
Dir of Rts, Spec Sales & Intl Dist: Maria Kjoller
School & Lib Mktg Dir: Lois Wallentine
School & Lib Sales Mgr: Brad Richason
Founded: 1959
ISBN Prefix(es): 978-0-87614; 978-1-58013; 978-0-8225; 978-0-7613; 978-1-57505; 978-0-92937; 978-0-93049; 978-1-58196
Number of titles published annually: 450 Print
Total Titles: 4,800 Print; 3,800 E-Book
Imprints: Bumba Books; Carolrhoda Books Inc; Carolrhoda Lab™; Darby Creek Publishing; ediciones Lerner; First Avenue Editions; Graphic Universe™; Hungary Tomato; Kar-Ben Publishing; Lerner Digital; Lerner Publications; LernerClassroom; Millbrook Press; Twenty-First Century Books
Divisions: Kar-Ben Publishing; Lerner Books UK; Lerner Publisher Services
Distributor for Andersen Press USA; Columbus Zoo; Walter Foster Publishing; Gecko Press; JR Comics; The Kane Press; Kar-Ben Partners; MVP Books; Red Chair Press; Sandy Creek; Scobre Educational; Stoke Books; We Do Listen
Foreign Rep(s): Bravo (Kar-Ben) (UK & the continent); INT Books (Australia); J Appleseed, A Division of Saunders (Canada); Mazeltov Books (Kar-Ben) (Australia); Monarch Books of Canada/Trade (Canada); Phambili Agencies (Botswana, Lesotho, Namibia, South Africa, Swaziland, Zimbabwe); Publishers Marketing Services (Brunei, Malaysia, Singapore); Saunders Book Co/Education (Canada); South Pacific Books (New Zealand)
Foreign Rights: Japan Foreign-Rights Center (Japan); Korea Copyright Center (KCC) (Korea); Michelle Lapautre Agence Junior (France); Literarische Agentur Silke Weniger (Germany)
Warehouse: 1251 Washington Ave N, Minneapolis, MN 55401, Mgr: Ken Rued
See separate listing for:
Carolrhoda Books
Carolrhoda Lab™
ediciones Lerner
First Avenue Editions
Graphic Universe™
Kar-Ben Publishing
Lerner Publications
LernerClassroom
Millbrook Press
Twenty-First Century Books

LernerClassroom
Imprint of Lerner Publishing Group Inc
241 First Ave N, Minneapolis, MN 55401
Tel: 612-332-3344 *Toll Free Tel:* 800-328-4929 *Fax:* 612-332-7615 *Toll Free Fax:* 800-332-1132
E-mail: info@lernerbooks.com; custserve@lernerbooks.com
Web Site: www.lernerbooks.com; www.facebook.com/lernerbooks
Key Personnel
Chmn: Harry J Lerner
CFO & EVP: Margaret Thomas
Pres & Publr: Adam Lerner
EVP, Sales: David Wexler
VP, Ed-in-Chief: Patricia M Stockland
Dir of Rts, Spec Sales & Intl Dist: Maria Kjoller
Group Mktg Dir: Jill Braithwaite
School & Lib Mktg Dir: Lois Wallentine
Dir, HR: Cyndi Radant
Nonfiction children's publications with teaching guides.
Total Titles: 860 Print; 55 E-Book
Foreign Rep(s): INT Books (Australia); Monarch Books of Canada (Canada); Phambili (Southern Africa); Publishers Marketing Services (Brunei, Malaysia, Singapore); South Pacific Books (New Zealand)
Foreign Rights: Japan Foreign-Rights Centre (Japan); Korea Copyright Center (Korea); Michelle Lapautre Agence Junior (France); Literarische Agentur Silke Weniger (Germany)
Warehouse: Lerner Publishing Group, 1251 Washington Ave N, Minneapolis, MN 55401, Mgr: Ken Rued

Lessiter Media
16655 W Wisconsin Ave, Brookfield, WI 53005
Mailing Address: PO Box 624, Brookfield, WI 53008-0624
Tel: 262-782-4480 *Toll Free Tel:* 800-645-8455 *Fax:* 262-782-1252; 262-786-5564
E-mail: info@lessitermedia.com
Web Site: www.lesspub.com; lessitermedia.com
Key Personnel
Chmn & Edit Dir: Frank Lessiter *E-mail:* lessitef@lesspub.com
Pres: Mike Lessiter *E-mail:* mlessiter@lessitermedia.com
Founded: 1981
Animals, farm equipment, business, sports, veterinary science (equine hoof care).
ISBN Prefix(es): 978-0-944079; 978-0-944605
Number of titles published annually: 6 Print
Total Titles: 35 Print

Letterbox/Papyrus of London Publishers USA
10501 Broom Hill Dr, Suite 1-F, Las Vegas, NV 89134-7339
Tel: 702-256-3838
E-mail: lb27383@cox.net
Key Personnel
Mng Dir: Anthony Wade
Ed-in-Chief: Geoffrey Hutchison-Cleaves, MA
Fin Offr: Josef Kase *Tel:* 702-256-3838 ext 2
Spec Orders Mgr: Erica Neubauer *Tel:* 702-256-3838 ext 1

Rts & Perms: Mrs H Neubauer *Tel:* 702-256-3838 ext 8
Founded: 1946 (at Penley Court, 173 Strand, London EC4)
No submissions accepted.
ISBN Prefix(es): 978-0-943698
Number of titles published annually: 4 Print
Total Titles: 138 Print
Imprints: Challenges of Aging (instruction booklets); Difficult Subjects Made Easy (instruction booklets)
Advertising Agency: ShowKase Advertising & Public Relations, 3250 S Fort Apache Rd, Suite 217, Las Vegas, NV 89117, Acct Exec: Ms Robin Lindsay
Distribution Center: Amazon.com
Baker & Taylor Books, PO Box 8888, Momence, IL 60954 *Tel:* 908-541-7459
Barnes & Noble

Letterbox Service, see Letterbox/Papyrus of London Publishers USA

Lexington Books
Imprint of Rowman & Littlefield Publishing Group
4501 Forbes Blvd, Suite 200, Lanham, MD 20706
Tel: 301-459-3366 *Fax:* 301-429-5749
Web Site: www.lexingtonbooks.com
Key Personnel
VP & Publr: Julie Kirsch *E-mail:* jkirsch@rowman.com
Mktg Mgr: Dave Horvath *E-mail:* dhorvath@rowman.com
Premier publisher of scholarly monographs & textbooks. Subjects include classics, political science, political theory, philosophy, history, international relations, literary studies, public policy, sociology, anthropology, religion, communications, cultural studies, education, psychology, linguistics & area studies.
ISBN Prefix(es): 978-0-7391; 978-1-4985
Number of titles published annually: 500 Print; 500 E-Book
Total Titles: 4,000 Print; 2,500 E-Book
Foreign Rep(s): APD Singapore Pte Ltd (Brunei, Cambodia, Indonesia, Laos, Malaysia, Singapore, Thailand, Vietnam); Asia Publishers Service Ltd (China, Hong Kong, Korea, Philippines, Taiwan); Avicenna Partnership Ltd (Afghanistan, Algeria, Armenia, Bahrain, Cyprus, Egypt, Iran, Iraq, Jordan, Kuwait, Lebanon, Libya, Morocco, Oman, Palestine, Qatar, Saudi Arabia, Sudan, Syria, Tunisia, United Arab Emirates, Yemen); Co Info Pty Ltd (Australia, New Zealand, Papua New Guinea); Cranbury International LLC (Caribbean, Central America, Mexico, Pakistan, Puerto Rico, South America); Durnell Marketing Ltd (Austria, Baltic States, Belgium, Czech Republic, Denmark, Finland, France, Germany, Greece, Hungary, Iceland, Italy, Malta, Netherlands, Norway, Poland, Portugal, Slovakia, Slovenia, Spain, Sweden, Switzerland); Juta & Co Ltd (Botswana, Lesotho, Namibia, South Africa, Swaziland, Zimbabwe); Overleaf (Bangladesh, Bhutan, India, Nepal, Sri Lanka); Quantum Publishing Solutions Ltd (UK); Tahir Lodhi Publishers' Representatives (Pakistan); United Publishers Service Ltd (Japan); Wise Book Solutions (Korea)
Foreign Rights: Clare Cox (worldwide)
Orders to: Rowman & Littlefield Publishing Group, 15200 NBN Way, Blue Ridge Summit, PA 17214 *Tel:* 717-794-3800 *Toll Free Tel:* 800-462-6420 *Fax:* 717-794-3803 *E-mail:* custserv@rowman.com
Membership(s): AAP

§LexisNexis®
Division of RELX Group PLC
230 Park Ave, Suite 7, New York, NY 10169
SAN: 202-6317
Tel: 212-309-8100 *Toll Free Fax:* 800-437-8674
Web Site: www.lexisnexis.com
Key Personnel
CEO: Mike Walsh
Founded: 1897
Multivolume legal reference works, state codes & single-volume legal texts, treatises & casebooks. Most material also in online versions.
ISBN Prefix(es): 978-0-409; 978-0-87215; 978-0-672; 978-0-87473; 978-0-406; 978-0-327; 978-0-88063; 978-0-930273; 978-1-55834; 978-1-56257
Imprints: Michie
Shipping Address: Broome Corp Park, 136 Carlin Rd, Conklin, NY 13748 *Tel:* 607-772-2600 *Toll Free Fax:* 800-323-9608

§LexisNexis® Matthew Bender®
Member of The LexisNexis® Group
701 E Water St, Charlottesville, VA 22902
Tel: 434-972-7600
Web Site: www.lexisnexis.com
Founded: 1887
Treatises, text & form books, newsletters, periodicals & manuals for the legal, accounting, insurance, banking & related professions, selected libraries on CD-ROM.
Branch locations also in New York City & Dayton, OH.
ISBN Prefix(es): 978-0-8205; 978-1-4224
Total Titles: 577 Print; 277 CD-ROM; 27 Online; 277 E-Book
Branch Office(s)
Immaculata Hall, 32 S Ewing St, Helena, MT 59601 *Toll Free Tel:* 800-227-9597

Liberty Fund Inc
8335 Allison Pointe Trail, Suite 300, Indianapolis, IN 46250-1684
SAN: 202-6740
Tel: 317-842-0880 *Toll Free Tel:* 800-955-8335; 800-866-3520; 800-368-7897 ext 6069 (cust serv) *Fax:* 317-577-9067; 317-579-6060 (cust serv); 708-534-7803
E-mail: books@libertyfund.org; info@libertyfund.org
Web Site: www.libertyfund.org
Key Personnel
VP, Publg: Patricia Gallagher
Mng Ed: Dan Kirklin
Mktg & Fulfillment Coord: Michele Roberts *Tel:* 317-842-0880 ext 0020 *E-mail:* mroberts@libertyfund.org
Founded: 1960
A publisher of print & electronic scholarly resources including new editions of classic works in American constitutional history, European history, natural law, law, modern political thought, economics & education.
ISBN Prefix(es): 978-0-913966; 978-0-86597; 978-1-61487
Number of titles published annually: 10 Print; 100 Online
Total Titles: 360 Print; 1,450 Online; 1 Audio
Foreign Rep(s): Academic Sales & Marketing (Andrew Jones) (Midlands, Northern England); Jim Biaho (Italy); Mara Cheli (Italy); Peter Couzens (Asia); Everybodys Book's (Warren Halford) (Southern Africa); Export Sales Agency (Ted Dougherty) (Austria, Germany, Switzerland); Four Corners Sales Agency (Charlotte Kelly) (Ireland, London, Scotland, Southern England, Wales); Gazelle Academic (Mark Trotter) (London); Charles Gibbes (Cyprus, Greece); Iberian Book Services (Charlotte Prout) (Gibraltar, Portugal, Spain); Iberian Book Services (Peter Prout); Marketing Solutions LLP (Andrew Wallace) (Central London, UK, East Anglia, England); Maya Publishers Pvt Ltd (India); Tony Moggach (Eastern Europe); David Towle (Baltic States, Northern Europe, Scandinavia)
Distribution Center: Scholarly Book Services, 289 Ridgeland Ave, Unit 105, Toronto, ON M6A 1Z6, Canada *Toll Free Tel:* 800-847-9736
Membership(s): AAP; ALA

Libraries Unlimited
Imprint of ABC-CLIO
130 Cremona Dr, Santa Barbara, CA 93117
Mailing Address: PO Box 1911, Santa Barbara, CA 93116-1911
Tel: 805-968-1911 *Toll Free Tel:* 800-368-6868 *Fax:* 805-685-9685 *Toll Free Fax:* 866-270-3856
E-mail: customerservice@abc-clio.com
Web Site: www.abc-clio.com
Founded: 1964
Library science textbooks, annotated bibliographies, reference books, professional books for school media specialists as well as resource & activity books for librarians & teachers; storytelling resources & collections.
ISBN Prefix(es): 978-0-313; 978-0-87287; 978-1-56308; 978-1-59158
Number of titles published annually: 80 Print
Total Titles: 600 Print; 5 Audio
Imprints: Linworth Publishing
See separate listing for:
Linworth Publishing

The Library of America
14 E 60 St, New York, NY 10022-1006
SAN: 286-9918
Tel: 212-308-3360 *Fax:* 212-750-8352
E-mail: info@loa.org
Web Site: www.loa.org
Key Personnel
Pres: Max Rudin
COO: Daniel W Baker
Assoc Publr: Brian McCarthy
Dir, Mktg: David Cloyce Smith
Prodn Ed: Trish Hoard
Cust Serv Mgr: Laura Gazlay
Founded: 1979
Collected editions of classic American authors; literature, history, philosophy, drama, poetry & journalism.
ISBN Prefix(es): 978-0-940450; 978-1-883011; 978-1-931082; 978-1-59853
Number of titles published annually: 14 Print
Total Titles: 300 Print
Distributed by Penguin Group USA, A Penguin Random House Company
Foreign Rep(s): Penguin Random House Canada (Canada); United Publishers Service (Japan)
Warehouse: Penguin Group USA, A Penguin Random House Company, One Grosset Dr, Kirkwood, NY 13795

Mary Ann Liebert Inc
140 Huguenot St, 3rd fl, New Rochelle, NY 10801-5215
Tel: 914-740-2100 *Toll Free Tel:* 800-654-3237 *Fax:* 914-740-2101
E-mail: info@liebertpub.com
Web Site: www.liebertonline.com
Key Personnel
Publr & CEO: Mary Ann Liebert
SVP: Harriet I Matysko
Ad Prodn Mgr: Kathleen De Souza
Ad Prodn: Wanda Sanchez *E-mail:* wsanchez@genengnews.com
Founded: 1980
Medical & sci-tech journals, books & newspapers. Additional subjects include: biomedical research, integrative medicine (CAM), public policy, public health/policy, gender & population studies, regenerative medicine, clinical medicine, biotechnology, environmental studies, humanities, life sciences, allied health & surgery.

ISBN Prefix(es): 978-0-913113; 978-1-934854
Number of titles published annually: 3 Print; 3 Online
Total Titles: 65 Print; 70 Online
Divisions: Genetic Engineering & Biotechnology News
Foreign Office(s): Impress Media, Carrington Kirk, Carrington, Midlothian EH23 4LR, United Kingdom, Contact: Hilary Turnbull *Tel:* (01875) 825700 *Fax:* (01875) 825701 *E-mail:* hturnbull@genengnews.com

Life Cycle Books
Division of Life Cycle Books Ltd (Canada)
PO Box 799, Fort Collins, CO 80522
SAN: 692-7173
Toll Free Tel: 800-214-5849 *Toll Free Fax:* 888-690-8532
E-mail: orders@lifecyclebooks.com; support@lifecyclebooks.com
Web Site: www.lifecyclebooks.com
Key Personnel
Founder & Pres: Paul Broughton *E-mail:* paulb@lifecyclebooks.com
Founded: 1973
Books, pamphlets, brochures & audiovisuals on human life issues.
ISBN Prefix(es): 978-0-919225
Number of titles published annually: 6 Print
Total Titles: 41 Print

Light-Beams Publishing
36 Blandings Way, Biddeford, ME 04005
Tel: 603-659-1300
E-mail: info@light-beams.com
Web Site: www.light-beams.com
Key Personnel
Mktg Mgr & Trade Contact: Mark Forman *E-mail:* mforman@light-beams.com
Founded: 2000
Specialize in & publishes award-winning children's books & videos for children ages 3 & up.
ISBN Prefix(es): 978-0-9708104; 978-0-9766289
Number of titles published annually: 8 Print
Distribution Center: Independent Publishers Group, 814 N Franklin St, Chicago, IL 60610 (exclusive dist to the book trade) *Toll Free Tel:* 800-888-4741 *Web Site:* www.ipgbook.com

Light Publications
Hope Artiste Village, 1005 Main St, Suite 1212, Pawtucket, RI 02806
Mailing Address: PO Box 2462, Providence, RI 02906
Tel: 401-484-0228
E-mail: info@lightpublications.com
Web Site: lightpublications.com
Key Personnel
Pres: Stephen Brendan *E-mail:* stephen@lightpublications.com
Founded: 1999
ISBN Prefix(es): 978-0-9702642; 978-0-9824707; 978-1-940060
Number of titles published annually: 2 Print; 5 Online; 3 E-Book; 1 Audio
Total Titles: 20 Print; 25 Online; 20 E-Book; 8 Audio
Membership(s): Independent Book Publishers Association

Light Technology Publishing
4030 E Huntington Dr, Flagstaff, AZ 86004
Mailing Address: PO Box 3540, Flagstaff, AZ 86003-3540
Tel: 928-526-1345 *Toll Free Tel:* 800-450-0985 *Fax:* 928-714-1132
E-mail: publishing@lighttechnology.net
Web Site: www.lighttechnology.com
Key Personnel
Owner & Publr: O'Ryin Swanson
Sidona Journal, metaphysical publications, mostly channelled.
ISBN Prefix(es): 978-1-891824; 978-1-929385
Number of titles published annually: 15 Print
Total Titles: 150 Print
Foreign Rights: Hagenbach & Bender GmbH (worldwide exc USA)
Membership(s): AAP

Lighthouse Publishing of the Carolinas
2333 Barton Oaks Dr, Raleigh, NC 27614-7940
Tel: 919-562-8439
E-mail: lighthousepublishingcarolinas@gmail.com
Web Site: lighthousepublishingofthecarolinas.com
Key Personnel
Founder & CEO: Eddie Jones
Mng Ed, Straight Street Books & Sonrise Devotionals: Cindy Sproles
ISBN Prefix(es): 978-0-9833196; 978-0-9822065; 978-0-9847655; 978-1-938499
Number of titles published annually: 40 Print
Total Titles: 132 Print; 40 E-Book
Imprints: Bling!; Brimstone; Firefly; Heritage Beacon; Straight Street Books; Sonrise Devotionals

Liguori Publications
One Liguori Dr, Liguori, MO 63057-1000
Tel: 636-464-2500 *Toll Free Tel:* 866-848-2492; 800-325-9521 *Fax:* 636-464-8449 *Toll Free Fax:* 800-325-9526 (sales)
E-mail: liguori@liguori.org (sales & cust serv)
Web Site: www.liguori.org/contact-us.html
Key Personnel
Pres: Fr Byron Miller
Publr: Virgil Tipton, III
Dir, Fin & Busn Opers: Tracey Kane
Acqs Ed: Julia DiSalvo
Founded: 1947
Academic & trade books on religion (Catholic) & spirituality, inspirational & educational resources for parishes & schools, devotional music, bulletins, pamphlets, Liguorian magazine.
ISBN Prefix(es): 978-0-89243; 978-0-7648
Number of titles published annually: 50 Print
Total Titles: 600 Print; 14 CD-ROM
Imprints: Libros Liguori; Liguori/Triumph
Distributor for Redemptorist Publications
Foreign Rep(s): Majellan (Australia); Novalis (Canada); Redemptorist Publications Book Services (England)

Limelight Editions
Imprint of Hal Leonard Performing Arts Publishing Group
33 Plymouth St, Suite 302, Montclair, NJ 07042
Tel: 973-337-5034 *Fax:* 973-337-5227
Web Site: limelighteditions.com
Key Personnel
Group Publr: John Cerullo
Full service trade publisher that produces books, book/CDs & DVDs on the performing arts including cinema, dance & theater.
ISBN Prefix(es): 978-0-87910
Number of titles published annually: 8 Print; 2 Audio
Total Titles: 260 Print; 5 Audio
Sales Office(s): 7777 W Bluemound Rd, Milwaukee, WI 53213 *Toll Free Tel:* 800-554-0626
Distributed by Hal Leonard Corp
Foreign Rep(s): Publishers Group UK (Europe, UK)
Billing Address: 960 E Mark St, Winona, MN 55987 *Tel:* 507-454-2920 *Fax:* 507-454-9334
Orders to: 7777 W Bluemound Rd, Milwaukee, WI 53213 *Toll Free Tel:* 800-554-0626
Returns: 1210 Innovation Dr, Winona, MN 55987 *Tel:* 507-454-2920 *Fax:* 507-454-8334
Warehouse: 1210 Innovation Dr, Winona, MN 55987 *Tel:* 507-454-2920 *Fax:* 507-454-8334
Distribution Center: 960 E Mark St, Winona, MN 55987 *Tel:* 507-454-2920 *Fax:* 507-454-8334

Linden Publishing Co Inc
2006 S Mary St, Fresno, CA 93721
Tel: 559-233-6633 *Toll Free Tel:* 800-345-4447 (orders) *Fax:* 559-233-6933
Web Site: lindenpub.com
Key Personnel
Pres & Publr: Richard Sorsky *E-mail:* richard@lindenpub.com
Founded: 1977
ISBN Prefix(es): 978-0-941936; 978-1-933502; 978-1-884956; 978-1-884995
Number of titles published annually: 12 Print; 5 E-Book
Total Titles: 200 Print; 50 E-Book
Imprints: Craven Street Books; Pace Press; Quill Driver Books
Foreign Rights: Books Crossing Borders (worldwide)
Distribution Center: Ingram Publisher Services, One Ingram Blvd, La Vergne, TN 37086
Membership(s): ABA; Independent Book Publishers Association

Lindisfarne Books
Imprint of SteinerBooks
610 Main St, Great Barrington, MA 01230
Mailing Address: PO Box 749, Great Barrington, MA 01230
Tel: 413-528-8233 *Fax:* 413-528-8826
E-mail: service@steinerbooks.org
Web Site: www.steinerbooks.org
Key Personnel
CEO & Pres: Eugene Gollogly *E-mail:* gene@steinerbooks.org
Ed-in-Chief: Christopher Bamford
Founded: 1979
Fine quality books in the areas of philosophy, psychology, new sciences, comparative theology, art & literature, emphasizing the synthesis of science, religion & art.
ISBN Prefix(es): 978-0-940262; 978-1-58420; 978-0-9701097
Number of titles published annually: 5 Print
Total Titles: 103 Print
Distributed by Floris Books
Foreign Rep(s): Floris Books (UK)
Orders to: PO Box 960, Herndon, VA 20172 *Tel:* 703-661-1594 *Toll Free Tel:* 800-856-8664 *Fax:* 703-661-1501
Warehouse: PO Box 960, Herndon, VA 20172 *Tel:* 703-661-1594

LinguaText LLC
103 Walker Way, Newark, DE 19711
SAN: 238-0307
Tel: 302-453-8695
E-mail: text@linguatextbooks.com
Web Site: www.linguatextbooks.com
Key Personnel
Owner & Publr: Michael Bolan
Founded: 1978
Publish foreign language textbooks, Hispanic monographs & classics of Spanish & French literature designed for the English-speaking college student.
ISBN Prefix(es): 978-0-936388; 978-0-942566; 978-1-58871; 978-1-58977
Number of titles published annually: 15 Print
Total Titles: 400 Print; 3 CD-ROM; 2 E-Book
Imprints: Cervantes & Co (Spanish classics series); Juan de la Cuesta Hispanic Monographs (literary criticism, monographs, critical editions); Moliere & Co (French classics series)
Distribution Center: GOBI® Library Solutions, 999 Maple St, Contoocook, NH 03229 *Tel:* 603-746-3102 *Toll Free Tel:* 800-258-3774 *Fax:* 603-746-5628 *Web Site:* gobi.ebsco.com
Baker & Taylor, 2550 W Tyvola Rd, Suite 300, Charlotte, NC 28217 *Toll Free Tel:* 800-775-1800 *E-mail:* btinfo@baker-taylor.com

Ingram, One Ingram Blvd, La Vergne, TN 37086 *Toll Free Tel:* 866-400-5351 *E-mail:* ips@ingramcontent.com
Membership(s): Textbook & Academic Authors Association

§The Linick Group Inc
Linick Bldg, 7 Putter Lane, Middle Island, NY 11953
Mailing Address: PO Box 102, Middle Island, NY 11953-0102
Tel: 631-924-3888; 631-775-6075 *Fax:* 631-924-8555
E-mail: linickgroup@gmail.com; andrew@asklinick.com
Web Site: www.andrewlinickdirectmarketing.com/Publishers-Advice.html; www.newworldpressbooks.com
Key Personnel
Lib Sales Dir: Jill Reynolds
Founded: 1968
Specialized health titles, health care, weight loss, exercise, fitness, martial arts/self-defense, wine & spirits, mature market, multicultural & bilingual picture; multimedia, workbooks & instructional material, public relations, restaurants & travel & tourism; confidential reports, foreign countries, newsletters, business & direct response advertising & marketing, communications, subscription & mail order, photography, psychology, ecommerce, ebooks, epublishing, Internet interactive campaigns, targeted epublic relations on a guaranteed placement basis.
This publisher has indicated that 50% of their product line is author subsidized.
ISBN Prefix(es): 978-0-917098 (New World Press)
Number of titles published annually: 25 Print; 10 CD-ROM; 450 Online; 50 E-Book
Total Titles: 125 Print; 120 CD-ROM; 950 Online; 350 E-Book
Imprints: CCA; Isshin-Ryu Productions; LKA Inc; National Association of Photo Sellers™; New World Press
Distributed by New World Press Books; Okinawan Kobujutsu Kyokai Association (OKKA)
Distributor for Linick International; LKA Inc; National Association of Photo Sellers™
Advertising Agency: LK Advertising Agency, 7 Putter Lane, PO Box 102, Middle Island, NY 11953-0102, EVP: Roger Dextor *Tel:* 631-924-3888; 631-924-8555 *Fax:* 631-924-8555 *E-mail:* printmedia4less@gmail.com *Web Site:* www.newworldpressbooks.com
Distribution Center: Bookmasters, 30 Amberwood Pkwy, Ashland, OH 44805
See separate listing for:
Copywriter's Council of America™ (CCA)

Linworth Publishing
Imprint of Libraries Unlimited
130 Cremona Dr, Santa Barbara, CA 93117
Mailing Address: PO Box 1911, Santa Barbara, CA 93116-1911
Tel: 805-968-1911 *Toll Free Tel:* 800-368-6868 *Fax:* 805-685-9685 *Toll Free Fax:* 866-270-3856
E-mail: customerservice@abc-clio.com
Web Site: www.abc-clio.com
Key Personnel
Pres & Publr: Marlene Woo-Lun
Founded: 1982
Professional book & magazine publishing for school library media specialists.
ISBN Prefix(es): 978-0-938865; 978-1-58683
Number of titles published annually: 20 Print
Total Titles: 100 Print
Imprints: Linworth Learning

§Lippincott Williams & Wilkins
Unit of Wolters Kluwer Health
333 Seventh Ave, New York, NY 10001
Toll Free Tel: 800-950-2035
E-mail: orders@lww.com
Web Site: www.lww.com
Key Personnel
Dir, Corp Communs, Health Learning, Res & Practice: Connie Hughes *Tel:* 646-674-6348 *E-mail:* connie.hughes@wolterskluwer.com
Founded: 1792
Medicine, dentistry life sciences, nursing, allied health, veterinary medicine books, journals, textbooks, looseleaf, newsletters & media.
ISBN Prefix(es): 978-0-8021; 978-0-397; 978-0-316; 978-0-683; 978-0-7817; 978-1-4698; 978-1-60929; 978-1-60831; 978-0-8067; 978-1-60547; 978-1-881063; 978-0-88167; 978-0-89004; 978-0-89313; 978-0-89640; 978-0-911216
Total Titles: 4,000 E-Book
Branch Office(s)
2 Commerce Sq, 2001 Market St, Philadelphia, PA 19103 *Tel:* 215-521-8300 *Fax:* 215-521-8902
351 W Camden St, Baltimore, MD 21201 *Tel:* 410-528-4000
Foreign Office(s): Lippincott Williams & Wilkins Pty Ltd, 101 Waterloo Rd, Level 2, North Ryde, NSW 2113, Australia *Tel:* (02) 9857 1313 *Fax:* (02) 9857 1304
Lippincott Williams & Wilkins Asia Ltd, 15/F, W Sq, 314-324 Hennessy Rd, Wan Chai, Hong Kong *Tel:* 2610 7000 *Fax:* 2610 7098
250 Waterloo Rd, London SE1 8RD, United Kingdom *Tel:* (020) 7981 0600 *Fax:* (020) 7981 0601
Warehouse: 16522 Hunters Green Pkwy, Hagerstown, MD 21740 *Tel:* 301-223-2300 *Fax:* 301-223-2400
Distribution Center: 16522 Hunters Green Pkwy, Hagerstown, MD 21740 *Tel:* 301-223-2300 *Fax:* 301-223-2400

Listen & Live Audio Inc
1700 Manhattan Ave, Union City, NJ 07087
Mailing Address: PO Box 817, Roseland, NJ 07068-0817
Tel: 201-558-9000 *Toll Free Tel:* 800-653-9400 (orders) *Fax:* 201-558-9800
Web Site: www.listenandlive.com
Key Personnel
Pres: Alfred C Martino *E-mail:* alfred@listenandlive.com
Publr: Alisa Weberman *E-mail:* alisa@listenandlive.com
Founded: 1995
Strictly audiobooks, self-help, fiction, motivational & men's adventure.
ISBN Prefix(es): 978-1-885408; 978-1-931953; 978-1-59316
Number of titles published annually: 10 Audio
Total Titles: 600 Audio
Membership(s): Audio Publishers Association; Independent Book Publishers Association

Little Bee Books
Imprint of Bonnier Publishing
853 Broadway, Suite 2014, New York, NY 10003
E-mail: info@littlebeebooks.com
Web Site: www.littlebeebooks.com
Key Personnel
Pres: Shimul Tolia
Publr: Sonali Fry
Fin & Opers Dir: Tom Morgan
Dir, Mktg & Publicity: Gayley Avery
Mng Ed: Dave Barrett
Sr Ed, Licensed Publg: Joy Bean
Edit Asst: Charlie Ilgunas
Sr Designer: Rob Wall
Designer: David DeWitt
Mgr, Mktg & Publicity: Caitlin Casey
Sr Publicist: Crystal McCoy
Prodn Mgr: Barbara Cho
Prodn Coord: Jade Yeung
Sales & Mktg Asst: Shefali Lohia
Founded: 2014
Creative & fun books for busy little bees ages 0-12 designed to entertain, inspire & educate.
Agented submissions only. No unsol mss accepted.
ISBN Prefix(es): 978-1-4998
Number of titles published annually: 150 Print
Total Titles: 46 Print
Distributed by Simon & Schuster, Inc
Foreign Rep(s): Bonnier Publishing (James Tavendale) (worldwide)
Foreign Rights: Bonnier Publishing (Nick Franklin) (worldwide)
Billing Address: Simon & Schuster, Inc, 100 Front St, Riverside, NJ 08075
Orders to: Simon & Schuster, Inc, 100 Front St, Riverside, NJ 08075 *Toll Free Tel:* 800-223-2336
Returns: Simon & Schuster, Inc, c/o Jacobson Logistics, 4406 Industrial Park Rd, Bldg 7, Camp Hill, PA 17011
Shipping Address: Simon & Schuster, Inc, 100 Front St, Riverside, NJ 08075
Warehouse: Simon & Schuster, Inc, 100 Front St, Riverside, NJ 08075
Distribution Center: Simon & Schuster, Inc, 100 Front St, Riverside, NJ 08075
Membership(s): AAP

§Little, Brown and Company
Division of Hachette Book Group
1290 Avenue of the Americas, New York, NY 10019
Tel: 212-364-1100 *Fax:* 212-364-0952
E-mail: firstname.lastname@hbgusa.com
Web Site: www.littlebrown.com; www.HachetteBookGroup.com
Key Personnel
SVP, HBG & Publr, Little, Brown and Company: Reagan Arthur
VP, Deputy Publr: Craig Young
VP, Ed-in-Chief: Judy Clain
VP, Publr, Digital & Pbk: Terry Adams
VP, Edit Dir, Mulholland Books & Exec Ed, Little, Brown and Company: Josh Kendall
VP, Subs Rts, HBG: Nancy Wiese
VP, Patterson Publg Dir: Ned Rust
VP, Edit Dir, Lee Boudreaux Books: Lee Boudreaux
VP, Creative Dir: Mario Pulice
Exec Dir, Publicity: Sabrina Callahan
Dir, Intl Rts: Tracy Williams
Fin Dir: Paul Boccardi
Sr Mng Ed: Mary Tondorf-Dick
Founded: 1837
Little, Brown and Company, the adult trade division of Hachette Book Group, is one of the country's oldest & most distinguished publishing houses. Unsol/unagented mss not accepted.
ISBN Prefix(es): 978-0-316
Number of titles published annually: 279 Print
Total Titles: 2,023 Print
Imprints: Back Bay Books; BookShots; Lee Boudreaux Books; Mulholland Books; jimmy patterson
Sales Office(s): Hachette Book Group, 1290 Avenue of the Americas, New York, NY 10019 (spec mkts) *Toll Free Tel:* 800-222-6747 *Toll Free Fax:* 800-477-5925
Foreign Rights: Agencia Literaria Carmen Balcells SA (Portugal, Spain); Bardon-Chinese Media Agency (China, Taiwan); BMSR Ag Literaria (Brazil); The Italian Literary Agency srl (Italy); JLM Literary Agency (Greece); Nurcihan Kesim Literary Agency (Turkey); The KM Agency (Netherlands); Agence Michelle Lapautre (France); Mohrbooks Agency (Germany); Andrew Nurnberg Associates Ltd (Baltic States, Bulgaria, Croatia, Czech Republic, Hungary, Poland, Romania, Russia & former USSR); I Pitarski Ltd Literary Agency (Israel); Sane Toregard Agency (Scandinavia); Tuttle-Mori Agency Inc (Japan); Eric Yang Agency (Korea)

Orders to: Hachette Book Group, 53 State St, Boston, MA 02109 *Toll Free Tel:* 800-759-0190 *Toll Free Fax:* 800-286-9471
Returns: Hachette Book Group, 322 S Enterprise Blvd, Lebanon, IN 46052
Shipping Address: Hachette Book Group, 121 N Enterprise Blvd, Lebanon, IN 46052

Little, Brown Books for Young Readers
Division of Hachette Book Group
1290 Avenue of the Americas, New York, NY 10019
SAN: 200-2205
Tel: 212-364-1100 *Toll Free Tel:* 800-759-0190 (cust serv)
Web Site: www.HachetteBookGroup.com
Key Personnel
EVP, HBG & Publr, Little, Brown Books for Young Readers: Megan Tingley
VP, Integrated Mktg: Melanie Chang
VP, Edit Dir, Picture Books: Andrea Spooner
VP & Ed-in-Chief: Alvina Ling
VP, Creative Dir: David Caplan
Edit Dir, Poppy & Nonfiction: Farrin Jacobs
Exec Dir, School & Lib Mktg: Victoria Stapleton
Exec Dir, Mktg: Emilie Polster
Exec Edit Dir, Brand, Licensed & Media Tie in Publg: Kara Sargent
Publicity Dir: Jessica Shoffel
Dir, Subs Rts: Kristin Dulaney
Busn Mgr: Roberto Velez
Founded: 1837
Specializes in board books, novelty items, picture books, middle reader, young adult fiction & nonfiction & selected media tie-ins.
ISBN Prefix(es): 978-0-316
Number of titles published annually: 284 Print
Total Titles: 1,845 Print
Imprints: LBKids; Poppy
Orders to: Hachette Book Group, 53 State St, Boston, MA 02109 *Toll Free Tel:* 800-759-0190 *Toll Free Fax:* 800-286-9471
Shipping Address: Hachette Book Group Distribution Center, 121 N Enterprise Blvd, Lebanon, IN 46052 *Tel:* 765-483-9900 *Fax:* 765-483-0706
Membership(s): AAP; ALA; The Children's Book Council; Women's National Book Association

The Little Entrepreneur
Imprint of Harper Arrington Publishing & Media
c/o Harper Arrington Media, 18701 Grand River, Suite 105, Detroit, MI 48223
Toll Free Tel: 888-435-9234 *Fax:* 248-281-0373
E-mail: info@harperarringtonmedia.com
Web Site: www.thelittlee.com
Key Personnel
Co-Founder & Publr: Jay Arrington; Michael Harper
Media Rel: John Thomas
Media Contact: Lance Smith
Founded: 2004
ISBN Prefix(es): 978-0-9764161
Number of titles published annually: 3 Print; 1 CD-ROM
Total Titles: 4 Print; 2 CD-ROM; 1 Online
Distributed by Harper Arrington Publishing

Little Simon, see Simon & Schuster Children's Publishing

§Liturgical Press
Division of The Order of St Benedict Inc
PO Box 7500, St John's Abbey, Collegeville, MN 56321-7500
SAN: 202-2494
Tel: 320-363-2213 *Toll Free Tel:* 800-858-5450 *Fax:* 320-363-3299 *Toll Free Fax:* 800-445-5899
E-mail: sales@litpress.org
Web Site: www.litpress.org
Key Personnel
Dir: Peter Dwyer *Tel:* 320-363-2533 *E-mail:* pdwyer@osb.org
Assoc Publr, Parish Mkt: Michelle Verkuilen *Tel:* 320-363-2227 *E-mail:* mverkuilen@osb.org
Fin Dir: Sandra Eiynck *Tel:* 320-363-2225 *E-mail:* seiynck@csbsju.edu
Sales & Mktg Mgr: Brian Woods *Tel:* 320-363-3953 *E-mail:* bwoods@csbsju.edu
Founded: 1926
Began publishing for the church in 1926 & continues to sustain the original mission of proclaiming the good news of Jesus Christ. Liturgical Press is a trusted publisher of liturgy, scripture, theology & spirituality evolving to serve the changing needs of the church.
ISBN Prefix(es): 978-0-87907; 978-0-8146
Number of titles published annually: 90 Print; 50 E-Book
Total Titles: 1,500 Print; 10 CD-ROM; 50 E-Book; 20 Audio
Imprints: Cistercian Publications; Michael Glazier Books; Liturgical Press Books; Pueblo Books
Foreign Rep(s): B Broughton Co Ltd (Canada); The Catholic Bookshop (South Africa); Claretian Publications (Philippines); Columba Book Service (European Union, Ireland, UK); John Garratt Publishing (Australia); Katong Catholic Book Centre Pte Ltd (Malaysia, Singapore); Pleroma Christian Supplies (New Zealand); Spring Arbor/Ingram (Tennessee)
Advertising Agency: Liturgical Advertising Agency
See separate listing for:
Cistercian Publications

Liturgy Training Publications
Subsidiary of Archdiocese of Chicago
3949 S Racine Ave, Chicago, IL 60609-2523
SAN: 670-9052
Tel: 773-579-4900 *Toll Free Tel:* 800-933-1800 (US & CN only orders) *Fax:* 773-579-4929 *Toll Free Fax:* 800-933-7094 (US & CN only orders)
E-mail: orders@ltp.org
Web Site: www.ltp.org
Key Personnel
Acting Dir & Edit Dir: Deanna M Keefe *Tel:* 773-579-4900 ext 3570 *E-mail:* dkeefe@ltp.org
Mktg & Sales Mgr: Kathleen Sommers Garcia *Tel:* 773-579-4900 ext 3535 *E-mail:* ksommers@ltp.org
Sales Supv & Trade Rep: Irene Sanchez *Tel:* 773-579-4900 ext 3566 *E-mail:* isanchez@ltp.org
Founded: 1964
Books & periodicals on Roman Catholic liturgy, worship & prayer in the home & church.
ISBN Prefix(es): 978-0-929650; 978-1-56854; 978-1-59525
Number of titles published annually: 30 Print; 2 CD-ROM; 20 E-Book; 2 Audio
Total Titles: 500 Print; 6 CD-ROM; 80 E-Book; 7 Audio
Imprints: Catechesis of the Good Shepherd Publications; Hillenbrand Books
Distributor for United States Catholic Conference Publications (select titles)
Foreign Rep(s): The Catholic Bookshop (South Africa); Garrett Publishing (Australia); Katong Catholic Book Centre (Malaysia, Philippines); McCrimmons Bookstore/Publisher (UK exc Ireland); Pleroma Christian Supplies (New Zealand)
Membership(s): Association of Catholic Publishers Inc

The Live Oak Press LLC
PO Box 60036, Palo Alto, CA 94306-0036
Tel: 650-853-0197 *Fax:* 815-366-8205
E-mail: info@liveoakpress.com
Web Site: www.liveoakpress.com
Key Personnel
Founder & Pres: David M Hamilton
Founded: 1982
Publishes California literary history.
ISBN Prefix(es): 978-0-931095; 978-0-931378
Number of titles published annually: 3 Print
Total Titles: 14 Print
Membership(s): ALA; Association of College & Research Libraries; The Authors Guild; Independent Book Publishers Association; Publishing Professionals Network; Society for Scholarly Publishing

Living Language
Imprint of Penguin Random House Audio Publishing
c/o Penguin Random House Inc, 1745 Broadway, New York, NY 10019
Tel: 212-782-9000 *Toll Free Tel:* 800-733-3000 (orders) *Toll Free Fax:* 800-659-2436
E-mail: livinglanguage@randomhouse.com
Web Site: www.livinglanguage.com
Key Personnel
SVP & Publr: Amanda D'Acierno
Assoc Dir, Mng Edit: Alison Skrabek
Mktg Dir: Heather Dalton
Dir, Publicity: Katherine Fleming Punia
Sr Mgr, Subs Rts: Maren McCamley
Founded: 1946
Self-study foreign language & ESL. Online courses, apps & digital content; Sign Language & dictionaries.
Penguin Random House Inc & its publishing entities are not accepting unsol submissions, proposals, mss, or submission queries via e-mail at this time.
ISBN Prefix(es): 978-0-609; 978-0-307
Number of titles published annually: 12 Print
Total Titles: 22 Print; 122 Audio
Returns: Random House LLC, 1019 N State Rd 47, Crawfordsville, IN 47933
Distribution Center: Random House LLC, c/o Library & School Servs, 400 Hahn Rd, Westminster, MD 21157 *Toll Free Tel:* 800-940-7046

§Living Stream Ministry (LSM)
2431 W La Palma Ave, Anaheim, CA 92801
Mailing Address: PO Box 2121, Anaheim, CA 92814-0121
Tel: 714-991-4681 *Toll Free Tel:* 800-549-5164 *Fax:* 714-236-6005
E-mail: books@lsm.org
Web Site: www.lsm.org
Key Personnel
Intl Rts Contact: Yorke Warden *E-mail:* yorke@lsm.org
Lib Sales Dir: John Pester
Founded: 1963
Religious publications.
ISBN Prefix(es): 978-0-87083; 978-1-57593; 978-0-7363
Number of titles published annually: 50 Print
Total Titles: 1,500 Print

Livingston Press
Division of University of West Alabama
University of West Alabama, Sta 22, Livingston, AL 35470
SAN: 851-917X
Tel: 205-652-3470
Web Site: www.livingstonpress.uwa.edu
Key Personnel
Dir: Joe Taylor *E-mail:* jwt@uwa.edu
Founded: 1984
ISBN Prefix(es): 978-0-942979; 978-0-930501; 978-1-931982; 978-1-60489
Number of titles published annually: 8 Print; 8 E-Book; 2 Audio
Total Titles: 140 Print; 90 E-Book; 2 Audio
Imprints: Swallow's Tale Press
Distributor for Swallow's Tale Press

Distribution Center: Small Press Distribution (SPD), 1341 Seventh St, Berkeley, CA 94710-1409 *Tel:* 510-524-1668 *Toll Free Tel:* 800-869-7553 *E-mail:* spd@spdbooks.org *Web Site:* www.spdbooks.org
Membership(s): Community of Literary Magazines & Presses; Independent Book Publishers Association

Llewellyn Publications
Division of Llewellyn Worldwide Ltd
2143 Wooddale Dr, Woodbury, MN 55125
SAN: 201-100X
Tel: 651-291-1970 *Toll Free Tel:* 800-843-6666 *Fax:* 651-291-1908
E-mail: publicity@llewellyn.com; customerservice@llewellyn.com
Web Site: www.llewellyn.com
Key Personnel
Publr: Bill Krause
Dir, Sales & Mktg: Tom Lund *E-mail:* toml@llewellyn.com
Sr Publicist: Kat Sanborn *Tel:* 651-312-8452 *E-mail:* kats@llewellyn.com
Founded: 1901
Body, mind, spirit. Trade publisher.
ISBN Prefix(es): 978-0-87542; 978-1-56718; 978-0-7387
Number of titles published annually: 110 Print; 10 CD-ROM
Total Titles: 900 Print
Imprints: Midnight Ink (mystery, trade, fiction, paperback)
Distributor for Blue Angel; Lo Scarabeo
Foreign Rep(s): PGUK (Ireland, UK)
Foreign Rights: Oxana Schroeder (worldwide)

The Local History Co
112 N Woodland Rd, Pittsburgh, PA 15232-2849
Tel: 412-362-2294 *Toll Free Tel:* 866-362-0789 (orders) *Fax:* 412-362-8192
E-mail: info@thelocalhistorycompany.com; sales@thelocalhistorycompany.com; editor@thelocalhistorycompany.com
Web Site: www.thelocalhistorycompany.com
Founded: 2001
Publishers of history & heritage.
ISBN Prefix(es): 978-0-9711835; 978-0-9744715; 978-0-9770429
Number of titles published annually: 10 Print
Total Titles: 25 Print
Imprints: Towers Maguire Publishing
Membership(s): Independent Book Publishers Association

Locks Art Publications/Locks Gallery
Division of Locks Gallery
600 Washington Sq S, Philadelphia, PA 19106
Tel: 215-629-1000
E-mail: info@locksgallery.com
Web Site: www.locksgallery.com
Key Personnel
Dir: Sueyun Locks
Founded: 1968
Exhibition catalogue, monographs on contemporary art.
ISBN Prefix(es): 978-1-879173; 978-0-9623799
Number of titles published annually: 8 Print
Total Titles: 45 Print

Loft Press Inc
9293 Fort Valley Rd, Fort Valley, VA 22652
Tel: 540-933-6210 *Fax:* 540-933-6523
E-mail: Books@LoftPress.com
Web Site: www.loftpress.com
Key Personnel
Pres & Publr: Stephen R Hunter
Ed-in-Chief: Ann A Hunter
Founded: 1987
ISBN Prefix(es): 978-0-9630797; 978-1-893846
Number of titles published annually: 3 Print; 2 CD-ROM; 1 E-Book
Total Titles: 137 Print; 2 CD-ROM; 1 E-Book
Imprints: Eschat Press (religion); Far Muse Press; Merry Muse Press; Punch Press
Subsidiaries: AAH Graphics Inc
Advertising Agency: AAH Advertising *Tel:* 540-933-6211
Membership(s): Washington Book Publishers

Logos Press
Imprint of thinkBiotech LLC
3909 Witmer Rd, Suite 416, Niagara Falls, NY 14305
Fax: 815-346-3514
E-mail: info@logos-press.com
Web Site: www.logos-press.com
Key Personnel
Ed: Yali Friedman
Founded: 2003
Specialize in reference & textbooks addressing the use of knowledge to make intelligent strategic decisions. Target audiences include college & advanced courses, business managers, directors & C-level executives. The objective is to help advanced students & decision makers implement their ideas based on solid fundamentals.
ISBN Prefix(es): 978-0-9734676; 978-1-934899
Number of titles published annually: 4 Print; 4 Online
Total Titles: 12 Print; 4 Online

Lonely Planet
150 Linden St, Oakland, CA 94607
Tel: 510-893-8555; 510-250-6400 *Toll Free Tel:* 800-275-8555 (orders) *Fax:* 510-893-8572
E-mail: info@lonelyplanet.com
Web Site: www.lonelyplanet.com
Key Personnel
CEO: Daniel Houghton
Dir, Mktg (US): Rana Freedman
Dir, Sales (Americas) & Gen Mgr: Patricia Kelly
Sr Design Mgr: Gerilyn Attebery
Sr Sales Mgr & Children's Specialist: Peg O'Donnell
Global Mktg Mgr, Busn Devt: Jennifer Pentes
Founded: 1973
Create & deliver the most compelling & comprehensive travel content in the world, giving travellers trustworthy information, engaging opinions, powerful images & informed perspectives on destinations around the globe. While known primarily for its 600+ travel guidebooks, we also offer an award-winning web site, photographic image library, television production, distribution & digital travel content licensing.
ISBN Prefix(es): 978-0-908086; 978-0-86442
Number of titles published annually: 100 Print
Total Titles: 600 Print
Foreign Office(s): 90 Maribyrnong St, Footscray, Victoria 3011, Australia *Tel:* (03) 8379 8000 *Fax:* (03) 8379 8111
302 DLF City Ct, Sikanderpurj Gurgaon 122002, India *Tel:* 124 423 1645
240 Blackfriars Rd, London SE1 8NW, United Kingdom *Tel:* (020) 3771 5100 *Fax:* (020) 3771 5101
Foreign Rep(s): A B E Marketing (Poland); Altair (Spain); Asia Books Co Ltd (Thailand); Asia Publishers' Services Ltd (China, Hong Kong, Taiwan); David Bateman Ltd (New Zealand); The Book Centre (Pakistan); Booktraders Ltd (Cyprus, Czech Republic, Greece, Israel, Malta, Middle East, Turkey); Brettschneider (Germany); CDE (sales: English & French editions) (France); Centralivros (Portugal); TB Clarke (Overseas Pty Ltd) (Fiji); CLB Marketing Services (Croatia, Hungary, Montenegro, Romania, Serbia, Slovenia); CV Java Books (Indonesia); Dinternal (Russia); Electra Media Group Pty Ltd (Guam, Micronesia, Philippines); Eleftheroudakis SA (Greece); Faradawn (South Africa); Freytag & Berndt U Artaria KG (Austria); Geocentre ILH (Germany); Geographical Tours Ltd (Israel); IMA Distribution (East Asia); India Book Distributors (Bombay) Ltd (India, Nepal); Intercontinental Marketing Corp (Japan); International Educational Library (Greece); Kartbutiken (Sweden); Lannoo Publishers (Belgium); Logos Art Srl (Italy); MPH Distributors (Malaysia, Singapore); Nilsson & Lamm Bv (Netherlands); Olf SA (Switzerland); Raincoast Books (Canada); Cav Giovanni Russano SAS (Italy); Scanvik Books Aps (Denmark, Finland, Iceland, Norway); Jana Seta (Latvia); Shoestring International (Korea); Sklep Podroznika (Poland); Sodis (dist) (France); Text Book Centre Ltd (Kenya); Trak Trade Centre (Estonia); The Travel Bookshop (Switzerland); Vijitha Yapa Bookshop (Pvt) Ltd (Sri Lanka); Westland Sundries Ltd (Kenya); Yab Yay Yayimcilik Sanayi (Turkey)

§Long River Press
Imprint of Sinomedia International Group
360 Swift Ave, Suite 48, South San Francisco, CA 94080
Tel: 650-872-7718 (ext 312) *Fax:* 650-872-7808
E-mail: info@longriverpress.com
Web Site: www.chinabooks.com
Key Personnel
Exec Ed: Chris Robyn *E-mail:* chris@chinabooks.com
Founded: 2002
Trade & academic titles on any aspect of China or Chinese history, culture & society.
ISBN Prefix(es): 978-1-59265
Number of titles published annually: 10 Print; 5 E-Book
Total Titles: 120 Print; 20 E-Book
Distribution Center: China Books, 360 Swift Ave, Suite 48, South San Francisco, CA 94706 *Toll Free Tel:* 800-818-2017 *E-mail:* orders@chinabooks.com
Membership(s): Association for Asian Studies

Looseleaf Law Publications Inc
Division of Warodean Corp
43-08 162 St, Flushing, NY 11358
Mailing Address: PO Box 650042, Fresh Meadows, NY 11365-0042
Tel: 718-359-5559 *Toll Free Tel:* 800-647-5547 *Fax:* 718-539-0941
E-mail: info@looseleaf.com
Web Site: www.looseleaflaw.com
Key Personnel
Owner: Michael L Loughrey
VP & Edit: Mary Loughrey
Sales Dir: Hilary McKeon
Founded: 1967
Law books; study aids for law enforcement, students, attorneys & court personnel.
ISBN Prefix(es): 978-0-930137; 978-1-889031; 978-1-932777
Number of titles published annually: 200 Print
Total Titles: 25 CD-ROM

§Lorenz Educational Press
Division of The Lorenz Corp
501 E Third St, Dayton, OH 45402
Mailing Address: PO Box 802, Dayton, OH 45401-0802
Tel: 937-228-6118 *Toll Free Tel:* 800-444-1144 *Fax:* 937-223-2042
E-mail: order@lorenz.com
Web Site: www.lorenzeducationalpress.com
Key Personnel
VP: Debra Kaiser *E-mail:* debk@lorenz.com
Founded: 2008
Educational publishing division includes visual resources, instructional guides & reproducibles, elementary supplementals.
ISBN Prefix(es): 978-1-42911
Number of titles published annually: 10 Print
Total Titles: 75 Print; 75 E-Book; 7 Audio
Membership(s): Education Market Association

Lost Classics Book Company LLC
411 N Wales Dr, Lake Wales, FL 33853-3881
Tel: 863-632-1981 (edit off)
E-mail: mgeditor@lostclassicsbooks.com
Web Site: www.lostclassicsbooks.com
Key Personnel
Owner: Michael Alan Fitterling
Founded: 1996
Republish late 19th & early 20th century literature & textbooks to aid parents & teachers in educating children.
ISBN Prefix(es): 978-0-9652735; 978-1-890623
Number of titles published annually: 8 Print
Total Titles: 43 Print
Imprints: Road Dog Publications (motorcycling books)
Distribution Center: National Book Network, 15200 NBN Way, Blue Ridge Summit, PA 17214 *Tel:* 717-794-3800 *Fax:* 717-794-3828 *E-mail:* customercare@nbnbooks.com *Web Site:* www.nbnbooks.com
Membership(s): Independent Book Publishers Association

Lost Horse Press
105 Lost Horse Lane, Sandpoint, ID 83864
Tel: 208-255-4410
E-mail: losthorsepress@mindspring.com
Web Site: www.losthorsepress.org
Key Personnel
Publr: Christine Holbert
Founded: 1998
Nonprofit independent press that publishes poetry titles of emerging as well as published poets & makes available fine contemporary literature through cultural, educational & publishing programs & activities.
ISBN Prefix(es): 978-0-9668612; 978-0-9717265; 978-0-9762114; 978-0-9800289
Number of titles published annually: 10 Print; 1 CD-ROM; 1 Audio
Total Titles: 110 Print; 2 CD-ROM; 1 Audio
Distributed by University of Washington Press
Distribution Center: University of Washington Press, 4333 Brooklyn Ave NE, Seattle, WA 98195 *Tel:* 410-516-6956 *Toll Free Tel:* 800-537-5487 *Fax:* 410-516-6998 *E-mail:* hfscustserv@press.jhu.edu *Web Site:* www.washington.edu/uwpress
Membership(s): Community of Literary Magazines & Presses

Lotus Light Publications, see Lotus Press

Lotus Press
Division of Lotus Brands Inc
PO Box 325, Twin Lakes, WI 53181-0325
Tel: 262-889-8561 *Toll Free Tel:* 800-824-6396 (orders) *Fax:* 262-889-8591
E-mail: lotuspress@lotuspress.com
Web Site: www.lotuspress.com
Key Personnel
Pres: Santosh Krinsky *E-mail:* santosh@lotuspress.com
Founded: 1981
Health, yoga, Native American & New Age metaphysics, Vedic astrology.
ISBN Prefix(es): 978-0-941524; 978-0-910261; 978-0-914955; 978-0-940985; 978-0-940676; 978-0-930736
Number of titles published annually: 6 Print; 2 CD-ROM; 2 Online; 15 E-Book; 3 Audio
Total Titles: 325 Print; 5 CD-ROM; 10 Online; 175 E-Book; 42 Audio
Imprints: Arcana Publishing; DIPTI; Shangri-La; Specialized Software
Distributor for Back to Eden Books; Dipti; East West Cultural Center; Les Editions ETC; Inner Worlds Music; November Moon; SABDA; Sadhana Publications; Samata Books; Sri Aurobindo Ashram; Star Sounds
Warehouse: 1100 Lotus Dr, Bldg 3, Silver Lake, WI 53170

Louisiana State University Press
338 Johnston Hall, Baton Rouge, LA 70803
Tel: 225-578-6294 *Fax:* 225-578-6461
E-mail: lsupress@lsu.edu
Web Site: lsupress.org
Key Personnel
Dir: MaryKatherine Callaway *Tel:* 225-578-6144 *E-mail:* mkc@lsu.edu
Asst Dir & Design & Prodn Mgr: Laura Gleason *Tel:* 225-578-6469 *E-mail:* lgleasn@lsu.edu
Mktg Mgr: Erin Rolfs *Tel:* 225-578-8282 *E-mail:* erolfs@lsu.edu
Mng Ed: Lee Sioles *Tel:* 225-578-6467 *E-mail:* lsioles@lsu.edu
Fulfillment Opers Mgr: Becky Brown *Tel:* 225-578-6415 *E-mail:* rbrown1@lsu.edu
Founded: 1935
Scholarly, regional, general; humanities & social sciences; southern history & literature; poetry; government & political science; music; paperbacks; fiction.
ISBN Prefix(es): 978-0-8071
Number of titles published annually: 85 Print
Total Titles: 1,000 Print; 4 CD-ROM
Foreign Rep(s): East-West Export Books (Asia, Australia, Japan, New Zealand, The Pacific); Scholarly Book Services (Canada)
Foreign Rights: McIntosh & Otis
Orders to: Longleaf Services Inc, 116 S Boundary St, Chapel Hill, NC 27514-3808 *Tel:* 919-966-7449 *Toll Free Tel:* 800-848-6224 *Fax:* 919-962-2704 *Toll Free Fax:* 800-272-6817 *E-mail:* customerservice@longleafservices.org *Web Site:* www.longleafservices.org
Returns: Longleaf Services Inc, c/o Ingram Publisher Services, 1210 Ingram Blvd, Chambersburg, PA 17202 *E-mail:* credit@longleafservices.org
Warehouse: Longleaf Services Inc, c/o Ingram Publisher Services, 1210 Ingram Blvd, Chambersburg, PA 17202
Membership(s): American Association of University Presses

Love Inspired Books
Imprint of Harlequin Enterprises Ltd
233 Broadway, Suite 1001, New York, NY 10279
SAN: 200-2450
Tel: 212-553-4200 *Fax:* 212-227-8969
E-mail: customer_service@harlequin.ca
Web Site: www.harlequin.com
Key Personnel
CEO & Publr: Craig Swinwood
EVP, Global Publg & Strategy: Loriana Sacilotto
Exec Ed: Tina James
Ed: Emily Rodmell
Founded: 1997
Inspirational romance novels, romantic suspense & women's fiction.
ISBN Prefix(es): 978-0-373
Number of titles published annually: 192 Print
Imprints: Love Inspired; Love Inspired Historical; Love Inspired Suspense
Distribution Center: 3010 Walden Ave, Depew, NY 14043

Love Publishing Co
9101 E Kenyon Ave, Suite 2200, Denver, CO 80237
SAN: 205-2482
Tel: 303-221-7333 *Toll Free Tel:* 877-240-6396 *Fax:* 303-221-7444
E-mail: lpc@lovepublishing.com
Web Site: www.lovepublishing.com
Key Personnel
Pres & Publr: Stanley F Love
Founded: 1968
College textbooks, journals & professional books in counseling, social work & special needs education.
ISBN Prefix(es): 978-0-89108
Number of titles published annually: 8 Print; 1 E-Book
Total Titles: 125 Print; 1 E-Book
Foreign Rep(s): Eurospan (Africa, Europe, UK); Publishers Marketing Service (Malaysia, Singapore)
Returns: PSSC, 660 S Mansfield, Ypsilanti, MI 48197
Membership(s): AAP

§Loving Healing Press Inc
5145 Pontiac Trail, Ann Arbor, MI 48105
SAN: 255-7770
Tel: 734-417-4266 *Toll Free Tel:* 888-761-6268 (US & CN) *Fax:* 734-663-6861
E-mail: info@lovinghealing.com; info@lhpress.com
Web Site: www.lovinghealing.com; www.modernhistorypress.com (imprint)
Key Personnel
Pres: Prof Victor R Volkman *E-mail:* victor@lhpress.com
Founded: 2003
Dedicated to producing books about innovative & rapid therapies to empower authors in redefining what is possible for healing the mind & spirit.
ISBN Prefix(es): 978-1-932690
Number of titles published annually: 15 Print; 15 E-Book
Total Titles: 250 Print; 250 E-Book
Imprints: AMI Press (official press of Applied Metapsychology International); Future Psychiatry Press (rethinking psychiatry & pharmacology); Marvelous Spirit Press (dedicated to helping your spiritual transformation & growth); Modern History Press (memoirs of people who have lived through significant events); Rocky Mountain Region Disaster Mental Health Institute Press (leading the way for strategic management of crisis response, first responders & rural responders); Victorian Heritage Press (showcasing the best of 19th century contemporary histories)
Foreign Rep(s): Ingram International (Australia, Europe, UK & Commonwealth)
Foreign Rights: IPR Licensing (worldwide exc USA)
Membership(s): Independent Book Publishers Association

Loyola Press
3441 N Ashland Ave, Chicago, IL 60657
SAN: 211-6537
Tel: 773-281-1818 *Toll Free Tel:* 800-621-1008 *Fax:* 773-281-0555 (cust serv); 773-281-4129 (edit)
E-mail: customerservice@loyolapress.com
Web Site: www.loyolapress.com
Key Personnel
Pres: Terry Locke
Exec Ed & Acqs: Joseph Durepos *E-mail:* durepos@loyolapress.com
Digital Rts Mgr & Foreign Rep: Andrew Yankech
Founded: 1912
Catholic publisher of books for elementary schools, parishes & the general trade.
ISBN Prefix(es): 978-0-8294
Number of titles published annually: 25 Print; 5 Audio
Total Titles: 350 Print
Returns: 677 Brighton Beach Rd, Menasha, WI 54952

§LPD Press
925 Salamanca NW, Los Ranchos de Albuquerque, NM 87107-5647
Tel: 505-344-9382 *Fax:* 505-345-5129
E-mail: lpdpress@q.com
Web Site: nmsantos.com
Key Personnel
Sr Partner: Barbe Awalt; Paul Rhetts

Founded: 1984
Publisher of books on the American Southwest & a quarterly magazine on the art & culture of the American Southwest.
ISBN Prefix(es): 978-0-9641542; 978-1-890689; 978-1-943681; 978-1-936744; 978-1-936745
Number of titles published annually: 18 Print; 10 E-Book
Total Titles: 150 Print; 1 CD-ROM; 60 E-Book
Imprints: Rio Grande Books
Membership(s): Independent Book Publishers Association; New Mexico Book Association; New Mexico Book Co-op

§LRP Publications
360 Hiatt Dr, Palm Beach Gardens, FL 33418
Mailing Address: PO Box 24668, West Palm Beach, FL 33416-4668
Tel: 561-622-6520 *Toll Free Tel:* 800-341-7874 *Fax:* 561-622-2423
E-mail: custserve@lrp.com
Web Site: www.lrp.com
Key Personnel
Pres: Kenneth F Kahn
Founded: 1977
Legal & general nonfiction in the areas of education, bankruptcy, employment, disability, workers compensation, personal injury & human resources.
ISBN Prefix(es): 978-0-934753
Number of titles published annually: 500 Print; 10 CD-ROM; 95 Online; 5 Audio
Total Titles: 9,000 Print; 10 CD-ROM; 95 Online; 8 Audio
Subsidiaries: LRP Magazine Group
Divisions: Jury Verdict Research
Branch Office(s)
747 Dresher Rd, Suite 500, Horsham, PA 19044 *Tel:* 215-784-0941 *Fax:* 215-784-9639

LRS
Division of Library Reproduction Service
19146 Van Ness Ave, Torrance, CA 90501
Tel: 310-354-2610 *Toll Free Tel:* 800-255-5002 *Fax:* 310-354-2601
E-mail: largeprintsb@aol.com
Web Site: lrs-largeprint.com
Key Personnel
Pres: Peter Jones
Founded: 1946
Large print books for adults & children including classics & fiction.
ISBN Prefix(es): 978-1-58118
Number of titles published annually: 10 Print
Total Titles: 150 Print

Lucent Books®
Imprint of The Rosen Publishing Group Inc
29 E 21 St, New York, NY 10010
Toll Free Tel: 800-237-9932 *Toll Free Fax:* 888-436-4643
Web Site: www.rosenpublishing.com
Founded: 1988
Curriculum-related nonfiction books aimed at the junior high level that explore current issues, historical topics, health, science/technology & biography. Active series include: *Diseases & Disorders, Hot Topics, People in the News, Technology 360 & World History*.
ISBN Prefix(es): 978-1-56006; 978-1-59018
Number of titles published annually: 85 Print; 60 E-Book
Distributor for Greenhaven Press; KidHaven Press

§Lucky Marble Books
Imprint of PageSpring Publishing
2671 Bristol Rd, Columbus, OH 43221
Mailing Address: PO Box 21133, Columbus, OH 43221
Tel: 614-264-5588
E-mail: sales@pagespringpublishing.com
Web Site: www.luckymarblebooks.com
Key Personnel
Ed: Katherine Matthews *Tel:* 614-327-3676 *E-mail:* yaeditor@pagespringpublishing.com
Sales & Mktg Dir: Lynn Bartels
Founded: 2012
Independent publisher. Specialize in high quality fiction for young adult & middle grade readers.
ISBN Prefix(es): 978-1-939403
Number of titles published annually: 3 Print; 3 E-Book

Luminis Books Inc
1950 E Greyhound Pass, Suite 18, PMB 280, Carmel, IN 46033
Tel: 317-840-5838
E-mail: editor@luminisbooks.com
Web Site: www.luminisbooks.com
Founded: 2008
Publish young adult, middle grade & literary fiction.
ISBN Prefix(es): 978-1-935462
Number of titles published annually: 7 Print; 7 E-Book
Total Titles: 10 Print; 10 E-Book
Advertising Agency: JKS Communications
Orders to: Independent Publishers Group, 814 N Franklin St, Chicago, IL 60610 *Tel:* 312-337-0747 *Toll Free Tel:* 800-888-4741 *Fax:* 312-337-5985 *Web Site:* www.ipgbook.com
Returns: Independent Publishers Group, 814 N Franklin St, Chicago, IL 60610 *Tel:* 312-337-0747 *Toll Free Tel:* 800-888-4741 *Fax:* 312-337-5985 *Web Site:* www.ipgbook.com
Distribution Center: Independent Publishers Group, 814 N Franklin St, Chicago, IL 60610 *Tel:* 312-337-0747 *Toll Free Tel:* 800-888-4741 *Fax:* 312-337-5985 *Web Site:* www.ipgbook.com
Membership(s): Society of Children's Book Writers & Illustrators

Luna Bisonte Prods
137 Leland Ave, Columbus, OH 43214
Tel: 614-846-4126
Web Site: www.johnmbennett.net; www.lulu.com/spotlight/lunabisonteprods
Key Personnel
Head & Intl Rts: John M Bennett *E-mail:* bennettjohnm@gmail.com
Founded: 1974
Avant-garde to experimental literature & poetry.
ISBN Prefix(es): 978-0-935350; 978-1-892280
Number of titles published annually: 25 Print; 2 Audio
Total Titles: 400 Print; 53 Audio

Lutheran Braille Workers Inc
13471 California St, Yucaipa, CA 92399
Mailing Address: PO Box 5000, Yucaipa, CA 92399-1450
Tel: 909-795-8977 *Toll Free Tel:* 800-925-6092 *Fax:* 909-795-8970
E-mail: lbw@lbwinc.org
Web Site: www.lbwinc.org
Key Personnel
Pres: Rev Dennis Stueve
Founded: 1943
Produce & distribute free braille & large print biblical & Christian literature in more than 30 languages for the blind & visually impaired in over 120 countries.
Number of titles published annually: 5 Print
Total Titles: 200 Print

Lyndon B Johnson School of Public Affairs
University of Texas at Austin, 2315 Red River St, Austin, TX 78712-1536
Mailing Address: University of Texas at Austin, PO Box Y, Austin, TX 78713-8925
Tel: 512-471-3200 *Fax:* 512-471-4697
E-mail: lbjdeansoffice@austin.utexas.edu
Web Site: www.utexas.edu/lbj
Key Personnel
Asst Dean, Communs: Susan Binford *E-mail:* susan.binford@austin.utexas.edu
Founded: 1972
Working papers; public service monographs; policy research projects; conference proceedings.
Return policy: No refunds; replace damaged books only. All sales are final. Prepayment usually required.
ISBN Prefix(es): 978-0-89940
Number of titles published annually: 8 Print
Total Titles: 300 Print

Lynx House Press
420 W 24 St, Spokane, WA 99203
Tel: 509-624-4894
E-mail: lynxhousepress@gmail.com
Web Site: www.lynxhousepress.org
Key Personnel
Dir & Ed-in-Chief: Christopher Howell *E-mail:* cnhowell@ewu.edu
Assoc Ed: Kristina Morgan
Intl Rts: John Orr
Founded: 1972
Fiction & poetry.
ISBN Prefix(es): 978-0-89924
Number of titles published annually: 4 Print
Total Titles: 160 Print
Distributed by University of Washington Press
Distribution Center: Hopkins Fulfillment Services, c/o Maple Logistics Solutions, Lebanon Distribution Center, 704 Legionaire Dr, Fredericksburg, PA 17026 *Tel:* 410-516-6956

The Lyons Press
Imprint of The Globe Pequot Press
246 Goose Lane, Guilford, CT 06437
Tel: 203-458-4500 *Fax:* 203-458-4668
E-mail: info@rowman.com
Web Site: rowman.com/page/lyonspress
Key Personnel
Subs Rts Dir: Clare Cox *E-mail:* ccox@rowman.com
Founded: 1978
Outdoors, natural history, sports, fitness, cooking, military history, fishing, hunting, equine, nonfiction, fiction, practical, Americana, outdoor skills, pets, nautical, survival & adventure.
ISBN Prefix(es): 978-1-55821; 978-0-8329; 978-1-58574; 978-1-59228; 978-0-936644; 978-0-941130
Number of titles published annually: 180 Print
Total Titles: 1,500 Print
Distribution Center: National Book Network, 4501 Forbes Blvd, Suite 200, Lantham, MD 20706 *Tel:* 301-459-3366 *Web Site:* nbnbooks.com

M U Press, see Marquette University Press

MAA Press, see The Mathematical Association of America

Pat MacKay Projects, see Quite Specific Media Group Ltd

§Macmillan
Subsidiary of Verlagsgruppe Georg von Holtzbrinck GmbH
175 Fifth Ave, New York, NY 10010
Tel: 646-307-5151
E-mail: press.inquiries@macmillan.com
Web Site: www.macmillan.com
Key Personnel
CEO: John Sargent
COO: Andrew Weber
Pres, Macmillan Publishers US: Don Weisberg
Pres & Publr, Macmillan Children's Publishing Group: Jonathan Yaged
Pres & Publr, Macmillan Audio: Mary Beth Roche

Pres & Publr, Farrar, Straus & Giroux: Jonathan Galassi
Pres & Publr, Henry Holt & Company: Stephen Rubin
Pres & Publr, St Martin's Press: Sally Richardson
Pres & Publr, Tom Doherty Associates: Thomas Doherty
Pres, Sales Div: Alison Lazarus
EVP, Edit Devt & Content Innovation: Will Schwalbe
EVP, Digital Publg & Strategic Technol: Fritz Foy
SVP & Gen Coun: Paul Sleven
SVP, Fin: Edward Garrett
SVP, Fin & Strategy: Dan Schwartz
SVP, Group Strategy & M&A: Kenneth Eng
SVP of Opers, MPS: Michael Shareck
VP, Dir of HR: Helaine Ohl
VP & Dir, Academic & Lib Mktg: Peter Janssen
VP, Client Publr Sales & Dist: Nora Flaherty
VP, Client Publr Servs: Liz Tzetzo
VP, Fin Planning & Admin: Cathy Goodfriend
VP, Supply Chain & Sales Opers: Tom Stouras
Dir, Busn Planning: Esther Kim
Ebook Channel Assoc Dir: Jonathan Hollingsworth
Intl Sales Mgr: Holly Ruck
Ed-at-Large: John Sterling
Founded: 1986
Macmillan is the administrative, sales, distribution & information technology arm of the Macmillan group in the US, which includes Bedford, Freeman & Worth Publishing Group, LLC (W H Freeman, Worth Publishers & Bedford/St Martin's); Tom Doherty Associates, LLC (Tor & Forge Books); Faber & Faber Inc; Farrar, Straus & Giroux, LLC; Feiwel & Friends; First Second; Hayden McNeil; Henry Holt and Company, LLC; Macmillan Audio; Nature America Inc; Palgrave Macmillan; Picador; Roaring Brook Press; St Martin's Press, LLC; Scientific American Inc; Square Fish.
Distribution Center: MPS Distribution Center, 16365 James Madison Hwy, Gordonsville, VA 22942 *Toll Free Tel:* 888-330-8477 *Fax:* 540-672-7540 (cust serv) *Toll Free Fax:* 800-672-2054 (orders) *E-mail:* orders@mpsvirginia.com
See separate listing for:
Tom Doherty Associates, LLC
Farrar, Straus & Giroux, LLC
Henry Holt and Company, LLC
Macmillan Learning
Picador
St Martin's Press, LLC

Macmillan Audio
Division of Macmillan
175 Fifth Ave, New York, NY 10010
Tel: 646-307-5151 *Toll Free Tel:* 888-330-8477 (cust serv) *Fax:* 917-534-0980
Web Site: www.macmillanaudio.com
Key Personnel
Pres, Macmillan Publishers US: Don Weisberg
Pres & Publr: Mary Beth Roche
Assoc Publr: Robert Allen
Sr Art Dir: Margo Goody
Dir, Prodn: Laura Wilson
Mktg Dir: Samantha Edelson
Founded: 1987
ISBN Prefix(es): 978-1-55927; 978-0-7927; 978-0-940687; 978-1-59397; 978-1-4272
Number of titles published annually: 100 Audio
Orders to: MPS Order Dept, 16365 James Madison Hwy, Gordonsville, VA 22942-8501 *Toll Free Tel:* 888-330-8477 *Fax:* 540-672-7540 *Toll Free Fax:* 800-672-2054
Membership(s): Audio Publishers Association; Publishers' Publicity Association

Macmillan Higher Education, see Macmillan Learning

§Macmillan Learning
Formerly Macmillan Higher Education
Subsidiary of Macmillan
41 Madison Ave, New York, NY 10010
Tel: 212-576-9400 *Fax:* 212-689-2383
Web Site: www.macmillanlearning.com
Key Personnel
CEO: Ken Michaels
COO: Ken Brooks
CTO: Chelsea Valentine
Chief Learning Offr: Dr Adam Black
SVP, Fin: Simon Horrer
SVP, Sales: Craig Bleyer
VP, Communs: Kate Geraghty
VP, Strategy: Elizabeth Widdicombe
Mng Dir: Susan Winslow
Dir, Content Mgmt Solutions: Susan Brown
Founded: 1999
Imprints: Bedford, Freeman & Worth High School Publishers; Bedford/St Martin's; W H Freeman; Hayden-McNeil; Worth Publishers
See separate listing for:
Bedford/St Martin's
W H Freeman
Worth Publishers

§Macmillan Reference USA™
Imprint of Gale
27500 Drake Rd, Farmington Hills, MI 48331-3535
Tel: 248-699-4253 *Toll Free Tel:* 800-877-4253 *Toll Free Fax:* 877-363-4253
E-mail: gale.customercare@cengage.com
Web Site: www.gale.cengage.com/macmillan
Key Personnel
SVP, Gen Mgr: Paul Gazzolo
SVP, Mng Dir, Intl: Terry Robinson
SVP, Sales North America: Brian McDonough
VP, Mktg & Communs: Harmony Faust
ISBN Prefix(es): 978-0-02
Number of titles published annually: 22 E-Book
Total Titles: 92 E-Book

Mage Publishers Inc
1408 35 St NW, Washington, DC 20007
Tel: 202-342-1642
Web Site: www.mage.com
Key Personnel
Art Dir: Najmieh Batmanglij *E-mail:* nb@mage.com
Publr & Ed: Mohammad Batmanglij *E-mail:* mb@mage.com
Asst to Publr & Rts Contact: Amin Sepehri *E-mail:* as@mage.com
Founded: 1985
Persian literature, art & culture in English; poetry, fiction, art & history.
ISBN Prefix(es): 978-0-934211; 978-1-933823
Number of titles published annually: 4 Print
Total Titles: 75 Print
Imprints: Mage Persian Editions
Returns: 1708A Crossroads Dr, Odenton, MD 21113
Warehouse: Tasco, 9 Jay Gould Ct, Waldorf, MD 20602
Distribution Center: University of Toronto Press, 5201 Dufferin St, Toronto M3H 5T8, Canada *Tel:* 416-667-6791 *Toll Free Tel:* 800-565-5923 *Fax:* 416-667-7832 *Toll Free Fax:* 800-221-9885 *Web Site:* www.utpress.utoronto.ca
Membership(s): AAP

The Magni Co
Subsidiary of The Magni Group Inc
7106 Wellington Point Rd, McKinney, TX 75070
Tel: 972-540-2050 *Fax:* 972-540-1057
E-mail: sales@magnico.com; info@magnico.com
Web Site: www.magnico.com
Key Personnel
CEO: Evan B Reynolds *E-mail:* ereynolds@magnico.com
Co-CEO: Darlene Reynolds
Founded: 1982
Health & beauty, weight loss, informative & organizer books.
ISBN Prefix(es): 978-1-882330
Number of titles published annually: 5 Print; 1 CD-ROM; 3 Online; 50 E-Book; 2 Audio
Total Titles: 65 Print; 2 CD-ROM; 50 Online; 52 E-Book; 9 Audio
Imprints: MAGNI
Membership(s): ABA

Maharishi University of Management Press
Subsidiary of Maharishi University of Management
1000 N Fourth St, Dept 1155, Fairfield, IA 52557-1155
Tel: 641-472-1101 *Toll Free Tel:* 800-831-6523 *Fax:* 641-472-1122
E-mail: mumpress@mum.edu
Web Site: www.mumpress.com
Key Personnel
Dir: Harry Bright
Founded: 1974
Specialize in books about transcendental meditation.
ISBN Prefix(es): 978-0-9616944; 978-0-923569
Number of titles published annually: 5 Print
Total Titles: 50 Print; 4 Audio
Distributed by Penguin Group USA, A Penguin Random House Company (select titles)

Management Advisory Services & Publications (MASP)
PO Box 81151, Wellesley Hills, MA 02481-0001
SAN: 203-8692
Tel: 781-235-2895 *Fax:* 781-235-5446
E-mail: info@masp.com
Web Site: www.masp.com
Key Personnel
Principal & Ed: Jay Kuong *E-mail:* jaykmasp@aol.com
Founded: 1972
A well established publications & advisory & training services company with a concentration in enterprise governance, internal controls, information technology security, auditing & contingency planning & business continuity fields. This includes reference books, journals & practitioners' manuals. Under the enterprise governance field, MASP publishes books on Sarbanes-Oxley compliance. Additionally, as part of the diversification efforts, we publish a few literary fiction books.
ISBN Prefix(es): 978-0-940706
Number of titles published annually: 10 Print
Total Titles: 75 Print
Foreign Office(s): Santa Fe Ave, Buenos Aires, Argentina, Contact: D Ramos *E-mail:* dramos@satlink.com

§Management Sciences for Health
200 Rivers Edge Dr, Medford, MA 02155
Tel: 617-250-9500 *Fax:* 617-250-9090
E-mail: bookstore@msh.org
Web Site: www.msh.org
Key Personnel
Deputy Dir, Pubns: Barbara K Timmons *Tel:* 617-250-9291 *E-mail:* btimmons@msh.org
Procurement Offr: Natasha Mahoney *Tel:* 617-250-9262
Founded: 1971
Established to assist, promote, evaluate, manage & perform research on the delivery of health care, establish methods & procedures leading to the improvement of health & social services & conduct education & publishing in these areas. MSH's publications unit develops & distributes books & a quarterly periodical to further MSH's mission, which is to help close the gap between knowledge about public health problems & action to solve them.

MSH currently stocks about 3 dozen products, most of which are books (including monographs, manuals & handbooks, some are available on CD-ROM). Many are available in languages other than English. Major products are The Manager continuing education quarterly; Managing Drug Supply (first published in 1981); instructional manuals (CORE, MOST, HOSPICAL, FIMAT); the Lessons from MSH & Stubbs monograph series; the series of success stories (20-page color booklets that present the highlights of successful programs) & books ranging from textbooks to syntheses of research.
MHS has offices in Afghanistan, Angola, Guinea, Haiti, Indonesia, Malawi, Philippines & Senegal.
ISBN Prefix(es): 978-0-913723
Number of titles published annually: 2 Print; 1 CD-ROM
Total Titles: 39 Print; 4 CD-ROM
Branch Office(s)
4301 N Fairfax Dr, Suite 400, Arlington, VA 22203-1627, Contact: Keith Johnson *Tel:* 703-524-6575
Distributed by Kumarian Press
Membership(s): Independent Book Publishers Association

Mandala Earth
Imprint of Insight Editions
800 "A" St, San Rafael, CA 94901
Tel: 415-526-1370 *Toll Free Fax:* 866-509-0515
E-mail: info@mandalapublishing.com
Web Site: www.mandalaeartheditions.com
Key Personnel
CEO & Publr: Raoul Goff *E-mail:* raoul@insighteditions.com
Sales Dir: Julie Hamilton *E-mail:* j.hamilton@insighteditions.com
Sales Mgr: Jacqui Goff *E-mail:* j.goff@insighteditions.com
Full color coffee table books & minibooks, as well as decks, calendars, journals, greeting cards, art prints & incense. Topics include: environmental issues, women's studies, Asian art, music, philosophy, cross-cultural issues & Hinduism. Cutting-edge environmental & cultural topics that feature the unique voices & new concepts of leading thinkers, environmentalists, photojournalists, cultural commentators & artists.
ISBN Prefix(es): 978-1-886069; 978-1-932771; 978-1-60109; 978-0-945475
Number of titles published annually: 15 Print; 2 Audio
Total Titles: 300 Print; 200 Online; 10 Audio
Foreign Rep(s): Bill Bailey Publishers Representatives (Europe); Book Promotions (Jonathan Ball) (South Africa); Gilles Fauveau (Japan, Korea); Jaime Gregorio (Philippines); NewSouth Books (Australia, New Zealand); Penguin Books India (Bangladesh, India, Maldives, Nepal, Pakistan, Sri Lanka); Perseus International (Suk Lee) (Malaysia, Singapore); Perseus International (Edison Garcia) (Caribbean, Latin America, Middle East, North Africa); June Poonpanich (Cambodia, Indonesia, Laos, Thailand, Vietnam); Publishers Group UK (UK); Wei Zhao (China, Hong Kong, Taiwan)
Shipping Address: Publishers Group West, 210 American Dr, Jackson, TN 38301
Warehouse: Publishers Group West, 210 American Dr, Jackson, TN 38301
Distribution Center: Publishers Group West, 210 American Dr, Jackson, TN 38301

Manhattan Publishing Co
Division of US & Europe Books Inc
670 White Plains Rd, Scarsdale, NY 10583
Tel: 914-472-4650 *Fax:* 914-472-4316
E-mail: coe@manhattanpublishing.com
Web Site: www.manhattanpublishing.com
Key Personnel
Pres: Kenneth Polin
Lib Sales Dir: Cathy Polin
Founded: 1938
Import sales for Council of Europe, European Court of Human Rights.
Number of titles published annually: 200 Print
Total Titles: 3,000 Print; 20 CD-ROM

Manic D Press Inc
250 Banks St, San Francisco, CA 94110
Mailing Address: PO Box 410804, San Francisco, CA 94141
Tel: 415-648-8288
E-mail: info@manicdpress.com
Web Site: www.manicdpress.com
Key Personnel
Publr & Intl Rts: Jennifer Joseph
Founded: 1984
Poetry & unusual fiction & alternative travel books, emphasis on innovative, new & established styles, writers & artists, paperbacks, general adult books.
ISBN Prefix(es): 978-0-916397; 978-1-933149
Number of titles published annually: 6 Print
Total Titles: 200 Print
Foreign Rep(s): Perseus (worldwide exc Canada & Europe); Publishers Group Canada (Canada); Turnaround Distribution (Europe)
Distribution Center: Consortium Book Sales & Distribution, The Keg House, 34 13 Ave NE, Suite 101, Minneapolis, MN 55413-1007 *Tel:* 612-746-2600 *Toll Free Tel:* 800-283-3572 (cust serv) *Fax:* 612-746-2606 *Web Site:* www.cbsd.com

Manning Publications Co
PO Box 761, Shelter Island, NY 11964
Tel: 203-626-1510
E-mail: sales@manning.com; support@manning.com (cust serv)
Web Site: www.manning.com
Key Personnel
Publr: Marjan Bace *E-mail:* maba@manning.com
Assoc Publr: Michael Stephens
Dir, Prodn: Mary Piergies
Busn Mgr: Kimberly Dickinson *Tel:* 856-375-2597 *E-mail:* kidi@manning.com
Founded: 1990
Full-scale company whose titles are distributed in the US, Europe & Asia.
ISBN Prefix(es): 978-1-884777; 978-1-930110; 978-1-932394; 978-1-933988; 978-1-61729; 978-1-935182; 978-1-63343
Number of titles published annually: 25 Print; 10 E-Book
Total Titles: 300 Print; 20 CD-ROM; 200 E-Book
Distributed by Dreamtech Press; Pearson Education
Distribution Center: O'Reilly Media Inc, 1005 Granvenstein Hwy N, Sebastopol, CA 95472 (US & CN) *Tel:* 707-829-1515 *Toll Free Tel:* 800-998-9939 *Toll Free Fax:* 800-997-9901 *E-mail:* retailics@oreilly.com *Web Site:* www.oreilly.com
Woodslane Pty Ltd, Unit 7/5 Vuko Place, Warriewood, NSW 2102, Australia (Australia, New Zealand, Pacific Islands) *Tel:* (02) 9970 5111 *Fax:* (02) 9970 5002 *E-mail:* info@woodslane.com.au *Web Site:* www.woodslane.com.au
Dreamtech Press, 19-A, Ansari Rd, Darya Ganj, New Delhi 110 002, India (Bangladesh, Bhutan, India, Maldives, Nepal, Pakistan, Sri Lanka) *Tel:* (011) 43551180 *E-mail:* info@dreamtechpress.com *Web Site:* dreamtechpress.com
Pansing Distribution Pte Ltd, 438 Ang Mo Kio Industrial Park 1, Off Ang Mo Kio Ave 10, Singapore, Singapore (Hong Kong, Malaysia, Singapore, South Korea, Taiwan, Thailand) *Tel:* 6319 9939 *Fax:* 6459 4931 *E-mail:* infobooks@pansing.com
Pearson Education, Edinburgh Gate, Harlow, Essex CM20 2JE, United Kingdom (Africa, Europe, UK) *Tel:* (01279) 623928 *Fax:* (01279) 414130 *E-mail:* enq.orders@pearsoned-ema.com *Web Site:* www.pearson-books.com

MapEasy Inc
PO Box 80, Wainscott, NY 11975-0080
Tel: 631-537-6213 *Fax:* 631-537-4541
E-mail: info@mapeasy.com
Web Site: www.mapeasy.com
Key Personnel
Owner: Gary Bradhering; Chris Harris *E-mail:* charris@mapeasy.com
Founded: 1990
Guidemaps & location guides to cities in North America, Western Europe & Asia.
ISBN Prefix(es): 978-1-878979; 978-1-929038
Number of titles published annually: 4 Print
Total Titles: 72 Print

MAR*CO Products Inc
PO Box 686, Hatfield, PA 19440
Tel: 215-956-0313 *Toll Free Tel:* 800-448-2197 *Fax:* 215-956-9041
E-mail: help@marcoproducts.com
Web Site: www.marcoproducts.com
Key Personnel
Pres: Arden Martenz
VP: Cameon Funk
Opers Mgr: Warren Funk
Founded: 1977
Educational guidance materials for elementary & secondary counselors, psychologists & social workers.
ISBN Prefix(es): 978-1-884063; 978-1-57543
Number of titles published annually: 12 Print; 20 Online; 25 E-Book
Total Titles: 300 Print; 400 Online
Distributed by ASCA; Boulden Publishing; Burnell Books; Calloway House; Career Kids FYI; CFKR Career; Character Development; Community Intervention; Courage to Change; Cress Productions Co; EDU Reference; Educational Media Corp; Incentive Plus; Jist; Mental Health Resources; National Center for Youth Issues/STARS; National Professional Resources; National Resource Center Youth Services; Paperbacks for Educators; School Speciality; SourceResource; WRS Group; Youth-Light Inc
Distributor for Boulden; Educational Media; HarperCollins; National Center for Youth Issues/STARS
Distribution Center: NIMCO Bookstore

Marathon Press
1500 Square Turn Blvd, Norfolk, NE 68701
Mailing Address: PO Box 407, Norfolk, NE 68702-0407
Tel: 402-371-5040 *Toll Free Tel:* 800-228-0629 *Fax:* 402-371-9382
Web Site: www.marathonpress.com
Key Personnel
Owner: Rex Alewel
Pres: Bruce Price
Founded: 1974
Books on professional photography.
ISBN Prefix(es): 978-0-934420
Number of titles published annually: 5 Print
Total Titles: 30 Print

Maren Green Publishing Inc
5630 Memorial Ave N, Suite 3, Oak Park Heights, MN 55082
Tel: 651-439-4500 *Toll Free Tel:* 800-287-1512 *Fax:* 651-439-4532
E-mail: info@marengreen.com
Web Site: www.marengreen.com
Key Personnel
Owner & Pres: Todd Snow *E-mail:* toddsnow@marengreen.com
Founded: 2006

Fiction & nonfiction books for children newborn to age 9.
This publisher has indicated that 100% of their product line is author subsidized.
ISBN Prefix(es): 978-1-934277
Number of titles published annually: 5 Print
Total Titles: 19 Print
Imprints: Books Good For Young Children™
Distributed by Crabtree Publishing Inc
Foreign Rights: Sylvia Hayse Literary Agency (worldwide)
Membership(s): ABA; Independent Book Publishers Association

Marick Press
PO Box 36253, Grosse Pointe Farms, MI 48236
Tel: 313-407-9236
E-mail: orders@marickpress.com
Web Site: www.marickpress.com
Key Personnel
Founding Publr: Mariela Griffor
E-mail: mgriffor@marickpress.com
Art Dir: Sean Tai
Assoc Ed: Christine Howson; Scott Minar
A not-for-profit literary publisher founded to preserve the best work by poets around the world including many under published women poets. We seek out & publish the best new work from an eclectic range of aesthetics - work that is technically accomplished, distinctive in style & thematically fresh.
ISBN Prefix(es): 978-0-9779703; 978-1-934851
Number of titles published annually: 6 Print
Total Titles: 45 Print

Marine Education Textbooks
124 N Van Ave, Houma, LA 70363-5895
SAN: 215-9651
Tel: 985-879-3866 *Fax:* 985-879-3911
E-mail: email@marineeducationtextbooks.com
Web Site: www.marineeducationtextbooks.com
Key Personnel
Mgr: Gwen M Block *E-mail:* gwen@ourmet.com
Ed: Richard A Block
Founded: 1970
Training & educational books for preparation of USCG exams. Marine safety signs, nautical charts.
ISBN Prefix(es): 978-0-934114; 978-1-879778
Number of titles published annually: 6 Print
Total Titles: 40 Print
Imprints: Marine Survey Press

Marine Techniques Publishing
311 W River Rd, Augusta, ME 04330-3991
SAN: 298-7805
Tel: 207-622-7984
E-mail: promariner@roadrunner.com; sales@marinetechpublishing.com; promariner@roadrunner.com
Web Site: marinetechpublishing.com; www.groups.yahoo.com/group/marinetechniquespublishing
Key Personnel
Owner & Pres: James L Pelletier
Founded: 1983
Industry specific directories; maritime/worldwide merchant marine; naval architecture; marine biology, chemistry, geology; civil, marine engineering; electrical, electronic marine engineering; energy, oil & gas offshore; mechanical marine engineering; transportation, marine. Commercial merchant marine - worldwide directories, *Mariner's Employment Guide* & maritime autobiographies (true maritime stories).
This publisher has indicated that 100% of their product line is author subsidized.
ISBN Prefix(es): 978-0-9644915; 978-0-9798008
Number of titles published annually: 5 Print; 245 Online; 2 E-Book; 2 Audio
Total Titles: 100 Print; 8 CD-ROM; 245 Online; 2 E-Book; 2 Audio
Distributed by Elsevier Science, Technology & Business Books; PennWell Business & Industrial Division
Distributor for Academic Press; Best Publishing Co; Butterworth-Heinemann; Clarkson Research Services Ltd; Elsevier, Science & Technology Books; Focal Press; Gulf Professional Publishers; PennWell Business & Industrial Division; W B Saunders Co; Waterfront Soundings Productions; Witherby Seamanship International Ltd
Foreign Rep(s): Chapters Inc (Canada); W H Everett & Sons Ltd (England, London, UK); Lavoisier (France)
Distribution Center: BooksXYZ.com
Follett School Solutions Inc, 1340 Ridgeview Dr, McHenry, IL 60050 *Tel:* 815-759-1700 *Toll Free Tel:* 888-511-5114 (cust serv) *Fax:* 815-759-9831 *Toll Free Fax:* 800-852-5458 *E-mail:* info@follettlearning.com *Web Site:* www.follettlearning.com SAN: 169-1902
Baker, Lyman & Co Inc, 5250 Veterans Memorial Blvd, Metairie, LA 70006 *Toll Free Tel:* 800-535-6956 *E-mail:* sales@bakerlyman.com *Web Site:* www.bakerlyman.com
The Book House Inc, 208 W Chicago St, Jonesville, MI 49250 *Toll Free Tel:* 800-248-1146 *Toll Free Fax:* 800-858-9716 *Web Site:* www.thebookhouse.com
Emery-Pratt Co, 1966 W Main St, Owosso, MI 48867 *Toll Free Tel:* 800-248-3887 *Toll Free Fax:* 800-523-6379 *Web Site:* www.emery-pratt.com
Membership(s): American Maritime Association; American Society of Naval Engineers; Association of Marine Engineers; The Association of Publishers for Special Sales; Independent Book Publishers Association; Independent Publishers of New England; Lloyd's Maritime Information Register; Women's Maritime Association

Marion Street Press LLC
4207 SE Woodstock Blvd, No 168, Portland, OR 97206-6267
Tel: 503-888-4624 *Toll Free Fax:* 866-571-8359
E-mail: marionbooks@outlook.com
Web Site: www.marionstreetpress.com
Key Personnel
Publr: Kel Winter
Founded: 1993
Books for writers & journalists, students, educators & financial professionals.
ISBN Prefix(es): 978-0-9665176; 978-0-9729937; 978-1-933338; 978-0-9710050; 978-1-936863
Number of titles published annually: 12 Print
Total Titles: 60 Print
Foreign Rep(s): IPG (Canada)
Membership(s): The Association of Publishers for Special Sales; Independent Book Publishers Association; National Association of Independent Publishers

Markowski International Publishers
One Oakglade Circle, Hummelstown, PA 17036-9525
Tel: 717-566-0468
E-mail: info@possibilitypress.com
Web Site: www.possibilitypress.com; www.aeronauticalpublishers.com
Key Personnel
Publr: Mike Markowski
Founded: 1981
Books on personal development, business, success, motivation, aviation & model aviation.
ISBN Prefix(es): 978-0-938716
Number of titles published annually: 6 Print
Total Titles: 40 Print
Imprints: Aeronautical Publishers; Possibility Press
Membership(s): Independent Book Publishers Association

Marquette University Press
Division of Marquette University
1415 W Wisconsin Ave, Milwaukee, WI 53233
Mailing Address: PO Box 3141, Milwaukee, WI 53201-3141
Tel: 414-288-1564 *Fax:* 414-288-7813
Web Site: www.marquette.edu/mupress
Key Personnel
Dir: Dr Andrew Tallon *E-mail:* andrew.tallon@marquette.edu
Mgr: Maureen Kondrick *E-mail:* maureen.kondrick@marquette.edu
Founded: 1916
Publications in the humanities by scholars of international reputation. Specialize in philosophy, theology, humanities & history in addition to regional studies relating to the city of Milwaukee & the state of Wisconsin.
ISBN Prefix(es): 978-0-87462; 978-1-62600
Number of titles published annually: 12 Print; 10 E-Book
Total Titles: 500 Print; 275 E-Book
Foreign Rep(s): Eurospan (Africa, Europe, Middle East); Scholarly Book Services (Canada)
Orders to: Bookmasters, 30 Amberwood Pkwy, Ashland, OH 44805, Contact: Elaine Lattanzi *Tel:* 419-281-1802 ext 1408 *Toll Free Tel:* 800-247-6553 *Fax:* 419-281-6883 *E-mail:* orders@bookmasters.com *Web Site:* www.bookmasters.com/shop/publisher/marquette-university-press
Returns: Bookmasters, 30 Amberwood Pkwy, Ashland, OH 44805, Contact: Elaine Lattanzi *Tel:* 419-281-1802 ext 1408 *Toll Free Tel:* 800-247-6553 *Fax:* 419-281-6883 *Web Site:* www.bookmasters.com
Distribution Center: Bookmasters, 30 Amberwood Pkwy, Ashland, OH 44805, Contact: Elaine Lattanzi *Tel:* 419-281-1802 ext 1408 *Toll Free Tel:* 800-247-6553 *Fax:* 419-281-6883 *E-mail:* orders@bookmasters.com *Web Site:* www.bookmasters.com
Membership(s): American Association of University Presses; Association of Jesuit University Presses

Marquis Who's Who
Imprint of Marquis Who's Who Ventures LLC
100 Connell Dr, Suite 2300, Berkeley Heights, NJ 07922
Tel: 908-673-0100 *Toll Free Tel:* 844-394-6946 *Fax:* 908-356-0184
E-mail: info@marquisww.com; customerservice@marquisww.com (cust serv, sales)
Web Site: www.marquiswhoswho.com
Key Personnel
CEO: Fred Marks
Founded: 1899
Publisher of comprehensive biographical references available in print, online & mailing list. Major Marquis Who's Who publications include *Who's Who in America*, *Who's Who in the World* & *Who's Who of American Women*.
ISBN Prefix(es): 978-0-8379
Number of titles published annually: 8 Print
Total Titles: 12 Print; 1 Online

Marriage Transformation LLC
PO Box 249, Harrison, TN 37341
Tel: 423-599-0153
Web Site: www.marriagetransformation.com
Key Personnel
Pres: Susanne M Alexander *E-mail:* susanne@marriagetransformation.com
Relationship & marriage education.
This publisher has indicated that 90% of their product line is author subsidized.
ISBN Prefix(es): 978-0-9726893
Number of titles published annually: 3 Print; 6 E-Book
Total Titles: 10 Print; 6 E-Book
Distributed by Barringer; Longman
Membership(s): National Association for Relationship & Marriage Education

Marshall & Swift
777 S Fiqueroa St, 12th fl, Los Angeles, CA 90017
Tel: 213-683-9000 *Toll Free Tel:* 800-544-2678 *Fax:* 213-683-9043
Web Site: www.marshallswift.com
Key Personnel
Res Supv: Gary Miller
Founded: 1932
Building cost databases for the construction market & insurance industry.
ISBN Prefix(es): 978-1-56842; 978-0-930458
Number of titles published annually: 10 Print
Total Titles: 21 Print
Imprints: Valuation Press
Distributed by McGraw-Hill Book Co
Warehouse: 1625 W Temple, Los Angeles, CA 90026

Marshall Cavendish Corp
Member of Times International Publishing Group
99 White Plains Rd, Tarrytown, NY 10591-9001
Tel: 914-332-8888 *Toll Free Tel:* 800-821-9881 *Fax:* 914-332-8102
E-mail: mce@marshallcavendish.com
Web Site: www.marshallcavendish.com; www.mceducation.us
Key Personnel
Dir, US: Vivian Cheng
Sales & Busn Devt Dir: Scott Burns
Busn Devt Mgr (Intl): Hoover Herrera
Mktg Mgr: Jennifer Feldman
Sr Accountant: Richard Moore
Accountant: Jay Lee
Accts Payable/Accts Receivable Assoc: Imelda Guarin
Sr Educ Consultant: Christopher Coyne
Educ/Sales Consultant: Thomas Corbia; Peter Iandiorio; Ellen Lauterbach; Jessica Shelley
Sr Cust Serv: Norma Palazzo
Founded: 1970
International publisher of books, directories, magazines & digital platforms. Products reach across the globe in 13 languages & our publishing network spans Asia & the US. Dedicated to the promotion of lifelong learning & self-development.
ISBN Prefix(es): 978-1-85435; 978-0-7614
Number of titles published annually: 320 Print; 10 Online; 300 E-Book
Total Titles: 1,200 Print; 57 Online; 590 E-Book
Imprints: Marshall Cavendish Adult Trade; Marshall Cavendish Benchmark; Marshall Cavendish Digital; Marshall Cavendish Education; Marshall Cavendish Reference
Distributed by Marshall Cavendish Ltd (UK)
Foreign Rep(s): Peter Pal Library Suppliers (Australia)
Warehouse: Swan Packaging, 415 Hamburg Tpke, Wayne, NJ 07470
Membership(s): ALA; The Children's Book Council

Martindale-Hubbell, see Martindale LLC

§Martindale LLC
121 Chanlon Rd, Suite 110, New Providence, NJ 07974
SAN: 205-8863
Mailing Address: PO Box 1001, Summit, NJ 07902-1001
Tel: 908-464-6800; 908-771-7777 (intl)
Toll Free Tel: 800-526-4902 *Fax:* 908-771-8704
E-mail: info@martindale.com
Web Site: www.martindale.com
Founded: 1868
Publisher of the *Martindale-Hubbell Law Directory* in hard copy, on CD-ROM & available online; containing listings of over 1 million lawyers & law firms worldwide. Other publications include *Law Digest*, a summary of laws from each of the 50 states & 80 countries; *Martindale-Hubbell International Law Directory*, designed for the international legal community & *Martindale-Hubbell Bar Register of Preeminent Lawyers*, listing of over 8,900 law practices designated as outstanding by members of the legal community.
ISBN Prefix(es): 978-1-56160; 978-1-934528; 978-1-60366
Number of titles published annually: 5 Print; 1 CD-ROM; 1 Online
Total Titles: 5 Print; 1 CD-ROM; 1 Online
Imprints: Martindale-Hubbell®

Martingale®
19021 120 Ave NE, Suite 102, Bothell, WA 98011
Tel: 425-483-3313 *Toll Free Tel:* 800-426-3126 *Fax:* 425-486-7596
E-mail: info@martingale-pub.com
Web Site: www.martingale-pub.com
Key Personnel
Publr: Jennifer Kelpner
CFO: Keith Brants
Content Dir: Karen Foltys
Dir, Mktg: Karen Johnson *Tel:* 425-483-3313 ext 1387
Dir, Sales: Wendy Jacobson
Founded: 1976
Quilting, knitting & crafting.
ISBN Prefix(es): 978-1-56477; 978-0-943574; 978-1-60468
Number of titles published annually: 55 Print; 55 E-Book
Total Titles: 250 Print; 300 E-Book
Imprints: That Patchwork Place

Maryland Historical Society
201 W Monument St, Baltimore, MD 21201
Tel: 410-685-3750 *Fax:* 410-385-2105
Web Site: www.mdhs.org
Key Personnel
Dir, Pubns & Lib Servs: Patricia Anderson, PhD *Tel:* 410-685-3750 ext 317 *E-mail:* panderson@mdhs.org
Founded: 1844
Publish historical books.
ISBN Prefix(es): 978-0-938420; 978-0-9842135; 978-0-9965944
Number of titles published annually: 5 Print
Total Titles: 35 Print
Distributed by Johns Hopkins University Press

Maryland History Press
PO Box 206, Fruitland, MD 21826-0206
Tel: 410-742-2682
E-mail: sales@marylandhistorypress.com
Web Site: www.marylandhistorypress.com
Key Personnel
Pres: Elaine Patterson
Founded: 1999
Editing, proofreading for almost any topic/web site. Publish books on diversified topics by various authors to help celebrate America's uniqueness...people, events, culture & environs. Services provided are publishing services, author-subsidy program, consignments, distribution services via national company, book searches & web site exposure through major online booksellers.
This publisher has indicated that 85% of their product line is author subsidized.
ISBN Prefix(es): 978-0-9703802
Number of titles published annually: 3 Print
Total Titles: 11 Print; 11 Online
Distributor for Dogwood Ridge Books; Tapestry Press Ltd
Warehouse: 109 Clyde Ave, Fruitland, MD 21826
Distribution Center: Follett School Solutions Inc, 1340 Ridgeview Dr, McHenry, IL 60050, Contact: Gail Wieczorek *Tel:* 815-759-1700 *E-mail:* gail.wieczorek@flr.follett.com *Web Site:* www.follett.com SAN: 169-1902
Baker & Taylor, PO Box 8888, Momemce, IL 60954
Membership(s): The Association of Publishers for Special Sales

Marymark Press
45-08 Old Millstone Dr, East Windsor, NJ 08520
Tel: 609-443-0646
Key Personnel
Publr & Ed: Mark Sonnenfeld
Founded: 1994
Independent small press publishing vehicle; various size chapbooks, broadsides, writing samplers, give-out sheets, single sheets, audio sound collages. Experimental writing. Prefer automatic writing/avant-garde genre.
ISBN Prefix(es): 978-0-9632820; 978-1-887379; 978-0-9844182; 978-0-9798819
Number of titles published annually: 10 Print
Total Titles: 400 Print; 35 Audio

Mason Crest Publishers
Imprint of National Highlights
450 Parkway Dr, Suite D, Broomall, PA 19008
Tel: 610-543-6200 *Toll Free Tel:* 866-MCP-BOOK (627-2665) *Fax:* 610-543-3878
Web Site: www.masoncrest.com
Key Personnel
Pres: Louis Cohen *Tel:* 917-763-7760 *E-mail:* lcohen@nationalhighlights.com
Cont: Diana Daniels *Tel:* 610-543-6200 ext 109 *E-mail:* ddaniels@nationalhighlights.com
Cust Serv: Grace Baffa *Tel:* 610-543-6200 ext 113 *E-mail:* gbaffa@nationalhighlights.com
Founded: 2001
Mason Crest Publishers is committed to publishing the finest nonfiction school, library & curriculum products available today. Our titles are full-color & include a glossary, index, further reading section, Internet resources & are library bound. Subjects include reality shows.
ISBN Prefix(es): 978-1-59084; 978-1-4222; 978-1-59482
Number of titles published annually: 300 Print; 1,500 E-Book
Total Titles: 2,000 Print; 2,500 E-Book
Foreign Rep(s): INT Books (Tom Danby) (Australia); Mare Nostrum Distributors (Maura Brescia) (Argentina, Chile, Uruguay); Missing Link Education CC (Farida Adam & Moreblessing Ngwenya) (South Africa); Morgan and Mann cc (David Sharon) (South Africa); PSI/Publishers' Services International Inc (James Schmelzer) (worldwide); Saunders Book Company (James Saunders) (Canada); Target Book Sales (Jonathan Brooks) (UK)
Returns: 701 Ashland Ave, Bays 1 & 2, Folcroft, PA 19032, Opers Mgr: Lee Wark *Tel:* 610-583-0211 *Fax:* 610-583-0212 *E-mail:* lee6250@aol.com
Shipping Address: 701 Ashland Ave, Bays 1 & 2, Folcroft, PA 19032, Opers Mgr: Lee Wark *Tel:* 610-583-0211 *Fax:* 610-583-0212 *E-mail:* lee6250@aol.com
Warehouse: 701 Ashland Ave, Bays 1 & 2, Folcroft, PA 19032, Opers Mgr: Lee Wark *Tel:* 610-583-0211 *Fax:* 610-583-0212 *E-mail:* lee6250@aol.com
Distribution Center: 701 Ashland Ave, Bays 1 & 2, Folcroft, PA 19032, Opers Mgr: Lee Wark *Tel:* 610-583-0211 *Fax:* 610-583-0212 *E-mail:* lee6250@aol.com
Membership(s): Friends of Libraries of USA; Independent Book Publishers Association

The Massachusetts Historical Society
1154 Boylston St, Boston, MA 02215-3695
Tel: 617-536-1608 *Fax:* 617-859-0074
E-mail: publications@masshist.org
Web Site: www.masshist.org

Key Personnel
Dir, Pubns: Ondine E Le Blanc *Tel:* 617-646-0524 *E-mail:* oleblanc@masshist.org
Founded: 1792
Scholarly historical regional publications.
ISBN Prefix(es): 978-0-934909; 978-0-9652584; 978-1-936520
Number of titles published annually: 4 Print
Total Titles: 500 Print
Distributed by University of Virginia Press

Massachusetts Institute of Technology Libraries
77 Massachusetts Ave, Bldg 14-S, Rm 0551, Cambridge, MA 02139-4307
Tel: 617-253-5671
E-mail: docs@mit.edu
Web Site: libraries.mit.edu/docs
Key Personnel
Dir, Libs: Chris Bourg *Tel:* 617-253-5297 *E-mail:* cbourg@mit.edu
Assoc Dir, Admin: Keith Glavash *Tel:* 617-253-7059 *E-mail:* kglavash@mit.edu
Devt & Communs Assoc, Admin: Ann Adelsberger *Tel:* 617-324-0131 *E-mail:* aadels@mit.edu
Founded: 1863
MIT theses, dissertations, technical reports & working papers.
ISBN Prefix(es): 978-0-911379
Number of titles published annually: 2,000 Print
Total Titles: 15,000 Print

§Master Books®
Imprint of New Leaf Publishing Group Inc
3142 Hwy 103 N, Green Forest, AR 72638
Mailing Address: PO Box 726, Green Forest, AR 72638
Tel: 870-438-5288 *Fax:* 870-438-5120
E-mail: submissions@newleafpress.net; info@nlpg.com
Web Site: www.nlpg.com
Key Personnel
Edit Asst: Craig Froman
Founded: 1975
Publish Biblically-based, scientifically sound creation materials & curriculum.
ISBN Prefix(es): 978-0-89051
Number of titles published annually: 25 Print; 20 E-Book
Total Titles: 425 Print; 3 CD-ROM; 70 E-Book; 2 Audio

Mastery Education
Subsidiary of Peoples Educational Holdings Inc
PO Box 513, Saddle Brook, NJ 07663-0513
Tel: 201-712-0090 *Toll Free Tel:* 800-822-1080 *Fax:* 201-712-0045
E-mail: cs@masteryeducation.com
Web Site: masteryeducation.com; www.measuringuplive2.com
Founded: 1990
Publisher & marketer of print & electronic educational materials for the K-12 school market. We focus our efforts in test preparation, assessment & instruction & college preparation.
ISBN Prefix(es): 978-1-61526; 978-1-61527; 978-1-936025; 978-1-936027; 978-1-936028; 978-1-936029; 978-1-936030; 978-1-61602; 978-1-61734; 978-1-60979; 978-1-936026; 978-1-936031; 978-1-56256; 978-1-58984; 978-1-4138
Number of titles published annually: 50 Print
Total Titles: 2,000 Print
Imprints: Asante®; Measuring Up®
Membership(s): International Society for Technology in Education

Materials Research Society
506 Keystone Dr, Warrendale, PA 15086-7537
SAN: 686-0125
Tel: 724-779-3003 *Fax:* 724-779-8313
E-mail: info@mrs.org
Web Site: www.mrs.org
Key Personnel
Dir, Communs: Eileen Kiley *E-mail:* kiley@mrs.org
Founded: 1973
Scientific reports on leading edge topics in materials research.
ISBN Prefix(es): 978-0-931837; 978-1-55899
Number of titles published annually: 30 Print
Total Titles: 1,100 Print

Math Solutions®
Unit of Houghton Mifflin Harcourt
One Harbor Dr, Suite 101, Sausalito, CA 94965
Tel: 415-332-4181 *Toll Free Tel:* 800-868-9092 *Fax:* 415-331-1931 *Toll Free Fax:* 877-942-8837
E-mail: info@mathsolutions.com; orders@mathsolutions.com
Web Site: www.mathsolutions.com
Key Personnel
Founder & Math Educ Consultant: Marilyn Burns
CEO & Pres: Christine Willig
VP: Patricio Dujan
Exec Ed: Jamie Cross
Sr Mktg Mgr: Kelli Cook
Founded: 1994
Dedicated to improving the teaching of mathematics by providing professional development of the highest quality to teachers & administrators.
ISBN Prefix(es): 978-0-941355; 978-1-935099
Number of titles published annually: 10 Print
Total Titles: 80 Print
Shipping Address: 1805 S McDowell Blvd, Petaluma, CA 94954, Contact: Taber Auren *Tel:* 707-769-0722
Warehouse: 1805 S McDowell Blvd, Petaluma, CA 94954, Contact: Taber Auren *Tel:* 707-769-0722
Membership(s): ASCD; National Council of Teachers of Mathematics

Math Teachers Press Inc
4850 Park Glen Rd, Minneapolis, MN 55416
Tel: 952-545-6535 *Toll Free Tel:* 800-852-2435 *Fax:* 952-546-7502
E-mail: info@movingwithmath.com
Web Site: www.movingwithmath.com
Key Personnel
Founder & Pres: Caryl K Pierson *E-mail:* cpierson@movingwithmath.com
Founded: 1980
PreK-12 manipulative-based math curriculum.
ISBN Prefix(es): 978-0-933383; 978-1-891192; 978-1-931106; 978-1-59167
Number of titles published annually: 3 Print
Total Titles: 70 Print

§The Mathematical Association of America
1529 18 St NW, Washington, DC 20036-1358
SAN: 203-9737
Tel: 202-387-5200 *Toll Free Tel:* 800-741-9415 *Fax:* 202-265-2384
E-mail: maahq@maa.org; advertising@maa.org (pubns)
Web Site: www.maa.org
Key Personnel
Exec Dir: Michael Pearson *E-mail:* mpearson@maa.org
Dir, Pubns: Jim Angelo *E-mail:* jangelo@maa.org
Assoc Dir, Pubns: Carol Baxter *E-mail:* cbaxter@maa.org
Acqs Ed: Steve Kennedy *E-mail:* kennedy@maa.org
Founded: 1915
Mathematical books & journals.
ISBN Prefix(es): 978-0-88385; 978-0-9835005; 978-1-939512; 978-1-61444
Number of titles published annually: 15 Print; 2 CD-ROM
Total Titles: 200 Print; 2 CD-ROM
Distributed by Cambridge University Press
Foreign Rep(s): Cambridge University Press (Africa, Europe, Middle East)
Orders to: MAA Service Center, PO Box 91112, Washington, DC 20090-1112 *Tel:* 301-617-7800 *Toll Free Tel:* 800-331-1622 *Fax:* 240-396-5647 *E-mail:* maaservice@maa.org

§Maven House Press
4 Snead Ct, Palmyra, VA 22963
Tel: 610-883-7988 *Toll Free Fax:* 888-894-3403
E-mail: info@mavenhousepress.com
Web Site: mavenhousepress.com
Key Personnel
Publr & Ed-in-Chief: Jim Pennypacker *E-mail:* jim@mavenhousepress.com
Desktop Publr, Ed & Indexer: Deborah Weiss
Founded: 2012
Publisher of business & self-help books.
ISBN Prefix(es): 978-1-938548
Number of titles published annually: 4 Print; 4 E-Book
Total Titles: 16 Print; 16 E-Book; 2 Audio
Foreign Rights: Russo Rights (worldwide)
Distribution Center: Ingram Publisher Services, 210 American Dr, Jackson, TN 38301 *Toll Free Tel:* 800-343-4499 *Toll Free Fax:* 800-351-5073 *E-mail:* orderentry@perseusbooks.com
Membership(s): The Association of Publishers for Special Sales; Independent Book Publishers Association; SLA

§Mazda Publishers Inc
One Park Plaza, Suite 600, Irvine, CA 92614
SAN: 658-120X
Mailing Address: PO Box 2603, Costa Mesa, CA 92628
Tel: 714-751-5252 *Fax:* 714-751-4805
E-mail: mazdapub@aol.com
Web Site: www.mazdapublishers.com
Key Personnel
Publr & CEO: Dr Ahmad Jabbari
VP: Fay Zamani
Ed-at-Large: Noel Silver; Ann West; Diane L Wilcox
Acqs Ed: Hilary Eastwood
Founded: 1980
Publishes scholarly books dealing with the Middle East, Central Asia & North Africa; critical reviews of poetry; Central Asia including art & architecture.
ISBN Prefix(es): 978-1-56859
Number of titles published annually: 32 Print
Total Titles: 280 Print
Imprints: Blind Owl Press

McBooks Press Inc
ID Booth Bldg, 520 N Meadow St, Ithaca, NY 14850
Tel: 607-272-2114
E-mail: mcbooks@mcbooks.com
Web Site: www.mcbooks.com
Key Personnel
Publr & Intl Rts Contact: Alexander Skutt *E-mail:* alex@mcbooks.com
Art Dir: Panda Musgrove *E-mail:* panda@mcbooks.com
Founded: 1979
Trade books. Specialize in historical fiction, vegetarianism, New York State regional books, period nautical, military fiction, sports including boxing.
ISBN Prefix(es): 978-1-59013
Number of titles published annually: 6 Print; 6 E-Book
Total Titles: 185 Print; 145 E-Book
Foreign Rep(s): Gazelle Book Services Ltd (Europe, UK)
Orders to: Independent Publishers Group, 814 N Franklin St, Chicago, IL 60610 *Tel:* 312-337-0747 *Toll Free Tel:* 800-888-4741 *Fax:* 312-337-5985 *Toll Free Fax:* 800-338-4550

E-mail: orders@ipgbook.com *Web Site:* www.ipgbook.com
Distribution Center: Independent Publishers Group, 814 N Franklin St, Chicago, IL 60610 *Tel:* 312-337-0747 *Toll Free Tel:* 800-888-4741 *Fax:* 312-337-5985 *Toll Free Fax:* 800-338-4550 *E-mail:* orders@ipgbook.com *Web Site:* www.ipgbook.com
Membership(s): AAP

McClanahan Publishing House Inc
107 W Main, Princeton, KY 42445
Tel: 270-963-9005
E-mail: books@kybooks.com
Web Site: kybooks.com
Key Personnel
Pres & Exec Ed: Michelle Stone *E-mail:* mstone@kybooks.com
Founded: 1983
Full service publisher offering art services & artist illustration, jacket design, book design & layout. Self-publishing division provides these services as well for authors who want to retain control of their work.
ISBN Prefix(es): 978-0-913383; 978-0-9758788; 978-1-934898; 978-0-9836687; 978-0-9829785; 978-0-9847933; 978-0-9895424; 978-0-9897078
Number of titles published annually: 15 Print
Total Titles: 140 Print
Imprints: Four Rivers Press

McCutchan Publishing Corp
2694 Ohart Rd, Richmond, CA 94806
SAN: 203-9486
Tel: 510-758-5510 *Toll Free Tel:* 800-227-1540 *Fax:* 510-758-6078
E-mail: mccutchanpublish@sbcglobal.net
Web Site: www.mccutchanpublishing.com
Key Personnel
Pres & Publr: Nancy Runyon
ISBN Contact & Rts & Perms: Kim Sharrar
Founded: 1963
College textbooks & professional books in education, hotel & restaurant management & law enforcement education.
ISBN Prefix(es): 978-0-8211
Number of titles published annually: 3 Print
Total Titles: 100 Print

The McDonald & Woodward Publishing Co
695 Tall Oaks Dr, Newark, OH 43055
Tel: 740-641-2691 *Toll Free Tel:* 800-233-8787 *Fax:* 740-641-2692
E-mail: mwpubco@mwpubco.com
Web Site: www.mwpubco.com
Key Personnel
Publr & Intl Rts Mgr: Jerry N McDonald *E-mail:* jmcd@mwpubco.com
Mktg Mgr: Trish Newcomb *E-mail:* tnewcomb@mwpubco.com
Founded: 1986
Books (primarily adult) in natural history & cultural history; co-publish with educational & governmental entities.
ISBN Prefix(es): 978-0-939923
Number of titles published annually: 8 Print
Total Titles: 70 Print

Margaret K McElderry Books, see Simon & Schuster Children's Publishing

McFarland
960 NC Hwy 88 W, Jefferson, NC 28640
Mailing Address: PO Box 611, Jefferson, NC 28640-0611
Tel: 336-246-4460 *Toll Free Tel:* 800-253-2187 (orders) *Fax:* 336-246-5018; 336-246-4403 (orders)
E-mail: info@mcfarlandpub.com
Web Site: www.mcfarlandpub.com
Key Personnel
Founder & Ed-in-Chief: Robert Franklin *E-mail:* rfranklin@mcfarlandpub.com
Pres: Rhonda Herman *E-mail:* rherman@mcfarlandpub.com
VP & Edit Dir: Steve Wilson *E-mail:* swilson@mcfarlandpub.com
VP, Sales & Mktg: Karl-Heinz Roseman *E-mail:* kroseman@mcfarlandpub.com
Subs & Intl Rights: Beth Cox *E-mail:* bcox@mcfarlandpub.com
Sr Acqs Ed: Gary Mitchem *E-mail:* gmitchem@mcfarlandpub.com
Acqs Ed: Charles Perdue *E-mail:* cperdue@mcfarlandpub.com
Founded: 1979
A leading independent publisher of academic & nonfiction books, known for covering popular topics in a serious fashion & for manufacturing books to meet high library standards.
ISBN Prefix(es): 978-0-89950; 978-0-7864
Number of titles published annually: 400 Print; 390 E-Book
Total Titles: 5,500 Print; 3,500 E-Book
Subsidiaries: McFarland & Co Ltd Publishers (London, UK)
Foreign Rep(s): Eurospan (Africa, Asia-Pacific, Australia, Europe, India, Middle East)
Returns: 961 NC Hwy 88 W, Jefferson, NC 28640
Shipping Address: 961 NC Hwy 88 W, Jefferson, NC 28640

§McGraw-Hill Career Education
Division of McGraw-Hill Higher Education
1333 Burr Ridge Pkwy, Burr Ridge, IL 60527
Tel: 630-789-4000 *Toll Free Tel:* 800-338-3987 (cust serv) *Fax:* 630-789-5523; 614-755-5645 (cust serv)
Web Site: www.mhhe.com
Key Personnel
VP & Natl Sales Mgr: Alan Hensley *E-mail:* alan.hensley@mheducation.com
Mng Dir: Scott Davidson *Tel:* 314-439-6862 *E-mail:* scott.davidson@mheducation.com
Founded: 2001
Provides textbooks & educational materials to post-secondary, trade & career schools.
ISBN Prefix(es): 978-0-697; 978-0-256; 978-0-07
Number of titles published annually: 100 Print; 7 CD-ROM; 50 Online; 75 E-Book
Total Titles: 2,315 Print; 250 Online; 350 E-Book
Branch Office(s)
McGraw-Hill Learning Solutions, 8900 Keystone at the Crossing, Suite 950, Indianapolis, IN 46240
Returns: 860 Taylor Station Rd, Blacklick, OH 43004-0539
Distribution Center: 860 Taylor Station Rd, Blacklick, OH 43004-0539

McGraw-Hill Contemporary Learning Series
Division of McGraw-Hill Higher Education
501 Bell St, Dubuque, IA 52001
SAN: 201-3460
Toll Free Tel: 800-243-6532
Web Site: www.mhcls.com
Key Personnel
Pres, Sci, Engg & Mathematics: Kurt Strand *Tel:* 563-584-6633 *Fax:* 563-584-6600 *E-mail:* kurt_strand@mcgraw-hill.com
SVP, Sales MHHE: Doug Hughes *Tel:* 630-789-5121 *Fax:* 630-789-6944 *E-mail:* doug_hughes@mcgraw-hill.com
VP, Creative Solutions: Mr Christian Perlee *Tel:* 732-275-1251 *E-mail:* christian.perlee@mheducation.com
Founded: 1971
Thought-provoking series of supplements & online web sites appropriate for college-level courses or for library purchase. Materials span over 20 disciplines & cover compelling, current topics & issues. The publications include annual discipline readers, debate style readers, online readers, geographic/atlas readers & college textbooks.
ISBN Prefix(es): 978-0-07; 978-0-697; 978-0-87967; 978-1-56134; 978-0-7024; 978-0-7235; 978-1-25
Number of titles published annually: 50 Print; 50 Online; 125 E-Book
Total Titles: 350 Print; 350 Online; 246 E-Book

McGraw-Hill Create
Division of McGraw-Hill Higher Education
2 Penn Plaza, New York, NY 10121
Toll Free Tel: 800-962-9342
E-mail: mhhe.create@mheducation.com
Web Site: create.mheducation.com; shop.mheducation.com
Key Personnel
Dir, Content & Opers: Cat Mattura *Tel:* 201-618-2497 *E-mail:* cat.mattura@mheducation.com
Dir, Print Solutions, The McGraw Hill Cos: Beth Kundert
Custom products derived from McGraw-Hill copyrighted material; college textbook & ebook adaptations; supplemental materials.
ISBN Prefix(es): 978-1-308; 978-1-309
Distribution Center: The McGraw-Hill Companies Distribution Center, 860 Taylor Station Rd, Blacklick, OH 43004-0504

McGraw-Hill/Dushkin, see McGraw-Hill Contemporary Learning Series

§McGraw-Hill Education
2 Penn Plaza, New York, NY 10121-2298
Tel: 212-904-2000
E-mail: customer.service@mheducation.com; international_cs@mheducation.com
Web Site: www.mheducation.com
Key Personnel
Pres & CEO: David Levin
CFO & Chief Admin Offr: Patrick Milano
Chief Communs Offr: Catherine J Mathis
Chief Digital Offr: Stephen Laster
CIO: Angelo T DeGenaro
Group Pres, US Educ: Peter Cohen
Pres, K-12 Group: Christine Willig
Pres, McGraw-Hill Education Higher Educ: Sally Shankland
Pres, McGraw-Hill International & Professional: Mark Dorman
SVP & Gen Coun: David Stafford
SVP, Govt Aff & Educ Policy: Heath Morrison
SVP, HR: Maryellen Valaitis
SVP, Strategy & Busn Devt: Teresa Martin-Retortillo
Sr Fellow, Digital Learning: Ulrik Juul Christensen, MD
Founded: 1989
McGraw-Hill Education, a division of The McGraw-Hill Companies (NYSE: MHP), is a leading global provider of instructional, assessment & reference solutions that empower professionals & students of all ages. McGraw-Hill Education has offices in numerous countries & publishes in more than 40 languages.
ISBN Prefix(es): 978-1-259; 978-1-260; 978-1-264; 978-1-265; 978-1-266
Imprints: Glencoe/McGraw-Hill; The Grow Network/McGraw-Hill; Macmillan/McGraw-Hill; McGraw-Hill Contemporary; McGraw-Hill Create; McGraw-Hill Education Australia, New Zealand & South Africa; McGraw-Hill Education Europe, Middle East and Africa; McGraw-Hill Education Latin America; McGraw-Hill Education Mexico; McGraw-Hill Education Spain; McGraw-Hill Humanities, Social Sciences, Languages; McGraw-Hill/Irwin; McGraw-Hill Professional; McGraw-Hill Professional Development; McGraw-Hill Ryerson; McGraw-Hill School Education Group; McGraw-Hill Science, Engineering, Mathematics; SRA/McGraw-Hill; Tata/McGraw-Hill

Distribution Center: The McGraw-Hill Companies Distribution Center, 2460 Kerper Blvd, Dubuque, IA 52001-0545
The McGraw-Hill Companies Distribution Center, 860 Taylor Station Rd, Blacklick, OH 43004-0504
Membership(s): AAP
See separate listing for:
McGraw-Hill Higher Education
McGraw-Hill International & Professional Publishing Group
McGraw-Hill School Education Group

§McGraw-Hill Higher Education
Division of McGraw-Hill Education
1333 Burr Ridge Pkwy, Burr Ridge, IL 60527
Tel: 630-789-4000 *Toll Free Tel:* 800-338-3987 (cust serv) *Fax:* 614-755-5645 (cust serv)
Web Site: www.mhhe.com
Key Personnel
Group Pres, US Educ: Peter Cohen
SVP, MHHE Fin: Mona Leung *E-mail:* mona.leung@mheducation.com
SVP, Prods & Mkts: Kurt Strand *Tel:* 563-584-6633 *Fax:* 563-584-6600 *E-mail:* kurt.strand@mheducation.com
SVP, Sales: Doug Hughes *Tel:* 630-789-5121 *E-mail:* doug.hughes@mheducation.com
VP, Content Prodn & Tech Servs: Kim David *Tel:* 563-584-6650 *Fax:* 563-584-6701 *E-mail:* kim.david@mheducation.com
VP, MHHE Global Publg: Michael Hays *Tel:* 212-904-5979 *Fax:* 212-904-5974 *E-mail:* michael.hays@mheducation.com
Founded: 1996
College texts.
ISBN Prefix(es): 978-0-07; 978-0-697; 978-0-256; 978-0-87; 978-1-25
Number of titles published annually: 1,100 Print; 50 CD-ROM; 750 Online; 800 E-Book; 5 Audio
Total Titles: 12,000 Print; 1,600 CD-ROM; 6,000 Online; 6,000 E-Book; 120 Audio
Imprints: McGraw-Hill Create; McGraw-Hill/Irwin; McGraw-Hill Learning Solutions; McGraw-Hill Science, Engineering, Mathematics
Divisions: McGraw-Hill Contemporary Learning Series; McGraw-Hill Humanities, Social Sciences, Languages
Orders to: The McGraw-Hill Companies, Distribution Center, 860 Taylor Station Rd, Blacklick, OH 43004-0539 *Toll Free Tel:* 800-338-3987 *Fax:* 614-755-5654
Returns: The McGraw-Hill Companies, Distribution Center, 860 Taylor Station Rd, Blacklick, OH 43004-0539 *Toll Free Tel:* 800-338-3987 *Fax:* 614-755-5654
Shipping Address: The McGraw-Hill Companies, Distribution Center, 860 Taylor Station Rd, Blacklick, OH 43004-0539 *Toll Free Tel:* 800-338-3987 *Fax:* 614-755-5654
Warehouse: The McGraw-Hill Companies, Distribution Center, 860 Taylor Station Rd, Blacklick, OH 43004-0539 *Toll Free Tel:* 800-338-3987 *Fax:* 614-755-5654
Distribution Center: The McGraw-Hill Companies, Distribution Center, 860 Taylor Station Rd, Blacklick, OH 43004-0539 *Toll Free Tel:* 800-338-3987 *Fax:* 614-755-5654
See separate listing for:
McGraw-Hill Career Education
McGraw-Hill Contemporary Learning Series
McGraw-Hill Create
McGraw-Hill Humanities, Social Sciences, Languages
McGraw-Hill/Irwin
McGraw-Hill Science, Engineering, Mathematics

McGraw-Hill Humanities, Social Sciences, Languages
Division of McGraw-Hill Higher Education
2 Penn Plaza, 21st fl, New York, NY 10121
Tel: 212-904-2000 *Toll Free Tel:* 800-338-3987 (cust serv) *Fax:* 614-755-5645 (cust serv)
Web Site: www.mhhe.com
Key Personnel
SVP, Prods & Mkts: Kurt Strand *Tel:* 563-584-6633 *Fax:* 563-584-6600 *E-mail:* kurt.strand@mheducation.com
SVP, Sales: Doug Hughes *Tel:* 630-789-5121 *Fax:* 630-789-6944 *E-mail:* doug.hughes@mheducation.com
VP & Ed-in-Chief: Mike Ryan *Tel:* 212-904-3044 *Fax:* 212-904-3813 *E-mail:* michael.ryan@mheducation.com
VP, Content Prodn & Tech Servs: Kim David *Tel:* 563-584-6650 *Fax:* 563-584-6701 *E-mail:* kim.david@mheducation.com
Founded: 1944
Publishes college textbooks & numerous ebooks.
ISBN Prefix(es): 978-0-07; 978-0-697; 978-0-87; 978-1-25
Number of titles published annually: 300 Print; 11 CD-ROM; 225 Online; 275 E-Book; 15 Audio
Total Titles: 3,500 Print; 150 CD-ROM; 2,500 Online; 2,500 E-Book; 225 Audio
Returns: 860 Taylor Station Rd, Blacklick, OH 43004-0539
Distribution Center: 860 Taylor Station Rd, Blacklick, OH 43004-0539

§McGraw-Hill International & Professional Publishing Group
Division of McGraw-Hill Education
2 Penn Plaza, New York, NY 10121
Tel: 646-766-2000
Web Site: www.mheducation.com
Key Personnel
CFO, Americas: Jennifer Grunebaum
Pres: Mark Dorman
VP, Fin & Opers (Latin America): Juan Ortego
Mng Dir, EMEA: Jill Jones
Mng Dir, India: Kaushik Bellani
Mng Dir, Latin America (Mexico): Eric Descombes
Mng Dir, North America: Aaron Yverski
Edit Dir, Busn Group: Donya Dickerson
ISBN Prefix(es): 978-0-07

§McGraw-Hill/Irwin
Division of McGraw-Hill Higher Education
1333 Burr Ridge Pkwy, Burr Ridge, IL 60527
Tel: 630-789-4000 *Toll Free Tel:* 800-338-3987 (cust serv) *Fax:* 630-789-6942; 614-755-5645 (cust serv)
Web Site: www.mhhe.com
Key Personnel
SVP, Prods & Mkts: Kurt Strand *Tel:* 563-584-6633 *E-mail:* kurt.strand@mheducation.com
VP & Natl Sales Mgr: Doug Hughes *Tel:* 630-789-5121 *E-mail:* doug_hughes@mcgraw-hill.com
VP, Content Prodn & Tech Servs: Kim David *Tel:* 563-584-6650 *E-mail:* kim_david@mcgraw-hill.com
Founded: 1933
College textbooks & numerous ebook titles.
ISBN Prefix(es): 978-0-07; 978-0-697; 978-0-256
Number of titles published annually: 230 Print; 57 CD-ROM; 200 Online; 200 E-Book
Total Titles: 2,100 Print; 630 CD-ROM; 1,500 Online; 1,500 E-Book; 1 Audio
Returns: 860 Taylor Station Rd, Blacklick, OH 43004-0539
Distribution Center: 860 Taylor Station Rd, Blacklick, OH 43004-0539

McGraw-Hill School Education Group
Division of McGraw-Hill Education
8787 Orion Place, Columbus, OH 43240
Tel: 614-430-4000 *Toll Free Tel:* 800-848-1567
Web Site: www.mheducation.com
Key Personnel
Group Pres, US Educ: Peter Cohen
Pres, School: Christine Willig
SVP, Sales: Sean Ryan
Founded: 1971
Educational materials for elementary, middle school & high school.
ISBN Prefix(es): 978-0-02; 978-0-07; 978-0-31; 978-0-39; 978-0-53; 978-0-65; 978-0-67; 978-0-80; 978-0-84; 978-0-89; 978-0-93; 978-0-96; 978-1-57; 978-1-58; 978-1-88
Imprints: Glencoe (grades 6-12); Macmillan (grades PreK-5)
Branch Office(s)
303 E Wacker Dr, Chicago, IL 60601 *Tel:* 312-233-6500
2 Penn Plaza, New York, NY 10121 *Tel:* 212-904-2000
Foreign Rep(s): The McGraw-Hill Companies (worldwide); McGraw-Hill Ryerson Limited (Canada)
Orders to: 860 Taylor Station Rd, Blacklick, OH 43004-0543, SVP, Cust Opers: Gerald A Salters *Tel:* 614-759-3825 ext 3825 *Toll Free Tel:* 800-334-7344 *Fax:* 614-759-3670 *E-mail:* gary_salters@mcgraw-hill.com
Returns: 6405 Commerce Ct, Groveport, OH 43125
Shipping Address: 6405 Commerce Ct, Groveport, OH 43125, Sr Dir, Dist: Richard Sestrich *Tel:* 614-835-2302 *Fax:* 614-835-2303
Distribution Center: 6405 Commerce Ct, Groveport, OH 43125 *Toll Free Tel:* 800-334-7344

§McGraw-Hill Science, Engineering, Mathematics
Division of McGraw-Hill Higher Education
501 Bell St, Dubuque, IA 52001
Tel: 563-584-6000 *Toll Free Tel:* 800-338-3987 (cust serv) *Fax:* 614-755-5645 (cust serv)
Web Site: www.mhhe.com
Key Personnel
SVP, Prods & Mkts: Kurt Strand *Tel:* 563-584-6633 *Fax:* 563-584-6600 *E-mail:* kurt.strand@mheducation.com
SVP, Sales: Doug Hughes *Tel:* 630-789-5121 *Fax:* 630-789-6944 *E-mail:* doug.hughes@mheducation.com
VP & Gen Mgr: Marty Lange *Tel:* 563-584-6648 *Fax:* 563-584-6601 *E-mail:* marty.lange@mheducation.com
VP, Content Prodn & Tech Servs: Kim David *Tel:* 563-584-6650 *Fax:* 563-584-6701 *E-mail:* kim.david@mheducation.com
Founded: 1944
College textbook publisher.
ISBN Prefix(es): 978-0-07; 978-0-697; 978-1-25
Number of titles published annually: 260 Print; 8 CD-ROM; 240 Online; 240 E-Book
Total Titles: 1,790 Print; 337 CD-ROM; 2,000 Online; 2,000 E-Book
Imprints: McGraw-Hill
Branch Office(s)
1333 Burr Ridge Pkwy, Burr Ridge, IL 60527 *Tel:* 630-789-4000 *Fax:* 630-789-5030
Returns: 860 Taylor Station Rd, Blacklick, OH 43004-0539
Distribution Center: 860 Taylor Station Rd, Blacklick, OH 43004-0539

McPherson & Co
148 Smith Ave, Kingston, NY 12401
SAN: 203-0632
Mailing Address: PO Box 1126, Kingston, NY 12402-1126
Tel: 845-331-5807 *Fax:* 845-331-5807
E-mail: bmcphersonco@gmail.com
Web Site: www.mcphersonco.com
Key Personnel
Publr & Ed-in-Chief: Bruce R McPherson
Founded: 1973
Fiction, anthropology, belles lettres & avant-garde art.

ISBN Prefix(es): 978-0-914232; 978-0-929701; 978-1-878352 (Saroff Editions); 978-1-62054
Number of titles published annually: 5 Print; 5 E-Book
Total Titles: 134 Print; 8 E-Book
Imprints: Documentext; Recovered Classics; Saroff Editions; Treacle Press
Foreign Rights: Agnese Incisa Agenzia Literaria (Italy); Kerigan-Moro Literary (Portugal, Spain); La Nouvelle Agence (France); Prava i prevodi (Bulgaria, Czech Republic, Hungary, Poland, Serbia, Slovenia); Literarische Agentur Simon (Germany)
Orders to: PO Box 1126, Kingston, NY 12402-1126
Distribution Center: Central Books Ltd, One Heath Park Industrial Estate, Freshwater Rd, Dagenham RM8 1RX, United Kingdom (UK only) *Tel:* (020) 8525 8800 *Fax:* (020) 8599 2694 *E-mail:* contactus@centralbooks.com *Web Site:* www.centralbooks.com
Membership(s): Community of Literary Magazines & Presses

McSweeney's Publishing
849 Valencia St, San Francisco, CA 94110
Tel: 415-642-5609 (cust serv)
Web Site: www.mcsweeneys.net
Key Personnel
Publr & Ed: Jordan Bass
Publicity Dir: Ruby Perez
Ed: Andi Winnette
Founded: 1998
ISBN Prefix(es): 978-1-936365
Number of titles published annually: 25 Print
Total Titles: 150 Print
Foreign Rights: The Wylie Agency (worldwide)
Distribution Center: Publishers Group West, 1700 Fourth St, Berkeley, CA 94710 *Tel:* 510-809-3700 *Fax:* 510-809-3777 *E-mail:* info@pgw.com *Web Site:* www.pgw.com

MDR, A D&B Co
6 Armstrong Rd, Suite 301, Shelton, CT 06484
Tel: 203-926-4800 *Toll Free Tel:* 800-333-8802 *Fax:* 203-225-4603 *Toll Free Fax:* 866-532-7097
E-mail: mdrinfo@dnb.com
Web Site: www.schooldata.com
Key Personnel
Gen Mgr: Aaron Stibel *Tel:* 203-225-4827
VP, Mktg: Kristina James *Tel:* 312-345-4356
VP, Sales & Mktg: Steve Gatland *Tel:* 312-345-4357
Founded: 1969
First choice for marketing information & services for the K-12, higher education, library, early childhood & related education markets. Powered by the most complete, current & accurate education databases available in the industry, MDR provides e-mail contacts & deployment, direct mail lists, sales contact & lead solutions, along with web & social media marketing services.
ISBN Prefix(es): 978-1-57953; 978-1-943664
Number of titles published annually: 53 Print
Branch Office(s)
20 S Clark St, Suite 2100, Chicago, IL 60603 *Tel:* 312-263-4169 *Fax:* 312-345-4360

Meadowbrook Press
6110 Blue Circle Dr, Suite 237, Minnetonka, MN 55343
SAN: 207-3404
Toll Free Tel: 800-338-2232 *Fax:* 952-930-1940
E-mail: info@meadowbrookpress.com
Web Site: www.meadowbrookpress.com
Key Personnel
Pres & Publr: Bruce Lansky
Busn Mgr: Robyn Beck
Prodn Mgr: Tami Peterson
Founded: 1975
Trade paperbacks; baby & child care, parenting, health, children's activities, humor, parties & games, children's poetry, adult light verse & business travel.
ISBN Prefix(es): 978-0-915658; 978-0-88166
Number of titles published annually: 5 Print
Total Titles: 75 Print
Distributed by Simon & Schuster
Foreign Rep(s): Chris Lloyd Sales & Marketing Services (UK); Monarch Books of Canada (Canada)
Foreign Rights: AM-USA (Seiko Uyeda) (Japan); Arrowsmith Agency (Nina Arrowsmith) (Germany); Big Apple Agency Inc (Wendy King) (China, Taiwan); The Book Publishers Association of Israel (Shoshi Grajower) (Israel); Bridge Communications Co (Pat Akkarasawrt) (Thailand); Iris Literary Agency (Catherine Fragou) (Greece); Alexander Korzhenevski Agency (Alexander Korzhenevski) (Russia); Maxima Creative Agency (Santo Manurung) (Indonesia); Montreal Contacts/The Rights Agency (Luc Jutras) (Canada); Montreal Contacts/The Rights Agency (Anne Confuron) (Canada (French-speaking), France); Kristin Olson Literary Agency (Kristin Olson) (Czech Republic); Publishing & Data Services (Sue Francis) (Australia); RDC Agencia Literaria (Beatriz Coll) (Latin America, Portugal, Spain); Margit Schaleck Literary Agency (Margit Schaleck) (Denmark); Tuttle-Mori Agency Inc (Thailand); WNET (H Katia Schumer) (Brazil); Eric Yang Agency (Henry Shin) (Korea)

me+mi publishing inc
400 S Knoll St, Suite B, Wheaton, IL 60187
Toll Free Tel: 888-251-1444 *Fax:* 630-588-9804
E-mail: rw@rosawesley.com
Web Site: www.memima.com
Key Personnel
Principal & Publr: Gladys Rosa-Mendoza; Mark Wesley
Founded: 2002
Independent publisher dedicated to creating the highest quality books available in two or more languages for infants & toddlers.
ISBN Prefix(es): 978-0-9679748; 978-1-931398
Number of titles published annually: 5 Print
Total Titles: 33 Print
Imprints: The English Spanish Foundation Series
Membership(s): Independent Book Publishers Association

§R S Means from The Gordian Group
1099 Hingham St, Suite 201, Rockland, MA 02370
Tel: 781-422-5000 *Toll Free Tel:* 800-448-8182 *Fax:* 781-585-8814 *Toll Free Fax:* 800-632-6701
Web Site: www.rsmeans.com
Key Personnel
VP, Sales: Scott Smith
Prod Mgr, RS Means Books: Andrea Sillah
Founded: 1942
A leader in construction cost estimating data, analytics & life cycle cost analysis available in 4 convenient formats: online, books, ebooks +/or CDs.
ISBN Prefix(es): 978-0-911950; 978-0-87629; 978-1-936335
Number of titles published annually: 25 Print
Total Titles: 150 Print
Divisions: Cost Annuals
Distributed by John Wiley & Sons Inc
Advertising Agency: The Stancliff Agency

MedBooks
Division of Professional Education Workshops & Seminars
101 W Buckingham Rd, Richardson, TX 75081-4802
Tel: 972-643-1809 *Fax:* 972-643-1859
E-mail: medbooks@medbooks.com
Web Site: www.medbooks.com
Key Personnel
Owner & Pres: Patrice Morin-Spatz
Gen Mgr: Mark Lerner
Founded: 1985
Specialize in books on health insurance coding & processing for medical offices, insurance companies & other health professions.
ISBN Prefix(es): 978-0-923369; 978-0-9762699; 978-0-9822597; 978-0-9773154; 978-0-9831904; 978-0-9790318; 978-0-9797234; 978-0-9800627; 978-1-937816
Number of titles published annually: 5 Print
Total Titles: 25 Print
Distributed by JA Majors
Membership(s): Independent Book Publishers Association; Textbook & Academic Authors Association

Medical Group Management Association (MGMA)
104 Inverness Terr E, Englewood, CO 80112-5306
Tel: 303-799-1111; 303-799-1111 (ext 1888, book orders) *Toll Free Tel:* 877-275-6462
E-mail: support@mgma.com; infocenter@mgma.com
Web Site: www.mgma.com
Founded: 1926
Specialize in medical practice management.
ISBN Prefix(es): 978-1-56829; 978-0-933948
Number of titles published annually: 8 Print; 4 CD-ROM; 1 E-Book
Total Titles: 150 Print; 15 CD-ROM; 1 E-Book; 2 Audio
Branch Office(s)
Government Affairs, 1717 Pennsylvania Ave NW, No 600, Washington, DC 20006, Contact: Anders Gilberg *Tel:* 202-293-3450 *E-mail:* govaff@mgma.org
Distributor for American Medical Association; Aspen Publishers; Greenbranch; HAP (Health Adminstration Press); Jones & Bartlett Learning; J Wiley & Sons

Medical Physics Publishing Corp (MPP)
4555 Helgesen Dr, Madison, WI 53718
Tel: 608-262-4021; 608-224-4508 *Toll Free Tel:* 800-442-5778 (cust serv) *Fax:* 608-224-5016
E-mail: mpp@medicalphysics.org
Web Site: www.medicalphysics.org
Key Personnel
Gen Mgr & Intl Rts: Ms Bobbett Shaub *Tel:* 608-224-4508 *E-mail:* bobbett@medicalphysics.org
Ed: Todd Hanson *E-mail:* todd@medicalphysics.org
Founded: 1985
Publish & distribute books in medical physics & related fields.
ISBN Prefix(es): 978-0-944838; 978-1-930524
Number of titles published annually: 6 Print; 6 E-Book
Total Titles: 100 Print; 8 CD-ROM; 35 Online; 35 E-Book

Medieval Institute Publications
Division of Medieval Institute of Western Michigan University
WMU East Campus, 100-E Walwood Hall, Kalamazoo, MI 49008
Mailing Address: 1903 W Michigan Ave, Kalamazoo, MI 49008-5432
Tel: 269-387-8754 *Fax:* 269-387-8750
Web Site: www.wmich.edu/medievalpublications
Key Personnel
Dir & Ed-in-Chief: Simon Forde
Founded: 1978
Academic publications on late antique & medieval studies.

ISBN Prefix(es): 978-1-918720; 978-1-879288; 978-1-58044
Number of titles published annually: 14 Print
Total Titles: 215 Print
Membership(s): Association of American University Presses

§MedMaster Inc
3337 Hollywood Oaks Dr, Fort Lauderdale, FL 33312
Mailing Address: PO Box 640028, Miami, FL 33164-0028
Tel: 954-962-8414 *Toll Free Tel:* 800-335-3480 *Fax:* 954-962-4508
E-mail: mmbks@aol.com
Web Site: www.medmaster.net
Key Personnel
Founder & Pres: Stephen Goldberg *E-mail:* stgoldberg@aol.com
VP & Secy: Michael Goldberg
Founded: 1979
Medical book & software publishers; medical subjects for education of medical students & other health professionals.
This publisher has indicated that 100% of their product line is author subsidized.
ISBN Prefix(es): 978-0-940780; 978-1-935660
Number of titles published annually: 1 Print; 2 E-Book
Total Titles: 33 Print; 9 E-Book
Returns: PO Box 640028, Miami, FL 33164-0028
Warehouse: 360 NE 191 St, Miami, FL 33179

The Russell Meerdink Co Ltd
1555 S Park Ave, Neenah, WI 54956
SAN: 249-1680
Tel: 920-725-0955 *Toll Free Tel:* 800-635-6499 *Fax:* 920-725-0709
E-mail: questions@horseinfo.com
Web Site: www.horseinfo.com
Key Personnel
Mng Dir & Intl Rts Contact: Jan Meerdink *E-mail:* jmeerdink@horseinfo.com
Founded: 1980
Equine titles & thoroughbred data services. Distribution & mail order sales of equine titles.
ISBN Prefix(es): 978-0-929346
Number of titles published annually: 8 Print; 2 CD-ROM
Total Titles: 33 Print; 4 CD-ROM

Mel Bay Publications Inc
4 Industrial Dr, Pacific, MO 63069-0066
Tel: 636-257-3970 *Toll Free Tel:* 800-863-5229 *Fax:* 636-257-5062 *Toll Free Fax:* 800-660-9818
E-mail: email@melbay.com
Web Site: www.melbay.com
Key Personnel
Pres: Bill Bay
Sales Supv: Nancy Oliver-Vallely
Info Systems Supv: Sharon Feldmann
Founded: 1947
Innovative instructional & performance material for most instruments.
ISBN Prefix(es): 978-0-7866; 978-0-87166; 978-1-56222; 978-8-83206; 978-1-60974; 978-1-61065; 978-1-61911; 978-1-5134
Number of titles published annually: 200 Print
Total Titles: 4,500 Print
Imprints: Building Excellence; Cathedral Music Press; Editions Classicae; Creative Keyboard; First Lessons; Getting Into; Gig Savers; Qwikguide; School of the Blues; You Can Teach Yourself
Divisions: Cathedral Music Press; Creative Keyboard Publications
Distributor for AcuTab Publications Inc; AMA; Chanterelle; Stefan Grossman's Guitar Workshop; Hardie Press; Learn Roots Music; Maggies Music; Malley's; Registry of Guitar Tutors (RGT); RGB Arte Visual; Scott's Highland Services; Voggenreiter Publishers; Walton's; SR Wheat
Foreign Rep(s): ATN Inc (Japan); Chorus Productions (Finland); Mel Bay Music Ltd (Belgium, Central Germany, Croatia, Czech Republic, Denmark, Eastern Africa, Eastern Europe exc Estonia, Latvia, Lithuania & Russia); Music Sales (Australia, New Zealand); People's Music Publishing House (China)
Advertising Agency: Mel Bay Licensing, Industrial Dr, No 4, Pacific, MO 63069 *Tel:* 678-772-0021 *E-mail:* licensing@melbay.com *Web Site:* www.licensing.melbay.com
Membership(s): ABA

The Edwin Mellen Press
415 Ridge St, Lewiston, NY 14092
Mailing Address: PO Box 450, Lewiston, NY 14092-0450 SAN: 207-110X
Tel: 716-754-2266; 716-754-1400 (mktg); 716-754-2788 (order fulfillment) *Fax:* 716-754-4056
E-mail: editor@mellenpress.com
Web Site: www.mellenpress.com
Key Personnel
Founder & Publr: Herbert Richardson
Dir & Acqs: Dr John Rupnow *E-mail:* jrupnow@mellenpress.com
Fulfillment Dir: Irene Miller *E-mail:* imiller@mellenpress.com
Prodn Mgr & Perms Ed: Patricia Schultz *E-mail:* pschultz@mellenpress.com
Founded: 1974
Non-subsidy academic publisher of books in the humanities of social sciences. Publish monographs, critical editions, collections, translations, revisionist studies, constructive essays, bibliographies, dictionaries, reference guides & dissertations.
ISBN Prefix(es): 978-0-88946; 978-0-7734; 978-0-935106; 978-0-7799; 978-1-4955
Number of titles published annually: 40 Print
Total Titles: 600 Print
Imprints: Mellen Biblical Press; Mellen Poetry Press; Tribunal for Administrative Justice
Foreign Office(s): The Edwin Mellen Press Ltd, 16 College St, Lampeter, Ceredigion SA48 7DY, United Kingdom, Mgr, Wales/UK Off: Iona Williams *Tel:* (01570) 423 356 *Fax:* (01570) 423 775 *E-mail:* emp@mellenpress.co.uk *Web Site:* www.mellenpress.co.uk
Advertising Agency: Lewiston Business Services

Menasha Ridge Press Inc
Imprint of AdventureKEEN
2204 First Ave S, Suite 102, Birmingham, AL 35233
Toll Free Tel: 888-604-4537 *Fax:* 205-326-1012
E-mail: info@adventurewithkeen.com
Web Site: www.menasharidge.com
Key Personnel
COO: Molly B Merkle *Tel:* 205-443-7993
Publr: Robert W Sehlinger
Mktg & Publicity: Tanya Sylvan *E-mail:* tanya@adventurewithkeen.com
Founded: 1982
Outdoor recreation, travel, nature & reference guides.
ISBN Prefix(es): 978-0-89732; 978-1-63404
Number of titles published annually: 35 Print; 35 E-Book
Total Titles: 140 Print; 100 E-Book
Orders to: Publishers Group West, 1700 Fourth St, Berkeley, CA 94710 *Tel:* 510-809-3700 *Toll Free Tel:* 800-788-3123 *Fax:* 510-809-3733 *E-mail:* tom.lupoff@pgw.com *Web Site:* www.pgw.com
Returns: Keen Communications, Returns Dept, 1700 Madison Rd, Cincinnati, OH 45206
Membership(s): ABA; Southern Independent Booksellers Alliance

§MennoMedia
1251 Virginia Ave, Harrisonburg, VA 22802-2434
Toll Free Tel: 800-245-7894 (orders & cust serv US) *Toll Free Fax:* 877-271-0760
E-mail: info@mennomedia.org
Web Site: www.mennomedia.org
Key Personnel
Dir: Amy Gingerich *E-mail:* amyg@mennomedia.org
Mng Ed: Melodie Davis
Founded: 1878
An agency of Mennonite Church USA & Mennonite Church Canada. Small denominational publisher. Specialize in the production of innovative Christian education resources for children, youth, young adults, adults & intergenerational groups. Topics of interest include materials on peace & justice, evangelism, Christian service & radical Christian discipleship.
ISBN Prefix(es): 978-0-8361 (Herald Press); 978-1-5138
Number of titles published annually: 10 Print
Imprints: Herald Press
Branch Office(s)
718 N Main St, Newton, KS 67114 *Tel:* 316-281-4412 *Fax:* 316-283-0454
50 Kent Ave, Suite 204, Kitchener, ON N2G 3R1, Canada *Fax:* 519-747-5721
See separate listing for:
Herald Press

Mercer University Press
368 Orange St, Macon, GA 31201
Mailing Address: 1400 Coleman Ave, Macon, GA 31207 SAN: 220-0716
Tel: 478-301-2880 *Toll Free Tel:* 866-895-1472 *Fax:* 478-301-2585
E-mail: mupressorders@mercer.edu
Web Site: www.mupress.org
Key Personnel
Dir: Marc Jolley *Tel:* 478-301-2880 *E-mail:* jolley_ma@mercer.edu
Publg Asst: Marsha Luttrell *Tel:* 478-301-4266 *E-mail:* luttrell_mm@mercer.edu
Mktg Dir: Mary Beth Kosowski *Tel:* 478-301-4262 *E-mail:* kosowski_mb@mercer.edu
Cust Serv Assoc: Candice E Morris *Tel:* 478-301-4261 *E-mail:* morris_ce@mercer.edu
Busn Off: Jenny Toole *Tel:* 478-301-4267 *E-mail:* toole_rw@mercer.edu
Founded: 1979
History, philosophy, religion, Southern studies, Southern literature, literary studies, regional interest.
ISBN Prefix(es): 978-0-86554; 978-0-88146
Number of titles published annually: 40 Print
Total Titles: 1,400 Print
Foreign Rep(s): East-West Export Books (Royden Muranaka) (Asia, Australia, New Zealand); The Eurospan Group (Africa, Central Asia, Europe, Middle East, UK)
Warehouse: 1701 Seventh St, Macon, GA 31206
Membership(s): American Association of University Presses

Merit Publishing International Inc
6839 Villas Dr S, Boca Raton, FL 33433
Tel: 561-350-0329
E-mail: merituk@aol.com
Web Site: www.meritpublishing.com
Key Personnel
Owner & Pres: Gene Evans
Owner & VP: Dr Marta Garrido
Founded: 1986 (in UK, 1992 in US)
Medical publishing & marketing in all clinical areas. Questions & answers series, visual diagnosis self-tests series, customized books, slide kits, newsletters, proceedings & monographs, new perspectives series, guides to families & children series.
ISBN Prefix(es): 978-1-873413
Number of titles published annually: 13 Print; 3 CD-ROM

Total Titles: 65 Print; 3 CD-ROM; 3 Online
Foreign Office(s): 30 Wey Barton, Byfleet, Surrey KT14 7EF, United Kingdom, Contact: Mrs Gene Evans *Tel:* (01932) 844526 *Fax:* (01932) 820419
Foreign Rep(s): Gazelle Book Services Ltd (UK); Momento Medico (Italy)
Foreign Rights: J & C Ediciones Medicas (Latin America, Spain)
Membership(s): Independent Book Publishers Association

Meriwether Publishing
Division of Pioneer Drama Service Inc
c/o Pioneer Drama Service, 9707-A E Easter Lane, Englewood, CO 80112
Mailing Address: PO Box 4267, Englewood, CO 80155 SAN: 990-2856
Tel: 303-779-4035 *Toll Free Tel:* 800-333-7262 *Fax:* 303-779-4315
E-mail: books@pioneerdrama.com
Web Site: www.pioneerdrama.com
Key Personnel
Publr: Steven Fendrich *E-mail:* steve@pioneerdrama.com
Exec Ed: Debra Fendrich *E-mail:* debra@pioneerdrama.com
Book Dept Coord: Karen Bullock
Founded: 1960
Books on theater, drama, performing arts, costuming, stagecraft, theatre games, play anthologies, plays, musicals, theatre arts DVDs, theatre/drama education.
ISBN Prefix(es): 978-0-916260; 978-1-56608
Number of titles published annually: 4 Print
Total Titles: 200 Print
Foreign Rep(s): Gazelle Book Services Ltd (Europe, UK); Hanbury Plays (UK)
Membership(s): Publishers Association of the West

§Merriam Press
133 Elm St, Suite 3R, Bennington, VT 05201-2250
Tel: 802-447-0313
Web Site: www.merriam-press.com
Key Personnel
Owner: Ray Merriam *E-mail:* ray@merriam-press.com
Founded: 1988
Primarily World War II/military history, memoirs & some fiction; also some non-military history, fiction, memoirs, poetry, children.
This publisher has indicated that 90% of their product line is author subsidized.
ISBN Prefix(es): 978-1-57638
Number of titles published annually: 50 Print; 20 CD-ROM; 50 E-Book
Total Titles: 250 Print; 150 CD-ROM; 150 E-Book

§Merriam-Webster Inc
Subsidiary of Encyclopaedia Britannica Inc
47 Federal St, Springfield, MA 01102
Mailing Address: PO Box 281, Springfield, MA 01102-0281
Tel: 413-734-3134 *Toll Free Tel:* 800-828-1880 (orders & cust serv) *Fax:* 413-731-5979 (sales)
E-mail: support@merriam-webster.com
Web Site: www.merriam-webster.com
Key Personnel
Pres & Publr: John M Morse
CFO: Caryl Schivley
VP & Dir, Sales: Jed Santoro *E-mail:* jsantoro@m-w.com
VP, Busn Devt: Matthew Dube
Dir, Eng Lang Learning Publg: Jane Mairs
Dir, Mktg: Meghan Lunghi *E-mail:* mlunghi@m-w.com
Dir, Mktg Design: Joanne Watson
Founded: 1831
Dictionaries & language reference products.
ISBN Prefix(es): 978-0-87779; 978-1-68150
Number of titles published annually: 4 Print
Total Titles: 102 Print; 7 CD-ROM; 2 Online; 2 E-Book
Divisions: Federal Street Press
See separate listing for:
Federal Street Press

Mesorah Publications Ltd
4401 Second Ave, Brooklyn, NY 11232
SAN: 213-1269
Tel: 718-921-9000 *Toll Free Tel:* 800-637-6724 *Fax:* 718-680-1875
E-mail: info@artscroll.com; orders@artscroll.com
Web Site: www.artscroll.com
Key Personnel
Pres & Gen Ed: Meir Zlotowitz
Publr: Nosson Scherman
Contact: Jacob Brander
Founded: 1976
Judaica, Bible study, liturgical materials, juvenile, history, Holocaust, Talmud, novels.
ISBN Prefix(es): 978-0-89906; 978-1-57819; 978-1-4226
Number of titles published annually: 50 Print
Total Titles: 850 Print
Imprints: Art Scroll Series; Shaar Press; Tamar Books
Distributor for NCSY Publications
Foreign Rep(s): Stephen Blitz (Israel)
Returns: 222 44 St, Brooklyn, NY 11232

§Messianic Jewish Publishers
Division of Messianic Jewish Communications
6120 Day Long Lane, Clarksville, MD 21029
Tel: 410-531-6644 *Toll Free Tel:* 800-410-7367 (orders) *Fax:* 410-531-9440; 717-761-7273 (orders) *Toll Free Fax:* 800-327-0048 (orders)
E-mail: editor@messianicjewish.net; customerservice@messianicjewish.net; permissions@messianicjewish.net (rights & perms)
Web Site: messianicjewish.net/publish
Key Personnel
Pres & Publr: Barry Rubin
Founded: 1949
Publish & distribute Messianic Jewish books & other products.
ISBN Prefix(es): 978-1-880226; 978-1-936716
Number of titles published annually: 12 Print; 6 E-Book
Total Titles: 82 Print; 40 E-Book
Divisions: Lederer Books
Distributor for Chosen People Ministries; First Fruits of Zion; Jewish New Testament Publications
Foreign Rep(s): Winfried Bluth (Europe)
Foreign Rights: Winfried Bluth (Europe)
Membership(s): CBA: The Association for Christian Retail; Evangelical Christian Publishers Association
See separate listing for:
Lederer Books

Metropolitan Classics
Division of Fort Ross Inc
26 Arthur Place, Yonkers, NY 10701
Tel: 914-375-6448
Web Site: www.fortrossinc.com
Key Personnel
Pres & Exec Dir: Dr Vladimir Kartsev *E-mail:* vkartsev2000@yahoo.com
Founded: 1992
Books in Russian. Russia, Ukraine, Kazakhstan-related books in English, co-publishing.
ISBN Prefix(es): 978-1-57480
Number of titles published annually: 4 Print; 4 Online; 4 E-Book
Total Titles: 50 Print; 4 Online; 4 E-Book
Foreign Rep(s): Nova Littera (Baltic States, Belarus, Eastern Europe, Russia, Ukraine)

§The Metropolitan Museum of Art
1000 Fifth Ave, New York, NY 10028
SAN: 202-6279
Tel: 212-879-5500; 212-570-3725 (edit) *Fax:* 212-396-5062
E-mail: editorial@metmuseum.org
Web Site: www.metmuseum.org
Key Personnel
CEO & Dir: Thomas P Campbell
Pres: Daniel Weiss
Publr & Ed-in-Chief: Mark Polizzotti
Assoc Publr & Gen Mgr, Pubns: Gwen Roginsky
Chief Prodn Mgr: Peter Antony
Founded: 1870
Art books, exhibition catalogs, quarterly bulletin, annual journal.
ISBN Prefix(es): 978-0-87099; 978-1-58839
Number of titles published annually: 30 Print
Total Titles: 300 Print; 5 CD-ROM
Distributed by Yale University Press
Foreign Rep(s): Yale University Press
Warehouse: Middle Village, Queens, NY 11381-0001

MFA Publications
Imprint of Museum of Fine Arts Boston
465 Huntington Ave, Boston, MA 02115
Tel: 617-369-4233 *Fax:* 617-369-3459
E-mail: publications@mfa.org
Web Site: www.mfa.org/publications
Key Personnel
Publr: Emiko Usui *Tel:* 617-369-4231 *E-mail:* eusui@mfa.org
Head, Prodn & Design: Terry McAweeney
Pubns Coord: Hope Stockton *E-mail:* hstockton@mfa.org
Founded: 1877
Exhibition & collection catalogues; general interest & trade arts publications, children's books. No returns accepted.
ISBN Prefix(es): 978-0-87846
Number of titles published annually: 12 Print
Total Titles: 80 Print
Imprints: ArtWorks
Distributed by Thames & Hudson (outside of North America)
Warehouse: c/o PSSC, 46 Development Rd, Fitchburg, MA 01420
Distribution Center: Distributed Art Publishers (DAP), 155 Sixth Ave, 2nd fl, New York, NY 10013 (North America)

MGI Management Institute Inc
12 Skyline Dr, Hawthorne, NY 10532
Tel: 914-428-6500 *Toll Free Tel:* 800-932-0191 *Fax:* 914-428-0773
E-mail: mgiusa@aol.com
Web Site: www.mgi.org
Key Personnel
Mgr: Sandra Wacht
Founded: 1968
Home study guides.
Number of titles published annually: 60 Print
Total Titles: 60 Print; 5 Online

Michelin Maps & Guides
Division of Michelin North America Inc
One Parkway S, Greenville, SC 29615-5022
Tel: 864-458-5565 *Fax:* 864-458-5665 *Toll Free Fax:* 866-297-0914; 888-773-7979
E-mail: orders@americanmap.com (orders)
Web Site: www.michelintravel.com; www.michelinguide.com
Key Personnel
Dir, B2B Sales & Mktg: Christopher Aufmuth
Sales Employee Training Mgr: Steve Hunt
Dir of Sales: Eileen Osteen *E-mail:* eileen.osteen@us.michelin.com
Founded: 1900
Specialize in travel publications; hotel & restaurant guides.
ISBN Prefix(es): 978-2-06

Number of titles published annually: 50 Print
Total Titles: 175 Print
Distributed by Editions du Renouveau Pedagogique (French titles in Canada); Langenscheidt Publishing Group; MAPART Publishing (CN only); NBN (guides for North America); Penguin Canada (English titles in Canada)
Orders to: PO Box 19001, Greenville, SC 29615 *Toll Free Tel:* 800-423-0485 *Toll Free Fax:* 800-378-7471

Michigan Municipal League
Affiliate of National League of Cities
1675 Green Rd, Ann Arbor, MI 48105
Mailing Address: PO Box 1487, Ann Arbor, MI 48106-1487
Tel: 734-662-3246 *Toll Free Tel:* 800-653-2483
E-mail: contact@mml.org
Web Site: www.mml.org
Key Personnel
Ed: Kim Cekola *Tel:* 734-669-6321 *E-mail:* kcekola@mml.org; Tawny Pearson *Tel:* 734-669-6301 *E-mail:* tpearson@mml.org
Founded: 1899
Municipal topics & newsletters, services & publications for local governments in Michigan.
ISBN Prefix(es): 978-1-929923
Number of titles published annually: 6 Print
Distributor for Crisp Books

§Michigan State University Press (MSU Press)
Division of Michigan State University
Manly Miles Bldg, Suite 25, 1405 S Harrison Rd, East Lansing, MI 48823-5245
SAN: 202-6295
Tel: 517-355-9543 *Fax:* 517-432-2611
Web Site: msupress.org
Key Personnel
Dir: Gabriel Dotto *Tel:* 517-884-6900 *E-mail:* dotto@msu.edu
Asst Dir & Ed-in-Chief: Julie L Loehr *Tel:* 517-884-6905 *E-mail:* loehr@msu.edu
Mktg & Sales Mgr: Julie K Reaume *Tel:* 517-884-6920 *E-mail:* reaumej@msu.edu
Mng Ed: Kristine M Blakeslee *Tel:* 517-884-6912 *E-mail:* blakes17@msu.edu
Digital Prodn Specialist: Annette K Tanner *Tel:* 517-884-6910 *E-mail:* tanneran@msu.edu
Busn & Fin Offr: Julie Wrzesinski *Tel:* 517-884-6922 *E-mail:* wrzesin2@msu.edu
Founded: 1947
Scholarly works & general nonfiction trade books.
ISBN Prefix(es): 978-0-944311; 978-0-937191; 978-0-87013; 978-1-62896; 978-1-62895; 978-1-60917; 978-1-61186; 978-1-938065; 978-1-941258; 978-0-9967252
Number of titles published annually: 40 Print; 2 CD-ROM; 10 E-Book
Total Titles: 650 Print; 4 CD-ROM; 59 E-Book
Distributed by UBC Press, Canada
Distributor for Mackinac Historic Parks; MSU Museum; University of Alberta Press; University of Manitoba Press
Foreign Rep(s): East-West Export Books (Royden Muranaka) (Asia, Australia, Far East, Hawaii, New Zealand, Pacific Islands); Eurospan (Europe); Raincoast Books-University of British Columbia Press (Canada)
Orders to: Chicago Distribution Center, 11030 S Langley Ave, Chicago, IL 60628 *Tel:* 773-702-7000 *Toll Free Tel:* 800-621-2736 *Fax:* 773-702-7212 *Toll Free Fax:* 800-621-8476 *E-mail:* orders@press.uchicago.edu *Web Site:* www.press.uchicago.edu
Returns: Chicago Distribution Center, 11030 S Langley Ave, Chicago, IL 60628 *Tel:* 773-702-7000 *Toll Free Tel:* 800-621-2736 *Fax:* 773-702-7212 *Toll Free Fax:* 800-621-8476 *E-mail:* orders@press.uchicago.edu *Web Site:* www.press.uchicago.edu
Distribution Center: Chicago Distribution Center, 11030 S Langley Ave, Chicago, IL 60628 *Tel:* 773-702-7000 *Toll Free Tel:* 800-621-2736 *Fax:* 773-702-7212 *Toll Free Fax:* 800-621-8476 *E-mail:* orders@press.uchicago.edu *Web Site:* www.press.uchicago.edu
Membership(s): American Association of University Presses; Society for Scholarly Publishing

Midmarch Arts Press
300 Riverside Dr, New York, NY 10025-5239
SAN: 200-8882
Tel: 212-666-6990
Web Site: midmarchartspress.org
Key Personnel
Dir: Cynthia Navaretta
Founded: 1973
Books.
ISBN Prefix(es): 978-1-877675; 978-0-9602476
Number of titles published annually: 3 Print
Total Titles: 118 Print
Returns: 19 Deep Six Dr, East Hampton, NY 11937
Warehouse: 19 Deep Six Dr, East Hampton, NY 11937
Membership(s): College Art Association; International Association of Art Critics

Midnight Marquee Press Inc
9721 Britinay Lane, Baltimore, MD 21234
Tel: 410-665-1198
E-mail: mmarquee@aol.com
Web Site: www.midmar.com
Key Personnel
Pres: Gary Svehla
VP & Lib Sales Dir: Susan Svehla
Founded: 1995
Publisher of books, two magazines, graphic novels with the main focus on film history, biographies & mysteries.
ISBN Prefix(es): 978-1-887664; 978-1-936168
Number of titles published annually: 6 Print
Total Titles: 150 Print

§Mighty Media Press
1201 Currie Ave, Minneapolis, MN 55403
Tel: 612-455-0252 *Fax:* 612-338-4817
Web Site: www.mightymediapress.com
Key Personnel
Publr & Creative Dir: Nancy Tuminelly *Tel:* 612-338-2075 *E-mail:* nancy@mightymedia.com
Mktg Dir & Publicity: Sammy Bosch *E-mail:* sammy@mightymedia.com
Founded: 2005
Delivers captivating books & media that ignite a child's curiosity, imagination, social awareness & sense of adventure.
ISBN Prefix(es): 978-0-9765201; 978-0-9798249; 978-0-9824584; 978-0-9830219; 978-1-938063
Number of titles published annually: 10 Print; 10 E-Book
Total Titles: 36 Print; 40 E-Book
Imprints: Mighty Media Junior Readers (middle grade literature); Mighty Media Kids (picture books & first reader/beginner books); Red Portal Press
Foreign Rights: Letter Soup Rights Agency (Allison Olson) (worldwide)
Returns: Perseus Distribution, Returns Dept, 193 Edwards Dr, Jackson, TN
Distribution Center: Perseus Distribution, 1094 Flex Dr, Jackson, TN 38301 *Toll Free Tel:* 800-343-4499 *Web Site:* www.perseusdistribution.com
Publishers Group West, 1700 Fourth St, Berkeley, CA 94710 *Tel:* 510-809-3700 *Toll Free Tel:* 800-788-3123
Membership(s): ABA; The Children's Book Council; Midwest Independent Booksellers Association; Midwest Independent Publishing Association; Minnesota Book Publishers Roundtable; Minnesota Bookbuilders; Society of Children's Book Writers & Illustrators

Mike Murach & Associates Inc
4340 N Knoll Ave, Fresno, CA 93722
SAN: 264-2255
Tel: 559-440-9071 *Toll Free Tel:* 800-221-5528 *Fax:* 559-440-0963
E-mail: murachbooks@murach.com
Web Site: www.murach.com
Key Personnel
Pres: Ben Murach
Mktg: Cynthia Vasquez *Tel:* 559-440-9071 ext 18 *E-mail:* cyndi@murach.com
Founded: 1974
Computer books.
ISBN Prefix(es): 978-0-911625; 978-1-890774; 978-1-943872; 978-1-943873
Number of titles published annually: 5 Print
Total Titles: 50 Print
Distributed by Shroff Publishers (reprints)
Foreign Rep(s): BPB Publications Ltd (India); Gazelle Book Services Ltd (Continental Europe, UK); Woodslane Pty Ltd (Australia, New Zealand)

§Milady
Division of Cengage Learning
Executive Woods, 5 Maxwell Dr, Clifton Park, NY 12065-2919
Tel: 518-348-2300 *Toll Free Tel:* 800-998-7498 *Fax:* 518-373-6309
E-mail: info@milady.com
Web Site: milady.cengage.com
Key Personnel
Exec Dir: Sandra Bruce
Sr Dir, Sales & Mktg: Gerard McAvey
Prod Dir: Corina Santoro
Founded: 1928
Textbooks, workbooks, exam reviews, digital solutions & instructional videos, newsletters, cosmetology & beauty education.
ISBN Prefix(es): 978-0-8273; 978-1-56253; 978-0-7668; 978-0-87350; 978-1-4018; 978-1-4180
Number of titles published annually: 20 Print
Total Titles: 50 Print
Foreign Office(s): Cengage Learning-Australia, 80 Dorcas St, Level 7, South Melbourne, Victoria 3205, Australia *Tel:* (03) 9685 4111 *Fax:* (03) 9685 4199
Cengage Learning-Latin America, Av Santa Fe 505 piso 12, Col Cruz Manca Sante Fe, Cuajimalpa CP, 05349 Mexico, DF, Mexico *Tel:* 55 1500 6000
Cengage Learning-EMEA, Cheriton House, North Way, Andover, Hampshire SP10 5BE, United Kingdom *Tel:* (01264) 332424 *Fax:* (01264) 342763
Distribution Center: 10650 Toebben Dr, Independence, KY 41051
Membership(s): American Association of Cosmetology Schools; National Association of Barber Boards of America; The National-Interstate Council of State Boards of Cosmetology Inc; Professional Beauty Association

Military Info Publishing
PO Box 41211, Plymouth, MN 55442
Tel: 763-533-8627 *Fax:* 763-533-8627
E-mail: publisher@military-info.com
Web Site: www.military-info.com
Key Personnel
Publr: Bruce A Hanesalo
Founded: 1987
Reprint historical military technology, including 34 books, 11,000 photocopies & 400 other items.
ISBN Prefix(es): 978-1-886848
Number of titles published annually: 4 Print
Total Titles: 34 Print

Military Living Publications
Division of Military Marketing Services Inc
333 Maple Ave E, Suite 3130, Vienna, VA 22180-4717
Tel: 703-237-0203 *Fax:* 703-552-7552

E-mail: customerservice@militaryliving.com
Web Site: www.militaryliving.com
Key Personnel
CEO: William R Crawford, Sr
Founded: 1969
Publisher of military travel atlases, maps & directories; for military only.
ISBN Prefix(es): 978-0-914862; 978-1-931424
Number of titles published annually: 8 Print
Total Titles: 12 Print
Foreign Rep(s): US Forces Exchanges

Milkweed Editions
1011 Washington Ave S, Suite 300, Minneapolis, MN 55415-1246
Tel: 612-332-3192 *Toll Free Tel:* 800-520-6455 *Fax:* 612-215-2550
Web Site: milkweed.org
Key Personnel
CEO & Publr: Daniel Slager
Mng Dir: Patrick Thomas *E-mail:* patrick_thomas@milkweed.org
Ed: Joey McGarvey
Warehouse Mgr: Celia Mattison
Engagement Coord: Abby Travis
Founded: 1980
Literary, nonprofit, independent press.
ISBN Prefix(es): 978-0-915943; 978-1-57131
Number of titles published annually: 18 Print; 18 E-Book; 1 Audio
Total Titles: 250 Print; 10 E-Book; 5 Audio
Distribution Center: Publishers Group West, 1700 Fourth St, Berkeley, CA 94710 *Tel:* 510-809-3700 *Toll Free Tel:* 800-788-3123 *Fax:* 510-528-3444
Membership(s): ABA; The Children's Book Council; Community of Literary Magazines & Presses; Independent Book Publishers Association; Midwest Independent Booksellers Association; Southern Independent Booksellers Alliance

Millbrook Press
Imprint of Lerner Publishing Group Inc
241 First Ave N, Minneapolis, MN 55401
Tel: 612-332-3344 *Toll Free Tel:* 800-328-4929 (US only) *Fax:* 612-332-7615 *Toll Free Fax:* 800-332-1132
E-mail: info@lernerbooks.com; custserve@lernerbooks.com
Web Site: www.lernerbooks.com; www.facebook.com/millbrookpress
Key Personnel
Chmn: Harry J Lerner
CFO & EVP: Margaret Thomas
Pres & Publr: Adam Lerner
EVP, Sales: David Wexler
VP, Ed-in-Chief: Patricia M Stockland
Edit Dir: Carol Hinz
Dir of Rts, Spec Sales & Intl Dist: Maria Kjoller
Group Mktg Dir: Jill Braithwaite
School & Lib Mktg Dir: Lois Wallentine
Dir, HR: Cyndi Radant
Founded: 1989
ISBN Prefix(es): 978-1-56294; 978-1-878841; 978-0-7613; 978-1-878137
Total Titles: 630 Print; 775 E-Book
Foreign Rep(s): INT Press Distribution (Australia); Monarch (Canada); Phambili (Southern Africa); Publishers Marketing Services (Brunei, Malaysia, Singapore); Saunders (Canada); South Pacific Books (New Zealand)
Foreign Rights: Japan Foreign-Rights Centre (Japan); Korea Copyright Center (Korea); Michelle Lapautre Agence Junior (France); Literarische Agentur Silke Weniger (Germany)
Warehouse: Lerner Publishing Group, 1251 Washington Ave N, Minneapolis, MN 55401, Mgr: Ken Rued

Richard K Miller Associates
4132 Atlanta Hwy, Suite 110, Loganville, GA 30052
Toll Free Tel: 888-928-RKMA (928-7562) *Toll Free Fax:* 877-928-7562
Web Site: rkma.com
Key Personnel
Pres: Richard K Miller *E-mail:* richard.miller@rkma.com
Founded: 1972
Market research reference handbooks for college & corporate libraries. Subjects include consumer behavior, marketing, retail, travel, healthcare, entertainment & restaurants.
ISBN Prefix(es): 978-1-57783
Number of titles published annually: 6 Print; 6 Online; 1 E-Book
Total Titles: 12 Print; 12 Online; 12 E-Book

Robert Miller Gallery
524 W 26 St, New York, NY 10001
Tel: 212-366-4774 *Fax:* 212-366-4454
E-mail: rmg@robertmillergallery.com
Web Site: www.robertmillergallery.com
Key Personnel
Dir: Betsy Miller
Founded: 1977
Art books on artwork by represented artists.
ISBN Prefix(es): 978-0-944680
Number of titles published annually: 3 Print
Total Titles: 30 Print

§Milliken Publishing Co
Division of The Lorenz Corp
501 E Third St, Dayton, OH 45402
Mailing Address: PO Box 802, Dayton, OH 45401-0802
Tel: 937-228-6118 *Toll Free Tel:* 800-444-1144 *Fax:* 937-223-2042
E-mail: order@lorenz.com
Web Site: www.lorenzeducationalpress.com
Key Personnel
VP, Mktg: Debra Kaiser *E-mail:* debk@lorenz.com
Founded: 1960
Educational publishing division includes visual resources, instructional guides & reproducibles; elementary supplementals.
ISBN Prefix(es): 978-0-88335; 978-1-55863; 978-1-4291; 978-0-7877
Number of titles published annually: 20 Print
Total Titles: 400 Print; 20 CD-ROM; 400 E-Book; 6 Audio
Membership(s): Education Market Association

§The Minerals, Metals & Materials Society (TMS)
Affiliate of AIME
5700 Corporate Dr, Suite 750, Pittsburgh, PA 15237
Tel: 724-776-9000 *Toll Free Tel:* 800-759-4867 *Fax:* 724-776-3770
E-mail: publications@tms.org (orders)
Web Site: www.tms.org/bookstore (orders); www.tms.org
Key Personnel
Exec Dir: James J Robinson *E-mail:* robinson@tms.org
Content Sr Mgr: Matt Baker *E-mail:* mbaker@tms.org
Founded: 1871
Leading professional society dedicated to the development & dissemination of scientific & engineering knowledge for materials-centered technology. The society is the only professional organization that encompasses the entire spectrum of materials & engineering, from minerals processing through the advanced applications of materials.
ISBN Prefix(es): 978-0-87339
Number of titles published annually: 20 Print
Total Titles: 200 Print

Minnesota Historical Society Press
Division of Minnesota Historical Society
345 Kellogg Blvd W, St Paul, MN 55102-1906
SAN: 202-6384
Tel: 651-259-3205 *Toll Free Tel:* 800-621-2736 (warehouse) *Fax:* 651-297-1345 *Toll Free Fax:* 800-621-8476 (warehouse)
E-mail: info-mnhspress@mnhs.org
Web Site: www.mnhs.org/mnhspress
Key Personnel
Dir & Intl Rts: Pamela McClanahan *Tel:* 651-259-3210 *E-mail:* pamela.mcclanahan@mnhs.org
Ed-in-Chief: Ann Regan *Tel:* 651-259-3206 *E-mail:* ann.regan@mnhs.org
Mng Ed: Shannon M Pennefeather *Tel:* 651-259-3212 *E-mail:* shannon.pennefeather@mnhs.org
Acqs Ed: Josh Leventhal *E-mail:* josh.leventhal@mnhs.org
Mktg & Sales Mgr: Mary Poggione *Tel:* 651-259-3204 *E-mail:* mary.poggione@mnhs.org
Sales Mgr: Jerry Bileak *E-mail:* jerry.bileak@mnhs.org
Founded: 1849
Scholarly & trade books on Upper Midwest history & prehistory.
ISBN Prefix(es): 978-0-87351; 978-1-68134
Number of titles published annually: 20 Print; 10 E-Book
Total Titles: 430 Print; 140 E-Book; 6 Audio
Foreign Rep(s): Gazelle Book Services Ltd (Europe, UK)
Warehouse: Chicago Distribution Center, 11030 S Langley Ave, Chicago, IL 60628 *Toll Free Tel:* 800-621-2736 (orders) *Toll Free Fax:* 800-621-8476 (orders)
Membership(s): American Association of University Presses

MIT List Visual Arts Center
MIT E 15-109, 20 Ames St, Cambridge, MA 02139
Tel: 617-253-4400; 617-253-4680 *Fax:* 617-258-7265
E-mail: mlinga@mit.edu
Web Site: listart.mit.edu
Key Personnel
Dir: Paul C Ha
Founded: 1966
Contemporary art.
ISBN Prefix(es): 978-0-938437
Number of titles published annually: 6 Print
Distribution Center: Distributed Art Publishers (DAP), 155 Sixth Ave, 2nd fl, New York, NY 10013 *Tel:* 212-627-1999 *Fax:* 212-627-9484 *E-mail:* orders@artbook.com

§The MIT Press
One Rogers St, Cambridge, MA 02142
SAN: 202-6414
Tel: 617-253-5255 *Toll Free Tel:* 800-207-8354 (orders) *Fax:* 617-258-6779; 617-577-1545 (orders)
Web Site: mitpress.mit.edu
Key Personnel
Cont: Charles Hale *Tel:* 617-258-0577 *E-mail:* chale@mit.edu
Dir: Amy Brand *Tel:* 617-253-4078 *E-mail:* amybrand@mit.edu
Dir, Fin & Opers & Assoc Dir: Brent Oberlin *Tel:* 617-253-5250 *E-mail:* brento@mit.edu
Dir, Intl Property Licensing: William Smith
Dir, Journals & Open Access: Nick Lindsay *Tel:* 617-258-0594 *E-mail:* nlindsay@mit.edu
Mktg Dir: Katie Hope *Tel:* 617-258-0603 *E-mail:* khope@mit.edu
Dir, Sales: David Goldberg *Tel:* 617-253-8838 *E-mail:* davidgol@mit.edu
Dir, Technol: Bill Trippe *Tel:* 617-452-3747 *E-mail:* trippe@mit.edu
Edit Dir: Gita Manaktala *Tel:* 617-253-3172 *E-mail:* manak@mit.edu
Exec Ed: Marie Lee *Tel:* 617-253-1558 *E-mail:* marielee@mit.edu

Mng Ed: Michael Sims *Tel:* 617-253-2080 *E-mail:* msims@mit.edu
Exec Ed: Roger L Conover *Tel:* 617-253-1677 *E-mail:* conover@mit.edu; Robert Prior *Tel:* 617-253-1584 *E-mail:* prior@mit.edu
Sr Acqs Ed: John S Covell *Tel:* 617-253-3757 *E-mail:* jcovell@mit.edu; Phil Laughlin *Tel:* 617-252-1636 *E-mail:* laughlin@mit.edu; Douglas Sery *Tel:* 617-253-5187 *E-mail:* dsery@mit.edu
Acqs Ed: Beth Clevenger *Tel:* 617-253-4113 *E-mail:* eclev@mit.edu
Acqs Ed, Physical Sciences, Engg & Math: Jermey Matthews
Ad & Digital Mktg Mgr: Anar Badalov *Tel:* 617-253-3516 *E-mail:* badalov@mit.edu
Design Mgr: Yasuyo Iguchi *Tel:* 617-253-8034 *E-mail:* iguchi@mit.edu
Digital Mgr: Anna Pollock-Nelson *Tel:* 617-258-0556 *E-mail:* annapn@mit.edu
Exhibits Mgr: John Costello *Tel:* 617-258-5764 *E-mail:* jcostell@mit.edu
Prodn Mgr: Janet Rossi *Tel:* 617-253-2882 *E-mail:* janett@mit.edu
Promos & Direct Mail Mgr: Astrid Baehrecke *Tel:* 617-253-7297 *E-mail:* baehreck@mit.edu
Publicity Mgr: Colleen Lanick *Tel:* 617-253-2874 *E-mail:* colleenl@mit.edu
Subs Rts Mgr: Cristina Sanmartin *Tel:* 617-253-0629 *E-mail:* csan@mit.edu
Textbook Promos Mgr: Michelle Pullano *Tel:* 617-253-3620 *E-mail:* mpullano@mit.edu
Asst Journals Mgr & Journals Busn Mgr: June McCaull *Tel:* 617-258-0593 *E-mail:* jmccaull@mit.edu
Bookstore Mgr: John Jenkins *Tel:* 617-253-5249 *E-mail:* jjenkins@mit.edu
Founded: 1962
Scholarly & professional books, advanced textbooks, nonfiction trade books & reference books; architecture & design, cognitive sciences & linguistics, computer science & artificial intelligence, economics & management sciences, environmental studies; philosophy, neuroscience; technology studies; new media; paperbacks, journals.
ISBN Prefix(es): 978-0-262; 978-0-89706
Number of titles published annually: 250 Print
Total Titles: 8,000 Print; 5 CD-ROM; 2 Online; 1 E-Book
Imprints: Bradford Books
Foreign Office(s): The MIT Press Ltd, One Duchess St, Suite 2, London W1W 6AN, United Kingdom *Tel:* (020) 7306 0603 *Fax:* (020) 7306 0604 *E-mail:* info@mitpress.org.uk
Distributor for AAAI Press; Afterall Books; Canadian Centre for Architecture; Semiotext(e); Zone Books
Foreign Rep(s): APD Singapore Pte Ltd (Ian Pringle) (Brunei, Cambodia, Indonesia, Laos, Malaysia, Myanmar, Philippines, Singapore, Thailand, Vietnam); Aromix Books Company Ltd (Jane Lam & Nick Wonn) (Hong Kong); Avicenna Partnership Ltd (Claire de Gruchy) (Algeria, Cyprus, Israel, Jordan, Malta, Morocco, Palestine, Tunisia, Turkey); Avicenna Partnership Ltd (Bill Kennedy) (Bahrain, Egypt, Iran, Iraq, Kuwait, Lebanon, Libya, Oman, Qatar, Saudi Arabia, Syria, United Arab Emirates, Yemen); Book Marketing Services (S Janakiraman) (Bangladesh, India, Sri Lanka); Cranbury International LLC (Renato Reichmann) (Brazil); Cranbury International LLC (Patricia Nelson) (British Columbia, CN); Cranbury International LLC (John Eklund) (Canada exc British Columbia); Cranbury International LLC (John Atkin) (Caribbean); Cranbury International LLC (Jose Rios) (Central America, Mexico, South America); Cranbury International LLC (David Rivera) (Dominican Republic, Puerto Rico); Cranbury International LLC (Patrice Ammon-Jagdco) (Trinidad and Tobago); Everest International Publishing Services (Wei Zhao) (China); Footprint Books Pty Ltd (Australia, New Zealand); IMA (Tony Moggach) (Africa, Cameroon, Ethiopia, The Gambia, Ghana, Kenya, Malawi, Mauritius, Nigeria, Rwanda, Tanzania, Uganda, Zambia); Information & Culture Korea (ICK) (Se-Yung Jun & Min-Hwa Yoo) (South Korea); BK Norton (Chiafeng Peng) (Taiwan); Rockbook Inc (Akiko Iwamoto & Gilles Fauveau) (Japan); University Press Group (Dominique Bartshukoff) (Austria, Croatia, Czech Republic, Germany, Greece, Hungary, Netherlands, Portugal, Slovenia, Spain); University Press Group (Peter Jacques) (Belgium, Europe, France, Italy, Poland, Scandinavia, Switzerland); University Press Group (Ben Mitchell) (Europe, Ireland, UK); World Press (Saleem Malik) (Pakistan)
Foreign Rights: Agencia Literaria Carmen Balcells SA (Maribel Luque) (Spain); Bardon-Chinese Media Agency (Joanne Yang) (Taiwan); The Berlin Agency (Frauke Jung-Lindemann) (Germany); The English Agency (Tsutomu Yawata) (Japan); Graal Literary Agency (Lukasz Wrobel) (Poland); The Deborah Harris Agency (Ilana Kurshan) (Israel); The Kayi Agency (Dilek Kayi) (Turkey); KCC (Sageun Lee) (Korea); Alexander Korzheneveski Agency (Alexander Korzheneveski) (Russia); OA Literary Agency (Michael Avramides) (Greece); Reiser Literary Agency (Roberto Gilodi) (Italy); Agencia Riff (Joao Riff) (Brazil)
Warehouse: Triliteral LLC, 100 Maple Ridge Dr, Cumberland, RI 02864 *Tel:* 401-658-4226 *Toll Free Tel:* 800-405-1619 *Fax:* 401-658-4193 *Toll Free Fax:* 800-406-9145 *E-mail:* orders@triliteral.org
Membership(s): AAP; Association of American University Presses

Mitchell Lane Publishers Inc
PO Box 196, Hockessin, DE 19707
SAN: 858-3749
Tel: 302-234-9426 *Toll Free Tel:* 800-814-5484 *Fax:* 302-234-4742 *Toll Free Fax:* 866-834-4164
E-mail: orders@mitchelllane.com
Web Site: www.mitchelllane.com
Key Personnel
Pres & Publr: Barbara J Mitchell *E-mail:* barbaramitchell@mitchelllane.com
VP, Sales & Mktg: Robert P Mitchell *Tel:* 302-250-2880 *E-mail:* robertmitchell@mitchelllane.com
Founded: 1993
Nonfiction for children & young adults.
ISBN Prefix(es): 978-1-883845; 978-1-58415; 978-1-61228; 978-1-68020
Number of titles published annually: 80 Print; 80 E-Book
Total Titles: 1,200 Print; 300 E-Book
Editorial Office(s): 1104 Kelly Dr, Newark, DE 19711
Foreign Rep(s): CrossCan Educational (Canada); Edu-Reference (Canada); David Hall (Africa, Australia, Continental Europe, Ireland, Malaysia, Singapore, South Africa)
Orders to: 1104 Kelly Dr, Newark, DE 19711
Warehouse: 20 Shea Way, Suite 205, Newark, DE 19713
Membership(s): Educational Book & Media Association

Mobility International USA
132 E Broadway, Suite 343, Eugene, OR 97401
Tel: 541-343-1284 *Fax:* 541-343-6812
E-mail: info@miusa.org
Web Site: www.miusa.org
Key Personnel
CEO & Exec Dir: Susan Sygall
Founded: 1981
The mission of Mobility International USA (MIUSA) is to empower people with disabilities through international exchange & international development to achieve their human rights.
MIUSA manages the National Clearinghouse on Disability & Exchange (NCDE), a project sponsored by the Bureau of Educational and Cultural Affairs of the US Department of State.
ISBN Prefix(es): 978-1-880034
Number of titles published annually: 4 Print
Total Titles: 6 Print

§Modern Language Association of America (MLA)
85 Broad St, Suite 500, New York, NY 10004-2434
SAN: 202-6422
Tel: 646-576-5000 *Fax:* 646-458-0030
Web Site: www.mla.org
Key Personnel
Exec Dir: Paula Krebs
Head, Mktg & Sales: Kathleen M Hansen *E-mail:* khansen@mla.org
Head, Publg Opers: Angela Gibson *E-mail:* agibson@mla.org
Founded: 1883
Research & teaching tools in languages & literature; professional publications for college teachers.
ISBN Prefix(es): 978-0-87352; 978-1-60329
Number of titles published annually: 12 Print
Total Titles: 300 Print; 1 CD-ROM; 1 Online

§Modern Memoirs
34 Main St, No 6, Amherst, MA 01002-2367
Tel: 413-253-2353
Web Site: www.modernmemoirs.com; www.whitepoppypress.com
Key Personnel
Founder & Pres: Kitty Axelson-Berry *E-mail:* kitty@modernmemoirs.com
Assoc Publr: Vinsula Hastings *E-mail:* vinsula@modernmemoirs.com
Founded: 1994
Private publishing services for discerning clients.
This publisher has indicated that 100% of their product line is author subsidized.
ISBN Prefix(es): 978-0-9662602; 978-0-9772337; 978-0-9856595; 978-0-9834752; 978-0-9905709
Number of titles published annually: 12 Print
Total Titles: 200 Print
Imprints: White Poppy Press
Membership(s): Association of Personal Historians; Independent Book Publishers Association

Modern Publishing
Division of Kappa Books Publishers LLC
6198 Butler Pike, Suite 200, Blue Bell, PA 19422
Tel: 215-643-6385 *Fax:* 215-628-3571
Web Site: www.modernpublishing.com
Key Personnel
Pres: Andrew Steinberg *E-mail:* asteinberg@modernpublishing.com
Founded: 1969
Juvenile, reference books; general nonfiction, humor, puzzle books.
This publisher has indicated that 25% of their product line is author subsidized.
ISBN Prefix(es): 978-0-7666

MoMA, see The Museum of Modern Art (MoMA)

The Monacelli Press
236 W 27 St, 4th fl, New York, NY 10001
Tel: 212-229-9925 (ext 25)
E-mail: contact@monacellipress.com
Web Site: www.monacellipress.com
Key Personnel
Publr: Gianfranco Monacelli
Exec Ed, Fine & Applied Arts: Victoria Craven
Prodn Dir: Michael Vagnetti

Mng Ed: Elizabeth White
Sr Ed, Architecture & Design: Alan Rapp
Consulting Ed: Nancy Green
Publicity & Mktg Mgr: Jaime Nelson Noven
Founded: 1994
High-quality, illustrated, hardcover & paperback books on art, architecture, decorative arts, interior design, fashion, photography, landscape, urbanism & graphic design.
ISBN Prefix(es): 978-1-58093; 978-1-885254
Imprints: Monacelli Studio (applied arts)
Foreign Rep(s): Penguin Random House Canada (Canada); Publishers Group UK (Ireland, UK)
Orders to: Penguin Random House Publisher Services (PRHPS), 400 Hahn Rd, Westminster, MD 21157 *Toll Free Tel:* 800-733-3000 *Toll Free Fax:* 800-659-2436 *E-mail:* distribution@penguinrandomhouse.com

Mondial
203 W 107 St, Suite 6-C, New York, NY 10025
Tel: 646-807-8031 *Fax:* 208-361-2863
E-mail: contact@mondialbooks.com
Web Site: www.mondialbooks.com
Key Personnel
Owner: Uday K Dhar
Publr: Ulrich Becker
Founded: 2004
Specialize in fiction & nonfiction translated into English from other languages or originally written in English or German. All kinds of publications (fiction & nonfiction) in the international language Esperanto.
ISBN Prefix(es): 978-1-59569
Number of titles published annually: 15 Print; 15 E-Book
Total Titles: 220 Print; 1 CD-ROM; 110 E-Book

Mondo Publishing
980 Avenue of the Americas, New York, NY 10018
Tel: 212-268-3560 *Toll Free Tel:* 888-88-MONDO (886-6636) *Toll Free Fax:* 888-532-4492
E-mail: info@mondopub.com
Web Site: www.mondopub.com
Key Personnel
Pres: Mark Vineis
Edit Dir: Ellen Ungaro
Mktg: Sonya Fleming
Founded: 1986
K-5 literacy materials & professional development services.
ISBN Prefix(es): 978-1-879531; 978-1-57255; 978-1-58653; 978-1-59034; 978-1-59336; 978-1-60201; 978-1-60715; 978-1-61736; 978-1-62889; 978-1-63060; 978-1-63061; 978-1-68156
Number of titles published annually: 200 Print
Total Titles: 500 Print
Imprints: Mondo
Warehouse: 200 Sherwood Ave, Farmingdale, NY 11735
Membership(s): The Children's Book Council

Money Market Directories
Unit of Standard & Poor's
401 E Market St, Charlottesville, VA 22902
Mailing Address: PO Box 1608, Charlottesville, VA 22902-1608
Tel: 434-977-1450 *Toll Free Tel:* 800-446-2810 *Fax:* 434-979-9962
E-mail: mmdsales@spcapitaliq.com
Web Site: www.mmdwebaccess.com
Key Personnel
Mng Dir, S&P Capital IQ: Jay Zacter
Dir, Prodn & Edit Servs: Jehu Martin
Direct Mktg Specialist: Misty Combs *E-mail:* misty.combs@spcapitaliq.com
Founded: 1970
Financial information regarding pension funds, nonprofits & service providers plus investment managers & consultants. Publications available as e-directories & online.
ISBN Prefix(es): 978-0-939712
Number of titles published annually: 3 Print; 2 CD-ROM; 1 Online; 4 E-Book
Total Titles: 3 Print; 2 CD-ROM, 1 Online, 4 E-Book
Foreign Office(s): International Commerce Ctr, One Austin Rd W, Unit 6901, Level 69, Kowloon, Hong Kong *Tel:* 2532 8020 *Fax:* 2532 3577
20 Canada Sq, 12th fl, London, United Kingdom *Tel:* (020) 7176 3449 *Fax:* (020) 7176 1203

The Mongolia Society Inc
Indiana University, 322 Goodbody Hall, 1011 E Third St, Bloomington, IN 47405-7005
Tel: 812-855-4078 *Fax:* 812-855-4078
E-mail: monsoc@indiana.edu
Web Site: www.mongoliasociety.org
Key Personnel
Pres: Dr Alicia Campi
VP: Dr Christopher Atwood
Exec Dir: Susie Drost
Mng Ed: David Bade
Secy: Dr Peter Marsh
Treas: Tserenchunt Ledges
Founded: 1961
Interests, culture & language of Mongolia.
ISBN Prefix(es): 978-0-910980
Number of titles published annually: 4 Print
Total Titles: 60 Print

Monkfish Book Publishing Co
22 E Market St, Suite 304, Rhinebeck, NY 12572
Tel: 845-876-4861
E-mail: monkfish@monkfishpublishing.com
Web Site: www.monkfishpublishing.com
Key Personnel
Publr: Paul Cohen *E-mail:* paul@monkfishpublishing.com
Founded: 2002
Publisher of spirituality & religion titles. Also operates a self-publishing company.
ISBN Prefix(es): 978-0-9823246; 978-0-9766843; 978-0-9726357; 978-0-9798828; 978-0-9749359; 978-0-9789427; 978-0-9824530; 978-0-9825255; 978-0-9826441; 978-0-9830517; 978-0-9833589; 978-1-936940; 978-1-939681; 978-1-944037
Number of titles published annually: 6 Print; 4 Online; 6 E-Book
Total Titles: 45 Print; 32 Online; 32 E-Book
Divisions: Epigraph Publishing Service (subsidy publishers)
Orders to: Consortium Book Sales & Distribution, 3413 13 Ave NE, Suite 101, Minneapolis, MN 55413-1007 *Toll Free Tel:* 800-283-3572
Distribution Center: Consortium Book Sales & Distribution, 3413 13 Ave NE, Suite 101, Minneapolis, MN 55413-1007 *Tel:* 612-746-2600 *Toll Free Tel:* 800-283-3572 *Fax:* 612-746-2606

Montana Historical Society Press
Capitol Complex, 225 N Roberts St, Helena, MT 59620
Mailing Address: PO Box 201201, Helena, MT 59620-1201
Tel: 406-444-0090 (edit); 406-444-2890 (orders/mktg); 406-444-2694 *Toll Free Tel:* 800-243-9900 *Fax:* 406-444-2696 (orders/mktg)
Web Site: mhs.mt.gov/pubs
Key Personnel
Ed & Dir, Pubns: Molly Holz *E-mail:* mholz@mt.gov
Busn Mgr: Tammy Ryan *E-mail:* tryan@mt.gov
Membership Coord: Rebecca Baumann *Tel:* 406-444-2918 *E-mail:* mhsmembership@mt.gov
Asst Ed: Christy Eckerle *E-mail:* ceckerle@mt.gov
Founded: 1891
ISBN Prefix(es): 978-0-917298; 978-0-9721522; 978-0-9759196; 978-0-9801292; 978-1-940527
Number of titles published annually: 5 Print
Total Titles: 50 Print; 1 Online; 1 Audio
Distribution Center: National Book Network (NBN), 15200 NBN Way, Blue Ridge Summit, PA 17214 *Tel:* 717-794-3800 *Toll Free Tel:* 800-462-6420 *Fax:* 717-794-3828 *Toll Free Fax:* 800-338-4550 *E-mail:* customercare@nbnbooks.com *Web Site:* www.nbnbooks.com

Montemayor Press
663 Hyland Hill Rd, Washington, VT 05675
Mailing Address: PO Box 546, Montpelier, VT 05601
Tel: 802-552-0750
E-mail: mail@montemayorpress.com
Web Site: www.montemayorpress.com
Key Personnel
Publr: Edward Myers
Exec Ed: Edith Poor
Founded: 1999
Independent publisher whose mission is to print & distribute quality fiction & nonfiction to adult, young adult & juvenile audiences.
ISBN Prefix(es): 978-0-9674477; 978-1-932727
Number of titles published annually: 4 Print; 2 E-Book
Total Titles: 24 Print; 4 E-Book
Membership(s): Community of Literary Magazines & Presses; Independent Book Publishers Association

Monthly Review Press
Division of Monthly Review Foundation Inc
146 W 29 St, Suite 6W, New York, NY 10001
SAN: 202-6481
Tel: 212-691-2555 *Toll Free Tel:* 800-670-9499 *Fax:* 212-727-3676
E-mail: mreview@igc.org
Web Site: monthlyreview.org
Key Personnel
Mng Dir: Martin Paddio
Edit Dir: Michael D Yates
Mktg Publicity Mgr: Susie Day
Founded: 1949
Economics, politics, history, sociology & world affairs.
ISBN Prefix(es): 978-0-85345; 978-1-58367
Number of titles published annually: 15 Print
Total Titles: 550 Print
Distributed by New York University Press
Billing Address: New York University Press, 838 Broadway, 3rd fl, New York, NY 10003
Orders to: New York University Press, 838 Broadway, 3rd fl, New York, NY 10003 *Toll Free Tel:* 800-996-6987 *Fax:* 212-995-3833 *E-mail:* orders@nyupress.org
Returns: Maple Logistics Solutions, Lebanon Distribution Ctr, 704 Legionaire Dr, Fredericksburg, PA 17026
Warehouse: Maple Logistics Solutions, Lebanon Distribution Ctr, 704 Legionaire Dr, Fredericksburg, PA 17026

Moody Publishers
Affiliate of Ministry of Moody Bible Institute
820 N La Salle Blvd, Chicago, IL 60610
SAN: 202-5604
Tel: 312-329-4000 *Toll Free Tel:* 800-678-8812 (cust serv) *Fax:* 312-329-2019
E-mail: mpcustomerservice@moody.edu
Web Site: www.moodypublishers.com
Key Personnel
SVP, Media: Greg Thornton
VP: Wade Koenig
Publicity Mgr: Janis Backing
Acqs Ed, Chapman: John Hinkley
Founded: 1894
Religion (interdenominational).
ISBN Prefix(es): 978-0-8024; 978-1-881273 (Northfield Publishing)

Number of titles published annually: 75 Print
Total Titles: 1,000 Print; 10 Audio
Imprints: Northfield Publishing; River North Fiction; WingSpread Publishers
Foreign Rep(s): Biblicum AS (Norway); Bookhouse Australia Ltd (Australia); Challenge Bookshops (Nigeria); Christian Art Wholesale (South Africa); Christian Literature Crusade (Hong Kong); David C Cook Distribution (Canada); Editeurs de Litterature Biblique (Germany); Euro-Outreach Ministries (East Africa, Kenya, Nairobi); Hong Kong Tien Dao Publishing House Ltd (Belgium); Kesho Publications (Zimbabwe); Matopo Book Room (Philippines); Overseas Missionary Fellowship (Canada); Rhema Boekimport (Singapore); S & U Book Centre (New Zealand); S-U Wholesale
Shipping Address: 215 W Locust St, Chicago, IL 60610

Morehouse Publishing
Imprint of Church Publishing Inc
19 E 34 St, New York, NY 10016
SAN: 202-6511
Tel: 212-592-1800 *Toll Free Tel:* 800-672-1789 (retail orders only); 800-251-3320 (wholesale orders only)
Web Site: www.morehousepublishing.com; www.churchpublishing.org
Key Personnel
VP, Prodn: Lorraine Simonello
Founded: 1884
Spirituality, religious, lay ministry, liturgy, church supplies, music CDs, all from an Episcopal/Anglican perspective. No illustrated children's books.
ISBN Prefix(es): 978-0-8192
Number of titles published annually: 40 Print; 35 E-Book
Total Titles: 800 Print; 650 E-Book
Distributed by Cokesbury (retail orders only); Abingdon Press (wholesale orders only)
Foreign Rep(s): Bayard Novalis Distribution (Canada); Norwich Books & Music (Europe)
Warehouse: UMPH Distribution Center, Nashville, TN

Morgan James Publishing
5 Penn Plaza, 23rd fl, New York, NY 10001
Tel: 212-655-5470 *Toll Free Tel:* 800-485-4943 *Fax:* 516-908-4496
E-mail: csauer@morganjamespublishing.com
Web Site: www.morganjamespublishing.com
Key Personnel
Founder: David L Hancock *E-mail:* david@morganjamespublishing.com
Founded: 2003
Provides entrepreneurs with the vital information, inspiration & guidance they need to be successful.
ISBN Prefix(es): 978-0-9746133; 978-0-9758570; 978-0-9760901; 978-0-9768491; 978-1-933596; 978-1-60037; 978-0-9815058; 978-0-9817906; 978-0-9820750; 978-0-9823793; 978-0-9835013; 978-0-9840316; 978-1-938467; 978-0-9846170; 978-0-9828590; 978-0-9833715; 978-1-61448; 978-0-9837125; 978-1-63047; 978-1-63195
Number of titles published annually: 130 Print; 90 E-Book
Total Titles: 2,000 Print
Imprints: Secure American Management (SAM) Institute
Returns: IPS Warehouse, 1280 Ingram Dr, Chambersburg, PA 17201
Membership(s): AAP

Morgan Kaufmann
Imprint of Elsevier Inc
50 Hampshire St, 5th fl, Cambridge, MA 02139
Toll Free Tel: 866-607-1417 *Fax:* 617-661-7061
Web Site: www.mkp.com; www.elsevier.com
Key Personnel
Publr: Jonathan Simpson
Founded: 1984
Computer science book publishers including database, networking, architecture, engineering, graphics & artificial intelligence.
ISBN Prefix(es): 978-1-55860
Number of titles published annually: 65 Print
Total Titles: 552 Print; 606 E-Book
Orders to: 3251 Riverport Lane, Maryland Heights, MO 63040
Returns: 3251 Riverport Lane, Maryland Heights, MO 63040
Warehouse: 3251 Riverport Lane, Maryland Heights, MO 63040

Morgan Reynolds Publishing
620 S Elm St, Suite 387, Greensboro, NC 27406
Tel: 336-275-1311 *Toll Free Tel:* 800-535-1504 *Fax:* 336-275-1152 *Toll Free Fax:* 800-535-5725
E-mail: editorial@morganreynolds.com; sales@morganreynolds.com
Web Site: www.morganreynolds.com
Key Personnel
Founder & Publr: John Riley
Mktg Dir: Anita Richardson *E-mail:* anita@morganreynolds.com
Founded: 1993
Hardcover trade & library-bound editions.
ISBN Prefix(es): 978-1-883846; 978-1-931798; 978-1-59935
Number of titles published annually: 50 Print
Total Titles: 300 Print

Moriah Books
PO Box 1094, Casper, WY 82602
Web Site: moriahbook.com
Founded: 2014
Independent publisher of Rocky Mountain regional, history, historical fiction & religious titles.
ISBN Prefix(es): 978-0-9970417
Number of titles published annually: 6 Print
Total Titles: 3 Print

Morning Sun Books Inc
1200 County Rd 523, Flemington, NJ 08822
Tel: 908-806-6216 *Fax:* 908-237-2407
E-mail: sales.morningsunbooks@gmail.com
Web Site: morningsunbooks.com
Key Personnel
Pres: Robert J Yanosey
Founded: 1986
Color photography of railroads during 1940-1970 period.
ISBN Prefix(es): 978-1-878887; 978-1-58248
Number of titles published annually: 36 Print
Total Titles: 500 Print
Editorial Office(s): 9 Pheasant Lane, Scotch Plains, NJ 07076

William Morrow & Co Inc, see HarperCollins Publishers

Morton Publishing Co
925 W Kenyon Ave, Unit 12, Englewood, CO 80110
SAN: 210-9174
Tel: 303-761-4805 *Fax:* 303-762-9923
E-mail: contact@morton-pub.com; returns@morton-pub.com
Web Site: www.morton-pub.com
Key Personnel
Pres: David Ferguson *E-mail:* davidf@morton-pub.com
VP, Opers: Chrissy DeMier *E-mail:* chrissyd@morton-pub.com
VP, Sales & Mktg: Carter Fenton *E-mail:* carterf@morton-pub.com
Returns: Heather Herman *E-mail:* heatherh@morton-pub.com
Founded: 1977
Allied health, biology, pharmacy, computer information technology, speech & educational.
ISBN Prefix(es): 978-0-89582; 978-1-61731
Number of titles published annually: 10 Print
Total Titles: 50 Print
Foreign Rep(s): Northrose Associates (Canada)

Mount Olive College Press
Affiliate of University of Mount Olive
634 Henderson St, Mount Olive, NC 28365
Tel: 919-658-2502 *Fax:* 919-658-7180
Web Site: www.umo.edu
Founded: 1990
Poetry, drama, biography, devotional, travel, essay, novel, cookbook, photography, children's books, literary criticism.
ISBN Prefix(es): 978-0-9627087; 978-1-880994; 978-1-59761
Number of titles published annually: 5 Print
Total Titles: 75 Print

Mountain n' Air Books
2947-A Honolulu Ave, La Crescenta, CA 91214
Mailing Address: PO Box 12540, La Crescenta, CA 91224-5540
Tel: 818-248-9345 *Toll Free Tel:* 800-446-9696 *Toll Free Fax:* 800-303-5578
Web Site: www.mountain-n-air.com
Key Personnel
Pres: Gilberto d'Urso *E-mail:* gilberto@mountain-n-air.com
Publr & Ed: Mary K d'Urso
Off Mgr: Elvira Sakalenka *E-mail:* elvira@mountain-n-air.com
Founded: 1985
Outdoor guides, nonfiction, cookbooks & travel adventures, maps.
ISBN Prefix(es): 978-1-879415
Number of titles published annually: 6 Print
Total Titles: 99 Print
Imprints: Mountain Air Books
Distributor for Tom Harrison Cartography

Mountain Press Publishing Co
1301 S Third W, Missoula, MT 59801
SAN: 202-8832
Mailing Address: PO Box 2399, Missoula, MT 59806-2399
Tel: 406-728-1900 *Toll Free Tel:* 800-234-5308 *Fax:* 406-728-1635
E-mail: info@mtnpress.com
Web Site: www.mountain-press.com
Key Personnel
History Ed: Gwen McKenna
Natural History & Roadside Geology Series Ed: Jennifer Carey
Gen Mgr: John Rimel *E-mail:* johnargyle@aol.com
Busn Mgr: Rob Williams
Mktg Mgr: Anne Iverson *Tel:* 406-728-1900 ext 131 *E-mail:* anne@mtnpress.com
Graphic Design: Jeannie Painter
Founded: 1948
ISBN Prefix(es): 978-0-87842; 978-0-9632562; 978-0-9626999; 978-1-886370; 978-1-889921; 978-1-892784; 978-0-9676747; 978-0-9717748; 978-0-9724827
Number of titles published annually: 20 Print
Total Titles: 150 Print
Imprints: Geology Underfoot Series; Mountain Sports Press Series; Roadside Geology Series; Roadside History Series; Tumbleweed Series
Distributor for Bucking Horse Books; Clark City Press; Hops Press; Npustin Press; RainStone Press; Western Edge Press

The Mountaineers Books
Division of The Mountaineers
1001 SW Klickitat Way, Suite 201, Seattle, WA 98134

Tel: 206-223-6303 *Toll Free Tel:* 800-553-4453 *Fax:* 206-223-6306 *Toll Free Fax:* 800-568-7604
E-mail: mbooks@mountaineersbooks.org; customerservice@mountaineersbooks.org
Web Site: www.mountaineersbooks.org
Key Personnel
Publr: Helen Cherullo *Tel:* 206-223-6303 ext 122
Ed-in-Chief: Kate Rogers *Tel:* 206-223-6303 ext 109
Sr Ed: Mary Metz *Tel:* 206-223-6303 ext 119
Dir, Sales & Mktg: Doug Canfield *Tel:* 206-223-6303 ext 114
Publicist: Emily White *Tel:* 206-223-6303 ext 138
Sales Rep: Darryl Booker
Founded: 1961
Mountaineering, backpacking, hiking, cross-country skiing, bicycling, canoeing, kayaking, trekking, nature, conservation, green living & sustainability; outdoor how-to, guidebooks & maps; nonfiction adventure-travel accounts; biographies of outdoor people; reprint editions of mountaineering classics; adventure narratives.
ISBN Prefix(es): 978-0-89886; 978-0-916890; 978-0-938567; 978-1-59485; 978-1-63374; 978-1-68051
Number of titles published annually: 30 Print
Total Titles: 550 Print
Imprints: Braided River; Skipstone
Distributor for Adventure Cycling Association; The American Alpine Club Press; Colorado Mountain Club Press
Foreign Rep(s): Cordee Publishing (UK)

§De Gruyter Mouton
Imprint of Walter de Gruyter GmbH & Co KG
125 Pearl St, Boston, MA 02110
Mailing Address: 121 High St, 3rd fl, Boston, MA 02110
Tel: 857-284-7073 *Fax:* 857-284-7358
E-mail: service@degruyter.com
Web Site: www.degruyter.com
Key Personnel
Ed: Lara Wysong *Tel:* 857-284-7073 ext 106 *E-mail:* laura.wysong@degruyter.com
Founded: 1956
Scholarly books & journals.
ISBN Prefix(es): 978-0-311
Number of titles published annually: 100 Print; 2 Online
Total Titles: 2,500 Print; 3 CD-ROM; 10 Online
Foreign Office(s): Walter de Gruyter GmbH & Co KG, Genthinerstr 13, 10785 Berlin, Germany *Tel:* (030) 260 05-0 *Fax:* (030) 260 05-251
Distributed by Walter de Gruyter Inc
Foreign Rep(s): Allied Publishers Ltd (India, Nepal, Sri Lanka); Book Club International (Bangladesh); Combined Representatives Worldwide Inc (Philippines); D A Books & Journals (Australia, New Zealand); Walter de Gruyter Inc (Canada, Mexico); Verlags und Kommissionsbuchhandlung Dr Franz Hain (Austria); Kumi Trading (South Korea); Kweilin Bookstore (Taiwan); Maruzen Co Ltd (Japan); Pak Book Corp (Pakistan); Parry's Book Center (Sendjrjan Berhad) (Brunei, Malaysia, Singapore); Swinden Book Co Ltd (Hong Kong)
Orders to: PPF c/o Walter de Gruyter, PO Box 830350, Birmingham, AL 35202-0350 *Tel:* 205-995-1567 *Toll Free Tel:* 800-633-4931 *Fax:* 205-995-1588; TriLiteral LLC, 100 Maple Ridge Dr, Cumberland, RI 02864 *Tel:* 401-531-2800 *Toll Free Tel:* 800-405-1619 *Fax:* 401-531-2801 *Toll Free Fax:* 800-406-9145 *E-mail:* customer.care@triliteral.org

Moznaim Publishing Corp
4304 12 Ave, Brooklyn, NY 11219
SAN: 214-4123
Tel: 718-438-7680 *Fax:* 718-438-1305
E-mail: sales@moznaim.com
Web Site: www.moznaim.com
Key Personnel
Pres: Menachem Wagshal
VP: Moshe Sternlicht
Founded: 1981
Judaica books in Hebrew, English & Spanish.
ISBN Prefix(es): 978-0-940118; 978-1-885220
Number of titles published annually: 7 Print
Total Titles: 200 Print
Foreign Office(s): 10 Telmie Yosef St, Mishor Adumim, Israel *Tel:* (02) 5333441 *Fax:* (02) 5354345
Distributor for Avamra Institute; Breslov Research Institute; Red Wheel/Weiser/Conari

MRTS
Imprint of Arizona Center for Medieval & Renaissance Studies (ACMRS)
PO Box 874402, Tempe, AZ 85287-4402
Tel: 480-727-6503 *Toll Free Tel:* 800-621-2736 (orders) *Fax:* 480-965-1681 *Toll Free Fax:* 800-621-8476 (orders)
E-mail: mrts@asu.edu
Web Site: acmrs.org/publications/mrts
Key Personnel
Mng Ed: Roy Rukkila *E-mail:* roy.rukkila@asu.edu
Scholarly/academic press. Specialize in medieval & Renaissance texts & studies.
ISBN Prefix(es): 978-0-86698
Number of titles published annually: 24 Print
Total Titles: 492 Print
Sales Office(s): Chicago Distribution Center, 11030 S Langley Ave, Chicago, IL 60628 *Tel:* 773-702-7000 *Toll Free Tel:* 800-621-2736 *Fax:* 773-702-7212 *Toll Free Fax:* 800-621-8476 *E-mail:* orders@press.uchicago.edu *Web Site:* www.press.uchicago.edu
Billing Address: Chicago Distribution Center, 11030 S Langley Ave, Chicago, IL 60628 *Tel:* 773-702-7000 *Toll Free Tel:* 800-621-2736 *Fax:* 773-702-7212 *Toll Free Fax:* 800-621-8476 *E-mail:* orders@press.uchicago.edu *Web Site:* www.press.uchicago.edu
Orders to: Chicago Distribution Center, 11030 S Langley Ave, Chicago, IL 60628 *Tel:* 773-702-7000 *Toll Free Tel:* 800-621-2736 *Fax:* 773-702-7212 *Toll Free Fax:* 800-621-8476 *E-mail:* orders@press.uchicago.edu *Web Site:* www.press.uchicago.edu
Returns: Chicago Distribution Center, 11030 S Langley Ave, Chicago, IL 60628 *Tel:* 773-702-7000 *Toll Free Tel:* 800-621-2736 *Fax:* 773-702-7212 *Toll Free Fax:* 800-621-8476 *E-mail:* orders@press.uchicago.edu *Web Site:* www.press.uchicago.edu
Distribution Center: Chicago Distribution Center, 11030 S Langley Ave, Chicago, IL 60628 *Tel:* 773-702-7000 *Toll Free Tel:* 800-621-2736 *Fax:* 773-702-7212 *Toll Free Fax:* 800-621-8476 *E-mail:* orders@press.uchicago.edu *Web Site:* www.press.uchicago.edu

§Multicultural Publications Inc
Subsidiary of Making Education Reform Imperative Today Inc (MERIT)
1939 Manchester Rd, Akron, OH 44314
Mailing Address: PO Box 8001, Akron, OH 44320-0001
Tel: 330-865-9578 *Fax:* 330-865-9578
E-mail: multiculturalpub@prodigy.net
Web Site: www.multiculturalpub.net
Key Personnel
Pres & CEO: Bobby L Jackson
Dir, Mktg & Promos & Intl Rts: James Lynell
Lib Sales Dir: Rae Neal
Founded: 1992
Books, greeting cards, dolls & stuffed toys, multimedia.
ISBN Prefix(es): 978-0-9634932; 978-1-884242
Number of titles published annually: 1 Print; 1 CD-ROM; 1 Online
Total Titles: 28 Print; 2 CD-ROM; 28 Online; 4 Audio
Branch Office(s)
1907 Massillon Rd, Akron, OH 44312
Returns: 1939 Manchester Rd, Akron, OH 44314
Shipping Address: 1939 Manchester Rd, Akron, OH 44314

Multnomah
Imprint of Crown Publishing Group
10807 New Allegiance Dr, Suite 500, Colorado Springs, CO 80921
Tel: 719-590-4999 *Toll Free Tel:* 800-603-7051 (orders) *Fax:* 719-590-8977 *Toll Free Fax:* 800-294-5686 (orders)
E-mail: info@waterbrookmultnomah.com
Web Site: waterbrookmultnomah.com
Founded: 2006
Publishes Christian books that proclaim the Gospel & equip followers of Jesus to make disciples. Seek timeless messages from trusted Christian voices that challenge readers to approach life from a Biblical perspective.
ISBN Prefix(es): 978-1-59052; 978-1-60142
Number of titles published annually: 19 Print
Membership(s): Evangelical Christian Publishers Association

§Mundania Press LLC
6457 Glenway Ave, Suite 109, Cincinnati, OH 45211
SAN: 255-013X
Tel: 513-404-7357 *Fax:* 513-598-9220 *Toll Free Fax:* 888-460-4752
E-mail: books@mundania.com; inquiry@mundania.com
Web Site: www.mundania.com
Key Personnel
Pres: Bob Sanders *E-mail:* bob@mundania.com
Art Dir: Niki Browning
Founded: 2012
Provides authors with publishing & distribution worldwide. Submissions are currently open & actively look for any fiction with exception being poetry. All other specifics are listed on the web site.
ISBN Prefix(es): 978-0-9723670; 978-1-59426
Number of titles published annually: 500 Print; 100 CD-ROM; 500 Online; 900 E-Book; 5 Audio
Total Titles: 700 Print; 200 CD-ROM; 700 Online; 900 E-Book; 1 Audio
Imprints: Awe-Struck; Hard Shell Word Factory; Mundania Press; Phaze Books
Foreign Rep(s): Lightning Source (UK, USA)
Membership(s): Electronically Published Internet Connection; Independent Book Publishers Association

Municipal Analysis Services Inc
PO Box 13453, Austin, TX 78711-3453
Tel: 512-704-7194
E-mail: munilysis@gmail.com
Web Site: sites.google.com/site/gregmichels/home
Key Personnel
Pres: Greg Michels
Founded: 1983
Analysis of local governments.
ISBN Prefix(es): 978-1-55507; 978-0-31738
Number of titles published annually: 82 Print; 40 CD-ROM; 80 E-Book
Total Titles: 2,200 Print; 200 CD-ROM; 540 E-Book

The Museum of Modern Art (MoMA)
11 W 53 St, New York, NY 10019
SAN: 202-5809
Tel: 212-708-9443 *Fax:* 212-333-6575
E-mail: moma_publications@moma.org
Web Site: www.moma.org
Key Personnel
Publr: Christopher Hudson
Assoc Publr: Charles R Kim
Edit Dir: David Frankel
Prodn Dir: Marc Sapir

Founded: 1929
Art, architecture, design, photography, film.
ISBN Prefix(es): 978-0-87070; 978-1-63345
Number of titles published annually: 18 Print
Total Titles: 1,250 Print
Distributed by Distributed Art Publishers (DAP) (US & CN only)
Foreign Rep(s): Thames & Hudson Ltd (worldwide exc Canada & USA)
Warehouse: South River Distribution, South River, NJ 08882
Membership(s): American Alliance of Museums; American Association of University Presses; CAA

§Museum of New Mexico Press
Unit of New Mexico State Department of Cultural Affairs
725 Camino Lejo, Suite C, Santa Fe, NM 87505
SAN: 202-2575
Mailing Address: PO Box 2087, Santa Fe, NM 87504-2087
Tel: 505-476-1155; 505-272-7777 (orders); 505-277-4810 *Toll Free Tel:* 800-249-7737 (orders) *Fax:* 505-476-1156 *Toll Free Fax:* 800-622-8667 (orders)
Web Site: www.mnmpress.org
Key Personnel
Dir: Anna Gallegos *Tel:* 505-476-1154 *E-mail:* anna.gallegos@state.nm.us
Art Dir & Prodn Mgr: David Skolkin *Tel:* 505-476-1159 *E-mail:* david.skolkin@state.nm.us
Edit Dir: Lisa Pachaco *Tel:* 505-476-1157 *E-mail:* lisa.pachaco@state.nm.us
Mktg & Sales Dir: Janet L Dick *E-mail:* janet.dick@state.nm.us
Founded: 1951
Publications related to Native America, Hispanic Southwest, 20th century art, photography, folk art & folklore, nature & gardening, architecture & the Americas.
ISBN Prefix(es): 978-0-89013
Number of titles published annually: 15 Print
Total Titles: 140 Print
Distributed by University of New Mexico Press
Foreign Rep(s): Codasat Canada Ltd (Canada); East-West Export Books (Asia-Pacific); Gazelle Book Services Ltd (Europe)
Orders to: University of New Mexico Press, 1312 Basehart Rd SE, Albuquerque, NM 87106-4363
Warehouse: University of New Mexico Press, 1312 Basehart Rd SE, Albuquerque, NM 87106-4363

Mutual Publishing LLC
1215 Center St, Suite 210, Honolulu, HI 96816
Tel: 808-732-1709 *Fax:* 808-734-4094
E-mail: info@mutualpublishing.com
Web Site: www.mutualpublishing.com
Key Personnel
Dir, Sales & Mktg: Gay Wong *E-mail:* gaywong@mutualpublishing.com
Founded: 1974
Publishing, print brokering & packaging. Editorial & design services; trade, mass market paperback, coffee table & souvenir books.
ISBN Prefix(es): 978-1-56647; 978-0-935180
Number of titles published annually: 30 Print
Total Titles: 330 Print

Mystic Seaport Museum Inc
PO Box 6000, Mystic, CT 06355-0990
SAN: 213-7550
Tel: 860-572-5302; 860-572-0711 (visitor serv) *Toll Free Tel:* 800-248-1066 (wholesale orders only); 800-331-2665 (retail orders only) *Fax:* 860-572-5321
E-mail: info@mysticseaport.org
Web Site: www.mysticseaport.org
Key Personnel
Pres: Stephen C White *E-mail:* administration@mysticseaport.com
EVP: Susan Funk; Marcy Withington
Dir, Busn Devt: Mary Anne Stets
Founded: 1929
Scholarly & trade books on American maritime history & art.
ISBN Prefix(es): 978-0-913372; 978-0-939510
Number of titles published annually: 3 Print
Total Titles: 84 Print
Distributor for Glencannon; Ten Pound Island Books
Foreign Rep(s): Nimbus (Canada); Dalton Young Assoc (UK)

NAB, see National Association of Broadcasters (NAB)

NACE International
15835 Park Ten Place, Houston, TX 77084
Tel: 281-228-6200; 281-228-6223 *Toll Free Tel:* 800-797-NACE (797-6223) *Fax:* 281-228-6300
E-mail: firstservice@nace.org
Web Site: www.nace.org
Key Personnel
Exec Dir: Bob Chalker *Tel:* 281-228-6250
Pubns Dir: Gretchen Jacobson *Tel:* 281-228-6207 *E-mail:* gretchen.jacobson@nace.org
Founded: 1943
Publishes technical books on corrosion control & prevention & materials selection, design & degradation issues. Books are developed by individual authors/editors utilizing corrosion experts to contribute text. Compilations of technical papers from NACE conferences & symposia are also issued on an annual basis.
ISBN Prefix(es): 978-1-877914; 978-0-915567; 978-1-57590
Number of titles published annually: 50 Print
Total Titles: 425 Print; 30 CD-ROM; 4 Online; 80 Audio
Foreign Office(s): Suite 14-7, Level 14, Wisma UOA 11, Jl Pinang, 50450 Kuala Lumpur, Malaysia *Tel:* (03) 2027-4656 *Fax:* (03) 2181-3121 *E-mail:* tommy.tan@nace.org
Distributed by Australasian Corrosion Association Inc
Distributor for ASM International; ASTM; AWS; Butterworth-Heinemann; Cambridge University Press; CASTI Publishing; Compass Publications; CRC Press; Marcel Dekker Inc; E&FN Spon; Elsevier Science Publishers; Gulf Publishing; Industrial Press; Institute of Materials; ISO; McGraw-Hill; MTI; Prentice Hall; Professional Publications; SSPC; Swedish Corrosion Institute; John Wiley & Sons Inc
Foreign Rep(s): ABI (India); ATP (Europe); BI Publications (Asia); IBS (India)

NACE Press, see NACE International

NASW Press
Division of National Association of Social Workers (NASW)
750 First St NE, Suite 800, Washington, DC 20002
SAN: 202-893X
Tel: 202-408-8600 *Fax:* 203-336-8312
E-mail: press@naswdc.org
Web Site: www.naswpress.org
Key Personnel
Publr: Cheryl Bradley *Tel:* 202-408-8600 ext 214 *E-mail:* cbradley@naswdc.org
Mng Ed, Journals & Books: Julie Gutin *Tel:* 202-408-8600 ext 281 *E-mail:* jgutin@naswdc.org
Sr Ed: Sarah Lowman *Tel:* 202-408-8600 ext 398 *E-mail:* slowman@naswdc.org
Founded: 1955
Professional & scholarly books & journals in the social sciences.
ISBN Prefix(es): 978-0-87101
Number of titles published annually: 6 Print; 2 CD-ROM
Total Titles: 100 Print
Billing Address: PBD Worldwide Fulfillment Services, 1650 Bluegrass Lakes Pkwy, Alpharetta, GA 30004 *Tel:* 770-238-0450 *Toll Free Tel:* 800-227-3590 *Fax:* 770-442-9742 *Toll Free Fax:* 866-494-1499
Orders to: PBD Worldwide Fulfillment Services, 1650 Bluegrass Lakes Pkwy, Alpharetta, GA 30004 *Tel:* 770-238-0450 *Toll Free Tel:* 800-227-3590 *Fax:* 770-442-9742 *Toll Free Fax:* 866-494-1499
Returns: PBD Worldwide Fulfillment Services, 1650 Bluegrass Lakes Pkwy, Alpharetta, GA 30004 *Tel:* 770-238-0450 *Toll Free Tel:* 800-227-3590 *Fax:* 770-442-9742 *Toll Free Fax:* 866-494-1499
Distribution Center: PBD Worldwide Fulfillment Services, 1650 Bluegrass Lakes Pkwy, Alpharetta, GA 30004 *Tel:* 770-238-0450 *Toll Free Tel:* 800-227-3590 *Fax:* 770-442-9742 *Toll Free Fax:* 866-494-1499

Nataraj Books
7967 Twist Lane, Springfield, VA 22153
Tel: 703-455-4996 *Fax:* 703-455-4001
E-mail: nataraj@erols.com; orders@natarajbooks.com; natarajbooks@gmail.com
Web Site: www.natarajbooks.com
Key Personnel
Pres: Vinod Mahajan
Founded: 1986
Books from South Asia.
ISBN Prefix(es): 978-1-881338
Number of titles published annually: 7 Print
Total Titles: 70 Print
Orders to: 7073 Brookfield Plaza, Springfield, VA 22150

§National Academies Press (NAP)
Division of National Academies
Lockbox 285, 500 Fifth St NW, Washington, DC 20001
SAN: 202-8891
Tel: 202-334-3313 *Fax:* 202-334-2451 (cust serv); 202-334-2793 (mktg dept)
E-mail: customer_service@nap.edu
Web Site: www.nap.edu
Key Personnel
Deputy Exec Dir, Communs: Ann Merchant *Tel:* 202-334-3117 *E-mail:* amerchan@nas.edu
Exec Ed: Stephen Mautner *Tel:* 202-334-3336 *E-mail:* smautner@nas.edu
Dir, Publg Opers: Sandra Adams
Dir, Publg Servs: Dottie Lewis *Tel:* 202-334-2409 *E-mail:* dlewis@nas.edu
Art Dir: Francesca Moghari *Tel:* 202-334-3323 *E-mail:* fmoghari@nas.edu
Founded: 1863
Science, technology & health, scholarly & trade books.
ISBN Prefix(es): 978-0-309
Number of titles published annually: 200 Print
Total Titles: 3,500 Print; 1,000 E-Book
Imprints: Joseph Henry Press
Foreign Office(s): Cumnor Hill, 12 Hid's Copse Rd, Oxford 0X2 9JJ, United Kingdom
Foreign Rep(s): Durnell Marketing Ltd (Europe, Ireland); Kinokuniya (Japan); Marston Book Services Ltd (Africa, Middle East, UK, Western Europe); Maruzen Co Ltd (Japan); US PubRep (Craig Falk) (Caribbean including Puerto Rico, Central America, Mexico, South America); World Scientific Publishing Co Pte Ltd (Brunei, China, Hong Kong, India, Indonesia, Korea, Malaysia, Philippines, Singapore, Taiwan, Thailand)
Orders to: Marston Book Service Ltd, PO Box 269, Abingdon, Oxon OX14 4YN, United Kingdom (for UK & Europe) *Tel:* (01235) 465500 *Fax:* (01235) 465555 *Web Site:* www.marston.co.uk
Returns: 22883 Quicksilver Dr, Dulles, VA 20166
Membership(s): AAP

The National Alliance Research Academy
Division of The National Alliance for Insurance Education & Research
3630 N Hills Dr, Austin, TX 78755
Mailing Address: PO Box 27027, Austin, TX 78755 2027
Tel: 512-345-7932 *Toll Free Tel:* 800-633-2165 *Fax:* 512-349-6194
E-mail: alliance@scic.com
Web Site: www.scic.com/academy
Key Personnel
Pres & CEO, National Alliance for Insurance Education & Research: William T Hold, PhD
VP: William J Hold
Founded: 1983
Insurance research & education.
ISBN Prefix(es): 978-1-878204
Number of titles published annually: 4 Print
Total Titles: 15 Print; 1 CD-ROM; 1 Audio

National Association for Music Education (NAfME)
1806 Robert Fulton Dr, Reston, VA 20191
Tel: 703-860-4000 *Toll Free Tel:* 800-462-6420 (orders & returns); 800-336-3768 *Fax:* 703-860-1531
Web Site: www.menc.org; www.nafme.org
Founded: 1907
Books on all phases of music education in schools & communities; professional philosophy & practical techniques, the arts & art education as a whole; current issues in music teaching & learning; music education advocacy.
ISBN Prefix(es): 978-0-940796; 978-1-56545
Number of titles published annually: 15 Print; 3 Online
Total Titles: 151 Print; 3 Online
Editorial Office(s): Rowman & Littlefield Publishing Group Inc, 4501 Forbes Blvd, Lanham, MD 20706
Distributed by Rowman & Littlefield Education
Orders to: Rowman & Littlefield Publishing Group Inc, 15200 NBN Way, Blue Ridge Summit, PA 17214 *Tel:* 717-794-3800 *Toll Free Tel:* 800-462-6420 *Fax:* 717-794-3803 *Toll Free Fax:* 800-338-4550 *E-mail:* orders@rowman.com
Distribution Center: National Book Network, 4501 Forbes Blvd, Suite 200, Lanham, MD 20706 *Web Site:* www.nbnbooks.com

National Association of Broadcasters (NAB)
1771 "N" St NW, Washington, DC 20036
Tel: 202-429-5300
E-mail: nab@nab.org
Web Site: www.nab.org
Key Personnel
CEO & Pres: Gordon H Smith
EVP, Mktg & Communs: Michelle Lehman *Tel:* 202-429-5444 *E-mail:* mlehman@nab.org
EVP, Conventions & Busn Opers: Mr Chris Brown
Trade association representing radio & television stations & companies that serve the broadcasting industry.
ISBN Prefix(es): 978 0 89324
Number of titles published annually: 15 Print
Total Titles: 71 Print
Distributed by Allyn & Bacon; Lawrence Erlbaum Associates; Focal Press; Macmillan; Tab Books

§National Association of Insurance Commissioners
1100 Walnut St, Suite 1500, Kansas City, MO 64106-2197
Tel: 816-842-3600; 816-783-8300 (cust serv) *Fax:* 816-783-8175; 816-460-7593 (cust serv)
E-mail: prodserv@naic.org
Web Site: www.naic.org
Key Personnel
Supv II, Strategic Busn Initiative: Latonya Buchanan *Tel:* 816-783-8944
Founded: 1871
ISBN Prefix(es): 978-0-89382; 978-1-59917
Number of titles published annually: 110 Print
Total Titles: 356 Print; 110 Online; 110 E-Book
Branch Office(s)
NAIC Government Relations, Hall of the States, Suite 701, 4444 N Capitol St NW, Washington, DC 20001, Dir: Ethan Sonnichsen *Tel:* 202-471-3990 *Fax:* 816-460-7493
Capital Markets & Investment Analysis Office, One New York Plaza, Suite 4210, New York, NY 10004, Dir: Chris Evangel *Tel:* 212-398-9000 *Fax:* 212-382-4207

National Association of Secondary School Principals (NASSP)
1904 Association Dr, Reston, VA 20191-1537
Tel: 703-860-0200 *Toll Free Tel:* 800-253-7746
E-mail: sales@nassp.org; publications2@nassp.org (communs & devt); membership@nassp.org
Web Site: www.nassp.org
Key Personnel
Dir, Pub Aff: Bob Farrace *Tel:* 703-909-4661 *E-mail:* farraceb@nassp.org
Founded: 1916
Journals, magazines, monographs, newsletters, videos & software.
ISBN Prefix(es): 978-0-88210
Number of titles published annually: 6 Print
Total Titles: 74 Print
Imprints: NASSP
Advertising Agency: YGS Group

National Book Co
Division of Educational Research Associates
PO Box 19069, Portland, OR 97280-0069
SAN: 212-4661
Tel: 503-228-6345 *Fax:* 810-885-5811
E-mail: info@eralearning.com
Web Site: www.eralearning.com
Key Personnel
Dir, Spec Materials: Mark R Salser
Prodn Mgr: Ward J Stroud
Founded: 1965
Individualized mastery learning programs for elementary, secondary & college levels, consisting of multimedia materials in business education, home economics, language skills, mathematics, science, shorthand skills, social studies, general & vocational education; special trade publications, particularly in subjects relating to education. Computer software, reference books, Black/Afro-American history, ESL.
ISBN Prefix(es): 978-0-89420
Number of titles published annually: 25 Print
Total Titles: 175 Print; 100 Audio
Imprints: Halcyon House

National Braille Press
88 Saint Stephen St, Boston, MA 02115-4302
Tel: 617-266-6160 *Toll Free Tel:* 800-548-7323 (cust serv); 888-965-8965 *Fax:* 617-437-0456
E-mail: orders@nbp.org; contact@nbp.org
Web Site: www.nbp.org
Key Personnel
Pres: Brian A MacDonald *E-mail:* bmacdonald@nbp.org
VP, Braille Pubns: Tony Grima *Tel:* 617-266-6160 ext 429 *E-mail:* agrima@nbp.org
VP, Devt & Major Gifts: Joseph Quintanilla
VP, Prodn: Jackie Sheridan
Dir, Sales: Nicole Noble
Founded: 1929
Braille books & magazines.
ISBN Prefix(es): 978-0-939173
Number of titles published annually: 30 Print; 15 E-Book
Total Titles: 50 Print; 1 CD-ROM; 14 E-Book

National Catholic Educational Association
1005 N Glebe Rd, Suite 525, Arlington, VA 22201
Tel: 571-257-0010 *Toll Free Tel:* 800-711-6232 *Fax:* 703-243-0025
E-mail: nceaadmin@ncea.org
Web Site: www.ncea.org
Key Personnel
PR Mgr: Margaret Kaplow *E-mail:* mkaplow@ncea.org
Mktg Communs Mgr: Kisha Bricsoe *E-mail:* kbriscoe@ncea.org
Graphic Design & Prodn Mgr: Bea Ruiz *E-mail:* ruiz@ncea.org
Nonfiction: educational trends, methodology, innovative programs, teacher education & inservice, research, technology, financial & public relations programs, management systems all applicable to nonpublic education.
ISBN Prefix(es): 978-1-55833
Number of titles published annually: 25 Print
Total Titles: 225 Print

§National Center for Children in Poverty
Division of Mailman School of Public Health at Columbia University
215 W 125 St, 3rd fl, New York, NY 10027
Tel: 646-284-9600 *Fax:* 646-284-9623
E-mail: info@nccp.org
Web Site: www.nccp.org
Key Personnel
Dir: Renee Wilson-Simmons
Founded: 1989
Nonprofit publisher of monographs, reports, statistical updates, working papers & issue briefs concerning children under 6 who live in poverty in the US. Topics cover impact of poverty on child health & development; statistical profiles of poor children & their families; research programs on the effects of poverty; research on policies that could reduce the young child poverty rate; integrated social & human services (private & public) for low-income families. Welfare reform & children, research forum on children, families & the new federalism.
ISBN Prefix(es): 978-0-926582
Number of titles published annually: 24 Print
Total Titles: 40 Print; 20 E-Book

National Center For Employee Ownership (NCEO)
1629 Telegraph Ave, Suite 200, Oakland, CA 94612
Tel: 510-208-1300 *Fax:* 510-272-9510
E-mail: customerservice@nceo.org
Web Site: www.nceo.org
Key Personnel
Exec Dir: Loren Rodgers *Tel:* 510-208-1307 *E-mail:* lrodgers@nceo.org
Dir, Publg & Info Technol: Scott Rodrick *Tel:* 510-208-1315 *E-mail:* srodrick@nceo.org
Founded: 1981
Employee ownership books, pamphlets & newsletter.
ISBN Prefix(es): 978-0-926902; 978-1-932924; 978-1-938220
Number of titles published annually: 8 Print; 8 E-Book
Total Titles: 60 Print

National Conference of State Legislatures (NCSL)
7700 E First Place, Denver, CO 80230
Tel: 303-364-7700 *Fax:* 303-364-7800
E-mail: books@ncsl.org
Web Site: www.ncsl.org
Key Personnel
Exec Dir: William T Pound
Dir, Communs: Karen Hansen

Prog Principal: Stacy Householder *Tel:* 303-364-7700 ext 1352 *E-mail:* stacy.householder@ncsl.org
Founded: 1975
Books, magazines, series of papers & issue briefs on state public policy issues.
ISBN Prefix(es): 978-1-55516; 978-1-58024; 978-0-941336
Number of titles published annually: 100 Print
Total Titles: 200 Print
Branch Office(s)
444 N Capitol St NW, Suite 515, Washington, DC 20001 *Tel:* 202-624-5400 *Fax:* 202-737-1069

National Council of Teachers of English (NCTE)
1111 W Kenyon Rd, Urbana, IL 61801-1096
Tel: 217-328-3870 *Toll Free Tel:* 877-369-6283 (cust serv) *Fax:* 217-328-9645
E-mail: orders@ncte.org
Web Site: www.ncte.org
Key Personnel
Exec Dir: Emily Kirkpatrick *Tel:* 217-278-3601
Sr Dir, Opers: Lynn Neal *Tel:* 217-278-3646 *E-mail:* lneal@ncte.org
Div Dir, Pubns & Perms Coord: Kurt Austin *Tel:* 217-278-3619 *E-mail:* permissions@ncte.org
Sr Ed: Bonny Graham *Tel:* 217-278-3618
Purch & Prodn Mgr: Charles Hartman *Tel:* 217-278-3664
Founded: 1911
Nonprofit professional association of educators in English studies, literacy & language arts. Specialize in the teaching of English & the language arts at all grade levels; research reports; guidelines & position statements; journals; professional development books.
ISBN Prefix(es): 978-0-8141
Number of titles published annually: 10 Print; 10 E-Book
Total Titles: 240 Print; 2 CD-ROM; 28 E-Book
Imprints: Principles in Practice

§National Council of Teachers of Mathematics (NCTM)
1906 Association Dr, Reston, VA 20191-1502
SAN: 202-9057
Tel: 703-620-9840 *Toll Free Tel:* 800-235-7566 *Fax:* 703-476-2970
E-mail: nctm@nctm.org
Web Site: www.nctm.org
Key Personnel
Exec Dir: Bob Doucette
Assoc Exec Dir, Communs: Kenneth Krehbiel *E-mail:* kkrehbiel@nctm.org
Sr Dir, Pubns: Joanne Hodges *Tel:* 703-620-9840 ext 2129
Founded: 1920
Professional publications, including books (printed & online), monographs & yearbooks. Members include individuals, institutions, students, teachers & educators. Multiyear plans available to individual & institutional members.
ISBN Prefix(es): 978-0-87353; 978-1-68054
Number of titles published annually: 15 Print
Total Titles: 175 Print
Distributed by Eric Armin Inc Education Ctr; Delta Education; Didax Educational Resources; Educators Outlet; ETA Cuisenaire; Lakeshore Learning Materials; NASCO; Spectrum
Distribution Center: Copyright Clearance Center Inc, 222 Rosewood Dr, Danvers, MA 01923 *Tel:* 978-750-8400

National Education Association (NEA)
1201 16 St NW, Washington, DC 20036-3290
Tel: 202-833-4000 *Fax:* 202-822-7974
Web Site: www.nea.org
Key Personnel
Pres: Lily Eskelsen Garcia
VP: Becky Pringle
Secy/Treas: Princess R Moss
Exec Dir: John C Stocks
Dir, PR: Ramona Oliver
Founded: 1857
Professional development publications for K-12 & higher education & AV materials for educators. Web site with resources & general information for educators & the general public.
ISBN Prefix(es): 978-0-8106
Number of titles published annually: 7 Print; 2 CD-ROM; 2 Online
Total Titles: 189 Print; 2 CD-ROM; 9 Online
Imprints: NEA Professional Library

§National Gallery of Art
Sixth & Constitution Ave NW, Washington, DC 20565
Mailing Address: 2000 S Club Dr, Landover, MD 20785
Tel: 202-737-4215; 202-842-6480 *Fax:* 202-842-6733
E-mail: casva@nga.gov
Web Site: www.nga.gov
Key Personnel
Deputy Publr & Prodn Mgr: Chris Vogel
Ed-in-Chief: Judy Metro
Founded: 1941
Exhibition catalogues, catalogues of the collection & scholarly monographs.
ISBN Prefix(es): 978-0-89468
Number of titles published annually: 15 Print
Total Titles: 112 Print; 2 CD-ROM; 1 Online
Distributed by Abrams; DAP; Lund Humphries/Ashgate; Prestel-Del Monico Books; Princeton University Press; Thames & Hudson; University of Chicago Press; Yale University Press

National Geographic Books
Division of National Geographic Society
1145 17 St NW, Washington, DC 20036-4688
SAN: 202-8956
Tel: 202-857-7000 *Toll Free Tel:* 877-866-6486
E-mail: ngbooks@cdsfulfillment.com
Web Site: www.nationalgeographic.com/books/; ngbooks.buysub.com
Key Personnel
Chief Media Offr, NGS: Declan Moore
Chief Educ Offr: Melinda Gerosa Bellows
SVP & Gen Mgr, Book Publg Group: Hector Sierra *E-mail:* hsierra@ngs.org
VP, Sales & Mktg, Books: Heidi Vincent
Publr & Edit Dir, Adult Books: Lisa Thomas
Sr Dir, Digital Book Publg: Rachel Graham
Dir, Photog, Books: Susan Blair
Deputy Ed: Hilary Black
Sr Ed: Bridget English
Proj Mgr: Anne Smyth
Founded: 1888
Nonfiction general illustrated reference, travel, photography, history, science. Children's nonfiction with emphasis on school & library markets.
ISBN Prefix(es): 978-0-7922; 978-0-87044; 978-1-4262; 978-1-4263
Number of titles published annually: 180 Print
Total Titles: 700 Print; 15 E-Book
Imprints: National Geographic Adventure Classics; National Geographic Adventure Press; National Geographic Children's Books; National Geographic Directions
Distributed by Penguin Random House (worldwide exc UK); PGUK/Hi Marketing (United Kingdom)
Foreign Rights: Maeyee Lee (worldwide); Rachel Love (worldwide); Mary Jo Slazak (USA)
Membership(s): AAP; The Children's Book Council

National Geographic Learning
Unit of Cengage Learning
20 Channel Center St, Boston, MA 02210
Tel: 617-289-7796
E-mail: schoolcustomerservice@cengage.com
Web Site: www.ngl.cengage.com/school
Founded: 1980
Provides quality PreK-12, academic & adult education instructional solutions for reading, science, social studies, mathematics, world languages, ESL/ELD, advanced, honors & electives, career & technical education & professional development. Catalog available online at ngl.cengage.com/assets/html/catalogs.
ISBN Prefix(es): 978-0-917837; 978-1-56334
Number of titles published annually: 10 CD-ROM; 10 Online
Membership(s): AAP

§National Golf Foundation
501 N Hwy A1A, Jupiter, FL 33477-4577
Tel: 561-744-6006 *Toll Free Tel:* 888-275-4643 *Fax:* 561-744-6107
E-mail: general@ngf.org
Web Site: www.ngf.org
Key Personnel
Pres: Dr Joseph Beditz
Founded: 1936
Premier publisher of research & information for the business of golf. Over 200 publications are offered on golf consumer research, industry & market trends, golf facility development & operations, golf range development, instruction & player development.
ISBN Prefix(es): 978-0-9638647; 978-1-57701
Number of titles published annually: 4 Print
Total Titles: 100 Print; 1 CD-ROM; 2 Online; 1 Audio

National Information Standards Organization (NISO)
3600 Clipper Mill Rd, Suite 302, Baltimore, MD 21211
Tel: 301-654-2512 *Fax:* 410-685-5278
E-mail: nisohq@niso.org
Web Site: www.niso.org
Key Personnel
Exec Dir: Todd Carpenter *E-mail:* tcarpenter@niso.org
Assoc Dir: Nettie Lagace *E-mail:* nlagace@niso.org
Memb Servs & Engagement Mgr: DeVonne Parks *E-mail:* dparks@niso.org
Founded: 1939
Maintain & develop technical standards for libraries, publishers & information services.
ISBN Prefix(es): 978-1-880124; 978-1-937522
Number of titles published annually: 6 Print; 6 E-Book
Total Titles: 60 Print; 3 Online; 60 E-Book
Imprints: NISO Press

National Institute for Trial Advocacy (NITA)
1685 38 St, Suite 200, Boulder, CO 80301-2735
Tel: 720-890-4860 *Toll Free Tel:* 877-648-2632; 800-225-6482 (orders & returns) *Fax:* 720-890-7069
E-mail: info@nita.org
Web Site: www.nita.org
Key Personnel
Exec Dir: Karen Lockwood *E-mail:* klockwood@nita.org
Dir, Sales & Mktg: Daniel McHugh *E-mail:* dmchugh@nita.org
Publr: Jennifer Schneider *E-mail:* jschneider@nita.org
Mng Ed: Eric H Sorensen *E-mail:* esorensen@nita.org
Founded: 1970
Legal & litigation training.
ISBN Prefix(es): 978-1-55681; 978-1-60156
Number of titles published annually: 20 Print; 1 CD-ROM
Total Titles: 350 Print; 2 CD-ROM; 12 Audio

National Learning Corp
212 Michael Dr, Syosset, NY 11791
Tel: 516-921-8888 *Toll Free Tel:* 800-632-8888
Fax: 516-921-8743
E-mail: info@passbooks.com
Web Site: www.passbooks.com
Key Personnel
Pres & CEO: Michael P Rudman
Founded: 1967
Basic competency tests for college, high school & occupations; functional literacy; career, general, vocational & technical, adult & continuing, special, cooperative & community education; professional licensure; test preparation books for civil service, postal service, government careers, armed forces, high school & college equivalency; college, graduate & professional school enhancement; certification & licensing in engineering & technical careers, teaching, law, dentistry, medicine & allied health professions.
ISBN Prefix(es): 978-0-8373; 978-0-8293
Number of titles published annually: 3 Print
Total Titles: 5,000 Print
Imprints: Admission Test Series; AP Placement Test Series; Career Examination Series; Certified Nurse Examination Series (CN); College Level Examination Series; College Proficiency Examination Series; Dante Series; General Aptitude & Abilities Series; Graduate Record Examination Series; National Teacher Examination Series; Occupational Competency Examination Series; Passbooks; Regents External Degree Series; Teachers Lesson Plan Book Series; Test Your Knowledge Books; Undergraduate Program Field Test Series
Subsidiaries: Delaney Books Inc; Frank Merriwell Inc
Membership(s): AAP

National Notary Association (NNA)
9350 De Soto Ave, Chatsworth, CA 91311-4926
Mailing Address: PO Box 541032, Los Angeles, CA 90054-1032
Tel: 818-739-4000 *Toll Free Tel:* 800-876-6827
Toll Free Fax: 800-833-1211
E-mail: nna@nationalnotary.org
Web Site: www.nationalnotary.org
Key Personnel
Pres & CEO: Thomas A Heymann
CFO: Rob Clark
VP & CIO/CTO: Dave Stephenson
EVP: Deborah M Thaw
VP, Busn Devt: Chris Sturdivant
VP, Mktg: Thomas K Hayden
Founded: 1957
Publish books, periodical, videos, seminars.
ISBN Prefix(es): 978-0-9600158; 978-0-933134; 978-1-891133; 978-1-59767
Number of titles published annually: 15 Print
Total Titles: 40 Print

National Register Publishing, see NRP Direct

National Resource Center for Youth Services (NRCYS)
Division of University of Oklahoma-Outreach
Schusterman Ctr, Bldg 4W, 4502 E 41 St, Tulsa, OK 74135-2512
Tel: 918-660-3700 *Toll Free Tel:* 800-274-2687
Fax: 918-660-3737
Web Site: www.nrcys.ou.edu
Key Personnel
Dir: Peter R Correia, III *E-mail:* pcorreia@ou.edu
Assoc Dir: Kristi Charles *E-mail:* klcharles@ou.edu
Founded: 1985
Curricula & resource manuals for professionals & volunteers who work with foster care & at-risk teenagers.
ISBN Prefix(es): 978-1-878848
Number of titles published annually: 3 Print
Total Titles: 20 Print

National Science Teachers Association (NSTA)
1840 Wilson Blvd, Arlington, VA 22201-3000
Tel: 703-312-9205 *Toll Free Tel:* 800-277-5300 (orders) *Toll Free Fax:* 888-433-0526 (orders)
E-mail: publisher@nsta.org (gen info); orders@nsta.org
Web Site: www.nsta.org/store
Key Personnel
Publr & Assoc Exec Dir: David Beacom
Tel: 703-312-9207 *Fax:* 703-841-0250
E-mail: dbeacom@nsta.org
Founded: 1944
Books & periodicals.
ISBN Prefix(es): 978-0-87355; 978-1-93353; 978-1-936137; 978-1-935155; 978-1-936959; 978-1-938946; 978-1-941316
Number of titles published annually: 25 Print; 25 E-Book
Total Titles: 350 Print; 350 E-Book
Imprints: NSTA Ebooks+; NSTA Kids; NSTA Press
Foreign Rep(s): Alkem (Southeast Asia); Eurospan (worldwide exc Canada & Southeast Asia); University of Toronto Press (Canada)
Foreign Rights: Cat Russo (worldwide)
Orders to: PO Box 90214, Washington, DC 20090-5300
Returns: 3280 Summit Ridge Pkwy, Duluth, GA 30096
Membership(s): AAP; AAP PreK-12 Learning Group; Association Media & Publishing; Independent Book Publishing Professionals Group

The National Underwriter Co
Division of ALM Media LLC
4157 Olympic Blvd, Suite 225, Erlanger, KY 41018
Tel: 859-692-2100 *Toll Free Tel:* 800-543-0874
Fax: 859-692-2289
E-mail: customerservice@nuco.com
Web Site: www.nationalunderwriter.com
Founded: 1897
ISBN Prefix(es): 978-0-87218; 978-1-936362; 978-1-938130; 978-1-939829; 978-1-941627
Number of titles published annually: 11 Print

The Nautical & Aviation Publishing Co of America Inc
845-A Lowcountry Blvd, Mount Pleasant, SC 29464
SAN: 213-3431
Tel: 843-856-0561 *Fax:* 843-856-3164
Web Site: www.nauticalandaviation.com
Key Personnel
Pres: Jan W Snouck-Hurgronje
Founded: 1979
Military history & aviation.
ISBN Prefix(es): 978-1-877853; 978-0-933852
Number of titles published annually: 4 Print; 2 Audio
Total Titles: 47 Print; 2 Audio
Imprints: N & A
Warehouse: REO Distribution, One Solutions Way, Waynesboro, VA 22980

§Naval Institute Press
Division of US Naval Institute
291 Wood Rd, Annapolis, MD 21402-5034
SAN: 202-9006
Tel: 410-268-6110 *Toll Free Tel:* 800-233-8764
Fax: 410-295-1084; 410-571-1703 (cust serv)
E-mail: webmaster@navalinstitute.org; customer@navalinstitute.org (cust serv)
Web Site: www.nip.org; www.usni.org
Key Personnel
CEO: Peter H Daly
Press Dir: Rick Russell *E-mail:* rrussell@usni.org
Sales & Mktg Dir: Claire Noble *Tel:* 410-295-1039 *E-mail:* cnoble@usni.org
Mng Ed: Susan Corrado *Tel:* 410-295-1032
E-mail: scorrado@usni.org
Sr Acqs Ed: Thomas Cutler *E-mail:* tcutler@usni.org
Subs Rts Ed: Susan Todd Brook *E-mail:* sbrook@usni.org
Sales Mgr: Robin Noonan
Publicist: Judy Heise *Tel:* 410-295-1028
E-mail: jheise@usni.org
Cust Serv: Jaemellah Kemp
Founded: 1873
Naval & maritime subjects: professional, biography, science, history, ship & aviation references, US Naval Institute magazines; literature.
ISBN Prefix(es): 978-0-87021; 978-1-55750; 978-1-59114; 978-1-61251; 978-1-68247
Number of titles published annually: 65 Print
Total Titles: 800 Print
Distributed by Publishers Group West (digital only)
Foreign Rep(s): Eurospan Group (Africa, Asia, Australia, Europe, India, Middle East, Oceania, UK); Scholarly Book Services (Canada)
Warehouse: US Naval Institute, 2427 Bond St, University Park, IL 60466
Membership(s): Association of American University Presses

NavPress Publishing Group
Division of The Navigators
3820 N 30 St, Colorado Springs, CO 80904
SAN: 211-5352
Tel: 719-598-1212 *Toll Free Tel:* 800-323-9400; 855-277-9400 (cust serv) *Toll Free Fax:* 800-684-0247
Web Site: www.navpress.com
Key Personnel
Publr: Don Pape
Founded: 1975
Paperbacks, mass market & trade, hardcovers, periodicals; religious (Protestant) materials.
ISBN Prefix(es): 978-0-89109; 978-1-57683; 978-1-60006; 978-1-61521; 978-1-61747; 978-1-61291; 978-1-63146
Number of titles published annually: 15 Print
Total Titles: 600 Print; 2 Audio
Imprints: NavPress
Distributed by Tyndale House Publishers Inc
Orders to: Tyndale House Publishers Inc, 351 Executive Dr, Carol Stream, IL 60188 *Toll Free Tel:* 800-323-9400 *Web Site:* www.tyndale.com

NBM Publishing Inc
160 Broadway, E Wing, Suite 700, New York, NY 10038
SAN: 210-0835
Tel: 646-559-4681 *Toll Free Tel:* 800-886-1223
Fax: 212-643-1545
E-mail: admin@nbmpub.com
Web Site: www.nbmpub.com
Key Personnel
Pres & Publr: Terry Nantier
Off Mgr: May Wong *E-mail:* mayw@nbmpub.com
Founded: 1976
Graphic novels.
ISBN Prefix(es): 978-0-918348; 978-1-56163; 978-1-68112
Number of titles published annually: 20 Print; 20 E-Book
Total Titles: 250 Print; 100 E-Book
Imprints: Amerotica (erotic graphic novels from North American authors); ComicsLit (best fiction in graphic novels from around the world); Eurotica (erotic graphic novels from European authors); Forever Nuts (reprints of classic comic strips)
Foreign Rep(s): IPG (Canada); Turnaround (Europe, UK)
Orders to: IPG Distribution Center, 600 N Pulaski Rd, Chicago, IL 60624 *Toll Free Tel:* 800-888-IPG1 (888-4741)

Returns: IPG Distribution Center, 600 N Pulaski Rd, Chicago, IL 60624
Warehouse: IPG Distribution Center, 600 N Pulaski Rd, Chicago, IL 60624
Distribution Center: IPG Distribution Center, 600 N Pulaski Rd, Chicago, IL 60624
Membership(s): AAP; The Children's Book Council; Independent Book Publishers Association

Neibauer Press
Division of Louis Neibauer Co Inc
20 Industrial Dr, Warminster, PA 18974
Tel: 215-322-6200 *Toll Free Tel:* 800-322-6203 (orders) *Fax:* 215-322-2495
E-mail: info@neibauer.com
Web Site: www.neibauer.com; www.churchsupplier.com (orders)
Key Personnel
Pres: Nathan Neibauer *E-mail:* nathan@neibauer.com
Founded: 1967
ISBN Prefix(es): 978-1-878259
Number of titles published annually: 5 Print
Total Titles: 30 Print
Divisions: ChurchSupplier.com
Membership(s): CBA: The Association for Christian Retail

§New City Press
Division of Focolare Movement
202 Comforter Blvd, Hyde Park, NY 12538
SAN: 203-7335
Tel: 845-229-0335 *Toll Free Tel:* 800-462-5980 (orders only) *Fax:* 845-229-0351
E-mail: info@newcitypress.com
Web Site: www.newcitypress.com
Key Personnel
Publr & Gen Mgr: Jim Webber
Accts Payable: Ms Soki Stanczyk *E-mail:* accountant@newcitypress.com
Cust Serv: Nick Cianfarani
Founded: 1964
Publishes spiritual works of all Christian eras, including the Church Fathers, the spiritual masters of the middle-ages, as well as publications of contemporary spirituality & theology.
ISBN Prefix(es): 978-0-911782; 978-1-56548
Number of titles published annually: 20 Print
Total Titles: 220 Print
Imprints: NCP
Distributor for Ciudad Nueva (Argentina, Spain); New City (Great Britain)
Foreign Rep(s): Enderle Book Co (Japan); John Garratt Publishing (Australia); Jerome's Specialist Booksellers (New Zealand); Joseph's Inspirational (Canada); New City (China, England, Ireland, Philippines); Preca Bookshop (Malta)

§New Concepts Publishing
5202 Humphreys Rd, Lake Park, GA 31636
E-mail: newconcepts@newconceptspublishing.com
Web Site: www.newconceptspublishing.com
Key Personnel
Pres & PR: Madris De Pasture *E-mail:* madris@newconceptspublishing.com
Founded: 1996
ISBN Prefix(es): 978-1-58608; 978-1-891020; 978-1-60394
Number of titles published annually: 50 Print; 192 Online; 144 E-Book
Total Titles: 200 Print; 700 Online; 700 E-Book

New Directions Publishing Corp
80 Eighth Ave, New York, NY 10011
SAN: 202-9081
Tel: 212-255-0230 *Fax:* 212-255-0231
E-mail: newdirections@ndbooks.com
Web Site: ndbooks.com
Key Personnel
Pres & Publr: Barbara Epler *E-mail:* bepler@ndbooks.com
EVP: Laurie Callahan *E-mail:* lcallahan@ndbooks.com
Art Dir & Prodn Mgr: Erik Rieselbach *E-mail:* erieselbach@ndbooks.com
Founded: 1936
Modern literature, poetry, criticism & belles lettres.
ISBN Prefix(es): 978-0-8112
Number of titles published annually: 30 Print
Total Titles: 930 Print
Distributed by W W Norton & Company Inc
Foreign Rep(s): APAC Publisher's Services Pte Ltd (Indonesia, Malaysia, Singapore, Thailand); Delaney Global Publishers Services Inc (Guam, Philippines); MK International Ltd (Japan); B K Norton Ltd (Korea, Taiwan); W W Norton Ltd (Africa, Europe, Ireland, Middle East, UK); Pearson Education (New Zealand); Penguin Random House Canada (Canada); Transglobal Publishers Services Ltd (Hong Kong); US PubRep (Caribbean, Central America, Mexico, South America); John Wiley & Sons (Australia)
Foreign Rights: Agencia Literaria Carmen Balcells SA (Spain); The Italian Literary Agency srl (Italy); Laurence Pollinger Ltd (British Commonwealth)
Warehouse: National Book Co, 800 Keystone Industrial Park, Scranton, PA 18512 *Tel:* 212-790-9453 *Toll Free Tel:* 800-233-4830 *Toll Free Fax:* 800-458-6515

§New Forums Press Inc
1018 S Lewis St, Stillwater, OK 74074
Mailing Address: PO Box 876, Stillwater, OK 74076-0876
Tel: 405-372-6158 *Toll Free Tel:* 800-606-3766 *Fax:* 405-377-2237
E-mail: submissions@newforums.com
Web Site: www.newforums.com
Key Personnel
Pres: Douglas Dollar *E-mail:* ddollar@newforums.com
Founded: 1981
Practical & innovative academic journals, newsletters & books for educators in colleges & universities. Textbooks are also a primary interest.
ISBN Prefix(es): 978-0-913507; 978-1-58107
Number of titles published annually: 25 Print; 1 Online; 3 E-Book
Total Titles: 250 Print; 1 Online; 5 E-Book
Advertising Agency: Copy & Art, 219 E Greenvale Ct, Stillwater, OK 74075 *Tel:* 405-377-8224
Membership(s): The Association of Publishers for Special Sales

New Harbinger Publications Inc
5674 Shattuck Ave, Oakland, CA 94609
Tel: 510-652-0215 *Toll Free Tel:* 800-748-6273 (orders only) *Fax:* 510-652-5472 *Toll Free Fax:* 800-652-1613
E-mail: nhhelp@newharbinger.com; customerservice@newharbinger.com
Web Site: www.newharbinger.com
Key Personnel
Publr: Matthew (Matt) McKay, PhD *E-mail:* matt.mckay@newharbinger.com
Assoc Publr: Catharine A Meyers *E-mail:* catharine@newharbinger.com
Prodn Mgr: Michele Waters *E-mail:* michele@newharbinger.com
Intl Rts: Dorothy Smyk *E-mail:* dorothy@newharbinger.com
Founded: 1973
We offer the best in self-help psychology; real tools for real change. Now offering spirituality titles from our Non-Duality Press & Reveal Press imprints, which offer new wisdom for living consciously in our modern world.
ISBN Prefix(es): 978-1-57224; 978-0-934986; 978-1-879237; 978-1-60882; 978-1-62625
Number of titles published annually: 60 Print; 60 E-Book
Total Titles: 800 Print; 450 E-Book; 20 Audio
Imprints: Context Press; Impact; Instant Help; Noetic Books; Non-Duality Press; Reveal Press
Foreign Rights: Bookreps NZ Ltd (New Zealand); Little, Brown Book Group (Europe, UK); Raincoast Books (Canada, UK); Real Books (South Africa); John Reed Book Distributors (Australia); Southern Publishers Group (New Zealand)
Returns: 660 S Mansfield St, Ypsilanti, MI 48197

New Horizon Press
PO Box 669, Far Hills, NJ 07931-0669
SAN: 677-119X
Tel: 908-604-6311
E-mail: nhp@newhorizonpressbooks.com
Web Site: www.newhorizonpressbooks.com
Key Personnel
VP, Fin & Mktg: JoAnne C Thomas *E-mail:* jct@newhorizonpressbooks.com
Founded: 1982
True stories of uncommon heroes, true crime, social issues, behavioral, political science & psychologically-oriented nonfiction, trade paper, children's self-help, helping children deal with crisis.
ISBN Prefix(es): 978-0-88282; 978-1-933893
Number of titles published annually: 12 Print; 12 E-Book
Total Titles: 340 Print; 62 Online
Imprints: Small Horizons
Foreign Rights: Books Crossing Borders (Betty Ann Crawford) (worldwide)
Orders to: Publishers Group West (Perseus Distribution), 1700 Fourth St, Berkeley, CA 94710 *Toll Free Tel:* 800-788-3123 *Fax:* 510-809-3777 *Toll Free Fax:* 800-351-5073 *Web Site:* www.pgw.com
Returns: Perseus Distribution Returns Dept, 1700 Fourth St, Berkeley, CA 94710 *Toll Free Tel:* 800-788-3123 *Toll Free Fax:* 800-351-5073
Distribution Center: Publishers Group West (Perseus Distribution), 1700 Fourth St, Berkeley, CA 94710 *Tel:* 510-809-3700 *Toll Free Tel:* 800-788-3123 *Fax:* 510-809-3777 *Toll Free Fax:* 800-351-5073 *E-mail:* info@pgw.com *Web Site:* www.pgw.com

New Issues Poetry & Prose
Affiliate of Western Michigan University
c/o Western Michigan University, 1903 W Michigan Ave, Kalamazoo, MI 49008-5463
Tel: 269-387-8185
E-mail: new-issues@wmich.edu
Web Site: www.wmich.edu/newissues
Key Personnel
Mng Ed: Kimberly Kolbe
Ed-in-Chief: William Olsen
Founded: 1996
ISBN Prefix(es): 978-1-930974; 978-0-932826; 978-1-936970
Number of titles published annually: 6 Print
Total Titles: 180 Print
Distribution Center: University Press of New England (UPNE), One Court St, Suite 250, Lebanon, NH 03766, Contact: Sherri Strickland *Toll Free Tel:* 800-421-1561 *E-mail:* sherri.strickland@dartmouth.edu *Web Site:* www.upne.com

New Leaf Press
Imprint of New Leaf Publishing Group Inc
3142 Hwy 103 N, Green Forest, AR 72638-2233
Mailing Address: PO Box 726, Green Forest, AR 72638-0726

Tel: 870-438-5288 *Toll Free Tel:* 800-999-3777 *Fax:* 870-438-5120
E-mail: nlp@newleafpress.net; submissions@newleafpress.net
Web Site: www.nlpg.com/imprint/new-leaf-press; www.nlpg.com
Key Personnel
Pres, New Leaf Publishing Group: Tim Dudley
VP, Mktg & Sales, New Leaf Publishing Group: Bob Minortti
Publicity, New Leaf Publishing Group: Katie Gumm
Asst Ed: Craig Froman
Founded: 1975
Christian living & creation books; evangelical, devotionals.
ISBN Prefix(es): 978-0-89221
Number of titles published annually: 35 Print; 25 E-Book
Total Titles: 425 Print; 200 E-Book

New Poets Series, see BrickHouse Books Inc

The New Press
38 Greene St, 4th fl, New York, NY 10013
Tel: 212-629-8802 *Toll Free Tel:* 800-343-4489 (orders) *Fax:* 212-629-8617 *Toll Free Fax:* 800-351-5073 (orders)
E-mail: newpress@thenewpress.com
Web Site: www.thenewpress.com
Key Personnel
Exec Dir: Diane Wachtell
Publr: Ellen Adler
Exec Ed: Marc Favreau
Sr Mng Ed: Maury Botton
Dir, Publicity & Mktg: Brian Ulicky
Edit Dir: Carl Bromley
Fin Dir: Carline Yup
Prodn Dir: Fran Forte
Founded: 1990
Nonprofit publisher in the public interest; politics, education, current affairs, history, biography, economics, international fiction in translation.
ISBN Prefix(es): 978-1-56584; 978-1-59558; 978-1-62097
Number of titles published annually: 50 Print
Total Titles: 800 Print; 200 E-Book
Foreign Rep(s): MK International Ltd (Japan); W W Norton & Company Ltd (USA); I B Taurus & Co Ltd (worldwide); University of Toronto Press (Canada)
Foreign Rights: Agencia Literaria Carmen Balcells SA (Spain); Ursula Bender (Germany); Ann Christine Danielsson (Scandinavia); Cristina de Mello e Souza; Beth Elon (Israel); Mary Kling (France); William Miller (Japan); Susanna Zevi (Italy)

New Readers Press
Division of ProLiteracy
104 Marcellus, Syracuse, NY 13204
SAN: 202-1064
Tel: 315-422-9121 *Toll Free Tel:* 800-448-8878 *Toll Free Fax:* 866-894-2100
E-mail: nrp@proliteracy.org
Web Site: www.newreaderspress.com
Key Personnel
Sales & Busn Dir: Susan Willey *Tel:* 315-422-9121 ext 2470
ISBN Contact: Mike Shaffer
Founded: 1965
Books & periodicals for adults & young adult reading at a 0-8 reading level, basic reading & writing materials, ESL, mathematics & GED prep.
ISBN Prefix(es): 978-0-88336; 978-1-56420; 978-1-56853; 978-0-929631; 978-1-944057
Number of titles published annually: 20 Print
Total Titles: 400 Print; 41 Audio
Foreign Rights: Laubach Literacy Ontario (Canada)

New Rivers Press
c/o Minnesota State University Moorhead, 1104 Seventh Ave S, Moorhead, MN 56563
Tel: 218-477-5870 *Fax:* 218-477-2236
E-mail: nrp@mnstate.edu
Web Site: www.newriverspress.com; www.mnstate.edu/newriverspress
Key Personnel
Mng Ed: Nathan Rundquist
Sr Ed: Dr Alan Davis *Tel:* 218-477-4681 *E-mail:* davisa@mnstate.edu
Founded: 1968
Books of poetry, short stories & novellas, creative nonfiction, memoirs.
ISBN Prefix(es): 978-0-912284; 978-0-89823
Number of titles published annually: 6 Print; 6 E-Book
Total Titles: 340 Print
Distribution Center: Small Press Distribution, 1341 Seventh St, Berkeley, CA 94710 *Toll Free Tel:* 800-869-7553 *E-mail:* spd@spdbooks.org *Web Site:* www.spdbooks.org
Membership(s): Association of Writers and Writing Programs; Community of Literary Magazines & Presses

New Strategist Press LLC
26 Austin Ave, Amityville, NY 11701
Mailing Address: PO Box 635, Amityville, NY 11701
Tel: 631-608-8795 *Toll Free Tel:* 800-848-0842 *Fax:* 631-691-1770
E-mail: demographics@newstrategist.com; info@newstrategist.com
Web Site: www.newstrategist.com
Key Personnel
Edit Dir: Cheryl Russell
Founded: 1990
Publish reference books; demographics & consumer spending.
ISBN Prefix(es): 978-1-885070; 978-1-933588; 978-1-935775; 978-0-9628092; 978-1-937737; 978-1-935114; 978-1-940308
Number of titles published annually: 20 Print; 20 Online
Total Titles: 32 Print; 32 Online

New Win Publishing
Division of Academic Learning Co LLC
9682 Telstar Ave, Suite 110, El Monte, CA 91731
SAN: 217-1201
Tel: 626-448-3448 *Fax:* 626-602-3817
E-mail: info@academiclearningcompany.com
Web Site: newwinpublishing.com; wbusinessbooks.com
Key Personnel
Publr: Arthur Chou
Founded: 1988
General nonfiction: business books for sales, marketing & entrepreneurship, crafts, reference, health & nutrition, healthy gourmet cooking, career development, outdoor sports, hunting, shooting, fishing, decoys & dogs.
ISBN Prefix(es): 978-0-8329; 978-0-87691
Number of titles published annually: 25 Print
Total Titles: 70 Print
Imprints: WBusiness Books; Winchester Press; ZHealth Books

New World Library
Division of Whatever Publishing Inc
14 Pamaron Way, Novato, CA 94949
SAN: 211-8777
Tel: 415-884-2100 *Toll Free Tel:* 800-227-3900 (ext 52, retail orders); 800-972-6657 *Fax:* 415-884-2199
E-mail: escort@newworldlibrary.com
Web Site: www.newworldlibrary.com
Key Personnel
Pres: Marc Allen *E-mail:* marc@newworldlibrary.com
Edit Dir: Georgia Hughes *E-mail:* georgia@newworldlibrary.com
Mktg Dir & Assoc Publr: Munro Magruder *E-mail:* munro@newworldlibrary.com
Prodn Dir: Tona Pearce Meyers *E-mail:* tona@newworldlibrary.com
Publicity Dir: Monique Muhlenkamp *E-mail:* monique@newworldlibrary.com
Exec Ed: Jason Gardner *E-mail:* jason@newworldlibrary.com
Submissions Ed: Joel Prin *E-mail:* joel@newworldlibrary.com
Foreign Rts Mgr: Danielle Galat *E-mail:* danielle@newworldlibrary.com
Soc Media Mgr & Sr Publicist: Kim Corbin *E-mail:* kim@newworldlibrary.com
Spec Sales Mgr: Ami Parkerson *E-mail:* ami@newworldlibrary.com
Founded: 1977
Publisher of books on self-improvement, personal growth & spirituality, health & wellness, pets & animals, psychology & women's interest.
ISBN Prefix(es): 978-0-915811; 978-0-931432; 978-1-880032; 978-0-945934; 978-1-57731; 978-1-882591; 978-1-930722; 978-1-932073; 978-1-60868
Number of titles published annually: 35 Print; 35 E-Book; 2 Audio
Total Titles: 600 Print; 470 E-Book; 35 Audio
Imprints: Amber-Allen Publishing; Nataraj
Divisions: HJ Kramer Inc
Foreign Rep(s): Akasha Books (New Zealand); Brumby Books (Australia); Dempsey-Your Distributor (Canada); Perseus International (Continental Europe, India, Japan, Korea, Latin America, Middle East, Philippines, South America, Southeast Asia, Taiwan); Publishers Group Canada (Canada); Publishers Group UK (UK); Real Books (South Africa)
Distribution Center: Publishers Group West, 193 Edwards Dr, Jackson, TN 38301-7795 *Toll Free Tel:* 800-788-3123 *Web Site:* www.pgw.com
Membership(s): AAP; Publishers Association of the West; Publishing Professionals Network
See separate listing for:
HJ Kramer Inc

New York Academy of Sciences (NYAS)
7 World Trade, 40th fl, 250 Greenwich St, New York, NY 10007-2157
SAN: 203-753X
Tel: 212-298-8600 *Toll Free Tel:* 800-843-6927 *Fax:* 212-298-3668
E-mail: nyas@nyas.org; annals@nyas.org; customerservice@nyas.org
Web Site: www.nyas.org
Key Personnel
CEO & Pres: Ellis Rubenstein *Tel:* 212-298-8686 *E-mail:* erubenstein@nyas.org
EVP & COO: T C Wescott *Tel:* 212-298-8695 *E-mail:* tcwescott@nyas.org
VP & Chief Admin Offr: Wendy Caruso Schneider *Tel:* 212-298-8680 *E-mail:* wschneider@nyas.org
Exec Dir, Opers: Erica Cullmann *Tel:* 212-298-8619 *E-mail:* ecullman@nyas.org
Exec Dir, Sci Pubns & Ed-in-Chief, Annals of the NYAS: Douglas Braaten, PhD *Tel:* 212-298-8634 *E-mail:* dbraaten@nyas.org
Assoc Ed: David Alvaro, PhD *E-mail:* dalvaro@nyas.org; Azra Jaferi, PhD *E-mail:* ajaferi@nyas.org
Founded: 1817
Annals & transactions of the New York Academy of Sciences; also publish *Update Magazine*.
ISBN Prefix(es): 978-0-89072; 978-0-89766; 978-1-57331
Number of titles published annually: 28 Print
Total Titles: 333 Print
Distributed by Wiley Blackwell Publishers

The New York Botanical Garden Press
Division of The New York Botanical Garden

2900 Southern Blvd, Bronx, NY 10458-5126
Tel: 718-817-8721 *Fax:* 718-817-8842
E-mail: nybgpress@nybg.org
Web Site: www.nybgpress.org
Founded: 1896
Dissemination of information on the scientific study of plants.
ISBN Prefix(es): 978-0-89327
Number of titles published annually: 10 Print
Total Titles: 244 Print
Warehouse: Maple Logistics Solutions, York Distribution Ctr, PO Box 15100, York, PA 17405
Distribution Center: Maple Logistics Solutions, York Distribution Ctr, PO Box 15100, York, PA 17405
Membership(s): AAP

§New York State Bar Association
One Elk St, Albany, NY 12207
SAN: 226-1952
Tel: 518-463-3200 *Toll Free Tel:* 800-582-2452 *Fax:* 518-487-5517
E-mail: mrc@nysba.org
Web Site: www.nysba.org
Key Personnel
Pubns Dir: Daniel J McMahon *E-mail:* dmcmahon@nysba.org
Pubns Coord: Naomi Pitts *E-mail:* npitts@nysba.org; Leslie Scully *E-mail:* lscully@nysba.org
Founded: 1985
Legal publications, including hardbound, looseleaf, softbound & ebooks.
ISBN Prefix(es): 978-0-942954; 978-1-57969
Number of titles published annually: 110 Print; 6 CD-ROM
Total Titles: 600 Print; 500 Online

New York University Press
838 Broadway, 3rd fl, New York, NY 10003-4812
SAN: 658-1293
Tel: 212-998-2575 (edit) *Toll Free Tel:* 800-996-6987 (orders) *Fax:* 212-995-4798 (orders)
E-mail: information@nyupress.org; nyupressinfo@nyu.edu; orders@nyupress.org
Web Site: www.nyupress.org
Key Personnel
Publr: Ellen Chodosh
Mktg & Sales Dir: Mary Beth Jarrad
Assoc Dir & Ed-in-Chief: Eric Zinner
Prodn Mgr: Charles Hames
Exec Ed: Ilene Kalish
Mng Ed: Eorotha Halliday
Ed: Jennifer Hammer
Publicist: Betsy Steve
Order Fulfillment & Spec Sales Supv: Kevin Cooper
Founded: 1916
Publish a wide array of provocative & compelling titles, as well as works of lasting scholarly & reference value.
ISBN Prefix(es): 978-0-8147; 978-1-4798
Number of titles published annually: 125 Print
Total Titles: 2,000 Print
Distributor for Combined Academic Publishers Ltd; Footprint Books; Monthly Review Press
Returns: Maple Logistics Solutions, Lebanon Distribution Ctr, 704 Legionaire Dr, Fredricksburg, PA 17026 *Tel:* 717-865-7600 *Fax:* 717-865-7800
Warehouse: Maple Logistics Solutions, Lebanon Distribution Ctr, 704 Legionaire Dr, Fredricksburg, PA 17026 *Tel:* 717-865-7600 *Fax:* 717-865-7800
Membership(s): AAP; Association of American University Presses

Newbury Street Press
Imprint of New England Historic Genealogical Society
99-101 Newbury St, Boston, MA 02116
Tel: 617-536-5740 *Toll Free Tel:* 888-296-3447 (NEHGS membership) *Fax:* 617-536-7307
E-mail: sales@nehgs.org
Web Site: www.americanancestors.org
Key Personnel
CEO & Pres: D Brenton Simons
VP & COO: Ryan Woods *Tel:* 617-226-1205 *E-mail:* rwoods@nehgs.org
Publg Dir: Penny Stratton *Tel:* 617-226-1210 *E-mail:* pstratton@nehgs.org
Dir, Pubns: Scott C Steward *Tel:* 617-226-1208 *E-mail:* scott.steward@nehgs.org
Dir, Devt: Ted MacMahon *Tel:* 617-226-1218 *E-mail:* tmacmahon@nehgs.org
Sales Coord: Rick Park *Tel:* 617-226-1212 *E-mail:* rpark@nehgs.org
Founded: 1996
A special publications division of The New England Historic Genealogical Society which publishes scholarly books & compiled genealogies.
ISBN Prefix(es): 978-0-88082
Number of titles published annually: 15 Print
Total Titles: 100 Print

NewSouth Books
Imprint of NewSouth Inc
105 S Court St, Montgomery, AL 36104
Tel: 334-834-3556 *Fax:* 334-834-3557
E-mail: info@newsouthbooks.com
Web Site: www.newsouthbooks.com
Key Personnel
Co-Founder & Publr: Suzanne La Rosa
Co-Founder & Ed-in-Chief: Randall Williams
Mng Ed: Brian Seidman *E-mail:* brian@newsouthbooks.com
Founded: 2000
Independent book publisher, publishing 15-20 titles per year, including literary fiction & nonfiction, with a special emphasis on books about the history & culture of the South.
ISBN Prefix(es): 978-1-58838; 978-1-60306
Number of titles published annually: 20 Print; 10 Online; 10 E-Book
Total Titles: 175 Print; 30 Online; 30 E-Book
Imprints: Court Street Press; Junebug Books
Distributed by John F Blair Publisher
Billing Address: Ingram Publisher Services (IPS)
Returns: Ingram Publisher Services (IPS)
Shipping Address: Ingram Publisher Services (IPS)
Warehouse: Ingram Publisher Services (IPS)
Distribution Center: Ingram Publisher Services (IPS) *Toll Free Tel:* 800-215-2608 *E-mail:* ips@ingramcontent.com
Membership(s): Southern Independent Booksellers Alliance

§Nightingale-Conant
Bldg 300, Suite 103, 1400 S Wolf Rd, Wheeling, IL 60090
Tel: 847-647-0306 *Toll Free Tel:* 800-557-1660 (sales); 800-560-6081 (cust serv)
Web Site: www.nightingale.com
Key Personnel
Chmn: Vic Conant
Founded: 1960
Audio, video books & CD-ROMs in the areas of sales, skills, wealth building, spiritual growth, foreign language & personal development.
ISBN Prefix(es): 978-1-55525; 978-0-935300
Number of titles published annually: 3 Print; 1 CD-ROM; 74 Audio
Total Titles: 190 Print; 5 CD-ROM; 400 Audio
Subsidiaries: Nightingale-Conant (UK)
Distributed by William Morrow

§Nilgiri Press
Division of Blue Mountain Center of Meditation
3600 Tomales Rd, Tomales, CA 94971
Mailing Address: PO Box 256, Tomales, CA 94971
Tel: 707-878-2369
E-mail: info@easwaran.org
Web Site: www.easwaran.org
Key Personnel
Press Coord: Debbie McMurray *E-mail:* debbie.mcmurray@nilgiripress.org
Intl Rts: Jennifer Jones *E-mail:* jennifer.jones@nilgiripress.org
Founded: 1972
Timeless wisdom for daily living books, videos, audios & online courses.
ISBN Prefix(es): 978-0-915132; 978-1-888314; 978-1-58638
Number of titles published annually: 3 Print; 10 E-Book; 10 Audio
Total Titles: 28 Print
Foreign Rep(s): Publishers Group West
Foreign Rights: Publishers Group West (Canada)

No Frills Buffalo
119 Dorchester Rd, Buffalo, NY 14213
Tel: 716-510-0520
E-mail: contact@nofrillsbuffalo.com; submissions@nofrillsbuffalo.com
Web Site: www.nofrillsbuffalo.com
Key Personnel
Founder: Mark Pogodzinski
Founded: 2009
Publishing new & engaging authors. Provides editorial services, interior & cover design, publicity & a chance to succeed. Accepting submissions in all genres, fiction, nonfiction, poetry, short stories, children's books.
ISBN Prefix(es): 978-0-615; 978-0-578; 978-0-692
Number of titles published annually: 5 Print; 5 E-Book
Total Titles: 50 Print; 40 E-Book
Imprints: Amelia Press (children's books); NFB
Distributed by Createspace; NFB Distribution
Membership(s): AAP

§No Starch Press
245 Eighth St, San Francisco, CA 94103
Tel: 415-863-9900 *Toll Free Tel:* 800-420-7240 *Fax:* 415-863-9950
E-mail: info@nostarch.com; sales@nostarch.com
Web Site: www.nostarch.com
Key Personnel
Founder: William Pollock
Sales Mgr: Julia Borden
Ed: Tyler Ortman
Founded: 1994
Carefully crafts the finest in geek entertainment. The growing list of award-winning No Starch Press best sellers covers topics like LEGO, hacking, STEM, programming, science, & math. Our titles have personality, our authors are passionate & our books tackle topics that people care about.
ISBN Prefix(es): 978-1-886411; 978-1-59627
Number of titles published annually: 30 Print; 30 E-Book
Total Titles: 250 Print; 300 E-Book
Distributed by O'Reilly Media
Distribution Center: Penguin Random House Publisher Services, 400 Hahn Rd, Westminster, MD 21157 *E-mail:* distribution@penguinrandomhouse.com *Web Site:* www.penguinrandomhouse.com
Membership(s): AAP; Independent Book Publishers Association

§NOLO
Subsidiary of Internet Brands Inc
7031 Koll Center Pkwy, Suite 100, Pleasanton, CA 94566
SAN: 206-7935
Web Site: www.nolo.com
Founded: 1971
Leading provider of plain-English legal & business books, software, online forms & information for consumers & businesses. Founded by 2 legal aid attorneys, Nolo products help you handle many legal matters yourself. All books

are written in concise, conversational English by Nolo's team of lawyer editors & regularly revised & updated to comply with changes in the law & technology. With over 50 web properties, the Nolo Network is one of the Web's largest libraries of free consumer-friendly legal information. Nolo also offers a Lawyer Directory for consumers & small businesses that want to find a local lawyer to handle or consult on a particular legal problem.
This publisher has indicated that 100% of their product line is author subsidized.
ISBN Prefix(es): 978-0-87337; 978-1-41330
Number of titles published annually: 60 Print; 200 Online; 140 E-Book
Total Titles: 140 Print; 200 Online; 140 E-Book
Distribution Center: Ingram Publisher Services, One Ingram Blvd, La Vergne, TN 37086 *Toll Free Tel:* 855-802-8230 *Toll Free Fax:* 800-838-1149 *E-mail:* customerservice@ingrampublisherservices.com *Web Site:* www.ingrampublisherservices.com
Membership(s): ALA; Independent Book Publishers Association

The Noontide Press
Imprint of Legion for the Survival of Freedom
PO Box 2719, Newport Beach, CA 92659-1319
Tel: 714-593-9725
E-mail: orders@noontidepress.com
Web Site: www.noontidepress.com
Key Personnel
Pres: Mark Weber
Founded: 1968
Publisher & mail-order distributor of books, disks & tapes.
ISBN Prefix(es): 978-0-939482; 978-0-911038
Number of titles published annually: 3 Print; 3 Audio
Total Titles: 20 Print; 2 CD-ROM; 50 Audio

Norilana Books
PO Box 209, Highgate Center, VT 05459-0209
SAN: 851-8556
E-mail: service@norilana.com
Web Site: www.norilana.com
Key Personnel
Owner & Publr: Vera Nazarian
Founded: 2006
Beautifully produced & packaged editions, primarily classics of world literature & quality originals.
ISBN Prefix(es): 978-1-934169; 978-1-934648; 978-1-60762
Number of titles published annually: 3 Print
Total Titles: 300 Print
Imprints: Curiosities; Leda; Spirit; The Sword of Norilana; TaLeKa; YA Angst

§North Atlantic Books
Division of Society for the Study of Native Arts & Sciences
2526 Martin Luther King Jr Way, Berkeley, CA 94704
SAN: 203-1655
Tel: 510-549-4270 *Fax:* 510-549-4276
Web Site: www.northatlanticbooks.com
Key Personnel
Founding Publr: Richard Grossinger
Interim Publr: Tim McKee
Sr Dir, Sales & Dist: Janet Levin *Tel:* 510-549-4270 ext 35 *E-mail:* jlevin@northatlanticbooks.com
Contracts Mgr: Susan Bumps *Tel:* 510-549-4270 ext 13 *E-mail:* sbumps@northatlanticbooks.com
Creative Mgr: Jasmine Hromjak *E-mail:* jhromijak@northatlanticbooks.com
Foreign Rts & Perms Mgr: Sarah Serafimidis *Tel:* 510-549-4270 ext 16 *E-mail:* sserafimidis@northatlanticbooks.com
Founded: 1974
North Atlantic Books has been located in Berkeley, California since 1977. Over this period, North Atlantic has become a leading publisher of alternative health, nutrition, bodywork, martial arts & spiritual titles.
ISBN Prefix(es): 978-1-883319; 978-0-913028; 978-0-938190; 978-1-55643; 978-1-58394 (Frog Ltd Books); 978-0-942941
Number of titles published annually: 50 Print; 50 E-Book; 10 Audio
Total Titles: 1,000 Print; 600 E-Book; 10 Audio
Imprints: Blue Snake Books; Evolver Editions; Frog Books
Distributor for DharmaCafe; Energy Arts; Ergos Institute; Heaven & Earth Publications; New Pacific Press
Foreign Rep(s): Faradawn (South Africa); Penguin Random House Canada (Canada); Penguin Random House Inc International Sales Div (worldwide); Publishers Group UK (UK)
Orders to: Penguin Random House Publisher Services (PRHPS), 400 Hahn Rd, Westminster, MD 21157 (bookstore orders) *Toll Free Tel:* 800-733-3000 *Toll Free Fax:* 800-659-2436 *E-mail:* customerservice@penguinrandomhouse.com *Web Site:* www.penguinrandomhouse.com
Returns: Penguin Random House Returns Dept, 1019 N State Rd 47, Crawfordsville, IN 47933
Distribution Center: Penguin Random House Publisher Services (PRHPS), 400 Hahn Rd, Westminster, MD 21157
Membership(s): Book Promotion Forum

North Carolina Office of Archives & History
Historical Publications Branch, 4610 Mail Service Ctr, Raleigh, NC 27699-4610
Tel: 919-807-7290
E-mail: historical.publications@ncdcr.gov
Web Site: www.ncdcr.gov
Key Personnel
Admin: Michael Ray Hill *Tel:* 919-807-7288 *E-mail:* michael.hill@ncdcr.gov
Founded: 1903
State government agency that publishes nonfiction hardcover & trade paperback books relating to North Carolina as well as the *North Carolina Historical Review*, a quarterly scholarly journal of history.
ISBN Prefix(es): 978-0-86526
Number of titles published annually: 8 Print
Total Titles: 152 Print
Distribution Center: University of North Carolina Press, 116 S Boundary St, Chapel Hill, NC 27514-3808 *Toll Free Tel:* 800-848-6224 *Toll Free Fax:* 800-272-6817 *Web Site:* www.uncpress.org

North Country Books Inc
220 Lafayette St, Utica, NY 13502-4312
Tel: 315-735-4877 *Toll Free Tel:* 800-342-7409 (orders) *Fax:* 315-738-4342
E-mail: ncbooks@verizon.net
Web Site: www.northcountrybooks.com
Key Personnel
Owner & Pres: Robert B Igoe, Jr *E-mail:* rbigoe@verizon.net
Gen Mgr: Zach Steffen
Founded: 1965
Book publisher & distributor of New York State regional titles to bookstores, schools & libraries, booksellers & non-traditional outlets.
ISBN Prefix(es): 978-0-932052; 978-0-925168; 978-0-9601158; 978-1-59531
Number of titles published annually: 5 Print
Total Titles: 140 Print
Imprints: North Country Books; North Country Classics

North Country Press
126 Main St, Unity, ME 04988
SAN: 247-9680
Mailing Address: PO Box 501, Unity, ME 04988
Tel: 207-948-2208 *Fax:* 207-948-9000
E-mail: info@northcountrypress.com
Web Site: www.northcountrypress.com
Key Personnel
Publr: Patricia Newell
Founded: 1977
Regional press dealing with New England (specializing in Maine) subjects. Three lines: outdoor (hunting, fishing, etc); humor, lore; literature (mysteries, essays, poetry).
ISBN Prefix(es): 978-0-945980; 978-1-943424
Number of titles published annually: 9 Print
Total Titles: 60 Print

North Point Press
Imprint of Farrar, Straus & Giroux, LLC
18 W 18 St, 8th fl, New York, NY 10011
Tel: 212-741-6900 *Toll Free Tel:* 888-330-8477 *Fax:* 212-633-9385
Web Site: www.fsgbooks.com
Key Personnel
SVP, Mktg & Publicity: Jeff Seroy *Tel:* 212-741-6900 ext 6323
VP, Contracts & Perms: Erika Seidman
Dir, Publicity & Promo: Sarita Varma
Founded: 1981
Nonfiction, environment, nature, design, food, spirituality.
ISBN Prefix(es): 978-0-86547
Number of titles published annually: 10 Print
Foreign Rep(s): HarperCollins Publishers (Canada); Jacaranda Wiley Ltd (Australia); Orion Ltd (worldwide)
Foreign Rights: ANA Baltic (Tatjana Zoldnere) (Estonia, Latvia, Lithuania); AnatoliaLit Agency (Amy Spangler & Eda Caca) (Turkey); Anthea Agency (Katalina Sabeva) (Bulgaria); L'Autre Agence (Corinne Marotte & Marie Lannurien) (France); Bardon-Chinese Media Agency (David Tsai) (China, Taiwan); Anoukh Foerg Agency (Germany); Deborah Harris Agency (Geula Geurts) (Israel); International Copyright Agency (Simon Kessler & Marina Adriana) (Romania); The Italian Literary Agency srl (Claire Sabatie-Garat) (Italy); Anna Jarota Agency (Dominika Bojanowska) (Poland); Katai & Bolza (Peter Bolza) (Hungary); KCC (Kyung Kang) (Korea); MB Agencia Literaria (Monica Martin & Ines Planells) (Latin America, Spain); Kristin Olson Literary Agency sro (Czech Republic); Plima Literary Agency (Vuk Perisic) (Albania, Croatia, Serbia, Slovenia); Read 'n Right Agency (Nike Davarinou) (Greece); Riff Agency (Laura & Joao Paulo Riff) (Brazil); Sebes & Bisseling Literary Agency (Paul Sebes) (Netherlands); Synopsis Literary Agency (Olga Zasetskaya) (Russia); Tuttle-Mori Agency Inc (Asako Kawachi) (Japan)

North River Press Publishing Corp
27 Rosseter St, Great Barrington, MA 01230
SAN: 202-1048
Mailing Address: PO Box 567, Great Barrington, MA 01230-0567
Tel: 413-528-0034 *Toll Free Tel:* 800-486-2665 *Fax:* 413-528-3163 *Toll Free Fax:* 800-BOOK-FAX (266-5329)
E-mail: info@northriverpress.com
Web Site: www.northriverpress.com
Key Personnel
Pres: Laurence Gadd
VP: Amy Gallagher
Founded: 1971
General nonfiction, business books, hardcovers & paperback.
ISBN Prefix(es): 978-0-88427
Number of titles published annually: 6 Print
Total Titles: 40 Print; 1 Audio

North Star Editions Inc
2297 Waters Dr, Mendota Heights, MN 55120

SAN: 990-2325
Tel: 651-204-3515 *Toll Free Tel:* 888-417-0195 *Fax:* 952-582-1000
E-mail: sales@northstareditions.com
Web Site: www.northstareditions.com
Key Personnel
Mktg Communs Mgr: Megan Naidl *Tel:* 952-446-7239 *E-mail:* mnaidl@northstareditions.com
Sales Mgr: Joe Riley *Tel:* 651-342-8181 *E-mail:* jriley@northstareditions.com
Sales Coord: Sam Temple *E-mail:* stemple@northstareditions.com
Founded: 2016
ISBN Prefix(es): 978-0-7387; 978-0-9848801; 978-0-9886491; 978-1-939967; 978-1-63163; 978-1-63517; 978-1-63583
Number of titles published annually: 125 Print; 125 E-Book; 4 Audio
Total Titles: 222 Print; 240 E-Book; 4 Audio
Imprints: Flux (young adult fiction); Focus Readers (juvenile nonfiction); Jolly Fish Press (hybrid)
Foreign Rep(s): INT Books (Australia, New Zealand); Roundhouse Group (Europe, Ireland, UK); Saunders Book Co (Canada)

North Star Press of Saint Cloud Inc
PO Box 451, St Cloud, MN 56302-0451
Tel: 320-558-9062
E-mail: info@northstarpress.com
Web Site: www.northstarpress.com
Key Personnel
Owner: Corinne A Dwyer
Busn Mgr: Curtis Weinrich
Ed: Anne Rasset
Founded: 1969
Regional, Minnesota history & fiction, general fiction, poetry.
ISBN Prefix(es): 978-0-87839
Number of titles published annually: 30 Print; 25 E-Book
Total Titles: 1,000 Print; 300 E-Book
Shipping Address: 19485 Estes Rd, Clearwater, MN 55320
Membership(s): Midwest Independent Publishing Association; Minnesota Library Association

North Star Way, see Gallery Books

Northeast-Midwest Institute
50 "F" St NW, Suite 950, Washington, DC 20001
Tel: 202-544-5200 *Fax:* 202-544-0043
E-mail: info@nemw.org
Web Site: www.nemw.org
Key Personnel
Pres & CEO: Michael Goff *Tel:* 202-464-4010 *E-mail:* mgoff@nemw.org
Dir, Fin & Admin: J T Fletcher *Tel:* 202-464-4007 *E-mail:* jfletcher@nemw.org
Admin Mgr: Hope Ratner *Tel:* 202-464-4019 *E-mail:* hratner@nemw.org
Founded: 1976
Energy, environment, economic development, human resources.
ISBN Prefix(es): 978-1-882061
Number of titles published annually: 3 Print
Total Titles: 50 Print

Northern Illinois University Press
2280 Bethany Rd, DeKalb, IL 60115
SAN: 202-8875
Tel: 815-753-1075 *Fax:* 815-753-1845
Web Site: www.niupress.niu.edu
Key Personnel
Dir: Linda Manning *Tel:* 815-753-9899 *E-mail:* lamanning2@niu.edu
Mng Ed: Nathan Holmes *Tel:* 815-753-9908 *E-mail:* nholmes1@niu.edu
Busn Mgr: Cara Carlson *Tel:* 815-753-1826 *E-mail:* ccarlso2@niu.eu
Mktg Mgr: Lori Propheter *Tel:* 815-753-9905 *E-mail:* lpropheter@niu.edu
Acqs Ed: Amy Farranto *E-mail:* afarranto@niu.edu
Founded: 1965
Publishes scholarly & trade books on a variety of topics in the humanities & social sciences. In fulfilling its educational mission, the Press publishes books for both specialists & general readers.
ISBN Prefix(es): 978-0-87580; 978-1-60909
Number of titles published annually: 25 Print
Total Titles: 600 Print
Imprints: Switchgrass Books (literary fiction)
Distributed by University of Chicago Press
Foreign Rep(s): Footprint Books Pty Ltd (Australia, Fiji, New Zealand, Papua New Guinea); United Publishers Service Ltd (Japan); John Wiley & Sons Ltd (Africa, Europe, India, Middle East, Pakistan, UK)
Distribution Center: Chicago Distribution Center, 11030 S Langley Ave, Chicago, IL 60628 *Toll Free Tel:* 800-621-2736 *Toll Free Fax:* 800-621-8476 *E-mail:* orders@press.uchicago.edu
Membership(s): American Association for the Advancement of Slavic Studies; American Association of University Presses; American Historical Association; Organization of American Historians

Northwestern University Press
629 Noyes St, Evanston, IL 60208-4210
SAN: 202-5787
Tel: 847-491-2046 *Toll Free Tel:* 800-621-2736 (orders only) *Fax:* 847-491-8150
E-mail: nupress@northwestern.edu
Web Site: www.nupress.northwestern.edu
Key Personnel
Dir: Jane Bunker *Tel:* 847-491-8111 *E-mail:* j-bunker@northwestern.edu
Asst Dir & Sr Ed: Henry L Carrigan, Jr *Tel:* 847-491-8112 *E-mail:* h-carrigan@northwestern.edu
Creative Dir: Marianne Jankowski *Tel:* 847-467-5368 *E-mail:* ma-jankowski@northwestern.edu
Dir, Mktg & Sales: JD Wilson *Tel:* 847-467-0319 *E-mail:* jdwilson@northwestern.edu
Busn Mgr: Kirstie Felland *Tel:* 847-491-8310 *E-mail:* kfelland@northwestern.edu
Mktg Mgr: Greta Bennion *Tel:* 847-491-5315 *E-mail:* g-bennion@northwestern.edu
Prodn Mgr: Morris (Dino) Robinson *Tel:* 847-467-3392 *E-mail:* morris-robinson@northwestern.edu
Sales & Subs Rts Mgr: Parneshia Jones *Tel:* 847-491-7420 *E-mail:* p-jones3@northwestern.edu
Ed-in-Chief: Gianna Mosser *Tel:* 847-467-1279 *E-mail:* g-barbera@northwestern.edu
Mng Ed: Anne Gendler *Tel:* 847-491-3844 *E-mail:* a-gendler@northwestern.edu
Acqs Ed: Jill Petty
Spec Proj Ed: Nathan MacBrien *Tel:* 847-467-7362 *E-mail:* nathan.macbrien@northwestern.edu
Acqs Coord: Maggie Grossman *Tel:* 847-491-8113 *E-mail:* m-grossman@northwestern.edu
Digital Content & Systems Coord: Emily Dalton *Tel:* 847-476-2434 *E-mail:* emily.dalton@northwestern.edu
Intellectual Property Specialist: Liz Hamilton *Tel:* 847-491-2458 *E-mail:* emhamilton@northwestern.edu
Founded: 1958
Part of Northwestern University, the Press publishes mostly scholarly books, with an emphasis on literature & language, philosophy, works in translation & theater, as well as trade books in the areas of fiction, poetry & play scripts.
ISBN Prefix(es): 978-0-8101
Number of titles published annually: 65 Print
Imprints: Curbstone Books; TriQuarterly Books (contemporary American fiction & poetry)
Distributor for Lake Forest College Press (Chicago area studies); Tia Chucha Press
Orders to: Chicago Distribution Center, 11030 S Langley, Chicago, IL 60628 *Toll Free Tel:* 800-621-2736 *Toll Free Fax:* 800-621-8476
Distribution Center: Chicago Distribution Center, 11030 S Langley, Chicago, IL 60628 *Toll Free Tel:* 800-621-2736 *Toll Free Fax:* 800-621-8476
Membership(s): Association of American University Presses
See separate listing for:
TriQuarterly Books

§W W Norton & Company Inc
500 Fifth Ave, New York, NY 10110-0017
SAN: 202-5795
Tel: 212-354-5500 *Toll Free Tel:* 800-233-4830 (orders & cust serv) *Fax:* 212-869-0856 *Toll Free Fax:* 800-458-6515
E-mail: orders@wwnorton.com
Web Site: books.wwnorton.com
Key Personnel
Chmn: W Drake McFeely
Pres: Julia Reidhead
CFO & VP: Stephen King
VChair & VP, Coll Dept: Roby Harrington
VChmn & Publg Dir: Jeannie Luciano
VP & Exec Art Dir: Ingsu Liu
VP & Exec Dir, Publicity & PR: Louise Brockett
VP & Dir, Opers: Jorie Krumpfer
VP & Dir, Natl Accts: Deirdre F Dolan
VP & Dir, Prodn Dept: Tim McGuire
VP & Dir, Sales & Mktg, Coll Dept: Stephen P Dunn
VP & Dir, Trade Prodn: Julia Druskin
VP & Corp Art Dir: Debra Morton Hoyt
VP & Assoc Publg Dir: Nomi Victor
VP & Dir, Coll Sales: Michael Wright
VP & Dir, Digital Learning Systems: April Lange
VP & Dir, Intl Sales: Dorothy M Cook
VP & Dir, Subs Rts: Elisabeth Kerr
VP & Sr Publicity Dir: Elizabeth Riley
VP & Edit Dir, Digital Media: Karl Bakeman
VP & Exec Ed: Alane Mason
VP & Exec Ed, Trade Dept: Jill Bialosky
VP & Sr Ed: Tom Mayer
VP & Sr Ed, Trade Dept: Amy Cherry
VP & Ed-in-Chief, Trade Dept: John Glusman
VP & Mng Ed, Trade Dept: Nancy K Palmquist
VP & Ed, Coll Dept: Carol Stiles Bemis; Jon Durbin; Marilyn Moller; Maribeth Payne; Jack Repcheck; Peter J Simon
VP & Ed, Digital Media: Steve Hoge
VP & Electronic Media Ed: Cliff Landesman *E-mail:* c.landesman@wwnorton.com
VP, Spec Accts: Rick Raeber
VP, Trade Sales & Mktg: Brendan Curry
Dir, Trade Sales: Steven Pace
Dom Rts Dir: Felice Mello
Mktg Dir: Kevin Olsen
Publicity Dir: Erin Lovett; Rachel Salzman
Publr & Ed-in-Chief, Liveright & Co: Robert Weil
Dir, Mktg-Trade Dept: Meredith McGinnis
Edit Dir, Prof Books Dept: Deborah A Malmud
Sr Ed: Matt Weiland
Ed, Coll Dept: Erik Fahlgren; Sheri Snavely; Betsy Twitchell
Ed, Liveright & Co: Katie Henderson Adams
Trade Ed: Quynh Do
E-Commerce Mgr: Emily Turner-Julier
HR Mgr: Jamie Finkelman
Perms Mgr: Elizabeth Clementson
Perms & Copyright Mgr: Claire Reinertsen
Asst Mgr, Subs Rts: Mary Kate Skehan
Sr Publicist: Kyle Radler; Alice Rha
Publicist: Lauren Opper
Founded: 1923
General nonfiction & fiction; trade paperbacks; college texts, professional books, architecture & interior design.
No unsol mss accepted.
ISBN Prefix(es): 978-0-393; 978-0-87140 (Liveright & Co); 978-1-324

Number of titles published annually: 400 Print; 110 E-Book
Total Titles: 4,800 Print; 75 CD-ROM; 600 E-Book
Imprints: The Countryman Press; Liveright & Co
Foreign Office(s): W W Norton & Company Ltd, Castle House, 75/76 Wells St, London W1T 3QT, United Kingdom, Mng Dir & VP: Edward Crutchley *Tel:* (020) 7323 1579 *Fax:* (020) 7436 4553 *E-mail:* academic@wwnorton.co.uk *Web Site:* www.wwnorton.co.uk
Distributor for Airphoto International Ltd/Odyssey Publications; Albatross Publishing House; Atlas & Co; Blue Guides Ltd; George Braziller Inc; Chess Information & Research Center; Dalkey Archive Press; Fantagraphics Books; Kales Press; New Directions Publishing Corp; Ontario Review Press; The Overlook Press; Peace Hill Press; Pegasus Books; Persea Books Inc; Pushcart Press; Quantuck Lane Press; Skyhorse Publishing; Thames & Hudson; Tilbury House Publishing; Tin House Books
Foreign Rep(s): Everest International Publishing Services (Wei Zhao) (China); Hardy Bigfoss International Co Ltd (Cambodia, Laos, Myanmar, Thailand, Vietnam); M K International Ltd (Japan); B K Norton Ltd (Korea, Taiwan); W W Norton & Company Ltd (UK) (Africa, Europe, India, Ireland, Middle East, UK); Pansing Distribution Pte Ltd (Brunei, Malaysia, Singapore); Penguin Random House Canada (Canada); Transglobal Publishers Services Ltd (Hong Kong, Macau); US PubRep (Caribbean, Central America, Mexico, South America); John Wiley & Sons Australia Ltd (Australia, New Zealand)
Foreign Rights: Akcali Copyright Agency (Turkey); L'Autre Agence (France); Bardon-Chinese Media Agency (China, Taiwan); Casanovas & Lynch (Portugal, Spain); Graal Literary Agency (Poland); The Deborah Harris Agency (Israel); International Copyright Agency (Romania); Japan UNI Agency (Japan); Katai & Bolza (Hungary); Duran Kim Agency (Korea); Mohrbooks (Germany); Nordin Agency (Scandinavia); Andrew Nurnberg Associates (Baltic States, Bulgaria, Russia); Kristin Olson Literary Agency sro (Czech Republic); The Riff Agency (Brazil); Roberto Santachiara Literary Agency (Italy); Marianne Schoenbach Literary Agency BV (Netherlands)
Advertising Agency: Verso Advertising
Shipping Address: National Book Co Inc, Keystone Industrial Park, Scranton, PA 18512
See separate listing for:
The Countryman Press

Norwood House Press
PO Box 316598, Chicago, IL 60631
Tel: 773-467-0837 *Toll Free Tel:* 866-565-2900 *Fax:* 773-467-9686 *Toll Free Fax:* 866-565-2901
E-mail: customerservice@norwoodhousepress.com
Web Site: www.norwoodhousepress.com
Founded: 2005
Specialize in children's books for the school & library.
ISBN Prefix(es): 978-1-59953; 978-1-60357
Number of titles published annually: 100 Print; 100 E-Book
Total Titles: 200 Print; 200 E-Book

Nova Press
9058 Lloyd Place, West Hollywood, CA 90069
Tel: 310-275-3513 *Fax:* 310-281-5629
E-mail: novapress@aol.com
Web Site: www.novapress.net
Key Personnel
Pres & Electronic Publg: Jeff Kolby
Founded: 1993
Publishes test prep books, software, phone apps & online courses for the SAT, ACT, GRE, LSAT, GMAT, MCAT & TOEFL.
ISBN Prefix(es): 978-1-889057
Number of titles published annually: 6 Print; 6 Online
Total Titles: 30 Print; 6 CD-ROM; 30 Online; 30 E-Book

Nova Science Publishers Inc
400 Oser Ave, Suite 1600, Hauppauge, NY 11788-3619
Tel: 631-231-7269 *Fax:* 631-231-8175
E-mail: main@novapublishers.com
Web Site: www.novapublishers.com
Key Personnel
Pres: Nadia Columbus
Founded: 1985
Scientific, technical, medical & social sciences publishing; trade books - hardcover & softcover.
ISBN Prefix(es): 978-0-941743; 978-1-56072; 978-1-59033; 978-1-59454; 978-1-60021; 978-1-60456; 978-1-60692; 978-1-60741; 978-1-60876; 978-1-61668; 978-1-61728; 978-1-61761; 978-1-61122; 978-1-61209; 978-1-61324; 978-1-61470; 978-1-62100; 978-1-61942; 978-1-62081; 978-1-62257; 978-1-62417; 978-1-62618; 978-1-62808; 978-1-62948; 978-1-63117; 978-1-63321; 978-1-63463; 978-1-63482; 978-1-63483; 978-1-63484; 978-1-63485; 978-1-5361
Number of titles published annually: 2,000 Print; 10 CD-ROM
Total Titles: 25,000 Print
Imprints: Noel Press; Nova Biomedical Press; Nova Global Affairs Press; Nova History Press; Nova Music; Nova Science Books; Novinka Books; Snova Books; Troitsa Books

NPS, see BrickHouse Books Inc

NRP Direct
Formerly National Register Publishing
430 Mountain Ave, Suite 403, New Providence, NJ 07974
Tel: 908-517-0780 *Toll Free Tel:* 844-592-4197 *Fax:* 908-608-3012 (cust serv)
E-mail: sales@nrpdirect.com
Web Site: www.nrpdirect.com
Founded: 1915
Publisher of business information directories available in print, online & mailing list for commercial & reference use.
ISBN Prefix(es): 978-0-87217
Number of titles published annually: 5 Print
Total Titles: 5 Print; 1 Online

Nursesbooks.org, The Publishing Program of ANA
Division of American Nurses Association
8515 Georgia Ave, Suite 400, Silver Spring, MD 20910-3492
SAN: 851-3481
Tel: 301-628-5000 *Toll Free Tel:* 800-274-4262; 800-637-0323 (orders) *Fax:* 301-628-5342
E-mail: anp@ana.org
Web Site: www.Nursesbooks.org; www.NursingWorld.org
Key Personnel
Publr: Joe Vallina *Tel:* 301-628-5118 *E-mail:* joseph.vallina@ana.org
Ed & Proj Mgr: Eric Wurzbacher *Tel:* 301-628-5212 *E-mail:* eric.wurzbacher@ana.org
Sr Mktg Specialist: Novella Green *Tel:* 301-628-5072 *E-mail:* novella.green@ana.org
Publishes books on ANA core issues & programs, including ethics, leadership, quality, specialty practice, advanced practice & the profession's enduring legacy. Best known for the foundational documents of the profession on nursing ethics, scope & standards of practice & social policy, Nursebooks.org is the publisher for the professional, career-oriented nurse, reaching & serving nurse educators, administrators, managers & researchers as well as staff nurses in the course of their professional development.
ISBN Prefix(es): 978 1 55810
Number of titles published annually: 14 Print; 10 E-Book
Total Titles: 95 Print; 60 E-Book
Imprints: ANCC Magnet Recognition Program; Nursing Knowledge Center
Sales Office(s): American Nurses Association (ebook site license sales), Busn Opers Specialist, Publg: Tony Ward *Tel:* 301-628-5194 *E-mail:* tony.ward@ana.org *Web Site:* www.nursesbooks.com/quick-links/electronic.aspx
ANA Nursing Knowledge Center (pubn sales integrated with other prods & servs), Specialist, Prod Sales & Servs: Mary Louise Cobb *Tel:* 301-628-5274 *E-mail:* marylouise.cobb@ana.org
Distribution Center: PBD Worldwide Inc, 1650 Bluegrass Lakes Pkwy, Alpharetta, GA 30004, Acct Coord: Lisa Johansen *Tel:* 770-280-0105 *E-mail:* lisa.johansen@pbd.com *Web Site:* www.pbd.com
Membership(s): Association Media & Publishing

NYBG Press, see The New York Botanical Garden Press

§Nystrom Education
Division of Social Studies School Service
10200 Jefferson Blvd, Culver City, CA 90232
Mailing Address: PO Box 802, Culver City, CA 90232
Tel: 310-839-2436 *Toll Free Tel:* 800-421-4246 *Fax:* 310-839-2249 *Toll Free Fax:* 800-944-5432
E-mail: access@nystromeducation.com; customerservice@nystromeducation.com
Web Site: www.nystromeducation.com
Key Personnel
Natl Sales Dir: Jennifer Carlson *E-mail:* jcarlson@nystromeducation.com
Founded: 1903
Social studies, history & geography programs, maps, globes, atlases & multimedia.
ISBN Prefix(es): 978-0-7825; 978-0-88463
Number of titles published annually: 3 Print
Total Titles: 50 Print; 5 CD-ROM; 1 E-Book

NYU Press, see New York University Press

§OAG Worldwide
3025 Highland Pkwy, Suite 200, Downers Grove, IL 60515-5561
Tel: 630-515-5300 *Toll Free Tel:* 800-342-5624 (cust serv)
E-mail: contactus@oag.com
Web Site: www.oag.com
Founded: 1929
Supplier of independent travel info.
ISBN Prefix(es): 978-0-9776295
Number of titles published annually: 7 Print; 5 CD-ROM; 5 Online
Total Titles: 11 Print; 5 CD-ROM; 5 Online
Foreign Office(s): 18F, Caroline Centre, Lee Gardens Two, 28 Yun Ping Rd, Causeway Bay, Hong Kong *Tel:* 2965 1700 *Fax:* 2965 1777 *E-mail:* custsvcaspac@oag.com
Toranomon, 40 MT Bldg 9F, 5-13-1 Toranomon, Minato-ku, Tokyo 105-0001, Japan *Tel:* 36402 7301 *Fax:* 36402 7302 *E-mail:* acustsvcjpn@oag.com
3 Lim Teck Kim Rd, No 10-01, Singapore Technologies Bldg, Singapore 088934, Singapore *Tel:* 6395-5868 *Fax:* 6293-6566 *E-mail:* custsvcsaspac@oag.com
Church St, Dunstable, Bedfordshire LU5 4HB, United Kingdom (headquarters) *Tel.* (01582) 600111 *Fax.* (01582) 695230 *E-mail:* customers@oag.com

Oak Knoll Press
310 Delaware St, New Castle, DE 19720
Tel: 302-328-7232 *Toll Free Tel:* 800-996-2556 *Fax:* 302-328-7274
E-mail: oakknoll@oakknoll.com; publishing@oakknoll.com
Web Site: www.oakknoll.com
Key Personnel
Pres: Robert D Fleck *E-mail:* bob@oakknoll.com
Mng Ed: Matthew Young
Antiquarian & Lib Sales: Robert Fleck, III *E-mail:* rob@oakknoll.com
Founded: 1976
Publish scholarly books (books about books), bibliographies, book arts & book history.
ISBN Prefix(es): 978-1-884718; 978-1-58456; 978-1-872116; 978-0-938768
Number of titles published annually: 25 Print
Total Titles: 1,100 Print; 1 CD-ROM
Distributor for American Antiquarian Society; Bibliographical Society of America; Bibliographical Society of University of Virginia; The Bibliographical Society (UK); Block Museum; Boston College; John Carter Brown Library; Bryn Mawr College; Catalpa Press; Caxton Club; Center for Book Arts; Chapin Library; Fondation Custodia; The Grolier Club; Hes & De Graaf; Historic New Orleans Collection; Library of Congress-Center for the Book; The Manuscript Society; New England Bibliographies; Providence Athenaeum; Rivendale Press; Tate Galleries; Texas State Historical Association; Typophiles; Winterthur Museum; Yushodo Press
Membership(s): AAP; Antiquarian Booksellers Association of America; International League of Antiquarian Booksellers

Oak Tree Press
1700 Dairy Ave, No 149, Corcoran, CA 93212
Tel: 217-824-6500
E-mail: publisher@oaktreebooks.com; info@oaktreebooks.com; query@oaktreebooks.com; pressdept@oaktreebooks.com; bookorders@oaktreebooks.com
Web Site: www.oaktreebooks.com; www.otpblog.blogspot.com
Key Personnel
Publr: Billie Johnson
PR Mgr: Jeana Thompson *Tel:* 217-825-4489
Ed: Marilyn Olsen *E-mail:* coptaleseditor@oaktreebooks.com
Acqs Ed: Marilyn Olsen
Off Mgr: Nancy Jacoby *E-mail:* weeklyroundup.items@gmail.com
Founded: 1998
Independent press that publishes fiction & nonfiction. Emphasis on mysteries & romances with series potential, business books, self-help & how-to.
ISBN Prefix(es): 978-1-892343; 978-1-61009
Number of titles published annually: 60 Print; 48 E-Book
Total Titles: 430 Print; 325 E-Book
Imprints: Acorn (children's books); Coptales (stories by & about law enforcement professionals-cops, medical examiners, criminal defense attorneys, DAs); Dark Oak Mysteries (all mystery genres, from amateur sleuths to hard-boiled detectives); Mystic Oaks (paranormal mysteries & romances); Oak Tree Books (mainstream fiction, how-to, memoir, self-help); Timeless Love (all romance genres, from sweet to steamy); Wild Oak (western)
Membership(s): Sisters in Crime

The Oaklea Press
41 Old Mill Rd, Richmond, VA 23226-3111
Tel: 804-218-2394
Web Site: oakleapress.com
Founded: 1995
Trade book publisher.
ISBN Prefix(es): 978-1-892538; 978-0-9646601; 978-0-9664098
Number of titles published annually: 6 Print; 8 E-Book; 6 Audio
Total Titles: 45 Print; 8 E-Book; 6 Audio
Imprints: New Marketplace
Sales Office(s): Delphi Distribution, 1263 Southwest Blvd, Kansas City, KS 66103, Contact: Amanda Garcia *Toll Free Tel:* 866-463-8541 *E-mail:* agarcia@delphidistribution.com *Web Site:* www.delphidistribution.com
Distribution Center: Delphi Distribution, 1263 Southwest Blvd, Kansas City, KS 66103, Contact: Amanda Garcia *Toll Free Tel:* 866-463-8541 *E-mail:* agarcia@delphidistribution.com *Web Site:* www.delphidistribution.com
Membership(s): Independent Book Publishers Association

Oberlin College Press
Subsidiary of Oberlin College
50 N Professor St, Oberlin, OH 44074-1091
SAN: 212-1883
Tel: 440-775-8408 *Fax:* 440-775-8124
E-mail: oc.press@oberlin.edu
Web Site: www.oberlin.edu/ocpress
Key Personnel
Mng Ed & Intl Rts Contact: Marco Wilkinson
First Ed: David Young
Ed: David Walker
Assoc Ed: Pamela Alexander; Kazim Ali; DeSales Harrison; Shane McCrae
Ed-at-Large: Martha Collins
Founded: 1969
Poetry in translation; contemporary American poetry.
ISBN Prefix(es): 978-0-932440
Number of titles published annually: 3 Print
Total Titles: 55 Print
Distributed by University Press of New England (UPNE)
Orders to: University Press of New England (UPNE), One Court St, Suite 250, Lebanon, NH 03766 *Toll Free Tel:* 800-421-1561 *Fax:* 603-448-9429 *Web Site:* www.upne.com
Returns: University Press of New England (UPNE), c/o Maple Logistics Solutions, Lebanon Distribution Ctr, 704 Legionaire Dr, Fredericksburg, PA 17026 *Tel:* 603-448-1533 ext 503 *Fax:* 603-448-9429
Membership(s): Community of Literary Magazines & Presses

Ocean Press
c/o CBSD The Keg House, 34 13 Ave NE, Suite 101, Minneapolis, MN 55413-1007
E-mail: info@oceanbooks.com.au; orders@oceanbooks.com.au (orders only); rights@oceanbooks.com.au
Web Site: www.oceanbooks.com.au
Key Personnel
Dir & Publr: Deborah Shnookal
Founded: 1990
ISBN Prefix(es): 978-1-875284; 978-1-876175; 978-1-920888; 978-1-921235
Number of titles published annually: 30 Print
Total Titles: 260 Print
Foreign Office(s): PO Box 1015, North Melbourne, Victoria 3051, Australia *Tel:* (03) 9326 4280 *Fax:* (03) 9329 5040
Distribution Center: Consortium Book Sales & Distribution
Publishers Group Canada (CN)
Turnaround Publisher Services Ltd (Europe & UK)

Ocean Tree Books
1325 Cerro Gordo Rd, Santa Fe, NM 87501
Mailing Address: PO Box 1295, Santa Fe, NM 87504 SAN: 241-0478
Tel: 505-983-1412 *Fax:* 505-983-0899
Web Site: www.oceantree.com
Key Personnel
Dir: Richard Polese *E-mail:* richard@oceantree.com
Publicity & Mktg: Hudson White
Off Mgr: Martin Burch
Founded: 1983
General trade with emphasis on Southwestern & Southern travel, faith & spirit & peacemaking. Distribution Centers: Baker & Taylor, Books West LLC & New Leaf Distributing Co.
ISBN Prefix(es): 978-0-943734; 978-0-9712548
Number of titles published annually: 5 Print
Total Titles: 60 Print
Imprints: Adventure Roads Travel; OTB Legacy Editions; Peacewatch Editions
Distributed by Treasure Chest Books
Foreign Rep(s): Blessingway Author Services (worldwide)
Foreign Rights: Blessingway Author Services
Distribution Center: Baker & Taylor
Books West LLC
New Leaf Distributing Co
Membership(s): Independent Book Publishers Association; New Mexico Book Association; Publishers Association of the West

Oceanview Publishing
CEO Center at Mediterranean Plaza, Suite 120-G, 595 Bay Isles Rd, Longboat Key, FL 34228
Tel: 941-387-8500
Web Site: oceanviewpub.com
Key Personnel
Publg Mgr: Lee Randall
Edit Asst: Emily Baar *E-mail:* emilyb@oceanviewpub.com
Founded: 2006
ISBN Prefix(es): 978-1-933515; 978-1-60809
Number of titles published annually: 13 Print
Total Titles: 52 Print
Distribution Center: Ingram Publisher Services, Cust Serv, Box 631, 14 Ingram Blvd, La Vergne, TN 37086 *Toll Free Tel:* 866-400-5351 *E-mail:* ips@ingramcontent.com
Membership(s): International Thriller Writers Inc; Mystery Writers of America

§OCP
5536 NE Hassalo St, Portland, OR 97213
Tel: 503-281-1191 *Toll Free Tel:* 800-548-8749 *Fax:* 503-282-3486 *Toll Free Fax:* 800-843-8181
E-mail: liturgy@ocp.org
Web Site: www.ocp.org
Key Personnel
Publr: John Limb *E-mail:* johnl@ocp.org
Mktg Mgr: Monica Rada *E-mail:* monicar@ocp.org
Cust Serv Mgr: Tim Dooley *Tel:* 503-460-5329 *E-mail:* timd@ocp.org
Founded: 1922
Books of music & liturgy.
ISBN Prefix(es): 978-0-915531; 978-0-9602378; 978-0-912405; 978-1-56929; 978-0-915903; 978-1-57992
Number of titles published annually: 25 Print; 25 Audio
Total Titles: 500 Print; 1 CD-ROM; 1 Online; 2,500 Audio
Imprints: Pastoral Press
Foreign Rights: Decani Music; Rainbow Book Agencies (Australia); Universal Songs (England, Europe, Ireland, UK)
Membership(s): CBA; Church Music Publishers Association

Octane Press
809 S Lamar Blvd, Suite H, Austin, TX 78704
Tel: 512-334-9441 *Fax:* 512-852-4737
E-mail: info@octanepress.com; orders@octanepress.com; sales@octanepress.com
Web Site: octanepress.com

Key Personnel
Founder & Publr: Lee Klancher *E-mail:* lee@octanepress.com
Graphic Designer: Tom Heffron *E-mail:* tom@octanepress.com
Mfg Specialist, Print Prodn: Joe Sita *E-mail:* joe@octanepress.com
Founded: 2010
Niche book publisher.
ISBN Prefix(es): 978-0-9821733; 978-0-9829131; 978-1-937747
Number of titles published annually: 10 Print; 5 E-Book
Total Titles: 18 Print; 10 E-Book
Foreign Rep(s): Publishers Group UK; Star Book Sales (Dennis Buckingham) (Europe)
Returns: 217 Etak Dr, Brainerd, MN 56401
Warehouse: 217 Etak Dr, Brainerd, MN 56401
Membership(s): Independent Book Publishers Association

Odyssey Books
Division of The Ciletti Publishing Group Inc
2421 Redwood Ct, Longmont, CO 80503-8155
Tel: 720-494-1473 *Fax:* 720-494-1471
E-mail: books@odysseybooks.net
Key Personnel
Pres & Publr: Barbara Ciletti
Promo: Erin Jones
Founded: 1995
Provides fiction & nonfiction for the retail trade, library, education & consumer markets.
ISBN Prefix(es): 978-0-9768655
Number of titles published annually: 20 Print
Membership(s): ABA; ALA; CMN; Independent Book Publishers Association; International Literacy Association; National Council of Teachers of English; National Science Teachers Association

§OECD Washington Center
Division of Organization for Economic Cooperation & Development (France)
1776 "I" St NW, Suite 450, Washington, DC 20006
Tel: 202-785-6323 *Toll Free Tel:* 800-456-6323 (dist ctr/pubns orders) *Fax:* 202-785-0350
E-mail: washington.contact@oecd.org
Web Site: www.oecd-ilibrary.org
Key Personnel
Sales & Mktg Mgr: Iain Williamson *Tel:* 202-822-3870 *E-mail:* iain.williamson@oecd.org
Founded: 1961
Periodicals, books, online services & statistical data.
ISBN Prefix(es): 978-92-64; 978-92-821; 978-92-65; 978-0-9501741
Number of titles published annually: 450 Print; 50 CD-ROM; 450 Online; 450 E-Book
Total Titles: 3,500 Print; 50 CD-ROM; 6,500 Online; 1,200 E-Book
Imprints: International Energy Agency; Nuclear Energy Agency
Foreign Office(s): 2 rue Andre-Pascal, 75775 Paris Cedex 16, France *Tel:* 01 45 24 82 00 *Fax:* 01 45 24 85 00
Distributor for International Energy Agency; International Transportation Forum; Nuclear Energy Agency
Orders to: Turpin Distribution Services Ltd, The Bleachery, 143 West St, New Milford, CT 06776 *Toll Free Tel:* 800-456-6323 *Fax:* 860-350-0039 *E-mail:* oecdma@turpin-distribution.com
Distribution Center: Turpin Distribution Services Ltd, The Bleachery, 143 West St, New Milford, CT 06776 *Toll Free Tel:* 800-456-6323 *Fax:* 860-350-0039

Ohio Genealogical Society
611 State Rte 97 W, Bellville, OH 44813-8813
Tel: 419-886-1903 *Fax:* 419-886-0092
E-mail: ogs@ogs.org
Web Site: www.ogs.org
Key Personnel
Pres: Margaret Cheney *E-mail:* president@ogs.org
Lib Dir: Thomas Stephen Neel *E-mail:* tneel@ogs.org
Founded: 1959
Family history library & society.
ISBN Prefix(es): 978-0-935057
Number of titles published annually: 3 Print
Total Titles: 25 Print

Ohio State University Foreign Language Publications
Division of Ohio State University Foreign Language Center
198 Hagerty Hall, 1775 College Rd, Columbus, OH 43210-1309
Tel: 614-292-3838 *Toll Free Tel:* 800-678-6999
E-mail: flpubs@osu.edu
Web Site: flpubs.osu.edu
Key Personnel
Pubns Mgr: Lauren Barrett
Founded: 1972
Foreign language individualized instruction materials for less commonly taught languages.
ISBN Prefix(es): 978-0-87415
Number of titles published annually: 5 Print
Total Titles: 280 Print

The Ohio State University Press
180 Pressey Hall, 1070 Carmack Rd, Columbus, OH 43210-1002
Tel: 614-292-6930 *Fax:* 614-292-2065 *Toll Free Fax:* 800-621-8476
E-mail: info@osupress.org
Web Site: ohiostatepress.org
Key Personnel
Dir: Tony Sanfilippo *Tel:* 614-292-7818 *E-mail:* tony@osupress.org
Asst Dir: Kathy Edwards *Tel:* 614-292-3692 *E-mail:* kathy@osupress.org
Mktg Dir: Laurie Avery *Tel:* 614-292-1462 *E-mail:* laurie@osupress.org
Mng Ed: Tara Cyphers *Tel:* 614-292-3667 *E-mail:* tara@osupress.org
Founded: 1957
General scholarly & trade nonfiction & fiction; classics.
ISBN Prefix(es): 978-0-8142
Number of titles published annually: 40 Print
Total Titles: 300 Print
Distribution Center: University of Chicago Distribution Center, 11030 S Langley Ave, Chicago, IL 60628 *Tel:* 773-568-1550 *Toll Free Tel:* 800-621-2736 *Fax:* 773-702-7212

Ohio University Press
31 S Court St, Suite 143, Athens, OH 45701-2979
Fax: 740-593-4536
Web Site: www.ohioswallow.com
Key Personnel
Dir & Ed-in-Chief: Gillian Berchowitz *Tel:* 740-593-1159 *E-mail:* berchowi@ohio.edu
Acqs Ed: Ricky S Huard *Tel:* 740-593-1157 *E-mail:* huard@ohio.edu
Mng Ed: Nancy Basmajian *Tel:* 740-593-1161 *E-mail:* basmajia@ohio.edu
Busn Mgr: Omar Aziz *Tel:* 740-593-1156 *E-mail:* azizo@ohio.edu
Acqs & Perms Admin: Sally Welch *E-mail:* welchs@ohio.edu
Founded: 1964
Publisher of scholarly & trade books.
ISBN Prefix(es): 978-0-8214; 978-0-8040; 978-0-89680; 978-0-940717
Number of titles published annually: 50 Print
Total Titles: 600 Print
Imprints: Swallow Press
Foreign Rep(s): Combined Academic Publishers Ltd (UK); East-West Export Books (Asia, Australia, New Zealand, Pacific Region); Scholarly Book Services Inc (Canada)
Orders to: Chicago Distribution Center, 11030 S Langley Ave, Chicago, IL 60628 *Tel:* 773-702-7212 *Toll Free Tel:* 800-621-2736 *Fax:* 773-702-7212 *Toll Free Fax:* 800-621-8476
Warehouse: Chicago Distribution Center, 11030 S Langley Ave, Chicago, IL 60628 *Tel:* 773-702-7212 *Toll Free Tel:* 800-621-2736 *Toll Free Fax:* 800-621-8476
Membership(s): American Association of University Presses
See separate listing for:
Swallow Press

§Olde & Oppenheim Publishers
3219 N Margate Place, Chandler, AZ 85224
E-mail: olde_oppenheim@hotmail.com
Key Personnel
Dir, Mktg: Mike Gratz
Animation, satire, slice-of-life.
ISBN Prefix(es): 978-0-944861
Number of titles published annually: 3 Print; 2 CD-ROM; 5 Online; 2 E-Book
Total Titles: 13 Print

The Oliver Press Inc
Charlotte Sq, 5707 W 36 St, Minneapolis, MN 55416-2510
Tel: 952-926-8981 *Toll Free Tel:* 800-8-OLIVER (865-4837) *Fax:* 952-926-8965
E-mail: orders@oliverpress.com
Web Site: www.oliverpress.com
Key Personnel
Publr & Ed: Mark Lerner *E-mail:* mark@oliverpress.com
Admin: Charles Helgesen
Founded: 1991
Nonfiction children's books.
ISBN Prefix(es): 978-1-881508
Number of titles published annually: 8 Print
Total Titles: 100 Print
Imprints: Clara House Books
Foreign Rights: INT Books (Australia)

OMNI Publishers Inc
PO Box 408, Bulverde, TX 78163
Tel: 210-778-4437 *Fax:* 830-438-4645
Web Site: www.omnipublishers.com; educatorsethicsseries.com
Key Personnel
Owner & Pres: Ruth Lansing
Mng Partner: Jim Lansing *E-mail:* jim@omnipublishers.com
Founded: 1989
Books on law & real estate, national education products, Texas law.
ISBN Prefix(es): 978-1-891172
Number of titles published annually: 25 Print
Total Titles: 65 Print

Omnibus Press
Imprint of Music Sales Group
257 Park Ave S, 20th fl, New York, NY 10010
Tel: 212-254-2100 *Toll Free Tel:* 800-431-7187 *Fax:* 212-254-2013 *Toll Free Fax:* 800-345-6842
E-mail: info@omnibuspress.com
Web Site: www.omnibuspress.com; www.musicsales.com
Key Personnel
Off Mgr: Kari Shannon
Founded: 1976
Pop culture, music & film books.
ISBN Prefix(es): 978-0-8256; 978-0-7119; 978-0-86001; 978-1-84449
Number of titles published annually: 40 Print
Total Titles: 500 Print
Distributor for Big Meteor; Gramophone
Distribution Center: Music Sales Distribution Center, 445 Bellvale Rd, Chester, NY 10918 *Tel:* 845-469-4699 *Toll Free Tel:* 800-431-

7187 *Fax:* 845-469-7544 *Toll Free Fax:* 800-345-6842 *E-mail:* info@musicsales.com *Web Site:* www.musicsales.com

Omnidawn Publishing
1632 Elm Ave, Richmond, CA 94805-1614
SAN: 299-3236
Tel: 510-237-5472 *Toll Free Tel:* 800-792-4957 *Fax:* 510-232-8525
E-mail: manager@omnidawn.com
Web Site: www.omnidawn.com
Key Personnel
Founder & Publr: Kenneth Keegan *E-mail:* kkeegan@omnidawn.com; Rusty Morrison *E-mail:* rusty@omnidawn.com
Mng Ed: Gillian Hamel *E-mail:* ghamel@omnidawn.com
Founded: 1996
Publishers of poetry, fabulist & new wave fabulist fiction.
ISBN Prefix(es): 978-1-890650
Number of titles published annually: 14 Print
Total Titles: 100 Print
Orders to: University Press of New England (UPNE), One Court St, Suite 250, Lebanon, NH 03766 *Toll Free Tel:* 800-421-1561 *Fax:* 603-448-9429 *Web Site:* www.upne.com
Shipping Address: UPNE Fulfillment, c/o Maple Logistics Solutions, Lebanon Distribution Ctr, 704 Legionaire Dr, Fredericksburg, PA 17026
Distribution Center: University Press of New England (UPNE), One Court St, Suite 250, Lebanon, NH 03766 *Toll Free Tel:* 800-421-1561 *Fax:* 603-448-9429 *Web Site:* www.upne.com

§Omnigraphics Inc
615 Griswold, Suite 901, Detroit, MI 48226
SAN: 249-2520
Tel: 610-461-3548 *Toll Free Tel:* 800-234-1340 (cust serv) *Fax:* 610-532-9001 *Toll Free Fax:* 800-875-1340 (cust serv)
E-mail: contact@omnigraphics.com; customerservice@omnigraphics.com
Web Site: omnigraphics.com
Key Personnel
Founder & Chmn: Frederick G Ruffner, Jr
Founder & Publr: Peter E Ruffner
Opers Mgr: Kevin Hayes
Founded: 1985
Reference books, directories, periodicals & journals for libraries & schools.
ISBN Prefix(es): 978-1-55888; 978-0-7808
Number of titles published annually: 40 Print; 1 Online
Total Titles: 400 Print; 1 Online
Advertising Agency: Marley & Cratchit
Orders to: PO Box 8002, Aston, PA 19014-8002; Edu Reference Publisher Direct Inc, 109 Woodbine Downs Blvd, Unit 3, Toronto, ON M9W 6Y1, Canada *Tel:* 416-674-8622 *Fax:* 416-674-6215 *E-mail:* sales@educanmedia.ca *Web Site:* www.educanmedia.ca
Returns: 105 Commerce Dr, Aston, PA 19014

Omohundro Institute of Early American History & Culture
Swem Library, Ground fl, 400 Landrum Dr, Williamsburg, VA 23185
Mailing Address: PO Box 8781, Williamsburg, VA 23187-8781 SAN: 201-5161
Tel: 757-221-1110 *Fax:* 757-221-1047
E-mail: ieahc1@wm.edu
Web Site: oieahc.wm.edu
Key Personnel
Dir: Karin A Wulf *Tel:* 757-221-1133 *E-mail:* kawulf@wm.edu
Books Ed: Paul W Mapp *Tel:* 757-221-1118 *E-mail:* pwmapp@wm.edu
Founded: 1943
Scholarly books on early American history culture & literature 1500-1815. Founded & still sponsored jointly by the College of William & Mary & the Colonial Williamsburg Foundation.
ISBN Prefix(es): 978-0-910776
Number of titles published annually: 4 Print
Total Titles: 205 Print
Distributed by The University of North Carolina Press

One On One Book Publishing/Film-Video Publications
Formerly Film-Video Publications/One on One Book Publishing
7944 Capistrano Ave, West Hills, CA 91304
SAN: 211-1527
Tel: 818-340-6620; 818-340-0175 *Fax:* 818-340-6620
E-mail: onebookpro@aol.com
Key Personnel
Pres & Publr: Alan Gadney
VP & Exec Ed: Carolyn Porter
Ed: Nancy Gadney
Founded: 1974
Reference books, directories & audio/video cassettes on film, video, photography, TV/radio broadcasting, writing, theater, business & finance, performing arts, publishing.
ISBN Prefix(es): 978-0-930828
Number of titles published annually: 22 Print; 3 E-Book; 10 Audio
Total Titles: 25 Print; 3 E-Book; 16 Audio
Foreign Rep(s): Australia & New Zealand Book Co (Australia); Fitzhenry & Whiteside (Canada); Reed Methuen Publishers (New Zealand)
Advertising Agency: Carolyn Chadwick Advertising
Membership(s): The Association of Publishers for Special Sales; Book Publicists of Southern California; Independent Book Publishers Association

§Ooligan Press
Portland State University, 369 Neuberger Hall, 724 SW Harrison St, Portland, OR 97201
Tel: 503-725-9748 *Fax:* 503-725-3561
E-mail: ooligan@ooliganpress.pdx.edu
Web Site: ooligan.pdx.edu
Key Personnel
Publr: Abbey Gaterud
Founded: 2001
ISBN Prefix(es): 978-1-932010
Number of titles published annually: 4 Print; 4 E-Book
Total Titles: 30 Print
Orders to: Ingram Publisher Services, One Ingram Blvd, La Vergne, TN 37086-1986 *Toll Free Tel:* 866-400-5351
Membership(s): Association of Writers and Writing Programs; Publishers Association of the West

§Open Books Press
Imprint of Pen & Publish Inc
4735 S State Rd 446, Bloomington, IN 47401
Tel: 314-827-6567; 812-837-9226
E-mail: info@openbookspress.com
Web Site: openbookspress.com
Key Personnel
Publr: Jennifer Geist *E-mail:* jennifer@openbookspress.com
Co-Founder & Pres: Paul Burt *E-mail:* paul@penandpublish.com
Co-Founder: Dee Burt *E-mail:* dee@penandpublish.com
Founded: 2010
Publish quality trade paperbacks & ebooks worldwide, including adult nonfiction & fiction for all ages.
Number of titles published annually: 4 Print; 4 E-Book
Total Titles: 24 Print; 14 E-Book
Membership(s): Independent Book Publishers Association

Open Court
Division of Carus Publishing Co, dba Cricket Media
70 E Lake St, Suite 800, Chicago, IL 60601
Tel: 312-701-1720 *Toll Free Tel:* 800-815-2280 *Fax:* 312-701-1728
E-mail: opencourt@cricketmedia.com
Web Site: www.opencourtbooks.com
Key Personnel
Edit Dir: David Ramsay Steele
Ed: Kerri Mommer
Founded: 1887
Publisher of academic philosophy, popular culture & philosophy books.
ISBN Prefix(es): 978-0-87548; 978-0-912050; 978-0-89688; 978-0-8126
Number of titles published annually: 12 Print
Total Titles: 350 Print

Open Horizons Publishing Co
PO Box 2887, Taos, NM 87571
Tel: 575-751-3398
E-mail: info@bookmarket.com
Web Site: www.bookmarket.com
Key Personnel
Owner & Publr: John Kremer *E-mail:* johnkremer@bookmarket.com
Founded: 1982
Books for publishers & direct marketers.
ISBN Prefix(es): 978-0-912411
Number of titles published annually: 3 Print; 3 CD-ROM; 3 Online; 40 E-Book; 3 Audio
Total Titles: 21 Print; 16 CD-ROM; 6 Online; 43 E-Book; 12 Audio
Distribution Center: National Book Network, 4720 Boston Way, No A, Lanham, MD 20706-4310, Pres: Jed Lyons *Tel:* 301-459-3366 *Fax:* 301-459-2118
Membership(s): The Association of Publishers for Special Sales; Independent Book Publishers Association

Open Road Publishing
32 Turkey Lane, Cold Spring Harbor, NY 11724
Tel: 631-692-7172
E-mail: jopenroad@aol.com
Web Site: www.openroadguides.com
Key Personnel
Publr: Jonathan Stein
Founded: 1993
Travel, domestic & foreign, how-to, biographies, current events, sports, fantasy & commentary.
ISBN Prefix(es): 978-1-892975; 978-1-59360
Number of titles published annually: 22 Print
Total Titles: 62 Print
Imprints: Cold Spring Press
Distributed by Simon & Schuster

§OPIS/STALSBY Directories & Databases
Division of IHS Markit
3349 Hwy 138, Bldg D, Suite D, Wall, NJ 07719
Tel: 732-901-8800 *Toll Free Tel:* 800-275-0950 *Toll Free Fax:* 800-450-5864
E-mail: opisstalsbylistings@opisnet.com
Web Site: www.opisnet.com
Key Personnel
Dir, Prodn: Renee Ortner *E-mail:* rortner@opisnet.com
Supervising Ed: Bonnie Walling *Tel:* 732-730-2536 *E-mail:* bwalling@opisnet.com
Founded: 1980
ISBN Prefix(es): 978-0-911299
Number of titles published annually: 2 Print; 1 CD-ROM
Total Titles: 2 Print; 1 CD-ROM

The Optical Society (OSA)
2010 Massachusetts Ave NW, Washington, DC 20036-1023
Tel: 202-223-8130 *Toll Free Tel:* 800-766-4672
E-mail: custserv@osa.org
Web Site: www.osa.org
Key Personnel
Chief Publg Offr: Elizabeth Nolan *Tel:* 202-416-1949 *E-mail:* enolan@osa.org
CIO: Sean Bagshaw *Tel:* 202-416-1905 *E-mail:* sbagsh@osa.org
Sr Publr: Kelly Cohen *Tel:* 202-416-1917 *E-mail:* kcohen@osa.org
Sr Dir, Publg Sales & Mktg: Daphne Greenwood *Tel:* 202-416-1405 *E-mail:* dgreen@osa.org
Dir, Intl Sales: Randy Kiefer *Tel:* 202-416-1906 *E-mail:* rkiefer@osa.org
Dir, Sales Americas: Alan N Tourtlotte *Tel:* 202-416-1908 *Fax:* 202-416-1408 *E-mail:* atourt@osa.org
Rts & Perms: Susannah Lehman *Tel:* 202-416-1901 *E-mail:* slehman@osa.org
Founded: 1916
Journal publishing, meetings & technical membership.
ISBN Prefix(es): 978-1-55752
Number of titles published annually: 20 Online
Total Titles: 230 Online
Foreign Rep(s): David Charles e-Licensing (Europe); Globe Publication Pvt Ltd (India); iGroup (Asia exc India & Japan, Australia, New Zealand); Kinokuniya (Japan); Shinwon Datanet (South Korea)
Membership(s): American Institute of Physics

Optometric Extension Program Foundation
2300 York Rd, Suite 113, Timonium, MD 21093
Tel: 410-561-3791
E-mail: oep@oep.org
Web Site: www.oepf.org
Key Personnel
Exec Dir: Kelin Kushin *E-mail:* kelin.kushin@oep.org
Off Mgr & Clinical Curriculum Coord: Karen Ruder *E-mail:* karen.ruder@oep.org
Founded: 1928
Books, journals, pamphlets, catalogs & directories.
ISBN Prefix(es): 978-0-943599; 978-0-929780
Number of titles published annually: 10 Print; 1 CD-ROM
Total Titles: 150 Print; 3 CD-ROM

§OptumInsight™
13625 Technology Dr, Eden Prairie, MN 55334
Tel: 952-833-7100 *Toll Free Tel:* 888-445-8745; 800-765-6713
E-mail: info@optum.com
Web Site: www.optum.com
Key Personnel
CEO: Bill Miller
Founded: 1983
Books & software for health care professionals.
ISBN Prefix(es): 978-1-56337; 978-1-56329
Number of titles published annually: 90 Print; 5 Online
Total Titles: 90 Print; 8 CD-ROM; 5 Online
Branch Office(s)
1755 Telstar Dr, Suite 400, Colorado Springs, CO 80920 *Tel:* 719-277-7545 *Toll Free Tel:* 800-341-6141 *Fax:* 719-277-0254
400 Capital Blvd, Rocky Hill, CT 06067 *Tel:* 860-221-0054 *Toll Free Tel:* 800-367-2427 *Fax:* 860-221-0209
2525 Lake Park Blvd, Salt Lake City, UT 84120 *Tel:* 801-982-3000 *Toll Free Tel:* 800-464-3649 *Fax:* 801-982-4000
12018 Sunrise Valley Dr, Suite 400, Reston, VA 20191 *Tel:* 571-521-7661 *Toll Free Tel:* 800-464-3649 *Fax:* 571-521-7237
10701 W Research Dr, Wauwatosa, WI 53226-3452 *Toll Free Tel:* 800-651-8313 *Fax:* 414-443-4331
Distributed by American Medical Association; Mosby
Distributor for American Medical Association; Medical Economics; Mosby

Orange Frazer Press Inc
37 1/2 W Main St, Wilmington, OH 45177
Mailing Address: PO Box 214, Wilmington, OH 45177-0214
Tel: 937-382-3196 *Toll Free Tel:* 800-852-9332 (orders) *Fax:* 937-383-3159
E-mail: ofrazer@erinet.com
Web Site: www.orangefrazer.com
Key Personnel
Publr: Marcy Hawley
Ed: John Baskin
Proj Mgr: Sarah Hawley
Founded: 1987
Regional book publisher specializing in Ohio nonfiction (reference, sports, commentary, travel, nature, etc). Production & design is considered "high-end".
This publisher has indicated that 80% of their product line is author subsidized.
ISBN Prefix(es): 978-1-882203; 978-0-9619637; 978-1-933197
Number of titles published annually: 16 Print
Total Titles: 60 Print

Orbis Books
Division of Maryknoll Fathers & Brothers
Price Bldg, Box 302, Maryknoll, NY 10545-0302
Tel: 914-941-7636 *Toll Free Tel:* 800-258-5838 (orders) *Fax:* 914-941-7005
E-mail: orbisbooks@maryknoll.org
Web Site: orbisbooks.com
Key Personnel
Publr & Ed-in-Chief: Robert Ellsberg *E-mail:* rellsberg@maryknoll.org
Assoc Publr & Mktg Mgr: Bernadette B Price *E-mail:* bprice@maryknoll.org
Busn Mgr: William Medeot *E-mail:* bmedeot@maryknoll.org
Sales Mgr: Michael Lawrence *E-mail:* mlawrence@maryknoll.org
Ed-at-Large: Michael Leach *E-mail:* mleach@maryknoll.org
Rts & Perms: Doris Goodnough *E-mail:* dgoodnough@maryknoll.org
Founded: 1970
Offering a wide range of books on prayer, spirituality, Catholic life, theology, mission & current affairs.
ISBN Prefix(es): 978-0-88344; 978-1-57075; 978-1-60833; 978-1-62698
Number of titles published annually: 50 Print; 50 E-Book
Total Titles: 780 Print; 470 E-Book
Foreign Rep(s): Alban Books (Europe, UK); Bayard/Novalis Distribution (Canada); Catholic Book Shop (South Africa); Garratt Publishing (Australia)
Advertising Agency: Roth Advertising, PO Box 96, Sea Cliff, NY 11579-0096, Pres: Daniel Roth *Tel:* 516-674-8603 *Fax:* 516-368-3885 *E-mail:* dan@rothadvertising.com
Warehouse: Maryknoll Center Warehouse, 79 Ryder Rd, Ossining, NY 10562, Warehouse Mgr: Paul Lonce *Tel:* 914-941-7636 ext 2458
Membership(s): Association of Catholic Publishers Inc

Orbit
Division of Hachette Book Group
1290 Avenue of the Americas, New York, NY 10019
Tel: 212-364-1100 *Toll Free Tel:* 800-759-0190
Web Site: www.orbitbooks.net
Key Personnel
SVP, HBG & Publr, Orbit: Tim Holman
VP & Deputy Publr: Anne Clarke
Sr Ed: Will Hinton
Assoc Ed, Asst to Will Hinton: Lindsey Hall
Assoc Ed, Asst to Anne Clarke: Brit Hvide
Mktg & Publicity Dir: Alex Lencicki
Sr Publicist: Ellen Wright
Online Mktg Mgr: Laura Fitzgerald
Mktg Designer: Derrick Kennelty-Cohen
Creative Dir: Lauren Panepinto
Sr Designer: Lisa Marie Pompillo
Designer: Crystal Ben
Busn Mgr: Jillian Amirault
Admin Asst: Nivia Evans
Founded: 2008
Orbit is a leading publisher of science fiction & fantasy with imprints in the UK, US & Australia. We publish across the spectrum of science fiction & fantasy—from action-packed urban fantasy to widescreen space opera; from sweeping epic adventures to near-future thrillers.
Number of titles published annually: 80 Print
Total Titles: 400 Print
Imprints: Redhook
Orders to: Hachette Book Group, 53 State St, Boston, MA 02109 *Toll Free Tel:* 800-759-0190 *Toll Free Fax:* 800-286-9471
Shipping Address: Hachette Book Group Distribution Center, 121 N Enterprise Blvd, Lebanon, IN 46052 *Tel:* 765-483-9900 *Fax:* 765-483-0706

Orca Book Publishers
PO Box 468, Custer, WA 98240-0468
Tel: 250-380-1229 *Toll Free Tel:* 800-210-5277 *Fax:* 250-380-1892 *Toll Free Fax:* 877-408-1551
E-mail: orca@orcabook.com
Web Site: www.orcabook.com
Key Personnel
Publr: Andrew Wooldridge *E-mail:* andrew.wooldridge@orcabook.com
Pres: Bob Tyrrell *E-mail:* tyrrell@orcabook.com
Founded: 1984
Children & young adult literature.
ISBN Prefix(es): 978-1-55143; 978-0-920501
Number of titles published annually: 65 Print
Total Titles: 730 Print
Branch Office(s)
PO Box 5626, Sta B, Victoria, BC V8R 6S4, Canada
Distributor for The Book Publishing Co; Coteau Books; Creative Book Publishing; Formac Publishing; Lobster Press; James Lorimer & Co; Nimbus Publishing; Polestar Calendars; Second Story Press; 7th Generation; Sono Nis Press; Sumach Press; Tradewind Books; Tuckamore Books; Tudor House
Foreign Rights: Transatlantic Literary Agency (Amy Tompkins) (worldwide exc North America)
Warehouse: 7056 Portal Way, Bldg E, Ferndale, WA 98248
Membership(s): ABA; ALA; Association of Book Publishers of British Columbia; Association of Canadian Publishers; Canadian Booksellers Association; Educational Book & Media Association

Orchises Press
PO Box 320533, Alexandria, VA 22320-4533
Tel: 703-683-1243
E-mail: orchises@gmail.com
Key Personnel
Pres & Ed-in-Chief: Roger Lathbury *E-mail:* lathbury@gmu.edu
Founded: 1983
Small press.
ISBN Prefix(es): 978-0-914061; 978-1-932535
Number of titles published annually: 3 Print; 1 E-Book
Total Titles: 61 Print; 1 E-Book

Oregon Catholic Press, see OCP

Oregon State University Press
121 The Valley Library, Corvallis, OR 97331-4501
SAN: 202-8328
Tel: 541-737-3166 *Toll Free Tel:* 800-621-2736 (orders)
Key Personnel
Dir: Faye Chadwell *E-mail:* faye.chadwell@oregonstate.edu
Assoc Dir: Tom Booth *Tel:* 503-796-0547 *E-mail:* thomas.booth@oregonstate.edu
Acqs Ed: Mary Elizabeth Braun *E-mail:* mary.braun@oregonstate.edu
EDP Mgr: Ms Micki Reaman *Tel:* 541-737-4620 *E-mail:* micki.reaman@oregonstate.edu
Founded: 1961
ISBN Prefix(es): 978-0-87071
Number of titles published annually: 20 Print
Total Titles: 225 Print
Distribution Center: Chicago Distribution Center, 11030 S Langley Ave, Chicago, IL 60628

O'Reilly Media Inc
1005 Gravenstein Hwy N, Sebastopol, CA 95472
Tel: 707-827-7000; 707-827-7019 (cust support) *Toll Free Tel:* 800-998-9938; 800-889-8969 *Fax:* 707-829-0104; 707-824-8268
E-mail: orders@oreilly.com
Web Site: www.oreilly.com
Key Personnel
Founder & CEO: Tim O'Reilly
Founded: 1978
Technical computer book publisher, conference provider.
ISBN Prefix(es): 978-0-937175; 978-1-56592; 978-0-596
Number of titles published annually: 140 Print; 65 E-Book
Total Titles: 800 Print
Branch Office(s)
2 Ave de Lafayette, 6th fl, Boston, MA 02111 *Tel:* 617-354-5800 *Fax:* 617-661-1116
Foreign Office(s): O'Reilly Beijing, Cheng Ming Mansion, Bldg C, Suite 807, No 2 Xizhimen South St, Xicheng District, Beijing 100035, China, Contact: Michelle Chen *Tel:* (010) 88097475 *Fax:* (010) 88097463 *E-mail:* orb@oreilly.com *Web Site:* www.oreilly.com.cn
Intelligent Plaza, Bldg 1-F, 12-22, Yotsuyasaka-machi, Shinjuku-ku, Tokyo 160-0002, Japan, General Dept Section, Sales: Kenji Watari *E-mail:* japan@oreilly.co.jp *Web Site:* www.oreilly.co.jp
5 St George's Yard, Farnham, Surrey GU9 7LW, United Kingdom *Tel:* (01252) 721284 *Fax:* (01252) 722337 *E-mail:* information@oreilly.co.uk
Distributor for Packt Publishing (technol ebook prog)
Foreign Rep(s): WoodsLane (Australia, New Zealand)

Organization for Economic Cooperation & Development (OECD), see OECD Washington Center

Oriental Institute Publications
Division of University of Chicago
1155 E 58 St, Chicago, IL 60637
Tel: 773-702-5967 *Fax:* 773-702-9853
E-mail: oi-publications@uchicago.edu
Web Site: oi.uchicago.edu
Key Personnel
Mng Ed, Pubns: Thomas Urban *E-mail:* turban@uchicago.edu
Founded: 1919
Academic publications.
ISBN Prefix(es): 978-0-918986; 978-1-885923
Number of titles published annually: 10 Print; 10 Online
Total Titles: 250 Print; 1,000 Online
Orders to: Casemate | academic, 1950 Lawrence Rd, Havertown, PA 19083 *Tel:* 610-853-9131 *Fax:* 610-853-9146 *E-mail:* info@casemateacademic.com *Web Site:* www.oxbowbooks.com/dbbc
Distribution Center: Casemate | academic, 1950 Lawrence Rd, Havertown, PA 19083 *Tel:* 610-853-9131 *Fax:* 610-853-9146 *E-mail:* info@casemateacademic.com *Web Site:* www.oxbowbooks.com/dbbc

The Original Falcon Press
1753 E Broadway Rd, No 101-277, Tempe, AZ 85282
Tel: 602-708-1409
E-mail: info@originalfalcon.com
Web Site: www.originalfalcon.com
Key Personnel
Pres: Nicholas Tharcher *E-mail:* nick@originalfalcon.com
Founded: 1982
Books, CDs & DVDs.
ISBN Prefix(es): 978-1-935150; 978-1-61869
Number of titles published annually: 10 Print; 10 E-Book; 10 Audio
Total Titles: 50 Print; 40 E-Book; 30 Audio
Imprints: Falcon Press; Golden Dawn Publications; New Falcon Publications
Distribution Center: New Leaf Distributing Co, 401 Thornton Rd, Lithia Springs, GA 30122-1557 *Tel:* 770-948-7845 *Fax:* 770-944-2313 *E-mail:* newleaf@newleaf-dist.com *Web Site:* www.newleaf-dist.com
Quanta Distribution, 3251 Kennedy Rd, Unit 20, Toronto, ON M1V 2J9, Canada *Tel:* 416-410-9411 *Toll Free Tel:* 888-436-7962 *Fax:* 416-291-8764 *E-mail:* quantamail@quanta.ca *Web Site:* www.quanta.ca
John Reed Book Distribution, 2/11 Yandala St, Tea Garden, NSW 2324, Australia, Dir: John Reed *Tel:* (02) 4997 2936 *Fax:* (02) 4997 2937 *E-mail:* sales@johnreedbooks.com.au *Web Site:* www.johnreedbooks.com.au
Gazelle Book Services Ltd, White Cross Mills, Hightown, Lancaster, Lancs LA1 4XS, United Kingdom *Tel:* (0152) 528500 *Fax:* (0152) 528510 *E-mail:* sales@gazellebookservices.co.uk *Web Site:* www.gazellebookservices.co.uk

Original Publications
PO Box 236, Old Beth Page, NY 11804
SAN: 133-0225
Tel: 516-605-0547 *Toll Free Tel:* 888-622-8581 *Fax:* 516-605-0549
E-mail: originalpub@aol.com
Web Site: www.occult1.com
Key Personnel
Publr & Dist: Mark Benezra
Founded: 1962
African religion, New Age, spirituality, Santeria & occult books.
ISBN Prefix(es): 978-0-942272
Number of titles published annually: 40 Print
Total Titles: 50 Print

ORO editions
31 Commercial Blvd, Suite F, Novato, CA 94949
Tel: 415-883-3300 *Fax:* 415-883-3309
E-mail: info@oroeditions.com
Web Site: www.oroeditions.com
Key Personnel
Contact: Gordon Goff *E-mail:* gordon@oroeditions.com
Founded: 2003
ISBN Prefix(es): 978-0-9746800; 978-0-9774672; 978-0-9793801; 978-0-9795395; 978-0-9814628; 978-0-9820607; 978-0-9819857; 978-0-9826226; 978-0-935935
Number of titles published annually: 50 Print; 4 E-Book

Other Press
267 Fifth Ave, 6th fl, New York, NY 10016
Tel: 212-414-0054 *Toll Free Tel:* 877-843-6843 *Fax:* 212-414-0939
E-mail: editor@otherpress.com; marketing@otherpress.com; publicity@otherpress.com
Web Site: www.otherpress.com
Key Personnel
Publr: Judith Gurewich
CFO: Bill Foo
Edit Dir: Janice Goldklang
Dir, Mktg: Terrie Akers
Dir, Subs Rts: Lauren Shekari
Publicity Dir: Jessica Greer
Opers Mgr: Iisha Stevens
Assoc Ed: Alexandra Poreda
Prodn Ed: Yvonne Cardenas
Publicist: Maria Whelan
Assoc Publicist: Esther Kim
Mktg Asst: Christie Michel
Founded: 1998
Publish literary fiction, literature in translation, trade nonfiction, memoirs, cultural studies, biographies & other subjects.
ISBN Prefix(es): 978-1-892746; 978-1-59051
Number of titles published annually: 25 Print; 25 E-Book
Foreign Rep(s): AnatoliaLit Agency (Amy Marie Spangler) (Turkey); Donatella D'Ormesson (France); The English Agency Ltd (Hamish Macaskill) (Japan); The Deborah Harris Agency (Rena Rossner) (Israel); Danny Hong Agency (Danny Hong) (Korea); Iris Literary Agency (Catherine Fragou) (Greece); Marc Koralnik Liepman AG (Germany); Prava i prevodi (Milena Kaplarevic) (Baltic States, Eastern Europe); Vicki Satlow Literary Agency (Vicki Satlow) (Italy)
Foreign Rights: MB Agencia Literaria (Monica Martin) (Brazil, Catalonia, Portugal, Spain); Peony Literary Agency (Marysia Juszczakiewicz & Tina Chou) (China, Taiwan)
Distribution Center: Penguin Random House Inc, Customer Service, 400 Hahn Rd, Westminster, MD 21157 *Toll Free Tel:* 800-733-3000 *Toll Free Fax:* 800-659-2436 *E-mail:* csorders@penguinrandomhouse.com *Web Site:* www.penguinrandomhouse.biz
Penguin Random House Inc, International Sales, 1745 Broadway, New York, NY 10019 *Fax:* 212-572-6045 *E-mail:* international@penguinrandomhouse.com
Penguin Random House Canada, Customer Service, 320 Front St W, Suite 1400, Toronto, ON M5V 3B6, Canada *Toll Free Tel:* 888-523-9292 *Toll Free Fax:* 888-562-9924 *E-mail:* csorders@penguinrandomhouse.com *Web Site:* www.penguinrandomhouse.biz
Membership(s): ABA; Community of Literary Magazines & Presses; Independent Book Publishers Association

§Our Sunday Visitor Publishing
Division of Our Sunday Visitor Inc
200 Noll Plaza, Huntington, IN 46750
SAN: 202-8344
Tel: 260-356-8400 *Toll Free Tel:* 800-348-2440 (orders) *Fax:* 260-356-8472 *Toll Free Fax:* 800-498-6709
E-mail: osvbooks@osv.com (book orders)
Web Site: www.osv.com
Key Personnel
Chmn of the Bd: Bishop Kevin C Rhoades
Assoc Publr & Ed: Owen Campion *E-mail:* ocampion@osv.com
Exec Asst: Michelle Hogan *E-mail:* mhogan@osv.com
Founded: 1912
Religious books: trade, adult & juvenile general interest & reference, hardcover & paperback, early childhood school; newsweekly, religious magazines & newspapers, CD-ROM.

ISBN Prefix(es): 978-0-87973; 978-1-931709; 978-0-9707756; 978-1-59276; 978-1-61278; 978-1-68192
Number of titles published annually: 60 Print
Total Titles: 600 Print; 6 CD-ROM; 8 Audio
Foreign Rep(s): Baker & Taylor (worldwide exc Canada, France, Malta, New Zealand, South Africa & UK); B Broughton (Canada); Catholic Supplies (New Zealand); Preca (Malta); Veritas (UK); Veritas Co Ltd (Ireland); Grace Wing (worldwide exc Australia); Word of Life (Australia)

§Out of Your Mind...and Into the Marketplace™
13381 White Sand Dr, Tustin, CA 92780-4565
Tel: 714-544-0248 *Toll Free Tel:* 800-419-1513 *Fax:* 714-730-1414
Web Site: www.business-plan.com
Key Personnel
Owner & Co-Publr: Linda Pinson *E-mail:* lpinson@aol.com
Co-Publr: Ndaba Mdhlongwa *E-mail:* nxm1673@yahoo.com
Admin Asst: Julie Filppi *E-mail:* jfilppi@aol.com
Founded: 1986
Publisher of entrepreneurial books & business plan software.
This publisher has indicated that 80% of their product line is author subsidized.
ISBN Prefix(es): 978-0-944205
Number of titles published annually: 2 Print; 1 CD-ROM; 6 E-Book
Total Titles: 7 Print; 1 CD-ROM; 6 E-Book
Distribution Center: Independent Publishers Group (IPG), 814 N Franklin St, Chicago, IL 60610 *Toll Free Tel:* 800-888-4741 *Web Site:* ipg.com
Membership(s): Independent Book Publishers Association

The Overlook Press
Subsidiary of Peter Mayer Publishers Inc
141 Wooster St, Suite 4-B, New York, NY 10012
SAN: 202-8360
Tel: 212-673-2210; 845-679-6838 (orders & dist) *Fax:* 212-673-2296
E-mail: sales@overlookny.com (orders)
Web Site: www.overlookpress.com
Key Personnel
Pres & Publr: Peter Mayer
Founded: 1971
Fiction, general nonfiction, theatre, biography, art, architecture, history, design, film, popular culture, hardcover reprints & trade paperbacks.
ISBN Prefix(es): 978-0-87951; 978-1-58567; 978-1-59020; 978-1-46830; 978-1-46831
Number of titles published annually: 100 Print
Total Titles: 1,000 Print
Imprints: Ardis Russian Literature; Duckworth; Elephant's Eye; Tusk Ivory; Tusk Paperbacks
Distributed by W W Norton & Company Inc
Foreign Rights: Akcali Copyright Agency (Turkey); Agencia Literaria Carmen Bal cells SA (Portugal, South America, Spain); Book/Lab Literary Agency (Poland); The Deborah Harris Agency (Israel); The Italian Literary Agency (Italy); Agence Michelle Lapautre (Belgium, France); Licht & Burr Literary Agency APS (Scandinavia); Liepman AG Literary Agency (Austria, Germany, Switzerland); Andrew Nurnberg Associates (Bulgaria, China, Croatia, Czech Republic, Estonia, Hungary, Latvia, Lithuania, Montenegro, Romania, Russia, Serbia, Taiwan); Agencia Riff (Lucia Riff) (Brazil); Sebes & Bisseling Literary Agency (Netherlands); Tuttle-Mori Agency Inc (Japan); Eric Yang Agency (Korea)
Membership(s): AAP; National Book Foundation

The Overmountain Press
Division of Sabre Industries Inc
PO Box 1261, Johnson City, TN 37605-1261
SAN: 687-6641
Tel: 423-926-2691 *Toll Free Tel:* 800-992-2691 (orders) *Fax:* 423-929-2464
E-mail: orders@overmtn.com; submissions@overmtn.com
Web Site: www.overmtn.com
Key Personnel
Sr Ed: Sherry Lewis *E-mail:* sherry@overmtn.com
Mktg: Karin O'Brien *E-mail:* karino@overmtn.com
Founded: 1970
Exhibit at trade shows, festivals, conventions. Subjects include Southern Appalachian nonfiction, history & children.
ISBN Prefix(es): 978-0-932807; 978-1-57072; 978-1-935692
Number of titles published annually: 5 Print
Total Titles: 320 Print
Imprints: Silver Dagger Mysteries

Richard C Owen Publishers Inc
PO Box 585, Katonah, NY 10536-0585
Tel: 914-232-3903 *Toll Free Tel:* 800-336-5588 *Fax:* 914-232-3977
Web Site: www.rcowen.com
Key Personnel
Pres & Publr: Richard C Owen *E-mail:* richardowen@rcowen.com
Founded: 1982
Education, language arts & literacy.
ISBN Prefix(es): 978-0-913461; 978-1-878450; 978-1-57274
Number of titles published annually: 5 Print
Total Titles: 378 Print
Warehouse: 243 Rte 100, Somers, NY 10589

Owl About Books Publisher Inc
1632 Royalwood Circle, Joshua, TX 76058
Mailing Address: PO Box 867, Joshua, TX 76058
Tel: 682-553-9078 *Fax:* 817-558-8983
E-mail: owlaboutbooks@gmail.com
Web Site: www.owlaboutbooks.com
Key Personnel
Pres: Dorota Harrington
Founded: 2011
Privately owned & devoted to publishing literature for children. Educational series philosophy is best described by the company's motto "Children's learning has no limits." Specialize in beautifully illustrated reading resources for parents & children with special needs. Well-placed fun facts accompany most of the stories & provide educational benefit.
ISBN Prefix(es): 978-1-937752
Number of titles published annually: 7 Print; 7 Online
Total Titles: 14 Print; 14 Online
Membership(s): Independent Book Publishers Association

§Oxford University Press USA
Division of University of Oxford
198 Madison Ave, New York, NY 10016
SAN: 202-5892
Tel: 212-726-6000 *Toll Free Tel:* 800-451-7556 (orders); 800-445-9714 (cust serv) *Fax:* 919-677-1303
E-mail: custserv.us@oup.com
Web Site: www.oup.com/us
Key Personnel
CEO: Nigel Portwood
CFO: Kevin Allison
Pres, OUP USA & Publr, Academic & Trade: Niko Pfund
VP & Publr, Higher Educ: John Challice
VP, Global Mktg: Colleen Scollans
VP, Publr Rel: Casper Grathwohl
Head, Academic Publg Div: Tim Barton
Head, Design, Global Academic Busn: Linda Secondari
Head, US Content Opers: Deborah Shor
Head, US Dictionaries: Katherine Martin
Edit Dir, Higher Educ: Patrick Lynch
Edit Dir, Ref Acqs: Damon Zucca
Ed-in-Chief, Academic/Trade Edit: Suzanne Ryan
Ed-in-Chief, History & Religion: Theo Calderara
Ed-in-Chief, Social Sciences: David McBride
Dir, Academic/Trade/Mkt, Medical & Law: Kim Craven
Cust Serv Dir: Cheryl Ammons-Longtin
Dir, Direct Mktg: Rose Pintaudi-Jones
Dir, Dist, Cary, NC: Simon Clark
Dir, Fin: Dottie Warlick
Dir, Global Online Mktg: Sarah Ultsch
Dir, Higher Educ Mktg & Sales: Frank Mortimer
Dir, HR: Rosann Ashe
Dir, HR, Cary, NC: Cherlynn Hoover
Dir, Instl Sales: Rebecca Seger
Opers Dir: Laurea Salvatore
Dir, Publicity: Sarah Russo
Divisional Systems Mgr: James Martin
Facilities/Off Supv Mgr, NY: Lorraine Betancourt
Warehouse Mgr: Todd Hayes
Gen Coun: Barbara Cohen
Founded: 1896 (1478 in UK)
Scholarly, professional & reference books in the humanities, science, medicine & social studies; nonfiction trade, Bibles, college textbooks, music, ESL, paperbacks, children's books, journals, online reference & online scholarly. Prospective authors should consult the Oxford University Press web site for submission guidelines & proposal submission policy.
ISBN Prefix(es): 978-0-19
Number of titles published annually: 3,000 Print; 6 CD-ROM; 200 Online; 500 E-Book; 30 Audio
Total Titles: 26,000 Print; 27 CD-ROM; 400 Online; 700 E-Book; 250 Audio
Imprints: Clarendon Press
Foreign Office(s): Great Clarendon St, Oxford OX2 6DP, United Kingdom (worldwide headquarters) *Tel:* (018165) 556-767
Distributor for The American Chemical Society; American University in Cairo; Arnold Clarendon; Cold Spring Harbor Laboratory Press; Engineering Press; Getty; Greenwich Medical Media; Grove Dictionaries; Hurst; IRL; Kodansha; Roxbury Publishing; Saunders; Stamford University Press; Thomson Publishing
Foreign Rights: Gersh Agency
Returns: 2001 Evans Rd, Cary, NC 27513 *Toll Free Tel:* 800-451-7556 *Web Site:* www.oup.com/us
Warehouse: 2001 Evans Rd, Cary, NC 27513 *Toll Free Tel:* 800-451-7556 *Web Site:* www.oup.com/us
Distribution Center: 2001 Evans Rd, Cary, NC 27513 *Toll Free Tel:* 800-451-7556 *Web Site:* www.oup.com/us
Membership(s): AAP; American Association of University Presses; BISG

Oxmoor House
Imprint of Time Inc Books
4100 Old Montgomery Hwy, Birmingham, AL 35209
SAN: 205-3462
Tel: 205-445-6000 *Toll Free Tel:* 800-366-4712; 888-891-8935 (cust serv); 800-765-6400 (orders)
Web Site: www.oxmoorhouse.com
Key Personnel
Edit Dir: Anja Schmidt
Sr Ed: Rachel West *E-mail:* rachel_west@timeinc.com
Founded: 1968
General interest books; cooking, gardening, decorating, home improvement, travel, entertaining, health, motion film companions, custom products, celebrity how-to, crafts, art, hobbies; book & binder programs.
ISBN Prefix(es): 978-0-8487

Number of titles published annually: 250 Print
Total Titles: 329 Print
Imprints: Coastal Living Books; Cooking Light Books; Health Books; Southern Living Books; Sunset Books
Distributed by H B Fenn (Canada); Leisure Arts Inc
Foreign Rep(s): Beckett Sterling (New Zealand); General Publishing Co (Canada); Little, Brown & Co, UK (Europe, UK); Struik Book Distributers (South Africa); Transworld Publishers (Australia)

Ozark Mountain Publishing Inc
PO Box 754, Huntsville, AR 72740-0754
Tel: 479-738-2348 *Toll Free Tel:* 800-935-0045 *Fax:* 479-738-2448
E-mail: info@ozarkmt.com
Web Site: www.ozarkmt.com
Key Personnel
CEO: Julia Degan *E-mail:* julia@ozarkmt.com
Gen Mgr: Nancy Vernon *E-mail:* nancy@ozarkmt.com
Gen Mgr Asst: Brandy McDonald *E-mail:* brandy@ozarkmt.com
Founded: 1992
Publish nonfiction New Age/metaphysical & spiritual type books.
ISBN Prefix(es): 978-0-9632776; 978-1-886940; 978-1-940265
Number of titles published annually: 10 Print; 10 E-Book; 2 Audio
Total Titles: 126 Print; 111 E-Book; 8 Audio
Foreign Rights: Ajatus Publishing Co (Finland); The English Agency (Japan); Gill (Ireland); Jaico (India); Luciernaga Oceano (Spain); Lyubka Mihailova (Bulgaria); Stigmarion (Russia)

Ozark Publishing Inc
PO Box 228, Prairie Grove, AR 72753-0228
Tel: 479-595-9522 *Toll Free Tel:* 800-321-5671 *Fax:* 479-846-2843
E-mail: srg304@yahoo.com
Web Site: www.ozarkpublishing.us
Key Personnel
Mng Ed: Dave Sargent
Mgr: Dave Sargent, Jr
Founded: 1988
Children & young adult books. All books have a moral; the children's books include both fact & fiction.
ISBN Prefix(es): 978-1-56763
Number of titles published annually: 60 Print
Total Titles: 1,100 Print; 80 Audio
Distributed by Econo-Clad Books; Gumdrop Books
Shipping Address: 13062 Butler, Prairie Grove, AR 72753
Distribution Center: Amazon.com
Apple
Barnes & Noble
Bound to Stay Bound Books Inc
Follett School Solutions Inc, 1340 Ridgeview Dr, McHenry, IL 60050 *Tel:* 815-759-1700 *Toll Free Tel:* 888-551-5114 (cust serv) *Fax:* 815-759-9831 *Toll Free Fax:* 800-852-5458 *E-mail:* info@follettlearning.com *Web Site:* www.follettlearning.com SAN: 169-1902

P & R Publishing Co
1102 Marble Hill Rd, Phillipsburg, NJ 08865
SAN: 205-3918
Mailing Address: PO Box 817, Phillipsburg, NJ 08865
Tel: 908-454-0505 *Toll Free Tel:* 800-631-0094 *Fax:* 908-859-2390
E-mail: sales@prpbooks.com; info@prpbooks.com
Web Site: www.prpbooks.com
Key Personnel
Pres: Bryce H Craig *E-mail:* bryce@prpbooks.com
VP: Ian M Thompson *E-mail:* ian@prpbooks.com
Sr Proj Mgr: Aaron Gottier *E-mail:* aarong@prpbooks.com
Founded: 1930
Christian books for all ages (Reformed Theology).
ISBN Prefix(es): 978-0-87552; 978-1-59638
Number of titles published annually: 60 Print; 100 E-Book
Total Titles: 750 Print; 1 CD-ROM; 200 E-Book
Foreign Rights: F J Rudy & Associates (Fred Rudy) (worldwide)
Membership(s): Evangelical Christian Publishers Association

Pace University Press
Unit of Pace University
Dept of Publishing, Rm 805-E, 551 Fifth Ave, New York, NY 10176
Tel: 212-346-1417 *Fax:* 212-346-1165
Web Site: www.pace.edu/press
Key Personnel
Dir: Sherman Raskin *E-mail:* sraskin@pace.edu
Assoc Dir: Manuela Soares *E-mail:* msoares@pace.edu
Founded: 1988
Academic books in the humanities.
ISBN Prefix(es): 978-0-944473
Number of titles published annually: 6 Print
Total Titles: 55 Print

Pacific Press Publishing Association
Division of Seventh-Day Adventist Church
1350 N Kings Rd, Nampa, ID 83687-3193
Mailing Address: PO Box 5353, Nampa, ID 83653-5353
Tel: 208-465-2500 *Toll Free Tel:* 800-447-7377 *Fax:* 208-465-2531
Web Site: www.pacificpress.com
Key Personnel
CIO: Ed Bahr *Tel:* 208-465-2630 *E-mail:* ed.bahr@pacificpress.com
Pres & Gen Mgr: Dale Galusha *Tel:* 208-465-2501 *E-mail:* dale.galusha@pacificpress.com
VP, Fin: Martin Ytreberg *Tel:* 208-465-2536 *E-mail:* martin.ytreberg@pacificpress.com
VP, Mktg & Sales: Doug Church *Tel:* 208-465-2505 *E-mail:* doug.church@pacificpress.com
VP, Prodn: Robert Congleton *Tel:* 208-465-2611 *E-mail:* robert.congleton@pacificpress.com
VP, Prod Devt: Jerry Thomas *E-mail:* jerry.thomas@pacificpress.com
Mktg Dir: Beverly Logan *Tel:* 208-465-2550 *E-mail:* beverly.logan@pacificpress.com
Dir, Publicity: Karen Pearson *Tel:* 208-465-2518 *E-mail:* karen.pearson@pacificpress.com
Sales Mgr: Dave Gatton *Tel:* 208-465-2618 *E-mail:* dave.gatton@pacificpress.com
Magazine Sr Ed: Marvin Moore *Tel:* 208-465-2577 *E-mail:* marvin.moore@pacificpress.com
Magazine Juv Ed: Aileen Andres Sox *Tel:* 208-465-2580 *E-mail:* aileen.sox@pacificpress.com
Ad: Bonnie Laing *Tel:* 208-465-2524 *E-mail:* bonnie.laing@pacificpress.com
Intl Rts: Carolyn Curtis *Tel:* 208-465-2511 *E-mail:* carolyn.curtis@pacificpress.com
Founded: 1874
Religion (Seventh-day Adventist).
ISBN Prefix(es): 978-0-8163; 978-1-5180
Number of titles published annually: 39 Print
Total Titles: 350 Print; 2 CD-ROM; 675 Online; 2 Audio

Paintbox Press
275 Madison Ave, Suite 600, New York, NY 10016
Tel: 212-878-6610
E-mail: info@paintboxpress.com
Web Site: www.paintboxpress.com
Key Personnel
Owner: Pamela Pease
PR: Kelly Smith
Founded: 1998
Pop-ups & books on art & design.
ISBN Prefix(es): 978-0-966943; 978-0-977790
Number of titles published annually: 4 Print
Total Titles: 10 Print
Membership(s): AIGA, the professional association for design; The Children's Book Council; Society of Illustrators

Paladin Press
Division of Paladin Enterprises Inc
5540 Central Ave, Suite 200, Boulder, CO 80301
SAN: 212-0305
Tel: 303-443-7250 *Toll Free Tel:* 800-392-2400 *Fax:* 303-442-8741
E-mail: service@paladin-press.com
Web Site: www.paladin-press.com
Key Personnel
Edit Dir & Sr Ed: Donna Duvall *E-mail:* donnad@paladin-press.com
Art Dir: Barbara Beasley
Sales & Mktg Mgr: Brad Efting
Cust Rel, Trade & Mail Order Sales: Jeanne Vaughan
Founded: 1970
New titles & reprints on military science & history, weaponry, martial arts & self-defense, survival, police science, terrorism & general interest.
ISBN Prefix(es): 978-0-87364; 978-1-58160
Number of titles published annually: 60 Print
Total Titles: 800 Print
Imprints: C E P Inc; Flying Machines Press; Sycamore Island Books
Advertising Agency: J S O Advertising Inc
Distribution Center: Amazon.com
Barnes & Noble
Borders
Membership(s): Independent Book Publishers Association

§Palgrave Macmillan
Imprint of Springer Nature
One New York Plaza, Suite 4500, New York, NY 10004-1562
Tel: 212-726-9200
E-mail: sales-ny@springernature.com; sales@palgrave-usa.com
Web Site: www.palgrave.com
Key Personnel
Exec Ed, Prof Busn & Fin: Laurie Harting *E-mail:* laurie.harting@palgrave-usa.com
Sales Dir, Channel Sales: Marit Vagstad
Founded: 1952
Scholarly & trade publisher - cross market publisher.
ISBN Prefix(es): 978-0-312; 978-0-333; 978-1-4039; 978-0-230
Number of titles published annually: 3,200 Print; 2 Online; 850 E-Book
Total Titles: 28,000 Print
Distributor for Berg Publishers; British Film Institute; Manchester University Press; Pluto Press; I B Tauris & Co Ltd; Zed Books
Membership(s): AAP Professional & Scholarly Publishing Division

Palladium Books Inc
39074 Webb Ct, Westland, MI 48185
SAN: 294-9504
Tel: 734-721-2903 (orders) *Fax:* 734-721-1238
Web Site: www.palladiumbooks.com
Key Personnel
Pres: Kevin Siembieda *E-mail:* ksiembieda@palladiumbooks.com
Sr Ed: Alex Marciniszyn *E-mail:* alex@palladiumbooks.com
Founded: 1981
Role-playing game books & supplements.

ISBN Prefix(es): 978-0-916211; 978-1-57457
Number of titles published annually: 12 Print
Total Titles: 200 Print

§Palm Island Press
411 Truman Ave, Key West, FL 33040
SAN: 298-4024
Tel: 305-296-3102
E-mail: pipress2@gmail.com
Key Personnel
Gen Mgr: Donald Langille
Founded: 1994
ISBN Prefix(es): 978-0-9643434; 978-0-9743524
Number of titles published annually: 3 Print; 2 E-Book
Total Titles: 15 Print; 2 E-Book
Membership(s): Florida Authors & Publishers Association Inc; Independent Book Publishers Association

Palmetto Bug Books
121 N Hibiscus Dr, Miami Beach, FL 33139
Tel: 305-531-9813 *Fax:* 305-604-1516
E-mail: palmettobugbooks@gmail.com
Key Personnel
Pres: Reginald Roach
Founded: 1992
Small publisher of fiction with a slant toward South Florida.
ISBN Prefix(es): 978-0-9634499
Number of titles published annually: 4 Print; 1 Online; 1 E-Book
Total Titles: 4 Print; 4 Online; 4 E-Book

Pangaea Publications
402 Church St, Wisconsin Dells, WI 53965
Tel: 651-226-2032 *Fax:* 651-226-2032
E-mail: info@pangaea.org
Web Site: pangaea.org
Key Personnel
Pres: Bonnie Hayskar *E-mail:* bonzi@pangaea.org
Founded: 1991
Publisher for nature & peoples of the earth.
ISBN Prefix(es): 978-0-9630180; 978-1-929165
Number of titles published annually: 4 Print
Total Titles: 32 Print

Pantheon Books/Schocken Books
Imprint of Knopf Doubleday Publishing Group
c/o Penguin Random House Inc, 1745 Broadway, New York, NY 10019
SAN: 202-862X
Tel: 212-751-2600
Web Site: knopfdoubleday.com/imprint/pantheon
Key Personnel
SVP & Assoc Publr: Christine Gillespie
SVP, Prodn & Design: Andy Hughes
VP & Publr: Jennifer Brown
VP & Dir, Edit: Daniel Frank
VP & Exec Ed: Erroll McDonald
Mng Ed & Dir, Edit, Schocken Books: Altie Karper
Publg Dir, AA Knopf: Patricia Johnson
Dir, Ad: Katie Burns
Dir, Dom Rts (Reprint Rts): Sean Yule
Dir, Publicity: Michiko Clark
Assoc Dir, Publicity: Josie Kals
Asst Dir, Mktg: Sara Eagle; Danielle Plafsky
Sr Ed: Deborah Garrison
Sr Ed, Pantheon Books: Shelley Wanger
Ed: Diana Tejerina Miller
Mktg Mgr: Julianne Clancy; Dani Toth
Assoc Mktg Mgr: Emily Murphy
Asst Mgr, Foreign Rts: Suzanne Smith
Founded: 1942
Fiction & nonfiction.
Penguin Random House Inc & its publishing entities are not accepting proposals, mss or submission queries via e-mail at this time.
ISBN Prefix(es): 978-0-679; 978-0-8052; 978-0-375
Imprints: Pantheon Books; Schocken Books
Foreign Rep(s): Century Hutchinson Group (South America); Colt Associates (Africa exc South Africa); Steve Franklin (Israel); India Book Distributors (India); International Publishers Representatives (Middle East exc Israel); Pandemic Ltd (Continental Europe exc Scandinavia); Penguin Random House Canada (Canada); Penguin Random House New Zealand (New Zealand); Penguin Random House UK (UK); Periodical Management Group Inc (Mexico); Random Century (Australia); Saga Books ApS (Scandinavia); Sonrisa Book Service (Latin America exc Mexico); Yohan (Japan)
Foreign Rights: Arts & Licensing International (China); Agencia Literaria Carmen Balcells SA (Spain); Agencia Literaria BMSR (Brazil); DRT International (Korea); The English Agency (Japan); Graal Literary Agency (Poland); JLM Literary Agency (Greece); Katai & Bolza (Hungary); Agence Michelle Lapautre (France); Licht & Licht Agency (Scandinavia); Literarni Agentura (Czech Republic); Roberto Santachiara (Italy); Sebes & Bisseling Literary Agency (Netherlands)

§Pants On Fire Press
2062 Harbor Cove Way, Winter Garden, FL 34787
Tel: 863-546-0760
E-mail: submission@pantsonfirepress.com
Web Site: www.pantsonfirepress.com
Key Personnel
Publr: David Powers *E-mail:* david@pantsonfirepress.com
Dir, Mktg: Cris Francet *E-mail:* cris@pantsonfirepress.com
Founded: 2007
Award-winning book publisher of picture, middle grade, young adult & new adult books.
ISBN Prefix(es): 978-0-9827271
Number of titles published annually: 12 Print; 8 E-Book
Total Titles: 39 Print; 39 E-Book
Foreign Rights: The Gersh Agency (Joe Veltre) (worldwide)
Distribution Center: INscribe Digital, 55 Francisco St, Suite 710, San Francisco, CA 94133 *Tel:* 415-489-7000 *Fax:* 415-489-7049
Membership(s): Independent Book Publishers Association

Papercutz
160 Broadway, E Wing, Suite 700, New York, NY 10038
Tel: 646-559-4681 *Toll Free Tel:* 800-886-1223 *Fax:* 212-643-1545
E-mail: papercutz@papercutz.com
Web Site: www.papercutz.com
Key Personnel
Pres & CEO: Terry Nantier
Ed-in-Chief: Jim Salicup
Founded: 2005
Graphic novels for ages 7-14.
ISBN Prefix(es): 978-1-59707; 978-1-62991
Number of titles published annually: 75 Print; 60 E-Book
Total Titles: 350 Print; 200 E-Book
Imprints: Charmz (early crush comics for girls ages 10-14); SuperGenius (graphic novels for teens & older)
Distributed by Macmillan
Orders to: MPS Distribution Center, 16365 James Madison Hwy, Gordonsville, VA 22942 *Toll Free Tel:* 888-330-8477 *Toll Free Fax:* 800-672-2054
Warehouse: MPS Distribution Center, 16365 James Madison Hwy, Gordonsville, VA 22942 *Toll Free Tel:* 888-330-8477 *Toll Free Fax:* 800-672-2054
Distribution Center: MPS Distribution Center, 16365 James Madison Hwy, Gordonsville, VA 22942 *Toll Free Tel:* 888-330-8477 *Toll Free Fax:* 800-672-2054
Membership(s): AAP; The Children's Book Council

Papyrus Publishers, see Letterbox/Papyrus of London Publishers USA

Parachute Publishing LLC
Division of Parachute Properties LLC
157 Columbus Ave, Suite 518, New York, NY 10023
Tel: 212-691-1421
Web Site: www.parachutepublishing.com
Key Personnel
Chmn & CEO: Joan Waricha *E-mail:* jwaricha@parachutepublishing.com
Chair: Jane Stine *Tel:* 212-691-1421 *E-mail:* jstine@parachutepublishing.com
Founded: 1983
Children's & adult fiction & nonfiction: original books & series, books from licensed properties.
ISBN Prefix(es): 978-0-938753
Number of titles published annually: 100 Print
Total Titles: 1,000 Print
Distributed by Bantam; Bendon; Berkley; Dorling Kindersley; Grosset; Harcourt; HarperCollins; HarperEntertainment; Kensington; Little, Brown; Penguin Random House Inc; Pocket; Running Press; Scholastic; Simon & Schuster, Inc
Membership(s): American Book Producers Association; The Children's Book Council

Paraclete Press Inc
36 Southern Eagle Cartway, Brewster, MA 02631
SAN: 282-1508
Mailing Address: PO Box 1568, Orleans, MA 02653-1568
Tel: 508-255-4685 *Toll Free Tel:* 800-451-5006 *Fax:* 508-255-5705
E-mail: mail@paracletepress.com
Web Site: www.paracletepress.com
Founded: 1981
Spirituality, personal testimonies, devotionals, literary fiction, new editions of classics & CDs.
ISBN Prefix(es): 978-1-55725; 978-0-941478
Number of titles published annually: 38 Print
Total Titles: 145 Print; 3 Audio
Distributor for Abbey of Saint Peter of Solesmes; Gloriae Dei Cantores
Distribution Center: Bookmasters, 30 Amberwood Pkwy, Ashland, OH 44805 (US & CN) *Tel:* 419-281-5100 *Toll Free Tel:* 800-537-6727 *Fax:* 419-281-0200 *E-mail:* info@bookmasters.com *Web Site:* www.bookmasters.com
Membership(s): CBA; Evangelical Christian Publishers Association

§Paradigm Publications
Division of Redwing Book Co
202 Bendix Dr, Taos, NM 87571
Tel: 575-758-7758 *Toll Free Tel:* 800-873-3946 (US); 888-873-3947 (CN) *Fax:* 575-758-7768
E-mail: info@paradigm-pubs.com
Web Site: www.paradigm-pubs.com; www.redwingbooks.com
Key Personnel
Publr: Robert L Felt *E-mail:* bob@paradigm-pubs.com
Founded: 1980
Scholarly books on traditional Chinese medicine & acupuncture.
ISBN Prefix(es): 978-0-912111; 978-0-9908698
Number of titles published annually: 2 Print
Total Titles: 60 Print; 12 E-Book; 1 Audio

Paradise Cay Publications Inc
120 Monda Way, Blue Lake, CA 95525
Mailing Address: PO Box 29, Arcata, CA 95518-0029
Tel: 707-822-9063 *Toll Free Tel:* 800-736-4509 *Fax:* 707-822-9163

E-mail: info@paracay.com
Web Site: www.paracay.com
Key Personnel
Owner & Dir: Jim Morehouse *E-mail:* james@paracay.com
Founded: 1977
Nautical books, videos, art prints, cruising guides & software.
ISBN Prefix(es): 978-0-939837; 978-0-9646036; 978-1-937196; 978-1-929214
Number of titles published annually: 6 Print
Total Titles: 82 Print; 4 Audio
Imprints: Pardey Publications
Foreign Rep(s): Boat Books (Australia); Islamorado Internacional (Panama); The Nautical Mind (Canada); Transpacific Marine (New Zealand)

Paragon House
3600 Labore Rd, Suite 1, St Paul, MN 55110-4144
Tel: 651-644-3087 *Toll Free Tel:* 800-447-3709 *Fax:* 651-644-0997
E-mail: paragon@paragonhouse.com
Web Site: www.paragonhouse.com
Key Personnel
Pres: Gordon L Anderson
Acqs Mgr & Opers Coord: Rosemary Yokoi
Founded: 1982
Nonfiction; reference, academic/scholarly monographs, trade & college paperbacks. History, religion, philosophy, New Age & government.
ISBN Prefix(es): 978-1-55778; 978-0-913729; 978-0-913757; 978-0-89226; 978-0-943852; 978-0-88702; 978-1-885118
Number of titles published annually: 10 Print
Total Titles: 400 Print
Imprints: Life Wisdom; PWPA Books
Distributed by Bloomsbury International Publishing USA (fulfillment by Macmillan)
Distributor for Professors World Peace Academy
Foreign Rep(s): Roundhouse Publishing (Europe, UK)
Orders to: MPS, PO Box 470, Gordonsville, VA 22942-8501 *Tel:* 540-672-7600 *Toll Free Tel:* 888-330-8477 *Fax:* 540-672-7703 *Toll Free Fax:* 800-672-2054 *E-mail:* orders@mpsvirginia.com

§Parallax Press
Division of Unified Buddhist Church
2236-B Sixth St, Berkeley, CA 94710
Mailing Address: PO Box 7355, Berkeley, CA 94707-0355
Tel: 510-540-6411 *Toll Free Tel:* 800-863-5290 (orders) *Fax:* 510-981-1157
Web Site: www.parallax.org
Key Personnel
Publr: Rachel Neumann *E-mail:* rachel.neumann@parallax.org
Acqs Dir: Hisae Matsuda *E-mail:* hisae@parallax.org
Art & Prodn Dir: Terri Saul *E-mail:* terri@parallax.org
Digital Content Dir: Stephen Houghton *E-mail:* stephen.houghton@parallax.org
Mktg Dir: Nancy Fish *E-mail:* nancy@parallax.org
Sales & Inventory Mgr: Heather Harrison *E-mail:* heather@parallax.org
Assoc Ed: Terry Barber *E-mail:* terry@parallax.org
Acqs Ed: Jacob Surpin *E-mail:* jacob@parallax.org
Publicist: Earlita Chenault *Tel:* 510-944-9032 *E-mail:* earlita@parallax.org
Founded: 1986
Nonprofit organization publishing books about mindfulness, justice & joy.
ISBN Prefix(es): 978-0-938077; 978-1-888375; 978-1-935209; 978-0-9846271; 978-1-937006; 978-1-941529
Number of titles published annually: 24 Print
Total Titles: 200 Print; 7 Audio
Imprints: Palm Leaves Press (scholarly Buddhist titles); Plum Blossom Books (mindfulness books for children)
Foreign Rights: Cecile Barendsma (worldwide exc Germany, India, Thailand & Vietnam); Brother Phap Kham (Vietnam); Literaturmanufaktur (Ursula Richard) (Germany); Plum Village Foundation (Thailand); Shantum Seth (India)
Distribution Center: Penguin Random House Publisher Services (PRHPS), 400 Hahn Rd, Westminster, MD 21157 *Toll Free Tel:* 800-659-2436 *E-mail:* distribution@penguinrandomhouse.com *Web Site:* www.penguinrandomhouse.biz/publisherservices
Penguin Random House Publisher Services (PRHPS), 1745 Broadway, New York, NY 10019 *Fax:* 212-572-4961 *E-mail:* distribution@penguinrandomhouse.com *Web Site:* www.penguinrandomhouse.biz/publisherservices
Penguin Random House Canada, 320 Front St W, Suite 1400, Toronto, ON M5V 3B6, Canada *Web Site:* www.penguinrandomhouse.ca SAN: 201-3975

Paramount Market Publishing Inc
950 Danby Rd, Suite 136, Ithaca, NY 14850
Tel: 607-275-8100
E-mail: editors@paramountbooks.com
Web Site: www.paramountbooks.com
Founded: 1999
Marketing, market research, market segments & brand management.
ISBN Prefix(es): 978-0-9571439; 978-0-9725290; 978-0-9766973; 978-0-9786602; 978-0-9801745; 978-0-9819869; 978-0-9830436
Number of titles published annually: 6 Print; 6 E-Book
Total Titles: 85 Print; 60 E-Book
Imprints: PMP

Parenting Press Inc
Imprint of Chicago Review Press
13751 Lake City Way NE, Suite 110, Seattle, WA 98125
Mailing Address: PO Box 75267, Seattle, WA 98175-0267
Tel: 206-364-2900 *Toll Free Tel:* 800-99-BOOKS (992-6657) *Fax:* 206-364-0702
E-mail: office@parentingpress.com; marketing@parentingpress.com
Web Site: www.parentingpress.com
Founded: 1979
Parenting, social skill building, personal safety for children, discipline, feelings, temperament, development, boundaries, problem solving, social relations.
ISBN Prefix(es): 978-0-943990; 978-0-9602862 (co-published with Raefield-Roberts); 978-1-884734; 978-1-936903
Number of titles published annually: 6 Print; 26 Online; 2 E-Book
Total Titles: 85 Print; 5 Online; 44 E-Book
Distribution Center: Independent Publishers Group (IPG), 814 N Franklin St, Chicago, IL 60610 *Tel:* 312-337-0747 *Toll Free Tel:* 800-888-4741 *Fax:* 312-337-5985 *Web Site:* www.ipgbook.com
Membership(s): Book Publishers of the Northwest; Independent Book Publishers Association; Publishers Association of the West

Park Place Publications
591 Lighthouse Ave, Suite 10, Pacific Grove, CA 93950
SAN: 297-5238
Mailing Address: PO Box 722, Pacific Grove, CA 93950-0722
Tel: 831-649-6640
E-mail: publishingbiz@sbcglobal.net
Web Site: www.parkplacepublications.com
Key Personnel
Owner & Publr: Patricia Hamilton
Founded: 1991
Provides book publishing, graphic design & prepress services. Founded on the premise that "Books make a world of difference" (the company slogan).
This publisher has indicated that 90% of their product line is author subsidized.
ISBN Prefix(es): 978-1-935530; 978-1-943887
Number of titles published annually: 15 Print; 15 Online; 10 E-Book
Total Titles: 75 Print; 15 Online; 10 E-Book
Imprints: Alamos Press (American & Mexican culture & bilingual); At Home on the Road (travel); Keepers of Our Culture (personal & historical stories, memoirs)
Distribution Center: Ingram Content Group, One Ingram Blvd, La Vergne, TN 37086 *Tel:* 615-793-5000 *Web Site:* www.ingramcontent.com
Membership(s): Association of Personal Historians; The Association of Publishers for Special Sales; Independent Book Publishers Association; Small Publishers, Artists & Writers Network

§Parmenides Publishing
3753 Howard Hughes Pkwy, Suite 200, Las Vegas, NV 89169
SAN: 254-4342
Tel: 702-892-3934 *Fax:* 702-892-3939
E-mail: info@parmenides.com
Web Site: www.parmenides.com
Key Personnel
Publr & CEO: Sara Hermann *E-mail:* sherman@parmenides.com
VP & Sales Dir: Gale Carr *E-mail:* gcarr@parmenides.com
Founded: 2000
Independent publishing house. Specialize in literature on philosophy, especially ancient Greek philosophy for the academic & trade markets.
ISBN Prefix(es): 978-1-930972
Number of titles published annually: 10 Print; 10 Online; 4 Audio
Total Titles: 40 Print; 40 Online; 4 Audio
Divisions: ParmenidesAudio™; ParmenidesFiction™
Foreign Rep(s): APAC (Tom Cassidy) (Brunei, Cambodia, China, Hong Kong, Indonesia, Malaysia, Myanmar, Singapore, Taiwan, Thailand, Vietnam)
Orders to: The University of Chicago Press Distribution Center, 1427 E 60 St, Chicago, IL 60637 *Toll Free Tel:* 800-621-2736 *Fax:* 773-702-9756 *E-mail:* orders@press.uchicago.edu
Returns: The University of Chicago Press Distribution Center, 11030 S Langley, Chicago, IL 60628 *Tel:* 773-702-7700 *Fax:* 773-702-9756 *Toll Free Fax:* 800-621-8476 *E-mail:* orders@press.uchicago.edu
Shipping Address: The University of Chicago Press Distribution Center, 11030 S Langley, Chicago, IL 60628 *Tel:* 773-702-7700 *Fax:* 773-702-9756 *Toll Free Fax:* 800-621-8476 *E-mail:* orders@press.uchicago.edu
Warehouse: The University of Chicago Press Distribution Center, 11030 S Langley, Chicago, IL 60628 *Tel:* 773-702-7700 *Fax:* 773-702-9756 *Toll Free Fax:* 800-621-8476 *E-mail:* orders@press.uchicago.edu
Distribution Center: The University of Chicago Press Distribution Center, 11030 S Langley, Chicago, IL 60628 *Tel:* 773-702-7700 *Toll Free Tel:* 800-621-8476 (orders) *Fax:* 773-702-9756 *Toll Free Fax:* 800-621-8476 *E-mail:* orders@press.uchicago.edu
Membership(s): AAP

Path Press Inc
708 Washington St, Evanston, IL 60202
SAN: 630-2041

Tel: 847-492-0177
E-mail: pathpressinc@aol.com
Key Personnel
Pres: Bennett J Johnson
Founded: 1962
Books for African-American & Third World people.
ISBN Prefix(es): 978-0-910671
Number of titles published annually: 3 Print
Total Titles: 43 Print
Subsidiaries: African-American Book Distributors Inc
Membership(s): Independent Book Publishers Association

Pathfinder Publishing Inc
120 S Houghton Rd, Suite 138, Tucson, AZ 85748
SAN: 694-2571
Tel: 520-647-0158
Web Site: www.pathfinderpublishing.com
Key Personnel
CEO & Pres: Bill Mosbrook *E-mail:* bill@pathfinderpublishing.com
Treas: Evelyn Mosbrook *E-mail:* evelyn@pathfinderpublishing.com
Founded: 1985
Books & audiobooks. Specialize in music, psychology, nautical & military history.
ISBN Prefix(es): 978-0-934793
Number of titles published annually: 3 Print; 1 Audio
Total Titles: 50 Print; 3 Audio
Membership(s): Independent Book Publishers Association

Patria Press Inc
PO Box 752, Carmel, IN 46082
Tel: 317-577-1321 *Toll Free Tel:* 888-859-8221 *Fax:* 413-215-8030
E-mail: moreinfo@patriapress.com
Web Site: www.patriapress.com; www.facebook.com/YoungPatriotsBooks; twitter.com/kidsbios
Key Personnel
Pres & Publr: Florrie Binford Kichler
Founded: 1999
Publisher of the Young Patriots Series of children's historical fiction.
ISBN Prefix(es): 978-1-882859; 978-1-935731
Number of titles published annually: 2 Print; 2 E-Book
Total Titles: 14 Print; 14 E-Book
Imprints: Young Patriots Series
Sales Office(s): Independent Publishers Group (IPG), 814 N Franklin St, Chicago, IL 60610
Billing Address: Independent Publishers Group (IPG), 814 N Franklin St, Chicago, IL 60610
Orders to: Independent Publishers Group (IPG), 814 N Franklin St, Chicago, IL 60610 *Tel:* 312-337-0747 *Toll Free Tel:* 800-888-4741 *Fax:* 312-337-5985 *E-mail:* orders@ipgbook.com *Web Site:* www.ipgbook.com
Returns: Independent Publishers Group (IPG), 814 N Franklin St, Chicago, IL 60610
Shipping Address: Independent Publishers Group (IPG), 814 N Franklin St, Chicago, IL 60610 *Tel:* 312-337-0747 *Toll Free Tel:* 800-888-4741 *Fax:* 312-337-5985 *E-mail:* orders@ipgbook.com *Web Site:* www.ipgbook.com
Warehouse: Independent Publishers Group (IPG), 814 N Franklin St, Chicago, IL 60610
Membership(s): BISG; The Children's Book Council; Independent Book Publishers Association; Women's National Book Association

Paul Dry Books
1700 Sansom St, Suite 700, Philadelphia, PA 19103
Tel: 215-231-9939 *Fax:* 215-231-9942
E-mail: editor@pauldrybooks.com
Web Site: www.pauldrybooks.com
Key Personnel
Owner & Publr: Paul Dry *E-mail:* pdry@pauldrybooks.com
Mng Ed: John Corenswet *E-mail:* jcorenswet@pauldrybooks.com
Assoc Ed: William Schofield
Literary publications: fiction, history & essays.
ISBN Prefix(es): 978-0-9664913; 978-0-9679675; 978-1-58988
Number of titles published annually: 8 Print
Total Titles: 100 Print

Pauline Books & Media
Division of Daughters of St Paul
50 Saint Paul's Ave, Boston, MA 02130
SAN: 203-8900
Tel: 617-522-8911 *Toll Free Tel:* 800-876-4463 (orders); 800-836-9723 (cust serv) *Fax:* 617-541-9805
E-mail: editorial@paulinemedia.com (ms submissions); orderentry@pauline.org (cust serv)
Web Site: www.pauline.org/publishing; www.pauline.org/PBMPublishing
Key Personnel
Publr & Edit Dir: Sr Mary Mark Wickenhiser
Promo Mgr: Sr Mary Martha Moss
Adult Acqs Ed: Sr Maria Grace Denato; Sr Christina Wegendt
Children's & Teen Ed: Sr Marlyn Evangelina Monge; Patricia Szczebak
Book Center Acqs: Anthony Ruggiero
Edit Asst, Acqs: Courtney Ward
Digital: Sr Kathryn James Hermes
Intl Rts & Perms: Elizabeth Doyle
Founded: 1932
Spirituality, prayer books, teachers' resources for religious education, liturgical books, church documents, adult religious instruction, saints lives, faith & culture, music & music CDs.
ISBN Prefix(es): 978-0-8198
Number of titles published annually: 60 Print; 50 E-Book; 1 Audio
Total Titles: 600 Print; 72 Audio
Imprints: Catholic Approach Series; Encounter the Saints Series (children); Faith & Culture; Pauline Comics & Graphic Novels (children & teens); Pauline Teen; The Saints Series; Theology of the Body Series
Membership(s): Association of Catholic Publishers Inc; Catholic Press Association; Society of Children's Book Writers & Illustrators

§Paulist Press
997 Macarthur Blvd, Mahwah, NJ 07430-9990
SAN: 202-5159
Tel: 201-825-7300 *Toll Free Tel:* 800-218-1903 *Fax:* 201-825-6921 *Toll Free Fax:* 800-836-3161
E-mail: info@paulistpress.com; publicity@paulistpress.com
Web Site: www.paulistpress.com
Key Personnel
Pres & Publr: Mark-David Janus, CSP *E-mail:* mdjanus@paulistpress.com
VP & Gen Mgr: Kevin Maguire
Dir, Sales: Bob Byrns *Tel:* 201-825-7300 ext 231 *E-mail:* bbyrns@paulistpress.com
Dir, Mktg: Gloria Capik *E-mail:* gcapik@paulistpress.com
Prodn Dir: Kimberly Bernard *E-mail:* kbernard@paulistpress.com
Mng Ed: Donna Crilly *E-mail:* dcrilly@paulistpress.com
Ed-in-Chief: Trace Murphy *E-mail:* tmurphy@paulistpress.com
Ed-at-Large: Christopher Bellitto
Rts & Intl Rts: Angela Ekroth *E-mail:* aekroth@paulistpress.com
Founded: 1865
Resources with emphasis on biblical studies, Christian, Catholic & ecumenical formation & education, ethics & social issues, pastoral ministry, personal growth, spirituality, philosophy, theology.
ISBN Prefix(es): 978-0-8091
Number of titles published annually: 60 Print
Total Titles: 1,650 Print; 1,000 E-Book; 3 Audio
Imprints: The Newman Press; Stimulus Books
Foreign Rep(s): Alban Books Ltd (Europe); Bayard Novalis Distribution (Canada); Brumby Sunstate (Australia); Claretian Communications Inc (India, Philippines); Katong Book Centre (Singapore); KCBS Inc (Korea); Pleroma Christian Supplies (New Zealand)
Warehouse: 39 Ramapo Valley Rd, Mahwah, NJ 07430
Membership(s): Association of Catholic Publishers Inc

Peabody Museum Press
Unit of Peabody Museum of Archaeology & Ethnology, Harvard University
11 Divinity Ave, Cambridge, MA 02138
Tel: 617-495-4255; 617-495-3938 (edit) *Fax:* 617-495-7535
E-mail: peapub@fas.harvard.edu
Web Site: www.peabody.harvard.edu/publications
Key Personnel
Dir, Pubns: Joan O'Donnell *E-mail:* jkodonn@fas.harvard.edu
Proj Mgr: Donna Dickerson *E-mail:* ddickers@fas.harvard.edu
Founded: 1888
ISBN Prefix(es): 978-0-87365
Number of titles published annually: 9 Print
Total Titles: 140 Print
Distributed by Harvard University Press
Orders to: Harvard University Press, c/o TriLiteral LLC, 100 Maple Ridge Dr, Cumberland, RI 02864-1769 *Tel:* 401-531-2300 *Toll Free Tel:* 800-405-1619 *Fax:* 401-531-2801 *Toll Free Fax:* 800-406-9145 *E-mail:* customer.care@triliteral.org

Peace Hill Press
18021 The Glebe Lane, Charles City, VA 23030
Tel: 804-829-5043 *Toll Free Tel:* 877-322-3445 (orders) *Fax:* 804-829-5704
E-mail: info@peacehillpress.com
Web Site: www.peacehillpress.com
Key Personnel
CEO: Jay Wise
Ed-in-Chief: Susan Wise Bauer
Exec Admin: Kim Norton
Founded: 2001
Publish educational books for home school families & schools & books for the well-trained mind.
ISBN Prefix(es): 978-0-9714129; 978-1-933339; 978-0-9728603; 978-1-942968
Number of titles published annually: 5 Print
Total Titles: 24 Print
Distributed by W W Norton & Company Inc
Foreign Rights: Richard Henshaw (Central America, South America)

§Peachpit Press
Imprint of Pearson Education Ltd
1301 Sansome St, San Francisco, CA 94111
Toll Free Tel: 800-283-9444
E-mail: info@peachpit.com; ask@peachpit.com
Web Site: www.peachpit.com
Key Personnel
VP & Publr: Nancy Ruenzel
Assoc Publr: Neil Edde
Exec Ed: Clifford Colby
Ed-in-Chief: Nancy Davis
Digital Opers Mgr: Keasley Jones
Sr Ed: Nikki McDonald; Susan Rimerman
Sr Acqs Ed: Karyn Johnson
Ed: Nancy Peterson
Assoc Ed: Valerie Witte
Founded: 1986

ISBN Prefix(es): 978-0-201; 978-1-56609; 978-0-321; 978-0-938151
Number of titles published annually: 180 Print
Total Titles: 400 Print

Peachtree Publishers
1700 Chattahoochee Ave, Atlanta, GA 30318-2112
SAN: 212-1999
Tel: 404-876-8761 *Toll Free Tel:* 800-241-0113 *Fax:* 404-875-2578 *Toll Free Fax:* 800-875-8909
E-mail: hello@peachtree-online.com
Web Site: www.peachtree-online.com
Key Personnel
VP & Foreign Rts: Kathy Landwehr
Sales: Laura Palermo *Tel:* 404-876-8761 ext 114
Subs Rts: Farah Gehy *E-mail:* gehy@peachtree-online.com
Founded: 1977
Children's fiction & nonfiction, self-help & health/parenting & regional guides.
ISBN Prefix(es): 978-0-931948; 978-0-934601; 978-1-56145; 978-1-68263
Number of titles published annually: 40 Print
Total Titles: 400 Print
Imprints: Freestone; Peachtree Jr
Foreign Rep(s): Fitzhenry & Whiteside Publishers (Canada); Jacqueline Miller Agency (France)

§Pearson
1900 E Lake Ave, Glenview, IL 60025
Tel: 847-729-3000 *Toll Free Tel:* 800-535-4391 (Midwest) *Fax:* 847-729-8910
Web Site: www.pearsonschool.com
Total Titles: 100 Print

Pearson Allyn & Bacon
Imprint of Pearson Higher Education
501 Boylston St, Boston, MA 02116
Tel: 617-848-6000 *Toll Free Tel:* 800-428-4466 *Fax:* 617-848-6016
Web Site: home.pearsonhighered.com
Founded: 1868
College textbook publisher focusing on a select number of social science, education & humanities disciplines.
ISBN Prefix(es): 978-0-205; 978-0-321
Number of titles published annually: 310 Print
Total Titles: 2,300 Print

Pearson Arts & Sciences
Division of Pearson Education Ltd
221 River St, Hoboken, NJ 07030
Tel: 917-981-2200
Web Site: www.pearsonhighered.com
Number of titles published annually: 200 Print

Pearson Benjamin Cummings
Imprint of Pearson Higher Education
1301 Sansome St, San Francisco, CA 94111-1122
Tel: 415-402-2500 *Toll Free Tel:* 800-922-0579 (orders) *Toll Free Fax:* 800-445-6991 (orders)
E-mail: question@aol.com
Web Site: home.pearsonhighered.com
Key Personnel
VP & Dir, Media Strategy: Stacy Treco
Specialize in anatomy & physiology, biology, health & kinesiology, microbiology.
ISBN Prefix(es): 978-0-201; 978-0-582; 978-0-8053; 978-0-321; 978-0-8465

§Pearson Business Publishing
Unit of Pearson Higher Education
225 River St, Hoboken, NJ 07030-4772
Tel: 201-236-7000
Web Site: www.pearsonhighered.com

Pearson Career, Health, Education & Technology
Division of Pearson Education Ltd
225 River St, Hoboken, NJ 07030-4772
Tel: 201-236-7000 *Toll Free Tel:* 800-848-9500 *Fax:* 201-236-7755

§Pearson Education International Group
225 River St, Hoboken, NJ 07030-4772
Tel: 201-236-7000
Number of titles published annually: 6 Print

Pearson Education Ltd
225 River St, Hoboken, NJ 07030-4772
Tel: 201-236-7000 *Fax:* 201-236-6549
E-mail: communications@pearsoned.com
Web Site: www.pearsoned.com
ISBN Prefix(es): 978-0-582
See separate listing for:
Pearson Arts & Sciences
Pearson Career, Health, Education & Technology
Pearson ELT
Pearson Higher Education
Pearson School

Pearson ELT
Division of Pearson Education Ltd
221 River St, Hoboken, NJ 07030
Toll Free Tel: 877-202-4572 *Toll Free Fax:* 800-445-6991
E-mail: english@pearson.com
Web Site: www.pearsonelt.com
Number of titles published annually: 100 Print
Foreign Office(s): Edinburgh Gate, Harlow, Essex CM20 2JE, United Kingdom *Tel:* (01279) 623623 *Fax:* (01279) 621330 *E-mail:* eltinquiries@pearson.com

Pearson Higher Education
Division of Pearson Education Ltd
225 River St, Hoboken, NJ 07030-4772
Tel: 201-236-7000
Web Site: www.pearson.com/us/higher-education.html
Key Personnel
EVP: Logan Campbell
ISBN Prefix(es): 978-0-13; 978-0-205; 978-0-8428; 978-0-87618; 978-0-87619; 978-0-87628; 978-0-89303
Imprints: Pearson Allyn & Bacon; Pearson Benjamin Cummings
See separate listing for:
Pearson Allyn & Bacon
Pearson Benjamin Cummings
Pearson Business Publishing
Pearson Humanities & Social Sciences
Pearson Learning Solutions

§Pearson Humanities & Social Sciences
Unit of Pearson Higher Education
225 River St, Hoboken, NJ 07030-4772
Tel: 201-236-7000
Key Personnel
VP, Fin: Robert Santini
Dir, Print, Prodn & Mfg: Barbara Kittle
Publr: Charlyce Jones Owen
Sr Devt Mgr: Susanna Lesan
Total Titles: 250 Print

Pearson Learning Solutions
Unit of Pearson Higher Education
501 Boyleston St, Suite 900, Boston, MA 02116
SAN: 214-0225
Toll Free Tel: 800-428-4466 (orders); 800-635-1579 *Fax:* 201-784-6131
Web Site: www.pearsoned.com
Key Personnel
Pres, Pearson North America: Donald Kilburn *Tel:* 617-671-3300
ISBN Prefix(es): 978-0-8087; 978-0-536; 978-1-4386; 978-0-555; 978-0-558; 978-1-256; 978-1-269; 978-1-323
Branch Office(s)
Pearson Custom Publishing, 7110 Ohms Lane, Edina, MN 55439-2143 *Tel:* 952-831-1881 *Toll Free Tel:* 800-922-2579 *Fax:* 952-831-3167

Pearson School
Unit of Pearson Education Ltd
221 River St, Hoboken, NJ 07030
Tel: 201-236-7000 *Toll Free Tel:* 800-848-9500 (K-12 prods)
Web Site: www.pearsonschool.com
ISBN Prefix(es): 978-0-13; 978-0-205; 978-0-556; 978-0-8224

T H Peek Publisher
Division of Clearweave Corp
PO Box 7406, Ann Arbor, MI 48107
SAN: 693-9708
Tel: 734-222-8205 *Fax:* 734-661-0136
E-mail: info@thpeekpublisher.com
Web Site: www.thpeekpublisher.com
Key Personnel
Owner: Colin D O'Brien
Founded: 1966
Ms acquisition, editorial, art, design, distribution, advertising & promotion.
ISBN Prefix(es): 978-0-917962; 978-1-935770
Number of titles published annually: 3 Print
Total Titles: 10 Print
Imprints: Alice Greene & Co

Pelican Publishing Co
1000 Burmaster St, Gretna, LA 70053-2246
SAN: 212-0623
Tel: 504-368-1175 *Toll Free Tel:* 800-843-1724 *Fax:* 504-368-1195
E-mail: sales@pelicanpub.com (sales); office@pelicanpub.com (permission); promo@pelicanpub.com (publicity)
Web Site: www.pelicanpub.com
Key Personnel
Pres & Publr: Kathleen Calhoun Nettleton *Tel:* 504-368-1175 ext 312
Promo Dir: Antoinette de Alteriis
Dir, Sales: Don Anderson
Ed & ISBN Contact: Nina Kooij *E-mail:* editorial@pelicanpub.com
Rts & Perms: Sally Boitnott *Tel:* 504-368-1175 ext 310
Founded: 1926
General, motivational, inspirational, nostalgia, note cards, almanacs, business & children's.
ISBN Prefix(es): 978-0-911116; 978-0-88289; 978-1-56554; 978-1-58980; 978-1-4556
Number of titles published annually: 50 Print; 25 E-Book
Total Titles: 2,600 Print; 12 CD-ROM; 1,100 E-Book; 35 Audio
Imprints: Dove Inspirational Press
Subsidiaries: Pelican International Corp
Distributor for Hope Publishing House; Marmac Publishing Co; SelfHelp Success Books
Foreign Rights: Everybody's Books Cc (South Africa); Gazelle Agency (Europe, Ireland, UK); John M Reed (Australia, New Zealand)
Membership(s): Museum Store Association; Southern Independent Booksellers Alliance

§Pen & Publish Inc
4735 S State Rd 446, Bloomington, IN 47401
Tel: 314-827-6567
E-mail: info@penandpublish.com
Web Site: www.penandpublish.com
Key Personnel
Publr: Jennifer Geist *E-mail:* jennifer@penandpublish.com
Co-Founder & Pres: Paul Burt *E-mail:* paul@penandpublish.com
Co-Founder: Dee Burt *E-mail:* dee@penandpublish.com
Founded: 2004
Publishes books by & for schools & nonprofits. It also offers author services to help writers with

self-publishing, editing, design & more. It's traditional imprints include Brick Mantel Books, Open Books Press & Transformation Media Books.
This publisher has indicated that 50% of their product line is author subsidized.
ISBN Prefix(es): 978-1-941799; 978-0-9768391; 978-0-9779530; 978-0-9790446; 978-0-9800429; 978-0-9817264; 978-0-9823850; 978-0-9842258; 978-0-9844600; 978-0-9845751; 978-0-9846359; 978-0-9852737; 978-0-9859367
Number of titles published annually: 3 Print; 3 E-Book
Total Titles: 100 Print; 14 E-Book
Imprints: Brick Mantel Books (literary fiction & poetry); Open Books Press (fiction for all ages & nonfiction for adults); Transformation Media Books (body/mind/spirit)
Membership(s): Independent Book Publishers Association; St Louis Publishers Association
See separate listing for:
Brick Mantel Books
Open Books Press

Pen-L Publishing
12 W Dickson St, No 4455, Fayetteville, AR 72702
Web Site: www.pen-l.com
Key Personnel
Publr: Kimberly Pennell *E-mail:* kimberly@pen-l.com
Founded: 2012
ISBN Prefix(es): 978-1-942428; 978-1-942428; 978-1-68313
Number of titles published annually: 24 Print; 24 E-Book; 4 Audio
Total Titles: 91 Print; 91 E-Book; 6 Audio
Membership(s): International Thriller Writers Inc; Society of Children's Book Writers & Illustrators; Western Writers of America

Pendragon Press
Subsidiary of Camelot Publishing Co Inc
52 White Hill Rd, Hillsdale, NY 12529-5839
Mailing Address: PO Box 190, Hillsdale, NY 12529
Tel: 518-325-6100 *Toll Free Tel:* 877-656-6381 (orders)
E-mail: editor@pendragonpress.com
Web Site: www.pendragonpress.com
Key Personnel
Mng Ed: Robert J Kessler
Founded: 1972
Reference works on books & musicology including music/aesthetics, biographies, music theory, organ, harpsichord, historic brass, 20th century music, French opera, music & religion.
ISBN Prefix(es): 978-0-918728; 978-0-945193; 978-1-57647
Number of titles published annually: 10 Print
Total Titles: 400 Print
Distributed by LIM Editrice SRL (Italy); G Ricordi (Italy)
Distributor for Croatian Musicological Society
Foreign Rep(s): Eurospan Ltd (Europe)

Penfield Books
215 Brown St, Iowa City, IA 52245
SAN: 221-6671
Tel: 319-337-9998 *Toll Free Tel:* 800-728-9998 *Fax:* 319-351-6846
E-mail: penfield@penfieldbooks.com
Web Site: www.penfieldbooks.com
Key Personnel
Publr: Joan Liffring-Zug Bourret
Returns Assoc: John Johnson *Tel:* 319-337-0570
Founded: 1979 (as Penfield Press)
Ethnic titles including Czech, Danish, Dutch, Finnish, French, German, Irish, Italian, Mexican, Norwegian, Polish, Scandinavian, Scottish, Slovak, Swedish & Ukrainian; cookbooks; crafts & folk art; history; ethnic cultural cookbooks, cookbooks of the states. No unsol mss.
ISBN Prefix(es): 978-0-941016; 978-1-932043; 978-1-57216
Number of titles published annually: 6 Print; 6 CD-ROM, 20 E-Book
Total Titles: 174 Print; 268 Online; 75 E-Book
Distribution Center: Amazon.ca (CN)
Amazon.com
Bergquist
Book Marketing Plus
Createspace.com
Kindle

Penguin Books
Imprint of Penguin Group USA, A Penguin Random House Company
375 Hudson St, New York, NY 10014
Tel: 212-366-2000
E-mail: penguinpublicity@us.penguingroup.com
Web Site: www.penguinclassics.com; www.penguin.com
Key Personnel
Pres & Publr, Penguin Books, Publr, Plume & VP, Penguin Group USA: Kathryn Court
SVP & Creative Art Dir: Paul Buckley
VP, Ed-in-Chief, Assoc Publr: Patrick Nolan
VP & Dir, Mktg, Penguin/Exec Dir, Academic Sales & Mktg: John Fagan
VP & Publr, Penguin Classics: Elda Rotor
Exec Mng Ed: Matt Giarratano
Exec Ed: Meg Leder
Exec Ed, Penguin Classics & Sr Ed, Penguin Books: John Siciliano
Sr Ed: Lindsey Schwoeri; Paul Slovak
Ed: Sarah Stein
Asst Ed: Shannon Kelly; Matt Klise; Victoria Savanh
Dir, Ad & Promo: Dennis Swaim
Assoc Dir, Publicity: Shannon Twomey
Publicity Mgr, Viking/Penguin: Rebecca Marsh
Publicity Mgr: Kristin Matzen
Sr Publicist: Tony Forde; Alison Klooster
Publicist: Chris Smith
Assoc Publicist: Brianna Linden
Digital Mktg Mgr: Ryan Murphy
Mktg Coord: Nora McCarthy
Founded: 1935
ISBN Prefix(es): 978-0-14
Number of titles published annually: 244 Print
Total Titles: 4,425 Print
Imprints: Penguin; Penguin Classics; Penguin Compass; Penguin 20th Century Classics
Advertising Agency: Spier NY

Penguin Group USA, A Penguin Random House Company
375 Hudson St, New York, NY 10014
SAN: 282-5074
Tel: 212-366-2000 *Toll Free Tel:* 800-847-5515 (inside sales); 800-631-8571 (cust serv) *Fax:* 212-366-2666; 607-775-4829 (inside sales)
E-mail: online@us.penguingroup.com
Web Site: www.penguin.com
Key Personnel
Pres & Publr, Penguin & Publr, Plume: Kathryn Court
Pres & Publr, Penguin Press: Ann Godoff
Pres & Publr, Portfolio & Sentinel Books: Adrian Zackheim
Pres & Publr, Viking: Brian Tart
Pres, Penguin Young Readers: Jen Loja
Pres, Putnam & Dutton: Ivan Held
SVP & Dir, Sales for Penguin Young Readers Group: Felicia Frazier
SVP & Dir, Strategy & Fin: Allison Dobson
SVP & Dir, Subs Rts: Leigh Butler
SVP, Dist: James C Clark
VP, Secy & Gen Coun: Karen Mayer
VP & Assoc Publr, Pbks (Putnam/Dutton): Benjamin Lee
VP & Corp Dir, HR: Carol Peterson
VP & Dir, Bldg Admin: Heidi Kagan
VP & Dir, Opers: Yvette Dano
VP & Dir of Sales, Pbk & Berkley/NAL: Lauren Monaco
VP & Print Prodn Dir: Vincenzo Ruggiero
VP, HR: Paige McInerney
VP, Order Fulfillment: Linda Bay
Edit Dir, Plume: Philip Budnick
Dir, Mfg Procurement: Mike Gallagher
Dir, Intellectual Property Group: Peter Harris
Dir, Publicity & Assoc Dir, Mktg, Portfolio, Sentinel & Current: Tara Gilbride
Media Rel Mgr: Erica Glass
Ed-in-Chief, Avery: Caroline Sutton
Ed-in-Chief, Viking: Andrea Schulz
Exec Ed, Portfolio, Sentinel & Current: Eric Nelson
Sr Ed, Portfolio, Sentinel & Current: Stephanie Frerich
Sr Ed, Portfolio/Sentinel: Bria Sanford
Ed, Viking: Melanie Tortoroli
Assoc Ed: Sam Raim
Assoc Ed, Avery: Gigi Campo
Assoc Ed, Dutton: Stephanie Kelly
Asst Ed, Pam Dorman Books & Viking: Jeramie Orton
Asst Ed, Penguin: Shannon Kelly
Asst Ed, Putnam: Sofie Brooks
Mgr, Busn Devt: Casey Blue James
Assoc Dir, Publicity: Shannon Twomey
Sr Publicist: Tony Forde
Publicity Mgr: Rebecca Marsh
Publicity Mgr, Portfolio/Sentinel: Margot Stamas
Founded: 1996
Publisher of consumer books in both hardcover & paperback for adults & children. Also produces maps, calendars, audiobooks & mass merchandise products.
Adult: hardcover, trade paperbacks & mass market paperbacks (originals & reprints)
Children: hardcover picture books, paperback picture books, board & novelty books
Young Adult: hardcover & trade paperback
Mass merchandise products.
ISBN Prefix(es): 978-0-201; 978-0-89529; 978-0-425; 978-0-441; 978-0-515; 978-1-57297; 978-0-14; 978-0-8037; 978-0-525; 978-0-452; 978-0-917657; 978-1-55611; 978-0-7232; 978-0-399; 978-0-698; 978-0-448; 978-1-58184; 978-0-89586; 978-0-912656; 978-1-55788; 978-0-87477; 978-0-451; 978-0-453; 978-0-670; 978-0-7860; 978-0-8431; 978-1-57395; 978-1-55773; 978-1-57322; 978-1-58333
Imprints: Ace (pbk); Ace/Putnam (hardcover); Avery; Current; DAW (hardcover & pbk); Dial Books for Young Readers (children's); Pam Dorman Books; Dutton (hardcover); Dutton Children's Books (children's); Grosset & Dunlap (children's); Grosset/Putnam (hardcover); HPBooks (pbk); InterMix; Jove (pbk); Minedition; Onyx (paperback); PaperStar (children's); Penguin (pbk); Penguin Classics (pbk); The Penguin Press; Penguin Workshop; Philomel Books (children's); Plume (pbk); Portfolio; Price Stern Sloan Inc (hardcover, pbk & children's); Puffin (children's); Putnam (hardcover); Razorbill; Riverhead Books (hardcover & pbk); ROC (pbk); Sentinel; Signet (pbk); Signet Classics (pbk); Studio; Tarcher Perigee; Topaz (pbk); Viking (hardcover); Viking Children's Books (children's); Viking Compass (hardcover); Frederick Warne (children's); Wee Sing (children's)
Divisions: Berkley Publishing Group
Distributor for Arkangel; Bibli O'Phile; Consumer Guide/PIL; DAW Books Inc; Dream Works; Granta; HighBridge Audio; Kensington Publishing Corp; The Library of America; The Monacelli Press
Foreign Rights: Penguin (Australia, Canada, India, New Zealand, South Africa, UK); Penguin Putnam International Sales
Advertising Agency: Mesa Group; Spier NY
Membership(s): AAP

See separate listing for:
Avery
Berkley Publishing Group
Celebra
DAW Books Inc
Dial Books for Young Readers
DK Publishing
Dutton
Dutton Children's Books
Grosset & Dunlap
HPBooks
Penguin Books
The Penguin Press
Penguin Young Readers Group
Philomel
Plume
Portfolio
Prentice Hall Press
Puffin Books
GP Putnam's Sons (Hardcover)
Riverhead Books
TarcherPerigee
Viking
Viking Children's Books
Viking Studio
Frederick Warne

The Penguin Press
Imprint of Penguin Group USA, A Penguin Random House Company
375 Hudson St, New York, NY 10014
Web Site: thepenguinpress.com
Key Personnel
Pres & Ed-in-Chief: Ann Godoff
VP & Publr: Scott Moyers
VP & Exec Dir, Copyediting: Tory Klose
VP, Art Dir: Darren Haggar
Publicity Dir: Sarah Hutson
Asst Publicity Dir: Juliana Kiyan
Asst Mktg Dir: Caitlin O'Shaughnessy
Exec Mng Ed, Penguin Group USA: Tricia Conley
Exec Ed: Ed Park
Sr Ed: Virginia Smith Younce
Ed: Emily Cunningham; William Heyward; Christopher Richards; Lindsay Whalen
Publicity Mgr: Gail Brussel
Mktg Coord: Grace Fisher
Founded: 2003
Publishers of literary fiction & select nonfiction.
ISBN Prefix(es): 978-1-59420
Number of titles published annually: 38 Print
Total Titles: 127 Print

Penguin Random House Audio Publishing
Subsidiary of Penguin Random House Inc
1745 Broadway, New York, NY 10019
E-mail: audio@penguinrandomhouse.com
Web Site: www.penguinrandomhouseaudio.com
Key Personnel
SVP & Publr: Amanda D'Acierno
VP, Opers: Sue Daulton
VP, Content Prodn: Dan Zitt
VP, Mktg: Heather Dalton
VP, Publicity: Katie Punia
Asst Dir, Content Prodn: Karen Dzienkonski
Exec Prodr: Linda Korn
Exec Prodr & Audio Spec Projs Mgr: Julie Wilson
Prodr: Nick Martorelli
Sr Acqs Ed, Audio & Large Print: Catherine Bucaria
Sr Mktg Mgr, Audio, Books on Tape & Living Language: Jennifer Rubins
Sr Publicist, Audio & Living Language: Nicole Morano
Asst Mgr, Rts & Perms: Tara Hart
Penguin Random House Inc & its publishing entities are not accepting unsol submissions, proposals, mss, or submission queries via e-mail at this time.
ISBN Prefix(es): 978-0-7393; 978-0-375
Number of titles published annually: 500 Print; 300 Audio
Total Titles: 2,000 Print; 894 Audio
See separate listing for:
Living Language
Random House Reference/Random House Puzzles & Games

§Penguin Random House Inc
1745 Broadway, New York, NY 10019
SAN: 202-5507
Tel: 212-782-9000 *Toll Free Tel:* 800-726-0600
Web Site: www.penguinrandomhouse.com
Key Personnel
Chmn: Philip Hoffman
CEO: Markus Dohle
COO & Pres, Sales, Opers & Digital: Madeline McIntosh
Chief HR Offr: Frank Steinert
Chmn, Knopf: Sonny Mehta
Pres & Publr, Crown Publishing Group: Maya Mavjee
Pres & Publr, Random House Children's Books: Barbara Marcus
Pres & Publr, Random House Publishing Group: Gina Centrello
Pres, Knopf Publishing Group: Tony Chirico
EVP & Gen Coun: Anke Steinecke
EVP & Publr, Ballantine Bantam Dell: Kara Welsh
EVP, Dir, Publg Devt & Author Platforms: Nina von Moltke
SVP & Deputy Gen Coun: Matthew Martin
SVP, Publr Digital Content: Scott Shannon
SVP, Strategic Busn Planning, US Digital Prod Devt, Audio & Fodor's: Susan Livingston
VP & Dir, Partnerships, Consumer Events & Apps: Katherine McCahill
VP & Dir, Retail Sales: Kim Shannon
VP & Dir, Strategy & Devt, Spec Mkts: Sarah Williams
VP & Imprint Sales Dir: Christopher Dufault
VP & Publr, Crown Books for Young Readers: Emily Easton
VP, Content Mktg: Kristen Fritz
VP, Corp Projs: Brendan Cahill
VP, Dir Digital Strategy & Assoc Publr, Digital: Matt Schwartz
VP, Edit Dir (Digital) & Assoc Publr (Romance): Gina Wachtel
VP, Educ Sales & Strategy: Brent Gordon
VP, Lib Mktg, Adult Lib Group: Jennifer Childs
VP, Lib Sales & Head, Adult Lib Group: Skip Dye
VP, Publg Innovation Dept: Alison Rich
VP, Sales Devt: Randi Rosenkranz
VP, Strategy & Corp Devt: Divya Sawhney
Sr Dir, Digital Video: John Clinton
Dir, Intl Online & Digital Sales: Richard Callison
Dir, Partnerships: Lilly Kim
Publg Dir, Vintage Espanol: Cristobal Pera
Sales Dir, Higher Educ: Kimberly Woods
Sales Dir, K-12 School Educ: Travis Temple
Assoc Dir, Publg Devt & Author Platforms: Andrea Bachofen
Mgr, Content Devt & Soc Media: Emily Hughes
Mgr, Publg Devt & Author Platforms: Phillip Stamper-Halpin
Publg Mgr, Vintage Espanol: Ingrid Paredes
Assoc Mng Ed, Crown Children's: Megan Williams
Assoc Ed, Alibi: Randall Klein
Assoc Ed, Hydra: Sarah Peed
Asst Ed, Knopf Books for Young Readers: Karen Greenberg
Ed-at-Large, Flirt & Loveswept: Sue Grimshaw
Ed-at-Large, Knopf Doubleday: Peter Gethers
Penguin Random House Inc & its publishing entities are not accepting unsol submissions, proposals, mss, or submission queries via e-mail at this time.
ISBN Prefix(es): 978-0-307; 978-0-679; 978-0-553; 978-0-676; 978-0-375; 978-0-87665; 978-0-805
Imprints: Alibi (mystery, thriller, suspense); Anchor Bible Commentary; Anchor Bible Dictionary; Anchor Bible Reference Library; Anchor Books; AtRandom.com; Ballantine Books; Ballantine Wellspring; Bantam Books; Bantam Hardcover; Bantam Mass Market; Bantam Skylark; Bantam Starfire; Bantam Trade Paperback; BDD Audio Publishing; Bell Tower; Children's Classics; Children's Media; Clarkson Potter; Crescent Books; Crimeline; Crown Books for Young Readers; Crown Publishers Inc; CTW Publishing; Currency; David Fickling Books; Del Rey; Delacorte Books for Young Readers; Delacorte Press; Dell; Dell Laurel Leaf; Dell Yearling; Delta; Derrydale; The Dial Press; Discovery Books; Disney Books for Young Readers; Domain; Doubleday; Doubleday Bible Commentary; Doubleday Books for Young Readers; Doubleday/Galilee; Doubleday/Image; Dragonfly Books; DTP; Everyman's Library; Fanfare; Fawcett; First Choice Chapter Books; Flirt (new adult); Golden Books; Gramercy Books; Harmony Books; House of Collectibles; Hydra (science fiction & fantasy); Island; Ivy; Alfred A Knopf; Knopf Books for Young Readers; Knopf Guides; Laurel Leaf Books; Library of Contemporary Thought; Living Language; Loveswept (digital only romance); Main Street Books; Modern Library; The Monacelli Press; The New Jerusalem Bible; One World; Pantheon Books; Picture Yearling; The Princeton Review; Random House; Random House Books for Young Readers; Random House Children's Publishing; Random House Digital; Random House Large Print Publishing; Random House Reference & Information Publishing; Razorbill; Schocken Books; Schwartz & Wade Books; Shaye Areheart Books; Sierra Club Adult Books; Skylark; Spectra; Nan A Talese; Testament Books; Three Rivers Press; Times Books; Villard Books; Vintage Books; Vintage Espanol; Wendy Lamb Books; Wings Books; Yearling
Branch Office(s)
WaterBrook Press, 5446 N Academy, Suite 200, Colorado Springs, CO 80918 *Tel:* 719-590-4999 *Fax:* 719-590-8977
Penguin Random House Canada, 2775 Mattheson Blvd E, Mississauga, ON L4W 4P7, Canada *Tel:* 905-624-0672 *Toll Free Tel:* 888-523-9292 (orders) *Fax:* 905-624-6217 *Web Site:* www.randomhouse.ca
Bantam Books Canada Inc, One Toronto St, Suite 300, Toronto, ON M5C 2V6, Canada *Tel:* 416-364-4449 *Fax:* 416-364-6863
Doubleday Canada, One Toronto St, Suite 300, Toronto, ON M5C 2V6, Canada *Tel:* 416-364-4449 *Fax:* 416-364-6863
Editorial Office(s): One Toronto St, Suite 300, Toronto, ON M5C 2V6, Canada *Tel:* 416-777-9477 *Fax:* 416-777-9470
Foreign Office(s): Random House Australia Pty Ltd, 16 Dalmore Dr, Scoresby, Victoria 3153, Australia *Tel:* (03) 9753-4511 *Fax:* (03) 9753-3944
Random House Australia Pty Ltd, 20 Alfred St, Milsons Point, Sydney, NSW 2061, Australia *Tel:* (02) 9954-9966 *Fax:* (02) 9954-4562
Random House New Zealand Ltd, 18 Poland Rd, Glenfield, Auckland 0627, New Zealand *Tel:* (09) 444-7197 *Fax:* (09) 444-7524
Random House South Africa Pty Ltd, Endulini, East Wing, 5A Jubilee Rd, Parktown, Sandton 2193, South Africa *Tel:* (011) 484-3538 *Fax:* (011) 484-6180
Tiptree Book Services, Colchester Rd, Frating Green, Colchester, Essex C07 7DW, United Kingdom *Tel:* (01206) 256000 *Fax:* (01206) 255916

Grantham Book Services, Alma Park Industrial Estate, Isaac Newton Way, Grantham, Lincs NG31 9SD, United Kingdom *Tel:* (01476) 541000 *Fax:* (01476) 590223
Doubleday London, 61-63 Uxbridge Rd, Ealing, London W5 5SA, United Kingdom *Tel:* (020) 8231 6717 *Fax:* (020) 8231 6718
Random House UK Ltd, 20 Vauxhall Bridge Rd, London SW1V 2SA, United Kingdom *Tel:* (020) 7840 8400 *Fax:* (020) 7233 8791
Transworld Publishers Ltd, 61-63 Uxbridge Rd, Ealing, London W5 5SA, United Kingdom *Tel:* (020) 8579-2652 *Fax:* (020) 8579-5479
Transworld Publishers Ltd, Sanders Rd, Finedon Rd Industrial Estate, Wellingborough, Northants NN8 4BU, United Kingdom (dist ctr) *Tel:* (0193) 322-5761 *Fax:* (0193) 327-1235
Distributor for Karen Brown's Guides; Mondadori Spanish Language; National Geographic; Princeton Review; Rizzoli; Rugged Land; Shambhala; Smithsonian Books; Soho Press; Steerforth Press; The Taunton Press; Ten Speed Press; Wizards of the Coast
Shipping Address: Westminster Distribution Center, 400 Hahn Rd, Westminster, MD 21157 *Tel:* 410-848-1900 *Fax:* 410-386-7013
Membership(s): AAP; BISG
See separate listing for:
Books on Tape®
House of Collectibles
Penguin Random House Audio Publishing
Penguin Random House Large Print
Random House Children's Books
Razorbill

Penguin Random House Large Print
Division of Penguin Random House Inc
1745 Broadway, New York, NY 10019
Tel: 212-782-9000
Web Site: www.penguinrandomhouse.com
Key Personnel
Edit Dir: Amy Metsch
Founded: 1990
Acquires & publishes general interest fiction & nonfiction in large print editions.
Penguin Random House Inc & its publishing entities are not accepting unsol submissions, proposals, mss, or submission queries via e-mail at this time.
ISBN Prefix(es): 978-0-679
Number of titles published annually: 40 Print
Total Titles: 300 Print

Penguin Young Readers Group
Division of Penguin Group USA, A Penguin Random House Company
345 Hudson St, New York, NY 10014
Tel: 212-366-2000; 212-414-3553 *Fax:* 212-414-3340
Web Site: www.penguin.com/children
Key Personnel
Pres: Jen Loja
Pres & Publr, Nancy Paulsen Books: Nancy Rose Paulsen
SVP & Dir, Sales: Felicia Frazier
VP & Assoc Publr: Jennifer Haller; Jocelyn Schmidt
VP & Exec Dir, Prodn: Nadine Britt
VP & Exec Dir, Publicity: Shanta Newlin
VP & Dir, Contracts & Busn Aff: George Schumacher
VP & Creative Mktg Dir: Erin Berger
VP & Dir, Subs Rts: Helen Boomer
VP & Dir, Trade Sales: Debra Polansky
VP, Digital Content Devt: Adam Royce
VP, Mktg: Emily Romero
Exec Dir, Licensing: Lori Burke
Exec Dir, Publicity: Elyse Marshall
Dir, Natl Accts: Cristi Navarro
Dir, Preschool & Young Readers Mktg: Jed Bennett
Founded: 1997
Children's hardcover picture books; fiction & nonfiction; trade paperbacks; picture book paperbacks; board & novelty books; calendars.
ISBN Prefix(es): 978-0-201; 978-0-14; 978-0-8037; 978-0-525; 978-0-7232; 978-0-399; 978-0-698; 978-0-448; 978-1-58184; 978-0-670; 978-0-8431
Imprints: Kathy Dawson Books; Dial Books for Young Readers; Firebird; Grosset & Dunlap; Nancy Paulsen Books; Penguin Workshop; Philomel; Price Stern Sloan; PSS; Puffin Books; G P Putnam's Sons; Razorbill; Speak; Viking Children's Books; Frederick Warne
Distribution Center: Penguin Group Distribution Center, One Grosset Dr, Kirkwood, NY 13795 *Tel:* 607-775-1740
See separate listing for:
Price Stern Sloan
GP Putnam's Sons (Children's)

Peninsula Publishing
1630 Post Rd E, Unit 312, Westport, CT 06880
E-mail: sales@peninsulapublishing.com
Web Site: www.peninsulapublishing.com
Key Personnel
Publr: Charles Wiseman *E-mail:* cwiseman@peninsulapublishing.com
Off Mgr: Hannah Wiseman
Founded: 1978
Publish new titles & reprints in the field of acoustics & sound.
ISBN Prefix(es): 978-0-932146
Number of titles published annually: 3 Print
Total Titles: 25 Print
Distributed by Scitech Publishing Inc
Membership(s): Acoustical Society of America; American Institute of Physics

Pennsylvania Historical & Museum Commission
Subsidiary of The Commonwealth of Pennsylvania
Commonwealth Keystone Bldg, 400 North St, Harrisburg, PA 17120-0053
SAN: 282-1532
Tel: 717-783-8946; 717-787-5526 (orders)
E-mail: ra-shoppaheritage@pa.gov
Web Site: www.shoppaheritage.com; www.phmc.pa.gov
Key Personnel
Exec Dir: James M Vaughan *E-mail:* jvaughan@pa.gov
Founded: 1945
Books, booklets & references on Pennsylvania prehistory, history, culture & natural history, both scholarly & popular.
ISBN Prefix(es): 978-0-911124; 978-0-89271
Number of titles published annually: 5 Print
Total Titles: 145 Print

§Pennsylvania State Data Center
Subsidiary of Institute of State & Regional Affairs
Penn State Harrisburg, 777 W Harrisburg Pike, Middletown, PA 17057-4898
Tel: 717-948-6336 *Fax:* 717-948-6754
E-mail: pasdc@psu.edu
Web Site: pasdc.hbg.psu.edu
Key Personnel
Dir: Susan Copella *Tel:* 717-948-6427 *E-mail:* sdc3@psu.edu
Founded: 1981
Policy, demographical analytical reports, hard copy & computer discs.
ISBN Prefix(es): 978-0-939667; 978-1-58036
Number of titles published annually: 5 Print; 5 CD-ROM
Total Titles: 130 Print; 130 CD-ROM; 1 E-Book

The Pennsylvania State University Press
Division of Pennsylvania State University Libraries & Scholarly Communications
University Support Bldg 1, Suite C, 820 N University Dr, University Park, PA 16802-1003
SAN: 213-5760
Tel: 814-865-1327 *Toll Free Tel:* 800-326-9180 *Fax:* 814-863-1408 *Toll Free Fax:* 877-778-2665
E-mail: info@psupress.org
Web Site: www.psupress.org
Key Personnel
Dir: Patrick Alexander *Tel:* 814-867-2209 *E-mail:* pha3@psu.edu
Assoc Press Dir, Design & Prodn Mgr: Jennifer Norton *Tel:* 814-863-8061 *E-mail:* jsn4@psu.edu
Sales & Mktg Dir: Brendan Coyne *Tel:* 814-863-5994 *E-mail:* bbc5228@psu.edu
Busn Mgr: Tina Laychur *Tel:* 814-863-5993 *E-mail:* txs17@psu.edu
IT Mgr: Ed Spicer *E-mail:* res122@psu.edu
Ed-in-Chief: Kendra Boileau *Tel:* 814-863-0524 *E-mail:* klb60@psu.edu
Mng Ed: Laura Reed-Morrisson *Tel:* 814-865-1606 *E-mail:* lxr168@psu.edu
Mng Ed, Journals: Astrid Meyer *Tel:* 814-863-3830 *E-mail:* aum38@psu.edu
Exec Ed: Eleanor Goodman *E-mail:* ehg11@psu.edu
Prodn Coord: Patricia Mitchell *Tel:* 814-867-2216 *E-mail:* pam18@psu.edu
Chief Designer: Steven Kress *E-mail:* srk5@psu.edu
Founded: 1956
Scholarly books & journals; art & architectural history; literature & literary criticism, philosophy, religion, social sciences, law, history, Latin American studies, regional books on Mid-Atlantic area; Special Series: Literature & Philosophy; Penn State Series in the History of the Book; Re-Reading the Canon; Keystone Books (regional); American & European Philosophy; Magic in History; Rural Studies; Refiguring Modernism; Buildings, Landscapes & Societies.
ISBN Prefix(es): 978-0-271
Number of titles published annually: 60 Print; 45 E-Book
Total Titles: 1,400 Print; 3 CD-ROM; 12 Online; 400 E-Book
Imprints: Keystone Books; Metalmark
Foreign Rep(s): NBN International (Africa, Continental Europe, Ireland, Israel, Middle East, UK); University of Toronto Press (Canada); US PubRep (Craig Falk) (Caribbean, Central America, Mexico, South America)
Membership(s): AAP; Association of American University Presses

PennWell Books
Division of PennWell
1421 S Sheridan Rd, Tulsa, OK 74112
Mailing Address: PO Box 21288, Tulsa, OK 74121-1288
Tel: 918-831-9421 *Toll Free Tel:* 800-752-9764 *Fax:* 918-831-9555 *Toll Free Fax:* 877-218-1348
E-mail: sales@pennwell.com
Web Site: www.pennwellbooks.com
Key Personnel
CEO: Mark Wilmoth
Dir: Mary McGee *E-mail:* marym@pennwell.com
Edit Mgr: Marla Patterson *E-mail:* marlap@pennwell.com
Mktg Mgr: Sarah De Vos *E-mail:* sarahd@pennwell.com
Opers Mgr: Andrew Kantola
Prodn Mgr: Sheila Brock *E-mail:* bookprodeditor@pennwell.com
Mktg Coord: Jane Green *E-mail:* jgreen@pennwell.com
Sales & Mktg Coord: Holly Fournier
Founded: 1973
Publish both technical & nontechnical books for petroleum, power & fire services industries. Written by selected industry experts, our books

will help you broaden your expertise in your current field, understand other related disciplines & provide quick-glance references as a topic arrives in your daily routine. Our products make excellent classroom, seminar & inhouse training texts.
ISBN Prefix(es): 978-0-912212; 978-0-87814; 978-1-59370; 978-0-9795633
Number of titles published annually: 20 Print
Total Titles: 400 Print; 5 Audio
Divisions: Fire Engineering Books & Videos
Foreign Rep(s): Cranbury International LLC (Ethan Atkin) (Caribbean, Central America, South America); Disvan Enterprises (Ish Dawar) (India); Eurospan (Africa, Asia, Australasia, Europe, Middle East); Tahir M Lodhi (Pakistan); Tony Poh (Southeast Asia)
See separate listing for:
Fire Engineering Books & Videos

§Pentecostal Publishing House
Subsidiary of United Pentecostal Church International
8855 Dunn Rd, Hazelwood, MO 63042
SAN: 219-3817
Tel: 314-837-7300 *Toll Free Tel:* 866-819-7667 *Fax:* 314-837-6574 (orders)
Web Site: www.pentecostalpublishing.com; wordaflamepress.com
Key Personnel
Chief Admin Offr: Billy Babb
Ed-in-Chief & Publr: Mr Robin Johnston *E-mail:* rjohnston@upci.org
Asst Ed: Lee Ann Alexander *E-mail:* lalexander@upci.org
Purch: Terri Miller
Founded: 1945
Trade paperbacks, periodicals, bibliographies; religion (Protestant), Bibles, foreign languages, crafts, self-help.
ISBN Prefix(es): 978-0-912315; 978-0-932581; 978-1-56722; 978-0-7577
Number of titles published annually: 10 Print; 10 CD-ROM
Total Titles: 400 Print; 35 CD-ROM
Imprints: WAP Academic; WAP Children; Word Aflame Press
Distributed by Anchor Distributors; Christian Network International; Innovative Marketing; Spring Arbor

Penton Media Inc
9800 Metcalf Ave, Overland Park, KS 66212
SAN: 204-3416
Mailing Address: PO Box 12901, Overland Park, KS 66212
Tel: 913-967-1719; 913-341-1300 *Toll Free Tel:* 800-262-1954 (cust serv) *Toll Free Fax:* 800-633-6219
E-mail: bookorders@penton.com
Web Site: www.penton.com
Publisher of repair manuals for motorcycles, ATV, PWC, boats, outdoor power equipment, snowmobiles & tractors, as well as valuation guides.
ISBN Prefix(es): 978-0-89287; 978-0-87288; 978-0-918371; 978-1-59969
Number of titles published annually: 25 Print
Total Titles: 532 Print
Imprints: Ac-u-Kwik; EC&M Books; Electrical Wholesaling; The Electronics Source Book; EquipmentWatch; I&T Shop Service; Penton Price Digests
Shipping Address: Smart Warehouse, 1869 N Topping Ave, Kansas City, MO 64120

Peradam Press
Subsidiary of The Center for Cultural & Naturalist Studies
PO Box 6, North San Juan, CA 95960-0006
Tel: 530-277-9324 *Fax:* 530-559-0754
E-mail: peradam@earthlink.net
Key Personnel
Pres & Sr Ed: Linda Birkholz
Exec Ed: Corinne Boyle
Ed: Patricia Hicks
Founded: 1993
General trade books hardcover & paperbacks.
ISBN Prefix(es): 978-1-885420
Number of titles published annually: 10 Print
Total Titles: 81 Print
Shipping Address: 19074 Oak Tree Rd, Nevada City, CA 95959

Perfection Learning Corp
1000 N Second Ave, Logan, IA 51546
Mailing Address: PO Box 500, Logan, IA 51546-0500
Tel: 712-644-2831 *Toll Free Tel:* 800-831-4190 *Toll Free Fax:* 800-543-2745
E-mail: orders@perfectionlearning.com
Web Site: perfectionlearning.com
Key Personnel
Design Dir: Randy Messer *E-mail:* rmesser@plconline.com
Edit Dir, Elem: Sue Thies *E-mail:* sthies@plconline.com
Mktg Opers Dir: Mark Hagenberg *E-mail:* mhagenberg@plconline.com
Founded: 1926
Elementary & secondary product line covers such content areas as reading, literature, math, test preparation, writing, vocabulary, handwriting, spelling & more.
ISBN Prefix(es): 978-0-89598; 978-0-7807; 978-0-7891; 978-0-8124; 978-1-56312; 978-0-7569; 978-1-60686; 978-1-63419; 978-1-62974; 978-1-62766; 978-1-61563; 978-1-61383; 978-1-61384; 978-1-62299; 978-1-62359; 978-1-62765; 978-1-68064; 978-1-68065; 978-1-68240
Number of titles published annually: 30 Print
Total Titles: 500 Print
Imprints: Cover Craft; Cover-to-Cover; Literature & Thought; Passages; Retold Classics; Summit Books; Tale Blazers
Distributor for Abrams; Ace Books; Airmont; Annick Press; Archway; Atheneum; Baker Books; Ballantine; Bantam; Barrons; Berkley; Blake Books; Candlewick Press; Charlesbridge Press; Chelsea House; Children's Press; Chronicle Books; Crabtree Publishing; Crown; Disney Press; Distri Books; DK; Doubleday; Dutton; F+W Media Inc; Farrar, Straus & Giroux Inc; Fawcett; Firefly; First Avenue; Free Spirit; Fulcrum; Golden Books; Greenhaven Press Inc; Hammond; Hayes; Gareth Stevens; Frederick Warne
Foreign Rep(s): School Book Fairs Ltd (Ron Grant) (Canada)

The Permanent Press
4170 Noyac Rd, Sag Harbor, NY 11963
Tel: 631-725-1101
E-mail: info@thepermanentpress.com
Web Site: www.thepermanentpress.com
Key Personnel
Co-Publr: Chris Knopf *E-mail:* chrisk@mintz.hoke; Judith Shepard *E-mail:* judith@thepermanentpress.com; Martin Shepard *E-mail:* shepard@thepermanentpress.com
Mng Ed: Cathy Suter *E-mail:* cathy@thepermanentpress.com
ISBN Prefix(es): 978-1-877946; 978-0-932966; 978-1-57962
Number of titles published annually: 16 Print
Total Titles: 450 Print
Imprints: Second Chance Press
See separate listing for:
Second Chance Press

Persea Books
277 Broadway, Suite 708, New York, NY 10007
SAN: 212-8233
Tel: 212-260-9256 *Fax:* 212-267-3165
E-mail: info@perseabooks.com
Web Site: www.perseabooks.com
Key Personnel
Pres & Publr: Michael Braziller
VP & Edit Dir: Karen Braziller
Poetry Ed: Gabriel Fried *E-mail:* poetry@perseabooks.com
Publicity: Jonah Fried *E-mail:* publicity@perseabooks.com
Founded: 1975
ISBN Prefix(es): 978-0-89255
Number of titles published annually: 12 Print; 10 E-Book
Total Titles: 500 Print; 40 E-Book
Imprints: A Karen & Michael Braziller Book
Distributed by W W Norton & Company Inc (worldwide exc Canada); Penguin Random House Canada (CN only)
Orders to: W W Norton & Company Inc, 500 Fifth Ave, New York, NY 10110 *Toll Free Tel:* 800-233-4830
Distribution Center: W W Norton & Company Inc c/o National Book Co, Keystone Industrial Park, Scranton, PA 18512 *Toll Free Fax:* 800-233-4830

§Perseus Books
Division of Hachette Book Group
250 W 57 St, 15th fl, New York, NY 10107
Tel: 212-340-8100 *Toll Free Tel:* 800-343-4499 (cust serv) *Fax:* 212-340-8105
Web Site: www.perseusbooks.com
Key Personnel
SVP, HBG & Publr, Perseus Books: Susan Weinberg
SVP, HBG & Publr, Da Capo Press: John Radziewicz
VP, HBG & Publr, Running Press: Kristin Kiser
VP, HBG & Publr, Avalon Press: Bill Newlin
VP, HBG & Publr, PublicAffairs: Clive Priddle
VP, HBG & Publr, Basic Books: Lara Heimert
VP, Acqs, Avalon Press: Grace Fujimoto
VP, Sr Edit Dir, Avalon Press: Kevin McLain
VP, HBG & Publr, Westview Press: Cathleen Tetro
VP, HBG & Assoc Publr, Avalon Press: Donna Galassi
VP, HBG & Dir of Mktg & Sales, Basic Books: Elizabeth Tzetzo
VP, HBG & Assoc Publr, Basic Books: TJ Kelleher
VP, HBG & Sr Dir, Publicity, Da Capo Press: Lissa Warren
VP, HBG & Assoc Publr & Publicity Dir, PublicAffairs: Jaime Leifer
VP, Prodn, Avalon Press: Jane Musser
Dir, Publicity & Mktg, Basic Books: Betsy DeJesu
Creative Dir, Da Capo Press: Alex Camlin
Sr Ed, Moon: Sabrina Young; Kathryn Ettinger; Leah Gordon
Sr Ed, Intl Rel & Area Studies, Westview Press: Katharine Moore
Sr Ed, Rick Steves: Madhu Prasher
Sr Ed, Westview Press: Ada Fung
Sr Acq Ed, Sociology & Digital Initiatives, Westview Press: James Sherman
Ed, Rick Steves: Jamie Andrade
Acqs Ed, Westview Press: Nikki Ioakimedes
Assoc Ed, Moon: Kimberly Ehart; Kristi Mitsuda
Asst Ed, Moon: Rachel Feldman
Assoc Ed, Rick Steves: Sierra Machado
Assoc Mng Ed, Westview Press: Krista Anderson
Mktg Dir, Avalon Press: Jaimee Callaway
Mktg Assoc, Avalon Press: Katie Mock; Clare Haugh
Digital Mktg Mgr, Avalon Press: Kimi Owens
Sales & Mktg Mgr, Westview Press: Renee Malis
Online Mktg Coord, Avalon Press: Crystal Turnau
Assoc Publicist, Avalon Press: Holly Birchfield
Publg Technologies Mgr, Avalon: Darren Alessi
Publg Assoc, Westview Press: Ravina Schneider

Sr Prodn Designer, Avalon Press: Rue Flaherty
Sr Mktg Mgr, Westview Press: Victoria Henson
Cartography Dir, Avalon: Michael Morgenfeld
Sr Cartography Ed, Avalon Press: Albert Angulo
Exec Ed, Basic Books: John Kulka
Sr Cartographer, Avalon Press: Katherine Bennett
Cartographer, Avalon Press: Brian Shotwell
Sr Ed, Basic Books: Dan Gerstle
Ed, Basic Books: Brian Distelberg; Leah Stecher
Asst Ed, Basic Books: Helene Barthelemy
Gen Asst to the SVP, Perseus Books, Admin Support, PublicAffairs: Megan Byrd
Edit Asst, Basic Books: Alia Massoud; Carrie Napolitano
Designer, Basic Books: Chelsea Hunter
Sr Mktg Mgr, Basic Books: Allison Finkel
Mktg Asst, Basic Books: Connie Capone
Asst Dir, Publicity, Basic Books: Courtney Nobile
Sr Publicist, Basic Books: Carrie Majer
Publicist, Basic Books: Kait Howard
Publicity Asst, Basic Books: Isadora Johnson
Exec Ed, Da Capo Press: Bob Pigeon; Ben Schafer
Exec Dir, Lifelong & Seal Press: Renee Sedliar
Exec Ed, Seal Press: Laura Mazer
Sr Ed, Seal Press: Stephanie Knapp
Sr Ed, Da Capo Press: Dan Ambrosio
Mng Ed, Da Capo Press: Fred Francis
Edit Asst, Da Capo Press: Justin Lovell; Miriam Riad
Creative Dir, Da Capo Press: Alex Camlin
Designer, Da Capo Press: Kerry Rubenstein
Publicity Mgr, Da Capo Press: Michael Giarratano
Assoc Publicist, Da Capo Press: Raquel Hitt
Dir of Mktg, Da Capo Press: Kevin Hanover
Assoc Dir of Mktg, Da Capo Press: Matt Weston
Mktg Mgr, Da Capo Press: Quinn Fariel
Sr Ed, PublicAffairs: Benjamin Adams; Colleen Lawrie
Group Mng Ed, Basic Books & PublicAffairs: Melissa Raymond
Asst Mng Ed, PublicAffairs: Katherine Haigler
Asst Ed, PublicAffairs: Athena Bryan
Sr Publicist, PublicAffairs: Josie Urwin
Publicist, PublicAffairs: Kristina Fazzalaro
Mktg Dir, PublicAffairs: Lindsay Fradkoff
Mktg Coord, PublicAffairs: Miguel Cervantes
Edit Dir, Running Press: Jennifer Kasius
Sr Ed, Running Press: Cindy De La Hoz; Kristen Wiewora; Jordana Tusman
Asst to the Publr, Running Press: Tina Camma
Acqs Ed, Running Press: Shannon Connors
Edit Asst, Running Press: Sarah Nodarse
Edit Dir, RP Kids: Julie Matysik
Assoc Ed, RP Kids: Adrienne Szpyrka
Design Dir & Creative Dir for RP Kids: Frances Soo Ping Chow
Assoc Design Dir, Running Press: Joshua McDonnell
Sr Designer, Running Press: Susan Van Horn; Amanda Richmond; Jason Kayser; Ashley Todd
Dim Designer/Sampler, Running Press: Mark Governa
Designer, RP Kids: Teresa Bonaddio
Dir, Miniature Editions & Licensing, Running Press: Jennifer Leczkowski
Assoc Mng Ed & Assoc Ed, Running Press: Jessica Fromm
Prodn Mgr, Miniature Editions, Running Press: Frank Sipala
Mktg & Publicity Dir, Running Press: Jessica Schmidt
Publicity Mgr, Running Press: Seta Zink
Mktg Mgr, Running Press: Geri DiTella
Sr Publicist, Running Press: Amy Cianfrone
Sr Mktg Designer, Running Press: Daniel Cantada
Children's Publicity & Mktg Mgr, Running Press: Valerie Howlett
Assoc Mgr, Digital Mktg & Social Media, Running Press: Cassie Drumm
Founded: 1997
ISBN Prefix(es): 978-0-465 (Basic Books); 978-0-306 (Da Capo Press); 978-1-161 (PublicAffairs); 978-0-762 (Running Press); 978-1-580 (Seal Press); 978-1-602 (Weinstein Books); 978-0-813 (Westview Press); 978-1-631 (Avalon Travel)
Number of titles published annually: 50 Print
Total Titles: 530 Print
Imprints: Avalon Travel (includes Moon, Rick Steves & Westview Press); Basic Books (includes Basic Civitas); Da Capo Press (includes Da Capo Lifelong, Seal Press & Weinstein Books); PublicAffairs (includes Nation Books); Running Press (includes Running Press Kids & Running Press Miniatures)
Orders to: 1094 Flex Dr, Jackson, TN 38301 *Toll Free Tel:* 800-343-4499 *Toll Free Fax:* 800-351-5073
Membership(s): AAP; National Book Foundation

Peter Pauper Press, Inc
202 Mamaroneck Ave, Suite 400, White Plains, NY 10601-5376
SAN: 204-9449
Tel: 914-681-0144 *Fax:* 914-681-0389
E-mail: customerservice@peterpauper.com; orders@peterpauper.com; marketing@peterpauper.com
Web Site: www.peterpauper.com
Key Personnel
CEO: Laurence Beilenson *E-mail:* lbeilenson@peterpauper.com
VP: John Hartley *E-mail:* jhartley@peterpauper.com
Creative Dir: Heather Zschock *E-mail:* hzschock@peterpauper.com
Dir, Spec Sales: Esther Beilenson
Publr: Evelyn L Beilenson *E-mail:* ebeilenson@peterpauper.com
Founded: 1928
Decorated hardcover gift, inspirational; quotations, miniatures, journals, photo albums, children's picture books, children's activity books, travel guides.
ISBN Prefix(es): 978-0-88088; 978-1-59359; 978-1-44130
Number of titles published annually: 60 Print; 15 E-Book
Total Titles: 500 Print; 270 E-Book
Imprints: Inspire Books
Foreign Rep(s): For Arts Sake (Australia, New Zealand); Alejandra Garza (Mexico); Saskia Knobbe (Netherlands); Bara Kristinsdottir (Iceland); Peter Pauper Press UK (UK); Phambili (Southern Africa); Israel Ring (Brazil); Sunstate Books (Australia, New Zealand)
Returns: Conri Services Inc, 5 Skyline Dr, Hawthorne, NY 10532
Shipping Address: Conri Services Inc, 5 Skyline Dr, Hawthorne, NY 10532, Contact: Connie Levene *Tel:* 914-592-2300 *Fax:* 914-592-2174
Warehouse: Conri Services Inc, 5 Skyline Dr, Hawthorne, NY 10532, Contact: Connie Levene *Tel:* 914-592-2300 *Fax:* 914-592-2174

§Peterson Institute for International Economics (PIIE)
1750 Massachusetts Ave NW, Washington, DC 20036-1903
SAN: 293-2865
Tel: 202-328-9000 *Fax:* 202-328-5432; 202-659-3225
E-mail: orders@petersoninstitute.org; media@piie.com
Web Site: www.petersoninstitute.org
Key Personnel
Pres: Adam Posen
VP, Pubns & Communs: Steven R Weisman *Tel:* 202-454-1331
Dir: C Fred Bergsten
Founded: 1981
Trade & textbooks on key economic, monetary, trade & investment issues.
ISBN Prefix(es): 978-0-88132
Number of titles published annually: 15 Print; 14 Online
Total Titles: 300 Print; 200 Online; 35 E-Book
Sales Office(s): Terry Associates
Trim Associates
Parson Weems
Distributor for Center for Global Development
Foreign Rep(s): The Eurospan Group (Africa, Eastern Europe, Iran, Israel, Russia, Turkey, Western Europe)
Orders to: PO Box 960, Herndon, VA 20172 *Toll Free Tel:* 800-522-9139 *Fax:* 703-661-1501 *E-mail:* petersonmail@presswarehouse.com *Web Site:* bookstore.petersoninstitute.org
Returns: 22883 Quicksilver Dr, Dulles, VA 20166
Distribution Center: Books International, PO Box 605, Herndon, VA 20172
Membership(s): AAP; Society for Scholarly Publishing; Washington Book Publishers

§Peterson's, a Nelnet Company
3 Columbia Circle, Suite 205, Albany, NY 12203-5158
Tel: 609-896-1800 (ext 53277) *Toll Free Tel:* 800-338-3282
E-mail: pubmarketing@petersons.com
Web Site: www.petersonspublishing.com
Key Personnel
Publg Dir: Bernadette Webster
Founded: 1966
Education, career books, software & CD-ROM, data licensing, test preparation, financial aid & adult education, online lead generation.
ISBN Prefix(es): 978-0-87866; 978-1-56079; 978-0-7689
Number of titles published annually: 50 Print; 2 E-Book
Total Titles: 120 Print; 2 E-Book
Imprints: Peterson's/Pacesetter Books
Foreign Rights: Ann-Christine Daniellsson Agency (Scandinavia); International Editors' Co (Latin America, Spain); Frederique Parretta Agency (Canada (French-speaking), France); Pikarski (Israel); Tuttle-Mori Agency Inc (Japan, Thailand)
Orders to: Hachette Book Group, 1290 Avenue of the Americas, New York, NY 10019 (intl orders) *Tel:* 212-364-1325 *Fax:* 212-364-0933 *E-mail:* international@hbgusa.com; Hachettte Book Group, 53 State St, Boston, MA 02109 (US & CN) *Toll Free Tel:* 800-759-0190 *Toll Free Fax:* 800-286-9471
Membership(s): BISG

§Petroleum Extension Service (PETEX)
Unit of University of Texas Division of Continuing & Innovative Education
JJ Pickle Research Campus, 10100 Burnet Rd, Bldg 2, Austin, TX 78758-4445
Tel: 512-471-5940 *Toll Free Tel:* 800-687-4132 *Fax:* 512-471-9410 *Toll Free Fax:* 800-687-7839
E-mail: info@petex.utexas.edu
Web Site: cee.utexas.edu/ce/petex/
Key Personnel
Dir of Publg, Communs & Branding: Debby Denehy
Founded: 1944
Develops, produces & delivers technical & non-technical training courses, publications & e-product solutions for employees in various sectors of the petroleum industry.
ISBN Prefix(es): 978-0-88698
Number of titles published annually: 10 Print
Total Titles: 400 Print
Branch Office(s)
4702 N Sam Houston Pkwy W, Suite 800, Houston, TX 77086

§Pflaum Publishing Group
Division of Peter Li Inc
2621 Dryden Rd, Suite 300, Dayton, OH 45439

Tel: 937-293-1415 *Toll Free Tel:* 800-543-4383 (sales) *Fax:* 937-293-1310 *Toll Free Fax:* 800-370-4450
E-mail: service@pflaum.com
Web Site: pflaum.com
Key Personnel
VP & Dir, Mktg: Terry Perkins *Tel:* 212-818-0700 *Fax:* 212-818-0708 *E-mail:* tperkins@peterli.com
VP & Dir, Sales: Michael Raffio *Tel:* 937-293-1415 ext 1107 *E-mail:* mraffio@peterli.com
Founded: 1885
Weekly liturgical magazines for PreK-8. Sacramental preparation for children & teens, catechetical resources for PreK-12, religious educators & youth ministers. Branch offices in Phoenix, AZ & New York, NY.
ISBN Prefix(es): 978-0-937997; 978-0-89837; 978-1-933178; 978-1-935042; 978-1-939105
Number of titles published annually: 20 Print
Total Titles: 75 Print
Membership(s): Association of Catholic Publishers Inc; National Catholic Education Association; National Catholic Educational Exhibitors

Phaidon
65 Bleecker St, 8th fl, New York, NY 10012
Tel: 212-652-5400 *Toll Free Tel:* 800-759-0190 (cust serv) *Fax:* 212-652-5410 *Toll Free Fax:* 800-286-9471 (cust serv)
E-mail: ussales@phaidon.com
Web Site: www.phaidon.com
Key Personnel
CEO: Keith Fox
COO: Philip Ruppel
VP & Group Publr: Deborah Aaronson
VP, Global Mktg & Communs: Linda Brennan *Tel:* 212-652-5207 *E-mail:* lbrennan@phaidon.com
Publr: Emilia Terragni
Publg Dir, Children's Books: Cecily Kaiser
Art Dir, Children's Books: Meagan Bennett
Dir, Busn Devt: Amy Hordes *Tel:* 646-400-4584 *E-mail:* ahordes@phaidon.com
Publicity Dir: Meg Parsont *Tel:* 212-652-5411 *E-mail:* mparsont@phaidon.com
Exec Commissioning Ed, Food: Emily Takoudes
Proj Ed, Food: Olga Massov
Founded: 1923
Illustrated books on fine art, architecture, design, photography, fashion, travel & decorative arts; cookbooks; children's books.
ISBN Prefix(es): 978-0-7148
Number of titles published annually: 80 Print
Total Titles: 1,500 Print
Foreign Office(s): Phaidon Sarl, 55 rue Traversiere, 75012 Paris, France *Tel:* 01 55 28 38 38 *Fax:* 01 55 28 38 39
Phaidon Verlag, Innstr 30, 10243 Berlin, Germany *Tel:* (030) 28 04 08 35 *Fax:* (030) 28 04 48 79
Phaidon Press Ltd, 18 Regents Wharf, All Saints St, London N1 9PA, United Kingdom *Tel:* (020) 7843 1000 *Fax:* (020) 7843 1010 *E-mail:* enquiries@phaidon.com *Web Site:* www.phaidon.com

Phi Delta Kappa International®
1525 Wilson Blvd, Suite 705, Arlington, VA 22209
Mailing Address: PO Box 13090, Arlington, VA 22219
Tel: 812-339-1156 *Toll Free Tel:* 800-766-1156 *Fax:* 812-339-0018
E-mail: memberservices@pdkintl.org
Web Site: www.pdkintl.org
Key Personnel
CEO: Josh Starr
Dir, Mktg & Communs: Ashley McDonald Kinkaid
Founded: 1906
International professional association of educators.
ISBN Prefix(es): 978-0-87367
Number of titles published annually: 8 Print
Total Titles: 12 Print; 1 CD-ROM
Foreign Rep(s): Unifacmann Trading Co (Taiwan)

Philadelphia Museum of Art
2525 Pennsylvania Ave, Philadelphia, PA 19130
Tel: 215-684-7250 *Fax:* 215-235-8715
Web Site: www.philamuseum.org
Key Personnel
Prodn Mgr: Rich Bonk
Ed: Mary Cason; Kathleen Krattenmaker; David Updike
Assoc Ed: Sarah Noreika
Founded: 1901
Illustrated scholarly works on the permanent collection & exhibitions at the museum.
ISBN Prefix(es): 978-0-87633
Number of titles published annually: 7 Print
Total Titles: 80 Print
Distributed by Yale University Press

Philomel
Imprint of Penguin Group USA, A Penguin Random House Company
345 Hudson St, New York, NY 10014
Tel: 212-366-2000
Key Personnel
Pres & Publr: Michael Green
Assoc Publr & Exec Mng Ed: David Briggs
Art Dir: Semadar Megged
Edit Dir: Jill Santopolo
Founded: 1980
Number of titles published annually: 41 Print
Total Titles: 367 Print

Philosophical Library Inc
275 Central Park W, Suite 12D, New York, NY 10024
Tel: 212-886-1873 *Fax:* 212-873-6070
E-mail: editors@philosophicallibrary.com
Web Site: philosophicallibrary.com
Key Personnel
Mgr: Regeen Runes Najar
Founded: 1941
Comprehensive collection of mid-level reference books. A consistent source for serious readers, libraries, academic institutions & booksellers worldwide. Also have a program for print on demand.
ISBN Prefix(es): 978-0-8022
Number of titles published annually: 70 Print; 170 E-Book; 75 Audio
Total Titles: 500 Print; 300 E-Book
Distributed by Open Road Integrated Media

Philosophy Documentation Center
PO Box 7147, Charlottesville, VA 22906-7147
Tel: 434-220-3300 *Toll Free Tel:* 800-444-2419 *Fax:* 434-220-3301
E-mail: order@pdcnet.org
Web Site: www.pdcnet.org
Key Personnel
Dir: George Leaman *E-mail:* leaman@pdcnet.org
Assoc Dir: Pamela K Swope *E-mail:* pkswope@pdcnet.org
Electronic Publg & Mktg: Susanne Mueller-Grote *E-mail:* smg@pdcnet.org
Founded: 1966
Scholarly, nonprofit publisher of peer-reviewed journals, book series, conference proceedings & specialized reference materials. Provides a range of publishing services, including online hosting of full-text content, secure access solutions, membership management, order fulfillment for print or electronic publications & rights management.
ISBN Prefix(es): 978-0-912632; 978-1-889680; 978-1-63435
Number of titles published annually: 15 Print; 30 Online; 10 E-Book
Total Titles: 150 Print; 200 Online; 30 E-Book
Distributor for Zeta Books (online access)
Membership(s): Society for Scholarly Publishing

Phoenix Society for Burn Survivors
1835 R W Berends Dr SW, Grand Rapids, MI 49519-4955
Tel: 616-458-2773 *Toll Free Tel:* 800-888-BURN (888-2876)
E-mail: info@phoenix-society.org
Web Site: www.phoenix-society.org
Key Personnel
Exec Dir: Amy Acton
Ed: Maureen Kalil
Founded: 1977
Books regarding burns.
Number of titles published annually: 3 Print
Total Titles: 35 Print; 35 E-Book

Piano Press
1425 Ocean Ave, Suite 5, Del Mar, CA 92014
Mailing Address: PO Box 85, Del Mar, CA 92014-0085
Tel: 619-884-1401 *Fax:* 858-755-1104
E-mail: pianopress@pianopress.com
Web Site: www.pianopress.com
Key Personnel
Owner & Ed: Elizabeth C Axford *E-mail:* lizaxford@pianopress.com
Music Typesetter: David Murray; Mark So
Audio Engr: John Dawes; Denny Martin; Matthew Dela Pola; Peter Sprague; Kris Stone
Webmaster & Mktg: Frank Tranfaglia
Edit Asst: Kathy Alward; Carol Buckley; Katie Cook; Dee Rome; Gay Salo
Founded: 1998
Publishes songbooks & CDs as well as music-related coloring books & poetry for the educational & family markets.
ISBN Prefix(es): 978-0-9673325; 978-1-931844
Number of titles published annually: 6 Print; 1 Audio
Total Titles: 100 Print
Membership(s): The American Society of Composers, Authors and Publishers; The Recording Academy; Society of Children's Book Writers & Illustrators

Picador
Subsidiary of Macmillan
175 Fifth Ave, 19th fl, New York, NY 10010
Tel: 646-307-5151 *Fax:* 212-253-9627
Web Site: www.picadorusa.com
Key Personnel
VP & Publr: Stephen Morrison *E-mail:* stephen.morrison@picadorusa.com
VP, Sales & Mktg: Darin Keesler *E-mail:* darin.keesler@picadorusa.com
Exec Dir, Publicity: James Meader *E-mail:* james.meader@picadorusa.com
Creative Dir: Henry Yee *E-mail:* henry.yee@picadorusa.com
Exec Ed: Anna deVries *E-mail:* anna.devries@picadorusa.com
Ed: Elizabeth Bruce
Sr Designer: LeeAnn Falciani *E-mail:* leeann.falciani@picadorusa.com
Sr Publicist: Marlena Brown *E-mail:* marlena.brown@picadorusa.com; Declan Taintor *E-mail:* declan.taintor@picadorusa.com
Publicist: Brianna Scharfenberg
Assoc Publicist: Isabella Alimonti *E-mail:* isabella.alimonti@picadorusa.com
Publicity Coord: Sara DeLozier
Mktg Assoc: Molly Fessenden
Founded: 1995
ISBN Prefix(es): 978-0-312
Number of titles published annually: 90 Print
Total Titles: 7,000 Print
Distribution Center: MPS Distribution Center, 16365 James Madison Hwy, Gordonsville, VA 22942-8501 *Toll Free Tel:* 888-330-8477 *Fax:* 540-672-7540 (cust serv) *Toll Free Fax:* 800-672-2054 (orders)

Picasso Project
Division of Alan Wofsy Fine Arts
1109 Geary Blvd, San Francisco, CA 94109
Tel: 415-292-6500 *Fax:* 415-292-6594
E-mail: editeur@earthlink.net (edit); picasso@art-books.com (orders)
Web Site: www.art-books.com
Key Personnel
Mgr: Adios Butler
Ed: Alan Hyman
Founded: 1990
Publish & distribute comprehensive catalogues on the works of Pablo Picasso. Distribution center located in Ashland, OH.
ISBN Prefix(es): 978-0-915346; 978-1-55660
Number of titles published annually: 6 Print; 4 CD-ROM
Total Titles: 75 Print; 12 CD-ROM
Imprints: Beauxarts; Collegium Graphicum
Distributed by Alan Wofsy Fine Arts
Distributor for Cramer (Switzerland); Kornfeld (Switzerland); Ramie (France)
Billing Address: PO Box 2210, San Francisco, CA 94126-2110
Membership(s): AAP

Piccadilly Books Ltd
PO Box 25203, Colorado Springs, CO 80936-5203
SAN: 665-9969
Tel: 719-550-9887
E-mail: orders@piccadillybooks.com
Web Site: www.piccadillybooks.com
Key Personnel
Publr: Bruce Fife *E-mail:* bruce@piccadillybooks.com
Founded: 1985
Health & nutrition, entertainment, performing arts, humorous skits & sketches, writing.
ISBN Prefix(es): 978-0-941599; 978-1-936709
Number of titles published annually: 3 Print
Total Titles: 83 Print; 44 E-Book; 2 Audio
Foreign Rep(s): Gazelle Book Services Ltd (Europe)
Membership(s): Independent Book Publishers Association

§Picton Press
Subsidiary of Picton Corp
814 E Elkcam Circle, Marco Island, FL 34145-2558
Mailing Address: 1637 Briarwood Ct, Marco Island, FL 34145-4007
Tel: 239-970-2442
E-mail: sales@pictonpress.com (orders)
Web Site: www.pictonpress.com
Key Personnel
Pres: Lewis Bunker Rohrbach *E-mail:* lewisrohrbach@hotmail.com
Founded: 1973
Genealogical & historical books.
ISBN Prefix(es): 978-0-89725
Number of titles published annually: 15 Print; 25 CD-ROM
Total Titles: 1,000 Print; 1,000 CD-ROM; 1 E-Book
Imprints: New England History Press; Penobscot Press

Pie in the Sky Publishing LLC
8031 E Phillips Circle, Centennial, CO 80112
Tel: 303-773-0851 *Fax:* 303-773-0851
E-mail: pieintheskypublishing@msn.com
Web Site: www.pieintheskypublishing.com
Key Personnel
Pres: Ann Simmons
Publr: Nancy L Mills *Tel:* 303-221-1551
Founded: 1998
Publishers of high quality, brightly illustrated children's picture books. Most stories are written for both the reader & listener.
ISBN Prefix(es): 978-1-893815
Number of titles published annually: 3 Print; 3 E-Book
Total Titles: 15 Print; 5 E-Book; 1 Audio

Pieces of Learning Inc
1990 Market Rd, Marion, IL 62959-8976
SAN: 298-461X
Tel: 618-964-9426 *Toll Free Tel:* 800-729-5137 *Toll Free Fax:* 800-844-0455
E-mail: info@piecesoflearning.com
Web Site: www.piecesoflearning.com
Key Personnel
Pres: Tyler Young
Founded: 1989
Teacher supplementary educational books; mail order.
ISBN Prefix(es): 978-1-880505; 978-0-9623835; 978-1-931334; 978-1-934358; 978-1-937113
Number of titles published annually: 16 Print
Total Titles: 350 Print; 50 E-Book
Distributed by A W Peller & Associates; Prufrock Press Inc
Membership(s): Education Market Association

The Pilgrim Press/United Church Press
700 Prospect Ave, Cleveland, OH 44115-1100
Tel: 216-736-2100 *Toll Free Tel:* 800-537-3394 (orders) *Fax:* 216-736-2207 (orders)
E-mail: permissions@thepilgrimpress.com; store@ucc.org
Web Site: www.thepilgrimpress.com; www.uccresources.com
Key Personnel
Publr: Rev Timothy Staveteig
Dir, Communs: Ann Poston *Tel:* 216-736-2173 *E-mail:* postona@ucc.org
Dir, Sales & Dist: Marie Tyson *Tel:* 216-736-3777 *E-mail:* tysonm@ucc.org
Graphic Designer: Robyn Nordstrom *Tel:* 216-736-3758 *E-mail:* nordstrr@ucc.org
Mktg Assoc: Aimee Jannsohn *Tel:* 216-736-3761 *E-mail:* jannsoha@ucc.org
Mktg & Soc Media Assoc: Tiffany French *Tel:* 216-736-3759 *E-mail:* frencht@ucc.org
Admin Asst to Dir, Communs: Juliet Dombos *Tel:* 216-736-3766 *E-mail:* dombosj@ucc.org
Founded: 1608
Alternative spiritualities; peace & justice; world religions; contemporary ministry.
ISBN Prefix(es): 978-0-8298
Number of titles published annually: 20 Print
Total Titles: 485 Print

Pineapple Press Inc
PO Box 3889, Sarasota, FL 34230-3889
Tel: 941-706-2507 *Toll Free Tel:* 866-766-3850 (orders) *Fax:* 941-706-2509 *Toll Free Fax:* 800-838-1149 (orders)
E-mail: info@pineapplepress.com; customer.service@ingrampublisherservices.com
Web Site: www.pineapplepress.com
Key Personnel
Pres: David M Cussen *E-mail:* david@pineapplepress.com
Exec Ed: June Cussen *E-mail:* june@pineapplepress.com
Founded: 1982
ISBN Prefix(es): 978-0-910923; 978-1-56164; 978-1-68334
Number of titles published annually: 25 Print
Total Titles: 300 Print
Warehouse: Ingram Publisher Services, 1210 Ingram Dr, Chambersburg, PA 17202

Pinnacle Books, see Kensington Publishing Corp

Pippin Press
229 E 85 St, New York, NY 10028
Mailing Address: PO Box 1347, Gracie Sta, New York, NY 10028
Tel: 212-288-4920 *Fax:* 908-237-2407
Key Personnel
Pres, Publr & Ed-in-Chief: Barbara Francis
Mng Ed & Rts Dir: Gregory Filling
Sr Ed: Joyce Segal
Sales Mgr & Lib Sales Dir: Alan Frese
Founded: 1987
Small chapter books for ages 7-10, humorous fiction for all ages, novels for ages 8-12 & unusual nonfiction for ages 6-12.
ISBN Prefix(es): 978-0-945912
Number of titles published annually: 4 Print
Total Titles: 55 Print
Foreign Rep(s): Baker & Taylor Books (Canada); Baker & Taylor International (worldwide exc Canada)
Orders to: Whitehurst & Clark Book Fulfillment Inc, 1200 County Rd, Rte 523, Flemington, NJ 08822 *Tel:* 908-782-2323 *Toll Free Tel:* 800-488-8040
Returns: Whitehurst & Clark Book Fulfillment Inc, 1200 County Rd, Rte 523, Flemington, NJ 08822 *Tel:* 908-782-2323 *Toll Free Tel:* 800-488-8040
Shipping Address: Whitehurst & Clark Book Fulfillment Inc, 1200 County Rd, Rte 523, Flemington, NJ 08822 *Tel:* 908-782-2323 *Toll Free Tel:* 800-488-8040
Warehouse: Whitehurst & Clark Book Fulfillment Inc, 1200 County Rd, Rte 523, Flemington, NJ 08822 *Tel:* 908-782-2323 *Toll Free Tel:* 800-488-8040
Distribution Center: Whitehurst & Clark Book Fulfillment Inc, 1200 County Rd, Rte 523, Flemington, NJ 08822 *Tel:* 908-782-2323 *Toll Free Tel:* 800-488-8040
Membership(s): ALA

Planert Creek Press
E4843 395 Ave, Menomonie, WI 54751
SAN: 855-7454
Tel: 715-235-4110
E-mail: publisher@planertcreekpress.com
Web Site: www.planertcreekpress.com
Key Personnel
Publr: David Tank
Founded: 2008
Specialize in 3D books & topics related to West Central Wisconsin.
This publisher has indicated that 100% of their product line is author subsidized.
ISBN Prefix(es): 978-0-9815064; 978-0-9962218
Number of titles published annually: 3 Print; 3 Online
Total Titles: 8 Print; 3 Online; 1 Audio
Membership(s): National Stereoscopic Association; Society of Children's Book Writers & Illustrators

Platinum Press LLC
281 Hicks St, Brooklyn, NY 11201
Tel: 718-875-4092 *Fax:* 718-875-5065
Key Personnel
Pres: Herbert J Cohen *E-mail:* herbertjcohen@aol.com
Founded: 1990
Publish nonfiction; book producer & packager; appointment books, diaries, date books, journals, blankbooks & joke books.
ISBN Prefix(es): 978-1-879582
Number of titles published annually: 12 Print
Total Titles: 145 Print; 2 E-Book

Platypus Media LLC
725 Eighth St SE, Washington, DC 20003
Tel: 202-546-1674 *Toll Free Tel:* 877-PLATYPS (752-8977) *Fax:* 202-546-2356
E-mail: info@platypusmedia.com
Web Site: www.platypusmedia.com
Key Personnel
Pres & Dir: Dia L Michels
Founded: 2000

An independent publisher creating books for families, teachers & parenting professionals.
ISBN Prefix(es): 978-1-930775
Number of titles published annually: 7 Print
Total Titles: 32 Print; 1 Audio
Distribution Center: National Book Network, 4501 Forbes Blvd, Suite 200, Lanham, MD 20706 *Tel:* 301-459-3366 *Toll Free Tel:* 800-464-6420 *Fax:* 301-459-5746 *Toll Free Fax:* 800-338-4550 *Web Site:* www.nbnbooks.com
Membership(s): The Association of Publishers for Special Sales; The Children's Book Council; Independent Book Publishers Association; Washington Book Publishers; Women's National Book Association

§Players Press Inc
PO Box 1132, Studio City, CA 91614-0132
Tel: 818-789-4980
E-mail: playerspress@att.net
Key Personnel
VP, Ed: David Wainright
VP, Opers: Chris Cordero
Busn Mgr: David Cole
Sales Mgr: M Cohen
Sr Ed: Robert Gordon
Founded: 196
Publisher of plays, musicals & performing arts textbooks & Sherlock Holmes. Represents world rights for other publishers of performing arts books (film, theater, television). Distributes English Speaking World for other publishers of entertainment books & Sherlockian. Publishes costume books in English & German.
ISBN Prefix(es): 978-0-88734; 978-1-85729
Number of titles published annually: 45 Print; 5 CD-ROM
Total Titles: 4,000 Print; 62 CD-ROM; 4 Audio
Imprints: Healthwatch; Players Press; Showcase
Divisions: Players Press (Canada); Player Press A/Z Ltd; Players Press GmbH; Player Press Ltd (UK)
Distributor for Camelion Plays; Garland-Clark Editors; Macmillan Education (UK); Preston Editions
Foreign Rep(s): Players Press Germany GmbH; Players Press UK Ltd (UK)
Foreign Rights: Players Press International (Europe)
Membership(s): ABA

Pleasure Boat Studio: A Literary Press
201 W 89 St, New York, NY 10024
Tel: 212-362-8563; 413-337-5346 *Fax:* 413-677-0085
E-mail: pleasboat@nyc.rr.com
Web Site: www.pleasureboatstudio.com
Key Personnel
Publr: Lauren Grosskopf *E-mail:* lrslate88@gmail.com
Founded: 1996
Fiction, nonfiction & poetry.
ISBN Prefix(es): 978-0-9651413; 978-1-929355; 978-0-912887
Number of titles published annually: 10 Print; 5 E-Book
Total Titles: 120 Print; 20 E-Book
Imprints: Aequitas Books (nonfiction only); Caravel Books (mysteries only)
Divisions: Empty Bowl Press
Distributor for Empty Bowl Press
Foreign Rights: Books Crossing Borders (worldwide)
Membership(s): Community of Literary Magazines & Presses; Independent Book Publishers Association

§Plexus Publishing, Inc
Affiliate of Information Today, Inc
143 Old Marlton Pike, Medford, NJ 08055
Tel: 609-654-6500 *Fax:* 609-654-4309
E-mail: info@plexuspublishing.com
Web Site: www.plexuspublishing.com
Key Personnel
Pres & CEO: Thomas H Hogan, Sr
VP, Mktg & Busn Devt: Thomas Hogan, Jr
Mktg & Exhibits Mgr: Robert Colding *Tel:* 609-654-6500 ext 330 *E-mail:* rcolding@plexuspublishing.com
Sales & Admin: Deb Kranz *Tel:* 609-654-6500 ext 117 *E-mail:* dkranz@plexuspublishing.com
HR Dir: Mary S Hogan *E-mail:* shogan@plexuspublishing.com
Founded: 1977
Regional book publisher specializing in nature, history & fiction for readers interested in the NJ Pinelands, Atlantic City/Jersey shore, Philadelphia & surrounds. No children's books, poetry, religion, or calendars.
ISBN Prefix(es): 978-0-937548; 978-0-9666748
Number of titles published annually: 3 Print
Total Titles: 50 Print; 25 E-Book; 2 Audio
Imprints: Medford Press (trade book titles, nationally dist by IPG); Plexus Books (regional titles/NJ topics especially Southern NJ history, nature/Pinelands, fiction)
Distribution Center: Independent Publishers Group (IPG) (Medford Press imprint only)
Membership(s): Independent Book Publishing Professionals Group; Mystery Writers of America

§Plough Publishing House
151 Bowne Dr, Walden, NY 12586-2832
SAN: 202-0092
Mailing Address: PO Box 398, Walden, NY 12586-0398
Tel: 845-572-3455 *Toll Free Tel:* 800-521-8011 *Fax:* 845-572-3472
E-mail: info@plough.com
Web Site: www.plough.com
Key Personnel
Mgr: Sam Hine
Founded: 1920
Religion (Anabaptist), church history, children's education, Christian communal living; music; social justice, radical Christianity; social issues.
ISBN Prefix(es): 978-0-87486
Number of titles published annually: 10 Print; 10 Online; 10 E-Book; 1 Audio
Total Titles: 59 Print; 59 Online; 55 E-Book; 5 Audio
Foreign Office(s): 4188 Gwydir Hwy, Elsmore, NSW 2360, Australia
Brightling Rd, Robertsbridge, East Sussex TN32 5DR, United Kingdom *E-mail:* contact@ploughbooks.co.uk
Distribution Center: Ingram Publisher Services, One Ingram Blvd, La Vergne, TN 37086 *Toll Free Tel:* 866-400-5351 *E-mail:* ips@ingramcontent.com *Web Site:* www.ingramcontent.com

Ploughshares
Subsidiary of Ploughshares Inc
Emerson College, 120 Boylston St, Boston, MA 02116
Tel: 617-824-3757
E-mail: pshares@pshares.org
Web Site: www.pshares.org
Key Personnel
Dir & Ed-in-Chief: Ladette Randolph
Founded: 1971
Journal publishing.
ISBN Prefix(es): 978-0-933277; 978-1-933058; 978-1-62608
Number of titles published annually: 3 Print
Total Titles: 118 Print; 9 E-Book
Membership(s): Combined Book Exhibit

§Plowshare Media
405 Vincente Way, La Jolla, CA 92037
SAN: 857-2933
Mailing Address: PO Box 278, La Jolla, CA 92038
E-mail: sales@plowsharemedia.com
Web Site: plowsharemedia.com
Key Personnel
Mng Partner: Maryann Callery *E-mail:* mc@plowsharemedia.com; Thomas P Tweed *E-mail:* tt@plowsharemedia.com
Founded: 2008
Handle all aspects of book publishing including acquisition, editing, typesetting, cover design, printing, marketing & promotion.
ISBN Prefix(es): 978-0-9860428; 978-0-9821145
Number of titles published annually: 2 Print; 2 E-Book
Total Titles: 10 Print; 8 E-Book
Imprints: RELS Press (nonprofit)
Membership(s): Independent Book Publishers Association

§Plum Tree Books
Imprint of Classical Academic Press
2151 Market St, Camp Hill, PA 17011
Tel: 717-730-0711 *Fax:* 717-730-0721
E-mail: info@classicalsubjects.com
Web Site: www.plumtreebooks.com
Key Personnel
Publr: Christopher Perrin *E-mail:* cperrin@classicalsubjects.com
Founded: 2012
Old Virtues, New Stories™ - children's stories presented entirely through digital formats.
ISBN Prefix(es): 978-1-60051
Number of titles published annually: 10 E-Book

§Plume
Division of Penguin Group USA, A Penguin Random House Company
375 Hudson St, New York, NY 10014
Tel: 212-366-2000 *Fax:* 212-243-6002
Web Site: www.penguin.com/publishers/plume
Key Personnel
VP, Assoc Publr & Dir, Mktg & Publicity: Aileen Boyle
Exec Mng Ed: Matt Giarratano
Exec Ed: Becky Cole
Exec Publicist: Marian Brown
Publicity Mgr: Gwyneth Stansfield
Sr Ed: Kate Napolitano
Ed: Nina Shield
Mktg Coord: Molly Pieper
Founded: 1970
Penguin Random House Inc & its publishing entities are not accepting unsol submissions, proposals, mss, or submission queries via e-mail at this time.
ISBN Prefix(es): 978-0-452
Number of titles published annually: 100 Print
Total Titles: 700 Print

§Plunkett Research Ltd
PO Drawer 541737, Houston, TX 77254-1737
Tel: 713-932-0000 *Fax:* 713-932-7080
E-mail: customersupport@plunkettresearch.com
Web Site: www.plunkettresearch.com
Key Personnel
CEO & Publr: Jack W Plunkett *E-mail:* jack_plunkett@plunkettresearch.com
Founded: 1985

Provider of business & industry information to corporate, library, academic & government markets. Plunkett's unique reference books are the only complete sources written in lay language for readers of all types. In many cases, these valuable resources are the only comprehensive guides covering the specific industries involved. Publish in print & electronic formats.
ISBN Prefix(es): 978-0-9638268; 978-1-891775; 978-1-59392; 978-1-60879; 978-1-62831
Number of titles published annually: 34 Print; 29 CD-ROM; 30 Online; 34 E-Book
Total Titles: 34 Print; 30 CD-ROM; 30 Online; 34 E-Book

Pocket Books, see Gallery Books

§Pocket Press Inc
PO Box 25124, Portland, OR 97298-0124
Toll Free Tel: 888-237-2110 *Toll Free Fax:* 877-643-3732
E-mail: sales@pocketpressinc.com
Web Site: www.pocketpressinc.com
Key Personnel
Pres: Bruce Coorpender
Sales & Mktg: Bob Born
Founded: 1992
Reference books for law enforcement.
ISBN Prefix(es): 978-1-884493; 978-1-61371
Number of titles published annually: 120 Print
Total Titles: 120 Print

Pocket Star, see Gallery Books

Pocol Press
6023 Pocol Dr, Clifton, VA 20124-1333
SAN: 253-6021
Tel: 703-830-5862
E-mail: info@pocolpress.com
Web Site: www.pocolpress.com
Key Personnel
Owner & Publr: J Thomas Hetrick
Founded: 1999
Leaders in short fiction & baseball history from first time non-agented authors. Several books used as college textbooks. All titles also ebooks available from Amazon for Kindle.
ISBN Prefix(es): 978-1-929763
Number of titles published annually: 4 Print; 4 E-Book
Total Titles: 64 Print; 64 E-Book
Membership(s): The Association of Publishers for Special Sales

Pointed Leaf Press
136 Baxter St, New York, NY 10013
Tel: 212-941-1800 *Fax:* 212-941-1822
E-mail: info@pointedleafpress.com
Web Site: www.pointedleafpress.com
Key Personnel
Publr & Edit Dir: Suzanne Slesin
Founded: 2002
This publisher has indicated that 50% of their product line is author subsidized.
ISBN Prefix(es): 978-0-9727661; 978-0-9777875; 978-0-9823585; 978-0-9833889; 978-1-938461
Number of titles published annually: 9 Print

Poisoned Pen Press
6962 E First Ave, Suite 103, Scottsdale, AZ 85251
Tel: 480-945-3375 *Toll Free Tel:* 800-421-3976 *Fax:* 480-949-1707
E-mail: info@poisonedpenpress.com
Web Site: www.poisonedpenpress.com
Key Personnel
Pres & Publr: Robert Rosenwald *E-mail:* robert@poisonedpenpress.com
Asst Publr: Diane DiBiase *E-mail:* diane@poisonedpenpress.com
Dir, Mktg: Raj Dayal *E-mail:* raj@poisonedpenpress.com
Ed-in-Chief: Barbara Peters *E-mail:* barbara@poisonedpenpress.com
Ed: Annette Rogers *E-mail:* annette@poisonedpenpress.com
Data Entry Specialist: Kacie Blackburn *E-mail:* kacie@poisonedpenpress.com
Founded: 1997
Publishing high quality works in the field of mystery. Interested in publishing books that we think booksellers everywhere & especially independent mystery booksellers would want to have available to sell. Electronic submissions only. Visit www.poisonedpenpress.com, click on Submission for guidelines & information.
ISBN Prefix(es): 978-1-890208; 978-1-929345 (The Poisoned Pencil); 978-1-59058; 978-1-46420; 978-1-61595 (ebooks)
Number of titles published annually: 60 Print; 60 E-Book
Total Titles: 600 Print; 500 E-Book
Imprints: Poisoned Pen Press (adult mystery); The Poisoned Pencil (young adult mystery)
Foreign Rep(s): Baror International (worldwide)
Foreign Rights: Danny Baror (worldwide)
Distribution Center: Ingram Publisher Services (IPS), One Ingram Blvd, La Vergne, TN 37086 *Tel:* 617-793-5000 *Toll Free Tel:* 866-400-5351 (orders) *E-mail:* ips@ingramcontent.com *Web Site:* www.ingramcontent.com
Membership(s): AAP; Independent Book Publishers Association; Publishers Association of the West

§Polar Bear & Company
Imprint of Solon Center for Research & Publishing
PO Box 311, Solon, ME 04979-0311
SAN: 858-8902
Tel: 207-643-2795
Web Site: www.polarbearandco.com
Key Personnel
Exec Dir: Paul Cornell du Houx
Founded: 1997
To help build community with quality books & art.
ISBN Prefix(es): 978-1-882190
Number of titles published annually: 6 Print; 6 E-Book
Total Titles: 60 Print; 8 E-Book
Orders to: Ingram Lightning Source Inc, 1246 Heil Quaker Blvd, La Vergne, TN 37086 *E-mail:* inquiry@lightningsource.com *Web Site:* www.lightningsource.com
Distribution Center: Ingram Lightning Source Inc, 1246 Heil Quaker Blvd, La Vergne, TN 37086 *Toll Free Tel:* 800-509-4156 *E-mail:* inquiry@lightningsource.com *Web Site:* www.lightningsource.com
Membership(s): Independent Publishers of New England; Maine Writers & Publishers Alliance

Polebridge Press
Division of Westar Institute
PO Box 346, Farmington, MN 55024
Tel: 651-200-2372
E-mail: orders@westarinstitute.org
Web Site: www.westarinstitute.org
Key Personnel
Publr: Arthur J Dewey
Art Dir & Prodn Mgr: Robaire Ream *E-mail:* robaire.ream@westarinstitute.org
Opers Dir & Dist Mgr: Bill Lehto *E-mail:* bill.lehto@westarinstitute.org
Mng Ed: Char Matejovsky *E-mail:* char@westarinstitute.org
Acqs Ed: David Galston *Tel:* 905-577-5726 *E-mail:* dgalston@westarinstitute.org
Developmental Ed: Cassandra Farrin *Tel:* 208-954-6848 *E-mail:* cfarrin@westarinstitute.org
Founded: 1981
Publishes up-to-date reference works for biblical scholars, primarily in support of research on the historical Jesus & the origins of Christianity as well as philosophical theology; scholarly books produced by Westar seminars, research projects & by individual scholars; books & periodicals that disseminate the results of critical scholarship on religion to the public.
ISBN Prefix(es): 978-1-59815; 978-0-944344
Number of titles published annually: 10 Print; 6 E-Book; 3 Audio
Total Titles: 110 Print; 30 E-Book; 93 Audio
Returns: 660 S Mansfield, Ypsilanti, MI 48197 *Tel:* 651-605-5275

Police Executive Research Forum
1120 Connecticut Ave NW, Suite 930, Washington, DC 20036
Tel: 202-466-7820
Web Site: www.policeforum.org
Key Personnel
Exec Dir: Chuck Wexler *Tel:* 202-454-8326 *E-mail:* cwexler@policeforum.org
Dir, Communs: Craig Fischer *Tel:* 202-454-8332 *E-mail:* cfischer@policeforum.org
Chief of Staff: Andrea Luna *Tel:* 202-454-8346 *E-mail:* aluna@policeforum.org
Communs Coord: James McGinty *Tel:* 202-454-8310 *E-mail:* jmcginty@policeforum.org
Founded: 1977
Community policing, POP, police research & management, police & criminal justice.
ISBN Prefix(es): 978-1-878734; 978-1-934485
Number of titles published annually: 7 Print
Total Titles: 70 Print
Distribution Center: Whitehurst & Clark, 1200 Rte 523, Flemington, NJ 08822, Contact: Brad Searles *Toll Free Tel:* 888-202-4563 *Fax:* 908-237-2407 *E-mail:* wcbooks@aol.com

Polis Books
1201 Hudson St, No 211S, Hoboken, NJ 07030
E-mail: info@polisbooks.com; submissions@polisbooks.com
Web Site: www.polisbooks.com; facebook.com/PolisBooks; twitter.com/PolisBooks
Key Personnel
Publr: Jason Pinter *E-mail:* jpinter@polisbooks.com
Founded: 2013
Publishing primarily commercial fiction in adult, young adult & middle grade.
ISBN Prefix(es): 978-1-940610
Number of titles published annually: 30 Print; 50 E-Book; 40 Audio
Foreign Rights: Biagi Literary Management (worldwide)
Distribution Center: Publishers Group West, 1700 Fourth St, Berkeley, CA 94710 *Toll Free Tel:* 800-788-3123 SAN: 202-8522
Membership(s): International Thriller Writers Inc; Mystery Writers of America; Society of Children's Book Writers & Illustrators

Pomegranate Communications Inc
19018 NE Portal Way, Portland, OR 97230
Tel: 503-328-6500 *Toll Free Tel:* 800-227-1428 *Fax:* 503-328-9330 *Toll Free Fax:* 800-848-4376
E-mail: contactus@pomegranate.com
Web Site: www.pomegranate.com
Key Personnel
Pres & Intl Rts: Thomas F Burke
Publr: Katie Burke
Exec Dir: Darius Burke
Sales & Mktg Dir: Leslie Davisson
Founded: 1968
Fine arts publisher of books, calendars, puzzles, stationery & children's products.
ISBN Prefix(es): 978-0-87654; 978-1-56640; 978-0-7649
Number of titles published annually: 12 Print

Total Titles: 120 Print
Imprints: PomegranateKids
Foreign Rep(s): Ashton International (Far East, Middle East); Canadian Manda (Canada); Hardie Grant Books (Australia, New Zealand); Pomegranate Europe Ltd (Europe, UK); Pomegranate International Sales (Africa, Latin America)
Membership(s): American Specialty Toy Retailing Association; APPL; Art Libraries Society of North America; MSA; Pacific Northwest Booksellers Association; Publishers Association of the West; Toy International Association

Portfolio
Subsidiary of Penguin Group USA, A Penguin Random House Company
375 Hudson St, New York, NY 10014
Web Site: www.penguin.com/meet/publishers/portfolio
Key Personnel
Pres & Publr: Adrian Zackheim
VP, Deputy Publr & Mktg Dir: William Weisser
VP & Exec Dir, Copyediting: Tory Klose
Art Dir: Christopher Sergio
Edit Dir: Niki Papadopoulos
PR Dir & Assoc Dir, Mktg: Tara Gilbride
Exec Mng Ed, Penguin Group USA: Tricia Conley
Exec Ed: Stephanie Frerich
Sr Ed, Portfolio/Sentinel: Bria Sandford
Ed: Natalie Horbachevsky
Assoc Ed: Jesse Maeshiro; Leah Trouwborst
Assoc Ed, Portfolio/Sentinel: Kaushik Viswanath
Publicity Mgr: Stefanie Rosenblum
Founded: 2001
Specialize in management, leadership, marketing, business narrative, investing, personal finance, economics, technology, sales, entrepreneurship & career advice.
Penguin Random House Inc & its publishing entities are not accepting unsol submissions, proposals, mss, or submission queries via e-mail at this time.
ISBN Prefix(es): 978-1-59184
Number of titles published annually: 78 Print
Total Titles: 286 Print

Potomac Books Inc
Imprint of University of Nebraska Press
University of Nebraska-Lincoln, 1111 Lincoln Mall, Suite 400, Lincoln, NE 68508
Mailing Address: PO Box 880630, Lincoln, NE 68588-0630
Tel: 402-472-3581 *Fax:* 402-472-6214
Web Site: www.nebraskapress.unl.edu
Founded: 1984 (as Brassey's Inc until 2005)
ISBN Prefix(es): 978-1-57488; 978-1-59797; 978-1-61234
Number of titles published annually: 80 Print; 50 E-Book
Total Titles: 550 Print; 400 E-Book
Foreign Rep(s): Casemate UK Ltd (Andrew Tarring) (Europe, UK); Codasat Canada (Canada); Peribo (Australia, New Zealand)
Foreign Rights: The Asano Agency Inc (Japan); CA-LINK International LLC (China); Graal Literary Agency (Eastern Europe, Poland); Natoli, Stefan & Oliva (Italy); La Nouvelle Agence (France); Julio F Yanez Agencia Literaria SL (Spanish)
Orders to: c/o Longleaf Services Inc, 116 S Boundary St, Chapel Hill, NC 27514-3808 *Tel:* 919-966-7449 *Toll Free Tel:* 800-848-6224 *Fax:* 919-962-2704 *Toll Free Fax:* 800-272-6817 *E-mail:* customerservice@longleafservices.org
Membership(s): NAIPR

Clarkson Potter Publishers
Imprint of Crown Publishing Group
1745 Broadway, New York, NY 10019
Tel: 212-782-9000
Web Site: crownpublishing.com/imprint/clarkson-potter
Founded: 1959
Dedicated lifestyle group within Penguin Random House, home to a community of award-winning & bestselling chefs, cooks, designers, arts & writers-visionaries who see to entertain, engage & teach. Commercial & literary diverse list, including cookbooks, illustrated gift books & a growing line of paper products such as journals, postcards, stationery & games.
ISBN Prefix(es): 978-0-609; 978-0-307; 978-1-4000; 978-0-517
Number of titles published annually: 145 Print
Total Titles: 1,000 Print
Imprints: Clarkson Potter
Foreign Rep(s): Penguin Random House Inc (worldwide)
Orders to: Penguin Random House Inc, 400 Hahn Rd, Westminster, MD 21157 *Toll Free Tel:* 800-733-3000 *E-mail:* csorders@randomhouse.com; Penguin Random House of Canada Inc, Diversified Sales, 2775 Mattheson Blvd E, Mississauga, ON L4W 4P4, Canada *Toll Free Tel:* 800-668-4247 *Fax:* 905-624-8091

powerHouse Books
Imprint of powerHouse Cultural Entertainment Inc
37 Main St, Brooklyn, NY 11201
Tel: 212-604-9074
E-mail: info@powerhousebooks.com
Web Site: www.powerhousebooks.com
Key Personnel
CEO: Daniel Power
Publr: Craig Cohen *E-mail:* craig@powerhousebooks.com
Founded: 1995
Contemporary art, photography & image-based cultural books.
ISBN Prefix(es): 978-1-57687
Number of titles published annually: 35 Print; 1 E-Book
Total Titles: 550 Print; 3 E-Book; 1 Audio
Imprints: Miss Rosen Edition
Distributor for Antinous Press; Juno Books; MTV Press; Throckmorton Press; VH1 Press; Vice Books
Foreign Rep(s): Bookwise International Pty Ltd (Australia); Critiques Livres (France); Peter Hyde Associates (South Africa); Perseus Books Group (Canada); Shimada (Japan); Turnaround (Austria, Eastern Europe, Germany, Ireland, Mediterranean, Scandinavia, Switzerland, UK)
Foreign Rights: Bookwise International Pty Ltd (Australia); Critiques Livres (France); Turnaround (UK)
Warehouse: Random House
Distribution Center: Penguin Random House Publisher Services (PRHPS)

§Practice Management Information Corp (PMIC)
4727 Wilshire Blvd, Suite 300, Los Angeles, CA 90010
SAN: 139-438X
Tel: 323-954-0224 *Fax:* 323-954-0253
E-mail: customer.service@pmiconline.com
Web Site: pmiconline.stores.yahoo.net
Key Personnel
Publr & Pres: James B Davis
Founded: 1986
Books & software for physicians, hospitals, insurance companies & other healthcare professionals on medical coding, reimbursement, practice management, financial management & medical risk management.
ISBN Prefix(es): 978-1-878487 (Health Information Press); 978-1-57066; 978-1-885987; 978-1-936977; 978-1-939852; 978-1-943009
Number of titles published annually: 35 Print
Total Titles: 35 Print
Imprints: Health Information Press (HIP)
Sales Office(s): 200 W 22 St, Suite 253, Lombard, IL 60148 *Toll Free Tel:* 800-633-4215; 800-MEDSHOP (orders) *Toll Free Fax:* 800-633-6556 (orders)

§Practising Law Institute
1177 Avenue of the Americas, New York, NY 10036
SAN: 203-0136
Tel: 212-824-5700 *Toll Free Tel:* 800-260-4PLI (260-4754, cust serv) *Fax:* 212-265-4742 (intl) *Toll Free Fax:* 800-321-0093 (local)
E-mail: info@pli.edu (cust serv)
Web Site: www.pli.edu
Key Personnel
CFO & Treas: Frank De Vivo *Tel:* 212-824-5709 *E-mail:* fdevivo@pli.edu
CIO: Christopher Rousseau *Tel:* 212-824-5878 *E-mail:* crousseau@pli.edu
Chief Sales & Mktg Offr: Don Berbary *Tel:* 212-590-8839 *E-mail:* dberbary@pli.edu
Pres: Anita C Shapiro *Tel:* 212-824-5701 *Fax:* 212-824-5843 *E-mail:* ashapiro@pli.edu
EVP: Sandra R Geller *Tel:* 212-824-5796 *E-mail:* sgeller@pli.edu
VP, Publg: William Cubberley *Tel:* 212-824-5761 *E-mail:* wcubberl@pli.edu
VP, HR: Joan Sternberg *Tel:* 212-824-5764 *E-mail:* jsternberg@pli.edu
VP, Progs: Laura Shields *Tel:* 212-824-5797 *E-mail:* lshields@pli.edu
Founded: 1933
Professional books for lawyers; CDs, DVDs, CD-ROMs, programs.
ISBN Prefix(es): 978-0-87224; 978-1-4024
Number of titles published annually: 210 Print
Total Titles: 330 Print; 4 CD-ROM; 330 Online
Imprints: PLI
Branch Office(s)
685 Market St, Suite 100, San Francisco, CA 94105-4202 *Tel:* 415-498-2800
Shipping Address: PMDS, 1780A Crossroads Dr, Odenton, MD 21113 *Tel:* 301-604-3305

Prayer Book Press Inc
Subsidiary of Media Judaica Inc
221 E 48 St, New York, NY 10017
SAN: 282-1788
Tel: 212-319-6666 *Fax:* 212-688-8597
E-mail: mediajudaica@aol.com
Key Personnel
Pres & Ed: Jonathan D Levine
VP & Sales & Dist Mgr: Walter B Stern
Founded: 1933
Religion (Jewish); prayer books, textbooks, gift editions & reference.
ISBN Prefix(es): 978-0-87677
Number of titles published annually: 5 Print; 1 Audio
Total Titles: 50 Print; 5 Audio
Imprints: Center for Contemporary Judaica

PRB Productions
963 Peralta Ave, Albany, CA 94706-2144
Tel: 510-526-0722 *Fax:* 510-527-4763
E-mail: prbprdns@aol.com
Web Site: www.prbmusic.com
Key Personnel
Prop & Publr: Peter R Ballinger; Leslie J Gold
Founded: 1989
Specialize in publishing high-quality performing editions of instrumental & vocal music from the Baroque & Classical eras, along with original contemporary works for early & contemporary instruments & voices. Customized music typesetting services available by special arrangement.
ISBN Prefix(es): 978-1-56571
Number of titles published annually: 10 Print
Total Titles: 300 Print

Prentice Hall Press
Division of Penguin Group USA, A Penguin Random House Company
375 Hudson St, New York, NY 10014
Tel: 212-366-2000 *Fax:* 212-366-2666
Key Personnel
Publr, Busn, Self-Help & Health: John Duff
Ed: Jeanette Shaw
Founded: 1913
ISBN Prefix(es): 978-0-7352
Number of titles published annually: 7 Print
Total Titles: 134 Print

PREP Publishing
Subsidiary of PREP Inc
3528 Turnberry Circle, Fayetteville, NC 28303
Tel: 910-483-6611 *Toll Free Tel:* 800-533-2814
E-mail: preppub@aol.com
Web Site: www.prep-pub.com
Key Personnel
Publr: Anne McKinney
Lib Sales Dir: Frances Sweeney
Founded: 1994
Books designed to enrich people's lives & help optimize the human experience. Publisher of general trade books, fiction & nonfiction, especially books related to careers, job hunting, government jobs & business planning, marketing & entrepreneurship. Fiction titles include mysteries, Christian fiction & romance.
ISBN Prefix(es): 978-1-885288
Number of titles published annually: 8 Print
Total Titles: 52 Print
Imprints: Business Success Series; Government Jobs Series; Judeo Christian Ethics Series; Anne McKinney Career Series
Advertising Agency: McKinney Communications, PO Box 66, Fayetteville, NC 28302-0066, Contact: Pat Mack
Warehouse: 435 W Russell St, Fayetteville, NC 28301
Membership(s): Community of Literary Magazines & Presses; Independent Book Publishers Association; Southern Independent Booksellers Alliance

Presbyterian Publishing Corp (PPC)
100 Witherspoon St, Louisville, KY 40202
Tel: 502-569-5000 *Toll Free Tel:* 800-523-1631 (US only) *Fax:* 502-569-5113
E-mail: ppcmail@presbypub.com
Web Site: www.ppcbooks.com
Key Personnel
Pres & Publr: Marc Lewis *E-mail:* mlewis@wjkbooks.com
VP & COO: Monty Anderson *E-mail:* manderson@wjkbooks.com
VP & Exec Dir of Publg: David Dobson *Tel:* 502-569-5394 *E-mail:* ddobson@wjkbooks.com
VP, Mktg & eCommerce: Alicia Samuels *E-mail:* asamuels@wjkbooks.com
Founded: 1838
Biblical studies, academic & scholarly textbooks, general trade religious books.
ISBN Prefix(es): 978-0-664; 978-0-8042
Number of titles published annually: 60 Print; 2 CD-ROM; 100 E-Book; 10 Audio
Total Titles: 2,100 Print; 5 CD-ROM
Imprints: Geneva Press; Westminster John Knox Press (WJK)
Distributor for Epworth; SCM
Foreign Rep(s): SCM Press (Europe, UK)
Distribution Center: Spring Arbor Distributors *Toll Free Tel:* 800-395-4340 *Toll Free Fax:* 800-876-0186 *E-mail:* orders@springarbor.com
Membership(s): AAP; PCPA
See separate listing for:
Westminster John Knox Press (WJK)

The Press at California State University, Fresno
Unit of California State University, Fresno
2380 E Keats, M/S MB 99, Fresno, CA 93740-8024
Tel: 559-278-3056 *Fax:* 559 278 6758
E-mail: press@csufresno.edu
Web Site: shop.thepressatcsufresno.com; thepressatcsufresno.com
Key Personnel
Gen Mgr: Gail Freeman
Founded: 1982
Art, architecture, drama, music, film & the media, New Age politics, business, autobiography, Armenian history, Fresno history & literary magazine. Peer reviewed multidisciplinary victimology journal.
ISBN Prefix(es): 978-0-912201
Number of titles published annually: 4 Print; 1 Online
Total Titles: 30 Print

Prestel Publishing
900 Broadway, Suite 603, New York, NY 10003
Tel: 212-995-2720 *Fax:* 212-995-2733
E-mail: sales@prestel-usa.com
Web Site: prestelpublishing.randomhouse.de
Key Personnel
VP: Stephen Hulburt *Tel:* 212-995-2720 ext 22 *E-mail:* shulburt@prestel-usa.com
Mktg & Spec Sales Mgr: Raya Thoma *E-mail:* rthoma@prestel-usa.com
Acqs Ed: Holly La Due
Publicist: Anne Wu *E-mail:* awu@prestel-usa.com
Founded: 1999
ISBN Prefix(es): 978-3-7913
Number of titles published annually: 150 Print
Total Titles: 1,000 Print
Distributor for Die Gestalten Verlag (DGV); Figure 1 Publishing; Loft; Lars Mueller Publishers GmbH; Periscope; Schirmer/Mosel
Warehouse: Innovative Logistics, 406 Wyckoff Mills Rd, East Windsor, NJ 08520 *Tel:* 732-363-5679 *Fax:* 732-363-0338 *Toll Free Fax:* 877-372-8892

§Prevention Products & Services Inc dba The Bureau for At-Risk Youth
PO Box 170, Farmingville, NY 11738
Toll Free Tel: 800-99YOUTH (999-6884) *Fax:* 631-389-2511
Web Site: www.at-risk.com
Key Personnel
Owner: Carmine Russo
Founded: 1988
Educational materials on at-risk children's issues for educators, counselors, parents & children.
ISBN Prefix(es): 978-1-56688
Number of titles published annually: 15 Print
Total Titles: 250 Print
Returns: c/o Karol Media, 375 Stewart Rd, Wilkes-Barre, PA 18706-1246

Mathew Price International Inc
2404 W Main St, Wailuku, HI 96793
Tel: 808-244-9585
E-mail: info@mathewprice.com
Web Site: www.mathewprice.com
Key Personnel
Pres: Mathew Price *E-mail:* mathewp@mathewprice.com
Founded: 1983
ISBN Prefix(es): 978-1-84248; 978-0-9516844
Number of titles published annually: 15 Print
Total Titles: 300 Print

Price Stern Sloan
Imprint of Penguin Young Readers Group
345 Hudson St, New York, NY 10014
SAN: 282-5074
Tel: 212-366-2000
E-mail: online@penguinputnam.com
Web Site: www.penguinrandomhouse.com; www.penguin.com/meet/publishers/grossetdunlap
Key Personnel
Pres & Publr: Francesco Sedita
Founded: 1963
ISBN Prefix(es): 978-0-201; 978-0-8431
Number of titles published annually: 29 Print
Total Titles: 319 Print
Imprints: Crazy Games; Doodle Art; Serendipity; Troubador Press; Wee Sing

§Price World Publishing
3971 Hoover Rd, Suite 77, Columbus, OH 43123-2839
Toll Free Tel: 888-234-6896 *Fax:* 216-803-0350
E-mail: info@priceworldpublishing.com
Web Site: www.priceworldpublishing.com
Key Personnel
Pres & Exec Ed: Robert Price, Esq *Tel:* 888-234-6896 ext 713 *E-mail:* rprice@priceworldpublishing.com
Founded: 2001
Bringing books & ebooks to global markets.
ISBN Prefix(es): 978-1-932549; 978-0-9724102; 978-1-61984; 978-1-93691
Number of titles published annually: 3 Print; 3 E-Book
Total Titles: 81 Print; 2 CD-ROM; 387 E-Book
Distributed by David Bateman Ltd (New Zealand); Cardinal Publishers Group (US)
Foreign Rep(s): Gazelle Book Services Ltd (UK); Monarch Books of Canada (Canada); John Reed Books (Australia); Rights & Distribution Inc (Brunei, Hong Kong, Malaysia, New Zealand, Philippines, Singapore, South Africa, Thailand)
Foreign Rights: Rights & Distribution Inc
Orders to: Cardinal Publishers Group, 2402 Shadeland Ave, Suite A, Indianapolis, IN 46219, Pres: Tom Doherty *Tel:* 317-352-8200 *Fax:* 317-352-8202 *E-mail:* tdoherty@cardinalpub.com *Web Site:* www.cardinalpub.com
Membership(s): American Bar Association; Independent Book Publishers Association

Prima Games
Imprint of DK Publishing
3000 Lava Ridge Ct, Roseville, CA 95661
SAN: 289-5609
Tel: 916-787-7000
Web Site: www.primagames.com
Key Personnel
Digital Publg Dir: Julie Asbury
Sr Ed: Christopher Buffa
Founded: 1984
Computer & video game guides.
Penguin Random House Inc & its publishing entities are not accepting unsol submissions, proposals, mss, or submission queries via e-mail at this time.
ISBN Prefix(es): 978-0-914629; 978-1-55958; 978-0-7615; 978-1-4000
Number of titles published annually: 150 Print
Total Titles: 1,100 Print

Primary Research Group Inc
2753 Broadway, Suite 156, New York, NY 10025
Tel: 212-736-2316 *Fax:* 212-412-9097
E-mail: primaryresearchgroup@gmail.com
Web Site: www.primaryresearch.com
Key Personnel
Pres: James Moses
Founded: 1989
Monographs, books, surveys & research reports on library science industry, economics, publishing (book, electronic & magazine), telecommunication, entertainment & higher education.
ISBN Prefix(es): 978-0-9626749; 978-1-57440
Number of titles published annually: 50 Print
Total Titles: 300 Print

Distributed by Academic Book Center; Ambassador Books; The Book House; Coutts Library Service; Croft House Books; Eastern Book Company; MarketResearch.com; Midwest Library Service; OPAMP Technical Books; Emory Pratt; Research & Markets; Rittenhouse Book Distributors; Total Information; Yankee Book Peddler

Princeton Architectural Press
37 E Seventh St, New York, NY 10003
Tel: 212-995-9620 *Toll Free Tel:* 800-722-6657 (dist); 800-759-0190 (sales) *Fax:* 212-995-9454
E-mail: sales@papress.com
Web Site: www.papress.com
Key Personnel
Publr: Kevin C Lippert *Tel:* 212-995-9620 ext 203 *E-mail:* lippert@papress.com
Mng Ed: Tom Cho
Acqs Dir: Jennifer Lippert *E-mail:* jennifer@papress.com
Design Dir: Paul Wagner *E-mail:* paul@papress.com
Prodn Dir: Janet Behning *E-mail:* behning@papress.com
Prog Dir, Paper & Goods: Sara McKay
Publicity Dir: Diane Levinson
Sales & Mktg Dir: Lia Hunt
Publicity Mgr: Susan Hershberg; Wes Seeley
Founded: 1981
Publisher of high quality books in architecture, graphic design & visual culture, arts & photography, children's & stationery.
ISBN Prefix(es): 978-0-910413; 978-1-878271; 978-1-56898; 978-1-61689
Number of titles published annually: 75 Print; 50 E-Book
Total Titles: 1,000 Print
Distributed by Chronicle Books
Distributor for Balcony Press; Hyphen Press
Foreign Rep(s): Abrams UK (Ewen Robertson) (Europe, Ireland, UK); Chronicle Books (Central America, South America, USA); Sonya Jeffery (Australia); Raincoast Books (Canada)
Distribution Center: Chronicle Books, 680 Second St, San Francisco, CA 94107 *Toll Free Tel:* 800-759-0190 *Toll Free Fax:* 800-286-9471 *E-mail:* order.desk@hbgusa.com *Web Site:* www.chroniclebooks.com

§Princeton Book Co Publishers
15 West Front St, Trenton, NJ 08608
Tel: 609-426-0602 *Toll Free Tel:* 800-220-7149 *Fax:* 609-426-1344
E-mail: pbc@dancehorizons.com
Web Site: www.dancehorizons.com
Key Personnel
Pres & Rts & Perms: Charles Woodford
Ed-in-Chief: Connie Woodford
Founded: 1975
Specialize in dance.
ISBN Prefix(es): 978-0-916622; 978-0-87127; 978-0-903102; 978-0-85418; 978-0-932582; 978-0-7121; 978-0-8463; 978-0-340
Number of titles published annually: 6 Print; 3 E-Book
Total Titles: 150 Print; 14 E-Book
Imprints: Dance Horizons; Dance Horizons Video; Elysian Editions (adult nonfiction)
Distributed by Dance Books Ltd
Distributor for Dance Books Ltd; Dance Notation Bureau
Foreign Rep(s): Dance Books Ltd (UK); John Reed Book Distribution (Australia)

§The Princeton Review
Imprint of Random House Children's Books
c/o Penguin Random House Inc, 1745 Broadway, New York, NY 10019
Toll Free Tel: 800-273-8439
Web Site: www.princetonreview.com
Key Personnel
Publg Dir: Alison Stoltzfus
Founded: 1981
Test preparation, college & graduate school guides, career guides & general study aids.
Penguin Random House Inc & its publishing entities are not accepting unsol submissions, proposals, mss, or submission queries via e-mail at this time.
ISBN Prefix(es): 978-0-9715750; 978-1-59908
Number of titles published annually: 75 Print; 12 CD-ROM
Total Titles: 230 Print; 15 CD-ROM

Princeton University Press
41 William St, Princeton, NJ 08540-5237
Tel: 609-258-4900 *Fax:* 609-258-6305
Web Site: press.princeton.edu
Key Personnel
CIO: Dennis Langlois
Dir: Christie Henry
Assoc Dir & Cont: Patrick Carroll *Tel:* 609-258-2486 *E-mail:* patrick_carroll@press.princeton.edu
Assoc Publg Dir: Al Bertrand *Tel:* 609-258-5775 *E-mail:* al_bertrand@press.princeton.edu
Asst Dir, Ed-in-Chief & Exec Ed: Brigitta van Rheinberg *Tel:* 609-258-4935 *E-mail:* brigitta_vanrheinberg@press.princeton.edu
Dir, Contracts: Shaquona Crews
Dir, Digital Sales: Priscilla Treadwell *Tel:* 609-258-9387 *E-mail:* priscilla_treadwell@press.princeton.edu
Publicity Dir: Andrew DeSio *Tel:* 609-258-5165 *E-mail:* andrew_desio@press.princeton.edu
Sales Dir: Timothy Wilkins *Tel:* 609-258-4877 *E-mail:* timothy_wilkins@press.princeton.edu
UK Intl Rts Dir: Kim Williams
Asst Dir, Publicity: Julia Haav
Asst Press Dir & Mktg Dir: Adam Fortgang *Tel:* 609-258-4896 *E-mail:* adam_fortgang@press.princeton.edu
Publr, Field Guides & Exec Ed (biology, natural history, ornithology): Robert Kirk *Tel:* 609-258-4884 *E-mail:* robert_kirk@press.princeton.edu
Exec Ed (anthropology, religion): Fred Appel *Tel:* 609-258-2484 *E-mail:* fred_appel@press.princeton.edu
Exec Ed (American history, political science): Eric Crahan *Tel:* 609-258-4922 *E-mail:* eric_crahan@press.princeton.edu
Exec Ed (architecture, art): Michelle Komie
Exec Ed (literature): Anne Savarese *Tel:* 609-258-4937 *E-mail:* anne_savarese@press.princeton.edu
Exec Ed (ancient world, philosophy, political theory): Robert Tempio *Tel:* 609-258-0843 *E-mail:* robert_tempio@press.princeton.edu
Sr Ed (economics): Joe Jackson
Sr Ed (biology, earth sciences): Alison Kalett *Tel:* 609-258-9232 *E-mail:* alison_kalett@press.princeton.edu
Sr Ed (psychology, sociology): Meagan Stacey Levinson
Assoc Ed (physical & earth sciences): Eric Henney
Asst Ed: Ryan Mulligan
Exhibits Mgr: Melissa Burton *Tel:* 609-258-4915 *E-mail:* melissa_burton@press.princeton.edu
Proj & Systems Mgr: Steven Peter
Sr Publicist: James Schneider
Publicist: Sara Henning-Stout
Assoc Publicist: Jodi Price
Founded: 1905
Scholarly, scientific & trade books on all subjects.
ISBN Prefix(es): 978-0-691
Number of titles published annually: 250 Print; 125 E-Book
Total Titles: 4,000 Print; 2,000 E-Book
Imprints: Bollingen Series
Foreign Office(s): 6 Oxford St, Woodstock, Oxon OX20 1TW, United Kingdom, Publg Dir, Europe: Caroline Priday *Tel:* (01993) 814500 *Fax:* (01993) 814504 *E-mail:* cpriday@pupress.co.uk
Foreign Rep(s): African Moon Press (Chris Reinders) (South Africa); Avicenna Partnership Ltd (Bill Kennedy) (Bahrain, Egypt, Iran, Iraq, Kuwait, Lebanon, Libya, Oman, Qatar, Saudi Arabia, Syria, United Arab Emirates); Avicenna Partnership Ltd (Claire de Gruchy) (Algeria, Cyprus, Jordan, Libya, Malta, Morocco, Palestine, Tunisia, Turkey); Dominique Bartshukoff (Austria, Croatia, Czech Republic, Germany, Greece, Holland, Hungary, Portugal, Slovenia, Spain); Book Marketing Services (S Janakiraman) (Bangladesh, India, Sri Lanka); Craig Faulk (Caribbean, Central America, South America); Footprint Books Pty Ltd (Australia, New Zealand); Peter Jacques (Belgium, France, Italy, Poland, Scandinavia, Switzerland); Lexa Publishers Representatives (Mical Moser) (Canada); University Press Group (Africa, Europe, India, Israel, Middle East, Pakistan, UK); Kelvin van Hasselt Publishing Services (Africa exc North & South Africa); World Press (Saleem Malik) (Pakistan)
Foreign Rights: Akcali Copyright (Atilla Izgi Turgur) (Turkey); ANAW Literary Agency (Aleksandra Matuszak) (Poland); L'Autre Agency (Corinne Marotte) (France); Agencia Literaria Carmen Balcells SA (Maribel Luque) (Latin America, Spain); Bardon-Chinese Media Agency (David Tsai) (China); Dar Cherlin (Amelie Cherlin) (Arab Middle East); Ilidio Da Fonseca Matos (Portugal); The English Agency (Tsutomu Yawata) (Japan); Paul & Peter Fritz AG (Christian Dittus) (Germany); Roberto Gilodi (Italy); JLM Literary Agency (John Moukakos) (Greece); Andrew Nurnberg Associates (Judit Hermann) (Croatia, Hungary); Andrew Nurnberg Associates (Petra Tobiskova) (Czech Republic, Slovakia, Slovenia); Andrew Nurnberg Associates (Anna Droumeva) (Bulgaria, Romania); Andrew Nurnberg Associates (Tatjana Zoldnere) (Estonia, Latvia, Lithuania); I Pikarski Literary Agency (Gabi Hertzmann) (Israel); Prava i prevodi (Nada Popovic) (Montenegro, Serbia); Agencia RIFF (Joao Paulo Riff) (Brazil); Marianne Schoenbach Literary Agency (Netherlands); Synopsis Literary Agency (Olga Zasetskaya) (Russia); Eric Yang Agency (Sue Yang) (Korea)
Orders to: Perseus Distribution, Attn: Customer Service, 210 American Dr, Jackson, TN 38301 (US, CN, Asia (except Japan), Australia & Latin America) *Toll Free Tel:* 800-343-4499 *Toll Free Fax:* 800-351-5073 *E-mail:* orderentry@perseusbooks.com; c/o John Wiley & Sons Ltd, European Distribution Centre, New Era Estate, Oldlands Way, Bognor Regis, West Sussex P022 9NQ, United Kingdom (UK, Africa, Europe, India, Middle East & Pakistan) *Tel:* (01243) 843291 *Fax:* (01243) 843302 *E-mail:* customer@wiley.com
Membership(s): AAP; American Association of University Presses; BISG

§Printing Industries of America
301 Brush Creek Rd, Warrendale, PA 15086-7529
Tel: 412-741-6860 *Toll Free Tel:* 800-910-4283 *Fax:* 412-741-2311
E-mail: info@printing.org
Web Site: www.printing.org
Key Personnel
Digital Content Mgr: Sam Shea *E-mail:* sshea@printing.org
Founded: 1924
Textbooks & reference books on graphic communications techniques & technology.
ISBN Prefix(es): 978-0-88362
Number of titles published annually: 3 Print; 2 E-Book

Total Titles: 200 Print; 10 E-Book
Branch Office(s)
1001 "G" St NW, Suite 800, Washington, DC 20001 *Tel:* 202-627-6924

Printing Industries Press, see Printing Industries of America

Privacy Journal
PO Box 28577, Providence, RI 02908
Tel: 401-274-7861
E-mail: orders@privacyjournal.net
Web Site: www.privacyjournal.net
Key Personnel
Publr: Robert Ellis Smith
Founded: 1974
Also publishes a monthly newsletter.
ISBN Prefix(es): 978-0-930072
Number of titles published annually: 1 Print; 1 CD-ROM; 1 E-Book
Total Titles: 12 Print; 1 CD-ROM; 5 E-Book
Membership(s): The Association of Publishers for Special Sales; The Authors Guild; Independent Book Publishers Association; Independent Publishers of New England

PRO-ED Inc
8700 Shoal Creek Blvd, Austin, TX 78757-6897
SAN: 222-1349
Tel: 512-451-3246 *Toll Free Tel:* 800-897-3202 *Fax:* 512-451-8542 *Toll Free Fax:* 800-397-7633
E-mail: general@proedinc.com; info@proedinc.com
Web Site: www.proedinc.com
Key Personnel
COO & Gen Coun: Robert Lum *Tel:* 512-451-3246 ext 664 *E-mail:* blum@prodinc.com
Exec Ed: Kathy Synatschk *E-mail:* ksynatschk@proedinc.com
Founded: 1977
College & professional reference books, tests, student materials, journals in education & psychology.
ISBN Prefix(es): 978-0-936104; 978-0-89079; 978-0-88744; 978-1-933014; 978-1-944480; 978-1-4164
Number of titles published annually: 50 Print
Total Titles: 1,500 Print

Pro Lingua Associates Inc
74 Cotton Mill Hill, Suite A-315, Brattleboro, VT 05301
SAN: 216-0579
Tel: 802-257-7779 *Toll Free Tel:* 800-366-4775 *Fax:* 802-257-5117
E-mail: info@prolinguaassociates.com
Web Site: www.prolinguaassociates.com
Key Personnel
Pres & Publr: Arthur A Burrows *E-mail:* andy@prolinguaassociates.com
VP & Ed: Raymond C Clark
Treas & Lib Sales Dir: Elise C Burrows
Secy: Mike Jerald
Founded: 1980
Teacher resource handbooks, language teacher training handbooks, English language & foreign language texts.
ISBN Prefix(es): 978-0-86647
Number of titles published annually: 7 Print
Total Titles: 120 Print; 44 Audio
Foreign Rep(s): English Central (Canada); English Language Bookshop (England); Foreign Language Bookshop (Australia); Foreign Language Ltd (Korea); Independent Publishers International (Japan); Nellie's Group Ltd (Japan)
Membership(s): The Children's Book Council; TESOL International Association

§Productivity Press
Imprint of CRC Press
711 Third Ave, 8th fl, New York, NY 10017
Tel: 212-216-7800 *Toll Free Tel:* 800-634-7064 (orders); 800-797-3803
E-mail: orders@taylorandfrancis.com
Web Site: www.productivitypress.com
Key Personnel
Sr Acqs Ed: Kristine Mednansky *Tel:* 630-482-9886 *E-mail:* kristine.mednansky@productivitypress.com; Michael Sinocchi *Tel:* 212-216-7867 *E-mail:* michael.sinocchi@taylorandfrancis.com
Sr Channel Mktg Mgr: Christopher Manion *E-mail:* chris.manion@taylorandfrancis.com
Assoc Ed: Lara Zoble *Tel:* 212-216-7863 *E-mail:* lara.zoble@productivitypress.com
Founded: 1983
Books & AV programs. Publishes & distributes materials on productivity, quality improvement, product development, corporate management, profit management & employee involvement for business & industry. Many products are direct source materials from Japan that have been translated into English for the first time.
ISBN Prefix(es): 978-0-915299; 978-1-56327; 978-0-527
Number of titles published annually: 12 Print
Total Titles: 200 Print; 4 CD-ROM
Imprints: Healthcare Performance Press; Productivity Press Spanish Imprint
Foreign Rep(s): Asia Pacific Research Center (Singapore); Books Aplenty (South Africa); Learning & Productivity (Australia); OCAPT Inc (Canada); Prism Books Private Ltd (India); Productivity Editorial Consultores SPD CV (Mexico)

Professional Communications Inc
1223 W Main, Suite 1427, Caddo, OK 74702-1427
Tel: 580-745-9838 *Toll Free Tel:* 800-337-9838 *Fax:* 580-745-9837
E-mail: info@pcibooks.com
Web Site: www.pcibooks.com
Key Personnel
Pres & Publr: J Malcolm Beasley *Tel:* 631-661-2852 *Fax:* 631-661-2167 *E-mail:* jmbpci@earthlink.net
VP: Phyllis Jones Freeny
Founded: 1992
Medicine.
ISBN Prefix(es): 978-1-884735; 978-0-9632400; 978-0-932610; 978-1-943236
Number of titles published annually: 5 Print
Total Titles: 55 Print
Branch Office(s)
Bulk Sales only, 400 Center Bay Dr, West Islip, NY 11795

§The Professional Education Group LLC (PEG)
700 Twelve Oaks Center Dr, Suite 716, Wayzata, MN 55391
Tel: 952-933-9990 *Toll Free Tel:* 800-229-2531 *Fax:* 952-933-7784
E-mail: orders@proedgroup.com
Web Site: www.proedgroup.com
Key Personnel
Pres: Henry Lake *E-mail:* henry@proedgroup.com
Founded: 1981
Continuing legal education materials; audio & video programs & books.
ISBN Prefix(es): 978-0-943380; 978-1-932831
Number of titles published annually: 6 Print; 1 CD-ROM; 6 Online; 5 Audio
Total Titles: 43 Print; 40 CD-ROM; 40 Online; 43 Audio
Distributed by American Bar Association; American Law Institute
Distributor for American Bar Association; American Law Institute; ASPEN
Membership(s): Association for Continuing Legal Education

§Professional Publications Inc (PPI)
1250 Fifth Ave, Belmont, CA 94002
SAN: 264-6315
Tel: 650-593-9119 *Fax:* 650-592-4519
E-mail: acquisitions@ppi2pass.com
Web Site: ppi2pass.com; feprep.com
Key Personnel
Pres: Michael Lindeburg
Edit Dir: Heather Subba *Tel:* 650-593-9119 ext 139 *E-mail:* hsubba@ppi2pass.com
Dir, Mktg: Thomas Hayward *Tel:* 650-593-9119 ext 1010 *E-mail:* thayward@ppi2pass.com
Dir, Prod Devt: Sarah Hubbard *Tel:* 650-593-9119 ext 128 *E-mail:* shubbard@ppi2pass.com
Founded: 1981
Provider of exam review books, online products & live & online classes in the fields of engineering, land surveying, LEED, architecture, interior design & landscape architecture. Specialty engineering areas include civil, structural, seismic, mechanical, electrical, environmental, chemical, nuclear, geotechnical & industrial engineering fields.
ISBN Prefix(es): 978-0-932276; 978-0-912045; 978-1-888577; 978-1-59126
Number of titles published annually: 10 Print; 1 CD-ROM; 2 Online; 5 E-Book
Total Titles: 120 Print; 20 Online; 20 E-Book
Distributor for American Association of State Highway & Transportation Officials; American Wood Council (American Forest & Paper Association) (National Design Specification for Wood Construction (NDS) & others); International Code Council; McGraw-Hill Professional (green building, design & construction titles, LEED titles); National Council of Examiners for Engineering & Surveying; SmartPros; Transportation Research Board Code; US Green Building Council (LEED reference guides)
Membership(s): American Society of Civil Engineers; American Society of Engineering Educators; American Society of Mechanical Engineers; National Society of Professional Engineers; US Green Building Council

Professional Resource Press
Imprint of Professional Resource Exchange Inc
1958 Barber Rd, Sarasota, FL 34240
SAN: 240-1223
Mailing Address: PO Box 3197, Sarasota, FL 34230-3197
Tel: 941-343-9601 *Toll Free Tel:* 800-443-3364 (orders & cust serv) *Fax:* 941-343-9201 *Toll Free Fax:* 866-804-4843 (orders only)
E-mail: cs.prpress@gmail.com
Web Site: www.prpress.com
Key Personnel
Pres: Judith W Ritt *E-mail:* jwrprp@gmail.com
Mktg & Lib Sales Dir: J M Warinner *E-mail:* judew61@gmail.com
Mng Ed: Laurie Girsch
Cust Serv: Jeff Klosterman *E-mail:* jdkprp@gmail.com
Founded: 1980
Books on clinical & forensic psychology, CD-ROMs, DVDs, continuing education programs & texts for mental health & health care professionals. Includes medicine & nursing.
ISBN Prefix(es): 978-0-943158; 978-1-56887
Number of titles published annually: 15 Print; 5 CD-ROM; 4 E-Book; 3 Audio
Total Titles: 230 Print; 10 CD-ROM; 4 E-Book; 17 Audio
Membership(s): The Association of Publishers for Special Sales

Progressive Press
3716 37 St, San Diego, CA 92105-2409
SAN: 222-5395
Tel: 619-892-7781 *Fax:* 619-892-7781
E-mail: info@progressivepress.com
Web Site: www.progressivepress.com

Key Personnel
Owner: John-Paul Leonard
Founded: 1973
Small publisher of political trade paperbacks. Also provides distribution for one Canadian publisher & several self-published authors. Frontlist: politics, backlist: New Age.
ISBN Prefix(es): 978-0-930852; 978-1-61577
Number of titles published annually: 6 Print
Total Titles: 60 Print
Imprints: Arthritis Research; Banned Books; Collections Livrier; Leaves of Healing; Prensa Pensar; Progressive Press; Tree of Life Books
Distributor for Global Research
Foreign Rep(s): Gazelle Book Services Ltd (UK); New Horizons (South Africa); Woodslane (Australia)
Foreign Rights: Beniamino Soressi (Italy); Thinkers Library (Malaysia); Gerhard Wisnewski (Germany)
Membership(s): The Imaging Alliance; Independent Book Publishers Association

Prometheus Books
59 John Glenn Dr, Amherst, NY 14228-2119
SAN: 202-0289
Tel: 716-691-0133 *Fax:* 716-691-0137
E-mail: marketing@prometheusbooks.com; editorial@prometheusbooks.com; rights@prometheusmail.com
Web Site: www.prometheusbooks.com
Key Personnel
Publr: Jonathan Kurtz *E-mail:* jkurtz@prometheusbooks.com
VP, Busn & Admin Dir: Lynette Nisbet *E-mail:* lnisbet@prometheusbooks.com
VP, Mktg: Jill Maxick *Tel:* 716-691-0133 ext 219 *E-mail:* jmaxick@prometheusbooks.com
Dir, Rts: Gretchen Kurtz
Edit Dir, Pyr: Rene Sears *E-mail:* rsears@prometheusbooks.com
Edit Dir, Seventh Street Books: Dan Mayer *E-mail:* dmayer@prometheusbooks.com
Ed-in-Chief: Steven L Mitchell *E-mail:* smitchell@prometheusbooks.com
Mgr, Print-on-Demand Div: Patrick Martin *E-mail:* pmartin@prometheusbooks.com
Founded: 1969
Provocative, progressive & independent nonfiction press publishing under 4 imprints, including 2 genre fiction imprints.
ISBN Prefix(es): 978-0-87975; 978-1-57392; 978-1-59102; 978-1-61614
Number of titles published annually: 85 Print; 85 E-Book
Total Titles: 2,800 Print; 1,800 E-Book
Imprints: Humanity Books (scholarly/academic); Pyr (science fiction/fantasy); Seventh Street Books (crime fiction, mystery, thriller)
Distributed by Penguin Random House
Foreign Rep(s): Penguin Random House Publisher Services (PRHPS) (worldwide)

§ProQuest LLC
Subsidiary of Cambridge Information Group Inc
789 E Eisenhower Pkwy, Ann Arbor, MI 48108
Mailing Address: PO Box 1346, Ann Arbor, MI 48106-1346
Tel: 734-761-4700 *Toll Free Tel:* 800-521-0600
Web Site: www.proquest.com
Key Personnel
CEO: Matti Shem Tov
SVP & CFO: Robert VanHees
CIO: Rich Belanger
SVP & Gen Mgr, ProQuest Books: Kevin Sayar
SVP & Gen Mgr, Workflow Solutions: John "JG" Chirapurath
SVP, Global HR: Kellie Teal-Guess
SVP, Global Sales, Mktg & Cust Experience: James Holmes
SVP, Mktg: Lynda James-Gilboe *E-mail:* lynda.james-gilboe@proquest.com
Founded: 1872
Publisher, distributor & aggregator of value-added information to libraries, government, universities & schools in over 160 countries. Access to information in periodicals, newspapers, doctoral dissertations & out of print books (retrospective scholarly works). Produce & publish Dissertation Abstracts International.
ISBN Prefix(es): 978-0-912380; 978-0-88692; 978-0-89093; 978-1-55655; 978-0-8357; 978-0-608; 978-0-7837; 978-0-591; 978-0-9702937; 978-0-599; 978-1-931694; 978-1-59399; 978-0-496; 978-0-542; 978-1-4247; 978-0-9778091; 978-1-4345; 978-0-549; 978-1-60205; 978-1-109; 978-1-124; 978-1-267; 978-1-303; 978-1-321; 978-1-339
Number of titles published annually: 56 Print
Total Titles: 56 Print
Subsidiaries: R R Bowker LLC
Branch Office(s)
699 James L Hart Pkwy, Ypsilanti, MI 48197 *Tel:* 734-879-5300 *Fax:* 734-879-5301
161 E Evelyn Ave, Mountain View, CA 94041 *Tel:* 650-475-8700 *Fax:* 650-475-8881
16855 W Bernardo Dr, Suite 100, San Diego, CA 92127 *Tel:* 858-674-6103 *Fax:* 858-674-6384
750 Park of Commerce Blvd, Suite 200, Boca Raton, FL 33487
620 S Third St, Suite 400, Louisville, KY 40202 *Tel:* 502-583-4111
One N Charles St, Suite 2305, Baltimore, MD 21201 *Tel:* 410-563-2378
7500 Old Georgetown Rd, Suite 1400, Bethesda, MD 20814
1155 W Fourth St, Suite 212, Reno, NV 89503 *Tel:* 775-327-4105
630 Central Ave, New Providence, NJ 07974 *Tel:* 908-286-1090 *Toll Free Tel:* 888-269-5371 *Fax:* 908-219-0182
888 Seventh Ave, 17th fl, New York, NY 10019 *Tel:* 212-331-7700
Stratford Hall, Suite 200, 1009 Slater Rd, Durham, NC 27703 *Tel:* 919-804-6493; 919-804-6193 *Fax:* 919-804-6410
5252 N Edgewood Dr, Suite 125, Provo, UT 84604 *Tel:* 801-765-1737
501 N 34 St, Suite 300, Seattle, WA 98103-8645 *Tel:* 206-545-9056
Foreign Office(s): The Quorum, Barnwell Rd, Cambridge CB5 8SW, United Kingdom *Tel:* (01223) 215 512 *Fax:* (01223) 215 513
607 St Kilda Rd, 1st fl, Melbourne, Victoria 3004, Australia *Tel:* (03) 8517 8388 *Fax:* (03) 8517 8322
Av das Americas 700, bl1 salas 114 e 115, Barra da Tijuca, 22640-100 Rio de Janeiro-RJ, Brazil *Tel:* (021) 2132 7230
Unit 804, Tower E1, Beijing Oriental Plaza, No 1 E Chang An Ave, Dong Cheng District, Beijing 100738, China *Tel:* (010) 8460 8861 *Fax:* (010) 8518 8848
Oranienburger Str 32, 10117 Berlin, Germany *Tel:* (030) 240 88 23-0 *Fax:* (030) 240 88 23 29
16A W Sq, 318 Hennessy Rd, Wanchai, Hong Kong *Tel:* 2836 5636 *Fax:* 2834 7133
315, AKD Tower, Near HUDA Off, Sector 14, Gurgaon 122 001, India *Tel:* (0124) 4100615
Mitsubishi Juko Yokohama Bldg, 3-3-1, Minatomiral, Nishi-ku, Yokohama-shi, Kanagawa 220-8401, Japan *Tel:* (045) 342 4780 *Fax:* (045) 342 4784
B909, Phileo Damansara 1, No 9 Jl 16/11, 46350 Pelaling Jaya, Selangor, Malaysia *Tel:* (03) 7954 2880 *Fax:* (03) 7958 3446
Modemstr 2, 1033 RW Amsterdam, Netherlands *Tel:* (020) 6353190 *Fax:* (020) 6337765
Daeyoung Bldg, 2nd fl, Seocho-gu, Seoul 137-070, South Korea *Tel:* (02) 733-5119 *Fax:* (02) 734-5120
Velazquez 100-5 D, 28006 Madrid, Spain *Tel:* 91 575 5597 *Fax:* 91 575 9885
Al-Thurayya II, Off 1304, PO Box 502568, Dubai, United Arab Emirates *Tel:* (04) 4331810 *Fax:* (04) 369 7646
The Quorum, Barnwell Rd, Cambridge CB5 8SW, United Kingdom *Tel:* (01223) 215 512 *Fax:* (01223) 215 513
3 Dorset Rise, 5th fl, London EC4Y 8EN, United Kingdom *Tel:* (020) 7832 1700 *Fax:* (020) 7832 1710
See separate listing for:
R R Bowker LLC

§Prospect Park Books
2359 Lincoln Ave, Altadena, CA 91001
Tel: 626-793-9796
E-mail: info@prospectparkbooks.com
Web Site: www.prospectparkbooks.com
Key Personnel
Publr & Founding Partner: Colleen Dunn Bates
Founded: 2006
Trade publisher.
ISBN Prefix(es): 978-0-9753939; 978-0-9844102; 978-0-9834594; 978-1-938849
Number of titles published annually: 10 Print; 8 E-Book
Total Titles: 50 Print; 40 E-Book
Imprints: Raymond Press
Foreign Rights: Kaplan/DeFiore Rights (worldwide)
Warehouse: Perseus Distribution, 193 Edwards Dr, Jackson, TN 38301 *Toll Free Tel:* 800-343-4499
Distribution Center: Consortium Book Sales & Distribution, The Keg House, 34 13 Ave NE, Suite 101, Minneapolis, MN 55413-1007 *Web Site:* www.cbsd.com SAN: 200-6049
Membership(s): AAP; Community of Literary Magazines & Presses; International Association of Culinary Professionals; Publishers Association of the West; Southern California Independent Booksellers Association

ProStar Publications Inc
3 Church Circle, Suite 109, Annapolis, MD 21401
SAN: 210-525X
Mailing Address: 514 W Florence Ave, Englewood, CA 90301
Toll Free Tel: 800-481-6277 *Toll Free Fax:* 800-487-6277
E-mail: editor@prostarpublications.com
Web Site: www.prostarpublications.com
Key Personnel
Pres & Publr: Peter L Griffes *E-mail:* peter@prostarpublications.com
Founded: 1965
Books about boating: regional guides, planning, navigation data, nautical charts, marine fauna, how-to, travel, technical, general fiction & music.
ISBN Prefix(es): 978-0-930030; 978-1-57785; 978-1-942388
Number of titles published annually: 145 Print
Total Titles: 440 Print; 30 CD-ROM
Imprints: Atlantic Boating Almanac; Lighthouse Press; Pacific Boating Almanac; US Coast Pilot

§The PRS Group Inc
5800 Heritage Landing Dr, Suite E, East Syracuse, NY 13057-9358
Tel: 315-431-0511 *Fax:* 315-431-0200
E-mail: custserv@prsgroup.com
Web Site: www.prsgroup.com
Key Personnel
Pres & CEO: Christopher McKee
Circ Mgr: Patti Davis
Asst to Pres: Dianna Spinner *E-mail:* dspinner@prsgroup.com
Founded: 1979
Over 100 reports, newsletters, journals & volumes per year for international business. No returns without prior approval.
ISBN Prefix(es): 978-1-933539; 978-1-931077; 978-1-941119; 978-1-936241
Number of titles published annually: 3 Print

Total Titles: 20 Print; 100 CD-ROM; 100 Online; 100 E-Book
Imprints: International Country Risk Guide; Political Risk Services

Prufrock Press
PO Box 8813, Waco, TX 76714-8813
SAN: 851-9188
Tel: 254-756-3337 *Toll Free Tel:* 800-998-2208 *Fax:* 254-756-3339 *Toll Free Fax:* 800-240-0333
E-mail: info@prufrock.com
Web Site: www.prufrock.com
Key Personnel
Publr & Mktg Dir: Joel McIntosh *E-mail:* jmcintosh@prufrock.com
Sr Ed: Lacy Compton *E-mail:* lcompton@prufrock.com
Asst Ed & Perms Coord: Katy McDowall *E-mail:* kmcdowall@prufrock.com
Founded: 1977
Publish supplementary text books & teacher guides for grades K-12, including gifted educational materials.
ISBN Prefix(es): 978-1-883055; 978-1-882664; 978-0-931724; 978-1-59363; 978-1-61821
Number of titles published annually: 20 Print
Total Titles: 566 Print
Editorial Office(s): 5926 Balcones Dr, Suite 220, Austin, TX 78731 *Tel:* 512-300-2220 *Fax:* 512-300-2221
Membership(s): Independent Book Publishers Association

PSMJ Resources Inc
10 Midland Ave, Newton, MA 02458
Tel: 617-965-0055 *Toll Free Tel:* 800-537-7765 *Fax:* 617-965-5152
E-mail: info@psmj.com
Web Site: www.psmj.com
Founded: 1980
Books, survey reports & digital toolbox programs for architects, engineers, interior designers, urban designers, planners, landscape architects on business & financial management; marketing; time & personnel management; legal topics; project management; human resources; newsletters; consulting & educational seminars.
ISBN Prefix(es): 978-1-55538
Number of titles published annually: 5 Print; 12 E-Book
Total Titles: 50 Print; 15 E-Book
Foreign Office(s): PO Box 773, Artarmon, NSW 2064, Australia *Tel:* (02) 9411 4819 *Fax:* (02) 9419 6044 *E-mail:* egoullet@psmj.com
242 Dorcas St, South Melbourne, Victoria 3205, Australia *Tel:* (03) 9686-3846 *Fax:* (03) 9682-5169 *E-mail:* cnelson@psmj.com

§Psychological Assessment Resources Inc (PAR)
16204 N Florida Ave, Lutz, FL 33549
Tel: 813-968-3003; 813-449-4065 *Toll Free Tel:* 800-331-8378 *Fax:* 813-968-2598; 813-961-2196 *Toll Free Fax:* 800-727-9329
E-mail: custsup@parinc.com
Web Site: www4.parinc.com
Key Personnel
Chmn & CEO: R Bob Smith, III *E-mail:* bsmith@parinc.com
COO & Pres: Kay Cunningham *E-mail:* kcunningham@parinc.com
VP, Mktg & Sales: Eric Jesson *E-mail:* ejesson@parinc.com
VP, R&D: Travis White *E-mail:* twhite@parinc.com
Mgr, Cust Serv: Daniel McFadden *E-mail:* dmcfadden@parinc.com
Exec Asst to CEO: Vicki King
Founded: 1978
Career, psychological, neuropsychology, educational & clinical assessments products; software.
ISBN Prefix(es): 978-0-911907
Number of titles published annually: 10 Print; 2 CD-ROM; 1 Online
Total Titles: 150 Print; 20 CD-ROM; 3 Online; 5 Audio
Distributed by ACER; Pro-Ed; Western Psychological Service
Distributor for American Guidance Service; Pro-Ed; Rorschach Workshops
Foreign Rep(s): ACER (Australia); Tea Ediciones (Spain); Testzentrale (Germany)
Returns: 16130 N Florida Ave, Lutz, FL 33549 *E-mail:* gpresson@parinc.com
Warehouse: 16130 N Florida Ave, Lutz, FL 33549 *E-mail:* gpresson@parinc.com

Public Citizen
1600 20 St NW, Washington, DC 20009
Tel: 202-588-1000 *Fax:* 202-588-7798
E-mail: public_citizen@citizen.org
Web Site: www.citizen.org
Key Personnel
CFO: Joe Stoshak
Pres: Robert Weissman
Founded: 1971
Books & reports; consumer advocacy organization.
ISBN Prefix(es): 978-0-937188; 978-1-58231
Number of titles published annually: 47 Print
Total Titles: 48 Print
Divisions: Congress Watch; Democracy Is For People; Energy Program; Global Trade Watch; Health Research Group; Litigation Group
Branch Office(s)
215 Pennsylvania Ave SE, Washington, DC 20003 *Tel:* 202-546-4996
1303 San Antonio St, Austin, TX 78701 *Tel:* 512-477-1155
Distributed by Addison Wesley; Simon & Schuster Pocket Books
Foreign Rights: Random House-Pantheon

§Publication Consultants
8370 Eleusis Dr, Anchorage, AK 99502
Tel: 907-349-2424 *Fax:* 907-349-2426
E-mail: books@publicationconsultants.com
Web Site: www.publicationconsultants.com
Key Personnel
Owner & Publr: Evan Swensen *E-mail:* evan@publicationconsultants.com
Founded: 1978
This publisher has indicated that 40% of their product line is author subsidized.
ISBN Prefix(es): 978-0-9644809; 978-1-888125; 978-1-59433
Number of titles published annually: 25 Print; 30 E-Book
Total Titles: 280 Print; 280 E-Book
Membership(s): Alaska Writers Guild; Better Business Bureau

Publications International Ltd (PIL)
7373 N Cicero Ave, Lincolnwood, IL 60712
Tel: 847-676-3470 *Fax:* 847-676-3671
E-mail: customer_service@pubint.com
Web Site: pilbooks.com
Key Personnel
CEO: Louis Weber
VP, Acqs & Proj Mgmt: Jenny Barney
Dir, Natl Accts: Scott Cox
Founded: 1967
ISBN Prefix(es): 978-0-88176; 978-1-56173; 978-1-68022
Number of titles published annually: 400 Print

§Puffin Books
Imprint of Penguin Group USA, A Penguin Random House Company
345 Hudson St, New York, NY 10014
Tel: 212-366-2000
Web Site: www.penguin.com/publishers/puffin
Key Personnel
Pres & Publr: Eileen Bishop Kreit
Assoc Publr & Mng Ed: Gerard Mancini
VP & Exec Art Dir, Penguin Young Readers Design Group: Deborah Kaplan
ISBN Prefix(es): 978-0-14
Number of titles published annually: 150 Print
Membership(s): The Children's Book Council

Purdue University Press
Stewart Ctr 190, 504 W State St, West Lafayette, IN 47907-2058
SAN: 203-4026
Tel: 765-494-2038 *Fax:* 765-496-2442
E-mail: pupress@purdue.edu
Web Site: www.thepress.purdue.edu
Key Personnel
Ed: Katherine Purple
Prodn Mgr: Bryan Shaffer
Founded: 1960
Publisher of scholarly titles with emphasis on business, veterinary medicine, health issues & the humanities.
ISBN Prefix(es): 978-0-911198; 978-1-55753
Number of titles published annually: 25 Print; 25 E-Book
Total Titles: 350 Print; 50 E-Book
Foreign Rep(s): The Eurospan Group (Continental Europe, Israel, Middle East, UK)
Orders to: Bookmasters, 30 Amberwood Pkwy, Ashland, OH 44805 *Toll Free Tel:* 800-247-6553 *Fax:* 419-281-6883 *Web Site:* www.bookmasters.com/purduepress
Returns: Bookmasters, 30 Amberwood Pkwy, Ashland, OH 44805 *Toll Free Tel:* 800-247-6553 *Fax:* 419-281-6883 *Web Site:* www.bookmasters.com/purduepress
Warehouse: Bookmasters, 30 Amberwood Pkwy, Ashland, OH 44805 *Toll Free Tel:* 800-247-6553 *Fax:* 419-281-6883 *Web Site:* www.bookmasters.com/purduepress
Distribution Center: Bookmasters, 30 Amberwood Pkwy, Ashland, OH 44805 *Toll Free Tel:* 800-247-6553 *Fax:* 419-281-6883 *Web Site:* www.bookmasters.com/purduepress
Membership(s): American Association of University Presses

Purple House Press
Imprint of Purple House Inc
8100 US Hwy 62 E, Cynthiana, KY 41031
Mailing Address: PO Box 787, Cynthiana, KY 41031
Tel: 859-235-9970
Web Site: www.purplehousepress.com
Key Personnel
Publr: Jill Morgan *E-mail:* jill@purplehousepress.com
Dir, Cust Fulfillment, Managed Info Servs: Ray Sanders *E-mail:* ray@purplehousepress.com
Prepress & Clerical: Hayley Morgan-Sanders *E-mail:* hayley@purplehousepress.com
Founded: 2000
Reissue of children's classics from the 1920s-1990s.
ISBN Prefix(es): 978-1-930900
Number of titles published annually: 8 Print; 3 E-Book
Total Titles: 70 Print; 20 E-Book

Purple Mountain Press Ltd
1060 Main St, Fleischmanns, NY 12430
Mailing Address: PO Box 309, Fleischmanns, NY 12430-0309 SAN: 222-3716
Tel: 845-254-4062 *Toll Free Tel:* 800-325-2665 (orders) *Fax:* 845-254-4476
E-mail: purple@catskill.net
Web Site: www.catskill.net/purple
Key Personnel
Pres & Publr: Wray Rominger

Founded: 1973
Publish adult nonfiction books about colonial history & New York State; history, natural history, folklore, the arts, outdoor recreation, a few regional mysteries, also maritime books.
ISBN Prefix(es): 978-0-935796; 978-0-916346; 978-1-930098
Number of titles published annually: 6 Print
Total Titles: 150 Print
Divisions: Harbor Hill Books
Distributor for Carmania Press London (North America only)

Pushcart Press
PO Box 380, Wainscott, NY 11975-0380
SAN: 202-9871
Tel: 631-324-9300
Key Personnel
Pres: Bill Henderson
Founded: 1972
Trade books, literary anthologies.
ISBN Prefix(es): 978-0-916366; 978-1-888889
Number of titles published annually: 6 Print
Total Titles: 65 Print
Distributed by W W Norton & Company Inc
Distribution Center: 500 Fifth Ave, New York, NY 10110

GP Putnam's Sons (Children's)
Member of Penguin Young Readers Group
345 Hudson St, New York, NY 10014
SAN: 282-5074
Tel: 212-366-2000 *Fax:* 212-414-3393
Web Site: www.penguin.com/publishers/gpputnamssonsbooksforyoungread
Key Personnel
Pres & Publr, Nancy Paulsen Books: Nancy Paulsen
Pres & Publr, Putnam Books for Young Readers: Jennifer Besser
VP & Art Dir: Cecilia Yung
Assoc Publr & Exec Mng Ed: David Briggs
Assoc Edit Dir: Susan Kochan
Exec Ed: Arianne Lewin
Sr Ed: Stacey Barney
Ed, Nancy Paulsen Books: Sara LaFleur
Assoc Ed: Katherine Perkins
Asst Ed: Kate Meltzer
Edit Asst: Amalia Frick
Founded: 1838
ISBN Prefix(es): 978-0-399; 978-0-698
Number of titles published annually: 51 Print
Total Titles: 386 Print
Membership(s): The Children's Book Council

GP Putnam's Sons (Hardcover)
Imprint of Penguin Group USA, A Penguin Random House Company
375 Hudson St, New York, NY 10014
Tel: 212-366-2000 *Fax:* 212-366-2643
E-mail: online@penguinputnam.com
Web Site: www.penguin.com/publishers/gpputnamssons
Key Personnel
Pres: Ivan Held
EVP, Assoc Publr & Ed-in-Chief: Neil S Nyren
SVP & Publr: Christine Ball
SVP & Dir, Publg Mgmt: Catharine Lynch
VP & Publr, Marian Wood Books: Marian Wood
VP & Assoc Publr, Paperbacks: Benjamin Lee
VP & Dir, Publicity: Alexis Welby
VP & Edit Dir: Sally Kim
VP & Prodn Dir: William Peabody
VP & Exec Ed: Christine Pepe; Mark Tavani
Art Dir: Claire Vaccaro
Dir, Copy Editing: Linda Rosenberg
Mktg Dir, Putnam: Ashley Pattison McClay
Mktg Dir, Putnam/Dutton: Carrie Swetonic
Exec Ed: Kerri Kolen
Sr Ed: Tara Singh Carlson; Sara Minnich
Asst Ed: Danielle Springer
Mktg Mgr, Putnam/Dutton: Katie Parry
Publicity Mgr: Ashley Hewlett
Asst Mktg Mgr, Putnam: Anna Romig
Founded: 1838
Fiction & general nonfiction.
ISBN Prefix(es): 978-0-399
Number of titles published annually: 65 Print
Total Titles: 208 Print
Imprints: Putnam; Marian Wood Books
Advertising Agency: Mesa Group

Pyncheon House
6 University Dr, Suite 105, Amherst, MA 01002
SAN: 297-6269
Key Personnel
Ed-in-Chief: David R Rhodes
Founded: 1991
Fine editions & trade books; contemporary poetry, short fiction, novels & essays; member of Library of Congress CIP Program.
ISBN Prefix(es): 978-1-881119
Number of titles published annually: 4 Print
Total Titles: 16 Print

Quail Ridge Press
101 Brooks Dr, Brandon, MS 39042
Mailing Address: PO Box 123, Brandon, MS 39043 SAN: 214-2201
Tel: 601-825-2063 *Toll Free Tel:* 800-343-1583 *Fax:* 601-825-3091 *Toll Free Fax:* 800-864-1082
E-mail: info@quailridge.com
Web Site: quailridge.com
Key Personnel
COO: Terresa Ray *E-mail:* tray@quailridge.com
Publr: Barney McKee *E-mail:* bmckee@quailridge.com
Sales Dir: Lacy Ward *E-mail:* lward@quailridge.com
Ed-in-Chief: Gwen McKee *E-mail:* gmckee@quailridge.com
Founded: 1978
Cookbooks, general interest, regional, health.
ISBN Prefix(es): 978-0-937552; 978-1-893062; 978-1-938879; 978-1-934193
Number of titles published annually: 4 Print
Total Titles: 150 Print
Imprints: QRP Books

§Quality Medical Publishing Inc
2248 Welsch Industrial Ct, St Louis, MO 63146-4222
Tel: 314-878-7808 *Toll Free Tel:* 800-348-7808 *Fax:* 314-878-9937
E-mail: qmp@qmp.com; customerservice@qmp.com
Web Site: www.qmp.com
Key Personnel
Pres & CEO: Andrew Berger *E-mail:* aberger@qmp.com
Founded: 1986
Medical books (especially surgery); plastic, neurological, spine & orthopaedics.
ISBN Prefix(es): 978-0-942219; 978-1-57626
Number of titles published annually: 16 Print
Total Titles: 145 Print; 2 CD-ROM
Imprints: QMP

Quarto Publishing Group USA Inc
Subsidiary of Quarto Group Inc (London, UK)
400 First Ave N, Suite 400, Minneapolis, MN 55401
SAN: 289-7148
Tel: 612-344-8100 *Toll Free Tel:* 800-328-0590 (sales); 800-458-0454 *Fax:* 612-344-8691
E-mail: sales@quartous.com
Web Site: www.quartoknows.com
Key Personnel
CEO & Exec Dir: Marcus Leaver
COO: Ken Fund
VP & Group Publr: Bryan Trandem
VP & Dir, Intl Sales: Wendy Friedman
VP & Sales Dir: Tara Catogge *E-mail:* tara.catogge@quartous.com
Adult Mktg Dir: Kristine Anderson
Children's Mktg Dir: Diane Naughton
Dir, Dist Servs & Specialty Mktg: John Groton *E-mail:* john.groton@quartous.com
Dir, New Busn Devt: Tim Lampley *E-mail:* tim.lampley@quartous.com
Dir, Opers: Joe Cella *E-mail:* joe.cella@quartous.com
Dir, Seagrass Press: Josalyn Moran
Assoc Dir, Children's Book Mktg, Publicity & Soc Media: Michelle Bayuk
Opers Mgr: Brad Runyan *E-mail:* brad.runyan@quartous.com
Founded: 2004
Represents a dynamic group of imprints dedicated to providing quality & excellence to its readers. Each imprint embodies the breadth & scope of its specialty topics.
ISBN Prefix(es): 978-0-86573; 978-0-7603; 978-1-59253; 978-0-929261; 978-1-56010; 978-1-59233; 978-1-58923; 978-1-59186; 978-1-61673; 978-1-61058; 978-1-61059; 978-1-61060; 978-1-62788; 978-0-89738; 978-0-912612; 978-1-63159; 978-0-9640392; 978-1-888608; 978-1-930604; 978-1-936309; 978-1-60058; 978-1-937994; 978-1-939581; 978-1-63106; 978-1-63322; 978-1-942875
Number of titles published annually: 300 Print
Total Titles: 4,000 Print
Imprints: Cool Springs Press; Creative Publishing International; Fair Winds Press; Walter Foster Jr; Walter Foster Publishing; Harvard Common Press; Moondance Press; Motorbooks; Quarry Books; QDS; Race Point Publishing; Rock Point Gift & Stationery; Rockport Publishers; Seagrass Press; Voyageur Press; Wellfleet Press; Zenith Press
Divisions: Book Sales Inc; Quayside Distribution Services
Distributed by Allen & Unwin (Australia & New Zealand)
See separate listing for:
Book Sales
Fair Winds Press
Walter Foster Publishing Inc
The Harvard Common Press

Quicksilver Productions
PO Box 340, Ashland, OR 97520-0012
Tel: 541-482-5343 *Toll Free Fax:* 888-974-6462
E-mail: celestialcalendars@email.com
Web Site: www.quicksilverproductions.com
Key Personnel
Prop: Jim Maynard
Asst: Rachell Grubbs
Founded: 1973
Publisher of calendars & cookbooks.
ISBN Prefix(es): 978-0-930356 (cookbooks); 978-1-935482 (astrological calendars)
Number of titles published annually: 4 Print
Total Titles: 8 Print

Quincannon Publishing Group
PO Box 8100, Glen Ridge, NJ 07028-8100
Tel: 973-380-9942
E-mail: editors@quincannongroup.com
Web Site: www.quincannongroup.com
Key Personnel
Ed-in-Chief: Alan Quincannon
Ed: Holly Benedict
Consulting Ed: Jeanne Wilcox
Lib Sales Dir & Admin Asst: Patricia Drury
Publicity: Loretta Bolger
Founded: 1990
Regional mystery novels made unique by involving some element of a region's history (i.e. the story's setting & time frame or the mystery's origin); custom tailored books for local & regional museums.
ISBN Prefix(es): 978-1-878452
Number of titles published annually: 3 Print

Total Titles: 18 Print; 17 Online
Imprints: Compass Point Mysteries; Jersey Yarns; Learning & Coloring Books; Rune-Tales; Tory Corner Editions
Foreign Rep(s): International Titles
Foreign Rights: International Titles (Loris Essary) (worldwide)

§Quintessence Publishing Co Inc
4350 Chandler Dr, Hanover Park, IL 60133
SAN: 215-9783
Tel: 630-736-3600 *Toll Free Tel:* 800-621-0387 *Fax:* 630-736-3633
E-mail: contact@quintbook.com; service@quintbook.com
Web Site: www.quintpub.com
Key Personnel
Pres: H W Haase
EVP: William Hartman *Tel:* 630-736-3600 ext 413 *E-mail:* whartman@quintbook.com
Founded: 1950
Professional & scholarly books, journals, medicine, dentistry, health & nutrition, medical history.
ISBN Prefix(es): 978-0-931386; 978-0-86715; 978-1-85097; 978-1-883695
Number of titles published annually: 20 Print; 2 CD-ROM
Total Titles: 410 Print; 80 CD-ROM; 250 Audio
Imprints: Quintessence Books; Quintessence of Dental Technology; Quintessence Pockets
Foreign Office(s): 2-4 Ifenpfad, 12107 Berlin, Germany *Tel:* (030) 761-805 *Fax:* (030) 761-80693 *E-mail:* info@quintessenz.de *Web Site:* www.quintessenz.de
Quint House Bldg, 326 Hongo, Bunkyo-ku Tokyo, Japan *Tel:* (03) 5842-2270 *Fax:* (03) 5800-7598 *E-mail:* info@quint-j.co.jp *Web Site:* www.quint-j.co.jp
2 Graston Rd, New Malden, Surrey KT3 3AB, United Kingdom *Tel:* (020) 8949-6087 *Fax:* (020) 8336-1484 *E-mail:* info@quintpub.co.uk *Web Site:* www.quintpub.co.uk
Distributor for Quintessence Publishing Co Ltd (Japan); Quintessence Publishing Ltd (London); Quintessence Verlags GmbH
Advertising Agency: QPC Advertising Inc

Quirk Books
215 Church St, Philadelphia, PA 19106
Tel: 215-627-3581 *Fax:* 215-627-5220
E-mail: general@quirkbooks.com
Web Site: www.quirkbooks.com
Key Personnel
Owner & CEO, Quirk Productions: David Borgenicht
Pres: Brett Cohen
Publr: Jason Rekulak
VP, Sales: Moneka Hewlett
Dir, Digital & Print Prodn: John McGurk
Dir, Publicity & Mktg: Nicole De Jackmo
Mng Ed: Mary Ellen Wilson
Mktg & Soc Media Coord: Julie Leung
Edit Asst: Jane Morley
Sales Asst: Kate Brown
Founded: 2002
Publishing list focuses on irreverent pop-culture, humor, gift, self-help & "impractical" reference books. The actual subject matter of our books is quite diverse. Publish everything from childcare tips & magic tricks to advice on stain removal. All of our books have a distinct sense of style, a refreshing sense of humor & innovative production values.
ISBN Prefix(es): 978-1-931686; 978-1-59474
Number of titles published annually: 25 Print
Total Titles: 150 Print
Distribution Center: Penguin Random House Publisher Services, 1745 Broadway, New York, NY 10019 *E-mail:* distribution@penguinrandomhouse.com

Quite Specific Media Group Ltd
Division of Silman-James Press Inc
141 N Clark Dr, Unit 1, West Hollywood, CA 90048
Tel: 310-205-0665
E-mail: info@silmanjamespress.com
Web Site: www.quitespecificmedia.com; www.silmanjamespress.com
Key Personnel
Publr: Ralph Pine
Founded: 1967
Publish original books as well as co-publish with foreign publishers. Specialize in costumes, fashion & theatre.
ISBN Prefix(es): 978-0-89676
Number of titles published annually: 8 Print
Total Titles: 380 Print
Imprints: By Design Press; Costume & Fashion Press; Drama Publishers; EntertainmentPro; Jade Rabbit; Pat MacKay Projects
Foreign Rep(s): Nick Hern Books (UK)
Orders to: Silman-James Press Inc *Tel:* 323-661-9922 *Toll Free Tel:* 877-SJP-BOOK (757-2665) *Fax:* 323-661-9933 *E-mail:* info@silmanjamespress.com
Distribution Center: Silman-James Press Inc *Fax:* 323-214-7943 *E-mail:* info@silmanjamespress.com

Quixote Press
3544 Blakslee St, Wever, IA 52658
Tel: 319-372-7480 *Toll Free Tel:* 800-571-2665 *Fax:* 319-372-7485
E-mail: heartsntummies@gmail.com
Key Personnel
Pres: Bruce Carlson
Founded: 1985
Regional paperback books of humor or folklore & cookbooks. Consulting work for self-publishers.
ISBN Prefix(es): 978-1-878488; 978-1-57166
Number of titles published annually: 30 Print
Total Titles: 350 Print
Divisions: Black Iron Cookin' Co; Hearts 'n Tummies Cookbook Co; Kid Help Publishing Co; PYO (Publish Your Own Co); Raise the Dough in 30 Days Co
See separate listing for:
Hearts 'n Tummies Cookbook Co

§Radix Press
Subsidiary of UGF/OR
11715 Bandlon Dr, Houston, TX 77072
Tel: 281-879-5688
Web Site: www.vvfh.org; www.specialforcesbooks.com
Key Personnel
Dir: Stephen Sherman *E-mail:* sherman1@flash.net
Founded: 1983
Directories, reference books. All unsol mss sent will be discarded.
ISBN Prefix(es): 978-0-9624009; 978-0-9623992; 978-1-929932
Number of titles published annually: 3 Print; 1 CD-ROM; 2 E-Book
Total Titles: 60 Print; 14 CD-ROM; 9 E-Book
Imprints: Electric Strawberry Press

§Rainbow Books Inc
PO Box 430, Highland City, FL 33846
SAN: 221-9859
Tel: 863-648-4420 *Fax:* 863-647-5951
E-mail: info@rainbowbooksinc.com; rbibooks@aol.com
Web Site: www.rainbowbooksinc.com
Key Personnel
Publr: Betsy Wright Lampe
Opers Dir: C Marzen Lampe *E-mail:* clampe@aol.com
Founded: 1978
How-to & self-help for both the adult lay & the juvenile markets; mystery & women's fiction titles for adults.
ISBN Prefix(es): 978-0-935834; 978-1-56825
Number of titles published annually: 10 Print; 10 E-Book
Total Titles: 120 Print; 23 E-Book
Foreign Rep(s): Hagenbach & Bender (worldwide exc USA)
Foreign Rights: HBG Productions & International Publishers Alliance (worldwide exc USA)
Returns: 5435 Highlands Vue Lane, Lakeland, FL 33812 (must get prior authorization. Location is residential), Opers Mgr: Charles Lampe
Warehouse: Publishers Storage & Shipping Corp, 660 S Mansfield St, Ypsilanti, MI 48197-5167, Contact: Donna Moore *Tel:* 734-487-9720 *Fax:* 734-487-1890 *E-mail:* dmoore@psscmi.com *Web Site:* www.pssc.com
Membership(s): AAP; Florida Authors & Publishers Association Inc

§Rainbow Publishers
4733 Torrance Blvd, No 259, Torrance, CA 90503
Mailing Address: PO Box 261129, San Diego, CA 92196
Tel: 858-277-1167 *Toll Free Tel:* 800-323-7337; 800-532-4278 *Fax:* 310-353-2116 *Toll Free Fax:* 800-331-0297
E-mail: info@rainbowpublishers.com; editor@rainbowpublishers.com (edit dept); orders@rainbowpublishers.com
Web Site: www.rainbowpublishers.com
Key Personnel
CEO: Daniel Miley
Founded: 1951
Christian education books.
ISBN Prefix(es): 978-0-937282; 978-1-885358; 978-1-58411
Number of titles published annually: 12 Print
Total Titles: 250 Print
Imprints: Legacy Press

Ram Publishing Co
Subsidiary of Garrett Electronics
1881 W State St, Garland, TX 75042
Tel: 972-494-6151 *Toll Free Tel:* 800-527-4011 *Fax:* 972-494-1881
E-mail: sales@garrett.com
Web Site: www.garrett.com
Key Personnel
Ed: Steve Moore
Founded: 1967
Nonfiction on treasure hunting with a metal detector & metal detector security.
ISBN Prefix(es): 978-0-915920
Number of titles published annually: 3 Print
Total Titles: 15 Print

§RAND Corp
1776 Main St, Santa Monica, CA 90407-2138
Mailing Address: PO Box 2138, Santa Monica, CA 90407-2138
Tel: 310-393-0411 *Fax:* 310-393-4818
Web Site: www.rand.org
Key Personnel
Dir, Strategic Communs: Jeremy Rawitch *E-mail:* jrawitch@rand.org
Mng Ed: Steve Kistler *E-mail:* skistler@rand.org
Mgr, Busn: Laura Shaw *E-mail:* lshaw@rand.org
Mgr, Publg Servs: Paul Murphy *E-mail:* murphy@rand.org
Print & Dist Mgr: Tim Erickson *E-mail:* tim@rand.org
Cust Serv Supv: Amy Majczyk *Tel:* 412-683-2300 ext 4604 *E-mail:* amajczyk@rand.org
Founded: 1948
Public policy research.
ISBN Prefix(es): 978-0-8330
Number of titles published annually: 140 Print; 100 Online; 30 E-Book

Total Titles: 30,000 Print; 24,000 Online; 1,550 E-Book
Divisions: Office of External Affairs
Foreign Rep(s): Aditya Books Pvt Ltd (India); Booknet Co Ltd (Cambodia, Laos, Myanmar, Thailand, Vietnam); ChoiceTEXTS Ltd (Indonesia, Singapore); iCaves Ltd (Hong Kong); IG Knowledge Services Ltd (Taiwan); iGroup (Brunei, China, Hong Kong, India, Indonesia, Malaysia, Philippines, Singapore, Taiwan); iGroup Press Co Ltd (China); Inbooks (Australia); Information Development Consultancy (IDC) (Korea); MegaTEXTS Phil Inc (Philippines); NBN Canada (Canada); NBN/DA Trade (Australia, New Zealand); NBN International (Europe, Middle East, UK)
Orders to: RAND Distribution Services, 4570 Fifth Ave, Pittsburgh, PA 15213, Cust Serv Mgr: Amy Majczyk *Tel:* 412-683-2300 *Toll Free Tel:* 877-584-8642 *Fax:* 412-802-4981 *E-mail:* order@rand.org
Distribution Center: National Book Network, 4720 Boston Way, Blue Ridge Summit, PA 17214 *Tel:* 717-794-3800 *Toll Free Tel:* 800-462-6420 *Toll Free Fax:* 800-338-4550 *E-mail:* mcozy@nbnbooks.com *Web Site:* www.nbnbooks.com
Membership(s): AIGA, the professional association for design; American Association of University Presses; Public Relations Society of America; Society for Scholarly Publishing

§Rand McNally
9855 Woods Dr, Skokie, IL 60077
SAN: 203-3917
Mailing Address: PO Box 7600, Chicago, IL 60680-7600
Tel: 847-329-8100
E-mail: ctsales@randmcnally.com; mediarelations@randmcnally.com
Web Site: www.randmcnally.com
Key Personnel
CEO: Stephen Fletcher
CTO: Yusuf Ozturk
VP, Mktg: Kendra Ensor
Design Dir: Joerg Metzner
Dir, Prod Educ: Ryan Walker
Mktg Mgr: Christine Devane
Prod Mgr: Mastan Holtzer
Founded: 1856
Road atlases & maps; world atlases; mileage & routing publications & software; educational maps, atlases; children's atlases, maps, books; electronic multimedia products; retail & online stores; online travel services, travel software.
Publisher of the *Thomas Guide* atlas series.
ISBN Prefix(es): 978-0-528
Number of titles published annually: 20 Print
Total Titles: 100 Print; 5 CD-ROM
Imprints: Rand McNally for Kids
Warehouse: 106 Hi-Lane, Richmond, KY 40475

Peter E Randall Publisher
5 Greenleaf Woods Dr, Suite 102, Portsmouth, NH 03801
Mailing Address: PO Box 4726, Portsmouth, NH 03802-4726
Tel: 603-431-5667 *Fax:* 603-431-3566
E-mail: media@perpublisher.com
Web Site: www.perpublisher.com
Key Personnel
Owner & CEO: Deidre C Randall
E-mail: deidre@perpublisher.com
Founded: 1970
This publisher has indicated that 100% of their product line is author subsidized.
ISBN Prefix(es): 978-0-914339; 978-1-931807; 978-0-9817898; 978-0-9828236; 978-1-937721
Number of titles published annually: 20 Print; 5 E-Book

Random House Children's Books
Division of Penguin Random House Inc
1745 Broadway, 10th fl, New York, NY 10019
Tel: 212-782-9000
Web Site: www.randomhousekids.com
Key Personnel
Pres & Publr: Barbara Marcus
Pres & Publr, Beginner Books & Dr Seuss Publg Prog: Cathy Goldsmith
EVP, Publg Opers: Rich Romano
SVP & Publr, Delacorte Press: Beverly Horowitz
SVP & Publr, Random House/Golden Books, Doubleday & Crown Books for Young Readers Group: Mallory Loehr
SVP & Assoc Publr: Judith Haut
SVP, Mktg: John Adamo
VP & Publr, Crown Books for Young Readers: Phoebe Yeh
VP & Publr, Knopf Books for Young Readers: Jennifer M Brown
VP & Publg Dir, Knopf/Crown: Nancy Hinkel
VP & Publg Dir, Schwartz & Wade Books: Anne Schwartz; Lee Wade
VP & Publg Dir, Wendy Lamb Books: Wendy Lamb
VP & Exec Dir, Publicity & Corp Communs: Dominique Cimina
VP & Exec Mng Ed: Denise DeGennaro
VP & Dir, Brand/Category Mgmt: Enid Chaban
VP & Dir, Children's Retail Sales: Becky Green
VP & Dir, Natl Accts, Mass Mdse Sales: Christina Jeffries
VP & Prodn Dir: Linda Palladino
VP, Group Sales Dir & Dir, Mass Mdse Sales: Mark Santella
VP, Mktg, Licensed & Proprietary Brands: Kerri Benvenuto
VP, Subs Rts Mkts: Pam White
Exec Dir, Art & Design, Knopf Delacorte Dell Young Readers Group: Isabel Warren-Lynch
Exec Dir, Mktg & Design Opers: Mary Beth Kilkelly
Exec Dir, Mktg Prodn & Opers: Beth Conte
Exec Dir, Publicity: Noreen Herits
Dir, Category Mktg: Diana Blough
Dir, Content Devt: Lynn Kestin
Dir, Digital Mktg: Kate Keating
Dir, Digital Strategy & Busn Devt: Sam Im
Dir, Mktg: Kimberly Lauber
Dir, School & Lib Mktg: Adrienne Waintraub
Assoc Publg Dir, Random House/Golden Books Group: Michelle Nagler
Assoc Publg Dir & Exec Ed, Knopf/Crown: Nancy Siscoe
Assoc Dir, Publicity: Casey Lloyd; Mary McCue
Dir, Publicity Events: Casey Ward
Exec Art Dir, Licensed Publg: Tracy Tyler
Sr Art Dir: Alison Impey; Maureen McLaughlin
Art Dir: Maria Middleton
Art Dir, Mktg Design: Sharon Burkle
Art Dir, Random House Books for Young Readers: Jan Gerardi
Art Dir, Random House/Golden Books for Young Readers: Jason Zamajtuk
Assoc Art Dir, KDD Art Group: Stephanie Moss
Assoc Art Dir: Nicole de las Heras; Sarah Hokanson
Asst Art Dir: Catherine Mucciardi
Sr Exec Ed, Delacorte Press: Wendy Loggia; Krista Marino
Exec Ed: Alice Jonaitis
Exec Ed, Doubleday: Francoise Bui
Edit Dir, Picture Books: Maria Modugno
Mng Ed, Random House Children's/Golden Books: Cindy Johnson
Sr Mktg Mgr: Stephanie O'Cain
Sr Mktg Mgr, Digital: Cayla Rasi
Sr Mktg Mgr, Licensed & Proprietary Brands: Robby Brown
Sr Mgr, Publicity: Jillian Vandall
Sr Prodn Mgr: Mary Ellen Owens
Sr Publicist: Lydia Finn; Allison Judd
Publicist & Online Media Specialist: Meg O'Brien
Publicist: Emily Pourciau; Josh Redlich; Elizabeth Zajac
Assoc Publicist: Emily Bamford; Sam Terris
Assoc Dir, Subs Rts: Kim Wrubel
Assoc Mktg Dir, Events Strategist: Joseph Scalora
Edit Dir, Sesame Workshop, Random House Books for Young Readers: Naomi Kleinberg
Ed-in-Chief & Exec Dir, Licensed Publg, Golden Books: Chris Angelilli
Sr Exec Ed, Knopf Children's: Erin Clarke
Exec Ed, Disney Books for Young Readers: Andrea Posner-Sanchez
Exec Ed, Random House Books for Young Readers: Heidi Kilgras
Exec Ed, Random House Books for Young Readers/Golden Books Group: Mary Man-Kong
Exec Creative Dir: Martha Rago
Edit Dir, Novelty, Random House/Golden Books Young Readers Group: Dennis Shealy
Dir, Licensing: Rachel Bader
Dir, Mktg, Licensed & Proprietary Brands: Derek Elmer
Dir, Mktg, New Media: Linda Leonard
Assoc Dir, Digital Content Strategy: Elizabeth Ward
Assoc Publg Dir, Knopf Children's: Melanie Cecka
Mng Ed, Knopf Children's: Dawn Ryan
Asst Mng Ed: Megan Williams
Sr Ed: Chelsea Eberly
Sr Ed, Knopf Books for Young Readers: Michele Burke; Allison Worchte
Sr Ed, Licensing: Frank Berrios
Sr Ed, Random House/Golden Books Young Readers Group: Diane Landolf
Sr Ed, Schwartz & Wade Books: Annie Kelley
Ed: Rachel Poloski
Ed, Knopf Books for Young Readers: Julia Maguire
Ed, Knopf Children's: Katherine Harrison
Assoc Ed: Meika Hashimoto; Michael Joosten; Jenna Lettice; Anna Membrino
Assoc Ed, Delacorte Press: Kelsey Horton
Assoc Ed, Golden Books: Courtney Carbone
Assoc Ed, Knopf Books for Young Readers: Kelly Delaney
Asst Ed: Samantha Gentry
Asst Ed, Delacorte Press: Monica Jean
Asst Ed, Knopf Books for Young Readers: Stephen Brown
Asst Ed, Schwartz & Wade: Stephanie Pitts
Copy Ed: Stephanie Bay
Assoc Copy Ed: Madelin Stone
Prodn Mgr: Thomas Marshall; Jennifer Moreno
Assoc Mgr, Digital Mktg: Julianne Conlon
Assoc Mgr, Subs Rts Dept: Mariana Ramos
Assoc Prodn Mgr: Shameiza Ally; Natalia Dextre
Soc Media Mgr: Chelsea Hassman
Mktg Mgr: Lauren Adams
Assoc Mktg Mgr: Nora MacDonald
Assoc Mktg Mgr, Licensed & Proprietary Brand: Robby Imfeld
Asst Mgr, Mktg Opers: Mallory Matney
Asst Mktg Mgr: Hannah Black; Nick Elliot; Sarah Wharton
Asst Mktg Mgr, Trade: Ashley Woodfolk
Asst Mgr, Subs Rts: Lauren Morgan
Mktg Coord: Alissa Nigro; Colleen Nuccio; Danielle Rollins
Mktg Coord, Licensed & Proprietary Brands: Tara Greico
Educ Mktg Assoc: Emily Petrick
Mktg Assoc: Linda Camacho
Lib Coord, School & Lib Mktg: Kristin Schultz
Subs Rts Coord: Kristina Forest
Mng Prodr, Content Devt & Mktg: Alison Folino
Content Prodr: Hanna Lee
Prodr: Santhana Souksamrane
Prodn Supv: Elizabeth Peskin; Alice Rahaeuser
Prodn Coord: Shay Brown
Prodn Assoc: Maggie Gibson
Publg Consultant: Robin Corey
Sr Designer: Krister Engstrom; Regina Flath; Ray Shappel
Designer: Bob Bianchini; Jaclyn Whalen

Designer, Trade Mktg Design Team: Michael Caiati
Jr Designer: Jinna Shin
ISBN Prefix(es): 978-0-679; 978-0-307; 978-0-676; 978-0-375; 978-1-4000; 978-1-58836
Imprints: Bluefire; Delacorte Press; Dragonfly; Ember; Golden Books; Alfred A Knopf Books for Young Readers; Laurel-Leaf; The Princeton Review; Random House Books for Young Readers; Schwartz & Wade Books; Sylvan Learning; Wendy Lamb Books; Yearling Books
Warehouse: Crawfordsville Distribution Center, 1019 N State Rd 47, Crawfordsville, IN 47933
Distribution Center: Crawfordsville Distribution Center, 1019 N State Rd 47, Crawfordsville, IN 47933
See separate listing for:
The Princeton Review

Random House Publishing Group
Division of Penguin Random House Inc
1745 Broadway, New York, NY 10019
SAN: 214-1175
Toll Free Tel: 800-200-3552
Web Site: atrandom.com
Key Personnel
CFO, Penguin Random House: Milena Alberti
Pres & Publr: Gina Centrello
EVP & Publr, Random House & Dial Press: Susan Kamil
EVP & Publr, Digital Content: Scott Shannon
SVP & Deputy CFO, Penguin Random House: James Johnston
Publr, Spiegel & Grau: Julie Grau; Cindy Spiegel
Publr & Ed-in-Chief, One World: Christopher Jackson
Deputy Publr, Nonfiction & Publr, Modern Library: Thomas Perry
Assoc Publr & Edit Strategy: Gina Wachtel
Assoc Publr, Spiegel & Grau & Dir, Mktg, Random House, Spiegel & Grau, Dial Press & Modern Library: Leigh Merchant
COO & EVP: Nihar Malaviya
Group EVP & Dir, Publg: Bill Takes
EVP & Dir, Mktg: Sanyu Dillon
EVP & Dir, Publicity: Theresa Zoro
Group SVP & Creative Dir: Paolo Pepe
EVP & Publr, Ballantine Bantam Dell: Kara Welsh
EVP, Assoc Publr & Exec Edit Dir: Kate Medina
EVP, Corp Communs: Claire von Schilling
SVP & Dir, Publg Opers: Lisa Feuer
SVP & Dir, Penguin Random House Intl Sales & Mktg & Dir, East Asia Busn Devt: Cyrus Kheradi
SVP & Deputy Publr, Ballantine Bantam Dell: Kim Hovey
SVP & Sr Dir, Subs Rts: Denise Cronin
SVP & Dir, Digital Marketplace Devt: Amanda Close
SVP & Dir, Spec Events & Event Partnerships: Sally Marvin
SVP & Edit Dir, Ballantine: Linda Marrow
SVP & Ed-in-Chief, Ballantine Bantam Dell: Jennifer Hershey
SVP: Nina von Moltke
VP & Assoc Publr, Del Rey/VP & Assoc Publr, Mass Mkt, Ballantine Bantam Dell: Keith Clayton
VP & Deputy Publr, Fiction: Avideh Bashirrad
VP & Sr Dir, Copy: Grant Neumann
VP & Dir, Digital Strategy: Matt Schwartz
VP & Edit Dir, Bantam Books/Delacorte Press: Kate Miciak
VP & Edit Dir, Nonfiction: Andy Ward
VP & Edit Dir, Nonfiction, Ballantine Bantam Dell: Jennifer Tung
VP & Deputy Dir, Media Coaching & Publicity: Barbara Fillon
Exec Dir, Art/Design: Robbin Schiff
Sr Dir, Art/Design: Beck Stvan
Sr Art Dir: Joe Perez
Exec Ed, Ballantine: Pamela Cannon; Marnie Cochran; Susanna Porter
Exec Ed, Ballantine Bantam Dell: Tracy Devine; Andra Miller; Brendan Vaughan
Exec Ed, Random House: Noah Eaker; Ben Greenberg; Susan Mercandetti; Will Murphy; Hilary Redmon; Andrea Walker
Dir, Ad & Promo: Stacey Witcraft
Dir, Creative Servs: Annette Melvin
Dir, Dom Rts: Rachel Bernstein
Dir, Interior Design: Carole Lowenstein
Dir, Partnerships & Busn Devt: Melissa Milsten
Dir, Publicity, Random House, Spiegel & Grau & The Dial Press: Maria Braeckel
Group Sales Dir: Cynthia Lasky
Imprint Sales Dir: Allyson Pearl
Deputy Dir, Digital Mktg: Susana Zialcita
Deputy Dir, Publicity: London King; David Moench; Cindy Murray
Assoc Dir, Publicity: Melanie DeNardo; Jennifer Garza
Asst Dir, Publicity: Michelle Jasmine; Greg Kubie; Lucy Silag
Assoc Dir, Foreign Rts: Rachel Kind
Asst Dir, Mktg, Random House, Spiegel & Grau & One World: Andrea Dewerd
Sr Mng Ed, Random House & Copy Chief: Benjamin Dreyer
Sr Mgr, Ad & Promos: Elizabeth Fabian
Sr Mktg Mgr: Erika Greber
Mktg Mgr: Maggie Oberrender
Publicity Mgr: Alison Masciovecchio
Publicity Mgr, Spec Events & Partnerships: Jenna Friedman
Sr Publicist: Christine Mykityshyn
Publicist: Emily Isayeff; Lindsay Kennedy
Publicist, Partnerships & Spec Events: Abbey Corey
Soc Media Publicist: Danielle Siess
Assoc Publicist: Alex Coumbis; Allyson Lord; Ella Maslin; Katie McNally; Catherine Mikula; Dhara Parikh
Sr Ed, Ballantine Bantam Dell: Sara Weiss
Sr Ed, Del Rey: Elizabeth Schaefer
Sr Ed, Spiegel & Grau: Emi Ikkanda
Ed: Kate Collins; Anne Groell; Dana Isaacson; Caitlin McKenna; Kaela Myers; Sam Nicholson; Tricia Pasternak; Anna Pitoniak; Shauna Summers
Ed, Ballantine Bantam Dell: Anne Speyer
Ed, One World: Victory Matsui
Ed, Spiegel & Grau: Annie Chagnot
Assoc Ed: Mika Kasuga; Molly Turpin
Assoc Ed, Alibi: Randall Klein
Assoc Ed, Ballantine Bantam Dell: Sarah Murphy
Assoc Ed, Hydra: Sarah Reed
Asst Ed, Ballantine Bantam Dell: Julia Maguire; Elana Seplow-Jolley
Asst Ed, One World: Nicole Counts
Ed-at-Large, Ballantine Bantam Dell: Alino Cho
Ed-at-Large, Del Rey/Ballantine: Shelly Shapiro
Ed-at-Large, Flirt & Loveswept: Sue Grimshaw
Founded: 1925
General fiction & nonfiction hardcover, trade & mass market paperbacks.
Penguin Random House Inc & its publishing entities are not accepting unsol submissions, proposals, mss, or submission queries via e-mail at this time.
ISBN Prefix(es): 978-0-307; 978-0-679; 978-0-89141; 978-0-345; 978-0-449; 978-0-8129; 978-0-375; 978-1-4000; 978-1-58836; 978-0-8041
Number of titles published annually: 700 Print; 150 E-Book
Total Titles: 5,900 Print; 1,100 E-Book
Imprints: Alibi (mystery, thriller, suspense); Ballantine Books; Bantam Books; Del Rey; Dell; The Dial Press; Flirt (new adult); Hydra (science fiction & fantasy); Loveswept (digital only romance); Modern Library; One World; Presidio Press; Random House; Spiegel & Grau; Triumph Books; Villard; Zinc Ink
Warehouse: 400 Hahn Rd, Westminster, MD 21157

Random House Reference/Random House Puzzles & Games
Imprint of Penguin Random House Audio Publishing
c/o Penguin Random House Inc, 1745 Broadway, New York, NY 10019
Tel: 212-782-9000
Web Site: www.penguinrandomhouse.com
Key Personnel
SVP & Publr: Amanda D'Acierno
Publishes reference, crossword puzzle books & chess books & price guides for collectibles.
Penguin Random House Inc & its publishing entities are not accepting unsol submissions, proposals, mss, or submission queries via e-mail at this time.
ISBN Prefix(es): 978-0-8129; 978-0-375
Total Titles: 215 Print
Imprints: Boston Globe Puzzle Books; Chicago Tribune Crosswords; House of Collectibles; Los Angeles Times Crosswords; Random House Webster's; Washington Post Crosswords

Rational Island Publishers
Division of The Re-evaluation Counseling Communities
719 Second Ave N, Seattle, WA 98109
Tel: 206-284-0311 *Fax:* 206-284-8429
E-mail: ircc@rc.org
Web Site: www.rc.org
Key Personnel
Ed: Lisa Kauffman
Founded: 1954
Articles about Re-evaluation Counseling (Co-Counseling) - the theory, the practice, the applications & implications.
ISBN Prefix(es): 978-0-911214; 978-0-913937; 978-1-885357; 978-1-58429; 978-1-893165
Number of titles published annually: 6 Print
Total Titles: 263 Print

§Rattapallax Press
217 Thompson St, Suite 353, New York, NY 10012
E-mail: info@rattapallax.com
Web Site: www.rattapallax.com
Key Personnel
Pres & Publr: Ram Devineni
Founded: 2000
ISBN Prefix(es): 978-1-892494
Number of titles published annually: 4 Print; 1 CD-ROM; 15 Online; 15 E-Book; 15 Audio
Total Titles: 15 Print; 1 CD-ROM; 15 Online; 15 E-Book; 15 Audio
Distribution Center: Small Press Distribution, 1341 Seventh St, Berkeley, CA 94710-1409 *Tel:* 510-524-1668 *Toll Free Tel:* 800-869-7553 *E-mail:* spd@spdbooks.org *Web Site:* www.spdbooks.org
Membership(s): Community of Literary Magazines & Presses

Raven Productions Inc
34 S Second Ave, Suite 204, Ely, MN 55731
Mailing Address: PO Box 188, Ely, MN 55731
Tel: 218-365-3375
E-mail: raven@ravenwords.com; order@ravenwords.com
Web Site: www.ravenwords.com
Founded: 1999
ISBN Prefix(es): 978-0-9677057; 978-0-9766264; 978-0-9794202; 978-0-9801045; 978-0-9819307; 978-0-9883508; 978-0-9835189
Number of titles published annually: 3 Print
Total Titles: 25 Print
Imprints: Rosebud Books

Warehouse: R & R, 420 N 15 Ave E, Ely, MN 55731
Distribution Center: Baker & Taylor, 501 S Gladiolus St, Momence, IL 60954-1799, Mdse Admin: Ms Robin Bright *Tel:* 908-541-7425 *Toll Free Tel:* 800-775-2300 *Fax:* 815-802-2444 *Toll Free Fax:* 800-411-8433 *E-mail:* pc@baker-taylor.com *Web Site:* www.baker-taylor.com
North Country Books, 220 Lafayette St, Utica, NY 13502 *Tel:* 315-735-4877 *Toll Free Tel:* 800-342-7409 *Fax:* 315-738-4342 *E-mail:* ncbooks@verizon.net *Web Site:* www.northcountrybooks.com
Membership(s): Independent Book Publishers Association; Midwest Independent Publishing Association

Raven Publishing Inc
125 Cherry Creek Rd, Norris, MT 59745
SAN: 254-5861
Mailing Address: PO Box 2866, Norris, MT 59745
Tel: 406-685-3545 *Toll Free Tel:* 866-685-3545
E-mail: info@ravenpublishing.net
Web Site: www.ravenpublishing.net
Key Personnel
Founder & Pres: Janet Muirhead Hill *E-mail:* janet@ravenpublishing.net
Founded: 2001
ISBN Prefix(es): 978-0-9714161; 978-0-9772525; 978-0-9820893; 978-0-9827377; 978-1-937849
Number of titles published annually: 4 Print; 4 E-Book
Total Titles: 32 Print; 33 E-Book; 2 Audio
Billing Address: PO Box 2866, Norris, MT 59745
Membership(s): Independent Book Publishers Association

§Ravenhawk™ Books
Division of The 6DOF Group
8364 E Balfour Place, Tucson, AZ 85710
Tel: 520-296-4491 *Fax:* 520-296-4491
E-mail: the6dofcompany@gmail.com
Key Personnel
Publr: Karl Lasky
Founded: 1998
Royalty publisher. Specialize in general trade, hard/softcover, fiction, nonfiction, self-help, teaching texts for professionals, crime, mystery & suspense fiction. Ebooks, CD/DVD audiobooks. Ms submissions are by invitation only through acknowledged literary agents.
ISBN Prefix(es): 978-1-893660
Number of titles published annually: 6 Print; 4 CD-ROM; 6 Online; 12 E-Book; 5 Audio
Total Titles: 48 Print; 6 Online; 6 E-Book
Distribution Center: Baker & Taylor Inc, 2550 W Tyvola Rd, Suite 300, Charlotte, NC 28217 *Tel:* 704-998-3100 *Fax:* 704-998-3319 *E-mail:* btinfo@baker-taylor.com *Web Site:* www.baker-taylor.com
Ingram Content Group Inc, One Ingram Blvd, La Vergne, TN 37086-1986 *Tel:* 615-793-5000 *Web Site:* www.ingramcontent.com
Membership(s): Interactive Creative Artists Network; National Writers Association; Society of Southwestern Authors

Razorbill
Imprint of Penguin Random House Inc
345 Hudson St, New York, NY 10014
Tel: 212-366-2000
Web Site: www.penguin.com/meet/publishers/razorbill
Key Personnel
Pres & Publr: Ben Schrank
Founded: 2004
ISBN Prefix(es): 978-1-59514
Number of titles published annually: 42 Print
Total Titles: 159 Print

Reader's Digest Trade Publishing
Division of Trusted Media Brands Inc
44 S Broadway, White Plains, NY 10601
SAN: 240-9720
Tel: 914-238-1000
Web Site: www.rdtradepublishing.com
Key Personnel
VP & Assoc Publr: Rosanne McManus
Founded: 1971
Illustrated trade (retail) reference books on home maintenance & repair, gardening, home decorating, crafts, art instruction, cooking, health & fitness, pet care, music, family reference, religion & inspiration, science & nature, travel & atlases, humor.
ISBN Prefix(es): 978-0-7621; 978-1-61765; 978-1-62145
Number of titles published annually: 100 Print
Total Titles: 350 Print
Distributed by Simon & Schuster

Reader's Digest USA Select Editions
Division of Trusted Media Brands Inc
44 S Broadway, 7th fl, White Plains, NY 10601
Tel: 914-238-1000 *Toll Free Tel:* 800-304-2807 (cust serv) *Fax:* 914-831-1560
Key Personnel
Exec Ed: Jim Menick
Founded: 1950
Publishers of current fiction & general nonfiction in condensed form. Selections are licensed from original publisher.
ISBN Prefix(es): 978-0-89577

Recorded Books Inc, an RBmedia company
270 Skipjack Rd, Prince Frederick, MD 20678
SAN: 677-8887
Tel: 410-535-5590 *Toll Free Tel:* 877-732-2898 *Fax:* 410-535-5499
E-mail: customerservice@recordedbooks.com
Web Site: www.recordedbooks.com
Key Personnel
Pres & CEO: Rich Freese
COO: Edward Longo *E-mail:* elongo@recordedbooks.com
CFO: Neil Tress *E-mail:* ntress@recordedbooks.com
CIO & CTO: Mike Pyland
Dir, Acqs: Brian Sweany *E-mail:* bsweany@recordedbooks.com
Dir, Mktg: Patrick Deering *E-mail:* pdeering@recordedbooks.com
Sr Acqs Ed: Bob Podrasky
Founded: 1979
Independent publisher of unabridged audiobooks & distributor of films & other media content delivered in CD & downloadable formats, to consumers, libraries & schools.
ISBN Prefix(es): 978-0-7887; 978-1-4025; 978-1-55690; 978-1-84197; 978-1-4193; 978-1-84505; 978-1-4281; 978-1-4361; 978-1-4407; 978-1-4498; 978-1-4561; 978-1-4618; 978-1-4640; 978-1-4703; 978-1-4906; 978-1-5019
Number of titles published annually: 700 Print; 250 CD-ROM; 100 Online; 50 E-Book; 787 Audio
Total Titles: 8,000 Print; 1,000 CD-ROM; 100 Online; 50 E-Book; 5,808 Audio
Imprints: Classics Library; Clipper Audio (UK); Film Movement; The Great Courses; Griot Audio; Harlequin; ITK (In the Know) Audio; Lone Star Audio; Maple Leaf Audio; Pimlseur Language Programs; RB Mystery; RB Shorts; Recorded Books Audiolibros; Recorded Books Development; Recorded Books Inspirational; Romantic Sounds Audio; Sci-Fi Audio; Southern Voices Audio; Western Audio; Your Coach in a Box
Foreign Office(s): WF Howes, Unit 4, Rearsby Business Park, Gaddesby Lane, Rearsby, Leics LE7 4YH, United Kingdom (recorded books) *Tel:* (01664) 423000 *Fax:* (01664) 423005 *E-mail:* info@wfhowes.co.uk *Web Site:* www.wfhowes.co.uk
Membership(s): Audio Publishers Association

Red Chair Press
PO Box 333, South Egremont, MA 01258-0333
Tel: 413-528-2398 (edit off) *Toll Free Tel:* 800-328-4929 (orders & cust serv) *Toll Free Fax:* 800-332-1132
E-mail: info@redchairpress.com
Web Site: www.redchairpress.com
Key Personnel
CFO: David P Sheehan *Tel:* 917-608-6198 *E-mail:* david@redchairpress.com
Pres & Publr: Keith Garton *E-mail:* keith@redchairpress.com
Art Dir: Jeff Dinardo *Tel:* 978-371-0111 ext 1 *E-mail:* jeff@redchairpress.com
Founded: 2009
Fiction & nonfiction books & ebooks; social & emotional learning with an emphasis on good decision-making for ages 3-10. No unsol mss.
ISBN Prefix(es): 978-1-936163; 978-1-937529; 978-1-63440
Number of titles published annually: 30 Print; 24 E-Book
Total Titles: 150 Print; 32 CD-ROM; 120 E-Book
Imprints: Rocking Chair Kids (picture books ages 5 & under)
Foreign Rep(s): Lerner Publishing (Maria Kjoller) (worldwide exc Canada & USA)
Distribution Center: Lerner Publisher Services, 1251 Washington Ave N, Minneapolis, MN 55401 (USA) *Toll Free Tel:* 800-328-4929
Membership(s): AAP PreK-12 Learning Group; The Association of Publishers for Special Sales; Independent Book Publishers Association; Society of Children's Book Writers & Illustrators

Red Dust Inc
1148 Fifth Ave, New York, NY 10128
SAN: 203-3860
Tel: 212-348-4388
Web Site: www.reddustbooks.com
Key Personnel
Pres & Publr: Joanna Gunderson *E-mail:* reddustjg@aol.com
Founded: 1961
Works by new writers; fiction, poetry, nonsequential texts.
ISBN Prefix(es): 978-0-87376
Number of titles published annually: 3 Print
Total Titles: 100 Print
Editorial Office(s): 845 Hancock St, Brooklyn, NY 11233, Mng Ed: Donald Breckenridge *Tel:* 347-721-7790 *E-mail:* dpbreckenridge@yahoo.com

Red Hen Press
1335 N Lake Ave, Suite 200, Pasadena, CA 91104
Mailing Address: PO Box 40820, Pasadena, CA 91114
Tel: 626-356-4760 *Fax:* 626-356-9974
Web Site: www.redhen.org
Key Personnel
Publr: Mark E Cull *E-mail:* mark@redhen.org
Mng Ed: Kate Gale *E-mail:* kategale@verizon.net
Founded: 1994
Publish perfect bound collections of poetry, short stories & books of a literary nature. Also sponsor several literary awards, along with the literary journal *The Los Angeles Review.*
ISBN Prefix(es): 978-0-9890361; 978-1-888996; 978-1-59709
Number of titles published annually: 22 Print
Total Titles: 350 Print
Imprints: Arktoi Books; Boreal Books; Hybrid Nation; Pighog Books; Story Line Press; Xeno Books
Distribution Center: Chicago Distribution Center, 11030 S Langley, Chicago, IL 60628 *Toll Free*

Tel: 800-621-2736 *Toll Free Fax:* 800-621-8476
E-mail: orders@press.uchicago.edu
Membership(s): Association of Writers and Writing Programs; Community of Literary Magazines & Presses

Red Moon Press
PO Box 2461, Winchester, VA 22604-1661
Tel: 540-722-2156
Web Site: www.redmoonpress.com
Key Personnel
Owner: Jim Kacian *E-mail:* jim.kacian@redmoonpress.com
Founded: 1993
Largest & most prestigious publisher of English-language haiku & related forms in the world.
ISBN Prefix(es): 978-1-9657818; 978-1-893959; 978-1-936848
Number of titles published annually: 15 Print
Total Titles: 250 Print
Imprints: Pond Frog Editions; Soffietto Editions

Red Rock Press
205 W 57 St, Suite 8B, New York, NY 10019
Tel: 212-362-8304 *Fax:* 212-362-6216
E-mail: info@redrockpress.com; sales@redrockpress.com; rights@redrockpress.com
Web Site: www.redrockpress.com
Key Personnel
Creative Dir: Ilene Barth
Busn Mgr: Richard Barth *E-mail:* richard@redrockpress.com
Founded: 1998
Gift books.
ISBN Prefix(es): 978-0-9714372; 978-1-933176; 978-0-9669573
Number of titles published annually: 8 Print
Total Titles: 50 Print

Red Sea Press Inc
541 W Ingham Ave, Suite B, Trenton, NJ 08638
Tel: 609-695-3200 *Fax:* 609-695-6466
E-mail: customerservice@africaworldpressbooks.com
Web Site: www.africaworldpressbooks.com
Key Personnel
Pres & Publr: Kassahun Checole
Opers Mgr: Senait Kassahun
Founded: 1985
Publisher of books on the Horn of Africa, Latin America; distributor of books on the Third World.
ISBN Prefix(es): 978-0-932415; 978-1-56902
Number of titles published annually: 100 Print
Total Titles: 1,200 Print
Imprints: Karnak House
Foreign Rights: Turnaround Publisher Services (Europe, London)

Red Wheel/Weiser/Conari
65 Parker St, Suite 7, Newburyport, MA 01950
Tel: 978-465-0504 *Toll Free Tel:* 800-423-7087 (orders) *Fax:* 978-465-0243
E-mail: info@rwwbooks.com
Web Site: www.redwheelweiser.com
Key Personnel
Pres & CEO: Michael Kerber *Tel:* 978-465-0504 ext 1115 *E-mail:* mkerber@rwwbooks.com
Assoc Publr: Greg Brandenburgh
Creative Dir: Kathryn Sky-Peck
Publicity Dir: Bonni Hamilton
Publicist: Eryn Eaton
Mng Ed: Jane Hagaman
Sr Acqs Ed: Christine LeBlond
Prodn Mgr: Michael Conlon
Founded: 1957
Self-help, spirituality, inspiration, women's interest & esoteric subjects from many traditions.
ISBN Prefix(es): 978-0-943233 (Conari); 978-0-87728 (Weiser); 978-1-57863 (Weiser); 978-1-59003 (Red Wheel); 978-1-57324 (Conari)
Number of titles published annually: 50 Print
Total Titles: 1,200 Print
Imprints: Disinformation Books; Hampton Roads Publishing
Distributor for Cleis Press; Nicolas Hays Inc; Viva Editions
Foreign Rep(s): Brumby Books (Australia); Deep Books (UK); Georgetown Publications (Canada)
Foreign Rights: Linda Biagi (translation)
Warehouse: Books International Inc, 22883 Quicksilver Dr, Dulles, VA 20166
Membership(s): ABA
See separate listing for:
Hampton Roads Publishing Co

Redleaf Press
Division of Think Small
10 Yorkton Ct, St Paul, MN 55117
SAN: 212-8691
Tel: 651-641-0508 *Toll Free Tel:* 800-423-8309 *Toll Free Fax:* 800-641-0115
E-mail: customerservice@redleafpress.org
Web Site: www.redleafpress.org
Key Personnel
Dir: David Heath *E-mail:* dheath@redleafpress.org
Dir, Mktg: Eric Johnson *E-mail:* ejohnson@redleafpress.org
Sales Mgr: Sue Ostfield
Founded: 1973
Resources for early childhood professionals including. early childhood curriculum, professional development, family child care business, record keeping & parenting.
ISBN Prefix(es): 978-0-934140; 978-1-884834; 978-1-929610; 978-1-933653; 978-1-60554
Number of titles published annually: 32 Print; 3 CD-ROM; 50 E-Book
Total Titles: 270 Print; 15 CD-ROM; 5 Online; 50 E-Book
Distributed by Pademelon Press Pty Ltd (Australia)
Foreign Rights: Perseus (worldwide)
Distribution Center: Consortium Book Sales & Distribution, The Keg House, Suite 101, 34 13th Ave NE, Minneapolis, MN 55413 (US book trade & libs) *Tel:* 612-746-2600 *Toll Free Tel:* 800-283-3572 (cust serv) *Fax:* 612-746-2606 *Web Site:* www.cbsd.com
Monarch Books of Canada, 5000 Dufferin St, Downsview, ON M3H 5T5, Canada
Pademelon Press Pty Ltd, Unit 7/3 Packard Ave, Castle Hill, NSW 2154, Australia *Tel:* (02) 9634 4655 *Fax:* (02) 9680 4634
Eurospan Group, 3 Henrietta St, London WC2E 8LU, United Kingdom (UK, Continental Europe, Africa, Asia & Middle East) *Tel:* (01767) 604972 *Fax:* (01767) 601640 *E-mail:* eurospan@turpin-distribution.com
Membership(s): Education Market Association

Robert D Reed Publishers
PO Box 1992, Bandon, OR 97411-1192
Tel: 541-347-9882 *Fax:* 541-347-9883
E-mail: 4bobreed@msn.com
Web Site: rdrpublishers.com
Key Personnel
Publr: Robert D Reed
Founded: 1977
All types of publications for trade, educational institutions, individuals & corporations.
ISBN Prefix(es): 978-1-889710; 978-1-885003; 978-1-931741
Number of titles published annually: 25 Print
Total Titles: 225 Print
Foreign Rep(s): Sylvia Hayse Literary Agency

Reedswain Inc
88 Wells Rd, Spring City, PA 19475
Tel: 610-495-9578 *Toll Free Tel:* 800-331-5191 *Fax:* 610-495-6632
E-mail: orders@reedswain.com
Web Site: www.reedswain.com
Key Personnel
Pres & Foreign Rts: Richard Kentwell
Founded: 1987
Soccer coaching books.
ISBN Prefix(es): 978-1-59164; 978-0-9651020; 978-1-890946
Number of titles published annually: 10 Print
Total Titles: 190 Print

Referee Books
Imprint of Referee Enterprises Inc
2017 Lathrop Ave, Racine, WI 53405
Tel: 262-632-8855 *Toll Free Tel:* 800-733-6100 *Fax:* 262-632-5460
E-mail: questions@referee.com
Web Site: www.referee.com
Key Personnel
Pres: Barry Mano *E-mail:* bmano@naso.org
Dir, Admin: Corey Ludwin
Founded: 1976
Publish sports officiating publications; magazines, books, manuals & booklets on officiating, umpiring, baseball, basketball, football, soccer, softball & athletics referee books.
ISBN Prefix(es): 978-1-58208; 978-0-9660209
Number of titles published annually: 30 Print
Total Titles: 75 Print

Reference Publications Inc
218 Saint Clair River Dr, Algonac, MI 48001
SAN: 208-4392
Mailing Address: PO Box 344, Algonac, MI 48001-0344
Tel: 810-794-5722
E-mail: referencepub@sbcglobal.net
Key Personnel
Pres & Ed: Marie Aline Irvine
Founded: 1975
Mail order & reference books. Specialize in botanical & medicinal plants, Americana, Amerindian & African reference books & botanical works.
ISBN Prefix(es): 978-0-917256
Number of titles published annually: 2 Print
Total Titles: 24 Print
Imprints: Encyclopaedia Africana
Sales Office(s): PO Box 344, Algonac, MI 48001-0344

ReferencePoint Press Inc
17150 Via del Campo, Suite 205, San Diego, CA 92127
Mailing Address: PO Box 27779, San Diego, CA 92198
Tel: 858-618-1314 *Toll Free Tel:* 888-479-6436 *Fax:* 858-618-1730
E-mail: info@referencepointpress.com
Web Site: www.referencepointpress.com
Key Personnel
Pres & Publr: Dan Leone *Tel:* 858-618-1314 ext 102 *E-mail:* dan@referencepointpress.com
Founded: 2006
Publish series nonfiction for young adults: current issues, health, science & paranormal.
ISBN Prefix(es): 978-1-60152; 978-1-68282
Number of titles published annually: 75 Print; 75 E-Book
Total Titles: 400 Print; 300 E-Book
Foreign Rep(s): Saunders Book Co (Canada)
Returns: Bang Fulfillment, 217 Etak Dr, Brainerd, MN 56401
Warehouse: Bang Fulfillment, 217 Etak Dr, Brainerd, MN 56401, Contact: Perry Gienger *Toll Free Tel:* 800-328-0450 *Fax:* 218-829-7145 *E-mail:* perryg@bangprinting.com

Reformation Heritage Books
2965 Leonard St NE, Grand Rapids, MI 49525
Tel: 616-977-0889 *Fax:* 616-285-3246
E-mail: orders@heritagebooks.org
Web Site: www.heritagebooks.org

Key Personnel
Chmn: Joel R Beeke
Contact: Jonathan Engelsma
Founded: 1994
Sell new & used religious books with emphasis on experiential religion. Also republish out-of-print Puritan works.
ISBN Prefix(es): 978-1-892777; 978-1-60178
Number of titles published annually: 40 Print
Total Titles: 250 Print; 70 E-Book

§Regal Crest Enterprises
1042 Mount Lebanon Rd, Maryville, TN 37804
Tel: 409-527-1188 *Toll Free Fax:* 866-294-9628
E-mail: info@regalcrestbooks.biz
Web Site: www.regalcrest.biz
Key Personnel
Owner: Cathy C Bryerose
Founded: 2003 (originally in 1999 as Renaissance Alliance Publishing Inc)
Traditional royalty publisher using innovative print technology.
ISBN Prefix(es): 978-1-932300; 978-1-935053; 978-1-61929
Number of titles published annually: 25 Print; 25 E-Book
Total Titles: 150 Print; 168 E-Book
Imprints: Blue Beacon Books (nonfiction); Mystic Books (paranormal); Quest Books (action, adventure, mystery, police procedure, detective); Regal Crest (drama & general fiction); Silver Dragon Books (science fiction/fantasy); Troubadour Books (poetry, short story, anthology); YA Books (young adult); Yellow Rose Books (romance)
Foreign Rep(s): Bella Distribution Inc (worldwide); Ingram (worldwide)
Distribution Center: Bella Distribution Inc, 1041 Aenon Church Rd, Tallahassee, FL 32302 *Toll Free Tel:* 800-533-1973
Ingram, One Ingram Blvd, La Vergne, TN 17202

Regal House Publishing
1723 Hickory Overlook Trail, No 110, Raleigh, NC 27607
Tel: 305-360-5969
E-mail: info@regalhousepublishing.com
Web Site: regalhousepublishing.com
Key Personnel
Founder & CEO: Jaynie Royal *E-mail:* editor@regalhousepublishing.com
Sr Ed: Ruth Feiertag
Ed: Michelle Esquillo; Amanda Irle; Kimberly Willardson
Founded: 2014
Passionately dedicated to the furtherance of exquisitely written literary works & the writers who pen them. Traditional publishing house accepting submissions directly from writers. Provide extensive editorial support for writers & formulate a marketing partnership pre- & post-publication.
ISBN Prefix(es): 978-0-9912612
Number of titles published annually: 16 Print; 16 Online; 16 E-Book
Total Titles: 4 Print; 4 Online; 4 E-Book
Imprints: Fitzroy Books (middle grade, new adult & young adult fiction); Pact Press (anthologies, poetry & short story collections, full-length & literary fiction)
Branch Office(s)
1678 Parkside Circle, Lafayette, CO 80026
Distribution Center: Ingram Books/IngramSpark, One Ingram Blvd, La Vergne, TN 37086 *Tel:* 615-793-5000
Membership(s): Community of Literary Magazines & Presses

Regnery Publishing
Subsidiary of Salem Media Group
300 New Jersey Ave NW, Washington, DC 20001
Tel: 202-216-0600 *Toll Free Tel:* 888-219-4747 *Fax:* 202-393-1795
Web Site: www.regnery.com
Key Personnel
Pres & Publr: Marjory G Ross
Dir, Publicity: Alyssa Cordova *E-mail:* alyssa.cordova@regnery.com
Dir, Sales: Mark Bloomfield
Exec Ed: Harry W Crocker, III
Foreign Rts: Matt Maschino *E-mail:* matthew.maschino@regnery.com
Perms: Will Hudson *E-mail:* william.hudson@regnery.com
Founded: 1947
Trade book publisher.
ISBN Prefix(es): 978-0-89526; 978-1-59698; 978-1-62157
Number of titles published annually: 50 Print; 50 E-Book
Total Titles: 1,000 Print; 800 E-Book
Imprints: Gateway Editions; Regnery; Regnery Faith; Regnery Fiction (thrillers); Regnery History; Regnery Kids
Distribution Center: Perseus Distribution Services, 193 Edwards Dr, Jackson, TN 38301

Regular Baptist Press
Division of General Association of Regular Baptist Churches
3715 N Ventura Dr, Arlington Heights, IL 60004
Tel: 847-843-1600 *Toll Free Tel:* 800-727-4440; 800-727-4440 (cust serv) *Fax:* 847-843-3757
E-mail: rbp@garbc.org
Web Site: regularbaptistpress.org
Key Personnel
Busn Dir: Tony Randolph
HR Asst: Meredith DeKock *E-mail:* mdekock@garbc.org
Founded: 1952
Curriculum & Christian books.
ISBN Prefix(es): 978-0-87227; 978-1-59402; 978-1-60776; 978-1-62940
Number of titles published annually: 6 Print
Imprints: Regular Baptist Books (trade books)

Renaissance House
Imprint of Laredo Publishing Co Inc
465 Westview Ave, Englewood, NJ 07631
Tel: 201-408-4048
E-mail: info@renaissancehouse.net
Web Site: www.renaissancehouse.net
Key Personnel
Pres: Sam Laredo *E-mail:* laredo@renaissancehouse.net
VP & Exec Ed: Raquel Benatar *E-mail:* raquel@renaissancehouse.net
Founded: 1991
Book developer & publisher of high quality illustrated children's books. Specialize in Spanish bilingual market. Works with more than 60 illustrators. Offers editorial services, translations, illustrations, project development & management.
ISBN Prefix(es): 978-1-56492
Number of titles published annually: 30 Print
Total Titles: 150 Print

Research & Education Association (REA)
61 Ethel Rd W, Piscataway, NJ 08854
Tel: 732-819-8880 *Fax:* 732-819-8808 (orders)
E-mail: info@rea.com
Web Site: www.rea.com
Key Personnel
Publr: Pamela Weston *E-mail:* pweston@rea.com
Founded: 1959
Professional books, secondary & college study guides & test preparation books, biology, business, engineering, mathematics, general science, history, social sciences, accounting & computer science.
ISBN Prefix(es): 978-0-87891; 978-0-7386
Number of titles published annually: 50 Print; 10 CD-ROM; 5 Audio
Total Titles: 1,200 Print; 26 CD-ROM; 7 Audio

Research Press
2612 N Mattis Ave, Champaign, IL 61822
SAN: 203-381X
Mailing Address: PO Box 7886, Dept 11-W, Champaign, IL 61826
Tel: 217-352-3273 *Toll Free Tel:* 800-519-2707 *Fax:* 217-352-1221
E-mail: rp@researchpress.com; orders@researchpress.com
Web Site: www.researchpress.com
Key Personnel
Chmn of the Bd: Cynthia Parkinson Martin
Pres: Judy Parkinson *E-mail:* jparkinson@researchpress.com
Mng Ed & Rts & Perms: Karen Steiner
Busn Mgr: Deborah Wilcoxon
Prodn Mgr: Jeff Helgesen
Founded: 1968
ISBN Prefix(es): 978-0-87822
Number of titles published annually: 4 Print
Total Titles: 200 Print; 2 Audio
Foreign Rep(s): Eurospan (Africa, Asia-Pacific, Caribbean, Europe, Latin America, Middle East, UK)

Resilient Publishing
406 S Third St, Boise, ID 83702
Tel: 208-258-9544
E-mail: submissions@resilientpublishing.com
Web Site: www.resilientpublishing.com; www.facebook.com/ResilientPub
Key Personnel
CEO: Lynn Hardy
Mktg & PR Support: Kate Delano-Condax Decker
Tech Ed: Phil Athens; Angela Gaudioso
Graphic Designer & Tech Support: Robert Morrissey
Cover Artist: Jeff Sharpton
Founded: 2009
Commitment fee $299. Authors receive 75% of income from bound book sales & 65% of income from ebook sales.
ISBN Prefix(es): 978-1-936408; 978-0-9841902; 978-1-937703; 978-0-9843669; 978-0-9845045
Number of titles published annually: 15 Print; 15 Online; 15 E-Book; 2 Audio
Total Titles: 40 Print; 40 Online; 40 E-Book
Distributor for Anderson Design; Brynwood Publishing
Membership(s): Idaho Writers Guild

§Revell
Division of Baker Publishing Group
PO Box 6287, Grand Rapids, MI 49516-6287
SAN: 203-3801
Tel: 616-676-9185 *Toll Free Tel:* 800-877-2665; 800-679-1957 *Fax:* 616-676-9573
Web Site: www.bakerpublishinggroup.com
Key Personnel
Pres: Dwight Baker
Edit Dir: Jennifer Leep
Mng Ed: Kristin Kornoelje
Prodn & ISBN Contact: Robert Bol
Rts & Perms & Intl Rts: Marilyn Gordon
Founded: 1870
Religious publisher.
ISBN Prefix(es): 978-0-8007
Number of titles published annually: 100 Print
Total Titles: 5 Audio
Imprints: Spire Books
Foreign Rep(s): Christian Art (South Africa); David C Cook Distribution (Canada); Marston Book Services Ltd (Europe, UK); Soul Distributors Ltd (New Zealand)
Shipping Address: 6030 E Fulton Rd, Ada, MI 49301

§Review & Herald Publishing Association
55 W Oak Ridge Dr, Hagerstown, MD 21740
Tel: 301-393-3000 *Toll Free Tel:* 800-234-7630; 800-456-3991 *Fax:* 301-393-3222 (book div)
Web Site: www.reviewandherald.com; www.rhpa.org
Key Personnel
Pres: Mark B Thomas
Founded: 1849
Religion (Seventh-day Adventist), health, nutrition & education.
ISBN Prefix(es): 978-0-8280
Number of titles published annually: 43 Print
Total Titles: 1,600 Print; 2 CD-ROM; 10 Audio
Foreign Rep(s): Stanborough Press Ltd (England)
Membership(s): Music Publishers Association

Lynne Rienner Publishers Inc
1800 30 St, Suite 314, Boulder, CO 80301
SAN: 683-1869
Tel: 303-444-6684 *Fax:* 303-444-0824
E-mail: questions@rienner.com; cservice@rienner.com
Web Site: www.rienner.com
Key Personnel
CEO & Pres: Lynne C Rienner
Dir, Mktg & Sales: Sally Glover *E-mail:* sglover@rienner.com
Sr Acqs Ed, Political Sci & Intl Rel: Marie-Claire Antoine
Cust Serv Mgr: Patty Troiano
Founded: 1984
Scholarly & reference books & journals, college textbooks; comparative politics, US politics, international relations, sociology, Third World literature & literary criticism.
ISBN Prefix(es): 978-1-56549; 978-0-931477; 978-1-55587; 978-0-89410; 978-1-58826; 978-1-935049 (FirstForumPress); 978-1-62637
Number of titles published annually: 70 Print
Total Titles: 1,050 Print
Divisions: FirstForumPress (scholarly monographs); Kumarian Press
Distributor for Center for US-Mexican Studies; Ayebia Clarke Publishing Ltd (African lit); St Andrews Center for Syrian Studies
Foreign Rep(s): China Publishers Marketing (China, Hong Kong, Taiwan); Co Info Pty Ltd (Australia); Cranbury International LLC (Caribbean, Latin America); Far Eastern Booksellers (Japan); Kinokuniya Co Ltd (Japan); KL Book Distributors (Malaysia); Maruzen Co Ltd (Japan); PMS Publishers Services Pte Ltd (Brunei, Indonesia, Malaysia, Singapore); Turpin Distribution (Europe); Viva (India)
Warehouse: 22883 Quicksilver Dr, Dulles, VA 20166, Contact: Vartan Ajamian
Membership(s): AAP
See separate listing for:
Kumarian Press

Rio Nuevo Publishers
451 N Bonita Ave, Tucson, AZ 85745
Mailing Address: PO Box 5250, Tucson, AZ 85703
Tel: 520-623-9558 *Toll Free Tel:* 800-969-9558 *Fax:* 520-624-5888 *Toll Free Fax:* 800-715-5888
E-mail: info@rionuevo.com (cust serv)
Web Site: www.rionuevo.com
Founded: 1999
Publisher of fine regional southwestern photographic, cooking & historical books & quality Native American books.
ISBN Prefix(es): 978-1-887896; 978-1-933855; 978-0-918080; 978-1-940322; 978-0-9700750
Number of titles published annually: 12 Print
Total Titles: 125 Print
Imprints: Rio Chico (educ & children's books)
Membership(s): Society of Children's Book Writers & Illustrators

Rising Sun Publishing
PO Box 70906, Marietta, GA 30007-0906
Tel: 770-518-0369 *Toll Free Tel:* 800-524-2813 *Fax:* 770-587-0862
E-mail: info@rspublishing.com
Web Site: www.rspublishing.com
Key Personnel
CFO: Mychal Wynn
Founded: 1982
Primary focus is educational training & materials.
ISBN Prefix(es): 978-1-880463
Number of titles published annually: 5 Print
Total Titles: 32 Print; 4 Audio

River City Publishing LLC
1719 Mulberry St, Montgomery, AL 36106
Tel: 334-265-6753 *Fax:* 334-265-8880
E-mail: sales@rivercitypublishing.com
Web Site: rivercitypublishing.com
Key Personnel
Publr: Carolyn Newman *E-mail:* cjnewman@rivercitypublishing.com
Ed: Fran Norris *E-mail:* fnorris@rivercitypublishing.com
Sales Mgr: Preston Williams *E-mail:* pwilliams@rivercitypublishing.com
Founded: 1989
Acquisition, editing, design, composition, marketing & sales of new books. Regional fiction & narrative nonfiction, especially books about the South, civil rights, folk art, contemporary fiction, regionally related travel history.
ISBN Prefix(es): 978-1-881320; 978-0-9622815; 978-1-57966; 978-0-913515; 978-1-880216
Number of titles published annually: 4 Print; 4 E-Book
Total Titles: 200 Print
Imprints: Elliott & Clark Publishing; River City Kids; Starrhill Press
Membership(s): Southern Independent Booksellers Alliance

River Road Press LLC
9 Dakin, New Orleans, LA 70121
Mailing Address: PO Box 125, Metairie, LA 70001
Tel: 504-722-8139
Web Site: riverroadpress.com
Key Personnel
Publr: Scott Campbell *E-mail:* scott@riverroadpress.com
Prodn Dir: Terry Callaway
Ed: Katy Doll; Lyndsey Reynolds
Illus: Julie Dupre Buckner
Founded: 2014
Boutique publisher, committed to publishing the highest quality books, encouraging collaboration & artistic partnership with its authors, illustrators, photographers & artists. Seek titles that appeal to niche markets. Full service company, from ms to finished book, including ms review, editing, proofreading, typesetting & formatting, design & illustration, paper printing & binding, shipping, warehousing, publicity & distribution. Assists authors & illustrators with conducting successful interviews & getting the most out of book signings.
ISBN Prefix(es): 978-1-941879
Number of titles published annually: 10 Print
Total Titles: 7 Print
Warehouse: Gallagher Records Management, 5301 Jefferson Hwy, New Orleans, LA 70123, Contact: Mike Barattini *Tel:* 504-940-1252 *E-mail:* records@galtrans.com
Distribution Center: Forest Sales & Distributing Co, 139 Jean Marie St, Reserve, LA 70084, Contact: Rob Schauffler *Tel:* 958-479-1456

§Riverdale Avenue Books (RAB)
5676 Riverdale Ave, Bronx, NY 10471
Tel: 212-279-6418
E-mail: customerservice@riverdaleavebooks.com
Web Site: www.riverdaleavebooks.com
Key Personnel
Publr: Lori Perkins
Founded: 2012
Hybrid publisher of fiction & nonfiction, epubns, print & audio.
ISBN Prefix(es): 978-1-936833 (Magnus); 978-1-62601 (RAB)
Number of titles published annually: 60 Print; 60 Online; 60 E-Book; 10 Audio
Total Titles: 230 Print; 230 Online; 230 E-Book; 20 Audio
Imprints: Dagger (mystery/thriller); Holler; RAB Afraid; RAB Desire (erotica & romance); RAB Gaming; RAB Pop (pop culture); RAB SFF (science fiction fantasy); RAB Sports; RAB Truth (erotic memoir line); RAB Verve (lifestyle); Riverdale/Magnus (LGBTQ titles)
Foreign Rights: Linda Biagli (worldwide)

§Riverhead Books
Imprint of Penguin Group USA, A Penguin Random House Company
375 Hudson St, New York, NY 10014
Tel: 212-366-2000
Web Site: www.penguin.com/publishers/riverhead
Key Personnel
Pres & Publr: Geoffrey Kloske
VP & Edit Dir: Rebecca Saletan
VP & Ed-in-Chief: Sarah McGrath
VP & Exec Ed: Cal Morgan
Exec Ed: Jake Morrissey; Courtney Young
VP, Assoc Publr & Dir, Mktg: Kate Stark
VP, Assoc Publr & Dir, Publicity: Jynne Dilling Martin
Art Dir: Helen Yentus
Assoc Dir, Publicity: Katharine Freeman
Asst Dir, Publicity: Claire McGinnis
Sr Publicity Mgr: Liz Hohenadel
Publicist: Glory Plata
Ed: Laura Perciasepe
Founded: 1994
ISBN Prefix(es): 978-1-57322
Number of titles published annually: 40 Print
Total Titles: 115 Print
Advertising Agency: Mesa Group

Riverside Publishing, see Houghton Mifflin Harcourt Assessments

Rizzoli International Publications Inc
Subsidiary of RCS Rizzoli Corp New York
300 Park Ave S, 4th fl, New York, NY 10010-5399
Tel: 212-387-3400 *Toll Free Tel:* 800-522-6657 (orders only) *Fax:* 212-387-3535
E-mail: publicity@rizzoliusa.com
Web Site: www.rizzoliusa.com
Key Personnel
VP & Publr: Charles Miers
VP, Sales & Mktg Opers: Jennifer deForest Pierson
Exec Dir, Publicity: Pam Sommers
Assoc Publr, HLLA, Universe & Welcome Books: Jim Muschett
Assoc Publr, Universe Books, Calendars & Licensing: Robb Pearlman
Creative Dir: Dung Ngo
Dir, Prodn: Maria Pia Gramaglia
Dir, Spec Sales & Fulfillment: Tracey Petitt
Assoc Publr: David Morton
Assoc Dir, Prodn: Kaija Markoe
Intl Sales Dir: Shanta Inshiqaq
Trade Sales Dir: John Deen
Assoc Dir, Publicity: Jessica Napp
Client Publr Sales Mgr: Sarah Carstens
Mktg Mgr, Creative Servs & Soc/New Media: Linda Pricci
Foreign Sales Mgr: Jerry Hoffnagle
Intl Sales Mgr: Susan Masry
Prodn Mgr: Susan Masry
Sr Ed, Ex Libris: Alessandra Lusardi

Publicist: Nora Heneghan
Founded: 1974
Fine arts, architecture, photography, decorative arts, cookbooks, gardening & landscape design, fashion & sports.
ISBN Prefix(es): 978-0-8478; 978-0-941807; 978-1-932183; 978-1-59962
Number of titles published annually: 100 Print
Imprints: Ex Libris; Flammarion; Hardie Grant; Marsilio; RCS Libri; Rizzoli, New York; Skira Rizzoli; Universe; Welcome Enterprises Inc
Distributed by Penguin Random House
Distributor for Editions Flammarion; Skira Editore; Smith Street Books
Advertising Agency: Rizzoli Graphic Studios
Orders to: Penguin Random House Publisher Services, 400 Hahn Rd, Westminster, MD 21157 *Toll Free Tel:* 800-733-3000 *Toll Free Fax:* 800-659-2436; Penguin Random House of Canada Ltd, 2775 Mattheson Blvd E, Mississaugua, ON L4W 4P7, Canada *Toll Free Tel:* 800-733-3000 *Toll Free Fax:* 800-659-2436
Returns: Penguin Random House, 1019 N State Rd 47, Crawfordsville, IN 47933; Penguin Random House of Canada Ltd, 2775 Mattheson Blvd E, Mississaugua, ON L4W 4P7, Canada *Toll Free Tel:* 800-733-3000 *Toll Free Fax:* 800-659-2436
See separate listing for:
Universe Publishing
Welcome Enterprises Inc

The RoadRunner Press
124 NW 32 St, Oklahoma City, OK 73118
Mailing Address: PO Box 2564, Oklahoma City, OK 73101
Tel: 405-524-6205 *Fax:* 405-524-6312
E-mail: info@theroadrunnerpress.com; orders@theroadrunnerpress.com
Web Site: www.theroadrunnerpress.com
Key Personnel
Publr & Ed: Jeanne Devlin *E-mail:* jeanne@theroadrunnerpress.com
Dir, Sales & Mktg: Michael Hollman
Founded: 2011
Small indie publishing house specializing in quality young adult fiction & regional nonfiction as well as select nonfiction & literary fiction with an emphasis on Native American voices from the American West.
ISBN Prefix(es): 978-1-937054
Number of titles published annually: 10 Print; 6 E-Book; 1 Audio
Total Titles: 29 Print; 8 E-Book
Imprints: Max Books; Red River Books
Foreign Rep(s): Fitzhenry & Whiteside (Canada)
Billing Address: PO Box 2564, Oklahoma City, OK 73101
Returns: Aero Corp, 1377 Tefft Ct, Saline, MI 48176
Warehouse: Aero Corp, 1377 Tefft Ct, Saline, MI 48176
Membership(s): ALA; The Children's Book Council; Independent Book Publishers Association; Midwest Independent Publishing Association; Mountains & Plains Independent Publishers Association; New Mexico Book Association; Publishers Association of the West; Western Writers of America

Roaring Brook Press
Member of Macmillan Children's Publishing Group
175 Fifth Ave, New York, NY 10010
Tel: 646-307-5151
Web Site: us.macmillan.com/publishers/roaring-brook-press
Key Personnel
Publr: Simon Boughton
Edit & Creative Dir: Mark Siegel
Exec Ed: Connie Hsu
Exec Ed, First Second Books: Calista Brill *Tel:* 646-307-5386
Assoc Ed: Emily Feinberg
Asst Ed: Claire Dorsett
Founded: 2002
ISBN Prefix(es): 978-0-7613; 978-1-59643
Number of titles published annually: 50 Print
Imprints: First Second Books

Roaring Forties Press
1053 Santa Fe Ave, Berkeley, CA 94706
Tel: 510-527-5461
E-mail: info@roaringfortiespress.com
Web Site: www.roaringfortiespress.com
Key Personnel
Founder & Publr: Deirdre Greene *E-mail:* dmg@roaringfortiespress.com; Nigel Quinney *E-mail:* nq@roaringfortiespress.com
Publisher of literary nonfiction & travel books with a twist.
ISBN Prefix(es): 978-0-9766706; 978-0-9777429; 978-0-9823410; 978-1-938901; 978-0-9843165
Number of titles published annually: 4 Print; 4 E-Book
Total Titles: 21 Print; 70 E-Book
Distribution Center: Legato Publishers Group/PGW, 1700 Fourth St, Berkeley, CA 94710 *Tel:* 510-809-3700 *Toll Free Tel:* 800-788-3123 *Fax:* 510-809-3777 *Web Site:* www.pgw.com
Perseus Books Group UK, 69-70 Temple Chambers, 3-7 Temple Ave, London EC4Y 0HP, United Kingdom *Tel:* (020) 7353 7771 *Fax:* (020) 7353 7786 *E-mail:* enquiries@perseusbooks.co.uk *Web Site:* www.perseusbooks.com
Membership(s): Independent Book Publishers Association

RockBench Publishing Corp
6101 Stillmeadow Dr, Nashville, TN 37211-6518
SAN: 855-5559
Tel: 615-831-2277 *Fax:* 615-831-2212
E-mail: info@rockbench.com
Key Personnel
Acqs Ed: David C Baker *E-mail:* david@rockbench.com
Circ Mgr: Jane Lawrence
Royalties: Julie Warren
Founded: 2008
Publish courageous thought leadership content for the business community.
ISBN Prefix(es): 978-1-60544
Number of titles published annually: 7 Print; 5 E-Book; 2 Audio
Total Titles: 14 Print; 5 E-Book
Advertising Agency: faceoutstudio, 520 SW Powerhouse Dr, Suite 628, Bend, OR 97702-1295, Pres: Mr Torrey Sharp *Tel:* 541-323-3220 *Fax:* 541-323-3221 *E-mail:* torrey@faceoutstudio.com *Web Site:* www.faceoutstudio.com
Membership(s): The Association of Publishers for Special Sales; Independent Book Publishers Association

The Rockefeller University Press
Unit of Rockefeller University
950 Third Ave, 2nd fl, New York, NY 10022
Tel: 212-327-7938 *Fax:* 212-319-1081
E-mail: rupress@rockefeller.edu
Web Site: www.rupress.org
Key Personnel
Fin Dir: Ray Fastiggi *Tel:* 212-327-8567 *E-mail:* fastigg@rockefeller.edu
Prodn Dir: Robert J O'Donnell *Tel:* 212-327-8545 *E-mail:* odonner@rockefeller.edu
Mktg Assoc: Laraine Karl *E-mail:* lkarl@rockefeller.edu
Founded: 1906
Currently publishes biomedical journals & books.
ISBN Prefix(es): 978-0-87470
Number of titles published annually: 1 Print
Total Titles: 8 Print; 3 Online; 6 Audio
Foreign Rep(s): iGroup Asia Pacific Ltd (Asia-Pacific)
Membership(s): AAP Professional & Scholarly Publishing Division; Association of American University Presses; Association of Learned & Professional Society Publishers; Society for Scholarly Publishing

RockHill Publishing LLC
PO Box 62241, Virginia Beach, VA 23466-2241
Tel: 757-692-2021
E-mail: jlh@rockhillpublishing.com
Web Site: rockhillpublishing.com
Key Personnel
Publr: James L Hill *E-mail:* jlhill@rockhillpublishing.com
Founded: 2013
Independent publishing house.
ISBN Prefix(es): 978-1-945286
Number of titles published annually: 3 Print; 3 Online; 3 E-Book
Total Titles: 7 Print; 7 Online; 7 E-Book
Distributed by The Ishmael Tree (titles in Arabic)
Foreign Rights: ARC Mohammed International LLC (Gigi Ishmael) (worldwide)
Membership(s): Independent Book Publishers Association

Rocky Mountain Mineral Law Foundation
9191 Sheridan Blvd, Suite 203, Westminster, CO 80031
Tel: 303-321-8100 *Fax:* 303-321-7657
E-mail: info@rmmlf.org
Web Site: www.rmmlf.org
Key Personnel
Exec Dir: Stevia Walther *Tel:* 303-321-8100 ext 101
Dir, Pubns: Margo MacDonnell *Tel:* 303-321-8100 ext 116
Assoc Dir: Frances Hartogh *Tel:* 303-321-8100 ext 107; Mark Holland *Tel:* 303-321-8100 ext 106 *E-mail:* mholland@rmmlf.org
Founded: 1955
Natural resources & legal education.
ISBN Prefix(es): 978-0-929047; 978-1-882047; 978-1-943497
Number of titles published annually: 10 Print
Total Titles: 81 Print; 1 CD-ROM

Rod & Staff Publishers Inc
Hwy 172, Crockett, KY 41413
Mailing Address: PO Box 3, Crockett, KY 41413-0003
Tel: 606-522-4348 *Fax:* 606-522-4896 *Toll Free Fax:* 800-643-1244 (US orders)
Key Personnel
Busn Mgr: John Martin
Founded: 1958
Religious storybooks; church, Sunday & Christian school materials & tracts.
ISBN Prefix(es): 978-0-7399
Number of titles published annually: 20 Print
Total Titles: 700 Print

Rodale Inc
400 S Tenth St, Emmaus, PA 18049
SAN: 200-2477
Tel: 610-967-5171 *Toll Free Tel:* 866-387-0509
E-mail: bookmarketing@rodale.com; bookpublicity@rodale.com
Web Site: www.rodale.com
Key Personnel
Chmn & CEO: Maria Rodale
EVP & COO: Beth Beuhler
EVP & CFO: Stephen Twilliger
Chief Ad Offr: Ronan Gardiner
Chief Content Offr: Adam Campbell
VP & Publr: Gail Gonzales
Assoc Publr & Dir, Mktg & Publicity: Jason Wells
EVP, Gen Coun & Chief Admin Offr: Paul McGinley

SVP, Mktg: Joyce Shirer
Group Edit Dir: Bill Strickland
Online Ed, RodaleWellness.com: Suzee Skwiot
Sr Mgr, Communs: Susan Turner
Founded: 1932 (by J I Rodale)
Adult trade titles in health & wellness, fitness & sports, cooking, gardening, spirituality & nature.
ISBN Prefix(es): 978-0-87857; 978-1-57954; 978-0-87596; 978-1-59486; 978-1-59486; 978-1-60529; 978-1-60961; 978-1-62336
Number of titles published annually: 75 Print
Imprints: Rodale Kids; Rodale Wellness
Branch Office(s)
733 Third Ave, 8th fl, New York, NY 10017-3204 *Tel:* 212-697-2040 *Fax:* 212-682-2237
Distributed by Macmillan (US); Pan Macmillan (worldwide exc Canada & US)
Orders to: MPS Distribution Center, 16365 James Madison Hwy, Gordonsville, VA 22942-8501 *Toll Free Tel:* 888-330-8477 *Toll Free Fax:* 800-672-2054; Raincoast Books, 2440 Viking Way, Richmond, BC V6V 1N2, Canada *Toll Free Tel:* 800-663-5714 *Toll Free Fax:* 800-565-3770 *E-mail:* customerservice@raincoast.com

Roman Catholic Books
Division of Catholic Media Apostolate Inc
PO Box 2286, Fort Collins, CO 80522-2286
Tel: 970-490-2735 *Fax:* 904-493-8781
Web Site: www.booksforcatholics.com
Key Personnel
Pres: Roger A McCaffrey *E-mail:* cxpeditor@gmail.com
VP, Mktg: Maureen Williamson *E-mail:* maureen@intrepidgroup.com
Founded: 1981
Traditional Catholic books.
ISBN Prefix(es): 978-0-912141; 978-1-929291; 978-0-9793540; 978-1-934888
Number of titles published annually: 10 Print
Total Titles: 270 Print

Roncorp Music
Division of Northeastern Music Publications Inc
PO Box 517, Glenmoore, PA 19343
Tel: 610-942-2370 *Toll Free Tel:* 866-385-8446 *Fax:* 610-942-0660
E-mail: info@nemusicpub.com
Web Site: www.nemusicpub.com
Key Personnel
Pres: Randy Navarre
Founded: 1978
Music & music texts.
ISBN Prefix(es): 978-0-939103
Number of titles published annually: 15 Print
Total Titles: 300 Print

Ronin Publishing Inc
PO Box 3436, Oakland, CA 94609
Tel: 510-420-3669 *Fax:* 510-420-3672
E-mail: ronin@roninpub.com
Web Site: www.roninpub.com
Key Personnel
Publr: Dr Beverly Potter *E-mail:* beverly@roninpub.com
Founded: 1983
Small, independent publisher in San Francisco Bay Area.
ISBN Prefix(es): 978-0-914171; 978-1-57951
Number of titles published annually: 8 Print; 8 E-Book
Total Titles: 125 Print; 100 E-Book; 2 Audio
Imprints: And/Or Press; Books for Independent Minds
Foreign Rep(s): PGW (worldwide)
Distribution Center: Publishers Group West, 1700 Fourth St, Berkeley, CA 94710 *Tel:* 510-809-3700 *Fax:* 510-809-3777 *E-mail:* info@pgw.com *Web Site:* www.pgw.com

The Rosen Publishing Group Inc
29 E 21 St, New York, NY 10010
SAN: 203-3720
Toll Free Tel: 800-237-9932 *Toll Free Fax:* 888-436-4643
E-mail: info@rosenpub.com
Web Site: www.rosenpublishing.com
Key Personnel
Pres: Roger Rosen
Founded: 1950
Hardcover, library editions, vocational guidance; personal guidance; music & art catalogs; drug abuse prevention, self-esteem development, values & ethics, new international writing, multicultural, African heritage, graphic nonfiction, curriculum related nonfiction. Grades PreK-12.
ISBN Prefix(es): 978-0-8239; 978-1-4042; 978-1-4358; 978-1-60851; 978-1-60852; 978-1-60853; 978-1-60854; 978-1-61511; 978-1-61512; 978-1-61513; 978-1-61514; 978-1-61530; 978-1-61531; 978-1-61532; 978-1-61533; 978-1-4488; 978-1-4777; 978-1-4824; 978-1-4994; 978-1-68048; 978-1-5081
Number of titles published annually: 200 Print
Total Titles: 2,000 Print
Imprints: Brittanica Educational Publishing; Editorial Buenas Letras; KidHaven Press; Gareth Stevens Publishing; Greenhaven Press®; Lucent Books®; Power Kids Press; Rosen Central; Rosen Digital; Rosen Young Adult; Windmall Books
Divisions: Rosen Classroom Books & Materials
Warehouse: Maple Logistics Solutions, York Distribution Ctr, 60 Grumbacher Rd, York, PA 17405
See separate listing for:
Gareth Stevens Publishing
Greenhaven Press®
Lucent Books®

§RosettaBooks
55 Broadway, Suite 2002, New York, NY 10006
Tel: 646-274-1970 *Fax:* 212-977-5997 (e-fax)
E-mail: rights@rosettabooks.com; production@rosettabooks.com
Web Site: www.rosettabooks.com
Key Personnel
CEO: Arthur Klebanoff
Founded: 2001
ISBN Prefix(es): 978-0-7953
Number of titles published annually: 10 Print; 50 E-Book; 10 Audio
Total Titles: 25 Print; 800 E-Book; 40 Audio
Distribution Center: Ingram Publisher Services, One Ingram Blvd, La Vergne, TN 37086 *Toll Free Tel:* 866-400-5351 *E-mail:* ips@ingramcontent.com *Web Site:* www.ingramcontent.com SAN: 631-8630

§Ross Books
PO Box 4340, Berkeley, CA 94704-0340
Tel: 510-841-2474 *Fax:* 510-295-2531
E-mail: sales@rossbooks.com
Web Site: www.rossbooks.com
Key Personnel
Owner & Pres: Franz H Ross *E-mail:* franz@rossbooks.com
Sales: Benny Juarez
Founded: 1977
General trade books & ebooks.
ISBN Prefix(es): 978-0-89496
Number of titles published annually: 4 Print; 1 CD-ROM; 3 E-Book; 1 Audio
Total Titles: 26 Print; 2 CD-ROM; 2 Online; 6 E-Book; 2 Audio
Imprints: Baldar
Membership(s): Book Promotion Forum

§Rothstein Associates Inc
4 Arapaho Rd, Brookfield, CT 06804-3104
Tel: 203-740-7400 *Toll Free Tel:* 888-768-4783 *Fax:* 203-740-7401
E-mail: info@rothstein.com
Web Site: www.rothstein.com; www.rothsteinpublishing.com
Key Personnel
Pres & CEO: Philip Jan Rothstein *E-mail:* pjr@rothstein.com
Chief Mktg Offr: Mr Glyn Davies *Tel:* 415-259-9137 *E-mail:* glyndavies@rothstein.com
Exec Ed: Kristen Noakes-Fry *Tel:* 727-258-8389 *E-mail:* knfwriter@rothstein.com
Founded: 1985
Publisher of digital & print content in business continuity, risk management, crisis communications, crisis management & emergency management for professionals & students.
ISBN Prefix(es): 978-0-9641648; 978-1-931332; 978-1-944480
Number of titles published annually: 15 Print; 9 CD-ROM; 25 E-Book
Total Titles: 80 Print; 36 CD-ROM; 30 E-Book
Divisions: NDY Publishing; Rothstein Publishing
Foreign Rep(s): iGroup.net (Asia-Pacific, Australasia)

§The Rough Notes Co Inc
Subsidiary of Insurance Publishing Plus Corp
11690 Technology Dr, Carmel, IN 46032-5600
Tel: 317-582-1600 *Toll Free Tel:* 800-428-4384 (cust serv) *Fax:* 317-816-1000 *Toll Free Fax:* 800-321-1909
E-mail: rnc@roughnotes.com
Web Site: www.roughnotes.com
Key Personnel
EVP & COO: Sam Berman
Ad & Natl Sales Dir: Eric Hall *E-mail:* ehall@roughnotes.com
Founded: 1878
Technical/educational reference material specific to the property/casualty insurance industry.
ISBN Prefix(es): 978-1-56461; 978-0-942326; 978-1-877723
Number of titles published annually: 10 Print
Total Titles: 40 Print; 4 Online
Advertising Agency: AdCom Group

Round Table Companies
Subsidiary of Writers of the Round Table Press Inc
1027 Kenton Rd, Deerfield, IL 60015
Mailing Address: PO Box 511, Highland Park, IL 60035
Tel: 949-375-1006 *Fax:* 815-346-2398
Web Site: www.roundtablecompanies.com
Key Personnel
Pres: Corey Michael Blake *Tel:* 847-682-3493 *E-mail:* corey@roundtablecompanies.com
Organizational Off Architect: Mike Winicour *E-mail:* mike@roundtablecompanies.com
Founded: 1996
Round Table Companies (RTC) support leaders interested in changing the world. Clients see their purpose brought to life while their thought leadership brand infrastructure is executed & their community built. Core values are brilliance, love, joy, courage, momentum, honesty, community & growth which create an atmosphere where transformation occurs through the magic of storytelling & the impact of human connection.
This publisher has indicated that 90% of their product line is author subsidized.
ISBN Prefix(es): 978-0-61066; 978-0-9814545; 978-0-9822206; 978-1-939418
Number of titles published annually: 6 Print; 6 E-Book
Total Titles: 99 Print; 66 E-Book
Imprints: Round Table Comics
Foreign Rights: Graal Literary Agency (Albania, Bulgaria, Croatia, Czech Republic, Estonia, Hungary, Latvia, Lithuania, Poland, Romania, Serbia, Slovakia, Slovenia); Grayhawk Agency (China, Indonesia, Taiwan, Thailand, Vietnam); Dany Hong Agency (Korea); International Ed-

itors' Co (Argentina, Brazil, Portugal, Spain); Tuttle-Mori Agency Inc (Japan)
Shipping Address: Lightning Source Inc, 1246 Heil Quaker Blvd, La Vergne, TN 37086, Content Acq Publr Sales Rep: Pam Dover *Tel:* 615-213-4437 *Fax:* 615-213-4735 *E-mail:* pam.dover@ingramcontent.com
Distribution Center: Lightning Source Inc, 14 Ingram Blvd, PO Box 3006, La Vergne, TN 37086-1986, Content Acq Publr Sales Rep: Pam Dover *Tel:* 615-213-4437 *Fax:* 615-213-4735 *E-mail:* pam.dover@ingramcontent.com
Membership(s): Independent Book Publishers Association

Routledge
Member of Taylor & Francis Group, an Informa Business
711 Third Ave, New York, NY 10017
SAN: 213-196X
Tel: 212-216-7800 *Toll Free Tel:* 800-634-7064 (order enquiries, cust servs) *Fax:* 212-564-7854
Web Site: www.routledge.com
Founded: 1836
Academic books in the humanities, social & behavioral sciences. Academic reference. Professional titles in architecture, education & the behavioral sciences.
ISBN Prefix(es): 978-0-915202 (formerly Accelerated Development); 978-1-55959 (formerly Accelerated Development); 978-0-87630 (formerly Brunner-Routledge); 978-1-57958 (formerly Fitzroy Dearborn); 978-0-8240 (formerly Garland); 978-0-8153 (formerly Garland); 978-0-415; 978-0-87830 (Theatre Arts); 978-1-85000 (formerly RoutledgeFalmer); 978-0-7007 (formerly Routledge Curzon); 978-0-419 (formerly Spon); 978-0-946653 (formerly Europa); 978-1-85743 (formerly Europa); 978-0-7494 (formerly Kogan Page); 978-90-5701 (formerly Gordon & Breach); 978-1-58391 (formerly Brunner-Routledge); 978-1-88496 (formerly Fitzroy Dearborn); 978-90-5702 (formerly Harwood Academic); 978-3-7186 (formerly Harwood Academic); 978-90-5823 (formerly Harwood Academic); 978-0-19713 (formerly Routledge Curzon); 978-0-72860 (formerly Routledge Curzon); 978-0-75070 (formerly RoutledgeFalmer)
Number of titles published annually: 2,000 Print; 2,000 Online; 2,000 E-Book
Total Titles: 33,000 Print; 21,000 Online; 21,000 E-Book
Imprints: CRC Press; Garland Science
Sales Office(s): Taylor & Francis, 6000 Broken Sound Pkwy, Suite 300, Boca Raton, FL 33487, VP, Sales: Dennis Weiss *Tel:* 561-994-0555 *Toll Free Tel:* 800-272-7737 *Fax:* 561-989-8732 *Toll Free Fax:* 800-374-3401
Foreign Office(s): 2 Park Sq, Milton Park, Abingdon Oxon OX14 4RN, United Kingdom, Group Sales Dir: Christoph Chesher *Tel:* (020) 7017 6000 *Fax:* (020) 7017 6699 *E-mail:* book.orders@tandf.co.uk
Warehouse: Taylor & Francis, 7625 Empire Dr, Florence, KY 41042-2919 *Toll Free Tel:* 800-634-7064 *Toll Free Fax:* 800-248-4724 *E-mail:* orders@taylorandfrancis.com

Rowman & Littlefield Publishers Inc
4501 Forbes Blvd, Suite 200, Lanham, MD 20706
SAN: 208-5143
Tel: 301-459-3366 *Toll Free Tel:* 800-462-6420 (cust serv) *Fax:* 301-429-5748
Web Site: rowman.com
Key Personnel
Group CEO & Pres: Jed Lyons
CFO: George Franzak
Pres, Academic & Prof Div: Oliver Gadsby
EVP, Fin & Opers: Robert Marsh
SVP & Exec Ed: Jonathan Sisk *E-mail:* jsisk@rowman.com
Trade Publr: Jim Childs
Rts & Perms Dir: Clare Cox *E-mail:* ccox@rowman.com
Sales Dir: Sheila Burnettt *Tel:* 301-459-3366 ext 5606 *E-mail:* sburnett@rowman.com
Exec Ed: Charles Harmon
Sr Acqs Ed: Leanne Silverman *Tel:* 303-543-7835 ext 312 *E-mail:* lsilverman@rowman.com
Founded: 1949
Policy studies; supplemental books & monographs, academic publisher.
ISBN Prefix(es): 978-0-8476; 978-1-56699; 978-0-7425; 978-1-4422; 978-0-87471; 978-0-9632978; 978-1-888051; 978-1-931890; 978-1-933494; 978-1-936283; 978-1-61281; 978-1-4616; 978-1-4617; 978-1-62093
Number of titles published annually: 350 Print
Total Titles: 2,000 Print
Foreign Office(s): 10 Thornbury Rd, Plymouth, Devon PL6 7PP, United Kingdom, Contact: Suzanne Wheatley *Tel:* (05602) 698234 *Fax:* (05602) 698234 *E-mail:* swheatley@rowman.com
Foreign Rep(s): APD Singapore Pte Ltd (Brunei, Cambodia, Indonesia, Laos, Malaysia, Singapore, Thailand, Vietnam); Aristotle House (Simons Watts) (Cameroon, Ethiopia, The Gambia, Ghana, Kenya, Malawi, Mauritius, Nigeria, Tanzania, Uganda); Asia Publishers Service Ltd (China, Hong Kong, Philippines, Taiwan); Avicenna Partnership Ltd (Middle East, North Africa); Co Info Pty Ltd (Australia, New Zealand, Papua New Guinea); Cranbury International LLC (Caribbean, Central America, Mexico, Puerto Rico, South America); Durnell Marketing Ltd (Andrew Durnell) (Europe); Juta & Co Ltd (Botswana, Lesotho, Namibia, South Africa, Swaziland, Zimbabwe); Overleaf (Bangladesh, Bhutan, India, Nepal, Sri Lanka); Publishers Representatives (Tahir Lodhi) (Pakistan); Quantum Publishing Solutions Ltd (Jim Chalmers) (UK); United Publishers Services Ltd (Japan); Wise Book Solutions (Korea)
Warehouse: 15200 NBN Way, Warehouse C, Blue Ridge Summit, PA 17214 *Tel:* 717-794-3800 *Fax:* 717-794-3803

Royal Fireworks Press
PO Box 399, Unionville, NY 10988
Tel: 845-726-4444 *Fax:* 845-726-3824
E-mail: mail@rfwp.com
Web Site: www.rfwp.com
Key Personnel
Dir, Order Dept & Cust Rel: Margaret Foley
Founded: 1977
Educational materials for gifted children, their parents & teachers; reading materials; adult literacy/education materials; fiction series for middle school: mystery & adventure; novels of growing up; young adult science fiction; youth against violence early childhood program (K-3).
ISBN Prefix(es): 978-0-89824; 978-0-88092
Number of titles published annually: 80 Print
Total Titles: 1,000 Print; 120 E-Book
Distributor for KAV Books; Silk Label Books; Trillium Press

Russell Sage Foundation
112 E 64 St, New York, NY 10065
SAN: 201-4521
Tel: 212-750-6000 *Toll Free Tel:* 800-524-6401 *Fax:* 212-371-4761
E-mail: info@rsage.org
Web Site: www.russellsage.org
Key Personnel
Pres: Sheldon Danzinger
Dir, Communs: David Haproff *Tel:* 212-750-6037
Dir, Pubns: Suzanne Nichols
Founded: 1907
Sociology, economics, political science.
ISBN Prefix(es): 978-0-87154; 978-1-61044
Number of titles published annually: 20 Print
Total Titles: 1,000 Print
Shipping Address: Chicago Distribution Center, 11030 S Langley Ave, Chicago, IL 60628 *Tel:* 773-702-7010 *Toll Free Fax:* 800-621-8476 *Web Site:* press.uchicago.edu

§Russian Information Services Inc
PO Box 567, Montpelier, VT 05601
Tel: 802-223-4955 *Toll Free Tel:* 800-639-4301
E-mail: orders@russianlife.com
Web Site: www.russianlife.com
Key Personnel
Pres & Publr: Paul E Richardson *E-mail:* paulr@russianlife.com
Founded: 1990
Publish magazines (including *Russian Life*), books, info, maps for business & independent travel to Russia.
ISBN Prefix(es): 978-1-880100
Number of titles published annually: 3 Print; 3 E-Book
Total Titles: 30 Print; 30 E-Book
Imprints: Edward & Dee

Rutgers University Press
Division of Rutgers, The State University of New Jersey
106 Somerset St, 3rd fl, New Brunswick, NJ 08901
SAN: 203-364X
Tel: 848-445-7762 *Toll Free Tel:* 800-848-6224 (orders only) *Fax:* 732-745-4935 (acqs, edit, mktg, perms & prodn) *Toll Free Fax:* 800-272-6817 (fulfillment)
Web Site: rutgerspress.rutgers.edu
Key Personnel
Dir: Micah Kleit
Assoc Dir & Ed-in-Chief: Leslie Mitchner *Tel:* 848-445-7787 *E-mail:* lmitch@rutgers.edu
Mktg & Sales Dir: Jeremy Grainger *Tel:* 848-445-7781 *E-mail:* jeremy.grainger@rutgers.edu
Prepress Dir: Marilyn A Campbell *Tel:* 848-445-7756 *E-mail:* marilync@rutgers.edu
Sr Promos Mgr: Brice Hammack *Tel:* 848-445-7765 *E-mail:* bhammack@rutgers.edu
Busn Mgr: David Flum *Tel:* 848-445-7763 *E-mail:* dflum@rutgers.edu
Cust Serv Mgr: Penny Burke *Tel:* 848-445-7788 *E-mail:* pborden@rutgers.edu
Asst to the Dir, Perms & Subs Rts Mgr & Ebook Coord: Elisabeth Maselli *Tel:* 848-445-7785 *E-mail:* esm102@rutgers.edu
Exec Ed: Kimberly Guinta *Tel:* 848-445-7786
Exec Ed, Clinical Health & Medicine: Dana Dreibelbis *Tel:* 848-445-7792 *E-mail:* dana.dreibelbis@rutgers.edu
Sr Ed: Peter Mickulas *Tel:* 848-445-7752 *E-mail:* mickulas@rutgers.edu
Prodn Ed: Carrie Hudak *Tel:* 848-445-7755 *E-mail:* carrie.hudak@rutgers.edu
Asst Ed: Lisa Boyajian *Tel:* 848-445-7791 *E-mail:* lmb333@rutgers.edu
Sr Prodn Coord: Anne Hegeman *Tel:* 848-445-7761 *E-mail:* hegeman@rutgers.edu
Prodn Coord: Jennifer Blanc-Tal *Tel:* 848-445-7764 *E-mail:* jfb131@scarletmail.rutgers.edu
Exhibit Coord/Mktg Asst: Victoria Verhowsky *Tel:* 848-445-7782 *E-mail:* victoria.verhowsky@rutgers.edu
Founded: 1936
Since its founding as a nonprofit publisher, Rutgers University Press has been dedicated to the advancement & dissemination of knowledge to scholars, students & the general reading public. An integral part of one of the leading public research & teaching universities in the US, the Press reflects & is essential to the University's missions of research, instruction & service. To carry out these goals, books are published in electronic & print format in a broad array of disciplines across the humanities, social sciences & sciences. Fulfilling its mandate to serve the people of New Jersey, books of

scholarly & popular interest on the state & surrounding region are also published. Working with authors throughout the world, the Press seeks books that meet high editorial standards, facilitate the exchange of ideas, enhance teaching & make scholarship accessible to a wide range of readers. It celebrates & affirms its role as a major cultural institution that contributes significantly to the ideas that shape the critical issues of our day.
ISBN Prefix(es): 978-0-8135
Number of titles published annually: 90 Print; 80 Online; 80 E-Book
Total Titles: 3,500 Print; 1,600 Online; 1,600 E-Book
Foreign Rep(s): Eurospan (Europe, Ireland, UK); Scholarly Book Services Inc (Canada)
Foreign Rights: McIntosh & Otis Inc (worldwide)
Returns: Ingram Book Group, One Ingram Blvd, La Vergne, TN 37086-1986 *Tel:* 615-793-5000 *Web Site:* www.ingramcontent.com
Warehouse: Ingram Book Group, One Ingram Blvd, La Vergne, TN 37086-1986 *Tel:* 615-793-5000 *Web Site:* www.ingramcontent.com
Distribution Center: Longleaf Services Inc, 116 S Boundary St, Chapel Hill, NC 27514-3808 *Tel:* 919-966-7449 *Toll Free Tel:* 800-848-6224 *Fax:* 919-962-2704 *Toll Free Fax:* 800-272-6817 *E-mail:* customerservice@longleafservices.org *Web Site:* www.longleafservices.org
Membership(s): American Association of University Presses

§Saddleback Educational Publishing
3120-A Pullman St, Costa Mesa, CA 92626
SAN: 860-0902
Tel: 714-640-5200 *Toll Free Tel:* 888-SDLBACK (735-2225); 800-637-8715 *Fax:* 714-640-5297 *Toll Free Fax:* 888-734-4010
E-mail: contact@sdlback.com
Web Site: www.sdlback.com
Key Personnel
Pres: Arianne McHugh
Founded: 1982
Publish high-interest, low-readabilty material for middle school & high school. Solutions for struggling learners.
ISBN Prefix(es): 978-1-56254; 978-1-59905; 978-1-61651; 978-1-60291; 978-1-62250; 978-1-62670; 978-1-63078; 978-1-68021
Number of titles published annually: 200 Print; 10 CD-ROM; 20 E-Book; 10 Audio
Total Titles: 2,000 Print; 150 CD-ROM; 400 E-Book; 150 Audio
Distributed by Children's Plus; Delaney
Distribution Center: Follett School Solutions Inc, 1340 Ridgeview Dr, McHenry, IL 60050 *Tel:* 815-759-1700 *Toll Free Tel:* 888-511-5114 (cust serv) *Fax:* 815-759-9831 *Toll Free Fax:* 800-852-5458 *E-mail:* info@follettlearning.com *Web Site:* www.follettlearning.com SAN: 169-1902
Saunders Book Co, PO Box 308, Collingwood, ON L9Y 3Z7, Canada *Tel:* 705-445-4777 *Toll Free Tel:* 800-461-9120 *Fax:* 705-445-9569 *Toll Free Fax:* 800-561-1763 *E-mail:* info@saundersbooks.ca
Membership(s): American Educational Publishers; Educational Book & Media Association

§William H Sadlier Inc
9 Pine St, New York, NY 10005
SAN: 204-0948
Tel: 212-227-2120 *Toll Free Tel:* 800-221-5175 (cust serv) *Fax:* 212-312-6080
E-mail: customerservice@sadlier.com
Web Site: www.sadlier.com
Key Personnel
Chmn of the Bd: Frank S Dinger
Treas: Raymond Sagan
Pres: William S Dinger
VP & Dir, Mktg: Alexandra Rivas-Smith
VP & Natl Field Sales Mgr: John Bonenberger
VP & Natl Sales Admin: Kevin O'Donnell
Creative Dir: Vincent Gallo
Gen Coun: Angela Dinger
Cust Serv: Melissa Gibbons
Founded: 1832
Preschool, elementary & secondary textbooks on catechetics, sacraments, reading/language arts, mathematics; adult catechetical programs.
ISBN Prefix(es): 978-0-87105; 978-0-8215; 978-1-4217
Number of titles published annually: 4 Print
Divisions: Sadlier; Sadlier-Oxford

§SAE (Society of Automotive Engineers International)
400 Commonwealth Dr, Warrendale, PA 15096-0001
SAN: 216-0811
Tel: 724-776-4841; 724-776-4970 (outside US & CN) *Toll Free Tel:* 877-606-7323 (cust serv) *Fax:* 724-776-0790 (cust serv)
E-mail: publications@sae.org; customerservice@sae.org
Web Site: www.sae.org
Key Personnel
CEO: David L Schutt
Pres: Donald Hillebrand
Founded: 1905
Scientific & technical publications.
ISBN Prefix(es): 978-0-89883; 978-1-56091; 978-0-7680; 978-1-4686
Number of titles published annually: 150 Print
Total Titles: 650 Print; 23 CD-ROM; 1 Online; 15 E-Book; 1 Audio
Branch Office(s)
1200 "G" St NW, Suite 800, Washington, DC 20005 *Tel:* 202-463-7318 *Fax:* 202-463-7319
Automotive Headquarters, 755 W Big Beaver Rd, Suite 1600, Troy, MI 48084 *Tel:* 248-273-2455 *Fax:* 248-273-2494
5 Research Dr, Greenville, SC 29607 *Tel:* 724-776-4841
Foreign Office(s): SAE International China Off, Rm 2503, Litong Plaza, No 1350 N Sichuan Rd, Hongkou District, Shanghai 200080, China *Tel:* (021) 6140 8900 *Fax:* (021) 6140 8901
Aerospace Standards Europe Off, One York St, London W1U 6PA, United Kingdom *Tel:* (020) 7034 1250 *Fax:* (020) 7034 1257
Distributor for Coordinating Research Council Inc
Foreign Rep(s): Aeromarine Vehicles (Singapore); Allied Publishers Pvt Ltd (India); Booknet Co Ltd (Thailand); Catarac (China); China National Publications (China); China Publishers Marketing (China); EBSCO Korea (Korea); Eurospan (Marc Bedwell) (Asia-Pacific exc China); Eurospan Group (Africa, Asia-Pacific, Australasia, Brazil, Europe, Middle East, Oceania); Eurospan India (India); GDI Co Ltd (Korea); IHS de Mexico (Latin America, Mexico); Kinokuniya Co Ltd (Japan); Maruzen Co Book Division (Japan); Normdocs (Russia); Pak Book Corp (Pakistan); PB for Books (Pathumthani) Co Ltd (Thailand); SAE Australasia (Australasia, Oceania); SAE Brasil (Brazil); SAE of Japan (Japan); Ta Tong Book Co Ltd (Taiwan); UBS Library Services Pte Ltd (Singapore); UBSD Distribution Sdn Bhd (Malaysia); Unifacamanu Trading Co Ltd (Taiwan); YPJ Publications & Distributors Sdn Bhd (Malaysia)

Safari Press
15621 Chemical Lane, Bldg B, Huntington Beach, CA 92649
Tel: 714-894-9080 *Toll Free Tel:* 800-451-4788 *Fax:* 714-894-4949
E-mail: info@safaripress.com
Web Site: www.safaripress.com
Key Personnel
CEO: Ludo J Wurfbain
Chief Ed: Jacque Neufeld
Founded: 1984
Specialize in big-game hunting, firearms, wingshooting, Africana & sporting; hardcover trade & limited editions.
ISBN Prefix(es): 978-0-940143; 978-1-57157
Number of titles published annually: 10 Print
Total Titles: 300 Print
Distributor for Quiller

Safer Society Foundation Inc
29 Union St, Brandon, VT 05733
Mailing Address: PO Box 340, Brandon, VT 05733-0340
Tel: 802-247-3132 *Fax:* 802-247-4233
E-mail: info@safersociety.org
Web Site: www.safersociety.org
Founded: 1985
Specialize in titles relating to the prevention & treatment of sexual abuse.
ISBN Prefix(es): 978-1-884444
Number of titles published annually: 4 Print
Total Titles: 80 Print
Imprints: Safer Society Press
Foreign Rep(s): Open Leaves Books (Australia); Visions Book Store Ltd (Canada)
Membership(s): Independent Book Publishers Association

Saga Press, see Simon & Schuster Children's Publishing

Sagamore Publishing LLC
1807 N Federal Dr, Urbana, IL 61801
SAN: 292-5788
Tel: 217-359-5940 *Toll Free Tel:* 800-327-5557 (orders) *Fax:* 217-359-5975
E-mail: web@sagamorepub.com
Web Site: www.sagamorepub.com
Key Personnel
CEO & Publr: Dr Joseph J Bannon, Sr *E-mail:* jjbannon@sagamorepub.com
Pres & Intl Rts: Peter L Bannon *E-mail:* pbannon@sagamorepub.com
Dir, Prodn & Devt: Susan M Davis *E-mail:* sdavis@sagamorepub.com
Sales & Mktg Mgr: Emily Wakefield *E-mail:* ewakefield@sagamorepub.com
Founded: 1974
ISBN Prefix(es): 978-0-915611; 978-1-57167; 978-1-58382
Number of titles published annually: 13 Print
Total Titles: 210 Print; 6 Online
Distributor for American Academy for Park & Recreation Administration
Foreign Rep(s): Gazelle Book Services Ltd (Continental Europe, Ireland, UK); HM Leisure Planning (Australia, New Zealand)

SAGE Publishing
2455 Teller Rd, Thousand Oaks, CA 91320
Toll Free Tel: 800-818-7243 *Toll Free Fax:* 800-583-2665
E-mail: info@sagepub.com
Web Site: www.sagepublishing.com
Key Personnel
Founder & Exec Chmn: Sara Miller McCune
Pres & CEO: Blaise R Simqu
Founded: 1965
SAGE Publishing is an independent company that disseminates journals, books & library products for the educational, scholarly & professional markets.
ISBN Prefix(es): 978-0-8039
Number of titles published annually: 800 Print
Imprints: Corwin Press; CQ Press; Learning Matters; Adam Matthew
Subsidiaries: Corwin Press Inc
Foreign Office(s): SAGE Publications India Pvt Ltd, B1/I-1 Mohan Cooperative Industrial Area, Mathura Rd, New Delhi 110 044, India *Tel:* (011) 4053 9222 *Fax:* (011) 4053 9234
SAGE Publications Asia-Pacific Pte Ltd, 3 Church St, Samsung Hub, Unit 10-04, Sin-

gapore 049483, Singapore *Tel:* 6220-1800 *Fax:* 6438-1008 *E-mail:* apac-librarysales@sagepub.co.uk
SAGE Publications Ltd, One Oliver's Yard, 55 City Rd, London EC1Y 1SP, United Kingdom *Tel:* (020) 7324 8500 *Fax:* (020) 7324 8600
Foreign Rep(s): Sage Publications India Pvt Ltd (India, South Asia); Sage Publications Ltd (Africa, Asia-Pacific, Europe, Middle East, UK); United Publishers Services Ltd (Japan, Korea)
See separate listing for:
CQ Press

St Andrews University Press
Subsidiary of St Andrews University
1700 Dogwood Mile, Laurinburg, NC 28352-5598
Tel: 910-277-5555 *Toll Free Tel:* 800-763-0198 *Fax:* 910-277-5020
Web Site: www.sa.edu/st-andrews-university-press
Key Personnel
Asst Ed: Madge McKeithen
Founded: 1969
ISBN Prefix(es): 978-0-932662; 978-1-879934
Number of titles published annually: 5 Print
Total Titles: 82 Print

St Augustine's Press Inc
PO Box 2285, South Bend, IN 46680-2285
Tel: 574-291-3500 *Fax:* 574-291-3700
E-mail: bruce@staugustine.net
Web Site: www.staugustine.net
Key Personnel
Pres & Publr: Bruce Fingerhut *E-mail:* bruce@staugustine.net
Prodn: Benjamin Fingerhut *Tel:* 773-983-8471 *E-mail:* benjaminfingerhut@yahoo.com
Founded: 1996
Scholarly & trade publishing in humanities.
ISBN Prefix(es): 978-1-890318; 978-1-883357; 978-1-58731
Number of titles published annually: 35 Print
Total Titles: 600 Print; 4 E-Book
Imprints: Carthage Reprints
Editorial Office(s): 17917 Killington Way, South Bend, IN 46614-9773, Contact: Bruce Fingerhut *Tel:* 574-291-3500 *E-mail:* bruce@staugustine.net
Sales Office(s): University of Chicago Press, Sales Dept, 1429 E 60 St, Chicago, IL 60637-2954, Sales Dir: John Kessler *Tel:* 773-702-7248 *Fax:* 773-702-9756 *E-mail:* jkessler@press.uchicago.edu
Distributed by University of Chicago Press
Distributor for Dumb Ox Books (publishes the Aristotelian Commentaries of Thomas Aquinas & like works); Hardwood Press (trade books, mostly in sports & regional works); New Criterion Books (poetry prize)
Foreign Rights: Jeremy Beer (worldwide exc USA)
Advertising Agency: Design Promotion
Billing Address: Chicago Distribution Center, 11030 S Langley Ave, Chicago, IL 60628-3893
Orders to: Chicago Distribution Center, 11030 S Langley Ave, Chicago, IL 60628-3893, Karen Hyzy *Tel:* 773-702-7000 *Toll Free Tel:* 800-621-2736 *Fax:* 773-702-7212 *Toll Free Fax:* 800-621-8476 *E-mail:* kh@press.uchicago.edu
Returns: Chicago Distribution Center, 11030 S Langley Ave, Chicago, IL 60628-3893
Shipping Address: Chicago Distribution Center, 11030 S Langley Ave, Chicago, IL 60628-3893, Contact: Karen Hyzy *Tel:* 773-702-7000 *Toll Free Tel:* 800-621-2736 *Fax:* 773-702-7212 *Toll Free Fax:* 800-621-8476 *E-mail:* kh@press.uchicago.edu
Warehouse: Chicago Distribution Center, 11030 S Langley Ave, Chicago, IL 60628-3893
Distribution Center: Chicago Distribution Center, 11030 S Langley Ave, Chicago, IL 60628-3893 *Toll Free Tel:* 800-621-8471 *Toll Free Fax:* 800-621-8471 *E-mail:* kh@press.uchicago.edu

Saint Herman Press
Subsidiary of Brotherhood of Saint Herman of Alaska
10 Beegum Gorge Rd, Platina, CA 96076
SAN: 661-583X
Mailing Address: PO Box 70, Platina, CA 96076-0070
Tel: 530-352-4430 *Fax:* 530-352-4432
E-mail: stherman@stherman.com
Web Site: www.stherman.com
Key Personnel
CFO: Nicholas Liebmann
Pres: Abbott Damascene
Secy: Paisius Bjerke
Founded: 1963
Publisher of books about the Orthodox Christian faith & Orthodox monasticism. Special emphasis on recent saints & spirituality, curriculum & textbooks.
ISBN Prefix(es): 978-0-938635; 978-1-887904
Number of titles published annually: 3 Print
Total Titles: 74 Print
Imprints: Brotherhood of Saint Herman of Alaska; Fr Seraphim Rose Foundation; St Herman Press; St Xenia Skete; Valaam Society of America
Distributed by Light & Life Publishing Co
Foreign Rep(s): Vladimir Ivlenkov (Australia); Orthodox Christian Books Ltd (Nicholas Chapman) (England)
Shipping Address: 4430 Hwy 36 W, Platina, CA 96076

§St James Press®
Imprint of Gale
27500 Drake Rd, Farmington Hills, MI 48331-3535
Tel: 248-699-4253 *Toll Free Tel:* 800-877-4253 (orders) *Toll Free Fax:* 877-363-4253
E-mail: gale.customerservice@cengage.com
Web Site: solutions.cengage.com/gale/publishers/imprints
Founded: 1968
ISBN Prefix(es): 978-1-55862; 978-0-912289
Number of titles published annually: 8 E-Book
Total Titles: 303 Print

Saint Johann Press
315 Schraalenburgh Rd, Haworth, NJ 07641
Tel: 201-387-1529 *Fax:* 201-501-0698
Web Site: www.stjohannpress.com
Key Personnel
Pres: David Biesel *E-mail:* d.biesel@verizon.net
VP: Diane Biesel
Dir, Sales & Promos: Deborah Brugger
Mgr, Acctg: Barbara Stinnett
Founded: 1990
Started as a book packager & consultant. Began publishing in 1998.
ISBN Prefix(es): 978-1-878282; 978-1-937943
Number of titles published annually: 12 Print
Total Titles: 120 Print
Membership(s): ALA; Combined Book Exhibit; Independent Book Publishers Association; USMC Combat Correspondents Association

St Joseph's University Press
5600 City Ave, Philadelphia, PA 19131-1395
SAN: 240-8368
Tel: 610-660-3402 *Fax:* 610-660-3412
E-mail: sjupress@sju.edu
Web Site: www.sjupress.com
Key Personnel
Dir: Mr Carmen R Croce *E-mail:* ccroce@sju.edu
Edit Dir of the Press: Rev Joseph F Chorpenning *Tel:* 610-660-1214 *E-mail:* jchorpen@sju.edu
Founded: 1971
Scholarly books on early modern Catholicism & the visual arts, regional studies (Philadelphia & environs), Jesuit studies (history, visual arts).
ISBN Prefix(es): 978-0-916101
Number of titles published annually: 5 Print
Total Titles: 78 Print
Membership(s): American Association of University Presses; Association of Jesuit University Presses

St Martin's Press, LLC
Subsidiary of Macmillan
175 Fifth Ave, New York, NY 10010
SAN: 200-2132
Tel: 646-307-5151
Web Site: us.macmillan.com/smp
Key Personnel
Pres & Publr: Sally Richardson
EVP & COO, Macmillan Trade Publg: Steve Cohen
EVP, Publr & Ed: Jennifer Enderlin
EVP, Mktg & Digital Media Strategy: Jeff Dodes
SVP, Publr of Minotaur: Andrew Martin
VP & Assoc Publr: Lisa Senz
VP, Dir of Fin: Thomas Cronin
VP, Exec Ed: Peter Wolverton
VP, Fin & Acctg: John Cusack
VP, Assoc Publr & Publg Dir, SMP Swerve: Anne Marie Tallberg
VP, Dir of Prodn/Mfg: Karen Gillis
VP, Mktg, Communs & Audience Devt: Brant Janeway
VP, Publicity & Independent Bookseller Liaison: Dori Weintraub
VP, Creative Dir, Pbks: Michael Storrings
VP, Creative Servs & Ad: Tom Thompson
Div VP, Publg Opers: Sidney Conde
Div VP, Dir of Publicity: John Murphy
Div VP, Creative Dir, Trade: Stephen Snider
Div VP, Ed-in-Chief, Trade: George Witte
Assoc Publr, Nonfiction: Laura Clark
Exec Art Dir, SMP/Minotaur: David Rotstein
Dir, Subs Rts: Kerry Nordling
Dir, Quick & Dirty Tips: Kathy Doyle
Edit Dir & Assoc Publr, Minotaur Books: Kelley Ragland
Edit Dir, Political & Current Aff: Adam Bellow
Edit Dir, Wednesday Books: Sara Goodman
Art Dir: Jimmy Iacobelli
Mktg Dir: Nancy Sheppard
Assoc Publicity Dir, Pbk/Ref Group: John Karle
Head, Thomas Dunne Books: Thomas Dunne
Sr Exec Mng Ed, Trade: Amelie Littell
Exec Mng Ed, Pbk/Ref Group: John Rounds
Exec Ed, Pbk/Ref Group: Marc Resnick
Exec Ed & Edit Dir, Romance: Monique Patterson
Exec Ed, Mgr of Concept Devt: Jennifer Weis
Exec Ed: Elizabeth Beier; Laurie Chittenden; Brenda Copeland; Hope Dellon; Elisabeth Dyssegaard; Michael Flamini; Keith Kahla; Marcia Markland; Charles Spicer; Karen Wolny
Exec Ed, Thomas Dunne Books: Stephen Power
Exec Ed-at-Large: Leslie Gelbman
Sr Ed: Emily Carleton; Michael Homler; Daniela Rapp
Sr Ed, Minotaur Books: Catherine Richards
Ed: Holly Ingraham; Meredith Mennitt
Ed, Thomas Dunne Books: Anne Brewer
Assoc Ed: Courtney Littler; April Osborn
Asst Ed: Alicia Clancy; Jaime Coyne; Sylvan Creekmore; Sara Thwaite
Assoc Dir, Mktg: Christine Catarino
Assoc Dir, Publicity: Gabrielle Gantz
Mgr, SMP Swerve & Ed: Eileen Rothschild
Sr Mktg Mgr: Karlyn Hixson
Mktg Mgr: Courtney Reed
Assoc Mktg Mgr: John Nicholas
Sr Publicity Mgr: Jessica Lawrence; Sarah Melnyk
Publicity Mgr: Rebecca Lang; Jessica Preeg
Sr Publicist: Katie Bassel; Justin Velella
Publicist: Staci Burt; Brittani Hilles
Founded: 1952

General nonfiction, fiction, reference, scholarly, mass market, travel, children's books.
ISBN Prefix(es): 978-0-312; 978-1-4039; 978-0-230; 978-1-4272; 978-1-250; 978-1-1370; 978-1-4299; 978-1-4668
Number of titles published annually: 1,000 Print
Imprints: All Points Books; Thomas Dunne Books; Golden Books Adult Publishing; Golden Guides; LA Weekly Books; Minotaur Books; Priddy Books; Renaissance Books; St Martin's Castle Point; St Martin's Dead Letter; St Martin's Griffin; St Martin's Paperbacks; St Martin's Press; St Martin's True Crime; St Martin's True Crime Classics; Stonewall Inn Editions; Swerve; Truman Talley Books; Wednesday Books
Foreign Rep(s): H B Fenn & Co Ltd (Canada); Macmillan India (India); Macmillan New Zealand (New Zealand); Melia UK (Ireland, UK); Pan Macmillan Australia (Australia); Pan Macmillan-Hong Kong (Asia, Middle East); Pan Macmillan South Africa (South Africa); Pan Macmillan UK (Caribbean, Europe, Israel, Latin America)
Foreign Rights: Big Apple Agency Inc (China, Taiwan); The Book Publishers Association of Israel (Israel); Eliane Benisti (France); International Editors' Co (Portugal, South America, Spain); Nurcihan Kesim Literary Agency Inc (Turkey); Lex Copyright Office (Hungary); Literary Services (Italy); Prava i prevodi (Eastern Europe, Greece); Sane Toregard Agency (Denmark, Finland, Iceland, Norway, Sweden); Thomas Schlueck GmbH (Germany); Tuttle-Mori Agency Inc (Thailand)
Distribution Center: MPS Distribution Center, 16365 James Madison Hwy, Gordonsville, VA 22942-8501 *Toll Free Tel:* 888-330-8477 *Toll Free Fax:* 800-672-2054
Membership(s): AAP

Saint Mary's Press
Subsidiary of Christian Brothers Publications
702 Terrace Heights, Winona, MN 55987-1318
SAN: 203-073X
Tel: 507-457-7900 *Toll Free Tel:* 800-533-8095 *Fax:* 507-457-7990 *Toll Free Fax:* 800-344-9225
E-mail: smpress@smp.org
Web Site: www.smp.org
Key Personnel
CEO & Pres: John M Vitek
Exec Dir, Delivery: Caren Yang
Libn & ISBN Contact: Connie Jensen
Founded: 1943
High school curriculum, paperbound & digital; religion (Catholic); Bibles, youth ministry resources.
ISBN Prefix(es): 978-0-88489; 978-1-59982
Number of titles published annually: 25 Print; 8 E-Book
Total Titles: 500 Print; 30 E-Book
Distributor for Group Publishing
Foreign Rep(s): The Bible Society (New Zealand); B Broughton Ltd (Canada); Catholic News, Books & Media (Singapore); John Garratt Publishing (Australia); Herald Publications Sdn Bhd (Malaysia); Pleroma Christian Supplies (New Zealand); Redemptorist Publications (UK)

Saint Nectarios Press
10300 Ashworth Ave N, Seattle, WA 98133-9410
SAN: 159-0170
Tel: 206-522-4471 *Toll Free Tel:* 800-643-4233
E-mail: orders@stnectariospress.com
Web Site: www.stnectariospress.com
Founded: 1977
Traditional Eastern Orthodox books.
ISBN Prefix(es): 978-0-913026
Number of titles published annually: 3 Print
Total Titles: 70 Print

St Pauls
Division of The Society of Saint Paul
2187 Victory Blvd, Staten Island, NY 10314-6603
SAN: 201-2405
Tel: 718-761-0047 (edit & prodn); 718-698-2759 (mktg & billing) *Toll Free Tel:* 800-343-2522 *Fax:* 718-761-0057
E-mail: sales@stpauls.us; marketing@stpauls.us
Web Site: www.stpauls.us
Key Personnel
Ed-in-Chief & Contact, ISBN & Rts & Perms: Br Zbigniew Gawron *E-mail:* editor@stpauls.us
Treas: Br Marco Bulgarelli
Prodn Mgr & Art Dir: Br Edward Donaher *E-mail:* edonaher@aol.com
Copy Ed: Br Frank Sadowski
Mktg: Fr Tony Bautista *Tel:* 718-698-2759
Founded: 1961
Religion (Catholic), bible, education, pastoral care, prayer books, biography, spirituality, psychology, philosophy, theology, Spanish titles (Roman Catholic), bereavement, church, ethics, homilies, liturgy, marriage & family life, prayer, religious education, saints' lives, scripture, cassettes & videos.
ISBN Prefix(es): 978-0-8189
Number of titles published annually: 24 Print; 10 CD-ROM; 20 Online; 20 E-Book
Total Titles: 425 Print; 85 CD-ROM; 105 Online; 105 E-Book
Foreign Office(s): Edizioni Paoline, Piazza Soncino 5, 520092 Cinisello Balsamo MI, Italy

Salaam Reads, see Simon & Schuster Children's Publishing

Salem Press Inc
Imprint of Grey House Publishing Inc™
2 University Plaza, Suite 310, Hackensack, NJ 07601
SAN: 208-838X
Tel: 201-968-0500 *Toll Free Tel:* 800-221-1592; 800-221-1592 *Fax:* 201-968-0511
E-mail: csr@salempress.com
Web Site: salempress.com
Key Personnel
Gen Mgr: Jim Wright *E-mail:* jwright@salempress.com
Founded: 1949
Reference books & online products for middle school, secondary school, colleges & public libraries.
ISBN Prefix(es): 978-0-89356; 978-1-58765
Number of titles published annually: 50 Print; 50 Online; 50 E-Book
Total Titles: 300 Print; 200 Online; 200 E-Book
Imprints: Magill's Choice
Foreign Rep(s): Aditya Books Pvt Ltd (Bangladesh, India, Nepal, Pakistan, Sri Lanka); Alkem Co (S) Pte Ltd (Brunei, Hong Kong, Indonesia, Korea, Malaysia, Philippines, Singapore, Taiwan, Thailand, Vietnam); Eurospan Ltd (Africa, Europe, Middle East, UK); Grey House Publishing Canada (Canada); Yushodo Co Ltd (Japan)

Salina Bookshelf Inc
3120 N Caden Ct, Suite 4, Flagstaff, AZ 86004
SAN: 253-0503
Toll Free Tel: 877-527-0070 *Fax:* 928-526-0386
Web Site: www.salinabookshelf.com
Key Personnel
Pres: Eric Lockard *Tel:* 877-527-0700 ext 425 *E-mail:* elockard@salinabookshelf.com
Art Dir: Baje Whitethorne, Jr *Tel:* 877-527-0700 ext 202
Founded: 1994
Publisher of multicultural books with a strong focus on the stories of the Navajo people. Our textbooks, children's picture books & electronic media in Navajo & English are resources for the home, library & classroom. We recognize the importance of portraying traditional language & culture & of making this knowledge accessible to a broad spectrum of curious minds.
ISBN Prefix(es): 978-1-893354; 978-0-9644189
Number of titles published annually: 10 Print; 3 Audio
Total Titles: 85 Print; 1 CD-ROM; 6 Audio
Membership(s): American Indian Library Association; The Children's Book Council; Independent Book Publishers Association; Publishers Association of the West

SAMS Technical Publishing LLC
Division of AGS Capital Inc
9850 E 30 St, Indianapolis, IN 46229
Toll Free Tel: 800-428-7267 *Toll Free Fax:* 800-552-3910
E-mail: customercare@samswebsite.com
Web Site: www.samswebsite.com
Founded: 1946
Publisher of Quickfact & Photofact® service manuals.
ISBN Prefix(es): 978-0-7906
Number of titles published annually: 150 Print
Total Titles: 4,800 Print
Imprints: Indy-Tech Publishing; Photofact®; Quickfact®
Distributor for Butterworth Heinemann; McGraw-Hill; Prompt Publications

San Diego State University Press
Division of San Diego State University Foundation
Arts & Letters 283/MC 6020, 5500 Campanile Dr, San Diego, CA 92182-6020
Tel: 619-594-6220 (orders)
E-mail: memo@sdsu.edu
Web Site: sdsupress.sdsu.edu
Key Personnel
Ed/Dir: Dr Bill Nericcio *Tel:* 619-594-1524 *E-mail:* bnericci@mail.sdsu.edu
Ed: Prof Harry Polkinhorn *E-mail:* hpolkinh@mail.sdsu.edu
Founded: 1959
Scholarly & trade, monographs.
ISBN Prefix(es): 978-0-916304; 978-1-879691
Number of titles published annually: 5 Print; 2 Online
Imprints: Binational Press; Hyperbole
Distributor for Institute for Regional Studies of the Californias

Sandlapper Publishing Inc
1281 Amelia St NE, Orangeburg, SC 29115-5475
SAN: 203-2678
Mailing Address: PO Box 730, Orangeburg, SC 29116-0730
Tel: 803-531-1658 *Toll Free Tel:* 800-849-7263 (orders only) *Fax:* 803-534-5223 *Toll Free Fax:* 800-337-9420
E-mail: sales@sandlapperpublishing.com
Web Site: www.sandlapperpublishing.com
Key Personnel
Owner & Pres: Amanda Gallman *E-mail:* agallman@sandlapperpublishing.com
Founded: 1982
Nonfiction material about South Carolina.
ISBN Prefix(es): 978-0-87844
Number of titles published annually: 10 Print
Total Titles: 100 Print

§Santa Monica Press LLC
215 S Hwy 101, Suite 110, Solana Beach, CA 92075
SAN: 298-1459
Mailing Address: PO Box 850, Solana Beach, CA 92075
Tel: 858-793-1890 *Toll Free Tel:* 800-784-9553
E-mail: books@santamonicapress.com
Web Site: www.santamonicapress.com

Key Personnel
Publr: Jeffrey Goldman *E-mail:* jgoldman@santamonicapress.com
Founded: 1994
Publish an eclectic line of books. Our critically acclaimed titles are sold in retail outlets around the world. Our authors are recognized experts who receive coverage both nationally & internationally. We're not afraid to cast a wide editorial net. Our list of lively & modern nonfiction titles includes books in such categories as popular culture, film history, photography, humor, biography, travel & reference.
ISBN Prefix(es): 978-0-9639946; 978-1-891661; 978-1-59580
Number of titles published annually: 12 Print; 12 E-Book
Total Titles: 135 Print; 85 E-Book
Foreign Rep(s): The Perseus Books Group (all other territories); Turnaround Publisher Services Ltd (Europe, UK)
Foreign Rights: The Perseus Books Group (Jennifer Thompson) (all other territories)
Orders to: Legato Publishers Group, 210 American Dr, Jackson, TN 38301 *Toll Free Tel:* 800-343-4499 *Toll Free Fax:* 800-351-5073 *Web Site:* www.legatopublishersgroup.com
Returns: Perseus Distribution, 210 American Dr, Jackson, TN 38301 *Toll Free Tel:* 800-343-4499 *Toll Free Fax:* 800-351-5073 *Web Site:* www.perseusdistribution.com
Warehouse: Perseus Distribution, 210 American Dr, Jackson, TN 38301 *Toll Free Tel:* 800-343-4499 *Toll Free Fax:* 800-351-5073 *Web Site:* www.perseusdistribution.com
Distribution Center: Legato Publishers Group, 210 American Dr, Jackson, TN 38301 *Toll Free Tel:* 800-343-4499 *Toll Free Fax:* 800-351-5073 *Web Site:* www.legatopublishersgroup.com

Santillana USA Publishing Co
Subsidiary of Grupo Santillana
2023 NW 84 Ave, Doral, FL 33122
SAN: 205-1133
Tel: 305-591-9522 *Toll Free Tel:* 800-245-8584
E-mail: customerservice@santillanausa.com
Web Site: www.santillanausa.com
Key Personnel
Pres & CEO: Miguel A Tapia *E-mail:* mtapia@santillanausa.com
COO: Marta Moldes Gomez *E-mail:* mmoldes@santillanausa.com
CTO: Javier Cabrera *E-mail:* jcabrera@santillanausa.com
Dir, Children's Books Div: Isabel Mendoza *E-mail:* imendoza@santillanausa.com
Natl Sales Dir: Arturo Castillon *E-mail:* acastillon@santillanausa.com
Mktg Dir: Kathy Jimenez *Tel:* 305-591-9522 ext 247 *E-mail:* kjimenez@santillanausa.com
Prodn Mgr: Jacqueline Rivera *E-mail:* jrivera@santillanausa.com
Founded: 1972
Educational & Spanish language trade books; ESL & bilingual textbooks; Spanish as a foreign language.
ISBN Prefix(es): 978-0-88272; 978-1-56014; 978-1-58105; 978-1-58986; 978-1-59437; 978-1-59820; 978-1-60396; 978-1-61605; 978-1-61435; 978-1-62263; 978-1-63113
Number of titles published annually: 50 Print; 3 CD-ROM; 5 Audio
Total Titles: 1,200 Print; 3 CD-ROM; 15 Audio
Membership(s): AAP

SAR Press, see School for Advanced Research Press

Sarabande Books Inc
2234 Dundee Rd, Suite 200, Louisville, KY 40205
Tel: 502-458-4028 *Fax:* 502-458-4065
E-mail: info@sarabandebooks.org
Web Site: www.sarabandebooks.org
Key Personnel
Pres & Ed-in-Chief: Sarah Gorham *E-mail:* sgorham@sarabandebooks.org
Dir, Mktg & Publicity: Ariel Lewiton
Dir, Opers & Outreach: Kristen Miller *E-mail:* kmiller@sarabandebooks.org
Founded: 1994
Short fiction, poetry & literary nonfiction collections.
ISBN Prefix(es): 978-1-889330; 978-1-932511; 978-0-9641151; 978-1-936747; 978-1-941411
Number of titles published annually: 10 Print; 1 E-Book
Total Titles: 220 Print; 1 E-Book
Branch Office(s)
112 W 27 St, Suite 607, New York, NY 10001, Mktg & Publicity Dir: Ariel Lewiton *Tel:* 917-923-3109 *E-mail:* kristen@sarabandebooks.org
Distribution Center: Consortium/Perseus Distribution, 1094 Flex Dr, Jackson, TN 38301-5070 *Toll Free Tel:* 800-283-3572 *Toll Free Fax:* 800-351-5073
Membership(s): ABA; Academy of American Poets; Association of Writers and Writing Programs; Community of Literary Magazines & Presses; PEN Center USA

SAS Publishing
Imprint of SAS Institute Inc
100 SAS Campus Dr, Cary, NC 27513-2414
Tel: 919-677-8000 *Toll Free Tel:* 800-727-0025 *Fax:* 919-677-4444
E-mail: saspress@sas.com
Web Site: www.sas.com/publishing
Key Personnel
Ed-in-Chief: Julie M Platt *E-mail:* julie.platt@sas.com
Founded: 1976
Books about SAS or JMP software.
ISBN Prefix(es): 978-1-55544; 978-0-917382; 978-1-58025; 978-1-59047; 978-1-61290; 978-1-59994; 978-1-60764; 978-1-62959; 978-1-62960
Number of titles published annually: 50 Print
Distributed by John Wiley & Sons Inc
Distributor for AMACOM Books; Breakfast Communications; CRC Press; Duxbury; Harcourt; Harvard Business School Press; McGraw-Hill; Oxford; Prentice-Hall; Springer; John Wiley & Sons Inc

Sasquatch Books
1904 S Third Ave, Suite 710, Seattle, WA 98101
SAN: 289-0208
Tel: 206-467-4300 *Toll Free Tel:* 800-775-0817 *Fax:* 206-467-4301
E-mail: custserv@sasquatchbooks.com
Web Site: www.sasquatchbooks.com
Key Personnel
Chmn, Chief Creative Offr & CEO: Gary Luke *Tel:* 206-826-4304 *E-mail:* gluke@sasquatchbooks.com
Pres & COO: Sarah Hanson *Tel:* 206-826-4303 *E-mail:* shanson@sasquatchbooks.com
Acqs Ed: Hannah Elnan
Founded: 1986
Nonfiction of & from the West Coast.
ISBN Prefix(es): 978-0-934007; 978-0-912365; 978-1-57061
Number of titles published annually: 40 Print
Total Titles: 390 Print; 3 Audio
Imprints: Best Places® Guidebooks Series; Paws IV
Foreign Rep(s): Publishers Group Canada (Canada)
Foreign Rights: Park Literary & Media
Distribution Center: Penguin Random House Publisher Services, 400 Hahn Rd, Westminster, MD 21157 (Attn: order entry) *Toll Free Tel:* 800-788-3123 *Fax:* 510-528-3444

§Satya House Publications
22 Turkey St, Hardwick, MA 01037
Mailing Address: PO Box 122, Hardwick, MA 01037
Tel: 413-477-8743
E-mail: info@satyahouse.com; orders@satyahouse.com
Web Site: www.satyahouse.com
Key Personnel
Publr: Julie Murkette *E-mail:* julie@satyahouse.com
Founded: 2003
Independent publishing company.
This publisher has indicated that 25% of their product line is author subsidized.
ISBN Prefix(es): 978-0-9729191; 978-0-9818720; 978-1-9358740
Number of titles published annually: 4 Print; 4 E-Book
Total Titles: 20 Print; 1 CD-ROM; 9 E-Book
Foreign Rep(s): Gazelle Book Services Ltd (UK)
Foreign Rights: Sylvia Hayse Literary Agency LLC (worldwide exc USA)
Distribution Center: Midpoint Trade Books, 27 W 20 St, Suite 1102, New York, NY 10011 *Tel:* 212-727-0190 *Web Site:* www.midpointtrade.com
Membership(s): Independent Book Publishers Association; Independent Publishers of New England

Savant Books & Publications LLC
2630 Kapiolani Blvd, Suite 1601, Honolulu, HI 96826
Tel: 808-941-3927 *Fax:* 808-941-3927
E-mail: savantbooks@gmail.com; savantdistribution@gmail.com
Web Site: www.savantbooksandpublications.com; www.savantdistribution.com
Key Personnel
Owner: Daniel S Janik
Ed-in-Chief: David Shinsato
Founded: 2007
Publishes unpublished, post-modern works of enduring value "with a twist" for English readers throughout the world. Special interest areas include: fiction (novels - all genres), nonfiction (transformative education, memoirs, academic theses & dissertations of note, single-author textbooks & workbooks). Under Aignos Publishing LLC (an imprint) publishes avant garde, experimental & innovative works that "push the leading edge" of all genres of fiction & nonfiction.
ISBN Prefix(es): 978-0-9841175 (Savant); 978-0-9845552 (Savant); 978-0-9829987 (Savant); 978-0-9832861 (Savant); 978-0-9852506 (Savant); 978-0-9886640 (Savant); 978-0-9915622 (Savant); 978-0-9963255 (Savant); 978-0-9972472 (Savant); 978-0-9860233 (Aignos); 978-0-9895191 (Aignos); 978-0-9904322 (Aignos); 978-0-9970020 (Aignos)
Number of titles published annually: 15 Print; 1 CD-ROM; 15 Online; 15 E-Book; 1 Audio
Total Titles: 110 Print; 1 CD-ROM; 110 Online; 100 E-Book; 5 Audio
Imprints: Aignos Publishing (avant garde)
Distribution Center: Ingram Content Group LLC, One Ingram Blvd, La Vergne, TN 37086 *Tel:* 615-793-5000 *Web Site:* www.ingramcontent.com
Membership(s): Independent Book Publishers Association

SBL Press
Unit of Society of Biblical Literature
The Luce Ctr, Suite 350, 825 Houston Mill Rd, Atlanta, GA 30329
Tel: 404-727-3100 *Fax:* 404-727-3101 (corp)
E-mail: sbl@sbl-site.org
Web Site: www.sbl-site.org

Key Personnel
Exec Dir: John F Kutsko *E-mail:* john.kutsko@sbl-site.org
Dir, Pubns: Bob Buller *E-mail:* bob.buller@sbl-site.org
Mktg Mgr: Kathie Klein *Tel:* 404-727-2325 *E-mail:* kathie.klein@sbl-site.org
Sales Mgr: Heather McMurray *Tel:* 404-727-3096 *E-mail:* heather.mcmurray@sbl-site.org
Founded: 1880
Publishing program of the Society of Biblical Literature, a learned society whose purpose is to stimulate the critical investigation of Biblical literature.
ISBN Prefix(es): 978-0-89130; 978-0-7885; 978-0-88414; 978-1-58983
Number of titles published annually: 43 Print; 43 Online; 43 E-Book
Total Titles: 850 Print; 200 Online; 200 E-Book
Distributor for Brown Judaic Studies; Sheffield Phoenix Press
Orders to: PO Box 2243, Williston, VT 05495-2243 *Tel:* 802-864-6185 *Toll Free Tel:* 877-725-3334 *Fax:* 802-864-7626
Returns: 82 Winter Sport Lane, Williston, VT 05495 *Tel:* 802-864-6185 *Toll Free Tel:* 877-725-3334 *Fax:* 802-864-7626
Warehouse: 82 Winter Sport Lane, Williston, VT 05495 *Tel:* 802-864-6185 *Toll Free Tel:* 877-725-3334 *Fax:* 802-864-7626

SBPRA, see Strategic Book Publishing & Rights Agency (SBPRA)

Scarecrow Press Inc
Imprint of Rowman & Littlefield Publishing Group
4501 Forbes Blvd, Suite 200, Lanham, MD 20706
Tel: 301-459-3366 *Fax:* 301-429-5748
Web Site: www.scarecrowpress.com
Key Personnel
CEO & Pres: Jed Lyons *E-mail:* jlyons@rowman.com
VP, Mktg & Sales: Linda May
Rts & Perms Dir: Clare Cox
Sales Dir: Sheila Burnett
Exec Ed: Charles Harmon
Founded: 1950
Reference books & texts in music, film, information technology, theater, performing arts, history, religion & cultural studies. Professional & reference books in library & information sciences & government regulatory areas. Co-publishing with Rutgers Jazz Institute, Music Library Association, American Theological Library Association & Children's Literature Association.
New titles to be released under the Rowman & Littlefield imprint.
ISBN Prefix(es): 978-0-8108; 978-1-57886
Number of titles published annually: 175 Print; 2 CD-ROM; 10 Online; 5 E-Book
Total Titles: 5,000 Print; 6 CD-ROM; 100 Online; 30 E-Book
Distribution Center: 15200 NBN Way, PO Box 191, Blue Ridge Summit, PA 17214 *Toll Free Tel:* 800-462-6420 *Toll Free Fax:* 800-338-4550

Scepter Publishers
PO Box 360694, Strongsville, OH 44149
Tel: 212-354-0670 *Toll Free Tel:* 800-322-8773 *Fax:* 212-354-0736
Web Site: www.scepterpublishers.org
Key Personnel
Assoc Publr: Robert Singerline *E-mail:* robert@scepterpublishers.org
Orders & Cust Serv: Kevin Lay *E-mail:* kevin@scepterpublishers.org
Founded: 1954
Catholic book publishing including doctrinal works, theology & liturgy.
ISBN Prefix(es): 978-0-933932; 978-0-1889334; 978-1-594170
Number of titles published annually: 10 Print
Total Titles: 170 Print

Schaffner Press
PO Box 41567, Tucson, AZ 85717
E-mail: tim@schaffnerpress.com
Web Site: www.schaffnerpress.com
Key Personnel
Assoc Ed: Sean Murphy *Tel:* 520-869-7632 *E-mail:* sean@schaffnerpress.com
Founded: 2001
Independent publisher of books of social relevance for the discerning reader.
ISBN Prefix(es): 978-0-9710598; 978-0-9801394; 978-0-9824332; 978-1-936182; 978-1-943156
Number of titles published annually: 8 Print; 8 E-Book
Total Titles: 40 Print; 40 E-Book
Foreign Rights: Susan Schulman Literary Agency LLC
Distribution Center: Independent Publishers Group, 814 N Franklin St, Chicago, IL 60610 *Tel:* 312-337-0747 *Toll Free Tel:* 800-888-4741 *Fax:* 312-337-5985 *Web Site:* www.ipgbook.com

Schiffer Publishing Ltd
4880 Lower Valley Rd, Atglen, PA 19310
SAN: 208-8428
Tel: 610-593-1777 *Fax:* 610-593-2002
E-mail: info@schifferbooks.com
Web Site: www.schifferbooks.com
Key Personnel
Pres & Ed-in-Chief: Pete Schiffer
EVP: Nancy Schiffer
Spec Sales: Joe Langman
Founded: 1974
Collecting, art books, antiques, architecture, toys, woodcarving, hobbies, weaving, color, metaphysics, aviation, military books, automotive books, design & fashion.
ISBN Prefix(es): 978-0-87033; 978-0-916838; 978-0-88740; 978-0-7643; 978-0-89538; 978-0-978278; 978-1-5073
Number of titles published annually: 300 Print
Total Titles: 5,000 Print
Imprints: Canal Press; Cornell Maritime Press; Geared Up Publications; Kaiser-Barlow; LW Books; Para Research; Schiffer; Schiffer Fashion Press; Schiffer Ltd; Schiffer Military History; Tidewater Publishers; Whitford Press
Distributor for The Donning Co
Foreign Rights: Bushwood Books (Europe)
See separate listing for:
Cornell Maritime Press Inc

G Schirmer Inc/Associated Music Publishers Inc
Unit of The Music Sales Group
180 Madison Ave, 24th fl, New York, NY 10016
Tel: 212-254-2100 *Fax:* 212-254-2013
E-mail: schirmer@schirmer.com; info@musicsales.com
Web Site: www.musicsalesclassical.com
Key Personnel
CEO: Tomas Wise
EVP & CFO: John Castaldo
Pres: Robert Thompson
Founded: 1935
Committed to intelligent, educational & entertaining books about all aspects of music, especially the recording arts, music business, genre histories & musician biographies.
ISBN Prefix(es): 978-0-8256; 978-0-7119
Number of titles published annually: 25 Print
Total Titles: 300 Print
Branch Office(s)
2 Old Rte 17, Chester, NY 10918 *Tel:* 845-469-4699 *Fax:* 845-469-7544
1247 Sixth St, Los Angeles, CA 90401 *Tel:* 310-393-9900 *Fax:* 310-393-9925
Distributor for Big Meteor Publishing; Independent Music Press
Membership(s): ABA; American Society of Journalists & Authors; Independent Book Publishers Association; Women's National Book Association

§Schlager Group Inc
325 N Saint Paul, Suite 3425, Dallas, TX 75201
Toll Free Tel: 888-416-5727 *Fax:* 214-347-9469
E-mail: info@schlagergroup.com
Web Site: www.schlagergroup.com
Key Personnel
Pres: Neil Schlager *Tel:* 888-416-5727 ext 801 *E-mail:* neil@schlagergroup.com
Creative Dir: Benjamin Painter *Tel:* 888-416-5727 ext 802 *E-mail:* benjamin@schlagergroup.com
Dir, Sales: Andrea Kesterke *Tel:* 888-416-5727 ext 805 *E-mail:* akesterke@milestonedocuments.com
Mng Ed: Sarah Robertson *Tel:* 888-416-5727 ext 804 *E-mail:* sarah@schlagergroup.com
Founded: 1997
Publisher of books & Internet materials for history instructors & students. Foreign Reps in Africa, Australia, Bangladesh, Canada, Europe, India, Japan, Mexico, Middle East, Nepal, New Guinea, New Zealand, Pakistan, Southeast Asia, Sri Lanka & UK, all via Salem Press Inc distributors & representatives.
ISBN Prefix(es): 978-9-797758; 978-9-35306
Number of titles published annually: 2 Print; 1 Online; 2 E-Book
Total Titles: 5 Print; 1 Online; 5 E-Book
Divisions: Milestone Documents
Distributed by Salem Press (ref books only)
Orders to: Salem Press, 2 University Plaza, Suite 121, Hackensack, NJ 07601 (ref books only)
Returns: Salem Press, 2 University Plaza, Suite 121, Hackensack, NJ 07601 (ref books only)
Shipping Address: Salem Press, 2 University Plaza, Suite 121, Hackensack, NJ 07601 (ref books only) *Toll Free Tel:* 800-221-1592 *Fax:* 201-968-1411 *E-mail:* csr@salempress.com *Web Site:* www.salempress.com
Membership(s): American Historical Association; Organization of American Historians

Schocken Books, see Pantheon Books/Schocken Books

Scholastic Education
Division of Scholastic Inc
557 Broadway, New York, NY 10012
Tel: 212-343-6100 *Fax:* 212-343-6189
Web Site: www.scholastic.com
Key Personnel
Pres: Greg Worrell
Chief Academic Offr: Michael Haggen
EVP, Consumer & Prof Publg: Hugh Roome
VP & Gen Mgr, Scholastic Lib Publg: Allison Henderson
VP of Digital & Strategic Initiatives: Evan St Lifer
VP of Mktg: Danielle Mirsky
Ed-in-Chief, Scholastic Classroom Magazines: Elliott Rebhun
SVP: Jennifer Boykins
SVP of Learning Supports & FACE: Ron Mirr
SVP & Publr: Janelle Cherrington
VP & Publr: Lois Bridges
Scholastic Education is a leading provider of comprehensive literacy solutions & responsive partner of schools & districts. Through instructional reading & writing, professional learning, family & community engagement & learning supports, Scholastic Education provides teachers, families & communities with the tools they need to support each & every child. Scholastic Consumer & Professional Publishing is a

leading print & digital publisher of classroom magazines & children's reference materials for school & public libraries, which include digital brands such as BookFlix® & TrueFlix® & Scholastic GO!® as well as the prestigious imprints Children's Press® & Franklin Watts®.
ISBN Prefix(es): 978-0-516; 978-0-590; 978-0-531; 978-0-7172; 978-0-439; 978-0-926891; 978-1-55998; 978-1-57809; 978-1-59009; 978-0-545
Imprints: Children's Press®; Franklin Watts®; Grolier Online®
Divisions: Assessment; Curriculum Solutions; Early Childhood Education; Professional Development; Publishing Services; Research; Sales & Marketing; Technology

Scholastic Inc
557 Broadway, New York, NY 10012
Tel: 212-343-6100 *Toll Free Tel:* 800-SCHOLASTIC (724-6527)
Web Site: www.scholastic.com
Key Personnel
Chmn, Pres & CEO: Richard Robinson
EVP, Chief Admin Offr & CFO: Maureen O'Connell
EVP, Gen Coun: Andrew Hedden
Pres, Trade Publg: Ellie Berger
EVP, Pres, Reading Club & E-Commerce: Judy A Newman
Pres, Scholastic Book Fairs: Alan Boyko
EVP & Pres, Consumer & Prof Publg: Hugh Roome
Pres, Scholastic Education: Greg Worrell
EVP & Pres, Intl: Nelson Hitchcock
SVP, Corp Communs & Media Rel: Kyle Good
Chief, Strategy: Iole Lucchese
Founded: 1920
Scholastic Corporation (NASDAQ: SCHL) is the world's largest publisher & distributor of children's books, a leading provider of print & digital instructional materials for PreK to grade 12, & a producer of educational & entertaining children's media. The company creates quality books & ebooks, print & technology-based learning materials & programs, classroom magazines & other products that, in combination, offer schools customized solutions to support children's learning both at school & at home. The company also makes quality, affordable books available to all children through school-based book clubs & book fairs. With a 95 year history of service to schools & families, Scholastic continues to carry out its commitment to "Open a World of Possible" for all children. Learn more at www.scholastic.com.
ISBN Prefix(es): 978-0-590; 978-0-439
Distribution Center: 2931 E McCarty St, Jefferson City, MO 65101
100 Plaza Drive W, Secaucus, NJ 07094
Membership(s): AAP; ALA; The Children's Book Council; The Council of Chief State School Officers; Council of Great City Schools; Data & Marketing Association; Education Commission of the States; International Literacy Association; National Governor's Association; New York Women in Communications Inc; Social-Media.org; Software & Information Industry Association
See separate listing for:
Scholastic Education
Scholastic International
Scholastic Trade Division

§Scholastic International
Division of Scholastic Inc
557 Broadway, New York, NY 10012
Tel: 212-343-6100; 646-330-5288 (intl cust serv) *Toll Free Tel:* 800-SCHOLASTIC (724-6527) *Fax:* 646-837-7878
E-mail: international@scholastic.com
Key Personnel
EVP & Pres, Intl: Nelson Hitchcock
VP, Intl Fin: Joe Macca
VP, Export Sales & Mktg: Anne Boynton-Trigg
Sr Prod Mgr: Alison Lytton
VP, New Busn Devt: Carol Sakoian
Scholastic International includes the publication & distribution of products & services outside the US by the company's international operations & its export sales business. Scholastic has operations in Canada, the UK, Australia, New Zealand & Asia, & export sales representatives in the rest of the world.
ISBN Prefix(es): 978-0-590; 978-0-439; 978-0-545
Subsidiaries: Scholastic Asia (with cos in China, India, Malaysia & Singapore & sales offs in Indonesia, Philippines, Taiwan & Thailand); Scholastic Australia Pty Ltd; Scholastic Canada Ltd; Scholastic Ltd UK; Scholastic New Zealand Ltd

Scholastic Trade Division
Division of Scholastic Inc
557 Broadway, New York, NY 10012
Tel: 212-343-6100; 212-343-4685 (export sales) *Fax:* 212-343-4714 (export sales)
Web Site: www.scholastic.com
Key Personnel
Pres, Trade Publg: Ellie Berger
SVP, Gen Mgr, Klutz: Stacy Lellos
SVP, Fin & Strategic Initiatives: David Ascher
SVP, Mktg: Mindy Stockfield
VP, Digital Publr & Pres of Weston Woods & Scholastic Audio: Lori Benton
VP & Publr, Arthur A Levine Books: Arthur A Levine
VP, Publr & Edit Dir, Scholastic Press: David Levithan
VP, Publr: Debra Dorfman
VP & Edit Dir, The Blue Sky Press: Bonnie Verburg
VP, Ed-at-Large: Andrea Pinkney
VP, Creative Dir & Edit Dir, Graphix: David Saylor
VP, Trade Sales: Alan Smagler
VP, Edit Dir, Orchard Books, Scholastic Press Picture Books & Cartwheel Books: Ken Geist
VP, Publicity & Edit Mktg: Tracy van Straaten
VP, Consumer Prods: Gary Hymowitz
VP, Fin: Ken Yamamoto
VP, Publg Opers: JoAnne Mojica
VP & Mng Ed: Leslie Garych
Exec Ed & Mgr, Scholastic en espanol: Maria Dominguez
Dir, Global Prog Sales & Mdsg: Anthony Kosiewska
Scholastic Trade Books is an award-winning publisher of original children's books. Scholastic publishes more than 600 new hardcover, paperback & novelty books each year & brings beloved stories & characters to life beyond the printed page via virtually every platform or screen kids access.
ISBN Prefix(es): 978-0-590; 978-0-439; 978-0-545
Number of titles published annually: 600 Print
Total Titles: 6,000 Print
Imprints: Arthur A Levine Books; The Blue Sky Press; Cartwheel Books; Chicken House; David Fickling Books; Graphix; Klutz; Little Shepherd; Orchard Books; Point; PUSH; Scholastic Audio; Scholastic en Espanol; Scholastic Inc; Scholastic Licensed Publishing; Scholastic Nonfiction; Scholastic Paperbacks; Scholastic Press; Scholastic Reference; Weston Woods
Distribution Center: 2931 E McCarty St, Jefferson City, MO 65102 *Tel:* 573-635-5881

Schonfeld & Associates Inc
1931 Lynn Circle, Libertyville, IL 60048
SAN: 255-2361
Tel: 847-816-4870 *Toll Free Tel:* 800-205-0030 *Fax:* 847-816-4872
E-mail: saiinfo@saibooks.com
Web Site: www.saibooks.com
Key Personnel
Pres: Carol Greenhut *E-mail:* cgreenhut@saibooks.com
Founded: 1977
Author statistical reference works.
ISBN Prefix(es): 978-1-878339; 978-1-932024; 978-0-989055; 978-0-996048; 978-0-996248; 978-1-945225
Number of titles published annually: 9 Print; 12 CD-ROM; 12 E-Book
Total Titles: 10 Print; 12 CD-ROM; 12 E-Book

School for Advanced Research Press
660 Garcia St, Santa Fe, NM 87505
Mailing Address: PO Box 2188, Santa Fe, NM 87504-2188
Tel: 505-954-7206 *Toll Free Tel:* 888-390-6070
E-mail: press@sarsf.org
Web Site: sarweb.org
Key Personnel
Acqs Ed: Sarah Soliz
Founded: 1907
Scholarly & general-interest books on anthropology, archaeology, Native American art & the American Southwest.
ISBN Prefix(es): 978-1-930618; 978-0-933452
Number of titles published annually: 12 Print
Total Titles: 142 Print
Distributed by University of New Mexico Press
Orders to: University of New Mexico Press, Order Dept, 1312 Basehart Rd SE, Albuquerque, NM 87106-4363 *Tel:* 505-272-7777 *Toll Free Tel:* 800-249-7737 *Fax:* 505-272-7778 *Toll Free Fax:* 800-622-8667 *Web Site:* www.unmpress.com

School Guide Publications
606 Halstead Ave, Mamaroneck, NY 10543
Tel: 914-632-1220 *Toll Free Tel:* 800-433-7771 *Fax:* 914-632-3412
E-mail: info@religiousministries.com
Web Site: www.graduateguide.com; www.schoolguides.com; www.religiousministries.com
Key Personnel
Pres & Publr: Myles Ridder *E-mail:* mridder@schoolguides.com
Founded: 1886
Directories for colleges, institutions & religious communities.
Number of titles published annually: 5 Print; 3 Online
Total Titles: 15 Print; 3 Online
Membership(s): Copywriter's Council of America™; National Association of College Admission Counseling

School of Government
Division of The University of NC Chapel Hill
University of North Carolina, CB 3330, Chapel Hill, NC 27599-3330
Tel: 919-966-4119 *Fax:* 919-962-2709
Web Site: www.sog.unc.edu
Key Personnel
Mktg & Communs Specialist: Matthew McKirahan *E-mail:* mckirahan@sog.unc.edu
Founded: 1931
Textbooks, casebooks, manuals & guidebooks, monographs, reports, ebooks & bulletins.
ISBN Prefix(es): 978-1-56011
Number of titles published annually: 20 Print; 1 CD-ROM; 5 Online; 1 E-Book
Total Titles: 200 Print

§School Zone Publishing Co
1819 Industrial Dr, Grand Haven, MI 49417
Tel: 616-846-5030 *Toll Free Tel:* 800-253-0564 *Fax:* 616-846-6181 *Toll Free Fax:* 800-550-4618 (orders only)
Web Site: www.schoolzone.com
Key Personnel
Pres: Jonathan Hoffman

VP, Retail Sales: Sharon Winningham *Tel:* 616-846-5030 ext 217 *E-mail:* sharonw@schoolzone.com
Founded: 1979
Instructional materials for early childhood, PreK to 6th grade; educational workbooks, flashcards & software.
ISBN Prefix(es): 978-0-88743; 978-0-938256; 978-1-58947; 978-1-60041; 978-1-68147; 978-1-60159
Number of titles published annually: 12 Print; 12 CD-ROM
Total Titles: 350 Print; 50 CD-ROM

Schreiber Publishing
PO Box 4193, Rockville, MD 20849
SAN: 203-2465
Tel: 301-589-5831 *Toll Free Tel:* 800-296-1961 (sales) *Fax:* 667-309-6993
E-mail: publisher@schreiberpublishing.net
Web Site: schreiberlanguage.com; shengold.com
Key Personnel
Pres & Dir: Jeremy Kay
Founded: 1954 (as Shengold Publishers)
Books on language & translation, Judaica history, Holocaust memoirs, juveniles, reference books, fiction, art books.
ISBN Prefix(es): 978-0-88400; 978-1-887563
Number of titles published annually: 10 Print; 7 E-Book; 1 Audio
Total Titles: 145 Print; 32 E-Book; 1 Audio
Imprints: Shengold Publishers
Foreign Rights: Bet Alim (Israel); Gazelle Book Services Ltd (Europe, UK); Importadora Agrimen (Latin America)
Shipping Address: Casemate | IPM, 1950 Lawrence Rd, Havertown, PA 19083, Contact: Christine Wolf *Tel:* 610-853-9131 *Fax:* 610-853-9146 *E-mail:* casemate@casematepublishers.com *Web Site:* www.casemateipm.com
Distribution Center: Casemate | IPM, 1950 Lawrence Rd, Havertown, PA 19083 *Tel:* 610-853-9131 *Fax:* 610-853-9146 *E-mail:* casemate@casematepublishers.com *Web Site:* www.casemateipm.com

§Science & Humanities Press
Subsidiary of Banis & Associates
63 Summit Point, St Charles, MO 63301-0571
Tel: 636-394-4950
Web Site: sciencehumanitiespress.com; beachhousebooks.com; macroprintbooks.com; earlyeditionsbooks.com; heuristicsbooks.com
Key Personnel
CEO & Publr: Robert J Banis *E-mail:* banis@sciencehumanitiespress.com
Founded: 1994
Publish books with a mission. Titles include adapting to living with a disability, computer capabilities, education & specialized medical/wellness topics. Most interested in books that have enduring human value, promoting the kind of world we all want to live in. Prefer inquiries by e-mail. No unsol mss; author guidelines on web site (sciencehumanitiespress.com).
ISBN Prefix(es): 978-1-888725; 978-1-59630
Number of titles published annually: 20 Print; 20 E-Book; 1 Audio
Total Titles: 110 Print; 10 Online; 60 E-Book; 4 Audio
Imprints: BeachHouse Books; Early Editions Books; Heuristic Books; MacroPrintBooks
Membership(s): Independent Book Publishers Association; St Louis Publishers Association

Science, Naturally
Affiliate of Platypus Media
725 Eighth St SE, Washington, DC 20003
Tel: 202-465-4798 *Toll Free Tel:* 866-724-9876 *Fax:* 202-558-2132
E-mail: info@sciencenaturally.com
Web Site: www.sciencenaturally.com
Key Personnel
Pres: Dia L Michels
Founded: 2001
Committed to creating & distributing engaging & educational STEM books for kids.
ISBN Prefix(es): 978-0-9678020; 978-0-9700106; 978-1-938492
Number of titles published annually: 5 Print; 5 E-Book
Total Titles: 11 Print; 7 E-Book
Distribution Center: National Book Network, 4501 Forbes Blvd, Lanham, MD 20706 *Tel:* 301-459-3366 *Fax:* 301-429-5746 *E-mail:* customercare@nbnbooks.com

ScienceThrillers Media
PO Box 601392, Sacramento, CA 95860-1392
Tel: 916-712-3334
E-mail: query@sciencethrillersmedia.com
Web Site: www.sciencethrillersmedia.com
Key Personnel
Publr: Dr Amy Rogers *E-mail:* publisher@sciencethrillersmedia.com
Founded: 2014
Specialize in page-turning stories (fiction or nonfiction) that feature science, technology, engineering, math, or medicine in the plot, or a protagonist in one of those fields.
ISBN Prefix(es): 978-1-940419
Number of titles published annually: 3 Print; 3 E-Book; 1 Audio
Membership(s): California Writers Club; Independent Book Publishers Association; International Thriller Writers Inc; Northern California Publishers & Authors Association

Scobre Press Corp
2255 Calle Clara, La Jolla, CA 92037
Fax: 858-551-1232
E-mail: info@scobre.com
Web Site: www.scobre.com; scobre.bookbuddyaudio.com
Key Personnel
Owner & Pres: Scott Blumenthal
Owner: Brett Hodus
Founded: 1999
ISBN Prefix(es): 978-0-9741695; 978-1-933423; 978-0-9708992; 978-0-9741997; 978-0-9766240; 978-1-934713; 978-1-61570; 978-1-62920; 978-1-93471
Number of titles published annually: 6 Print
Total Titles: 32 Print
Imprints: Scobre Educational
Distribution Center: Lerner Publishing Group, 1251 Washington Ave N, Minneapolis, MN 55401 *Toll Free Tel:* 800-328-4929 *Toll Free Fax:* 800-332-1132 *Web Site:* www.lernerbooks.com

Scout Press, see Gallery Books

Scribner
Imprint of Scribner Publishing Group
1230 Avenue of the Americas, New York, NY 10020
Key Personnel
Pres: Susan Moldow *Tel:* 212-698-7182 *E-mail:* susan.moldow@simonandschuster.com
SVP, Publr: Nan Graham *Tel:* 212-632-4930 *E-mail:* nan.graham@simonandschuster.com
VP, Assoc Publr: Roz Lippel *Tel:* 212-698-7666 *E-mail:* roz.lippel@simonandschuster.com
VP, Ed-in-Chief: Colin Harrison *Tel:* 212-632-4942 *E-mail:* colin.harrison@simonandschuster.com
VP, Dir of Subs Rts: Paul O'Halloran *Tel:* 212-698-7367 *E-mail:* paul.o'halloran@simonandschuster.com
VP, Dir of Publicity: Brian Belfiglio *Tel:* 212-632-4945 *E-mail:* brian.belfiglio@simonandschuster.com
Art Dir: Jaya Miceli *Tel:* 212-632-4959 *E-mail:* jaya.miceli@simonandschuster.com
Ed, Assoc Mktg Dir: Kara Watson *Tel:* 212-632-4936 *E-mail:* kara.watson@simonandschuster.com
Deputy Dir of Publicity: Katie Monaghan *Tel:* 212-632-4950 *E-mail:* katie.monaghan@simonandschuster.com; Kate Lloyd *Tel:* 212-632-4951 *E-mail:* kate.lloyd@simonandschuster.com
VP, Exec Ed: Rick Horgan *Tel:* 212-698-1129 *E-mail:* rick.horgan@simonandschuster.com
Exec Ed: Kathryn Belden *Tel:* 212-632-4932 *E-mail:* kathryn.belden@simonandschuster.com; Valerie Steiker *Tel:* 212-698-7652 *E-mail:* valerie.steiker@simonandschuster.com
Assoc Ed: Daniel Loedel *Tel:* 212-698-1226 *E-mail:* daniel.loedel@simonandschuster.com
Edit Asst: Sarah Goldberg *Tel:* 212-632-4903 *E-mail:* sarah.goldberg@simonandschuster.com; Sally Howe *Tel:* 212-698-2445 *E-mail:* sally.howe@simonandschuster.com; Emily Greenwald *Tel:* 212-632-4921 *E-mail:* emily.greenwald@simonandschuster.com
Online Mktg Mgr: Ashley Gilliam *Tel:* 212-698-2889 *E-mail:* ashley.gilliam@simonandschuster.com
Publg Mgr: Julia Lee McGill *Tel:* 212-698-2286 *E-mail:* julia.lee.mcgill@simonandschuster.com
Asst to the Publr: Tamar McCollom *Tel:* 212-632-4920 *E-mail:* tamar.mccollom@simonandschuster.com
ISBN Prefix(es): 978-0-684; 978-0-7432
Number of titles published annually: 70 Print
Imprints: Scribner Classics; Scribner Poetry

Scripta Humanistica Publishing International
Subsidiary of Brumar Communications
1383 Kersey Lane, Potomac, MD 20854
Tel: 301-294-7949 *Fax:* 301-424-9584
E-mail: info@scriptahumanistica.com
Web Site: www.scriptahumanistica.com
Key Personnel
Chmn of the Bd & Publr: Prof Bruno M Damiani *Tel:* 301-340-1095 *E-mail:* damiani@cua.edu
Founded: 1984
Publish reference books in the Humanities.
ISBN Prefix(es): 978-0-916379
Number of titles published annually: 5 Print
Total Titles: 175 Print; 175 Online
Editorial Office(s): Dept of Romance Languages, 512 Williams Hall, Philadelphia, PA 19104-6305, Gen Ed: Jose M Regueiro *Tel:* 215-898-5124 *Fax:* 215-898-0933 *E-mail:* jregueir@sas.upenn.edu
Foreign Rep(s): Grant & Cutler Ltd (Northern Europe, UK); Leader Books SA (Greece, Middle East); Portico (Africa, Southern Europe, Spain); Scripta Humanistica (Caribbean, Latin America); Spain Shobo Co Inc (Asia, Australia, New Zealand)
Distribution Center: Baker & Taylor, 501 S Gladiolus Ave, Momence, IL 60954-1799 *Tel:* 815-472-2444
Ingram/Lightning Source, 7315 Innovation Blvd, Fort Wayne, IN 46818-1371 *E-mail:* csacademic@ingramcontent.com *Web Site:* www.ingramcontent.com
Midwest Library Service, 11443 Saint Charles Rock Rd, Bridgeton, MO 63044-2789 *Tel:* 314-739-3100 *Fax:* 314-739-1326 *E-mail:* madden@midwestls.com *Web Site:* www.midwestls.com
Yankee Book Peddler Inc, 999 Maple St, Contoocook, NH 03229-3374 *Tel:* 603-746-3102 *Fax:* 603-746-5628
Scripta Humanistica, Calle Union 657, Miramar 00907, Puerto Rico *Tel:* 809-723-2445
Leader Books SA, 62 Koniaristr, 115 21 Ampelokipi, Greece *Tel:* 210 6452825 *Fax:* 210 6449924
Spain Shobo Co Ltd, Yamoto, PO Box 12, Miyagui 981-0503, Japan *Tel:* (0225) 84-1280

Fax: (0225) 84-1283 *E-mail:* info@spainshobo.co.jp
Portico Librerias SA, Calle Munoz Seca 6, 50005 Zaragoza, Spain *Tel:* 976 55 70 39 *Fax:* 976 35 32 26 *E-mail:* jalcrudo@porticolibrerias.es
Grant & Cutler Ltd, 55-57 Great Marlborough St, London W1V 1DD, United Kingdom *Tel:* (0171) 734-2012

The Scriptural Research & Publishing Co Inc
344 E Johnson Ave, Cheshire, CT 06410
Mailing Address: PO Box 725, New Britain, CT 06050-0725
Tel: 203-272-1780 *Fax:* 203-272-2296
E-mail: src1@srpublish.org
Web Site: www.scripturalresearch.com
Key Personnel
Admin: Joseph R Poulin
Founded: 1995
Religious & scripturally-based books.
ISBN Prefix(es): 978-1-57277
Number of titles published annually: 2 Print; 1 E-Book
Total Titles: 50 Print; 1 Audio

Search Institute Press®
Division of Search Institute
The Banks Bldg, Suite 125, 615 First Ave NE, Minneapolis, MN 55413
Tel: 612-376-8955; 612-692-5520 *Toll Free Tel:* 800-888-7828 *Fax:* 612-692-5553
E-mail: si@search-institute.org
Web Site: www.search-institute.org
Key Personnel
Co-Chair: Jeff Peterson; Ann Curme Shaw
Contracts & Proj Mgr: Jan DeWall *E-mail:* jand@search-institute.org
Provide practical, hope-filled books to create a world in which young people are valued & thrive. Content is based on Search Institute's 50 years of research & focuses on the 40 Developmental Assets®, a framework of qualities, experiences & relationships youth need to succeed. Publishes resources for adults & youth that help strengthen communities by nurturing parents, concerned & caring adults, young people, educators & youth, family & community service professionals.
ISBN Prefix(es): 978-1-57482
Number of titles published annually: 4 Print; 4 E-Book
Total Titles: 110 Print; 50 E-Book
Distribution Center: Independent Publishers Group (IPG), 814 N Franklin St, Chicago, IL 60610 *Tel:* 312-337-0747 *Toll Free Tel:* 800-888-4741 (orders) *Fax:* 312-337-5985 *E-mail:* orders@ipgbook.com *Web Site:* www.ipgbook.com
Membership(s): ABC

Second Chance Press
Imprint of The Permanent Press
4170 Noyac Rd, Sag Harbor, NY 11963
SAN: 213-1633
Tel: 631-725-1101
E-mail: info@thepermanentpress.com
Web Site: www.thepermanentpress.com
Key Personnel
Co-Publr: Judith Shepard *E-mail:* judith@thepermanentpress.com; Martin Shepard *E-mail:* shepard@thepermanentpress.com
Mng Ed: Cathy Suter *E-mail:* cathy@thepermanentpress.com
Assoc Ed: Brian Skulnik *E-mail:* brian@thepermanentpress.com
Typesetting, Design & Prodn: Susan Ahlquist *E-mail:* susan@thepermanentpress.com
Founded: 1977
Originals & reprints of literary works in hardcover & paperback.
ISBN Prefix(es): 978-0-933256
Number of titles published annually: 16 Print
Total Titles: 475 Print
Foreign Rights: Nike Davarinou (Greece); Kira Dominguez (Australia); Lora Fountain Agency (France); Jill Hughes (Eastern Europe); International Editors (Jennifer Houge) (Portugal, Spain); Jane Judd (UK); Andrew Nurnberg Associates (China); ONK Agency Ltd (Turkey); Thomas Schlueck GmbH (Germany); Rita Vivian (Italy); Eric Yang (Korea)

Seedling Publications Inc
Imprint of Continental Press
520 E Bainbridge St, Elizabethtown, PA 17022
Toll Free Tel: 800-233-0759 *Toll Free Fax:* 888-834-1303
E-mail: info@continentalpress.com
Web Site: www.continentalpress.com
Key Personnel
CEO: Daniel Raffensperger
Pres: Eric Beck *E-mail:* ebeck@continentalpress.com
VP & Publr: Megan Bergonzi
VP, Mktg: Robyn Matus
Founded: 1992
Books for beginning readers in 8-16 page format; leveled readers-parental involvement materials.
ISBN Prefix(es): 978-0-8454
Number of titles published annually: 15 Print
Total Titles: 275 Print
Distributed by Kendall Hunt Publishing
Foreign Rep(s): PSI

SelectBooks Inc
87 Walker St, Suite B1, New York, NY 10013
Tel: 212-206-1997 *Fax:* 212-206-3815
E-mail: info@selectbooks.com
Web Site: www.selectbooks.com
Key Personnel
Founder & Publr: Kenzi Sugihara *E-mail:* kenzi@selectbooks.com
Publicity Mgr: Kenichi Sugihara *E-mail:* kenichi@selectbooks.com
Founded: 2001
ISBN Prefix(es): 978-1-59079
Number of titles published annually: 25 Print; 5 E-Book; 2 Audio
Total Titles: 100 Print; 5 E-Book; 3 Audio
Sales Office(s): Midpoint Trade Books, 27 W 20 St, Suite 1102, New York, NY 10011 *Tel:* 212-727-0190 *Fax:* 212-727-0195 *E-mail:* midpointny1@aol.com
Foreign Rights: Waterside Productions (worldwide)
Orders to: Midpoint Trade Books, 27 W 20 St, Suite 1102, New York, NY 10011 *Tel:* 212-727-0190 *Fax:* 212-727-0195 *E-mail:* orders@midpt.com *Web Site:* www.midpointtrade.com
Returns: Midpoint Trade Books, 27 W 20 St, Suite 1102, New York, NY 10011 *Tel:* 212-727-0190 *Fax:* 212-727-0195 *E-mail:* orders@midpt.com *Web Site:* www.midpointtrade.com
Distribution Center: Midpoint Trade Books, 27 W 20 St, Suite 1102, New York, NY 10011 *Tel:* 212-727-0190 *Fax:* 212-727-0195 *Web Site:* www.midpointtrade.com
Baker & Taylor, 2550 W Tyvola Rd, Suite 300, Charlotte, NC 28217 *Tel:* 704-998-3100 *Toll Free Tel:* 800-775-1800 *Web Site:* www.btol.com
Ingram Content Group Inc, One Ingram Blvd, La Vergne, TN 37086 *Tel:* 615-793-5000 *E-mail:* inquiry@ingramcontent.com *Web Site:* www.ingramcontent.com
Membership(s): Independent Book Publishers Association

Self-Realization Fellowship Publishers
3208 Humboldt St, Los Angeles, CA 90031
SAN: 204-5788
Tel: 323-276-6002 *Toll Free Tel:* 888-773-8680 *Fax:* 323-927-1624
E-mail: sales@yogananda-srf.org
Web Site: www.yogananda-srf.org; bookstore.yogananda-srf.org/ (orders)
Key Personnel
Sales Mgr: Phil Gray
Mktg: Mike Baake *E-mail:* mikeb@yogananda-srf.org
Founded: 1920 (by Paramahansa Yogananda)
Publisher for the complete works of Paramahansa Yogananda.
ISBN Prefix(es): 978-0-87612
Number of titles published annually: 10 Print; 7 Audio
Returns: 3233 N San Fernando Rd, Unit 2, Los Angeles, CA 90065, Contact: Mark Russell *Tel:* 323-276-6000 *E-mail:* markr@yogananda-srf.org SAN: 204-5688
Membership(s): Independent Book Publishers Association

Sentient Publications LLC
PO Box 7204, Boulder, CO 80306
Tel: 303-443-2188 *Fax:* 303-381-2538
E-mail: contact@sentientpublications.com
Web Site: www.sentientpublications.com
Key Personnel
Publr: Connie Shaw *E-mail:* cshaw@sentientpublications.com
Founded: 2001
Ecology, education, health, science, spirituality. Publish quality nonfiction books that arise from the spirit of inquiry & the richness of the inherent dialogue between writer & reader.
ISBN Prefix(es): 978-0-9710786; 978-1-59181
Number of titles published annually: 5 Print; 5 E-Book
Total Titles: 105 Print; 130 E-Book; 10 Audio
Foreign Rights: ANA Sofia Ltd (Bulgaria, Romania); Asli Karasuil Telif Haklari Ajansi (Turkey); Book Publishers Association of Israel (Israel); Giro di Parole (Italy); The English Agency (Japan); International Editors' Co (Spain); JLM Literary Agency (Greece); Michelle Lapautre Literary Agency (France); Maxima Creative Agency (Indonesia); Andrew Nurnberg (China); Piper & Poppenhusen (Germany); H Katia Schumer (Brazil); Silkroad Publishers Agency (Thailand)
Orders to: National Book Network, 4720 Boston Way, Lanham, MD 20706 *Tel:* 301-459-3366 *Toll Free Tel:* 800-462-6420 *Fax:* 301-459-1705 *Web Site:* www.nbnbooks.com
Shipping Address: National Book Network, 4720 Boston Way, Lanham, MD 20706 *Tel:* 301-459-3366 *Toll Free Tel:* 800-462-6420 *Fax:* 301-459-1705 *Web Site:* www.nbnbooks.com
Distribution Center: National Book Network, 4720 Boston Way, Lanham, MD 20706 *Tel:* 301-459-3366 *Toll Free Tel:* 800-462-6420 *Fax:* 301-459-1705 *Web Site:* www.nbnbooks.com
Membership(s): Publishers Association of the West

Serindia Publications
PO Box 10335, Chicago, IL 60610-0335
Fax: 312-664-4389
E-mail: info@serindia.com
Web Site: www.serindia.com
Key Personnel
Publr: Shane Suvikapakornkul
Founded: 1976 (in London)
ISBN Prefix(es): 978-1-932476
Number of titles published annually: 11 Print
Total Titles: 60 Print
Distributed by Art Media Resources Inc (US & CN)
Foreign Rep(s): Kodansha Europe (Europe, UK); Paragon Asia Co Ltd (Singapore, Southeast Asia, Thailand); United Century Book Service (Hong Kong, Mainland China); The Variety Book Depot (Bhutan, India, Nepal, South Asia)

Seven Stories Press
140 Watts St, New York, NY 10013
Tel: 212-226-8760 *Toll Free Tel:* 800-733-3000 (orders) *Fax:* 212-226-1411
E-mail: info@sevenstories.com
Web Site: www.sevenstories.com
Key Personnel
Publr: Daniel Simon
Dir, Mktg & Publicity, Triangle Square Books: Ruth Weiner *E-mail:* ruth@sevenstories.com
Opers Dir: Jon Gilbert *E-mail:* jon@sevenstories.com
Rts Dir: Silvia Stramenga
Mng Ed: Rachel Nam
Sr Ed: Veronica Liu
Asst Ed: Lauren Hooker
Founded: 1995
Publish original hardcover & paperback books for the general reader in the area of literature, literature in translation, popular culture, politics, media studies, health & nutrition & sports. No unsol mss.
ISBN Prefix(es): 978-1-58322; 978-1-888363; 978-1-60980
Number of titles published annually: 50 Print; 15 E-Book; 2 Audio
Total Titles: 560 Print; 370 E-Book
Imprints: Siete Cuentos Editorial (Spanish lang); Triangle Square Books for Young Readers
Foreign Rep(s): Penguin Random House (all other territories); Turnaround Distribution (UK)
Foreign Rights: AnatoliaLit Agency (Turkey); Big Apple Agency (China, Taiwan); Paul & Peter Fritz Agency (Germany); Deborah Harris Literary Agency (Israel); Japan Uni Agency Inc (Japan); Katai & Bolza Agency (Hungary); Duran Kim Agency (Korea); MB Agencia Literaria (Spain, Spanish Latin America); Piergiorgio Nicolazzini Literary Agency (Italy); Sandorf Literary Agency (Croatia, Serbia, Slovenia); Ludmilla Shuskova (Russia); Villas-Boas & Moss Agencia Literaria (Brazil, Portugal)
Distribution Center: Penguin Random House, 400 Hahn Rd, Westminster, MD 21157 *Tel:* 612-746-2600 *Toll Free Tel:* 800-283-3572 (cust serv) *Fax:* 612-746-2606 *Web Site:* www.penguinrandomhouse.com

1765 Productions
PO Box 4151, Fairfax, VA 22124-8151
Tel: 202-813-9421
E-mail: 1765productions@gmail.com
Key Personnel
Publr & Prodr: Patrick G Finegan, Jr
Founded: 1990
Subject specialties include finance, film scripts & screenplays.
ISBN Prefix(es): 978-1-878905
Number of titles published annually: 4 Print
Total Titles: 6 Print

§Shadow Mountain
PO Box 30178, Salt Lake City, UT 84130-0178
Tel: 801-534-1515 *Toll Free Tel:* 800-453-3876 *Fax:* 801-517-3119
E-mail: submissions@shadowmountain.com
Web Site: shadowmountain.com
Key Personnel
Edit Mgr & Acqs Ed: Lisa Mangum
Subs Rts Mgr: Jack Newman
Founded: 1985
US-based publisher committed to providing books (print, electronic & audio) that offer value-based messages for readers of all ages. Publish quality children's fantasy & numerous bestsellers in the inspiration, fiction, history & business genres.
ISBN Prefix(es): 978-0-88494; 978-0-87747; 978-1-59038; 978-1-57345; 978-1-57008; 978-0-87579; 978-1-60908; 978-1-60641; 978-1-60907; 978-1-62972; 978-1-62973
Number of titles published annually: 25 Print, 2 Online; 25 E-Book; 10 Audio
Total Titles: 200 Print; 2 Online; 70 E-Book; 80 Audio
Imprints: Proper Romance
Distribution Center: Baker & Taylor, 2550 W Tyvola Rd, Suite 300, Charlotte, NC 28217 *Tel.* 704-998-3100 *Web Site:* www.btol.com
Ingram Content Group, One Ingram Blvd, La Vergne, TN 37086 *Tel:* 615-793-5000 *Web Site:* www.ingramcontent.com
Membership(s): ABC; The Children's Book Council; Independent Book Publishers Association; Mountains & Plains Independent Publishers Association; Romance Writers of America

§Shambhala Publications Inc
4720 Walnut St, Boulder, CO 80301
SAN: 203-2481
Tel: 303-222-9598 *Toll Free Tel:* 866-424-0030 (off); 888-424-2329 (cust serv) *Fax:* 303-200-9406
E-mail: customercare@shambhala.com
Web Site: www.shambhala.com
Key Personnel
Founder & Ed-in-Chief: Samuel Bercholz
Owner, EVP, Publr of Roost Books: Sara Bercholz
Owner, EVP & Course Prodn Mgr: Ivan Bercholz
Pres: Nikko Odiseos
VP & Assoc Publr: Jonathan Green
Cont & HR Dir: Lisa Reusser
Dir, Publicity: Steven Pomije
Prodn & Design Dir: Lora Zorian
Mng Ed: Liz Shaw
Asst Mng Ed: John Golebiewski
Sr Ed: David O'Neal
Ed: Beth Frankl
Ed, Roost Books: Jennifer Urban-Brown
Sr Mktg Mgr: Claire Kelley
Rts Mgr: Oliver Glosband
Sales & Mktg Mgr: KJ Grow
Sr Designer: Jim Zaccaria
Sr Designer, Roost Books: Daniel Urban-Brown
Founded: 1969
Trade books; art, literature, comparative religion, philosophy, science, psychology & related subjects.
ISBN Prefix(es): 978-0-307; 978-0-87773; 978-1-56957; 978-1-57062; 978-1-59030; 978-1-61180
Number of titles published annually: 85 Print; 50 Online
Total Titles: 1,050 Print; 50 Online
Imprints: Bala Kids; Roost Books; Snow Lion
Distributed by Penguin Random House Inc
Foreign Rep(s): Airlift Books (UK); Penguin Random House Australia Ltd (Australia); Penguin Random House of Canada Ltd (Canada); Penguin Random House of New Zealand (New Zealand)
Foreign Rights: ACER (Spain); The English Agency (Japan); Anoukh Foerg (Germany); La Nouvelle Agence (Vanessa Kling) (France); Schindler's Literary Agency (Brazil)
Advertising Agency: Vermillion Graphics, Boulder, CO 80302
Returns: Penguin Random House, Returns Dept, 400 Bennett Dr, Westminster, MD 21157
Shipping Address: Penguin Random House Distribution Center, 400 Hahn Rd, Westminster, MD 21157
See separate listing for:
Snow Lion

Shenanigan Books
84 River Rd, Summit, NJ 07901
Tel: 908-219-4275 *Fax:* 908-219-4485
Web Site: www.shenaniganbooks.com
Key Personnel
Founder & Creative Dir: Mary Watson
Founded: 2005
Children's literature: craft/picture/board books.
ISBN Prefix(es): 978-0-9726614; 978-1-934860
Number of titles published annually: 6 Print
Membership(s): ALA; The Children's Book Council; Independent Book Publishers Association

Shengold Publishers, see Schreiber Publishing

Shen's Books
Imprint of Lee & Low Books
95 Madison Ave, Suite 1205, New York, NY 10016
Tel: 212-779-4400 *Fax:* 212-683-1894
E-mail: general@leeandlow.com
Web Site: www.leeandlow.com
Founded: 1985
Children's books.
ISBN Prefix(es): 978-1-885008
Number of titles published annually: 3 Print
Total Titles: 25 Print
Membership(s): ABA; Independent Book Publishers Association

Shepard Publications
PO Box 280, Friday Harbor, WA 98250
Web Site: www.shepardpub.com
Key Personnel
Owner & Pres: Aaron Shepard
ISBN Prefix(es): 978-0-938497; 978-1-62035; 978-0-9849616
Number of titles published annually: 4 Print; 10 E-Book
Total Titles: 45 Print; 45 E-Book
Imprints: Islander Images (photography); Islander Press; Shepard & Piper (literary fiction & nonfiction); Simple Productions (nonviolence, lifestyle alternatives, music); Skyhook Press (children's)

Sherman Asher Publishing
126 Candelario St, Santa Fe, NM 87501
Tel: 505-988-7214
E-mail: westernedge@santa-fe.net
Web Site: www.shermanasher.com; www.westernedgepress.com
Key Personnel
Owner & Publr: James Mafchir
Founded: 1995
Literary books that include Spanish, English & bilingual memoirs & Judaica.
ISBN Prefix(es): 978-0-9644196; 978-1-890932
Number of titles published annually: 3 Print
Total Titles: 29 Print
Imprints: Western Edge Press
Distribution Center: SCB Distributors, 15608 S New Century Dr, Gardena, CA 90248 *Tel:* 310-532-9400 *Toll Free Tel:* 800-729-6423 *Fax:* 310-532-7001
See separate listing for:
Western Edge Press

Sheron Enterprises Inc
1035 S Carley Ct, North Bellmore, NY 11710
Tel: 516-783-5885
E-mail: sheronent1@msn.com
Web Site: www.longislandbookpublisher.com
Key Personnel
Owner & Pres: Sheryl Perry
Secy: Ronald Perry
Founded: 1996
Publish college textbooks, lab manuals & study aids for college professors with small & large print runs as well as helping unknown authors get published: poetry.
ISBN Prefix(es): 978-1-891877
Number of titles published annually: 5 Print
Total Titles: 42 Print

§Show What You Know® Publishing, A Lorenz Company
c/o The Lorenz Corp, 501 E Third St, Dayton, OH 45402

Mailing Address: PO Box 802, Dayton, OH 45401-0802
Tel: 614-764-1211; 937-228-6118
Toll Free Tel: 877-PASSING (727-7464)
Fax: 937-233-2042
E-mail: info@lorenz.com
Web Site: www.lorenzeducationalpress.com
Key Personnel
Chmn: Geoff Lorenz
CEO: Reiff Lorenz
Pres: Barbara Meeks
Mktg Assoc: Katherine LeVan
Educational publisher of K-12 supplemental test-preparation books & other materials.
ISBN Prefix(es): 978-1-884183; 978-1-59230
Number of titles published annually: 30 Print
Total Titles: 275 Print

SIAM, see Society for Industrial & Applied Mathematics

Side Street, see BrickHouse Books Inc

Siglio
PO Box 111, Catskill, NY 12414
Tel: 310-857-6935
E-mail: publisher@sigliopress.com
Web Site: sigliopress.com
Key Personnel
Publr: Lisa Pearson
Founded: 2008
Dedicated to publishing uncommon books that live at the intersection of art & literature.
ISBN Prefix(es): 978-0-9799562; 978-1-938221
Number of titles published annually: 4 Print
Total Titles: 26 Print

Signalman Publishing
3700 Commerce Blvd, Kissimmee, FL 34741
Tel: 407-504-4103 *Toll Free Tel:* 888-907-4423
E-mail: info@signalmanpublishing.com
Web Site: www.signalmanpublishing.com
Key Personnel
Pres: John McClure *E-mail:* john@signalmanpublishing.com
Ed: Urmila McClure *E-mail:* urmila@signalmanpublishing.com
Founded: 2008
Specialize in bringing nonfiction works to the Kindle format. Have also branched out into trade paper with both nonfiction & fiction works.
This publisher has indicated that 45% of their product line is author subsidized.
ISBN Prefix(es): 978-0-9840614; 978-1-935991; 978-1-940145
Number of titles published annually: 12 Print; 14 E-Book
Total Titles: 56 Print; 76 E-Book
Imprints: Trinity Grace Press
Orders to: Lightning Source, 1246 Heil Quaker Blvd, La Vergne, TN 37086, Contact: Justine Bylo *Tel:* 212-714-9000 *Fax:* 615-213-4725 *E-mail:* justine.bylo@ingramcontent.com
Shipping Address: Lightning Source, 1246 Heil Quaker Blvd, La Vergne, TN 37086, Contact: Justine Bylo *Tel:* 212-714-9000 *Fax:* 615-213-4725 *E-mail:* justine.bylo@ingramcontent.com
Membership(s): The Association of Publishers for Special Sales; Christian Small Publishers Association

Signature Books Publishing LLC
564 W 400 N, Salt Lake City, UT 84116-3411
SAN: 217-4391
Tel: 801-531-1483 *Fax:* 801-531-1488
E-mail: people@signaturebooks.com
Web Site: www.signaturebooks.com; www.signaturebookslibrary.org
Key Personnel
Pres & Publr: George D Smith
Mng Dir & Sr Ed: Ronald L Priddis
Mktg Dir: Tom Kimball
Busn Mgr: Keiko Jones *Tel:* 801-531-1483 ext 102 *E-mail:* keiko@signaturebooks.com
Shipping Mgr: Greg Jones
Prodn & Design: Jason Francis
Founded: 1980
Western Americana.
ISBN Prefix(es): 978-0-941214; 978-1-56085
Number of titles published annually: 5 Print; 5 E-Book
Total Titles: 173 Print; 1 CD-ROM; 173 E-Book
Distribution Center: Chicago Distribution Center, 11030 S Langley Ave, Chicago, IL 60628 *Tel:* 773-702-7000 *Toll Free Tel:* 800-621-2736 *Fax:* 773-702-7212 *Toll Free Fax:* 800-621-8476 *E-mail:* orders@press.uchicago.edu *Web Site:* www.press.uchicago.edu

§SIL International
7500 W Camp Wisdom Rd, Dallas, TX 75236-5629
Tel: 972-708-7400; 972-708-7404 *Fax:* 972-708-7350; 972-708-7363
E-mail: publications_intl@sil.org
Web Site: www.sil.org; www.ethnologue.com
Key Personnel
Asst Mgr, Bookstore: Darryl Johnson
Founded: 1934
ISBN Prefix(es): 978-0-88312; 978-1-55671
Number of titles published annually: 6 Print
Total Titles: 160 Print; 2 CD-ROM; 3 Online; 3 E-Book

Silicon Press
25 Beverly Rd, Summit, NJ 07901
Tel: 908-273-8919 *Fax:* 908-273-6149
E-mail: info@silicon-press.com
Web Site: www.silicon-press.com
Key Personnel
CEO: Indu Gehani
Founded: 1987
Books about computers & technology/fiction.
ISBN Prefix(es): 978-0-929306; 978-0-9615336
Number of titles published annually: 10 Print; 4 Audio
Total Titles: 45 Print

Silman-James Press Inc
141 N Clark Dr, Unit 1, West Hollywood, CA 90048
Tel: 310-205-0665 *Fax:* 323 214-7943
E-mail: info@silmanjamespress.com
Web Site: www.silmanjamespress.com
Key Personnel
Publr: Gwen Feldman *E-mail:* gwen@silmanjamespress.com; Jim Fox *E-mail:* jim@silmanjamespress.com
Founded: 1990
Publisher of books on film, filmmaking, the motion picture industry & the performing arts.
ISBN Prefix(es): 978-1-879505; 978-1-935247
Number of titles published annually: 5 Print
Total Titles: 150 Print; 45 E-Book
Divisions: Quite Specific Media; Siles Press (chess & nonfiction titles)
Distributed by Codasat Canada Ltd
Foreign Rep(s): Gazelle Book Services Ltd (Continental Europe, UK)
Returns: 660 S Mansfield, Ypsilanti, MI 48197
See separate listing for:
Quite Specific Media Group Ltd

Silver Leaf Books LLC
13 Temi Rd, Holliston, MA 01746
Mailing Address: PO Box 6460, Holliston, MA 01746
E-mail: sales@silverleafbooks.com; editor@silverleafbooks.com; customerservice@silverleafbooks.com
Web Site: www.silverleafbooks.com
Key Personnel
Mng Dir & Dir, Fin: Clifford B Bowyer
E-mail: cbbowyer@silverleafbooks.com
Edit Mgr: Brett Fried
Sales Mgr: Marilyn Fried
Founded: 2003
ISBN Prefix(es): 978-0-9744354; 978-0-9787782; 978-1-60975
Number of titles published annually: 20 Print; 25 E-Book
Total Titles: 84 Print; 112 E-Book

Simcha Press
Imprint of Health Communications Inc
3201 SW 15 St, Deerfield Beach, FL 33442-8190
Tel: 954-360-0909 ext 212 *Toll Free Tel:* 800-851-9100 ext 212 *Toll Free Fax:* 800-424-7652
E-mail: simchapress@hcibooks.com
Web Site: www.hcibooks.com
Key Personnel
Dir, Communs & Mgr: Kim Weiss
E-mail: kimw@hcibooks.com
Founded: 1999
Nonfiction titles for those on the path of Jewish enrichment. Jewish interest, spirituality, inspirational, mysticism & recovery.
ISBN Prefix(es): 978-0-932194; 978-1-55874; 978-0-7573
Number of titles published annually: 4 Print; 4 Online; 4 E-Book
Total Titles: 13 Print; 13 Online; 8 E-Book

Simon & Schuster
Imprint of Simon & Schuster Publishing Group
1230 Avenue of the Americas, New York, NY 10020
Tel: 212-698-7000 *Toll Free Tel:* 800-223-2348 (cust serv); 800-223-2336 (orders)
Toll Free Fax: 800-943-9831 (orders)
Web Site: www.simonandschuster.com
Key Personnel
Pres & Publr: Jonathan Karp
VP & Assoc Publr: Richard Rhorer
VP & Ed-in-Chief: Marysue Rucci
VP & Edit Dir: Alice E Mayhew
VP & Exec Ed: Priscilla Painton; Robert Bender
VP & Dir, Publicity, Sr Ed: Cary Goldstein
VP & Exec Art Dir, Trade Art: Jackie Seow
Dir of Subs Rts: Marie Florio
Exec Ed: Jofie Ferrari-Adler; Ben Loehnen
Sr Ed: Karyn Marcus; Ira Silverberg; Christine Pride
Ed: Emily Graff; Jonathan Cox
Assoc Ed: Johanna Li
Deputy Dir, Publicity: Julia Prosser
Assoc Dir, Publicity: Larry Hughes; Anne Pearce
Sr Publicity Mgr: Sarah Reidy
Publicity Mgr: Amanda Lang; Erin Reback
Publicist: Leah Johanson; Elizabeth Gay
Assoc Dir, Mktg: Dana Trocker
Sr Mktg Mgr: Stephen Bedford
Mktg Mgr: Ebony LaDelle
Asst Mktg Mgr: Nicole McArdle
Mktg Asst: Elizabeth Breeden
Assoc Art Dir: Alison Forner
Mng Ed: Kristen Lemire
Asst Mng Ed: Allison Har-zvi
Subs Rts Mgr: Sandy Hill
Subs Rts Asst: Emma del Valle
Asst Ed: Stuart Roberts; Julianna Haubner; Megan Hogan; Amar Deol
Edit Asst: Zach Knoll
Publicity Asst: Lauren Carsley; Lindsay Means; Samantha O'Hara
ISBN Prefix(es): 978-0-684
Number of titles published annually: 125 Print
Imprints: Adams Media; Folger Shakespeare Library; Free Press
Foreign Rights: Akali Copyright Agency (Turkey); Antonella Antonelli Agenzia (Italy); Book Publishers Association of Israel (Israel); Japan UNI Agency (Japan); JLM Literary Agency (Greece); KCC (Korea Copyright

Center) (Korea); Mohrbooks Literary Agency (Germany); La Nouvelle Agence (France); Andrew Nurnberg Associates (Bulgaria, Croatia, Czech Republic, Estonia, Hungary, Latvia, Lithuania, Montenegro, Poland, Romania, Serbia, Slovakia, Slovenia); Sane Toregard Agency (Denmark, Finland, Iceland, Norway); Sebes & Bisseling Literary Agency (Netherlands); Tuttle-Mori Agency Inc (Thailand)
See separate listing for:
Adams Media

Simon & Schuster Audio
Division of Simon & Schuster, Inc
1230 Avenue of the Americas, New York, NY 10020
Web Site: audio.simonandschuster.com
Key Personnel
Pres & Publr: Chris Lynch
VP, Audio Prodn: Elisa Shokoff
VP & Edit Dir: Tom Spain
VP, Pimsleur Language Programs: Tom McLean
VP, Mktg Dir: Sarah Lieberman
Sr Publicity, Media & Mktg Mgr: Lauren Pires
Audiobooks & Pimsleur Language Programs.
ISBN Prefix(es): 978-0-684; 978-0-7435; 978-0-671; 978-1-4423
Number of titles published annually: 100 Audio
Imprints: Audioworks; Beyond Words; Encore; Pimsleur; Sound Ideas
Distributor for Monostereo
Shipping Address: Total Warehouse Services, 2207 Radcliffe St, Bristol, PA 19007

Simon & Schuster Books for Young Readers, see Simon & Schuster Children's Publishing

§Simon & Schuster Children's Publishing
Division of Simon & Schuster, Inc
1230 Avenue of the Americas, New York, NY 10020
Tel: 212-698-7000
Web Site: www.simonandschuster.com/kids; www.simonandschuster.com/teen; simonandschuster.net; simonandschuster.biz
Key Personnel
Pres & Publr: Jon Anderson
VP & Publr, S&S Books for Young Readers, Atheneum, McElderry Books, Saga Press: Justin Chanda
VP & Publr, Simon Pulse, Aladdin: Mara Anastas
VP & Publr, Licensed & Novelty Publg, Simon Spotlight, Little Simon: Valerie Garfield
VP & Publr, Paula Wiseman Books: Paula Wiseman
VP & Publr, Beach Lane Books: Allyn Johnston
VP & Deputy Publr, S&S Books for Young Readers, Atheneum, McElderry, Saga Press, Paula Wiseman Books, Beach Lane Books: Anne Zafian
VP & Edit Dir, S&S Books for Young Readers: David Gale
VP & Edit Dir, Atheneum, Caitlyn Dlouhy Books: Caitlyn Dlouhy
VP, Edit Dir, McElderry Books: Karen Wojtyla
VP, Edit Dir, Simon Pulse & Assoc Edit Dir, Aladdin: Liesa Abrams
VP & Creative Dir: Dan Potash
Edit Dir, Saga Press: Joe Monti
Edit Dir, Aladdin: Fiona Simpson
Edit Dir, Little Simon: Jeffrey Salane
Edit Dir, Simon Spotlight: Siobhan Ciminera
Exec Ed, S&S Books for Young Readers/Salaam Reads: Zareen Jaffrey
Exec Ed, Atheneum: Reka Simonsen
Exec Ed, Aladdin: Karen Nagel
Sr Ed, Beach Lane Books: Andrea Welch
Sr Ed, McElderry: Ruta Rimas
Exec Art Dir, Simon Pulse, Atheneum (novels), McElderry (novels): Russell Gordon
Exec Art Dir, Atheneum (picture books), McElderry (picture books), Beach Lane Books: Ann Bobco
Exec Art Dir, Little Simon, Simon Spotlight: Channi Yammer
Exec Art Dir, S&S Books for Young Readers, Paula Wiseman Books: Lizzy Bromley
Exec Art Dir, Aladdin: Karin Paprocki
VP & Exec Mng Ed: Lisa Donovan
VP, Subs Rts: Stephanie Voros
VP, Dir of Mktg & Publicity: Lauren Hoffman
VP, Dir of Educ & Lib Mktg: Michelle Leo
Sr Mktg Dir: Chrissy Noh
Sr Dir, Publicity: Nicole Russo
Dir of Publicity: Lisa Moraleda
Assoc Mktg Dir, Aladdin, Simon Pulse, Simon Spotlight, Little Simon: Carolyn Swerdloff
Preschool through young adult, hardcover & paperback fiction, nonfiction, trade, library, mass market titles & novelty books.
ISBN Prefix(es): 978-0-02; 978-0-609; 978-0-689; 978-0-7434; 978-1-4169
Number of titles published annually: 750 Print
Total Titles: 4,329 Print
Imprints: Aladdin; Atheneum Books for Young Readers (includes Caitlyn Dlouhy Books); Beach Lane Books; Little Simon; Margaret K McElderry Books; Saga Press (adult science-fiction/fantasy/horror); Salaam Reads; Simon & Schuster Books for Young Readers; Simon Pulse; Simon Spotlight; Paula Wiseman Books

§Simon & Schuster, Inc
Division of CBS Corporation
1230 Avenue of the Americas, New York, NY 10020
SAN: 200-2450
Tel: 212-698-7000 *Fax:* 212-698-7007
E-mail: firstname.lastname@simonandschuster.com
Web Site: www.simonandschuster.com
Key Personnel
Pres & CEO: Carolyn K Reidy
EVP & Gen Coun: Hazel-Ann Mayers
EVP, Opers & CFO: Dennis Eulau
EVP, Sales & Mktg: Michael Selleck
Pres & Publr, Simon & Schuster Audio: Chris Lynch
Pres & Publr, Children's Publishing Div: Jon Anderson
Pres & Publr, Simon & Schuster Publishing Group: Jonathan Karp
Pres & Publr, Scribner Publishing Group: Susan Moldow
Pres & Publr, Atria Publishing Group: Judith Curr
Pres & Publr, Simon & Schuster Canada: Kevin Hanson
SVP & Publr, Gallery Publishing Group: Jennifer Bergstrom
Chief Exec & Publr, Simon & Schuster UK Ltd: Ian Chapman
Mng Dir, Simon & Schuster (Australia) Pty Ltd: Dan Ruffino
Mng Dir, Simon & Schuster India: Rahul Srivastava
EVP, Chief Mktg Offr: Liz Perl
SVP, Corp Communs: Adam Rothberg
SVP, HR: Carolyn Connolly
VP, Group Cont: Deepak Daswani
VP, Busn Opers: Frank Nunez
VP, Gen Mgr, Adult, Children's & Audio: Craig Mandeville
VP, Client Publr Servs: Stephen Black
VP, Global Ebook Mkt Devt & Strategy: Doug Stambaugh
VP, Client Mgmt & Busn Devt: Joe Bulger
VP, Exec Mng Ed, Prodn & Copy Editing: Irene Kheradi
VP, Design & Digital Content Devt: Samantha Cohen
VP, Dist & Fulfillment: Dave Schaeffer
VP, Contracts & Perms: Jeff Wilson
VP, Dir, Ad & Promo: Mark Speer
VP, Dir of Mktg, Adult Trade: Wendy Sheanin
VP, Dir of Educ & Lib Mktg: Michelle Leo
VP, Digital Content: Sue Fleming
VP, Digital Mktg: Sienna Farris
VP, Digital Prod: David Krivda
VP, Digital Technol: Stephen Morgan
Founded: 1924
ISBN Prefix(es): 978-1-55850; 978-0-02; 978-0-941831; 978-1-885223; 978-0-7867; 978-0-13; 978-1-878990; 978-0-7318; 978-0-669; 978-0-86417; 978-0-88708; 978-0-7434; 978-1-58270; 978-1-86842; 978-0-7435; 978-1-4169; 978-1-4165; 978-1-59337; 978-1-904027; 978-0-89256; 978-0-9674601; 978-0-9711953; 978-1-58229; 978-1-59309; 978-1-60061; 978-1-84737; 978-1-84738; 978-1-84739; 978-0-684; 978-0-7432; 978-0-689; 978-0-671; 978-1-4391; 978-1-903650; 978-1-4423; 978-1-4424; 978-1-4516; 978-1-84983; 978-0-9870685; 978-1-84970; 978-1-921470; 978-0-85720; 978-0-85707; 978-1-62266; 978-1-4711; 978-1-4767; 978-1-4814; 978-1-922052; 978-1-925030; 978-0-85783; 978-0-85941; 978-0-87605; 978-1-5011; 978-1-925184; 978-1-59869; 978-1-60550; 978-1-4405; 978-1-925310; 978-1-5082; 978-1-925368; 978-1-925456; 978-1-5072; 978-0-932102; 978-0-9714010; 978-1-5344; 978-1-936399; 978-1-4972; 978-1-925384; 978-1-925533; 978-1-925596; 978-1-925640; 978-1-935562; 978-81-933552
Branch Office(s)
Beach Lane Books, 5666 La Jolla Blvd, No 154, La Jolla, CA 92037 *Tel:* 858-551-0860 *Fax:* 858-551-0492
Pimsleur, 30 Monument Sq, Concord, MA 01742 *Tel:* 978-369-7525
Adams Media, 57 Littlefield St, Avon, MA 02322 *Tel:* 508-427-7100 *Fax:* 508-427-6790
Simon & Schuster, 1639 Rte 10 E, Parsippany, NJ 07054 (royalties, accts payable, fin) *Tel:* 973-656-6000 *Fax:* 973-656-6070
Simon & Schuster Canada, 116 King St E, Suite 300, Toronto, ON M5A 1J3, Canada *Tel:* 647-427-8882 *Fax:* 647-430-9446
Foreign Office(s): Simon & Schuster Australia Pty Ltd, 450 Miller St, Suite 19a, Level 1, Bldg C, Cammeray, NSW 2062, Australia *Tel:* (02) 9983 6600 *Fax:* (02) 9988 4232 (sales & mktg) *E-mail:* cservice@simonandschuster.com.au *Web Site:* www.simonandschuster.com.au/
Simon & Schuster Publishers India Pvt Ltd, 2316, Tower–A, The Corenthum A -41, Sector -62, Noida, Uttar Pradesh 201301, India
Simon & Schuster UK Ltd, 222 Gray's Inn Rd, 1st fl, London WC1X 8HB, United Kingdom *Tel:* (020) 7316-1900 *Fax:* (020) 7316-0333 *E-mail:* enquiries@simonandschuster.co.uk *Web Site:* www.simonandschuster.co.uk
Distributor for Andrews McMeel Publishing LLC; Backlist LLC (div of Chicken Soup for the Soul Publishing); Baen Books; Baseball America; Beyond Words; BL Publishing (div of Games Workshop); Boom! Studios; Cardoza Publishing; Cernunnos; Chicken Soup for the Soul Publishing; Cider Mill Press Book Publishers LLC (including Applesauce Press imprint); Downtown Bookworks; Frederator Books LLC; Gallup (worldwide); Games Workshop; Harlequin Enterprises Ltd (billing only); Hooked on Phonics (Sandviks HOP Inc/Sandvik Publishing); Inner Traditions/Bear & Company; Insight Editions; Kaplan Publishing (including Manhattan Prep); Katalitix Media; Kinfolk; Little Bee Books; Meadowbrook Press; Merck Publishing; Moll Anderson Productions; NorthSouth Books (div of NordSued Verlag); Omnific Publishing; Open Road Publishing; Permuted Press LLC; Piggyback Interactive; Pikachu Press (Pokemon Company International); Post Hill Press LLC; Reader's Digest Books (div of Trusted Media Brands Inc); Rebellion Publishing; Regan Arts; Ripley Entertainment Inc (Ripley's Believe it or Not); Ry-

land, Peters & Small (including CICO Books); Start Publishing LLC; Studio Fun International (div of Trusted Media Brands Inc); TC Media Books; To The Stars Inc; Tuttle Publishing; Ubisoft; Uncrate LLC; Victory Belt Publishing; VIZ Media; Weldon Owen; Wisdom Publications; World Almanac (div of Facts on File); Yilin Press (Mandarin ebooks)
Returns: Simon & Schuster, c/o Jacobson Companies, 4406 Industrial Park Rd, Bldg 7, Camp Hill, PA 17011 (by appt; to schedule call 717-730-5212 ext 5316)
Shipping Address: Riverside Distribution Center, 100 Front St, Riverside, NJ 08075 (trade, children's, audio, mass-market & dist clients) *Tel:* 856-461-6500 *Fax:* 856-824-2402; Bristol Distribution Center, 2207 Radcliffe St, Bristol, PA 19007 *Tel:* 215-785-0531 *Fax:* 215-826-3002
Membership(s): AAP; BISG
See separate listing for:
Simon & Schuster Audio
Simon & Schuster Children's Publishing
Simon & Schuster Sales Division

Simon & Schuster Sales Division
Division of Simon & Schuster, Inc
1230 Avenue of the Americas, New York, NY 10020
Tel: 212-698-7000
Key Personnel
EVP, Sales & Mktg: Michael Selleck *Tel:* 212-698-7420 *E-mail:* michael.selleck@simonandschuster.com
VP & Exec Dir, Dist Sales & Retail Mktg: Gary Urda *Tel:* 212-698-7389 *E-mail:* gary.urda@simonandschuster.com
VP & Dir, Children's Sales: Christina Pecorale *Tel:* 212-698-1126 *E-mail:* christina.pecorale@simonandschuster.com
VP & Dir, Retail Sales: Paula Amendolara *Tel:* 212-698-7069 *E-mail:* paula.amendolara@simonandschuster.com
VP & Dir, Global Digital & Online Sales: Colin Shields *Tel:* 212-698-7536 *E-mail:* colin.shields@simonandschuster.com
VP & Dir, Intl Sales: Mr Seth Russo *Tel:* 212-698-7422 *E-mail:* seth.russo@simonandschuster.com
VP & Dir, Sales & Client Communs: Eileen Gentillo *Tel:* 212-698-7470 *E-mail:* eileen.gentillo@simonandschuster.com
VP & Dir, Client Sales & Servs: Michael Perlman *Tel:* 212-698-7061 *E-mail:* michael.perlman@simonandschuster.com
VP & Dir, Spec Mkts: Sumya Ojakli *Tel:* 212-698-7202 *E-mail:* sumya.ojakli@simonandschuster.com
Distributor for Andrews McMeel Publishing LLC; Applesauce Press (children's); Baen Books; Baseball America; Boom! Studios; Cardoza; Cernunnos; Chicken Soup for the Soul; Cider Mill Press Book Publishers LLC; Downtown Bookworks; Frederator Books LLC; Gallup (worldwide); Games Workshop; Hazelden; Hooked On Phonics; Insight Editions; Juniper Publishing; Kaplan Publishing; Katalitix; Kinfolk; little bee books; Manhattan Prep; Meadowbrook Press; Merck Publishing; North South Books; Omnific; Open Road; Permuted Press LLC; Piggyback Interactive; Post Hill Press LLC; Reader's Digest Children's Books; Rebellion; Regan Arts; Ripley Entertainment; To the Stars Inc; Uncrate LLC; VIZ Media; Weldon Owen; World Almanac (div of Facts on File)

Simon Pulse, see Simon & Schuster Children's Publishing

Simon Spotlight, see Simon & Schuster Children's Publishing

§Sinauer Associates Inc
23 Plumtree Rd, Sunderland, MA 01375
SAN: 203-2392
Mailing Address: PO Box 407, Sunderland, MA 01375-0407 SAN: 203-2392
Tel: 413-549-4300 *Fax:* 413-549-1118
E-mail: publish@sinauer.com; orders@sinauer.com
Web Site: sinauer.com
Key Personnel
Pres & Ed: Andrew D Sinauer
VP & Mktg Dir: Dean H Scudder
Busn Mgr: Jeannine LeBlanc
Prodn Mgr: Christopher Small
Biology Acqs Ed: Rachel Meyers
Psych/Neurosci Acqs Ed: Sydney Carroll
Rts & Perms: Sherri Ellsworth
Founded: 1969
College textbooks & reference works in the biological & behavioral sciences.
ISBN Prefix(es): 978-0-87893; 978-1-60535
Number of titles published annually: 10 Print
Total Titles: 100 Print; 10 CD-ROM; 7 Online
Foreign Rep(s): Alkem (Bangladesh, Brunei, Cambodia, Hong Kong, Indonesia, Laos, Malaysia, Myanmar, Philippines, Singapore, Taiwan, Thailand); FUNPEC-Editora (Brazil); Palgrave Macmillan (Africa, Australia, Brazil, Caribbean, China, Europe, Japan, Latin America, Middle East, Nepal, New Zealand, Pakistan, Russia, Sri Lanka, UK); Panima Educational Book Agency (India); Shinil Books Co Ltd (Korea); World Science Publishing Co (Korea)
Warehouse: Publishers Storage & Shipping Corp, 46 Development Rd, Fitchburg, MA 01420 *Tel:* 978-345-2121 *Fax:* 978-348-1233

Six Gallery Press
PO Box 90145, Pittsburgh, PA 15224-0545
Web Site: www.sixgallerypress.com
Key Personnel
Publr & Ed: Che Elias *E-mail:* rocketsconstrue@yahoo.com; Michael Hafftka *E-mail:* michael@sixgallerypress.com
Founded: 2000
Independent press producing & marketing experimental literature. We promote these books through reviews in journals, online & through author readings as well as special events including bookfairs.
ISBN Prefix(es): 978-0-9703840; 978-0-9726301; 978-0-9810091; 978-0-9782962; 978-0-9746033; 978-0-9776242
Number of titles published annually: 10 Print
Total Titles: 50 Print
Imprints: Convergence
Distribution Center: Small Press Distribution, 1341 Seventh St, Berkeley, CA 94710-1409

§SkillPath Publications
Division of The Graceland University Center for Professional Development & Lifelong Learning Inc
6900 Squibb Rd, Mission, KS 66202
Mailing Address: PO Box 2768, Mission, KS 66201-2768
Tel: 913-362-3900 *Toll Free Tel:* 800-873-7545 *Fax:* 913-362-4241
E-mail: customercare@skillpath.com; products@skillpath.com
Web Site: www.skillpath.com
Founded: 1989
Books, audio programs, computer based training.
ISBN Prefix(es): 978-1-878542; 978-1-57294; 978-1-929874; 978-1-934589; 978-1-60811
Number of titles published annually: 10 Print
Total Titles: 50 Print; 4 Audio
Divisions: CompuMaster
Branch Office(s)
100 Armstrong Ave, Georgetown, ON L7G 5S4, Canada *Fax:* 913-362-4241 *Web Site:* www.skillpath.ca
Foreign Office(s): GPO Box 1747, Melbourne, Victoria 3001, Australia *Tel:* (0800) 145 231 *Fax:* (0800) 145 244 *Web Site:* www.skillpath.com.au
FreePost 105776, PO Box 742, Wellington 6140, New Zealand *Tel:* (0800) 447 301 *Fax:* (0800) 447 304 *Web Site:* www.skillpath.co.nz
PO Box 203, Chessington KT9 9BZ, United Kingdom *Tel:* (0800) 328 1140 *Fax:* (0800) 892972 *Web Site:* www.skillpath.co.uk
Distributor for Franklin Covey; Pearson Technology; Thomson Publishing; John Wiley & Sons Inc

Skinner House Books
Imprint of Unitarian Universalist Assn
c/o Unitarian Universalist Assn, 24 Farnsworth St, Boston, MA 02210-1409
Tel: 617-742-2100 *Fax:* 617-948-6466
E-mail: skinnerhouse@uua.org
Web Site: www.skinnerhouse.org
Key Personnel
Edit Dir: Mary Benard
Edit Asst: Betsy Martin *Tel:* 617-948-4644 *E-mail:* betsymartin@uua.org
Founded: 1975
Specialize in spirituality, inspirational literature, books on church resources for religious liberals.
ISBN Prefix(es): 978-0-933840; 978-1-55896
Number of titles published annually: 15 Print; 15 E-Book
Total Titles: 265 Print
Sales Office(s): Red Wheel/Weiser/Conari, 65 Parker St, Suite 7, Newburyport, MA 01950 *Tel:* 978-465-0504 *Toll Free Tel:* 800-423-7087 *Fax:* 978-465-0243 *E-mail:* orders@redwheelweiser.com *Web Site:* redwheelweiser.com
Returns: Red Wheel/Weiser/Conari, 65 Parker St, Suite 7, Newburyport, MA 01950 *Tel:* 978-465-0504 *Toll Free Tel:* 800-423-7087 *Fax:* 978-465-0243 *E-mail:* orders@redwheelweiser.com *Web Site:* redwheelweiser.com
Distribution Center: Red Wheel/Weiser/Conari, 65 Parker St, Suite 7, Newburyport, MA 01950 *Tel:* 978-465-0504 *Toll Free Tel:* 800-423-7087 *Fax:* 978-465-0243 *E-mail:* info@redwheelweiser.com *Web Site:* redwheelweiser.com

Sky Pony Press
Imprint of Skyhorse Publishing Inc
307 W 36 St, 11th fl, New York, NY 10018
Tel: 212-643-6816 *Fax:* 212-643-6819
E-mail: skypony@skyhorsepublishing.com; info@skyhorsepublishing.com; submissions@skyhorsepublishing.com
Web Site: www.skyponypress.com
Key Personnel
Ed-in-Chief: Alison Weiss
Ed: Becky Herrick
Asst Ed: Rachel Stark
Founded: 2011
ISBN Prefix(es): 978-1-61145; 978-1-60239; 978-1-61608; 978-1-62087; 978-1-63220; 978-1-62914; 978-1-62873; 978-1-5107
Number of titles published annually: 80 Print
Foreign Rights: Biagi Literary Management (Linda Biagi) (worldwide)
Orders to: Perseus Distribution, 250 W 57 St, 15th fl, New York, NY 10107 *E-mail:* orderentry@perseusbooks.com
Warehouse: 210 American Dr, Jackson, TN 38301
Distribution Center: Perseus Distribution, 250 W 57 St, 15th fl, New York, NY 10107 *E-mail:* orderentry@perseusbooks.com

SkyLight Paths
Imprint of Turner Publishing Co
4507 Charlotte Ave, Suite 100, Nashville, TN 37209
SAN: 134-5621

Tel: 615-255-BOOK (255-2665) *Fax:* 615-255-5081
E-mail: marketing@turnerpublishing.com
Web Site: www.skylightpaths.com; www.turnerpublishing.com
Key Personnel
Pres & Publr, Turner Publishing Co: Todd Bottorff
Founded: 1999
General trade books for seekers & believers of all faith traditions. Subject areas include spirituality, children's, self-help, crafts, interfaith, spiritual living, eastern & western religion.
ISBN Prefix(es): 978-1-893361; 978-1-59473
Number of titles published annually: 5 Print; 5 E-Book
Total Titles: 350 Print; 350 E-Book

§SLACK® Incorporated, A Wyanoke Group Company
6900 Grove Rd, Thorofare, NJ 08086-9447
SAN: 201-8632
Tel: 856-848-1000 *Toll Free Tel:* 800-257-8290 *Fax:* 856-848-6091
E-mail: sales@slackinc.com; editor@slackinc.com; customerservice@slackinc.com
Web Site: www.healio.com/books
Key Personnel
SVP, Sales: Mike Graziani
VP, Mktg, Health Care Books & Journals: Michelle Gatt
VP, Mktg & Audience Devt: Lee Gaymon
VP, Digital Innovation & Busn Devt: Christine Martynick
VP, Prod: April Underwood
Head of Global Mktg: Kelly Watkins
Ed-in-Chief: Katrina Altersitz Wells
Exec Ed: John Schoen
Edit Dir, Health Care Books & Journals: Karen G Stanwood
Mng Ed: Gina Brockenbrough
Founded: 1960
Academic textbooks & professional reference books: medicine, occupational therapy, physical therapy, ophthalmology, gastroenterology, orthopedics, athletic training, pediatrics, nursing & other areas.
ISBN Prefix(es): 978-1-55642
Number of titles published annually: 35 Print; 35 E-Book
Total Titles: 250 Print; 250 E-Book
Foreign Rep(s): EuroSpan (Europe); Login Canada (Canada)
Foreign Rights: John Scott Co
Advertising Agency: Alcyon Advertising
Distribution Center: 200 Richardson Ave, Bldg B, Swedesboro, NJ 08085

Sleeping Bear Press™
2395 S Huron Pkwy, Suite 200, Ann Arbor, MI 48104
Toll Free Tel: 800-487-2323 *Fax:* 734-929-2649
E-mail: customerservice@sleepingbearpress.com
Web Site: www.sleepingbearpress.com
Key Personnel
Publr: Heather Hughes
Publicity: Audrey Mitnick
Sales & Mktg: Amy Patrick *E-mail:* amy.patrick@sleepingbearpress.com
Founded: 1998
Publisher of children's books infants to young adults.
ISBN Prefix(es): 978-1-57504; 978-1-886947; 978-1-58536
Number of titles published annually: 40 Print
Total Titles: 500 Print
Membership(s): ALA; Association of Children's Booksellers; International Literacy Association

§Small Beer Press
150 Pleasant St, No 306, Easthampton, MA 01027
Tel: 413-203-1636 *Fax:* 413-203-1636
E-mail: info@smallbeerpress.com
Web Site: smallbeerpress.com
Key Personnel
Founder & Publr: Gavin J Grant
Founder: Kelly Link
CTO: Michael J Deluca
Founded: 2000
ISBN Prefix(es): 978-1-931520; 978-1-61873
Number of titles published annually: 10 Print; 10 E-Book
Total Titles: 90 Print; 150 E-Book
Sales Office(s): Consortium Book Sales & Distribution, 34 13 Ave N, Suite 101, Minneapolis, MN 55413
Foreign Rights: Cooke Agency International
Billing Address: Consortium Book Sales & Distribution, 34 13 Ave N, Suite 101, Minneapolis, MN 55413
Orders to: Consortium Book Sales & Distribution, 34 13 Ave N, Suite 101, Minneapolis, MN 55413
Returns: Consortium Book Sales & Distribution, 34 13 Ave N, Suite 101, Minneapolis, MN 55413
Shipping Address: Consortium Book Sales & Distribution, 34 13 Ave N, Suite 101, Minneapolis, MN 55413
Warehouse: Consortium Book Sales & Distribution, 34 13 Ave N, Suite 101, Minneapolis, MN 55413
Distribution Center: Consortium Book Sales & Distribution, 34 13 Ave N, Suite 101, Minneapolis, MN 55413
Membership(s): Community of Literary Magazines & Presses

Small Business Advisors Inc
11 Franklin Ave, Hewlett, NY 11557
Tel: 516-374-1387 *Fax:* 516-374-1175
Web Site: www.smallbusinessadvice.com
Key Personnel
CEO & Founder: Joe Gelb *E-mail:* joe@smallbusinessadvice.com
Pres: Arthur VanDam *E-mail:* arthurvandam1@gmail.com
Contact: Eric Gelb *E-mail:* eric@smallbusinessadvice.com
Founded: 1991
Publisher of books, ebooks & blogs on small business, finance & marketing/copyrighting.
ISBN Prefix(es): 978-1-890158
Number of titles published annually: 4 Print
Total Titles: 20 Print; 1 Audio
Membership(s): ALA; Independent Book Publishers Association

Smith & Kraus Publishers Inc
40 Walch Dr, Portland, ME 04103
Mailing Address: 177 Lyme Rd, Hanover, NH 03755
Tel: 207-523-2585 *Toll Free Tel:* 877-668-8680 *Fax:* 207-699-3698
E-mail: editor@smithandkraus.com
Web Site: www.smithandkraus.com
Key Personnel
Pres & Publr: Marisa Smith Kraus
Founded: 1990
Drama books, monologues, books of interest to our theatrical community, play anthologies.
ISBN Prefix(es): 978-0-9622722; 978-1-880399; 978-1-57525
Number of titles published annually: 35 Print
Total Titles: 500 Print
Imprints: In an Hour Books LLC (playwrights); Smith & Kraus Books For Kids (young adult fiction)
Subsidiaries: Smith & Kraus Global (world affairs)

§M Lee Smith Publishers
Division of BLR®-Business & Legal Resources
100 Winners Circle, Suite 300, Brentwood, TN 37027
Mailing Address: PO Box 5094, Brentwood, TN 37024-5094
Tel: 615-373-7517 *Toll Free Tel:* 800-274-6774; 800-727-5257
E-mail: custserv@mleesmith.com; service@blr.com
Web Site: www.mleesmith.com; www.blr.com
Key Personnel
CEO: Dan Oswald
CFO: Lawton Miller
VP, Training & Legal: Brad Forrister
Dir, Cust Serv & Circ: Kim Mesecher
Founded: 1975
Legal newsletters/legal book related titles.
ISBN Prefix(es): 978-0-925773; 978-1-60029; 978-0-9605796
Number of titles published annually: 130 Print
Total Titles: 2 CD-ROM; 60 Online

Steve Smith Autosports
PO Box 11631, Santa Ana, CA 92711-1631
Tel: 714-639-7681 *Fax:* 714-639-9741
Web Site: www.stevesmithautosports.com
Key Personnel
Pres & Publr: Steve Smith *E-mail:* steve@ssapubl.com
Founded: 1971
Specialize in auto racing technical books.
ISBN Prefix(es): 978-0-936834
Number of titles published annually: 5 Print
Total Titles: 200 Print

Smithsonian Scholarly Press
Division of Smithsonian Institution
Aerospace Bldg, 704-A, MRC 957, Washington, DC 20013
Mailing Address: PO Box 37012, Washington DC, DC 20013-7012
Tel: 202-633-3017 *Fax:* 202-633-6877
E-mail: scholarlypress@si.edu
Web Site: www.scholarlypress.si.edu
Key Personnel
Prog Asst: Stephanie Summerhays
Founded: 1966
General trade & adult nonfiction.
ISBN Prefix(es): 978-0-87474; 978-1-56098; 978-1-58834
Number of titles published annually: 8 Print
Total Titles: 800 Print
Distributed by Penguin Random House Inc

§Smyth & Helwys Publishing Inc
6316 Peake Rd, Macon, GA 31210-3960
Tel: 478-757-0564 *Toll Free Tel:* 800-747-3016 (orders only); 800-568-1248 (orders only) *Fax:* 478-757-1305
E-mail: information@helwys.com
Web Site: www.helwys.com
Key Personnel
Pres & CEO: Cecil P Staton, Jr
Publr & EVP: Keith Gammons *E-mail:* keith@helwys.com
Founded: 1990
Christian books, literature, Sunday school books (curriculum).
ISBN Prefix(es): 978-1-880837; 978-0-9628455; 978-1-57312
Number of titles published annually: 30 Print
Total Titles: 330 Print
Foreign Rep(s): Grace Wing Publishers (England)

Snow Lion
Imprint of Shambhala Publications Inc
4720 Walnut St, Boulder, CO 80301
Tel: 617-236-0030 *Fax:* 303-200-9406
E-mail: customercare@shambhala.com
Web Site: www.shambhala.com/snowlion
Key Personnel
Sales & Mktg Mgr: KJ Grow
Founded: 1980

Trade & scholarly books on Tibetan Buddhism & Tibet.
ISBN Prefix(es): 978-0-937938; 978-1-55939
Number of titles published annually: 20 Print; 20 E-Book
Total Titles: 350 Print; 250 E-Book; 1 Audio

Society for Human Resource Management (SHRM)
1800 Duke St, Alexandria, VA 22314
Tel: 703-548-3440 *Toll Free Tel:* 800-444-5006 (orders) *Fax:* 703-535-6490
E-mail: shrm@shrm.org; shrmstore@shrm.org
Web Site: www.shrm.org
Founded: 1948
Professional association with more than 275,000 members in over 160 countries.
ISBN Prefix(es): 978-1-58644
Number of titles published annually: 12 Print; 12 E-Book
Total Titles: 90 Print; 60 E-Book

§Society for Industrial & Applied Mathematics
3600 Market St, 6th fl, Philadelphia, PA 19104-2688
Tel: 215-382-9800 *Toll Free Tel:* 800-447-7426 *Fax:* 215-386-7999
E-mail: siambooks@siam.org
Web Site: www.siam.org
Key Personnel
Publr: David K Marshall *E-mail:* marshall@siam.org
Prodn Mgr: Donna Witzleben *E-mail:* witzleben@siam.org
Pubns Mgr: Mitch Chernoff *E-mail:* chernoff@siam.org
Exec Ed: Elizabeth Greenspan *E-mail:* greenspan@siam.org
Mng Ed: Kelly Thomas *E-mail:* thomas@siam.org
Sr Pubns Coord: Heather Blythe *E-mail:* blythe@siam.org
Prodn Coord: Cally Shrader *E-mail:* shrader@siam.org
Founded: 1952
Journals, books, conferences & reprints in mathematics/computer science/statistics/physical science.
ISBN Prefix(es): 978-0-89871; 978-1-61197
Number of titles published annually: 20 Print
Total Titles: 450 Print; 400 E-Book

§Society for Mining, Metallurgy & Exploration
12999 E Adam Aircraft Circle, Englewood, CO 80112
Tel: 303-948-4200 *Toll Free Tel:* 800-763-3132 *Fax:* 303-973-3845
E-mail: cs@smenet.org; books@smenet.org
Web Site: www.smenet.org
Key Personnel
Exec Dr: Dave Kanagy
Sr Ed: Bill Gleason *Tel:* 303-948-4234 *E-mail:* gleason@smenet.org; Georgene Renner *Tel:* 303-948-4254 *E-mail:* renner@smenet.org
Pubns Ed: Steve Kral *Tel:* 303-948-4245 *E-mail:* kral@smenet.org
Founded: 1871
Publish mining related monthly magazine, quarterly journal, trade books, hardbound & paperback.
ISBN Prefix(es): 978-0-87335
Number of titles published annually: 3 Print; 5 E-Book
Total Titles: 80 Print; 15 CD-ROM
Foreign Rep(s): Affiliated East-West Press (India); Australian Mineral Foundation (Australia)

The Society for Protective Coatings, see SSPC: The Society for Protective Coatings

Society of American Archivists
17 N State St, Suite 1425, Chicago, IL 60602-4061
SAN: 211-7614
Tel: 312-606-0722 *Toll Free Tel:* 866-722-7858 *Fax:* 312-606-0728
Web Site: www.archivists.org
Key Personnel
Dir, Publg: Teresa Brinati *E-mail:* tbrinati@archivists.org
Edit & Prodn: Abigail Christian *E-mail:* achristian@archivists.org
Founded: 1936
Archival literature; preservation.
ISBN Prefix(es): 978-0-931828; 978-1-931666
Number of titles published annually: 5 Print
Total Titles: 72 Print

Society of Automotive Engineers International, see SAE (Society of Automotive Engineers International)

Society of Biblical Literature, see SBL Press

Society of Environmental Toxicology & Chemistry (SETAC)
229 S Baylen St, 2nd fl, Pensacola, FL 32502
Tel: 850-469-1500 *Toll Free Fax:* 888-296-4136
E-mail: setac@setac.org; etc@setac.org (edit)
Web Site: www.setac.org
Key Personnel
Sr Publg Mgr: Mimi Meredith *Tel:* 850-469-1500 ext 113 *E-mail:* mimi.meredith@setac.org
Pubns Mgr: Jen Lynch *Tel:* 850-469-1500 ext 109 *E-mail:* jen.lynch@setac.org
Founded: 1979
Supports publications of scientific value relating to environmental topics. Proceedings of technical workshops that explore current & prospective environmental issues are published as peer-reviewed technical documents. Publications are used by scientists, engineers & managers because of their technical basis & comprehensive, state-of-the-science reviews; association press; nonprofit, professional society.
ISBN Prefix(es): 978-1-880611
Number of titles published annually: 8 Print; 1 CD-ROM
Total Titles: 105 Print; 5 CD-ROM
Imprints: SETAC Press
Foreign Office(s): Av de la Toison d'Or 67 b 6, 1060 Brussels, Belgium *Tel:* (02) 772 72 81 *Fax:* (02) 770 53 86 *E-mail:* setaceu@setac.org

§Society of Exploration Geophysicists
8801 S Yale Ave, Tulsa, OK 74137
Mailing Address: PO Box 702740, Tulsa, OK 74170-2740
Tel: 918-497-5500 *Fax:* 918-497-5557
E-mail: web@seg.org
Web Site: www.seg.org
Key Personnel
Dir, Pubns: Ted Bakamjian *Tel:* 918-497-5506 *E-mail:* tbakamjian@seg.org
Sr Mgr, Journals & Books: Jennifer Cobb *Tel:* 918-497-5537 *E-mail:* jcobb@seg.org
Founded: 1930
Textbooks, videos, technical journals, magazines & meeting papers.
ISBN Prefix(es): 978-1-56080; 978-0-931839
Number of titles published annually: 5 Print; 5 Online; 5 E-Book
Total Titles: 80 Print; 9 CD-ROM; 125 Online; 125 E-Book

§Society of Manufacturing Engineers
One SME Dr, Dearborn, MI 48121
SAN: 203-2376
Tel: 313-425-3000 *Toll Free Tel:* 800-733-4763 (cust serv) *Fax:* 313-425-3400
E-mail: publications@sme.org
Web Site: www.sme.org
Key Personnel
CEO & Exec Dir: Jeffrey Krause *Tel:* 313-425-3100 *E-mail:* jkrause@sme.org
Dir, Prof Devt: Jeannine Kunz
SME Resource Ctr: Carol Selleck *Tel:* 313-425-3152
E-Libn: Carol Tower *Tel:* 313-425-3288 *E-mail:* ctower@sme.org
Founded: 1932
Professional engineering association.
ISBN Prefix(es): 978-0-87263; 978-1-62104
Number of titles published annually: 3 Print
Total Titles: 150 Print; 21 CD-ROM
Branch Office(s)
7100 Woodbine Ave, Suite 312, Markham, ON L3R 5J2, Canada *Tel:* 905-752-4415 *Toll Free Tel:* 888-322-7333 *Fax:* 905-479-0113 *E-mail:* canadasales@sme.org
Distributed by American Technical Publishers Inc; McGraw-Hill; Productivity Press
Distributor for Industrial Press; McGraw-Hill; Prentice Hall; John Wiley & Sons Inc
Foreign Rights: American Technical Publishers (UK); DA Books Pty Ltd (Australia); Elsevier Science Publishers (Netherlands)

The Society of Naval Architects & Marine Engineers (SNAME)
99 Canal Center Plaza, Suite 310, Alexandria, VA 22314
SAN: 202-0572
Tel: 703-997-6701 *Toll Free Tel:* 800-798-2188 *Fax:* 703-997-6702
Web Site: www.sname.org
Key Personnel
Dir, Content: Susan Evans Grove *E-mail:* sevans@sname.org
Pubns Coord: Kristin Walker *Tel:* 703-997-6710 *E-mail:* kwalker@sname.org
Reference books, directories, periodicals, technical research reports & bulletins on naval architecture, marine engineering & ocean engineering.
ISBN Prefix(es): 978-0-9603048; 978-0-939773; 978-1-941762
Number of titles published annually: 3 Print
Total Titles: 29 Print

Soho Press Inc
853 Broadway, New York, NY 10003
SAN: 202-5531
Tel: 212-260-1900
E-mail: soho@sohopress.com; publicity@sohopress.com; contact@sohopress.com
Web Site: www.sohopress.com
Key Personnel
Publr: Bronwen Hruska *E-mail:* bhruska@sohopress.com
Assoc Publr: Juliet Grames
Dir, Publicity & Mktg: Paul Oliver *E-mail:* poliver@sohopress.com
Sr Ed: Mark Doten *E-mail:* mdoten@sohopress.com
Asst Ed: Amara Hoshijo
Sr Mktg Mgr: Rudy Martinez *E-mail:* rmartinez@sohopress.com
Sr Publicist: Abby Koski
Digital Media Mgr: Kevin Murphy *E-mail:* kmurphy@sohopress.com
Sales Mgr: Carin Siegfried
Founded: 1986 (first books published in 1987)
Hard & softcover trade books: fiction, mysteries, general nonfiction, history & social history.
ISBN Prefix(es): 978-0-939149; 978-1-56947; 978-1-61695
Number of titles published annually: 90 Print; 68 E-Book
Total Titles: 350 Print
Imprints: Soho Crime; Soho Press; Soho Teen
Foreign Rights: ACER Agencia Literaria (Elizabeth Atkins) (Spain); AnatoliaLit Agency (Amy Spangler) (Turkey); English Agency

(Corinne Shioji) (Japan); Grayhawk Agency (Gray Tan) (Taiwan); Deborah Harris Agency (Ilana Kurshan) (Israel); International Editors Co (Flavia Sala) (Brazil); Leonardt & Hoier Literary Agency (Anneli Hoier) (Denmark, Finland, Norway, Sweden); Michael Meller Literary Agency (Franka Zastrow) (Germany); Jan Michael (Belgium, Netherlands); Daniela Micura Literary Services (Italy); PLS (Publishing Language Service) (Yang Young Chul) (Korea); Prava i prevodi (Nada Popovic) (Bulgaria, Croatia, Czech Republic, Estonia, Hungary, Latvia, Lithuania, Poland, Romania, Russia, Serbia, Slovakia, Slovenia); Read N' Right Agency (Nike Davarinou) (Greece)
Orders to: Penguin Random House Publisher Services (PRHPS), 400 Hahn Rd, Westminster, MD 21157 *Toll Free Tel:* 800-733-3000; 800-669-1536 (electronic orders) *Toll Free Fax:* 800-659-2436 *Web Site:* www.penguinrandomhouse.biz SAN: 631-760X; Penguin Random House Canada, 2775 Matheson Blvd E, Mississauga, ON L4W 4P7, Canada *Toll Free Tel:* 888-523-9292; 800-258-4233 (electronic orders) *Toll Free Fax:* 888-562-9924 *Web Site:* www.penguinrandomhouse.ca
Distribution Center: Penguin Random House Publisher Services (PRHPS), 400 Hahn Rd, Westminster, MD 21157 *Toll Free Tel:* 800-733-3000; 800-669-1536 (electronic orders) *Toll Free Fax:* 800-659-2436 *Web Site:* www.penguinrandomhouse.biz SAN: 631-760X
Penguin Random House Canada, 2775 Matheson Blvd E, Mississauga, ON L4W 4P7, Canada *Toll Free Tel:* 888-523-9292; 800-258-4233 (electronic orders) *Toll Free Fax:* 888-562-9924 *Web Site:* www.penguinrandomhouse.ca

Soil Science Society of America
5585 Guilford Rd, Madison, WI 53711-5801
Tel: 608-273-8080
Web Site: www.soils.org
Key Personnel
CEO: Ellen Bergfeld *Tel:* 608-268-4979 *E-mail:* ebergfeld@soils.org
CFO: Wes Meixelsperger *Tel:* 608-268-4958 *E-mail:* meixelsperger@soils.org
Pubns Dir: Bill Cook *Tel:* 608-268-4974 *E-mail:* bcook@soils.org
Pubns Mktg Coord: Tricia Newell *Tel:* 608-268-4967 *E-mail:* tnewell@soils.org
Founded: 1936
Technical books for professionals in soil science.
ISBN Prefix(es): 978-0-89118
Number of titles published annually: 5 Print
Total Titles: 90 Print

Solano Press Books
PO Box 773, Point Arena, CA 95468
Tel: 707-884-4508 *Toll Free Tel:* 800-931-9373 *Fax:* 707-884-4109
E-mail: spbooks@solano.com
Web Site: www.solano.com
Key Personnel
Publr: Ling-Yen Jones
Acqs Ed: Natalie Macris
Asst to Publr: Nancy McLaughlin
Founded: 1984
Professional books: law, public administration, real estate, land use, environment, urban planning, environmental analysis & management.
ISBN Prefix(es): 978-0-9614657; 978-0-923956; 978-1-938166
Number of titles published annually: 4 Print
Total Titles: 25 Print; 3 E-Book

Solution Tree
555 N Morton St, Bloomington, IN 47404
Tel: 812-336-7700 *Toll Free Tel:* 800-733-6786 *Fax:* 812 336 7790
E-mail: pubs@solution-tree.com
Web Site: www.solution-tree.com
Key Personnel
Dist Rel: Cindy Johnson *E-mail:* cindy.johnson@solution-tree.com
Founded: 1987
Provide tested & proven resources that help those who work with youth create safe & caring schools, agencies & communities where all children succeed.
ISBN Prefix(es): 978-1-879639; 978-1-932127
Number of titles published annually: 20 Print
Total Titles: 400 Print; 2 Audio
Imprints: Solution Tree Press

SOM Publishing
Division of School of Metaphysics
163 Moon Valley Rd, Windyville, MO 65783
SAN: 159-5423
Tel: 417-345-8411 *Fax:* 417-345-6668
E-mail: som@som.org; dreams@dreamschool.org
Web Site: www.som.org; www.dreamschool.org
Key Personnel
CEO, Dist & Mktg: Dr Barbara Condron
Pres: Dr Christine Spretnjak
Founded: 1973
Publish books in the fields of dream interpretation, Kundalini, holistic health, visualization, interfaith studies, meditation, Christian religion, past life recall & spiritual enlightenment.
ISBN Prefix(es): 978-0-944386
Number of titles published annually: 4 Print
Total Titles: 30 Print
Distribution Center: New Leaf Distributing Co, 401 Thornton Rd, Lithia Springs, GA 30122-1557 *Tel:* 770-948-7845 *Fax:* 770-944-2313 *E-mail:* newleaf@newleaf-dist.com *Web Site:* www.newleaf-dist.com

Somerset Hall Press
416 Commonwealth Ave, Suite 612, Boston, MA 02215
Tel: 617-236-5126
E-mail: info@somersethallpress.com
Web Site: www.somersethallpress.com
Key Personnel
Publr: Dean Papademetriou
Founded: 2003
Independent press specializing in literary & scholarly titles with a special interest in Greek studies.
ISBN Prefix(es): 978-0-9724661; 978-0-9774610; 978-1-935244
Number of titles published annually: 3 Print
Total Titles: 20 Print

Soncino Press Ltd
123 Ditmas Ave, Brooklyn, NY 11218
Tel: 718-972-6200 *Toll Free Tel:* 800-972-6201 *Fax:* 718-972-6204
E-mail: info@soncino.com
Web Site: www.soncino.com
Key Personnel
Pres: Gloria Goldman
Mng Ed: Norman Shapiro
Bible, Talmud & Judaism.
ISBN Prefix(es): 978-1-871055; 978-0-900689
Number of titles published annually: 20 Print
Total Titles: 100 Print

Sophia Institute Press®
522 Donald St, Unit 3, Bedford, NH 03110
Mailing Address: PO Box 5284, Manchester, NH 03108 SAN: 657-7172
Tel: 603-836-5505 *Toll Free Tel:* 800-888-9344 *Fax:* 603-641-8108 *Toll Free Fax:* 888-288-2259
E-mail: orders@sophiainstitute.com
Web Site: www.sophiainstitute.com
Key Personnel
Pres: Charlie McKinney *E-mail:* cmckinney@sophiainstitute.com
Dir, Mktg: Aja McCarthy *E-mail:* amccarthy@sophiainstitute.com
Dir, Sales: Michael DeMonico *E-mail:* mdemonico@sophiainstitute.com
Prodn Mgr: Sheila M Perry *E-mail:* production@sophiainstitute.com
Founded: 1983
Books on religion (Roman Catholicism).
ISBN Prefix(es): 978-0-918477; 978-1-928832; 978-1-933184
Number of titles published annually: 15 Print
Total Titles: 150 Print
Foreign Rep(s): Cenacle House Ltd (UK); Family Life International (New Zealand); John XXIII Fellowship (Australia); Redemptorist Publications (UK); St Joseph's Workshops (Canada); Sunrise Marion Center (Canada)

§Soul Mate Publishing
3210 Sherwood Dr, Walworth, NY 14568
Tel: 585-598-4791
E-mail: submissions@soulmatepublishing.com
Web Site: www.soulmatepublishing.com
Key Personnel
Founder & Sr Ed: Deborah Gilbert *E-mail:* debby@soulmatepublishing.com
Founded: 2011
ISBN Prefix(es): 978-1-61935
Number of titles published annually: 100 E-Book
Total Titles: 15 Print; 120 E-Book
Membership(s): Romance Writers of America

§Sound Feelings Publishing
18375 Ventura Blvd, No 8000, Tarzana, CA 91356
Tel: 818-757-0600
E-mail: information@soundfeelings.com
Web Site: www.soundfeelings.com
Key Personnel
Founder & Pres: Howard Richman
This publisher has indicated that 80% of their product line is author subsidized.
ISBN Prefix(es): 978-0-9615963; 978-1-882060
Number of titles published annually: 3 Print; 3 E-Book; 2 Audio
Total Titles: 15 Print; 10 E-Book; 11 Audio
Foreign Rep(s): Gazelle Book Services Ltd (Europe)

Sounds True Inc
413 S Arthur Ave, Louisville, CO 80027
Tel: 303-665-3151 *Toll Free Tel:* 800-333-9185
E-mail: customerservice@soundstrue.com; sales@soundstrue.com
Web Site: www.soundstrue.com
Key Personnel
Founder & Publr: Tami Simon
Acqs Ed: Melissa Valentine
Freelance Ed-at-Large: Jen Adams; Caroline Pincus
Founded: 1985
ISBN Prefix(es): 978-1-56455; 978-1-59179; 978-1-60407; 978-1-62203
Number of titles published annually: 30 Print; 30 E-Book; 40 Audio
Total Titles: 200 Print; 150 E-Book; 800 Audio
Distributor for Eckhart Teachings Inc; New Earth Records; Relaxation Co

§Sourcebooks Inc
1935 Brookdale Rd, Suite 139, Naperville, IL 60563
SAN: 666-7864
Mailing Address: PO Box 4410, Naperville, IL 60567-4410
Tel: 630-961-3900 *Toll Free Tel:* 800-432-7444 *Fax:* 630-961-2168
E-mail: info@sourcebooks.com; customersupport@sourcebooks.com
Web Site: www.sourcebooks.com
Key Personnel
CEO & Publr: Dominique Raccah
COO & SVP: Barbara Briel
SVP & Dir, Technol & Content Delivery: Lynn Dilger

VP & Edit Dir: Todd Stocke *Tel:* 630-536-0543 *E-mail:* todd.stocke@sourcebooks.com
Art Dir: Brittany Vibbert
Art Dir, Entertainment & Gift Group: John Aardema
Edit Dir, Sourcebooks Casablanca: Deb Werksman *Tel:* 203-876-9790 *E-mail:* deb.werksman@sourcebooks.com
Edit Dir, Sourcebooks Children's Books: Steve Geck *Tel:* 212-414-1701 ext 2226 *E-mail:* steve.geck@sourcebooks.com
Edit Dir, Sourcebooks Children's Nonfiction: Kelly Barrales-Saylor
Edit Dir, Sourcebooks Landmark: Shana Drehs *Tel:* 630-536-0535 *E-mail:* shana.drehs@sourcebooks.com
Dir, Sales & Mktg: Chris Bauerle *E-mail:* chris.bauerle@sourcebooks.com
Assoc Creative Dir: Kelly Lawler
Mng Ed: Bret Kehoe
Sr Ed: Anna Michels
Sr Prodn Ed: Rachel Gilmer; Heather Hall
Ed, Sourcebooks Casablanca: Cat Clyne
Assoc Ed, Sourcebooks Jabberwocky & Fire: Kate Prosswimmer
Asst Ed, College Ref: Chris Francis
Sr Mgr, Specialty Retail: Ilene Schreider
Busn Devt Mgr, Spec Mkts: Shane White
Cust Serv Mgr: Suzanne Walker
E-Commerce Opers Mgr: Brad Hentz
Edit Mgr, Sourcebooks Fire: Annette Pollert *Tel:* 212-414-1701 ext 2229 *E-mail:* annette.pollert@sourcebooks.com
HR Mgr: Amy Hayes
Mktg & Publicity Mgr, Sourcebooks Casablanca: Beth Sochacki
Mktg Mgr, Libs: Beth Oleniczak
Mktg Mgr, Retail & Lib Mkts: Valerie Pierce *Tel:* 630-961-3900 ext 233 *E-mail:* valerie.pierce@sourcebooks.com
Natl Accts Mgr, Gift & Regl: Liz Otte
Online Mktg Mgr: James Hegberg
Publicity Mgr: Heather Moore *Tel:* 630-536-0553 *E-mail:* heather.moore@sourcebooks.com
Publg Mgr, Entertainment Group: Karen Shapiro
Sr Publicist, Children's & Young Adult: Katy Lynch
Publicist: Stephany Daniel
Ebook Prodn Coord: Jessica Zulli
Mktg Coord: Stephanie Graham
Mktg Coord, E-Commerce Div: Molly Fletcher
Sr Designer: Heather Morris
Graphic Designer: Allison Sundstrom
Jr Graphic Designer, E-Commerce Div: Kandi Rich
Assoc Print Buyer: Cristina Wilson
Mfg Assoc: Susan Busch
Royalty Assoc, Acctg: Lauren McClearn
Founded: 1987
Nonfiction, fiction, romance novels, children's books, young adult, gift books & calendars.
ISBN Prefix(es): 978-0-942061; 978-1-57071; 978-1-57248; 978-0-913825; 978-1-883518; 978-0-9629162; 978-1-887166; 978-1-4022; 978-1-4926
Number of titles published annually: 400 Print; 270 E-Book
Total Titles: 3,000 Print; 1,700 E-Book
Imprints: Cumberland House (nonfiction gift, history & cooking); Little Pickle Press (children's nonfiction); Sourcebooks Casablanca (romance fiction); Sourcebooks Fire (young adult); Sourcebooks Jabberwocky (children's books); Sourcebooks Landmark (fiction); Sourcebooks MediaFusion (multimedia books)
Branch Office(s)
18 Cherry St, Suite 1W, Milford, CT 06460 *Tel:* 203-876-9790
Sourcebooks New York, 232 Madison Ave, Suite 805, New York, NY 10018 *Tel:* 212-414-1701
Distributor for Prufrock Press
Foreign Rep(s): Eliane Benisti Literary Agency (Eliane Benisti) (France); The Deborah Harris Agency (Israel); Inter-Ko (Korea); Nurcihan Kesim Literary Agency Inc (Turkey); Maxima Creative Agency (Indonesia); Piergiorgio Nicolazzini (Italy); Nova Littera Ltd (Russia); Prava i prevodi (Eastern Block, Slovakia); Schindler's Literary Agency (Brazil); Tuttle-Mori Agency Inc (Japan, Thailand); Yanez Agencia Literaria (Spain)
Returns: RR Donnelley, 677 Brighton Beach Rd, Menasha, WI 54952
Warehouse: RR Donnelley, N9234 Lake Park Rd, Appleton, WI 54915 *Tel:* 920-969-6400 *Fax:* 920-969-6441
Distribution Center: Baker & Taylor Global Publishers Services (GPS), 2550 W Tyvola Rd, Chicago, IL 28217 *E-mail:* gps@baker-taylor.com
Raincoast Books, 2440 Viking Way, Richmond, BC V6V 1N2, Canada *Toll Free Tel:* 800-663-5714 *Toll Free Fax:* 800-565-3770 *E-mail:* info@raincoast.com
Melia Publishing Services, One St Peter's Rd, Maidenhead, Berks SL6 7QU, United Kingdom
See separate listing for:
Cumberland House

Sourced Media Books
15 Via Picato, San Clemente, CA 92673
Tel: 949-813-0182
E-mail: editor@sourcedmediabooks.com
Web Site: sourcedmediabooks.com
Key Personnel
Publr: Amy Cook, PhD
Sr Ed: Jennifer Durrant
Ed: J'Nel Wright
Asst Ed: Hayley Tyler
Founded: 2009
ISBN Prefix(es): 978-0-9841068; 978-1-937458
Number of titles published annually: 10 Print; 15 Online; 15 E-Book
Total Titles: 45 Print; 18 Online; 18 E-Book
Distributed by Gibbs-Smith; Many Hats Media
Distribution Center: Brigham Distributing, 110 S 800 W, Brigham City, UT 84302

South Carolina Bar
Continuing Legal Education Div, 950 Taylor St, Columbia, SC 29201
Mailing Address: PO Box 608, Columbia, SC 29202-0608
Tel: 803-799-6653 *Toll Free Tel:* 800-768-7787 *Fax:* 803-799-4118
E-mail: scbar-info@scbar.org
Web Site: www.scbar.org
Key Personnel
Pubns Dir: Alicia Hutto *E-mail:* ahutto@scbar.org
Continuing Legal Educ Dir: Terry Burnett *Tel:* 803-799-6653 ext 152 *E-mail:* tburnett@scbar.org
Founded: 1979
Law materials, legal treatises, manuals & software.
ISBN Prefix(es): 978-0-943856
Number of titles published annually: 10 Print
Total Titles: 100 Print

South Dakota Historical Society Press
900 Governors Dr, Pierre, SD 57501
Tel: 605-773-6009 *Fax:* 605-773-6041
E-mail: info@sdshspress.com; orders@sdshspress.com
Web Site: sdshspress.com
Key Personnel
Dir & Ed-in-Chief: Nancy Tystad Koupal *Tel:* 605-773-4371 *E-mail:* Nancy.Koupal@state.sd.us
Mktg Dir & Assoc Ed: Jennifer McIntyre *Tel:* 605-773-8161 *E-mail:* Jennifer.McIntyre@state.sd.us
Mng Ed: Jeanne Ode *Tel:* 605-773-6008 *E-mail:* Jeanne.Ode@state.sd.us
Founded: 1997
The South Dakota Historical Society Press is committed to producing books that reflect the rich & varied history of South Dakota & the region.
ISBN Prefix(es): 978-0-9622621; 978-0-9715171; 978-0-9749195; 978-0-9777955; 978-0-9798940; 978-0-9845041; 978-0-9846505; 978-0-9852905; 978-0-9860355; 978-1-941813; 978-0-9822749; 978-0-9852817
Number of titles published annually: 7 Print
Total Titles: 55 Print
Foreign Rep(s): Eurospan Group (worldwide exc North America)

South Platte Press
PO Box 163, David City, NE 68632-0163
Tel: 402-367-3554
E-mail: railroads@windstream.net
Web Site: www.southplattepress.net
Key Personnel
Publr: James J Reisdorff
Founded: 1982
Railroad related titles.
ISBN Prefix(es): 978-0-942035
Number of titles published annually: 5 Print
Total Titles: 25 Print

Southern Historical Press Inc
375 W Broad St, Greenville, SC 29601
Mailing Address: PO Box 1267, Greenville, SC 29602-1267
Tel: 864-233-2346 *Toll Free Tel:* 800-233-0152
E-mail: southernhistoricalpress@gmail.com
Web Site: www.southernhistoricalpress.com
Key Personnel
Pres: LaBruce M S Lucas
Founded: 1967
Historical & genealogical books.
ISBN Prefix(es): 978-0-89308
Number of titles published annually: 20 Print
Total Titles: 370 Print

Southern Illinois University Press
Division of Southern Illinois University
1915 University Press Dr, SIUC Mail Code 6806, Carbondale, IL 62901-4323
SAN: 203-3623
Tel: 618-453-2281 *Fax:* 618-453-1221
E-mail: custserv@press.uchicago.edu; rights@siu.edu
Web Site: www.siupress.com
Key Personnel
Dir: Barbara Martin *Tel:* 618-453-6614 *E-mail:* bbmartin@siu.edu
Mktg & Sales Mgr: Amy Etcheson *Tel:* 618-453-6623 *E-mail:* aetcheson@siu.edu
Rts & Perms Mgr: Angela Moore-Swafford *Tel:* 618-453-6619 *E-mail:* angmoore@siu.edu
Acqs Ed: Kristine Priddy *Tel:* 618-453-6631 *E-mail:* mkpriddy@siu.edu
Founded: 1956
Scholarly nonfiction, educational material, rhetoric & composition, aviation, history, theatre, regional history & poetry.
ISBN Prefix(es): 978-0-8093
Number of titles published annually: 40 Print; 40 E-Book
Total Titles: 1,400 Print; 2 CD-ROM; 400 E-Book; 17 Audio
Foreign Rep(s): East West Export Books (Royden Muranaka) (Asia, Australia, Pacific Rim); Eurospan (Andrew Wong) (Europe, Middle East); Scholarly Book Services Inc (Laura Rust) (Canada)
Distribution Center: Chicago Distribution Center, 11030 S Langley Ave, Chicago, IL 60628-3830 *Toll Free Tel:* 800-621-2736 *Toll Free Fax:* 800-621-8476
Membership(s): Association of American University Presses

Soyinfo Center
PO Box 234, Lafayette, CA 94549-0234
SAN: 212-8411
Tel: 925-283-2991
Web Site: www.soyinfocenter.com
Key Personnel
Pres & Ed-in-Chief: William Shurtleff
Founded: 1976
Books & bibliographies on all aspects of soybeans & soyfoods; industry & marketing studies. All books since 2008 published in PDF format on the web free of charge.
ISBN Prefix(es): 978-0-933332; 978-1-928914
Number of titles published annually: 10 Print; 10 Online
Total Titles: 162 Print; 60 Online
Shipping Address: 1021 Dolores Dr, Lafayette, CA 94549

Sparkhouse, see Augsburg Fortress Publishers, Publishing House of the Evangelical Lutheran Church in America

Sparkhouse Family, see Augsburg Fortress Publishers, Publishing House of the Evangelical Lutheran Church in America

Specialty Press Inc
300 NW 70 Ave, Suite 102, Plantation, FL 33317
SAN: 251-6977
Tel: 954-792-8100 *Toll Free Tel:* 800-233-9273 *Fax:* 954-792-8545
E-mail: websales@addwarehouse.com
Web Site: addwarehouse.com
Key Personnel
CEO & Intl Rts: Harvey Parker *E-mail:* hparker@addwarehouse.com
Founded: 1990
Selections related to children with special needs.
ISBN Prefix(es): 978-0-9621629; 978-1-886941; 978-1-937761
Number of titles published annually: 3 Print
Total Titles: 40 Print; 4 E-Book
Distributed by Boys Town Press; Child Play; MHS
Distributor for Bantam; Guilford Press; Plenum; Simon & Schuster; Slossen; Woodbine House

§SPIE
1000 20 St, Bellingham, WA 98225-6705
Mailing Address: PO Box 10, Bellingham, WA 98227-0010
Tel: 360-676-3290 *Toll Free Tel:* 888-504-8171 (orders) *Fax:* 360-647-1445
E-mail: help@spie.org; customerservice@spie.org (orders)
Web Site: www.spie.org
Key Personnel
Pubns Dir: Eric Pepper *Tel:* 360-685-5473 *E-mail:* eric@spie.org
Pubns Busn Devt Mgr: Mary Summerfield *Tel:* 360-685-5588 *E-mail:* marysu@spie.org
SPIE Press Mgr: Tim Lamkins *Tel:* 360-685-5475 *E-mail:* timl@spie.org
Journals Mgr: Karolyn Labes *Tel:* 360-685-5421 *E-mail:* karolyn@spie.org
Founded: 1955
Scientific, technical books & journals, proceedings of symposia.
ISBN Prefix(es): 978-0-8194
Number of titles published annually: 450 Print; 450 Online; 25 E-Book
Total Titles: 200 CD-ROM; 250 E-Book
Imprints: Proceedings of SPIE (spie.org/publications/conference-proceedings); SPIE Journals (spie.org/journals); SPIE Press
Membership(s): Copyright Clearance Center; CrossRef

SPIE, The International Society for Optics & Photonics, see SPIE

Spinsters Ink
Imprint of Bella Books
PO Box 10543, Tallahassee, FL 32302
Tel: 850-576-2370 *Toll Free Tel:* 800-729-4992
E-mail: info@bellabooks.com
Web Site: www.bellabooks.com/Publisher-spinsters-ink-cat.html
Key Personnel
Publr: Linda Hill
Founded: 1978
Novels & nonfiction by women about LGBT lives & issues, including social justice.
ISBN Prefix(es): 978-1-935226; 978-1-883523
Number of titles published annually: 8 Print; 12 E-Book
Total Titles: 100 Print; 24 E-Book
Imprints: Grave Issues
Foreign Rep(s): Airlift Book Co (Europe); Bulldog Distribution (Australia)
Distribution Center: Bella Distribution

Spizzirri Publishing Inc
PO Box 9397, Rapid City, SD 57709-9397
Tel: 605-348-2749 *Toll Free Tel:* 800-325-9819 *Fax:* 605-348-6251 *Toll Free Fax:* 800-322-9819
E-mail: spizzpub@aol.com
Web Site: www.spizzirri.com
Key Personnel
Pres: Linda Spizzirri
Founded: 1978
Educational coloring books, book-CD packages, activity books, workbooks & how-to-draw books. PreK-5th grade featuring realistic illustrations & museum curator approved texts on topics, including everything from dinosaurs to space.
ISBN Prefix(es): 978-0-86545
Number of titles published annually: 3 Print
Total Titles: 200 Print

§Springer
Subsidiary of Springer Science+Business Media
233 Spring St, New York, NY 10013-1578
Tel: 212-460-1500 *Toll Free Tel:* 800-SPRINGER (777-4643) *Fax:* 212-460-1700
E-mail: customerservice@springer.com
Web Site: www.springer.com
Key Personnel
Cont: Ned Woods
VP, Applied Sci: Dieter Merkle
VP, HR: Eileen Purelis *E-mail:* eileen.purelis@springer.com
VP, Prodn: Henry Krell
VP, Publg Devt & Head, Edit Dept, Astronomy: Harry Blom
Edit Dir: Antoinette Cimino *E-mail:* antoinette.cimino@springer.com
Edit Dir, Biomedicine: Carolyn Honour
Edit Dir, Clinical Medicine: Richard Lansing *E-mail:* richard.lansing@springer.com
Edit Dir, Computer Sci & Engg: Jennifer Evans
Founded: 1842 (1964 NY office)
Scientific, medical, technical, research, reference books & periodicals.
ISBN Prefix(es): 978-0-387
Number of titles published annually: 6,500 Print; 6,000 E-Book
Total Titles: 70,000 Print; 36,000 Online; 38,000 E-Book
Imprints: Apress; BioMed Central; Birkhauser Science; Copernicus; Current Medicine Group; Humana Press; Springer Healthcare
Foreign Office(s): Heidelberger Platz 3, 14197 Berlin, Germany
Tiergartenstr 17, 69121 Heidelberg, Germany
Van Godewijckstr 30, 3311 GX Dordrecht, Netherlands
Membership(s): International Association of Scientific, Technical & Medical Publishers

§Springer Publishing Co
11 W 42 St, 15th fl, New York, NY 10036-8002
SAN: 203-2236
Tel: 212-431-4370 *Toll Free Tel:* 877-687-7476 *Fax:* 212-941-7842
E-mail: marketing@springerpub.com; cs@springerpub.com (orders); editorial@springerpub.com
Web Site: www.springerpub.com
Key Personnel
CEO: Mary E Gatsch *E-mail:* mgatsch@springerpub.com
VP, Journal Pubns: James C Costello *E-mail:* jcostello@springerpub.com
VP, Sales & Mktg: Jason Roth *E-mail:* jroth@springerpub.com
Edit Dir: Nancy Hale *E-mail:* nhale@springerpub.com
Dir, Spec Sales & Rts: Annette Imperati *E-mail:* aimperati@springerpub.com
Sr Sales Dir: Kathy Weiss *E-mail:* kweiss@springerpub.com
Nursing Publr: Margaret Zuccarini *E-mail:* mzuccarini@springerpub.com
Exec Ed: Sheri W Sussman *E-mail:* swsussman@springerpub.com
Exec Ed, Nursing: Elizabeth Nieginski *E-mail:* enieginski@springerpub.com
Sr Acqs Ed: Joseph Morita *E-mail:* jmorita@springerpub.com
Acqs Ed: Stephanie Drew *E-mail:* sdrew@springerpub.com
Founded: 1950 (Feb 2004, acquired by Mannheim Holdings, LLC, subsidiary of Mannheim Trust)
Professional books, encyclopedias, college textbooks & journals; nursing, psychology, gerontology/geriatrics, medical education, public health, rehabilitation, social work & scholarly health sciences.
ISBN Prefix(es): 978-0-8261
Number of titles published annually: 100 Print
Total Titles: 700 Print
Divisions: Demos Medical Publishing
Foreign Rep(s): Cranbury International LLC (Ethan Atkin) (Latin America); The Eurospan Group (Africa, Europe, Middle East, UK); Footprint Books Pty Ltd (Australia, New Zealand); Login Canada (Canada); Taylor & Francis Asia Pacific (Asia); Taylor & Francis Books India Pvt Ltd (Bangladesh, India, Pakistan, Sri Lanka)
Shipping Address: Ingram Publishers Services, One Ingram Blvd, La Vergne, TN 37006 *Tel:* 978-345-2121 *Toll Free Tel:* 877-687-7476 *Fax:* 978-348-1233 *Web Site:* www.ingrampublisherservices.com
Warehouse: Ingram Publishers Services, One Ingram Blvd, La Vergne, TN 37006 *Tel:* 978-345-2121 *Toll Free Tel:* 877-687-7476 *Fax:* 978-348-1233 *Web Site:* www.ingrampublisherservices.com
Membership(s): AAP; American Medical Publishers Association; STM
See separate listing for:
Demos Medical Publishing

Spry Publishing
315 E Eisenhower Pkwy, Suite 2, Ann Arbor, MI 48108
Tel: 734-531-7600 *Toll Free Tel:* 877-722-2264
E-mail: info@sprypub.com
Web Site: www.sprypub.com
Key Personnel
Publr & COO: Lynne Johnson *E-mail:* ljohnson@sprypub.com
Dir, Busn Devt: Jeremy Sterling
Mktg & Publicity Mgr: Katie Spence *E-mail:* kspence@sprypub.com
Founded: 1999
ISBN Prefix(es): 978-1-58726; 978-1-93817
Number of titles published annually: 20 Print
Total Titles: 120 Print
Imprints: Mitten Press

Square One Publishers Inc
115 Herricks Rd, Garden City Park, NY 11040
Tel: 516-535-2010 *Toll Free Tel:* 877-900-BOOK (900-2665) *Fax:* 516-535-2014
E-mail: sq1publish@aol.com
Web Site: www.squareonepublishers.com
Key Personnel
Pres & Publr: Rudy Shur
Art Dir: Jeannie Tudor
VP, Mktg, PR & Rts: Anthony Pomes
Sales Dir: Ken Kaiman
Mgr, Opers: Robert Love
Exec Ed: Joanne Abrams
Sr Ed: Marie Caratozzolo
Founded: 2000
Specialize in adult nonfiction books. Topics covered include collectibles, cooking, general interest, history, how-to, parenting, self-help & health.
ISBN Prefix(es): 978-0-7570
Number of titles published annually: 25 Print
Total Titles: 500 Print; 1 Audio
Imprints: Ocean Publishing
Distributed by Thomas Allen & Son
Distributor for InnoVision Health Media; Rainbow Ridge Books
Foreign Rep(s): Thomas Allen & Son (Canada); Brumby Books (Australia, New Zealand); G D Daby (Southeast Asia); Deep Books (Europe, UK); Trinity Books (South Africa)
Membership(s): ABA; ALA; The Association of Publishers for Special Sales; Independent Book Publishers Association

§SSPC: The Society for Protective Coatings
800 Trumbull Dr, Pittsburgh, PA 15220-4365
Tel: 412-281-2331 *Toll Free Tel:* 877-281-7772 (US only) *Fax:* 412-281-9992
E-mail: info@sspc.org
Web Site: www.sspc.org
Key Personnel
Exec Dir: William Worms *Tel:* 412-281-2331 ext 2230 *E-mail:* worms@sspc.org
Memb Servs Fulfillment Coord: Nicole Lourette *Tel:* 412-281-2331 ext 2204 *E-mail:* lourette@sspc.org
Mktg Specialist: Michael Kline *Tel:* 412-281-2331 ext 2207 *E-mail:* kline@sspc.org
Founded: 1950
Technical publications; CD-ROMs, standards for industry.
ISBN Prefix(es): 978-0-938477; 978-1-889060
Number of titles published annually: 12 Print
Total Titles: 80 Print
Distributed by Technology Publishing Co

§ST Media Group Book Division
Division of ST Media Group International
11262 Cornell Park Dr, Cincinnati, OH 45242
SAN: 204-5974
Tel: 513-421-2050 *Toll Free Tel:* 866-265-0954 *Fax:* 513-263-6999
E-mail: books@stmediagroup.com
Web Site: www.stmediagroup.com
Key Personnel
Dir: Mark Kissling *Tel:* 800-925-1110 ext 399 *E-mail:* mark.kissling@stmediagroup.com
Founded: 1906
Books, magazines, buyers' guides: sign, screen printing, visual merchandising & store design industries, large format digital printing & package design.
ISBN Prefix(es): 978-0-911380; 978-0-944094
Number of titles published annually: 3 Print
Total Titles: 44 Print

§Stackpole Books
5067 Ritter Rd, Mechanicsburg, PA 17055
SAN: 202-5396
Tel: 717-796-0411 *Toll Free Tel:* 800-732-3669 *Fax:* 717-796-0412
Web Site: www.stackpolebooks.com
Key Personnel
Publr & Acting CEO: Judith Schnell *E-mail:* jschnell@stackpolebooks.com
VP & Dir, Creative Servs & Prodn: Tracy Patterson
Fulfillment Mgr & Warehouse Supv: Anne Lodge
Ed & Rts: Mark Allison *Tel:* 717-796-0411 ext 153
Ed: Kyle Weaver
Founded: 1933
Trade book publisher with a proud, 80 plus year history of publishing titles in the categories of outdoor sports, nature, crafts, history, military reference & regional. Strong in fly fishing, nature guides, military history & military reference, we publish deep in our niche areas. Presently expanding into the fast-growing world of ebooks while continuing to produce alternative, high-quality hardcovers, trade paperbacks & ebooks.
ISBN Prefix(es): 978-0-8117
Number of titles published annually: 100 Print; 5 CD-ROM
Total Titles: 2,000 Print; 5 CD-ROM
Foreign Rights: Bardon-Chinese Media Agency (Phillip Chen) (China); Alex Korzheneuski (Russia); Hana Whitton (Eastern Europe)
Distribution Center: National Book Network, 15200 NBN Way, Blue Ridge Summit, PA 17214 *Tel:* 717-794-3800 *Fax:* 717-794-3828

Standard International Media Holdings
568 Ninth St S, Suite 201, Naples, FL 34102-7336
Tel: 239-248-5550 *Fax:* 239-649-5832 *Toll Free Fax:* 866-948-7883
E-mail: sales@standardinternationalmedia.com
Web Site: www.standardinternationalmedia.com
Key Personnel
CFO: Connie Miller *E-mail:* connie@standardinternationalmedia.com
Pres: Simon Bailey *Tel:* 844-502-6657 *E-mail:* simon@standardinternationalmedia.com
Intl Sales Dir: Elaine Evans *Tel:* 844-502-6657 *E-mail:* elaine@standardinternationalmedia.com
Founded: 1994
Book publisher & distributor.
ISBN Prefix(es): 978-1-888777; 978-1-58279; 978-1-86091
Number of titles published annually: 7 Print
Total Titles: 200 Print
Imprints: Chef Express; Chef Success; Trident Reference

Standard Publishing
4050 Lee Vance View, Colorado Springs, CO 80918
SAN: 110-5515
Tel: 513-931-4050 *Toll Free Tel:* 800-323-7543 *Fax:* 513-931-0950 *Toll Free Fax:* 800-323-0726
E-mail: customerservice@standardpub.com
Web Site: www.standardpub.com
Key Personnel
Dir, Sales: Ken Lorenz
Mng Ed: James Nieman
Ed, Children's: Karen Cain
Ed, Christian Standard: Mark Taylor
Asst Ed, The Lookout: Sheryl Overstreet
Magazine Prodn Coord, Christian Standard: Diane Jones
Rts & Perms Consultant: Joann VanMeter
Founded: 1866
Religious children's books, Sunday school literature & supplies, youth & adult trade books.
ISBN Prefix(es): 978-0-87239; 978-0-87403; 978-0-7847
Number of titles published annually: 75 Print
Total Titles: 700 Print; 30 CD-ROM
Imprints: Happy Day Books
Foreign Rights: Foundation Distributing Inc (Canada); Omega (New Zealand); Salvation Book Centre (Malaysia); Scripture Press Foundation Ltd (UK)

§Standard Publishing Corp
10 High St, Boston, MA 02110
Tel: 617-457-0600 *Toll Free Tel:* 800-682-5759 *Fax:* 617-457-0608
Web Site: www.spcpub.com
Key Personnel
Pres & Publr: John C Cross, Esq
Edit Dir: Katherine Allnutt Panikian, Esq
Mktg Mgr: Susanne Edes Dillman *E-mail:* s.dillman@spcpub.com
Founded: 1865
Information for insurance professionals.
ISBN Prefix(es): 978-0-923240
Number of titles published annually: 10 Print
Total Titles: 10 Print; 3 CD-ROM
Subsidiaries: John Liner Organization
Branch Office(s)
Insurance Record, 9601 White Rock Trail, Suite 213, Dallas, TX 75238
Distributed by LexisNexis®; Silverplume, a Vertafore Co

Stanford University Press
425 Broadway St, Redwood City, CA 94063-3126
SAN: 203-3526
Tel: 650-723-9434 *Fax:* 650-725-3457
E-mail: info@www.sup.org; publicity@www.sup.org
Web Site: www.sup.org
Key Personnel
Publr: Michael Keller
Publg Dir & Ed-in-Chief: Kate Wahl *E-mail:* kwahl@stanford.edu
Dir: Dr Alan Harvey *E-mail:* aharvey@stanford.edu
Dir, Edit, Design & Prodn: Patricia Myers *E-mail:* pmyers@stanford.edu
Dir, Fin & Opers: Jean H Kim *E-mail:* plcmnkim@stanford.edu
Art Dir: Robert Ehle *E-mail:* ehle@stanford.edu
Exec Ed: Emily-Jane Cohen
Sr Ed: Margo Beth Fleming *E-mail:* mbfleming@stanford.edu
Acqs Ed: Jenny Gavacs *E-mail:* jgavacs@stanford.edu; Margo Irvin; Michelle Lipinski *E-mail:* mlipinski@stanford.edu; Friederike Sundaram
Sr Contracts & Rts Mgr: Ariane de Pree-Kajfez
Mktg Mgr: Stephanie Adams
Prodn Mgr: Mike Sagara *E-mail:* msagara@stanford.edu
Publicity & PR Mgr: Mary Kate Maco
Sales & Exhibits Mgr: Kate Templar
Publicist: Ryan Furtkamp
Founded: 1925
ISBN Prefix(es): 978-0-8047
Number of titles published annually: 150 Print; 40 E-Book
Total Titles: 2,500 Print; 400 E-Book
Imprints: Redwood Press; Stanford Briefs; Stanford Business Books; Stanford Economics & Finance; Stanford Law Books; Stanford Security Studies
Foreign Rep(s): East-West Export Books (Asia, Australia, New Zealand, The Pacific); Marston Book Services Ltd (Africa, Europe, Middle East, UK)
Returns: Chicago Distribution Center, 11030 S Langley Ave, Chicago, IL 60628 *Tel:* 773-702-7010 *Toll Free Tel:* 800-621-2736 *Toll Free Fax:* 800-621-8476 *E-mail:* custserv@press.uchicago.edu
Warehouse: Chicago Distribution Center, 11030 S Langley Ave, Chicago, IL 60628 *Tel:* 773-702-7010 *Toll Free Tel:* 800-621-2736 *Toll Free Fax:* 800-621-8476 *E-mail:* custserv@press.uchicago.edu

Distribution Center: Chicago Distribution Center, 11030 S Langley Ave, Chicago, IL 60628 *Tel:* 773-702-7010 *Toll Free Tel:* 800-621-2736 *Toll Free Fax:* 800-621-8476 *E-mail:* custserv@press.uchicago.edu
Membership(s): AAP; Association of American University Presses

Star Bright Books Inc
13 Landsdowne St, Cambridge, MA 02139
Tel: 617-354-1300 *Fax:* 617-354-1399
E-mail: info@starbrightbooks.com; orders@starbrightbooks.com
Web Site: www.starbrightbooks.org
Key Personnel
Publr: Deborah Shine
Founded: 1994
Independent children's book publisher.
ISBN Prefix(es): 978-1-887734; 978-1-932065; 978-1-59572
Number of titles published annually: 16 Print
Total Titles: 400 Print
Membership(s): ABA; ALA; Independent Book Publishers Association

Star Publishing Co Inc
PO Box 5165, Belmont, CA 94002-5165
SAN: 212-6958
Tel: 650-591-3505 *Fax:* 650-752-9212
Web Site: www.starpublishing.com
Key Personnel
Publr: Stuart A Hoffman
Founded: 1978
College/university textbooks, laboratory manuals; reference books; professional books; California history/local history.
ISBN Prefix(es): 978-0-89863
Number of titles published annually: 14 Print
Total Titles: 450 Print
Imprints: Encore Editions

STARbooks Press
Affiliate of Florida Literary Foundation (FLF)
PO Box 711612, Herndon, VA 20171
E-mail: publish@starbookspress.com
Web Site: www.starbookspress.com
Key Personnel
Sr Edit Dir: Eric Summers
Founded: 1989
ISBN Prefix(es): 978-1-877978; 978-1-891855
Number of titles published annually: 8 Print
Total Titles: 30 Print; 1 Audio
Imprints: Florida Literary Foundation (FLF) Press; Starbooks

§Starcrafts LLC
334-A Calef Hwy, Epping, NH 03042
SAN: 208-5380
Tel: 603-734-4300 *Toll Free Tel:* 866-953-8458 (24/7 message ctr) *Fax:* 603-734-4311
E-mail: astrosales@astrocom.com
Web Site: acspublications.com; www.starcraftseast.com; www.astrocom.com
Key Personnel
Owner & Publr: Maria K Simms *E-mail:* maria@starcraftpublishing.com
Cust Serv: Thomas Canfield *E-mail:* tom@astrocom.com
Founded: 1973
Astrology: ephemerides, chart interpretation.
ISBN Prefix(es): 978-0-935127; 978-0-917086; 978-0-9762422; 978-1-934976
Number of titles published annually: 4 Print; 1 CD-ROM
Total Titles: 60 Print; 5 CD-ROM; 1 Audio
Imprints: ACS Publications; Starcrafts Publishing
Foreign Rep(s): The Rights Agency (Canada)
Distribution Center: New Leaf Distributing Co, 401 Thornton Rd, Lithia Springs, GA 30122-1557 *Tel:* 770-948-7845 *Fax:* 770-944-2313 *E-mail:* newleaf@newleaf-dist.com *Web Site:* www.newleaf-dist.com

Stargazer Publishing Co
958 Stanislaus Dr, Corona, CA 92881
Mailing Address: PO Box 77002, Corona, CA 92877-0100
Tel: 951-898-4619 *Toll Free Tel:* 800-606-7895 (orders) *Fax:* 951-898-4633
E-mail: stargazer@stargazerpub.com; orders@stargazerpub.com
Web Site: www.stargazerpub.com
Founded: 1995
ISBN Prefix(es): 978-0-9643853; 978-1-933277; 978-0-9713756
Number of titles published annually: 10 Print; 5 CD-ROM; 5 E-Book
Total Titles: 44 Print; 5 CD-ROM; 5 E-Book
Warehouse: Publishers Storage & Shipping Corp, 660 S Mansfield, Ypsilanti, MI 48197
Membership(s): Independent Book Publishers Association; National Association of College Stores; Publishers Association of Los Angeles

StarGroup International Inc
1194 Old Dixie Hwy, Suite 201, West Palm Beach, FL 33413
Tel: 561-547-0667 *Fax:* 561-843-8530
E-mail: info@stargroupinternational.com
Web Site: stargroupinternational.com
Key Personnel
Pres & CEO: Brenda Star *E-mail:* brenda@stargroupinternational.com
Creative Dir: Mel Abfier
Head Writer & Film/Video Prodr: Gwen Carden; Linda Haas
Internet Mktg Coord: Butch Butler
Mktg, Media & Website Devt: Rusty Durham
Media Specialist: Sam Smyth
Founded: 1983
Create books to be used as marketing & media tools. For over 2 decades have maintained access to the best researchers, writers, editors, proofreaders, designers & printers in the industry, while offering public relations & marketing services. Specialize in creating books for clients to enhance their credibility & position them as experts in their field.
This publisher has indicated that 75% of their product line is author subsidized.
ISBN Prefix(es): 978-1-884886
Number of titles published annually: 25 Print
Total Titles: 150 Print
Membership(s): Florida Authors & Publishers Association Inc; Independent Book Publishers Association

State University of New York Press
10 N Pearl St, 4th fl, Albany, NY 12207
SAN: 760-7261
Tel: 518-944-2800 *Toll Free Tel:* 877-204-6073 (orders) *Fax:* 518-320-1592 *Toll Free Fax:* 877-204-6074 (orders)
E-mail: info@sunypress.edu (edit off); suny@presswarehouse.com (orders)
Web Site: www.sunypress.edu
Key Personnel
Co-Dir: Donna Dixon *Tel:* 518-944-2802 *E-mail:* donna.dixon@sunypress.edu; James Peltz *Tel:* 518-944-2815 *E-mail:* james.peltz@sunypress.edu
Assoc Dir & Dir, Sales & Busn Devt: Daniel Flynn *Tel:* 518-944-2823 *E-mail:* daniel.flynn@sunypress.edu
Dir, Mktg & Publicity: Fran Keneston *Tel:* 518-944-2807 *E-mail:* fran.keneston@sunypress.edu
Rts & Perms: Sharla Clute *Tel:* 518-944-2803 *E-mail:* sharla.clute@sunypress.edu
Founded: 1966
Scholarly nonfiction, especially works in philosophy, psychology, African American studies, gender/sexuality studies, American Indian studies, museum/archival science, Asian studies & religious studies.
ISBN Prefix(es): 978-0-87395; 978-0-88706; 978-0-7914; 978-1-4384
Number of titles published annually: 150 Print; 140 Online; 140 E-Book; 2 Audio
Total Titles: 5,670 Print; 3,500 Online; 3,500 E-Book; 2 Audio
Imprints: Excelsior Editions
Distributor for Albany Institute of History & Art; Codhill Press; Samuel Dorsky Museum of Art; Mount Ida Press; Muswell Hill Press; New Netherland Institute; Rockefeller Institute Press; Uncrowned Queens
Foreign Rep(s): Cassidy & Associates Inc (China, Hong Kong, Taiwan); Lexa Publishers' Representatives (Canada); MHM Limited (Japan); US PubRep (Caribbean, Central America, Mexico, Puerto Rico, South America)
Billing Address: PO Box 960, Herndon, VA 20172-0960, Cust Serv *Tel:* 703-661-1575 *Fax:* 703-996-1010
Orders to: PO Box 960, Herndon, VA 20172-0960, Cust Serv *Tel:* 703-661-1575 *Fax:* 703-996-1010
Returns: 22883 Quicksilver Dr, Dulles, VA 20166, Cust Serv *Tel:* 703-661-1575 *Fax:* 703-996-1010
Shipping Address: 22835 Quicksilver Dr, Dulles, VA 20166 *Tel:* 703-661-1575 *Fax:* 703-996-1010
Warehouse: PO Box 960, Herndon, VA 20172-0960, Cust Serv *Tel:* 703-661-1575 *Fax:* 703-996-1010
Distribution Center: NBN International, Estover Rd, Plymouth PL6 7PY, United Kingdom *Tel:* (01752) 202-301 *Fax:* (01752) 202-233 *E-mail:* orders@nbninternational.com
Membership(s): ABA; Association of American University Presses
See separate listing for:
Excelsior Editions

Steerforth Press
45 Lyme Rd, Suite 208, Hanover, NH 03755-1222
Tel: 603-643-4787 *Fax:* 603-643-4788
E-mail: info@steerforth.com
Web Site: www.steerforth.com
Key Personnel
Founder & Publr: Chip Fleischer *E-mail:* chip@steerforth.com; Alan Lelchuk; Thomas Powers
Dir, Publg Opers & Foreign Rts: Helga Schmidt *E-mail:* helga@steerforth.com
Fiction Ed: Roland Pease *E-mail:* roland@steerforth.com
Founded: 1993
ISBN Prefix(es): 978-1-883642; 978-0-944072; 978-1-58195; 978-1-58642
Number of titles published annually: 18 Print
Total Titles: 250 Print
Imprints: Zoland Books
Foreign Rights: Big Apple Agency Inc (Taiwan); Agence Bookman (Scandinavia); The English Agency (Japan); Anouk H Foerg; Harris-Elon Agency (Israel); International Editors' Co SA (Argentina, Brazil, Latin America, Portugal, Spain); Katai & Bolza (Hungary); David Marshall; Daniela Micura Literary Services (Italy); Onk Agency (Turkey)
Distribution Center: Penguin Random House Distribution Center, 400 Hahn Rd, Westminster, MD 21157 *Toll Free Tel:* 800-733-3000 *Toll Free Fax:* 800-659-2436
Membership(s): ABA; Independent Book Publishers Association; New England Independent Booksellers Association

§SteinerBooks
610 Main St, Great Barrington, MA 01230
Tel: 413-528-8233 *Fax:* 413-528-8826
E-mail: friends@steinerbooks.org
Web Site: steiner.presswarehouse.com
Key Personnel
CEO & Pres: Gene Gollogly *Tel:* 212-414-2275

ext 11 *Fax:* 212-414-2412 *E-mail:* gene@steinerbooks.org
Edit & Art Dir: Mary Giddens *E-mail:* mary@steinerbooks.org
Ed-in-Chief: Christopher Bamford
Founded: 1928
American & English editions of works by Rudolf Steiner & related authors.
ISBN Prefix(es): 978-0-910142; 978-0-88010
Number of titles published annually: 29 Print
Total Titles: 451 Print
Imprints: Bell Pond Books; Lindisfarne Books
Distributed by Rudolf Steiner Press UK
Distributor for Chiron Publications; Clairview Books; Floris Books; Hawthorn Press; Lantern Books; Rudolph Steiner Press; Temple Lodge Publishing
Foreign Rep(s): Ceres (New Zealand); Peter Hyde & Associates (South Africa); Rudolf Steiner Press (UK)
Orders to: PO Box 960, Herndon, VA 20172-0960 *Tel:* 703-661-1594 *Fax:* 703-661-1501 *E-mail:* service@steinerbooks.org SAN: 201-1824
See separate listing for:
Lindisfarne Books

Stellar Publishing
2114 S Live Oak Pkwy, Wilmington, NC 28403
SAN: 860-2298
Tel: 910-269-7444
Web Site: www.stellar-publishing.com
Key Personnel
Publr: Jasper Williams *E-mail:* publisher@stellar-publishing.com
Founded: 2000
This publisher has indicated that 50% of their product line is author subsidized.
ISBN Prefix(es): 978-0-970341
Number of titles published annually: 3 Print
Total Titles: 9 Print

Stemmer House Publishers Inc
Division of Pathway Book Service
4 White Brook Rd, Gilsum, NH 03448
SAN: 207-9623
Mailing Address: PO Box 89, Gilsum, NH 03448
Tel: 603-357-0236 *Toll Free Tel:* 800-345-6665 *Fax:* 603-965-2181
E-mail: pbs@pathwaybook.com
Web Site: www.stemmer.com
Key Personnel
Pres & Publr: Judith Peter
Founded: 1975
Books in the arts & crafts, audio CDs, illustrated books, multicultural studies & children's books on the environment.
ISBN Prefix(es): 978-0-916144; 978-0-88045
Number of titles published annually: 10 Print
Total Titles: 150 Print; 5 Audio
Imprints: International Design Library®; NaturEncyclopedia Series
Foreign Rep(s): Gazelle Book Services Ltd (Europe, UK); John Reed Books (Australia, New Zealand)
Returns: Pathway Book Service, 4 White Brook Rd, Gilsum, NH 03448
Shipping Address: Pathway Book Service, 4 White Brook Rd, Gilsum, NH 03448
Warehouse: Pathway Book Service, 4 White Brook Rd, Gilsum, NH 03448
Distribution Center: Pathway Book Service, 4 White Brook Rd, Gilsum, NH 03448

§Stenhouse Publishers
Division of Highlights for Children Education Group
480 Congress St, Portland, ME 04101-3451
Tel: 207-253-1600 *Toll Free Tel:* 888-363-0566 *Fax:* 207-253-5121 *Toll Free Fax:* 800-833-9164
E-mail: customerservice@stenhouse.com
Web Site: www.stenhouse.com
Key Personnel
Mng Ed: William Varner *E-mail:* wvarner@stenhouse.com
Founded: 1993
Professional books for teachers.
ISBN Prefix(es): 978-1-57110
Number of titles published annually: 20 Print; 3 Online; 15 E-Book
Total Titles: 350 Print; 250 E-Book; 3 Audio
Distributor for Pembroke Publishers
Foreign Rep(s): Curriculum Corp (Australia, New Zealand); Eurospan (Africa, Central America, China, Europe, Hong Kong, India, Japan, Korea, South America, Taiwan, UK); Pembroke Publishers (Canada); Publishers Marketing Services (Southeast Asia)
Billing Address: PO Box 11020, Portland, ME 04104-7020, Opers Mgr: Elaine Cyr *E-mail:* ecyr@stenhouse.com
Warehouse: 4200 Parkway Ct, Hilliard, OH 43026, Contact: Vicki Woolwhine *Tel:* 614-487-2883 *Fax:* 614-529-0670

Sterling Publishing Co Inc
Subsidiary of Barnes & Noble Inc
1166 Avenue of the Americas, 17th fl, New York, NY 10036
SAN: 211-6324
Tel: 212-532-7160 *Toll Free Tel:* 800-367-9692 *Fax:* 212-213-2495
Web Site: www.sterlingpublishing.com
Key Personnel
Pres: Theresa Thompson
VP, Fin: Tom Allen
VP, Publg Opers: Adria Dougherty *Tel:* 646-688-2444 *E-mail:* adougherty@sterlingpub.com
Dir, Edit & Subs Rts: Marilyn Kretzer
Dir, HR: Kerri Cuocci
Dir, North American Trade: Trudi Bartow
Dir, Spec Sales: Nicole Vines Verlin
Founded: 1949
Publisher of quality nonfiction & fiction books for adults & children. Subject categories include art & photography, cookbooks, wine, self-improvement, mind/body/spirit, business, history, reference, science & nature, home reference, gardening, music, sports, lifestyle & design, hobbies, crafts, classics, study guides, puzzles & games, children's nonfiction, picture, board & humor books.
This publisher has indicated that 50% of their product line is author subsidized.
ISBN Prefix(es): 978-0-7607; 978-0-937274 (Lark Books); 978-1-887374 (Lark Books); 978-1-57990 (Lark Books); 978-0-8069; 978-1-895569 (Sterling/Tamos); 978-1-4027; 978-1-58816 (Hearst); 978-1-58663 (SparkNotes); 978-1-59308 (Barnes & Noble Classics); 978-1-60059 (Lark Books); 978-1-4114 (SparkNotes); 978-1-934618 (Begin Smart); 978-1-4351 (Fall River Press); 978-1-4547 (Lark Books); 978-1-4549; 978-1-60736 (Ecosystem); 978-1-61837 (Hearst)
Number of titles published annually: 800 Print
Total Titles: 5,000 Print
Imprints: Flashkids; Hearst Books; Lark Crafts; Puzzlewright Press; Sterling; Sterling Children's Books; Sterling Epicure; Sterling Ethos
Distributor for Boxer Books (selected titles); Brooklyn Botanic Garden (selected titles); Carlton Books (selected titles); Davis Publications (selected titles); Sally Milner (selected titles); Pavilion (selected titles); Salaryia (selected titles); Sixth & Spring; White Star Publishers (selected titles)
Foreign Rep(s): Angell Eurosales (Scandinavia); David Bateman Ltd (New Zealand); Guia Representaciones de Mexico (Mexico); Guild of Master Craftsman (Central Europe, Eastern Europe, Italy, Malaysia, Malta, Middle East, Philippines, Portugal, Singapore, Spain, Taiwan, UK); Hardy Bigfoss International Co Ltd (Cambodia, Laos, Thailand, Vietnam); JCC Enterprises (Caribbean); NewSouth Books (Australia); Penguin India (Bangladesh, India, Nepal, Sri Lanka); Phambili Agencies (South Africa)
Foreign Rights: ANA Sofia Ltd (Bulgaria, Romania, Southeast Europe); Agence Litteraire Lora Fountain (France); Graal Literary Agency (Poland); Katai & Bolza Literary Agents (Hungary); Ute Korner Literary Agent (Portugal, Spain); Alexander Korzhenevski (Russia); Kristin Olson Literary Agency (Czech Republic); Literarische Agentur Silke Weniger (Germany)
Warehouse: RR Donnelley-Lark Park, N9234 Lake Park Rd, Appleton, WI 54915
See separate listing for:
Lark Crafts

Stewart, Tabori & Chang
Imprint of Harry N Abrams Inc
115 W 18 St, 6th fl, New York, NY 10011
SAN: 239-0361
Tel: 212-519-1200; 212-206-7715 *Fax:* 212-519-1210
E-mail: abrams@abramsbooks.com
Web Site: www.abramsbooks.com/imprints/stc
Key Personnel
CEO & Pres: Michael Jacobs
VP & Publr: Michael Sand *E-mail:* msand@abramsbooks.com
VP, Sales, Mktg & Publicity: Mary Wowk *E-mail:* mwowk@abramsbooks.com
Mktg Dir: Erin Hotchkiss
Sr Ed: Liana Allday
Founded: 1981
Art, illustrated gift books, gardening, cookbooks, African American history, interior design, New Age, photography, popular culture, humor, weddings.
ISBN Prefix(es): 978-1-55670; 978-0-941434; 978-1-58479
Number of titles published annually: 80 Print
Total Titles: 350 Print
Foreign Rep(s): Ralph & Sheila Summers (Southeast Asia); Paul Walton (South Africa); David Williams (South America)
Foreign Rights: General Publishing (Canada); HI Marketing Ltd (Europe, UK); Korea Copyright Center (Korea); New Holland (Australia); Onslow Books Ltd (Europe); Sigma Literary Agency (Korea); Southern Publishers Group (New Zealand); Tuttle-Mori Agency Inc (Japan); David Williams (South America)

§Stipes Publishing LLC
204 W University Ave, Champaign, IL 61820
Mailing Address: PO Box 526, Champaign, IL 61824-0526
Tel: 217-356-8391 *Fax:* 217-356-5753
E-mail: stipes01@sbcglobal.net
Web Site: www.stipes.com
Key Personnel
Partner & Electronic Publg: Benjamin Watts
Partner: J L Hecker
Founded: 1927
Primarily educational, some overlap trade publishing in music & horticulture.
ISBN Prefix(es): 978-0-87563; 978-1-58874
Number of titles published annually: 15 Print
Total Titles: 550 Print; 2 CD-ROM; 1 Online; 1 E-Book; 2 Audio

STM Learning Inc
1220 Paddock Dr, Florissant, MO 63033
Tel: 314-434-2424
E-mail: info@stmlearning.com; orders@stmlearning.com
Web Site: www.stmlearning.com
Key Personnel
Pres: Marianne Whaley *E-mail:* marianne@stmlearning.com

VP: Glenn Whaley *E-mail:* glenn@stmlearning.com
Founded: 1993
STM Learning is the expert in publishing leading clinical research for professionals who are in positions to serve & protect victims of abuse. Our customers consider STM Learning products to be the most trusted scientific, technical & medical resources available to aid in their efforts to identify, report, treat & prevent child maltreatment & domestic violence.
ISBN Prefix(es): 978-1-878060; 978-1-936590
Number of titles published annually: 10 Print; 10 E-Book
Total Titles: 50 Print; 7 CD-ROM; 50 E-Book
Foreign Rep(s): CoreSource (worldwide); Eurospan (worldwide)
Advertising Agency: GW Graphics & Publishing
Distribution Center: Amazon.com
Barnes & Noble
Rittenhouse Book Distributors Inc, 511 Feheley Dr, King of Prussia, PA 19406 *Toll Free Tel:* 800-345-6425 *Toll Free Fax:* 800-223-7488 *Web Site:* www.rittenhouse.com

STOCKCERO Inc
3785 NW 82 Ave, Suite 302, Doral, FL 33166
Tel: 305-722-7628 *Fax:* 305-477-5794
E-mail: academicservices@stockcero.com; sales@stockcero.com
Web Site: www.stockcero.com
Key Personnel
CEO: Pablo Agrest Berge *E-mail:* pagrest@stockcero.com
Founded: 2000
Committed to building an ever expanding collection of significant books, comprising Spanish literature, both Peninsular & Latin American. Our editions are conceived with modern nonnative Spanish speaking readers & students in mind, so they include updated & sharply focused footnotes, prefaces & bibliographies written by scholarly literary editors.
ISBN Prefix(es): 978-1-934768
Number of titles published annually: 14 Print
Total Titles: 164 Print; 140 Online

§Stone Bridge Press Inc
1393 Solano Ave, Suite C, Albany, CA 94706
Mailing Address: PO Box 8208, Berkeley, CA 94706
Tel: 510-524-8732
E-mail: sbp@stonebridge.com; sbpedit@stonebridge.com
Web Site: www.stonebridge.com
Key Personnel
Founder & Publr: Peter Goodman
Founded: 1989
Books on Japan & Asia.
ISBN Prefix(es): 978-0-89346 (Heian International); 978-1-880656; 978-0-9628137; 978-1-933330; 978-1-61172
Number of titles published annually: 6 Print; 10 Online; 10 E-Book
Total Titles: 120 Print; 15 Online; 75 E-Book
Imprints: Heian International (children's & crafts); Three L Media
Foreign Rep(s): Perseus International (Australia)
Distribution Center: Consortium Book Sales & Distribution Inc (US & CN) *Toll Free Tel:* 800-283-3572
Membership(s): Independent Book Publishers Association
See separate listing for:
Heian

Stone Pier Press
PO Box 170572, San Francisco, CA 94117
Tel: 415-484-2821
E-mail: hello@stonepierpress.org
Web Site: www.stonepierpress.org
Key Personnel
Publr: Clare Ellis *E-mail:* clare@stonepierpress.org
Dir, Partnerships & Devt: Faith Lemon *E-mail:* faith@stonepierpress.org
Founded: 2017
Nonprofit mission-oriented publisher with books about good food that highlight the difference that choosing climate-sensitive, sustainably produced food could make to the health of our communities & our planet. Aim to support the move to a less meat-intensive, more environmentally sustainable diet. Lean toward narrative nonfiction, but open to memoirs, biographies, children's books, fiction & guidebooks.
ISBN Prefix(es): 978-0-9988623
Number of titles published annually: 8 Print; 8 E-Book
Distributed by Chelsea Green Publishing

Stonewall, see BrickHouse Books Inc

Stoneydale Press Publishing Co
523 Main St, Stevensville, MT 59870-2839
Mailing Address: PO Box 188, Stevensville, MT 59870-0188
Tel: 406-777-2729 *Toll Free Tel:* 800-735-7006 *Fax:* 406-777-2521
E-mail: stoneydale@stoneydale.com
Web Site: www.stoneydale.com
Key Personnel
Publr: Dale A Burk
Founded: 1976
Outdoor recreation, regional history & reminisces of Northern Rockies region.
ISBN Prefix(es): 978-0-912299; 978-1-931291; 978-1-938707
Number of titles published annually: 8 Print
Total Titles: 190 Print
Membership(s): Mountains & Plains Booksellers Association; Pacific Northwest Booksellers Association

Storey Publishing LLC
210 MASS MoCA Way, North Adams, MA 01247
SAN: 203-4158
Tel: 413-346-2100 *Toll Free Tel:* 800-441-5700 (orders); 800-793-9396 (edit) *Fax:* 413-346-2199; 413-346-2196 (edit)
E-mail: sales@storey.com
Web Site: www.storey.com
Key Personnel
Publr: Deborah Balmuth *E-mail:* deborah.balmuth@storey.com
Mng Ed & Dir, Contracts: Jennifer Travis
Dir, Publicity: Amy Greeman *E-mail:* amy.greeman@storey.com
Rts Dir: Maribeth Casey *Tel:* 413-346-2135 *E-mail:* maribeth.casey@storey.com
Design Mgr: Carolyn Eckert
HR & Opers Mgr: Marci Saunders *E-mail:* marci.saunders@storey.com
Trade & Spec Sales Mgr: Janea Brachfeld
Trade, Gift & Ebook Sales Mgr: Adrienne Franceschi
Book Designer: Michaela Jebb
Copywriter & Asst to the Publr: Michal Lumsden
Founded: 1983
How-to books on country living, gardening, cooking, natural health, home building, country business, crafts, small-scale livestock, pets, beer & wine, children's nonfiction.
ISBN Prefix(es): 978-0-945352; 978-0-88266; 978-1-58017
Number of titles published annually: 50 Print
Total Titles: 600 Print
Distributed by Workman Publishing Co Inc
Foreign Rep(s): Thomas Allen & Sons Ltd (Canada); Bill Bailey Publishers' Representatives (Europe); Bookreps NZ Ltd (Susan Holmes) (New Zealand); Capricorn Link Australia Pty Ltd (Australia); Michelle Morrow Curreri (Asia, Middle East); IMA/Intermediaamericana Ltd (David Williams) (Caribbean, Latin America); Melia Publishing Services (UK); Trinity Books CC (South Africa)

Story Monsters LLC
Formerly Five Star Publications Inc
4696 W Tyson St, Chandler, AZ 85226-2903
Tel: 480-940-8182 *Fax:* 480-940-8787
Web Site: www.StoryMonsters.com; www.DragonflyBookAwards.com; www.AuthorsandExperts.com; www.SchoolBookings.com
Key Personnel
Pres: Linda F Radke *E-mail:* Linda@StoryMonsters.com
Founded: 1985
Dedicated to helping authors of all genres strive for excellence with book production, marketing & promotion. Publish the award-winning *Story Monsters Ink*® magazine. Provide publishers support services in areas such as editing, cover design & publicity. Sponsor of the Dragonfly Book Awards.
ISBN Prefix(es): 978-0-9619853; 978-1-877749; 978-1-58985
Number of titles published annually: 10 Print
Total Titles: 36 Print; 12 E-Book
Imprints: School Express Press (publishing plan for schools, teachers & librarians); Story Monsters Press (children's books)
Divisions: AuthorsandExperts.com; SchoolBookings.com
Membership(s): Arizona Professional Writers; The Children's Book Council; Independent Book Publishers Association; National Federation of Press Women; New Mexico Publishers Association; Small Publishers, Artists & Writers Network

§The Story Plant
Division of Studio Digital CT LLC
PO Box 4331, Stamford, CT 06907
Tel: 203-722-7920
E-mail: thestoryplant@thestoryplant.com
Web Site: www.thestoryplant.com
Key Personnel
Publr: Lou Aronica *E-mail:* lou.aronica@thestoryplant.com
Assoc Publr: Mitchell Maxwell *E-mail:* mitchell.maxwell@thestoryplant.com
Founded: 2008
Independent publisher of commercial fiction. The focus is on author development & building publishing programs for each author.
ISBN Prefix(es): 978-1-61188
Number of titles published annually: 25 Print; 25 E-Book; 5 Audio
Total Titles: 150 Print; 150 E-Book; 10 Audio
Distribution Center: National Book Network, 4501 Forbes Boulevard, Lanham, MD 20706 *Tel:* 301-459-3366
Membership(s): AAP; ABA

Strata Publishing Inc
PO Box 1303, State College, PA 16804
SAN: 298-9794
Tel: 814-234-8545
Web Site: www.stratapub.com
Key Personnel
Publr: Kathleen Domenig
Gen Mgr: Brian Henry
Founded: 1990
Books in communication & journalism for midlevel & advanced college courses, scholars & professionals. Return authorization required.
ISBN Prefix(es): 978-0-9634489, 978-1-891136
Number of titles published annually: 3 Print
Total Titles: 16 Print

Strategic Book Publishing & Rights Agency (SBPRA)
12620 FM W 1960, Suite A-4507, Houston, TX 77065
SAN: 853-8492
Tel: 703-637-6006
Web Site: sbpra.net; www.facebook.com/sbpra.us
Founded: 2007
Provides book publishing, marketing & ebook services to writers around the world. Catalog of more than 5,000 authors. Books are available through Ingram as well as in bookstores such as Barnes & Noble & all online channels. Attends & exhibits at the major book expositions in London, New York, China & Germany each year.
This publisher has indicated that 50% of their product line is author subsidized.
ISBN Prefix(es): 978-1-61204
Number of titles published annually: 475 Print; 85 E-Book
Total Titles: 2,786 Print; 3,062 Online; 336 E-Book

§Strategic Media Books LLC
782 Wofford St, Rock Hill, SC 29730
Tel: 803-366-5440
E-mail: contact@strategicmediabooks.com
Web Site: strategicmediabooks.com
Key Personnel
Pres: Ron Chepesiuk
VP: Barbara Casey
Tech Opers: Al Casey
Founded: 2010
Publisher of crime, true crime & southern interest books.
ISBN Prefix(es): 978-0-9852440; 978-1-939521
Number of titles published annually: 8 Print; 8 Online; 8 E-Book; 3 Audio
Total Titles: 28 Print; 25 Online; 25 E-Book; 3 Audio
Foreign Rep(s): Cardinal Publishers Group (UK)
Membership(s): Independent Book Publishers Association

§Stress Free Kids®
Imprint of Stress Free Publishers
2561 Chimney Springs Dr, Marietta, GA 30062
Tel: 678-642-9555 *Toll Free Fax:* 866-302-2759
E-mail: media@stressfreekids.com
Web Site: www.stressfreekids.com
Key Personnel
Founder: Lori Lite; Rick Lite
Founded: 1996
Books, CDs (physical & digital formats), lesson plans to help children & teens manage stress, lower anxiety & decrease anger, while improving self-esteem.
ISBN Prefix(es): 978-0-9708633; 978-0-9787781; 978-0-9800328
Number of titles published annually: 2 Print; 5 Online; 4 E-Book; 4 Audio
Total Titles: 35 Print; 12 Audio

The Jesse Stuart Foundation (JSF)
4440 13 St, Ashland, KY 41102
SAN: 245-8837
Mailing Address: PO Box 669, Ashland, KY 41105-0669
Tel: 606-326-1667 *Fax:* 606-325-2519
E-mail: jsf@jsfbooks.com
Web Site: www.jsfbooks.com
Key Personnel
CEO & Sr Ed: James M Gifford, PhD
Founded: 1979
Publisher of Appalachia-Kentuckiana. Not accepting unsol mss at this time.
ISBN Prefix(es): 978-0-945084
Number of titles published annually: 4 Print
Total Titles: 75 Print

Stylus Publishing LLC
22883 Quicksilver Dr, Sterling, VA 20166-2012
SAN: 299-1853
Mailing Address: PO Box 605, Herndon, VA 20172-0605
Tel: 703-661-1504 (edit & sales)
Toll Free Tel: 800-232-0223 (orders & cust serv) *Fax:* 703-661-1547
E-mail: stylusmail@presswarehouse.com (orders & cust serv); stylusinfo@styluspub.com
Web Site: www.styluspub.com
Key Personnel
Pres & Publr: John von Knorring *E-mail:* jvk@styluspub.com
VP, Mktg & Busn Devt: Andrea Ciecierski *E-mail:* andrea@styluspub.com
Sales Mgr: Jean Westcott *Tel:* 703-661-1541 *E-mail:* jean.westcott@styluspub.com
Founded: 1996
Publish books for faculty & administrators in higher education. Distributes books in the areas of art, business, training, psychology & psychotherapy as well as educational & scholarly titles & books on Third World development & the environment.
ISBN Prefix(es): 978-1-57922; 978-1-62036
Number of titles published annually: 30 Print; 30 E-Book
Total Titles: 400 Print; 2 CD-ROM; 150 E-Book
Distributor for American Association for Higher Education; Cabi Books; Campus Compact; Commonwealth Scientific & Industrial Research Organization (CSIRO); Global Professional Publishing; Greenleaf Publishing; Institute of Education; The Institution of Engineering & Technology (IET); Karnac Books; Latin America Bureau; Mercury Learning & Information; National Resource Center First Year Experience; Oxfam Publishing; Practical Action; River Publishers; SciTech; Trentham Books Ltd; World Health Organization (WHO)
Foreign Rep(s): Cranbury International (Central America, South America); Eurospan (Asia, Australia, Europe, Middle East, UK)
Distribution Center: Books International Inc, 22883 Quicksilver Dr, Dulles, VA 20166

Success Advertising & Publishing
Division of The Success Group
3419 Dunham Rd, Warsaw, NY 14569
SAN: 678-9501
Tel: 585-786-5663
Key Personnel
Pres & Publr: Allan H Smith *E-mail:* allan33001@aol.com
VP: Ginger B Smith
Book Ed: Robin Garretson
Founded: 1978
How-to, self-help, crafts, business, home-based business.
ISBN Prefix(es): 978-0-931113
Number of titles published annually: 7 Print
Total Titles: 58 Print
Divisions: Academy of Continuing Education; National Doll Society of America; Success Advertising

Summer Institute of Linguistics Inc, see SIL International

§Summertime Publications Inc
4115 E Palo Verde Dr, Phoenix, AZ 85018
Tel: 480-409-1554
E-mail: handell@summertimepublications.com
Web Site: www.summertimepublications.com
Key Personnel
CEO & Dir, Pubns: Laurel Leffmann
Founded: 2009
Small press. Quality books about France; also memoirs, history, science fiction, short story, literary fiction & nonfiction.
ISBN Prefix(es): 978-0-9823698; 978-1-940333
Number of titles published annually: 3 Print; 4 E-Book
Total Titles: 9 Print; 14 E-Book
Imprints: PWN; Summertime
Distributor for ACHCBYZ (Paris academic press specializing in Byzantine history)
Foreign Rights: IPR License Ltd (worldwide exc China); Rightol Media (China)
Membership(s): Independent Book Publishers Association

§Summit University Press
63 Summit Way, Gardiner, MT 59030-9314
Tel: 406-848-9742; 406-848-9500 (retail orders)
Toll Free Tel: 800-245-5445 (retail orders)
Fax: 406-848-9744
E-mail: info@summituniversitypress.com; marketing@summituniversitypress.com; production@summituniversitypress.com; rights@summituniversitypress.com
Web Site: www.summituniversitypress.com
Key Personnel
Edit Dir: Peter Duffy *E-mail:* peter@summituniversitypress.com
Intl Rts Dir: Phyllis Blain
Mktg Dir: Thomas Schumacher
Prodn Dir: Christopher Allen
Sales Dir (English): Norman N Millman *E-mail:* director@summituniversitypress.com
Sales Dir (Spanish): Natalia Zabala *E-mail:* director@supespanol.com
Founded: 1975
Global publisher of fine books, ebooks, audiobooks & DVDs on spirituality. Very active foreign rights sales. Specialize in New Age & mind, body & spirit.
ISBN Prefix(es): 978-0-916766; 978-0-922729; 978-1-932890; 978-1-60988
Number of titles published annually: 4 Print; 45 Online; 45 E-Book
Total Titles: 100 Print; 20 CD-ROM; 45 Online; 47 E-Book; 70 Audio
Distribution Center: National Book Network, 15200 NBN Way, Blue Ridge Summit, PA 17214 *Tel:* 717-794-3800 *Toll Free Tel:* 800-462-6420 *Toll Free Fax:* 800-338-4550 *E-mail:* customercare@nbnbooks.com *Web Site:* www.nbnbooks.com
NBN Canada/Rowman & Littlefield Publishing Group, 67 Mowat Ave, Suite 241, Toronto, ON M6K 3E3, Canada *Tel:* 416-534-1660 *Toll Free Tel:* 877-626-2665 *Fax:* 416-534-3699 *Web Site:* www.nbnbooks.com
NBN International, Plymbridge House, Estover Rd, Plymouth, Devon PL6 7PY, United Kingdom *Tel:* (01752) 202300 *Fax:* (01752) 202330 *E-mail:* enquiries@nbninternational.com
Membership(s): Independent Book Publishers Association

Sun Books, see Sun Publishing Company

Sun Publishing Company
Division of The Sun Companies
PO Box 5588, Santa Fe, NM 87502-5588
SAN: 206-1325
Tel: 505-471-5177; 505-473-4161
Toll Free Tel: 877-849-0051
E-mail: info@sunbooks.com
Web Site: www.sunbooks.com
Key Personnel
Pres & Rts/Perms: Skip Whitson
Founded: 1973
Motivational, success, business, recovery, inspirational, history, self-help, new thought, philosophy, western mysticism, scholarly; oriental philosophy & studies. No unsol mss. Query first by e-mail.
ISBN Prefix(es): 978-0-89540
Number of titles published annually: 10 Print
Total Titles: 400 Print
Imprints: Far West Publishing; Sun Books
Advertising Agency: Sun Agency

Sunbelt Publications Inc
1250 Fayette St, El Cajon, CA 92020-1511
SAN: 630-0790
Tel: 619-258-4911 *Toll Free Tel:* 800-626-6579 (cust serv) *Fax:* 619-258-4916
E-mail: service@sunbeltpub.com; info@sunbeltpub.com
Web Site: www.sunbeltbooks.com
Key Personnel
CEO: Lowell Lindsay *Tel:* 619-258-4911 ext 111 *E-mail:* llindsay@sunbeltpub.com
Pres: Diana Lindsay *Tel:* 619-258-4911 ext 104 *E-mail:* dlindsay@sunbeltpub.com
Acctg & Opers Mgr: Terry Cochran *Tel:* 619-258-4905 ext 110 *E-mail:* tcochran@sunbeltpub.com
Pubns Mgr: Debi Young *Tel:* 619-258-4905 ext 103 *E-mail:* dyoung@sunbeltpub.com
Founded: 1984
Publisher & distributor of natural history, science, pictorial & travel specializing in Alta & Baja, California.
ISBN Prefix(es): 978-0-932653; 978-0-916251
Number of titles published annually: 10 Print
Total Titles: 75 Print
Imprints: First Choice
Distributor for Abbott Publishing; Alti Corporation; Amaroma Ediciones (Mexican architectural & design publisher); Anza-Borrego Foundation; W H Berger; Bobolink Media; Joan Brady; California Sea Grant; Paul Douglas Campbell; Dawsons Book Shop; Leland Fetzer; Fun Places Publishing; Jeffrey Garcia; Maureen Gilmer; Glove Pequot; Green Grass Press; Healey Publishing; Huckleberry House LLC; Intellect Publishing; Island Paradise Publishing; Jaguar Tales; Scott G Kyle; Lawtech Publishing; Little Oak Press; Mission San Juan Capistrano Women's Guild; Newtona LLC; Northcross Books; Nelson Papucci; Bette L Pegas; Linda Pequegnat; Picaro Publishing; Planeta Peninsula (Mexican publisher); Phil R Pryde; Quick Reference Publishing; R & B Food & Culture Production; Random House; Renegade Enterprises; San Diego Architecture Foundation; San Diego Association of Geologists; San Diego City Works Press; San Diego Natural History Museum; San Diego Police Historical Association; San Dieguito River Park Joint Powers Authority; Save Our Heritage Organization; Surf Angel Publications; Trail Wisdom; University of California Press; Armand Vallee; Wigton Publishing; Wilderness Press; Wolf Water Press
Membership(s): Association of Earth Science Editors; Independent Book Publishers Association; Outdoor Writers Association of America; Publishers Association of the West

Sundance/Newbridge Publishing
Division of Rowman & Littlefield Publishing Group
33 Boston Post Rd W, Suite 440, Marlborough, MA 01752
Toll Free Tel: 888-200-2720; 800-343-8204 (Sundance cust serv & orders); 800-867-0307 (Newbridge cust serv & orders) *Toll Free Fax:* 800-456-2419 (orders)
E-mail: info@sundancepub.com; info@newbridgeonline.com
Web Site: www.sundancepub.com; www.newbridgeonline.com
Key Personnel
Pres: Paul Konowitch *E-mail:* pkonowitch@sundancepub.com
SVP, Sales: John Atkocaitis *E-mail:* jatkocaitis@sundancepub.com
Founded: 1981
Supplemental educational publisher for PreK-8 that creates standards-based classroom materials for reading in the content areas.
ISBN Prefix(es): 978-1-56784; 978-1-58273; 978-1-4007
Number of titles published annually: 150 Print; 36 Audio
Total Titles: 680 Print; 118 Audio
Imprints: Early Math; Early Science; Early Social Studies; GoFacts Guided Writing; Kids Corner; Newbridge Discovery Links; Ranger Rick Science Program; Thinking Like a Scientist
Foreign Rep(s): Schmelzer PSI
Membership(s): AAP; International Literacy Association; National Science Teachers Association

§Sunrise River Press
Affiliate of Cartech Books/Specialty Press
838 Lake St S, Forrest Lake, MN 55025
Tel: 651-277-1400 *Toll Free Tel:* 800-895-4585 *Fax:* 651-277-1203
E-mail: info@sunriseriverpress.com; sales@sunriseriverpress.com
Web Site: www.sunriseriverpress.com
Key Personnel
Sales & Mktg: Bob Wilson
Publisher of consumer books & books for the professional healthcare market with an emphasis on self-help, weight loss, nutrition, diet, food & recipes with additional focus on family health, fitness & specific diseases such as cancer, anorexia, Alzheimer's, autism & depression.
ISBN Prefix(es): 978-0-9624814; 978-1-934716
Number of titles published annually: 10 Print

Sunstone Press
Imprint of The Sunstone Corp
PO Box 2321, Santa Fe, NM 87504-2321
SAN: 214-2090
Tel: 505-988-4418 *Toll Free Tel:* 800-243-5644 *Fax:* 505-988-1025 (orders only)
Web Site: www.sunstonepress.com
Key Personnel
Pres & Treas: James Clois Smith, Jr
Dir, Opers & Sales: Carl Daniel Condit
Founded: 1971
Mainstream & Southwestern US titles, general nonfiction, fiction & how-to craft books.
ISBN Prefix(es): 978-0-913270; 978-0-86534; 978-1-61139 (ebooks); 978-1-63293
Number of titles published annually: 100 Print; 300 E-Book
Total Titles: 1,600 Print; 1,500 E-Book
Foreign Rights: Daniel Bial Literary Agency
Membership(s): New Mexico Book Association

SUNY Press, see State University of New York Press

Superintendent of Documents, see US Government Publishing Office (GPO)

Surrey Books
Imprint of Agate Publishing
1328 Greenleaf St, Evanston, IL 60202
SAN: 275-8857
Tel: 847-475-4457 *Toll Free Tel:* 800-326-4430
Web Site: agatepublishing.com/surrey
Key Personnel
Pres & Publr: Doug Seibold *E-mail:* seibold@agatepublishing.com
Founded: 1982
Trade books. Specialize in nonfiction: cooking, health & lifestyle.
ISBN Prefix(es): 978-0-940625; 978-1-57284
Number of titles published annually: 20 Print
Total Titles: 120 Print
Distribution Center: Publishers Group West, 1700 Fourth St, Berkeley, CA 94710 *Tel:* 510-809-3700 *Toll Free Tel:* 800-788-3123 (cust serv) *Fax:* 510-809-3777 *E-mail:* info@pgw.com *Web Site:* www.pgw.com
Membership(s): International Association of Culinary Professionals

§Swallow Press
Imprint of Ohio University Press
31 S Court St, Suite 143, Athens, OH 45701
Tel: 740-593-1155 *Toll Free Tel:* 800-621-2736 *Fax:* 740-593-4536
Web Site: www.ohioswallow.com
Key Personnel
Dir: Gillian Berchowitz *Tel:* 740-593-1159 *E-mail:* berchowi@ohio.edu
Mng Ed: Nancy Basmajian *Tel:* 740-593-1161 *E-mail:* basmajia@ohio.edu
Acqs Ed: Ricky S Huard *Tel:* 740-593-1157 *E-mail:* huard@ohio.edu
Acqs & Perms Admin: Sally R Welch *Tel:* 740-593-1154 *E-mail:* welchs@ohio.edu
Busn Mgr: Omar Aziz *Tel:* 740-593-1156 *E-mail:* azizo@ohio.edu
Founded: 1940
Publisher of scholarly & trade books.
ISBN Prefix(es): 978-0-8214; 978-0-8040
Number of titles published annually: 45 Print
Total Titles: 600 Print
Foreign Rep(s): Combined Academic Publishers (Africa, Europe, Middle East, Pacific Rim)
Orders to: Chicago Distribution Center, 11030 S Langley Ave, Chicago, IL 60628 *Toll Free Tel:* 800-621-2736 *Toll Free Fax:* 800-621-8476
Warehouse: Chicago Distribution Center, 11030 S Langley Ave, Chicago, IL 60628 *Toll Free Tel:* 800-621-2736 *Toll Free Fax:* 800-621-8476

Swan Isle Press
11030 S Langley Ave, Chicago, IL 60628
Tel: 773-728-3780 (edit); 773-702-7000 (cust serv) *Toll Free Tel:* 800-621-2736 (cust serv) *Fax:* 773-702-7212 (cust serv) *Toll Free Fax:* 800-621-8476 (cust serv)
E-mail: info@swanislepress.com
Web Site: www.swanislepress.com
Key Personnel
Founder, Dir & Ed: David Rade
Founded: 1999
Not-for-profit, 501(c)(3) literary publisher, dedicated to publishing fiction, nonfiction & poetry in translation.
ISBN Prefix(es): 978-0-9678808; 978-0-9748881
Number of titles published annually: 4 Print; 2 E-Book
Total Titles: 30 Print; 3 E-Book
Distributed by University of Chicago Press
Foreign Rep(s): University of Chicago Press (worldwide)
Orders to: Baker & Taylor, 2550 W Tyvola Rd, Suite 300, Charlotte, NC 28217 *Tel:* 704-998-3100 *Toll Free Tel:* 800-775-1800 *E-mail:* btinfo@baker-taylor.com *Web Site:* www.btol.com; Ingram Book Co, One Ingram Blvd, La Vergne, TN 37086 *Tel:* 615-793-5000 *Toll Free Tel:* 800-937-8200 *E-mail:* customer.service@ingrambook.com *Web Site:* www.ingrambook.com
Membership(s): AAP

Swedenborg Foundation
320 N Church St, West Chester, PA 19380
SAN: 202-5280
Tel: 610-430-3222 *Toll Free Tel:* 800-355-3222 (cust serv) *Fax:* 610-430-7982
E-mail: info@swedenborg.com
Web Site: www.swedenborg.com
Key Personnel
Opers Mgr: Morgan Beard *Tel:* 610-430-3222 ext 102 *E-mail:* mbeard@swedenborg.com
Ed: John Connolly *Tel:* 610-430-3222 ext 101 *E-mail:* jconnolly@swedenborg.com
Mktg Coord: Amy Acquarola *Tel:* 610-430-3222 ext 103 *E-mail:* aacquarola@swedenborg.com
Founded: 1849
Books & DVDs by, or relating to, the theological works & spiritual insights of Emanuel Swedenborg & related literature.
ISBN Prefix(es): 978-0-87785
Number of titles published annually: 10 Print

Total Titles: 200 Print
Orders to: Continental Sales Inc (CSI), 213 W Main St, Barrington, IL 60010 *Tel:* 847-381-6530 *Fax:* 847-382-0419 *E-mail:* bookreps@wybel.com; Wybel Marketing Group Inc, 213 W Main St, Barrington, IL 60010 *Tel:* 847-382-0384 *Fax:* 847-382-0385 *E-mail:* bookreps@wybel.com; Melman-Moster Associates Inc, 43 Yawpo Ave, Suite 6, Oakland, NJ 07436 *Tel:* 201-651-9400 *Fax:* 201-651-9440 *E-mail:* books@melman-moster.com; Faherty & Associates, 6665 SW Hampton St, Suite 100, Portland, OR 97223 *Tel:* 503-639-3113 *Fax:* 503-598-9850 *E-mail:* faherty@fahertybooks.com; Southern Territory Associates, 4508 64 St, Lubbock, TX 79414 *Tel:* 806-799-9997 *Fax:* 806-799-9777 *E-mail:* sta77@suddenlink.net; Rainbow Book Agencies, 303 Arthur St, Fairfield 3078, Australia *Tel:* (0613) 9481 6611 *Fax:* (0613) 9481 2371 *E-mail:* rba@rainbowbooks.com.au *Web Site:* www.rainbowbooks.com.au
Returns: University of Chicago Press/The Chicago Distribution Center, 11030 S Langley Ave, Chicago, IL 60628
Distribution Center: University of Chicago Press/The Chicago Distribution Center, 11030 S Langley Ave, Chicago, IL 60628

§SYBEX Inc
Division of John Wiley & Sons Inc
111 River St, Hoboken, NJ 07030-5774
SAN: 211-1667
Tel: 201-748-6000 *Fax:* 201-748-6088
E-mail: info@wiley.com
Web Site: www.sybex.com; www.wiley.com
Founded: 1976
For beginning, intermediate & advanced users of all types of software & hardware, including how-to books on various networking, word processing, database, graphics & spreadsheet software, certification, as well as computer games & Internet books, graphics & programming.
ISBN Prefix(es): 978-0-89588; 978-0-7821; 978-0-47028
Number of titles published annually: 150 Print
Total Titles: 601 Print; 2 CD-ROM
Branch Office(s)
One Montgomery St, Suite 1200, San Francisco, CA 94104 *Tel:* 415-433-1740 *Fax:* 415-433-0499
10475 Crosspoint Blvd, Indianapolis, IN 46256 *Tel:* 317-572-3000
Foreign Rep(s): Robert Blake (Central America, Mexico); Phillip Bowie (Caribbean); Computercollectief (Netherlands); Lidel Edicoes Tecnicas Lda (Portugal); Ledy Martinez (Brazil, South America); John Wiley & Sons Canada Ltd (Canada); John Wiley & Sons Ltd (Natalie Lord) (Europe exc Austria, Germany & Switzerland, UK); John Wiley & Sons Singapore Pte Ltd (Singapore); Wiley-VCH Verlag GmbH (Austria, Germany, Switzerland)

§Synapse Information Resources Inc
1247 Taft Ave, Endicott, NY 13760
Tel: 607-748-4145 *Toll Free Tel:* 888-SYN-CHEM (796-2436) *Fax:* 607-786-3966
E-mail: salesinfo@synapseinfo.com
Web Site: www.synapseinfo.com
Key Personnel
Owner & Pres: Irene Ash *E-mail:* iash@synapseinfo.com
Owner: Michael Ash
Founded: 1981
Chemical database references for industry. Publish both books & CD-ROMs in industrial chemistry. Reference books & software serving the industrial chemical market.
ISBN Prefix(es): 978-1-890595
Number of titles published annually: 3 Print; 3 CD-ROM
Total Titles: 20 Print; 23 CD-ROM

§SynergEbooks
948 New Hwy 7, Columbia, TN 38401
SAN: 254-4962
Tel: 931-548-2494
E-mail: synergebooks@aol.com
Web Site: www.synergebooks.com
Key Personnel
Publr & Exec Ed: Debra Staples
Founded: 1999
Electronic publishing house & bookstore that also include CD-ROMs, audiobooks & trade paperbacks. Genres include fiction, nonfiction, romance, young adults fantasy, science fiction, poetry, humor, mystery/suspense, inspiration, cookbooks, self-help/reference, business, true crime, New Age, Native American & a children's section.
ISBN Prefix(es): 978-0-9702; 978-0-7443; 978-1-931540
Number of titles published annually: 35 Print; 48 E-Book
Total Titles: 180 Print; 360 Online; 360 E-Book; 4 Audio
Imprints: SynErotica (erotic titles); YourSpecs (self-publishing ebook conversion service)
Membership(s): Electronically Published Internet Connection; Independent Book Publishers Association

Syracuse University Press
621 Skytop Rd, Suite 110, Syracuse, NY 13244-5290
SAN: 206-9776
Tel: 315-443-5534 *Toll Free Tel:* 800-365-8929 (cust serv) *Fax:* 315-443-5545
E-mail: supress@syr.edu
Web Site: syracuseuniversitypress.syr.edu
Key Personnel
Dir: Alice Randal Pfeiffer *Tel:* 315-443-5535 *E-mail:* arpfeiff@syr.edu
Ed-in-Chief: Suzanne Guiod *Tel:* 315-443-5539 *E-mail:* seguiod@syr.edu
Acqs Ed: Deborah Manion *Tel:* 315-443-5647 *E-mail:* dmmanion@syr.edu; Alison Shay *Tel:* 315-443-5543 *E-mail:* amshay@syr.edu
Edit & Prodn Mgr: Kay Steinmetz *Tel:* 315-443-9155 *E-mail:* kasteinm@syr.edu
Sr Busn Mgr: Karen Lockwood *Tel:* 315-443-5536 *E-mail:* kflockwo@syr.edu
Sr Designer: Lynn Wilcox *Tel:* 315-443-1975 *E-mail:* lphoppel@syr.edu
Mktg Coord: Lisa Kuerbis *Tel:* 315-443-5546 *E-mail:* lkuerbis@syr.edu
Acctg Asst: Bobbi Clapps *Tel:* 315-443-5538 *E-mail:* baclaps@syr.edu
Founded: 1943
Scholarly, general & regional nonfiction; Middle East, Irish studies, medieval, women's studies, Iroquois studies, television, religion & politics, geography, sports & leisure, space, place & society, literature, Jewish studies (fiction & nonfiction).
ISBN Prefix(es): 978-0-8156
Number of titles published annually: 50 Print; 50 E-Book
Total Titles: 1,800 Print; 400 E-Book
Distributed by Arlen House; Dedalus Press
Distributor for Arlen House; Dedalus Press; Pucker Gallery
Foreign Rep(s): David Diehl (Western USA); Eurospan University Press Group Ltd (Africa, Continental Europe, Middle East, UK); EWEB (Royden Muranaka) (Asia, Australia, Far East, Hawaii, India, New Zealand, Pakistan); Hand Associates (Western USA); Rob Igoe Jr (New York State); Miller Trade Book Marketing (Midwestern States); Scholarly Book Services Inc (Canada); UMG Publishers Representatives (David K Brown) (Eastern States)
Orders to: Longleaf Services Inc, 116 S Boundary St, Chapel Hill, NC 27514-8895 *Tel:* 919-966-7449 *Toll Free Tel:* 800-848-6224 *Fax:* 919-962-2704 *Toll Free Fax:* 800-272-6817 *E-mail:* customerservice@longleafservices.org *Web Site:* www.longleafservices.org
Returns: Longleaf Services Inc, c/o Ingram Publisher Services, 1550 Heil Quaker Blvd, Suite 200, La Vergne, PA 37086 *Tel:* 919-966-7449 *Toll Free Tel:* 866-400-5351 *Fax:* 919-962-2704 *Toll Free Fax:* 800-272-6817 *E-mail:* credit@longleafservices.org
Distribution Center: Longleaf Services Inc, 116 S Boundary St, Chapel Hill, NC 27514-8895 *Tel:* 919-966-7449 *Toll Free Tel:* 800-848-6224 *Fax:* 919-962-2704 *Toll Free Fax:* 800-272-6817 *E-mail:* customerservice@longleafservices.org *Web Site:* www.longleafservices.org
Membership(s): American Association of University Presses

Tachyon Publications LLC
1459 18 St, No 139, San Francisco, CA 94107
Tel: 415-285-5615
E-mail: tachyon@tachyonpublications.com
Web Site: www.tachyonpublications.com
Key Personnel
Publr & Ed: Jacob Weisman *E-mail:* jw@tachyonpublications.com
Mng Ed: Jill Roberts *E-mail:* jill@tachyonpublications.com
Publicist: James DeMaiolo *E-mail:* jim@tachyonpublications.com
Soc Media: Rick Klaw *Tel:* 512-777-9036 *E-mail:* rick@tachyonpublications.com
Founded: 1995
Science fiction, fantasy & genre publishing.
ISBN Prefix(es): 978-0-9648320; 978-1-892391; 978-1-61696
Number of titles published annually: 10 Print; 6 E-Book
Total Titles: 173 Print; 56 E-Book
Foreign Rights: JABberwocky Literary Agency (Joshua Bilmes) (worldwide)
Orders to: Ingram/Publishers Group West (PGW)/Legato, 1700 Fourth St, Berkeley, CA 94710 *Tel:* 615-793-5000 *Toll Free Tel:* 800-937-8000 *Toll Free Fax:* 800-937-8000 *E-mail:* customerservice@ingramcontent.com *Web Site:* www.ingramcontent.com/contact
Shipping Address: Publishers Group West via IPS, 210 American Dr, Jackson, TN 38301, Contact: Jennifer Pascal *Tel:* 510-809-3700 *E-mail:* jennifer.pascal@pgw.com
Warehouse: Publishers Group West via IPS, 210 American Dr, Jackson, TN 38301, Contact: Jennifer Pascal *Tel:* 510-809-3700 *E-mail:* jennifer.pascal@pgw.com
Distribution Center: Ingram/Publishers Group West (PGW)/Legato, 1700 Fourth St, Berkeley, CA 94710, Contact: Sarah Armstrong *Tel:* 510-809-3700 *E-mail:* sarah.armstrong@ingramcontent.com *Web Site:* www.pgw.com
Membership(s): Science Fiction & Fantasy Writers of America

§Tahrike Tarsile Qur'an Inc
80-08 51 Ave, Elmhurst, NY 11373
Tel: 718-446-6472 *Fax:* 718-446-4370
E-mail: read@koranusa.org
Web Site: www.koranusa.org
Key Personnel
Pres: Aun Ali Khalfan
Publishers & distributors of the Holy Quran & other Islamic books, videos & CDs.
ISBN Prefix(es): 978-0-940368; 978-1-879402
Number of titles published annually: 125 Print
Total Titles: 150 Print

§TAN Books
Imprint of Saint Benedict Press LLC
PO Box 410487, Charlotte, NC 28241
Tel: 704-731-0651 *Toll Free Tel:* 800-437-5876 *Fax:* 815-226-7770

E-mail: customerservice@tanbooks.com
Web Site: www.tanbooks.com
Key Personnel
Chmn & CEO: Robert Gallagher
Publr: Conor Gallagher
Dir: Brian Kennelly
Dir, Mktg: Christian Tappe
Founded: 1967
Publish traditional Catholic books, especially reprint classic works.
ISBN Prefix(es): 978-0-89555
Number of titles published annually: 15 Print
Total Titles: 550 Print

T&T Clark International
Imprint of Bloomsbury Publishing PLC
1385 Broadway, 5th fl, New York, NY 10018
Key Personnel
Mktg: Nicholas Stewart
Founded: 1821
Biblical studies, theology & church history.
ISBN Prefix(es): 978-0-8264; 978-1-56338; 978-0-334; 978-0-7162; 978-0-567
Number of titles published annually: 100 Print
Total Titles: 2,200 Print
Foreign Rep(s): Codasat (Canada)

Tanglewood Publishing
1060 N Capitol Ave, Suite E-395, Indianapolis, IN 46204
Tel: 812-877-9488 *Toll Free Tel:* 800-788-3123 (orders)
E-mail: info@tanglewoodbooks.com; orders@tanglewoodbooks.com
Web Site: www.tanglewoodbooks.com
Key Personnel
Publr: Peggy Tierney *E-mail:* ptierney@tanglewoodbooks.com
Dir, Mktg: Ayanna Coleman *E-mail:* ayanna@tanglewoodbooks.com
Acqs Ed: Kairi Hamlin *E-mail:* khamlin@tanglewoodbooks.com
Founded: 2003
ISBN Prefix(es): 978-0-9749303; 978-1-933718
Number of titles published annually: 5 Print; 1 Audio
Total Titles: 37 Print; 2 Audio
Distribution Center: Publishers Group West (PGW), 1700 Fourth St, Berkeley, CA 94710 *Tel:* 510-809-3700 *Toll Free Tel:* 800-788-3123 *Fax:* 510-809-3777 *E-mail:* info@pgw.com *Web Site:* www.pgw.com

Tantor Media Inc
Division of Recorded Books
6 Business Park, Old Saybrook, CT 06475
Toll Free Tel: 877-782-6867 *Toll Free Fax:* 888-782-7821
Web Site: www.tantor.com
Key Personnel
Dir, Acqs: Ron Formica *Tel:* 877-782-6867 ext 31 *E-mail:* ron@tantor.com
Founded: 2001
Independent publisher & producer of audiobooks.
Number of titles published annually: 1,000 Online; 1,000 Audio
Total Titles: 7,000 Online; 7,000 Audio
Imprints: Tantor Audio; Tantor Media
Foreign Rep(s): IPS (worldwide)
Membership(s): ALA; Audio Publishers Association; Public Library Association

Tapestry Press Ltd
19 Nashoba Rd, Littleton, MA 01460
Tel: 978-486-0200 *Toll Free Tel:* 800-535-2007 *Fax:* 978-486-0244
E-mail: publish@tapestrypress.com
Web Site: www.tapestrypress.com
Key Personnel
Pres: Michael J Miskin
Publr: Elizabeth A Larsen
VP & Ed-in-Chief: Sara E Hofeldt
Founded: 1988
College textbooks & journals; custom textbooks & anthologies.
ISBN Prefix(es): 978-0-924234; 978-1-56888; 978-1-59830
Number of titles published annually: 70 Print
Total Titles: 75 Print

Taplinger Publishing Co Inc
PO Box 175, Marlboro, NJ 07746-0175
SAN: 213-6821
Tel: 305-256-7880 *Fax:* 305-256-7816
E-mail: taplingerpub@yahoo.com (rts & perms, edit, corp only)
Key Personnel
CEO: Theodore D Rosenfeld
Founded: 1955
General nonfiction, including art, biography, calligraphy, graphic arts, history, music.
ISBN Prefix(es): 978-0-8008
Number of titles published annually: 4 Print
Total Titles: 100 Print
Imprints: Crescendo
Foreign Rep(s): Baker & Taylor International (Africa, Asia, Europe, South Africa, South America)
Orders to: Parkwest Publications LLC, PO Box 310251, Miami, FL 33231-0251, Dir: Brian Squire *Tel:* 305-256-7880 *E-mail:* mail@parkwestpubs.com *Web Site:* www.parkwestpubs.com
Returns: Parkwest Publications LLC, 14332 SW 142 Ave, Miami, FL 33186, Dir: Brian Squire *Tel:* 305-256-7880
Warehouse: Parkwest Publications LLC, 14332 SW 142 Ave, Miami, FL 33186, Dir: Brian Squire *Tel:* 305-256-7880
Distribution Center: Parkwest Publications LLC, PO Box 310251, Miami, FL 33231-0251, Dir: Brian Squire *Tel:* 305-256-7880 *E-mail:* mail@parkwestpubs.com *Web Site:* www.parkwestpubs.com

TarcherPerigee
Imprint of Penguin Group USA, A Penguin Random House Company
375 Hudson St, New York, NY 10014
Tel: 212-366-2000 *Fax:* 212-366-2643
E-mail: customerservice@penguinrandomhouse.com (cust serv); TarcherPerigeePublicity@penguinrandomhouse.com (media queries)
Web Site: www.tarcherbooks.com; www.facebook.com/TarcherPerigee/; www.penguin.com/publishers/tarcherperigee
Key Personnel
VP & Publr: Joel Fotinos
Assoc Publr & Exec Dir, Publicity & Mktg: Brianna Yamashita
VP, Exec Ed & Dir, Backlist & Reissues: Mitch Horowitz
Edit Dir: Sara Carder; Marian Lizzi
Sr Ed: Stephanie Bowen
Ed: Joanna Ng
Nonfiction Ed: Amanda Shih
Assoc Ed: Lauren Appleton
Mktg & Publicity Coord: Tyler Fields
Founded: 2015
Core publishing areas include self-improvement, creativity, parenting, spirituality & gift/inspiration.
ISBN Prefix(es): 978-0-399
Number of titles published annually: 73 Print
Total Titles: 517 Print
Advertising Agency: Spier NY

Taschen America
6671 Sunset Blvd, Suite 1508, Los Angeles, CA 90028
Tel: 323-463-4441 *Toll Free Tel:* 888-TASCHEN (827-2436) *Fax:* 323-463-4442
E-mail: contact-us@taschen.com
Web Site: www.taschen.com
Key Personnel
Busn Mgr: Meghan Clarke *E-mail:* m.clarke@taschen.com
Founded: 1996
Publishers of high-quality, reasonably priced illustrated books on the subjects of art, architecture, design, photography, erotica, gay interest & popular culture.
ISBN Prefix(es): 978-3-8228; 978-3-8365
Number of titles published annually: 80 Print
Total Titles: 500 Print
Imprints: Taschen GmbH
Distribution Center: Ingram, One Ingram Blvd, La Vergne, TN 37086 *Toll Free Tel:* 888-558-2624

§The Taunton Press Inc
63 S Main St, Newtown, CT 06470
SAN: 210-5144
Mailing Address: PO Box 5506, Newtown, CT 06470-5506
Tel: 203-426-8171 *Toll Free Tel:* 800-477-8727 (cust serv); 800-888-8286 (orders) *Fax:* 203-426-3434
E-mail: booksales@taunton.com
Web Site: www.taunton.com
Key Personnel
CEO: Dan McCarthy
Dir, Book Sales: John Bacigalupi
Founded: 1975
Woodworking, home building, fiber arts, cooking & gardening books, magazines, DVDs & web sites.
ISBN Prefix(es): 978-0-918804; 978-0-942391; 978-1-56158; 978-1-60085; 978-1-63186
Number of titles published annually: 25 Print; 10 CD-ROM; 25 E-Book; 1 Audio
Total Titles: 525 Print; 100 CD-ROM; 10 Online; 300 E-Book; 1 Audio
Distributor for Guild of Master Craftsman (North America); Lucky Spool (North America & Australia)
Foreign Rep(s): Thomas Allen & Sons; Guild of Master Craftsman
Warehouse: 141 Sheridan Dr, Naugatuck, CT 06770
Distribution Center: Ingram Publisher Services, One Ingram Blvd, La Vergne, TN 37086 *Tel:* 615-793-5000

Taylor & Francis Inc
530 Walnut St, Suite 850, Philadelphia, PA 19106
Tel: 215-625-8900 *Toll Free Tel:* 800-354-1420 *Fax:* 215-207-0050; 215-207-0046 (cust serv)
E-mail: support@tandfonline.com
Web Site: www.taylorandfrancis.com
Key Personnel
CEO: Annie Callanan
Pres: Kevin J Bradley
VP, Prodn: Ed Cilurso *E-mail:* ed.cilurso@taylorandfrancis.com
Global Publg Dir, Journals: Leon Heward-Mills
Journals Mktg Dir: Deborah Lovell *E-mail:* deborah.lovell@taylorandfrancis.com
Founded: 1974
Journals in engineering, physical science, psychology, sociology, physics, chemistry, mathematics, environmental science, business, public health, marketing, arts, anthropology, political science, library science & LGBT studies.
ISBN Prefix(es): 978-1-56032; 978-0-87630; 978-0-86377; 978-0-8448; 978-0-85066; 978-0-85109; 978-0-905273; 978-1-85000
Number of titles published annually: 585 Print
Total Titles: 1,500 Print
Imprints: Cogent OA; CRC Press; Garland Science; Routledge; Taylor & Francis Asia Pacific; Taylor & Francis Books
Foreign Office(s): Taylor & Francis Group, Milton Park, 2 & 4 Park Sq, Abingdon, Oxon OX14 4RN, United Kingdom *Tel:* (020) 7017 6000 *Fax:* (020) 7017 6699 *E-mail:* enquiries@taylorandfrancis.com

Orders to: 7625 Empire Dr, Florence, KY 41042-2929 *Tel:* 859-727-5000 *Toll Free Tel:* 800-634-7064 *Fax:* 859-647-4029 *Toll Free Fax:* 800-248-4724 *E-mail:* orders@taylorandfrancis.com; Bookpoint, 130 Milton Park, Abingdon, Oxon OX14 4SB, United Kingdom (Africa, Asia, Australia, Europe) *Tel:* (01235) 400 400 *Fax:* (01235) 400 401 *E-mail:* book.orders@tandf.co.uk
Distribution Center: 7625 Empire Dr, Florence, KY 41042 *Tel:* 859-727-5000 *Toll Free Tel:* 800-634-7064 *Fax:* 859-647-4029 *Toll Free Fax:* 800-248-4724 *E-mail:* orders@taylorandfrancis.com

Taylor-Dth Publishing
108 Caribe Isle, Novato, CA 94949
Tel: 415-299-1087
Web Site: www.taylor-dth.com
Key Personnel
Owner: Harold Miller *E-mail:* hmiller@taylor-dth.com
Founded: 2001
Limited book publisher.
ISBN Prefix(es): 978-0-9747532; 978-0-9727583; 978-0-9774431
Number of titles published annually: 4 Print
Total Titles: 40 Print

TCU Press
3000 Sandage Ave, Fort Worth, TX 76109
Mailing Address: TCU Box 298300, Fort Worth, TX 76129
Tel: 817-257-7822 *Toll Free Tel:* 800-826-8911 (orders) *Fax:* 817-257-5075
Web Site: www.prs.tcu.edu
Key Personnel
Dir: Dan Williams *Tel:* 817-257-5907 *E-mail:* d.e.williams@tcu.edu
Prodn Mgr: Melinda Esco *Tel:* 817-257-6874 *E-mail:* m.esco@tcu.edu
Mktg Coord: Rebecca Allen *Tel:* 817-257-6872 *E-mail:* rebecca.a.allen@tcu.edu
Ed: Kathy S Walton *Tel:* 817-257-5074 *E-mail:* k.s.walton@tcu.edu
Off Mgr: Molly Spain *E-mail:* molly.spain@fcu.edu
Founded: 1947
History & literature of Texas & the American West.
ISBN Prefix(es): 978-0-912646; 978-0-87565
Number of titles published annually: 15 Print; 20 Online
Total Titles: 440 Print; 20 Online; 100 E-Book; 1 Audio
Distributed by Texas A&M University Press
Foreign Rep(s): Texas A&M University Press
Shipping Address: Texas A&M University Press, Lewis St, Lindsy Bldg, College Station, TX 77843-4354, Mgr, Cust Rel: Sharon Mills
Warehouse: Texas A&M University Press, Lewis St, Lindsy Bldg, College Station, TX 77843-4354, Mgr, Cust Rel: Sharon Mills
Membership(s): Association of American University Presses

Teach Me Tapes Inc
10400 N Enterprise Dr, Mequon, WI 53092
Mailing Address: PO Box 698, Mequon, WI 53092
Toll Free Tel: 800-456-4656
E-mail: marie@teachmetapes.com
Web Site: www.teachmetapes.com
Key Personnel
Owner & Pres: Judy Mahoney *E-mail:* judy@teachmetapes.com
Founded: 1985
Offers a series of books with CDs that introduce children to new languages using familiar songs & stories.
ISBN Prefix(es): 978-0-934633; 978-1-59972
Number of titles published annually: 3 Print
Total Titles: 100 Print; 37 Audio
Distribution Center: Amazon.com
Follett School Solutions Inc, 1340 Ridgeview Dr, McHenry, IL 60050 *Tel:* 815-759-1700 *Toll Free Tel:* 888-511-5114 (cust serv) *Fax:* 815-759-9831 *Toll Free Fax:* 800-852-5458 *E-mail:* info@follettlearning.com *Web Site:* www.follettlearning.com SAN: 169-1902

Teacher Created Resources Inc
12621 Western Ave, Garden Grove, CA 92481
Tel: 714-891-7895 *Toll Free Tel:* 800-662-4321; 888-343-4335 *Toll Free Fax:* 800-525-1254
E-mail: custserv@teachercreated.com
Web Site: www.teachercreated.com
Key Personnel
Founder & Pres: Mary Dupuy Smith
Founded: 1977
Publishes PreK-12 curriculum programs, supplemental resource materials & technology products. Also provides professional staff development for teachers.
ISBN Prefix(es): 978-1-55734; 978-1-57690; 978-1-4206; 978-1-4570
Number of titles published annually: 250 Print
Total Titles: 1,500 Print

§Teachers College Press
Affiliate of Teachers College, Columbia University
1234 Amsterdam Ave, New York, NY 10027
SAN: 213-263X
Mailing Address: PO Box 20, Williston, VT 05495-0020
Tel: 212-678-3929 *Toll Free Tel:* 800-575-6566 *Fax:* 212-678-4149; 802-864-7626
E-mail: tcpress@tc.columbia.edu; tcp.orders@aidcvt.com (orders)
Web Site: www.teacherscollegepress.com
Key Personnel
Dir: Carole Saltz
Exec Acqs Ed: Brian Ellerbeck *E-mail:* ellerbeck@tc.edu
Founded: 1904
Professional books & textbooks in education; tests, classroom materials & reference works.
ISBN Prefix(es): 978-0-8077
Number of titles published annually: 60 Print; 1 CD-ROM
Total Titles: 1,123 Print; 1 CD-ROM
Foreign Rep(s): Eurospan Ltd (worldwide exc Canada & USA); Guidance Center (Canada)
Orders to: University of Toronto Press-Guidance Centre, 5201 Dufferin St, Toronto, ON M3H 5T8, Canada (CN) *Toll Free Tel:* 800-565-9523 *Toll Free Fax:* 800-221-9958 *E-mail:* utpbooks@utpress.utoronto.ca *Web Site:* www.utpress.utoronto.ca; Eurospan, c/o Turpin Distribution, Stratton Business Park, Pegasus Dr Biggleswade, Beds SG18 8TQ, United Kingdom (worldwide exc CN & US) *Tel:* (01767) 604972 *Fax:* (01767) 601640 *E-mail:* eurospan@turpin-distribution.com *Web Site:* www.eurospanbookstore.com/tcp
Returns: Returns Dept, 82 Wintersport Lane, Williston, VT 05495
Membership(s): AAP; American Association of University Presses; BISG

§Teacher's Discovery
Division of American Eagle Co Inc
2741 Paldan Dr, Auburn Hills, MI 48326
Toll Free Tel: 800-832-2437 *Toll Free Fax:* 800-287-4509
E-mail: help@teachersdiscovery.com
Web Site: www.teachersdiscovery.com
Key Personnel
Owner: Skip McWilliams
Mktg Mgr: Steve Giroux
Founded: 1968
Sell supplemental classroom teaching materials for Spanish, French, German, English & Social Studies. See www.vocesdigital.com for prize-winning digital courseware (e-textbooks).
ISBN Prefix(es): 978-1-884473; 978-0-7560
Number of titles published annually: 200 Print

Teachers of English to Speakers of Other Languages Inc, see TESOL International Association

§Teaching & Learning Co
501 E Third St, Dayton, OH 45402
Mailing Address: PO Box 802, Dayton, OH 45401-0802
Tel: 937-228-6118 *Toll Free Tel:* 800-444-1144 *Fax:* 937-223-2042
E-mail: info@lorenz.com
Web Site: www.lorenzeducationalpress.com
Key Personnel
VP, Mktg: Debra Kaiser *E-mail:* debk@lorenz.com
Founded: 1994
Educational publishing division includes visual resources, instructional guides & reproducibles, elementary supplementals.
ISBN Prefix(es): 978-1-57310
Number of titles published annually: 35 Print
Total Titles: 400 Print; 325 E-Book; 10 Audio
Membership(s): Education Market Association

§Teaching Strategies LLC
4500 East-West Hwy, Suite 300, Bethesda, MD 20814
Tel: 301-634-0818 *Toll Free Tel:* 800-637-3652 *Fax:* 301-657-0250; 301-634-0833
E-mail: info@teachingstrategies.com
Web Site: www.teachingstrategies.com
Founded: 1988
Curriculum, assessment & training materials for early childhood education (birth-age 8) & parent's guides; web subscription service.
ISBN Prefix(es): 978-1-879537; 978-0-9602892; 978-1-60617
Number of titles published annually: 5 Print
Total Titles: 66 Print
Distributor for Gryphon House
Orders to: PO Box 42243, Washington, DC 20015
Returns: Teaching Strategies Inc, c/o RRD P & F, 1077 Prospect Lane, Kaukauna, WI 54130

§Temple University Press
Division of Temple University of the Commonwealth System of Higher Education
1852 N Tenth St, Philadelphia, PA 19122-6099
SAN: 202-7666
Tel: 215-926-2140 *Toll Free Tel:* 800-621-2736 *Fax:* 215-926-2141
E-mail: tempress@temple.edu
Web Site: www.temple.edu/tempress
Key Personnel
Dir: Mary Rose Muccie *E-mail:* maryrose.muccie@temple.edu
Asst Dir & Mktg Dir: Ann-Marie Anderson *E-mail:* anderson@temple.edu
Ed-in-Chief: Aaron Javsicas *E-mail:* aaron.javsicas@temple.edu
Ad & Promo Mgr: Irene Imperio Kull *E-mail:* irene.imperio@temple.edu
Busn Mgr: Karen Baker *E-mail:* karen.baker@temple.edu
Publicity Mgr: Gary Kramer *E-mail:* gkramer@temple.edu
Rts & Perms & Intl Rts: Nikki Miller *E-mail:* m.d.miller@temple.edu
Founded: 1969
Scholarly books; all regional interests.
ISBN Prefix(es): 978-0-87722; 978-1-56639; 978-1-59213; 978-1-4399
Number of titles published annually: 45 Print
Total Titles: 1,450 Print
Foreign Rep(s): Baker & Taylor Ltd (Asia, The Pacific, worldwide exc Canada); Combined Academic Publishing (CAP) (Europe); East-

West Export Books (Royden Muranaka) (Asia, The Pacific); Lynn McClory (Canada)
Returns: Temple University Press Chicago Distribution Center, 11030 S Langley, Chicago, IL 60628 *Tel:* 773-702-7000 *Fax:* 773-702-7000 *Toll Free Fax:* 800-621-8476
Warehouse: Temple University Press Chicago Distribution Center, 11030 S Langley, Chicago, IL 60628, Contact: Sue Tranchita *Tel:* 773-702-7000 *Fax:* 773-702-7000 *Toll Free Fax:* 800-621-8476
Membership(s): Association of American University Presses; Society for Scholarly Publishing

Templegate Publishers
302 E Adams St, Springfield, IL 62701
SAN: 123-0115
Mailing Address: PO Box 5152, Springfield, IL 62705-5152
Tel: 217-522-3353 (edit & sales)
Toll Free Tel: 800-367-4844 (orders only)
E-mail: wisdom@templegate.com; orders@templegate.com (sales)
Web Site: www.templegate.com
Key Personnel
Dir & Owner: Thomas M Garvey *E-mail:* tmg@templegate.com
Exec Ed, Rts & Perms & Publicity: John Fisher
Sales & Ad Mgr, ISBN & Lib Sales Dir: Elaine Garvey
Founded: 1947
Nonfiction.
ISBN Prefix(es): 978-0-87243
Number of titles published annually: 4 Print
Total Titles: 225 Print
Imprints: Octavo Press
Foreign Rep(s): Gracewing (Europe)

Templeton Press
Subsidiary of John Templeton Foundation
300 Conshohocken State Rd, Suite 665, West Conshohocken, PA 19428
Tel: 484-531-8380 *Fax:* 484-531-8382
E-mail: tpinfo@templetonpress.org
Web Site: www.templetonpress.org
Key Personnel
Publr: Susan Arellano *E-mail:* sarellano@templetonpress.org
Edit & Soc Media Content Coord: Angelina Horst
Mktg & Ad Coord: Ryan Klein
Edit/Prodn & Cust Serv Mgr: Trish Vergilio
Edit Asst: Tomas Puyans
Founded: 1997
Focus on science & religion, spirituality & health, character development & business.
ISBN Prefix(es): 978-1-890151; 978-1-932031; 978-1-59947
Number of titles published annually: 12 Print; 12 E-Book
Total Titles: 347 Print; 347 E-Book; 14 Audio
Billing Address: Chicago Distribution Center, 11030 S Langley Ave, Chicago, IL 60628 *Tel:* 773-702-7000 *Toll Free Tel:* 800-621-2736 *Fax:* 773-702-7212 *Toll Free Fax:* 800-621-8476 *Web Site:* press.uchicago.edu/cdc
Orders to: Chicago Distribution Center, 11030 S Langley Ave, Chicago, IL 60628 *Tel:* 773-702-7000 *Toll Free Tel:* 800-621-2736 *Fax:* 773-702-7212 *Toll Free Fax:* 800-621-8476 *Web Site:* press.uchicago.edu/cdc
Returns: Chicago Distribution Center, 11030 S Langley Ave, Chicago, IL 60628 *Tel:* 773-702-7000 *Toll Free Tel:* 800-621-2736 *Fax:* 773-702-7212 *Toll Free Fax:* 800-621-8476 *Web Site:* press.uchicago.edu/cdc
Shipping Address: Chicago Distribution Center, 11030 S Langley Ave, Chicago, IL 60628 *Tel:* 773-702-7000 *Toll Free Tel:* 800-621-2736 *Fax:* 773-702-7212 *Toll Free Fax:* 800-621-8476 *Web Site:* press.uchicago.edu/cdc
Warehouse: Chicago Distribution Center, 11030 S Langley Ave, Chicago, IL 60628 *Tel:* 773-702-7000 *Toll Free Tel:* 800-621-2736 *Fax:* 773-702-7212 *Toll Free Fax:* 800-621-8476 *Web Site:* press.uchicago.edu/cdc
Distribution Center: Chicago Distribution Center, 11030 S Langley Ave, Chicago, IL 60628 *Tel:* 773-702-7000 *Toll Free Tel:* 800-621-2736 *Fax:* 773-702-7212 *Toll Free Fax:* 800-621-8476 *Web Site:* press.uchicago.edu/cdc
Membership(s): Independent Book Publishers Association

Temporal Mechanical Press
Division of Enos Mills Cabin Museum & Gallery
6760 Hwy 7, Estes Park, CO 80517-6404
Tel: 970-586-4706
E-mail: info@enosmills.com
Web Site: www.enosmills.com
Key Personnel
Owner: Elizabeth M Mills; Eryn Mills
ISBN Prefix(es): 978-1-928878
Number of titles published annually: 3 Print
Total Titles: 32 Print

Ten Speed Press
Imprint of Crown Publishing Group
6001 Shellmound St, Suite 600, Emeryville, CA 94608
Tel: 510-285-3000 *Toll Free Tel:* 800-841-BOOK (841-2665)
Web Site: crownpublishing.com/imprint/ten-speed-press
Founded: 1971
Illustrated books. Actively seeks out new & established authors who are authorities & tastemakers in the world of food, drink, design, reference & humor. Create cookbooks, illustrated gift titles, popular business titles & groundbreaking self-help titles.
ISBN Prefix(es): 978-1-58761; 978-1-58091; 978-1-58008; 978-1-60774
Number of titles published annually: 100 Print
Total Titles: 587 Print
Imprints: Food52 Works; Lorena Jones Books (cooking & lifestyle)
Foreign Rep(s): Penguin Random House Inc (worldwide)
Orders to: Penguin Random House Inc, 400 Hahn Rd, Westminster, MD 21157 *Toll Free Tel:* 800-733-3000 *E-mail:* csorders@randomhouse.com; Penguin Random House of Canada Inc, Diversified Sales, 2775 Mattheson Blvd E, Mississauga, ON L4W 4P4, Canada *Toll Free Tel:* 800-668-4247 *Fax:* 905-624-8091

Teora USA LLC
505 Hampton Park Blvd, Unit G, Capitol Heights, MD 20743
SAN: 256-1220
Tel: 301-986-6990 *Fax:* 301-350-5480
E-mail: 2010@teora.com
Web Site: www.teora.com
Key Personnel
Busn Mgr: Teodor Raducanu
Founded: 2003
ISBN Prefix(es): 978-1-59496
Number of titles published annually: 6 Print
Total Titles: 60 Print
Imprints: Teora
Distribution Center: Fitzhenry & Whiteside, 195 Allstate Pkwy, Markham, ON L3R 4T8, Canada *Tel:* 904-477-9700 *Toll Free Fax:* 800-260-9777
Membership(s): Independent Book Publishers Association

Terra Nova Books
33 Alondra Rd, Santa Fe, NM 87508
Tel: 505-670-9319 *Fax:* 509-461-9333
E-mail: publisher@terranovabooks.com; marketing@terranovabooks.com
Web Site: www.terranovabooks.com
Key Personnel
Co-Owner & Publr: Scott Gerber
Co-Owner & Ed: Marty Gerber *Tel:* 505-470-6797 *E-mail:* editor@terranovabooks.com
VP, Mktg: Joanna V Hill *Tel:* 267-304-8521
Founded: 2012
Innovative independent book publisher actively developing fresh new titles & authors titles across a wide range of genres.
ISBN Prefix(es): 978-1-938288
Number of titles published annually: 16 Print; 15 E-Book
Total Titles: 47 Print; 35 E-Book
Sales Office(s): SBC Distributors, 15608 S New Century Dr, Gardena, CA 90248, Sales & Mktg Mgr: Gabriel Wilmoth *Tel:* 310-532-9400 *Toll Free Tel:* 800-729-6423 *E-mail:* gabriel@scbdistributors.com *Web Site:* scbdistributors.com
Foreign Rep(s): SCB Distributors (Steve Paton) (Western Canada); SCB Distributors (Terry Fernihough) (New Brunswick, CN, Nova Scotia, CN, Ontario, CN, Prince Edward Island, CN); SCB Distributors (Karen Stacey) (Quebec, CN)
Orders to: SBC Distributors, 15608 S New Century Dr, Gardena, CA 90248, Sales & Mktg Mgr: Gabriel Wilmoth *Tel:* 310-532-9400 *Toll Free Tel:* 800-729-6423 *E-mail:* gabriel@scbdistributors.com *Web Site:* scbdistributors.com
Returns: SBC Distributors, 15608 S New Century Dr, Gardena, CA 90248, Sales & Mktg Mgr: Gabriel Wilmoth *Tel:* 310-532-9400 *Toll Free Tel:* 800-729-6423 *E-mail:* gabriel@scbdistributors.com *Web Site:* scbdistributors.com
Distribution Center: SBC Distributors, 15608 S New Century Dr, Gardena, CA 90248, Sales & Mktg Mgr: Gabriel Wilmoth *Tel:* 310-532-9400 *Toll Free Tel:* 800-729-6423 *E-mail:* gabriel@scbdistributors.com *Web Site:* scbdistributors.com

TESOL International Association
Formerly Teachers of English to Speakers of Other Languages Inc
1925 Ballenger Ave, Alexandria, VA 22314-6820
Tel: 703-836-0774 *Fax:* 703-836-7864; 703-836-6447
E-mail: publications@tesol.org; info@tesol.org; members@tesol.org
Web Site: www.tesol.org
Key Personnel
Exec Dir & CEO: Rosa Aronson, PhD *Tel:* 703-836-0774 ext 505 *E-mail:* raronson@tesol.org
Founded: 1966
Education association & publisher of professional education books & products for the ESL teaching profession.
ISBN Prefix(es): 978-0-939791; 978-1-1931; 978-1-931185; 978-1-942223; 978-1-942799; 978-1-945351
Number of titles published annually: 6 Print
Total Titles: 90 Print; 1 CD-ROM
Distributed by Alta Book Center Publishers; Delta Systems Inc; New Readers Press; Saddleback Educational
Foreign Rep(s): Eurospan Group (worldwide)
Orders to: PO Box 79283, Baltimore, MD 21279 *Tel:* 240-646-7037 *Toll Free Tel:* 888-891-0041 *Fax:* 301-206-9789 *E-mail:* tesolpubs@brightkey.net
Distribution Center: BrightKey Inc, 9050 Junction Dr, Annapolis Junction, MD 20701 *E-mail:* tesolpubs@brightkey.net

Teton NewMedia Inc
90 E Simpson, Suite 110, Jackson, WY 83001
Mailing Address: PO Box 4833, Jackson, WY 83001
Tel: 307-732-0028 *Toll Free Tel:* 877-306-9793 *Fax:* 307-734-0841
E-mail: sales@tetonnm.com
Web Site: www.tetonnm.com

Key Personnel
Owner: John F Spahr *Tel:* 877-306-9793 ext 103 *E-mail:* lodgepole@tetonnm.com
Pres & Ed-in-Chief: Carroll C Cann *Tel:* 610-594-7634 *E-mail:* ccann@tetonnm.com
Creative Dir: Sue Haun *Tel:* 307-883-5640 *E-mail:* sue@fiftysixforty.com
Mktg Mgr: Sara Scartz-Montesano *Tel:* 307-732-0028 ext 101 *E-mail:* sara@tetonnm.com
Prod Mgr: Mike Albiniak *Tel:* 307-883-5640 *E-mail:* mike@fiftysixforty.com
Founded: 1999 (by John Sphar & Carroll Cann)
Health science publisher that focuses on producing high quality, affordable veterinary text & reference books.
ISBN Prefix(es): 978-1-893441; 978-1-59161
Number of titles published annually: 6 Print; 2 CD-ROM
Total Titles: 25 Print; 18 CD-ROM
Distributed by Blackwells; LifeLearn; Logan Brothers; Rittenhouse; Yankee
Distributor for LifeLearn

Texas A&M University Press
Division of Texas A&M University
John H Lindsey Bldg, Lewis St, 4354 TAMU, College Station, TX 77843-4354
SAN: 207-5237
Tel: 979-845-1436 *Toll Free Tel:* 800-826-8911 (orders) *Fax:* 979-847-8752 *Toll Free Fax:* 888-617-2421 (orders)
E-mail: bookorders@tamu.edu
Web Site: www.tamupress.com
Key Personnel
Dir: Dr Shannon Davies *Tel:* 979-458-3980 *E-mail:* sdavies@tamu.edu
Lib Sales Dir & Mktg Mgr: Gayla Christiansen *Tel:* 979-845-0148 *E-mail:* gayla-c@tamu.edu
Ed-in-Chief & Mng Ed: Dr Jay Dew *Tel:* 979-845-0759 *E-mail:* jaydew@tamu.edu
Mgr, Cust Rel: Sharon Mills *Tel:* 979-458-3994 *E-mail:* sharon-mills@tamu.edu
Design Mgr: Mary Ann Jacob *Tel:* 979-845-3694 *E-mail:* m-jacob@tamu.edu
Fin Mgr: Dianna Sells *Tel:* 979-845-0146 *E-mail:* d-sells@tamu.edu
Publicity & Ad Mgr: Christine Brown *Tel:* 979-458-3982 *E-mail:* christinebrown@tamu.edu
Trade Sales: David Neel *Tel:* 979-458-3981 *E-mail:* d-neel@tamu.edu
Founded: 1974
Scholarly nonfiction, regional studies, economics, history, natural history, presidential studies, anthropology, US-Mexican borderlands studies, women's studies, nautical archaeology, military studies, agriculture, Texas history & archaeology.
ISBN Prefix(es): 978-0-89096; 978-1-58544; 978-1-60344; 978-1-60344
Number of titles published annually: 60 Print; 1 CD-ROM
Total Titles: 1,400 Print; 2 CD-ROM; 900 E-Book; 4 Audio
Distributor for Stephen F Austin State University Press; McWhiney Foundation Press/State House Press; Texas Christian University Press; Texas Review Press; Texas State Historical Association; University of North Texas Press
Foreign Rep(s): Eurospan Group (Europe, UK); EWEB (Asia, Australia, Middle East, New Zealand, Pacific Islands); Scholarly Book Services (Laura Rust) (Canada); US PubRep (Craig Falk) (Latin America)
Foreign Rights: Tamu Press
Membership(s): Association of American University Presses

Texas Christian University Press, see TCU Press

Texas State Historical Association
3001 Lake Austin Blvd, Suite 3.116, Austin, TX 78703
Tel: 512-471-2600 *Fax:* 512-473-8691
Web Site: www.tshaonline.org
Key Personnel
Mng Ed: Ryan R Schumacher *Tel:* 512-471-5862 *E-mail:* ryan.schumacher@tshaonline.org
Founded: 1897
Books & articles related to Texas history.
ISBN Prefix(es): 978-0-87611; 978-1-62511
Number of titles published annually: 4 Print; 4 E-Book
Total Titles: 100 Print; 33 E-Book
Distributed by Texas A&M University Press

Texas Tech University Press
1120 Main St, 2nd fl, Lubbock, TX 79401
SAN: 218-5989
Mailing Address: PO Box 41037, Lubbock, TX 79409-1037 SAN: 218-5989
Tel: 806-742-2982 *Toll Free Tel:* 800-832-4042 *Fax:* 806-742-2979
E-mail: ttup@ttu.edu
Web Site: www.ttupress.org
Key Personnel
Dir: Courtney Burkholder *E-mail:* courtney.burkholder@ttu.edu
Ed-in-Chief: Joanna Conrad *E-mail:* joanna.conrad@ttu.edu
Mng Ed: Amanda Werts *E-mail:* amanda.werts@ttu.edu
Cust Serv Mgr: Isabel Williams *E-mail:* isabel.williams@ttu.edu
Design & Prodn Mgr: Kasey McBeath *E-mail:* kasey.mcbeath@ttu.edu
Mktg Mgr: John Brock *E-mail:* john.brock@ttu.edu
Warehouse Mgr: LaTisha Roberts *E-mail:* latisha.roberts@ttu.edu
Founded: 1971
Scholarly books & journals: History, culture & natural history of Texas, the Southwest & the Great Plains; photography; military history; sports history; American roots music; memoirs, especially of the American West; sustainability studies; gender in the American West.
ISBN Prefix(es): 978-0-89672; 978-1-68283; 978-1-945797 (Texas Tech University Libraries)
Number of titles published annually: 25 Print; 15 E-Book
Total Titles: 410 Print; 100 E-Book
Distributor for National Ranching Heritage Center
Distribution Center: Chicago Distribution Center, 11030 S Langley Ave, Chicago, IL 60628 SAN: 202-5280
Membership(s): Association of American University Presses; Publishers Association of the West

§University of Texas Press
Division of University of Texas
3001 Lake Austin Blvd, 2.200, Austin, TX 78703
SAN: 212-9876
Mailing Address: PO Box 7819, Austin, TX 78713-7819
Tel: 512-471-7233 *Fax:* 512-232-7178
E-mail: utpress@uts.cc.utexas.edu; info@utpress.utexas.edu
Web Site: www.utexaspress.com
Key Personnel
CFO: Joyce Lewandoski
Dir, Press: Dave Hamrick
Ed-in-Chief: Robert Bevens
Acq Ed: Jim Burr
Mgr & Intl Rts Contact: Ines ter Horst
Ad, Exhibits Mgr: Chris Farmer
Credit Mgr & Cust Serv: Brenda Jo Hoggutt
Prodn Mgr: Ellen McKie
Sales Mgr: Gianna La Norte
Asst Mktg Mgr: Nancy Bryan
Founded: 1950
General scholarly nonfiction, Latin America, Middle Eastern studies, Southwest regional, social sciences, humanities & science, linguistics, architecture, classics, natural history, Latin American literature in translation.
ISBN Prefix(es): 978-0-292
Number of titles published annually: 100 Print
Total Titles: 2,200 Print; 1 CD-ROM; 1 Online
Distributor for Bat Conservation International; Institute for Mesoamerican Studies; Menil Foundation; Rothko Chapel; Texas Parks & Wildlife Department
Foreign Rep(s): Codash (Canada); Combined Academic Publisher (Australia, New Zealand); Nicholas Esson (Europe, UK); Marketing Dept, University of Texas (Caribbean)
Membership(s): AAP; Association of American University Presses

Texas Western Press
Affiliate of University of Texas at El Paso
c/o University of Texas at El Paso, 500 W University Ave, El Paso, TX 79968-0633
SAN: 202-7712
Tel: 915-747-5688 *Toll Free Tel:* 800-488-3798 (orders only) *Fax:* 915-747-7515
E-mail: twpress@utep.edu
Web Site: twp.utep.edu
Key Personnel
Dir: Robert Stakes *Tel:* 915-747-7895 ext 6710
Founded: 1952
Scholarly books on the history, art, photography & culture of the American Southwest.
ISBN Prefix(es): 978-0-87404
Number of titles published annually: 2 Print
Total Titles: 63 Print; 1 Audio
Imprints: Southwestern Studies
Distributed by University of Texas Press

TFH Publications Inc
Subsidiary of Central Garden & Pet Corp
PO Box 427, Neptune, NJ 07754
SAN: 202-7720
Toll Free Tel: 855-273-7527 (cust serv) *Fax:* 732-988-5466 (cust serv); 732-776-8763 (sales)
E-mail: info@tfh.com (cust serv); sales@tfh.com
Web Site: www.tfhpublications.com; www.tfh.com; www.facebook.com/TfhPetBooks
Key Personnel
Pres & CEO: Glen Axelrod
Founded: 1952
Pet care reference books & specialty magazines.
ISBN Prefix(es): 978-0-87666; 978-0-86622; 978-0-7938; 978-1-890087 (Microcosm Books); 978-0-9820262 (Microcosm Books)
Number of titles published annually: 40 Print; 40 E-Book
Total Titles: 1,200 Print; 200 E-Book
Imprints: Microcosm Books
Divisions: Nylabone Products
Foreign Rep(s): Brooklands Aquarium Ltd (New Zealand); Fitzhenry & Whiteside (Canada); Rolf C Hagen Ltd (Canada); Interpet Publishing (England); TFH Pty Ltd (Australia); Trinity Books (South Africa)
Foreign Rights: R&G Media (Richard Gay) (worldwide)

Thames & Hudson
500 Fifth Ave, New York, NY 10110
SAN: 202-5795
Tel: 212-354-3763 *Toll Free Tel:* 800-233-4830 *Fax:* 212-398-1252
E-mail: bookinfo@thames.wwnorton.com
Web Site: www.thamesandhudsonusa.com
Key Personnel
CEO: Rolf Grisebach
Pres & Publr: Will Balliett
Assoc Edit Dir: Elizabeth Keene
Assoc Mktg Dir: Lauren Miller
Ed-at-Large: Christopher Sweet
Publicity: Harry Burton
Publicity Assoc: Sarah Thegeby
Founded: 1977

Nonfiction trade, quality paperbacks & college texts on art, archaeology, architecture, crafts, history & photography.
ISBN Prefix(es): 978-0-500
Number of titles published annually: 150 Print
Total Titles: 1,000 Print
Distributed by W W Norton & Company Inc
Advertising Agency: Verso
Shipping Address: National Book Co Inc, Keystone Industrial Park, Scranton, PA 18512
Membership(s): AAP

Theatre Communications Group
520 Eighth Ave, 24th fl, New York, NY 10018-4156
Tel: 212-609-5900 *Fax:* 212-609-5901
E-mail: tcg@tcg.org
Web Site: www.tcg.org
Key Personnel
Publr: Terence Nemeth *E-mail:* tnemeth@tcg.org
Edit Dir & Ed: Kathy Sova
Founded: 1961
Performing arts, dramatic literature.
ISBN Prefix(es): 978-0-930452; 978-1-55936
Number of titles published annually: 24 Print; 20 E-Book
Total Titles: 450 Print; 200 E-Book
Distributor for Aurora Metro Publications; 53rd State Press; Nick Hern Books; Oberon Books; Padua Playwrights Press; PAJ Publications; Playscripts Inc; Playwrights Canada Press; Martin E Segal Theatre Center Publications; Ubu Repertory Theatre Publications
Foreign Rep(s): Nick Hern Books (UK); Playwrights Canada Press (Canada)
Distribution Center: Consortium Book Sales & Distribution, The Keg House, 34 13 Ave NE, Suite 101, Minneapolis, MN 55413-1007 *Tel:* 612-746-2600 *Toll Free Tel:* 800-283-3572 (cust serv) *Fax:* 612-746-2606 *Web Site:* www.cbsd.com

§Theosophical University Press
Affiliate of Theosophical Society (Pasadena)
PO Box C, Pasadena, CA 91109-7107
SAN: 205-4299
Tel: 626-798-3378
E-mail: tupress@theosociety.org
Web Site: www.theosociety.org
Key Personnel
Dir: Randell C Grubb
Mgr & Intl Rts: Will Thackara
Cust Serv: Ina Belderis
Founded: 1886
Quality theosophical literature.
ISBN Prefix(es): 978-0-911500; 978-1-55700
Number of titles published annually: 2 Print; 5 Online; 2 E-Book
Total Titles: 86 Print; 1 CD-ROM; 115 Online; 84 E-Book; 7 Audio
Imprints: Sunrise Library
Foreign Office(s): Theosophischer Verlag GmbH, Brunnenstr 11, 56414 Hundsangen, Germany, Contact: Jochen Hannappel *Tel:* (06435) 96033 *Fax:* (06435) 96053 *E-mail:* info@theosophischer-verlag.de *Web Site:* www.theosophischer-verlag.de
Theosophical University Press Agency, Daal en Bergselaan 68, 2565 AG The Hague, Netherlands, Contact: Coen Vonk *Tel:* (070) 323 1776 *Fax:* (070) 325 7275 *E-mail:* tupa@theosofie.net *Web Site:* www.theosofie.net
Theosophical University Press South African Agency, PO Box 504, Constantia 7848, South Africa, Contact: Dewald Bester *Tel:* (021) 4342281 *E-mail:* besterdewald@gmail.com
The Theosophical Society, 43 Stephenson Grove, Rainhill, Merseyside L35 9AB, United Kingdom, Contact: Patrick Powell *E-mail:* ts-uk@talktalk.net *Web Site:* www.theosophical.org.uk/tup.html
Warehouse: 2416 N Lake Ave, Altadena, CA 91001

§Thieme Medical Publishers Inc
Subsidiary of Georg Thieme Verlag KG
333 Seventh Ave, 18th fl, New York, NY 10001
SAN: 202-7399
Tel: 212-760-0888 *Toll Free Tel:* 800-782-3488 *Fax:* 212-947-1112
E-mail: customerservice@thieme.com
Web Site: www.thieme.com
Key Personnel
Pres: Brian Scanlan *Tel:* 212-584-4707 *E-mail:* bscanlan@thieme.com
Sales Dir: Mike Roseman *Tel:* 631-365-4625 *E-mail:* mike.roseman@thieme.com
Founded: 1979
Electronic products, apps, books, journals, textbooks in clinical medicine, dentistry, speech & hearing, allied health, audiology, organic chemistry plus electronic products, medical education & databases.
ISBN Prefix(es): 978-0-913258; 978-0-86577; 978-1-58890; 978-1-60406; 978-1-62623
Number of titles published annually: 50 Print; 3 CD-ROM; 50 Online
Total Titles: 605 Print; 50 Online; 605 E-Book
Foreign Office(s): Thieme Publishers Rio, Argentina Bldg, 16th fl, Ala A, 228, Praia do Botafogo, 22250-040 Rio de Janeiro-RJ, Brazil, VP: Daniel Schiff *Tel:* (021) 3736-3631
Georg Thieme Verlag, PO Box 30 11 20, 70451 Stuttgart, Germany *Tel:* (0711) 89310 *Fax:* (0711) 8931410 *E-mail:* customerservice@thieme.de *Web Site:* www.thieme.de
Thieme Medical & Scientific Publishers Pvt Ltd, A-12, Sector 2, 2nd fl, Noida, Uttar Pradesh 201 301, India *Tel:* (0120) 427 4461 *Fax:* (0120) 427 4465 *E-mail:* customerservice@thieme.in
Distributor for AO Foundation
Foreign Rep(s): Login Canada (Canada); Woodslane (Australia)
Foreign Rights: Heike Schwabenthan (worldwide)
Warehouse: Mount Joy Distribution Center, 1000 Strickler Rd, Mount Joy, PA 17552
Membership(s): AAP; Independent Publishers Association; STM

Third World Press
7822 S Dobson Ave, Chicago, IL 60619
Mailing Address: PO Box 19730, Chicago, IL 60619
Tel: 773-651-0700 *Fax:* 773-651-7286
E-mail: twpress3@aol.com
Web Site: www.thirdworldpressfoundation.com
Key Personnel
Publr: Haki R Madhubuti
Ed: Gwendolyn Mitchell
Founded: 1967
Publishers of quality Black fiction, nonfiction, poetry, drama, young adult & children literature; primarily adult literature.
ISBN Prefix(es): 978-0-88378
Number of titles published annually: 10 Print
Total Titles: 140 Print
Distribution Center: Ingram Publisher Services, One Ingram Blvd, La Vergne, TN 37086 *Toll Free Tel:* 866-400-5351

Charles C Thomas Publisher Ltd
2600 S First St, Springfield, IL 62704
SAN: 201-9485
Tel: 217-789-8980 *Toll Free Tel:* 800-258-8980 *Fax:* 217-789-9130
E-mail: books@ccthomas.com
Web Site: www.ccthomas.com
Key Personnel
Pres: Michael Payne Thomas
Cont: Cheryl Steelman
Founded: 1927
Medicine, allied health sciences, science, technology, education, public administration, law enforcement, behavioral & social sciences, special education.
ISBN Prefix(es): 978-0-398
Number of titles published annually: 60 Print
Total Titles: 905 Print
Advertising Agency: Thomas Advertising Agency

§Thomas Nelson
Imprint of HarperCollins Christian Publishing
501 Nelson Place, Nashville, TN 37214
SAN: 209-3820
Mailing Address: PO Box 141000, Nashville, TN 37214-1000
Tel: 615-889-9000 *Toll Free Tel:* 800-251-4000 *Fax:* 615-902-1548
Web Site: www.thomasnelson.com
Key Personnel
Pres & CEO, Christian Publg Div: Mark Schoenwald
SVP, Author & Partnership Devt: Matt Baugher
SVP, Book Publg: David Moberg
SVP & Publr, Nelson Books: Brian Hampton
SVP & Publr, Bibles: John Kramp
SVP & Publr, Spanish: Larry Downs
SVP, Sales: Tom Knight
SVP, Specialty Publg: Laura Minchew
VP & Publr, W Publishing Group: Daisy Blackwell Hutton
VP, Mktg: Michael Aulisio
Publr, Emanate Books: Joel Kneedler
Publr, Fiction: Amanda Bostic
Publr, Harper Christian Specialty Div: LeeEric Fesko
Assoc Publr: Megan Jayne Dobson
Assoc Publr, Gift Books: MacKenzie Howard
Sr Mktg Dir: Tim Marshall
Dir, Corp Communs: Casey Harrell
Dir, Mktg: Karen Jackson
Dir of Mktg, W Publishing Group: Kristi Smith
Dir of Publicity, W Publishing Group: Becky Melvin
Founded: 1798
Bibles & Testaments, trade, Christian & inspirational books, gift books, children's books & videos.
ISBN Prefix(es): 978-0-8407; 978-1-4047
Number of titles published annually: 600 Print
Total Titles: 3,500 Print; 6 CD-ROM; 30 Audio
Imprints: Emanate Books; W Publishing Group
Distributed by Winston-Derek

Thomson Reuters Westlaw™
610 Opperman Dr, Eagan, MN 55123
Tel: 651-687-7000 *Toll Free Tel:* 888-728-7677 (sales); 800-328-4880 (cust serv)
E-mail: legalsolutions@thomsonreuters.com
Web Site: legalsolutions.thomsonreuters.com
Key Personnel
Sr Dir, Cust Serv Opers: Scott Morgan
Founded: 1804
Publisher of state statutes, attorney general opinions & practice manuals for the US & international.
ISBN Prefix(es): 978-0-8322; 978-0-7620; 978-0-8366; 978-0-87632
Number of titles published annually: 4 Print
Branch Office(s)
Aqueduct Bldg, Rochester, NY 14694 *Tel:* 585-546-5530 *Toll Free Tel:* 800-527-0430 *Fax:* 585-327-6269
Distributor for Law Library Microform Consortium
Returns: 545 Wescott Rd, Eagan, MN 55123

Thorndike Press
Imprint of Gale
10 Water St, Suite 310, Waterville, ME 04901
Toll Free Tel: 800-223-1244 (ext 4, cust serv/orders) *Toll Free Fax:* 800-558-4676 (orders)
E-mail: gale.printorders@cengage.com; international@cengage.com (cust orders outside US & CN)
Web Site: www.gale.com/thorndike

Key Personnel
Publr: Jamie Knobloch *E-mail:* jamie.knobloch@cengage.com
Edit Dir: Mary P Smith *Tel:* 207-861-7517 *E-mail:* mary.p.smith@cengage.com
Assoc Mktg Mgr: Barb Littlefield *Tel:* 207-861-7532 *E-mail:* barb.littlefield@cengage.com
Founded: 1980
Large print titles for the public library market.
ISBN Prefix(es): 978-0-7862; 978-1-4104; 978-1-58724; 978-1-59414; 978-1-59413; 978-1-59415
Number of titles published annually: 1,500 Print
Total Titles: 4,000 Print
Distributor for Grand Central/Hachette Large Print; HarperLuxe; Mills & Boon Large Print; Random House Large Print

Threshold Editions, see Gallery Books

ThunderStone Books
6575 Horse Dr, Las Vegas, NV 89131
E-mail: info@thunderstonebooks.com
Web Site: www.thunderstonebooks.com
Key Personnel
Mng Dir: Robert Noorda *E-mail:* robert.noorda@thunderstonebooks.com
Edit Dir: Rachel Noorda *E-mail:* rachel.noorda@thunderstonebooks.com
Founded: 2014
Specialize in children's books that have an educational aspect. We are not looking for curriculum for learning certain subjects, but rather stories that encourage learning for children, whether that be learning about a new language/culture or learning more about science & math in a fun, fictional format. We want to help children to gain a love for other languages & subjects so that they are curious about the world around them. We are currently accepting fiction & nonfiction submissions. In the area of language, our expertise lies in stories concerning Mandarin Chinese (language, culture, setting +/or mythology), but we are open to other languages as well. For submissions concerning other subjects, we are quite open to anything which creatively teaches & inspires, particularly in areas such as math or science. Fiction submissions that have an educational element are encouraged & welcome.
ISBN Prefix(es): 978-1-63411
Number of titles published annually: 6 Print; 6 E-Book
Total Titles: 5 Print; 5 E-Book
Foreign Office(s): 3B Bow St, Stirling FK8 1BS, United Kingdom *Tel:* (07825) 483348
Orders to: Ingram Content Group, One Ingram Blvd, La Vergne, TN 37086, Contact: Ron Smithson *Toll Free Tel:* 800-937-8222 ext 35176 *E-mail:* ron.smithson@ingramcontent.com
Returns: Ingram Content Group, One Ingram Blvd, La Vergne, TN 37086, Contact: Ron Smithson *Toll Free Tel:* 800-937-8222 ext 35176 *E-mail:* ron.smithson@ingramcontent.com
Shipping Address: Ingram Content Group, One Ingram Blvd, La Vergne, TN 37086, Contact: Ron Smithson *Toll Free Tel:* 800-937-8222 ext 35176 *E-mail:* ron.smithson@ingramcontent.com
Warehouse: Ingram Content Group, One Ingram Blvd, La Vergne, TN 37086, Contact: Ron Smithson *Toll Free Tel:* 800-937-8222 ext 35176 *E-mail:* ron.smithson@ingramcontent.com
Distribution Center: Ingram Content Group, One Ingram Blvd, La Vergne, TN 37086, Contact: Ron Smithson *Toll Free Tel:* 800-937-8222 ext 35176 *E-mail:* ron.smithson@ingramcontent.com

Tide-mark Press
22 Prestige Park Circle, East Hartford, CT 06108-1917
SAN: 222-1802
Tel: 860-310-3370 *Toll Free Tel:* 800-338-2508 *Fax:* 860-310-3654
E-mail: customerservice@tide-mark.com
Web Site: www.tidemarkpress.com
Key Personnel
Publr: Scott Kaeser *Tel:* 860-310-3370 ext 108 *E-mail:* scott@tide-mark.com
ISBN Prefix(es): 978-1-63114
Number of titles published annually: 4 Print
Total Titles: 24 Print
Foreign Rep(s): Gazelle Book Services Ltd (Europe)

Tiger Tales
5 River Rd, Suite 128, Wilton, CT 06897-4069
SAN: 253-6382
Tel: 920-387-2333 *Fax:* 920-387-9994
Web Site: www.tigertalesbooks.com
Key Personnel
Art Dir: Michelle Martinez
Sales Dir: Barb Knight *E-mail:* barbknight@tigertalesbooks.com
Ed: Tammi Salzano
Publg Admin: Jeannie Rubsam *Tel:* 203-834-0005 *Fax:* 203-834-0004 *E-mail:* jrubsam@tigertalesbooks.com
Founded: 2000
Tiger Tales publishes imaginative & entertaining hardcover picture books as well as board & novelty books for children 2-7. For ages 6 to 10, Tiger Tales publishes fiction series: *Pet Rescue Adventures & Animal Rescue Center. 360 Degrees*, an imprint of Tiger Tales is middle-grade nonfiction dedicated to building a broader view of our world. Tiger Tales remains steadfast in our commitment to publishing children's books that will capture the imagination of children.
ISBN Prefix(es): 978-1-58925; 978-1-68010; 978-1-944530 (360 Degrees)
Number of titles published annually: 100 Print
Total Titles: 650 Print
Sales Office(s): PO Box 70, Iron Ridge, WI 53035
Orders to: 1263 Southwest Blvd, Kansas City, KS 66103, Contact: Vanessa Ottens *Tel:* 913-362-7400 *Fax:* 913-362-7401 *E-mail:* vanessa@midpt.com
Returns: 1263 Southwest Blvd, Kansas City, KS 66103 *Tel:* 913-362-7400 *Fax:* 913-362-7401 *E-mail:* lreeder@tigertalesbooks.com
Shipping Address: 1263 Southwest Blvd, Kansas City, KS 66103, Contact: Vanessa Ottens *Tel:* 913-362-7400 *Toll Free Tel:* 888-454-0097 *Fax:* 913-362-7401 *E-mail:* vanessa@midpt.com
Warehouse: 1263 Southwest Blvd, Kansas City, KS 66103, Contact: Vanessa Ottens *Tel:* 913-362-7400 *Toll Free Tel:* 888-454-0097 *Fax:* 913-362-7401 *E-mail:* vanessa@midpt.com
Membership(s): ABA

Tilbury House Publishers
Imprint of WordSplice Studio LLC
12 Starr St, Thomaston, ME 04861
Tel: 207-582-1899 *Toll Free Tel:* 800-582-1899 (orders) *Fax:* 207-582-8227
E-mail: tilbury@tilburyhouse.com
Web Site: www.tilburyhouse.com
Key Personnel
Publr: Tristram Coburn; Jonathan Eaton
Children's Book Ed: Audrey Maynard
Founded: 1990
ISBN Prefix(es): 978-0-88448
Number of titles published annually: 10 Print
Total Titles: 100 Print
Distributed by W W Norton & Company Inc
Membership(s): ABA; Independent Book Publishers Association

Timber Press Inc
Subsidiary of Workman Publishing Co
133 SW Second Ave, Suite 450, Portland, OR 97204
SAN: 216-082X
Tel: 503-227-2878 *Toll Free Tel:* 800-327-5680 *Fax:* 503-227-3070
E-mail: info@timberpress.com
Web Site: www.timberpress.com
Key Personnel
Publr: Andrew Beckman
Ed-in-Chief: Tom Fischer
Trade & Spec Sales Mgr: Janea Brachfeld
Founded: 1976
Gardening, horticulture, botany, natural history, Pacific Northwest regional.
ISBN Prefix(es): 978-0-88192
Number of titles published annually: 40 Print
Total Titles: 300 Print
Imprints: Timber Press
Distributed by Thomas Allen & Son

TLC, see THE Learning Connection®

The Toby Press LLC
PO Box 8531, New Milford, CT 06776-8531
SAN: 253-9985
Tel: 203-830-8508 *Fax:* 203-830-8512
E-mail: toby@tobypress.com; sales@korenpub.com
Web Site: www.tobypress.com; www.korenpub.com
Key Personnel
Publr: Matthew Miller *E-mail:* publisher@tobypress.com
Sales Dir: Shlomo Peterseil *Tel:* 203-830-8509
Founded: 1999
Publish Jewish religious texts, Jewish philosophy, Holocaust memoirs.
ISBN Prefix(es): 978-1-902881; 978-1-59264
Number of titles published annually: 50 Print
Total Titles: 800 Print
Imprints: Koren Publishers (Hebrew Bibles & other Jewish religious texts); Maggid (contemporary Jewish thought); Steinsaltz (Talmud, Bible with commentary, Hassidism)
Distributor for Ofeq Books; Steinsaltz
Shipping Address: Focus Mailing, One Prindle Lane, Danbury, CT 06811 *Tel:* 203-830-8500 *Fax:* 203-830-2516 *Web Site:* www.focusmailing.com
Warehouse: Focus Mailing, One Prindle Lane, Danbury, CT 06811 *Tel:* 203-830-8500 *Fax:* 203-830-2516 *Web Site:* www.focusmailing.com
Distribution Center: Focus Mailing, One Prindle Lane, Danbury, CT 06811 *Tel:* 203-830-8500 *Fax:* 203-830-2516 *Web Site:* www.focusmailing.com
Baker & Taylor, 2550 W Tyvola Rd, Suite 300, Charlotte, NC 28217 *Tel:* 714-998-3100 *Toll Free Tel:* 800-775-1800 *Fax:* 704-998-3319
Brodart, 500 Arch St, Williamsport, PA 17701 *Tel:* 570-326-2461 *Toll Free Tel:* 800-999-6799 *Fax:* 570-326-1479
Ingram, One Ingram Blvd, La Vergne, TN 37086 *Toll Free Tel:* 800-400-5351

§Todd Publications
920 Dogwood Dr, No 461, Delray Beach, FL 33483
SAN: 207-0804
Tel: 561-910-0440 *Fax:* 561-910-0440
E-mail: toddpub@yahoo.com
Key Personnel
Ed/Publr: Barry Klein
Founded: 1973

Directories & reference books to the trade. Returns accepted within 30 days when in resalable condition.
ISBN Prefix(es): 978-0-87340; 978-0-915344; 978-0-873400
Number of titles published annually: 10 Print; 2 CD-ROM
Total Titles: 15 Print; 2 CD-ROM

Tommy Nelson
Imprint of HarperCollins Christian Publishing
501 Nelson Place, Nashville, TN 37214
Mailing Address: PO Box 141000, Nashville, TN 37214-1000
Tel: 615-889-9000; 615-902-1485 (cust serv) *Toll Free Tel:* 800-251-4000 *Fax:* 615-391-5225
Web Site: www.tommynelson.com
Key Personnel
Pres & CEO: Mark Schoenwald
Publr, Harper Christian Specialty Div: LeeEric Fesko
Assoc Publr, Children's Books: MacKenzie Howard
Sr Dir, Mktg: AnnJanette Toth
Founded: 1984
Inspirational children's books for evangelical & secular marketplace & other products.
ISBN Prefix(es): 978-0-8499; 978-1-4003
Number of titles published annually: 75 Print; 10 Audio
Total Titles: 200 Print; 8 E-Book; 50 Audio

§Top of the Mountain Publishing
Division of Powell Productions
4837 62 St N, St Petersburg, FL 33709
SAN: 287-590X
Tel: 727-391-3958
Web Site: www.topofthemountain.com
Key Personnel
Dir: Judith Powell; Tag Powell
Intl Rts & Lib Sales Dir: Sharon Boulder
PR: Lance Wilson
Founded: 1979
Exhibits at international, national bookfairs, BFA, Frankfurt Book Fairs; no unsol mss.
ISBN Prefix(es): 978-1-56087
Number of titles published annually: 30 Print; 100 Audio
Total Titles: 100 Print; 12 CD-ROM
Advertising Agency: Powell Productions
Distribution Center: New Leaf Distributing Co, 401 Thornton Rd, Lithia Springs, GA 30122-1557 *Tel:* 770-948-7845 *Fax:* 770-944-2313 *E-mail:* domestic@newleaf-dist.com *Web Site:* www.newleaf-dist.com

§Top Publications Ltd
2745 Dallas Pkwy, Suite 420, Plano, TX 75093
Tel: 972-628-6414 *Fax:* 972-233-0713
E-mail: info@toppub.com
Web Site: topfiction.net
Key Personnel
Mgr: Bill Manchee *E-mail:* info@toppub.com
Founded: 1999
ISBN Prefix(es): 978-0-9666366; 978-1-929976; 978-1-935722
Number of titles published annually: 3 Print; 2 CD-ROM; 3 E-Book
Total Titles: 58 Print; 19 CD-ROM; 58 E-Book; 19 Audio
Imprints: TOP
Orders to: Ingram Book Co, One Ingram Blvd, La Vergne, TN 37086-3650 *Web Site:* ipage.ingramcontent.com
Membership(s): Independent Book Publishers Association

Tor/Forge Books, see Tom Doherty Associates, LLC

Torah Aura Productions
4423 Fruitland Ave, Los Angeles, CA 90058
Tel: 323-585-7312 *Toll Free Tel:* 800-238-6724 *Fax:* 323-585-0327
E-mail: misrad@torahaura.com; orders@torahaura.com
Web Site: www.torahaura.com
Key Personnel
Pres: Alan Rowe *E-mail:* alan@torahaura.com
Founded: 1981
Textbooks, Judaica.
ISBN Prefix(es): 978-0-933873; 978-0-943527
Number of titles published annually: 10 Print
Total Titles: 500 Print
Distributor for Free Spirit (selected titles)

Torah Umesorah Publications
Division of Torah Umesorah-National Society for Hebrew Day Schools
620 Foster Ave, Brooklyn, NY 11230
Tel: 718-259-1223 *Fax:* 718-259-1795
E-mail: publications@torah-umesorah.org
Key Personnel
Dir, Pubns: Shmuel Yaakov Klein
Founded: 1946
Text teaching aids & visual aids for Yeshiva-day schools & Hebrew schools, students & teachers; posters & workbooks.
ISBN Prefix(es): 978-0-914131; 978-1-878895
Number of titles published annually: 5 Print
Total Titles: 82 Print

Tortuga Press
2777 Yulupa Ave, PMB 181, Santa Rosa, CA 95405
SAN: 299-1756
Tel: 707-544-4720 *Fax:* 707-595-5331
E-mail: info@tortugapress.com
Web Site: www.tortugapress.com
Key Personnel
Publr: Matthew Gollub *E-mail:* mg@tortugapress.com
Off Mgr: Simone Peters
Founded: 1997
Creator of award-winning children's literature & multimedia products to delight & open young people's minds.
ISBN Prefix(es): 978-1-889910
Number of titles published annually: 4 Print; 2 Audio
Total Titles: 24 Print; 7 Audio
Warehouse: CubeSmart, 220 Business Park Dr, Rohnert Park, CA 94928
Membership(s): California Association of Bilingual Education; California School Library Association; Independent Book Publishers Association; Texas Library Association

§TotalRecall Publications Inc
1103 Middlecreek, Friendswood, TX 77546
Tel: 281-992-3131
E-mail: sales@totalrecallpress.com
Web Site: www.totalrecallpress.com
Key Personnel
Pres: Bruce Moran *E-mail:* bruce@totalrecallpress.com
Mktg Dir: Terri Mitchem *Tel:* 352-596-1192
Founded: 1998
Publish nonfiction books in a variety of professional fields, including library science & library assistant/technician education (Learn Library Skills Series) & financial certification exam preparation, with many titles adopted as college texts. The exam preparation study guides offer free downloads of a proprietary interactive test engine that generates randomized mock exams designed to identify a candidate's strengths & weaknesses & determine where to allocate study time. These titles are also distributed electronically to libraries, corporations & government agencies via EBSCOHost, ebrary & Books24x7.com. The company has expanded into fiction, especially mystery/thrillers, along with self-help, travel & religion.
ISBN Prefix(es): 978-1-59095
Number of titles published annually: 50 Print; 10 Online; 50 E-Book
Total Titles: 400 Print; 120 Online; 250 E-Book

Touchstone
Imprint of Scribner Publishing Group
1230 Avenue of the Americas, New York, NY 10020
Key Personnel
Pres & Publr: Susan Moldow
VP, Assoc Publr: David Falk
VP & Dir, Subs Rts: Paul O'Halloran
VP, Dir of Publicity: Brian Belfiglio
Ed-in-Chief: Tara Parsons
VP, Exec Ed: Trish Todd
Sr Ed: Cara Bedick; Matthew Benjamin; Lauren Spiegel
Asst Ed: Kaitlin Olson
Edit Asst: Isabella Betita; Lara Blackman; Jessie Chasan-Taber
Sr Art Dir: Cherlynne Li
Art Mgr: Janetta Dancer
Assoc Mktg Dir: Meredith Vilarello
Digital Mktg Mgr: Kelsey Manning
Publg & Mktg Asst: Isabel DaSilva
Asst Dir, Publicity: Shida Carr
Publicity Mgr: Jessica Roth
Publicity Asst: Courtney Brach; Leah Morse; Charlotte O'Donnell
Assoc Mng Ed: Monica Oluwek
Mng Edit Asst: Julie Ficks
ISBN Prefix(es): 978-0-684
Number of titles published annually: 60 Print
Imprints: Libros en Espanol
Foreign Rights: Akcali Copyright Agency (Turkey); Antonella Antonelli Agenzia (Italy); Book Publishers Association of Israel (Israel); Japan UNI Agency (Japan); JLM Literary Agency (Greece); KCC (Korea Copyright Center); Mohrbooks Literary Agency (Germany); La Nouvelle Agence; Andrew Nurnberg Associates (Bulgaria, Croatia, Czech Republic, Estonia, Hungary, Latvia, Lithuania, Montenegro, Poland, Romania, Russia, Serbia, Slovakia, Slovenia); Sane Toregard Agency (Denmark, Finland, Iceland, Norway, Sweden); Sebes & Bisseling Literary Agency (Netherlands); Tuttle-Mori Agency Inc (Thailand)

§Tower Publishing Co
588 Saco Rd, Standish, ME 04084
Tel: 207-642-5400 *Toll Free Tel:* 800-969-8693 *Fax:* 207-264-3870
E-mail: info@towerpub.com
Web Site: www.towerpub.com
Key Personnel
Publr: Michael Lyons
Mng Ed: Mary Anne Hildreth
Business & manufacturing directories, law publications, business databases.
ISBN Prefix(es): 978-0-89442
Number of titles published annually: 20 Print

Tracks Publishing
140 Brightwood Ave, Chula Vista, CA 91910
Tel: 619-476-7125 *Toll Free Tel:* 800-443-3570 *Fax:* 619-476-8173
E-mail: tracks@cox.net
Web Site: www.startupsports.com
Key Personnel
Owner: Doug Werner
Founded: 1993
ISBN Prefix(es): 978-1-884654; 978-1-935937
Number of titles published annually: 2 Print; 6 E-Book
Total Titles: 45 Print; 135 E-Book
Distribution Center: Independent Publishers Group (IPG), 814 N Franklin St, Chicago, IL 60610 *Tel:* 312-337-0747 *Fax:* 312-337-

5985 *E-mail:* frontdesk@ipgbook.com *Web Site:* www.ipgbook.com
Membership(s): Independent Book Publishers Association

Trafalgar Square Books
388 Howe Hill Rd, North Pomfret, VT 05053
SAN: 213-8859
Mailing Address: PO Box 257, North Pomfret, VT 05053-0257
Tel: 802-457-1911 *Toll Free Tel:* 800-423-4525 *Fax:* 802-457-1913
E-mail: contact@trafalgarbooks.com
Web Site: www.trafalgarbooks.com; www.horseandriderbooks.com
Key Personnel
Pres & Publr: Caroline Robbins
Mng Dir: Martha Cook *E-mail:* mcook@trafalgarbooks.com
Dir, Mktg & Promo: Kim Cook *E-mail:* kcook@trafalgarbooks.com
Mng Ed: Rebecca Didier *E-mail:* rdidier@trafalgarbooks.com
Founded: 1972
ISBN Prefix(es): 978-0-943955; 978-1-57076
Number of titles published annually: 25 Print
Total Titles: 300 Print
Distributor for J A Allen; Kenilworth Press; Pferdia TV
Distribution Center: Ingram Publisher Services, One Ingram Blvd, La Vergne, TN 37086 *Tel:* 615-793-5000 *Toll Free Tel:* 855-867-1920 *Web Site:* www.ingramcontent.com

Trafford
Division of Author Solutions LLC
1663 Liberty Dr, Bloomington, IN 47403
Toll Free Tel: 888-232-4444
E-mail: customersupport@trafford.com; sales@trafford.com
Web Site: www.trafford.com
Key Personnel
SVP, Mktg: Keith Ogorek
SVP, Prodn Servs & Output Opers: Bill Becher
Founded: 1995
The first company in the world to offer an "on-demand publishing service" & led the independent publishing revolution since its establishment. One of the earliest publishers to utilize the Internet for selling books. More than 16,000 authors from over 120 countries have utilized Trafford's experience for self-publishing their books.
This publisher has indicated that 100% of their product line is author subsidized.
ISBN Prefix(es): 978-1-55369; 978-1-55212; 978-1-55395; 978-1-4120; 978-1-4122; 978-1-4251
Number of titles published annually: 800 Print
Total Titles: 2,243 Print
Distribution Center: Baker & Taylor Inc, 2550 W Tyvola Rd, Suite 300, Charlotte, NC 28217 *Tel:* 704-998-3100 *Toll Free Tel:* 800-775-1800 *E-mail:* btinfo@baker-taylor.com *Web Site:* www.btol.com
Ingram Book Group, One Ingram Blvd, La Vergne, TN 37086 *Tel:* 615-793-5000 *Toll Free Tel:* 800-937-8200 *E-mail:* customer.service@ingrambook.com *Web Site:* www.ingrambook.com
Membership(s): ABA; Canadian Booksellers Association

Trans-Atlantic Publications Inc
311 Bainbridge St, Philadelphia, PA 19147
SAN: 694-0234
Tel: 215-925-5083 *Fax:* 215-925-1912
Web Site: www.transatlanticpub.com; www.businesstitles.com
Key Personnel
Pres & Intl Rts: Ronald Smolin
Mgr: Jeff Goldstein *E-mail:* jeffgolds@comcast.net
Founded: 1984
Popular culture.
ISBN Prefix(es): 978-1-891696
Number of titles published annually: 200 Print
Total Titles: 2,500 Print
Imprints: BainBridgeBooks
Distributor for Book Guild; Book House; Financial Times Publishing; Hodder Education; Instituto Monsa de Ediciones SA (art books from Spain); Longman; Arnoldo Mondadori Electa; Nexus Special Interests; Pearson Education; Nelson Thornes

Trans Tech Publications Inc
c/o Enfield Distribution Co, 234 May St, Enfield, NH 03748
Mailing Address: PO Box 699, Enfield, NH 03748-0699
Tel: 603-632-7377 *Fax:* 603-632-5611
E-mail: info@enfieldbooks.com
Web Site: www.ttp.net
Key Personnel
Dir, US Dist: Linda Jones
Founded: 1967
Materials sciences & engineering.
ISBN Prefix(es): 978-0-87849; 978-3-908450
Number of titles published annually: 150 Print
Total Titles: 1,200 Print
Imprints: Scitec Publications
Foreign Office(s): Kreuzstr 10, 8635 Durnten-Zurich, Switzerland *Tel:* (041) 44922 1033
Distributed by Curran Associates Inc; Yankee Book Peddler
Distributor for Enfield Publishers

Transaction Publishers Inc
10 Corporate Place S, Suite 102, Piscataway, NJ 08854
Tel: 732-445-2280; 703-661-1589 (orders) *Toll Free Tel:* 888-999-6778 (dist ctr) *Fax:* 732-445-3138
E-mail: trans@transactionpub.com; orders@transactionpub.om
Web Site: www.transactionpub.com
Key Personnel
Pres: Mary E Curtis *E-mail:* mcurtis@transactionpub.com
Mktg Mgr: Mindy Waizer *E-mail:* mwaizer@transactionpub.com
Rts & Perms Mgr: Jeffrey Stetz *E-mail:* jstetz@transactionpub.com
Admin, Sales & Ordering: Susan Philipsheck *E-mail:* sphilipsheck@transactionpub.com
Founded: 1962
Independent publisher of books & serials in all disciplines of the social sciences & related areas.
ISBN Prefix(es): 978-0-202 (Aldine Transaction); 978-1-56000; 978-0-87855; 978-0-88738; 978-0-7658; 978-1-4128
Number of titles published annually: 120 Print; 100 E-Book
Total Titles: 6,200 Print
Imprints: Aldine Transaction; Center for Urban Policy Research; Transaction Large Print
Distributor for Bridge 21; IWGIA; The Netherlands Institute for Social Research; Editions Scholasticae; Studien Verlag
Foreign Rights: The Asano Agency (Mr Kiyoshi Asano) (Japan); Eliane Benisti Agent Litteraire (Eliane Benisti) (France); Big Apple Agency Inc (Lily Chen) (China, Taiwan); International Editors' Co (Isabel Monteagudo) (Spain); International Editors' Co (Rosa Bertan) (Argentina, Latin America); International Editors' Co (Flavia Sala) (Brazil); Korea Copyright Center Inc (Korea)
Advertising Agency: Paine-Whitman Agency
Returns: 22883 Quicksilver Dr, Dulles, VA 20166 *Fax:* 703-996-1010
Warehouse: PO Box 960, Herndon, VA 20172-0960 *Fax:* 703-996-1010

Transcontinental Music Publications (TMP)
Division of American Conference of Cantors (ACC)
1375 Remington Rd, Suite M, Schaumburg, IL 60173-4844
Tel: 847-781-7800 *Fax:* 847-781-7801
E-mail: tmp@accantors.org
Web Site: www.transcontinentalmusic.com
Key Personnel
COO: Rachel Roth
Founded: 1938
Publishers of Jewish music.
ISBN Prefix(es): 978-1-8074
Number of titles published annually: 50 Print; 5 Audio
Total Titles: 1,000 Print; 75 Audio
Imprints: Hazamir; Theophilis
Membership(s): MPA - The Association of Magazine Media; National Music Publishers' Association

§Transportation Research Board (TRB)
Division of The National Academies of Sciences, Engineering & Medicine
500 Fifth St NW, Washington, DC 20001
Tel: 202-334-3213 (orders); 202-334-3072 (subns) *Fax:* 202-334-2519
E-mail: trbsales@nas.edu
Web Site: trb.org
Key Personnel
Mgr, Pubn Sales & Affiliate Servs: Andrea Kisiner *Tel:* 202-334-3214
Founded: 1920
Research results, TRR (online journal), bibliographies & abstracts on books pertaining to civil engineering, public transit, aviation, freight, transportation administration & economics & transportation law.
ISBN Prefix(es): 978-0-309
Number of titles published annually: 150 Print; 5 CD-ROM; 100 Online
Total Titles: 2,600 Print; 40 CD-ROM; 1,000 Online
Orders to: Lockbox 936135, 3585 Atlanta Ave, Hapeville, GA 30354

Travel Keys
PO Box 160691, Sacramento, CA 95816-0691
SAN: 682-2452
Mailing Address: PO Box 162266, Sacramento, CA 95816-2266
Tel: 916-452-5200 *Fax:* 916-452-5200
Key Personnel
Publr & Ed: Peter B Manston
Ed: Robert C Bynum
Founded: 1984
How-to travel books & antique guides; travel books worldwide; newsletter about travel books.
ISBN Prefix(es): 978-0-931367
Number of titles published annually: 7 Print
Total Titles: 20 Print
Editorial Office(s): PO Box 160691, Sacramento, CA 95816-0691 SAN: 682-2452
Advertising Agency: Travel Key Media, 2510 "S" St, Sacramento, CA 95816-7307
Billing Address: PO Box 160691, Sacramento, CA 95816-0691 SAN: 682-2452
Orders to: PO Box 162266, Sacramento, CA 95816-2266
Returns: PO Box 162266, Sacramento, CA 95816-2266
Shipping Address: Travel Key Media, 2510 "S" St, Sacramento, CA 95816-7307, Contact: P Manuski

Travelers' Tales
Subsidiary of Solas House Inc
2320 Bowdoin St, Palo Alto, CA 94306
Tel: 650-462-2110 *Fax:* 650-462-6305
E-mail: ttales@travelerstales.com
Web Site: travelerstales.com

Key Personnel
Publr: James O'Reilly
Exec Ed: Larry Habegger
Ed-at-Large: Sean O'Reilly
Founded: 1992
Sponsors annual Solas Awards for Best Travel Writing. For more information see www.besttravelwriting.com.
ISBN Prefix(es): 978-1-885211; 978-1-932361
Number of titles published annually: 8 Print; 10 E-Book
Total Titles: 135 Print
Sales Office(s): Publishers Group West, 1700 Fourth St, Berkeley, CA 94710 *Tel:* 510-528-1444 *Fax:* 510-528-3444
Billing Address: Publishers Group West, 1700 Fourth St, Berkeley, CA 94710 *Tel:* 510-528-1444 *Fax:* 510-528-3444
Orders to: Publishers Group West, 1700 Fourth St, Berkeley, CA 94710 *Tel:* 510-528-1444 *Fax:* 510-528-3444
Shipping Address: Perseus PGW, 193 Edwards Dr, Jackson, TN 38301 *Toll Free Tel:* 800-343-4499
Warehouse: Publishers Group West, 1700 Fourth St, Berkeley, CA 94710 *Tel:* 510-528-1444 *Fax:* 510-528-3444
Distribution Center: Publishers Group West, 1700 Fourth St, Berkeley, CA 94710 *Tel:* 510-528-1444 *Fax:* 510-528-3444

Treasure Bay Inc
PO Box 119, Novato, CA 94948
Tel: 415-884-2888 *Fax:* 415-884-2840
E-mail: webothread@comcast.net
Web Site: www.webothread.com
Key Personnel
Pres: Don Panec
Founded: 1997
Publish educational children's books that specialize in books for parent involvement in reading.
ISBN Prefix(es): 978-1-891327; 978-1-60115
Number of titles published annually: 12 Print
Total Titles: 100 Print

Treehaus Communications Inc
PO Box 249, Loveland, OH 45140-0249
Tel: 513-683-5716 *Toll Free Tel:* 800-638-4287 (orders) *Fax:* 513-683-2882 (orders)
E-mail: treehaus@treehaus1.com
Web Site: www.treehaus1.com
Key Personnel
Publr & Owner: Gerard A Pottebaum
Founded: 1972
Children's books, liturgical & catechetical material for children & adults.
ISBN Prefix(es): 978-0-929496; 978-1-886510
Number of titles published annually: 6 Print
Total Titles: 55 Print

Triad Publishing Co
Imprint of Triad Communications Inc
PO Box 13355, Gainesville, FL 32604
Fax: 304-727-9345 *Toll Free Fax:* 800-854-4947
E-mail: orders@triadpublishing.com
Web Site: www.triadpublishing.com
Key Personnel
Pres & Dir: Lorna Rubin *E-mail:* lorna@triadpublishing.com
Order Dept & Cust Rel: Donna L Hamon *E-mail:* donna@triadpublishing.com
Founded: 1971
Consumer health & medical education for professionals.
ISBN Prefix(es): 978-0-937404
Total Titles: 18 Print; 2 CD-ROM; 2 E-Book
Returns: IFM Services, 2302 Kanawha Terr, St Albans, WV 25177
Shipping Address: IFM Services, 2302 Kanawha Terr, St Albans, WV 25177

Membership(s): The Association of Publishers for Special Sales; Independent Book Publishers Association; National Association of Science Writers

The Trinity Foundation
PO Box 68, Unicoi, TN 37692-0068
Tel: 423-743-0199 *Fax:* 423-743-2005
Web Site: www.trinityfoundation.org
Key Personnel
Pres & Dir: Thomas W Juodaitis *E-mail:* tjtrinityfound@aol.com
Founded: 1977
Scholarly Christian books.
ISBN Prefix(es): 978-0-940931; 978-1-891777
Number of titles published annually: 5 Print; 5 E-Book; 1 Audio
Total Titles: 75 Print; 1 CD-ROM; 17 E-Book; 2 Audio

Trinity University Press
Unit of Trinity University
One Trinity Place, San Antonio, TX 78212-7200
Tel: 210-999-8884 *Fax:* 210-999-8838
E-mail: books@trinity.edu
Web Site: www.tupress.org
Key Personnel
Dir: Thomas Payton
Mng Ed: Sarah Nawrocki
Busn Mgr: Lee Ann Sparks
Mktg Mgr: Ms Burgin Streetman
Asst Ed: Steffanie Mortis
Founded: 2002 (after 14 years of inoperation)
Publish titles for the general trade & academic markets.
ISBN Prefix(es): 978-1-59534; 978-0-911536
Number of titles published annually: 12 Print; 12 E-Book
Total Titles: 150 Print; 100 E-Book
Distribution Center: Publishers Group West, 1700 Fourth St, Berkeley, CA 94710 (booksellers & libraries) *Toll Free Tel:* 800-788-3123 *Fax:* 510-528-3614

TripBuilder Media Inc
180 Post Rd E, Suite 200, Westport, CT 06880
SAN: 297-7893
Tel: 203-227-1255 *Toll Free Tel:* 800-525-9745 *Fax:* 203-227-1257
E-mail: info@tripbuildermedia.com
Web Site: www.tripbuildermedia.com
Key Personnel
Pres: Nancy Judson *E-mail:* njudson@tripbuilder.com
EVP: Steven Tanzer
Founded: 1989
Travel guides.
ISBN Prefix(es): 978-1-56621
Number of titles published annually: 20 Print

TriQuarterly Books
Imprint of Northwestern University Press
629 Noyes St, Evanston, IL 60208
Tel: 847-491-7420 *Toll Free Tel:* 800-621-2736 (orders only) *Fax:* 847-491-8150
E-mail: nupress@northwestern.edu
Web Site: www.nupress.northwestern.edu
Key Personnel
Dir: Jane Bunker *Tel:* 847-491-8111 *E-mail:* j-bunker@northwestern.edu
Founded: 1989
Special attention to new writing talent, the noncommercial work of established writers & writing in translation. Special emphasis on poetry.
ISBN Prefix(es): 978-0-8101
Number of titles published annually: 8 Print
Total Titles: 75 Print

TRISTAN Publishing
2355 Louisiana Ave N, Minneapolis, MN 55427
Tel: 763-545-1383 *Toll Free Tel:* 866-545-1383 *Fax:* 763-545-1387
E-mail: info@tristanpublishing.com
Web Site: www.tristanpublishing.com
Key Personnel
Owner & Publr: Brett Waldman *E-mail:* bwaldman@tristanpublishing.com
Owner & VP Sales, Mktg & Relationships: Sheila Waldman *E-mail:* swaldman@tristanpublishing.com
Founded: 2002
Exquisite gift books that inspire, uplift & touch lives.
ISBN Prefix(es): 978-0-931674
Number of titles published annually: 6 Print
Total Titles: 60 Print; 2 Audio
Imprints: TRISTAN OUTDOORS; Waldman House Press

Triumph Books
814 N Franklin St, Chicago, IL 60610
Tel: 312-337-0747 *Toll Free Tel:* 800-888-4741 (cust serv) *Fax:* 312-280-5470; 312-337-5985
Web Site: www.triumphbooks.com
Key Personnel
Pres & Publr: Mitch Rogatz
Edit Dir: Tom Bast
Mktg Mgr: Tom Galvin
Publicist: Samantha Frontera
Founded: 1989
Leading publisher of sports titles & official rule books of NFL, NHL, MLB, NCAA, among others.
ISBN Prefix(es): 978-0-9624436; 978-1-880141; 978-1-57243; 978-1-892049 (Benchmark Press); 978-1-60078; 978-1-62368; 978-1-61749; 978-1-62937
Number of titles published annually: 95 Print; 75 E-Book
Total Titles: 600 Print; 450 E-Book
Imprints: Benchmark Press; Triumph Entertainment
Foreign Rep(s): Monarch Books of Canada (Canada); Peribo Pty Ltd (Australia, New Zealand)
Foreign Rights: RoundHouse Publishing Ltd (Europe, UK)
Returns: Independent Publishers Group (IPG), 600 N Pulaski Rd, Chicago, IL 60624
Distribution Center: Independent Publishers Group (IPG), 600 N Pulaski Rd, Chicago, IL 60624 *E-mail:* orders@ipgbook.com *Web Site:* www.ipgbook.com
Membership(s): ABA

§Triumph Learning LLC
Division of Haights Cross Communications®
136 Madison Ave, 7th fl, New York, NY 10016
Mailing Address: PO Box 1270, Littleton, MA 01460-4270
Tel: 212-652-0200 *Toll Free Tel:* 800-338-6519 (cust serv) *Toll Free Fax:* 866-805-5723
E-mail: info@triumphlearning.com; customerservice@triumphlearning.com
Web Site: www.triumphlearning.com
Key Personnel
CEO: Rick Noble
CFO: Ken Collins
CTO: Aoife Dempsey
Publr: Mike Morley
SVP, Sales: Bonnie Louque
VP, HR: Diane Curtin
Founded: 1964
Print & digital K-12 Common Core resources, standards-aligned instructional materials & effective literacy programs.
ISBN Prefix(es): 978-0-87694; 978-1-58620; 978-1-59823; 978-1-60471; 978-1-60824; 978-1-61997; 978-1-62362; 978-1-62928
Number of titles published annually: 150 Print; 40 CD-ROM
Total Titles: 1,000 Print; 40 CD-ROM

Imprints: Buckle Down; Coach; Jumpstart; Ladders; Options; Plugged-in to Reading; Waggle; Workout
Warehouse: One Beeman Rd, Northborough, MA 01532
Membership(s): AAP

Truman State University Press
Unit of Truman State University
100 E Normal Ave, Kirksville, MO 63501-4221
Tel: 660-785-7336 *Toll Free Tel:* 800-916-6802 *Fax:* 660-785-4480
E-mail: tsup@truman.edu
Web Site: tsup.truman.edu
Key Personnel
Dir & Ed-in-Chief: Barbara Smith-Mandell *E-mail:* bsm@truman.edu
Founded: 1986
University Press, scholarly, early modern studies, American studies, regional & general titles, contemporary nonfiction & poetry.
ISBN Prefix(es): 978-0-940474; 978-0-943549; 978-1-931112; 978-1-935503
Number of titles published annually: 14 Print; 14 E-Book
Total Titles: 200 Print; 80 E-Book
Foreign Rep(s): Gazelle Book Services Ltd (Europe)
Distribution Center: Longleaf Services Inc, 116 S Boundary St, Chapel Hill, NC 27514-3808 *Toll Free Tel:* 800-848-6224 *Toll Free Fax:* 800-272-6817 *E-mail:* orders@longleafservices.org *Web Site:* www.longleafservices.org

Trusted Media Brands Inc
750 Third Ave, 3rd fl, New York, NY 10017
SAN: 212-4416
Toll Free Tel: 800-310-6261 (cust serv)
E-mail: customercare@tmbi.com
Web Site: www.tmbi.com; www.rd.com
Key Personnel
Pres & CEO: Bonnie Kintzer
Chief Content Offr, Reader's Digest: Bruce Kelley
Chief Digital Offr: Vincent Errico
CFO: Dean D Durbin
Chief Mktg Offr: Alec Casey
Chief Revenue Offr, North America: Rich Sutton
SVP, Global HR & Communs: Phyllis Gebhardt
VP, Gen Coun & Secy: Mark Sirota
Divisions: Reader's Digest Trade Publishing
Branch Office(s)
44 S Broadway, White Plains, NY 10601 *Tel:* 914-238-1000
1610 N Second St, Suite 102, Milwaukee, WI 53212
Membership(s): AAP
See separate listing for:
Reader's Digest Trade Publishing

TSG Foundation, see TSG Publishing Foundation Inc

§TSG Publishing Foundation Inc
28641 N 63 Place, Cave Creek, AZ 85331
SAN: 250-6726
Mailing Address: PO Box 7068, Cave Creek, AZ 85327
Tel: 480-502-1909 *Fax:* 480-502-0713
E-mail: info@tsgfoundation.org
Web Site: www.tsgfoundation.org
Key Personnel
Founder, Pres & Dir: Gita Saraydarian *E-mail:* gita@tsgfoundation.org
Founded: 1987
Publish & sell books by Torkom Saraydarian, spiritual training center.
ISBN Prefix(es): 978-0-929874; 978-0-911794; 978-0-9656203
Number of titles published annually: 14 Print
Total Titles: 163 Print; 110 CD-ROM
Foreign Rep(s): TSG (UK) Ltd (Europe, UK)

Tudor Publishers Inc
Subsidiary of Cornwallis Press (young adult fiction & nonfiction)
3109 Shady Lawn Dr, Greensboro, NC 27408
Tel: 336-288-5395
E-mail: tudorpublishers@triad.rr.com
Key Personnel
Pres: Eugene E Pfaff, Jr
Sr Publr: Pamela Cocks
Assoc Ed: Nancy Strange
Founded: 1985
Specialize in adult fiction & nonfiction.
ISBN Prefix(es): 978-0-936389
Number of titles published annually: 12 Print
Total Titles: 80 Print

Tughra Books
Imprint of Blue Dome Inc
335 Clifton Ave, Clifton, NJ 07011
Tel: 973-777-2704 *Fax:* 973-457-7334
E-mail: info@tughrabooks.com
Web Site: www.tughrabooks.com
Key Personnel
Dir, Pubns: Huseyin Senturk *E-mail:* senturk@tughrabooks.com
Dir, Mktg: Ahmet Idil *E-mail:* agi@tughrabooks.com
Sr Ed: Yusuf Alan *E-mail:* alan@tughrabooks.com
Founded: 2001
Publishing, design & printing.
ISBN Prefix(es): 978-975-7388; 978-0-9704370; 978-1-59784
Number of titles published annually: 15 Print
Total Titles: 185 Print
Imprints: The Fountain; The Light
Foreign Rep(s): Gazelle Book Services Ltd (Europe, UK)
Distribution Center: National Book Network (NBN), 4501 Forbes Blvd, Suite 200, Lanham, MD 20706 *Tel:* 301-459-3366 *Fax:* 301-429-5746 *Web Site:* www.nbnbooks.com
Membership(s): AAP; ABA; Independent Book Publishers Association

Tumblehome Learning Inc
201 Newbury St, Suite 201, Boston, MA 02116
E-mail: info@tumblehomelearning.com
Web Site: www.tumblehomelearning.com
Key Personnel
Chair: Penny Noyce *E-mail:* penny@tumblehomelearning.com
Pres: Barnas Monteith *E-mail:* barnas@tumblehomelearning.com
Opers: Yuyi Ling *E-mail:* yuyi@tumblehomelearning.com
Founded: 2010
Helps kids imagine themselves as young scientists & engineers & encourages them to experience science through adventure & discovery. Publish science & adventure mystery stories, picture books & occasional nonfiction.
ISBN Prefix(es): 978-0-9850008; 978-0-9897924; 978-0-9907829; 978-1-943431
Number of titles published annually: 6 Print; 4 Online; 4 E-Book
Total Titles: 18 Print; 6 E-Book
Membership(s): The Children's Book Council; Independent Publishers Group; National Science Teachers Association

Tupelo Press Inc
243 Union St, Suite 305, North Adams, MA 01247
Mailing Address: PO Box 1767, North Adams, MA 01247 SAN: 254-3281
Tel: 413-664-9611 *Fax:* 413-664-9711
E-mail: info@tupelopress.org
Web Site: www.tupelopress.org
Key Personnel
Publr & Ed-in-Chief: Jeffrey Levine *E-mail:* publisher@tupelopress.org
Mng Ed: Jim Schley
Founded: 1999
Independent, nonprofit literary press.
ISBN Prefix(es): 978-1-932195; 978-1-936797
Number of titles published annually: 16 Print; 3 E-Book
Total Titles: 153 Print; 9 E-Book; 12 Audio
Membership(s): Association of Writers and Writing Programs; Community of Literary Magazines & Presses

Turner Publishing Co
4507 Charlotte Ave, Suite 100, Nashville, TN 37209
Tel: 615-255-BOOK (255-2665) *Fax:* 615-255-5081
E-mail: marketing@turnerpublishing.com; submissions@turnerpublishing.com
Web Site: www.turnerpublishing.com; www.facebook.com/turner.publishing
Key Personnel
Pres & Publr: Todd Bottorff
CFO: Angie Lithgow
Acqs & Rts: Stephanie Beard *Tel:* 615-255-2665 ext 105 *E-mail:* sbeard@turnerpublishing.com
Mng Ed: Jon O'Neal *E-mail:* editorial@turnerpublishing.com
Founded: 1984
Trade publisher.
ISBN Prefix(es): 978-0-943763 (GemStone Press); 978-1-879045 (Jewish Lights); 978-1-58023 (Jewish Lights); 978-1-893361 (SkyLight Paths); 978-1-59120 (Basic Health Publications); 978-1-59473 (SkyLight Paths); 978-1-56311
Number of titles published annually: 36 Print
Total Titles: 3,000 Print
Imprints: Ancestry; Basic Health Publications; Christian Journeys; Fieldstone Alliance; GemStone Press; Hunter House; Iroquois Press (fiction); Jewish Lights; Ramsey & Todd; SkyLight Paths; Turner; Wiley
Branch Office(s)
445 Park Ave, 9th fl, New York, NY 10022 *Tel:* 646-291-8961 *Fax:* 646-291-8962
Warehouse: c/o IPS, 1210 Ingram Dr, Chambersburg, PA 17202
Membership(s): AAP; ABA; Independent Book Publishers Association
See separate listing for:
Basic Health Publications
GemStone Press
Jewish Lights
SkyLight Paths

Turtle Point Press
208 Java St, 5th fl, Brooklyn, NY 11222-5748
Tel: 212-741-1393
E-mail: info@turtlepointpress.com
Web Site: www.turtlepointpress.com
Key Personnel
Pres & Intl Rts Contact: Ruth Greenstein *E-mail:* rg@turtlepointpress.com
Founded: 1990
Contemporary & rediscovered fiction, poetry, literary nonfiction.
ISBN Prefix(es): 978-0-9627987; 978-1-885983; 978-1-885583; 978-1-933527
Number of titles published annually: 10 Print
Total Titles: 120 Print
Imprints: Books & Co/Turtle Point; Helen Marx/Turtle Point; Turtle Point
Foreign Rep(s): Turnaround (UK)
Distribution Center: Consortium Book Sales & Distribution, 1094 Flex Dr, Jackson, TN 38301-5070 *Tel:* 612-746-2600 *Toll Free Tel:* 800-283-3572 (cust serv) *Toll Free Fax:* 800-351-5073 *E-mail:* info@cbsd.com *Web Site:* www.cbsd.com

§Tuttle Publishing
Member of Periplus Publishing Group

Airport Business Park, 364 Innovation Dr, North Clarendon, VT 05759-9436
SAN: 213-2621
Tel: 802-773-8930 *Toll Free Tel:* 800-526-2778 *Fax:* 802-773-6993 *Toll Free Fax:* 800-FAX-TUTL (329-8885)
E-mail: info@tuttlepublishing.com; orders@tuttlepublishing.com
Web Site: www.tuttlepublishing.com
Key Personnel
Secy & Owner: Michael Sargent
Pres & CEO: Eric Oey
Publg Dir: Ed Walters
Sales & Mktg Dir: Christopher Johns *E-mail:* cjohns@tuttlepublishing.com
Founded: 1948
Founded by Charles E Tuttle in Tokyo, Tuttle Publishing publishes books to span the East & West, publisher of high quality books & book kits on a wide range of topics including Asian culture, cooking, martial arts, spirituality, philosophy, travel, language, art, architecture & design.
ISBN Prefix(es): 978-0-8048; 978-4-333 (Kosei Publishing Co); 978-1-85391 (Merehurst Ltd); 978-0-460 (Everyman Paperbacks); 978-4-07 (Shufunotomo Co); 978-4-900737; 978-962-593 (Periplus Editions); 978-0-945971 (Periplus Editions); 978-0-935621 (Healing Tao Books); 978-0-933756 (Paperweight Press); 978-0-7946 (Periplus Editions); 978-0-970171 (Kotan); 978-1-840590 (Milet); 978-4-8053
Number of titles published annually: 152 Print
Total Titles: 2,000 Print; 20 Audio
Imprints: Everyman's Classic Library in Paperback; Kosei Publishing Co; Kotan Publishing Inc; Merehurst Ltd; Milet Publishing Ltd; Periplus Editions
Foreign Office(s): Yaekari Bldg, 3rd fl, 5-4-12 Osaki, 141-0032 Shinagawa-ku, Tokyo 141-0032, Japan *Tel:* (03) 5437 0171 *Fax:* (03) 5437 0755 *E-mail:* sales@tuttle.co.jp *Web Site:* www.tuttle.co.jp
Distributed by Publishers Group West (digital only)
Distributor for Healing Tao Books; Kosei Publishing Co; Kotan Publishing Inc; Milet Publishing Ltd; Paperweight Press; Periplus Editions; Shanghai Press; Shufunotomo Co; Tai Chi Foundation
Foreign Rep(s): Bill Bailey Publishers Representatives (Europe); Berkeley Books Pte Ltd (Southeast Asia); Humphrys Roberts Associates (Caribbean, Central America, Mexico); IMA/Intermediaamericana Ltd (David Williams) (South America); Publishers Group Canada (Canada); Publishers Group UK (UK); Trinity Books (South Africa); Van Ditmar Boekenimport BV (Netherlands); Ward Intl (Book Exports) Ltd (Richard Ward) (Middle East)

Tuxedo Press
546 E Springville Rd, Carlisle, PA 17015
Tel: 717-258-9733 *Fax:* 717-243-0074
E-mail: info@tuxedo-press.com
Web Site: tuxedo-press.com
Key Personnel
Publr: Thomas R Benjey *E-mail:* tom@tuxedo-press.com
Assoc Ed: Ann Fitch *E-mail:* ann@tuxedo-press.com
Founded: 2005
Small press of nonfiction books. Titles released to date have been historical in nature. Future releases may also include political topics. New releases are offset print; reprints are POD. Considering expansion to audiobooks. Titles are of US interest only.
ISBN Prefix(es): 978-0-9774486; 978-1-936161
Number of titles published annually: 3 Print
Total Titles: 15 Print; 3 E-Book

Advertising Agency: Anne Dozier & Associates, 313 E 84 St, Suite 1-B, New York, NY 10028, Contact: Anne Dozier *Tel:* 212-717-0276 *E-mail:* annedozier@aol.com
Orders to: Ingram Book Co, 14 Ingram Blvd, La Vergne, TN 37086 *Tel:* 615-213-5335 *Fax:* 615-213-5430
Distribution Center: Ingram Book Co, 14 Ingram Blvd, La Vergne, TN 37086 *Tel:* 615-213-5335 *Fax:* 615-213-5430
Membership(s): Independent Book Publishers Association

Twenty-First Century Books
Imprint of Lerner Publishing Group Inc
241 First Ave N, Minneapolis, MN 55401
Tel: 612-332-3344 *Toll Free Tel:* 800-328-4929 *Fax:* 612-332-7615 *Toll Free Fax:* 800-332-1132
E-mail: info@lernerbooks.com; custserve@lernerbooks.com
Web Site: www.lernerbooks.com; www.facebook.com/lernerbooks
Key Personnel
Chmn: Harry J Lerner
CFO & EVP: Margaret Thomas
Pres & Publr: Adam Lerner
EVP, Sales: David Wexler
VP, Ed-in-Chief: Patricia M Stockland
Edit Dir: Domenica Di Piazza
Dir of Rts, Spec Sales & Intl Dist: Maria Kjoller
Group Mktg Dir: Jill Braithwaite
School & Lib Mktg Dir: Lois Wallentine
Dir, HR: Cyndi Radant
Publisher of nonfiction books for the upper grades & young adults.
ISBN Prefix(es): 978-0-8050; 978-1-56294; 978-0-7613; 978-0-941477
Total Titles: 480 Print; 255 E-Book
Foreign Rep(s): INT Press Distribution (Australia); Phambili (Southern Africa); Publishers Marketing Service (Brunei, Malaysia, Singapore); South Pacific Books (New Zealand)
Foreign Rights: Sandra Bruna Agencia Literaria (Spain); Japan Foreign-Rights Centre (Japan); Korea Copyright Center (Korea); Michelle Lapautre Agence Junior (France)
Warehouse: Lerner Publishing Group, 1251 Washington Ave N, Minneapolis, MN 55401, Mgr: Ken Rued

§Twenty-Third Publications
Division of Bayard Inc
One Montauk Ave, Suite 200, New London, CT 06320
Tel: 860-437-3012 *Toll Free Tel:* 800-321-0411 (orders) *Toll Free Fax:* 800-572-0788
E-mail: resources@twentythirdpublications.com
Web Site: www.twentythirdpublications.com
Key Personnel
VP & Edit Dir: Dan Connors *E-mail:* dan.connors@bayard-inc.com
Publr: Therese Ratliff *E-mail:* tratliff@twentythirdpublications.com
Art Dir: Jeff McCall *E-mail:* jeff.mccall@bayard-inc.com
Mktg Dir: Dan Smart *E-mail:* dsmart@twentythirdpublications.com
Assoc Dir, Sales & Mktg: Kerry Moriarty
Founded: 1967
ISBN Prefix(es): 978-0-89622; 978-1-58595
Number of titles published annually: 45 Print; 6 CD-ROM
Total Titles: 450 Print; 24 CD-ROM
Distributed by Columba (UK); John Garrett (Australia); Novalis (Canada)
Distributor for Novalis (Canada)
Foreign Rights: Bayard Presse International (Asia, Central Europe, Eastern Europe)
Membership(s): Association of Catholic Publishers Inc; Catholic Press Association

§Twilight Times Books
PO Box 3340, Kingsport, TN 37664-0340
Tel: 423-323-0183 *Fax:* 423-323-0183
E-mail: publisher@twilighttimes.com
Web Site: www.twilighttimesbooks.com
Key Personnel
Publr: Lida E Quillen
Mng Ed: Ardy M Scott
Ed: Eric Olsen
Tech Support: Michael D Bobbitt
Founded: 1999
Royalty paying small press trade publisher of speculative fiction. Our mission is to promote excellence in writing & great literature. Currently publishing limited edition hardcover, first edition trade paperback books & ebooks as downloads in various formats.
ISBN Prefix(es): 978-1-931201; 978-1-933353; 978-1-60619
Number of titles published annually: 14 Print; 14 E-Book
Total Titles: 110 Print; 150 E-Book
Imprints: Paladin Timeless Books; Twilight Visions
Distribution Center: Brodart Co, 50 Arch St, Williamsport, PA 17701 *Tel:* 570-326-2461 *Toll Free Tel:* 800-474-9816 *Toll Free Fax:* 800-999-6799 *E-mail:* support@brodart.com *Web Site:* www.brodart.com
Follett Library Resources, 1340 Ridgeview Dr, McHenry, IL 60050-7048
Membership(s): AAP; The Association of Publishers for Special Sales; Electronically Published Internet Connection; Independent Book Publishers Association; Small Publishers, Artists & Writers Network; Speculative Literature Foundation

Two Thousand Three Associates
135 Chilean Ave, Palm Beach, FL 33480
Tel: 386-690-2503
E-mail: ttta1@att.net
Web Site: www.twothousandthree.com
Key Personnel
Intl Rts & Lib Sales Dir: Frederick B Smith
Mktg Dir: Hank Hankshaw
Publicity Dir: Barbara Brent
Asst to Pres: Geoffery Crawford Tell
Founded: 1995
Nonfiction including memoirs, humor, sports & travel.
ISBN Prefix(es): 978-0-9639905; 978-1-892285
Number of titles published annually: 4 Print
Total Titles: 16 Print
Membership(s): Independent Publishers Association; Independent Publishers Group

§Tyndale House Publishers Inc
351 Executive Dr, Carol Stream, IL 60188
SAN: 206-7749
Tel: 630-668-8300 *Toll Free Tel:* 800-323-9400 *Toll Free Fax:* 800-684-0247
Web Site: www.tyndale.com
Key Personnel
CEO & Chmn of the Bd: Mark Taylor
Pres & COO: Jeff Johnson
SVP & Group Publr: Ron Beers
VP, Publg Servs: CJ Van Wagner
Sr Dir, Digital Publg: Alan Huizenga
Dir, Intl Publg: James Elwell
PR Dir: Todd Starowitz
Spec Sales Mgr: Charlie Swaney
Founded: 1962
Religion: hardcover & paperback originals & reprints, ebooks, Bibles, reference, DVDs, audio CDs & software.
ISBN Prefix(es): 978-0-8423; 978-1-4143
Number of titles published annually: 125 Print; 1 CD-ROM; 73 Online; 75 E-Book; 25 Audio
Total Titles: 1,000 Print; 5 CD-ROM; 300 E-Book; 225 Audio
Imprints: BarnaBooks (George Barna titles); Living Books (mass mkt pbk); Resurgence

(Mars Hill Church); SaltRiver (deeper Christian thought); Tyndale Audio (adult audiobooks); Tyndale Entertainment (kids' audio/video products); Tyndale Kids (children's); Tyndale Momentum; Tyndale Ninos (Spanish children's)
Distributor for Focus on the Family; NavPress
Advertising Agency: Design Promotion
Membership(s): Evangelical Christian Publishers Association

UCLA Latin American Center Publications
UCLA Latin American Institute, 10343 Bunche Hall, Los Angeles, CA 90095
Mailing Address: PO Box 951447, Los Angeles, CA 90095-1447
Tel: 310-825-4571 *Fax:* 310-206-6859
E-mail: latinamctr@international.ucla.edu
Web Site: www.international.ucla.edu/lai
Key Personnel
Dir: Kevin Terraciano *E-mail:* terraciano@international.ucla.edu
Exec Dir: David Arriaza
Dir, Pubns: Orchid Mazurkiewicz
Founded: 1959
Scholarly books & journals in Latin American studies.
ISBN Prefix(es): 978-0-87903
Number of titles published annually: 6 Print; 1 CD-ROM; 1 Online
Total Titles: 124 Print; 1 CD-ROM; 1 Online

Ugly Duckling Presse
The Old American Can Factory, 232 Third St, Suite E303, Brooklyn, NY 11215
Tel: 347-948-5170
E-mail: info@uglyducklingpresse.org
Web Site: www.uglyducklingpresse.org
Key Personnel
Pres: Matvei Yankelevich
Mng Ed: Anna Moschovakis
Ed: Gregory L Ford; Emmalea Russo
Artist Book Ed: Ellie Ga
Founded: 1993
A nonprofit arts & publishing collective.
ISBN Prefix(es): 978-0-9727684
Number of titles published annually: 20 Print; 2 Audio
Total Titles: 200 Print
Imprints: Dossier; Emergency Gazette; Houston European Poetry Series; Knock-off Books; New York Nights; Senal; 6 x 6 Magazine
Distributor for United Artists
Membership(s): Community of Literary Magazines & Presses

Ulysses Press
PO Box 3440, Berkeley, CA 94703-0440
Tel: 510-601-8301 *Toll Free Tel:* 800-377-2542 *Fax:* 510-601-8307
E-mail: ulysses@ulyssespress.com
Web Site: www.ulyssespress.com
Key Personnel
Publr: Ray Riegert *E-mail:* rayriegert@ulyssespress.com
EVP: Bryce Willett *E-mail:* brycewillett@ulyssespress.com
Founded: 1983
Health & fitness books, cookbooks, pop culture & trivia, lifestyle, crafts & hobbies titles, mind, body & spirit.
ISBN Prefix(es): 978-0-915233; 978-1-56975
Number of titles published annually: 50 Print
Total Titles: 150 Print
Imprints: Hidden Travel Series; Seastone
Foreign Rep(s): Hi Marketing (Central America, Continental Europe, Far East, South Africa, South America, UK); Raincoast Book Distribution Ltd (Canada)
Foreign Rights: InterLicense
Shipping Address: 3286 Adeline St, Suite 1, Berkeley, CA 94703 *Toll Free Tel:* 800-377-2542
Distribution Center: Publishers Group West
Membership(s): Independent Book Publishers Association; SATW

Unarius Academy of Science Publications
Division of Unarius Educational Foundation
145 S Magnolia Ave, El Cajon, CA 92020-4522
SAN: 168-9614
Tel: 619-444-7062 *Toll Free Tel:* 800-475-7062 *Fax:* 619-444-9637
E-mail: uriel@unarius.org
Web Site: www.unarius.org
Key Personnel
Ed: Celeste Appel
Founded: 1954
Books, CDs/MP3s & DVDs/MP4s describing a new science of life, past life therapy, extraterrestrial civilizations, the prehistory of earth, the psychology of consciousness: a course in self-mastery. Unarius provides the foundation for personal growth that will lead to the development of self-mastery & the clairvoyant aptitudes of the mind. Classes in past-life therapy are webcast on Sunday & Wednesday 7pm PT.
ISBN Prefix(es): 978-0-932642; 978-0-935097
Number of titles published annually: 4 Print
Total Titles: 90 Print; 70 Audio
Divisions: Audio Books; Unarius Video Productions; Visionary Art

Editorial Unilit
Division of Spanish House Inc
8167 NW 84 St, Medley, FL 33166
Tel: 305-592-6136 *Toll Free Tel:* 800-767-7726 *Fax:* 305-592-0087
E-mail: info@editorialunilit.com; customerservice@editorialunilit.com
Web Site: www.editorialunilit.com
Key Personnel
Pres: David Ecklebarger
Sales Mgr: Mariana Tafura *E-mail:* mariana@editorialunilit.com
Mktg Coord: Hilda Urra *E-mail:* hilda@editorialunilit.com
Founded: 1989
Publishing for the Spanish family.
ISBN Prefix(es): 978-1-56063; 978-0-7899; 978-0-945792
Number of titles published annually: 120 Print
Total Titles: 800 Print
Membership(s): CBA; Evangelical Christian Publishers Association; SEPA

The United Educators Inc
900 W North Shore Dr, Suite 276, Lake Bluff, IL 60044
SAN: 204-8795
Tel: 847-234-3700 *Toll Free Tel:* 800-323-5875 *Fax:* 847-234-8705
Key Personnel
Pres: Peter Ewing
Secy: Christine Ewing
Founded: 1993
Encyclopedias & subscription books.
ISBN Prefix(es): 978-0-87566
Subsidiaries: Standard Educational Corp

§United Nations Publications
300 E 42 St, 9th fl, New York, NY 10017
SAN: 206-6718
Tel: 703-661-1571 *Fax:* 703-996-1010
E-mail: publications@un.org
Web Site: shop.un.org
Key Personnel
Chief: Sherri Aldis *E-mail:* aldis@un.org
Acqs Offr: Nicolas Bovay *E-mail:* bovay@un.org
Sales & Mktg Offr: Irina Lumelsky *E-mail:* lumelsky@un.org
Founded: 1946
Promotes the knowledge & work of the UN to scholars, information specialists, policy-makers & influencers. We publish approximately 500 new titles per year in economic & social development, international law & justice, peacekeeping & security, human rights & refugees, natural resources & more.
ISBN Prefix(es): 978-92-1 (United Nations Publications); 978-92-807 (UNEP); 978-92-808 (United Nations University); 978-92-806 (UNICEF); 978-88-000 (UNICEF); 978-184-966 (DESA); 978-1-849 (UNEP); 978-1-618 (UNFPA); 978-92-9137 (ITC)
Number of titles published annually: 500 Print; 60 Online
Total Titles: 2,300 Print; 35 CD-ROM; 160 E-Book
Sales Office(s): Books International, PO Box 960, Herndon, VA 20172
Distributor for Food & Agriculture Organization of the United Nations (FAO); International Atomic Energy Agency (IAEA); International Criminal Tribunal for Rwanda (UNICTR); International Criminal Tribunal for the former Yugoslavia (ICTY); International Organization for Migration (IOM); International Trade Centre (ITC); Office of the United Nations High Commissioner for Human Rights (OHCHR); United Nations Children's Fund (UNICEF); United Nations Development Programme (UNDP); United Nations Economic & Social Commission for Asia & the Pacific (ESCAP); United Nations Economic & Social Commission for Western Asia (ESCWA); United Nations Economic Commission for Africa (ECA); United Nations Economic Commission for Europe (ECE); United Nations Economic Commission for Latin America & the Caribbean (ECLAC); United Nations High Commissioner for Refugees (UNHCR); United Nations Human Settlements Programme (UN-HABITAT); United Nations Industrial Development Organization (UNIDO); United Nations Institute for Disarmament Research (UNIDIR); United Nations Institute for Training & Research (UNITAR); United Nations International Research & Training Institute for the Advancement of Women (INSTRAW); United Nations Interregional Crime & Justice Research Institute (UNICRI); United Nations Office for Project Services (UNOPS); United Nations Office for the Coordination of Humanitarian Affairs (OCHA); United Nations Office on Drugs & Crime (UNODC); United Nations Population Fund (UNFPA); United Nations Research Institute for Social Development (UNRISD); United Nations University (UNU)
Foreign Rep(s): Eurospan Group (Africa, Asia, China, Europe, Hong Kong, Middle East, Taiwan)
Returns: Books International, 22883 Quicksilver Dr, Dulles, VA 20166
Shipping Address: Books International, PO Box 960, Herndon, VA 20172
Warehouse: Books International, 22883 Quicksilver Dr, Dulles, VA 20166

§United States Holocaust Memorial Museum
100 Raoul Wallenberg Place SW, Washington, DC 20024-2126
Tel: 202-314-7837; 202-488-6144 (orders) *Toll Free Tel:* 800-259-9998 (orders) *Fax:* 202-479-9726; 202-488-0438 (orders)
E-mail: cahs_publications@ushmm.org
Web Site: www.ushmm.org
Key Personnel
Dir, Academic Pubns, Jack, Joseph & Morton Mandel Center for Advanced Holocaust Studies: Benton M Arnovitz *Tel:* 202-488-6117 *E-mail:* barnovitz@ushmm.org
Dir, Museum Bookstore & Holocaust Lib Sales Opers: Jerry Rehm
Emerging Scholars Prog Offr: Steven Feldman
Pubns Offr, Mandel Ctr Staff Applied Res Projs: Mel Hecker

Creative Servs, Prodn: Amy Donovan
Exhibitions Projs: Ted Phillips
Perms: Karen Coe
Founded: 1993
Co-publish original monographs, translations, classic reprints, testimonial materials & a scholarly journal; publish memoirs & related titles of Holocaust Publications' Holocaust Library imprint (assets acquired in 1993) as well as occasional papers, exhibition catalogues & related works.
ISBN Prefix(es): 978-0-89604
Number of titles published annually: 12 Print
Total Titles: 150 Print
Imprints: Holocaust Library
Foreign Rights: Goldfarb & Associates (selected titles)

United States Institute of Peace Press
2301 Constitution Ave NW, Washington, DC 20037
Tel: 202-457-1700 (edit); 703-661-1590 (cust serv) *Toll Free Tel:* 800-868-8064 (cust serv) *Fax:* 202-429-6063; 703-661-1501 (cust serv)
E-mail: usipmail@presswarehouse.com (orders)
Web Site: bookstore.usip.org
Key Personnel
Ed: James Rupert
Founded: 1989
Area of international peacebuilding, policy analysis & conflict resolution. Primarily publish research results from grants, fellowship & commissioned research.
This publisher has indicated that 100% of their product line is author subsidized.
ISBN Prefix(es): 978-1-878379; 978-1-929223; 978-1-601270
Number of titles published annually: 10 Print
Total Titles: 160 Print
Orders to: PO Box 605, Herndon, VA 20172-0605 (sales & returns/bookseller, wholesaler & instl) *E-mail:* usipmail@presswarehouse.com SAN: 254-6965
Shipping Address: 22883 Quicksilver Dr, Dulles, VA 20166 (indiv returns)

United States Pharmacopeia
12601 Twinbrook Pkwy, Rockville, MD 20852-1790
Tel: 301-881-0666 *Toll Free Tel:* 800-227-8772 *Fax:* 301-816-8237 (mktg)
E-mail: marketing@usp.org
Web Site: www.usp.org
Key Personnel
CEO: Ronald T Piervincenzi, PhD
Founded: 1820
Reference books & directories; Databases in print & electronic formats.
ISBN Prefix(es): 978-0-913595
Number of titles published annually: 5 Print
Total Titles: 25 Print; 2 CD-ROM
Distributed by Consumer Reports
Foreign Rep(s): Deutscher Apotheker Verlag (Austria, Germany, Switzerland); Login Canada (Canada); Maruzen Co Ltd (Japan); Pharmaceutical Society of Australia (Australia); Pharmasystems (Canada); Ernesto Reichmann Distribuidora de Livros Ltda (Brazil)
Distribution Center: Matthews Book Co, 11559 Rock Island Ct, Maryland Heights, MO 63043 *Tel:* 314-432-1400 *Toll Free Fax:* 800-421-8816
Rittenhouse Book Distributors, Inc, 522 Feheley Dr, King of Prussia, PA 19406 *Toll Free Tel:* 800-345-6425 *Toll Free Fax:* 800-223-7488
National Technical Information Service, 5285 Port Royal Rd, Springfield, VA 22161 *Tel:* 703-487-4825 *Fax:* 703-487-4098
Promachem LLC, PO Box 1126, 2931 Soldier Springs Rd, Laramie, WY 82070 *Tel:* 307-742-6343 *Fax:* 307-745-7936
Login Canada, 300 Saulteaux Crescent, Winnipeg, MB R3J 3T2, Canada *Tel:* 204-837-2987 (cust serv) *Toll Free Tel:* 800-665-1148 (cust serv) *Web Site:* lb.ca

United States Tennis Association
70 W Red Oak Lane, White Plains, NY 10604
Tel: 914-696-7000 *Fax:* 914-696-7027
Web Site: www.usta.com
Key Personnel
Dir, Publg: Richard S Rennert *E-mail:* rennert@usta.com
Founded: 1881
Tennis materials; books, magazines & souvenir programs.
ISBN Prefix(es): 978-0-938822
Number of titles published annually: 5 Print
Total Titles: 25 Print
Distributed by Triumph Books; Universe Publishing; H O Zimman Inc

Univelt Inc
Affiliate of American Astronautical Society
740 Metcalf St, No 13, Escondido, CA 92025
Mailing Address: PO Box 28130, San Diego, CA 92198-0130
Tel: 760-746-4005 *Fax:* 760-746-3139
E-mail: sales@univelt.com
Web Site: www.univelt.com; www.astronautical.org
Key Personnel
Pres & Publr: Robert H Jacobs
Founded: 1970
Publisher for American Astronautical Society, International Academy of Astronautics, Lunar & Planetary Society, National Space Society. Specialize in astronautics & aerospace engineering.
ISBN Prefix(es): 978-0-912183; 978-0-87703
Number of titles published annually: 10 Print; 6 CD-ROM
Total Titles: 363 Print
Distributor for Astronautical Society of Western Australia; US Space Foundation

Universal-Publishers Inc
23331 Water Circle, Boca Raton, FL 33486-8540
SAN: 299-3635
Tel: 561-750-4344 *Toll Free Tel:* 800-636-8329 (US only) *Fax:* 561-750-6797
Web Site: www.universal-publishers.com
Key Personnel
Publr & CEO: Jeffrey R Young
Artistic & Edit Dir: Shereen Siddiqui, PhD
Prodn Ed: Christie Mayer
Founded: 1997
Dictionaries, encyclopedias, textbooks-all, university presses. Scholarly books, reprints, professional books, paperbacks, directories & reference books.
ISBN Prefix(es): 978-1-58112; 978-1-59942; 978-1-61233; 978-1-62734
Number of titles published annually: 60 Print; 50 E-Book
Total Titles: 1,500 Print; 1,000 E-Book
Imprints: Brown Walker Press; Dissertation.com
Distribution Center: Ingram Book Group, One Ingram Blvd, La Vergne, TN 37086 *Tel:* 615-793-5000 *Web Site:* www.ingramcontent.com
Bertrams, One Broadland Business Park, Norwich NR7 0WF, United Kingdom *E-mail:* books@bertrams.com *Web Site:* www.bertrams.com
See separate listing for:
Dissertation.com

Universe Publishing
Imprint of Rizzoli International Publications Inc
300 Park Ave S, 4th fl, New York, NY 10010
Tel: 212-387-3400 *Fax:* 212-387-3535
Founded: 1956
Architecture, fine art, photography, illustrated gift books, fashion, culinary, popular culture, children's, design, style & calendars.
ISBN Prefix(es): 978-0-87663; 978-1-55550; 978-0-7893
Number of titles published annually: 60 Print
Imprints: Universe; Universe Calendars
Distributed by Random House
Foreign Rep(s): Bill Bailey (Central Europe), Bookport Associates (Southern Europe); Michelle Curreri (Asia); Hi Marketing (UK); IMA (Eastern Europe); IPR (Middle East); Marston Book Services Ltd (Europe, UK); Random House (Canada); Murray Sutton (Scandinavia); Cynthia Zimpfer (Latin America)

University Council for Educational Administration
University of Virginia, Curry School of Education, 405 Emmet St S, Ruffner Hall, Rm 400287, Charlottesville, VA 22903-2424
Tel: 434-243-1041
E-mail: ucea.org@gmail.com
Web Site: www.ucea.org
Key Personnel
Exec Dir: Michelle D Young *E-mail:* mdy8n@virginia.edu
Founded: 1947
Books, journals, monographs, newsletters.
ISBN Prefix(es): 978-1-55996
Number of titles published annually: 5 Print
Total Titles: 23 Print

University of Alabama Press
200 Hackberry Lane, 2nd fl, Tuscaloosa, AL 35487
Mailing Address: PO Box 870380, Tuscaloosa, AL 35487-0380
Tel: 205-348-5180 *Fax:* 205-348-9201
Web Site: www.uapress.ua.edu
Key Personnel
Dir: Linda Manning *Tel:* 205-348-1560 *E-mail:* lmanning@uapress.ua.edu
Ed-in-Chief: Daniel Waterman *Tel:* 205-348-5538 *E-mail:* dwaterman@uapress.ua.edu
Mng Ed: Vanessa Rusch *Tel:* 205-348-9708 *E-mail:* vrusch@uapress.ua.edu
Busn Mgr: Rosalyn Carr *Tel:* 205-348-1567 *E-mail:* rcarr@uapress.ua.edu
Prodn Mgr: W Richard Cook *Tel:* 205-348-1571 *E-mail:* rcook@uapress.ua.edu
Rts & Perms Mgr: Claire Lewis Evans *Tel:* 205-348-1561 *E-mail:* levans@uapress.ua.edu
Sales Mgr: Kristi Henson *Tel:* 205-348-9534 *E-mail:* khenson@uapress.ua.edu
Mktg Coord: Blanche Sarratt *Tel:* 205-348-3476 *E-mail:* bsarratt@uapress.ua.edu
Founded: 1945
American & Latin American history & culture, religious & ethnohistory, rhetoric & communications, African American & Native American studies, Judaic studies, Southern regional studies, theatre & regional trade titles.
ISBN Prefix(es): 978-0-8173; 978-0-914590; 978-0-932511; 978-1-57366
Number of titles published annually: 70 Print; 25 E-Book
Total Titles: 1,200 Print; 100 E-Book
Imprints: Fiction Collective 2 (FC2)
Foreign Rep(s): East-West Export Books (Asia, Australia, Hawaii, New Zealand); Eurospan (Europe); Scholarly Book Services (Canada)
Distribution Center: Chicago Distribution Center, 11030 S Langley, Chicago, IL 60628 (orders) *Tel:* 773-702-7000 (orders) *Toll Free Tel:* 800-621-2736 (orders) *Fax:* 773-702-7212 *Toll Free Fax:* 800-621-8476 SAN: 630-6047
See separate listing for:
Fiction Collective Two Inc (FC2)

§University of Alaska Press
1760 Westwood Way, Fairbanks, AK 99709
SAN: 203-3011

Mailing Address: PO Box 756240, Fairbanks, AK 99775-6240
Tel: 907-474-5831 *Toll Free Tel:* 888-252-6657 (US only) *Fax:* 907-474-5502
Web Site: www.alaska.edu/uapress
Key Personnel
Mgr: Amy Simpson *E-mail:* amy.simpson@alaska.edu
Sales & Mktg Mgr: Laura Walker *E-mail:* laura.walker@alaska.edu
Prodn Ed: Krista West *Tel:* 907-474-6413 *E-mail:* krista.west@alaska.edu
Founded: 1967
Emphasis on scholarly & nonfiction works related to Alaska, the circumpolar regions & the North Pacific rim.
ISBN Prefix(es): 978-0-912006; 978-1-889963; 978-1-60223
Number of titles published annually: 24 Print
Total Titles: 220 Print
Imprints: Alaska Writer Laureate Series; Classic Reprint Series; Geology & Geography of Alaska Series; Great Explorer Series; Lantern-Light Library; Literary Reprint Series; Oral Biography Series; Rasmuson Library Historical Translation Series; Snowy Owl Books
Distributor for Alaska Native Language Center; Alaska Quarterly Review; Alaska Sea Grant; Alutiiq Museum; Anchorage Museum Association; Anchorage Museum of Art History; Arctic Studies Center of the Smithsonian Museum; Far to the North Press; Geophysical Institute; Limestone Press; Spirit Mountain Press; UA Museum; Vanessapress
Distribution Center: Chicago Distribution Center, 11030 S Langley Ave, Chicago, IL 60628 (for orders outside Alaska) *Toll Free Tel:* 800-621-2736 *Toll Free Fax:* 800-621-8476
Membership(s): Alaska History Association; Alaska Library Association; Association of American University Presses; Independent Book Publishers Association; Pacific Northwest Booksellers Association

The University of Arizona Press
1510 E University Blvd, Tucson, AZ 85721
SAN: 205-468X
Mailing Address: PO Box 210055, Tucson, AZ 85721-0055
Tel: 520-621-1441 *Toll Free Tel:* 800-426-3797 (orders) *Fax:* 520-621-8899 *Toll Free Fax:* 800-426-3797
E-mail: uap@uapress.arizona.edu
Web Site: www.uapress.arizona.edu
Key Personnel
Dir: Kathryn Conrad *E-mail:* kconrad@uapress.arizona.edu
Ed-in-Chief: Kristen Buckles *E-mail:* kbuckles@uapress.arizona.edu
Sr Ed: Dr Allyson Carter *E-mail:* allysonc@uapress.arizona.edu
Editing & Prodn Mgr: Amanda Krause *E-mail:* akrause@uapress.arizona.edu
Publicity Mgr: Rosemary Brandt *Tel:* 520-621-3920 *E-mail:* rbrande@uapress.arizona.edu
Founded: 1959
Scholarly & regional nonfiction about Arizona, the American West & Mexico, Latino studies, Latin American studies, Native American studies, anthropology & environmental studies.
ISBN Prefix(es): 978-0-8165
Number of titles published annually: 55 Print
Total Titles: 783 Print
Foreign Rep(s): East-West Export Books (Asia, The Pacific); William Gills (Africa, Europe, Middle East); University of British Columbia Press (Canada)
Membership(s): American Association of University Presses; Arizona Book Publishing Association; Publishers Association of the West

The University of Arkansas Press
Division of The University of Arkansas
McIlroy House, 105 N McIlroy Ave, Fayetteville, AR 72701
Tel: 479-575-3246 *Toll Free Tel:* 800-626-0090 *Fax:* 479-575-6044
E-mail: info@uapress.com
Web Site: www.uapress.com
Key Personnel
Dir: Mike Bieker *Tel:* 479-575-3859 *E-mail:* mbieker@uark.edu
Mktg Dir: Melissa King *Tel:* 479-575-7715 *E-mail:* mak001@uark.edu
Busn & Dist Servs Mgr: Sam Ridge *Tel:* 479-575-3858 *E-mail:* sridge@uark.edu
Edit & Prodn Mgr: Brian King *Tel:* 479-575-6780 *E-mail:* brking@uark.edu
Sr Ed: David Scott Cunningham *Tel:* 479-575-5767 *E-mail:* dscunnin@uark.edu
Founded: 1980
General humanities: popular culture, Middle East studies, Civil War & civil rights studies.
ISBN Prefix(es): 978-0-938626; 978-1-55728; 978-0-912456
Number of titles published annually: 20 Print
Total Titles: 560 Print; 150 E-Book
Distributor for Butler Center for Arkansas Studies; Hearne Fine Art; Moon City Press; Ozark Society; Phoenix International
Foreign Rep(s): Eurospan Group (Africa, Asia-Pacific, Continental Europe, Middle East, UK); Scholarly Book Services (Bev Calder) (Canada)
Foreign Rights: Eurospan (Africa, Europe, Middle East, UK)
Advertising Agency: Ad Lib *Fax:* 479-575-6044
Distribution Center: Chicago Distribution Center, 11030 S Langley Ave, Chicago, IL 60628 *Tel:* 773-702-7000 *Toll Free Tel:* 800-621-2736 *Fax:* 773-702-7212 *E-mail:* orders@press.uchicago.edu
Membership(s): American Association of University Presses

University of California, ANR Publications, see ANR Publications University of California

§University of California Institute on Global Conflict & Cooperation
Subsidiary of University of California
9500 Gilman Dr, MC 0518, La Jolla, CA 92093-0518
Tel: 858-534-6106 *Fax:* 858-534-7655
E-mail: igcc-communications@ucsd.edu
Web Site: igcc.ucsd.edu
Key Personnel
Mng Ed: Lynne Bush *Tel:* 858-534-1979 *E-mail:* lbush@ucsd.edu
Founded: 1983
Policy briefs & newsletters, policy papers & books authored by members of the University of California faculty & other participants in sponsored research programs.
ISBN Prefix(es): 978-0-934637
Number of titles published annually: 2 Print
Total Titles: 74 Print; 60 E-Book
Distributed by Brookings Institution Press; Columbia International Affairs Online (CIAO); Cornell University Press; Garland Publishers; Lynn-Reinner Publishing; Penn State University Press; Princeton University Press; Transaction Publishers; University of Michigan Press; Westview Press

§University of California Press
155 Grand Ave, Suite 400, Oakland, CA 94612-3758
Tel: 510-883-8232 *Fax:* 510-836-8910
E-mail: customerservice@ucpressjournals.com
Web Site: www.ucpress.edu
Key Personnel
Mng Dir, UK & Europe: Andrew Brewer
Dir, Design & Prodn: Lia Pjandra
Dir, Digital Content Devt & Acqs Ed: Neal Christenson
Dir, Mktg & Sales: Elena McAnespia
Dir, Sales & Licensing: Clare Wellnitz
Edit Dir: Kim Robinson
Assoc Dir, Sales: Chris Cook
Exec Ed: Kim Robinson
Acqs Ed: Niels Hooper; Reed Malcolm; Kate Marshall; Eric A Schmidt; Naomi Schneider
Assoc Ed: Seth Bobris; Christopher Johnson; Nadine Little; Raina Polivka; Maura Roessner
Founded: 1893
Trade nonfiction, scholarly & scientific nonfiction, translations & journals; paperbacks, limited fiction (reprints).
ISBN Prefix(es): 978-0-520
Number of titles published annually: 260 Print; 10 Online; 10 E-Book
Total Titles: 4,200 Print; 60 Online; 60 E-Book
Imprints: The Ahmanson Foundation Humanities Endowment Fund; Ahmanson-Murphy (fine arts); The Atkinson Family Imprint (higher educ); Authors; The Stephen Bechtel Fund (ecology & the environment); The George Gund Foundation (African American studies); The Fletcher Jones Foundation (humanities); Philip E Lilienthal (Asian studies); Joan Palevsky (classical lit); Roth Family Foundation (music in America); A Naomi Schneider Book; Simpson (humanities); The S Mark Taper Foundation (Jewish studies)
Foreign Office(s): University Presses of California, Columbia & Princeton Ltd, One Oldlands Way, Bognor Regis, West Sussex P022 9SA, United Kingdom *Tel:* (01243) 843291 *Fax:* (01243) 820250 *E-mail:* sales@upccp.demon.co.uk
Distributor for art-SITES; British Film Institute; Sierra Club Books (adult trade)
Foreign Rep(s): Thomas V Cassidy (China); Adrian Greenwood (Europe, UK); Andrew & Atsuko Ishigami (Japan); David Stimpson (Australia, Canada)
Advertising Agency: Fiat Lux
Orders to: Perseus Distribution, Order Dept, 210 American Dr, Jackson, TN 38301 (Asia, North America & South America) *Toll Free Tel:* 800-343-4499 *Toll Free Fax:* 800-351-5073 *E-mail:* orderentry@perseusbooks.com
Distribution Center: Perseus Distribution, Order Dept, 210 American Dr, Jackson, TN 38301 (Asia, North America & South America) *Toll Free Tel:* 800-343-4499 *Toll Free Fax:* 800-351-5073 *E-mail:* orderentry@perseusbooks.com
Footprint Books Pty Ltd, 1/6A Prosperity Parade, Warriewood, NSW 2102, Australia (Australasia) *Tel:* (02) 9997 3973 *Fax:* (02) 9997 3185 *E-mail:* sales@footprint.com.au *Web Site:* www.footprint.com.au
John Wiley & Sons Ltd, European Distribution Ctr, New Era Estate, Oldlands Way, Bognor Regis, West Sussex PO22 9NQ, United Kingdom (Africa, Europe & Middle East) *Tel:* (01243) 843291 *Fax:* (01243) 843302 *E-mail:* customer@wiley.com
Membership(s): AAP

University of Chicago Press
1427 E 60 St, Chicago, IL 60637-2954
SAN: 202-5280
Tel: 773-702-7700; 773-702-7600 *Toll Free Tel:* 800-621-2736 (orders) *Fax:* 773-702-9756; 773-660-2235 (orders); 773-702-2708
E-mail: custserv@press.uchicago.edu; marketing@press.uchicago.edu
Web Site: www.press.uchicago.edu
Key Personnel
Dir: Garrett P Kiely *Tel:* 773-702-8878 *E-mail:* gkiely@uchicago.edu
Deputy Dir: Christopher Heiser *Tel:* 773-702-2998 *E-mail:* cheiser@uchicago.edu
Exec Dir, IT: Patti O'Shea *Tel:* 773-702-8521 *E-mail:* poshea@uchicago.edu
Dir, Intellectual Property: Laura Leichum

Journals Dir: Michael Magoulias *Tel:* 773-753-2669 *E-mail:* mmagoulias@uchicago.edu
Exec Ed: Susan Bielstein *Tel:* 773-702-7633 *E-mail:* smb1@uchicago.edu; T David Brent *Tel:* 773-702-7642 *E-mail:* tbrent@uchicago.edu; Douglas C Mitchell *Tel:* 773-702-0427 *E-mail:* dmitchel@uchicago.edu
Exec Ed, American History, Urban Studies & Regl Titles: Timothy Mennel *Tel:* 773-702-0158 *E-mail:* tmennel@uchicago.edu
Exec Ed, Sci Studies: Karen Merikangas Darling *Tel:* 773-702-7641 *E-mail:* darling@uchicago.edu
Edit Dir, Humanities & Sci: Alan G Thomas *Tel:* 773-702-7644 *E-mail:* athomas2@uchicago.edu
Intl Rts Mgr, Books: Beatrice Bourgogne *Tel:* 773-702-7741 *E-mail:* bbourgogne@uchicago.edu
Sr Ed: David Morrow *Tel:* 773-702-7465 *E-mail:* dmorrow@uchicago.edu
Sr Ed, Law & Political Sci: Chuck Myers
Sr Ed, Ref & Writing Guides: Mary Laur *Tel:* 773-702-7326 *E-mail:* mlaur@uchicago.edu
Ed: Elizabeth Branch Dyson *Tel:* 773-702-7637 *E-mail:* ebd@uchicago.edu; Marta Tonegutti *Tel:* 773-702-0427 *E-mail:* mtonegut@uchicago.edu
Ed, Anthropology & History: Priya Nelson *Tel:* 773-702-4759 *E-mail:* pnelson@uchicago.edu
Ed, Economics, Busn & Fin: Jane Macdonald
Pbk Ed: Maggie Hivnor *Tel:* 773-702-7649 *E-mail:* mhivnorl@uchicago.edu
Asst Ed: Randolph Petilos *Tel:* 773-702-7647 *E-mail:* rpetilos@uchicago.edu
UK Ed-at-Large: James Attlee
Asst to Dir: Ellen Zalewski *Tel:* 773-702-8879 *E-mail:* emz1@uchicago.edu
Founded: 1891
Scholarly, nonfiction, advanced texts, monographs, clothbound & paperback, scholarly & professional journals, reference books & atlases.
ISBN Prefix(es): 978-0-226
Number of titles published annually: 250 Print
Total Titles: 5,400 Print; 1 E-Book
Foreign Rep(s): Academic Book Promotions (Benelux, France, Scandinavia); The American University Press Group (Hong Kong, Japan, Korea, Taiwan); Thomas Cassidy (China); Ewa Ledochowicz (Eastern Europe); Uwe Ludemann (Austria, Germany, Italy, Switzerland); Mediamatics (India); Publishers Marketing & Research Associates (Caribbean, Latin America); Arie Ruitenbeek (Portugal, Spain); The University Press Group (Australia, Canada, New Zealand); Yale Representation Ltd (UK)
Distribution Center: Chicago Distribution Center (CDC), 11030 S Langley Ave, Chicago, IL 60628 *Toll Free Fax:* 800-621-8476 (US & CN)
John Wiley & Sons Ltd, European Dist Ctr, New Era Estate, Oldlands Way, Bognor Regis, West Sussex PO22 9NQ, United Kingdom *Tel:* (01243) 779777 *Fax:* (01243) 820250 *E-mail:* cs-books@wiley.co.uk
Membership(s): AAP; American Association of University Presses

University of Delaware Press
200A Morris Library, 181 S College Ave, Newark, DE 19717-5267
Tel: 302-831-1149 *Fax:* 302-831-6549
E-mail: ud-press@udel.edu
Web Site: library.udel.edu/udpress
Key Personnel
Chair, Bd of Eds: Prof Donald C Mell *E-mail:* dmell@udel.edu
Interim Dir: Prof Edward Larkin *E-mail:* elarkin@udel.edu
Sr Ed: Julia Oestreich *E-mail:* joestrei@udel.edu
Founded: 1922
Literary studies, especially Shakespeare, Renaissance & early modern literature; eighteenth-century studies, French literature, art history & history & cultural studies of Delaware & the Eastern Shore.
ISBN Prefix(es): 978-0-87413; 978-1-61149
Number of titles published annually: 37 Print
Total Titles: 1,053 Print
Distributed by Rowman & Littlefield
Distribution Center: Rowman & Littlefield, 15200 NBN Way, Blue Ridge Summit, PA 17214 *Toll Free Tel:* 800-462-6420 *Toll Free Fax:* 800-338-4550 *E-mail:* orders@rowman.com *Web Site:* rowmanlittlefield.com
Quantum Publishing Solutions Ltd, 2 Cheviot Rd, Paisley PA2 8AN, United Kingdom *Tel:* (07702) 831967
Durnell Marketing Ltd, 2 Linden Close, Tunbridge Wells TN4 8HH, United Kingdom (Europe including Ireland) *Tel:* (01892) 544272 *Fax:* (01892) 511152 *E-mail:* orders@durnell.co.uk

University of Georgia Press
Main Library, 3rd fl, 320 S Jackson St, Athens, GA 30602
Fax: 706-542-2558; 706-542-6770
Web Site: www.ugapress.org
Key Personnel
Dir: Lisa Bayer *Tel:* 706-542-0027 *E-mail:* lbayer@uga.edu
Dir, Mktg & Digital Initiatives: David E Des Jardines *Tel:* 706-542-9758 *E-mail:* ddesjard@uga.edu
Asst Dir for Acqs & Ed-in-Chief: Mick Gusinde-Duffy *Tel:* 706-542-9907 *E-mail:* mickgd@uga.edu
Asst Dir for Edit, Design & Prodn: Jon Davies *Tel:* 706-542-2101 *E-mail:* jdavies@uga.edu
Busn Mgr: Phyllis Wells *Tel:* 706-542-7250 *E-mail:* pwells@uga.edu
Asst Edit, Design & Prodn Mgr: Melissa Buchanan *Tel:* 706-542-4488 *E-mail:* melissa.buchanan@uga.edu
Founded: 1938
Publisher of scholarly works, creative & literary works, regional works & digital projects.
ISBN Prefix(es): 978-0-8203
Number of titles published annually: 70 Print; 60 E-Book
Total Titles: 2,000 Print; 600 E-Book
Foreign Rep(s): Codasat (Canada); Eurospan Group (worldwide exc Canada & USA)
Orders to: Longleaf Services Inc, 116 S Boundary St, Chapel Hill, NC 27514-3808 *Tel:* 919-966-7449 *Toll Free Tel:* 800-848-6224 *Fax:* 919-962-2704 *Toll Free Fax:* 800-272-6817 *E-mail:* orders@longleafservices.org *Web Site:* www.longleafservices.org
Returns: Longleaf Services - Returns, c/o Ingram Publisher Services, 1250 Ingram Dr, Chambersburg, PA 17202 *E-mail:* credit@longleafservices.org
Shipping Address: Longleaf Services Inc, 116 S Boundary St, Chapel Hill, NC 27514-3808 *Tel:* 919-966-7449 *Toll Free Tel:* 800-848-6224 *Fax:* 919-962-2704 *Toll Free Fax:* 800-272-6817 *E-mail:* customerservice@longleafservices.org *Web Site:* www.longleafservices.org
Warehouse: Longleaf Services Inc, 116 S Boundary St, Chapel Hill, NC 27514-3808 *Tel:* 919-966-7449 *Toll Free Tel:* 800-848-6224 *Fax:* 919-962-2704 *Toll Free Fax:* 800-272-6817 *E-mail:* customerservice@longleafservices.org *Web Site:* www.longleafservices.org
Membership(s): Association of American University Presses

University of Hawaii Press
2840 Kolowalu St, Honolulu, HI 96822
SAN: 202-5353
Tel: 808-956-8255 *Toll Free Tel:* 888-UHPRESS (847-7377) *Fax:* 808-988-6052 *Toll Free Fax:* 800-650-7811
E-mail: uhpbooks@hawaii.edu
Web Site: www.uhpress.hawaii.edu
Key Personnel
CFO: Joel Cosseboom *Tel:* 808-956-6292 *E-mail:* cosseboo@hawaii.edu
Dir: Michael Duckworth *E-mail:* mpd4@hawaii.edu
Dir, Devt & Outreach: Colins Kawai *Tel:* 808-956-6417 *E-mail:* ckawai@hawaii.edu
Interim Exec Ed: Pamela Kelley *Tel:* 808-956-6207 *E-mail:* pkelley@hawaii.edu
Acq Ed: Stephanie Chun *Tel:* 808-956-8695 *E-mail:* chuns@hawaii.edu; Masako Ikeda *Tel:* 808-956-8696 *E-mail:* masakoi@hawaii.edu; Nadine Little *Tel:* 808-956-6208 *E-mail:* nlittle@hawaii.edu
Digital Mgr & Interim Mktg Mgr: Trond Knutsen *Tel:* 808-956-6227 *E-mail:* tknutsen@hawaii.edu
Journals Mgr: Pamela Wilson *Tel:* 808-956-6790 *E-mail:* pwilson6@hawaii.edu
Prod Mgr: Steve Hirashima *Tel:* 808-956-8698 *E-mail:* stevehir@hawaii.edu
Prodn Mgr: Santos Barbasa *Tel:* 808-956-8277 *E-mail:* barbasa@hawaii.edu
Promo Mgr: Carol Abe *Tel:* 808-956-8697 *E-mail:* abec@hawaii.edu
Sales Mgr: Royden Muranaka *Tel:* 808-956-6214 *E-mail:* royden@hawaii.edu
IT Specialist: Collin Wong *Tel:* 808-956-6209 *E-mail:* cwong808@hawaii.edu
Founded: 1947
Scholarly & general books & monographs, particularly those dealing with the Pacific & Asia; regional books; journals.
ISBN Prefix(es): 978-0-8248; 978-0-87022
Number of titles published annually: 70 Print; 100 E-Book
Total Titles: 1,500 Print; 1,500 E-Book
Imprints: Kolowalu Books; Latitude 20
Subsidiaries: East-West Export Books
Distributor for Ateneo De Manila University Press; Cornell University East Asia Program; Huia Publishers; MerwinAsia; NIAS Press; The Numata Center; NUS Press; Renaissance Press; Seoul Selection; Shanghai Press; Three Pines Press; University of the Philippines Press
Foreign Rep(s): East-West Export Books (Asia, Australia, New Zealand); The Eurospan Group (Africa, Continental Europe, Middle East, UK); Scholarly Book Services (Canada)
Membership(s): American Association of University Presses

University of Illinois Press
Unit of University of Illinois
1325 S Oak St, MC-566, Champaign, IL 61820-6903
SAN: 202-5310
Tel: 217-333-0950 *Fax:* 217-244-8082
E-mail: uipress@uillinois.edu; journals@uillinois.edu
Web Site: www.press.uillinois.edu
Key Personnel
Dir & Ed-in-Chief: Laurie Matheson *Tel:* 217-244-4685 *E-mail:* lmatheso@uillinois.edu
Art Dir: Dustin Hubbart *Tel:* 217-333-9227 *E-mail:* dhubbart@uillinois.edu
Direct Mktg & Ad Mgr: Denise Peeler *Tel:* 217-244-4690 *E-mail:* dpeeler@uillinois.edu
Edit Design & Prodn Mgr: Jennifer Comeau *Tel:* 217-244-3279 *E-mail:* jlcomeau@uillinois.edu
Exhibits Mgr: Margo Chaney *Tel:* 217-244-6491 *E-mail:* mechaney@uillinois.edu
Journals Mgr: Clydette Wantland *Tel:* 217-244-6496 *E-mail:* cwantland@uillinois.edu
Mktg & Sales Mgr: Michael Roux *Tel:* 217-244-4683 *E-mail:* mroux@uillinois.edu

Prodn Mgr: Kristine Ding *Tel:* 217-244-4701
E-mail: kding@uillinois.edu
Publicity Mgr: Steven Fast *Tel:* 217-244-4689
E-mail: sfast@uillinois.edu
Founded: 1918
Working-class & ethnic studies, religion, architecture, film studies, communication & media studies, political science, folklore, Chicago, food studies, immigration studies, American history, women's history, music history, regional history, sport history, gender & sexuality studies.
ISBN Prefix(es): 978-0-252
Number of titles published annually: 100 Print
Total Titles: 2,200 Print; 10 Online; 850 E-Book
Foreign Rep(s): Combined Academic Publishers Ltd (Africa, Europe, Middle East, UK); Footprint (Australia); MHM Ltd (Japan); B K Norton (China, Hong Kong, Korea, Taiwan); Scholarly Book Services Inc (Canada)
Orders to: Chicago Distribution Center, 11030 S Langley Ave, Chicago, IL 60628 *Tel:* 773-702-7000 *Toll Free Tel:* 800-621-2736 *Fax:* 773-702-7212 *Toll Free Fax:* 800-621-8476
E-mail: orders@press.uchicago.edu
Returns: Chicago Distribution Center, 11030 S Langley Ave, Chicago, IL 60628 *Tel:* 773-702-7000 *Toll Free Tel:* 800-621-2736 *Fax:* 773-702-7212 *Toll Free Fax:* 800-621-8476
E-mail: orders@press.uchicago.edu
Warehouse: Chicago Distribution Center, 11030 S Langley Ave, Chicago, IL 60628 *Tel:* 773-702-7000 *Toll Free Tel:* 800-621-2736 *Fax:* 773-702-7212 *Toll Free Fax:* 800-621-8476
E-mail: orders@press.uchicago.edu
Membership(s): AAP; Association of American University Presses

University of Iowa Press
119 W Park Rd, 100 Kuhl House, Iowa City, IA 52242-1000
SAN: 282-4868
Tel: 319-335-2000 *Toll Free Tel:* 800-621-2736 (orders only) *Fax:* 319-335-2055
Toll Free Fax: 800-621-8476 (orders only)
E-mail: uipress@uiowa.edu
Web Site: www.uiowapress.org
Key Personnel
Dir: James McCoy *Tel:* 319-335-2013
E-mail: james-mccoy@uiowa.edu
Assoc Dir/Design & Prodn Mgr: Karen Copp *Tel:* 319-335-2014 *E-mail:* karen-copp@uiowa.edu
Founded: 1969
Poetry, short fiction & creative nonfiction. As the only university press in the state, Iowa is also dedicated to preserving the literature, history, culture, wildlife & natural areas of the Midwest.
ISBN Prefix(es): 978-0-87745; 978-1-58729; 978-1-60938
Number of titles published annually: 35 Print; 35 E-Book
Total Titles: 800 Print
Foreign Rep(s): Eurospan (Europe, UK); EWEB (Asia, Australia, New Zealand, The Pacific)
Orders to: Chicago Distribution Center, 11030 S Langley Ave, Chicago, IL 60628
E-mail: orders@press.uchicago.edu
Returns: Chicago Distribution Center, 11030 S Langley Ave, Chicago, IL 60628
E-mail: orders@press.uchicago.edu
Distribution Center: Chicago Distribution Center, 11030 S Langley Ave, Chicago, IL 60628 *Toll Free Tel:* 800-621-2736 *Toll Free Fax:* 800-621-8476 *E-mail:* orders@press.uchicago.edu
Membership(s): American Association of University Presses

University of Louisiana at Lafayette Press
PO Box 43558, Lafayette, LA 70504-3558
Tel: 337-482-6027 *Fax:* 337-482-6028
E-mail: ulpress@louisiana.edu
Web Site: www.ulpress.org
Key Personnel
Dir: Dr Michael Martin
Assoc Dir: James Wilson
Prodn Mgr: Mary Duhe
Founded: 1973
Publish titles on Louisiana culture & history.
ISBN Prefix(es): 978-0-940984; 978-1-887366; 978-1-935754
Number of titles published annually: 12 Print; 5 E-Book
Total Titles: 200 Print; 25 E-Book
Shipping Address: 302 E Saint Mary Blvd, Lafayette, LA 70504

University of Massachusetts Press
East Experiment Sta, 671 N Pleasant St, Amherst, MA 01003
Tel: 413-545-2217 *Fax:* 413-545-1226
E-mail: info@umpress.umass.edu
Web Site: www.umass.edu/umpress
Key Personnel
Dir: Mary V Dougherty *Tel:* 413-545-4990
E-mail: mvd@umpress.umass.edu
Busn Mgr: Yvonne Crevier *Tel:* 413-545-4994
E-mail: ycrevier@umpress.umass.edu
Exec Ed: Matt Becker *Tel:* 413-545-4989
E-mail: mbecker@umpress.umass.edu
Sr Ed: Brian Halley *Tel:* 617-287-5610
E-mail: brian.halley@umb.edu
Mktg Mgr: Courtney J Andree *E-mail:* cjandree@umpress.umass.edu
Assoc Prodn Mgr & Design: Sally Nichols *Tel:* 413-545-4997 *E-mail:* snichols@umpress.umass.edu
Founded: 1963
Scholarly works & serious nonfiction, including African American studies, American history, American studies, architecture & landscape design, disability studies, environmental studies, gender studies, history of the book, journalism & media studies, literary & cultural studies, Native American studies, technology studies, urban studies & books of regional interest.
ISBN Prefix(es): 978-0-87023; 978-1-55849; 978-1-62534
Number of titles published annually: 40 Print; 35 E-Book
Total Titles: 1,000 Print; 400 E-Book
Foreign Rep(s): East-West Export Books (Asia, Hawaii, The Pacific); Eurospan (Africa, Europe, Middle East, UK)
Distribution Center: Hopkins Fulfillment Services, PO Box 50370, Baltimore, MD 21211-4370 *Tel:* 410-516-6965 *Toll Free Tel:* 800-537-5487 (US & CN) *Fax:* 410-516-6998
E-mail: hfscustserv@press.jhu.edu *Web Site:* hfs.jhu.edu
Brunswick Books, 20 Maud St, Suite 303, Toronto, ON M5V 2M5, Canada *Tel:* 416-703-3598 *Fax:* 416-703-6561 *E-mail:* orders@brunswickbooks.ca *Web Site:* www.brunswickbooks.ca
Membership(s): Association of American University Presses

University of Michigan Press
Unit of University of Michigan
839 Greene St, Ann Arbor, MI 48104-3209
SAN: 202-5329
Tel: 734-764-4388 *Fax:* 734-615-1540
E-mail: esladmin@umich.edu
Web Site: www.press.umich.edu
Key Personnel
Dir: Charles Watkinson
Edit Dir: Mary Francis *Tel:* 734-763-4134
E-mail: mfranci@umich.edu
Dir, Mktg & Res: Renee Tambeau *Tel:* 734-936-0388 *E-mail:* rtambeau@umich.edu
Founded: 1930
Aims for diversity in its books & in its audiences.
ISBN Prefix(es): 978-0-472
Number of titles published annually: 110 Print; 90 E-Book
Total Titles: 3,500 Print; 1,100 E-Book; 24 Audio
Imprints: Ann Arbor Paperbacks; digitalculture
Distributor for Center for Chinese Studies, University of Michigan; Center for Japanese Studies, University of Michigan; Center for South & Southeast Asian Studies, University of Michigan
Foreign Rep(s): Eurospan (Europe)
Foreign Rights: University of Chicago Press
Returns: Chicago Distribution Center (CDC), 11030 S Langley Ave, Chicago, IL 60628 *Toll Free Tel:* 800-621-2736 *Toll Free Fax:* 800-621-8476 *E-mail:* orders@press.uchicago.edu
Distribution Center: Chicago Distribution Center (CDC), 11030 S Langley Ave, Chicago, IL 60628

University of Minnesota Press
Unit of University of Minnesota
111 Third Ave S, Suite 290, Minneapolis, MN 55401-2520
SAN: 213-2648
Tel: 612-301-1990 *Fax:* 612-301-1980
E-mail: ump@umn.edu
Web Site: www.upress.umn.edu
Key Personnel
Dir: Doug Armato
Edit Dir: Jason Weidemann
Asst Dir, Book Div & Mktg Dir: Emily Hamilton
Assoc Dir, MMPI: Beverly Kaemmer
Copy-Editing Mgr: Laura Westlund
Opers Mgr: Susan Doerr
Prodn Mgr: Daniel Ochsner
Sales Mgr: Matt Smiley
Regl Ed: Erik Anderson
Publicist: Heather Skinner
Intl Rts Contact: Jeff Moen
Direct Mail: Maggie Sattler
Founded: 1925
Recognized internationally for its innovative, boundary-breaking editorial program in the humanities & social sciences & as publisher of the Minnesota Multiphasic Personality Inventory (MMPI), the most widely used objective tests of personality in the world. Minnesota also maintains as part of its mission a strong commitment to publishing books on the people, history & natural environment of Minnesota & the upper Midwest.
Among the founding members of the Association of American University Presses (AAUP).
ISBN Prefix(es): 978-0-8166; 978-1-4529
Number of titles published annually: 110 Print; 95 E-Book
Total Titles: 3,360 Print; 2,899 E-Book
Distributor for Univocal Publishing
Foreign Rep(s): Lexa Publishers (Canada); NewSouth Books (Australia, New Zealand); United Publishers Services Ltd (Japan)
Returns: Chicago Distribution Center, 11030 S Langley Ave, Chicago, IL 60628
Shipping Address: Chicago Distribution Center, 11030 S Langley Ave, Chicago, IL 60628 *Tel:* 773-568-1550 *Toll Free Tel:* 800-621-2736 (orders only) *Toll Free Fax:* 800-621-8476 (orders only)
Warehouse: Chicago Distribution Center, 11030 S Langley Ave, Chicago, IL 60628 *Tel:* 773-702-7000 *Toll Free Tel:* 800-621-2736 *Fax:* 773-702-7212 *Toll Free Fax:* 800-621-8476
Membership(s): AAP; Association of American University Presses; CrossRef; Minnesota Book Publishers Roundtable

University of Missouri Press
113 Heinkel Bldg, 201 S Seventh St, Columbia, MO 65211
SAN: 203-3143
Tel: 573-882-7641 *Toll Free Tel:* 800-621-2736 (orders) *Fax:* 573-884-4498 *Toll Free Fax:* 800-621-8476 (orders)

E-mail: upress@missouri.edu
Web Site: upress.missouri.edu; press.umsystem.edu
Key Personnel
Dir: David M Rosenbaum *Tel:* 573-882-9478 *E-mail:* rosenbaumd@missouri.edu
Ed-in-Chief: Andrew J Davidson *Tel:* 573-882-9997 *E-mail:* davidsonaj@missouri.edu
Mng Ed: Sara Davis *Tel:* 573-882-8714 *Fax:* davissd@missouri.edu
Acqs Ed: Gary Kass *Tel:* 573-884-1277 *E-mail:* kassg@missouri.edu
Busn Mgr: Tracy Tritschler *Tel:* 573-882-9459 *E-mail:* tritschlert@missouri.edu
Mktg Mgr: Stephanie Williams *Tel:* 573-882-9672 *E-mail:* williamssteph@missouri.edu
Founded: 1958
Scholarly books, general trade, art, regional, intellectual thought, history, literary criticism, African-American, journalism, political science, sports & women's studies.
ISBN Prefix(es): 978-0-8262
Number of titles published annually: 30 Print
Total Titles: 900 Print
Distributor for Missouri History Museum; St Louis Mercantile Library
Foreign Rep(s): East-West Export Books (Asia, Australia, New Zealand, Pacific Islands); The Eurospan Group (Africa, Europe, Middle East); Scholarly Book Services (Canada)
Orders to: Chicago Distribution Center, 11030 S Langley Ave, Chicago, IL 60628 *E-mail:* orders@press.uchicago.edu

University of Nebraska Press
Division of University of Nebraska at Lincoln
1111 Lincoln Mall, Lincoln, NE 68588-0630
Tel: 402-472-3581; 919-966-7449 (cust serv & foreign orders) *Toll Free Tel:* 800-848-6224 (cust serv & US orders) *Fax:* 402-472-6214; 919-962-2704 (cust serv & foreign orders) *Toll Free Fax:* 800-526-2617 (cust serv & US orders)
E-mail: pressmail@unl.edu
Web Site: www.nebraskapress.unl.edu
Key Personnel
Dir: Donna Shear *Tel:* 402-472-2861 *E-mail:* dshear2@unl.edu
Ed-in-Chief: Alisa Plant *E-mail:* aplant2@unl.edu
Humanities Ed: Alicia Christensen *E-mail:* achristensen6@unl.edu
Publicity Mgr: Rosemary Vestal *Tel:* 402-472-7710 *E-mail:* rvestal2@unl.edu
Rts & Perms, Intl Rts: Leif Milliken *Tel:* 402-472-7702 *E-mail:* lmilliken2@unl.edu
Founded: 1941
General scholarly nonfiction, including anthropology, sports history, literature & criticism, history of the Trans-Mississippi West.
ISBN Prefix(es): 978-0-8032
Number of titles published annually: 150 Print; 150 E-Book
Total Titles: 4,000 Print; 1,000 E-Book
Imprints: Bison Books; Potomac Books
Distributor for Buros Institute; Society for American Baseball Research
Foreign Rep(s): Codasat Canada (Canada); Combined Academic Publishers Ltd (Europe)
Foreign Rights: Perseus Books Group (Jennifer Schaper)
Advertising Agency: Scholarly Press Advertising Services
Warehouse: Longleaf Services Inc, c/o Ingram Publisher Services, 1250 Ingram Dr, Chambersburg, PA 17202
Distribution Center: Longleaf Services Inc, 116 S Boundary St, Chapel Hill, NC 27514-3808 *Tel:* 919-966-7449 *Toll Free Tel:* 800-848-6224 *Fax:* 919-962-2704 *Toll Free Fax:* 800-272-6817 *E-mail:* customerservice@longleafservices.org *Web Site:* www.longleafservices.org
Membership(s): American Association of University Presses
See separate listing for:
Potomac Books Inc

University of Nevada Press
c/o University of Nevada, Continuing Educ Bldg, MS 0166, Reno, NV 89557-0166
SAN: 203-316X
Tel: 775-784-6573 *Fax:* 775-784-6200
Web Site: www.unpress.nevada.edu
Key Personnel
Dir: Justin Race *Tel:* 775-682-7389 *E-mail:* jrace@unpress.nevada.edu
Mktg & Sales Mgr: Caddie Dufurrena *Tel:* 775-682-7395 *E-mail:* cdufurrena@unpress.nevada.edu
Mktg Asst: Mayanne Coyne *Tel:* 775-682-7394 *E-mail:* mcoyne@unpress.nevada.edu
Design & Prodn Mgr: Virginia Fontana *Tel:* 775-682-7390 *E-mail:* vfontana@unpress.nevada.edu
Busn Mgr: JoAnne Banducci *Tel:* 775-682-7387 *E-mail:* jbanducci@unpress.nevada.edu
Founded: 1961
ISBN Prefix(es): 978-0-87417
Number of titles published annually: 20 Print; 20 E-Book
Total Titles: 400 Print
Foreign Rep(s): East-West Books (Asia-Pacific); Eurospan University Press Group (Africa, Central America, Europe, Middle East, South America, UK); Scholarly Book Service (Canada)
Orders to: Chicago Distribution Center, 11030 S Langley Ave, Chicago, IL 60628 *Toll Free Tel:* 800-621-2736 *Toll Free Fax:* 800-621-8476 *E-mail:* custserv@press.uchicago.edu
Warehouse: Chicago Distribution Center, 11030 S Langley Ave, Chicago, IL 60628 *Toll Free Tel:* 800-621-2736 *Toll Free Fax:* 800-621-8476 *E-mail:* custserv@press.uchicago.edu
Membership(s): American Association of University Presses; Publishers Association of the West

University of New Mexico Press
One University of New Mexico, Albuquerque, NM 87131-0001
SAN: 213-9588
Mailing Address: MSC05 3185, One University of New Mexico, Albuquerque, NM 87131-0001
Tel: 505-272-7777 *Fax:* 505-277-3343; 505-272-7778 (cust serv) *Toll Free Fax:* 800-622-8667 (orders only)
E-mail: unmpress@unm.edu; custserv@unm.edu (order dept)
Web Site: unmpress.com
Key Personnel
Dir: John W Byram *Tel:* 505-277-32800 *E-mail:* jbyram@unm.edu
Assoc Dir, Busn Opers: Richard Schuetz *Tel:* 505-277-3284 *E-mail:* rschuetz@unm.edu
Rts & Perms Coord: Briony Jones *Tel:* 505-925-9512 *E-mail:* briony@unm.edu
Sr Book Designer: Catherine Leonardo *Tel:* 505-277-3299 *E-mail:* davinci@unm.edu
Founded: 1929
General, scholarly & regional books, Latin American studies & native studies.
ISBN Prefix(es): 978-0-8263
Number of titles published annually: 75 Print
Total Titles: 1,750 Print
Distributor for Avanyu Publishing; Fresco Fine Art Publications LLC; La Frontera Publishing; West End Press
Foreign Rep(s): Codasat (Canada); Eurospan Ltd (Africa, Europe, Middle East, UK); EWEB (Asia, Australia); US PubRep (Craig Falk) (Caribbean including Puerto Rico, Central America, Latin America, Mexico)
Shipping Address: 1312 Basehart Rd SE, Albuquerque, NM 87106-4363
Membership(s): Association of American University Presses

§The University of North Carolina Press
116 S Boundary St, Chapel Hill, NC 27514-3808
SAN: 203-3151
Tel: 919-966-3561 *Fax:* 919-966-3829
E-mail: uncpress@unc.edu
Web Site: www.uncpress.unc.edu
Key Personnel
Dir: John Sherer
Sr Dir, Mktg & Digital Busn Devt: Dino Battista *Tel:* 919-962-0579 *E-mail:* dino_battista@unc.edu
Dir, Contracts & Subs Rts: Vicky Wells *Tel:* 919-962-0369 *E-mail:* vicky_wells@unc.edu
Dir, Publicity & ISBN Contact: Gina M Mahalek *Tel:* 919-962-0581 *E-mail:* gina_mahalek@unc.edu
Edit Dir: Mark Simpson-Vos *Tel:* 919-962-0535
Sales Dir: Michael Donatelli *Tel:* 919-962-0475 *E-mail:* michael_donatelli@unc.edu
Asst Dir & Sr Ed: Charles Grench *Tel:* 919-962-0481 *E-mail:* charles_grench@unc.edu
Mng Ed: Paul Betz *Tel:* 919-962-0530 *E-mail:* paul_betz@unc.edu
Sr Ed: Brandon Proia
Founded: 1922
General, scholarly, regional.
ISBN Prefix(es): 978-0-8078
Number of titles published annually: 100 Print
Total Titles: 776 E-Book
Distributor for Museum of Early Southern Decorative Arts; North Carolina Museum of Art; Southeastern Center for Contemporary Art; Valentine Museum
Foreign Rep(s): East-West Export Books (Asia, Australia, New Zealand, The Pacific); EDIREP (Caribbean, Central America, Mexico, South America); Eurospan University Press Group (Africa, Continental Europe, Middle East, UK); Scholarly Book Services (Canada)
Advertising Agency: Brimley Agency
Orders to: Long Leaf Services Inc, PO Box 8895, Chapel Hill, NC 27515-8895 *Toll Free Tel:* 800-848-6224 *Toll Free Fax:* 800-272-6817 *E-mail:* customerservice@longleafservices.org
Returns: Longleaf Returns, c/o Maple Logistics Solutions, Lebanon Distribution Ctr, 704 Legionaire Dr, Fredericksburg, PA 17026
Membership(s): AAP; BISG

University of North Texas Press
Willis Library, Rm 251, 1506 Highland St, Denton, TX 76203-5017
SAN: 249-4280
Mailing Address: 1155 Union Circle, No 311336, Denton, TX 76203-5017
Tel: 940-565-2142 *Fax:* 940-565-4590
Web Site: untpress.unt.edu
Key Personnel
Dir: Ronald Chrisman *E-mail:* ronald.chrisman@unt.edu
Asst Dir: Karen DeVinney *E-mail:* karen.devinney@unt.edu
Mktg Mgr: Bess Whitby *E-mail:* elizabeth.whitby@unt.edu
Founded: 1987
ISBN Prefix(es): 978-0-929398; 978-1-57441
Number of titles published annually: 16 Print; 5 Online; 16 E-Book
Total Titles: 300 Print; 75 Online; 100 E-Book
Foreign Rep(s): East-West Export Books (Asia, Australia, Hawaii, New Zealand, Pacific Islands); Eurospan Group (Europe); Scholarly Book Services (Canada); US PubRep (Latin America)
Distribution Center: Texas Book Consortium, John H Lindsey Bldg, Lewis St, 4354 Tamu,

College Station, TX 77843-4354 *Toll Free Tel:* 800-826-8911 *Toll Free Fax:* 888-617-2421
Membership(s): American Association of University Presses

University of Notre Dame Press
310 Flanner Hall, Notre Dame, IN 46556
SAN: 203-3178
Tel: 574-631-6346 *Fax:* 574-631-8148
E-mail: undpress@nd.edu
Web Site: www.undpress.nd.edu
Key Personnel
Dir: Stephen M Wrinn *Tel:* 574-631-3265 *E-mail:* swrinn@nd.edu
Sr Acqs Ed: Eli Bortz *Tel:* 574-631-4912 *E-mail:* ebortz@nd.edu
Acqs Ed: Stephen Little *Tel:* 574-631-4906 *E-mail:* slittle2@nd.edu
Mng Ed: Rebecca De Boer *Tel:* 574-631-4908 *E-mail:* rdeboer@nd.edu
Busn Mgr: Diane Schaut *Tel:* 574-631-4904 *E-mail:* dschaut@nd.edu
Mktg Mgr: Kathryn D Pitts *Tel:* 574-631-3267 *Fax:* 574631-4410 *E-mail:* pitts.5@nd.edu
Prodn & Design Mgr: Wendy McMillen *Tel:* 574-631-4907 *E-mail:* wmcmill@nd.edu
Coord, Off Servs: Gina Bixler *Tel:* 574-631-4915 *E-mail:* gbixler@nd.edu
Founded: 1949
Academic books, hardcover & paperback; philosophy, Irish studies, literature, theology, international relations, sociology & general interest.
ISBN Prefix(es): 978-0-268
Number of titles published annually: 50 Print
Total Titles: 1,200 Print
Foreign Rep(s): Eurospan; EWEB
Returns: Chicago Distribution Center, 11030 S Langley, Chicago, IL 60628 *Tel:* 773-702-7000 (rest of world) *Toll Free Tel:* 800-621-2736 (US & CN) *Fax:* 773-702-7212 (rest of world) *Toll Free Fax:* 800-621-8476 (US & CN)
Distribution Center: Chicago Distribution Center, 11030 S Langley Ave, Chicago, IL 60628 *Tel:* 773-702-7000 (rest of world) *Toll Free Tel:* 800-621-2736 (US & CN) *Fax:* 773-702-7212 (rest of world) *Toll Free Fax:* 800-621-8476 (US & CN)
Membership(s): Association of American University Presses

University of Oklahoma Press
2800 Venture Dr, Norman, OK 73069-8216
SAN: 203-3194
Tel: 405-325-2000 *Toll Free Tel:* 800-627-7377 (orders) *Fax:* 405-364-5798 (orders) *Toll Free Fax:* 800-735-0476 (orders)
E-mail: presscs@ou.edu
Web Site: www.oupress.com
Key Personnel
CFO, Rts & Perms & Fulfillment Mgr: Diane Cotts *Tel:* 405-325-3276 *E-mail:* dcotts@ou.edu
Dir: B Byron Price *Tel:* 405-325-5666 *E-mail:* b_byron_price@ou.edu
Dir, Sales & Mktg: Dale Bennie *Tel:* 405-325-3207 *E-mail:* dbennie@ou.edu
Ed-in-Chief: Charles Rankin *Tel:* 405-325-2873 *E-mail:* cerankin@ou.edu
Mng Ed: Steven Baker *Tel:* 405-325-1325 *E-mail:* steven.b.baker@ou.edu
Prodn Mgr: Tony Roberts *Tel:* 405-325-3186 *E-mail:* eezzell@ou.edu
Publicity Mgr: Sandy See *Tel:* 405-325-3200 *E-mail:* ssee@ou.edu
Founded: 1928
Scholarly & general interest books on Americana, Native American studies, Western history, regional interest, natural history, anthropology, archaeology, military history, literature, classical studies, women's studies & political science.
ISBN Prefix(es): 978-0-8061; 978-0-87062 (Arthur H Clark Co)
Number of titles published annually: 90 Print; 80 E-Book
Total Titles: 1,850 Print; 5 CD-ROM; 1,280 E-Book
Imprints: Arthur H Clark Co
Distributor for Cherokee Heritage Press; Dakota Institute; Denver Art Museum; Gilcrease Museum; Vanderbilt University Press
Membership(s): American Association of University Presses

§University of Pennsylvania Museum of Archaeology & Anthropology
Division of University of Pennsylvania
3260 South St, Philadelphia, PA 19104-6324
Tel: 215-898-6322; 215-898-4119
E-mail: publications@pennmuseum.org; info@pennmuseum.org
Web Site: www.penn.museum
Key Personnel
Head, Collections, Pubns & Digital Media: James R Mathieu, PhD *Tel:* 215-898-4050
Ed: Page Selinsky, PhD
Founded: 1887
ISBN Prefix(es): 978-0-934718; 978-0-924171; 978-1-931707
Number of titles published annually: 4 Print; 4 E-Book
Total Titles: 210 Print; 18 CD-ROM
Distributed by University of Pennsylvania Press
Billing Address: Hopkins Fulfillment Services, PO Box 50370, Hampden Sta, Baltimore, MD 21211-4370 *Toll Free Tel:* 800-537-5487 *Fax:* 410-516-6998 *E-mail:* hfscustserv@press.jhu.edu
Orders to: Hopkins Fulfillment Services, PO Box 50370, Hampden Sta, Baltimore, MD 21211-4370 *Toll Free Tel:* 800-537-5487 *Fax:* 410-516-6998 *E-mail:* hfscustserv@press.jhu.edu
Returns: Hopkins Fulfillment Services, PO Box 50370, Hampden Sta, Baltimore, MD 21211-4370 *Toll Free Tel:* 800-537-5487 *Fax:* 410-516-6998 *E-mail:* hfscustserv@press.jhu.edu
Shipping Address: Hopkins Fulfillment Services, PO Box 50370, Hampden Sta, Baltimore, MD 21211-4370 *Toll Free Tel:* 800-537-5487 *Fax:* 410-516-6998 *E-mail:* hfscustserv@press.jhu.edu

University of Pennsylvania Press
3905 Spruce St, Philadelphia, PA 19104
SAN: 202-5345
Tel: 215-898-6261 *Fax:* 215-898-0404
E-mail: custserv@pobox.upenn.edu
Web Site: www.pennpress.org
Key Personnel
Dir: Eric Halpern *Tel:* 215-898-6263 *E-mail:* ehalpern@upenn.edu
Mktg Dir: Laura Waldron *Tel:* 215-898-1673 *E-mail:* lwaldron@upenn.edu
Busn Mgr: Joseph Guttman *Tel:* 215-898-1670 *E-mail:* josephgg@upenn.edu
Editing & Prodn Mgr: Elizabeth Glover *Tel:* 215-898-1675 *E-mail:* gloverel@upenn.edu
Publicity & PR Mgr: Gigi Lamm *Tel:* 215-898-1674 *E-mail:* glamm@upenn.edu
Ed-in-Chief: Peter A Agree *Tel:* 215-573-3816 *E-mail:* agree@upenn.edu
Mng Ed: Lily Palladino *Tel:* 215-898-1678 *E-mail:* lilypall@upenn.edu
History Ed: Robert Lockhart *Tel:* 215-898-1677 *E-mail:* rlockhar@upenn.edu
Humanities Ed: Jerome E Singerman *Tel:* 215-898-1681 *E-mail:* singerma@upenn.edu
Consulting Ed: Damon Linker *Tel:* 610-613-4546 *E-mail:* linkerpennpress@gmail.com
Consulting Ed (UK): Deborah Blake *E-mail:* dcblake.pennpress@virginmedia.com
Founded: 1890
Scholarly & semipopular nonfiction, especially in history, literature & criticism, social sciences & human rights.
ISBN Prefix(es): 978-0-8122; 978-1-5128
Number of titles published annually: 120 Print; 120 Online
Total Titles: 1,200 Print; 800 E-Book
Imprints: Pine Street Books
Foreign Rep(s): Combined Academic Publishers (Africa, Arab Middle East, Asia, Austria, China, UK); Durnell Marketing Ltd (Continental Europe); Scholarly Book Services (Canada)
Orders to: Penn Press, c/o Hopkins Fulfillment Services, Hampden Sta, Box 50370, Baltimore, MD 21211 *Toll Free Tel:* 800-537-5487 *Fax:* 410-516-6998 *E-mail:* hfscustserv@press.jhu.edu
Returns: Penn Press, c/o Maple Logistics Solutions, Lebanon Distribution Ctr, 704 Legionaire Dr, Fredericksburg, PA 17026
Warehouse: Maple Logistics Solutions, Lebanon Distribution Ctr, PO Box 1287, 704 Legionaire Dr, Lebanon, PA 17042 *Tel:* 717-865-7600 *Web Site:* www.maplelogisticsssolutions.com
Marston Book Services Ltd, 160 Eastern Ave, Milton Park, Oxon OX14 4SB, United Kingdom, Asst Cust Servs & Trade Mgr: Donna Green *Tel:* (01235) 465630 *Fax:* (01235) 465555 *E-mail:* donna.green@marston.co.uk *Web Site:* www.marston.co.uk/home.htm
Membership(s): AAP Professional & Scholarly Publishing Division; American Association of University Presses

University of Pittsburgh Press
7500 Thomas Blvd, Pittsburgh, PA 15260
Tel: 412-383-2456 *Fax:* 412-383-2466
E-mail: info@upress.pitt.edu
Web Site: www.upress.pitt.edu
Key Personnel
Dir: Peter Kracht
Edit Dir: Sandy Crooms
Mktg Dir: David Baumann
Mng Ed: Alexander Wolfe *E-mail:* apw20@pitt.edu
Busn Mgr: Cindy Wessels *E-mail:* caw1@pitt.edu
Rts & Perms: Margie K Bachman *Tel:* 412-383-2544 *E-mail:* mkbachma@pitt.edu
Publicist: Maria Sticco *E-mail:* mes5@pitt.edu
Founded: 1936
Scholarly nonfiction, poetry, regional books, short fiction, Russian & East European studies, composition & rhetoric, Latin American studies, environmental history, urban studies, philosophy of science, political science.
ISBN Prefix(es): 978-0-8229
Number of titles published annually: 65 Print
Total Titles: 1,400 Print; 1,000 E-Book
Sales Office(s): Chicago Distribution Center, 11030 S Langley Ave, Chicago, IL 60628
Distributed by University of Chicago Press Distribution Center
Foreign Rep(s): East-West Export Books (Asia, The Pacific); Eurospan (Africa, Europe, Middle East, UK); Scholarly Book Services (Canada)
Billing Address: Chicago Distribution Center, 11030 S Langley Ave, Chicago, IL 60628
Returns: Chicago Distribution Center, 11030 S Langley Ave, Chicago, IL 60628
Warehouse: Chicago Distribution Center, 11030 S Langley Ave, Chicago, IL 60628 *Tel:* 773-702-7000 *Toll Free Tel:* 800-621-2736 *Fax:* 773-702-7212 *Toll Free Fax:* 800-621-8471
Distribution Center: Chicago Distribution Center, 11030 S Langley Ave, Chicago, IL 60628
Membership(s): Association of American University Presses

University of Puerto Rico Press
Subsidiary of University of Puerto Rico
Edificio La Editorial (level 2), Carr No 1, KM 12.0, Jardin Botanico Norte, San Juan, PR 00927
Mailing Address: PO Box 23322, Rio Pedras, PR 00931-3322 SAN: 208-1245
Tel: 787-250-0435; 787-250-0550 *Toll Free Tel:* 877-338-7788 *Fax:* 787-753-9116

E-mail: info@laeditorialupr.com
Web Site: www.laeditorialupr.com
Key Personnel
Admin Offr: Ruth Morales *E-mail:* ruth.morales3@upr.edu
Ed: Rosa Vanessa Otero *E-mail:* rosa.otero1@upr.edu
Sales: Jose Burgos *E-mail:* joseburgos73@gmail.com; Ramon Lugo
Founded: 1947
General fiction & nonfiction, reference books, college texts; Latin America.
ISBN Prefix(es): 978-0-8477
Number of titles published annually: 10 Print; 10 E-Book
Total Titles: 1,047 Print; 50 E-Book
Imprints: Coleccion Antologia Personal; Coleccion Aqui y Ahora; Coleccion Caribena; Coleccion Ciencias Naturales; Coleccion Clasicos No Tan Clasicos; Coleccion Cuadernos La Torre; Coleccion Cuentos de un Mundo Perdido; Coleccion Cultura Basica; Coleccion Obras Completas Eugenio Maria de Hostos (edicion critica); Coleccion Dos Lenguas; Coleccion Mujeres de Palabra; Coleccion Nueve Pececitos; Coleccion Puertorriquena; Coleccion San Pedrito
Foreign Rep(s): Baker & Taylor/Libros Sin Fronteras (USA); DESA (Latin America); Lectorum Publications (USA); Libreria La Trinitaria (Dominican Republic)
Membership(s): American Association of University Presses

University of Rochester Press
Affiliate of Boydell & Brewer Inc
668 Mount Hope Ave, Rochester, NY 14620-2731
Tel: 585-275-0419 *Fax:* 585-271-8778
E-mail: boydell@boydellusa.net
Web Site: www.urpress.com
Key Personnel
Edit Dir: Sonia Kane *E-mail:* sonia.kane@rochester.edu
Prodn Dir: Sue Smith *E-mail:* smith@boydellusa.net
Founded: 1989
Philosophy, music & African studies titles.
ISBN Prefix(es): 978-1-878822; 978-1-58046
Number of titles published annually: 25 Print
Total Titles: 132 Print
Foreign Office(s): PO Box 9, Woodbridge, Suffolk IP12 3DF, United Kingdom
Foreign Rep(s): Boydell & Brewer (Europe, Japan)
Warehouse: Publishers Storage & Shipping Corp, 231 Industrial Park, 46 Development Rd, Fitchburg, MA 01420-6019, Contact: John Salvey *Tel:* 978-345-2121 *Fax:* 978-348-1233

§University of South Carolina Press
Affiliate of University of South Carolina
1600 Hampton St, Suite 544, Columbia, SC 29208
SAN: 203-3224
Tel: 803-777-5245 *Toll Free Tel:* 800-768-2500 (orders) *Fax:* 803-777-0160 *Toll Free Fax:* 800-868-0740 (orders)
Web Site: www.sc.edu/uscpress
Key Personnel
Dir: Richard Brown
Asst Dir, Opers: Linda Haines Fogle *Tel:* 803-777-4848 *E-mail:* lfogle@mailbox.sc.edu
Busn Mgr: Vicki Sewell *Tel:* 803-777-7754 *E-mail:* sewellv@mailbox.sc.edu
Design & Prodn Mgr: Pat Callahan *Tel:* 803-777-2449 *E-mail:* mpcallah@mailbox.sc.edu
Mng Ed: William Adams *Tel:* 803-777-5075 *E-mail:* adamswb@mailbox.sc.edu
Asst to Dir: Vicki Bates *Tel:* 803-777-5245 *E-mail:* batesvc@mailbox.sc.edu
Founded: 1944
American history/studies, Southern studies, military history, maritime history, literary studies including contemporary American & British literature & modern world literature, religious studies, speech/communication, social work.
ISBN Prefix(es): 978-0-87249; 978-1-57003
Number of titles published annually: 50 Print
Total Titles: 700 Print; 2 CD-ROM; 2 Audio
Imprints: Story River Books (Southern fiction)
Distributor for McKissick Museum; Saraland Press; South Carolina Bar Association; South Carolina Historical Society
Foreign Rep(s): East-West Export Books (Asia, The Pacific); Eurospan University Press Group (Europe, UK); Scholary Book Services (Canada)
Warehouse: 718 Devine St, Columbia, SC 29208, Orders: Ms Lee Heckle *Tel:* 803-777-1774 *Fax:* 803-777-0026
Membership(s): American Association of University Presses; Southern Independent Booksellers Alliance

University of Tennessee Press
Division of University of Tennessee
110 Conference Center Bldg, 600 Henley St, Knoxville, TN 37996-4108
SAN: 212-9930
Tel: 865-974-3321 *Toll Free Tel:* 800-621-2736 (orders) *Fax:* 865-974-3724 *Toll Free Fax:* 800-621-8476 (orders)
E-mail: custserv@utpress.org
Web Site: www.utpress.org
Key Personnel
Dir: Scott Danforth *E-mail:* danforth@utk.edu
Mktg Dir: Tom Post *Tel:* 865-974-5466 *E-mail:* tpost@utk.edu
Busn Mgr: Lisa Davis *E-mail:* ldavis49@utk.edu
Acqs Ed: Kerry Webb *E-mail:* webbke@utk.edu; Thomas Wells *E-mail:* twells@utk.edu
Mktg Asst: Linsey Sims *Tel:* 865-974-4444 *E-mail:* lsims9@utk.edu
Founded: 1940
Scholarly & regional nonfiction.
ISBN Prefix(es): 978-0-87049; 978-1-57233; 978-1-62190
Number of titles published annually: 40 Print
Total Titles: 900 Print; 1 Online
Foreign Rep(s): East-West Export Books Inc (Asia, The Pacific); Eurospan Group (Africa, Central Asia, Europe, Middle East, UK)
Distribution Center: Chicago Distribution Center, 11030 S Langley, Chicago, IL 60628 *Toll Free Tel:* 800-621-2736 *Fax:* 773-702-7212
Membership(s): AAP; Association of American University Presses

University of Texas at Arlington College of Architecture, Planning & Public Affairs
601 S Nedderman Dr, Suite 203, Arlington, TX 76019
Fax: 817-272-5008
E-mail: cappa@uta.edu
Web Site: www.uta.edu/cappa
Key Personnel
Coord, Communs: Robert Rummel-Hudson *E-mail:* rhudson@uta.edu
Newsletter, working papers, books, reports on community revitalization, population projection, charter school evaluation, strategic planning, land use planning, transportation planning, social welfare policy, urban politics, social planning, urban public finance, consensus, building & dispute resolution, group facilitation, urban management, environmental planning & analysis.
ISBN Prefix(es): 978-0-936440
Number of titles published annually: 15 Print
Total Titles: 40 Print

§The University of Utah Press
Subsidiary of University of Utah
J Willard Marriott Library, Suite 5400, 295 S 1500 E, Salt Lake City, UT 84112-0860
SAN: 220-0023
Tel: 801-585-9786 *Fax:* 801-581-3365
E-mail: hannah.new@utah.edu
Web Site: www.uofupress.com
Key Personnel
Dir & Mng Ed: Glenda Cotter *E-mail:* glenda.cotter@utah.edu
Busn Mgr & Perms: Sharon Day *E-mail:* sharon.day@utah.edu
Prodn Mgr: Jessica Booth *E-mail:* jessica.booth@utah.edu
Founded: 1949
Scholarly books, regional studies, anthropology, archaeology, linguistics, Mesoamerican studies, natural history, Western history, outdoor recreation.
ISBN Prefix(es): 978-0-87480; 978-1-60781
Number of titles published annually: 32 Print
Total Titles: 550 Print
Imprints: Bonneville Books (trade)
Distributor for BYU Museum of Peoples & Cultures; BYU Studies; KUED (Utah PBS affiliate); Western Epics Publications
Foreign Rep(s): East-West Export Books (Asia, Australia, Hawaii, New Zealand, Oceania); Scholarly Book Services Inc (Canada)
Orders to: The Chicago Distribution Center, 11030 S Langley Ave, Chicago, IL 60628 *Tel:* 773-702-7000 *Toll Free Tel:* 800-621-2736 *Fax:* 773-702-7212 *Toll Free Fax:* 800-621-8741 *Web Site:* www.uofupress.com
Returns: The Chicago Distribution Center, 11030 S Langley Ave, Chicago, IL 60628

The University of Virginia Press
Affiliate of University of Virginia
PO Box 400318, Charlottesville, VA 22904-4318
Tel: 434-924-3468 (cust serv); 434-924-3469 (cust serv) *Toll Free Tel:* 800-831-3406 (orders) *Fax:* 434-982-2655 *Toll Free Fax:* 877-288-6400
E-mail: vapress@virginia.edu
Web Site: www.upress.virginia.edu
Key Personnel
Dir: Mark H Saunders *Tel:* 434-924-6064 *E-mail:* msaunders@virginia.edu
Asst Dir/Ed-in-Chief & Humanities Ed: Eric Brandt
Dir, Mktg & Sales: Jason Coleman *Tel:* 434-924-1450 *E-mail:* jgc3h@virginia.edu
Publicity Dir: Emily Grandstaff *Tel:* 434-982-2932 *E-mail:* ekg4a@virginia.edu
Mng Ed, Ms Edit/Design & Prodn: Ellen Satrom *Tel:* 434-924-6065 *E-mail:* esatrom@virginia.edu
Acqs Ed, Architecture & Environmental: Boyd Zenner *Tel:* 434-924-1373 *E-mail:* bz2v@virginia.edu
Acqs Ed, Soc Sci & History: Richard Holway *Tel:* 434-924-7301 *E-mail:* rkh2a@virginia.edu
Cust Serv Mgr: Brenda Fitzgerald *E-mail:* bwf@virginia.edu
Database Mgr: Mary MacNeil *E-mail:* mmm5w@virginia.edu
Founded: 1963
General scholarly nonfiction with emphasis on history, literature & regional books.
ISBN Prefix(es): 978-0-8139; 978-978-0
Number of titles published annually: 65 Print; 60 E-Book
Total Titles: 1,350 Print
Distributor for Colonial Society of Massachusetts; Mount Vernon Ladies Association
Foreign Rep(s): East-West Export Books (The Pacific); Eurospan (Europe); Scholarly Book Services (Canada)
Shipping Address: Longleaf Services, 116 S Boundary St, Chapel Hill, NC 27514-3808 *Toll Free Tel:* 800-848-6224 *Toll Free Fax:* 800-272-6817 *E-mail:* orders@longleafservices.org SAN: 203-3151
Membership(s): American Association of University Presses

§University of Washington Press
4333 Brooklyn Ave NE, Seattle, WA 98105-9570
SAN: 212-2502
Mailing Address: PO Box 359570, Seattle, WA 98195-9570
Tel: 206-543-4050 *Toll Free Tel:* 800-537-5487 (orders) *Fax:* 206-543-3932; 410-516-6998 (orders)
E-mail: uwapress@uw.edu
Web Site: www.washington.edu/uwpress
Key Personnel
Dir: Nicole Mitchell *Tel:* 206-685-9373 *E-mail:* nfmm@uw.edu
Art Dir: Katrina Noble
Mktg & Sales Dir: Rachael Levay *Tel:* 617-871-0295 *Fax:* 617-932-1178 *E-mail:* remann@uw.edu
Exec Ed: Lorri Hagman *E-mail:* lhagman@uw.edu
Ed-in-Chief: Larin McLaughlin *Tel:* 206-221-4995 *E-mail:* lmclaugh@uw.edu
Sr Acqs Ed: Catherine Cocks
Edit, Design & Prodn Mgr: Margaret Sullivan
Sr Designer: Tom Eykemans *Tel:* 206-221-7004 *E-mail:* eykemans@uw.edu
Founded: 1920
General scholarly nonfiction, reprints, imports.
ISBN Prefix(es): 978-0-295
Number of titles published annually: 68 Print
Total Titles: 1,500 Print; 1 CD-ROM
Foreign Rep(s): Combined Academic Publisher Ltd (UK); Douglas & McIntyre (Canada); University of British Columbia Press (Canada)

University of Wisconsin Press
Unit of The University of Wisconsin
1930 Monroe St, 3rd fl, Madison, WI 53711-2059
SAN: 501-0039
Tel: 608-263-0668 *Toll Free Tel:* 800-621-2736 (orders) *Fax:* 608-263-1173 *Toll Free Fax:* 800-621-2736 (orders)
E-mail: uwiscpress@uwpress.wisc.edu (main off); publicity@uwpress.wisc.edu
Web Site: uwpress.wisc.edu
Key Personnel
Dir: Dennis Lloyd *Fax:* 608-263-1120 *E-mail:* dlloyd2@wisc.edu
Communs Dir: Sheila M Leary *Tel:* 608-263-0734
Journals Mgr: Toni Gunnison *Tel:* 608-263-0667 *E-mail:* gunnison@wisc.edu
Prodn Mgr & ISBN Contact: Terry Emmrich *Tel:* 608-263-0731 *E-mail:* temmrich@wisc.edu
Sales & Mktg Mgr: Andrea Christofferson *Tel:* 608-263-0814 *Fax:* 608-263-1132 *E-mail:* aschrist@wisc.edu
Sr Acqs Ed: Raphael Kadushin *Tel:* 608-263-1062 *E-mail:* kadushin@wisc.edu
Founded: 1936
Academic press, including regional Midwest titles & trade titles.
ISBN Prefix(es): 978-0-87972; 978-0-299; 978-1-928755; 978-0-87020; 978-0-9671787; 978-1-931; 978-8-158; 978-0-9682722; 978-0-924119; 978-0-9655464; 978-0-9718963; 978-0-9624369; 978-0-932900; 978-1-931569
Number of titles published annually: 60 Print; 1 CD-ROM; 60 E-Book; 1 Audio
Total Titles: 1,480 Print; 2 CD-ROM; 1,100 E-Book; 10 Audio
Imprints: Popular Press; Terrace Books
Distributor for The Center for the Study of Upper Midwestern Culture; Dryad Press; Elvehjem Museum of Art; Max Kade Institute for German-American Studies; Spring Freshet Press; Wisconsin Academy of Sciences, Arts & Letters; Wisconsin Veterans Museum
Foreign Rights: East-West Export Books Inc (Asia, Australia, New Zealand, The Pacific); Eurospan Ltd (Africa, Continental Europe, Iceland, Ireland, Middle East, UK)
Advertising Agency: Ad Vantage *E-mail:* advertising@uwpress.wisc.edu
Orders to: Chicago Distribution Center, 11030 S Langley Ave, Chicago, IL 60628-3892 *Tel:* 773-702-7000 *Toll Free Tel:* 800-621-2736 *Fax:* 773-702-7212 *Toll Free Fax:* 800-621-8476 *E-mail:* custserv@press.uchicago.edu SAN: 202-5280
Returns: Chicago Distribution Center, 11030 S Langley Ave, Chicago, IL 60628-3892 SAN: 202-5280
Shipping Address: Chicago Distribution Center, 11030 S Langley Ave, Chicago, IL 60628-3892 *E-mail:* custserv@press.uchicago.edu SAN: 202-5280
Warehouse: Chicago Distribution Center, 11030 S Langley Ave, Chicago, IL 60628-3892 *E-mail:* custserv@press.uchicago.edu SAN: 202-5280
Distribution Center: East-West Export Books, c/o University of Hawaii Press, 2840 Kolowalu St, Honolulu, HI 96822 (Asia, Australia, New Zealand & the Pacific) *Tel:* 808-956-8830 *Fax:* 808-988-6052 *E-mail:* eweb@hawaii.edu
Chicago Distribution Center, 11030 S Langley Ave, Chicago, IL 60628-3892 *Tel:* 773-568-1550 *Toll Free Tel:* 800-621-2736 *Fax:* 773-660-2235 *Toll Free Fax:* 800-621-8476 SAN: 202-5280
Eurospan Group, c/o Turpin Distribution, Stratton Business Park, Pegasus Dr, Biggleswade, Beds SG18 8TQ, United Kingdom (Africa, Europe, Middle East, UK & Russia) *Tel:* (01767) 604972 *Fax:* (01767) 601640 *E-mail:* eurospan@turpin-distribution.com
Membership(s): Association of American University Presses; Midwest Independent Booksellers Association; Wisconsin Library Association

University Press of America Inc
4501 Forbes Blvd, Suite 200, Lanham, MD 20706
SAN: 200-2256
Tel: 301-459-3366 *Toll Free Tel:* 800-462-6420 *Fax:* 301-429-5748 *Toll Free Fax:* 800-338-4550
Web Site: www.univpress.com
Key Personnel
VP & Publr: Julie Kirsch *E-mail:* jkirsch@rowman.com
VP, Mfg & Prodn: Stephen Driver
Dir, Mktg: Dave Horvath *E-mail:* dhorvath@rowman.com
Mgr, Rts & Perms & Intl Rts Contact: Clare Cox *E-mail:* ccox@rowman.com
Acqs Ed: Holly Buchanan *E-mail:* hbuchanan@univpress.com
Founded: 1975
Scholarly monographs, college texts, conference proceedings, professional books & reprints in the social sciences & the humanities.
ISBN Prefix(es): 978-0-8191; 978-0-7618
Number of titles published annually: 100 Print; 100 E-Book
Total Titles: 10,000 Print; 2,000 E-Book
Branch Office(s)
67 Mowat Ave, Suite 241, Toronto, ON M6K 3E3, Canada, Contact: Les Petriw *Tel:* 416-534-1660 *Toll Free Tel:* 877-626-2665 *Fax:* 416-534-3699 *E-mail:* kstinson@rowmanlittlefield.com
Distributor for Atlantic Council; Center for National Policy Press; Harvard Center for International Affairs; International Law Institute; Joint Center for Political & Economic Studies Press; White Burkett Miller Center; Society of the Cincinnati
Foreign Rep(s): NBN Plymbridge (Europe, UK); United Publishers Services (Japan)
Foreign Rights: United Publishers Service (Japan)
Shipping Address: 15200 NBN Way, Blue Ridge Summit, PA 17214-0191 *Toll Free Tel:* 800-462-6420 *Fax:* 717-794-3812 *Toll Free Fax:* 800-338-4550
Membership(s): AAP

University Press of Colorado
5589 Arapahoe Ave, Suite 206-C, Boulder, CO 80303
SAN: 202-1749
Tel: 720-406-8849 *Toll Free Tel:* 800-621-2736 (orders) *Fax:* 720-406-3443
Web Site: www.upcolorado.com
Key Personnel
Dir: Darrin Pratt *E-mail:* darrin@upcolorado.com
Acqs Ed: Jessica d'Arbonne *E-mail:* jessica@upcolorardo.com
Founded: 1965
Scholarly & regional nonfiction.
ISBN Prefix(es): 978-0-87081; 978-1-60732
Number of titles published annually: 30 Print; 30 E-Book
Total Titles: 340 Print; 3 CD-ROM; 334 E-Book
Imprints: Utah State University Press
Distributor for Center for Literary Publishing; History Colorado; Western Press Books
Foreign Rep(s): Codasat Canada Ltd (Canada); NBN International (Australia, UK & the continent)
Returns: Chicago Distribution Center, Returns Processing Ctr, 11030 S Langley, Chicago, IL 60628 *Toll Free Tel:* 800-621-2736
Distribution Center: Chicago Distribution Center, 11030 S Langley, Chicago, IL 60628 *Toll Free Tel:* 800-621-2736
Membership(s): Association of American University Presses
See separate listing for:
Utah State University Press

University Press of Florida
Affiliate of State University System of Florida
15 NW 15 St, Gainesville, FL 32603-2079
SAN: 207-9275
Tel: 352-392-1351 *Toll Free Tel:* 800-226-3822 (orders only) *Fax:* 352-392-0590 *Toll Free Fax:* 800-680-1955 (orders only)
E-mail: press@upress.ufl.edu; orders@upress.ufl.edu
Web Site: www.upf.com
Key Personnel
Dir: Meredith Morris-Babb *E-mail:* mb@upress.ufl.edu
Assoc Dir & Busn Mgr: Kim Lake *E-mail:* kl@upress.ufl.edu
Assoc Dir & EDP Mgr: Michele Fiyak-Burkley *E-mail:* mf@upress.ufl.edu
Deputy Dir & Ed-in-Chief: Linda Bathgate
Ed-at-Large: Judith Knight
Founded: 1945
Scholarly & regional nonfiction.
ISBN Prefix(es): 978-0-8130
Number of titles published annually: 100 Print; 100 E-Book
Total Titles: 2,830 Print; 1,850 E-Book
Imprints: Orange Grove Textbooks; University of Florida Press
Foreign Rights: Eurospan Group (Africa, Europe, Middle East, UK); Scholary Book Service (Canada)
Membership(s): American Association of University Presses

§University Press of Kansas
2502 Westbrooke Circle, Lawrence, KS 66045-4444
SAN: 203-3267
Tel: 785-864-4154; 785-864-4155 (orders) *Fax:* 785-864-4586
E-mail: upress@ku.edu; upkorders@ku.edu (orders)
Web Site: www.kansaspress.ku.edu
Key Personnel
Interim Dir & Busn Mgr: Conrad Roberts *Tel:* 785-864-9158 *E-mail:* ceroberts@ku.edu
Ed-in-Chief: Joyce Harrison *Tel:* 785-864-9162 *E-mail:* joyce@ku.edu
Art Dir & Webmaster: Karl Janssen *Tel:* 785-864-9164 *E-mail:* kjanssen@ku.edu

Mktg & Sales Dir: Mike Kehoe *Tel:* 785-864-9165 *E-mail:* mkehoe@ku.edu
Direct Mail & Exhibits Mgr: Debra Diehl *Tel:* 785-864-9166 *E-mail:* ddiehl@ku.edu
Publicity Mgr: Derek Helms *Tel:* 785-864-9170 *E-mail:* helms@ku.edu
Acqs Ed: Kim Hogeland *Tel:* 785-864-9161 *E-mail:* khogeland@ku.edu
Founded: 1946
General scholarly nonfiction: American, environmental & Western history, government & political science, military history, legal history, regional, women's studies, cultural studies, presidential studies.
ISBN Prefix(es): 978-978-07006
Number of titles published annually: 50 Print
Total Titles: 1,250 Print; 1 CD-ROM
Foreign Rep(s): East-West Export Books (Asia, The Pacific); Eurospan Ltd (Africa, Europe, Middle East, UK); Scholarly Book Services Inc (Canada)
Returns: University Press of Kansas Warehouse, 2445 Westbrooke Circle, Lawrence, KS 66045-4440
Warehouse: University Press of Kansas Warehouse, 2445 Westbrooke Circle, Lawrence, KS 66045-4440
Membership(s): Association of American University Presses

The University Press of Kentucky
663 S Limestone St, Lexington, KY 40508-4008
SAN: 203-3275
Tel: 859-257-8400 *Fax:* 859-257-8481
Web Site: www.kentuckypress.com
Key Personnel
Dir, Editing, Design & Prodn: David Cobb *Tel:* 859-257-4252 *Fax:* 859-257-2984 *E-mail:* dlcobb2@email.uky.edu
Dir, Mktg & Sales: Amy Harris *Tel:* 859-257-4249 *Fax:* 859-323-4981 *E-mail:* ae.harris@uky.edu
Dir, Fin & Admin: Craig Wilkie *Tel:* 859-257-8436 *Fax:* 859-257-7975 *E-mail:* crwilk00@email.uky.edu
Asst Dir, Fin & Admin: Teresa Wells Collins *Tel:* 859-257-8405 *E-mail:* twell1@email.uky.edu
Sr Acqs Ed: Anne Dean Dotson *Tel:* 859-257-8434 *Fax:* 859-323-1873 *E-mail:* adwatk0@email.uky.edu
Founded: 1943
ISBN Prefix(es): 978-0-8131
Number of titles published annually: 60 Print; 70 E-Book
Total Titles: 1,200 Print; 550 E-Book
Distributor for Kentucky Historical Society
Foreign Rep(s): Eurospan (UK & the continent); Scholarly Book Services (Canada)
Orders to: Hopkins Fulfillment Services, PO Box 50370, Baltimore, MD 21211-4370 *Tel:* 410-516-6956 *Toll Free Tel:* 800-537-5487 *Fax:* 410-516-6998 *E-mail:* hfscustserv@press.jhu.edu
Returns: Hopkins Fulfillment Services, c/o Maple Logistics Solutions, Lebanon Distribution Ctr, 704 Legionaire Dr, Fredericksburg, PA 17026 *Toll Free Tel:* 800-537-5487 *Fax:* 410-516-6998 *E-mail:* hfscustserv@press.jhu.edu
Membership(s): AAP; Association of American University Presses

University Press of Mississippi
3825 Ridgewood Rd, Jackson, MS 39211-6492
SAN: 203-1914
Tel: 601-432-6205 *Toll Free Tel:* 800-737-7788 (orders & cust serv) *Fax:* 601-432-6217
E-mail: press@mississippi.edu
Web Site: www.upress.state.ms.us
Key Personnel
Dir: Craig Gill *E-mail:* cgill@mississippi.edu
Assoc Dir/Mktg Dir: Steve Yates *E-mail:* syates@mississippi.edu
Busn Mgr: Tonia Lonie *E-mail:* tlonie@mississippi.edu
Data Servs & Course Adoptions Mgr: Kathy Burgess *E-mail:* kburgess@mississippi.edu
Prodn & Design Mgr: Todd Lape *E-mail:* tlape@mississippi.edu
Proj Mgr: Mrs Shane Gong Stewart *E-mail:* sgong@mississippi.edu
Publicity & Ad Mgr: Clint Kimberling *E-mail:* ckimberling@mississippi.edu
Admin Asst/Rts & Perms Mgr: Cynthia Foster *E-mail:* cfoster@mississippi.edu
Cust Serv & Order Supv: Sandy Alexander *Tel:* 601-432-6704 *E-mail:* salexander@mississippi.edu
Acqs Ed: Vijay Shah *E-mail:* vshah@mississippi.edu
Proj Ed: Valerie Jones *E-mail:* vjones@mississippi.edu
Assoc Proj Ed: Kristi Ezernack *E-mail:* kezernack@mississippi.edu
Assoc Ed: Katie Keene *E-mail:* kkeene@mississippi.edu
Sr Book Designer: Pete Halverson *E-mail:* phalverson@mississippi.edu
Book Designer: Jennifer Mixon *E-mail:* jmixon@mississippi.edu
Electronic & Direct-to-Consumer Mktg Specialist: Kristin Kirkpatrick *E-mail:* kkirkpatrick@mississippi.edu
Edit Asst: Lisa McMurtray *E-mail:* lmcmurtray@mississippi.edu
Mktg Asst: Courtney McCreary *E-mail:* cmccreary@mississippi.edu
Asst to the Dir: Emily Bandy *E-mail:* ebandy@mississippi.edu
Founded: 1970
Publisher of trade & scholarly books, nonfiction, fiction & regional.
ISBN Prefix(es): 978-0-87805; 978-1-57806; 978-1-934110; 978-1-60473; 978-1-61703; 978-1-62103; 978-1-62846; 978-1-62674; 978-1-4968
Number of titles published annually: 80 Print; 80 E-Book
Total Titles: 2,000 Print; 1,500 E-Book
Foreign Rep(s): Eurospan (Africa, Asia-Pacific, Caribbean, Continental Europe, Indian subcontinent, Ireland, Latin America, Middle East, UK); Scholarly Book Services Inc (Canada)
Advertising Agency: PM Productions, 203 Summer Hill Rd, Madison, MS 39110, Designer: Patti Mitchell *E-mail:* pattipmpro@aol.com
Returns: Maple Logistics Solutions, Lebanon Distribution Ctr, 704 Legionaire Dr, Fredericksburg, PA 17026 (non-USPS deliveries); Maple Logistics Solutions, Lebanon Distribution Ctr, PO Box 1287, Lebanon, PA 17042 (all USPS deliveries)
Warehouse: Maple Logistics Solutions, Lebanon Distribution Ctr, 704 Legionaire Dr, Fredericksburg, PA 17026
Membership(s): Association of American University Presses

University Press of New England
One Court St, Suite 250, Lebanon, NH 03766
SAN: 203-3283
Tel: 603-448-1533 *Toll Free Tel:* 800-421-1561 (orders only) *Fax:* 603-448-7006; 603-448-9429 (orders only)
E-mail: university.press@dartmouth.edu
Web Site: www.upne.com
Key Personnel
Dir: Michael Burton *Tel:* 603-448-1533 ext 201
Dir, Mktg & Sales: Richard Henning *Tel:* 603-448-1533 ext 234
Assoc Dir, Opers: Thomas Johnson *Tel:* 603-448-1533 ext 251
Acqs Ed-in-Chief: Phyllis Deutsch *Tel:* 603-448-1533 ext 222
Acqs Ed: Stephen Hull *Tel.* 603-448-1533 ext 225; Richard Pult *Tel:* 603-448-1533 ext 226
Publicity & Subs Rts Mgr: Barbara Briggs *Tel:* 603-448-1533 ext 233
Sales & Trade Exhibits Mgr: Sherri Strickland *Tel:* 603-448-1533 ext 238
Founded: 1970
Scholarly, nonfiction, regional, New England fiction.
ISBN Prefix(es): 978-0-87451; 978-1-58465
Number of titles published annually: 60 Print
Total Titles: 825 Print; 300 E-Book
Imprints: Brandeis University Press; Dartmouth College Press; ForeEdge; Hardscrabble Books; Northeastern University Press; Tufts University Press; University of New Hampshire Press; University of Vermont Press
Distributor for Academia Press; Autumn House Press; Bauhan Publishing; Carnegie Mellon University Press; CavanKerry Press; Chipstone Foundation; Duquesne University Press; Four Way Books; Historic New England; International Polar Institute; New Issues Poetry & Prose; Nightboat Books; Northeastern University Press; Oberlin College Press; Omnidawn Publishing; Peter E Randall Publisher; Saturnalia Books; The Sheep Meadow Press; Tagus Press; University of New Hampshire Press; Vermont Folklife Center; Warring States Project; Wesleyan University Press
Foreign Rep(s): East-West Export Books (Asia, Australia, New Zealand, The Pacific); Oxbow Books Ltd (Europe, Middle East, UK); University of Toronto Press (Canada)
Advertising Agency: New England Imprints, One Court St, Lebanon, NH 03766, Contact: Sara J Carpenter *Tel:* 603-448-1533 ext 231
Returns: UPNE Fulfillment, c/o Maple Logistics Solutions, Lebanon Distribution Ctr, 704 Legionaire Dr, Fredericksburg, PA 17026 *Tel:* 603-448-1533 ext 503 *Fax:* 603-448-9429
Membership(s): Association of American University Presses; NEBA

University Publishing Group
6 W Washington St, Suite 302, Hagerstown, MD 21740
Tel: 240-420-0036 *Fax:* 240-718-7100
E-mail: orders@upgbooks.com
Key Personnel
Owner & Treas: Norman Quist
Pres: Leslie LeBlanc *E-mail:* leblanc@upgbooks.com
Cust Serv Mgr: Mary Gesford
Founded: 1985
Publish books in medicine, social sciences, philosophy & law.
ISBN Prefix(es): 978-1-55572
Number of titles published annually: 6 Print
Total Titles: 35 Print

University Publishing House
PO Box 1664, Mannford, OK 74044
Tel: 918-865-4726
E-mail: upub5@outlook.com
Web Site: www.universitypublishinghouse.net
Key Personnel
Owner & Pres: Randell Nyborg
Founded: 1987
Industrial & automotive, classic fiction reprints, mail order books & industrial processes.
ISBN Prefix(es): 978-1-877767; 978-1-57002
Number of titles published annually: 5 Print
Total Titles: 140 Print

University Science Books
20 Edgeshill Rd, Mill Valley, CA 94941
SAN: 213-8085
Tel: 703-661-1572 (cust serv, orders) *Fax:* 703-661-1572 (cust serv, orders)
E-mail: usbmail@presswarehouse.com (cust serv, orders)
Web Site: www.uscibooks.com

Key Personnel
Pres: Bruce Armbruster
VP & Intl Rts Contact: Kathy Armbruster
Assoc Publr/Edit: Jane Ellis *Tel:* 973-378-3900 *Fax:* 973-378-3925 *E-mail:* bjellis@igc.org
Founded: 1978
Intermediate level college textbooks & monographs in astronomy, chemistry, biochemistry & physics, environmental science, technical writing, biology, reference books, children's books.
ISBN Prefix(es): 978-0-935702; 978-1-891389
Number of titles published annually: 8 Print; 8 E-Book
Total Titles: 200 Print; 200 E-Book
Foreign Rep(s): Palgrave Macmillan (Africa exc Botswana & South Africa, Australia, Austria, The Balkans exc Bulgaria, Greece & Turkey, Baltic States, British Commonwealth, Central Europe, China, Continental Europe, Europe, Saudi Arabia, South America)
Foreign Rights: Eastern Book Service Inc (Japan); Palgrave/Macmillan's Global Academic Publishing (Europe, India)
Orders to: Books International Inc, PO Box 605, Herndon, VA 20172, Contact: Todd Riggleman *Tel:* 703-661-1572 *Fax:* 703-661-1501
Returns: Books International Inc, 22883 Quicksilver Dr, Dulles, VA 20166 (15% restocking fee, damaged books not accepted, books must be in original shrinkwrap for credit) *Tel:* 703-661-1572 *Fax:* 703-661-1501
Distribution Center: Books International Inc, 22883 Quicksilver Dr, Dulles, VA 20166 (15% discount on all web orders) *Tel:* 703-661-1572 *Fax:* 703-661-1501 *E-mail:* usbmail@presswarehouse.com

UnKnownTruths.com Publishing Co
8815 Conroy Windermere Rd, Suite 190, Orlando, FL 32835
SAN: 255-6375
Tel: 407-929-9207
E-mail: info@unknowntruths.com
Web Site: unknowntruths.com
Key Personnel
Pres: Walter Parks *E-mail:* hparks@cfl.rr.com
Founded: 2002
Formed to publish true stories of the unusual or of the previously unexplained. Stories typically provide radically different views from those that have shaped the understandings of our natural world, our religions, our science, our history & even the foundations of our civilizations. Also include stories of the very important life-extending medical breakthroughs: stem cell therapies, genetic therapies, cloning & other emerging findings that promise to change the very meaning of life.
ISBN Prefix(es): 978-0-9745393
Number of titles published annually: 12 Print; 4 Online
Advertising Agency: James Brooke & Associates, 2660 Second St, Suite 1, Santa Monica, CA 90405, PR: Cherie Carter *Tel:* 310-396-8070 *Fax:* 310-396-8071 *E-mail:* cherie@unknowntruths.com
Distribution Center: New Leaf Distributing Co, 401 Thornton Rd, Lithia Springs, GA 30122 *Tel:* 770-948-7845 *Fax:* 770-944-2313
Quality Books Inc, 1003 W Pines Rd, Oregon, IL 61061 *Toll Free Tel:* 800-323-4241 *Fax:* 815-732-4499
Membership(s): The Association of Publishers for Special Sales; Independent Book Publishers Association

§Unlimited Publishing LLC
PO Box 99, Nashville, IN 47448
Tel: 206-666-5484
E-mail: acquisitions@unlimitedpublishing.com
Web Site: www.unlimitedpublishing.com
Founded: 2000
Bringing back out of print books & new nonfiction by professional writers. Visit web site for submission guidelines before sending a proposal. No simultaneous submissions; e-mail queries preferred, proposals sent by post will not be returned.
ISBN Prefix(es): 978-1-58832
Number of titles published annually: 25 Print; 25 Online; 25 E-Book
Total Titles: 250 Print
Membership(s): Independent Book Publishers Association

UNO Press
Division of University of New Orleans
University of New Orleans Metro College, 2000 Lakeshore Dr, New Orleans, LA 70148
Tel: 504-280-7457
E-mail: unopress@uno.edu
Web Site: unopress.org
Key Personnel
Mng Ed: George Darby
Founded: 2000
ISBN Prefix(es): 978-0-9728143; 978-0-9706190; 978-1-60801
Number of titles published annually: 4 Print; 3 E-Book
Total Titles: 40 Print; 3 E-Book
Distribution Center: Hopkins Fulfillment Services, PO Box 50370, Baltimore, MD 21211-4370 *Tel:* 410-516-6965 *Toll Free Tel:* 800-537-5487 *Fax:* 410-516-6998 *E-mail:* hfscustserv@press.jhu.edu *Web Site:* hfs.jhu.edu
Membership(s): Independent Book Publishers Association

Unveiled Media LLC
PO Box 930463, Verona, WI 53593
Tel: 707-986-8345
Web Site: www.unveiledmedia.com
Key Personnel
Publr: Michael Seelen *E-mail:* mseelen@unveiledmedia.com
Founded: 2012
Boutique publisher. Specialize in photography, works of fiction & children's books.
ISBN Prefix(es): 978-0-9776385
Number of titles published annually: 3 Print; 3 E-Book
Total Titles: 3 Print; 3 E-Book
Imprints: Cotton Candy Press; Iron Icon Books
Distribution Center: Create Space
Lightning Source
Membership(s): Independent Book Publishers Association

W E Upjohn Institute for Employment Research
300 S Westnedge Ave, Kalamazoo, MI 49007-4686
Tel: 269-343-5541; 269-343-4330 (pubns) *Toll Free Tel:* 888-227-8569 *Fax:* 269-343-7310
E-mail: publications@upjohn.org; communications@upjohn.org
Web Site: www.upjohn.org
Key Personnel
Mgr, Pubns: Richard Wyrwa
Founded: 1959
Labor economics & industrial relations.
ISBN Prefix(es): 978-0-88099; 978-0-911558
Number of titles published annually: 12 Print; 8 E-Book
Total Titles: 160 Print; 80 E-Book
Imprints: Upjohn Press
Membership(s): Association of American University Presses

§Upper Access Inc
87 Upper Access Rd, Hinesburg, VT 05461
SAN: 667-1195
Tel: 802-482-2988 *Toll Free Tel:* 800-310-8320 (orders) *Fax:* 802-417-3002
E-mail: info@upperaccess.com
Web Site: www.upperaccess.com
Key Personnel
VP & Publr: Stephen T Carlson *E-mail:* steve@upperaccess.com
Assoc Publr: Thomas Gray
Devt Dir: Ron Lawrence *Tel:* 802-899-2276 *Fax:* 802-899-1291 *E-mail:* ron@pubassist.com
Sales Dir: Kristen Lewis
Founded: 1986
Publisher of nonfiction books to improve the quality of life. Also publish business software.
ISBN Prefix(es): 978-0-942679
Number of titles published annually: 3 Print; 2 E-Book
Total Titles: 57 Print; 8 E-Book
Imprints: Upper Access Books; Publishers' Assistant (software & related servs)
Orders to: Midpoint National, 1263 Southwest Blvd, Kansas City, KS 66103 (trade sales & returns) *Tel:* 913-362-7400 *E-mail:* info@midpt.com *Web Site:* www.midpt.com
Returns: Midpoint National, 1263 Southwest Blvd, Kansas City, KS 66103 (trade sales & returns) *Tel:* 913-362-7400 *E-mail:* info@midpt.com *Web Site:* www.midpt.com
Shipping Address: Midpoint Trade Books, 27 W 20 St, Suite 1102, New York, NY 10011 (trade sales & returns) *Tel:* 212-727-0190 *Fax:* 212-727-0195 *E-mail:* nina@midpointtrade.com *Web Site:* www.midpointtrade.com
Warehouse: Midpoint Trade Books, 1550 Heil Quaker Blvd, La Vergne, TN 37086 (trade sales & returns) *Tel:* 212-616-2021 *E-mail:* julie@midpointtrade.com *Web Site:* www.midpointtrade.com
Distribution Center: Midpoint National, 1263 Southwest Blvd, Kansas City, KS 66103 (trade sales & returns) *Tel:* 913-362-7400 *E-mail:* info@midpt.com *Web Site:* www.midpt.com
Membership(s): The Association of Publishers for Special Sales; Independent Book Publishers Association; Independent Publishers of New England; Publishers North

§Upper Room Books
Division of The Upper Room
1908 Grand Ave, Nashville, TN 37212
SAN: 203-3364
Tel: 615-340-7200 *Toll Free Tel:* 800-972-0433 *Fax:* 615-340-7266
Web Site: books.upperroom.org
Key Personnel
Asst Ed & Admin Coord: Joanna Bradley *E-mail:* jbradley@umcdiscipleship.org
Dir, Prodn & Scheduling: Debbie Gregory *Tel:* 615-340-7224
Founded: 1935
Prayer & devotional life publications. No fiction or poetry accepted.
ISBN Prefix(es): 978-0-8358
Number of titles published annually: 20 Print; 20 E-Book
Imprints: Fresh Air Books
Foreign Rights: Riggins International Rights (worldwide exc North America)
Warehouse: PBD Inc, 1650 Bluegrass Pkwy, Alpharetta, GA 30201
Membership(s): ABA; CBA: The Association for Christian Retail; Evangelical Christian Publishers Association
See separate listing for:
Fresh Air Books

Upstart Books™
Division of Demco Inc
4810 Forest Run Rd, Madison, WI 53704
Mailing Address: PO Box 14410, Madison, WI 53708-0410

Tel: 608-241-1201 *Toll Free Tel:* 800-448-4887 (orders) *Toll Free Fax:* 800-448-5828
E-mail: custsvc@upstartpromotions.com
Web Site: www.demco.com/category/upstart-promotions
Key Personnel
Dir, Educ Mkts: Matt Mulder *E-mail:* mattm@demco.com
Founded: 1990
Reading activities & library skills for teachers & children's librarians; storytelling activity books & Internet resources.
ISBN Prefix(es): 978-0-917846; 978-0-913853; 978-1-57950; 978-1-932146
Number of titles published annually: 12 Print
Total Titles: 100 Print

§The Urban Institute
2100 "M" St NW, Washington, DC 20037
SAN: 203-3380
Tel: 202-833-7200
Web Site: www.urban.org
Founded: 1968
Public policy, economics, government, social sciences.
ISBN Prefix(es): 978-0-87766
Number of titles published annually: 10 Print
Membership(s): American Association of University Presses

Urim Publications
527 Empire Blvd, Brooklyn, NY 11225-3121
Tel: 718-972-5449 *Fax:* 718-972-6307
E-mail: publisher@urimpublications.com; editor@urimpublications.com
Web Site: urimpublications.com
Key Personnel
Publr: Tzvi Mauer
Children's Book Ed: Shari Dash Greenspan *E-mail:* children@urimpublications.com
Founded: 1997
Publisher & worldwide distributor of new & classic books with Jewish content.
ISBN Prefix(es): 978-965-7108
Number of titles published annually: 8 Print
Total Titles: 35 Print
Editorial Office(s): HaUman, 9 HaUman St, 2nd fl, PO Box 52287, Jerusalem 91521, Israel *Tel:* (02) 679-7633 *Fax:* (02) 679-7634
Distribution Center: Independent Publishers Group (IPG), 814 N Franklin St, Chicago, IL 60610 *Toll Free Tel:* 800-888-4741

Urzone Inc, see Zone Books

US Conference of Catholic Bishops
USCCB Publishing, 3211 Fourth St NE, Washington, DC 20017
Tel: 202-541-3090 *Toll Free Tel:* 800-235-8722 *Fax:* 202-722-8709 (orders)
E-mail: css@usccb.org; publications@usccb.org
Web Site: store.usccb.org
Founded: 1938
The official publisher for the US Catholic Bishop & Vatican documents; English & Spanish.
ISBN Prefix(es): 978-1-55586; 978-1-57455
Number of titles published annually: 20 Print
Total Titles: 820 Print
Returns: USCCB Returns, 3570 Blatensburg Rd, Brentwood, MD 20722
Membership(s): Association of Catholic Publishers Inc

US Games Systems Inc
179 Ludlow St, Stamford, CT 06902
SAN: 206-1368
Tel: 203-353-8400 *Toll Free Tel:* 800-54-GAMES (544-2637) *Fax:* 203-353-8431
E-mail: info@usgamesinc.com
Web Site: www.usgamesinc.com
Key Personnel
Founder & Chmn: Stuart R Kaplan *Tel:* 203-353-8400 ext 301
VP, Export Sales: Barbara Bensaid
Treas: Ricky Cruz
Art Dir: Paula Palmer
Founded: 1968
Popular & scholarly works in the field of tarot, wellness, inspiration, spirituality, educational games & the history of symbolism of playing cards; reprints of historical tarot decks & playing cards from the past five centuries.
ISBN Prefix(es): 978-0-913866; 978-0-88079; 978-1-57281
Number of titles published annually: 20 Print
Total Titles: 400 Print
Imprints: Cove Press
Distributor for Blue Angel Publishing; KonigsFurt
Foreign Rep(s): KonigsFurt (Germany); Koppenhol Agenturen (Netherlands); Lion Playing Card Co (Israel); Publishers Group (UK); David Westnedge Ltd (UK)

§US Government Publishing Office (GPO)
Division of US Government
Superintendent of Documents, 732 N Capitol St NW, Washington, DC 20401
Tel: 202-512-1800 *Toll Free Tel:* 866-512-1800 (orders) *Fax:* 202-512-2104
E-mail: contactcenter@gpo.gov
Web Site: www.gpo.gov; bookstore.gpo.gov (sales)
Key Personnel
Chief PR Offr: Gary Somerset
Acting Superintendent, Documents: Laurie Hall
Dir: Davita Vance-Cooks
Dir, Sales & Mktg: Jeffrey Turner *Tel:* 202-512-1055
Founded: 1861
Distributor & printer of federal government publications & public documents in various formats including ebooks; military, space exploration, political science.
ISBN Prefix(es): 978-0-16
Number of titles published annually: 250 Print; 15 Online
Total Titles: 2,500 Print; 140 CD-ROM
Imprints: Energy Information Administration (EIA)
Orders to: PO Box 979050, St Louis, MO 63197-9000
See separate listing for:
Energy Information Administration (EIA)

Utah Geological Survey
Division of Utah Department of Natural Resources
1594 W North Temple, Suite 3110, Salt Lake City, UT 84116-3154
Mailing Address: PO Box 146100, Salt Lake City, UT 84114-6100
Tel: 801-537-3300 *Toll Free Tel:* 888-UTAH-MAP (882-4627 bookstore) *Fax:* 801-537-3400
E-mail: geostore@utah.gov
Web Site: geology.utah.gov
Key Personnel
Geological Pubns Ed: Vicky Clarke *Tel:* 801-537-3330 *E-mail:* vickyclarke@utah.gov
Founded: 1935
ISBN Prefix(es): 978-1-55791
Number of titles published annually: 30 Print; 15 CD-ROM; 5 Online
Total Titles: 702 Print

Utah State University Press
Imprint of University Press of Colorado
3078 Old Main Hill, Logan, UT 84322-3078
Tel: 435-797-1362
Web Site: www.usupress.com
Key Personnel
Dir: Darrin Pratt *E-mail:* darrin@upcolorado.com
Founded: 1972
ISBN Prefix(es): 978-0-87421; 978-1-60732
Number of titles published annually: 20 Print
Total Titles: 250 Print
Membership(s): Association of American University Presses

VanDam Inc
The VanDam Bldg, 121 W 27 St, New York, NY 10001
Tel: 212-929-0416 *Toll Free Tel:* 800-UNFOLDS (863-6537) *Fax:* 212-929-0426
E-mail: info@vandam.com
Web Site: www.vandam.com
Key Personnel
Pres/Creative Dir: Stephan Van Dam *Tel:* 212-929-0416 ext 10 *E-mail:* stephan@vandam.com
VP, Sales: Bob Troast *Tel:* 212-929-0416 ext 12 *E-mail:* bob@vandam.com
Founded: 1984
Publisher of UNFOLDS®, StreetSmart & Pop-Up maps; licensor of patented folding technology used to produce UNFOLDS® products.
ISBN Prefix(es): 978-0-931141; 978-1-932527; 978-1-934395
Number of titles published annually: 50 Print
Total Titles: 250 Print
Imprints: @tlas®; Smartmaps®; UNFOLDS®
Divisions: VanDam Publishing
Foreign Rep(s): LAC (Italy); RV Verlag (Germany)

Vandamere Press
3580 Morris St N, St Petersburg, FL 33713
SAN: 657-3088
Mailing Address: PO Box 149, St Petersburg, FL 33731
Tel: 727-556-0950 *Toll Free Tel:* 800-551-7776 *Fax:* 727-556-2560
E-mail: orders@vandamere.com
Web Site: www.vandamere.com
Key Personnel
Publr & Ed-in-Chief: Arthur Brown *E-mail:* abrown@vandamere.com
Dir, Spec Sales: Stephanie Brown
Sr Book Ed & Acq Ed: Jerry Frank
Wholesale Sales: John Cabin
Founded: 1984
ISBN Prefix(es): 978-0-918339
Number of titles published annually: 8 Print
Total Titles: 70 Print
Distributor for ABI Professional Publications (non-exclusive); JMC Press (exclusive to trade); NRH Press (non-exclusive); Quodlibetal Features

Vanderbilt University Press
Division of Vanderbilt University
2014 Broadway, Suite 320, Nashville, TN 37203
SAN: 202-9308
Mailing Address: VU Sta B, No 351813, Nashville, TN 37235-1813
Tel: 615-322-3585 *Toll Free Tel:* 800-627-7377 (orders only) *Fax:* 615-343-8823 *Toll Free Fax:* 800-735-0476 (orders only)
E-mail: vupress@vanderbilt.edu
Web Site: www.vanderbiltuniversitypress.com
Key Personnel
Dir: Michael Ames
Mng Ed: Joell Smith Borne
Design & Prodn Mgr: Dariel Mayer *E-mail:* dariel.mayer@vanderbilt.edu
Busn Mgr & Rts & Perms: Gretta Thomas
Sales & Mktg Mgr: Betsy Phillips *E-mail:* betsy.phillips@vanderbilt.edu
Mktg & New Media Assoc: Jenna Phillips
Founded: 1940
Scholarly nonfiction, humanities, social sciences, literary criticism, history, regional studies.
ISBN Prefix(es): 978-0-8265
Number of titles published annually: 20 Print
Total Titles: 350 Print; 2 CD-ROM; 200 E-Book
Imprints: Country Music Foundation Press

Distributed by University of Oklahoma Press
Distributor for Country Music Foundation Press
Foreign Rep(s): Royden Muranaka (Australia, China, Hong Kong, India, Japan, Korea, New Zealand, Pacific Islands, Pakistan, Philippines, Southeast Asia, Taiwan)

Vault.com Inc
132 W 31 St, 16th fl, New York, NY 10001
Tel: 212-366-4212 *Toll Free Tel:* 800-535-2074 *Fax:* 212-366-6117 (cust serv)
E-mail: editors@vault.com; customerservice@vault.com
Web Site: www.vault.com
Key Personnel
Sr Fin Ed: Derek Loosvelt
Law Ed: Matt Moody
Consulting Ed: Phil Stott
Assoc Prodr: Cathy Vandewater
Founded: 1997
"Insider" career development for professionals.
ISBN Prefix(es): 978-1-58131
Number of titles published annually: 4 Print; 10 Online
Total Titles: 61 Print; 124 Online

Vedanta Press
Subsidiary of Vedanta Society of Southern California
1946 Vedanta Place, Hollywood, CA 90068
Tel: 323-960-1327 *Toll Free Tel:* 800-816-2242 (catalog) *Fax:* 323-465-9568
E-mail: vpress@vedanta.org
Web Site: www.vedanta.com
Key Personnel
Mgr: Robert Adjemian *E-mail:* bob@vedanta.org
Founded: 1945
ISBN Prefix(es): 978-81-85301 (Advaita Ashrama); 978-0-87481; 978-81-8172 (Ramakrishna Math); 978-81-7505
Number of titles published annually: 1 CD-ROM; 5 Online
Total Titles: 17 CD-ROM; 25 Online
Distributor for Advaita Ashrama; Ananda Ashrama; Ramakrishna Math; Ramakrishna-Vivkanana
Membership(s): Independent Book Publishers Association

Velazquez Press
Division of Academic Learning Co LLC
9682 Telstar Ave, Suite 110, El Monte, CA 91731
Tel: 626-448-3448 *Fax:* 626-602-3817
E-mail: info@academiclearningcompany.com
Web Site: www.velazquezpress.com
Key Personnel
Mng Dir: Arthur Chou
Dir, Busn Devt: Jonathan Ruiz *E-mail:* jruiz@academiclearningcompany.com
Founded: 2003
Publisher of bilingual dictionaries.
ISBN Prefix(es): 978-1-59495
Number of titles published annually: 4 Print
Total Titles: 10 Print

The Vendome Press
244 Fifth Ave, Suite 2043, New York, NY 10001
Tel: 212-737-1857
E-mail: info@vendomepress.com
Web Site: www.vendomepress.com
Key Personnel
Chmn: Alexis Gregory
Pres: Mark Magowan
Prodn Dir: Jim Spivey
Ed: Jackuelen Decter
Founded: 1981
Illustrated art, architecture & lifestyle books.
ISBN Prefix(es): 978-0-86565
Number of titles published annually: 10 Print
Total Titles: 85 Print
Distributed by Abrams Books
Distributor for Thames & Hudson

Venture Publishing Inc
1999 Cato Ave, State College, PA 16801
SAN: 240-897X
Tel: 814-234-4561 *Fax:* 814-234-1651
E-mail: vpublish@venturepublish.com
Web Site: www.venturepublish.com
Key Personnel
Pres: Frank Guadagnolo
Mgr: Kay Whiteside *E-mail:* cawhiteside@venturepublish.com
Ed: Geoffrey Godbey
Prodn: George Lauer *E-mail:* glauer@venturepublish.com; Richard Yocum
Founded: 1979
Parks & recreation, social sciences & sociology, leisure studies, long-term care, therapeutic recreation.
ISBN Prefix(es): 978-0-910251; 978-1-892132
Number of titles published annually: 8 Print
Total Titles: 86 Print
Foreign Rep(s): Creative & More Inc (Taiwan); HM Leisure Planning Pty Ltd (Australia, Canada, New Zealand)

Vernon Press
Imprint of Vernon Art & Science Inc
1000 N West St, Suite 1200, Wilmington, DE 19801
Tel: 302-250-4440
E-mail: info@vernonpress.com
Web Site: www.vernonpress.com
Key Personnel
Dir: Rosario Batana
ISBN Prefix(es): 978-1-62273
Number of titles published annually: 10 Print

Verso
20 Jay St, Suite 1010, Brooklyn, NY 11201
Tel: 718-246-8160 *Fax:* 718-246-8165
E-mail: verso@versobooks.com
Web Site: www.versobooks.com
Key Personnel
Mng Dir: Jacob Stevens
Creative Dir: Rachel Rosenfelt
Mktg Mgr: Anne Rumberger
Founded: 1970
Nonfiction, progressive studies on politics, history, society & culture.
ISBN Prefix(es): 978-0-86091; 978-0-85984; 978-0-84467
Number of titles published annually: 80 Print
Total Titles: 2,000 Print
Foreign Office(s): 6 Meard St, London W1F OE6, United Kingdom
Distributed by Penguin (Canada)
Foreign Rep(s): Verso (England)
Foreign Rights: Verso (worldwide)
Shipping Address: Marston Book Services, Kemp Hall Bindery, Osney Mead, Oxford, United Kingdom

Vesuvian Books
Division of Vesuvian Media Group Inc
2817 West End Ave, Nashville, TN 37203
Mailing Address: 711 Dolly Parton Pkwy, No 4313, Sevierville, TN 37864
E-mail: info@vesuvianmedia.com
Web Site: www.vesuvianbooks.com
Key Personnel
CEO/Founder: Italia Gandolfo *E-mail:* italia@vesuvianmedia.com
Dir of Opers: Liana Gardner *E-mail:* liana@vesuvianmedia.com
Exec Chmn: Thomas N Ellsworth
Dir of Acqs: Elizabeth Isaacs
Dir of Busn Devt: Gareth Worthington
Art Dir: Sam Shearon
Creative Dir: Michael J Canales
Founded: 2015
A multimedia corporation dedicated to creating quality entertainment across literary & visual arts. Vesuvian Books does not accept unsol submissions. Prospective authors & illustrators must submit their work through an agent.
ISBN Prefix(es): 978-1-944109
Number of titles published annually: 15 Print; 15 E-Book
Total Titles: 12 Print; 15 E-Book
Foreign Rights: Books Crossing Borders (Betty Anne Crawford) (worldwide exc USA)
Billing Address: 711 Dolly Parton Pkwy, No 4313, Sevierville, TN 37864 *Tel:* 502-836-1201
Warehouse: Pathway Book Services, 34 Production Ave, Keene, NH 03431, Contact: Julie Ballou *Tel:* 603-357-0236 *Toll Free Tel:* 800-345-6665 *Fax:* 603-965-2181 *E-mail:* julie.ballou@pathwaybook.com *Web Site:* pathwaybook.com
Distribution Center: Ingram, One Ingram Blvd, La Vergne, TN 37086 *Tel:* 615-793-5000 *Web Site:* www.ingramcontent.com
Membership(s): Horror Writers Association; Independent Book Publishers Association

Victory in Grace Press
Division of Victory in Grace Ministries
60 Quentin Rd, Lake Zurich, IL 60047
Tel: 847-438-4494 *Toll Free Tel:* 800-78-GRACE (784-7223) *Fax:* 847-438-4232
E-mail: feedback@victoryingrace.org
Web Site: www.victoryingrace.org
Key Personnel
Founder: Dr James A Scudder
Founded: 2000
Publish conservative evangelical books, audio series, magazines & tracts.
ISBN Prefix(es): 978-0-9679145; 978-0-9719262
Number of titles published annually: 3 Print; 4 E-Book; 3 Audio
Total Titles: 9 Print; 4 E-Book; 15 Audio

Viking
Imprint of Penguin Group USA, A Penguin Random House Company
375 Hudson St, New York, NY 10014
Tel: 212-366-2000 *Fax:* 212-243-6002
Web Site: www.penguin.com/publishers/vikingbooks
Key Personnel
Pres & Publr: Brian Tart
SVP & Creative Art Dir: Paul Buckley
VP & Publr, Pamela Dorman Books: Pamela Dorman
VP, Assoc Publr & Dir, Mktg: Kate Stark
VP, Assoc Publr & Edit Dir (Nonfiction): Wendy Wolf
VP & Exec Dir, Copyediting: Tory Klose
VP & Exec Ed: Paul Slovak
VP & Exec Ed, Viking/Penguin: Carole DeSanti
VP & Exec Publicist: Carolyn Coleburn
Exec Dir, Ad & Promo: Dennis Swaim
Dir, Publicity: Lindsay Prevette
Assoc Dir, Publicity: Shannon Twomey
Publicity Mgr, Viking/Penguin: Rebecca Marsh
Sr Publicist: Tony Forde; Alison Klooster; Olivia Taussig
Publicist: Chris Smith
Assoc Publicist: Andrea Lam; Brianna Linden
Ed-in-Chief: Andrea Schulz
Exec Mng Ed: Tricia Conley
Exec Ed: Carolyn Carlson; Joy de Menil; Rick Kot; Allison Lorentzen; Laura Tisdel
Ed: Emily Wunderlich
Asst Ed: Georgia Bodnar; Diego Nunez; Jeramie Orton
Founded: 1925
ISBN Prefix(es): 978-0-670
Number of titles published annually: 75 Print
Total Titles: 250 Print
Imprints: Viking Compass
Advertising Agency: Spier NY

Viking Children's Books
Imprint of Penguin Group USA, A Penguin Random House Company
345 Hudson St, New York, NY 10014
Fax: 212-414-3393
E-mail: youngreaderspublicity@us.penguingroup.com
Web Site: www.penguin.com/publishers/vikingchildrensbooks
Key Personnel
VP & Publr: Ken Wright
VP & Art Dir: Denise Cronin
Assoc Publr & Mng Ed: Gerard Mancini
Edit Dir, Picture Books: Tracy Gates
Exec Ed: Kendra Levin
Asst Ed: Maggie Rosenthal
Ed-at-Large: Regina Hayes
Founded: 1933
ISBN Prefix(es): 978-0-670
Number of titles published annually: 60 Print
Membership(s): The Children's Book Council

Viking Studio
Imprint of Penguin Group USA, A Penguin Random House Company
375 Hudson St, New York, NY 10014
Tel: 212-366-2000 *Fax:* 212-366-2636
E-mail: averystudiopublicity@us.penguingroup.com
Web Site: www.penguin.com
Key Personnel
Pres & Publr: Brian Tart
Founded: 1988
ISBN Prefix(es): 978-0-14; 978-0-670
Number of titles published annually: 4 Print
Total Titles: 40 Print
Advertising Agency: Spier NY

Carl Vinson Institute of Government
University of Georgia, 201 N Milledge Ave, Athens, GA 30602
Tel: 706-542-2736 *Fax:* 706-542-9301
Web Site: www.cviog.uga.edu
Key Personnel
Dir: Laura Meadows *Tel:* 706-542-6192 *E-mail:* lmeadows@uga.edu
Communs Dir: Jana Wiggins *Tel:* 706-542-6221 *E-mail:* wigginsj@uga.edu
Founded: 1927
Instruction, technical assistance, research & publications for state & local governments & communities.
ISBN Prefix(es): 978-0-89854
Number of titles published annually: 10 Print; 2 CD-ROM
Total Titles: 70 Print; 3 CD-ROM

Vintage Books
Imprint of Knopf Doubleday Publishing Group
c/o Penguin Random House Inc, 1745 Broadway, New York, NY 10019
Tel: 212-572-2420
E-mail: vintageanchorpublicity@randomhouse.com
Web Site: knopfdoubleday.com/imprint/vintage
Key Personnel
EVP & Publr: Anne Messitte
SVP & Edit Dir: Luann Walther
VP & Assoc Publr: Beth Lamb
VP & Exec Dir, Publicity & Soc Media: Russell Perreault
VP & Exec Ed: Edward Kastenmeier
Design Dir: Claudia Martinez
Dir, Ad & Promo: Irena Vukov-Kendes
Dir, Digital Mktg: Paige Smith
Dir, Digital Publg & Busn Devt: Laura Crisp
Dir, Publicity: Kate Runde
Mng Ed: Barbara Richard
Sr Ed: Lexy Bloom
Ed: Margaux Weisman
Publicity Mgr: Angie Venezia
Founded: 1954
ISBN Prefix(es): 978-0-307; 978-0-679; 978-0-375; 978-1-4000; 978-0-394
Number of titles published annually: 175 Print; 190 E-Book
Total Titles: 2,650 Print; 1,750 E-Book
Imprints: Vintage Shorts (ebooks)
Foreign Rights: Anthea Agency (Katalina Sabeva) (Bulgaria); Bardon-Chinese Media Agency (Xu Weiguang) (China); Bardon-Chinese Media Agency (Yu Shiuan Chen & David Tsai) (Taiwan); The English Agency (Hamish Macaskill & Junzo Sawa) (Japan); Graal Literary Agency (Maria Strarz-Kanska) (Poland); The Deborah Harris Agency (Ilana Kurshan) (Israel); JLM Literary Agency (Nelly Moukakou) (Greece); Katai & Bolza Literary (Peter Bolza) (Croatia, Hungary, Serbia); Simona Kessler Agency (Simona Kessler) (Romania); Korea Copyright Center (MiSook Hong) (Korea); Licht & Burr Literary Agency (Trine Licht) (Scandinavia); La Nouvelle Agence (Vanessa Kling) (France); Kristin Olson Literary Agency (Kristin Olson) (Czech Republic); Agenzia Letteraria Santachiara (Roberto Santachiara) (Italy); Sebes & Bisseling Literary Agency (Holland)

Visible Ink Press®
43311 Joy Rd, Suite 414, Canton, MI 48187-2075
Tel: 734-667-3211 *Fax:* 734-667-4311
E-mail: info@visibleinkpress.com
Web Site: www.visibleinkpress.com
Key Personnel
Publr: Roger Janecke
Founded: 1989
Popular reference publisher specializing in handy answer books, spiritual phenomena & encyclopedias.
ISBN Prefix(es): 978-0-8103; 978-0-7876; 978-1-57859
Number of titles published annually: 10 Print; 10 E-Book
Total Titles: 100 Print; 300 E-Book
Distribution Center: Legato Publishers Group, 1814 William St, River Forest, IL 60305 *Tel:* 630 947-2217 *Toll Free Tel:* 800-343-4499 *Web Site:* www.legatopublishersgroup.com

§Visual Profile Books Inc
389 Fifth Ave, Suite 1105, New York, NY 10016
SAN: 213-1552
Tel: 212-279-7000
Web Site: www.visualprofilebooks.com
Key Personnel
Publr: Larry Fuersich *Tel:* 212-279-7000 ext 314 *E-mail:* larry@visualprofilebooks.com
Edit Dir: Roger Yee *E-mail:* rhtyee@gmail.com
Founded: 1931
Architecture, interior & graphic design.
ISBN Prefix(es): 978-0-9825989
Number of titles published annually: 15 Print
Total Titles: 568 Print
Foreign Rights: Larry Fuersich
Distribution Center: National Book Network, 15200 NBN Way, Blue Ridge Summit, PA 17214 *Tel:* 717-794-3800 *Fax:* 717-794-3828 *E-mail:* customercare@nbnbooks.com *Web Site:* nbnbooks.com

Viva Editions, see Cleis Press

Volcano Press
21496 National St, Volcano, CA 95689
Mailing Address: PO Box 270, Volcano, CA 95689-0270 SAN: 220-0015
Tel: 209-296-7989
E-mail: sales@volcanopress.com
Web Site: www.volcanopress.com
Key Personnel
Publr: Adam Gottstein *E-mail:* adam@volcanopress.com
Founded: 1969
Domestic violence, general trade, professional books, Spanish language books; medicine, health & nutrition, psychology, social sciences, women's studies.
ISBN Prefix(es): 978-0-912078; 978-1-884244
Number of titles published annually: 3 Print; 3 E-Book
Total Titles: 50 Print; 1 Audio
Imprints: Kazan Media
Sales Office(s): PO Box 270, Volcano, CA 95689-0270 SAN: 220-0015
Billing Address: PO Box 270, Volcano, CA 95689-0270 SAN: 220-0015

Ludwig von Mises Institute
518 W Magnolia Ave, Auburn, AL 36832
Tel: 334-321-2100 *Fax:* 334-321-2119
E-mail: info@mises.org
Web Site: www.mises.org
Key Personnel
CEO: Lew Rockwell
Bookstore Mgr: Brandon Hill *E-mail:* brandon@mises.org
Founded: 1982
Nonprofit educational organization devoted to the Austrian School of Economics.
ISBN Prefix(es): 978-0-945466; 978-1-933550; 978-1-61016
Number of titles published annually: 7 Print; 8 Audio
Total Titles: 54 Print

§Voyager Sopris Learning Inc
Imprint of Cambium Learning Inc
17855 Dallas Pkwy, Suite 400, Dallas, TX 75287
Tel: 303-651-2829 *Toll Free Tel:* 800-547-6747 *Fax:* 303-776-5934 *Toll Free Fax:* 888-819-7767
E-mail: customerservice@voyagersopris.com
Web Site: www.voyagersopris.com
Founded: 1978
Training, development materials for educators.
ISBN Prefix(es): 978-0-944584; 978-1-57035; 978-1-59318
Number of titles published annually: 100 Print
Total Titles: 350 Print

Wake Forest University Press
A5 Tribble Hall, Wake Forest University, Winston-Salem, NC 27109
Mailing Address: PO Box 7333, Winston-Salem, NC 27109-7333
Tel: 336-758-5448 *Fax:* 336-758-5636
E-mail: wfupress@wfu.edu
Web Site: wfupress.wfu.edu
Key Personnel
Founder & Advising Ed: Dillon Johnston
Dir & Ed: Jefferson Holdridge
Mgr: Amanda Keith
Founded: 1975
Contemporary Irish poetry.
ISBN Prefix(es): 978-0-916390; 978-1-930630
Number of titles published annually: 5 Print
Total Titles: 100 Print

Walch Education
40 Walch Dr, Portland, ME 04103-1286
SAN: 203-0268
Tel: 207-772-2846 *Toll Free Tel:* 800-558-2846 *Fax:* 207-772-3105 *Toll Free Fax:* 888-991-5755
E-mail: customerservice@walch.com
Web Site: www.walch.com
Key Personnel
Pres: Al Noyes *E-mail:* anoyes@walch.com
VP, Educ: Jill Rosenblum *E-mail:* jrosenblum@walch.com
Founded: 1927
Educational books & supplementary materials for middle school through adult.
ISBN Prefix(es): 978-0-8251

Number of titles published annually: 100 Print; 75 Online
Total Titles: 1,700 Print; 850 Online
Membership(s): ASCD; International Literacy Association; National Council for the Social Studies; National Council of Teachers of English; National Council of Teachers of Mathematics; National Science Teachers Association

Walch Publishing, see Walch Education

Waldorf Publishing
2140 Hall Johnson Rd, No 102-345, Grapevine, TX 76051
Tel: 972-674-3131
E-mail: info@waldorfpublishing.com
Web Site: www.waldorfpublishing.com
Key Personnel
Owner & Publr: Barbara Terry
Founded: 2014
ISBN Prefix(es): 978-1-68419; 978-1-943275; 978-1-943277; 978-1-944245; 978-1-945173
Number of titles published annually: 55 Print; 55 CD-ROM; 55 Online; 55 E-Book; 55 Audio
Total Titles: 200 Print; 200 CD-ROM; 200 Online; 200 E-Book; 200 Audio
Foreign Rights: Susan Schulman Literary Agency (worldwide)
Distribution Center: Bookmasters, 30 Amberwood Pkwy, Ashland, OH 44805 (worldwide)

Frederick Warne
Imprint of Penguin Group USA, A Penguin Random House Company
375 Hudson St, New York, NY 10014
SAN: 282-5074
Tel: 212-366-2000
Web Site: www.penguin.com
Founded: 1865
ISBN Prefix(es): 978-0-7232
Number of titles published annually: 22 Print
Total Titles: 201 Print
Foreign Rep(s): Bardon-Chinese Media Agency (China); DRT International (Korea); ICBS (Netherlands, Scandinavia); International Press Agency (South Africa); The Italian Literary Agency srl (Italy); Japan UNI (Japan); Literari Agentura (Czech Republic); Mohrbooks (Germany); La Nouvelle Agence (France); I Pikarski Ltd Literary Agency (Israel)

Warner Press
Affiliate of Church of God
1201 E Fifth St, Anderson, IN 46018
Tel: 765-644-7721 *Toll Free Tel:* 800-741-7721 (orders) *Fax:* 765-640-8005 *Toll Free Fax:* 800-347-6411
E-mail: wporders@warnerpress.org
Web Site: www.warnerpress.org
Key Personnel
Pres: Eric King
VP, Sales: Connie Crist
VP, Prod Mktg: Regina Jackson
Founded: 1881
Specialize in religious books, activity books, coloring books & greeting cards.
ISBN Prefix(es): 978-0-87162; 978-1-59317
Number of titles published annually: 6 Print

Warren Communications News Inc
2115 Ward Ct NW, Washington, DC 20037
Tel: 202-872-9200 *Toll Free Tel:* 800-771-9202 *Fax:* 202-293-3435; 202-318-8350
E-mail: info@warren-news.com; newsroom@warren-news.com
Web Site: www.warren-news.com
Key Personnel
Chmn & Publr: Paul Warren
Pres & Ed: Daniel Warren *E-mail:* dwarren@warren-news.com
Exec Ed: Jonathan Make
NY Bureau Chief: Paul Gluckman
Founded: 1945
Newsletters & directories.
ISBN Prefix(es): 978-0-911486
Number of titles published annually: 7 Print
Total Titles: 7 Print

Washington State University Press
Division of Washington State University
Cooper Publications Bldg, Grimes Way, Pullman, WA 99164-5910
SAN: 206-6688
Mailing Address: PO Box 645910, Pullman, WA 99164-5910
Tel: 509-335-3518; 509-335-7880 (order fulfillment) *Toll Free Tel:* 800-354-7360 (orders) *Fax:* 509-335-8568
E-mail: wsupress@wsu.edu
Web Site: wsupress.wsu.edu
Key Personnel
Dir: Edward Sala *E-mail:* sala@wsu.edu
Prodn Ed & NW Sci Ed: Nancy Grunewald *Tel:* 509-335-5817 *E-mail:* grunewan@wsu.edu
Mktg Mgr: Caryn Lawton *Tel:* 509-335-7877 *E-mail:* lawton@wsu.edu
Founded: 1928
Trade & scholarly books focusing on the history, natural history, military history, culture & politics of the greater Pacific Northwest region (Washington, Idaho, Oregon, Western Montana, British Columbia & Alaska). Refer to web site for submission guidelines.
ISBN Prefix(es): 978-0-87422
Number of titles published annually: 10 Print
Total Titles: 182 Print
Sales Office(s): Hand Associates, 408 30 Ave, Seattle, WA 98122, Sales Rep: David Diehl *Tel:* 206-328-0295 *E-mail:* david_diehl@mindspring.com
Wholesale Solutions, 1959 NW Dock Place, Suite 3002, Seattle, WA 98107, Contact: David Diehl *Tel:* 206-310-9207 *E-mail:* david_diehl@mindspring.com
Hand Associates, 16 Nelson Ave, Mill Valley, CA 94941-2120, Sales Rep: David Diehl *Tel:* 415-383-3883 *E-mail:* david_diehl@mindspring.com
Hand Associates, 3851 Daisy Circle, Seal Beach, CA 90740-2901, Sales Rep: David Diehl *Tel:* 562-431-0771 *E-mail:* david_diehl@mindspring.com
Distributor for The Hutton Settlement (single title); Oregon California Trails Assn; Oregon Writers Colony (single title); Pacific Institute (single title); Washington State Historical Society (single title); WSU Museum of Art
Distribution Center: Baker & Taylor Books, PO Box 8888, Momence, IL 60954 (US & CN) *Toll Free Tel:* 800-775-1100 *Toll Free Fax:* 800-775-7480
Ingram Book Co, One Ingram Blvd, La Vergne, TN 37086 (US & CN) *Toll Free Tel:* 800-937-8000
Membership(s): Association of American University Presses

Water Environment Federation
601 Wythe St, Alexandria, VA 22314-1994
Tel: 703-684-2400 *Toll Free Tel:* 800-666-0206 (cust serv) *Fax:* 703-684-2492
E-mail: inquiry@wef.org
Web Site: www.wef.org
Key Personnel
Pubns: Jessica Rozek *Tel:* 703-684-2400 ext 7552 *E-mail:* jrozek@wef.org
Founded: 1928
Scientific publisher of environmental titles. Seeks authors of sound, state-of-the-art environmental material.
ISBN Prefix(es): 978-0-943244; 978-1-881369
Number of titles published annually: 15 Print
Total Titles: 220 Print

§Water Resources Publications LLC
PO Box 630026, Highlands Ranch, CO 80163-0026
SAN: 209-9136
Tel: 720-873-0171 *Toll Free Tel:* 800-736-2405 *Fax:* 720-873-0173 *Toll Free Fax:* 800-616-1971
E-mail: info@wrpllc.com
Web Site: www.wrpllc.com
Key Personnel
Busn Mgr: Jennie Campbell
Founded: 1971
Publishing & distributing books & computer software on water resources & related fields.
ISBN Prefix(es): 978-0-918334; 978-1-887201
Number of titles published annually: 10 Print
Total Titles: 220 Print; 35 CD-ROM
Distributor for ASAE; ASCE
Shipping Address: 10607 Flatiron Rd, Littleton, CO 80124 *Toll Free Fax:* 844-270-6832
Warehouse: 10607 Flatiron Rd, Littleton, CO 80124 *Toll Free Fax:* 844-270-6832

WaterBrook
Imprint of Crown Publishing Group
10807 New Allegiance Dr, Suite 500, Colorado Springs, CO 80921
Tel: 719-590-4999 *Toll Free Tel:* 800-603-7051 (orders) *Fax:* 719-590-8977 *Toll Free Fax:* 800-294-5686 (orders)
E-mail: info@waterbrookmultnomah.com
Web Site: waterbrookmultnomah.com
Founded: 1996
Publishes Christian books that seek to intensify & satisfy a reader's elemental thirst for a deeper relationship with God. Seek messages that draw on the Bible, experiential learning, story, practical guidance & inspiration to help readers thrive in their faith.
ISBN Prefix(es): 978-1-57856; 978-0-7352; 978-1-4000; 978-1-60142
Number of titles published annually: 41 Print
Imprints: Shaw Books
Membership(s): Evangelical Christian Publishers Association

Watermark Publishing
1000 Bishop St, Suite 806, Honolulu, HI 96813
Tel: 808-587-7766 *Toll Free Tel:* 866-900-BOOK (900-2665) *Fax:* 808-521-3461
E-mail: info@bookshawaii.net
Web Site: www.bookshawaii.net
Key Personnel
Dir, Sales & Mktg: Dawn Sakamoto *Tel:* 808-534-7170 *E-mail:* dawn@bookshawaii.net
ISBN Prefix(es): 978-0-9720932; 978-0-9705787; 978-0-9631154; 978-0-9753740; 978-0-9779143; 978-0-9790647; 978-0-9796769; 978-0-9815086
Number of titles published annually: 8 Print
Total Titles: 55 Print

Watson-Guptill Publications
Imprint of Crown Publishing Group
c/o Ten Speed Press, 6001 Shellmount St, Suite 600, Emeryville, CA 94608
Web Site: crownpublishing.com/imprint/watson-guptill
Founded: 1937
Hard-working & influential illustrated art books. Seeks out respected authorities who instruct & inspire artists in a wide range of art & craft. List covers both fine art & practical art instruction in traditional disciplines such as drawing, painting, sculpture & printmaking. Also publish modern books focused on artistic pursuits such as craft, collage, mixed media, comics, sequential art, cartooning, manga & animation.
ISBN Prefix(es): 978-0-8230; 978-0-8174; 978-1-58065
Number of titles published annually: 60 Print
Total Titles: 800 Print

Orders to: Penguin Random House Inc, 400 Hahn Rd, Westminster, MD 21157 *Toll Free Tel:* 800-733-3000 *E-mail:* csorders@randomhouse.com; Penguin Random House of Canada Inc, Diversified Sales, 2775 Mattheson Blvd E, Mississauga, ON L4W 4P4, Canada *Toll Free Tel:* 800-668-4247 *Fax:* 905-624-8091

Watson Publishing International LLC
PO Box 1240, Sagamore Beach, MA 02562-1240
Tel: 508-888-9113
E-mail: orders@watsonpublishing.com; orders@shpusa.com
Web Site: www.shpusa.com; www.watsonpublishing.com
Key Personnel
Pres & CEO: Neale W Watson, Esq *E-mail:* nww@shpusa.com
Founded: 1971
Scholarly books on the history, philosophy & sociology of science, technology & medicine.
ISBN Prefix(es): 978-0-88135
Number of titles published annually: 5 Print
Total Titles: 120 Print
Imprints: Prodist; Science History Publications USA; Neale Watson Academic Publications
Shipping Address: Publishers Storage & Shipping Corp, 46 Development Rd, Fitchburg, MA 01420-6020, Publr Rep: Donna Machonis *Tel:* 978-345-2121 ext 380

Waveland Press Inc
4180 IL Rte 83, Suite 101, Long Grove, IL 60047-9580
SAN: 209-0961
Tel: 847-634-0081 *Fax:* 847-634-9501
E-mail: info@waveland.com
Web Site: www.waveland.com
Key Personnel
Pres & Publr: Neil Rowe
Ed: Carol Rowe
Ed & Mktg Mgr: Thomas Curtin
Ed, Prodn Mgr, & Intl Rts: Don Rosso
Founded: 1975
College textbooks & supplements.
ISBN Prefix(es): 978-0-88133; 978-0-917974; 978-1-57766; 978-1-4786
Number of titles published annually: 40 Print
Total Titles: 700 Print
Subsidiaries: Sheffield Publishing Co
Warehouse: 9009 Antioch Rd, Salem, WI 53168, Gen Mgr: Steve Nelson

Wayne State University Press
Leonard N Simons Bldg, 4809 Woodward Ave, Detroit, MI 48201-1309
SAN: 202-5221
Tel: 313-577-6120 *Toll Free Tel:* 800-978-7323 *Fax:* 313-577-6131
E-mail: bookorders@wayne.edu
Web Site: www.wsupress.wayne.edu
Key Personnel
Dir: Jane Ferreyra *Tel:* 313-577-4220
Assoc Dir & Ed-in-Chief: Kathryn Wildfong *Tel:* 313-577-6070
Mgr, Sales & Mktg: Emily Nowak *Tel:* 313-577-6128
Busn Mgr: Andrew Kaufman *Tel:* 313-577-3671
Order Fulfillment Mgr: Theresa Martinelli *Tel:* 313-577-6126
Edit, Design & Prodn: Kristin Harpster *Tel:* 313-577-4604
Founded: 1941
Scholarly & trade books in African American studies, film & television, women's studies, Jewish studies, poetry, speech & language pathology, fairy tales & folklore, regional studies & urban studies.
ISBN Prefix(es): 978-0-8143
Number of titles published annually: 40 Print
Total Titles: 2,500 Print; 2 CD-ROM
Imprints: Great Lakes Books; Painted Turtle Books (general interest trade)
Distributor for Cranbrook Institute of Science; Detroit Institute of Arts
Foreign Rep(s): Eurospan (Africa, Europe, Middle East, UK); EWEB (Far East); Scholarly Book Services (Canada)
Warehouse: 40 W Hancock St, Detroit, MI 48201
Membership(s): Association of American University Presses

Wayside Publishing
262 US Route 1, Suite 2, Freeport, ME 04032
Toll Free Tel: 888-302-2519
E-mail: sales@waysidepublishing.com
Web Site: www.waysidepublishing.com
Key Personnel
Pres: Greg Greuel
Founded: 1988
Humanities, English & foreign language textbooks & history.
ISBN Prefix(es): 978-1-877653
Number of titles published annually: 5 Print
Total Titles: 54 Print

Welcome Books®, see Welcome Enterprises Inc

Welcome Enterprises Inc
Formerly Welcome Books®
Imprint of Rizzoli International Publications Inc
300 Park Ave S, New York, NY 10010
Tel: 212-387-3400
Web Site: www.rizzoliusa.com
Founded: 1980
Illustrated books for adult trade & gift market.
ISBN Prefix(es): 978-0-941807
Number of titles published annually: 8 Print
Total Titles: 100 Print
Distributed by Random House
Distributor for AAP; Cerf & Peterson; Music Sales; Zeke Holdings Ltd
Distribution Center: Random House, 400 Hahn Rd, Westminster, MD 21157 *Toll Free Tel:* 800-733-3000 *Toll Free Fax:* 800-659-2436
Membership(s): American Book Producers Association

Welcome Rain Publishers LLC
217 Thompson St, Suite 473, New York, NY 10012
Tel: 212-686-1909
Web Site: welcomerain.com
Key Personnel
Publr: John Weber
Founded: 1997
General trade publisher.
ISBN Prefix(es): 978-1-56649
Number of titles published annually: 21 Print
Total Titles: 95 Print
Distribution Center: National Book Network (NBN), 15200 NBN Way, Blue Ridge Summit, PA 17214 *Tel:* 717-794-3800 *Fax:* 717-794-3828

Wellington Press
Division of BooksUPrint.com Inc
9601-30 Miccosukee Rd, Tallahassee, FL 32309
E-mail: peacegames@aol.com
Web Site: www.peacegames.com
Key Personnel
Pres & Intl Rts: David W Felder, PhD
Founded: 1982
Publish philosophy books, including texts, & role play peacegames that examine conflicts of all types.
ISBN Prefix(es): 978-0-910959; 978-1-57501
Number of titles published annually: 10 Print; 10 E-Book
Total Titles: 85 Print; 90 Online; 100 E-Book

Eliot Werner Publications Inc
31 Willow Lane, Clinton Corners, NY 12514
Mailing Address: PO Box 268, Clinton Corners, NY 12514
Tel: 845-266-4241 *Fax:* 845-266-3317
E-mail: eliotwerner@optonline.net
Web Site: www.eliotwerner.com
Founded: 2001
Academic & scholarly books in anthropology, archaeology, psychology, sociology & related fields; writing, editing & contract publishing.
ISBN Prefix(es): 978-0-9712427; 978-0-9719587; 978-0-9752738; 978-0-9797731; 978-0-9898249
Number of titles published annually: 6 Print
Total Titles: 54 Print
Imprints: Percheron Press
Distribution Center: Ian Stevens Distribution, 70 Enterprise Dr, No 2, Bristol, CT 06010, Fin & Off Mgr: Melanie Palleria *Tel:* 860-584-6546 *Fax:* 860-516-4873 *E-mail:* melanie@isdistribution.com *Web Site:* www.isdistribution.com

Wesleyan Publishing House
Division of Wesleyan Church Corp
13300 Olio Rd, Fishers, IN 46037
Mailing Address: PO Box 50434, Indianapolis, IN 46250
Tel: 317-774-3853 *Toll Free Tel:* 800-493-7539 *Fax:* 317-774-3865 *Toll Free Fax:* 800-788-3535
E-mail: wph@wesleyan.org
Web Site: www.wesleyan.org/books
Key Personnel
Proj Mgr: Susan LeBaron *E-mail:* lebarons@wesleyan.org
Founded: 1968
ISBN Prefix(es): 978-0-89827
Number of titles published annually: 40 Print
Total Titles: 60 Print
Membership(s): CBA: The Association for Christian Retail; Christian Holiness Partnership; Evangelical Christian Publishers Association; Holiness Publisher's Association; Protestant Church-Owned Publishers Association

Wesleyan University Press
215 Long Lane, Middletown, CT 06459-0433
Tel: 860-685-7711 *Fax:* 860-685-7712
Web Site: www.wesleyan.edu/wespress
Key Personnel
Dir & Ed-in-Chief: Suzanna L Tamminen *Tel:* 860-685-7727 *E-mail:* stamminen@wesleyan.edu
Mktg Mgr: Jaclyn Wilson *Tel:* 860-685-7725 *E-mail:* jwilson05@wesleyan.edu
Acqs Ed: Marla Zubel *Tel:* 860-685-7730 *E-mail:* mzubel@wesleyan.edu
Publicist: Stephanie Elliott *Tel:* 860-685-7723 *E-mail:* selliott@wesleyan.edu
Founded: 1957
Editorial program which has been awarded 6 Pulitzer Prizes; distinguished history of publishing scholarly & trade books that have influenced American poetry & critical thought over the last four decades.
ISBN Prefix(es): 978-0-8195
Number of titles published annually: 25 Print
Total Titles: 425 Print
Imprints: Early Classics of Science Fiction; Music/Culture; Wesleyan Poetry
Foreign Rep(s): East-West Export Books (Asia, Australia, New Zealand, The Pacific); Oxbow Books Ltd (Europe, Middle East, UK); University of Toronto Press (Canada)
Shipping Address: UPNE, One Court St, Suite 250, Lebanon, NH 03766-1358 *Tel:* 603-448-1533 *Toll Free Tel:* 800-421-1561 *Fax:* 603-448-9429 *E-mail:* university.press@dartmouth.edu
Distribution Center: University Press of New England, One Court St, Suite 250, Lebanon,

NH 03766 *Tel:* 603-448-1533 *Fax:* 603-643-1540 *E-mail:* university.press@dartmouth.edu
Membership(s): AAP; Association of American University Presses; NEBA

§West Academic Publishing
444 Cedar St, Suite 700, St Paul, MN 55101
Toll Free Tel: 877-888-1330
E-mail: customerservice@westacademic.com; support@westacademic.com; media@westacademic.com
Web Site: www.westacademic.com
Key Personnel
Sr Natl & Intl Acct Mgr: Scott Duckson *Tel:* 651-202-4764 *E-mail:* scott.duckson@westacademic.com
Founded: 1953
Law school casebook, statute, study aid & career success publisher.
ISBN Prefix(es): 978-0-1590; 978-0-3141
Number of titles published annually: 50 Print; 2 CD-ROM
Total Titles: 375 Print; 10 CD-ROM; 60 Audio
Imprints: Foundation Press; Gilbert
See separate listing for:
Foundation Press

West Virginia University Press
West Virginia University, PO Box 6295, Morgantown, WV 26506-6295
Tel: 304-293-8400 *Fax:* 304-293-6585
Web Site: www.wvupress.com
Key Personnel
Dir/Acqs Ed (Nonfiction): Derek Krissoff *E-mail:* derek.krissoff@mail.wvu.edu
Sales & Mktg Dir: Abby Freeland *E-mail:* abby.freeland@mail.wvu.edu
Mng Ed: Jason Gosnell *E-mail:* jmgosnell@mail.wvu.edu
Acqs Ed, Vandalia Press (Fiction): Abby Freeland *E-mail:* abby.freeland@mail.wvu.edu
Prodn & Design Mgr: Than Saffel *Tel:* 304-293-8400 ext 4 *E-mail:* than.saffel@mail.wvu.edu
Off Mgr: Floann Downey *Tel:* 304-293-8400 ext 1 *E-mail:* fdowney2@mail.wvu.edu
Founded: 1965
ISBN Prefix(es): 978-1-933202; 978-0-937058
Number of titles published annually: 12 Print; 1 CD-ROM; 1 Audio
Total Titles: 75 Print; 8 CD-ROM; 2 Audio
Imprints: Vandalia Press
Orders to: Chicago Distribution Center, 11030 S Langley Ave, Chicago, IL 60628 *Toll Free Tel:* 800-621-2736 *Toll Free Fax:* 800-621-8476 *E-mail:* orders@press.chicago.edu
Distribution Center: Chicago Distribution Center, 11030 S Langley Ave, Chicago, IL 60628 *Tel:* 773-702-7000 (intl) *Toll Free Tel:* 800-621-2736 *Fax:* 773-702-7212 (intl) *Toll Free Fax:* 800-621-8476
Membership(s): Association of American University Presses

Western Edge Press
Imprint of Sherman Asher Publishing
126 Candelario St, Santa Fe, NM 87501
Tel: 505-988-7214
E-mail: westernedge@santa-fe.net
Web Site: www.westernedgepress.com
Key Personnel
Owner & Publr: James Mafchir
Founded: 1995
Western nonfiction, art, history, archaeology & Spanish/English bilingual oral history.
ISBN Prefix(es): 978-1-890932
Number of titles published annually: 3 Print
Total Titles: 30 Print
Distribution Center: Mountain Press, Missoula, MT 59806 *Toll Free Tel:* 800-234-5308 *Fax:* 310-532-7001 *E-mail:* mtnpress@montana.com *Web Site:* www.mountainpresspublish.com

Western Pennsylvania Genealogical Society
4400 Forbes Ave, Pittsburgh, PA 15213-4080
Tel: 412-687-6811 (answering machine)
E-mail: info@wpgs.org
Web Site: www.wpgs.org
Founded: 1974
ISBN Prefix(es): 978-0-9745162
Number of titles published annually: 10 Print; 1 CD-ROM; 40 Online
Total Titles: 40 Print
Membership(s): National Genealogical Society

Western Reflections Publishing Co
951B N Hwy 149, Lake City, CO 81235
Mailing Address: PO Box 1149, Lake City, CO 81235-1149
Tel: 970-944-0110
E-mail: publisher@westernreflectionspublishing.com
Web Site: www.westernreflectionspublishing.com
Key Personnel
Pres: P David Smith
Founded: 1996
History & culture of the western US with an emphasis on Colorado.
ISBN Prefix(es): 978-1-890437; 978-1-932738
Number of titles published annually: 6 Print
Total Titles: 210 Print

Westernlore Press
PO Box 35305, Tucson, AZ 85740-5305
SAN: 202-9650
Tel: 520-297-5491
Key Personnel
Pres & Ed: Lynn R Bailey
Treas & ISBN Contact: Anne G Bailey
Founded: 1941
History & biography, anthropology, historic archaeology & historic sites & ethnohistory pertaining to the greater American West.
ISBN Prefix(es): 978-0-87026
Number of titles published annually: 4 Print
Total Titles: 65 Print

§Westminster John Knox Press (WJK)
Imprint of Presbyterian Publishing Corp (PPC)
100 Witherspoon St, Louisville, KY 40202-1396
SAN: 202-9669
Toll Free Tel: 800-523-1631 (US only) *Fax:* 502-569-5113 *Toll Free Fax:* 800-541-5113 (US & CN)
E-mail: wjk@wjkbooks.com; customer_service@wjkbooks.com
Web Site: www.wjkbooks.com
Key Personnel
COO: Monty Anderson *E-mail:* manderson@wjkbooks.com
Pres & Publr: Marc Lewis *E-mail:* mlewis@wjkbooks.com
Exec Dir, Publg & Edit Dir: David Dobson *E-mail:* ddobson@wjkbooks.com
Mktg Mgr: Emily Kiefer *E-mail:* ekiefer@wjkbooks.com
Rts & Perms: Michele Blum *E-mail:* mblum@wjkbooks.com
Founded: 1838
With a publishing heritage that dates back more than 160 years, WJK Press publishes religious & theological books & resources for scholars, clergy, laity & general readers. The publisher employs the motto "Challenging the Mind, Nourishing the Soul".
ISBN Prefix(es): 978-0-664; 978-0-8042
Number of titles published annually: 150 Print
Total Titles: 1,100 Print; 2 CD-ROM; 2 Audio
Foreign Office(s): 13 Hellesdon Park Rd, Norwich Norfolk NR6 5DR, United Kingdom *Tel:* (01603) 612 914 *E-mail:* orders@norwichbooksandmusic.co.uk
Distributor for SCM
Foreign Rep(s): Academic Books for Seminaries (Rocky C L Chen) (Taiwan); Africa Christian Textbooks (Nigeria); Canaanland Distributors Sdn Bhd (Malaysia); Christian Book Discounters (South Africa); Claretian Communications Inc (Philippines); Cross Communications Ltd (Alexander Y C Lee) (Hong Kong); Import-Export & Wholesale Center (India); Korea Christian Book Service Inc (South Korea); Methodist Publishing House (South Africa); Omega Distributors Ltd (New Zealand); SKS Books Warehouse (Lek Eng Khiang) (Singapore)
Distribution Center: Presbyterian Publishing Corp (PPC), 341 Great Circle Rd, Nashville, TN 37228 *Toll Free Tel:* 800-227-2872 *Toll Free Fax:* 800-541-5113 *Web Site:* www.ppcpub.com

Wheatherstone Press
Subsidiary of Dickinson Consulting Group
11595 SW Butner Rd, No 22, Portland, OR 97225
Tel: 503-244-8929
E-mail: relocntr@nwlink.com
Web Site: www.wheatherstonepress.com
Key Personnel
Pres & CEO: Jan Dickinson
Founded: 1983
Publishes handbooks & step-by-step guides covering all phases of relocation, including internationally.
ISBN Prefix(es): 978-0-9613011
Number of titles published annually: 3 Print
Total Titles: 49 Print

§Whiskey Creek Press
Imprint of Start Publishing LLC
c/o Start Publishing LLC, 101 Hudson St, 37th fl, Suite 3705, Jersey City, NJ 07302
Tel: 212-431-5455 *Fax:* 917-464-6394
E-mail: publisher@whiskeycreekpress.com
Web Site: whiskeycreekpress.com
Key Personnel
Mng Ed: Ashley Noelle *E-mail:* noelle@start-media.com
Founded: 2003
Traditional royalty-paying small press, publishing fiction in ebook & print formats. Titles can be purchased through Amazon Kindle, Barnes & Noble Nook & Apple ITunes.
ISBN Prefix(es): 978-1-60313; 978-1-61160
Number of titles published annually: 50 Print; 200 E-Book
Total Titles: 500 Print; 1,350 E-Book
Imprints: Torrid Books (sensual & erotic romances)

§Whitaker House
1030 Hunt Valley Circle, New Kensington, PA 15068
Tel: 724-334-7000 *Fax:* 724-334-1200
E-mail: publisher@whitakerhouse.com
Web Site: www.whitakerhouse.com
Key Personnel
Mng Dir: Tom Cox
Founded: 1970
ISBN Prefix(es): 978-0-88368; 978-1-60374; 978-1-62911
Number of titles published annually: 70 Print; 1 CD-ROM; 70 E-Book; 8 Audio
Total Titles: 500 Print; 20 CD-ROM; 400 E-Book; 40 Audio
Imprints: Banner Publishing
Foreign Rep(s): Donna Rowley
Warehouse: Anchor Distributors, 1030 Hunt Valley Circle, New Kensington, PA 15068, Mgr: Dave Brennan
Membership(s): American Christian Fiction Writers; CBA; Evangelical Christian Publishers Association

White Cloud Press
300 E Hersey St, Suite 11, Ashland, OR 97520

Mailing Address: PO Box 3400, Ashland, OR 97520
Tel: 541-488-6415 *Fax:* 541-482-7708
E-mail: info@whitecloudpress.com
Web Site: www.whitecloudpress.com
Key Personnel
Publr: Steve Scholl *E-mail:* scholl@whitecloudpress.com
Prodn Mgr: Christy Collins *E-mail:* christy@whitecloudpress.com
Founded: 1993
General trade, emphasis on religion & fiction.
ISBN Prefix(es): 978-1-883991; 978-0-9745245
Number of titles published annually: 6 Print
Total Titles: 60 Print; 40 E-Book; 4 Audio
Imprints: Caveat Press; Confluence Books; River-Wood Books
Subsidiaries: Confluence Book Services
Foreign Rights: Danny Baror; Nigel Yorwerth
Distribution Center: Publishers Group West, 1700 Fourth St, Berkeley, CA 94710 *Toll Free Tel:* 800-788-3123 *Toll Free Fax:* 800-351-5073 *E-mail:* orderentry@perseusbooks.com *Web Site:* www.pgw.com
Publishers Group Canada, 300-76 Stafford St, Toronto, ON M6J 2S1, Canada *Toll Free Tel:* 800-747-8147 *Fax:* 416-934-1410 *E-mail:* info@pgcbooks.ca *Web Site:* pgcbooks.ca
Membership(s): Independent Book Publishers Association

White Pine Press
PO Box 236, Buffalo, NY 14201
Tel: 716-627-4665 *Fax:* 716-627-4665
E-mail: wpine@whitepine.org
Web Site: www.whitepine.org
Key Personnel
Mng Dir: Elaine La Mattina
Publr & Ed: Dennis Maloney *E-mail:* dennismaloney@yahoo.com
Founded: 1973
Specialize in poetry, essays, fiction, literature in translation.
ISBN Prefix(es): 978-0-934834; 978-1-877727; 978-1-877800; 978-1-893996
Number of titles published annually: 10 Print
Total Titles: 160 Print
Subsidiaries: Springhouse Editions
Distributor for Springhouse Editions
Distribution Center: Consortium Book Sales & Distribution, The Keg House, Suite 101, 34 13 Ave NE, Minneapolis, MN 55413-1007 *Tel:* 612-746-2600 *Toll Free Tel:* 800-283-3572 (cust serv) *Fax:* 612-746-2606 *Web Site:* www.cbsd.com

Whitman, Albert & Co, see Albert Whitman & Co

§Whittier Publications Inc
3115 Long Beach Rd, Oceanside, NY 11572
Tel: 516-432-8120 *Toll Free Tel:* 800-897-TEXT (897-8398) *Fax:* 516-889-0341
E-mail: info@whitbooks.com
Web Site: www.whitbooks.com
Key Personnel
Pres: Judith Etra
Founded: 1990
Textbooks, trade, self-help.
ISBN Prefix(es): 978-1-878045; 978-1-57604
Number of titles published annually: 200 Print

§Whole Person Associates Inc
101 W Second St, Suite 203, Duluth, MN 55802
Tel: 218-727-0500 *Toll Free Tel:* 800-247-6789 *Fax:* 218-727-0505
E-mail: books@wholeperson.com
Web Site: www.wholeperson.com
Key Personnel
Owner: Jack Kosmach
Publr: Carlene Sippola
Founded: 1980
Stress management & wellness promotion.
ISBN Prefix(es): 978-0-938586; 978-1-57025
Number of titles published annually: 8 Print
Total Titles: 210 Print; 29 CD-ROM; 38 Audio
Imprints: Whole Person Associates
Membership(s): Independent Book Publishing Professionals Group

§Wide World of Maps Inc
2626 W Indian School Rd, Phoenix, AZ 85017
Tel: 602-279-2323 (ext 1) *Toll Free Tel:* 800-279-7654 *Fax:* 602-433-0695
E-mail: sales@maps4u.com
Web Site: www.maps4u.com
Key Personnel
Pres: James L Willinger *E-mail:* james@maps4u.com
Founded: 1975
Atlases, charts, guide books, maps, map software, map accessories & more.
ISBN Prefix(es): 978-0-938448; 978-1-887749
Number of titles published annually: 6 Print; 2 CD-ROM
Total Titles: 20 Print; 2 CD-ROM
Imprints: Yellow 1
Divisions: Desert Charts; Metro Maps; Phoenix Mapping Service
Distributed by Rand McNally
Distributor for Benchmark Maps; Big Sky Maps; Franko Maps; MacVan Maps (Colorado Springs); Metro Maps; Rand McNally

Wide World Publishing
PO Box 476, San Carlos, CA 94070-0476
SAN: 211-1462
Tel: 650-593-2839 *Fax:* 650-595-0802
E-mail: wwpbl@aol.com
Web Site: wideworldpublishing.com
Key Personnel
Partner & Intl Rts: Elvira Monroe
Founded: 1976
Trade paperbacks, cookbooks, mathematics books/calendars, travel books & guides.
ISBN Prefix(es): 978-0-933174; 978-1-884550
Number of titles published annually: 6 Print
Total Titles: 38 Print
Imprints: Math Products Plus; Wide World Publishing/Tetra
Foreign Rep(s): Publishers Group West (Asia, Canada, Europe)
Distribution Center: Ingram Content Services, One Ingram Blvd, La Vergne, TN 37086 *Tel:* 615-795-5000 *Web Site:* www.ingramcontent.com
Perseus Distribution, 193 Edwards Dr, Jackson, TN 38301 *Toll Free Tel:* 800-343-4499 *Toll Free Fax:* 800-351-5073 *Web Site:* www.perseusdistribution.com
Publishers Group West, 1700 Fourth St, Berkeley, CA 94710 SAN: 202-8522

Markus Wiener Publishers Inc
231 Nassau St, Princeton, NJ 08542
SAN: 282-5465
Tel: 609-921-1141 *Fax:* 609-921-1140
E-mail: publisher@markuswiener.com
Web Site: www.markuswiener.com
Key Personnel
Pres: M Markus Wiener
VP: Shelley Frisch
Founded: 1981
Independent publisher of academic & trade books & journals in the areas of world history, Latin American & Caribbean history, Middle Eastern & African history & culture. Its publications also include related topics in music, religion, women's history, Jewish history, western civilization & slavery.
ISBN Prefix(es): 978-0-910129; 978-0-945179; 978-1-55876
Number of titles published annually: 25 Print
Total Titles: 300 Print
Foreign Rep(s): Eurospan (Europe)

Michael Wiese Productions
12400 Ventura Blvd, No 1111, Studio City, CA 91604
Tel: 818-379-8799 *Toll Free Tel:* 800-833-5738 (orders) *Fax:* 818-986-3408
E-mail: mwpsales@mwp.com; fulfillment@portcity.com
Web Site: www.mwp.com
Key Personnel
Founder & Publr: Michael Wiese
VP: Ken Lee *Tel:* 206-283-2948 *E-mail:* kenlee@mwp.com
Spec Sales: Michele Chong *Tel:* 818-841-4123
Founded: 1981
Publisher of books on screenwriting & filmmaking.
ISBN Prefix(es): 978-0-941188
Number of titles published annually: 15 Print
Total Titles: 250 Print
Imprints: Divine Arts
Distribution Center: Ingram Publisher Services, One Ingram Blvd, La Vergne, TN 37086 *Toll Free Tel:* 866-400-5351 *E-mail:* customerservice@ingrampublisherservices.com *Web Site:* www.ingrampublisherservices.com

Wilderness Adventures Press Inc
45 Buckskin Rd, Belgrade, MT 59714
Tel: 406-388-0112 *Toll Free Tel:* 866-400-2012
E-mail: books@wildadvpress.com
Web Site: store.wildadvpress.com
Key Personnel
Pres & Prodn Ed: Chuck Johnson *Tel:* 406-388-0112 ext 12 *Fax:* 406-388-0120 *E-mail:* chuck@wildadvpress.com
Secy & Treas: Blanche Johnson *Tel:* 406-388-0112 ext 14 *Fax:* 406-388-0120 *E-mail:* blanche@wildadvpress.com
Founded: 1994
Outdoor guidebooks, sporting books & cookbooks, fly fishing, dog training & big game hunting, plus maps.
ISBN Prefix(es): 978-1-885106; 978-1-932098; 978-1-940239
Number of titles published annually: 6 Print
Total Titles: 90 Print
Distributed by American West Books; Angler's Book Supply; Raymond C Rumpf & Son Inc
Distribution Center: Baker & Taylor, 2550 W Tyvola Rd, Suite 300, Charlotte, NC 28217 *Tel:* 704-998-3100 *Toll Free Tel:* 800-775-1800 *Web Site:* www.btol.com
Ingram Publisher Services, One Ingram Blvd, La Vergne, TN 37086 *Toll Free Tel:* 866-400-5351 *E-mail:* customerservice@ingrampublisherservices.com *Web Site:* www.ingrampublisherservices.com
Barnes & Noble *Tel:* 516-338-8000 *Web Site:* bn.com

Wildflower Press
Affiliate of Oakbrook Press
c/o Oakbrook Press, 3301 S Valley Dr, Rapid City, SD 57703
Mailing Address: PO Box 3362, Rapid City, SD 57709
Tel: 605-381-6385
E-mail: info@wildflowerpress.org
Web Site: www.wildflowerpress.org
Key Personnel
Pres: L J Bryant *E-mail:* wildflowerpress@live.com
Publicity Dir: Robert E Fuchs *E-mail:* pr@wildflowerpress.org
Literary Agent: Charlene Caulfield
Sales: Jordan Dadah
Edit: Leisette Fox
Billing: Christina MacLachlan
Founded: 2010

Small press specializing in publishing works of fiction with a significant message. Not a vanity press; no funds required to publish.
ISBN Prefix(es): 978-0-9835332
Number of titles published annually: 5 Print; 5 E-Book
Total Titles: 12 Print; 13 E-Book
Membership(s): Independent Book Publishers Association

Wildlife Education Ltd
2418 Noyes St, Evanston, IL 60201
Tel: 859-261-2556 *Toll Free Tel:* 800-477-5034 *Fax:* 859-261-2355
Web Site: www.zoobooks.com; wildlife-ed.com
Key Personnel
Pres & CEO: John Toraason
Publr: Ed Shadek
Edit Dir: Renee C Burch; Marjorie Shaw
Sales Mgr: Kurt Von Hertsenberg *E-mail:* kurt@zoobooks.com
Founded: 1980
Books on wildlife & animals. Publisher of *Zoobooks* magazine.
ISBN Prefix(es): 978-0-937934; 978-1-888153
Number of titles published annually: 27 Print; 27 E-Book
Total Titles: 200 Print; 200 E-Book
Membership(s): AAP PreK-12 Learning Group

Wildside Press LLC
9710 Traville Gateway Dr, Suite 234, Rockville, MD 20850
Tel: 301-762-1305 *Fax:* 301-762-1306
E-mail: wildside@wildsidepress.com; wildsidepress@yahoo.com
Web Site: wildsidepress.com
Key Personnel
Publr: John Betancourt
Dir, Publg Opers: Carla Coupe
Founded: 1989
Reprints of classic science fiction, fantasy, mystery, reference & mainstream.
ISBN Prefix(es): 978-1-880448; 978-1-58715; 978-1-59224
Number of titles published annually: 1,500 Print; 400 E-Book; 100 Audio
Total Titles: 16,000 Print; 1,400 E-Book; 800 Audio
Imprints: Borgo Press; Owlswick Press
Foreign Rights: Donald Maass Literary Agency (worldwide exc USA)

§Wiley-Blackwell
Imprint of John Wiley & Sons Inc
111 River St, Hoboken, NJ 07030-5774
Tel: 201-748-6000 *Fax:* 201-748-6088
E-mail: info@wiley.com
Web Site: www.wiley.com
Founded: 1984
General, scholarly, reference & college texts, with an emphasis on the humanities, social sciences & business. Also medical allied health, veterinary, earth & life sciences, environment & engineering.
ISBN Prefix(es): 978-0-631; 978-0-85520; 978-0-86216; 978-1-55786; 978-1-57718
Number of titles published annually: 500 Print
Total Titles: 4,500 Print

§John Wiley & Sons Inc
111 River St, Hoboken, NJ 07030-5774
SAN: 202-5183
Tel: 201-748-6000 *Toll Free Tel:* 800-225-5945 (cust serv) *Fax:* 201-748-6088
E-mail: info@wiley.com
Web Site: www.wiley.com
Key Personnel
Chmn of the Bd & Interim CEO: Matthew Kissner
Corp Cont & SVP: Edward J Melando
Corp Secy: Joanna Jia
CFO & EVP, Technol & Opers: John Kritzmacher
EVP & Chief HR Offr: Archana Singh
EVP & Chief Mktg Offr: Clay Stobaugh
EVP & Chief Strategy Offr: John Semel
EVP & Gen Coun: Gary M Rinck
EVP, Intl Devt & GR Sales: Reed Elfenbein
EVP, Knowledge & Learning: Joan O'Neil
EVP, Res: Judy Verses
EVP, Talent Solutions & Educ Servs: Jeffrey Sugerman
SVP & Treas: Vincent Marzano
Mgr, Busn Devt: Jesse C Wiley
Founded: 1807
Global publisher of print & electronic products specializing in professional & consumer books & subscription services; scientific, technical, medical books & journals; textbooks & educational materials for undergraduate & graduate students as well as lifelong learners. Wiley has publishing, marketing & distribution centers in the US, Canada, Europe, Asia & Australia.
ISBN Prefix(es): 978-0-470; 978-0-471; 978-0-442; 978-0-8436; 978-0-87055
Number of titles published annually: 1,500 Print
Total Titles: 15,000 Print
Imprints: American Geophysical Union; Architectural Graphic Standards; Capstone; Cochrane Library; CrossKnowledge; Culinary Institute of America; Current Protocols; Ernst & Sohn; Essential Evidence Plus; Everything DiSC®; For Dummies®; GIT Verlag; Jacaranda; Jossey-Bass; JK Lasser; The Leadership Challenge®; Merck; MOAC; RSMeans; Spectroscopy Now; Sybex; Teach Yourself Visually; Wiley-Blackwell; Wiley Custom Select; Wiley Global Education; Wiley-IEEE Press; Wiley Online Library; Wiley Science Solutions; Wiley-VCH; Wiley Visualizing; WileyPLUS; Workplace Learning Solutions; Wrightbooks; Wrox™
Branch Office(s)
One Montgomery St, Suite 1200, San Francisco, CA 94104 *Tel:* 415-433-1740 *Fax:* 415-433-0499
4500 Cherry Creek Dr S, Suite 350, Denver, CO 80246 *Tel:* 303-316-2200 *Fax:* 303-329-7999
851 Trafalgar Dr, Suite 420, Maitland, FL 32751
1415 W 22 St, Suite 500, Oak Brook, IL 60523 *Tel:* 630-366-2900 *Fax:* 630-528-3101
10475 Crosspoint Blvd, Indianapolis, IN 46256 (cust care ctr/consumer accts) *Tel:* 317-572-3000; 317-572-3994 (consumer tech support) *Fax:* 317-572-4000
1606 Golden Aspen Dr, Suite 104, Ames, IA 50010 *Tel:* 515-292-0140 *Fax:* 515-292-3348
350 Main St, Commerce Place, Malden, MA 02148 *Tel:* 781-388-8200 *Fax:* 781-388-8210
400 Hwy 169, Suite 300, Minneapolis, MN 55426 *Tel:* 763-765-2222 *Fax:* 763-765-2276
5205 Lake Shore Dr, Waco, TX 76710 *Tel:* 254-751-1644
90 Eglington Ave E, Suite 300, Toronto, ON M4P 2Y3, Canada *Tel:* 416-236-4433 *Toll Free Tel:* 800-567-4797 *Fax:* 416-236-8743 *Toll Free Fax:* 800-565-6802 *E-mail:* canada@wiley.com
Distribution Center: One Wiley Dr, Somerset, NJ 08875-1272 (US cust care opers/trade & wholesale) *Fax:* 732-302-2300 *E-mail:* custserv@wiley.com
Membership(s): AAP
See separate listing for:
Wiley-Blackwell
John Wiley & Sons Inc Global Education
John Wiley & Sons Inc Professional Development

§John Wiley & Sons Inc Global Education
Division of John Wiley & Sons Inc
111 River St, Hoboken, NJ 07030-5774
Tel: 201-748-6000 *Toll Free Tel:* 800-225-5945 (cust serv) *Fax:* 201-748-6008
E-mail: info@wiley.com
Web Site: www.wiley.com
Key Personnel
VP, Cust Engagement: Susan Elbe
Total Titles: 615 Print

§John Wiley & Sons Inc Professional Development
Division of John Wiley & Sons Inc
111 River St, Hoboken, NJ 07030-5774
Tel: 201-748-6000 *Toll Free Tel:* 800-225-5945 (cust serv) *Fax:* 201-748-6088
E-mail: info@wiley.com
Web Site: www.wiley.com
Global brands include For Dummies, Jossey-Bass, Bloomberg Press, Sybex, Wrox, Pfeiffer, Fisher Investments Press, J K Lasser, Leadership Challenge, Wiley Learning Institute, Therascribe & Wiley CPA Exam Review.

John Wiley & Sons Inc Scientific, Technical, Medical & Scholarly (STMS), see Wiley-Blackwell

William Carey Library Publishers
Division of Frontier Ventures
1605 E Elizabeth St, Pasadena, CA 91104
Tel: 626-720-8210 *Toll Free Tel:* 866-732-6657 (orders & cust serv)
E-mail: assistant@wclbooks.com
Web Site: www.missionbooks.org
Key Personnel
Gen Mgr: Jeff Minard *E-mail:* manager@wclbooks.com
Founded: 1969
Cross-cultural Christian mission work & experiences in frontier countries.
ISBN Prefix(es): 978-0-87808
Number of titles published annually: 15 Print
Total Titles: 250 Print; 3 CD-ROM
Imprints: Mandate Press
Orders to: STL Distribution, 100 Biblica Way, Elizabethton, TN 37643 *Toll Free Tel:* 800-647-7466
Membership(s): Evangelical Christian Publishers Association; Independent Book Publishers Association

§Williams & Company Book Publishers
1317 Pine Ridge Dr, Savannah, GA 31406
Tel: 912-352-0404
E-mail: bookpub@comcast.net
Web Site: www.pubmart.com
Key Personnel
Publr & Ed-in-Chief: Thomas A Williams, PhD
Founded: 1989
Niche market nonfiction.
ISBN Prefix(es): 978-1-878853
Number of titles published annually: 15 Print
Total Titles: 25 Print
Imprints: Venture Press; Williams & Co Publishers
Warehouse: Juliana Group, 1110 Staley Ave, Savannah, GA 31405
Membership(s): Independent Publishers Association

Willow Creek Press
9931 Hwy 70 W, Minocqua, WI 54548
Mailing Address: PO Box 147, Minocqua, WI 54548
Tel: 715-358-7010 *Toll Free Tel:* 800-850-9453 *Fax:* 715-358-2807
E-mail: info@willowcreekpress.com
Web Site: www.willowcreekpress.com
Key Personnel
Publr & Ed-in-Chief: Tom Petrie
VP, Sales: Jeremy Petrie *E-mail:* jpetrie@willowcreekpress.com
Founded: 1986
Publish high quality books most specifically related to nature, animals, wildlife, hunting, fishing & gardening. The company also offers a unique line of cookbooks & has established a niche in the pet book market. The company

also publishes high quality nature, wild life, fishing, pet & sporting calendars.
ISBN Prefix(es): 978-1-57223
Number of titles published annually: 24 Print
Total Titles: 130 Print; 3 Audio
Membership(s): AAM; AAP

Wilshire Book Co
22647 Ventura Blvd, No 314, Woodland Hills, CA 91364-1416
SAN: 205-5368
Tel: 818-700-1522
E-mail: sales@mpowers.com
Web Site: www.mpowers.com
Key Personnel
Pres & Rts & Perms: Marcia Powers
Founded: 1967 (by Melvin Powers)
Psychological, self-help, motivational & inspirational books, adult fables; mail order, business, advertising & marketing; horse, bridge; originals & reprints.
ISBN Prefix(es): 978-0-87980
Number of titles published annually: 3 Print
Total Titles: 23 Print

Wimmer Cookbooks
Division of Mercury Printing, an RR Donnelley Co
4650 Shelby Air Dr, Memphis, TN 38118
Toll Free Tel: 800-548-2537 *Fax:* 901-363-1771
E-mail: info@wimmerco.com
Web Site: www.wimmerco.com
Key Personnel
Acct Coord: Robyn Hite
Sales & Mktg: Terry Rayner *Tel:* 214-676-2444 *E-mail:* terry.s.rayner@rrd.com
Founded: 1946
Development, publishing, manufacturing, marketing & distribution of community & self-published cookbooks.
ISBN Prefix(es): 978-1-879958
Number of titles published annually: 50 Print
Total Titles: 300 Print
Imprints: Tradery House

§Wind Canyon Books
PO Box 7035, Stockton, CA 95267
Tel: 209-956-1600 *Toll Free Tel:* 800-952-7007 *Fax:* 209-956-9424 *Toll Free Fax:* 888-289-7086
E-mail: books@windcanyonbooks.com
Web Site: www.windcanyonbooks.com
Key Personnel
Owner: George Jaquith
Founded: 1996
ISBN Prefix(es): 978-0-943691; 978-1-891118
Number of titles published annually: 5 Print
Total Titles: 70 Print

Windsor Books
Division of Windsor Marketing Corp
260 W Main St, Suite 5, Bayshore, NY 11706
SAN: 203-2945
Mailing Address: PO Box 280, Brightwaters, NY 11718
Tel: 631-665-6688 *Toll Free Tel:* 800-321-5934
E-mail: windsor.books@att.net
Web Site: www.windsorpublishing.com
Key Personnel
Founder: Alfred Schmidt
Mng Ed: Jeff Schmidt
Founded: 1968
Business, economics & investment.
ISBN Prefix(es): 978-0-930233
Number of titles published annually: 5 Print
Advertising Agency: A Schmidt Agency

Windward Publishing
Imprint of Finney Company Inc
5995 149 St W, Suite 105, Apple Valley, MN 55124
Tel: 952-469-6699 *Toll Free Tel:* 800-846-7027 *Fax:* 952-469-1968 *Toll Free Fax:* 800-330-6232
E-mail: info@finneyco.com
Web Site: www.finneyco.com
Key Personnel
Pres: Alan E Krysan
Founded: 1973
Publishes books with educational value; children's books & trade books. Topics covered are natural history/science, nature & outdoor recreation.
ISBN Prefix(es): 978-0-89317
Number of titles published annually: 5 Print
Total Titles: 42 Print

§Wings Press
627 E Guenther, San Antonio, TX 78210-1134
Tel: 210-271-7805
E-mail: press@wingspress.com
Web Site: www.wingspress.com
Key Personnel
Publr & Ed: Bryce Milligan *E-mail:* milligan@wingspress.com
Founded: 1975
Literary book publishing.
ISBN Prefix(es): 978-0-916727; 978-0-930324
Number of titles published annually: 12 Print; 12 E-Book; 1 Audio
Total Titles: 230 Print; 4 CD-ROM; 200 E-Book; 4 Audio
Foreign Rights: Independent Publisher's Group (Susan M Sewall)
Orders to: Independent Publisher's Group (IPG), 814 N Franklin St, Chicago, IL 60624 *Tel:* 312-337-0747 *Toll Free Tel:* 800-888-0747 *Fax:* 312-337-5985 *E-mail:* orders@ipgbook.com
Returns: Independent Publisher's Group Distribution Center, 600 N Pulaski Rd, Chicago, IL 60624 *Tel:* 312-337-0747 *Fax:* 312-337-5985 *Toll Free Fax:* 800-888-0747 *E-mail:* frontdesk@ipgbook.com
Shipping Address: Independent Publisher's Group Distribution Center, 600 N Pulaski Rd, Chicago, IL 60624 *Tel:* 312-337-0747 *Fax:* 312-337-5985 *E-mail:* orders@ipgbook.com
Warehouse: Independent Publisher's Group Distribution Center, 600 N Pulaski Rd, Chicago, IL 60624 *Tel:* 312-337-0747 *Fax:* 312-337-5985 *E-mail:* orders@ipgbook.com
Distribution Center: Independent Publisher's Group Distribution Center, 600 N Pulaski Rd, Chicago, IL 60624 *Tel:* 312-337-0747 *Toll Free Tel:* 800-888-0747 *Fax:* 312-337-5985 *E-mail:* orders@ipgbook.com
Membership(s): Association of Writers and Writing Programs; Community of Literary Magazines & Presses

Winters Publishing
705 E Washington St, Greensburg, IN 47240
SAN: 298-1645
Mailing Address: PO Box 501, Greensburg, IN 47240
Tel: 812-663-4948 *Toll Free Tel:* 800-457-3230 *Fax:* 812-663-4948
E-mail: winterspublishing@gmail.com
Web Site: www.winterspublishing.com
Key Personnel
Owner & Publr: Mr Tracy Winters
Founded: 1988
Produces high-quality, custom books for individuals & groups. We publish community & corporate history books for cities & organizations celebrating centennials, bicentennials & other milestone events. We also work with individual authors & publish children's books, books for the Christian market, cookbooks for the bed & breakfast industry & a variety of other fiction & nonfiction books.
ISBN Prefix(es): 978-0-9625329; 978-1-883651
Number of titles published annually: 15 Print; 2 E-Book
Total Titles: 75 Print; 2 E-Book
Imprints: Faith Press
Distribution Center: Ingram Book Co, One Ingram Blvd, La Vergne, TN 37086 *Tel:* 615-793-5000

Winterthur Museum, Garden & Library
5105 Kennett Pike, Winterthur, DE 19735
Tel: 302-888-4663 *Toll Free Tel:* 800-448-3883 *Fax:* 302-888-4950
Web Site: www.winterthur.org
Key Personnel
Contact: Onie Rollins
ISBN Prefix(es): 978-0-912724
Number of titles published annually: 4 Print
Total Titles: 80 Print
Distributed by Antique Collectors Club; Monacelli Press; W W Norton & Company Inc; University of Pennsylvania Press; University Press of New England
Membership(s): ABA; American Alliance of Museums; Art Libraries Society

§Wisconsin Department of Public Instruction
125 S Webster St, Madison, WI 53703
Mailing Address: PO Box 7841, Madison, WI 53707-7841
Tel: 608-266-2188 *Toll Free Tel:* 800-441-4563 *Fax:* 608-267-9110
Web Site: pubsales.dpi.wi.gov
Key Personnel
State Superintendent of Public Instruction: Tony Evers, PhD
Communs Dir: Thomas McCarthy *Tel:* 608-266-3559 *E-mail:* thomas.mccarthy@dpi.wi.gov
Pubn Sales Mktg Specialist: Joy Martell *Tel:* 800-243-8782 *E-mail:* joy.martell@dpi.wi.gov
Specialize in English, math, science & social studies, character education, driver education & traffic safety, career & technical education, world languages & teaching strategies.
ISBN Prefix(es): 978-1-57337
Number of titles published annually: 8 Print; 4 CD-ROM
Total Titles: 120 Print; 10 CD-ROM

Wisdom Publications Inc
199 Elm St, Somerville, MA 02144
Tel: 617-776-7416 *Toll Free Tel:* 800-272-4050 (orders) *Fax:* 617-776-7841
E-mail: info@wisdompubs.org; submission@wisdompubs.org
Web Site: www.wisdompubs.org
Key Personnel
Publr & CEO: Timothy McNeill
Publr: Daniel Aitken *Tel:* 617-776-7416 ext 22
Promo: Lydia Anderson *E-mail:* promo@wisdompubs.org
Founded: 1976
Books on Buddhism published in various series encompassing theory & practice, biography, history, art & culture.
ISBN Prefix(es): 978-0-86171
Number of titles published annually: 30 Print
Total Titles: 300 Print
Imprints: Pali Text Society
Distributed by Simon & Schuster
Foreign Rep(s): PPUK (England)
Foreign Rights: ACER (Spain); Eliane Benisti (France); Chinese Connection Agency (China); Fritz Literary Agency (Germany); Eric Yang Agency (Korea)
Orders to: Simon & Schuster, 100 Front St, Riverside, NJ 08075 *Toll Free Tel:* 800-223-2336 *Toll Free Fax:* 800-943-9831

Paula Wiseman Books, see Simon & Schuster Children's Publishing

Wittenborn Art Books
Division of Alan Wofsy Fine Arts
1109 Geary Blvd, San Francisco, CA 94109
Tel: 415-292-6500 *Toll Free Tel:* 800-660-6403 *Fax:* 415-292-6594
E-mail: wittenborn@art-books.com
Web Site: www.art-books.com
Key Personnel
Ed: Alan Hyman *E-mail:* editeur@earthlink.net
Opers Mgr: J Thrombly
Acqs: Lancelot Andrewes *E-mail:* beauxarts@earthlink.net
Rts: Mark Hyman *Tel:* 510-666-1150 *E-mail:* art-books.com@jps.net
Prodn: Duke Mantee *Tel:* 510-482-3677
Founded: 1939
Publish deluxe edition art reference books & artist books. Subject specialties include art, bibliography & decorative arts.
ISBN Prefix(es): 978-0-8150
Number of titles published annually: 9 Print; 4 CD-ROM
Total Titles: 180 Print; 30 CD-ROM
Imprints: Documents of Modern Art; George Wittenborn
Distributor for Cramer; Kornfeld; Menil Foundation (Houston, TX)
Billing Address: PO Box 2210, San Francisco, CA 94126
Warehouse: Ashland, OH 44805
Membership(s): AAP

Wizards of the Coast LLC
Subsidiary of Hasbro Inc
1600 Lind Ave SW, Suite 400, Renton, WA 98057-3305
Mailing Address: PO Box 707, Renton, WA 98057-0707
Tel: 425-226-6500
E-mail: press@wizards.com
Web Site: company.wizards.com; www.wizards.com
Founded: 1975 (as TSR Inc)
Publisher of fantasy, science fiction & horror novels. Young adult game material; role-playing games, trading card games, board games & books, makers of Dungeons & Dragons. Not seeking proposals for our shared world lines at this time.
ISBN Prefix(es): 978-0-88038; 978-1-56076; 978-0-7869
Number of titles published annually: 50 Print; 60 E-Book
Total Titles: 300 Print
Distributed by Penguin Random House

Alan Wofsy Fine Arts
1109 Geary Blvd, San Francisco, CA 94109
SAN: 207-6438
Mailing Address: PO Box 2210, San Francisco, CA 94126-2210
Tel: 415-292-6500 *Toll Free Tel:* 800-660-6403 *Fax:* 415-292-6594 (off & cust serv); 510-251-1840 (acctg)
E-mail: order@art-books.com (orders); editeur@earthlink.net (edit); beauxarts@earthlink.net (cust serv)
Web Site: www.art-books.com
Key Personnel
Chmn of the Bd: Lord Cohen
CEO: Alan Wofsy
Art Dir: Zeke Greenberg
Ed, French Books: Charles DuPont
Ed, German Books: Willi Rahm
PR Mgr: Milton J Goldbaum
Website Mgr: Steven Barich
Website & Imaging: Matt Novack
Mktg: Andy Redkin
Libn: Adios Butler
Coun: Judith Mazia
Rts: Elizabeth Regina Snowden
Founded: 1969
Art reference books, bibliographies, art books, iconographies, prints, posters & note cards.
ISBN Prefix(es): 978-0-915346; 978-1-55660
Number of titles published annually: 20 Print; 5 CD-ROM; 60 Online
Total Titles: 350 Print; 10 CD-ROM; 500 Online
Imprints: Beauxarts; Collegium Graphicum; The Picasso Project
Divisions: Wittenborn Art Books
Branch Office(s)
401 China Basin St, Suite 202, San Francisco, CA 94158-2133 (sales & cust serv)
Distributor for Bora; Brusberg (Berlin); Cramer (Geneva); Huber; Ides et Calendes; Kornfeld & Co (Bern); Welz; Wittenborn Art Books
Warehouse: Ashland, OH 44805
Distribution Center: Ashland, OH 44805
Membership(s): AAP
See separate listing for:
Picasso Project
Wittenborn Art Books

Wolters Kluwer US Corp
Subsidiary of Wolters Kluwer NV (The Netherlands)
2700 Lake Cook Rd, Riverwoods, IL 60015
Tel: 847-267-7000 *Fax:* 847-580-5192
E-mail: info@wolterskluwer.com
Web Site: www.wolterskluwer.com
Key Personnel
CEO & Chmn of the Bd: Nancy McKinstry
CFO: Kevin Entricken
Dir, Mktg Communs: Linda Gharib *E-mail:* linda.gharib@wolterskluwer.com
Medical books & journals, law books, business & tax publications.
Total Titles: 5,000 Print
Imprints: Adis International; Aspen Publishers Incorporated; CCH INCORPORATED; CT Corporation; Lippincott, Williams & Wilkins
Foreign Office(s): Zuidpoolsingel 2, PO Box 1030, 2400 BA Alphen aan den Rijn, Netherlands (headquarters) *Tel:* (0172) 641 400 *Fax:* (0172) 474 889

Woodbine House
6510 Bells Mill Rd, Bethesda, MD 20817
SAN: 692-3445
Tel: 301-897-3570 *Toll Free Tel:* 800-843-7323 *Fax:* 301-897-5838
E-mail: info@woodbinehouse.com
Web Site: www.woodbinehouse.com
Key Personnel
Publr: Fran Marinaccio
Mktg Mgr & Intl Rts: Fran M Marinaccio *E-mail:* fmarinaccio@woodbinehouse.com
Mktg & Sales Mgr: Beth Binns *E-mail:* bbinns@woodbinehouse.com
Ed & Perms: Susan S Stokes *E-mail:* sstokes@woodbinehouse.com
Acqs Ed: Nancy Gray Paul *E-mail:* ngpaul@woodbinehouse.com
Founded: 1985
Trade nonfiction, hardcover & paperback.
ISBN Prefix(es): 978-0-933149; 978-1-890627; 978-1-60613
Number of titles published annually: 10 Print; 8 E-Book
Total Titles: 90 Print; 35 E-Book
Foreign Rep(s): Gazelle Book Services Ltd (Europe, UK); Silvereye Educational Publications (Australia); University of Toronto Press Guidance Centre (Canada)
Foreign Rights: Writer's House
Returns: IFC, 3570 Bladensburg Rd, Brentwood, MD 20722 *Tel:* 301-779-4660
Warehouse: Woodbine House, c/o IFC, 3570 Bladensburg Rd, Brentwood, MD 20722

Woodland Publishing Inc
515 S 700 E, Suite 2D, Salt Lake City, UT 84102
SAN: 219-3531
Toll Free Tel: 800-277-3243
E-mail: info@woodlandpublishing.com
Web Site: www.woodlandpublishing.com
Key Personnel
Ed: Sarah Beale
Founded: 1975
General trade & paperbacks, professional books; health & nutrition.
ISBN Prefix(es): 978-0-89557; 978-1-58054
Number of titles published annually: 50 Print
Total Titles: 200 Print
Distributed by Summit Beacon
Warehouse: 500 N 1030 W, Lindon, UT 84042 *Toll Free Tel:* 800-777-2665 *Fax:* 801-785-8511
Distribution Center: New Leaf Distributing Co, 401 Thornton Rd, Lithia Springs, GA 30122-1557 *Tel:* 770-948-7845 *Toll Free Tel:* 800-326-2665 *Fax:* 770-944-2313 *Web Site:* www.newleaf-dist.com
Nutri-Books, 790 W Tennessee Ave, Denver, CO 80217 *Toll Free Tel:* 800-279-2048

Woodrow Wilson Center Press
Division of The Woodrow Wilson International Center for Scholars
One Woodrow Wilson Plaza, 1300 Pennsylvania Ave NW, Washington, DC 20004-3027
Tel: 202-691-4000 *Fax:* 202-691-4001
Web Site: wilsoncenter.org
Founded: 1988
Humanities & social sciences; policy studies.
ISBN Prefix(es): 978-0-943875; 978-1-930365
Number of titles published annually: 8 Print; 8 E-Book
Total Titles: 200 Print
Imprints: Wilson Center Press; Woodrow Wilson Center Press/Johns Hopkins University Press; Woodrow Wilson Center Press/Stanford University Press; Woodrow Wilson Center Press/Columbia University Press
Distributed by Columbia University Press; The Johns Hopkins University Press; Stanford University Press; University of California Press
Membership(s): AAP; Association of American University Presses

WoodstockArts
PO Box 1342, Woodstock, NY 12498
Tel: 845-679-8111 *Fax:* 419-793-3452
E-mail: info@woodstockarts.com
Web Site: woodstockarts.com
Key Personnel
Founder: Julia Blelock; Weston Blelock
Founded: 1999
Dedicating memories of Woodstock artists.
ISBN Prefix(es): 978-0-9679268
Number of titles published annually: 3 Print
Total Titles: 5 Print
Membership(s): Independent Book Publishers Association

Workers Compensation Research Institute
955 Massachusetts Ave, Cambridge, MA 02139
Tel: 617-661-9274 *Fax:* 617-661-9284
E-mail: wcri@wcrinet.org
Web Site: www.wcrinet.org
Key Personnel
Pubns Specialist: Sarah Solorzano
Founded: 1983
Workers compensation public policy research.
ISBN Prefix(es): 978-0-935149
Number of titles published annually: 40 Print
Total Titles: 500 Print

§Workman Publishing Co Inc
225 Varick St, 9th fl, New York, NY 10014-4381
SAN: 203-2821
Tel: 212-254-5900 *Toll Free Tel:* 800-722-7202 *Fax:* 212-254-8098
E-mail: info@workman.com
Web Site: www.workman.com

Key Personnel
Exec Chair of the Bd & Pres: Carolan Workman
CEO: Dan Reynolds
COO: Glenn D'Agnes *Tel:* 212-614-7798 *E-mail:* glenn@workman.com
Cont: Bill Jackson *Tel:* 212-614-7552 *E-mail:* bill@workman.com
Publr & Edit Dir: Susan Bolotin *Tel:* 212-614-7514 *E-mail:* susan@workman.com
Publr, Children's Group: Daniel Nayeri
Assoc Publr: Page Edmunds *Tel:* 212-614-7528 *E-mail:* page@workman.com
Group Creative Dir: David Schiller
Exec Dir, Digital Opers: Kate Travers
Exec Dir, New Busn Devt: Jenny Mandel *Tel:* 212-614-7508 *E-mail:* jenny@workman.com
Exec Dir, Publicity & Mktg: Selina Meere *E-mail:* selina@workman.com
Exec Dir, Sales: James Wehrle
Exec Dir, Spec Projs: Ann Bramson
Art Dir, Children's Dept: Colleen Venable
Creative Dir: Vaughn Andrews
Dir, Digital Mktg & Strategy: Thea James
Dir, Gift & Mass Merchant Sales: Jodi Weiss *Tel:* 212-614-7529 *E-mail:* jodiw@workman.com
Dir, Gift Field Sales: Marilyn Barnett *Tel:* 212-614-7737 *E-mail:* marilyn@workman.com
Dir, Intl Sales & Licensing: Kristina Peterson *Tel:* 212-614-5617 *E-mail:* kristina@workman.com
Dir, Online Retail Accts: Randall Lotowycz
Dir, Publicity: Rebecca Carlisle
Dir, Spec Mkts & Custom Publg: Emily Krasner
Licensing Dir: Pat Upton *Tel:* 212-614-7588 *E-mail:* pat@workman.com
Assoc Dir, Field Sales: Jenny Lui
Assoc Dir of Mktg, Adult Trade: Moira Kerrigan
Publicity Mgr: Chloe Puton
Sr Publicist: John Jenkinson
Publicist & Mktg Assoc, Children's: Estelle Hallick
Assoc Publicist: Jenny Lee
Exec Ed: Suzanne Rafer *Tel:* 212-614-7516 *E-mail:* suzanne@workman.com
Exec Ed, Children's Group: Nathalie Le Du
Mng Ed: Claire McKean
Sr Ed: Mary Ellen O'Neill; Maisie Tivnan; Bruce Tracy
Sr Ed, Children's: Carol Burrell
Ed, Children's: Justin Krasner
Assoc Ed, Children's: Olivia Swomley
Ed-at-Large: Raquel Jaramillo
Gen Mgr: Jill Salayi *Tel:* 212-614-7532 *E-mail:* jill@workman.com
Sr Mgr, Digital Opers: Cheryl Clayton
Adult Lib Mktg Mgr: Annie Mazes
Digital Content & Soc Media Community Mgr: Louisa Hager
Intl Rts Mgr: Allison Huggins
Mgr, Cust Serv: Shirley Ortiz *Tel:* 212-614-7583 *E-mail:* shirley@workman.com
Mgr, Digital Opers & Analytics: Steven Whitener
Prodn Mgr: Doug Wolff *Tel:* 212-614-7595 *E-mail:* doug@workman.com
Promos Mgr: Megan Harley
Assoc Mgr, Natl Accts: Caitlin Kleinschmidt
Asst Mgr, Cust Serv: Natalya Pilguy *Tel:* 212-614-7555 *E-mail:* natalya@workman.com
Asst Mgr, Digital Mktg: Laura DiNardo
Asst Mgr, Mail Order, Specialty Wholesale & Online Retail: Kayla Burson
Asst Mgr, Sales Opers: Vanessa Karalis
Asst Mgr, Web Opers: Cialina Temena-Husemann
Asst Mktg Mgr: Lauren Southard
Digital Mktg Coord: Zelina Bennett
Natl Accts Sales Assoc: J T Green
Founded: 1967
General nonfiction, calendars.
ISBN Prefix(es): 978-0-89480; 978-1-56305; 978-0-7611
Number of titles published annually: 345 Print
Divisions: Algonquin Books; Artisan; Storey Publishing; Timber Press; Workman Speakers Bureau
Distributor for Duo Press; The Experiment; Greenwich Workshop Press
Foreign Rep(s): Thomas Allen & Son Ltd (Canada); Bookreps New Zealand (New Zealand); Hardie Grant Books (Australia); Melia Publishing Services (Ireland, UK)
Foreign Rights: Big Apple Agency Inc (China, Taiwan); Graal Literary Agency (Poland); Japan UNI Agency (Japan); JLM Literary Agency (Greece); Katai & Bolza Literary Agency (Hungary); KCC (Korea); Alexander Korahenevski Agency (Russia); Kristin Olson Literary Agency (Czech Republic); Mickey Pikarski (Israel); Sebes & Bisseling Literary Agency (Netherlands); Julio F Yanez Agencia Literaria (Latin America, Portugal, Spain)
Returns: RR Donnelley Fulfillment, 655 Brighton Beach Rd, Menasha, WI 54952
Warehouse: RR Donnelley Fulfillment, N9234 Lake Park Rd, Appleton, WI 54915, Mgr, Cust Serv: Kim Rose *Tel:* 920-969-6411 *Fax:* 920-969-6441 *E-mail:* kim.m.rose@rrd.com
Membership(s): AAP
See separate listing for:
Algonquin Books
Artisan Books
Timber Press Inc

World Almanac®
Imprint of Infobase Learning
132 W 31 St, New York, NY 10001
SAN: 211-6944
Toll Free Tel: 800-322-8755
E-mail: almanac@infobaselearning.com
Web Site: www.worldalmanac.com
Key Personnel
Sr Ed: Sarah Janssen *E-mail:* sjanssen@infobaselearning.com
Rts & Licensing: Ben Jacobs *E-mail:* bjacobs@infobaselearning.com
Founded: 1868
Annual juvenile & adult reference books.
ISBN Prefix(es): 978-1-60057
Number of titles published annually: 6 Print
Total Titles: 9 Print; 3 E-Book
Foreign Rep(s): Adnkronos Libri SRL (Italy)

§World Bank Publications
Member of The World Bank Group
Office of the Publisher, 1818 "H" St NW, U-11-1104, Washington, DC 20433
Tel: 202-458-4497; 202-473-1000 *Toll Free Tel:* 800-645-7247 (cust serv) *Fax:* 202-522-2631
E-mail: books@worldbank.org; pubrights@worldbank.org (foreign rts)
Web Site: www.worldbank.org/en/publication/reference
Key Personnel
Pres, World Bank Group & Chmn of the Bd of Dirs: Dr Jim Yong Kim
Founded: 1944
Publish over 200 new titles annually in support of the World Bank's mission to fight poverty & distributes them globally in both print & electronic formats; electronic online subscription database; international affairs.
ISBN Prefix(es): 978-0-8213
Number of titles published annually: 200 Print; 10 CD-ROM; 3 Online; 30 E-Book
Total Titles: 2,000 Print; 50 CD-ROM; 3 Online; 50 E-Book
Imprints: World Bank
Foreign Rep(s): Africa Connection (Guy Simpson) (Sub-Saharan Africa); African Moon Press (Chris Reinders) (Southern Africa); Co Info Pty Ltd (Australia, New Zealand); Eurospan Group (Africa, Central Asia, East Asia, Europe, Ireland, Middle East, UK); Far Eastern Booksellers (East Asia, Japan); International Publishers Representatives (Middle East, North Africa); Viva Books Pvt Ltd (South Asia)
Membership(s): AAP

§World Book Inc
Subsidiary of The Scott Fetzer Co
180 N LaSalle, Suite 900, Chicago, IL 60601
SAN: 201-4815
Tel: 312-729-5800 *Toll Free Tel:* 800-967-5325 (consumer sales, US); 800-463-8845 (consumer sales, CN); 800-975-3250 (school & lib sales, US); 800-837-5365 (school & lib sales, CN); 866-866-5200 (web sales) *Fax:* 312-729-5600; 312-729-5606 *Toll Free Fax:* 800-433-9330 (school & lib sales, US); 888-690-4002 (school lib sales, CN)
E-mail: customercare@worldbook.com
Web Site: www.worldbook.com
Key Personnel
Pres: Jim O'Rourke
VP, Edit & Ed-in-Chief: Paul A Kobasa
Founded: 1917
Publisher of high-quality, award-winning, educational reference & nonfiction publications for the school & library market & home market, in print & online formats.
ISBN Prefix(es): 978-0-7166
Number of titles published annually: 40 Print
Total Titles: 350 Print; 10 Online
Imprints: Bright Connections Media
See separate listing for:
Bright Connections Media, A World Book Encyclopedia Company

World Citizens
Affiliate of Cinema Investments Co Inc
PO Box 131, Mill Valley, CA 94942-0131
Tel: 415-380-8020 *Toll Free Tel:* 800-247-6553 (orders only)
Key Personnel
Ed-in-Chief: Joan Ellen
Ed: John Ballard
Assoc Ed: Jack Henry
Sales Mgr & Intl Rts: Steve Ames
Founded: 1984
Cross cultural & multicultural novels & texts. Adult, educational, trade & young adult divisions.
ISBN Prefix(es): 978-0-932279
Number of titles published annually: 6 Print; 4 CD-ROM; 6 E-Book; 4 Audio
Total Titles: 18 Print
Imprints: Classroom Classics; New Horizons Book Publishing Co; Skateman Publications
Distributed by Inland
Distribution Center: Bookmasters, PO Box 388, Ashland, OH 44805-0388 *Fax:* 419-201-6883

§World Resources Institute
10 "G" St NE, Suite 800, Washington, DC 20002
Tel: 202-729-7600 *Fax:* 202-729-7610
Web Site: www.wri.org
Key Personnel
Dir, Pubns: Hyacinth Billings *Tel:* 202-729-7712
Founded: 1982
Professional, scholarly & general interest publications, including energy, the environment, agriculture, forestry, natural resources, economics, geography, climate, biotechnology & development. Some titles co-published with university presses & commercial publishers.
ISBN Prefix(es): 978-0-915825; 978-1-56973
Number of titles published annually: 10 Print
Total Titles: 420 Print; 2 CD-ROM

§World Scientific Publishing Co Inc
27 Warren St, Suite 401-402, Hackensack, NJ 07601
Tel: 201-487-9655 *Fax:* 201-487-9656
E-mail: wspc_us@wspc.com; sales@wspc.com; mkt@wspc.com; editor@wspc.com
Web Site: www.worldscientific.com

Key Personnel
Chmn & Ed-in-Chief: K K Phuna
Group Mng Dir: Doreen Kiu
Mng Dir: Max Phua
Founded: 1981
ISBN Prefix(es): 978-1-944659
Number of titles published annually: 400 Print
Total Titles: 5,000 Print
Subsidiaries: Imperial College Press
Foreign Office(s): World Scientific Publishing (Beijing), B1505, Caizhi International Bldg, No 18 Zhongguancun E Rd, Haidan District, Beijing 100083, China *Tel:* (010) 82601201 *E-mail:* wspbj@wspc.com
Global Consultancy (Shanghai) Pte Ltd, Shanghai Bund International Tower, Rm 2003, No 99, Huangpu Rd, Shanghai 200080, China *Tel:* (021) 63254982 *Fax:* (021) 63254985 *E-mail:* shanghai@worldscientific.com.cn
World Scientific Publishing Co Pte Ltd, Theresienstr 66, 80333 Munich, Germany *Tel:* (089) 12414-770 *Fax:* (089) 12414-7710 *E-mail:* munich@wspc.com
World Scientific Publishing (HK) Co Ltd, PO Box 72482, Kowloon Central Post Office, Hong Kong, Hong Kong *Tel:* 2771 8791 *Fax:* 2771 8155 *E-mail:* hongkong@worldscientific.com.hk
World Scientific Publishing Co Pte Ltd, No 16 SW Boag Rd, T Nagar, Chennai 600 017, India *Tel:* (044) 52065464 *Fax:* (044) 52065464
World Scientific Publishing Co, Kiriat Hatikshoret-Neve Ilan, Suite 226, Harei, 90805 Yehuda, Israel *Tel:* (054) 4403728 *Fax:* (02) 5791532; (02) 5791533 *E-mail:* rspindel@wspc.com
World Scientific Publishing Co, c/o Science Press Tokyo, 2F, No 3 Katou Bldg, 23-2 Yushima 2-chome, Bunkyo-ku, Tokyo 113-0034, Japan *Tel:* (080) 81080-6881 *E-mail:* wspc_japan@wspc.com
World Scientific Publishing Co Pte Ltd, 5 Toh Tuck Link, Singapore 596224, Singapore *Tel:* 6466 5775 *Fax:* 6467 7667 *E-mail:* wspc@wspc.com.sg
World Scientific Publishing Co Pte Ltd, 8F, No 162, Sec 4, Roosevelt Rd, Taipei 10091, Taiwan *Tel:* (02) 2369-1366 *Fax:* (02) 2366-0460 *E-mail:* wsptw@ms13.hinet.net
World Scientific Publishing (UK) Ltd, 57 Shelton St, London WC2H 9HE, United Kingdom *Tel:* (020) 7836 0888 *Fax:* (020) 7836 2020 *E-mail:* sales@wspc.co.uk
Warehouse: 46 Development Rd, Fitchburg, MA 01420

§World Trade Press
800 Lindberg Lane, Suite 190, Petaluma, CA 94952
Tel: 707-778-1124 *Toll Free Tel:* 800-833-8586 *Fax:* 707-778-1329
Web Site: www.worldtradepress.com
Key Personnel
Publr & CEO: Edward G Hinkelman *Tel:* 707-778-1124 ext 204 *E-mail:* egh@worldtradepress.com
Founded: 1990
Professional books for international trade & business travel.
ISBN Prefix(es): 978-0-9631864; 978-1-885073
Number of titles published annually: 8 Print; 240 Online; 26 E-Book
Total Titles: 118 Print
Distributed by Reference Press

WorldTariff
Division of FedEx Corp
220 Montgomery St, Suite 448, San Francisco, CA 94104-3410
Tel: 415-391-7501 *Toll Free Tel:* 866-268-7602
Web Site: ftn.fedex.com/wtonline
Founded: 1961
Publish customs duty & tax information.
ISBN Prefix(es): 978-1-56745
Number of titles published annually: 100 Print
Total Titles: 22 Online
Foreign Office(s): Eurotariff, National House, 60-66 Wardour St, 6th fl, London W1V 3HP, United Kingdom

§Worth Publishers
Imprint of Macmillan Learning
41 Madison Ave, 37th fl, New York, NY 10010
Tel: 212-576-9400; 212-375-7000 *Fax:* 212-561-8281
E-mail: press.inquiries@macmillan.com
Web Site: www.macmillanlearning.com
Key Personnel
VP, Strategy: Elizabeth Widdicombe
Founded: 1966
Social science texts for the higher education market & advanced high school courses.
ISBN Prefix(es): 978-1-57259; 978-1-4292; 978-0-7167
Number of titles published annually: 10 E-Book
Total Titles: 300 Print
Foreign Rep(s): Macmillan East Asia (China, Hong Kong, Indonesia, Korea, Philippines, Singapore, Thailand, Vietnam); Macmillan Publishers (Taiwan); Palgrave Macmillan (Australia, New Zealand); Palgrave Macmillan UK (Africa, Caribbean, Europe, India, Japan, Latin America, Middle East, Pakistan, UK); USBD Distribution Sdn Bhd (Malaysia)
Warehouse: MPS Distribution Center, 16365 James Madison Hwy (US Rte 15), Gordonsville, VA 22942 *Toll Free Tel:* 888-330-8477 *Fax:* 540-672-7540 (cust serv) *Toll Free Fax:* 800-672-2054 (orders)

WorthyKids/Ideals
Imprint of Worthy Publishing Group
6100 Tower Circle, Suite 210, Franklin, TN 37067
Tel: 615-932-7600
E-mail: idealsinfo@worthypublishing.com
Web Site: www.idealsbooks.com
Key Personnel
VP & Assoc Publr: Peggy Schaefer *E-mail:* peggys@worthypublishing.com
Founded: 1944 (acquired by Worthy Media Inc in 2014)
Publisher of *IDEALS* magazine, children's books & board books.
ISBN Prefix(es): 978-0-8249; 978-1-885593; 978-1-61795; 978-1-945470
Number of titles published annually: 35 Print
Total Titles: 200 Print
Imprints: Ideals Annuals; Williamson Books

Write Stuff Enterprises LLC
1001 S Andrews Ave, Suite 120, Fort Lauderdale, FL 33316
Tel: 954-462-6657 *Toll Free Tel:* 800-900-2665 *Fax:* 954-462-6023
E-mail: legends@writestuffbooks.com
Web Site: www.writestuffbooks.com
Key Personnel
Founder & CEO: Jeffrey L Rodengen
Leading publisher of historical works focusing on industry & technology.
ISBN Prefix(es): 978-0-945903; 978-1-932022
Number of titles published annually: 4 Print; 4 E-Book
Imprints: Write Stuff®
Membership(s): ABA; Independent Book Publishers Association

WriteLife LLC
2323 S 171 St, Suite 202, Omaha, NE 68130
Tel: 402-934-1412 *Toll Free Tel:* 877-974-8354
E-mail: info@writelife.com
Web Site: www.writelife.com; www.facebook.com/WriteLife
Key Personnel
Publr: Cindy Grady
Sr Ed & In-House Agent: Erin Reel
Mktg Dir: Kristl Finnes
Founded: 2008
ISBN Prefix(es): 978-1-60808
Number of titles published annually: 12 Print; 12 E-Book
Total Titles: 81 Print; 11 E-Book
Membership(s): Independent Book Publishers Association; Midwest Independent Booksellers Association; Mountains & Plains Independent Booksellers Association

Writer's AudioShop
1316 Overland Stage Rd, Dripping Springs, TX 78620
Tel: 512-476-1616
E-mail: wrtaudshop@aol.com
Web Site: www.writersaudio.com
Key Personnel
Publr: Elaine Davenport
Founded: 1985
Audio publisher.
ISBN Prefix(es): 978-1-880717
Number of titles published annually: 4 Audio
Total Titles: 35 Audio
Membership(s): Audio Publishers Association

Writer's Digest
Imprint of F+W Media Inc
10151 Carver Rd, Suite 200, Blue Ash, OH 45242
Tel: 513-531-2690 *Toll Free Tel:* 800-289-0963
E-mail: writersdigest@fwmedia.com (edit)
Web Site: www.writersdigest.com
Key Personnel
CEO: Thomas Beusse
Pres: Sara Domville
Prodn Dir: Phil Graham
Rts & Perms: Stephanie McKenna *E-mail:* stephanie.mckenna@fwcommunity.com
Top-quality instructional & reference books to help creative people find personal satisfaction & professional success. Topics covered include writing, publishing, songwriting & personal growth.
ISBN Prefix(es): 978-0-89879; 978-1-58297
Number of titles published annually: 28 Print
Total Titles: 150 Print
Foreign Rep(s): David Bateman Ltd (New Zealand); BookMovers Group (Canada); Capricorn Link (Australia); David & Charles Ltd (UK); Real Books (South Africa); Marta Schooler (Asia, Central America, Mexico, Middle East, South America)
Returns: Aero Fulfillment Services, 2800 Henkle Dr, Lebanon, OH 45036

WRP, see Water Resources Publications LLC

Wyndham Hall Press
5050 Kerr Rd, Lima, OH 45806
SAN: 686-6743
Tel: 419-648-9124 *Toll Free Tel:* 866-895-0977 *Fax:* 419-648-9124; 413-208-2409
Web Site: www.wyndhamhallpress.com
Key Personnel
Mng Ed: Mark S McCullough *E-mail:* mark@wyndhamhallpress.com
Founded: 1981
Scholarly monographs & textbooks.
ISBN Prefix(es): 978-1-55605; 978-0-932269
Number of titles published annually: 8 Print
Total Titles: 240 Print

XanEdu Publishing Inc, see Copley Custom Textbooks

§Xist Publishing
PO Box 61593, Irvine, CA 92602

Tel: 949-478-2568
E-mail: info@xistpublishing.com
Web Site: www.xistpublishing.com
Key Personnel
COO: Jacob Lee
Pres: Calee Lee
Founded: 2010
Digital-first publisher. Specialize in children's ebooks for every major device.
ISBN Prefix(es): 978-1-62395; 978-1-5324
Number of titles published annually: 50 Print; 200 E-Book; 30 Audio
Total Titles: 300 Print; 1,000 E-Book; 60 Audio
Foreign Rep(s): Sylvia Hayse (worldwide)
Membership(s): Society of Children's Book Writers & Illustrators

Xlibris Corp
Division of Author Solutions LLC
1663 Liberty Dr, Suite 200, Bloomington, IN 47403
Toll Free Tel: 888-795-4274 *Fax:* 610-915-0294
E-mail: info@xlibris.com
Web Site: www.xlibris.com
Key Personnel
CEO: Andrew Phillips
SVP & COO: Kevin G Gregory
SVP, Mktg: Keith Ogorek
SVP, Prodn Servs & Output Opers: Bill Becher
Founded: 1997
One of the leading publishing services providers for authors, Xlibris provides authors with a broad set of publishing options including hardcover, trade paperback, custom leather bound & full-color formats. In addition, Xlibris offers its authors the widest selection of professional, marketing & bookselling services. Since its founding, Xlibris has published more than 25,000 titles.
This publisher has indicated that 100% of its product line is author subsidized.
ISBN Prefix(es): 978-0-7388; 978-0-9663501; 978-1-4010; 978-1-4134; 978-1-59926; 978-1-4257; 978-1-4363; 978-1-4415
Number of titles published annually: 5,100 Print
Total Titles: 25,000 Print
Distribution Center: Baker & Taylor Inc, 2550 W Tyvola Rd, Suite 300, Charlotte, NC 28217 *Tel:* 704-998-3100 *Toll Free Tel:* 800-775-1800 *Web Site:* www.btol.com
Ingram Book Group, One Ingram Blvd, La Vergne, TN 37086 *Tel:* 615-793-5000 *Web Site:* www.ingramcontent.com
Membership(s): ABA; Canadian Booksellers Association

§XML Press
Subsidiary of R L Hamilton & Associates LLC
24310 Moulton Pkwy, Suite O-175, Laguna Hills, CA 92637
Tel: 970-231-3624
E-mail: publisher@xmlpress.net
Web Site: xmlpress.net
Key Personnel
Publr: Richard Hamilton *E-mail:* hamilton@xmlpress.net
Founded: 2008
Specialize in publications for technical communicators, content strategists, managers & marketers, with an emphasis on XML technology, social media & management. Also provides publication services to corporations that want to make their technical documentation available in print form through retail channels.
ISBN Prefix(es): 978-0-9822191; 978-1-937434
Number of titles published annually: 12 Print; 5 E-Book
Total Titles: 20 Print
Distribution Center: Ingram, One Ingram Blvd, La Vergne, TN 37086
Membership(s): Organization of Advancement of Structured Information Standards; Society for Technical Communication

Yale Center for British Art
1080 Chapel St, New Haven, CT 06510-2302
Mailing Address: PO Box 208280, New Haven, CT 06520-8280
Tel: 203-432-2800 *Fax:* 203-432-4538
Web Site: britishart.yale.edu
Key Personnel
Dir: Amy Meyers *E-mail:* ycba.director@yale.edu
Founded: 1977
Exhibition catalogues.
ISBN Prefix(es): 978-0-930606
Number of titles published annually: 4 Print
Total Titles: 61 Print

§Yale University Press
Division of Yale University
302 Temple St, New Haven, CT 06511-8909
SAN: 203-2740
Mailing Address: PO Box 209040, New Haven, CT 06520-9040
Tel: 203-432-0960; 203-432-0966 (sales); 401-531-2800 (cust serv) *Toll Free Tel:* 800-405-1619 (cust serv) *Fax:* 203-432-0948; 203-432-8485 (sales); 401-531-2801 (cust serv) *Toll Free Fax:* 800-406-9145 (cust serv)
E-mail: sales.press@yale.edu (sales); customer.care@triliteral.org (cust serv)
Web Site: www.yalebooks.com; yalepress.yale.edu/yupbooks
Key Personnel
COO: Kate Brown
Publr: John Donatich
Publr, Art & Architecture: Patricia Fidler
Deputy Dir, Fin & Opers: John D Rollins
Art Dir: Nancy Ovedovitz
Dir, Mktg & Promo: Heather D'Auria
Dir, Publg Opers: Christina Coffin
Edit Dir: Seth Ditchik
Publicity Dir: Brenda King
Sales Dir: Jay Cosgrove
Sr Exec Ed, Sci & Medicine: Jean E Thomson Black
Exec Ed: Jennifer Banks; William Frucht
Exec Ed, History & Current Events: Christopher Rogers
Exec Ed-at-Large: Steve Wasserman
Mng Ed: Jenya Weinreb
Sr Ed, Sci & Technol: Joseph Calamia
Ed, Art & Architecture: Katherine Boller
Ed, Lang, Lit & Performing Arts: Sarah Miller
Assoc Ed, Art & Architecture: Amy Canonico
Assoc Ed, World History, Geopolitics & Intl Rel: Jaya Aninda Chatterjee
Asst Ed & Mktg Mgr: Travis Kimbel
Asst Ed, Religion: Heather Gold
Edit Asst: Eva Skewes
Consulting Ed-at-Large: John Loudon; Benjamin Schwarz
Sr Sales Mgr, Art & Digital Publg: Stephen Cebik
Educ Mktg Mgr: Debra Bozzi
Mgr, Ad & Exhibits: Ellen Freiler
Mktg Mgr, Art & Architecture: Jessica Holahan
Online Mktg Mgr: Michael Hoak
Sr Publicist: Jennifer Doerr; Liz Pelton; Robert Pranzatelli
Publicist: Alden Ferro
Publicist, Art & Architecture: Courtney Andree; Joshua Machat
Founded: 1908
Scholarly publications.
ISBN Prefix(es): 978-0-300
Number of titles published annually: 350 Print
Total Titles: 5,000 Print
Foreign Office(s): 47 Bedford Sq, London WC1B 3DP, United Kingdom, Head, Rts: Anne Bihan *Tel:* (020) 7079-4900 *Fax:* (020) 7079-4901 *E-mail:* sales@yaleup.co.uk *Web Site:* www.yalebooks.co.uk
Distributor for Addison Gallery of American Art, Phillips Academy; The Art Institute of Chicago; The Bard Graduate Center, Dallas Museum of Art; Harvard University Art Museums; Japan Society; The Jewish Museum; Kimbell Art Museum; Paul Mellon Centre; The Menil Collection; The Metropolitan Museum of Art; National Gallery, London; National Gallery of Art (Washington, DC); Philadelphia Museum of Art; Princeton University Art Museum; Sterling & Francine Clark Art Institute; Whitney Museum of American Art; Yale Center for British Art; Yale University Art Gallery
Foreign Rep(s): Rockbook (Japan, South Korea, Taiwan); David Stimpson (Australia, Canada, New Zealand)
Foreign Rights: Ann Bihan (England); Craig Falk (Latin America, Mexico, South America)
Shipping Address: TriLiteral LLC, 100 Maple Ridge Dr, Cumberland, RI 02864-1769 *Tel:* 401-658-4226
Membership(s): AAP; Association of American University Presses

§Yard Dog Press
710 W Redbud Lane, Alma, AR 72921-7247
Tel: 479-632-4693 *Fax:* 479-632-4693
Web Site: www.yarddogpress.com
Key Personnel
Owner & Ed-in-Chief: Selina Rosen *E-mail:* selinarosen@cox.net
Tech Ed & Orders Contact: Lynn Rosen *E-mail:* lynnstran@cox.net
Founded: 1995
Micro press specializing in science fiction, fantasy & horror. Closed to unsol submissions. Special pricing for bulk orders.
ISBN Prefix(es): 978-1-893687; 978-0-9824704; 978-1-937105; 978-1-945941
Number of titles published annually: 4 Print; 4 E-Book
Total Titles: 130 Print; 130 E-Book
Imprints: Double Dog (flip books - two short novels); Fantasy Writers' Asylum; Just Cause (non-genre books)
Membership(s): Science Fiction & Fantasy Writers of America

YBK Publishers Inc
39 Crosby St, New York, NY 10013
Tel: 212-219-0135
E-mail: readmybook@ybkpublishers.com; info@ybkpublishers.com
Web Site: www.ybkpublishers.com
Key Personnel
Pres: Otto Barz *E-mail:* obarz@ybkpublishers.com
Founded: 2001
Print-on-demand; general trade & nonfiction.
ISBN Prefix(es): 978-0-9703923; 978-0-9764359; 978-1-936411; 978-0-9790972; 978-0-9800508; 978-0-9824012
Number of titles published annually: 7 Print
Total Titles: 90 Print; 5 E-Book
Distribution Center: Lightning Source, 1246 Heil Quaker Blvd, La Vergne, TN 37086 *Tel:* 615-213-5815 *Fax:* 615-213-4426 *E-mail:* info@ybkpublishers.com
Membership(s): AAP; PEN American Center

Yeshiva University Press
500 W 185 St, New York, NY 10033
Mailing Address: KTAV Publishing House Inc, 888 Newark Ave, Jersey City, NJ 07306
Tel: 212-960-5400 *Fax:* 212-960-0043
Web Site: www.yu.edu
Key Personnel
Pres: Richard Joel *Tel:* 212-960-5300 *E-mail:* president@yu.edu
ISBN Prefix(es): 978-0-87068; 978-0-88125; 978-1-60280
Number of titles published annually: 10 Print
Total Titles: 71 Print
Distributed by KTAV Publishing House Inc

YMAA Publication Center Inc
PO Box 480, Wolfeboro, NH 03894
SAN: 665-2077
Tel: 603-569-7988 *Toll Free Tel:* 800-669-8892 *Fax:* 603-569-1889
E-mail: info@ymaa.com
Web Site: www.ymaa.com
Key Personnel
Publr: David Ripianzi
Prodn Mgr: Tim Comrie
Sales Rep: David Silver
Founded: 1984
Publisher of in-depth books, videos & DVDs on martial arts, meditation, traditional Chinese medicine & alternative health therapies.
ISBN Prefix(es): 978-0-940871; 978-1-886969; 978-1-59439
Number of titles published annually: 10 Print; 10 E-Book
Total Titles: 80 Print; 50 E-Book; 4 Audio
Distributor for Wind Records (Chinese healing music)
Foreign Rep(s): Big Apple Agency (Maggie Han) (China, Taiwan); The Book Publishers Association of Israel (Shoshi Grajower) (Israel); Graal Literary Agency (Madga Cabajewska) (Poland); Imprima Korea Agency (Joseph Lee) (Korea); International Copyright Agency (Simona Kessler) (Romania); Japan Uni Agency (Taeko Nagatsuka) (Japan); JS Literary & Media Agency (Somjai Raksasee) (Thailand); Nurcihan Kesim Literary Agency Inc (Filiz Karaman) (Turkey); Maxima Creative Agency (Santo Manurung) (Indonesia); Nova Littera SL (Konstantin Paltchikov) (Russia); Andrew Nurnberg Associates (Tatjana Zoldnere) (Latvia, Lithuania, Ukraine); Andrew Nurnberg Associates (Anna Droumeva) (Bulgaria); Andrew Nurnberg Associates (Petra Tobiskova) (Czech Republic); OA Literary Agency (Michael Avramides) (Greece); Plima Literary Agency (Mila Perisic) (Croatia, Serbia, Slovenia); Schindler's Literary Agency (Suely Pedro Dos Santos) (Brazil); Ralph & Sheila Summers (Hong Kong, Korea, Malaysia, Philippines, Singapore, Taiwan, Thailand); Tuttle-Mori Agency Inc (Fumi Nishijima) (Japan); Julio F Yanez Agencia Literaria SL (Montse F Yanez) (Mexico, Spain)
Foreign Rights: Agencia Literaria (Brazil, Portugal); Big Apple Agency Inc (China, Taiwan); Bookman (Denmark, Finland, Iceland, Norway, Sweden); Imprima Korea Agency (Korea); Jarir Bookstore (Egypt, Middle East, Saudi Arabia); JS Literary & Media Agency (Thailand); La Nouvelle Agency (Belgium, Switzerland); Nova Littera Ltd (Russia); Andrew Nurnberg Associates (Baltic States); Andrew Nurnberg Associates Sofia (Bulgaria); OA Literary Agency (Greece); Permissions & Rights (Albania, Croatia, Montenegro, Serbia, Slovenia); Tuttle-Mori Agency Inc (Japan); Julio F Yanez Agencia Literaria SL (Mexico, Spain, Spanish, Spanish Latin America)
Orders to: Baker & Taylor, 2550 W Tyvola Rd, Charlotte, NC *Toll Free Tel:* 800-775-1800 *Fax:* 704-998-3100 *Web Site:* www.btol.com; Ingram Book Co, One Ingram Blvd, La Vergne, TN *Tel:* (615) 793-5000 *Toll Free Tel:* 800-937-8200 *Web Site:* www.ingrambook.com; National Book Network, 15200 NBN Way, Blue Ridge Summit, PA 17214 *Tel:* 717-794-3800 *Toll Free Tel:* 800-462-6420 *Toll Free Fax:* 800-338-4550 *E-mail:* custserv@nbnbooks.com *Web Site:* www.nbnbooks.com; New Leaf Distributing Co, 401 Thornton Rd, Lithia Springs, GA 30122-1557 *Tel:* 770-948-7845 *Toll Free Tel:* 800-944-2313 *Fax:* 770-994-2313 *E-mail:* newleaf@newleaf-dist.com *Web Site:* www.newleaf-dist.com
Distribution Center: National Book Network, 15200 NBN Way, Blue Ridge Summit, PA 07214 *Tel:* 717-794-3800 *Toll Free Tel:* 800-338-4550 *Toll Free Fax:* 800-338-4550 *E-mail:* custserv@nbnbooks.com *Web Site:* www.nbnbooks.com
Membership(s): ABA; Independent Book Publishers Association

§Yotzeret Publishing
PO Box 18662, St Paul, MN 55118-0662
Tel: 651-470-3853 *Fax:* 651-224-7447
E-mail: info@yotzeretpublishing.com; orders@yotzeretpublishing.com
Web Site: yotzeretpublishing.com
Key Personnel
Publr: Sheyna Galyan
Founded: 2002
Adult & children's books & ebooks from a Jewish perspective.
ISBN Prefix(es): 978-1-59287
Number of titles published annually: 2 Print; 2 E-Book; 1 Audio
Total Titles: 10 Print; 7 E-Book
Orders to: Itasca Books, 5120 Cedar Lake Rd, Minneapolis, MN 55416, Dist Mgr: Mark Jung *Tel:* 952-345-4488 *Toll Free Tel:* 800-901-3480 *Fax:* 952-920-0541 *E-mail:* orders@itascabooks.com *Web Site:* www.itascabooks.com
Distribution Center: Itasca Books, 5120 Cedar Lake Rd, Minneapolis, MN 55416, Dist Mgr: Mark Jung *Tel:* 952-342-4888 ext 118 *Toll Free Tel:* 800-901-3480 ext 118 *Fax:* 952-920-0541 *E-mail:* orders@itascabooks.com *Web Site:* www.itascabooks.com
Membership(s): Independent Book Publishers Association; Midwest Independent Publishing Association; Minnesota Book Publishers Roundtable

YWAM Publishing
Division of Youth With A Mission
PO Box 55787, Seattle, WA 98155-0787
Tel: 425-771-1153 *Toll Free Tel:* 800-922-2143 *Fax:* 425-775-2383
E-mail: books@ywampublishing.com
Web Site: www.ywampublishing.com
Key Personnel
Mktg Dir: Wenche Warren *E-mail:* marketing@ywampublishing.com
Founded: 1960
Books on missions, evangelism & discipleship & also religious classics.
ISBN Prefix(es): 978-0-927545
Number of titles published annually: 10 Print; 2 CD-ROM
Total Titles: 260 Print; 15 CD-ROM; 10 Audio
Distributor for Emerald Books
Shipping Address: 7825 230 St SW, Edmonds, WA 98026
Warehouse: 7825 230 St SW, Edmonds, WA 98026

§Zagat Survey LLC
76 Ninth Ave, 4th fl, New York, NY 10011
SAN: 289-4777
Toll Free Tel: 800-540-9609
E-mail: feedback@zagat.com
Web Site: www.zagat.com
Key Personnel
Co-Founder, Co-Chair & CEO: Tim Zagat
Co-Founder & Co-Chair: Nina S Zagat *E-mail:* nina@zagat.com
Founded: 1979
Provider of consumer survey-based information on where to eat, drink, stay & play worldwide.
ISBN Prefix(es): 978-1-57006; 978-1-60478
Number of titles published annually: 49 Online

Zaner-Bloser Inc
Subsidiary of Highlights for Children Inc
1201 Dublin Rd, Columbus, OH 43215
Tel: 614-486-0221 *Toll Free Tel:* 800-421-3018 (cust serv) *Toll Free Fax:* 800-992-6087 (orders)
E-mail: zbcsd@zaner-bloser.com; international@zaner-bloser.com
Web Site: www.zaner-bloser.com
Key Personnel
Pres: Donna Schultz
Founded: 1888
Elementary textbooks for critical thinking, whole language, substance abuse prevention, spelling & handwriting; modality (learning styles) kit, professional education books, storytelling kits & early childhood education.
ISBN Prefix(es): 978-0-88309; 978-0-88085
Number of titles published annually: 200 Print
Foreign Rep(s): Children's Press
Advertising Agency: EDPUB
Orders to: PO Box 16764, Columbus, OH 43216-6764
Warehouse: 4200 Parkway Ct, Hilliard, OH 43026

Zarahemla Books
869 E 2680 N, Provo, UT 84604
Tel: 801-368-7374
Web Site: www.zarahemlabooks.com
Key Personnel
Publr: Christopher Bigelow
Founded: 2006
Alternative Mormon-themed fiction & memoir.
ISBN Prefix(es): 978-0-9787971; 978-0-9843603
Number of titles published annually: 3 Print
Total Titles: 22 Print

Zebra Books, see Kensington Publishing Corp

Zeig, Tucker & Theisen Inc
2632 E Thomas Rd, Suite 200, Phoenix, AZ 85016
Tel: 480-389-4342 *Fax:* 602-944-8118
E-mail: marketing@zeigtucker.com
Web Site: www.zeigtucker.com
Key Personnel
Pres: Jeffrey K Zeig, PhD *Tel:* 602-944-6529 *E-mail:* jeff@zeigtucker.com
Busn Mgr: Stacey Moore *E-mail:* stacey@zeigtucker.com
Mng Ed: Chuck Lakin *E-mail:* chuck@zeigtucker.com
Founded: 1998
Independent publisher in the behavioral sciences.
ISBN Prefix(es): 978-1-891944; 978-1-932462
Number of titles published annually: 10 Print
Total Titles: 45 Print; 8 Audio
Editorial Office(s): 3606 N 24 St, Phoenix, AZ 86015
Billing Address: Longleaf Services Inc, 116 S Boundary St, Chapel Hill, NC 27514-3808 *Toll Free Tel:* 800-848-6224 *Toll Free Fax:* 800-272-6817 *Web Site:* www.longleafservices.org
Orders to: Longleaf Services Inc, 116 S Boundary St, Chapel Hill, NC 27514-3808 *Tel:* 607-277-2211 *Toll Free Tel:* 800-848-6224 *Toll Free Fax:* 800-272-6817 *Web Site:* www.longleafservices.org
Returns: Longleaf Services Inc, 116 S Boundary St, Chapel Hill, NC 27514-3808 *Toll Free Tel:* 800-848-6224 *Toll Free Fax:* 800-272-6817 *Web Site:* www.longleafservices.org
Shipping Address: Longleaf Services Inc, 116 S Boundary St, Chapel Hill, NC 27514-3808 *Toll Free Tel:* 800-848-6224 *Toll Free Fax:* 800-272-6817 *Web Site:* www.longleafservices.org
Warehouse: Longleaf Services Inc, 116 S Boundary St, Chapel Hill, NC 27514-3808 *Toll Free Tel:* 800-848-6224 *Toll Free Fax:* 800-272-6817 *Web Site:* www.longleafservices.org
Distribution Center: Longleaf Services Inc, 116 S Boundary St, Chapel Hill, NC 27514-3808 *Toll Free Tel:* 800-848-6224 *Toll Free Fax:* 800-272-6817 *Web Site:* www.longleafservices.org

Zephyr Press, see Chicago Review Press

Zest Books
2443 Stillman St, Suite 340, San Francisco, CA 94115
Tel: 415-777-8654; 510-984-0841 *Fax:* 415-777-8653
E-mail: info@zestbooks.net; publicity@zestbooks.net
Web Site: zestbooks.net
Key Personnel
Publr & Creative Dir: Hallie Warshaw *E-mail:* hallie@zestbooks.net
Publg Dir: Daniel Harmon
Mktg & Publicity Mgr: Emma Boyer
Founded: 2006
ISBN Prefix(es): 978-0-9772660
Number of titles published annually: 14 Print; 14 E-Book
Total Titles: 60 Print
Distributed by Quarto (Ireland, North America & UK)

§Zondervan
Imprint of HarperCollins Christian Publishing
3900 Sparks Dr, Grand Rapids, MI 49546
SAN: 203-2694
Tel: 616-698-6900 *Toll Free Tel:* 800-226-1122; 800-727-1309 (retail orders) *Fax:* 616-698-3350 *Toll Free Fax:* 800-698-3256 (retail orders)
E-mail: zinfo@zondervan.com
Web Site: www.zondervan.com
Key Personnel
SVP & Ed-in-Chief: Stan Gundry
SVP, Sales: Tom Knight
VP & Publr, Nonfiction Trade Books: David Morris
VP of Mktg: Michael Aulisio
VP of Mktg, Church, Academic, Ref & Reflective Publg: Jesse Hillman
VP of Mktg, Trade Books: Tom Dean
Assoc Publr, Bibles: Melinda Bourma
Sr Mktg Dir, Gift Books: Tim Marshall
Sr Mktg Dir, Kidz Bibles & Storybook Bibles: Kevin Traub
Mktg Dir of Online Learning, Academic Div: Kent Hendricks
PR Dir, Nonfiction Trade: Robin Barnett
Sr Acqs Ed, Digital, Ref & Reflective Titles: Madison Trammel
Sr Ed: Joey Paul
Sr Ed, Biblical Langs, Textbooks & Ref Tools: Christopher Beetham
Acqs Ed, Zonderkidz: Robyn Burwell
Acqs Ed, Zonderkidz Bibles: Sara Bierling
Sr Publicity Mgr: Trinity McFadden
Founded: 1931
A world leader in Christian communications & the leading Christian publishing brand. For more than 75 years, Zondervan has delivered transformational Christian experiences through general & academic resources authored by influential leaders & emerging voices & been honored with more Christian Book Awards than any other publisher. Headquartered in Grand Rapids, MI, with offices in San Diego & Miami, Zondervan conducts events & publishes its bestselling Bibles, books, audio, video, curriculum, software & digital products through its Zondervan, eZondervan, Zonderkidz, Youth Specialties, Editorial Vida & National Pastors Convention brands. Zondervan resources are sold worldwide through retail stores, online & by Zondervan ChurchSource & are translated into nearly 200 languages in more than 60 countries.
ISBN Prefix(es): 978-0-310
Number of titles published annually: 200 Print; 4 CD-ROM; 30 Online; 50 E-Book; 50 Audio
Total Titles: 5,000 Print; 30 CD-ROM; 300 Online; 300 E-Book; 400 Audio
Divisions: Zonderkidz
Returns: 2205 E Lincoln Way, La Porte, IN 46350
Membership(s): AAP; ABA; Audio Publishers Association; Better Business Bureau; BISG; CBA; Chamber of Commerce; Evangelical Christian Publishers Association; Evangelical Press Association; Society of Bible Literature; Society of Children's Book Writers & Illustrators; Software & Information Industry Association

Zone Books
633 Vanderbilt St, Brooklyn, NY 11218
Tel: 718-686-0048 *Toll Free Tel:* 800-405-1619 (orders & cust serv) *Fax:* 718-686-9045
E-mail: orders@triliteral.org
Web Site: www.zonebooks.org
Key Personnel
Dir: Meighan Gale *E-mail:* mgale@zonebooks.org
Asst Ed: Michael Newton *E-mail:* mnewton@zonebooks.org
Founded: 1985
Publish books in the arts, humanities & social sciences.
ISBN Prefix(es): 978-0-942299; 978-1-890951
Number of titles published annually: 6 Print
Total Titles: 59 Print
Distributed by The MIT Press
Foreign Rights: Casanovas & Lynch Agencia Literaria (Maria Lynch) (Brazil, France, Greece, Netherlands, Portugal, Spain); English Agency (Kohei Hattori) (Japan); Paul & Peter Fritz Agency (Antonia Fritz) (Germany); Graal Literary Agency (Filip Wojciechowski) (Eastern Europe); Imprima Agency (Terry Kim) (South Korea); Agnese Incisa Agenzia Litteraria (Agnese Incisa) (Italy)

Zumaya Publications LLC
3209 S IH 35, Suite 1086, Austin, TX 78741
Tel: 512-537-3145 *Fax:* 512-276-6745
E-mail: acquisitions@zumayapublications.com
Web Site: www.zumayapublications.com
Key Personnel
CFO: Marianne Moul
Exec Ed/Publr: Liz Burton
Partner: Joyanne Moul
Acqs Ed: Rie Sheridan Rose
Founded: 2001
Trade paperback & ebook formats offering full-length works of fiction & nonfiction.
ISBN Prefix(es): 978-1-93413; 978-1-93484
Number of titles published annually: 20 Print; 20 E-Book
Total Titles: 200 Print; 200 E-Book
Imprints: Arcane (mysteries of the spirit); Boundless; Embraces; Enigma; Otherworlds (speculative fiction, science fiction, fantasy & paranormal suspense); Thresholds (imagination); Yesterdays (journeys into the past - both real & imaginary)
Membership(s): Independent Book Publishers Association

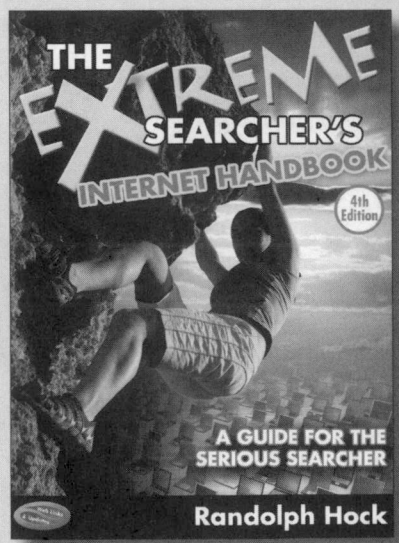

U.S. Publishers — Geographic Index

COLORADO

CONNECTICUT

DELAWARE

DISTRICT OF COLUMBIA

FLORIDA

MINNESOTA

MISSISSIPPI

MISSOURI

MONTANA

NEBRASKA

NEVADA

NEW HAMPSHIRE

NEW JERSEY

NEW MEXICO

NEW YORK

NORTH CAROLINA

NORTH DAKOTA

OHIO

OKLAHOMA

OREGON

PENNSYLVANIA

RHODE ISLAND

SOUTH CAROLINA

SOUTH DAKOTA

TENNESSEE

TEXAS

UTAH

VERMONT

VIRGINIA

WASHINGTON

WEST VIRGINIA

WISCONSIN

WYOMING

PUERTO RICO

U.S. Publishers — Type of Publication Index

ASSOCIATION PRESSES

AUDIOBOOKS

AV MATERIALS

BELLES LETTRES

BIBLES

BIBLIOGRAPHIES

Bureau of Economic Geology, University of Texas at Austin, pg 45
Center for East Asian Studies (CEAS), pg 51
Clearfield Co Inc, pg 57
Crumb Elbow Publishing, pg 65
Cypress House, pg 66
Walter De Gruyter Inc, pg 69
Goose River Press, pg 94
Gospel Publishing House (GPH), pg 94
Helm Book Publishing, pg 106
Homa & Sekey Books, pg 110
The International Institute of Islamic Thought, pg 119
George Kurian Reference Books, pg 128
Libraries Unlimited, pg 133
The Linick Group Inc, pg 135
Management Advisory Services & Publications (MASP), pg 140
The Edwin Mellen Press, pg 148
Merriam Press, pg 149
Military Info Publishing, pg 150
Modern Language Association of America (MLA), pg 152
The Mongolia Society Inc, pg 153
National Center for Children in Poverty, pg 157
The New York Botanical Garden Press, pg 161
Nova Science Publishers Inc, pg 165
Oak Knoll Press, pg 166
Omnigraphics Inc, pg 168
Open Horizons Publishing Co, pg 168
Pennsylvania Historical & Museum Commission, pg 179
Picasso Project, pg 183
Picton Press, pg 183
RockBench Publishing Corp, pg 200
Routledge, pg 202
Saint Johann Press, pg 204
Scarecrow Press Inc, pg 207
The Scriptural Research & Publishing Co Inc, pg 210
Soyinfo Center, pg 219
Transportation Research Board (TRB), pg 234
Tuttle Publishing, pg 236
United Nations Publications, pg 238
University of Wisconsin Press, pg 246
Watermark Publishing, pg 252
Markus Wiener Publishers Inc, pg 255
Wisconsin Department of Public Instruction, pg 257
Wittenborn Art Books, pg 258
Alan Wofsy Fine Arts, pg 258

BRAILLE BOOKS

American Printing House for the Blind Inc, pg 13
The Christian Science Publishing Society, pg 55
Faith Alive Christian Resources, pg 81
Forward Movement, pg 87
Kazi Publications Inc, pg 125
The Linick Group Inc, pg 135
Lutheran Braille Workers Inc, pg 139
National Braille Press, pg 157

CD-ROM, EBOOKS

A-R Editions Inc, pg 1
AAAI Press, pg 1
AAPG (American Association of Petroleum Geologists), pg 1
Abbeville Press, pg 2
ABC-CLIO, pg 2
Abingdon Press, pg 2
Abrams Learning Trends, pg 3
Academic Press, pg 3
Accuity, pg 3
Adams Media, pg 4
Adventures Unlimited Press (AUP), pg 5
AFB Press, pg 5
African American Images, pg 5
Ageless Press, pg 5
AICPA Professional Publications, pg 6
ALA Neal-Schuman, pg 6
Alfred Music Publishing, pg 7
All Things That Matter Press, pg 7
Allium Press of Chicago, pg 7
Allworth Press, pg 8
Alpha Books, pg 8
AMACOM Books, pg 8
Amakella Publishing, pg 9
Ambassador International, pg 9
American Academy of Orthopaedic Surgeons (AAOS), pg 9
American Anthropological Association (AAA), pg 10
American Association for Vocational Instructional Materials, pg 10
American Association of Blood Banks, pg 10
American Bible Society, pg 10
American Carriage House Publishing, pg 10
The American Ceramic Society, pg 10
American Diabetes Association, pg 11
American Geosciences Institute (AGI), pg 11
American Historical Association (AHA), pg 12
American Institute for Economic Research (AIER), pg 12
American Institute of Chemical Engineers (AIChE), pg 12
American Law Institute, pg 12
American Law Institute Continuing Legal Education (ALI CLE), pg 12
The American Library Association (ALA), pg 12
American Printing House for the Blind Inc, pg 13
American Psychiatric Association Publishing, pg 14
American Society for Quality (ASQ), pg 14
American Society of Agricultural & Biological Engineers (ASABE), pg 14
American Society of Civil Engineers (ASCE), pg 15
American Society of Health-System Pharmacists (ASHP), pg 15
American Society of Mechanical Engineers (ASME), pg 15
American Water Works Association (AWWA), pg 15
Amherst Media Inc, pg 15
Ampersand Inc/Professional Publishing Services, pg 16
Andrews McMeel Publishing LLC, pg 16
Angelus Press, pg 17
ANR Publications University of California, pg 17
APS PRESS, pg 19
Arbordale Publishing, pg 19
Ariel Press, pg 20
Ariel Starr Productions Inc, pg 20
Artech House Inc, pg 21
Artisan Bookworks, pg 22
ASCD, pg 22
ASM International, pg 23
ASM Press, pg 23
Aspatore Books, pg 23
Association for Computing Machinery, pg 24
ASTM International, pg 24
Atlantic Publishing Group Inc, pg 25
Atlas Publishing, pg 25
Augsburg Fortress Publishers, Publishing House of the Evangelical Lutheran Church in America, pg 25
Authorlink Press, pg 26
Avention Inc, pg 27
Awe-Struck Publishing, pg 27
Bagwyn Books, pg 28
Baker Books, pg 28
BearManor Media, pg 31
Belltown Media, pg 32
BenBella Books Inc, pg 32
Bentley Publishers, pg 33
Berrett-Koehler Publishers Inc, pg 34
Bess Press, pg 34
Bhaktivedanta Book Trust (BBT), pg 34
George T Bisel Co Inc, pg 35
Bisk Education, pg 35
Bitingduck Press LLC, pg 35
BJU Press, pg 36
Black Mountain Press, pg 36
Bloch Publishing Co, pg 37
Blue Poppy Press, pg 38
BoardSource, pg 39
Bolchazy-Carducci Publishers Inc, pg 39
Bold Strokes Books Inc, pg 39
Bondfire Books, pg 39
BookLogix, pg 40
Boson Books, pg 40
Bradford Publishing Co, pg 41
Brick Mantel Books, pg 42
Brill Inc, pg 43
Brookes Publishing Co Inc, pg 44
The Brookings Institution Press, pg 44
Bureau of Economic Geology, University of Texas at Austin, pg 45
Business & Legal Resources Inc, pg 45
Business Research Services Inc, pg 45
Cambridge Educational, pg 46
Cambridge University Press, pg 46
Candlewick Press, pg 46
Cardiotext Publishing, pg 47
Caribe Betania Editores, pg 47
Cascade Pass Inc, pg 49
Catholic Book Publishing Corp, pg 49
CCH, a Wolters Kluwer business, pg 49
Cedar Grove Books, pg 50
Cengage Learning, pg 50
Center for Futures Education Inc, pg 51
Chain Store Guide (CSG), pg 52
Channel Photographics, pg 52
The Charles Press, Publishers, pg 53
Chelsea Green Publishing Co, pg 53
Cheng & Tsui Co Inc, pg 53
The Child's World Inc, pg 54
China Books, pg 54
Christian Liberty Press, pg 55
The Christian Science Publishing Society, pg 55
Circlet Press Inc, pg 56
Clearfield Co Inc, pg 57
Clinical Laboratory & Standards Institute (CLSI), pg 57
CN Times Books, pg 57
Coachlight Press LLC, pg 58
Cold Spring Harbor Laboratory Press, pg 58
The College Board, pg 58
Columbia Books & Information Services (CBIS), pg 58
Columbia University Press, pg 59
Comex Systems Inc, pg 59
The Connecticut Law Tribune, pg 60
Copper Canyon Press, pg 60
Copywriter's Council of America™ (CCA), pg 61
Corwin, a Sage Co, pg 61
Cosimo Inc, pg 62
Council for Exceptional Children (CEC), pg 62
The Countryman Press, pg 63
Covenant Communications Inc, pg 63
Crabtree Publishing Co, pg 63
Craftsman Book Co, pg 63
CRC Press, pg 64
The Creative Co, pg 64
Cricket Cottage Publishing LLC, pg 64
Cross-Cultural Communications, pg 64
The Crossroad Publishing Co, pg 65
Crown House Publishing Co LLC, pg 65
Crystal Clarity Publishers, pg 65
CSLI Publications, pg 66
Cup of Tea Books, pg 66
Dante University Press, pg 67
The Dartnell Corporation, pg 67
Data Trace Publishing Co (DTP), pg 67
Davies Publishing Inc, pg 68
F A Davis Co, pg 68
DAW Books Inc, pg 68
Walter De Gruyter Inc, pg 69
Deep River Books LLC, pg 69
Demos Medical Publishing, pg 69
Deseret Book Co, pg 69
DEStech Publications Inc, pg 69
Destiny Image Inc, pg 69
Dewey Publications Inc, pg 70
Discovery House Publishers, pg 70
Dogwise Publishing, pg 71
Dover Publications Inc, pg 72
Dragon Door Publications, pg 72
Dragonfairy Press, pg 73
Dun & Bradstreet, pg 73
Dustbooks, pg 74
Eifrig Publishing LLC, pg 76
Elderberry Press Inc, pg 76
The Electrochemical Society (ECS), pg 77
Elsevier Inc, pg 77
EMC Publishing LLC, pg 77
Encyclopaedia Britannica Inc, pg 78
Enfield Publishing & Distribution Co, pg 79
Enslow Publishing LLC, pg 79
Environmental Law Institute, pg 79
Etruscan Press, pg 80
Evan-Moor Educational Publishers, pg 80
Facts On File, pg 81
Faith Alive Christian Resources, pg 81
Faith Library Publications, pg 82
Faithlife Corp, pg 82
Familius, pg 82
Farcountry Press, pg 82
Father & Son Publishing Inc, pg 83
Federal Bar Association, pg 83
Ferguson Publishing, pg 84

CHILDREN'S BOOKS

COMPUTER SOFTWARE

DATABASES

DICTIONARIES, ENCYCLOPEDIAS

DIRECTORIES, REFERENCE BOOKS

FINE EDITIONS, ILLUSTRATED BOOKS

FOREIGN LANGUAGE & BILINGUAL BOOKS

GENERAL TRADE BOOKS - HARDCOVER

JUVENILE & YOUNG ADULT BOOKS

LARGE PRINT BOOKS

MAPS, ATLASES

PAPERBACK BOOKS - MASS MARKET

PAPERBACK BOOKS - TRADE

PERIODICALS, JOURNALS

PROFESSIONAL BOOKS

REPRINTS

SCHOLARLY BOOKS

SIDELINES

SUBSCRIPTION & MAIL ORDER BOOKS

TEXTBOOKS - ELEMENTARY

TEXTBOOKS - SECONDARY

TEXTBOOKS - COLLEGE

TRANSLATIONS

UNIVERSITY PRESSES

VIDEOS, DVDS

U.S. Publishers — Subject Index

AGRICULTURE

ALTERNATIVE

AMERICANA, REGIONAL

ANIMALS, PETS

ANTHROPOLOGY

ANTIQUES

ARCHAEOLOGY

ARCHITECTURE & INTERIOR DESIGN

ART

ASIAN STUDIES

ASTROLOGY, OCCULT

ASTRONOMY

AUTOMOTIVE

BEHAVIORAL SCIENCES

BIBLICAL STUDIES

BIOGRAPHY, MEMOIRS

BIOLOGICAL SCIENCES

BUSINESS

CAREER DEVELOPMENT

CHEMISTRY, CHEMICAL ENGINEERING

CHILD CARE & DEVELOPMENT

CIVIL ENGINEERING

COMMUNICATIONS

COMPUTER SCIENCE

COMPUTERS

COOKERY

CRAFTS, GAMES, HOBBIES

CRIMINOLOGY

DEVELOPING COUNTRIES

DISABILITY, SPECIAL NEEDS

DRAMA, THEATER

EARTH SCIENCES

ECONOMICS

EDUCATION

ELECTRONICS, ELECTRICAL ENGINEERING

ENERGY

ENGINEERING (GENERAL)

ENGLISH AS A SECOND LANGUAGE

ENVIRONMENTAL STUDIES

EROTICA

ETHNICITY

FASHION

FICTION

FILM, VIDEO

FINANCE

FOREIGN COUNTRIES

GARDENING, PLANTS

GENEALOGY

GEOGRAPHY, GEOLOGY

GOVERNMENT, POLITICAL SCIENCE

HEALTH, NUTRITION

HISTORY

HOUSE & HOME

HOW-TO

HUMAN RELATIONS

HUMOR

INSPIRATIONAL, SPIRITUALITY

JOURNALISM

LABOR, INDUSTRIAL RELATIONS

LANGUAGE ARTS, LINGUISTICS

LAW

LGBTQ

LIBRARY & INFORMATION SCIENCES

LITERATURE, LITERARY CRITICISM, ESSAYS

MANAGEMENT

MARITIME

MARKETING

MATHEMATICS

MECHANICAL ENGINEERING

MEDICINE, NURSING, DENTISTRY

MILITARY SCIENCE

MUSIC, DANCE

MYSTERIES, SUSPENSE

NATIVE AMERICAN STUDIES

NATURAL HISTORY

NONFICTION (GENERAL)

OUTDOOR RECREATION

PARAPSYCHOLOGY

PHILOSOPHY

PHOTOGRAPHY

PHYSICAL SCIENCES

PHYSICS

POETRY

POP CULTURE

PSYCHOLOGY, PSYCHIATRY

PUBLIC ADMINISTRATION

PUBLISHING & BOOK TRADE REFERENCE

RADIO, TV

REAL ESTATE

REGIONAL INTERESTS

RELIGION - BUDDHIST

RELIGION - CATHOLIC

RELIGION - HINDU

RELIGION - ISLAMIC

RELIGION - JEWISH

RELIGION - PROTESTANT

RELIGION - OTHER

ROMANCE

SCIENCE (GENERAL)

SCIENCE FICTION, FANTASY

SECURITIES

SELF-HELP

SOCIAL SCIENCES, SOCIOLOGY

SPORTS, ATHLETICS

TECHNOLOGY

THEOLOGY

TRANSPORTATION

TRAVEL & TOURISM

VETERINARY SCIENCE

WESTERN FICTION

WINE & SPIRITS

WOMEN'S STUDIES

Imprints, Subsidiaries & Distributors

A Cappella Books, *imprint of* Chicago Review Press

A G Fiction™, *imprint of* American Girl Publishing

A-R Editions Inc, *distributor for* AIM (American Institute of Musicology)

AAAI Press, *imprint of* Association for the Advancement of Artificial Intelligence, *distributed by* The MIT Press

AAH Graphics Inc, *subsidiary of* Loft Press Inc

A&D Xtreme, *imprint of* ABDO Publishing Group

AAP, *distributed by* Welcome Enterprises Inc

AAPG (American Association of Petroleum Geologists), *distributor for* Geological Society of London, *distributed by* Affiliated East-West Press Private Ltd, Canadian Society of Petroleum Geologists, Geological Society of London

AATEC Publications, *distributed by* Chelsea Green Publishing Co

Abaris Books, *division of* Opal Publishing Corp

Abbeville Kids, *imprint of* Abbeville Publishing Group

Abbeville Press, *imprint of* Abbeville Publishing Group

Abbey of Saint Peter of Solesmes, *distributed by* Paraclete Press Inc

Abbott Publishing, *distributed by* Sunbelt Publications Inc

ABC International Group Inc, *imprint of* Kazi Publications Inc

Abdo & Daughters Publishing, *imprint of* ABDO Publishing Group

Abdo Kids, *imprint of* ABDO Publishing Group

ABDO Publishing Group, *subsidiary of* Abdo Consulting Group Inc (ACGI), Abdo Consulting Group Inc (ACGI), *distributed by* Rockbottom Book Co

The Aberdeen Group, *distributor for* Craftsman Book Co

ABI Professional Publications, *distributed by* Vandamere Press

Abingdon Press, *imprint of* The United Methodist Publishing House, *distributor for* Church Publishing Inc, Judson Press, Morehouse Publishing, Upper Room Books

Abjad Books, *imprint of* Kazi Publications Inc

Ableton, *distributed by* Hal Leonard Corp

Abrams, *distributor for* National Gallery of Art, *distributed by* Perfection Learning Corp

Abrams & Chronicle Books, *distributor for* Harry N Abrams Inc

Abrams Appleseed, *imprint of* Harry N Abrams Inc

Abrams Books, *imprint of* Harry N Abrams Inc, *distributor for* The Vendome Press

Abrams Books for Young Readers, *imprint of* Harry N Abrams Inc

Abrams ComicArts, *imprint of* Harry N Abrams Inc

Harry N Abrams Inc, *distributed by* Hachette Book Group

Harry N Abrams Inc, *subsidiary of* La Martiniere Groupe, *distributor for* American Federation of Arts, Booth-Clibborn Editions, The Colonial Williamsburg Foundation, Editions Alain Ducasse, 5 Continents Editions, Getty Publications, Museum of Modern Art Children's Books, SelfMadeHero, Tate Publishing, V&A Publishing, The Vendome Press, *distributed by* Abrams & Chronicle Books (Great Britain), Editions Alain

Abrams Image, *imprint of* Harry N Abrams Inc

Abrams Learning Trends, *subsidiary of* Learning Trends LLC, *distributor for* General Education Services (New Zealand)

Abrams Noterie, *imprint of* Harry N Abrams Inc

Abrams Press, *imprint of* Harry N Abrams Inc

The ABS Group, *distributed by* American Academy of Environmental Engineers & Scientists™

ACA, *imprint of* American Counseling Association

Academia Press, *distributed by* University Press of New England

Academic Book Center, *distributor for* Primary Research Group Inc

Academic Press, *imprint of* Elsevier BV, *distributed by* Marine Techniques Publishing

Academy Chicago, *imprint of* Chicago Review Press

Academy Chicago Publishers, *imprint of* Chicago Review Press

Academy of Continuing Education, *division of* Success Advertising & Publishing

Academy of Natural Sciences, *distributed by* Diane Publishing Co

Academy of Nutrition & Dietetics, *distributed by* Small Press United (Eat Right Press)

ACC Distribution, *division of* Antique Collectors' Club Ltd

ACC Editions, *imprint of* Antique Collectors' Club Ltd

Accord Publishing, *imprint of* Andrews McMeel Publishing LLC

Accuity, *division of* Reed Business Information Ltd

Ace, *imprint of* Penguin Group USA, A Penguin Random House Company

Ace Books, *imprint of* Berkley Publishing Group, *distributed by* Perfection Learning Corp

Ace/Putnam, *imprint of* Penguin Group USA, A Penguin Random House Company

ACER, *distributor for* Psychological Assessment Resources Inc (PAR)

ACHCBYZ, *distributed by* Summertime Publications Inc

Acorn, *imprint of* Oak Tree Press

Acoustica, *distributed by* Hal Leonard Corp

Acres USA, *division of* Acres USA Inc, Acres USA Inc

Acropolis Books, *distributed by* DeVorss & Co

ACS Publications, *imprint of* Starcrafts LLC

ACTA Publications, *distributor for* Grief Watch, Veritas

Action Language Learning, *distributed by* Cheng & Tsui Co Inc

ACU Press, *affiliate of* Abilene Christian University

Ac-u-Kwik, *imprint of* Penton Media Inc

AcuTab Publications Inc, *distributed by* Mel Bay Publications Inc

Ad Infinitum Books, *distributor for* Cross-Cultural Communications

Ad Infinitum Press, *distributed by* Cross-Cultural Communications

Adams Business, *imprint of* Adams Media

Adams Media, *imprint of* Simon & Schuster

Adapted Classics, *imprint of* ArtWrite Productions

ADASI Publishing Co, *distributor for* Wall & Thompson

ADC the Map People, *subsidiary of* American Map Corp, *distributed by* Hagstrom Map

Addison Gallery of American Art, Phillips Academy, *distributed by* Yale University Press

Addison Wesley, *distributor for* Public Citizen

Adis International, *imprint of* Wolters Kluwer US Corp

Admission Test Series, *imprint of* National Learning Corp

Advaita Ashrama, *distributed by* Vedanta Press

Adventure Cycling Association, *distributed by* The Mountaineers Books

Adventure Guides, *imprint of* Hunter Publishing Inc

Adventure Publications, *imprint of* Adventure-KEEN

Adventure Roads Travel, *imprint of* Ocean Tree Books

AdventureKEEN, *distributor for* Blacklock Nature Photography, Kollath-Stensaas, Nodin Press, Pocket Guides Publishing

Adventures in Odyssey, *imprint of* Focus on the Family

Adventures Unlimited Press (AUP), *distributor for* Eagle Wing Books, EDFU Books, Yelsraek Publishing

The AEI Press, *division of* American Enterprise Institute, *distributed by* MIT (selected titles)

Aequitas Books, *imprint of* Pleasure Boat Studio: A Literary Press

Aerie Books, *imprint of* Tom Doherty Associates, LLC

Aeronautical Publishers, *imprint of* Markowski International Publishers

AF Editions, *distributed by* Casemate | publishers

AFB Press, *imprint of* American Foundation for the Blind, American Foundation for the Blind (AFB)

Affiliated East-West Press Private Ltd, *distributor for* AAPG (American Association of Petroleum Geologists)

African-American Book Distributors Inc, *subsidiary of* Path Press Inc

African American Islamic Institute, *distributed by* Fons Vitae

Editions d'Afrique du Nord, *distributed by* Edgewise Press Inc

Afterall Books, *distributed by* The MIT Press

Aftershocks Media, *division of* Epicenter Press Inc

Agape, *division of* Hope Publishing Co

Agathon Press, *imprint of* Algora Publishing

Agenda Publishing, *distributed by* Columbia University Press

Agronomy Publications, *imprint of* Hobar Publications

AHA (American Hospital Association), *imprint of* Health Forum Inc

aha! Chinese, *distributed by* Cheng & Tsui Co Inc

Aha Communications, *distributed by* Gryphon House Inc

AHLP Books, *imprint of* Africana Homestead Legacy Publishers Inc

AHLP Communications, *imprint of* Africana Homestead Legacy Publishers Inc

The Ahmanson Foundation Humanities Endowment Fund, *imprint of* University of California Press

Ahmanson-Murphy, *imprint of* University of California Press

AICPA Professional Publications, *subsidiary of* American Institute of Certified Public Accountants, *distributor for* Wiley, *distributed by* CCH, Practitioners Publishing Co, Thomson Reuters

Aignos Publishing, *imprint of* Savant Books & Publications LLC

AIM (American Institute of Musicology), *distributed by* A-R Editions Inc

Keith Ainsworth Pty Ltd, *distributor for* Interweave Press LLC

Air Sea Media, *distributed by* Casemate | publishers

Air War Publications, *distributed by* Casemate | publishers

Airfile Publications, *distributed by* Casemate | publishers

Airmont, *distributed by* Perfection Learning Corp

Airphoto International Ltd/Odyssey Publications, *distributed by* W W Norton & Company Inc

AirTurn, *distributed by* Hal Leonard Corp

AK Press Distribution, *subsidiary of* AK Press Inc, AK Press Inc, *distributor for* Arbeiter Ring, Autonomedia, Crimethinc, Freedom Press, Charles H Kerr, Kersplebedelo

ALA Neal-Schuman, *imprint of* The American Library Association (ALA)

Aladdin, *imprint of* Simon & Schuster Children's Publishing

Editions Alain, *distributor for* Harry N Abrams Inc

Alamos Press, *imprint of* Park Place Publications

Alan Wofsy Fine Arts, *distributor for* Bora, Brusberg (Berlin), Cramer (Geneva), Huber, Ides et Calendes, Kornfeld & Co (Bern), Picasso Project, Welz, Wittenborn Art Books

Alaska Native Language Center, *division of* University of Alaska Fairbanks, *distributed by* University of Alaska Press

Alaska Northwest Books®, *imprint of* Graphic Arts Books

Alaska Quarterly Review, *distributed by* University of Alaska Press

Alaska Sea Grant, *distributed by* University of Alaska Press

Alaska Writer Laureate Series, *imprint of* University of Alaska Press

Albany Institute of History & Art, *distributed by* Excelsior Editions, State University of New York Press

Albatross Publishing House, *distributed by* W W Norton & Company Inc

Albert Whitman & Co, *distributed by* Open Road

Alchemical Press, *imprint of* Holmes Publishing Group LLC

Aldine Transaction, *imprint of* Transaction Publishers Inc

Alexandrian Press, *imprint of* Holmes Publishing Group LLC

Alfred Music Publishing, *distributor for* Daisy Rock Girl Guitars, Dover Publications, Drum Channel, Faber Music, MakeMusic Inc, Penguin, WEA

Algonquin Books, *division of* Workman Publishing Co Inc, *distributor for* Fearless Critic Media, Greenwich Workshop Press, HighBridge Audio, *distributed by* Workman Publishing Co Inc

Algonquin Young Readers, *imprint of* Algonquin Books

Alibi, *imprint of* Penguin Random House Inc, Random House Publishing Group

Alice James Books, *division of* Alice James Poetry Cooperative Inc

Alive Guides, *imprint of* Hunter Publishing Inc

All Points Books, *imprint of* St Martin's Press, LLC

All Rights Reserved Ltd, *distributed by* Gingko Press Inc

Allen & Unwin, *distributor for* Quarto Publishing Group USA Inc

J A Allen, *distributed by* Trafalgar Square Books

Thomas Allen & Son, *distributor for* Square One Publishers Inc, Timber Press Inc

Alloy Entertainment LLC, *member of* Warner Bros Entertainment Group, *distributed by* Avon Books, HarperCollins, Hyperion, Little, Brown & Co, Penguin Group USA, A Penguin Random House Company, Penguin Random House Inc, Scholastic Books, Simon & Schuster

Allworth Press, *imprint of* Skyhorse Publishing Inc

Allyn & Bacon, *distributor for* National Association of Broadcasters (NAB)

Alma Little, *imprint of* Elva Resa Publishing

Alpha Books, *subsidiary of* DK Publishing

Alta Book Center Publishers, *distributor for* TESOL International Association

AltaMira Press, *imprint of* Rowman & Littlefield Publishing Group, *distributor for* American Association for State & Local History

Alti Corporation, *distributed by* Sunbelt Publications Inc

Alutiiq Museum, *distributed by* University of Alaska Press

AMA, *distributed by* Mel Bay Publications Inc

AMA Research, *distributed by* FurnitureCore

AMACOM Books, *division of* American Management Association (AMA), American Management Association® (AMA), *distributor for* J J Keller & Associates, Inc, *distributed by* SAS Publishing

Amadeus Press, *imprint of* Hal Leonard Books, *distributed by* Hal Leonard Corp

Amadeus Press/Hal Leonard Performing Arts Publishing Group, *division of* Hal Leonard Performing Arts Publishing Group

Amaroma Ediciones, *distributed by* Sunbelt Publications Inc

Frank Amato Publications Inc, *distributor for* Haugen Enterprises (cooking & hunting titles)

Ambassador Books, *distributor for* Primary Research Group Inc

Ambassador International, *division of* Emerald House Inc

Amber-Allen Publishing, *imprint of* New World Library

Amber Books, *distributed by* Casemate | publishers

Amberley, *distributed by* Casemate | publishers

Amble Press, *imprint of* Bywater Books

AMC Discover Series, *imprint of* Appalachian Mountain Club Books

AMC Nature Walks Series, *imprint of* Appalachian Mountain Club Books

AMC Quiet Water Guides, *imprint of* Appalachian Mountain Club Books

AMC River Guides, *imprint of* Appalachian Mountain Club Books

AMC Trail Guides, *imprint of* Appalachian Mountain Club Books

Amelia Press, *imprint of* No Frills Buffalo

America West Publishers, *subsidiary of* Global Insights Inc

American Academy for Park & Recreation Administration, *distributed by* Sagamore Publishing LLC

American Academy of Environmental Engineers & Scientists™, *distributor for* The ABS Group, CRC Press, McGraw-Hill, Pearson Education, Prentice Hall, John Wiley & Sons Inc

American Academy of Orthopaedic Surgeons (AAOS), *distributed by* Jones & Bartlett Publishers

The American Alpine Club Press, *division of* The American Alpine Club, *distributed by* Mountaineers Books, The Mountaineers Books

American Anthropological Association (AAA), *distributed by* Wiley-Blackwell

American Antiquarian Society, *distributed by* Oak Knoll Press

American Association for Higher Education, *distributed by* Stylus Publishing LLC

American Association for State & Local History, *distributed by* AltaMira Press

American Association for Vocational Instructional Materials, *distributor for* Southeastern Cooperative Wildlife Disease Study

American Association of State Highway & Transportation Officials, *distributed by* Professional Publications Inc (PPI)

American Bar Association, *distributor for* The Professional Education Group LLC (PEG), *distributed by* The Professional Education Group LLC (PEG)

American Carriage House Publishing, *distributed by* Faith Works Books

American Ceramic Society (ACerS), *distributor for* American Society for Nondestructive Testing

The American Chemical Society, *distributor for* Royal Society of Chemistry, *distributed by* Oxford University Press, Oxford University Press USA

American College of Healthcare Executives Management Series, *imprint of* Health Administration Press

American College of Surgeons, *distributed by* Cine-Med Inc, Scientific American Medicine

American Council for an Energy Efficient Economy (ACEEE), *distributed by* Chelsea Green Publishing Co

American Council on Education, *distributed by* Rowman & Littlefield

American Dust Publications, *distributed by* Dustbooks

American Federation of Arts, *distributed by* Harry N Abrams Inc, Delmonico/Prestel, Distributed Art Publishers, D Giles Ltd, Hudson Hills Press Inc, Scala Publishers, Skira Rizzoli Publishers, University of Washington Press, Yale University Press

American Geophysical Union, *imprint of* John Wiley & Sons Inc

American Geosciences Institute (AGI), *distributed by* W H Freeman, It's About Time Inc, Prentice Hall

American Girl Library®, *imprint of* American Girl Publishing

American Girl Publishing, *subsidiary of* Mattel

The American Girls Collection®, *imprint of* American Girl Publishing

American Guidance Service, *distributed by* Psychological Assessment Resources Inc (PAR)

American Heritage Dictionary, *imprint of* Houghton Mifflin Harcourt Trade & Reference Division

American Historical Association (AHA), *affiliate of* Center for the Study of Film & History

American Institute of Buddhist Studies, *distributed by* Columbia University Press

American Institute of Chemical Engineers (AIChE), *distributor for* ASM International (selected titles), Dechema (selected titles), Engineering Foundation, IchemE (selected titles), *distributed by* Dechema (selected titles)

American Institute of Physics, *distributed by* Springer-Verlag

American Institute of Physics (AIP), *distributor for* The Electrochemical Society (ECS)

American Law Institute, *distributor for* The Professional Education Group LLC (PEG), *distributed by* The Professional Education Group LLC (PEG)

American Law Institute Continuing Legal Education (ALI CLE), *affiliate of* American Law Institute

American Map Corp, *member of* Kappa Map Group, Kappa Map Group LLC, *distributor for* De Lorme Atlas, Kappa Map Group, RV Guides, Stubs Magazine, *distributed by* Arrow Maps Inc, Creative Sales Corp, Hagstrom Map

American Maritain Association, *distributed by* The Catholic University of America Press

American Mathematical Society, *distributor for* Annales de la faculte des sciences de Toulouse mathematiques, Bar-Ilan University, Brown University, European Mathematical Society, Hindustan Book Agency, Independent University of Moscow, International Press, Mathematica Josephina, Mathematical Society of Japan, Narosa Publishing House, Ramanujan Mathematical Society, Science Press New York & Science Press Beijing, Societe Mathematique de France, Tata Institute of Fundamental Research, Theta Foundation of Bucharest, University Press, Vieweg Verlag Publications

American Medical Association, *distributor for* OptumInsight™, *distributed by* Medical Group Management Association (MGMA), OptumInsight™

American Milestones, *imprint of* Gallopade International Inc

American Philosophical Society, *distributed by* Diane Publishing Co

American Poetry Review/Honickman, *distributed by* Copper Canyon Press

American Products Publishing Co, *division of* American Products Corp

American Psychiatric Association (APA), *distributed by* American Psychiatric Association Publishing

American Psychiatric Association Publishing, *division of* American Psychiatric Association (APA), *distributor for* American Psychiatric Association (APA), Group for the Advancement of Psychiatry

American School of Classical Studies at Athens, *imprint of* ASCSA Publications

American Society for Mechanical Engineers (ASME), *distributor for* American Society for Nondestructive Testing

American Society for Metals (ASM), *distributor for* American Society for Nondestructive Testing

American Society for Nondestructive Testing, *distributed by* American Ceramic Society (ACerS), American Society for Mechanical Engineers (ASME), American Society for Metals (ASM), The American Welding Society (AWS), ASTM, Edison Welding Institute, Mean Free Path

American Society for Quality (ASQ), *distributed by* GOAL/QPC, IEEE Computer Society Press, McGraw-Hill Professional Publishing, Productivity Press

American Society of Association Executives, *distributor for* BoardSource

American Sports Publishing, *imprint of* Athletic Guide Publishing

American Swedish Historical Museum, *distributed by* Diane Publishing Co

American Technical Publishers Inc, *distributor for* Craftsman Book Co, Society of Manufacturing Engineers

American University in Cairo, *distributed by* Oxford University Press USA

American Water Works Association (AWWA), *distributor for* CRC Press, McGraw-Hill, John Wiley & Sons

The American Welding Society (AWS), *distributor for* American Society for Nondestructive Testing

American West Books, *distributor for* Wilderness Adventures Press Inc

American Wood Council (American Forest & Paper Association), *distributed by* Professional Publications Inc (PPI)

The Americas Review, *subsidiary of* Arte Publico Press

Amerotica, *imprint of* NBM Publishing Inc

AMI Press, *imprint of* Loving Healing Press Inc

Amicus Ink, *imprint of* Amicus, *distributed by* Chronicle Books LLC

Amistad, *imprint of* HarperCollins Children's Books, HarperCollins General Books Group

Amphoto Books, *imprint of* Crown Publishing Group

AMS, *distributor for* International Press of Boston Inc

Amulet Books, *imprint of* Harry N Abrams Inc

An Inc Original, *imprint of* Greenleaf Book Group LLC

Anacus Press, *imprint of* Finney Company Inc

Ananda Ashrama, *distributed by* Vedanta Press

ANCC Magnet Recognition Program, *imprint of* Nursesbooks.org, The Publishing Program of ANA

Ancestry, *imprint of* Turner Publishing Co

Anchor Bible Commentary, *imprint of* Penguin Random House Inc

Anchor Bible Dictionary, *imprint of* Penguin Random House Inc

Anchor Bible Reference Library, *imprint of* Penguin Random House Inc

Anchor Books, *imprint of* Knopf Doubleday Publishing Group, Penguin Random House Inc

Anchor Distributors, *distributor for* Pentecostal Publishing House

Anchorage Museum Association, *distributed by* University of Alaska Press

Anchorage Museum of Art History, *distributed by* University of Alaska Press

Ancient City Press, *imprint of* Gibbs Smith Publisher

Ancient Faith Publishing, *division of* Ancient Faith Ministries, *distributor for* Light & Life, *distributed by* Light & Life, St Vladimir's

And/Or Press, *imprint of* Ronin Publishing Inc

Andersen Press USA, *distributed by* Lerner Publishing Group Inc

Anderson Design, *distributed by* Resilient Publishing

Andrea Press, *distributed by* Casemate | publishers

Andrews McMeel Publishing LLC, *division of* Andrews McMeel Universal, *distributor for* Gooseberry Patch (North America), Signatures Network, Sporting News, Universe Publishing Calendars, Vegan Heritage Press, *distributed by* Simon & Schuster, Inc, Simon & Schuster Sales Division

Andrews University Press, *division of* Andrews University

Andy Cohen Books, *imprint of* Henry Holt and Company, LLC

Angel Books, *distributed by* Dufour Editions Inc

Angelus Press, *distributed by* Catholic Treasures, Fatima Crusader

Angler's Book Supply, *distributor for* Wilderness Adventures Press Inc

Anglican Book Centre, *distributed by* Forward Movement

Animal Media Group LLC, *subsidiary of* Animal Inc

Ann Arbor Paperbacks, *imprint of* University of Michigan Press

Annales de la faculte des sciences de Toulouse mathematiques, *distributed by* American Mathematical Society

Annick Press, *distributed by* Perfection Learning Corp

Anomaly Press, *distributed by* Chelsea Green Publishing Co

Another Great Achiever Series, *imprint of* Advance Publishing Inc

Anqa Press, *distributed by* Fons Vitae

ANR Publications University of California, *division of* Agriculture & Natural Resources, University of California

Antares, *distributed by* Hal Leonard Corp

Antinous Press, *distributed by* powerHouse Books

Antique Collectors Club, *distributor for* Winterthur Museum, Garden & Library

Antique Collectors' Club Ltd, *division of* Antique Collectors Club Ltd (England), Antique Collectors Club Ltd (England), *distributor for* George Braziller Inc

Antique Trader, *imprint of* Krause Publications Inc

Antique Trader Books, *imprint of* F+W Media Inc, Krause Publications Inc

Coleccion Antologia Personal, *imprint of* University of Puerto Rico Press

Anvil Series, *imprint of* Krieger Publishing Co

Anza-Borrego Foundation, *distributed by* Sunbelt Publications Inc

AO Foundation, *distributed by* Thieme Medical Publishers Inc

AOCS Press, *division of* American Oil Chemists' Society

AP Placement Test Series, *imprint of* National Learning Corp

APA Books®, *imprint of* American Psychological Association

APA Planners Press, *imprint of* American Planning Association

Aperture, *distributed by* Fons Vitae

Aperture Books, *division of* Aperture Foundation Inc, *distributed by* Farrar, Straus & Giroux Inc

Aperture Monographs, *imprint of* Aperture Books

The Apex Press, *imprint of* Rowman & Littlefield Publishers Inc, Rowman & Littlefield Publishing Group

Aphrodisia, *imprint of* Kensington Publishing Corp

Apogee, *distributed by* Hal Leonard Corp

Apostrofa Publishers, *distributed by* Central European University Press

Appalachian, *distributor for* Faith Library Publications

Appalachian Mountain Club Books, *division of* Appalachian Mountain Club, *distributed by* The Globe Pequot Press

Appell Publishing, *distributed by* Epicenter Press Inc

Applause Books, *distributed by* Hal Leonard Corp

Applause Theatre & Cinema Books, *imprint of* Hal Leonard Books, Hal Leonard Performing Arts Publishing Group, *distributor for* The Working Arts Library, Glenn Young Books, *distributed by* Hal Leonard LLC

Applesauce Press, *imprint of* Cider Mill Press Book Publishers LLC, *distributed by* Simon & Schuster Sales Division

Appraisal Institute, *distributed by* Dearborn Trade

Apress, *imprint of* Springer

Apress Media LLC, *subsidiary of* Springer Science+Business Media LLC

APS PRESS, *imprint of* The American Phytopathological Society (APS)

AQS, *imprint of* American Quilter's Society

Aquarius, *distributed by* Hal Leonard Corp

Coleccion Aqui y Ahora, *imprint of* University of Puerto Rico Press

Arba Sicula, *distributed by* Cross-Cultural Communications

Arbeiter Ring, *distributed by* AK Press Distribution

ARC (Magazine & Press), *imprint of* Cross-Cultural Communications

Arcade Publishing Inc, *imprint of* Skyhorse Publishing Inc

Arcadia Books Ltd (London), *distributed by* Dufour Editions Inc

Arcadia Publishing Inc, *distributor for* Cool Springs Press, Voyageur Press

Arcana Publishing, *imprint of* Lotus Press

Arcane, *imprint of* Zumaya Publications LLC

Archetype, *distributed by* Fons Vitae

Archimap, *distributed by* Gingko Press Inc

Architectural Graphic Standards, *imprint of* John Wiley & Sons Inc

Archival, *distributed by* Donald M Grant Publisher Inc

Archway, *distributed by* Perfection Learning Corp

Arctic Studies Center of the Smithsonian Museum, *distributed by* University of Alaska Press

Arcturus Publishing, *imprint of* Black Rabbit Books

Arcturus Publishing Ltd, *distributor for* Big Guy Books Inc

Arcus, *distributed by* Franklin, Beedle & Associates Inc

Ardis Russian Literature, *imprint of* The Overlook Press

ARE Press, *division of* The Association for Research & Enlightenment Inc (ARE), The Association for Research & Enlightenment Inc (ARE)

Ariel Press, *subsidiary of* Light, *distributor for* Enthea Press, Kudzu House

The Arion Press, *division of* Lyra Corp

Arkangel, *distributed by* Penguin Group USA, A Penguin Random House Company

Arktoi Books, *imprint of* Red Hen Press

Arlen House, *distributor for* Syracuse University Press, *distributed by* Syracuse University Press

Eric Armin Inc Education Ctr, *distributor for* National Council of Teachers of Mathematics (NCTM)

Jason Aronson Inc, *imprint of* Rowman & Littlefield Publishing Group

Arrangers Publishing, *distributed by* Hal Leonard Corp

Arrow Maps Inc, *subsidiary of* American Map Corp, *distributor for* American Map Corp, *distributed by* Hagstrom Map

ARSIS Audio, *imprint of* ECS Publishing Corp

Arsis Press, *imprint of* Empire Publishing Service, *distributed by* Empire Publishing Service

Art Image Publications, *division of* GB Publishing Inc

The Art Institute of Chicago, *distributed by* Yale University Press

Art Media Resources Inc, *distributor for* Serindia Publications

Art Power, *distributed by* Gingko Press Inc

Art Scroll Series, *imprint of* Mesorah Publications Ltd

art-SITES, *distributed by* University of California Press

Art String Publishing, *distributed by* Hal Leonard Corp

Art Treasures, *imprint of* Branden Books

Artabras, *imprint of* Abbeville Publishing Group

ArtAge Publications, *distributor for* Heinemann, Hal Leonard

Arte Publico Press, *affiliate of* University of Houston, *distributor for* Bilingual Review Press, Latin American Review Press, *distributed by* Empire Publishing Service

Artech House Inc, *subsidiary of* Horizon House Publications Inc, Horizon House Publications Inc

Artemis Books, *imprint of* Gateways Books & Tapes

Arthritis Research, *imprint of* Progressive Press

Arthur A Levine Books, *imprint of* Scholastic Trade Division

Artisan, *division of* Workman Publishing Co Inc

Artisan Books, *division of* Workman Publishing Co Inc, *distributor for* Greenwich Workshop Press

ArtWorks, *imprint of* MFA Publications

As Sabr, *imprint of* Imago Press

ASAE, *distributed by* Water Resources Publications LLC

Asante®, *imprint of* Mastery Education

ASCA, *distributor for* MAR*CO Products Inc

ASCD, *distributor for* Council for Exceptional Children (CEC)

ASCE, *distributed by* Water Resources Publications LLC

ASCE Press, *imprint of* American Society of Civil Engineers (ASCE)

ASCP Press, *subsidiary of* American Society for Clinical Pathology

Ash Tree Publishing, *distributed by* Brumby Sunstate, Dempsey Your Distributor, New Leaf, Nutri-Books

Ashgate, *distributed by* William S Hein & Co Inc

Ashland Creek Press, *imprint of* Ashland Creek Press

Ashley Music, *distributed by* Hal Leonard Corp

ASI Books, *imprint of* Information Today, Inc

Asian Humanities Press, *imprint of* Jain Publishing Co

AsiaPac, *distributed by* China Books

ASIS&T Monograph Series, *imprint of* Information Today, Inc

Aslan Publishing, *division of* Renaissance Book Services Corp

ASM International, *distributed by* American Institute of Chemical Engineers (AIChE), NACE International

ASM Press, *division of* American Society for Microbiology

ASME Press, *imprint of* American Society of Mechanical Engineers (ASME)

Aspatore Books, *division of* Thomson Reuters

Aspatore Thought Leadership, *imprint of* Aspatore Books

ASPEN, *distributed by* William S Hein & Co Inc, The Professional Education Group LLC (PEG)

Aspen Publishers, *distributed by* Medical Group Management Association (MGMA)

Aspen Publishers Incorporated, *imprint of* Wolters Kluwer US Corp

Assessment, *division of* Scholastic Education

Associated University Presses, *distributor for* Susquehanna University Press

Association for Information Science & Technology (ASIS&T), *distributed by* Information Today, Inc, John Wiley & Sons Inc

Association for Talent Development (ATD) Press, *distributed by* Cengage Learning Asia Pte Ltd (Asia), Eurospan Group (Europe, Middle East & the former Soviet Bloc), Knowledge Resources (South Africa), National Book Network (NBN) (US, CN, Australia & New Zealand)

Association of College & Research Libraries (ACRL), *division of* The American Library Association (ALA)

ASTM, *distributor for* American Society for Nondestructive Testing, *distributed by* NACE International

Astragal Press, *imprint of* Finney Company Inc

Astronautical Society of Western Australia, *distributed by* Univelt Inc

ASVP, *imprint of* Elsevier, Health Sciences Division

At Home on the Road, *imprint of* Park Place Publications

Ateneo De Manila University Press, *distributed by* University of Hawaii Press

Atheneum, *distributed by* Perfection Learning Corp

Atheneum Books for Young Readers, *imprint of* Simon & Schuster Children's Publishing

The Atkinson Family Imprint, *imprint of* University of California Press

Atlantic Boating Almanac, *imprint of* ProStar Publications Inc

Atlantic Books Ltd, *imprint of* Grove Atlantic Inc

Atlantic Council, *distributed by* University Press of America Inc

Atlantic Law Book Co, *division of* Peter Kelsey Publishing Inc, Peter Kelsey Publishing Inc

Atlantic Monthly Press, *imprint of* Grove Atlantic Inc

@tlas®, *imprint of* VanDam Inc

Atlas & Co, *distributed by* W W Norton & Company Inc

AtRandom.com, *imprint of* Penguin Random House Inc

Atria Books, *imprint of* Atria Publishing Group

Atria Trade Paperback, *imprint of* Atria Books

Attara, *distributed by* Hachai Publishing

Attic Press, *distributed by* Dufour Editions Inc

Audio Books, *division of* Unarius Academy of Science Publications

Audioworks, *imprint of* Simon & Schuster Audio

Augsburg Books, *imprint of* Augsburg Fortress Publishers, Publishing House of the Evangelical Lutheran Church in America

August House Audio, *imprint of* August House Inc

August House Little Folk, *imprint of* August House Inc

August House Story Cove, *imprint of* August House Inc

Augustinian Press, *distributed by* Diane Publishing Co

AUPHA Press/Health Administration Press, *imprint of* Health Administration Press

Aurora Metro Publications, *distributed by* Theatre Communications Group

Stephen F Austin State University Press, *distributed by* Texas A&M University Press

Australasian Corrosion Association Inc, *distributor for* NACE International

Austrian Film Museum Books, *distributed by* Columbia University Press

Auteur Publishing, *distributed by* Columbia University Press

AuthorHouse, *division of* Author Solutions LLC

Authorlink Press, *imprint of* Authorlink®

Authors, *imprint of* University of California Press

AuthorsandExperts.com, *division of* Story Monsters LLC

Autonomedia, *distributed by* AK Press Distribution

Autumn House Press, *distributed by* University Press of New England

Avalon House, *distributed by* Chelsea Green Publishing Co

Avalon Travel, *imprint of* Perseus Books

Avamra Institute, *distributed by* Moznaim Publishing Corp

Avant-Guide, *imprint of* Empire Press Media/Avant-Guide

Avanyu Publishing, *distributed by* University of New Mexico Press

Ave Maria Press, *imprint of* Ave Maria Press

Avery, *imprint of* Penguin Group USA, A Penguin Random House Company, Penguin Group USA, A Penguin Random House Company

AVF Modeller, *distributed by* Casemate | publishers

Aviaeology, *distributed by* Casemate | publishers

Avid, *distributed by* Hal Leonard Corp

Avon, *imprint of* HarperCollins General Books Group

Avon Books, *distributor for* Alloy Entertainment LLC

Avon Impulse, *imprint of* HarperCollins General Books Group

Avon Inspire, *imprint of* HarperCollins General Books Group

Avon Red, *imprint of* HarperCollins General Books Group

Awe-Struck, *imprint of* Mundania Press LLC

Awe-Struck Publishing, *imprint of* Mundania Press LLC

AWS, *distributed by* NACE International

AWWA, *imprint of* American Water Works Association (AWWA)

Axe Heauen, *distributed by* Hal Leonard Corp

Artes Monte Azul, *imprint of* Blue Mountain Arts Inc

Back Bay Books, *imprint of* Little, Brown and Company

Back to Eden Books, *distributed by* Lotus Press

Backbeat Books, *imprint of* Hal Leonard Books, Hal Leonard Performing Arts Publishing Group, *distributed by* Hal Leonard Corp

Backlist LLC, *distributed by* Simon & Schuster, Inc

BADM Books, *distributed by* Father & Son Publishing Inc

Baen Books, *distributed by* Simon & Schuster, Inc, Simon & Schuster Sales Division

Baen Publishing Enterprises, *distributed by* Simon & Schuster

Bagwyn Books, *imprint of* Arizona Center for Medieval & Renaissance Studies (ACMRS)

Baha'i Publishing, *subsidiary of* The National Spiritual Assembly of the Baha'is of the United States, The National Spiritual Assembly of the Baha'is of the United States

BainBridgeBooks, *imprint of* Trans-Atlantic Publications Inc

Baker Books, *division of* Baker Publishing Group, *distributor for* Focus on the Family, *distributed by* Perfection Learning Corp

Baker's Plays, *distributor for* Samuel French Inc, *distributed by* Samuel French Inc

Bala Kids, *imprint of* Shambhala Publications Inc

Balboa Press, *division of* Hay House Inc

Balcony Press, *distributed by* Princeton Architectural Press

Baldar, *imprint of* Ross Books

Ball Publishing, *imprint of* Chicago Review Press

Ballantine, *distributed by* Perfection Learning Corp

Ballantine Books, *imprint of* Penguin Random House Inc, Random House Publishing Group

Ballantine Wellspring, *imprint of* Penguin Random House Inc

Baltos Lankos, *distributed by* Central European University Press

Balzer + Bray, *imprint of* HarperCollins Children's Books

Bancroft-Sage Publishing, *imprint of* Finney Company Inc

B&H Publishing Group, *imprint of* LifeWay Christian Resources

Bandit Books, *distributed by* John F Blair Publisher

Banned Books, *imprint of* Progressive Press

Banner Publishing, *imprint of* Whitaker House

Bantam, *distributor for* Parachute Publishing LLC, *distributed by* Perfection Learning Corp, Specialty Press Inc

Bantam Books, *imprint of* Penguin Random House Inc, Random House Publishing Group

Bantam Hardcover, *imprint of* Penguin Random House Inc

Bantam Mass Market, *imprint of* Penguin Random House Inc

Bantam Skylark, *imprint of* Penguin Random House Inc

Bantam Starfire, *imprint of* Penguin Random House Inc

Bantam Trade Paperback, *imprint of* Penguin Random House Inc

Bar Ilan, *distributed by* Gefen Books

Bar-Ilan University, *distributed by* American Mathematical Society

Barbary Coast Books, *subsidiary of* Berkeley Slavic Specialties

Barbour Books, *imprint of* Barbour Publishing Inc

The Bard Graduate Center, *distributed by* Yale University Press

BarnaBooks, *imprint of* Tyndale House Publishers Inc

Barnes & Noble Classics, *imprint of* Fine Creative Media, Inc

Barricade Books, *imprint of* Barricade Books Inc

Barringer, *distributor for* Marriage Transformation LLC

Barringer Publishing, *division of* Schlesinger Advertising & Marketing

Barrons, *distributed by* Perfection Learning Corp

Bartleby Press, *subsidiary of* Jackson Westgate Publishing Group

Basch, *distributor for* Business Research Services Inc

Baseball America, *distributed by* Simon & Schuster, Inc, Simon & Schuster Sales Division

Basheer, *distributed by* Gingko Press Inc

Bashu Publishing, *distributed by* CN Times Books

Basic Books, *imprint of* Perseus Books, *distributed by* HarperCollins Publishers

Basic Health Guides, *imprint of* Basic Health Publications

Basic Health Publications, *imprint of* Turner Publishing Co

Randol Bass Music, *distributed by* ECS Publishing Corp

Bat Conservation International, *distributed by* University of Texas Press

David Bateman Ltd, *distributor for* Interweave Press LLC, Price World Publishing

Battlebridge, *distributed by* Franklin, Beedle & Associates Inc

Bauhan Publishing, *distributed by* University Press of New England

Bayard, *distributed by* Crabtree Publishing Co

Baylor University Press, *distributed by* The Johns Hopkins University Press

BDD Audio Publishing, *imprint of* Penguin Random House Inc

Beach Lane Books, *imprint of* Simon & Schuster Children's Publishing

Beach Lloyd Publishers LLC, *distributor for* Le Chambon-sur-Lignon, CIDEB (Italy), Fondation pour la Memoire de la Shoah (Paris), Kar-Ben Publishing, Kiron Editions du Felin (Paris), JP Lattes (Paris), Le Manuscrit (Paris), Oxford University Press (NYC), *distributed by* Tralco (CN)

BeachHouse Books, *imprint of* Science & Humanities Press

Beacon Hill Press of Kansas City, *subsidiary of* Nazarene Publishing House

Bear & Co Inc, *imprint of* Inner Traditions International Ltd

Bear Cub Books, *imprint of* Inner Traditions International Ltd

Bear Meadows Research Group, *imprint of* Crumb Elbow Publishing

BearManor Bare, *imprint of* BearManor Media

BearManor Fiction, *imprint of* BearManor Media

Beauxarts, *imprint of* Picasso Project, Alan Wofsy Fine Arts

Bebop Books, *imprint of* Lee & Low Books Inc

The Stephen Bechtel Fund, *imprint of* University of California Press

Bedford, Freeman & Worth High School Publishers, *imprint of* Macmillan Learning

Bedford/St Martin's, *imprint of* Macmillan Learning

Beech Tree Books, *imprint of* HarperCollins Publishers

Beekman Books Inc, *distributor for* C W Daniel, Gomer Press, Music Sales Corp, Kogan Page

Begell-Atom LLC, *subsidiary of* Begell House Inc Publishers

Behrman House Inc, *distributor for* Rossel Books

Belknap Press, *imprint of* Harvard University Press

Bell Bridge Books, *imprint of* BelleBooks

Bell Pond Books, *imprint of* SteinerBooks

Bell Tower, *imprint of* Penguin Random House Inc

Bella Books, *distributed by* Turnaround (London)

Belle Isle Books, *imprint of* Brandylane Publishers Inc

Belwin, *imprint of* Alfred Music Publishing

Benchmark Maps, *distributed by* Wide World of Maps Inc

Benchmark Press, *imprint of* Triumph Books

Bendon, *distributor for* Parachute Publishing LLC

John Benjamins North America Inc, *subsidiary of* John Benjamins Publishing Co

Bentley Publishers, *division of* Robert Bentley Inc, Robert Bentley Inc

BePuzzled, *division of* University Games

Berg Publishers, *distributed by* Palgrave Macmillan

Berger Books, *imprint of* Dark Horse Comics

W H Berger, *distributed by* Sunbelt Publications Inc

Berghahn Books Ltd (UK), *division of* Berghahn Books

Berklee Press, *imprint of* Hal Leonard Corp, *distributed by* Hal Leonard Corp

Berkley, *distributor for* Parachute Publishing LLC, *distributed by* Perfection Learning Corp

Berkley Books, *imprint of* Berkley Publishing Group

Berkley Publishing Group, *division of* Penguin Group USA, A Penguin Random House Company, Penguin Group USA, A Penguin Random House Company

Bernan, *imprint of* Rowman & Littlefield Publishing Group

Leonard Bernstein, *distributed by* Hal Leonard Corp

Berrett-Koehler Publishers, *distributed by* Dreamscape Media LLC

Bertrams UK, *distributor for* Dissertation.com

Bess Press, *distributed by* The Islander Group (TIG) (Hawaii wholesaler/book dist)

Best Books International, *subsidiary of* Empire Publishing Service

Best Places® Guidebooks Series, *imprint of* Sasquatch Books

Best Publishing Co, *distributed by* Marine Techniques Publishing

Emily Bestler Books, *imprint of* Atria Books

Beta Books, *imprint of* Bandanna Books

Bethany House Publishers, *division of* Baker Publishing Group

Bethlehem Books, *affiliate of* Bethlehem Community, *distributed by* Ignatius Press

Betterway Books, *imprint of* F+W Media Inc

Betty Crocker®, *imprint of* Houghton Mifflin Harcourt Trade & Reference Division

Between the Lines, *distributed by* Dufour Editions Inc

Beyond Words, *imprint of* Atria Books, Simon & Schuster Audio, *distributed by* Simon & Schuster, Inc

Bibli O'Phile, *distributed by* Penguin Group USA, A Penguin Random House Company

Biblio, *distributed by* Bloch Publishing Co

Bibliographical Society of America, *distributed by* Oak Knoll Press

Bibliographical Society of University of Virginia, *distributed by* Oak Knoll Press

The Bibliographical Society (UK), *distributed by* Oak Knoll Press

Bider Technology, *distributed by* Cheng & Tsui Co Inc

Big Buddy Books, *imprint of* ABDO Publishing Group

Big Guy Books Inc, *distributed by* Arcturus Publishing Ltd (United Kingdom), Bookwise International (Australia), Independent Publishers Group (handles all trade dist in the US), Scholastic New Zealand (New Zealand), Iwasaki Shoten (Japanese translation)

Big Meteor, *distributed by* Omnibus Press

Big Meteor Publishing, *distributed by* G Schirmer Inc/Associated Music Publishers Inc

Big Picture Press, *imprint of* Candlewick Press

Big Sky Maps, *distributed by* Wide World of Maps Inc

Big Sky Publishing, *distributed by* Casemate | publishers

Big Tree Books, *imprint of* Easy Money Press

Bigwig Briefs, *imprint of* Aspatore Books

Bilingual Review Press, *distributed by* Arte Publico Press

Binational Press, *imprint of* San Diego State University Press

Bindu Books, *imprint of* Inner Traditions International Ltd

Biographical Publishing Co, *distributor for* Eagles Landing Publishing, Spyglass Books LLC

BioMed Central, *imprint of* Springer

BioTechniques Books, *division of* Informa Business Information

Birch Brook Impressions, *subsidiary of* Birch Brook Press

Birch Brook Press, *distributor for* Carpenter Gothic Press, Natural Heritage Press, Persephone Press

Bird Dog Publishing, *imprint of* Bottom Dog Press

Birkhauser Science, *imprint of* Springer

Birlinn, *distributed by* Casemate | publishers

Bisk Education, *distributed by* Bisk Publishing Co

Bisk Publishing Co, *distributor for* Bisk Education

Bison Books, *imprint of* University of Nebraska Press

BJU Press, *unit of* BJU Education Group

BL Publishing, *distributed by* Simon & Schuster, Inc

Black & White Publishing (UK), *distributed by* Interlink Publishing Group Inc

Black Cat, *imprint of* Grove Atlantic Inc

Black Classic Press, *distributed by* Publishers Group West (PGW)

Black Coral, *imprint of* Genesis Press Inc

Black Dog & Leventhal, *imprint of* Hachette Books

Black Heritage: Celebrating Culture, *imprint of* Gallopade International Inc

Black Iron Cookin' Co, *division of* Quixote Press

Black Sparrow, *imprint of* David R Godine Publisher Inc

Black Squirrel Books, *imprint of* Kent State University Press

Blacklock Nature Photography, *distributed by* AdventureKEEN

Blackstaff Press Ltd, *distributed by* Dufour Editions Inc

Blackwells, *distributor for* Teton NewMedia Inc

John F Blair Publisher, *distributor for* Bandit Books, Bright Mountain Books, Carolina Wren Press, The Colonial Williamsburg Foundation, Down Home Press, Eno Publishers, Hub City Press, Looking Glass Books, Lookout Books, NewSouth Books, Niche Publishing, Pennywell Press, Upper Ohio Valley Books

Blake Books, *distributed by* Perfection Learning Corp

The Blaxis, *imprint of* Cedar Grove Books

Blind Owl Press, *imprint of* Mazda Publishers Inc

Bling!, *imprint of* Lighthouse Publishing of the Carolinas

Bliss, *imprint of* Entangled Publishing

Bloch Publishing Co, *distributor for* Biblio, Menorah, Scarf Press, Sephardic House, Soncino

Block Museum, *distributed by* Oak Knoll Press

Bloodaxe Books Ltd, *distributed by* Dufour Editions Inc

Bloody Brits Press, *imprint of* Bywater Books

Bloomberg BNA Books, *division of* Bloomberg BNA

Bloom's Literary Criticism, *imprint of* Infobase Learning

Bloomsbury, *imprint of* Bloomsbury Publishing Inc

Bloomsbury Academic, *distributor for* Paragon House, Spring Publications

Bloomsbury International Publishing USA, *distributor for* Paragon House

Bloomsbury Press, *imprint of* Bloomsbury Publishing Inc

Bloomsbury Publishing Inc, *distributed by* Macmillan

Bloomsbury USA, *imprint of* Bloomsbury Publishing Inc

Blue & Gray, *imprint of* Book Sales

Blue Angel, *distributed by* Llewellyn Publications

Blue Angel Publishing, *distributed by* US Games Systems Inc

Blue Apple Books, *distributed by* Chronicle Books LLC

Blue Beacon Books, *imprint of* Regal Crest Enterprises

Blue Guides Ltd, *distributed by* W W Norton & Company Inc

Blue Microphones, *distributed by* Hal Leonard Corp

Blue Mountain Press®, *imprint of* Blue Mountain Arts Inc

Blue Note, *imprint of* Blue Note Publications Inc

Blue Note Books, *imprint of* Blue Note Publications Inc

Blue Poppy Press, *division of* Blue Poppy Enterprises Inc, *distributed by* China Books, New Leaf Books, Partner's Book Distributing Inc, Partner's/West Book Distributing Inc, Redwing Book Co, Satas

Blue Sky Gallery, *distributed by* Franklin, Beedle & Associates Inc

The Blue Sky Press, *imprint of* Scholastic Trade Division

Blue Snake Books, *imprint of* North Atlantic Books

BlueBridge, *imprint of* United Tribes Media Inc

Bluefire, *imprint of* Random House Children's Books

BNI Publications, *distributor for* Craftsman Book Co, *distributed by* Craftsman Book Co

BoardSource, *distributed by* American Society of Association Executives

Boatwhistle Books, *distributed by* Dufour Editions Inc

Bobolink Media, *distributed by* Sunbelt Publications Inc

Fred Bock Music Company, *distributed by* Hal Leonard Corp

Bollingen Series, *imprint of* Princeton University Press

Bonneville Books, *imprint of* Cedar Fort Inc, The University of Utah Press

Book Guild, *distributed by* Trans-Atlantic Publications Inc

Book House, *distributor for* Business Research Services Inc, *distributed by* Trans-Atlantic Publications Inc

The Book House, *distributor for* Primary Research Group Inc

Book Marketing Works, *subsidiary of* Book Marketing Works LLC

Book Peddlers, *distributed by* Gryphon House Inc

Book Publishing Co, *distributor for* Cherokee Publications, Crazy Crow, CRCS Publications, Critical Path, Gentle World, Hippocrates Publications, Magni Co, Sproutman Publications

The Book Publishing Co, *distributed by* Orca Book Publishers

Book Sales, *division of* Quarto Publishing Group USA Inc

Book Sales Inc, *division of* Quarto Publishing Group USA Inc

Booklines Hawaii, *distributor for* Centerstream Publishing LLC

Books Alive, *imprint of* Book Publishing Co

Books Americana, *imprint of* Krause Publications Inc

Books & Co/Turtle Point, *imprint of* Turtle Point Press

Books for Independent Minds, *imprint of* Ronin Publishing Inc

Books Good For Young Children™, *imprint of* Maren Green Publishing Inc

Books In Motion, *division of* Classic Ventures Ltd, Classic Ventures Ltd

Books on Tape®, *imprint of* Penguin Random House Audio Publishing, Penguin Random House Inc, *distributor for* Listening Library®

BookShots, *imprint of* Little, Brown and Company

Bookwise International, *distributor for* Big Guy Books Inc

Boom! Studios, *distributed by* Simon & Schuster, Inc, Simon & Schuster Sales & Marketing, Simon & Schuster Sales Division

Boone & Crockett Club, *distributed by* The Globe Pequot Press

Boosey & Hawkes, *distributed by* Hal Leonard Corp

Booth-Clibborn Editions, *distributed by* Harry N Abrams Inc

Bora, *distributed by* Alan Wofsy Fine Arts

Borden Publishing, *distributed by* Gem Guides Book Co

Boreal Books, *imprint of* Red Hen Press

Borgo Press, *imprint of* Wildside Press LLC

Boson Books, *imprint of* Bitingduck Press LLC

Boston College, *distributed by* Oak Knoll Press

Boston Globe Puzzle Books, *imprint of* Random House Reference/Random House Puzzles & Games

Botanica Press, *imprint of* Book Publishing Co

Bottom Dog Press, *distributor for* The Firelands Writing Center (Heartlands Magazine)

Lee Boudreaux Books, *imprint of* Little, Brown and Company

Boulden, *distributed by* MAR*CO Products Inc

Boulden Publishing, *distributor for* MAR*CO Products Inc

Boundless, *imprint of* Zumaya Publications LLC

Bourbon Street Books, *imprint of* HarperCollins General Books Group

R R Bowker LLC, *subsidiary of* ProQuest LLC

R R Bowker's Books in Print Series, *imprint of* Grey House Publishing Inc™

Boxer Books, *distributed by* Sterling Publishing Co Inc

Boydell & Brewer Inc, *affiliate of* Boydell & Brewer Ltd (UK)

Boyds Mills Press, *division of* Highlights for Children Inc, *subsidiary of* Highlights for Children Inc

Boye Knives Press, *distributed by* Chelsea Green Publishing Co

Boynton/Cook Publishers, *imprint of* Heinemann, *distributed by* Pearson Australia-Schools Division, Pearson Education Canada, Pearson New Zealand-Schools Division

Boys Town Press, *division of* Boys Town, *distributor for* Specialty Press Inc, *distributed by* Deep Books Ltd (Europe & UK), Footprint Books (Australia & New Zealand), University of Toronto Press (Canada)

BPI Records, *imprint of* Bridge Publications Inc

Bradford Books, *imprint of* The MIT Press

Brady, *distributed by* Fire Engineering Books & Videos

Joan Brady, *distributed by* Sunbelt Publications Inc

Braided River, *imprint of* The Mountaineers Books

Brandeis University Press, *imprint of* University Press of New England

Branden Books, *subsidiary of* Branden Publishing Co, *distributor for* Dante University of America Press Inc

Branden Publishing Co, *distributor for* Dante University Press

Brandon Books, *distributed by* Dufour Editions Inc

Brandon Books Cinematic Novels, *imprint of* Branden Books

Brashear Music Co, *imprint of* Branden Books

Deya Brashears, *distributed by* Gryphon House Inc

Brava, *imprint of* Kensington Publishing Corp

Brazen, *imprint of* Entangled Publishing

George Braziller Inc, *distributed by* Antique Collectors' Club Ltd, W W Norton & Company Inc, W W Norton & Company Inc

A Karen & Michael Braziller Book, *imprint of* Persea Books

Breakfast Communications, *distributed by* SAS Publishing

Breakthrough Publications, *imprint of* Breakthrough Publications Inc

Nicholas Brealey Publishing, *imprint of* John Murray (Publishers) Ltd, John Murray (Publishers) Ltd (UK), *distributed by* Hachette Book Group

Breslov Research Institute, *distributed by* Moznaim Publishing Corp

Brethren Press, *division of* Church of the Brethren

Brewers Publications, *division of* Brewers Association

Brick Mantel Books, *imprint of* Pen & Publish Inc

Brick Tower Press, *subsidiary of* J T Colby & Co Inc

Bridge, *imprint of* Bridge-Logos

Bridge Audio, *imprint of* Bridge Publications Inc

Bridge-Logos, *distributor for* Warboys LLC

Bridge 21, *distributed by* Transaction Publishers Inc

Brief Books, *imprint of* Birch Brook Press

Bright Connections Media, *imprint of* World Book Inc

Bright Connections Media, A World Book Encyclopedia Company, *imprint of* World Book Inc

Bright Mountain Books, *distributed by* John F Blair Publisher

Bright Ring Publishing, *distributed by* Gryphon House Inc

Brigids Books, *subsidiary of* Leilah Publications

Brill Inc, *subsidiary of* Koninklijke Brill NV

Brilliance Audio, *subsidiary of* Amazon.com, Amazon.com Inc

Brimstone, *imprint of* Lighthouse Publishing of the Carolinas

British Film Institute, *distributed by* Palgrave Macmillan, University of California Press

Brittanica Educational Publishing, *imprint of* The Rosen Publishing Group Inc

Broadside Books, *imprint of* HarperCollins General Books Group

Broadstone Books, *distributed by* Fons Vitae

Broadway Books, *imprint of* Crown Publishing Group

Brookings Institution Press, *distributor for* Council on Foreign Relations Press, University of California Institute on Global Conflict & Cooperation

The Brookings Institution Press, *division of* Brookings Institution, *distributed by* The Johns Hopkins University Press

Brooklands Books Ltd, *distributed by* CarTech Inc

Brooklyn Botanic Garden, *distributed by* Sterling Publishing Co Inc

Brookes, *distributed by* Council for Exceptional Children (CEC)

Brotherhood of Saint Herman of Alaska, *imprint of* Saint Herman Press

Brown Bear Books, *imprint of* Black Rabbit Books

Brown Books Agency, *division of* Brown Books Publishing Group

Brown Books Kids, *division of* Brown Books Publishing Group

John Carter Brown Library, *distributed by* Oak Knoll Press

Brown Judaic Studies, *distributed by* SBL Press

Brown University, *distributed by* American Mathematical Society

Brown Walker Press, *imprint of* Universal-Publishers Inc

Karen Brown's Guides, *distributed by* Penguin Random House Inc

Brumby Sunstate, *distributor for* Ash Tree Publishing

Brusberg (Berlin), *distributed by* Alan Wofsy Fine Arts

Bryn Mawr College, *distributed by* Oak Knoll Press

Bryn Mawr Commentaries, *distributed by* Hackett Publishing Co Inc

Brynmorgen Press, *distributed by* Gem Guides Book Co

Brynwood Publishing, *distributed by* Resilient Publishing

Bucking Horse Books, *distributed by* Mountain Press Publishing Co

Buckle Down, *imprint of* Triumph Learning LLC

Bucknell University Press, *distributed by* Rowman & Littlefield

Buddy Books, *imprint of* ABDO Publishing Group

Barbara Budrich Publishers, *distributed by* Columbia University Press

Editorial Buenas Letras, *imprint of* The Rosen Publishing Group Inc

Bufflehead Books, *imprint of* Down The Shore Publishing Corp

BuilderBooks.com, *division of* National Association of Home Builders (NAHB), *distributor for* National Association of Home Builders (NAHB)

Builders Book Inc, *distributor for* Craftsman Book Co, *distributed by* Craftsman Book Co

Building Blocks, *distributed by* Gryphon House Inc

Building Excellence, *imprint of* Mel Bay Publications Inc

Building News Inc, *distributed by* Craftsman Book Co

Bulgarian-American Cultural Society ALEKO, *subsidiary of* Cross-Cultural Communications

Bullfrog Books, *imprint of* Jump!

Bumba Books, *imprint of* Lerner Publishing Group Inc

Bureau of Economic Geology, University of Texas at Austin, *division of* University of Texas at Austin, *distributor for* Gulf Coast Association of Geological Societies, Gulf Coast Section, Texas Memorial Museum (selected titles)

Burnell Books, *distributor for* MAR*CO Products Inc

Burns Archive Press, *imprint of* Burns Archive Photographic Distributors Ltd

Buros Institute, *distributed by* University of Nebraska Press

Business & Research Associates, *distributed by* FurnitureCore

Business Expert Press, *subsidiary of* IGroup

Business Research Services Inc, *distributor for* Riley & Johnson, *distributed by* Basch, Book House, Coutts, Gale Research Inc, Midwest Library Service

Business Success Series, *imprint of* PREP Publishing

Butler Center for Arkansas Studies, *distributed by* The University of Arkansas Press

Butterworth Heinemann, *distributed by* SAMS Technical Publishing LLC

Butterworth-Heinemann, *distributed by* Marine Techniques Publishing, NACE International

Butterworths, *distributed by* William S Hein & Co Inc

By Design Press, *imprint of* Quite Specific Media Group Ltd

Byte Level Books, *imprint of* Ashland Creek Press

BYU Museum of Peoples & Cultures, *distributed by* The University of Utah Press

BYU Studies, *distributed by* The University of Utah Press

C E P Inc, *imprint of* Paladin Press

Cabi Books, *distributed by* Stylus Publishing LLC

Caissa Editions, *affiliate of* Dale A Brandreth Books

Cakewalk, *distributed by* Hal Leonard Corp

Cal-Earth, *distributed by* Chelsea Green Publishing Co

Caliber, *imprint of* Berkley Publishing Group

Calico, *imprint of* ABDO Publishing Group

California Sea Grant, *distributed by* Sunbelt Publications Inc

Calkins Creek, *imprint of* Boyds Mills Press

Calloway House, *distributor for* MAR*CO Products Inc

Cambridge Educational, *imprint of* Infobase Learning

Cambridge University Press, *division of* University of Cambridge, *distributor for* The Mathematical Association of America, *distributed by* NACE International

Camden House, *imprint of* Boydell & Brewer Inc

Camel Press, *distributed by* Epicenter Press Inc

Camelion Plays, *distributed by* Players Press Inc

Camerapix Publishers International, *distributed by* Interlink Publishing Group Inc

Georgina Campbell Guides (Ireland), *distributed by* Interlink Publishing Group Inc

Paul Douglas Campbell, *distributed by* Sunbelt Publications Inc

Campus Compact, *distributed by* Stylus Publishing LLC

Canadian Centre for Architecture, *distributed by* The MIT Press

Canadian Society of Petroleum Geologists, *distributor for* AAPG (American Association of Petroleum Geologists)

Canal Press, *imprint of* Schiffer Publishing Ltd

Candied Plums, *imprint of* Paper Republic LLC

Candle Books, *distributed by* Kregel Publications

Candlewick Entertainment, *imprint of* Candlewick Press

Candlewick Press, *subsidiary of* Walker Books Ltd (London), *distributed by* Perfection Learning Corp

Candlewick Studio, *imprint of* Candlewick Press

C&T Publishing Inc, *distributed by* Watson-Guptill Publications

Gloriae Dei Cantores, *distributed by* Paraclete Press Inc

Capall-Bann, *distributed by* Holmes Publishing Group LLC

Capital Enquiry Inc, *distributor for* Center for Investigative Reporting

Capstone, *imprint of* John Wiley & Sons Inc

Capstone Press, *imprint of* Capstone Publishers™

Capstone Young Readers, *imprint of* Capstone Publishers™

Caravel Books, *imprint of* Pleasure Boat Studio: A Literary Press

Cardinal Publishers Group, *distributor for* Price World Publishing

Cardoza, *distributed by* Simon & Schuster Sales Division

Cardoza Publishing, *distributor for* Simon & Schuster, *distributed by* Simon & Schuster, Inc

Career Examination Series, *imprint of* National Learning Corp

Career Kids FYI, *distributor for* MAR*CO Products Inc

Caress, *imprint of* Kensington Publishing Corp

Caribe Betania Editores, *division of* Grupo Nelson Inc

Coleccion Caribena, *imprint of* University of Puerto Rico Press

Carina Press, *imprint of* Harlequin Enterprises Ltd

Carlton Books, *distributed by* Sterling Publishing Co Inc

Carmania Press London, *distributed by* Purple Mountain Press Ltd

Carnegie Mellon University Press, *distributed by* University Press of New England

Carolina Wren Press, *distributed by* John F Blair Publisher

Carolrhoda Books, *imprint of* Lerner Publishing Group Inc

Carolrhoda Books Inc, *imprint of* Lerner Publishing Group Inc

Carolrhoda Lab™, *imprint of* Lerner Publishing Group Inc

Carpe Diem Professional Calendars, *imprint of* Flying Pen Press LLC

Carpenter Gothic Press, *distributed by* Birch Brook Press

Carson-Dellosa Publishing LLC, *distributor for* Key Education, Mark Twain Media

CarTech Inc, *distributor for* Brooklands Books Ltd, Wolfgang Publications

Carthage Reprints, *imprint of* St Augustine's Press Inc

Cartwheel Books, *imprint of* Scholastic Trade Division

Casa Bautista, *distributed by* Editorial Bautista Independiente

Casa Bautista de Publicaciones, *affiliate of* Southern Baptist Convention, *distributed by* LifeWay Christian Resources

Casa Creation, *imprint of* Charisma Media

Cascade Expeditions, *imprint of* Crumb Elbow Publishing

Cascade Geographic Society, *imprint of* Crumb Elbow Publishing

Casemate, *distributed by* Casemate | publishers

Casemate | publishers, *division of* Casemate Group, *distributor for* AF Editions, Air Sea Media, Air War Publications, Airfile Publications, Amber Books (UK), Amberley (UK), Andrea Press, AVF Modeller, Aviaeology, Big Sky Publishing, Birlinn (UK), Casemate (USA), Chipotle Publishing, Claymore Press, Clear Vue Publishing, Colourpoint, Compendium (UK), Compendium Films, D-Day Publishing (Belgium), Fighting High Publishing, Fonthill Media, Formac (Canada), Foundry, Front Street Press (USA), Frontline Books, Greenhill Books, Grub Street Publishing (UK), Harpia Publishing, Heimdal, Helion & Co (UK), Helion & Co/CG Books, Editions Charles Herissey (France), Histoire & Collections (France), Historical Indexes (USA), History Facts, Kagero, De Krijger (Belgium), Lombardy Studios, Lorimer, LRT Editions, Military History Press, MMP-Books (UK/Poland), Model Centrum Progres, Moselle River, Panzerwrecks, PeKo Publishing, PelikaanPers, Pen & Sword (UK), Pen & Sword Digital, Philedition, Pool of London Press, Pritzker Military Museum & Library, Riebel-Roque, RN Publishing (USA), S I Publicaties BV, Sabrestorm Publishing, Savas Beatie (USA), Savas Publishing, Scarab Miniatures, Seaforth Publishing, Tattered Flag, 30 Degrees South Publishers, WAG Books, Warlord Games

CASTI Publishing, *distributed by* NACE International

Castle Books, *imprint of* Book Sales

Catalpa Press, *distributed by* Oak Knoll Press

Catapult, *imprint of* Counterpoint Press LLC

Catechesis of the Good Shepherd Publications, *imprint of* Liturgy Training Publications

Cathedral Music Press, *division of* Mel Bay Publications Inc, *imprint of* Mel Bay Publications Inc

Catholic Approach Series, *imprint of* Pauline Books & Media

Catholic Treasures, *distributor for* Angelus Press

Catholic University of America Press, *distributed by* The Johns Hopkins University Press

The Catholic University of America Press, *distributor for* American Maritain Association, Institute for the Psychological Sciences Press (IPS), Sapientia Press

CavanKerry Press, *distributed by* University Press of New England

Caveat Press, *imprint of* White Cloud Press

Caxton Club, *distributed by* Oak Knoll Press

Caxton Press, *division of* The Caxton Printers Ltd, The Caxton Printers Ltd, *distributor for* Hambleton Publishing, Historic Idaho Series, Photosmith Books, Snake Country Pub lishing, University of Idaho Asian American Comparative Collection, University of Idaho Press

CBP/EMH, *imprint of* Casa Bautista de Publicaciones

CCA, *imprint of* Copywriter's Council of America™ (CCA), The Linick Group Inc

CCH, *distributor for* AICPA Professional Publications

CCH, a Wolters Kluwer business, *subsidiary of* Wolters Kluwer

CCH INCORPORATED, *imprint of* Wolters Kluwer US Corp

CCH Peterson, *subsidiary of* CCH, a Wolters Kluwer business

CCH Riverwoods, *subsidiary of* CCH, a Wolters Kluwer business

CCH St Petersburg, *subsidiary of* CCH, a Wolters Kluwer business

CCH Tax Compliance, *subsidiary of* CCH, a Wolters Kluwer business

CCH Washington DC, *subsidiary of* CCH, a Wolters Kluwer business

CD Sheet Music, *distributed by* Hal Leonard Corp

Cedar Fort Inc, *distributor for* Horizon Publishers & Distributors Inc

Cedar Grove Books, *subsidiary of* Inkbaby Intermedia

CEF Press, *subsidiary of* Child Evangelism Fellowship Inc, Child Evangelism Fellowship Inc

Celebra, *imprint of* Penguin Group USA, A Penguin Random House Company, Penguin Group USA, A Penguin Random House Company

Celebrity Profiles Publishing, *division of* Edison & Kellogg

Cengage Learning Asia Pte Ltd, *distributor for* Association for Talent Development (ATD) Press

Cengage Learning Australia, *distributed by* Cheng & Tsui Co Inc

Centaur Books, *imprint of* Joshua Tree Publishing

Center for Book Arts, *distributed by* Oak Knoll Press

Center for Chinese Studies, University of Michigan, *distributed by* University of Michigan Press

Center for Contemporary Judaica, *imprint of* Prayer Book Press Inc

Center for Creative Leadership LLC, *affiliate of* Smith Richardson Foundation, *distributor for* Free Press, Harvard Business School Press, Jossey-Bass, Lominger Inc, John Wiley & Sons Inc, *distributed by* Jossey-Bass, John Wiley & Sons Inc

Center for East Asian Studies (CEAS), *subsidiary of* Western Washington University

Center for Global Development, *distributed by* Peterson Institute for International Economics (PIIE)

Center for Investigative Reporting, *distributed by* Capital Enquiry Inc

Center for Japanese Studies, University of Michigan, *distributed by* University of Michigan Press

The Center for Learning, *division of* Social Studies School Service

Center for Literary Publishing, *distributed by* University Press of Colorado

Center for National Policy Press, *distributed by* University Press of America Inc

Center for South & Southeast Asian Studies, University of Michigan, *distributed by* University of Michigan Press

Center for Talented Youth, *distributed by* The Johns Hopkins University Press

Center for the Child Care Workforce, *distributed by* Gryphon House Inc

The Center for the Study of Upper Midwestern Culture, *distributed by* University of Wisconsin Press

Center for US-Mexican Studies, *distributed by* Lynne Rienner Publishers Inc

Center for Urban Policy Research, *imprint of* Transaction Publishers Inc

Center of Emigrants from Serbia, *distributed by* Cross-Cultural Communications

Center Street, *imprint of* Hachette Nashville

Centerbrook Publishing, *subsidiary of* Centerstream Publishing LLC

Centerstream Publications, *imprint of* Hal Leonard Corp, *distributed by* Hal Leonard Corp

Centerstream Publishing LLC, *distributed by* Booklines Hawaii, Hal Leonard Corp

Central European University Press, *distributor for* Apostrofa Publishers, Baltos Lankos, Helena History Press, International Debate Education Association, Open Society Institute, *distributed by* University of Toronto Press (Canada)

Central Recovery Press (CRP), *unit of* Central Recovery Treatment

The Century Foundation Press, *division of* The Century Foundation

Cerf & Peterson, *distributed by* Welcome Enterprises Inc

Cernunnos, *distributed by* Simon & Schuster, Inc, Simon & Schuster Sales Division

Certified Nurse Examination Series (CN), *imprint of* National Learning Corp

Cervantes & Co, *imprint of* LinguaText LLC

CFI, *imprint of* Cedar Fort Inc

CFKR Career, *distributor for* MAR*CO Products Inc

CGN, *imprint of* Cedar Grove Books

Chalice Press, *division of* Christian Board of Publications, *distributed by* Cokesbury

Challenges of Aging, *imprint of* Letterbox/Papyrus of London Publishers USA

Le Chambon-sur-Lignon, *distributed by* Beach Lloyd Publishers LLC

Chanterelle, *distributed by* Mel Bay Publications Inc

Chapin Library, *distributed by* Oak Knoll Press

Chapter Books, *imprint of* ABDO Publishing Group

Character Development, *distributor for* MAR*CO Products Inc

CharismaLife, *distributed by* CharismaLife Publishers

CharismaLife Publishers, *distributor for* CharismaLife

The Charles Press, Publishers, *subsidiary of* Oxbridge Corp, The Oxbridge Corp

Charles River Media, *imprint of* Cengage Learning

Charles Scribner's Sons®, *imprint of* Gale

Charlesbridge Press, *distributed by* Perfection Learning Corp

Charlesbridge Publishing Inc, *distributor for* EarlyLight Books

Charmz, *imprint of* Papercutz

Chartwell Books, *imprint of* Book Sales

Chatterbox Press, *distributed by* Gryphon House Inc

Cheap Bastards, *imprint of* The Globe Pequot Press

Checkerboard Library, *imprint of* ABDO Publishing Group

Chef Express, *imprint of* Standard International Media Holdings

Chef Success, *imprint of* Standard International Media Holdings

Chelsea Clubhouse, *imprint of* Chelsea House Publishers

Chelsea Green Publishing, *distributor for* Stone Pier Press

Chelsea Green Publishing Co, *distributor for* AATEC Publications, American Council for an Energy Efficient Economy (ACEEE), Anomaly Press, Avalon House, Boye Knives Press, Cal-Earth, Earth Pledge, Eco Logic Books, Ecological Design Institute, Ecological Design Press, Empowerment Institute, Filaree Productions, Flower Press, Foundation for Deep Ecology, Fox Maple Press, Green Books, Green Building Press, Green Man Publishing, Groundworks, Hand Print Press, Holmgren Design Services, Jenkins Publishing, Knossus Project, Left To Write Press, Madison Area Community Supported Agriculture Coalition, Marion Institute, marketumbrella.org, Metamorphic Press, Moneta Publications, Ottographics, Peregrinzilla, Permanent Publications, Daniela Piazza Editore, Polyface, Rainsource Press, Raven Press, Anita Roddick Publications, Rural Science Institute, Seed Savers, Service Employees International Union, Slow Food Editore, Solar Design Association, Stonefield Publishing, Sun Plans Inc, Sustainability Press, Trailblazer Press, Trust for Public Land, Yes Books

Chelsea House, *distributed by* Perfection Learning Corp

Chelsea House Publishers, *imprint of* Infobase Learning

Chelsea Publishing Co Inc, *imprint of* American Mathematical Society

Chemical Heritage Foundation, *distributed by* Diane Publishing Co

Cheng & Tsui Co Inc, *distributor for* Action Language Learning, aha! Chinese, Bider Technology, Cengage Learning Australia, China International Book Trading Co (Beijing, selected titles only), China Soft, China Sprout, Crabtree Publishing, Curriculum Corp, Facets Video, Ilchokak Publishers, Italian School of East Asian Studies, JPT America Inc, Oxford University Press, Pan Asian Publications, Panmun Academic Services, Panpac Education, Paradigm Busters, Pearson Australia, Royal Asiatic Society (Korea Branch), SMC Publishing, Sogang University Institute, Stone Bridge Press, SUP Publishing Logistics, Tuttle Publishing, US International Publishing, White Rabbit Press, Yale University Press, Zeitgeist Films

Cherokee Heritage Press, *distributed by* University of Oklahoma Press

Cherokee Publications, *distributed by* Book Publishing Co

Cherry Lane Music Co, *imprint of* Hal Leonard Corp, *distributed by* Hal Leonard Corp

Chesapeake Bay Maritime Museum, *distributed by* Cornell Maritime Press Inc

Chess Information & Research Center, *distributed by* W W Norton & Company Inc

Chester Book Co, *division of* Finney Company Inc

Chestnut Hills Press, *imprint of* BrickHouse Books Inc

Chicago Review Press, *distributed by* Gryphon House Inc

Chicago Tribune Crosswords, *imprint of* Random House Reference/Random House Puzzles & Games

Chicken House, *imprint of* Scholastic Trade Division

Chicken Soup for the Soul, *distributed by* Simon & Schuster Sales Division

Chicken Soup for the Soul Publishing, *distributed by* Simon & Schuster, Inc

Child Play, *distributor for* Specialty Press Inc

Children's Book Press, *imprint of* Lee & Low Books, Lee & Low Books Inc

Children's Classics, *imprint of* Penguin Random House Inc

Children's Media, *imprint of* Penguin Random House Inc

Children's Plus, *distributor for* Saddleback Educational Publishing

Children's Press, *distributed by* Perfection Learning Corp

Children's Press®, *imprint of* Scholastic Education

Children's Resources International, *distributed by* Gryphon House Inc

Child's Play®, *affiliate of* Child's Play (International) Ltd

Child's Play International, *distributed by* Heimburger House Publishing Co

The Child's World Inc, *distributor for* Tradition Books

Chilton Book Co, *distributed by* J J Keller & Associates, Inc

China Books, *division of* Sinomedia International Group, *distributor for* AsiaPac, Blue Poppy Press, CIBTC, Commercial Press, Foreign Languages Press, Joint Publishers, New World Press, Panda Books, Peace Books, Red Mansions Publishing

China Encyclopedia Publishing House, *distributed by* Homa & Sekey Books

China Institute, *distributed by* EastBridge

China Intercontinental Press, *distributed by* Homa & Sekey Books

China International Book Trading Co, *distributed by* Cheng & Tsui Co Inc

China Soft, *distributed by* Cheng & Tsui Co Inc

China Sprout, *distributed by* Cheng & Tsui Co Inc

China Zhejiang Publishing United Group, *distributed by* Homa & Sekey Books

Chinese University Press, *distributed by* Columbia University Press

Chipotle Publishing, *distributed by* Casemate | publishers

Chipstone Foundation, *distributed by* University Press of New England

Chiral House, *imprint of* Joshua Tree Publishing

Chiron Publications, *distributed by* SteinerBooks

Choi's Gallery, *distributed by* Gingko Press Inc

ChordBuddy, *distributed by* Hal Leonard Corp

Chosen Books, *division of* Baker Publishing Group

Chosen People Ministries, *distributed by* Lederer Books, Messianic Jewish Publishers

Christ Church-Philadelphia, *distributed by* Diane Publishing Co

Christian Classics, *imprint of* Ave Maria Press

Christian Journeys, *imprint of* Turner Publishing Co

Christian Large Print, *imprint of* Gale

Christian Network International, *distributor for* Pentecostal Publishing House

Christian Press, *division of* Brown Books Publishing Group

The Christian Science Publishing Society, *division of* First Church of Christ, Scientist, The First Church of Christ, Scientist

Chronicle, *distributor for* Country Music Foundation Press

Chronicle Books, *distributor for* Handprint Books Inc, Princeton Architectural Press, *distributed by* Hachette Book Group, Perfection Learning Corp

Chronicle Books LLC, *distributor for* Amicus Ink, Blue Apple Books, Handprint Books, Hardie Grant Books, Laurence King Publishing, Moleskine, Princeton Architectural Press, Quadrille Publishing, SmartLab, SmartsCo

Chronology Books, *imprint of* History Publishing Co LLC

Church Publishing Inc, *distributed by* Abingdon Press

ChurchSupplier.com, *division of* Neibauer Press

CIBTC, *distributed by* China Books

CIDEB, *distributed by* Beach Lloyd Publishers LLC

Cider Mill Press, *imprint of* Cider Mill Press Book Publishers LLC

Cider Mill Press Book Publishers LLC, *distributed by* Simon & Schuster, Simon & Schuster, Inc, Simon & Schuster Sales Division

Coleccion Ciencias Naturales, *imprint of* University of Puerto Rico Press

Cine-Med Inc, *distributor for* American College of Surgeons

Circle Time Publishers, *distributed by* Gryphon House Inc

Circlet Press Inc, *distributed by* SCB Distributors

Circumflex, *imprint of* Circlet Press Inc

Cistercian Publications, *imprint of* Liturgical Press, *distributed by* Liturgical Press

Citadel, *imprint of* Kensington Publishing Corp

Ciudad Nueva, *distributed by* New City Press

Civitas, *distributed by* HarperCollins Publishers

Clairview Books, *distributed by* SteinerBooks

Clara House Books, *imprint of* The Oliver Press Inc

Arnold Clarendon, *distributed by* Oxford University Press USA

Clarendon Press, *imprint of* Oxford University Press USA

Clarion Books, *imprint of* Houghton Mifflin Harcourt, Houghton Mifflin Harcourt Trade & Reference Division, *distributed by* Houghton Mifflin Harcourt

Clarity Sound & Light, *imprint of* Crystal Clarity Publishers

Arthur H Clark Co, *imprint of* University of Oklahoma Press

Clark City Press, *distributed by* Mountain Press Publishing Co

Ayebia Clarke Publishing Ltd, *distributed by* Lynne Rienner Publishers Inc

Clarkson Potter, *imprint of* Crown Publishing Group, Penguin Random House Inc, Clarkson Potter Publishers

Clarkson Potter Publishers, *imprint of* Crown Publishing Group, *distributor for* The Colonial Williamsburg Foundation

Clarkson Research Services Ltd, *distributed by* Marine Techniques Publishing

Coleccion Clasicos No Tan Clasicos, *imprint of* University of Puerto Rico Press

Classic Reprint Series, *imprint of* University of Alaska Press

Editions Classicae, *imprint of* Mel Bay Publications Inc

Classics Library, *imprint of* Recorded Books Inc, an RBmedia company

Classics With a Twist, *imprint of* Empire Publishing Service

Classroom Classics, *imprint of* World Citizens

Claymore Press, *distributed by* Casemate | publishers

Clear Creek Publishing, *distributed by* Gem Guides Book Co

Clear Day Books, *imprint of* Clarity Press Inc

Clear Vue Publishing, *distributed by* Casemate | publishers

Clearfield, *distributed by* Ericson Books

Clearfield Co Inc, *subsidiary of* Genealogical Publishing Co

Cleartype American Map Corp, *imprint of* American Map Corp

Cleis Press, *imprint of* Start Publishing LLC, *distributed by* Red Wheel/Weiser/Conari

Sydney Gurewitz Clemens, *distributed by* Gryphon House Inc

Clerc Books, *imprint of* Gallaudet University Press

Clerisy Press, *imprint of* AdventureKEEN

CLIE, *distributed by* Editorial Bautista Independiente

Client Distribution Services, *distributor for* Harvard Business Review Press

CliffNotes™, *imprint of* Houghton Mifflin Harcourt Trade & Reference Division

Clipper Audio (UK), *imprint of* Recorded Books Inc, an RBmedia company

Clo Iar-Chonnachta, *distributed by* Dufour Editions Inc

Clockroot Books, *imprint of* Interlink Publishing Group Inc

Cloister Recordings, *distributed by* Gateways Books & Tapes

Close Up Publishing, *division of* Close Up Foundation

Closson Press, *distributor for* Hearthside Books, Darvin Martin CDs, Retrospect Publishing, *distributed by* Janaway Publishing, Masthof Press

CMC, *distributor for* dbS Productions

CN Times Books, *imprint of* CN Times Inc, *distributor for* Bashu Publishing, Foreign Language Press, Intercontinental Press, Phoenix Publishing

Coach, *imprint of* Triumph Learning LLC

Coastal Living Books, *imprint of* Oxmoor House

Coastal New England Publications, *imprint of* Harvest Hill Press

Coastal Publishing, *distributed by* Epicenter Press Inc

Cochrane Library, *imprint of* John Wiley & Sons Inc

Codagen Guides USA, *imprint of* Interlink Publishing Group Inc

Codasat Canada Ltd, *distributor for* Silman-James Press Inc

Codhill Press, *distributed by* State University of New York Press, SUNY Press

Coffeetown Press, *distributed by* Epicenter Press Inc

Cogent OA, *imprint of* Taylor & Francis Inc

Cokesbury, *distributor for* Chalice Press, Morehouse Publishing

Cold Spring Harbor Laboratory Press, *division of* Cold Spring Harbor Laboratory, *distributed by* Oxford University Press USA

Cold Spring Press, *imprint of* Open Road Publishing

Collections Livrier, *imprint of* Progressive Press

The College Board, *distributed by* Macmillan

College Level Examination Series, *imprint of* National Learning Corp

College Proficiency Examination Series, *imprint of* National Learning Corp

Collegium Graphicum, *imprint of* Picasso Project, Alan Wofsy Fine Arts

Collins Press, *distributed by* Dufour Editions Inc

Colonial Society of Massachusetts, *distributed by* The University of Virginia Press

Colonial Williamsburg, *imprint of* The Colonial Williamsburg Foundation

The Colonial Williamsburg Foundation, *distributed by* Harry N Abrams Inc, John F Blair Publisher, Clarkson Potter Publishers, Lexington Books, National Geographic, Ohio University Press, Quite Specific Media Group Ltd, Rodale, Rowman & Littlefield, Scholastic Inc, Stackpole Books, Texas Tech University Press, The University of Virginia Press, University Press of New England, Yale University Press

Colorado Mountain Club Press, *distributed by* The Mountaineers Books

Colorprint American Map Corp, *imprint of* American Map Corp

Colourpoint, *distributed by* Casemate | publishers

Columba, *distributor for* Twenty-Third Publications

Columba Press, *distributed by* Dufour Editions Inc

Columbia Books on Architecture & the City, *distributed by* Columbia University Press

Columbia Business School Publishing, *imprint of* Columbia University Press

Columbia International Affairs Online (CIAO), *distributor for* University of California Institute on Global Conflict & Cooperation

Columbia University Press, *distributor for* Agenda Publishing, American Institute of Buddhist Studies, Austrian Film Museum Books, Auteur Publishing, Barbara Budrich Publishers, Chinese University Press, Columbia Books on Architecture & the City, Columbia University Press (Hitchcock Annual), Maria Curie-Sklodowska University Press, Harrington Park Press (frontlist titles), Hong Kong University Press, ibidem Press (English lang titles exc China & India), Jagiellonian University Press, Peterson Institute for International Economics, Slovenian Cinematheque, Social Science Research Council, Transcript Verlag, Tulika Books, University of Tokyo Press, Woodrow Wilson Center Press, *distributed by* Columbia University Press

Columbus Zoo, *distributed by* Lerner Publishing Group Inc

Combined Academic Publishers Ltd, *distributed by* New York University Press

ComicsLit, *imprint of* NBM Publishing Inc

Commercial Press, *distributed by* China Books

Common Courage Press, *distributor for* Odonian Press, Real Story Series

Commonwealth Editions, *imprint of* Applewood Books Inc

Commonwealth Scientific & Industrial Research Organization (CSIRO), *distributed by* Stylus Publishing LLC

Community Intervention, *distributor for* MAR*CO Products Inc

Companion Guides, *imprint of* Boydell & Brewer Inc

Companion House Press, *imprint of* Fox Chapel Publishing Co Inc

Compass, *imprint of* Brigantine Media

Compass American Guides, *imprint of* Fodor's Travel Publications

Compass Point Books, *imprint of* Capstone Publishers™

Compass Point Mysteries, *imprint of* Quincannon Publishing Group

Compass Publications, *distributed by* International Book Centre Inc, NACE International

Compendium, *distributed by* Casemate | publishers

Compendium Films, *distributed by* Casemate | publishers

Compu-Tek, *distributed by* Copywriter's Council of America™ (CCA)

CompuMaster, *division of* SkillPath Publications

Computer Connections, *imprint of* THE Learning Connection®

Comstock Publishing Associates, *imprint of* Cornell University Press

Conari Press, *distributed by* Gryphon House Inc

Concord Library, *imprint of* Beacon Press

Concordia Academic Press, *division of* Concordia Publishing House

Concordia Publishing House, *subsidiary of* The Lutheran Church, Missouri Synod, The Luthern Church, Missouri Synod

Confluence Book Services, *subsidiary of* White Cloud Press

Confluence Books, *imprint of* White Cloud Press

Congress Watch, *division of* Public Citizen

The Connecticut Law Tribune, *division of* ALM Media LLC

Consciousness Classics, *imprint of* Gateways Books & Tapes

Consortium, *distributor for* Enchanted Lion Books

Conspire Creative, *division of* Everything Goes Media LLC

Consumer Guide/PIL, *distributed by* Penguin Group USA, A Penguin Random House Company

Consumer Reports, *distributor for* United States Pharmacopeia

Consumertronics, *affiliate of* Top Secret Consumertronics Global (TSC-Global)

Context Press, *imprint of* New Harbinger Publications Inc

Continental AfrikaPublishers, *division of* Afrikamawu Miracle Mission, AMI Inc

Contra/Thought, *imprint of* Holmes Publishing Group LLC

Convergence, *imprint of* Six Gallery Press

Convergent Books, *imprint of* Crown Publishing Group

Thomas Cook Publishing, *distributed by* The Globe Pequot Press

Cooking Light Books, *imprint of* Oxmoor House

Cool Springs Press, *imprint of* Quarto Publishing Group USA Inc, *distributed by* Arcadia Publishing Inc

Coordinating Research Council Inc, *distributed by* SAE (Society of Automotive Engineers International)

Copernicus, *imprint of* Springer

Copley Custom Textbooks, *imprint of* XanEdu Publishing Inc

Copley Editions, *imprint of* Copley Custom Textbooks

Copley Publishing Group, *imprint of* Copley Custom Textbooks

Copper Canyon Press, *distributor for* American Poetry Review/Honickman

Copper Raven Press, *distributed by* Epicenter Press Inc

Coptales, *imprint of* Oak Tree Press

Copywriter's Council of America™ (CCA), *division of* The Linick Group Inc, *distributor for* Compu-Tek, National Association of Photo Sellers, PictureProfits® Tool Kit, World Dating Consultants™

Corbey Books, *imprint of* ACTA Publications

Core Library, *imprint of* ABDO Publishing Group

Cormorant Books, *imprint of* Down The Shore Publishing Corp

Cormorant Calendars, *imprint of* Down The Shore Publishing Corp

Cornell Maritime Press, *imprint of* Schiffer Publishing Ltd

Cornell Maritime Press Inc, *imprint of* Schiffer Publishing Ltd, *distributor for* Chesapeake Bay Maritime Museum, Independent Seaport Museum, Literary House Press, Maryland Historical Trust Press, Maryland Sea Grant Program

Cornell Southeast Asia Program (SEAP) Publications, *distributed by* Cornell University Press

Cornell University East Asia Program, *distributed by* University of Hawaii Press

Cornell University Press, *division of* Cornell University, *distributor for* Cornell Southeast Asia Program (SEAP) Publications, Leuven University Press, University of California Institute on Global Conflict & Cooperation

Cortina Institute of Languages, *division of* Cortina Learning International Inc, Cortina Learning International Inc (CLI)

Corwin, *distributed by* Council for Exceptional Children (CEC)

Corwin, a Sage Co, *distributor for* SAGE UK Resources for Educators

Corwin Press, *imprint of* SAGE Publishing

Corwin Press Inc, *subsidiary of* SAGE Publishing

Cosimo Books, *imprint of* Cosimo Inc

Cosimo Classics, *imprint of* Cosimo Inc

Cosimo Reports, *imprint of* Cosimo Inc

Cost Annuals, *division of* R S Means from The Gordian Group

Costume & Fashion Press, *imprint of* Quite Specific Media Group Ltd

Coteau Books, *distributed by* Orca Book Publishers

Cotsen Institute of Archaeology Press, *division of* University of California, Los Angeles

Cotton Candy Press, *imprint of* Unveiled Media LLC

Council for Exceptional Children (CEC), *distributor for* Brookes (selected titles), Corwin (selected titles), Free Spirit (selected titles), Guilford (selected titles), National Professional Resources (selected titles), *distributed by* ASCD, National Professional Resources (selected titles)

The Council for Research in Values & Philosophy, *imprint of* Council for Research in Values & Philosophy (RVP)

Council Oak Books, *distributed by* Gryphon House Inc

Council on Foreign Relations Press, *division of* Council on Foreign Relations, *distributed by* Brookings Institution Press

Counterpoint, *imprint of* Counterpoint Press LLC, *distributed by* HarperCollins Publishers

Country Bumpkin, *distributed by* Krause Publications Inc

Country Music Foundation Press, *division of* Country Music Hall of Fame® & Museum, *imprint of* Vanderbilt University Press, *distributed by* Chronicle, Oxford University Press Inc, Providence Publishing, Universe, Vanderbilt University Press

The Countryman Press, *division of* W W Norton & Company Inc, *imprint of* W W Norton & Company Inc, *distributed by* W W Norton & Company Inc, Penguin Books (CN only)

Courage to Change, *distributor for* MAR*CO Products Inc

Court Street Press, *imprint of* NewSouth Books

Coutts, *distributor for* Business Research Services Inc

Coutts Library Service, *distributor for* Primary Research Group Inc

Cove Press, *imprint of* US Games Systems Inc

Cover Craft, *imprint of* Perfection Learning Corp

Cover-to-Cover, *imprint of* Perfection Learning Corp

Covet, *imprint of* Entangled Publishing

Franklin Covey, *distributed by* SkillPath Publications

Coyote Press, *affiliate of* Archaeological Consulting

CQ Press, *imprint of* SAGE Publications, SAGE Publishing

Crabtree Publishing, *distributed by* Cheng & Tsui Co Inc, Perfection Learning Corp

Crabtree Publishing Co, *distributor for* Bayard, Maren Green

Crabtree Publishing Co Ltd, *subsidiary of* Crabtree Publishing Co

Crabtree Publishing Inc, *distributor for* Maren Green Publishing Inc

Craftsman Book Co, *distributor for* BNI Publications, Builders Book Inc, Building News Inc, Home Builders Press, *distributed by* The Aberdeen Group, American Technical Publishers Inc, BNI Publications, Builders Book Inc

Cramer, *distributed by* Wittenborn Art Books

Cramer (Geneva), *distributed by* Alan Wofsy Fine Arts

Cramer (Switzerland), *distributed by* Picasso Project

Cranbrook Institute of Science, *distributed by* Wayne State University Press

Craven Street Books, *imprint of* Linden Publishing Co Inc

Crazy Crow, *distributed by* Book Publishing Co

Crazy Games, *imprint of* Price Stern Sloan

CRC Press, *imprint of* Routledge, Taylor & Francis Group, an Informa Business, Taylor & Francis Inc, *distributor for* The Fairmont Press Inc, *distributed by* American Academy of Environmental Engineers & Scientists™, American Water Works Association (AWWA), NACE International, SAS Publishing

CRCS Publications, *distributed by* Book Publishing Co

Createspace, *distributor for* No Frills Buffalo

Creation House, *imprint of* Charisma Media

Creative Book Publishing, *distributed by* Orca Book Publishers

Creative Editions, *imprint of* The Creative Co

Creative Education, *imprint of* The Creative Co

Creative Homeowner, *imprint of* Fox Chapel Publishing Co Inc

Creative Keyboard, *imprint of* Mel Bay Publications Inc

Creative Keyboard Publications, *division of* Mel Bay Publications Inc

Creative Paperbacks, *imprint of* The Creative Co

Creative Publishing International, *imprint of* Quarto Publishing Group USA Inc

Creative Sales Corp, *subsidiary of* American Map Corp, *distributor for* American Map Corp, *distributed by* Hagstrom Map

Creighton University Press, *distributed by* Fordham University Press

Crescendo, *imprint of* Taplinger Publishing Co Inc

Crescent Books, *imprint of* Penguin Random House Inc

Cress Productions Co, *distributor for* MAR*CO Products Inc

Crestline, *imprint of* Book Sales

Cricket Cottage Publishing LLC, *unit of* Justice & Chaos Entertainment LLC

Crickhollow Books, *imprint of* Great Lakes Literary LLC

Crimeline, *imprint of* Penguin Random House Inc

Crimethinc, *distributed by* AK Press Distribution

Crimson Romance, *imprint of* Adams Media, F+W Media Inc

Crisp Books, *distributed by* Michigan Municipal League

Critical Path, *distributed by* Book Publishing Co

Croatian Musicological Society, *distributed by* Pendragon Press

Crocodile Books, *imprint of* Interlink Publishing Group Inc

Croft House Books, *distributor for* Primary Research Group Inc

Cross-Cultural Communications, *division of* Cross-Cultural Literary Editions Inc, *distributor for* Ad Infinitum Press, Arba Sicula (Magazine, US), Center of Emigrants from Serbia (Serbia), Decalogue Books (US), The Feral Press (US), Greenfield Review Press (US), Hochelaga (Canada), Immagine&Poesia (Italy), Legas Publishers (CN), Lips (Magazine & Press) (US), Pholiota Press Inc (England), The Seventh Quarry Press (Wales), Shabdaguchha (Magazine & Press) (Bangladesh & US), Sicilia Parra (Magazine, US), Word & Quill Press (US), *distributed by* Ad Infinitum Books, Hochelaga (Canada)

Cross-Cultural Prototypes, *imprint of* Cross-Cultural Communications

CrossKnowledge, *imprint of* John Wiley & Sons Inc

Crossquarter Breeze, *imprint of* Crossquarter Publishing Group

Crossroad, *imprint of* The Crossroad Publishing Co

CrossTIME, *imprint of* Crossquarter Publishing Group

Crossway, *division of* Good News Publishers

Crown, *distributed by* Perfection Learning Corp

Crown Archetype, *imprint of* Crown Publishing Group

Crown Books for Young Readers, *imprint of* Penguin Random House Inc

Crown Business, *imprint of* Crown Publishing Group

Crown Forum, *imprint of* Crown Publishing Group

Crown House Publishing Co LLC, *division of* Crown House Publishing Ltd, Crown House Publishing Ltd (UK Co), *distributor for* Developing Press Co, Human Alchemy Publications, Institute Press, Transforming Press

Crown Publishers, *imprint of* Crown Publishing Group

Crown Publishers Inc, *imprint of* Penguin Random House Inc

Crown Publishing Group, *division of* Penguin Random House LLC

CSI Publications, *imprint of* Christian Schools International

The CSIS Press, *division of* Center for Strategic & International Studies, *distributed by* Rowman & Littlefield

CSLI Publications, *distributed by* University of Chicago Press

CSWE Press, *division of* Council on Social Work Education

CT Corporation, *imprint of* Wolters Kluwer US Corp

CTW Publishing, *imprint of* Penguin Random House Inc

Coleccion Cuadernos La Torre, *imprint of* University of Puerto Rico Press

Coleccion Cuentos de un Mundo Perdido, *imprint of* University of Puerto Rico Press

Culinary Institute of America, *imprint of* John Wiley & Sons Inc

Coleccion Cultura Basica, *imprint of* University of Puerto Rico Press

Cumberland House, *imprint of* Sourcebooks Inc

CUNY Journalism Press, *division of* CUNY Graduate School of Journalism, *distributed by* OR Books

Cup of Tea Books, *imprint of* PageSpring Publishing

Curbstone Books, *imprint of* Northwestern University Press

Maria Curie-Sklodowska University Press, *distributed by* Columbia University Press

Curiosities, *imprint of* Norilana Books

Curnow Music, *distributed by* Hal Leonard Corp

Currach Press, *distributed by* Dufour Editions Inc

Curran Associates Inc, *distributor for* Trans Tech Publications Inc

Currency, *imprint of* Crown Publishing Group, Penguin Random House Inc

Current, *imprint of* Penguin Group USA, A Penguin Random House Company

Current Medicine Group, *imprint of* Springer

Current Protocols, *imprint of* John Wiley & Sons Inc

Curriculum Corp, *distributed by* Cheng & Tsui Co Inc

Curriculum Solutions, *division of* Scholastic Education

James Curry Ltd, *imprint of* Boydell & Brewer Inc

Fondation Custodia, *distributed by* Oak Knoll Press

Custom House, *imprint of* HarperCollins General Books Group

CWLA Press, *imprint of* Child Welfare League of America (CWLA)

CyberAge Books, *imprint of* Information Today, Inc

Cycle Publishing, *imprint of* Cycle Publishing LLC

Cynthia Publishing Co, *distributor for* HarperCollins Publishers

CYPI, *distributed by* Gingko Press Inc

Cypress House, *imprint of* Comp-Type Inc, *affiliate of* QED Press

D'Asia Vu Reprint Library, *imprint of* EastBridge

D-Day Publishing, *distributed by* Casemate | publishers

Da Capo Press, *imprint of* Perseus Books

Dafina, *imprint of* Kensington Publishing Corp

Dagger, *imprint of* Riverdale Avenue Books (RAB)

Daisy Rock Girl Guitars, *distributed by* Alfred Music Publishing

Dakota Institute, *distributed by* University of Oklahoma Press

Dalkey Archive Press, *distributed by* W W Norton & Company Inc

Dallas Museum of Art, *distributed by* Yale University Press

Dance Books Ltd, *distributor for* Princeton Book Co Publishers, *distributed by* Princeton Book Co Publishers

Dance Horizons, *imprint of* Princeton Book Co Publishers

Dance Horizons Video, *imprint of* Princeton Book Co Publishers

Dance Notation Bureau, *distributed by* Princeton Book Co Publishers

D&B Publishing, *distributed by* The Globe Pequot Press

C W Daniel, *distributed by* Beekman Books Inc

John Daniel & Co, *division of* Daniel & Daniel Publishers Inc, Daniel & Daniel Publishers Inc, *distributor for* Fithian Press, Perseverance Press

Dante Series, *imprint of* National Learning Corp

Dante University of America Press Inc, *distributed by* Branden Books

Dante University Press, *distributed by* Branden Publishing Co

DAP, *distributor for* National Gallery of Art

Dar Nun, *distributed by* Fons Vitae

Darby Creek Publishing, *imprint of* Lerner Publishing Group Inc

Dark Horse Books, *imprint of* Dark Horse Comics

Dark Horse Comics, *affiliate of* Dark Horse Entertainment, *distributed by* LPC Group Inc

Dark Oak Mysteries, *imprint of* Oak Tree Press

Darling & Co, *imprint of* Laughing Elephant

Dartmouth College Press, *imprint of* University Press of New England

The Dartnell Corporation, *subsidiary of* Eli Research Inc

Darwin® Books, *imprint of* The Darwin Press Inc

The Darwin Press Inc, *imprint of* Darwin® Books

David & Charles, *imprint of* F+W Media Inc, *distributed by* Krause Publications Inc

David Fickling Books, *imprint of* Penguin Random House Inc, Scholastic Trade Division

David Publishing, *distributor for* Fire Engineering Books & Videos

Davis Publications, *distributed by* Sterling Publishing Co Inc

DAW, *imprint of* Penguin Group USA, A Penguin Random House Company

DAW Books Inc, *imprint of* Penguin Group USA, A Penguin Random House Company, Penguin Group USA, A Penguin Random House Company, *distributed by* Penguin Group USA, A Penguin Random House Company, Penguin Group USA, A Penguin Random House Company

DAW/Fantasy, *imprint of* DAW Books Inc

DAW/Fiction, *imprint of* DAW Books Inc

DAW/Science Fiction, *imprint of* DAW Books Inc

The Dawn Horse Press, *division of* Avataric Pan-Communion of Adidam

Dawn Sign Press, *distributed by* Gryphon House Inc

DawnSignPress, *distributor for* Gallaudet University Press, MIT Press, Penguin Random House Inc, *distributed by* Gryphon House

Kathy Dawson Books, *imprint of* Penguin Young Readers Group

Dawsons Book Shop, *distributed by* Sunbelt Publications Inc

Day Hike Books Inc, *distributed by* The Globe Pequot Press

The Day That Was Different, *imprint of* Gallopade International Inc

DBI Books, *imprint of* Krause Publications Inc

dbS Productions, *distributed by* CMC

DC Comics, *imprint of* DC Entertainment

DC Entertainment, *division of* Warner Bros Entertainment, Warner Bros Entertainment Co

DC Nation, *imprint of* DC Entertainment

Walter De Gruyter Inc, *division of* Walter de Gruyter GmbH & Co KG, Walter de Gruyter GmbH & Co KG, *distributor for* De Gruyter Mouton

De Haske Publications, *distributed by* Hal Leonard Corp

Coleccion Obras Completas Eugenio Maria de Hostos, *imprint of* University of Puerto Rico Press

Juan de la Cuesta Hispanic Monographs, *imprint of* LinguaText LLC

De Lorme Atlas, *distributed by* American Map Corp, Hagstrom Map

Dearborn Trade, *distributor for* Appraisal Institute

Decalogue Books, *distributed by* Cross-Cultural Communications

Dechema, *distributor for* American Institute of Chemical Engineers (AIChE), *distributed by* American Institute of Chemical Engineers (AIChE)

B C Decker, *imprint of* Elsevier, Health Sciences Division

Dedalus Press, *distributor for* Syracuse University Press, *distributed by* Syracuse University Press

Deep Books Ltd, *distributor for* Boys Town Press

Deep River Books, *imprint of* Deep River Books LLC

Marcel Dekker Inc, *distributed by* NACE International

Del Rey, *imprint of* Penguin Random House Inc, Random House Publishing Group

Delacorte Books for Young Readers, *imprint of* Penguin Random House Inc

Delacorte Press, *imprint of* Penguin Random House Inc, Random House Children's Books

Delaney, *distributor for* Saddleback Educational Publishing

Delaney Books Inc, *subsidiary of* National Learning Corp

Delano Publishing, *distributed by* Epicenter Press Inc

Dell, *imprint of* Penguin Random House Inc, Random House Publishing Group

Dell Laurel Leaf, *imprint of* Penguin Random House Inc

Dell Yearling, *imprint of* Penguin Random House Inc

Delmar Publishers Inc, *distributed by* Gryphon House Inc

Delmonico/Prestel, *distributor for* American Federation of Arts

Delphinium Books, *distributed by* HarperCollins, HarperCollins Publishers

Delta, *imprint of* Penguin Random House Inc

Delta Education, *distributor for* National Council of Teachers of Mathematics (NCTM)

Delta Systems Inc, *distributor for* TESOL International Association

Democracy Is For People, *division of* Public Citizen

Demos Health, *imprint of* Demos Medical Publishing

Demos Medical Publishing, *division of* Springer Publishing Co

Dempsey Your Distributor, *distributor for* Ash Tree Publishing

Denver Art Museum, *distributed by* University of Oklahoma Press

Derrydale, *imprint of* Penguin Random House Inc

Deseret Book, *imprint of* Deseret Book Co

Deseret Book Co, *subsidiary of* Deseret Management Corp, Deseret Management Corp

Desert Charts, *division of* Wide World of Maps Inc

Design Originals, *imprint of* Fox Chapel Publishing Co Inc

Destiny Books, *imprint of* Inner Traditions International Ltd

Destiny Image Inc, *subsidiary of* Nori Media Group

Destiny Recordings, *imprint of* Inner Traditions International Ltd

Detroit Institute of Arts, *distributed by* Wayne State University Press

Developing Press Co, *distributed by* Crown House Publishing Co LLC

DeVorss & Co, *distributor for* Acropolis Books (Joel S Goldsmith titles), Touch for Health, White Eagle Publishing Trust (England)

Dey Street Books, *imprint of* HarperCollins General Books Group, HarperCollins Publishers

DharmaCafe, *distributed by* North Atlantic Books

Michael di Capua Books, *imprint of* Disney-Hyperion Books

Dial Books for Young Readers, *imprint of* Penguin Group USA, A Penguin Random House Company, Penguin Group USA, A Penguin Random House Company, Penguin Young Readers Group

The Dial Press, *imprint of* Penguin Random House Inc, Random House Publishing Group

Diamond Books, *imprint of* Berkley Publishing Group

Diane Publishing Co, *distributor for* Academy of Natural Sciences, American Philosophical Society, American Swedish Historical Museum, Augustinian Press, Chemical Heritage Foundation, Christ Church-Philadelphia, Friends of University of Princeton, Geneological Society of Pennsylvania, Library Company of Philadelphia, University of Pennsylvania Libraries

Dictionary Series, *imprint of* Bandanna Books

Didax Educational Resources, *distributor for* National Council of Teachers of Mathematics (NCTM)

Die Gestalten Verlag (DGV), *distributed by* Prestel Publishing

Dietz Press, *distributed by* Ericson Books

Difficult Subjects Made Easy, *imprint of* Letterbox/Papyrus of London Publishers USA

digitalculture, *imprint of* University of Michigan Press

Dipti, *imprint of* Lotus Press, *distributed by* Lotus Press

DiscoverNet Publishing, *division of* DiscoverNet

Discovery Books, *imprint of* Penguin Random House Inc

Discovery House Publishers, *division of* Our Daily Bread Ministries

Disinformation Books, *imprint of* Red Wheel/Weiser/Conari

Disney Book Group, *distributed by* Hachette Book Group

Disney Books for Young Readers, *imprint of* Penguin Random House Inc

Disney Children's Book Group, *division of* Disney Publishing Worldwide

Disney Editions, *imprint of* Disney Publishing Worldwide

Disney-Hyperion, *imprint of* Disney Publishing Worldwide

Disney-Hyperion Books, *imprint of* Disney Book Group

Disney Lucasfilm Press, *imprint of* Disney Publishing Worldwide

Disney Press, *division of* The Walt Disney Co, *imprint of* Disney Publishing Worldwide, *distributed by* Hachette Book Group (USA), Perfection Learning Corp

Disney Publishing Worldwide, *subsidiary of* The Walt Disney Co

Dissertation.com, *imprint of* Universal-Publishers Inc, *distributed by* Bertrams UK

Distri Books, *distributed by* Perfection Learning Corp

Distributed Art Publishers, *distributor for* American Federation of Arts

Distributed Art Publishers (DAP), *distributor for* The Museum of Modern Art (MoMA)

Diversion Books, *distributor for* Zubaan Books

Divine Arts, *imprint of* Michael Wiese Productions

DJ Inkers, *imprint of* Carson-Dellosa Publishing LLC

DK, *distributed by* Perfection Learning Corp

DK Publishing, *division of* Penguin Group USA, A Penguin Random House Company, Penguin Group USA, A Penguin Random House Company

Documentary Media, *distributed by* Epicenter Press Inc

Documentext, *imprint of* McPherson & Co

Documents of Modern Art, *imprint of* Wittenborn Art Books

Dogwise Publishing, *division of* Direct Book Service Inc

Dogwood Ridge Books, *distributed by* Maryland History Press

Tom Doherty Associates, LLC, *subsidiary of* Macmillan, *distributed by* Macmillan

Domain, *imprint of* Penguin Random House Inc

Domus Latina Publishing, *distributed by* Focus

The Donning Co, *distributed by* Schiffer Publishing Ltd

The Donning Company Publishers, *subsidiary of* Walsworth

Doodle Art, *imprint of* Price Stern Sloan

Dordt College Press, *affiliate of* Dordt College

Dorland Health, *division of* DecisionHealth LLC

Dorling Kindersley, *distributor for* Parachute Publishing LLC

Pam Dorman Books, *imprint of* Penguin Group USA, A Penguin Random House Company

Samuel Dorsky Museum of Art, *distributed by* State University of New York Press

Coleccion Dos Lenguas, *imprint of* University of Puerto Rico Press

Dossier, *imprint of* Ugly Duckling Presse

Dots & Lines Inc, *distributed by* Hal Leonard Corp

Double Dog, *imprint of* Yard Dog Press

Doubleday, *imprint of* Penguin Random House Inc, *distributed by* Perfection Learning Corp

Doubleday Bible Commentary, *imprint of* Penguin Random House Inc

Doubleday Books for Young Readers, *imprint of* Penguin Random House Inc

Doubleday/Galilee, *imprint of* Penguin Random House Inc

Doubleday/Image, *imprint of* Penguin Random House Inc

Doubleday/Nan A Talese, *imprint of* Knopf Doubleday Publishing Group

Dove Inspirational Press, *imprint of* Pelican Publishing Co

Dover Publications, *distributed by* Alfred Music Publishing

Down East Books, *imprint of* The Globe Pequot Press, *distributor for* Nimbus Publishing Ltd (selected titles, CN sales only)

Down Home Press, *distributed by* John F Blair Publisher

Downtown Bookworks, *distributed by* Simon & Schuster, Inc, Simon & Schuster Sales Division

Downtown Press, *imprint of* Gallery Books

Drache Publications, *distributed by* Finney Company Inc, Hobar Publications

Dragonfairy Press, *imprint of* Dragonfairy Press LLC

DragonFish Comics, *imprint of* Gauthier Publications Inc

Dragonfly, *imprint of* Random House Children's Books

Dragonfly Books, *imprint of* Penguin Random House Inc

Drama Publishers, *imprint of* Quite Specific Media Group Ltd

Drawn & Quarterly, *distributed by* Farrar, Straus & Giroux, LLC

Dream Works, *distributed by* Penguin Group USA, A Penguin Random House Company

Dreaming Robot Press, *imprint of* Studio Weaver

Dreamscape Media LLC, *division of* Midwest Tapes, *distributor for* Berrett-Koehler Publishers, Gildan Media, HarperCollins, Ideal Audiobooks, Penguin Random House Inc, Radio Archives

Dreamtech Press, *distributor for* Manning Publications Co

Drum Channel, *distributed by* Alfred Music Publishing

Dryad Press, *distributed by* University of Wisconsin Press

DTP, *imprint of* Penguin Random House Inc

Editions Alain Ducasse, *distributed by* Harry N Abrams Inc

Duckworth, *imprint of* The Overlook Press

Dufour Editions' Distributed Presses, *imprint of* Dufour Editions Inc

Dufour Editions Inc, *distributor for* Angel Books, Arcadia Books Ltd (London) (including Black-Amber, Bliss Books, Eurocrime & The Maia Press Ltd), Attic Press (including Atrium), Between the Lines, Blackstaff Press Ltd, Bloodaxe Books Ltd, Boatwhistle Books, Brandon Books, Clo Iar-Chonnachta, Collins Press, Columba Press, Currach Press, Eland Books/Sickle Moon Books, Flyleaf Press, Gill, Goblinshead, The Liffey Press, Lilliput Press Ltd, Little Toller Books, Y Lolfa (including Alcemi), Mercier, Messenger Publications, New Island Books, Norvik Press, O'Brien Press, Orpen Press, Persephone Books, Portnoy Publishing, Route, Salmon Poetry, Sandstone Press, Smokestack Books, Colin Smythe Ltd, Stinging Fly Press, University College Dublin Press, Vagabond Voices, Veritas, The Waywiser Press, Wordwell Books

Tim Duggan Books, *imprint of* Crown Publishing Group

Duke University Press, *distributor for* Forest History Society

Dumb Ox Books, *distributed by* St Augustine's Press Inc

Dumbarton Oaks, *distributed by* Harvard University Press

Thomas Dunne Books, *imprint of* St Martin's Press, LLC

Dunstan House, *distributed by* ECS Publishing Corp

Duo Press, *distributed by* Workman Publishing Co Inc

Duquesne University Press, *distributed by* University Press of New England

Editions Durand, *distributed by* Hal Leonard Corp

Dustbooks, *affiliate of* Associated Writing Programs, *distributor for* American Dust Publications

Dutton, *division of* Penguin Group USA, A Penguin Random House Company, Penguin Group USA, A Penguin Random House Company, *imprint of* Dutton Children's Books, Penguin Group USA, A Penguin Random House Company, *distributed by* Perfection Learning Corp

Dutton Children's Books, *imprint of* Penguin Group USA, A Penguin Random House Company, Penguin Group USA, A Penguin Random House Company

Duxbury, *distributed by* SAS Publishing

Eagan Press, *imprint of* AACC International

Eagle Editions, *imprint of* Heritage Books Inc

Eagle Wing Books, *distributed by* Adventures Unlimited Press (AUP)

Eagles Landing Publishing, *distributed by* Biographical Publishing Co

Eagle's View Publishing, *subsidiary of* Westwind Inc, Westwind Inc

Eakin Press, *imprint of* Wild Horse Media Group

Eamon Dolan Books, *imprint of* Houghton Mifflin Harcourt Trade & Reference Division

E&FN Spon, *distributed by* NACE International

Early Childhood Education, *division of* Scholastic Education

Early Classics of Science Fiction, *imprint of* Wesleyan University Press

Early Editions Books, *imprint of* Science & Humanities Press

Early Educator's Press, *distributed by* Gryphon House Inc

Early English Text Society, *imprint of* Boydell & Brewer Inc

Early Math, *imprint of* Sundance/Newbridge Publishing

Early Science, *imprint of* Sundance/Newbridge Publishing

Early Social Studies, *imprint of* Sundance/Newbridge Publishing

EarlyLight Books, *distributed by* Charlesbridge Publishing Inc

Earth Love Publishing, *distributed by* Gem Guides Book Co

Earth Pledge, *distributed by* Chelsea Green Publishing Co

Earthling Press, *subsidiary of* Awe-Struck Publishing

East Asian Legal Studies Program (EALSP), *division of* University of Maryland School of Law

East West Cultural Center, *distributed by* Lotus Press

East-West Export Books, *subsidiary of* University of Hawaii Press

EastBridge, *distributor for* China Institute, John Helde, International Christian University Foundation, Nippon Foundation, Yosifumi Taguchi

Eastern Book Company, *distributor for* Primary Research Group Inc

Eastland Press, *imprint of* Terence Dalton Ltd, *distributor for* Journal of Chinese Medicine Publications

Easy Money Press, *subsidiary of* Wolford & Associates

EC&M Books, *imprint of* Penton Media Inc

Ecco, *imprint of* HarperCollins General Books Group

Eckhart Teachings Inc, *distributed by* Sounds True Inc

Eco Logic Books, *distributed by* Chelsea Green Publishing Co

Ecological Design Institute, *distributed by* Chelsea Green Publishing Co

Ecological Design Press, *distributed by* Chelsea Green Publishing Co

Econo-Clad Books, *distributor for* Ozark Publishing Inc

Ecopress, *imprint of* Finney Company Inc

Ecosystem Research Group, *imprint of* Crumb Elbow Publishing

ECS Publishing Corp, *distributor for* Randol Bass Music, Dunstan House, Edition Delrieu, Gaudia Music & Arts, Stainer & Bell Ltd, Vireo Press

EDC Publishing, *division of* Educational Development Corp, Educational Development Corp, *distributor for* Usborne Publishing Ltd

Edda Publishing, *distributed by* Holmes Publishing Group LLC

Edda USA, *division of* Edda Publishing Ltd, Edda Publishing Ltd (Iceland)

EDFU Books, *distributed by* Adventures Unlimited Press (AUP)

Edgewise Press Inc, *distributor for* Editions d'Afrique du Nord, Libri Canali Bassi, Paolo Torti degli Alberti

ediciones Lerner, *imprint of* Lerner Publishing Group Inc

Edison Welding Institute, *distributor for* American Society for Nondestructive Testing

Edition Delrieu, *distributed by* ECS Publishing Corp

Editions du Signe, *distributed by* Gem Guides Book Co

Les Editions ETC, *distributed by* Lotus Press

Editions Orphee Inc, *distributed by* Theodore Presser Co

Editorial Bautista Independiente, *division of* Baptist Mid-Missions, *distributor for* Casa Bautista, CLIE, Portavoz

Editorial Concordia, *division of* Concordia Publishing House

Editorial Portavoz, *division of* Kregel Publications, *imprint of* Kregel Publications

EDU Reference, *distributor for* MAR*CO Products Inc

Educational Impressions Inc, *distributed by* Newbridge Communications Inc, Scholastic Inc, Scholastic-Tab Publications

Educational Insights, *subsidiary of* Learning Resources

Educational Media, *distributed by* MAR*CO Products Inc

Educational Media Corp, *distributor for* MAR*CO Products Inc

Educators for Social Responsibility, *distributed by* Gryphon House Inc

Educators Outlet, *distributor for* National Council of Teachers of Mathematics (NCTM)

Edupress Inc, *division of* Demco Inc

Edward & Dee, *imprint of* Russian Information Services Inc

Eerdmans Books for Young Readers, *imprint of* Wm B Eerdmans Publishing Co

Eifrig Publishing, *imprint of* Eifrig Publishing LLC

Eland Books/Sickle Moon Books, *distributed by* Dufour Editions Inc

Elbow Books, *imprint of* Crumb Elbow Publishing

Elderberry Press Inc, *distributor for* Poison Vine Books, Red Anvil Press

Electric Strawberry Press, *imprint of* Radix Press

Electrical Wholesaling, *imprint of* Penton Media Inc

The Electrochemical Society (ECS), *distributed by* American Institute of Physics (AIP) (journals), John Wiley & Sons (monographs)

The Electronics Source Book, *imprint of* Penton Media Inc

Elephant's Eye, *imprint of* The Overlook Press

Elite Books, *division of* Author's Publishing Cooperative (APC)

Elliott & Clark Publishing, *imprint of* River City Publishing LLC

Elsevier, *distributed by* Gulf Publishing Co

Elsevier Engineering Information (Ei), *subsidiary of* Elsevier Inc

Elsevier, Health Sciences Division, *division of* RELX Group PLC, *distributor for* G W Medical Publisher

Elsevier Inc, *subsidiary of* RELX Group PLC

Elsevier, Science & Technology Books, *distributed by* Marine Techniques Publishing

Elsevier Science Publishers, *distributed by* NACE International

Elsevier Science, Technology & Business Books, *distributor for* Marine Techniques Publishing

Elstreet Educational, *imprint of* Bartleby Press

Elva Resa, *imprint of* Elva Resa Publishing

Elvehjem Museum of Art, *distributed by* University of Wisconsin Press

Elysian Editions, *imprint of* Princeton Book Co Publishers

EM Books, *distributed by* Hal Leonard Corp

Emanate Books, *imprint of* Thomas Nelson

Ember, *imprint of* Random House Children's Books

Embrace, *imprint of* Entangled Publishing

Embraces, *imprint of* Zumaya Publications LLC

EMC Publishing LLC, *division of* New Mountain Learning LLC, *distributor for* Sybex Inc

Emerald Books, *affiliate of* YWAM Publishing, *distributed by* YWAM Publishing

Emergency Gazette, *imprint of* Ugly Duckling Presse

EMI Christian, *distributed by* Hal Leonard Corp

Emmaus Road Publishing Inc, *division of* St Paul Center for Biblical Theology

EMP, *imprint of* Easy Money Press

Empire, *imprint of* Empire Press Media/Avant-Guide

Empire Press Media/Avant-Guide, *unit of* Empire Press Media Inc

Empire Publishing Service, *division of* The Empire, The Empire (media group), *distributor for* Arsis Press, Arte Publico Press, Ian Henry Publications, ISH Group (worldwide exc Australia), Paul Mould Publishing

Empire State Editions, *imprint of* Fordham University Press

Empowerment Institute, *distributed by* Chelsea Green Publishing Co

Empty Bowl Press, *division of* Pleasure Boat Studio: A Literary Press, *distributed by* Pleasure Boat Studio: A Literary Press

Enchanted Lion Books, *distributed by* Consortium, Farrar, Straus & Giroux, LLC

Encore, *imprint of* Simon & Schuster Audio

Encore Editions, *imprint of* Star Publishing Co Inc

Encounter the Saints Series, *imprint of* Pauline Books & Media

Encyclopaedia Africana, *imprint of* Reference Publications Inc

Energy Arts, *distributed by* North Atlantic Books

Energy Information Administration (EIA), *imprint of* US Government Publishing Office, US Government Publishing Office (GPO), *distributed by* EPO, NTIS

Energy Program, *division of* Public Citizen

Energy Psychology Press, *division of* Energy Psychology Group

Enfield Publishers, *distributed by* Trans Tech Publications Inc

Engineering Foundation, *distributed by* American Institute of Chemical Engineers (AIChE)

Engineering Press, *distributed by* Oxford University Press USA

The English Spanish Foundation Series, *imprint of* me+mi publishing inc

Enigma, *imprint of* Zumaya Publications LLC

Enliven, *imprint of* Atria Books

Eno Publishers, *distributed by* John F Blair Publisher

Ensign Peak, *imprint of* Deseret Book Co

Enslow, *imprint of* Enslow Publishing LLC

Enslow Elementary, *imprint of* Enslow Publishing LLC

Entangled Edge, *imprint of* Entangled Publishing

Entangled Publishing, *distributed by* Macmillan

Entangled Select, *imprint of* Entangled Publishing

Entangled Teen, *imprint of* Entangled Publishing

EntertainmentPro, *imprint of* Quite Specific Media Group Ltd

Enthea Press, *imprint of* Ariel Press, *distributed by* Ariel Press

Entomological Society of America, *distributed by* Oxford University Press

Environmental Law Institute, *distributed by* Island Press

Epicenter Press Inc, *distributor for* Appell Publishing, Camel Press, Coastal Publishing, Coffeetown Press, Copper Raven Press, Delano Publishing, Documentary Media, Far North Press, Five Star Misadventures, Gold Fever Press, Joyful Productions, McRoy & Blackburn, Publishers, Meditation Press, Old Seattle Press, Patos Island Press, Raising Lucy Studios LLC, Raleigh Press, Reach for the Sky Publishing, RLO Media Productions, Saltry Press, Sprucehaven Publishing, Westridge Art, Winternights Publishing, Yamhill Press

Epigraph Publishing Service, *division of* Monkfish Book Publishing Co

EPO, *distributor for* Energy Information Administration (EIA)

EPS/School Specialty Literacy & Intervention, *division of* School Specialty Inc

Epworth, *distributed by* Presbyterian Publishing Corp (PPC)

EquipmentWatch, *imprint of* Penton Media Inc

Ergos Institute, *distributed by* North Atlantic Books

Ericson Books, *distributor for* Clearfield, Dietz Press, Southern Historical Press, *distributed by* Mountain Press, Byron Sistler

Lawrence Erlbaum Associates, *distributor for* National Association of Broadcasters (NAB)

Ernst & Sohn, *imprint of* John Wiley & Sons Inc

Eschat Press, *imprint of* Loft Press Inc

Editions Max Eschig, *distributed by* Hal Leonard Corp

Eshel Books, *imprint of* Bartleby Press

Essential Evidence Plus, *imprint of* John Wiley & Sons Inc

Essential Library, *imprint of* ABDO Publishing Group

ETA Cuisenaire, *distributor for* National Council of Teachers of Mathematics (NCTM)

Europa Editions, *distributed by* Penguin Random House Canada, Penguin Random House Inc

Europa World Noir, *imprint of* Europa Editions

European Mathematical Society, *distributed by* American Mathematical Society

Eurospan Group, *distributor for* Association for Talent Development (ATD) Press

The Eurospan Group, *distributor for* Health Professions Press

Eurotica, *imprint of* NBM Publishing Inc

M Evans & Company, *imprint of* Rowman & Littlefield Publishing Group

Evergreen Pacific Publishing, *imprint of* Evergreen Pacific Publishing Ltd

Evergreen Press, *distributed by* Heimburger House Publishing Co

Everyman Chess, *distributed by* The Globe Pequot Press

Everyman's Classic Library in Paperback, *imprint of* Tuttle Publishing

Everyman's Library, *imprint of* Penguin Random House Inc

Everything, *imprint of* Adams Media

Everything DiSC®, *imprint of* John Wiley & Sons Inc

Everything Goes Media, *imprint of* Everything Goes Media LLC

Evolver Editions, *imprint of* North Atlantic Books

Ex Libris, *imprint of* Rizzoli International Publications Inc

Excelsior Editions, *imprint of* State University of New York Press, *distributor for* Albany Institute of History & Art, Uncrowned Queens

Executive Essentials, *imprint of* Health Administration Press

Executive Reports, *imprint of* Aspatore Books

The Experiment, *distributed by* Workman Publishing, Workman Publishing Co Inc

Explorer Publishing, *distributed by* The Globe Pequot Press

Exploring Community History Series, *imprint of* Krieger Publishing Co

Expressive Editions, *imprint of* Cross-Cultural Communications

Faber Music, *distributed by* Alfred Music Publishing

Faber Music Ltd, *distributed by* Hal Leonard Corp

Facets Video, *distributed by* Cheng & Tsui Co Inc

Fact Publishers, *imprint of* Cross-Cultural Communications

Facts On File, *imprint of* Infobase Learning

Fair Winds Press, *imprint of* Quarto Publishing Group USA, Quarto Publishing Group USA Inc

Fairchild Books, *division of* Bloomsbury Publishing PLC

Fairfax Genealogical Society, *distributed by* Heritage Books Inc

Fairleigh Dickinson University Press, *affiliate of* Rowman & Littlefield, *distributed by* Rowman & Littlefield

The Fairmont Press Inc, *distributed by* CRC Press, Taylor & Francis

Faith Alive, *imprint of* Faith Alive Christian Resources

Faith Alive Christian Resources, *imprint of* Christian Reformed Church in North America

Faith & Culture, *imprint of* Pauline Books & Media

Faith & Fellowship Publishing, *subsidiary of* Church of the Lutheran Brethren

Faith Library Publications, *subsidiary of* RHEMA Bible Church, *distributed by* Appalachian, Harrison House, Spring Arbor, Whitaker

Faith Press, *imprint of* Winters Publishing

Faith Works Books, *distributor for* American Carriage House Publishing

faithQuest, *imprint of* Brethren Press

FaithWalk Publishing, *imprint of* CSS Publishing Co Inc

FaithWords, *imprint of* Hachette Nashville

Falcon®, *imprint of* The Globe Pequot Press

Falcon Press, *imprint of* The Original Falcon Press

Family Center of Nova University, *distributed by* Gryphon House Inc

Family Communications, *distributed by* Hal Leonard Corp

Family Films, *division of* Concordia Publishing House

Family Tree Books, *imprint of* Betterway Books

Famous Artists School, *division of* Cortina Learning International Inc

Famous Writers School, *division of* Cortina Learning International Inc

F+W Media Inc, *distributed by* Perfection Learning Corp

Fanfare, *imprint of* Penguin Random House Inc

Fantagraphics Books, *distributed by* W W Norton & Company Inc

Fantasy Writers' Asylum, *imprint of* Yard Dog Press

Far Muse Press, *imprint of* Loft Press Inc

Far North Press, *distributed by* Epicenter Press Inc

Far to the North Press, *distributed by* University of Alaska Press

Far West Publishing, *imprint of* Sun Publishing Company

Farrar, Straus & Giroux Books for Young Readers, *imprint of* Farrar, Straus & Giroux, LLC, Macmillan Children's Publishing Group

Farrar, Straus & Giroux Inc, *distributor for* Aperture Books, *distributed by* Perfection Learning Corp

Farrar, Straus & Giroux, LLC, *subsidiary of* Macmillan, *distributor for* Drawn & Quarterly, Enchanted Lion Books, Gray Wolf Books

Father & Son Publishing Inc, *distributor for* BADM Books

Fatima Crusader, *distributor for* Angelus Press

Favorable Impressions, *affiliate of* The Lincoln Library (now part of the FactCite family of databases)

Fawcett, *imprint of* Penguin Random House Inc, *distributed by* Perfection Learning Corp

Fearless Critic Media, *distributed by* Algonquin Books

Federal Street Press, *division of* Merriam-Webster Inc

Feldheim Publishers, *distributor for* Hamadia Publishing, Jerusalem Publications

Feldheim Publishers USA, *imprint of* Feldheim Publishers

Jean Feldman, *distributed by* Gryphon House Inc

H B Fenn, *distributor for* Oxmoor House

Fenris Brothers, *imprint of* Crossquarter Publishing Group

The Feral Press, *distributed by* Cross-Cultural Communications

Margaret Ferguson Books, *imprint of* Holiday House Inc

Ferguson Publishing, *imprint of* Infobase Learning

Leland Fetzer, *distributed by* Sunbelt Publications Inc

Fiction Collective 2 (FC2), *imprint of* University of Alabama Press

Fiction Collective Two Inc (FC2), *imprint of* University of Alabama Press, *distributed by* University of Alabama Press

Fieldstone Alliance, *imprint of* Turner Publishing Co

53rd State Press, *distributed by* Theatre Communications Group

Fighting High Publishing, *distributed by* Casemate | publishers

Figure 1 Publishing, *distributed by* Prestel Publishing

Filaree Productions, *distributed by* Chelsea Green Publishing Co

Film Movement, *imprint of* Recorded Books Inc, an RBmedia company

Filmakers Library, *imprint of* Alexander Street, a ProQuest Company

The Final Edition, *imprint of* Crumb Elbow Publishing

Financial Executives Research Foundation Inc (FERF), *affiliate of* Financial Executives International (FEI)

Financial Ratings Series, *imprint of* Grey House Publishing Inc™

Financial Times Press, *imprint of* Pearson Education Ltd

Financial Times Publishing, *distributed by* Trans-Atlantic Publications Inc

FineEdge.com LLC, *distributed by* Heritage House, Sunbelt Publications Inc

Finney Company Inc, *distributor for* Drache Publications, Joyce Shellhart

Fire Engineering Books & Videos, *division of* PennWell Books, *distributor for* Brady, Idea Bank, IFSTA, Mosby, *distributed by* David Publishing, Fire Protection Publications

Fire Protection Publications, *distributor for* Fire Engineering Books & Videos

Firebird, *imprint of* Penguin Young Readers Group

Firefly, *imprint of* Lighthouse Publishing of the Carolinas, *distributed by* Perfection Learning Corp

Firefly Books Ltd, *distributed by* Heimburger House Publishing Co

The Firelands Writing Center (Heartlands Magazine), *distributed by* Bottom Dog Press

Fireside Fiction, *imprint of* Heritage Books Inc

First Avenue, *distributed by* Perfection Learning Corp

First Avenue Editions, *imprint of* Lerner Publishing Group Inc

First Choice, *imprint of* Sunbelt Publications Inc

First Choice Chapter Books, *imprint of* Penguin Random House Inc

First Fruits of Zion, *distributed by* Lederer Books, Messianic Jewish Publishers

First Lessons, *imprint of* Mel Bay Publications Inc

First Second Books, *imprint of* Roaring Brook Press

FirstForumPress, *division of* Lynne Rienner Publishers Inc

Fish Pond, *imprint of* Deep River Books LLC

Fisher Productions, *imprint of* Franciscan Media

Fithian Press, *distributed by* John Daniel & Co

Fitzroy Books, *imprint of* Regal House Publishing

5 Continents Editions, *distributed by* Harry N Abrams Inc

Five Star™, *imprint of* Gale

Five Star Misadventures, *distributed by* Epicenter Press Inc

Flammarion, *imprint of* Rizzoli International Publications Inc

Editions Flammarion, *distributed by* Rizzoli International Publications Inc

Flashkids, *imprint of* Sterling Publishing Co Inc

Fleamarket Music, *distributed by* Hal Leonard Corp

Flirt, *imprint of* Penguin Random House Inc, Random House Publishing Group

Florida Academic Press, *division of* FAP Books Inc, *distributor for* Publisher's Stone Publications

Florida Literary Foundation (FLF) Press, *imprint of* STARbooks Press

Floris Books, *distributor for* Lindisfarne Books, *distributed by* Gryphon House Inc, SteinerBooks

Flower Press, *distributed by* Chelsea Green Publishing Co

Flux, *imprint of* North Star Editions Inc

Flying Machines Press, *imprint of* Paladin Press

Flying Pen Press Colorado, *imprint of* Flying Pen Press LLC

Flying Pen Press Park Trek, *imprint of* Flying Pen Press LLC

Flying Pen Press Rocky Mountain West, *imprint of* Flying Pen Press LLC

Flying Pen Press Science Fiction, *imprint of* Flying Pen Press LLC

Flying Pen Press Southwest, *imprint of* Flying Pen Press LLC

Flying Pen Press Travel Guides, *imprint of* Flying Pen Press LLC

Flying Piggybank Press, *imprint of* Flying Pen Press LLC

Flyleaf Press, *distributed by* Dufour Editions Inc

FMP, *imprint of* Forward Movement

Focal Press, *distributor for* National Association of Broadcasters (NAB), *distributed by* Marine Techniques Publishing

Focus, *imprint of* Hackett Publishing Co Inc, *distributor for* Domus Latina Publishing

Focus on the Family, *distributed by* Baker Books, Moody Press, Tyndale House Publishers, Tyndale House Publishers Inc, Zondervan

Focus Readers, *imprint of* North Star Editions Inc

Fodor's, *imprint of* Fodor's Travel Publications

Fodor's Travel Publications, *division of* Internet Brands Inc

Folger Shakespeare Library, *imprint of* Simon & Schuster

Fondation pour la Memoire de la Shoah, *distributed by* Beach Lloyd Publishers LLC

Fons Vitae, *distributor for* African American Islamic Institute, Anqa Press (UK), Aperture (NY), Archetype (UK), Broadstone Books, Dar Nun, Golganooza Press (UK), Islamic Texts Society (UK), Matheson Trust, Parabola, Paragon, Parvardigar Press, Sophia Perennis, Pir Press (NY), Qiblah Books, Quilliam Press (UK), Sandala Productions, Sri Lanka Institute of Traditional Studies, Thesaurus Islamicus Foundation, Tradigital, White Thread Press (US), Wisdom Foundation, World Wisdom (US), Zaytuna Institute Press (US)

Fonthill Media, *distributed by* Casemate | publishers

Food & Agriculture Organization of the United Nations (FAO), *distributed by* United Nations Publications

Food52 Works, *imprint of* Ten Speed Press

The Food Paper, *division of* Gault Millau Inc/ Gayot Publications

Footprint Books, *distributor for* Boys Town Press, *distributed by* New York University Press

Footprint Books Pty Ltd, *distributor for* Health Professions Press

For Dummies®, *imprint of* John Wiley & Sons Inc

Fordham University Press, *distributor for* Creighton University Press, Institute for Advanced Study in the Theatre Arts (IASTA), Little Room Press, The Reconstructionist Press, Rockhurst University Press, St Bede's Publications, University of San Francisco Press, *distributed by* Heimburger House Publishing Co, Oxford University Press (US & CN)

ForeEdge, *imprint of* University Press of New England

Foreign Affairs Information Service, *imprint of* George Kurian Reference Books

Foreign Language Press, *distributed by* CN Times Books

Foreign Languages Press, *distributed by* China Books

Forest History Society, *distributed by* Duke University Press

Forest of Peace, *imprint of* Ave Maria Press

Forever, *imprint of* Grand Central Publishing

Forever Nuts, *imprint of* NBM Publishing Inc

Forever Regency, *imprint of* ImaJinn Books

Forever Yours, *imprint of* Grand Central Publishing

Forge Books, *imprint of* Tom Doherty Associates, LLC

Formac, *distributed by* Casemate | publishers

Formac Publishing, *distributed by* Orca Book Publishers

Fortress Press, *imprint of* Augsburg Fortress Publishers, Publishing House of the Evangelical Lutheran Church in America

Forward Movement, *affiliate of* The Episcopal Church, *distributor for* Anglican Book Centre

Frances Foster Books, *imprint of* Farrar, Straus & Giroux Books for Young Readers

Walter Foster Jr, *imprint of* Quarto Publishing Group USA Inc

Walter Foster Publishing, *imprint of* Quarto Publishing Group USA Inc, *distributed by* Lerner Publishing Group Inc

Walter Foster Publishing Inc, *imprint of* Quarto Publishing Group USA, Quarto Publishing Group USA Inc

G T Foulis, *distributed by* Haynes Manuals Inc

Foundation for Deep Ecology, *distributed by* Chelsea Green Publishing Co

Foundation Press, *imprint of* West Academic Publishing

Foundry, *distributed by* Casemate | publishers

The Fountain, *imprint of* Tughra Books

Four Rivers Press, *imprint of* McClanahan Publishing House Inc

Four Seas, *imprint of* Branden Books

Four Way Books, *distributed by* University Press of New England

4th Dimension Press, *imprint of* ARE Press

Fowler Museum at UCLA, *distributed by* University of Washington Press

Fox Chapel Publishing Co Inc, *distributor for* Reader's Digest, Taunton Sterling Dover

Fox Maple Press, *distributed by* Chelsea Green Publishing Co

Franciscan Communications, *imprint of* Franciscan Media, *distributed by* Franciscan Media

Franciscan Media, *distributor for* Franciscan Communications (books & videos), Ikonographics (videos)

Franklin, Beedle & Associates Inc, *distributor for* Arcus, Battlebridge, Blue Sky Gallery, Photolucida Book, Ringing Bell Press, Tayo Press, Wordstock

Franklin Street Books, *imprint of* Inkwater Press

Franklin Watts®, *imprint of* Scholastic Education

Franko Maps, *distributed by* Wide World of Maps Inc

Frederator Books LLC, *distributed by* Simon & Schuster, Inc, Simon & Schuster Sales Division

Free Press, *imprint of* Simon & Schuster, *distributed by* Center for Creative Leadership LLC

Free Spirit, *distributed by* Council for Exceptional Children (CEC), Perfection Learning Corp, Torah Aura Productions

Freedom Fox Press, *imprint of* Dancing Lemur Press LLC

Freedom Press, *distributed by* AK Press Distribution

Freeform, *imprint of* Disney Publishing Worldwide

W H Freeman, *imprint of* Macmillan Learning, *distributor for* American Geosciences Institute (AGI)

Freestone, *imprint of* Peachtree Publishers

Samuel French Inc, *distributor for* Baker's Plays, Samuel French Ltd (UK), *distributed by* Baker's Plays, Samuel French Ltd (UK)

Samuel French Ltd, *distributor for* Samuel French Inc, *distributed by* Samuel French Inc

Fresco Fine Art Publications LLC, *distributed by* University of New Mexico Press

Fresh Air Books, *imprint of* Upper Room Books

Friends of University of Princeton, *distributed by* Diane Publishing Co

Friends United Press, *subsidiary of* Friends United Meeting

Friendship Bible Studies, *imprint of* Faith Alive Christian Resources

Frog Books, *imprint of* North Atlantic Books

Frog Legs Ink, *imprint of* Gauthier Publications Inc

Front Street Press, *distributed by* Casemate | publishers

Front Table Books, *imprint of* Cedar Fort Inc

La Frontera Publishing, *distributed by* University of New Mexico Press

Frontline Books, *distributed by* Casemate | publishers

FT Press, *imprint of* Financial Times Press

Fulcrum, *distributed by* Perfection Learning Corp

Fulgur Ltd, *distributed by* Holmes Publishing Group LLC

Fun For All, *imprint of* Kidsbooks LLC

Fun Places Publishing, *distributed by* Sunbelt Publications Inc

FurnitureCore, *distributor for* AMA Research, Business & Research Associates

Future Psychiatry Press, *imprint of* Loving Healing Press Inc

G Q Publishing, *imprint of* Great Quotations Inc

G-unit, *imprint of* Gallery Books

G W Medical Publisher, *distributed by* Elsevier, Health Sciences Division

Galaxy Audio, *imprint of* Galaxy Press

Galaxy Music Corp, *imprint of* ECS Publishing Corp

Gale, *division of* Cengage Learning, *unit of* Cengage Learning, *subsidiary of* Cengage Learning

Gale Research Inc, *distributor for* Business Research Services Inc

Gallaudet University Press, *distributor for* Signum Verlag, *distributed by* DawnSignPress

Gallery Books, *imprint of* Gallery Publishing Group

Gallery 13, *imprint of* Gallery Books

Gallup, *distributed by* Simon & Schuster, Inc, Simon & Schuster Sales Division

Games Workshop, *distributed by* Simon & Schuster, Inc, Simon & Schuster Sales Division

Jeffrey Garcia, *distributed by* Sunbelt Publications Inc

Garden Art Press, *imprint of* Antique Collectors' Club Ltd

Gareth Stevens Publishing, *imprint of* The Rosen Publishing Group Inc

Garland-Clark Editors, *distributed by* Players Press Inc

Garland Publishers, *distributor for* University of California Institute on Global Conflict & Cooperation

Garland Science, *imprint of* Routledge, Taylor & Francis Inc

Garland Science Publishing, *imprint of* Taylor & Francis Group, an Informa Business

John Garrett, *distributor for* Twenty-Third Publications

Gaslight Publications, *imprint of* Empire Publishing Service

Gateway Editions, *imprint of* Regnery Publishing

Gateway to Healthcare Management, *imprint of* Health Administration Press

Gateways Books & Tapes, *division of* Institute for the Development of the Harmonious Human Being Inc, Institute for the Development of the Harmonious Human Being Inc, *distributor for* Cloister Recordings (audio & video tapes)

Gateways Fine Art Series, *imprint of* Gateways Books & Tapes

Gaudia Music & Arts, *distributed by* ECS Publishing Corp

Gault Millau, *imprint of* Gault Millau Inc/Gayot Publications

Gault Millau Inc/Gayot Publications, *distributed by* Publishers Group West

GAYOT, *imprint of* Gault Millau Inc/Gayot Publications

Geared Up Publications, *imprint of* Schiffer Publishing Ltd

Gecko Press, *distributed by* Lerner Publishing Group Inc

Gefen Books, *distributor for* Bar Ilan, Magnes Press

Gem Guides Book Co, *distributor for* Borden Publishing, Brynmorgen Press, Clear Creek Publishing, Earth Love Publishing, Editions du Signe, GemStone Press, Golden West Books, Grand Canyon Association, Heaven & Earth Press, Hexagon Press, International Jewelry Publications, George R Jezek Photography, Cy Johnson & Son, KC Publications Inc, Many Moons Press, Naturegraph, Nevada Publications, Out of This World Press, Pinyon Publishing, Primer Publications, Ram Publishing, Recreation Sales, Shortfuse Press, Sierra Press, Delos Toole, Trees Co, Tri-Star Boze Books, Weseanne Publications, *distributed by* Nevada Publications

Gembooks, *imprint of* Gem Guides Book Co

GemStone Press, *imprint of* Turner Publishing Co, *distributed by* Gem Guides Book Co

Gender Genre, *imprint of* Bandanna Books

Genealogical Publishing Co, *subsidiary of* Genealogical.com

Geneological Society of Pennsylvania, *distributed by* Diane Publishing Co

General Aptitude & Abilities Series, *imprint of* National Learning Corp

General Education Services (New Zealand), *distributed by* Abrams Learning Trends

Genetic Engineering & Biotechnology News, *division of* Mary Ann Liebert Inc

Geneva Press, *imprint of* Presbyterian Publishing Corp (PPC)

Gennadeion Monographs, *imprint of* ASCSA Publications

Gentle World, *distributed by* Book Publishing Co

Geological Society of London, *distributor for* AAPG (American Association of Petroleum Geologists), *distributed by* AAPG (American Association of Petroleum Geologists)

Geology & Geography of Alaska Series, *imprint of* University of Alaska Press

Geology Underfoot Series, *imprint of* Mountain Press Publishing Co

Geophysical Institute, *distributed by* University of Alaska Press

Georgetown University Press, *distributed by* The Johns Hopkins University Press

The Georgia Literary Association, *imprint of* Blood Moon Productions Ltd

GetFitNow.com Books, *imprint of* Hatherleigh Press Ltd

Getting Into, *imprint of* Mel Bay Publications Inc

Getting Smart, *imprint of* Eifrig Publishing LLC

Getty, *distributed by* Oxford University Press USA

Getty Publications, *distributed by* Harry N Abrams Inc, University of Chicago Press (US only)

Gibbs-Smith, *distributor for* Sourced Media Books

Gifted Psychology Press, *imprint of* Great Potential Press Inc

Gig Savers, *imprint of* Mel Bay Publications Inc

Gilbert, *imprint of* West Academic Publishing

Gilcrease Museum, *distributed by* University of Oklahoma Press

Gildan Media, *distributed by* Dreamscape Media LLC, Hachette Book Group

D Giles Ltd, *distributor for* American Federation of Arts

Gill, *distributed by* Dufour Editions Inc

Maureen Gilmer, *distributed by* Sunbelt Publications Inc

Gingko Press, *distributed by* Gingko Press Inc

Gingko Press Inc, *distributor for* All Rights Reserved Ltd, Archimap, Art Power, Basheer, Choi's Gallery, CYPI, Gingko Press, Rebel Arts, Sandu Publications, Sendpoints Books Co Ltd, Upper Playground, Victionary, Wax Facts Press, Zero+ Publishing

GIT Verlag, *imprint of* John Wiley & Sons Inc

Gival Press, *imprint of* Gival Press LLC

Michael Glazier Books, *imprint of* Liturgical Press

Glencannon, *distributed by* Mystic Seaport Museum Inc

Glencoe, *imprint of* McGraw-Hill School Education Group

Glencoe/McGraw-Hill, *imprint of* McGraw-Hill Education

Peter Glenn Publications, *division of* Blount Communications Corp

Global Professional Publishing, *distributed by* Stylus Publishing LLC

Global Research, *distributed by* Progressive Press

Global Trade Watch, *division of* Public Citizen

Globe Pequot, *imprint of* The Globe Pequot Press

Globe Pequot Press, *distributed by* Heimburger House Publishing Co

The Globe Pequot Press, *division of* Rowman & Littlefield Publishing Group, *distributor for* Appalachian Mountain Club Books, Boone & Crockett Club, Thomas Cook Publishing, D&B Publishing, Day Hike Books Inc, Everyman Chess, Explorer Publishing, Globetrotter, Good Sam's, Jonglez Publishing, Montana Historical Society Press, New Holland Publishers (UK) Ltd, Oval Books (UK), Alastair Sawday Publishing (co-publr), Stoecklein Publishing, 30 Words, Trailblazer Publications, Western Horseman Books

Globetrotter, *distributed by* The Globe Pequot Press

Glove Pequot, *distributed by* Sunbelt Publications Inc

GOAL/QPC, *distributor for* American Society for Quality (ASQ)

Goblinshead, *distributed by* Dufour Editions Inc

Godwin Books, *imprint of* Henry Holt and Company, LLC

GoFacts Guided Writing, *imprint of* Sundance/Newbridge Publishing

Gold Fever Press, *distributed by* Epicenter Press Inc

Golden Books, *imprint of* Penguin Random House Inc, Random House Children's Books, *distributed by* Perfection Learning Corp

Golden Books Adult Publishing, *imprint of* St Martin's Press, LLC

Golden Dawn Publications, *imprint of* The Original Falcon Press

Golden Guides, *imprint of* St Martin's Press, LLC

Golden West Books, *distributed by* Gem Guides Book Co

Golden West Cookbooks, *division of* American Traveler Press

Golganooza Press, *distributed by* Fons Vitae

Gollehon Books, *imprint of* Gollehon Press Inc

Gomer Press, *distributed by* Beekman Books Inc

Good Sam's, *distributed by* The Globe Pequot Press

Gooseberry Patch, *imprint of* The Globe Pequot Press, *distributed by* Andrews McMeel Publishing LLC

Goosebottom Books, *imprint of* Goosebottom Books LLC

Gorgias Press LLC, *distributor for* Yeshiva University Museum Press

Gospel Publishing House, *imprint of* Gospel Publishing House (GPH)

Gospel Publishing House (GPH), *division of* General Council of the Assemblies of God

Government Jobs Series, *imprint of* PREP Publishing

Gower, *imprint of* Elsevier, Health Sciences Division

Colin Gower, *distributed by* Krause Publications Inc

GPC/Gollehon, *imprint of* Gollehon Press Inc

GPP® Travel, *imprint of* The Globe Pequot Press

Grab a Pencil Press, *imprint of* Applewood Books Inc

Graduate Record Examination Series, *imprint of* National Learning Corp

Gramercy Books, *imprint of* Penguin Random House Inc

Gramophone, *distributed by* Omnibus Press

Grand Canyon Association, *distributed by* Gem Guides Book Co

Grand Central/Hachette Large Print, *distributed by* Thorndike Press

Grand Central Life & Style, *imprint of* Grand Central Publishing

Grand Central Publishing, *division of* Hachette Book Group

Grand Harbor Press, *imprint of* Brilliance Audio

Donald M Grant Publisher Inc, *distributor for* Archival, Oswald Train

Granta, *distributed by* Penguin Group USA, A Penguin Random House Company

Graphia, *imprint of* Houghton Mifflin Harcourt Trade & Reference Division

Graphic Arts Books, *unit of* Ingram Content Group Inc

Graphic Planet, *imprint of* ABDO Publishing Group

Graphic Universe™, *imprint of* Lerner Publishing Group Inc

Graphix, *imprint of* Scholastic Trade Division

Grave Issues, *imprint of* Spinsters Ink

Gray Wolf Books, *distributed by* Farrar, Straus & Giroux, LLC

Great Books of the Islamic World, *imprint of* Kazi Publications Inc

The Great Courses, *imprint of* Recorded Books Inc, an RBmedia company

Great Explorer Series, *imprint of* University of Alaska Press

Great Lakes Books, *imprint of* Wayne State University Press

Great Outdoors Publishing Co, *imprint of* Finney Company Inc

Great Potential Press Inc, *division of* Anodyne Inc, Anodyne Inc

The Greeley Co, *subsidiary of* HCPro Inc

Green Books, *distributed by* Chelsea Green Publishing Co

Green Building Press, *distributed by* Chelsea Green Publishing Co

Green Grass Press, *distributed by* Sunbelt Publications Inc

Green Knees, *imprint of* Azro Press

Green Man Publishing, *distributed by* Chelsea Green Publishing Co

Green Tiger Press, *imprint of* Laughing Elephant

Greenberg Books, *imprint of* Kalmbach Publishing Co

Greenbranch, *distributed by* Medical Group Management Association (MGMA)

Alice Greene & Co, *imprint of* T H Peek Publisher

Greenfield Review Press, *distributed by* Cross-Cultural Communications

Greenhaven Press, *distributed by* Lucent Books®

Greenhaven Press®, *imprint of* The Rosen Publishing Group Inc

Greenhaven Press Inc, *distributed by* Perfection Learning Corp

Greenhill Books, *distributed by* Casemate | publishers

Greenleaf Book Group Press, *imprint of* Greenleaf Book Group LLC

Greenleaf Publishing, *distributed by* Stylus Publishing LLC

Greenway Music Press, *imprint of* A-R Editions Inc

Greenwich Medical Media, *distributed by* Oxford University Press USA

Greenwich Workshop Press, *distributed by* Algonquin Books, Artisan Books, Workman Publishing Co Inc

Greenwillow Books, *imprint of* HarperCollins Children's Books

Greenwood Publishing Group, *imprint of* ABC-CLIO

Greenwood Research Books & Software, *division of* Greenwood Research

Grey House, *imprint of* Grey House Publishing Inc™

Grey House Publishing Canada, *division of* Grey House Publishing Inc™

Grief Watch, *distributed by* ACTA Publications

Griffin Technology, *distributed by* Hal Leonard Corp

Griot Audio, *imprint of* Recorded Books Inc, an RBmedia company

Griot Enterprises, *imprint of* Cedar Grove Books

The Grolier Club, *distributed by* Oak Knoll Press

Grolier Online®, *imprint of* Scholastic Education

Grosset, *distributor for* Parachute Publishing LLC

Grosset & Dunlap, *imprint of* Penguin Group USA, A Penguin Random House Company, Penguin Group USA, A Penguin Random House Company, Penguin Young Readers Group

Grosset/Putnam, *imprint of* Penguin Group USA, A Penguin Random House Company

Stefan Grossman's Guitar Workshop, *distributed by* Mel Bay Publications Inc

Groundworks, *distributed by* Chelsea Green Publishing Co

Group Cares, *imprint of* Group Publishing Inc

Group for the Advancement of Psychiatry, *distributed by* American Psychiatric Association Publishing

Group Publishing, *distributed by* Saint Mary's Press

Grove Dictionaries, *distributed by* Oxford University Press USA

Grove Press, *imprint of* Grove Atlantic Inc

The Grow Network/McGraw-Hill, *imprint of* McGraw-Hill Education

Grub Street Publishing, *distributed by* Casemate | publishers

B R Gruener Publishing Co, *imprint of* John Benjamins Publishing Co

Gryphon House, *distributor for* DawnSignPress, *distributed by* Teaching Strategies LLC

Gryphon House Inc, *subsidiary of* Kaplan Early Learning Co, *distributor for* Aha Communications, Book Peddlers, Deya Brashears, Bright Ring Publishing, Building Blocks, Center for the Child Care Workforce, Chatterbox Press, Chicago Review Press, Children's Resources International, Circle Time Publishers, Sydney Gurewitz Clemens, Conari Press, Council Oak Books, Dawn Sign Press, Delmar Publishers Inc, Early Educator's Press, Educators for Social Responsibility, Family Center of Nova University, Jean Feldman, Floris Books, Hawthorne Press, Hunter House Publishers, Kaplan Press, Miss Jackie Inc, Monjeu Press, National Center Early Childhood Workforce, New England AEYC, New Horizons, Nova Southeastern University, Pademelon Press, Partner Press, Pollyanna Productions, Robins Lane Press, School Renaissance, Southern Early Childhood Association, Steam Press, Syracuse University Press, Teaching Strategies, Telshare Publishing

GT Publishing, *distributed by* HarperCollins Publishers

Guild of Master Craftsman, *distributed by* The Taunton Press Inc

Guilford, *distributed by* Council for Exceptional Children (CEC)

Guilford Press, *distributed by* Specialty Press Inc

Guitar World, *distributed by* Hal Leonard Corp

Gulf Coast Association of Geological Societies, *distributed by* Bureau of Economic Geology, University of Texas at Austin

Gulf Coast Section, *distributed by* Bureau of Economic Geology, University of Texas at Austin

Gulf Professional Publishers, *distributed by* Marine Techniques Publishing

Gulf Publishing, *distributed by* NACE International

Gulf Publishing Co, *distributor for* Elsevier, Pennwell, Simon & Schuster, Editions Technip, Wiley

Gumdrop Books, *distributor for* Ozark Publishing Inc

Gun Digest® Books, *imprint of* Krause Publications Inc

The George Gund Foundation, *imprint of* University of California Press

Haase House, *imprint of* Easy Money Press

Hachai Publishing, *distributor for* Attara, Kerem, Living Lessons

Hachette Audio, *division of* Hachette Book Group

Hachette Book Group, *division of* Hachette Livre, *subsidiary of* Hachette Livre, *distributor for* Harry N Abrams Inc, Nicholas Brealey Publishing, Chronicle Books, Disney Book Group, Disney Press, Gildan Media, Hachette UK, Houghton Mifflin Harcourt, Houghton Mifflin Harcourt Trade & Reference Division, Kids Can Press, Marvel Worldwide Inc, Moleskine, Octopus Books, Peterson's, Phaidon Press, Phoenix International Publications (PiKids), Quarto Publishing Group, Quercus Books, Time Inc Books, Yen Press

Hachette Books, *division of* Hachette Book Group

Hachette Nashville, *division of* Hachette Book Group

Hachette UK, *distributed by* Hachette Book Group

Hackett Publishing Co Inc, *distributor for* Bryn Mawr Commentaries

Hagstrom Map, *subsidiary of* American Map Corp, *distributor for* ADC The Map People, American Map Corp, Arrow Maps Inc, Creative Sales Corp, De Lorme Atlas, Hammond World Atlas Corp, RV International Maps & Atlases, Stubs Guides, Trakker Maps Inc

Hagstrom Map Co Inc, *subsidiary of* American Map Corp

Hal Leonard Books, *imprint of* Hal Leonard Performing Arts Publishing Group

Hal Leonard Corp, *distributor for* Ableton, Acoustica, AirTurn, Amadeus Press, Antares, Apogee, Applause Books, Aquarius, Arrangers Publishing, Art String Publishing, Ashley Music, Avid, Axe Heauen, Backbeat Books, Berklee Press, Leonard Bernstein, Blue Microphones, Fred Bock Music Company, Boosey & Hawkes, Cakewalk, CD Sheet Music, Centerstream Publications, Centerstream Publishing LLC, Cherry Lane Music Co, ChordBuddy, Curnow Music, De Haske Publications, Dots & Lines Inc, Editions Durand, EM Books, EMI Christian, Editions Max Eschig, Faber Music Ltd, Family Communications, Fleamarket Music, Griffin Technology, Guitar World, Hamilton Stands, Hartke, G Henle Verlag, Homespun Tapes, Hudson Music, IK Multimedia, Lauren Keiser Music, Lorie Lane, Limelight Editions, Line 6, M-Audio, Ashley Mark Publishing Co, Edward B Marks Music, Meredith Music, Mighty Bright, Modern Drummer Publications, Music Minus One, Music Sales America, Musicians Institute Press, Noteflight, Peermusic Classical, PreSonus, Professional Music Institute, Propellerhead, PWM Editions, QSC, Ricordi, Lee Roberts Publications, Rock House, Rubank Publications, St Nicolas Music Inc, Editions Salabert, Samson Audio, G Schirmer Inc (Associated Music Publishers), Schott Music, Shawnee Press, Sibelius, Sikorski, Sony, Steinberg, Sterling Publishing, String Letter Publishing, Tara Publications, Tycoon Percussion, Vintage Guitar, Voyageur Press, Waltons Irish Music, Willis Music, XLN Audio, Yamaha

Hal Leonard LLC, *distributor for* Applause Theatre & Cinema Books

Hal Leonard Performing Arts Publishing Group, *division of* Hal Leonard Corp

Halcyon House, *imprint of* National Book Co

Hamadia Publishing, *distributed by* Feldheim Publishers

Hambleton Publishing, *distributed by* Caxton Press

Hamewith, *imprint of* Baker Books

Hamilton Books, *imprint of* Rowman & Littlefield Publishing Group

Hamilton Stands, *distributed by* Hal Leonard Corp

Hammond, *distributed by* Perfection Learning Corp

Hammond World Atlas Corp, *subsidiary of* American Map Corp, *distributed by* Hagstrom Map

Hampton Roads Publishing, *imprint of* Red Wheel/Weiser/Conari

Hampton Roads Publishing Co, *imprint of* Red Wheel/Weiser/Conari, *distributed by* Red Wheel/Weiser/Conari

Hand Print Press, *distributed by* Chelsea Green Publishing Co

Handprint Books, *distributed by* Chronicle Books LLC

Handprint Books Inc, *imprint of* Chronicle Books LLC, *distributed by* Chronicle Books

Hanover Square Press, *imprint of* Harlequin Enterprises Ltd

Hanser Publications LLC, *subsidiary of* Carl Hanser Verlag GmbH & Co KG, *distributor for* Hanser Publishers

Hanser Publishers, *distributed by* Hanser Publications LLC

HAP (Health Adminstration Press), *distributed by* Medical Group Management Association (MGMA)

Happy Day Books, *imprint of* Standard Publishing

Harbor Hill Books, *division of* Purple Mountain Press Ltd

Harbor Lights, *imprint of* LangMarc Publishing

Harcourt, *distributor for* Parachute Publishing LLC, *distributed by* Learning Links Inc, SAS Publishing

Harcourt Children's, *imprint of* Houghton Mifflin Harcourt Trade & Reference Division

Hard Shell Word Factory, *imprint of* Mundania Press LLC

Hardie Grant, *imprint of* Rizzoli International Publications Inc

Hardie Grant Books, *distributed by* Chronicle Books LLC

Hardie Press, *distributed by* Mel Bay Publications Inc

Hardscrabble Books, *imprint of* University Press of New England

Hardwood Press, *distributed by* St Augustine's Press Inc

Harlequin, *imprint of* Harlequin Enterprises Ltd, Recorded Books Inc, an RBmedia company

Harlequin Enterprises Ltd, *division of* HarperCollins, *distributed by* Simon & Schuster, Simon & Schuster, Inc

Harlequin Teen, *imprint of* Harlequin Enterprises Ltd

Harmony Books, *imprint of* Crown Publishing Group, Penguin Random House Inc

Harper, *imprint of* HarperCollins General Books Group

Harper Arrington Publishing, *distributor for* The Little Entrepreneur

Harper Business, *imprint of* HarperCollins General Books Group

Harper Design, *imprint of* HarperCollins General Books Group

Harper Luxe, *imprint of* HarperCollins General Books Group

Harper Paperbacks, *imprint of* HarperCollins General Books Group

Harper Perennial, *imprint of* HarperCollins General Books Group

Harper Voyager, *imprint of* HarperCollins General Books Group

Harper Wave, *imprint of* HarperCollins General Books Group

HarperAudio, *imprint of* HarperCollins Children's Books, HarperCollins General Books Group

HarperBibles, *imprint of* HarperCollins General Books Group

HarperCollins, *imprint of* HarperCollins General Books Group, HarperCollins Publishers, *distributor for* Alloy Entertainment LLC, Delphinium Books, Parachute Publishing LLC, *distributed by* Dreamscape Media LLC, Heimburger House Publishing Co, Learning Links Inc, MAR*CO Products Inc

HarperCollins Children's Books, *division of* HarperCollins Publishers

HarperCollins e-books, *imprint of* HarperCollins Children's Books, HarperCollins General Books Group

HarperCollins General Books Group, *division of* HarperCollins Publishers

HarperCollins Publishers, *subsidiary of* News Corporation, *distributor for* Basic Books, Civitas, Counterpoint, Delphinium Books, GT Publishing, Perseus (Addison Wesley Trade), Public Affairs, TV Books, *distributed by* Cynthia Publishing Co, Ingram Publisher Services/Spring Arbor (Christian market)

HarperCollins 360, *imprint of* HarperCollins General Books Group

HarperElixir, *imprint of* HarperCollins General Books Group

HarperEntertainment, *distributor for* Parachute Publishing LLC

HarperFestival, *imprint of* HarperCollins Children's Books

HarperLuxe, *distributed by* Thorndike Press

HarperOne, *imprint of* HarperCollins General Books Group

Harpia Publishing, *distributed by* Casemate | publishers

Harrington Park Press, *distributed by* Columbia University Press

Harrison House, *distributor for* Faith Library Publications

Tom Harrison Cartography, *distributed by* Mountain n' Air Books

Hartke, *distributed by* Hal Leonard Corp

Harvard Art Museums, *distributed by* Yale University Press

Harvard Business Reference, *imprint of* Harvard Business Review Press

Harvard Business Review Press, *division of* Harvard Business Publishing, *distributed by* Client Distribution Services

Harvard Business School Press, *distributed by* Center for Creative Leadership LLC, SAS Publishing

Harvard Center for International Affairs, *distributed by* University Press of America Inc

Harvard Center for Middle Eastern Studies, *distributed by* Harvard University Press

Harvard Center for Population Studies, *distributed by* Harvard University Press

Harvard Center for the Study of World Religions, *distributed by* Harvard University Press

Harvard College Library, *distributed by* Harvard University Press

Harvard Common Press, *imprint of* Quarto Publishing Group USA Inc

The Harvard Common Press, *imprint of* Quarto Publishing Group USA Inc

Harvard Department of Sanskrit & Indian Studies, *distributed by* Harvard University Press

Harvard Department of the Classics, *distributed by* Harvard University Press

Harvard Education Letter, *imprint of* Harvard Education Publishing Group

Harvard Education Press, *imprint of* Harvard Education Publishing Group

Harvard Education Publishing Group, *division of* Harvard Graduate School of Education

Harvard Educational Review, *imprint of* Harvard Education Publishing Group

Harvard Ukrainian Research Institute, *subsidiary of* Business History Review, Harvard University, *distributed by* Harvard University Press

Harvard University Art Museums, *distributed by* Yale University Press

Harvard University Asia Center, *distributed by* Harvard University Press

Harvard University David Rockefeller Center for Latin American Studies, *distributed by* Harvard University Press

Harvard University Press, *distributor for* Dumbarton Oaks, Harvard Center for Middle Eastern Studies, Harvard Center for Population Studies, Harvard Center for the Study of World Religions, Harvard College Library (including Houghton Library Judaica division), Harvard Department of Sanskrit & Indian Studies, Harvard Department of the Classics, Harvard Ukrainian Research Institute, Harvard University Asia Center, Harvard University David Rockefeller Center for Latin American Studies, Harvard-Yenching Institute, Peabody Museum of Archaeology & Ethnology, Peabody Museum Press

Harvard-Yenching Institute, *distributed by* Harvard University Press

Harvest Hill Press, *distributed by* University Press of New England

Hatherleigh Press Ltd, *distributed by* Penguin Random House Inc

Haugen Enterprises, *distributed by* Frank Amato Publications Inc

Haven, *imprint of* Bridge-Logos

Hawthorn Press, *distributed by* SteinerBooks

Hawthorne Press, *distributed by* Gryphon House Inc

Hayden-McNeil, *imprint of* Macmillan Learning

Hayes, *distributed by* Perfection Learning Corp

Haynes Manuals Inc, *division of* The Haynes Publishing Group, *distributor for* G T Foulis, Haynes Owners Workshop Manuals, Oxford Illustrated Press, *distributed by* Motorbooks International

Haynes Owners Workshop Manuals, *distributed by* Haynes Manuals Inc

Nicolas Hays Inc, *distributed by* Red Wheel/Weiser/Conari

Hazamir, *imprint of* Transcontinental Music Publications (TMP)

Hazelden, *distributed by* Simon & Schuster Sales Division

Hazelden/Johnson Institute, *imprint of* Hazelden Publishing

Hazelden/Keep Coming Back, *imprint of* Hazelden Publishing

Hazelden-Pittman Archives Press, *imprint of* Hazelden Publishing

Hazelden Publishing, *division of* The Hazelden Betty Ford Foundation, Hazelden Foundation, *distributor for* Obsessive Anonymous, *distributed by* Health Communications Inc (trade), Simon & Schuster

HCI Books, *imprint of* Health Communications Inc

HCI Printing & Publishing, *division of* Health Communications Inc

HCI Teens, *imprint of* Health Communications Inc

Healey Publishing, *distributed by* Sunbelt Publications Inc

Healing Arts Press, *imprint of* Inner Traditions International Ltd

Healing Tao Books, *distributed by* Tuttle Publishing

Health Administration Press, *division of* Foundation of the American College of Healthcare Executives

Health Books, *imprint of* Oxmoor House

Health Communications Inc, *distributor for* Hazelden Publishing

Health Forum Inc, *subsidiary of* American Hospital Association

Health Information Press (HIP), *imprint of* Practice Management Information Corp (PMIC)

Health Professions Press, *division of* Paul H Brookes Publishing Co Inc, Brookes Publishing Co Inc, *subsidiary of* Brookes Publishing Co Inc, *distributed by* The Eurospan Group (Africa, Europe & Middle East), Footprint Books Pty Ltd (Australia, Fiji, New Zealand & Papua New Guinea), Login Canada (Canada), Unifacmanu Trading Co Ltd (Taiwan)

Health Research Group, *division of* Public Citizen

Healthcare Performance Press, *imprint of* Productivity Press

HealthCheques, *imprint of* Appletree Press Inc

Healthwatch, *imprint of* Players Press Inc

Healthy Living, *imprint of* Book Publishing Co

Healthy Living Books, *imprint of* Hatherleigh Press Ltd

Hearne Fine Art, *distributed by* The University of Arkansas Press

Hearst Books, *imprint of* HarperCollins Publishers, Sterling Publishing Co Inc

Hearthside Books, *distributed by* Closson Press

Hearts 'n Tummies Cookbook Co, *division of* Quixote Press

HeatWave Romance, *subsidiary of* Awe-Struck Publishing

Heaven & Earth Press, *distributed by* Gem Guides Book Co

Heaven & Earth Publications, *distributed by* North Atlantic Books

Hebrew Union College Press, *division of* Hebrew Union College, *distributed by* Wayne State University Press

Heian, *imprint of* Stone Bridge Press Inc

Heian International, *imprint of* Stone Bridge Press Inc

Heimburger House Publishing Co, *distributor for* Child's Play International, Evergreen Press, Firefly Books Ltd, Fordham University Press, Globe Pequot Press, HarperCollins, Johns Hopkins University Press, Houghton Mifflin Harcourt, Iconografix, Indiana University Press, Kalmbach Publishing, Krause Publications, Motorbooks International, National Book Network, New York University Press, W W Norton & Company Inc, Penguin Putnam Inc, Pictorial Histories Publishing Co, Steam Passages Publishing, Sterling Publishing, Sugar Cane Press, Syracuse University Press, Thunder Bay Press, University of Minnesota Press, John Wiley & Sons

Heimdal, *distributed by* Casemate | publishers

William S Hein & Co Inc, *distributor for* Ashgate, Aspen, Butterworths, Sweet & Maxwell, John Wiley & Sons Inc

Heinemann, *division of* Houghton Mifflin Harcourt, *distributed by* ArtAgc Publications, Pearson (Canada, Australia & New Zealand)

Heinemann Raintree, *division of* Capstone Publishers™, *imprint of* Capstone Publishers™

Heinle, *subsidiary of* Cengage Learning

John Helde, *distributed by* EastBridge

Helena History Press, *distributed by* Central European University Press

Heliconia Press, *imprint of* Fox Chapel Publishing Co Inc

Helion & Co, *distributed by* Casemate | publishers

Helion & Co/CG Books, *distributed by* Casemate | publishers

Hellgate Press, *imprint of* L & R Publishing

G Henle Verlag, *distributed by* Hal Leonard Corp

Henry Holt, *imprint of* Henry Holt and Company, LLC

Henry Holt Books for Younger Readers, *imprint of* Henry Holt and Company, LLC

Ian Henry Publications, *distributed by* Empire Publishing Service

Joseph Henry Press, *imprint of* National Academies Press (NAP)

Herald Press, *imprint of* MennoMedia

Herald Publishing House, *division of* Community of Christ

Herb & Spice, *imprint of* Crossquarter Publishing Group

Herder & Herder, *imprint of* The Crossroad Publishing Co

Here & Now, *imprint of* Gallopade International Inc

Editions Charles Herissey, *distributed by* Casemate | publishers

Heritage Beacon, *imprint of* Lighthouse Publishing of the Carolinas

Heritage Books, *imprint of* Heritage Books Inc

Heritage Books Inc, *distributor for* Fairfax Genealogical Society, National Genealogical Society, Virginia Genealogical Society

Heritage Builders, *imprint of* Focus on the Family

Heritage House, *distributor for* FineEdge.com LLC

Nick Hern Books, *distributed by* Theatre Communications Group

Heroes & Helpers, *imprint of* Gallopade International Inc

Heroides Publishing, *imprint of* Joshua Tree Publishing

Hes & De Graaf, *distributed by* Oak Knoll Press

Hesperia, *imprint of* ASCSA Publications

Heuristic Books, *imprint of* Science & Humanities Press

Hewitt Homeschooling Resources, *division of* Hewitt Research Foundation

Hexagon Press, *distributed by* Gem Guides Book Co

Hidden Travel Series, *imprint of* Ulysses Press

High Tide Monograph Series, *imprint of* High Tide Press

High Tide Press, *subsidiary of* The Trinity Foundation

HighBridge Audio, *distributed by* Algonquin Books, Penguin Group USA, A Penguin Random House Company

Highgate Press, *imprint of* ECS Publishing Corp

Highland/Etling, *imprint of* Alfred Music Publishing

Highlights Press, *imprint of* Highlights for Children

Hill & Wang, *division of* Farrar, Straus & Giroux, LLC, *imprint of* Farrar, Straus & Giroux, LLC

Lawrence Hill Books, *imprint of* Chicago Review Press

Hillenbrand Books, *imprint of* Liturgy Training Publications

Hillsdale College Press, *division of* Hillsdale College

Himalayan Institute Press, *division of* Himalayan International Institute of Yoga Science & Philosophy

Hindustan Book Agency, *distributed by* American Mathematical Society

Hippocrates Publications, *distributed by* Book Publishing Co

Histoire & Collections, *distributed by* Casemate | publishers

Historic Idaho Series, *distributed by* Caxton Press

Historic New England, *distributed by* University Press of New England

Historic New Orleans Collection, *distributed by* Oak Knoll Press

Historical Indexes, *distributed by* Casemate | publishers

History Colorado, *distributed by* University Press of Colorado

History Facts, *distributed by* Casemate | publishers

History Press, *imprint of* Arcadia Publishing Inc

History Publishing Company, *imprint of* History Publishing Co LLC

HMH Franchise, *imprint of* Houghton Mifflin Harcourt Trade & Reference Division

Hoard's Dairyman Magazine, *imprint of* W D Hoard & Sons Co

Hobar Publications, *division of* Finney Company Inc, *distributor for* Drache Publications

Hobbes End Publishing LLC, *subsidiary of* Hobbes End Entertainment LLC

Hobble Creek Press, *imprint of* Cedar Fort Inc

Hochelaga, *distributor for* Cross-Cultural Communications, *distributed by* Cross-Cultural Communications

Hodder Education, *distributed by* Trans-Atlantic Publications Inc

Hogarth, *imprint of* Crown Publishing Group

Verlag Hans Huber Hogrefe AG, *distributed by* Hogrefe Publishing Corp

Hogrefe Publishing Corp, *subsidiary of* Hogrefe Verlag GmbH & Co Kg, *distributor for* Verlag Hans Huber Hogrefe AG (Switzerland), Hogrefe Verlag (Germany)

Hogrefe Verlag, *distributed by* Hogrefe Publishing Corp

Hohm Press, *subsidiary of* HSM LLC

Holler, *imprint of* Riverdale Avenue Books (RAB)

Holloway House, *imprint of* Kensington Publishing Corp

Holmes Publishing Group, *imprint of* Holmes Publishing Group LLC

Holmes Publishing Group LLC, *distributor for* Capall-Bann (UK), Edda Publishing (Sweden), Fulgur Ltd (UK), Jerusalem Press (UK), Starfire Publishing (UK), Theion Publishing (Germany), Three Hands Press (US), Xoanon Publishing (US)

Holmgren Design Services, *distributed by* Chelsea Green Publishing Co

Holocaust Library, *imprint of* United States Holocaust Memorial Museum

Henry Holt and Company, LLC, *division of* Macmillan, Macmillan

Holt Paperbacks, *imprint of* Henry Holt and Company, LLC

Holy Cross Orthodox Press, *division of* Hellenic College Holy Cross

Homa & Sekey Books, *distributor for* China Encyclopedia Publishing House, China Intercontinental Press, China Zhejiang Publishing United Group

Home Builders Press, *distributed by* Craftsman Book Co

Homespun Tapes, *distributed by* Hal Leonard Corp

Homestead Publishing, *affiliate of* Book Design Ltd

Hong Kong University Press, *distributed by* Columbia University Press

Hooked On Phonics, *distributed by* Simon & Schuster, Inc, Simon & Schuster Sales Division

Hoover Institution Press, *subsidiary of* Hoover Institution on War, Revolution & Peace

Hoover's Business Press, *imprint of* Hoover's Inc

Hoover's Handbooks, *imprint of* Hoover's Inc

Hoover's Inc, *subsidiary of* Dun & Bradstreet

Hope Publishing House, *distributed by* Pelican Publishing Co

Johns Hopkins University Press, *distributor for* Inter-American Development Bank, International Food Policy Research Institute, Maryland Historical Society, *distributed by* Heimburger House Publishing Co

Hops Press, *distributed by* Mountain Press Publishing Co

Horizon Publishers, *imprint of* Cedar Fort Inc

Horizon Publishers & Distributors Inc, *distributed by* Cedar Fort Inc

Horse Latitudes Press, *imprint of* Crumb Elbow Publishing

Horticulture Books, *imprint of* Betterway Books

Hospital & Healthcare Compensation Service, *subsidiary of* John R Zabka Associates Inc, John R Zabka Associates Inc

Houghton Mifflin Books for Children, *imprint of* Houghton Mifflin Harcourt Trade & Reference Division

Houghton Mifflin Harcourt, *imprint of* Houghton Mifflin Harcourt Trade & Reference Division, *distributor for* Clarion Books, The Old Farmer's Almanac, *distributed by* Hachette Book Group, Heimburger House Publishing Co

Houghton Mifflin Harcourt Assessments, *subsidiary of* Houghton Mifflin Harcourt, Houghton Mifflin Harcourt Publishing Co

Houghton Mifflin Harcourt K-12 Publishers, *division of* Houghton Mifflin Harcourt

Houghton Mifflin Harcourt Publishing Company, *distributed by* Learning Links Inc

Houghton Mifflin Harcourt Trade & Reference Division, *division of* Houghton Mifflin Harcourt, *distributor for* Larausse, Old Farmers Almanac, *distributed by* Hachette Book Group

Hourglass, *imprint of* Baker Books

House of Collectibles, *imprint of* Penguin Random House Inc, Random House Reference/ Random House Puzzles & Games

House to House Publications, *division of* DOVE International

Houston European Poetry Series, *imprint of* Ugly Duckling Presse

HOW Books, *imprint of* F+W Media Inc

Howard Books, *imprint of* Atria Publishing Group

Howard University Press, *distributed by* The Johns Hopkins University Press

HPBooks, *imprint of* Berkley Publishing Group, Penguin Group USA, A Penguin Random House Company, Penguin Group USA, A Penguin Random House Company

HQ, *imprint of* Harlequin Enterprises Ltd

HQN Books, *imprint of* Harlequin Enterprises Ltd

HRD Press, *distributed by* Training & Development Materials of Canada (Canada)

HSWF, *imprint of* Hard Shell Word Factory

Hub City Press, *distributed by* John F Blair Publisher

Huber, *distributed by* Alan Wofsy Fine Arts

Huckleberry House LLC, *distributed by* Sunbelt Publications Inc

Hudson Hills Press Inc, *distributor for* American Federation of Arts

Hudson Music, *distributed by* Hal Leonard Corp

Huia Publishers, *distributed by* University of Hawaii Press

Human Alchemy Publications, *distributed by* Crown House Publishing Co LLC

Human Rights Watch Books, *imprint of* Human Rights Watch

Humana Press, *imprint of* Springer

Humanity Books, *imprint of* Prometheus Books

Humanix Books LLC, *division of* Newsmax Media

Bruce Humphries, *imprint of* Branden Books

Hungary Tomato, *imprint of* Lerner Publishing Group Inc

Hungry Goat Press, *imprint of* Gauthier Publications Inc

Hunter House, *imprint of* Turner Publishing Co

Hunter House Publishers, *distributed by* Gryphon House Inc

Karen Hunter Publishing, *imprint of* Gallery Books

Hurst, *distributed by* Oxford University Press USA

The Hutton Settlement, *distributed by* Washington State University Press

Hybrid Nation, *imprint of* Red Hen Press

Hydra, *imprint of* Penguin Random House Inc, Random House Publishing Group

Hyperbole, *imprint of* San Diego State University Press

Hyperion, *distributor for* Alloy Entertainment LLC

Hyperion Books for Children, *imprint of* Disney Publishing Worldwide

Hypermedia Inc, *imprint of* Frederic C Beil Publisher Inc

Hyphen Press, *distributed by* Princeton Architectural Press

I&T Shop Service, *imprint of* Penton Media Inc

IBEX Press, *imprint of* Ibex Publishers

Ibex Publishers, *distributor for* Farhang Moaser

IBFD North America Inc (International Bureau of Fiscal Documentation), *division of* IBFD Foundation

ibidem Press, *distributed by* Columbia University Press

IchemE, *distributed by* American Institute of Chemical Engineers (AIChE)

ICLE, *imprint of* Institute of Continuing Legal Education

Iconografix, *distributed by* Heimburger House Publishing Co

Idea Bank, *distributed by* Fire Engineering Books & Videos

Ideal Audiobooks, *distributed by* Dreamscape Media LLC

Ideals Annuals, *imprint of* WorthyKids/Ideals

Ides et Calendes, *distributed by* Alan Wofsy Fine Arts

IEE, *imprint of* IET USA Inc

IEEE Computer Society Press, *distributor for* American Society for Quality (ASQ)

IEEE Press, *division of* Institute of Electrical & Electronics Engineers Inc (IEEE), *distributed by* John Wiley & Sons Inc

IFSTA, *distributed by* Fire Engineering Books & Videos

Ignatius Press, *division of* Guadalupe Associates Inc, Guadalupe Associates Inc, *distributor for* Bethlehem Books, Veritas

Ignite, *imprint of* Entangled Publishing

IHS Jane's, *subsidiary of* IHS Markit

IIP Consumers Series, *imprint of* Independent Information Publications

IK Multimedia, *distributed by* Hal Leonard Corp

Ikonographics, *imprint of* Franciscan Media, *distributed by* Franciscan Media

Ilchokak Publishers, *distributed by* Cheng & Tsui Co Inc

Illinois State Museum Society, *affiliate of* Illinois State Museum

Illuminating Engineering Society of North America (IES), *distributor for* Taylor & Francis, Techstreet

ILR Press, *imprint of* Cornell University Press

Image Books, *imprint of* Crown Publishing Group

Imagine Publishing, *imprint of* Charlesbridge Publishing Inc

Imago Mundi, *imprint of* David R Godine Publisher Inc

ImaJinn Books, *imprint of* BelleBooks

IMM Lifestyle Books, *imprint of* Fox Chapel Publishing Co Inc

Immagine&Poesia, *distributed by* Cross-Cultural Communications

Immedium, *imprint of* Immedium Inc

Impact, *imprint of* New Harbinger Publications Inc

Impact Publications/Development Concepts Inc, *distributed by* National Book Network

Imperial College Press, *subsidiary of* World Scientific Publishing Co Inc

In an Hour Books LLC, *imprint of* Smith & Kraus Publishers Inc

In Extenso Press, *imprint of* ACTA Publications

In the Garden Publishing, *division of* What Would Love Do Intl

Incentive Plus, *distributor for* MAR*CO Products Inc

Independence Press, *imprint of* Herald Publishing House

Independent Information Publications, *division of* Computing!

Independent Music Press, *distributed by* G Schirmer Inc/Associated Music Publishers Inc

Independent Publishers Group, *division of* Chicago Review Press, *distributor for* Big Guy Books Inc

Independent Seaport Museum, *distributed by* Cornell Maritime Press Inc

Independent University of Moscow, *distributed by* American Mathematical Society

Indiana University Press, *distributed by* Heimburger House Publishing Co

Indigo, *imprint of* Genesis Press Inc

Indigo Love Spectrum, *imprint of* Genesis Press Inc

Indigo Vibe, *imprint of* Genesis Press Inc

Indulgence, *imprint of* Entangled Publishing

Industrial Press, *distributed by* NACE International, Society of Manufacturing Engineers

Indy-Tech Publishing, *imprint of* SAMS Technical Publishing LLC

Infinitum Nihil, *imprint of* HarperCollins General Books Group

Influence Resources, *imprint of* Gospel Publishing House (GPH)

Information Gatekeepers Inc (IGI), *division of* IGI Group Inc

Information Today Books, *imprint of* Information Today, Inc

Information Today, Inc, *distributor for* Association for Information Science & Technology (ASIS&T)

Ingram Publisher Services/Spring Arbor, *distributor for* HarperCollins Publishers

Inkwater Press, *imprint of* Firstbooks.com Inc, Firstbooks.com Inc

Inland, *distributor for* World Citizens

Inner Traditions, *imprint of* Inner Traditions International Ltd

Inner Traditions/Bear & Company, *distributed by* Simon & Schuster, Inc

Inner Traditions en espanol, *imprint of* Inner Traditions International Ltd

Inner Traditions India, *imprint of* Inner Traditions International Ltd

Inner Worlds Music, *distributed by* Lotus Press

Innovation & Tourisms (INTO), *imprint of* Cognizant Communication Corp

Innovative Marketing, *distributor for* Pentecostal Publishing House

innovativeKids®, *division of* Innovative USA® Inc, Innovative USA® Inc

InnoVision Health Media, *distributed by* Square One Publishers Inc

Inprint Editions, *imprint of* Black Classic Press

Inside the Minds, *imprint of* Aspatore Books

Insight Editions, *distributed by* Simon & Schuster, Simon & Schuster, Inc, Simon & Schuster Sales Division

Insight Media, *imprint of* Alexander Street, a ProQuest Company

Inspec, *imprint of* IET USA Inc

Inspire Books, *imprint of* Peter Pauper Press, Inc

Instant Help, *imprint of* New Harbinger Publications Inc

Institute for Advanced Study in the Theatre Arts (IASTA), *distributed by* Fordham University Press

Institute for Mesoamerican Studies, *distributed by* University of Texas Press

Institute for Regional Studies of the Californias, *distributed by* San Diego State University Press

Institute for the Psychological Sciences Press (IPS), *distributed by* The Catholic University of America Press

Institute of Education, *distributed by* Stylus Publishing LLC

Institute of Governmental Studies, *subsidiary of* University of California, Berkeley

Institute of Materials, *distributed by* NACE International

Institute of Mathematical Geography, *division of* Arlinghaus Enterprises LLC

Institute of Police Technology & Management, *division of* University of North Florida

Institute Press, *distributed by* Crown House Publishing Co LLC

The Institution of Engineering & Technology (IET), *distributed by* Stylus Publishing LLC

Instituto Monsa de Ediciones SA, *distributed by* Trans-Atlantic Publications Inc

Integrity Music, *division of* David C Cook

Intellect Publishing, *distributed by* Sunbelt Publications Inc

Inter-American Development Bank, *division of* Multilateral Development Bank, *distributed by* Johns Hopkins University Press

Inter-University Consortium for Political & Social Research (ICPSR), *affiliate of* University of Michigan Institute for Social Research

Intercontinental Press, *distributed by* CN Times Books

Intercultural Press Inc, *division of* Nicholas Brealey Publishing

Interlink Books, *imprint of* Interlink Publishing Group Inc

Interlink Publishing Group Inc, *distributor for* Black & White Publishing (UK), Camerapix Publishers International, Georgina Campbell Guides (Ireland), Macmillan Caribbean (UK), Quartet Books (UK), Rucksack Readers (UK), Serif Publishing Ltd (UK), Sheldrake Press (UK), Signal Books (UK), Waverley Books (UK), Neil Wilson Publishing (UK)

InterMix, *imprint of* Penguin Group USA, A Penguin Random House Company

International Air Transport Association, *distributed by* J J Keller & Associates, Inc

International Atomic Energy Agency (IAEA), *distributed by* United Nations Publications

International Book Centre Inc, *distributor for* Compass Publications, Library du Liban (Lebanon), New Readers Press, Oxford University Press, Pro Lingua Associates, Stacey International Ltd (London), University of Michigan

International Christian University Foundation, *distributed by* EastBridge

International Code Council, *distributed by* Professional Publications Inc (PPI)

International Country Risk Guide, *imprint of* The PRS Group Inc

International Criminal Tribunal for Rwanda (UNICTR), *distributed by* United Nations Publications

International Criminal Tribunal for the former Yugoslavia (ICTY), *distributed by* United Nations Publications

International Debate Education Association, *distributed by* Central European University Press

International Design Library®, *imprint of* Stemmer House Publishers Inc

International Energy Agency, *imprint of* OECD Washington Center, *distributed by* OECD Washington Center

International Food Policy Research Institute, *member of* Consultative Group on International Agricultural Research (CGIAR), *distributed by* Johns Hopkins University Press

International Jewelry Publications, *distributed by* Gem Guides Book Co

International Law Institute, *distributed by* University Press of America Inc

International Organization for Migration (IOM), *distributed by* United Nations Publications

International Pocket Library, *imprint of* Branden Books

International Polar Institute, *distributed by* University Press of New England

International Press, *distributed by* American Mathematical Society

International Press of Boston Inc, *distributed by* AMS

International Trade Centre (ITC), *distributed by* United Nations Publications

International Transportation Forum, *distributed by* OECD Washington Center

InterVarsity Press, *division of* InterVarsity Christian Fellowship/USA

Interweave, *imprint of* F+W Media Inc

Interweave Press LLC, *imprint of* F+W Media Inc, *distributed by* Keith Ainsworth Pty Ltd (Australia), David Bateman Ltd (New Zealand), Search Press (UK)

Ione Press, *imprint of* ECS Publishing Corp

Iranbooks Press, *imprint of* Ibex Publishers

Iris Press, *imprint of* The Iris Publishing Group Inc

IRL, *distributed by* Oxford University Press USA

Iron Icon Books, *imprint of* Unveiled Media LLC

Iroquois Press, *imprint of* Turner Publishing Co

ISH Group, *distributed by* Empire Publishing Service

The Ishmael Tree, *distributor for* RockHill Publishing LLC

ISI Books, *imprint of* Intercollegiate Studies Institute Inc

Islamic Texts Society, *distributed by* Fons Vitae

Island, *imprint of* Penguin Random House Inc

Island Paradise Publishing, *distributed by* Sunbelt Publications Inc

Island Press, *distributor for* Environmental Law Institute, IUCN, Techne Press

Islander Group, *distributor for* Kamehameha Publishing

The Islander Group (TIG), *distributor for* Bess Press

Islander Images, *imprint of* Shepard Publications

Islander Press, *imprint of* Shepard Publications

ISO, *distributed by* NACE International

IsraBook, *subsidiary of* Gefen Books

Isshin-Ryu Productions, *imprint of* The Linick Group Inc

Issues Press, *imprint of* Idyll Arbor Inc

Italian School of East Asian Studies, *distributed by* Cheng & Tsui Co Inc

ITK (In the Know) Audio, *imprint of* Recorded Books Inc, an RBmedia company

It's About Time Inc, *distributor for* American Geosciences Institute (AGI)

IUCN, *distributed by* Island Press

iUniverse, *division of* Author Solutions LLC

IVP Academic, *imprint of* InterVarsity Press

IVP Books, *imprint of* InterVarsity Press

IVP Connect, *imprint of* InterVarsity Press

IVP Crescendo, *imprint of* InterVarsity Press

IVP Praxis, *imprint of* InterVarsity Press

Ivy, *imprint of* Penguin Random House Inc

IWGIA, *distributed by* Transaction Publishers Inc

Jacaranda, *imprint of* John Wiley & Sons Inc

Jade Rabbit, *imprint of* Quite Specific Media Group Ltd

Jagiellonian University Press, *distributed by* Columbia University Press

Jaguar Tales, *distributed by* Sunbelt Publications Inc

Janaway Publishing, *distributor for* Closson Press

Japan Publications Inc, *distributed by* Kodansha USA Inc

Japan Publications Trading Co Inc, *distributed by* Kodansha USA Inc

Japan Society, *distributed by* Yale University Press

JayJo Books LLC, *subsidiary of* The Guidance Group

Jems, *imprint of* Elsevier, Health Sciences Division

Jenkins Publishing, *distributed by* Chelsea Green Publishing Co

Jersey Yarns, *imprint of* Quincannon Publishing Group

Jerusalem Press, *distributed by* Holmes Publishing Group LLC

Jerusalem Publications, *distributed by* Feldheim Publishers

Jeter Publishing, *imprint of* Gallery Books

Jewish Lights, *imprint of* Turner Publishing Co

The Jewish Museum, *distributed by* Yale University Press

Jewish New Testament Publications, *distributed by* Lederer Books, Messianic Jewish Publishers

Jewish Publication Society, *distributed by* University of Nebraska Press

George R Jezek Photography, *distributed by* Gem Guides Book Co

Jhpiego, *affiliate of* The Johns Hopkins University

Jist, *distributor for* MAR*CO Products Inc

JIST Career Solutions, *imprint of* JIST Publishing

JIST Publishing, *division of* EMC Publishing LLC

JMC Press, *distributed by* Vandamere Press

The JOC Group Inc, *division of* IHS Markit

John Deere Publishing, *division of* Deere & Co

John Macrae Books, *imprint of* Henry Holt and Company, LLC

Johns Hopkins Aids Service, *distributed by* The Johns Hopkins University Press

Johns Hopkins University Press, *distributor for* Inter-American Development Bank, International Food Policy Research Institute, Maryland Historical Society, *distributed by* Heimburger House Publishing Co

The Johns Hopkins University Press, *affiliate of* The Johns Hopkins University, *distributor for* Baylor University Press, The Brookings Institution Press, Catholic University of America Press, Center for Talented Youth, Georgetown University Press, Howard University Press, Johns Hopkins Aids Service, Maryland Historical Society, Resources for the Future, University of Massachusetts Press, University of Pennsylvania Museum, University of Pennsylvania Press, University of Washington Press, The University Press of Kentucky, Urban Institute Press, The Woodrow Wilson Center Press, Woodrow Wilson Center Press, World Resources Institute

Cy Johnson & Son, *distributed by* Gem Guides Book Co

Joint Center for Political & Economic Studies Press, *distributed by* University Press of America Inc

Joint Publishers, *distributed by* China Books

Jolly Fish Press, *imprint of* North Star Editions Inc

Jones & Bartlett Learning, *distributed by* Medical Group Management Association (MGMA)

Jones & Bartlett Learning LLC, *division of* Ascend Learning

Jones & Bartlett Publishers, *distributor for* American Academy of Orthopaedic Surgeons (AAOS)

The Fletcher Jones Foundation, *imprint of* University of California Press

Lorena Jones Books, *imprint of* Ten Speed Press

Jonglez Publishing, *distributed by* The Globe Pequot Press

Jossey-Bass, *imprint of* John Wiley & Sons Inc, *distributor for* Center for Creative Leadership LLC, *distributed by* Center for Creative Leadership LLC

Journal of Chinese Medicine Publications, *distributed by* Eastland Press

JourneyForth Books, *division of* BJU Press, *imprint of* BJU Press

Jove, *imprint of* Berkley Publishing Group, Penguin Group USA, A Penguin Random House Company

Joy Publishing Co, *division of* California Clock Co, California Clock Co

Joyful Productions, *distributed by* Epicenter Press Inc

JPT America Inc, *distributed by* Cheng & Tsui Co Inc

JR Comics, *distributed by* Lerner Publishing Group Inc

Judeo Christian Ethics Series, *imprint of* PREP Publishing

Judson Press, *division of* American Baptist Churches in the USA, *distributed by* Abingdon Press

Juloya, *imprint of* Elva Resa Publishing

Jump!, *distributed by* myON, a division of Capstone

Jump at the Sun, *imprint of* Disney-Hyperion Books, Disney Publishing Worldwide

Jumpstart, *imprint of* Triumph Learning LLC

Junebug Books, *imprint of* NewSouth Books

Juniper Publishing, *distributed by* Simon & Schuster Sales Division

Juno Books, *distributed by* powerHouse Books

Jury Verdict Research, *division of* LRP Publications

Just Cause, *imprint of* Yard Dog Press

K A Publishing, *imprint of* Hobar Publications

Kabbalah Publishing, *division of* Kabbalah Centre International

Max Kade Institute for German-American Studies, *distributed by* University of Wisconsin Press

Kaeden Books, *imprint of* Kaeden Corp

Kagero, *distributed by* Casemate | publishers

Kaiser-Barlow, *imprint of* Schiffer Publishing Ltd

Kales Press, *distributed by* W W Norton & Company Inc

Kalindi Press, *imprint of* Hohm Press

Kalmbach Books, *imprint of* Kalmbach Publishing Co

Kalmbach Publishing, *distributed by* Heimburger House Publishing Co

Kalmbach Publishing Co, *distributed by* Publishers Group West (PGW)

Kalmus, *imprint of* Alfred Music Publishing

Kamehameha Publishing, *division of* Kamehameha Schools, *distributed by* Islander Group

Kamehameha Schools Press, *imprint of* Kamehameha Publishing

Kane Miller Books, *division of* Educational Development Corp, Educational Development Corp

The Kane Press, *distributed by* Lerner Publishing Group Inc

Kaplan Press, *distributed by* Gryphon House Inc

Kaplan Publishing, *distributed by* Simon & Schuster, Inc, Simon & Schuster Sales Division

Kappa Map Group, *distributed by* American Map Corp

Kar-Ben Partners, *distributed by* Lerner Publishing Group Inc

Kar-Ben Publishing, *division of* Lerner Publishing Group Inc, *imprint of* Lerner Publishing Group Inc, *distributed by* Beach Lloyd Publishers LLC

Karnac Books, *distributed by* Stylus Publishing LLC

Karnak House, *imprint of* Red Sea Press Inc

Katalitix, *distributed by* Simon & Schuster Sales Division

Katalitix Media, *distributed by* Simon & Schuster, Inc

KAV Books, *distributed by* Royal Fireworks Press

Kazan Media, *imprint of* Volcano Press

KC Publications Inc, *distributed by* Gem Guides Book Co

Keepers of Our Culture, *imprint of* Park Place Publications

Lauren Keiser Music, *distributed by* Hal Leonard Corp

J J Keller & Associates, Inc, *distributor for* Chilton Book Co, International Air Transport Association, National Archives & Records Administration, National Institute of Occupational Safety & Health, Office of the Federal Register, Research & Special Programs Administration of the US Department of Transportation, John Wiley & Sons Inc, *distributed by* AMACOM Books

Kendall Green, *imprint of* Gallaudet University Press

Kendall Hunt Publishing, *distributor for* Seedling Publications Inc

Kenilworth Press, *distributed by* Trafalgar Square Books

Kennedy Information Inc, *division of* Bloomberg BNA

Kensington, *distributor for* Parachute Publishing LLC

Kensington Books, *imprint of* Kensington Publishing Corp

Kensington Hardcover, *imprint of* Kensington Publishing Corp

Kensington Mass-Market, *imprint of* Kensington Publishing Corp

Kensington Publishing Corp, *distributor for* Urban Books, *distributed by* Penguin Group USA, A Penguin Random House Company, Penguin Group USA, A Penguin Random House Company

Kensington Trade Paperback, *imprint of* Kensington Publishing Corp

Kentucky Historical Society, *distributed by* The University Press of Kentucky

Kerem, *distributed by* Hachai Publishing

Charles H Kerr, *distributed by* AK Press Distribution

Kersplebedelo, *distributed by* AK Press Distribution

Kessinger Publishing®, *imprint of* Kessinger Publishing LLC

Key Education, *distributed by* Carson-Dellosa Publishing LLC

Keynote Speakers Today, *imprint of* Empire Press Media/Avant-Guide

Keystone Books, *imprint of* The Pennsylvania State University Press

Keywords Press, *imprint of* Atria Books

Kid Help Publishing Co, *division of* Quixote Press

KidHaven Press, *imprint of* The Rosen Publishing Group Inc, *distributed by* Lucent Books®

Kids Can Press, *distributed by* Hachette Book Group

Kids Corner, *imprint of* Sundance/Newbridge Publishing

KidsBooks, *imprint of* Kidsbooks LLC

Kimani, *imprint of* Harlequin Enterprises Ltd

Kimbell Art Museum, *distributed by* Yale University Press

Kinfolk, *distributed by* Simon & Schuster, Inc, Simon & Schuster Sales Division

Laurence King Publishing, *distributed by* Chronicle Books LLC

The King Legacy, *imprint of* Beacon Press

Kingswell, *imprint of* Disney Publishing Worldwide

Kiron Editions du Felin, *distributed by* Beach Lloyd Publishers LLC

Klutz, *division of* Scholastic Corp, *imprint of* Scholastic Trade Division

Wolters Kluwer Law & Business, *subsidiary of* Wolters Kluwer, Wolters Kluwer

Knock-off Books, *imprint of* Ugly Duckling Presse

Alfred A Knopf, *imprint of* Penguin Random House Inc

Alfred A Knopf Books for Young Readers, *imprint of* Random House Children's Books

Alfred A Knopf/Everyman's Library, *imprint of* Knopf Doubleday Publishing Group

Knopf Books for Young Readers, *imprint of* Penguin Random House Inc

Knopf Guides, *imprint of* Penguin Random House Inc

Knossus Project, *distributed by* Chelsea Green Publishing Co

Knowledge Resources, *distributor for* Association for Talent Development (ATD) Press

Kodansha, *distributed by* Oxford University Press USA

Kodansha America, *imprint of* Kodansha USA Inc

Kodansha Globe, *imprint of* Kodansha USA Inc

Kodansha International, *imprint of* Kodansha USA Inc

Kodansha USA Inc, *subsidiary of* Kodansha Ltd (Japan), Kodansha Ltd (Japan), *distributor for* Japan Publications Inc, Japan Publications Trading Co Inc, *distributed by* Oxford University Press

Kollath-Stensaas, *distributed by* AdventureKEEN

Kolowalu Books, *imprint of* University of Hawaii Press

Konecky & Konecky (K&K), *imprint of* Konecky & Konecky LLC

Konecky & Konecky LLC, *distributor for* Octavo Editions

KonigsFurt, *distributed by* US Games Systems Inc

Koren Publishers, *imprint of* The Toby Press LLC

Kornfeld, *distributed by* Wittenborn Art Books

Kornfeld & Co (Bern), *distributed by* Alan Wofsy Fine Arts

Kornfeld (Switzerland), *distributed by* Picasso Project

Kosei Publishing Co, *imprint of* Tuttle Publishing, *distributed by* Tuttle Publishing

Kotan Publishing Inc, *imprint of* Tuttle Publishing, *distributed by* Tuttle Publishing

HJ Kramer Inc, *division of* New World Library

Krause Publications, *imprint of* F+W Media Inc, *distributed by* Heimburger House Publishing Co

Krause Publications Inc, *subsidiary of* F+W Media Inc, *distributor for* Country Bumpkin, David & Charles, Colin Gower, Quarto Books

Pam Krauss Books, *imprint of* Avery

Kregel Academic & Professional, *imprint of* Kregel Publications

Kregel Classics, *imprint of* Kregel Publications

Kregel Kidzone, *imprint of* Kregel Publications

Kregel Publications, *division of* Kregel Inc, Kregel Inc, *imprint of* Kregel Publications, *distributor for* Candle Books, Monarch Books

De Krijger, *distributed by* Casemate | publishers

KTAV Publishing House Inc, *distributor for* Yeshiva University Press

KTeen, *imprint of* Kensington Publishing Corp

Kudzu House, *imprint of* Ariel Press, *distributed by* Ariel Press

KUED, *distributed by* The University of Utah Press

Kumarian Press, *division of* Lynne Rienner Publishers Inc, *distributor for* Management Sciences for Health

Scott G Kyle, *distributed by* Sunbelt Publications Inc

LA Weekly Books, *imprint of* St Martin's Press, LLC

Ladders, *imprint of* Triumph Learning LLC

Lady Fern Press, *imprint of* Crumb Elbow Publishing

Lake Claremont Press, *imprint of* Everything Goes Media LLC

Lake Forest College Press, *distributed by* Northwestern University Press

Lakeshore Learning Materials, *distributor for* National Council of Teachers of Mathematics (NCTM)

Lorie Lane, *distributed by* Hal Leonard Corp

Peter Lang Publishing Inc, *subsidiary of* Peter Lang AG (Switzerland), Peter Lang AG (Switzerland)

Langenscheidt Publishing Group, *distributor for* Michelin Maps & Guides

Lantern Books, *division of* Booklight Inc, *distributed by* SteinerBooks

LanternLight Library, *imprint of* University of Alaska Press

Larausse, *distributed by* Houghton Mifflin Harcourt Trade & Reference Division

Large Print Press™, *imprint of* Gale

Lark Crafts, *imprint of* Sterling Publishing Co Inc

JK Lasser, *imprint of* John Wiley & Sons Inc

Latin America Bureau, *distributed by* Stylus Publishing LLC

Latin American Review Press, *distributed by* Arte Publico Press

Latitude 20, *imprint of* University of Hawaii Press

JP Lattes, *distributed by* Beach Lloyd Publishers LLC

Laurel-Leaf, *imprint of* Random House Children's Books

Laurel Leaf Books, *imprint of* Penguin Random House Inc

Law Library Microform Consortium, *distributed by* Thomson Reuters Westlaw™

Lawtech Publishing, *distributed by* Sunbelt Publications Inc

LBKids, *imprint of* Little, Brown Books for Young Readers

The Leadership Challenge®, *imprint of* John Wiley & Sons Inc

Leafwood Publishers, *imprint of* ACU Press

Learn Roots Music, *distributed by* Mel Bay Publications Inc

Learning & Coloring Books, *imprint of* Quincannon Publishing Group

Learning Challenge, *imprint of* Kidsbooks LLC

The Learning Company, *division of* Houghton Mifflin Harcourt

Learning Links Inc, *distributor for* Harcourt, HarperCollins, Houghton Mifflin Harcourt Publishing Company, Little, Brown & Company, Penguin Group USA, A Penguin Random House Company, Penguin Random House Inc, Scholastic, Simon & Schuster

Learning Matters, *imprint of* SAGE Publishing

LearningExpress, *imprint of* LearningExpress LLC

LearningExpress LLC, *distributed by* National Book Network

Leaves of Healing, *imprint of* Progressive Press

Leda, *imprint of* Norilana Books

Lederer Books, *division of* Messianic Jewish Publishers, *distributor for* Chosen People Ministries, First Fruits of Zion, Jewish New Testament Publications

Left To Write Press, *distributed by* Chelsea Green Publishing Co

Legacy Press, *imprint of* Rainbow Publishers

Legas Publishers, *distributed by* Cross-Cultural Communications

Legendary Locals, *imprint of* Arcadia Publishing Inc

Dennis Lehane Books, *imprint of* HarperCollins General Books Group

Lehigh University Press, *affiliate of* Rowman & Littlefield Publishing Group (RLPG), *distributed by* Rowman & Littlefield

Leisure Arts Inc, *division of* Liberty Media, *distributor for* Oxmoor House

The Lentz Leadership Institute LLC, *imprint of* The Refractive Thinker Press

Hal Leonard, *distributed by* ArtAge Publications

Hal Leonard Corp, *distributor for* Ableton, Acoustica, AirTurn, Amadeus Press, Antares, Apogee, Applause Books, Aquarius, Arrangers Publishing, Art String Publishing, Ashley Music, Avid, Axe Heauen, Backbeat Books, Berklee Press, Leonard Bernstein, Blue Microphones, Fred Bock Music Company, Boosey & Hawkes, Cakewalk, CD Sheet Music, Centerstream Publications, Centerstream Publishing LLC, Cherry Lane Music Co, ChordBuddy, Curnow Music, De Haske Publications, Dots & Lines Inc, Editions Durand, EM Books, EMI Christian, Editions Max Eschig, Faber Music Ltd, Family Communications, Fleamarket Music, Griffin Technology, Guitar World, Hamilton Stands, Hartke, G Henle Verlag, Homespun Tapes, Hudson Music, IK Multimedia, Lauren Keiser Music, Lorie Lane, Limelight Editions, Line 6, M-Audio, Ashley Mark Publishing Co, Edward B Marks Music, Meredith Music, Mighty Bright, Modern Drummer Publications, Music Minus One, Music Sales America, Musicians Institute Press, Noteflight, Peermusic Classical, PreSonus, Professional Music Institute, Propellerhead, PWM Editions, QSC, Ricordi, Lee Roberts Publications, Rock House, Rubank Publications, St Nicolas Music Inc, Editions Salabert, Samson Audio, G Schirmer Inc (Associated Music Publishers), Schott Music, Shawnee Press, Sibelius, Sikorski, Sony, Steinberg, Sterling Publishing, String Letter Publishing, Tara Publications, Tycoon Percussion, Vintage Guitar, Voyageur Press, Waltons Irish Music, Willis Music, XLN Audio, Yamaha

Lerner Books UK, *division of* Lerner Publishing Group Inc

Lerner Digital, *imprint of* Lerner Publishing Group Inc

Lerner Publications, *imprint of* Lerner Publishing Group Inc

Lerner Publisher Services, *division of* Lerner Publishing Group Inc

Lerner Publishing Group Inc, *division of* Lerner Universal Corp, *distributor for* Andersen Press USA, Columbus Zoo, Walter Foster Publishing, Gecko Press, JR Comics, The Kane Press, Kar-Ben Partners, MVP Books, Red Chair Press, Sandy Creek, Scobre Educational, Stoke Books, We Do Listen

LernerClassroom, *imprint of* Lerner Publishing Group Inc

The Letter People®, *imprint of* Abrams Learning Trends

Leuven University Press, *distributed by* Cornell University Press

Lexington Books, *imprint of* Rowman & Littlefield Publishing Group, *distributor for* The Colonial Williamsburg Foundation

LexisNexis®, *division of* RELX Group PLC, *distributor for* Standard Publishing Corp

LexisNexis® Matthew Bender®, *member of* The LexisNexis® Group

Liaison, *imprint of* Kensington Publishing Corp

Libraries Unlimited, *imprint of* ABC-CLIO

Library Company of Philadelphia, *distributed by* Diane Publishing Co

Library du Liban (Lebanon), *distributed by* International Book Centre Inc

The Library of America, *distributed by* Penguin Group USA, A Penguin Random House Company, Penguin Group USA, A Penguin Random House Company

Library of Congress-Center for the Book, *distributed by* Oak Knoll Press

Library of Contemporary Thought, *imprint of* Penguin Random House Inc

Library of Islam, *imprint of* Kazi Publications Inc

Libri Canali Bassi, *distributed by* Edgewise Press Inc

Libros Desafio, *imprint of* Faith Alive Christian Resources

Libros en Espanol, *imprint of* Touchstone

Libros Liguori, *imprint of* Liguori Publications

Life Cycle Books, *division of* Life Cycle Books Ltd (Canada)

Life on the Edge, *imprint of* Focus on the Family

Life Wisdom, *imprint of* Paragon House

LifeGuide Bible Studies, *imprint of* InterVarsity Press

LifeLearn, *distributor for* Teton NewMedia Inc, *distributed by* Teton NewMedia Inc

Lifetree™, *imprint of* Group Publishing Inc

LifeWay Christian Resources, *distributor for* Casa Bautista de Publicaciones

The Liffey Press, *distributed by* Dufour Editions Inc

The Light, *imprint of* Tughra Books

Light & Life, *distributor for* Ancient Faith Publishing, *distributed by* Ancient Faith Publishing

Light & Life Publishing Co, *distributor for* Saint Herman Press

Lighthouse Press, *imprint of* ProStar Publications Inc

Lightning Rod Press, *imprint of* American Philosophical Society

Liguori Publications, *distributor for* Redemptorist Publications

Liguori/Triumph, *imprint of* Liguori Publications

L'il Acorns, *imprint of* Cedar Grove Books

Philip E Lilienthal, *imprint of* University of California Press

Lillenas Publishing Co, *imprint of* Beacon Hill Press of Kansas City

Lilliput Press Ltd, *distributed by* Dufour Editions Inc

LIM Editrice SRL (Italy), *distributor for* Pendragon Press

Limelight Editions, *imprint of* Hal Leonard Books, Hal Leonard Performing Arts Publishing Group, *distributed by* Hal Leonard Corp

Limestone Press, *distributed by* University of Alaska Press

Lindisfarne Books, *imprint of* SteinerBooks, SteinerBooks, *distributed by* Floris Books

Line by Line, *imprint of* Aspatore Books

Line 6, *distributed by* Hal Leonard Corp

John Liner Organization, *subsidiary of* Standard Publishing Corp

The Linick Group Inc, *distributor for* Linick International, LKA Inc, National Association of Photo Sellers™, *distributed by* New World Press Books, Okinawan Kobujutsu Kyokai Association (OKKA)

Linick International, *distributed by* The Linick Group Inc

Linux Journal Press, *imprint of* Belltown Media

Linworth Learning, *imprint of* Linworth Publishing

Linworth Publishing, *imprint of* ABC-CLIO, Libraries Unlimited

Lippincott Williams & Wilkins, *unit of* Wolters Kluwer Health

Lippincott, Williams & Wilkins, *imprint of* Wolters Kluwer US Corp

Lips (Magazine & Press), *distributed by* Cross-Cultural Communications

LIS (Legal Information Services), *subsidiary of* CCH, a Wolters Kluwer business

Listening Library®, *division of* Books on Tape®, *imprint of* Books on Tape®, *distributed by* Books on Tape®

Literary House Press, *distributed by* Cornell Maritime Press Inc

Literary Reprint Series, *imprint of* University of Alaska Press

Literature & Thought, *imprint of* Perfection Learning Corp

Litigation Group, *division of* Public Citizen

little bee books, *imprint of* Bonnier Publishing, *distributed by* Simon & Schuster, Inc, Simon & Schuster Sales Division

Little, Brown, *distributor for* Parachute Publishing LLC

Little, Brown & Co, *distributor for* Alloy Entertainment LLC

Little, Brown & Company, *distributed by* Learning Links Inc

Little, Brown and Company, *division of* Hachette Book Group

Little, Brown Books for Young Readers, *division of* Hachette Book Group

The Little Entrepreneur, *imprint of* Harper Arrington Publishing & Media, *distributed by* Harper Arrington Publishing

Little Oak Press, *distributed by* Sunbelt Publications Inc

Little Pickle Press, *imprint of* Sourcebooks Inc

Little Room Press, *distributed by* Fordham University Press

Little Shepherd, *imprint of* Scholastic Trade Division

Little Simon, *imprint of* Simon & Schuster Children's Publishing

Little Toller Books, *distributed by* Dufour Editions Inc

Liturgical Press, *division of* The Order of St Benedict Inc, *distributor for* Cistercian Publications

Liturgical Press Books, *imprint of* Liturgical Press

Liturgy Training Publications, *subsidiary of* Archdiocese of Chicago, *distributor for* United States Catholic Conference Publications (select titles)

Liveright & Co, *imprint of* W W Norton & Company Inc

Living Books, *imprint of* Tyndale House Publishers Inc

Living Language, *imprint of* Penguin Random House Audio Publishing, Penguin Random House Inc

Living Lessons, *distributed by* Hachai Publishing

Livingston Press, *division of* University of West Alabama, *distributor for* Swallow's Tale Press

LKA Inc, *imprint of* The Linick Group Inc, *distributed by* The Linick Group Inc

Llewellyn Publications, *division of* Llewellyn Worldwide Ltd, *distributor for* Blue Angel, Lo Scarabeo

Lobster Press, *distributed by* Orca Book Publishers

Locks Art Publications/Locks Gallery, *division of* Locks Gallery

Loft, *distributed by* Prestel Publishing

Logan Brothers, *distributor for* Teton NewMedia Inc

Login Canada, *distributor for* Health Professions Press

Logion Press, *imprint of* Gospel Publishing House (GPH)

Logos, *imprint of* Bridge-Logos

Logos Press, *imprint of* thinkBiotech LLC

Y Lolfa, *distributed by* Dufour Editions Inc

Lombardy Studios, *distributed by* Casemate | publishers

Lominger Inc, *distributed by* Center for Creative Leadership LLC

Lone Oak Press, *imprint of* Finney Company Inc

Lone Star Audio, *imprint of* Recorded Books Inc, an RBmedia company

Long River Press, *imprint of* Sinomedia International Group

Longman, *distributor for* Marriage Transformation LLC, *distributed by* Trans-Atlantic Publications Inc

Looking Glass Books, *distributed by* John F Blair Publisher

Looking Glass Library, *imprint of* ABDO Publishing Group

Lookout Books, *distributed by* John F Blair Publisher

Looseleaf Law Publications Inc, *division of* Warodean Corp

Lorenz Educational Press, *division of* The Lorenz Corp

Lorimer, *distributed by* Casemate | publishers

James Lorimer & Co, *distributed by* Orca Book Publishers

Los Angeles Times Crosswords, *imprint of* Random House Reference/Random House Puzzles & Games

Lost Coast Press, *imprint of* Cypress House

Lost Horse Press, *distributed by* University of Washington Press

Lothrop, Lee & Shepard Books, *imprint of* HarperCollins Publishers

Lotus Press, *division of* Lotus Brands Inc, Lotus Brands Inc, *distributor for* Back to Eden Books, Dipti, East West Cultural Center, Les Editions ETC, Inner Worlds Music, November Moon, SABDA, Sadhana Publications, Samata Books, Sri Aurobindo Ashram, Star Sounds

Love Inspired, *imprint of* Love Inspired Books

Love Inspired Books, *imprint of* Harlequin Enterprises Ltd

Love Inspired Historical, *imprint of* Love Inspired Books

Love Inspired Suspense, *imprint of* Love Inspired Books

Lovestruck, *imprint of* Entangled Publishing

Loveswept, *imprint of* Penguin Random House Inc, Random House Publishing Group

LPC Group Inc, *distributor for* Dark Horse Comics

LRP Magazine Group, *subsidiary of* LRP Publications

LRS, *division of* Library Reproduction Service

LRT Editions, *distributed by* Casemate | publishers

Lucent Books®, *imprint of* The Rosen Publishing Group Inc, *distributor for* Greenhaven Press, KidHaven Press

Lucky Marble Books, *imprint of* PageSpring Publishing

Lucky Spool, *distributed by* The Taunton Press Inc

Luna Books, *imprint of* Harlequin Enterprises Ltd

Lund Humphries/Ashgate, *distributor for* National Gallery of Art

Luster Editions, *imprint of* Circlet Press Inc

LW Books, *imprint of* Schiffer Publishing Ltd

Lynn-Reinner Publishing, *distributor for* University of California Institute on Global Conflict & Cooperation

Lynx House Press, *distributed by* University of Washington Press

The Lyons Press, *imprint of* The Globe Pequot Press

Lyrical Press, *imprint of* Kensington Publishing Corp

Lyrical Shine, *imprint of* Kensington Publishing Corp

Lyrical Underground, *imprint of* Kensington Publishing Corp

M & H Type, *division of* The Arion Press

M-Audio, *distributed by* Hal Leonard Corp

Pat MacKay Projects, *imprint of* Quite Specific Media Group Ltd

Mackinac Historic Parks, *distributed by* Michigan State University Press (MSU Press)

Macmillan, *subsidiary of* Verlagsgruppe Georg von Holtzbrinck GmbH, Verlagsgruppe Georg von Holtzbrinck GmbH, *imprint of* McGraw-Hill School Education Group, *distributor for* Bloomsbury Publishing Inc, The College Board, Tom Doherty Associates, LLC, Entangled Publishing, National Association of Broadcasters (NAB), Papercutz, Rodale Inc

Macmillan Audio, *division of* Macmillan, Macmillan Holdings, LLC

Macmillan Caribbean (UK), *distributed by* Interlink Publishing Group Inc

Macmillan Education (UK), *distributed by* Players Press Inc

Macmillan Learning, *subsidiary of* Macmillan

Macmillan/McGraw-Hill, *imprint of* McGraw-Hill Education

Macmillan Reference USA™, *imprint of* Gale

MacroPrintBooks, *imprint of* Science & Humanities Press

MacVan Maps, *distributed by* Wide World of Maps Inc

MAD Books, *imprint of* DC Entertainment

Madison Area Community Supported Agriculture Coalition, *distributed by* Chelsea Green Publishing Co

Mage Persian Editions, *imprint of* Mage Publishers Inc

Maggid, *imprint of* The Toby Press LLC

Maggies Music, *distributed by* Mel Bay Publications Inc

Magic Readers, *imprint of* ABDO Publishing Group

Magill's Choice, *imprint of* Salem Press Inc

Magnes Press, *distributed by* Gefen Books

MAGNI, *imprint of* The Magni Co

Magni Co, *distributed by* Book Publishing Co

The Magni Co, *subsidiary of* The Magni Group Inc

Maharishi University of Management Press, *subsidiary of* Maharishi University of Management, *distributed by* Penguin Group USA, A Penguin Random House Company (select titles)

Main Street Books, *imprint of* Penguin Random House Inc

JA Majors, *distributor for* MedBooks

Make Prophetz, *imprint of* Cedar Grove Books

MakeMusic Inc, *distributed by* Alfred Music Publishing

Malley's, *distributed by* Mel Bay Publications Inc

Management Sciences for Health, *distributed by* Kumarian Press

Manchester University Press, *distributed by* Palgrave Macmillan

Mandala Earth, *imprint of* Insight Editions

Mandate Press, *imprint of* William Carey Library Publishers

Manhattan Prep, *distributed by* Simon & Schuster Sales Division

Manhattan Publishing Co, *division of* US & Europe Books Inc

Manning Publications Co, *distributed by* Dreamtech Press, Pearson Education

The Manuscript Society, *distributed by* Oak Knoll Press

Le Manuscrit, *distributed by* Beach Lloyd Publishers LLC

Many Hats Media, *distributor for* Sourced Media Books

Many Moons Press, *distributed by* Gem Guides Book Co

MAPART Publishing, *distributor for* Michelin Maps & Guides

Maple Leaf Audio, *imprint of* Recorded Books Inc, an RBmedia company

MAR*CO Products Inc, *distributor for* Boulden, Educational Media, HarperCollins, National Center for Youth Issues/STARS, *distributed by* ASCA, Boulden Publishing, Burnell Books, Calloway House, Career Kids FYI, CFKR Career, Character Development, Community Intervention, Courage to Change, Cress Productions Co, EDU Reference, Educational Media Corp, Incentive Plus, Jist, Mental Health Resources, National Center for Youth Issues/STARS, National Professional Resources, National Resource Center Youth Services, Paperbacks for Educators, School Speciality, SourceResource, WRS Group, YouthLight Inc

Marble Arch, *imprint of* Atria Books

Maren Green, *distributed by* Crabtree Publishing Co

Maren Green Publishing Inc, *distributed by* Crabtree Publishing Inc

Marine Survey Press, *imprint of* Marine Education Textbooks

Marine Techniques Publishing, *distributor for* Academic Press, Best Publishing Co, Butterworth-Heinemann, Clarkson Research Services Ltd, Elsevier, Science & Technology Books, Focal Press, Gulf Professional Publishers, PennWell Business & Industrial Division, W B Saunders Co, Waterfront Soundings Productions, Witherby Seamanship International Ltd, *distributed by* Elsevier Science, Technology & Business Books, PennWell Business & Industrial Division

Mariner Books, *imprint of* Houghton Mifflin Harcourt Trade & Reference Division

Marion Institute, *distributed by* Chelsea Green Publishing Co

Ashley Mark Publishing Co, *imprint of* Hal Leonard Corp, *distributed by* Hal Leonard Corp

marketumbrella.org, *distributed by* Chelsea Green Publishing Co

MarketResearch.com, *distributor for* Primary Research Group Inc

Edward B Marks Music, *distributed by* Hal Leonard Corp

Marmac Publishing Co, *distributed by* Pelican Publishing Co

Marquette University Press, *division of* Marquette University

Marquis Who's Who, *imprint of* Marquis Who's Who Ventures LLC

Marriage Transformation LLC, *distributed by* Barringer, Longman

Carole Marsh Books, *imprint of* Gallopade International Inc

Carole Marsh Mysteries, *imprint of* Gallopade International Inc

Marshall & Swift, *distributed by* McGraw-Hill Book Co

Marshall Cavendish Adult Trade, *imprint of* Marshall Cavendish Corp

Marshall Cavendish Benchmark, *imprint of* Marshall Cavendish Corp

Marshall Cavendish Corp, *member of* Times International Publishing Group, *distributed by* Marshall Cavendish Ltd (UK)

Marshall Cavendish Digital, *imprint of* Marshall Cavendish Corp

Marshall Cavendish Education, *imprint of* Marshall Cavendish Corp

Marshall Cavendish Ltd, *distributor for* Marshall Cavendish Corp

Marshall Cavendish Reference, *imprint of* Marshall Cavendish Corp

Marsilio, *imprint of* Rizzoli International Publications Inc

Darvin Martin CDs, *distributed by* Closson Press

Rux Martin Books, *imprint of* Houghton Mifflin Harcourt Trade & Reference Division

Martindale-Hubbell®, *imprint of* Martindale LLC

Marvel, *imprint of* Disney Publishing Worldwide

Marvel Worldwide Inc, *distributed by* Hachette Book Group

Marvelous Spirit Press, *imprint of* Loving Healing Press Inc

Helen Marx/Turtle Point, *imprint of* Turtle Point Press

Maryland Historical Society, *distributed by* Johns Hopkins University Press, The Johns Hopkins University Press

Maryland Historical Trust Press, *distributed by* Cornell Maritime Press Inc

Maryland History Press, *distributor for* Dogwood Ridge Books, Tapestry Press Ltd

Maryland Sea Grant Program, *distributed by* Cornell Maritime Press Inc

Mason Crest Publishers, *imprint of* National Highlights

The Massachusetts Historical Society, *distributed by* University of Virginia Press

Master Books®, *imprint of* New Leaf Publishing Group Inc

Masters of Photography, *imprint of* Aperture Books

Mastery Education, *subsidiary of* Peoples Educational Holdings Inc

Masthof Press, *distributor for* Closson Press

Math Products Plus, *imprint of* Wide World Publishing

Math Solutions®, *unit of* Houghton Mifflin Harcourt

Mathematica Josephina, *distributed by* American Mathematical Society

The Mathematical Association of America, *distributed by* Cambridge University Press

Mathematical Society of Japan, *distributed by* American Mathematical Society

Matheson Trust, *distributed by* Fons Vitae

Adam Matthew, *imprint of* SAGE Publishing

Maunsel & Co Publishers, *imprint of* Academica Press

Max Books, *imprint of* The RoadRunner Press

MCD/FSG, *imprint of* Farrar, Straus & Giroux, LLC

Margaret K McElderry Books, *imprint of* Simon & Schuster Children's Publishing

McFarland & Co Ltd Publishers, *subsidiary of* McFarland

McGraw-Hill, *imprint of* McGraw-Hill Science, Engineering, Mathematics, *distributor for* Society of Manufacturing Engineers, *distributed by* American Academy of Environmental Engineers & Scientists™, American Water Works Association (AWWA), NACE International, SAMS Technical Publishing LLC, SAS Publishing, Society of Manufacturing Engineers

McGraw-Hill Book Co, *distributor for* Marshall & Swift

McGraw-Hill Career Education, *division of* McGraw-Hill Higher Education

McGraw-Hill Contemporary, *imprint of* McGraw-Hill Education

McGraw-Hill Contemporary Learning Series, *division of* McGraw-Hill Higher Education

McGraw-Hill Create, *division of* McGraw-Hill Higher Education, *imprint of* McGraw-Hill Education, McGraw-Hill Higher Education

McGraw-Hill Education Australia, New Zealand & South Africa, *imprint of* McGraw-Hill Education

McGraw-Hill Education Europe, Middle East and Africa, *imprint of* McGraw-Hill Education

McGraw-Hill Education Latin America, *imprint of* McGraw-Hill Education

McGraw-Hill Education Mexico, *imprint of* McGraw-Hill Education

McGraw-Hill Education Spain, *imprint of* McGraw-Hill Education

McGraw-Hill Higher Education, *division of* McGraw-Hill Education

McGraw-Hill Humanities, Social Sciences, Languages, *division of* McGraw-Hill Higher Education, *imprint of* McGraw-Hill Education

McGraw-Hill International & Professional Publishing Group, *division of* McGraw-Hill Education

McGraw-Hill/Irwin, *division of* McGraw-Hill Higher Education, *imprint of* McGraw-Hill Education, McGraw-Hill Higher Education

McGraw-Hill Learning Solutions, *imprint of* McGraw-Hill Higher Education

McGraw-Hill Professional, *imprint of* McGraw-Hill Education, *distributed by* Professional Publications Inc (PPI)

McGraw-Hill Professional Publishing, *distributor for* American Society for Quality (ASQ)

McGraw-Hill Ryerson, *imprint of* McGraw-Hill Education

McGraw-Hill School Education Group, *division of* McGraw-Hill Education, *imprint of* McGraw-Hill Education

McGraw-Hill Science, Engineering, Mathematics, *division of* McGraw-Hill Higher Education, *imprint of* McGraw-Hill Education, McGraw-Hill Higher Education

McGraw-Hill Professional Development, *imprint of* McGraw-Hill Education

Anne McKinney Career Series, *imprint of* PREP Publishing

McKissick Museum, *distributed by* University of South Carolina Press

McRoy & Blackburn, Publishers, *distributed by* Epicenter Press Inc

McWhiney Foundation Press/State House Press, *distributed by* Texas A&M University Press

Md Books, *imprint of* May Davenport Publishers

MDR, A D&B Co, *division of* Dun & Bradstreet Corp

Meadow Creek Press, *imprint of* Crumb Elbow Publishing

Meadowbrook Press, *distributed by* Simon & Schuster, Simon & Schuster, Inc, Simon & Schuster Sales Division

Mean Free Path, *distributor for* American Society for Nondestructive Testing

R S Means from The Gordian Group, *distributed by* John Wiley & Sons Inc

Measuring Up®, *imprint of* Mastery Education

MedBooks, *division of* Professional Education Workshops & Seminars, *distributed by* JA Majors

Medford Press, *imprint of* Plexus Publishing, Inc

Medical Economics, *distributed by* OptumInsight™

Medical Group Management Association (MGMA), *distributor for* American Medical Association, Aspen Publishers, Greenbranch, HAP (Health Adminstration Press), Jones & Bartlett Learning, J Wiley & Sons

Medical Publishing (Gefen), *division of* Gefen Books

Medieval Institute Publications, *division of* Medieval Institute of Western Michigan University

Meditation Press, *distributed by* Epicenter Press Inc

Mel Bay Publications Inc, *distributor for* AcuTab Publications Inc, AMA, Chanterelle, Stefan Grossman's Guitar Workshop, Hardie Press, Learn Roots Music, Maggies Music, Malley's, Registry of Guitar Tutors (RGT), RGB Arte Visual, Scott's Highland Services, Voggenreiter Publishers, Walton's, SR Wheat

Mellen Biblical Press, *imprint of* The Edwin Mellen Press

Mellen Poetry Press, *imprint of* The Edwin Mellen Press

Paul Mellon Centre, *distributed by* Yale University Press

Memoirs, *imprint of* American Philosophical Society

Menasha Ridge Press, *imprint of* AdventureKEEN

Menasha Ridge Press Inc, *imprint of* AdventureKEEN

The Menil Collection, *distributed by* Yale University Press

Menil Foundation, *distributed by* University of Texas Press, Wittenborn Art Books

Menorah, *distributed by* Bloch Publishing Co

Mental Health Resources, *distributor for* MAR*CO Products Inc

Mercier, *distributed by* Dufour Editions Inc

Merck, *imprint of* John Wiley & Sons Inc

Merck Publishing, *distributed by* Simon & Schuster, Inc, Simon & Schuster Sales Division

Mercury Learning & Information, *distributed by* Stylus Publishing LLC

Meredith Music, *distributed by* Hal Leonard Corp

Merehurst Ltd, *imprint of* Tuttle Publishing

Merit Press Books, *imprint of* F+W Media Inc

Meriwether Publishing, *division of* Pioneer Drama Service Inc

Merriam-Webster Inc, *subsidiary of* Encyclopaedia Britannica Inc

Frank Merriwell Inc, *subsidiary of* National Learning Corp

Merry Muse Press, *imprint of* Loft Press Inc

MerwinAsia, *distributed by* University of Hawaii Press

Mesorah Publications Ltd, *distributor for* NCSY Publications

Messenger Publications, *distributed by* Dufour Editions Inc

Messianic Jewish Publishers, *division of* Messianic Jewish Communications, *distributor for* Chosen People Ministries, First Fruits of Zion, Jewish New Testament Publications

Metalmark, *imprint of* The Pennsylvania State University Press

Metamorphic Press, *distributed by* Chelsea Green Publishing Co

Metro Maps, *division of* Wide World of Maps Inc, *distributed by* Wide World of Maps Inc

Metropolitan Books, *imprint of* Henry Holt and Company, LLC

Metropolitan Classics, *division of* Fort Ross Inc

The Metropolitan Museum of Art, *distributed by* Yale University Press

MFA Publications, *imprint of* Museum of Fine Arts Boston, *distributed by* Thames & Hudson (outside of North America)

MHS, *distributor for* Specialty Press Inc

Michelin Maps & Guides, *division of* Michelin North America Inc, *distributed by* Langenscheidt Publishing Group, MAPART Publishing (CN only), NBN (guides for North America), Editions du Renouveau Pedagogique (French titles in Canada), Penguin Canada (English titles in Canada)

Michie, *imprint of* LexisNexis®

Michigan Municipal League, *affiliate of* National League of Cities, *distributor for* Crisp Books

Michigan State University Press (MSU Press), *division of* Michigan State University, *distributor for* Mackinac Historic Parks, MSU Museum, University of Alberta Press, University of Manitoba Press, *distributed by* UBC Press, Canada

Microcosm Books, *imprint of* TFH Publications Inc

Microtraining Associates, *imprint of* Alexander Street, a ProQuest Company

Midewin Series, *imprint of* High Tide Press

Midnight Editions, *imprint of* Cleis Press

Midnight Ink, *imprint of* Llewellyn Publications

Midnight Marquee Press Inc, *affiliate of* Luminary Press

Midrashic Editions, *imprint of* Cross-Cultural Communications

Midwest Library Service, *distributor for* Business Research Services Inc, Primary Research Group Inc

Mighty Bright, *distributed by* Hal Leonard Corp

Mighty Media Junior Readers, *imprint of* Mighty Media Press

Mighty Media Kids, *imprint of* Mighty Media Press

Mike Murach & Associates Inc, *distributed by* Shroff Publishers (reprints)

Milady, *division of* Cengage Learning

Milestone Documents, *division of* Schlager Group Inc

Milet Publishing Ltd, *imprint of* Tuttle Publishing, *distributed by* Tuttle Publishing

Military History Press, *distributed by* Casemate | publishers

Military Living Publications, *division of* Military Marketing Services Inc, Military Marketing Services Inc

Millbrook Press, *imprint of* Lerner Publishing Group Inc

White Burkett Miller Center, *distributed by* University Press of America Inc

Milliken Publishing Co, *division of* The Lorenz Corp, The Lorenz Corp

Mills & Boon Large Print, *distributed by* Thorndike Press

Sally Milner, *distributed by* Sterling Publishing Co Inc

Minedition, *imprint of* Penguin Group USA, A Penguin Random House Company

The Minerals, Metals & Materials Society (TMS), *affiliate of* AIME

Minnesota Historical Society Press, *division of* Minnesota Historical Society

Minotaur Books, *imprint of* St Martin's Press, LLC

MIRA, *imprint of* Harlequin Enterprises Ltd

Miranda Press Trade Division, *imprint of* Cognizant Communication Corp

Miss Jackie Inc, *distributed by* Gryphon House Inc

Miss Rosen Edition, *imprint of* powerHouse Books

Mission San Juan Capistrano Women's Guild, *distributed by* Sunbelt Publications Inc

The Missionary Enterprise in Asia, *imprint of* EastBridge

Missouri History Museum, *distributed by* University of Missouri Press

MIT, *distributor for* The AEI Press

MIT Press, *distributed by* DawnSignPress

The MIT Press, *distributor for* AAAI Press, Afterall Books, Canadian Centre for Architecture, Semiotext(e), Zone Books

Mitten Press, *imprint of* Spry Publishing

MJF Books, *imprint of* Fine Creative Media, Inc

MMPBooks, *distributed by* Casemate | publishers

MOAC, *imprint of* John Wiley & Sons Inc

Farhang Moaser, *distributed by* Ibex Publishers

Model Centrum Progres, *distributed by* Casemate | publishers

Modern Drummer Publications, *distributed by* Hal Leonard Corp

Modern History Press, *imprint of* Loving Healing Press Inc

Modern Learning Press, *imprint of* EPS/School Specialty Literacy & Intervention

Modern Library, *imprint of* Penguin Random House Inc, Random House Publishing Group

Modern Masters, *imprint of* Abbeville Publishing Group

Modern Publishing, *division of* Kappa Books Publishers LLC

Moleskine, *distributed by* Chronicle Books LLC, Hachette Book Group

Moliere & Co, *imprint of* LinguaText LLC

Moll Anderson Productions, *distributed by* Simon & Schuster, Inc

Monacelli Press, *distributor for* Winterthur Museum, Garden & Library

The Monacelli Press, *imprint of* Penguin Random House Inc, *distributed by* Penguin Group USA, A Penguin Random House Company

Monacelli Studio, *imprint of* The Monacelli Press

Monarch Books, *distributed by* Kregel Publications

Arnoldo Mondadori Electa, *distributed by* Trans-Atlantic Publications Inc

Mondadori Spanish Language, *distributed by* Penguin Random House Inc

Mondo, *imprint of* Mondo Publishing

Moneta Publications, *distributed by* Chelsea Green Publishing Co

Money Market Directories, *unit of* Standard & Poor's

Monjeu Press, *distributed by* Gryphon House Inc

Monostereo, *distributed by* Simon & Schuster Audio

Montana Historical Society Press, *distributed by* The Globe Pequot Press

Monthly Review Press, *division of* Monthly Review Foundation Inc, Monthly Review Foundation Inc, *distributed by* New York University Press

Moody Press, *distributor for* Focus on the Family

Moody Publishers, *affiliate of* Ministry of Moody Bible Institute

Moon City Press, *distributed by* The University of Arkansas Press

Moondance Press, *imprint of* Quarto Publishing Group USA Inc

Morehouse Publishing, *imprint of* Church Publishing Inc, *distributed by* Abingdon Press (wholesale orders only), Cokesbury (retail orders only)

Morgan Kaufmann, *imprint of* Elsevier Inc

Morrow Junior Books, *imprint of* HarperCollins Publishers

William Morrow, *imprint of* HarperCollins General Books Group, *distributor for* Nightingale-Conant

William Morrow Cookbooks, *imprint of* HarperCollins General Books Group

William Morrow Paperbacks, *imprint of* HarperCollins General Books Group

Mosby, *imprint of* Elsevier, Health Sciences Division, *distributor for* OptumInsight™, *distributed by* Fire Engineering Books & Videos, OptumInsight™

Moselle River, *distributed by* Casemate | publishers

Motorbooks, *imprint of* Quarto Publishing Group USA Inc

Motorbooks International, *distributor for* Haynes Manuals Inc, *distributed by* Heimburger House Publishing Co

Paul Mould Publishing, *imprint of* Empire Publishing Service, *distributed by* Empire Publishing Service

Mount Blue, *imprint of* Genesis Press Inc

Mount Ida Press, *distributed by* State University of New York Press

Mt Nittany Press, *imprint of* Eifrig Publishing LLC

Mount Olive College Press, *affiliate of* University of Mount Olive

Mount Vernon Ladies Association, *distributed by* The University of Virginia Press

Mountain Air Books, *imprint of* Mountain n' Air Books

Mountain Biking Press, *imprint of* FineEdge.com LLC

Mountain n' Air Books, *distributor for* Tom Harrison Cartography

Mountain Press, *distributor for* Ericson Books

Mountain Press Publishing Co, *distributor for* Bucking Horse Books, Clark City Press, Hops Press, Npustin Press, RainStone Press, Western Edge Press

Mountain Sports Press Series, *imprint of* Mountain Press Publishing Co

Mountaineers Books, *distributor for* The American Alpine Club Press

The Mountaineers Books, *division of* The Mountaineers, *distributor for* Adventure Cycling Association, The American Alpine Club Press, Colorado Mountain Club Press

De Gruyter Mouton, *imprint of* Walter de Gruyter GmbH & Co KG, Walter de Gruyter GmbH & Co KG, *distributed by* Walter de Gruyter Inc

Moznaim Publishing Corp, *distributor for* Avamra Institute, Breslov Research Institute, Red Wheel/Weiser/Conari

MRTS, *imprint of* Arizona Center for Medieval & Renaissance Studies (ACMRS)

MSU Museum, *distributed by* Michigan State University Press (MSU Press)

MTI, *distributed by* NACE International

MTV Books, *imprint of* Gallery Books

MTV Press, *distributed by* powerHouse Books

Mudborn Press, *imprint of* Bandanna Books

Coleccion Mujeres de Palabra, *imprint of* University of Puerto Rico Press

Mulberry Books, *imprint of* HarperCollins Publishers

Mulholland Books, *imprint of* Little, Brown and Company

Lars Mueller Publishers GmbH, *distributed by* Prestel Publishing

Multicultural Publications Inc, *subsidiary of* Making Education Reform Imperative Today Inc (MERIT)

Multnomah, *imprint of* Crown Publishing Group

Mundania Press, *imprint of* Mundania Press LLC

Museum of Early Southern Decorative Arts, *distributed by* The University of North Carolina Press

The Museum of Modern Art (MoMA), *distributed by* Distributed Art Publishers (DAP) (US & CN only)

Museum of Modern Art Children's Books, *distributed by* Harry N Abrams Inc

Museum of New Mexico Press, *unit of* New Mexico State Department of Cultural Affairs, *distributed by* University of New Mexico Press

Music/Culture, *imprint of* Wesleyan University Press

Music Inc, *imprint of* Alfred Music Publishing

Music Minus One, *distributed by* Hal Leonard Corp

Music Sales, *distributed by* Welcome Enterprises Inc

Music Sales America, *distributed by* Hal Leonard Corp

Music Sales Corp, *distributed by* Beekman Books Inc

Musicians Institute Press, *imprint of* Hal Leonard Corp, *distributed by* Hal Leonard Corp

Muswell Hill Press, *distributed by* State University of New York Press

MVP Books, *distributed by* Lerner Publishing Group Inc

My Healthy Church, *imprint of* Gospel Publishing House (GPH)

Mycroft & Moran, *imprint of* Arkham House Publishers Inc

myON, a division of Capstone, *distributor for* Jump!

MyReportLinks.com Books, *imprint of* Enslow Publishing LLC

The Mysterious Press, *imprint of* Grove Atlantic Inc

Mystic Books, *imprint of* Regal Crest Enterprises

Mystic Oaks, *imprint of* Oak Tree Press

Mystic Seaport Museum Inc, *distributor for* Glencannon, Ten Pound Island Books

N & A, *imprint of* The Nautical & Aviation Publishing Co of America Inc

NACE International, *distributor for* ASM International, ASTM, AWS, Butterworth-Heinemann, Cambridge University Press, CASTI Publishing, Compass Publications, CRC Press, Marcel Dekker Inc, E&FN Spon, Elsevier Science Publishers, Gulf Publishing, Industrial Press, Institute of Materials, ISO, McGraw-Hill, MTI, Prentice Hall, Professional Publications, SSPC, Swedish Corrosion Institute, John Wiley & Sons Inc, *distributed by* Australasian Corrosion Association Inc

Narosa Publishing House, *distributed by* American Mathematical Society

NASCO, *distributor for* National Council of Teachers of Mathematics (NCTM)

NASSP, *imprint of* National Association of Secondary School Principals (NASSP)

NASW Press, *division of* National Association of Social Workers (NASW)

Nataraj, *imprint of* New World Library

National Academies Press (NAP), *division of* National Academies

The National Alliance Research Academy, *division of* The National Alliance for Insurance Education & Research

National Archives & Records Administration, *distributed by* J J Keller & Associates, Inc

National Association for Music Education (NAfME), *distributed by* Rowman & Littlefield Education

National Association of Broadcasters (NAB), *distributed by* Allyn & Bacon, Lawrence Erlbaum Associates, Focal Press, Macmillan, Tab Books

National Association of Home Builders (NAHB), *distributed by* BuilderBooks.com

National Association of Photo Sellers, *imprint of* Copywriter's Council of America™ (CCA), *distributed by* Copywriter's Council of America™ (CCA)

National Association of Photo Sellers™, *imprint of* The Linick Group Inc, *distributed by* The Linick Group Inc

National Book Co, *division of* Educational Research Associates

National Book Network, *distributor for* Impact Publications/Development Concepts Inc, LearningExpress LLC, *distributed by* Heimburger House Publishing Co

National Book Network (NBN), *distributor for* Association for Talent Development (ATD) Press

National Center Early Childhood Workforce, *distributed by* Gryphon House Inc

National Center for Children in Poverty, *division of* Mailman School of Public Health at Columbia University

National Center for Youth Issues/STARS, *distributor for* MAR*CO Products Inc, *distributed by* MAR*CO Products Inc

National Council of Examiners for Engineering & Surveying, *distributed by* Professional Publications Inc (PPI)

National Council of Teachers of Mathematics (NCTM), *distributed by* Eric Armin Inc Education Ctr, Delta Education, Didax Educational Resources, Educators Outlet, ETA Cuisenaire, Lakeshore Learning Materials, NASCO, Spectrum

National Doll Society of America, *division of* Success Advertising & Publishing

National Farm Book Co, *division of* Hobar Publications

National Gallery, London, *distributed by* Yale University Press

National Gallery of Art, *distributed by* Abrams, DAP, Lund Humphries/Ashgate, Prestel-Del Monico Books, Princeton University Press, Thames & Hudson, University of Chicago Press, Yale University Press

National Genealogical Society, *distributed by* Heritage Books Inc

National Geographic, *distributor for* The Colonial Williamsburg Foundation, *distributed by* Penguin Random House Inc

National Geographic Adventure Classics, *imprint of* National Geographic Books

National Geographic Adventure Press, *imprint of* National Geographic Books

National Geographic Books, *division of* National Geographic Society, *distributed by* Penguin Random House (worldwide exc UK), PGUK/Hi Marketing (United Kingdom)

National Geographic Children's Books, *imprint of* National Geographic Books

National Geographic Directions, *imprint of* National Geographic Books

National Geographic Learning, *unit of* Cengage Learning

National Institute of Occupational Safety & Health, *distributed by* J J Keller & Associates, Inc

National Professional Resources, *distributor for* Council for Exceptional Children (CEC), MAR*CO Products Inc, *distributed by* Council for Exceptional Children (CEC)

National Ranching Heritage Center, *distributed by* Texas Tech University Press

National Resource Center First Year Experience, *distributed by* Stylus Publishing LLC

National Resource Center for Youth Services (NRCYS), *division of* University of Oklahoma-Outreach

National Resource Center Youth Services, *distributor for* MAR*CO Products Inc

National Teacher Examination Series, *imprint of* National Learning Corp

The National Underwriter Co, *division of* ALM Media LLC

Native Ink Press, *imprint of* Ink Smith Publishing

Native Voices, *imprint of* Book Publishing Co

Natural Heritage Press, *distributed by* Birch Brook Press

Nature Study Guides, *imprint of* AdventureKEEN

Naturegraph, *distributed by* Gem Guides Book Co

NaturEncyclopedia Series, *imprint of* Stemmer House Publishers Inc

Naval Institute Press, *division of* US Naval Institute, *distributed by* Publishers Group West (digital only)

NavPress, *imprint of* NavPress Publishing Group, *distributed by* Tyndale House Publishers Inc

NavPress Publishing Group, *division of* The Navigators, *distributed by* Tyndale House Publishers Inc

Nazarene Publishing House, *imprint of* Beacon Hill Press of Kansas City

NBN, *distributor for* Michelin Maps & Guides

NCP, *imprint of* New City Press

NCSY Publications, *distributed by* Mesorah Publications Ltd

NDY Publishing, *division of* Rothstein Associates Inc

NEA Professional Library, *imprint of* National Education Association (NEA)

Near Eastern Press, *imprint of* Holmes Publishing Group LLC

Nefu Books, *imprint of* Africana Homestead Legacy Publishers Inc

Neibauer Press, *division of* Louis Neibauer Co Inc, Louis Neibauer Co Inc

The Netherlands Institute for Social Research, *distributed by* Transaction Publishers Inc

Nevada Publications, *distributor for* Gem Guides Book Co, *distributed by* Gem Guides Book Co

New American Fiction Series, *imprint of* Green Integer

New American Poetry Series, *imprint of* Green Integer

The New Careers Center, *division of* Finney Company Inc

New City, *distributed by* New City Press

New City Press, *division of* Focolare Movement, *distributor for* Ciudad Nueva (Argentina, Spain), New City (Great Britain)

New Criterion Books, *distributed by* St Augustine's Press Inc

New Directions Publishing Corp, *distributed by* W W Norton & Company Inc

New Earth Records, *distributed by* Sounds True Inc

New England AEYC, *distributed by* Gryphon House Inc

New England Bibliographies, *distributed by* Oak Knoll Press

New England History Press, *imprint of* Picton Press

New Falcon Publications, *imprint of* The Original Falcon Press

New Forest Press, *imprint of* Black Rabbit Books

New Harvest, *imprint of* Houghton Mifflin Harcourt Trade & Reference Division

New Holland Publishers (UK) Ltd, *distributed by* The Globe Pequot Press

New Horizons, *distributed by* Gryphon House Inc

New Horizons Book Publishing Co, *imprint of* World Citizens

New Island Books, *distributed by* Dufour Editions Inc

New Issues Poetry & Prose, *affiliate of* Western Michigan University, *distributed by* University Press of New England

The New Jerusalem Bible, *imprint of* Penguin Random House Inc

New Leaf, *distributor for* Ash Tree Publishing

New Leaf Books, *distributor for* Blue Poppy Press

New Leaf Press, *imprint of* New Leaf Publishing Group Inc

New Marketplace, *imprint of* The Oaklea Press

New Netherland Institute, *distributed by* State University of New York Press

New Pacific Press, *distributed by* North Atlantic Books

New Page Books, *imprint of* The Career Press Inc

New Poets Series, *imprint of* BrickHouse Books Inc

New Readers Press, *division of* ProLiteracy, ProLiteracy, *distributor for* TESOL International Association, *distributed by* International Book Centre Inc

New Traditions, *imprint of* Gallopade International Inc

New Voices, *imprint of* Florida Academic Press

New Win Publishing, *division of* Academic Learning Co LLC

New World Library, *division of* Whatever Publishing Inc, Whatever Publishing Inc

New World Paperbacks, *imprint of* International Publishers Co Inc

New World Press, *imprint of* Copywriter's Council of America™ (CCA), The Linick Group Inc, *distributed by* China Books

New World Press Books, *distributor for* The Linick Group Inc

New York Academy of Sciences (NYAS), *distributed by* Wiley Blackwell Publishers

The New York Botanical Garden Press, *division of* New York Botanical Garden, The New York Botanical Garden

New York Nights, *imprint of* Ugly Duckling Presse

New York University Press, *distributor for* Combined Academic Publishers Ltd, Footprint Books, Monthly Review Press, *distributed by* Heimburger House Publishing Co

Newbridge Communications Inc, *distributor for* Educational Impressions Inc

Newbridge Discovery Links, *imprint of* Sundance/Newbridge Publishing

Newbury Street Press, *imprint of* New England Historic Genealogical Society

The Newman Press, *imprint of* Paulist Press

Newmarket Press for It Books, *imprint of* HarperCollins General Books Group

NewSouth Books, *imprint of* NewSouth Inc, *distributed by* John F Blair Publisher

Newtona LLC, *distributed by* Sunbelt Publications Inc

Nexus Special Interests, *distributed by* Trans-Atlantic Publications Inc

NFB, *imprint of* No Frills Buffalo

NFB Distribution, *distributor for* No Frills Buffalo

NIAS Press, *distributed by* University of Hawaii Press

Niche Publishing, *distributed by* John F Blair Publisher

Nightboat Books, *distributed by* University Press of New England

Nightingale-Conant, *distributed by* William Morrow

Nightingale-Conant (UK), *subsidiary of* Nightingale-Conant

Nightingale Editions, *imprint of* Cross-Cultural Communications

Nilgiri Press, *division of* Blue Mountain Center of Meditation

Nimbus Publishing, *distributed by* Orca Book Publishers

Nimbus Publishing Ltd, *distributed by* Down East Books

Nippon Foundation, *distributed by* EastBridge

NISO Press, *imprint of* National Information Standards Organization (NISO)

No Frills Buffalo, *distributed by* Createspace, NFB Distribution

No Starch Press, *distributed by* O'Reilly Media

Nodin Press, *distributed by* AdventureKEEN

Noel Press, *imprint of* Nova Science Publishers Inc

Noesis Press, *imprint of* The Davies Group Publishers

Noetic Books, *imprint of* New Harbinger Publications Inc

NOLO, *subsidiary of* Internet Brands Inc

Non-Duality Press, *imprint of* New Harbinger Publications Inc

Nonpareil Books, *imprint of* David R Godine Publisher Inc

The Noontide Press, *imprint of* Legion for the Survival of Freedom

North Atlantic Books, *division of* Society for the Study of Native Arts & Sciences, *distributor for* DharmaCafe, Energy Arts, Ergos Institute, Heaven & Earth Publications, New Pacific Press

North Carolina Museum of Art, *distributed by* The University of North Carolina Press

North Country Books, *imprint of* North Country Books Inc

North Country Classics, *imprint of* North Country Books Inc

North Light Books, *imprint of* F+W Media Inc

North Point Press, *imprint of* Farrar, Straus & Giroux, LLC

North South Books, *distributed by* Simon & Schuster Sales Division

North Star Way, *imprint of* Gallery Books

Northcross Books, *distributed by* Sunbelt Publications Inc

Northeastern University Press, *imprint of* University Press of New England, *distributed by* University Press of New England

Northern Illinois University Press, *distributed by* University of Chicago Press

Northfield Publishing, *imprint of* Moody Publishers

NorthSouth Books, *distributed by* Simon & Schuster, Inc

Northwestern University Press, *distributor for* Lake Forest College Press (Chicago area studies), Tia Chucha Press

W W Norton & Company Inc, *distributor for* Airphoto International Ltd/Odyssey Publications, Albatross Publishing House, Atlas & Co, Blue Guides Ltd, George Braziller Inc, Chess Information & Research Center, The Countryman Press, Dalkey Archive Press, Fantagraphics Books, Kales Press, New Directions Publishing Corp, Ontario Review Press, The Overlook Press, Peace Hill Press, Pegasus Books, Persea Books, Persea Books Inc, Pushcart Press, Quantuck Lane Press, Skyhorse Publishing, Thames & Hudson, Tilbury House Publishers, Tilbury House Publishing, Tin House Books, Winterthur Museum, Garden & Library, *distributed by* Heimburger House Publishing Co

Norvik Press, *distributed by* Dufour Editions Inc

Norwalk Press, *imprint of* Book Publishing Co

Nosy Crow, *imprint of* Candlewick Press

Noteflight, *distributed by* Hal Leonard Corp

Nova Biomedical Press, *imprint of* Nova Science Publishers Inc

Nova Global Affairs Press, *imprint of* Nova Science Publishers Inc

Nova History Press, *imprint of* Nova Science Publishers Inc

Nova Music, *imprint of* Nova Science Publishers Inc

Nova Science Books, *imprint of* Nova Science Publishers Inc

Nova Southeastern University, *distributed by* Gryphon House Inc

Novalis, *distributor for* Twenty-Third Publications, *distributed by* Twenty-Third Publications

Novel-Ties Study Guides, *imprint of* Learning Links Inc

November Moon, *distributed by* Lotus Press

Novinka Books, *imprint of* Nova Science Publishers Inc

Npustin Press, *distributed by* Mountain Press Publishing Co

NRH Press, *distributed by* Vandamere Press

NSTA Ebooks+, *imprint of* National Science Teachers Association (NSTA)

NSTA Kids, *imprint of* National Science Teachers Association (NSTA)

NSTA Press, *imprint of* National Science Teachers Association (NSTA)

NTIS, *distributor for* Energy Information Administration (EIA)

Nuclear Energy Agency, *imprint of* OECD Washington Center, *distributed by* OECD Washington Center

Coleccion Nueve Pececitos, *imprint of* University of Puerto Rico Press

The Numata Center, *distributed by* University of Hawaii Press

Number Success, *imprint of* Advance Publishing Inc

Numismatics Books, *imprint of* Betterway Books

Nursesbooks.org, The Publishing Program of ANA, *division of* American Nurses Association

Nursing Knowledge Center, *imprint of* Nursesbooks.org, The Publishing Program of ANA

NUS Press, *distributed by* University of Hawaii Press

Nutri-Books, *distributor for* Ash Tree Publishing

Nylabone Products, *division of* TFH Publications Inc

Nystrom Education, *division of* Social Studies School Service

Oak Knoll Press, *distributor for* American Antiquarian Society, Bibliographical Society of America, Bibliographical Society of University of Virginia, The Bibliographical Society (UK), Block Museum, Boston College, John Carter Brown Library, Bryn Mawr College, Catalpa Press, Caxton Club, Center for Book Arts, Chapin Library, Fondation Custodia, The Grolier Club, Hes & De Graaf, Historic New Orleans Collection, Library of Congress-Center for the Book, The Manuscript Society, New England Bibliographies, Providence Athenaeum, Rivendale Press, Tate Galleries, Texas State Historical Association, Typophiles, Winterthur Museum, Yushodo Press

Oak Tree Books, *imprint of* Oak Tree Press

Oberlin College Press, *subsidiary of* Oberlin College, *distributed by* University Press of New England, University Press of New England (UPNE)

Oberon Books, *distributed by* Theatre Communications Group

O'Brien Press, *distributed by* Dufour Editions Inc

Obsessive Anonymous, *distributed by* Hazelden Publishing

Obsidian, *imprint of* Genesis Press Inc

Occupational Competency Examination Series, *imprint of* National Learning Corp

Ocean Publishing, *imprint of* Square One Publishers Inc

Ocean Tree Books, *distributed by* Treasure Chest Books

Octavo Editions, *distributed by* Konecky & Konecky LLC

Octavo Press, *imprint of* Templegate Publishers

Octopus Books, *distributed by* Hachette Book Group

Odonian Press, *distributed by* Common Courage Press

Odyssey Books, *division of* The Ciletti Publishing Group Inc

OECD Washington Center, *division of* Organization for Economic Cooperation & Development (France), *distributor for* International Energy Agency, International Transportation Forum, Nuclear Energy Agency

Ofeq Books, *distributed by* The Toby Press LLC

Office of External Affairs, *division of* RAND Corp

Office of the Federal Register, *distributed by* J J Keller & Associates, Inc

Office of the United Nations High Commissioner for Human Rights (OHCHR), *distributed by* United Nations Publications

Ohio State University Foreign Language Publications, *division of* Ohio State University Foreign Language Center

Ohio University Press, *distributor for* The Colonial Williamsburg Foundation

Okinawan Kobujutsu Kyokai Association (OKKA), *distributor for* The Linick Group Inc

Old Farmers Almanac, *distributed by* Houghton Mifflin Harcourt Trade & Reference Division

The Old Farmer's Almanac, *distributed by* Houghton Mifflin Harcourt

Old Kings Road Press, *imprint of* Athletic Guide Publishing

Old Seattle Press, *distributed by* Epicenter Press Inc

Olive Branch Press, *imprint of* Interlink Publishing Group Inc

Omnibus Press, *imprint of* Music Sales Group, *distributor for* Big Meteor, Gramophone

Omnidawn Publishing, *distributed by* University Press of New England

Omnific, *distributed by* Simon & Schuster Sales Division

Omnific Publishing, *distributed by* Simon & Schuster, Inc

Omohundro Institute of Early American History & Culture, *distributed by* The University of North Carolina Press

On My Own, *imprint of* Appletree Press Inc

1000 Readers, *imprint of* Gallopade International Inc

One World, *imprint of* Penguin Random House Inc, Random House Publishing Group

Ontario Review Press, *distributed by* W W Norton & Company Inc

Onyx, *imprint of* Penguin Group USA, A Penguin Random House Company

OPAMP Technical Books, *distributor for* Primary Research Group Inc

Open Books Press, *imprint of* Pen & Publish Inc

Open Court, *division of* Carus Publishing Co, dba Cricket Media

Open Road, *distributor for* Albert Whitman & Co, *distributed by* Simon & Schuster Sales Division

Open Road Integrated Media, *distributor for* Philosophical Library Inc

Open Road Publishing, *distributed by* Simon & Schuster, Simon & Schuster, Inc

Open Scroll, *imprint of* Bridge-Logos

Open Society Institute, *distributed by* Central European University Press

OPIS/STALSBY Directories & Databases, *division of* IHS Markit

Options, *imprint of* Triumph Learning LLC

OptumInsight™, *distributor for* American Medical Association, Medical Economics, Mosby, *distributed by* American Medical Association, Mosby

Opus Communications, *imprint of* HCPro Inc

OR Books, *distributor for* CUNY Journalism Press

Oral Biography Series, *imprint of* University of Alaska Press

Orange Grove Textbooks, *imprint of* University Press of Florida

Orb Books, *imprint of* Tom Doherty Associates, LLC

Orbis Books, *division of* Maryknoll Fathers & Brothers

Orbit, *division of* Hachette Book Group

Orbit Series, *imprint of* Krieger Publishing Co

Orca Book Publishers, *distributor for* The Book Publishing Co, Coteau Books, Creative Book Publishing, Formac Publishing, Lobster Press, James Lorimer & Co, Nimbus Publishing, Polestar Calendars, Second Story Press, 7th Generation, Sono Nis Press, Sumach Press, Tradewind Books, Tuckamore Books, Tudor House

Orchard Books, *imprint of* Scholastic Trade Division

Oregon California Trails Assn, *distributed by* Washington State University Press

Oregon Fever Books, *imprint of* Crumb Elbow Publishing

Oregon River Watch, *imprint of* Crumb Elbow Publishing

Oregon Writers Colony, *distributed by* Washington State University Press

O'Reilly Media, *distributor for* No Starch Press

O'Reilly Media Inc, *distributor for* Packt Publishing (technol ebook prog)

Oriental Institute Publications, *division of* University of Chicago

Orpen Press, *distributed by* Dufour Editions Inc

Orphiflamme Press™, *imprint of* Blue Mountain Arts Inc

Osprey Publishing, *imprint of* Bloomsbury Publishing Inc

Ostrich Editions, *imprint of* Cross-Cultural Communications

OTB Legacy Editions, *imprint of* Ocean Tree Books

Otherworlds, *imprint of* Zumaya Publications LLC

Christy Ottaviano Books, *imprint of* Henry Holt and Company, LLC

Ottographics, *distributed by* Chelsea Green Publishing Co

Our Sunday Visitor Publishing, *division of* Our Sunday Visitor Inc

Out of This World Press, *distributed by* Gem Guides Book Co

Outdoor Books & Maps, *imprint of* Adler Publishing Inc

Oval Books, *distributed by* The Globe Pequot Press

The Overlook Press, *subsidiary of* Peter Mayer Publishers Inc, Peter Mayer Publishers Inc, *distributed by* W W Norton & Company Inc

The Overmountain Press, *division of* Sabre Industries Inc, Sabre Industries Inc

Owlswick Press, *imprint of* Wildside Press LLC

Oxfam Publishing, *distributed by* Stylus Publishing LLC

Oxford, *distributed by* SAS Publishing

Oxford Illustrated Press, *distributed by* Haynes Manuals Inc

Oxford University Press, *distributor for* The American Chemical Society, Entomological Society of America, Fordham University Press, Kodansha USA Inc, *distributed by* Beach Lloyd Publishers LLC, Cheng & Tsui Co Inc, International Book Centre Inc

Oxford University Press Inc, *distributor for* Country Music Foundation Press

Oxford University Press USA, *division of* University of Oxford, *distributor for* The American Chemical Society, American University in Cairo, Arnold Clarendon, Cold Spring Harbor Laboratory Press, Engineering Press, Getty, Greenwich Medical Media, Grove Dictionaries, Hurst, IRL, Kodansha, Roxbury Publishing, Saunders, Stamford University Press, Thomson Publishing

Oxmoor House, *imprint of* Time Inc Books, *distributed by* H B Fenn (Canada), Leisure Arts Inc

Oyinde Publishing, *imprint of* Africana Homestead Legacy Publishers Inc

Ozark Publishing Inc, *distributed by* Econo-Clad Books, Gumdrop Books

Ozark Society, *distributed by* The University of Arkansas Press

Pace Press, *imprint of* Linden Publishing Co Inc

Pace University Press, *unit of* Pace University

Pacific Boating Almanac, *imprint of* ProStar Publications Inc

Pacific Institute, *distributed by* Washington State University Press

Pacific Press Publishing Association, *division of* Seventh-Day Adventist Church

Packt Publishing, *distributed by* O'Reilly Media Inc

Pact Press, *imprint of* Regal House Publishing

Pademelon Press, *distributed by* Gryphon House Inc

Pademelon Press Pty Ltd, *distributor for* Redleaf Press

Padua Playwrights Press, *distributed by* Theatre Communications Group

Kogan Page, *distributed by* Beekman Books Inc

Painted Turtle Books, *imprint of* Wayne State University Press

PAJ Publications, *distributed by* Theatre Communications Group

PAKS-Parents & Kids, *imprint of* THE Learning Connection®

Paladin Press, *division of* Paladin Enterprises Inc

Paladin Timeless Books, *imprint of* Twilight Times Books

Joan Palevsky, *imprint of* University of California Press

Palgrave Macmillan, *imprint of* Springer Nature, *distributor for* Berg Publishers, British Film Institute, Manchester University Press, Pluto Press, I B Tauris & Co Ltd, Zed Books

Pali Text Society, *imprint of* Wisdom Publications Inc

Palm Leaves Press, *imprint of* Parallax Press

Pan Asian Publications, *distributed by* Cheng & Tsui Co Inc

Pan Macmillan, *distributor for* Rodale Inc

Panda Books, *distributed by* China Books

Panmun Academic Services, *distributed by* Cheng & Tsui Co Inc

Panpac Education, *distributed by* Cheng & Tsui Co Inc

Pantheon Books, *imprint of* Pantheon Books/Schocken Books, Penguin Random House Inc

Pantheon Books/Schocken Books, *imprint of* Knopf Doubleday Publishing Group

Panzerwrecks, *distributed by* Casemate | publishers

Paolo Torti degli Alberti, *distributed by* Edgewise Press Inc

Paperbacks for Educators, *distributor for* MAR*CO Products Inc

Papercutz, *distributed by* Macmillan

PaperStar, *imprint of* Penguin Group USA, A Penguin Random House Company

Paperweight Press, *distributed by* Tuttle Publishing

Nelson Papucci, *distributed by* Sunbelt Publications Inc

Para Research, *imprint of* Schiffer Publishing Ltd

Parabola, *distributed by* Fons Vitae

Parachute Publishing LLC, *division of* Parachute Properties LLC, *distributed by* Bantam, Bendon, Berkley, Dorling Kindersley, Grosset, Harcourt, HarperCollins, HarperEntertainment, Kensington, Little, Brown, Penguin Random House Inc, Pocket, Running Press, Scholastic, Simon & Schuster, Inc

Paraclete Press Inc, *division of* Creative Joys Inc, *distributor for* Abbey of Saint Peter of Solesmes, Gloriae Dei Cantores

Paradigm Busters, *distributed by* Cheng & Tsui Co Inc

Paradigm Publications, *division of* Redwing Book Co

Paradigm Publishing Inc, *division of* EMC Publishing LLC

Paragon, *distributed by* Fons Vitae

Paragon House, *distributor for* Professors World Peace Academy, *distributed by* Bloomsbury Academic, Bloomsbury International Publishing USA (fulfillment by Macmillan)

Parallax Press, *division of* Unified Buddhist Church

Paraview Pocket Books, *imprint of* Cosimo Inc

Paraview Press, *division of* Cosimo Inc

Paraview Special Editions, *imprint of* Cosimo Inc

Pardey Publications, *imprint of* Paradise Cay Publications Inc

Parenting Press, *imprint of* Chicago Review Press

Parenting Press Inc, *imprint of* Chicago Review Press

Park Row Books, *imprint of* Harlequin Enterprises Ltd

Park Street Press, *imprint of* Inner Traditions International Ltd

ParmenidesAudio™, *division of* Parmenides Publishing

ParmenidesFiction™, *division of* Parmenides Publishing

Partner Press, *distributed by* Gryphon House Inc

Partner's Book Distributing Inc, *distributor for* Blue Poppy Press

Partner's/West Book Distributing Inc, *distributor for* Blue Poppy Press

Partnership Publications, *imprint of* House to House Publications

Parvardigar Press, *distributed by* Fons Vitae

Passages, *imprint of* Perfection Learning Corp

Passbooks, *imprint of* National Learning Corp

Pastoral Press, *imprint of* OCP

Patos Island Press, *distributed by* Epicenter Press Inc

jimmy patterson, *imprint of* Little, Brown and Company

Pauline Books & Media, *division of* Daughters of St Paul

Pauline Comics & Graphic Novels, *imprint of* Pauline Books & Media

Pauline Teen, *imprint of* Pauline Books & Media

Nancy Paulsen Books, *imprint of* Penguin Young Readers Group

Pavilion, *distributed by* Sterling Publishing Co Inc

Paws IV, *imprint of* Sasquatch Books

Peabody Museum of Archaeology & Ethnology, *distributed by* Harvard University Press

Peabody Museum Press, *unit of* Peabody Museum of Archaeology & Ethnology, Peabody Museum of Archaeology & Ethnology, Harvard University, *distributed by* Harvard University Press

Peace Books, *distributed by* China Books

Peace Hill Press, *distributed by* W W Norton & Company Inc

Peacewatch Editions, *imprint of* Ocean Tree Books

Peachpit Press, *imprint of* Pearson Education Ltd

Peachtree Jr, *imprint of* Peachtree Publishers

Pearson, *distributor for* Heinemann

Pearson Allyn & Bacon, *imprint of* Pearson Higher Education

Pearson Arts & Sciences, *division of* Pearson Education Ltd

Pearson Australia, *distributed by* Cheng & Tsui Co Inc

Pearson Australia-Schools Division, *distributor for* Boynton/Cook Publishers

Pearson Benjamin Cummings, *imprint of* Pearson Higher Education

Pearson Business Publishing, *unit of* Pearson Higher Education

Pearson Career, Health, Education & Technology, *division of* Pearson Education Ltd

Pearson Education, *distributor for* Manning Publications Co, *distributed by* American Academy of Environmental Engineers & Scientists™, Trans-Atlantic Publications Inc

Pearson Education Canada, *distributor for* Boynton/Cook Publishers

Pearson ELT, *division of* Pearson Education Ltd

Pearson Higher Education, *division of* Pearson Education Ltd

Pearson Humanities & Social Sciences, *unit of* Pearson Higher Education

Pearson Learning Solutions, *unit of* Pearson Higher Education

Pearson New Zealand-Schools Division, *distributor for* Boynton/Cook Publishers

Pearson School, *unit of* Pearson Education Ltd

Pearson Technology, *distributed by* SkillPath Publications

Editions du Renouveau Pedagogique, *distributor for* Michelin Maps & Guides

T H Peek Publisher, *division of* Clearweave Corp

Peermusic Classical, *distributed by* Hal Leonard Corp

Bette L Pegas, *distributed by* Sunbelt Publications Inc

Pegasus Books, *distributed by* W W Norton & Company Inc

PeKo Publishing, *distributed by* Casemate | publishers

Pelican International Corp, *subsidiary of* Pelican Publishing Co

Pelican Publishing Co, *distributor for* Hope Publishing House, Marmac Publishing Co, Self-Help Success Books

PelikaanPers, *distributed by* Casemate | publishers

A W Peller & Associates, *distributor for* Pieces of Learning Inc

Pembroke Publishers, *distributed by* Stenhouse Publishers

Pen & Sword, *distributed by* Casemate | publishers

Pen & Sword Digital, *distributed by* Casemate | publishers

Pendragon Press, *subsidiary of* Camelot Publishing Co Inc, Camelot Publishing Co Inc, *distributor for* Croatian Musicological Society, *distributed by* LIM Editrice SRL (Italy), G Ricordi (Italy)

Penguin, *imprint of* Penguin Books, Penguin Group USA, A Penguin Random House Company, *distributor for* Verso, *distributed by* Alfred Music Publishing

Penguin Books, *imprint of* Penguin Group USA, A Penguin Random House Company, Penguin Group USA, A Penguin Random House Company, *distributor for* The Countryman Press

Penguin Canada, *distributor for* Michelin Maps & Guides

Penguin Classics, *imprint of* Penguin Books, Penguin Group USA, A Penguin Random House Company

Penguin Compass, *imprint of* Penguin Books

Penguin Group USA, A Penguin Random House Company, *distributor for* Alloy Entertainment LLC, Arkangel, Bibli O'Phile, Consumer Guide/PIL, DAW Books Inc, Dream Works, Granta, HighBridge Audio, Kensington Publishing Corp, The Library of America, Maharishi University of Management Press, The Monacelli Press, *distributed by* Learning Links Inc

The Penguin Press, *imprint of* Penguin Group USA, A Penguin Random House Company, Penguin Group USA, A Penguin Random House Company

Penguin Putnam Inc, *distributed by* Heimburger House Publishing Co

Penguin Random House, *distributor for* National Geographic Books, Prometheus Books, Rizzoli International Publications Inc, Wizards of the Coast LLC

Penguin Random House Audio Publishing, *division of* Penguin Random House Inc, *subsidiary of* Penguin Random House Inc

Penguin Random House Canada, *distributor for* Europa Editions, Persea Books

Penguin Random House Inc, *distributor for* Alloy Entertainment LLC, Karen Brown's Guides, Europa Editions, Hatherleigh Press Ltd, Mondadori Spanish Language, National Geographic, Parachute Publishing LLC, Princeton Review, Rizzoli, Rugged Land, Shambhala, Shambhala Publications Inc, Smithsonian Books, Smithsonian Scholarly Press, Soho Press, Steerforth Press, The Taunton Press, Ten Speed Press, Wizards of the Coast, *distributed by* DawnSignPress, Dreamscape Media LLC, Learning Links Inc

Penguin Random House Large Print, *division of* Penguin Random House Inc

Penguin 20th Century Classics, *imprint of* Penguin Books

Penguin Workshop, *imprint of* Penguin Group USA, A Penguin Random House Company, Penguin Young Readers Group

Penguin Young Readers Group, *division of* Penguin Group USA, A Penguin Random House Company, Penguin Group USA, A Penguin Random House Company

Peninsula Publishing, *distributed by* Scitech Publishing Inc

PenMark Press, *imprint of* The Davies Group Publishers

Penn State University Press, *distributor for* University of California Institute on Global Conflict & Cooperation

Pennsylvania Historical & Museum Commission, *subsidiary of* The Commonwealth of Pennsylvania

Pennsylvania State Data Center, *subsidiary of* Institute of State & Regional Affairs

The Pennsylvania State University Press, *division of* Pennsylvania State University Libraries & Scholarly Communications

Pennwell, *distributed by* Gulf Publishing Co

PennWell Books, *division of* PennWell

PennWell Business & Industrial Division, *distributor for* Marine Techniques Publishing, *distributed by* Marine Techniques Publishing

Pennywell Press, *distributed by* John F Blair Publisher

Pennywyse Press, *imprint of* Imago Press

Penobscot Press, *imprint of* Picton Press

Pensiero Press, *imprint of* The Lentz Leadership Institute LLC

Pentecostal Publishing House, *subsidiary of* United Pentecostal Church International, *distributed by* Anchor Distributors, Christian Network International, Innovative Marketing, Spring Arbor

Penton Price Digests, *imprint of* Penton Media Inc

Linda Pequegnat, *distributed by* Sunbelt Publications Inc

Peradam Press, *subsidiary of* The Center for Cultural & Naturalist Studies

Percheron Press, *imprint of* Eliot Werner Publications Inc

Peter Peregrinus Ltd, *imprint of* IET USA Inc

Peregrinzilla, *distributed by* Chelsea Green Publishing Co

Sophia Perennis, *distributed by* Fons Vitae

Perfection Learning Corp, *distributor for* Abrams, Ace Books, Airmont, Annick Press, Archway, Atheneum, Baker Books, Ballantine, Bantam, Barrons, Berkley, Blake Books, Candlewick Press, Charlesbridge Press, Chelsea House, Children's Press, Chronicle Books, Crabtree Publishing, Crown, Disney Press, Distri Books, DK, Doubleday, Dutton, F+W Media Inc, Farrar, Straus & Giroux Inc, Fawcett, Firefly, First Avenue, Free Spirit, Fulcrum, Golden Books, Greenhaven Press Inc, Hammond, Hayes, Gareth Stevens, Frederick Warne

Perigee, *imprint of* Berkley Publishing Group

Periplus Editions, *imprint of* Tuttle Publishing, *distributed by* Tuttle Publishing

Periscope, *distributed by* Prestel Publishing

Permanent Publications, *distributed by* Chelsea Green Publishing Co

Permuted Press LLC, *distributed by* Simon & Schuster, Inc, Simon & Schuster Sales Division

Persea Books, *distributed by* W W Norton & Company Inc (worldwide exc Canada), Penguin Random House Canada (CN only)

Persea Books Inc, *distributed by* W W Norton & Company Inc

Persephone Books, *distributed by* Dufour Editions Inc

Persephone Press, *imprint of* Birch Brook Press, *distributed by* Birch Brook Press

Perseus (Addison Wesley Trade), *distributed by* HarperCollins Publishers

Perseus Books, *division of* Hachette Book Group

Perseverance Press, *distributed by* John Daniel & Co

Personal Profiles, *division of* Brown Books Publishing Group

Peterson Institute for International Economics, *distributed by* Columbia University Press

Peterson Institute for International Economics (PIIE), *distributor for* Center for Global Development

Peterson's, *distributed by* Hachette Book Group

Peterson's/Pacesetter Books, *imprint of* Peterson's, a Nelnet Company

Petroleum Extension Service (PETEX), *unit of* University of Texas Division of Continuing & Innovative Education

Pferdia TV, *distributed by* Trafalgar Square Books

Pflaum Publishing Group, *division of* Peter Li Inc

PGUK/Hi Marketing, *distributor for* National Geographic Books

Phaidon Press, *distributed by* Hachette Book Group

Phantom Books & Music, *imprint of* Empire Publishing Service

Phaze Books, *imprint of* Mundania Press LLC

Philadelphia Museum of Art, *distributed by* Yale University Press

Philedition, *distributed by* Casemate | publishers

Philomel, *imprint of* Penguin Group USA, A Penguin Random House Company, Penguin Group USA, A Penguin Random House Company, Penguin Young Readers Group

Philomel Books, *imprint of* Penguin Group USA, A Penguin Random House Company

Philosophical Library Inc, *distributed by* Open Road Integrated Media

Philosophy Documentation Center, *distributor for* Zeta Books (online access)

Phoenix International, *distributed by* The University of Arkansas Press

Phoenix International Publications, *distributed by* Hachette Book Group

Phoenix Mapping Service, *division of* Wide World of Maps Inc

Phoenix Publishing, *distributed by* CN Times Books

Pholiota Press Inc, *distributed by* Cross-Cultural Communications

Phonics Adventure, *imprint of* Advance Publishing Inc

Photofact®, *imprint of* SAMS Technical Publishing LLC

Photolucida Book, *distributed by* Franklin, Beedle & Associates Inc

Photosmith Books, *distributed by* Caxton Press

Daniela Piazza Editore, *distributed by* Chelsea Green Publishing Co

Picador, *subsidiary of* Macmillan

Picaro Publishing, *distributed by* Sunbelt Publications Inc

Picasso Project, *division of* Alan Wofsy Fine Arts, Alan Wofsy Fine Arts, *distributor for* Cramer (Switzerland), Kornfeld (Switzerland), Ramie (France), *distributed by* Alan Wofsy Fine Arts

The Picasso Project, *imprint of* Alan Wofsy Fine Arts

Picton Press, *subsidiary of* Picton Corp

Pictorial Histories Publishing Co, *distributed by* Heimburger House Publishing Co

PictureProfits® Tool Kit, *distributed by* Copywriter's Council of America™ (CCA)

Picture Window Books, *imprint of* Capstone Publishers™

Picture Yearling, *imprint of* Penguin Random House Inc

Pieces of Learning Inc, *distributed by* A W Peller & Associates, Prufrock Press Inc

Pierrepont Street Press, *imprint of* Italica Press

Piggyback Interactive, *distributed by* Simon & Schuster, Inc, Simon & Schuster Sales Division

Pighog Books, *imprint of* Red Hen Press

Pikachu Press, *distributed by* Simon & Schuster, Inc

Pimlseur Language Programs, *imprint of* Recorded Books Inc, an RBmedia company

Pimsleur, *imprint of* Simon & Schuster Audio

Pinata Books, *imprint of* Arte Publico Press

Pine Street Books, *imprint of* University of Pennsylvania Press

Pine Winds Press, *imprint of* Idyll Arbor Inc

Pinnacle Books, *imprint of* Kensington Publishing Corp

Pinyon Publishing, *distributed by* Gem Guides Book Co

Pioneer Press, *imprint of* Cedar Fort Inc

Pir Press, *distributed by* Fons Vitae

Plain Sight Publishing, *imprint of* Cedar Fort Inc

Planeta Peninsula, *distributed by* Sunbelt Publications Inc

Player Press A/Z Ltd, *division of* Players Press Inc

Player Press Ltd (UK), *division of* Players Press Inc

Players Press, *imprint of* Players Press Inc

Players Press (Canada), *division of* Players Press Inc

Players Press GmbH, *division of* Players Press Inc

Players Press Inc, *distributor for* Camelion Plays, Garland-Clark Editors, Macmillan Education (UK), Preston Editions

Playscripts Inc, *distributed by* Theatre Communications Group

Playwrights Canada Press, *distributed by* Theatre Communications Group

Pleasure Boat Studio: A Literary Press, *distributor for* Empty Bowl Press

Plenum, *distributed by* Specialty Press Inc

Plexus Books, *imprint of* Plexus Publishing, Inc

Plexus Publishing, Inc, *affiliate of* Information Today, Inc

PLI, *imprint of* Practising Law Institute

Ploughshares, *subsidiary of* Ploughshares Inc

Plugged-in to Reading, *imprint of* Triumph Learning LLC

Plum Blossom Books, *imprint of* Parallax Press

Plum Tree Books, *imprint of* Classical Academic Press

Plumbago Books, *imprint of* Boydell & Brewer Inc

Plume, *division of* Penguin Group USA, A Penguin Random House Company, Penguin Group USA, A Penguin Random House Company, *imprint of* Penguin Group USA, A Penguin Random House Company

Pluto Press, *distributed by* Palgrave Macmillan

PMP, *imprint of* Paramount Market Publishing Inc

Pocket, *distributor for* Parachute Publishing LLC

Pocket Books Trade Paperback, *imprint of* Gallery Books

Pocket Guides Publishing, *distributed by* AdventureKEEN

Pocket Star, *imprint of* Gallery Books

Pogo, *imprint of* Jump!

Pogo Press, *imprint of* Finney Company Inc

Point, *imprint of* Scholastic Trade Division

Poison Vine Books, *imprint of* Elderberry Press Inc, *distributed by* Elderberry Press Inc

Poisoned Pen Press, *imprint of* Poisoned Pen Press

The Poisoned Pencil, *imprint of* Poisoned Pen Press

Polar Bear & Company, *imprint of* Solon Center for Research & Publishing

Polebridge Press, *division of* Westar Institute

Polestar Calendars, *distributed by* Orca Book Publishers

Political Risk Services, *imprint of* The PRS Group Inc

Pollyanna Productions, *distributed by* Gryphon House Inc

Polyface, *distributed by* Chelsea Green Publishing Co

PomegranateKids, *imprint of* Pomegranate Communications Inc

Pond Frog Editions, *imprint of* Red Moon Press

Pool of London Press, *distributed by* Casemate | publishers

Poplar Books, *imprint of* Book Sales

Poppy, *imprint of* Little, Brown Books for Young Readers

Popular Press, *imprint of* University of Wisconsin Press

Popular Technology, *imprint of* Branden Books

Popular Woodworking Books, *imprint of* Betterway Books

Portavoz, *distributed by* Editorial Bautista Independiente

Neal Porter Books, *imprint of* Holiday House Inc

Portfolio, *subsidiary of* Penguin Group USA, A Penguin Random House Company, Penguin Group USA, A Penguin Random House Company, *imprint of* Penguin Group USA, A Penguin Random House Company

Portnoy Publishing, *distributed by* Dufour Editions Inc

Portraits of America, *imprint of* The Donning Company Publishers

Possibility Press, *imprint of* Markowski International Publishers

Post Hill Press LLC, *distributed by* Simon & Schuster, Inc, Simon & Schuster Sales Division

Potomac Books, *imprint of* University of Nebraska Press

Potomac Books Inc, *imprint of* University of Nebraska Press

Clarkson Potter Publishers, *imprint of* Crown Publishing Group, *distributor for* The Colonial Williamsburg Foundation

Power Kids Press, *imprint of* The Rosen Publishing Group Inc

powerHouse Books, *division of* PowerHouse Cultural Entertainment Inc, *imprint of* powerHouse Cultural Entertainment Inc, *distributor for* Antinous Press, Juno Books, MTV Press, Throckmorton Press, VH1 Press, Vice Books

Practical Action, *distributed by* Stylus Publishing LLC

Practitioners Publishing Co, *distributor for* AICPA Professional Publications

Praeger, *imprint of* ABC-CLIO

Emory Pratt, *distributor for* Primary Research Group Inc

Prayer Book Press Inc, *subsidiary of* Media Judaica Inc, Media Judaica Inc

Prensa Pensar, *imprint of* Progressive Press

Prentice Hall, *distributor for* American Geosciences Institute (AGI), *distributed by* American Academy of Environmental Engineers & Scientists™, NACE International, Society of Manufacturing Engineers

Prentice-Hall, *distributed by* SAS Publishing

Prentice Hall Press, *division of* Penguin Group USA, A Penguin Random House Company, Penguin Group USA, A Penguin Random House Company, *imprint of* Berkley Publishing Group

PREP Publishing, *subsidiary of* PREP Inc, PREP Inc

Presbyterian Publishing Corp (PPC), *distributor for* Epworth, SCM

Presidio Press, *imprint of* Random House Publishing Group

PreSonus, *distributed by* Hal Leonard Corp

The Press at California State University, Fresno, *unit of* California State University, Fresno

The Press for Humanitarian Causes, *imprint of* Flying Pen Press LLC

Theodore Presser Co, *distributor for* Editions Orphee Inc

Prestel-Del Monico Books, *distributor for* National Gallery of Art

Prestel Publishing, *distributor for* Die Gestalten Verlag (DGV), Figure 1 Publishing, Loft, Lars Mueller Publishers GmbH, Periscope, Schirmer/Mosel

Preston Editions, *distributed by* Players Press Inc

Price Stern Sloan, *imprint of* Penguin Young Readers Group

Price Stern Sloan Inc, *imprint of* Penguin Group USA, A Penguin Random House Company

Price World Publishing, *distributed by* David Bateman Ltd (New Zealand), Cardinal Publishers Group (US)

Priddy Books, *imprint of* St Martin's Press, LLC

Prima Games, *imprint of* DK Publishing

Primary Research Group Inc, *distributed by* Academic Book Center, Ambassador Books, The Book House, Coutts Library Service, Croft House Books, Eastern Book Company, MarketResearch.com, Midwest Library Service, OPAMP Technical Books, Emory Pratt, Research & Markets, Rittenhouse Book Distributors, Total Information, Yankee Book Peddler

Primary Source Media™, *imprint of* Gale

Prime Crime, *imprint of* Berkley Publishing Group

Primer Publications, *distributed by* Gem Guides Book Co

Princeton Architectural Press, *distributor for* Balcony Press, Hyphen Press, *distributed by* Chronicle Books, Chronicle Books LLC

Princeton Book Co Publishers, *distributor for* Dance Books Ltd, Dance Notation Bureau, *distributed by* Dance Books Ltd

Princeton Review, *distributed by* Penguin Random House Inc

The Princeton Review, *imprint of* Penguin Random House Inc, Random House Children's Books

Princeton University Art Museum, *distributed by* Yale University Press

Princeton University Press, *distributor for* National Gallery of Art, University of California Institute on Global Conflict & Cooperation

Principles in Practice, *imprint of* National Council of Teachers of English (NCTE)

Pritzker Military Museum & Library, *distributed by* Casemate | publishers

Pro-Ed, *distributor for* Psychological Assessment Resources Inc (PAR), *distributed by* Psychological Assessment Resources Inc (PAR)

Pro Lingua Associates, *distributed by* International Book Centre Inc

Proceedings, *imprint of* American Philosophical Society

Proceedings of SPIE, *imprint of* SPIE

Process Media, *imprint of* Feral House

Prodist, *imprint of* Watson Publishing International LLC

Productivity Press, *imprint of* CRC Press, *distributor for* American Society for Quality (ASQ), Society of Manufacturing Engineers

Productivity Press Spanish Imprint, *imprint of* Productivity Press

Professional Development, *division of* Scholastic Education

The Professional Education Group LLC (PEG), *distributor for* American Bar Association, American Law Institute, ASPEN, *distributed by* American Bar Association, American Law Institute

Professional Music Institute, *distributed by* Hal Leonard Corp

Professional Practices, *imprint of* Krieger Publishing Co

Professional Publications, *distributed by* NACE International

Professional Publications Inc (PPI), *distributor for* American Association of State Highway & Transportation Officials, American Wood Council (American Forest & Paper Association) (National Design Specification for Wood Construction (NDS) & others), International Code Council, McGraw-Hill Professional (green building, design & construction titles, LEED titles), National Council of Examiners for Engineering & Surveying, SmartPros, Transportation Research Board Code, US Green Building Council (LEED reference guides)

Professional Resource Press, *imprint of* Professional Resource Exchange Inc

Professors World Peace Academy, *distributed by* Paragon House

Progressive Press, *imprint of* Progressive Press, *distributor for* Global Research

Prologue Books, *imprint of* F+W Media Inc

Prometheus Books, *distributed by* Penguin Random House

Prompt Publications, *distributed by* SAMS Technical Publishing LLC

Propellerhead, *distributed by* Hal Leonard Corp

Proper Romance, *imprint of* Shadow Mountain

ProQuest LLC, *subsidiary of* Cambridge Information Group Inc

Providence Athenaeum, *distributed by* Oak Knoll Press

Providence Press, *division of* Hope Publishing Co

Providence Publishing, *distributor for* Country Music Foundation Press

Prufrock Press, *distributed by* Sourcebooks Inc

Prufrock Press Inc, *distributor for* Pieces of Learning Inc

Phil R Pryde, *distributed by* Sunbelt Publications Inc

PS&E Publications, *imprint of* Bartleby Press

PSG, *imprint of* Elsevier, Health Sciences Division

PSS, *imprint of* Grosset & Dunlap, Penguin Young Readers Group

Psychological Assessment Resources Inc (PAR), *distributor for* American Guidance Service, Pro-Ed, Rorschach Workshops, *distributed by* ACER, Pro-Ed, Western Psychological Service

Public Affairs, *distributed by* HarperCollins Publishers

Public Citizen, *distributed by* Addison Wesley, Simon & Schuster Pocket Books

Public History, *imprint of* Krieger Publishing Co

PublicAffairs, *imprint of* Perseus Books

Publishers' Assistant, *imprint of* Upper Access Inc

Publishers Group West, *distributor for* Gault Millau Inc/Gayot Publications, Naval Institute Press, Tuttle Publishing

Publishers Group West (PGW), *distributor for* Black Classic Press, Kalmbach Publishing Co

Publisher's Stone Publications, *distributed by* Florida Academic Press

Publishers Trade Secrets Library, *imprint of* Copywriter's Council of America™ (CCA)

Publishing Services, *division of* Scholastic Education

Pucker Gallery, *distributed by* Syracuse University Press

Pueblo Books, *imprint of* Liturgical Press

Coleccion Puertorriquena, *imprint of* University of Puerto Rico Press

Puffin, *imprint of* Penguin Group USA, A Penguin Random House Company

Puffin Books, *imprint of* Penguin Group USA, A Penguin Random House Company, Penguin Group USA, A Penguin Random House Company, Penguin Young Readers Group

Punch Press, *imprint of* Loft Press Inc

Purple House Press, *imprint of* Purple House Inc

Purple Mountain Press Ltd, *distributor for* Carmania Press London (North America only)

PUSH, *imprint of* Scholastic Trade Division

Pushcart Press, *distributed by* W W Norton & Company Inc

Putnam, *imprint of* Penguin Group USA, A Penguin Random House Company, GP Putnam's Sons (Hardcover)

G P Putnam's Sons, *imprint of* Penguin Young Readers Group

GP Putnam's Sons (Children's), *member of* Penguin Young Readers Group

GP Putnam's Sons (Hardcover), *imprint of* Penguin Group USA, A Penguin Random House Company, Penguin Group USA, A Penguin Random House Company

Puzzlewright Press, *imprint of* Sterling Publishing Co Inc

PWM Editions, *distributed by* Hal Leonard Corp

PWN, *imprint of* Summertime Publications Inc

PWPA Books, *imprint of* Paragon House

PYO (Publish Your Own Co), *division of* Quixote Press

Pyr, *imprint of* Prometheus Books

QDS, *imprint of* Quarto Publishing Group USA Inc

QED Press, *imprint of* Cypress House

Qiblah Books, *distributed by* Fons Vitae

QMP, *imprint of* Quality Medical Publishing Inc

QRP Books, *imprint of* Quail Ridge Press

QSC, *distributed by* Hal Leonard Corp

Quadrille Publishing, *distributed by* Chronicle Books LLC

Quantuck Lane Press, *distributed by* W W Norton & Company Inc

Quarry Books, *imprint of* Indiana University Press, Quarto Publishing Group USA Inc

Quartet Books (UK), *distributed by* Interlink Publishing Group Inc

Quarto, *distributor for* Zest Books

Quarto Books, *distributed by* Krause Publications Inc

Quarto Publishing Group, *distributed by* Hachette Book Group

Quarto Publishing Group USA Inc, *subsidiary of* Quarto Group Inc, Quarto Group Inc (London, UK), *distributed by* Allen & Unwin (Australia & New Zealand)

Quayside Distribution Services, *division of* Quarto Publishing Group USA Inc

Quercus Books, *distributed by* Hachette Book Group

Quest Books, *imprint of* Regal Crest Enterprises

Quest for Success, *imprint of* Advance Publishing Inc

Quick Reference Publishing, *distributed by* Sunbelt Publications Inc

Quickfact®, *imprint of* SAMS Technical Publishing LLC

Quill Driver Books, *imprint of* Linden Publishing Co Inc

Quill House Publishers, *imprint of* Kirk House Publishers

Quill Trade Paperbacks, *imprint of* HarperCollins Publishers

Quiller, *distributed by* Safari Press

Quilliam Press, *distributed by* Fons Vitae

Quintessence Books, *imprint of* Quintessence Publishing Co Inc

Quintessence of Dental Technology, *imprint of* Quintessence Publishing Co Inc

Quintessence Pockets, *imprint of* Quintessence Publishing Co Inc

Quintessence Publishing Co Inc, *distributor for* Quintessence Publishing Co Ltd (Japan), Quintessence Publishing Ltd (London), Quintessence Verlags GmbH

Quintessence Publishing Co Ltd (Japan), *distributed by* Quintessence Publishing Co Inc

Quintessence Publishing Ltd (London), *distributed by* Quintessence Publishing Co Inc

Quintessence Verlags GmbH, *distributed by* Quintessence Publishing Co Inc

Quite Specific Media, *division of* Silman-James Press Inc

Quite Specific Media Group Ltd, *division of* Silman-James Press Inc, *distributor for* The Colonial Williamsburg Foundation

Quodlibetal Features, *distributed by* Vandamere Press

Qwikguide, *imprint of* Mel Bay Publications Inc

R & B Food & Culture Production, *distributed by* Sunbelt Publications Inc

RAB Afraid, *imprint of* Riverdale Avenue Books (RAB)

RAB Desire, *imprint of* Riverdale Avenue Books (RAB)

RAB Gaming, *imprint of* Riverdale Avenue Books (RAB)

RAB Pop, *imprint of* Riverdale Avenue Books (RAB)

RAB SFF, *imprint of* Riverdale Avenue Books (RAB)

RAB Sports, *imprint of* Riverdale Avenue Books (RAB)

RAB Truth, *imprint of* Riverdale Avenue Books (RAB)

RAB Verve, *imprint of* Riverdale Avenue Books (RAB)

Rabbit's Foot Press™, *imprint of* Blue Mountain Arts Inc

Race Point Publishing, *imprint of* Quarto Publishing Group USA Inc

Radiant Life Curriculum, *imprint of* Gospel Publishing House (GPH)

Radio Archives, *distributed by* Dreamscape Media LLC

Radio Theatre, *imprint of* Focus on the Family

Radix Press, *subsidiary of* UGF/OR

Rainbow Bridge Publishing, *imprint of* Carson-Dellosa Publishing LLC

Rainbow Ridge Books, *distributed by* Square One Publishers Inc

Rainsource Press, *distributed by* Chelsea Green Publishing Co

RainStone Press, *distributed by* Mountain Press Publishing Co

Raise the Dough in 30 Days Co, *division of* Quixote Press

Raising Lucy Studios LLC, *distributed by* Epicenter Press Inc

Raleigh Press, *distributed by* Epicenter Press Inc

Ram Publishing, *distributed by* Gem Guides Book Co

Ram Publishing Co, *subsidiary of* Garrett Electronics

Ramakrishna Math, *distributed by* Vedanta Press

Ramakrishna-Vivkanana, *distributed by* Vedanta Press

Ramanujan Mathematical Society, *distributed by* American Mathematical Society

Ramie (France), *distributed by* Picasso Project

Ramsey & Todd, *imprint of* Turner Publishing Co

Rand McNally, *distributor for* Wide World of Maps Inc, *distributed by* Wide World of Maps Inc

Rand McNally for Kids, *imprint of* Rand McNally

Peter E Randall Publisher, *distributed by* University Press of New England

Random House, *imprint of* Penguin Random House Inc, Random House Publishing Group, *distributor for* Universe Publishing, Welcome Enterprises Inc, *distributed by* Sunbelt Publications Inc

Random House Books for Young Readers, *imprint of* Penguin Random House Inc, Random House Children's Books

Random House Children's Books, *division of* Penguin Random House Inc

Random House Children's Publishing, *imprint of* Penguin Random House Inc

Random House Digital, *imprint of* Penguin Random House Inc

Random House Large Print, *distributed by* Thorndike Press

Random House Large Print Publishing, *imprint of* Penguin Random House Inc

Random House Publishing Group, *division of* Penguin Random House Inc

Random House Reference & Information Publishing, *imprint of* Penguin Random House Inc

Random House Reference/Random House Puzzles & Games, *imprint of* Penguin Random House Audio Publishing

Random House Webster's, *imprint of* Random House Reference/Random House Puzzles & Games

Ranger Rick Science Program, *imprint of* Sundance/Newbridge Publishing

Rasmuson Library Historical Translation Series, *imprint of* University of Alaska Press

Rational Island Publishers, *division of* The Reevaluation Counseling Communities

Raven Press, *distributed by* Chelsea Green Publishing Co

Ravenhawk™ Books, *division of* The 6DOF Group, The 6DOF Group

Raymond Press, *imprint of* Prospect Park Books

Rayo, *imprint of* HarperCollins Children's Books

Razorbill, *imprint of* Penguin Group USA, A Penguin Random House Company, Penguin Random House Inc, Penguin Young Readers Group

RB Mystery, *imprint of* Recorded Books Inc, an RBmedia company

RB Shorts, *imprint of* Recorded Books Inc, an RBmedia company

RCS Libri, *imprint of* Rizzoli International Publications Inc

RDV Books, *imprint of* Akashic Books

Reach for the Sky Publishing, *distributed by* Epicenter Press Inc

Reader's Digest, *distributed by* Fox Chapel Publishing Co Inc

Reader's Digest Books, *distributed by* Simon & Schuster, Inc

Reader's Digest Children's Books, *distributed by* Simon & Schuster Sales Division

Reader's Digest Trade Publishing, *division of* Trusted Media Brands Inc, *distributed by* Simon & Schuster

Reader's Digest USA Select Editions, *division of* Trusted Media Brands Inc

Reading Success, *imprint of* Advance Publishing Inc

Read'n Run Books, *imprint of* Crumb Elbow Publishing

REAL Phonics™, *imprint of* Broden Books LLC

Real Story Series, *distributed by* Common Courage Press

Rebel Arts, *imprint of* Gingko Press Inc, *distributed by* Gingko Press Inc

Rebel Base Books, *imprint of* Kensington Publishing Corp

Rebellion, *distributed by* Simon & Schuster Sales Division

Rebellion Publishing, *distributed by* Simon & Schuster, Inc

The Reconstructionist Press, *distributed by* Fordham University Press

Recorded Books Audiolibros, *imprint of* Recorded Books Inc, an RBmedia company

Recorded Books Development, *imprint of* Recorded Books Inc, an RBmedia company

Recorded Books Inspirational, *imprint of* Recorded Books Inc, an RBmedia company

Recovered Classics, *imprint of* McPherson & Co

Recreation Sales, *distributed by* Gem Guides Book Co

Red Anvil Press, *imprint of* Elderberry Press Inc, *distributed by* Elderberry Press Inc

Red Chair Press, *distributed by* Lerner Publishing Group Inc

Red Dress Ink, *imprint of* Harlequin Enterprises Ltd

Red Lead Press, *imprint of* Dorrance Publishing Co Inc

Red Mansions Publishing, *distributed by* China Books

Red Portal Press, *imprint of* Mighty Media Press

Red River Books, *imprint of* The RoadRunner Press

Red Wheel/Weiser/Conari, *distributor for* Cleis Press, Hampton Roads Publishing Co, Nicolas Hays Inc, Viva Editions, *distributed by* Moznaim Publishing Corp

Redemptorist Publications, *distributed by* Liguori Publications

Redhook, *imprint of* Orbit

Redleaf Press, *division of* Think Small, *distributed by* Pademelon Press Pty Ltd (Australia)

Redwing Book Co, *distributor for* Blue Poppy Press

Redwood Press, *imprint of* Stanford University Press

Referee Books, *imprint of* Referee Enterprises Inc

Reference Press, *distributor for* World Trade Press

Regal Crest, *imprint of* Regal Crest Enterprises

Regan Arts, *distributed by* Simon & Schuster, Inc, Simon & Schuster Sales Division

Regents External Degree Series, *imprint of* National Learning Corp

Registry of Guitar Tutors (RGT), *distributed by* Mel Bay Publications Inc

Regnery, *imprint of* Regnery Publishing

Regnery Faith, *imprint of* Regnery Publishing

Regnery Fiction, *imprint of* Regnery Publishing

Regnery History, *imprint of* Regnery Publishing

Regnery Kids, *imprint of* Regnery Publishing

Regnery Publishing, *subsidiary of* Salem Media Group

Regular Baptist Books, *imprint of* Regular Baptist Press

Regular Baptist Press, *division of* General Association of Regular Baptist Churches

Relaxation Co, *distributed by* Sounds True Inc

RELS Press, *imprint of* Plowshare Media

Renaissance Books, *imprint of* St Martin's Press, LLC

Renaissance House, *imprint of* Laredo Publishing Co Inc

Renaissance Press, *distributed by* University of Hawaii Press

Renegade Enterprises, *distributed by* Sunbelt Publications Inc

Research, *division of* Scholastic Education

Research & Markets, *distributor for* Primary Research Group Inc

Research & Special Programs Administration of the US Department of Transportation, *distributed by* J J Keller & Associates, Inc

Research Centrex, *imprint of* Crumb Elbow Publishing

Resilient Publishing, *distributor for* Anderson Design, Brynwood Publishing

Resources for the Future, *distributed by* The Johns Hopkins University Press

Resurgence, *imprint of* Tyndale House Publishers Inc

Resurrection Press, *imprint of* Catholic Book Publishing Corp

Retold Classics, *imprint of* Perfection Learning Corp

Retro Science Fiction, *imprint of* Gateways Books & Tapes

Retrospect Publishing, *distributed by* Closson Press

Reveal Press, *imprint of* New Harbinger Publications Inc

Revell, *division of* Baker Publishing Group

RGB Arte Visual, *distributed by* Mel Bay Publications Inc

Ribbits, *imprint of* Focus on the Family

Ricordi, *distributed by* Hal Leonard Corp

G Ricordi (Italy), *distributor for* Pendragon Press

Riebel-Roque, *distributed by* Casemate | publishers

Lynne Rienner Publishers Inc, *distributor for* Center for US-Mexican Studies, Ayebia Clarke Publishing Ltd (African lit), St Andrews Center for Syrian Studies

Rigby, *imprint of* Houghton Mifflin Harcourt K-12 Publishers

Riley & Johnson, *distributed by* Business Research Services Inc

Ringing Bell Press, *distributed by* Franklin, Beedle & Associates Inc

Rio Chico, *imprint of* Rio Nuevo Publishers

Rio Grande Books, *imprint of* LPD Press

Rick Riordan Presents, *imprint of* Disney-Hyperion Books

Ripley Entertainment, *distributed by* Simon & Schuster Sales Division

Ripley Entertainment Inc, *distributed by* Simon & Schuster, Inc

Rittenhouse, *distributor for* Teton NewMedia Inc

Rittenhouse Book Distributors, *distributor for* Primary Research Group Inc

Rivendale Press, *distributed by* Oak Knoll Press

River City Kids, *imprint of* River City Publishing LLC

River Grove Books, *imprint of* Greenleaf Book Group LLC

River North Fiction, *imprint of* Moody Publishers

River Publishers, *distributed by* Stylus Publishing LLC

Riverdale/Magnus, *imprint of* Riverdale Avenue Books (RAB)

Riverhead Books, *imprint of* Penguin Group USA, A Penguin Random House Company, Penguin Group USA, A Penguin Random House Company

Riverhead Books (Paperback), *imprint of* Berkley Publishing Group

RiverWood Books, *imprint of* White Cloud Press

Rizzoli, *distributed by* Penguin Random House Inc

Rizzoli International Publications Inc, *subsidiary of* RCS Rizzoli Corp New York, RCS Rizzoli Corp New York, *distributor for* Editions Flammarion, Skira Editore, Smith Street Books, *distributed by* Penguin Random House

Rizzoli, New York, *imprint of* Rizzoli International Publications Inc

RLO Media Productions, *distributed by* Epicenter Press Inc

RN Publishing, *distributed by* Casemate | publishers

Road Dog Publications, *imprint of* Lost Classics Book Company LLC

Roadside Geology Series, *imprint of* Mountain Press Publishing Co

Roadside History Series, *imprint of* Mountain Press Publishing Co

Roaring Brook Press, *member of* Macmillan Children's Publishing Group

Lee Roberts Publications, *distributed by* Hal Leonard Corp

Robins Lane Press, *distributed by* Gryphon House Inc

Roc, *imprint of* Berkley Publishing Group, Penguin Group USA, A Penguin Random House Company

Rock House, *distributed by* Hal Leonard Corp

Rock Point Gift & Stationery, *imprint of* Quarto Publishing Group USA Inc

Rockbottom Book Co, *distributor for* ABDO Publishing Group

Rockefeller Institute Press, *distributed by* State University of New York Press

The Rockefeller University Press, *unit of* Rockefeller University

RockHill Publishing LLC, *distributed by* The Ishmael Tree (titles in Arabic)

Rockhurst University Press, *distributed by* Fordham University Press

Rocking Chair Kids, *imprint of* Red Chair Press

Rockport Publishers, *imprint of* Quarto Publishing Group USA Inc

Rocky Mountain Region Disaster Mental Health Institute Press, *imprint of* Loving Healing Press Inc

Rodale, *distributor for* The Colonial Williamsburg Foundation

Rodale Inc, *distributed by* Macmillan (US), Pan Macmillan (worldwide exc Canada & US)

Rodale Kids, *imprint of* Rodale Inc

Rodale Wellness, *imprint of* Rodale Inc

Anita Roddick Publications, *distributed by* Chelsea Green Publishing Co

Roman Catholic Books, *division of* Catholic Media Apostolate Inc

Romantic Sounds Audio, *imprint of* Recorded Books Inc, an RBmedia company

Roncorp Music, *division of* Northeastern Music Publications Inc

Roost Books, *imprint of* Shambhala Publications Inc

Rorschach Workshops, *distributed by* Psychological Assessment Resources Inc (PAR)

Rose Dog Books, *imprint of* Dorrance Publishing Co Inc

Fr Seraphim Rose Foundation, *imprint of* Saint Herman Press

Rosebud Books, *imprint of* Raven Productions Inc

Rosen Central, *imprint of* The Rosen Publishing Group Inc

Rosen Classroom Books & Materials, *division of* The Rosen Publishing Group Inc

Rosen Digital, *imprint of* The Rosen Publishing Group Inc

Rosen Young Adult, *imprint of* The Rosen Publishing Group Inc

Rossel Books, *distributed by* Behrman House Inc

Roth Family Foundation, *imprint of* University of California Press

Rothko Chapel, *distributed by* University of Texas Press

Rothstein Publishing, *division of* Rothstein Associates Inc

The Rough Notes Co Inc, *subsidiary of* Insurance Publishing Plus Corp, Insurance Publishing Plus Corp

Round Table Comics, *imprint of* Round Table Companies

Round Table Companies, *subsidiary of* Writers of the Round Table Press Inc

Route, *distributed by* Dufour Editions Inc

Routledge, *member of* Taylor & Francis Group, an Informa Business, *imprint of* Taylor & Francis Inc

Rowman & Littlefield, *distributor for* American Council on Education, Bucknell University Press, The Colonial Williamsburg Foundation, The CSIS Press, Fairleigh Dickinson University Press, Lehigh University Press, University of Delaware Press

Rowman & Littlefield Education, *distributor for* National Association for Music Education (NAfME)

Rowman & Littlefield Publishers Inc, *imprint of* Rowman & Littlefield Publishing Group

Roxbury Publishing, *distributed by* Oxford University Press USA

Royal Asiatic Society (Korea Branch), *distributed by* Cheng & Tsui Co Inc

Royal Fireworks Press, *distributor for* KAV Books, Silk Label Books, Trillium Press

Royal Historical Society, *imprint of* Boydell & Brewer Inc

Royal Society of Chemistry, *distributed by* The American Chemical Society

RSMeans, *imprint of* John Wiley & Sons Inc

Rubank Publications, *distributed by* Hal Leonard Corp

Rucksack Readers (UK), *distributed by* Interlink Publishing Group Inc

Rugged Land, *distributed by* Penguin Random House Inc

Raymond C Rumpf & Son Inc, *distributor for* Wilderness Adventures Press Inc

Rune-Tales, *imprint of* Quincannon Publishing Group

Running Press, *imprint of* Perseus Books, *distributor for* Parachute Publishing LLC

Rural Science Institute, *distributed by* Chelsea Green Publishing Co

Rutgers University Press, *division of* Rutgers, The State University of New Jersey

RV Guides, *distributed by* American Map Corp

RV International Maps & Atlases, *distributed by* Hagstrom Map

Ryland, Peters & Small, *distributed by* Simon & Schuster, Inc

S-A Design Books, *imprint of* CarTech Inc

S I Publicaties BV, *distributed by* Casemate | publishers

SABDA, *distributed by* Lotus Press

Sabrestorm Publishing, *distributed by* Casemate | publishers

Saddleback Educational, *distributor for* TESOL International Association

Saddleback Educational Publishing, *distributed by* Children's Plus, Delaney

Sadhana Publications, *distributed by* Lotus Press

Sadlier, *division of* William H Sadlier Inc

Sadlier-Oxford, *division of* William H Sadlier Inc

SAE (Society of Automotive Engineers International), *distributor for* Coordinating Research Council Inc

Safari Press, *distributor for* Quiller

Safer Society Press, *imprint of* Safer Society Foundation Inc

Saga Press, *imprint of* Simon & Schuster Children's Publishing

Sagamore Publishing LLC, *distributor for* American Academy for Park & Recreation Administration

Sage, *imprint of* Genesis Press Inc

SAGE UK Resources for Educators, *distributed by* Corwin, a Sage Co

St Andrews Center for Syrian Studies, *distributed by* Lynne Rienner Publishers Inc

St Andrews University Press, *subsidiary of* St Andrews University

St Augustine's Press Inc, *distributor for* Dumb Ox Books (publishes the Aristotelian Commentaries of Thomas Aquinas & like works), Hardwood Press (trade books, mostly in sports & regional works), New Criterion Books (poetry prize), *distributed by* University of Chicago Press

St Bede's Publications, *distributed by* Fordham University Press

Saint Herman Press, *subsidiary of* Brotherhood of Saint Herman of Alaska, *distributed by* Light & Life Publishing Co

St Herman Press, *imprint of* Saint Herman Press

St James Press®, *imprint of* Gale

St Louis Mercantile Library, *distributed by* University of Missouri Press

St Martin's Castle Point, *imprint of* St Martin's Press, LLC

St Martin's Dead Letter, *imprint of* St Martin's Press, LLC

St Martin's Griffin, *imprint of* St Martin's Press, LLC

St Martin's Paperbacks, *imprint of* St Martin's Press, LLC

St Martin's Press, *imprint of* St Martin's Press, LLC

St Martin's Press, LLC, *subsidiary of* Macmillan

St Martin's True Crime, *imprint of* St Martin's Press, LLC

St Martin's True Crime Classics, *imprint of* St Martin's Press, LLC

Saint Mary's Press, *subsidiary of* Christian Brothers Publications, *distributor for* Group Publishing

St Nicolas Music Inc, *distributed by* Hal Leonard Corp

St Pauls, *division of* The Society of Saint Paul

St Vladimir's, *distributor for* Ancient Faith Publishing

St Xenia Skete, *imprint of* Saint Herman Press

The Saints Series, *imprint of* Pauline Books & Media

Salaam Reads, *imprint of* Simon & Schuster Children's Publishing

Editions Salabert, *distributed by* Hal Leonard Corp

Salaryia, *distributed by* Sterling Publishing Co Inc

Salem Press, *imprint of* Grey House Publishing Inc™, *distributor for* Schlager Group Inc

Salem Press Inc, *imprint of* Grey House Publishing Inc™

Sales & Marketing, *division of* Scholastic Education

Salmon Poetry, *distributed by* Dufour Editions Inc

SaltRiver, *imprint of* Tyndale House Publishers Inc

Saltry Press, *distributed by* Epicenter Press Inc

Salubris Resources, *imprint of* Gospel Publishing House (GPH)

Samata Books, *distributed by* Lotus Press

SAMS Technical Publishing LLC, *division of* AGS Capital Inc, *distributor for* Butterworth Heinemann, McGraw-Hill, Prompt Publications

Samson Audio, *distributed by* Hal Leonard Corp

San Diego Architecture Foundation, *distributed by* Sunbelt Publications Inc

San Diego Association of Geologists, *distributed by* Sunbelt Publications Inc

San Diego City Works Press, *distributed by* Sunbelt Publications Inc

San Diego Natural History Museum, *distributed by* Sunbelt Publications Inc

San Diego Police Historical Association, *distributed by* Sunbelt Publications Inc

San Diego State University Press, *division of* San Diego State University Foundation, *distributor for* Institute for Regional Studies of the Californias

San Dieguito River Park Joint Powers Authority, *distributed by* Sunbelt Publications Inc

Coleccion San Pedrito, *imprint of* University of Puerto Rico Press

Sandala Productions, *distributed by* Fons Vitae

Sandcastle, *imprint of* ABDO Publishing Group

Sandpiper, *imprint of* Houghton Mifflin Harcourt Trade & Reference Division

Sandstone Press, *distributed by* Dufour Editions Inc

The Sandstone Press, *imprint of* Frederic C Beil Publisher Inc

Sandu Publications, *distributed by* Gingko Press Inc

Sandy Creek, *distributed by* Lerner Publishing Group Inc

Santillana USA Publishing Co, *subsidiary of* Grupo Santillana

Sapientia Press, *distributed by* The Catholic University of America Press

Sapling, *imprint of* Cedar Grove Books

Saraland Press, *distributed by* University of South Carolina Press

Saroff Editions, *imprint of* McPherson & Co

Sarto House, *imprint of* Angelus Press

SAS Publishing, *imprint of* SAS Institute Inc, *distributor for* AMACOM Books, Breakfast Communications, CRC Press, Duxbury, Harcourt, Harvard Business School Press, McGraw-Hill, Oxford, Prentice-Hall, Springer, John Wiley & Sons Inc, *distributed by* John Wiley & Sons Inc

Satas, *distributor for* Blue Poppy Press

Saturnalia Books, *distributed by* University Press of New England

Saunders, *imprint of* Elsevier, Health Sciences Division, *distributed by* Oxford University Press USA

W B Saunders Co, *distributed by* Marine Techniques Publishing

Savas Beatie, *distributed by* Casemate | publishers

Savas Publishing, *distributed by* Casemate | publishers

Save Our Heritage Organization, *distributed by* Sunbelt Publications Inc

Alastair Sawday Publishing, *distributed by* The Globe Pequot Press

Saxon, *imprint of* Houghton Mifflin Harcourt K-12 Publishers

SBL Press, *unit of* Society of Biblical Literature, *distributor for* Brown Judaic Studies, Sheffield Phoenix Press

Scala Publishers, *distributor for* American Federation of Arts

Scandalous, *imprint of* Entangled Publishing

Scarab Miniatures, *distributed by* Casemate | publishers

Lo Scarabeo, *distributed by* Llewellyn Publications

Scarecrow Press Inc, *imprint of* Rowman & Littlefield Publishing Group

Scarf Press, *distributed by* Bloch Publishing Co

SCB Distributors, *distributor for* Circlet Press Inc

Schiffer, *imprint of* Schiffer Publishing Ltd

Schiffer Fashion Press, *imprint of* Schiffer Publishing Ltd

Schiffer Ltd, *imprint of* Schiffer Publishing Ltd

Schiffer Military History, *imprint of* Schiffer Publishing Ltd

Schiffer Publishing Ltd, *distributor for* The Donning Co

E C Schirmer Music Co, *imprint of* ECS Publishing Corp

G Schirmer Inc (Associated Music Publishers), *distributed by* Hal Leonard Corp

G Schirmer Inc/Associated Music Publishers Inc, *unit of* The Music Sales Group, *distributor for* Big Meteor Publishing, Independent Music Press

Schirmer/Mosel, *distributed by* Prestel Publishing

Schirmer Reference™, *imprint of* Gale

Schlager Group Inc, *distributed by* Salem Press (ref books only)

A Naomi Schneider Book, *imprint of* University of California Press

Schocken Books, *imprint of* Pantheon Books/ Schocken Books, Penguin Random House Inc

Scholarly Digital Editions, *imprint of* Boydell & Brewer Inc

Scholarly Resources Inc, *imprint of* Gale

Scholastic, *distributor for* Parachute Publishing LLC, *distributed by* Learning Links Inc

Scholastic Asia, *subsidiary of* Scholastic International

Scholastic Audio, *imprint of* Scholastic Trade Division

Scholastic Australia Pty Ltd, *subsidiary of* Scholastic International

Scholastic Books, *distributor for* Alloy Entertainment LLC

Scholastic Canada Ltd, *subsidiary of* Scholastic International

Scholastic Education, *division of* Scholastic Inc

Scholastic en Espanol, *imprint of* Scholastic Trade Division

Scholastic Inc, *imprint of* Scholastic Trade Division, *distributor for* The Colonial Williamsburg Foundation, Educational Impressions Inc

Scholastic International, *division of* Scholastic Inc

Scholastic Licensed Publishing, *imprint of* Scholastic Trade Division

Scholastic Ltd UK, *subsidiary of* Scholastic International

Scholastic New Zealand, *distributor for* Big Guy Books Inc

Scholastic New Zealand Ltd, *subsidiary of* Scholastic International

Scholastic Nonfiction, *imprint of* Scholastic Trade Division

Scholastic Paperbacks, *imprint of* Scholastic Trade Division

Scholastic Press, *imprint of* Scholastic Trade Division

Scholastic Reference, *imprint of* Scholastic Trade Division

Scholastic-Tab Publications, *distributor for* Educational Impressions Inc

Scholastic Trade Division, *division of* Scholastic Inc

Editions Scholasticae, *distributed by* Transaction Publishers Inc

School Express Press, *imprint of* Story Monsters LLC

School for Advanced Research Press, *distributed by* University of New Mexico Press

School of the Blues, *imprint of* Mel Bay Publications Inc

School of Government, *division of* The University of NC Chapel Hill

School Renaissance, *distributed by* Gryphon House Inc

School Speciality, *distributor for* MAR*CO Products Inc

SchoolBookings.com, *division of* Story Monsters LLC

Schott Music, *distributed by* Hal Leonard Corp

Schwartz & Wade Books, *imprint of* Penguin Random House Inc, Random House Children's Books

Sci-Fi Audio, *imprint of* Recorded Books Inc, an RBmedia company

Science & Humanities Press, *subsidiary of* Banis & Associates

Science History Publications USA, *imprint of* Watson Publishing International LLC

Science, Naturally, *affiliate of* Platypus Media

Science Press New York & Science Press Beijing, *distributed by* American Mathematical Society

Scientific American, *imprint of* Farrar, Straus & Giroux, LLC

Scientific American Medicine, *distributor for* American College of Surgeons

Scitec Publications, *imprint of* Trans Tech Publications Inc

SciTech, *distributed by* Stylus Publishing LLC

Scitech Publishing Inc, *distributor for* Peninsula Publishing

SCM, *distributed by* Presbyterian Publishing Corp (PPC), Westminster John Knox Press (WJK)

Scobre Educational, *imprint of* Scobre Press Corp, *distributed by* Lerner Publishing Group Inc

John Scognamiglio Books, *imprint of* Kensington Publishing Corp

Scottish Text Society, *imprint of* Boydell & Brewer Inc

Scott's Highland Services, *distributed by* Mel Bay Publications Inc

Scout Press, *imprint of* Gallery Books

Scribner, *imprint of* Scribner Publishing Group

Scribner Classics, *imprint of* Scribner

Scribner Poetry, *imprint of* Scribner

Scripta Humanistica Publishing International, *subsidiary of* Brumar Communications

Scythian Books, *imprint of* Berkeley Slavic Specialties

Sea-to-Sea Publishing, *imprint of* Black Rabbit Books

Seaforth Publishing, *distributed by* Casemate | publishers

Seagrass Press, *imprint of* Quarto Publishing Group USA Inc

Sealife Research Alliance, *imprint of* Crumb Elbow Publishing

Search Institute Press®, *division of* Search Institute

Search Press, *distributor for* Interweave Press LLC

Seastone, *imprint of* Ulysses Press

Second Chance Press, *imprint of* The Permanent Press

Second Story Press, *distributed by* Orca Book Publishers

Secure American Management (SAM) Institute, *imprint of* Morgan James Publishing

Seed Savers, *distributed by* Chelsea Green Publishing Co

Seedling Publications Inc, *imprint of* Continental Press, Continental Press Inc, *distributed by* Kendall Hunt Publishing

Martin E Segal Theatre Center Publications, *distributed by* Theatre Communications Group

SelfHelp Success Books, *distributed by* Pelican Publishing Co

SelfMadeHero, *distributed by* Harry N Abrams Inc

Semiotext(e), *distributed by* The MIT Press

Senal, *imprint of* Ugly Duckling Presse

Sendpoints Books Co Ltd, *distributed by* Gingko Press Inc

Sensation, *imprint of* Berkley Publishing Group

Sentinel, *imprint of* Penguin Group USA, A Penguin Random House Company

Seoul Selection, *distributed by* University of Hawaii Press

Sephardic House, *distributed by* Bloch Publishing Co

Serendipity, *imprint of* Price Stern Sloan

Serif Publishing Ltd (UK), *distributed by* Interlink Publishing Group Inc

Serindia Publications, *distributed by* Art Media Resources Inc (US & CN)

Servant Books, *imprint of* Franciscan Media

Service Employees International Union, *distributed by* Chelsea Green Publishing Co

SETAC Press, *imprint of* Society of Environmental Toxicology & Chemistry (SETAC)

7th Generation, *imprint of* Book Publishing Co, *distributed by* Orca Book Publishers

The Seventh Quarry, *imprint of* Cross-Cultural Communications

The Seventh Quarry Press, *imprint of* Cross-Cultural Communications, *distributed by* Cross-Cultural Communications

Seventh Street Books, *imprint of* Prometheus Books

Shaar Press, *imprint of* Mesorah Publications Ltd

Shabdaguchha (Magazine & Press), *distributed by* Cross-Cultural Communications

Shadow Mountain, *imprint of* Deseret Book Co

Shakespeare Playbooks, *imprint of* Bandanna Books

Shambhala, *distributed by* Penguin Random House Inc

Shambhala Publications Inc, *distributed by* Penguin Random House Inc

Shanghai Press, *distributed by* Tuttle Publishing, University of Hawaii Press

Shangri-La, *imprint of* Lotus Press

Shaw Books, *imprint of* WaterBrook

Shawnee Press, *distributed by* Hal Leonard Corp

Shaye Areheart Books, *imprint of* Penguin Random House Inc

Shearwater Books, *imprint of* Island Press

The Sheep Meadow Press, *distributed by* University Press of New England

Sheffield Phoenix Press, *distributed by* SBL Press

Sheffield Publishing Co, *subsidiary of* Waveland Press Inc

Sheldrake Press (UK), *distributed by* Interlink Publishing Group Inc

Joyce Shellhart, *distributed by* Finney Company Inc

Shengold Publishers, *imprint of* Schreiber Publishing

Shen's Books, *imprint of* Lee & Low Books, Lee & Low Books Inc

Shepard & Piper, *imprint of* Shepard Publications

W B Sheridan, *imprint of* Academica Press

Shiloh Kidz, *imprint of* Barbour Publishing Inc

Shiloh Run Press, *imprint of* Barbour Publishing Inc

G Shirmer, *imprint of* Hal Leonard Corp

Short Tales, *imprint of* ABDO Publishing Group

Shortfuse Press, *distributed by* Gem Guides Book Co

Iwasaki Shoten, *distributor for* Big Guy Books Inc

Showcase, *imprint of* Players Press Inc

ShowForth Videos, *division of* BJU Press, *imprint of* BJU Press

Shroff Publishers, *distributor for* Mike Murach & Associates Inc

Shufunotomo Co, *distributed by* Tuttle Publishing

Sibelius, *distributed by* Hal Leonard Corp

Sicilia Parra, *distributed by* Cross-Cultural Communications

Side Street, *imprint of* BrickHouse Books Inc

Sierra Club Adult Books, *imprint of* Penguin Random House Inc

Sierra Club Books, *imprint of* Counterpoint Press LLC, *distributed by* University of California Press

Sierra College Press, *imprint of* Heyday Books

Sierra Press, *distributed by* Gem Guides Book Co

Siete Cuentos Editorial, *imprint of* Seven Stories Press

Signal Books (UK), *distributed by* Interlink Publishing Group Inc

Signature Books, *imprint of* EastBridge

Signatures Network, *distributed by* Andrews McMeel Publishing LLC

Signet, *imprint of* Berkley Publishing Group, Penguin Group USA, A Penguin Random House Company

Signet Classics, *imprint of* Penguin Group USA, A Penguin Random House Company

Signum Verlag, *distributed by* Gallaudet University Press

Sikorski, *distributed by* Hal Leonard Corp

Siles Press, *division of* Silman-James Press Inc

Silhouette, *imprint of* Harlequin Enterprises Ltd

Silhouette Imprints, *imprint of* Crumb Elbow Publishing

Silk & Magic, *imprint of* ImaJinn Books

Silk Label Books, *distributed by* Royal Fireworks Press

Silman-James Press Inc, *distributed by* Codasat Canada Ltd

Siloam Press, *imprint of* Charisma Media

Silver Dagger Mysteries, *imprint of* The Overmountain Press

Silver Dragon Books, *imprint of* Regal Crest Enterprises

Silverplume, a Vertafore Co, *distributor for* Standard Publishing Corp

Simcha Press, *imprint of* Health Communications Inc

Simon & Schuster, *imprint of* Simon & Schuster Publishing Group, *distributor for* Alloy Entertainment LLC, Baen Publishing Enterprises, Cider Mill Press Book Publishers LLC, Harlequin Enterprises Ltd, Hazelden Publishing, Insight Editions, Meadowbrook Press, Open Road Publishing, Reader's Digest Trade Publishing, Wisdom Publications Inc, *distributed by* Cardoza Publishing, Gulf Publishing Co, Learning Links Inc, Specialty Press Inc

Simon & Schuster Audio, *division of* Simon & Schuster, Inc, *distributor for* Monostereo

Simon & Schuster Books for Young Readers, *imprint of* Simon & Schuster Children's Publishing

Simon & Schuster Children's Publishing, *division of* Simon & Schuster, Inc

Simon & Schuster, Inc, *division of* CBS Corporation, *distributor for* Andrews McMeel Publishing LLC, Backlist LLC (div of Chicken Soup for the Soul Publishing), Baen Books, Baseball America, Beyond Words, BL Publishing (div of Games Workshop), Boom! Studios, Cardoza Publishing, Cernunnos, Chicken Soup for the Soul Publishing, Cider Mill Press Book Publishers LLC (including Applesauce Press imprint), Downtown Bookworks, Frederator Books LLC, Gallup (worldwide), Games Workshop, Harlequin Enterprises Ltd (billing only), Hooked on Phonics (Sandviks HOP Inc/Sandvik Publishing), Inner Traditions/Bear & Company, Insight Editions, Kaplan Publishing (including Manhattan Prep), Katalitix Media, Kinfolk, Little Bee Books, Meadowbrook Press, Merck Publishing, Moll Anderson Productions, NorthSouth Books (div of NordSued Verlag), Omnific Publishing, Open Road Publishing, Parachute Publishing LLC, Permuted Press LLC, Piggyback Interactive, Pikachu Press (Pokemon Company International), Post Hill Press LLC, Reader's Digest Books (div of Trusted Media Brands Inc), Rebellion Publishing, Regan Arts, Ripley Entertainment Inc (Ripley's Believe it or Not), Ryland, Peters & Small (including CICO Books), Start Publishing LLC, Studio Fun International (div of Trusted Media Brands Inc), TC Media Books, To The Stars Inc, Tuttle Publishing, Ubisoft, Uncrate LLC, Victory Belt Publishing, VIZ Media, Weldon Owen, Wisdom Publications, World Almanac (div of Facts on File), Yilin Press (Mandarin ebooks)

Simon & Schuster Pocket Books, *distributor for* Public Citizen

Simon & Schuster Sales & Marketing, *distributor for* Boom! Studios

Simon & Schuster Sales Division, *division of* Simon & Schuster, Inc, *distributor for* Andrews McMeel Publishing LLC, Applesauce Press (children's), Baen Books, Baseball America, Boom! Studios, Cardoza, Cernunnos, Chicken Soup for the Soul, Cider Mill Press Book Publishers LLC, Downtown Bookworks, Frederator Books LLC, Gallup (worldwide), Games Workshop, Hazelden, Hooked On Phonics, Insight Editions, Juniper Publishing, Kaplan Publishing, Katalitix, Kinfolk, little bee books, Manhattan Prep, Meadowbrook Press, Merck Publishing, North South Books, Omnific, Open Road, Permuted Press LLC, Piggyback Interactive, Post Hill Press LLC, Reader's Digest Children's Books, Rebellion, Regan Arts, Ripley Entertainment, To the Stars Inc, Uncrate LLC, VIZ Media, Weldon Owen, World Almanac (div of Facts on File)

Simon Pulse, *imprint of* Simon & Schuster Children's Publishing

Simon Spotlight, *imprint of* Simon & Schuster Children's Publishing

Simple Productions, *imprint of* Shepard Publications

Simply Youth Ministry, *imprint of* Group Publishing Inc

Simpson, *imprint of* University of California Press

Singing Dragon, *imprint of* Jessica Kingsley Publishers Inc

Sisra Music Publishing, *imprint of* Empire Publishing Service

Byron Sistler, *distributor for* Ericson Books

6 x 6 Magazine, *imprint of* Ugly Duckling Presse

Six House, *subsidiary of* Gallopade International Inc

Sixth & Spring, *distributed by* Sterling Publishing Co Inc

Skateman Publications, *imprint of* World Citizens

SkillPath Publications, *division of* The Graceland University Center for Professional Development & Lifelong Learning Inc, *distributor for* Franklin Covey, Pearson Technology, Thomson Publishing, John Wiley & Sons Inc

SkillsTutor, *division of* Houghton Mifflin Harcourt

Skinner House Books, *imprint of* Unitarian Universalist Assn, Unitarian Universalist Association

SkipJack Press, *imprint of* Finney Company Inc

Skipstone, *imprint of* The Mountaineers Books

Skira Editore, *distributed by* Rizzoli International Publications Inc

Skira Rizzoli, *imprint of* Rizzoli International Publications Inc

Skira Rizzoli Publishers, *distributor for* American Federation of Arts

Sky Pony Press, *imprint of* Skyhorse Publishing Inc

Skybound Books, *imprint of* Atria Books

Skyhook Press, *imprint of* Shepard Publications

Skyhorse Publishing, *distributed by* W W Norton & Company Inc

Skylark, *imprint of* Penguin Random House Inc

SkyLight Paths, *imprint of* Turner Publishing Co

Slossen, *distributed by* Specialty Press Inc

Slovenian Cinematheque, *distributed by* Columbia University Press

Slow Food Editore, *distributed by* Chelsea Green Publishing Co

Small Horizons, *imprint of* New Horizon Press

Small Press United, *distributor for* Academy of Nutrition & Dietetics

Smart Apple Media, *imprint of* Black Rabbit Books

Smart Pop, *imprint of* BenBella Books Inc

Smart Sex Stuff for Kids, *imprint of* Gallopade International Inc

SmartLab, *distributed by* Chronicle Books LLC

Smartmaps®, *imprint of* VanDam Inc

SmartPros, *distributed by* Professional Publications Inc (PPI)

SmartsCo, *distributed by* Chronicle Books LLC

SMC Publishing, *distributed by* Cheng & Tsui Co Inc

Smith & Kraus Books For Kids, *imprint of* Smith & Kraus Publishers Inc

Smith & Kraus Global, *subsidiary of* Smith & Kraus Publishers Inc

M Lee Smith Publishers, *division of* BLR®-Business & Legal Resources

Smith Street Books, *distributed by* Rizzoli International Publications Inc

Smithsonian Books, *distributed by* Penguin Random House Inc

Smithsonian Scholarly Press, *division of* Smithsonian Institution, *distributed by* Penguin Random House Inc

Smokestack Books, *distributed by* Dufour Editions Inc

Colin Smythe Ltd, *distributed by* Dufour Editions Inc

Snake Country Publishing, *distributed by* Caxton Press

Snova Books, *imprint of* Nova Science Publishers Inc

Snow Lion, *imprint of* Shambhala Publications Inc

Snowy Owl Books, *imprint of* University of Alaska Press

Social Science Research Council, *distributed by* Columbia University Press

Societe Mathematique de France, *distributed by* American Mathematical Society

Society for American Baseball Research, *distributed by* University of Nebraska Press

Society of Manufacturing Engineers, *distributor for* Industrial Press, McGraw-Hill, Prentice Hall, John Wiley & Sons Inc, *distributed by* American Technical Publishers Inc, McGraw-Hill, Productivity Press

Society of the Cincinnati, *distributed by* University Press of America Inc

Soffietto Editions, *imprint of* Red Moon Press

Soft Skull Press, *imprint of* Counterpoint Press LLC

Sogang University Institute, *distributed by* Cheng & Tsui Co Inc

Soho Crime, *imprint of* Soho Press Inc

Soho Press, *imprint of* Soho Press Inc, *distributed by* Penguin Random House Inc

Soho Teen, *imprint of* Soho Press Inc

Solar Design Association, *distributed by* Chelsea Green Publishing Co

Solution Tree Press, *imprint of* Solution Tree

SOM Publishing, *division of* School of Metaphysics

Somerset Press, *division of* Hope Publishing Co

Somerville House USA, *imprint of* Grosset & Dunlap

Sommer-Time Story Classics Series, *imprint of* Advance Publishing Inc

Sommer-Time Story Series, *imprint of* Advance Publishing Inc

Soncino, *distributed by* Bloch Publishing Co

Sono Nis Press, *distributed by* Orca Book Publishers

Sonrise Devotionals, *imprint of* Lighthouse Publishing of the Carolinas

Sony, *distributed by* Hal Leonard Corp

Sorin Books, *imprint of* Ave Maria Press

Sound Ideas, *imprint of* Simon & Schuster Audio

SoundForth Music, *division of* BJU Press, *imprint of* BJU Press

Sounds True Inc, *distributor for* Eckhart Teachings Inc, New Earth Records, Relaxation Co

Sourcebooks Casablanca, *imprint of* Sourcebooks Inc

Sourcebooks Fire, *imprint of* Sourcebooks Inc

Sourcebooks Inc, *distributor for* Prufrock Press

Sourcebooks Jabberwocky, *imprint of* Sourcebooks Inc

Sourcebooks Landmark, *imprint of* Sourcebooks Inc

Sourcebooks MediaFusion, *imprint of* Sourcebooks Inc

Sourced Media Books, *distributed by* Gibbs-Smith, Many Hats Media

SourceResource, *distributor for* MAR*CO Products Inc

South Carolina Bar Association, *distributed by* University of South Carolina Press

South Carolina Historical Society, *distributed by* University of South Carolina Press

Southeastern Center for Contemporary Art, *distributed by* The University of North Carolina Press

Southeastern Cooperative Wildlife Disease Study, *distributed by* American Association for Vocational Instructional Materials

Southern Early Childhood Association, *distributed by* Gryphon House Inc

Southern Historical Press, *distributed by* Ericson Books

Southern Illinois University Press, *division of* Southern Illinois University

Southern Living Books, *imprint of* Oxmoor House

Southern Voices Audio, *imprint of* Recorded Books Inc, an RBmedia company

Southwestern Studies, *imprint of* Texas Western Press

Sparkhouse, *imprint of* Augsburg Fortress Publishers, Publishing House of the Evangelical Lutheran Church in America

Speak, *imprint of* Penguin Young Readers Group

Speaker's Corner, *imprint of* Fulcrum Publishing Inc

Specialized Software, *imprint of* Lotus Press

Specialty Press Inc, *distributor for* Bantam, Guilford Press, Plenum, Simon & Schuster, Slossen, Woodbine House, *distributed by* Boys Town Press, Child Play, MHS

Spectra, *imprint of* Penguin Random House Inc

Spectroscopy Now, *imprint of* John Wiley & Sons Inc

Spectrum, *distributor for* National Council of Teachers of Mathematics (NCTM)

SPIE Journals, *imprint of* SPIE

SPIE Press, *imprint of* SPIE

Spiegel & Grau, *imprint of* Random House Publishing Group

Spinsters Ink, *imprint of* Bella Books

Spire Books, *imprint of* Revell

Spirit, *imprint of* Norilana Books

Spirit Mountain Press, *distributed by* University of Alaska Press

Sporting News, *distributed by* Andrews McMeel Publishing LLC

Sports Collectors Digest, *imprint of* Betterway Books

SportsZone, *imprint of* ABDO Publishing Group

Spotlight, *imprint of* ABDO Publishing Group

Spotlight Books, *imprint of* Empire Publishing Service

Jack Spratt Choral Music, *imprint of* Empire Publishing Service

Spring Arbor, *distributor for* Faith Library Publications, Pentecostal Publishing House

Spring Freshet Press, *distributed by* University of Wisconsin Press

Spring Publications, *distributed by* Bloomsbury Academic

Springer, *subsidiary of* Springer Science+Business Media, *distributed by* SAS Publishing

Springer Healthcare, *imprint of* Springer

Springer-Verlag, *distributor for* American Institute of Physics

Springhouse Editions, *subsidiary of* White Pine Press, *distributed by* White Pine Press

Sproutman Publications, *distributed by* Book Publishing Co

Sprucehaven Publishing, *distributed by* Epicenter Press Inc

Spyglass Books LLC, *distributed by* Biographical Publishing Co

Square One Publishers Inc, *distributor for* Inno-Vision Health Media, Rainbow Ridge Books, *distributed by* Thomas Allen & Son

SRA/McGraw-Hill, *imprint of* McGraw-Hill Education

Sri Aurobindo Ashram, *distributed by* Lotus Press

Sri Lanka Institute of Traditional Studies, *distributed by* Fons Vitae

SSPC, *distributed by* NACE International

SSPC: The Society for Protective Coatings, *distributed by* Technology Publishing Co

ST Media Group Book Division, *division of* ST Media Group International

Stacey International Ltd (London), *distributed by* International Book Centre Inc

Stackpole Books, *distributor for* The Colonial Williamsburg Foundation

Stainer & Bell Ltd, *distributed by* ECS Publishing Corp

Stamford University Press, *distributed by* Oxford University Press USA

Standard Educational Corp, *subsidiary of* The United Educators Inc

Standard Publishing Corp, *distributed by* Lexis-Nexis®, Silverplume, a Vertafore Co

Stanford Briefs, *imprint of* Stanford University Press

Stanford Business Books, *imprint of* Stanford University Press

Stanford Economics & Finance, *imprint of* Stanford University Press

Stanford Security Studies, *imprint of* Stanford University Press

Stanford Law Books, *imprint of* Stanford University Press

Stanford University Press, *distributor for* Woodrow Wilson Center Press

Star Sounds, *distributed by* Lotus Press

Star Trek®, *imprint of* Gallery Books

Starbooks, *imprint of* STARbooks Press

STARbooks Press, *affiliate of* Florida Literary Foundation (FLF)

Starcrafts Publishing, *imprint of* Starcrafts LLC

Starfire Publishing, *distributed by* Holmes Publishing Group LLC

Stargazer Books, *imprint of* Black Rabbit Books

Starrhill Press, *imprint of* River City Publishing LLC

Starscape, *imprint of* Tom Doherty Associates, LLC

Start Publishing LLC, *distributed by* Simon & Schuster, Inc

State Experience, *imprint of* Gallopade International Inc

State Stuff, *imprint of* Gallopade International Inc

State University of New York Press, *distributor for* Albany Institute of History & Art, Codhill Press, Samuel Dorsky Museum of Art, Mount Ida Press, Muswell Hill Press, New Netherland Institute, Rockefeller Institute Press, Uncrowned Queens

Steam Passages Publishing, *distributed by* Heimburger House Publishing Co

Steam Press, *distributed by* Gryphon House Inc

Steeple Hill, *imprint of* Harlequin Enterprises Ltd

Steerforth Press, *distributed by* Penguin Random House Inc

Steinberg, *distributed by* Hal Leonard Corp

Rudolf Steiner Press UK, *distributor for* Steiner-Books

Rudolph Steiner Press, *distributed by* Steiner-Books

SteinerBooks, *distributor for* Chiron Publications, Clairview Books, Floris Books, Hawthorn Press, Lantern Books, Rudolph Steiner Press, Temple Lodge Publishing, *distributed by* Rudolf Steiner Press UK

Steinsaltz, *imprint of* The Toby Press LLC, *distributed by* The Toby Press LLC

Stemmer House Publishers Inc, *division of* Pathway Book Service

Stenhouse Publishers, *division of* Highlights for Children Education Group, *distributor for* Pembroke Publishers

Sterling, *imprint of* Sterling Publishing Co Inc

Sterling & Francine Clark Art Institute, *distributed by* Yale University Press

Sterling Children's Books, *imprint of* Sterling Publishing Co Inc

Sterling Epicure, *imprint of* Sterling Publishing Co Inc

Sterling Ethos, *imprint of* Sterling Publishing Co Inc

Sterling Publishing, *distributed by* Hal Leonard Corp, Heimburger House Publishing Co

Sterling Publishing Co Inc, *subsidiary of* Barnes & Noble Inc, *distributor for* Boxer Books (selected titles), Brooklyn Botanic Garden (selected titles), Carlton Books (selected titles), Davis Publications (selected titles), Sally Milner (selected titles), Pavilion (selected titles), Salaryia (selected titles), Sixth & Spring, White Star Publishers (selected titles)

Gareth Stevens, *distributed by* Perfection Learning Corp

Stewart, Tabori & Chang, *imprint of* Harry N Abrams Inc

Stimulus Books, *imprint of* Paulist Press

Stinging Fly Press, *distributed by* Dufour Editions Inc

Stoecklein Publishing, *distributed by* The Globe Pequot Press

Stoke Books, *distributed by* Lerner Publishing Group Inc

Stone Arch Books, *imprint of* Capstone Publishers™

Stone Bridge Press, *distributed by* Cheng & Tsui Co Inc

Stone Pier Press, *distributed by* Chelsea Green Publishing

Stonefield Publishing, *distributed by* Chelsea Green Publishing Co

Stonewall, *imprint of* BrickHouse Books Inc

Stonewall Inn Editions, *imprint of* St Martin's Press, LLC

Storey Publishing, *division of* Workman Publishing Co Inc

Storey Publishing LLC, *distributed by* Workman Publishing Co Inc

Story Line Press, *imprint of* Red Hen Press

Story Monsters Press, *imprint of* Story Monsters LLC

The Story Plant, *division of* Studio Digital CT LLC

Story River Books, *imprint of* University of South Carolina Press

Straight Street Books, *imprint of* Lighthouse Publishing of the Carolinas

Strebor Books, *imprint of* Atria Books

Stress Free Kids®, *imprint of* Stress Free Publishers

String Letter Publishing, *distributed by* Hal Leonard Corp

Strong Books, *imprint of* Book Marketing Works LLC

Lyle Stuart Books, *imprint of* Kensington Publishing Corp

Stubs Guides, *distributed by* Hagstrom Map

Stubs Magazine, *distributed by* American Map Corp

Studien Verlag, *distributed by* Transaction Publishers Inc

Studio, *imprint of* Penguin Group USA, A Penguin Random House Company

Studio Fun International, *distributed by* Simon & Schuster, Inc

Stylus Publishing LLC, *distributor for* American Association for Higher Education, Cabi Books, Campus Compact, Commonwealth Scientific & Industrial Research Organization (CSIRO), Global Professional Publishing, Greenleaf Publishing, Institute of Education, The Institution of Engineering & Technology (IET), Karnac Books, Latin America Bureau, Mercury Learning & Information, National Resource Center First Year Experience, Oxfam Publishing, Practical Action, River Publishers, SciTech, Trentham Books Ltd, World Health Organization (WHO)

Success Advertising, *division of* Success Advertising & Publishing

Success Advertising & Publishing, *division of* The Success Group

Suffolk Records Society, *imprint of* Boydell & Brewer Inc

Sugar Cane Press, *distributed by* Heimburger House Publishing Co

Sumach Press, *distributed by* Orca Book Publishers

Summertime, *imprint of* Summertime Publications Inc

Summertime Publications Inc, *distributor for* ACHCBYZ (Paris academic press specializing in Byzantine history)

Summit Beacon, *distributor for* Woodland Publishing Inc

Summit Books, *imprint of* Perfection Learning Corp

Sun & Moon Classics, *imprint of* Green Integer

Sun Books, *imprint of* Sun Publishing Company

Sun Plans Inc, *distributed by* Chelsea Green Publishing Co

Sun Publishing Company, *division of* The Sun Companies

Sunbelt Publications Inc, *distributor for* Abbott Publishing, Alti Corporation, Amaroma Ediciones (Mexican architectural & design publisher), Anza-Borrego Foundation, W H Berger, Bobolink Media, Joan Brady, California Sea Grant, Paul Douglas Campbell, Dawsons Book Shop, Leland Fetzer, FineEdge.com LLC, Fun Places Publishing, Jeffrey Garcia, Maureen Gilmer, Glove Pequot, Green Grass Press, Healey Publishing, Huckleberry House LLC, Intellect Publishing, Island Paradise Publishing, Jaguar Tales, Scott G Kyle, Lawtech Publishing, Little Oak Press, Mission San Juan Capistrano Women's Guild, Newtona LLC, Northcross Books, Nelson Papucci, Bette L Pegas, Linda Pequegnat, Picaro Publishing, Planeta Peninsula (Mexican publisher), Phil R Pryde, Quick Reference Publishing, R & B Food & Culture Production, Random House, Renegade Enterprises, San Diego Architecture Foundation, San Diego Association of Geologists, San Diego City Works Press, San Diego Natural History Museum, San Diego Police Historical Association, San Dieguito River Park Joint Powers Authority, Save Our Heritage Organization, Surf Angel Publications, Trail Wisdom, University of California Press, Armand Vallee, Wigton Publishing, Wilderness Press, Wolf Water Press

Sundance/Newbridge Publishing, *division of* Rowman & Littlefield Publishing Group

Sunrise Library, *imprint of* Theosophical University Press

Sunrise River Press, *affiliate of* Cartech Books/Specialty Press

Sunset Books, *imprint of* Oxmoor House

Sunstone Press, *imprint of* The Sunstone Corp

SUNY Press, *distributor for* Codhill Press

SUP Publishing Logistics, *distributed by* Cheng & Tsui Co Inc

Super Sandcastle, *imprint of* ABDO Publishing Group

SuperGenius, *imprint of* Papercutz

Supplement Editions, *imprint of* Bandanna Books

Sure Fire Press, *imprint of* Holmes Publishing Group LLC

Surf Angel Publications, *distributed by* Sunbelt Publications Inc

Surrey Books, *imprint of* Agate Publishing

Susquehanna University Press, *distributed by* Associated University Presses

Sustainability Press, *distributed by* Chelsea Green Publishing Co

Swallow Press, *imprint of* Ohio University Press

Swallow's Tale Press, *imprint of* Livingston Press, *distributed by* Livingston Press

Swan Books, *division of* Learning Links Inc

Swan Isle Press, *distributed by* University of Chicago Press

Swedish Corrosion Institute, *distributed by* NACE International

Sweet & Maxwell, *distributed by* William S Hein & Co Inc

Sweetwater Books, *imprint of* Cedar Fort Inc

Swerve, *imprint of* St Martin's Press, LLC

Switchgrass Books, *imprint of* Northern Illinois University Press

The Sword of Norilana, *imprint of* Norilana Books

Sybex, *imprint of* John Wiley & Sons Inc

Sybex Inc, *division of* John Wiley & Sons Inc, *distributed by* EMC Publishing LLC

Sycamore Island Books, *imprint of* Paladin Press

Sylvan Learning, *imprint of* Random House Children's Books

Synergy, *imprint of* Bridge-Logos

SynErotica, *imprint of* SynergEbooks

Syracuse University Press, *distributor for* Arlen House, Dedalus Press, Pucker Gallery, *distributed by* Arlen House, Dedalus Press, Gryphon House Inc, Heimburger House Publishing Co

Tab Books, *distributor for* National Association of Broadcasters (NAB)

Tabard Press, *imprint of* Konecky & Konecky LLC

Tabernacle Publishing, *division of* Hope Publishing Co

The TAFT Group®, *imprint of* Gale

Yosifumi Taguchi, *distributed by* EastBridge

Tagus Press, *distributed by* University Press of New England

Tai Chi Foundation, *distributed by* Tuttle Publishing

Talc Blazers, *imprint of* Perfection Learning Corp

TaLeKa, *imprint of* Norilana Books

Nan A Talese, *imprint of* Penguin Random House Inc

Tamar Books, *imprint of* Mesorah Publications Ltd

Tamesis Books, *imprint of* Boydell & Brewer Inc

TAN Books, *imprint of* Saint Benedict Press LLC

T&T Clark International, *imprint of* Bloomsbury Publishing PLC

Tantor Audio, *imprint of* Tantor Media Inc

Tantor Media, *imprint of* Tantor Media Inc

Tantor Media Inc, *division of* Recorded Books

The S Mark Taper Foundation, *imprint of* University of California Press

Tapestry Press Ltd, *distributed by* Maryland History Press

Tara Publications, *distributed by* Hal Leonard Corp

Tarcher Perigee, *imprint of* Penguin Group USA, A Penguin Random House Company

TarcherPerigee, *imprint of* Penguin Group USA, A Penguin Random House Company, Penguin Group USA, A Penguin Random House Company

Taschen GmbH, *imprint of* Taschen America

Tastes Newsletter, *subsidiary of* Gault Millau Inc/Gayot Publications

Tata Institute of Fundamental Research, *distributed by* American Mathematical Society

Tata/McGraw-Hill, *imprint of* McGraw-Hill Education

Tate Galleries, *distributed by* Oak Knoll Press

Tate Publishing, *distributed by* Harry N Abrams Inc

Tattered Flag, *distributed by* Casemate | publishers

The Taunton Press, *distributed by* Penguin Random House Inc

The Taunton Press Inc, *distributor for* Guild of Master Craftsman (North America), Lucky Spool (North America & Australia)

Taunton Sterling Dover, *distributed by* Fox Chapel Publishing Co Inc

I B Tauris & Co Ltd, *distributed by* Palgrave Macmillan

Taylor & Francis, *distributor for* The Fairmont Press Inc, *distributed by* Illuminating Engineering Society of North America (IES)

Taylor & Francis Asia Pacific, *imprint of* Taylor & Francis Inc

Taylor & Francis Books, *imprint of* Taylor & Francis Inc

Taylor Trade, *imprint of* The Globe Pequot Press

Tayo Press, *distributed by* Franklin, Beedle & Associates Inc

TC Media Books, *distributed by* Simon & Schuster, Inc

TCU Press, *distributed by* Texas A&M University Press

Teach Yourself Visually, *imprint of* John Wiley & Sons Inc

Teachers College Press, *affiliate of* Teachers College, Columbia University

Teacher's Discovery, *division of* American Eagle Co Inc

Teachers Lesson Plan Book Series, *imprint of* National Learning Corp

Teaching Strategies, *distributed by* Gryphon House Inc

Teaching Strategies LLC, *distributor for* Gryphon House

Techne Press, *distributed by* Island Press

Editions Technip, *distributed by* Gulf Publishing Co

Technology, *division of* Scholastic Education

Technology Publishing Co, *distributor for* SSPC: The Society for Protective Coatings

Techstreet, *distributed by* Illuminating Engineering Society of North America (IES)

Katherine Tegen Books, *imprint of* HarperCollins Children's Books

Telshare Publishing, *distributed by* Gryphon House Inc

Templar Books, *imprint of* Candlewick Press

Temple Lodge Publishing, *distributed by* SteinerBooks

Temple University Press, *division of* Temple University of the Commonwealth System of Higher Education

Templeton Press, *subsidiary of* John Templeton Foundation

Temporal Mechanical Press, *division of* Enos Mills Cabin Museum & Gallery

Ten Pound Island Books, *distributed by* Mystic Seaport Museum Inc

Ten Speed Press, *imprint of* Crown Publishing Group, *distributed by* Penguin Random House Inc

Teora, *imprint of* Teora USA LLC

Terrace Books, *imprint of* University of Wisconsin Press

Terrapin Greetings, *imprint of* Down The Shore Publishing Corp

TESOL International Association, *distributed by* Alta Book Center Publishers, Delta Systems Inc, New Readers Press, Saddleback Educational

Test Your Knowledge Books, *imprint of* National Learning Corp

Testament Books, *imprint of* Penguin Random House Inc

Teton NewMedia Inc, *distributor for* LifeLearn, *distributed by* Blackwells, LifeLearn, Logan Brothers, Rittenhouse, Yankee

Texas A&M University Press, *division of* Texas A&M University, Texas A&M University, *distributor for* Stephen F Austin State University Press, McWhiney Foundation Press/State House Press, TCU Press, Texas Christian University Press, Texas Review Press, Texas State Historical Association, University of North Texas Press

Texas Christian University Press, *distributed by* Texas A&M University Press

Texas Memorial Museum, *distributed by* Bureau of Economic Geology, University of Texas at Austin

Texas Parks & Wildlife Department, *distributed by* University of Texas Press

Texas Review Press, *distributed by* Texas A&M University Press

Texas State Historical Association, *distributed by* Oak Knoll Press, Texas A&M University Press

Texas Tech University Press, *distributor for* The Colonial Williamsburg Foundation, National Ranching Heritage Center

University of Texas Press, *division of* University of Texas, *distributor for* Bat Conservation International, Institute for Mesoamerican Studies, Menil Foundation, Rothko Chapel, Texas Parks & Wildlife Department, Texas Western Press

Texas Western Press, *affiliate of* University of Texas at El Paso, *distributed by* University of Texas Press

TFH Publications Inc, *subsidiary of* Central Garden & Pet Corp

Thames & Hudson, *distributor for* MFA Publications, National Gallery of Art, *distributed by* W W Norton & Company Inc, The Vendome Press

That Patchwork Place, *imprint of* Martingale®

That the World May Know, *imprint of* Focus on the Family

Theatre Communications Group, *distributor for* Aurora Metro Publications, 53rd State Press, Nick Hern Books, Oberon Books, Padua Playwrights Press, PAJ Publications, Playscripts Inc, Playwrights Canada Press, Martin E Segal Theatre Center Publications, Ubu Repertory Theatre Publications

Theion Publishing, *distributed by* Holmes Publishing Group LLC

Theology of the Body Series, *imprint of* Pauline Books & Media

Theophilis, *imprint of* Transcontinental Music Publications (TMP)

Theosophical University Press, *affiliate of* Theosophical Society (Pasadena)

Thesaurus Islamicus Foundation, *distributed by* Fons Vitae

Theta Books, *imprint of* Bridge Publications Inc

Theta Foundation of Bucharest, *distributed by* American Mathematical Society

Thieme Medical Publishers Inc, *subsidiary of* Georg Thieme Verlag KG, *distributor for* AO Foundation

Thinking Like a Scientist, *imprint of* Sundance/Newbridge Publishing

30 Degrees South Publishers, *distributed by* Casemate | publishers

37 Ink, *imprint of* Atria Books

30 Words, *distributed by* The Globe Pequot Press

Thomas Nelson, *imprint of* HarperCollins Christian Publishing, *distributed by* Winston-Derek

Thomson Publishing, *distributed by* Oxford University Press USA, SkillPath Publications

Thomson Reuters, *distributor for* AICPA Professional Publications

Thomson Reuters Westlaw™, *distributor for* Law Library Microform Consortium

Thorndike Press, *subsidiary of* Cengage Learning, *imprint of* Gale, *distributor for* Grand Central/Hachette Large Print, HarperLuxe, Mills & Boon Large Print, Random House Large Print

Thorndike Press®, *imprint of* Gale

Nelson Thornes, *distributed by* Trans-Atlantic Publications Inc

Three Hands Press, *distributed by* Holmes Publishing Group LLC

Three L Media, *imprint of* Stone Bridge Press Inc

Three Pines Press, *distributed by* University of Hawaii Press

Three Rivers Press, *imprint of* Crown Publishing Group, Penguin Random House Inc

Threshold Editions, *imprint of* Gallery Books

Thresholds, *imprint of* Zumaya Publications LLC

Throckmorton Press, *distributed by* powerHouse Books

Thunder Bay Press, *distributed by* Heimburger House Publishing Co

Tia Chucha Press, *distributed by* Northwestern University Press

Tidewater Publishers, *imprint of* Cornell Maritime Press Inc, Schiffer Publishing Ltd

Tilbury House Publishers, *imprint of* WordSplice Studio LLC, *distributed by* W W Norton & Company Inc

Tilbury House Publishing, *distributed by* W W Norton & Company Inc

Timber Press, *division of* Workman Publishing Co Inc, *imprint of* Timber Press Inc

Timber Press Inc, *subsidiary of* Workman Publishing Co, Workman Publishing Co Inc, *distributed by* Thomas Allen & Son

Timerberline Productions, *imprint of* Crumb Elbow Publishing

Time Inc Books, *distributed by* Hachette Book Group

Timeless Love, *imprint of* Oak Tree Press

Times Books, *imprint of* Henry Holt and Company, LLC, Penguin Random House Inc

Tin House Books, *distributed by* W W Norton & Company Inc

To the Stars Inc, *distributed by* Simon & Schuster, Inc, Simon & Schuster Sales Division

The Toby Press LLC, *distributor for* Ofeq Books, Steinsaltz

Toccata Press, *imprint of* Boydell & Brewer Inc

Today's Books, *imprint of* History Publishing Co LLC

Today's Titles, *imprint of* History Publishing Co LLC

TOKYOPOP, *imprint of* HarperCollins Children's Books

Tommy Nelson, *imprint of* HarperCollins Christian Publishing

Tonga Books, *imprint of* Europa Editions

Delos Toole, *distributed by* Gem Guides Book Co

TOP, *imprint of* Top Publications Ltd

Top of the Mountain Publishing, *division of* Powell Productions

Topaz, *imprint of* Penguin Group USA, A Penguin Random House Company

Tor, *imprint of* Tom Doherty Associates, LLC

Tor Classics, *imprint of* Tom Doherty Associates, LLC

Tor Teen, *imprint of* Tom Doherty Associates, LLC

Torah Aura Productions, *distributor for* Free Spirit (selected titles)

Torah Umesorah Publications, *division of* Torah Umesorah-National Society for Hebrew Day Schools

Torrid Books, *imprint of* Whiskey Creek Press

Tory Corner Editions, *imprint of* Quincannon Publishing Group

Total Information, *distributor for* Primary Research Group Inc

Touch for Health, *distributed by* DeVorss & Co

Touchstone, *imprint of* Scribner Publishing Group

Tourism Dynamic, *imprint of* Cognizant Communication Corp

Towers Maguire Publishing, *imprint of* The Local History Co

Tradery House, *imprint of* Wimmer Cookbooks

Tradewind Books, *distributed by* Orca Book Publishers

Tradigital, *distributed by* Fons Vitae

Tradition Books, *imprint of* The Child's World Inc, *distributed by* The Child's World Inc

Trafalgar Square Books, *distributor for* J A Allen, Kenilworth Press, Pferdia TV

Trafford, *division of* Author Solutions LLC

Trail Wisdom, *distributed by* Sunbelt Publications Inc

Trailblazer Press, *distributed by* Chelsea Green Publishing Co

Trailblazer Publications, *distributed by* The Globe Pequot Press

Oswald Train, *distributed by* Donald M Grant Publisher Inc

Training & Development Materials of Canada, *distributor for* HRD Press

Trakker Maps Inc, *subsidiary of* American Map Corp, *distributed by* Hagstrom Map

Tralco, *distributor for* Beach Lloyd Publishers LLC

Trans-Atlantic Publications Inc, *distributor for* Book Guild, Book House, Financial Times Publishing, Hodder Education, Instituto Monsa de Ediciones SA (art books from Spain), Longman, Arnoldo Mondadori Electa, Nexus Special Interests, Pearson Education, Nelson Thornes

Trans Tech Publications Inc, *distributor for* Enfield Publishers, *distributed by* Curran Associates Inc, Yankee Book Peddler

Transaction Large Print, *imprint of* Transaction Publishers Inc

Transaction Publishers, *distributor for* University of California Institute on Global Conflict & Cooperation

Transaction Publishers Inc, *distributor for* Bridge 21, IWGIA, The Netherlands Institute for Social Research, Editions Scholasticae, Studien Verlag

Transactions, *imprint of* American Philosophical Society

Transcontinental Music Publications (TMP), *division of* American Conference of Cantors (ACC)

Transcript Verlag, *distributed by* Columbia University Press

Transformation Media Books, *imprint of* Pen & Publish Inc

Transforming Press, *distributed by* Crown House Publishing Co LLC

Transportation Research Board (TRB), *division of* The National Academies of Sciences, Engineering & Medicine

Transportation Research Board Code, *distributed by* Professional Publications Inc (PPI)

Travelers' Tales, *subsidiary of* Solas House Inc

Traveling Pen Press, *imprint of* Flying Pen Press LLC

Treacle Press, *imprint of* McPherson & Co

Treasure Chest Books, *distributor for* Ocean Tree Books

Tree of Life Books, *imprint of* Progressive Press

Trees Co, *distributed by* Gem Guides Book Co

Trentham Books Ltd, *distributed by* Stylus Publishing LLC

Tri-Star Boze Books, *distributed by* Gem Guides Book Co

Triad Publishing Co, *imprint of* Triad Communications Inc

Triangle Square Books for Young Readers, *imprint of* Seven Stories Press

Tribunal for Administrative Justice, *imprint of* The Edwin Mellen Press

Trident Reference, *imprint of* Standard International Media Holdings

Trillium Mountain Productions, *imprint of* Crumb Elbow Publishing

Trillium Press, *distributed by* Royal Fireworks Press

Trinity Grace Press, *imprint of* Signalman Publishing

Trinity University Press, *unit of* Trinity University

TriQuarterly Books, *imprint of* Northwestern University Press

TRISTAN OUTDOORS, *imprint of* TRISTAN Publishing

Triumph Books, *imprint of* Random House Publishing Group, *distributor for* United States Tennis Association

Triumph Entertainment, *imprint of* Triumph Books

Triumph Learning, *division of* Haights Cross Communications®

Triumph Learning LLC, *division of* Haights Cross Communications®

Troitsa Books, *imprint of* Nova Science Publishers Inc

Troubador Press, *imprint of* Price Stern Sloan

Troubadour Books, *imprint of* Regal Crest Enterprises

Truman State University Press, *unit of* Truman State University

Truman Talley Books, *imprint of* St Martin's Press, LLC

Trust for Public Land, *distributed by* Chelsea Green Publishing Co

Trusted Books, *imprint of* Deep River Books LLC

Tu Books, *imprint of* Lee & Low Books Inc

Tuckamore Books, *distributed by* Orca Book Publishers

Tudor House, *distributed by* Orca Book Publishers

Tudor Publishers Inc, *subsidiary of* Cornwallis Press, Cornwallis Press (young adult fiction & nonfiction)

Tufts University Press, *imprint of* University Press of New England

Tughra Books, *imprint of* Blue Dome Inc

Tulika Books, *distributed by* Columbia University Press

Tumbleweed Series, *imprint of* Mountain Press Publishing Co

Turnaround (London), *distributor for* Bella Books

Turner, *imprint of* Turner Publishing Co

Turtle Point, *imprint of* Turtle Point Press

Tusk Ivory, *imprint of* The Overlook Press

Tusk Paperbacks, *imprint of* The Overlook Press

Tuttle Publishing, *member of* Periplus Publishing Group, *distributor for* Healing Tao Books, Kosei Publishing Co, Kotan Publishing Inc, Milet Publishing Ltd, Paperweight Press, Periplus Editions, Shanghai Press, Shufunotomo Co, Tai Chi Foundation, *distributed by* Cheng & Tsui Co Inc, Publishers Group West (digital only), Simon & Schuster, Inc

TV Books, *distributed by* HarperCollins Publishers

Mark Twain Media, *distributed by* Carson-Dellosa Publishing LLC

Twelve, *imprint of* Grand Central Publishing

Twenty-First Century Books, *imprint of* Lerner Publishing Group Inc

Twenty-Third Publications, *division of* Bayard Inc, *distributor for* Novalis (Canada), *distributed by* Columba (UK), John Garrett (Australia), Novalis (Canada)

Twilight Visions, *imprint of* Twilight Times Books

TwoDot®, *imprint of* The Globe Pequot Press

Tycoon Percussion, *distributed by* Hal Leonard Corp

Tyee Press, *imprint of* Crumb Elbow Publishing

Tyndale Audio, *imprint of* Tyndale House Publishers Inc

Tyndale Entertainment, *imprint of* Tyndale House Publishers Inc

Tyndale House Publishers, *distributor for* Focus on the Family

Tyndale House Publishers Inc, *distributor for* Focus on the Family, NavPress, NavPress Publishing Group

Tyndale Kids, *imprint of* Tyndale House Publishers Inc

Tyndale Momentum, *imprint of* Tyndale House Publishers Inc

Tyndale Ninos, *imprint of* Tyndale House Publishers Inc

Typophiles, *distributed by* Oak Knoll Press

U X L™, *imprint of* Gale

UA Museum, *distributed by* University of Alaska Press

UBC Press, Canada, *distributor for* Michigan State University Press (MSU Press)

Ubisoft, *distributed by* Simon & Schuster, Inc

Ubu Repertory Theatre Publications, *distributed by* Theatre Communications Group

Udig, *imprint of* Andrews McMeel Publishing LLC

Ugly Duckling Presse, *distributor for* United Artists

The Ultra Violet Library, *imprint of* Circlet Press Inc

Unarius Academy of Science Publications, *division of* Unarius Educational Foundation

Unarius Video Productions, *division of* Unarius Academy of Science Publications

Uncrate LLC, *distributed by* Simon & Schuster, Inc, Simon & Schuster Sales Division

Uncrowned Queens, *distributed by* Excelsior Editions, State University of New York Press

Undergraduate Program Field Test Series, *imprint of* National Learning Corp

UNFOLDS®, *imprint of* VanDam Inc

Unifacmanu Trading Co Ltd, *distributor for* Health Professions Press

Editorial Unilit, *division of* Spanish House Inc

United Artists, *distributed by* Ugly Duckling Presse

United Nations Children's Fund (UNICEF), *distributed by* United Nations Publications

United Nations Development Programme (UNDP), *distributed by* United Nations Publications

United Nations Economic & Social Commission for Asia & the Pacific (ESCAP), *distributed by* United Nations Publications

United Nations Economic & Social Commission for Western Asia (ESCWA), *distributed by* United Nations Publications

United Nations Economic Commission for Africa (ECA), *distributed by* United Nations Publications

United Nations Economic Commission for Europe (ECE), *distributed by* United Nations Publications

United Nations Economic Commission for Latin America & the Caribbean (ECLAC), *distributed by* United Nations Publications

United Nations High Commissioner for Refugees (UNHCR), *distributed by* United Nations Publications

United Nations Human Settlements Programme (UN-HABITAT), *distributed by* United Nations Publications

United Nations Industrial Development Organization (UNIDO), *distributed by* United Nations Publications

United Nations Institute for Disarmament Research (UNIDIR), *distributed by* United Nations Publications

United Nations Institute for Training & Research (UNITAR), *distributed by* United Nations Publications

United Nations International Research & Training Institute for the Advancement of Women (INSTRAW), *distributed by* United Nations Publications

United Nations Interregional Crime & Justice Research Institute (UNICRI), *distributed by* United Nations Publications

United Nations Office for Project Services (UNOPS), *distributed by* United Nations Publications

United Nations Office for the Coordination of Humanitarian Affairs (OCHA), *distributed by* United Nations Publications

United Nations Office on Drugs & Crime (UNODC), *distributed by* United Nations Publications

United Nations Population Fund (UNFPA), *distributed by* United Nations Publications

United Nations Publications, *distributor for* Food & Agriculture Organization of the United Nations (FAO), International Atomic Energy Agency (IAEA), International Criminal Tribunal for Rwanda (UNICTR), International Criminal Tribunal for the former Yugoslavia (ICTY), International Organization for Migration (IOM), International Trade Centre (ITC), Office of the United Nations High Commissioner for Human Rights (OHCHR), United Nations Children's Fund (UNICEF), United Nations Development Programme (UNDP), United Nations Economic & Social Commission for Asia & the Pacific (ESCAP), United Nations Economic & Social Commission for Western Asia (ESCWA), United Nations Economic Commission for Africa (ECA), United Nations Economic Commission for Europe (ECE), United Nations Economic Commission for Latin America & the Caribbean (ECLAC), United Nations High Commissioner for Refugees (UNHCR), United Nations Human Settlements Programme (UN-HABITAT), United Nations Industrial Development Organization (UNIDO), United Nations Institute for Disarmament Research (UNIDIR), United Nations Institute for Training & Research (UNITAR), United Nations International Research & Training Institute for the Advancement of Women (INSTRAW), United Nations Interregional Crime & Justice Research Institute (UNICRI), United Nations Office for Project Services (UNOPS), United Nations Office for the Coordination of Humanitarian Affairs (OCHA), United Nations Office on Drugs & Crime (UNODC), United Nations Population Fund (UNFPA), United Nations Research Institute for Social Development (UNRISD), United Nations University (UNU)

United Nations Research Institute for Social Development (UNRISD), *distributed by* United Nations Publications

United Nations University (UNU), *distributed by* United Nations Publications

United States Catholic Conference Publications, *distributed by* Liturgy Training Publications

United States Pharmacopeia, *distributed by* Consumer Reports

United States Tennis Association, *distributed by* Triumph Books, Universe Publishing, H O Zimman Inc

Univelt Inc, *affiliate of* American Astronautical Society, *distributor for* Astronautical Society of Western Australia, US Space Foundation

Universe, *imprint of* Rizzoli International Publications Inc, Universe Publishing, *distributor for* Country Music Foundation Press

Universe Calendars, *imprint of* Universe Publishing

Universe Publishing, *imprint of* Rizzoli International Publications Inc, *distributor for* United States Tennis Association, *distributed by* Random House

Universe Publishing Calendars, *distributed by* Andrews McMeel Publishing LLC

University College Dublin Press, *distributed by* Dufour Editions Inc

University of Alabama Press, *distributor for* Fiction Collective Two Inc (FC2)

University of Alaska Press, *distributor for* Alaska Native Language Center, Alaska Quarterly Review, Alaska Sea Grant, Alutiiq Museum, Anchorage Museum Association, Anchorage Museum of Art History, Arctic Studies Center of the Smithsonian Museum, Far to the North Press, Geophysical Institute, Limestone Press, Spirit Mountain Press, UA Museum, Vanessapress

University of Alberta Press, *distributed by* Michigan State University Press (MSU Press)

The University of Arkansas Press, *division of* The University of Arkansas, *distributor for* Butler Center for Arkansas Studies, Hearne Fine Art, Moon City Press, Ozark Society, Phoenix International

University of California Institute on Global Conflict & Cooperation, *subsidiary of* University of California, *distributed by* Brookings Institution Press, Columbia International Affairs Online (CIAO), Cornell University Press, Garland Publishers, Lynn-Reinner Publishing, Penn State University Press, Princeton University Press, Transaction Publishers, University of Michigan Press, Westview Press

University of California Press, *distributor for* artSITES, British Film Institute, Sierra Club Books (adult trade), Woodrow Wilson Center Press, *distributed by* Sunbelt Publications Inc

University of Chicago Press, *distributor for* CSLI Publications, Getty Publications, National Gallery of Art, Northern Illinois University Press, St Augustine's Press Inc, Swan Isle Press

University of Chicago Press Distribution Center, *distributor for* University of Pittsburgh Press

University of Delaware Press, *distributed by* Rowman & Littlefield

University of Florida Press, *imprint of* University Press of Florida

University of Hawaii Press, *distributor for* Ateneo De Manila University Press, Cornell University East Asia Program, Huia Publishers, MerwinAsia, NIAS Press, The Numata Center, NUS Press, Renaissance Press, Seoul Selection, Shanghai Press, Three Pines Press, University of the Philippines Press

University of Idaho Asian American Comparative Collection, *distributed by* Caxton Press

University of Idaho Press, *distributed by* Caxton Press

University of Illinois Press, *unit of* University of Illinois

University of Manitoba Press, *distributed by* Michigan State University Press (MSU Press)

University of Massachusetts Press, *distributed by* The Johns Hopkins University Press

University of Michigan, *distributed by* International Book Centre Inc

University of Michigan Press, *unit of* University of Michigan, *distributor for* Center for Chinese Studies, University of Michigan, Center for Japanese Studies, University of Michigan, Center for South & Southeast Asian Studies, University of Michigan, University of California Institute on Global Conflict & Cooperation

University of Minnesota Press, *unit of* University of Minnesota, *distributor for* Univocal Publishing, *distributed by* Heimburger House Publishing Co

University of Missouri Press, *distributor for* Missouri History Museum, St Louis Mercantile Library

University of Nebraska Press, *division of* University of Nebraska at Lincoln, *distributor for* Buros Institute, Jewish Publication Society, Society for American Baseball Research

University of New Hampshire Press, *imprint of* University Press of New England, *distributed by* University Press of New England

University of New Mexico Press, *distributor for* Avanyu Publishing, Fresco Fine Art Publications LLC, La Frontera Publishing, Museum of New Mexico Press, School for Advanced Research Press, West End Press

The University of North Carolina Press, *distributor for* Museum of Early Southern Decorative Arts, North Carolina Museum of Art, Omohundro Institute of Early American History & Culture, Southeastern Center for Contemporary Art, Valentine Museum

University of North Texas Press, *distributed by* Texas A&M University Press

University of Oklahoma Press, *distributor for* Cherokee Heritage Press, Dakota Institute, Denver Art Museum, Gilcrease Museum, Vanderbilt University Press

University of Pennsylvania Libraries, *distributed by* Diane Publishing Co

University of Pennsylvania Museum, *distributed by* The Johns Hopkins University Press

University of Pennsylvania Museum of Archaeology & Anthropology, *division of* University of Pennsylvania, *distributed by* University of Pennsylvania Press

University of Pennsylvania Press, *distributor for* University of Pennsylvania Museum of Archaeology & Anthropology, Winterthur Museum, Garden & Library, *distributed by* The Johns Hopkins University Press

University of Pittsburgh Press, *distributed by* University of Chicago Press Distribution Center

University of Puerto Rico Press, *subsidiary of* University of Puerto Rico

University of Rochester Press, *imprint of* Boydell & Brewer Inc, *affiliate of* Boydell & Brewer Inc

University of San Francisco Press, *distributed by* Fordham University Press

University of South Carolina Press, *affiliate of* University of South Carolina, *distributor for* McKissick Museum, Saraland Press, South Carolina Bar Association, South Carolina Historical Society

University of Tennessee Press, *division of* University of Tennessee

University of Texas Press, *division of* University of Texas, *distributor for* Bat Conservation International, Institute for Mesoamerican Studies, Menil Foundation, Rothko Chapel, Texas Parks & Wildlife Department, Texas Western Press

University of the Philippines Press, *distributed by* University of Hawaii Press

University of Tokyo Press, *distributed by* Columbia University Press

University of Toronto Press, *distributor for* Boys Town Press, Central European University Press

The University of Utah Press, *subsidiary of* University of Utah, *distributor for* BYU Museum of Peoples & Cultures, BYU Studies, KUED (Utah PBS affiliate), Western Epics Publications

University of Vermont Press, *imprint of* University Press of New England

The University of Virginia Press, *affiliate of* University of Virginia, *distributor for* Colonial Society of Massachusetts, The Colonial Williamsburg Foundation, Mount Vernon Ladies Association

University of Virginia Press, *distributor for* The Massachusetts Historical Society

University of Washington Press, *distributor for* American Federation of Arts, Fowler Museum at UCLA, Lost Horse Press, Lynx House Press, *distributed by* The Johns Hopkins University Press

University of Wisconsin Press, *unit of* The University of Wisconsin, *distributor for* The Center for the Study of Upper Midwestern Culture, Dryad Press, Elvehjem Museum of Art, Max Kade Institute for German-American Studies, Spring Freshet Press, Wisconsin Academy of Sciences, Arts & Letters, Wisconsin Veterans Museum

University Press, *distributed by* American Mathematical Society

University Press of America Inc, *distributor for* Atlantic Council, Center for National Policy Press, Harvard Center for International Affairs, International Law Institute, Joint Center for Political & Economic Studies Press, White Burkett Miller Center, Society of the Cincinnati

University Press of Colorado, *distributor for* Center for Literary Publishing, History Colorado, Western Press Books

University Press of Florida, *affiliate of* State University System of Florida

The University Press of Kentucky, *distributor for* Kentucky Historical Society, *distributed by* The Johns Hopkins University Press

University Press of Maryland, *imprint of* CDL Press

University Press of New England, *distributor for* Academia Press, Autumn House Press, Bauhan Publishing, Carnegie Mellon University Press, CavanKerry Press, Chipstone Foundation, The Colonial Williamsburg Foundation, Duquesne University Press, Four Way Books, Harvest Hill Press, Historic New England, International Polar Institute, New Issues Poetry & Prose, Nightboat Books, Northeastern University Press, Oberlin College Press, Omnidawn Publishing, Peter E Randall Publisher, Saturnalia Books, The Sheep Meadow Press, Tagus Press, University of New Hampshire Press, Vermont Folklife Center, Warring States Project, Wesleyan University Press, Winterthur Museum, Garden & Library

University Press of New England (UPNE), *distributor for* Oberlin College Press

Univocal Publishing, *distributed by* University of Minnesota Press

UNO Press, *division of* University of New Orleans

Unofficial Guides, *imprint of* AdventureKEEN

Upjohn Press, *imprint of* W E Upjohn Institute for Employment Research

Upper Access Books, *imprint of* Upper Access Inc

Upper Ohio Valley Books, *distributed by* John F Blair Publisher

Upper Playground, *distributed by* Gingko Press Inc

Upper Room Books, *division of* The Upper Room, *imprint of* Abingdon Press, *distributed by* Abingdon Press

Upstart Books™, *division of* Demco Inc

Urban Books, *imprint of* Kensington Publishing Corp, *distributed by* Kensington Publishing Corp

Urban Christian, *imprint of* Kensington Publishing Corp

Urban Institute Press, *distributed by* The Johns Hopkins University Press

Urban Renaissance, *imprint of* Kensington Publishing Corp

US Coast Pilot, *imprint of* ProStar Publications Inc

US Games Systems Inc, *distributor for* Blue Angel Publishing, KonigsFurt

US Government Publishing Office (GPO), *division of* US Government

US Green Building Council, *distributed by* Professional Publications Inc (PPI)

US International Publishing, *distributed by* Cheng & Tsui Co Inc

US Space Foundation, *distributed by* Univelt Inc

Usborne Books, *imprint of* EDC Publishing

Usborne Publishing Ltd, *distributed by* EDC Publishing

User's Guides, *imprint of* Basic Health Publications

Utah Geological Survey, *division of* Utah Department of Natural Resources

Utah State University Press, *imprint of* University Press of Colorado

Vagabond Voices, *distributed by* Dufour Editions Inc

Valaam Society of America, *imprint of* Saint Herman Press

Valentine Museum, *distributed by* The University of North Carolina Press

Armand Vallee, *distributed by* Sunbelt Publications Inc

Valuation Press, *imprint of* Marshall & Swift

Van der Plas Publications, *imprint of* Cycle Publishing LLC

V&A Publishing, *distributed by* Harry N Abrams Inc

Vandalia Press, *imprint of* West Virginia University Press

VanDam Publishing, *division of* VanDam Inc

Vandamere Press, *distributor for* ABI Professional Publications (non-exclusive), JMC Press (exclusive to trade), NRH Press (non-exclusive), Quodlibetal Features

Vanderbilt University Press, *division of* Vanderbilt University, *distributor for* Country Music Foundation Press, *distributed by* University of Oklahoma Press

Vanessapress, *distributed by* University of Alaska Press

Varlik, *subsidiary of* Cross-Cultural Communications

Vedanta Press, *subsidiary of* Vedanta Society of Southern California, *distributor for* Advaita Ashrama, Ananda Ashrama, Ramakrishna Math, Ramakrishna-Vivkanana

Vegan Heritage Press, *distributed by* Andrews McMeel Publishing LLC

Vegas Lit, *imprint of* Huntington Press Publishing

Velazquez Press, *division of* Academic Learning Co LLC

The Vendome Press, *distributor for* Thames & Hudson, *distributed by* Abrams Books, Harry N Abrams Inc

Venture Press, *imprint of* Williams & Company Book Publishers

Verba Mundi, *imprint of* David R Godine Publisher Inc

Veritas, *distributed by* ACTA Publications, Dufour Editions Inc, Ignatius Press

Vermont Folklife Center, *distributed by* University Press of New England

Vernon Press, *imprint of* Vernon Art & Science Inc

Verso, *distributed by* Penguin (Canada)

Vertigo, *imprint of* DC Entertainment

Vesuvian Books, *division of* Vesuvian Media Group Inc

VH-1, *imprint of* Gallery Books

VH1 Press, *distributed by* powerHouse Books

Vice Books, *distributed by* powerHouse Books

Victionary, *distributed by* Gingko Press Inc

Victorian Heritage Press, *imprint of* Loving Healing Press Inc

Victory Belt Publishing, *distributed by* Simon & Schuster, Inc

Victory History of the Counties of England, *imprint of* Boydell & Brewer Inc

Victory in Grace Press, *division of* Victory in Grace Ministries

Vieweg Verlag Publications, *distributed by* American Mathematical Society

Viking, *imprint of* Penguin Group USA, A Penguin Random House Company, Penguin Group USA, A Penguin Random House Company

Viking Children's Books, *imprint of* Penguin Group USA, A Penguin Random House Company, Penguin Group USA, A Penguin Random House Company, Penguin Young Readers Group

Viking Compass, *imprint of* Penguin Group USA, A Penguin Random House Company, Viking

Viking Studio, *imprint of* Penguin Group USA, A Penguin Random House Company, Penguin Group USA, A Penguin Random House Company

Villard, *imprint of* Random House Publishing Group

Villard Books, *imprint of* Penguin Random House Inc

Vintage Books, *imprint of* Knopf Doubleday Publishing Group, Penguin Random House Inc

Vintage Espanol, *imprint of* Penguin Random House Inc

Vintage Guitar, *imprint of* Hal Leonard Corp, *distributed by* Hal Leonard Corp

Vintage Shorts, *imprint of* Vintage Books

Vireo Press, *distributed by* ECS Publishing Corp

Virginia Genealogical Society, *distributed by* Heritage Books Inc

Vision, *imprint of* Grand Central Publishing

Visionary Art, *division of* Unarius Academy of Science Publications

Vital Resources, *imprint of* Gospel Publishing House (GPH)

Viva Editions, *imprint of* Cleis Press, *distributed by* Red Wheel/Weiser/Conari

VIZ Media, *distributed by* Simon & Schuster, Inc, Simon & Schuster Sales Division

Voggenreiter Publishers, *distributed by* Mel Bay Publications Inc

Voices of Asia, *imprint of* EastBridge

Volo, *imprint of* Disney-Hyperion Books

Voyage, *imprint of* Brigantine Media

Voyager Sopris Learning Inc, *imprint of* Cambium Learning Inc

Voyageur Press, *imprint of* Quarto Publishing Group USA Inc, *distributed by* Arcadia Publishing Inc, Hal Leonard Corp

W Publishing Group, *imprint of* Thomas Nelson

Wadsworth, *subsidiary of* Cengage Learning

WAG Books, *distributed by* Casemate | publishers

Waggle, *imprint of* Triumph Learning LLC

Walden Pond Press, *imprint of* HarperCollins Children's Books

Waldman House Press, *imprint of* TRISTAN Publishing

Wall & Thompson, *distributed by* ADASI Publishing Co

Wallflower Press, *imprint of* Columbia University Press

Walton's, *distributed by* Mel Bay Publications Inc

Waltons Irish Music, *distributed by* Hal Leonard Corp

WAP Academic, *imprint of* Pentecostal Publishing House

WAP Children, *imprint of* Pentecostal Publishing House

Warboys LLC, *distributed by* Bridge-Logos

Warlord Games, *distributed by* Casemate | publishers

Warman's, *imprint of* F+W Media Inc, Krause Publications Inc

Frederick Warne, *imprint of* Penguin Group USA, A Penguin Random House Company, Penguin Group USA, A Penguin Random House Company, Penguin Young Readers Group, *distributed by* Perfection Learning Corp

Warner/Chappell Music Inc, *imprint of* Alfred Music Publishing

Warner Press, *affiliate of* Church of God

Warring States Project, *distributed by* University Press of New England

Washington Post Crosswords, *imprint of* Random House Reference/Random House Puzzles & Games

Washington Service Bureau, *subsidiary of* CCH, a Wolters Kluwer business

Washington Square Press, *imprint of* Atria Books

Washington State Historical Society, *distributed by* Washington State University Press

Washington State University Press, *division of* Washington State University, *distributor for* The Hutton Settlement (single title), Oregon California Trails Assn, Oregon Writers Colony (single title), Pacific Institute (single title), Washington State Historical Society (single title), WSU Museum of Art

Water Resources Publications LLC, *distributor for* ASAE, ASCE

WaterBrook, *imprint of* Crown Publishing Group

Waterfall Press, *imprint of* Brilliance Audio

Waterfront Soundings Productions, *distributed by* Marine Techniques Publishing

WaterLife Books, *imprint of* Deep River Books LLC

Watersport Books, *imprint of* Aqua Quest Publications Inc

Watson-Guptill, *imprint of* Crown Publishing Group

Watson-Guptill Publications, *imprint of* Crown Publishing Group, *distributor for* C&T Publishing Inc

Neale Watson Academic Publications, *imprint of* Watson Publishing International LLC

Waverley Books (UK), *distributed by* Interlink Publishing Group Inc

Wax Facts Press, *distributed by* Gingko Press Inc

Wayne State University Press, *distributor for* Cranbrook Institute of Science, Detroit Institute of Arts, Hebrew Union College Press

The Waywiser Press, *distributed by* Dufour Editions Inc

WBusiness Books, *imprint of* New Win Publishing

We Do Listen, *distributed by* Lerner Publishing Group Inc

WEA, *distributed by* Alfred Music Publishing

Wednesday Books, *imprint of* St Martin's Press, LLC

Wee Sing, *imprint of* Penguin Group USA, A Penguin Random House Company, Price Stern Sloan

Irene Weinberger Books, *imprint of* Hamilton Stone Editions

Welcome Enterprises Inc, *imprint of* Rizzoli International Publications Inc, *distributor for* AAP, Cerf & Peterson, Music Sales, Zeke Holdings Ltd, *distributed by* Random House

Weldon Owen, *distributed by* Simon & Schuster, Inc, Simon & Schuster Sales Division

Wellfleet Press, *imprint of* Quarto Publishing Group USA Inc

Wellington Press, *division of* BooksUPrint.com Inc

Welz, *distributed by* Alan Wofsy Fine Arts

Wendy Lamb Books, *imprint of* Penguin Random House Inc, Random House Children's Books

Weseanne Publications, *distributed by* Gem Guides Book Co

Wesleyan Poetry, *imprint of* Wesleyan University Press

Wesleyan Publishing House, *division of* Wesleyan Church Corp, Wesleyan Church Corporation

Wesleyan University Press, *distributed by* University Press of New England

West End Press, *distributed by* University of New Mexico Press

Western Audio, *imprint of* Recorded Books Inc, an RBmedia company

Western Edge Press, *imprint of* Sherman Asher Publishing, Sherman Asher Publishing, *distributed by* Mountain Press Publishing Co

Western Epics Publications, *distributed by* The University of Utah Press

Western Horseman, *imprint of* The Globe Pequot Press

Western Horseman Books, *distributed by* The Globe Pequot Press

Western Press Books, *distributed by* University Press of Colorado

Western Psychological Service, *distributor for* Psychological Assessment Resources Inc (PAR)

Westminster John Knox Press (WJK), *imprint of* Presbyterian Publishing Corp (PPC), *distributor for* SCM

Weston Woods, *imprint of* Scholastic Trade Division

Westridge Art, *distributed by* Epicenter Press Inc

Westview Press, *distributor for* University of California Institute on Global Conflict & Cooperation

WestWinds Press®, *imprint of* Graphic Arts Books

SR Wheat, *distributed by* Mel Bay Publications Inc

Wheatherstone Press, *subsidiary of* Dickinson Consulting Group

Wheeler Publishing™, *imprint of* Gale

Whiskey Creek Press, *imprint of* Start Publishing LLC

Whitaker, *distributor for* Faith Library Publications

White Eagle Publishing Trust (England), *distributed by* DeVorss & Co

White Pine Press, *distributor for* Springhouse Editions

White Poppy Press, *imprint of* Modern Memoirs

White Rabbit Press, *distributed by* Cheng & Tsui Co Inc

White Star Publishers, *distributed by* Sterling Publishing Co Inc

White Thread Press, *distributed by* Fons Vitae

Whitford Press, *imprint of* Schiffer Publishing Ltd

Whitney Museum of American Art, *distributed by* Yale University Press

Whole Person Associates, *imprint of* Whole Person Associates Inc

Wide World of Maps Inc, *distributor for* Benchmark Maps, Big Sky Maps, Franko Maps, MacVan Maps (Colorado Springs), Metro Maps, Rand McNally, *distributed by* Rand McNally

Wide World Publishing/Tetra, *imprint of* Wide World Publishing

Wigton Publishing, *distributed by* Sunbelt Publications Inc

Wildcat Canyon Press, *imprint of* Council Oak Books LLC

Wild Mountain Press, *imprint of* Crumb Elbow Publishing

Wild Oak, *imprint of* Oak Tree Press

Wilderness Adventures Press Inc, *distributed by* American West Books, Angler's Book Supply, Raymond C Rumpf & Son Inc

Wilderness Press, *imprint of* AdventureKEEN, *distributed by* Sunbelt Publications Inc

Wildflower Press, *affiliate of* Oakbrook Press

Wildlife Research Group, *imprint of* Crumb Elbow Publishing

Wiley, *imprint of* Turner Publishing Co, *distributed by* AICPA Professional Publications, Gulf Publishing Co

Wiley-Blackwell, *imprint of* John Wiley & Sons Inc, *distributor for* American Anthropological Association (AAA)

Wiley Blackwell Publishers, *distributor for* New York Academy of Sciences (NYAS)

Wiley Custom Select, *imprint of* John Wiley & Sons Inc

Wiley Global Education, *imprint of* John Wiley & Sons Inc

Wiley-IEEE Press, *imprint of* IEEE Press, John Wiley & Sons Inc

J Wiley & Sons, *distributed by* Medical Group Management Association (MGMA)

John Wiley & Sons, *distributor for* The Electrochemical Society (ECS), *distributed by* American Water Works Association (AWWA), Heimburger House Publishing Co

John Wiley & Sons Inc, *distributor for* Association for Information Science & Technology (ASIS&T), Center for Creative Leadership LLC, IEEE Press, R S Means from The Gordian Group, SAS Publishing, *distributed by* American Academy of Environmental Engineers & Scientists™, Center for Creative Leadership LLC, William S Hein & Co Inc, J J Keller & Associates, Inc, NACE International, SAS Publishing, SkillPath Publications, Society of Manufacturing Engineers

John Wiley & Sons Inc Global Education, *division of* John Wiley & Sons Inc, John Wiley & Sons Inc

John Wiley & Sons Inc Professional Development, *division of* John Wiley & Sons Inc

Wiley Online Library, *imprint of* John Wiley & Sons Inc

Wiley Science Solutions, *imprint of* John Wiley & Sons Inc

Wiley-VCH, *imprint of* John Wiley & Sons Inc

Wiley Visualizing, *imprint of* John Wiley & Sons Inc

WileyPLUS, *imprint of* John Wiley & Sons Inc

William Carey Library Publishers, *division of* Frontier Ventures

William, James & Co, *imprint of* Franklin, Beedle & Associates Inc

Williams & Co Publishers, *imprint of* Williams & Company Book Publishers

Williamson Books, *imprint of* WorthyKids/Ideals

Willis Music, *distributed by* Hal Leonard Corp

Willow Bend Books, *imprint of* Heritage Books Inc

Wilson Center Press, *imprint of* Woodrow Wilson Center Press

H W Wilson, *imprint of* Grey House Publishing Inc™

Neil Wilson Publishing (UK), *distributed by* Interlink Publishing Group Inc

Wimmer Cookbooks, *division of* Mercury Printing, an RR Donnelley Co

Winchester Press, *imprint of* New Win Publishing

Wind Records, *distributed by* YMAA Publication Center Inc

Windflower Press, *imprint of* Crumb Elbow Publishing

Windmall Books, *imprint of* The Rosen Publishing Group Inc

Windsor Books, *division of* Windsor Marketing Corp, Windsor Marketing Corp

Windward Publishing, *imprint of* Finney Company Inc

Kelley Wingate Publications, *imprint of* Carson-Dellosa Publishing LLC

Wings Books, *imprint of* Penguin Random House Inc

WingSpread Publishers, *imprint of* Moody Publishers

Winston-Derek, *distributor for* Thomas Nelson

Wintergreen/Orchard House Inc, *imprint of* Houghton Mifflin Harcourt Assessments

Winternights Publishing, *distributed by* Epicenter Press Inc

Winterthur Museum, *distributed by* Oak Knoll Press

Winterthur Museum, Garden & Library, *distributed by* Antique Collectors Club, Monacelli Press, W W Norton & Company Inc, University of Pennsylvania Press, University Press of New England

Wisconsin Academy of Sciences, Arts & Letters, *distributed by* University of Wisconsin Press

Wisconsin Veterans Museum, *distributed by* University of Wisconsin Press

Wisdom Foundation, *distributed by* Fons Vitae

Wisdom Publications, *distributed by* Simon & Schuster, Inc

Wisdom Publications Inc, *distributed by* Simon & Schuster

Paula Wiseman Books, *imprint of* Simon & Schuster Children's Publishing

Witherby Seamanship International Ltd, *distributed by* Marine Techniques Publishing

Witness Impulse, *imprint of* HarperCollins General Books Group

Wittenborn Art Books, *division of* Alan Wofsy Fine Arts, *distributor for* Cramer, Kornfeld, Menil Foundation (Houston, TX), *distributed by* Alan Wofsy Fine Arts

George Wittenborn, *imprint of* Wittenborn Art Books

Wizards of the Coast, *distributed by* Penguin Random House Inc

Wizards of the Coast LLC, *subsidiary of* Hasbro Inc, *distributed by* Penguin Random House

Alan Wofsy Fine Arts, *distributor for* Bora, Brusberg (Berlin), Cramer (Geneva), Huber, Ides et Calendes, Kornfeld & Co (Bern), Picasso Project, Welz, Wittenborn Art Books

Wolf Water Press, *distributed by* Sunbelt Publications Inc

Wolfe, *imprint of* Elsevier, Health Sciences Division

Wolfgang Publications, *distributed by* CarTech Inc

Wolters Kluwer US Corp, *subsidiary of* Wolters Kluwer NV (The Netherlands)

Women In Nontraditional Careers, *imprint of* Her Own Words LLC

Women's Publications, *imprint of* Consumer Press

Marian Wood Books, *imprint of* GP Putnam's Sons (Hardcover)

Woodbine House, *distributed by* Specialty Press Inc

S Woodhouse Books, *imprint of* Everything Goes Media LLC

Woodland Publishing Inc, *distributed by* Summit Beacon

The Woodrow Wilson Center Press, *distributed by* The Johns Hopkins University Press

Woodrow Wilson Center Press, *division of* The Woodrow Wilson International Center for Scholars, Woodrow Wilson International Center for Scholars, *distributed by* Columbia University Press, The Johns Hopkins University Press, Stanford University Press, University of California Press

Woodrow Wilson Center Press/Columbia University Press, *imprint of* Woodrow Wilson Center Press

Woodrow Wilson Center Press/Johns Hopkins University Press, *imprint of* Woodrow Wilson Center Press

Woodrow Wilson Center Press/Stanford University Press, *imprint of* Woodrow Wilson Center Press

Word Aflame Press, *imprint of* Pentecostal Publishing House

Word & Quill Press, *distributed by* Cross-Cultural Communications

WordSong, *imprint of* Boyds Mills Press

Wordstock, *distributed by* Franklin, Beedle & Associates Inc

Wordwell Books, *distributed by* Dufour Editions Inc

The Working Arts Library, *distributed by* Applause Theatre & Cinema Books

Workman Publishing, *distributor for* The Experiment

Workman Publishing Co Inc, *distributor for* Algonquin Books, Duo Press, The Experiment, Greenwich Workshop Press, Storey Publishing LLC

Workman Speakers Bureau, *division of* Workman Publishing Co Inc

Workout, *imprint of* Triumph Learning LLC

Workplace Learning Solutions, *imprint of* John Wiley & Sons Inc

World Almanac, *distributed by* Simon & Schuster, Inc, Simon & Schuster Sales Division

World Almanac®, *imprint of* Infobase Learning

World Bank, *imprint of* World Bank Publications

World Bank Publications, *member of* The World Bank Group

World Book Inc, *subsidiary of* The Scott Fetzer Co

World Catholic Press, *imprint of* Catholic Book Publishing Corp

World Citizens, *affiliate of* Cinema Investments Co Inc, *distributed by* Inland

World Dating Consultants™, *distributed by* Copywriter's Council of America™ (CCA)

World Health Organization (WHO), *distributed by* Stylus Publishing LLC

World Literature Ministries, *imprint of* Faith Alive Christian Resources

World Resources Institute, *distributed by* The Johns Hopkins University Press

World Trade Press, *distributed by* Reference Press

World Wisdom, *distributed by* Fons Vitae

World Wrestling Entertainment, *imprint of* Gallery Books

The World's Largest Publishing Co, *subsidiary of* Gallopade International Inc

WorldTariff, *division of* FedEx Corp

Worth Publishers, *imprint of* Macmillan Learning

WorthyKids/Ideals, *imprint of* Worthy Publishing Group

Wrightbooks, *imprint of* John Wiley & Sons Inc

Write Stuff®, *imprint of* Write Stuff Enterprises LLC

Writers & Artists on Photography Series, *imprint of* Aperture Books

Writer's Digest, *imprint of* F+W Media Inc

Writer's Digest Books, *imprint of* F+W Media Inc

Wrox™, *imprint of* John Wiley & Sons Inc

WRS Group, *distributor for* MAR*CO Products Inc

WSU Museum of Art, *distributed by* Washington State University Press

Wyrick & Co, *imprint of* Gibbs Smith Publisher

Xemplar, *imprint of* Crossquarter Publishing Group

Xeno Books, *imprint of* Red Hen Press

Xlibris Corp, *division of* Author Solutions LLC

XLN Audio, *distributed by* Hal Leonard Corp

XML Press, *subsidiary of* R L Hamilton & Associates LLC

Xoanon Publishing, *distributed by* Holmes Publishing Group LLC

Xpat Fiction, *imprint of* Franklin, Beedle & Associates Inc

YA Angst, *imprint of* Norilana Books

YA Books, *imprint of* Regal Crest Enterprises

YACK!, *imprint of* Eifrig Publishing LLC

Yale Center for British Art, *distributed by* Yale University Press

Yale University Art Gallery, *distributed by* Yale University Press

Yale University Press, *division of* Yale University, *distributor for* Addison Gallery of American Art, Phillips Academy, American Federation of Arts, The Art Institute of Chicago, The Bard Graduate Center, The Colonial Williamsburg Foundation, Dallas Museum of Art, Harvard Art Museums, Harvard University Art Museums, Japan Society, The Jewish Museum, Kimbell Art Museum, Paul Mellon Centre, The Menil Collection, The Metropolitan Museum of Art, National Gallery, London, National Gallery of Art, National Gallery of Art (Washington, DC), Philadelphia Museum of

Art, Princeton University Art Museum, Sterling & Francine Clark Art Institute, Whitney Museum of American Art, Yale Center for British Art, Yale University Art Gallery, *distributed by* Cheng & Tsui Co Inc

Yamaha, *distributed by* Hal Leonard Corp

Yamhill Press, *distributed by* Epicenter Press Inc

Yankee, *distributor for* Teton NewMedia Inc

Yankee Book Peddler, *distributor for* Primary Research Group Inc, Trans Tech Publications Inc

Year Book, *imprint of* Elsevier, Health Sciences Division

Yearling, *imprint of* Penguin Random House Inc

Yearling Books, *imprint of* Random House Children's Books

Yellow Books, *imprint of* Leadership Directories

Yellow 1, *imprint of* Wide World of Maps Inc

Yellow Rose Books, *imprint of* Regal Crest Enterprises

Yelsraek Publishing, *distributed by* Adventures Unlimited Press (AUP)

Yen Press, *distributed by* Hachette Book Group

Yes Books, *distributed by* Chelsea Green Publishing Co

Yeshiva University Museum Press, *distributed by* Gorgias Press LLC

Yeshiva University Press, *distributed by* KTAV Publishing House Inc

Yesterdays, *imprint of* Zumaya Publications LLC

Yilin Press, *distributed by* Simon & Schuster, Inc

YMAA Publication Center Inc, *distributor for* Wind Records (Chinese healing music)

York Medieval Press, *imprint of* Boydell & Brewer Inc

You Can Teach Yourself, *imprint of* Mel Bay Publications Inc

Glenn Young Books, *distributed by* Applause Theatre & Cinema Books

Young Patriots Series, *imprint of* Patria Press Inc

Your Coach in a Box, *imprint of* Recorded Books Inc, an RBmedia company

YourSpecs, *imprint of* SynergEbooks

YouthLight Inc, *distributor for* MAR*CO Products Inc

Yugen Press, *imprint of* In the Garden Publishing

Yushodo Press, *distributed by* Oak Knoll Press

YWAM Publishing, *division of* Youth With A Mission, *distributor for* Emerald Books

Zahava Publications, *imprint of* Judaica Press Inc

Zak Books, *imprint of* Black Rabbit Books

Zaner-Bloser Inc, *subsidiary of* Highlights for Children Inc

Zaytuna Institute Press, *distributed by* Fons Vitae

Zebra Books, *imprint of* Kensington Publishing Corp

Zebra Shout, *imprint of* Kensington Publishing Corp

Zed Books, *distributed by* Palgrave Macmillan

Zeitgeist Films, *distributed by* Cheng & Tsui Co Inc

Zeke Holdings Ltd, *distributed by* Welcome Enterprises Inc

Zenith Press, *imprint of* Quarto Publishing Group USA Inc

Zephyr Press, *imprint of* Chicago Review Press

Zero+ Publishing, *distributed by* Gingko Press Inc

Zest Books, *distributed by* Quarto (Ireland, North America & UK)

Zeta Books, *distributed by* Philosophy Documentation Center

ZHealth Books, *imprint of* New Win Publishing

H O Zimman Inc, *distributor for* United States Tennis Association

Zinc Ink, *imprint of* Random House Publishing Group

Zoland Books, *imprint of* Steerforth Press

Zonderkidz, *division of* Zondervan

Zondervan, *imprint of* HarperCollins Christian Publishing, *distributor for* Focus on the Family

Zone Books, *distributed by* The MIT Press

Zubaan Books, *distributed by* Diversion Books

Zumaya Publications LLC, *imprint of* eXtasy Books

Canadian Publishers

Listed in alphabetical order are those Canadian publishers that have reported to *LMP* that they produce an average of three or more books annually. Publishers that have appeared in a previous edition of *LMP*, but whose output currently does not meet our defined rate of activity, will be reinstated when their annual production reaches the required level. It should be noted that this rule of publishing activity does not apply to publishers of dictionaries, encyclopedias, atlases or Braille books or to university presses.

The definition of a book excludes charts, pamphlets, folding maps, sheet music and material with stapled bindings. Publishers that make their titles available only in electronic or audio format are included if they meet the stated criteria. In the case of packages, the book must be of equal or greater importance than the accompanying piece. With few exceptions, new publishers are not listed prior to having published at least three titles within a year.

§ before the company name indicates those publishers involved in electronic publishing.

ACTA Press
2451 Dieppe Ave SW, Bldg B1, Suite 230, Calgary, AB T3E 7K1
Tel: 403-288-1195 *Fax:* 403-247-6851
E-mail: journals@actapress.com; publish@actapress.com; sales@actapress.com
Web Site: www.actapress.com
Key Personnel
Owner & Mng Dir: Dr Mohamed H Hamza
Sr Publr & Graphic Designer: Debbie Quinton
Founded: 1972
Scientific & technical conference proceedings & journals; Computers, control & power systems, information technology, robotics, signal & image processing.
Publishes in English.
ISBN Prefix(es): 978-0-88986
Number of titles published annually: 50 Print; 50 CD-ROM
Total Titles: 900 Print; 50 CD-ROM
Branch Office(s)
1811 W Katella Ave, No 101, Anaheim, CA 92804, United States, US Rep: Sunny Yacenda *Tel:* 714-778-3230 *Fax:* 714-778-5463 *E-mail:* usa@iasted.org

Annick Press Ltd
15 Patricia Ave, Toronto, ON M2M 1H9
SAN: 115-0065
Tel: 416-221-4802 *Fax:* 416-221-8400
E-mail: annickpress@annickpress.com
Web Site: www.annickpress.com
Key Personnel
Dir: Rick Wilks
Mktg Mgr: Brigitte Waisberg *E-mail:* brigittew@annickpress.com
Sales & Rts Mgr: Gayna Theophilus *E-mail:* gaynat@annickpress.com
Founded: 1975
Fiction & nonfiction for children & young adults.
Publishes in English, French.
ISBN Prefix(es): 978-0-920236; 978-0-920303; 978-1-55037; 978-1-55451
Number of titles published annually: 24 Print
Total Titles: 425 Print
U.S. Rep(s): Ian Booth; Nicholas Booth; Bob Ditter; Rachel Ginsburg; Tom Hamburg; Larry Hollern; David Lewis; Ted Lucia; Thomas Martin; Thomas J McFadden Associates; McLemore/Hollern & Associates Inc; Parisa Michailidis (spec sales); Kevin T Monahan; Frank Porter; Ann Quinn; Sirak & Sirak; Jennifer Sorensen (spec sales); Michael R Watson; Karen Winters; Debra Woodward; Karen Woodward
Foreign Rep(s): CSH Educational Resources Pte Ltd (Singapore); Jay Books (New Zealand); Lexsys Ltd (Caribbean); John Reed Book Distribution (Australia); Ediciones Samara (Mexico)
Foreign Rights: Bardon-Chinese Media Agency (Jian-Mei Wang) (China); Bardon-Chinese Media Agency (Cynthia Chang) (Hong Kong, Taiwan); The Deborah Harris Agency (Efrat Lev) (Israel); International Editors' Co (Flavia Sala) (Brazil); International Editors' Co (Liliana Costa) (Latin America); International Editors' Co (Jennifer Hoge) (Portugal, Spain); Japan UNI Agency Inc (May Fujinaga) (Japan); Simona Kessler Agency (Romania); Agency Lapautre (Catherine Lapautre) (France); Literarische Agentur & Medienservice (Barbara Kuper) (Germany); Servizi Editoriali Guido Lagomarsino (Anna Spadolini) (Italy)
Distribution Center: University of Toronto Press, 5201 Dufferin St, Toronto, ON M3H 5T8 *Tel:* 416-667-7791 *Toll Free Tel:* 800-565-9523 *Fax:* 416-667-7832 *Toll Free Fax:* 800-221-9885 *E-mail:* utpbooks@utpress.utoronto.ca *Web Site:* www.utpress.utoronto.ca
Membership(s): Association of Canadian Publishers; Ontario Arts Council; Organization of Book Publishers of Ontario

Anvil Press Publishers
278 E First Ave, Vancouver, BC V5T 1A6
Mailing Address: PO Box 3008, MPO, Vancouver, BC V6B 3X5
Tel: 604-876-8710 *Fax:* 604-879-2667
E-mail: info@anvilpress.com
Web Site: www.anvilpress.com
Key Personnel
Publr: Brian Kaufman
Asst Publr & Mktg Coord: Karen Green
Publg Asst: Kara Lang
Founded: 1988
Literary, all genres; theatre & modern contemporary literature. Mostly Canadian authored titles only.
Publishes in English.
ISBN Prefix(es): 978-1-895636; 978-1-897535; 978-1-927380
Number of titles published annually: 12 Print
Total Titles: 90 Print
Distribution Center: Raincoast Books, 2440 Viking Way, Richmond, BC V6V 1N3 *Toll Free Tel:* 800-663-5714 *Fax:* 604-270-7161 *Toll Free Fax:* 800-565-3770 *E-mail:* orders@raincoast.com
Small Press Distribution, 1341 Seventh St, Berkeley, CA 94710-1409, United States *Tel:* 510-524-1668 *Toll Free Tel:* 800-869-7553 (US) *Fax:* 510-524-0852 *E-mail:* spd@spdbooks.org
Membership(s): Association of Book Publishers of British Columbia; Association of Canadian Publishers; Literary Press Group

§Aquila Communications Inc
281 rue Alice-Carriere St, Beaconsville, QC H9W 6E6
Toll Free Tel: 800-667-7071 *Fax:* 514-505-4579 *Toll Free Fax:* 866-338-1948
Web Site: www.aquilacommunications.com
Key Personnel
Founder & Pres: Sami Kelada
Contact: Mike Kelada *E-mail:* mike@aquilacommunications.com
Founded: 1970
High-interest/low-vocabulary readers for learners of French as a second language, grades 4 through college. Also, short humorous situational dialogues in comic book format for kids & teens. Funny episodes of daily life of North American kids & teens (home & school).
Publishes in French.
ISBN Prefix(es): 978-0-88510; 978-2-89054
Number of titles published annually: 15 Print
Total Titles: 500 Print; 100 Audio
Imprints: Scaramouche
Distributed by Aquila Communications Ltd

Arsenal Pulp Press
211 E Georgia St, No 202, Vancouver, BC V6A 1Z6
Tel: 604-687-4233 *Toll Free Tel:* 888-600-PULP (600-7857) *Fax:* 604-687-4283
E-mail: info@arsenalpulp.com
Web Site: www.arsenalpulp.com
Key Personnel
Publr: Brian Lam
Assoc Publr: Robert Ballantyne *E-mail:* robert@arsenalpulp.com
Mktg Mgr: Cynara Geissler
Prodn Mgr: Oliver McPartlin
Assoc Ed: Susan Safyan
Founded: 1982 (as Pulp Press Book Publishers)
Literary press.
Publishes in English.
ISBN Prefix(es): 978-0-88978; 978-1-55152
Number of titles published annually: 20 Print
Total Titles: 360 Print
Imprints: Advance Editions; Little Sister's Classics; Pulp Press; Robin's Egg Books; Tillacum Library
U.S. Rep(s): Consortium Book Sales & Distribution
Foreign Rep(s): NewSouth Books (Australia, New Zealand); Turnaround Publisher Services (Europe, UK)
Distribution Center: University of Toronto Press Distribution, 5201 Dufferin St, Toronto, ON M3H 5T8 *Toll Free Tel:* 800-565-9523 *Toll Free Fax:* 800-221-9985 *E-mail:* utpbooks@utpress.utoronto.ca *Web Site:* www.utpress.utoronto.ca
Consortium Book Sales & Distribution, c/o Perseus Distribution, 1094 Flex Dr, Jackson, TN 38301-5070, United States *Toll Free Tel:* 800-283-3572 *Toll Free Fax:* 800-351-5073 *E-mail:* orderentry@perseusbooks.com *Web Site:* www.cbsd.com

Editions ASTED
Subsidiary of Association pour l'Avancement des Sciences et des Techniques de la Documentation
2065 rue Parthenais, Bureau 387, Montreal, QC H2K 3T1
Tel: 514-281-5012 *Fax:* 514-281-8219
E-mail: editions@asted.org; info@asted.org

Web Site: www.asted.org
Key Personnel
Exec Dir: Lionel Villalonga *E-mail:* lvillalonga@asted.org
Founded: 1973
Publishes in French.
ISBN Prefix(es): 978-2-921548; 978-2-89055; 978-2-923563; 978-2-89123; 978-2-89224
Number of titles published annually: 3 Print

Athabasca University Press
Edmonton Learning Ctr, Peace Hills Trust Tower, 1200, 10011-109 St, Edmonton, AB T5J 3S8
Tel: 780-497-3412 *Fax:* 780-421-3298
E-mail: aupress@athabascau.ca
Web Site: www.aupress.ca
Key Personnel
Mktg & Prodn Coord & Acting Dir: Megan Hall *E-mail:* director.aupress@athabascau.ca
Sr Ed: Pamela Holway *E-mail:* editor.aupress@athabascau.ca
Founded: 2008
This publisher has indicated that 25% of their product line is author subsidized.
Publishes in English, French.
ISBN Prefix(es): 978-0-919737; 978-0-920982; 978-1-897425; 978-1-926836; 978-1-927356
Number of titles published annually: 20 Print
Distribution Center: UBC Press, c/o UTP Distribution, 5201 Dufferin St, Toronto, ON M3H 5T8 *Tel:* 416-667-7791 *Toll Free Tel:* 800-565-9523 *Fax:* 416-667-7832 *Toll Free Fax:* 800-221-9985 *E-mail:* utpbooks@utpress.utoronto.ca
University of Washington Press, c/o Hopkins Fulfillment Services, PO Box 50370, Baltimore, MD 21211-4370, United States *Tel:* 410-516-6956 *Toll Free Tel:* 800-537-5487 *E-mail:* hfscustserv@press.jhu.edu
Eurospan Group, c/o Turpin Distribution, Pegasus Dr, Stratton Business Park, Biggleswade, Beds SG18 8TQ, United Kingdom (Africa, Europe, Middle East, UK) *Tel:* (01767) 604972 *Fax:* (01767) 601640 *E-mail:* eurospan@turpin-distribution.com

B & B Publishing
4823 Sherbrooke St W, Off 275, Westmount, QC H3Z 1G7
Tel: 514-932-9466 *Fax:* 514-932-5929
E-mail: editions@ebbp.ca
Key Personnel
Publr: Paul Beullac
Founded: 1996
Publisher of educational materials; books & wall maps for schools across Canada.
Publishes in English, French.
ISBN Prefix(es): 978-0-88537; 978-2-7615
Number of titles published annually: 10 Print
Total Titles: 400 Print
Distributed by Brault & Bouthillier Ltee; Brault & Bouthillier School Supplies
Foreign Rep(s): Bricolux (Belgium); Canada Ortho (France); Intelligence Insight LLP (Singapore); Wesco (France)
Distribution Center: 700, ave Beaumont, Montreal, QC H3N 1V5 *Tel:* 514-273-9186 *Fax:* 514-273-8627

Banff Centre Press
107 Tunnel Mountain Dr, Banff, AB T1L 1H5
Mailing Address: Box 1020, Banff, AB T1L 1H5
Tel: 403-762-6408
E-mail: press@banffcentre.ca
Web Site: www.banffcentre.ca/press
Founded: 1995
Publisher of books on contemporary art & culture.
Publishes in English, French.
ISBN Prefix(es): 978-0-920159; 978-1-894773
Number of titles published annually: 4 Print
Total Titles: 41 Print; 2 CD-ROM; 4 E-Book
Orders to: LitDistCo, 8300 Lawson Rd, Milton, ON L9T 0A4 *Toll Free Tel:* 800-591-6250 *Toll Free Fax:* 800-591-6251 *E-mail:* ordering@litdistco.ca *Web Site:* www.litdistco.ca
Returns: LitDistCo, 8300 Lawson Rd, Milton, ON L9T 0A4 *Toll Free Tel:* 800-591-6250 *Toll Free Fax:* 800-591-6251 *Web Site:* www.litdistco.ca
Warehouse: LitDistCo, 8300 Lawson Rd, Milton, ON L9T 0A4 *Toll Free Tel:* 800-591-6250 *Toll Free Fax:* 800-591-6251 *Web Site:* www.litdistco.ca
Distribution Center: LitDistCo, 8300 Lawson Rd, Milton, ON L9T 0A4 *Toll Free Tel:* 800-591-6250 *Toll Free Fax:* 800-591-6251 *E-mail:* ordering@litdistco.ca *Web Site:* www.litdistco.ca
Membership(s): Book Publishers Association of Alberta; Literary Press Group of Canada

§Bayeux Arts Inc
119 Stratton Crescent SW, Calgary, AB T3H 1T7
E-mail: mail@bayeux.com
Web Site: bayeux.com
Key Personnel
Co-Publr & Dir: Swapna Gupta
Co-Publr: Ashis Gupta *E-mail:* agupta@bayeux.com
Ed, Children's Lit: Judd Palmer *E-mail:* jpalmer@bayeux.com
Ed, Fiction/Nonfiction/Poetry: Mercedes Batiz-Benet *E-mail:* mercedes@bayeux.com
Founded: 1994
Committed to producing books of beauty that build bridges across cultures.
Publishes in English.
ISBN Prefix(es): 978-1-896209; 978-1-897411
Number of titles published annually: 10 Print
Imprints: Alebrije; Gondolier; Odd Little Books; Rosencrantz Comics
Distribution Center: LitDistCo, 8300 Lawson Rd, Milton, ON L9T 0A4 *Toll Free Tel:* 800-591-6250 *Toll Free Fax:* 800-591-6251 *E-mail:* ordering@litdistco.ca *Web Site:* www.litdistco.ca
Chicago Distribution Center, 11030 S Langley Ave, Chicago, IL 60628, United States *Tel:* 773-702-7010 *Toll Free Fax:* 800-621-8476
Membership(s): Literary Press Group of Canada

Beliveau Editeur
567 rue Bienville, Boucherville, QC J4B 2Z5
Tel: 450-679-1933
Web Site: www.beliveauediteur.com
Key Personnel
Pres & CEO: Mathieu Beliveau *E-mail:* mbeliveau@beliveauediteur.com
Asst Ed: Diane Perreault *E-mail:* dperreault@beliveauediteur.com
Founded: 1975
Specialize in recovery, geopolitics & self-help, medicine, taxation & motivation.
Publishes in French.
ISBN Prefix(es): 978-2-89092
Number of titles published annually: 30 Print
Total Titles: 250 Print
Foreign Rep(s): DG Diffusion (France); Servidis (Switzerland)
Distribution Center: Prologue Inc, 1650, Lionel-Bertrand, Boisbriand, QC J7H 1N7 *Toll Free Tel:* 800-363-2864

Between the Lines
401 Richmond St W, No 277, Toronto, ON M5V 3A8
SAN: 115-0189
Tel: 416-535-9914 *Toll Free Tel:* 800-718-7201 *Fax:* 416-535-1484
E-mail: info@btlbooks.com
Web Site: btlbooks.com
Key Personnel
Art Dir & Prodn Mgr: Jennifer Tiberio
Accts Mgr: Paula Brill
Mktg & Sales Mgr: Renee Knapp
Mng Ed: Amanda Crocker
Publicist: Matthew Adams *E-mail:* publicity@btlbooks.com
Founded: 1977
Nonfiction, social, economic & political works dealing with international development issues & Canadian social issues.
Publishes in English.
ISBN Prefix(es): 978-0-919946; 978-0-921284; 978-1-896357; 978-1-897071; 978-1-926662; 978-1-77113
Number of titles published annually: 16 Print
Total Titles: 263 Print
U.S. Rep(s): Brunswick Books
Foreign Rep(s): Brunswick Books (Canada)
Orders to: Brunswick Books, 20 Maud St, Suite 303, Toronto, ON M5V 2M5 *Tel:* 416-703-3598; Central Books Ltd, One Heath Park Industrial Estate, Freshwater Rd, Dagenham RM8 1RX, United Kingdom *Tel:* (020) 8525 8800 *Fax:* (020) 8599 2694 *E-mail:* contactus@centralbooks.com *Web Site:* www.centralbooks.com
Membership(s): Canada Council for the Arts; Ontario Arts Council

Black Rose Books Ltd
CP 35788 Succ Leo Pariseau, Montreal, QC H2X 0A4
SAN: 115-2653
Tel: 514-844-4076 *Toll Free Tel:* 800-565-9523 (orders) *Toll Free Fax:* 800-221-9985 (orders)
E-mail: info@blackrosebooks.net
Web Site: blackrosebooks.net
Key Personnel
Mktg Promo: Lucia Kowaluk
Edit Admin: Robert Dollins
Founded: 1970
Politics, book & journal publishing in the social sciences & humanities.
Publishes in English.
ISBN Prefix(es): 978-0-919618; 978-0-919619; 978-0-920057; 978-0-921689; 978-1-55164; 978-1-895431
Number of titles published annually: 15 Print; 20 Online; 30 E-Book
Total Titles: 585 Print; 300 E-Book
Distributed by University of Toronto Press

Blue Bike Books
58 Lodgepole Crescent, St Albert, AB T8N 2R7
Tel: 780-435-2376
E-mail: info@bluebikebooks.com
Web Site: www.bluebikebooks.com
Key Personnel
Publr: Peter J Boer *E-mail:* peterb@bluebikebooks.com
Founded: 2005
Publish humor & trivia books. Large number of regional trivia titles as well as national ones.
Publishes in English.
ISBN Prefix(es): 978-1-897278; 978-0-9739116
Number of titles published annually: 5 Print; 5 E-Book
Total Titles: 85 Print; 15 E-Book
Distributed by Lone Pine Publishing
Orders to: Lone Pine Publishing, 11414 119 St, Edmonton, AB T5G 2X6 *Tel:* 780-433-9333 *Toll Free Tel:* 800-661-9017 *Fax:* 780-433-9646 *Toll Free Fax:* 800-424-7173 *E-mail:* accounts@lonepinepublishing.com *Web Site:* www.lonepinepublishing.com
Shipping Address: Lone Pine Publishing, 11414 119 St, Edmonton, AB T5G 2X6 *Tel:* 780-433-9333 *Toll Free Tel:* 800-661-9017 *Fax:* 780-433-9646 *Toll Free Fax:* 800-424-7173 *E-mail:* accounts@lonepinepublishing.com *Web Site:* www.lonepinepublishing.com
Distribution Center: Lone Pine Publishing, 11414 119 St, Edmonton, AB T5G 2X6 *Tel:* 780-433-9333 *Toll Free Tel:* 800-661-9017

Fax: 780-433-9646 *Toll Free Fax:* 800-424-7173 *E-mail:* accounts@lonepinepubishing.com *Web Site:* www.lonepinepublishing.com
Membership(s): Book Publishers Association of Alberta

Editions du Bois-de-Coulonge
1140 Ave de Montigny, Sillery, QC G1S 3T7
Tel: 418-683-6332
Web Site: www.ebc.qc.ca
Key Personnel
Owner & Pres: Dr Richard Leclerc, PhD
Founded: 1995
Publish & distribute books about music, multimedia, television & movies.
Publishes in French.
ISBN Prefix(es): 978-2-9801397
Number of titles published annually: 1 Print
Total Titles: 7 Print
Membership(s): Association for the Export of Canadian Books

§Books We Love Ltd
100 Chinook Winds Place SW, Unit 4407, Airdrie, AB T4B 4B4
Tel: 403-710-4869
E-mail: bookswelove@telus.net
Web Site: bookswelove.net; www.facebook.com/Books.We.Love.Ltd
Key Personnel
Pres: Brian Roberts
Publr: Judith Pittman *E-mail:* judepittman@telus.net
Sr Ed: Jess Poettcker
Founded: 2010
Publisher of genre fiction written by Canadian, American & international authors, including historical fiction, romance (in all forms), mystery, suspense, thrillers, fantasy, paranormal, young adult, science fiction, western & more.
Publishes in English.
ISBN Prefix(es): 978-1-927476
Number of titles published annually: 300 Print; 600 E-Book
Total Titles: 300 Print; 500 E-Book
Membership(s): Romance Writers of America

§Borealis Press Ltd
8 Mohawk Crescent, Nepean, ON K2H 7G6
Tel: 613-829-0150 *Toll Free Tel:* 877-696-2585 *Fax:* 613-829-7783
E-mail: drt@borealispress.com
Web Site: www.borealispress.com
Founded: 1972
Canadian-oriented general titles of most types. No unsol mss, query first. Include synopsis +/or outline & sample chapter with SASE.
Publishes in English, French.
ISBN Prefix(es): 978-0-88887; 978-1-896133; 978-0-919594; 978-0-919662
Number of titles published annually: 24 Print
Subsidiaries: Tecumseh Press
Distributed by Blackwell; Dawson; EBSCO; Ex Libris; Hein

The Boston Mills Press
Division of Firefly Books Ltd
50 Staples Ave, Unit 1, Richmond Hill, ON L4B 0A7
Tel: 416-499-8412 *Toll Free Tel:* 800-387-6192 *Fax:* 416-499-8313 *Toll Free Fax:* 800-450-0391
E-mail: service@fireflybooks.com
Web Site: www.fireflybooks.com
Key Personnel
Dir, Prodn & Co-Editions: Jacqueline Hope Raynor
Founded: 1974
Canadian & American history, guide books, large format colour photograph books.
Publishes in English.
ISBN Prefix(es): 978-0-919822; 978-0-919783; 978-1-55046
Number of titles published annually: 20 Print
Total Titles: 200 Print
Distributed by Firefly Books Ltd

BPS Books
Division of Bastian Publishing Services Ltd
47 Anderson Ave, Toronto, ON M5P 1H6
Tel: 416-609-2004
Web Site: www.bpsbooks.com
Key Personnel
Publr & Ed-in-Chief: Donald G Bastian
Founded: 2007
Print-on-demand publisher of original & reprint trade paperbacks for the US, Canadian & UK markets via bookstore web sites such as the Amazon sites in all three countries. No unsol mss, query first using online form.
This publisher has indicated that 90% of their product is author subsidized.
Publishes in English, French.
ISBN Prefix(es): 978-1-926645; 978-0-9784402; 978-0-9809231; 978-1-927483; 978-0-9783286
Number of titles published annually: 15 Print; 10 E-Book
Total Titles: 75 Print; 26 E-Book
Membership(s): Word Guild

Brault & Bouthillier
Division of B & B School Supplies
700 ave Beaumont, Montreal, QC H3N 1V5
Tel: 514-273-9186 *Toll Free Tel:* 800-361-0378 *Fax:* 514-273-8627 *Toll Free Fax:* 800-361-0378
E-mail: ventes@bb.ca
Web Site: bb.ca
Key Personnel
Pres: Paul LeBrun *E-mail:* paullebrun@bb.ca
VP, Busn Devt: Yves Brault *Tel:* 514-273-9186 ext 219 *E-mail:* yvesbrault@bb.ca
VP, Mktg: Ms Josee Legault *E-mail:* jlegault@bb.ca
Sales Dir: Claude Vaillancourt *Tel:* 514-273-9186 ext 227 *E-mail:* cvaillancourt@bb.ca
Founded: 1944
Pedagogical & scientific.
Publishes in English, French.
ISBN Prefix(es): 978-0-88537; 978-2-7615
Number of titles published annually: 100 Print
Branch Office(s)
150 Brittania Rd E, Unit 7, Mississauga, ON L4Z 2A4 *Tel:* 905-890-0404 *Toll Free Tel:* 800-668-1108 *Fax:* 905-890-7999 *Toll Free Fax:* 800-839-7718
Distributed by DPLU Inc (Montreal); B B Jocus (Toronto)

Breakwater Books Ltd
One Stamp's Lane, St John's, NL A1C 6E6
Mailing Address: PO Box 2188, St John's, NL A1C 6E6
Tel: 709-722-6680 *Toll Free Tel:* 800-563-3333 (orders) *Fax:* 709-753-0708
E-mail: info@breakwaterbooks.com; orders@breakwaterbooks.com
Web Site: www.breakwaterbooks.com
Key Personnel
Owner & Pres: Rebecca Rose
Founded: 1973
Books primarily about education & trade books.
Publishes in English, French.
ISBN Prefix(es): 978-0-919519; 978-0-919948; 978-0-920911; 978-1-55081
Number of titles published annually: 16 Print
Total Titles: 600 Print

Brick Books
Box 20081, 431 Boler Rd, London, ON N6K 4G6
Tel: 519-657-8579
E-mail: brick.books@sympatico.ca
Web Site: www.brickbooks.ca
Key Personnel
Gen Mgr: Kitty Lewis
Prodn Mgr: Alayna Munce
Founded: 1975
Publish poetry collections by Canadian authors.
Publishes in English.
ISBN Prefix(es): 978-0-919626; 978-1-894078; 978-1-77131
Number of titles published annually: 7 Print
Total Titles: 210 Print; 186 E-Book
Distribution Center: LitDistCo, 8300 Lawson Rd, Milton, ON L9T 0A4 *Toll Free Tel:* 800-591-6250 *Toll Free Fax:* 800-591-6251 *E-mail:* ordering@litdistco.ca *Web Site:* www.litdistco.ca
Membership(s): Association of Canadian Publishers; Literary Press Group of Canada

Brindle & Glass Publishing Ltd
Imprint of TouchWood Editions
1075 Pendergast St, Suite 103, Victoria, BC V8V 0A1
Tel: 250-360-0829 *Fax:* 250-386-0829
E-mail: info@brindleandglass.com
Web Site: www.brindleandglass.com
Key Personnel
Publr: Taryn Boyd
Founded: 2001
Literary press.
Publishes in English.
ISBN Prefix(es): 978-1-897142; 978-0-9732481; 978-1-926972; 978-1-927366
Number of titles published annually: 4 Print
Total Titles: 110 Print
Foreign Rep(s): Heritage Group (Canada); Publishers Group West (PGW) (USA)
Distribution Center: Heritage Group Distribution, 19272 96 Ave, Suite 8, Surrey, BC V4N 4C1 *Tel:* 604-881-7067 *Toll Free Tel:* 800-665-3302 *Fax:* 604-881-7068 *Toll Free Fax:* 800-566-3336 *E-mail:* orders@hgdistribution.com *Web Site:* www.hgdistribution.com
Membership(s): Canada Council for the Arts

§Broadview Press
280 Perry St, Unit 5, Peterborough, ON K9J 2J4
SAN: 115-6772
Mailing Address: PO Box 1243, Peterborough, ON K9J 7H5
Tel: 705-743-8990 *Fax:* 705-743-8353
E-mail: customerservice@broadviewpress.com
Web Site: www.broadviewpress.com
Key Personnel
Founder & CEO: Don Le Pan *Tel:* 250-824-5015 *Fax:* 250-824-5001 *E-mail:* don.lepan@broadviewpress.com
Pres: Leslie Dema *Tel:* 519-821-0706 *Fax:* 519-265-6544 *E-mail:* dema@broadviewpress.com
Mng Ed: Tara Lowes *E-mail:* taralowes@broadviewpress.com
Accts Mgr: LeeAnna Dykstra *E-mail:* ldykstra@broadviewpress.com
Exam Copies Coord: Lisa Reid *E-mail:* examcopies@broadviewpress.com
Founded: 1985
The word "broadview" expresses a great deal about the approach that guides our publishing program. Our focus is very much on English studies & philosophy, but within those two core subject areas we are open to a broad range of academic approaches & political viewpoints. We are proud to publish pedagogically valuable books that make a real contribution to scholarship. We welcome feminist perspectives & we have a strong commitment to the environment. Our publishing program is internationally oriented & our individual titles often appeal to a broad readership; we publish many titles that are of as much interest to the general reader as they are to academics & students.
Publishes in English.

ISBN Prefix(es): 978-0-921149; 978-1-55111; 978-1-55481
Number of titles published annually: 45 Print; 40 E-Book
Total Titles: 600 Print; 425 E-Book
Branch Office(s)
10 Douglas St, Suite B, Guelph, ON N1H 2S9 *Tel:* 519-821-2171 *Fax:* 519-265-6544
515-815 First St SW, Calgary, AB T2P 1N3 *Tel:* 403-232-1443 *Fax:* 403-233-0001 *E-mail:* broadview@broadviewpress.com
555 Riverwalk Pkwy, Tonawanda, NY 14150, United States
U.S. Rep(s): Brad DeVetten
Returns: 555 Riverwalk Pkwy, Tonawanda, NY 14150, United States

Broquet Inc
97-B, Montee des Bouleaux, St-Constant, QC J5A 1A9
Tel: 450-638-3338 *Fax:* 450-638-4338
E-mail: info@broquet.qc.ca
Web Site: www.broquet.qc.ca
Key Personnel
Pres & Ed: Antoine Broquet
Artistic Dir: Brigit Levesque
Prodn Dir: Ms Josee Fortin
Founded: 1979
Nature books & astronomy.
Publishes in French.
ISBN Prefix(es): 978-2-89000; 978-2-89654
Number of titles published annually: 100 Print; 12 E-Book
Total Titles: 800 Print; 40 E-Book
Foreign Rep(s): Dilisco (Benelux, France); Servidis (Switzerland)
Distribution Center: Prologue Inc, 1650, blvd Lionel-Bertrand, Boisbriand, QC J7H 1N7 *Tel:* 450-434-0306 *Toll Free Tel:* 800-363-2864 *Fax:* 450-434-2627 *Toll Free Fax:* 800-361-8088

Brush Education Inc
6531-111 St, Edmonton, AB T6H 4R5
SAN: 115-0324
Tel: 780-989-0910 *Toll Free Tel:* 855-283-0900 *Fax:* 780-989-0930 *Toll Free Fax:* 855-283-6947
E-mail: contact@brusheducation.ca
Web Site: www.brusheducation.ca
Key Personnel
Partner: Glenn Rollans *E-mail:* glenn.rollans@brusheducation.ca
Mng Ed: Lauri Seidlitz *E-mail:* lauri.seidlitz@brusheducation.ca
Founded: 1975
Independent publisher of books for college, university & professional audiences. Our publishing program includes medial & health sciences, education & K9 training.
Publishes in English.
ISBN Prefix(es): 978-0-920490; 978-1-55059
Number of titles published annually: 17 Print; 15 E-Book
Total Titles: 120 Print; 50 E-Book
Distributed by University of Toronto Press
Orders to: University of Toronto Press, 5201 Dufferin St, Toronto, ON M3H 5T8 (CN & US) *Tel:* 416-667-7791 *Toll Free Tel:* 800-565-9523 *Fax:* 416-667-7832 *Toll Free Fax:* 800-221-9985 *E-mail:* utpbooks@utpress.utoronto.ca
Membership(s): Association of Canadian Publishers; Book Publishers Association of Alberta

Callawind Publications Inc
3551 St Charles Blvd, Suite 179, Kirkland, QC H9H 3C4
Tel: 514-685-9109
E-mail: info@callawind.com
Web Site: www.callawind.com
Key Personnel
Mktg: Pamela Carmen *E-mail:* pamela@callawind.com
Founded: 1995
Custom book publisher. Specialize in cookbooks, children's books & book fundraising projects.
This publisher has indicated that 100% of their product line is author subsidized.
Publishes in English.
ISBN Prefix(es): 978-1-896511
Number of titles published annually: 15 Print
Total Titles: 85 Print
Membership(s): The Association of Publishers for Special Sales; Independent Book Publishers Association

§Canada Law Book®
Division of Thomson Reuters Canada Ltd
One Corporate Plaza, 2075 Kennedy Rd, Toronto, ON M1T 3V4
Tel: 416-609-3800 (cust rel & orders) *Toll Free Tel:* 800-387-5351 (cust rel, CN & US only); 800-347-5164 (cust rel & orders, CN & US) *Fax:* 416-298-5082 (cust rel & orders, Toronto) *Toll Free Fax:* 877-750-9041 (cust rel & orders, CN only)
E-mail: customersupport.legaltaxcanada@thomsonreuters.com; printorders.legaltaxcanada@thomsonreuters.com
Web Site: www.carswell.com
Founded: 1855 (as Upper Canada Law Journal)
Law books.
Publishes in English.
ISBN Prefix(es): 978-0-88804
Number of titles published annually: 50 Print; 3 CD-ROM; 3 E-Book
Total Titles: 480 Print; 25 CD-ROM; 40 Online; 9 E-Book
Subsidiaries: Canadian Lawyer/Law Times Media, a Thomson Reuters business
Returns: 245 Bartley Dr, Toronto, ON M4A 2V8
Distribution Center: 245 Bartley Dr, Toronto, ON M4A 2V8

Canadian Bible Society
10 Carnforth Rd, Toronto, ON M4A 2S4
SAN: 112-5559
Tel: 416-757-4171 *Toll Free Tel:* 800-465-2425 *Fax:* 416-757-3376
E-mail: custserv@biblesociety.ca
Web Site: www.biblescanada.com; www.biblesociety.ca
Founded: 1904
Bibles, new testaments, scripture portions, selections; scriptures in foreign languages.
Publishes in English, French.
ISBN Prefix(es): 978-0-88834
Number of titles published annually: 20 Print; 5 Audio
Total Titles: 2,500 Print; 50 Audio
U.S. Publishers Represented: American Bible Society
Foreign Rep(s): United Bible Societies (worldwide)
Membership(s): United Bible Societies

Canadian Circumpolar Institute (CCI) Press
Imprint of University of Alberta Press
University of Alberta, Ring House 2, Edmonton, AB T6G 2E1
Tel: 780-492-3662 *Fax:* 780-492-0719
Web Site: www.uap.ualberta.ca
Founded: 1960 (as Boreal Institute for Northern Studies; reconfigured & renamed 1990 as CCI; acquired 2013 by University of Alberta Press)
Publishes in English.
ISBN Prefix(es): 978-1-896445; 978-0-919058
Number of titles published annually: 2 Print; 2 E-Book
Total Titles: 140 Print
Sales Office(s): Ampersand Canada's Book & Gift Agency Inc, 321 Carlaw Ave, Suite 213, Toronto, ON M4M 2S1, Contact: Saffron Beckwith *Tel:* 416-703-0666 ext 124 *Fax:* 416-703-4745 *E-mail:* saffronb@ampersandinc.ca *Web Site:* www.ampersandinc.ca
U.S. Rep(s): Wayne State University Press
Billing Address: University of Toronto Press, 5201 Dufferin St, Toronto, ON M3H 5T8 *Tel:* 416-667-7841 *Toll Free Tel:* 800-565-9523 *Fax:* 416-667-7832 *Toll Free Fax:* 800-221-9985 *E-mail:* utpbooks@utpress.utoronto.ca *Web Site:* www.utpress.utoronto.ca
Orders to: University of Toronto Press, 5201 Dufferin St, Toronto, ON M3H 5T8 *Tel:* 416-667-7841 *Toll Free Tel:* 800-565-9523 *Fax:* 416-667-7832 *Toll Free Fax:* 800-221-9985 *E-mail:* utpbooks@utpress.utoronto.ca *Web Site:* www.utpress.utoronto.ca
Returns: University of Toronto Press, 5201 Dufferin St, Toronto, ON M3H 5T8 *Tel:* 416-667-7841 *Toll Free Tel:* 800-565-9523 *Fax:* 416-667-7832 *Toll Free Fax:* 800-221-9985 *E-mail:* utpbooks@utpress.utoronto.ca *Web Site:* www.utpress.utoronto.ca
Shipping Address: University of Toronto Press, 5201 Dufferin St, Toronto, ON M3H 5T8 *Tel:* 416-667-7841 *Toll Free Tel:* 800-565-9523 *Fax:* 416-667-7832 *Toll Free Fax:* 800-221-9985 *E-mail:* utpbooks@utpress.utoronto.ca *Web Site:* www.utpress.utoronto.ca
Distribution Center: University of Toronto Press, 5201 Dufferin St, Toronto, ON M3H 5T8, Client Service Rep: Jackie Courtney *Tel:* 416-667-7841 *Toll Free Tel:* 800-565-9523 *Fax:* 416-667-7832 *Toll Free Fax:* 800-221-9985 *E-mail:* utpbooks@utpress.utoronto.ca *Web Site:* www.utpress.utoronto.ca
Wayne State University Press (WSUP), Shipping& Receiving, 40 W Hancock, Detroit, MI 48201-1309, United States (does not carry all CCI Press titles) *Tel:* 313-577-6120 *Fax:* 313-577-6131 *E-mail:* bookorders@wayne.edu *Web Site:* wsupress.wayne.edu
Gazelle Book Services Ltd, White Cross Mills, Hightown, Lancaster, Lancs LA1 4XS, United Kingdom *Tel:* (01524) 528500 *Fax:* (01524) 528510 *E-mail:* sales@gazellebookservices.co.uk *Web Site:* www.gazellebookservices.co.uk

Canadian Council on Social Development (Conseil canadien de developpement social)
190 O'Connor St, Suite 100, Ottawa, ON K2P 2R3
Mailing Address: PO Box 13713, Kanata, ON K2K 1X6
Tel: 613-236-8977 *Fax:* 613-236-2750
E-mail: info@ccsd.ca
Web Site: www.ccsd.ca
Key Personnel
Pres & CEO: Peggy Taillon *Tel:* 613-236-8977 ext 22 *E-mail:* taillon@ccsd.ca
VP, Res & Policy: Katherine Scott *Tel:* 613-236-8977 ext 21 *E-mail:* scott@ccsd.ca
Founded: 1920
Social policy, poverty, retirement, income security, economics, sustainable development self-help & aboriginal peoples,
Publishes in English, French.
ISBN Prefix(es): 978-0-88810
Number of titles published annually: 12 Print
Total Titles: 100 Print
Distributed by Renouf Publishing Ltd

Canadian Energy Research Institute
3512 33 St NW, Suite 150, Calgary, AB T2L 2A6
Tel: 403-282-1231 *Fax:* 403-284-4181
E-mail: info@ceri.ca
Web Site: www.ceri.ca
Key Personnel
CEO & Pres: Allan Fogwill
Exec Asst: Megan Murphy *Tel:* 403-220-2370 *Fax:* 403-220-9579 *E-mail:* mmurphy@ceri.ca
Founded: 1975
Energy research, conferences.

Publishes in English.
ISBN Prefix(es): 978-0-920522; 978-1-896091
Number of titles published annually: 5 Print
Total Titles: 156 Print

Canadian Institute of Chartered Accountants (CICA) (L'Institut Canadien des Comptables Agrees), see Chartered Professional Accountants of Canada (CPA Canada)

Canadian Institute of Resources Law (L'Institut canadien du droit des ressources)
Faculty of Law, University of Calgary, 2500 University Dr NW, MFH 3353, Calgary, AB T2N 1N4
Tel: 403-220-3200 *Fax:* 403-282-6182
E-mail: cirl@ucalgary.ca
Web Site: www.cirl.ca
Key Personnel
Admin Coord: Jane Rowe *E-mail:* jrowe@ucalgary.ca
Founded: 1979
Leading national centre of expertise on legal & policy issues relating to Canada's natural resources.
Publishes in English.
ISBN Prefix(es): 978-0-919269
Number of titles published annually: 4 Print; 3 Online
Total Titles: 96 Print; 64 Online

Canadian Institute of Ukrainian Studies Press
Division of Canadian Institute of Ukrainian Studies
University of Toronto, 256 McCaul St, Rm 308, Toronto, ON M5T 1W5
Tel: 416-946-7326 *Fax:* 416-978-2672
E-mail: cius@ualberta.ca
Web Site: www.ciuspress.com
Key Personnel
Exec Dir: Marko R Stech *E-mail:* m.stech@utoronto.ca
Founded: 1976
Publisher of scholarly works in Ukranian studies & Ukranian Canadian studies.
Publishes in English, French.
ISBN Prefix(es): 978-0-920862; 978-1-895571; 978-1-894865; 978-1-894301
Number of titles published annually: 5 Print
Total Titles: 180 Print
U.S. Rep(s): Baker & Taylor Books
Orders to: University of Alberta, 4-30 Pembina Hall, Edmonton, AB T6G 2H8 *Tel:* 780-492-2973 *Fax:* 780-492-4967 *E-mail:* cius@ualberta.ca
Returns: University of Alberta, 4-30 Pembina Hall, Edmonton, AB T6G 2H8 *Tel:* 780-492-2973 *Fax:* 780-492-4967 *E-mail:* cius@ualberta.ca

Canadian Museum of History (Musee canadien de l'histoire)
100 Laurier St, Gatineau, QC K1A 0M8
Tel: 819-776-7000 *Toll Free Tel:* 800-555-5621 (North American orders only) *Fax:* 819-776-7187
Web Site: www.historymuseum.ca
Key Personnel
VP, Corp Aff & Devt: Claudette Levesque *Tel:* 819-776-7162 *E-mail:* claudette.levesque@historymuseum.ca
Acting Mgr, Publg & Corp Prods: Lee Wyndham *Tel:* 819-776-8385 *E-mail:* lee.wyndham@historymuseum.ca
Founded: 1968 (as the National Museum of Man)
Publications in the subject areas of museology, anthropology, archaeology, ethnology, folk culture, history, contemporary Native & Inuit art, native studies.
Publishes in English, French.
Number of titles published annually: 15 Print
Total Titles: 400 Print; 8 CD-ROM
Distribution Center: University of Toronto Press, 5201 Dufferin St, Toronto, ON M3H 5T8 *Toll Free Tel:* 800-565-9523 *E-mail:* utpbooks@utpress.utoronto.ca SAN: 115-1134
Membership(s): Association for the Export of Canadian Books; Association of Canadian Publishers; Canadian Booksellers Association

Canadian Poetry Press
Dept of English, University of Western Ontario, London, ON N6A 3K7
Tel: 519-661-2111 (ext 85813); 519-661-2111 (ext 85834) *Fax:* 519-661-3776
E-mail: canadianpoetry@uwo.ca
Web Site: canadianpoetry.org
Key Personnel
Gen Ed: D M R Bentley *E-mail:* dbentley@uwo.ca
Gen Mgr: Susan Bentley
Founded: 1986
Publish scholarly editions of early Canadian long poems, editions of the work of the Confederation poets & critical studies of Canadian poetry.
Publishes in English.
ISBN Prefix(es): 978-0-921243
Number of titles published annually: 3 Print; 4 Online
Total Titles: 30 Print; 40 Online

§Canadian Scholars' Press Inc
425 Adelaide St W, Suite 200, Toronto, ON M5V 3C1
SAN: 118-9484
Tel: 416-929-2774 *Toll Free Tel:* 800-463-1998 *Fax:* 416-929-1926
E-mail: info@cspi.org; info@canadianscholars.ca; editorial@canadianscholars.ca; orders@canadianscholars.ca
Web Site: www.canadianscholars.ca; www.womenspress.ca
Key Personnel
Pres: Andrew Wayne *Tel:* 416-929-2774 ext 220 *E-mail:* awayne@canadianscholars.ca
VP: Drew Hawkins *Tel:* 416-929-2774 ext 225 *E-mail:* dhawkins@canadianscholars.ca
Dir, Publg: Lily Bergh *Tel:* 416-929-2774 ext 218 *E-mail:* lily.bergh@canadianscholars.ca
Mktg Mgr: Emma Melnyk *Tel:* 416-929-2774 ext 232 *E-mail:* emma.melnyk@canadianscholars.ca
Prodn Mgr: Caley Clements *Tel:* 416-929-2774 ext 222 *E-mail:* caley.clements@canadianscholars.ca
Founded: 1986
Scholarly books & texts for post-secondary education. Trade books-feminist orientation.
Publishes in English, French.
ISBN Prefix(es): 978-0-921627; 978-1-55130; 978-0-921881; 978-0-88961 (Women's Press); 978-1-89418
Number of titles published annually: 24 Print; 10 E-Book
Total Titles: 400 Print; 6 CD-ROM; 80 E-Book
Divisions: Women's Press
Distribution Center: Eurospan Group, 3 Henrietta St, London WC2E 8LU, United Kingdom (Africa, Asia Pacific, Caribbean, Europe, Latin America, Middle East & UK) *Tel:* (01767) 604972 *Fax:* (01767) 601640 *E-mail:* eurospan@turpin-distribution.com
Membership(s): Association of Canadian Publishers; Canada Council for the Arts; Ontario Arts Council; Organization of Book Publishers of Ontario

Captus Press Inc
1600 Steeles Ave W, Units 14 & 15, Concord, ON L4K 4M2
Tel: 416-736-5537 *Fax:* 416-736-5793
E-mail: info@captus.com
Web Site: www.captus.com
Key Personnel
Pres: Randy Hoffman *E-mail:* randy@captus.com
Mgr: Pauline Lai *E-mail:* pauline@captus.com
Accts Admin & Intl Rts: Lily Chu *E-mail:* lily@captus.com
Founded: 1987
Publication of textbooks, scholarly books, professional books, nonfiction trade books & multimedia Internet courses. Publishes in French & Spanish also.
Publishes in English, French.
ISBN Prefix(es): 978-0-921801; 978-1-896691; 978-1-895712; 978-1-55322
Number of titles published annually: 34 Print; 2 Online; 3 E-Book
Total Titles: 158 Print; 6 Online; 6 E-Book
Imprints: Captus Press; Captus University Publications; University Press of Canada

§Carswell
Division of Thomson Reuters Canada Ltd
One Corporate Plaza, 2075 Kennedy Rd, Toronto, ON M1T 3V4
Tel: 416-298-5141; 416-609-3800 *Toll Free Tel:* 800-387-5164 (CN & US) *Fax:* 416-298-5094; 416-298-5082 *Toll Free Fax:* 877-750-9041 (CN only)
E-mail: carswell.customerrelations@thomsonreuters.com; carswell.orders@thomsonreuters.com
Web Site: www.carswell.com
Founded: 1864
Canada's leading provider of specialized information & electronic research solutions to the legal, tax, accounting & human resources markets. Headquartered in Toronto, ON, Carswell provides integrated information in a range of formats, including books, looseleaf services, journals, newsletters, CD-ROMs & online. Carswell is a business within The Thomson Corporation.
Publishes in English, French.
ISBN Prefix(es): 978-0-459; 978-0-88820; 978-0-7798
Number of titles published annually: 100 Print
Total Titles: 1,113 Print; 10 Online
Imprints: Richard De Boo
Branch Office(s)
430 rue St Pierre, Montreal, QC H2Y 2M5 *Tel:* 514-842-3937 *Toll Free Tel:* 800-363-3047 *Fax:* 514-842-7144
Distributor for Australian Tax Practice (ATP); Editions Yvon Blais; Brookers; Compu-Mark; Editorial Aranrzadi; ELLIS Publications; Fakta Info Direkt; Federal & State Government Printers; Forlaget Thomson; Foundation Press; GEE Publishing; W Green; Incorporated Council (London); IOB; La Ley; Lawbook Co; Legal Solutions USA; McGill University Air & Space Institute (Montreal); Native Law Center University of Saskatchewan; Professional Publishing (London); Provincial Government Printers; Research Institute of America; Round Hall Ltd; The Stationary Office (London); Sweet & Maxwell Asia; Sweet & Maxwell Group; Sweet & Maxwell UK; Thomson Legal & Regulatory; Thomson Tax Ltd (London); Transactive SARL; West Group
U.S. Publishers Represented: Research Institute of America; West
Foreign Rep(s): Brookers (New Zealand, Pacific Islands, Solomon Islands); Legal & Regulatory Australia (Australia); Sweet & Maxwell (Africa, Europe, Middle East); Sweet & Maxwell Hong Kong (China, Hong Kong, Japan, Korea, Macau, Taiwan); Sweet & Maxwell Malaysia (Brunei, Indonesia, Malaysia, Singapore)
Returns: 245 Bartley Dr, Toronto, ON M4A 2V8
Distribution Center: 245 Bartley Dr, Toronto, ON M4A 2V8
See separate listing for:
Editions Yvon Blais

CCI Press, see Canadian Circumpolar Institute (CCI) Press

Centre for Reformation & Renaissance Studies (CRRS)
71 Queen's Park Crescent E, Toronto, ON M5S 1K7
Tel: 416-585-4465 *Fax:* 416-585-4430 (attn: CRRS)
E-mail: crrs.publications@utoronto.ca
Web Site: crrs.ca
Key Personnel
Dir: Ethan Matt Kavaler *E-mail:* crrs.director@utoronto.ca
Graduate Fellow, Pubns & Promos: Leslie Wexler
Founded: 1965
Specialty library & academic publisher.
Publishes in English, French.
ISBN Prefix(es): 978-0-7727; 978-0-9697512
Number of titles published annually: 10 Print
Total Titles: 102 Print
Imprints: Dovehouse Press

Centre Franco-Ontarien de Ressources en Alphabetisation (Centre FORA)
PO Box 56, Hanmer, ON P3P 1S9
Tel: 705-524-3672 *Toll Free Tel:* 888-814-4422 (orders, CN only) *Fax:* 705-524-8535
E-mail: info@centrefora.on.ca
Web Site: www.centrefora.on.ca
Founded: 1989
Nonprofit organization that publishes learning materials for adult literacy & distribute education materials for all ages.
Publishes in French.
ISBN Prefix(es): 978-2-921706; 978-1-895336; 978-2-89567
Number of titles published annually: 20 Print
Total Titles: 150 Print

The Charlton Press Corp
Division of Charlton International Inc
991 Victoria St N, Kitchener, ON N2B 3C7
Tel: 416-962-2665 *Toll Free Tel:* 866-663-8827 *Fax:* 519-579-0532
E-mail: chpress@charltonpress.com
Web Site: www.charltonpress.com
Key Personnel
Owner: Marc Drake *Tel:* 416-964-1632
Founded: 1952
Specialize in 20th century numismatics.
Publishes in English.
ISBN Prefix(es): 978-0-88968; 978-2-9800475
Number of titles published annually: 4 Print
Total Titles: 12 Print

Chartered Professional Accountants of Canada (CPA Canada)
Formerly Canadian Institute of Chartered Accountants (CICA) (L'Institut Canadien des Comptables Agrees)
277 Wellington St W, Toronto, ON M5V 3H2
Tel: 416-977-3222 *Toll Free Tel:* 800-268-3793 *Fax:* 416-977-8585
E-mail: member.services@cpacanada.ca
Web Site: www.cpacanada.ca; www.facebook.com/CPACanada/
Key Personnel
Pres & CEO: Joy Thomas
Dir, Pubns: Liz Cram *Tel:* 416-204-3433
Founded: 1917
Taxation, accounting, auditing, financial.
Publishes in English, French.
ISBN Prefix(es): 978-0-88800; 978-1-55385
Number of titles published annually: 15 Print
Total Titles: 200 Print
Branch Office(s)
100-4200 N Fraser Way, Burnaby, BC V5J 5K7 *Tel:* 604-669-3555 *Toll Free Tel:* 800-663-1529 *Fax:* 604-689-5845
1201-350 Sparks St, Ottawa, ON K1R 7S8 *Tel:* 613-789-7771 *Fax:* 613-789-7772
680, rue Sherbrooke W, 17th fl, Montreal, QC H3A 2M7

§ChemTec Publishing
38 Earswick Dr, Toronto, ON M1E 1C6
Tel: 416-265-2603 *Fax:* 416-265-1399
E-mail: orderdesk@chemtec.org
Web Site: www.chemtec.org
Key Personnel
CEO: Anna Wypych
Circ Mgr: Anna Fox
Founded: 1988
Additives, blends, polymers, recycling & rheology.
Publishes in English.
ISBN Prefix(es): 978-1-895198
Number of titles published annually: 7 Print
Total Titles: 80 Print; 10 CD-ROM

Cheneliere Education Inc
Division of TC Media
5800, rue St Denis, bureau 900, Montreal, QC H2S 3L5
Tel: 514-273-1066 *Toll Free Tel:* 800-565-5531 *Fax:* 514-276-0324 *Toll Free Fax:* 800-814-0324
E-mail: info@cheneliere.ca
Web Site: www.cheneliere.ca
Key Personnel
Gen Mgr: Patrick Lutzy *E-mail:* patrick.lutzy@tc.tc
Founded: 1971
School, college & university textbooks; vocational; French Immersion; teaching skills & book packaging (French & English languages).
Publishes in French.
ISBN Prefix(es): 978-2-89310; 978-2-89461; 978-2-7650
Number of titles published annually: 200 Print
Imprints: Beauchemin; Gaetan Morin Editeur; Graficor
U.S. Publishers Represented: McGraw-Hill Inc
Warehouse: McGraw-Hill Ryerson Limited, 300 Water St, Whitby, ON L1N 9B6
See separate listing for:
Gaetan Morin Editeur

Chestnut Publishing Group Inc
44 Stubbs Dr, Suite 207, Toronto, ON M2L 2R3
Tel: 416-224-5824 *Fax:* 416-224-0595
Web Site: www.chestnutpublishing.com
Key Personnel
Pres: Stanley Starkman *E-mail:* sharkstark@sympatico.ca
VP, Publg: Grace Yang
VP, Fin: Allan Goldbach *Tel:* 416-499-1253 *Fax:* 416-499-1652 *E-mail:* agoldbach@on.aibn.com
Founded: 2001
Publish education, school & college, trade, adult, children, juvenile, young adult & ESL titles.
Publishes in English, French.
ISBN Prefix(es): 978-1-894601; 978-1-894929; 978-0-9689522; 978-0-9688946
Number of titles published annually: 20 Print; 4 CD-ROM; 3 Audio
Total Titles: 220 Print; 20 CD-ROM; 20 Audio
Imprints: Chestnut Publishing; Doyen Publishing (el-hi books; mathematics); Lynx Publishing (ESL); Patnor Publishing (books for reluctant readers & ESL)
Foreign Rights: INT Press (Australia, New Zealand)
Warehouse: TTS Distributing Inc, 155 Edward St, Aurora, ON L4G 1W3, Contact: Duncan Stewart *Tel:* 905-841-3898 *Fax:* 905-841-3026 *E-mail:* dstewart@ttsdistributing.com *Web Site:* www.ttsdistributing.com
Membership(s): Organization of Book Publishers of Ontario

Chouette Publishing
1001 Lenoir St, Suite B-238, Montreal, QC H4C 2Z6
Tel: 514-925-3325 *Fax:* 514-925-3323
E-mail: info@editions-chouette.com
Web Site: www.chouette-publishing.com
Key Personnel
Publr & Ed: Anne Paradis
Founded: 1987
Produce children's books adapted to each age group from birth to age six, with the well-known Caillou character.
Publishes in English, French.
ISBN Prefix(es): 978-2-9800909; 978-2-921198; 978-2-89450; 978-2-89718
Number of titles published annually: 30 Print
Distributed by PGW/Legato Publishers Group
U.S. Rep(s): Client Distribution Services
Foreign Rep(s): Simon Payette
Warehouse: PGW/Legato Publishers Group, 210 American Dr, Jackson, TN 38301, United States *Toll Free Tel:* 800-343-4499 (Perseus) *Toll Free Fax:* 800-351-5073 *E-mail:* orderentry@perseusbooks.com
Distribution Center: Canadian Manda Group, 165 Dufferin St, Toronto, ON M6K 3H6 *Tel:* 416-516-0911 *Fax:* 416-516-0917 *E-mail:* info@mandagroup.com *Web Site:* www.canadianmandagroup.ca
PGW/Legato Publishers Group, 210 American Dr, Jackson, TN 38301, United States *Toll Free Tel:* 800-343-4499 (Perseus) *Toll Free Fax:* 800-351-5073 *E-mail:* orderentry@perseusbooks.com

CIUS Press, see Canadian Institute of Ukrainian Studies Press

Coach House Books
80 bpNichol Lane, Toronto, ON M5S 3J4
Tel: 416-979-2217 *Toll Free Tel:* 800-367-6360 (outside Toronto) *Fax:* 416-977-1158
E-mail: mail@chbooks.com
Web Site: www.chbooks.com
Key Personnel
Founder & Publr: Stan Bevington *E-mail:* stan@chbooks.com
Edit Dir: Alana Wilcox *E-mail:* alana@chbooks.com
Digital & Prodn Mgr: Norman Nehmetallah *E-mail:* norman@chbooks.com
Publicist: Jessica Rattray *E-mail:* jessica@chbooks.com
Founded: 1965
Literary small press specializing in experimental fiction & poetry.
Publishes in English.
ISBN Prefix(es): 978-1-55245
Number of titles published annually: 16 Print; 5 Online
Total Titles: 140 Print; 60 Online
Foreign Rights: Amo Agency (Amo Noh) (South Korea); AnatoliaLit Agency (Amy Spangler) (Turkey); Sandra Bruna Agencia Literaria SL (Natalia Berenguer) (Portugal, Spain); English Agency Japan (Hamish Macaskill) (Japan); The Grayhawk Agency (Lora Fountain) (China, Taiwan); Mohr Books Literary Agency (Annelie Geissler) (Germany); Piergiorgio Nicolazzini Literary Agency (Maura Solinas) (Italy); Sandrine Paccher (France)
Distribution Center: Publishers Group Canada, 76 Stafford St, Suite 300, Toronto, ON M6J 2S1 (CN orders), Sales Dir: Lori Richardson *Tel:* 416-934-9900 *Fax:* 416-934-1410 *E-mail:* info@pgcbooks.ca *Web Site:* www.pgcbooks.ca
Consortium Book Sales & Distribution, The Keg House, 34 13 Ave NE, Suite 101, Minneapolis, MN 55413-1007, United States (US orders) *Toll Free Tel:* 800-283-3572 *Toll Free*

Fax: 800-351-5073 *E-mail:* sales.orders@cbsd.com *Web Site:* www.cbsd.com
Membership(s): Association of Canadian Publishers; Community of Literary Magazines & Presses; Literary Press Group

Collector Grade Publications Inc
PO Box 1046, Cobourg, ON K9A 4W5
Tel: 905-342-3434 *Fax:* 905-342-3688
E-mail: info@collectorgrade.com
Web Site: www.collectorgrade.com
Key Personnel
Pres: R Blake Stevens
Founded: 1979
Accurate, in-depth studies of modern small arms. Technical reference books.
Publishes in English.
ISBN Prefix(es): 978-0-88935
Number of titles published annually: 3 Print
Total Titles: 60 Print

Company's Coming Publishing Ltd
87 E Pender St, Vancouver, BC V6A 1S9
Tel: 780-450-6223 (orders & inquiries)
Toll Free Tel: 800-661-9017 (CN); 800-518-3541 (US) *Fax:* 780-450-1857
E-mail: info@companyscoming.com
Web Site: www.companyscoming.com
Key Personnel
Pres: Grant Lovig
Founded: 1981
Publish cookbooks, craft books & stationery products.
Publishes in English.
ISBN Prefix(es): 978-0-9690695; 978-0-9693322; 978-1-895455; 978-1-896891; 978-1-897069; 978-1-897477; 978-1-927126
Number of titles published annually: 25 Print
Total Titles: 200 Print
Distribution Center: Booklogic, 2311 96 St, Edmonton, AB T6N 1G3

Comptables professionnels agrees du Canada, see Chartered Professional Accountants of Canada (CPA Canada)

Conseil canadien de developpement social, see Canadian Council on Social Development (Conseil canadien de developpement social)

The Continuing Legal Education Society of British Columbia (CLEBC)
500-1155 W Pender St, Vancouver, BC V6E 2P4
Tel: 604-669-3544; 604-893-2121 (cust serv)
Toll Free Tel: 800-663-0437 (CN) *Fax:* 604-669-9260
E-mail: custserv@cle.bc.ca
Web Site: www.cle.bc.ca
Key Personnel
CEO: Ron Friesen *Tel:* 604-893-2114
E-mail: rfriesen@cle.bc.ca
Dir, Pubns: Susan Munro *Tel:* 604-893-2106
E-mail: smunro@cle.bc.ca
Mktg Mgr: Adam Simpkins *Tel:* 604-893-2168
E-mail: adams@cle.bc.ca
Founded: 1976
Publish course materials, practice manuals & case digests.
Publishes in English.
ISBN Prefix(es): 978-0-86504; 978-1-55258
Number of titles published annually: 35 Print; 35 Online
Total Titles: 50 Print; 1 CD-ROM; 48 Online
Imprints: CLEBC

Cormorant Books Inc
10 St Mary St, Suite 615, Toronto, ON M4Y 1P9
Tel: 416-925-8887
E-mail: info@cormorantbooks.com
Web Site: www.cormorantbooks.com
Key Personnel
Pres & Publr, Cormorant Books: Marc Cote
E-mail: m.cote@cormorantbooks.com
Assoc Publr, Cormorant Books & Publr, DCB/Dancing Cat Books: Barry Jowett *E-mail:* b.jowett@cormorantbooks.com
Founded: 1986
Independent literary publisher of Canadian authors.
Publishes in English.
ISBN Prefix(es): 978-0-920953; 978-1-896951; 978-1-896332; 978-1-897151
Number of titles published annually: 26 Print; 26 Online; 26 E-Book
Total Titles: 150 Print; 150 Online; 82 E-Book
Imprints: DCB; The Riverbank Press
Distribution Center: University of Toronto Press, 5201 Dufferin St, Toronto, ON M3H 5T8
Tel: 416-667-7791 *Toll Free Tel:* 800-565-9523
Fax: 416-667-7832 *Toll Free Fax:* 800-221-9985 *E-mail:* utpbooks@utpress.utoronto.ca
Web Site: www.utpress.utoronto.ca

Coteau Books
Division of Thunder Creek Publishing Co-operative
2517 Victoria Ave, Regina, SK S4P 0T2
SAN: 115-1037
Tel: 306-777-0170 *Toll Free Tel:* 800-440-4471 (CN only) *Fax:* 306-522-5152
E-mail: coteau@coteaubooks.com
Web Site: www.coteaubooks.com
Key Personnel
Publr: John Agnew *E-mail:* publisher@coteaubooks.com
Design & Prodn: Susan Buck
E-mail: production@coteaubooks.com
Mktg & Publicity: MacKenzie Hamon
E-mail: publicist@coteaubooks.com
Founded: 1975
Publish & promote examples of the best fiction, poetry, drama & young readers' fiction written in Canada.
Publishes in English.
ISBN Prefix(es): 978-0-919926; 978-0-55050; 978-0-9780316
Number of titles published annually: 12 Print; 12 E-Book
Total Titles: 130 Print; 150 E-Book
Orders to: Publishers Group Canada, Raincoast Books, 2440 Viking Way, Richmond, BC V6V 1N2 *Toll Free Tel:* 800-663-5714 *Toll Free Fax:* 800-565-3770 *E-mail:* customerservice@raincoast.com
Distribution Center: Publishers Group Canada, Raincoast Books, 2440 Viking Way, Richmond, BC V6V 1N2 *Toll Free Tel:* 800-663-5714 *Toll Free Fax:* 800-565-3770
E-mail: customerservice@raincoast.com

La Courte Echelle
4388, rue Saint-Denis, Suite 315, Montreal, QC H2J 2L1
Tel: 514 312 6950
E-mail: info@courteechelle.com
Web Site: courteechelle.groupecourteechelle.com
Key Personnel
Gen Dir: Marieve Talbot
Artistic Dir: Julie Massy
Literary Dir & Children's Ed: Carole Tremblay
Edit Asst: Celine Comtois
Communs Coord: Melina Schoenborn
Sales Coord: Marianne Dalpe
Graphic Designer: Catherine Charbonneau
Founded: 1978
Children's, young adult & adult fiction. No unsol mss accepted.
Publishes in French.
ISBN Prefix(es): 978-2-89021; 978-1-894731; 978-2-89651; 978-2-89695
Number of titles published annually: 50 Print
Total Titles: 545 Print
Distribution Center: Hachette Canada, 9001 de l'Acadie, bureau 1002, Montreal, QC H4N 3H5
Tel: 514-382-3034 *Toll Free Tel:* 888-422-4388
Fax: 514-381-5088 *E-mail:* info@hachette.qc.ca *Web Site:* www.hachette.qc.ca
Socadis Inc, 420 rue Stinson, Montreal, QC H4N 3L7 *Tel.* 514-331-3300 *Toll Free Tel:* 800-361-2847 *Fax:* 514-745-3282
Librairie du Quebec a Paris, Diffusion du Nouveau Monde (DNM), 30, rue Gay-Lussac, 75005 Paris, France (France & Europe)
Tel: 01 43 54 49 02 *Fax:* 01 43 54 39 15
E-mail: dnm@librairieduquebec.fr *Web Site:* www.librairieduquebec.fr

§Crabtree Publishing Co Ltd
Subsidiary of Crabtree Publishing Co (USA)
616 Welland Ave, St Catharines, ON L2M 5V6
SAN: 115-1436
Tel: 905-682-5221 *Toll Free Tel:* 800-387-7650
Fax: 905-682-7166 *Toll Free Fax:* 800-355-7166
E-mail: custserv@crabtreebooks.com; sales@crabtreebooks.com; orders@crabtreebooks.com
Web Site: www.crabtreebooks.com
Key Personnel
Pres: Peter A Crabtree *E-mail:* peter_c@crabtreebooks.com
Publr: Bobbie Kalman *E-mail:* bobbiek@crabtreebooks.com
VP, Edit: Kathy Middleton *E-mail:* kathy_m@crabtreebooks.com
VP, Mktg: Julie Alguire *E-mail:* julie_a@crabtreebooks.com
VP, Opers: Craig Culliford *E-mail:* craig_c@crabtreebooks.com
Dir, New Media: Rob MacGregor
E-mail: rob_m@crabtreebooks.com
Dir, Sales: Andrea Crabtree *E-mail:* andrea_c@crabtreebooks.com
Cust Serv Mgr: Linda Wade *E-mail:* linda_w@crabtreebooks.com
Warehouse Mgr: Karl Kasper
E-mail: warehouse@crabtreebooks.com
Founded: 1978
Children's nonfiction & fiction, library binding & paperback for school & trade.
Publishes in English, French.
ISBN Prefix(es): 978-0-86505; 978-0-7787; 978-1-4271
Number of titles published annually: 300 Print; 150 E-Book
Total Titles: 4,612 Print; 1,665 E-Book; 105 Audio
Imprints: Look, Listen & Learn Audio Books
Distributor for Bayard; Maren Green
Foreign Rep(s): Everybody's Books (Namibia, South Africa); INT Press (Australia); Roundhouse Group (European Union, UK); South Pacific Books (New Zealand)
Membership(s): ABA; ALA; American Alliance of Museums; American Marketing Association; Association of Canadian Publishers; Canadian Booksellers Association; Educational Book & Media Association; National Science Teachers Association; Ontario Library Association

CRRS, see Centre for Reformation & Renaissance Studies (CRRS)

§Database Directories
588 Dufferin Ave, London, ON N6B 2A4
Tel: 519-433-1666 *Fax:* 519-430-1131
E-mail: mail@databasedirectory.com
Web Site: www.databasedirectory.com
Key Personnel
CEO: Lesley Classic *E-mail:* lclassic@databasedirectory.com
Founded: 1995
Directories & e-files on libraries, schools, colleges, universities, academic retailers & municipalities.

Publishes in English.
ISBN Prefix(es): 978-1-896537
Number of titles published annually: 3 Print; 4 CD-ROM; 4 Online
Total Titles: 10 Print; 10 CD-ROM; 4 Online

§DC Canada Education Publishing (DCCED)
180 Metcalfe St, Suite 204, Ottawa, ON K2P 1P5
Tel: 613-565-8885 *Toll Free Tel:* 888-565-0262 *Fax:* 613-565-8881
E-mail: info@dc-canada.ca
Web Site: www.dc-canada.ca
Key Personnel
Publg Dir: Mei Dang
Founded: 1995
Publishes in English.
ISBN Prefix(es): 978-0-9738439; 978-0-9738440; 978-0-9808816; 978-0-9810549; 978-1-926776
Number of titles published annually: 6 Print

§Double Dragon Publishing Inc
1-5762 Hwy 7 E, Markham, ON L3P 7Y4
Mailing Address: PO Box 54016, Markham, ON L3P 7Y4
E-mail: sales@double-dragon-ebooks.com
Web Site: www.double-dragon-ebooks.com
Key Personnel
CEO & Publr: Deron Douglas
Founded: 2001
Publishes ebooks & trade paperbacks in the fantasy, science fiction, speculative fiction, horror & suspense genres. Established with the goal of building a Canadian-based publishing venue for the growing number of good but unpublished fiction writers around the world. Dedicated to publishing quality works of fiction & nonfiction & will continue to publish works in various genres in both the ebook & traditional paper book formats. Make special efforts to publish a specific number of works written by North American Aboriginal authors each year.
Publishes in English.
ISBN Prefix(es): 978-1-894841; 978-1-55404
Number of titles published annually: 40 Print; 100 E-Book
Total Titles: 40 Print; 125 E-Book
Imprints: Blood Moon Publishing; Carnal Desires Publishing; DDP Literary Press; Double Dragon eBooks; Double Dragon Press; Dragon Dance; Dragon Tooth Fantasy; Dragon's Heart Romance

Doubleday Canada
Imprint of Penguin Random House Canada
320 Front St W, Suite 1400, Toronto, ON M5V 3B6
SAN: 115-0340
Tel: 416-364-4449 *Fax:* 416-598-7764
Web Site: www.penguinrandomhouse.ca
Key Personnel
Pres & Publr, PRHC: Kristin Cochrane
Pres & CEO: Brad Martin
EVP & CFO: Barry Gallant
SVP & COO: Robert Wheaton
SVP & Dir, Mktg & Corp Communs: Tracey Turriff
SVP & Dir, Prodn: Janine Laporte
Assoc Publr: Amy Black
Ed-in-Chief: Martha Kanya-Forstner
Sr Ed: Bhavna Chauhan
Ed: Kiara Kent; Zoe Maslow
Founded: 1937
General trade nonfiction (current affairs, politics, business, sports); fiction, children's illustrated.
Penguin Random House Canada & its publishing entities are not accepting unsol submissions, proposals, mss, or submission queries via e-mail at this time.
Publishes in English.
ISBN Prefix(es): 978-0-385; 978-0-7704
Number of titles published annually: 60 Print; 5 E-Book
Total Titles: 1,172 Print; 41 E-Book
Imprints: Anchor Canada; Bond Street Books; Seal Books
Membership(s): Canadian Booksellers Association; Canadian Publishers' Council

Douglas & McIntyre (2013) Ltd
4437 Rondeview Rd, Madeira Park, BC V0N 2H1
Mailing Address: PO Box 219, Madeira Park, BC V0N 2H0
Toll Free Tel: 800-667-2988
E-mail: info@douglas-mcintyre.com
Web Site: www.douglas-mcintyre.com
Key Personnel
Interim Publr: Howard White
Founded: 1970
Focus on biographies, native art & history, architecture, literary fiction & cookbooks.
Publishes in English.
ISBN Prefix(es): 978-0-88894; 978-1-55054; 978-1-55365; 978-1-77100; 978-0-920841; 978-1-55051; 978-1-926812; 978-1-926685; 978-1-926706
Number of titles published annually: 90 Print
Total Titles: 1,500 Print
Distributed by University of Toronto Press
Membership(s): AAP; Association for the Export of Canadian Books; Association of Book Publishers of British Columbia; Association of Canadian Publishers; Canadian Booksellers Association

Dundurn Press Ltd
3 Church St, Suite 500, Toronto, ON M5E 1M2
SAN: 115-0359
Tel: 416-214-5544 *Fax:* 416-214-5556
E-mail: info@dundurn.com
Web Site: www.dundurn.com
Key Personnel
Pres & Publr: Kirk Howard *E-mail:* khoward@dundurn.com
Founded: 1972
Specialize in Canadian history, social sciences, some biography & art, fiction & mysteries.
Publishes in English.
ISBN Prefix(es): 978-0-919670; 978-0-9690454; 978-0-88924; 978-0-88882; 978-1-55488; 978-1-4597
Number of titles published annually: 100 Print
Foreign Rep(s): Gazelle Book Services Ltd (Europe)
Distribution Center: University of Toronto Press Distribution, 5201 Dufferin St, Toronto, ON M3H 5T8 *Tel:* 416-978-2239 *Fax:* 416-978-4738 *Web Site:* www.utpress.utoronto.ca
Ingram Publisher Services, One Ingram Blvd, La Vergne, TN 37086-1986, United States *Toll Free Tel:* 866-400-5351
Membership(s): Association of Canadian Publishers

Ecrits des Forges
992-A rue Royale, Trois-Rivieres, QC G9A 4H9
Tel: 819-840-8492
E-mail: ecritsdesforges@gmail.com
Web Site: www.ecritsdesforges.com
Key Personnel
Admin Dir: Etienne Poirier
Literary Dir: Bernard Pozier
Founded: 1971
Publish poetry.
Publishes in French.
ISBN Prefix(es): 978-2-89046
Number of titles published annually: 50 Print
Total Titles: 1,125 Print
Distributed by DCR; Prologue
Membership(s): Association Nationale des Editeurs de Livres

ECW Press
665 Gerrard St E, Toronto, ON M4M 1Y2
SAN: 115-1274
Tel: 416-694-3348
E-mail: info@ecwpress.com
Web Site: www.ecwpress.com
Key Personnel
Co-Publr: Jack David *E-mail:* jack@ecwpress.com
Founded: 1974
Publishes in English.
ISBN Prefix(es): 978-0-920763; 978-1-55022; 978-0-920802; 978-1-77041
Number of titles published annually: 50 Print
Total Titles: 1,200 Print; 400 E-Book
Imprints: misFit
Foreign Rights: David Caron (worldwide exc Canada & USA)
Membership(s): Association of Canadian Publishers; Literary Press Group

EDGE Science Fiction & Fantasy Publishing Inc
Imprint of Hades Publications Inc
PO Box 1714, Calgary, AB T2P 2L7
Tel: 403-254-0160 *Fax:* 403-254-0456
E-mail: admin@hadespublications.com
Web Site: www.edgewebsite.com
Key Personnel
Pres & Publr: Brian Hades *E-mail:* publisher@hadespublications.com
Mktg: Janice Shoults
Founded: 1996
Encourage, produce & promote thought-provoking science fiction & fantasy & horror literature by "bringing the magic alive-one world at a time" with each new book released. Independent publisher of science fiction & fantasy novels in hardcover or trade paperback format. Produce high-quality books with lots of attention to detail & lots of marketing effort.
Publishes in English.
ISBN Prefix(es): 978-1-894063; 978-1-896944; 978-1-77053
Number of titles published annually: 8 Print
Total Titles: 87 Print; 1 Audio
Imprints: Absolute XPress; Tesseract Books
U.S. Rep(s): Baker & Taylor; Fitzhenry & Whiteside; Ingram Book Co
Distribution Center: Fitzhenry & Whiteside, 195 Allstate Pkwy, Markham, ON L3R 4T8 (CN & US) *Toll Free Tel:* 800-387-9776 *Toll Free Fax:* 800-260-9777 *E-mail:* bookinfo@fitzhenry.ca
Membership(s): Book Publishers Association of Alberta; The Imaging Alliance; Independent Book Publishers Association; IPAC

Les Editions Alire
120 cote du Passage, Levis, QC G6V 5S9
Tel: 418-835-4441 *Fax:* 418-838-4443
E-mail: info@alire.com
Web Site: www.alire.com
Key Personnel
Admin Dir: Melanie Bissonnette *E-mail:* melanie.bissonnette@alire.com
Edit Dir: Jean Pettigrew *E-mail:* jean.pettigrew@alire.com
Dir, Sales: Louise Alain *E-mail:* louise.alain@alire.com
Founded: 1996
Publish French Canadian popular genre fiction.
Publishes in French.
ISBN Prefix(es): 978-2-922145; 978-2-89615; 978-2-9801068
Number of titles published annually: 10 Print
Total Titles: 131 Print
Distribution Center: Messageries ADP, 2315, rue de la Province, Longueuil, QC J4G 1G4 (CN & US) *Tel:* 450-640-1237 *Fax:* 450-674-6237
Interforum Editis, Immeuble Paryseine, 3, allee de la Seine, 94854 Ivry Cedex, France *Tel:* 02 38 32 71 00 *Fax:* 02 28 32 71 28

E-mail: cdes-export@interforum.fr *Web Site:* www.interforum.fr
Membership(s): Association Nationale des Editeurs de Livres

Les Editions Caractere
Division of TC Media
5800, rue St-Denis, bureau 900, Montreal, QC H2S 3L5
Tel: 514-273-1066 *Fax:* 514-276-0324
E-mail: caractere@tc.tc
Web Site: www.editionscaractere.com
Founded: 2004
Publishes in French.
ISBN Prefix(es): 978-2-923351; 978-2-89642; 978-2-89643
Number of titles published annually: 130 Print
Distribution Center: Prologue Inc, 1650, Lionel Bertrand, Boisbriand, QC J7H 1N7 *Tel:* 450-434-0306 *Toll Free Tel:* 800-363-2864 *Fax:* 450-434-4135 *Toll Free Fax:* 800-361-8088

Editions de la Pleine Lune
223 34 Ave, Lachine, QC H8T 1Z4
Tel: 514-634-7954
E-mail: editpllune@videotron.ca
Web Site: www.pleinelune.qc.ca
Key Personnel
Literary Dir: Marie-Madeleine Raoult
Media Rel: Caroline St Louis *Tel:* 514-918-2481 *E-mail:* carostlo@virgolia.com
Founded: 1975
Publishes in French.
ISBN Prefix(es): 978-2-89024
Number of titles published annually: 8 Print
Total Titles: 185 Print
Distribution Center: Diffusion Dimedia, 539, Lebau Blvd, St-Laurent, QC H4N 1S2 *Tel:* 514-336-3941 *Fax:* 514-331-3916 *E-mail:* general@dimedia.qc.ca *Web Site:* www.dimedia.com
La Librairie du Quebec a Paris et DNM, 30, rue Gay Lussac, 75005 Paris, France *Tel:* 01 43 54 49 02 *Fax:* 01 43 54 39 15 *Web Site:* www.librairieduquebec.fr
Membership(s): Association Nationale des Editeurs de Livres

Les Editions de l'Hexagone
Division of Groupe Ville Marie Litterature
1055, blvd Rene Levesque Est, Bureau 300, Montreal, QC H2L 4S5
Tel: 514-523-7993 *Fax:* 514-849-1388
Web Site: www.edhexagone.com
Key Personnel
Literary Dir & VP: Martin Balthazar
Literary Ed, Essays: Alain-Nicolas Renaud *E-mail:* alain.nicolas.renaud@groupevml.com
Exec Asst: Sylvie Briere *Tel:* 514-523-1182 ext 4213 *E-mail:* sylvie.briere@groupevml.com
Founded: 1953
Publishes in French.
ISBN Prefix(es): 978-2-89006; 978-2-89295; 978-2-89648; 978-0-88508
Number of titles published annually: 30 Print
Total Titles: 35 Print
Foreign Office(s): Immeuble Paryseine, 3, allee de la Seine, 94854 Ivry Cedex, France *Tel:* 01 49 59 12 40 *Fax:* 06 16 94 14 38
Orders to: Messageries ADP, 2315 rue de la Province, Longueuil, QC J4G 1G4 *Tel:* 450-640-1234 *Toll Free Tel:* 800-771-3022 *Fax:* 450-640-1251 *Toll Free Fax:* 800-603-0433 *E-mail:* adpcommandes@messageries-adp.com *Web Site:* www.messageries-adp.com
Warehouse: Messageries ADP, 2315 rue de la Province, Longueuil, QC J4G 1G4 *Tel:* 450-640-1234 *Toll Free Tel:* 800-771-3022 *Fax:* 450-640-1251 *Toll Free Fax:* 800-603-0433 *Web Site:* www.messageries-adp.com

Les Editions de Mortagne
CP 116, Boucherville, QC J4B 5E6
Tel: 450-641-2387 *Fax:* 450-655-6092
E-mail: info@editionsdemortagne.com
Web Site: www.editionsdemortagne.com
Key Personnel
Founder & Pres: Max Permingeat
VP, Admin & Prodn: Alexandra Pellerin
VP, Editions & Promo: Sandy Pellerin
Founded: 1978
Novels.
Publishes in French.
ISBN Prefix(es): 978-2-89074
Number of titles published annually: 15 Print
Total Titles: 15 Print
Foreign Office(s): BP 13, 16700 Ruffec, France *Tel:* 05 45 85 79 00
Distribution Center: Prologue, 1650 blvd Lionel-Bertrand, Broisbriand, QC J7N 1N7 *Tel:* 450-434-0306 *Toll Free Tel:* 800-363-2864 *Fax:* 450-434-2627 *Toll Free Fax:* 800-361-8088 *E-mail:* prologue@prologue.ca *Web Site:* www.prologue.ca
DG Diffusion, Zl de Bogues, 31750 Escalquens, France *Tel:* 05 55 51 80 00 *Fax:* 05 55 62 17 39
Distribution Servidis, Chemin des Chalets 7, 1279 Chavannes-de-Bogis, Switzerland *Tel:* (022) 960 95 23 *Fax:* (022) 960 95 77 *Web Site:* www.servidis.ch
Membership(s): Association Nationale des Editeurs de Livres

Les Editions du Ble
340, blvd Provencher, St Boniface, MB R2H 0G7
Tel: 204-237-8200 *Fax:* 204-233-8182
E-mail: direction@editionsduble.ca
Web Site: ble.avoslivres.ca
Key Personnel
Dir Gen: Emmanuelle Rigaud
Founded: 1974
Publish books in French (novels, essays, poetry) pertaining mainly to the Canadian West (but not exclusively).
Publishes in French.
ISBN Prefix(es): 978-2-921347; 978-2-923673
Number of titles published annually: 6 Print
Total Titles: 100 Print
Distribution Center: Diffusion Dimedia Inc, 539 Blvd Lebeau, Saint-Laurent, QC H4N 1S2 *Tel:* 514-336-3941 *Web Site:* www.dimedia.com

Les Editions du Boreal
4447, rue St-Denis, Montreal, QC H2J 2L2
Tel: 514-287-7401 *Fax:* 514-287-7664
E-mail: boreal@editionsboreal.qc.ca
Web Site: www.editionsboreal.qc.ca
Key Personnel
Dir Gen: Pascal Assathiany
Dir: Jean Bernier
Founded: 1963
General literature, essays, history, translations, children's & philosophy.
Publishes in French.
ISBN Prefix(es): 978-2-89052; 978-2-7646; 978-0-88503
Number of titles published annually: 70 Print
Total Titles: 1,700 Print
Distributed by Editions Du Seuil (Europe)
Foreign Rights: AMV Agencia Literaria (Eduardo Melon Vallat) (Portugal, Spain); AnatoliaLit Literary & Copyright Agency (Amy Spangler) (Turkey); Balla & Co Literary Agents (Catherine Balla) (Hungary); Berla & Griffini Rights Agency (Erica Berla) (Italy); Bureau des Copyrights Francais (Corinne Quentin) (Japan); The Grayhawk Agency (Nicolas Wu) (Taiwan); Anastasia Lester (Belarus, Bosnia and Herzegovina, Bulgaria, Croatia, Czech Republic, Estonia, Kosovo, Latvia, Lithuania, Macedonia, Montenegro, Poland, Russia, Serbia, Slovakia, Slovenia, Ukraine); Liepman AG Literary Agency (Marc Koralnik) (Germany); Rightol Media Ltd (Zoe Luo) (China); 2 Seas Agency (Marleen Seegers) (Iceland, Netherlands, Scandinavia, USA)
Distribution Center: Exportlivre Inc, 289, blvd Desaulniers, St-Lambert, QC J4P 1M8 (US) *Tel:* 450-671-3888 *Fax:* 450-671-2121 *E-mail:* order@exportlivre.com *Web Site:* www.exportlivre.com
Diffusion Dimedia, 539, blvd Lebeau, Ville St-Laurent, QC H4N 1S2 *Tel:* 514-336-3941 *Fax:* 514-331-3916 *E-mail:* info@dimedia.qc.ca *Web Site:* www.dimedia.com
Volumen, 25, blvd Romain Rolland, CS 21418, 75993 Paris Cedex 14, France (Europe) *Tel:* 01 41 48 84 60 *Fax:* 01 64 48 49 63 *E-mail:* volumen@volumen.fr

Editions du CHU Sainte-Justine
Unit of Direction de l'enseignement
3175, chemin de la Cote-Sainte-Catherine, Montreal, QC H3T 1C5
Tel: 514-345-4671 *Fax:* 514-345-4631
E-mail: edition.hsj@ssss.gouv.qc.ca
Web Site: www.editions-chu-sainte-justine.org
Key Personnel
Publg Dir: Marise Labrecque *Tel:* 514-345-7743 *E-mail:* marise.labrecque.hsj@ssss.gouv.qc.ca
Sales Dir: Jean-Francois Hebert *Tel:* 514-345-4931 ext 5541 *E-mail:* jean-francois.hebert.hsj@ssss.gouv.qc.ca
Ed: Marie-Eve Lefebvre *Tel:* 514-345-2350 *E-mail:* marie-eve.lefebvre.hsj@ssss.gouv.qc.ca
ISBN Prefix(es): 978-2-921215; 978-2-921858; 978-2-922770; 978-2-89619
Number of titles published annually: 20 Print
Distribution Center: Prologue, 1650 blvd Lionel-Bertrand, Boisbriand, QC J7H 1N7 *Tel:* 450-434-0306 *Toll Free Tel:* 800-363-2864 *Fax:* 450-434-2627 *Toll Free Fax:* 800-361-8088 *E-mail:* prologue@prologue.ca *Web Site:* www.prologue.ca
SDL La Caravelle, Rue du Pre-aux-oies, 303, 1130 Brussels, Belgium (Belgium & Luxembourg) *Tel:* (02) 240 93 08 *Fax:* (02) 216 35 98 *E-mail:* info@sdlcaravelle.com
Daudin Distribution, One, rue Guynemer, 78114 Magny-les Hameaux, France *Tel:* 01 30 48 74 74 *Fax:* 01 34 98 02 44 *E-mail:* commandes@daudin.fr
Servidis, Chemin des chalets, 1279 Chavannes-de-Bogis, Switzerland *Tel:* (022) 960 95 32 *Fax:* (022) 960 95 77 *E-mail:* commande@servidis.ch

§Les Editions du Noroit
4609, rue D'Iberville, espace 202, Montreal, QC H2H 2L9
Tel: 514-727-0005
E-mail: lenoroit@lenoroit.com
Web Site: www.lenoroit.com
Key Personnel
Literary Dir: Paul Belanger
Founded: 1971
Poetry.
Publishes in French.
ISBN Prefix(es): 978-2-89018; 978-0-88524
Number of titles published annually: 25 Print
Total Titles: 730 Print; 1 CD-ROM; 10 Audio
Distribution Center: Diffusion Dimedia Inc, 539 blvd Lebeau, Montreal, QC H4N 1S2 *Tel:* 514-336-3941 *Fax:* 514-331-3916 *E-mail:* general@dimedia.qc.ca *Web Site:* www.dimedia.com

Les Editions du Remue-Menage
La Maison Parent-Roback, 110 rue Sainte-Therese, bureau 303, Montreal, QC H2Y 1E6
Tel: 514-876-0097 *Fax:* 514-876-7951
E-mail: info@editions-rm.ca
Web Site: www.editions-rm.ca
Key Personnel
Ed: Rachel Bedard; Valerie Lefebvre-Faucher *E-mail:* vlf@editions-rm.ca; Anne Migner-Laurin *E-mail:* amlaurin@editions-rm.ca

Edit Asst: Camille Simard *E-mail:* camille.simard@editions-rm.ca
Founded: 1976
Specialize in feminist books.
Publishes in English, French.
ISBN Prefix(es): 978-2-89091
Number of titles published annually: 15 Print
Total Titles: 170 Print
Distributed by Export Livre (Europe, US); Hushion House Publishing Ltd (CN, US); Librarie du Quebec (France)
Foreign Rep(s): Library Plaisir (Egypt); S A Vander (Belgium)
Distribution Center: Diffusion Dimedia, 539 blvd Lebeau, St-Laurent, QC H4N 1S2 *Tel:* 514-336-3941 *Fax:* 514-331-3916 *Toll Free Fax:* 800-667-3941 *E-mail:* commandes@dimedia.qc.ca
Membership(s): Association Nationale des Editeurs de Livres

Les Editions du Septentrion
835 Turnbull Ave, Quebec City, QC G1R 2X4
Tel: 418-688-3556 *Fax:* 418-527-4978
E-mail: info@septentrion.qc.ca
Web Site: www.septentrion.qc.ca
Key Personnel
Pres & Publr: Denis Vaugeois
Dir Gen & Ed: Gilles Herman
Founded: 1988
Full service publisher.
Publishes in English, French.
ISBN Prefix(es): 978-2-89448; 978-0-89664; 978-0-88514; 978-0-921114; 978-0-89011
Number of titles published annually: 30 Print
Total Titles: 700 Print
Divisions: Hamac
Distributed by Baraka Books
Distribution Center: Dimedia, 539 blvd Lebeau, St-Laurent, QC H4N 1S2

Les Editions du Vermillon
305, rue St-Patrick, Ottawa, ON K1N 5K4
Tel: 613-241-4032 *Fax:* 613-241-3109
E-mail: leseditionsduvermillon@rogers.com
Web Site: www.leseditionsduvermillon.ca
Key Personnel
Founder & Edit Dir: Jacques Flamand
CEO: Monique Bertoli
Founded: 1982
Poetry, novels, children's books, textbooks, essays.
Publishes in English, French.
ISBN Prefix(es): 978-0-919925; 978-1-895873; 978-1-894547; 978-1-897058; 978-1-926628; 978-2-89040; 978-1-77120
Number of titles published annually: 12 Print
Total Titles: 400 Print
Foreign Rep(s): Diffusion Albert-le-Grand (Switzerland); Librairie du Quebec (France)
Foreign Rights: Montreal-Contacts (worldwide)
Distribution Center: Librairie du Quebec, 300, rue Gay Lussac, 75005 Paris, France *Tel:* 01 43 54 49 02 *Fax:* 01 43 54 39 15 *E-mail:* liquebec@noos.fr
Diffusion Albert le Grand SA, 20, rue de Beaumont, 1701 Fribourg, Switzerland *Tel:* (026) 425 85 95 *Fax:* (026) 425 85 90 *E-mail:* diffusion@albert-le-grand.ch
Membership(s): Canada Council for the Arts; Ontario Arts Council

Les Editions Fides
Subsidiary of Coopsco
7333 place des Roseraies, bureau 100, Anjou, QC H1M 2X6
Tel: 514-745-4290 *Fax:* 514-745-4299
E-mail: editions@groupefides.com
Web Site: www.editionsfides.com
Key Personnel
CEO: Claude Rheaume
Edit Dir: Michel Maille *Tel:* 514-745-4290 ext 355
Edit Dir, Fides Educ: M Jean-Pierre Albert *Tel:* 514-745-4290 ext 352 *E-mail:* jean-pierre.albert@groupefides.com
Dir, Fin & Admin: Michel Perreault
Mktg: David Senechal
Founded: 1937
Publishes in French.
ISBN Prefix(es): 978-0-7755; 978-2-7621; 978-2-87374; 978-2-89007; 978-2-923989
Number of titles published annually: 60 Print
Total Titles: 2,000 Print
Distribution Center: Socadis, 420 rue Stinson, Ville St-Laurent, QC H4N 3L7 *Tel:* 514-331-3300 *Toll Free Tel:* 800-361-2847 *Fax:* 514-745-3282 *Toll Free Fax:* 866-803-5422 *E-mail:* socinfo@socadis.com
Sofedis, 11, rue Soufflot, 75005 Paris, France (Europe) *Tel:* 01 53 10 25 25 *Fax:* 01 53 10 25 26 *E-mail:* info@sofedis.fr

Editions FouLire
4339, rue des Becassines, Quebec, QC G1G 1V5
Tel: 418-628-4029 *Toll Free Tel:* 877-628-4029 (CN & US) *Fax:* 418-628-4801
E-mail: info@foulire.com; edition@foulire.com
Web Site: www.foulire.com
Key Personnel
Ed: Yvon Brochu
Head, Communs & Soc Media: Marc Proulx
Prodn & Mktg: Danielle Lajeunesse
Founded: 2002
Publishers of books for children.
Publishes in French.
ISBN Prefix(es): 978-2-89591
Number of titles published annually: 30 Print
Total Titles: 3,500 Print
Foreign Rights: Ambre Communication (Pascale Patte-Wilbert) (France)
Distribution Center: Prologue Inc, 1650, blvd Lionel-Bertrand, Boisbriand, QC J7H 1N7 *Tel:* 450-434-0306 *Toll Free Tel:* 800-363-2864 *Fax:* 450-434-2627 *Toll Free Fax:* 800-361-8088 *E-mail:* prologue@prologue.ca
Librairie du Quebec, 30, rue Gay-Lussac, 75005 Paris, France *Tel:* 01 43 54 49 02 *Fax:* 01 43 54 39 15 *E-mail:* liquebec@noos.fr

Les Editions Ganesha Inc
CP 484, succursale d'Youville, Montreal, QC H2P 2W1
Tel: 450-641-2395
E-mail: courriel@editions-ganesha.qc.ca
Web Site: www.editions-ganesha.qc.ca
Key Personnel
Publr: Andre Beaudoin
Founded: 1978
Publishes in French.
ISBN Prefix(es): 978-2-89145
Number of titles published annually: 3 Print
Total Titles: 68 Print

Les Editions Goelette Inc
1350 Marie-Victorin, St-Bruno-de-Montarville, Quebec, QC J3V 6B9
Tel: 450-653-1337 *Toll Free Tel:* 800-463-4961 *Fax:* 450-653-9924
E-mail: info@boutiquegoelette.com
Web Site: www.boutiquegeolette.com
Key Personnel
Pres: Alain Delorme
Publr: Ingrid Remazeilles
Dir, Prodn: Chantel Morisset
Founded: 1997
Publishes in English, French.
ISBN Prefix(es): 978-2-9804941; 978-2-9806291; 978-2-922983; 978-2-89638; 978-2-89690
Number of titles published annually: 200 Print
Total Titles: 2,000 Print
Distribution Center: Les Messageries ADP, 2315, rue de la Province, Longueuil, QC J4G 1G4 *Tel:* 450-640-1234 *Toll Free Tel:* 800-771-3022 *Fax:* 450-640-1251 *Toll Free Fax:* 800-603-0433

Les Editions Heritage Inc
1101, ave Victoria, St-Lambert, QC J4R 1P8
Tel: 514-875-0327
Key Personnel
CEO & Pres of the Council: Jacques Payette
Pres: Sylvie Payette
Founded: 1968
Juvenile, adult & French language.
Publishes in French.
ISBN Prefix(es): 978-0-7773; 978-2-7625
Number of titles published annually: 250 Print
Total Titles: 2,000 Print
Foreign Rights: Barbara Creary
Membership(s): Association for Canadian Publishers in the US

Editions Hurtubise
Division of Groupe HMH
1815, ave De Lorimier, Montreal, QC H2K 3W6
Tel: 514-523-1523 *Toll Free Tel:* 800-361-1664 *Fax:* 514-523-9969
Web Site: www.editionshurtubise.com
Key Personnel
Pres: Herve Foulon
VP, Publg & Opers: Arnaud Foulon *E-mail:* arnaud.foulon@groupehmh.com
VP, Sales & Mktg: Alexandrine Foulon *E-mail:* alexandrine.foulon@groupehmh.com
Prodn Mgr: Dominique Lemay *E-mail:* dominique.lemay@editionshurtubise.com
Publg Mgr: Andre Gagnon *E-mail:* andre.gagnon@editionshurtubise.com
Rts Mgr: Sandra Felteau *E-mail:* sandra.felteau@groupehmh.com
Sr Ed: Sandrine Lazure *E-mail:* sandrine.lazure@editionshurtubise.com
Founded: 1960
French Canadian publishing house. Fiction & nonfiction, adult & young adult.
Publishes in French.
ISBN Prefix(es): 978-2-89045; 978-2-89428; 978-2-89647; 978-0-7758; 978-2-89723; 978-2-89781
Number of titles published annually: 80 Print; 60 E-Book; 10 Audio
Total Titles: 1,200 Print; 700 E-Book; 10 Audio
Imprints: Bibliotheque Quebecoise (BQ)
Distributor for Bibliotheque Quebecoise; Marcel Didier; Editions MultiMondes; Editions XYZ
Warehouse: Distribution HMH, 1815, ave De Lorimier, Montreal, QC H2K 3W6, Head of Dist: Guylaine Halle *E-mail:* guylaine.halle@distributionhmh.com *Web Site:* www.distributionhmh.com
Distribution Center: Distribution HMH, 1815, ave De Lorimier, Montreal, QC H2K 3W6, Head of Dist: Guylaine Halle *E-mail:* guylaine.halle@distributionhmh.com *Web Site:* www.distributionhmh.com

Les Editions JCL
Member of Bertrand Publishing Group
688, rue St-Joseph, Marieville, QC J3M 1H1
Tel: 450-460-4438
E-mail: info@jcl.qc.ca
Web Site: www.jcl.qc.ca
Key Personnel
Pres & Publr: Daniel Bertrand *E-mail:* dbertrand@jcl.qc.ca
Chief Commercial Offr: Elsa Galardo
Consulting Publr: Jean-Claude Larouche
Dir, Publg: Stephanie Roy
Founded: 1977
Novels & nonfiction.
Publishes in French.
ISBN Prefix(es): 978-2-920176; 978-2-89431; 978-2-89432

Number of titles published annually: 26 Print
Total Titles: 500 Print
Distribution Center: Messageries ADP, 2315, rue de la Province, Longueuil, QC J4G 1G4 *Tel:* 450-640-1234 *Toll Free Tel:* 800-771-3022 *Fax:* 450-640-1251 *Toll Free Fax:* 800-603-0433
Librairie du Quebec, 30, rue Gay Lussac, 75005 Paris, France (France & Europe) *Tel:* 01 45 54 49 02 *Fax:* 01 43 54 39 15 *E-mail:* libraires@librairiequebec.fr *Web Site:* www.librairieduquebec.fr
Membership(s): Association Nationale des Editeurs de Livres

Editions Le Dauphin Blanc Inc
825, blvd Lebourgneuf, Suite 125, Quebec, QC G2J 0B9
Tel: 418-845-4045 *Fax:* 418-845-1933
E-mail: info@dauphinblanc.com
Web Site: www.dauphinblanc.com
Key Personnel
CEO: Alain Williamson
E-mail: alainwilliamson@dauphinblanc.com
Asst Dir & Prodn Mgr: Annie Sauvgeau
Founded: 1991
Publishes in French.
ISBN Prefix(es): 978-2-89436
Number of titles published annually: 50 Print
Distribution Center: Prologue Inc, 1650, blvd Lionel-Bertrand, Boisbriand, QC J7H 1N7 *Tel:* 450-434-0306 *Toll Free Tel:* 800-363-2864 *Fax:* 450-434-2627 *Web Site:* www.prologue.ca
DG Diffusion, Zl de Bogues, 31750 Escalquens, France (Belgium & France) *Tel:* 05 61 00 09 99 *Fax:* 05 61 00 23 12 *E-mail:* adv@dgdiffusion.com *Web Site:* www.dgdiffusion.com
Diffusion Transat/Servidis, Chemin des Chalets 7, 1279 Chavannes-de-Bogis, Switzerland *Tel:* (022) 42 77 40 *Fax:* (022) 43 46 46 *E-mail:* transat@transatdiffusion.ch

Editions Marie-France
CP 32263 BP Waverly, Montreal, QC H3L 3X1
Tel: 514-329-3700 *Toll Free Tel:* 800-563-6644 (CN) *Fax:* 514-329-0630
E-mail: editions@marie-france.qc.ca
Web Site: www.marie-france.qc.ca
Key Personnel
Pres: Jean Lachapelle
VP: Joanne Lacombe
Founded: 1977
School, kindergarten, elementary & secondary adult & university in French, natural sciences, human sciences, music, economic education & physics. Some titles in both French & English.
Publishes in English, French.
ISBN Prefix(es): 978-2-89168
Number of titles published annually: 25 Print
Total Titles: 1,001 Print
Membership(s): Association Nationale des Editeurs de Livres

§Editions Mediaspaul
3965, blvd Henri-Bourassa E, Montreal, QC H1H 1L1
Tel: 514-322-7341 *Fax:* 514-322-4281
E-mail: editeur@mediaspaul.ca
Web Site: mediaspaul.ca
Key Personnel
Exec Dir: Joseph Sciortino *E-mail:* jsciortino@mediaspaul.ca
Publr: Gilles Collicelli
Founded: 1975
Religious & photographic books.
Publishes in French.
ISBN Prefix(es): 978-2-7122; 978-0-88840; 978-2-89039; 978-2-89420
Number of titles published annually: 20 Print
Total Titles: 300 Print
Foreign Rep(s): Paul Johnston
Distribution Center: Sodis, 128 Ave du Marechal de Lattre de Tassigny, 77400 Lagny-sur-Marne, France *Web Site:* www.sodis.fr

Editions Michel Quintin
2259 Papineau Ave, Suite 104, Montreal, QC H2K 4J5
SAN: 116-5356
Tel: 514-379-3774
E-mail: info@editionsmichelquintin.ca
Web Site: www.editionsmichelquintin.ca
Key Personnel
Pres: Michel Quintin
VP: Collette Dufresne
Founded: 1982
Nonfiction on fauna, nature, environment.
Publishes in French.
ISBN Prefix(es): 978-2-920438; 978-2-89435
Number of titles published annually: 60 Print
Total Titles: 700 Print
Branch Office(s)
4770 rue Foster, Waterloo, QC J0E 2N0 *Tel:* 450-539-3774
Editorial Office(s): PO Box 340, Waterloo, QC J0E 2N0
Foreign Rep(s): Bacon & Hughes (Canada); Interforum Editis
Distribution Center: Les Messageries ADP, 1261-A rue Shearer, Montreal, QC H3K 3G4 *Tel:* 514-523-1182 *Fax:* 514-939-0705

Editions MultiMondes
Affiliate of Groupe HMH
1815, Avenue de Lorimier, Montreal, QC H2K 3W6
Tel: 514-523-1523 *Toll Free Tel:* 800-361-1664 *Fax:* 514-523-9969
Web Site: www.multim.com
Key Personnel
Exec Dir: Dominique Lemay *E-mail:* dominique.lemay@editionsmultimondes.com
Edit Dir: Raymond Lemieux *E-mail:* raymond.lemieux@editionsmultimondes.com
Edit Asst: Sarah Jalbert *E-mail:* jalbert@editionsmultimondes.com
Founded: 1988
Books on science & the environment.
Publishes in English, French.
ISBN Prefix(es): 978-2-921146; 978-2-89544
Number of titles published annually: 20 Print
Total Titles: 200 Print
Distribution Center: GEODIF, One, rue Thenard, Paris 75005, France (Europe) *E-mail:* geodif@eyolles.com

Les Editions Phidal Inc
5740 Ferrier, Montreal, QC H4P 1M7
Tel: 514-738-0202 *Toll Free Tel:* 800-738-7349 *Fax:* 514-738-5102
E-mail: info@phidal.com; customer@phidal.com (sales & export)
Web Site: www.phidal.com
Key Personnel
Publr: Lionel Soussan
Founded: 1979
Full service publisher.
Publishes in English, French.
ISBN Prefix(es): 978-2-89393; 978-2-7643; 978-2-920129
Number of titles published annually: 55 Print

Les Editions Pierre Tisseyre
155, rue Maurice, Rosemere, QC J7A 2S8
Tel: 514-335-0777 *Fax:* 514-335-6723
E-mail: info@edtisseyre.ca
Web Site: www.tisseyre.ca
Key Personnel
Pres: Charles Tisseyre
Mng Ed: Michelle Tisseyre *E-mail:* mtisseyre@edtisseyre.ca
Sr Ed: Genevieve Mativat; Melanie Perreault
Founded: 1947
Primarily publish novels, novellas, essays, memoirs, novels for young people & children's literature.
Publishes in French.
ISBN Prefix(es): 978-2-89051; 978-2-89633; 978-0-7753
Number of titles published annually: 55 Print
Total Titles: 800 Print
Distribution Center: Prologue, 1650, Blvd Lionel-Bertrand, Boisbriand, QC J7H 1N7 *Tel:* 450-434-0306 *Toll Free Tel:* 800-363-2864 *E-mail:* prologue@prologue.ca

Editions Trecarre
Imprint of Groupe Librex
La Tourelle, 1055, blvd Rene-Levesque E, Bureau 300, Montreal, QC H2L 4S5
Tel: 514-849-5259 *Fax:* 514-849-1388
Web Site: www.editions-trecarre.com
Key Personnel
Rts Mgr: Carole Boutin *Tel:* 514-373-2743
E-mail: carol.boutin@groupelibrex.com
Founded: 1982
How-to books, cookbooks, practical books, health & lifestyle.
Publishes in French.
ISBN Prefix(es): 978-2-89249; 978-2-89568
Number of titles published annually: 15 Print
Total Titles: 700 Print; 100 E-Book
Warehouse: Les Messageries ADP, 2315, de la province, Longueuil, QC J4G 1G4 *Tel:* 450-640-1234 *Toll Free Tel:* 800-361-4806

§Les Editions Un Monde Different
3905 Isabelle, bureau 101, Brossard, QC J4Y 2R2
Mailing Address: CP 51546, Greenfield Park, QC J4V 3N8
Tel: 450-656-2660 *Toll Free Tel:* 800-443-2582 *Fax:* 450-659-9328
E-mail: info@umd.ca
Web Site: www.umd.ca
Key Personnel
Owner & Ed: Michel Ferron
Asst Ed: Manon Martel
Cust Serv/Promo & Mktg: Monique Duchesneau
E-mail: mduchesneau@umd.ca
Founded: 1977
Motivational & inspirational books.
Publishes in French.
ISBN Prefix(es): 978-2-89225; 978-2-920000
Number of titles published annually: 25 Print
Total Titles: 750 Print
Distribution Center: Messageries ADP, 2315, rue de la Province, Longueuil, QC J4G 1G4 *Tel:* 450-640-1234 *Fax:* 450-640-1251
Interforum Editis, Immeuble Paryseine, 3, alle de la Seine, 94854 Ivry, Cedex, France (Europe) *Tel:* 01 49 59 11 56 *Fax:* 01 49 59 11 91

Les Editions Vents d'Ouest
109, rue Wright, bureau 202, Gatineau, QC J8X 2G7
Tel: 819-770-6377
E-mail: info@ventsdouest.ca
Web Site: www.ventsdouest.ca
Key Personnel
Pres: Michel Tessier
VP: Gilles Parent
Dir, Gen Lit: Jeanne Duhaime; Pierre Gregoire; Jacques Michaud
Coord & Dir, Young Adult Lit: Michel Lavoie
Founded: 1993
Novels, short stories, history.
Publishes in French.
ISBN Prefix(es): 978-2-921603; 978-2-89537
Number of titles published annually: 18 Print
Total Titles: 220 Print
Distribution Center: Prologue Inc, 1650 Blvd Lionel-Bertrand, Boisbriand, QC J7H 1N7 *Tel:* 450-434-0306 *Toll Free Tel:* 800-363-2864

Fax: 450-434-2627 *Toll Free Fax:* 800-361-8088
Librairie du Quebec a Paris, 30, rue Gay-Lussac, 750005 Paris, France *Tel:* 01 43 54 49 02 *Fax:* 01 43 54 39 15

Les Editions XYZ inc
Affiliate of Groupe HMH
1815, ave De Lorimier, Montreal, QC H2K 3W6
Tel: 514-525-2170 *Fax:* 514-525-7537
E-mail: info@editionsxyz.com
Web Site: www.editionsxyz.com
Key Personnel
Dir Gen & Publr: Pascal Genet *Tel:* 514-525-2170 ext 260 *E-mail:* pascal.genet@editionsxyz.com
Prodn Mgr: Nathalie Tasse *Tel:* 514-525-2170 ext 255 *E-mail:* nathalie.tasse@editionsxyz.com
Ed: Marie-Pierre Barathon *Tel:* 514-525-2170 ext 270 *E-mail:* marie-pierre.barathon@editionsxyz.com
Founded: 1985
Novels, short stories & essays on literature.
Publishes in French.
ISBN Prefix(es): 978-2-89261; 978-2-89772
Number of titles published annually: 20 Print; 20 E-Book
Total Titles: 457 Print; 175 Online; 145 E-Book
Distribution Center: Distribution HMH, 1815, Ave de Lorimier, Montreal, QC H2K 3W6 *Tel:* 514-523-1523 *Toll Free Tel:* 800-361-1664 *Fax:* 514-523-9969 *Web Site:* www.distributionhmh.com
Distribution du Nouveau Monde (DNM), 30, rue Gay Lussac, 75005 Paris, France *Tel:* 01 43 54 50 24 *Fax:* 01 43 54 39 15
Membership(s): Association Nationale des Editeurs de Livres

§Editions Yvon Blais
Member of Carswell
75 rue Queen, Bureau 4700, Montreal, QC H3C 2N6
Toll Free Tel: 800-363-3047 *Fax:* 450-263-9256
E-mail: editionsyvonblais.commandes@thomsonreuters.com (cust serv)
Web Site: www.editionsyvonblais.com
Key Personnel
Dir, Pubns: Marie-Noelle Guay
Founded: 1978
Legal publishing.
Publishes in French.
ISBN Prefix(es): 978-2-89073; 978-2-89451; 978-2-89635
Number of titles published annually: 30 Print
Total Titles: 800 Print
Returns: 245 Bartley Dr, Toronto, ON M4A 2V8

Emond Montgomery Publications Ltd
60 Shaftesbury Ave, Toronto, ON M4T 1A3
Tel: 416-975-3925 *Toll Free Tel:* 888-837-0815 *Fax:* 416-975-3924
E-mail: orders@emp.ca
Web Site: www.emp.ca
Key Personnel
Pres: D Paul Emond *Tel:* 416-975-3925 ext 233 *E-mail:* pemond@emp.ca
VP, Educ Div: Anthony Rezek *Tel:* 416-975-3925 ext 229 *E-mail:* arezek@emp.ca
VP, Prodn & Admin: Paula Pike *Tel:* 416-975-3925 ext 223 *E-mail:* ppike@emp.ca
Mktg Mgr: Holly Penick *Tel:* 416-975-3925 ext 246 *E-mail:* hpenick@emp.ca
Founded: 1978
Academic publisher.
Publishes in English.
ISBN Prefix(es): 978-0-920722; 978-1-55239
Number of titles published annually: 30 Print; 40 E-Book
Total Titles: 200 Print; 40 E-Book
Returns: 240 Industrial Pkwy S, Unit 4, Door 1, Aurora, ON L4G 3V6, Contact: Judith Lynn *E-mail:* jlynn@emp.ca
Warehouse: 240 Industrial Pkwy S, Unit 4, Door 1, Aurora, ON L4G 3V6, Contact: Judith Lynn *E-mail:* jlynn@emp.ca

ERPI, see Pearson ERPI

§Fairwinds Press
PO Box 668, Lions Bay, BC V0N 2E0
Tel: 604-913-0649
E-mail: orders@fairwinds-press.com
Web Site: www.fairwinds-press.com
Key Personnel
Publr & Intl Rts: Leslie Nolin *E-mail:* leslie@fairwinds-press.com
Founded: 1997
Publishes in English.
ISBN Prefix(es): 978-0-9682149; 978-0-9780974; 978-0-9881081
Number of titles published annually: 3 Print; 2 E-Book
Total Titles: 17 Print; 6 E-Book
Membership(s): Independent Publishers Association

Fernwood Publishing
32 Oceanvista Lane, Black Point, NS B0J 1B0
Tel: 902-857-1388 *Fax:* 902-857-1328
E-mail: info@fernpub.ca; roseway@fernpub.ca
Web Site: fernwoodpublishing.ca
Key Personnel
Co-Publr: Wayne Antony *E-mail:* wayne@fernpub.ca; Errol Sharpe *E-mail:* errol@fernpub.ca
Prodn Coord & Publr/Mng Ed, Roseway: Beverly Rach *E-mail:* bev@fernpub.ca
Mktg Mgr, Academic Titles: Nancy Malek
Mktg Mgr, Trade Titles: Curran Faris
Mng Ed: Candida Hadley *E-mail:* candida@fernpub.ca
Fin, Perms & Rts: James Patterson
Founded: 1991
Social sciences & humanities, emphasizing labour studies, women's studies, gender studies, critical theory & research, political economy, cultural studies & social work for use in undergraduate courses in colleges & universities.
Publishes in English.
ISBN Prefix(es): 978-1-895686; 978-1-55266
Number of titles published annually: 30 Print
Total Titles: 500 Print
Imprints: Roseway Publishing
Branch Office(s)
748 Broadway Ave, Winnipeg, MB R3G 0X3 *Tel:* 204-474-2958 *Fax:* 204-475-2813
U.S. Rep(s): Brunswick Books
Foreign Rep(s): Central Books Ltd (UK)
Orders to: Brunswick Books, 20 Maud St, Suite 303, Toronto, ON M5V 2M5 (North America & Australia) *Tel:* 416-703-3598 *Fax:* 416-703-6561 *E-mail:* orders@brunswickbooks.ca *Web Site:* www.brunswickbooks.ca; Central Books Ltd, One Heath Park Industrial Estate, Freshwater Rd, Dagenham RM8 1RX, United Kingdom (UK & Europe) *Tel:* (020) 8525 8800 *Fax:* (020) 8599 2694 *E-mail:* contactus@centralbooks.com *Web Site:* www.centralbooks.com
Returns: Brunswick Books, c/o TTS Distributing, 155 Edward St, Aurora, ON L4G IW3

Fifth House Publishers
Division of Fitzhenry & Whiteside Limited
195 Allstate Pkwy, Markham, ON L3R 4T8
Tel: 905-477-9700 *Toll Free Tel:* 800-387-9776 *Toll Free Fax:* 800-260-9777
E-mail: godwit@fitzhenry.ca; bookinfo@fitzhenry.ca (cust serv)
Web Site: www.fitzhenry.ca/fifthhouse.aspx
Key Personnel
Publr: Tracey Dettman *E-mail:* tdettman@fitzhenry.ca
Founded: 1982
Trade publisher focusing on Western Canadian interest books & First Nations titles.
Publishes in English, French.
ISBN Prefix(es): 978-0-920079; 978-1-895618; 978-1-894004; 978-1-894856; 978-1-897252; 978-1-927083
Number of titles published annually: 18 Print
Total Titles: 211 Print; 1 CD-ROM; 5 E-Book; 1 Audio
Distributed by Fitzhenry & Whiteside Limited
Orders to: Firefly Books, 50 Staples Ave, Unit 1, Richmond Hill, ON L4B 0A7 (US only) *E-mail:* service@fireflybooks.com
Returns: Firefly Books, c/o Frontier Distributing, 145 Gruner Rd, Cheektowaga, NY 14227, United States (US only)
Membership(s): Book Publishers Association of Alberta

Firefly Books Ltd
50 Staples Ave, Unit 1, Richmond Hill, ON L4B 0A7
Tel: 416-499-8412 *Toll Free Tel:* 800-387-6192 (CN); 800-387-5085 (US) *Fax:* 416-499-8313 *Toll Free Fax:* 800-450-0391 (CN); 800-565-6034 (US)
E-mail: info@fireflybooks.com
Web Site: www.fireflybooks.com
Key Personnel
Pres: Lionel Koffler
EVP: Leon Gouzoules
Lib Sales Dir: Ann Quinn *Tel:* 416-499-8412 ext 134 *E-mail:* annq@fireflybooks.com
Publicity Dir: Melissa Cilberberg *Tel:* 416-499-8412 ext 128 *E-mail:* melissa@fireflybooks.com
Rts & Contracts Mgr: Parisa Michailidis *Tel:* 416-499-8412 ext 157 *E-mail:* parisa.fireflybooks@gmail.com
Founded: 1977
Books & calendars.
Publishes in English.
ISBN Prefix(es): 978-0-920668; 978-1-895565; 978-1-896284; 978-1-55209; 978-1-55297; 978-1-55407; 978-1-77085
Number of titles published annually: 220 Print
Total Titles: 2,000 Print; 25 Online
Divisions: The Boston Mills Press
Branch Office(s)
8514 Long Canyon Dr, Austin, TX 78730-2183, United States *Tel:* 512-372-8500 *Fax:* 512-372-2499
Distributor for Boston Mills Press; Cottage Life; Kiddy Chronicles Publishing; Mikaya Press; Robert Rose Inc
Foreign Rep(s): Angell Eurosales (Gill Angell & Stewart Siddall) (Denmark, Finland, Iceland, Norway, Scandinavia, Sweden); Ashton International Marketing Services (Julian Ashton) (Asia); Baccus Books (Owen Early) (South Africa, Sub-Saharan Africa); Bookport Associates (Joe Portelli) (Greece, Italy, Malta, Portugal, Southern Europe, Spain); Cranbury International LLC (Ethan Atkin) (Caribbean, Latin America); European Marketing Services (Anselm Robinson) (Austria, Belgium, France, Germany, Switzerland, Western Europe); IMA (Anthony Moggach) (East Africa, Eastern Europe, West Africa); Chris Lloyd Sales & Marketing Services (Northern Europe, UK); Peribo Pty Ltd (Australia); Butler Sims Ltd (Ireland)
Returns: c/o Frontier Distributing, 145 Gruner Rd, Cheektowaga, NY 14227, United States
Membership(s): ABA; Association of Canadian Publishers; Canadian Booksellers Association
See separate listing for:
The Boston Mills Press

Fitzhenry & Whiteside Limited
195 Allstate Pkwy, Markham, ON L3R 4T8
SAN: 115-1444
Tel: 905-477-9700 *Toll Free Tel:* 800-387-9776 *Fax:* 905-477-2834 *Toll Free Fax:* 800-260-9777
E-mail: bookinfo@fitzhenry.ca; godwit@fitzhenry.ca
Web Site: www.fitzhenry.ca
Key Personnel
COO: Holly Doll *E-mail:* hdoll@fitzhenry.ca
CFO: Peter Stubbs
Pres: Sharon Fitzhenry *Tel:* 905-477-9700 ext 228 *E-mail:* sfitz@fitzhenry.ca
Compt: Earl Leibovitch *E-mail:* earll@fitzhenry.ca
Mktg Dir: Winston Stilwell *E-mail:* winston@fitzhenry.ca
Mgr, Cust Serv: Judy Ghoura *E-mail:* jghoura@fitzhenry.ca
Publr Rel: Sonya Gilliss *E-mail:* sonya.gilliss@fitzhenry.ca
Founded: 1966
Trade, reference & children's books, educational material for elementary, high school & college.
Publishes in English.
ISBN Prefix(es): 978-0-88902; 978-1-55005; 978-1-55041; 978-1-55285; 978-1-894004 (Fifth House); 978-1-894856 (Fifth House); 978-0-88995; 978-1-55455; 978-1-77050
Number of titles published annually: 70 Print
Total Titles: 1,100 Print
Divisions: Fifth House Publishers; Red Deer Press Inc; Whitecap Books
Distributor for Black Moss Press; Boulder Publications; ChiZine Publications; Clockwise Press; DC Books; The Glenbow Museum; Grub Street Publishing; Hades - Edge Science Fiction & Fantasy Publishing; Icon Empire Press; Inhabit Media Inc; Veronica Lane Books; Lee & Low Books; Manor House Publishing; Mosaic Press; New Internationalist Publications; Nunavut Arctic College; Annika Parance Publishing; Peachtree Publishers; Pemmican Publications; Railfare DC Books; Royal British Columbia Museum Press; Sands Press; Thirty Six Peonies Publishing; Tilbury House Publishers; Tradewind Books; Tree House Press Inc; Whitecap Books
U.S. Publishers Represented: Arbordale Publishing; ArtScroll Mesorah; Dawn Publications; Epicenter Press; Lee & Low Books; McDonald & Woodward; MVP Kids; Peachtree Publishers; Road Runner Press; Star Bright Books; teNeues; Tilbury House Publishers; Tundra Books
U.S. Rep(s): Firefly Books
Returns: Firefly Books Ltd, c/o Frontier Distributing, 145 Gruner Rd, Cheektowaga, NY 14227, United States
See separate listing for:
Fifth House Publishers
Red Deer Press Inc
Whitecap Books

Flammarion Quebec
375 Ave Laurier W, Montreal, QC H2V 2K3
Tel: 514-277-8807 *Fax:* 514-278-2085
E-mail: info@flammarion.qc.ca
Web Site: www.flammarion.qc.ca
Key Personnel
Publr: Louise Loiselle *E-mail:* lloiselle@flammarion.qc.ca
Gen Dir, Dist: Guy Gougeon
Founded: 1974
Best sellers, translations, Quebec literature, novels.
Publishes in French.
ISBN Prefix(es): 978-2-89077
Number of titles published annually: 20 Print
Total Titles: 286 Print
Imprints: Advenir; Bis (Pocket Book)
Distributor for AB Ludis; Alibi; Ambre SA; Amethis-Grenouille; Ariane; Arola; Art Global; Art Lys; Art Lys Jeunesse; Atelier 10; Artemis; Aubier; Auzou; Autrement; Beaux-Arts mag; Belize; Des Bulles dans l'Ocean; Casterman; Centre Georges Pompidou; Centre Pompidou Jeunesse; Champs; Chariot d'or; Climats; Contre-dires; De Courberon; Courrier du Livre; Dangles; Dervy; DG Duffuseur; Le Dilettante; Documents; Ego Comme X; Ensba; Esprit du livre; Exergue; Eveil et Decouvertes; Eyrolles; Fablus; Flammarion; Fluide Glacial; Genex Editions; GF; Grancher; Viviane Hamy; Harlequin; Hoebeke; Horay; J'ai lu; Jouvence Bussiere; Jungle; Lacroix; Nicole Lambert; Lerelie; De L'Herne; Librio; Lux; Josette Lyon; McGray; Medicis; Mic Mac; MK2 Editions; Musee du quai Branly; Neige-Galerie; Neopol; Nouveau Projet; Nova; Organisation-Management; Paquet; La Pasteque; Le Petit Fute; Pierre de soleil; Piktos; La Presse; Profil Sante; Pygmalion; Editions Retrouvees; Rizzoli International Publications; RMN Adulte; RMN Jeunesse; Rogers; Rue de Sevre; Sarbacane; Sarbacane BD; Sassi; Leo Scheer; Septembre Inc; Septembre Jeunesse; Skira Editore; Editions Societe du Figaro; Somogy; Sophia Publications; Spice Box; Steinkis; La Tengo; 13e Note Editions; Tom'poche; Trajectoire; Guy Tredaniel; Ullman; VDB; Vega; Vox Populi; Warum-Vraoum; Zeste
Warehouse: 420 Stinson, St-Laurent, QC H4N 2E9

Flanker Press Ltd
1243 Kenmount Rd, Unit 1, Paradise, NL A1L 0V8
Mailing Address: PO Box 2522, Sta C, St John's, NL A1C 6K1
Tel: 709-739-4477 *Toll Free Tel:* 866-739-4420 *Fax:* 709-739-4420
E-mail: info@flankerpress.com; sales@flankerpress.com
Web Site: www.flankerpress.com
Key Personnel
Pres: Garry Cranford *Tel:* 709-739-4477 ext 23
Mgr: Bob Woodworth *Tel:* 709-739-4477 ext 21
Prodn Mgr: Jerry Cranford *Tel:* 709-739-4477 ext 30
Digital Coord: Peter Hanes *Tel:* 709-739-4477 ext 29
Mktg & Publicity Coord: Laura Cameron *Tel:* 709-739-4477 ext 24
Sales Rep: Jennifer Konieczny *Tel:* 709-739-4477 ext 22
Founded: 1994
Wholly Canadian-owned trade book publisher.
Publishes in English.
ISBN Prefix(es): 978-0-9698767; 978-1-894463; 978-1-897317; 978-1-926881; 978-1-77117
Number of titles published annually: 20 Print; 20 E-Book
Imprints: Brazen Books; Flanker Press; Pennywell Books
Membership(s): Association of Canadian Publishers; Atlantic Publishers Marketing Association

Flowerpot Press
2160 S Service Rd W, Oakville, ON L6L 5N1
Tel: 416-479-0695 *Toll Free Tel:* 866-927-5001
E-mail: info@flowerpotpress.com; order@flowerpotpress.com
Web Site: www.flowerpotpress.com
Founded: 2005
Publish titles for young readers ages 4-12.
Publishes in English.
ISBN Prefix(es): 978-1-77093; 978-1-4867; 978-1-926988
Number of titles published annually: 60 Print; 60 E-Book
Total Titles: 200 Print; 350 E-Book
Editorial Office(s): 142 Second Ave N, Franklin, TN 37064, United States

Folklore Publishing
11717-9B Ave NW, Unit 2, Edmonton, AB T6J 7B7
Tel: 780-435-2376
E-mail: submissions@folklorepublishing.com (ms submissions)
Web Site: www.folklorepublishing.com
Key Personnel
Pres & Publr: Faye Boer *E-mail:* fboer@folklorepublishing.com
Founded: 2001
Publisher of popular history of North America & humor.
Publishes in English.
ISBN Prefix(es): 978-1-894864; 978-1-897206 (iThink Books); 978-1-926677
Number of titles published annually: 5 Print; 5 E-Book
Total Titles: 97 Print; 14 Online; 14 E-Book
Imprints: Full Court Press (sports history); ICON Press (celebrity bios); iThink Books (children's educ titles)
Sales Office(s): Canada Book Distributors/BookLogic, 11414 119 St NW, Edmonton, AB T5G 2X6 *Tel:* 780-433-9333 *Toll Free Tel:* 800-661-9017 *Fax:* 780-433-9646 *Toll Free Fax:* 800-424-7173 *E-mail:* info@lonepinepublishing.com *Web Site:* www.lonepinepublishing.com
Distributed by Canada Book Distributors/BookLogic
U.S. Rep(s): Lone Pine Publishing
Foreign Rep(s): Canada Book Distributors/BookLogic (Canada (English-speaking)); Gazelle Book Services Ltd (UK & the continent)
Billing Address: Canada Book Distributors/BookLogic, 11414 119 St NW, Edmonton, AB T5G 2X6 *Tel:* 780-433-9333 *Toll Free Tel:* 800-661-9017 *Fax:* 780-433-9646 *Toll Free Fax:* 800-424-7173 *E-mail:* accounts@lonepinepublishing.com *Web Site:* www.lonepinepublishing.com
Orders to: Canada Book Distributors/BookLogic, 11414 119 St NW, Edmonton, AB T5G 2X6 *Tel:* 780-433-9333 *Toll Free Tel:* 800-661-9017 *Fax:* 780-433-9646 *Toll Free Fax:* 800-424-7173 *E-mail:* accounts@lonepinepublishing.com *Web Site:* www.lonepinepublishing.com
Returns: Canada Book Distributors/BookLogic, 11414 119 St NW, Edmonton, AB T5G 2X6 *Tel:* 780-433-9333 *Toll Free Tel:* 800-661-9017 *Fax:* 780-433-9646 *Toll Free Fax:* 800-424-7173 *E-mail:* info@lonepinepublishing.com *Web Site:* www.lonepinepublishing.com
Distribution Center: Canada Book Distributors/BookLogic, 11414 119 St NW, Edmonton, AB T5G 2X6 *Tel:* 780-433-9333 *Toll Free Tel:* 800-661-9017 *Fax:* 780-433-9646 *Toll Free Fax:* 800-424-7173 *E-mail:* accounts@lonepinepublishing.com *Web Site:* www.lonepinepublishing.com
Membership(s): Book Publishers Association of Alberta

Gaetan Morin Editeur
Imprint of Cheneliere Education Inc
5800, rue St-Denis, bureau 900, Montreal, QC H2S 3L5
Tel: 514-273-1066 *Toll Free Tel:* 800-565-5531 *Fax:* 514-276-0324 *Toll Free Fax:* 800-814-0324
E-mail: info@cheneliere.ca
Web Site: www.cheneliere.ca
Key Personnel
Gen Mgr: Patrick Lutzy *E-mail:* patrick.lutzy@tc.tc
Founded: 1977
Textbooks, college, university & professional books.
Publishes in French.
ISBN Prefix(es): 978-2-89105; 978-0-88612; 978-2-910749; 978-2-89632
Number of titles published annually: 20 Print; 1 CD-ROM
Total Titles: 300 Print; 2 CD-ROM

Golden Meteorite Press
Subsidiary of Golden Meteorite Press Ltd
11919 82 St NW, Suite 103, Edmonton, AB T5B 2W4
Tel: 780-378-0063 *Fax:* 780-378-0063
Key Personnel
Ed & Lib Sales Dir: Austin Mardon *E-mail:* aamardon@yahoo.ca
Intl Rts: C Curry
Founded: 1989
Preferred submission is outline. Canadian SASE or IRC is required or else material is recycled. Accept fiction & nonfiction mss in all categories & genres. Submit to editor. Response in 12 weeks on all complete ms submissions. No phone calls please.
Publishes in English, French.
ISBN Prefix(es): 978-1-895385; 978-1-897; 978-1-894573; 978-0-929024; 978-1-897480
Number of titles published annually: 11 Print
Total Titles: 85 Print

Goose Lane Editions
500 Beaverbrook Ct, Suite 330, Fredericton, NB E3B 5X4
SAN: 115-3420
Tel: 506-450-4251 *Toll Free Tel:* 888-926-8377 *Fax:* 506-459-4991
E-mail: info@gooselane.com; customerservice@gooselane.com
Web Site: www.gooselane.com
Key Personnel
Publr: Susanne Alexander *Tel:* 506-450-4251 ext 222 *E-mail:* s.alexander@gooselane.com
Creative Dir: Julie Scriver *Tel:* 506-450-4251 ext 223 *E-mail:* jscriver@gooselane.com
Publicity Mgr: Kathleen Peacock *Tel:* 506-450-4251 ext 230 *E-mail:* publicity@gooselane.com
Fiction Ed: Bethany Gibson *E-mail:* bgibson@gooselane.com
Poetry Ed: Ross Leckie *E-mail:* rleckie@gooselane.com
Prodn Ed: Martin Ainsley *Tel:* 506-450-4251 ext 226 *E-mail:* mainsley@gooselane.com
Publg Asst: Angela Williams *Tel:* 506-450-4251 ext 225 *E-mail:* awilliams@gooselane.com
Founded: 1954
Primarily deal with Canadian authors. Submissions not accepted from outside of Canada.
Publishes in English.
ISBN Prefix(es): 978-0-920110; 978-0-919197; 978-0-86492
Number of titles published annually: 20 Print; 20 E-Book
Total Titles: 310 Print; 20 E-Book
Distributed by University of Toronto Press
Distribution Center: University of Toronto Press Distribution, 5201 Dufferin St, Toronto, ON M3H 5T8 *Tel:* 416-667-7791 *Fax:* 416-667-7832 *E-mail:* utpbooks@utpress.utoronto.ca
University of Toronto Press Distribution, 2250 Military Rd, Tonawanda, NY 14150, United States *Toll Free Tel:* 800-221-9523 *Toll Free Fax:* 800-221-9985
Membership(s): American Audiobook Publishers Association; Association of Canadian Publishers; Atlantic Publishers Marketing Association; Literary Press Group of Canada

Greystone Books Ltd
Affiliate of The Heritage Group
343 Railway St, Suite 201, Vancouver, BC V6A 1A4
Tel: 604-875-1550 *Fax:* 604-875-1556
E-mail: info@greystonebooks.com
Web Site: www.greystonebooks.com
Key Personnel
Publr: Rob Sanders *Tel:* 604-875-1550 ext 205 *E-mail:* rob.sanders@greystonebooks.com
Assoc Publr: Nancy Flight *Tel:* 604-875-1550 ext 210 *E-mail:* nancy.flight@greystonebooks.com
Sales & Mktg Dir: Jen Gauthier *Tel:* 604-875-1550 ext 202 *E-mail:* jenniferg@greystonebooks.com
Founded: 1993
Publishes in English.
ISBN Prefix(es): 978-0-88894; 978-1-55054; 978-1-55365; 978-0-88833; 978-1-77100; 978-1-927435; 978-1-77164
Number of titles published annually: 30 Print
Total Titles: 400 Print
Distributed by University of Toronto Press
U.S. Rep(s): Publishers Group West
Foreign Rights: Eliane Benisti (France); Silvia Brunelli (Italy); Marysia Juszczakiewicz (China); Yukiko Kurioka (Japan); Angela Reynolds (Portugal, Spain)
Orders to: University of Toronto Press Distribution, 5201 Dufferin St, Toronto, ON M3H 5T8 (through Pubnet) *Tel:* 416-667-7791 *Toll Free Tel:* 800-565-9523 *Fax:* 416-667-7832 *Toll Free Fax:* 800-221-9985 *E-mail:* utpbooks@utpress.utoronto.ca SAN: 115-1134; Publishers Group West/Ingram Publisher Services, 210 American Dr, Jackson, TN 38301, United States (submit orders to sales rep via IPS Cart on iPage) *Toll Free Tel:* 866-400-5351 *Toll Free Fax:* 800-838-1149 *E-mail:* ips@ingramcontent.com *Web Site:* www.ingramcontent.com; Publishers Group West/Perseus International, 250 W 57 St, 15th fl, New York, NY 10107, United States (intl orders) *Tel:* 212-581-7839 *E-mail:* intlorders@perseusbooks.com
Membership(s): AAP; Association for the Export of Canadian Books; Association of Book Publishers of British Columbia; Association of Canadian Publishers

Groundwood Books
Subsidiary of House of Anansi Press Inc
128 Sterling Rd, Lower Level, Toronto, ON M6R 2B7
Tel: 416-363-4343 *Fax:* 416-363-1017
E-mail: genmail@groundwoodbooks.com
Web Site: www.houseofanansi.com
Key Personnel
Chair: Scott Griffin
Pres & Publr: Sarah MacLachlan
VP, Fin: Allan Ibarra
VP, Publg Opers: Matt Williams
VP, Sales & Licensing: Barbara Howson
Dir, Cross-Media Dept: Erin Mallory
Edit Dir: Janie Yoon
Mktg Dir: Carolyn McNeillie
Publicity Dir: Laura Meyer
Mktg Mgr: Fred Horler
Mng Ed: Maria Golikova
Founded: 1978
Publish children's books, picture books, novels, nonfiction & folktales; publishes in Spanish also.
Publishes in English.
ISBN Prefix(es): 978-0-88899; 978-1-55498
Number of titles published annually: 25 Print
Total Titles: 500 Print
Sales Office(s): Martin & Associates Sales Agency, 594 Windermere Ave, Toronto, ON M6S 3L8 (Atlantic, ON & QC), Contact: Michael Martin *Tel:* 416-769-3947 *Toll Free Tel:* 866-225-3439 *Fax:* 416-769-5967 *E-mail:* memartin@interlog.com
Foreign Rights: Bardon Media Agency (Jianmei Wang & Cynthia Chang) (China); Japan Uni Agency Inc (Maiko Fujinaga) (Japan)
Distribution Center: University of Toronto Press Distribution Division, 5201 Dufferin St, Toronto, ON M3H 5T8 *Tel:* 416-667-7791 *Toll Free Tel:* 800-565-9523 *Fax:* 416-667-7832 *Toll Free Fax:* 800-221-9985 SAN: 115-1134
Publishers Group West/Ingram, 1700 Fourth St, Berkeley, CA 94710, United States *Toll Free Tel:* 800-343-4499 *Toll Free Fax:* 800-351-5073 *E-mail:* orderentry@ingram.com *Web Site:* www.perseusdistribution.com
Membership(s): Association of Canadian Publishers; International Board on Books for Young People; Organization of Book Publishers of Ontario

§Groupe Educalivres Inc
955, rue Bergar, Laval, QC H7L 4Z6
Tel: 514-334-8466 *Toll Free Tel:* 800-567-3671 (info serv) *Fax:* 514-334-8387
E-mail: infoservice@grandduc.com
Web Site: www.educalivres.com
Key Personnel
VP, Fin & Admin: Joe Cristofaro
Founded: 1992
School & professional textbooks.
Publishes in English, French.
ISBN Prefix(es): 978-2-7607; 978-0-03
Number of titles published annually: 3 Print

Groupe Modulo
Imprint of TC Media Books Inc
c/o TC Media Books Inc, 5800 St Denis St, Suite 900, Montreal, QC H2S 3L5
Tel: 514-273-1066 *Toll Free Tel:* 800-565-5531 *Fax:* 514-276-0234 *Toll Free Fax:* 800-814-0324
Web Site: www.groupemodulo.com
Founded: 1975
School books, dictionaries, children's books, professional & technical textbooks.
Publishes in English, French.
ISBN Prefix(es): 978-2-920922; 978-2-89443; 978-2-89113; 978-2-920210; 978-2-89593; 978-0-88560
Number of titles published annually: 100 Print
Total Titles: 2,000 Print

Groupe Sogides Inc
Division of Groupe Livre Quebecor Media Inc
955 rue Amherst, Montreal, QC H2L 3K4
Tel: 514-523-1182 *Fax:* 514-597-0370
Web Site: www.sogides.com
Key Personnel
Pres, Sogides: Celine Massicotte
VP, Publg, Grouphomme: Pierre Bourdon
Rts & Perms, Grouphomme: Florence Bisch
Founded: 1967
Practical books, cookbooks, biographies, general interest books, popular psychology, art books, poetry, diaries, art calendars & stationery, novels, drama.
Publishes in French.
ISBN Prefix(es): 978-2-7619; 978-0-7760; 978-2-89026; 978-2-89194; 978-2-89044; 978-2-89043; 978-2-89347
Number of titles published annually: 150 Print
Total Titles: 2,000 Print
Imprints: Les Editions de l'Homme; Le Jour Editeur; Utilis
Subsidiaries: Le Groupe Ville-Marie Litterature; Quinze
Branch Office(s)
Les Editions de l'Homme, c/o Messageries ADP, Immeuble Paryseine, 3 Allee de la Seine, 94854 Ivry Cedex, France, Contact: Anne Da Cunha-Guillegault *Tel:* 01 49 59 11 56 *Fax:* 01 49 59 11 33
Distributed by Vivendi Universal Publishing
Distributor for Actif; Atlas; Berlitz Fixot; Chouette; Le Cri; Edimag; Fleuve Noir; Gault & Millau; Heritage; De L'Homme; Hors Collection; JCL; Albin Michel Jeunesse; Julliard; Robert Laffont; Langues pour tous; Albin Michel; Albin Michel Education; Editions Modus Vivendi; Nathan; Nathan Education; Option Sante; Olivier Orban; Perrin; Plon; Pocket; La Presse; Presses de la Cite (Poche); Presses de la Cite Litterature; Presses Libres; Michel Quintin; Quinze; Du Rocher; Rouge & Or; Seghers; Selection du Reader's Digest; Solar; Time-Life; Trapeze; Usborne; Claire Vigne; VLB; XYZ (Typo Seulement)
U.S. Publishers Represented: Reader's Digest

Guerin Editeur Ltee
800, Blvd Industriel, bureau 200, St-Jean-sur-Richelieu, QC J3B 8G4
Tel: 514-842-3481 *Fax:* 514-842-4923
Web Site: www.guerin-editeur.qc.ca
Key Personnel
Pres. France Larochelle *E-mail:* france.larochelle@guerin-editeur.qc.ca
VP: Claude Legault
Secy: Ginette Laperriere
Founded: 1970
Publisher of books for schools from kindergarten to university.
Publishes in English, French.
ISBN Prefix(es): 978-2-7601
Number of titles published annually: 80 Print; 2 Audio
Total Titles: 2,300 Print; 43 Audio
Foreign Rep(s): Librairie du Quebec (France); Librairie Pelagie (Eastern Canada); Patrimoine SPRL (Belgium); Servidis SA (Switzerland); Sopodriff Sarl (Africa); Pierre Carme Yves Levy (Haiti)

§Guernica Editions Inc
1569 Heritage Way, Oakville, ON L6M 2Z7
Tel: 905-599-5304
E-mail: info@guernicaeditions.com
Web Site: www.guernicaeditions.com
Key Personnel
Publr & Chief Admin Offr: Connie McParland *E-mail:* conniemcparland@guernicaeditions.com
Publr & Ed-in-Chief: Michael Mirolla *E-mail:* michaelmirolla@guernicaeditions.com
Admin Asst/Publicist: Anna Geisler *E-mail:* annageisler@guernicaeditions.com
Founded: 1978
Literary press specializing in Canadian writing (prose, poetry, literary criticism, drama & social studies), translation into English, some foreign publications in the English language.
Publishes in English.
ISBN Prefix(es): 978-0-919349; 978-0-920717; 978-2-89135; 978-1-55071; 978-1-77183
Number of titles published annually: 25 Print
Total Titles: 450 Print
Sales Office(s): Literary Press Group, 425 Adelaide St W, Suite 700, Toronto, ON M5V 3C1, Sales Mgr & US Rep: Tan Light *Tel:* 416-483-1321 *Fax:* 416-483-2510 *E-mail:* sales@lpg.ca *Web Site:* www.lpg.ca
Distribution Center: University of Toronto Press, 5201 Dufferin St, Toronto, ON M3H 5T8 *Toll Free Tel:* 800-565-9523 *Toll Free Fax:* 800-221-9985
Gazelle Book Services Ltd, White Cross Mills, Hightown, Lancaster, Lancs LA1 1XS, United Kingdom *Tel:* (01524) 68765 *Fax:* (01524) 63232 *E-mail:* sales@gazellebookservices.co.uk *Web Site:* www.gazellebookservices.co.uk

Hancock House Publishers Ltd
19313 Zero Ave, Surrey, BC V3S 9R9
Mailing Address: 1431 Harrison Ave, Blaine, WA 98230-5005, United States
Tel: 604-538-1114 *Toll Free Tel:* 800-938-1114 *Fax:* 604-538-2262 *Toll Free Fax:* 800-983-2262
E-mail: sales@hancockhouse.com; info@hancockhouse.com
Web Site: www.hancockhouse.com
Key Personnel
Pres: David Hancock
Founded: 1975
Biographical nature guide books.
Publishes in English.
ISBN Prefix(es): 978-0-88839; 978-0-919654; 978-1-55205
Number of titles published annually: 20 Print
Total Titles: 450 Print
Foreign Rep(s): Gazelle Book Services Ltd (UK)

Harbour Publishing Co Ltd
4437 Rondeview Rd, Madeira Park, BC V0N 2H0
Mailing Address: PO Box 219, Madeira Park, BC V0N 2H0
Tel: 604-883-2730 *Toll Free Tel:* 800-667-2988 *Fax:* 604-883-9451
E-mail: info@harbourpublishing.com
Web Site: www.harbourpublishing.com
Key Personnel
Publr: Howard White
Mktg Mgr: Marisa Alps
Prodn Coord: Anna Comfort
Founded: 1972
History & culture of British Columbia & West Coast, including fiction, nonfiction & poetry by Canadian authors.
Publishes in English.
ISBN Prefix(es): 978-0-920080; 978-1-55017
Number of titles published annually: 20 Print; 1 CD-ROM; 1 Audio
Total Titles: 600 Print; 1 CD-ROM; 5 Audio
Imprints: Lost Moose Books
Distributor for Nightwood Editions
Foreign Rep(s): Ampersand Inc (Canada); Gazelle Book Services Ltd (Eastern Europe, Ireland, UK, Western Europe)
Orders to: 12672 Lagoon Rd, Madeira Park, BC V0N 2H0 *E-mail:* orders@harbourpublishing.com
Warehouse: 12672 Lagoon Rd, Madeira Park, BC V0N 2H0 *Tel:* 604-883-2460
Distribution Center: 12672 Lagoon Rd, Madeira Park, BC V0N 2H0

Harlequin Enterprises Ltd
Division of HarperCollins
225 Duncan Mill Rd, Don Mills, ON M3B 3K9
SAN: 115-3749
Mailing Address: PO Box 603, Fort Erie, ON L2A 5X3
Tel: 416-445-5860 *Toll Free Tel:* 888-432-4879; 800-370-5838 (ebook inquiries)
E-mail: customerservice@harlequin.com
Web Site: www.harlequin.com
Key Personnel
CEO & Publr: Craig Swinwood
COO, Intl: Steve Miles
CFO: Andrew Wright
EVP, Direct to Consumer: Christina Clifford
EVP, Global Publg & Strategy: Loriana Sacilotto
EVP, Mktg & Digital: Brent Lewis
VP, Opers & Admin: Jim Robinson
VP, Retail Sales: Alex Osuszek
VP & CIO Info Systems: Margaret Morrison
VP, Series Edit & Subs Rts: Dianne Moggy
VP, Gen Coun & Secy: Karen Louie
Dir, Digital Prods: Farah Mullick
Dir, Overseas Publg Strategy: Emily Martin
Dir, Subs Rts & Harlequin Audio: Reka Rubin
Dir, Young Adult Prod: Amy Jones
Edit Dir, Carina Press: Angela James
Edit Dir, Harlequin Teen: Natashya Wilson
Edit Dir, HQN Books & Graydon House Books: Susan Swinwood
Edit Dir, MIRA: Nicole Brebner
Edit Dir, Park Row Books: Erika Imranyi
Global Mng Ed: Roxanne Finkelstein
Asst Mng Ed: Punam Patel
Mng Edit Coord, NY/Toronto: Beth Attwood
Edit Coord, MIRA: Margot Mallinson
Sr Ed, HQN, LUNA & Teen: Margo Lipschultz
Ed: Adrienne Macintosh; Karen Reid
Ed, Graydon House Books: Melanie Fried
Assoc Ed: Dana Grimaldi
Assoc Ed, Kimani: Rachel Burkot
Asst Ed, Harlequin American, Blaze, Worldwide Library, BAC: Dana Hopkins
Asst Ed, Harlequin Romantic Suspense: Dana Hamilton
Asst Ed, HQN: Brittany Lavery; Kate Studer
Asst Ed, MIRA: Michelle Venditti
Asst Ed, Superromance & DTC: Piya Campana
Sr Mgr, PR: Michelle Renaud *E-mail:* publicrelations@harlequin.ca
Mgr, Author Engagement: Miranda Indrigo
Founded: 1949 (in Winnipeg, MB, CN)
Publishes in 34 languages in 110 international markets on 6 continents.
Publishes in English, French.
ISBN Prefix(es): 978-0-373; 978-1-55166; 978-0-7783; 978-1-58314; 978-1-55254; 978-1-4268; 978-1-4603; 978-1-4592
Number of titles published annually: 1,320 Print; 30 Online; 1,530 E-Book; 75 Audio
Total Titles: 30 Online; 1,850 E-Book; 95 Audio
Imprints: Carina Press (digital-first); Graydon House Books (commercial women's fiction); Harlequin Books (series romance); Harlequin HQN (romance fiction); Harlequin Kimani Arabesque; Harlequin Kimani Press (African-American); Harlequin Kimani TRU; Harlequin LUNA (fantasy/paranormal); Harlequin MIRA; Harlequin Teen (young adult fiction); HQ; Love Inspired Books (inspirational romance); Rogue Angel; Silhouette Books (series romance); Spice (erotic fiction); Worldwide Library (mystery fiction); Worldwide Mystery
Branch Office(s)
233 Broadway, Suite 1001, New York, NY 10279, United States *Tel:* 212-553-4200 *Fax:* 212-227-8969 SAN: 200-2450
Foreign Office(s): Harlequin Mills & Boon, 18-24 Paradise Rd, Richmond, Surrey TW9 1SR, United Kingdom *Tel:* (020) 8288 2800 *Fax:* (020) 8288 2899 *Web Site:* www.millsandboon.co.uk
Advertising Agency: Vickers & Benson-Direct
Distribution Center: 3010 Walden Ave, Depew, NY 14043, United States
Membership(s): AAP; Association of Canadian Publishers; BISG
See separate listing for:
Worldwide Library

§HarperCollins Canada Ltd
Division of HarperCollins Publishers
2 Bloor St E, 20th fl, Toronto, ON M4W 1A8
Tel: 416-975-9334 *Fax:* 416-975-5223
E-mail: hcorder@harpercollins.com
Web Site: www.harpercollins.ca
Key Personnel
SVP & Exec Publr: Iris Tupholme *Tel:* 416-975-9334 ext 123 *E-mail:* Iris.Tupholme@HarperCollins.com
VP, Mktg & Sales: Leo MacDonald
Publr, Patrick Crean Editions: Patrick Crean
Sr Dir, Publicity & Communs: Rob Firing *Tel:* 416-975-9334 ext 141 *E-mail:* Rob.Firing@HarperCollins.com
Sr Coun & Dir, Legal Aff: Jeremy Rawlings
Dir, Subs Rts & Publg Opers: Lisa Rundle
Founded: 1989
Literary & commercial fiction, nonfiction, children's books, cookbooks, reference & spiritual books. Distribute for all HarperCollins companies in the US, UK & Australia.
Publishes in English.
ISBN Prefix(es): 978-1-4434
Number of titles published annually: 100 Print
Total Titles: 1,500 Print
Imprints: Collins; Patrick Crean Editions; Harper Avenue; HarperCollins Canada; Harper Perennial; HarperWeekend

Heritage House Publishing Co Ltd
Member of The Heritage Group
1075 Pendergast St, No 103, Victoria, BC V8V 0A1
Tel: 250-360-0829 *Fax:* 250-386-0829
E-mail: heritage@heritagehouse.ca
Web Site: www.heritagehouse.ca
Key Personnel
Publr: Rodger Touchie
Sr Ed: Lara Kordic
Publicity: Leslie Kenny

Founded: 1969
Publishes in English.
ISBN Prefix(es): 978-1-895811; 978-1-894384; 978-1-894974; 978-0-919214; 978-0-9690546; 978-1-926613; 978-1-926936; 978-1-927051; 978-1-927527
Number of titles published annually: 30 Print
Total Titles: 175 Print
Orders to: Heritage Group Distribution, 19272 96 Ave, Suite 8, Surrey, BC V4N 4C1 *Tel:* 604-881-7067 *Toll Free Tel:* 800-665-3302 *Fax:* 604-881-7068 *Toll Free Fax:* 800-566-3336 *E-mail:* orders@hgdistribution.com
Distribution Center: Heritage Group Distribution, 19272 96 Ave, Suite 8, Surrey, BC V4N 4C1 *Tel:* 604-881-7067 *Toll Free Tel:* 800-665-3302 *Fax:* 604-881-7068 *Toll Free Fax:* 800-566-3336 *E-mail:* orders@hgdistribution.com
Membership(s): Association of Book Publishers of British Columbia; Association of Canadian Publishers

Les Heures bleues
560, rue Mercier, St-Lambert, QC J4P 1Z5
Tel: 450-671-7718 *Fax:* 450-671-7718
E-mail: info@heuresbleues.com
Web Site: www.heuresbleues.com
Key Personnel
Pres: Rene Bonenfant
Founded: 1996
Publishes in French.
ISBN Prefix(es): 978-2-922265
Number of titles published annually: 8 Print
Total Titles: 90 Print; 40 E-Book
Distribution Center: Dimedia, 539, blvd Lebeau, St-Laurent, QC H4N 1S2
Membership(s): Association Nationale des Editeurs de Livres

§House of Anansi Press Inc
128 Sterling Rd, Lower Level, Toronto, ON M6R 2B7
Tel: 416-363-4343 *Fax:* 416-363-1017
E-mail: customerservice@houseofanansi.com
Web Site: www.houseofanansi.com
Key Personnel
Pres & Publr: Sarah MacLachlan
VP, Publg Opers: Matt Williams
VP, Sales & Licensing: Barbara Howson
Dir, Cross-Media Group: Erin Mallory
Edit Dir: Janie Yoon
Mktg Dir: Carolyn McNeillie
Publicity Dir: Laura Meyer
Ed: Douglas Richmond
Sr Publicist: Cindy Ma
Publicist: Lindsay Holung
Intl Sales Assoc: Caryn Cathcart
Founded: 1967
Literary publishing; fiction, poetry, criticism & belles lettres.
Publishes in English.
ISBN Prefix(es): 978-0-88784; 978-1-77089; 978-1-48700
Number of titles published annually: 30 Print
Total Titles: 200 Print
Imprints: Ambrosia; Anansi International; Arachnide Editions; Astoria; Spiderline (crime fiction)
Subsidiaries: Groundwood Books
Foreign Rights: Akcali Copyright Agency (Atilla Turgut) (Turkey); Anthea Agency (Zlatka Paskaleva) (Bulgaria); Bestun Agency (Yumi Chun) (Korea); Big Apple Agency (Amanda Chen) (Mainland China); Big Apple Agency (Chris Lin) (Taiwan); Paul & Peter Fritz Agency (Antonia Fritz) (Germany); Japan Uni Agency Inc (Yukiko Kurioka) (Japan); Antonia Kerrigan Agency (Antonia Kerrigan) (Latin America, Spain); Simona Kessler Agency (Simona Kessler) (Romania)
Distribution Center: Publishers Group West/ Perseus Books Group, 1700 Fourth St, Berkeley, CA 94710, United States (US orders) *Tel:* 510-809-3700 *Toll Free Tel:* 800-343-4499 *Fax:* 510-809-3777 *Toll Free Fax:* 800-351-5073 *Web Site:* www.pgw.com
See separate listing for:
Groundwood Books

C D Howe Institute
67 Yonge St, Suite 300, Toronto, ON M5E 1J8
Tel: 416-865-1904 *Fax:* 416-865-1866
E-mail: cdhowe@cdhowe.org
Web Site: www.cdhowe.org
Key Personnel
Pres & CEO: William B P Robson *E-mail:* bill_robson@cdhowe.org
SVP & COO: Duncan Munn *E-mail:* dmunn@cdhowe.org
VP, Media & Ed: James Fleming *Tel:* 416-865-1904 ext 9216 *E-mail:* jfleming@cdhowe.org
Founded: 1958
Economics & social policy studies.
Publishes in English, French.
ISBN Prefix(es): 978-0-88806
Number of titles published annually: 48 Print
Total Titles: 150 Print
Distributed by Renouf Publishing Co (Ottawa)

Inclusion Press International
47 Indian Trail, Toronto, ON M6R 1Z8
Tel: 416-658-5363 *Fax:* 416-658-5067
E-mail: inclusionpress@inclusion.com
Web Site: www.inclusion.com
Key Personnel
Founding Publr: Marsha Forest; Jack Pearpoint *E-mail:* jack@inclusion.com
Founded: 1989
Inclusion, change, diversity & community.
Publishes in English.
ISBN Prefix(es): 978-1-895418
Number of titles published annually: 5 Print; 2 CD-ROM; 2 E-Book
Total Titles: 100 Print; 10 CD-ROM; 4 E-Book
Distribution Center: Inclusion Distribution, United Kingdom

Insomniac Press
520 Princess Ave, London, ON N6B 2B8
Tel: 519-266-3556
Web Site: www.insomniacpress.com
Key Personnel
Publr: Mike O'Connor *E-mail:* mike@insomniacpress.com
Mng Ed: Dan Varrette *E-mail:* dan@insomniacpress.com
Founded: 1992
General trade publisher of fiction, nonfiction & poetry.
Publishes in English.
ISBN Prefix(es): 978-1-895837; 978-1-894663; 978-1-897178; 978-1-897414; 978-1-897415; 978-1-926582; 978-1-55483
Number of titles published annually: 16 Print
Total Titles: 235 Print
Orders to: LitDistCo, 8300 Lawson Rd, Milton, ON L9T 0A4 (CN & US) *Toll Free Tel:* 800-591-6250 *Toll Free Fax:* 800-591-6251 *E-mail:* ordering@litdistco.ca *Web Site:* www.litdistco.ca; The Literary Press Group of Canada, 425 Adelaide St W, Suite 700, Toronto, ON M5V 3C1 (CN & US) *Tel:* 416-483-1321 *Fax:* 416-483-2510 *Web Site:* www.lpg.ca; Wakefield Press, One The Parade West, Kent Town, SA 5067, Australia (Australia) *Tel:* (08) 8362 8800 *Fax:* (08) 8362 7592 *Web Site:* www.wakefieldpress.com.au; BookWise Asia Pte Ltd, D'Centennial, Suite 03-02, 100 Lorong 23 Geylang, Singapore 388398, Singapore (Southeast Asia) *Tel:* 6743 2815 *Fax:* 6743 2817 *Web Site:* www.bookwise.com.au/publishers; Gazelle Book Services Ltd, White Cross Mills, Hightown, Lancaster, Lancs LA1 4XS, United Kingdom (UK & Europe) *Tel:* (01524) 528500 *Fax:* (01524) 528510 *E-mail:* sales@gazellebookservices.co.uk *Web Site:* www.gazellebookservices.co.uk
Membership(s): Literary Press Group of Canada

L'Institut canadien du droit des ressources, see Canadian Institute of Resources Law (L'Institut canadien du droit des ressources)

Institute for Research on Public Policy (IRPP)
1470 Peel St, No 200, Montreal, QC H3A 1T1
Tel: 514-985-2461 *Fax:* 514-985-2559
E-mail: irpp@irpp.org
Web Site: irpp.org
Key Personnel
Pres & CEO: Graham Fox *E-mail:* gfox@irpp.org
VP, Opers: Suzanne Ostiguy McIntyre *Tel:* 514-787-0740 *E-mail:* smcintyre@irpp.org
VP, Res: France St-Hilaire *E-mail:* fsthilaire@irpp.org
Res Dir: Joanne Castonguay *E-mail:* jcastonguay@irpp.org; Stephen Tapp *E-mail:* stapp@irpp.org
Edit Coord: Francesca Worrall *E-mail:* fworrall@irpp.org
Founded: 1972
Research on public policy.
Publishes in English, French.
ISBN Prefix(es): 978-0-88645; 978-0-920380
Number of titles published annually: 200 Online
Total Titles: 500 Print

Institute of Intergovernmental Relations
Queen's University, Robert Sutherland Hall, Rm 301, Kingston, ON K7L 3N6
Tel: 613-533-2080 *Fax:* 613-533-6868
E-mail: iigr@queensu.ca
Web Site: www.queensu.ca/iigr
Key Personnel
Dir: Dr Elizabeth Goodyear-Grant
Pubns Coord & Admin Secy: Mary Kennedy
Founded: 1965
Publish research & other scholarly work on Canadian federalism & intergovernmental relations; ethnicity, government & political science.
Publishes in English, French.
ISBN Prefix(es): 978-1-55339
Number of titles published annually: 4 Print
Total Titles: 96 Print
Distribution Center: McGill-Queen's University Press, Georgetown Terminal Warehouses, 34 Armstrong Ave, Georgetown, ON L7G 4R9 *Tel:* 905-873-2750 *Fax:* 905-873-6170

Institute of Psychological Research, Inc.
76 Ave, Mozart W, Montreal, QC H2S 1C4
Tel: 514-382-3000 *Toll Free Tel:* 800-363-7800 *Fax:* 514-382-3007 *Toll Free Fax:* 888-382-3007
E-mail: info@irpcanada.com
Web Site: www.irpcanada.com
Founded: 1958 (incorporated in 1964)
Psychological tests & materials.
Publishes in English, French.
ISBN Prefix(es): 978-0-88509; 978-2-89109
Number of titles published annually: 10 Print
Imprints: IPR; IRP
Distributed by Editions Editest (Belgium); Librairie du Quebec a Paris (France)
Distributor for Aseba (CN); Hogrefe France (CN); Hans Huber (Rorschach only)
U.S. Publishers Represented: Academic Therapy Publications; American Orthopsychiatric; Behavior Sciences Systems; Editions Behaviora; Martin M Bruce; Cardall Associates; Center for Psychological Services; Clinical Psychology Publishing; Nigel Cox; Educational & Clinical Publications; Educational Industrial Testing Service; Educational Performance Associate; Educators Publishing Services; Granada Learning; Guidance Associates of Delaware; Harvard University Press; Hogrefe UK; Industrial Psychology; Institute for Personality & Ability Testing; International Tests; Lafayette

Instrument; Language Research Associates; Multi Health Systems; National Foundation for Educational Research; Pacific Book; Pro Ed; Psychological Assessment Resources; Psychological Test Specialists; Psychologists & Educators; Research Psychologist Press; Sheridan Psychological Services; Stoelting; Western Psychological Services

Institute of Public Administration of Canada
1075 Bay St, Suite 401, Toronto, ON M5S 2B1
Tel: 416-924-8787 *Fax:* 416-924-4992
E-mail: ntl@ipac.ca
Web Site: www.ipac.ca
Key Personnel
CEO: Robert Taylor, PhD *Tel:* 416-924-8787 ext 230 *E-mail:* rtaylor@ipac.ca
Mng Ed: Christy Paddick *Tel:* 905-447-6351 (cell) *E-mail:* cpaddick@ipac.ca
Ed: Evert A Lindquist
Founded: 1947
National bilingual English/French nonprofit organization, concerned with the theory & practice of public management, with 20 regional groups across Canada. Provide networks & forums regionally, nationally & internationally. Specialize in political science, Canadian history & Canadian law.
Publishes in English, French.
ISBN Prefix(es): 978-0-919400; 978-0-920715; 978-0-919696; 978-1-55061
Number of titles published annually: 10 Print; 5 E-Book
Total Titles: 600 Print; 50 Online; 10 E-Book; 5 Audio

International Travel Maps & Books, see ITMB Publishing Ltd

Irwin Law Inc
14 Duncan St, Suite 206, Toronto, ON M5H 3G8
SAN: 810-0144
Tel: 416-862-7690 *Toll Free Tel:* 888-314-9014 *Fax:* 416-862-9236
Web Site: www.irwinlaw.com
Key Personnel
Pres & Publr: Jeffrey Miller *Tel:* 416-862-7690 ext 23 *E-mail:* jmiller@irwinlaw.com
VP: Alisa Posesorski *E-mail:* aposes@irwinlaw.com
Founded: 1996
Publisher of books & other material for lawyers & law students.
Publishes in English.
ISBN Prefix(es): 978-1-55221
Number of titles published annually: 20 Print; 20 E-Book
Total Titles: 200 Print; 100 E-Book
Distributor for The Federation Press (North America only)
Foreign Rep(s): The Federation Press (Australia, New Zealand)
Distribution Center: Gaunt Inc, Gaunt Bldg, 3011 Gulf Dr, Holmes Beach, FL 34217, United States *Tel:* 941-778-5211 *Toll Free Tel:* 800-942-8683 *Fax:* 941-778-5252 SAN: 202-9413
Membership(s): Association of Canadian Publishers; Organization of Book Publishers of Ontario

ITMB Publishing Ltd
12300 Bridgeport Rd, Richmond, BC V6V 1J5
Tel: 604-273-1400 *Fax:* 604-273-1488
E-mail: itmb@itmb.com
Web Site: www.itmb.com
Key Personnel
Pres: Jack Joyce
Founded: 1983
Publisher/distributor of international travel maps & atlases.
Publishes in English.
ISBN Prefix(es): 978-1-55341; 978-0-921463; 978-1-895907
Number of titles published annually: 30 Print
Total Titles: 425 Print
Distributor for Borch; Freytag & Bernot; Gizi; National Geographic; Nelles; Rand McNally
Membership(s): International Map Industry Association

Ivey Publishing, see Richard Ivey School of Business

Richard Ivey School of Business
Division of Ivey Management Services
Ivey Business School at Western University, 1255 Western Rd, London, ON N6G 0N1
Tel: 519-661-3206; 519-661-3208 *Toll Free Tel:* 800-649-6355 *Fax:* 519-661-3485; 519-661-3882
E-mail: cases@ivey.uwo.ca
Web Site: www.iveycases.com; www.ivey.uwo.ca
Founded: 1923
Publish business case studies for university business courses.
Publishes in English, French.
ISBN Prefix(es): 978-0-919534
Number of titles published annually: 200 Print
Total Titles: 3,500 Print
Distributed by Caseplace (The Aspen Institute's Centre for Business Education); Cengage Learning (USA); Centrale de Cas et de Medias Pedagogiques (CCMP) (Paris, France); College of Commerce (National Chengchi University, Taiwan); European Case Clearing House (ECCH) (UK); IESE Publishing (Spain); Institute for International Studies and Training (IIST) (Japan); LAD Publishing (USA); McGraw-Hill (USA); National Archive Publishing (USA); Pearson Custom Publishing (USA); Study.Net (USA); University Readers Inc (USA)
Distributor for Asian Business Case Center/Nanyang Business School at Nanyang Technological University; China-Europe International Business School (CEIBS); China Management Case Sharing Centre; China University of Hong Kong; College of Commerce (National Chengchi University, Taiwan); Darden Business School; Gordon Institute of Business Science (University of Pretoria, South Africa); Harvard Business Review; Harvard Business School Publishing; Indian Institute of Management Bangalore; Indian School of Business (India); Ivey Business Journal (reprints); National University of Singapore; Northeastern University; Peking University (China); Thunderbird School of Global Management; Tsinghua University (China); University of Regina-Paul J Hill School of Business; University of West Indies; Yonsei University (Korea; Harvard Business School cases & Harvard Business Review reprints)
U.S. Rep(s): Harvard Business School Publishing (case studies & HBR reprints)
Foreign Rep(s): European Case Clearing House (Europe)

Kids Can Press Ltd
Division of Corus Entertainment Inc
25 Dockside Dr, Toronto, ON M5A 0B5
Tel: 416-479-7000 *Toll Free Tel:* 800-265-0884 *Fax:* 416-960-5437
E-mail: info@kidscan.com; customerservice@kidscan.com
Web Site: www.kidscanpress.com; www.kidscanpress.ca
Key Personnel
Pres: Lisa Lyons Johnston
Cont, Corus Entertainment: June Samms
Assoc Publr: Semareh Al-Hillal
Art Dir: Marie Bartholomew
Edit Dir: Yvette Ghione
Mktg Dir: Naseem Hrab
Rts Dir: Adrienne Tang
Sales Dir: Molly Helferty
Digital Busn Devt Mgr: Amelie Roberge
Mng Ed: Jennifer Grimbleby
Sr Ed: Yasemin Ucar
Ed: Jennifer Stokes
Founded: 1973
Books for children exclusively.
Publishes in English.
ISBN Prefix(es): 978-0-919964; 978-1-55074; 978-1-55337; 978-0-921103; 978-1-55453; 978-1-77138; 978-1-5253
Number of titles published annually: 75 Print; 75 Online; 70 E-Book
Total Titles: 500 Print; 715 Online; 240 E-Book
Imprints: CitizenKid™; Franklin the Turtle; KCP Loft; Kids Can Do It; Scaredy Squirrel
Distributed by Hachette Book Group
Orders to: Hachette Book Group, 185 N Mount Zion Rd, Lebanon, IN 46052, United States *Toll Free Tel:* 800-759-0190 *Toll Free Fax:* 800-286-9471 *Web Site:* www.hachettebookgroup.com
Returns: Hachette Book Group, c/o GTW, 34 Armstrong Ave, Georgetown, ON L7G 4R9 (CN) *Tel:* 905-873-2750 *Fax:* 905-873-6171 *E-mail:* orders@gtwcanada.com *Web Site:* gtwcanada.com; Hachette Book Group, 322 S Enterprise Group, Lebanon, IN 46052, United States (US) *Toll Free Tel:* 800-759-0190 *Toll Free Fax:* 800-286-9471 *Web Site:* www.hachettebookgroup.com
Shipping Address: Hachette Book Group, 185 N Mount Zion Rd, Lebanon, IN 46052, United States *Toll Free Tel:* 800-759-0190 *Toll Free Fax:* 800-286-9471 *Web Site:* www.hachettebookgroup.com
Distribution Center: Hachette Book Group, 185 N Mount Zion Rd, Lebanon, IN 46052, United States *Toll Free Tel:* 800-759-0190 *Toll Free Fax:* 800-286-9471 *Web Site:* www.hachettebookgroup.com
Membership(s): Association of Canadian Publishers; The Children's Book Council; Organization of Book Publishers of Ontario

Kindred Productions
Division of Mennonite Brethren Church
1310 Taylor Ave, Winnipeg, MB R3M 3Z6
Tel: 204-669-6575 *Toll Free Tel:* 800-545-7322 *Fax:* 204-654-1865
E-mail: kindred@mbchurches.ca
Web Site: www.kindredproductions.com
Key Personnel
Cust Serv Rep: Helga Kasdorf
Founded: 1982
Denominational material, Low German Bible, trade books & church resources.
Publishes in English, French.
ISBN Prefix(es): 978-0-919797; 978-0-921788; 978-1-894791
Number of titles published annually: 15 Print
Total Titles: 250 Print

Kinesiology Books Publisher
Subsidiary of Sport Books Publisher
212 Robert St (side basement door), Toronto, ON M5S 2K7
Tel: 416-323-9438 *Fax:* 416-966-9022
E-mail: sbp@sportbookspub.com; kbp@kinesiology101.com
Web Site: www.sportbookspub.com
Key Personnel
Pres: Dr Peter Klavora *E-mail:* peter.klavora@utoronto.ca
Exec Dir: Tania Klavora
Founded: 1983
Activity books, sports books & DVDs; subjects include physical education, exercise science textbooks & kinesiology. Orders accepted by mail, fax or online. Returns accepted if in mint condition.

Publishes in English, French.
ISBN Prefix(es): 978-0-920905
Number of titles published annually: 5 Print; 1 CD-ROM
Total Titles: 48 Print; 3 CD-ROM
Branch Office(s)
PO Box 2583, Niagara Falls, NY 14302, United States

Knopf Canada
Imprint of Penguin Random House Canada
320 Front St W, Suite 1400, Toronto, ON M5V 3B6
SAN: 201-3975
Tel: 416-364-4449 *Toll Free Tel:* 888-523-9292 *Fax:* 416-598-7764
Web Site: www.penguinrandomhouse.ca
Key Personnel
Pres & Publr, PRHC: Kristin Cochrane
Exec Publr & EVP, PRHC: Louise Dennys
Pres & CEO: Brad Martin
EVP & CFO: Barry Gallant
SVP & COO: Robert Wheaton
SVP, Corp Communs & VP, Publicity: Tracey Turriff
SVP & Dir, Prodn: Janine Laporte
VP & Deputy Publr, PRHC: Marion Garner
VP & Publr, KRC: Anne Collins
Publg Dir, KC: Lynn Henry
Founded: 1991
Penguin Random House Canada & its publishing entities are not accepting unsol submissions, proposals, mss, or submission queries via e-mail at this time.
Publishes in English.
ISBN Prefix(es): 978-0-307; 978-0-676
Number of titles published annually: 40 Print
Imprints: Vintage Canada
Distributed by Penguin Random House Canada
Shipping Address: Penguin Random House Canada, 6971 Columbus Rd, Mississauga, ON L5T 1K1
Membership(s): Canadian Booksellers Association; Canadian Publishers' Council

Laurier Books Ltd
PO Box 8493, Ottawa, ON K1G 3H9
SAN: 168-2806
Tel: 613-738-2163 *Toll Free Fax:* 855-736-9160
E-mail: laurierbooks@yahoo.com
Key Personnel
Pres: L Marthe
Lib Sales Dir: R Lalwani
Founded: 1975
All foreign language dictionaries, Native American publications, annuals, bibliographic products, business directories, distribution, publishing, mail orders.
Publishes in English.
ISBN Prefix(es): 978-1-895959; 978-1-55394
Number of titles published annually: 15 Print
Total Titles: 3,000 Print
U.S. Rep(s): IBD Ltd

§LexisNexis® Canada Inc
Member of The LexisNexis® Group
111 Gordon Baker Rd, Suite 900, Toronto, ON M2H 3R1
Tel: 905-479-2665 *Toll Free Tel:* 800-668-6481; 800-387-0899 (cust care); 800-255-5174 (sales)
E-mail: service@lexisnexis.ca (cust serv); sales@lexisnexis.ca
Web Site: www.lexisnexis.ca
Key Personnel
Dir, Training & Cust Care: Jeff Morrison *E-mail:* jeff.morrison@lexisnexis.ca
Cust Serv Mgr, Print & CD-ROM Div: Barbara Brumwell *Tel:* 905-415-5816 *E-mail:* barbara.brumwell@lexisnexis.ca
Prog Coord: Luc Meloche *E-mail:* luc.meloche@lexisnexis.ca
Founded: 1912
Books, looseleaf services, newsletters, journals, legal publishing & online services.
Publishes in English, French.
ISBN Prefix(es): 978-0-409; 978-0-433
Number of titles published annually: 80 Print; 20 CD-ROM
Branch Office(s)
112 Kent St, Suite 700, Ottawa, ON K1P 5P2 *Tel:* 613-238-3499 *Toll Free Tel:* 800-387-0899
1200 Ave McGill College, Suite 1100, Montreal, QC H3B 4G7 *Tel:* 514-287-0339

Lidec Inc
800, blvd Industriel, bureau 202, Saint-Jean-sur-Richlieu, QC J3B 8G4
Tel: 514-843-5991 *Toll Free Tel:* 800-350-5991 (CN only) *Fax:* 514-843-5252
E-mail: lidec@lidec.qc.ca
Web Site: www.lidec.qc.ca
Founded: 1965
Publisher of school books.
Publishes in English, French.
ISBN Prefix(es): 978-2-7608
Number of titles published annually: 30 Print
Total Titles: 1,500 Print

Life Cycle Books Ltd
11 Progress Ave, Unit 6, Toronto, ON M1P 4S7
SAN: 110-8417
Toll Free Tel: 866-880-5860 *Toll Free Fax:* 866-260-8172
E-mail: orders@lifecyclebooks.ca; billing@lifecyclebooks.ca; support@lifecyclebooks.ca
Web Site: www.lifecyclebooks.com
Key Personnel
Founder & Pres: Paul Broughton *E-mail:* paulb@lifecyclebooks.com
Founded: 1973
Human life issues.
Publishes in English, French.
ISBN Prefix(es): 978-0-919225
Number of titles published annually: 3 Print
Total Titles: 41 Print
Branch Office(s)
PO Box 799, Fort Collins, CO 80522, United States *Toll Free Tel:* 800-214-5849

Lone Pine Publishing
87 E Pender, Vancouver, BC V6A 1S9
SAN: 115-4125
Mailing Address: 11414 119 St NW, Edmonton, AB T5G 2X6
Tel: 780-433-9333 *Toll Free Tel:* 800-661-9017 *Fax:* 780-433-9646 *Toll Free Fax:* 800-424-7173
E-mail: info@lonepinepublishing.com
Web Site: www.lonepinepublishing.com
Key Personnel
Pres: Shane Kennedy
US Sales Mgr: Michael O Campbell
Founded: 1980
Natural history, travel, recreation, popular history, bird guides & gardening.
Publishes in English.
ISBN Prefix(es): 978-1-55105; 978-1-894877 (Ghost House Books); 978-0-919433
Number of titles published annually: 30 Print
Total Titles: 800 Print; 25 E-Book
Imprints: Ghost House Books
Branch Office(s)
1808 "B" St NW, Suite 140, Auburn, WA 98001, United States, Sales Mgr: Michael Campbell *Tel:* 253-394-0400 *Toll Free Tel:* 800-518-3541 *Fax:* 253-394-0405 *Toll Free Fax:* 800-548-1169 *E-mail:* mikec@lonepinepublishing.com
Distributor for Blue Bike Books; Dragon Hill Publishing; Eschia Books; Folklore Publishing; Editions de la Montagne Verte; Partners Publishing; Quagmire Press; Red Deer College Press
U.S. Rep(s): Baker & Taylor; Benjamin News; Book People; Ingram Book Co; Sunbelt

James Lorimer & Co Ltd, Publishers
117 Peter St, Suite 304, Toronto, ON M5V 0M3
Tel: 416-362-4762 *Fax:* 416-362-3939
Web Site: www.lorimer.ca
Key Personnel
Pres & Publr: James Lorimer
Promos: Jess Morgan
Founded: 1970
Hardcover & paperback trade; business, economics, finance, history, politics; children's books; social sciences & sociology; cookbooks; illustrated history.
Publishes in English.
ISBN Prefix(es): 978-1-55028; 978-0-88862; 978-1-55277; 978-1-4594
Number of titles published annually: 12 Print
Total Titles: 600 Print
Orders to: Formac Distributing, 5502 Atlantic St, Halifax, NS B3H 1G4 *Toll Free Tel:* 800-565-1975 *Fax:* 902-425-0166 *E-mail:* orderdesk@formac.ca
Warehouse: Formac Distributing, 5502 Atlantic St, Halifax, NS B3H 1G4 *Tel:* 902-421-7022 *Toll Free Tel:* 800-565-1975 *Fax:* 902-425-0166 *E-mail:* orderdesk@formac.ca *Web Site:* www.formac.ca

Lugus Publications
Division of Lugus Productions Ltd
28 Industrial St, Studio 203, Toronto, ON M4G 1Y9
Tel: 416-467-0924
Web Site: www.thestudio203.com
Key Personnel
Pres: Gethin James *E-mail:* james.gethin@gmail.com
Secy: Jacqueline James
Founded: 1981
Educational & trade publishing.
Publishes in English, French.
ISBN Prefix(es): 978-0-921633
Number of titles published annually: 5 Print
Total Titles: 120 Print
U.S. Publishers Represented: Blackwells North America

Madison Press Books
155 Edward St, Suite 1, Aurora, ON L4G 1W3
Mailing Address: PO Box 239, Cannington, ON L0E 1E0
E-mail: info@madisonpressbooks.com
Web Site: www.madisonpressbooks.com
Key Personnel
Pres & Publr: Oliver Salzmann *E-mail:* osalzmann@madisonpressbooks.com
Founded: 1979
Book producer for the international publishing community; illustrated nonfiction co-editions, narrative nonfiction, books for young readers, history, culinary, humour, reference, contemporary culture, fine art.
Publishes in English.
ISBN Prefix(es): 978-1-895892; 978-1-897330
Number of titles published annually: 20 Print
Total Titles: 250 Print

Madison Press Ltd, see Madison Press Books

Madonna House Publications
2888 Dafoe Rd, Combermere, ON K0J 1L0
Tel: 613-756-3728 *Toll Free Tel:* 888-703-7110 *Fax:* 613-756-0103 *Toll Free Fax:* 877-717-2888
E-mail: publications@madonnahouse.org
Web Site: www.madonnahouse.org/publications
Founded: 1988
Publishes in English, French.
ISBN Prefix(es): 978-0-921440; 978-1-897145
Number of titles published annually: 4 Print; 2 Audio
Total Titles: 68 Print; 68 Online; 15 Audio

Branch Office(s)
879-431 State St, Ogdensburg, NY 13669, United States
Membership(s): Catholic Publishers Association; CMN

§Master Point Press
214 Merton St, Suite 205, Toronto, ON M4S 1A6
Tel: 647-956-4933
E-mail: info@masterpointpress.com
Web Site: www.masterpointpress.com; www.ebooksbridge.com (ebook sales)
Key Personnel
Founder & Co-Owner: Ray Lee
Co-Owner: Linda Lee
Founded: 1994
Books on contract bridge.
Publishes in English.
ISBN Prefix(es): 978-0-9698461; 978-1-894154; 978-1-897106; 978-1-55494; 978-1-77140
Number of titles published annually: 20 Print; 20 E-Book
Total Titles: 250 Print; 10 CD-ROM; 300 E-Book
Distributor for Better Bridge Now
U.S. Rep(s): Strauss Consultants, 45 Main St, Brooklyn, NY 11201, United States
Foreign Rep(s): The Bridge Shop (Australia); Orca Book Services (UK)
Orders to: Georgetown Terminal Warehouses Ltd, 34 Armstrong Ave, Georgetown, ON L7G 4R9 *Tel:* 905-873-2750 *Fax:* 905-873-6170 *E-mail:* orders@gtwcanada.com *Web Site:* www.gtwcanada.com; Baker & Taylor, 2550 W Tyvola Rd, Suite 300, Charlotte, NC 28217, United States *Tel:* 704-998-3100 *Toll Free Tel:* 800-775-1800 *E-mail:* btinfo@btol.com *Web Site:* www.btol.com; Ingram Book Group, One Ingram Blvd, La Vergne, TN 37086, United States *Tel:* 615-793-5000 *Toll Free Tel:* 800-937-8200 *E-mail:* customer.service@ingramcontent.com; Orca Book Services, 160 Eastern Ave, Milton Park, Abingdon, Oxon OX14 4SB, United Kingdom *Tel:* (01235) 465500 *E-mail:* tradeorders@orcabookservices.co.uk *Web Site:* www.orcabookservices.co.uk
Shipping Address: Georgetown Terminal Warehouses Ltd, 34 Armstrong Ave, Georgetown, ON L7G 4R9

§Mawenzi House Publishers Ltd
39 Woburn Ave (B), Toronto, ON M5W 1K5
Tel: 416-483-7191
E-mail: info@mawenzihouse.com
Web Site: www.mawenzihouse.com
Key Personnel
Publr: Ms Nurjehan Aziz
Founded: 1985 (as TSAR Publications)
Canadian literature, multicultural & international literature. No unsol mss, query first.
Publishes in English.
ISBN Prefix(es): 978-0-920661; 978-1-894770
Number of titles published annually: 8 Print
Total Titles: 101 Print
U.S. Rep(s): Small Press Distribution Inc, 1341 Seventh St, Berkeley, CA 94710, United States
Distribution Center: University of Toronto Press Inc, 5201 Dufferin St, Toronto, ON M3H 5T8 (CN & US) *Tel:* 416-667-7791 *Toll Free Tel:* 800-565-9523 *Fax:* 416-667-7832 *Toll Free Fax:* 800-221-9985 *E-mail:* utpbooks@utpress.utoronto.ca
Small Press Distribution Inc, 1341 Seventh St, Berkeley, CA 94710, United States *Tel:* 510-524-1668 *Toll Free Tel:* 800-869-7553 *Fax:* 510-524-0852
Membership(s): Literary Press Group

McClelland & Stewart Ltd
Imprint of Penguin Random House Canada
320 Front St W, Suite 1400, Toronto, ON M5V 3B6
Tel: 416-364-4449 *Fax:* 416-598-7764
E-mail: customerservicescanada@penguinrandomhouse.com; publicity@ca.penguingroup.com
Web Site: penguinrandomhouse.ca/imprints/mcclelland-stewart
Key Personnel
Publr: Jared Bland
Publr, Signal: Douglas Pepper
Publg Mgr: Kelly Joseph
Ed-in-Chief: Martha Kanya-Forstner
Sr Ed: Jenny Bradshaw
Sr Ed & Assoc Publr, Emblem Editions: Anita Chong
Poetry Ed: Dionne Brand
Founded: 1906
Publishes in English.
ISBN Prefix(es): 978-0-7710
Number of titles published annually: 70 Print
Total Titles: 2,000 Print
Imprints: Signal (nonfiction)
Divisions: Tundra Books

McGill-Queen's University Press
Imprint of Combined Academic Publishers
1010 Sherbrooke W, Suite 1720, Montreal, QC H3A 2R7
Tel: 514-398-3750 *Fax:* 514-398-4333
E-mail: mqup@mqup.ca
Web Site: www.mqup.ca
Key Personnel
Exec Dir: Philip Cercone *Tel:* 514-398-2910 *E-mail:* philip.cercone@mcgill.ca
Assoc Dir & Mktg Dir: Susan McIntosh *Tel:* 514-398-6306 *E-mail:* susan.mcintosh@mcgill.ca
Ed-in-Chief: Jonathan Crago *Tel:* 514-398-7480 *E-mail:* jonathan.crago@mcgill.ca
Mng Ed: Ryan Van Huijstee *Tel:* 514-398-3922 *E-mail:* ryan.vanhuijstee@mcgill.ca
Asst Mng Ed: Kathleen Fraser *Tel:* 514-398-2068 *E-mail:* kathleen.fraser@mcgill.ca
Sr Ed: Kyla Madden *Tel:* 514-398-2056 *E-mail:* kyla.madden@mcgill.ca
Acqs Ed: Khadija Coxon *Tel:* 613-533-2155 *E-mail:* khadija.coxon@queensu.ca
Prodn Mgr: Elena Goranescu McAdam *Tel:* 514-398-7395 *E-mail:* elena.goranescu@mcgill.ca
Rts & Projs Mgr: Natalie Blachere *Tel:* 514-398-2121 *E-mail:* natalie.blachere@mcgill.ca
Sales Mgr: Jack Hannan *Tel:* 514-398-5165 *E-mail:* jack.hannan@mcgill.ca
Founded: 1970
Original peer-reviewed, high-quality books in all areas of social sciences & humanities. Our emphasis is on providing an outlet for Canadian authors & scholarship. Publish authors from around the world.
Publishes in English, French.
ISBN Prefix(es): 978-0-88629; 978-0-88911; 978-0-7735; 978-0-7709; 978-1-55240; 978-0-9690334
Number of titles published annually: 120 Print
Total Titles: 3,000 Print; 5 CD-ROM
Branch Office(s)
Douglas Library Bldg, 93 University Ave, Kingston, ON K7L 5C4 *Tel:* 613-533-2155 *Fax:* 613-533-6822 *E-mail:* mqup@queensu.ca
Distributor for CIGI Press; John Deutsch Institute for the Study of Economic Policy; Fontanus Monograph Series; Institute for Research on Public Policy; McCord Museum; Queen's Policy Studies Series; Les Editions du Septentrion (English titles)
Foreign Rep(s): The African Moon Press (Chris Reinders) (South Africa); Avicenna Partnership Ltd (Bill Kennedy) (Middle East); Colin Flint Ltd (Ben Greig, Steven Haslemere & Wilf Jones) (Denmark, Finland, Iceland, Norway, Sweden); Claire De Gruchy (Middle East); East-West Export Books (Royden Muranaka) (Asia, Australia, New Zealand, The Pacific); Charles Gibbes (Cyprus, Greece); Mare Nostrum (Katie Machin) (Belgium, France, Luxembourg, Netherlands); Mare Nostrum (Frauke Feldmann) (Austria, Germany, Switzerland); Mare Nostrum (Francesca Pollard & David Pickering) (Italy); Mare Nostrum (Cristina De Lara Ruiz) (Portugal, Spain); Tony Moggach (Africa exc South Africa, Eastern Europe); Quantum Publishing Solutions Ltd (Jim Chalmers) (England, Ireland, Scotland, Wales); Research Press (India, Indian subcontinent)
Distribution Center: c/o Georgetown Terminal Warehouses, 34 Armstrong Ave, Georgetown, ON L7G 4R9 *Tel:* 905-873-9781 *Toll Free Tel:* 877-864-8477 *Fax:* 905-873-6170 *Toll Free Fax:* 877-864-4272 *E-mail:* orders@gtwcanada.com
Chicago Distribution Center, 11030 S Langley Ave, Chicago, IL 60628, United States *Tel:* 773-702-7000 *Toll Free Tel:* 800-621-2736 *Fax:* 773-702-7212 *Toll Free Fax:* 800-621-8476 *E-mail:* orders@press.uchicago.edu SAN: 202-5280
Research Press, FF21 Megacity Mall, M G Rd, Gurgaon, Haryana 122 011, India *Tel:* (0124) 4040017 *Fax:* (011) 23281819 *E-mail:* marketing@researchpress.co.in
Marston Book Services Ltd, 160 Eastern Ave, Milton Park, Abingdon, Oxon OX14 4SB, United Kingdom *Tel:* (01235) 465500 *Fax:* (01235) 465555 *E-mail:* trade.orders@marston.co.uk *Web Site:* www.pubeasy.com
Membership(s): American Association of University Presses; Association of Canadian Publishers; Association of Canadian University Presses

§McGraw-Hill Ryerson Limited
Division of McGraw-Hill Education
300 Water St, Whitby, ON L1N 9B6
SAN: 115-060X
Tel: 905-430-5000 *Toll Free Tel:* 800-565-5758 (cust serv) *Fax:* 905-430-5020 *Toll Free Fax:* 800-463-5885
Web Site: www.mheducation.ca
Founded: 1971 (as McGraw-Hill Book Co)
Publishes & distributes educational & professional products in both print & non-print media.
Publishes in English.
ISBN Prefix(es): 978-0-07; 978-0-7700
Number of titles published annually: 70 Print; 40 CD-ROM; 30 Online
Total Titles: 1,300 Print; 150 CD-ROM; 200 Online; 50 E-Book
Imprints: McGraw-Hill Ryerson
Distributed by McGraw-Hill Publishing Cos
Distributor for Glencoe/McGraw-Hill; Jamestown Education; McGraw-Hill; McGraw-Hill/Irwin; MedMaster Inc; Open Court; Osborne; Schaum's; SRA; Wright Group
U.S. Publishers Represented: The McGraw-Hill Cos
Membership(s): Canadian Educational Resources Council; Canadian Publishers' Council

Modus Vivendi Publishing Inc
55, rue Jean-Talon Ouest, 2e etage, Montreal, QC H2R 2W8
Tel: 514-272-0433 *Fax:* 514-272-7234
E-mail: info@groupemodus.com
Web Site: www.groupemodus.com
Key Personnel
Founder & CEO: Marc Alain
Dir, Sales & Ed: Isabelle Jodoin
Founded: 1992
General trade publishing.
Publishes in French.
ISBN Prefix(es): 978-2-921556; 978-2-89523; 978-2-89543 (Presses Aventure); 978-2-923720 (Editions Bravo!); 978-2-89670 (Editions Bravo!)
Number of titles published annually: 200 Print
Divisions: Editions Bravo!; Editions Rouge; Presses Aventure

Distribution Center: Georgetown Publications, 34 Armstrong Ave, Georgetown, ON L7G 4R9 (English) *Tel:* 905-702-7093
Les Messageries ADP, 2315, rue de la Province, Longueuil, QC J4G 1G4 (French) *Tel:* 450-640-1237 *Toll Free Tel:* 866-874-1237 *Fax:* 450-674-6237 *Toll Free Fax:* 866-874-6237 *E-mail:* adpcommandes@sogides.com

Moose Hide Books
Imprint of Moose Enterprise Book & Theatre Play Publishing
684 Walls Rd, Prince Township, ON P6A 6K4
Tel: 705-779-3331 *Fax:* 705-779-3331
E-mail: mooseenterprises@on.aibn.com
Web Site: www.moosehidebooks.com
Key Personnel
Owner & Publr: Richard Mousseau
E-mail: rmousseau@moosehidebooks.com
Ed: Edmond Alcid *E-mail:* ealcid@moosehidebooks.com
Book & theatre play publishing. Full author royalties paid. 90% of authors are new. House assists new first time authors.
This publisher has indicated that 50% of their product line is author subsidized.
Publishes in English.
ISBN Prefix(es): 978-1-894650
Number of titles published annually: 7 Print; 7 E-Book; 1 Audio
Total Titles: 200 Print; 100 Online; 25 E-Book; 1 Audio

§Mosaic Press
1252 Speers Rd, Units 1 & 2, Oakville, ON L6L 5N9
Tel: 905-825-2130
E-mail: info@mosaic-press.com
Web Site: www.mosaic-press.com
Key Personnel
Publr: Howard Aster
Founded: 1975
Literary scholarly books. No unsol mss.
ISBN Prefix(es): 978-0-88962; 978-1-77161
Number of titles published annually: 20 Print
Total Titles: 502 Print
Distribution Center: Fitzhenry & Whiteside, 195 Allstate Pkwy, Markham, ON L3R 4T8 *Tel:* 905-477-9700 *Toll Free Tel:* 800-387-9776 *Fax:* 905-477-2834 *Toll Free Fax:* 800-387-9777 *E-mail:* bookinfo@fitzhenry.ca *Web Site:* www.fitzhenry.ca
Bookmasters, 30 Amberwood Pkwy, Ashland, OH 44805, United States *Toll Free Tel:* 800-266-5564 *E-mail:* order@bookmasters.com *Web Site:* www.bookmasters.com
Gazelle Book Services Ltd, White Cross Mills, Hightown, Lancaster, Lancs LA1 4XS, United Kingdom *Tel:* (01524) 528500 *Fax:* (01524) 528510 *E-mail:* sales@gazellebookservices.co.uk *Web Site:* www.gazellebookservices.co.uk

Musee canadien de l'histoire, see Canadian Museum of History (Musee canadien de l'histoire)

Narada Press
3165-133 Weber St N, Waterloo, ON N2J 3G9
Tel: 519-886-1969
Founded: 1993
General books on economics, development studies, Asian studies, Vietnamese studies. Directories, reference books, foreign language, scholarly books, college textbooks.
Publishes in English.
ISBN Prefix(es): 978-1-895938
Number of titles published annually: 5 Print

National Gallery of Canada Boutique
380 Sussex Dr, Ottawa, ON K1N 9N4
Mailing Address: PO Box 427, Sta A, Ottawa, ON K1N 9N4
Tel: 613-990-0962 (mail order sales)
E-mail: ngcbook@gallery.ca
Web Site: www.gallery.ca
Founded: 1980
Exhibition catalogues, monographs, permanent collection series, books on photography, posters.
Publishes in English, French.
ISBN Prefix(es): 978-0-88884
Number of titles published annually: 4 Print
U.S. Rep(s): ABC Art Books Canada

Nelson Education Ltd
Affiliate of Cengage Learning
1120 Birchmount Rd, Scarborough, ON M1K 5G4
Tel: 416-752-9100 *Toll Free Tel:* 800-268-2222 (cust serv) *Fax:* 416-752-8101 *Toll Free Fax:* 800-430-4445
E-mail: peopleandengagement@nelson.com
Web Site: www.nelson.com
Key Personnel
Pres & CEO: Steven Brown
CFO: Stephen Aubert
SVP, Media & Prodn Servs: Susan Cline
SVP & Mng Dir, K-20: Jessica Mosher
VP, People & Engagement: Jessica Phinn
Founded: 1914
School, college, test, professional & reference.
Publishes in English.
ISBN Prefix(es): 978-0-919913; 978-1-896081; 978-0-7705; 978-0-17; 978-0-7725; 978-1-85032
Number of titles published annually: 700 Print
Total Titles: 11,864 Print; 30 CD-ROM; 30 E-Book; 100 Audio
U.S. Publishers Represented: American Technical Publishers Inc (ATP); Aseba; Brooks-Cole Publishing; Canada Housing & Mortgage Corp (CMHC); Centennial Press; Course Technology Inc; Craftsman; DC Heath Canada Ltd (school & coll); Delmar Publishers Inc; Douglas & McIntyre; Duxbury Press; Exclusive; Goodheart Willcox; Great Source Educational; Groupe Beauchemin; HarperCollins; Heinemann; Heinle & Heinle Publishers Inc; Houghton Mifflin Harcourt Publishing Company (school, coll & trade); Indigo Instrument; Industrial Press; International Thomson Publishing Services; Irwin Publishing; Learning Media Co; McDougall Littell & Co; Mondo; Nelson Thomson Learning; Nelson Thomson Learning Australia; Norbry; Peterson's; Phoenix Learning Resources; PWS Publishing; Reidmore Publishing; The Riverside Publishing Co; William H Sadlier; Scott Jones; South Western Education & College Publishing; Texere; Thomas Learning Asia; VideoActive Production; Wadsworth Publishers; West Publishing (educ prods only); West Virginia University (FIT)
Membership(s): Canadian Educational Resources Council; Canadian Publishers' Council

§New Author Publishing
4 E Fulford Place, Brockville, ON K6V 2Z8
Tel: 613-865-7471
Web Site: www.newauthorpublishing.com
Key Personnel
Owner: Gary Wolfe *E-mail:* gary@newauthorpublishing.com
Founded: 2013
Print on demand & ebook publishing.
Publishes in English.
ISBN Prefix(es): 978-1-928045
Number of titles published annually: 8 Print; 8 Online; 8 E-Book
Total Titles: 14 Print; 14 Online; 14 E-Book

New Star Books Ltd
107-3477 Commercial St, Vancouver, BC V5N 4E8
SAN: 115-1908
Tel: 604-738-9429
E-mail: info@newstarbooks.com
Web Site: www.newstarbooks.com
Key Personnel
Pres & Publr: Rolf Maurer
Founded: 1970
Social issues & current affairs, fiction, literary, history, international politics, labor, feminist, gay/lesbian studies & poetry. Emphasis on British Columbia & Western Canada.
Publishes in English.
ISBN Prefix(es): 978-0-919888; 978-0-919573; 978-0-921586; 978-1-55420; 978-0-96860
Number of titles published annually: 10 Print
Total Titles: 110 Print
Branch Office(s)
1574 Gulf Rd, No 1517, Point Roberts, WA 98281, United States
Distribution Center: Brunswick Books, 20 Maud St, Suite 303, Toronto, ON M5V 2M5 *Tel:* 416-703-3598 *Fax:* 416-703-6561 *E-mail:* info@brunswickbooks.ca
Membership(s): Literary Press Group

§New World Publishing (Canada)
PO Box 36075, Halifax, NS B3J 3S9
Tel: 902-576-2055 (inquiries) *Toll Free Tel:* 877-211-3334 (orders) *Fax:* 902-576-2095
Web Site: www.newworldpublishing.com
Key Personnel
Owner & Mng Ed: Dr Francis Mitchell
E-mail: francis@newworldpublishing.com
Founded: 1995
Publishes in English.
ISBN Prefix(es): 978-1-895814
Number of titles published annually: 4 Print; 1 E-Book; 1 Audio
Total Titles: 53 Print; 7 CD-ROM; 5 Online; 5 E-Book; 5 Audio
Distributed by Glen Margaret Publishing (most independent & gift stores in Maritimes)
Returns: 19 Frenchman's Rd, Oakfield, NS B2T-1A9 *E-mail:* nwp1@eastlink.ca
Warehouse: JEM Enterprises, 79 Jackson Rd, Apt 3, Dartmouth, NS B3A 4A7, Shipper: Ms Jacqui E Mitchell *Tel:* 902-449-7552 *E-mail:* nwp1@eastlink.ca
Membership(s): Atlantic Publishers Marketing Association; Canadian Booksellers Association

NeWest Press
8540 109 St, No 201, Edmonton, AB T6G 1E6
Tel: 780-432-9427 *Fax:* 780-433-3179
E-mail: info@newestpress.com; orders@newestpress.com
Web Site: www.newestpress.com
Key Personnel
Gen Mgr: Matt Bowes
Mktg & Prodn Coord: Claire Kelly
Founded: 1977
Committed to developing & publishing first-time writers, as well as ensuring the availability of Canadian classics.
Publishes in English.
ISBN Prefix(es): 978-0-920316; 978-0-920897; 978-1-896300; 978-1-897126; 978-1-927063
Number of titles published annually: 12 Print
Total Titles: 140 Print
Sales Office(s): Literary Press Group, 425 Adelaide St W, Suite 700, Toronto, ON M5V 3C1, Sales Mgr: Tan Light *Tel:* 416-483-1321 *Fax:* 416-483-2510 *E-mail:* sales@lpg.ca
Foreign Rep(s): Gazelle Book Services Ltd (Europe, UK)
Distribution Center: LitDistCo, 8300 Lawson Rd, Milton, ON L9T 0A4 *Toll Free Tel:* 800-591-6250 *Toll Free Fax:* 800-591-6251 *E-mail:* ordering@litdistco.ca *Web Site:* www.litdistco.ca

Membership(s): Association of Canadian Publishers; Book Publishers Association of Alberta; Canadian Booksellers Association; Crime Writers of Canada; Literary Press Group of Canada

Nimbus Publishing Ltd
3731 Mackintosh St, Halifax, NS B3K 5A5
SAN: 115-0685
Mailing Address: PO Box 9166, Halifax, NS B3K 5M8
Tel: 902-455-4286 *Toll Free Tel:* 800-NIMBUS9 (646-2879) *Fax:* 902-455-5440 *Toll Free Fax:* 888-253-3133
E-mail: customerservice@nimbus.ca
Web Site: www.nimbus.ca
Key Personnel
Sr Ed: Whitney Moran *E-mail:* editorial@nimbus.ca
Prodn Mgr: Heather Bryan *E-mail:* hbryan@nimbus.ca
Sales Mgr & Foreign Rts: Terrilee Bulger *Tel:* 902-455-4286 ext 223 *E-mail:* tbulger@nimbus.ca
Mktg Coord: Matt McNeill *Tel:* 902-455-4286 ext 226 *E-mail:* mmcneill@nimbus.ca
Billing: Phyllis Murray
Founded: 1978
Regional nonfiction books, relevant to the Atlantic-Canadian experience, social & natural history, children's books, cookbooks, travel, biography, photography & nautical.
Publishes in English, French.
ISBN Prefix(es): 978-0-920852; 978-0-919380; 978-0-921054; 978-0-921128; 978-1-55109; 978-1-77108
Number of titles published annually: 45 Print
Total Titles: 1,000 Print
Imprints: Nimbus; Vagrant Press (fiction)
Distributor for Acadiensis Press; Acorn Press; Bouton D'or Acadie; Breton Books; Bunim & Bannigan; Cape Breton University Press; Down East; Heritage House; Maritime Lines; Pottersfield Press
U.S. Publishers Represented: Down East; Flat Hammock Press; Mystic Seaport Museum Inc; Sheridan House; Wooden Boat
U.S. Rep(s): Downeast Books
Membership(s): Association for the Export of Canadian Books; Association of Canadian Publishers; Atlantic Publishers Marketing Association; Canadian Booksellers Association; NEBA

Novalis Publishing
Division of Bayard Canada
10 Lower Spadina Ave, Suite 400, Toronto, ON M5V 2Z2
Tel: 416-363-3303 *Toll Free Tel:* 877-702-7773 *Fax:* 416-363-9409 *Toll Free Fax:* 877-702-7775
E-mail: books@novalis.ca
Web Site: www.novalis.ca
Key Personnel
Edit Dir: Simon Appoloni *E-mail:* simon.appoloni@novalis.ca
Publg Dir: Joseph Sinasac *E-mail:* joseph.sinasac@novalis.ca
Mktg Mgr: Matthew Sottile
Sales Mgr: Maria Medeiros
Founded: 1936
Religious children's & adult books, periodicals & religious books (Catholic/Christian).
Publishes in English, French.
ISBN Prefix(es): 978-2-89088; 978-2-89507; 978-2-89646; 978-0-88587; 978-1-895195
Number of titles published annually: 30 Print
Total Titles: 360 Print
Distributor for Canterbury Press; Catholic Health Alliance of Canada (CHAC); Church House Publishing; Columba Press; Creative Communications for the Parish; Crossroad Publishing; Jewish Lights Publishing/Skylight Paths; Liguori Publications; Loyola Press; Morehouse Publishing/Church Publishing/Seabury; Orbis Books; Paulist Press; Penguin Random House; Pflaum Publishing Group; Printery House; Saint Mary's Press; St Vladimir Seminary Press; SCM Press; Editions du Signe; Twenty Third Publications; Wild Goose Publications
U.S. Publishers Represented: Creative Communications for the Parish; Jewish Lights Publishing; Orbis Books; Paulist Press; Pflaum Gospel Weeklies; Saint Mary's Press; Twenty-Third Publications
Billing Address: BND Distribution, 4475 Frontenac St, Montreal, QC H2H 2S2 *Tel:* 514-278-3020 *Toll Free Tel:* 800-387-7164 *Fax:* 514-278-3030 *Toll Free Fax:* 800-204-4140 *Web Site:* www.novalis.com
Orders to: BND Distribution, 4475 Frontenac St, Montreal, QC H2H 2S2 *Tel:* 514-278-3020 *Toll Free Tel:* 800-387-7164 *Fax:* 514-278-3030 *Toll Free Fax:* 800-204-4140 *Web Site:* www.novalis.com
Returns: BND Distribution, 4475 Frontenac St, Montreal, QC H2H 2S2 *Tel:* 514-278-3020 *Toll Free Tel:* 800-387-7164 *Fax:* 514-278-3030 *Toll Free Fax:* 800-204-4140 *Web Site:* www.novalis.com
Shipping Address: BND Distribution, 4475 Frontenac St, Montreal, QC H2H 2S2 *Tel:* 514-278-3020 *Toll Free Tel:* 800-387-7164 *Fax:* 514-278-3030 *Toll Free Fax:* 800-204-4140 *Web Site:* www.novalis.com
Warehouse: BND Distribution, 4475 Frontenac St, Montreal, QC H2H 2S2 *Tel:* 514-278-3020 *Toll Free Tel:* 800-387-7164 *Fax:* 514-278-3030 *Toll Free Fax:* 800-204-4140 *Web Site:* www.novalis.com

Oberon Press
145 Spruce St, Suite 205, Ottawa, ON K1R 6P1
SAN: 115-0723
Tel: 613-238-3275 *Fax:* 613-238-3275
E-mail: oberon@sympatico.ca
Web Site: www.oberonpress.ca
Key Personnel
Pres: Michael Macklem
VP & Gen Mgr: Nicholas Macklem
Founded: 1966
Canadiana, fiction, history, biography, poetry & travel.
Publishes in English.
ISBN Prefix(es): 978-0-88750; 978-0-7780
Number of titles published annually: 7 Print
Total Titles: 671 Print

One Act Play Depot
618 Memorial Dr, PO Box 335, Spiritwood, SK S0J 2M0
E-mail: plays@oneactplays.net; orders@oneactplays.net
Web Site: oneactplays.net
Key Personnel
Mng Ed: Fraser MacFarlane
Ed: K Balvenie
Founded: 2002
Publication, sale & distribution of one-act plays. Orders ship within 24 hours. Accept submissions only in Feb of each year.
Publishes in English.
ISBN Prefix(es): 978-1-894910; 978-1-926849
Number of titles published annually: 10 Print; 5 E-Book
Total Titles: 167 Print; 22 E-Book

Oolichan Books
PO Box 2278, Fernie, BC V0B 1M0
SAN: 115-4680
Tel: 250-423-6113
E-mail: info@oolichan.com
Web Site: www.oolichan.com
Key Personnel
Founder & Ed: Ronald Smith
Publr: Randal Macnair
Consulting Ed: Pat Smith
Asst to the Publr: Carolyn Nikodym
Founded: 1974
Publishers of literary fiction, poetry & literary nonfiction. Publish only Canadian authors.
Publishes in English.
ISBN Prefix(es): 978-0-88982
Number of titles published annually: 10 Print
Total Titles: 160 Print
Shipping Address: 542 B Second Ave, Fernie, BC V0B 1M0
Distribution Center: University of Toronto Press, 5201 Dufferin St, Toronto, ON M3H 5T8 *Toll Free Tel:* 800-565-9523 *E-mail:* utpbooks@utpress.utoronto.ca
Membership(s): Association of Book Publishers of British Columbia; Association of Canadian Publishers; Literary Press Group

Owlkids Books Inc
Division of Bayard Canada
10 Lower Spadina Ave, Suite 400, Toronto, ON M5V 2Z2
Tel: 416-340-2700 *Fax:* 416-340-9769
E-mail: owlkids@owlkids.com
Web Site: www.owlkidsbooks.com
Key Personnel
Publr: Karen Boersma
Edit Dir: Karen Li
Dir, Sales & Mktg: Judy Brunsek
Founded: 1976
Award-winning publisher of books for children ages 3-13.
Publishes in English.
ISBN Prefix(es): 978-0-920775; 978-1-895688; 978-1-894379; 978-1-897066; 978-1-897349; 978-1-926973; 978-0-919872; 978-1-926818
Number of titles published annually: 25 Print
Total Titles: 150 Print; 50 E-Book
Orders to: University of Toronto Press, 5201 Dufferin St, Toronto, ON M3H 5T8 *Tel:* 416-667-7791 *Toll Free Tel:* 800-565-9523 *Fax:* 416-667-7832 *Toll Free Fax:* 800-221-9985 *E-mail:* utpbooks@utpress.utoronto.ca *Web Site:* www.utpress.utoronto.ca; Publishers Group West, 1700 Fourth St, Berkeley, CA 94710, United States *Toll Free Tel:* 866-400-5351 *Toll Free Fax:* 800-838-1149 *E-mail:* ips@ingramcontent.com *Web Site:* www.pgw.com

Pacific Educational Press
Imprint of University of British Columbia Press
c/o UBC Press, 2029 West Mall, Vancouver, BC V6T 1Z2
Tel: 604-822-5959; 604-827-2232 (cust serv) *Toll Free Tel:* 855-827-2232
E-mail: pep.admin@ubc.ca; pep.sales@ubc.ca
Web Site: pacificedpress.ca
Founded: 1971
Textbooks for teacher education programs, education materials, materials which are generally used in classrooms or educational institutes, books on education topics & issues for a general readership.
Publishes in English.
ISBN Prefix(es): 978-0-88865; 978-1-895766
Number of titles published annually: 6 Print
Total Titles: 104 Print; 16 E-Book
Distributor for Critical Thinking Consortium (TC2)
Distribution Center: Georgetown Terminal Warehouse, 34 Armstrong Ave, Georgetown, ON L7G 4R9 *Tel:* 905-873-9781 *Toll Free Tel:* 877-864-8477 (CN only) *Fax:* 905-873-6170 *Toll Free Fax:* 877-864-4272 (CN only) *E-mail:* orders@gtwcanada.com
Membership(s): Association of Book Publishers of British Columbia; Association of Canadian Publishers

Palimpsest Press
1171 Eastlawn Ave, Windsor, ON N8S 3J1

Tel: 519-259-2112
E-mail: info@palimpsestpress.ca
Web Site: www.palimpsestpress.ca
Key Personnel
Publr/Ed: Aimee Parent Dunn *E-mail:* aimee@palimpsestpress.ca
Poetry Ed & Graphic Designer: Dawn Kresan *E-mail:* dawnkresan@palimpsestpress.ca
Founded: 2000
Publish poetry collections, nonfiction, essays, literary fiction.
Publishes in English.
ISBN Prefix(es): 978-0-9733952; 978-1-926794; 978-0-9784917
Number of titles published annually: 6 Print
Total Titles: 30 Print
Sales Office(s): Literary Press Group, 425 Adelaide St W, Suite 700, Toronto, ON M5V 3C1 *Tel:* 416-483-1321 *Fax:* 416-483-2510 *E-mail:* sales@lpg.ca *Web Site:* www.lpg.ca
Orders to: LitDistCo, 8300 Lawson Rd, Milton, ON L9T 0A4 *Toll Free Tel:* 800-591-6250 *Toll Free Fax:* 800-591-6251 *E-mail:* ordering@litdistco.ca *Web Site:* www.litdistco.ca
Shipping Address: LitDistCo, 8300 Lawson Rd, Milton, ON L9T 0A4 *Toll Free Tel:* 800-581-6250 *Toll Free Fax:* 800-581-6251 *Web Site:* www.litdistco.ca
Warehouse: LitDistCo, 8300 Lawson Rd, Milton, ON L9T 0A4 *Toll Free Tel:* 800-581-6250 *Toll Free Fax:* 800-581-6251 *Web Site:* www.litdistco.ca
Distribution Center: LitDistCo, 8300 Lawson Rd, Milton, ON L9T 0A4 *Toll Free Tel:* 800-591-6250 *Toll Free Fax:* 800-591-6251 *E-mail:* ordering@litdistco.ca *Web Site:* www.litdistco.ca
Membership(s): Association of Canadian Publishers; Literary Press Group of Canada

§Paulines Editions
5610 rue Beaubien est, Montreal, QC H1T 1X5
Tel: 514-253-5610 *Fax:* 514-253-1907
E-mail: fsp-paulines@videotron.ca
Web Site: www.editions.paulines.qc.ca
Key Personnel
Dir & Intl Rts Contact: Vanda Salvador
Lib Sales Dir: Lucille Paradis
Founded: 1956
Religious books.
Publishes in English, French.
ISBN Prefix(es): 978-2-920912
Number of titles published annually: 4 Print
Total Titles: 60 Print
Distributed by Mediaspaul (Montreal)

§Pearson Education Canada
Division of Pearson Canada Inc
26 Prince Andrew Place, North York, ON M3C 2H4
SAN: 115-0022
Tel: 416-447-5101 *Toll Free Tel:* 800-263-9965 *Fax:* 416-443-0948 *Toll Free Fax:* 800-263-7733; 888-465-0536
Web Site: www.pearsoncanada.ca
Founded: 1966
Educational textbooks, trade, reference.
Publishes in English, French.
ISBN Prefix(es): 978-0-201
Total Titles: 5,700 Print
Imprints: Addison Wesley; Allyn & Bacon; Copp Clark; Benjamin Cummings; Ginn; Longman; Prentice Hall
Orders to: Pearson Education Operations Centre, PO Box 335, Newmarket, ON L3Y 4X7 *Toll Free Tel:* 800-567-3800 (cust serv); 800-361-6128 (school) *Toll Free Fax:* 800-236-7733 (cust serv); 800-563-9196 (school)
Returns: Pearson Education Operations Centre, PO Box 335, Newmarket, ON L3Y 4X7 *Toll Free Tel:* 800-567-3800 (cust serv); 800-361-6128 (school) *Toll Free Fax:* 800-236-7733 (cust serv); 800-563-9196 (school)
Distribution Center: 195 Harry Walker Pkwy, Newmarket, ON L3Y 7B3 *Tel:* 905-853-7888 *Fax:* 905-853-7865

Pearson ERPI
Division of Pearson PLC
1611 Cremazie Blvd E, 10th fl, Montreal, QC H2M 2P2
Tel: 514-334-2690 *Toll Free Tel:* 800-263-3678 *Fax:* 514-334-4720 *Toll Free Fax:* 800-643-4720
E-mail: erpidlm@erpi.com
Web Site: www.erpi.com; pearsonplc.ca
Key Personnel
Artistic Dir: Helene Cousineau *E-mail:* helene.cousineau@pearsonerpi.com
Intl Rts: Lise Barras *Tel:* 514-334-2690 ext 2445 *E-mail:* lise.barras@pearsonerpi.com
Founded: 1965
Textbooks.
Publishes in English, French.
ISBN Prefix(es): 978-2-7613; 978-0-7767
Number of titles published annually: 50 Print; 12 CD-ROM; 50 Online
Total Titles: 950 Print; 15 CD-ROM; 50 Online
Imprints: PEARSON ERPI
Distributed by De Boeck; Pearson Education France
Distributor for Campus Press France; Duculot; Pearson Canada (ESL series); Prentice-Hall
Membership(s): Association Nationale des Editeurs de Livres

Pembroke Publishers Ltd
538 Hood Rd, Markham, ON L3R 3K9
Tel: 905-477-0650 *Toll Free Tel:* 800-997-9807 *Fax:* 905-477-3691 *Toll Free Fax:* 800-339-5568
Web Site: www.pembrokepublishers.com
Key Personnel
Pres & Intl Rts: Mary Macchiusi *E-mail:* mary@pembrokepublishers.com
Mng Dir: Claudia Connolly
Founded: 1985
Educational books.
Publishes in English.
ISBN Prefix(es): 978-0-921217; 978-1-55138
Number of titles published annually: 10 Print
Total Titles: 300 Print; 100 E-Book
Distributor for Stenhouse Publishers
U.S. Publishers Represented: Stenhouse Publishers
U.S. Rep(s): Stenhouse Publishers
Foreign Rep(s): Eurospan (UK); Hawker Brownlow Education (Australia, New Zealand); PMS (Singapore); Stenhouse Publishers (USA)
Distribution Center: Eurospan, 3 Henrietta St, Covent Garden, London WC2E 8LU, United Kingdom
Membership(s): Organization of Book Publishers of Ontario

Pemmican Publications Inc
150 Henry Ave, Winnipeg, MB R3B 0J7
SAN: 115-1657
Tel: 204-589-6346 *Fax:* 204-589-2063
E-mail: pemmican@pemmican.mb.ca
Web Site: www.pemmicanpublications.ca
Key Personnel
Mng Ed: Randal McIlroy
Founded: 1980
Books of Metis & native concern, juvenile & young adult books, trade paperbacks, scholarly books. Submissions outside Canada must include international reply coupons.
Publishes in English, French.
ISBN Prefix(es): 978-0-919143; 978-0-921827; 978-1-894717
Number of titles published annually: 5 Print
Total Titles: 120 Print

Penguin Books Canada Limited, see Penguin Group (Canada)

§Penguin Group (Canada)
Imprint of Penguin Random House Canada
320 Front St W, Suite 1400, Toronto, ON M5V 3B6
Tel: 416-364-4449 *Fax:* 416-598-7764
E-mail: customerservicescanada@penguinrandomhouse.com; publicity@ca.penguingroup.com
Web Site: penguinrandomhouse.ca/imprints/penguin-canada
Key Personnel
Chmn: Rob Prichard
COO: Barry Gallant
Pres & Publr: Nicole Winstanley
VP, Fin: Helena Hung
VP, HR: Ann Wood
Dir, Prodn: Janette Lush
Rts & Contracts Mgr: David Whiteside
Founded: 1974
General trade & paperback books, hardcover & classics.
Publishes in English.
ISBN Prefix(es): 978-0-14; 978-0-452; 978-0-451; 978-0-453; 978-0-7214; 978-0-216
Number of titles published annually: 3,280 Print
Total Titles: 76,500 Print
Imprints: A&C Black UK; Ace; Albatross; Alpha Books; Arden; Arkana; Atlantic Books; Avery; BBC Children's Books; Berkley; Berkshire House; Bibli O'Phile; Bloomberg Press; Bloomsbury UK; Bloomsbury USA; Blue Hen; Boulevard; Callaway; Canongate; Celebra; Chamberlain Brothers; Children's High Level Group; Corinthian Books; The Countryman Press; Current; Dalkey Archive Press; DAW; Dial Books for Young Readers; Dutton; Dutton Children's Books; Europa Editions; Faber & Faber Ltd; Fig Tree; Firebird; Foul Play Press; Gotham Books; GP Putnam & Sons; Grosset & Dunlap; Hamish Hamilton; Hamish Hamilton Canada; Hamish Hamilton Juvenile; Heat; Hippocrene Books; Home; HP Books; Hudson Street Press; Humanity Books; Icon Books; Michael Joseph; Michael Joseph Juvenile; Jove; Kales Press; Ladybird; Allen Lane; Library of America; Liveright; Meridian; Methuen Canadian List; Minedition; Modern Gems; New Directions; Noah Publications; W W Norton & Company Inc; Onyx; Overlook Press; Peace Hill Press; Pegasus Books; Penguin Audio UK; Penguin Australia; Penguin Canada; Penguin Classics; Penguin Compass; Penguin 007; Penguin India; Penguin Ireland; Penguin New Zealand; Penguin Paperbacks; Penguin Press; Penguin South Africa; Penguin UK; Perigee; Persea Books; Philomel Books; Pi Press; Planet Dexter; Plume; Portfolio; Prentice Hall Cda; Prentice Hall Press; Price Stern Sloan; Price Stern Sloan Merchandise; Prime Crime; Profile Books; Prometheus Books; Puffin Canada; Puffin UK; Puffin USA; Pushcart Press; Putnam Audio; PYR Books; Quantuck Lane; Razorbill; Rose Reisman; Riverhead; Roadside Amusements; Roc; Screen Press Books; Sentinel; Short Books; Signet; Smithsonian; Speak; Tarcher; Thames & Hudson; Time Out Guides Ltd; Tusk/Ivories; Verso Press Canada; Verso Press UK; Verso Press USA; Viking Canada; Viking Children's Books; Viking Penguin Audio; Viking Studio; Viking UK; Viking UK Juvenile; Viking USA; Walting Street; Frederick Warne; Wee Sing; Which Books; Wizard Books
Distributor for Alpha Books; Arkangel; Atlantic Books; Avery; BBC Children's Books; Berkley Publishing; Bibli O'Phile; Bloomsbury Press; Callaway; Canongate; DAW; Dutton; Europa Editions; Faber & Faber Ltd; Fig Tree; Gotham Books; Hamish Hamilton; Hamish Hamilton Canada; Hippocrene Books; Hudson Street

Press; Icon Books; Michael Joseph; Ladybird; Allen Lane; Library of America; Michelin North America (Canada) (English titles in Canada); New American Library; W W Norton & Company Inc; Overlook Press; Penguin Audio UK; Penguin Australia; Penguin Books USA; Penguin Canada; Penguin India; Penguin New Zealand; Penguin Press; Penguin Random House Audio Publishing; Penguin South Africa; Penguin UK; Penguin Young Readers; Plume; Portfolio; Prometheus Books; Puffin Canada; Putnam; Rose Reisman; Verso Press USA; Viking Canada; Viking Penguin Audio; Viking USA; Frederick Warne; Which Book
Distribution Center: Pearson Canada Distribution Centre, 195 Harry Walker Pkwy, Newmarket, ON L3Y 7B4 *Tel:* 905-713-3852 *Toll Free Tel:* 800-399-6858 *Toll Free Fax:* 800-363-2665 *Web Site:* www.pearsoned.ca

Penguin Random House Canada
Division of Penguin Random House Inc
320 Front St W, Suite 1400, Toronto, ON M5V 3B6
SAN: 201-3975
Tel: 416-364-4449 *Toll Free Tel:* 888-523-9292 (cust serv) *Fax:* 416-598-7764
Web Site: www.penguinrandomhouse.ca
Key Personnel
Pres & CEO: Brad Martin
EVP & CFO: Barry Gallant
Pres & Publr, PRHC: Kristin Cochrane
VP, PRHC & Publr, Penguin Canada: Nicole Winstanley
SVP & COO: Robert Wheaton
Exec Publr, EVP, PRHC: Louise Dennys
SVP, Dir, Corp Communs & VP, Dir, Publicity, PRHC: Tracey Turriff
SVP, Dir, Prodn: Janine Laporte
VP & Publr, Appetite by Random House: Robert McCullough
VP, Mktg: Beth Lockley
Founded: 1944
Penguin Random House Canada & its publishing entities are not accepting unsol submissions, proposals, mss, or submission queries via e-mail at this time.
Publishes in English.
ISBN Prefix(es): 978-0-307; 978-0-679; 978-0-553; 978-0-385; 978-0-7704; 978-0-345; 978-0-449; 978-0-676
Imprints: Anchor Canada; Appetite by Random House; Bond Street Books; Doubleday Canada; Emblem Editions; Fenn; Douglas Gibson Books; Hamish Hamilton Canada; Knopf Canada; Allen Lane Canada; McClelland & Stewart; Penguin Canada; Portfolio Penguin Canada; Puffin Canada; Random House Canada; Razorbill Canada; Seal Books; Signal; Tundra Books; Viking Canada; Vintage Canada
Warehouse: 6971 Columbus Rd, Mississauga, ON L5T 1K1
Membership(s): Canadian Booksellers Association; Canadian Publishers' Council
See separate listing for:
Doubleday Canada
Knopf Canada
McClelland & Stewart Ltd
Penguin Group (Canada)
Tundra Books

Pippin Publishing
Division of University of Toronto Press
5201 Dufferin St, Toronto, ON M3H 5T8
Tel: 416-667-8731; 426-667-7791 (CN warehouse) *Toll Free Tel:* 800-565-9523 (CN warehouse) *Fax:* 416-667-7832 *Toll Free Fax:* 800-221-9985 (CN warehouse)
E-mail: utpbooks@utpress.utoronto.ca (CN warehouse)
Web Site: www.utpguidancecentre.com
Key Personnel
Mgr: Cindy Hall *E-mail:* chall@utpress.utoronto.ca
Founded: 1995
Educational books: English as a foreign language; English language teaching, books for teachers & students. Also trade military memoirs.
Publishes in English.
ISBN Prefix(es): 978-0-88751
Number of titles published annually: 6 Print
Total Titles: 85 Print
Imprints: Dominie Press (CN)
Distributed by University of Toronto Press (worldwide)
Foreign Rep(s): NBN International (Africa, Europe, UK)
Warehouse: University of Toronto Press, 2250 Military Rd, Tonawanda, NY 14150, United States

Pontifical Institute of Mediaeval Studies, Department of Publications
59 Queen's Park Crescent E, Toronto, ON M5S 2C4
SAN: 115-0804
Tel: 416-926-7142 *Fax:* 416-926-7258
Web Site: www.pims.ca
Key Personnel
Ed-in-Chief: Fred R Unwalla *E-mail:* unwalla@chass.utoronto.ca
Founded: 1936
Scholarly publishing on the Middle Ages.
Publishes in English, French.
ISBN Prefix(es): 978-0-88844
Number of titles published annually: 10 Print
Total Titles: 350 Print
Orders to: University of Toronto Press, 5201 Dufferin St, Toronto, ON M3H 5T8 *Tel:* 416-667-7791 *Toll Free Tel:* 800-565-9523 *Fax:* 416-667-7832 *Toll Free Fax:* 800-221-9985 *E-mail:* orders@utpress.utoronto.ca *Web Site:* www.utpress.utoronto.ca
Distribution Center: University of Toronto Press, 5201 Dufferin St, Toronto, ON M3H 5T8 *Tel:* 416-667-7791 *Toll Free Tel:* 800-565-9523 *Fax:* 416-667-7832 *Toll Free Fax:* 800-221-9985 *E-mail:* orders@utpress.utoronto.ca *Web Site:* www.utpress.utoronto.ca

§Porcupine's Quill Inc
68 Main St, Erin, ON N0B 1T0
Mailing Address: PO Box 160, Erin, ON N0B 1T0
Tel: 519-833-9158
E-mail: pql@sentex.net
Web Site: porcupinesquill.ca
Key Personnel
Publr: Tim Inkster
Founded: 1974
Modern Canadian literature, poetry & art.
Publishes in English.
ISBN Prefix(es): 978-0-88984
Number of titles published annually: 10 Print
Total Titles: 100 Print
U.S. Rep(s): University of Toronto Press
Membership(s): Association of Canadian Publishers; Canada Council for the Arts; Literary Press Group; Ontario Arts Council

Portage & Main Press
318 McDermot, Suite 100, Winnipeg, MB R3A 0A2
Tel: 204-987-3500 *Toll Free Tel:* 800-667-9673 *Fax:* 204-947-0080 *Toll Free Fax:* 866-734-8477
E-mail: books@portageandmainpress.com
Web Site: www.portageandmainpress.com
Key Personnel
Owner, Publr, Rts & Perms: Catherine Gerbasi
Edit Dir: Annalee Greenberg
Dir, Mktg: Kirsten Phillips
Founded: 1967 (as Peguis Publishers)
Educational resource (K-12).
Publishes in English.
ISBN Prefix(es): 978-0-919566; 978-0-920541; 978-1-895411; 978-1-894110; 978-1-55379; 978-0-9699032; 978-0-9694264
Number of titles published annually: 14 Print
Total Titles: 200 Print
Imprints: HighWater Press

Pottersfield Press
248 Leslie Rd, East Lawrencetown, NS B2Z 1T4
SAN: 115-0790
Toll Free Tel: 800-646-2879 (orders only) *Toll Free Fax:* 888-253-3133
Web Site: www.pottersfieldpress.com
Key Personnel
Pres & Publr: Lesley Choyce *E-mail:* lchoyce@ns.sympatico.ca
Founded: 1979
Fiction, books about the sea, books of Atlantic & Canada; nonfiction, books of literary travel.
Publishes in English.
ISBN Prefix(es): 978-0-919001; 978-1-895900; 978-1-897426; 978-1-988286
Number of titles published annually: 6 Print; 16 E-Book
Total Titles: 170 Print; 2 CD-ROM; 16 E-Book; 4 Audio
Imprints: Atlantic Classics Series
Distributed by Nimbus Publishing
U.S. Rep(s): Nimbus Publishing
Orders to: c/o Nimbus Publishing, Box 9166, Halifax, NS B3K 5M8 *Toll Free Tel:* 800-646-2879 *Toll Free Fax:* 888-253-3133 *E-mail:* customerservice@nimbus.ca *Web Site:* www.nimbus.ca
Shipping Address: c/o Nimbus Publishing, 3731 MacIntosh St, Halifax, NS B3K 5A5 *Tel:* 904-455-4286-orders only *Toll Free Tel:* 800-646-2879 *Toll Free Fax:* 888-253-3133 *E-mail:* customerservice@nimbus.ca *Web Site:* www.nimbus.ca
Membership(s): Atlantic Publishers Marketing Association

PrairieView Press Ltd
PO Box 460, Gretna, MB R0G 0V0
Tel: 204-327-6543 *Toll Free Tel:* 800-477-7377 *Toll Free Fax:* 866-480-0253
Web Site: www.prairieviewpress.com
Key Personnel
Owner & Pres: Chester Goossen
Secy: Darleen Loewen
Contact: Chad Goossen
Founded: 1968
Quality reading material for children & adults; songbooks. Over 2,000 titles in distribution, listed in catalog.
Publishes in English.
ISBN Prefix(es): 978-0-920035; 978-1-896199; 978-1-897080
Number of titles published annually: 36 Print
Total Titles: 1,450 Print
Branch Office(s)
PO Box 88, Neche, ND 58265-0088, United States

Les Presses de l'Université d'Ottawa, see University of Ottawa Press (Presses de l'Université d'Ottawa)

Les Presses de l'Universite du Quebec
Division of Universite du Quebec
2875 blvd Laurier, Suite 450, Quebec, QC G1V 2M2
Tel: 418-657-4399 *Fax:* 418-657-2096
E-mail: puq@puq.ca
Web Site: www.puq.ca
Founded: 1969
University press.
Publishes in English, French.

ISBN Prefix(es): 978-2-7605; 978-0-7770; 978-2-920073
Number of titles published annually: 80 Print
Total Titles: 1,300 Print
Distributor for Figura; Imaginaire du Nord; Tele-Universite
Distribution Center: Prologue Inc, 1650, blvd Lionel-Bertrand, Boisbriand, QC J7H 1N7 *Toll Free Tel:* 800-363-2864 *Toll Free Fax:* 800-361-8088 *E-mail:* sac@prologue.ca *Web Site:* www.prologue.ca
Independent Publishers Group, 814 N Franklin St, Chicago, IL 60610, United States (English titles only) *Toll Free Tel:* 800-888-4741 *Fax:* 312-337-5985 *E-mail:* frontdesk@ipgbook.com *Web Site:* www.ipgbook.com
Patrimoine SPRL, Milcamps Ave 119 B, 1030 Brussels, Belgium *Tel:* (02) 7366847 *Fax:* (02) 7366847 *E-mail:* patrimoine@telenet.be
Sodis SARL, 128 Ave du Marechal de Lattre de Tassigny, 77400 Lagny-sur-Marne, France *Tel:* 01 60 07 82 99 *Fax:* 01 64 30 32 27 *E-mail:* portail@sodis.fr *Web Site:* www.sodis.fr
Servidis SA, Chemin des Chalets 7, 1279 Chavannes-de-Bogis, Switzerland *Tel:* (022) 940 95 32 *Fax:* (022) 960 95 77 *E-mail:* pgavillet@servidis.ch *Web Site:* www.servidis.ch

§Les Presses de l'Universite Laval
Division of Universite du Quebec
2180, Chemin Sainte-Foy, 1st fl, Quebec, QC G1V 0A6
Tel: 418-656-2803 *Fax:* 418-656-3305
E-mail: presses@pul.ulaval.ca
Web Site: www.pulaval.com
Key Personnel
Gen Dir: Denis Dion *E-mail:* denis.dion@pul.ulaval.ca
Gen Ed: Andre Baril *E-mail:* andr.baril@sympatico.ca
Ed: Andre Baril *E-mail:* andr.baril@sympatico.ca; Helene Cormier *E-mail:* helene.cormier@pul.ulaval.ca; Denis Dion *E-mail:* denis.dion@pul.ulaval.ca
Admin: Sylvie Hudon *E-mail:* sylvie.hudon@pul.ulaval.ca
Communs: Sylvie Servant *E-mail:* sylvie.servant@pul.ulaval.ca
Prodn: Jocelyne Naud *E-mail:* jocelyne.naud@pul.ulaval.ca
Dir Asst: Dominique Gingras *E-mail:* dominique.gingras@pul.ulaval.ca
Founded: 1950
Books in the humanities & social sciences with an emphasis on subjects of interest in Quebec & Canada, administration, economy.
Publishes in French.
ISBN Prefix(es): 978-2-7637; 978-0-7746
Number of titles published annually: 120 Print
Foreign Rights: Librairie du Quebec (France); Patrimoine SPRL (Belgium); Servidis (Switzerland)
Distribution Center: Prologue Inc, 1650, blvd Lionel-Bertrand, Boisbriand, QC J7H 1N7 (CN & US) *Tel:* 450-434-0306 *Toll Free Tel:* 800-363-2864 *E-mail:* prologue@prologue.ca *Web Site:* www.prologue.ca

Prise de parole Inc
109 Elm St, Suite 205, Sudbury, ON P3C 1T4
Mailing Address: CP 550, Sudbury, ON P3E 4R2
Tel: 705-675-6491 *Fax:* 705-673-1817
E-mail: info@prisedeparole.ca
Web Site: www.prisedeparole.ca
Key Personnel
Co-Exec Dir & Dir, Publg: Denise Truax *E-mail:* dtruax@prisedeparole.ca
Co-Exec Dir & Dir, Mktg: Stephane Cormier *E-mail:* scormier@prisedeparole.ca
Cont: Alain Mayotte *E-mail:* amayotte@prisedeparole.ca
Founded: 1973
Poetry, novels, drama, textbooks, essays.
Publishes in French.
ISBN Prefix(es): 978-2-89423; 978-2-89744; 978-2-921573; 978-2-920814
Number of titles published annually: 18 Print
Total Titles: 386 Print; 545 Online; 211 E-Book
Distribution Center: Diffusion Dimedia, 1650, blvd Lionel-Bertrand, Boisbriand, QC J7H 1N7 *Tel:* 450-434-0306
Membership(s): Association Nationale des Editeurs de Livres; Regroupement des Editeurs Canadiens-Francais

Productive Publications
7-B Pleasant Blvd, Unit 1210, Toronto, ON M4T 1K2
SAN: 117-1712
Mailing Address: PO Box 7200, Sta A, Toronto, ON M5W 1X8
Tel: 416-483-0634 *Toll Free Tel:* 877-879-2669 (orders) *Fax:* 416-322-7434
E-mail: productivepublications@rogers.com
Web Site: www.productivepublications.ca
Key Personnel
Owner & Pres: Iain Williamson
Founded: 1985
Trade paperback books; business, finance, communications, computers, management, marketing, taxation, personal finance, entrepreneurship, self-help.
Publishes in English.
ISBN Prefix(es): 978-0-920847; 978-1-896210; 978-1-55270
Number of titles published annually: 28 Print
Total Titles: 180 Print

§Les Publications du Quebec
1000, rte de l'Eqalise, Bureau 500, Quebec, QC G1V 3V9
Tel: 418-643-5150 *Toll Free Tel:* 800-463-2100 (Quebec province only) *Fax:* 418-643-6177 *Toll Free Fax:* 800-561-3479
E-mail: publicationsduquebec@cspq.gouv.qc.ca
Web Site: www.publicationsduquebec.gouv.qc.ca
Key Personnel
Dir: Sylvie Ferland
Founded: 1982
Government publications.
Publishes in English, French.
ISBN Prefix(es): 978-2-550; 978-2-551; 978-0-7754
Number of titles published annually: 200 Print; 20 Online
Total Titles: 4,000 Print; 100 Online

§QA International (QAI)
Division of Groupe Quebec Amerique
329 De la Commune W, 3rd fl, Montreal, QC H2Y 2E1
Tel: 514-499-3000 *Fax:* 514-499-3010
Web Site: www.qa-international.com
Key Personnel
Founder & CEO: Jacques Fortin
Dir, Busn Devt: Rossana Sommaruga
Founded: 1989
Create, develop & produce editorial content built around state-of-the-art computer images for publication in print & electronic media throughout the world.
Publishes in French.
ISBN Prefix(es): 978-2-7644
Number of titles published annually: 60 Print
Total Titles: 770 Print

Quattro Books Inc
12 Concord Ave, 2nd fl, Toronto, ON M6H 2P1
Tel: 647-748-7484
E-mail: info@quattrobooks.ca
Web Site: www.quattrobooks.ca
Key Personnel
Exec Dir & Publr: Luciano Iacobelli *E-mail:* luciano@quattrobooks.ca
Assoc Publr: Sonia D'Agostino
Publishes in English.
ISBN Prefix(es): 978-0-9782806; 978-0-9810186; 978-1-926802
Number of titles published annually: 16 Print; 16 E-Book
Imprints: Fourfront Editions
Distribution Center: LitDistCo, 8300 Lawson Rd, Milton, ON L9T 0A4 *E-mail:* ordering@litdistco.ca *Web Site:* www.litdistco.ca
Membership(s): Literary Press Group of Canada

Quebec Dans Le Monde
335, rue Saint-Joseph E, bureau 600, Quebec, QC G1K 3B4
SAN: 116-8657
Fax: 418-659-4143
E-mail: info@quebecmonde.com
Web Site: www.quebecmonde.com
Founded: 1983
Databases, guides & reference books on Quebec at large.
Publishes in French.
ISBN Prefix(es): 978-2-9801130; 978-2-921309
Number of titles published annually: 7 Print
Total Titles: 21 Print; 15 E-Book
Distribution Center: Librairie du Quebec a Paris, 30 rue Gay Lussac, 75005 Paris, France *Tel:* 01 43 54 49 02

Reader's Digest Association Canada ULC (Selection du Reader's Digest Canada SRI)
1100 Rene Levesque Blvd W, 8th fl, Suite 822, Montreal, QC H3B 5H5
Tel: 514-940-0751 *Toll Free Tel:* 888-459-3333 (cust serv) *Fax:* 514-940-3637
E-mail: erdcustserv@cdsfulfillment.com
Web Site: www.readersdigest.ca
Founded: 1943
Magazine subscriptions, fiction & general nonfiction books in condensed form.
Publishes in English, French.
ISBN Prefix(es): 978-0-89577; 978-0-88850; 978-0-276; 978-2-7098; 978-0-7621; 978-1-55475
Number of titles published annually: 12 Print
Total Titles: 12 Print
Warehouse: 3010 Walden Ave, Depew, NY 14043, United States
Membership(s): Canadian Marketing Association

Red Deer Press Inc
Division of Fitzhenry & Whiteside Limited
195 Allstate Pkwy, Markham, ON L3R 4T8
Tel: 905-477-9700 *Toll Free Tel:* 800-387-9776 (orders)
E-mail: rdp@reddeerpress.com; bookinfo@fitzhenry.ca
Web Site: www.reddeerpress.com
Key Personnel
Publr: Richard Dionne *Tel:* 800-387-9776 ext 248 *E-mail:* dionne@reddeerpress.com
Dir, Sales: Sonya Gilliss *Tel:* 800-387-9776 ext 250 *E-mail:* sonya.gilliss@fitzhenry.ca
Children's Ed: Peter Carver
Promos: Winston Stillwell *Tel:* 800-387-9776 ext 258 *E-mail:* winston.stillwell@fitzhenry.ca
Cust Serv: Judy Ghoura *Tel:* 800-387-9776 ext 225
Founded: 1975
Publishes in English.
ISBN Prefix(es): 978-0-88995
Number of titles published annually: 15 Print
Total Titles: 400 Print
Imprints: Robert J Sawyer Books
Distribution Center: Firefly Books Ltd, 50 Staples Ave, Unit 1, Richmond Hill, ON L4B 0A7 *Tel:* 416-499-8412 *Toll Free Tel:* 800-387-6192 *Fax:* 416-499-8313 *Toll Free Fax:* 800-450-0391 *E-mail:* service@fireflybooks.com *Web Site:* www.fireflybooks.com

Rocky Mountain Books Ltd (RMB)
Member of The Heritage Group
103-1075 Pendergast St, Victoria, BC V8V 0A1
Tel: 250-360-0829 *Fax:* 250-386-0829
Web Site: www.rmbooks.com
Key Personnel
Publr, Acqs, Foreign Rts, Sales & Mktg: Don Gorman *E-mail:* don@rmbooks.com
Art Dir: Chyla Cardinal *E-mail:* chyla@rmbooks.com
Sr Ed: Joe Wilderson *E-mail:* joe@rmbooks.com
Publr Asst, Admin & Publicity: Rick Wood *E-mail:* rick@rmbooks.com
Founded: 1979
Regional publisher of books on outdoor activities, mountain literature & mountain biographies.
Publishes in English.
ISBN Prefix(es): 978-0-9690038; 978-0-921102; 978-1-894765; 978-1-897522; 978-1-926855; 978-1-927330; 978-1-77160
Number of titles published annually: 30 Print
Total Titles: 188 Print
Branch Office(s)
414 13 Ave NE, Calgary, AB T2E 1C2 (design & edit) *Tel:* 403-271-3145 *Fax:* 403-249-2968
Orders to: Heritage Group Distribution, 19272 96 Ave, Suite 8, Surrey, BC V4N 4C1 *Tel:* 604-881-7067 *Toll Free Tel:* 800-665-3302 *Fax:* 604-881-7068 *Toll Free Fax:* 800-566-3336 *E-mail:* orders@hgdistribution.com *Web Site:* www.hgdistribution.com
Distribution Center: Heritage Group Distribution, 19272 96 Ave, Suite 8, Surrey, BC V4N 4C1 *Tel:* 604-881-7067 *Toll Free Tel:* 800-665-3302 *Fax:* 604-881-7068 *Toll Free Fax:* 800-566-3336 *E-mail:* orders@hgdistribution.com *Web Site:* www.hgdistribution.com
Membership(s): Book Publishers Association of Alberta

Ronsdale Press Ltd
3350 W 21 Ave, Vancouver, BC V6S 1G7
SAN: 116-2454
Tel: 604-738-4688 *Fax:* 604-731-4548
E-mail: ronsdale@shaw.ca
Web Site: ronsdalepress.com
Key Personnel
Dir & Intl Rts: Ronald Hatch
Lib Sales Dir: Veronica Hatch
Founded: 1988
Literary press, children's, history, literary & regional. Specialize in Canadian authors.
Publishes in English.
ISBN Prefix(es): 978-0-921870; 978-1-55380
Number of titles published annually: 12 Print; 12 E-Book
Total Titles: 265 Print
Distribution Center: LitDistCo, 8300 Lawson Rd, Milton, ON L9T 0A4 (US only) *Toll Free Tel:* 800-591-6250 *Toll Free Fax:* 800-591-6251 *Web Site:* www.litdistco.ca
Raincoast Books, 2440 Viking Way, Richmond, BC V6V 1N2 *Toll Free Tel:* 800-663-5714 *Toll Free Fax:* 800-565-3770 *E-mail:* customerservice@raincoast.com *Web Site:* www.raincoast.com
Small Press Distribution, 1341 Seventh St, Berkeley, CA 94710-1409, United States *Tel:* 510-524-1668 *Toll Free Tel:* 800-869-7553 *Fax:* 510-524-0852 *E-mail:* spd@spdbooks.org *Web Site:* www.spdbooks.org
Baker & Taylor, 2550 W Tyvola Rd, Suite 300, Charlotte, NC 28217, United States *Tel:* 704-998-3100 *Toll Free Tel:* 800-775-1800 *E-mail:* btinfo@baker-taylor.com *Web Site:* www.btol.com
Ingram Content Group, One Ingram Blvd, La Vergne, TN 37086, United States *Tel:* 615-793-5000 *E-mail:* inquiry@ingramcontent.com *Web Site:* www.ingramcontent.com
Gazelle Book Services Ltd, White Cross Mills, Hightown, Lancaster, Lancs LA1 4XS, United Kingdom (UK & Europe) *Tel:* (01524) 528500 *Fax:* (01524) 528510 *E-mail:* sales@gazellebookservices.co.uk *Web Site:* www.gazellebookservices.co.uk
Membership(s): Association of Book Publishers of British Columbia; Association of Canadian Publishers; Literary Press Group of Canada

Robert Rose Inc
120 Eglinton Ave E, Suite 800, Toronto, ON M4P 1E2
Tel: 416-322-6552 *Fax:* 416-322-6936
Web Site: www.robertrose.ca
Founded: 1995
Publishes in English.
ISBN Prefix(es): 978-1-896503; 978-0-7788
Number of titles published annually: 25 Print
Total Titles: 285 Print
Distributed by Firefly Books Ltd

§Royal Ontario Museum Press
100 Queen's Park, Toronto, ON M5S 2C6
Tel: 416-586-8000 *Fax:* 416-586-5642
E-mail: info@rom.on.ca
Web Site: www.rom.on.ca
Key Personnel
Dir & CEO: John Basseches
Founded: 1912
Scholarly & general books on art, archaeology & sciences.
Publishes in English, French.
ISBN Prefix(es): 978-0-88854
Number of titles published annually: 8 Print
Total Titles: 100 Print
U.S. Rep(s): University of Toronto Press (NY)
Warehouse: University of Toronto Press, 5201 Dufferin St, Toronto, ON M3H 5T8, Contact: Carol Trainor *Tel:* 416-667-7791 *Toll Free Tel:* 800-565-9523 *Fax:* 416-667-7832 *E-mail:* utpbooks@utpress.utoronto.ca *Web Site:* www.utpress.utoronto.ca
Distribution Center: University of Toronto Press, 5201 Dufferin St, Toronto, ON M3H 5T8, Contact: Carol Trainor *Tel:* 416-667-7791 *Toll Free Tel:* 800-565-9523 *Fax:* 416-667-7832 *E-mail:* utpbooks@utpress.utoronto.ca *Web Site:* www.utpress.utoronto.ca

Guy Saint-Jean Editeur Inc
4490, rue Garand, Laval, QC H7L 5Z6
Tel: 450-663-1777
E-mail: info@saint-jeanediteur.com
Web Site: saint-jeanediteur.com
Key Personnel
Pres: Nicole Saint-Jean *E-mail:* nicole@saint-jeanediteur.com
VP, Publg: Marie-Claire Saint-Jean *E-mail:* mclaire@saint-jeanediteur.com
Mng Dir: Jean Pare *E-mail:* jean.pare@saint-jeanediteur.com
Prodn/Opers Dir: Jacques Frechette *E-mail:* jacques@saint-jeanediteur.com
Founded: 1981
Publishes in English, French.
ISBN Prefix(es): 978-2-920340; 978-2-89455
Number of titles published annually: 30 Print; 10 E-Book
Total Titles: 550 Print
Imprints: Green Frog Publishing
Foreign Office(s): Saint-Jean Editeur (France), 30-32 rue de Lappe, 75011 Paris, France, Contact: Christian Richard *Tel:* 01 39 76 99 43 *Fax:* 01 39 76 21 78 *E-mail:* gsj.editeur@free.fr
U.S. Publishers Represented: CDS
Foreign Rep(s): INT Press (Australia, New Zealand); Christian Richard (Europe)
Foreign Rights: Elizabeth Brayne (Europe)
Distribution Center: Prologue, 1650, blvd Lionel-Bertrand, Boisbriand, QC J7H 1N7 *Tel:* 450-434-0306 *Toll Free Tel:* 800-363-2864 *Web Site:* www.prologue.ca
Librairie du Quebec, 30, rue Gay Lussac, 75005 Paris, France *Tel:* 01 43 54 49 02 *Fax:* 01 43 54 39 15 *E-mail:* libraires@librairieduquebec.fr
Servidis SA, Chemin des Chalets 7, 1279 Chavannes-de-Bogis, Switzerland *Tel:* (022) 960 95 23 *Fax:* (022) 960 95 77 *Web Site:* www.servidis.ch
Membership(s): Association Nationale des Editeurs de Livres

§Sara Jordan Publishing
Division of Jordan Music Productions Inc
RPO Lakeport Box 28105, St Catharines, ON L2N 7P8
Tel: 905-938-5050 *Toll Free Tel:* 800-567-7733 *Fax:* 905-938-9970 *Toll Free Fax:* 800-229-3855
Web Site: www.sara-jordan.com
Key Personnel
Pres: Sara Jordan
Founded: 1990
Publish educational resources.
Publishes in English, French.
ISBN Prefix(es): 978-1-895523; 978-1-894262; 978-1-55386
Number of titles published annually: 6 Print; 2 Audio
Total Titles: 100 Print; 60 Audio
Distribution Center: Gazelle Book Services Ltd, White Cross Mills, Hightown, Lancaster, Lancs LA1 4XS, United Kingdom *Tel:* (01524) 528500 *Fax:* (01524) 528510 *E-mail:* sales@gazellebookservices.co.uk *Web Site:* www.gazellebookservices.co.uk
Membership(s): Association of Canadian Publishers

Scholastic Canada Ltd
Subsidiary of Scholastic Inc
604 King St W, Toronto, ON M5V 1E1
SAN: 115-5164
Tel: 905-887-7323 *Toll Free Tel:* 800-268-3860 (CN) *Toll Free Fax:* 866-387-4944
E-mail: custserve@scholastic.ca
Web Site: www.scholastic.ca
Key Personnel
Pres, Fin, Opers & Admin: Anne Browne *Tel:* 905-887-7323 ext 4396 *E-mail:* abrown@scholastic.ca
Pres, Mktg & Publg: Nancy Pearson *Tel:* 416-915-3515 *E-mail:* npearson@scholastic.ca
VP, Book Fairs: Brigitte Birtch *Tel:* 905-887-7323 ext 4322 *E-mail:* bbirtch@scholastic.ca
VP, Educ: Wendy Graham *Tel:* 905-887-7323 ext 4299 *E-mail:* wgraham@scholastic.ca
VP, French Div: Chantale Gravel Lalonde *Tel:* 416-915-3510 *E-mail:* clalonde@scholastic.ca
VP, Publg: Diane Kerner *Tel:* 416-915-3523 *E-mail:* dkerner@scholastic.ca
VP, Reading Clubs: Vicki Pasternak *Tel:* 416-915-3516 *E-mail:* vpasternak@scholastic.ca
VP, Trade: Kathy Goncharenko *Tel:* 416-915-3517 *E-mail:* kgoncharenko@scholastic.ca
Rts & Contracts: Maral Maclagan *Tel:* 416-915-3524 *E-mail:* mmaclagan@scholastic.ca
Founded: 1957
Publish & distribute children's books & educational materials in both official languages.
Publishes in English, French.
ISBN Prefix(es): 978-0-590; 978-0-439; 978-0-7791; 978-1-55268; 978-0-545; 978-1-4431; 978-1-338
Imprints: Les Editions Scholastic; North Winds Press; Scholastic Canada
Divisions: Scholastic Book Fairs Canada Inc
Branch Office(s)
175 Hillmount Rd, Markham, ON L6C 1Z7
Distributor for Blue Sky Press (exclusive in CN); Cartwheel Books (exclusive in CN); Chicken House (exclusive in CN); Children's Press (exclusive in CN); Franklin Watts (US) (exclusive in CN); Grolier (exclusive in CN); Klutz (ex-

clusive in CN); Arthur A Levine Books (exclusive in CN); Orchard Books (exclusive in CN); Scholastic en Espanol (exclusive in CN); Scholastic Graphix (exclusive in CN); Scholastic Nonfiction (exclusive in CN); Scholastic Paperbacks (exclusive in CN); Scholastic Press (exclusive in CN); Scholastic Reference (exclusive in CN)
U.S. Publishers Represented: Scholastic Inc
U.S. Rep(s): Scholastic Inc
Foreign Rights: Akcali Copyright Agency (Bengu Ayfer) (Turkey); Bardon-Chinese Media Agency (Electra Chang & Shirley Viva Chang) (Mainland China); Bardon-Chinese Media Agency (Cynthia Chang) (Taiwan); Marcin Biegaj (Poland); Sandra Bruna Agencia Literaria (Sandra Bruna) (Spain); JLM Literary Agency (Nelly, Tatiana & John Moukakos) (Greece); Simona Kessler Agency (Adriana Marina) (Romania); Maxima Creative Agency (Santo Manurung) (Indonesia); Nika Literary Agency (Vania Kadiyska) (Bulgaria); Schindler's Literary Agency (Brazil); Seibel Publishing Services Ltd (Patricia Seibel) (Brazil); Shinwon Agency Co (Yona Kang) (Korea); Tuttle-Mori Agency Inc (Solan Natsume) (Japan); Tuttle-Mori Agency Inc (Pimolporn Yutisri) (Thailand)

§Seal Books
Imprint of Penguin Random House Canada
320 Front St W, Suite 1400, Toronto, ON M5V 3B6
SAN: 201-3975
Tel: 416-364-4449 *Toll Free Tel:* 888-523-9292 (order desk) *Fax:* 416-598-7764
Web Site: www.penguinrandomhouse.ca
Key Personnel
Pres & Publr, PRHC: Kristin Cochrane
Pres & CEO: Brad Martin
EVP & CFO: Barry Gallant
SVP & COO: Robert Wheaton
SVP, Corp Communs & VP, Publicity: Tracey Turriff
VP & Dir, Mktg Strategy & Assoc Publr, RHC: Scott Sellers
SVP & Dir, Prodn: Janine Laporte
Assoc Dir, Prodn: Carla Kean
Founded: 1977
No unsol mss; prefer queries in advance from potential authors.
Publishes in English.
ISBN Prefix(es): 978-0-7704
Number of titles published annually: 18 Print
Membership(s): Canadian Booksellers Association; Canadian Publishers' Council

§Second Story Press
20 Maud St, Suite 401, Toronto, ON M5V 2M5
Tel: 416-537-7850 *Fax:* 416-537-0588
E-mail: info@secondstorypress.ca
Web Site: secondstorypress.ca
Key Personnel
Publr, Owner & Pres: Margie Wolfe
Gen Mgr: Phuong Truong
Prodn Mgr: Melissa Kaita
Mktg & Promos Mgr: Emma Rodgers
Mktg & Promos Coord: Allie Chenoweth
Founded: 1988
Feminist-inspired books for adults & young readers.
Publishes in English.
ISBN Prefix(es): 978-0-929005; 978-1-896764; 978-1-897187; 978-0-921299
Number of titles published annually: 14 Print
Total Titles: 108 Print
Distributor for The Azrieli Foundation; The Book Publishing Co; Desputeaux & Aubin (aka The Caillou Books) (English-speaking CN)
U.S. Rep(s): Orca Books (children's books)
Orders to: University of Toronto Press, 5201 Dufferin St, North York, ON M3H 5T8 *Tel:* 416-667-7791 *Toll Free Tel:* 800-565-9523 *Fax:* 416-667-7832 *Toll Free Fax:* 800-221-9985; Orca Book Publishers, PO Box 468, Custer, WA 98240-0468, United States (US, children's books) *Toll Free Tel:* 800-210-5277 *Fax:* 250-380-1892 *Web Site:* www.us.orcabook.com; Gazelle Book Services Ltd, White Cross Mills, Hightown, Lancaster, Lancs LA1 4XS, United Kingdom *Tel:* (01524) 528500 *Fax:* (01524) 528510 *E-mail:* sales@gazellebookservices.co.uk *Web Site:* www.gazellebookservices.co.uk
Shipping Address: University of Toronto Press, 5201 Dufferin St, North York, ON M3H 5T8 *Tel:* 416-667-7791 *Toll Free Tel:* 800-565-9523 *Fax:* 416-667-7832 *Toll Free Fax:* 800-221-9985
Distribution Center: University of Toronto Press, 5201 Dufferin St, North York, ON M3H 5T8 *Tel:* 416-667-7791 *Toll Free Tel:* 800-565-9523 *Fax:* 416-667-7832 *Toll Free Fax:* 800-221-9985

Selection du Reader's Digest Canada SRI, see Reader's Digest Association Canada ULC (Selection du Reader's Digest Canada SRI)

§Self-Counsel Press Inc
1481 Charlotte Rd, North Vancouver, BC V7J 1H1
SAN: 115-0545
Tel: 604-986-3366 *Toll Free Tel:* 800-663-3007
E-mail: orders@self-counsel.com; sales@self-counsel.com
Web Site: www.self-counsel.com
Founded: 1971
Legal, business & reference books.
Publishes in English, French.
ISBN Prefix(es): 978-1-55180; 978-1-77040
Number of titles published annually: 24 Print; 5 CD-ROM
Total Titles: 230 Print
Foreign Rights: Atmarr Agency Services (China, France, Germany, Japan, Korea, Philippines, Taiwan, Thailand)
Membership(s): ALA

J Gordon Shillingford Publishing Inc
PO Box 86, RPO Corydon Ave, Winnipeg, MB R3M 3S3
Tel: 204-779-6967
Web Site: www.jgshillingford.com
Key Personnel
Pres & Publr: Gordon Shillingford
Founded: 1992
Primarily a literary publisher (drama & poetry), but also 3-4 nonfiction titles per year. Publish works of Canadian citizens only.
Publishes in English.
ISBN Prefix(es): 978-0-9689709; 978-0-920486; 978-1-896239; 978-0-9697261; 978-1-897289; 978-1-927922
Number of titles published annually: 12 Print
Total Titles: 272 Print
Sales Office(s): Canadian Manda Group, 165 Dufferin St, Toronto, ON M6K 3H6 *Tel:* 416-516-0911 *Fax:* 416-516-0917 *E-mail:* info@mandagroup.com *Web Site:* www.mandagroup.com
The Literary Press Group of Canada, 425 Adelaide St W, Suite 700, Toronto, ON M5V 2C1 (US Rep), Contact: Tan Light *Tel:* 416-483-1321 ext 3 *Fax:* 416-483-2510 *E-mail:* sales@lpg.ca
Distribution Center: University of Toronto Press, 5210 Dufferin St, Toronto, ON M3H 5T8 (CN) *Tel:* 416-667-7791 *Toll Free Tel:* 800-565-9523 *Toll Free Fax:* 800-221-9985 *E-mail:* utpbooks@utpress.utoronto.ca
University of Toronto Press, 2250 Military Rd, Tonowanda, NY 14150, United States (US) *Tel:* 416-667-7791 *Toll Free Tel:* 800-565-9523 *Fax:* 416-667-7832 *Toll Free Fax:* 800-221-9985 *E-mail:* utpbooks@utpress.utoronto.ca
Membership(s): Association of Canadian Publishers; Association of Manitoba Book Publishers; Literary Press Group

Shoreline Press
23 Rue Sainte-Anne, Ste-Anne-de-Bellevue, QC H9X 1L1
SAN: 116-9564
Tel: 514-457-5733
E-mail: info@shorelinepress.ca
Web Site: shorelinepress.ca
Key Personnel
Owner & Sr Ed: Judith Isherwood
Founded: 1991
Publishes in English, French.
ISBN Prefix(es): 978-0-9695180; 978-0-9698752; 978-1-896754; 978-1-926953
Number of titles published annually: 5 Print
Total Titles: 125 Print
Orders to: Coutts Information Services Ltd, 6900 Kinsman Ct, Niagara Falls, ON L2E 7E7 *Tel:* 905-356-6382
Distribution Center: Coutts Information Services Ltd, 6900 Kinsman Ct, Niagara Falls, ON L2E 7E7 *Tel:* 905-356-6382
Membership(s): Association of English-language Publishers of Quebec; Quebec Library Association

Signature Editions
PO Box 206, RPO Corydon, Winnipeg, MB R3M 3S7
Tel: 204-779-7803
E-mail: submissions@signature-editions.com; orders@signature-editions.com
Web Site: www.signature-editions.com
Key Personnel
Publr: Karen Haughian *E-mail:* khaughian@signature-editions.com
Mystery Ed: Doug Whiteway
Poetry Ed: Garry Thomas Morse
Founded: 1986 (as Nuage Editions)
Literary publisher which publishes Canadian authors in the genres of fiction, nonfiction, poetry & drama.
Publishes in English.
ISBN Prefix(es): 978-0-921833; 978-1-897109; 978-1-927426; 978-1-773240
Number of titles published annually: 10 Print; 5 E-Book
Total Titles: 170 Print; 65 E-Book; 10 Audio
Distributor for Cyclops Press
Foreign Rep(s): The Literary Press Group of Canada (Tan Light) (USA)
Orders to: University of Toronto Press (UTP), 5201 Dufferin St, North York, ON M3H 5T8 *Tel:* 416-667-7791 *Toll Free Tel:* 800-565-9523 *Fax:* 416-667-7832 *Toll Free Fax:* 800-221-9985 *E-mail:* utpbooks@utpress.utoronto.ca; University of Toronto Press (UTP), 2250 Military Rd, Tonawanda, NY 14150, United States *Tel:* 416-667-7791 *Toll Free Tel:* 800-565-9523 *Fax:* 416-667-7832 *Toll Free Fax:* 800-221-9985 *E-mail:* utpbooks@utpress.utoronto.ca
Returns: University of Toronto Press (UTP), 5201 Dufferin St, North York, ON M3H 5T8 *Tel:* 416-667-7791 *Toll Free Tel:* 800-565-9523 *Fax:* 416-667-7832 *Toll Free Fax:* 800-221-9985 *E-mail:* utpbooks@utpress.utoronto.ca
Shipping Address: University of Toronto Press (UTP), 5201 Dufferin St, North York, ON M3H 5T8 *Tel:* 416-667-7791 *Toll Free Tel:* 800-565-9523 *Fax:* 416-667-7832 *Toll Free Fax:* 800-221-9985 *E-mail:* utpbooks@utpress.utoronto.ca
Distribution Center: University of Toronto Press (UTP), 5201 Dufferin St, North York, ON M3H 5T8 *Tel:* 416-667-7791 *Toll Free Tel:* 800-565-9523 *Fax:* 416-667-7832 *Toll Free Fax:* 800-221-9985 *E-mail:* utpbooks@utpress.utoronto.ca

University of Toronto Press (UTP), 2250 Military Rd, Tonawanda, NY 14150, United States *Tel:* 416-667-7791 *Toll Free Tel:* 800-565-9523 *Fax:* 416-667-7832 *Toll Free Fax:* 800-221-9985 *E-mail:* utpbooks@utpress.utoronto.ca
Membership(s): Association of Canadian Publishers; Association of Manitoba Book Publishers; Literary Press Group of Canada

Simon & Pierre Publishing Co Ltd
Imprint of The Dundurn Group
3 Church St, Suite 500, Toronto, ON M5E 1M2
Tel: 416-214-5544
E-mail: info@dundurn.com
Web Site: www.dundurn.com
Key Personnel
Pres & Publr: J Kirk Howard *E-mail:* khoward@dundurn.com
Founded: 1991
Fiction.
Publishes in English.
ISBN Prefix(es): 978-0-9690454; 978-0-88924
Number of titles published annually: 80 Print
Total Titles: 133 Print
Distributed by Dundurn Press
Distribution Center: University of Toronto Press, 5201 Dufferin St, Toronto, ON M3H 5T8 *Tel:* 416-667-7791 *Toll Free Tel:* 800-565-9523 *Fax:* 416-667-7832 *Toll Free Fax:* 800-221-9985 *E-mail:* utpbooks@utpress.utoronto.ca *Web Site:* www.utpress.utoronto.ca
Ingram Publisher Services, PO Box 3006, La Vergne, TN 37086-1986, United States *Toll Free Tel:* 855-802-8228 *Toll Free Fax:* 800-838-1149 *E-mail:* customer.service@ingrampublisherservices.com *Web Site:* www.ingrampublisherservices.com
Ingram Publisher Services, Chapter House, Pitfield, Kiln Farm, Milton Keynes MK11 3LW, United Kingdom (UK & Europe) *Tel:* 0800 136-0600 *E-mail:* ipsuksupport@ingramcontent.com

§Simon & Schuster Canada
Subsidiary of Simon & Schuster, Inc
166 King St E, Suite 300, Toronto, ON M5A 1J3
Tel: 647-427-8882 *Toll Free Tel:* 800-387-0446; 800-268-3216 (orders) *Fax:* 647-430-9446 *Toll Free Fax:* 888-849-8151 (orders)
E-mail: info@simonandschuster.ca
Web Site: www.simonandschuster.ca
Key Personnel
Pres & Publr: Kevin Hanson *E-mail:* kevin.hanson@simonandschuster.ca
VP, Sales & Mktg: David Millar *E-mail:* david.millar@simonandschuster.ca
VP, Sales: Nancy Purcell *E-mail:* nancy.purcell@simonandschuster.ca
VP, Mktg & Publicity: Felicia Quon *E-mail:* felicia.quon@simonandschuster.ca
VP, Edit Dir: Nita Pronovost *E-mail:* nita.pronovost@simonandschuster.ca
Dir, Busn Aff: Kien Vuong *E-mail:* kien.vuong@simonandschuster.ca
Dir, Publicity: Adria Iwasutiak *E-mail:* adria.iwasutiak@simonandschuster.ca
Mng Ed: Patricia Ocampo *E-mail:* patricia.ocampo@simonandschuster.ca
Assoc Ed: Brendan May *E-mail:* brendan.may@simonandschuster.ca
Publishes in English.
Distributor for Andrews McMeel Publishing LLC; Baen Books; Baseball America; Black Library; Blue Heeler Books; Cardoza; Chicken Soup for the Soul; Cider Mill Press Book Publishers LLC; Downtown Books; Games Workshop; Good Books; Hooked on Phonics; Kaplan Publishing; KinFolk; John Locke Publishing; Merck; Open Road Press; Rebellion; Ripley's Publishing; Simon & Schuster; Viz; Weldon Owen Inc; World Almanac

Simply Read Books
501-5525 West Blvd, Vancouver, BC V6M 3W6
Tel: 604-727-2960
E-mail: go@simplyreadbooks.com
Web Site: www.simplyreadbooks.com
Founded: 2001
Our approach to illustrated children's books follows the finest publishing tradition & spirit with inspired content, extraordinary artwork, outstanding graphic design form & quality production. We introduce contemporary books with a modern appeal & fresh outlook & offer a careful selection of timeless stories that link the past with the present. We specialize in high-quality, unique picture books & fiction. Before submitting, please browse our web site, bookstores & libraries to look at & read what we publish. This will give you an idea of whether or not your story or illustrations would fit with our list.
Publishes in English, French.
ISBN Prefix(es): 978-1-894965; 978-0-9688768; 978-1-897476; 978-1-927018
Number of titles published annually: 20 Print
Total Titles: 200 Print
Sales Office(s): Ingram Content Group, One Ingram Blvd, La Vergne, TN 37086, United States *Tel:* 615-793-5000 *E-mail:* inquiry@ingramcontent.com *Web Site:* www.ingramcontent.com
Orders to: Ingram Content Group, One Ingram Blvd, La Vergne, TN 37086, United States *Tel:* 615-793-5000 *E-mail:* inquiry@ingramcontent.com *Web Site:* www.ingramcontent.com
Returns: Ingram Publisher Services, 1210 Ingram Dr, Chambersburg, PA 17202, United States *Tel:* 717-262-4860 *E-mail:* customerservice@ingrampublisherservices.com
Warehouse: Ingram Content Group, One Ingram Blvd, La Vergne, TN 37086, United States *Tel:* 615-793-5000 *E-mail:* inquiry@ingramcontent.com *Web Site:* www.ingramcontent.com
Distribution Center: Ingram Content Group, One Ingram Blvd, La Vergne, TN 37086, United States *Tel:* 615-793-5000 *E-mail:* inquiry@ingramcontent.com *Web Site:* www.ingramcontent.com
Membership(s): Association for Canadian Publishers in the US; Independent Book Publishers Association

Gordon Soules Book Publishers Ltd
2372 Haywood Ave, West Vancouver, BC V7V 1X7
SAN: 115-0987
Tel: 604-922-6588 *Fax:* 604-922-6574
E-mail: books@gordonsoules.com
Web Site: www.gordonsoules.com
Key Personnel
Pres: Gordon Soules
Founded: 1965
Publishers & distributors of high quality trade books.
Publishes in English.
ISBN Prefix(es): 978-0-919574; 978-1-894661; 978-0-920045
Number of titles published annually: 4 Print
Total Titles: 65 Print

Summerthought Publishing
PO Box 2309, Banff, AB T1L 1C1
Tel: 403-762-0535 *Fax:* 403-762-3095 *Toll Free Fax:* 800-762-3095 (orders)
E-mail: info@summerthought.com; sales@summerthought.com
Web Site: summerthought.com
Key Personnel
Co-Owner & Publr: Andrew Hempstead
Sales, Mktg & Opers: Dianne Melton *E-mail:* dianne@summerthought.com
Founded: 1971
Publisher of Canadian Rockies nonfiction books.
Publishes in English.
ISBN Prefix(es): 978-0-9782375; 978-0-9699732; 978-0-9811491; 978-0-919934; 978-1-926983
Number of titles published annually: 3 Print; 3 E-Book
Total Titles: 30 Print; 9 E-Book
Imprints: EJH Literary Enterprises
Foreign Rep(s): Cordee (UK); Freytag & Berndt (Europe)

Synaxis Press
37323 Hawkins Rd, Dewdney, BC V0M 1H0
Tel: 604-826-9336
E-mail: synaxis@new-ostrog.org
Web Site: synaxispress.ca
Key Personnel
Illus: Vasili Novakshonoff
Ed: Archbishop Lazar Puhalo
Founded: 1972
Theology for the Orthodox church & children's books.
Publishes in English, French.
ISBN Prefix(es): 978-0-919672
Number of titles published annually: 6 Print
Total Titles: 90 Print
Distributed by Light & Life Publishing Co

TCP Press
Imprint of The Communication Project
20200 Marsh Hill Rd, Uxbridge, ON L9P 1R3
Tel: 905-852-3777 *Toll Free Tel:* 800-772-7765
E-mail: tcp@tcpnow.com
Web Site: www.tcppress.com
Key Personnel
Dir, Publg: Brian Puppa
Founded: 1984
Trade & educational books for both children & adults.
Publishes in English, French.
ISBN Prefix(es): 978-1-896232
Number of titles published annually: 4 Print; 1 CD-ROM; 5 E-Book; 1 Audio
Total Titles: 26 Print; 3 CD-ROM; 6 E-Book; 3 Audio
Membership(s): Independent Publishers Association

Tecumseh Press, see Borealis Press Ltd

Theytus Books Ltd
Subsidiary of Okanagan Indian Educational Resources Society
RR 2, Green Mountain Rd, Site 50, Comp 8, Lot 45, Penticton, BC V2A 6J7
SAN: 115-1517
Tel: 250-493-7181 *Fax:* 250-493-5302
E-mail: order@theytus.com
Web Site: www.theytus.com
Key Personnel
Publr: Greg Younging *Tel:* 250-493-7181 ext 201
Founded: 1980
Native history, culture, politics, education & literature.
Publishes in English, French.
ISBN Prefix(es): 978-0-919441; 978-1-894778
Number of titles published annually: 8 Print; 2 CD-ROM
Total Titles: 76 Print; 3 CD-ROM
Distribution Center: Sandhill Book Marketing, Mill Crook Industrial Park, Unit 4, 3308 Appaloosa Rd, Kelowna, BC V1V 2G9 (AB & BC), Contact: Nancy Wise *Tel:* 250-491-1446 *Toll Free Tel:* 800-667-3848 *Fax:* 250-491-4066 *E-mail:* info@sandhillbooks.com
University of Toronto Press, 5201 Dufferin St, North York, ON M3H 5T8 (CN exc AB & BC) *Tel:* 416-667-7791 *Toll Free Tel:* 800-565-9523 *Fax:* 416-667-7832 *E-mail:* utpbooks@utpress.utoronto.ca *Web Site:* www.utpress.utoronto.ca
University of Toronto Press, 2250 Military Rd, Tonawanda, NY 14150, United States *Tel:* 416-667-7791 *Toll Free Tel:* 800-565-9523

Fax: 416-667-7832 *Toll Free Fax:* 800-221-9985 *E-mail:* utpbooks@utpress.utoronto.ca
Web Site: www.utpress.utoronto.ca
Membership(s): Association of Canadian Publishers

Thistledown Press
410 Second Ave, Saskatoon, SK S7K 2C3
SAN: 115-1061
Tel: 306-244-1722 *Fax:* 306-244-1762
E-mail: tdpress@thistledownpress.com; editorial@thistledownpress.com; marketing@thistledownpress.com
Web Site: www.thistledownpress.com
Key Personnel
Owner & Publr: Allan Forrie
Publg & Prodn Mgr: Jackie Forrie
Sales, Fulfillment, Promos & Edit: Nicole Haldoupis
Founded: 1975
Poetry, fiction & nonfiction by Canadian authors; Irish poetry; fiction for young adults.
Publishes in English.
ISBN Prefix(es): 978-0-920066; 978-0-920633; 978-1-895449; 978-1-894345; 978-1-897235
Number of titles published annually: 14 Print
Total Titles: 250 Print
U.S. Rep(s): Amazon.com; University of Toronto Press
Distribution Center: University of Toronto Press, 5201 Dufferin St, Toronto, ON M3H 5T8 *Tel:* 416-667-7791 *Toll Free Tel:* 800-565-9523 (CN & US) *Fax:* 416-667-7832 *Toll Free Fax:* 800-221-9985 (CN & US) *E-mail:* utpbooks@utpress.utoronto.ca *Web Site:* www.utpress.utoronto.ca

Thompson Educational Publishing Inc
20 Ripley Ave, Toronto, ON M6S 3N9
Tel: 416-766-2763 (admin & orders) *Toll Free Tel:* 877-366-2763 *Fax:* 416-766-0398 (admin & orders)
E-mail: info@thompsonbooks.com
Web Site: www.thompsonbooks.com
Key Personnel
Pres: Keith Thompson
VP, Teacher & Student Success: Faye Thompson
Busn Dir: Rowan Thompson
Founded: 1989
High school, college & university textbooks.
Publishes in English.
ISBN Prefix(es): 978-1-55077; 978-0-921332
Number of titles published annually: 6 Print
Total Titles: 170 Print
Distribution Center: University of Toronto Press Distribution, 5201 Dufferin St, Toronto, ON M3H 5T8 (CN orders, higher educ) *Toll Free Tel:* 800-565-9523 *Toll Free Fax:* 800-221-9985 *E-mail:* utpbooks@utpress.utoronto.ca *Web Site:* www.utpress.utoronto.ca
University of Toronto Press Distribution, 2250 Military Rd, Tonawanda, NY 14150, United States (US orders, higher educ) *Toll Free Tel:* 800-565-9523 *Toll Free Fax:* 800-221-9985 *E-mail:* utpbooks@utpress.utoronto.ca *Web Site:* utpress.utoronto.ca
Membership(s): Association of Canadian Publishers; Ontario Business Educator's Association; Organization of Book Publishers of Ontario

TouchWood Editions
Member of The Heritage Group
103-1075 Pendergast St, Victoria, BC V8V 0A1
Tel: 250-360-0829 *Fax:* 250-386-0829
E-mail: info@touchwoodeditions.com
Web Site: www.touchwoodeditions.com
Key Personnel
Publr: Taryn Boyd *E-mail:* taryn@touchwoodeditions.com
Founded: 1985
Publishes in English.
ISBN Prefix(es): 978-1-894898; 978-1-926741; 978-1-926971; 978-0-920663; 978-1-927129; 978-1-77151
Number of titles published annually: 12 Print; 18 E-Book
Total Titles: 224 Print; 170 E-Book
Imprints: Brindle & Glass
Orders to: Heritage Group Distribution, 19272-96 Ave, Suite 8, Surrey, BC V4N 4C1 *Tel:* 604-881-7067 *Toll Free Tel:* 800-665-3302 *Fax:* 604-881-7068 *Toll Free Fax:* 800-566-3336 *E-mail:* orders@hgdistribution.com *Web Site:* www.hgdistribution.com
Returns: Heritage Group Distribution, 19272-96 Ave, Suite 8, Surrey, BC V4N 4C1 *Tel:* 604-881-7067 *Toll Free Tel:* 800-665-3302 *Fax:* 604-881-7068 *Toll Free Fax:* 800-566-3336 *E-mail:* orders@hgdistribution.com *Web Site:* www.hgdistribution.com
Shipping Address: Heritage Group Distribution, 19272-96 Ave, Suite 8, Surrey, BC V4N 4C1 *Tel:* 604-881-7067 *Toll Free Tel:* 800-665-3302 *Fax:* 604-881-7068 *Toll Free Fax:* 800-566-3336 *E-mail:* orders@hgdistribution.com *Web Site:* www.hgdistribution.com
Warehouse: Heritage Group Distribution, 19272-96 Ave, Suite 8, Surrey, BC V4N 4C1 *Tel:* 604-881-7067 *Toll Free Tel:* 800-665-3302 *Fax:* 604-881-7068 *Toll Free Fax:* 800-566-3336 *E-mail:* orders@hgdistribution.com *Web Site:* www.hgdistribution.com
Distribution Center: Heritage Group Distribution, 19272-96 Ave, Suite 8, Surrey, BC V4N 4C1 *Tel:* 604-881-7067 *Toll Free Tel:* 800-665-3302 *Fax:* 604-881-7068 *Toll Free Fax:* 800-566-3336 *E-mail:* orders@hgdistribution.com *Web Site:* www.hgdistribution.com
Membership(s): Association of Book Publishers of British Columbia; Association of Canadian Publishers
See separate listing for:
Brindle & Glass Publishing Ltd

Townson Publishing Co Ltd
Affiliate of General Publishing Inc
PO Box 1404, Sta A, Vancouver, BC V6C 2P7
Tel: 604-886-0594
E-mail: townsonpublishing@gmail.com
Web Site: generalpublishing.co.uk
Key Personnel
Chmn: Donald Townson
Ed & Rts: Jackson House
Founded: 1977
General trade books, literature in translation.
Publishes in English, French.
ISBN Prefix(es): 978-0-920822
Number of titles published annually: 4 Print; 2 E-Book
Total Titles: 16 Print; 16 E-Book
Imprints: General Publishing; Townson Publishing; translatedbooks.com
Subsidiaries: Associated Merchandisers Inc (USA)
Foreign Rep(s): Associated Merchandisers Inc (UK, USA)

Tradewind Books
202-1807 Maritime Mews, Vancouver, BC V6H 3W7
Tel: 604-662-4405
E-mail: tradewindbooks@yahoo.com; tradewindbooks@gmail.com
Web Site: www.tradewindbooks.com
Key Personnel
Owner & Publr: Michael Katz
Art Dir & Co-Publr: Carol Frank
Ed: Kim Aippersbach
Copy-Ed: Viktoria Cseh
Founded: 1996
Children's picture books, chapter books & young adults novels.
Publishes in English.
ISBN Prefix(es): 978-1-896580; 978-1-926890
Number of titles published annually: 8 Print
Total Titles: 95 Print
Distributed by Fitzhenry & Whiteside (CN); Orca Book Publishers (US)
U.S. Rep(s): Orca Books
Foreign Rep(s): John Reed Book Distribution (Australia, New Zealand); Turnaround Publisher Services Ltd (UK)
Distribution Center: John Reed Book Distribution, 11 Yandala St, PO Box 257, Tea Gardens, NSW 2324, Australia (Australia & New Zealand) *Tel:* (02) 4997 2936 *Fax:* (02) 4997 2937 *E-mail:* johnmreed@johnreedbooks.com.au
Turnaround Publisher Services Ltd, Olympia Trading Estate, Unit 3, Coburg Rd, Wood Green, London N22 6TZ, United Kingdom *Tel:* (020) 8829 3000 *Fax:* (020) 8881 5088 *E-mail:* enquirie@turnaround-uk.com
Membership(s): Association of Book Publishers of British Columbia; Association of Canadian Publishers

§Tralco-Lingo Fun
PO Box 79008, RPO Garth, Hamilton, ON L9C 7N6
Tel: 905-575-5717 *Toll Free Tel:* 888-487-2526
E-mail: contact_tralco@tralco.com; sales@tralco.com
Web Site: www.tralco.com
Key Personnel
Owner & Pres: Karen Traynor *E-mail:* karen@tralco.com
Founded: 1982
Publisher & distributor of second language educational materials.
Publishes in French.
ISBN Prefix(es): 978-0-921376; 978-1-55409
Number of titles published annually: 10 Print; 12 CD-ROM
Total Titles: 300 Print
Branch Office(s)
3909 Witmer Rd, No 856, Niagara Falls, NY 14305, United States
Distributor for Languages for Kids
Membership(s): Education Market Association

Tundra Books
Imprint of Penguin Random House Canada
320 Front St W, Suite 1400, Toronto, ON M5V 3B6
SAN: 115-5415
Tel: 416-364-4449 *Toll Free Tel:* 888-523-9292 (orders); 800-588-1074 *Fax:* 416-598-7764 *Toll Free Fax:* 888-562-9924 (orders)
E-mail: tundra@mcclelland.com
Web Site: tundrabooks.wordpress.com
Key Personnel
Publr: Tara Walker *Tel:* 416-364-4449 ext 813951
Founded: 1967
Children's books.
Publishes in English, French.
ISBN Prefix(es): 978-0-88776
Number of titles published annually: 50 Print
Total Titles: 350 Print
Branch Office(s)
Tundra Books of Northern New York, PO Box 1030, Plattsburgh, NY 12901, United States
Distributed by Everybody's Books CC (South Africa); Forrester Books NZ Ltd (New Zealand); El Hombre de la Mancha (Costa Rica & Panama); El Hormiguero (Guatemala)
U.S. Publishers Represented: Tundra Books of Northern New York
U.S. Rep(s): Jack Eichkorn & Associates Inc; R&R Book Co; Southern Territory Associates Inc; Nancy Suib & Associates
Foreign Rights: Cooke Agency International
Orders to: Penguin Random House Canada, 6971 Columbus Rd, Mississauga, ON L5T 1K1; Random House Inc - Distribution Center, 400 Hahn Rd, Westminster, MD 21157, United

States *Toll Free Tel:* 800-726-0600; 800-733-3000 *Toll Free Fax:* 800-659-2436
Returns: Random House Inc, 1019 N State Rd 47, Crawfordsville, IN 47933, United States
Warehouse: Random House Inc - Distribution Center, 400 Hahn Rd, Westminster, MD 21157, United States *Toll Free Tel:* 800-726-0600 *Toll Free Fax:* 800-659-2436
Membership(s): ABA; ALA; Association of Booksellers for Children; International Board on Books for Young People

Turnstone Press
Artspace Bldg, 206-100 Arthur St, Winnipeg, MB R3B 1H3
SAN: 115-1096
Tel: 204-947-1555 *Toll Free Tel:* 888-363-7718 *Fax:* 204-942-1556
E-mail: info@turnstonepress.com
Web Site: www.turnstonepress.com
Key Personnel
Assoc Publr & Intl Rts: Jamis Paulson
Founded: 1976
Literary press including fiction, nonfiction, poetry, literary criticism, biography, travel fiction & adventure all with a strong Canadian focus.
Publishes in English.
ISBN Prefix(es): 978-0-88801
Number of titles published annually: 10 Print
Total Titles: 300 Print
Imprints: Ravenstone Books
Returns: LitDistCo, 8300 Lawson Rd, Milton, ON L9T 0A4 *Toll Free Tel:* 800-591-6250 *Toll Free Fax:* 800-591-6251 *E-mail:* orders@litdistco.ca *Web Site:* www.litdistco.ca
Distribution Center: LitDistCo, 8300 Lawson Rd, Milton, ON L9T 0A4 *Toll Free Tel:* 800-591-6250 *Toll Free Fax:* 800-591-6251 *E-mail:* orders@litdistco.ca *Web Site:* www.litdistco.ca
Membership(s): Literary Press Group of Canada

UBC Press, see University of British Columbia Press

Ulysses Travel Guides
4176, rue Saint-Denis, Montreal, QC H2W 2M5
Tel: 514-843-9882 (ext 2232); 514-843-9447 (bookstore) *Toll Free Tel:* 800-748-9171 *Fax:* 514-843-9448
E-mail: info@ulysses.ca; st-denis@ulysses.ca
Web Site: www.ulyssesguides.com
Key Personnel
Pres: Daniel Desjardins *Tel:* 514-843-9447 ext 2224 *E-mail:* daniel@ulysses.ca
VP, Publg: Claude Morneau *E-mail:* claude@ulysses.ca
Founded: 1980
Travel books.
Publishes in English, French.
ISBN Prefix(es): 978-2-921444; 978-2-89464; 978-2-9801872; 978-1-894676
Number of titles published annually: 25 Print; 25 E-Book; 2 Audio
Total Titles: 175 Print; 175 E-Book; 2 Audio
Imprints: Guides de Voyage Ulysses
Branch Office(s)
560, Ave du President-Kennedy, Montreal, QC H3A 1J9 *Tel:* 514-843-7222 *E-mail:* pk@ulysse.ca *Web Site:* www.guidesulysse.com
Distributor for A A Publications; Dakota; Footprint Handbooks; Editions Syvain Harvey; Hunter Publishing; ITMB Publishing Ltd; Odyssey Publications; PassPorter Travel Press; Rother Walking Guides; Trans Canada Trail Foundation; Vacation Works Publications

University of Alberta Press
Ring House 2, Edmonton, AB T6G 2E1
SAN: 118-9794
Tel: 780-492-3662 *Fax:* 780-492-0719
Web Site: www.uap.ualberta.ca
Key Personnel
Dir: Linda Cameron *Tel:* 780-492-0717 *E-mail:* linda.cameron@ualberta.ca
Assoc Dir: Cathie Crooks *Tel:* 780-492-5820 *E-mail:* ccrooks@ualberta.ca
Mng Ed: Mary Lou Roy *Tel:* 780-492-9488 *E-mail:* marylou.roy@ualberta.ca
Acq Ed: Peter Midgley *Tel:* 780-492-7714 *E-mail:* pmidgley@ualberta.ca
Busn Administrator: Basia Kowal *E-mail:* bkowal@ualberta.ca
Prodn & Designer: Alan Brownoff *Tel:* 780-492-8285 *E-mail:* abrownof@ualberta.ca
Founded: 1969
The UAP publishes in the areas of biography, history, language, literature, natural history, regional interest, native studies, travel narratives & reference books. UAP contributes to the intellectual & cultural life of Alberta & Canada by publishing well-edited, research-based knowledge & creative thought.
Publishes in English.
ISBN Prefix(es): 978-0-88864; 978-1-77212
Number of titles published annually: 22 Print; 15 E-Book
Total Titles: 600 Print; 88 E-Book; 2 Audio
Imprints: CCI Press; Gutteridge Books; Pica Pica Books
Sales Office(s): Ampersand Canada's Book & Gift Agency Inc, 321 Carlaw Ave, Suite 213, Toronto, ON M4M 2S1, Contact: Saffron Beckwith *Tel:* 416-703-0666 ext 124 *Fax:* 416-703-4745 *E-mail:* saffronb@ampersandinc.ca *Web Site:* www.ampersand.ca
U.S. Rep(s): Wayne State University Press
Foreign Rep(s): Gazelle Academic (Albania, Andorra, Armenia, Austria, Bahrain, Belarus, Belgium, Bosnia and Herzegovina, Botswana, Bulgaria, Cambodia, China, Continental Europe, Croatia, Cyprus, Czech Republic, Denmark, Egypt, Ethiopia, Europe, Finland, France, Georgia, Germany, Gibraltar, Greece, Hungary, Iceland, India, Indonesia, Iran, Iraq, Ireland, Israel, Italy, Japan, Jordan, Kenya, Laos, Latvia, Liechtenstein, Lithuania, Luxembourg, Macedonia, Malaysia, Malta, Moldova, Monaco, Montenegro, Mozambique, Myanmar, Namibia, Netherlands, Norway, Oman, Poland, Portugal, Qatar, Romania, Russia, Serbia, Slovakia, Slovenia, South Africa, Spain, Sweden, Switzerland, Taiwan, Turkey, Uganda, Ukraine, United Arab Emirates, UK, UK & the continent, UK Commonwealth)
Orders to: University of Toronto Press, 5201 Dufferin St, Toronto, ON M3H 5T8 *Tel:* 416-667-7841 *Toll Free Tel:* 800-565-9523 *Fax:* 416-667-7832 *Toll Free Fax:* 800-221-9985 *E-mail:* utpbooks@utpress.utoronto.ca *Web Site:* www.utpress.utoronto.ca
Returns: University of Toronto Press, 5201 Dufferin St, Toronto, ON M3H 5T8 *Tel:* 416-667-7841 *Toll Free Tel:* 800-565-9523 *Fax:* 416-667-7832 *Toll Free Fax:* 800-221-9985 *E-mail:* utpbooks@utpress.utoronto.ca *Web Site:* www.utpress.utoronto.ca
Shipping Address: University of Toronto Press, 5201 Dufferin St, Toronto, ON M3H 5T8 *Tel:* 416-667-7841 *Toll Free Tel:* 800-565-9523 *Fax:* 416-667-7832 *Toll Free Fax:* 800-221-9985 *E-mail:* utpbooks@utpress.utoronto.ca *Web Site:* www.utpress.utoronto.ca
Warehouse: University of Toronto Press, 5201 Dufferin St, Toronto, ON M3H 5T8 *Tel:* 416-667-7841 *Toll Free Tel:* 800-565-9523 *Fax:* 416-667-7832 *Toll Free Fax:* 800-221-9985 *E-mail:* utpbooks@utpress.utoronto.ca *Web Site:* www.utpress.utoronto.ca
Distribution Center: University of Toronto Press, 5201 Dufferin St, Toronto, ON M3H 5T8 *Tel:* 416-667-7841 *Toll Free Tel:* 800-565-9523 *Fax:* 416-667-7832 *Toll Free Fax:* 800-221-9985 *E-mail:* utpbooks@utpress.utoronto.ca *Web Site:* www.utpress.utoronto.ca
Wayne State University Press (WSUP), Shipping& Receiving, 40 W Hancock, Detroit, MI 48201-1309, United States *Tel:* 313-577-6120 *Fax:* 313-577-6131 *E-mail:* bookorders@wayne.edu *Web Site:* wsupress.wayne.edu
Gazelle Book Services Ltd, White Cross Mills, Hightown, Lancaster, Lancs LA1 4XS, United Kingdom *Tel:* (01524) 528500 *Fax:* (01524) 528510 *E-mail:* sales@gazellebookservices.co.uk *Web Site:* www.gazellebookservices.co.uk
Membership(s): Association of American University Presses; Association of Canadian Publishers; Association of Canadian University Presses; Book Publishers Association of Alberta
See separate listing for:
Canadian Circumpolar Institute (CCI) Press

University of British Columbia Press
2029 West Mall, Vancouver, BC V6T 1Z2
SAN: 115-1118
Tel: 604-822-5959 *Toll Free Tel:* 877-377-9378 *Fax:* 604-822-6083 *Toll Free Fax:* 800-668-0821
E-mail: frontdesk@ubcpress.ca
Web Site: www.ubcpress.ca
Key Personnel
Dir: Melissa Pitts *Tel:* 604-822-6376 *E-mail:* pitts@ubcpress.ca
Asst Dir, Prodn & Edit Servs: Holly Keller *Tel:* 604-822-4545 *E-mail:* keller@ubcpress.ca
Sr Ed (Kelowna): Randy Schmidt *Tel:* 250-764-4761 *Fax:* 250-764-4709 *E-mail:* schmidt@ubcpress.ca
Sr Ed (Toronto): James MacNevin *Tel:* 289-779-2414 *E-mail:* macnevin@ubcpress.ca
Publicity & Events Mgr: Kerry Kilmartin *Tel:* 604-822-8244 *E-mail:* kilmartin@ubcpress.ca
Edit Coord: Nadine Pedersen *Tel:* 604-827-1795 *E-mail:* pedersen@ubcpress.ca
Ed: Megan Brand *Tel:* 604-822-5885 *E-mail:* brand@ubcpress.ca; Leslie Erickson *Tel:* 604-822-4548 *E-mail:* erickson@ubcpress.ca; Ann Macklem *Tel:* 604-822-0093 *E-mail:* macklem@ubcpress.ca
Academic Mktg Mgr: Harmony Johnson *Tel:* 604-822-1978 *E-mail:* johnson@ubcpress.ca
Mktg Mgr: Laraine Coates *Tel:* 604-822-6486 *E-mail:* coates@ubcpress.ca
Founded: 1971
Academic & scholarly publications; native studies, law & society, military history, northern studies, sexuality, political science & forestry.
Publishes in English.
ISBN Prefix(es): 978-0-88865; 978-0-7748
Number of titles published annually: 70 Print
Total Titles: 900 Print; 2 CD-ROM; 1 E-Book
Imprints: On Campus; On Point Press; Pacific Education Press; Purich Books; UBC Press
Branch Office(s)
587 Markham St, 2nd fl, Toronto, ON M6G 2L7 *Fax:* 416-535-9677
Distributed by University of Washington Press
Distributor for Art Gallery of New South Wales; Athabasca University Press (worldwide); Canadian Forest Service (worldwide); Editors Canada (worldwide); Fowler Museum at UCLA; International Sculpture Center; Island Press; Jessica Kingsley Publishers; Laval University Press (worldwide, English lang books); Lost Horse Press; Lynx House Press; Museum for African Art; National Gallery of Australia; Oregon State University Press; Power Publications; Silkworm Books; UCLA Chicano Studies Research Center Press; University of Arizona Press; University of Washington Press; Western Geographical Press (worldwide)
U.S. Publishers Represented: Island Press; Last Horse Press; Lynx House Press; Oregon State University Press; University of Arizona Press; University of Washington Press; Western Geographical Press (worldwide)
U.S. Rep(s): University of Washington Press

Foreign Rep(s): Combined Academic Publishers (Africa, Europe, Middle East, UK); East-West Export Books (Royden Muranaka) (Asia-Pacific); Special Book Services Ltd (South America)
Orders to: University of Toronto Press Distribution, 5201 Dufferin St, Toronto, ON M3H 5T8 *Tel:* 416-667-7791 *Toll Free Tel:* 800-565-9523 *Fax:* 416-667-7832 *Toll Free Fax:* 800-221-9985 *E-mail:* utpbooks@utpress.utoronto.ca; University of Washington Press, c/o Hopkins Fulfillment Services, PO Box 50370, Baltimore, MD 21211-4370, United States *Tel:* 410-516-6956 *Toll Free Tel:* 800-537-5487 (US) *Fax:* 410-516-6998 *E-mail:* hfscustserv@press.jhu.edu
Distribution Center: University of Toronto Press Distribution, 5201 Dufferin St, Toronto, ON M3H 5T8 *Tel:* 416-667-7791 *Toll Free Tel:* 800-565-9523 *Fax:* 416-667-7832 *Toll Free Fax:* 800-221-9985 *E-mail:* utpbooks@utpress.utoronto.ca
Membership(s): Association of American University Presses; Association of Book Publishers of British Columbia; Association of Canadian Publishers; Association of Canadian University Presses; International Association of Scholarly Publishers
See separate listing for:
Pacific Educational Press

University of Calgary Press
2500 University Dr NW, Calgary, AB T2N 1N4
Tel: 403-220-7578 *Fax:* 403-282-0085
E-mail: ucpress@ucalgary.ca
Web Site: press.ucalgary.ca
Key Personnel
Dir: Brian Scivener *Tel:* 403-220-3511 *E-mail:* brian.scivener@ucalgary.ca
Edit & Mktg Coord: Helen Hajnoczky *Tel:* 403-220-4208 *E-mail:* helen.hajnoczky@ucalgary.ca
Mktg Specialist: Alison Cobra *Tel:* 403-220-3979 *E-mail:* alison.cobra@ucalgary.ca
Founded: 1981
Specialize in scholarly books that make a difference. Series subjects include history, parks & protected areas, regional history, Northern studies, Africa, cinema studies, cultural studies, Canadian military & military history & communications studies.
Publishes in English, French.
ISBN Prefix(es): 978-0-919813; 978-1-895176; 978-1-55238
Number of titles published annually: 20 Print; 2 CD-ROM; 10 Online; 20 E-Book
Total Titles: 400 Print; 5 CD-ROM; 25 Online; 150 E-Book
U.S. Rep(s): Michigan State University Press
Foreign Rep(s): Gazelle Book Services Ltd (Europe, UK)
Foreign Rights: Roli Books (New Delhi)
Distribution Center: Georgetown Terminal Warehouses, 34 Armstrong Ave, Georgetown, ON L7G 4R9 *Toll Free Tel:* 877-864-8477 *Toll Free Fax:* 877-864-4272 *E-mail:* orders@gtwcanada.com *Web Site:* www.gtwcanada.com
Longleaf Services Inc, 116 S Boundary St, Chapel Hill, NC 27514-3808, United States *Tel:* 919-966-7449 *Toll Free Tel:* 800-848-6224 *Fax:* 919-962-2704 *Toll Free Fax:* 800-272-6817 *E-mail:* customerservice@longleafservices.org *Web Site:* www.longleafservices.org
Gazelle Book Services Ltd, White Cross Mills, Hightown, Lancaster, Lancs LA1 4XS, United Kingdom (Asia, Europe, Middle East, South Africa & UK) *Tel:* (01524) 68765 *Fax:* (01524) 63232 *E-mail:* sales@gazellebookservices.co.uk *Web Site:* www.gazellebookservices.co.uk
Membership(s): Association for Canadian Publishers in the US; Association of Canadian Publishers; Book Publishers Association of Alberta

University of Manitoba Press
University of Manitoba, 301 St Johns College, 92 Dysart Rd, Winnipeg, MB R3T 2M5
SAN: 115-5474
Tel: 204-474-9495 *Fax:* 204-474-7566
E-mail: uofmpress@umanitoba.ca
Web Site: uofmpress.ca
Key Personnel
Dir: David Carr *Tel:* 204-474-9242 *E-mail:* carr@cc.umanitoba.ca
Mng Ed: Glenn Bergen *Tel:* 204-474-7338 *E-mail:* d.bergen@umanitoba.ca
Acqs Ed: Jill McConkey *Tel:* 204-474-8804 *E-mail:* jill.mcconkey@umanitoba.ca
Sales & Mktg Supv: David Larsen *Tel:* 204-474-9998 *E-mail:* david.larsen@umanitoba.ca
Promos & Publicity Coord: Ariel Gordon *Tel:* 204-474-8408 *E-mail:* ariel.gordon@umanitoba.ca
Founded: 1967
Scholarly & general titles in humanities & social sciences; western Canadian history & native studies.
Publishes in English.
ISBN Prefix(es): 978-0-88755
Number of titles published annually: 14 Print
Total Titles: 120 Print
Distributed by University of Toronto Press (Canadian sales); Michigan State University Press (US sales)
Distribution Center: University of Toronto Press, 5201 Dufferin St, Toronto, ON M3H 5T8 *Tel:* 416-667-7791 *Toll Free Tel:* 800-565-9523 *Fax:* 416-667-7856 *Toll Free Fax:* 800-221-9985 *E-mail:* utpbooks@utpress.utoronto.ca
Michigan State University Press, c/o Chicago Distribution Center, 11030 S Langley Ave, Chicago, IL 60628, United States *Toll Free Tel:* 800-621-2736 *Toll Free Fax:* 800-621-8476 *E-mail:* orders@press.chicago.edu *Web Site:* www.msupress.org

University of Ottawa Press (Presses de l'Université d'Ottawa)
Affiliate of University of Ottawa
542 King Edward Ave, Ottawa, ON K1N 6N5
Tel: 613-562-5246 *Fax:* 613-562-5247
E-mail: puo-oup@uottawa.ca
Web Site: press.uottawa.ca
Key Personnel
Dir: Lara Mainville, MA *Tel:* 613-562-5663 *E-mail:* lara.mainville@uottawa.ca
Acqs Ed: Dominike Thomas *Tel:* 613-562-5800 ext 3065 *E-mail:* dthomas@uottawa.ca
Prodn Mgr: Suzanne Cloutier *Tel:* 613-562-5800 ext 2853 *E-mail:* scloutier@uottawa.ca; Elizabeth Schwaiger *Tel:* 613-562-5800 ext 3064 *E-mail:* eschwaig@uottawa.ca
Admin Asst: Sonia Rheault
Founded: 1936
Scholarly & trade books. The oldest francophone university press & only fully bilingual university press in North America.
Publishes in English, French.
ISBN Prefix(es): 978-0-7766; 978-2-7603
Number of titles published annually: 22 Print; 22 E-Book
Total Titles: 450 Print; 400 E-Book
Foreign Rep(s): Ampersand Inc (Canada (English-speaking)); CEDIF (France); Durnell Marketing (Europe exc UK); Oxford Publicity Partnership (UK); Patrimoine Diffusion SPRL (Belgium, Luxembourg, Netherlands); Prologue Inc (Canada (French-speaking)); Servidis (Switzerland)
Distribution Center: University of Toronto Press (UTP), 5201 Dufferin St, North York, ON M3H 5T8 (English titles to CN) *Tel:* 416-667-7791 *Toll Free Tel:* 800-565-9523 *Fax:* 416-667-7832 *Toll Free Fax:* 800-221-9985 *E-mail:* utpbooks@utpress.utoronto.ca *Web Site:* www.utpress.utoronto.ca
Prologue Inc, 1650 Lionel-Bertrand Blvd, Boisbriand, QC J7H 1N7 (French titles to CN) *Tel:* 450-434-0306 *Toll Free Tel:* 800-363-2864 *Toll Free Fax:* 800-361-8088 *E-mail:* prologue@prologue.ca *Web Site:* www.prologue.ca
Patrimoine Diffusion SPRL, 119 Milcamps Ave, 1030 Brussels, Belgium, Contact: Eric Durigneux *Tel:* (02) 736 68 47 *Fax:* (02) 736 68 47 *E-mail:* patrimoine@telenet.be
Distribution du Nouveau Monde, 30 rue Guy Lussac, 75005 Paris, France (French titles to France) *Tel:* 01 43 54 49 02 *Fax:* 01 43 54 39 15 *E-mail:* dnm@librairieduquebec.fr *Web Site:* www.librairieduquebec.fr
Servidis SA, Chemin des Chalets 7, 1279 Chavannes-de-Bogis, Switzerland (French titles to Switzerland) *Tel:* (022) 960 95 25 *Fax:* (022) 776 63 64 *E-mail:* commande@servidis.ch *Web Site:* www.servidis.ch
Marston Book Services Ltd, 160 Milton Park, PO Box 269, Abingdon, Oxon OX14 4YN, United Kingdom (English titles to Europe & UK) *Tel:* (01235) 465521 *Fax:* (01235) 465555 *E-mail:* direct.orders@marston.co.uk *Web Site:* www.marston.co.uk
Membership(s): American Association of University Presses; Association Nationale des Editeurs de Livres; Association of Canadian Publishers; Association of Canadian University Presses

University of Regina Press
2 Research Dr, Suite 246, Regina, SK S4S 7H9
SAN: 115-0278
Mailing Address: University of Regina, 3737 Wascana Pkwy, Regina, SK S4S 0A2
Tel: 306-585-4758 *Fax:* 306-585-4699
E-mail: uofrpress@uregina.ca
Web Site: uofrpress.ca
Key Personnel
Publr & Dir: Bruce Walsh *Tel:* 306-585-4795 *E-mail:* bruce.walsh@uregina.ca
Sr Ed: Donna Grant *Tel:* 306-585-4787 *E-mail:* donna.grant@uregina.ca
Ed: David McLennan *Tel:* 306-585-4789 *E-mail:* david.mclennan@uregina.ca
Media & Publicity: Melissa Shirley *Tel:* 647-389-9510 *E-mail:* melissa.shirley@uregina.ca
Founded: 1973
Scholarly paperbacks & hardcovers on cultural & economic development & history of Canadian Plains & western Canada.
Publishes in English, French.
ISBN Prefix(es): 978-0-88977
Number of titles published annually: 15 Print
Total Titles: 90 Print; 1 CD-ROM
Distribution Center: University of Toronto Press Distribution, 5201 Dufferin St, Toronto, ON M3H 5T8 *Tel:* 416-667-7791 *Toll Free Tel:* 800-565-9523 (CN & US) *Fax:* 416-667-7832 *Toll Free Fax:* 800-221-9985 (CN & US) *E-mail:* utpbooks@utpress.utoronto.ca *Web Site:* www.utpress.utoronto.ca
Ingram Publisher Services, c/o Customer Service, 14 Ingram Blvd, Box 631, La Vergne, TN 37086, United States *Toll Free Tel:* 866-400-5351 *Toll Free Fax:* 800-838-1149 *E-mail:* ips@ingramcontent.com *Web Site:* www.ipage.ingramcontent.com
Gazelle Book Services, White Cross Mills, Hightown, Lancaster, Lancs LA1 4XS, United Kingdom *Tel:* (01524) 528500 *Fax:* (01524) 528510 *E-mail:* sales@gazellebookservices.co.uk *Web Site:* www.gazellebookservices.co.uk
Membership(s): Association of Canadian Publishers; Association of Canadian University Presses; Saskatchewan Publishers Group

§University of Toronto Press
Division of Multicultural History Society of Canada
10 St Mary St, Suite 700, Toronto, ON M4Y 2W8

Tel: 416-978-2239 *Fax:* 416-978-4738
E-mail: info@utpress.utoronto.ca
Web Site: www.utpress.utoronto.ca; www.utppublishing.com
Key Personnel
Pres, CEO & Publr: John Yates *Tel:* 416-978-2239 ext 2222 *E-mail:* jyates@utpress.utoronto.ca
VP, Dist & MIS: Hamish Cameron *Tel:* 416-667-7773 *E-mail:* hcameron@utpress.utoronto.ca
VP, Scholarly Publg: Lynn Fisher *Tel:* 416-978-2239 ext 2243 *E-mail:* lfisher@utpress.utoronto.ca
Sales & Mktg Mgr: Brian MacDonald *Tel:* 416-978-2239 ext 2253 *E-mail:* brianm@utpress.utoronto.ca
Founded: 1901
Publisher, distributor & university bookstore.
Publishes in English.
ISBN Prefix(es): 978-0-8020; 978-0-7727; 978-1-4426
Number of titles published annually: 200 Print; 100 E-Book
Total Titles: 3,500 Print; 500 E-Book
Imprints: Rotman-UTP Publishing; University of Toronto
Divisions: Pippin Publishing; University of Toronto Press Guidance Centre; University of Toronto Press Journals Division
Branch Office(s)
2250 Military Rd, Tonawanda, NY 14150, United States *Tel:* 716-693-2768 *Fax:* 716-693-2167
Distributor for Anvil Press; Ashlar House; Aspasia Books; Baltray Books; Between the Lines; Black Rose Books; Book Publishing Co; The British Library (CN only); Canadian Museum of Nature; Caslon Publishing; CAW/TCA Canada; Central European University Press; Centre for Urban & Community Studies, University of Toronto; Codasat Canada Ltd; Cormorant Books; Diamond Mind Enterprises; Douglas & McIntyre; DreamCatcher Publishing Co; The Dundurn Group; Faculty of Applied Science & Engineering; G7 Funds; Goose Lane Editions; Great Plains Publishing Ltd; Greystone Books; Guernica Editions; Guidance Centre; Help...We've Got Kids; Integrative Leadership International Ltd; ISSI; Journals-Canadian Theatre Review; Jump Math; KapableKidz Inc; Edgar Kent; Kids Can Press; Knowledge Bureau; Wilfrid Laurier University Press; Legas Publishing; Lobster Press Ltd; Mage Publishers; Mayant Press; McDonald & Woodward Publishing Co; McGilligan Books; La Montage Secrete; Multicultural History Society of Ontario; Multilingual Matters (North America only); National Museum of Science & Technology; New Society Publishers; OISE Press; Oolichan Books; Penn State University Press; Pippin Publishing; Porcupine's Quill; Princess Margaret Hospital Foundation; Quill Driver Books/Word Dancer Press Inc; RDR Books; Royal Ontario Museum; RREES Inc; Elysa Schwartzman; Second Story Press; Secret Mountain; Seraphim Editions; J Gordon Shillingford Publishing Inc; Signature Editions; Sister Vision Press; Square One Publishing Inc; Subway Books Ltd; Sumach Press; Teachers College Press; Theytus Books Ltd; Thompson Educational Publishing; Toronto Heschel School; TSAR Publications; Twin Guinep Ltd; University of British Columbia Press; University of Manitoba Press; University of Ottawa Press; University of Toronto Center for Public Management; University of Toronto Press-Higher Education; Wall & Emerson Inc; Wolsak & Wynn Publishers; Word of Mouth Production
U.S. Rep(s): Book Traveler (Roger Sauls) (Southeast); Terry & Read LLC (Southwest coast); Ben Schrager (Northeast); Trim Associates (Gary Trim) (Midwest)
Foreign Rep(s): Cranbury International LLC (Ethan Atkin) (Caribbean, Central America, South America); Durnell Marketing Ltd (Andrew Durnell) (Europe, Iceland, Ireland, Israel, Northern Ireland, Russia); East-West Export Books (Royden Muranaka) (Australia, New Zealand, Pacific Islands, South Korea, Southeast Asia); Everest International Publishing Services (Wei Zhao) (China); Oxford Publicity Partnership Ltd (Gary Hall) (UK); Viva Books Pvt Ltd (India)
Returns: 5201 Dufferin St, North York, ON M3H 5T8 (worldwide exc CN, India, Japan, UK/Europe & US)
Warehouse: 2250 Military Rd, Tonawanda, NY 14150, United States
5201 Dufferin St, North York, ON M3H 5T8 (worldwide exc CN, India, Japan, UK/Europe & US)
Distribution Center: 5201 Dufferin St, North York, ON M3H 5T8 (worldwide exc CN, India, Japan, UK/Europe & US) *Tel:* 416-667-7791 *Toll Free Tel:* 800-565-9523 *Fax:* 416-667-7832 *Toll Free Fax:* 800-221-9985 *E-mail:* utpbooks@utpress.utoronto.ca
2250 Military Rd, Tonawanda, NY 14150, United States *Tel:* 716-693-2768
Viva Books Pvt Ltd, 4737/23 Ansari Rd, Darya Ganj, New Delhi 110 002, India *Tel:* (011) 42242200 *Fax:* (011) 42242240 *E-mail:* viva@vivagroupindia.net
MHM Ltd, 1-1-13-4F Kanda Jimbocho, Chiyoda-ku, Tokyo 101-0051, Japan *Tel:* (03) 3518-9181 *Fax:* (03) 3518-9523 *E-mail:* sales@mhmlimited.co.jp
NBN International, Airport Business Ctr, 10 Thornbury Rd, Plymouth, Devon PL6 7PP, United Kingdom (UK & Europe) *Tel:* (01752) 202301 *Fax:* (01752) 202333 *E-mail:* orders@nbninternational.com *Web Site:* distribution.nbni.co.uk
Membership(s): American Association of University Presses; Association of Canadian Publishers; Association of Canadian University Presses; Organization of Book Publishers of Ontario
See separate listing for:
Pippin Publishing

Vehicule Press
PO Box 42094, CP Roy, Montreal, QC H2W-2T3
Tel: 514-844-6073 *Fax:* 514-844-7543
E-mail: vp@vehiculepress.com; admin@vehiculepress.com
Web Site: www.vehiculepress.com
Key Personnel
Publr & Gen Ed: Simon Dardick; Nancy Marrelli
Mng Ed: Vicki Marcok
Ed, Esplanade Books: Dimitri Nasrallah
Ed, Signal Editions: Carmine Starnino
Mktg & Promos Mgr: Maya Assouad
Founded: 1973
Paperback trade; fiction, jazz, biography, literature, poetry, translation.
Publishes in English.
ISBN Prefix(es): 978-0-919890; 978-1-55065
Number of titles published annually: 14 Print
Total Titles: 530 Print
Imprints: Esplanade Books (fiction); Signal Editions (poetry)
U.S. Rep(s): IPG (Independent Publishers Group)
Returns: LitDistCo, 8300 Lawson Rd, Milton, ON L9T 0A4 *Toll Free Tel:* 800-591-6250 *Toll Free Fax:* 800-591-6251 *Web Site:* www.litdistco.ca
Shipping Address: LitDistCo, 8300 Lawson Rd, Milton, ON L9T 0A4 *Toll Free Tel:* 800-591-6250 *Toll Free Fax:* 800-591-6251 *Web Site:* www.litdistco.ca
Distribution Center: LitDistCo, 8300 Lawson Rd, Milton, ON L9T 0A4 *Toll Free Tel:* 800-591-6250 *Toll Free Fax:* 800-591-6251 *E-mail:* ordering@litdistco.ca *Web Site:* www.litdistco.ca
Membership(s): Association of Canadian Publishers; Literary Press Group of Canada

VLB Editeur Inc
Division of Groupe Ville-Marie Litterature
1055, boul Rene-Levesque Est, bureau 300, Montréal, QC H2L 4S5
Tel: 514-849-5259 *Fax:* 514-849-1388
Web Site: www.edvlb.com
Key Personnel
Pres: Christian Jette
VP, Publg & Ed: Martin Balthazar
Literary Dir for Essays: Alain-Nicolas Renaud
Asst Ed: Ariane Caron-Lacoste *E-mail:* ariane.caron.l@groupevml.com
Founded: 1976
Publishes in French.
ISBN Prefix(es): 978-2-89005
Number of titles published annually: 20 Print; 18 E-Book
Total Titles: 600 Print; 250 E-Book
Distribution Center: Messageries ADP, 2315 Rue de la Province, Longueuil, QC J4G 1G4

Weigl Educational Publishers Ltd
6325 Tenth St SE, Calgary, AB T2H 2Z9
SAN: 115-1312
Tel: 403-233-7747 *Toll Free Tel:* 800-668-0766 *Fax:* 403-233-7769 *Toll Free Fax:* 866-449-3445
E-mail: orders@weigl.com
Web Site: www.weigl.ca; av2books.com
Key Personnel
Pres & Publr: Linda Weigl *E-mail:* linda@weigl.com
Founded: 1979
School library resources & textbooks for grades K-12 in English & French. Emphasis on: Canadian history, social studies & public affairs; science; multiculturalism; career/vocational/life management; distance education; books & guides for teachers.
Publishes in English.
ISBN Prefix(es): 978-0-919879; 978-1-896990; 978-1-55388
Number of titles published annually: 40 Print
Total Titles: 200 Print
Branch Office(s)
350 Fifth Ave, 59th fl, New York, NY 10118, United States *Toll Free Tel:* 866-649-3445 *E-mail:* av2books@weigl.com
Distributed by The Creative Co (US); Rourke Publishing; Saunders Book Co (CN); Smart Apple Media (US)

Whitecap Books
Division of Fitzhenry & Whiteside Limited
314 W Cordova St, Suite 209, Vancouver, BC V6B 1E8
Tel: 604-681-6181 *Toll Free Tel:* 800-387-9776 *Toll Free Fax:* 800-260-9777
Web Site: www.whitecap.ca
Key Personnel
Publr: Nick Rundall *Tel:* 905-477-9700 ext 244 *E-mail:* nickr@whitecap.ca
Ed: Patrick Geraghty *E-mail:* patrickg@whitecap.ca
Designer: Andrew Bagatella *E-mail:* andrewb@whitecap.ca
Founded: 1977
Trade books, photography, cookery, regional, gardening, outdoor guide books, natural history, juvenile nonfiction & illustrated children's books, juvenile fiction.
Publishes in English.
ISBN Prefix(es): 978-1-55110; 978-1-55285; 978-1-77050
Number of titles published annually: 85 Print
Total Titles: 480 Print
Imprints: Walrus Books
U.S. Rep(s): Firefly Books
Returns: Fitzhenry & Whiteside, 195 Allstate Pkwy, Markham, ON L3R 4T8

John Wiley & Sons Canada Ltd
Subsidiary of John Wiley & Sons Inc
90 Eglinton Ave E, Suite 300, Toronto, ON M4P 2Y3
Tel: 416-236-4433 *Toll Free Tel:* 800-225-5945 (orders only) *Fax:* 416-236-8743 (cust serv); 416-236-4447 *Toll Free Fax:* 800-565-6802 (orders)
E-mail: canada@wiley.com
Web Site: www.wiley.ca
Founded: 1968
Textbooks for colleges & universities; trade, professional & reference.
Publishes in English, French.
ISBN Prefix(es): 978-0-470; 978-0-471
Number of titles published annually: 50 Print
Total Titles: 600 Print
Distributor for John Wiley & Sons Inc
Distribution Center: 6045 Freemont Blvd, Mississauga, ON L5R 4J3 *Tel:* 416-236-4433 *Fax:* 416-236-8743

Wilfrid Laurier University Press
75 University Ave W, Waterloo, ON N2L 3C5
Tel: 519-884-0710 *Toll Free Tel:* 866-836-5551 (CN & US) *Fax:* 519-725-1399
E-mail: press@wlu.ca
Web Site: www.wlupress.wlu.ca
Key Personnel
Dir: Lisa Quinn *Tel:* 519-884-0710 ext 2843 *E-mail:* lquinn@wlu.ca
Mng Ed: Rob Kohlmeier *Tel:* 519-884-0710 ext 6119 *E-mail:* rkohlmeier@wlu.ca
Sr Ed: Siobhan McMenemy *Tel:* 519-884-0710 ext 3782 *E-mail:* smcmenemy@wlu.ca
Sales & Mktg Coord: Clare Hitchens *Tel:* 519-884-0710 ext 2665 *E-mail:* chitchens@wlu.ca
Digital Projs Coord: Murray Tong *Tel:* 519-884-0710 ext 3029 *E-mail:* mtong@wlu.ca
Prodn Coord: Mike Bechthold *Tel:* 519-884-0710 ext 6122 *E-mail:* mbechthold@wlu.ca
Founded: 1974
Publish scholarly & general interest books in the social sciences & humanities.
Publishes in English.
ISBN Prefix(es): 978-0-88920; 978-1-55458; 978-0-921821
Number of titles published annually: 30 Print; 30 Online
Total Titles: 416 Print; 400 Online
Imprints: Laurier Digital
Distributor for Laurier Centre for Military Strategic & Disarmament Studies; Toronto International Film Festival
Foreign Rep(s): Blue4Books Inc (Midwest USA, Southeast USA, Southwest USA); CRW Marketing Services for Publishers (Tony Sagun) (Philippines, Thailand); Terry Fernihough (Ontario, CN); Gazelle Book Services Ltd (Caribbean, Continental Europe, India, Ireland, Israel, Japan, Latin America, Middle East, South Africa, Southeast Asia, Sub-Saharan Africa, UK); Hargreaves, Fuller & Paton (Terry Fernihough) (Ontario, CN); Hargreaves, Fuller & Paton (Karen Stacey) (Quebec, CN); Hargreaves, Fuller & Paton (Alberta, CN, British Columbia, CN, Manitoba, CN, Northwest Territories, CN, Saskatchewan, CN, West Toronto, ON, CN, Yukon, CN); Bob Rosenberg Group (Western USA); Ben Schrager (Northeast USA); Karen Stacey (Quebec, CN); Leona & Jerry Trainer (Eastern Canada)
Orders to: University of Toronto Press Distribution, 5201 Dufferin Street, Toronto, ON M3H 5T8 *Toll Free Tel:* 800-565-9523 *Toll Free Fax:* 800-221-9985 *E-mail:* utpbooks@utpress.utoronto.ca; Ingram Publisher Services, 14 Ingram Blvd, La Vergne, TN 37086, United States *Toll Free Tel:* 866-400-5351; Gazelle Book Services Ltd, White Cross Mills, Hightown, Lancaster, Lancs LA1 4XS, United Kingdom (outside North America) *Tel:* (01524) 68765 *Fax:* (01524) 63232 *E-mail:* sales@gazellebooks.co.uk
Membership(s): Association of American University Presses; Association of Canadian Publishers; Association of Canadian University Presses; Canadian Booksellers Association; Organization of Book Publishers of Ontario

WLU Press, see Wilfrid Laurier University Press

Wood Lake Publishing Inc
485 Beaver Lake Rd, Kelowna, BC V4V 1S5
Tel: 250-766-2778 *Toll Free Tel:* 800-663-2775 (orders & cust serv) *Fax:* 250-766-2736 *Toll Free Fax:* 888-841-9991 (orders & cust serv)
E-mail: info@woodlake.com; customerservice@woodlake.com
Web Site: www.woodlakebooks.com
Key Personnel
Pres & Publr: Patty Berube
Mktg Promos & Sales: Samantha Michaels *E-mail:* samantham@woodlake.com
Founded: 1980
Books, church curriculum & periodicals.
Publishes in English.
ISBN Prefix(es): 978-1-55145; 978-0-919599; 978-0-929032
Number of titles published annually: 8 Print
Total Titles: 135 Print
Imprints: CopperHouse; Seasons of the Spirit; Whole People of God Online; Wood Lake
Distributed by Augsburg Canada; Presbyterian Church of Canada; United Church of Canada
Distributor for Northstone

§Worldwide Library
Imprint of Harlequin Enterprises Ltd
225 Duncan Mill Rd, Don Mills, ON M3B 3K9
Mailing Address: PO Box 603, Fort Erie, ON L2A 5X3
Tel: 416-445-5860 *Toll Free Tel:* 888-432-4879
E-mail: customerservice@harlequin.com
Web Site: www.harlequin.com
Founded: 1982
Mass market fiction.
Publishes in English.
ISBN Prefix(es): 978-0-373
Number of titles published annually: 5 Print; 9 E-Book
Imprints: Gold Eagle Books; Worldwide Mystery
Branch Office(s)
PO Box 9049, Buffalo, NY 14269-9049, United States
Foreign Rights: Booklink (Europe)
Warehouse: 3010 Walden Ave, Depew, NY 14043, United States

Small Presses

Listed here, in alphabetical order, are U.S. & Canadian publishers who were not eligible to be listed in the sections covering U.S. Publishers or Canadian Publishers. Many of these publishers are new or offer distinctive titles they wish to make known to the users of *Literary Market Place*. Entries in this section are paid listings.

Publishers interested in participating in this section in future editions of LMP are invited to contact **Lauri Rimler, Advertising Sales** by e-mail at lwrimler@infotoday.com, by phone at 800-409-4929 (press 1) or 908-219-0088, or by mail at Information Today, Inc., 121 Chanlon Road, Suite G-20, New Providence, NJ 07974-2195.

Acroterion Books
5305 Harvard Rd, Lawrence, KS 66049-4781
Tel: 785-917-0773
E-mail: info@acroterionbooks.com
Web Site: www.acroterionbooks.com
Key Personnel
Edit Dir: Charles Anthony Silvestri
Artistic Dir: Anne Horjus *Tel:* 608-355-0481
Founded: 2013
Our mission is to offer picture books of the highest quality, combining words with music & illustrations & create powerful connections between these different forms of art.
Titles include *SLEEP (ISBN: 978-1-4803-5402-9)*
Distributed by Amazon.com; Barnes & Noble; Hal Leonard; J W Pepper; Sheet Music Plus

Adams-Pomeroy Press
103 N Jackson St, Albany, WI 53502
Mailing Address: PO Box 189, Albany, WI 53502
Tel: 608-862-3645 *Toll Free Tel:* 877-862-3645 *Fax:* 608-862-3647
E-mail: adamspomeroy@tds.net
Founded: 1996
Adams-Pomeroy Press publishes books in the areas of education, multicultural nonfiction, juvenile fiction & fiction.
Titles include *Basic Level Literacy Programs for English-Speaking and Non-English-Speaking Adults: A Variety of Options*; *Haunted Hill (A Sam & Stephanie Mystery)*; *How Big Is Your Class? Practical Tips for Teaching Small and Large Primary Grade Classes*; *Missing What's-Her-Name*; *Mixed Heritage: Your Source for Books for Children and Teens about Persons and Families of Mixed Racial, Ethnic, and/or Religious Heritage*; *My Reading Buddy Is a Dog!: Your Resource for Creating and Running a Canine Reading Buddy Program*
ISBN Prefix(es): 978-0-9661009
Membership(s): The Association of Publishers for Special Sales; Colorado Independent Publishers Association; Independent Book Publishers Association

AIC Publications
PO Box 181467, Arlington, TX 76002-1467
E-mail: submissions@aicpublications.com
Web Site: aicpublications.com
Key Personnel
Pres: M Hamzah
Our literature focuses on adult nonfiction, young adult fiction & children's picture book stories highlighting the unique & diverse experiences of Blacks in America & Africa designed to promote positive advancement, socioeconomic empowerment & literacy rates. We take real community issues presented in fiction, offer solutions for them while providing the positive end result of success. Our nonfiction provides a historical understanding & analysis for community growth in a fast changing world. We want our readers to Attain the knowledge, Innovate for success & take Command of their future!
Titles include *A Worthy Muslim: Quranic Tools Needed to Overcome Oppression and Imperialism in Order to Institute Justice*
ISBN Prefix(es): 978-0-9799464
Membership(s): Independent Book Publishers Association

Alazar Press
Imprint of Royal Swan Enterprises Inc
201 Orchard Lane, Carrboro, NC 27510
SAN: 853-0521
Tel: 919-274-0653
E-mail: alazar.press@gmail.com
Web Site: www.alazar-press.com
Key Personnel
Publr: Rosemarie Gulla *E-mail:* rgulla@nc.rr.com
Mgr: Joseph Gulla
Founded: 2007
Focused on engaging young people with ideas, Alazar Press is dedicated to producing quality books for children of all ages & is aligned with the mission of Royal Swan Enterprises.
Royal Swan Enterprises offers high quality literature & accompanying ideas in a vital & relevant manner in order to best serve the developing minds of young people. Royal Swan acknowledges the inherent worth & dignity of all children & works to equip them with the tools of a literate & reflective society. Asserting the primacy of building true emotional engagement to learning, Royal Swan develops books, story frameworks, methods, products & services for young learners & their families.
Titles include *The Artist and the King*; *By Trolley Past Trimbledon Bridge*; *I'm Going to Sing, Black American Spirituals Volume Two*; *On the Wings of the Swan*; *PAR-TAY: Dance of the Veggies (And Their Friends)*; *The Thumbtack Dancer*; *Walk Together Children, Black American Spirituals Volume One*
ISBN Prefix(es): 978-0-9793000; 978-0-9977720
Distributed by Independent Publishers Group (IPG)
Membership(s): International Literacy Association; North Carolina Reading Association; Triangle Reading Council

Class Action Ink
1300 NE 16 Ave, Suite 712, Portland, OR 97232-1483
Tel: 503-280-2448
E-mail: pamg0822@gmail.com
Web Site: www.classactionink.com
Key Personnel
Owner/Publr: Pam Glenn
Founded: 2009
Publishes literary fiction & poetry for mature, culturally savvy readers.
Titles include *All the Wrong Places—Mrs. Frog's Improbable Search for Love*; *Barter World*; *Even As We Speak: Selected Poems*; *What you least expect: selected poems 1980-2011*
ISBN Prefix(es): 978-0-9841530
Membership(s): Independent Book Publishers Association

Dreaming Publications LLC
1126 Bel Air Dr, Santa Barbara, CA 93103
SAN: 859-4333
Tel: 661-776-5152; 310-560-4732
E-mail: dreamingpublications@gmail.com
Web Site: dreamingpublications.com
Key Personnel
Dir of Innovative Opers: Carrie West, MFA *E-mail:* carriekc00@gmail.com
Dir of Creative & Visionary Devt: Lyn Marsh, PhD *E-mail:* lynmarshphd@gmail.com
Founded: 2010
Dreaming Publications LLC publishes adult & juvenile fiction & nonfiction. Our focus is to publish works that inspire new dreams & future visions, as well as creative/innovative thinking & imagination.
Titles include *Conversations with Einstein in His Afterlife*; *The Grand Tree (2nd ed) (book 1 of 3 in the Rainbow Crystal series)*
ISBN Prefix(es): 978-0-9844495
Membership(s): Independent Book Publishers Association

Filsinger & Company Ltd
288 W 12 St, Suite 2R, New York, NY 10014
Tel: 212-243-7421 (by appt)
E-mail: filsingercompany@gmail.com
Web Site: www.filsingerco.com
Key Personnel
Pres: Cheryl Filsinger
Founded: 1974
Publisher of museum-quality children's books including the NEIGHBORS series.
Retail availability: *Bummer* at Sustenance Books, Murphys, CA; *NEIGHBORS* series at Teich Toys+Books (NYC), Book Hampton, Canio's, Harbor Books, & South Fork Natural History Museum (Hamptons, NY); *Philippe The Black Sheep* at Albertine, Book Culture on Columbus, & McNally Jackson (NYC), Book Hampton (Hamptons, NY).
Titles include *Bummer (print & ebook)*; *The Children's Pack of Frames*; *NEIGHBORS The Water Critters*; *NEIGHBORS The Yard Critters Book 1*; *NEIGHBORS The Yard Critters TOO*; *Philippe The Black Sheep (print ed in English, ebooks in English & French)*
ISBN Prefix(es): 978-0-916754
Distributed by Amazon.com (print & ebooks); Baker & Taylor (print); Follett School Solutions (print); kobo.com (ebooks)

4Kidz Publishing
265 El Dorado Blvd, No 1712, Webster, TX 77598
Tel: 601-467-2743
E-mail: info@4kidzpublishing.com
Web Site: www.facebook.com/4kidzpublishing/
Key Personnel
Owner: Andrew Fairchild
Mktg Consultant: Simon Salinas *E-mail:* marketing@4kidzpublishing.com
Founded: 2013
We at 4Kidz Publishing pride ourselves in creating award-winning books in children's literature. Though we are a small press company, our service & dedication to helping authors achieve their publishing goals is our number one commitment. We provide access to award-winning editors & illustrators while developing a publishing time line & market-

ing strategy that is within the author's budget. We also provide assistance with press releases, query letters & submissions to exclusive children's magazines & bloggers for review. To learn what we can do for you, contact us at info@4kidzpublishing.com.
Titles include *The Adventures of Hairy Goat*; *Have You Seen My Egg?*; *Rose and Her Amazing Nose*
ISBN Prefix(es): 978-1-5136
Distributed by Lightning Source

Granite Peak Publications
5131 NE 201 Place, Lake Forest Park, WA 98155
Tel: 206-417-2861
E-mail: publicity@yellowstonetreasures.com
Web Site: www.yellowstonetreasures.com
Key Personnel
Ed & Publr: Beth Chapple *E-mail:* beth@yellowstonetreasures.com
Founded: 2000
Granite Peak Publications publishes well researched adult trade books on Greater Yellowstone.
Titles include *Through Early Yellowstone: Adventuring by Bicycle, Covered Wagon, Foot, Horseback, and Skis*; *Visiting Geyserland*; *Yellowstone Treasures: The Traveler's Companion to the National Park*
ISBN Prefix(es): 978-0-9706873; 978-0-9858182
Distributed by Independent Publishers Group (IPG)
Membership(s): Publishers Association of the West

Moonstone Press LLC
4816 Carrington Circle, Sarasota, FL 34243
SAN: 852-5625
Tel: 301-765-1081 *Fax:* 301-765-0510
E-mail: mazeprod@erols.com
Web Site: www.moonstonepress.net
Key Personnel
Publr: Stephanie Maze
Founded: 2001
Publishes quality photography-based books in English & Spanish for ages 3 & up. Award-winning book titles include: *Healthy Foods from A to Z/Comida sana de la A a la Z*; *Keeping Fit from A to Z/Mantente en forma de la A a la Z*; *Breastfeeding Around the World/Amamantar alrededor del mundo*; *Moments in the Wild/Momentos en el reino animal* (4 title series); *With Ballet in My Soul: Adverntures of a Globetrotting Impresario* (ISBN: 978-0-9834983-8-4).
ISBN Prefix(es): 978-0-9707768; 978-0-9769542; 978-0-9834983
Distributed by IPG/Small Press United
Membership(s): Independent Book Publishers Association; White House Press Photogaphers Association

Painted Hills Publishing
16500 Dakota Ridge Rd, Longmont, CO 80503
Tel: 303-823-6642
E-mail: cw@livingimagescjw.com
Web Site: www.wildhoofbeats.com; www.livingimagescjw.com
Key Personnel
Owner: Carol Walker
Founded: 2008
Publishes photography books on wild horses with the purpose of educating the public about the wild horse situation in the US. Also publishes books on the techniques of photographing domestic & wild horses.
Titles include *Galloping to Freedom: Saving the Adobe Town Appaloosas*; *Horse Photography: The Dynamic Guide for Horse Lovers*; *Wild Hoofbeats: America's Vanishing Wild Horses*
ISBN Prefix(es): 978-0-9817936
Distributed by Baker & Taylor; Gazelle International; Greenleaf Book Group
Membership(s): Independent Book Publishers Association; PPA

Ransom Note Press
143 E Ridgewood Ave, Box 419, Ridgewood, NJ 07451
Tel: 201-835-2790
E-mail: editorial@ransomnotepress.com
Web Site: www.ransomnotepress.com
Key Personnel
Publr: Christian Alighieri
Sr Ed: Emily Marlowe
Publicist: Max St John
Founded: 2005
Ransom Note Press publishes modern & traditional mysteries & novels of suspense. Query via e-mail with descriptive letter & first 25 pages. No pet mysteries, serial killers or short story collections. We are interested only in novels that offer gripping story lines & well-executed plots. In general, we prefer novels in which the author has attempted to do something different to break from tradition & explore new ground.
Titles include *Never Kill a Friend*; *Nine Man's Murder*; *The Outsmarting of Criminals: A Mystery Introducing Miss Felicity Prim*
ISBN Prefix(es): 978-0-9773787
Distributed by Baker & Taylor; Brodart Books; Midpoint Trade Books
Membership(s): Independent Book Publishers Association

Rivendell Books
PO Box 29348, St Louis, MO 63126-0348
SAN: 854-1531
Tel: 314-609-6534
E-mail: butch@rivendellbooks.com
Web Site: www.rivendellbooks.com
Key Personnel
Publr: Butch Drury
Founded: 2008
Rivendell Books is a narrowly focused, niche publisher for the lone writer of creative nonfiction books that explore the Transcendent Function or collaboration of the conscious & the unconscious—the process at the heart of Carl Jung's theory of psychological growth, by which one is guided, thru Active Imagination or dialogue with the unconscious, toward the person one is meant to be.
Titles include *A Different Kind of Sentinel*
ISBN Prefix(es): 978-0-9797023
Distributed by Amazon.com; Barnes & Noble (online); Ingram; Lightning Source
Membership(s): The C G Jung Society of Saint Louis; Independent Book Publishers Association; The International Hearing Voices Network; Missouri Writers' Guild; St Louis Publishers Association; St Louis Writers Guild

Thompson Mill Press

Thompson Mill Press LLC
2110 S Eagle Rd, No 368, Newtown, PA 18940
Tel: 215-431-1424
E-mail: bob.regan@thompsonmillpress.com
Web Site: www.thompsonmillpress.com; www.KobeeManatee.com
Key Personnel
Principal: Bob Regan
Founded: 2012
Located in the northern suburbs of Philadelphia, Thompson Mill Press LLC focuses on the development, publishing & distribution of children's educational picture books containing anthropomorphic characters. Our initial plans for distribution include all of North America. Future distribution plans include Asia, Australia, Central & South America, Europe & Mexico.
We do not accept unsol material.
Titles include *Kobee Manatee: A Wild Weather Adventure*; *Kobee Manatee: Heading Home to Florida*; *Kobee Manatee: Shipwreck Sea Friends*
ISBN Prefix(es): 978-0-9883269; 978-0-9971239
Distributed by Small Press United (through Independent Publishers Group)
Membership(s): ABA; The Children's Book Council; Independent Book Publishers Association

Three Wishes Publishing Company
26500 W Agoura Rd, Suite 102-754, Calabasas, CA 91302
Tel: 818-878-0902 *Fax:* 818-878-1805
E-mail: Alva710@aol.com
Web Site: www.threewishespublishing.com
Founded: 2007
Children's book publisher.
Titles include *Circus Fever*; *Dear Master Dragon*; *I'm 5*; *On Your Mark, Get Set, Go!*
ISBN Prefix(es): 978-0-9796380
Distributed by Amazon.com; Baker & Taylor; Barnes & Noble; Follett School Solutions Inc
Membership(s): ALA; Angels of the Alliance; Association of Jewish Libraries of Southern California; California Literary Arts Society; California School Library Association; Children's Literature Council; Independent Book Publishers Association; Reading Is Fundamental of Southern California; Society of Children's Book Writers & Illustrators

TJ Publishers Inc
PO Box 702701, Dallas, TX 75370
Toll Free Tel: 800-999-1168 *Fax:* 972-416-0944
E-mail: TJPubinc@aol.com
Key Personnel
Pres: T Patrick O'Rourke
Founded: 1978
Publisher & distributor of quality books, DVDs & other materials related to sign language & deafness including several best sellers.
Titles include *A Basic Course in American Sign Language (2nd ed)*; *From Mime to Sign*; *Student Study Guide to A Basic Course in American Sign Language*
ISBN Prefix(es): 978-0-932666

Worthy & James Publishing
PO Box 362015, Milpitas, CA 95036
SAN: 852-5765
Tel: 408-945-3963
E-mail: worthy1234@sbcglobal.net; mail@worthyjames.com
Web Site: www.worthyjames.com
Key Personnel
Mgr: Diane James
Mgr/Author: Greg Mostyn
Founded: 2006
Publications in basic accounting, basic finance & basic math.
Titles include *Basic Accounting Concepts, Principles, and Procedures (vols 1 & 2, 2nd ed)*
ISBN Prefix(es): 978-0-9914231
Membership(s): Independent Book Publishers Association

Editorial Services & Agents

Editorial Services — Activity Index

FACT CHECKING

GHOSTWRITING

INDEXING

INTERVIEWING

LINE EDITING

MANUSCRIPT ANALYSIS

PERMISSIONS

PHOTO RESEARCH

PROOFREADING

RESEARCH

REWRITING

SPECIAL ASSIGNMENT WRITING

STATISTICS

TECHNICAL WRITING

TRANSCRIPTION EDITING

TYPEMARKING

Editorial Services

For information on other companies who provide services to the book industry, see **Consultants, Book Producers, Typing & Word Processing Services** and **Artists & Art Services.**

A+ English LLC/Book-Editing.com/Book Editing Associates
PO Box 1369, Mansfield, TX 76063
Tel: 469-789-3030
E-mail: editingnetwork@gmail.com
Web Site: www.editing-writing.com; www.book-editing.com; www.helpwithstatistics.com; www.apawriting.com; childrensbookeditors.com; www.christianeditorsnetwork.com; dissertationwriting.com; statisticstutors.com
Key Personnel
Freelance Network Coord: Lynda Lotman
Founded: 1976
Serving writers (unpublished, published), publishers (mainstream, genre, trade, academic), agents, researchers & businesses. Ms evaluations, copy-editing, developmental editing, submission materials (query letters, book proposals), mentoring & ghostwriting. We work with fiction, nonfiction, medical/scientific/technical material, business documents & textbooks.
Membership(s): Science Fiction & Fantasy Writers of America

A Westport Wordsmith
101 Winfield St, Norwalk, CT 06855
Tel: 203-939-9484
E-mail: pj104daily@aol.com
Key Personnel
Prop: Peggy Daily
Founded: 1999
Proofreading (nonfiction & fiction) & indexing of trade books. Americanization.
Membership(s): American Society for Indexing; Editorial Freelancers Association

AAA Photos
401 Ocean Dr, Unit 804, Miami Beach, FL 33139
Tel: 305-534-0804
Web Site: www.photosphotos.net
Key Personnel
Pres: Jeff Greenberg *E-mail:* jeffreygreenberg@aol.com
Provides photos to tourism bureau, book publishers, magazine publishers, newspapers, travel publications, web sites & by assignment & stock.

AAH Graphics Inc
Subsidiary of Loft Press Inc
9293 Fort Valley Rd, Fort Valley, VA 22652-2020
Tel: 540-933-6211 *Fax:* 540-933-6523
E-mail: srhunter@aahgraphics.com
Web Site: www.aahgraphics.com
Key Personnel
Pres: Ann A Hunter
Founded: 1973
Complete editorial through production serving publishers & individuals. Design of text, jackets & covers, composition & production management through manufacturing.

Aaron-Spear
PO Box 42, Brooksville, ME 04617
Tel: 207-326-8764
Key Personnel
Prop: Jody Spear
Developmental editing & copy-editing of scholarly mss in the humanities. Rewriting for style & sensibility as well as clarity, consistency & accuracy. Specialize in art history & environmental studies.

About Books Inc
1001 Taurus Dr, Colorado Springs, CO 80906
Tel: 719-445-8875 *Fax:* 719-213-2602
Web Site: www.about-books.com
Key Personnel
Owner & Pres: Debi Flora *E-mail:* debiflora@about-books.com
Owner & VP: Scott Flora *E-mail:* scott@about-books.com
Founded: 1977
Complete writing, editorial & book development services: editing; cover & interior design; ebooks & print books; specialize in nonfiction books on all subjects.
Membership(s): The Association of Publishers for Special Sales

Access Editorial Services
1133 Broadway, Suite 528, New York, NY 10010
Tel: 212-255-7306
E-mail: wiseword@juno.com
Key Personnel
Dir: Louise Weiss
Founded: 1990
Services include travel writing.
Membership(s): The Authors Guild; New York Travel Writers Association; SATW; Toastmasters International

Accurate Writing & More
16 Barstow Lane, Hadley, MA 01035
Tel: 413-586-2388
Web Site: www.accuratewriting.com; www.frugalmarketing.com; www.goingbeyondsustainability.com; www.transformpreneur.com; www.greenandprofitable.com; www.twitter.com/shelhorowitz
Key Personnel
Owner & Dir: Shel Horowitz *E-mail:* shel@principledprofit.com
Dir: Dina Friedman
Founded: 1981
Advertising & promotion copywriting, ghostwriting, editing, publishing consulting, interviewing, ms analysis, research, rewriting, special assignment writing & publishing consulting for authors, publishers & green businesses.
Membership(s): Connecticut Authors & Publishers Association; Independent Book Publishers Association; Independent Publishers of New England; National Writers Union; Western New England Editorial Freelancers Network

J Adel Art & Design
586 Ramapo Rd, Teaneck, NJ 07666
Tel: 201-836-2606
E-mail: jadelnj@aol.com
Key Personnel
Creative Dir: Judith Adel
Founded: 1985
Freelance copy, illustration & design services for publishers.

AEIOU Inc
894 Piermont Ave, Piermont, NY 10968
Tel: 845-680-5380
Key Personnel
Pres: Cynthia Crippen *E-mail:* ccrippen@verizon.net
Founded: 1976

Rodelinde Albrecht
PO Box 444, Lenox Dale, MA 01242-0444
Tel: 413-243-4350
E-mail: rodelinde@gmail.com
Founded: 1979
Full editorial services; scanning; copy/line editing (hard copy/electronic); rewriting; castoff, typemarking; proofreading; proof-checking & consulting.

AllWrite Advertising & Publishing
241 Peachtree St NE, Suite 400, Atlanta, GA 30303
Mailing Address: PO Box 1071, Atlanta, GA 30301
Tel: 404-221-0703 *Fax:* 770-284-8986
E-mail: questions@allwritepublishing.com
Web Site: www.e-allwrite.com
Key Personnel
Pres & Publr: Annette R Johnson *Tel:* 770-284-8956 *E-mail:* annette@allwritepublishing.com
Founded: 1996
A conventional publisher that also offers editorial services for self-publishers & those who need promotional documents or materials, including booklets & brochures. Provides comprehensive editing & proofreading services: checking syntax, grammar, punctuation & style; & offering substantive/line editing, developmental editing & production editing. Get a free online quote at www.e-allwrite.com.
Membership(s): Writers Guild of America, East

Jeanette Almada
452 W Aldine, Unit 215, Chicago, IL 60657
Tel: 773-404-9350
E-mail: jmalmada@sbcglobal.net
Writer, reporter, editor. Rewrite, co-author or author any story for publication as a book, article, newsletter or brochure. Areas of research & writing interest include urban affairs & lifestyle; organic standards & organic consumer topics; slow & local food; corporate cultural issues & corporate profiles, land use & conservation; neighborhood or community development & other nonfiction topics.

Ampersand Group
12 Morenz Terr, Kanata, ON K2K 3G9, Canada
Tel: 613-435-5066
Key Personnel
Pres: Ed Matheson *E-mail:* ematheson@bell.net
Book publishing consultants for publishers, business, government & individuals with publishing problems. Specialize in project management, general book design & production.

Joyce L Ananian
25 Forest Circle, Waltham, MA 02452-4719
Tel: 781-894-4330
E-mail: jlananian@hotmail.com
Founded: 1981
Copy-editing, fact checking, indexing, proofreading & line editing.

EDITORIAL SERVICES

Barbara S Anderson
706 W Davis Ave, Ann Arbor, MI 48103-4855
Tel: 734-995-0125
E-mail: bsa@watercolorbarbara.com
Rewriting, proofreading, ms analysis & line editing. For related services, see listing in Artists & Art Services.

Denice A Anderson
210 E Church St, Clinton, MI 49236
Tel: 517-456-4990 *Fax:* 517-456-4990
E-mail: deniceanderson@frontier.com
Founded: 1984
Copy-editing, line editing & proofreading; fiction & nonfiction; art, history, medical, legal, business, newspapers, journals & directories.
Membership(s): Editorial Freelancers Association

Jim Anderson
77 S Second St, Brooklyn, NY 11249
Tel: 718-388-1083
E-mail: jim.and@att.net

Patricia Anderson, PhD, Editor & Literary Consultant
1489 Marine Dr, Suite 515, West Vancouver, BC V7T 1B8, Canada
Tel: 604-740-0805
E-mail: query@helpingyougetpublished.com; patriciaanderson@helpingyougetpublished.com
Web Site: www.helpingyougetpublished.com
Key Personnel
Literary Consultant: Dr Patricia Anderson, PhD
Founded: 1998 (online since 1999)
Offering ms assessment, book editing, proofreading, query letters, book proposals & market research. Specialist in personalized writing & publishing strategies for emerging novelists & authors of book-length nonfiction.
Membership(s): The Authors Guild; Editors' Association of Canada/Association canadienne des reviseurs; The Writers' Union of Canada

Angel Editing Services
PO Box 752, Mountain Ranch, CA 95246
Tel: 209-728-8364
E-mail: info@stephaniemarohn.com
Web Site: www.stephaniemarohn.com
Key Personnel
Owner & Ed: Stephanie Marohn
Founded: 1993
Full range of editorial services, from developmental editing through copy-editing. Specialize in nonfiction trade books, particularly psychospiritual topics, metaphysics, natural medicine & other alternative thought.
Membership(s): Bay Area Editors' Forum

Angels Editorial Services
1630 Main St, Suite 41, Coventry, CT 06238
Tel: 860-742-5279
E-mail: angelsus@aol.com
Key Personnel
Pres: Prof Claire Connelly, PhD
Founded: 1969
Ms or disk: counseling & psychotherapy, science & computers, textbooks, LGBT, fiction & nonfiction, animals.
Membership(s): American Copy Editors Society; Society for Technical Communication

Aptara Inc
3110 Fairview Park Dr, Suite 900, Falls Church, VA 22042
Tel: 703-352-0001
E-mail: moreinfo@aptaracorp.com
Web Site: www.aptaracorp.com
Key Personnel
Pres: Samir Kakar
SVP, Busn & Contact Ctr Opers: Ashish Madan
SVP, Fin & Cont: Prashant Kapoor
Busn Devt: Michael Scott *E-mail:* michael.scott@aptaracorp.com
Liaison for complete or any combination of production services, ranging from simple 1-color to complex 4-color projects & copy-editing. Offer ebook conversions & end-to-end solutions publishing services in print & digital.

Archon Editorial LLC
815 King St, Suite 204, Alexandria, VA 22314
Tel: 703-838-1650
E-mail: stoddardbc@gmail.com
Web Site: www.archoneditorial.com
Key Personnel
Owner: Brooke C Stoddard *E-mail:* brooke@archoneditorial.com
Founded: 1983
Magazine & book writing & editing. Can handle design & production.
Membership(s): American Society of Journalists & Authors; The Authors Guild; Editorial Freelancers Association; National Press Club

ASJA Freelance Writer Search
Affiliate of American Society of Journalists & Authors Inc
355 Lexington Ave, 15th fl, New York, NY 10017
Tel: 212-997-0947
E-mail: asjaoffice@asja.org
Web Site: www.freelancewritersearch.com
Key Personnel
Exec Dir: Alexandra Owens
Founded: 1948
Vital resource for anyone seeking the services of professional writers for articles, books, book proposals, brochures, annual reports, speeches, TV & film scripts, advertising copy, publicity campaigns, corporate communications & more. Free, private listing service goes only to the 1,300 professional members of ASJA.

Associated Editors
27 W 96 St, New York, NY 10025
Tel: 212-662-9703 *Fax:* 212-662-9703
Key Personnel
Contact: Lynne Glasner *E-mail:* lyngla1@gmail.com
Copy-editing, rewriting, proofreading, indexing, research, developmental editing. Specialize in elementary & secondary textbooks; nonfiction trade books.

Astor Indexers
22 S Commons, Kent, CT 06757
Tel: 860-592-0225; 570-534-8951 (cell)
Key Personnel
Owner: Jane Farnol *E-mail:* bjfarnol@snet.net
Founded: 1970
Indexing is our only business. Staff handles all subjects; hard copy, e-mail or disk. Quality, speed & accuracy are our trademarks.

Audrey Owen
494 Eaglecrest Dr, Gibsons, BC V0N 1V8, Canada
E-mail: editor@writershelper.com
Web Site: www.writershelper.com
Founded: 2002
Besides the editing services offered by other agencies, I also specialize in educative editing that becomes a mini tutorial designed for, but is not restricted to, self-publishing writers. Also offer substantive editing.
Membership(s): Editors' Association of Canada/Association canadienne des reviseurs; Federation of British Columbia Writers; Society of Children's Book Writers & Illustrators

The Author's Friend
548 Ocean Blvd, No 12, Long Branch, NJ 07740

Tel: 732-571-8051
Key Personnel
Prop: Judith Stein *E-mail:* jstein@panix.com
Founded: 1976
Copy & line editing, proofreading & transcription editing. Specialize in religion & spirituality, psychology, medicine, self-help, bibliographies & esoterica.

Backman Writing & Communications
32 Hillview Ave, Rensselaer, NY 12144
Tel: 518-449-4985
Web Site: www.backwrite.com
Key Personnel
Principal: John Backman *E-mail:* johnb@backwrite.com
Founded: 1986
Articles, blogs, advertising & marketing copy. Areas of focus: Spirituality, higher education, engineering, financial services & generally making the complex simple.

Baldwin Literary Services
935 Hayes St, Baldwin, NY 11510-4834
Tel: 516-546-8338 *Fax:* 516-546-8338
Key Personnel
Pres: Marjorie Gillette Jones
Founded: 1982
Creative writing courses. Specialize in novels, historical novels, autobiographies, medical, gardening & nature, spiritual.
Membership(s): International Women's Writing Guild

Kathleen Barnes
238 W Fourth St, Suite 3-C, New York, NY 10014
Tel: 212-924-8084
E-mail: kbarnes@compasscommunications.org
Writing, rewriting, line editing, copy-editing & proofreading.

Melinda Barrett
37915 Sundance Dr, Coarsegold, CA 93614
Tel: 559-641-0944
E-mail: mbarrett_3@netzero.net
Founded: 1989
Copy-editing, proofreading, rewriting & special assignment writing.

Diana Barth
535 W 51 St, Suite 3-A, New York, NY 10019
Tel: 212-307-5465
E-mail: diabarth@juno.com
Founded: 1970
All subjects; specialize in performing arts, health, psychology, education & travel. Feature & ghostwriter.

Anita Bartholomew
16650 SE Sunridge Lane, Portland, OR 97267
Tel: 941-358-0495
E-mail: anita@anitabartholomew.com
Web Site: www.anitabartholomew.com
Founded: 1993
Developmental editor. Specialize in fiction & narrative nonfiction. Have ghosted fiction & nonfiction. Co-authored a leading OB-GYN's award-winning memoir. Clients include authors (typically referred by their literary agents), publishers & nonprofits. Endorsements/testimonials available on web site & LinkedIn profile.

Mark E Battersby
PO Box 527, Ardmore, PA 19003
Tel: 610-924-9157 *Fax:* 610-924-9159
E-mail: mebatt12@earthlink.net
Web Site: www.thetaxscribe.com
Founded: 1971
Freelance writer. Specialize in tax & financial features, columns, web content & white papers.

Beaver Wood Associates
655 Alstead Center Rd, Alstead, NH 03602
Mailing Address: PO Box 717, Alstead, NH 03602
Tel: 603-835-7900
Web Site: www.beaverwood.com
Key Personnel
Owner: Jeanne C Moody *E-mail:* jcmoody@beaverwood.com
Founded: 1985
Indexing, copy-editing & proofreading.
Membership(s): American Society for Indexing

Barbara Bergstrom MA LLC
13 Stockton Way, Howell, NJ 07731
Tel: 732-363-8372
Offers complete editorial services: copy-editing, ms analysis, critique, development of mss, proofreading, research, revision, rewriting, condensations, copy fitting, writing, ghostwriting, transcription editing, project development & management, production services & editing for publishers, authors, academics, medical professionals, psychologists, businesses, public figures, associations & organizations. Act as publisher-author liaison, or as author's agent, full project management for publishers with mss needing copy-editing, revision +/or editor to work with author, or for self-publishing authors. Will travel to meet with authors to develop & edit mss. Meticulous editor (former university faculty) will copy-edit Masters Thesis & Doctoral Dissertation, or we can help you to prepare your ms for publication. Business, medical, psychological & technical writing, editing of user manuals into clearly understood English, project management & editing of in-house publications. Transcribe & edit books to tape. Special expertise in psychology, comparative literature, fiction, nonfiction, autobiography & memoirs, biography, art, art history, history, East Asian culture (China, Korea, Japan), Eastern philosophy & religions (Buddhism, Taoism, Confucianism, Shinto), T'ai Ch'i, martial arts, women's studies, natural healing, New Age, Native American, alternative healing sciences, meditation, "how-to", health & fitness, self-help, English, ESL & more. ESL authors welcome. We are the editing/contracting agency for Dr Fred Penzel whose books include the award-winning *Obsessive-Compulsive Disorders: A Complete Guide to Getting Well and Staying Well* & *The Hair-Pulling Problem: A Complete Guide to Trichotillomania*. We also edited Jae Woong Kim's *Polishing the Diamond Enlightening the Mind*. Call before submitting mss. Leave your name, number & brief message about your project. Ask about our specials. Also see listing under Consultants.

Jean Brodsky Bernard
4609 Chevy Chase Blvd, Chevy Chase, MD 20815-5343
Tel: 301-654-8914
E-mail: dranreb@starpower.net
Founded: 1982

Daniel Bial & Associates
41 W 83 St, Suite 5-C, New York, NY 10024
Tel: 212-721-1786
E-mail: dbialagency@msn.com
Web Site: www.danielbialagency.com
Key Personnel
Founder & Prop: Daniel Bial
Founded: 1991
Creating, designing & producing illustrated el-hi & adult books; emphasis on reference sports.

Bibliogenesis
152 Coddington Rd, Ithaca, NY 14850
Tel: 607-277-9660
Web Site: www.bibliogenesis.com
Key Personnel
Owner: Marian Hartman Rogers
E-mail: mrogers@lightlink.com
Founded: 1987
Full editorial services encompassing all aspects of ms development: analysis, writing, rewriting, content editing, copy-editing, line editing, proofreading, fact checking, research & special assignment writing. Specialize in scholarly works (classical & medieval studies, European history & literature, anthropology & gender studies, Middle Eastern studies, geography & travel); languages (French, German, Greek, Latin).

Bloom Ink
3497 Bennington Ct, Bloomfield Hills, MI 48301
Tel: 248-291-0370
E-mail: info@bloomwriting.com
Web Site: www.bloomwriting.com
Key Personnel
Founder & Principal: Barbara Bloom
Founded: 2008
Provides a range of editing & publishing services including copy-editing, developmental editing, audio abridgements (fiction, nonfiction), book proposals, query letters & ghostwriting as well as assistance with self-publishing, book layout & design.
Membership(s): Editorial Freelancers Association

Heidi Blough, Book Indexer
502 Tanager Rd, St Augustine, FL 32086
Tel: 904-797-6572
E-mail: indexing@heidiblough.com
Web Site: www.heidiblough.com
Key Personnel
Owner: Heidi Blough
Founded: 2001
Indexing diverse topics that include: aerospace; biography; business, cooking, food & nutrition; engineering; general trade subjects; health & hospital administration; history, government & politics; how-to; maritime & transportation subjects.
Membership(s): American Society for Indexing

Blue & Ude Writers' Services
4249 Nuthatch Way, Clinton, WA 98236
Mailing Address: PO Box 145, Clinton, WA 98236-0145
Tel: 360-341-1630
E-mail: blueyude@whidbey.com
Web Site: www.blueudewritersservices.com
Key Personnel
Partner: Marian Blue; Wayne Ude
Founded: 1991
Provides all aspects of creative & technical writing & editing, including critiques, revisions & promotional copy.

Book Editing Associates, see A+ English LLC/Book-Editing.com/Book Editing Associates

Book-Editing.com, see A+ English LLC/Book-Editing.com/Book Editing Associates

BookCrafters LLC
Box C, Convent Station, NJ 07961
Tel: 973-984-7880
Web Site: bookcraftersllc.com
Key Personnel
Founder, Pres & Ed: Elizabeth Zack
E-mail: ezack@bookcraftersllc.com
Founded: 2003

Specialize in ms development & editing. Offers services for published authors, literary agents & first-time writers from creating a marketable book proposal to fine-tuning a ms. The editor has over 23 years of experience in book publishing.

The Bookmill
501 Palisades Dr, No 315, Pacific Palisades, CA 90272-2848
Tel: 310-459-0190
E-mail: thebookmill1@verizon.net
Web Site: www.thebookmill.us
Key Personnel
Dir & Ed: Barbara Marinacci
Founded: 1982
Ms critiques; developmental editing for books, articles; preparing queries & proposals; word processing; contacts with agents, editors & publishers; blurb writing, book doctoring, proposals, restructuring & revising, transcribing.

Boston Informatics
35 Byard Lane, Westborough, MA 01581
Tel: 508-366-8176
Web Site: www.bostoninformatics.com
Key Personnel
Principal: M (May) H Hasso *E-mail:* mhsh2009@verizon.net
Founded: 2002
Provides indexing services for ebooks, databases, web & back of the book. Subjects covered include: business, finance & management, nutrition, health & allied sciences, social sciences, technology & engineering. Other services include taxonomy development, fact checking, information searching & word processing.
Membership(s): American Society for Indexing

Boston Road Communications
227 Boston Rd, Groton, MA 01450-1959
Tel: 978-448-8133
Web Site: www.bostonrdcom.com
Key Personnel
Owner: Christine R Lindemer
E-mail: crlindemer@gmail.com
Founded: 2002
Indexing business, computer technology, quality management, project management, health care, history, agriculture, cookbooks, how-to, literary criticism & other subjects. Over 400 books indexed.
Membership(s): American Society for Indexing

bradylit
81 Town Farm Hill, Hartland Four Corners, VT 05049
Mailing Address: PO Box 64, Hartland Four Corners, VT 05049
Tel: 802-436-2455
Key Personnel
Owner: Sally R Brady *E-mail:* bradylit@vermontel.net
Founded: 1988
Ms analysis, conceptual, developmental & line editing, book doctoring, rewriting; trade fiction & nonfiction; contacts with agents, editors & publishers. Work on a fee +/or percentage basis.

Hilary R Burke
59 Sparks St, Ottawa, ON K1P 6C3, Canada
Mailing Address: Box 133, Sta B, Ottawa, ON K1P 6C3, Canada
Tel: 613-237-4658
E-mail: hburke99@yahoo.com
Promotional writing of fiction & nonfiction.

BZ/Rights & Permissions Inc
145 W 86 St, New York, NY 10024
Tel: 212-924-3000 *Fax:* 212-924-2525
E-mail: info@bzrights.com
Web Site: www.bzrights.com
Key Personnel
Pres: Barbara Zimmerman *E-mail:* bz@bzrights.com
Founded: 1980
Clears rights for literary materials, music, film & TV clips, photos, art, celebrities for educational projects - printed textbooks, spoken word recordings, new electronic media, DVDs/videocassettes. Work with film & TV producers & ad agencies. Publisher of *The Mini-Encyclopedia of Public Domain Songs & They Never Renewed: Songs You Never Dreamed Were in the Public Domain.*
Membership(s): Association of Independent Music Publishers; Copyright Society of the USA; Independent Book Publishers Association

Carpe Indexum
1960 Deer Run Rd, LaFayette, NY 13084
Tel: 315-677-3030
E-mail: info@carpeindexum.com
Web Site: www.carpeindexum.com
Key Personnel
Owner: Michele Combs *E-mail:* mrothen2@twcny.rr.com
Founded: 2004
Services include back-of-book & XML indexing services; research & fact checking; editing at various levels; copywriting & work-for-hire; XML/XSLT consulting.
Membership(s): American Society for Indexing; Editorial Freelancers Association; Society of American Archivists

R E Carsch, MS-Consultant
1453 Rhode Island St, San Francisco, CA 94107-3248
Tel: 415-641-1095 *Fax:* 415-641-1095
E-mail: recarsch@mzinfo.com
Founded: 1973
Full-range, custom information editorial services including, fact checking, interviewing, ms analysis, proofreading, research & industry overviews.
Membership(s): Art Libraries Society

Anne Carson Associates
3323 Nebraska Ave NW, Washington, DC 20016
Tel: 202-244-6679
Key Personnel
Ed-in-Chief: Anne Conover Carson
Founded: 1976
Proofreading, research, rewriting, special assignment writing, ms analysis. Specialize in Latin American culture & history, biographies of women & 20th century expats in Paris.
Membership(s): Academy of American Poets; The Authors Guild; MLA; National Coalition of Independent Scholars; National Press Club

Carol Cartaino
2000 Flat Run Rd, Seaman, OH 45679
Tel: 937-764-1303 *Fax:* 937-764-1303
E-mail: cartaino@aol.com
Founded: 1986
Content, developmental & line editing; ms analysis; rewriting & collaboration; development & packaging of book ideas & book programs. Nonfiction & selected fiction including how-to, self-help, reference, humorous & highly illustrated books. Also expert assistance of all kinds for self-publishers & solutions for problem mss.

Claudia Caruana
PO Box 654, Murray Hill Sta, New York, NY 10016
Tel: 516-488-5815
E-mail: ccaruana29@hotmail.com
Copy-editing, ms analysis, rights & permissions, picture search, proofreading, research, rewriting, special assignment writing, magazine photography.

Angela M Casey
42 Nathaniel Blvd, Delmar, NY 12054
Tel: 518-729-2693
E-mail: casey.angela.m@gmail.com
Founded: 2000
Book editing & ghostwriting for established authors. Categories include psychology, health, diet, exercise & relationships. Advertising & promotion copywritten for print & for web according to search engine optimization (SEO) standards.

Catalyst Communication Arts
94 Chuparrosa Dr, San Luis Obispo, CA 93401
Tel: 805-235-2351 *Fax:* 805-543-7140
Web Site: www.sonsieconroy.com
Key Personnel
Owner: Sonsie Carbonara Conroy
E-mail: sconroy@slonet.org
Founded: 1980
Specialize in indexing college textbooks, cookbooks, self-help, trade nonfiction.

Catalyst Creative Services
619 Marion Plaza, Palo Alto, CA 94301-4251
Tel: 650-325-1500
E-mail: afriendlyghostwriter@gmail.com
Web Site: www.catalystcreative.us
Key Personnel
Owner & Chief Catalyst: Dennis Alan Briskin
E-mail: chief@catalystcreative.us
Founded: 1975
Our clients get published. We offer complete editorial services (fiction & nonfiction), from intelligent strategy (you must aim at the right target) to the structure, composition, revisions & final polish. We help companies & nonprofessional writers clarify, craft & publish their work for educated adult readers. We also ghostwrite for well-funded individuals with a story to tell or a cause to promote. (We respect academic integrity.) Writing contains both art & technique. We can show you the art & teach you the technique. We accept debit/credit cards.
Membership(s): Association of Ghostwriters; National Writers Union

Jeanne Cavelos Editorial Services
PO Box 75, Mont Vernon, NH 03057
Tel: 603-673-6234
Web Site: jeannecavelos.com
Key Personnel
Owner: Jeanne Cavelos *E-mail:* jcavelos@comcast.net
Founded: 1994
Published, best-selling writer & former senior editor at major publishing house. Full editorial services for publishers, book packagers, businesses, agents & authors. From line edit to thorough edit, to heavy edit. Detailed reader's reports. Book proposal doctoring. Editorial consulting, creative development. Newsletters, magazine articles, novelizations. Handle the full range of fiction & nonfiction. Specialize in thrillers, literary fiction, fantasy, science fiction, horror, popular culture, self-help, health & science.
Membership(s): Horror Writers Association; Science Fiction & Fantasy Writers of America

CeciBooks Editorial & Publishing Consultation
7057 26 Ave NW, Seattle, WA 98117
Mailing Address: PO Box 17229, Seattle, WA 98127
Tel: 206-706-9565
E-mail: cecibooks@gmail.com
Web Site: www.cecibooks.com

Key Personnel
Owner: Ceci Miller
Founded: 1988
Provide complete book development & production from concept & content to finished book. Innovative in assembling teams of experts to develop, write, edit, design & produce superior products. Specialty is kids nonfiction (both trade & curriculum), but we also do adult books on topics such as history, biography, science, how-to & business. We do education (textbooks, teacher resources, reference), focusing on social sciences, literacy & soft science. Produce publisher-initiated titles as well as original books. Will work with other packagers to co-produce books.
Membership(s): Book Publishers of the Northwest; Pacific Northwest Writers Association; Society of Children's Book Writers & Illustrators; Women's Business Exchange

Cenveo Publisher Services
555 Virginia Dr, Fort Washington, PA 19034
Tel: 215-591-9125
E-mail: info.psg@cenveo.com
Web Site: cenveopublisherservices.com
Key Personnel
VP: Harry J Nesbitt, III *E-mail:* harry.nesbitt@cenveo.com
Dir, Technol: Bruce Nesbitt *E-mail:* bruce.nesbitt@cenveo.com
Sr Prodn Coord: Harry F Druding *E-mail:* harry.druding@cenveo.com
Founded: 1998
Our school division offers complete PreK-12 educational publishing services including conceptual development, prototype development, research, writing, content editing, copy-editing, fact checking & production editing. Editorial expertise includes mathematics, science/health & reading/language arts. Extensive experience creating student & teacher's editions, alternative programs, supplemental materials, assessment, curriculum alignment, state customizations, correlations & professional developmental materials. Our higher education division provides expert full service management for college, medical, nursing, allied health & scholarly publications. Production services for both school & higher education include instructional design, page layouts, art creation & art services, photo research/shoots, electronic composition & prepress services.
Branch Office(s)
3575 Hempland Rd, Lancaster, PA 17601 *Toll Free Tel:* 800-724-4400
5457 Twin Knolls Rd, Suite 200, Columbia, MD 21045 *Tel:* 267-640-9158
2905 Byrdhill Rd, Richmond, VA 23228 *Tel:* 804-515-5147

Margaret Cheasebro
246 Rd 2900, Aztec, NM 87410
Tel: 505-334-2869
E-mail: mwriter4571@yahoo.com
Web Site: www.wordsandwellness.com
Founded: 1986
Freelance writer. Specialize in articles about people, places & issues of the Four Corners area, nonfiction books about alternative healing & related subjects.
Membership(s): The Authors Guild; National Federation of Press Women; New Mexico Press Women

Ruth Chernia
198 Victor Ave, Toronto, ON M4K 1B2, Canada
Tel: 416-466-0164
E-mail: rchernia@editors.ca; rchernia@sympatico.ca
Web Site: www.editors.ca/profile/444/ruth-chernia
Founded: 1983
Provides professional editorial & publishing consultation to companies & individuals.
Membership(s): Editors' Association of Canada/Association canadienne des reviseurs

Clear Concepts
1329 Federal Ave, Suite 6, Los Angeles, CA 90025
Tel: 323-285-0325
Key Personnel
Owner: Karen Kleiner
Founded: 1986
Provides writing, substantive editing & research. Specializes in holistic health, fiction, children's books, technology & business. Owner holds BA from UCLA in Communication Studies.
Membership(s): Society for Technical Communication

Clerical Plus
97 Blueberry Lane, Shelton, CT 06484
Tel: 203-225-0879 *Fax:* 203-225-0879
E-mail: clericalplus@aol.com
Web Site: www.clericalplus.net
Key Personnel
Pres: Rose Brown
Founded: 1990
Transcription/office support service company.

Clotilde's Secretarial & Management Services
PO Box 871926, New Orleans, LA 70187
Tel: 504-242-2912; 504-800-4853 (cell)
E-mail: elcsy58@aol.com; elcsy58@att.net
Key Personnel
Pres & Admin Mgr: Elvira C Sylve
Asst: Lillian Gail Tillman
Founded: 1989
Proofread & edit journals, newsletters, mss, research papers & medical documents. Specialize in preparing & typing research papers, grant proposals, medical & legal documents. Legal course work—Louisiana laws: briefs, business law, computer research & software, family law, interviewing, legal writing, litigation & researching in Westlaw.
Membership(s): American Health Information Management Association; National Association of Legal Assistants

Dwight Clough
311 W Main St, Sun Prairie, WI 53590
Tel: 608-834-8291
E-mail: lmp@dwightclough.com
Web Site: dwightclough.com
Founded: 1983
Serving authors & publishers.

Coastside Editorial
PO Box 181, Moss Beach, CA 94038
E-mail: bevjoe@pacific.net
Key Personnel
Contact: Beverly McGuire
Membership(s): Editcetera

Robert L Cohen
182-12 Horace Harding Expwy, Suite 2M, Fresh Meadows, NY 11365
Tel: 718-762-1195 *Toll Free Tel:* 866-EDITING (334-8464)
E-mail: wordsmith@sterlingmp.com
Web Site: www.rlcwordsandmusic.com; www.linkedin.com/in/robertcohen17
Copy, line (substantive) & developmental editing of academic, trade, & reference books; editing & rewriting of public policy books/reports/policy briefs/newsletters/monographs; lexicography; radio & AV scriptwriting; speechwriting & other contract writing. Specialize in international relations (especially Middle East & related countries & regions), history (including military history) & social sciences, urban affairs & public policy, politics & government, psychology & education, media & communications, Judaica & religion, music, sports. Also writing coach & teacher for businesses/nonprofits/individuals.
Membership(s): American Society for Jewish Music; Cambridge Academic Editors Network; Editorial Freelancers Association

Cohesion®
511 W Bay St, Suite 480, Tampa, FL 33606
Tel: 813-999-3111 *Toll Free Tel:* 877-774-3000
E-mail: info@cohesion.com
Web Site: www.cohesion.com
Key Personnel
Pres, Fin & Opers: John Owens *Tel:* 813-999-3100
Pres, Sales & Mktg: John Larson *Tel:* 813-999-3100
Founded: 1982
Complete book & journal content development & production services: writing, copy-editing, developmental editing, indexing, proofreading; project management; abstracting, advertising & promotion copywriting, bibliographies, fact checking, interviewing, developmental editing, ms analysis, rewriting, special assignment writing, transcription editing; design, art rendering, photo research, covers & jackets; permissions; in-house composition as well as development of electronic publishing products, including HTML & XML coding & supervising printing. Online editing experts (visit EditExpress.com). Specialize in technical subject areas: college, medical & allied health, computer science, law, physical & life sciences & engineering.
Branch Office(s)
4780 Ashford Dunwoody Rd, Suite A-245, Atlanta, GA 30338 *Toll Free Tel:* 866-727-6800
6760 Alexander Bell Dr, Suite 120, Columbia, MD 21046 *Toll Free Tel:* 800-560-0630
1500 District Ave, Burlington, MA 01803, EVP: Tess Kastning *Tel:* 781-273-6300
5151 Pfeiffer Rd, Suite 105, Cincinnati, OH 45242 *Tel:* 513-587-7700
156 Granville St, Columbus, OH 43230 *Tel:* 614-423-5272

Copywriter's Council of America™ (CCA)
Division of The Linick Group Inc
CCA Bldg, 7 Putter Lane, Middle Island, NY 11953-1920
Mailing Address: PO Box 102, Middle Island, NY 11953-0102
Tel: 631-924-3888; 631-775-6075 *Fax:* 631-924-8555
E-mail: cca4dmcopy@gmail.com
Web Site: www.andrewlinickdirectmarketing.com/Copywriters-Council.html; www.newworldpressbooks.com
Key Personnel
Chmn, Consulting Group: Andrew S Linick, PhD *E-mail:* andrew@asklinick.com
EVP: Roger Dextor
Dir, Spec Projs: Barbara Deal
Over 35,000 freelance advertising copywriters, editors, communication specialists & journalists; covering publishing, Internet direct response/direct mail field for health, physical fitness, gourmet, how-to, martial arts, self improvement, travel & tourism, photography, sports & recreation, business communications & high tech for books, magazines, manuals, newsletters, in-house organs & courses. Marketing, research, rewriting, special assignment writing, copy-editing, indexing, proofreading, ms analysis; video production, audio-video news releases; interviews & profiles; rights & permissions. Also offer annual seminars, workshops & trade show to writers/editors who would like to increase their income. Phone consultation available. Provide comprehensive

graphic redesign/new web site content development, interactive services with web site marketing makeover advice for first-time authors, self-publishers, professionals & entrepreneurs. Specializes in online advertising/PR, links to top search engines, consulting on a 100% satisfaction guarantee. Free site evaluation marketing checklist (a $250 value) for LMP readers.

Corbett Gordon Co
6 Fort Rachel Place, Mystic, CT 06355
Tel: 860-536-4108 *Fax:* 860-536-3732
E-mail: corbettgordon@comcast.net
Key Personnel
Owner: Rose Corbett Gordon
Fine art & historical research for books, book covers & exhibits. Art copyright expertise.

Course Crafters Inc
PO Box 100, Amesbury, MA 01913
Tel: 978-372-3446
E-mail: info@coursecrafters.com
Web Site: www.coursecrafters.com
Key Personnel
Publr & CEO: Lise B Ragan
Founded: 1993
Full service development house & packager of educational materials, K-adult, with a unique focus in the growing English Language Learner (ELL) market. Specialize in ESL, bilingual education & literacy material for English language learners, their teachers & parents. Provide services to publishers in market research, consulting, conceptualizing, writing/editing, production, translation & developing marketing/sales plans. Also can develop customized materials for schools. Print, audio, video & multimedia in ESL & Spanish; professional development, instructional materials & assessment.

Creative Freelancers Inc
PO Box 366, Tallevast, FL 34270
Toll Free Tel: 800-398-9544
Web Site: www.freelancers1.com
Key Personnel
Pres: Marilyn Howard
Freelance copy & art services for publishing & advertising. Designers, artists, copy-editors, all creative areas, translations.

Creative Inspirations Inc
6203 Old Springville Rd, Pinson, AL 35126
Mailing Address: PO Box 362, Clay, AL 35048
Web Site: www.manuscriptcritique.com
Key Personnel
Pres: Michael Garrett *E-mail:* mike@manuscriptcritique.com
Founded: 1995
Editorial services for aspiring authors, including line edit & content evaluation.

CS International Literary Agency
43 W 39 St, New York, NY 10018
Tel: 212-921-1610; 212-391-9208
E-mail: query@csliterary.com; csliterary08@gmail.com
Web Site: www.csliterary.com
Key Personnel
Literary Agent: Cynthia Neesemann
Ms analysis, evaluation & agent representation available for nonfiction, fiction & screenplays. We assist writers in developing strategies to achieve ms publication or film production & to find the writing niche that suits their talents & personality in general or specialized markets. We are particularly responsive to helping beginning writers to improve their writing skills & style with suggestions for better plotting, characterization, dialogue & structure. Fees are very reasonable. Interests extend to full range of topics whether fact or fantasy, including international, occult, ethnic, political, historical & religious subjects, mysteries & comedies. Query with short synopsis of project.

Cultural Studies & Analysis
1123 Montrose St, Philadelphia, PA 19147-3721
Tel: 215-592-8544
E-mail: info@culturalanalysis.com
Web Site: www.culturalanalysis.com
Key Personnel
Dir: Margaret J King, PhD *E-mail:* mjking9@comcast.net
Sr Analyst: Jamie O'Boyle
Founded: 1994
Specialize in cultural analysis; identify consumer values & decision making. We do not provide novel writing.

Cypress House
155 Cypress St, Fort Bragg, CA 95437
Tel: 707-964-9520 *Toll Free Tel:* 800-773-7782 *Fax:* 707-964-7531
E-mail: cypresshouse@cypresshouse.com
Web Site: www.cypresshouse.com
Key Personnel
Pres: Cynthia Frank *E-mail:* cynthia@cypresshouse.com
Mng Ed: Joe Shaw *E-mail:* joeshaw@cypresshouse.com
Complete editorial, design, production, marketing & promotion services to independent publishers. Editorial services include ms evaluation, editing, rewriting, copymarking & proofing. Production services include book, cover & page design & make-up to camera-ready. Marketing & promotion services for selected titles.
Membership(s): ABA; Bay Area Independent Publishers Association; Independent Book Publishers Association; Northern California Independent Booksellers Association; Pacific Northwest Booksellers Association

John M Daniel Literary Services
PO Box 2790, McKinleyville, CA 95519
Tel: 707-839-3495 *Fax:* 707-839-3242
E-mail: jmd@danielpublishing.com
Web Site: www.danielpublishing.com/litserv.htm
Key Personnel
Ed: John M Daniel
Specialize in fiction & memoir.

Darla Bruno Writing Coach, Developmental Editor
PO Box 243, Madison, NJ 07940
E-mail: editor@darlabruno.com
Web Site: www.darlabruno.com
Developmental editing, rewriting, critiques, marketing, coaching. Specialize in memoir & literary fiction, as well as self-help, personal development, spiritual, health & wellness.

Suzanne B Davidson
8084 N 44 St, Brown Deer, WI 53223
Tel: 414-355-6640
E-mail: davidson@milwpc.com
Founded: 1984
College texts, scholarly works; law & criminal justice, business & finance, politics, public policy, history, social sciences, genealogy.

Mari Lynch Dehmler, see Fine Wordworking

Christina Di Martino Literary Services
139 Sandpiper Ave, Royal Palm Beach, FL 33411
Tel: 212-996-9086
E-mail: writealotmail@gmail.com
Key Personnel
Owner: Christina Di Martino
Full book line services, collaboration of book projects, freelance writing for national magazines & teaching of writing.

DK Research Inc
14 Mohegan Lane, Commack, NY 11725
Tel: 631-543-5537 *Fax:* 631-543-5549
E-mail: dkresearch@optimum.net
Web Site: www.dkresearchinc.com
Key Personnel
Owner & Pres: Diane Kraut
Founded: 1993
Handle all phases of text permission clearance. Also available for ms assessments & review for permission items. Photo research services also available.
Membership(s): Editorial Freelancers Association

Double Play
303 Hillcrest Rd, Belton, MO 64012-1852
Tel: 816-651-7118
E-mail: wlloydj@lyahoo.com
Key Personnel
Pres: Lloyd Johnson *E-mail:* wlloydj@yahoo.com
VP: Connie Johnson
Writing & research about baseball; sports, baseball museum consultant, exhibits; working on database of professional baseball.
Membership(s): Society for American Baseball Research

Drennan Communications
6 Robin Lane, East Kingston, NH 03827
Tel: 603-642-8002 *Fax:* 603-642-8002
Key Personnel
Pres & Edit Dir: William D Drennan
VP & Sr Ed: Christina L Drennan
Founded: 1980
Line editing, copy-editing, ms analysis, proofreading, rewriting, ghostwriting, special assignment writing, condensations, typemarking, abstracting, fact checking, interviewing, research, advertising & promotion copywriting.

Drummond Books
2111 Cleveland St, Evanston, IL 60202
Tel: 847-302-2534
E-mail: drummondbooks@gmail.com
Key Personnel
Owner: Siobhan Drummond
Editorial & production services for web, print & ebooks, editorial management, project management from raw ms to finished book, copy-editing, substantive editing, proofreading & indexing.

DWJ BOOKS LLC
46 Cliff Dr, Sag Harbor, NY 11963
Mailing Address: PO Box 996, Sag Harbor, NY 11963
Tel: 631-899-4500
E-mail: info@dwjbooks.com
Web Site: www.dwjbooks.com
Key Personnel
EVP: Lauren Fedorko *E-mail:* lfedorko@dwjbooks.com
Edit Dir: Darrell Kozlowski
Founded: 2005 (developing & packaging original content since 1988)
Full service book & electronic development of large scale nonfiction projects & single titles for library & general reference publishing, test prep publishing, & curriculum-aligned publishing. Editorial services include: proposals, consulting, hiring of freelance staffs, writing, research, line & content editing, copy-editing, proofreading, indexing, fact checking, translat-

ing, special assignment writing, preparing files for print & online products.
Membership(s): ALA; American Book Producers Association

Earth Edit
PO Box 114, Maiden Rock, WI 54750
Tel: 715-448-3009
Key Personnel
Contact: George Dyke *E-mail:* gmdyke@gmail.com
Copy-editing & proofreading of earth science & geography texts.

East Mountain Editing Services
PO Box 1895, Tijeras, NM 87059-1895
Tel: 505-281-8422
Web Site: www.spanishindexing.com
Key Personnel
Mgr: Francine Cronshaw *E-mail:* cronshaw@nmia.com
Founded: 1992
Indexing (back-of-the-book) in Spanish or English. Also French, Italian & Portuguese. Expert witness on Spanish surnames. Special attention to Canadian editions. Consulting on bilingual or Spanish language editions. For experience, see web site.
Membership(s): American Society for Indexing

EditAndPublishYourBook.com
PO Box 2965, Nantucket, MA 02584-2965
E-mail: michaeltheauthor@yahoo.com
Web Site: www.editandpublishyourbook.com
Key Personnel
Principal: Michael Wells Glueck
Founded: 2002
Services offered include abstracting, condensations, copy-editing, interviewing, line editing, ms analysis, proofreading, rewriting, special assignment writing & transcription editing. Can also submit work to a reasonably priced subsidy publisher, shepherd it through the publication process & monitor online booksellers' web sites to make sure that it remains available for purchase, that they list it correctly & that the listing includes a front-cover photograph & other features. Can also suggest unorthodox but effective marketing techniques & write & submit reviews to online booksellers' web sites.
Recent projects include arranging online distribution for Donald E DeMarco's *Nantucket Taste Memories: The DeMarco Restaurant Cookbook* (self-published Oct 2007); as well as both writing & editing reviews for the Fictional Rome web site linked to the Richard Stockton College of New Jersey.

Edit Etc
26 Country Lane, Brunswick, ME 04011
Tel: 914-715-5849
E-mail: atkedit@cs.com
Web Site: www.anntkeene.com
Key Personnel
Pres: Ann T Keene
Founded: 1985
Editing, writing, copywriting, research, photo research.
Membership(s): The Authors Guild

Edit Resource LLC
Division of Stanford Creative Services LLC
19265 Lincoln Green Lane, Monument, CO 80132
Tel: 719-290-0757
E-mail: info@editresource.com
Web Site: www.editresource.com
Key Personnel
Owner: Elisa Stanford *E-mail:* elisa@editresource.com; Eric Stanford *E-mail:* eric@editresource.com
Founded: 1998
A writing & editing services provider.

EditAmerica
115 Jacobs Creek Rd, Ewing, NJ 08628
Tel: 609-882-5852
Web Site: www.editamerica.com; www.linkedin.com/in/PaulaPlantier
Key Personnel
Owner/Founder/Ed/Proofer/Fact Checker: Paula Plantier *E-mail:* paula@editamerica.com
Founded: 1979
Expert copy-editing, line editing, ms editing, rewriting/revising/repurposing, fact checking & proofreading of written communications in the areas of accounting, advertising, bibliography, biography, brochures, business, college application essays, company annual reports, cover letters, curricula vitae, dissertations, education, finance, Forms 10-K and 10-Q, marketing, medicine, newsletters, news releases, peer-reviewed & refereed medical/scientific journal articles, pharmaceutics, pharmacology, press releases, religious treatises, resumes, theses, user's manuals & web site content. Strict adherence to client-set deadlines. Satisfaction guaranteed for editorial services performed.
Membership(s): American Copy Editors Society; Editorial Freelancers Association

Editcetera
2034 Blake St, Suite 5, Berkeley, CA 94704
Tel: 510-849-1110 *Fax:* 510-900-6141
E-mail: info@editcetera.com
Web Site: www.editcetera.com
Key Personnel
Dir: Barbara Fuller
Founded: 1971
Association of freelance publishing professionals. Clients include authors, packagers, trade publishers, el-hi & college textbook publishers, self-publishers, computer companies (software & hardware) & corporations. Services available include production management from mss through bound books as well as writing, rewriting, developmental editing, copy-editing, coaching of writers, proofreading, indexing & web editing. Rigorous testing & review of all members.

EditCraft Editorial Services
422 Pine St, Grass Valley, CA 95945
Tel: 530-273-3934
Web Site: www.editcraft.com
Key Personnel
Prop: Eric W Engles, PhD *E-mail:* eric@editcraft.com
Founded: 1986
Editorial services for publishers, independent authors, scholars & technology companies.
Membership(s): Bay Area Editors' Forum

The Editorial Department LLC
7650 E Broadway, Suite 308, Tucson, AZ 85710
Tel: 520-546-9992 *Fax:* 520-979-3408
E-mail: admin@editorialdepartment.com
Web Site: www.editorialdepartment.com
Key Personnel
Founder: Renni Browne
Pres & Dir, Edit Servs: Ross Browne *E-mail:* rsb@editorialdepartment.com
Lead Ed, Romance & Women's Fiction: Lindsay Guzzardo
Founded: 1980
Ms critique & evaluation, line & copy-editing, novelizations & adaptations, book proposals, agent referral service, book cover design, book illustration, interior layout, ebook formatting, book/author marketing, publishing consultation, screenplay critique & consultation.

The Editors Circle
462 Grove St, Montclair, NJ 07043
Tel: 862-596-9709
E-mail: query@theeditorscircle.com
Web Site: www.theeditorscircle.com
Key Personnel
Ed: Bonny Fetterman *Tel:* 718-739-1057 *E-mail:* bvfetterman@aol.com; Rob Kaplan *Tel:* 914-736-7182 *E-mail:* robkaplan@optonline.net; Beth Lieberman *Tel:* 310-403-1602 *E-mail:* liebermanedit@socal.rr.com; John Paine *E-mail:* jpaine@johnpaine.com; Susan Schwartz *Tel:* 212-877-3211 *E-mail:* susan.sas22@gmail.com
Founded: 2005
A group of independent editors & publishing consultants with many years of in-house & freelance experience providing a wide range of editorial services for both fiction & nonfiction books, including: evaluating & critiquing book proposals & partial or complete mss; developing & editing book proposals, query letters & mss; ghostwriting, rewriting, or collaborating on book proposals & mss; consulting on self-publishing & digital publishing opportunities; providing referrals to suitable agents & publishers.

Diane Eickhoff
3808 Genessee St, Kansas City, MO 64111
Tel: 816-561-6693
E-mail: diane.eickhoff@gmail.com
Founded: 2000

Irene Elmer
2806 Cherry St, Berkeley, CA 94705-2310
Tel: 510-841-0466
E-mail: ielmer@earthlink.net
Founded: 1969
Rewriting, line editing & copy-editing of trade fiction & nonfiction, textbooks & scholarly works. Specialize in difficult rewrites, dialogue & lively presentation of difficult material. Special assignment writing of adult texts; trade nonfiction; high-interest, low-readability el-hi texts (fiction, drama, nonfiction).
Membership(s): Editcetera

Catherine C Elverston ELS
9 Red Bay Lane, Kitty Hawk, NC 27949-3307
Tel: 352-222-0625 (cell)
E-mail: celverston@gmail.com
All aspects of editing, preparing mss for publication, information research & retrieval. Also an agent.
Membership(s): American Medical Writers Association; Board of Editors in the Life Sciences

R Elwell Indexing
193 Main St, Cold Spring, NY 10516
Tel: 845-667-1036
E-mail: r.elwell.indexing@gmail.com
Founded: 1975
Indexing.

Enough Said
3959 NW 29 Lane, Gainesville, FL 32606
Tel: 352-262-2971 *Fax:* 352-372-5747 (call first)
E-mail: enoughsaid@cox.net
Web Site: users.navi.net/~heathlynn
Key Personnel
Owner & Ed: Ms Heath Lynn Silberfeld
Founded: 1984
Full range of hard copy & electronic editorial services for nonfiction trade, mass market, textbook & self-publishing projects.

Farrar Writing & Editing
4638 Manchester Rd, Mound, MN 55364
Tel: 952-472-6874 *Fax:* 952-472-6874 (call first)
Web Site: www.writeandedit.net

Key Personnel
Freelance Writer & Ed: Amy E Farrar
E-mail: amyfarrar@mchsi.com
Founded: 1999
Published book author (educational books for K-12 readers & general nonfiction); journalistic writing; book editor (copy-editing to substantive editing & rewriting). Clients include book publishers, nonprofits, magazines, newspapers & general businesses. Subjects include environmental, social, travel & health/medical. Interested parties with book projects in need of editing, send e-mail with synopsis of book, type of editorial service being sought, budget & deadline.
Membership(s): Professional Editors Network

Betsy Feist Resources
140 E 81 St, Unit 7-E, New York, NY 10028-1875
Tel: 212-861-2014
E-mail: bfresources@rcn.com
Key Personnel
Pres: Betsy Feist
Complete editorial services, including development, writing, project management & editorial/production coordination. Specialize in instructional & informational materials.

Jerry Felsen
3960 NW 196 St, Miami Gardens, FL 33055-1869
Tel: 305-625-5012
E-mail: jfelsen0@att.net
Web Site: beatthemarket.org
Computer science, artificial intelligence, information systems & computer applications in business & investing; professional papers & business reports.

Fine Wordworking
PO Box 3041, Monterey, CA 93942-3041
Tel: 831-375-6278
E-mail: info@finewordworking.com
Web Site: marilynch.com
Key Personnel
Owner: Mari Lynch Dehmler
Founded: 1981
Writing, editing & proofreading of literary, business, personal & other material. Ghostwriting, collaborative writing & editing of adult, young adult & children's nonfiction books. Editing & proofreading of fiction. Well versed in Chicago style. Web content development & design collaboration. Interviewing, research & other support. Phone calls welcome.

Richard A Flom, see Lynn C Kronzek & Richard A Flom

Focus Strategic Communications Inc
2474 Waterford St, Oakville, ON L6L 5E6, Canada
Tel: 905-825-8757 *Toll Free Tel:* 866-263-6287 *Fax:* 905-825-5724 *Toll Free Fax:* 866-613-6287
E-mail: info@focussc.com
Web Site: www.focussc.com
Key Personnel
Dir: Adrianna Edwards *E-mail:* aedwards@focussc.com; Ron Edwards *E-mail:* redwards@focussc.com
Founded: 1988
Provide complete book development & production from concept & content to finished book. Innovative in assembling teams of experts to develop, write, edit, design & produce superior products. Specialty is children's nonfiction (both trade & curriculum) but also do adult books on topics such as history, biography, science, how-to & business. Also education (textbooks, teacher resources, reference), focusing on social sciences, literacy & soft science. Produce publisher-initiated titles as well as original books. Will work with other packagers to co-produce books.
Membership(s): AAP; AAP PreK-12 Learning Group; American Book Producers Association; Association of Canadian Publishers; International Literacy Association; International Society for Technology in Education; National Association for the Education of Young Children; National Council for the Social Studies; National Council of Teachers of English; National Science Teachers Association; TESOL International Association

Foster Travel Publishing
1623 Martin Luther King, Berkeley, CA 94709
Tel: 510-549-2202
Web Site: www.fostertravel.com
Key Personnel
Owner & Pres: Lee Foster *E-mail:* lee@fostertravel.com
Founded: 1970
Picture search, research, writing; travel (emphasizing locations, history, wine, nature). Specialize in Northern California, the West, Mexico-Baja, Europe, the Orient. Writing & photography available on web site. Provides travel writing/photography services for print & web editorial markets.
Membership(s): Bay Area Travel Writers; SATW

Sandi Frank
8 Fieldcrest Ct, Cortlandt Manor, NY 10567
Tel: 914-739-7088
E-mail: sfrankmail@aol.com
Specialize in nonfiction in many disciplines, including textbooks, bibliographies, medical texts & journals, social sciences, scholarly material & cookbooks.
Membership(s): American Society for Indexing

Fromer Editorial Services
1606 Noyes Dr, Silver Spring, MD 20910-2224
Tel: 301-585-8827
Key Personnel
Pres: Margot J Fromer *E-mail:* margotfromer@erols.com
Founded: 1980
Writing, rewriting & consultation in all aspects of health care & medicine; ms analysis, special assignment writing.
Membership(s): American Medical Writers Association; Science Writers' Association

Diane Gallo
49 Hilton St, Gilbertsville, NY 13776
Mailing Address: PO Box 106, Gilbertsville, NY 13776
Tel: 607-783-2386 *Fax:* 607-783-2386
E-mail: dgallo@stny.rr.com
Web Site: www.dianegallo.com
Interviewing & video scripts.

Michael Garrett, see Creative Inspirations Inc

The Gary-Paul Agency
1549 Main St, Stratford, CT 06615
Tel: 203-345-6167
Web Site: www.thegarypaulagency.com; www.nutmegpictures.com
Key Personnel
Owner: Gary Maynard *E-mail:* garret@thegarypaulagency.com
Founded: 1994
Literary agency that represents & promotes screenplays. Specialize in script development. WGAe Signatory.
Branch Office(s)
127 Horseshoe Rd, Fayston, VT 05660 *Tel:* 203-556-8671
Membership(s): Writers Guild of America, East

Fred Gebhart
PO Box 111, Gold Hill, OR 97525
Tel: 541-855-8975
E-mail: fgebhart@pobox.com
Web Site: www.fredgebhart.com
Founded: 1981
Editorial & advertorial writing. Specialize in business, consumer education, travel, healthcare, foreign countries, medicine, science, transportation, wine & spirits.
Membership(s): American Medical Writers Association; American Society of Journalists & Authors; International Society of Travel Medicine; National Association of Science Writers

Gelles-Cole Literary Enterprises
135 John Joy Rd, Woodstock, NY 12498-0341
Web Site: www.literaryenterprises.com
Key Personnel
Founder & Pres: Sandi Gelles-Cole
E-mail: sandigc@aol.com
Founded: 1983
Editorial consultant (book doctor) specializing in commercial fiction & nonfiction serving authors, publishers & literary agents; writing coach; consultant for self-publishing authors, collaboration. Editorial specialty is development of concept & character development. Provide an intense word by word tutorial focusing on concept, style, voice, pace & characterization & for nonfiction, structure. Offers help to experts & other authors developing their material for the general public. Also have small publishing arm. Soft spot for first novels.

Nancy C Gerth PhD
1431 Harlan's Trail, Sagle, ID 83860
Tel: 208-304-9066
E-mail: docnangee@nancygerth.com
Web Site: www.nancygerth.com
Founded: 2005
Freelance indexing & related services. Index focus: Scholarly specializing in American history, indigenous studies, postmodernism. PhD in philosophy (Cornell University). Providing information services since 1988.
Membership(s): American Society for Indexing; Pacific Northwest Chapter of American Society for Indexing

GGP Publishing Inc
105 Calvert St, Suite 201, Harrison, NY 10528-3138
Tel: 914-834-8896 *Fax:* 914-834-7566
Web Site: www.GGPPublishing.com
Key Personnel
Pres & Publg Dir: Generosa Gina Protano
E-mail: GGProtano@GGPPublishing.com
Founded: 1991
Packager for trade & educational publishers. All editorial, art & design, production & printing services—from concept to bound books or any segment(s) of this publishing process. Trade (fiction & nonfiction) & children's books, textbooks (el-hi, college & adult education), professional, reference & how-to books, cookbooks, audiotapes, videotapes & CDs. Specialize in the development of materials for the study of foreign languages (such as French, German, Italian, Japanese, Latin, Portuguese, Russian & Spanish) & ESL, as well as in the development of materials for bilingual education & language arts. In addition, we translate complete or partial programs from & into the

various languages & act as literary agents & foreign publisher representatives.
Membership(s): American Book Producers Association

Cathe Giffuni, see Research Research

Sheri Gilbert
123 Van Voorhis Ave, Rochester, NY 14617
Tel: 585-342-0331
E-mail: shergilb@aol.com
Web Site: www.permissionseditor.com
Reviews mss for permissions identification; preparing permissions reports; obtaining permissions for text, art, photographs & song lyrics. Creating credit lines & source notes.

Michael Wells Glueck, see EditAndPublishYourBook.com

Gold Leaf Press
3670 Morrissey Ave, Warren, MI 48091
Tel: 313-331-3571
Web Site: www.goldleafpress.com
Key Personnel
Publr & Publg Consultant: Rebecca J Ensign *E-mail:* rensign2014@gmail.com
Founded: 1994
Independent publisher & publishing services provider to the trade, corporate & academic markets. Our proprietary publishing program, for qualifying works & authors, emphasizes editorial development for market worthiness. Through our services, Gold Leaf Press has edited, published & represented fiction & nonfiction titles & authors in a variety of genres, from scholarly works, autobiographies & company training manuals to corporate identity publications, self-help books & novels.

Donald Goldstein
1500 E 17 St, Brooklyn, NY 11230
Tel: 718-375-9346
E-mail: dgoldsbkyn@aol.com
Founded: 1988
Sports, sociology, American politics, the labor movement, Israel, Jewish related subjects; research, interviewing, copy-editing, rewriting, special assignment writing & proofreading.

Robert M Goodman
140 West End Ave, Unit 11-J, New York, NY 10023
Tel: 917-439-1097
E-mail: bobbybgood@gmail.com
Membership(s): Editorial Freelancers Association

P M Gordon Associates Inc
2115 Wallace St, Philadelphia, PA 19130
Tel: 215-769-2525
E-mail: pmga@pond1.net
Web Site: www.pmgordonassociates.com
Key Personnel
Pres: Peggy M Gordon
VP: Douglas C Gordon
Founded: 1982
Developmental editing, rewriting & copy-editing for trade, text & corporate books; indexing. Complete design & production services.

Sherry Gottlieb
Unit of wordservices.com
4900 Dunes St, Oxnard, CA 93035
Tel: 805-382-3425
E-mail: writer@wordservices.com
Web Site: www.wordservices.com
Founded: 1991
Private editorial service that specializes in fiction & screenplays. Edited over 450 book mss, mostly fiction. Several clients have sold their books to major publishers.

Graphic World Publishing Services
Division of Graphic World Inc
11687 Adie Rd, St Louis, MO 63043
Tel: 314-567-9854 *Fax:* 314-567-7178
E-mail: quote@gwinc.com
Web Site: www.gwinc.com
Key Personnel
Pres & CEO: Kevin P Arrow
EVP, Opers: Michael J Loomis *E-mail:* mike.loomis@gwinc.com
EVP, Technol: Andrew R Vosburgh *E-mail:* a.vosburgh@gwinc.com
Dir, Publg & Media Servs: Suzanne Kastner
Complete editorial & project management services from ms through final files, including interior & cover design, composition services, electronic publishing services & art rendering.

Paul Greenland Communications Inc
Formerly Paul Greenland Editorial Services
9184 Longfellow Lane, Machesney Park, IL 61115
Tel: 815-240-4108 *Toll Free Tel:* 888-798-7786
Web Site: www.paulgreenland.com
Key Personnel
Owner: Paul R Greenland
Services include writing, ghostwriting & collaboration, research, editing & proofreading. Published nonfiction author, marketing/communications professional & former senior editor of national business magazine. Contributor to many leading reference books (Cengage Learning, University of Chicago Press, Facts on File). Interview subjects include celebrities, athletes & leading business executives. Specialize in reference, business, biography & history. References available upon request.
Membership(s): Editorial Freelancers Association

Paul Greenland Editorial Services, see Paul Greenland Communications Inc

Rosemary F Gretton
1029 El Capitan Dr, Danville, CA 94526
Tel: 925-336-0003 *Fax:* 925-336-0003
E-mail: rgretton@lyricism.ca
Web Site: www.lyricism.ca
Founded: 2003
Writing, editing & research services for publishers, government, business, nonprofit organizations & individuals. Specializes in copywriting, copy-editing, fact checking, line editing, proofreading, research & rewriting.
Membership(s): American Copy Editors Society; Editorial Freelancers Association; Editors' Association of Canada/Association canadienne des reviseurs

Joan K Griffitts Indexing
3909 W 71 St, Indianapolis, IN 46268-2257
Tel: 317-297-7312
E-mail: jkgriffitts@gmail.com
Web Site: www.joankgriffittsindexing.com
Founded: 1989
Indexing & proofreading of textbooks, trade books, reference books, technical documentation, catalogs & newspapers by former librarian. Most subjects; specialize in business, science, sports, gardening, computer science, library science, education, taxation & social science. Various computer formats & e-mail delivery. Technical editing of various types of books & magazines including crochet, knit, weaving, etc.
Membership(s): American Society for Indexing

Anne Hebenstreit
20 Tip Top Way, Berkeley Heights, NJ 07922
Tel: 908-665-0536
Copy-editing & proofreading of el-hi & college texts & trade books.

Helm Editorial Services
707 SW Eighth Way, Fort Lauderdale, FL 33315
Tel: 954-525-5626
E-mail: lynnehelm12@aol.com
Freelance writing, line editing & publishing for executives & authors.

Herr's Indexing Service
76-340 Kealoha St, Kailua Kona, HI 96740
Tel: 808-365-4348
E-mail: lindahallinger@gmail.com
Web Site: www.herrsindexing.com
Key Personnel
Owner: Linda Herr Hallinger *E-mail:* linda@herrsindexing.com
Founded: 1944
Provide quality & affordable indexes for a variety of topics. Specialize in medical books.
Membership(s): American Medical Writers Association; American Society for Indexing; Editorial Freelancers Association

L Anne Hirschel DDS
5990 Highgate Ave, East Lansing, MI 48823
Tel: 517-333-1748
E-mail: alicerichard@comcast.net
Medicine & dentistry, consumer/patient information, continuing education & editing for foreign speaking scientists.
Membership(s): American Dental Association; Medical Writers Association

Burnham Holmes
182 Lakeview Hill Rd, Poultney, VT 05764-9179
Tel: 802-287-9707 *Fax:* 802-287-9707 (computer fax/modem)
E-mail: burnham.holmes@castleton.edu
Founded: 1990
Write textbooks, fiction & general nonfiction, juvenile, young adult, plays & children's books.
Membership(s): The Authors Guild; League of Vermont Writers

Henry Holmes Literary Agent/Book Publicist/Marketing Consultant
Mitchell Heights, Apt 205, 2100 S Main St, Fall River, MA 02724
Tel: 508-672-2258
Key Personnel
Pres & Literary Agent: Henry Holmes
Founded: 1997
Nonfiction: biography, business, education, law, health, history, sports, etc. Exclusive literary agent/book publicist for authors. Authors must present complete book proposal with SASE when submitting. Impeccable presentation is a must. Prefer books targeted at general audiences rather than an exclusive or limited market. Send letter with a good hook & a list of publishers you have contacted in the past. Do not send any spiral bound proposals; word count must be stated. Include past publicity & endorsement(s). Commission 15%. Contract must be signed. Upon receipt of signed contract, author will be sent a media portfolio with marketing data, tip sheet & full compliment of media contact listings. Professional consultation related to all media, freelance assignments, interviewing celebrities, professional athletes, musicians, political figures & other famous people.

Imagefinders Inc
6101 Utah Ave NW, Washington, DC 20015
Fax: 202-244-3237

Key Personnel
Pres: Elisabeth M Hartjens *E-mail:* hartjens@erols.com
Founded: 1985
Photo & illustration research & editing; fact checking, information research. Specialize in Washington public domain sources.

IndexEmpire Indexing Services
16740 Orville Wright Dr, Riverside, CA 92518
Tel: 951-697-2819
E-mail: indexempire@gmail.com
Web Site: www.indexempire.com
Key Personnel
Indexer: Jean F Middleton
Founded: 1999
Provides back-of-the-book indexes for nonfiction books of all types.
Membership(s): American Society for Indexing

Indexing by the Book
PO Box 12513, Tucson, AZ 85732-2513
Tel: 520-750-8439
E-mail: indextran@cox.net
Web Site: www.indexingbythebook.com
Key Personnel
Indexer: Cynthia J Coan
Founded: 2003
Index books & serials. Subject specialties include health/medicine, history (especially Arizona/Southwest), education, language studies, library science, social sciences & psychology. Index adult, children's & Spanish language titles. Also translate print materials from Spanish & Swedish into English.
Membership(s): American Society for Indexing; ATA; National Council on Interpreting in Health Care

Integra Software Services Inc
Division of Integra Software Services Pvt Ltd
1110 Jorie Blvd, Suite 200, Oak Brook, IL 60523
Tel: 630-586-2579 *Fax:* 630-586-2599
E-mail: marketing@integra.co.in
Web Site: www.integra.co.in
Key Personnel
Dir, Edit Devt: Ingrid Benson *E-mail:* ingrid.benson@integra.co.in
Design Mgr: Emily Friel *E-mail:* emily.friel@integra.co.in
Founded: 1991
Project management, development & production support for book publishers. Full range of publishing services, including developmental editing, design, rights & permissions, photo research, copy-editing & indexing, proofreading, language polishing, typesetting, XML & conversion, illustrations & artwork, ebooks & digital services. Specialty areas are business & economics, computer science, mathematics, science, history, English, medical & education texts.

Iridescent Orange Press, see Wambtac Communications

Jan Williams Indexing Services
300 Dartmouth College Hwy, Lyme, NH 03768-3207
Tel: 603-795-4924
Web Site: www.janwilliamsindexing.com
Key Personnel
Prop: Jan Williams
Founded: 1998
Back-of-book indexes for trade, scholarly, reference & textbooks; database/online indexes for journals.
Membership(s): American Society for Indexing

Jenkins Group Inc
1129 Woodmere Ave, Suite B, Traverse City, MI 49686
Tel: 231-933-0445 *Toll Free Tel:* 800-706-4636 *Fax:* 231-933-0448
E-mail: info@bookpublishing.com
Web Site: www.bookpublishing.com
Key Personnel
CEO: Jerrold R Jenkins *Tel:* 231-933-0445 ext 1008 *E-mail:* jrj@bookpublishing.com
Pres & COO: James Kalajian *Tel:* 231-933-0445 ext 1006 *E-mail:* jjk@bookpublishing.com
Dir, Consulting & Mktg Servs: Kim Hornyak *Tel:* 231-933-0445 ext 1013 *E-mail:* khornyak@bookpublishing.com
Mng Ed, Independent Publisher Online: Jim Barnes *E-mail:* jimb@bookpublishing.com
Book Prodn Mgr: Leah Nicholson *Tel:* 231-933-0445 ext 1015 *E-mail:* lnicholson@bookpublishing.com
Founded: 1990
Full service custom book publishing services for corporations, independent authors, organizations & small press publishers. Services include registrations, typesetting, cover design, color separations, ghostwriting, illustration & photo placement, galley preparation & print management.

JFE Editorial
8425 Doreen Ave, Fort Worth, TX 76116-4922
Tel: 817-560-7018
Founded: 1987
Founded by Ms Ford, a nationally published author, ghostwriter, project manager, editor & proofreader. Focus includes: writing, ghostwriting, rewriting, special assignment writing; developmental, copy, line, style & content editing; proofreading; ms analysis; permissions, interviewing; fact checking; database research, coding, editing. Published in genres ranging from children's, trade & true crime to scholastic, self-help & sports books; also a variety of magazine articles. Coordinator of many high-dollar projects & extremely successful at transforming complex material into easily understood information. Ms Ford is a speaker for grades 3-12, universities & conferences. Fax number provided upon request.

JL Communications
10205 Green Holly Terr, Silver Spring, MD 20902
Tel: 301-593-0640
Key Personnel
Writer, Ed & Poet: Joyce Eileen Latham
Founded: 1996

Cliff Johnson & Associates
10867 Fruitland Dr, Studio City, CA 91604
Tel: 818-761-5665 *Fax:* 818-761-9501
E-mail: quest543@yahoo.com
Key Personnel
Pres: Cliff Johnson
Founded: 1976
Nonfiction specialists (primarily medical, psychology, religious, self-help & philosophical books).

Just Creative Writing & Indexing Services (JCR)
301 Wood Duck Dr, Greensboro, MD 21639
Tel: 410-482-6337
E-mail: support@justcreativewriting.com
Web Site: www.justcreativewriting.com
Key Personnel
Sole Prop: Judith Reveal *E-mail:* 19editor45@gmail.com
Founded: 2005
Provides editorial services for fiction & nonfiction; professional back-of-the-book indexing; auto ethnographic dissertation editing; book reviews.
Membership(s): Eastern Shore Writers' Association; Editorial Freelancers Association; Greensboro Business & Civic Association

Sharon Kapnick
185 West End Ave, New York, NY 10023-5547
Tel: 212-787-7231
Web Site: sharonswineline.wordpress.com
Food & wine articles for magazines, web sites, newspapers & books.

Ann T Keene, see Edit Etc

Keim Publishing
66 Main St, Suite 807, Yonkers, NY 10701
Tel: 917-655-7190
Key Personnel
Owner & Pres: Betty Keim *E-mail:* mieklb@gmail.com
Founded: 1985
Books & art catalogs, corporate reports, newsletters, brochures, pamphlets, electronic materials (e.g., web sites, advertisements, etc), promotional items, reference books, production & design, line editing, copy-editing, indexing, permissions, photo research, proofreading, reference assignments, research, rewriting, typemarking, special assignment writing. All subjects; specialize in art, broadcasting, history, literature, science, mathematics & music.

Jascha Kessler
218 16 St, Santa Monica, CA 90402-2216
Tel: 310-393-7968 *Fax:* 310-393-7968 (by request only)
E-mail: urim.urim@gmail.com
Web Site: www.jfkessler.com; www.xlibris.com
Freelance reviews of poetry, fiction, history, philosophy, current affairs. Criticism as well as "cultural commentary" on the arts, theater & dance.
Membership(s): The American Society of Composers, Authors and Publishers

Theodore Knight PhD
RockCliff Farm, 40 Old Louisquisset Pike, Unit 101A, North Smithfield, RI 02896
Tel: 401-597-6982
E-mail: tedknight1@cox.net
Founded: 1989
Editorial & project management for trade, textbook, university press & reference.

Bill Koehnlein
236 E Fifth St, New York, NY 10003-8545
Tel: 212-674-9145
E-mail: koehnlein.bill@gmail.com
Founded: 1982
Indexing & editing: all subjects, especially current affairs, social science, American labor & radical history, radical political movements & theory: socialism, Marxism, anarchism. Also food & nutrition issues, especially vegetarianism & veganism.

Barry R Koffler
Featherside, 14 Ginger Rd, High Falls, NY 12440
Tel: 845-687-9851
E-mail: barkof@feathersite.com
Founded: 1979
Indexing, proofreading, editing. Writing most subjects (including encyclopedic). Specialize in popular & scientific works on animals & natural history.

KOK Edit
15 Hare Lane, East Setauket, NY 11733-3606
Tel: 631-997-8191 *Fax:* 631-474-9849

E-mail: editor@kokedit.com
Web Site: www.kokedit.com; twitter.com/kokedit; www.facebook.com/K.OmooreKlopf; www.linkedin.com/in/kokedit; www.editor-mom.blogspot.com
Key Personnel
Owner: Katharine O'Moore-Klopf
Founded: 1995
Medical editor providing copy-editing & substantive editing to publishers of medical textbooks, professional books & journal articles & providing English-language editing to researcher-authors who are non-native English speakers. Certified by the Board of Editors in the Life Sciences.
Membership(s): American Medical Writers Association; Board of Editors in the Life Sciences; Council of Science Editors; Editorial Freelancers Association; World Association of Medical Editors

Kraft & Kraft
40 Memorial Hwy, Apt 23-C, New Rochelle, NY 10801
Tel: 914-319-3320
Web Site: www.erickraft.com
Key Personnel
Owner & Edit Dir: Eric Kraft *E-mail:* eric-kraft@post.harvard.edu
Contact: Madeline Kraft
Founded: 1975
Design & development of educational materials.

Eileen Kramer
336 Great Rd, Stow, MA 01775
Tel: 978-897-4121
E-mail: kramer@tiac.net
Copy editor/proofreader/ESL teacher/curriculum developer. Specialties include academic journals & textbooks for STEM.

Lynn C Kronzek & Richard A Flom
Affiliate of Lynn C Kronzek & Associates
145 S Glenoaks Blvd, Suite 240, Burbank, CA 91502
Tel: 818-768-7688 *Fax:* 818-768-7648
Key Personnel
Principal: Lynn C Kronzek *E-mail:* lckronzek@sbcglobal.net
Founded: 1989
Nonfiction writing & editorial services, with particular expertise in history, multicultural & Judaic studies, government/public affairs & religion. Affiliated with the National Council on Public History, American Association for State & Local History & the Rabbinical Assembly.

Polly Kummel LLC
624 Boardman Rd, Aiken, SC 29803
Tel: 803-641-6831
E-mail: editor@amazinphrasin.com; pollyk1@msn.com
Web Site: www.amazinphrasin.com
Founded: 1990
Nonfiction (all subjects; trade & academic): copyediting; substantive/developmental editing; coaching. Specialties: journalism, history, political science, memoir, equestrian subjects. Dissertation/thesis help for humanities grad students; electronic editing. More than 35 years of experience.

Lachina Publishing Services Inc
3791 S Green Rd, Cleveland, OH 44122
Tel: 216-292-7959
E-mail: info@lachina.com
Web Site: www.lachina.com
Key Personnel
Founder & Pres: Jeffrey A Lachina
Founded: 1989
Project management, editorial development, copyediting, biomedical illustration, indexing, page composition, book & jacket design, proofreading, technical illustration.

Lynne Lackenbach Editorial Services
31 Pillsbury Rd, East Hampstead, NH 03826
Tel: 603-329-8133
E-mail: lynnelack@gmail.com
Full line of editorial services to college & professional publishers. Specialize in scientific & technical material.

Bob Land, see Land on Demand

Land on Demand
20 Long Crescent Dr, Bristol, VA 24201
Tel: 423-366-0513
E-mail: landondemand@gmail.com
Web Site: boblandedits.blogspot.com
Key Personnel
Prop & Ed: Bob Land
Founded: 1994
Editing, indexing, proofreading. Full-time freelancer since 1994; freelancer since 1986; full-time editor, writer, proofreader 1981-1994.

LaurelTech
Subsidiary of diacriTech Inc
4 S Market St, 4th fl, Boston, MA 02109-6201
Tel: 617-600-3366 *Fax:* 617-848-2938
Web Site: www.diacritech.com
Key Personnel
EVP: Madhu Rajamani *E-mail:* madhu@diacritech.com
Dir, Prodn & Edit Servs: Maureen Ross *E-mail:* m.ross@diacritech.com
Founded: 1997
Specialize in meeting educational publishing needs. Full service development includes project management, editorial & content development services, print & digital production, art & prepress services. In-house staff of over 800 are experienced with all phases & disciplines of K-12, college & STM. Facilities in Boston, MA & in Chennai, Madurai, Kottayam in India.

The Learning Source Ltd
644 Tenth St, Brooklyn, NY 11215
Tel: 718-768-0231 (ext 10) *Fax:* 718-369-3467
E-mail: info@learningsourceltd.com
Web Site: www.learningsourceltd.com
Key Personnel
Dir: Gary Davis; Wendy Davis
Mng Ed: Brian Ableman
Provides a full range of editorial & book-producing services from concept through ms & design to film & bound book. Specialty areas include children's fiction & nonfiction, adult reference & nonfiction series & classroom materials. Sister company to Ivy Gate Books.
Membership(s): American Book Producers Association; International Literacy Association; National Council of Teachers of Mathematics

Debra Lemonds
Affiliate of Lemon Turtle Hawk Press
PO Box 5516, Pasadena, CA 91117-0516
Tel: 626-844-9363
E-mail: dlemonds@zoho.com
Founded: 1984
Photo editing. Graphic design.
Membership(s): ASPP

Andrew S Linick PhD, The Copyologist®
Subsidiary of The Linick Group Inc
Linick Bldg, 7 Putter Lane, Middle Island, NY 11953
Mailing Address: PO Box 102, Middle Island, NY 11953-0102
Tel: 631-924-3888; 631-775-6075 *Fax:* 631-924-8555
E-mail: linickgroup@gmail.com; topmarketingadvisor@gmail.com
Web Site: www.andrewlinickdirectmarketing.com/The-Copyologist.html; www.newworldpressbooks.com
Key Personnel
CEO & Creative Dir: Andrew S Linick, PhD *E-mail:* andrew@asklinick.com
EVP: Roger Dextor
Founded: 1968
Complete editorial & copywriting services: copy analysis & line editing, research, rewriting for direct response, direct mail, mail order, sales promotions; specialize in newsletters, newspapers, magazines, house organs & seminars; catalog writing, business & consumer launch packages & in-house seminars on how to sell what you write; articles, nonfiction books & manuals. Phone consultation available; consumer, trade, business to business, all markets, media & subjects; ms analysis & development, proofreading, special assignment writing, ghostwriting, e-mail marketing campaigns for publishers. Provide comprehensive graphic redesign/new web site content development, interactive services with web site marketing makeover advice for first-time authors, self-publishers, professionals & entrepreneurs. Specializes in flash, animation, merchant accounts, online advertising/PR, links to top search engines, consulting on a 100% satisfaction guarantee. Free site evaluation marketing checklist (a $250 value) for LMP readers. For over 49 years we have helped first-time authors & best-selling authors/publishers/entrepreneurs successfully promote books. Call for help today.
Membership(s): Independent Book Publishers Association

Elliot Linzer
126-10 Powells Cove Blvd, College Point, NY 11356
Tel: 718-353-1261
E-mail: elinzer@juno.com
Founded: 1971
Indexing of trade books, textbooks, reference books & scholarly books. Fifty years experience.
Membership(s): American Society for Indexing; Editorial Freelancers Association

Little Chicago Editorial Services
154 Natural Tpke, Ripton, VT 05766
Mailing Address: PO Box 185, Ripton, VT 05766
Tel: 802-388-9782
Web Site: andreachesman.com
Key Personnel
Writer & Ed: Andrea Chesman *E-mail:* andreachesman@gmail.com
Membership(s): International Association of Culinary Professionals

Lumina Datamatics Inc
Affiliate of Datamatics Global Services (Mumbai)
4 Collins Ave, Plymouth, MA 02360
Tel: 508-746-0300 *Fax:* 508-746-3233
Web Site: luminadatamatics.com
Key Personnel
SVP, Busn Devt: Jack Mitchell *Tel:* 508-415-6158 (cell) *E-mail:* jack.mitchell@luminad.com
SVP, Content Technol: John Wheeler *E-mail:* john.wheeler@luminad.com
SVP, Prod Devt: Gordon Laws *Tel:* 508-746-0300 ext 212 *E-mail:* gordon.laws@luminad.com
SVP, Sales: Prashant Prabhu *E-mail:* prashant.prabhu@luminad.com

VP, Fin & Acctg: John Chappell *Tel:* 508-746-0300 ext 304 *E-mail:* john.chappell@luminad.com
Founded: 2005
Content & solutions provider that specializes in partnering with publishers, learning companies, assessment providers & others to automate & produce results-driven learning solutions. Offers a full service solution, or can partner with you & your most valued resources to help you achieve game-changing advantages over your closest competitors. Beyond the traditional production & delivery services that include everything from authoring & development to the complete production process, specializes in assessment authoring, AIG (automatic item generation), adaptive assessment, analytics, instructional design, simulation-based learning (with reporting engine), print & digital permissions (enterprise platform & service), audio/video & more. Employs over 1,800 US & offshore resources. Areas of specialization include K-12, higher education, professional & scholarly publishing, as well as accessibility & ADA compliance. All disciplines served including, but not limited to, mathematics, history, social studies, reading, social sciences, political science, humanities, hard sciences, computer science, business, engineering, world languages, English language teaching, ESL & technical trades & workforce readiness.
Branch Office(s)
31572 Industrial Rd, Livonia, MI 48150 *Toll Free Tel:* 800-717-9153 *Fax:* 734-525-4455
510 Thornall St Metropark, Suite 100, Edison, NJ 08837 (sales) *Toll Free Tel:* 888-772-5532 *Fax:* 732-635-0600
345 Seventh Ave, 4th fl, New York, NY 10001 *Tel:* 646-453-1000 *Fax:* 212-564-8285
1797 Seddon Ct, Ashland, OH 44805 (prof, journals) *Tel:* 419-289-0558 *Fax:* 418-289-8923
3265 Farmtrail Rd, York, PA 17406 *Tel:* 717-764-4000
Ascendas International Tech Park, Taramani Rd, 12th fl, Phase II, Chennai 600 113, India

Mari Lynch, see Fine Wordworking

Elizabeth Lyon
3530 E Game Farm Rd, No 39, Springfield, OR 97477
Tel: 541-357-4181
E-mail: elyon123@comcast.net
Web Site: www.elizabethlyon.com
Founded: 1988
Full-time freelance book editor. Specialize in novels, memoirs, nonfiction books & proposals. Advises writers about how to write, connect with literary agents &, should 'Plan A' not succeed, how to successfully self-publish an ebook +/or print-on-demand. Over 60 writers have found publication with large publishers & small presses, while dozens have "gone indie," some to great success & acclaim. Edits query letters & synopses for clients. Has written 6 books on writing, including the bestsellers *Nonfiction Book Proposals Anybody Can Write* & *Manuscript Makeover. Writing Subtext* is the first in a booklet series, sold as an ebook & in paperback.
Membership(s): Oregon Writers Colony; Williamette Writers Association

Phyllis Manner
17 Springdale Rd, New Rochelle, NY 10804
Tel: 914-834-4707 *Fax:* 914-834-4707
E-mail: pmanner@aol.com; manneredit@gmail.com
Specialize in medicine, biochemistry & archeology.
Membership(s): American Society for Indexing; Archeological Institute of America

Danny Marcus Word Worker
Division of D M Enterprises
62 Washington St, Suite 2, Marblehead, MA 01945-3553
Tel: 781-631-3886; 781-290-9174 (cell) *Fax:* 781-631-3886
E-mail: emildanelle@yahoo.com
Founded: 1984
Proofreading, line editing & copy-editing. Specialize in politics, income taxes, government, history, current events, all kinds of fiction & general nonfiction.
Membership(s): Cambridge Academic Editors Network

Joy Matkowski
212 Ridge Hill Rd, Mechanicsburg, PA 17050
Tel: 717-620-8490
E-mail: jmatkowski1@comcast.net
Copy-editing & proofreading.

Peter Mayeux
8148 Regent Dr, Lincoln, NE 68507-3366
Tel: 402-466-8547
E-mail: pm41923@windstream.net
Resumes, original research, writing papers & projects, Power Point presentations, broadcast commercial writing, textbooks & media scripts.

Anita D McClellan Associates
464 Common St, Suite 142, Belmont, MA 02478-2704
Tel: 617-575-9203
E-mail: adm@anitamcclellan.com
Web Site: www.anitamcclellan.com
Key Personnel
Mng Dir: Anita D McClellan
Founded: 1988
Developmental editing, nonfiction proposal development, revising, restructuring, book doctoring, fiction & nonfiction.
Membership(s): The Authors Guild; Bay Area Editors' Forum; Cape Cod Writers Center; Editorial Freelancers Association; Independent Book Publishers Association; Independent Publishers of New England; International Women's Writing Guild; National Book Critics Circle; Sisters in Crime; Society of Children's Book Writers & Illustrators; Women's National Book Association

Pamela Dittmer McKuen
87 Tanglewood Dr, Glen Ellyn, IL 60137
Tel: 630-545-0867 *Fax:* 630-545-0868
E-mail: pmckuen@gmail.com
Web Site: www.pamelamckuen.com; www.allthewriteplaces.com
Special assignment writing, editorial & corporate projects, periodicals, copy-editing, interviewing & research.
Membership(s): Association of Women in Journalism; National Association of Real Estate Editors

Pat McNees
10643 Weymouth St, Suite 204, Bethesda, MD 20814
Tel: 301-897-8557
E-mail: patmcnees@gmail.com
Web Site: www.patmcnees.com; www.writersandeditors.com
Founded: 1971
Articles, books, photohistories. Specialize in memoirs, personal histories, biographies & organizational histories, especially in fields of medicine & psychiatry. Teach life story & legacy writing; do substantial editing, rewriting & book doctoring. Theme anthologies & stories about food, dancing & travel.
Membership(s): American Society of Journalists & Authors; Association of Health Care Journalists; Association of Personal Historians; The Authors Guild; Biographers International Organization; Independent Book Publishers Association; National Association of Science Writers; PEN International; Society for Technical Communication

MC2 Solutions LLC
5101 Violet Lane, Madison, WI 53714
Tel: 608-240-4959
Key Personnel
Writer/Ed: Mark Crawford *E-mail:* mark.crawford@charter.net
Founded: 1995
Servicing all audiences including academic, technical, science, corporate & public relations. Additional services include: substantive editing, promotional writing & writing of corporate histories, business writing, marketing & communications, feature writing, editing & proofreading.

Barbara A Mele
2525 Holland Ave, New York, NY 10467-8703
Tel: 718-654-8047 *Fax:* 718-654-8047
E-mail: bannmele@aol.com
Freelance permissions.

Tom Mellers Publishing Services (TMPS)
60 Second Ave, New York, NY 10003
Tel: 212-254-4958
E-mail: tmps71@yahoo.com
Comprehensive rights & permissions administration, acquiring & granting rights for text of all kinds, photos, art, video, film, music, spoken word. Acquiring services range from consulting with rightseekers, to evaluating permissionable material, setting up projects, sending & tracking requests, negotiating fees, preparing acknowledgments, administering payment & righting contracts. Granting services include drafting contracts, negotiating & collecting fees & preparing records (edit-in). Copyright registration. Specialize in literary estates. All subjects & media. Extensive editing & editorial services, from author consultation to ms analysis, fact checking & rewriting to project supervision (including typemarking, book design, line editing, copy-editing, proofreading). Ghostwriting & special assignment writing, author representation & photo research, drafting contracts, image research & international work with museums.
Branch Office(s)
4629 Vestal Pkwy E, Vestal, NY 13850 *Tel:* 607-798-7994

Fred C Mench Professor of Classics Emeritus
207 Saint Martins Lane, Smyrna, TN 37167
Tel: 615-459-0765
E-mail: fmench@earthlink.net
Text editing, especially classical antiquity or English literature. Past projects included reading drafts of Roman historical novels for content & form, writing reviews of scholarly & fictional works (especially on ancient Rome). Book review editor of the journal *Classical World* for 15 years, involving extensive condensing of submitted texts. Special areas: Julius Caesar, Roman republic, Latin texts, the Bible, Greek mythology & G B Shaw. Also available for general editing.
Membership(s): American Philological Association

Metropolitan Editorial & Writing Service
Subsidiary of Metropolitan Research Co
4455 Douglas Ave, Riverdale, NY 10471
Tel: 718-549-5518
Key Personnel
Pres: Chauncey G Olinger, Jr *E-mail:* cgolinger@verizon.net
Founded: 1982

Editing, ms analysis, rewriting & restyling of general, professional & scholarly writing, especially in economics, business, social sciences, humanities, medicine & pharmacy. Specialize in editorial collaboration with authors; oral history interviewing.

Susan T Middleton
366-A Norton Hill Rd, Ashfield, MA 01330-9601
Tel: 413-628-4039
E-mail: smiddle@crocker.com
Founded: 1985
Book revision, collaboration, developmental & copy-editing for individuals & for trade & college markets primarily in the sciences.
Membership(s): Western New England Editorial Freelancers Network

Stephen M Miller Inc
15727 S Madison Dr, Olathe, KS 66062
Tel: 913-768-7997
Web Site: www.stephenmillerbooks.com
Key Personnel
Pres: Stephen M Miller *E-mail:* steve@stephenmillerbooks.com
Founded: 1994
Writing, editing; bible specialty & health subspecialty. Full-time freelance writer & former editor, books, magazines & newspaper. Seminary & journalism school graduate, Kansas City area. Clientele of top national book publishers & magazines.
Membership(s): CBA: The Association for Christian Retail; Evangelical Christian Publishers Association; Society of Bible Literature; Wesleyan Theological Society

Kathleen Mills Editorial Services
327 E King St, Chardon, OH 44024
Tel: 440-285-4347
E-mail: mills_edit@yahoo.com
Key Personnel
Edit Dir: Kathleen Mills
Founded: 1990
More than 30 years of publishing experience. Editing, indexing, writing, author liaison & project management. Arts & humanities, social sciences, technical, reference, medical, college, business, general nonfiction & web sites. Clients include the Cleveland Museum of Art, Western Reserve Historical Society, Case Western Reserve University, ASM International, UCLA & many others.

Sondra Mochson
18 Overlook Dr, Port Washington, NY 11050
Tel: 516-883-0961
All subjects, text & trade.

Mary Mueller
516 Bartram Rd, Moorestown, NJ 08057
Tel: 856-778-4769
E-mail: mamam49@aol.com
Abstracting, copy-editing, ghostwriting, indexing, proofreading, rewriting & book reviewing-publicity. Specialize in consumer education, gardening, health, nutrition, house & home organizing, science & technology, hobby art & craft books & how-to-books.

Nina Neimark Editorial Services
543 Third St, Brooklyn, NY 11215
Tel: 718-499-6804
E-mail: pneimark@hotmail.com
Key Personnel
Pres: Nina Neimark
Founded: 1965
Specialize in scholarly books & college texts on environmental issues, history, art, music, social sciences; also general nonfiction. Mss analysis & development, content & photo research, rewriting, copy-editing, proofreading, production editing & complete book packaging services.

Newgen North America Inc
Subsidiary of Newgen KnowledgeWorks
2714 Bee Cave Rd, Suite 201, Austin, TX 78746
Tel: 512-478-5341 *Fax:* 512-476-4756
Web Site: www.newgen.co
Key Personnel
Pres: Maran Elancheran *Tel:* 512-870-7106 (cell) *E-mail:* maran@newgen.co
VP, Cust Support: Bill M Grosskopf *E-mail:* bill@newgen.co
Sales Dir, USA: Linda Thomas *Tel:* 703-297-1473 *E-mail:* lindat@newgen.co
Founded: 1955
Prepares project material for copy-editor, supervises the copy-editing, serves as liaison with the author, reviews the final ms & makes sure that all elements of the project are complete & ready to be turned over to a designer. Ensures that file conversions, coding & cleanup properly prepare book material for each stage in the process. Convert files to ebook formats. Scan printed books to prepare new print file & ebook files.

Sue Newton
1385 Cypress Point Lane, Suite 202, Ventura, CA 93003
Tel: 805-765-4412; 805-827-1961
E-mail: sue.edit@gmail.com
Ms & line editing services including the correction of spelling errors, grammar, punctuation, syntax & consistency. Minor rewrites. 20 years experience in the publishing industry including fiction, nonfiction, autobiographies, textbooks, medical records & advertising.
Membership(s): Small Publishers, Artists & Writers Network; Ventura County Writers Club

Donald Nicholson-Smith
50 Plaza St E, Apt 1D, Brooklyn, NY 11238
Tel: 718-636-4732
E-mail: mnr.dns@verizon.net
French-English literary translation.
Membership(s): Translators Association (London)

Veronica Oliva
304 Lily St, San Francisco, CA 94102-5608
Tel: 415-337-7707
E-mail: veronicaoliva@sbcglobal.net
Founded: 1994
Permissions editor: Trade & educational publishers. Specialty: French, Spanish & Italian college level textbooks.
Membership(s): Bay Area Editors' Forum

Oyster River Press
36 Oyster River Rd, Durham, NH 03824-3029
Tel: 603-868-5006
E-mail: oysterriverpress@comcast.net
Web Site: www.facebook.com/OysterRiverPress/
Key Personnel
Publr & Ed: Cicely Buckley
Founded: 1987
Interviewing, special assignment writing, translating services to/from French, Spanish, Russian, Polish.
Membership(s): New Hampshire Writers Project

Pacific Publishing Services
PO Box 1150, Capitola, CA 95010-1150
Tel: 831-476-8284 *Fax:* 831-476-8294
E-mail: pacpubs@attglobal.net
Key Personnel
Pres: Albert Lee Strickland
Assoc: Lynne Ann De Spelder
Research, editorial & writing services for trade, text & corporate publications.

Karen L Pangallo
27 Buffum St, Salem, MA 01970
Tel: 978-744-8796
E-mail: pangallo@noblenet.org

Diane Patrick
140 Carver Loop, No 21A, Bronx, NY 10475-2954
E-mail: dpatrickediting@aol.com
Web Site: www.dianepatrick.net
Expert who creates & polishes written materials for publishers, editors, agents, academics, legal professionals, entertainers & business owners.
Membership(s): ALA; International Women's Writing Guild; New York Association of Black Journalists

PeopleSpeak
25401 Alicia Pkwy, Suite L-512, Laguna Hills, CA 92653
Tel: 949-581-6190 *Fax:* 949-581-4958
E-mail: pplspeak@att.net
Web Site: www.detailsplease.com/peoplespeak
Key Personnel
Sr Ed: Sharon Goldinger
Founded: 1985
An eye for details. Copy-editing; specialize in nonfiction mss, marketing materials, newsletters, directories.
Membership(s): Independent Book Publishers Association; Publishers Association of Los Angeles; San Diego Professional Editors Network

Rebecca Pepper
434 NE Floral Place, Portland, OR 97232
Tel: 503-236-5802
E-mail: rpepper@rpepper.net
Web Site: pepperedit.com
Founded: 1986
Membership(s): Editcetera; Editorial Freelancers Association; Northwest Independent Editors Guild

The Permissions Group Inc
401 S Milwaukee Ave, Suite 180, Wheeling, IL 60090
Tel: 847-635-6550 *Toll Free Tel:* 800-374-7985 *Fax:* 847-635-6968
E-mail: info@permissionsgroup.com
Web Site: www.permissionsgroup.com
Key Personnel
Dir: Sherry Hoesly *E-mail:* sherry_hoesly@permissionsgroup.com
Founded: 1990
Full service copyright & permissions consulting company. Specialize in ms review & analysis, rights negotiation, individualized consulting.

Elsa Peterson Ltd
41 East Ave, Norwalk, CT 06851-3919
Tel: 203-846-8331
E-mail: epltd@earthlink.net
Founded: 1984
Offer a full range of editorial services personalized to your project: developmental editing, substantive editing, writing, rights clearance, picture research, translation (Spanish to English).
Membership(s): Association for Psychological Science; Editorial Freelancers Association; Textbook & Academic Authors Association

Evelyn Walters Pettit
114 S Park Ave, Suite E, Winter Park, FL 32789-7012
Tel: 407-620-0131 (cell); 407-644-1711 *Fax:* 407-644-1711
E-mail: bookseller@brandywinebooks.com
Copy & line editing, rewriting & proofreading. Specialize in professional & reference books, journal articles & magazines & books in gen-

eral. Experience in subjects ranging from social & biological sciences to engineering & mathematics to business.

Meredith Phillips
4127 Old Adobe Rd, Palo Alto, CA 94306
Tel: 650-857-9555
E-mail: mphillips0743@comcast.net
Former author & award-nominated mystery publisher (Perseverance Press). Editing (developmental, line, copy), researching, fact checking, proofreading of trade books (fiction or nonfiction).

PhotoEdit Inc
3505 Cadillac Ave, Suite P-101, Costa Mesa, CA 92626
Toll Free Tel: 888-450-0946 *Fax:* 714-434-5937 *Toll Free Fax:* 800-804-3707
E-mail: sales@photoeditinc.com
Web Site: www.photoeditinc.com
Key Personnel
Photo Edit Dir: Tashauna Johnson *Tel:* 714-434-5935 *E-mail:* tashauna.johnson@photoeditinc.com
Founded: 1987
Photographers; large stock on hand.

Pictures & Words Editorial Services
3100 "B" Ave, Anacortes, WA 98221
Tel: 360-293-8476
E-mail: editor@picturesandwords.com
Web Site: www.picturesandwords.com/words
Key Personnel
Owner: Kristi Hein
Founded: 1995
Versatile generalist with decades of experience serving trade publishers & authors. Expertise in cookbooks, health & well-being, gardening (ornamental & food), nature & environment, education, consumer interest & activism, business & fiction.
Membership(s): Bay Area Editors' Forum; Northwest Independent Editors Guild

Caroline Pincus Book Midwife
101 Wool St, San Francisco, CA 94110
Tel: 415-516-6206
E-mail: caroline@carolinepincus.com
Web Site: carolinepincus.com
Key Personnel
Book Midwife: Caroline Pincus
Founded: 1998
Ms development & book doctoring for the general trade. Specialize in health, personal growth, women's issues & narrative nonfiction.

J P Pochron Writer for Hire
830 Lake Orchid Circle, No 203, Vero Beach, FL 32962
Tel: 772-569-2967
E-mail: hotwriter15@hotmail.com
Key Personnel
Owner & Writer: J P Pochron
Former editor, reporter & freelance writer, with marketing, advertising & public relations experience. Press releases, promotional copy, commercials, personal & business letter writing are services offered. Eight years library reference experience to assist with research.

Wendy Polhemus-Annibell
PO Box 464, Peconic, NY 11958
Tel: 631-276-0684
E-mail: wannibell@gmail.com
Founded: 1987
Freelance copy-editing, line editing, developmental editing, proofreading, project management. Specialize in college textbooks (particularly English/grammar/writing/rhetoric texts) & fiction/nonfiction trade books, with an emphasis on editorial excellence.

The Professional Writer
175 W 12 St, Suite 6D, New York, NY 10011
Tel: 212-414-0188; 917-658-1946 (cell)
E-mail: paul@theprofessionalwriter.com
Web Site: www.theprofessionalwriter.com
Key Personnel
Owner: Paul Wisenthal *E-mail:* paulwisenthal@gmail.com
Founded: 1989
Book networking to the industry, book development—includes creative writing/editing, writer's block, project preparation. Copywriting for brochures, media kits, newsletters, business & investment proposals, writers coach & grants. Script writing, script doctor for TV/film/radio. Speech writing. Youth market specialists. Story development workshops.
Membership(s): The Authors Guild; National Writers Union

Pronk Media Inc
PO Box 340, Beaverton, ON L0K 1A0, Canada
Tel: 416-441-3760
E-mail: info@pronk.com
Web Site: www.pronk.com
Key Personnel
Pres: Gord Pronk *Tel:* 416-441-3760 ext 203 *E-mail:* gord@pronk.com
Founded: 1981 (as Pronk & Associates Inc)
Print design & production, including product conceptualization & prototypes, design & art direction, photo research & licensing, infographics, charts, graphs, technical art, page design, layout & production.

Proofed to Perfection Editing Services
6519 Sherrill Baggett Rd, Godwin, NC 28344
Tel: 919-908-1912
E-mail: inquiries@proofedtoperfection.com
Web Site: www.proofedtoperfection.com
Key Personnel
Sr Ed & Proj Coord: Pamela Cangioli *E-mail:* pamg@proofedtoperfection.com
Founded: 2006
Full service editing company specializing in comprehensive, professional book editing. We offer proofreading, copy-editing, developmental editing, book critiques & book proposals at competitive rates. We hire editors with experience in the industry & guarantee personal, quality service. All new clients are offered a free sample edit & book critique.
Membership(s): American Christian Fiction Writers; Editorial Freelancers Association; Evangelical Christian Publishers Association

Generosa Gina Protano Publishing, see GGP Publishing Inc

Publishing Resources Inc
425 Carr 693, PMB 160, Dorado, PR 00646
Tel: 787-647-9342
E-mail: pri@chevako.net
Key Personnel
Pres: Ronald J Chevako
EVP & Ed: Anne W Chevako
Prodn: Jay A Chevako
Founded: 1982
Complete services including ms development, research, writing, translation (Spanish-English; English-Spanish), indexing, content editing & line editing by US trained professionals & full production services.

Publishing Synthesis Ltd
39 Crosby St, New York, NY 10013
Tel: 212-219-0135 *Fax:* 212-219-0136
E-mail: mainmail@pubsyn.com
Web Site: www.pubsyn.com
Key Personnel
Pres: Otto H Barz *E-mail:* obarz@pubsyn.com
VP & Spec Projs Coord: Ellen Small *E-mail:* esmall@pubsyn.com
Founded: 1975
Editing, design, typesetting & prepress production of college text & highly technical trade books.
Membership(s): Book Industry Guild of New York; Independent Book Publishers Association

Jerry Ralya
7909 Vt Rte 14, Craftsbury Common, VT 05827
Tel: 802-586-7514
E-mail: jerryralya@gmail.com
Editing, development & indexing of trade, technical, medical & reference books. Specialties include computers, behavioral sciences & the humanities. Twenty-five years of experience.
Membership(s): Editorial Freelancers Association

The Reading Component
3900 Parkview Lane, 3B, Irvine, CA 92612-2003
Mailing Address: 2155 N Bellflower Blvd, PMB 169, Long Beach, CA 90815
Tel: 949-387-6330
Key Personnel
Owner: Helen M Winton *E-mail:* hmwinton@outlook.com
Founded: 1994

Research Research
240 E 27 St, Suite 20-K, New York, NY 10016-9238
Tel: 212-779-9540 *Fax:* 212-779-9540
E-mail: ehtac@msn.com
Key Personnel
Pres: Cathe Giffuni
Founded: 1987

Judith Riven Literary Agent LLC
250 W 16 St, Suite 4F, New York, NY 10011
Tel: 212-255-1009 *Fax:* 212-255-8547
E-mail: rivenlitqueries@gmail.com
Web Site: rivenlit.com
Key Personnel
Owner & Pres: Judith Riven
Founded: 1993
Editorial consultation, developmental & structural editing, line editing, ms analysis.

The Roberts Group
12803 Eastview Curve, Apple Valley, MN 55124
Tel: 952-322-4005
E-mail: info@editorialservice.com
Web Site: www.editorialservice.com
Key Personnel
Owner: Sherry Roberts; Tony Roberts
Founded: 1990
Book design, production, editorial services & web development. A one-stop creative resource for quality interior book design, typesetting, editing, proofreading, indexing, Kindle & e-pub formatting. Serving established presses & self-publishers. Competitive prices. We pay attention to details & will work to meet your deadlines. See web site for more info & samples.
Membership(s): Independent Book Publishers Association; Midwest Independent Publishing Association; Professional Editors Network

Peter Rooney
332 Bleecker St, PMB X-6, New York, NY 10014-2980
Tel: 917-376-1792 *Fax:* 212-226-8047
E-mail: magnetix@ix.netcom.com
Web Site: www.magneticreports.com

Indexer, programmer/consultant for indexes, databases, directories, catalogues raisonnes. Large & small projects.
Membership(s): American Society for Indexing

Dick Rowson
4701 Connecticut Ave NW, Suite 503, Washington, DC 20008
Tel: 202-244-8104
E-mail: rcrowson2@aol.com
Helps authors find good publishers & appraise mss.

Sachem Publishing Associates Inc
402 W Lyon Farm Dr, Greenwich, CT 06831
Tel: 203-813-3077
E-mail: sachempub@optonline.net
Key Personnel
Pres & Ed: Stephen P Elliott
Founded: 1974
Complete trade & mail order book preparation & packaging; editorial services, from concept to finished books. Specialize in consumer & educational reference books, including encyclopedias & dictionaries.

Salmon Bay Indexing
PO Box 2362, Vashon, WA 98070
Tel: 206-612-3993
Web Site: salmonbayindexing.com
Key Personnel
Indexer: Beth Nauman-Montana *E-mail:* beth@salmonbayindexing.com
Founded: 2002
Professional indexer. Provides indexes for books & ebooks in all subject areas. Every project is delivered on time & according to client guidelines.

Barbara S Salz LLC Photo Research
127 Prospect Place, South Orange, NJ 07079
Tel: 646-734-5949
E-mail: bsalz.photo@gmail.com
Image research & permissions for books, magazines, exhibitions & advertising.
Membership(s): ASPP

Paul Samuelson
117 Oak Dr, San Rafael, CA 94901
Tel: 415-459-5352; 415-517-0700 (cell) *Fax:* 415-459-5352
E-mail: paul@storywrangler.com
Web Site: www.storywrangler.com
Also consults on narrative material & screenplays.

C J Scheiner Books
PO Box 96, Brooklyn, NY 11226-0096
Tel: 718-469-1089
Key Personnel
Owner: C J Scheiner
Literature searches, special assignment writing, fact checking, research, photo research illustrations provided, bibliographies & source lists, text & introduction writing. Specialize in erotica, curiosa & sexology.

Schoolhouse Indexing
10-B Parade Ground Rd, Etna, NH 03750
Tel: 603-643-1617
Web Site: schoolhouseindexing.com
Key Personnel
Owner & Indexer: Christine Hoskin *E-mail:* christine@schoolhousefarm.net
Schoolhouse Indexing is a freelance indexing business. Professional indexing services offered include the fields of law & legal issues, education (in both English & French), business & economics, children's elementary education/nonfiction, travel, hospitality & tourism, social sciences & culture, health & psychology, history & biography, environmental sciences, geology, engineering, construction & architecture. Indexing queries regarding general indexing information, rates & availability are welcome.
Membership(s): American Society for Indexing

Schoolhouse Network
PO Box 1518, Northampton, MA 01061
Tel: 480-427-4836
E-mail: schoolhousenetwork@gmail.com
Key Personnel
Pres: Marilyn Greco
Dir, Curriculum: Mary K Messick
Founded: 1998
Provides a comprehensive range of editorial service & products to educational publishers, development groups, schools & other educational institutions for PreK, K-12 & college in both print & electronic media in the areas of reading/language arts, ESL, literature, social studies, health & science. Develop student & teacher editions, leveled readers, children's books, graphic novels, fiction & nonfiction, trade book publications which include memoir, poetry, travel with accompanying art & photography.
Membership(s): Editorial Freelancers Association; International Literacy Association; National Association for the Education of Young Children; TESOL International Association

Schroeder Indexing Services
23 Camilla Pink Ct, Bluffton, SC 29909
Tel: 843-705-9779
E-mail: sanindex@schroederindexing.com
Web Site: www.schroederindexing.com
Key Personnel
Owner & CEO: Sandi Schroeder
Produce custom indexes using dedicated indexing software. Company web site includes current information on clients & titles indexed, information on planning an index, downloadable Project Information Sheet & request for an estimate.
Membership(s): American Society for Indexing

Franklin L Schulaner
PO Box 507, Kealakekua, HI 96750-0507
Tel: 808-322-3785
E-mail: fschulaner@hawaii.rr.com

Sherri Schultz/Words with Grace
1631 16 Ave, Seattle, WA 98122
Tel: 206-323-3348
E-mail: WordsWithGraceEditorial@gmail.com
Founded: 1992
Experienced copy-editor & proofreader of fiction & nonfiction books, web content, & more. Works with clients around the country. Special expertise in politics, environment, travel, literary nonfiction & art.

Scribendi Inc
405 Riverview Dr, Chatham, ON N7M 0N3, Canada
Tel: 519-351-1626 (cust serv) *Fax:* 519-354-0192
E-mail: customerservice@scribendi.com
Web Site: www.scribendi.com
Key Personnel
Pres: Chandra Clarke *Tel:* 519-351-1626 ext 706 *E-mail:* chandra.clarke@scribendi.com
VP: Terence Johnson, MA *Tel:* 519-351-1626 ext 707 *E-mail:* terry@scribendi.com
Founded: 1997
On demand proofreading & editing services available 24/7. Web site offers instant quotes on all standard services; call or e-mail for special project quotes or long-term arrangements.

SDP Publishing Solutions LLC
36 Captain's Way, East Bridgewater, MA 02333
Tel: 617-775-0656
Web Site: www.sdppublishingsolutions.com
Key Personnel
Publr & Agent: Lisa Akoury-Ross *E-mail:* lross@sdppublishing.com
Developmental Ed, Copyeditor, Proofreader & Ghostwriter: Kathleen A Tracy
Developmental Ed & Copyeditor: Kathy Bruins; Ashley Fedor; Lisa Schleifer
Prof Proofreader/Proofchecker: Karen Grennan
Artist: Randy Jennings
Cover & Interior Designer: Howard Johnson
Admin Asst: Kim Sexton
Founded: 2009
Specialize in editorial services for all genres including fiction, nonfiction, memoirs, business books, children's books & more. Our business is designed to review mss & determine the best editorial approach for each author. From ghostwriting, developmental editing, copy-editing & proofreading, we help our authors become better writers! We also write effective marketing kits, query letters, analysis of the competitive marketplace, along with the marketing & media landscape for those who wish to pitch to literary agents & traditional publishers. We offer optimal publishing solutions for authors worldwide from literary agency representation, to worldwide marketing, including international rights & independent publishing.

Richard Selman
14 Washington Place, New York, NY 10003
Tel: 212-473-1874 *Fax:* 212-473-1875
Multimedia & electronic desktop publishing, advertising & promotional copywriting; fact checking, line editing, permissions, research, photo research, proofreading, ms analysis, bibliographies, copy-editing, interviewing, rewriting, special assignment writing, transcript editing, indexing, audio/video text.

Alexa Selph
4300 McClatchey Circle, Atlanta, GA 30342
Tel: 404-256-3717
E-mail: lexa101@aol.com

Barry Sheinkopf
c/o The Writing Ctr, 601 Palisade Ave, Englewood Cliffs, NJ 07632
Tel: 201-567-4017 *Fax:* 201-567-7202
E-mail: bsheinkopf@optonline.net
Founded: 1977
Trade, scholarly & professional publications, book design & self-publishing.
Membership(s): The Authors Guild; Mystery Writers of America

Monika Shoffman-Graves
70 Transylvania Ave, Key Largo, FL 33037
Tel: 305-451-1462 *Fax:* 305-451-1462
E-mail: keysmobill@earthlink.net; mograv@gmail.com
Indexing, ms analysis, proofreading & research.

Roger W Smith
59-67 58 Rd, Maspeth, NY 11378-3211
Tel: 718-416-1334
E-mail: brandeis106@gmail.com
Founded: 1982
Membership(s): Editorial Freelancers Association

Stackler Editorial Agency
200 Woodland Ave, Summit, NJ 07901

Tel: 510-912-9187
E-mail: ed.stackler@gmail.com
Web Site: www.fictioneditor.com
Key Personnel
Owner: Ed Stackler
Founded: 1996
Editorial services for novelists of crime, thriller & suspense fiction.

Nancy Steele
2210 Pine St, Philadelphia, PA 19103-6516
Tel: 215-732-5175
E-mail: Nancy.Steele.Edits@gmail.com
Founded: 1999
Versatile, intuitive editor with more than 20 years of experience in editing nonfiction. Expertise in American art & antiques, anthologies, biographies & memoirs, business & technology, psychology, reference & illustrated books. Special interest in the arts of Japan.
Membership(s): National Association of Science Writers

Sterling Media Productions LLC, see Robert L Cohen

Jeri L Stolk
8 Rush Vine Ct, Owings Mills, MD 21117
Tel: 410-864-8109
E-mail: jeristolk@gmail.com
Edit journals & books, especially academic.

Vivian Sudhalter
1202 Loma Dr, No 117, Ojai, CA 93023
Tel: 805-640-9737
E-mail: vivians09@att.net
Freelance editor specializing in fiction & nonfiction books on women's studies, holistic health, memoirs & other genres. I improve finished mss by copy-editing for good grammar, flow, punctuation, usage & consistency, while maintaining the author's authentic voice. I also help shape books from inception by working with authors to create the structure that will best serve their vision. Having been in the book publishing industry for more than 4 decades, I provide insights into the publication process, whether conventional or POD. Contact by e-mail preferred.

Fraser Sutherland
39 Helena Ave, Toronto, ON M6G 2H3, Canada
Tel: 416-652-5735
E-mail: rodfrasers@gmail.com
Founded: 1970
General editorial services. Specialize in dictionaries & reference books (lexicography), ms analysis & rewriting.
Membership(s): Dictionary Society of North America; Editors' Association of Canada/Association canadienne des reviseurs; PEN Canada

Thodestool Fiction Editing
40 McDougall Rd, Waterloo, ON N2L 2W5, Canada
Web Site: www.thodestool.com
Key Personnel
Owner: Vanessa Ricci-Thode
E-mail: vanessariccithode@gmail.com
Founded: 2010
Focus on providing editing services for fiction of varying lengths, with a specialty in speculative fiction (science fiction, fantasy, horror) & a focus on structural/developmental editing & ms evaluations.
Membership(s): Canadian Author's Association; Editors' Association of Canada/Association canadienne des reviseurs

Susan Thornton
6090 Liberty Ave, Vermilion, OH 44089
Tel: 440-967-1757
E-mail: allenthornton@earthlink.net
Key Personnel
Freelance Copy Ed: Allen Thornton; Susan Thornton
Medical, technical, mathematics, university press, college text, reference, trade nonfiction & journals on hard copy & on disk.

Twin Oaks Indexing
Division of Twin Oaks Community
138 Twin Oaks Rd, Suite W, Louisa, VA 23093
Tel: 540-894-5126
Web Site: www.twinoakscommunity.org
Key Personnel
Mgr: Rachel Nishan
Founded: 1981

Visuals Unlimited Inc
27 Meadow Dr, Hollis, NH 03049
Tel: 603-465-3340 *Fax:* 603-465-3360
E-mail: staff@visualsunlimited.com
Web Site: www.visualsunlimited.com
Key Personnel
VP & Busn Devt Mgr, Ad: Robert Folz
E-mail: rfolz@visualsunlimited.com
Dir: Shelly Folz *E-mail:* sfolz@visualsunlimited.com
Photo agent, photo research & stock agency.

Wambtac Communications
1512 E Santa Clara Ave, Santa Ana, CA 92705
Tel: 714-954-0580 *Toll Free Tel:* 800-641-3936
E-mail: wambtac@wambtac.com
Web Site: www.wambtac.com; claudiasuzanne.com (prof servs)
Key Personnel
Owner, Founder & Creative Partner: Claudia Suzanne *E-mail:* claudiasuzanne@gmail.com
Founded: 1995
Book writing & publishing.
Membership(s): Independent Book Publishers Association

WC Publishing, see Wambtac Communications

Toby Wertheim
240 E 76 St, New York, NY 10021
Tel: 212-472-8587
E-mail: tobywertheim@yahoo.com
Research/editor.

Rosemary Wetherold
4507 Cliffstone Cove, Austin, TX 78735
Tel: 512-892-1606
E-mail: roses@ix.netcom.com
Founded: 1985
Copy-editing, substantitive editing, desktop publishing. Varied subjects, including biological sciences & natural history.

WFS, see Write for Success Editing Services

Helen Rippier Wheeler
1909 Cedar St, Suite 212, Berkeley, CA 94709-2037
Tel: 510-549-2970
E-mail: pen136@dslextreme.com
Consulting & professional development training. Sole proprietor of Womanhood Media.
Membership(s): Writers Guild of America

Barbara Mlotek Whelehan
7064 SE Cricket Ct, Stuart, FL 34997
Tel: 954-554-0765 (cell); 772-463-0818 (home)
E-mail: barbarawhelehan@bellsouth.net
More than 20 years of publishing experience. All subjects; specialize in personal finance, investments, mutual funds, business & consumer topics. Also copy-edit fiction.

Martin L White
10511 Preston St, Westchester, IL 60154-5311
Tel: 708-492-1253 *Fax:* 708-492-1253
E-mail: mlw@mlwindexing.com
Web Site: www.mlwindexing.com
Founded: 1990
Book & journal indexing.
Membership(s): American Society for Indexing; Society for Scholarly Publishing; Society for Technical Communication

White Oak Editions, see Carol Cartaino

Eleanor B Widdoes
417 W 120 St, New York, NY 10027
Tel: 917-886-6401 (cell)
E-mail: widdoese@aa.org
Indexing, proofreading, research, bibliographies & newsletters.

Windhaven®
466 Rte 10, Orford, NH 03777
Tel: 603-512-9251 (cell)
Web Site: www.windhavenpress.com
Key Personnel
Dir & Ed: Nancy C Hanger *E-mail:* nhanger@windhavenpress.com
Ed & Consultant: Andrew V Phillips
E-mail: andrew@windhavenpress.com
Founded: 1985
Consulting & developmental editing, line editing, copy-editing, proofreading.
Membership(s): Editorial Freelancers Association; National Writers Union

Wolf Pirate Project Inc
337 Lost Lake Dr, Divide, CO 80814
Tel: 305-333-3186
E-mail: contact@wolfpiratebooks.com; workshop@wolfpiratebooks.com
Web Site: www.wolf-pirate.com
Key Personnel
Founder & Pres: Catherine Rudy
E-mail: catherinerudy@wolfpiratebooks.com
VP: Bryan Rudy
Volunteer Ed: May Bestall *E-mail:* maybestall@wolfpiratebooks.com
Founded: 2010
Nonprofit company established to mentor, educate, develop & promote new writers & artists & focus on the general public to instill a desire to read for leisure. Fiction/nonfiction literary; content & development blue line edit. Service offered only through acceptance into the workshop. Otherwise online class is open to all at no cost & editors are available to answer questions.

WordCo Indexing Services Inc
49 Church St, Norwich, CT 06360
Tel: 860-886-2532 *Toll Free Tel:* 877-WORDCO-3 (967-3263) *Fax:* 860-886-1155
E-mail: office@wordco.com
Web Site: www.wordco.com
Key Personnel
Owner & CEO: Stephen Ingle *E-mail:* sringle@wordco.com
Proj Coord: Amy Moriarty *E-mail:* amoriarty@wordco.com
Founded: 1988
Since 1988, WordCo has completed thousands of thorough & accurate indexes in hundreds of subject areas for many major publishers. WordCo's in-house team of professionally trained indexers has the experience & capability to complete your indexing projects professionally & on time. Rush service & ebook indexing available.
Membership(s): American Society for Indexing; Bookbuilders of Boston

WordForce Communications
35 Ormskirk Ave, Suite 805, Toronto, ON M6S 1A8, Canada
Tel: 416-534-9881
E-mail: info@wordforce.ca
Web Site: www.wordforce.ca
Key Personnel
CEO & Pres: Maja Rehou *E-mail:* mrehou@wordforce.ca
Founded: 2003
Provide editing, writing & consulting services to help engineers, scientists, lawyers, web developers & business professionals improve the effectiveness & profitability of their technical documents & marketing materials.

Words into Print
208 Java St, 6th fl, Brooklyn, NY 11222
E-mail: query@wordsintoprint.org
Web Site: wordsintoprint.org
Key Personnel
Ed: Jeff Alexander *E-mail:* jeffale73@gmail.com; Becky Cabaza *E-mail:* rtcbooks@gmail.com; Anne Cole Norman *E-mail:* acole157@gmail.com; Jane Fleming Fransson *E-mail:* jffeditor@gmail.com; Ruth Greenstein *E-mail:* rg@greenlinepublishing.com; Emily Loose *E-mail:* emilylooselit@gmail.com; Julie Miesionczek *E-mail:* julie@writewithjulie.com
Founded: 1998
An alliance of top New York publishing professionals who offer a broad range of editorial services to authors, publishers, literary agents, book packagers & content providers.

Words with Grace, see Sherri Schultz/Words with Grace

WordWitlox
1261 Ashland Dr, Cobourg, ON K9A 5S5, Canada
Tel: 647-505-9673
Web Site: www.wordwitlox.com
Key Personnel
Copy Ed: Cathy Witlox *E-mail:* cathy@wordwitlox.com
Founded: 2004
Editing professionally since 1998, including 6-1/2 years full-time in-house experience copy-editing for a large North American fiction publisher. WordWitlox is outside Toronto.
Membership(s): American Copy Editors Society; Editors' Association of Canada/Association canadienne des reviseurs

Working With Words
5320 SW Mayfair Ct, Beaverton, OR 97005
Tel: 503-644-4317
E-mail: editor@zzz.com
Key Personnel
Owner: Sue Mann
Founded: 1985
Freelance editorial services. General trade, nonfiction. Subjects include children's, cookbooks, creativity, historical, inspirational, memoirs, self-help, spiritual, training. Substantive editing. Online & hard copy.
Membership(s): Northwest Independent Editors Guild

Wright Information Indexing Services
PO Box 658, Sandia Park, NM 87047
Tel: 505-281-2600
Web Site: www.wrightinformation.com
Key Personnel
Owner & Pres: Jan C Wright *E-mail:* jancw@wrightinformation.com
Founded: 1991
Book, ebook & online indexing services, specializing in single-source publications; 2009 winner of H W Wilson Award for Excellence in Indexing.
Membership(s): American Society for Indexing

Write for Success Editing Services
PO Box 292153, Los Angeles, CA 90029-8653
Tel: 323-356-8833
E-mail: writeforsuccess@yahoo.com
Web Site: www.write-for-success.com
Key Personnel
Owner/Ed: Christine Van Zandt *E-mail:* christine@write-for-success.com
Ed: Michael Biehl *E-mail:* michael@write-for-success.com; Patricia Fox *E-mail:* patricia@write-for-success.com
Founded: 2009
Full service professional editing, from creation to publication. Insider knowledge of the current marketplace. Editors with Masters' degrees in English who are published writers, detail-oriented & committed to providing quality editing services. Based in Hollywood; editors in San Francisco & Minneapolis. Self-publishing, freelance & agented authors welcome. Assistance at any stage. All genres & categories, adult & children's considered. Responsive communication with competitive pricing. See web site for more information.
Membership(s): Bay Area Editors' Forum; Editorial Freelancers Association; The Greater Los Angeles Writers Society; Independent Book Publishers Association; Society of Children's Book Writers & Illustrators

The Write Way
3048 Horizon Lane, Suite 1102, Naples, FL 34109
Tel: 239-273-9145
E-mail: darekane@gmail.com
Key Personnel
Pres: Roberta Kane
Also handle advertising & marketing.

Writers Anonymous Inc
1302 E Coronado Rd, Phoenix, AZ 85006
Tel: 602-256-2830 *Fax:* 602-256-2830
Web Site: writersanonymousinc.blogspot.com
Key Personnel
Pres: Jordan Richman *E-mail:* jordanp.richman@gmail.com
Edit Dir: Vita Richman
Substantive editing, scholarly, education, humanities, social science, environment, philosophy, music, art, literature, health, general science, medical, legal.
Membership(s): Editorial Freelancers Association

The Writer's Lifeline Inc
400 S Burnside Ave, Suite 11B, Los Angeles, CA 90036
Tel: 323-932-1685 *Fax:* 323-932-1220
Web Site: www.thewriterslifeline.com
Key Personnel
CEO: Kenneth Atchity, PhD *E-mail:* kja@thewriterslifeline.com
EVP: Lisa Cerasoli
Founded: 1996
A full service editorial company, providing nonfiction book writers, novelists, business, professional, technical & screenwriters with assistance in storytelling, mentoring, perfecting their style & craft, style-structure-concept-line editing, ghostwriting, publishing consulting, development, translation, advertising & promotion, printing & self-publishing, distribution & research.
Sister companies: Atchity Entertainment International Inc; Atchity Productions; Story Merchant; Story Merchant Books.
Membership(s): American Comparative Literature Association; The Authors Guild; National Academy of Television Arts & Sciences; PEN American Center; Women in Film; Writers Guild of America

Writer's Relief, Inc
207 Hackensack St, Wood-Ridge, NJ 07075
Tel: 201-641-3003 *Toll Free Tel:* 866-405-3003 *Fax:* 201-641-1253
E-mail: info@wrelief.com
Web Site: www.WritersRelief.com
Key Personnel
Pres: Ronnie L Smith *E-mail:* ronnie@wrelief.com
Founded: 1994
Don't have time to submit your writing? We can help. Submission leads & cover/query letter guidelines. Join the 50,000+ writers who subscribe to *Submit Write Now*, our free e-publication.

Wyman Indexing
1311 Delaware Ave SW, No S332, Washington, DC 20024
Tel: 443-336-5497
Web Site: www.wymanindexing.com
Key Personnel
Owner & Chief Indexer: Pilar Wyman *E-mail:* pilarw@wymanindexing.com
Founded: 1990
Freelance indexing & consulting (specialties include medicine, technology & current events). Also provide Spanish-to-English translation services.
Membership(s): American Medical Writers Association; American Society for Indexing

Zebra Communications
230 Deerchase Dr, Woodstock, GA 30188-4438
Tel: 770-924-0528
Web Site: www.zebraeditor.com
Key Personnel
Owner: Bobbie Christmas *E-mail:* bobbie@zebraeditor.com
Founded: 1992
Editorial services that specialize in fiction & nonfiction books.
Membership(s): Atlanta Writers Club; Florida Writers Association; Georgia Writers Association; International Guild of Professional Business Consultants; Society for the Preservation of English Language Literature; South Carolina Writers Workshop; Southeastern Writers Association; The Writers' Network

Robert Zolnerzak
101 Clark St, Unit 20-K, Brooklyn, NY 11201
Tel: 718-522-0591
E-mail: rzolnerzak@gmail.com
Computer-assisted indexing for medical, scientific & computer science textbooks & journals since 1973.
Membership(s): American Society for Indexing; Editorial Freelancers Association

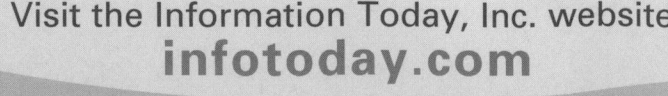

Literary Agents

The agents listed here are among the most active in the field. Prior to obtaining a listing in *LMP*, potential entrants are required to submit verifiable references from publishers with whom they have placed titles. Letters in parentheses following the agency name indicate fields of activity:

(L)–Literary Agent (D)–Dramatic Agent (L-D)–Literary & Dramatic Agent

Those individuals who are members of the Association of Authors' Representatives are identified by the presence of (AAR) after their name.

Authors seeking literary representation are advised that some agents request a nominal reading fee that may be applied to the agent's commission upon representation. Other agencies may charge substantially higher fees which may not be applicable to a future commission and which are not refundable. The recommended course is to first send a query letter with an outline, sample chapter, and a self-addressed stamped envelope (SASE). Should an agent express interest in handling the manuscript, full details of fees and commissions should be obtained in writing before the complete manuscript is sent. Should an agency require significant advance payment from an author, the author is cautioned to make a careful investigation to determine the agency's standing in the industry before entering an agreement. The author should always retain a copy of the manuscript in his or her possession.

AAA Books Unlimited (L)
3060 Blackthorn Rd, Riverwoods, IL 60015
Tel: 847-444-1220 *Fax:* 847-607-8335
Web Site: www.aaabooksunlimited.com
Key Personnel
Principal: Nancy Rosenfeld *E-mail:* nancy@aaabooksunlimited.com
Founded: 1993
Full service literary agency to provide clients with first class service "over & above" what normally is handled by a literary agency. We offer content-copy-line editing services. No unsol mss, query first.
Titles recently placed: *A Couple's Guide to Sexual Addiction: A Step-by-Step Plan to Rebuild Trust and Restore Intimacy*, Paldrom Catharine Collins, George N Collins, MA; *A Woman's Framework for a Successful Career and Life*, James Hamerstone, Lindsay Musser Hough; *An Introduction to Mozart: "The Music, The Man, The Myths"*, Roye E Wates, PhD; *Attached at the Heart: 8 Proven Parenting Principles for Raising Connected and Compassionate Children*, Barbara Nicholson, Lysa Parker; *Baseball and American Culture*, John Rossi; *Belief To Die For*, James Alcock, PhD; *Breaking the Cycle: Free Yourself from Sex Addiction, Porn Obsession, and Shame*, George N Collins, MA, Andrew Adleman, MA; *Celebrity Obsession*, Michael S Levy, PhD; *Children of Separation and Loss: Picking Up the Pieces After Hitler*, Dr Gertrude Pollitt; *Circus Lab*, Jackie Leigh Davis; *Do You Mind if I Order the Cheeseburger?*, Sherry F Colb, PhD; *Freedom of Assembly and Petition: The First Amendment: Its Constitutional History and the Contemporary Debate (Bill of Rights series)*, Margaret M Russell; *Gotta Get Out of My Own Way*, Abraham Twerski; *I'm Not a Mind Reader: Using Three-Dimensional Communication to Make Your Relationship Better*, Marty Babits, LCSW, BCD; *Jacob's Courage: A Holocaust Love Story (reprint)*, Charles S Weinblatt; *Let's Talk About Death*, Steve Gordon, Irene Kacandes; *Many Seconds Into the Future*, John J Clayton; *Mindfulness for Borderline Personality Disorder*, Blaise Aguirre, MD, Dr Gillian Galen; *Minyan: Ten Overlapping Stories*, John J Clayton; *Mitzvah Man (Modern Jewish Literature and Culture)*, John J Clayton; *Mood: The Key to Understanding Ourselves and Others*, Patrick M Burke, PhD; *Negroes with Guns: The Black Tradition of Arms*, Nicholas Johnson; *Overcoming Destructive Anger*, Bernard Golden, PhD; *Parenting Your Child with Autism: Practical Solutions, Strategies, and Advice for Helping Your Family*, M Anjali Sastry, PhD, Blaise Aguirre, MD; *Quantum Leaps in the Wrong Direction*, Arthur W Wiggins, Charles M Wynn, PhD, Sidney Harris; *Reimagining Men's Cancers*, Mark Boguski, MD, Michelle Berman, MD, David Tabatsky; *Reimagining Women's Cancers*, Mark Boguski, MD, Michelle Berman, MD, David Tabatsky; *Rx for Hope: A Cancer Care Model to Optimize the Immune System Integrating Low Dose Chemotherapy and Complementary Medicine*, Nick Chen, MD, PhD, David Tabatsky; *Searches and Seizures: The Fourth Amendment: Its Constitutional History and Contemporary Debate (Bill of Rights series)*, Cynthia Lee; *Survival to Growth*, Sam A Hout, PhD; *Teshuvah and Recovery*, Abraham J Twerski, MD; *The Gift of Mortality*, Steve Gordon, Irene Kacandes; *The Human Side of Science*, Arthur W Wiggins, Charles M Wynn, PhD, Sidney Harris; *The Nature of Nature: 200,000 Years of History of Science*, Demetris Nicolaides, PhD; *The Nun's Rabbi: The Rabbi-Psychiatrist and the Sisters of St Francis*, Abraham J Twerski, MD; *The Politics of Joint University-Community Housing Development in Cambridge, Boston and Beyond*, Richard Sobel; *The Problem Was Me: How to End Negative Self-Talk and Take Your Life to a New Level*, Thomas Gagliano, Abraham J Twerski, MD; *The Truth About Cardiovascular Health*, Jay N Cohn, MD; *The Unlikeliest of Places: How Nachman Libeskind Survived the Nazis, the Gulags and Soviet Communism*, Annette Libeskind Berkovits; *Transparency in Government: What it Means and How You Can Make it Happen*, Donald Gordon; *Under a Dark Eye: A Family Story*, Sharon Dunn; *Wrestling with Angels: New & Collected Stories*, John J Clayton

The Aaland Agency (L)
PO Box 849, Inyokern, CA 93527-0849
Tel: 760-384-3910
Web Site: www.the-aaland-agency.com
Key Personnel
Dir & Fiction/Nonfiction: Jo Ann Krueger
Foreign Rep, CN & Europe: Richard Allan
Romance/Adventure: Mitzi Rhone
Founded: 1991
Adult fiction & nonfiction. One-inch margins & space & a half. Any format, e-mail file attachment, hard copy or CD is acceptable (e-mail file preferred). Crime drama, romance/adventure, children's stories, biographies & textbooks gladly accepted. No fees for ms review/evaluation. Complete ms or first 3 chapters. No unsol mss, query first.
Titles recently placed: *Cypher*, T R Dawson; *The Hydra Brief*, William Davison; *USS Kitty Hawk: The Last Warrior*, Marty S Bourdon

Dominick Abel Literary Agency Inc (L)
146 W 82 St, Suite 1-A, New York, NY 10024
Tel: 212-877-0710 *Fax:* 212-595-3133
E-mail: agency@dalainc.com
Web Site: www.dalainc.com
Key Personnel
Pres: Dominick Abel (AAR) *E-mail:* dominick@dalainc.com
Founded: 1975
Adult fiction & nonfiction. Handle film & TV rights. No unsol mss, query first by e-mail; no reading fee. Representatives in Hollywood & all major foreign countries.
Foreign Rep(s): Akcali Agency (Turkey); Big Apple Agency Inc (China, Indonesia, Malaysia, Taiwan, Vietnam); The Buckman Agency (Israel, Scandinavia); The English Agency (Japan); David Grossman Literary Agency (UK Commonwealth); The Italian Literary Agency (Italy); Korean Copyright Center (Korea); Lex Copyright Agency (Hungary); La Nouvelle Agence (France); Prava i prevodi (Eastern Europe, Greece, Russia, Ukraine); Lennart Sane Agency (Brazil, Central America, Netherlands, Portugal, South America, Spain); Thomas Schlueck GmbH (Germany); Tuttle-Mori Agency Inc (Thailand)
Membership(s): The Authors Guild; Authors Registry; Copyright Clearance Center; Mystery Writers of America

Abrams Artists Agency (L-D)
275 Seventh Ave, 26th fl, New York, NY 10001
Tel: 646-486-4600 *Fax:* 646-486-0100
E-mail: literary@abramsartny.com
Web Site: www.abramsartists.com
Key Personnel
Dir, Book Div: Steve Ross
Dir, Foreign Rts: David Doerrer
Literary Agent: Sarah L Douglas; Katie Gamelli; Max Grossman; Ron Gwiazda; Ben Izzo; Charles Kopelman; Amy Wagner
Founded: 1977
Plays, screenplays, film & TV rights. No unsol mss, query first. Submit synopsis. No reading fee.
Branch Office(s)
9200 Sunset Blvd, 11th fl, Los Angeles, CA 90069, Contact: Norma Robbins *Tel:* 310-859-0625 *E-mail:* contactla@abramsartists.com

Acacia House Publishing Services Ltd (L)
51 Chestnut Ave, Brantford, ON N3T 4C3, Canada
Tel: 519-752-0978 *Fax:* 519-752-0978
Key Personnel
Mng Dir: Bill Hanna *E-mail:* bhanna.acacia@rogers.com
Founded: 1985
Adult fiction; no science fiction, occult, horror; most nonfiction. Handle film & TV rights for authors. Handle foreign rights for 4 client publishers. Territories handled directly by Acacia

include Territories handled directly by Acacia include Australia, Bulgaria, Canada (English-speaking), Czechia, Estonia, Latvia, Lithuania, Slovak Republic, UK, USA. No unsol mss, query first; submit outline & first 50 pages. Only typed, double-spaced mss may be submitted with return postage. No reading fee. Fee charged for photocopying & postage or courier.
Foreign Rights: Akcali (Turkey); Argosy Agency (fiction only) (Italy); Agencia Literaria Carmen Balcells SA (Portugal, Spain); Big Apple Agency Inc (China, Hong Kong, Malaysia, Taiwan, Vietnam); Paul & Peter Fritz AG (Austria, Germany); Graal Literary Agency (Poland); Harris-Elon Agency (Ilana Kurshan) (Israel); International Literatuur Bureau BV (Netherlands); International Press Agency (South Africa); Japan UNI Agency Inc (Japan); Katai & Bolza (Bosnia and Herzegovina, Croatia, Hungary, Montenegro, Serbia, Slovenia); Simona Kessler (Romania); Duran Kim Agency (Korea); Alexander Korzhenevski (Russia); Maxima Creative Agency (Santo Manarung) (Indonesia); Daniela Micura Literary Services (nonfiction only) (Italy); Montreal-Contact (worldwide French-speaking Territories); A Nicolaissen Agency (Scandinavia); Read n' Right (Greece); Silk Road Agency (Thailand)

Aevitas Creative Management (L-D)
Formerly Kuhn Projects; Zachary Shuster Harmsworth Agency
19 W 21 St, Suite 501, New York, NY 10010
Tel: 212-765-6900
Web Site: aevitascreative.com
Key Personnel
Mng Partner: Esmond Harmsworth; David Kuhn (AAR); Todd Shuster
Sr Partner: Jennifer Gates; Laura Nolan (AAR); Janet Silver; Lane Zachary
Partner: Rick Richter; Jane von Mehren
Agent: Elias Altman; Sarah Bowlin; Michelle Brower; Nick Chiles; Ariel Foxman; Lori Galvin; David Granger; Albert Lee; Sarah Levitt; William LoTurco; Jen Marshall; Bridget Wagner Matzie; Lauren Sharp; Becky Sweren; Nan Thornton; Susan Zanger
Subs Rts Dir: Chelsey Heller
Literary, commercial & genre fiction & nonfiction, mystery, thriller, non-category romance, science fiction, biography, current affairs, business, psychology, memoir, science & history, young adult, children's. No unsol mss, e-mail only query letters, full plot; synopsis or detailed chapters summary plus 3 sample chapters up to 50 pages. No mss returned without SASE. No reading fee.
Branch Office(s)
3532 Hayden Ave, Culver Sity, CA 90232
Tel: 310-270-9096
601 "I" St NW, Washington, DC 20001 *Tel:* 202-836-8923
545 Boylston St, 11th fl, Boston, MA 02116
Tel: 617-262-2400
Foreign Rights: Agencia Riff (Laura & Joao Paulo Riff) (Brazil); ELST Literary Agency (Kalina Stefanova) (Bulgaria); Ersilia Literary Agency (Greece); Grayhawk Agency (China, Indonesia, Taiwan, Thailand, Vietnam); Agence Hoffman (Andrea Wildgruber) (Germany); Agence Michelle Lapautre (France); Prava i prevodi (Eastern Europe); Sebes & Bisseling Literary Agency (Netherlands)

Agency Chicago (L-D)
332 S Michigan Ave, Suite 1032, No A600, Chicago, IL 60604
E-mail: ernsant@aol.com
Key Personnel
Owner: Ernest Santucci
Assoc: Shelly Chou
Founded: 1988
Professional & cross-over writers. No unsol mss, query letter first; handle film, stage & TV rights; no reading fee. True crime & police procedural, historical fiction, humor, politics, Southwest & general wellness.

Agency for the Performing Arts Inc, see APA Talent & Literary Agency

Agent's Ink (L)
PO Box 4956, Fresno, CA 93744-4956
Tel: 559-438-1883 *Fax:* 559-438-8289
Web Site: agents-ink.com
Key Personnel
Owner/Dir: Sydney H Harriet, PhD
E-mail: sydharriet@yahoo.com
Founded: 1988
Health-related nonfiction, business, cookbooks, sports, fiction, mystery, psychology, how-to & literary for medical & mental health professionals; no unsol mss, query first; send outline or sample chapters with a SASE; no phone or e-mail queries, query by mail only. No reading fee or monthly fee for representation. Marketing fee of $300 covers mailing, production, postage, phone calls, etc. Commission of 15%.
Titles recently placed: *I Got Caught Cheating! How Can I Save My Marriage?*, Dr Othniel Seiden, Jane L Bilett PhD; *I'm "Heeling" One Day at a Time*, Carole Brody Fleet
Branch Office(s)
9400 E Iliff Ave, Suite 361, Denver, CO 80231
Tel: 720-369-1851

The Ahearn Agency Inc (L)
2021 Pine St, New Orleans, LA 70118
Tel: 504-861-8395 *Fax:* 504-866-6434
Web Site: www.ahearnagency.com
Key Personnel
Pres: Pamela G Ahearn *E-mail:* pahearn@aol.com
Founded: 1992
General fiction, adult; no poetry, plays, young adult, articles or autobiographies. Specialize in women's fiction & suspense. No unsol mss, query first with SASE. No reading fee. Do not send attachments with e-mail queries unless requested.
Titles recently placed: *A Mortal Likeness*, Laura Joh Rowland; *A Season to Lie*, Emily Littlejohn; *Just a Breath Away*, Carlene Thompson; *Married at Midnight*, Gerri Russell; *Mister Tender's Girl*, Carter Wilson; *The Pleasures of Passion*, Sabrina Jeffries; *Washington Power Play*, Allan Topol
Foreign Rights: Lorella Belli Agency (Lorella Belli) (UK); Agence Eliane Benisti (Eliane Benisti) (France); Prava i prevodi (Eastern Europe); Thomas Schluek GmbH (Germany)
Membership(s): International Thriller Writers Inc; Mystery Writers of America; Romance Writers of America

Aitken Alexander Associates LLC (L)
30 Vandam St, Suite 5A, New York, NY 10013
Web Site: www.aitkenalexander.co.uk
Founded: 2009
Independent NY branch of the established London-based Aitken Alexander Associates Ltd specializing in literary fiction & narrative nonfiction. No unsol mss, query first. No fees charged.
Titles recently placed: *Asunder*, Chloe Aridjis; *Goliath*, Max Blumenthal; *I Want to Show You More*, Jamie Quatro; *Kill Chain*, Andrew Cockburn; *Leaving the Atocha Station*, Ben Lerner; *Longbourn*, Jo Baker; *Love Me Back*, Merritt Tierce; *Panorama City*, Antoine Wilson; *Revenge*, Yoko Ogawa; *Salvation for a Saint*, Keigo Higashino; *Suddenly a Knock on the Door*, Etgar Keret; *The Butterfly Cabinet*, Bernie McGill; *The Free*, Willy Vlautin; *The Lady's Handbook for Her Mysterious Illness*, Sarah Ramsey; *The People in the Trees*, Hanya Yanagihara; *The Story of My Purity*, Francesco Pacifico; *The Unknowns*, Gabriel Roth; *The Virgins*, Pamela Erens; *Under the Sun: The Letters of Bruce Chatwin*, Bruce Chatwin; *Unremarried Widow*, Artis Henderson; *Where'd You Go Bernadette*, Maria Semple; *Winter King*, Tom Penn

Betsy Amster Literary Enterprises (L)
6312 SW Capitol Hwy, No 503, Portland, OR 97239
Tel: 503-496-4007
E-mail: rights@amsterlit.com (rts inquiries); b.amster.assistant@gmail.com (adult book queries); b.amster.kidsbooks@gmail.com (children & young adult book queries)
Web Site: www.amsterlit.com
Key Personnel
Pres: Betsy Amster (AAR)
Agent, Children's & Young Adult: Mary Cummings
Founded: 1992
Literary fiction, upscale commercial fiction (specifically mysteries/thrillers & women's fiction) & adult nonfiction. Subject areas of interest: narrative nonfiction (especially by journalists), travelogues, psychology, self-help, social issues, popular culture, cultural criticism, history, art & design, health, parenting, careers, lifestyle, cookbooks, gardening, gift books; no unsol mss. Handle film & TV rights for client book properties via co-agents; no reading fee. For fiction or memoirs, embed the first 3 pages in the body of your e-mail; for nonfiction, embed your proposal. Do not represent screenplays, poetry, western, fantasy, science fiction, action adventure, techno thrillers, spy capers, apocalyptic scenarios or political or religious arguments. We do not open attachments unless we have requested them; no phone, fax or snail mail queries.
Foreign Rights: Big Apple Agency Inc (China); Donatella d'Ormesson (France); The English Agency (Japan) Ltd (Japan); Japan Uni (Japan); Asli Karasuil Literary Agency (Asli Ermis) (Turkey); Korea Copyright Center (KCC) (MiSook Hong) (Korea); Mohrbooks (Germany); Prava i prevodi (Bulgaria, Croatia, Czech Republic, Estonia, Greece, Hungary, Latvia, Lithuania, Macedonia, Poland, Romania, Russia, Serbia, Slovakia, Slovenia); Lennart Sane Agency AB (Philip Sane) (Brazil, Holland, Portugal, Scandinavia, Spain, Spanish Latin America); Vicki Satlow (Italy); Abner Stein Agency (UK)
Membership(s): PEN Center USA

Anderson Literary Management LLC (L)
244 Fifth Ave, 11th fl, New York, NY 10001
Tel: 212-645-6045 *Fax:* 212-741-1936
E-mail: info@andersonliterary.com
Web Site: www.andersonliterary.com
Key Personnel
Pres: Kathleen Anderson (AAR)
E-mail: kathleen@andersonliterary.com
Represents quality fiction & nonfiction (adult, young adult & middle grade) for print, electronic, film & television.
Membership(s): PEN American Center

Andy Ross Literary Agency (L)
767 Santa Ray Ave, Oakland, CA 94610
Tel: 510-238-8965
E-mail: andyrossagency@hotmail.com
Web Site: www.andyrossagency.com
Key Personnel
Agent: Andy Ross (AAR)
Founded: 2008
Specialize in narrative nonfiction, journalism, history, current events, literary, commercial & young adult fiction.

Queries: send by e-mail only including "query" in the title header. Letters should be kept to a half page. State the project category in the first sentence & provide a very brief description. Proposals: submit by e-mail only. See web site for additional query & proposal guidelines. No fees.
Titles recently placed: *Beauty of the Broken*, Tawni Waters; *Not Your Mothers Slow Cooker Book*, Beth Hensperger; *Snowball in a Blizzard*, Steven Hatch; *The Arab of Warsaw*, Randall Platt; *The Tango War*, Mary Jo McConahay; *To the Secretary: Leaked Embassy Cables and America's Foreign Policy Disconnect*, Mary Thompson-Jones; *You Don't Own Me: The Life and Times of Lesley Gore*, Trevor Tolliver; *Zionism: The Birth and Transformation of an Ideal*, Milton Viorst

APA Talent & Literary Agency (L-D)
405 S Beverly Dr, Beverly Hills, CA 90212
Tel: 310-888-4200 *Fax:* 310-888-4242
Web Site: www.apa-agency.com
Key Personnel
Owner: Lee Dinstman
SVP (Nashville): Steve Lassiter
Agent: David Saunders
Agent (Nashville): Frank Wing
Founded: 1962
Handle film & TV rights. No unsol mss; query first. Submit outline & sample chapters & SASE. No reading fee; 10% commission. Represent writers & producers.
Branch Office(s)
135 W 50 St, 17th fl, New York, NY 10020 *Tel:* 212-205-4320 *Fax:* 212-245-5062
150 Fourth Ave N, Suite 2300, Nashville, TN 37219 *Tel:* 615-297-0100 *Fax:* 615-297-5434

Arcadia (L)
31 Lake Place N, Danbury, CT 06810
Tel: 203-797-0993
E-mail: arcadialit@sbcglobal.net
Key Personnel
Pres: Victoria Gould Pryor (AAR)
Founded: 1986
Not seeking new clients.
Foreign Rights: Japan UNI Agency Inc (Japan); Barbara Levy Agency (UK); The Marsh Agency (translation)
Membership(s): The Authors Guild

Arthur Pine Associates Inc, see InkWell Management

Aurous Inc (L)
Formerly Pimlico/Aurous Inc
PO Box 20490, New York, NY 10017
Tel: 212-628-9729 *Fax:* 212-535-7861
Key Personnel
Pres: Kay McCauley *E-mail:* kaymcc25@aol.com
Busn Mgr: Christopher Shepard
Agent: Kirby McCauley
Founded: 1974
Adult fiction & nonfiction. Motion picture & TV rights from book properties only. No unsol mss. Projects by referral only. No reading fee. Agents in all principal foreign countries.
Foreign Rights: ZENO Agency

The Axelrod Agency (L)
55 Main St, Chatham, NY 12037
Mailing Address: PO Box 357, Chatham, NY 12037
Tel: 518-392-2100
Key Personnel
Pres: Steven Axelrod (AAR) *E-mail:* steve@axelrodagency.com
Foreign Rts Dir: Lori Antonson *E-mail:* lori@axelrodagency.com
Founded: 1983
Fiction & nonfiction, film & TV rights. No unsol mss, query first. No reading fee. E-mail queries receive attention first.

Elizabeth H Backman (L)
86 Johnnycake Hollow Rd, Pine Plains, NY 12567
Mailing Address: PO Box 762, Pine Plains, NY 12567-0762
Tel: 518-398-9344 *Fax:* 518-398-6368
E-mail: bethcountry@fairpoint.net
Key Personnel
Owner: Elizabeth H Backman
Ad Serv: Donn King Potter
Founded: 1981
Literary & commercial fiction; nonfiction; current events, politics, business, biography, the arts, cooking, diet, health, sports, gardening, history, science, self-help & psychology; audio & video cassettes. Author representatives, consulting editors, advertising & promotion copywriters. No unsol mss, query first with SASE; submit introduction, cover letter, chapter by chapter outline or table of contents, 3 sample chapters & authors bio or complete ms with cover letter & author's bio. Reading fees: $100 for proposals, $500 for complete mss; 15% agency fee plus expenses (phone, mail, photocopying, etc). Handle film & TV rights.
Foreign Rights: Lennart Sane (Netherlands, Portugal, Scandinavia, Spain); Thomas Schlueck GmbH (Germany); Tuttle-Mori Agency Inc (Japan)

Malaga Baldi Literary Agency (L-D)
233 W 99, Suite 19C, New York, NY 10025
Tel: 212-222-3213
E-mail: baldibooks@gmail.com
Web Site: www.baldibooks.com
Key Personnel
Pres: Malaga Baldi
Founded: 1986
Cultural history, nonfiction & literary-edgy fiction. No unsol mss, query first with SASE; no reading fee.
Titles recently placed: *All the Rage*, Martin Moran; *Anslinger Nation*, Alexandra Chasin; *How Dogs Work*, Ramond Coppinger, Mark Epstein; *In the Mood: An Almanack*, Mary Cappello; *Jazz Moon*, Joe Okonkwo; *Something in the Blood*, David J Skal; *Sticking It Out*, Patti Niemi; *The Butterfly Hours*, Patty Dann; *The Castle Cross the Magnet Carter*, Kia Corthron; *The Contender*, William J Mann; *The Detective's Garden*, Janyce Stefan-Cole; *The War of the Roosevelts*, William J Mann; *What Is a Dog?*, Raymond Coppinger, Lorna Coppinger
Foreign Rep(s): Abner Stein (UK)
Foreign Rights: Eliane Benisti (France); Marsh Agency (Europe); Owls Agency Inc (Japan)

A Richard Barber/Peter Berinstein & Associates (L)
60 E Eighth St, Suite 21-N, New York, NY 10003
Tel: 212-737-7266 *Fax:* 860-927-3942
E-mail: barberrich@aol.com
Key Personnel
Pres: A Richard Barber
Sr Assoc: Peter Berinstein
Handle software, film & TV rights. Specialize in fiction & nonfiction. No fees. No unsol mss, query first by mail (include SASE). No fax or e-mail submissions.
Branch Office(s)
80 N Main St, Kent, CT 06757-0887 *Tel:* 860-927-4911

Baror International Inc (L)
PO Box 868, Armonk, NY 10504-0868
Tel: 914-273-9199 *Fax:* 914-273-5058
Web Site: www.barorint.com
Key Personnel
Pres: Danny Baror *E-mail:* danny@barorint.com
Literary Agent: Heather Baror-Shapiro *E-mail:* heather@barorint.com
Specialize in international & domestic representation of literary works in both fiction & nonfiction ranging in genre including commercial fiction, literary titles, science fiction, fantasy, young adult & more. No unsol mss.

Loretta Barrett Books Inc (L)
220 E 23 St, 11th fl, New York, NY 10010
Tel: 212-242-3420
E-mail: lbbquery@gmail.com
Web Site: www.lorettabarrettbooks.com
Key Personnel
Pres: Nick Mullendore
Founded: 1990
Fiction & nonfiction. Handle film, TV & multimedia rights. No poetry or children's literature, no screenplays; no unsol mss, query first by e-mail only. Submit outlines, sample chapters & bio (nonfiction); synopsis & bio (fiction). Representatives on the West Coast & in all major foreign countries. No reading fee.
Foreign Rights: Akcali Copyright Agency (Turkey); Eliane Benisti Agency (France); Capel & Land Ltd (Australia, UK); The Italian Literary Agency srl (Italy); Andrew Nurnberg Associates International Ltd (Mainland China, Taiwan); Prava i prevodi (Baltic States, Czech Republic, Eastern Europe, Slovakia, Ukraine); Lennart Sane Agency AB (Scandinavia); Thomas Schlueck GmbH (Germany); Synopsis Literary Agency (Russia); Tuttle-Mori Agency Inc (Japan); Eric Yang Agency (Korea)

Meredith Bernstein Literary Agency Inc (L)
2095 Broadway, Suite 505, New York, NY 10023
Tel: 212-799-1007 *Fax:* 212-799-1145
E-mail: MGoodBern@aol.com
Web Site: www.meredithbernsteinliteraryagency.com
Key Personnel
Agent: Meredith Bernstein (AAR)
Adult fiction (commercial & literary) & nonfiction; memoirs, current events, biography, health & fitness, women's issues, mysteries & special projects; crafts & creative endeavors. No poetry or screenplays. No unsol mss, query first online (no attachments) or by mail (include SASE). For fiction submit a 1 page query letter; nonfiction send 1 page query letter, table of contents & information on why you are an expert in this field. Handle film & TV rights only for books represented. Representatives in foreign countries & on the West Coast. No reading fee.
Membership(s): The Authors Guild; Sisters in Crime; Women's Media Group

The Bethel Agency (L-D)
PO Box 21043, Park West Sta, New York, NY 10025
Tel: 212-864-4510
E-mail: bethelagcy@aol.com
Key Personnel
Pres: Lewis R Chambers
Founded: 1967
Books & articles, fiction & nonfiction; stage plays, motion picture & TV properties; foreign & domestic. Represents photojournalists. Handles film & TV rights. No unsol mss, query first. No initial reading fee. Submissions of proposals are accepted via "snail mail" ONLY.

Vicky Bijur Literary Agency (L-D)
27 W 20 St, Suite 1003, New York, NY 10011
Tel: 212-580-4108
E-mail: queries@vickybijuragency.com
Web Site: www.vickybijuragency.com

Key Personnel
Agent: Vicky Bijur (AAR)
Founded: 1988
Adult fiction & nonfiction. No children's books, poetry, science fiction, fantasy or horror. No unsol mss. Fiction: query first; paste first chapter in body of e-mail. Nonfiction: query first. No phone queries. If query by hard copy, include SASE for response. If material to be returned, include SASE large enough to contain pages. No reading fee. Agents in all principal foreign countries. Handle film & TV rights.
Titles recently placed: *BraveTart: Iconic American Desserts*, Stella Parks; *Devil's Breath*, G M Malliet; *Food Lab*, Kenji Lopez-Alt; *Long Upon the Land*, Margaret Maron; *Still Alice*, Lisa Genova; *Unpunished*, Lisa Black; *Widows of Malabar Hill*, Sujata Massey; *Wilde Lake*, Laura Lippman; *Willnot*, James Sallis
Foreign Rights: AnatoliaLit Agency (Turkey); The English Agency Japan (Japan); The Grayhawk Agency (China, Taiwan); The Deborah Harris Agency (Israel); The Italian Literary Agency SRL (Italy); Agence Michelle Lapautre (France); Lennart Sane Agency (Argentina, Brazil, Denmark, Finland, Holland, Norway, Portugal, Spain, Sweden); Liepman Agency AG (Germany); Maxima Creative Agency (Indonesia); Prava i prevodi (Bulgaria, Czech Republic, Estonia, Greece, Hungary, Poland, Russia, Serbia, Slovakia); Abner Stein Agency (England); Tuttle-Mori Agency Inc (Thailand); Eric Yang Agency (Korea)

David Black Agency (L-D)
Subsidiary of Black Inc
335 Adams St, 27th fl, Suite 2707, Brooklyn, NY 11201
Tel: 718-852-5500 *Fax:* 718-852-5539
Web Site: www.davidblackagency.com
Key Personnel
Pres: David Black (AAR) *E-mail:* dblack@dblackagency.com
Agent: Rica Allannic *E-mail:* rallannic@dblackagency.com; Jennifer Herrera *E-mail:* jherrera@dblackagency.com; Heather Jackson *E-mail:* hjackson@dblackagency.com; Gary Morris *Tel:* 718-852-5518 *E-mail:* gmorris@dblackagency.com; Susan Raihofer *Tel:* 718-852-5542 *E-mail:* sraihofer@dblackagency.com; Sarah Smith *E-mail:* ssmith@dblackagency.com; Joy Tutela *Tel:* 718-852-5533 *E-mail:* jtutela@dblackagency.com
Founded: 1990
Literary & commercial fiction & nonfiction, especially sports, politics, business, health, fitness, romance, parenting, psychology & social issues. No poetry. No unsol mss, query first with SASE. No reading fee. Agents in all principal foreign countries. Handle film & TV rights. No mysteries or thrillers.
Foreign Rights: Bardon-Chinese Media Agency (Ming-Ming Liu) (China); Eliane Benisti Agent Litteraire (Eliane Benisti & Noemi Rollet) (France); The Deborah Harris Agency (Efrat Lev) (Israel); International Editors' Co (Spanish) (Latin America, Spain); The Italian Literary Agency srl (Italy); Katai & Bolza Literary Agents (Peter Bolza) (Hungary); Maxima Creative Agency (Santo Manurung) (Indonesia); Mohrbooks (Sabine Ibach, Bettina Kaufmann, Sebastian Ritscher & Cristina Uytiepo) (Germany); Prava i prevodi (Milena Lukic, Ana Milenkovic & Jelena Todosijevic) (Bulgaria, Croatia, Czech Republic, Estonia, Greece, Latvia, Lithuania, Poland, Russia, Serbia, Slovenia); Agencia Riff (JP, Laura & Lucia Riff) (Brazil, Portugal); Sebes & Bisseling Literary Agency (Paul Sebes) (Netherlands); Abner Stein Agency (Caspian Dennis) (Australia, UK); Tuttle-Mori Agency Inc (Japan, Thailand); Eric Yang Agency (Sue Yang) (Korea)

Bleecker Street Associates Inc (L)
215 Thompson St, Suite 519, New York, NY 10012
Tel: 212-677-4492 *Fax:* 212-388-0001
Key Personnel
Pres: Agnes Birnbaum (AAR)
Founded: 1984
No unsol mss, query first about book project & author with SASE (cannot respond nor return materials without SASE). Do not query via e-mail, phone or fax. Handle film & TV rights for clients' own work only. Fiction & nonfiction; no poetry, plays or screenplays; handle magazine articles by book clients only. No reading fee.
Titles recently placed: *Handy Forensics Answer Book*, Patricia Barnes-Svarney, Thomas V Svarney; *Harlen Ellison Biography*, Nat Segaloff; *Haunted: Malevolent Ghosts, Threatening Phantoms*, Brad Steiger, Sherry Steiger; *Jimmy & Fay*, Michael W Mayo; *St Catherine of Sienna*, Shelley Emling; *Under a Flaming Sky*, Daniel James Brown
Foreign Rights: Bookman (Netherlands, Scandinavia); The English Agency (Japan) Ltd (Japan); International Editors' Co (Portugal, South America, Spain); The Italian Literary Agency srl (Italy); Thomas Schlueck GmbH (Germany); Abner Stein Agency (British Commonwealth)

Reid Boates Literary Agency (L-D)
69 Cooks Crossroad, Pittstown, NJ 08867-0328
Mailing Address: PO Box 328, Pittstown, NJ 08867-0328
Tel: 908-797-8087
E-mail: reid.boates@gmail.com
Key Personnel
Sole Prop: Reid Boates
Founded: 1985
Narrative +/or how-to nonfiction, health, spirituality, wellness, business & sports. Handle film & TV rights. No fiction. Most new clients by referral. No reading fee. Agents in all major foreign markets. No unsol mss, submit written query with SASE.
Titles recently placed: *Most Intimate*, Roshi Pat Enkyo O'Hara; *Soul Fury and Kindness*, Coleman Barks; *The Shambhala Principle*, Sakyong Mipham Rinpoche
Foreign Rep(s): Agence Litteraire Eliane Benisti (France); Raquel de la Concha (Spain); Michael Meller (Eastern Europe, Germany, UK); Owls Agency Inc (Japan)

Alison Bond Literary Agency (L)
171 W 79 St, No 143, New York, NY 10024
Key Personnel
Principal: Alison M Bond *E-mail:* alison@bondlit.com
Founded: 1982
Literary fiction, memoir/biography, women's issues, foodie & narrative nonfiction. Accepting few new writers at present. Agents in most European countries. No science fiction, fantasy or genre categories.
Membership(s): Women's Media Group

Bond Literary Agency (L)
4340 E Kentucky Ave, Suite 471, Denver, CO 80246
Tel: 303-781-9305
E-mail: queries@bondliteraryagency.com
Web Site: bondliteraryagency.com
Key Personnel
Owner & Agent: Sandra Bond *E-mail:* sandra@bondliteraryagency.com
Assoc Agent: Becky LeJeune *E-mail:* becky@bondliteraryagency.com
Founded: 1998
Specialize in adult commercial & literary fiction including mysteries & women's fiction (no romance, children's picture books, health or poetry); juvenile fiction; narrative nonfiction, science, biography & business. Becky is looking for adult & young adult horror, fantasy, science fiction. Talented, previously unpublished writers will be considered. Nonfiction authors must have excellent credentials & a strong platform. No unsol mss, query by e-mail first to queries@bondliteraryagency.com (letter in the body of the e-mail, no attachments). Preferably no snail mail. No phone calls please. Ms submissions by request only. Sell foreign & film/TV rights through subagents. No fees charged.
Titles recently placed: *Amelia Earhart: Beyond the Grave*, W C Jameson; *Among the Lesser Gods*, Margo Catts; *Betrayal at IGA: A Hiro Hattori Mystery*, Susan Spann; *Border Bandits, Border Raids*, W C Jameson; *Imagine*, Federico Pena; *Life in a Fish Bowl*, Len Vlahos; *Lost Canyon of Gold*, W C Jameson; *Sticks & Stones / Steel & Glass*, Anthony Poon; *Texas Train Robberies*, W C Jameson; *The Ninja's Daughter: A Hiro Hattori Mystery*, Susan Spann; *The Past Is Never*, Tiffany Quay Tyson; *We Have Your Daughter*, Paula Woodward

BookEnds Literary Agency (L)
136 Long Hill Rd, Gillette, NJ 07933
Web Site: www.bookendsliterary.com
Key Personnel
Owner & Literary Agent: Jessica H Faust (AAR) *E-mail:* jfsubmissions@bookendsliterary.com
Agent: Jessica Alvarez (AAR) *E-mail:* jasubmissions@bookendsliterary.com; Rachel Brooks; Kim Lionetti (AAR) *E-mail:* klsubmissions@bookendsliterary.com
Agent & Subs Rts Dir: Moe Ferrara *E-mail:* mfsubmissions@bookendsliterary.com
Dir, Digital Content: Bill Harris
Literary Agent: Tracy Marchini *E-mail:* tmsubmissions@bookendsliterary.com
Asst Literary Agent: Beth Campbell *E-mail:* bcsubmissions@bookendsliterary.com
Founded: 1999
Founded by former editors from Berkley Publishing, BookEnds is a literary agency that represents fiction & nonfiction for adults, children & teens. No unsol mss, query first. Review web site for submission instructions & get tips on queries & proposals. No fees.
Titles recently placed: *A Family Under the Christmas Tree*, Terri Reed; *A Witch Before Dying*, Heather Blake; *At His Mercy*, Shelly Bell; *Bedding Lord Ned*, Sally Mackenzie; *Bought by the Boss*, Stacey Kennedy; *Buried in a Bog*, Sheila Connolly; *Chapter & Hearse: A Booktown Mystery*, Lorna Barrett; *Due or Die: A Library Mystery*, Jenn McKinlay; *Every Trick in the Book*, Lucy Arlington; *Final Catcall*, Sofie Kelly; *Fire Kissed*, Erin Kellison; *Get Off Easy*, Sara Brookes; *Immortally Yours*, Angie Fox; *Miles Away From You*, A B Rutledge; *Never Entice an Earl*, Lily Dalton; *One Hot Murder*, Lorraine Bartlett; *Reborn (Shadow Falls: After Dark)*, C C Hunter; *Shark-Nate-O*, Tara Luebbe, Becky Cattie; *Silent Rescue*, Melinda Di Lorenzo; *Sleep Over*, Heidi Bleackley; *Some Enchanted Éclair*, Bailey Cates; *The Coffin Maker*, Breeann Allison; *The Retail Doctor's Guide to Growing Your Business*, Bob Phibbs; *Unicorns are Jerks*, Theo Nicole Lorenz; *Webb Glass Shop Mysteries 4-6*, Cheryl Hollon; *Wed to a Spy*, Sharon Cullen; *Worth Waiting For*, Wendy Qualls
Foreign Rep(s): The Book Project Agency (nonexclusive) (Greece); Book/lab (Poland); The English Agency (Japan); Deborah Harris Agency (Israel); Imprima Korea Agency (Korea); Kayi Literary Agency (Turkey); Agence Michelle Lapautre (France); Andrew Nurnberg (China, Czech Republic, Slovakia, Slovenia, Taiwan); Tuttle-Mori Agency Inc (Japan); Julio F Yanez Agencia Literaria SL (Portugal, Spain)

Membership(s): Mystery Writers of America; Romance Writers of America; Science Fiction & Fantasy Writers of America; Society of Children's Book Writers & Illustrators

Books & Such (L)
52 Mission Circle, Suite 122, PMB 170, Santa Rosa, CA 95409-5370
Tel: 707-538-4184
Web Site: booksandsuch.com
Key Personnel
Founder & Pres: Janet Kobobel Grant *E-mail:* janet@booksandsuch.com
VP: Wendy Lawton *E-mail:* wendy@booksandsuch.com
Literary Agent, Adult Fiction, Nonfiction & Teen: Rachelle Gardner *E-mail:* rachelle@booksandsuch.com
Literary Agent, Teens, Twenties & Thirties: Rachel Kent *E-mail:* rachel@booksandsuch.com
Literary Agent: Cynthia Ruchti
Founded: 1996
Handles fiction & nonfiction. Submission by e-mail (no attachments). No phone calls. No unsol mss, query first. No fees.
Titles recently placed: *Coastal Guardians*, Dani Pettrey; *Deliver Us from Bullying*, Paul Coughlin; *Engraved on the Heart*, Tara Johnson; *Fresh Eyes*, Doug Newton; *Holy Hustle*, Cyrstal Stine; *Manual to Middle School*, Jonathan Catherman; *Tarpon Springs*, Judith Miller; *The Shaker*, Ann Gabhart; *The Turquoise Table*, Kristin Schell; *World's Okayest Mom*, Natalie Gwyn
Branch Office(s)
PO Box 1227, Hilmar, CA 95324-1227 *Tel:* 209-634-1913
Membership(s): Advanced Writers & Speakers Association; American Christian Fiction Writers; CBA; Romance Writers of America

BookStop Literary Agency LLC (L)
67 Meadow View Rd, Orinda, CA 94563
E-mail: info@bookstopliterary.com
Web Site: www.bookstopliterary.com
Key Personnel
CEO & Pres: Kendra Marcus
Foreign Rts Coord: Ilse Craane
Literary Agent: Ms Minju Chang
Founded: 1984
Juvenile & young adult mss only (fiction & nonfiction) & illustration for children's books, especially humorous voices, diverse perspectives, intense young adult fiction, clever middle grade & topics & mss for the Hispanic, African-American, Asian-American juvenile markets in the US. Accept unsol mss. Submit full mss for picture books; first 10 pages for fiction; sample chapters & outline for nonfiction. See web site for additional submission information. No reading fee.
Titles recently placed: *Echo*, Pam Munoz Ryan; *Hensel and Gretel: Ninja Chicks*, Corey Schwartz, Rebecca Gomez; *My New Mom & Me*, Renata Galindo; *This is Not a Werewolf Story*, Sandra Evans

Georges Borchardt Inc (L-D)
136 E 57 St, New York, NY 10022
Tel: 212-753-5785
E-mail: georges@gbagency.com
Web Site: www.gbagency.com
Key Personnel
Founder & Pres: Georges Borchardt (AAR)
Founder: Anne Borchardt (AAR)
VP & Foreign Rts Dir: Valerie Borchardt (AAR) *E-mail:* valerie@gbagency.com
Agent: Samantha Shea *E-mail:* samantha@gbagency.com
Foreign Rts Asst: Emma Gougeon *E-mail:* emma@gbagency.com
Asst: Will Vunderink *E-mail:* will@gbagency.com
Founded: 1967
Fiction & nonfiction. No unsol mss; handle film & TV rights & software. No fees charged.
Titles recently placed: *Because Uncertainty Arises*, Rachel Arndt; *Benneville*, Jane Delury; *Bhagavad Gita*, Amit Majmudar; *Brodsky Among Us*, Ellendea Teasley; *Commotion of the Birds*, John Ashbery; *Dreamcatcher's Daughter*, Jennifer Haupt; *Houdini*, Adam Begley; *House of Stone*, Novuyo Tshuma; *Into the Middle Country*, Michael Meyer; *Literature & Memory*, Saul Friedlander; *Marriage of Dreamers*, Adam Hochschild; *Nutshell*, Ian McEwan; *Remember to Forget Me*, Kerry Bakken; *Shadow Child*, Reiko Rizzuto; *Sisters*, Lily Tuck; *Sour Heart*, Jenny Zhang; *The Cowboy King*, Jerome Charyn; *The Relive Box*, TC Boyle
Foreign Rights: Agencia Literaria Carmen Balcells (Maribel Luque) (Spain); Bardon-Chinese Media Agency (Ming-Ming Lui) (Chinese); Tassy Barham Associates (Brazil); English Agency (Junzo Sawa) (Japanese); Graal Literary Agency (Marcin Biegaj) (Polish); Deborah Harris Agency (Efrat Lev) (Israel); The Italian Literary Agency srl; Japan UNI Agency (Miko Yamanouchi) (Japanese); JLM Agency (Nelly & John Moukakou) (Greek); Asli Karasuil Literary Agency (Turkish); Katai & Bolza (Peter Bolza) (Hungarian); Korean Copyright Center (Misook Hong) (Korean); Agence Michelle Lapautre (Catherine Lapautre) (France); Mohrbooks (Sabine Ibach & Sebastian Ritscher) (German); Andrew Nurnberg Associates (Kristine Shatrovska) (Baltic States); Andrew Nurnburg Associates (Anna Droumeva) (Bulgarian & Romanian); Andrew Nurnberg Associates (Ludmilla Sushkova) (Russian); Kristin Olson Literary Agency sro (Kristin Olson) (Czech); RDC Agencia Literaria (Raquel de la Concha) (Portuguese) (Portugal); Marianne Schoenbach Literary Agency BV (Marianne Schoenbach) (Dutch); Sheil Land Associates (Vivien Green) (British); Sane Toregard Agency (Ulf Toregard) (Scandinavia); Tuttle-Mori Agency Inc (Asako Kawachi) (Japanese)

Bradford Literary Agency (L)
5694 Mission Center Rd, Suite 347, San Diego, CA 92108
Tel: 619-521-1201
E-mail: queries@bradfordlit.com
Web Site: www.bradfordlit.com
Key Personnel
Agent: Laura Bradford (AAR) *E-mail:* laura@bradfordlit.com; Natalie Lakosil *E-mail:* natalie@bradfordlit.com; Sarah LaPolla (AAR) *E-mail:* sarah@bradfordlit.com; Monica Odom *E-mail:* monica@bradfordlit.com; Kari Sutherland *E-mail:* kari@bradfordlit.com
Founded: 2001
A boutique agency offering a full range of representation services to authors, both published & pre-published. We are an editorial-focused agency & prefer to work closely with our authors in helping to build strong, sustainable careers. We believe the best author-agent relationships extend beyond making sales; in order to best serve our client's needs, we must also be a partner, advisor, a careful listener, a troubleshooter & an advocate.
We are currently acquiring fiction: romance (historical, romantic suspense, paranormal, category, contemporary, erotic), urban fantasy, women's fiction, mystery, thrillers, young adult, middle grade & picture books (Natalie & Kari only). Also nonfiction: business, relationships, biography/memoir, self-help, parenting, narrative humor, pop culture, illustrated/graphic design, food & cooking, history & social issues. We are not currently acquiring: poetry, screenplays, short stories, westerns, horror, New Age, religion, crafts.
We accept unsol mss. Queries are accepted by e-mail only to queries@bradfordlit.com. We do not open e-mail attachments, unless specifically requested by an agent. Your entire submission must appear in the body of the e-mail & not as an attachment. The subject line should begin as follows: QUERY: (The title of the ms or any short message you would like us to see should follow). For fiction: Please e-mail a query letter along with the first chapter of your ms & a synopsis. Please be sure to include the genre & word count in your cover letter. For nonfiction: submit a book proposal including an outline, sample material, author bio & competitive survey. No fees.
Titles recently placed: *A Daring Arrangement*, Joanna Shupe; *Aftermath*, Clara Kensie; *Alex, Approximately*, Jenn Bennett; *All the Lies We Tell*, Megan Hart; *Allegedly*, Tiffany Jackson; *Alterations*, Stephanie Scott; *Diablo Lake: Protected*, Lauren Dane; *Forbidden Promises*, Katee Robert; *Girl in a Bad Place*, Kaitlin Ward; *Gray Wolf Island*, Tracey Neithercott; *Guarding Mr. Fine*, HelenKay Dimon; *His Alone*, Alexa Riley; *His Ex's Well-Kept Secret*, Joss Wood; *In A Daze Work*, Siobhan Gallagher; *In His Hands*, Adriana Anders; *Midtown Masters*, Cara McKenna; *Nico*, Sarah Castille; *Piper Morgan Plans a Party*, Stephanie Faris; *Ring In The Year with Murder*, Auralee Wallace; *Seducing Mr. Sykes*, Maggie Robinson; *Siege of Shadows*, Sarah Raughley; *The Fixer*, HelenKay Dimon; *The Silver Gate*, Kristin Bailey; *The Star Thief*, Lindsey Becker; *Too Hot to Handle*, Tessa Bailey; *Trains Don't Sleep*, Andria Rosenbaum; *Vanguard*, Ann Aguirre; *Whiskey Sharp: Unravelled*, Lauren Dane; *Witchtown*, Cory Putman Oakes; *Wives of War*, Soraya Lane
Foreign Rights: Taryn Fagerness Agency (Taryn Fagerness) (Albania, Argentina, Australia, Brazil, Bulgaria, Canada, China, Croatia, Czech Republic, Denmark, Estonia, Finland, France, Germany, Greece, Hungary, Iceland, India, Indonesia, Israel, Italy, Japan, Korea, Latvia, Lithuania, Mexico, Netherlands, Norway, Poland, Portugal, Romania, Russia, Serbia, Slovakia, Spain, Sweden, Taiwan, Thailand, Turkey, Ukraine, UK, Vietnam)
Membership(s): ALA; Romance Writers of America; Society of Children's Book Writers & Illustrators

Brandt & Hochman Literary Agents Inc (L)
1501 Broadway, Suite 2310, New York, NY 10036
Tel: 212-840-5760 *Fax:* 212-840-5776
Web Site: brandthochman.com
Key Personnel
Pres: Gail Hochman (AAR) *E-mail:* ghochman@bromasite.com
Agent & Foreign Rts: Marianne Merola (AAR) *E-mail:* mmerola@bromasite.com
Agent: Bill Contardi (AAR) *E-mail:* bill@billcontardi.com; Emily Forland (AAR) *E-mail:* eforland@bromasite.com; Emma Patterson (AAR) *E-mail:* epatterson@bromasite.com; Jody Kahn (AAR) *E-mail:* jkahn@bromasite.com; Henry Thayer (AAR) *E-mail:* hthayer@bromasite.com
Audio Rts & Perms Contact: Lina Granada *E-mail:* reply@bromasite.com
Represents fiction & nonfiction, including literary, mystery/thriller, memoir, narrative nonfiction, journalism, history, current affairs, health, science, pop culture, lifestyle, art history & children's books. No screenplays or textbooks. No unsol mss, query first by e-mail or regular mail. Responses to e-mailed queries not guaranteed. Queries limited to 2 pages. Include SASE if sending by regular mail. See web site for specific submission preferences for each

agent. No reading fee. Fee charged for making copies & book/galley purchases. Co-agents in most foreign countries.

The Joan Brandt Agency (L)
788 Wesley Dr NW, Atlanta, GA 30305
Tel: 404-351-8877 *Fax:* 404-351-0068
Key Personnel
Pres: Joan Brandt
Founded: 1990
Fiction & nonfiction (no science fiction, horror, fantasy, historical or romance). No unsol mss, query first with SASE; submit letter plus brief synopsis. Agents present in all principal countries.

Barbara Braun Associates Inc (L)
7 E 14 St, Suite 19F, New York, NY 10003
Tel: 212-604-9023
Web Site: www.barbarabraunagency.com
Key Personnel
Pres: Barbara Braun (AAR) *E-mail:* barbara@barbarabraunagency.com
Assoc: John F Baker
Founded: 1994
Represents both literary & commercial fiction as well as serious nonfiction, including memoir, biography, cultural history, women's issues, pop culture, art & architecture. Fiction is strong on stories for women, art-related fiction, historical & multicultural stories & mysteries & thrillers. Interested in narrative nonfiction & current affairs. No unsol mss, query first by e-mail to bbasubmissions@gmail.com. Include brief summary of book, word count, genre, any relevant publishing experience & first 5 pages of ms pasted into the body of the e-mail. No reading or other fees.
Foreign Rights: Jean V Naggar Literary Agency (Jennifer Weltz) (worldwide)
Membership(s): The Authors Guild; PEN American Center

M Courtney Briggs Esq, Authors Representative (L)
Chase Tower, 28th fl, 100 N Broadway Ave, Oklahoma City, OK 73102
Key Personnel
Author's Rep: M Courtney Briggs
Founded: 1994
Fiction & nonfiction, adult & juvenile with emphasis on children's books, including picture books, middle grade & young adult books. Represent authors & illustrators of trade books of all types. Handle film & TV rights. No unsol mss, query first by regular mail with SASE, include publishing history; published authors only; no reading fees.
Membership(s): Society of Children's Book Writers & Illustrators

Brockman Inc (L)
260 Fifth Ave, 10th fl, New York, NY 10001
Tel: 212-935-8900 *Fax:* 212-935-5535
E-mail: rights@brockman.com
Web Site: www.brockman.com
Key Personnel
Chmn: John Brockman
CEO: Max Brockman
Pres: Katinka Matson
VP: Russell Weinberger
Literary & software agency. No unsol mss. Deal direct in all foreign markets. No fees charged.

Curtis Brown Ltd (L-D)
10 Astor Place, New York, NY 10003
Tel: 212-473-5400
Web Site: www.curtisbrown.com
Key Personnel
CEO: Timothy F Knowlton (AAR)
Pres: Peter L Ginsberg (AAR)
EVP & Book Agent: Ginger Knowlton (AAR)
SVP & Book Agent: Maureen Walters (AAR)
VP & Book Agent: Elizabeth Harding (AAR); Laura Blake Peterson (AAR)
Dir, Foreign Rts & Book Agent: Jonathan Lyons (AAR)
Foreign Rts Mgr: Sarah Perillo (AAR)
Book Agent: Noah Ballard (AAR); Ginger Clark (AAR); Katherine Fausset (AAR); Mitchell Waters (AAR); Monika Woods
Assoc Book Agent: Kerry D'Agostino (AAR); Steven Salpeter (AAR)
Film & TV Rts: Holly Frederick (AAR)
Founded: 1914
Handle general trade fiction & nonfiction, juvenile. No unsol mss, query first with SASE. Submit outline or sample chapters. No reading fee. Other fees charged (for photocopies, express mail, etc). Handle film & TV rights & merchandising & multimedia. No playwrights. Representatives in all major foreign countries.
Branch Office(s)
1750 Montgomery St, San Francisco, CA 94111 *Tel:* 415-954-8566

Marie Brown Associates (L)
412 W 154 St, New York, NY 10032
Tel: 212-939-9725
E-mail: submissions.mbrownlit@gmail.com
Key Personnel
Owner & Pres: Marie D Brown
Founded: 1984
Adult & juvenile fiction & nonfiction. Handle film & TV rights through representatives in Hollywood. No unsol mss, query first; submit outline & sample chapters or full ms on request, 12-point, double-spaced, one-sided only, typed, white paper & unbound. Include SASE. E-mail queries accepted. No reading fee.

Browne & Miller Literary Associates (L)
410 S Michigan Ave, Suite 460, Chicago, IL 60605
Tel: 312-922-3063
E-mail: mail@browneandmiller.com
Web Site: www.browneandmiller.com
Key Personnel
Pres & Owner: Danielle Egan-Miller (AAR) *E-mail:* danielle@browneandmiller.com
Agent & Internship Coord: Joanna MacKenzie (AAR) *E-mail:* joanna@browneandmiller.com
Founded: 1971
General adult trade fiction, nonfiction & young adult. No horror, science fiction, or children's books. No unsol mss, query first by e-mail; no reading fee.
Foreign Rep(s): Agence Eliane Benisti (Eliane Benisti) (France); Big Apple Agency Inc (China, Taiwan); Book Publishers Association of Israel (Israel); The English Agency (Japan) Ltd (Japan); International Copyright Agency Ltd (Simona Kessler) (Romania); Japan UNI Agency Inc (Japan); KCBS Literary Agency (Hosung Maeng) (Korea); The Marsh Agency UK (Netherlands, Poland, Scandinavia); Natoli, Stefan & Oliva (Roberta Oliva) (Italy); Andrew Nurnberg Associates Baltic (Tatjana Zoldnere) (Baltic States); Andrew Nurnberg Associates (Hungary); O A Literary Agency (Greece); Prava i prevodi (Croatia, Montenegro, Serbia, Slovenia); Riff Agency (Brazil); Thomas Schlueck GmbH (Germany); Tuttle-Mori Agency Inc (Japan); Julio F Yanez Agencia Literaria (Montse F Yanez) (Mexico, South America, Spain); Eric Yang Agency (Korea)
Foreign Rights: Andrew Nurnberg Literary Agency (Liudmilla Sushkova) (Russia)
Membership(s): The Authors Guild; Mystery Writers of America; Romance Writers of America

J B Bryans Literary (L)
7 Meetinghouse Ct, Indian Mills, NJ 08088
Tel: 609-922-0369
E-mail: info@brylit.com
Web Site: brylit.com
Key Personnel
Pres: John B Bryans *E-mail:* john@brylit.com
Founded: 2017
Literary agency & consultancy founded to provide close personal attention to the needs of a small stable of established & emerging authors. Adult commercial & literary fiction & nonfiction. Fiction: historical, adventure, mystery & culturally relevant novels distinguished by quirky, relatable characters & plenty of belly laughs. Nonfiction: history, politics, environment, true crime, regional (NJ), business, cyberculture, library & information science, education, biography, music, & humor. No unsol mss, query first. Send e-mail with working title in the subject line & short description of the work in the message body. We will reply to request ms or sample chapters if interested. No fees charged.

Don Buchwald & Associates Inc (L)
10 E 44 St, New York, NY 10017
Tel: 212-867-1200 *Fax:* 212-867-2434
E-mail: info@buchwald.com
Web Site: www.buchwald.com
Key Personnel
Pres & CEO (NY): Don Buchwald *E-mail:* don@buchwald.com
VP & CFO: Stephen Fisher *E-mail:* steve@buchwald.com
EVP, Legal & Admin Aff: Richard Basch *E-mail:* richard@buchwald.com
Agent (NY): David Lewis *E-mail:* davidl@buchwald.com; Jonathan Mason *E-mail:* jmason@buchwald.com; Joanne Nici *E-mail:* jonici@buchwald.com
Talent representatives & literary agency: TV, film, commercial, theatre & broadcasting. No unsol mss, query first. No reading fee.
Branch Office(s)
6500 Wilshire Blvd, Suite 2200, Los Angeles, CA 90048 *Tel:* 323-665-7400 *Fax:* 323-665-7470

Judith Buckner Literary Agency (L-D)
12721 Hart St, North Hollywood, CA 91605
Tel: 818-982-8202 *Fax:* 818-764-6844
Key Personnel
Pres: Judith Buckner *E-mail:* jbuckner@pacbell.net
Founded: 1970
Handle commercial & literary fiction & nonfiction, some film & TV scripts. No children's, young adult, romance, science fiction or horror. No unsol mss; query first by letter or e-mail. No reading fee. Commission 15% domestic, 20% foreign. Handle film & TV rights. If invited to submit, for fiction send first fifty pages & brief synopsis of remainder. For nonfiction, send proposal including overview, target market, outline or table of contents, sample chapter, author's bio, survey of competition & reasons why your book is superior & marketing plan.

The Bukowski Agency Ltd (L)
14 Prince Arthur Ave, Suite 202, Toronto, ON M5R 1A9, Canada
Tel: 416-928-6728 *Fax:* 416-963-9978
E-mail: info@bukowskiagency.com
Web Site: www.bukowskiagency.com
Key Personnel
Pres & Primary Agent: Denise Bukowski
Founded: 1986
Adult trade except genre fiction by Canadian authors. No unsol mss, query first by regular mail. Submit proposal & sample for nonfiction; query & sample for fiction. No reading fees. Commission plus disbursements.
Foreign Rights: AJA Literary Agency (Anna Jarota) (France); Akcali Copyright Agency

(Atilla Izgi Turgut) (Istanbul); Big Apple Agency (Vincent Lin) (China, Taiwan); The Foreign Office (Teresa Vilarrubla) (Latin America, Portugal, Spain); Graal Liteary Agency (Filip Wojciechowski) (Eastern Europe, Poland); Grandi & Associati (Alessandra Mele) (Italy); The Deborah Harris Agency (Ilana Kurshan) (Israel); A M Heath & Co Ltd (Bill Hamilton) (UK); Japan UNI Agency Inc (Cecilia Kashiwamura) (Japan); JLM Literary Agency (John Moukakou) (Greece); Katai & Bolza Literary Agents (Peter Bolza) (Hungary); Duran Kim Agency (Duran Kim) (Korea); Licht & Burr (Trine Licht) (Scandinavia); Mohrbooks AG (Annelie Geissler) (Germany); Marianne Schoenbach Literary Agency (Marianne Schoenbach) (Holland); The Van Lear Agency (Elizabeth Van Lear) (Russia)

Sheree Bykofsky Associates Inc (L)
PO Box 706, Brigantine, NJ 08203
E-mail: submitbee@aol.com
Web Site: www.shereebee.com
Key Personnel
Pres & Agent: Sheree Bykofsky (AAR)
Founded: 1991
Adult trade & mass market nonfiction & fiction. No unsol mss, send e-query in body of e-mail to submitbee@aol.com. Handle film & TV rights through subagents. No fees.
Foreign Rights: Bardon-Chinese Media Agency (China, Taiwan); Eliane Benisti Agency (France); BookLab (Poland); Dalia Ever Hadani (Israel); Japan Uni Agency Inc (Japan); Alexander Korzhenevski (Russia); Piergiorgio Nicolazzini (Italy); OA Literary Agency (Greece); Kristin Olson Literary Agency (Czech Republic, Slovakia); Onk Agency Ltd (Eastern Europe, Greece, Turkey); Plima Literary Agency (Croatia, Serbia, Slovenia); RDC Agencia Literaria SL (Latin America, Portugal, Spain); Thomas Schlueck GmbH (Germany); Marianne Schoenbach Literary Agency (Netherlands); Abner Stein Agency (UK); Eric Yang (Korea); Pimolporn Yutsiri (Indonesia, Thailand, Vietnam)
Membership(s): The Authors Guild; North American Travel Journalists Association

Cambridge Literary Associates (L-D)
Division of Valentino Enterprises Inc
135 Beach Rd, Unit C-3, Salisbury, MA 01952
Tel: 978-499-0374 *Fax:* 978-499-9774
Web Site: www.cambridgeliterary.com
Key Personnel
Pres: Michael Valentino
VP: Ralph Valentino
Full literary agency. Fiction & nonfiction: action, mystery, romance, science fiction, screenplays. No unsol mss, query first with letter. No reading fee. Fee of $3 per page for editing.

Kimberley Cameron & Associates LLC (L)
1550 Tiburon Blvd, Suite 704, Tiburon, CA 94920
Tel: 415-789-9191 *Fax:* 415-789-9177
Web Site: www.kimberleycameron.com
Key Personnel
Pres & Literary Agent: Kimberley Cameron (AAR) *E-mail:* kimberley@kimberleycameron.com
Literary Agent: Lisa Abellera *E-mail:* lisa@kimberleycameron.com; Amy Cloughly *E-mail:* amy@kimberleycameron.com; Elizabeth Krach *E-mail:* elizabeth@kimberleycameron.com; Douglas Lee *E-mail:* doug@kimberleycameron.com; Ms Dorian Maffei *E-mail:* dorian@kimberleycameron.com; Pooja Menon; Mary Moore *E-mail:* mary@kimberleycameron.com
Founded: 1957
Represent quality writing in book-length fiction & nonfiction, including memoirs, biographies, literary fiction, mainstream fiction, science fiction, mysteries & thrillers. Do not handle screenplays, poetry or children's literature. Handle film & TV rights. E-mail all queries. For fiction, include one-page synopsis & first 50 pages as separate attachments. For nonfiction, send complete proposal including sample chapters. No fees charged Please submit through the individual agent's page at our web site.
Foreign Rights: The Fielding Agency (Whitney Lee) (worldwide)
Membership(s): Sisters in Crime

Carlisle & Co LLC, see InkWell Management

Maria Carvainis Agency Inc (L)
Rockefeller Center, 1270 Avenue of the Americas, Suite 2320, New York, NY 10020
Tel: 212-245-6365 *Fax:* 212-245-7196
E-mail: mca@mariacarvainisagency.com
Web Site: mariacarvainisagency.com
Key Personnel
Pres: Maria Carvainis (AAR)
Contracts & Subs Rts Mgr: Martha Guzman (AAR)
Assoc Agent: Elizabeth Copps (AAR)
Literary Asst: Samantha Brody
Founded: 1977
Represents a wide range of fiction & nonfiction with special interest in literary & mainstream fiction, mystery & suspense, thrillers, historicals, contemporary women's fiction, young adult & middle grade, memoir, biography, history, business, psychology, pop culture & popular science. We do not represent screenplays, children's picture books, science fiction, or poetry. If you would like to query the agency, please send a query letter, a synopsis of the work, first 5-10 pages & note of any writing credentials. The agency prefers e-mailed queries: mca@mariacarvainisagency.com.
Titles recently placed: *Anything for You*, Kristan Higgins; *Blue for the Water*, Sonja Yoerg; *Friction*, Sandra Brown; *If You Only Knew*, Kristan Higgins; *Palindrome*, Ephraim Rinsky; *Ruby Clyde*, Corabel Shofner; *The Infinite*, Nicholas Mainieri; *The Survivor's Club*, Mary Balogh
Membership(s): ABA; The Authors Guild; International Thriller Writers Inc; Mystery Writers of America; Romance Writers of America; Society of Children's Book Writers & Illustrators

Linda Chester Literary Agency (L-D)
630 Fifth Ave, Suite 2000, New York, NY 10111
Tel: 212-218-3350
E-mail: submissions@lindachester.com
Web Site: www.lindachester.com
Key Personnel
Principal: Linda Chester (AAR)
Exec Mgr: Gary Jaffe *E-mail:* gjaffe@lindachester.com
Quality adult fiction & nonfiction. Handle film & TV rights. No reading fes; no unsol mss, query first.
Branch Office(s)
1525 Arch St, Suite 3, Berkeley, CA 94708, Contact: Laurie Fox *Tel:* 510-704-0971 *E-mail:* laurie@lindachester.com
Foreign Rights: The Fielding Agency LLC (Whitney Lee)

Faith Childs Literary Agency Inc (L)
111 John St, Suite 1620, New York, NY 10038
Tel: 212-995-9600
Web Site: faithchildsliteraryagency.com
Key Personnel
Pres: Faith Hampton Childs (AAR) *E-mail:* faith@faithchildsliteraryagency.com
Subs Rts Assoc: Diana Lachatanere *E-mail:* dianalachatanere@faithchildsliteraryagency.com
Asst: Rachel Sandberg *E-mail:* rachel@faithchildslitereryagency.com
Founded: 1990
Specialize in fiction & nonfiction film & TV rights. No unsol mss, queries or unreferred clients accepted. Agents in all principal countries.
Foreign Rep(s): The English Agency (Japan) Ltd (Japan)

Chinese Connection Agency (L-D)
Division of The Yao Enterprises LLC
67 Banksville Rd, Armonk, NY 10504
Tel: 914-765-0296 *Fax:* 914-765-0297
Web Site: www.yaollc.com
Key Personnel
Pres: Mei C Yao
Founded: 1995
Translation rights sales of adult fiction & nonfiction, professional/business management books, college books, personal development, leisure books, etc. No unsol mss, query first (e-mail queries welcome). No reading fee. Handle software & film & TV rights.

Cine/Lit Representation (L-D)
PO Box 802918, Santa Clarita, CA 91380-2918
Tel: 661-513-0268
E-mail: cinelit@att.net
Key Personnel
Partner: Anna Cottle; Mary Alice Kier (AAR)
Founded: 1991
Commercial & literary fiction & nonfiction. Emphasis in mainstream thrillers, suspense/mysteries, supernatural, horror & speculative. Nonfiction interest in narrative environmental, travel & pop culture. Not accepting submissions at this time. No reading fee. Representatives in all major foreign markets. Handle film & TV rights.
Membership(s): British Academy of Film & Television Arts/Los Angeles; Independent Film Project/West

Wm Clark Associates (L)
186 Fifth Ave, 2nd fl, New York, NY 10010
Tel: 212-675-2784
E-mail: general@wmclark.com
Web Site: www.wmclark.com
Key Personnel
Principal: William Clark (AAR) *E-mail:* wmclark@wmclark.com
Founded: 1999
Represents mainstream & literary fiction & quality nonfiction to the book publishing, motion picture, television & new media fields. No reading fees; handle film & TV rights for books written by clients only; does not represent screenplays. In addition to selling directly in the global English language markets, translation rights are sold directly in the German, Italian, Spanish, Portuguese, Latin American, French, Dutch, & Scandinavian territories; in association with Andrew Nurnberg Associates Ltd (UK) through offices in China, Bulgaria, Czech Republic, Latvia, Poland & Hungary; & through corresponding agents in Russia, Ukraine, Japan, Greece, Israel, Turkey, Korea, Taiwan & Thailand. Other network partners provide services including editorial consultation, media training, lecture booking, marketing support & public relations. Queries sent by any method other than through web site query page will be discarded unread.
Titles recently placed: *Interior Design Master Class*, Carl J Dellatore; *Marilyn: The Passion and the Paradox*, Lois Banner; *Modern Monopolies: What It Takes to Dominate the 21st Century Economy*, Alex Moazed, Nicholas

Johnson; *Political Animals: How Our Stone Age Brain Gets in the Way of Politics*, Rick Shenkman; *Strange Stones: Dispatches from East to West*, Peter Hessler
Foreign Rights: Andrew Nurnberg Associates Ltd (China, Eastern Europe, Taiwan)
Membership(s): The Authors Guild; PEN International

Collier Associates (L)
37 Marina Gardens Dr, Palm Beach Gardens, FL 33410
Mailing Address: PO Box 20149, West Palm Beach, FL 33416
Tel: 561-514-6548
E-mail: dmccabooks@gmail.com
Key Personnel
Pres & Agent: Dianna Collier
Founded: 1976
Fiction & nonfiction adult books. Fiction: war novels, mysteries, true crime, romance, contemporary & historical. Nonfiction: biographies & autobiographies of well-known people, popular works of political subjects & history, exposes, popular works on medical & scientific subjects, finance, popular reference & how-to books, health, beauty & motherhood. Also handle film & TV rights for adult books only with co-agents. No unsol mss, query first with SASE; submit outline, sample chapters & bio; no reading fee for published authors of trade books, may charge fee for full-length book mss for unpublished authors; charge cost of copying ms; submission postage; books ordered for subsidiary rights. When ms is submitted it should meet the Chicago Manual of Style Guidelines, along with a sample chapter by chapter outline & SASE. Submissions must be in Microsoft Word format, one sided pages, all pages numbered at bottom center, header with author & title right justified, double spaced, Courier font, 12 pt. All others submissions may be discarded. Include cover proposal letter & chapter-by-chapter outline. Co-agents on West Coast & in many foreign countries.
Foreign Rep(s): Big Apple Agency Inc (China, Japan, Taiwan); International Literature Bureau BV (Netherlands); Johnson & Alcock Ltd (British Commonwealth); Mohrbooks AG (Austria, Germany, Switzerland); Tuttle-Mori Agency Inc (Japan); Julio F Yanez Agencia Literaria (Portugal, South America, Spain)
Foreign Rights: Agence Michelle Lapautre (France); Light & Burr (Denmark, Finland, Iceland, Norway, Sweden)
Membership(s): Mystery Writers of America

Frances Collin Literary Agency (L)
PO Box 33, Wayne, PA 19087
Tel: 610-254-0555
E-mail: queries@francescollin.com
Web Site: www.francescollin.com
Key Personnel
Owner: Frances Collin (AAR)
Literary Agent: Sarah Yake *E-mail:* sarah@francescollin.com
Founded: 1948
Successor to Marie Rodell-Frances Collin Literary Agency (1975).
Trade fiction & nonfiction; no original screenplays. Special interest in the following areas: literary fiction, biography, history, travel, environmental, nature, memoir, fantasy/science fiction. No unsol mss, query via e-mail to queries@francescollin.com. Send query letter describing your project (text in the body of the e-mail only, e-mails with unsol attachments will be deleted unread). Handle film & TV rights through sub-agents; representatives in all foreign markets. No fees.

Don Congdon Associates Inc (L)
110 William St, Suite 2202, New York, NY 10038-3914
Tel: 212-645-1229 *Fax:* 212-727-2688
E-mail: dca@doncongdon.com
Web Site: www.doncongdon.com
Key Personnel
Agent: Cristina Concepcion (AAR); Michael Congdon (AAR); Katie Grimm (AAR); Katie Kotchman (AAR); Maura Kye-Casella (AAR); Susan Ramer (AAR)
Founded: 1983
Handle any & all trade books. Handle film & TV rights for regular clients. No unsol mss, query first with a one page synopsis of your work & relevant background & SASE or e-mail without attachments. In heading include "Query" & agent's full name. Include a sample chapter in body of e-mail. Now accepting new & professional authors. No reading fee.
Foreign Rep(s): AnatoliaLit Agency (Turkey); Big Apple Agency Inc (China, Indonesia, Taiwan, Thailand, Vietnam); Nurichan Kesim Literary Agency Inc (Turkey); Agence Michelle Lapautre (France); Andrew Nurnberg Associates (Eastern Europe, Germany, Russia); Read n' Right Agency (Greece); Vicki Satlow Literary Agency (Italy); Sebes & Bisseling Agency (Scandinavia); Abner Stein Agency (UK); Tuttle-Mori Agency Inc (Japan); Julio F Yanez (Latin America, Portugal, Spain); Eric Yang Agency (Korea)

The Doe Coover Agency (L)
PO Box 668, Winchester, MA 01890
Tel: 781-721-6000 *Fax:* 781-721-6727
E-mail: info@doecooveragency.com
Web Site: www.doecooveragency.com
Key Personnel
Pres: Doe Coover
Agent: Colleen Mohyde
Assoc: Frances Kennedy
Founded: 1986
Nonfiction & fiction. Specialize in literary fiction, business, history & biography, psychology, science & health, cooking & food writing, gardening, humor, sports & music. No poetry, fantasy, science fiction or screenplays. E-mail queries only; see web site for submission guidelines.
Handle film & TV rights on agency projects only. 15% commission.
Titles recently placed: *A Girl's Guide to Missiles*, Karen Piper; *Biography of Garry Trudeau*, Steve Weinberg; *Canal House Kitchen Basics*, Christopher Hirsheimer, Melissa Hamilton; *Lessons from a Grandfather*, Jacques Pepin; *Living with Cancer: A Step-by-Step Guide for Coping Medically and Emotionally with your Diagnosis*, Dr Vicki Jackson, Dr Patrick Ryan, Michelle Seaton; *The Life She Wished to Live: Biography of Marjorie Kinnan Rawlings*, Ann McCutchan; *Where the Wild Coffee Grows*, Jeff Koehler
Foreign Rights: The English Agency (Japan) Ltd (Japan); The Marsh Agency (Europe); Abner Stein Agency (UK)

CreativeWell Inc (L)
PO Box 3130, Memorial Sta, Upper Montclair, NJ 07043
Tel: 973-783-7575 *Fax:* 973-783-7530
E-mail: info@creativewell.com
Web Site: www.creativewell.com
Key Personnel
Pres: George M Greenfield *E-mail:* george@creativewell.com
Founded: 2003
Primarily nonfiction, film & TV rights. No unsol mss. No reading fee; other fees charged (for photocopies, express mail, etc). Representatives in principal foreign countries. Also offers full service lecture representation.

Titles recently placed: *52 Reasons to Vote for Hillary*, Bernard Whitman, Brittany L Stalsburg PhD; *Finding Calm Clarity*, Due Quach; *First They Killed My Father: A Daughter of Cambodia Remembers*, Loung Ung; *Lincoln's Gamble: The Tumultuous Six Months That Gave America the Emancipation Proclamation and Changed the Course of the Civil War*, Todd Brewster; *Metaphors Be With You*, Dr Mardy Grothe; *Nobody: Casualties of America's War on the Vulnerable from Ferguson to Flint and Beyond*, Marc Lamont Hill; *The Art of Movement*, Ken Browar, Deborah Ory; *To Hell and Back: The Last Train from Hiroshima*, Charles Pellegrino

Crichton & Associates Inc (L)
6940 Carroll Ave, Takoma Park, MD 20912
Tel: 301-495-9663
E-mail: cricht1@aol.com
Web Site: www.crichton-associates.com
Key Personnel
Pres: Sha-Shana Crichton
Founded: 2002
For fiction, submit first 3 chapters with synopsis & bio. For nonfiction, submit proposal with bio. No fees charged. Send queries to query@crichton-associates.com.
Membership(s): Romance Writers of America

Richard Curtis Associates Inc (L)
200 E 72 St, Suite 28J, New York, NY 10021
Tel: 212-772-7363 *Fax:* 212-772-7393
E-mail: info@curtisagency.com
Web Site: www.curtisagency.com
Key Personnel
Pres: Richard Curtis (AAR) *E-mail:* rcurtis@curtisagency.com
Founded: 1979
No stage plays or screenplays, short fiction, articles or poetry. Handle film & TV rights. No unsol mss, query first via US mail with SASE or via e-mail at info@curtisagency.com.
Foreign Rights: Baror International Inc (worldwide exc USA)
Membership(s): Mystery Writers of America; Romance Writers of America; Science Fiction & Fantasy Writers of America

Darhansoff & Verrill (L)
133 W 72 St, Rm 304, New York, NY 10023
Tel: 917-305-1300
E-mail: permissions@dvagency.com
Web Site: www.dvagency.com
Key Personnel
Agent: Liz Darhansoff
Agent & Rights Dir: Michele Mortimer
Agent: Chuck Verrill
Off Mgr: Eric Amling
Founded: 1975
Fiction & nonfiction, literary fiction, young adult, memoirs, sophisticated suspense, history, science, biography, pop culture & current affairs. No theatrical plays or film scripts. No unsol mss, query first with SASE or by e-mail via submissions@dvagency.com. Film & TV rights handled by Los Angeles associates, Lynn Pleshette, Richard Green & UTA. Agents in many foreign countries. No fees charged.
Foreign Rights: Alkcali Copyright Agency (Ozgur Emir) (Turkey); Bardon-Chinese Media Agency (Joanne Yang) (China); Eliane Benisti Agency (France); The Book Publishers Association of Israel (Dalia Ever Hadani) (Israel); The English Agency (Hamish Macaskill) (Japan); Graal Literary Agency (Maria Strarz-Kanska) (Poland); International Copyrights Agency (Simona Kessler) (Romania); Interrights (Svetlana Stefanova) (Bulgaria); The Italian Literary Agency srl (Italy); JLM Literarary Agency (John Moukakis) (Greece); Katai & Bolza (Peter Bolza) (Hungary); Licht & Burr

(Trine Licht) (Scandinavia); Zvonimir Majdak (Croatia); Mohrbooks (Sebastian Ritscher) (Germany); Andrew Nurnberg Agency (Lumilla Shushkova) (Russia); Andrew Nurnberg Association Baltic (Tatjana Zoldnere) (Latvia); Kristin Olson Literary Agency (Kristin Olson) (Czech Republic); Agencia Riff (Laura Riff & Joao Paulo Riff) (Brazil, Portugal); The Sayle Agency (Rachel Calder) (UK); Sebes & Bisseling Literary Agency (Paul Sebes) (Holland); Shin Won Agency (Tae Kim) (Korea); Yanez Agencia Literaria (Montse F Yanez) (Spain)

Liza Dawson Associates (L)
350 Seventh Ave, Suite 2003, New York, NY 10001
Tel: 212-465-9071 *Fax:* 212-947-0460
Web Site: www.lizadawsonassociates.com
Key Personnel
CFO & Foreign Rts Mgr: Havis Dawson *E-mail:* queryhavis@lizadawsonassociates.com
Pres: Liza Dawson (AAR) *E-mail:* queryliza@lizadawsonassociates.com
Literary Agent & Audio Rts Mgr: Caitie Flum *E-mail:* querycaitie@lizadawson.com
Literary Agent: Caitlin Blasdell *E-mail:* querycaitlin@lizadawsonassociates.com; Hannah Bowman *E-mail:* queryhannah@lizadawsonassociates.com; Jennifer Johnson-Blalock *E-mail:* queryjennifer@lizadawson.com
Founded: 1996
Liza Dawson: Fiction, both literary & commercial. Nonfiction: strong narratives, history, psychology, memoirs, parenting & business books. No poetry, westerns or children's books.
Caitlin Blasdell: science fiction, fantasy, romance & young adult.
Hannah Bowman: science fiction, fantasy, young adult. Nonfiction: math, science, religion.
Jennifer Johnson-Blalock: women's fiction, mysteries, thrillers, contemporary romance, young adult & middle grade. Nonfiction: current events, social sciences, women's issues, law, business, history, the arts & pop culture, lifestyle, sports & food, including cookbooks & health/wellness.
Caitie Flum: women's fiction, mysteries, thrillers, contemporary romance, book club fiction, young adult science fiction & fantasy, young adult & middle grade. Nonfiction: narrative nonfiction, especially history, books on pop culture, theater, current events, women's issues & humor.
No unsol mss. Send query letter via e-mail. Agents in Hollywood, CA & all foreign countries.
Foreign Rights: Akcali Copyright Agency (Atilla Izgi Turgut) (Turkey); Eliane Benisti Agency (Leon de la Menadiere, science fiction/fantasy only) (France); Graal Literary Agency (Marcin Biegaj) (Albania, Baltic States, Bulgaria, Greece, Hungary, Iceland, Macedonia, Poland, Romania, Serbia, Slovenia); The Grayhawk Agency (Gray Tan) (China, Taiwan, Thailand, Vietnam); Danny Hong Agency (Danny Hong) (Korea); Alexander Korzhenevski Agency (Alexander Korzhenevski) (Russia); Piergiorgio Nicollazzini Agency (Maura Solinas, science fiction/fantasy only) (Italy); Kristin Olson Literary Agency (Kristin Olson) (Czech Republic); Thomas Schlueck GmbH (Bastian Schlueck, science fiction/fantasy only) (Germany); Tuttle-Mori Agency Inc (Manami Tamaoki, nonfiction) (Japan); Tuttle-Mori Agency Inc (Misa Morikawa, fiction) (Japan)
Membership(s): Women's Media Group

J de S Associates Inc (L)
9 Shagbark Rd, South Norwalk, CT 06854
Tel: 203-838-7571 *Fax:* 203-866-2713
Web Site: www.jdesassociates.com
Key Personnel
Pres: Jacques de Spoelberch *E-mail:* jdespoel@aol.com
Founded: 1975
Fiction & nonfiction. No unsol mss, query first. Send outline & 2 sample chapters; no reading fee. Agents & film representatives in major foreign countries.

The Jennifer DeChiara Literary Agency (L)
299 Park Ave, 6th fl, New York, NY 10171
Tel: 212-739-0803
Web Site: www.jdlit.com
Key Personnel
Owner, Pres & Agent: Jennifer DeChiara *E-mail:* jenndec@aol.com
Sr Literary Agent: Stephen Fraser *E-mail:* fraserstephena@gmail.com
Film/TV Mgr: Kimberly Guidone
Assoc Agent: Cari Lamba *E-mail:* cari.jdlit@gmail.com; Marie Lamba *E-mail:* marie.jdlit@gmail.com; Damian McNicholl *E-mail:* damianmcnichollvarney@gmail.com; Victoria Selvaggio *E-mail:* vselvaggio@windstream.net; Alexandra Weiss *E-mail:* alexandra.weiss@loop.colum.edu; Roseanne Wells *E-mail:* roseannelitagent@gmail.com
Founded: 2001
Accepting queries in the following areas: children's books for every age (picture books, middle grade & young adult), adult fiction & nonfiction in a wide range of genres. Accept e-mail queries only, with "Query" in the subject line; no attachments. Co-agents in every country. No fees.
Titles recently placed: *Annika Riz, Math Whiz*, Claudia Mills; *Bees In The Trees*, Ruth Horowitz; *Daughter of Australia*, Harmony Verna; *Eliza Bing Is (Not) A Big, Fat Quitter*, Carmella Van Vleet; *Fannie Never Flinches*, Mary Cronk Farrell; *Girl*, M-E Girard; *Guts For Glory*, JoAnna Lapati; *Hazy Bloom*, Jennifer Hamburg; *Honestly, Ben*, Bill Konigsberg; *I Only Know Who I Am When I Am Somebody Else*, Danny Aiello; *I'll Be Damned*, Eric Braeden; *Irena's Children*, Mary Cronk Farrell; *Izzy Barr, Running Star*, Claudia Mills; *Luke Veracruz Saves The Day*, Jeff Anderson; *My Days...Happy and Otherwise*, Marion Ross; *Not Young, Still Restless: My Life So Far*, Jeanne Cooper; *Omega Days*, John L Campbell; *Openly Straight*, Bill Konigsberg; *Peanut Butter and Brains*, Joe McGee; *Quack*, Jennifer Hamburg; *Sitting Next to Jesus*, Carol Lynch Williams; *Skynned Alive: Keeping the Best in Lynyrd Skynyrd, America's Greatest Rock 'n' Roll Band*, Artimus Pyle; *Stuck In My Sister's Fat*, Carol Lynch Williams; *The Ed Lucas Story*, Ed Lucas, Christopher Lucas; *The Hole Story of the Doughnut*, Pat Miller; *The Jumbie Seed*, Tracey Baptiste; *The Jumbies*, Tracey Baptiste; *The Nora Notebooks*, Claudia Mills; *The One-Way Bridge*, Cathie Pelletier; *The Porcupine of Truth*, Bill Konigsberg; *The Quantum League*, Matthew Kirby; *The Summer Experiment*, Cathie Pelletier; *The Write-Brain Workbook (10th anniversary ed)*, Bonnie Neubauer; *The Year After Henry*, Cathie Pelletier; *Three Truths and a Lie*, Brent Hartinger; *Tippi*, Tippi Hedren; *To The Stars! The Story of Kathy Sullivan, First American Woman to Walk in Space*, Carmella Van Vleet, Kathy Sullivan; *Toni Tennille, A Memoir*, Toni Tennille; *Waggers*, Stacy A Nyikos; *Whistle Root*, Christopher Pennell
Foreign Rights: Books Crossing Borders (Betty Anne Crawford) (USA)

DeFiore and Company Literary Management Inc (L)
47 E 19 St, 3rd fl, New York, NY 10003
Tel: 212-925-7744 *Fax:* 212-925-9803
E-mail: info@defliterary.com; submissions@defliterary.com
Web Site: www.defliterary.com
Key Personnel
Founder & Pres: Brian DeFiore (AAR) *E-mail:* querybrian@defliterary.com
Dir, Busn Aff: Adam Schear (AAR) *E-mail:* adam@defliterary.com
Dir, Foreign Rts: Linda Kaplan
Literary Agent & UK Rts Dir: Meredith Kaffel Simonoff (AAR) *E-mail:* meredith@defliterary.com
Literary Agent: Laurie Abkemeier (AAR) *E-mail:* laurie@defliterary.com; Miriam Altschuler (AAR) *E-mail:* querymiriam@defliterary.com; Ashley Collom *E-mail:* ashley@defliterary.com; Reiko Davis *E-mail:* reiko@defliterary.com; Matthew Elblonk *E-mail:* matthew@defliterary.com; Lisa Gallagher *E-mail:* lgsubmissions@defliterary.com; Karen Gerwin; Caryn Karmatz Rudy (AAR) *E-mail:* caryn@defliterary.com; Rebecca Strauss (AAR) *E-mail:* rebecca@defliterary.com; Nicole Tourtelot *E-mail:* nicole@defliterary.com
Founded: 1999
Handles mainstream fiction, suspense fiction, business, self-help, narrative nonfiction, cookbooks & memoirs.
Titles recently placed: *Celebrate*, Lauren Conrad; *Down the Rabbit Hole*, Holly Madison; *Rise of the Rocket Girls*, Nathalia Holt; *So Sad Today*, Melissa Broder; *The Cheese Trap*, Neal Barnard; *The Fat Artist and Other Stories*, Benjamin Hale
Foreign Rep(s): Gillon Aitken Associates (UK); Andrew Nurnberg Associates
Foreign Rights: The Book Publishers Association of Israel (Delia Ever Hadani) (Israel); JLM Literary Agency (John Moukakos) (Greece); Kayi Agency (Dilek Kayi) (Turkey); Andrew Nurnberg Associates (Sabine Pfannenstiel, London) (Germany); Andrew Nurnberg Associates (Claire Anouchian, London) (France, Quebec, CN); Andrew Nurnberg Associates (Lucy Flynn) (Latin America exc Brazil, Portugal, Spain); Andrew Nurnberg Associates (Barbara Barbieri) (Brazil, Italy); Andrew Nurnberg Associates (Marei Pittner, London) (Netherlands, Scandinavia); Andrew Nurnberg Associates (Anna & Mira Droumeva, Sofia) (Bulgaria, Romania, Serbia); Andrew Nurnberg Associates (Petra Tobiskova & Jana Borovanova, Prague) (Czech Republic, Slovakia, Slovenia); Andrew Nurnberg Associates (Aleksandra Lapinska & Renata Paczewska, Warsaw) (Poland); Andrew Nurnberg Associates (Judit Hermann, Budapest) (Croatia, Hungary); Andrew Nurnberg Associates (Ludmilla Sushkova, Moscow) (Russia); Andrew Nurnberg Associates (Tatjana Zoldnere, Latvia) (Estonia, Latvia, Lithuania, Ukraine); Andrew Nurnberg Associates (Jackie Huang, Beijing) (China); Andrew Nurnberg Associates (Whitney Hsu, Taipei) (Taiwan); Tuttle-Mori Agency Inc (Ken Mori & Manami Tamaoki) (Japan); Tuttle-Mori Agency Inc (Thananchai Pandey, Bangkok) (Thailand); Eric Yang Agency (Henry Shin) (Korea)

Joelle Delbourgo Associates Inc (L)
101 Park St, Montclair, NJ 07042
Tel: 973-773-0836 (call only during standard business hours)
Web Site: www.delbourgo.com
Key Personnel
Founder & Pres, Agent & Consultant: Joelle Delbourgo (AAR) *E-mail:* joelle@delbourgo.com
Assoc Agent & Ed: Carrie Cantor *Tel:* 973-783-1005 *E-mail:* cantor.carrie@gmail.com
Ed: John Paine *E-mail:* jpaine@johnpaine.com; Fran Schumer *E-mail:* frannyrs2@gmail.com
Publicity Consultant: Jennifer Prost *E-mail:* jennifer@delbourgo.com

Agent: Jacquie Flynn *Tel:* 973-783-6800 ext 3 *E-mail:* jacquie@delbourgo.com
Founded: 2000
Boutique firm handling a wide range of adult fiction (literary & commercial) & nonfiction (narrative, prescriptive, reference). Young adult & middle grade fiction. E-mail queries only accepted, but check submission guidelines on web site. Materials will not be returned.
Titles recently placed: *After Anatevka*, Alexandra Silber; *Bering Sea Strong*, Laura Hartema; *Cold Hard Truth About You and Me*, Anne Greenwood Brown; *Lift and Separate*, Marilyn Simon Rothstein; *Love Wins*, Debbie Cenziper, Jim Obergefell; *Mashed*, Holly Herrick; *My Part-Time Paris Life*, Lisa Anselmo; *Otherwise Engaged*, Lindsey J Palmer; *Rescued*, Peter Zheutlin; *Secrets of Mindful Beauty*, Elizabeth Reid-Boyd, Jessica Boyd-Moncrieff; *Shame Nation*, Sue Scheff; *Superbug*, Geeta Anand; *The Gospel of Mary*, Philip Freeman; *The Mindful Woman*, Caroline S Welch; *The Power of Presence*, Kristi Hedges; *The Prisoner*, Ben H Winters; *The Secret Letters Project*, Julie Merrick; *The Winged Herds of Anok*, Jennifer Alvarez; *Witness: Lessons from Elie Wiesel's Classroom*, Ariel Burger; *Women on the Front Lines*, Eileen Rivers
Foreign Rights: Duran Kim Agency (Korea); Maxima Agency (Indonesia); Jenny Meyer Literary Agency (worldwide exc Asia); Andrew Nurnberg Associates Inc (China); Tuttle-Mori Agency Inc (Japan)
Membership(s): Women's Media Group

D4EO Literary Agency (L-D)
7 Indian Valley Rd, Weston, CT 06883
Tel: 203-544-7180 *Fax:* 203-544-7160
Web Site: www.d4eoliteraryagency.com; www.publishersmarketplace.com/members/d4eo/; twitter.com/d4eo
Key Personnel
Principal: Robert (Bob) G Diforio *E-mail:* bob@d4eo.com
Founded: 1991
Represent trade books of all types, fiction, nonfiction, business. No unsol mss, query first with SASE. Submit outline & sample chapters, if requested. No reading fee. Handle film & TV rights. Prefer recommendation from client or publisher. For middle grade & young adult: query with query letter & first 5 pages of your project in the body of the e-mail, no attachments.
Foreign Rep(s): Agence Litteraire Eliane Benisti (France); Nabu International Literary & Film Agency (Italy)
Foreign Rights: Anthea Agency (Katalena Sabeva) (Bulgaria); Agence Litteraire Eliane Benisti (Eliane Benisti) (France); Michael Meller Literary Agency GmbH (Michael Meller) (Germany); Nabu International Literary & Film Agency (Silvia Brunelli) (Italy); Tuttle-Mori Agency Inc (Ken Mori) (Japan)

Sandra Dijkstra Literary Agency (L)
1155 Camino del Mar, PMB 515, Del Mar, CA 92014-2605
E-mail: queries@dijkstraagency.com
Web Site: dijkstraagency.com
Key Personnel
Pres & Agent: Sandra Dijkstra
Agency Mgr & Agent: Elise Capron *Tel:* 858-755-3115 ext 100 *E-mail:* elise@dijkstraagency.com
Fin & Agent: Thao Le *Tel:* 858-755-3115 ext 106 *E-mail:* thao@dijkstraagency.com
Agent: Suzy Evans *E-mail:* suzy@dijkstraagency.com; Roz Foster *E-mail:* roz@dijkstraagency.com; Jill Marr *Tel:* 858-755-3115 ext 108 *E-mail:* jmsubmissions@dijkstraagency.com; Jessica Watterson *E-mail:* jessica@dijkstraagency.com
Asst & Agent: Jennifer Kim *Tel:* 858-755-3115 ext 101 *E-mail:* jennifer@dijkstraagency.com
Founded: 1981
Fiction: contemporary, women's, literary, suspense, thrillers, science fiction & fantasy. Nonfiction: narrative, history, business, psychology, self-help, science & memoir/biography. Works in conjunction with foreign & film agents. E-mail submissions only. See web site for most up-to-date guidelines. No reading fee.
Foreign Rights: Bardon-Chinese Media Agency (China, Taiwan); Sandra Bruna Agencia Literaria (Portugal, Spain); The English Agency (Japan) Ltd (Japan); Graal Literary Agency (Poland); The Italian Literary Agency srl (Italy); Katai & Bolza (Hungary); Licht & Burr (Scandinavia); Maxima Creative Agency (Indonesia); La Nouvelle Agence (France); ONK Agency (Turkey); Prava i prevodi (Eastern Europe); Sebes & Bisseling Literary Agency (Netherlands); Abner Stein Agency (UK); Synopsis Agency (Baltic States, Russia); TBPAI (Israel); Tuttle-Mori Agency Inc (Thailand); Eric Yang Agency (Korea)
Membership(s): The Authors Guild

Donadio & Olson Inc (L-D)
40 W 27 St, 5th fl, New York, NY 10001
Tel: 212-691-8077 *Fax:* 212-633-2837
E-mail: mail@donadio.com
Web Site: donadio.com
Key Personnel
Agent: Edward Hibbert; Neil Olson (AAR)
Founded: 1969
Fiction, nonfiction & young adult. Handle film & TV rights for clients. No fees.
Foreign Rights: AnatoliaLit Agency (Amy Spangler) (Turkey); Agence Litteraire Eliane Benisti (Noemie Rollet) (France); Big Apple Agency Inc (Luc Kwanten) (China, Thailand); Paul & Peter Fritz AG (Christian Dittus) (Germany); The Deborah Harris Agency (Efrat Lev) (Israel); The Italian Literary Agency SRL (Italy); Japan Uni Agency (Miko Yamanouchi) (Japan); JLM Literary Agency (John Moukakos) (Greece); Korea Copyright Center (KCC) (Misun Kwon) (Korea); Licht & Burr (Trine Licht) (Denmark, Finland, Iceland, Norway, Sweden); MB Agencia Literaria (Monica Martin) (Catalonia, Portugal, Spain); Andrew Nurnberg Associates (Mira Droumeva, Sofia) (Albania, Macedonia, Romania, Serbia); Andrew Nurnberg Associates (Judit Hermann) (Croatia, Hungary); Andrew Nurnberg Associates (Aleksandra Matuszak, Warsaw) (Poland); Andrew Nurnberg Associates (Ludmilla Sushkova) (Russia); Andrew Nurnberg Associates (Tatjana Zoldnere, Baltic) (Estonia, Latvia, Lithuania, Ukraine); Andrew Nurnberg Associates (Petra Tobiskova, Prague) (Czech Republic); The Riff Agency (Laura Riff) (Brazil); Marianne Schoenbach Literary Agency (Marianne Schoenbach) (Netherlands)

Janis A Donnaud & Associates Inc (L)
77 Bleecker St, No C1-25, New York, NY 10012
Tel: 212-431-2663 *Fax:* 212-431-2667
E-mail: jdonnaud@aol.com
Key Personnel
Pres: Janis A Donnaud (AAR)
Founded: 1993
Nonfiction by experts in their fields: biography, business, history, mind/body/spirit, health, lifestyle, cookbooks/food writing, African-American, popular science, memoir, narrative nonfiction, cultural subjects, animal books, contemporary social issues, "Big Think" Books, women's issues. Does not handle fiction. Query letter by e-mail – sample material only on request. Handle film, TV & international rights. No phone calls.
Titles recently placed: *Arthritis: Taming the Flame*, Susan Blum, MD; *Dinner*, Melissa Clark; *Forks Over Knives Global Flavors*, Brian Wendel, Darshana Ghacker; *Skinnytaste Fast and Slow*, Gina Homolka; *The Blue Apron Cookbook*, Blue Apron; *The Little Dogist*, Elias Weiss Friedman
Foreign Rights: Agence Litteraire Eliane Benisti (France); Berla & Griffini (Italy); Big Apple Agency Inc (China, Taiwan); Graal Literary Agency (Eastern Europe); Kalem Agency (Turkey); Liepman Agency (Germany); Lennart Sane Agency (Scandinavia, Spanish & Portuguese); Sebes & Bisseling (Netherlands); Shinwon Agency (Korea); Abner Stein Agency (UK & Commonwealth); Tuttle-Mori Agency Inc (Japan)
Membership(s): The Authors Guild

Jim Donovan Literary (L)
5635 SMU Blvd, Suite 201, Dallas, TX 75206
Tel: 214-696-9411
E-mail: jdlqueries@sbcglobal.net
Key Personnel
Owner & Pres: Jim Donovan
Agent: Melissa Shultz
Founded: 1993
Literary & commercial fiction & nonfiction, especially biography, health, history, popular culture & sports. No poetry, short stories or children's. Accept unsol mss only with SASE. For nonfiction, query first with letter & SASE. For fiction, submit first 30-40 pages & synopsis with SASE. May query with e-mail, no attachments, response only if interested. No online submissions accepted. Handle film & TV rights for clients only. Agents in Hollywood & major foreign countries. No fees, 15% commission on monies earned.
Titles recently placed: *As Good as Dead*, Stephen Moore; *Cataclysm*, Tim Washburn; *Grace Under Pressure*, Allen Barra; *James Monroe*, Tim McGrath; *Resurrection Pass*, Kurt Anderson; *The Earth Is All That Lasts*, Mark Gardner; *The Greatest Fury*, William C Davis; *The Hamilton Affair*, Elizabeth Cobbs; *The Swamp Fox*, John Oller; *Their Backs Against the Sea*, Bill Sloan; *Vagabonds*, Jeff Guin

Drennan Literary Agency (L)
6 Robin Lane, East Kingston, NH 03827
Tel: 603-642-8002 *Fax:* 603-642-8002
Key Personnel
Pres: William D Drennan
Contact: Christina L Drennan
Founded: 1980
Scholarly only. No unsol mss, query first with outline & SASE. No reading fee.

Dunham Literary Inc (L)
110 William St, Suite 2202, New York, NY 10038
Tel: 212-929-0994
Web Site: dunhamlit.com
Key Personnel
Founder, Pres & Agent: Jennie Dunham (AAR)
Agent: Bridget Smith (AAR)
Founded: 2000
Literary fiction & nonfiction, children's book writers & illustrators. No plays or screenplays. Handle film & TV rights for books represented. No unsol mss, query letter first with SASE. No fax or e-mail queries. No reading fee.
Foreign Rights: Taryn Fagerness Agency (worldwide exc USA)
Membership(s): Society of Children's Book Writers & Illustrators

Dunow, Carlson & Lerner Literary Agency Inc (L)
27 W 20 St, Suite 1107, New York, NY 10011
Tel: 212-645-7606
E-mail: mail@dclagency.com
Web Site: www.dclagency.com

Key Personnel
Literary Agent: Jennifer Carlson (AAR); Arielle Datz (AAR); Stacia Decker (AAR); Henry Dunow (AAR); Erin Hosier; Amy Hughes; Eleanor Jackson; Julia Kenny (AAR); Betsy Lerner; Edward Necarsulmer, IV (AAR); Yishai Seidman (AAR)
Founded: 2005
Query first, fiction & nonfiction. Handle film & TV rights. Agents in all foreign territories. Submit outlines & sample chapters with SASE. No reading fee.
Foreign Rights: Akcali Copyright Agency (Turkey); Big Apple Agency Inc (China, Taiwan); The English Agency (Japan); Grayhawk Agency (China, Taiwan); The Deborah Harris Agency (Israel); David Higham Associates (UK); JLM Literary Agency (Greece); Andrew Nurnberg Associates (Eastern Europe, Europe, Russia, South America); Owls Agency Inc (Japan); Abner Stein Agency (UK); Tuttle-Mori Agency Inc (Japan); Eric Yang (Korea)

Dupree, Miller & Associates Inc (L)
100 Highland Park Village, Suite 350, Dallas, TX 75205
Tel: 214-559-2665 *Fax:* 214-559-7243
E-mail: editorial@dupreemiller.com
Web Site: www.dupreemiller.com
Key Personnel
Pres: Jan Miller *E-mail:* jmr@dupreemiller.com
EVP: Shannon Marven
Agent: Nena Madonia
Fiction & nonfiction. No children's, science fiction, fantasy, horror, short stories, poetry or screenplays. No unsol mss; accept query letter only, with SASE enclosed for reply. No fees. Market & promote own books both regionally & nationally.

Dystel & Goderich Literary Management, see Dystel, Goderich & Bourret LLC

Dystel, Goderich & Bourret LLC (L-D)
Formerly Dystel & Goderich Literary Management
One Union Sq W, Suite 904, New York, NY 10003
Tel: 212-627-9100 *Fax:* 212-627-9313
Web Site: www.dystel.com
Key Personnel
Pres & Partner: Jane Dystel (AAR)
Agent & Partner: Michael Bourret (AAR) *E-mail:* mbourret@dystel.com; Miriam Goderich *Tel:* 212-627-9100 ext 16 *E-mail:* miriam@dystel.com
VP, Subs Rts Dir & Agent: Lauren E Abramo *Tel:* 212-627-9100 ext 13 *E-mail:* labramo@dystel.com
VP, Sr Agent: Jim McCarthy (AAR) *Tel:* 212-627-9100 ext 15 *E-mail:* jmccarthy@dystel.com
VP & Agent: Stacey Kendall Glick *E-mail:* sglick@dystel.com
Proj Mgr, Ebook Prog & Agent: Sharon Pelletier *Tel:* 212-627-9100 ext 25 *E-mail:* spelletier@dystel.com
Royalties Mgr & Agent: Michael Hoogland *Tel:* 212-627-9100 ext 14 *E-mail:* mhoogland@dystel.com
Agent: Jessica Papin *E-mail:* jpapin@dystel.com; John Rudolph *E-mail:* jrudolph@dystel.com
Asst & Agent: Erin Young *E-mail:* eyoung@dystel.com
Asst: Amy Elizabeth Bishop *Tel:* 212-627-9100 ext 10 *E-mail:* abishop@dystel.com
Subs Rts & Royalties Asst: Kemi Faderin *Tel:* 212-627-9100 ext 11 *E-mail:* kfaderin@dystel.com
Founded: 1994 (as Jane Dystel Literary Management)
General fiction & nonfiction, also cookbooks & children's books. No unsol mss, query letter or e-mail query with outline & first 50 pages. No reading fee. Handle film & TV rights. Firm also has a West Coast office staffed by Michael Bourret & Erin Young (e-mail queries only).
Titles recently placed: *100 Days*, Nicole McInnes; *Adnan's Story*, Rabia Chaudry; *All Better Now*, Emily Wing Smith; *As I Descended*, Robin Talley; *Bad Boy*, Elliot Wake; *Cooking Solo*, Klancy Miller; *Epitaph*, Mary Doria Russell; *Essential Oils for Healing*, Vannoy Gentles Fite; *Fat Boy vs the Cheerleaders*, Geoff Herbach; *Filthy Rich*, Raine Miller; *Good as Gone*, Amy Gentry; *If I Stay*, Gayle Forman; *In a French Kitchen*, Susan Loomis; *Inspector of the Dead*, David Morrell; *Invisible Man, Got the Whole World Watching*, Mychal Denzel Smith; *Irena's Children*, Tilar Mazzeo; *It Ends With Us*, Colleen Hoover; *Junk*, Allison Stewart; *Making It Right*, Catherine Bybee; *Miranda and Caliban*, Jacqueline Carey; *My Sweet Angel*, John Glatt; *Smashed, Mashed, Boiled & Baked*, Raghavan Iyer; *Strange Glow*, Timothy J Jorgensen; *The All-Star Antes Up*, Nancy Herkness; *The Duration*, Dave Fromm; *The Glittering Court*, Richelle Mead; *The Leper Spy*, Ben Montgomery; *The One Real Thing*, Samantha Young; *The Remedy*, Suzanne Young; *The Remember Balloons*, Jessie Oliveros; *The Seasoned Life*, Ayesha Curry; *The Storyteller*, Aaron Starmer; *The Thunder Beneath Us*, Nicole Blades; *The Ugly Dumpling*, Stephanie Campisi; *The Valley*, Helen Bryan; *The Vanilla Bean Baking Book*, Sarah Kieffer; *The World From Up Here*, Cecilia Galante; *Trusting You and Other Lies*, Nicole Williams; *Until Friday Night*, Abbi Glines; *Up in Flames*, Abbi Glines; *Vegetarian India*, Madhur Jaffrey; *Zeroboxer*, Fonda Lee
Foreign Rep(s): Ali (Italy); ANAW (Poland); Agence Litteraire Eliane Benisti (France); Big Apple Agency Inc (China); EAJ (Japan); International Editors' Co (Latin America, Spain); Kayi Literary (Turkey); Mohrbooks (Germany); Andrew Nurnberg (Eastern Europe); Read 'n' Right (Greece); Agencia Riff (Brazil); Sebes & Bisseling Literary Agency (Netherlands); Abner Stein Agency (UK); TBPAI (Israel); Ulf Toregard Agency (Scandinavia); Tuttle-Mori Agency Inc (Thailand); Eric Yang Agency (Korea)

Anne Edelstein Literary Agency LLC (L)
404 Riverside Dr, New York, NY 10025
Tel: 212-414-4923
E-mail: info@aeliterary.com; rights@aeliterary.com
Web Site: www.aeliterary.com
Key Personnel
Pres: Anne Edelstein (AAR)
Literary Asst: Sarah Cohen
Founded: 1990
Literary fiction & narrative nonfiction (including memoir, history, psychology, religion & culinary); handle film & TV rights; agents in all principal foreign countries.
No unsol mss.
Foreign Rights: AM Heath (Victoria Hobbs) (UK); Anatolia Lit (Turkey); L'Autre Agence (Corinne Marotte) (France); Silvia Bastos Agencia Literaria SL (Pau Centellas) (Spain); Petra Eggers Agency (Petra Eggers) (Germany); The English Agency (Japan); The Grayhawk Agency (China, Taiwan); The Harris Agency (Efrat Lev) (Israel); Danny Hong Agency (Danny Hong) (Korea); The Italian Literary Agency srl (Italy); Prava i prevodi (Eastern Europe); Sebes & Bisseling (Holland, Scandinavia); The Van Lear Agency (Russia); Villas-Boas & Moss Literary Agency (Brazil)
Membership(s): The Authors Guild

Educational Design Services LLC (L)
5750 Bou Ave, Suite 1508, North Bethesda, MD 20852
Tel: 301-881-8611
Web Site: www.educationaldesignservices.com
Key Personnel
Pres: Bertram L Linder *E-mail:* blinder@educationaldesignservices.com
Founded: 1981
Materials for the el-hi & professional education market. Accept unsol mss with SASE, prefer query by e-submission first. Submit outline & sample chapter. No reading fee.
Titles recently placed: *Better Writing*, Travis Koll; *Bully Nation*, Susan Eva Porter; *Fire Up Your Life in Retirement*, Catherine DePino; *Individualized Learning with Technology*, Chris Bernat, Richard J Mueller; *Making a Difference in the Classroom*, Charlese E Brown; *Standardized Testing Skills*, Guinevere Durham; *Success in Schools*, Susan Andres, Felicity Pines; *The Teachers' Lounge (Uncensored)*, Kelly Flynn

The Lisa Ekus Group LLC (L)
57 North St, Hatfield, MA 01038
Tel: 413-247-9325 *Fax:* 413-247-9873
E-mail: info@lisaekus.com
Web Site: lisaekus.com
Key Personnel
Principal & Pres: Lisa Ekus (AAR) *E-mail:* lisaekus@lisaekus.com
Mgr & Literary Assoc: Sally Ekus *E-mail:* sally@lisaekus.com
Founded: 1982
Since our inception in 1982, we have been helping both new & established authors & chefs make their mark on the culinary landscape. All of our nationally recognized culinary promotions are built on the same foundation: to create innovative strategies, pay meticulous attention to client needs & effectively & productively network across the culinary, media & publishing industries.
In 2000 we expanded our award-winning expertise to include author representation & literary agent services. Within 8 years, our literary agency facilitated more than 150 book deals, representing over 90 authors & numerous leading publishers internationally.
We offer comprehensive media training programs designed for authors, chefs, spokespeople, show hosts & food professionals & orchestrate creative partnerships between individuals & corporations in the culinary industry. Specialty areas include: food, nutrition, health & wine & spirit.
Accept unsol mss. Submissions should be in the form of a complete proposal & we provide detailed guidelines on our web site. No fees, clients are billed for expenses.
Titles recently placed: *Gluten-Free Cooking for Two: 125 Favorites*, Carol Fenster; *How to Eat a Lobster and Other Edible Enigmas Explained*, Ashley Blom; *PNW Veg: 100 Vegetable Recipes Inspired by the Local Bounty of the Pacific Northwest*, Kim O'Donnel; *Recipes from the Herbalist's Kitchen: Delicious, Nourishing Food for Lifelong Health and Well-Being*, Brittany Wood Nickerson; *Sweet, Savory, and Free: Insanely Delicious Plant-Based Recipes without Any of the Top 8 Food Allergens*, Debbie Adler; *The Healthy Meal Prep Cookbook: Easy and Wholesome Meals to Cook, Prep, Grab, and Go*, Toby Amidor; *The Migraine Relief Plan: An 8-Week Transition to Better Eating, Fewer Headaches, and Optimal Health*, Stephanie Weaver; *The Ultimate Vegan Cookbook for Your Instant Pot: 80 Easy and Delicious Plant-Based Recipes That You Can Make in Half the Time*, Kathy Hester; *The Wellness Project: How I Learned to Do Right by My Body, Without Giving Up My Life*, Phoebe Lapine; *Weeknight Paleo: 100+ Easy and Delicious Family-Friendly Meals*, Julie

Mayfield, Charles Mayfield; *Welcome to the Farm: How-to Wisdom from The Elliott Homestead*, Shaye Elliott
Foreign Rights: The Jean V Naggar Literary Agency
Membership(s): International Association of Culinary Professionals; Women Presidents' Organization

Ethan Ellenberg Literary Agency (L)
155 Suffolk St, Suite 2R, New York, NY 10002
Tel: 212-431-4554
E-mail: agent@ethanellenberg.com
Web Site: www.ethanellenberg.com
Key Personnel
Pres & Agent: Ethan Ellenberg (AAR)
Agent: Evan Gregory (AAR)
Off Mgr & Subs Rts Assoc: BiBi Lewis
Founded: 1984
Commercial & literary fiction & nonfiction. Fiction: specialize in science fiction, fantasy, romance & all women's fiction. Suspense, thriller, mystery, first novels, all children's books including new adult & middle grade. Nonfiction: narrative nonfiction, history, adventure, science. Accepting new clients, both published & unpublished. No reading fees; accept unsol submissions with SASE. E-mail submissions without attachments accepted, but prefer submissions by mail. For fiction: first 3 chapters, synopsis & SASE. For nonfiction: proposal, including outline & author bio, sample chapters, if available. Co-agents in Hollywood & all principal foreign countries.
Titles recently placed: *Alphaville (series)*, Christine Warren; *Andromedan Dark (series)*, Ian Douglas; *At the Table of Wolves*, Kay Kenyon; *Bulldozer Helps Out*, Candace Fleming; *Danger Sweetheart*, MaryJanice Davidson; *Dangerous Grounds*, Sharon Shinn; *Deja Who*, MaryJanice Davidson; *Dreaming of Antigone*, Robin Bridges; *Frontlines (series)*, Marko Kloos; *Java Jive (series)*, Caroline Fardig; *Jennifer Wilde Estate*, Jennifer Wilde; *Life After Coffee*, Virginia Franken; *Rocked by Love*, Christine Warren; *Sam Sorts*, Marthe Jocelyn; *Shadow of Empire*, Jay Allan; *The Falcon Throne*, Karen Miller; *The Oncoming Storm*, Christopher Nuttall; *The Undoing*, Shelly Laurenston; *Twelve Book Deal with Tor*, John Scalzi; *Twilight Dreams*, Amanda Ashley; *Undead and Done*, MaryJanice Davidson; *Under a Blood Red Sun*, John Domagalski
Foreign Rights: Agence Litteraire Eliane Benisti (France); Berla & Griffini (Italy); Big Apple Agency Inc (China); Book Publishers Association of Israel (Israel); BookCosmos Agency (Korea); The English Agency (Japan); Alexander Korzhenevski Agency (Russia); Mo Literary Agency (Holland); Prava i prevodi (Eastern Europe); RDC Agencia Literaria SL (Spain); Thomas Schlueck GmbH (Germany)
Membership(s): The Authors Guild; Authors Registry; Mystery Writers of America; Romance Writers of America; Science Fiction & Fantasy Writers of America; Society of Children's Book Writers & Illustrators

Nicholas Ellison Agency (L)
469 W 147 St, Apt 1, New York, NY 10031
Web Site: www.thenicholasellisonagency.com
Key Personnel
Pres: Nicholas Ellison
Founded: 1932
Fiction & narrative nonfiction (all subjects). No children's or science fiction. No unsol mss, query first. Submit sample chapters. Include a cover letter & brief synopsis of first 20 pages of mss. Handle film & TV rights. Fees charged for photocopying & books ordered. Agents in principal foreign countries.

Felicia Eth Literary Representation (L)
555 Bryant St, Suite 350, Palo Alto, CA 94301
Tel: 415-970-9717
E-mail: feliciaeth.literary@gmail.com
Web Site: www.ethliterary.com
Key Personnel
Pres: Felicia Eth (AAR)
Founded: 1989
Diverse nonfiction including narrative, psychology, health & popular science; including women's issues, investigative journalism & biography. Selective mainstream literary fiction. No unsol mss, query first for fiction, proposal for nonfiction. No discs, no files by e-mail. Handle film & TV rights for clients, books only through sub-agents in LA. No reading fee. Xeroxing costs & overseas mail, FedEx charged to client, $75 for full-length ms to cover mailing. Commission is 15% domestic & 20% foreign. Foreign rights agents in all major territories.
Titles recently placed: *Citizen Kane - A Filmmaker's Journey*, Harlan Lebo; *Fastest Things on Wings*, Terry Masear; *Tales of Alpine Obsession*, Daniel Arnold; *The Collapse of Parenting*, Leonard Sax; *The Memory Thief*, Emily Coin

Mary Evans Inc (L)
242 E Fifth St, New York, NY 10003-8501
Tel: 212-979-0880 *Fax:* 212-979-5344
E-mail: info@maryevansinc.com
Web Site: www.maryevansinc.com
Key Personnel
Pres: Mary Evans (AAR)
VP: Julia Kardon (AAR)
Literary fiction, narrative nonfiction, commercial fiction, self-help, science & history, graphic novels & memoirs. Nonfiction should be submitted in proposal form & fiction with a query letter, a synopsis & 3 sample chapters, SASE required. Accept unsol mss. Handle film & TV rights, no reading fee.
Foreign Rights: Akcali Copyright Agency (Ozgur Emir) (Turkey); Berla and Griffini Rights Agency (Erica Berla) (Italy); The Book Publishers Association of Israel (Dalia Ever-Hadani) (Israel); Chandler Crawford Agency (Holland); The Grayhawk Agency (Gray Tan) (China, Taiwan); International Editors (Maru de Montserrat) (Portugal, Spain); LEX Copyright Office (Norbert Uzseka) (Hungary); Licht & Burr (Trine Licht) (Scandinavia); Liepman Agency (Mark Koralnik) (Germany); La Nouvelle Agence (Michele Kanonidis) (France); Andrew Nurnberg Associates (Ludmilla Sushkova) (Russia); Owls Agency Inc (Mario Tauchi) (Japan); Prava i prevodi (Ana Milenkovic) (Eastern Europe, Greece); Riff Agency (Lauri Riff) (Brazil); Eric Yang Agency (Henry Shin) (Korea)

Feigenbaum Publishing Consultants Inc (L)
61 Bounty Lane, Jericho, NY 11753
Tel: 516-647-8314 (cell)
Key Personnel
Pres: Laurie Feigenbaum
E-mail: lauriefeigenbaum@gmail.com
Founded: 1991
Contract negotiations & review, agenting, trademark & copyright registration, permissions clearance & general publishing advice. Expertise in book publishing & electronic publishing. No unsol mss, query first. Hourly fee or commission. Contracts negotiation, $95 per hour for contracts review, negotiation, trademark & copyright registration & permissions.

Robert L Fenton (L)
Affiliate of Fenton Entertainment Group Inc
PO Box 300885, Waterford, MI 48330
Tel: 248-855-8780
Founded: 1984
Specialize in nonfiction, fiction, women's fiction, historical romances, action & suspense; limited poetry, children's photographic books. Handle film & TV scripts. No unsol mss, preliminary letter or telephone call first. Submit outline & sample chapters. Reading fee: $350. Frequently charge an additional retainer along with a percentage if there is an agreement of representation. Extensive experience in all areas of publishing, film & TV. Producer at Universal Studios & 20th Century Fox; produced several feature films & Movies of the Week; published three best selling novels; Literary Guild, Doubleday Book-of-the-Month. Founded 1960. Writer's Workshop on Holland America Cruise Lines, Adjunct Professor, Creative Writing at Marygrove College, Detroit, MI; Writer's Digest Presents; The RLF Writer's Workshop on cruise lines, 2000; 1999 Guest Lecturer, Entertainment Law Seminar, University of MI Law School, April 1998. Mr Fenton prefers English but has limited working knowledge of French, Spanish, German & Russian. Will only represent seven or eight new writers each year. There is a waiting list.

FinePrint Literary Management (L)
207 W 106 St, Suite 1D, New York, NY 10025
Tel: 212-279-6214
E-mail: assist@fineprint.com
Web Site: www.fineprintlit.com
Key Personnel
CEO: Peter Rubie (AAR) *E-mail:* peter@fineprintlit.com
In-House Subs Rts Dir: Jacqueline Murphy *E-mail:* jacqueline@fineprintlit.com
Agent: Lauren Bieker *Tel:* 212-279-1412 *E-mail:* lauren@fineprintlit.com; June Clark *E-mail:* june@fineprintlit.com; Laura Wood (AAR) *E-mail:* laura@fineprintlit.com
Founded: 2007 (formed by the merger of the Peter Rubie Agency & the Imprint Agency)
High quality fiction & nonfiction. Handle film, TV & foreign rights through sub-agents. No unsol mss, query first. Submit outline & first two chapters with one page query letter & proposal. No reading fees. Photocopying fees. Some foreign mailing charges. Please send queries to the appropriate e-mail for the agent you wish to query.
Titles recently placed: *30 Days a Black Man*, Bill Steigerwald; *A Secret History of Witches*, Louisa Morgan (aka Louise Marley); *Ants Among Elephants*, Sujatha Gidla; *Apprenticed to Venus*, Tristine Rainer; *August Snow*, Stephen M Jones; *Ayurveda Lifestyle Medicine*, Acharya Shunya; *Charlie Henry: Rob Thy Neighbor*, David Thurlo; *Chest of Bone*, Vicki Stiefel; *Dangers of Dating a Rebound Vampire*, Molly Harper White; *Death is a Bargain*, Noreen Smith; *Donny's Inferno*, P W Catanese; *Dreamland*, Sam Quinones; *Eccentrics, Mavericks, and Outsiders at War*, Jason Ridler; *Evolution Underground*, Anthony J Martin; *Fizzopolis*, Patrick Carman; *Floors*, Patrick Carman; *Graphene*, Les Johnson; *Grim Expectations*, K W Jeter; *Hummus and Homicide*, Tina Kashian; *Jane on the Brain*, Wendy S Jones; *Mask of the Sun*, John Dvorak; *Napoleon III: The Last Emperor of France*, Alan Straus-Schom; *Red Sky*, Chris Goff; *Signal*, Patrick Lee; *The Divided City*, Luke McCallin; *The End of Breast Cancer*, Kathleen Ruddy; *The Equity Culture*, B Mark Smith; *The First Circumnavigators: Unsung Heroes of the Age of Discovery*, Harry Kelsey; *The Invasive*, Michael Hodges; *The Runner Up Presidency*, Mark Weston; *Undercover Warrior*, Aimee Thurlo, David Thurlo; *Wonderlandscape*, John Clayton
Foreign Rep(s): Lorella Belli (UK); The Book Publishers' Association of Israel (Israel); Donatella d'Ormesson (France); The English Agency (Japan); Grayhawk Agency (China,

Taiwan); International Editors (Latin America, Spain); Japan Uni Agency (Japan); Nurcihan Kesim (Turkey); Lennart Sane Agency AB (Scandinavia); Lex Copywright Agency (Hungary); Maxima Creative Agency (Indonesia); PNLA (Italy); Prava i prevodi (Eastern Europe); Agencia Literaria Riff (Brazil); Thomas Schlueck GmbH (Germany); Tuttle-Mori Agency Inc (Malaysia, Thailand, Vietnam); Eric Yang Agency (Korea)

The Fischer-Harbage Agency Inc (L)
540 President St, 3rd fl, Brooklyn, NY 11215
Tel: 212-695-7105
E-mail: info@fischerharbage.com
Web Site: www.fischerharbage.com
Key Personnel
Pres: Ryan Fischer-Harbage
Assoc Agent: Christopher Hermelin
Founded: 2007
Full service boutique literary agency specializing in fiction, memoir, narrative nonfiction & current events. No unsol mss, query first with a short description, bio & first chapter of your book in the body of an e-mail to submissions@fischerharbage.com. No fees, standard commission paid.
Titles recently placed: *A Crash of Rhinos: and other wild animal groups*, Greg Danylyshyn, Stephan Lomp; *American Spies: Modern Surveillance, Why You Should Care, and What to Do About It*, Jennifer Granick; *Contrary Motion: A Novel*, Andy Mozina; *Forever Painless: End Chronic Pain and Reclaim Your Life in 30 Minutes a Day*, Miranda Esmonde-White; *Liar: A Memoir*, Rob Roberge; *Literary Starbucks: Fresh-Brewed, Half-Caf, No-Whip Bookish Humor*, Nora Katz, Wilson Josephson, Jill Poskanzer; *Lord of the Swallows: A Malko Linge Novel*, Gérard de Villiers; *Raising an Entrepreneur: 10 Rules for Nurturing Risk Takers, Problem Solvers, and Changemakers*, Margot Machol Bisnow; *Surface to Air: A Malko Linge Novel*, Gérard de Villiers; *Surpassing Certainty: What My Twenties Taught Me*, Janet Mock; *Testimony*, Robbie Robertson
Foreign Rights: Linda Biagi Rights Management (worldwide)

Flannery Literary (L)
1140 Wickfield Ct, Naperville, IL 60563
Web Site: flanneryliterary.com
Key Personnel
Owner: Jennifer Flannery *E-mail:* jennifer@flanneryliterary.com
Founded: 1992
Represents authors of books written for children & young adults. No unsol mss, query first via e-mail. No snail mail or phone queries. No fees.
Membership(s): ABA; ALA; Chicago Women in Publishing; International Literacy Association; National Council of Teachers of English; Society of Children's Book Writers & Illustrators

Peter Fleming Agency (L)
PO Box 458, Pacific Palisades, CA 90272
Tel: 310-454-1373
E-mail: peterfleming@earthlink.net
Key Personnel
Pres: Peter Fleming
Nonfiction: that rare expertise so vital in America that nonbook readers will buy it, read it! Includes populist, contrarian, dissent, suppressed information overlooked or avoided by mainstream media (ex: corporate/political crimes). Interested in authors with strong platforms, web sites, blogs & seminar experience. No unsol mss, query first with SASE. Submit outline. No reading fee. Clients billed for major postage, FedEx, foreign communication & other pre-approved expenses.

Sheldon Fogelman Agency Inc (L)
420 E 72 St, New York, NY 10021
Tel: 212-532-7250 *Fax:* 212-685-8939
E-mail: info@sheldonfogelmanagency.com
Web Site: sheldonfogelmanagency.com
Key Personnel
Pres & Literary Agent: Sheldon Fogelman
Asst Agent/Foreign Rts Mgr: Janine Hauber
Asst Agent: Amy Stern
Founded: 1975
Juvenile trade books of all types. Handle all rights, including film, TV, & foreign. Query with full picture book mss or first chapters & synopsis of novel. E-mail only. Include publishing history. No reading fee.

The Foley Literary Agency (L)
34 E 38 St, Suite 1B, New York, NY 10016
Tel: 212-686-6930
Key Personnel
Partner: Joan Foley
Founded: 1961
Fiction & nonfiction books. No unsol mss, query first with SASE & brief outline. No reading fee. 10% sales commission, 15% foreign rights fees. Rare but occasional fees for phone, mail or copying. ICM handles film & TV rights. Agents in all major European countries.

Folio Literary Management (L)
The Film Center Bldg, 630 Ninth Ave, Suite 1101, New York, NY 10036
Tel: 212-400-1494 *Fax:* 212-967-0977
Web Site: www.foliolit.com
Key Personnel
Founding Partner: Scott Hoffman; Jeff Kleinman (AAR)
Partner: Claudia Cross (AAR)
SVP, Dir, Opers & Agent: Frank Weimann
SVP & Agent: Erin Niumata; Steve Troha (AAR); Emily van Beek
Agent & Dir, Folio Unbound: Annie Hwang
Dir, Intl Rts & Agent: Melissa White
Contracts Mgr & Agent: Michael Harriot
Agent: Jamie Chambliss; John Cusick; Dado Derviskadic; Erin Harris; Katherine Latshaw; Marcy Posner; Jeff Silberman (AAR)
Literary & Dramatic Rts Agent: Ruth Pomerance
Founded: 2006
A full service literary agency with co-agents around the world. No unsol mss, query first via e-mail. No fees.
Titles recently placed: *10-Day Green Smoothie Cleanse*, J J Smith; *A Psalm for Lost Girls*, Katie Bayerl; *Anchor & Sophia*, Tommy Wallach; *But Enough About Me*, Burt Reynolds; *Deep Nutrition*, Dr Cate Shanahan; *Ginny Moon*, Benjamin Ludwig; *Girls on the Verge*, Sharon Biggs Waller; *Hustle*, Neal Patel, Patrick Vlaskovits, Jonas Koffler; *I'm Judging You*, Luvvie Ajay; *Jackie's Girl*, Kathy McKeon; *Maybe a Mermaid*, Josephine Cameron; *Only Child*, Rhiannon Navin; *Saints and Misfits*, S K Ali; *Seven Deadly Shadows*, Courtney Alameda, Valynne Maetani; *The Ballerina Body*, Misty Copeland; *The Grown-Up's Guide to Teenage Humans*, Josh Shipp; *The Marsh King's Daughter*, Karen Dionne; *The Pieces of Piper Perish*, Kayla Cagan; *The Reminders*, Val Emmich; *The River at Night*, Erica Ferencik; *The Seven Torments of Amy and Craig*, Don Zolidis; *The Wellness Mama Cookbook*, Katie Spears; *Tia and Tamera Mowry*, Twintuition; *Wallis in Love*, Andrew Morton; *Warren Buffett's Ground Rules*, Jeremy Miller; *Where the Light Gets In*, Kimberly Williams-Paisley
Foreign Rights: Berla & Griffini (Italy); The Book Publishers Association of Israel (Israel); Catherine Fragou (Greece); Graal Literary Agency (Poland); The Grayhawk Agency (China, Taiwan); Danny Hong Agency (Korea); IECO (Portugal); Asli Karasuil Telif Haklari (Turkey); Michelle Lapautre Agency (France); Maxima Creative Agency (Indonesia); Prava i prevodi (Czech Republic, Russia, Serbia); Riff Agency (Brazil); Thomas Schlueck GmbH (Germany); Marianne Schoenbach Literary Agency (Netherlands); Livia Stoia Literary Agency (Romania); Ulf Toregard Agency (Scandinavia); Tuttle-Mori Agency Inc (Japan, Thailand, Vietnam); Susanna Zevi Agenzia Letteraria (Italy)

Fort Ross Inc - International Representation for Artists (L)
Division of Fort Ross Inc
26 Arthur Place, Yonkers, NY 10701
Tel: 914-375-6448
Web Site: www.fortrossinc.com
Key Personnel
Pres & Exec Dir: Dr Vladimir P Kartsev *E-mail:* vkartsev2000@gmail.com
Founded: 1992
Fiction: romance, mysteries, science fiction, fantasy, adventure. Provide American publishers with illustrations from Russia. Find European publishers for American book authors & illustrators. No unsol mss, query first.
Foreign Rep(s): Nova Littera (Baltic States, Belarus, Russia, Ukraine)

Lynn C Franklin Associates Ltd (L)
1350 Broadway, Suite 2015, New York, NY 10018
Tel: 212-868-6311 *Fax:* 212-868-6312
E-mail: agency@franklinandsiegal.com
Key Personnel
Pres & Agent: Lynn C Franklin (AAR)
Rts Mgr: Claudia Nys
Adult commercial & literary fiction; middle grade & young adult fiction; & general nonfiction with special interest in self-help, health, psychology, personal growth & biographies, as well as current international affairs. No unsol mss, query e-mail (no attachments). No reading fee. Representatives in Hollywood & in all major foreign countries. Handle film & TV rights.
Titles recently placed: *The Book of Forgiving: The Four-Fold Path of Healing for Ourselves and Our World*, Desmond M Tutu, Mpho A Tutu; *The Customer Rules: The 39 Essential Rules for Delivering Sensational Service*, Lee Cockerell; *The Wahls Protocol*, Terry Wahls, MD, Eve Adamson
Foreign Rights: ACER Agencia Literaria (Elizabeth Atkins) (Portugal, Spain, Spanish Latin America); Eliane Benisti Literary Agency (France); Book Publishers Association of Israel (Israel); Chinese Connection Agency (China, Taiwan); Mary Clemmey Literary Agency (Mary Clemmey) (Australia, New Zealand, UK); The English Agency (Japan) Ltd (Japan); Fritz Agency (Germany); Graal Literary Agency (Poland); Berla e Griffini (Erica Berla) (Italy); Katai & Bolza (Hungary); Simona Kessler International Copyright Agency (Romania); Maxima Creative (Indonesia); Andrew Nurnberg Associates (Russia); Kristin Olson (Czech Republic); Prava i prevodi (Bulgaria, Croatia, Montenegro, Serbia, Slovenia); Read n' Right Agency (Greece); Agencia Riff (Brazil); Lennart Sane Agency (Netherlands, Scandinavia); Eric Yang Agency (Korea)

Jeanne Fredericks Literary Agency Inc (L)
221 Benedict Hill Rd, New Canaan, CT 06840
Tel: 203-972-3011 *Fax:* 203-972-3011
E-mail: jeanne.fredericks@gmail.com (no unsol attachments)
Web Site: jeannefredericks.com
Key Personnel
Pres: Jeanne Fredericks (AAR)
Founded: 1997 (purchased assets of Susan P Urstadt Inc in May 1997)

Adult nonfiction only, especially practical popular reference, health & medical, gardening, business, travel, practical how-to, biography, antiques & decorative arts, sports, natural history, cookbooks, women's issues, history. No unsol mss, query first by e-mail or by mail with SASE. If requested, submit proposal, author biography (including previous publishing history), detailed outline & sample chapters by e-mail or by mail with SASE. Do not require signature for delivery. Handle film & TV rights with co-agent. No reading fee.
Titles recently placed: *Behind the Therapy Door: Simple Strategies to Transform Your Life*, Dr Randy Kamen; *Chefs & Company*, Maria Isabella; *Colorful Landscaping in Drought, Desert & Dry Times*, Maureen Gilmer; *For Sale - American Paradise*, Willie Drye; *Herb Gardening: How to Prepare Soil, Choose Your Plants, and Care For, Harvest and Use Your Herbs*, Melissa Snyder; *Propel to Quality Healthcare: Six Steps to Improve Patient Care, Staff Engagement, and the Bottom Line*, Tom Muha; *Stonewall Jackson's Little Sorrel*, Sharon Smith; *The Greenhouse Gardener's Manual*, Roger Marshall; *The New England Catch*, Martha Murphy; *Yoga Nidra for Stress Relief*, Julie Lusk; *Yoga Therapy*, Eden Goldman, DC, Terra Gold, DOM, Larry Payne, PhD
Foreign Rep(s): Books Crossing Borders (worldwide)
Membership(s): The Authors Guild

Robert A Freedman Dramatic Agency Inc (D)
1501 Broadway, Suite 2310, New York, NY 10036
Tel: 212-840-5760 *Fax:* 212-840-5776
Key Personnel
Pres: Robert A Freedman (AAR)
E-mail: rfreedmanagent@aol.com
SVP: Marta Praeger (AAR)
Agent: Samara Anderson
Founded: 1928 (as Harold Freedman Brandt & Brandt Dramatic Department Inc, until 1981)
Dramatic scripts for stage, motion picture & TV. No unsol mss, query first. No reading fee. Material placed for production/publication is subject to 10% commission. Agents in all European countries. Will co-agent with literary agents to handle film rights & books.

Samuel French Inc (D)
235 Park Ave S, 5th fl, New York, NY 10003
Tel: 212-206-8990 *Toll Free Tel:* 866-598-8449 *Fax:* 212-206-1429
E-mail: info@samuelfrench.com
Web Site: www.samuelfrench.com
Key Personnel
Pres: Nate Collins *E-mail:* ncollins@samuelfrench.com
VP & Dir, Opers: Kenneth Dingledine
E-mail: kdingledine@samuelfrench.com
Literary Dir: Amy Rose Marsh *E-mail:* amarsh@samuelfrench.com
Founded: 1830
Plays for publication & agency representation. Accept unsol mss, standard US play form. No reading fee. Handle film & TV rights for published works only. Send $4 for guidelines (recommended mss format).
Branch Office(s)
Samuel French Bookshop, 7623 Sunset Blvd, Hollywood, CA 90046
Foreign Office(s): Samuel French Ltd, 52 Fitzroy St, London W1T 5JR, United Kingdom, Opers Dir: David Webster *Tel:* (020) 7387 9373 *Fax:* (020) 7387 2161 *E-mail:* theatre@samuelfrench-london.co.uk *Web Site:* www.samuelfrench-london.co.uk

Sarah Jane Freymann Literary Agency LLC (L)
59 W 71 St, Suite 9-B, New York, NY 10023
Tel: 212-362-9277
E-mail: submissions@sarahjanefreymann.com
Web Site: www.sarahjanefreymann.com
Key Personnel
Owner & Agent: Sarah Jane Freymann
E-mail: sarah@sarahjanefreymann.com
Assoc: Katharine Sands *Tel:* 212-751-8892; Steven Schwartz *Tel:* 212-362-1998 *E-mail:* steve@sarahjanefreymann.com; Jessica Sinsheimer *E-mail:* jessica@sarahjanefreymann.com
Founded: 1974
Represents book-length fiction & general nonfiction. Fiction: popular fiction plus quality mainstream, literary fiction & young adult. Nonfiction: spiritual/inspirational, psychology, self-help; women's/men's issues; health (conventional & alternative); cookbooks; narrative nonfiction, natural science, nature, memoirs, biography; current events, multicultural issues, popular culture; illustrated books, lifestyle, garden, design, architecture, humor, sports, travel & business. No unsol mss, query first with SASE. Handle film & TV rights with subagents. Representation in all foreign markets. No reading fee.
Titles recently placed: *Falling Under*, Gwen Hayes

Fredrica S Friedman & Co Inc (L)
136 E 57 St, 14th fl, New York, NY 10022
Tel: 212-829-9600 *Fax:* 212-829-9669
E-mail: info@fredricafriedman.com; submissions@fredricafriedman.com
Web Site: www.fredricafriedman.com
Key Personnel
Pres: Fredrica S Friedman
Founded: 2000
Literary management firm that represents best selling & award-winning authors. General nonfiction & fiction. No poetry, plays, screenplays, children's picture books, science fiction/fantasy or horror. No unsol mss-query first. Send all queries by e-mail, no attachments. See web site for detailed submission information. Hard copy materials will not be returned; no fees.
Foreign Rep(s): Georges Borchardt Inc
Foreign Rights: Georges Borchardt Inc

Candice Fuhrman Literary Agency (L)
10 Cypress Hollow Dr, Tiburon, CA 94920
Tel: 415-383-1014
E-mail: fuhrmancandice@gmail.com
Key Personnel
Pres & Owner: Candice Fuhrman
Nonfiction: health, memoir, psychology, women's issues, how-to & self-help; literary & commercial fiction. No unsol mss.
Currently not accepting new clients.
Foreign Rights: Jenny Meyer Literary Agency

The Garamond Agency Inc (L)
12 Horton St, Newburyport, MA 01950
E-mail: query@garamondagency.com
Web Site: www.garamondagency.com
Key Personnel
Dir: Lisa Adams; David Miller
Adult nonfiction, all subjects. No unsol mss, query by e-mail first. Submit cover letter, outline, synopsis, author bio & SASE. No reading fees. Handle TV & movie rights.
Foreign Rights: AnatoliaLit Agency (Turkey); Bardon-Chinese Media Agency (China, Taiwan); Berla & Griffini Rights Agency (Italy); Raquel de la Concha Agencia Literaria (Portugal, Spain); Graal Literary Agency (Poland); Anna Jarota Agency (France); Katai & Bolza Literary Agents (Hungary); Duran Kim Agency (Korea); Mo Literary Services (Netherlands, Scandinavia); Mohrbooks (Germany); Andrew Nurnberg Association Sofia (Bulgaria); Andrew Nurnberg Literary Agency (Russia & former USSR); The Riff Agency (Brazil); Agentia Literara Sun (Romania); Tuttle-Mori Agency Inc (Japan)
Membership(s): The Authors Guild

Max Gartenberg Literary Agency (L)
912 N Pennsylvania Ave, Yardley, PA 19067
Tel: 215-295-9230
Web Site: www.maxgartenberg.com
Key Personnel
Agent: Anne G Devlin *E-mail:* agdevlin@aol.com
Founded: 1954
Children & adult nonfiction books. No unsol mss, query first. Submit formal book proposal, outline & sample as requested. No reading fee. Handle film & TV rights. Agents in all principal foreign markets.
Titles recently placed: *Beethovan for Kids: His Life and Music*, Helen Bauer; *Everything a New Elementary School Teacher REALLY Needs to Know*, Otis Kreigel; *Gangsters to Governors*, David Clary; *Starved*, Anne McTiernan; *Step Into Reading: Penguins!*, David Salomon; *The Enlightened College Applicant*, Andrew Belasco, Dave Bergman; *The New Senior Man*, Thelma Reese, Barbara Fleisher; *What to Believe When You're Expecting*, Jonathan Schaffir
Foreign Rights: International Editors' Co (Argentina); Mohrbooks AG, Literary Agency (Switzerland); La Nouvelle Agence (France); Pollinger Ltd (UK); Lennart Sane (Sweden); Tuttle-Mori Agency Inc (Japan)

Gelfman Schneider/ICM Partners (L)
Affiliate of John Farquharson Ltd
850 Seventh Ave, Suite 903, New York, NY 10019
Tel: 212-245-1993 *Fax:* 212-245-8678
E-mail: mail@gelfmanschneider.com
Web Site: gelfmanschneider.com
Key Personnel
Contact: Jane Gelfman (AAR); Deborah Schneider (AAR)
General trade fiction & nonfiction. Queries by mail only, no e-mail queries will be considered. No unsol mss, query first with SASE. Submit sample chapters & outline. Handle film & TV rights. No reading fee.
Foreign Rights: Curtis Brown Ltd (translation, UK)
Membership(s): The Authors Guild; Authors Registry

The Gersh Agency (TGA) (L-D)
41 Madison Ave, 33rd fl, New York, NY 10010
Tel: 212-997-1818
Web Site: gershbooks.com
Key Personnel
Partner & Head of Books Dept: J Joseph Veltre, III
Agent: Allison Cohen *E-mail:* acohen@gersh.com
Books Dept Coord: Alice Lawson
Founded: 2007 (1949 as talent agency)
Fiction, nonfiction, adult & juvenile, film & TV rights & plays. No unsol mss. Unsol materials will not be accepted or considered. No online submission unless requested. No reading fee.
Branch Office(s)
9465 Wilshire Blvd, Suite 600, Beverly Hills, CA 90212 (talent div) *Tel:* 310-274-6611

GGP Publishing Inc (L)
105 Calvert St, Suite 201, Harrison, NY 10528-3138
Tel: 914-834-8896 *Fax:* 914-834-7566
Web Site: www.GGPPublishing.com
Key Personnel
Pres & Publg Dir: Generosa Gina Protano
E-mail: GGProtano@GGPPublishing.com
Founded: 1991
Fiction & nonfiction; educational materials, English & foreign languages. Handle film & TV

rights. No unsol mss, query first. Reading fees on all submissions, refundable from commission; fee charged for photocopying & postage or courier. Editorial & translation services also available.
Membership(s): American Book Producers Association

Susan Gleason (L)
325 Riverside Dr, Suite 41, New York, NY 10025
Tel: 212-662-3876 *Fax:* 212-864-3298
E-mail: sgleasonliteraryagent@gmail.com
Founded: 1992
Adult trade & mass market, fiction & nonfiction. No unsol mss, query first with SASE.
Handle film & TV rights, foreign rights. No reading fees.
Membership(s): International Women's Writing Guild

Global Lion Intellectual Property Management Inc (L-D)
Affiliate of Millennium Lion Inc
PO Box 669238, Pompano Beach, FL 33066
Tel: 754-222-6948 *Fax:* 754-222-6948
E-mail: queriesgloballionmgt@gmail.com
Web Site: www.globallionmanagement.com
Key Personnel
Pres: Peter Miller *E-mail:* peter@globallionmgt.com
Assoc: Gail Shivel *E-mail:* gailgloballionmgt@gmail.com; Zachary Yerian *E-mail:* zackgloballionmgt@gmail.com
Media Coord: Sage Gee
Represents transformational & spiritual nonfiction, young adult, commercial fiction, nonfiction, true crime & celebrity books. Handles film & TV rights. Represent literary & film properties internationally. No unsol mss, query first. Submit one page synopsis or finished treatment & author bio. See web site for additional submission guidelines. Co-agents in select foreign territories & deal directly with foreign publishers. Affiliate packages & produces feature films & TV. No fees charged.
Titles recently placed: *Creative Schools*, Sir Ken Robinson; *Cubanisms*, Pedro Menocal; *Red Wine*, Mike DeSimone, Jeff Jenssen; *Ten Prayers That Changed the World*, Jean-Pierre Isbouts; *Ten Things You Should Know About Educating Your Children*, Sir Ken Robinson; *The Essentials of the Bible*, Jean-Pierre Isbouts; *The Wonder Wall*, Peter Gamwell; *Young Leonardo*, Jean-Pierre Isbouts
Foreign Rep(s): Big Apple Agency Inc (China); Peter Bolza (Hungary); Tuttle-Mori Agency Inc (Japan)

Globo Libros Literary Agency (L)
450 E 63 St, New York, NY 10065
Web Site: www.globo-libros.com; www.publishersmarketplace.com/members/dstockwell
Key Personnel
Literary Agent: Diane Stockwell *E-mail:* diane.stockwell@globo-libros.com
Founded: 2006
Specialize in nonfiction authors from the US & abroad. Looking for compelling narrative nonfiction, current events, history, cookbooks, memoir, biography, parenting & self-help by authors of any background. We also offer book length & short translations from Spanish into English. Query by e-mail only with a detailed summary of the project & author bio in the body of the message. No attachments. No fees charged.
Titles recently placed: *Against the Inquisition*, Marcos Aguinis; *Om to Amen*, Sharon Koenig; *Slaves for Peanuts*, Jori Lewis; *There Goes the Neighborhood: How Communities Overcome Prejudice and Meet the Challenge of US Immigration*, Ali Noorani; *We Built the Wall: How the US Shuts Out Asylum Seekers*, Eileen Truax
Membership(s): The Authors Guild

Goldfarb & Associates (L-D)
721 Gibbon St, Alexandria, VA 22314
Tel: 202-466-3030 *Fax:* 703-836-5644
E-mail: rlglawlit@gmail.com
Web Site: www.ronaldgoldfarb.com
Key Personnel
Founder & Owner: Ronald L Goldfarb
Literary Agent/Off Mgr: Ms Gerrie Lipson Sturman
Literary Agent: Robbie Anna Hare
Founded: 1966
Only select new clients accepted. Fiction & serious nonfiction; no romance or science fiction. No unsol mss, query first with e-mail/letter, outline or synopsis, sample of best chapter, bio & SASE. No reading fee.
Branch Office(s)
177 Ocean Lane Dr, Suite 1101, Key Biscayne, FL 33149

Frances Goldin Literary Agency, Inc (L-D)
214 W 29 St, Suite 410, New York, NY 10001
Tel: 212-777-0047 *Fax:* 212-228-1660
E-mail: agency@goldinlit.com
Web Site: www.goldinlit.com
Key Personnel
Principal & Agent: Frances Goldin
VP & Sr Agent: Ellen Geiger (AAR); Sam Stoloff (AAR)
Sr Agent & Rts Dir: Matt McGowan (AAR) *E-mail:* mm@goldinlit.com
Assoc Agent: Caroline Eisenmann
Coun: Ria Julien
Literary Asst: Nina Cochran
Founded: 1977
No unsol mss or work previously submitted to publishers, query first with letter & SASE. No racist, sexist, agist, homophobic or pornographic material considered. Adult literary fiction & serious progressive nonfiction. Agents in Hollywood & all major foreign countries. No software. Handle film & TV rights. No reading fee.
Foreign Rep(s): Eliane Benisti (France); The English Agency (Japan) Ltd (Hamish Macaskill) (Japan); Graal Literary Agency (Maria Starz-Kanska) (Poland); David Grossman Literary Agency Ltd (David Grossman) (England, UK); International Editors' Co (Isabel Monteagudo) (Spain); International Editors' Co (Nicholas Costa) (Argentina); International Editors' Co (Flavia Sala) (Brazil); Jia-Xi Books (Gray Tan) (China, Taiwan); JLM Literary Agency (John L Moukakos) (Greece); Nurcihan Kesim Literary Agency Inc (Asli Karasuil) (Istanbul, Turkey); Ruth Liepman Agency (Ruth Weibel) (Germany); Living Literary Agency (Elfriede Pexa) (Italy); Jovan Milenkovic (Vuk Perisic) (Montenegro, Serbia); Kristin Olson Literary Agency (Kristin Olson) (Czech Republic); Pikarski Literary Agency Ltd (Gal Pikarski) (Israel); Lennart Sane Agency (Lennart Sane) (Iceland, Netherlands, Scandinavia, Sweden); Synopsis Literary Agency (Natalia Sanina) (Russia); Tuttle-Mori Agency Inc (Supanya Pratum) (Indonesia, Thailand, Vietnam); The Eric Yang Agency (Sue Yang) (Korea)

Goodman Associates (L)
500 West End Ave, New York, NY 10024
Tel: 212-873-4806
Key Personnel
Pres: Arnold P Goodman (AAR)
VP: Elise Simon Goodman
Founded: 1976
Adult book-length fiction & nonfiction. No plays, screenplays, poetry, textbooks, science fiction, children's books. No unsol mss, query first with SASE. No fees. Handle film & TV rights for clients' published materials. Representatives in Hollywood & major foreign markets. Accepting new clients by recommendation only.

Irene Goodman Literary Agency (L)
27 W 24 St, Suite 700B, New York, NY 10010
Tel: 212-604-0330
E-mail: queries@irenegoodman.com
Web Site: www.irenegoodman.com
Key Personnel
Pres: Irene Goodman (AAR) *E-mail:* irene.queries@irenegoodman.com
VP: Miriam Kriss *E-mail:* miriam.queries@irenegoodman.com; Barbara Poelle *E-mail:* barbara.queries@irenegoodman.com
Agent: Rachel Ekstrom *E-mail:* rachel.queries@irenegoodman.com; Victoria Marini (AAR) *E-mail:* victoria.queries@irenegoodman.com; Kim Perel *E-mail:* kim.queries@irenegoodman.com
Assoc Agent: Brita Lundberg *E-mail:* brita.queries@irenegoodman.com
Founded: 1978
Commercial & literary fiction & nonfiction including mysteries, romance, women's fiction, thrillers & suspense. No poetry, inspirational fiction, screenplays or children's picture books. Handle film & TV rights through Steven Fisher in Los Angeles. No unsol mss, query first with first 10 pages & synopsis via e-mail. No snail mail. See web site under submission guidelines for each agent's preferences. No reading fee.
Foreign Rep(s): Danny Baror
Foreign Rights: Baror International Agency

Doug Grad Literary Agency Inc (L)
68 Jay St, Suite W11, Brooklyn, NY 11201-1189
Tel: 718-788-6067
E-mail: query@dgliterary.com
Web Site: www.dgliterary.com
Key Personnel
Pres: Doug Grad *E-mail:* doug.grad@dgliterary.com
Founded: 2008
Commercial fiction & nonfiction in a wide variety of genres & subjects. See web site for additional information. Send cover letter only with brief description of book. Will ask to see more material if interested, via e-mail only to query@dgliterary.com. Do not send hard copies of proposals or mss. No fees.
Titles recently placed: *A Vision of Ice: Book Two of the EarthEnd Saga*, Gillian Anderson, Jeff Rovin; *Abandoned in Hell: The Fight for Vietnam's Fire Base Kate*, William Albracht, Marvin J Wolf; *Arch Enemy*, Leo Maloney; *Bounty*, Michael Byrnes; *Breaking the Ice: My Journey and Evolution through Hockey*, Pat LaFontaine, Allan Kreda; *El Guettar: America's First Victory Against the Nazi War Machine*, Leo Barron; *Igniting the American Revolution: 1773-1775*, Derek W Beck; *Lords of an Empty Land*, Randy Denmon; *Pet Friendly*, Sue Pethick; *Plantation Shudders*, Ellen Byron; *Storm's Thunder*, Brandon Boyce; *Totally Scripted: The Guide to Hollywood Idioms, Phrases, Quotes and Words That Have Changed the English Language*, Josh Chetwynd; *Where Divers Dare: The Hunt for the Last U-Boat*, Randall Peffer
Foreign Rep(s): Alice Bauer (worldwide)
Foreign Rights: Alice Bauer (worldwide)

Graham Agency (D)
115 W 45 St, Suite 505, New York, NY 10036
Tel: 212-489-7730
Key Personnel
Prop: Earl Graham
Founded: 1971
Full-length stage plays & musicals only. No unsol mss, query by mail first. Submit brief description. No reading fee, 10% commission.

Sanford J Greenburger Associates Inc (L)
55 Fifth Ave, New York, NY 10003
Tel: 212-206-5600 *Fax:* 212-463-8718
Web Site: greenburger.com; www.sjga.com
Key Personnel
Pres: Heide Lange (AAR) *E-mail:* queryhl@sjga.com
Dir, Intl Rts: Stefanie Diaz *Tel:* 221-206-5628 *E-mail:* sdiaz@greenburger.com
Dir, Intl Scouting Dept: Agnes Krup *E-mail:* akrup@sjga.com
Agent: Matt Bialer *E-mail:* querymb@sjga.com; Brenda Bowen (AAR) *E-mail:* querybb@sjga.com; Faith Hamlin (AAR) *E-mail:* fhamlin@sjga.com; Daniel Mandel *E-mail:* querydm@sjga.com; Rachel Dillon-Fried *E-mail:* rfried@sjga.com
Assoc Agent: Stephanie Delman (AAR) *E-mail:* sdelman@sjga.com; Edward Maxwell *E-mail:* emaxwell@sjga.com
Sr Scout: Mary Kate Skeehan
Sr Scout, Adult Fiction & Nonfiction: Megan Reid *E-mail:* mreid@sjga.com
Sr Scout, Children's & Young Adult: Hanna Masaryk *E-mail:* hmasaryk@sjga.com
Scout: John Bowers
Founded: 1932
Fiction, nonfiction, young adult & children's. No unsol mss, physical or phone queries. Query e-mail first. Submit outline or synopsis & sample chapter. No reading fee. Copying fee. Agents in all principal foreign countries.
Foreign Rights: Graal Literary Agency (Poland); Deborah Harris Agency (Israel); The Italian Literary Agency SRL (Italy); Licht & Burr (Scandinavia); MB Agencia Literaria (Brazil, Catalonia, Galicia, Portugal, Spain); Mohrbooks (Germany); La Nouvelle Agence (France, Quebec, CN); Andrew Nurnberg Associates (Netherlands); Andrew Nurnberg Associates (Baltic) (Estonia, Latvia, Lithuania, Ukraine); Andrew Nurnberg Associates (Bucharest) (Romania); Andrew Nurnberg Associates (Budapest) (Croatia, Hungary); Andrew Nurnberg Associates International Ltd (China, Taiwan); Andrew Nurnberg Associates (Prague) (Czech Republic, Slovakia, Slovenia); Andrew Nurnberg Associates (Sofia) (Albania, Bulgaria, Macedonia, Serbia); Andrew Nurnberg Literary Agency (Russia); Read n Right Agency (Greece); Abner Stein Agency (UK); Tuttle-Mori Agency Inc (Indonesia, Japan, Thailand, Vietnam); Eric Yang Agency (Korea)

Jill Grinberg Literary Management LLC (L)
392 Vanderbilt Ave, Brooklyn, NY 11238
Tel: 212-620-5883
E-mail: info@jillgrinbergliterary.com
Web Site: www.jillgrinbergliterary.com
Key Personnel
Pres: Jill Grinberg (AAR) *E-mail:* jill@jillgrinbergliterary.com
Agent: Katelyn Detweiler (AAR) *E-mail:* katelyn@jillgrinbergliterary.com
Agent & Dir, Foreign & Subs Rts: Cheryl Pientka (AAR) *E-mail:* cheryl@jillgrinbergliterary.com
Founded: 1999
Send query letter to info@jillgrinbergliterary.com. For fiction, attach first 50 pages; for nonfiction, send proposal (Word document). Regular mail accepted but e-mail preferred.

Jill Grosjean Literary Agency (L)
1390 Millstone Rd, Sag Harbor, NY 11963
Tel: 631-725-7419 *Fax:* 631-725-8632
E-mail: JillLit310@aol.com
Key Personnel
Owner & Literary Agent: Jill Grosjean
Founded: 1999
Literary fiction, mystery/suspense, women's fiction. No unsol mss, query first; e-mail queries preferred, no downloads or attachments. No fees charged. Foreign rights in UK, France, Italy, Spain, Netherlands, South America.
Titles recently placed: *A Spark of Death*, Bernadette Pajer; *A Thread So Thin*, Marie Bostwick; *Beating the Babushka*, Tim Maleeny; *Comfort and Joy*, Marie Bostwick; *Emma and the Vampires*, Wayne Josephson; *Fatal Induction*, Bernadette Pajer; *Jump*, Tim Maleeny; *Murder in Time*, Julie McElwain; *Nectar*, David Fickett; *Snow Angels*, Marie Bostwick; *Spectres in the Smoke*, Tony Broadbent; *Spun Tales*, Felicia Donovan; *Stealing the Dragon*, Tim Maleeny; *The Black Widow Agency*, Felicia Donovan; *The Edison Effect*, Bernadette Pajer; *The Reluctant Journey of David Connors*, Don Locke; *The Silver Gun*, L A Chandlar; *The Smoke*, Tony Broadbent; *Thread of Truth*, Marie Bostwick; *Threading the Needle*, Marie Bostwick; *Tim Cratchit's Christmas Carol*, Jim Piecuch; *Twist in Time*, Julie McEwain

Laura Gross Literary Agency Ltd (L)
PO Box 610326, Newton Highlands, MA 02461
Tel: 617-964-2977 *Fax:* 617-964-3023
E-mail: query@lg-la.com
Web Site: www.lg-la.com
Key Personnel
Pres: Laura Gross (AAR)
Founded: 1988
No unsol mss, query or e-mail first. On web site, submit query using form: lg-la.com/contact. Fiction, commercial & literary; nonfiction, serious topics, social, political, cultural issues & psychology. Include list of previous publications & bio. No reading fee.
Foreign Rights: Teri Tobias Agency LLC (worldwide exc UK)

The Charlotte Gusay Literary Agency (L-D)
10532 Blythe Ave, Los Angeles, CA 90064
Tel: 310-559-0831 *Fax:* 310-559-2639
E-mail: gusay1@ca.rr.com (queries only)
Web Site: www.gusay.com
Founded: 1988
Fiction & nonfiction, screenplay, children & adult, humor, parenting; crossover literary/commercial fiction; gardening, women's & men's issues, feminism, psychology, memoir, biography, travel. Handle film & TV rights. Represent selected illustrators, especially children's. No unsol mss, query first with SASE; ONLY when agency requests, submit one-page synopsis & first 3 chapters or first 50 pages (for fiction); proposal (for nonfiction). Include SASE. No reading fee. For borderline queries we sometimes give prospective clients the benefit of the doubt & impose a nominal processing fee allowing the prospective clients to decide whether to submit their material or not. Once client is signed, client is responsible for providing agency hard copies of mss (as necessary) & shipping expenses (as necessary).
Titles recently placed: *Dancing in the Baron's Shadow*, Fabienne Josaphat; *Everything I Need to Know I Learned in the Twilight Zone*, Mark Dawidziak (ed); *Mark Twain for Cat Lovers*, Mark Dawidziak (ed); *Mark Twain for Dog Lovers*, Kent Rasmussen (ed); *Mark Twain's Guide to Diet, Exercise, Beauty, Fashion, Investment, Romance, Health and Happiness*, Mark Dawidziak (ed); *Outrageous Fortune: Growing Up at Leeds Castle*, Anthony Russell; *The Burma Spring: Aung San Suu Kyi and the Struggle for the Soul of Burma*, Rena Pederson; *The Reputation Economy*, Michael Fertik, David Thompson; *US (a)*, Saul Williams
Foreign Rep(s): The Fielding Agency (Whitney Lee) (worldwide)
Membership(s): The Authors Guild; PEN American Center; PEN Center USA West; Writers Guild of America, West

Lisa Hagan Literary (L)
110 Martin Dr, Bracey, VA 23919
Tel: 434-636-4138
E-mail: LisaHaganLiterary@yahoo.com
Web Site: www.publishersmarketplace.com/members/LisaHagan/
Key Personnel
Owner, Pres & Agent: Lisa Hagan
Founded: 1985
Business/investing/finance, health, mind/body/spirit, science & self-help. No unsol mss, query first with letter. Handles film & TV rights. No fee charged.
Titles recently placed: *501 Ways to Roll Out the Red Carpet for Your Customers*, Donna Cutting; *A Little Bit of Angels*, Elaine Clayton; *Ask Dr. Nandi: 5 Steps to Becoming your Own #HealthHero for Longevity, Well-being and a Joyful Life*, Partha Nandi, MD; *Connecting with Coincidence*, Dr Bernard Beitman; *It's Not About Time: How to Thrive and Get the Results You Want at Work and in Life!*, Nan S Russell; *Secret Societies: The Complete Guide to Histories, Rites, and Rituals*, Nick Redfern; *Spirit Drumming: A Guide to the Healing Power of Rhythm*, Gabriel Horn, White Deer of Autumn; *The E-Word: Ego, Enlightenment & Other Essentials*, Cate Montana; *The Emergency Survival Guide*, Marie D Jones; *The Five Gifts: Uncommon Wisdom for Troubling Times*, Laurie Nadel, PhD; *The Heart of Wellness: Bridging Western and Eastern Medicine to Transform Your Relationship with Habits, Lifestyle and Health*, Kavitha M Chinnaiyan, MD; *The Holistic Heart Book: A Preventive Cardiologist's Guide to Halt Heart Disease Now*, Joel K Kahn, MD; *The Illuminati: The Secret Society That Hijacked the World*, Jim Marrs; *The New Alpha: Join the Rising Movement of Influencers and Changemakers Who are Redefining Leadership*, Danielle Harlan, PhD; *Turbo Metabolism: Preventing and Reversing Diabetes and Other Metabolic Diseases by Treating the Causes*, Pankaj Vij, MD; *Use the Force: The Jedi Science Behind the Law of Attraction*, Joshua Warren; *Way Out There: Adventures of a Wilderness Trekker*, J Robert Harris

The Joy Harris Literary Agency Inc (L)
1501 Broadway, Suite 2310, New York, NY 10036
Tel: 212-924-6269 *Fax:* 212-840-5776
E-mail: contact@joyharrisliterary.com
Web Site: www.joyharrisliterary.com
Key Personnel
Pres: Joy Harris (AAR) *E-mail:* joy@joyharrisliterary.com
Agent & Subs Rts: Adam Reed (AAR) *E-mail:* adam@joyharrisliterary.com
Translation Rts: Marianne Merola *E-mail:* mmerola@bromasite.com
No unsol mss, query first. No poetry, screenplays or self-help.

Hartline Literary Agency LLC (L)
123 Queenston Dr, Pittsburgh, PA 15235
Web Site: www.hartlineliterary.com
Key Personnel
Owner & CEO: Joyce Hart *E-mail:* joyce@hartlineliterary.com
VP & Agent: Jim Hart *E-mail:* jim@hartlineliterary.com
Agent: Diana Flegal *E-mail:* diana@hartlineliterary.com; Linda Glaz *E-mail:* linda@hartlineliterary.com; Andy Scheer *E-mail:* andy@hartlineliterary.com; Cyle Young *E-mail:* cyle@hartlineliterary.com
Founded: 1992
Advise clients on how to prepare proposals & advise them concerning what various publishers are looking for. Also help clients plan their literary careers. Our expertise is in the Christian

market & we also work in the general market. Looking for clean, wholesome fiction for adults & inspiring nonfiction. Mss reflecting a Christian worldview preferred, even for the general market. Fiction: romance, romantic suspense, women's fiction, mystery/suspense, humor, chick/mom lit & general fiction. Nonfiction: self-help, Christian living, prayer, health, humor & business.

Accepts unsol mss. Submit cover letter, author bio, marketing analysis, summary & 3 sample chapters. If submitting via e-mail, send as an attachment & send the entire submission in one file. We do not accept submissions in multiple files. We accept e-mail, US mail, UPS & FedEx submissions. See web site for complete submission details. No fees.

Titles recently placed: *21 Days of Grace*, Kathy Ide; *A Light in Bailey's Harbor*, Bethany Baker; *An Untimely Frost*, Penny Richards; *Anna's Crossing*, Suzanne Woods Fisher; *Bound Heart*, Dawn Crandall; *Death, Narnia & Songs of Innocence*, Kevin Ott; *Dubiosity*, Christy Barritt; *Hebrew Word Study, Revealing the Heart of God*, Chaim Bentorah; *His Precious Inheritance*, Dorothy Clark; *Imposter*, Suzanne Woods Fisher; *Mary, Mother of God*, Diana Wallis Taylor; *Memory Weaver*, Jane Kirkpatrick; *Missing*, Lisa Harris; *Mountain Hideaway*, Christy Barritt; *My Heart Belongs on Mackinac Island*, Carrie Fancett Pagels; *Not by Sight*, Kate Breslin; *Reclaiming Sanity*, Dr Laurel Shaler; *She Who Went First*, Jane Kirkpatrick; *Simple Lessons for a Better Life*, Charles E Dodgen; *Skirting Convention*, Kay Moser; *The Bravest You*, Adam Smith; *The Captive Imposter*, Dawn Crandall; *The Color of Justice*, Ace Collins; *The Devil's Daughter*, Cindy Sproles; *The Fruitcake Murders*, Ace Collins; *The Methuselah Project*, Rick Barry; *The Nanny's Secret Child*, Lorraine Beatty; *The Quieting*, Suzanne Woods Fisher; *The View Through Your Window*, Greg Singleton, Martha Singleton; *Unblemished*, Sara Ella; *Vendetta*, Lisa Harris; *Wedded for the Baby (Stand-In Brides series)*, Dorothy Clark; *What Ever Happened to Happily Ever After?*, David Clarke

Membership(s): American Christian Fiction Writers

John Hawkins and Associates Inc (L)
80 Maiden Lane, Suite 1503, New York, NY 10038
Tel: 212-807-7040
E-mail: jha@jhalit.com
Web Site: jhalit.com
Key Personnel
Pres & Foreign Rts Dir: Moses Cardona (AAR) *E-mail:* moses@jhalit.com
Agent: Warren Frazier (AAR) *E-mail:* frazier@jhalit.com; Anne Hawkins (AAR) *E-mail:* ahawkins@jhalit.com; William Reiss (AAR) *E-mail:* reiss@jhalit.com
Perms & Rts: Annie Kronenberg *E-mail:* annie@jhalit.com
Founded: 1893 (by Paul R Reynolds)
No unsol mss, query first. Submit 1-page bio & 1- to 3-page outline with SASE. No reading fee. Photocopy charges & fees for other services. Handle film & TV rights, software.
Titles recently placed: *A Book of American Martyrs*, Joyce Carol Oates; *Fortune Smiles*, Adam Johnson; *Friendly Fire*, John Gilstrap; *Grief Cottage*, Gail Godwin; *Perfume River*, Robert Olen Butler; *The Mask*, Taylor Stevens; *The Moth Catcher*, Ann Cleeves
Foreign Rep(s): Sara Menguc Inc (UK)

The Jeff Herman Agency LLC (L)
29 Park St, Stockbridge, MA 01262
Mailing Address: PO Box 1522, Stockbridge, MA 01262
Tel: 413-298-0077 *Fax:* 413-298-8188
E-mail: submissions@jeffherman.com
Web Site: www.jeffherman.com
Key Personnel
Pres: Jeffrey H Herman *E-mail:* jeff@jeffherman.com
VP: Deborah Levine
Founded: 1985
Nonfiction, reference, health, self-help, how-to business, technology, spirituality & textbooks. No unsol mss, query first with letter & SASE. No reading fee. Handle software, film & TV rights. Agents in all principal foreign countries.
Foreign Rep(s): Asano (Japan); De la Concha (Portugal, Spain)

Susan Herner Rights Agency Inc (L)
10 Upper Shad Rd, Pound Ridge, NY 10576
Tel: 914-234-2864 *Fax:* 914-234-2866
E-mail: shernerageney@optonline.net
Key Personnel
Pres: Susan N Herner
Founded: 1987
A full service literary agency representing a broad range of fiction & nonfiction authors. Not looking for new clients at the present time.

Hill Nadell Literary Agency (L)
6442 Santa Monica Blvd, Suite 201, Los Angeles, CA 90038
Tel: 310-860-9605 *Fax:* 323-380-5206
E-mail: queries@hillnadell.com; rights@hillnadell.com (rts & perms)
Web Site: www.hillnadell.com
Key Personnel
Pres: Bonnie Nadell
Agent: Dara Hyde
Founded: 1979
Literary & commercial fiction, narrative nonfiction, current affairs, memoirs & pop culture; film & TV rights only if handling the book. No unsol mss, query first with SASE. No reading fee. Co-agents in all foreign countries.
Titles recently placed: *A Stitch of Time*, Lauren Marks; *Graffiti Palace*, A G Lombardo; *Men Explain Things to Me*, Rebecca Solnit; *My Paris Kitchen*, David Lebovitz; *On Trails: An Exploration*, Robert Moor; *The Animators*, Kayla Rae Whitaker; *The Grim Sleeper*, Christine Pelisek; *The Only Living Boy*, David Gallaher, Steve Ellis; *The Tenth Island*, Diana Marcum; *The Widow Nash*, Jamie Harrison
Foreign Rights: ILA (Western Europe)

The Barbara Hogenson Agency Inc (L-D)
165 West End Ave, Suite 19-C, New York, NY 10023
Tel: 212-874-8084 *Fax:* 212-595-6748
E-mail: bhogenson@aol.com
Key Personnel
Pres: Barbara Hogenson (AAR)
Contract Mgr: Lori Styler
Founded: 1994
Recommendation by clients only. Literary fiction, nonfiction, full-length plays, consider some illustrated books. No screenplays or teleplays. No fees.
Membership(s): The Authors Guild; Authors Registry; The Dramatists Guild of America; Society of Stage Directors & Choreographers; Writers Guild of America

Henry Holmes Literary Agent/Book Publicist/Marketing Consultant (L)
Mitchell Heights, Apt 205, 2100 S Main St, Fall River, MA 02724
Tel: 508-672-2258
Key Personnel
Pres & Literary Agent: Henry Holmes
Founded: 1997
Nonfiction, no unsol mss, query first. Send query letter with chapters 1 & 2. If published, include past publicity, endorsement(s) etc. SASE. Ten mailings sent to preferred publishers via mss/CDs (this includes publisher research, query letter, packing, mailing, etc, at competitive rates. Independent of my representation, professional consultation via freelance assignments/project work would be based on involvement & duration of project based on competitive fees. Specialize in consulting, marketing, media publicity, talk show placement, etc. 15% standard commission. No reading fee. Retainer fee charged if ms is acceptable.

Hornfischer Literary Management LP (L)
PO Box 50544, Austin, TX 78763
Tel: 512-472-0011
E-mail: queries@hornfischerlit.com
Web Site: www.hornfischerlit.com
Key Personnel
Pres: Jim Hornfischer *E-mail:* jim@hornfischerlit.com
Founded: 2001
Quality narrative nonfiction, biography & autobiography, current events, US history, military history & world history, political & cultural subjects science, medicine/health, business/management/finance, academic writing & research that has a general-interest audience. No unsol mss; query first through e-mail, no longer accept queries through mail. No fees.
Titles recently placed: *A Curious Madness: An American Combat Psychiatrist, a Japanese War Crimes Suspect, and an Unsolved Mystery from World War II*, Eric Jaffe; *Area 51*, Annie Jacobsen; *Brothers, Rivals, Victors*, Jonathan Jordan; *Operation Paperclip: The Secret Intelligence Program that Brought Nazi Scientists to America*, Annie Jacobsen; *Outlaw Platoon*, Sean Parnell, John Bruning; *Running the Maze (Sniper)*, Jack Coughlin, Donald A Davis; *The Guerrilla Factory: The Making of Special Forces Officers, the Green Berets*, Tony Schwalm; *The Liberator*, Alex Kershaw; *The Possibility Dogs: What a Handful of "Unadoptables" Taught Me About Service, Hope, and Healing*, Susannah Charleston; *The Second Nuclear Age: Strategy, Danger, and the New Power Politics*, Paul Bracken; *The Trident: The Forging and Reforging of a Navy SEAL Leader*, Jason Redman, John Bruning; *Under Fire: The Untold Story of the Attack in Benghazi*, Fred Burton, Samuel M Katz; *Verdun: The Lost History of the Most Important Battle of World War I, 1914-1918*, John Mosier

ICM Partners (L-D)
65 E 55 St, New York, NY 10022
Tel: 212-556-5600
Web Site: www.icmtalent.com
Key Personnel
Partner: Kristine Dahl; Jennifer Joel; Sloan Harris; Alexandra Machinist; Esther Newberg; Amanda Urban
Literary Agent: Amelia "Molly" Atlas; Hillary Jacobson; Heather Karpas; Kristyn Keene; Dan Kirschen; Zoe Sandler; Anna Stein; Kari Stuart; Tina Wexler
Founded: 1975
Handle film & TV rights. No unsol mss, query first. No reading fee.
Branch Office(s)
10250 Constellation Blvd, Los Angeles, CA 90067 *Tel:* 310-550-4000

ICM/Sagalyn (L)
Affiliate of ICM Partners
2 Wisconsin Circle, Suite 650, Chevy Chase, MD 20815-7045
Tel: 240-802-2760
E-mail: info@sagalyn.com
Web Site: www.sagalyn.com
Key Personnel
Owner: Raphael Sagalyn (AAR)

Quality nonfiction & mainstream fiction. No romance, westerns, science fiction, poetry, children's books or screenplays. No unsol mss, query first with e-mail. Handle film & TV rights. No reading fee.
Foreign Rights: Curtis Brown UK (translation rights) (worldwide exc USA)

InkWell Management (L)
521 Fifth Ave, 26th fl, New York, NY 10175
Tel: 212-922-3500 *Fax:* 212-922-0535
E-mail: info@inkwellmanagement.com
Web Site: inkwellmanagement.com
Key Personnel
Founder & Pres: Michael Carlisle; Richard S Pine; Kim Witherspoon *E-mail:* kim@inkwellmanagement.com
Dir, Subs Rts: Alexis Hurley *E-mail:* alexis@inkwellmanagement.com
Agent: David Forrer; George Lucas
Busn Mgr: Jennifer Witherell *E-mail:* jwitherell@inkwellmanagement.com
Founded: 2004 (created through the merger of Arthur Pine Associates Inc, Carlisle & Co LLC & Witherspoon Associates Inc)
General nonfiction & fiction books. No screenplays, plays, poetry. Motion picture, TV & foreign rights. No unsol mss, query first with SASE; submissions must be on an exclusive basis. No fees.
Titles recently placed: *Antony & Cleopatra*, Colleen McCullough; *Knockemstiff*, Donald Ray Pollock; *Mister Pip*, Lloyd Jones; *Right is Wrong*, Arianna Huffington; *Sepulchre*, Kate Mosse; *The Ghost*, Robert Harris

InterLicense Ltd (L)
110 Country Club Dr, Suite A, Mill Valley, CA 94941
Tel: 415-381-9780 *Fax:* 415-381-6485
E-mail: interlicense@interlicense.net
Web Site: interlicense.net
Key Personnel
Exec Dir: Manfred Mroczkowski
Founded: 1981
Foreign & subsidiary rights agency representing independent authors & publishers.

International Titles (L)
931 E 56 St, Austin, TX 78751-1724
Tel: 512-909-2447
Web Site: www.internationaltitles.com
Key Personnel
Dir: Loris Essary *E-mail:* loris@internationaltitles.com
Represent all genres; primary emphasis on sales of foreign rights. No fees charged, no submission policy.

International Transactions Inc (L)
28 Alope Way, Gila, NM 88038
Mailing Address: PO Box 97, Gila, NM 88038
Tel: 845-373-9696 *Fax:* 480-393-5162
E-mail: info@intltrans.com
Web Site: www.intltrans.com
Key Personnel
Pres: Peter Riva *E-mail:* priva@intltrans.com
VP & Dir: Sandra Anne Riva *E-mail:* sriva@intltrans.com
Assoc Ed: JoAnn Collins *E-mail:* jcollins@intltrans.com
Founded: 1975
International literary & licensing agency. Specialize in nonfiction (including large projects), fiction, illustrated & children's. We cannot help every prospective author nor can we review every ms. Send a fiction submission query (only) to Submission-Fiction@IntlTrans.com. If, within three weeks, we are interested, we will call for more material. In the case of nonfiction authors, each query for submission must include a one-page summary of the book proposed as well as a brief description of the author's bona fides or expertise as author, including links to any media platform he or she may be able to employ. Send the nonfiction submission query to Submission-NonFiction@IntlTrans.com. Also handles film & TV rights. No fees.
Titles recently placed: *A California Closing*, Robert Wintner; *An Undisturbed Peace*, Mary Glickman; *Blitzkreig*, Niklas Zetterling; *Charleston, A Good Life*, Ned Brown; *Courting Death*, Paul J Heald; *Diary of a Citizen Scientist: Chasing Tiger Beetles and Other New Ways of Engaging the World*, Sharman Apt Russell; *Disappear Home*, Laura Hurwitz; *Ferrari 70 Years*, Dennis Adler; *Hemingway's Paris*, Robert Wheeler; *Humankind*, Sandy harcourt; *Liberty*, Christopher Webber; *Marijuana Nation*, Roger Roffman; *Misery Bay*, Chris Angus; *Nights in Tents*, Laura Love; *Orphan Hero*, John Babb; *Porsche: The Classic Era*, Dennis Adler; *Radical Virus*, Azeem Ibrahim; *Reef Libre*, Robert Wintner; *Some People Talk with God*, John Enright; *Styx*, Bavo Dhooge; *The Covenant*, Jeff Crook; *The Fourth Figure*, Pieter Aspe; *The Mechanic*, Alan Gold; *The Sixth Man*, Ron Lealos
Foreign Office(s): Rechtsanwalt Roth, Gewurzmuhlstr 5, 80538 Munich, Germany *Tel:* (089) 55 26 26 55

JABberwocky Literary Agency Inc (L)
49 W 45 St, 12th fl, New York, NY 10036
Tel: 917-388-3010 *Fax:* 917-388-2998
Web Site: www.awfulagent.com
Founded: 1994
Full line of fiction & nonfiction trade books, particularly genre fiction (science fiction, fantasy, mystery, horror), literary fiction, young adult & middle grade & serious nonfiction (biography, science, history). No unsol mss, query first with biographical information & SASE. Will request mss after reviewing query if interested. Handle film & TV rights for regular clients. No reading fee. No fax or e-mail queries & always check web site to see which agents are currently accepting queries.
Titles recently placed: *Alcatraz vs the Dark Talent (5th in The Alcatraz Smedry series)*, Brandon Sanderson; *All Rights Reserved*, Gret Katsoulis; *America Rising*, William C Dietz; *Dr DOA (10th in The Secret Histories series)*, Simon R Green; *Duskfall*, Christopher Husberg; *Mystic*, Jason Denzel; *Slotter Key*, Elizabeth Moon; *The Unnoticeables*, Robert Brockway
Foreign Rep(s): AnatoliaLit Agency (Turkey); ANAW (Poland); Anthea Agency (Albania, Bulgaria); Tassy Barham Associates (Brazil); Agence Eliane Benisti (France); Book Publishers Association (Israel); Bookman (Scandinavia); The English Agency (Japan) Ltd (Japan); Paul & Peter Fritz AG (Germany); The Grayhawk Agency (China, Indonesia, Taiwan, Thailand, Vietnam); Danny Hong Agency (Korea); Katai & Bolza (Croatia, Hungary, Serbia, Slovenia); Simona Kessler (Romania); Alexander Korzhenevski (Russia); Piergiorgio Nicolazzini (Italy); Andrew Nurnberg (Baltic States); Kristin Olson (Czech Republic); Read N Right (Greece); Julio F Yanez (Portugal, Spain); Zeno Agency Ltd (UK)
Membership(s): Science Fiction & Fantasy Writers of America

Melanie Jackson Agency LLC (L)
41 W 72 St, Suite 3F, New York, NY 10023
Tel: 212-873-3373
Key Personnel
Owner & Agent: Melanie Jackson
Perms: Matthew Dissen
No unsol mss, query first.
Foreign Rep(s): Liepman Agency (Germany); Rogers, Coleridge & White (UK); Roberto Santachiara (Italy)

James Peter Associates Inc (L)
PO Box 358, New Canaan, CT 06840
Tel: 203-972-1070
Web Site: www.jamespeterassociates.com
Key Personnel
Pres: Gene Brissie *E-mail:* gene_brissie@msn.com
Founded: 1971
Nonfiction only, all subject areas. Handle software, film & TV rights through sub-agents in many foreign countries. No unsol mss, query first with SASE. Submit brief description of book, potential market, chapter outline, one sample chapter, competitive titles & author's credentials. No reading fee.

Janklow & Nesbit Associates (L)
285 Madison Ave, 21st fl, New York, NY 10017
Tel: 212-421-1700 *Fax:* 212-355-1403
E-mail: info@janklow.com
Web Site: www.janklowandnesbit.com
Key Personnel
Sr Partner: Morton L Janklow
Partner: Lynn Nesbit
SVP: Anne Sibbald
Agent: Melissa Flashman; Allison Hunter; Lucas W Janklow; Kirby Kim; Stefanie Lieberman; Paul Lucas; P J Mark; Richard Morris; Emma Parry; Brooks Sherman; Marya Spence
Founded: 1989 (successor to Morton L Janklow Assoc Inc founded in 1975)
General fiction & nonfiction. Handle film & TV rights for book represented; no reading fee.
Foreign Office(s): Janklow & Nesbit (UK) Ltd, 13-A Hillgate St, London W87SP, United Kingdom, Contact: Rachel Balcombe *Tel:* (020) 7243 2975 *Fax:* (020) 7243 4339 *E-mail:* queries@janklow.co.uk *Web Site:* www.janklowandnesbit.co.uk

Janus Literary Agency (L)
PO Box 837, Methuen, MA 01844
Tel: 978-273-4227
E-mail: janusliteraryagency@gmail.com
Web Site: janusliteraryagency.com
Key Personnel
Owner: Lenny Cavallaro
Founded: 1980
No new clients at this time. No reading fee. Possible handling fees if agency represents author & deals with editors via hard copy; none for electronic submissions. Provide editing, ghostwriting services +/or rewrites for a fee; also consultation on digital publication & POD/self-publication. No unsol mss, query first by e-mail only without attachments unless requested. Nonfiction: prospectus, outline, sample chapter. No longer handling fiction. Will reply only if interested.

Jellinek & Murray Literary Agency (L-D)
47-231 Kamakoi Rd, Kaneohe, HI 96744
Tel: 808-239-8451
Key Personnel
Pres: Roger Jellinek *E-mail:* rgr.jellinek@gmail.com
Founded: 1995
General adult fiction & nonfiction. No genre fiction. No unsol mss, query first with an e-mail. Submit proposal, outline, 2 sample chapters, author bio & credentials & platform, by e-mail. No reading fees. Handle film & TV rights.

Carolyn Jenks Agency (L-D)
30 Cambridge Park Dr, Suite 3140, Cambridge, MA 02140

Tel: 617-233-9130
E-mail: queries@carolynjenksagency.com (submissions)
Web Site: www.carolynjenksagency.com
Key Personnel
Owner, CEO & Dir: Carolyn Jenks
E-mail: carolynjenks@comcast.net
Founded: 1979
Literary & commercial fiction & nonfiction. All genres. Theatre, film & screenwriters represented. Signatory to Writers Guild of America. Contact by e-mail or via web site. Electronic submissions only; prefer query via web site. No fees charged.
Titles recently placed: *Adrift in a Vanishing City*, Vincent Czyz; *Esther*, Rebecca Kanner; *Snafu*, Miryam Sifan; *The Christos Mosaic*, Vincent Czyz; *The Red Tent (20th anniversary ed)*, Anita Diamant; *True Surrealism*, Christopher Klim; *Two Maidens of the Sword*, Anne Echols
Membership(s): Writers Guild of America

JET Literary Associates Inc (L)
941 Calle Mejia, Suite 507, Santa Fe, NM 87501
Tel: 505-780-0721
E-mail: etp@jetliterary.com
Web Site: www.jetliterary.wordpress.com
Key Personnel
Pres (Austria off): Jim Trupin *E-mail:* jetlit@hotmail.com
VP: Elizabeth Trupin-Pulli *E-mail:* etp@jetliterary.com
Founded: 1975
General book-length fiction & nonfiction. Specialize in adult fiction & commercial nonfiction; no plays, poetry, science fiction/fantasy, young adult or books for young children. No unsol mss, query first, preferably via e-mail. No reading fees. Full representation in all foreign markets.
Foreign Office(s): Esterhazygasse 9A/26, 1060 Vienna, Austria *Tel:* (01) 587 0077 *Fax:* (01) 587 0077
Foreign Rep(s): Eliane Benisti (France); Big Apple Agency Inc (China); Educational Materials Enterprises (Greece); Fritz Agency (Germany); Nurcihan Kesim Literary Agency Inc (Turkey); Kohn (Netherlands); Lennart Sane (Sweden); Living Literary Agency (Italy); Tuttle-Mori Agency Inc (Japan); Julio F Yanez (Brazil, Spain)
Foreign Rights: Abner Stein Agency (UK)

JMW Group Inc (L)
347 Rte 6, No 867, Mahopac, NY 10541
Tel: 914-841-7105 *Fax:* 914-248-8861
E-mail: jmwgroup@jmwgroup.net
Web Site: jmwgroup.net
Key Personnel
Dir of Licensing: Sara Castle
VP, Rts: Pete Allen
Founded: 1949
Publisher, Rights agency; no fees charged.

Jody Rein Books Inc (L)
7741 S Ash Ct, Centennial, CO 80122
Tel: 303-694-9386
Web Site: www.jodyreinbooks.com
Key Personnel
Pres: Jody Rein (AAR) *E-mail:* jodyrein@jodyreinbooks.com
Founded: 1994
Specialize in adult narrative & commercial nonfiction. Some literary fiction. Handle film & TV rights through agents. Send query to assistant@jodyreinbooks.com. Agency responds if interested in project. See also Author Planet Publishing Services listing.
Titles recently placed: *Anzio: Desperate Valour*, Flint Whitlock; *Crazy Horse Weeps*, Joseph Marshall III; *You Can Draw It in Just 30 Minutes*, Mark Kistler
Foreign Rep(s): The English Agency (Japan); Grayhawk Agency (China, Taiwan); Japan UNI (Japan); Eric Yang Agency (Korea)
Foreign Rights: Judy Klein (worldwide exc China, Japan, Korea, Thailand & USA)
Membership(s): The Authors Guild

Jones Hutton Literary Associates (L)
140D Heritage Village, Southbury, CT 06488
Tel: 203-558-4478
E-mail: huttonbooks@hotmail.com
Key Personnel
Mng Ed: Caroline DuBois Hutton
Founded: 1994
Welcomes new & established writers. Will work closely with clients to get material into the best possible shape for presentation to editors at various publishing houses. Works with publishers both in the US & abroad. Handles mainly nonfiction in many categories, but always on the lookout for good new novels. Handles only a few authors at a time & gives to each the utmost personal attention. Turnaround time is short, usually less than two weeks. Earns fees from advances & royalties (15% domestic & 20% foreign sales). No reading or submission fees. For nonfiction, form for proposal may be e-mailed upon request. For fiction, a one- to two-page synopsis is required, as well as a short author's biography & two to three chapters of the novel. Please send all submissions by hard copy after first querying via e-mail. Affiliates in both editing & PR fields are available for referral.

The Karpfinger Agency (L)
357 W 20 St, New York, NY 10011-3379
Tel: 212-691-2690 *Fax:* 212-691-7129
E-mail: info@karpfinger.com (no queries or submissions)
Web Site: karpfinger.com
Key Personnel
Owner: Barney M Karpfinger
Foreign Rts Mgr: Cathy Jaque
Agent: Kate Garrick
Contact: Rowan Spencer
Founded: 1985
Quality fiction & nonfiction. No unsol mss. See web site for specific instructions for queries. No reading fee. Direct representation in all foreign markets.

Keller Media Inc (L)
578 Washington Blvd, No 745, Marina del Rey, CA 90292
Toll Free Tel: 800-278-8706
E-mail: query@kellermedia.com
Web Site: kellermedia.com/query
Key Personnel
CEO & Sr Agent: Wendy Keller
Literary Agent: Megan Close Zavala
Edit Dir: Alex Schnitzler
Founded: 1989
Represent nonfiction in these categories: business (sales, management, marketing); finance; self-help (parenting, women's issues, relationships, pop psychology, etc); health (alternative & allopathic); metaphysical/spiritual/inspirational (never religious); nature, science, archaeology, reference, how-to (do anything). Megan Close Zavala represents fiction titles in all categories except fantasy, science fiction & horror. Do not send poetry, scripts, your memoir unless you are a celebrity, religious or juvenile books, or first person accounts of overcoming some medical or mental condition. Most of agency's authors are either experts in their field, successful professional speakers, have their own radio, infomercial or television program, or are a household name. For best results, fill in the simple form on the web site. Please do not mail your self-published book unless we request it.
Titles recently placed: *Disruptive Marketing*, Geoffrey Colon; *Entrepreneurial Thinking*, Jeffrey Hayzlett; *In the Garden of Happiness*, Dodinsky; *The History of Television*, Seth Shapiro; *The Millionaire Master Plan*, Roger James Hamilton; *The People Equation: Innovation Implementation*, Deborah Perry Piscione
Membership(s): National Association for Female Executives; National Speakers Association; United States Women's Chamber of Commerce

Natasha Kern Literary Agency Inc (L)
PO Box 1069, White Salmon, WA 98672
Tel: 509-493-3803
E-mail: agent@natashakern.com
Web Site: www.natashakern.com
Key Personnel
Pres: Natasha Kern *E-mail:* natasha@natashakern.com
Busn & Translation Rts Mgr: Jack Lauer
Sr Agent: Susan Bower *E-mail:* susan@natashakern.com
Agent: Athena Kern *E-mail:* athena@natashakern.com
Founded: 1986
Represent commercial adult fiction, inspirational fiction & young adult fiction. Actively represent all women's fiction; multicultural fiction; mainstream fiction; inspirational, historical & contemporary romance; romantic suspense, thrillers, & all subgenres of mysteries from cozies to PIs. DO NOT represent children's, horror, science fiction, short stories, poetry, sports, scholarly or coffee-table books. Handle film & TV rights only on represented books. Represented in all principal foreign countries as well as in Hollywood. No unsol mss, query first via e-mail (queries@natashakern.com). Please look at web site for submission info. Queries by mail are not accepted. Will respond only if interested. Include a 2-3 page synopsis & the first chapter of the novel.
Titles recently placed: *By Your Side*, Candace Calvert; *Gunpowder Tea*, Margaret Brownley; *Indulgences: The Marriage of Martin Luther and Katharina Von Bora*, Jody Hedlund; *Once Upon A Plaid*, Mia Marlowe; *Saving Amelie*, Cathy Gohlke; *Soul of Fire*, Eliott Pattison; *Striking Distance*, Pamela Clare; *The Bracelet*, Dorothy Love; *The Miracle Thief*, Iris Anthony; *The Perfect Affair*, Lutishia Lovely; *The Sharp Hook of Love*, Sherry Jones; *The Summer of Me*, Angela Benson; *To Win Her Favor*, Tamera Alexander
Foreign Rep(s): Agencia Literaria Carmen Balcells SA (Spain); Agence Eliane Benisti (France); Phillip Chen (China, Taiwan); The Italian Literary Agency srl (Italy); Prava i prevodi (Eastern Europe); Lucia Riff (Brazil); Lennart Sane (Scandinavia); Junzo Sawa (Japan); Tom Schlueck (Germany); Lorna Soifer (Israel)

Louise B Ketz Agency (L)
414 E 78 St, Suite 1-B, New York, NY 10075
Tel: 212-249-0668
E-mail: ketzagency@aol.com
Key Personnel
Pres: Louise B Ketz
Founded: 1986
Nonfiction only: science, business, sports, reference, history. No unsol mss, query letter, chapter outline, table of contents, sample chapter, author biography. No reading fee.
Titles recently placed: *The Traveler's Guide to Space: For One-Way Settlers and Round-Trip Tourists*, Neil F Comins
Membership(s): Editorial Freelancers Association; National Association of Professional & Executive Women; United States Commission on Military History

Virginia Kidd Agency Inc (L)
538 E Harford St, PO Box 278, Milford, PA 18337
Tel: 570-296-6205
Web Site: vk-agency.com
Key Personnel
Literary Agent, Foreign & Translation Rts, Film Queries: Christine M Cohen *E-mail:* chrisco@ptd.net
Literary Agent, Ebooks, Contracts & Royalties: Vaughne L Hansen *E-mail:* vaughne@ptd.net
Literary Agent, Submission Queries & Perms: William D Reeve *E-mail:* wmreeve@ptd.net
Founded: 1965
We are seeking quality, marketable fiction with an eye toward strong character development & fresh storytelling. While our focus remains on speculative fiction, we are happy to consider works beyond that if the story is compelling. We consider science fiction/fantasy, dark fantasy, historical fiction, popular fiction & adventures. Cozy mystery & romance too. Overall, the characters & their story are more important than the genre.
Titles recently placed: *A Borrowed Man*, Gene Wolfe; *Aftertaste*, Andrew Post; *Alien: Covenant*, Alan Dean Foster; *Breath*, Jackson Creed; *Oshenerth*, Alan Dean Foster; *Star Wars: The Force Awakens*, Alan Dean Foster; *The Year's Best Science Fiction 35*, Gardner Dozois
Foreign Rep(s): Bardon Chinese Media Agency (China); The Book Publishers Association of Israel (Israel); Bridge Communications Co (Thailand); Paul & Peter Fritz AG (Germany); International Editors' Co (Portugal, South America, Spain); The Italian Literary Agency SRL (Italy); Alexander Korzhenevski (Estonia, Latvia, Lithuania, Russia); Agence Litteraire Lenclud (France); Prava i prevodi (Central Europe, Eastern Europe, Greece, Turkey); Lennart Sane (Netherlands, Scandinavia); Tuttle-Mori Agency Inc (Japan); Eric Yang Agency Inc (Korea)
Foreign Rights: LEX Copyright Office (Hungary)

Kirchoff/Wohlberg Inc (L)
897 Boston Post Rd, Madison, CT 06443
Tel: 203-245-7308 *Fax:* 203-245-3218
Web Site: www.kirchoffwohlberg.com
Key Personnel
Pres: Morris A Kirchoff
VP: Ronald P Zollshan *E-mail:* rzollshan@kirchoffwohlberg.com
Founded: 1974
Children & young adult fiction & nonfiction trade books only. Agency does not handle adult titles. No fees. Handle film & TV rights.
Membership(s): AIGA, the professional association for design; ALA; Book Industry Guild of New York; Bookbuilders of Boston; International Literacy Association; Society of Children's Book Writers & Illustrators; Society of Illustrators

Harvey Klinger Inc (L)
300 W 55 St, Suite 11V, New York, NY 10019
Tel: 212-581-7068 *Fax:* 212-315-3823
E-mail: queries@harveyklinger.com
Web Site: www.harveyklinger.com
Key Personnel
Pres: Harvey Klinger (AAR) *E-mail:* harvey@harveyklinger.com
Dir, Devt: Wendy Levinson *E-mail:* wendy@harveyklinger.com
Agent: David Dunton *E-mail:* david@harveyklinger.com; Andrea Somberg *E-mail:* andrea@harveyklinger.com; Rachel Ridout *E-mail:* rachel@harveyklinger.com
Founded: 1977
Mainstream adult & children's fiction & nonfiction. Handle film & TV rights. No unsol full mss or faxes; do not phone or fax; no reading fee. E-mail query with brief synopsis. First 5 pages ms pasted into body of e-mail also allowed. Representatives in Hollywood & all principal foreign countries.
Foreign Rights: Eliane Benisti (France); David Grossman Literary Agency Ltd (David Grossman) (UK); Daniela Micura Literary Services (Daniela Micura) (Italy); Prava i prevodi (Ana Milenkovic) (Eastern Europe, Russia); Lennart Sane (Philip Sane) (Brazil, Holland, Latin America, Portugal, Scandinavia, Spain); Thomas Schlueck GmbH (Thomas Schlueck) (Germany); Tuttle-Mori Agency Inc (Ken Mori) (Japan); Eric Yang Agency (Sue Yang) (Korea)
Membership(s): PEN Center USA

Kneerim & Williams Agency (L-D)
90 Canal St, Boston, MA 02114
Tel: 617-303-1650
Web Site: www.kwlit.com
Key Personnel
Agency Admin: Hope Denekamp *Tel:* 617-303-1651 *E-mail:* hope@kwlit.com
Partner: John Taylor "Ike" Williams *E-mail:* ike@kwlit.com
Mng Partner: Jill Kneerim *E-mail:* jill@kwlit.com
Agent: Katherine Flynn *E-mail:* kflynn@kwlit.com; Carol Franco *E-mail:* carolfranco@comcast.net
Affiliated Agent: Carolyn Savarese
Edit Mgr: Lucy Cleland *Tel:* 617-303-1654 *E-mail:* lucy@kwlit.com
Founded: 1990
Handles books, film & television rights. Does not handle children's picture books & genre fiction; no romance, western or science fiction & fantasy. No unsol mss, query first. Send query via e-mail to agent. Query should contain a cover letter explaining your book & why you are qualified to write it. You may include a two-page synopsis, one sample chapter, a curriculum vitae or history of your publications.
For dramatic rights inquiries, contact Lucy Cleland & Katherine Flynn. For other inquiries, contact Lucy Cleland & Hope Denekamp.
Titles recently placed: *Approaching Ali*, Davis Miller; *Brain Storms*, Jon Palfreman; *Breed of Heroes*, Julie Flavell; *Department of Experiments*, Amanda Claybaugh; *Do Your Om Thing*, Rebecca Pacheo; *Eat Drink and Remarry*, Margo Howard; *Evicted*, Matthew Desmond; *Existential Prescriptions*, Gordon Marino; *Extreme You*, Sarah Robb O'Hagan; *Formerly Known as Food*, Kristin Wartman Lawless; *Four Strong*, Rosann Sdoia; *Great Fire*, Lou Ureneck; *Honeydew*, Edith Pearlman; *How Did We Miss That?*, Amy Webb; *How Star Wars Conquered the Universe*, Chris Taylor; *More Than a Scarecrow: The Life of Ray Bolger*, Holly Van Leuven; *New World Inc*, John Butman, Simon Targett; *Self-Reg*, Stuart Shanker, Teresa Barker; *The Arsonist*, Sue Miller; *The Bettencourt Affair*, Tom Sancton; *The Feather Underground*, Kirk Johnson; *The Gates of Europe*, Serhii Plokhii; *The Last Great Day*, Jerald Walker; *The Mantle of Command, Commander in Chief*, Nigel Hamilton; *The Meaning of Human Existence*, E O Wilson; *The Power of Little Ideas*, David Robertson; *The President's Shadow*, Brad Meltzer; *The Quartet*, Joe Ellis; *The Shift*, Theresa Brown; *The Sirens of Mars*, Sarah Stewart Johnson; *The Story of Literature*, Martin Puchner; *The Virgin Vote*, Jon Grinspan; *The Worm at the Core*, Sheldon Solomon, Tom Pyszczynski, Jeff Greenberg
Foreign Rep(s): Baror International Inc (translation); Zoe Pagnamenta Agency (UK & Commonwealth)
Foreign Rights: Baror International Inc (translation); Zoe Pagnamenta Agency (UK & Commonwealth)

The Knight Agency Inc (L)
570 East Ave, Madison, GA 30650
E-mail: submissions@knightagency.net
Web Site: www.knightagency.net
Key Personnel
Owner & Pres: Deidre Knight
VP: Judson Knight
VP, Sales & Agent: Pamela Harty
VP, Opers & Agent: Elaine Spencer (AAR)
Mktg Dir: Jia Gayles
Agent: Melissa Jeglinski
Agent, CA Office: Nephele Tempest (AAR)
Agent, FL Office: Lucienne Diver
Submissions Coord: Kristy Hunter
Founded: 1996
Fiction: romance, women's fiction, commercial fiction, literary & multicultural fiction, young adult, science fiction & fantasy, middle grade fiction. In nonfiction: business, self-help, finance, music/entertainment, media-related, pop culture, how-to, psychology, travel, health, inspirational/religious, reference & holiday books. No anthology collections, short stories or poetry. No unsol mss, query first by sending a brief summary or proposal, author info & first five pages by e-mail (no attachments). Allow a two to four week response time for queries. Upon request only submit the following: for fiction: first three chapters, synopsis or outline & copy of original query; nonfiction: proposal or outline, first one to three chapters, summary of author's qualifications, unique marketing opportunities & copy of original query. Allow 8-12 weeks for ms review. No reading fee. 15% commission on domestic sales, 15-25% on foreign. May use sub-agent for sale or film & foreign rights. Screenplays not accepted.
Titles recently placed: *A Man to Hold on To*, Marilyn Pappano; *Archangel's Legion*, Nalini Singh; *Burning Dawn*, Gena Showalter; *Cal Leandros (series)*, Rob Thurman; *Chicagoland Vampire*, Chloe Neill; *Eversea*, Natasha Boyd; *Ghost Seer*, Robin Owens; *Ink*, Amanda Sun; *Linger*, Lauren Hawkeye; *Nexus*, Ramez Naam; *Risky Game*, Tracy Solheim; *Sanctuary Island*, Lily Everett; *Stupid Girl*, Cindy Miles; *Talk Dirty to Me*, Dakota Cassidy; *Teach Me a Lesson*, Jasmine Haynes; *The Deamon Prism*, Carol Berg; *The Duke Can Go to the Devil*, Erin Knightley; *The Golden City*, J Kathleen Cheney; *The Great Library*, Rachel Caine; *The Last Monster*, Ginger Garrett; *The Memory Child*, Steena Holmes; *Wickedly Powerful*, Deborah Blake
Branch Office(s)
14622 Ventura Blvd, No 785, Sherman Oaks, CA 91403
PO Box 2659, Land O Lakes, FL 34639
Foreign Rights: ANA Sofia Ltd (Bulgaria); The Fielding Agency (Whitney Lee) (Brazil, Bulgaria, China, Croatia, Czech Republic, Estonia, Greece, Hungary, Israel, Korea, Latvia, Lithuania, Poland, Portugal, Romania, Russia, Serbia, Slovakia, Slovenia, Taiwan, UK); Graal Literary Agency (Poland); Katai & Bolza Literary Agents (Hungary); Kayi Literary Agency Ltd (Turkey); The Lenclud Agency (France); Nova Littera (Russia); Kristin Olson Literary Agency (Czech Republic); PNLA / Piergiorgio Nicolazzini Literary Agency (Maura Solinas) (Italy); Read N Right Agency (Greece); Lennart Sane Agency (Scandinavia); Thomas Schlueck GmbH (Germany); Julio F Yanez Agency (Montse F Yanez) (Brazil, Portugal, Spain)
Membership(s): The Authors Guild; Mystery Writers of America; Romance Writers of America; Science Fiction & Fantasy Writers of America; Society of Children's Book Writers & Illustrators

Paul Kohner Agency (L-D)
9300 Wilshire Blvd, Suite 555, Beverly Hills, CA 90212
Tel: 310-550-1060 *Fax:* 310-276-1083
Key Personnel
Pres & Owner: Pearl Wexler
Literary Agent: Stephen Moore
Founded: 1938
Film & TV rights. No unsol mss, query first. No reading fee; fees for extensive copying or binding charges.

Linda Konner Literary Agency (L)
10 W 15 St, Suite 1918, New York, NY 10011
Tel: 212-691-3419 *Fax:* 212-691-0935
Web Site: www.lindakonnerliteraryagency.com
Key Personnel
Pres: Linda Konner (AAR) *E-mail:* ldkonner@cs.com
Founded: 1996
Health, nutrition, diet, relationships, sex, pop psychology, self-help, parenting, cookbooks, business & career/personal finance, celebrity/pop culture. No fiction, children's or memoir. No unsol mss, query first with one-page query & SASE or via e-mail. Submit outline & one to two sample chapters. No reading fee. 15% fee on US sales & up to 25% on foreign sales. One-time expense fee of $65, deducted from publisher's advance payment.
Titles recently placed: *80/20 Triathlon*, Matt Fitzgerald, David Warden; *Get Money: Learn How to Live the Life You Want, Not Just the Life You Can Afford*, Kristin Wong; *The Reducetarian Solution*, Brian Kateman; *Tiny Buddha's Gratitude Journal*, Lori Deschene
Foreign Rights: Books Crossing Borders (Betty Anne Crawford) (worldwide exc USA)
Membership(s): American Society of Journalists & Authors; The Authors Guild

Barbara S Kouts Literary Agency LLC (L)
PO Box 560, Bellport, NY 11713
Tel: 631-286-1278 *Fax:* 631-286-1538
E-mail: bkouts@aol.com
Key Personnel
Owner: Barbara S Kouts
Founded: 1980
Specialize in children's fiction & nonfiction. No unsol mss, query first. Submit synopsis or outline & sample chapters. No reading fee, but copy fees would apply, no software. Handle film & TV rights from sale of books. Agents in all principal foreign countries.
Membership(s): Society of Children's Book Writers & Illustrators

Stuart Krichevsky Literary Agency Inc (L)
6 E 39 St, Suite 500, New York, NY 10016
Tel: 212-725-5288 *Fax:* 212-725-5275
E-mail: query@skagency.com
Web Site: skagency.com
Key Personnel
Pres: Stuart Krichevsky (AAR)
Literary Agent & Rts Dir: Ross Harris (AAR)
Literary Agent & Busn Mgr: Hannah Schwartz
Literary Agent: Melissa Danaczko; David Patterson; Laura Usselman; Mackenzie Brady Watson
Founded: 1995
Fiction & nonfiction. No reading fee. No unsol mss, query first; prefer e-mail queries (no attachments) to query@skagency.com. Include query letter & synopsis. To submit to Shana Cohen include letter, synopsis & first 2 pages to SCquery@skagency.com.
Foreign Rights: Akcali Copyright Trade & Tourism Co Ltd (Turkey); The Deborah Harris Agency (Israel); Andrew Nurnberg Associates (China, Europe, South Africa); Tuttle-Mori Agency Inc (Japan); Eric Yang (Korea)

Edite Kroll Literary Agency Inc (L)
20 Cross St, Saco, ME 04072
Tel: 207-283-8797 *Fax:* 207-283-8799
Key Personnel
Pres: Edite Kroll *E-mail:* ekroll@maine.rr.com
Founded: 1981
Adult general & feminist nonfiction & humor; children's fiction, young adult & picture books. No unsol mss, query first by e-mail.
Titles recently placed: *Eqbal Achmed Biography*, Stuart Schaar; *Kate the Great (3 titles in series)*, Suzy Becker; *Pig in the Wig (4 titles in series)*, Emma Virjan
Foreign Rights: ACER (Brazil, Portugal); ACER (children's) (Spain, Spanish Latin America); Akcali (Turkey); IA Atterholm Agency (Scandinavia); Author Rights Agency (Estonia, Latvia, Russia); L'Autre Agence (France); Bardon-Chinese Media Agency (China); Big Apple (China); Book Publishers Association of Israel (Israel); Bookbank (adult) (Spain, Spanish Latin America); Silvia Donzelli Literary Agency (Italy); English Agency (Japan); David Grossman (adult) (UK); International Literatuur Bureau (Netherlands); JLM (Greece); Simona Kessler (Romania); Prava i prevodi (Bulgaria, Czech Republic, Estonia, Hungary, Montenegro, Poland, Serbia, Slovakia, Slovenia); Rights People (children's) (UK); Schlueck Agency (Germany); Eric Yang Agency (Korea)

Kuhn Projects, see Aevitas Creative Management

The LA Literary Agency (L)
PO Box 46370, Los Angeles, CA 90046
Tel: 323-654-5288
E-mail: laliteraryagency@mac.com; mail@laliteraryagency.com
Web Site: www.laliteraryagency.com
Key Personnel
Literary Agent: Ann Cashman *E-mail:* ann@laliteraryagency.com; Eric Lasher *E-mail:* eric.laliterary@mac.com; Maureen Lasher *E-mail:* maureen.laliterary@mac.com
Founded: 1980
Specialize in narrative nonfiction, commercial & literary fiction. Accept unsol mss. Nonfiction: query, qualifications & proposal; Fiction: query & 50 pages. See web site for books, clients & submission information.

Peter Lampack Agency Inc (L)
350 Fifth Ave, Suite 5300, New York, NY 10118
Tel: 212-687-9106 *Fax:* 212-687-9109
Web Site: www.peterlampackagency.com
Key Personnel
Pres: Peter A Lampack
Agent & Foreign Rts: Rema Dilanyan *E-mail:* rema@peterlampackagency.com
Agent: Andrew Lampack *E-mail:* andrew@peterlampackagency.com
Off Mgr: Christie Russell *E-mail:* christie@peterlampackagency.com
Founded: 1977
Commercial & literary fiction; nonfiction by recognized experts in a given field (especially autobiography, biography, law, finance, politics, history). Handle motion picture & TV rights from book properties only. No stageplays, teleplays or screenplays. No unsol mss. Query with letter which describes the nature of the ms plus author's credentials if any, sample chapter & synopsis by e-mail only.
Titles recently placed: *Built to Thrill*, Clive Cussler; *Frozen Fire*, Clive Cussler, Graham Brown; *Odessa Sea*, Clive Cussler, Dirk Cussler; *Oregon Files*, Clive Cussler, Boyd Morrison; *Police State*, Gerry Spence; *The Cutthroat*, Clive Cussler, Justin Scott; *The Pirate*, Clive Cussler, Robin Burcell; *The Schooldays of Jesus*, J M Coetzee
Foreign Rep(s): Big Apple Agency Inc (China, Taiwan); Prava i prevodi (Eastern Europe, Greece); Tuttle-Mori Agency Inc (Japan, Thailand); Eric Yang Agency (Korea)

Sarah Lazin Books (L)
19 W 21 St, Suite 501, New York, NY 10010
Tel: 212-989-5757 *Fax:* 212-989-1393
Key Personnel
Pres: Sarah Lazin (AAR)
General nonfiction, fiction & illustrated books. Handle film & TV rights. Domestic & foreign rights in all principal countries. No unsol mss, query first. No fees.
Foreign Rights: Bardon-Chinese Media Agency (Taiwan); The English Agency (Japan) Ltd (Japan); Graal Literary Agency (Poland); Katai & Bolza (Hungary); La Nouvelle Agence (France); Kristin Olson (Czech Republic); Owls Agency Inc (Japan); I Pikarski (Israel); Prava i prevodi (Croatia, Greece, Montenegro, Romania, Serbia, Slovenia, Turkey); Vicki Satlow Agency (Italy); Thomas Schlueck GmbH (Germany); Tuttle-Mori Agency Inc (Japan); Lucas Alexander Whitley (Australia, UK); Julio F Yanez (Portugal, Spain); Eric Yang Agency (Korea)

The Ned Leavitt Agency (L)
70 Wooster St, Suite 4-F, New York, NY 10012
Tel: 212-334-0999
Web Site: www.nedleavittagency.com
Key Personnel
Pres: Ned Leavitt (AAR) *E-mail:* ned@ndleavittagency.com
Agent: Britta Alexander; Jillian Sweeney
Literary & commercial fiction & nonfiction, books on spirituality & psychology. No unsol mss. Submissions by recommendation only. Rejections not returned, no reading fee.

Levine|Greenberg|Rostan Literary Agency (L)
307 Seventh Ave, Suite 2407, New York, NY 10001
Tel: 212-337-0934 *Fax:* 212-337-0948
Web Site: lgrliterary.com
Key Personnel
Principal: Daniel Greenberg (AAR) *E-mail:* dgreenberg@lgrliterary.com; James Levine (AAR) *E-mail:* jlevine@lgrliterary.com; Stephanie Rostan (AAR) *E-mail:* srostan@lgrliterary.com
Rts Dir: Elizabeth Fisher (AAR) *E-mail:* efisher@lgrliterary.com
Busn Mgr: Melissa Rowland *E-mail:* mrowland@lgrliterary.com
Agent & Digital Rts Mgr: Kerry Sparks (AAR) *E-mail:* ksparks@lgrliterary.com
Assoc Agent & Rts Mgr: Tim Wojcik *E-mail:* twojcik@lgrliterary.com
Agent: Lindsay Edgecombe (AAR) *E-mail:* ledgecombe@lgrliterary.com; Victoria Skurnick (AAR) *E-mail:* vskurnick@lgrliterary.com; Danielle Svetcov (AAR) *E-mail:* dsvetcov@lgrliterary.com; Monika Verma (AAR) *E-mail:* mverma@lgrliterary.com
Assoc Agent: Sarah Bedingfield *E-mail:* sbedingfield@lgrliterary.com
Agent-at-Large: Arielle Eckstut
Founded: 1989
Narrative nonfiction, business, technology, psychology, parenting, health, humor, women's, men's, sexuality, education & social issues, popular culture, narrative nonfiction, fiction, cookbooks, sports. Online queries via the How To Submit page on web site or e-mail queries to submit@levinegreenberg.com. Attachments limited to 50 pages. Handle software, film & TV rights. No reading fee.
Foreign Rights: AnatoliaLit Agency (Turkey); Bardon-Chinese Media Agency (China, Taiwan); Eliane Benisti Agence Litteraire

(France); The Book Publishers Association of Israel (Israel); Bridge Communications; The English Agency (Japan); Ersilia Literary Agency (Greece); The Foreign Office (Latin America, Portugal, Spain); Graal Literary Agency (Czech Republic, Eastern Europe, Poland); Agence Hoffmann (Germany); Internationaal Literatuur Bureau (Netherlands); Korea Copyright Center (KCC) (Korea); Maxima Creative Agency (Indonesia, Malaysia); Agencia Riff (Brazil); Vicki Satlow Agency (Italy); Abner Stein Agency (UK); Synopsis Literary Agency (Baltic States, Estonia, Russia); Ulf Toregard Agency (Scandinavia)

Robert Lieberman Agency (L)
Subsidiary of Ithaca Film & Writing Works
475 Nelson Rd, Ithaca, NY 14850
Tel: 607-273-8801
Web Site: www.kewgardensmovie.com/CUPeople/users/rhl10
Key Personnel
Pres: Robert H Lieberman *E-mail:* RHL10@cornell.edu
Founded: 1994
ABSOLUTELY NONFICTION ONLY! WILL NOT RESPOND TO FICTION QUERIES. Specialize in college level textbooks by established & recognized academics in all fields, as well as trade books in science, math, economics, engineering, medicine, psychology, computers & other academic areas that would be of general or popular interest. Represent producers of CD-ROM/multimedia/software, film & videos that fall into these categories. Submissions can be proposals +/or sample chapters, resume & table of contents. No unsol mss, query first (prefer e-mail query); will give quick response by e-mail but will accept mail query with SASE; handle software; no reading fee.

Literary & Creative Artists Inc (L)
3543 Albemarle St NW, Washington, DC 20008-4213
Tel: 202-362-4688 *Fax:* 202-362-8875
E-mail: lcadc@earthlink.net (queries, no attachments)
Web Site: www.lcadc.com
Key Personnel
Founder & Pres: Muriel G Nellis (AAR)
VP: Jane F Roberts
Founded: 1981
Specialize in adult trade fiction & nonfiction credentialed authors only. No poetry or academic/technical work. No unsol mss, query first by mail addressed to Muriel Nellis with SASE or by e-mail (no attachments). Require exclusive review period of 2-3 weeks. No reading fee. Visit the submission page on our web site for more information.
Membership(s): ABA; American Bar Association; The Authors Guild

Literary Artists Representatives (L)
575 West End Ave, Suite GRC, New York, NY 10024-2711
Tel: 212-679-7788
E-mail: litartists@aol.com
Key Personnel
Pres: Madeline Perrone
VP: Samuel Fleishman
Founded: 1993
Emphasizes adult trade, nonfiction (narrative, biography, memoir, current affairs, business, culture, history, how-to, film/TV, personal finance, sciences, sports, motivational). Handle film, TV electronic rights. Co-agents in Hollywood & other selected cities. No unsol mss, query first via e-mail. No fees.
Titles recently placed: *Disney U: How Disney University Develops the World's Most Engaged, Loyal, and Customer-Centric Employees*, Doug Lipp; *Financial Fitness Forever: 5 Steps to More Money, Less Risk, and More Peace of Mind*, Paul Merriman, Richard Buck; *First Over There: America's First Battle of World War I: The Attack on Cantigny May 28-31, 1918*, Matthew James Davenport; *Investment Mistakes Even Smart Investors Make and How to Avoid Them*, Larry E Swedroe, RC Balaban; *JFK in the Senate: Pathway to the Presidency*, John T Shaw; *Kaiten: Japan's Secret Manned Suicide Submarine and the First American Ship It Sank in WWI: The Untold Story*, Michael Mair, Joy Waldron; *Lady in the Dark: Iris Barry and the Art of Film*, Robert Sitton; *Political Mercenaries: How Fundraisers Allowed Billionaires to Take Over Politics*, Lindsay Mark Lewis, Jim Arkedis; *The $1,000 Challenge: How One Family Slashed Its Budget Without Moving Under a Bridge or Living on Government Cheese*, Brian J O'Connor; *The Intelligent Option Investor: Applying Value Investing to the World of Options*, Erik Kobayashi-Solomon; *The Women's Guide to Successful Investing: Achieving Financial Security and Realizing Your Goals*, Nancy Tengler; *Think, Act, and Invest Like Warren Buffett: The Winning Strategy to Help You Achieve Your Financial and Life Goals*, Larry Swedroe

Literary Management Group LLC (L)
521 Oakley Dr, Nashville, TN 37220
Tel: 615-812-4445
Web Site: www.literarymanagementgroup.com
Key Personnel
Pres & CEO: Bruce R Barbour
E-mail: brucebarbour@literarymanagementgroup.com
VP, Prod Devt: Karen Moore *Tel:* 614-266-2876
E-mail: karenmoorebarbour@gmail.com
Founded: 1997
Nonfiction: Christian, motivational & inspirational. No unsol mss, query first with letter prior to submission of ms for review. E-mail proposal, outline, sample chapters. We do not represent fiction, screenplays, children's, poetry, text or reference.
Membership(s): CBA: The Association for Christian Retail; Evangelical Christian Publishers Association

Lowenstein Associates Inc (L-D)
115 E 23 St, 4th fl, New York, NY 10010
Tel: 212-206-1630
E-mail: assistant@bookhaven.com (queries, no attachments)
Web Site: www.lowensteinassociates.com
Key Personnel
Pres: Barbara Lowenstein (AAR)
Agent, Contracts & Foreign Rts Mgr: Mary South (AAR) *E-mail:* mary@bookhaven.com
Founded: 1976
Electronic queries (no attachments). No westerns, textbooks, children's picture books or books needing translation. Fiction: submit via Authors.me or send a one-page query with first 10 pages in the body of the e-mail; nonfiction: submit via authors.me or send a one-page query, table of contents & a proposal (if available) in the body of the e-mail to assistant@bookhaven.com. Include the word QUERY & the project name in the subject line. Address the e-mail to the agent you want to consider your work. Visit our web site to find more information about each agent's interests. No reading fee.
Membership(s): Romance Writers of America

Donald Maass Literary Agency (L)
1000 Dean St, Suite 252, Brooklyn, NY 11238
Tel: 212-727-8383 *Fax:* 212-727-3271
E-mail: info@maassagency.com
Web Site: www.maassagency.com
Key Personnel
Pres: Donald Maass (AAR) *E-mail:* dmaass@maassagency.com
VP & Agent: Jennifer Jackson (AAR)
E-mail: jjackson@maassagency.com
Rts Dir & Agent: Katie Shea Boutillier (AAR)
E-mail: ksboutillier@maassagency.com
Agent: Michael Curry (AAR) *E-mail:* mcurry@maassagency.com; Cameron McClure (AAR) *E-mail:* cmcclure@maassagency.com; Caitlin McDonald (AAR); Paul Stevens (AAR)
Founded: 1980
Literary agency for professional novelists, representing more than 100 authors & selling more than 150 novels every year to major publishers in the US & overseas. Also handles book-to-film & TV rights. Leading clients include Anne Bishop, Jim Butcher, Diane Duane, Nnedi Okorafor, Anne Perry, Cherie Priest & Brent Weeks. See web site for submission guidelines. Query via e-mail with 1-page letter, first 5 pages of novel & 1- to 2-page synopsis, pasted into e-mail; no attachments.
Titles recently placed: *Binti: Home*, Nnedi Okorafor; *Brimstone*, Cherie Priest; *Cinder Spires 1: The Aeronaut's Windlass*, Jim Butcher; *Echoes of Sherlock Holmes*, Les Klinger; *Etched in Bone*, Anne Bishop; *Ghost Talkers*, Mary Robinette Kowal; *Lotus Wars: The Stone in the Skull*, Elizabeth Bear; *Raven Stratagem*, Yoon Ha Lee; *The Blood Mirror*, Brent Weeks; *The Divine Cities: City of Miracles*, Robert Jackson Bennett; *The Prey of Gods*, Nicky Drayden; *The Promise of Pierson Orchard*, Kate Brandes; *William Monk 22: Revenge in a Cold River*, Anne Perry
Foreign Rights: Book Publishers Association of Israel (Israel); Silvia Donzelli Agency (Italy); The English Agency (Japan) (Japan); Grayhawk Agency (China, Indonesia, Taiwan, Thailand, Vietnam); International Editors Co (Brazil, South America, Spain); Anna Jarota Agency (France); A Korzhenevski Agency (Russia); MBA Literary Agents Ltd (UK); ONK Agency Ltd (Turkey); Prava i prevodi (Bulgaria, Czech Republic, Montenegro, Poland, Romania, Serbia); Lennart Sane Agency AB (Denmark, Finland, Netherlands, Norway, Sweden); Thomas Schlueck GmbH (Germany); Eric Yang Agency (Korea)
Membership(s): Mystery Writers of America; Romance Writers of America; Science Fiction & Fantasy Writers of America

Gina Maccoby Literary Agency (L)
PO Box 60, Chappaqua, NY 10514-0060
Tel: 914-238-5630
E-mail: query@maccobylit.com
Web Site: www.publishersmarketplace.com/members/GinaMaccoby
Key Personnel
Principal: Gina Maccoby (AAR)
Founded: 1986
High quality fiction & nonficton for adults & children. Handle film & TV rights for clients' work only. No screenplays. No unsol mss; query first. E-mail queries preferred. Include SASE if querying by regular mail. Owing to the volume of queries received, we will only respond if interested. No reading fee. May recover the cost of books purchased for submissions; airmail shipping of books overseas; overnight shipping domestically if requested by client; bank fees incurred related to transfers of payments; legal fees incurred with prior client approval. Co-agents in Hollywood & overseas.
Foreign Rep(s): Anatolia Lit (Turkey); Big Apple Agency Inc (China); Graal Literary Agency (Poland); Mohrbooks (Germany); Andrew Nurnberg Associates (Bulgaria, Estonia, Latvia, Lithuania, Russia, Ukraine); Lennart Sane

Agency (Brazil, Portugal, Scandinavia, Spain, Spanish Latin America)
Membership(s): The Authors Guild; Society of Children's Book Writers & Illustrators

Ricia Mainhardt Agency, see RMA

Carol Mann Agency (L)
55 Fifth Ave, New York, NY 10003
Tel: 212-206-5635 *Fax:* 212-675-4809
E-mail: submissions@carolmannagency.com
Web Site: www.carolmannagency.com
Key Personnel
Pres: Carol Mann (AAR)
Agent: Laura Yorke; Gareth Esersky; Myrsini Stephanides; Lydia Shamah; Joanne Wyckoff; Tom Miller
Founded: 1977
Literary & commercial fiction, no genre fiction, general nonfiction & memoir. Subs-agents in Los Angeles & for all foreign languages. No unsol mss, query first. E-mail queries only (no attachments). Mailed queries no longer accepted. For fiction & memoir, send a synopsis, brief bio & first 25 pages of ms. All other nonfiction, submit synopsis & brief bio. No reading fee. Handle film & TV rights for book clients only.
Foreign Rights: Ackali Copyright Agency (Turkey); Am Oved (Dalia Ever-Hadani) (Israel); Anthea Agency (Bulgaria); Eliane Benisti Agency (France); Big Apple Agency Inc (China, Indonesia, Taiwan); Graal Literary Agency (Poland); The Italian Literary Agency srl (Italy); JLM Literary Agency (Greece); Katai & Bolza Literary Agents (Hungary); Simona Kessler International Copyright Agency (Romania); Licht & Burr Literary Agency (Trine Licht) (Denmark, Iceland, Norway, Sweden); Mohrbooks (Germany); Andrew Nurnberg Associates Baltic (Kristine Supe) (Latvia); Andrew Nurnberg Literary Agency (Ludmilla Sushkova) (Russia); Kristin Olson Literary Agency (Czech Republic); Prava i prevodi (Ana Milenkovic) (Serbia); Guillermo Schavelzon & Associados (Jacoba Casier) (Spain); Schindler's Literary Agency (Brazil); Sebes & Bisseling Literary Agency (Paul Sebes) (Netherlands); Abner Stein Associates (Arabella Stein) (England); Tuttle-Mori Agency Inc (Manami Tamaoki) (Japan); Tuttle-Mori Agency Inc (Pimolporn Yutisri) (Thailand); Shin Won Agency (Tae Eun Kim) (Korea)

Freya Manston Associates Inc (L)
145 W 58 St, New York, NY 10019
Tel: 212-247-3075
Key Personnel
Pres: Freya Manston
Fiction & nonfiction. No unsol mss; not accepting new queries at this time. Agents in all principal countries. No fees charged.

March Tenth Inc (L)
24 Hillside Terr, Montvale, NJ 07645
Tel: 201-387-6551 *Fax:* 201-387-6552
Web Site: www.march10th.com
Key Personnel
Pres: Sandra Choron *E-mail:* schoron@aol.com
VP: Harry Choron *E-mail:* hchoron@aol.com
Founded: 1980
General nonfiction & fiction; specialize in popular culture. No children's or young adult novels, plays, screenplays or poetry. No unsol mss, query first. E-mail queries accepted. If mailing hard copy, include a SASE for materials you want returned. See web site for additional information. No reading fee. Book production services available. Handle film & TV rights. 15% commission.
Titles recently placed: *It's Not About the Shark*, David Niven; *Shakespeare Saved My Life*, Laura Bates

Denise Marcil Literary Agency LLC (L)
483 Westover Rd, Stamford, CT 06902
Tel: 203-327-9970 *Fax:* 203-327-9970
E-mail: dmla@denisemarcilagency.com
Web Site: www.denisemarcilagency.com
Key Personnel
Mgr & Agent: Denise Marcil (AAR)
E-mail: dmla@denisemarcilagency.com
Agent: Anne Marie O'Farrell (AAR)
Tel: 516-365-6029 *E-mail:* annemarie@denisemarcilagency.com
Founded: 1977
Nonfiction: Personal growth, intelligent self-help & how-to's including mind-body-spirit, sports, business, careers, psychology & cookbooks. Send nonfiction e-mail queries to annemarie@denisemarciagency.com. Represents contemporary women's fiction & thrillers. Not accepting any new fiction queries or novelists. No unsol mss, query first, via e-mail. Subagents in all major countries.
Titles recently placed: *Discovering Vintage New York*, Mitch Broder; *Gratitude Prayers*, June Cotner; *Home to Seaview Key*, Sherryl Woods; *Idea Stormers, How To Lead and Inspire Creative Breakthroughs*, Bryan W Mattimore; *Sand Castle Bay*, Sherryl Woods; *Something About Sophie*, Mary Kay McComas; *Swinging '73, Baseball's Wildest Season*, Matthew Silverman; *The College Bound Organizer*, Anna Costaras, Gail Liss; *The Healthy Pregnancy Book*, William Sears, MD, Martha Sears, RN
Membership(s): The Authors Guild; Women's Media Group

Mildred Marmur Associates Ltd (L)
2005 Palmer Ave, PMB 127, Larchmont, NY 10538
Tel: 914-834-1170 *Fax:* 914-833-1175
E-mail: marmur@westnet.com
Key Personnel
Pres: Mildred Marmur (AAR)
Founded: 1987
Nonfiction only. No unsol mss; referrals only. Represented in Hollywood & foreign markets. Does not charge fees.
Membership(s): The Authors Guild

Marsal Lyon Literary Agency LLC (L)
665 San Rodolfo Dr, Suite 124, PMB 121, Solana Beach, CA 92075
Tel: 760-814-8507
Web Site: www.marsallyonliteraryagency.com
Key Personnel
Owner & Literary Agent: Kevan Lyon
E-mail: kevan@marsallyonliteraryagency.com; Jill Marsal *E-mail:* jill@marsallyonliteraryagency.com
Literary Agent: Shannon Hassan
E-mail: shannon@marsallyonliteraryagency.com; Patricia Nelson *E-mail:* patricia@marsallyonliteraryagency.com; Deborah Ritchken *E-mail:* deborah@marsallyonliteraryagency.com
Founded: 2009
Dedicated to helping authors successfully place their work. Members have many years of experience in the publishing industry & possess a diverse & unique skill set. Have worked with many bestselling & award-winning authors, as well as first-time authors.
Fiction genres & categories represented: commercial, mainstream, multicultural, mystery, suspense, thriller, women's fiction, romance (all genres), young adult & middle grade. Nonfiction represented: biography, business/economics/investing/finance, diet, fitness & health, history/politics/current events, investigative journalism, lifestyle, memoirs, narrative nonfiction, parenting, pets/animals, pop culture & music, psychology, relationships/advice, science & nature, self-help, sports, women's issues. No unsol ms, query first. Writers are encouraged to visit the web site to determine who might be the best fit for your work. For electronic submissions (preferred), send query letter & write QUERY in the subject line of the e-mail. Hard copy submissions: for fiction, send cover letter, one-page synopsis of work & first 10 pages of ms; for nonfiction, include either cover letter or cover letter & complete proposal. No fees.
The Taryn Fagerness Agency represents foreign, audio & film subsidiary rights.
Titles recently placed: *$6 Million in Cash*, Anthony M DeStefano; *A Better Man*, Candis Terry; *A Brazen Bargain*, Laura Trentham; *A Covert Affair*, Katie Reus; *A Father's Desperate Rescue*, Amelia Autin; *A License to Wed*, Diana Quincy; *A Peach of a Pair*, Kim Boykin; *A Perfect Plan*, Anna Sugden; *A Pressing Engagement*, Anna Lee Huber; *A Promise of Fire*, Amanda Bouchet; *A Second Chance at Murder*, Diana Orgain; *A Wild Highland Heart*, Kathleen Bittner Roth; *All the Good Parts*, Loretta Nyhan; *All There Is*, Violet Duke; *Almost Anywhere*, Krista Schlyer; *An Indecent Invitation*, Laura Trentham; *At the Edge*, Laura Griffin; *Beach House Brunch: 100 Delicious Ways to Start Your Long Summer Days*, Lei Shishak; *Beauty and the Highland Beast*, Lecia Cornwall; *Black Rose*, Jenna Ryan; *Bleeding Pixels*, Patrick Markey, Chris Ferguson; *Blind Spot*, Katana Collins; *Bound by Duty*, Cat Schield; *Breaking the Rules*, Katie McGarry; *Broken*, Candace Havens; *Bulletproof Badge*, Angi Morgan; *Camp So and So*, Mary McCoy; *Cat Got Your Diamonds*, Julie Chase; *Caught Up in the Touch*, Laura Trentham; *China's New Red Guard*, Jude Blanchette; *Christmas Joy*, Nancy Naigle; *Cliteracy*, Laurie Mintz; *Come on Closer*, Kendra Leigh Castle; *Counting Stars*, Kathleen Long; *Crude Nation*, Raul Gallegos; *Demon of Mine*, Rayna Vause; *Dial Em for Murder*, Marni Bates; *Die Young with Me*, Robert Rufus; *Dirtiest Secret*, J Kenner; *Ernesto: Hemingway's Years in Cuba*, Andrew Feldman; *Eternal Sonata*, Jamie Metzl; *Evenings in Paris*, Jeanne Mackin; *Every Yesterday*, Nancy Naigle; *Everywhere and Every Way*, Jennifer Probst; *Fatal Identity*, Marie Force; *Flawless*, Stefanie Little; *Flirting with Scandal*, Chanel Cleeton; *Fly with Me*, Chanel Cleeton; *Follow Me*, Tiffany Snow; *Forbidden Fling*, Skye Jordan; *Forever Beach*, Shelley Noble; *Forgetting August*, J L Berg; *Forgotten Secrets*, Robin Perini; *From Duke 'Til Dawn*, Eva Leigh; *Haunted Vintage Mystery*, Rose Pressey; *Haven*, A R Ivanovich; *Heart & Sell*, Shari Levitin; *Her Highland Rogue*, Violetta Rand; *Hide from Me*, Mary Lindsey; *Highland Vixen*, Mary Wine; *His Deception*, Patricia Rosemoor; *Hostage Rescue Hero*, Elizabeth Heiter; *House Trained*, Jackie Bouchard; *I See You*, Molly McAdams; *In Another Life*, Julie Christine Johnson; *In His Shadow*, Tiffany Snow; *It Had to Be Fate*, Tamra Baumann; *It Started with Goodbye*, Christina June; *It's in His Smile*, Shelly Alexander; *Karma Khullar's Mustache*, Kristi Wientge; *Last Call*, Kristen Lepionka; *Last Kiss of Summer*, Marina Adair; *Le French Oven*, Hillary Davis; *Leaving Amarillo*, Caisey Quinn; *Les Desserts*, Hillary Davis; *Let the Good Prevail*, Logan Miller, Noah Miller; *Listen to Me*, Kristen Proby; *Listen to the Moon*, Rose Lerner; *Little House in the Hollywood Hills*, Charlotte Stewart, Andy Demsky; *Monet's Palate Cookbook: The Artist and His Kitchen Garden at Giverny*, Aileen Bordman, Derek Fell; *Moonlight Over Paris*, Jennifer Robson; *My Dear Hamilton*, Laura

Kamoie, Stephanie Dray; *My Paris Market Cookbook: A Culinary Tour of Flavors and Seasonal Recipes*, Emily Dilling; *Nanny Makes Three*, Cat Schield; *Oblivion*, Jennifer L Armentrout; *Pill City*, Kevin Deutsch; *Ping Pong Heart*, Martin Limon; *Pippa's Magical Garden*, Pippa Rossi; *Portrait of a Conspiracy (book 1 of the Da Vinci's Disciples trilogy)*, Donna Russo Morin; *Power Play*, Tiffany Snow; *Rebels Like Us*, Liz Reinhardt; *Redeeming the Billionaire Seal*, Lauren Canan; *Relentless Protector*, Hope White; *Return to Marker Ranch*, Claire McEwen; *Ride Hard*, Laura Kaye; *Salem's Cipher*, Jess Lourey; *Seconds to Live*, Melinda Leigh; *Secrets of Nanreath Hall*, Alix Rickloff; *Seized*, Elizabeth Heiter; *Serving Trouble*, Sara Jane Stone; *Smart Girl*, Rachel Hollis; *Surviving Cancer*, David Palma; *Sweet Madness*, Trisha Leaver, Lindsay Currie; *Take Me Home Tonight*, Erika Kelly; *Terror in Taffeta*, Marla Cooper; *Texan's Baby*, Barb Han; *The Accidental Scot*, Patience Griffin; *The Betrayal of the Bonfire of the Vanities (book 3 of the Da Vinci's Disciples trilogy)*, Donna Russo Morin; *The Competition (book 2 of the Da Vinci's Disciples trilogy)*, Donna Russo Morin; *The Crows of Beara*, Julie Christine Johnson; *The Empress of Bright Moon (book 2 of The Moon in the Palace duology)*, Weina Dai Randel; *The Good Daughter*, Alexandra Burt; *The Heir Hunter*, Diane Capri; *The Invisible Shore*, Jacquelyn McShulskis; *The Irresistible Rogue*, Valerie Bowman; *The Kiss on Castle Road*, Lauren Christopher; *The Last August Rose*, Tessa Arlen; *The Memory Diet*, Judi Zucker, Shari Zucker; *The Moon in the Palace (book 1 of The Moon in the Palace duology)*, Weina Dai Randel; *The New Way We Make War*, Louis Del Monte; *The Other Mythology*, Bill Hansen; *The Perfectly Proper Paranormal Museum*, Kirsten Weiss; *The Portable Feast: Creative Meals for Work and Play*, Jeanne Kelley; *The Possibility of Somewhere*, Julia Day; *The Problem with Forever*, Jennifer L Armentrout; *The Puppy Proposal*, Katie Meyer; *The Secret Ingredient of Wishes*, Susan Bishop Crispell; *The Secret of Us*, Camille Di Maio; *The Sweetheart Racket*, Cheryl Ann Smith; *The Tao of Running*, Gary Dudney; *The World's Greatest Adventure Machine*, Frank L Cole; *Then He Kissed Me*, Laura Trentham; *This Loving Feeling*, Miranda Liasson; *This Victorian Life*, Sarah Chrisman; *To Kiss a Thief*, Susanna Craig; *To Steal a Heart*, K C Bateman; *Trail of Echoes*, Rachel Howzell Hall; *Trick or Deceit*, Shelley Freydont; *Turn Me Loose*, Rosalind James; *Unthinkable*, Nina Croft; *Upscale Downhome: Family Recipes, All Gussied Up*, Rachel Hollis; *Visibility Marketing*, David Avrin; *What the Waves Know*, Tamara Valentine; *Whispers in the Mist*, Lisa Alber; *Windy City Blues*, Renee Rosen; *With Love from the Inside*, Angela Pisel; *Worth the Trouble*, Jamie Beck; *Write Naked*, Jennifer Probst

Foreign Rights: Taryn Fagerness Agency LLC (Albania, Argentina, Australia, Brazil, Bulgaria, Canada, China, Croatia, Czech Republic, Denmark, Estonia, Finland, France, Germany, Greece, Hungary, Iceland, India, Indonesia, Israel, Italy, Japan, Korea, Latvia, Lithuania, Mexico, Netherlands, Norway, Poland, Portugal, Romania, Russia, Serbia, Slovakia, Slovenia, Spain, Sweden, Taiwan, Thailand, Turkey, Ukraine, UK, Vietnam)

Membership(s): Romance Writers of America

The Evan Marshall Agency (L)
One Pacio Ct, Roseland, NJ 07068-1121
Tel: 973-287-6216 *Fax:* 973-488-7910
Web Site: www.evanmarshallagency.com
Key Personnel
Pres: Evan S Marshall (AAR) *E-mail:* evan@evanmarshallagency.com
Founded: 1987
Literary management firm actively seeking new clients. Specialize in adult & young adult fiction. Handles a wide-ranging roster of writers in numerous genres, from romance to mystery & thriller to literary fiction. Titles regularly make national bestseller lists including Amazon, USA Today, Barnes & Noble, Publishers Weekly & The New York Times.
No unsol mss, query first. E-mail query letter, first 3 chapters & synopsis of entire novel in body of e-mail, with "project query" in subject line.
Titles recently placed: *A Love for Leah*, Emma Miller; *Death of a Bachelorette*, Laura Levine; *Highland Chieftain*, Hannah Howell; *No Place I'd Rather Be*, Cathy Lamb; *Pretend You're Safe*, Alexandra Ivy; *The Cowboy's Secret Baby*, Karen Rose Smith; *Three Weeks with a Princess*, Vanessa Kelly
Membership(s): Novelists Inc

The Martell Agency (L)
1350 Avenue of the Americas, Suite 1205, New York, NY 10019
Tel: 212-317-2672
Web Site: www.themartellagency.com
Key Personnel
Owner: Alice Fried Martell
Contact: Stephanie Finman
Founded: 1985
Fiction & nonfiction. Handle film & TV rights. No unsol mss, query first. Submit query letters by e-mail, sample material only on request. Include market analysis for nonfiction & author biography. No reading fee. Represented in foreign markets.
Foreign Rep(s): Eliane Benisti (France); Jill Hughes Agent (Eastern Europe, Greece, Middle East); Nurchian Kesim (Filiz Karaman) (Turkey); Liepman Agency (Germany, Switzerland); Maxima Creative Agency (Indonesia, Malaysia); Sara Menguc (Australia, UK); Natoli Stefan & Oliva SA (Italy); Andrew Nurnberg Associates International (Whitney Hsu) (Taiwan); Andrew Nurnberg Associates International (Jackie Huang) (China); Lennart Sane Agency (Netherlands, Scandinavia); Tuttle-Mori Agency Inc (Japan); Tuttle-Mori Agency Inc (Thananchai Pandey) (Thailand); Julio F Yanez Agencia Literaria (Montse Yanez) (Brazil, Portugal, Spain, Spanish Latin America); Eric Yang Agency (Henry Shin) (Korea)

Martin Literary Management (L)
15601 32 Ave SE, Mill Creek, WA 98012
Tel: 206-466-1773 (no queries) *Fax:* 206-466-1774
Web Site: www.martinliterarymanagement.com
Key Personnel
Literary Mgr & Agent: Sharlene Martin *E-mail:* sharlene@martinliterarymanagement.com
Agent: Clelia Gore *E-mail:* clelia@martinliterarymanagement.com
Assoc Literary Mgr: Adria Goetz
Founded: 2003
Nonfiction only. No unsol mss, query first. Now a "green agency," only e-mail queries (no attachments) will be accepted. No fees charged.
Titles recently placed: *Angels All Around Us*, Rebekah Gregory, Anthony Flacco; *Band Geeks*, Amy Cobb; *Breakthrough*, Jack Andraka, Matthew Lysiak; *Chasing Portraits*, Elizabeth Rynecki; *Dario and the Whale*, Cheryl Lawton; *Finding My Shine*, Nastia Liukin; *Geoengineering a New Climate*, Jennifer Swanson; *Horace J Edwards and the Time Keepers: Secret of the Scarab Beetle*, William Meyer; *Maximum Harm*, Michele McPhee; *The Art of the Con*, Anthony Amore; *Too Pretty to Live*, Dennis Brooks; *Wisteria Jane Hummel*, Amber Harris
Foreign Rights: Taryn Fagerness Agency (worldwide exc Canada & US Territories)

Martin-McLean Literary Associates LLC (L)
5023 W 120 Ave, Suite 228, Broomfield, CO 80020
Tel: 303-465-2056 *Fax:* 303-465-2057
E-mail: martinmcleanlit@aol.com
Web Site: www.martinmcleanlit.com; www.mcleanlit.com
Key Personnel
CEO & Agent: Lisa Ann Martin, PhD
Founded: 1986
Literary fiction, nonfiction, health issues, psychology, how-to, self-help, sports, new thought, critical thinking, scholarly, biographies, memoirs, autobiographies & murder mystery. No unsol mss. Query first with letter, synopsis, total word count of ms & e-mail address to the agency's street address or by e-mail. Requirements: send proposal with SASE, follow submission directions on web site, or call for agency brochure. No evaluation or reading fee; work at $60/hour. New writers welcome.
Services: editing, proposal development & critique. Book development available. Ghostwriters can be matched to author. Agents worldwide with Internet access.
Titles recently placed: *A Bird in the Hand*, Jerry Banks; *Angel Kisses: Kildare Beginnings*, Karen K Hoiland; *Angel Kisses: The Gift of Infirmity*, Karen K Hoiland; *Constellation Draco*, J R Bacon; *Diary of a Mad Seducer*, Paul de Vito; *How to Avoid the Over-diagnosis and Over-treatment of Prostate Cancer*, Anthony H Horan, MD; *Indian Zero to American Hero: An Incredible Story of a Slumdog Scientist*, Dr B Vithal Shetty; *Lighter Than Air: Painting with the Colors of the Wind*, Paul de Vito; *Mandy and Thelma*, Billie Thomas; *Mountains of Poetry: Colorado Poems by Colorado Kids*, Coyote Authors Club; *Pact of the Seven Stones: The Mist of Maletoc*, Kevin Cooke; *The Elements of Selling: Everyone Has Something to Sell*, Alan Zell; *The End of Days*, J R Bacon; *The Feral Pistillate*, Warner Bair II; *The Fifth Estate*, Steven Berger; *The Magic Law of Increase: Tithing Your Way to Prosperity*, Lisa Ann Martin, PhD; *The Sacred Agreements: Purpose. Passion. And the Power to Lead.*, Marsh Engle; *The Second District*, Jerry Banks; *The Three R's Make the World Go Around!*, Jade Martin, Dylan George, Kyra Mowry, Valerie Ulsh; *The Uncertain Believer*, Edward Correia; *Vulture Culture*, Eric Gerst; *Who Killed Public TV?*, Smith; *Winter is Upon Us*, Kevin Cooke

Margret McBride Literary Agency (L)
PO Box 9128, La Jolla, CA 92038
Tel: 858-454-1550
E-mail: staff@mcbridelit.com
Web Site: www.mcbrideliterary.com
Key Personnel
Owner & Pres: Margret McBride (AAR)
Founded: 1981
Specialize in fiction, nonfiction & business. No unsol mss, query first with synopsis or outline. E-mail submissions preferred. If submitting via regular mail, include SASE. No poetry, romance, children's or screenplays. Foreign rights sub-agents in all major countries.
Titles recently placed: *Adversaries into Allies*, Bob Burg; *Among Heroes: A US Navy SEAL's True Story of Friendship, Heroism, and the Ultimate Sacrifice*, Brandon Webb, John D Mann; *Red Flags: How to Spot Frenemies, Underminers, and Toxic People in Your Life*, Dr Wendy Patrick; *The Making of a Navy SEAL*, Brandon Webb; *Think to Win: Unleashing the Power of Strategic Thinking*, Paul Butler, John Manfredi,

Peter Klein; *Under the Hood: Fire up and Fine Tune Your Employee Culture*, Stan Slap; *What Works: Common Sense Solutions for a Stronger America*, Cal Thomas
Foreign Rights: Akcali Copyright (Turkey); The Asano Agency (Kiyoshi Asano) (Japan); Bardon-Chinese Media Agency (David Tsai) (China); Eliane Benisti Agency (France); Raquel De La Concha Agencia Literaria (Portugal, Spain, Spanish, Spanish & Portuguese, Spanish Latin America); KCC (Korea Copyright Center) (Korea); Licht & Burr (Scandinavia); Maxima Creative Agency (Santo Manarung) (Indonesia); I Pikarski (Israel); Pravi i prevodi (Eastern Europe)
Membership(s): Writers Guild of America

E J McCarthy Agency (L)
405 Maple St, Suite A, Mill Valley, CA 94941
Tel: 415-383-6639 *Fax:* 415-383-6639
E-mail: ejmagency@gmail.com
Web Site: www.publishersmarketplace.com/members/ejmccarthy
Key Personnel
Owner: E J McCarthy
Founded: 2003
Independent literary agency. Subject specialties: history, military history, politics, sports, biography, media, memoir, thrillers & other nonfiction. No reading fee. Query first by e-mail.
Titles recently placed: *American General*, John S D Eisenhower; *An Angel from Hell*, Ryan A Conklin; *Forty-Seven Days*, Mitchell Yockelson; *Guerilla Leader*, James Schneider; *Hell's Angels*, Jay A Stout; *Lincoln's Counsel*, Arthur Rizer; *One Bullet Away*, Nathaniel Fick; *Resilience*, Eric Greitens; *The Heart & the Fist*, Eric Greitens; *The Sling & the Stone*, Thomas X Hammes; *The Unforgiving Minute*, Craig M Mullaney; *Wanted Dead or Alive*, Benjamin Runkle; *War Play*, Corey Mead; *Why We Lost*, Daniel P Bolger

Gerard McCauley Agency Inc (L)
PO Box 844, Katonah, NY 10536-0844
Tel: 914-232-5700
Key Personnel
Pres: Gerard McCauley
E-mail: gerrymccauley44@gmail.com
Founded: 1970
Nonfiction; educational materials. No unsol mss. Representatives in all major foreign countries. Not currently considering new mss. Does not charge fees.

Anita D McClellan Associates (L)
464 Common St, Suite 142, Belmont, MA 02478-2704
Tel: 617-575-9203
E-mail: adm@anitamcclellan.com
Web Site: www.anitamcclellan.com
Key Personnel
Agent: Anita McClellan (AAR)
Founded: 1988
General fiction & nonfiction, including feminism. No unsol mss, query first by e-mail without attachments, no work previously submitted to publishers. Submit outline or synopsis & first 2,500 words. No software. No reading fees charged.
Membership(s): The Authors Guild; Bay Area Editors' Forum; Cape Cod Writers Center; Editorial Freelancers Association; Grub Street; Independent Book Publishing Professionals Group; International Women's Writing Guild; National Book Critics Circle; Sisters in Crime; Society of Children's Book Writers & Illustrators; Women's National Book Association

McIntosh & Otis Inc (L)
353 Lexington Ave, New York, NY 10016-0900
Tel: 212-687-7400 *Fax:* 212-687-6894
E-mail: info@mcintoshandotis.com
Web Site: www.mcintoshandotis.com
Key Personnel
Owner & CEO: Eugene H Winick
Pres & Sr Adult Agent: Elizabeth Winick Rubinstein (AAR)
Agent, Children's Dept: Christa Heschke (AAR)
Agent: Adam Muhlig
Royalty Admin: Alecia Douglas
Founded: 1928
Represent adult & juvenile fiction & nonfiction books. No unsol mss, query first via e-mail. See web site for instructions. No reading fees. Handle film & TV rights for represented clients only. Agents in most major foreign countries.
Foreign Rep(s): AnatoliaLit Agency (adult) (Turkey); Bardon-Chinese Media Agency (Mainland China, Taiwan); The Deborah Harris Agency (Israel); The Italian Literary Agency SRL (Italy); Japan Uni Agency Inc (Japan); Simona Kessler International Copyright Agency Ltd (Romania); Mohrbooks (Germany); La Nouvelle Agence (adult) (France); Andrew Nurnburg (Eastern Europe); Prava i prevodi (Croatia, Serbia); Read n Right Agency (Greece); Abner Stein Agency (UK); Julio F Yanez (Latin America, Portugal, Spain)

McLean Literary Associates, see
Martin-McLean Literary Associates LLC

Sally Hill McMillan LLC (L)
429 E Kingston Ave, Charlotte, NC 28203
Tel: 704-334-0897
E-mail: mcmagency@aol.com
Key Personnel
Pres: Sally Hill McMillan
Founded: 1990 (converted to LLC 2011)
Southern fiction & adult trade nonfiction; no unsol mss, query first & await further instructions. No science fiction, military, horror, fantasy/adventure children's books or cookbooks. No reading fee. Handle film, TV, foreign & electronic rights through sub-agents.
Titles recently placed: *Art of Arranging Flowers*, Lynne Hinton Branard; *Coastal Birds*, John Yow; *Traveling Light*, Lynne Hinton Branard
Foreign Rights: The Fielding Agency (all other territories); Thomas Schlueck GmbH (Germany)
Membership(s): Women's National Book Association

Mendel Media Group LLC (L)
115 W 30 St, Suite 800, New York, NY 10001
Tel: 646-239-9896 *Fax:* 212-685-4717
Web Site: www.mendelmedia.com
Key Personnel
Mng Partner: Scott Mendel (AAR)
E-mail: scott@mendelmedia.com
Founded: 2002
Represent nonfiction writers in most subject areas, from biography & serious history to health & relationships. Nonfiction clientele includes individual authors & institutions whose works, collections, archives, researchers +/or policy experts contribute to important public discussions & debates. Also represent more lighthearted nonfiction projects, when they suit the market particularly well. The agency's fiction writers principally write historical & contemporary multicultural fiction, contemporary thrillers & mainstream women's fiction. Do not accept fax or e-mail submissions. Submission guidelines are available on the web site. No fees.
Titles recently placed: *Agorafabulous!: Dispatches from My Bedroom*, Sara Benincasa; *Allah: The Biography*, Abbas Milani; *Aretha Franklin: The Queen of Soul*, Mark Bego; *Art Girls Are Easy*, Julie Klausner; *Great*, Sara Benincasa; *How to Exercise When You're Expecting*, Lindsay Brin; *How to Win at Everything*, Daniel Kibblesmith, Sam Weiner; *I Could Pee on This: And Other Poems by Cats*, Francesco Marciuliano; *I, Steve: Steve Jobs in His Own Words*, George Beahm; *Impatient Optimist: Bill Gates in His Own Words*, Lisa Rogak; *Off the Menu*, Stacey Ballis; *Our Man in the Dark*, Rashad Harrison; *Patient One*, Leonard Goldberg; *Slow Fire: The Beginner's Guide to Barbecue*, Ray "Dr BBQ" Lampe; *Super Boys: The Amazing Adventures of Jerry Siegel and Joe Shuster-the Creators of Superman*, Brad Ricca; *The Dogs of War: The Courage, Love, and Loyalty of Military Working Dogs*, Lisa Rogak; *The First Lady of Fleet Street: The Life, Fortune and Tragedy of Rachel Beer*, Yehuda Koren, Eilat Negev; *The King Whisperers: Power Behind the Throne, from Rasputin to Rove*, Kerwin Swint; *The March of the Bohemian Irregulars*, Peter Carlson; *The Raft*, S A Bodeen; *United Nations: A History*, Stanley Meisler; *Whitney Houston!: The Spectacular Rise and Tragic Fall of the Woman Whose Voice Inspired a Generation*, Mark Bego
Membership(s): American Association of University Professors; The Authors Guild; MLA; Mystery Writers of America; Romance Writers of America; Society of Children's Book Writers & Illustrators

Scott Meredith Literary Agency LP (L)
Exchange Plaza, 55 Broadway, Suite 2002, New York, NY 10006
Tel: 646-218-9240 *Fax:* 212-977-5997
E-mail: info@scottmeredith.com
Web Site: www.scottmeredith.com
Key Personnel
Pres: Arthur M Klebanoff *E-mail:* aklebanoff@rosettabooks.com
VP, Fin: Maxine Schweitzer
E-mail: mschweitzer@scottmeredith.com
Dir, Subs Rts: Mary Jo Anne Valko-Warner
E-mail: mjaz@ptd.net
Founded: 1946
More than 1,500 titles in print. No unsol mss, query first. No fees charged.

Metamorphosis Literary Agency (L)
12837 S Seminole Dr, Olathe, KS 66062
Tel: 646-397-1640
E-mail: info@metamorphosisliteraryagency.com
Web Site: www.metamorphosisliteraryagency.com
Key Personnel
Owner & Sr Agent: Stephanie Hansen *Tel:* 913-530-3304
Literary Agent: Jennifer Haskin
E-mail: jennhaskin.agent@gmail.com
Founded: 2016
Our mission is to help authors become traditionally published. We represent commercial fiction that is well-crafted, including fantasy, mystery, romance, science-fiction & young adult. Metamorphosis Literary Agency works closely with authors to ensure their book is in the best presentable form. Our publishing connections come from numerous conferences, luck & genuine care. We do not charge reading fees as we adhere to the AAR's Canon of Ethics.
No unsol mss, query first. Please send queries to info@metamorphosisliteraryagency.com for Stephanie & jennhaskin.agent@gmail.com for Jennifer. Include a query letter within the body of the e-mail & attach the first 3 chapters & synopsis. Please only query unpublished projects. Format the ms in a word document to size 12 either Times Roman or Arial font, justified align, no manual tabs, header top left (title & your name), page numbers beginning on page 2 bottom right, & a cover page with just the title & your name.
Titles recently placed: *Accidental Lawyer*, Kim Hamilton; *And Eve Said Yes*, Mark Scheel; *Baby Wolf's First Winter*, Madeline Stout;

But, But Veronica, Alvina Leder; *Claimed*, P J O'Dwyer; *Dawn of the Reaper*, Paul McGowan; *Death in Disguise*, Karen Neary; *Echelon*, Chris Pearson; *Immortal Sleepers | Blood Awakening*, Miranda Nichols; *Lyric Cal*, Missy Burke; *Mirror, Mirror*, Michelle Aimes; *Operation Santa*, Anitra Schutle; *Relentless*, Karen Lynch; *Runes*, Ednah Walters; *The Gorilla Picked Me!*, Michele McAvoy; *The Key of F*, Jennifer Haskin; *The Power Club*, Greg Gildersleeve; *Witches' Quarters*, Laura M Snider

Foreign Rep(s): AnatoliaLit Agency (Amy Marie Spangler) (Turkey); Lora Fountain Literary Agency (Lora Fountain) (Belgium (French-speaking), Brazil, Canada, France, Holland, Italy, Portugal, Spain, Switzerland)

The Miller Agency Inc (L)
630 Ninth Ave, Suite 1102, New York, NY 10036
Tel: 212-206-0913 *Fax:* 212-206-1473
Key Personnel
Contact: Sharon Bowers *E-mail:* sharon@mbgliterary.com; Angela Miller *E-mail:* angela@mbgliterary.com
Fiction & nonfiction. No unsol mss. Handle software, film & TV rights. No reading fee. Subagents in all principle foreign countries.

Montreal-Contacts/The Rights Agency (L)
1350 Sherbrooke St E, Suite 1, Montreal, QC H2L 1M4, Canada
Tel: 514-400-7075 *Fax:* 514-400-1045
Web Site: www.montreal-contacts.com/?lang=en
Key Personnel
Owner: Jean-Sebastien Dufresne *E-mail:* jsdufresne@montreal-contacts.com
Founded: 1981
Represents publishers +/or literary agents exclusively for foreign rights. No author representation. Does not handle original mss. Representation in all principal countries through 20 corresponding agents covering 50 languages. Representing full catalogues or selected titles with new online promotional platform eMediaRights.

Howard Morhaim Literary Agency Inc (L)
30 Pierrepont St, Brooklyn, NY 11201-3371
Tel: 718-222-8400 *Fax:* 718-222-5056
E-mail: info@morhaimliterary.com
Web Site: www.morhaimliterary.com
Key Personnel
Pres: Howard Morhaim (AAR) *E-mail:* howard@morhaimliterary.com
Agent: MacKenzie Fraser-Bub; Kate McKean (AAR) *E-mail:* kate@morhaimliterary.com; DongWon Song
General adult & young adult fiction & nonfiction. Howard Morhaim is not accepting unsol mss. Kate McKean is open to submissions. E-mail your query letter along with three sample chapters (for fiction) or full proposal (for nonfiction). No reading fee. Handle film & TV rights. Representatives in all principal foreign markets.
Foreign Rep(s): Baror International (worldwide exc Portugal, Spain & UK); The Gotham Group (Michael Prevett, film & TV); RDC Agencia Literaria (Portugal, Spain); Abner Stein Agency (UK)

Henry Morrison Inc (L)
PO Box 235, Bedford Hills, NY 10507-0235
Tel: 914-666-3500 *Fax:* 914-241-7846
E-mail: hmorrison1@aol.com
Key Personnel
Pres: Henry Morrison
Founded: 1965
Fiction & nonfiction. Handle film & TV rights. Accept unsol mss but must send query & outline first with SASE; no reading fee. Fee for ms copies, galleys, bound books for foreign & movie sales & ordering books for subsidiary rights.
Titles recently placed: *Barely Legal*, Parnell Hall, Stuart Woods; *The Bourne Initiative*, Eric Van Lustbader; *The Cutthroat*, Justin Scott, Clive Cussler

Moveable Type Management (L)
244 Madison Ave, Suite 334, New York, NY 10016
Web Site: www.movabletm.com
Founded: 2002
Full service literary agency representing writers of adult trade fiction & nonfiction.
After a brief stint at a renowned literary agency, Adam Chromy went out on his own to represent a novel written by a close friend. The gamble paid off & the book was sold on a preemptive offer. Since that auspicious start in 2002, Adam's fresh, rule-breaking approach has led to dozens of book deals at major publishing houses, a national & New York Times Bestseller & a number of film deals for his clients' projects.
No unsol mss, e-mail query first. Send e-mail with "query" in subject line & description of project & brief author bio. See web site for submission policies; no fees charged.
Titles recently placed: *Dead in the Water*, Annelise Ryan; *Glow Kids*, Dr Nicholas Kardaras; *Never Quit*, Jimmy Settle, Don Rearden; *Rage*, Zygmunt Miloszewski; *Sex in the Museum*, Sarah Forbes; *The Forever Summer*, Jamie Brenner; *The Last Days of Cafe Leila*, Donia Bijan

Bonnie Nadell Literary Agency, see Hill Nadell Literary Agency

Jean V Naggar Literary Agency Inc (JVNLA) (L)
216 E 75 St, Suite 1-E, New York, NY 10021
Tel: 212-794-1082
E-mail: jvnla@jvnla.com
Web Site: www.jvnla.com
Key Personnel
Pres: Jennifer Weltz (AAR) *E-mail:* jweltz@jvnla.com
Agent: Alice Tasman *E-mail:* atasman@jvnla.com
Founded: 1978
Trade & mass market fiction & nonfiction. Motion picture, TV & foreign representation, film & TV rights for the books represented. No unsol mss, query first (see web site for complete, up-to-date submission guidelines). No reading fee. Commissions: 15% domestic, 20% UK & foreign translation.
Please be advised that Jean Naggar is no longer accepting new clients.
Titles recently placed: *A Tragic Kind of Wonderful*, Eric Lindstrom; *Big Foot and Little Foot*, Ellen Potter; *D'Arc*, Robert Repino; *Marlene*, C W Gortner; *The Illustrated Book of Sayings*, Ella Frances Sanders; *The Not-Quite States of America*, Doug Mack; *There I Go Again*, William Daniels; *Third Victim*, Phillip Margolin; *This Phenomenal Life*, Misha Blaise
Foreign Rep(s): Akcali Copyright Agency (Turkey); Big Apple Agency (Mainland China, Taiwan); Graal Literary Agency (Poland); Greene & Heaton (UK); Deborah Harris Agency (Israel); Danny Hong Agency (Korea); International Editors Co (Brazil, Latin America, Portugal, Spain); The Italian Literary Agency SRL (Italy); JLM Agency (Greece); Katai & Bolza Literary Agency (Hungary); Simona Kessler International Copyright Agency (Romania); Michelle Lapautre Agency (France); Licht & Burr Literary Agency (Scandinavia); Liepman Agency (Germany); Maxima Creative Agency (Indonesia); Mo Literary Services (Netherlands); Andrew Nurnberg Literary Agency (Baltic States, Bulgaria, Czech Republic, Russia); PLIMA (Montenegro, Serbia); Silkroad Publishers Agency (Thailand); Tuttle-Mori Agency Inc (Japan)

BK Nelson Inc Literary Agency (L-D)
Division of BK Nelson Inc
6726 Moonriver St, Mira Loma, CA 91752-3428
Tel: 760-902-1868 *Fax:* 760-778-6242
E-mail: bknelson4@cs.com
Key Personnel
Pres & CEO: Bonita K Nelson
CFO: Corp Reed
VP: John W Benson
Edit Dir: Tony Pastor
Acctg Dept: Erv Rosenfeld
Founded: 1998
All subjects; handle books, films, TV rights & careers of authors for books, movies & lectures. Edit ms to prepare for publishing & negotiate movie rights for major film companies as well as television. Office at the American Film Market, BookExpo & Frankfurt Book Fair. Represent major film distributor. If we sell the movie for a book you have written, we will help put you on the lecture circuit.
Titles recently placed: *A Play on Words*, John Starcevich; *Creating Wealth Without Risk*, Marc Garrison; *Death Waltz*, Marc Garrison, Brenda Garrison; *Mansions of the Leopard Mistress*, Dr Ted Austin Telford; *People of the Bear Mother: Periphus of the Sea of Souls (book 1)*, Dr Ted Austin Telford; *Platypuss Trilogy*, Jovanka Bach; *The Adventures of Sebastian the Angel Kitty (vol 2)*, S J Knight
Foreign Rep(s): David Bolt Associates (England); Ulla Lohren Literary Agency (Scandinavia); McKee & Mouche (France, Germany); Tuttle-Mori Agency Inc (Japan)
Foreign Rights: Alexandra Chapman
Membership(s): American Association of University Women; The Authors Guild; The Dramatists Guild of America; Motion Picture Alliance; NACA

Nelson Literary Agency LLC (L)
1732 Wazee St, Suite 207, Denver, CO 80202-1284
Tel: 303-292-2805
E-mail: query@nelsonagency.com
Web Site: www.nelsonagency.com
Key Personnel
Pres & Sr Literary Agent: Kristin Nelson (AAR)
COO/CFO: Brian Nelson
Dir, Contracts & NLA Digital: Lori Bennett
Dir, Literary Devt: Angie Hodapp
Asian Rts & Submissions Mgr: James Persichetti
Royalty Auditor & NLA Digital Assoc: Sam Cronin
Founded: 2002
Accepts queries by e-mail only to query@nelsonagency.com. Represents fiction (literary, mainstream, women's, chick lit, romance, science fiction, fantasy, young adult, middle grade). No nonfiction, screenplays, short story collections, poetry, children's picture books, chapter books or Christian/inspirational. See web site for additional submission guidelines; no attachments, phone calls, postal mail or office visits. Some query letters & FAQs posted on web site. No fees charged.
Titles recently placed: *A Study in Scarlet Women*, Sherry Thomas; *Batman*, Marie Lu; *Beacon 23*, Hugh Howey; *Black Mad Wheel*, Josh Malerman; *Dust*, Hugh Howey; *Iron Sharpens Iron*, Scott Reintgen; *It Happened One Doomsday*, Laurence MacNaughton; *Judgment at the Verdant Court*, M C Planck; *Kingdom of Ashes*, Rhiannon Thomas; *Outrun the Moon*, Stacey Lee; *Perfect Liars*, Kimberly Reid; *Pretty Boys Must Die*, Kimberly Reid; *Rebel Mechanics*, Shanna Swendson; *Shift*, Hugh Howey; *Tell*

the Wind and Fire, Sarah Rees Brennan; *The Fourth Monkey*, J D Barker; *The Secret of a Heart Note*, Stacey Lee; *Vivian in Red*, Kristina Riggle; *Warcross*, Marie Lu
Foreign Rights: Jenny Meyer Literary Agency (Jenny Meyer) (worldwide exc Asia)
Membership(s): Romance Writers of America; Science Fiction & Fantasy Writers of America; Society of Children's Book Writers & Illustrators

Regula Noetzli Literary Agent (L)
Affiliate of Charlotte Sheedy Literary Agency Inc
2344 County Rte 83, Pine Plains, NY 12567
Tel: 518-398-6260
E-mail: regula@taconic.net; regula@sheedylit.com
Adult fiction & nonfiction only with special interest in mysteries, biographies, psychology, popular science, sociology & environmental issues. Query first with outline & sample chapter. Representatives in Hollywood & most major foreign countries. No reading fees, no software.

The Betsy Nolan Literary Agency (L)
Division of The Nolan/Lehr Group Inc
112 E 17 St, Suite 1W, New York, NY 10003
Tel: 212-967-8200 *Fax:* 212-967-7292
E-mail: dblehr@cs.com
Key Personnel
Founding Partner: Betsy Nolan
Pres: Donald Lehr
Agent: Carla Glasser
Off Mgr: Jennifer Alperen
Nonfiction, popular culture, child care, psychology, cookbooks, how-to, biography, African-American & Judaica. No poetry. No unsol mss, query first; submit outline, no more than three sample chapters & author background; no reading fee; SASE.
Titles recently placed: *Celebrate Everything*, Darcy Miller; *Seaside Houses*, Nick Voulgaris; *Simple Matters*, Erin Boyle; *Urban Farm Store's Guide for the Perplexed Chicken Keeper*, Robert & Hannah Litt

Harold Ober Associates Inc (L)
425 Madison Ave, New York, NY 10017
Tel: 212-759-8600 *Fax:* 212-759-9428
Web Site: www.haroldober.com
Key Personnel
Pres: Phyllis Westberg (AAR)
Agent, Film Rts: Don Laventhall
Agent (backlist), Perms: Craig Tenney (AAR) *Tel:* 212-759-8600 ext 216
Founded: 1929
General fiction & nonfiction. No screenplays or plays. No e-mail queries. No unsol mss, query first with letter & SASE. Queries are accepted by postal mail & must be addressed to a specific agent for consideration. Enclose concise cover letter, the first five pages of the ms or proposal & SASE for reply. No reading fee.
Foreign Rep(s): David Higham Associates Ltd (UK)

Objective Entertainment (L-D)
609 Greenwich St, 6th fl, New York, NY 10014
Tel: 212-431-5454 *Fax:* 917-464-6394
Web Site: www.objectiveent.com
Key Personnel
COO: Jarred Weisfeld *E-mail:* Jarred@objectiveent.com
Pres: Ian Kleinert *E-mail:* IK@objectiveent.com
Founded: 2007
Full service management company specializing in book publishing, dramatic writing, talent & television packaging. Handles literary, dramatic & film rights, all commerical & adult trade publishing. No unsol mss. Submit query letter. No fees charged.

Fifi Oscard Agency Inc (L-D)
1440 Broadway, 23rd fl, New York, NY 10018
Tel: 212-764-1100
E-mail: agency@fifioscard.com
Web Site: fifioscard.com
Key Personnel
Pres & Literary Agent: Peter Sawyer *Tel:* 212-764-1100 ext 3 *E-mail:* psawyer@fifioscard.com
VP & Literary Agent: Carmen La Via *Tel:* 212-764-1100 ext 2 *E-mail:* laviagent@fifioscard.com
Founded: 1955
General fiction & nonfiction, all areas; film & TV rights; scripts for stage, motion picture & TV. Have always represented talent as well. No fees charged. No unsol mss, query first; submit outline & sample chapter if requested. See web site for more instruction.
Foreign Rep(s): Bardon-Chinese Media Agency (China); Caroline Van Gelderan (Netherlands); Imprima Korea (Korea); The Italian Literary Agency srl (Italy); Agence Michelle Lapautre (France); Thomas Schlueck GmbH (Germany); Abner Stein Agency (England); Julio F Yanez Agencia Literaria (Spain)

Kathi J Paton Literary Agency (L)
Box 2236, Radio City Sta, New York, NY 10101-2236
Tel: 212-265-6586
E-mail: kjplitbiz@optonline.net
Web Site: www.patonliterary.com
Key Personnel
Owner: Kathi J Paton
Founded: 1987
Interested in biography, computers/technology, business/investing/finance, history, health, sports, science, literary fiction, parenting, Christian life & issues, popular culture, humor, investigative journalism & progressive politics/current affairs. No unsol mss; e-mail queries only with a brief description. If requested, e-mail proposal (nonfiction) or synopsis (fiction) & sample chapter. Sorry, no science fiction, horror, poetry, juvenile or self-published books. No reading fee. Subs-agents in all major foreign markets & Hollywood.
Titles recently placed: *Catholic Women Confront Their Church: Stories of Hurt and Hope*, Celia V Wexler; *Out of the News: Former Journalists Discuss a Profession in Crisis*, Celia V Wexler
Membership(s): The Authors Guild

PearlCo Literary Agency, LLC (L)
6596 Heronswood Cove, Memphis, TN 38119
Tel: 901-754-5276
Key Personnel
Owner & Agent: Susan Perlman Cohen *E-mail:* susanperlmancohen@gmail.com
No unsol mss. Query first by mail or e-mail. No fees.

Dan Peragine Literary Agency (L)
227 Beechwood Ave, Bogota, NJ 07603
Tel: 201-390-0468 *Fax:* 201-390-0468
E-mail: dpliterary@aol.com
Key Personnel
Owner & Pres: Dan Peragine *E-mail:* dannyperagine@aol.com
Founded: 1991
Specialize in behavioral sciences, biography, environment, history, Christian, inspirational, nonfiction, self-help, computers, sports, photography, all high school & college textbooks, advanced placement & testing, musical groups, World War I, World War II. Handle software, film & TV rights. Represent photographic archives & books of all types. No unsol mss, query first with a complete proposal; if sending fiction, include any type of readers report or outside review with the submission; submit sample chapters single page, double-spaced, or on disk (do not send by e-mail if it needs to be downloaded). No reading fees, fees charged for editorial development, re-writes, ghostwriters, publishing consulting, full book packaging & book marketing.
Membership(s): ABA; ASPP; National Press Photographers Association; PPA

Alison Picard Literary Agent (L-D)
PO Box 2000, Cotuit, MA 02635
Tel: 508-477-7192 *Fax:* 508-477-7192 (call first)
E-mail: ajpicard@aol.com
Founded: 1985
Representing adult & juvenile/young adult fiction & nonfiction. Beginners welcome. No unsol mss, query first with letter & SASE; no phone or fax queries. Upon positive response, submit double-spaced complete ms. No fees charged.
Titles recently placed: *365 Days of Slow Cooker Recipes*, Stephanie O'Dea; *Curse of the Jade Lily*, David Housewright; *Decided on the Battlefield*, David Johnson; *Fear of Beauty*, Susan Froetschel; *Not Your Mother's Freezer Cookbook*, Jessica Fisher; *Seconds (new ed)*, David Ely; *The Efficiency Trap: Finding a Better Way to Achieve a Sustainable Energy Future*, Steve Hallett; *The Finest Hours (middle grade ed)*, Michael Tougias, Casey Sherman; *Three Cheers for Girls*, Sara Hunt; *Torn*, Stephanie Guerra; *Totally Together: Shortcuts to an Organized Life*, Stephanie O'Dea
Foreign Rights: John Pawsey (Europe)

Pimlico Agency, see Aurous Inc

Pimlico/Aurous Inc, see Aurous Inc

Pinder Lane & Garon-Brooke Associates Ltd (L)
159 W 53 St, New York, NY 10019
Tel: 212-489-0880 *Fax:* 212-489-7104
E-mail: pinderlanegaronbrooke@gmail.com
Web Site: www.pinderlaneandgaronbrooke.com
Key Personnel
Owner & Agent: Dick Duane (AAR); Robert Thixton (AAR)
Founded: 1996
Fiction & nonfiction, film & TV rights. No unsol mss, query first. No reading fee. Submit short synopsis, double-spaced & unbound. Representatives in Hollywood & all foreign markets.
Titles recently placed: *War and Craft*, Tom Doyle
Foreign Rep(s): Abner Stein Agency (UK)

Pippin Properties Inc (L)
110 W 40 St, Suite 1704, New York, NY 10018
Tel: 212-338-9310 *Fax:* 212-338-9579
E-mail: info@pippinproperties.com
Web Site: www.pippinproperties.com; www.facebook.com/pippinproperties
Key Personnel
Pres & Creative Dir: Holly M McGhee *E-mail:* hmcghee@pippinproperties.com
Sr Agent: Elena Giovinazzo *E-mail:* egiovinazzo@pippinproperties.com
Agent, Audio Rts: Heather Alexander
Mgr, Subs Rts & Assoc Agent: Larissa Helena
Asst, Dramatic Rts & Perms: Courtney Stevenson
Founded: 1998
Represent authors & artists for children's picture books, middle grade novels, chapter books & young adult novels. To submit, e-mail query & first chapter. Handle film, TV & foreign rights.
Foreign Rep(s): Rights People (worldwide exc USA)

Pom Inc (L-D)
18-15 215 St, Bayside, NY 11360
Tel: 516-487-3441
Key Personnel
Pres: Dan Green *E-mail:* dangreen@pomlit.com

Founded: 1990
Fiction & general nonfiction. No unsol mss. Please do not fax or e-mail. Handle electronic, film & TV rights. No reading fee.
Titles recently placed: *Crucible of the West*, Brian Catlos; *Inventing Equality*, Michael Bellesile; *Juice*, Robert Bryce; *Thaddeus Stevens*, Bruce Levine; *The Republic in Peril*, Carol Berkin; *Thunder at the Gates*, Douglas Egerton

The Aaron M Priest Literary Agency Inc (L)
200 W 41 St, 21st fl, New York, NY 10036
Tel: 212-818-0344 *Fax:* 212-573-9417
E-mail: info@aaronpriest.com
Web Site: www.aaronpriest.com
Key Personnel
Pres & Agent: Aaron M Priest (AAR)
E-mail: querypriest@aaronpriest.com
Agent: Lucy Childs Baker (AAR)
E-mail: querychilds@aaronpriest.com; Mitch Hoffman *E-mail:* queryhoffman@aaronpriest.com; Lisa Erbach Vance (AAR) *E-mail:* queryvance@aaronpriest.com
Founded: 1974
Our agents are interested in the following:
Aaron Priest: thrillers, general fiction
Lisa Erbach Vance: general fiction, mystery, thrillers, upmarket women's fiction, historical fiction, narrative nonfiction, memoir
Lucy Childs Baker: literary & commercial fiction, historical fiction, memoir, edgy women's fiction
Mitch Hoffman: thrillers, suspense, crime fiction, literary fiction, narrative nonfiction, politics, popular science, history, memoir, current events, pop culture
For all agents: no poetry, no screenplays. The best way to query all agents is to submit a query letter via e-mail. The query should be about one page long describing your work as well as your background. No attachments, however a first chapter pasted into the body of an e-mail query is acceptable. Do not submit to more than one agent at a time at this agency (we urge you to consider each agent's emphasis before submitting). We will get back to you within 4 weeks, but only if interested. No fees are charged.

Prospect Agency (L)
285 Fifth Ave, PMB 445, Brooklyn, NY 11215
Tel: 718-788-3217 *Fax:* 718-360-9582
Web Site: www.prospectagency.com
Key Personnel
Founder, Pres & Literary Agent (NJ Off): Emily Sylvan Kim *E-mail:* esk@prospectagency.com
Literary Agent: Linda Camacho; Carrie Pestritto *E-mail:* carrie@prospectagency.com; Becca Stumpf *E-mail:* becca@prospectagency.com
Literary Agent (NJ Off): Rachel Orr *E-mail:* rko@prospectagency.com; Teresa Kietlinski *E-mail:* tk@prospectagency.com
Founded: 2005
Full service literary agency representing a range of fiction, nonfiction, illustrators, romance, literary fiction, middle grade fiction & picture books, adult commercial fiction, women's fiction & young adult titles. No unsol mss, query first via web. Only queries submitted through our web site are accepted. Queries sent by e-mail or regular mail not accepted. Send query letter, three chapters & a brief synopsis on web site. No fees charged. See web site for detailed submission guidelines.
Titles recently placed: *A Friend for Bo*, Elisabeth Zuniga; *A Weird and Wild Beauty*, Erin Peabody; *Ghost Hunters*, Jeff Cole, Johnathan Robson; *Have Mercy*, Shelley Ann Clark; *Play Me*, Tracy Wolff; *Pug & Pig*, Joyce Wan; *Ruined*, Tracy Wolff; *Shattered*, Tracy Wolff; *Shredded*, Tracy Wolff; *Sinful Rewards*, Cynthia Sax; *Snail and Worm*, Tina Kugler; *Swallow the Leader*, Kevin Sherry; *The Change Your Name Store*, Tina Kugler; *The Critter Club (books 10-12)*, Marsha Riti; *The Yeti Files (1 & 2)*, Kevin Sherry; *Unnatural Selection*, Sara Joiner; *Worth the Fall*, Claudia Connor; *Worth the Risk*, Claudia Connor
Branch Office(s)
551 Valley Rd, PMB 377, Upper Montclair, NJ 07043
Foreign Rights: The Fielding Agency (Whitney Lee) (worldwide)

Generosa Gina Protano Publishing, see GGP Publishing Inc

Puddingstone Literary, Authors' Agents (L-D)
Subsidiary of Cohen Group LLC
11 Mabro Dr, Denville, NJ 07834-9607
Tel: 973-366-3622
Key Personnel
Dir: Alec Bernard
Memb: Michael R Cohen
Contact: Eugenia Kielbicki
Founded: 1972
General trade & mass market fiction & nonfiction; motion picture scripts & teleplays. Handle film & TV rights. No unsol mss, query first with SASE. Submit outline & sample chapters. No reading fee. Representatives in Hollywood & foreign countries. Fee for ms copies, galleys & bound books for foreign & domestic submissions.

Raines & Raines (L-D)
103 Kenyon Rd, Medusa, NY 12120
Tel: 518-239-8311 *Fax:* 518-239-6029
Key Personnel
Partner: Joan Raines (AAR); Keith Korman
Founded: 1961
Handle film & TV rights. No unsol mss, query first; submit one page; no reading fee. Agents in all principal countries.
Foreign Rep(s): Agencia Literaria Carmen Balcells SA; Big Apple Agency Inc; Bookman; Campbell Thomson & McLaughlin; Fritz; The Italian Literary Agency srl; Lapautre; Nurnberg; Tuttle-Mori Agency Inc

Charlotte Cecil Raymond, Literary Agent (L)
32 Bradlee Rd, Marblehead, MA 01945
Tel: 781-631-6722 *Fax:* 781-631-6722
E-mail: raymondliterary@gmail.com
Adult nonfiction & literary fiction; no juvenile, young adult, poetry, short stories, fantasy, science fiction or screenplays. No unsol mss, query first with SASE; submit outline & sample chapters. No reading fee.

Rees Literary Agency (L)
14 Beacon St, Suite 710, Boston, MA 02108
Tel: 617-227-9014 *Fax:* 617-227-8762
Web Site: www.reesagency.com
Key Personnel
Agent: Mr Lorin Rees (AAR) *E-mail:* lorin@reesagency.com; Ann Collette *E-mail:* agent10702@aol.com; Rebecca Podos *E-mail:* rebecca@reesagency.com
Founded: 1983
Literary fiction, nonfiction, young adult, business, biography, health, history, self-help, psychology, current affairs, humor, mystery, thrillers, etc. For fiction, include query letter +/or synopsis & the first 3 chapters. For nonfiction, enclose a complete book proposal or substantial treatment. See web site for complete book list.
Foreign Rights: Taryn Fagerness (Albania, Argentina, Australia, Brazil, Bulgaria, Canada, China, Croatia, Czech Republic, Denmark, Estonia, Finland, France, Germany, Greece, Hungary, Iceland, India, Indonesia, Israel, Italy, Japan, Korea, Latvia, Lithuania, Mexico, Netherlands, Norway, Poland, Portugal, Romania, Russia, Serbia, Slovakia, Slovenia, Spain, Sweden, Taiwan, Thailand, Turkey, UK, Vietnam)
Membership(s): PEN American Center

Marian Reiner (L)
71 Disbrow Lane, New Rochelle, NY 10804
Tel: 914-235-7808 *Fax:* 914-576-1432
E-mail: mreinerlit@aol.com
Founded: 1963
Handle only work for children; fiction, nonfiction. No unsol mss. No online submissions. No new clients. No reading fee. Charge for photocopying & overseas phone & mail. Handle film & TV rights only for books agency sold.
Membership(s): The Authors Guild; Society of Authors & Illustrators; Society of Children's Book Writers & Illustrators

Renaissance Literary & Talent (L-D)
PO Box 17379, Beverly Hills, CA 90209
Tel: 323-848-8305 *Fax:* 424-298-2588
E-mail: query@renaissancemgmt.net
Web Site: renaissancemgmt.net
Key Personnel
Pres: Alan Nevins *E-mail:* alan@renaissancemgmt.net
Agent: Berta Treitl
Founded: 1993
Commercial fiction & nonfiction. Handle film & TV rights; novels. No unsol mss. Query first. Handle highly recommended mss. Submit outlines & sample chapters. No reading fee, 15% commission.

The Amy Rennert Agency Inc (L)
1550 Tiburon Blvd, Suite 302, Tiburon, CA 94920
Tel: 415-789-8955
E-mail: queries@amyrennert.com
Web Site: amyrennert.com
Key Personnel
Pres: Amy Rennert
Busn Mgr: Laura Velkei *E-mail:* lvelkei@frfllp.com
Assoc: Louise Kollenbaum *E-mail:* louise@amyrennert.com
Founded: 1999
The agency specializes in books that matter. Amy has spent more than 25 years in the publishing business, pursuing her passion for the written word. The agency represents a select group of quality fiction & nonfiction writers - many of them award-winners & dozens of agency books have been New York Times & national bestsellers. We provide career management for established & first time authors & our breadth of experience in many genres enables us to meet the needs of a diverse clientele. The agency has developed a reputation since its inception for a passionate commitment to agency writers. We are purposely a small organization to facilitate hands-on personalized service & attention to our authors & their books. We are not currently accepting unsol submissions.
Foreign Rights: Taryn Fagerness (worldwide)
Membership(s): The Authors Guild

Ann Rittenberg Literary Agency Inc (L)
15 Maiden Lane, Suite 206, New York, NY 10038
Tel: 212-684-6936 *Fax:* 212-684-6929
E-mail: info@rittlit.com
Web Site: www.rittlit.com
Key Personnel
Pres: Ann Rittenberg (AAR)
Assoc: Camille Goldin *E-mail:* camille@rittlit.com
Contact: Rosie Jonker *E-mail:* rosie@rittlit.com
Founded: 1992
Literary fiction & nonfiction; no genre fiction, no screenplays. Co-agents in all principal foreign countries as well as Hollywood. Query letter

& first 3 chapters of double-spaced ms with SASE; no queries by fax.
Membership(s): The Authors Guild

Judith Riven Literary Agent LLC (L)
250 W 16 St, Suite 4F, New York, NY 10011
Tel: 212-255-1009 *Fax:* 212-255-8547
E-mail: rivenlitqueries@gmail.com
Web Site: rivenlit.com
Key Personnel
Owner & Pres: Judith Riven
Founded: 1993
Fiction & nonfiction. Handle film & TV rights for book clients only. One page query letter describing material with SASE. Unless requested, no mss accepted. E-mail queries are accepted but no attachments. We are not currently accepting science fiction, fantasy, or horror submissions.
Titles recently placed: *Over There: America in The Great War, 1917-1918*, Lisa Davis; *The Divorce Diet (novel)*, Ellen Hawley; *The Reason for Flowers: How Flowers Changed Our World*, Stephen Buchmann

Riverside Literary Agency (L)
41 Simon Keets Rd, Leyden, MA 01337
Tel: 413-772-0067 *Fax:* 413-772-0969
E-mail: rivlit@sover.net
Web Site: www.riversideliteraryagency.com
Key Personnel
Pres: Susan Lee Cohen
Founded: 1990
Adult fiction & nonfiction. No unsol mss, query first with SASE. No reading fees. Handle film & TV rights & foreign rights with co-agents.

RLR Associates Ltd (L-D)
7 W 51 St, New York, NY 10019
Tel: 212-541-8641 *Fax:* 212-262-7084
Web Site: www.rlrassociates.net
Key Personnel
VP & Literary Agent: Scott Gould *E-mail:* sgould@rlrassociates.net
Founded: 1980
A boutique literary agency in Manhattan, representing fiction of all types (from genre to literary) & narrative nonfiction. No unsol mss; e-mail or regular mail query letters.

RMA (L)
85 Lincoln St, 1st fl, Meriden, CT 06451
Tel: 718-434-1893 *Fax:* 203-440-1013
Web Site: www.ricia.com
Key Personnel
Owner: Ricia Mainhardt *E-mail:* riciarma@gmail.com
Founded: 1987
Popular fiction, especially science fiction, fantasy, mystery, thriller, romance; nonfiction, especially pop culture, history & science. Do not accept poetry. Online submissions preferred. For fiction, submit query letter, brief one paragraph pitch & 1-2 page synopsis in body of the e-mail. Attach ms. For nonfiction, in the body of the e-mail with the cover letter, include a high concept pitch & a detailed table of contents. Include sample chapters or ms as an attachment. Handle audio & drama rights for client's books only. Affiliates handle translation, film & TV rights for client's books. No reading fee. Branch office in Hollywood, CA.
Membership(s): Mystery Writers of America; Romance Writers of America; Science Fiction & Fantasy Writers of America

Roam Agency (L)
45 Main St, Suite 727, Brooklyn, NY 11201-1076
E-mail: roam@roamagency.com
Web Site: www.roamagency.com
Key Personnel
Founder, Agent & Dir: Anthony Arnove
Agent: Roisin Davis *E-mail:* rdavis@roamagency.com; Jessie Kindig *E-mail:* kindig@roamagency.com
Founded: 2002
Adult nonfiction & fiction, handles all subsidiary rights. No unsol mss, query first by e-mail. No reading fee.
Titles recently placed: *The Ministry of Utmost Happiness*, Arundhati Roy; *What I Learned in a Thousand Towns*, Dar Williams; *Who Rules the World?*, Noam Chomsky
Foreign Rights: AnatoliaLit Agency (Turkey); BC Agency (Mr Mihai Taru) (Korea); Best Literary & Rights Agency (Korea); Big Apple Agency (Lily Chen & Dr Luc Kwanten) (China, Indonesia, Malaysia, Taiwan, Vietnam); Brandt New Agency (Carina Brandt) (Finland, Iceland, Netherlands, Norway, Sweden); The English Agency (Japan) Ltd (Tsutomu Yawata) (Japan); Paul & Peter Fritz AG Literatur Agentur (Christian Dittus) (Germany, Switzerland); David Grossman Literary Agency (David Grossman) (English outside North America); The Deborah Harris Agency (Rena Rossner) (Israel); International Editors' Co SA (Isabel Monteagudo) (Spanish); Korea Copyright Center Inc (Korea); Nabu International Literary Agency (Silvia Brunelli) (Italy); Prava i prevodi (Nada Popovic) (Albania, Bosnia and Herzegovina, Bulgaria, Croatia, Czech Republic, Estonia, Hungary, Latvia, Lithuania, Macedonia, Poland, Romania, Russia, Serbia, Slovakia, Slovenia, Ukraine); Read n' Right Agency (Nike Davarinou) (Greece); Riff Agency (Laura & Joao Paulo Riff) (Brazil, Portugal)

BJ Robbins Literary Agency (L)
5130 Bellaire Ave, North Hollywood, CA 91607
E-mail: robbinsliterary@gmail.com
Key Personnel
Owner & Pres: BJ Robbins (AAR)
Founded: 1992
Literary & commercial fiction, general nonfiction. Handle film & TV rights for agency clients only. E-mail queries accepted. No unsol attachments. Mailed submissions must include SASE.
Titles recently placed: *Blood Brothers*, Deanne Stillman; *Blood of the Tiger*, J A Mills; *Little Bighorn*, John Hough, Jr; *Mongrels*, Stephen Graham Jones; *Planet Earth, 2050*, J Maarten Troost; *Reliance*, Mary Volmer; *Shoot for the Moon*, James Donovan; *The Fiction Writer's Guide to Dialogue*, John Hough, Jr; *The Paris Deadline*, Max Byrd
Foreign Rights: The Marsh Agency (worldwide exc UK); Abner Stein Agency (UK)
Membership(s): PEN Center USA

Roger Williams Agency (L-D)
Division of New England Publishing Associates Inc
17 Paddock Dr, Lawrence Twp, NJ 08648
Mailing Address: PO Box 66066, Lawrenceville, NJ 08648-6066
Tel: 860-973-2439
E-mail: roger@rogerwilliamsagency.com
Web Site: www.rogerwilliamsagency.com
Key Personnel
Agent & Mng Dir: Roger S Williams (AAR)
Founded: 1983
No unsol mss, query first. See web site for submission details.
Foreign Rights: Books Crossing Borders (worldwide)
Membership(s): ABA; The Authors Guild; Organization of American Historians

Linda Roghaar Literary Agency LLC (L)
133 High Point Dr, Amherst, MA 01002
Tel: 413-256-1921
E-mail: contact@lindaroghaar.com
Web Site: www.lindaroghaar.com
Key Personnel
Owner & Pres: Linda L Roghaar (AAR) *E-mail:* linda@lindaroghaar.com
Founded: 1996
Full service agency handling mainly nonfiction; lifestyle, crafts, religion & spirituality, history, self-help. No romance, horror or science fiction. Manage comprehensive rights. No unsol mss, query with SASE first. No reading fee. Domestic sales commission: 15%.
Titles recently placed: *CatWise*, Pam Johnson-Bennett; *Complete Crochet Course*, Shannon Mullet-Bowlsby; *Cornell '77*, Peter Conners; *East-Meets-West Quilts*, Patricia Belyea; *Home Spa Lab*, Maya Pagan; *Little Book of Celtic Wisdom*, Carl McColman; *Sweaters Every Day*, Amy Herzog; *The Mitten Handbook*, Mary Scott Huff; *The Patterned Home*, Kristin Nicholas

The Roistacher Literary Agency (L)
545 W 111 St, Suite 7-J, New York, NY 10025
Tel: 212-222-1405
Key Personnel
Pres: Robert E Roistacher *E-mail:* rer41@columbia.edu
Founded: 1978
General nonfiction, especially journalism, social science & public policy. Literary fiction only from published writers. No unsol mss, query first. For nonfiction, submit prospectus, curriculum vitae, 2 sample chapters, chapter outline & table of contents. No reading fee.

The Rosenberg Group (L)
23 Lincoln Ave, Marblehead, MA 01945
Tel: 781-990-1341 *Fax:* 781-990-1344
E-mail: rosenberglitsubmit@icloud.com
Web Site: www.rosenberggroup.com
Key Personnel
Agent: Barbara Collins Rosenberg (AAR)
Founded: 1998
Representing romance & women's fiction; young adult & new adult fiction; trade nonfiction (check web site for areas of nonfiction interest); college level textbooks for the first & second year courses. No unsol mss, query first via e-mail. Representatives in all foreign markets.
Membership(s): Romance Writers of America

Rita Rosenkranz Literary Agency (L)
440 West End Ave, Suite 15D, New York, NY 10024-5358
Tel: 212-873-6333 *Fax:* 212-873-5225
Web Site: www.ritarosenkranzliteraryagency.com
Key Personnel
Agent: Rita Rosenkranz (AAR) *E-mail:* rrosenkranz@mindspring.com
Founded: 1990
Nonfiction, adult; no unsol mss, query first with SASE or via e-mail; no fees.
Membership(s): The Authors Guild; International Women's Writing Guild; Women's Media Group

Jane Rotrosen Agency LLC (L)
85 Broad St, 28th fl, New York, NY 10004
Tel: 212-593-4330 *Fax:* 212-935-6985
Web Site: janerotrosen.com
Key Personnel
Founder: Jane Rotrosen Berkey (AAR)
Agent: Andrea Cirillo *E-mail:* acirillo@janerotrosen.com; Christina Hogrebe *E-mail:* chogrebe@janerotrosen.com; Annelise Robey *E-mail:* arobey@janerotrosen.com; Meg Ruley *E-mail:* mruley@janerotrosen.com; Kathy Schneider; Amy Tannenbaum *E-mail:* atannenbaum@janerotrosen.com

Global Rts Mgr: Danielle Sickles
E-mail: dsickles@janerotrosen.com
Edit Asst: Rebecca Scherer *E-mail:* rscherer@janerotrosen.com
Founded: 1974
Fiction & nonfiction. No unsol mss or queries. Query by referral only. Handle film & TV rights. No reading fee. 15% commission in US & CN co-represented abroad & on the West Coast.
Membership(s): The Authors Guild

Regina Ryan Books (L)
251 Central Park W, Suite 7-D, New York, NY 10024
Tel: 212-787-5589
E-mail: queries@reginaryanbooks.com
Web Site: www.reginaryanbooks.com
Key Personnel
Pres: Regina Ryan (AAR) *E-mail:* reginaryan@reginaryanbooks.com
Founded: 1976
Book-length works of nonfiction for adult & juvenile markets. Specialize in narrative nonfiction, natural history, science (especially the brain), psychology, history, business, popular culture, cooking & food especially in relation to travel, wellness, diet & fitness, self-help, parenting, nature, gardening, pets, architecture, biography, women's issues. No poetry, screenplays or software. Query first, using the guidelines on our web site. Please no queries or follow-up by fax or phone. No reading fee. We handle film, TV & foreign rights. Representation in all foreign countries.
Titles recently placed: *7 Secrets of Persuasion: Leading-Edge Neuromarketing Techniques to Influence Anyone*, James C Crimmins; *Connecting in the Land of Dementia*, Deborah Shouse; *Craft Wine*, Richard Bender; *In Praise of Poison Ivy*, Anita Sanchez; *Itch!*, Anita Sanchez; *Listening to a Continent Sing*, Donald W Kroodsma; *Peterson Guide to Bird Sounds of North America*, Nathan Pieplow; *Peterson Guide to Finding Mammals*, Vladimir Dinets; *The Boy Who Became Buffalo Bill*, Andrea Warren; *The Friendly Orange Glow: The Untold Story of the PLATO System and the Dawn of Cyberculture*, Brian Dear; *What's Wrong With My Weed?*, David Deardorff, Kathryn Wadsworth; *Wildlife Spectacles: Mass Migration, Mating Rituals and Other Fascinating Animal Behaviors*, Vladimir Dinets
Foreign Rights: Books Crossing Borders (worldwide exc UK); Abner Stein Agency (UK & Commonwealth)
Membership(s): The Authors Guild; The Linnaean Society of New York; PEN American Center; Women's Media Group

Victoria Sanders & Associates LLC (L)
241 Avenue of the Americas, Suite 11-H, New York, NY 10014
Tel: 212-633-8811 *Fax:* 212-633-0525
E-mail: queriesvsa@gmail.com
Web Site: www.victoriasanders.com
Key Personnel
Pres: Victoria Sanders
Agent: Bernadette Baker-Baughman
Founded: 1992
Always interested in new material & welcome all genres: literary & commercial fiction, nonfiction, memoir, women's fiction, thrillers, humor, science fiction/fantasy, graphic novels & self-help/motivational, just to name a few. No unsol mss, query first. E-mail queries only. Please include first 3 chapters (or about 25 pages) pasted into the body of the e-mail. Consult web site for further information. Handle film & TV rights & translation rights. No reading fees.
Titles recently placed: *50 Mice*, Dan Pyne; *All the Happiness You Deserve*, Michael Piafsky; *Animus*, Kim Green; *Catching Air*, Sarah Pekkanen; *Children of the Jacaranda Tree*, Sahar Delijani; *Cop Town*, Karin Slaughter; *Delilah Dirk and the Blades of England*, Tony Cliff; *Descending Son*, Scott Shepherd; *Five Days Left*, Julie Lawson Timmer; *Safe With Me*, Sarah Pekkanen; *The Adventures of Super Hero Girl*, Faith Erin Hicks; *The Black Cabinet*, Jill Watts; *The Death Trail*, Sara Blaedel; *The Forgotten Girls*, Sara Blaedel; *The Gods of Tango*, Carolina De Robertis; *The Human Body Theatre*, Maris Wicks; *The Prey*, Tom Isbell; *The Seventh Day*, Scott Shepherd; *The Strange and Beautiful Sorrows of Ava Lavender*, Leslye Walton; *The Wedding Gift*, Marlen Suyapa Bodden; *The Wind is Not a River*, Brian Payton; *Those Above*, Daniel Polansky; *Three Years in Wonderland*, Todd James Pierce; *Til the Well Runs Dry*, Lauren Francis-Sharma; *Unseen*, Karin Slaughter; *Wanderers*, Susan Kim, Laurence Klavan; *Who We Be: The Colorization of America*, Jeff Chang
Branch Office(s)
440 Buck Rd, Stone Ridge, NY 12484 *Tel:* 845-687-6140
Foreign Rights: Chandler Crawford (worldwide)

Jack Scagnetti Talent & Literary Agency (L-D)
5136 Vineland Ave, North Hollywood, CA 91601
Tel: 818-762-3871
Web Site: www.jackscagnettiagency.com; www.facebook.com/jackscagnettiagency/
Key Personnel
Owner: Jack Scagnetti
Agent: David Goldman
Founded: 1974
Screenplays, TV & film treatments. No unsol mss, query first. Submit synopsis, first chapter for books; paragraph or one-page synopsis for scripts. No reading fee, charge one-way postage for multiple submissions, 10% commission. Detailed critique & consultation services available for books on hourly basis. Represented self in sale of 15 books which led to representing writer friends & others.
Membership(s): Television Academy; Writers Guild of America, West

Schiavone Literary Agency Inc (L-D)
236 Trails End, West Palm Beach, FL 33413-2135
Tel: 561-966-9294 *Fax:* 561-966-9294
E-mail: profschia@aol.com
Web Site: www.publishersmarketplace.com/members/profschia
Key Personnel
CEO: Dr James Schiavone
Pres (Bronx, NY off): Jennifer DuVall
E-mail: jendu77@aol.com
EVP (NY off): Kevin McAdams *E-mail:* kvn.mcadams@yahoo.com
Founded: 1996
Fiction & nonfiction, all genres: young adult, scholarly books, textbooks, business, motivational, advertising, marketing. Specialize in celebrity biography & autobiography & memoirs. No poetry or children's picture books. No unsol mss. No queries via phone, fax or post. Accept only e-mail queries consisting of one page (no attachments). No previously published work in any format. Query only one agent at the company. No fees. Commission: 15% domestic, 20% foreign. Representation in foreign markets. Send e-mail queries to individual personnel at their e-mail address noted. Also have offices in New York, NY.
Titles recently placed: *Accused*, Brittany Ducker; *Beautiful Old Dogs*, David Tabatsky; *Blending Families Successfully*, George Glass, MD; *Edwardian Cooking: 80 Recipes Inspired by Downton Abbey's Elegant Meals*, Larry Edwards; *Finding Jack: A Novel*, Gareth Crocker; *Get a Clue: Mystery Devotions for Kids*, Mark Littleton; *Hungry Love: Classy Eating, Trashy Reading*, Cindy Silvert; *The Last Meal: Defending an Accused Mass Murderer*, Dennis Shere; *The Overparenting Epidemic*, George Glass, MD, David Tabatsky; *Through the New Testament: Devotions for Kids*, Mark Littleton; *Trust Me: A Memoir*, George Kennedy; *Unlikely Liberal: Sarah Palin's Curious Record as Alaska's Governor*, Matthew Zencey
Branch Office(s)
Bronx, NY 10463-1139 (Jennifer DuVall only considers books on real estate. Kevin McAdams only considers work on contemporary music)
New York, NY (contact Kevin McAdams for musical entertainment titles, Francine Edelman for all other genres - special interest in business, marketing, advertising & self-help)
Foreign Rights: Chloe Ataroff (Central Europe, France); Asli Ermis (Turkey); Feliz Karaman (Turkey); Hamish Mackaskill (Japan); Radoslav Trenev (Bulgaria, Eastern Europe); Annisa Waharyudisti (Indonesia, Vietnam); Yang Young-Chul (Korea)
Membership(s): National Education Association

Wendy Schmalz Agency (L)
402 Union St, Unit 831, Hudson, NY 12534
Tel: 518-672-7697
E-mail: wendy@schmalzagency.com
Web Site: www.schmalzagency.com
Key Personnel
Owner: Wendy Schmalz (AAR)
Founded: 2002
Adult & children's fiction & nonfiction. No unsol mss, e-mail queries only. See web site for submission details.
Titles recently placed: *A Lie For a Lie*, Robin Morrow MacCready; *Caroline: Little House, Revisited*, Sarah Miller; *Snowbirds*, Crissa-Jean Chappell; *Summer of Salt and Magic*, Katrina Leno; *The White Van*, April Henry; *Threads*, Ami Polonsky; *Train I Ride*, Paul Mosier
Foreign Rights: Rights People (worldwide)

Harold Schmidt Literary Agency (L-D)
415 W 23 St, Suite 6-F, New York, NY 10011
Tel: 212-727-7473
Key Personnel
Pres: Harold D Schmidt (AAR) *E-mail:* hslanyc@aol.com
Specialize in book-length fiction & nonfiction. No unsol mss, query first by e-mail & include up to the first 5 pages of your book embedded in the e-mail; do not send as an attachment. Telephone queries not accepted. Do not send material through the mail unless requested. Representatives in Hollywood & in all principal foreign countries.

Susan Schulman Literary Agency LLC (L-D)
454 W 44 St, New York, NY 10036
Tel: 212-713-1633
E-mail: queries@schulmanagency.com; linda@schulmanagency.com (translation & audio rts)
Key Personnel
Owner: Susan Schulman (AAR) *E-mail:* susan@schulmanagency.com
Founded: 1980
Adult book-length genre & literary fiction & nonfiction especially women's studies, biography, psychology & the social sciences. No unsol mss. Query first with SASE or by e-mail. Submit outline & 3 sample chapters. No reading fee. Co-agent in all principal foreign countries. Handles film & TV rights for other agencies & individual titles.
Foreign Rep(s): ACER Agencia Literaria (Spain); Big Apple Agency Inc (China); Lora Fountain & Associates (France); The Italian Literary Agency SRL (Italy); Nurcihan Kesim Literary Agency Inc (Turkey); Korea Copyright Center (Korea); Leipman AG (Germany); Lennart Sane Agency (Sweden); Owls Agency

Inc (Japan); I Pikarski Literary Agency (Israel); Prava i prevodi (Eastern Europe); The Rights Agency (Canada (French-speaking)); Susanna Zevi Agenzia Letteraria (Italy)
Membership(s): The Authors Guild; The Dramatists Guild of America; Society of Children's Book Writers & Illustrators; Women in Film; Women's Media Group; Writers Guild of America, East

Laurens R Schwartz, Esquire (L-D)
5 E 22 St, Suite 15-D, New York, NY 10010-5325
Tel: 212-228-2614
Founded: 1981
Full service agency handling all media for all ages worldwide. No fees; standard commissions; WGA Signatory. No unsol mss, CD-ROMs, etc. Query first with synopsis of one project & resume. Also provide information relating to the project having been with other agents or shopped around. Enclose SASE. Require 4-week right of first refusal if request submission of entire project. Handle film, TV & licensing & merchandising rights.
Membership(s): Writers Guild of America

S©ott Treimel NY (L)
434 Lafayette St, New York, NY 10003-6943
Tel: 212-505-8353
E-mail: general@scotttreimelny.com
Web Site: scotttreimelny.com; scotttreimelny.blogspot.com
Key Personnel
Owner & Pres: Scott Treimel (AAR)
Asst: Christopher R Hoyt *E-mail:* ch@scotttreimelny.com
Founded: 1995
Sells & administers intellectual property rights - foreign, dramatic, electronic, broadcast, merchandise, promotion - for children's book creators. No unsol submissions.
Titles recently placed: *A Bike for Sergio*, Maribeth Boelts; *Dandy*, Ame Dyckman; *Flickers*, Arthur Slade; *Girl + Bot*, Ame Dyckman; *Girl + Gorilla*, Rick Walton; *Horrible Bear!*, Ame Dyckman; *Misunderstood Shark*, Ame Dyckman; *Other Wordly*, Yee-Lum Mak; *Pupunzel*, Maribeth Boelts; *Read the Book, Lemmings!*, Ame Dyckman; *The Fairy Dogmother*, Maribeth Boelts; *The Girls' Bible*, Barbara Diamond Goldin, Jane Yolen; *Wolfie the Bunny*, Ame Dyckman; *You Don't Want a Unicorn*, Ame Dyckman
Foreign Rep(s): Akcali Copyright (Turkey); Donatalla d'Ormesson Agent Litteraire (France); Japan Uni (Japan); Barbara Kuper Literarische Agentur + Medienservice (Germany)
Membership(s): The Authors Guild; Society of Children's Book Writers & Illustrators

Scovil Galen Ghosh Literary Agency Inc (L)
276 Fifth Ave, Suite 708, New York, NY 10001
Tel: 212-679-8686 *Fax:* 212-679-6710
E-mail: info@sgglit.com
Web Site: www.sgglit.com
Key Personnel
Pres: Russell Galen (AAR) *Fax:* 646-349-1868 *E-mail:* russellgalen@sgglit.com
Agent: Ann Behar *E-mail:* annbehar@sgglit.com
Founded: 1993
All types fiction & nonfiction, adult & juvenile. Handle film & TV rights. No unsol mss, query first. Submit outline & sample chapters. E-mailed queries preferred but without attachments. Does not charge fees.
Titles recently placed: *An Echo in the Bone*, Diana Gabaldon
Foreign Rep(s): Baror International Inc (worldwide exc USA)

Lynn Seligman (L)
400 Highland Ave, Upper Montclair, NJ 07043
Tel: 973-783-3631 *Fax:* 973-783-3691
E-mail: seliglit@aol.com
Founded: 1986
Adult & young adult fiction; adult nonfiction. Handle film & TV rights through agents in Hollywood. Submit letter or e-mail describing project with short sample pasted to e-mail if desired. No attachments or unsol mss; query first with SASE if snail mail.
Titles recently placed: *Stealing Jason Wilde*, Dee Ernst; *Thinking Parent, Thinking Child, 2nd edition*, Dr. Myrna B. Shure; *Waiting for an Earl Like You (Masters of Seduction)*, Alexandra Hawkins; *You Can't Always Get the Marquis You Want (Masters of Seduction)*, Alexandra Hawkins
Foreign Rights: Books Crossing Borders (Betty Anne Crawford) (worldwide)
Membership(s): Women's Media Group

Edythea Ginis Selman Literary Agency Inc (L-D)
14 Washington Place, New York, NY 10003
Tel: 212-473-1874 *Fax:* 212-473-1875
Key Personnel
Pres & Agent: Edythea Ginis Selman
VP & Electronic Rights: Richard Selman
Literary commercial fiction & serious issue-oriented narrative nonfiction. Selected children's fiction & young adult picture books, handles film & TV rights from adult novels & young adult (by referral only). No unsol mss, query first, only upon request (with SASE). Submit author bio, 2 sample chapters or 50 pages (nonfiction) or complete ms (fiction).
Foreign Rights: Eliane Benisti (France); David Grossman (England); Japan UNI Agency Inc (Japan); Ruth Liepman (Germany); Isabel Monteagudo (Spain); Andrew Nurnburg (Eastern Europe)
Membership(s): The Authors Guild; CSA; National Writers Union; PEN American Center; Society of Children's Book Writers & Illustrators; Women's National Book Association

Seventh Avenue Literary Agency (L)
2052 124 St, South Surrey, BC V4A 9K3, Canada
Tel: 604-538-7252 *Fax:* 604-538-7252
E-mail: info@seventhavenuelit.com
Web Site: www.seventhavenuelit.com
Key Personnel
Pres & Dir: Robert Mackwood *E-mail:* rmackwood@seventhavenuelit.com
Founded: 1974
Nonfiction agency representing international authors from a wide range of subjects & interests. No unsol mss, query first by e-mail; no fees charged.
Titles recently placed: *Great Companies Deserve Great Boards: A CEO's Guide to the Boardroom*, Beverly Behan; *Happy Healthy Gut: The Natural Diet Solution to Curing IBS and Other Chronic Digestive Disorders*, Jennifer Browne; *Route 66 Still Kicks: Driving America's Main Street*, Rick Antonson; *The Mom Shift: Women Share Their Thoughts of Career Success After Having Children*, Reva Seth; *Things That Must Not Be Forgotten: A Childhood in Wartime China (updated)*, Michael David Kwan; *Thrive Energy Cookbook: 150 Plant-Based Whole Food Recipes*, Brendan Brazier
Foreign Rights: Big Apple Agency Inc (Luc Kwantlen) (China, Indonesia, Taiwan); Fritz Agency (Christan Dittus) (Germany); Deborah Harris Agency (Ilana Kurshan) (Israel); Nurcihan Kesim Literary Agency (Dilek Kaya) (Turkey); Simona Kessler Agency (Adriana Marinara) (Romania); Korea Copyright Agency (Ms MiSook Hong) (Korea); Nova Littera Ltd (Daria Pridatkina) (Russia); Kristin Olson Agency (Czech Republic); The Riff Agency (Lucia Riff) (Brazil, Portugal); Sebes & Bisseling Literary Agency (Netherlands)

The Seymour Agency (L-D)
475 Miner Street Rd, Canton, NY 13617
Tel: 315-386-1831
Web Site: www.theseymouragency.com
Key Personnel
Sr Agent: Nicole Resciniti
Assoc Agent: Marisa Cleveland
Founded: 1992
Christian romance & women's fiction, nonfiction & secular romance.
Membership(s): The Authors Guild; Romance Writers of America; Writers Guild of America; Writers Guild of America, East

Charlotte Sheedy Literary Agency Inc (L)
928 Broadway, Suite 901, New York, NY 10010
Tel: 212-780-9800
Web Site: www.sheedylit.com
Key Personnel
Owner: Charlotte Sheedy *E-mail:* charlotte@sheedylit.com
Assoc: Evan Brown *E-mail:* evan@sheedylit.com
Agent/Rts & Perms: Joan Rosen *E-mail:* joan@sheedylit.com
Agent: Kevin O'Connor *E-mail:* kevin@sheedylit.com
Fiction & nonfiction film & TV rights. No unsol mss, query first (no screenplays); submit outline & sample chapters; no reading fee. Agents in all principal countries.
Titles recently placed: *All the Wrong Questions Series*, Lemony Snicket; *Hurry Up and Wait*, Daniel Handler, Maira Kalman; *Meanwhile, in San Francisco: The City in its Own Words*, Wendy MacNaughton; *The Blood of Emmett Till*, Timothy B Tyson; *The Firebrand and the First Lady*, Patricia Bell-Scott; *The Gutsy Girl*, Caroline Paul, Wendy MacNaughton (illus); *The Odd Woman and the City*, Vivian Gornick; *The Winner's Kiss*, Marie Rutkoski; *Thomas Jefferson: Life, Liberty and the Pursuit of Everything*, Maira Kalman; *Tyler Makes a Cake!*, Tyler Florence; *Viva Frida*, Yuyi Morales
Foreign Rep(s): The English Agency (Japan); Agnes Krup (Australia, Germany, Italy, Portugal, Switzerland); Lennart Sane (Netherlands, Scandinavia, Spain); Abner Stein Agency (England)

The Robert E Shepard Agency (L)
4804 Laurel Canyon Blvd, Box 592, Valley Village, CA 91607-3717
Web Site: www.shepardagency.com
Founded: 1994
Not currently accepting submissions.

Ken Sherman & Associates (L-D)
1275 N Hayworth, Suite 103, Los Angeles, CA 90046
Tel: 310-273-8840
E-mail: kenshermanassociates@gmail.com
Web Site: www.kenshermanassociates.com
Key Personnel
Owner & Pres: Ken Sherman
Founded: 1989
Fiction & nonfiction books plus screenplays, teleplays, film & TV rights to books & life rights. No unsol mss or screenplays. Accept by referral only. Submit outline & minimum three sample chapters. No reading fee. International Advisory Board member, The Christopher Isherwood Foundation.
Titles recently placed: *Good Manners for Nice People Who Sometimes Say F*ck*, Amy Alkon
Membership(s): American Film Institute Third Decade Council; British Academy of Film & Television Arts/Los Angeles; PEN International

Wendy Sherman Associates Inc (L)
27 W 24 St, Suite 700-B, New York, NY 10010
Tel: 212-279-9027
E-mail: submissions@wsherman.com
Web Site: www.wsherman.com
Key Personnel
Founder, Owner & Pres: Wendy Sherman (AAR) *E-mail:* wendy@wsherman.com
Founded: 1999
Represents a wide range of fiction & nonfiction. Literary & commercial fiction, including upmarket women's fiction; Nonfiction includes, memoir, narrative nonfiction, health & wellness, gender issues, practical, self-help, popular psychology, lifestyle, home & design, fashion. No unsol mss, query first with SASE. For fiction, a letter & synopsis. Paste first 10 pages, No attachments. For nonfiction, send proposal & 2 sample chapters. See web site for submission guidelines: No paper submissions. No poetry, screenplays, mysteries, romance, westerns, science fiction, fantasy or children's books.
Titles recently placed: *All Is Not Forgotten*, Wendy Walker; *Beautiful Gestures*, Therese Anne Fowler; *Crush*, Cathy Alter, Dave Singleton; *Crystal Energy Rituals for Intentional Living*, Heather Askinose, Timmi Jandro; *Dinner Chez Moi*, Elizabeth Bard; *Eight Flavors*, Sarah Lohman; *Finding Calm for the Expentant Mom*, Ali Domar; *How to Be You*, Jeffrey Marsh; *How to Live a Good Life*, Jonathan Fields; *November Project*, Brogan Graham, Bojan Mandaric, Caleb Daniloff; *Oh! You Pretty Things*, Shanna Mahin; *Poison Girls*, Cheryl Reed; *Raising the Transgender Child*, Dr Michele Angello, Ali Bowman; *Second House from the Corner*, Sadeqa Johnson; *Street of Eternal Happiness*, Rob Schmitz; *The Charm Bracelet*, Viola Shipman; *The Fatherless Daughter Project*, Denna Babul, Dr Karin Smithson; *The Power Greens Cookbook*, Dana Jacobi; *The Promise Kitchen*, Peggy Lampman; *Women Rocking Business*, Sage Lavine
Foreign Rights: Duran Kim Agency (Duran Kim) (Korea); Jenny Meyer Literary Agency (Jenny Meyer) (worldwide exc Asia); Andrew Nurnberg Associates Inc (Whitney Hsu) (Taiwan); Andrew Nurnberg Associates Inc (Jackie Huang) (China); Tuttle-Mori Agency Inc (Japan)
Membership(s): Women's Media Group

Side by Side Literary Productions Inc (L)
145 E 35 St, Suite 7FE, New York, NY 10016
Tel: 212-685-6831
Web Site: sidebysidelit.com
Key Personnel
Founder & Pres: Laurie Bernstein *E-mail:* laurie@sidebysidelit.com
Founded: 2004
Handles general trade fiction & nonfiction as well as select juvenile titles. Specialize in popular health, medicine, self-help, parenting, popular culture, diet & narrative nonfiction. No unsol mss, query first. Will review hard copy & digital submissions. Handles film & TV rights.

Irene Skolnick Literary Agency (L)
27 W 20 St, Suite 305, New York, NY 10011
Tel: 212-727-3648 *Fax:* 212-352-2059
E-mail: office@skolnickliterary.com (queries)
Web Site: www.skolnickagency.com
Key Personnel
CEO: Irene Skolnick (AAR) *E-mail:* irene@skolnickliterary.com
Asst: Sally Chabert
Founded: 1994
Literary & historical fiction, thrillers; narrative nonfiction: memoir, biography, history, travel, humor; YA, middle grade. Handle film & TV rights. Representation in all major countries & Hollywood through co-agents. No unsol mss, query first. Send queries via e-mail or mail with SASE. Include/attach outline & sample chapter.
Titles recently placed: *Give Me Everything You Have: On Being Stalked*, James Lasdun; *Love, Dishonor, Marry, Die, Cherish, Perish*, David Rakoff; *Middle School Cool*, Maiya Williams; *The Chalk Artist*, Allegra Goodman; *The Ice Cream Queen of Orchard Street*, Susan Jane Gilman; *The Long Shadow: The Great War and the Twentieth Century*, David Reynolds; *The Poe Annex*, Polly Shulman; *Where the Dead Pause and the Japanese Say Goodbye*, Marie Mutsuki Mockett
Foreign Rights: Lippincott Massie McQuilkin (Maria Massie)
Membership(s): PEN American Center; Women's Media Group

Beverley Slopen Literary Agency (L)
131 Bloor St W, Suite 711, Toronto, ON M5S 1S3, Canada
Tel: 416-964-9598 *Fax:* 416-921-7726
Web Site: www.slopenagency.com
Key Personnel
Owner: Beverley Slopen *E-mail:* beverley@slopenagency.ca
Founded: 1973
Serious fiction & nonfiction. No children's books, illustrated books, science fiction or fantasy. No software, no film or TV rights handled. Query letter & brief proposal sent by mail with Canadian postage if you want it returned, but e-mail queries preferred. Not taking on many new clients.
Titles recently placed: *20b*, Martyn Burke; *50 Canadians Who Changed the World*, Ken McGoogan; *Al Qaeda Declares War: The African Embassy Bombings and America's Search for Justice*, Tod Hoffman; *Believing: The Neuroscience of Fantasies, Fears, and Convictions*, Michael McGuire; *Beyond Intelligence: Secrets for Raising Happily Productive Kids*, Dona Matthews, Joanne Foster; *Butterfly of Venus*, Susan Ferrier MacKay; *City of Fallen Angels*, Howard Engel; *Is Work Killing You?: A Doctor's Prescription for Treating Workplace Stress*, David Posen, MD; *Life Class*, Ann Charney; *Mr Selden's Map of China: Decoding the Secrets of a Vanished Cartographer*, Tim Brook; *Music for Love or War*, Martyn Burke; *No Relation*, Terry Falles; *Perdita*, Hilary Scharper; *The Harem Midwife*, Roberta Rich; *The Hole in the Middle*, Kate Hilton; *The Memory Clinic*, Tiffany Chow
Foreign Rep(s): Akcali Copyright Agency (Turkey); Paul & Peter Fritz AG (Germany); The Grayhawk Agency (Gray Tan) (China); David Grossman Literary Agency Ltd (David Grossman) (UK); The Deborah Harris Agency (Israel); International Literatuur Bureau (Netherlands); The Italian Literary Agency srl (Italy); JLM Literary Agency (Greece); Katai & Bolza Literary Agency (Hungary); Alexander Korzhenevski (Russia); Agence Michelle Lapautre (Michelle Lapautre) (France); Licht & Burr Literary Agency (Scandinavia); Agencia Riff (Lucia Riff) (Brazil); Tuttle-Mori Agency Inc (Japan); Julio F Yanez Agencia Literaria SL (Julio F Yanez) (Spain); Eric Yang Agency (Korea)

Valerie Smith, Literary Agent (L)
1746 Rte 44-55, Modena, NY 12548
Tel: 845-883-5848
Key Personnel
Contact: Valerie Smith
Founded: 1978
Fiction & nonfiction; special interest in fantasy & science fiction. No unsol mss, query first; no reading fee. Outline & 3 sample chapters. Representatives in Hollywood & all principal foreign countries.

Michael Snell Literary Agency (L)
PO Box 1206, Truro, MA 02666-1206
Tel: 508-349-3718
Web Site: www.michaelsnellagency.com
Key Personnel
Pres & Edit Dir: Michael Snell
EVP: Patricia Snell *E-mail:* patricia@michaelsnellagency.com
Founded: 1978
Adult nonfiction; all levels of business & management from popular trade to professional reference; legal, medical, health, psychology, self-help & how-to books; animals & pets; women's issues in business, family & society; popular science & business; technical & scientific; professional & general computer books; parenting & relationships; project development & rewrite services. Welcome new authors. No unsol mss, query first. Submit outline, synopsis & up to 50 sample pages with SASE. Publication *How to Write a Book Proposal* available upon request with SASE, or consult Michael Snell's book *From Book Idea to Bestseller* (Prima Publishing). Write for information on purchasing a model book proposal. Consider new clients on an exclusive basis. No reading fee, but do arrange for developmental editors & ghostwriters who do charge a fee.
Titles recently placed: *Business Biologic*, William Schneider; *Business Etiquette*, Rosanne Thomas; *Career Coach*, Katie C Kelley; *Finding Peace in Your Heart When Your Heart is in Pieces*, Paul Coleman; *My Radio, Radio*, Jessie van Eerden; *Springboard: Launching Your Personal Search for Success*, G Richard Shell; *Sun House*, David James Duncan; *Tipping Sacred Cows: Kick the Bad Work Habits that Masquerade as Virtues*, Jake Breeden; *What Keeps Leaders Up at Night: Recognizing and Resolving Your Most Troubling Management Issues*, Nicole Lipkin

Sobel Weber Associates Inc (L)
146 E 19 St, New York, NY 10003-2404
Tel: 212-420-8585
E-mail: info@sobelweber.com
Web Site: www.sobelweber.com
Key Personnel
Principal: Nat Sobel; Judith Weber
Founded: 1970
General fiction & nonfiction. No unsol mss, query first with SASE, no electronic submissions. No reading fee. Handle film, TV & foreign rights; serialization & audio rights. Representatives on the West Coast & in all major foreign countries. Consult web site for submission guidelines & client list.
Titles recently placed: *Bishop's War*, Rafael Amadeus Hines; *The Refugees*, Viet Thanh Nguyen; *Trajectory: Stories*, Richard Russo
Foreign Rights: Akcali Copyright Agency (Turkey); Agencia Literaria Carmen Balcells SA (Maribel Luque) (Spain); Tassy Barham Associates (Brazil, Portugal); Paul & Peter Fritz Agency (Germany); The Deborah Harris Agency (Israel); Katai & Bolza (Hungary); Agence Michelle Lapautre (France); Andrew Nurnberg Associates International Ltd (China, Taiwan); Kristin Olson Agency (Czech Republic); Prava i prevodi (Eastern Europe exc Czech Republic, Hungary & Slovenia, Greece, Russia); Santachiara Literary Agency (Italy); Sobel Weber Associates Inc NY (Denmark, Finland, Netherlands, Norway, Sweden); The Abner Stein Agency (UK); Tuttle-Mori Agency Inc (Indonesia, Japan, Thailand, Vietnam); Eric Yang Agency (Korea)

Spectrum Literary Agency (L)
320 Central Park W, Suite 1-D, New York, NY 10025
Tel: 212-362-4323 *Fax:* 212-362-4562
Web Site: www.spectrumliteraryagency.com

Key Personnel
Pres & Agent: Eleanor Wood
Agent: Justin Bell
Founded: 1976
Science fiction, mysteries, thrillers, horror & fantasy. No unsol mss, query first with letter, synopsis, first 10 pages & SASE. No reading fee. Agents in all principal foreign countries.
Titles recently placed: *Penric's Demon*, Lois McMaster Bujold; *Spear of Light*, Brenda Cooper; *The Genius Plague*, David Walton
Foreign Rights: Big Apple Agency Inc (Mr Luc Kwanten) (China); Book Cosmos Agency (Mihai Taru) (Korea); The Book Publishers Association of Israel (Dalia Ever-Hadani) (Israel); Graal Literary Agency (Lukasz Wrobel) (Poland); Japan Uni Agency Inc (Miko Yamanouchi) (Japan); Katai & Bolza Literary Agents (Peter Bolza) (Hungary); Katai & Bolza Literary Agents (Reka Bartha) (Croatia, Serbia, Slovenia); Nurcihan Kesim Literary Agency Ltd (Dilek Kayi) (Turkey); Agence Litteraire Lenclud (Anne Lenclud & Pierre Lenclud) (France); Piergiorgio Nicolazzini Literary Agency (Maura Solinas) (Italy); Nova Littera Ltd (Konstantin Palchikov & Sergei Cheredov) (Russia); Andrew Nurnberg Associates Sofia (Mira Droumeva) (Bulgaria); Andrew Nurnberg Associates Sofia (Anna Droumeva & Mira Droumeva) (Romania); Kristin Olson Literary Agency SRO (Kristin Olson & Tereza Dubova) (Czech Republic); Prava i prevodi (Russia); Read n Right Agency (Nike Davarinou) (Greece); Thomas Schlueck GmbH (Thomas Schlueck & Franka Zastrow) (Germany); Sebes & Bisseling Literary Agency (Lester Hekking & Jeanine Langenberg) (Netherlands); Julio F Yanez Agencia Literaria SL (Montse F Yanez) (Portugal, Spain)
Membership(s): Mystery Writers of America; Science Fiction & Fantasy Writers of America

The Spieler Agency (L)
27 W 20 St, Suite 302, New York, NY 10011
Tel: 212-757-4439 *Fax:* 212-333-2019
E-mail: spieleragency@spieleragency.com
Key Personnel
Agent: Joseph Spieler
Nonfiction & literary fiction; thrillers, children's books including middle grade, young adult & new adult. Areas of interest include: environmental issues, business; women's issues; natural history & science for religious studies, psychology; health; history; biography. No unsol mss, query first with letter (prefer e-mail), first chapter/contents or detailed proposal. No phone queries. Submit author background, description of work & sample chapter with SASE. Handle film & TV rights only for book clients. No reading fee, only commissions.
Titles recently placed: *Escape From Mr Lemoncello's Library*, Chris Grabenstein; *Pity the Billionaire: The Hard-Times Swindle and the Unlikely Comeback of the Right*, Thomas Frank; *The $14 Billion Year*, Anne Thompson; *The Financial Crisis Inquiry Report*; *The Lost Mona Lisa: The Extraordinary True Story of the Greatest Art Theft in History*, R A Scotti
Foreign Rights: The Marsh Agency (Continental Europe); Abner Stein Agency (England)

Philip G Spitzer Literary Agency Inc (L)
50 Talmage Farm Lane, East Hampton, NY 11937
Tel: 631-329-3650 *Fax:* 631-329-3651
Web Site: www.spitzeragency.com
Key Personnel
Pres: Philip Spitzer (AAR) *E-mail:* spitzer516@aol.com
Mng Agent: Lukas Ortiz (AAR) *E-mail:* lukas.ortiz@spitzeragency.com
Off Mgr: Kim Lombardini *E-mail:* kim.lombardini@spitzeragency.com
Founded: 1969
Literary fiction, suspense/thriller, general nonfiction, sports, politics, social issues, biography, film & TV rights. No unsol mss, query first with SASE, submit outline & sample chapters. No reading fee, photocopying fee. Foreign rights agents in all major markets.
Titles recently placed: *Darkansas*, Jarret Middleton; *Lie in Wait*, Eric Rickstad; *Mexico: Stories*, Josh Barkan; *Signature Wounds*, Kirk Russell; *The Brain Defense*, Kevin Davis; *The Emerald Lie*, Ken Bruen; *The Ex*, Alafair Burke; *The Hanged Man*, Gary Inbinder; *The Jealous Kind*, James Lee Burke; *The Wrong Side of Goodbye*, Michael Connelly
Foreign Rights: Big Apple Agency Inc (Luc Kwanten & Lily Chen) (China, Malaysia, Taiwan, Vietnam); Big Apple Agency Inc (Erica Zhou) (Indonesia); ELST Literary Agency (Kalina Stefanova) (Bulgaria); The Deborah Harris Agency (Efrat Lev) (Israel); The Italian Literary Agency SRL (Italy); KALEM (Sedef Ilgic) (Turkey); Agence Michelle Lapautre (Catherine Lapautre) (France); Mohrbooks Literary Agency (Sebastian Ritcsher & Annelie Geissler) (Austria, Germany, Switzerland); Prava i prevodi (Anna Milenkovic) (Russia); Prava i prevodi (Milena Kaplarevic) (Eastern Europe exc Russia); Agencia Literaria Riff (Laura Riff & Joao Paulo Riff) (Brazil); Lennart Sane Agency AB (Philip Sane) (Holland, Latin America, Portugal, Scandinavia, Spain); Abner Stein Agency (Caspian Dennis) (UK); Tuttle-Mori Agency Inc (Misa Morikawa) (Japan); Eric Yang Agency (Sue Yang) (Korea)

Nancy Stauffer Associates (L)
30 Corbin Dr, Suite 1203, Darien, CT 06820
Mailing Address: PO Box 1203, Darien, CT 06820
Tel: 203-202-2500
Web Site: staufferliterary.com; publishersmarketplace.com/members/nstauffer
Key Personnel
Owner: Nancy Stauffer Cahoon *E-mail:* nancy@staufferliterary.com
Founded: 1989
Literary fiction, narrative nonfiction & young adult fiction. No mysteries, science fiction, fantasy, romance novels, screenplays or children's picture books. Query by e-mail only, with first 10 pages of your work. No attachments. Agents in all foreign markets.
Titles recently placed: *Our Souls at Night*, Kent Haruf; *You Don't Have to Say You Love Me: A Memoir*, Sherman Alexie
Membership(s): The Authors Guild

Michael Steinberg Literary Agent (L)
PO Box 274, Glencoe, IL 60022-0274
Tel: 847-626-1000 *Fax:* 847-626-1002
E-mail: michael14steinberg@comcast.net
Key Personnel
Principal: Michael Steinberg
Founded: 1980
Book-length fiction (mystery, science fiction) & nonfiction (business topics). No unsol mss, query first. Submit outline & first 3 chapters (hard copy). Will read only by personal reference from represented author or editor.
Titles recently placed: *All About Day Trading*, Jake Bernstein

Sterling Lord Literistic Inc (L)
115 Broadway, Suite 1602, New York, NY 10006
Tel: 212-780-6050 *Fax:* 212-780-6095
E-mail: info@sll.com
Web Site: www.sll.com
Key Personnel
Co-Chmn: Sterling Lord; Peter Matson
Pres: Philippa Brophy (AAR)
VP: Laurie Liss (AAR)
Mng Dir: Nadyne Pike
Agent: Elizabeth Bewley; Celeste Fine (AAR); Robert Guinsler; Sarah Landis; John Maas; Alison MacKeen; Neeti Madan; Martha Millard (AAR); Sarah Passick; Jim Rutman (AAR); Douglas Stewart
Assoc Agent: Mary Krienke; Jenny Stephens
Foreign Rts Mgr: Szilvia Molnar
Foreign Rts Assoc: Danielle Bukowski
Founded: 1952
Fiction & nonfiction; film & TV rights. No unsol mss, query first; submit outline & sample chapters with SASE. No reading fee.
Foreign Rep(s): AnatoliaLit Agency (Amy Spangler) (Turkey); Agence Eliane Benisti (Eliane Benisti) (France); Book/Lab Ltd (Agata Zabowska) (Poland); Paul & Peter Fritz Literary Agency (Antonia Fritz) (Austria, Germany); The Grayhawk Agency (Gray Tan) (China, Taiwan); The Grayhawk Agency (Itzel Hsu) (Indonesia, Thailand, Vietnam); The Deborah Harris Agency (Geula Geurts) (Israel); Danny Hong Agency (Danny Hong) (Korea); The Italian Literary Agency (Mariavittoria Puccetti) (Italy); JLM Literary (John Moukakos) (Greece); MB Agencia Literaria (Monica Martin) (Andorra, Catalonia, Portugal, Spain); Andrew Nurnberg Associates Baltic (Tatjana Zoldnere) (Estonia, Latvia, Lithuania, Ukraine); Andrew Nurnberg Associates Budapest (Blanka Enyi) (Croatia, Hungary); Andrew Nurnberg Associates Prague (Marta Soukopova) (Czech Republic, Slovakia, Slovenia); Andrew Nurnberg Associates Sofia (Mira Droumeva) (Albania, Bulgaria, Macedonia, Romania, Serbia); Riff Agency (Laura Riff) (Brazil); Marianne Schoenbach Literary Agency (Marianne Schoenbach) (Netherlands); Tuttle-Mori Agency Inc (Ken Mori) (Japan); The Van Lear Agency (Liz Van Lear) (Russia)

Miriam Stern, Entertainment Attorney/Literary Agent (L-D)
303 E 83 St, 20th fl, New York, NY 10028
Tel: 212-794-1289
Fiction & nonfiction. No unsol mss, call or letter query first. Submit finished mss, outlines with sample chapters when applicable. Negotiate for license or sale of motion picture rights for film & TV projects.

Stimola Literary Studio Inc (L)
308 Livingston Ct, Edgewater, NJ 07020
Tel: 201-945-9353 *Fax:* 201-945-9353; 201-490-5920
E-mail: info@stimolaliterarystudio.com
Web Site: www.stimolaliterarystudio.com
Key Personnel
Pres: Rosemary B Stimola (AAR) *Tel:* 201-945-9565 *E-mail:* rosemary@stimolaliterarystudio.com
Sr Agent: Erica Rand Silverman *Tel:* 917-734-3943 *E-mail:* erica@stimolaliterarystudio.com
Agent: Adriana Stimola *Tel:* 617-784-8770 *E-mail:* adriana@stimolaliterarystudio.com
Assoc Agent: Allison Remcheck
Founded: 1997
Specialize in fiction & nonfiction, preschool through young adult. Also representing cookbooks, farm to table, lifestyle. Queries via e-mail preferred. Respond only to those queries we wish to pursue further. No unsol attachments. See web site for submission guidelines. No fees.
Titles recently placed: *A Few Red Drops*, Claire Hartfield; *Apartment 1986*, Lisa Papademetriou; *Better Off Undead*, James Preller; *Florian Bates (series)*, James Ponti; *Girl Rising*, Tanya Lee Stone, Girl Rising; *Henry & Eva (series)*, Andrea Portes; *Last Seen Leaving*, Caleb Roehrig; *Midnight at the Electric*, Jodi Lynn Anderson; *One Amazing Elephant*, Linda Oat-

man High; *One of Us is Lying*, Katherine McManus; *Pete Without Pants*, Rowboat Watkins; *Piecing Me Together*, Renee Watson; *Red and Lulu*, Matt Tavares; *Simon Thorn (series)*, Aimee Carter; *The Remnant Chronicles*, Mary Pearson; *Vincent Can't Sleep*, Barb Rosenstock, Mary Grand Pre; *Wally Does Not Want a Haircut*, Amanda Driscoll; *Wolf in the Snow*, Matthew Cordell
Foreign Rep(s): Intercontinental Literary Agency (translation); Schleuck Agency (Germany)
Foreign Rights: Rights People (UK)
Membership(s): ALA; The Authors Guild; National Council of Teachers of English; PEN American Center; Society of Children's Book Writers & Illustrators

The Stonesong Press LLC (L)
270 W 39 St, No 201, New York, NY 10018
Tel: 212-929-4600
E-mail: editors@stonesong.com
Web Site: www.stonesong.com
Key Personnel
Partner & Literary Agent: Alison Fargis
Partner & Prodn Servs: Ellen Scordato
EVP & Literary Agent: Judy Linden
Literary Agent: Emmanuelle Morgen; Leila Campoli; Maria Ribas
Founded: 1979
Complete trade hardcover, paperback & ebook development, from concept to delivery. Represents commercial nonfiction & popular reference books on many subjects: cooking, business, how-to, self-help, memoir, beauty & fashion; also represents fiction, including middle grade, young adult, & adult titles. Consultants on backlist exploitation, acquisitions, publicity planning & editorial systems. Custom publishing for professional associations & magazines. No unsol mss, query first by e-mail. Include a brief synopsis & the first 10 pages of your work in the e-mail body. Complete submission guidelines are on our web site. No fees charged.
Titles recently placed: *Below the Belt*, Jeanette Murray; *Cook for Your Life*, Ann Ogden; *Love & Lemons*, Jeanine Donofrio; *Ruined*, Amy Tintera; *The Forest Feast*, Erin Gleeson; *The Forest Feast Gatherings*, Erin Gleeson; *The Forst Feast Children's Cookbook*, Erin Gleeson; *The Unquiet*, Ruth Dada writing as Mikaela Everett
Foreign Rep(s): Allen & Unwin (Australia, New Zealand); Commonwealth (China); Maxim Konyvkiado (Hungary); Oceana (Spain); Penguin Random House Canada (Canada); Piemme (Italy); Editora Record (Brazil); Jacqui Small (England)
Foreign Rights: The Fielding Agency (Whitney Lee) (worldwide)
Membership(s): American Book Producers Association

Straus Literary (L)
319 Lafayette St, Suite 220, New York, NY 10012
Tel: 646-843-9950 *Fax:* 646-390-3320
Web Site: www.strausliterary.com
Key Personnel
Agent: Jonah Straus *E-mail:* jonah@strausliterary.com
Founded: 2003
Focus on literary fiction, historical fiction, works in translation (especially Spanish & Portuguese), literary mystery & thriller, cookbooks, food & travel narratives, politics, history, international affairs, biography, memoir.
Straus Literary acts as English sub-agent for: Mertin Agency (Nicole Witt), Germany; Riff Agency, Brazil.
Branch office in San Francisco, CA.
Titles recently placed: *Arzak Secrets*, Juan Mari Arzak; *Bellini and the Sphinx*, Tony Bellotto; *Counternarratives*, John Keene; *Crow-Blue*, Adriana Lisboa, Alison Entrekin; *Death & Co (Cocktail Book)*, David Kaplan, Nick Fauchald; *Finding Mezcal: An Artist's Journey into Mexico's Liquid Soul*, Ron Cooper, Chantal Martineau; *Ingredient: The True Elements of Cooking*, Ali Bouzari; *Molly on the Range*, Molly Yeh; *Peru: The Cookbook*, Gaston Acurio; *Poison Spring: The Secret History of the EPA*, Evaggelos Vallianatos; *Smuggler's Cove: Cocktails, Rum and the Cult of Tiki*, Martin Cate; *The Cage: The Fight for Sri Lanka and the Last Days of the Tamil Tigers*, Gordon Weiss; *The Collected Poems of Carlos Drummond de Andrade*, Carlos Drummond de Andrade, Richard Zenith; *The Cruelest Gift: Inherited Disease in the Age of DNA*, Clark Blaise; *The Descartes Highlands*, Eric Gamalinda; *The House in Smyrna*, Tatiana Salem Levy; *The La Cocina Cookbook*, Caleb Zigas and Leticia Landa
Foreign Rights: AK Agency (Alex Korzhenevski) (Baltic States, Russia, Ukraine); Amo Agency (Amo Noh) (Korea); Silvia Bastos Agency (Pau Centellas) (Latin America exc Brazil, Portugal, Spain); Big Apple Agency (Luc Kwanten) (China, Southeast Asia, Thailand); DS Budapest (Szabolcs Torok) (Hungary); ELST Literary Agency (Kalina Stefanova) (Bulgaria); The English Agency (Tsutomu Yawata) (Japan); Graal Literary Agency (Filip Wojiechowski) (Poland); Deborah Harris Agency (Rena Rossner) (Israel); Iris Literary (Catherine Fragou) (Greece); Kalem Agency (Sedef Ligic) (Turkey); Simona Kessler International Copyright Agency (Adriana Marina) (Romania); Michelle Lapautre Agency (Catherine Lapautre) (France, Quebec, CN, Switzerland (French-speaking)); Michael Meller Agency (Regina Seitz) (Austria, Germany, Switzerland (German-speaking)); Andrew Nurnberg, Prague (Petra Tobiskova) (Czech Republic, Slovakia); Plima Literary (Vuk Perisic) (Albania, Bosnia and Herzegovina, Croatia, Macedonia, Montenegro, Serbia); Riff Agency (Joao Paulo Riff) (Brazil); Lennart Sane Agency (Philip Sane) (Netherlands, Scandinavia); Susanna Zevi Agency (Susanna Zevi) (Italy)

Robin Straus Agency Inc (L)
229 E 79 St, Suite 5A, New York, NY 10075
Tel: 212-472-3282 *Fax:* 212-472-3833
E-mail: info@robinstrausagency.com
Web Site: www.robinstrausagency.com
Key Personnel
Pres: Robin Straus (AAR) *E-mail:* robin@robinstrausagency.com
Jr Agent: Katelyn Hales
Founded: 1983
High quality fiction & nonfiction. Handle film & TV rights for represented clients' books. Foreign agents in all major foreign countries. No unsol mss, query first. No screenplays, plays, romance, westerns, horror, children's or poetry. E-mail query with outline or synopsis, short author biography & sample chapters; or send brief e-mail letter describing book project (no downloads). No reading fees.
Foreign Rights: AnatoliaLit Agency (Turkey); Deborah Harris (Israel); JLM Literary Agency (Greece); Andrew Nurnberg Associates (worldwide exc Greece, Japan, Korea, Thailand & Turkey); Tuttle-Mori Agency Inc (Japan, Thailand); Eric Yang Agency (Korea)

Marianne Strong Literary Agency (L)
65 E 96 St, New York, NY 10128
Tel: 212-249-1000 *Fax:* 212-831-3241
Web Site: stronglit.com
Key Personnel
Owner & Pres: Marianne Strong *E-mail:* mariannestrong@stronglit.com
Agent: Nicole Lowary
Founded: 1978
In addition to select fiction, we handle general nonfiction, how-to books, biographies, gossip, society & entertainment, celebrity books, social history, lifestyle, cookbooks, investigative biographies, mysteries, adventure, true crime fictionalized (or actual true crime), politics, self-help, inspirational, historic & memoirs. A separate service is provided that obtains assignments for professional writers. No fees charged; no unsol mss, query first with one page (no attachments) to mariannestrong@stronglit.com.
Titles recently placed: *Affirmed: The Last Triple Crown Winner*, Lou Sahadi; *Capital of the World: A Portrait of New York City in the Roaring Twenties*, David Wallace; *Night Harvest*, Michael Alexiades
Membership(s): The Authors Guild

Strothman Agency LLC (L)
63 E Ninth St, 10X, New York, NY 10003
E-mail: info@strothmanagency.com
Web Site: www.strothmanagency.com
Key Personnel
Principal & Agent: Wendy Strothman (AAR)
Agent: Lauren E MacLeod (AAR)
Founded: 2003
Dedicated to promoting authors of significant books through the entire publishing cycle. No unsol mss, query first by e-mail only. Submit query letter, synopsis & first 10 pages to strothmanagency@gmail.com, no attachments. Submissions will be acknowledged by an autoresponder. No fees charged.
Titles recently placed: *Adults in the Room*, Yanis Varoufakis; *Before She Ignites (Trilogy)*, Jodi Meadows; *Hunting for Hamilton*, Joanne Freeman; *Not the Girls You're Looking For*, Aminah Mae Safi; *The Field of Blood*, Joanne Freeman; *The Hue and Cry and Our House: A Year Remembered*, Benjamin Taylor; *The New Authoritarians*, Kevin O'Leary

Swagger Literary Agency (L)
601 Shenandoah Valley Dr, Front Royal, VA 22630
Tel: 540-636-7076
E-mail: swaggerlit@gmail.com
Web Site: www.swaggerliterary.com
Key Personnel
Owner & Literary Agent: Joseph Brendan Vallely
Founded: 2014
Represents upmarket nonfiction: current events, history, biography, sports & outdoors, word books & the occasional upscale project that doesn't easily fit into these categories. Submit query letter & book proposal by e-mail only. Representation on the West Coast & in foreign countries.
Titles recently placed: *iWar: War and Peace in the Information Age*, Bill Gertz; *Law & Disorder*, Charles Sevilla; *What So Proudly We Hailed: Francis Scott Key, A Life*, Marc Leepson
Foreign Rep(s): Anthea Literary Agency (Katalina Sabeva) (Bulgaria); Eliane Benisti Agent Litteraire (France); Big Apple Agency Inc (Grace Yang, Dr Luk Kwanten & Lily Chen) (China, Taiwan); Graal Literary Agency (Maria Strarz-Kanska) (Poland); International Copyright Agency Ltd (Simona Kessler) (Romania); International Editors' Co (Isabel Monteagudo) (Portugal, Spain); International Editors' Co (Nicolas Costa) (Argentina); International Editors' Co (Ms Flavia Sala) (Brazil, Portugal); The Italian Literary Agency srl (Italy); Japan UNI (Miko Yamanouchi) (Japan); JLM Literary Agency (Nelly Moukakou) (Greece); Katai & Bolza (Peter Bolza) (Hungary); Linda Kohn International Literatuur (Netherlands); Nurcihan Kesim® Literary Agency (Filiz Karaman) (Turkey); Kristin Olson Literary Agency

sro (Czech Republic); Ilana Pikarski Literary Agency (Ms Gal Pikarski) (Israel); Lennart Sane Agency SB (Lina Hammarling) (Scandinavia); Thomas Schlueck GmbH (Thomas Schlueck) (Bulgaria); Thomas Schlueck GmbH (Joachim Jessen) (Germany); Shin Won Agency (Eunja Beck, Mr Sang Hyung & Steve Yang) (Korea); Tuttle-Mori Agency Inc (Anongnard Podchanajun & Pimolporn Yutisri) (Thailand); Eric Yang Agency (Vince Baek) (Korea)

Carolyn Swayze Literary Agency Ltd (L)
7360 137 St, Suite 319, Surrey, BC V3W 1A3, Canada
Tel: 604-503-3895
E-mail: reception@swayzeagency.com
Web Site: www.swayzeagency.com
Key Personnel
Pres: Carolyn Swayze *E-mail:* carolyn@swayzeagency.com
Founded: 1994
Representing emerging & established authors of literary fiction, some commercial fiction, nonfiction, middle grade & young adult books. No science fiction, no self-help, no picture books. An inquiry must include an author bio, a short description of the available project & short sample. No fees charged. Authors may consult web site for current submission guidelines. Mostly Canadian authors & US Pacific Northwest.
Titles recently placed: *Crossing Home Ground: A Grassland Odyssey through Southern Interior British Columbia*, David Pitt-Brooke; *Dazzle Patterns*, Alison Watt; *Decision on the Rhine: First Canadian Army's Rhineland Campaign, February 8-March 10, 1945*, Mark Zuehlke; *Generation Robotq*, Terri Favro; *Ghost Warning*, Kara Stanley; *Is Canada Even Real?*, J C Villamere; *Lady of the Lake*, Laine Ferndale; *Russian Dolls*, W P Kinsella; *Sputnik's Daughter*, Terri Favro; *Sunset Bay Sanctuary*, Roxanne Snopek; *The Chocolate Cure*, Roxanne Snopek; *The Conjoined*, Jen Sookfong Lee; *The Turing Machinists*, Mary E Reid; *Undertow*, R M Greenaway; *What We Once Believed*, Andrea MacPherson
Foreign Rep(s): L'Autre Agence (Corinne Marotte) (France)
Foreign Rights: AM Heath & Co Ltd, Authors' Agents (UK); AnatoliaLit Agency (Turkey); L'Autre Agence (France); The Book Publishers Association of Israel (Dalia Ever Hadani) (Israel); Chinese Connection Agency (China, Taiwan); Paul Christoph Literary Agency (Brazil, Portugal); Silvia Donzelli Agency (Stefania Fietta) (Italy); ELST Literary Agency (Kalina Stefanova) (Bulgaria); International Copyright Agency (Simona Kessler) (Moldova, Romania); Duran Kim Agency (Korea); Lex Copyright (Hungary); Mo Literary Services (Netherlands); Mohr Books (Germany); Andrew Nurnberg Associates (Baltic States); O A Literary Agency (Greece); Maria Starz-Kanska (Poland); Tuttle-Mori Agency Inc (Japan)

Tessler Literary Agency LLC (L)
27 W 20 St, Suite 1003, New York, NY 10011
Tel: 212-242-0466
Web Site: www.tessleragency.com
Key Personnel
Pres: Michelle Tessler (AAR)
Founded: 2004
Full service boutique agency dedicated to writers of high quality fiction & nonfiction. Nonfiction list includes narrative, popular science, memoir, history, psychology, business, biography, food & travel. In fiction, represents literary, women's & commercial. No unsol mss, query first via web form. No fees charged.
Titles recently placed: *Are We Smart Enough to Know How Smart Animals Are?*, Frans de Waal; *Become Alien: A Hacker's Education*, Jeremy N Smith; *Blood & Ivy: The True Story of Money, Murder & the Trial That Shocked Harvard*, Paul Collins; *Breaking the Standard: The Upstarts and Underdogs Who Toppled Rockefeller*, Peter Doran; *Emotional First Aid: Practical Strategies for Treating Failure, Rejection, Guilt, and Other Everyday Psychological Injuries*, Guy Winch, PhD; *Lady Cop Makes Trouble*, Amy Stewart; *Part Time Paleo*, Leanne Ely; *Pounce*, Seth Casteel; *Salt Houses*, Hala Alyan; *Shanghai Grand: A True Tale of Forbidden Love, International Intrigue, and Doomed Glamour in Old Cathay*, Taras Grescoe; *The Alchemy of Algae: How Commonplace Creatures Created Us, Sustain Us, and Just Might Save Us*, Ruth Kassinger; *The Drunken Botanist*, Amy Stewart; *The Nearness of You*, Amanda Eyre Ward; *The Sleepwalker's Guide to Dancing*, Mira Jacob; *Thirsty Dragon: China's Lust for Bordeaux, A Story of Conquest, Crime, and Wine*, Suzanne Mustacich
Foreign Rights: The Deborah Harris Agency (Israel); Andrew Nurnberg & Associates (China, Europe, Latin America); Tuttle-Mori Agency Inc (Japan); Eric Yang Agency (Korea)

3 Seas Literary Agency (L)
PO Box 444, Sun Prairie, WI 53590
Tel: 608-834-9317
E-mail: threeseaslit@aol.com
Web Site: threeseasagency.com
Key Personnel
Literary Agent: Michelle Grajkowski (AAR); Cori Deyoe *E-mail:* cori@threeseaslit.com; Linda Scalissi
Founded: 2000
E-mail queries only. For fiction titles, query with first chapter & synopsis embedded in the e-mail. For nonfiction, query with complete proposal attached. For picture books, query with complete text. Illustrations are not necessary. Considers simultaneous submissions. Responds within one month to e-mail submissions. No snail mail queries. 3 Seas will not respond to queries that are sent to e-mail addresses other than queries@threeseaslit.com. Obtains most new clients through recommendations from others & conferences. No fees charged.
Titles recently placed: *A Navy SEAL'S Surprise Baby*, Laura Marie Altom; *A Time for Home*, Alexis Morgan; *Captive*, KM Fawcett; *Changed by His Son*, Robin Gianakopoulus; *Do or Diner: A Comfort Food Mystery*, Christine Wenger; *Every Breath She Takes*, Norah Wilson; *Forever Friday*, Timothy Lewis; *Haley's Mountain Man*, Tracy Madison; *Her Perfect Cowboy*, Trish Milburn; *His Uptown Girl*, Liz Talley; *How to Write a Book in 30 Days*, Karen Wiesner; *Jimmie Joe Johnson: Manwhore*, Lindsey Brookes; *Just Perfect*, JoMarie DeGioia; *Must Love Dukes*, Elizabeth Michaels; *One Night with the Sheikh*, Kristi Gold; *Passion and Pretense*, Susan Gee Heino; *Queen of Song and Souls*, C L Wilson; *Queen of the Sylphs*, L J McDonald; *Say It With Roses*, Devon Vaughn Archer; *Six Months Later*, Natalie D Richards; *The Art of Stealing Time*, Katie MacAlister; *The Bride Next Door*, Winnie Griggs; *The Casanova Code*, Donna MacMeans; *The Champion*, Carla Capshaw; *The Rancher's Homecoming*, Cathy McDavid; *The Sister Season*, Jennifer Brown; *The Vampire With a Dragon Tattoo*, Kerrelyn Sparks; *The Winter King*, C L Wilson; *Thousand Words*, Jennifer Brown; *Three Days on Mimosa Lane*, Anna DeStefano
Foreign Rights: Marleen Seegers (China, France, Holland, Scandinavia); Ingo Stein (Germany)
Membership(s): Romance Writers of America

The Tomasino Agency Inc (L)
70 Chestnut St, Dobbs Ferry, NY 10522
Tel: 914-674-9659 *Fax:* 914-693-0381
E-mail: info@tomasinoagency.com
Web Site: www.tomasinoagency.com
Key Personnel
Pres: Christine K Tomasino
Founded: 1998
Commercial & literary fiction & nonfiction. Represent all subrights for book clients only. Specialize in conventional & mind/body health, women's issues, self-improvement, spirituality/esoterica, narrative nonfiction, lifestyle, adult illustrated & packaged books, sports. Translation of nonbook content into book-related formats for corporate & nonprofit organizational clients such as major web businesses & museums. No poetry, genre fiction, plays, science fiction or purely scholarly work. Foreign agents in all major markets. No unsol mss, query first.

Transatlantic Agency (L)
2 Bloor St E, Suite 3500, Toronto, ON M4W 1A8, Canada
Tel: 416-488-9214
E-mail: info@transatlanticagency.com
Web Site: www.transatlanticagency.com
Key Personnel
Pres: David Bennett *E-mail:* david@transatlanticagency.com
VP: Lynn Bennett *E-mail:* lynn@transatlanticagency.com; Samantha Haywood *E-mail:* samantha@transatlanticagency.com
Partner & Agent: Shaun Bradley *E-mail:* shaun@transatlanticagency.com; Marie Campbell *E-mail:* marie@transatlanticagency.com
Assoc Agent: Stephanie Sinclair; Amy Tompkins *E-mail:* amy@transatlanticagency.com
Agent: Sandra Bishop (AAR); Andrea Cascardi; Fiona Kenshole (AAR) *E-mail:* fiona@transatlanticagency.com
Founded: 1993
Children's, adult literary fiction & literary nonfiction. Markets Canadian & American literary properties to English language publishers in the UK, US & CN & through sub-agents to publishers around the world. Handles film & TV rights for literary properties only: no film scripts or teleplays. No unsol mss; initial letter of inquiry essential. No reading fees. See web site for individual agents' submission details.
Titles recently placed: *Boundless*, Kathleen Winter; *McKenna - American Girl*, Mary Casanova; *Punishment*, Linden MacIntyre; *Tell It to the World*, Eliott Behar; *The Circus Dogs of Prague*, Rachelle Delaney; *The Devil You Know*, Elizabeth de Mariaffi; *The Gospel Truth*, Carolyn Pignat; *The Gypsy King*, Maureen Fergus; *The Silent Wife*, A S A Harrison; *The Unlikely Hero of 13B*, Teresa Toten; *They Left Us Everything*, Plum Johnson; *Walking Home*, Eric Walters; *Will Starling*, Ian Weir
Foreign Rights: Akcali Copyright (Turkey); ANAW Literary Agency (Poland); Berla & Griffini Rights Agency (Italy); The Book Publishers Association of Israel (Israel); ELST Literary Agency (Bulgaria); The English Agency (Japan) Ltd (Japan); Agence Litteraire Lora Fountain (France, Portugal, Spain); International Editors' Co (Spanish & Portuguese); Japan Uni Agency Inc (Japan); The Anna Jarota Agency (France); JLM Literary Agency (Greece); Katai & Bolza Literary Agents (Hungary); Liepman AG (Germany); Literarische Agentur+Medienservice (Germany); Mo Literary Services (Netherlands, Scandinavia); Andrew Nurnberg Associates International Ltd (China, Hong Kong, Taiwan); Kristin Olson Literary Agency sro (Czech Republic); Orange Agency (Korea); Agencia Literaria RIFF (Brazil); Shinwon Agency Co (Korea); THE agency (Korea); Tuttle-Mori Agency Inc (Indonesia, Japan, Malaysia, Thailand, Vietnam); Young Agency (Korea)

Treimel, S©ott, NY, see S©ott Treimel NY

TriadaUS Literary Agency (L)
PO Box 561, Sewickley, PA 15143
Tel: 412-401-3376
Web Site: www.triadaus.com
Key Personnel
Founder & Sr Agent: Dr Uwe Stender (AAR)
E-mail: uwe@triadaus.com
Agent & Subs Rts Mgr: Brent Taylor
E-mail: brent@triadaus.com
Assoc Agent: Laura Crockett *E-mail:* laura@triadaus.com
Asst Agent: Mallory Brown *E-mail:* mallory@triadaus.com; Lauren Spieller *E-mail:* lauren@triadaus.com
Founded: 2004
Full service literary agency including fiction & nonfiction. Also international sales, film & TV options. No unsol mss, query first.
Titles recently placed: *A Short History of the Girl Next Door*, Jared Reck; *Alan Cole is Not a Coward*, Eric Bell; *Chaotic Good*, Whitney Gardner; *Gettysburg Rebels*, Tom McMillan; *Here Comes Trouble*, Kate Hattemer; *Kiranmala and the Kingdom of Serpents*, Sayantani DasGupta; *Plants That Can Kill: 101 Toxic Species to Make You Think Twice*, Stacy Tornio; *Pretty Little World*, Elizabeth LaBan, Melissa DePino; *Project Pandora*, Aden Polydoros; *Seven Bad Cats*, Monique Bonneau; *Seven Days of Stone*, Dana Davis; *Sometime after Midnight*, L Philips; *Ten Past Closing*, Jessica Bayliss; *The Awkward Path of Getting Lucky*, Summer Heacock; *The Diminished*, Kaitlyn Sage Patterson; *The Italy List*, Deanna Romito; *The Principles Behind Flotation*, Alexandra Teague
Foreign Rights: Arika Interrights Agency (Indonesia, Thailand, Vietnam); Big Apple Agency (China); Blackbird Literary Agency (Netherlands); Book/lab Literary Agency (Poland); Corto Literary (Croatia); Donatella d'Ormesson Agent Litteraire (France); The Deborah Harris Agency (Israel); IMC Literary Agency (Mexico, Spain); Kalem Literary Agency (Turkey); Alexander Korzhenevski Agency (Baltic States, Russia); Agencia Das Letras (Portugal); Piergiorgio Nicolazzini Literary Agency (Italy); Plima Literary (Serbia); Riff Agency (Brazil); Tuttle-Mori Agency Inc (Japan); Eric Yang Agency (Korea)
Membership(s): AAP

Trident Media Group LLC (L)
41 Madison Ave, 36th fl, New York, NY 10010
Tel: 212-333-1511
E-mail: info@tridentmediagroup.com; press@tridentmediagroup.com
Web Site: www.tridentmediagroup.com
Key Personnel
Chmn: Robert Gottlieb
CEO: Daniel Strone
EVP: Ellen Levine (AAR); Scott Miller; John Silbersack
SVP: Don Fehr
VP: Claire Roberts
Dir, Foreign Rts: Sylvie Rosokoff; Dorothy Vincent
Audio Rts Agent: Meagan Cohen
Dom Agent: Sarah Bush Phair; Alex Slater
Foreign Rts Agent: Nicola DeRobertis-Theye
Literary Agent: Amanda O'Connor Annis; Mark Gottlieb; Alyssa Eisner Henkin; Erica Spellman-Silverman
Founded: 2000
General fiction & nonfiction. No unsol mss, query first by e-mail. Submit outline & sample chapters if requested. No reading fee. Handle film & TV rights for clients only. Representation in Hollywood.
Titles recently placed: *365 Days of Wonder: Mr Browne's Book of Precepts*, R J Palacio; *A Fall From Grace*, Adam Mitzner; *Alluring Indulgence*, Nicole Edwards; *Angel Killer*, Andrew Mayne; *Avenged*, Daniel Judson; *Bad Blood*, Mark Sennen; *Blacklist*, Sylvia Day; *Bound by Night*, Larissa Ione; *Breaking Nova*, Jessica Sorensen; *Call Me*, Kristina Knight; *Chained by Night*, Larissa Ione; *Cloud City: An Anna Strong Novella*, Jeanne Stein; *Collateral Damage*, Kyra Davis; *Cut Dead*, Mark Sennen; *Dangerous Alliance*, Kyra Davis; *Deceptive Innocence*, Kyra Davis; *Family by Design*, Kristina Knight; *Future Humans: The Ongoing Evolution of Homo Sapiens*, Prof Scott Solomon; *Green Girl*, Kate Zambreno; *Hemingway's War*, Terry Mort; *In Pursuit: The Saga of the Nazi Hunters*, Andrew Nagorski; *In the Skin of a Lion*, Michael Ondaatje; *Light My Fire*, Kristina Knight; *Music Class Today!*, David Weinstone; *Mystique*, Julie Berry; *No Time to Die*, Kira Peikoff; *Pics*, Nathan Jurgenson; *President Me: The America That's in My Head*, Adam Carolla; *Rebel Democracy: Digital Warriors and Islamic World*, Haroon Ullah; *Resistance*, Ryk Brown; *Ruin*, Rachel Van Dyken; *Running in the Family*, Michael Ondaatje; *Sistering*, Hannah Roberts-McKinnon; *Slow Burn (series)*, Maya Banks; *Starfire*, Dale Brown; *Start Me Up*, Kristina Knight; *The Birth of Capitalism in Islam*, Benedikt Koehler; *The Confessors' Club*, Jack Fredrickson; *The Distance Between Lost and Found*, Kathryn Holmes; *The Ever After of Ella and Micha*, Jessica Sorensen; *The Great Surge*, Steven Radelet; *The Julian Chapter: A Wonder Story*, R J Palacio; *The Last Days*, Joel Rosenberg; *The Last Jihad*, Joel Rosenberg; *The Last Rescue*, Howard Wasdin, Debbie Wasdin; *The Monet Murders*, Terry Mort; *The Mountain*, T Jefferson Parker; *The New Abolition*, Gary Dorrien; *The Other Side of Impossible: How to Let Go of the Life You Planned and Find a Happy Ending*, Tracey Cleantis; *The Rose Hotel*, Rahimeh Andalibian; *The Scandalous Sisterhood of Prickwillow Place*, Julie Berry; *The Struggle for Liberation*, Gary Dorrien; *The Winter Place*, Alexander Yates; *The Youngs: The Brothers Who Built AC/DC*, Jesse Fink; *Thieves Road: General George Custer and the Invasion of the Black Hills*, Terry Mort; *To Silence the Screaming Dead*, Jack Fredrickson; *Touch*, Mark Sennen; *Tower of Winds*, Ilana Myer; *Toxic*, Rachel Van Dyken; *Transit Girl*, Jamie Shupak; *Treading on Thin Air*, Dr Elizabeth Austin; *True Lies*, Monica Murphy; *Unspeakable Things*, Kathleen Spivack; *Welcome to Dog Beach*, Lisa Greenwald; *Werewolf Cop*, Andrew Klavan

2M Communications Ltd (L)
19 W 21 St, Suite 501, New York, NY 10010
Tel: 212-741-1509 *Fax:* 212-691-4460
Web Site: www.2mcommunications.com
Key Personnel
Pres: Madeleine Morel (AAR) *E-mail:* morel@2mcommunications.com
Founded: 1982
Only represent previously published ghostwriters & collaborators who work with platformed authors already represented by recognized literary agents or acquired by publishing houses. Numerous New York Times bestsellers but all confidential. No unsol mss, query first. Submit CV or resume.
Membership(s): PEN American Center; Women's Media Group

United Talent Agency (L-D)
9336 Civic Center Dr, Beverly Hills, CA 90210
Tel: 310-273-6700 *Fax:* 310-247-1111
Web Site: www.unitedtalent.com
Key Personnel
CEO: Jeremy Zimmer
Mng Dir: David Kramer
Head, Corp Communs: Chris Day
Agent & Dir, Foreign Rts Dept: Meredith Miller
Agent: Brandi Bowles
Founded: 1991
Fiction, nonfiction. Handle film & TV rights. No unsol mss, query first; reading fee.
Branch Office(s)
888 Seventh Ave, 9th fl, New York, NY 10106
Tel: 212-659-2600

Janis Vallely Literary Agency (L)
111 Raup Rd, Chatham, NY 12037
Tel: 518-392-0897
E-mail: janvall@aol.com
Web Site: www.janisvallely.com
Key Personnel
Owner & Literary Agent: Janis Vallely
Founded: 2014
Represents upscale commercial nonfiction: memoir, self-help, diet, narrative nonfiction, popular psychology & health. No unsol mss; no phone calls, no reading fee. Submit query letter & book proposal by e-mail only. Representation on the West Coast & in foreign countries.
Titles recently placed: *Eat Right 4 Your Type*, Dr Peter J Dadamo; *Staying Sharp*, Hennry Emmons, MD, David Alter, PhD; *The Microbiome Diet*, Raphael Kellman, MD; *The Whole Brain*, Raphael Kellman, MD
Foreign Rep(s): Anthea Literary Agency (Katalina Sabeva) (Bulgaria); Eliane Benisti Agent Litteraire (France); Big Apple Agency Inc (Grace Yang, Dr Luk Kwanten & Lily Chen) (China, Taiwan); Graal Literary Agency (Maria Strarz-Kanska) (Poland); International Copyright Agency Ltd (Simona Kessler) (Romania); International Editors' Co (Isabel Monteagudo) (Portugal, Spain); International Editors' Co (Nicolas Costa) (Argentina); International Editors' Co (Ms Flavia Sala) (Brazil, Portugal); The Italian Literary Agency srl (Italy); Japan UNI Agency Inc (Miko Yamanouchi) (Japan); JLM Literary Agency (Nelly Moukakou) (Greece); Katai & Bolza (Peter Bolza) (Hungary); Linda Kohn International Literatuur (Netherlands); Nurcihan Kesim® Literary Agency (Filiz Karaman) (Turkey); Kristin Olson Literary Agency sro (Czech Republic); I Pikarski Literary Agency (Ms Gal Pikarski) (Israel); Lennart Sane Agency SB (Lina Hammarling) (Scandinavia); Thomas Schlueck GmbH (Thomas Schlueck) (Bulgaria); Thomas Schlueck GmbH (Joachim Jessen) (Germany); Shin Won Agency (Eunja Beck, Mr Sang Hyung & Steve Yang) (Korea); Tuttle-Mori Agency Inc (Anongnard Podchanajun & Pimolporn Yutisri) (Thailand); Eric Yang Agency (Vince Baek) (Korea)

Wales Literary Agency Inc (L)
1508 Tenth Ave E, No 401, Seattle, WA 98102
Tel: 206-284-7114
E-mail: waleslit@waleslit.com
Web Site: www.waleslit.com
Key Personnel
Owner & Literary Agent: Elizabeth Wales (AAR)
Asst Agent & Foreign Rts: Neal Swain
Founded: 1990
Specialize in quality fiction & nonfiction. Does not handle screenplays, children's books, genre fiction or most category nonfiction. No unsol mss, query first by e-mail only (no attachments). No phone queries. Accept electronic submissions only. Simultaneous submissions accepted. Response provided within 3 weeks to queries, 3 months to mss.
Titles recently placed: *Growing a Revolution*, David Montgomery; *Mozart's Starling*, Lyanda Lynn Haupt; *Our Native Bees*, Paige Embry; *Victory Parade*, Leela Corman; *Witness Tree*, Lynda Mapes
Foreign Rights: Big Apple Agency Inc (China, Taiwan); Nurcihan Kesim Literary & Licensing Agency (Turkey); Agence Lapautre (France);

Mohrbooks Literary Agency (Austria, Germany, Switzerland); Andrew Nurnberg Associates (Croatia, Hungary); Reiser Agency (Italy); Sebes & Bisseling Literary Agency (Netherlands, Scandinavia); Shinwon Agency (Korea); Silk Road Agency (Thailand); Abner Stein Agency (UK); Tuttle-Mori Agency Inc (Japan)

The Wallace Literary Agency (L)
229 E 79 St, No 5A, New York, NY 10075
Tel: 212-472-3282 *Fax:* 212-472-3833
E-mail: info@wallaceliteraryagency.com
Key Personnel
Pres: Robin Straus *E-mail:* robin@wallaceliteraryagency.com
Asst: Katelyn Hales
Founded: 1988
Handle film & TV rights for agency clients only. No unsol mss. The agency is not accepting new clients.
Foreign Rights: AnatoliaLit Agency (Turkey); Deborah Harris (Israel); JLM Literary Agency (Greece); Andrew Nurnberg Associates (worldwide exc Greece, Israel, Japan, Korea & Turkey); Tuttle-Mori Agency Inc (Japan); Eric Yang Agency (Korea)

Ward & Balkin Agency, Inc, see Roam Agency

Warwick Associates (L)
18340 Sonoma Hwy, Sonoma, CA 95476
Tel: 707-939-9212 *Fax:* 707-938-3515
E-mail: warwick@vom.com
Web Site: www.warwickassociates.com
Key Personnel
Pres: Simon Warwick-Smith
Founded: 1985
A "one-stop" agency handling any or all parts of literary agenting through publicity & sales, etc. Specialize in spirituality, metaphysics, religion & psychology, celebrity memoirs, business & self-help, pop culture. Literary agent for a number of celebrity spiritual authors. No reading fee. Accept unsol mss, but query first with 2 chapters & SASE. No fiction or poetry.

Waterside Productions Inc (L)
2055 Oxford Ave, Cardiff, CA 92007
Tel: 760-632-9190 *Fax:* 760-632-9295
E-mail: admin@waterside.com
Web Site: www.waterside.com
Key Personnel
Founder & Literary Agent: Bill Gladstone *E-mail:* bgladstone@waterside.com
VP & Agent: Carole Jelen *Tel:* 925-968-9066 *E-mail:* carole@jelenpub.com
Sr Agent: Margot Maley Hutchison *Tel:* 858-483-0426 *E-mail:* mmaley@waterside.com
Foreign Rts Dir & Agent: Kimberly Brabec *E-mail:* kimberly@waterside.com
Agent: Jill Kramer *Tel:* 760-201-5737 *E-mail:* WatersideAgentJK@aol.com; Johanna Maaghul *E-mail:* johanna@waterside.com; David Nelson
Founded: 1982
Specialize in nonfiction. Professional how-to: technology, business, software, test prep, etc. General: self-help, spiritual, health, human interest, etc. No phone calls. No unsol mss. Submit a full book proposal per guidelines found at, or query through, the web site form. No reading fee. Handles software, film & TV rights with co-agents. In-house international division. Affiliations with PR agencies. Waterside now has its own print on demand & ebook publishing division at end of description of services.

Watkins/Loomis Agency Inc (L)
PO Box 20925, New York, NY 10025
Tel: 212-532-0080 *Fax:* 646-383-2449
E-mail: assistant@watkinsloomis.com
Web Site: www.watkinsloomis.com
Key Personnel
Pres: Gloria Loomis
Agent: Julia Masnik
Founded: 1908
Literary fiction, memoir, political nonfiction, biography. No unsol material.
Foreign Rights: The Marsh Agency; Abner Stein Agency (UK)

Waverly Place Literary Agency (L)
124 E 84 St, No 2D, New York, NY 10028-0918
Tel: 212-925-3721
E-mail: waverlyplaceliterary@aol.com
Web Site: www.waverlyplaceliterary.com; twitter.com/waverlyplacelit
Key Personnel
Literary Agent: Deborah Carter
Founded: 1998
Representing writing with charisma for adults, teens & children. No reading or editorial fees. Submissions not screened by assistants or interns. Expenses for photocopying & postage, if any, pre-approved by client. Interests include multicultural & international fiction relatable to American readers; narrative nonfiction in memoir/biography about extraordinary people & experiences; mysteries, thrillers & suspense novels; mainstream fiction (no romance, science fiction, fantasy, horror, religious/spiritual); historical fiction that's relevant to our lives today; literary novels; short story & poetry collections with popular appeal; children's & teen fiction. Send 1 to 2 paragraph synopsis & description of your background. E-mail queries only. In the subject line write Q: followed by a description of your book. Unsol mss sent by post will be discarded. Multiple submissions ok. If no response within 2 weeks, try again.
Titles recently placed: *Adventures of Molly Whuppie & Other Appalachian Folktales (Taiwan)*, Anne Shelby; *Homeplace (McGraw-Hill Spanish Kindergarten kit)*, Anne Shelby; *What to Do About Pollution/South Korea*, Anne Shelby
Foreign Rights: EntersKorea Agency (Lauren Kim) (Korea); Jiaxi Books (China, Taiwan)
Membership(s): Association of Writers and Writing Programs; The Authors Guild; Biographers International Organization; Historical Novel Society

Waxman Leavell Literary Agency (L)
Affiliate of Diversion Publishing Corp
443 Park Ave S, No 1004, New York, NY 10016
Tel: 212-675-5556 *Fax:* 212-675-1381
Web Site: www.waxmanleavell.com
Key Personnel
Founder & Agent: Scott Waxman; Byrd Leavell
Sr Agent: Larry Kirshbaum
Agent: Kirsten Carlton; Cassie Hanjian; Molly O'Neill; Fleetwood Robbins; Rachel Vogel
Founded: 1997
Fiction & nonfiction. No unsol mss, query first via e-mail. No reading fee, charge for reproductions.

Cherry Weiner Literary Agency (L)
925 Oak Bluff Ct, Dacula, GA 30019-6660
Tel: 732-446-2096 *Fax:* 732-792-0506
E-mail: cherry8486@aol.com
Key Personnel
Owner: Cherry Weiner
Founded: 1977
Science fiction, general fiction. No nonfiction. No unsol mss. Referred authors submit letter saying who referred. Submissions or recommendations only. Query letter where applicable, no downloads. No reading fee. Handle film & TV rights. Foreign representatives in England, Germany, Italy, Japan, Netherlands, Scandinavia, Russia, Spain, Eastern Europe & France.
Titles recently placed: *Black Wings 5 & 6*, S T Joshi; *Burning Sky*, Weston Ochse; *Cackle of Cthulhu*, Alex Shvartsman; *Castle Butte*, John Nesbitt; *Dead and Buried*, Tim Bryant; *Good Water*, John D Nesbitt; *Magic Forgotten*, Jack Hillman; *Resident Evil Novelization*, Tim Waggoner; *Snake Oil*, Marcus Galloway; *The Big Empty*, Jim Jones; *Tiny Bible Stories*, William C Bauers

The Weingel-Fidel Agency (L)
310 E 46 St, Suite 21-E, New York, NY 10017
Tel: 212-599-2959 *Fax:* 212-286-1986
E-mail: queries@theweingel-fidelagency.com
Key Personnel
Owner: Loretta Weingel-Fidel *E-mail:* lwf@theweingel-fidelagency.com
Founded: 1989
General fiction & nonfiction. Provide services to book authors/writers. No unsol mss, query first, by referral only; no reading fee.
Foreign Rep(s): Mary Clemmey (UK); Fritz Agency (Germany); Japan UNI (Japan); Michelle Lapautre (France); Lennart Sane (Netherlands, Scandinavia, Spain)
Foreign Rights: Jill Hughes (Albania, Bulgaria, Croatia, Estonia, Hungary, Latvia, Lithuania, Macedonia, Montenegro, Romania, Serbia, Slovakia, Slovenia)

Westwood Creative Artists Ltd (L)
138 Sussex Mews, Toronto, ON M5S-2K1, Canada
Tel: 416-964-3302 *Fax:* 416-964-3302
E-mail: wca_office@wcaltd.com
Web Site: www.wcaltd.com
Key Personnel
Founder & CEO: Bruce Westwood
Chmn: Michael Levine
Pres & COO: Jackie Kaiser
EVP: Hilary McMahon
Agent & Intl Rts Mgr: Carolyn Forde
Off Mgr & Literary Asst: Stephanie Thompson
Agent: John Pearce
Exec Asst & Intl Rts Asst: Meg Wheeler
Exec Asst: Liz Culotti
Founded: 1995
General trade fiction & nonfiction for international marketplace. Canadian authors only. No unsol mss, query first. Handle film & TV rights. No screenwriters. No reading fee. For submission guidelines, please visit us at www.wcaltd.com/submission-guidelines.
Foreign Rep(s): Akcali Copyright (Kezban Akcali & Atilla Izgi Turgut) (Turkey); Sandra Bruna Literary Agency (Sandra Bruna & Natalia Berenguer) (Brazil, Latin America, Portugal, Spain); The English Agency (Hamish Macaskill) (Japan); Graal Literary Agency (Marcin Biegal & Maria Starz-Kanska) (Poland); The Deborah Harris Agency (Efrat Lev) (Israel); International Copyright Agency (Simona Kessler) (Romania); The Italian Literary Agency SRL (Italy); Japan Uni Agency (Miko Suga Yamanouchi) (Japan); Anna Jarota Agency (Sandrine Bilan & Anna Jarota) (France); JLM Literary Agency (John Moukakos) (Greece); Katai & Bolza (Peter Bolza) (Hungary); Liepman Agency (Suzanne de Roche & Ruth Weibel) (Germany); Maxima Creative Agency (Santo Manurung) (Indonesia); NiKa (Vania Kadiyska) (Bulgaria); Andrew Nurnberg & Associates (Lisa Brannstrom & Eleonoora Kirk) (Netherlands, Scandinavia); Andrew Nurnberg Associates International (Whitney Hsu) (China); Kristin Olson (Czech Republic); PLIMA (Vuk Perisic) (Croatia, Serbia, Slovenia); Shin Won Agency (Tae Eun Kim) (Korea); Synopsis (Natalia Sanina) (Russia); Tuttle-Mori Agency Inc (Thananchai

Pandey) (Thailand); Tuttle-Mori Agency Inc (Ken Mori) (Japan)
Membership(s): Professional Association of Canadian Literary Agents

Rhoda Weyr Agency, see Dunham Literary Inc

Witherspoon Associates Inc, see InkWell Management

WME (L-D)
11 Madison Ave, 18th fl, New York, NY 10010
Tel: 212-586-5100
Web Site: www.wmeentertainment.com
Key Personnel
Partner: Tina Bennett; Dorian Karchmar (AAR)
Head, NY Lit Dept: Suzanne Gluck
EVP, Co-Head: Jennifer Rudolph Walsh
Dept Head: Eric Simonoff
Agent: Mel Berger *E-mail:* mmb@wmeentertainment.com; Margaret Riley King *E-mail:* mrk@wmeentertainment.com; Kathleen Nishimoto *E-mail:* kn@wmeentertainment.com
Contact: Jay Mandel
All subjects; handle software, film & TV rights. No unsol mss, query first; no reading fee.
Foreign Office(s): Center Point, 100 New Oxford St, London WC1A 1HB, United Kingdom *Tel:* (020) 7534 6800 *Fax:* (020) 7534 6900

Writers House (L)
21 W 26 St, New York, NY 10010
Tel: 212-685-2400 *Fax:* 212-685-1781
Web Site: www.writershouse.com
Key Personnel
Founder: Albert Zuckerman
Chmn & CEO: Amy Berkower (AAR)
Pres: Simon Lipskar (AAR)
EVP, Fiction & Nonfiction: Merrilee Heifetz (AAR)
VP & Dir, Juv & Young Adult: Susan Cohen (AAR)
Exec Dir, Global Licensing & Dom Partnerships: Cecelia de la Campa
Digital Dir: Daniel Berkowitz
Dir, Digital Rts: Julie Trelstad
Mng Dir, Global Licensing: Maja Nikolic
UK Rts Dir: Peggy Boulos Smith
Sr Agent: Stephen Barr; Dan Conaway (AAR); Susan Ginsburg; Dan Lazar (AAR) *E-mail:* dlazar@writershouse.com
Sr Agent, Juv & Young Adult: Jodi Reamer, Esq (AAR); Rebecca Sherman *E-mail:* rsherman@writershouse.com
Sr Agent, Mainstream Fiction & Nonfiction: Robin Rue (AAR)
Agent: Lisa DiMona; Susan Golomb (AAR); Brianne Johnson; Geri Thoma (AAR)
Licensing Mgr: James Munro; Kathryn Stuart
Founded: 1973
Represent trade books of all types, fiction & nonfiction, including all rights. Handle film & TV rights. No screenplays, teleplays or software. No unsol mss, query first with an intelligent one page letter stating what's wonderful about the book, what it's about & what background & experience you, as an author, bring to it. Queries generally responded to within 2 weeks & mss within 4 weeks. No reading fee.
Branch Office(s)
3368 Governor Dr, San Diego, CA 92122, Dir, Juv, Young Adult & Illus: Steven Malk *Tel:* 858-678-8767 *Fax:* 858-678-8530
Foreign Office(s): Writers House UK, c/o Good Business, 25 Gerrard St, London W1D 6JL, United Kingdom, Contact: Angharad Kowal *E-mail:* akowal@writershouse.com
Foreign Rep(s): Angharad Kowal (UK)
Foreign Rights: Ia Atterholm (Scandinavia); Bardon-Chinese Agency Inc (Taiwan); Eliane Benisti (France); Claude Choquette (Canada (French-speaking)); Raquel de la Concha (Portugal, Spain); DRT (Korea); The Italian Literary Agency srl (Italy); Japan Uni Agency Inc (juv & young adult) (Japan); JLM Literary Agency (Greece); Simona Kessler (Romania); Ulla Lohren (Scandinavia); Aleksandra Matuszak (Poland); Jovan Milenkovic (Croatia, Montenegro, Serbia); Andrew Nurnberg Associates (Baltic States); Owls Agency Inc (Japan); I Pikarski Literary Agency (Israel); Katalina Sabeva (Bulgaria); Schindler's Literary Agency (Brazil); Thomas Schlueck GmbH (Germany); Sebes & Bisseling Literary Agency (Netherlands); Synopsis Literary Agency (Russia); Petra Tobiskova (Czech Republic)

Writers' Productions (L-D)
PO Box 630, Westport, CT 06881-0630
Tel: 203-227-8199
Key Personnel
Owner & Pres: David L Meth *E-mail:* dlm67@mac.com
Founded: 1977
Literary quality fiction & nonfiction. Handle film, TV & licensing rights. Foreign reps available as & where needed. No fees. No unsol mss; not accepting new clients. No mss or samples by e-mail. No phone calls.
Membership(s): Academy of American Poets; The Dramatists Guild of America; PEN American Center

Writers' Representatives LLC (L)
116 W 14 St, 11th fl, New York, NY 10011-7305
Tel: 212-620-9009 *Fax:* 212-620-0023
E-mail: transom@writersreps.com
Web Site: www.writersreps.com
Key Personnel
Principal: Lynn Chu; Glen Hartley *E-mail:* glen@writersreps.com
Founded: 1985
Represents authors of book-length works of nonfiction & literary fiction for adults. Once WR agrees to represent an author, we give advice on how best to structure or edit a book proposal, discuss ideas for book pojects & comment on finished ms material, with the goal of placing a book with the right publisher on the best possible terms for our author. We also discuss our authors' backgrounds & interests with publishers to promote upcoming projects or to find new ones. We sell to major publishers in the US & abroad. Prefer to see ms material rather than synopses. Background about an author's professional experience, particularly that which is relevant to the book, as well as a list of previously published works. We respond within 4-6 weeks on average. We require that all authors fully advise us as to whether any project has been previously submitted to a publisher & what the response was & if the project has been submitted to another agent. Postal submissions should be accompanied by SASE. No reading fees.
Titles recently placed: *Falstaff: Give Me Life*, Harold Bloom; *The Road to Character*, David Brooks; *The Second World Wars*, Victor Davis Hanson
Foreign Rights: Agencia Literaria Carmen Balcells SA (Anna Bofill) (Portugal); Agencia Literaria Carmen Balcells SA (Maribel Luque) (Spain); Tassy Barham Associates (Tassy Barham) (Brazil); Eggers & Landwehr KG (Petra Eggers) (Germany); Japan Uni Agency (Miko Yamanouchi) (Japan); Susanna Zevi Agencia Letteraria (Susanna Zevi) (Italy)

The Wylie Agency LLC (L)
250 W 57 St, Suite 2114, New York, NY 10107
Tel: 212-246-0069 *Fax:* 212-586-8953
E-mail: mail@wylieagency.com
Web Site: www.wylieagency.com
Key Personnel
Founder & Pres: Andrew Wylie
Literary Agent: Jin Auh; Sarah Chalfant; Jeffrey Posternak
Founded: 1980
Literary fiction & nonfiction; no unsol mss; query first with SASE. Handle film & TV rights. Contact for fee information.
Foreign Office(s): The Wylie Agency (UK) Ltd, 17 Bedford Sq, London WC1B 3JA, United Kingdom *Tel:* (020) 7908 5900 *Fax:* (020) 7908 5901 *E-mail:* mail@wylieagency.co.uk
Foreign Rights: The Wylie Agency (UK) Ltd (UK)

The Young Agency (L)
115 W 29 St, 3rd fl, New York, NY 10001
Tel: 212-695-2431
Key Personnel
Prop: Marian Young
Founded: 1986
Fiction & nonfiction. No unsol mss; no reading fees. Handle film & TV rights after book is sold.

Zachary Shuster Harmsworth Agency, see Aevitas Creative Management

Barbara J Zitwer Agency (L-D)
525 West End Ave, Unit 11-H, New York, NY 10024
Tel: 212-501-8423
E-mail: zitwer@gmail.com
Key Personnel
Pres: Barbara J Zitwer *E-mail:* zitwer@gmail.com
Founded: 1991
Winner of 2016 International Literary Agent of the Year Award, specializing in fiction & narrative nonfiction by writers from all over the world. Represents the best writers from Korea including Booker short listed, Han Kang, Man Asian Prize winner, Kyouing sook Shin. We look for new, exciting literary voices from every country on the globe.
Titles recently placed: *Not Without Her Daughter*, Andrea Claudia Hoffmann; *Painter of the Wind*, J M Lee; *Raif Badawi: The Voice of Freedom*, Ensaf Haidar, Andrea Claudia Hoffmann; *Swallowing Mercury*, Wioletta Greg; *The Accusation*, Bandi; *The Girl Who Beat Isis*, Farida Khalaf, Claudia Andrea Hoffmann; *The Vegetarian*, Han Kang; *The White Book*, Han Kang
Foreign Rights: Gabriella Ambrosioni (Italy); Donatalla D'Ormesson (France); Anoukh Foerg Litteraire Agent (Germany); Deborah Harris Agency (Israel); KL Management (China, Japan, Korea); MO Literary Agency (Scandinavia); Andrew Nurnberg Agency (Whitney Hsu) (Taiwan); Prava i prevodi (Eastern Europe, Russia); SalmaiaLit (Portugal, Spanish)

Illustration Agents

Artists Associates
4416 La Jolla Dr, Bradenton, FL 34210-3927
Tel: 941-756-8445
Key Personnel
Dir: Bill Erlacher
Represents 9 artists.

Artworks Illustration
PO Box 453, New York, NY 10156
Tel: 212-239-4946
E-mail: artworksillustration@earthlink.net
Web Site: www.artworksillustration.com
Founded: 1990
Represents 30 artists.
Membership(s): Society of Illustrators

Carol Bancroft & Friends
PO Box 2030, Danbury, CT 06813
Tel: 203-730-8270 *Fax:* 203-730-8275
E-mail: cbfriends@sbcglobal.net
Web Site: www.carolbancroft.com
Key Personnel
Owner: Joy Elton Tricarico
Founded: 1972
Represents many fine illustrators specializing in art for children of all ages. Servicing the publishing industry including, but not limited to: picture/mass market books & educational materials. We work with packagers, studios, toy companies & corporations in addition to licensing art to related products. Promotional packets sent upon request. Unsol artwork not accepted.
Membership(s): Graphic Artists Guild; Society of Children's Book Writers & Illustrators; Society of Illustrators

Benoit & Associates
279 S Schuyler Ave, Kankakee, IL 60901
Tel: 815-932-2582 *Fax:* 815-932-2582
Web Site: www.benoit-associates.com
Key Personnel
Pres: Michael J Benoit *E-mail:* mbenoit@benoit-associates.com
Full service design & advertising studio. Specialize in technical & color airbrush illustration & computer generated art (Mac & IBM) design, art direction, in-house photography, elementary through college textbook cover & newsletters, brochures, letterheads & annual reports. High volume, high quality, quick turnaround & satisfaction guaranteed.

Bernstein & Andriulli Inc
190 Bowery, 3rd fl, New York, NY 10012
Tel: 212-682-1490 *Fax:* 212-286-1890
E-mail: info@ba-reps.com
Web Site: www.ba-reps.com
Key Personnel
Illustration: Louisa St Pierre
Commercial illustration & photography.
Represents 82 artists.
Branch Office(s)
Rm 207, Block 1, 427 Ju Men Rd, Huangl'u District, Shanghai 200023, China, Pres: Jonathan Tay *E-mail:* jonathan.tay@amanacliq.com
49 Borough High St, London SE1 1NB, United Kingdom, Illustration Rep: Sam Summerskill *Tel:* (0207) 645 3337 *E mail:* sam@ba-reps.com

Byer-Sprinzeles Agency
5800 Arlington Ave, Suite 16-C, Riverdale, NY 10471
Tel: 718-543-9399
Web Site: www.maggiebyersprinzeles.com
Key Personnel
Agent: Maggie Byer-Sprinzeles *E-mail:* maggie@maggiebyersprinzeles.com
Founded: 1991
Represents children's book illustrators.
Represents 27 artists.
Membership(s): Society of Children's Book Writers & Illustrators

Cornell & McCarthy LLC
2-D Cross Hwy, Westport, CT 06880
Tel: 203-454-4210
E-mail: contact@cmartreps.com
Web Site: www.cmartreps.com
Key Personnel
Partner: Merial Cornell; Pat McCarthy
Founded: 1989
Professional illustrators, specializing in the children's book markets; educational, trade & mass market. Representing over 35 artists with a variety of styles & techniques.
Membership(s): Graphic Artists Guild; Society of Children's Book Writers & Illustrators

Craven Design Inc
229 E 85 St, New York, NY 10028
Mailing Address: PO Box 282, New York, NY 10028-9998
Tel: 212-288-1022 *Fax:* 212-249-9910
E-mail: cravendesign@mac.com
Web Site: www.cravendesignstudios.com
Key Personnel
Artist Rep: Meryl Jones
Founded: 1981
Artist's representative: book illustration (text & trade), juvenile through adult; humorous, realistic, decorative & technical; maps, charts, graphs.
Represents 20 artists.

Deborah Wolfe Ltd
731 N 24 St, Philadelphia, PA 19130
Tel: 215-232-6666 *Fax:* 215-232-6585
E-mail: info@illustrationonline.com
Web Site: www.illustrationonline.com
Founded: 1978
Commercial illustrators & animators representative.
Represents 30 artists.

Fort Ross Inc - International Representation for Artists
Division of Fort Ross Inc
26 Arthur Place, Yonkers, NY 10701
Tel: 914-375-6448; 718-775-8340
Web Site: www.fortrossinc.com
Key Personnel
Pres & Exec Dir: Dr Vladimir P Kartsev *E-mail:* vkartsev2000@gmail.com
Founded: 1992
Foreign sales of secondary rights for illustrations, photographs & covers made by American & Canadian artists. Representation of Russian & East European artists & photographers in the US & CN.
Represents 50 artists.

Carol Guenzi Agents Inc
Subsidiary of Artagent.com
865 Delaware St, Denver, CO 80204
Tel: 303-820-2599 *Toll Free Tel:* 800-417-5120 *Fax:* 303-820-2598
E-mail: art@artagent.com
Web Site: www.artagent.com
Key Personnel
Pres: Carol Guenzi
Founded: 1984
A wide selection of talent in all areas of visual communications.
Represents 25 artists.
Membership(s): AIGA, the professional association for design; Art Directors Club of Denver

The Charlotte Gusay Literary Agency
10532 Blythe Ave, Los Angeles, CA 90064
Tel: 310-559-0831 *Fax:* 310-559-2639
E-mail: gusay1@ca.rr.com (queries only)
Web Site: www.gusay.com
Founded: 1988
Selectively represent children's book artists & illustrators.

Herman Agency
350 Central Park W, Apt 4I, New York, NY 10025
Tel: 212-749-4907
Web Site: www.hermanagencyinc.com
Key Personnel
Owner & Pres: Ronnie Ann Herman *E-mail:* ronnie@hermanagencyinc.com
Founded: 1999
Represent illustrators, authors & author/illustrators of children's books, trade & educational.
Represents 23 artists.
Membership(s): The Authors Guild; Society of Children's Book Writers & Illustrators

The Ivy League of Artists Inc
18 Edgemere Rd, Livingston, NJ 07039
Tel: 973-992-4048 *Fax:* 973-992-4049
E-mail: ilartists2@gmail.com
Key Personnel
Owner & Pres: Ivy Mindlin
Illustration, spot drawings, comps, storyboards, design, infographics, PowerPoint & mechanical art.

Levy Creative Management LLC
425 E 58 St, Suite 37F, New York, NY 10022
Tel: 212-687-6463 *Fax:* 212-661-4839
E-mail: info@levycreative.com
Web Site: www.levycreative.com
Key Personnel
Pres & Founder: Sari Schorr *E-mail:* sari@levycreative.com
Founded: 1996
Boutique agency representing only award-winning international artists.

Lindgren & Smith
888C Eighth Ave, No 329, New York, NY 10019
Tel: 212-397-7330
E-mail: info@lindgrensmith.com
Web Site: lindgrensmith.com
Key Personnel
Owner: Pat Lindgren *E-mail:* pat@lindgrensmith.com; Piper Smith *E-mail:* piper@lindgrensmith.com
Founded: 1987
Do not accept mss; examples of illustrator's work can be requested via e-mail. The best way to contact us is by e-mail.
Represents 25 artists.

Lott Representatives Ltd
PO Box 3607, New York, NY 10163
Tel: 212-755-5737
Web Site: www.lottreps.com
Key Personnel
Pres: Peter Lott *E-mail:* peter@lottreps.com
Represent commercial illustrators.

MB Artists
775 Sixth Ave, Suite 6, New York, NY 10001
Tel: 212-689-7830 *Fax:* 212-689-7829
Web Site: www.mbartists.com
Key Personnel
Pres & Agent: Mela Bolinao *E-mail:* mela@mbartists.com
Founded: 1986
Represents illustrators whose work is intended for juvenile market.
Represents 64 artists.
Membership(s): The Children's Book Council; Graphic Artists Guild; Society of Children's Book Writers & Illustrators; Society of Illustrators

Melissa Turk & the Artist Network
9 Babbling Brook Lane, Suffern, NY 10901
Tel: 845-368-8606
E-mail: melissa@melissaturk.com
Web Site: www.melissaturk.com
Key Personnel
Contact: Dorothy Ziff
Founded: 1986
Represents professional artists supplying quality illustration, calligraphy & cartography. Specialize in children's trade & educational illustration as well as natural science illustration (wildlife, botanical, medical, etc), publishing & interpretive signage.
Represents 12 artists.
Membership(s): Graphic Artists Guild; Society of Children's Book Writers & Illustrators

Morgan Gaynin Inc
149 Madison Ave, Suite 1140, New York, NY 10016
Tel: 212-475-0440
E-mail: info@morgangaynin.com
Web Site: www.morgangaynin.com
Key Personnel
Owner, Principal & Rep: Gail Gaynin
Rep: Kate Kelly
Founded: 1974
Illustrator's representative.
Represents 40 artists.
Membership(s): Graphic Artists Guild; Society of Children's Book Writers & Illustrators; Society of Illustrators

Wanda Nowak Creative Illustrators Agency
231 E 76 St, Suite 5-D, New York, NY 10021
Tel: 212-535-0438
E-mail: wanda@wandanow.com
Web Site: www.wandanow.com
Key Personnel
Pres: Wanda Nowak
Founded: 1995
Children's trade books, elementary & secondary textbook illustration & book cover illustration.
Represents 16 artists.

Painted-Words Inc
310 W 97 St, Suite 24, New York, NY 10025
Tel: 212-663-2311 *Fax:* 212-663-2891
E-mail: info@painted-words.com
Web Site: painted-words.com
Key Personnel
Agent: Claire Easton; Lori Nowicki
E-mail: lori@painted-words.com
Founded: 1992 (as Lori Nowicki & Associates)
Artist & literary agent.
Represents 41 artists.
Membership(s): Society of Children's Book Writers & Illustrators

Portfolio Solutions LLC
136 Jameson Hill Rd, Clinton Corners, NY 12514
Tel: 845-266-1001
Web Site: www.portfoliosolutionsllc.com
Key Personnel
Owner & Agent: Bernadette Szost *E-mail:* b.szost@portfoliosolutionsllc.com
Founded: 1999
Agency representing illustrators of children's books & related materials.
Represents 35 artists.
Membership(s): The Authors Guild; Society of Children's Book Writers & Illustrators

Gerald & Cullen Rapp
420 Lexington Ave, New York, NY 10170
Tel: 212-889-3337 *Fax:* 212-889-3341
E-mail: info@rappart.com
Web Site: www.rappart.com
Key Personnel
Rep: Nancy Moore *Tel:* 212-889-3337 ext 103
E-mail: nancy@rappart.com
Founded: 1944
Represent leading commercial illustrators on an exclusive basis. Sell to magazine & book publishers, ad agencies, design firms & major corporations.
Represents 60 artists.
Membership(s): Graphic Artists Guild; Society of Illustrators

Kerry Reilly: Representatives
1826 Asheville Place, Charlotte, NC 28203
Tel: 704-372-6007
E-mail: kerry@reillyreps.com
Web Site: www.reillyreps.com
Animation, illustration & photography.
Represents 25 artists.

Renaissance House
Imprint of Laredo Publishing Co Inc
465 Westview Ave, Englewood, NJ 07631
Tel: 201-408-4048
E-mail: laredo@renaissancehouse.net; contact@renaissancehouse.net
Web Site: www.renaissancehouse.net
Founded: 1991
Book developer that specializes in children's books, educational materials & bilingual market (English/Spanish). Represents illustrators who specialize in art for children that provide a wide variety of styles & techniques. Services the advertising & publishing industries, including children's books & educational materials. Multicultural artists are available. Promotional booklet sent upon request.
Represents 90 artists.

Rosenthal Represents
23725 Hartland St, West Hills, CA 91307
Tel: 818-222-5445
E-mail: eliselicenses@earthlink.net
Key Personnel
Pres: Elise Rosenthal
Sales & Mktg & Artists Rep: Neil Sandler
Founded: 1979
Illustrate book covers, children's & adult books. Licensing agents.
Represents 35 artists.
Membership(s): Licensing Industry Merchandisers' Association; Society of Illustrators

Salzman International
1751 Charles Ave, Arcata, CA 95521
Tel: 415-285-8267 *Fax:* 707-822-5500
Web Site: www.salzint.com
Key Personnel
Owner: Richard Salzman *E-mail:* rs@salzint.com
Founded: 1982
Agents for visual artists for educational & trade books specializing in art illustrators. Feature art for magazines & periodicals. Editorial services available.
Represents 25 artists.

Richard W Salzman Artists' Representative, see Salzman International

The Schuna Group Inc
1503 Briarknoll Dr, Arden Hills, MN 55112
Tel: 651-631-8480
Web Site: www.schunagroup.com
Key Personnel
Pres: Jo Anne Schuna *E-mail:* joanne@schunagroup.com
Represents 12 artists.

Storybook Arts Inc
414 Poplar Hill Rd, Dover Plains, NY 12522
Mailing Address: PO Box 672, Dover Plains, NY 12522
Tel: 845-877-3305
Web Site: www.storybookartsinc.com
Key Personnel
Owner & Pres: Janet De Carlo *E-mail:* janet@storybookartsinc.com
Founded: 2005
Artist representative agency.
Represents 26 artists.
Membership(s): Society of Children's Book Writers & Illustrators

Christina A Tugeau Artist Agency LLC
29 Newman Place, Fairfield, CT 06825
Tel: 917-434-3141
E-mail: chris@catugeau.com
Web Site: www.catugeau.com
Key Personnel
Owner & Rep: Christina Tugeau
Partner: Christy Ewers *E-mail:* christy@catugeau.com
Founded: 1994
Represents mostly North American illustrators for children's publishing: mass market & trade books, educational (preschool through young adult). Will view e-mail samples.
Represents 30 artists.
Membership(s): Society of Children's Book Writers & Illustrators

Tugeau 2 Inc
2231 Grandview Ave, Cleveland Heights, OH 44106
Tel: 216-707-0854
Web Site: www.tugeau2.com
Key Personnel
Owner: Nicole Tugeau *E-mail:* nicole@tugeau2.com
Founded: 2003
Agency for artist representation in the children's publishing industry.
Represents 35 artists.
Membership(s): Society of Children's Book Writers & Illustrators

WendyLynn & Co
504 Wilson Rd, Annapolis, MD 21401
Tel: 410-224-2729; 410-507-1059
Web Site: wendylynn.com
Key Personnel
Pres & Illustration Agent: Wendy Mays
E-mail: wendy@wendylynn.com
Busn Mgr & Illustration Agent: Janice Onken
E-mail: janice@wendylynn.com
Founded: 2002
Specialize in the children's publishing market. Represent & promote our illustrators to pub-

lishing companies which produce work for children & young adults.
Represents 25 artists.
Membership(s): Society of Children's Book Writers & Illustrators

Wilkinson Studios Inc
2955 Kelly Dr, Elgin, IL 60124-4349
Tel: 312-286-3683
Web Site: www.wilkinsonstudios.com
Key Personnel
Founder & Pres: Christine Wilkinson
E-mail: chris@wilkinsonstudios.com
VP: Lisa O'Hara *E-mail:* lisa@wilkinsonstudios.com
Founded: 1999
Specializing in representing illustrators & managing art programs for educational, trade book & mass market publishing, children's magazines, games & related fields. Over 100 illustrators offering age appropriate artwork for PreK-college in a wide range of styles, techniques & media, both conventional & electronic. Project management of large volume blackline or color illustration programs by dedicated staff with art & design backgrounds, working directly with the publisher or interfacing with design & development house vendors.
Represents 100 artists.
Membership(s): Graphic Artists Guild; Society of Children's Book Writers & Illustrators

Lecture Agents

Listed below are some of the most active lecture agents who handle tours and single engagements for writers.

American Program Bureau Inc
One Gateway Center, Suite 751, Newton, MA 02458
Tel: 617-614-1600 *Fax:* 617-965-6610
E-mail: apb@apbspeakers.com
Web Site: www.apbspeakers.com
Key Personnel
COO, Sales Dir: Andrew Walker *Tel:* 617-614-1611 *E-mail:* awalker@apbspeakers.com
Mktg Coord: Drew Sullivan *Tel:* 617-614-1638 *E-mail:* dsullivan@apbspeakers.com
Founded: 1965
Lecture representation/speakers bureau. Branches located in CA, IL & NJ.
Membership(s): International Association of Speakers Bureaus; NACA

The Barnabas Agency
Division of The B&B Media Group Inc
PO Box 3113, Corsicana, TX 75151-3113
Toll Free Tel: 800-927-0517
E-mail: info@barnabasagency.com
Web Site: www.barnabasagency.com
Key Personnel
Pres & CEO: Tina Jacobson *Tel:* 800-927-0517 ext 101 *E-mail:* tina@barnabasagency.com
VP & COO: Rick Roberson *Tel:* 800-927-0517 ext 100 *E-mail:* rick@barnabasagency.com
VP, PR: Diane Morrow *Tel:* 800-927-1517 *E-mail:* diane@barnabasagency.com
Founded: 2002
Objectives: To increase recognition of the client, his/her ministry, products & service; to establish client's credibility, help achieve long-term & short-term goals & help client develop a vision. Services range from consulting to full-scale personal management of the client & implementation of the various components of the campaign.
Membership(s): Public Relations Society of America

Burns Entertainment & Sports Marketing
820 Davis St, Suite 222, Evanston, IL 60201
Tel: 847-866-9400 *Fax:* 847-491-9778
E-mail: burnsl@burnsent.com
Web Site: burnsent.com
Key Personnel
CEO & COO: Bob Williams *E-mail:* bobwilliams@burnsent.com
Pres & Gen Coun: Marc Ippolito
Pres: Doug Shabelman
Founded: 1970
Sports & entertainment marketing, match corporations with talent celebrities for appearances, speeches & endorsements.
Branch Office(s)
333 Seventh Ave, Suite 1702, New York, NY 10001

CreativeWell Inc
PO Box 3130, Memorial Sta, Upper Montclair, NJ 07043
Tel: 973-783-7575 *Toll Free Tel:* 800-743-9182 *Fax:* 973-783-7530
E-mail: info@creativewell.com
Web Site: www.creativewell.com
Key Personnel
Pres: George M Greenfield *E-mail:* george@creativewell.com
Founded: 2003
Literary, lecture & arts management.

The Fischer Ross Group Inc
75 Holly Hill Lane, Suite 100, Greenwich, CT 06830
Tel: 203-622-4950 *Fax:* 203-531-4132
E-mail: frgstaff@frg-speakers.com
Web Site: www.frg-speakers.com
Key Personnel
Pres: Grada Fischer
Exclusive lecture agents for authors (fiction, nonfiction, trade) & journalists (print & broadcast), as well as nationally known celebrities & personalities. Arrange lecture tours, individual speaking engagements, product endorsements, public openings & appearances for the university, association & corporate markets.

Greater Talent Network Inc
437 Fifth Ave, New York, NY 10016
Tel: 212-645-4200 *Toll Free Tel:* 800-326-4211 *Fax:* 212-627-1471
E-mail: info@greatertalent.com
Web Site: www.greatertalent.com
Key Personnel
CEO: Don R Epstein
Founded: 1981
Exclusive lecture & entertainment management. Represent authors, journalists & nationally & internationally known individuals. Arrange speaking engagements & tours for corporations, associations, colleges & universities, town halls, hospitals & other organizations, as well as literary, motion picture, television & radio representation.
Membership(s): International Association of Speakers Bureaus

ICM Lecture Division
Division of International Creative Management
730 Fifth Ave, New York, NY 10019
Tel: 212-556-5600 *Fax:* 212-556-5665
Web Site: www.icmtalent.com
Key Personnel
Dir: Betsy Berg *Tel:* 212-556-5676
Exclusively represents a long list of authors, entertainers & distinguished clients & celebrities from all fields for lectures & personal appearances.
Branch Office(s)
10250 Constellation Blvd, Los Angeles, CA 90067 *Tel:* 310-550-4000
Marlborough House, 3rd fl, 10 Earlham St, London WC2H 9LN, United Kingdom *Tel:* (020) 7836 8564

International Entertainment Bureau
3612 N Washington Blvd, Indianapolis, IN 46205-3592
Tel: 317-926-7566
E-mail: ieb@prodigy.net
Key Personnel
Founder: David Leonards
Founded: 1972
Database, resource center & clearing house. Information on speakers, celebrities & entertainers available in the marketplace. Planning, consulting & booking.
Membership(s): Indiana Association of Fairs, Festivals & Events; Indiana Society of Association Executives; Meeting Professionals International

BK Nelson Inc Lecture Bureau
Division of BK Nelson Inc
6726 Moonriver St, Mira Loma, CA 91752-3428
Tel: 760-902-1868 *Fax:* 760-778-6242
E-mail: bknelson4@cs.com
Key Personnel
Pres & CEO: Bonita K Nelson
CFO: Corp Reed
VP: John W Benson
Edit Dir: Tony Pastor
Acctg Dept: Erv Rosenfeld
Founded: 1998
Book authors & personalities, experts in diverse fields. Arrange seminars & keynote speaking engagements. Speechwriting/coaching. Publish BK Nelson's Speaker's Directory with photos each year. Online booking. Certification status granted by New York State Department of Economic Development.
Membership(s): American Association of University Women; The Authors Guild; The Dramatists Guild of America; Motion Picture Alliance; NACA

Penguin Random House Speakers Bureau, A Penguin Random House Company
1745 Broadway, Mail Drop 13-1, New York, NY 10019
Tel: 212-572-2013
E-mail: speakers@penguinrandomhouse.com
Web Site: www.prhspeakers.com
Key Personnel
VP & Exec Dir: Tiffany Tomlin
Sr Agent Dir: Wade Lucas *Tel:* 212-572-6113 *E-mail:* walucas@randomhouse.com
Agent Dir: Jayme Boucher *Tel:* 212-572-7309 *E-mail:* jboucher@randomhouse.com; Mary Coyne *Tel:* 212-572-2247 *E-mail:* mcoyne@randomhouse.com; Kathy Dunn *Tel:* 631-283-5923 *E-mail:* kdunn@randomhouse.com; Kim Thornton Ingenito *Tel:* 212-572-2299 *E-mail:* kthornton@randomhouse.com; Caitlin McCaskey *Tel:* 212-572-8661 *E-mail:* cmccaskey@randomhouse.com
Agent Dir, Random House Children's: Christine Labov
Asst Agent Dir: Lisa Barnes
Assoc: Stasia Whalen
Sr Agent: Erin Simpson
Mgr: Elaine Trevorrow *Tel:* 212-572-2175 *E-mail:* etrevorrow@randomhouse.com
Mktg Mgr: Stefanie Von Beoczy *Tel:* 212-572-2398 *E-mail:* svonbeoczy@randomhouse.com
Coord: Jessie Garretson *Tel:* 212-572-2396 *E-mail:* jgarretson@randomhouse.com
Founded: 2006
Full service lecture agency that represents best-selling authors, literary legends, cutting-edge thinkers & current tastemakers.
Membership(s): International Association of Speakers Bureaus

Random House Speakers Bureau, see Penguin Random House Speakers Bureau, A Penguin Random House Company

Royce Carlton Inc
866 United Nations Plaza, Suite 587, New York, NY 10017-1880
Tel: 212-355-7700 *Toll Free Tel:* 800-LECTURE (532-8873) *Fax:* 212-888-8659
E-mail: info@roycecarlton.com
Web Site: www.roycecarlton.com

Key Personnel
Pres: Carlton Sedgeley *Tel:* 212-822-0999
E-mail: carlton@roycecarlton.com
EVP: Lucy Lepage *Tel:* 212-822-0979
E-mail: lucy@roycecarlton.com
VP: Helen Churko *Tel:* 212-822-0981
E-mail: helen@roycecarlton.com
Founded: 1968
Agents, managers & brokers for speakers.

Jodi Solomon Speakers Bureau
295 Huntington Ave, Suite 211, Boston, MA 02115
Tel: 617-266-3450 *Fax:* 617-266-5660
E-mail: inquiries@jodisolomonspeakers.com
Web Site: www.jodisolomonspeakers.com
Founded: 1990
Lecture & performing arts management.
Membership(s): NACA

The Tuesday Agency
132 1/2 E Washington St, Iowa City, IA 52240
Tel: 319-338-7080
E-mail: trinity@tuesdayagency.com
Web Site: tuesdayagency.com
Key Personnel
Pres: Trinity Ray
VP: Kevin Mills
Founded: 2011
Exclusive speaker representation.

World Class Speakers & Entertainers
5200 Kanan Rd, Suite 210, Agoura Hills, CA 91301
Tel: 818-991-5400
E-mail: wcse@wcspeakers.com
Web Site: www.wcspeakers.com
Key Personnel
Pres: Joseph I Kessler *E-mail:* jkessler@wcspeakers.com
Founded: 1970
Represents world class speakers & entertainers. Database of 25,000 speakers & entertainers; directory/guide available.

Writers' League of Texas (WLT)
611 S Congress Ave, Suite 200 A-3, Austin, TX 78704
Tel: 512-499-8914
E-mail: wlt@writersleague.org
Web Site: www.writersleague.org
Key Personnel
Prog Dir: Michael Noll *E-mail:* michael@writersleague.org
Founded: 1981

Associations, Events, Courses & Awards

Book Trade & Allied Associations — Index

LITERACY

LITERARY

MAGAZINE & PRESS

MEDIA - COMMUNICATIONS

PUBLISHING

PUBLISHING SERVICES

WRITERS

Book Trade & Allied Associations

Listed here are associations and organizations that are concerned with books, literacy, language and speech, media and communications as well as groups who provide services to the publishing community.

AAP PreK-12 Learning Group
Division of Association of American Publishers (AAP)
455 Massachusetts Ave NW, Suite 700, Washington, DC 20001
Tel: 267-351-4310 *Fax:* 267-351-4317
E-mail: prek12learning@publishers.org
Web Site: www.aepweb.org
Key Personnel
Exec Dir: Jay Diskey *Tel:* 202-220-4549 *E-mail:* jdiskey@publishers.org
Sr Dir: Susan Fletcher *Tel:* 202-220-4550 *E-mail:* sfletcher@publishers.org
Strategic Partnerships Exec: Jo-Ann McDevitt *Tel:* 267-351-4327 *E-mail:* jmcdevitt@publishers.org
Dir, Policy & Res: Julie Copty *Tel:* 202-220-4548 *E-mail:* jcopty@publishers.org
Edit Dir: Stacey Pusey *Tel:* 267-351-4331 *E-mail:* spusey@publishers.org
Dir of Digital Initiatives: Dave Gladney *Tel:* 267-351-4329 *E-mail:* dgladney@publishers.org
Awards Prog Mgr: Linda Swank *Tel:* 267-351-4322 *E-mail:* lswank@publishers.org
Membership Servs Mgr: Brittany Lawrence *Tel:* 267-351-4316 *E-mail:* blawrence@publishers.org
Admin/Mktg Assoc: Rachel Burgos *Tel:* 202-220-4550 *E-mail:* rburgos@publishers.org
Founded: 2013 (merger of AAP School Division & Association of Educational Publishers (AEP))
Supports educational publishing through its programs & member services.
Number of Members: 350
Meeting(s): Content in Context (CIC)
Branch Office(s)
455 Massachusetts Ave, Suite 700, Washington, DC 20001 *Tel:* 202-347-3375 *Fax:* 202-347-3690

AAR, see Association of Authors' Representatives Inc

ABAC/ALAC
368 Dalhousie St, Suite 301, Ottawa, ON K1N 7G3, Canada
Tel: 416-364-2376
E-mail: info@abac.org
Web Site: www.abac.org
Key Personnel
Pres: Liam McGahern
Treas: Michael Park
Founded: 1966
The association's aim is to foster an interest in rare books & mss & to maintain high standards in the antiquarian book trades.
Number of Members: 70
Publication(s): *ABAC/ALAC Membership Directory* (free by request)
Membership(s): International League of Antiquarian Booksellers

The Academy of American Poets Inc
75 Maiden Lane, Suite 901, New York, NY 10038
Tel: 212-274-0343 *Fax:* 212-274-9427
E-mail: academy@poets.org
Web Site: www.poets.org
Key Personnel
Exec Dir: Jennifer Benka
Prog Coord: Nikay Paredes *Tel:* 212-274-0343 ext 13 *E-mail:* nparedes@poets.org
Founded: 1934
The country's largest nonprofit association devoted to poetry. Sponsors the James Laughlin Award, Walt Whitman Award, Harold Morton Landon Translation Award, Wallace Stevens Award, Lenore Marshall Poetry Prize & annual college poetry prizes; award fellowship to American poets for distinguished poetic achievement. Publishes biannual journal. Also administers the National Poetry Month.
Number of Members: 6,000
Publication(s): *American Poet* (biannual, newsletter)

Academy of Motion Picture Arts & Sciences (AMPAS)
8949 Wilshire Blvd, Beverly Hills, CA 90211
Tel: 310-247-3000 *Fax:* 310-859-9619
E-mail: ampas@oscars.org
Web Site: www.oscars.org
Key Personnel
CEO: Dawn Hudson
To advance the arts & sciences of motion pictures & to foster cooperation among the creative leadership of the motion picture industry for cultural, educational & technological progress. Confer annual awards of merit, serving as a constant incentive within the industry & focusing public attention upon the best in motion pictures.
Number of Members: 5,024
Publication(s): *Academy Players Directory, Annual Index to Motion Picture Credits, Nominations & Winners, List of Eligible Releases* (bulletin)

Academy of Television Arts & Sciences (ATAS), see Television Academy

Access Copyright, The Canadian Copyright Licensing Agency
56 Wellesley St W, Suite 401A, Toronto, ON M5S 2S3, Canada
Tel: 416-868-1620 *Toll Free Tel:* 800-893-5777 *Fax:* 416-868-1621
E-mail: info@accesscopyright.ca
Web Site: www.accesscopyright.ca
Key Personnel
Exec Dir: Roanie Levy
Founded: 1988
Number of Members: 36
Publication(s): *Online Access* (quarterly, newsletter, free, electronic)
Membership(s): Book & Periodical Council; International Federation of Reproduction Rights Organizations

Advertising Research Foundation (ARF)
432 Park Ave S, 4th fl, New York, NY 10016-8013
Tel: 212-751-5656 *Fax:* 212-319-5265
E-mail: info@thearf.org; jar@thearf.org (edit)
Web Site: www.thearf.org
Key Personnel
CEO & Pres: Gayle Fuguitt
EVP, Digital: Ted McConnell
EVP, Res & Innovation: Don Gloeckler *Tel:* 646-465-5725
Ed-in-Chief: Geoffrey Precourt
Mng Ed: Nanette Burns *Tel:* 646-465-5728 *E-mail:* nanette@thearf.org
Leadership Progs Mgr: Zena Pagan *Tel:* 646-465-5721 *E-mail:* zena@thearf.org
Founded: 1936
Advertising research service trade association.
Meeting(s): The ARF Annual Convention & Insights Zone (also known as Re:think)
Publication(s): *Journal of Advertising Research (JAR)* (quarterly, $365 standard subn; includes 4 print issues & a 2 yr online archive)

AIGA, the professional association for design
233 Broadway, Suite 1740, New York, NY 10279
Tel: 212-807-1990 *Fax:* 212-807-1799
E-mail: general@aiga.org
Web Site: www.aiga.org
Key Personnel
CFO & COO: Hezron Gurley *Tel:* 212-710-3127
Exec Dir: Julie Anixter *Tel:* 212-710-3100
Mng Ed: Rebecca Sears *Tel:* 212-710-3123
Founded: 1914
National nonprofit organization for graphic design profession. Organizes competitions, exhibitions, publications, educational activities & projects in the public interest to promote excellence in the graphic design industry.
Number of Members: 25,000
New Election: Annually in June
2018 Meeting(s): AIGA Design Conference, Pittsburgh, PA, Oct 4-6, 2018

ALA, see The American Library Association (ALA)

Alcuin Society
PO Box 3216, Sta Terminal, Vancouver, BC V6B 3X8, Canada
Tel: 604-732-5403
E-mail: info@alcuinsociety.com; awards@alcuinsociety.com
Web Site: alcuinsociety.com
Key Personnel
Chair, Book Design Competition: Leah Gordon
Judges book design; publishes articles on book arts, collecting, typography, private presses, book collections, book binding.
Number of Members: 275
New Election: March 2018
Publication(s): *Amphora* (3 issues/yr, journal, $50/yr membs, $75 instns)

Alliance for Audited Media (AAM)
48 W Seegers Rd, Arlington Heights, IL 60005
Tel: 224-366-6939 *Fax:* 224-366-6949
Web Site: www.auditedmedia.com
Key Personnel
CEO, Pres & Mng Dir: Tom Drouillard *Tel:* 224-366-6500 *E-mail:* tom.drouillard@auditedmedia.com
Cooperative association of advertisers, advertising agencies & publishers of newspapers, magazines, farm & business publications. Audit & report circulation, web site & additional digital edition analytics, including mobile application activity for publisher brands in North America.
Number of Members: 4,500
Branch Office(s)
The Chanin Bldg, 122 E 42 St, Suite 807, New York, NY 10168-0899 *Tel:* 212-867-8992 *Fax:* 212-867-8947

151 Bloor St W, Suite 850, Toronto, ON M5S 1S4, Canada, VP & Gen Mgr: Joan Brehl *Tel:* 416-962-5840 *Fax:* 416-962-5844 *E-mail:* joan.brehl@auditedmedia.com *Web Site:* www.auditedmedia.com

Alliance for Audited Media (AAM), Canadian Office
151 Bloor St W, Suite 850, Toronto, ON M5S 1S4, Canada
Tel: 416-962-5840 *Fax:* 416-962-5844
Web Site: auditedmedia.com
Key Personnel
VP & Gen Mgr: Joan Brehl *Tel:* 416-962-5840 ext 224
Number of Members: 4,500

Alliance for Women in Media (AWM)
1250 24 St NW, Suite 300, Washington, DC 20037
Tel: 202-750-3664 *Fax:* 202-750-3664
E-mail: info@allwomeninmedia.org
Web Site: allwomeninmedia.org
Key Personnel
Exec Dir: Becky Brooks
Founded: 1951
For members of the electronic & media industries.
Number of Members: 3,000
Publication(s): *FastForward* (enewsletter)

American Academy of Arts & Sciences (AAAS)
Norton's Woods, 136 Irving St, Cambridge, MA 02138
Tel: 617-576-5000 *Fax:* 617-576-5050
E-mail: aaas@amacad.org
Web Site: www.amacad.org
Key Personnel
Pres: Jonathan Fanton
Promote interchange of ideas through seminars & publications.
Number of Members: 6,000
Publication(s): *Daedalus*

American Academy of Political & Social Science
202 S 36 St, Philadelphia, PA 19104-3806
Tel: 215-746-6500 *Fax:* 215-573-2667
Web Site: www.aapss.org
Key Personnel
Exec Dir: Tom Kecskemethy *Tel:* 215-746-7321 *E-mail:* thomask@asc.upenn.edu
Assoc Dir & Mng Ed: Emily Wood *Tel:* 215-898-5081 *E-mail:* ewood@asc.upenn.edu
Founded: 1889
Publication(s): *The Annals of American Academy of Political & Social Science* (6 issues/yr, $112/yr indivs, $898/yr instns, $824/yr instns (e-access), $916/yr (print & e-access))

American Antiquarian Society (AAS)
185 Salisbury St, Worcester, MA 01609-1634
Tel: 508-755-5221 *Fax:* 508-753-3311
E-mail: library@americanantiquarian.org
Web Site: www.americanantiquarian.org
Key Personnel
Pres: Ellen S Dunlap *Tel:* 508-471-2161 *E-mail:* edunlap@mwa.org
Founded: 1812
Maintain research library in American history & culture through 1876.
Number of Members: 1,028

American Association for the Advancement of Science (AAAS)
1200 New York Ave NW, Washington, DC 20005
Tel: 202-326-6400
Web Site: www.aaas.org
Key Personnel
Dir, Exec Off Aff: Gretchen Seiler
Founded: 1848
Mission is to further the work of scientists, to facilitate cooperation among them, foster scientific freedom & responsibility, improve effectiveness of science in the promotion of human welfare & to increase public understanding & appreciation of the importance & promise of the methods of science in human progress. There are many membership organizations & professional societies which have similar aims or have interest in supporting these objectives. For further information, contact the AAAS Office of News & Information at the above address. US regional divisions: Arctic; Caribbean; Pacific; Southwest & Rocky Mountains.
New Election: Annually in the Fall
2018 Meeting(s): Annual Meeting (Serving Society Through Science Policy), Austin, TX, Feb 15-19, 2018
2019 Meeting(s): Annual Meeting (Serving Society Through Science Policy), Washington, DC, Feb 14-18, 2019
2020 Meeting(s): Annual Meeting (Serving Society Through Science Policy), Seattle, WA, Feb 13-17, 2020
2021 Meeting(s): Annual Meeting (Serving Society Through Science Policy), Phoenix, AZ, Feb 11-14, 2021
2022 Meeting(s): Annual Meeting (Serving Society Through Science Policy), Philadelphia, PA, Feb 17-20, 2022
Publication(s): *Science* (weekly, journal, $10/issue, $135/yr prof rate); *Science Advances* (journal); *Science Immunology* (journal); *Science Signaling* (journal); *Science Translational Medicine* (journal)

American Auto Racing Writers & Broadcasters
922 N Pass Ave, Burbank, CA 91505
Tel: 818-842-7005 *Fax:* 818-842-7020
Key Personnel
Pres: Ms Dusty Brandel
Media people who cover auto racing.
Number of Members: 300

American Book Producers Association (ABPA)
31 W Eighth St, 2nd fl, New York, NY 10011
Tel: 212-675-1363 *Fax:* 212-675-1364
E-mail: office@abpaonline.org
Web Site: www.abpaonline.org
Key Personnel
Pres: Richard Rothschild
VP: Nancy Hall
Treas: Valerie Tomaselli
Bd of Dirs: Leslie Carola; Karen Matsu Greenberg; Susan Knopf
Founded: 1980
An organization of independent book producing companies in the US & CN.
Number of Members: 60
Publication(s): *Booknews* (membs only)

American Booksellers Association
333 Westchester Ave, Suite S202, White Plains, NY 10604
Tel: 914-406-7500 *Toll Free Tel:* 800-637-0037 *Fax:* 914-410-6297
E-mail: info@bookweb.org
Web Site: www.bookweb.org
Key Personnel
CEO: Oren Teicher *Tel:* 800-637-0037 ext 7511 *E-mail:* oren@bookweb.org
CFO: Robyn DesHotel
Content Offr: Dan Cullen *Tel:* 800-637-0037 ext 6660 *E-mail:* dan@bookweb.org
Meetings & Planning Offr: Jill Perlstein *Tel:* 800-637-0037 ext 6642 *E-mail:* jill@bookweb.org
Membership & Mktg Offr: Meg Z Smith *Tel:* 800-637-0037 ext 6641 *E-mail:* meg@bookweb.org
Sr Prog Offr: Joy Dallanegra-Sanger *Tel:* 800-637-0037 ext 6618 *E-mail:* joy@bookweb.org
Dir, Devt & Publr Rel: Matthew Zoni *Tel:* 800-637-0037 ext 6651 *E-mail:* matthew@bookweb.org
Dir, Public Policy & Advocacy: David Grogan
Technol Dir: Greg Galloway *Tel:* 800-637-0037 ext 6668 *E-mail:* greg@bookweb.org
ABC Group Mgr: Gen de Botton
Mgr, IndieCommerce: Geeta Nathan
Proj Mgr: Peter Reynolds
Soc Media Coord: Akira McKinzie
Founded: 1900
Trade organization representing independent booksellers. Sponsor of BookExpo.
Number of Members: 3,500
2018 Meeting(s): BookExpo, Jacob K Javits Convention Center, 655 W 43 St, New York, NY, May 30-June 1, 2018
Publication(s): *Book Buyers Handbook* (electronic); *Bookselling This Week* (electronic)
Membership(s): BISG

American Christian Writers
PO Box 110390, Nashville, TN 37222-0390
Tel: 615-331-8668 *Toll Free Tel:* 800-21-WRITE (219-7483)
E-mail: acwriters@aol.com
Web Site: regaforder.wordpress.com
Key Personnel
Pres: Reg A Forder
2018 Meeting(s): Mentoring Retreat, Nashville, TN, April 20-21, 2018; Mentoring Retreat, Grand Rapids, MI, June 8-9, 2018; Mentoring Retreat, Atlanta, GA, July 6-7, 2018; Mentoring Retreat, Minneapolis, MN, Aug 3-4, 2018; Mentoring Retreat, Phoenix, AZ, Sept 7-8, 2018; Mentoring Retreat, Nashville, TN, Oct 12-13, 2018; Mentoring Retreat, Orlando, FL, Nov 16-17, 2018
Membership(s): Evangelical Christian Publishers Association; Evangelical Press Association; Global Network of Christian Ministries

American Civil Liberties Union
125 Broad St, 18th fl, New York, NY 10004
Tel: 212-549-2500
E-mail: media@aclu.org
Web Site: www.aclu.org
Key Personnel
Pres: Susan N Herman
Exec Dir: Anthony D Romero
Communs Dir: Emily Tynes
Protection of constitutional rights & civil liberties through litigation, legislative lobbying & public education; 250 branch offices.
Number of Members: 500,000

American Council on Education
One Dupont Circle NW, Washington, DC 20036
Tel: 202-939-9300
Web Site: www.acenet.edu
Key Personnel
Pres: Molly Corbett Broad
Founded: 1918
The nation's major coordinating body for postsecondary education. Professional books & guides in higher education (special studies & reports on higher education).
Number of Members: 1,850
2018 Meeting(s): 100th Annual Meeting, Marriott Marquis, Washington, DC, March 10-13, 2018
Publication(s): *The Presidency* (3 issues/yr, $30/yr membs, $40/yr nonmembs)

American Forest & Paper Association (AF&PA)
1101 "K" St NW, Suite 700, Washington, DC 20005
Tel: 202-463-2700
E-mail: info@afandpa.org
Web Site: www.afandpa.org

Key Personnel
CEO & Pres: Donna A Harman
CFO & VP, Admin: Samuel Kerns
VP, Gen Coun & Corp Secy: Jan A Poling
Founded: 1993
National trade association of the forest products industry.
Number of Members: 120
2018 Meeting(s): Paper2018, Lotte New York Palace Hotel, 455 Madison Ave, New York, NY, March 11-13, 2018

American Institute of Graphic Arts, see AIGA, the professional association for design

American Jewish Committee (AJC)
Affiliate of Institute of Human Relations
Jacob Blaustein Bldg, 165 E 56 St, New York, NY 10022
Tel: 212-751-4000; 212-891-1456 (membership) *Fax:* 212-891-1450
Web Site: www.ajc.org
Key Personnel
Exec Dir: David A Harris *E-mail:* harrisd@ajc.org
Dir, Pubns: Lawrence Grossman *Tel:* 212-751-4000 ext 308 *E-mail:* grossmanl@ajc.org
Founded: 1906
Civic & religious rights of Jews in the US & abroad; intergroup relations & human rights.
Number of Members: 43,000
Publication(s): *AJC Journal* (6 issues/yr, free to membs); *American Jewish Year Book* ($30); *Commentary* (magazine, $19.95/yr)
Branch Office(s)
2027 Massachusetts Ave NW, Washington, DC 20036

The American Library Association (ALA)
50 E Huron St, Chicago, IL 60611
Tel: 312-944-6780; 312-280-4299 (memb & cust serv) *Toll Free Tel:* 800-545-2433 *Fax:* 312-440-9374
E-mail: ala@ala.org; customerservice@ala.org
Web Site: www.ala.org
Key Personnel
Exec Dir: Keith Michael Fiels *Tel:* 800-545-2433 ext 1392 *E-mail:* kfiels@ala.org
Founded: 1876
ALA is the oldest & largest library association in the world. ALA promotes the highest quality library & information services & public access to information. Offers professional services & publications to members & nonmembers.
Number of Members: 60,000
2018 Meeting(s): Midwinter Meeting, Denver, CO, Feb 9-13, 2018; National Library Week, Nationwide throughout the USA, April 8-14, 2018; Annual Conference, New Orleans, LA, June 21-26, 2018
2019 Meeting(s): Midwinter Meeting, Seattle, WA, Jan 25-29, 2019; National Library Week, Nationwide throughout the USA, April 7-13, 2019; Annual Conference, Washington, DC, June 20-25, 2019
2020 Meeting(s): Midwinter Meeting, Philadelphia, PA, Jan 17-21, 2020; National Library Week, Nationwide throughout the USA, April 19-25, 2020; Annual Conference, Chicago, IL, June 23-28, 2020
2021 Meeting(s): Midwinter Meeting, Indianapolis, IN, Jan 22-26, 2021; Annual Conference, Chicago, IL, June 24-29, 2021
2022 Meeting(s): Midwinter Meeting, San Antonio, TX, Jan 21-25, 2022; Annual Conference, Washington, DC, June 23-28, 2022
Publication(s): *American Libraries* (6 issues/yr, magazine, free to membs, $70/yr instns US & CN, $80/yr instns foreign)
Branch Office(s)
1615 New Hampshire Ave NW, 1st fl, Washington, DC 20009-2520 *Tel:* 202-628-8410 *Toll Free Tel:* 800-941-8478 *Fax:* 202-628-8419

American Literacy Council
1441 Mariposa Ave, Boulder, CO 80302
Tel: 303-440-7385
Web Site: www.americanliteracy.com
Key Personnel
Pres: Alan Mole *E-mail:* president@americanliteracy.com
Dir & Opers Mgr: Joseph R Little *Tel:* 212-663-4200 *E-mail:* spellingprogress@americanliteracy.com
Founded: 1876
To convey information on new solutions, innovative technologies & tools for engaging more boldly in the battle for literacy.
Number of Members: 12
Publication(s): *Sound-Write®* (free)

American Literary Translators Association (ALTA)
900 E Seventh St, PMB 266, Bloomington, IN 47405-3201
Tel: 972-883-2093 *Fax:* 972-883-6303
Web Site: www.literarytranslators.org
Key Personnel
Pres: Russell Valentino *E-mail:* russell.v@indiana.edu
Literary translation & translators.
Number of Members: 800
Publication(s): *Translation Review* (3 issues/yr, $100/yr indivs, $30/students)

American Management Association (AMA)
1601 Broadway, New York, NY 10019
Tel: 212-586-8100 *Toll Free Tel:* 877-566-9441 *Fax:* 212-903-8168; 518-891-0368
E-mail: customerservice@amanet.org
Web Site: www.amanet.org
Key Personnel
CEO & Pres: Edward T Reilly
SVP: Diane Laurenzo
PR Mgr: Roger Kelleher *Tel:* 212-903-7976 *E-mail:* rkelleher@amanet.org
Over 140 seminars in 20 areas including management, project management, time management, leadership, finance, interpersonal skills, communication, supervisory skills & human resources.
Number of Members: 700,000
New Election: Annually in March

American Marketing Association
130 E Randolph St, 22nd fl, Chicago, IL 60601
Tel: 312-542-9000 *Toll Free Tel:* 800-AMA-1150 (262-1150) *Fax:* 312-542-9001
E-mail: info@ama.org
Web Site: www.ama.org
Key Personnel
CEO: Russ Klein *E-mail:* ceo@ama.org
CFO: Beth Taylor *E-mail:* btaylor@ama.org
CTO: Bob Panger *E-mail:* bpanger@ama.org
Chief Mktg Offr: Nancy Costopulos *E-mail:* ncostopulos@ama.org
Chief Prof Devt Offr: Carol Arnold *E-mail:* carnold@ama.org
Dir, Digital Content: Christopher Bartone *Tel:* 312-542-9029 *E-mail:* cbartone@ama.org
Founded: 1937
A nonprofit, educational institution. Offers online marketing info. Sponsors seminars, conferences & student marketing clubs & doctoral consortium. Publish books, journals, magazines & proceedings of conferences.
Number of Members: 30,000
Publication(s): *Journal of International Marketing*; *Journal of Marketing*; *Journal of Marketing Research* (6 issues/yr); *Journal of Public Policy & Marketing* (semiannual); *Marketing Health Services* (quarterly); *Marketing Insights*; *Marketing News* (biweekly)

American Medical Association
AMA Plaza, 330 N Wabash, Suite 39300, Chicago, IL 60611-5885
Tel: 312-464-5000 *Toll Free Tel:* 800-621-8335 *Fax:* 312-464-4184
Web Site: www.ama-assn.org
Key Personnel
CEO & EVP: James L Madara, MD
SVP & Publr, Periodic Pubns: Thomas J Easley *Tel:* 312-464-5000 ext 5740
Promotes the science & art of medicine & betterment of public health. Association of physicians.
Publication(s): *JAMA: Dermatology* (monthly); *JAMA: Facial Plastic Surgery* (6 issues/yr); *JAMA: Internal Medicine* (monthly); *JAMA: Neurology* (monthly); *JAMA: Ophthalmology* (monthly); *JAMA: Otolaryngology* (monthly); *JAMA: Pediatrics* (monthly); *JAMA: Psychiatry* (monthly); *JAMA: Surgery* (monthly); *JAMA: The Journal of the American Medical Association* (weekly)
Branch Office(s)
119 Cherry Hill Rd, Parsippany, NJ 07054

American Medical Writers Association (AMWA)
30 W Gude Dr, Suite 525, Rockville, MD 20850-4357
Tel: 240-238-0940 *Fax:* 301-294-9006
E-mail: amwa@amwa.org
Web Site: www.amwa.org
Key Personnel
Exec Dir: Susan Krug *Tel:* 240-238-0940 ext 109 *E-mail:* skrug@amwa.org
Deputy Dir: Shari Rager *Tel:* 240-238-0940 ext 107 *E-mail:* srager@amwa.org
Founded: 1940
Professional organization for writers, editors & other communicators of medical information.
Number of Members: 5,300
2018 Meeting(s): Annual Conference, Renaissance DC Downtown Hotel, Washington, DC, Nov 1-3, 2018
2019 Meeting(s): Annual Conference, Sheraton San Diego Hotel & Marina, San Diego, CA, Nov 7-9, 2019
2020 Meeting(s): Annual Conference, Baltimore Marriott Waterfront Hotel, Baltimore, MD, Oct 12-14, 2020
Publication(s): *AMWA Journal* (quarterly, journal, free to membs, $75/yr nonmembs); *AMWA Membership Directory* (annual, directory); *Freelance Directory* (online, directory, free); *Jobs Online* (monthly, classified listing)

American Political Science Association
1527 New Hampshire Ave NW, Washington, DC 20036-1203
Tel: 202-483-2512 *Fax:* 202-483-2657
E-mail: apsa@apsanet.org
Web Site: www.apsanet.org
Key Personnel
Exec Dir: Steven Rathgeb Smith *E-mail:* smithsr@apsanet.org
Founded: 1903
Provide services to facilitate research, teaching & professional development in political science, including publications & services to assist college faculty, graduate students & researchers.
Number of Members: 15,000
2018 Meeting(s): Teaching & Learning Conference, Sheraton Inner Harbor Hotel, Baltimore, MD, Feb 2-4, 2018; Annual Meeting & Exhibition, Boston, MA, Aug 30-Sept 2, 2018
2019 Meeting(s): Annual Meeting & Exhibition, Washington, DC, Aug 29-Sept 1, 2019
2020 Meeting(s): Annual Meeting & Exhibition, San Francisco, CA, Sept 3-6, 2020
2021 Meeting(s): Annual Meeting & Exhibition, Seattle, WA, Sept 29-Oct 3, 2021

2022 Meeting(s): Annual Meeting & Exhibition, Montreal, QB, CN, Sept 14-18, 2022
Publication(s): *American Political Science Review* (quarterly); *Perspectives on Politics* (quarterly); *PS: Political Science & Politics* (quarterly)

American Printing History Association
PO Box 4519, Grand Central Sta, New York, NY 10163
Tel: 202-544-2422
E-mail: secretary@printinghistory.org
Web Site: printinghistory.org
Key Personnel
Pres: Nina Schneider
VP, Membership: Charles Cuykendall Carter
VP, Progs: Sara T Sauers
VP, Pubns: Katherine McCanless Ruffin
Treas: David Goodrich
Secy: Charles Cuykendall Carter
Local chapters in New York City, New England, Inland, Chesapeake, Southern & Northern California.
Number of Members: 700
New Election: Annually in Jan

American Psychological Association
750 First St NE, Washington, DC 20002-4242
Tel: 202-336-5500 *Toll Free Tel:* 800-374-2721
E-mail: order@apa.org
Web Site: www.apa.org
Key Personnel
Exec Publr: Jasper Simons
Publr, APA Books: Brenda Carter
Sr Dir, Prod Mgmt: Aaron Wood
Founded: 1892
Publish numerous periodicals & books in the field of psychology.
Number of Members: 130,000
Publication(s): *American Psychologist* (9 times/yr beginning in Jan); *APA Membership Register* (annual); *APA Monitor* (monthly); *Directory of the APA* (1 issue/4 yrs, directory)

American Public Human Services Association
1133 19 St NW, Suite 400, Washington, DC 20036
Tel: 202-682-0100 *Fax:* 202-289-6555
Web Site: www.aphsa.org
Key Personnel
Exec Dir: Tracy Wareing *Tel:* 202-682-0100 ext 231 *E-mail:* tracy.wareing@aphsa.org
Mgr, Membership & Mktg: Brittany Donald *Tel:* 202-682-0100 ext 276 *E-mail:* brittany.donald@aphsa.org
Founded: 1930
Membership organization of public human services professionals.
Number of Members: 5,000
New Election: Annually in Dec
Publication(s): *Policy & Practice* (6 issues/yr, directory, $65 single copy, $75 single copy intl, $400/yr, $475/yr intl); *This Week In Washington* (weekly when Congress is in session, newsletter, free, electronic)

American Society for Indexing Inc (ASI)
1628 E Southern Ave, Suite 9-223, Tempe, AZ 85282
Tel: 480-245-6750
E-mail: info@asindexing.org
Web Site: www.asindexing.org
Key Personnel
Exec Dir: Gwen Henson *E-mail:* gwen@asindexing.org
Founded: 1968
Educational programs for indexing field.
Number of Members: 450
New Election: Annually in May
Publication(s): *KeyWords* (monthly, magazine, free to membs, $40 nonmembs)

American Society of Composers, Authors & Publishers (ASCAP)
1900 Broadway, New York City, NY 10023
Tel: 212-621-6000 *Toll Free Tel:* 800-952-7227 *Fax:* 212-612-8453
E-mail: info@ascap.com
Web Site: www.ascap.com
Key Personnel
Chmn of the Bd & Pres: Paul Williams *E-mail:* pwilliams@ascap.com
CEO: John Lo Frumento
Founded: 1914
License nondramatic right of public performance of members' copyrighted musical compositions & distribute royalties to members on basis of performances. Members are composers, songwriters, lyricists & music publishers.
Number of Members: 500,000
Branch Office(s)
7920 W Sunset Blvd, 3rd fl, Los Angeles, CA 90046 *Tel:* 323-883-1000 *Fax:* 323-883-1049
420 Lincoln Rd, Suite 385, Miami Beach, FL 33139 *Tel:* 305-673-3446 *Fax:* 305-673-2446
950 Joseph E Lowery Blvd NW, Suite 23, Atlanta, GA 30318 *Tel:* 404-685-8699 *Fax:* 404-685-8701
Two Music Sq W, Nashville, TN 37203 *Tel:* 615-742-5000 *Fax:* 615-742-5020
Ave Martinez Nadal, c/ Hill Side 623, San Juan 00920, Puerto Rico *Tel:* 787-707-0782 *Fax:* 787-707-0783
8 Cork St, London W1S 3LJ, United Kingdom *Tel:* (020) 7439 0909 *Fax:* (020) 7434 0073

American Society of Journalists and Authors (ASJA)
355 Lexington Ave, 15th fl, New York, NY 10017-6603
Tel: 212-997-0947
Web Site: asja.org
Key Personnel
Exec Dir: Alexandra Owens *E-mail:* director@asja.org
Founded: 1948
Service organization providing exchange of ideas & market information. Regular meetings with speakers from the industry, annual writers conference; medical plans available. Professional referral service, annual membership directory; first amendment advocacy group.
Number of Members: 1,400
Publication(s): *ASJA Monthly* (11 times/yr online, printed quarterly, newsletter, membs only)

American Society of Magazine Editors (ASME)
757 Third Ave, 11th fl, New York, NY 10017
Tel: 212-872-3700 *Fax:* 212-906-0128
E-mail: asme@magazine.org
Web Site: www.magazine.org/asme
Key Personnel
Chief Exec: Sid Holt
Dir: Nina Fortuna *Tel:* 212-872-3737
Founded: 1963
Professional society for senior magazine editors. Sponsor the National Magazine Awards in association with the Columbia Journalism School; hold monthly luncheons for members & conduct periodic seminars.
Number of Members: 700
New Election: Annually in April

American Society of Media Photographers (ASMP)
PO Box 31207, Bethesda, MD 20804
Toll Free Tel: 877-771-2767 *Fax:* 231-946-6180
E-mail: info@asmp.org
Web Site: asmp.org
Key Personnel
Exec Dir: Thomas R Kennedy *E-mail:* kennedy@asmp.org
Founded: 1944
Maintain & promote high professional standards & ethics in photography; cultivate mutual understanding among professional photographers; protect & promote interests of photographers whose work is for publication.
Number of Members: 5,785
New Election: Jan 2018
Publication(s): *The ASMP Guide to New Markets in Photography* ($24.95); *ASMP Professional Business Practices in Photography, 7th Ed* ($23.21); *Digital Photography Best Practices & Workflow & Handbook* ($17.92 membs)

American Society of News Editors (ASNE)
209 Reynolds Journalism Institute, Missouri School of Journalism, Columbia, MO 65211
Tel: 573-882-2430 *Fax:* 573-884-3824
Web Site: asne.org
Key Personnel
Exec Dir: Teri Hayt *Tel:* 573-882-9854 *E-mail:* thayt@asne.org
Sr Advisor: Arnie Robbins *E-mail:* arobbins@asne.org
Dir, Youth Journalism Initiative: Le Anne Wiseman *E-mail:* lwiseman@asne.org
Sr Info Specialist: Megan Morrison *E-mail:* mschumacher@asne.org
Communs Coord: Jiyoung Won *E-mail:* jwon@asne.org
Founded: 1922
Nonprofit professional organization focused on leadership development & journalism-related issues.

American Sociological Association (ASA)
1430 "K" St NW, Suite 600, Washington, DC 20005-4701
Tel: 202-383-9005 *Fax:* 202-638-0882
E-mail: customer@asanet.org
Web Site: www.asanet.org
Key Personnel
Exec Offr: Sally Hillsman *Tel:* 202-383-9005 ext 316 *E-mail:* executive.office@asanet.org
Pubns Dir: Karen Gray Edwards *Tel:* 202-383-9005 ext 319 *E-mail:* publications@asanet.org
Founded: 1905
Nonprofit membership association dedicated to advancing sociology as a scientific discipline & profession serving the public good. Encompass sociologists who are faculty members at colleges & universities, researchers, practitioners & students.
Number of Members: 13,000
New Election: Annually in Aug
2018 Meeting(s): Annual Meeting, Pennsylvania Convention Center & Philadelphia Marriott, Philadelphia, PA, Aug 11-14, 2018
2019 Meeting(s): Annual Meeting, Hilton New York Midtown & Sheraton New York Times Square Hotel, New York, NY, Aug 10-13, 2019
2020 Meeting(s): Annual Meeting, Hilton San Francisco Union Square, San Francisco, CA, Aug 15-18, 2020
2021 Meeting(s): Annual Meeting, Hyatt Regency Chicago, Chicago, IL, Aug 14-17, 2021
2022 Meeting(s): Annual Meeting, Los Angeles Convention Center, Los Angeles, CA, Aug 13-16, 2022
2023 Meeting(s): Annual Meeting, Philadelphia Convention Center, Marriot & Loews, Philadelphia, PA, Aug 18-21, 2023
2024 Meeting(s): Annual Meeting, Palais des Congres de Montreal, Montreal, QB, CN, Aug 10-13, 2024
Publication(s): *American Sociological Review* (6 issues/yr, $45 membs, $30 student membs, $400 instns (print/online), $360 instns (online only)); *Contemporary Sociology* (6 issues/yr, $45 membs, $30 student membs, $382 instns (print/online), $344 instns (online only)); *Contexts* (quarterly, magazine, $45 membs, $30 student membs, $225 instns (print/online), $247 instns (online only)); *Footnotes* (monthly exc

July/Aug, Sept/Oct, May/June, newsletter, free online); *Journal of Health & Social Behavior* (quarterly, $45 membs, $30 student membs, $340 instns (print/online), $305 instns (online only)); *Social Psychology Quarterly* (quarterly, $45 membs, $30 student membs, $340 instns (print/online), $305 instns (online only)); *Sociological Methodology* (annual, $45 membs, $30 student membs, $365 instns (print/online), $330 instns (online only)); *Sociological Theory* (quarterly, $45 membs, $30 student membs, $370 instns (print/online), $334 instns (online only)); *Sociology of Education* (quarterly, $45 membs, $30 student membs, $340 instns (print/online), $305 instns (online only)); *Teaching Sociology* (quarterly, $45 membs, $30 student membs, $340 instns (print/online), $305 instns (online only))

American Speech-Language-Hearing Association (ASHA)
2200 Research Blvd, Rockville, MD 20850-3289
Tel: 301-296-5700 *Toll Free Tel:* 800-638-8255 (nonmembs); 800-498-2071 (membs) *Fax:* 301-296-5777; 301-296-8580
E-mail: actioncenter@asha.org
Web Site: www.asha.org
Founded: 1925
Membership organization for speech-language pathologists & audiologists. Provide consumers with information & referral on speech, language & hearing. Publish information brochures & packets.
Number of Members: 186,000
New Election: Annually in Sept
Publication(s): *American Journal of Audiology* (quarterly, journal, $15/single article for 24 hours, $30 for entire site for 24 hours, $110/yr electronic nonmembs, $270/yr electronic instns, $160/yr online archive nonmembs & instns); *American Journal of Speech-Language Pathology* (quarterly, journal, $15/single article for 24 hours, $30 for entire site for 24 hours, $110/yr electronic nonmembs, $270/yr electronic instns, $197/yr online archives nonmembs & instns); *The ASHA Leader* (monthly, newspaper, $129/yr nonmembs, $172/yr foreign nonmembs, $194/instns, $243 foreign instns); *Journal of Speech, Language & Hearing Research* (monthly, journal, $15/single article for 24 hours, $30 for entire site for 24 hours, $230/yr electronic nonmembs, $648/yr electronic instns, $461/yr online archives nonmembs & instns); *Language, Speech & Hearing Services In Schools* (quarterly, journal, $15/single article for 24 hours, $30 for entire site for 24 hours, $110/yr electronic nonmembs, $270/yr electronic instns, $197/yr online archives nonmembs & instns)
Branch Office(s)
444 N Capitol St NW, Suite 715, Washington, DC 20001 *Tel:* 202-624-5884

American Translators Association (ATA)
225 Reinekers Lane, Suite 590, Alexandria, VA 22314
Tel: 703-683-6100 *Fax:* 703-683-6122
E-mail: ata@atanet.org
Web Site: www.atanet.org
Key Personnel
Exec Dir: Walter W Barak, Jr
Founded: 1959
Membership consists of those professionally engaged in translating, interpreting or closely allied work, as well as those who are interested in these fields. Membership: $190/yr indivs, $350/yr corps, $235/yr instl, $80/yr student.
Number of Members: 11,000
2018 Meeting(s): Annual Conference, New Orleans, LA, Oct 24-27, 2018
2019 Meeting(s): Annual Conference, Palm Springs, CA, Oct 23-26, 2019
2020 Meeting(s): Annual Conference, Boston, MA, Oct 21-24, 2020
2021 Meeting(s): Annual Conference, Minneapolis, MN, Oct 27-30, 2021
Publication(s): *The ATA Chronicle* (11 issues/yr, $65, $90 CN & Mexico, $110 all other countries)
Membership(s): Federation of International Translators

Antiquarian Booksellers' Association of America (ABAA)
20 W 44 St, Suite 507, New York, NY 10036
Tel: 212-944-8291 *Fax:* 212-944-8293
E-mail: hq@abaa.org
Web Site: www.abaa.org
Key Personnel
Exec Dir: Susan Benne *E-mail:* sbenne@abaa.org
Founded: 1949
Chapters: Northern California, Southern California, Midwest, Middle Atlantic, New England, Southeast, Southwest & Pacific Northwest. Membership open to antiquarian booksellers only. ABAA sponsors 3 or 4 international book fairs per year in Los Angeles & San Francisco (alternately) in Midwinter; in NY in the Spring; in Boston in late Autumn.
Number of Members: 450
2018 Meeting(s): California International Antiquarian Book Fair, Pasadena Convention Center, 300 E Green St, Pasadena, CA, Feb 9-11, 2018; New York Antiquarian Book Fair, Park Avenue Armory, 643 Park Ave at 67 St, New York, NY, March 8-11, 2018
2019 Meeting(s): California International Antiquarian Book Fair, Oakland Marriott City Center, 1001 Broadway, Oakland, CA,, Feb 8-10, 2019
Publication(s): *Newsletter* (quarterly, free, electronic)

Antiquarian Booksellers' Association of Canada/Association de la Librairie Ancienne du Canada, see ABAC/ALAC

ASHA, see American Speech-Language-Hearing Association (ASHA)

Asian American Writers' Workshop
110-112 W 27 St, Suite 600, New York, NY 10001
Tel: 212-494-0061
E-mail: desk@aaww.org
Web Site: aaww.org
Key Personnel
Exec Dir: Ken Chen
Not-for-profit arts organization devoted to the creating, publishing, developing & disseminating of creative writing by Asian Americans.

Aspen Words
110 E Hallam St, Suite 116, Aspen, CO 81611
Tel: 970-925-3122 *Fax:* 970-920-5700
E-mail: aspenwords@aspeninstitute.org
Web Site: www.aspenwords.org
Key Personnel
Exec Dir: Adrienne Brodeur *Tel:* 646-461-3554 *E-mail:* adrienne.brodeur@aspeninstitute.org
Mng Dir: Jamie Kravitz *Tel:* 970-925-3122 ext 2 *E-mail:* jamie.kravitz@aspeninstitute.org
Sr Prog Assoc, Mktg & Communs: Caroline Tory *Tel:* 970-925-3122 ext 3 *E-mail:* caroline.tory@aspeninstitute.org
Founded: 1976
Program of the Aspen Institute. Encourages writers, inspires readers & connects people through the exchange of words, stories & ideas.
Meeting(s): Aspen Summer Words Writing Conference & Literary Festival, Aspen, CO, June

Associated Business Writers of America Inc
Division of National Writers Association
10940 S Parker Rd, Suite 508, Parker, CO 80134
Tel: 303-841-0246
E-mail: natlwritersassn@hotmail.com
Web Site: www.nationalwriters.com
Key Personnel
Exec Dir: Sandy Whelchel *E-mail:* authorsandy@hotmail.com
To help business writers & those seeking their services.
Number of Members: 80

Associated Press Broadcast
1100 13 St NW, Suite 700, Washington, DC 20005
Tel: 202-641-9000 *Toll Free Tel:* 800-821-4747 *Fax:* 202-370-2710
E-mail: info@ap.org
Web Site: www.ap.org
Number of Members: 5,800
Publication(s): *AP Stylebook* (annual, $20.95)

Association canadienne des reviseurs, see Editors' Association of Canada (Association canadienne des reviseurs)

Association des Editeurs de Langue Anglaise du Quebec, see The Association of English-Language Publishers of Quebec-AELAQ (Association des Editeurs de Langue Anglaise du Quebec)

Association des Libraires du Quebec (ALQ)
407 St-Laurent, bureau 801, Montreal, QC H2Y 2Y5, Canada
Tel: 514-526-3349 *Fax:* 514-526-3340
E-mail: info@alq.qc.ca
Web Site: www.alq.qc.ca
Key Personnel
CEO: Katherine Fafard *E-mail:* kfafard@alq.qc.ca
Founded: 1969
Quebec association of booksellers.
Number of Members: 95

Association for Information & Image Management International (AIIM)
1100 Wayne Ave, Suite 1100, Silver Spring, MD 20910
Tel: 301-587-8202 *Toll Free Tel:* 800-477-2446 *Fax:* 301-587-2711
E-mail: aiim@aiim.org; info@aiim.org
Web Site: www.aiim.org
Key Personnel
Ed & Community Mgr: Bryant Duhon *Tel:* 301-916-7182 *E-mail:* bduhon@aiim.org
Global association bringing together the users of document technologies with the providers of that technology.
Number of Members: 9,197
Branch Office(s)
8, Canalside, Lowesmoor Wharf, Worcester WR1 2RR, United Kingdom *Tel:* (01905) 727600 *Fax:* (01905) 727609

Association for Information Science & Technology (ASIS&T)
8555 16 St, Suite 850, Silver Spring, MD 20910
Tel: 301-495-0900 *Fax:* 301-495-0810
E-mail: asist@asist.org
Web Site: www.asist.org
Key Personnel
Exec Dir: Lydia Middleton
Dir of Fin & Admin, Webmaster: Jan Hatzakos *E-mail:* jhatzakos@asist.org
Dir of Meetings & Membership: Vanessa Foss *E-mail:* vfoss@asist.org
Membership Servs: Stephan Addo *E-mail:* saddo@asist.org
Acctg Asst & Meeting Registrar: Carline Haynes *E-mail:* chaynes@asist.org

Founded: 1937
To foster & lead the advancement of information science & technology.
Number of Members: 4,000
2018 Meeting(s): The IA Summit, Chicago, IL, March 21-25, 2018; ASIS&T Annual Meeting, Vancouver, CN, Nov 9-15, 2018
Publication(s): *Bulletin of the Association for Information Science & Technology* (6 issues/yr); *Journal of the Association for Information Science & Technology (JASIST)*

Association Media & Publishing (AM&P)
529 14 St, Suite 750, Washington, DC 20045
Tel: 202-591-2457
E-mail: info@associationmediaandpublishing.org
Web Site: associationmediaandpublishing.org
Key Personnel
Exec Dir: Meredith Taylor
Publr: Carla Kalogeridis *Tel:* 313-884-0988 *E-mail:* carlak@arion-media.com
Proj Mgr: Nate Bell *E-mail:* nbell@kellencompany.com
Founded: 1963 (as Society of National Association Publications)
A nonprofit professional society that serves the needs of association & society publications & their staff to represent, promote & advance the common interest of periodicals of voluntary associations & societies.
Number of Members: 1,400
Publication(s): *Signature* (6 issues/yr, magazine)

Association Nationale des Editeurs de Livres
2514, blvd Rosemont, Montreal, QC H1Y 1K4, Canada
Tel: 514-273-8130 *Toll Free Tel:* 866-900-ANEL (900-2635)
E-mail: info@anel.qc.ca
Web Site: www.anel.qc.ca
Key Personnel
Dir Gen: Richard Prieur *E-mail:* prieur@anel.qc.ca
Deputy Dir Gen: Karine Vachone *E-mail:* vachon@anel.qc.ca
Mgr, Memb Servs: Helene Letourneau *E-mail:* letourneau@anel.qc.ca
Founded: 1992
Professional association of French publishers in Canada.
Number of Members: 100

Association of American Editorial Cartoonists
PO Box 460673, Fort Lauderdale, FL 33346
Tel: 954-356-4945
Web Site: www.editorialcartoonists.com
Key Personnel
Pres: Adam Zyglis
Gen Mgr: Stephanie McMillan *E-mail:* steph@minimumsecurity.net
Founded: 1957
Professional association.
Number of Members: 260
Publication(s): *Notebook* (quarterly, free to membs, $40/yr nonmembs)

Association of American Publishers (AAP)
455 Massachusetts Ave NW, Suite 700, Washington, DC 20001-2777
Tel: 212-255-0200 *Fax:* 212-255-7007
E-mail: info@publishers.org
Web Site: publishers.org
Key Personnel
Pres & CEO: Maria Pallante
VP: Tina Jordan *Tel:* 212-255-0275 *E-mail:* tjordan@publishers.org
VP & Exec Dir, Prof & Scholarly Publg: John Tagler *Tel:* 212-255-1407 *E-mail:* jtagler@publishers.org
Gen Coun & VP, Govt Aff: Allan R Adler *Tel:* 202-220-4544 *E-mail:* adler@publishers.org
Exec Dir, PreK-12 Learning Group: Jay Diskey *Tel:* 202-220-4549 *E-mail:* jdiskey@publishers.org
Founded: 1970
Monitor & promote the USA publishing industry. Members: those actively engaged in the creation, publication & production of books, journals, electronic media, testing materials & a range of educational materials. Sponsor of BookExpo.
Number of Members: 450
Meeting(s): Annual Meeting
2018 Meeting(s): Annual Conference, Ritz-Carlton, Washington, DC, Feb 7-9, 2018; BookExpo, Jacob K Javits Convention Center, 655 W 43 St, New York, NY, May 30-June 1, 2018
Publication(s): *AAP Export Sales Report* (annual); *AAP StatShot* (monthly)
Branch Office(s)
325 Chestnut St, Suite 1110, Philadelphia, PA 19106-7761 *Tel:* 267-351-4310 *Fax:* 267-351-4317
Membership(s): BISG

Association of American University Presses (AAUP)
1412 Broadway, Suite 2135, New York, NY 10018
Tel: 212-989-1010 *Fax:* 212-989-0275
E-mail: info@aaupnet.org
Web Site: www.aaupnet.org
Key Personnel
Exec Dir: Peter Berkery *Tel:* 917-288-5594 *E-mail:* pberkery@aaupnet.org
Asst Dir & Cont: Tim Muench *Tel:* 917-244-1463 *E-mail:* tmuench@aaupnet.org
Dir, Mktg & Communs: Brenna McLaughlin *Tel:* 917-244-2051 *E-mail:* bmclaughlin@aaupnet.org
Membership Mgr: Susan Patton *Tel:* 917-244-1915 *E-mail:* spatton@aaupnet.org
Off Mgr & Prog Admin: Kim Miller *Tel:* 917-244-1264 *E-mail:* kmiller@aaupnet.org
Prog Asst: Bailey Bretz *Tel:* 917-244-2665 *E-mail:* bbretz@aaupnet.org
Communs Coord: John Michael Eadicicco *Tel:* 917-244-3859 *E-mail:* jeadicicco@aaupnet.org
Membership & affiliation consists of university presses in North America & abroad that function as the publishing arms of their respective universities, issuing some 11,000 titles & more than 600 journals annually. AAUP helps these presses do their work more economically, creatively & effectively through its own activities in professional development; fund raising; statistical research & analysis; promoting the value of university presses; community & institutional relations & through its marketing programs.
Number of Members: 141
2018 Meeting(s): Annual Meeting, Fairmont San Francisco, San Francisco, CA, June 17-19, 2018
2019 Meeting(s): Annual Meeting, Detroit Marriott at the Renaissance Center, Detroit, MI, June 11-13, 2019
Publication(s): *AAUP Book, Jacket & Journal Show* (catalog, $20 current yr, $15 past yrs); *Annual Directory* ($30); *The Exchange* (quarterly, newsletter, free); *University Press Books for Public & Secondary School Libraries* (annual, free)
Branch Office(s)
1775 Massachusetts Ave NW, Washington, DC 20036
Membership(s): BISG

Association of Authors' Representatives Inc
302A W 12 St, No 122, New York, NY 10014
Tel: 212-840-5770
E-mail: administrator@aaronline.org
Web Site: www.aaronline.org
Founded: 1991
Voluntary & elective professional association of literary & play agents whose individual members subscribe to certain ethical practices. Members meet to discuss industry developments & problems of mutual interest. Sponsor of BookExpo.
Number of Members: 386
New Election: Annually in June
2018 Meeting(s): BookExpo, Jacob K Javits Convention Center, 655 W 43 St, New York, NY, May 30-June 1, 2018

Association of Book Publishers of British Columbia
Affiliate of Association of Canadian Publishers
600-402 W Pender St, Vancouver, BC V6B 1T6, Canada
Tel: 604-684-0228 *Fax:* 604-684-5788
E-mail: admin@books.bc.ca
Web Site: www.books.bc.ca
Key Personnel
Exec Dir: Heidi Waechtler
Founded: 1974
Trade association representing the interests of Canadian-owned & operated book publishing companies based in BC.
Number of Members: 31
New Election: Annually in April

Association of Canadian Publishers (ACP)
174 Spadina Ave, Suite 306, Toronto, ON M5T 2C2, Canada
Tel: 416-487-6116 *Fax:* 416-487-8815
E-mail: admin@canbook.org
Web Site: publishers.ca
Key Personnel
Exec Dir: Kate Edwards *Tel:* 416-487-6116 ext 234 *E-mail:* kate_edwards@canbook.org
Founded: 1976
Association of English language Canadian owned book publishing companies in Canada. Sponsor professional development seminars for book publishers. Publish membership directories, studies & reports.
Number of Members: 135
Publication(s): *Membership Directory* (annual)

Association of Canadian University Presses
10 Saint Mary St, Suite 700, Toronto, ON M4Y 2W8, Canada
Tel: 416-978-2239 ext 237 *Fax:* 416-978-4738
Web Site: www.acup.ca
Key Personnel
Admin: Charley La Rose *E-mail:* clarose@utpress.utoronto.ca
Founded: 1972
Number of Members: 17
New Election: Annually in Autumn

Association of Catholic Publishers Inc
4725 Dorsey Hall Dr, Suite A, PMB 709, Elliott City, MD 21042
Tel: 410-988-2926 *Fax:* 410-571-4946
Web Site: www.catholicsread.org; www.catholicpublishers.org; www.midatlanticcongress.org
Key Personnel
Pres: Mary Beth Oria
VP: Peter Dwyer
Secy: Donna Crilly
Treas: Tom Hawley
Exec Dir: Therese Brown
Facilitate the sharing of professional information, networking, cooperation & friendship among those involved in Catholic book publishing in the US & abroad. Offers trade co-op catalog, mailing list, Catholic bestsellers, advertising insert program & professional skills workshops.
Number of Members: 100
New Election: Annually in Dec

2018 Meeting(s): Mid-Atlantic Congress, Baltimore Hilton Hotel, Baltimore, MD, Feb 15-17, 2018
Publication(s): *Promotional Brochure* (annually)

Association of College & University Printers (ACUP)
PO Box 285, Carrabelle, FL 32322
Tel: 850-570-5241
Web Site: www.acup-edu.org
Key Personnel
Admin Dir: Jennifer Bowers *E-mail:* jennifer.bowers@acup-edu.org
Number of Members: 300
2018 Meeting(s): Annual Conference, Harrah's Lake Tahoe, 15 Hwy 50, Stateline, NV, April 29-May 3, 2018

The Association of English-Language Publishers of Quebec-AELAQ (Association des Editeurs de Langue Anglaise du Quebec)
Atwater Library, 1200 Atwater Ave, Suite 3, Westmount, QC H3Z 1X4, Canada
Tel: 514-932-5633
E-mail: admin@aelaq.org
Web Site: aelaq.org
Key Personnel
Pres: Keith Henderson
Exec Dir: Julia Kater
Advance the publication, distribution & promotion of English language books from Quebec.
Number of Members: 18
Publication(s): *Montreal Review of Books* (3 times/yr, report, free)

Association of Free Community Papers (AFCP)
135 Old Cove Rd, Suite 210, Liverpool, NY 13090
Toll Free Tel: 877-203-2327 *Fax:* 781-459-7770
E-mail: afcp@afcp.org
Web Site: www.afcp.org
Key Personnel
Exec Dir: Loren Colburn *E-mail:* loren@afcp.org
Founded: 1950
Organization of publishers serving the free-circulation community publication industry.
Number of Members: 250
2018 Meeting(s): Annual Conference & Trade Show, Hyatt Regency Baltimore Inner Harbor, 300 Light St, Baltimore, MD, May 3-5, 2018
Publication(s): *Freepaper Ink* (monthly, newsletter, free)

Association of Jewish Libraries (AJL) Inc
Affiliate of American Library Association (ALA)
PO Box 1118, Teaneck, NJ 07666
Tel: 201-371-3255
E-mail: info@jewishlibraries.org
Web Site: jewishlibraries.org
Key Personnel
Pres: Amalia Warshenbrot
Member libraries in two divisions; RAS (Research Libraries, Archives & Special Collections) & SCC (Schools, Synagogues & Centers). Promote librarianship, services & standards in the field of Judaica. Affiliate of the American Library Association & the American Theological Library Association.
Number of Members: 600
2018 Meeting(s): Annual Conference, Boston, MA, June 18-20, 2018
Publication(s): *AJL Conference Proceedings* (annual); *AJL News* (quarterly); *AJL Reviews* (quarterly); *Judaica Librarianship* (semiannual, journal)

Association of Manitoba Book Publishers
100 Arthur St, Suite 404, Winnipeg, MB R3B 1H3, Canada
Tel: 204-947-3335 *Fax:* 204-956-4689
E-mail: ambp@mts.net
Web Site: ambp.ca
Key Personnel
Exec Dir: Michelle Peters
Projs Coord: Karen San Filippo
Founded: 1979
Publishing industry association.
Number of Members: 13
Publication(s): *Prairie Books Now* (3 issues/yr, magazine)
Membership(s): Association of Canadian Publishers

Association of Marketing Service Providers (AMSP), see Epicomm

The Association of Medical Illustrators (AMI)
201 E Main St, Suite 1405, Lexington, KY 40507
Toll Free Tel: 866-393-4264 *Fax:* 859-514-9166
E-mail: hq@ami.org
Web Site: www.ami.org
Key Personnel
Exec Dir, Ex-Officio: Melanie Bowzer *E-mail:* mbowzer@amrms.com
Founded: 1945
Promote the use of high-quality artwork in medical publications to advance medical education.
Number of Members: 850

Association of Publishers for Special Sales (APSS)
PO Box 715, Avon, CT 06001-0715
Tel: 860-675-1344
Web Site: www.spannet.org
Key Personnel
Exec Dir: Brian Jud *E-mail:* brianjud@bookapss.org
Busn Mgr: Kaye Krassner
A trade association for independent presses, self-publishers & pro-active authors who want to sell more books.
Publication(s): *The Sales Informer* (monthly)

Association of Writers & Writing Programs (AWP)
George Mason University, 4400 University Dr, MSN 1E3, Fairfax, VA 22030
Tel: 703-993-4301 *Fax:* 703-993-4302
E-mail: awp@awpwriter.org
Web Site: www.awpwriter.org
Key Personnel
Exec Dir: David W Fenza
Dir, Conferences: Christian Teresi
Dir, Devt: Pamela Mills
Dir, Membership Servs: Diane Zinna
Dir, Pubns: Supriya Bhatnagar
Assoc Ed: Jason Gray
Conference Events Coord: Abigail Campbell
Founded: 1967
Magazine, publications, directory, competitions for awards (including publication), advocacy for literature & education, annual meeting, job placement.
Number of Members: 34,000
2018 Meeting(s): Annual Conference & Bookfair, Tampa Convention Center & Marriott Tampa Waterside, Tampa, FL, March 7-10, 2018
2019 Meeting(s): Annual Conference & Bookfair, Oregon Convention Center, Portland, OR, March 27-30, 2019
2020 Meeting(s): Annual Conference & Bookfair, Henry B Gonzalez Convention Center, San Antonio, TX, March 4-7, 2020
2021 Meeting(s): Annual Conference & Bookfair, Kansas City Convention Center, Kansas City, MO, March 3-6, 2021
2022 Meeting(s): Annual Conference & Bookfair, Pennsylvania Convention Center, Philadelphia, PA,, March 23-26, 2022
Publication(s): *The Writer's Chronicle* (6 issues/yr, free to membs)

Association pour l'Avancement des Sciences et des Techniques de la Documentation
2065 rue Parthenais, Bureau 387, Montreal, QC H2K 3T1, Canada
Tel: 514-281-5012 *Fax:* 514-281-8219
E-mail: info@asted.org
Web Site: www.asted.org
Key Personnel
Exec Dir: Lionel Villalonga *E-mail:* lvillalonga@asted.org
Objective is the promotion of standards of excellence in the services & personnel of libraries, documentation & information centers.
Number of Members: 550
New Election: Annually during congress
Publication(s): *Documentation et Bibliotheques* (quarterly, $65/yr CN, $85/yr elsewhere)

ASTED, see Association pour l'Avancement des Sciences et des Techniques de la Documentation

Authors Alliance
2705 Webster St, No 5805, Berkeley, CA 94705
E-mail: info@authorsalliance.org
Web Site: www.authorsalliance.org
Key Personnel
Exec Dir: Brianna Schofield *E-mail:* brianna@authorsalliance.org
Communs & Opers Mgr: Erika Wilson *E-mail:* erika@authorsalliance.org
Further public interest in facilitating widespread access to works of authorship by assisting & representing authors who want to disseminate knowledge & products of the imagination broadly.

The Authors Guild
31 E 32 St, 7th fl, New York, NY 10016
Tel: 212-563-5904 *Fax:* 212-564-5363
E-mail: staff@authorsguild.org
Web Site: www.authorsguild.org
Key Personnel
Pres: Roxana Robinson
VP: Judy Blume; Richard Russo; James Shapiro
VP, Programming & Outreach: Paul Morris
Exec Dir: Mary Rasenberger
Founded: 1912
National membership organization for nonfiction & fiction book authors & freelance journalists. Deals with the business & professional interests of authors in such fields as book contracts, copyright, subsidiary rights, free expression, taxes & others. Offer free contract reviews, web site development & hosting & health insurance.
Number of Members: 9,000
Publication(s): *The Bulletin* (quarterly, free to membs)

The Authors League Fund
31 E 32 St, 7th fl, New York, NY 10016
Tel: 212-268-1208 *Fax:* 212-564-5363
E-mail: staff@authorsleaguefund.org
Web Site: www.authorsleaguefund.org
Key Personnel
Pres: Pat Cummings
VP: Sidney Offit
Exec Dir: Isabel Howe
Secy: Peter Straub
Treas: James B Stewart
Founded: 1917
Provides emergency assistance to professional writers facing financial hardship.
Number of Members: 900

The Authors League of America Inc, see The Authors Guild

The Authors Registry Inc
31 E 32 St, 7th fl, New York, NY 10016
Tel: 212-563-6920 *Fax:* 212-564-5363

E-mail: staff@authorsregistry.org
Web Site: www.authorsregistry.org
Key Personnel
Opers Dir: Terry King *E-mail:* tking@authorsregistry.org
A nonprofit corporation that provides a royalty collection & distribution service.
Number of Members: 40,000

The Baker Street Irregulars (BSI)
7938 Mill Stream Circle, Indianapolis, IN 46278
Tel: 317-293-2212; 317-956-6666 (cell)
Web Site: bakerstreetjournal.com
Key Personnel
Wiggins, Chmn: Michael F Whelan
Literary society with a small press operation including a quarterly journal with a Christmas annual & 3-4 published books annually.
Number of Members: 300
Publication(s): *The Baker Street Journal* (quarterly & Christmas annual, $41.95/yr, $55/yr foreign)

Before Columbus Foundation
The Raymond House, 655 13 St, Suite 302, Oakland, CA 94612
SAN: 159-2955
Tel: 916-425-7916
E-mail: info@beforecolumbusfoundation.com
Web Site: www.beforecolumbusfoundation.com
Key Personnel
Founder: Ishmael Reed
Founded: 1976
Provide information, research, consultation & promotional services for contemporary American multicultural writers & publishers. A nonprofit service organization that also sponsors classes, workshops, readings, public events & the annual American Book Awards.

Bibliographical Society of America
PO Box 1537, Lenox Hill Sta, New York, NY 10021-0043
Tel: 212-452-2710 *Fax:* 212-452-2710
E-mail: bsa@bibsocamer.org
Web Site: www.bibsocamer.org
Key Personnel
Pres: Martin Antonetti
Treas: G Scott Clemons
VP: John Chrichton
Exec Dir: Michele E Randall
Secy: Barbara Heritage
Sponsor short-term fellowships for bibliographic projects. Membership open to anyone interested in bibliographic projects & process.
Number of Members: 1,100
New Election: Annually in Jan
Meeting(s): Annual Meeting, New York, NY, Jan (Friday following the 4th Thursday)
Publication(s): *The Papers of the Bibliographical Society of America* (quarterly, free for membs)

Bibliographical Society of the University of Virginia
c/o Alderman Library, University of Virginia, McCormick Rd, Charlottesville, VA 22904
Mailing Address: PO Box 400152, Charlottesville, VA 22904-4152
Tel: 434-924-7013 *Fax:* 434-924-1431
E-mail: bibsoc@virginia.edu
Web Site: bsuva.org
Key Personnel
Pres: G Thomas Tanselle
Exec Secy-Treas: Anne G Ribble *E-mail:* ar3g@virginia.edu
Founded: 1947
Scholarly society promoting the study of books as physical objects, the history of the book & of printing & publishing.
Number of Members: 400
Publication(s): *Studies in Bibliography* (annual, $55)

Binding Industries Association (BIA)
Affiliate of Printing Industries of America
301 Brush Creek Rd, Warrendale, PA 15086-7529
Tel: 412-741-6860 *Toll Free Tel:* 800-910-4283 *Fax:* 412-741-2311
Web Site: www.printing.org/bia
Key Personnel
Dir: Michael Packard *Tel:* 412-741-6860 *E-mail:* mpackard@printing.org
Founded: 1955
Trade finishers & loose-leaf manufacturers united to conduct seminars, hold conventions, formulate & maintain industry standards. Bestow annual product of excellence awards.
Number of Members: 100
Publication(s): *The Binding Edge* (quarterly, magazine); *Bound for Excellence* (monthly, newsletter, membs only); *Membership Directory* (in print biennially & online, book)

BISG, see Book Industry Study Group Inc (BISG)

BlackPressUSA, see National Newspaper Publishers Association (NNPA)

BMI®
7 World Trade Ctr, 250 Greenwich St, New York, NY 10007-0030
Tel: 212-586-2000; 212-220-3000 *Toll Free Tel:* 888-689-5264 (sales); 800-925-8451 (cust rel) *Fax:* 212-246-2163
E-mail: foundation@bmi.com
Web Site: www.bmi.com
Key Personnel
CEO: Michael O'Neill
Pres: Del R Bryant
Sr Dir, Corp Mktg: Darlene Rosado
Founded: 1939
Secure & license the performing rights of music on behalf of its creators.
Number of Members: 600,000
Publication(s): *BMI MusicWorld Online* (monthly)
Branch Office(s)
8730 Sunset Blvd, 3rd fl W, West Hollywood, CA 90069-2211 *Tel:* 310-659-9109 *E-mail:* losangeles@bmi.com
1691 Michigan Ave, Suite 350, Miami Beach, FL 33139 *Tel:* 305-673-5148 *E-mail:* miami@bmi.com
3340 Peachtree Rd NE, Suite 570, Atlanta, GA 30326 *Tel:* 404-261-5151 *E-mail:* atlanta@bmi.com
10 Music Sq E, Nashville, TN 37203-4399 *Tel:* 615-401-2000 *E-mail:* nashville@bmi.com
San Jose Bldg, Suite 1008, 1250 Ave Ponce de Leon, Santurce 00907, Puerto Rico *Tel:* 787-754-6490
84 Harley House, Marylebone Rd, London NW1 5HN, United Kingdom *Tel:* (020) 7846 2036 *E-mail:* london@bmi.com

Book & Periodical Council (BPC)
192 Spadina Ave, Suite 107, Toronto, ON M5T 2C2, Canada
Tel: 416-975-9366 *Fax:* 416-975-1839
E-mail: info@thebpc.ca
Web Site: www.thebpc.ca
Key Personnel
Exec Dir: Anne McClelland
Founded: 1975
Umbrella organization for Canadian associations that are or whose members are primarily involved with the writing, editing, translating, publishing, producing, distributing, lending, marketing, reading & selling of written words.
Number of Members: 32
Publication(s): *Dividends: The Value of Public Libraries in Canada* (free); *Freedom to Read Kit* (annual); *When the Censor Comes* (free online)

Book Industry Guild of New York
PO Box 2001, New York, NY 10113-2001
E-mail: admin@bookindustryguildofny.org
Web Site: www.bookindustryguildofny.org
Key Personnel
Pres: Michael Weinstein
VP: Steve Bedney
Fin Secy & Book Show Comm Co-Chair: Emily Larsen *Tel:* 413-210-1275 *E-mail:* emily.larsen@gmail.com
Founded: 1926
For book publishing production, editorial, design & manufacturing people from the book community. Monthly dinner meetings, book show & educational seminars.
Number of Members: 800

Book Industry Study Group Inc (BISG)
1412 Broadway, Suite 2119, New York, NY 10018
Tel: 646-336-7141
E-mail: info@bisg.org
Web Site: bisg.org
Key Personnel
Exec Dir: Brian O'Leary
Opers Mgr: Kim Graff *E-mail:* kim@bisg.org
Founded: 1975
Trade association for policy, standards & research. The member-driven organization uniquely represents all segments of our industry, from publishers & e-publishers to paper manufacturers, libraries, authors, printers, wholesalers, retailers & e-tailers, as well as organizations concerned with the book industry as a whole. For over 40 years, BISG has provided a forum for all industry professionals to come together & efficiently address issues & concerns to advance the book community.
Number of Members: 150
New Election: Annually in Sept
2018 Meeting(s): BISG Annual Meeting of Members, April 27, 2018
Membership(s): AAP; ALA; Book Industry Communication; BookNetCanada; EDItEUR; Independent Book Publishers Association; National Information Standards Organization

Book Manufacturers' Institute Inc (BMI)
PO Box 731388, Ormond Beach, FL 32173
Tel: 386-986-4552 *Fax:* 386-986-4553
E-mail: info@bmibook.com
Web Site: www.bmibook.org
Key Personnel
EVP: Daniel N Bach *E-mail:* dbach@bmibook.com
Founded: 1933
BMI is the leading nationally recognized trade association of the book manufacturing industry.
Number of Members: 80
2018 Meeting(s): Management Conference, King & Prince, St Simons Island, GA, April 29-May 1, 2018; Annual Conference, Hyatt Regency Coconut Point, Bonita Springs, FL, Nov 4-6, 2018
Membership(s): Book Industry Guild of New York; National Association of Manufacturers

Book Publicists of Southern California
714 Crescent Dr, Beverly Hills, CA 90210
Tel: 323-461-3921 *Fax:* 323-461-0917
Web Site: www.bookpublicists.org
Key Personnel
Founder: Irwin Zucker *Tel:* 310-497-4001 (cell) *E-mail:* irwin@promotioninmotion.net
Pres: Bruce Braunstein
VP: Bill Frank
Membership: Valinda Rothman
Mktg: Melinda Sue Norin
Publicity: Rhonda Rees
Founded: 1976

Literary club. Bimonthly meetings at Sportsmen's Lodge, Studio City, CA, varied topics-anything pertinent to promotion of books & authors.
Number of Members: 1,200
New Election: Annually in Nov
Publication(s): *Know Thy Shelf* (6 issues/yr, newsletter, free to membs)

The Book Publishers Association of Alberta (BPAA)
Affiliate of Association of Canadian Publishers (ACP)
10523 100 Ave, Edmonton, AB T5J 0A8, Canada
Tel: 780-424-5060
E-mail: info@bookpublishers.ab.ca
Web Site: www.bookpublishers.ab.ca
Key Personnel
Exec Dir: Kieran Leblanc *E-mail:* kleblanc@bookpublishers.ab.ca
Sponsor professional development seminars, workshops & Alberta Book Industry Awards.
Number of Members: 32
Publication(s): *Membership Directory* (free)

Bookbuilders of Boston
115 Webster Woods Lane, North Andover, MA 01845
Tel: 781-378-1361 *Fax:* 419-821-2171
E-mail: office@bbboston.org
Web Site: www.bbboston.org
Key Personnel
Pres: Jamie Carter
Meetings, New England Book Show, seminars & scholarships; nonprofit organization.
New Election: Annually in April
Publication(s): *Directory* (annually, free)

Books for Everybody
111 Queen St E, Suite 320, Toronto, ON M5C 1S2, Canada
Tel: 416-364-3333 *Toll Free Tel:* 888-360-6658 *Fax:* 416-595-5415
Key Personnel
Assoc Publr: Attila Berki *Tel:* 416-364-3333 ext 3160 *E-mail:* aberki@booksforeverybody.com
Founded: 1937
Publish consumer catalogues for independent book stores.
Publication(s): *Books for Everybody* (annual); *Books for Everybody British Columbia Edition*; *Books for Everybody Young Readers Edition*
Membership(s): Canadian Booksellers Association

Boston Authors Club Inc
33 Brayton Rd, Brighton, MA 02135
Tel: 617-783-1357
E-mail: bostonauthors@aol.com
Web Site: www.bostonauthorsclub.org
Key Personnel
Pres: Alan Lawson *E-mail:* lawson@bc.edu
VP: Shirley Moskow *Tel:* 781-862-7697 *E-mail:* shirley.moskow@rtr.com
Founded: 1899
Nonprofit organization promoting discourse & community among authors with various programs & gives annual awards.
Number of Members: 140
New Election: Annually in May
Branch Office(s)
79 Moore Rd, Wayland, MA 01778 *Tel:* 508-358-4098

BPA Worldwide
100 Beard Sawmill Rd, 6th fl, Shelton, CT 06484
Tel: 203-447-2800 *Fax:* 203-447-2900
E-mail: info@bpaww.com
Web Site: www.bpaww.com
Key Personnel
CEO & Pres: Glenn J Hansen *E-mail:* ghansen@bpaww.com
SVP & Chief Quality Offr: Russell Haderer *E-mail:* rhaderer@bpaww.com
SVP, Auditing: Richard J Murphy *E-mail:* rmurphy@bpaww.com
SVP, Busn Devt: Peter D Black *E-mail:* pblack@bpaww.com
SVP, Fin & Admin: Doreen Castignoli *E-mail:* dcastignoli@bpaww.com
Founded: 1931
International, independent, not-for-profit organization whose membership consists of advertiser companies, advertising agencies & publications. Audit all-paid, all-controlled or any combination of paid & controlled circulation for more than 2,600 media properties including business, technical, professional publications, consumer magazines, newspapers, web sites, e-mail, newsletters & face-to-face events-expos & shows as well as more than 2,700 advertising & agency members.
Number of Members: 5,300
Branch Office(s)
CCAB (div of BPA Worldwide Inc), 111 Queen St E, No 450, Toronto, ON M5C 1S2, Canada, VP: Tim Peel *Tel:* 416-487-2418 *Fax:* 416-487-6405 *E-mail:* mpeel@bpaww.com
CCAB (div of BPA Worldwide Inc), 1 Ave Holiday, East Tower, Suite 501, Pointe-Claire, QC H9R 5N3, Canada, Dir: Matt Pasquale *Tel:* 514-845-0003 *Fax:* 514-845-0905 *E-mail:* mpasquale@bpaww.com
Suite 505, Bldg 4, China Central Place, 89 Jianguo Rd, Chaoyang District, Beijing 100025, China, Gen Mgr: Doreen Chan *Tel:* (010) 8591 0691 *Fax:* (010) 8591 0589 *E-mail:* dchan@bpaww.com
PO Box 502458, Dubai Media City, Dubai, United Arab Emirates, Dir: Rina Hariz *Tel:* (04) 3692468 *Fax:* (04) 3697073 *E-mail:* rhariz@bpaww.com
Central Working Shoreditch, 6-8 Bonhill St, London EC2A 4BX, United Kingdom, Dir, European Opers: Francis Stones *Tel:* (020) 3752 6844 *E-mail:* fstones@bpaww.com

Broadcast Music Inc, see BMI®

Business Forms Management Association (BFMA)
1147 Fleetwood Ave, Madison, WI 53716
Toll Free Tel: 888-367-3078
E-mail: bfma@bfma.org
Web Site: www.bfma.org
Key Personnel
CFO: Ray Killam
Pres: Kelly Halseth
VP, Membership: Mike Mulcahy
VP, Opers: Robin Miller
VP, Progs: Shantelle Boatright
Dir, Educ: J P Terry
Dir, Membership: Shannon Lerner
Founded: 1958
Sponsor professional training in all aspects of information resource management; classes are conducted in major cities in the US & CN. Bestow the association's highest award, the Jo Warner Award, to professionals in the information resources industry. Recipients do not have to be BFMA members.
Number of Members: 600

Business Marketing Association (BMA)
Division of Association of National Advertisers (ANA)
708 Third Ave, New York, NY 10017
Tel: 212-697-5950 *Fax:* 212-687-7310
E-mail: info@marketing.org
Web Site: www.marketing.org
Key Personnel
Exec Dir: Michael Palmer *Tel:* 646-369-4898 *E-mail:* mpalmer@marketing.org
Sr Dir: Arthur Tharpe *Tel:* 212-455-8004 *E-mail:* atharpe@marketing.org
Fin Dir: Lana Mavreshko *Tel:* 212-340-0087 *E-mail:* lmavreshko@marketing.org
Founded: 1922 (as National Industrial Advertising Association)
Provides information & resources to business-to-business marketers & marketing communicators.
Number of Members: 2,200
Publication(s): *BMA Buzz* (monthly, newsletter)

Canada Council for the Arts (Conseil des arts du Canada)
150 Elgin St, Ottawa, ON K1P 1L4, Canada
Mailing Address: PO Box 1047, Ottawa, NS K1P 5V8, Canada
Tel: 613-566-4414 *Toll Free Tel:* 800-263-5588 (CN only) *Fax:* 613-566-4390
E-mail: info@canadacouncil.ca
Web Site: www.canadacouncil.ca
Key Personnel
Admin Coord, Writing & Publg Section: Brigitte Fontille *Tel:* 613-566-4414 ext 4571 *E-mail:* brigitte.fontille@canadacouncil.ca
Federal cultural granting agency for Canadian literature. See web site for various awards, prize contests, fellowships & grants.

Canadian Authors Association (CAA)
6 West St N, Suite 203, Orillia, ON L3V 5B8, Canada
Tel: 705-325-3926
E-mail: admin@canadianauthors.org
Web Site: www.canadianauthors.org
Key Personnel
Exec Dir: Anita Purcell
Founded: 1921
Encourage & develop a climate favorable to the literary arts in Canada. Assistance to professional & emerging writers. Represent the concerns & interests of members.
Number of Members: 600
Publication(s): *Canadian Writers Guide* ($36)

Canadian Bookbinders and Book Artists Guild (CBBAG)
80 Ward St, Suite 207, Toronto, ON M6H 4A6, Canada
Tel: 416-581-1071
E-mail: cbbag@cbbag.ca
Web Site: www.cbbag.ca
Key Personnel
Pres: Mary MacIntyre
Founded: 1983
Presents workshops & courses on a wide variety of topics, including bookbinding, box making, paper making & decorating, letterpress printing, paper conservation & more. Also maintains a reference library & AV catalogue.
Number of Members: 600
Publication(s): *Book Arts arts du livre Canada* (May & Nov, magazine)

Canadian Cataloguing in Publication Program
Library & Archives Canada, 395 Wellington St, Ottawa, ON K1A 0N4, Canada
Tel: 819-994-6881 *Toll Free Tel:* 866-578-7777 (CN) *Fax:* 819-934-6777
E-mail: cip@lac-bac.gc.ca
Web Site: www.collectionscanada.gc.ca/cip/index-e.html
Voluntary program of cooperation between publishers & libraries.
Publication(s): *Livres a Paraitre/Forthcoming Books* (monthly, free)

Canadian Children's Book Centre
40 Orchard View Blvd, Suite 217, Toronto, ON M4R 1B9, Canada
Tel: 416-975-0010 *Fax:* 416-975-8970
E-mail: info@bookcentre.ca
Web Site: www.bookcentre.ca

Key Personnel
Exec Dir: Charlotte Teeple *E-mail:* charlotte@bookcentre.ca
Lib Coord: Meghan Howe *E-mail:* meghan@bookcentre.ca
Mktg & Web Site Coord: Camilia Kahrizi *E-mail:* camilia@bookcentre.ca
Prog Coord: Shannon Howe Barnes *E-mail:* shannon@bookcentre.ca
Founded: 1976
National not-for-profit organization to promote the reading, writing & illustrating of Canadian books for young readers. We provide programs, publications & resources for teachers, librarians, authors, illustrators, publishers, booksellers & parents.
Number of Members: 558
Publication(s): *Best Books for Kids & Teens* (semiannual, catalog, $5.95/issue); *Canadian Children's Book News* (quarterly, magazine, $4.95/issue, $24.95/single subn includes copies of Best Books for Kids & Teens)

Canadian Circulations Audit Board, see CCAB Inc

Canadian Education Association (Association canadienne d'education), see EdCan Network

Canadian Institute for Studies in Publishing
Simon Fraser University at Harbour Centre, 515 W Hastings St, Suite 3576, Vancouver, BC V6B 5K3, Canada
Tel: 778-782-5242
E-mail: pub-info@sfu.ca
Web Site: publishing.sfu.ca
Key Personnel
Prog Mgr: Jo-Anne Ray
Founded: 1987
Undergraduate, graduate & noncredit courses; research on print & digital publishing.

Canadian ISBN Agency
Unit of Library & Archives Canada
Library & Archives Canada, 395 Wellington St, Ottawa, ON K1A 0N4, Canada
Tel: 613-996-5115 *Toll Free Tel:* 866-578-7777 (CN & US) *Fax:* 613-995-6274
E-mail: isbn@lac-bac.gc.ca
Web Site: www.collectionscanada.gc.ca/ciss-ssci/index-e.html

Canadian Newspaper Association
890 Yonge St, Suite 200, Toronto, ON M4W 3P4, Canada
Tel: 416-923-3567; 416-482-1090 *Toll Free Tel:* 877-305-2262 *Fax:* 416-923-7206; 416-482-1908
E-mail: info@newspaperscanada.ca
Web Site: www.newspaperscanada.ca
Key Personnel
CEO & Pres: John Hinds *Tel:* 416-923-3567 ext 244 *E-mail:* jhinds@newspaperscanada.ca
Dir, Pub Aff: Adele Ritchie *E-mail:* aritchie@newspaperscanada.ca
Founded: 1996
An organization providing service to its members in the area of marketing, member services & contesting legislation that is potentially harmful to newspapers & freedom of the press in general. The association brings the wisdom & dedication of all its members to foster & nurture a free press committed to providing the best possible service to its readers.
Number of Members: 99

Canadian Publishers' Council (CPC)
250 Merton St, Suite 203, Toronto, ON M4S 1B1, Canada
Tel: 416-322-7011 *Fax:* 416-322-6999
Web Site: www.pubcouncil.ca
Key Personnel
Exec Dir, External Rel & Copyright: Jacqueline Hushion *Tel:* 416-322-7011 ext 222 *E-mail:* jhushion@pubcouncil.ca
Exec Dir, Trade & Higher Educ Publishers Groups: Colleen O'Neill *Tel:* 416-322-7011 ext 226 *E-mail:* coneill@pubcouncil.ca
Acctg Offr: Joanna Ames *Tel:* 416-322-7011 ext 228 *E-mail:* james@pubcouncil.ca
Founded: 1910
Represents the interests of Canadian publishing companies that publish books & other media for elementary & secondary schools, colleges & universities, professional & reference markets, the retail & library markets.
Number of Members: 20
New Election: Annually in Feb
Publication(s): *Publishing: A View from the Inside* ($2 plus GST); *Who Buys Books?* ($50 plus GST)
Membership(s): International Federation of Reproduction Rights Organizations; International Publishers Association

Canadian Society of Children's Authors, Illustrators & Performers (CANSCAIP)
720 Bathurst St, Suite 503, Toronto, ON M5S 2R4, Canada
Tel: 416-515-1559
E-mail: office@canscaip.org
Web Site: www.canscaip.org
Key Personnel
Pres: Sharon Jennings
VP: Jennifer Maruno
Admin Dir: Helena Aalto
Founded: 1977
Dedicated to the celebration & promotion of Canadian children's authors, illustrators & performers & their work. Provide promotional & networking opportunities.
Number of Members: 1,000
New Election: April even-numbered yrs
Meeting(s): Packaging Your Imagination, Toronto, Ontario, CN, annually in Nov
Publication(s): *CANSCAIP News* (quarterly, $45/yr nonmembs, free to membs, electronic)

CASW, see Council for the Advancement of Science Writing (CASW)

Catholic Book Publishers Association Inc, see Association of Catholic Publishers Inc

Catholic Library Association
8550 United Plaza Blvd, Suite 1001, Baton Rouge, LA 70809
Tel: 225-408-4417
E-mail: cla2@cathla.org
Web Site: cathla.org
Key Personnel
Pres: N Curtis LeMay
Exec Dir: Bland O'Connor *E-mail:* cla2@cathla.org
Founded: 1921
Initiate, foster & encourage activities & library programs that promote literature & libraries of a Catholic nature & of an ecumenical spirit.
Number of Members: 500
Publication(s): *Catholic Library World* (3 issues/yr, $100 nonmembs US; $140/yr foreign & $25 S&H)

Catholic Press Association of the United States & Canada
205 W Monroe St, Suite 470, Chicago, IL 60606
Tel: 312-380-6789 *Fax:* 312-361-0256
E-mail: journalist@catholicpress.org
Web Site: www.catholicpress.org
Key Personnel
Exec Dir: Timothy M Walter *E-mail:* twalter@catholicpress.org
Founded: 1911
Writing, publishing, advertising; all facets of publishing.
Number of Members: 800
2018 Meeting(s): Catholic Media Conference, Hyatt Regency Green Bay, 333 Main St, Green Bay, WI, June 13-15, 2018
Publication(s): *The Catholic Journalist* (monthly (exc Aug), $18/yr US, $24/yr CN & elsewhere); *Catholic Press Directory* (annual)

CBA: The Association for Christian Retail
1365 Garden of the Gods Rd, Suite 105, Colorado Springs, CO 80907
Tel: 719-265-9895 *Toll Free Tel:* 800-252-1950 *Fax:* 719-272-3508
E-mail: info@cbaonline.org
Web Site: cbaonline.org
Key Personnel
Chmn of the Bd: Sue Smith *E-mail:* sue.smith@bakerbookhouse.com
Vice Chair: Andrew Criswell, Sr *E-mail:* andrew@pdbcs.com
Pres: Curtis Riskey *E-mail:* criskey@cbaonline.org
Treas: Bill Covey *E-mail:* billc@dayspring.com
Secy: Robin Hogan *E-mail:* rhogan@cccinfo.org
Founded: 1950
Association members are Christian publishers, music publishers & gift houses.
Number of Members: 3,200
New Election: Annually in July
2018 Meeting(s): International Christian Retail Show (ICRS), Duke Energy Convention Center, 525 Elm St, Cincinnati, OH, July 8-11, 2018
Publication(s): *CBA Retailers+Resources* (monthly, magazine, $49.95/yr membs, $59.95/yr nonmembs)

CCAB Inc
Division of BPA Worldwide
One Concorde Gate, Suite 800, Toronto, ON M3C 3N6, Canada
Tel: 416-487-2418 *Fax:* 416-487-6405
E-mail: info@bpaww.com
Web Site: www.bpaww.com
Key Personnel
VP: Tim Peel *E-mail:* mpeel@bpaww.com
Founded: 1931
Number of Members: 550

The Center for Book Arts
28 W 27 St, 3rd fl, New York, NY 10001
Tel: 212-481-0295
E-mail: info@centerforbookarts.org
Web Site: www.centerforbookarts.org
Key Personnel
Exec Dir & Curator: Alexander Campos
Founded: 1974
Nonprofit, provides workspace, education, exhibitions & slide registry for book artists, hand papermakers & letter press printers; publication of fine art editions, lectures, outreach program.
Number of Members: 6,500
Publication(s): *Exhibition Catalogs* (4 issues/yr, $15 membs, $20 nonmembs)

The Center for Exhibition Industry Research (CEIR)
12700 Park Central Dr, Suite 308, Dallas, TX 75251
Tel: 972-687-9242 *Fax:* 972-692-6020
E-mail: info@ceir.org
Web Site: www.ceir.org
Key Personnel
CEO & Pres: Brian D Casey *Tel:* 972-687-9219 *E-mail:* bcasey@ceir.org
Exec Dir: Cathy Breden *Tel:* 972-687-9201 *E-mail:* cbreden@ceir.org
Promote the exhibition industry by promoting the value & benefits of exhibitions in an integrated

marketing program through research, information & communications.
Number of Members: 600

The Center for Fiction
17 E 47 St, New York, NY 10017
Tel: 212-755-6710 *Fax:* 212-826-0831
E-mail: info@centerforfiction.org
Web Site: centerforfiction.org/awards
Key Personnel
Chmn & Pres: Peter Ginna
Exec Dir: Noreen Tomassi *E-mail:* noreen@centerforfiction.org
Founded: 1820 (as the Mercantile Library)
Devoted to the vital art of fiction & to encourage people to read & value fiction. Circulating library of mainly fiction titles. Monthly programs, literary lectures & readings. Writers' studio. Inquiries invited.
Number of Members: 500
Publication(s): *The Literarian* (quarterly, newsletter, $5.95/issue (print), free online)

The Center for the Book in the Library of Congress
The Library of Congress, 101 Independence Ave SE, Washington, DC 20540-4920
Tel: 202-707-5221 *Fax:* 202-707-0269
E-mail: cfbook@loc.gov
Web Site: www.read.gov; www.read.gov/cfb
Key Personnel
Dir: John Y Cole *E-mail:* jcole@loc.gov
Communs Offr: Guy Lamolinara
Prog Offr: Anne Boni
Founded: 1977 (est by law)
Uses the influence & resources of the Library of Congress to stimulate public interest in books & reading & to encourage the study of books. Its program of symposia, projects, lectures, exhibitions & publications is supported by tax-deductible contributions from corporations & individuals. National reading promotion network includes more than 50 affiliated state centers & more than 80 educational & civic organizations.

Chicago Women in Publishing
PO Box 268107, Chicago, IL 60626
Tel: 773-508-0351 *Fax:* 303-942-7164
E-mail: info@cwip.org
Web Site: www.cwip.org
Key Personnel
Pres: Mejhann Workman *E-mail:* president@cwip.org
Secy: Fiona Saltmarsh *E-mail:* secretary@cwip.org
Founded: 1972
Jobline employment listing service, monthly newsletter, monthly program meetings, freelance directory, membership directory.
Number of Members: 300
New Election: May 2018

The Children's Book Council (CBC)
54 W 39 St, 14th fl, New York, NY 10018
Tel: 212-966-1990
E-mail: cbc.info@cbcbooks.org
Web Site: www.cbcbooks.org
Key Personnel
Exec Dir: Carl Lennertz *E-mail:* carl.lennertz@cbcbooks.org
Dir, Programming: Shaina Birkhead *E-mail:* shaina.birkhead@cbcbooks.org
Communs Coord: Emma Kantor *E-mail:* emma.kantor@cbcbooks.com
Founded: 1945
Nonprofit trade association of children's book publishers & related companies. Publish reading promotion display & informational materials. New electronic edition of Children's Books: Awards & Prizes; provides professional education & online member services.
Number of Members: 70
New Election: Annually in Sept
2018 Meeting(s): Children's Book Week, Nationwide across the USA, May 7-13, 2018
2019 Meeting(s): Children's Book Week, Nationwide across the USA, May 6-12, 2019
2020 Meeting(s): Children's Book Week, Nationwide across the USA, May 4-10, 2020
2021 Meeting(s): Children's Book Week, Nationwide across the USA, May 3-9, 2021
2022 Meeting(s): Children's Book Week, Nationwide across the USA, May 2-8, 2022
Publication(s): *Awards & Prizes Online* (online database, annual, $150); *CBC Features* (semiannual, $60 one-time charge)

Christian Booksellers Association, see CBA: The Association for Christian Retail

CIP Program, see Canadian Cataloguing in Publication Program

City & Regional Magazine Association
2512 Artesia Blvd, Suite 200, Redondo Beach, CA 90278
Tel: 310-379-8261 *Fax:* 310-379-8283
E-mail: admin@citymag.org
Web Site: www.citymag.org
Key Personnel
Pres: Gary Whitaker
VP: Bob Fernald
Secy: Remy Spreeuw
Treas: Chris Schulz
Exec Dir: C James Dowden *Tel:* 310-379-8261 ext 11
The purpose of the association is to facilitate professional development & training opportunities for member magazines & provide opportunities to exchange information & ideas. Also the sponsor of CRMA Awards Competition, The City & Regional Magazine Award Program at the University of Missouri School of Journalism; city & regional magazine competition as well as an annual conference.
Number of Members: 89
Publication(s): *CRMA Newsletter* (free to membs, electronic)

Colorado Authors' League
PO Box 24905, Denver, CO 80224
Web Site: coloradoauthors.org
Key Personnel
Pres: Denny Dressman
Founded: 1931
Organization of independent, professional writers united to further members' success.
Number of Members: 250

Committee On Scholarly Editions
Subsidiary of Modern Language Association of America (MLA)
c/o Modern Language Association of America, 26 Broadway, 3rd fl, New York, NY 10004-1789
Tel: 646-576-5044 *Fax:* 646-458-0030
Web Site: www.mla.org
Key Personnel
Sr Acqs Ed: James C Hatch
Founded: 1979
Assists editors & publishers in preparing reliable scholarly editions.
Number of Members: 9

Community of Literary Magazines & Presses (CLMP)
154 Christopher St, Suite 3C, New York, NY 10014-9110
Tel: 212-741-9110 *Fax:* 212-741-9112
E-mail: info@clmp.org
Web Site: www.clmp.org
Key Personnel
Exec Dir: Jeffrey Lependorf *Tel:* 212-741-9110 ext 14 *E-mail:* jlependorf@clmp.org
Dir, Membership: Ted Dodson
Progs Dir: Kathy Daneman *E-mail:* kdaneman@clmp.org
Founded: 1967
A national nonprofit organization that provides services to small independent literary magazine & book publishers, including technical assistance, various publications, marketing workshops, an online directory of literary magazines & granting programs for literary magazines & presses.
Number of Members: 500

Connecticut Authors & Publishers Association (CAPA)
PO Box 715, Avon, CT 06001-0715
Tel: 860-675-1344 *Fax:* 860-673-7650
Web Site: www.aboutcapa.com
Key Personnel
Founder: Brian Jud *E-mail:* brianjud@bookmarketing.com
Founded: 1994
Number of Members: 150
Meeting(s): Monthly Meeting, Avon Community Center, Avon, CT, 3rd Saturday of the month
Publication(s): *The Authority* (monthly, newsletter, free with membership)

Conseil des arts du Canada, see Canada Council for the Arts (Conseil des arts du Canada)

Copywriter's Council of America™ (CCA)
Division of The Linick Group Inc
CCA Bldg, 7 Putter Lane, Middle Island, NY 11953-1920
Mailing Address: PO Box 102, Middle Island, NY 11953-0102
Tel: 631-924-3888; 631-775-6075 *Fax:* 631-924-8555
E-mail: cca4dmcopy@gmail.com
Web Site: www.andrewlinickdirectmarketing.com/Copywriters-Council.html; www.newworldpressbooks.com
Key Personnel
Chmn, Consulting Group: Andrew S Linick, PhD *E-mail:* andrew@asklinick.com
Pres: Gaylen Andrews
EVP: Roger Dextor
Dir, Spec Projs: Barbara Deal
Freelance direct response advertising copywriters, direct marketing consultants, PR & communication specialists & marketing researchers. Cover business-to-business, consumer & industrial markets. Creative services covering all media, all products & services A-Z, e-commerce, e-marketing, e-targeted public relations. Provide comprehensive graphic redesign/new web site content development, interactive services with marketing web site makeover advice for first-time authors, self-publishers, professionals & entrepreneurs. Specializes in online advertising/PR, links to top search engines, consulting on a 100% satisfaction guarantee. Free site evaluation marketing checklist (a $250 value) for LMP readers.
Number of Members: 35,000
Publication(s): *The Digest* (quarterly, for membs only, ezine, $40)

Corporation for Public Broadcasting (CPB)
401 Ninth St NW, Washington, DC 20004-2129
Tel: 202-879-9600
Web Site: www.cpb.org
Key Personnel
CEO & Pres: Patricia de Stacy Harrison
COO & EVP: Vincent Curren
CFO & Treas: William P Tayman, Jr
EVP, Corp & Pub Aff: Michael Levy

SVP & Gen Coun: Westwood Smithers, Jr
SVP & Corp Secy: Teresa Safon
Support the nation's public TV & public radio industry through federally appropriated funds. Conduct support services & to stimulate the creation of programming on TV, radio & online.

Corporation of Professional Librarians of Quebec
1453, rue Beaubien Est, Bureau 215, Montreal, QC H2G 3C6, Canada
Tel: 514-845-3327 *Fax:* 514-845-1618
E-mail: info@cbpq.qc.ca
Web Site: www.cbpq.qc.ca
Key Personnel
Exec Dir: Regine Horinstein
Founded: 1969
Publications, continuing education for information professionals.
Number of Members: 700
Publication(s): *Argus* (3 issues/yr, $48 CN, $50 foreign)

Council for Advancement & Support of Education (CASE)
1307 New York Ave NW, Suite 1000, Washington, DC 20005-4701
Tel: 202-328-CASE (328-2273) *Fax:* 202-387-4973
E-mail: membersupportcenter@case.org
Web Site: www.case.org
Key Personnel
Pres: Sue Cunningham
VP, Busn & Fin: Donald Falkenstein *Tel:* 202-478-5637 *E-mail:* falkenstein@case.org
Dir, Communs: Pam Russell *Tel:* 202-478-5680 *E-mail:* russell@case.org
Founded: 1974
International association of educational institutions. Helps its members build stronger relationships with their alumni & donors, raise funds for campus projects, produce recruitment materials, market their institutions to prospective students, diversity the profession & foster public support of education.
Number of Members: 81,000
Publication(s): *Currents* (9 issues/yr (3 double issues), $150/yr, $220/2 yrs, $180/yr intl, $280/2 yrs intl)
Branch Office(s)
Berlin 18 4to piso, Colonia Juarez, Delegacion Cuauhtemoc, 06600 Mexico, DF, Mexico *Tel:* (0155) 2709 15 77 *E-mail:* americalatina@case.org
Shaw Foundation Alumni House, Unit 05-03, 11 Kent Ridge Dr, Singapore, Singapore *Tel:* 6778 3285 *Fax:* 6778 3286 *E-mail:* asia-pacific@case.org
Paxton House, 3rd fl, 30 Artillery Lane, London E1 7LS, United Kingdom *Tel:* (020) 7448 9940 *Fax:* (020) 7377 5944 *E-mail:* europe@case.org

Council for the Advancement of Science Writing (CASW)
PO Box 910, Hedgesville, WV 25427
Tel: 304-754-6786
Web Site: www.casw.org
Key Personnel
Exec Dir: Rosalind Reid *E-mail:* rosreid@gmail.com
Admin: Diane McGurgan *E-mail:* diane@casw.org
Founded: 1959
To advance science writing.
Meeting(s): New Horizons in Science, annually in Oct

CWA/SCA Canada
Affiliate of Canadian Labour Congress
2200 Prince of Wales Dr, Suite 301, Ottawa, ON K2E 6Z9, Canada
Tel: 613-820-9777 *Toll Free Tel:* 877-486-4292 *Fax:* 613-820-8188
E-mail: info@cwa-scacanada.ca
Web Site: www.cwa-scacanada.ca
Key Personnel
Pres: Martin O'Hanlon *Tel:* 613-820-8460 *E-mail:* mohanlon@cwa-scacanada.ca
Contracts Coord: Marj Botsford *E-mail:* mbotsford@cwa-scacanada.ca
Fin Coord: Joanne Scheel *E-mail:* jscheel@cwa-scacanada.ca
Founded: 1995 (as TNG Canada)
Media union representing members in Canada.
Affiliate of: The Newspaper Guild, Communication Workers of America (CWA) & Canadian Labour Congress.
Number of Members: 7,000

Data & Marketing Association (DMA)
Formerly Direct Marketing Association (DMA)
1333 Broadway, Suite 301, New York, NY 10018
SAN: 692-6487
Tel: 212-768-7277 *Fax:* 212-302-6714
E-mail: memberservices@the-dma.org
Web Site: thedma.org
Key Personnel
CEO: Thomas J Benton
Sr Dir, Memb Communs & Sr Ed: Susan Taplinger *Tel:* 212-790-1589
Dir, Educ & Prof Devt: Michelle Tiletnick
Founded: 1917
A member organization representing the direct marketing business to legislators, regulators & the media, also offering educational & networking experiences for members.
2018 Meeting(s): &THEN, MGM Grand, Las Vegas, NV, Oct 7-9, 2018
Publication(s): *3D-DMA Daily Digest* (3 times/wk)
Branch Office(s)
1615 "L" St NW, Suite 1100, Washington, DC 20036 *Tel:* 202-955-5030 *Fax:* 202-955-0085

Deadline Club
Division of Society of Professional Journalists
c/o Salmagundi Club, 47 Fifth Ave, New York, NY 10003
Tel: 646-481-7584
E-mail: info@deadlineclub.org
Web Site: www.deadlineclub.org
Key Personnel
Chairwoman: J Alex Tarquinio
Pres: Peter Szekely
Secy: Melissa Heule
VP, Awards Contest: Michael Arena
VP, Awards Dinner: Jacqueline Leo
VP, Membership: Polly Whittell
Founded: 1925
Monthly meetings. Membership includes professionals working in print, broadcast, online & journalism education. Professional membership $30, student membership $20. Must be SPJ member.
Number of Members: 300
Meeting(s): Annual Awards Dinner, Waldorf Astoria, New York, NY
Publication(s): *Deadliner Express* (newsletter); *Quill* (6 issues/yr, magazine, free to membs, $75/yr nonmembs); *SPJ Leads* (weekly, newsletter, free to membs)

Direct Marketing Association (DMA), see Data & Marketing Association (DMA)

Dog Writers' Association of America Inc (DWAA)
66 Adams St, Jamestown, NY 14701
Tel: 716-484-6155
E-mail: dogwriter@windstream.net
Web Site: www.dwaa.org
Key Personnel
Pres: Ida Estep, Esq *Tel:* 252-478-6088 *Fax:* 252-478-6089 *E-mail:* ida@dogwriters.org
VP & Contest Chair: Elaine Gerwitz *Tel:* 805-418-7899 *Fax:* 821-374-9231 *E-mail:* elaine@dogwriters.org
Treas: Marsha Pugh *E-mail:* marsha@dogwriters.org
Secy: Susan M Ewing *E-mail:* su@dogwriters.org
Founded: 1935
Provide information about dogs (sport, breeding & ownership) & assist writers in gaining access to exhibitions. Annual writing competition.
Number of Members: 545
Meeting(s): Annual Meeting, Hotel Pennsylvania, 401 Seventh Ave, New York, NY, Feb
Publication(s): *Ruff Drafts* (quarterly, newsletter, free to membs)

EdCan Network
Formerly Canadian Education Association (Association canadienne d'education)
60 St Clair Ave E, Suite 703, Toronto, ON M4T 1N5, Canada
Tel: 416-591-6300 *Toll Free Tel:* 866-803-9549 *Fax:* 416-591-5345 *Toll Free Fax:* 866-803-9549
E-mail: info@edcan.ca
Web Site: www.edcan.ca
Key Personnel
COO: Gilles Latour *Tel:* 416-591-6300 ext 237 *E-mail:* glatour@edcan.ca
Dir, Communs: Max Cooke *Tel:* 416-591-6300 ext 225 *E-mail:* mcooke@edcan.ca
Founded: 1891
A national bilingual, charitable organization that promotes transformation in education.
Number of Members: 304
New Election: Annually in Sept or Oct
Publication(s): *Education Canada* (4 issues/yr, magazine, free to membs; available for purchase through subn servs)

Editorial Freelancers Association (EFA)
71 W 23 St, 4th fl, New York, NY 10010-4102
Tel: 212-929-5400 *Toll Free Tel:* 866-929-5425 *Fax:* 212-929-5439 *Toll Free Fax:* 866-929-5439
E-mail: office@the-efa.org
Web Site: www.the-efa.org
Key Personnel
Exec: William P Keenan, Jr; J P Partland
Founded: 1970
A nonprofit, volunteer-based professional association of freelance editors, writers, copy editors, proofreaders, indexers, production specialists, researchers & translators. Provides job listing service, courses, member directory & related professional services. More than 20 chapters nationwide.
Number of Members: 2,300
Publication(s): *EFA Directory* (online, free); *EFA Newsletter* (6 issues/yr, newsletter, free to membs)

Editors' Association of Canada (Association canadienne des reviseurs)
27 Carlton St, Suite 505, Toronto, ON M5B 1L2, Canada
Tel: 416-975-1379 *Toll Free Tel:* 866-CAN-EDIT (226-3348) *Fax:* 416-975-1637
E-mail: info@editors.ca; info@reviseurs.ca
Web Site: www.editors.ca; www.reviseurs.ca
Key Personnel
Exec Dir: John Yip-Chuck *E-mail:* executivedirector@editors.ca
Sr Communs Mgr: Michelle Ou *E-mail:* communications@editors.ca
Founded: 1979
Promotes professional editing as key in producing effective communication. Our members work with individuals in the corporate, technical,

government, not-for-profit & publishing sectors. Sponsor professional development seminars, promotes & maintains high standards of editing & publishing in Canada, establishes guidelines to help editors secure fair pay & good working conditions, helps both in-house & freelance editors to network & cooperates with other publishing associations in areas of common concern. The association is incorporated federally as a not-for-profit organization & is governed at the national level by an executive council.
Number of Members: 1,500
New Election: Annually in June
Publication(s): *Active Voice (La Voix Active)* (semiannual, newsletter, free to membs)
Membership(s): Book & Periodical Council; Cultural Human Resources Council

Education Writers Association (EWA)
3516 Connecticut Ave NW, Washington, DC 20008
Tel: 202-452-9830 *Fax:* 202-452-9837
E-mail: ewa@ewa.org
Web Site: www.ewa.org
Key Personnel
COO: George Dieter *E-mail:* gdieter@ewa.org
Exec Dir: Caroline W Hendrie *E-mail:* chendrie@ewa.org
Asst Dir: Lori Crouch *E-mail:* lcrouch@ewa.org
Multimedia & Web Mgr: Michael Marriott *E-mail:* mmarriott@ewa.org
Founded: 1947
Professional organization of members of the media who cover education at all levels with a mission to increase the quality & quantity of education coverage to create a better informed society. Conferences, seminars, newsletters, publications, employment services, freelance referral, workshops & national awards.
Number of Members: 3,000
Publication(s): *Standards for Education Reporters* (free)

Educational Book & Media Association (EBMA)
11 Main St, Suite D, Warrenton, VA 20186
Mailing Address: PO Box 3363, Warrenton, VA 20188
Tel: 540-318-7770 *Fax:* 202-962-3939
E-mail: info@edupaperback.org
Web Site: www.edupaperback.org
Key Personnel
Pres: Jill Faherty
VP: Joyce Skokut
Treas: Nancy Stetzinger
Exec Dir: Brian Gorg
Meeting Mgr: Maureen Gelwicks
Founded: 1975
To develop better techniques & procedures for the sales, marketing & distribution of paperback books, prebound books & related media in the school & library markets. Regular membership consists of educational paperback & prebound book wholesalers; associate members are paperback publishers.
Number of Members: 125
2018 Meeting(s): EBMA Annual Meeting, Palm Springs, CA, Jan 8-10, 2018

Epicomm
1800 Diagonal Rd, Suite 320, Alexandria, VA 22314-2862
Tel: 703-836-9200
E-mail: webmaster@epicomm.org
Web Site: epicomm.org
Key Personnel
Pres & CEO: Ken Garner *Tel:* 703-972-2730 *E-mail:* kgarner@epicomm.org
EVP: Dean D'Ambrosi *Tel:* 201-523-6314 *E-mail:* ddambrosi@epicomm.org
SVP & Chief Economist: Andrew D Paparozzi *Tel:* 201-523-6353 *E-mail:* apaparozzi@epicomm.org
Founded: 2014 (through merger of AMSP, NAPL & NAQP)
Association for leaders in print, mail, fulfillment & marketing services. Epicomm provides management tools & learning & professional development opportunities to help make informed business decisions in an ever-changing market environment.
Number of Members: 3,600
Publication(s): *Bottom Line* (6 issues/yr, magazine); *Management Bulletin* (quarterly, newsletter); *Owner Operator* (quarterly, newsletter); *REVIEW* (monthly, newsletter, electronic); *State of the Industry Update* (quarterly, newsletter)
Branch Office(s)
One Meadowlands Plaza, Suite 1511, East Rutherford, NJ 07073 *Tel:* 201-634-9600

Evangelical Christian Publishers Association (ECPA)
5801 S McClintock Dr, Suite 104, Tempe, AZ 85283
Tel: 480-966-3998 *Fax:* 480-966-1944
E-mail: info@ecpa.org
Web Site: www.ecpa.org
Key Personnel
Exec Dir: Stan Jantz
Founded: 1974
Trade association supporting Christian publishers worldwide. Provides professional seminars, compiles statistical studies & presents religious book awards.
Number of Members: 280
2018 Meeting(s): Leadership Summit & Annual Member Meeting, Museum of the Bible, Washington, DC, May 1-2, 2018
Membership(s): BISG

Evangelical Press Association (EPA)
PO Box 1787, Queen Creek, AZ 85142
Toll Free Tel: 888-311-1731
E-mail: info@evangelicalpress.com
Web Site: www.evangelicalpress.com
Key Personnel
Exec Dir & CFO: Lamar Keener
Founded: 1948
Professional association of Christian freelancers, associates, magazines, newsletters, newspapers & content-rich web sites.
Number of Members: 329
2018 Meeting(s): Annual Convention, Orlando Airport Marriott Lakeside, Orlando, FL, April 4-6, 2018
Publication(s): *Liaison* (quarterly, newsletter)

FAPA, see Florida Authors & Publishers Association Inc (FAPA)

Federation of BC Writers
PO Box 16028, 617 Belmont St, New Westminster, BC V3M 6W6, Canada
E-mail: info@bcwriters.ca
Web Site: bcwriters.ca
Key Personnel
Pres: Coco Aders-Weremczuk
Exec Dir: Craig Spence
Founded: 1976
Not-for-profit organization established to contribute to a supportive environment for writing in the province. Writers of all levels working in all genres & specialties welcome. We publish a magazine & hold readings, workshops & literary competitions.
Number of Members: 400
New Election: Annually in May
Publication(s): *WordWorks*

Florida Authors & Publishers Association Inc (FAPA)
1702 N Woodland Blvd, Suite 116, Box 145, Deland, FL 32720
E-mail: member.services@floridapublishersassociation.com
Web Site: www.floridapublishersassociation.com
Key Personnel
Pres: Terri Gerrell *E-mail:* president@floridapublishersassociation.com
Founded: 1983
Networking seminars, newsletter, publishing, book shows, workshops, small presses, independents & self-publishers; annual President's Book Award competition. Affiliate of IBPA (Independent Book Publishers Association), AAP (Association of American Publishers) & APSS (Association of Publishers for Small Sales).
Number of Members: 144
Publication(s): *FAPA REaD* (monthly, newsletter, free to membs, media, booksellers, libraries & reviewers, electronic)

Florida Freelance Writers Association
Affiliate of Writers-Editors Network
45 Main St, North Stratford, NH 03590
Mailing Address: PO Box A, North Stratford, NH 03590
Tel: 603-922-8338 *Fax:* 603-922-8339
E-mail: ffwa@writers-editors.com; info@writers-editors.com
Web Site: www.writers-editors.com; www.ffwamembers.com
Key Personnel
Exec Dir: Dana K Cassell *E-mail:* dana@writers-editors.com
Founded: 1982
Network of freelance writers & editors, offering a job bank, Florida Markets directory, newsletter, etc.
Number of Members: 200
Publication(s): *Directory of Florida Markets for Writers* (newsletter & electronic formats, $35, free to membs); *Freelance Writer's Report* (monthly, free to membs); *Guide to WEN/FFWA Writers* (continuously updated, free to qualified publishing companies & businesses)

Florida Outdoor Writers Association Inc
24 NW 33 Ct, Suite A, Gainesville, FL 32607
Tel: 352-284-1763
E-mail: info@fowa.org
Web Site: www.fowa.org
Key Personnel
Chmn of the Bd: Ron Presley
Pres: Bob Wattendorf
1st VP: Jill Zima Borski
2nd VP: Rob Modys
Secy: Susan Young
Treas: Frank Morello
Exec Dir: Tommy Thompson
Founded: 1946
Not-for-profit 501(c)(3) statewide paid professional communicators organization made up of outdoor communicators who report & reflect upon Florida's diverse interests in the outdoors to educate & encourage the public in ways to protect & conserve our natural heritage.
Number of Members: 300
New Election: Annually in Sept
Publication(s): *The Market Edge* (6 issues/yr, newsletter, free to membs, electronic)

Florida Writers Association Inc
PO Box 66069, St Pete Beach, FL 33736-6069
Web Site: www.floridawriters.net
Key Personnel
Pres: Cheyenne Williams *E-mail:* ckwilliams@onlinebinding.com
EVP: Jade Kerrion
VP, Admin & Fin: Larry Kokko

VP, Fin: Robyn Weinbaum
Founded: 2001
Association of "writers helping writers" to improve writing skills, produce good work in all genres & successfully publish.
Number of Members: 1,500
Publication(s): *The Florida Writer* (quarterly, $4.95, free to membs)

Foil & Specialty Effects Association (FSEA)
2150 SW Westport Dr, Suite 101, Topeka, KS 66614
Tel: 785-271-5816 *Fax:* 785-271-6404
E-mail: info@fsea.com; fseamail@fsea.com
Web Site: www.fsea.com
Key Personnel
Exec Dir: Jeff Peterson *E-mail:* jeff@fsea.com
Asst Dir: Kym Conis *E-mail:* kym@fsea.com
Sales Dir: Gayla Peterson *E-mail:* gayla@petersonpublications.com
Founded: 1992
Trade association for graphics finishing industry.
Number of Members: 325
Publication(s): *Inside Finishing Magazine* (3 issues/yr)

La Fondation Emile Nelligan
100, rue Sherbrooke, Suite 202, Montreal, QC H2X 1C3, Canada
Tel: 514-278-4657 *Fax:* 514-278-1943
E-mail: info@fondation-nelligan.org
Web Site: www.fondation-nelligan.org
Key Personnel
CEO: Manon Gagnon
Pres: Michel Dallaire
VP: Marie-Andree Beaudet
Treas/Secy: Michel Gonneville
Founded: 1979
Sponsoring organization.
Number of Members: 1,000

4A's (American Association of Advertising Agencies)
1065 Avenue of the Americas, 16th fl, New York, NY 10018
Tel: 212-682-2500
Web Site: www.aaaa.org
Key Personnel
CEO & Pres: Nancy Hill *E-mail:* nhill@aaaa.org
COO & CFO: Laura J Bartlett *E-mail:* lbartlett@aaaa.org
EVP, Strategic Partnerships: Michael D Donahue *E-mail:* donahue@aaaa.org
Bd Secy: Michele Adams *E-mail:* adams@aaaa.org
Founded: 1917
National trade association for the advertising agency business.
Number of Members: 430
2018 Meeting(s): Transformation, Loews Miami Beach Hotel, 1601 Collins Ave, Miami Beach, FL, April 8-11, 2018
Branch Office(s)
9595 Wilshire Blvd, Suite 900, Beverly Hills, CA 90212, EVP, Western Reg: Jerry McGee *Tel:* 310-300-3422 *Fax:* 310-300-3421 *E-mail:* jmcgee@aaaa.org
1707 "L" St NW, Suite 600, Washington, DC 20036, EVP: Dick O'Brien *Tel:* 202-331-7345 *Fax:* 202-857-3675 *E-mail:* dobrien@aaaa.org
3050 Bellingrath Blvd, Roswell, GA 30076, VP, Agency Rel & Membership: Greg Walker *Tel:* 770-639-6720 (cell) *Fax:* 770-587-1217 *E-mail:* gwalker@aaaa.org
747 N Wabash Ave, Suite 902, Chicago, IL 60611, VP, Agency Rel & Membership: Laurie Stearn *Tel:* 312-388-7470 *E-mail:* lstearn@aaaa.org

The Graphic Artists Guild Inc
31 W 34 St, 8th fl, New York, NY 10001
Tel: 212-791-3400 *Fax:* 212-791-0333
E-mail: admin@graphicartistsguild.org; membership@graphicartistsguild.org
Web Site: www.graphicartistsguild.org
Key Personnel
Pres: Lara Kisielewska *E-mail:* president@graphicartistsguild.org
Founded: 1967
Labor organization which advocates the advancement of artists' rights. Members are illustrators, graphic designers, surface & textile designers, computer graphics artists, cartoonists & others.
Number of Members: 1,100
Publication(s): *Pricing & Ethical Guidelines, 14th ed* ($39.99)

Graphic Arts Show Company (GASC)
1899 Preston White Dr, Reston, VA 20191
Tel: 703-264-7200 *Fax:* 703-620-9187
E-mail: info@gasc.org
Web Site: www.gasc.org
Key Personnel
Pres: Ralph Nappi *Tel:* 703-264-7200 ext 227
Founded: 1982
Trade show management for printing, publishing & graphic communications events.
2018 Meeting(s): Graph Expo®, McCormick Place, South Hall, 2301 S Lake Shore Dr, Chicago, IL, Sept 30-Oct 3, 2018
2019 Meeting(s): Graph Expo®, Orange County Convention Center, North Hall, Orlando, FL, Sept 22-25, 2019
2021 Meeting(s): PRINT®, McCormick Place, South Hall, 2301 S Lake Shore Dr, Chicago, IL, Autumn 2021

Gravure Association of the Americas Inc
8281 Pine Lake Rd, Denver, NC 28037
Tel: 201-523-6042 *Fax:* 201-523-6048
E-mail: gaa@gaa.org
Web Site: www.gaa.org
Key Personnel
Exec Dir: Philip Pimlott *Tel:* 812-406-5434 *E-mail:* ppimlott@gaa.org
Dir, Planning & Admin: Pamela W Schenk *Tel:* 585-288-2297 *E-mail:* pwschenk@gaa.org
Foster the advancement of gravure printing industry. Sponsor of the Golden Cylinder Awards.
Number of Members: 250
Publication(s): *Gravure Magazine* (quarterly, free to qualified companies)

Great Lakes Graphics Association
Affiliate of Printing Industries of America
W232 N2950 Roundy Circle E, Pewaukee, WI 53072
Tel: 262-522-2210 *Toll Free Tel:* 855-522-2210 *Fax:* 262-522-2211
E-mail: admin@piw.org
Web Site: www.piw.org
Key Personnel
Pres: Joe Lyman *Tel:* 262-522-2212
Founded: 1886
Number of Members: 175
Publication(s): *NewScan* (electronic, newsletter, free to membs)

Guild of Book Workers
521 Fifth Ave, New York, NY 10175
Tel: 212-292-4444
E-mail: communications@guildofbookworkers.org
Web Site: www.guildofbookworkers.org
Key Personnel
Pres: Mark Andersson *Tel:* 520-682-7241 *E-mail:* president@guildofbookworkers.org
VP: Bexx Caswell *E-mail:* vicepresident@guildofbookworkers.org
Secy: Katy Baum *Tel:* 214-363-7946 *E-mail:* secretary@guildofbookworkers.org
Treas: Laura Bedford *E-mail:* treasurer@guildofbookworkers.org
Founded: 1906
A national nonprofit educational organization which fosters the hand book arts: binding, calligraphy, illumination, paper decorating. Sponsor exhibits, lectures, workshops. See web site for membership fee information.
Number of Members: 850
Publication(s): *Journal* (annual, free to membs); *Newsletter* (6 issues/yr, free to membs)

GWA: The Association for Garden Communicators
355 Lexington Ave, 15th fl, New York, NY 10017
Tel: 806-832-1870 *Fax:* 806-832-5244
E-mail: info@gardenwriters.org
Web Site: www.gardenwriters.org
Founded: 1948
Professional association garden communicators working as staff or freelance as newspaper columnists, magazine columnists, photographers & radio/TV hosts. Sponsor annual writer's contest & annual Garden Media award program for published articles or books, as well as an annual symposium.
Number of Members: 1,800
2018 Meeting(s): Annual Conference & Expo, Navy Pier, Chicago, IL, Aug 13-16, 2018
Publication(s): *Quill & Trowel* (6 issues/yr, newsletter)

Horror Writers Association (HWA)
c/o Horror Writers Association, PO Box 56687, Sherman Oaks, CA 91413
E-mail: hwa@horror.org
Web Site: horror.org
Key Personnel
Pres: Rocky Wood *E-mail:* president@horror.org
VP: Lisa Morton *E-mail:* vp@horror.org
Treas: Leslie Klinger *E-mail:* treasurer@horror.org
Secy: Joe McKinney *E-mail:* secretary@horror.org
Admin: Brad Hodson *E-mail:* admin@horror.org
Founded: 1985
To encourage public interest in & foster an appreciation of good horror & dark fantasy literature. Publishes monthly newsletter, provides online information & resources, Hardship Fund, Grievance Committee, scholarships. Sponsors Bram Stoker Awards & presents an annual Lifetime Achievement Award.
Membership fees: $69 indiv, $48 supporting, $115 corp, $89 family.
Number of Members: 600
Publication(s): *Horror Writers Association Newsletter* (monthly, electronic, free)

The Ibsen Society of America
University of California, Dept of Scandinavian, 6303 Dwinelle Hall, No 2690, Berkeley, CA 94720-2690
Tel: 510-642-4484 *Fax:* 510-642-6220
Web Site: www.ibsensociety.liu.edu
Founded: 1978
Nonprofit corporation which fosters an understanding of Ibsen's works through lectures, readings, performances, conferences & publications.
Number of Members: 250
Publication(s): *Ibsen News & Comment* (annual, newsletter, $15 libs & nonmembs, free to membs)

ICEA, see The Institute for Cooperation on Adult Education (Institut de Cooperation pour l'Education des Adultes-ICEA)

IDEAlliance®
1800 Diagonal Rd, Suite 320, Alexandria, VA 22314-2862
Tel: 703-837-1070 *Fax:* 703-837-1072
E-mail: registrar@idealliance.org
Web Site: www.idealliance.org

Key Personnel
Pres & CEO: David J Steinhardt *Tel:* 703-837-1066 *E-mail:* dsteinhardt@idealliance.org
EVP: Steve Bonoff *Tel:* 952-896-1908 *E-mail:* sbonoff@idealliance.org
VP, Opers & Mng Dir: Frank Balser *Tel:* 703-837-1089 *E-mail:* fbalser@idealliance.org
Founded: 1966
Represent printing, publishing, newspapers, suppliers, government organizations & advertising agencies. Seek productivity & technical improvement in creation & distribution of printed & digital materials.
Number of Members: 200

In-Plant Printing & Mailing Association (IPMA)
455 S Sam Barr Dr, Suite 203, Kearney, MO 64060
Tel: 816-919-1691
E-mail: ipmainfo@ipma.org
Web Site: www.ipma.org
Key Personnel
Exec Dir: Carma Goin *E-mail:* cgoin@ipma.org
Fin Coord & Off Asst: Jennifer Chambers *E-mail:* jchambers@ipma.org
Founded: 1964
Professional association dedicatd to the specific needs of all industry segments of in-house professionals who provide graphic design, copy, print, mail & distribution services to their organizations. Annual Educational Conference & Vendor Fair.
Number of Members: 500
Publication(s): *Inside Edge* (monthly, newsletter)

The Independent Book Publishers Association (IBPA)
1020 Manhattan Beach Blvd, Suite 204, Manhattan Beach, CA 90266
Tel: 310-546-1818 *Fax:* 310-546-3939
E-mail: info@ibpa-online.org
Web Site: www.ibpa-online.org
Key Personnel
CEO: Angela Bole *E-mail:* angela@ibpa-online.org
COO: Terry Nathan *E-mail:* terry@ibpa-online.org
Founded: 1983 (as Publishers Association of Southern California)
A national nonprofit publishers' co-operative which coordinates discounted participation in major book & library exhibits & trade shows throughout the country, as well as ad placement in major publications & direct mail programs. Sponsor workshops, awards & prizes.
Number of Members: 3,000
Publication(s): *IBPA Independent* (monthly, newsletter, free to membs, $60/yr nonmembs); *Membership & Service Directory* (free to membs)

Independent Writers of Chicago (IWOC)
332 S Michigan Ave, Suite 1032, Chicago, IL 60604
Toll Free Tel: 800-804-IWOC (804-4962)
E-mail: info@iwoc.org
Web Site: www.iwoc.org
Key Personnel
Pres: James Kepler *E-mail:* jkepler@adamspress.com
Monthly meetings, workshops & seminars dealing with the business aspects of independent writing. Writers' line job referral. Speakers' bureau.
Number of Members: 125
Publication(s): *Membership Directory* (annual, $10); *STET* (11 issues/yr, newsletter, $20/yr)

InScribe Christian Writers' Fellowship (ICWF)
PO Box 6201, Wetaskiwin, AB T9A 2E9, Canada
E-mail: inscribe.mail@gmail.com
Web Site: inscribe.org
Key Personnel
Pres: Ruth L Snyder *E-mail:* sun.beam3@yahoo.ca
Treas: Bobbi Junior *E-mail:* bobbi.junior@gmail.com
Secy: Sandi Somers *E-mail:* sksomers@shaw.ca
Founded: 1980 (as Alberta Christian Writers' Fellowship)
Stimulate, encourage & support Christians who write anywhere across Canada, to advance effective Christian writing & to promote the influence of all Christians who write.
Number of Members: 150
Meeting(s): Fall Conference, Annually last weekend in Sept
Publication(s): *FellowScript* (quarterly, newsletter, included with membership)

Institut de Cooperation pour l'Education des Adultes, see The Institute for Cooperation on Adult Education (Institut de Cooperation pour l'Education des Adultes-ICEA)

The Institute for Cooperation on Adult Education (Institut de Cooperation pour l'Education des Adultes-ICEA)
4321, ave Papineau, Montreal, QC H2H 1T3, Canada
Tel: 514-948-2044 *Fax:* 514-948-2046
E-mail: icae@icea.qc.ca
Web Site: www.icea.qc.ca
Key Personnel
Dir Gen: Daniel Baril *Tel:* 514-948-2044 ext 234 *E-mail:* dbaril@icea.qc.ca
Founded: 1946
Adult education lifelong learning.
Number of Members: 107
Publication(s): *ICAE News* (newsletter, free to membs)

Inter American Press Association (IAPA)
3511 NW 91 Ave, Miami, FL 33172
Tel: 305-634-2465 *Fax:* 305-635-2272
E-mail: info@sipiapa.org
Web Site: www.sipiapa.org
Key Personnel
Exec Dir: Ricardo Trotti *E-mail:* rtrotti@sipiapa.org
Founded: 1942
To guard freedom of speech & freedom of the press; to foster & protect the general & specific interests of the daily & periodical press of the Americas; to promote & maintain the dignity, rights & responsibilities of journalism; to encourage uniform standards of professional & business conduct; to exchange ideas & information which contribute to the cultural, material & technical development of the press; to foster a wider knowledge & greater interchange in support of the basic principles of a free society & individual liberty.
Number of Members: 1,300
Publication(s): *Hora de Cierre* (quarterly); *IAPA Annual Report* (annual); *IAPA News* (6 issues/yr); *Notisip* (quarterly)

International Association of Business Communicators (IABC)
155 Montgomery St, Suite 1210, San Francisco, CA 94104
Tel: 415-544-4700 *Toll Free Tel:* 800-776-4222 (US & CN) *Fax:* 415-544-4747
E-mail: leader_centre@iabc.com
Web Site: www.iabc.com
Key Personnel
Exec Dir: Carlos Fulcher *Tel:* 415-544-4706 *E-mail:* cfulcher@iabc.com
Founded: 1970
Communication association.
Number of Members: 14,000
2018 Meeting(s): World Conference, Palais des congres de Montreal, Montreal, QC, CN, June 3-6, 2018
Publication(s): *Communication World* (monthly)

International Association of Crime Writers Inc, North American Branch
243 Fifth Ave, Suite 537, New York, NY 10016
Tel: 212-243-8966 *Fax:* 815-361-1477
E-mail: info@crimewritersna.org
Web Site: www.crimewritersna.org
Key Personnel
Exec Dir: Mary A Frisque *E-mail:* mfrisque@igc.org
Pres: J Madison Davis
Secy-Treas: Jim Weikart
Secy: Steven Steinbock
Founded: 1987
Promote communication among crime writers worldwide & enhance awareness & encourage translations of the genre in the US & abroad.
Number of Members: 285
Publication(s): *Border Patrol* (quarterly, free to membs)

International Digital Enterprise Alliance, see IDEAlliance®

International Encyclopedia Society
3689 Campbell Ct, Yorktown Heights, NY 10598
Tel: 914-962-3287 *Fax:* 914-962-3287
Key Personnel
Pres & Ed: George Thomas Kurian *E-mail:* gtkurian@aol.com
Publication of books & journals; conferences; award of prizes.
Number of Members: 210

International Literacy Association (ILA)
800 Barksdale Rd, Newark, DE 19711-3204
Mailing Address: PO Box 8139, Newark, DE 19714-8139
Tel: 302-731-1600 *Toll Free Tel:* 800-336-7323 (US & CN) *Fax:* 302-731-1057
E-mail: customerservice@reading.org
Web Site: www.literacyworldwide.org; www.reading.org
Key Personnel
Exec Dir: Marcie Craig Post *E-mail:* mpost@reading.org
Founded: 1956
Conferences; publications, research, membership services; publications on reading & related topics; professional journals.
Number of Members: 60,000
2018 Meeting(s): Annual Conference, Austin, TX, July 20-23, 2018

International Society of Latino Authors
c/o Latino Literacy Now, 3445 Catalina Dr, Carlsbad, CA 92010
Tel: 760-434-1223 *Fax:* 760-434-7476
Key Personnel
COO: Kirk Whisler *E-mail:* kirk@whisler.com
Open to published & unpublished Latino authors or any author writing about the Latino experience/issues, all publishers & related service providers who support Latino literacy, nationally or internationally.

International Society of Weekly Newspaper Editors
Missouri Southern State University, 3950 E Newman Rd, Joplin, MO 64801-1595
Tel: 417-625-9736 *Fax:* 417-659-4445
Web Site: www.iswne.org
Key Personnel
Exec Dir: Dr Chad Stebbins *E-mail:* stebbins-c@mssu.edu
Founded: 1955

Help those in weekly press to improve standards of editorial writing & news reporting. Encourages strong independent editorial voices.
Number of Members: 300
2018 Meeting(s): ISWNE Conference, Lewis & Clark College, Portland, OR, July 11-15, 2018
Publication(s): *Grassroots Editor* (quarterly, $25/yr US & CN, $28 elsewhere)

International Standard Book Numbering (ISBN) US Agency, A Cambridge Information Group Co
Affiliate of R R Bowker LLC
630 Central Ave, New Providence, NJ 07974
Toll Free Tel: 877-310-7333 *Fax:* 908-219-0188
E-mail: isbn-san@bowker.com
Web Site: www.isbn.org
Coordinate implementation of the ISBN & SAN standards.
Number of Members: 120,000

The International Women's Writing Guild (IWWG)
5 Penn Plaza, 19th fl, PMB 19059, New York, NY 10001
Tel: 917-720-6959
E-mail: iwwgquestions@iwwg.org
Web Site: www.iwwg.org
Key Personnel
Exec Dir: Dixie King, PhD
Interim Opers Dir: Marj Hahne
Founded: 1976
Network for the empowerment of women through writing. Services include updated list of close to 35 literary agents, independent small presses & other writing services. Writing conferences & events annually, subscriptionn to the newsletter *Network*, regional clusters & opportunities for publications. IWWG is a supportive network open to any woman regardless of portfolio. As such, it has established a remarkable record of achievement in the publishing world as well as in circles where lifelong learning & personal information are valued for their own sake.
Number of Members: 5,000
Publication(s): *Network* (quarterly, free)

Investigative Reporters & Editors
Missouri School of Journalism, 141 Neff Annex, Columbia, MO 65211
Tel: 573-882-2042 *Fax:* 573-882-5431
E-mail: info@ire.org
Web Site: www.ire.org
Key Personnel
Exec Dir: Mark Horvit *Tel:* 573-882-1984 *E-mail:* mhorvit@ire.org
Founded: 1975
Nonprofit organization to improve the quality of investigative journalism.
Number of Members: 5,000
Publication(s): *The IRE Journal* (quarterly, free with membership, $70/yr nonmembs, $125/yr instns, $85/yr libs, $90/yr foreign nonmembs, $150/yr foreign instns)

Jewish Book Council
520 Eighth Ave, 4th fl, New York, NY 10018
Tel: 212-201-2920 *Fax:* 212-532-4952
E-mail: jbc@jewishbooks.org
Web Site: www.jewishbookcouncil.org
Key Personnel
Exec Dir: Naomi Firestone-Teeter
Prog Mgr, JBC Network & National Jewish Book Awards: Evie Saphire-Bernstein *E-mail:* evie@jewishbooks.org
Founded: 1925
Sponsors programs based on its conviction that books of Jewish interest are an invaluable contribution to the welfare of the Jewish people. Works to promote the reading, writing, publishing & distribution of worthy books of Jewish content. Honors excellence in all fields of Jewish literary endeavor with awards to writers & citations to publishers. Serves as a resource providing guidance, program tools & publications; acts as a clearinghouse for information on all aspects of Jewish literature & publishing in North America.
Publication(s): *Jewish Book Month Poster*; *Paper Brigade* (annually, journal, $25/yr)

The League of Canadian Poets
192 Spadina Ave, Suite 312, Toronto, ON M5T 2C2, Canada
Tel: 416-504-1657 *Fax:* 416-504-0096
Web Site: poets.ca
Key Personnel
Exec Dir: Lesley Fletcher *E-mail:* lesley@poets.ca
Asst Dir: Ingel Madrus *E-mail:* readings@poets.ca
Admin & Communs Coord: Barbara Erochina *E-mail:* admin@poets.ca
Founded: 1966
Promote Canadian poetry & poets.
Number of Members: 700
New Election: Annually in June
Publication(s): *Poetry Markets for Canadians* (online only, $20/yr public, $100/yr schools or libraries)

League of Vermont Writers
PO Box 5046, Burlington, VT 05402
Tel: 802-349-7475
E-mail: lvw@leaguevtwriters.org
Web Site: www.leagueofvermontwriters.org
Founded: 1929
Four meetings per year (Jan, April, July, Sept), reader & promotional services; occasional instructional seminars & workshops, publication of anthologies of members' work, writer's service.
Number of Members: 275
New Election: Annually in Jan
Publication(s): *League Lines* (quarterly, newsletter); *Vermont Voices Jubilee, 75th Anniversary Edition*; *Vermont Voices III, An Anthology*

Library Association of Alberta (LAA)
80 Baker Crescent NW, Calgary, AB T2L 1R4, Canada
Tel: 403-284-5818 *Toll Free Tel:* 877-522-5550 *Fax:* 403-282-6646
E-mail: info@laa.ca
Web Site: www.laa.ca
Key Personnel
Exec Dir/Conference Coord: Christine Sheppard
Founded: 1930
Nonprofit organization.
Number of Members: 625
2018 Meeting(s): Alberta Library Conference, Fairmont Jasper Park Lodge, Jasper, AB, CN, April 26-29, 2018
2019 Meeting(s): Alberta Library Conference, Fairmont Jasper Park Lodge, Jasper, AB, CN, April 25-28, 2019
2020 Meeting(s): Alberta Library Conference, Fairmont Jasper Park Lodge, Jasper, AB, CN, April 30-May 3, 2020

Library of American Broadcasting (LAB)
Unit of University of Maryland Libraries
University of Maryland, Hornbake Library, College Park, MD 20742
Tel: 301-405-9212
Web Site: www.lib.umd.edu/special/collections/massmedia/about-us
Key Personnel
Dir & Donor Rel: Chuck Howell *Tel:* 301-314-0401 *E-mail:* chuckh@umd.edu
Founded: 1972
Library devoted to history of public & commercial broadcasting including collections of audio & video recordings, books, pamphlets, periodicals, personal collections, oral histories, photographs, scripts & vertical files. Referral center to other sources of broadcast history.
Number of Members: 21
New Election: Annually in Nov
Publication(s): *Airwaves*

Linguistic Society of America
522 21 St NW, Suite 120, Washington, DC 20006-5012
Tel: 202-835-1714 *Fax:* 202-835-1717
E-mail: lsa@lsadc.org
Web Site: www.linguisticsociety.org
Key Personnel
Exec Dir: Alyson Reed *E-mail:* areed@lsadc.org
Dir, Communs: Brice Russ *E-mail:* bruss@lsadc.org
Dir, Membership & Meetings: David Robinson *E-mail:* drobinson@lsadc.org
Founded: 1924
Advancing the scientific study of language.
Number of Members: 5,000
New Election: Annually in Sept
Publication(s): *Language* (quarterly, free to membs, $140-190/yr organizations); *LSA Meeting Handbook* (annual, free, electronic)

The Literary Press Group of Canada
425 Adelaide St W, Suite 700, Toronto, ON M5V 3C1, Canada
Tel: 416-483-1321 *Fax:* 416-483-2510
Web Site: www.lpg.ca
Key Personnel
Exec Dir: Christen Thomas *Tel:* 416-483-1321 ext 1 *E-mail:* christen@lpg.ca
Busn Mgr: Barb Phillips *Tel:* 416-483-1321 ext 2 *E-mail:* barb@lpg.ca
Mktg Mgr: Tanya Snyder *Tel:* 416-483-1321 ext 3 *E-mail:* tsnyder@lpg.ca
Sales Mgr: Tan Light *Tel:* 416-483-1321 ext 4 *E-mail:* sales@lpg.ca
National trade association providing cooperative sales, marketing, advertising & publicity services to members.
Number of Members: 52
New Election: Annually in May

Literary Translators' Association of Canada
Concordia University, LB 601, 1455 De Maisonneuve W, Montreal, QC H3G 1M8, Canada
Tel: 514-848-2424 (ext 8702)
E-mail: info@attlc-ltac.org
Web Site: www.attlc-ltac.org
Key Personnel
Pres: Madeleine Stratford
Founded: 1975
Promote & protect interests of literary translators in Canada; occasional meetings with local universities & occasional workshops, lobby for funding, organize readings & other events.
Number of Members: 150
New Election: Annually in June

Livestock Publications Council
200 W Exchange Ave, Fort Worth, TX 76164
Tel: 817-336-1130 *Fax:* 817-232-4820
Web Site: www.livestockpublications.com
Key Personnel
Exec Dir: Diane E Johnson *E-mail:* diane@livestockpublications.com
Founded: 1974
A nonprofit organization designed to serve the livestock communications industry.
Number of Members: 195
New Election: Annually in July
Publication(s): *Actiongram* (monthly, newsletter)

Livres Canada Books
One Nicholas, Suite 504, Ottawa, ON K1N 7B7, Canada
Tel: 613-562-2324 *Fax:* 613-562-2329

E-mail: info@livrescanadabooks.com
Web Site: www.livrescanadabooks.com
Key Personnel
Exec Dir: Francois Charette *Tel:* 613-562-2324 ext 223 *E-mail:* fcharette@livrescanadabooks.com
Mgr, Digital Publg & Intl Mkts: Gabrielle Etcheverry *Tel:* 613-562-2324 ext 229 *E-mail:* getcheverry@livrescanadabooks.com
Mgr, Progs: Christy Doucet *Tel:* 613-562-2324 ext 225 *E-mail:* cdoucet@livrescanadabooks.com
As the only national trade association that connects English & French language publishers across Canada, Livres Canada Books has a mandate to foster Canadian publishers' export sales. Coordinates Canadian publishers' presence at international book fairs, promotes Canadian titles abroad through its catalogues, exhibits & web site, provides market intelligence & acts as a liaison between Canadian publishers & foreign buyers. Also assists the industry by providing funding assistance for Canadian publishers' international marketing strategies & activities.
Publication(s): *Canadian Studies Collection* (annual, free); *Rights Canada Catalogue* (annual, free)

Magazine Publishers of America, see MPA - The Association of Magazine Media

Magazines Canada (MC)
425 Adelaide St W, Suite 700, Toronto, ON M5V 3C1, Canada
Tel: 416-504-0274 *Fax:* 416-504-0437
E-mail: info@magazinescanada.ca
Web Site: www.magazinescanada.ca/development/magnet
Key Personnel
CEO: Mark Jamison *Tel:* 416-504-0274 ext 223 *E-mail:* mjamison@magazinescanada.ca
Gen Mgr & Publr: Barbara Zatyko *Tel:* 416-504-0274 ext 222 *E-mail:* bzatyko@magazinescanada.ca
Mgr, Communs: Brianne DiAngelo *Tel:* 416-504-0274 ext 227 *E-mail:* bdiangelo@magazinescanada.ca
Founded: 1973
Distribution, promotion, professional development & lobbying for Canadian magazines.
Number of Members: 350
2018 Meeting(s): MagNet, The Courtyard Downtown Toronto, 475 Yonge St, Toronto, ON, CN, April 23-28, 2018
Publication(s): *Small Magazine Advertising* ($25 membs); *Small Magazine Business* ($25 membs); *Small Magazine Circulation* ($25 membs); *Small Magazine Editorial* ($25 membs); *Small Magazine Human Resources* ($35 membs)

Maine Writers & Publishers Alliance
314 Forest Ave, Rm 318, Portland, ME 04101
Tel: 207-228-8263 *Fax:* 207-228-8150
E-mail: info@mainewriters.org
Web Site: mainewriters.org
Key Personnel
Exec Dir: Joshua Bodwell *E-mail:* director@mainewriters.org
Asst Dir: Stephen E Abbott *E-mail:* abbott@mainewriters.org
Founded: 1975
Writing retreats, writing workshops, information services.
Number of Members: 1,600
Publication(s): *Ex Libris Maine* (monthly, newsletter, membs, supporters & parenting organizations); *The Peavey* (weekly, newsletter, membs only)

Manitoba Arts Council
525-93 Lombard Ave, Winnipeg, MB R3B 3B1, Canada
Tel: 204-945-2237 *Toll Free Tel:* 866-994-2787 *Fax:* 204-945-5925
E-mail: info@artscouncil.mb.ca
Web Site: artscouncil.mb.ca
Key Personnel
Exec Dir: Douglas Riske *Tel:* 204-945-2239 *E-mail:* driske@artscouncil.mb.ca
Assoc Dir, Policy, Planning & Partnerships: Patricia Sanders *Tel:* 204-945-0422 *E-mail:* psanders@artscouncil.mb.ca
Communs Mgr: Leanne Foley *Tel:* 204-945-0646 *E-mail:* lfoley@artscouncil.mb.ca
Founded: 1965
Provincial arts council that funds professional Manitoban artists & arts organizations.

The Manitoba Writers' Guild Inc
218-100 Arthur St, Winnipeg, MB R3B 1H3, Canada
Tel: 204-944-8013
E-mail: info@mbwriter.mb.ca
Web Site: www.mbwriter.mb.ca
Key Personnel
Exec Dir: Carolyn Gray
Founded: 1981
Provides professional & personal support to Manitoba writers throughout their writing lives. Membership $60/yr regular, $30/yr students & low income.
Number of Members: 550

Media Alliance
2830 20 St, Suite 102, San Francisco, CA 94110
Tel: 415-746-9475
E-mail: information@media-alliance.org
Web Site: www.media-alliance.org
Key Personnel
Exec Dir: Tracy Rosenberg *Tel:* 510-684-6853 (cell) *E-mail:* tracy@media-alliance.org
Info Coord: Phavia Kujichagulia *E-mail:* jobfile@media-alliance.org
Educational programs in editing, writing & journalism skills. Media relations & advocacy & hands-on computer skills. Job listings & resources, media watchdog activities.
Number of Members: 3,200
Publication(s): *Media How-to Guide* (book, $15 membs, $20 nonmembs)

Media Coalition Inc
19 Fulton St, Suite 407, New York, NY 10038
Tel: 212-587-4025 *Fax:* 212-587-2436
E-mail: info@mediacoalition.org
Web Site: mediacoalition.org
Key Personnel
Exec Dir: David Horowitz *Tel:* 212-587-4025 ext 3 *E-mail:* horowitz@mediacoalition.org
Communs Coord: Kris Anne Bonifacio
Founded: 1973
Trade association, defends first amendment rights to produce & distribute constitutionally-protected books, magazines, recordings, home video & video games.
Number of Members: 12
Publication(s): *Sense and Censorship: The Vanity of Bonfires* (free online); *Shooting the Messenger: Why Censorship Won't Stop Violence* (free online)

The Melville Society
Johns Hopkins University Press, PO Box 19966, Baltimore, MD 21211-0966
Web Site: melvillesociety.org
Key Personnel
Pres: Geoffrey Sanborn
Treas: Steven Olsen-Smith
Ed, Leviathan: Samuel Otter
Exec Secy: Tony McGowan
Annual & special meetings & publications. Conferences in association with the Modern Language Association annual convention & American Literature Association annual convention.
Number of Members: 760
New Election: Annually in Spring
Publication(s): *Leviathan: A Journal of Melville Studies* (3 issues/yr, free with membership)

Metropolitan Lithographers Association Inc
c/o Pictorial Offset, 111 Amor Ave, Carlstadt, NJ 07072
Tel: 201-935-7100
Key Personnel
Pres: Gary Samuels
Multiemployer lithographic trade association active in collective bargaining, labor relations, management educational programs & public relations.
Number of Members: 7
New Election: Annually in Jan

Midwest Independent Booksellers Association (MIBA)
2355 Louisiana Ave N, Suite A, Golden Valley, MN 55427-3646
Tel: 763-544-2993 *Toll Free Tel:* 800-784-7522 *Fax:* 612-354-5728
E-mail: info@midwestbooksellers.org
Web Site: midwestbooksellers.org
Key Personnel
Exec Dir: Carrie Obry *E-mail:* carrie@midwestbooksellers.org
Founded: 1981
Association of independent bookstores in Midwest: Illinois, Iowa, Kansas, Minnesota, Missouri, Nebraska, North Dakota, South Dakota & Wisconsin. Annual trade show & meeting. Book catalog for member stores to use with consumers. Sponsors educational programs for booksellers, Spring meeting, Midwest Booksellers' Choice Awards & "Midwest Connections" regional marketing program.
Number of Members: 500
Publication(s): *Membership Directory* (online); *MIBA Trade Show Program* (annual); *Midwest Booksellers Association Winter Catalog* (annual)

Midwest Travel Writers Association
902 S Randall Rd, Suite C311, St Charles, IL 60174
Toll Free Tel: 888-551-8184
E-mail: admin@mtwa.org
Web Site: www.mtwa.org
Key Personnel
Admin Asst: Patti Ciccone
Founded: 1951
To promote & practice travel writing as a profession. Subjects addressed include: food, wine, music, dance, theater, photography, sports, recreation, travel & resorts.
Number of Members: 100
Publication(s): *MTWA Directory* (annual, $100 print, $150 print & electronic)

Miniature Book Society Inc
702 Rosecrans St, San Diego, CA 92106-3013
Tel: 619-226-4441 *Fax:* 619-226-4441
E-mail: minibook@cox.net
Web Site: www.mbs.org
Key Personnel
Pres: Stephen Byrne
Secy: Jim Brogan
Founded: 1983
Number of Members: 302
Publication(s): *Miniature Book Society Newsletter* (3 issues/yr, newsletter, $40/yr)
Membership(s): Fellowship of American Bibliophilic Societies

Modern Language Association of America (MLA)
85 Broad St, Suite 500, New York, NY 10004-2434
SAN: 202-6422
Tel: 646-576-5000 *Fax:* 646-458-0030
E-mail: convention@mla.org
Web Site: www.mla.org
Key Personnel
Exec Dir: Paula Krebs
Founded: 1883
Convention; employment information, professional organization, scholarly publications.
Number of Members: 30,000
2018 Meeting(s): Annual Convention, New York Hilton Midtown, Sheraton New York Times Square & New York Marriott Marquis, New York, NY, Jan 4-7, 2018
2019 Meeting(s): Annual Convention, Chicago, IL, Jan 3-6, 2019
2020 Meeting(s): Annual Convention, Seattle, WA, Jan 9-12, 2020
Publication(s): *MLA International Bibliography* (annual, inquire); *MLA Newsletter* (quarterly, free to membs); *PMLA* (5 issues/yr, $12/issue); *Profession* (annual, journal, free to membs, $7.50 nonmembs, online)

Motion Picture Association of America Inc (MPAA)
1600 "I" St NW, Washington, DC 20006
Tel: 202-293-1966 *Fax:* 202-296-7410
E-mail: contactus@mpaa.org
Web Site: www.mpaa.org
Key Personnel
Chmn & CEO: Christopher Dodd
VP: Patrick Kilcur
VP, Corp Communs: Kate Bedingfield *E-mail:* kate_bedingfield@mpaa.org
Founded: 1922
Trade association for the major motion picture producers & distributors. Administer motion picture industry's system of self-regulation & are spokespeople for production & distribution of motion pictures for theatrical, home video & TV use in the USA.
Number of Members: 60
Branch Office(s)
15301 Ventura Blvd, Bldg E, Sherman Oaks, CA 91403 *Tel:* 818-995-6600 *Fax:* 818-285-4403
500 Mamaroneck Ave, Suite 403, Harrison, NY 10528 *Tel:* 914-333-8892 *Fax:* 914-333-7541
1425 Greenway Dr, Suite 270, Irving, TX 75038 *Tel:* 972-756-9078 *Fax:* 972-756-9402
55 Saint Clair Ave W, Suite 210, Toronto, ON M4V 2Y7, Canada *Tel:* 416-961-1888 *Fax:* 416-968-1016 *E-mail:* info@mpa-canada.org *Web Site:* www.mpa-canada.org
FSA 74, Driver Ave, Moore Park, NSW 2021, Australia
Avenue des Arts 46, 8th fl, 1000 Brussels, Belgium *Tel:* (02) 778 27 11 *Fax:* (02) 778 27 00
Rua Jeronimo da Veiga, 45, Conj 121/122, 12th fl, Jardim Europa, 04536-000 Sao Paulo-SP, Brazil *Tel:* (011) 3667-2080 *Web Site:* www.mpaal.org.br
Rm 508, No 16 Bldg, Jianwai SOHO, 39 Dongsanhuan Zhonglu Rd, Beijing 100022, China
215 Atrium, A 206, Chakala, Andheri-Kurla Rd, Andheri (East), Mumbai 400 059, India
Nihon Seimei Ichibancho Bldg, 6F 23-3, Inchiben-Cho, Chiyoda-ku, Tokyo 102-0082, Japan
Lafontaine No 42, Chapultepec Polanco, 11560 Mexico, DF, Mexico *Tel:* (0155) 5280-6878; (0155) 5281-6090 (main)
No 04-07 Central Mall, No 1 Magazine Rd, Singapore 059567, Singapore *Tel:* 6253 1033 *Fax:* 6255 1838 *Web Site:* www.mpa-i.org
1007, 10th fl, Monaco Bldg, 1316-5 Seocho-dong, Seocho-gu, Seoul 137-856, South Korea

MPA - The Association of Magazine Media
757 Third Ave, 11th fl, New York, NY 10012
Tel: 212-872-3700 *Fax:* 212-888-4217
Web Site: www.magazine.org
Key Personnel
Pres & CEO: Linda Thomas Brooks *Tel:* 212-872-3710
VP, Creative Servs & Events: Patty Bogie *Tel:* 212-872-3729 *E-mail:* pbogie@magazine.org
Founded: 1919
Promote the value of magazines.
Number of Members: 265
Branch Office(s)
1211 Connecticut Ave NW, Washington, DC 20036, EVP, Govt Aff: James Cregan *Tel:* 202-296-7277 *Fax:* 202-296-0343 *E-mail:* jcregan@magazine.org

Music Publishers Association (MPA)
243 Fifth Ave, Suite 236, New York, NY 10016
Tel: 212-327-4044
E-mail: admin@mpa.org
Web Site: www.mpa.org
Founded: 1895
Foster trade & commerce in the interest of those in the music publishing business & encourage understanding of & compliance with the copyright law to protect musical works against piracies & infringements.
Number of Members: 300
New Election: Annually, first week of June

Mystery Writers of America (MWA)
1140 Broadway, Suite 1507, New York, NY 10001
Tel: 212-888-8171
E-mail: mwa@mysterywriters.org
Web Site: www.mysterywriters.org
Key Personnel
Admin Dir: Margery Flax
Founded: 1945
The premier organization for mystery writers & other professionals in the mystery field. MWA watches developments in legislation & tax laws, sponsors symposia & mystery conferences, presents the Edgar Awards® & provides information for mystery writers. Membership open to published authors, editors, screenwriters & other professionals in the field.
Number of Members: 3,000
Publication(s): *Mystery Writers of American Anthology*; *The Third Degree* (10 issues/yr, free to membs)

NAB, see National Association of Broadcasters (NAB)

NASW, see National Association of Science Writers (NASW)

National Association for Printing Leadership (NAPL), see Epicomm

National Association of Black Journalists (NABJ)
1100 Knight Hall, Suite 3100, College Park, MD 20742
Tel: 301-405-0248 *Fax:* 301-314-1714
E-mail: nabj@nabj.org
Web Site: www.nabj.org
Key Personnel
Exec Dir: Darryl R Matthews, Sr *E-mail:* drmatthews@nabj.org
Devt Dir: Denise Brooking *Tel:* 301-405-6986 *E-mail:* dbrooking@nabj.org
Fin Mgr: Nathaniel Chambers *Tel:* 301-405-0532 *E-mail:* nchambers@nabj.org
Membership Mgr: Veronique Dodson *Tel:* 301-405-0554 *E-mail:* vdodson@nabj.org
Prog Coord: Lisa Waldschmitt *Tel:* 301-405-2592 *E-mail:* lwaldschmitt@nabj.org
Founded: 1975
Organization of journalists, students & media-related professionals that provides quality programs & services to & advocates on behalf of black journalists worldwide.
Number of Members: 3,300
New Election: Biennially, odd-numbered yrs
2018 Meeting(s): NABJ Annual Convention & Career Fair, Detroit Marriott at the Renaissance Center, Detroit, MI, Aug 1-5, 2018
Publication(s): *NABJ Journal* (quarterly, journal)

National Association of Book Entrepreneurs (NABE)
PO Box 606, Cottage Grove, OR 97424
Tel: 541-942-7455
E-mail: nabe@bookmarketingprofits.com
Web Site: www.bookmarketingprofits.com
Key Personnel
Exec Dir: Al Galasso
Promo Dir: Russ Von Hoelscher
Assoc Dir: Ingrid Crawford
Founded: 1980
International book marketing organization of independent publishers & mail order entrepreneurs. Activities include NABE Combined Book Exhibits at national & regional conventions serving the book, educational, gift & business trade. Publishers Preview Mail Order Program, National Press Release, Electronic Marketing plus complete publisher consultation services for printing, promoting & marketing books.
Number of Members: 1,000
Publication(s): *Book Dealers World* (quarterly, circ 10,000, $5/sample, $50/yr & $90/semiannual membership)

National Association of Broadcasters (NAB)
1771 "N" St NW, Washington, DC 20036
Tel: 202-429-5300
E-mail: nab@nab.org
Web Site: www.nab.org
Key Personnel
CEO & Pres: Gordon H Smith
EVP, Conventions & Busn Opers: Mr Chris Brown
EVP, Mktg & Communs: Michelle Lehman *Tel:* 202-429-5444 *E-mail:* mlehman@nab.org
Trade association for radio & television stations. Provide products, publications (over 130) & other services related to broadcasting.
Number of Members: 9,000
2018 Meeting(s): NAB Show®, Las Vegas Convention Center, 3150 Paradise Rd, Las Vegas, NV, April 7-12, 2018

National Association of College Stores (NACS)
500 E Lorain St, Oberlin, OH 44074
Tel: 440-775-7777 *Toll Free Tel:* 800-622-7498 *Fax:* 440-775-4769
Web Site: www.nacs.org
Key Personnel
Dir of Expositions: Mary Adler-Kozak *Tel:* 800-622-7498 ext 2265 *E-mail:* madler-kozak@nacs.org
Dir, Meetings: Jodie Wilmot *Tel:* 800-622-7498 ext 2272 *E-mail:* jwilmot@nacs.org
Exhibit Sales & Serv Rep: Linda Vargo *Tel:* 800-622-7498 ext 2302 *E-mail:* lvargo@nacs.org
Trade association for college store industry.
Number of Members: 4,000
2018 Meeting(s): CAMEX (Campus Market Expo), Kay Bailey Hutchison Convention Center, Dallas, TX, March 2-6, 2018
2019 Meeting(s): CAMEX (Campus Market Expo), Henry B Gonzalez Convention Center, San Antonio, TX, Feb 22-26, 2019
Publication(s): *Campus Marketplace* (weekly, newsletter, online); *The College Store* (6 issues/yr, magazine); *Directory of Colleges &*

College Stores (annual); *The Torchlight* (semi-annual, newsletter)
Membership(s): BISG

National Association of Hispanic Publications Inc (NAHP)
529 14 St NW, Suite 1126, Washington, DC 20045
Tel: 202-662-7250
Web Site: www.nahp.org
Key Personnel
Pres: Eddie Escobedo, Jr *Tel:* 702-649-8553 *E-mail:* eddiejr.escobedo@yahoo.com
VP, Membership: Martha Montoya *Tel:* 714-366-3225 (cell) *E-mail:* martha@elmundous.com
Founded: 1982
Promote Hispanic media.
Number of Members: 100
Publication(s): *NAHP Newsletter* (quarterly)
Membership(s): Hispanic Association on Corporate Responsibility; National Hispanic Leadership Agenda; United States Hispanic Chamber of Commerce

National Association of Independent Publishers Representatives
111 E 14 St, PMB 157, New York, NY 10003
Tel: 267-546-6561 *Toll Free Tel:* 888-624-7779
Web Site: naipr.org
Key Personnel
Exec Dir: Robert Rooney *E-mail:* robert.rooney@naipr.org
Founded: 1990
Information & promotion of commission selling for book publishers.
Seasonal offering of Publishers Frontlist trade catalogs.
Number of Members: 850
Publication(s): *The Call Report*™ (monthly, newsletter, free); *Marketing Advice for the Very Small or Self-Publishers* (newsletter, free); *NAIPR News Online* (monthly, newsletter, free); *Selling on Commission* (free)

National Association of Printing Ink Manufacturers (NAPIM)
15 Technology Pkwy S, Peachtree Corners, GA 30092
Tel: 770-209-7289 *Fax:* 678-680-4920; 770-209-7217
E-mail: napim@napim.org
Web Site: www.napim.org
Key Personnel
Exec Dir: John Copeland *Tel:* 815-979-2341 *E-mail:* jcopeland@napim.org
Dir, Regulatory Aff & Technol: George Fuchs *Tel:* 770-209-7291 *E-mail:* gfuchs@napim.org
Memb Rel Mgr: Ben Hopper *E-mail:* bhopper@napim.org
Founded: 1916
Trade association representing the printing ink industry & providing information & assistance to members to better manage their business.
Number of Members: 82
2018 Meeting(s): Annual Convention, Fairmont Sonoma Mission Inn & Spa, Sonoma, CA, April 20-23, 2018
Publication(s): *Introduction to Printing Ink* ($6 membs, $10 nonmembs); *Printing Ink Handbook, 6th ed* ($90 membs, $150 nonmembs); *Raw Materials Data Handbook, 2nd ed* ($200 membs, $400 nonmembs)

National Association of Quick Printers (NAQP), see Epicomm

National Association of Real Estate Editors (NAREE)
1003 NW Sixth Terr, Boca Raton, FL 33486-3455
Tel: 561-391-3599 *Fax:* 561-391-0099
Web Site: www.naree.org
Key Personnel
Pres: Daniel Taub
Exec Dir: Mary Doyle-Kimball *E-mail:* madkimba@aol.com
Contact: David Kimball *E-mail:* dakimball@aol.com
Founded: 1929
Nonprofit professional association of writers Journalism Contest & seminars in winter, spring & fall; memberships active for journalists & associate for communications professionals. Bruss Real Estate Book Awards annual competition.
Number of Members: 650
2018 Meeting(s): NAREE Winter Meeting, Orange County Convention Center, Orlando, FL, Jan 9-11, 2018; Spring Real Estate Journalism Conference, Las Vegas, NV, June 13-16, 2018
Publication(s): *NAREE Directory* (annual, directory, free to membs); *NAREE News* (quarterly, free to membs); *Spring Conference Book* (free to membs)

National Association of Science Writers (NASW)
PO Box 7905, Berkeley, CA 94707
Tel: 510-647-9500
Web Site: www.nasw.org
Key Personnel
Exec Dir: Tinsley Davis *E-mail:* director@nasw.org
Founded: 1934
Professional development organization for science writers.
Number of Members: 2,200
New Election: Biennially, even-numbered yrs
Meeting(s): World Conference of Science Journalists
Publication(s): *ScienceWriters* (quarterly, magazine, free for membs)
Membership(s): World Federation of Science Journalists

National Cartoonists Society (NCS)
PO Box 592927, Orlando, FL 32859-2927
Tel: 407-994-6703 *Fax:* 407-442-0786
E-mail: info@reuben.org
Web Site: www.reuben.org
Key Personnel
Pres: Bill Morrison
Exec Dir: Phil Pyster *E-mail:* phil@crowsegal.com
Founded: 1946
Fraternal Organization of Cartoonists.
Number of Members: 500
Publication(s): *The Cartoonist*

National Coalition Against Censorship (NCAC)
19 Fulton St, Suite 407, New York, NY 10038
Tel: 212-807-6222 *Fax:* 212-807-6245
E-mail: ncac@ncac.org
Web Site: www.ncac.org
Key Personnel
Exec Dir: Joan E Bertin
Communs Dir: Michael O'Neil
Dir, Progs: Svetlana Mintcheva
Founded: 1974
Promote & defend free speech, inquiry & expression; monitor & publicize censorship incidents; sponsor public programs; assist in censorship controversies through advice, materials, contacts with local organizations & individuals. Membership is comprised of 50 national participating organizations. Reprints & informational materials available upon request.
Publication(s): *Censorship News* (semiannual, $30/yr)

National Coalition for Literacy (NCL)
PO Box 2932, Washington, DC 20013-2932
E-mail: ncl@ncladvocacy.org
Web Site: www.national-coalition-literacy.org
Key Personnel
Pres: Marty Finsterbusch *Tel:* 484-443-8457
Founded: 1981
A member organization made up of major service, research & policy organizations in adult education, family literacy & English language acquisition. NCL's mission is to advance adult education, family literacy & English language acquisition in the US - from the most basic skills proficiency level across a continuum of services including the transition into postsecondary education & job training.
Number of Members: 30
Publication(s): *NCL Update* (monthly, newsletter, free)

National Communication Association
1765 "N" St NW, Washington, DC 20036
Tel: 202-464-4622 *Fax:* 202-464-4600
E-mail: inbox@natcom.org
Web Site: www.natcom.org
Key Personnel
COO: Mark Fernando *Tel:* 202-534-1105 *E-mail:* mfernando@natcom.org
Exec Dir: Paaige K Turner, PhD *Tel:* 202-534-1120 *E-mail:* pturner@natcom.org
Founded: 1914
To promote effective & ethical communication.
Number of Members: 7,500
2018 Meeting(s): Annual Convention, Salt Palace Convention Center, Salt Lake City, UT, Nov 8-11, 2018
2019 Meeting(s): Annual Convention, Baltimore Convention Center, Baltimore, MD, Nov 14-17, 2019
2020 Meeting(s): Annual Convention, JW Marriott Indianapolis/Indianapolis Marriott Downtown, Indianapolis, IN, Nov 19-22, 2020
2021 Meeting(s): Annual Convention, Washington State Convention Center, Seattle, WA, Nov 18-21, 2021
Publication(s): *Communication and Critical/Cultural Studies*; *Communication Education* (quarterly); *Communication Monographs* (quarterly, journal); *Communication Teacher* (quarterly); *Critical Studies in Media Communication* (journal); *First Amendment Studies*; *Journal of Applied Communication Research*; *Journal of International & Intercultural Communication*; *The Quarterly Journal of Speech*; *Review of Communication*; *Text & Performance Quarterly* (journal)

National Council of Teachers of English (NCTE)
1111 W Kenyon Rd, Urbana, IL 61801-1096
Tel: 217-328-3870 *Toll Free Tel:* 877-369-6283 (cust serv) *Fax:* 217-328-9645
E-mail: public_info@ncte.org
Web Site: www.ncte.org
Key Personnel
Exec Dir: Emily Kirkpatrick *Tel:* 217-278-3601
Asst to Exec Dir: Lori Bianchini *Tel:* 217-278-3611 *Fax:* 217-328-0977 *E-mail:* lbianchini@ncte.org
Perms Coord: Kurt Austin *Tel:* 217-278-3619 *E-mail:* permissions@ncte.org
Founded: 1911
Focus on the major concerns of teachers of English & the language arts; offer teaching aids, advice, direction & guidance for members. Publish educational books, journals, pamphlets, research reports & position papers for all levels of the English teaching profession. Hold annual convention for members in November; sponsor conferences & workshops.
Number of Members: 25,000
2018 Meeting(s): NCTE Annual Convention, Houston, TX, Nov 15-18, 2018
Publication(s): *College Composition & Communication* (quarterly, journal, $75/yr, includes NCTE & CCCC membership); *College English* (6 times/yr, journal, $75/yr, includes NCTE

membership); *English Education* (quarterly, journal, $75/yr, includes NCTE & CEE membership); *English Journal* (6 times/yr, $75/yr, includes NCTE membership); *English Leadership Quarterly* (journal, $75/yr, includes NCTE & CEL membership); *Language Arts* (6 times/yr, journal, $75/yr, includes NCTE membership); *Research in the Teaching of English* (quarterly, journal, $75/yr, includes NCTE membership); *Talking Points* (semiannual, journal, $75/yr, includes NCTE & WLU membership); *Teaching English in the Two-Year College* (quarterly, journal, $75/yr, includes NCTE & TYCA membership); *Voices from the Middle* (quarterly, journal, $75/yr, includes NCTE membership)

National Education Association (NEA)
1201 16 St NW, Washington, DC 20036-3290
Tel: 202-833-4000 *Fax:* 202-822-7974
Web Site: www.nea.org
Key Personnel
Pres: Lily Eskelsen Garcia
VP: Becky Pringle
Secy/Treas: Princess R Moss
Exec Dir: John C Stocks
Founded: 1857
Professional employee organization for over 3 million educators, with affiliates in every state & in more than 14,000 communities committed to advancing the cause of public education.
Number of Members: 3,200,000
Publication(s): *Higher Education Advocate* (6 issues/yr, newsletter); *The NEA Almanac of Higher Education* (annual); *NEA Today* (quarterly, magazine); *NEA Today for NEA-Retired Members* (quarterly, magazine); *This Active Life* (6 issues/yr, magazine); *Thought & Action* (annual, journal); *Tomorrow's Teachers* (annual, magazine)

National Federation of Advanced Information Services (NFAIS)
801 Compass Way, Suite 201, Annapolis, MD 21401
Tel: 443-221-2980 *Fax:* 443-221-2981
E-mail: nfais@nfais.org
Web Site: www.nfais.org
Key Personnel
Exec Dir: Marcie Granahan *Tel:* 443-221-2980 ext 101 *E-mail:* mgranahan@nfais.org
Dir, Mktg & Communs: Barbara Meyers Ford *Tel:* 443-221-2980 ext 103 *E-mail:* bmeyersford@nfais.org
Dir, Prof Devt: Nancy Blair-DeLeon
Sponsors research; carries out a comprehensive program of continuing education; issues pertinent publications in all areas of documentation & information dissemination.
Number of Members: 60
Publication(s): *Membership Directory* (directory, online only); *NFAIS E Notes* (online only)
Membership(s): CENDI; ICSTI; National Information Standards Organization

National Federation of Press Women Inc (NFPW)
PO Box 3007, Mechanicsville, VA 23116-0026
Tel: 703-237-9804 *Fax:* 703-237-9808
E-mail: presswomen@aol.com
Web Site: www.nfpw.org
Key Personnel
Off Mgr: Carol Pierce
Founded: 1936
Organization of professional women & men pursuing careers across the communications spectrum.
Number of Members: 2,000
New Election: Annually in Sept
2018 Meeting(s): Communications Conference, Bethlehem, PA, Sept 6-8, 2018
Publication(s): *Agenda* (quarterly)

National Freedom of Information Coalition (NFOIC)
Affiliate of Missouri School of Journalism
101C Reynolds Journalism Institute, Columbia, MO 65211
Tel: 573-882-4856
Web Site: nfoic.org
Key Personnel
Prog Coord: Melissa MacGowan *Tel:* 573-882-3229 *E-mail:* macgowanm@missouri.edu
Founded: 1989 (as National Freedom of Information Assembly)
Nonpartisan alliance of state & regional affiliates promoting collaboration, education & advocacy for open government; transparency & freedom of information.
Number of Members: 62
Publication(s): *The FOI Advocate: The NFOIC News Blog*; *FOI InSight* (newsletter)

National Information Standards Organization (NISO)
3600 Clipper Mill Rd, Suite 302, Baltimore, MD 21211
Tel: 301-654-2512 *Fax:* 410-685-5278
E-mail: nisohq@niso.org
Web Site: www.niso.org
Key Personnel
Exec Dir: Todd Carpenter *E-mail:* tcarpenter@niso.org
Assoc Dir: Nettie Lagace *E-mail:* nlagace@niso.org
Memb Servs & Engagement Mgr: DeVonne Parks *E-mail:* dparks@niso.org
Founded: 1939
Developing, maintaining & publishing technical standards used by libraries, information services & publishers. Accredited by the American National Standards Institute.
Number of Members: 90
Publication(s): *Information Standards Quarterly (ISQ)* (online)

National League of American Pen Women Inc
The Pen Arts Bldg & Arts Museum, 1300 17 St NW, Washington, DC 20036-1973
Tel: 202-785-1997 *Fax:* 202-452-8868
E-mail: contact@nlapw.org
Web Site: www.nlapw.org
Key Personnel
Pres: Virginia Franklin Campbell
Founded: 1897
Scholarships, letters, art & music workshops, awards & prizes. Must send SASE for information.
Number of Members: 3,500
Publication(s): *The Pen Woman* (quarterly, magazine, $25/yr, free to membs)

National Music Publishers' Association (NMPA)
975 "F" St NW, Suite 315, Washington, DC 20004
Tel: 202-393-6672 *Fax:* 202-393-6673
E-mail: pr@nmpa.org
Web Site: www.nmpa.org
Key Personnel
CEO & Pres: David M Israelite
Founded: 1917
Trade association of American Music Publishers.
Number of Members: 3,000
Branch Office(s)
The Harry Fox Agency (HFA), 40 Wall St, 6th fl, New York, NY 10005-1344 *Tel:* 212-834-0100 *Fax:* 646-487-6779 *Web Site:* www.harryfox.com

National Newspaper Association
900 Community Dr, Springfield, IL 62703-5180
Tel: 217-241-1400 *Fax:* 217-241-1301
E-mail: nna@nna.org
Web Site: nnaweb.org
Key Personnel
Assoc Dir: Tony Scott *Tel:* 217-241-1400 ext 230 *E-mail:* tony@nna.org
Founded: 1885
Trade association with a mission to protect, promote & enhance America's community newspapers.
Number of Members: 2,500
2018 Meeting(s): Annual Convention & Trade Show, Norfolk Waterside Marriott, 235 E Main St, Norfolk, VA, Sept 27-29, 2018
Publication(s): *Publishers Auxiliary* (monthly, online)

National Newspaper Publishers Association (NNPA)
1816 12 St NW, Washington, DC 20009
Tel: 202-588-8764 *Fax:* 202-588-8960
E-mail: info@nnpa.org
Web Site: www.nnpa.org; www.blackpressusa.com
Key Personnel
Chmn: Cloves C Cambell, Jr
CEO & Pres: Bill Tompkins
Founded: 1941 (as the National Negro Publishers Association)
Federation of more than 200 black community newspapers from across the US.
Number of Members: 200

National Press Club (NPC)
529 14 St NW, 13th fl, Washington, DC 20045
Tel: 202-662-7500 *Fax:* 202-662-7569
E-mail: infocenter@npcpress.org
Web Site: www.press.org
Key Personnel
Club Pres: Myron Belkind
Lib Dir: Julie Schoo *E-mail:* jschoo@press.org
Gen Mgr: William McCarren
Founded: 1908
Private professional organization for journalists. Sponsors workshops, rap sessions with authors, press forums, morning newsmakers, famous speaker luncheons; awards prizes for consumer journalism, environmental reporting; freedom of the press; diplomatic writing, Washington coverage & newsletters; book & art exhibits; computerized reference library; annual Book Fair & Authors' Night.
Number of Members: 4,000
Publication(s): *The Record* (weekly)

National Press Club of Canada Foundation Inc
17 York St, Suite 201, Ottawa, ON K1N 9J6, Canada
E-mail: info@pressclubcanada.ca
Web Site: pressclubcanada.ca
Key Personnel
Pres: James Baxter
Dir: Phil Gibson; Lois Siegel; Hugh Winsor
Founded: 1928
Not-for-profit association for reporters, journalists & media-related people; organizes small & large events of interest to the media community in & around Ottawa's political circles; awards annual scholarships for journalism students.
Number of Members: 50

National Press Foundation
1211 Connecticut Ave NW, Suite 310, Washington, DC 20036
Tel: 202-663-7280
Web Site: nationalpress.org
Key Personnel
COO & Pres: Bob Meyers *E-mail:* bob@nationalpress.org
Dir, Opers: Jessica Jean-Francois *E-mail:* jessica@nationalpress.org
Dir, Progs: Linda Topping Streitfeld *E-mail:* linda@nationalpress.org
Digital Media Mgr: Reyna Abigale Levine *E-mail:* reyna@nationalpress.org
Founded: 1976

Provide all expenses paid educational programs to help journalists understand & report on complex topics in Washington, DC & around the world.

National Press Photographers Association Inc (NPPA)
3200 Croasdaile Dr, Suite 306, Durham, NC 27705
Tel: 919-383-7246 *Fax:* 919-383-7261
E-mail: info@nppa.org
Web Site: www.nppa.org
Key Personnel
Exec Dir: Chip Deale *E-mail:* cdeale@nppa.org
Prof Servs Dir: Thomas Kenniff *Tel:* 919-383-7246 ext 10 *E-mail:* tkenniff@nppa.org
Founded: 1946
To promote & protect integrity & excellence in visual journalism.
Number of Members: 5,500
Publication(s): *News Photographer Magazine* (monthly, free with membership)

National Society of Newspaper Columnists (NSNC)
PO Box 411532, San Francisco, CA 94141
Tel: 415-488-NCNC (488-6762) *Fax:* 484-297-0336
E-mail: director@columnists.com
Web Site: www.columnists.com
Key Personnel
Offr, Admin: Luenna Kim
Founded: 1977
Promotes professionalism & camaraderie among columnists & other writers of the serial essay, including bloggers. Advocates for columnists & free-press issues.
Number of Members: 500
Publication(s): *Newsletter* (monthly, free)

National Writers Association
10940 S Parker Rd, Suite 508, Parker, CO 80134
Tel: 303-841-0246
E-mail: natlwritersassn@hotmail.com
Web Site: www.nationalwriters.com
Key Personnel
Exec Dir & Ed: Sandy Whelchel
E-mail: authorsandy@hotmail.com
Founded: 1937
Nonprofit representative organization of new & established writers, serving freelance writers throughout the world.
Number of Members: 2,000
Publication(s): *Authorship* (quarterly, $20/yr); *NWA Newsletter* (monthly by e-mail only)

National Writers Union/UAW Local 1981
Affiliate of UAW International of the United Automobile Aerospace & Agricultural Implement Workers of America
256 W 38 St, Suite 703, New York, NY 10018
Tel: 212-254-0279 *Fax:* 212-254-0673
E-mail: nwu@nwu.org
Web Site: www.nwu.org/
Key Personnel
Pres: Larry Goldbetter
Founded: 1981
Organizing for better treatment of freelance writers by publishers; grievance procedures; negotiate union contracts with publishers; health insurance; conferences. Direct services include the Technical Writers Job Hotline & the Publication Rights Clearinghouse, a groundbreaking license fee collection system. National health insurance programs around the country; national grievance officers & contract advisors; agents database online for members; Authors Network, a Bed & Breakfast program for touring authors at over 160 sites throughout the country, including local reviewer's database, local press contacts & local bookstores/vendors.
Number of Members: 1,200
Publication(s): *local chapter newsletters* (quarterly, free to membs); *National Membership News* (monthly, newsletter, free to membs)

NCTA, see Northern California Translators Association

New England Independent Booksellers Association Inc (NEIBA)
1955 Massachusetts Ave, Cambridge, MA 02140
Web Site: www.newenglandbooks.org
Key Personnel
Exec Dir: Steven Fischer *E-mail:* steve@neba.org
Admin Coord: Nan Sorensen *E-mail:* nan@neba.org
Trade association. Fall trade show & conference annually in September or October; educational workshops, holiday gift catalog, book awards.
Number of Members: 300
Publication(s): *NEIBA News* (weekly, membs only)

New England Poetry Club
46 Wallace St, Somerville, MA 02144
Tel: 617-744-6034
E-mail: info@nepoetryclub.org
Web Site: www.nepoetryclub.org
Founded: 1915
Society for professional published poets. Sponsor various poetry contests & workshops. Workshops meet at the Yen Ching Institute (2 Divinity Ave Harvard Campus). Readings on first Monday, 7 pm at a location to be announced; workshops third Monday 7:30 pm; monthly from Sept May. Special programs at Longfellow House Sunday pm out of doors, $3,000 in prizes annually.
Number of Members: 500
Publication(s): *Writ* (semiannual, newsletter, free with annual dues)
Branch Office(s)
137 W Newton St, Boston, MA 02118 (inquiries on membership), Membership Chmn: Victor Howes

New Hampshire Writers' Project
2500 N River Rd, Manchester, NH 03106
Tel: 603-314-7980 *Fax:* 603-314-7981
E-mail: info@nhwritersproject.org
Web Site: www.nhwritersproject.org
Founded: 1988
Supports the development of individual writers & encourages an audience for literature in the state.
Number of Members: 780
Publication(s): *NH Writer* (6 issues/yr, newsletter)

New Mexico Book Association (NMBA)
1219 Luisa St, Suite 1, Santa Fe, NM 87505
Mailing Address: PO Box 1285, Santa Fe, NM 87504
Tel: 505-660-6357
E-mail: admin@nmbook.org
Web Site: www.nmbook.org
Key Personnel
Pres: Paula Lozar *Tel:* 505-473-3479
E-mail: lozarpaula@cs.com
Off Admin: Susan Waterman
Archivist & Sr Advisor: Richard Polese *Tel:* 505-983-1412 *E-mail:* richard@oceantree.com
Founded: 1994
Nonprofit association serving the interests of publishing, writing, designing, editing, selling & marketing for book professionals throughout New Mexico. Open to all involved in books or publishing. Need not be a resident of New Mexico.
Number of Members: 180
Publication(s): *LIBRO Book News* (6 issues/yr, newsletter, $50/yr membs)
Membership(s): The Association of Publishers for Special Sales; Independent Book Publishers Association; New Mexico Library Association; Publishers Association of the West

News Media Alliance
Formerly Newspaper Association of America (NAA)
4401 N Fairfax Dr, Suite 300, Arlington, VA 22203
Tel: 571-366-1000
E-mail: info@newsmediaalliance.org
Web Site: www.newsmediaalliance.org
Key Personnel
Pres & CEO: David Chavern *Tel:* 571-366-1100
E-mail: david@newsmediaalliance.org
CFO: Robert Walden *Tel:* 571-366-1140
E-mail: robert@newsmediaalliance.org
VP, HR & Opers: Sarah Burkman *Tel:* 571-366-1012 *E-mail:* sarah@newsmediaalliance.org
VP, Membership & Devt: Michelle Harris
Tel: 571-366-1115 *E-mail:* michellelindsey@newsmediaalliance.org
Mgr, Communs: Lindsey Loving *Tel:* 571-366-1009 *E-mail:* lindsey@newsmediaalliance.org
Serves newspapers & newspaper executives by working to advance the cause of a free press; to encourage the efficiency & economy of the newspaper publishing business in all departments & aspects; to engage in & promote research of use to newspapers; to gather & distribute among its member newspapers accurate, reliable & useful information about newspapers & their environment & to promote the highest standard of journalism.
Number of Members: 2,000
Publication(s): *Presstime* (weekly, membs only)

The NewsGuild - CWA
501 Third St NW, 6th fl, Washington, DC 20001-2797
Tel: 202-434-7177; 202-434-7162 (The Guild Reporter) *Fax:* 202-434-1472
E-mail: guild@cwa-union.org
Web Site: www.newsguild.org
Key Personnel
Pres: Bernard Lunzer
Ed, The Guild Reporter: Sally Davidow
E-mail: sdavidow@cwa-union.org
Founded: 1934
Labor union; AFL-CIO, CLC.
Number of Members: 26,000
Publication(s): *The Guild Reporter* (quarterly, free to membs, $20 subn rate nonmembs)

Newspaper Association of America (NAA), see News Media Alliance

North American Agricultural Journalists (NAAJ)
6434 Hurta Lane, Bryan, TX 77808
Tel: 979-845-2872
Web Site: www.naaj.net
Key Personnel
Exec Secy & Treas: Kathleen Phillips *E-mail:* ka-phillips@tamu.edu
Founded: 1952
Self-improvement seminars; annual writing contest for members & nonmembers.
Number of Members: 120
2018 Meeting(s): Annual Meeting, Washington, DC, April 2018
2019 Meeting(s): Annual Meeting, Washington, DC, April 2019
2020 Meeting(s): Annual Meeting, Washington, DC, April 2020
2021 Meeting(s): Annual Meeting, Washington, DC, April 2021
2022 Meeting(s): Annual Meeting, Washington, DC, April 2022
Publication(s): *NAAJ Newsletter* (varies/online to membs as needed)

North American Snowsports Journalists Association (NASJA)
11728 SE Madison St, Portland, OR 97216-3849
Tel: 503-255-3771 *Fax:* 503-255-3771
Web Site: www.nasja.org
Key Personnel
VP: Kristen Lummis *E-mail:* braveskimom@braveskimom.com
Exec Secy-Treas: Vicki Andersen *E-mail:* execsec@nasja.org
Founded: 1963 (founded as the US Ski Writers Association)
Professional group of writers, photographers, broadcasters, filmmakers, authors & editors who report ski & snowboard related news, info & features throughout the US & Canada.
Number of Members: 340
New Election: Annually in March
2018 Meeting(s): Western Winter Summit, Schweitzer, ID & Big White, BC, CN, Jan 21-26, 2018; Annual Meeting, Squaw Valley, CA, April 11-15, 2018

North Carolina Writers' Network
PO Box 21591, Winston-Salem, NC 27120-1591
Tel: 336-293-8844
Web Site: www.ncwriters.org
Key Personnel
Exec Dir: Ed Southern *E-mail:* ed@ncwriters.org
Founded: 1985
Nonprofit, statewide.
Number of Members: 1,500
Publication(s): *Writers' Network News* (semiannual, newspaper, free to membs)

Northern California Independent Booksellers Association (NCIBA)
651 Broadway, Sonoma, CA 95476
Mailing Address: PO Box 280, Sonoma, CA 95476
Tel: 415-561-7686 *Fax:* 415-561-7685
E-mail: info@nciba.com
Web Site: www.nciba.com
Key Personnel
Exec Dir: Calvin Crosby
Admin: Ann Seaton
Trade Show Mgr & Admin: Elsa Eder *E-mail:* elsa@nciba.com
Trade show, education seminars, collaborative advertising, regional holiday catalog. Special memberships for authors include mailing list on labels & e-blast discounts.
Number of Members: 500
Publication(s): *Holiday Catalog*; *Membership Directory* (free); *NCIBA News* (6 issues/yr, newsletter, free to membs); *Northern California Rep Directory* (annual, free)
Membership(s): ABA

Northern California Translators Association
2261 Market St, Suite 160, San Francisco, CA 94114-1600
Tel: 510-845-8712
E-mail: administrator@ncta.org
Web Site: www.ncta.org
Key Personnel
Pres: Sonia Wichmann
Admin: Juliet Viola Kniffen
Founded: 1978
Professional translators & interpreters association. Chapter of the American Translators Association. Online referral service.
Number of Members: 500
New Election: Annually in Feb
Publication(s): *Translorial* (2 issues/yr, print & online, journal, free to membs at www.translorial.com; free PDF access for *Translorial Reader* registrants at www.ncta.org)

Northwest Independent Editors Guild
7511 Greenwood Ave N, No 307, Seattle, WA 98103
E-mail: info@edsguild.org
Web Site: www.edsguild.org
Key Personnel
Admin: Rebecca Brinbury
Founded: 1997
Professional association of more than 300 editors in the Pacific Northwest. Members work on all types of communication projects, from brochures & newsletters to books & web sites. The Editors Guild connects clients with professional editors, fosters community among its members & provides resources for their career development.
Number of Members: 300

Northwest Territories Public Library Services
Unit of Department of Education, Culture & Employment
75 Woodland Dr, Hay River, NT X0E 1G1, Canada
Tel: 867-874-6531 *Toll Free Tel:* 866-297-0232 (CN) *Fax:* 867-874-3321
Web Site: www.nwtpls.gov.nt.ca
Key Personnel
Territorial Libn: Alison Hopkins *E-mail:* alison_hopkins@gov.nt.ca
Provide leadership in coordinating public library services throughout the Northwest Territories.

NPES The Association for Suppliers of Printing, Publishing & Converting Technologies
1899 Preston White Dr, Reston, VA 20191
Tel: 703-264-7200 *Fax:* 703-620-0994
E-mail: npes@npes.org
Web Site: www.npes.org
Key Personnel
Pres: Thayer Long
Sr Dir, Communs: Deborah Vieder *E-mail:* dvieder@npes.org
Founded: 1933 (as the National Printing Equipment Association)
Represent manufacturers & distributors of equipment, supplies, systems & software for printing, publishing & converting.
Number of Members: 600
2018 Meeting(s): Graph Expo 18, McCormick Place, South Hall, 2301 S Lake Shore Dr, Chicago, IL, Sept 30-Oct 3, 2018
2019 Meeting(s): Graph Expo 19, Orange County Convention Center, North Hall, Orlando, FL, Sept 22-25, 2019
Publication(s): *NPES Pressroom Safety Manual*; *Safe Cleaning of Offset Sheetfed Presses*; *Safe Cleaning of Offset Webfed Presses*

NPTA Alliance
330 N Wabash Ave, Suite 2000, Chicago, IL 60611
Tel: 312-321-4092 *Toll Free Tel:* 800-355-NPTA (355-6782) *Fax:* 312-673-6736
Web Site: www.gonpta.com
Key Personnel
CEO & Pres: Kevin Gammonley
Mgr, Membership Opers: Gretchen Fox
Founded: 1903
Trade association serving the printing, publishing, catalog, direct mail, imaging, retail & corporate markets.
Number of Members: 2,600
New Election: Annually in Autumn
Publication(s): *Paper Merchant Weekly* (newsletter, free to membs, electronic)
Membership(s): National Association of Wholesaler-Distributors

NWT Public Library Services, see Northwest Territories Public Library Services

Ontario Book Publishers Organization (OBPO)
One Rutton St, Suite 101, Toronto, ON M6P 0A1, Canada
Tel: 416-536-7584
E-mail: info@obpo.ca
Web Site: obpo.ca
Founded: 1990
Represent the needs, interests, concerns & issues of Ontario book publishers; facilitate information sharing & educational opportunities; facilitate group marketing projects.
Number of Members: 35

Ontario Library Association
2 Toronto St, 3rd fl, Toronto, ON M5C 2B6, Canada
Tel: 416-363-3388 *Toll Free Tel:* 866-873-9867 *Fax:* 416-941-9581
E-mail: info@accessola.com
Web Site: www.accessola.com
Key Personnel
Exec Dir: Shelagh Paterson *Tel:* 416-363-3388 ext 224 *E-mail:* spaterson@accessola.com
Founded: 1900
Memberships available: Personal membership (for one individual, based on salary earned in library work, whether full-time or part-time) $40-$120, Institutional Membership (for one or two-persons, transferable within an institution) $140-$190, Associate Membership (for businesses/corporations to provide support) $215.
Number of Members: 5,300
New Election: Annually in Dec
Publication(s): *The Teaching Librarian* (3 issues/yr, magazine, $36/yr CN)

Ordre des traducteurs, terminologues et interpretes agrees du quebec
Affiliate of Federation Internationale de Traducteurs
2021 Union Ave, Suite 1108, Montreal, QC H3A 2S9, Canada
Tel: 514-845-4411 *Toll Free Tel:* 800-265-4815 *Fax:* 514-845-9903
E-mail: info@ottiaq.org
Web Site: www.ottiaq.org
Key Personnel
Exec Dir: Johanne Boucher *Tel:* 514-845-4411 ext 227 *E-mail:* direction@ottiaq.org
Communs Coord: Catherine Guillemette-Bedard *Tel:* 514-845-4411 ext 225 *E-mail:* cgbedard@ottiaq.org
Bring translators together to exchange information, send out offers of employment to members. Promote profession & protect public interest. Conferences, annual meeting, social activities, seminars, continuing education. Newsletter for membs only.
Number of Members: 2,073
Publication(s): *Circuit* (quarterly, ezine, $42 CN, $50 elsewhere); *L'antenne Express* (newsletter)

Oregon Christian Writers (OCW)
1075 Willow Lake Rd N, Keizer, OR 97303
Tel: 503-393-3356
E-mail: contact@oregonchristianwriters.org
Web Site: www.oregonchristianwriters.org
Key Personnel
Pres: Marilyn Rhoades
Prog Chmn: Don White
Summer Conference Dir: Lindy Jacobs *E-mail:* summerconf@oregonchristianwriters.org
Registrar & Busn Mgr: Sue Miholer
Founded: 1963
Workshops & seminars for beginning & advanced writers; guest speakers & critiques by professional writers.
Number of Members: 375
New Election: Annually in Oct
2018 Meeting(s): Oregon Christian Writers Seminar, Chemeketa Community College, Salem, OR, Feb 24, 2018; Oregon Christian Writers Seminar, Eugene, OR, May 19, 2018; Summer Coaching Conference, Red Lion Hotel on the River-Jantzen Beach, Portland, OR, Aug 20-

23, 2018; Oregon Christian Writers Seminar, Portland, OR, Oct 2018
Publication(s): *Oregon Christian Writers Newsletter* (3 issues/yr)

Overseas Press Club of America (OPC)
40 W 45 St, New York, NY 10036
Tel: 212-626-9220 *Fax:* 212-626-9210
Web Site: www.opcofamerica.org
Key Personnel
Exec Dir: Patricia Kranz *E-mail:* patricia@opcofamerica.org
Founded: 1939
Maintain an international association of journalists, encourage professional skill & integrity of reportage, contribute to the freedom & independence of journalism & the press worldwide.
Number of Members: 440
New Election: Annually in Aug
Publication(s): *Bulletin* (monthly, newsletter, free to membs); *Dateline* (annual, magazine, free to membs)

Pacific Northwest Booksellers Association (PNBA)
338 W 11 Ave, Unit 108, Eugene, OR 97401
Tel: 541-683-4363 *Toll Free Tel:* 800-353-6764 *Fax:* 541-683-3910
E-mail: info@pnba.org
Web Site: www.pnba.org
Key Personnel
Exec Dir: Brian Juenemann *E-mail:* brian@pnba.org
Founded: 1965
Annual trade lists of publishing companies' sales reps; educational seminars; work with local literacy groups & anticensorship organizations; sponsor annual booksellers awards presented for books of exceptional quality by Northwest writers or publishers; sponsor workshops & prizes.
Number of Members: 300
Publication(s): *Footnotes* (monthly e-mail, newsletter, free to membs); *PNBA Member Handbook* (annual, free to membs, electronic)

Pacific Northwest Writers Association, see PNWA - a writer's resource

Pacific Printing Industries Association
Affiliate of Printing Industries of America
6825 SW Sandburg St, Portland, OR 97223
Mailing Address: PO Box 23575, Portland, OR 97281-3575
Tel: 503-221-3944 *Toll Free Tel:* 877-762-7742 *Fax:* 503-221-5691
E-mail: info@ppiassociation.org
Web Site: www.ppiassociation.org
Key Personnel
Exec Dir: Jules Van Sant *E-mail:* jules@ppiassociation.org
Membership Sales & Support: Chris Ryce
Trade association.
Number of Members: 230

Palm Springs Writers Guild
PO Box 947, Rancho Mirage, CA 92270-0947
Web Site: www.palmspringswritersguild.org
Key Personnel
Pres: Diana Miller-Castells *E-mail:* president.pswg@gmail.com
VP, Membership: Hillary Christiansen *E-mail:* vpmembership.pswg@gmail.com
Founded: 1977
Number of Members: 280

PEN American Center
Affiliate of PEN International
588 Broadway, Suite 303, New York, NY 10012
Tel: 212-334-1660 *Fax:* 212-334-2181
E-mail: info@pen.org
Web Site: pen.org
Key Personnel
Exec Dir: Suzanne Nossel *Tel:* 212-334-1600 ext 4811 *E-mail:* snossel@pen.org
Pres: Andrew Solomon
Intl Pres: John Ralston Saul
Sr Dir, Literary Progs & Dir, PEN World Voices Festival: Chip Rolley
Membership Coord: Daniel Guzman *Tel:* 212-334-1660 ext 4819 *E-mail:* daniel@pen.org
Asst Ed & Soc Media Assoc: Wei-Ling Woo *Tel:* 212-334-1660 ext 4832 *E-mail:* weiling@pen.org
An association of writers working to advance literature, defend free expression & foster international literary fellowship.
Number of Members: 4,000
Publication(s): *Grants & Awards Available to American Writers* (online directory, $12)

PEN Canada
24 Ryerson Ave, Suite 301, Toronto, ON M5T 2P3, Canada
Tel: 416-703-8448 *Fax:* 416-703-3870
E-mail: queries@pencanada.ca
Web Site: www.pencanada.ca
Key Personnel
Pres: Phillip Slayton
Exec Dir: Tasleem Thawar *Tel:* 416-703-8448 ext 24
Admin: Pari Rajagopalan *Tel:* 416-703-8448 ext 25
Progs & Communs Coord: Brendan De Cairns *Tel:* 416-703-8448 ext 21
Founded: 1926
Promotes freedom of expression through writing.
Number of Members: 500

PEN Center USA
Affiliate of PEN International
PO Box 6037, Beverly Hills, CA 90212
Tel: 323-424-4939 *Fax:* 323-424-4944
E-mail: pen@penusa.org
Web Site: penusa.org
Key Personnel
Exec Dir: Michelle Franke *Tel:* 323-424-4939 ext 1 *E-mail:* michelle@penusa.org
Founded: 1943
National association of poets, playwrights, screenwriters, essayists, editors, novelists, historians, critics, journalists & translators whose purpose is to foster a sense of community among writers in the Western US & to advance the freedom to write throughout the world.
Number of Members: 1,000
Publication(s): *ePen* (26 issues/yr, free); *Membership Directory* (annual, free for membs)

PEN New England
Unit of PEN American Center
MIT, 14N-221A, 77 Massachusetts Ave, Cambridge, MA 02139
Tel: 617-324-1729
E-mail: pen-newengland@mit.edu
Web Site: www.pen-ne.org/hemingway
Key Personnel
Exec Dir: Karen Wulf *E-mail:* kwulf@mit.edu
Advance the cause of literature & reading in New England & defending free expression everywhere.

Periodical & Book Association of America Inc (PBAA)
481 Eighth Ave, Suite 526, New York, NY 10001
Tel: 212-563-6502 *Fax:* 212-563-4098
Web Site: www.pbaa.net
Key Personnel
Exec Dir: Lisa W Scott *E-mail:* lisawscott@hotmail.com
Assoc Dir: Jose Cancio *E-mail:* jcancio@pbaa.net
Founded: 1965
Nonprofit organization for publishers, distributors, wholesalers, retailers, consultants & industry service providers.
Number of Members: 102

Photographic Society of America® (PSA®)
8241 S Walker Ave, Suite 104, Oklahoma City, OK 73139
Tel: 405-843-1437 *Toll Free Tel:* 855-PSA-INFO (772-4636) *Fax:* 405-843-1438
E-mail: hq@psa-photo.org
Web Site: www.psa-photo.org
Key Personnel
Opers Mgr: Kara Goodson
Founded: 1934
Sponsor workshops & awards for members.
Number of Members: 6,500
2018 Meeting(s): PSA® International Conference of Photography, Sheraton Salt Lake City Hotel, 150 W 500 S, Salt Lake City, UT, Sept 30-Oct 6, 2018
Publication(s): *PSA Journal* (monthly, free to membs)

Playwrights Guild of Canada
401 Richmond St W, Suite 350, Toronto, ON M5V 3A8, Canada
Tel: 416-703-0201 *Fax:* 416-703-0059
E-mail: info@playwrightsguild.ca
Web Site: www.playwrightsguild.ca
Key Personnel
Exec Dir: Robin Sokoloski *E-mail:* robin@playwrightsguild.ca
Membership & Prof Contracts Mgr: Rebecca Burton *E-mail:* membership@playwrightsguild.ca
Off & Progs Mgr: Tina Salek *E-mail:* tina@playwrightsguild.ca
Founded: 1982
Professional association. Contracts, amateur agent productions, script service, readings.
Number of Members: 735
Membership(s): Professional Association of Canadian Playwrights

PNWA - a writer's resource
1420 NW Gilman Blvd, Suite 8, PMB 2717, Issaquah, WA 98027
Tel: 425-673-2665 *Fax:* 425-961-0768
E-mail: pnwa@pnwa.org
Web Site: www.pnwa.org
Key Personnel
Pres: Pam Binder
Founded: 1955
Nonprofit association. Develops writing talent through education, accessibility to publishing industry & participation in a vital writer community.
Number of Members: 1,400

Poetry Society of America (PSA)
15 Gramercy Park, New York, NY 10003
Tel: 212-254-9628
Web Site: www.poetrysociety.org
Key Personnel
Pres: Kimiko Hahn
Exec Dir: Alice Quinn
Deputy Dir: Brett Fletcher Lauer *E-mail:* brett@poetrysociety.org
Membership & Devt Dir: Elsbeth Pancrazi *E-mail:* elsbeth@poetrysociety.org
Prog Dir: Laurin Macios *E-mail:* laurin@poetrysociety.org
Founded: 1910
Contests, readings, lectures, symposia, seminars, weekly workshops for members.
Number of Members: 2,900

Poets & Writers Inc
90 Broad St, Suite 2100, New York, NY 10004
Tel: 212-226-3586 *Fax:* 212-226-3963
E-mail: admin@pw.org
Web Site: www.pw.org

Key Personnel
Exec Dir: Elliot Figman
Dir, Fin & Acctg: William F Hayes
Mng Dir: Melissa Ford Gradel *Tel:* 212-226-3586 ext 223
Founded: 1970
A nonprofit organization which offers information, support & exposure to writers at all stages in their careers. Founded to foster the development of poets & fiction writers & to promote communication throughout the literary community. It publishes the bimonthly *Poets & Writers Magazine*, which delivers to its readers profiles of noted authors & publishing professionals, practical how-to articles, a comprehensive listing of grants & awards for writers & special sections on subjects ranging from small presses to writers conferences. The Readings/Workshops Program supports public literary events through matching grants to community organizations.
Publication(s): *Poets & Writers Magazine* (6 issues/yr, $15.95/yr, $25.95/2 yrs, $4.95 single copy 1999 forward; prior to 1999 $3.95)
Branch Office(s)
2035 Westwood Blvd, Suite 211, Los Angeles, CA 90025, Dir: Jamie Fitzgerald *Tel:* 310-481-7195 *Fax:* 310-481-7193 *E-mail:* calif@pw.org

PRIMIR, see Print Industries Market Information & Research Organization

Print Industries Market Information & Research Organization
Affiliate of NPES The Association for Suppliers of Printing, Publishing & Converting Technologies
1899 Preston White Dr, Reston, VA 20191
Tel: 703-264-7200 *Fax:* 703-620-0994
E-mail: npes@npes.org
Web Site: www.primir.org; www.npes.org/primirresearch/primir.aspx
Key Personnel
Mng Dir: Jacqueline M Bland *E-mail:* jbland@primir.org
Founded: 2005
Research association of the graphic arts industry; provide data & research to printers, publishers & manufacturers of equipment & supplies for the printing/publishing industry & converting industries.
Number of Members: 60
New Election: Annually in Dec

Printing & Graphics Association MidAtlantic (PGAMA)
9685 Gerwig Lane, Suite A, Columbia, MD 21046-1520
Tel: 410-319-0900 *Toll Free Tel:* 877-319-0906 *Fax:* 410-319-0905
E-mail: info@pgama.com
Web Site: www.pgama.com
Key Personnel
Pres: Kerry C Stackpole *E-mail:* kerry@pgama.com
Founded: 1894
Number of Members: 360

Printing Association of Florida Inc (PAF)
Affiliate of Printing Industries of America (PIA)
6250 Hazeltine National Dr, Suite 114, Orlando, FL 32822
Tel: 407-240-8009 *Toll Free Tel:* 800-331-0461 *Fax:* 407-240-8333
Web Site: www.flprint.org
Key Personnel
Dir, Communs: Monica Turner *E-mail:* monica@flprint.org
Dir, Membership & Pub Aff: Harold Yankelevitz *E-mail:* harold@flprint.org
Opers Mgr: Rich Bider *E-mail:* rich@flprint.org
Founded: 1937
Trade association for the graphic arts industry.
Number of Members: 380
2018 Meeting(s): Graphics of the Americas, Broward County Convention Center, 1950 Eisenhower Blvd, Fort Lauderdale, FL, Feb 22-24, 2018
Publication(s): *Graphics Update* (monthly, free to membs)

Printing Brokerage/Buyers Association International (PBBA)
74-5576 Pawai Place, No 599, Kailua Kona, HI 96740
Tel: 808-339-0880
E-mail: contactus@pbba.org
Web Site: pbba.org
Key Personnel
Chmn: Vincent Mallardi *E-mail:* vince@pbba.org
Founded: 1985
Trade association for printing, sales brokerage & purchasing.
Number of Members: 830
Publication(s): *Brokerage* (monthly, newsletter, free to membs); *Hot Markets for Print Demand Annual Rankings of Buyers, Print Products & Geographies* (annual, $995); *Hot Markets for Print Supply Annual Rankings of Providers, Intermediaries & Geographies* (annual, $995); *Law v. Print: Avoid Problems & Protect Opportunities Buying & Selling Prints* ($395); *Printing Brokerage in North America: The Survey* ($195); *Why Use a Printing Independent? Outsourcing is In* ($95)

Printing Industries of America
301 Brush Creek Rd, Warrendale, PA 15086-7529
Tel: 412-741-6860 *Toll Free Tel:* 800-910-4283 *Fax:* 412-741-2311
E-mail: printingind@comm.printing.org
Web Site: www.printing.org
Key Personnel
Pres & CEO: Michael F Makin *Tel:* 412-259-1777 *E-mail:* mmakin@printing.org
VP, Mktg: Lisa Rawa *E-mail:* lrawa@printing.org
Sr Mktg Mgr: Jenn Strang *Tel:* 412-259-1810 *E-mail:* jstrang@printing.org
Mgr, Mktg: Chrystal Kapanyko *E-mail:* ckapanyko@printing.org
Founded: 1887
Member organization providing research, educational & technical services to printing industry worldwide.
Number of Members: 14,000
Publication(s): *The Magazine* (10 issues/yr, free to membs); *Publications Catalog* (annual, free); *QC Catalog* (annual, free)
Branch Office(s)
601 13 St NW, Suite 350S, Washington, DC 20005-3807 *Tel:* 202-730-7970
1001 "G" St NW, Suite 800, Washington, DC 20001 *Tel:* 202-627-6924

Printing Industries Press, see Printing Industries of America

Printing Industry Association of the South (PIAS)
305 Plus Park Blvd, Nashville, TN 37217
Tel: 615-366-1094 *Fax:* 615-366-4192
E-mail: info@pias.org
Web Site: www.pias.org
Key Personnel
Pres: Ed Chalifoux
Provide services & support to the printing industry.
Number of Members: 400
Publication(s): *Print South* (monthly, magazine, free with membership)

Professional Writers Association of Canada (PWAC)
c/o Canadian Brownfields Network (CBN), 2800 14 Ave, Suite 210, Markham, ON L3R 0E4, Canada
Tel: 416-504-1645
E-mail: info@pwac.ca
Web Site: pwac.ca; www.writers.ca
Protect & promote the interests of freelance writers in Canada, develop & maintain professional standards in editor-writer relationships, lobby for higher standard fees for freelancers, sponsor professional development workshops & offset freelancers' isolation by circulating news, information & market data on the industry.
Number of Members: 625
Publication(s): *PWAC Guide to Editing as a Sideline* (book); *PWAC Guide to Roughing in the Market* (book)

Protestant Church-Owned Publishers Association
6631 Westbury Oaks Ct, Springfield, VA 22152
Tel: 703-220-5989
Web Site: www.pcpaonline.org
Key Personnel
Dir: Gary Mulder *E-mail:* mulder@pcpaonline.org
Founded: 1951
Number of Members: 40

Public Relations Society of America
33 Maiden Lane, 11th fl, New York, NY 10038-5150
Tel: 212-460-1400 *Fax:* 212-995-0757
Web Site: www.prsa.org
Key Personnel
CFO: Philip Bonaventura *Tel:* 212-460-1440 *E-mail:* philip.bonaventura@prsa.org
VP, Mktg: Nicole Zerillo *Tel:* 212-460-1417 *E-mail:* nicole.zerillo@prsa.org
VP, PR: Stephanie Cegielski *Tel:* 212-460-1495 *E-mail:* stephanie.cegielski@prsa.org
Dir, Memb Servs: Eileen Lintao *Tel:* 212-460-1490 *E-mail:* eileen.lintao@prsa.org
Founded: 1947
Association of public relations professionals dedicated to development & ethical practice of public relations.
Publication(s): *The Public Relations Strategist* (quarterly, $150/yr); *Public Relations Tactics* (monthly, $100/yr)

Publishers Association of the West Inc (PubWest)
17501 Hill Way, Lake Oswego, OR 97035
Tel: 503-901-9865
Web Site: pubwest.org
Key Personnel
Exec Dir: Kent Watson *E-mail:* executivedirector@pubwest.org
Founded: 1977
Members are small & medium-sized book publishers located throughout North America. Supply marketing & technical information to members; conduct annual educational seminars; promote sales in the region. Participates in BookExpo, MPBA & PNBA tradeshows. Publisher of the Huenefeld-PubWest Survey of Financial Operations.
Number of Members: 360
Publication(s): *The Endsheet* (quarterly, journal, free); *PubWest Membership Directory* (annual, directory, free to membs, $25 for nonmembs)

Publishers Information Bureau (PIB)®
Division of MPA - The Association of Magazine Media
757 Third Ave, 11th fl, New York, NY 10017
Tel: 212-872-3745; 212-872-3700 (MPA)
E-mail: infocenter@magazine.org
Web Site: www.magazine.org

Key Personnel
CEO & Pres: Mary Berner *Tel:* 212-872-3710 *E-mail:* president@magazine.org
CFO & SVP: William Wood *Tel:* 212-872-3722 *E-mail:* wwood@magazine.org
EVP, Communs: Meredith Wagner *Tel:* 212-872-3732 *E-mail:* mwagner@magazine.org
EVP, Mktg: Linda Mason *Tel:* 212-872-3734 *E-mail:* lmason@magazine.org
Dir, Info Servs: Sandy Jimenez *Tel:* 212-872-3795 *E-mail:* sjimenez@magazine.org
Measure advertising pages & rate card revenues in consumer magazines & newspaper supplements.
Number of Members: 250

Publishing Professionals Network
c/o Postal Annex, 274 Redwood Shores Pkwy, Box 129, Redwood City, CA 94065-1173
E-mail: operations@pubpronetwork.org
Web Site: www.pubpronetwork.org
Key Personnel
Treas: Tona Pearce Myers
Founded: 1969
Specialize in supporting the book publishing industry. Offers educational programs, seminars & scholarships. Produces an annual book show & has monthly dinner meetings.
Number of Members: 400
New Election: Annually in Jan
Publication(s): *Bookbuilders West Newsletter* (5 times/yr)

PubWest, see Publishers Association of the West Inc (PubWest)

Quebec Writers' Federation (QWF)
1200 Atwater Ave, Rm 3, Westmount, QC H3Z 1X4, Canada
Tel: 514-933-0878
E-mail: info@qwf.org
Web Site: www.qwf.org; www.hireawriter.ca
Key Personnel
Exec Dir: Lori Schubert *E-mail:* admin@qwf.org
Association of Quebec writers to promote English language writing in Quebec through literary awards, writing workshops, mentorship program & literary events.
Number of Members: 600

Reporters Committee for Freedom of the Press
1156 15 St NW, Suite 1250, Washington, DC 20005-1779
Tel: 202-795-9300 *Toll Free Tel:* 800-336-4243
E-mail: info@rcfp.org
Web Site: www.rcfp.org
Key Personnel
Exec Dir: Bruce Brown *Tel:* 703-807-2101
Communs Dir: Debra Gersh Hernandez *Tel:* 703-807-2104
Busn Mgr: Lois Loyd *Tel:* 571-481-9321
Founded: 1970
Legal defense & research services for journalists & media lawyers.
Publication(s): *Access to Electronic Communications* (handbook); *Access to Juror Questionnaires* (handbook); *Access to Juvenile Justice* (handbook); *Access to Police Records* (handbook); *Access to Terrorism Proceedings* (handbook); *Agents of Discovery* (report); *Alternative Dispute Resolution* (handbook); *Anonymous Juries* (report); *Federal FOIA Appeals Guide* (handbook); *Federal Open Government Guide* (handbook); *FERPA, HIPAA & DPPA* (handbook); *The First Amendment Handbook* (booklet); *Gag Orders* (handbook); *Grand Juries* (handbook); *Homefront Confidential* (report); *Judicial Speech* (handbook); *Jury Proceedings and Records* (handbook); *The Lost Stories* (handbook); *The News Media & the Law* (quarterly, magazine, $20/yr, free online a few weeks after released to subscribers); *Off Base: Military Court Dockets* (handbook); *Online Access to Plea Agreements* (handbook); *Open Courts Compendium* (handbook); *Open Government Guide, 6th ed* (handbook); *Photographers' Guide to Privacy* (handbook); *Police, Protesters and the Press* (handbook); *Private Eyes* (handbook); *Privatization v the Public's Right to Know* (handbook); *Privilege Compendium* (handbook); *A Reporter's Field Guide* (handbook); *A Reporter's Guide to American Indian Law* (handbook); *A Reporter's Guide to Medical Privacy Law* (handbook); *A Reporter's Guide to Military Justice* (handbook); *Reporter's Recording Guide* (handbook); *Secret Dockets* (handbook); *Secret Juries* (handbook); *SLAPP Stick* (handbook); *Sunshine Inc* (handbook); *Warrants & Wiretaps* (handbook); *White Paper: Military Dockets* (handbook)

Le Reseau EdCan, see EdCan Network

Romance Writers of America®
14615 Benfer Rd, Houston, TX 77069
Tel: 832-717-5200 *Fax:* 832-717-5201
E-mail: info@rwa.org
Web Site: www.rwa.org
Key Personnel
Exec Dir: Allison Kelley *Tel:* 832-717-5200 ext 124 *E-mail:* allison.kelley@rwa.org
Deputy Exec Dir: Carol Ritter *Tel:* 832-717-5200 ext 127 *E-mail:* carol.ritter@rwa.org
Ed & Pubns Mgr: Erin Fry *Tel:* 832-717-5200 ext 122 *E-mail:* erin.fry@rwa.org
Educ & Progs Mgr: Stephani Fry *Tel:* 832-717-5200 ext 126 *E-mail:* steph.fry@rwa.org
Membership Servs Rep: Donna Mathoslah *Tel:* 832-717-5200 ext 121 *E-mail:* donna.mathoslah@rwa.org
Founded: 1980
Romance Writers of America is dedicated to advancing the professional interests of career-focused romance writers through networking & advocacy.
Membership: $99/yr, $25 processing fee (new & reinstating).
Number of Members: 10,000
2018 Meeting(s): Annual Conference, Sheraton Denver Downtown Hotel, 1550 Court Place, Denver, CO, July 25-28, 2018
2019 Meeting(s): Annual Conference, New York Marriott® Marquis, 1535 Broadway, New York, NY, July 24-27, 2019
2020 Meeting(s): Annual Conference, San Francisco Marriott Marquis, 780 Mission St, San Francisco, CA, July 29-Aug 1, 2020
2021 Meeting(s): Annual Conference, Gaylord Opryland Resort & Convention Center, 2800 Opryland Dr, Nashville, TN, July 14-17, 2021
Publication(s): *Romance Writers Report* (monthly, magazine, free to membs)

SABEW, see Society of American Business Editors & Writers Inc (SABEW)

Saskatchewan Arts Board
1355 Broad St, Regina, SK S4R 7V1, Canada
Tel: 306-787-4056 *Toll Free Tel:* 800-667-7526 (CN) *Fax:* 306-787-4199
E-mail: info@saskartsboard.ca
Web Site: www.saskartsboard.ca
Key Personnel
CEO: Michael Jones
Dir, Admin: Gail Paul Armstrong
Founded: 1948
Provide consultation, advice, grants, programs +/or services to individual artists, arts groups & organizations & members of the public. Programs support & encourage the development of artists, arts groups & organizations in the literary, performing, visual, media & multidisciplinary arts. Also develop & maintain a permanent collection of original works by Saskatchewan artists.
Branch Office(s)
201 Avenue "B" S, Saskatoon, SK S7M 1M3, Canada *Tel:* 306-964-1155 *Fax:* 306-964-1167

Science Fiction & Fantasy Writers of America Inc (SFWA)
PO Box 3238, Enfield, CT 06083-3238
E-mail: office@sfwa.org
Web Site: www.sfwa.org
Key Personnel
Pres: Cat Rambo *E-mail:* cat.rambo@sfwa.org
VP: Erin M Hartshorn *E-mail:* erin.hortshorn@sfwa.org
Treas & CFO: Bud Sparhawk *E-mail:* bud.sparhawk@sfwa.org
Secy: Susan Forest *E-mail:* susan.forest@sfwa.org
Dir, Communs: Jaym Gates *E-mail:* communications@sfwa.org
Opers Mgr: Kate Baker
Founded: 1965
An organization of professional writers, editors, artists, agents & others in the science fiction & fantasy field.
Number of Members: 1,800
New Election: Annually in May
Publication(s): *Annual Membership Directory*; *SFWA Bulletin* (quarterly, $32/yr nonmembs, $48/yr foreign nonmembs, $38 CN/Mexico)

SF Canada
c/o Judy McCrosky, Secy-Treas, 516 Ninth St E, Saskatoon, SK S7N 0B1, Canada
Web Site: www.sfcanada.org
Key Personnel
Pres: Ira Nayman
VP: Donna McMahon
Secy-Treas: Judy McCrosky
Founded: 1989
Exists to foster a sense of community among Canadian writers of speculative fiction, to improve communication between Canadian writers of speculative fiction, to foster the growth of quality writing in Canadian speculative fiction, to lobby on behalf of Canadian writers of speculative fiction & to encourage the translation of Canadian speculative fiction. Supports positive social action.
Number of Members: 130

SHARP, see Society for the History of Authorship, Reading & Publishing Inc (SHARP)

SIBA, see Southern Independent Booksellers Alliance

Small Publishers, Artists & Writers Network (SPAWN)
323 E Matilija St, Suite 110, PMB 123, Ojai, CA 93023
Tel: 805-646-3045 *Fax:* 805-640-8213
E-mail: execdir@spawn.org
Web Site: www.spawn.org
Key Personnel
Exec Dir: Kathleen Sexton Kaiser
Secy-Treas: Mindy Reed
Membership Dir: Helen Gallagher
Founded: 1996
Number of Members: 200

Social Sciences & Humanities Research Council of Canada (SSHRC)
350 Albert St, Ottawa, ON K1P 6G4, Canada
Mailing Address: PO Box 1610, Ottawa, ON K1P 6G4, Canada
Tel: 613-992-0691
E-mail: research@sshrc-crsh.gc.ca
Web Site: www.sshrc.ca

Key Personnel
EVP: Ted Hewitt
VP, Future Challenges: Ursula Gobel
VP, Res Progs: Brent Herbert-Copley
Offers 2 programs of support for scholarly publishing: Aid to scholarly publication program, aid to research & transfer journal program. Only Canadian citizens or permanent residents of Canada are eligible to apply under either program. SSHRC is a Federal Crown Corporation.
Number of Members: 22

Sociedad Interamericana de Prensa (SIP), see Inter American Press Association (IAPA)

Society for Features Journalism (SFJ)
University of Maryland, Philip Merrill College of Journalism, 1100 Knight Hall, College Park, MD 20742
Tel: 301-314-2631 *Fax:* 301-314-9166
Web Site: featuresjournalism.org
Key Personnel
Exec Dir: Merrilee Cox *E-mail:* merrileesfj@gmail.com
Founded: 1947 (as AASFE - American Association of Sunday & Feature Editors)
Nonprofit trade association of Sunday & feature editors.
Number of Members: 250
Publication(s): *Style Magazine* (annual)

Society for Scholarly Publishing (SSP)
10200 W 44 Ave, Suite 304, Wheat Ridge, CO 80033-2840
Tel: 303-422-3914 *Fax:* 720-881-6101
E-mail: info@sspnet.org
Web Site: www.sspnet.org
Key Personnel
Exec Dir: Ann Mehan Crosse *Tel:* 720-881-6114 *E-mail:* amcrosse@kellencompany.com
Dir, Info Servs: Ruth Gleason Roth
Dir, Memb Servs: Kristi Klinke
Founded: 1978
Professional association for people in scholarly publishing industry; 12-16 seminars/workshops sponsored each year.
Number of Members: 1,000
2018 Meeting(s): Annual Meeting, Sheraton Chicago Hotel & Towers, Chicago, IL, May 30-June 1, 2018
2019 Meeting(s): Annual Meeting, Marriott Marquis San Diego Marina, San Diego, CA, May 29-May 31, 2019
2020 Meeting(s): Annual Meeting, Westin Waterfront, Boston, MA, May 27-May 29, 2020
2021 Meeting(s): Annual Meeting, Gaylord National Resort, National Harbor, MD, May 26-May 28, 2021
2022 Meeting(s): Annual Meeting, Sheraton Chicago Hotel & Towers, Chicago, IL, June 1-June 3, 2022
Publication(s): *Directory* (annual, membs only)

Society for Technical Communication
9401 Lee Hwy, Suite 300, Fairfax, VA 22031
Tel: 703-522-4114 *Fax:* 703-522-2075
E-mail: stc@stc.org
Web Site: www.stc.org
Key Personnel
Dir, Communs & Intercom Ed: Liz Pohland *Tel:* 571-366-1910 *E-mail:* liz.pohland@stc.org
Dir, Meetings & Educ: Molly Jin *Tel:* 571-366-1904 *E-mail:* molly.jin@stc.org
Founded: 1960 (as Society of Technical Writers & Publishers)
Professional society dedicated to the advancement of the theory & practice of technical communication in all media.
Number of Members: 15,000
Publication(s): *Intercom* (monthly, magazine, electronic version free to membs; print version $60/yr membs, $160/yr nonmembs, $185/yr nonmembs CN, $215/yr nonmembs elsewhere); *Technical Communication* (quarterly, journal, free to membs, $275/yr nonmembs, electronic)

Society for the History of Authorship, Reading & Publishing Inc (SHARP)
c/o The Johns Hopkins University Press, Journals Publishing Div, PO Box 19966, Baltimore, MD 21211-0966
Tel: 410-516-6987 *Toll Free Tel:* 800-548-1784 *Fax:* 410-516-3866
E-mail: members@sharpweb.org
Web Site: www.sharpweb.org
Key Personnel
Ed: Sydney Sharp *E-mail:* editor@sharpweb.org
Founded: 1993
Promotes the study of book history among academics & nonacademics. Publishing & scholarly attention to its history.
Number of Members: 1,175
Publication(s): *Book History* (annual, journal, included with individual membership, $73/yr instns); *SHARP News* (quarterly, included with membership); *SHARP Online Membership & Periodicals Directory* (annual, access to online included with membership)

Society of American Business Editors & Writers Inc (SABEW)
Walter Cronkite School of Journalism & Mass Communication, Arizona State University, 555 N Central Ave, Suite 406E, Phoenix, AZ 85004-1248
Tel: 602-496-7862 *Fax:* 602-496-7041
E-mail: sabew@sabew.org
Web Site: sabew.org
Key Personnel
Pres: Cory Schouten
Exec Dir: Kathleen Graham *Tel:* 602-496-5190 *E-mail:* kgraham@sabew.org
Spec Projs Mgr: Crystal Beasley *Tel:* 602-496-5188 *E-mail:* cbeasley@sabew.org
Founded: 1964
Professional development. Sponsor regional workshops. Specialize in business journalism.
Number of Members: 3,500
2018 Meeting(s): Spring Conference, Capital Hilton, Washington, DC, April 26-28, 2018

Society of American Travel Writers (SATW)
One Parkview Plaza, Suite 800, Oakbrook Terrace, IL 60181
Tel: 202-591-2476
E-mail: info@satw.org
Web Site: www.satw.org
Key Personnel
Exec Dir: Marla Schrager *Tel:* 312-420-6846 *E-mail:* mschrager@satw.org
Membership Coord/Convention Registrar: John Kingzette *Tel:* 847-686-2321 *E-mail:* jkingzette@satw.org
Founded: 1955
Promote responsible journalism, provide professional support & development for our members, encourage the conservation & preservation of travel resources worldwide.
Number of Members: 1,100
Publication(s): *Directory of Members* (annual, $250 print + $7.50 S&H)

Society of Children's Book Writers and Illustrators (SCBWI)
4727 Wilshire Blvd, Suite 301, Los Angeles, CA 90010
Tel: 323-782-1010 *Fax:* 323-782-1892
E-mail: scbwi@scbwi.org; membership@scbwi.org
Web Site: www.scbwi.org
Key Personnel
Pres: Stephen Mooser *E-mail:* stephenmooser@scbwi.org
Exec Dir: Lin Oliver *E-mail:* linoliver@scbwi.org
Dir, Community Mktg & Engagement: Tammy Brown
Dir, Opers & Membership Coord: Gee Cee Addison Bahador *E-mail:* gcaddison@scbwi.org
Founded: 1971
An organization of children's writers & illustrators & others devoted to the interests of children's literature; annual workshops & conferences throughout the world.
Number of Members: 22,000
Meeting(s): Summer Conference, annually in July/Aug
2018 Meeting(s): Winter Conference, Grand Hyatt New York, 109 E 42 St at Grand Central Terminal, New York, NY, Feb 2-4, 2018
Publication(s): *SCBWI Bulletin* (6 issues/yr, free to membs)

Society of Illustrators (SI)
128 E 63 St, New York, NY 10065
Tel: 212-838-2560 *Fax:* 212-838-2561
E-mail: info@societyillustrators.org
Web Site: www.societyillustrators.org
Key Personnel
Exec Dir: Anelle Miller *E-mail:* anelle@societyillustrators.org
Dir, Opers: John Capobiano *E-mail:* john@societyillustrators.org
Founded: 1901
Formed to promote the art of illustration. The society houses the Museum of American Illustration.
Number of Members: 950
New Election: Annually in June
Publication(s): *American Illustration* (annual, $45)

The Society of Midland Authors (SMA)
PO Box 10419, Chicago, IL 60610
E-mail: info@midlandauthors.com
Web Site: www.midlandauthors.com
Founded: 1915
Nonprofit writer's association that seeks to stimulate creative efforts & closer association among Midwest writers; maintain collections of writer's works & encourage interest in reading, literature & writing in cooperation with other educational & cultural institutions. Members are qualified authors & co-authors of works from recognized publishers or associates (nonvoting) who live in Illinois, Indiana, Kansas, Michigan, Minnesota, Missouri or Nebraska. Monthly literary & professional programs, annual awards dinner, $500 & recognition plaque, for best books of previous year in six categories: adult fiction, adult nonfiction, poetry, biography & memoirs (adult), children's fiction, children's nonfiction.
Number of Members: 400
Publication(s): *Literary License* (8 issues/yr, newsletter)

Society of Motion Picture & Television Engineers® (SMPTE®)
3 Barker Ave, 5th fl, White Plains, NY 10601
Tel: 914-761-1100 *Fax:* 914-761-3115
Web Site: www.smpte.org
Key Personnel
Exec Dir: Barbara Lange *Tel:* 914-205-2370
Dir, Events & Governance Liaison: Sally-Ann D'Amato *Tel:* 914-205-2375
Dir, Membership: Roberta Gorman *Tel:* 914-205-2376
Dir, Philanthropy: Mary Vinton *Tel:* 914-205-2380
Dir, Standards & Engg: Howard Lukk *Tel:* 914-205-2371
Mktg & Communs: Aimee Ricca *Tel:* 914-205-2381
Founded: 1916
To advance theory & practice of engineering in film, TV, motion imaging & allied arts & sci-

ences; establishment of standards & practices. Annual membership dues are $145.
Number of Members: 6,800
Publication(s): *SMPTE Motion Imaging Journal* (8 issues/yr, journal, $185/yr US & CN, $200/yr elsewhere, free to membs)

The Society of Southwestern Authors (SSA)
PO Box 30355, Tucson, AZ 85751-0355
E-mail: info@ssa-az.org
Web Site: www.ssa-az.org
Key Personnel
Pres: Chris Stern *E-mail:* azwritten@gmail.com
VP: Donna Young *E-mail:* karmaniranda@aol.com
Treas: Jay McCall *E-mail:* jmcca11415@msn.com
Recording Secy: Jean Young *E-mail:* migralaws@aol.com
Founded: 1972
Nonprofit association of writers & other publishing professionals. Sponsors a writing contest which includes three categories: short story, personal essay/memoirs & poetry.
Number of Members: 400
Publication(s): *The Write Word* (6 issues/yr, newsletter, free to membs)

Software & Information Industry Association (SIIA)
1090 Vermont Ave NW, 6th fl, Washington, DC 20005-4095
Tel: 202-289-7442 *Fax:* 202-289-7097
Web Site: www.siia.net
Key Personnel
Pres: Kenneth Wasch *Tel:* 202-789-4440
VP, Membership: Eric Fredell *Tel:* 202-789-4464
Principal trade association of the software & information industry.
Number of Members: 850
Publication(s): *Upgrade* (6 issues/yr, magazine, free to membs, $79 nonmembs)

Southern Independent Booksellers Alliance
3806 Yale Ave, Columbia, SC 29205
Tel: 803-994-9530 *Fax:* 309-410-0211
E-mail: info@sibaweb.com
Web Site: www.sibaweb.com
Key Personnel
Exec Dir: Wanda Jewell *E-mail:* wanda@sibaweb.com
Number of Members: 500
2018 Meeting(s): SIBA Discovery Show, Tampa, FL, Sept 13-15, 2018
Publication(s): *SEBA Holiday Catalog*

Special Libraries Association (SLA)
7918 Jones Branch Dr, Suite 300, McLean, VA 22102
Tel: 703-647-4900 *Fax:* 703-506-3266
Web Site: www.sla.org
Key Personnel
Deputy CEO: Doug Newcomb *Tel:* 703-647-4923 *E-mail:* dnewcomb1@sla.org
CFO: Linda N Broussard *Tel:* 703-647-4938 *E-mail:* lbroussard@sla.org
Exec Dir: Amy Lestition Burke
Dir, Membership: Paula Diaz *Tel:* 703-647-4926 *E-mail:* pdiaz@sla.org
Founded: 1909
Serial & nonserial publications; public relations; professional development; employment clearinghouse; resume referral service; computer-assisted, self-study programs; chapters, divisions, student groups & caucuses; government relations; fund development; scholarships; grants; honors & awards; annual conference & exhibit; winter meeting; information resources center.
Number of Members: 8,000
2018 Meeting(s): Annual Conference & INFO-EXPO, Baltimore, MD, June 11-13, 2018
Publication(s): *Information Outlook* (6 issues/yr, ezine, $240)

Specialized Information Publishers Association (SIPA)
Division of Software & Information Industry Association (SIIA)
1090 Vermont Ave NW, 6th fl, Washington, DC 20005-4095
Web Site: www.sipaonline.com
Key Personnel
Edit Dir: Ronn Levine *Tel:* 202-789-4491 *E-mail:* rlevine@siia.net
Members are subscription-based publishers representing small & large companies. Activities include e-mail, marketing, technical developments, copyright, business practices & editorial development.
Number of Members: 250
2018 Meeting(s): SIPA Annual Conference, Capital Hilton, Washington, DC, June 5-7, 2018
Publication(s): *SIPAlert Daily*

Specialty Graphic Imaging Association (SGIA)
10015 Main St, Fairfax, VA 22031-3489
Tel: 703-385-1335 *Toll Free Tel:* 888-385-3588 *Fax:* 703-273-0456
E-mail: sgia@sgia.org
Web Site: www.sgia.org
Key Personnel
Pres & CEO: Ford Bowers
Founded: 1992
Members are digital imaging producers, suppliers who sell to digital imagers & schools which teach digital imaging.
Number of Members: 900
2018 Meeting(s): SGIA Expo, Las Vegas Convention Center, Las Vegas, NV, Oct 18-20, 2018
2019 Meeting(s): SGIA Expo, Dallas, TX, Oct 23-25, 2019
Publication(s): *SGIA Journal Graphic Edition* (6 issues/yr, free to membs); *SGIA Journal Garment Edition* (quarterly, free to membs)

Jean Stein Book Award, see PEN American Center

Teachers & Writers Collaborative
520 Eighth Ave, Suite 2020, New York, NY 10018-4165
Tel: 212-691-6590 *Toll Free Tel:* 888-BOOKS-TW (266-5789) *Fax:* 212-675-0171
E-mail: info@twc.org
Web Site: www.twc.org
Key Personnel
Dir: Amy Swauger *E-mail:* aswauger@twc.org
Dir, Opers: Jade Triton *E-mail:* jtriton@twc.org
Educ Dir: Jordan Dann *E-mail:* jdann@twc.org
Founded: 1967
Information source for those interested in teaching writing & literary arts; publish books & magazines about creative writing; sponsor workshops. Basic annual membership: $35.
Publication(s): *Teachers & Writers* (quarterly, magazine, $20/yr or $35/2 yrs indiv, $45/yr instns & organizations)

Technical Association of the Pulp & Paper Industry (TAPPI)
15 Technology Pkwy S, Suite 115, Peachtree Corners, GA 30092
Tel: 770-446-1400 *Toll Free Tel:* 800-332-8686 (US); 800-446-9431 (CN) *Fax:* 770-446-6947
E-mail: memberconnection@tappi.org
Web Site: www.tappi.org
Key Personnel
CEO & Pres: Larry N Montague
VP, Opers: Eric Fletty *Tel:* 770-209-7535 *E-mail:* efletty@tappi.org
Press Mgr: Jeff Wells *Tel:* 770-209-7228 *E-mail:* jwells@tappi.org
Founded: 1915
Professional society of executives, operating managers, engineers, scientists & technologists serving the pulp, paper & allied industries.
Number of Members: 7,000
2018 Meeting(s): PaperCon 2018, Charlotte Convention Center, Charlotte, NC, April 15-18, 2018; TAPPI PEERS Conference, Hilton Portland, Portland, OR, Oct 28-31, 2018
2020 Meeting(s): TAPPI/AICC SuperCorrExpo®, Orange County Convention Center, Orlando, FL, Sept 14-17, 2020
Publication(s): *TAPPI JOURNAL* (monthly, free to membs, electronic)

Television Academy
5220 Lankershim Blvd, North Hollywood, CA 91601-3109
Tel: 818-754-2800 *Fax:* 818-761-2827
Web Site: www.emmys.com
Key Personnel
CEO & Chmn of the Bd: Bruce Rosenblum
CFO: Heather Cochran
Pres: Maury McIntyre
SVP, Awards: John Leverence
Founded: 1977
Organization for those involved in national television; bestows Emmy awards for excellence in television; college television awards & college internship program; inducts deserving individuals in "Television Academy Hall of Fame".
Number of Members: 20,000
Publication(s): *EMMY Magazine*

Texas Institute of Letters (TIL)
c/o 7748 Hwy 290 W, Austin, TX 78736-3202
E-mail: president@texasinstituteofletters.org; secretary@texasinstituteofletters.org
Web Site: www.texasinstituteofletters.org
Key Personnel
Pres: Steve Davis
VP: Carmen Tafolla
Treas: W K Stratton
Secy: Sergio Troncoso
Recording Secy: Joe Holley
Founded: 1936
Awards over $20,000 annually to recognize outstanding literary works in several categories. Cooperate in sponsorship of various writing fellowships.
Number of Members: 250
Publication(s): *Newsletter* (quarterly, membs only)

Texas Library Association (TLA)
3355 Bee Cave Rd, Suite 401, Austin, TX 78746-6763
Tel: 512-328-1518 *Toll Free Tel:* 800-580-2852 *Fax:* 512-328-8852
E-mail: tla@txla.org
Web Site: www.txla.org
Key Personnel
Exec Dir: Patricia A Smith *Tel:* 512-328-1518 x151 *E-mail:* pats@txla.org
Founded: 1902
TLA is the largest state library association in the country promoting librarianship & library service in Texas.
Number of Members: 7,200
2018 Meeting(s): Annual Conference, Dallas, TX, April 10-13, 2018
2019 Meeting(s): Annual Conference, Austin, TX, April 15-18, 2019
2020 Meeting(s): Annual Conference, Houston, TX, March 24-27, 2020
2021 Meeting(s): Annual Conference, San Antonio, TX, April 20-23, 2021
2022 Meeting(s): Annual Conference, Fort Worth, TX, April 5-8, 2022
Publication(s): *Texas Library Journal* (quarterly); *Texline* (irregular, enewsletter); *TLACast Newsletter* (irregular)

The Society of Professional Journalists (SPJ)
Eugene S Pulliam National Journalism Ctr, 3909 N Meridian St, Indianapolis, IN 46208
Tel: 317-927-8000 *Fax:* 317-920-4789
E-mail: spj@spj.org
Web Site: www.spj.org
Key Personnel
Exec Dir: Joe Skeel *Tel:* 317-927-8000 ext 216 *E-mail:* jskeel@spj.org
Assoc Exec Dir: Chris Vachon *Tel:* 317-927-8000 ext 207 *E-mail:* cvachon@spj.org
Creative Dir: Tony Peterson *Tel:* 317-927-8000 ext 214 *E-mail:* tpeterson@spj.org
Dir, Educ: Scott Leadingham *Tel:* 317-640-9304 (cell) *E-mail:* sleadingham@spj.org
Dir, Membership: Linda Hall *Tel:* 317-927-8000 ext 203 *E-mail:* lindah@spj.org
Awards Coord: Chad Hosier *Tel:* 317-927-8000 ext 210 *E-mail:* chosier@spj.org
Communs Coord: Ellen Kobe *Tel:* 317-927-8000 ext 205 *E-mail:* ekobe@spj.org
Founded: 1909 (as Sigma Delta Chi fraternity)
Professional organization that includes broadcast, print & online journalists, journalism educators & students interested in journalism as a career.
Number of Members: 9,000
2018 Meeting(s): Excellence in Journalism, Hilton Baltimore, 401 W Pratt St, Baltimore, MD, Sept 27-29, 2018
2019 Meeting(s): Excellence in Journalism, Grand Hyatt San Antonio, 600 E Market St, San Antonio, TX, Sept 5-7, 2019
2020 Meeting(s): Excellence in Journalism, Washington Hilton, 1919 Connecticut Ave NW, Washington, DC, Sept 10-12, 2020
Publication(s): *Quill* (6 times/yr, magazine, $75/yr, free for membs)

Theatre Library Association (TLA)
c/o The New York Public Library for the Performing Arts, 40 Lincoln Center Plaza, New York, NY 10023
E-mail: TheatreLibraryAssociation@gmail.com
Web Site: www.tla-online.org/awards/bookawards
Key Personnel
Pres: Nancy Friedland
VP: Angela Weaver
Exec Secy: Laurie Murphy
Treas: Colleen Reilly
Founded: 1937
Supports librarians & archivists affiliated with theatre, dance, popular entertainment, performance studies, motion picture & broadcasting collections.
Publication(s): *Performing Arts Resources* (irregularly, series)

United for Libraries
Division of The American Library Association (ALA)
859 W Lancaster Ave, Suite 2-1, Bryn Mawr, PA 19010
Tel: 312-280-2161 *Toll Free Tel:* 800-545-2433 (ext 2161) *Fax:* 484-698-7868
E-mail: united@ala.org
Web Site: www.ala.org/united
Key Personnel
Exec Dir: Beth Nawalinski *E-mail:* bnawalinski@ala.org
Mktg/PR Specialist: Jillian Wentworth *E-mail:* jwentworth@ala.org
Founded: 2009
Support citizens who govern, advocate & fundraise for all type of libraries.
Number of Members: 5,000

United Nations Association of the United States of America
1750 Pennsylvania Ave NW, Suite 300, Washington, DC 20006
Tel: 202-887-9040 *Fax:* 202-887-9021
Web Site: www.unausa.org
Key Personnel
Exec Dir: Chris Whatley *E-mail:* cwhatley@unausa.org
Deputy Exec Dir: Mary-Frances Wain *E-mail:* mwain@unausa.org
Membership Dir: Laura Giroux *E-mail:* lgiroux@unausa.org
Founded: 1946
Publications, nonprofit information & educational services about international affairs & organizations.
Number of Members: 25,000
Branch Office(s)
801 Second Ave, 9th fl, New York, NY 10017 *Tel:* 212-697-3315 *Fax:* 212-697-3316

US Board on Books For Young People (USBBY)
Division of International Board on Books for Young People (IBBY)
c/o V Ellis Vance, 5503 N El Adobe Dr, Fresno, CA 93711-2363
Tel: 559-351-6119
Web Site: www.usbby.org
Key Personnel
Exec Dir: V Ellis Vance *E-mail:* executive.director@usbby.org
Founded: 1953
To promote international understanding & goodwill through books for children & adolescents.
Number of Members: 500
Publication(s): *Bridges: A Publication of USBBY* (semiannual, newsletter)
Membership(s): ALA; The Children's Book Council; International Literacy Association; National Council of Teachers of English

USBE: United States Book Exchange
2969 W 25 St, Cleveland, OH 44113
Tel: 216-241-6960 *Fax:* 216-241-6966
E-mail: usbe@usbe.com
Web Site: www.usbe.com
Key Personnel
Mng Dir: John T Zubal; Marilyn Zubal
Redistribution of library materials to & from libraries.
Number of Members: 15,888

Visual Artists & Galleries Association Inc (VAGA)
111 Broadway, Suite 1006, New York, NY 10006
Tel: 212-736-6666 *Fax:* 212-736-6767
E-mail: info@vagarights.com
Web Site: vagarights.com
Key Personnel
Exec Dir: Robert Panzer *E-mail:* rpanzer@vagarights.com
Rts Specialist: Lucie Amour *E-mail:* lamour@vagarights.com
Protects artists copyrights; provides art licensing & reproduction rights clearances & royalties collection for artists. Have archive of color transparencies & B&W images.
Number of Members: 18,000

Visual Media Alliance (VMA)
665 Third St, Suite 500, San Francisco, CA 94107-1956
Tel: 415-489-7601 *Toll Free Tel:* 800-659-3363 *Toll Free Fax:* 800-824-1911
E-mail: info@vma.bz
Web Site: main.vma.bz
Key Personnel
Pres: Dan Nelson *Tel:* 415-489-7617 *E-mail:* dan@vma.bz
Trade association.
Number of Members: 950

Western Writers of America Inc (WWA)
271 CR 219, Encampment, WY 82325
Tel: 307-329-8942
Web Site: westernwriters.org
Key Personnel
Pres: Kirk Ellis *E-mail:* president@westernwriters.org
Exec Dir & Secy-Treas: Candy Moulton *E-mail:* wwa.moulton@gmail.com
Founded: 1953
Nonprofit confederation of professional writers of fiction & nonfiction pertaining to, or inspired by, tradition, legends, development & history of the American West.
Number of Members: 650
2018 Meeting(s): Annual Convention, Billings, MT, June 22-24, 2018
Publication(s): *Roundup Magazine* (6 times/yr, $40/yr)

Willamette Writers
5331 SW Macadam Ave, Suite 258, PMB 215, Portland, OR 97239
Tel: 901-200-5385
E-mail: wilwrite@willamettewriters.org
Web Site: willamettewriters.org
Key Personnel
VP & Secy: Gail Pasternack *E-mail:* secretary@willamettewriters.org
Monthly meeting (open to public); critique groups; writer referrals; monthly newsletter; annual writing contest & awards, annual conference.
Number of Members: 1,450
Publication(s): *The Willamette Writer* (monthly, free to membs)

Women Who Write Inc
PO Box 652, Madison, NJ 07940-0652
E-mail: info@womenwhowrite.org
Web Site: womenwhowrite.org
Key Personnel
Pres: Ginger Pate
VP, Membership: Amy Reade
VP, Progs: Debbie Gerrish
Ed, Writers' Notes: Michelle Hollander
Founded: 1988
Writing groups, writers' conference, workshops, readings, literary events, newsletter & literary magazine.
Number of Members: 130
Publication(s): *Goldfinch* (annual, magazine, $10); *Writers' Notes* (quarterly, newsletter)

Women's National Book Association Inc
PO Box 237, FDR Sta, New York, NY 10150-0231
Tel: 212-208-4629 (headquarters) *Fax:* 212-208-4629
E-mail: publicity@bookbuzz.com; info@wnba-books.org
Web Site: www.wnba-books.org; www.NationalReadingGroupMonth.org
Key Personnel
PR: Susannah Greenberg
Founded: 1917
Increase opportunities for women & recognition of women in the world of books. Sponsor WNBA Award (formerly Constance Lindsay Skinner Award), WNBA Pannell Award & WNBA Eastman Grant. Ten chapters: Boston, Charlotte, Detroit, Los Angeles, Nashville, New Orleans, New York, San Francisco, Seattle & Washington, DC.
Number of Members: 1,000
New Election: Biennially in May
Publication(s): *The Bookwoman* (3 issues/yr, free to membs)

Writers' Alliance of Newfoundland & Labrador
Haymarket Sq, 223 Duckworth St, Suite 208, St John's, NL A1C 6N1, Canada
Tel: 709-739-5215 *Toll Free Tel:* 866-739-5215
E-mail: wanl@nf.aibn.com
Web Site: wanl.ca

Key Personnel
Exec Dir: Alison Dyer
Founded: 1987
Not-for-profit, member-based organization established to contribute to a supportive environment for writing & serve the needs & protect the rights of writers in the province.
Number of Members: 350
New Election: Annually in Oct

Writers' Federation of Nova Scotia
1113 Marginal Rd, Halifax, NS B3H 4P7, Canada
Tel: 902-423-8116 *Fax:* 902-422-0881
E-mail: contact@writers.ns.ca
Web Site: writers.ns.ca
Key Personnel
Exec Dir: Jonathan Meakin *E-mail:* director@writers.ns.ca
Arts Educ & Admin Offr: Heidi Hallett *E-mail:* wits@writers.ns.ca
Communs & Devt Offr: Robin Spittal *E-mail:* programs@writers.ns.ca
Mentorship & Outreach Offr: Sue Goyette *E-mail:* events@writers.ns.ca
Founded: 1976
Foster creative writing & the profession of writing in the province of Nova Scotia; provide advice & assistance to writers at all stages of their careers; encourage greater public recognition of Nova Scotian writers & their achievements; enhance the literary arts in our regional & national culture.
Number of Members: 800
New Election: Annually in June
Publication(s): *Eastword* (6 issues/yr, newsletter, electronic version free to membs, hard copy $45/yr)

Writers' Guild of Alberta
11759 Groat Rd, Edmonton, AB T5M 3K6, Canada
Tel: 780-422-8174 *Toll Free Tel:* 800-665-5354 (AB only) *Fax:* 780-422-2663 (attn WGA)
E-mail: mail@writersguild.ca
Web Site: writersguild.ca
Key Personnel
Exec Dir: Carol Holmes *E-mail:* carol.holmes@writersguild.ca
Communs & Partnerships Coord: Ellen Kartz *E-mail:* ellen.kartz@writersguild.ca
Memb Servs Coord: Giorgia Severini
Progs Coord: Natalie Cook *E-mail:* natalie.cook@writersguild.ca; Julie Robinson *E-mail:* julie.robinson@writersguild.ca
Founded: 1980
Our mission is to support, encourage & promote writers & writing, to safeguard the freedom to write & to read & to advocate for the well-being of writers.
Number of Members: 1,000
Publication(s): *WestWord* (quarterly, magazine)
Branch Office(s)
505 21 Ave SW, Calgary, AB T2S 0G9, Canada, Prog Coord: Samantha Warwick *Tel:* 403-265-2226 *E-mail:* samathawarwick@writersguild.ca

Writers Guild of America, East (WGAE)
250 Hudson St, Suite 700, New York, NY 10013
Tel: 212-767-7800 *Fax:* 212-582-1909
Web Site: www.wgaeast.org
Key Personnel
Exec Dir: Lowell Peterson *Tel:* 212-767-7828 *E-mail:* lpeterson@wgaeast.org
Dir, Communs: Jason Gordon *Tel:* 212-767-7809 *E-mail:* jgordon@wgaeast.org
Dir, Progs: Dana Weissman *Tel:* 212-767-7835 *E-mail:* dweissman@wgaeast.org
Labor union representing professional writers in motion pictures, TV, radio, as well as digital media content. Membership available only through the sale of literary material or employment for writing services in one of these areas.
Number of Members: 4,200
New Election: Annually in Sept
Publication(s): *On Writing* (online web series)

Writers Guild of America, West (WGAW)
7000 W Third St, Los Angeles, CA 90048
Tel: 323-951-4000 *Toll Free Tel:* 800-548-4532 *Fax:* 323-782-4800
Web Site: www.wga.org
Key Personnel
Pres: Howard Rodman
VP: David Goodman
Secy & Treas: Aaron Mendelsohn
Labor union: Collective bargaining representation for film, TV broadcast, interactive & new media writers. Awards dinner & seminars (sometimes for public).
Number of Members: 12,000
Publication(s): *Written By Magazine* (6 issues/yr, $50/yr)

Writers' League of Texas (WLT)
611 S Congress Ave, Suite 200 A-3, Austin, TX 78704
Tel: 512-499-8914
E-mail: wlt@writersleague.org
Web Site: www.writersleague.org
Key Personnel
Exec Dir: Becka Oliver *E-mail:* becka@writersleague.org
Prog Dir: Michael Noll *E-mail:* michael@writersleague.org
Memb Servs Mgr: Jordan Smith *E-mail:* jordan@writersleague.org
Founded: 1981
Workshops, seminars, classes, library resource center, technical assistance, newsletter, monthly programs, educational programs for young people. Memberships: $50 (indiv/family), $100 & up (premium), $250 & up (businesses & organizations).
Number of Members: 1,200
Publication(s): *Footnotes* (26 issues/yr, newsletter, free, electronic); *Scribe* (blog)

The Writers' Union of Canada (TWUC)
600-460 Richmond St W, Toronto, ON M5V 1Y1, Canada
Tel: 416-703-8982 *Fax:* 416-504-9090
E-mail: info@writersunion.ca
Web Site: www.writersunion.ca
Key Personnel
Exec Dir: John Degen *Tel:* 416-703-8982 ext 221
Assoc Dir: Siobhan O'Connor *Tel:* 416-703-8982 ext 222 *E-mail:* soconnor@writersunion.ca
Off Admin: Valerie Laws *Tel:* 416-703-8982 ext 224
Specialize in service for members & nonmembers including publications, newsletter, contract advice, competitions, ms evaluation & advocacy.
Number of Members: 2,000

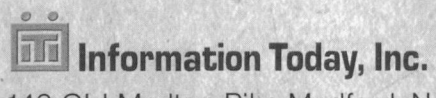

Foundations

Listed below are foundations that are closely affiliated with the book trade.

Bridge to Asia
1505 Juanita Way, Berkeley, CA 94702-1103
Tel: 510-665-3998
E-mail: asianet@bridge.org
Web Site: www.bridge.org
Key Personnel
Pres: Jeffrey Smith
VP: Newton Liu
Founded: 1987
A nonprofit book donation program, which provides donated books, journals & Internet based research services to developing countries in Asia. Primary book donors include members of the American Council of Learned Societies, the Nebraska Book Company, Follett Higher Education Group & several thousand individual book donors.

The Canadian Writers' Foundation Inc (La Fondation des Ecrivains Canadiens)
PO Box 13281, Kanata Sta, Ottawa, ON K2K 1X4, Canada
Tel: 613-256-6937 *Fax:* 613-256-5457
E-mail: info@canadianwritersfoundation.org
Web Site: www.canadianwritersfoundation.org
Key Personnel
Pres: Marianne Scott *Tel:* 613-733-4223 *Fax:* 613-733-8752
Exec Secy: Suzanne Williams *E-mail:* smw.enterprises@sympatico.ca
Founded: 1931
Benevolent trust. Provides financial assistance to distinguished senior Canadian writers in need.

La Foundation des Ecrivains Canadiens, see The Canadian Writers' Foundation Inc (La Fondation des Ecrivains Canadiens)

Graphic Arts Education & Research Foundation (GAERF)
1899 Preston White Dr, Reston, VA 20191
Tel: 703-264-7200 *Toll Free Tel:* 844-381-9839 *Fax:* 703-620-3165
E-mail: gaerf@npes.org
Web Site: www.gaerf.org
Key Personnel
Pres: Thayer Long
Dir: Judith B Durham *E-mail:* jdurham@npes.org
Founded: 1983
A major source of financial support for projects & programs designed to provide a graphic communications work force for the future.

John Simon Guggenheim Memorial Foundation
90 Park Ave, New York, NY 10016
Tel: 212-687-4470 *Fax:* 212-697-3248
E-mail: fellowships@gf.org
Web Site: www.gf.org
Key Personnel
CFO & VP: Coleen Higgins-Jacob
Pres: Edward Hirsch
SVP & Secy: Andre Bernard
Dir, Devt & PR: Richard W Hatter
Founded: 1925
Provide fellowships to further the development of scholars & artists by assisting them to engage in research in any field of knowledge & creation in any of the arts; awarded to persons who have already demonstrated exceptional capacity for productive scholarship or exceptional creative ability in the arts.

The Zora Neale Hurston/Richard Wright Foundation
840 First St NE, 3rd fl, Washington, DC 20002
Tel: 202-248-5051
E-mail: info@hurstonwright.org
Web Site: www.hurstonwright.org
Key Personnel
Co-Founder: Marita Golden; Clyde McElvane
Exec Dir: Deborah Heard
Founded: 1990
Dedicated to discovering, mentoring & honoring Black writers. Through workshops, master classes & readings, the organization preserves the voices of Black writers in the world literary canon, serves as a community for writers & continues a tradition of literary excellence in storytelling established by its namesakes. 501(c)(3) nonprofit.

National Endowment for the Arts
400 Seventh St SW, Washington, DC 20506-0001
Tel: 202-682-5400
Web Site: www.arts.gov
Key Personnel
Chmn: Jane Chu *Tel:* 202-682-5414 *E-mail:* chairman@arts.gov
Sr Deputy Chmn: Adriana Kertzer *Tel:* 202-682-5729 *E-mail:* kertzera@arts.gov
Dir, Admin Servs: Kathy Daum *Tel:* 202-682-5561 *E-mail:* daumk@arts.gov
Dir, Lit: Amy Stolls *Tel:* 202-682-5771 *E-mail:* stollsa@arts.gov
Dir, Pub Aff: Jessamyn Sarmiento *Tel:* 202-682-5759 *E-mail:* sarmientoj@arts.gov
Asst Dir, Press: Victoria Hutter *Tel:* 202-682-5692 *E-mail:* hutterv@arts.gov
Asst Dir, Pubns: Don Ball *Tel:* 202-682-5750 *E-mail:* balld@arts.gov
Founded: 1965
Independent federal agency. Grants to organizations & individuals.

Western States Arts Federation
1743 Wazee St, Suite 300, Denver, CO 80202
Tel: 303-629-1166 *Toll Free Tel:* 888-562-7232 *Fax:* 303-629-9717
E-mail: staff@westaf.org
Web Site: www.westaf.org
Key Personnel
Exec Dir: Anthony Radich *E-mail:* anthony.radich@westaf.org
Dir, Mktg & Communs: Leah Horn *E-mail:* leah.horn@westaf.org
Assoc Dir: Seyan Lucero *E-mail:* seyan.lucero@westaf.org
Fin Assoc: Michelle Baca *E-mail:* michelle.baca@westaf.org
Performing, visual & folk arts programs.

The H W Wilson Foundation
420 Lexington Ave, Suite 2450, New York, NY 10170
Tel: 212-972-6490
Web Site: www.thwwf.org
Key Personnel
Exec Dir: William Stanton
Pres: Harold Regan
VP & Treas: William Hayden
VP & Secy: James Matarazzo
Founded: 1952
Scholarship grants to ALA accredited library & information science programs.

Calendar of Book Trade & Promotional Events—Alphabetical Index of Sponsors

Calendar of Book Trade & Promotional Events—Alphabetical Index of Events

Calendar of Book Trade & Promotional Events

Arranged chronologically by year and month, this section lists book trade events worldwide. Preceding this section are two indexes: the Sponsor Index is an alphabetical list of event sponsors and includes the names and dates of the events they sponsor; the Event Index is an alphabetical list of events along with the dates on which they are held.

2017

NOVEMBER

Feria Internacional del Libro de Guadalajara
Av Alemania 1370, Colonia Moderna, 44190 Guadalajara, Jalisco, Mexico
Tel: (033) 3810 0331; (033) 3268 0900
E-mail: fil@fil.com.mx
Web Site: www.fil.com.mx
Key Personnel
Pres: Raul Padilla Lopez
Gen Dir: Marisol Schulz Manaut *E-mail:* marisol.schulz@fil.com.mx
Contents Mgmt: Laura Niembro Diaz *E-mail:* laura.niembro@fil.com.mx
Exhibitors Coord: Armando Montes de Santiago *E-mail:* armando.desantiago@fil.com.mx
Location: Centro de Exposiciones, Expo Guadalajara, Av Mariano Otero, 1499, Col Verde Valle, Guadalajara, Jalisco, Mexico
Nov 25-Dec 3, 2017

Karlsruher Buecherschau (Karlsruhe Book Fair)
Sponsored by Boersenverein des Deutschen Buchhandels, Landesverband Baden-Wuerttemberg eV (Association of Publishers & Booksellers in Baden-Wuerttemberg eV)
Paulinenstr 53, 70178 Stuttgart, Germany
Tel: (0711) 61941-0 *Fax:* (0711) 61941-44
E-mail: post@buchhandelsverband.de
Web Site: www.karlsruher-buecherschau.de; www.buchhandelsverband.de
Key Personnel
Contact: Carolin Schneider *Tel:* (0711) 61941-26 *E-mail:* schneider@buchhandelsverband.de
Location: Karlsruhe, Germany
Nov 10-Dec 3, 2017

Salon du Livre et de la Presse Jeunesse (SLPJ)
Sponsored by Centre de Promotion du Livre de Jeunesse (CPLJ)
3, rue Francois Debergue, 93100 Montreuil, France
Tel: 01 55 86 86 55 *Fax:* 01 48 57 04 62
E-mail: contact@slpj.fr
Web Site: www.salon-livre-presse-jeunesse.net
Key Personnel
Dir: Sylvie Vassallo
Leading publishing event dedicated to children's books.
Location: l'Espace Paris-Est-Montreuil, 128 rue de Montreuil, Paris, France
Nov 29-Dec 4, 2017

Stuttgarter Buchwochen (Stuttgart Book Weeks)
Sponsored by Boersenverein des Deutschen Buchhandels, Landesverband Baden-Wuerttemberg eV (Association of Publishers & Booksellers in Baden-Wuerttemberg eV)
Paulinenstr 53, 70178 Stuttgart, Germany
Tel: (0711) 61941-0 *Fax:* (0711) 61941-44
E-mail: post@buchhandelsverband.de
Web Site: www.buchwochen.de; www.buchhandelsverband.de
Key Personnel
Contact: Andrea Baumann *Tel:* (0711) 61941-28 *E-mail:* baumann@buchhandelsverband.de
Location: Haus de Wirtschaft, Willi-Bleicher-Str 19, Stuttgart, Germany
Nov 9-Dec 3, 2017

DECEMBER

Sofia International Book Fair
Sponsored by Bulgarian Book Association (BBA)
blvd Vitosha 64, 2nd fl, ap 4, 1463 Sofia, Bulgaria
Tel: (02) 958 15 25; (02) 958 92 11
E-mail: office@abk.bg
Web Site: www.abk.bg
Key Personnel
Event Mgr: Mariya Marinova *E-mail:* m.popstefanova@abk.bg
The first Sofia International Book fair was organized in 1968. Since then it brings together over 40,000 visitors yearly to meet with exhibiting companies from Bulgaria & abroad & offers unrivalled access to the national & international book publishing & bookseller communities.
Location: National Palace of Culture, One Bulgaria Blvd, Sofia, Bulgaria
Dec 12-17, 2017

2018

JANUARY

APE 2018
Sponsored by digiprimo GmbH & Co KG
Lutherstr 122, 14089 Berlin, Germany
Mailing Address: PO Box 22 01 16, 14061 Berlin, Germany
Tel: (030) 36 43 01 64 *Fax:* (030) 36 43 02 70
E-mail: info@digiprimo.com
Web Site: www.digiprimo.com
Location: Berlin, Germany
Jan 16-17, 2018

Football Writers Association of America Annual Meeting
Sponsored by Football Writers Association of America (FWAA)
18652 Vista del Sol, Dallas, TX 75287
Tel: 972-713-6198
Web Site: www.sportswriters.net/fwaa; twitter.com/thefwaa
Key Personnel
Exec Dir: Steve Richardson *E-mail:* tiger@fwaa.com
Location: Atlanta Marriott Marquis, Atlanta, GA, USA
Jan 5-8, 2018

IS&T Electronic Imaging Conference
Sponsored by Society for Imaging Science & Technology (IS&T)
7003 Kilworth Lane, Springfield, VA 22151
Tel: 703-642-9090 *Fax:* 703-642-9094
E-mail: info@imaging.org
Web Site: www.imaging.org
Key Personnel
Exec Dir: Suzanne E Grinnan *E-mail:* sgrinnan@imaging.org
Conference Prog Mgr: Diana Gonzalez *Tel:* 703-642-9090 ext 106 *E-mail:* dgonzalez@imaging.org
Exec Asst: Donna Smith *E-mail:* dsmith@imaging.org
Location: Hyatt Regency San Francisco Airport, Burlingame, CA, USA
Jan 28-Feb 1, 2018

MLA Annual Convention
Sponsored by Modern Language Association of America (MLA)
85 Broad St, Suite 500, New York, NY 10004-2434
SAN: 202-6422
Tel: 646-576-5266 (convention); 646-576-5000 *Fax:* 646-458-0030
E-mail: convention@mla.org
Web Site: www.mla.org/convention
Key Personnel
Assoc Dir of Convention Progs: Karin L Bagnall *E-mail:* kbagnall@mla.org
Location: New York Hilton Midtown, Sheraton New York Times Square & New York Marriott Marquis, New York, NY, USA
Jan 4-7, 2018

Remainder & Promotional Book Fair
Sponsored by Ciana Ltd
Rockholt, Ellimore Rd, Lustleigh, Newton Abbot TQ13 9TF, United Kingdom
Tel: (01626) 897 106 *Fax:* (01626) 897 107
E-mail: enquiries@ciana.co.uk
Web Site: www.ciana.co.uk
Key Personnel
Contact: Sarah Weedon; Robert Collie
Location: ILEC Conference Centre, 47 Lillie Rd, London, UK
Jan 21-22, 2018

FEBRUARY

American Library Association Midwinter Meeting
Sponsored by The American Library Association (ALA)
50 E Huron St, Chicago, IL 60611
Tel: 312-944-6780 *Toll Free Tel:* 800-545-2433 (ext 3223, conference servs) *Fax:* 312-440-9374
E-mail: ala@ala.org
Web Site: www.ala.org
Key Personnel
Registration & Housing Specialist: Alicia Babcock *Tel:* 800-545-2433 ext 3229 *E-mail:* ababcock@ala.org

Conference Dir: Paul Graller *Tel:* 800-545-2433 ext 3219 *E-mail:* pgraller@ala.org
Conference Mgr: Amy McGuigan *Tel:* 800-545-2433 ext 3226 *E-mail:* amcguigan@ala.org
Meetings, AV & Catering Coord: Yvonne McLean *Tel:* 800-545-2433 ext 3222 *E-mail:* ymclean@ala.org
Conference Coord: Lina Zabaneh *Tel:* 800-545-2433 ext 3227 *E-mail:* lzabaneh@ala.org
Meeting Coord: Alicia (Alee) Navarro *Tel:* 800-545-2433 ext 3216 *E-mail:* anavarro@ala.org
Location: Denver, CO, USA
Feb 9-13, 2018

California International Antiquarian Book Fair
Sponsored by Antiquarian Booksellers' Association of America (ABAA)
20 W 44 St, Suite 507, New York, NY 10036
Tel: 212-944-8291 *Fax:* 212-944-8293
E-mail: cafair@whiterainproductions.com
Web Site: www.cabookfair.com; www.abaa.org
Key Personnel
Exec Dir: Susan Benne *E-mail:* sbenne@abaa.org
Annual event co-sponsored by International League of Antiquarian Booksellers & managed by White Rain Productions.
Location: Pasadena Convention Center, 300 E Green St, Pasadena, CA, USA
Feb 9-11, 2018

Graphics of the Americas Expo & Conference (GOA)
Sponsored by Printing Association of Florida Inc (PAF)
Affiliate of Printing Industries of America (PIA)
6250 Hazeltine National Dr, Suite 114, Orlando, FL 32822
Tel: 407-240-8009 *Toll Free Tel:* 800-331-0461 *Fax:* 407-240-8323
E-mail: info@goaexpo.com
Web Site: www.goaexpo.com; www.flprint.org
Key Personnel
Pres: James Hernandez *Tel:* 407-845-0597 *E-mail:* gabe@flprint.org
Trade Show Dir: Adham Faltas *Tel:* 407-845-0600 *E-mail:* adham@flprint.org
Location: Broward County Convention Center, 1950 Eisenhower Blvd, Fort Lauderdale, FL, USA
Feb 22-24, 2018

IPA Congress
Sponsored by International Publishers Association (IPA)
23, ave de France, 1202 Geneva, Switzerland
Tel: (022) 704 18 20 *Fax:* (022) 704 18 21
E-mail: secretariat@internationalpublishers.org; info@internationalpublishers.org
Web Site: www.ipacongress.com; www.internationalpublishers.org
Key Personnel
Secy Gen: Jose Borghino *E-mail:* borghino@internationalpublishers.org
Hosted by the Federation of Indian Publishers (FIP). Held every 2 years.
Location: Taj Palace Hotel, New Delhi, India
Feb 11-13, 2018

PSP Annual Conference
Sponsored by Association of American Publishers (AAP)
455 Massachusetts Ave NW, Suite 700, Washington, DC 20001-2777
Tel: 212-255-0200 *Fax:* 212-255-7007
E-mail: info@publishers.org
Web Site: www.publishers.org
Key Personnel
VP & Exec Dir, Prof & Scholarly Publg: John Tagler *Tel:* 212-255-1407 *E-mail:* jtagler@publishers.org
Dir, Prof & Scholarly Publg: Sara Pinto *Tel:* 212-255-1716 *E-mail:* spinto@publishers.org
Location: Ritz-Carlton, Washington, DC, USA
Feb 7-9, 2018

SCBWI Winter Conference
Sponsored by Society of Children's Book Writers and Illustrators (SCBWI)
4727 Wilshire Blvd, Suite 301, Los Angeles, CA 90010
Tel: 323-782-1010 *Fax:* 323-782-1892
E-mail: scbwi@scbwi.org
Web Site: www.scbwi.org
Key Personnel
Pres: Stephen Mooser *E-mail:* stephenmooser@scbwi.org
Exec Dir: Lin Oliver *E-mail:* linoliver@scbwi.org
Location: Grand Hyatt New York, 109 E 42 St at Grand Central Terminal, New York, NY, USA
Feb 2-4, 2018

Texas Outdoor Writers Association Annual Conference
Sponsored by Texas Outdoor Writers Association (TOWA)
PO Box 151293, Austin, TX 78715-1293
Tel: 512-358-8000 *Fax:* 512-358-8010
E-mail: towa@towa.org
Web Site: www.towa.org
Key Personnel
Exec Dir: Burney Brown
Location: TX, USA
Feb 22-25, 2018

WestPack®
Sponsored by UBM Canon
2901 28 St, Suite 100, Santa Monica, CA 90405
Tel: 310-445-4200
E-mail: tsoperations@ubm.com
Web Site: ubmcanon.com
Location: Anaheim Convention Center, 800 W Katella Ave, Anaheim, CA, USA
Feb 6-8, 2018

MARCH

Adelaide Festival
Sponsored by Adelaide Festival Corp
Level 9, 33 King William St, Adelaide, SA 5000, Australia
Mailing Address: PO Box 8221, Station Arcade, Adelaide, SA 5000, Australia
Tel: (08) 8216 4444 *Fax:* (08) 8216 4455
E-mail: info@adelaidefestival.com.au
Web Site: www.adelaidefestival.com.au
Key Personnel
Artistic Dir: Neil Armfield; Rachel Healy
Assoc Prodr: Anne Wiberg
Prog Dir: Lesley Newton
Prodn Mgr: Adam Hornhardt
Annual event highlighting the arts, including literature. Adelaide Writers' Week is one of the high-profile events held during the festival.
Location: Adelaide's Central Business District, Adelaide, SA, Australia
March 2-18, 2018

AWP Annual Conference & Bookfair
Sponsored by Association of Writers & Writing Programs (AWP)
George Mason University, 4400 University Dr, MSN 1E3, Fairfax, VA 22030
Tel: 703-993-4301 *Fax:* 703-993-4302
E-mail: awp@awpwriter.org
Web Site: www.awpwriter.org/awp_conference/; www.awpwriter.org
Key Personnel
Exec Dir: David W Fenza
Dir, Conferences: Christian Teresi
Assoc Dir, Conferences: Cynthia Sherman
Location: Tampa Convention Center & Marriott Tampa Waterside, Tampa, FL, USA
March 7-10, 2018

Bologna Children's Book Fair
Sponsored by BolognaFiere SpA
Piazza Costituzione, 6, 40128 Bologna, Italy
Tel: (051) 282 111 *Fax:* (051) 637 4011
E-mail: bookfair@bolognafiere.it
Web Site: www.bolognachildrensbookfair.com
Key Personnel
Exhibition Mgr: Elena Pasoli *Tel:* (051) 282 966 *E-mail:* elena.pasoli@bolognafiere.it
Location: Bologna Fair Centre, Piazza Costituzione, 6, Bologna, Italy
March 26-29, 2018

CAMEX
Sponsored by National Association of College Stores (NACS)
500 E Lorain St, Oberlin, OH 44074
Tel: 440-775-7777 *Toll Free Tel:* 800-622-7498 *Fax:* 440-775-4769
E-mail: camex@nacs.org
Web Site: www.camex.org; www.nacs.org
Key Personnel
CEO: Bob Walton *Tel:* 800-622-7498 ext 2201 *E-mail:* rwalton@nacs.org
Dir, Meetings: Jodie Wilmot *Tel:* 800-622-7498 ext 2272 *E-mail:* jwilmot@nacs.org
Dir of Expositions: Mary Adler-Kozak *Tel:* 800-622-7498 ext 2265 *E-mail:* madler-kozak@nacs.org
Conference & trade show dedicated exclusively to the more than $10 billion collegiate retailing industry.
Location: Kay Bailey Hutchison Convention Center, Dallas, TX, USA
March 2-6, 2018

The IA Summit
Sponsored by Association for Information Science & Technology (ASIS&T)
8555 16 St, Suite 850, Silver Spring, MD 20910
Tel: 301-495-0900 *Fax:* 301-495-0810
E-mail: asist@asist.org
Web Site: www.asist.org
Key Personnel
Dir of Meetings & Membership: Vanessa Foss *E-mail:* vfoss@asist.org
Location: Chicago, IL, USA
March 21-25, 2018

Leipzig Book Fair (Leipziger Buchmesse)
Sponsored by Leipziger Messe GmbH
Messe-Allee 1, 04356 Leipzig, Germany
Mailing Address: Postfach 10 07 20, 04007 Leipzig, Germany
Tel: (0341) 678-0 *Fax:* (0341) 678-8762
E-mail: info@leipziger-buchmesse.de
Web Site: www.leipziger-buchmesse.de
Key Personnel
Dir: Oliver Zille *Tel:* (0341) 678-8240
Held annually in conjunction with The Leipzig Antiquarian Book Fair.
Location: Leipzig Exhibition Centre, Messe-Allee 1, Leipzig, Germany
March 15-18, 2018

Livre Paris (Book Paris)
Sponsored by Reed Expositions France
Subsidiary of Reed Exhibition Companies
52-54 quai de Dion-Bouton, CS 80001, 92806 Puteaux Cedex, France
Tel: 01 47 56 64 31 *Fax:* 01 47 56 64 44
E-mail: livre@reedexpo.fr
Web Site: www.livreparis.com
Key Personnel
Mktg & Commun Mgr: Marion Thomassin *E-mail:* marion.thomassin@reedexpo.fr

Annual international publishing event for publishers, booksellers, teachers & librarians. Open to the trade & the public.
Location: Paris Expo, Porte de Versailles, Paris, France
March 16-19, 2018

New York Antiquarian Book Fair
Sponsored by Antiquarian Booksellers' Association of America (ABAA)
20 W 44 St, Suite 507, New York, NY 10036
Tel: 212-944-8291 *Fax:* 212-944-8293
Web Site: www.nyantiquarianbookfair.com; www.abaa.org
Key Personnel
Exec Dir: Susan Benne *E-mail:* sbenne@abaa.org
Co-sponsored by International League of Antiquarian Booksellers (ILAB) & managed by Sanford L Smith & Associates Ltd.
Location: Park Avenue Armory, 643 Park Ave at 67 St, New York, NY, USA
March 8-11, 2018

Paper2018
Sponsored by American Forest & Paper Association (AF&PA)
1101 "K" St NW, Suite 700, Washington, DC 20005
Tel: 202-463-2700 *Fax:* 202-463-2708
E-mail: info@afandpa.org
Web Site: www.afandpa.org; www.paper2018.com
Key Personnel
Dir, Meetings: Susan Van Eaton
Sr Mgr, Meetings & Memb Servs: Kathy Smith
Co-hosted with the National Paper Trade Association (NPTA), this annual paper industry event offers participants access to decision makers from an impressive array of manufacturers, merchants, publishers, distributors of printing paper, packaging material & industrial material & supplies.
Location: Lotte New York Palace Hotel, 455 Madison Ave, New York, NY, USA
March 11-13, 2018

Virginia Festival of the Book
Sponsored by Virginia Foundation for the Humanities
145 Ednam Dr, Charlottesville, VA 22903
Tel: 434-924-3296 *Fax:* 434-296-4714
E-mail: vabook@virginia.edu
Web Site: www.vabook.org
Key Personnel
Prog Dir: Jane Kulow *Tel:* 434-924-7548
Annual public festival for children & adults featuring authors, illustrators, publishers, publicists, agents & other book professionals in panel discussions & readings. Most events are free. Hundreds of authors invited annually.
Location: Charlottesville, VA, USA
March 21-25, 2018

APRIL

Alberta Library Conference
Sponsored by Library Association of Alberta (LAA)
80 Baker Crescent NW, Calgary, AB T2L 1R4, Canada
Tel: 403-284-5818 *Toll Free Tel:* 877-522-5550 *Fax:* 403-284-5818
E-mail: info@laa.ca
Web Site: www.albertalibraryconference.com; www.laa.ca
Key Personnel
Exec Dir/Conference Coord: Christine Sheppard
Co-hosted by Alberta Library Trustees Association (ALTA).
Location: Fairmont Jasper Park Lodge, Jasper, AB, CN
April 26-29, 2018

ASQ World Conference on Quality & Improvement
Sponsored by American Society for Quality (ASQ)
600 N Plankinton Ave, Milwaukee, WI 53203
Mailing Address: PO Box 3005, Milwaukee, WI 53201-3005
Tel: 414-272-8575 *Toll Free Tel:* 800-248-1946 (US & CN) *Fax:* 414-272-1734
E-mail: help@asq.org
Web Site: www.asq.org
Key Personnel
Conference Mgr: Michael Dzick *E-mail:* mdzick@asq.org
Location: Washington State Convention Center, 705 Pike St, Seattle, WA, USA
April 30-May 2, 2018

BMI Management Conference
Sponsored by Book Manufacturers' Institute Inc (BMI)
PO Box 731388, Ormond Beach, FL 32173
Tel: 386-986-4552 *Fax:* 386-986-4553
Web Site: www.bmibook.org
Key Personnel
EVP: Daniel N Bach *E-mail:* dbach@bmibook.com
Conference Coord: Jackie Murray
Location: King & Prince, St Simons Island, GA, USA
April 29-May 1, 2018

EPA Annual Convention
Sponsored by Evangelical Press Association (EPA)
PO Box 1787, Queen Creek, AZ 85142
Toll Free Tel: 888-311-1731
Web Site: www.evangelicalpress.com
Key Personnel
Exec Dir & CFO: Lamar Keener
Annual convention for editors, publishers, writers & other staff (print & online publications). Workshop tracks & plenary sessions, opportunities for networking & fellowship.
Location: Orlando Airport Marriott Lakeside, Orlando, FL, USA
April 4-6, 2018

The Federation of Children's Book Groups Annual Conference
Sponsored by The Federation of Children's Book Groups (FCBG)
10 St Laurence Rd, Bradford on Avon BA15 1JG, United Kingdom
Tel: (0300) 102 1559
E-mail: info@fcbg.org.uk
Web Site: www.fcbg.org.uk; twitter.com/fcbgnews?lang=en; www.facebook.com/The-Federation-of-Childrens-Book-Groups-119682808115620/
Organized by one of our local children's book groups in collaboration with the national executive, this conference is an opportunity for authors, illustrators, parents, teachers, librarians & all interested children's book lovers to come together to promote their mission of bringing children & books together.
Location: Queenswood School, Hatfield, Hertfordshire, UK
April 13-15, 2018

International Children's Book Day
Sponsored by International Board on Books for Young People (IBBY)
Nonnenweg 12, Postfach, 4009 Basel, Switzerland
Tel: (061) 272 29 17 *Fax:* (061) 272 27 57
E-mail: ibby@ibby.org
Web Site: www.ibby.org
Key Personnel
Exec Dir: Liz Page *E-mail:* liz.page@ibby.org
Admin Asst: Luzmaria Stauffenegger-Lobato *E-mail:* luzmaria.stauffenegger@ibby.org
On Hans Christian Andersen's birthday, April 2nd, International Children's Book Day (ICBD) is celebrated to inspire a love of reading & to call attention to children's books. Each year a different national section has the opportunity to be the international sponsor. It decides upon a theme & invites a prominent author to write a message to the children of the world & a well-known illustrator to design a poster. These materials are used in different ways to promote books & reading around the world.
April 2, 2018

IS&T Archiving Conference
Sponsored by Society for Imaging Science & Technology (IS&T)
7003 Kilworth Lane, Springfield, VA 22151
Tel: 703-642-9090 *Fax:* 703-642-9094
E-mail: info@imaging.org
Web Site: www.imaging.org
Key Personnel
Exec Dir: Suzanne E Grinnan *E-mail:* sgrinnan@imaging.org
Conference Prog Mgr: Diana Gonzalez *Tel:* 703-642-9090 ext 106 *E-mail:* dgonzalez@imaging.org
Exec Asst: Donna Smith *E-mail:* dsmith@imaging.org
Location: Washington, DC, USA
April 17-20, 2018

The London Book Fair
Sponsored by Reed Exhibitions UK
Division of RELX Group PLC
Gateway House, 28 The Quadrant, Richmond, Surrey TW9 1DN, United Kingdom
Tel: (020) 8271 2124
E-mail: lbf.helpline@reedexpo.co.uk; lbfteam@reedexpo.co.uk
Web Site: www.londonbookfair.co.uk
Key Personnel
Conference Mgr: Orna O'Brien *Tel:* (020) 8910 7906 *E-mail:* orna.obrien@reedexpo.co.uk
The London Book Fair is the global marketplace for rights negotiation & the sale & distribution of content across print, audio, TV, film & digital channels. Taking place every spring in the world's premier publishing & cultural capital, it is a unique opportunity to hear from authors, enjoy the vibrant atmosphere & explore innovations shaping the publishing world of the future. The London Book Fair brings you 3 days of focused access to customers, content & emerging markets.
Location: Olympia London, Hammersmith Rd, Kensington, London, UK
April 10-12, 2018

Los Angeles Times Festival of Books
Sponsored by Los Angeles Times
Subsidiary of Tronc Inc
202 W First St, Los Angeles, CA 90012
Tel: 213-237-5000 *Toll Free Tel:* 800-528-4637 *Fax:* 213-237-2335
E-mail: eventinfo@latimes.com
Web Site: events.latimes.com/festivalofbooks
Location: The University of Southern California (USC), Los Angeles, CA, USA
April 21-23, 2018

MagNet
Sponsored by Magazines Canada (MC)
425 Adelaide St W, Suite 700, Toronto, ON M5V 3C1, Canada
Tel: 416-504-0274 *Fax:* 416-504-0437
E-mail: info@magazinescanada.ca; magnet@magazinescanada.ca

Web Site: www.magazinescanada.ca/development/magnet; twitter.com/magnetcanada
Key Personnel
Mgr, Events: Amanda Raponi Hart *Tel:* 416-504-0274 ext 224 *E-mail:* araponihart@magazinescanada.ca
Canada's magazine conference, MagNet is a jointly sponsored by Magazines Canada (MC), Canadian Society of Magazine Editors (CSME) & Circulation Management Association of Canada (CMC).
Location: The Courtyard Downtown Toronto, 475 Yonge St, Toronto, ON, CN
April 23-28, 2018

NAAJ Annual Meeting
Sponsored by North American Agricultural Journalists (NAAJ)
6434 Hurta Lane, Bryan, TX 77808
Tel: 979-845-2872 *Fax:* 979-862-1202
Web Site: www.naaj.net
Key Personnel
Exec Secy & Treas: Kathleen Phillips *E-mail:* kaphillips@tamu.edu
Annual meeting, writing awards & scholarship benefit dance.
Location: Washington, DC, USA
April 2018

NAPIM Annual Convention
Sponsored by National Association of Printing Ink Manufacturers (NAPIM)
15 Technology Pkwy S, Peachtree Corners, GA 30092
Tel: 770-209-7289 *Fax:* 678-680-4920; 770-209-7217
Web Site: www.napim.org
Key Personnel
Exec Dir: John Copeland *Tel:* 815-979-2341 *E-mail:* jcopeland@napim.org
Memb Rel Mgr: Ben Hopper *E-mail:* bhopper@napim.org
Location: Fairmont Sonoma Mission Inn & Spa, Sonoma, CA, USA
April 20-23, 2018

National Library Week
Sponsored by The American Library Association (ALA)
50 E Huron St, Chicago, IL 60611
Tel: 312-944-6780 *Toll Free Tel:* 800-545-2433 *Fax:* 312-440-9374
E-mail: ala@ala.org
Web Site: www.ala.org/nlw
Location: Nationwide throughout the USA
April 8-14, 2018

PaperCon
Sponsored by Technical Association of the Pulp & Paper Industry (TAPPI)
15 Technology Pkwy S, Suite 115, Peachtree Corners, GA 30092
Tel: 770-446-1400 *Toll Free Tel:* 800-332-8686 (US); 800-446-9431 (CN) *Fax:* 770-446-6947; 770-209-7206
E-mail: memberconnection@tappi.org
Web Site: www.papercon.org; www.tappi.org
Key Personnel
Dir of Mktg: Simona Marcellus *Tel:* 770-209-7293 *E-mail:* smarcellus@tappi.org
Location: Charlotte Convention Center, Charlotte, NC, USA
April 15-18, 2018

The Quest for Excellence® Conference
Sponsored by National Institute of Standards and Technology (NIST)
100 Bureau Dr, Stop 1070, Gaithersburg, MD 20899-1070
Tel: 301-975-2036 *Fax:* 301-948-3716
E-mail: baldrige@nist.gov
Web Site: www.nist.gov/baldrige/qe/index.cfm
Key Personnel
Conference Chair: Barbara Fischer *E-mail:* barbara.fischer@nist.gov
Official conference of the Malcolm Baldrige National Quality Award, held in partnership with American Society for Quality (ASQ) & Association for Talent Development (ATD).
Location: Baltimore Marriott Waterfront, 700 Aliceanna St, Baltimore, MD, USA
April 8-11, 2018

Society of American Business Editors & Writers Spring Conference
Sponsored by Society of American Business Editors & Writers Inc (SABEW)
Walter Cronkite School of Journalism & Mass Communication, Arizona State University, 555 N Central Ave, Suite 406E, Phoenix, AZ 85004-1248
Tel: 602-496-7862 *Fax:* 602-496-7041
E-mail: sabew@sabew.org
Web Site: sabew.org
Key Personnel
Exec Dir: Kathleen Graham *Tel:* 602-496-5190 *E-mail:* kgraham@sabew.org
Spec Projs Mgr: Crystal Beasley *Tel:* 602-496-5188 *E-mail:* cbeasley@sabew.org
Location: Capital Hilton, Washington, DC, USA
April 26-28, 2018

Southern Kentucky Book Fest
WKU Libraries, Cravens 106, 1906 College Heights Blvd, Bowling Green, KY 42101-1067
Tel: 270-745-4502 *Fax:* 270-745-6422
E-mail: sokybookfest@wku.edu
Web Site: www.sokybookfest.org
Key Personnel
Mtkg Coord: Jennifer Wilson *E-mail:* jennifer.wilson@wku.edu
The Southern Kentucky Book Fest is one of the state's largest literary events & is presented by WKU Libraries, Warren County Public Library & Barnes & Noble Booksellers. Book Fest is a fundraiser for the promotion of literacy in our community.
Location: Knicely Conference Center, 645 Campbell Lane, Bowling Green, KY, USA
April 20-21, 2018

Texas Library Association Annual Conference
Sponsored by Texas Library Association (TLA)
3355 Bee Cave Rd, Suite 401, Austin, TX 78746-6763
Tel: 512-328-1518 *Toll Free Tel:* 800-580-2852 *Fax:* 512-328-8852
E-mail: tla@txla.org
Web Site: www.txla.org
Key Personnel
Conference Mgr: Elise Walker *Tel:* 512-328-1518 x145 *E-mail:* elisew@txla.org
Location: Dallas, TX, USA
April 10-13, 2018

Transformation
Sponsored by 4A's (American Association of Advertising Agencies)
1065 Avenue of the Americas, 16th fl, New York, NY 10018
Tel: 212-682-2500
E-mail: eventhelp@aaaa.org
Web Site: transformation.aaaa.org; www.aaaa.org
Key Personnel
CEO & Pres: Nancy Hill *E-mail:* nhill@aaaa.org
Events Mgr: Jennifer Falik Rains *Tel:* 212-850-0733 *E-mail:* jfrains@aaaa.org
The annual gathering of C-level executives from various disciplines within the marketing, media & agency businesses.
Location: Loews Miami Beach Hotel, 1601 Collins Ave, Miami Beach, FL, USA
April 8-11, 2018

UKSG Annual Conference & Exhibition
Sponsored by UKSG (United Kingdom Serials Group)
Bowman & Hillier Bldg, The Old Brewery, Priory Lane, Burford, Oxon OX18 4SG, United Kingdom
Mailing Address: PO Box 5594, Newbury, Berks RG20 0YD, United Kingdom
Web Site: www.uksg.org
Key Personnel
Busn Mgr: Alison Whitehorn *Tel:* (01635) 254292 *Fax:* (01635) 253826 *E-mail:* alison@uksg.org
Admin: Karen Sadler *Tel:* (01865) 310834 *Fax:* (01865) 310834 *E-mail:* karen@uksg.org
Annual 3 day event open to everyone.
Location: Harrogate, UK
April 9-11, 2018

Xploration® 18
Sponsored by Xplor International
24156 State Rd 54, Suite 4, Lutz, FL 33559
Tel: 813-949-6170 *Fax:* 813-949-9977
E-mail: info@xplor.org
Web Site: www.xplor.org
Key Personnel
Mktg Mgr: Chad Henk *Tel:* 813-949-6171
Progs Mgr: Jennifer Smith
Location: Rosen Plaza, Orlando, FL, USA
April 17-19, 2018

MAY

BookExpo
Sponsored by ReedPOP
Division of Reed Exhibitions USA
383 Main Ave, Norwalk, CT 06851
Tel: 203-840-4800 *Toll Free Tel:* 800-840-5614 (cust serv)
E-mail: inquiry@bookexpoamerica.com (cust serv)
Web Site: www.bookexpoamerica.com; www.reedpop.com
Key Personnel
Event Dir: Brien McDonald *Tel:* 203-840-5483 *E-mail:* Brien@ReedPop.com
Produced & managed by ReedPop, BookExpo is sponsored by the American Booksellers Association (ABA), the Association of American Publishers Inc (AAP) & the Association of Authors' Representatives Inc (AAR).
Location: Jacob K Javits Convention Center, 655 W 43 St, New York, NY, USA
May 30-June 1, 2018

Children's Book Week
Sponsored by The Children's Book Council (CBC)
54 W 39 St, 14th fl, New York, NY 10018
Tel: 212-966-1990
E-mail: cbc.info@cbcbooks.org
Web Site: www.bookweekonline.com; www.cbcbooks.org
Key Personnel
Exec Dir: Carl Lennertz *E-mail:* carl.lennertz@cbcbooks.org
Dir, Programming: Shaina Birkhead *E-mail:* shaina.birkhead@cbcbooks.org
Location: Nationwide across the USA
May 7-13, 2018

SSP Annual Meeting
Sponsored by Society for Scholarly Publishing (SSP)
10200 W 44 Ave, Suite 304, Wheat Ridge, CO 80033-2840
Tel: 303-422-3914 *Fax:* 720-881-6101
E-mail: info@sspnet.org

Web Site: www.sspnet.org
Key Personnel
Exec/Meetings Asst: Jennifer Lanphere
Location: Sheraton Chicago Hotel & Towers, Chicago, IL, USA
May 30-June 1, 2018

JUNE

AAUP Annual Meeting
Sponsored by Association of American University Presses (AAUP)
1412 Broadway, Suite 2135, New York, NY 10018
Tel: 212-989-1010 *Fax:* 212-989-0275
E-mail: annualmeeting@aaup.org; info@aaupnet.org
Web Site: www.aaupnet.org
Key Personnel
Exec Dir: Peter Berkery *Tel:* 917-288-5594 *E-mail:* pberkery@aaupnet.org
Asst Dir & Cont: Tim Muench *Tel:* 917-244-1463 *E-mail:* tmuench@aaupnet.org
Dir, Mktg & Communs: Brenna McLaughlin *Tel:* 917-244-2051 *E-mail:* bmclaughlin@aaupnet.org
Off Mgr & Prog Admin: Kim Miller *Tel:* 917-244-1264 *E-mail:* kmiller@aaupnet.org
Location: Fairmont San Francisco, San Francisco, CA, USA
June 17-19, 2018

American Library Association Annual Conference
Sponsored by The American Library Association (ALA)
50 E Huron St, Chicago, IL 60611
Tel: 312-944-6780 *Toll Free Tel:* 800-545-2433 (ext 3223, conference servs) *Fax:* 312-440-9374
E-mail: ala@ala.org
Web Site: www.ala.org
Key Personnel
Registration & Housing Specialist: Alicia Babcock *Tel:* 800-545-2433 ext 3229 *E-mail:* ababcock@ala.org
Conference Dir: Paul Graller *Tel:* 800-545-2433 ext 3219 *E-mail:* pgraller@ala.org
Conference Mgr: Amy McGuigan *Tel:* 800-545-2433 ext 3226 *E-mail:* amcguigan@ala.org
Meetings, AV & Catering Coord: Yvonne McLean *Tel:* 800-545-2433 ext 3222 *E-mail:* ymclean@ala.org
Conference Coord: Lina Zabaneh *Tel:* 800-545-2433 ext 3227 *E-mail:* lzabaneh@ala.org
Meeting Coord: Alicia (Alee) Navarro *Tel:* 800-545-2433 ext 3216 *E-mail:* anavarro@ala.org
Location: New Orleans, LA, USA
June 21-26, 2018

Ann Arbor Book Festival
PO Box 4387, Ann Arbor, MI 48106
E-mail: info@aabookfestival.org
Web Site: aabookfestival.org
First held in 2004, Ann Arbor Book Festival is a community-wide celebration of reading, writing & literacy regional in scope & interest.
Location: Ann Arbor & Ypsilanti, MI, USA
June 2018

BookCon
Sponsored by ReedPOP
Division of Reed Exhibitions USA
383 Main Ave, Norwalk, CT 06851
Tel: 203-840-5632 (cust serv); 203-840-4800 *Toll Free Tel:* 800-777-8774
E-mail: inquiry@TheBookCon.com
Web Site: www.thebookcon.com; www.reedpop.com
Key Personnel
Global SVP: Lance Fensterman *E-mail:* Lance@ReedPOP.com
Event Dir: Brien McDonald *Tel:* 203-840-5483 *E-mail:* Brien@ReedPop.com
Consumer event following BookExpo.
Location: Jacob K Javits Convention Center, 655 W 43 St, New York, NY, USA
June 2-3, 2018

Catholic Media Conference
Sponsored by Catholic Press Association of the United States & Canada
205 W Monroe St, Suite 470, Chicago, IL 60606
Tel: 312-380-6789 *Fax:* 312-361-0256
Web Site: www.catholicpress.org
Key Personnel
Exec Dir: Timothy M Walter *E-mail:* twalter@catholicpress.org
Location: Hyatt Regency Green Bay, 333 Main St, Green Bay, WI, USA
June 13-15, 2018

EastPack®
Sponsored by UBM Canon
2901 28 St, Suite 100, Santa Monica, CA 90405
Tel: 310-445-4200
E-mail: tsoperations@ubm.com
Web Site: ubmcanon.com
Location: Jacob K Javits Convention Center, 655 W 43 St, New York, NY, USA
June 12-14, 2018

IABC World Conference
Sponsored by International Association of Business Communicators (IABC)
155 Montgomery St, Suite 1210, San Francisco, CA 94104
Tel: 415-544-4700 *Toll Free Tel:* 800-776-4222 (US & CN) *Fax:* 415-544-4747
E-mail: conference@iabc.com
Web Site: wc.iabc.com; www.iabc.com
Key Personnel
Dir, Content: Natasha Nicholson
Location: Palais des congres de Montreal, Montreal, QC, CN
June 3-6, 2018

Outdoor Writers Association of America Annual Conference
Sponsored by Outdoor Writers Association of America (OWAA)
615 Oak St, Suite 201, Missoula, MT 59801
Tel: 406-728-7434 *Fax:* 406-728-7445
E-mail: info@owaa.org
Web Site: www.owaa.org
Key Personnel
Membership & Conference Servs: Jessica (Pollett) Seitz *E-mail:* jseitz@owaa.org
The annual OWAA Conference is an opportunity for outdoor communicators & outdoor groups, businesses & agencies that are involved in the world of outdoor communication to learn & connect with others in the industry. It will give attendees a chance to network with other professionals, allow them to build crucial business outlets & help improve their skills. Attend sessions geared toward general business & newsmaker sessions, plus craft improvement in multiple genres of outdoor communication.
Location: Grand Wayne Convention Center, Fort Wayne, IN, USA
June 2-4, 2018

SIPA Annual Conference
Sponsored by Specialized Information Publishers Association (SIPA)
Division of Software & Information Industry Association (SIIA)
1090 Vermont Ave NW, 6th fl, Washington, DC 20005-4095
Tel: 202-289-7442 *Fax:* 202-289-7097
Web Site: www.sipaonline.com
Key Personnel
Prog Coord: Nevena Jovanovic *Tel:* 202-789-4491
Location: Capital Hilton, Washington, DC, USA
June 5-7, 2018

SLA Annual Conference & INFO-EXPO
Sponsored by Special Libraries Association (SLA)
7918 Jones Branch Dr, Suite 300, McLean, VA 22102
Tel: 703-647-4900 *Fax:* 703-506-3266
Web Site: www.sla.org
Key Personnel
Dir, Events: Mary Katherine Bilowus *E-mail:* mkbilowus@sla.org
Location: Baltimore, MD, USA
June 11-13, 2018

JULY

Hong Kong Book Fair
Sponsored by Hong Kong Trade Development Council
c/o Exhibition Dept, Unit 13, Expo Galleria, Hong Kong Convention & Exhibition Centre, Wan Chai, Hong Kong
Tel: 1830 670; 1830 668 (cust serv) *Fax:* 2824 0026; 2824 0249
E-mail: exhibitions@hktdc.org
Web Site: hkbookfair.hktdc.com; hkbookfair.hktdc.com/en/index.html (English)
Location: Hong Kong Convention & Exhibition Center, One Expo Dr, Wan Chai, Hong Kong
July 18-24, 2018

IAML Annual Conference
Sponsored by International Association of Music Libraries, Archives & Documentation Centres Inc (IAML)
c/o Gothenburg University Library, Music & Drama Library, Box 210, 405 30 Gothenburg, Sweden
Tel: (031) 786 40 57 *Fax:* (031) 786 40 59
E-mail: contact@iaml.info
Web Site: www.iaml.info
Key Personnel
Secy Gen: Pia Shekhter *E-mail:* secretary@iaml.info
Location: Leipzig, Germany
July 22-27, 2018

ILA Annual Conference
Sponsored by International Literacy Association (ILA)
800 Barksdale Rd, Newark, DE 19711-3204
Mailing Address: PO Box 8139, Newark, DE 19714-8139
Tel: 302-731-1600 *Toll Free Tel:* 800-336-7323 (US & CN) *Fax:* 302-731-1057
E-mail: customerservice@reading.org
Web Site: www.literacyworldwide.org
Key Personnel
Exec Dir: Marcie Craig Post *E-mail:* mpost@reading.org
Location: Austin, TX, USA
July 20-23, 2018

International Christian Retail Show (ICRS)
Sponsored by CBA: The Association for Christian Retail
1365 Garden of the Gods Rd, Suite 105, Colorado Springs, CO 80907
Tel: 719-265-9895 *Toll Free Tel:* 800-252-1950 *Fax:* 719-272-3508

E-mail: info@cbaonline.org
Web Site: christianretailshow.com; cbaonline.org
Key Personnel
Pres: Curtis Riskey *E-mail:* criskey@cbaonline.org
For over 50 years, the annual International Christian Retail Show has been our industry's single-most impacting week. During this week, people of the industry from all over the world meet face-to-face for buying & selling, education, inspiration, fellowship & future planning. Here individuals unite to further the mission of seeing Christian products impact lives for God's Kingdom the world over. At this unique gathering, our industry's strength is most evident & our goals are most clearly in focus. It is, in short, the most important week in the ministry of your business & of the industry as a whole.
Location: Gaylord Opryland Hotel & Convention Center, 2800 Opryland Dr, Nashville, TN, USA
July 8-11, 2018

Payson Book Festival
Sponsored by Arizona Professional Writers (APW)
PO Box 1495, Payson, AZ 85547
E-mail: info@paysonbookfestival.org
Web Site: www.paysonbookfestival.org; www.facebook.com/PaysonBookFestival
Key Personnel
Chair: Connie Cockrell
The Payson Book Festival is held to promote literacy & showcase Arizona authors. Our mission is to enhance the love of reading by providing a friendly environment that encourages personal interaction between Arizona authors & readers of all ages. Proceeds will benefit the scholarship funds of both the Payson High School & the Gila Community College. Over 80 Arizona authors participate by signing books & visiting with readers of all ages. Some will speak about their books & the craft of writing. There will be a full schedule of speakers & several workshops throughout the day.
Location: Mazatal Hotel & Casino Ballroom, Payson, AZ, USA
July 2018

Romance Writers of America Annual Conference
Sponsored by Romance Writers of America®
14615 Benfer Rd, Houston, TX 77069
Tel: 832-717-5200 *Fax:* 832-717-5201
E-mail: info@rwa.org
Web Site: www.rwa.org
Key Personnel
Exec Dir: Allison Kelley *Tel:* 832-717-5200 ext 124 *E-mail:* allison.kelley@rwa.org
Location: Sheraton Denver Downtown Hotel, 1550 Court Place, Denver, CO, USA
July 25-28, 2018

AUGUST

The Dorothy L Sayers Society Annual Convention
Sponsored by The Dorothy L Sayers Society
Witham Library, 18 Newland St, Witham CM8 2AQ, United Kingdom
Tel: (01376) 519625
E-mail: info@sayers.org.uk
Web Site: www.sayers.org.uk
Key Personnel
Convention Admin: Simon Medd
Membership Secy: Lenelle Davis
E-mail: membership@sayers.org.uk
Members only event.
Location: UK
Aug 2018

Edinburgh International Book Festival
5 Charlotte Sq, Edinburgh EH2 4DR, United Kingdom
Tel: (0131) 718 5666
E-mail: admin@edbookfest.co.uk
Web Site: www.edbookfest.co.uk
Each year we welcome over 800 international authors & over 200,000 visitors to the biggest book festival in the world, turning Edinburgh's Charlotte Square Gardens into a literary village for 18 days every August.
Location: Charlotte Square Gardens, Edinburgh, UK
Aug 11-27, 2018

EXPOLIT (Exposicion de Literatura Cristiana Book Fair)
Sponsored by Spanish Evangelical Publishers Association (SEPA)/Asociacion Evangelica espanola de Editores
8167 NW 84 St, Medley, FL 33166
Tel: 305-503-1191 *Toll Free Tel:* 866-782-3976 *Fax:* 305-717-6886
E-mail: info@expolit.com
Web Site: www.expolit.com
Key Personnel
Supv: Jessica Hernandez *E-mail:* jessica@expolit.com
Media & Promo Coord: Maria De La Cruz *E-mail:* medios@expolit.com
Exhibit Coord: Angela Peralta *E-mail:* exhibitor@expolit.com
Spanish Christian literature convention. Also sponsored by Editorial Unilit.
Location: DoubleTree by Hilton Hotel Miami Airport & Convention Center, 711 NW 72 Ave, Miami, FL, USA
Aug 9-12, 2018

GWA Annual Conference & Expo
Sponsored by GWA: The Association for Garden Communicators
355 Lexington Ave, 15th fl, New York, NY 10017
Tel: 212-297-2198 *Fax:* 212-297-2140
E-mail: info@gardenwriters.org
Web Site: www.gardenwriters.org; www.gwaa.org
Co-located with Independent Garden Center Show (IGC).
Location: Navy Pier, Chicago, IL, USA
Aug 13-16, 2018

IFLA World Library & Information Congress
Sponsored by International Federation of Library Associations & Institutions (IFLA) (Federation internationale des associations de bibliothecaires et des bibliotheques)
Prins Willem-Alexanderhof 5, 2595 BE The Hague, Netherlands
Mailing Address: Postbus 95312, 2509 CH The Hague, Netherlands
Tel: (70) 314 08 84 *Fax:* (70) 383 48 27
E-mail: ifla@ifla.org
Web Site: conference.ifla.org; www.ifla.org
Key Personnel
Secy Gen: Gerald Leitner
Mgr, Conferences & Busn Rel: Josche Ouwerkerk *E-mail:* josche.ouwerkerk@ifla.org
Held simultaneously with IFLA General Conference & Assembly.
Location: Kuala Lumpur, Malaysia
Aug 2018

The South African Booksellers Annual General Meeting
Sponsored by South African Booksellers Association (SABA)
29 Golf Course Rd, Sybrand Park, Rondebosch, South Africa
Mailing Address: PO Box 870, Bellville 7535, South Africa
Tel: (021) 697 1164 *Fax:* (021) 697 1410
E-mail: saba@sabooksellers.com
Web Site: www.sabooksellers.com
Location: Guateng, South Africa
Aug 2018

Swanwick: The Writers' Summer School
Sponsored by Writers' Summer School
130 Wood Lane, Hucknall, Notts NG15 6PN, United Kingdom
Tel: (01290) 552248
Web Site: www.swanwickwritersschool.org.uk
A weeklong residential writing school with top name speakers & tutors, plus informative panels, talks & discussion groups. Comfortable rooms with all meals & tuition included in the price. Open to everyone, from absolute beginners to published authors. Beautiful setting, licensed bar & evening entertainment. Believed to be the longest established residential writers' school in the world, Swanwick, held annually in August, is a must attend event in every writer's diary.
Location: The Hayes Conference Centre, Swanwick, Alfreton, Derbyshire, UK
Aug 11-17, 2018

AUTUMN

Louisiana Book Festival
Sponsored by Louisiana Center for the Book
Subsidiary of State Library of Louisiana
701 N Fourth St, Baton Rouge, LA 70802
Tel: 225-219-9503 *Fax:* 225-219-9840
Web Site: louisianabookfestival.org
Key Personnel
Dir: Jim Davis *Tel:* 225-342-9714
E-mail: jdavis@slol.lib.la.us
Asst Dir: Robert Wilson *E-mail:* rwilson@slol.lib.la.us
A free festival celebrating readers, writers & books representing a variety of genres & related events for all ages, food, music.
Location: State Library of Louisiana, Louisiana State Capitol, Capitol Park Museum & nearby locations, Baton Rouge, LA, USA
Autumn 2018

SEPTEMBER

Christian Resources Retailers & Suppliers Retreat
Sponsored by Christian Resources Together
Cedar Tree, 4 Ditchingham Close, Aylesbury, Bucks HP19 7SA, United Kingdom
Tel: (01296) 489860
Web Site: www.christianresourcestogether.co.uk
Location: The Hayes Conference Centre, Swanwick, Alfreton, Derbyshire, UK
Sept 11-12, 2018

Didac India
Sponsored by Worlddidac Association
Bollwerk 21, 3011 Bern, Switzerland
Tel: (031) 311 76 82 *Fax:* (031) 312 17 44
E-mail: info@worlddidac.org
Web Site: worlddidacindia.com; www.worlddidac.org
Key Personnel
Proj & Communs Mgr: Kateryna Schuetz
E-mail: schuetz@worlddidac.org

International exhibition for education, training, technology & supply.
Location: India
Sept 2018

Distripress Annual Congress
Sponsored by Distripress
Postfach 8034, Zurich, Switzerland
Tel: (020) 3865 3519
E-mail: info@distripress.org
Web Site: www.distripress.org
Key Personnel
Mng Dir: Tracy Jones *E-mail:* tracy.jones@distripress.net
Community Mgr: Anna Sponquiado *E-mail:* anna.sponquiado@distripress.org
Annual event sponsored by Distripress, a non-profit association for the promotion of international press distribution.
Location: Rome Cavalieri, Waldorf Astoria Hotels & Resorts, Rome, Italy
Sept 30-Oct 3, 2018

Excellence in Journalism
Sponsored by The Society of Professional Journalists (SPJ)
Eugene S Pulliam National Journalism Ctr, 3909 N Meridian St, Indianapolis, IN 46208
Tel: 317-927-8000 *Fax:* 317-920-4789
E-mail: convention@spj.org
Web Site: excellenceinjournalism.org; www.spj.org
Key Personnel
Assoc Exec Dir: Chris Vachon *Tel:* 317-927-8000 ext 207 *E-mail:* cvachon@spj.org
Events Coord: Abbi Martzall *Tel:* 319-920-4791 *E-mail:* amartzall@spj.org
Annual conference co-organized by The Native American Journalists Association (NAJA) & Radio Television Digital News Association (RTDNA).
Location: Hilton Baltimore, 401 W Pratt St, Baltimore, MD, USA
Sept 27-29, 2018

Goeteborg Book Fair
Sponsored by Bok & Bibliotek i Norden AB
Maessans Gata 20, 412 94 Gothenburg, Sweden
Tel: (031) 708 84 00 *Fax:* (031) 20 91 03
E-mail: info@goteborg-bookfair.com; info@bokmassan.se
Web Site: www.bokmassan.se
Key Personnel
CEO: Maria Kaellsson *E-mail:* maka@goteborg-bookfair.com
Sr Advisor: Anna Falck *E-mail:* af@goteborg-bookfair.com
Prog Coord: Anneli Jonasson *Tel:* (031) 708 84 03 *E-mail:* aj@goteborg-bookfair.com
Location: Gothenburg, Sweden
Sept 27-30, 2018

Graph Expo®
Sponsored by Graphic Arts Show Company (GASC)
1899 Preston White Dr, Reston, VA 20191
Tel: 703-264-7200 *Fax:* 703-620-9187
E-mail: info@gasc.org
Web Site: www.graphexpo.com; www.gasc.org
Key Personnel
VP, Meetings & Events: Kelly Kilga *Tel:* 703-264-7200 ext 213 *E-mail:* kkilga@gasc.org
Dir, Meetings & Events: Deedee (Diana) Tinkham *Tel:* 703-264-7200 ext 245 *E-mail:* dtinkham@gasc.org
Produced for NPES The Association for Suppliers of Printing, Publishing & Converting Technologies.
Location: McCormick Place, South Hall, 2301 S Lake Shore Dr, Chicago, IL, USA
Sept 30-Oct 3, 2018

International Board on Books for Young People Biennial Congress
Sponsored by International Board on Books for Young People (IBBY)
Nonnenweg 12, Postfach, 4009 Basel, Switzerland
Tel: (061) 272 29 17 *Fax:* (061) 272 27 57
E-mail: ibby@ibby.org
Web Site: www.ibby.org
Key Personnel
Exec Dir: Liz Page *E-mail:* liz.page@ibby.org
Admin Asst: Luzmaria Stauffenegger-Lobato *E-mail:* luzmaria.stauffenegger@ibby.org
IBBY's biennial congresses, hosted by different countries, are the most important meeting points for IBBY members & other people involved in children's books & reading development. They are wonderful opportunities to make contacts, exchange ideas & open horizons.
Location: Istanbul, Turkey
Sept 1-4, 2018

National Federation of Press Women Communications Conference
Sponsored by National Federation of Press Women Inc (NFPW)
PO Box 3007, Mechanicsville, VA 23116-0026
Tel: 804-746-1033
E-mail: info@nfpw.org
Web Site: www.nfpw.org
Location: Bethlehem, PA, USA
Sept 6-8, 2018

National Newspaper Association Annual Convention & Trade Show
Sponsored by National Newspaper Association
200 Little Falls St, Suite 405, Falls Church, VA 22046
Mailing Address: PO Box 50301, Arlington, VA 22205
Tel: 703-237-9802 *Toll Free Tel:* 800-829-4NNA (829-4662) *Fax:* 703-237-9808
Web Site: nnaweb.org
Key Personnel
Mng Dir: Carol Pierce *E-mail:* carol@nna.org
Dir, Memb Servs: Lynne Lance
Location: Norfolk Waterside Marriott, 235 E Main St, Norfolk, VA, USA
Sept 27-29, 2018

SIBA Discovery Show
Sponsored by Southern Independent Booksellers Alliance
3806 Yale Ave, Columbia, SC 29205
Tel: 803-994-9530 *Fax:* 309-410-0211
E-mail: info@sibaweb.com
Web Site: www.sibaweb.com/trade-show; www.sibaweb.com
Key Personnel
Exec Dir: Wanda Jewell *E-mail:* wanda@sibaweb.com
Members only event.
Location: Tampa, FL, USA
Sept 13-15, 2018

OCTOBER

ACP/CMA National College Media Convention
Sponsored by Associated Collegiate Press (ACP) Division of National Scholastic Press Association
2221 University Ave SE, Suite 121, Minneapolis, MN 55414
Tel: 612-625-8335
E-mail: info@studentpress.org
Web Site: www.studentpress.org; facebook.com/acpress; twitter.com/acpress
Key Personnel
Exec Dir, NSPA/ACP: Laura Widmer *Tel:* 612-625-6519
Co-sponsored by College Media Association.
Location: Galt House Hotel, Louisville, KY, USA
Oct 25-28, 2018

AIGA Design Conference
Sponsored by AIGA, the professional association for design
233 Broadway, Suite 1740, New York, NY 10279
Tel: 212-807-1990
Web Site: www.aiga.org
Key Personnel
Dir of Events: Jonathan Feinberg *Tel:* 212-710-3142
Prog Dir: Kathleen Budny *Tel:* 212-710-3144
Registrar & Events Coord: Susan Augenbraum *Tel:* 212-710-3133
Annual conference.
Location: Pittsburgh, PA, USA
Oct 4-6, 2018

American Translators Association Annual Conference
Sponsored by American Translators Association (ATA)
225 Reinekers Lane, Suite 590, Alexandria, VA 22314
Tel: 703-683-6100 *Fax:* 703-683-6122
E-mail: ata@atanet.org
Web Site: www.atanet.org
Key Personnel
Exec Dir: Walter W Barak, Jr
Meetings Mgr: Teresa C Kelly *Tel:* 703-683-6100 ext 3014 *E-mail:* teresak@atanet.org
Location: New Orleans, LA, USA
Oct 24-27, 2018

&THEN
Sponsored by Data & Marketing Association (DMA)
1333 Broadway, Suite 301, New York, NY 10018
SAN: 692-6487
Tel: 212-768-7277
Web Site: thedma.org
Key Personnel
Asst Conference Mgr: Jeremy A Ladson *Tel:* 212-790-1545 *E-mail:* jladson@thedma.org
Location: MGM Grand, Las Vegas, NV, USA
Oct 7-9, 2018

Frankfurt Book Fair
Sponsored by Frankfurter Buchmesse GmbH
Braubachstr 16, 60311 Frankfurt am Main, Germany
Mailing Address: Postfach 100116, 60001 Frankfurt am Main, Germany
Tel: (069) 21020 *Fax:* (069) 2102 277
E-mail: info@book-fair.com
Web Site: www.frankfurt-book-fair.com; www.book-fair.com
Key Personnel
CEO & Dir: Juergen Boos
Major international book & media fair attracting 7,100 exhibitors from over 100 countries & 275,000 visitors.
Location: Frankfurt Fairgrounds, Ludwig-Erhard-Anlage One, Frankfurt, Germany
Oct 10-14, 2018

Inter American Press Association General Assembly
Sponsored by Inter American Press Association (IAPA)
3511 NW 91 Ave, Miami, FL 33172
Tel: 305-634-2465 *Fax:* 305-860-4264
E-mail: info@sipiapa.org
Web Site: www.sipiapa.org
Key Personnel
Exec Dir: Ricardo Trotti *E-mail:* rtrotti@sipiapa.org

Gathering of important international figures for workshops, seminars & other related activities, while offering networking opportunities for those interested on press/media freedom & freedom of expression issues.
Location: Medellin, Colombia
Oct 2018

LIBER Feria Internacional del Libro
Sponsored by Federacion de Gremios de Editores de Espana (FGEE) (Spanish Association of Publishers Guilds)
Cea Bermudez, 44-2° Dcha, 28003 Madrid, Spain
Tel: 91 534 51 95 *Fax:* 91 535 26 25
E-mail: fgee@fge.es
Web Site: www.federacioneditores.org
Key Personnel
Exec Dir: Antonio Maria Avila
Location: Barcelona, Spain
Oct 3-5, 2018

NAIBA Fall Conference
Sponsored by New Atlantic Independent Booksellers Association (NAIBA)
2667 Hyacinth St, Westbury, NY 11590
Tel: 516-333-0681 *Fax:* 516-333-0689
E-mail: naibabooksellers@gmail.com
Web Site: www.naiba.com
Key Personnel
Exec Dir: Eileen Dengler *E-mail:* NAIBAeileen@gmail.com
Location: Baltimore, MD, USA
Oct 6-8, 2018

PACK EXPO International
Sponsored by PMMI: The Association for Packaging and Processing Technologies
11911 Freedom Dr, Suite 600, Reston, VA 20190
Tel: 571-612-3200 *Toll Free Tel:* 888-ASK-PMMI (275-7664) *Fax:* 703-243-8556
E-mail: expo@pmmi.org
Web Site: www.packexpointernational.com; www.packexpo.com; www.pmmi.org
Key Personnel
VP, Meetings & Events: Patti Fee *Tel:* 571-612-3193
Dir, Tradeshow Opers: Laura Thompson *Tel:* 571-612-3217
Dir, Tradeshow Mktg: Tina Scott *Tel:* 571-612-3203
Events Mgr: Anna Hudson *Tel:* 571-612-3198
Exhibitor Servs Sr Mgr: Merideth Newman *Tel:* 703-243-8555 *E-mail:* mnewman@pmmi.org
Exhibitor Servs & Sales Mgr: Beth Murray *Tel:* 571-612-3186 *E-mail:* bmurray@pmmi.org
Tradeshow Asst: Nina Sader *Tel:* 571-266-4409 *E-mail:* nsader@pmmi.org
Biennial event held in even-numbered years.
Location: McCormick Place, 2301 S Lake Shore Dr, Chicago, IL, USA
Oct 14-17, 2018

Poligrafia
Sponsored by Poznan International Fair Ltd
ul Glogowska 14, 60-734 Poznan, Poland
Tel: (61) 869 20 00 *Fax:* (61) 869 29 99
E-mail: poligrafia@mtp.pl; info@mtp.pl
Web Site: www.poligrafiaexpo.pl/en (English); www.poligrafiaexpo.pl/pl (Polish); www.mtp.pl/en/ (English); www.mtp.pl/pl/ (Polish)
Key Personnel
Proj Mgr: Konrad Flesman *Tel:* (61) 869 20 94 *E-mail:* konrad.flesman@mtp.pl
International fair of printing machines, materials & services.
Location: Poznan International Fair Grounds, Poznan, Poland
Oct 1-4, 2018

PSA® International Conference of Photography
Sponsored by Photographic Society of America® (PSA®)
8241 S Walker Ave, Suite 104, Oklahoma City, OK 73139
Tel: 405-843-1437 *Toll Free Tel:* 855-PSA-INFO (772-4636) *Fax:* 405-843-1438
E-mail: hq@psa-photo.org
Web Site: www.psa-photo.org
Key Personnel
Conference VP: Gregory Daley *E-mail:* conferencevp@psa-photo.org
Location: Sheraton Salt Lake City Hotel, 150 W 500 S, Salt Lake City, UT, USA
Sept 30-Oct 6, 2018

TAPPI PEERS Conference
Sponsored by Technical Association of the Pulp & Paper Industry (TAPPI)
15 Technology Pkwy S, Suite 115, Peachtree Corners, GA 30092
Tel: 770-446-1400 *Toll Free Tel:* 800-332-8686 (US); 800-446-9431 (CN) *Fax:* 770-446-6947
E-mail: memberconnection@tappi.org
Web Site: www.tappi.org
Key Personnel
Dir of Mktg: Simona Marcellus *Tel:* 770-209-7293 *E-mail:* smarcellus@tappi.org
Location: Hilton Portland, Portland, OR, USA
Oct 28-31, 2018

Twin Cities Book Festival
Sponsored by Rain Taxi
PO Box 3840, Minneapolis, MN 55403
Tel: 612-825-1528 *Fax:* 612-825-1528
E-mail: bookfest@raintaxi.com
Web Site: www.raintaxi.com/twin-cities-book-festival
Key Personnel
Dir: Eric Lorberer
Gala celebration of books, featuring large exhibition, author readings & signings, book art activities, panel discussions, used book sale & children's events.
Location: Minnesota State Fairgrounds, 1265 Snelling Ave N, St Paul, MN, USA
Oct 2018

Utah Humanities Book Festival
Sponsored by Utah Humanities Council
Affiliate of Utah Center for the Book
202 W 300 N, Salt Lake City, UT 84103
Tel: 801-359-9670 *Fax:* 801-531-7869
Web Site: utahhumanities.org
Key Personnel
Exec Dir: Cynthia Buckingham *E-mail:* buckingham@utahhumanities.org
Lit Prog Offr: Michael McLane *E-mail:* mclane@utahhumanities.org
Communs Dir: Deena Pyle *E-mail:* pyle@utahhumanities.org
Free literary event featuring national, regional & local authors held Oct 1-31 annually (National Book Month).
Location: Statewide, UT, USA
Oct 1-31, 2018

NOVEMBER

AMWA Annual Conference
Sponsored by American Medical Writers Association (AMWA)
30 W Gude Dr, Suite 525, Rockville, MD 20850-4357
Tel: 240-238-0940 *Fax:* 301-294-9006
E-mail: amwa@amwa.org
Web Site: www.amwa.org
Key Personnel
Conference Prog Mgr & Workshop Coord: Becky Phillips *Tel:* 240-238-0940 ext 103 *E-mail:* becky@amwa.org
Location: Renaissance DC Downtown Hotel, Washington, DC, USA
Nov 1-3, 2018

ASIS&T Annual Meeting
Sponsored by Association for Information Science & Technology (ASIS&T)
8555 16 St, Suite 850, Silver Spring, MD 20910
Tel: 301-495-0900 *Fax:* 301-495-0810
E-mail: asist@asist.org
Web Site: www.asist.org
Key Personnel
Dir of Meetings & Membership: Vanessa Foss *E-mail:* vfoss@asist.org
Location: Vancouver, BC, CN
Nov 9-15, 2018

BMI Annual Conference
Sponsored by Book Manufacturers' Institute Inc (BMI)
PO Box 731388, Ormond Beach, FL 32173
Tel: 386-986-4552 *Fax:* 386-986-4553
Web Site: www.bmibook.org
Key Personnel
EVP: Daniel N Bach *E-mail:* dbach@bmibook.com
Conference Coord: Jackie Murray
Location: Hyatt Regency Coconut Point, Bonita Springs, FL, USA
Nov 4-6, 2018

Jewish Book Month
Sponsored by Jewish Book Council
520 Eighth Ave, 4th fl, New York, NY 10018
Tel: 212-201-2920 *Fax:* 212-532-4952
E-mail: jbc@jewishbooks.org
Web Site: www.jewishbookcouncil.org; www.facebook.com/JewishBookCouncil; twitter.com/jewishbook
Key Personnel
Exec Dir: Naomi Firestone-Teeter
Dir: Carolyn Starman Hessel
Dedicated to the celebration of Jewish books held annually during the month leading up to Hanukkah.
Location: Nationwide throughout the USA
Nov 2-Dec 2, 2018

Miami Book Fair
Sponsored by Florida Center for the Literary Arts
c/o Miami Dade College, 300 NE Second Ave, Miami, FL 33132
Tel: 305-237-3258
E-mail: wbookfair@mdc.edu
Web Site: www.miamibookfair.com
Key Personnel
Dir of Opers: Delia Lopez
Exhibit Coord: Giselle Hernandez
Miami Book Fair is the largest event of its kind in the USA. For more than 30 years, the fair has been held over 8 days each November. In addition to readings by more than 400 authors from all over the world & the sale of thousands of books in many languages, the fair offers book-centered fun for children, panel discussions & writing classes in English & Spanish. For up to date information, call or visit the book fair web site at www.miamibookfair.com.
Location: Miami Dade College, Wolfson Campus, Miami, FL, USA
Nov 11-18, 2018

Salon du Livre de Montreal (Montreal Book Show)
Sponsored by Salon du Livre de Montreal

300, rue du St-Secrement, Suite 430, Montreal, QC H2Y 1X4, Canada
Tel: 514-845-2365 *Fax:* 514-845-7119
E-mail: slm.info@videotron.ca
Web Site: www.salondulivredemontreal.com
Key Personnel
Dir Gen: Francine Bois
Location: Place Bonaventure, Montreal, QC, CN
Nov 14-19, 2018

Texas Book Festival
610 Brazos, Suite 200, Austin, TX 78701
Tel: 512-477-4055 *Fax:* 512-322-0722
E-mail: bookfest@texasbookfestival.org
Web Site: www.texasbookfestival.org
Key Personnel
Exec Dir: Lois Kim *E-mail:* loiskim@texasbookfestival.org
Outreach Coord: Lea Bogner *E-mail:* lea@texasbookfestival.org
Devt Mgr: Claire Burrows *E-mail:* claire@texasbookfestival.com
Literary Dir: Julie Wernersbach *E-mail:* julie@texasbookfestival.org
Literary & Communs Coord: Lydia Melby *E-mail:* lydia@texasbookfestival.org
Admin Asst: Maris Finn *E-mail:* maris@texasbookfestival.org
The festival is a statewide program that promotes reading & literacy highlighted by a 2 day festival, held annually in the fall, featuring authors from Texas & across the USA. Money raised from the festival is distributed as grants to public libraries throughout the state.
Location: State Capitol Bldg, Austin, TX, USA
Nov 2018

Worlddidac Bern/Swissdidac Bern
Sponsored by Worlddidac Association
Bollwerk 21, 3011 Bern, Switzerland
Tel: (031) 311 76 82 *Fax:* (031) 312 17 44
E-mail: info@worlddidac.org
Web Site: www.worlddidac-bern.com; www.worlddidac.org
International exhibition for education, training, technology & supply. Held in conjunction with Didacta Schweiz Basel. Held biennially in even-numbered years.
Location: BERNEXPO, Mingerstrasse 6, Bern, Switzerland
Nov 7-9, 2018

2019

JANUARY

American Library Association Midwinter Meeting
Sponsored by The American Library Association (ALA)
50 E Huron St, Chicago, IL 60611
Tel: 312-944-6780 *Toll Free Tel:* 800-545-2433 (ext 3223, conference servs) *Fax:* 312-440-9374
E-mail: ala@ala.org
Web Site: www.ala.org
Key Personnel
Registration & Housing Specialist: Alicia Babcock *Tel:* 800-545-2433 ext 3229 *E-mail:* ababcock@ala.org
Conference Dir: Paul Graller *Tel:* 800-545-2433 ext 3219 *E-mail:* pgraller@ala.org
Conference Mgr: Amy McGuigan *Tel:* 800-545-2433 ext 3226 *E-mail:* amcguigan@ala.org
Meetings, AV & Catering Coord: Yvonne McLean *Tel:* 800-545-2433 ext 3222 *E-mail:* ymclean@ala.org
Conference Coord: Lina Zabaneh *Tel:* 800-545-2433 ext 3227 *E-mail:* lzabaneh@ala.org
Meeting Coord: Alicia (Alee) Navarro *Tel:* 800-545-2433 ext 3216 *E-mail:* anavarro@ala.org
Location: Seattle, WA, USA
Jan 25-29, 2019

MLA Annual Convention
Sponsored by Modern Language Association of America (MLA)
85 Broad St, Suite 500, New York, NY 10004-2434
SAN: 202-6422
Tel: 646-576-5266 (convention); 646-576-5000 *Fax:* 646-458-0030
E-mail: convention@mla.org
Web Site: www.mla.org/convention
Key Personnel
Assoc Dir of Convention Progs: Karin L Bagnall *E-mail:* kbagnall@mla.org
Location: Chicago, IL, USA
Jan 3-6, 2019

FEBRUARY

California International Antiquarian Book Fair
Sponsored by Antiquarian Booksellers' Association of America (ABAA)
20 W 44 St, Suite 507, New York, NY 10036
Tel: 212-944-8291 *Fax:* 212-944-8293
E-mail: cafair@whiterainproductions.com
Web Site: www.cabookfair.com; www.abaa.org
Key Personnel
Exec Dir: Susan Benne *E-mail:* sbenne@abaa.org
Annual event co-sponsored by International League of Antiquarian Booksellers & managed by White Rain Productions.
Location: Oakland Marriott City Center, 1001 Broadway, Oakland, CA, USA
Feb 8-10, 2019

CAMEX
Sponsored by National Association of College Stores (NACS)
500 E Lorain St, Oberlin, OH 44074
Tel: 440-775-7777 *Toll Free Tel:* 800-622-7498 *Fax:* 440-775-4769
E-mail: camex@nacs.org
Web Site: www.camex.org; www.nacs.org
Key Personnel
CEO: Bob Walton *Tel:* 800-622-7498 ext 2201 *E-mail:* rwalton@nacs.org
Dir, Meetings: Jodie Wilmot *Tel:* 800-622-7498 ext 2272 *E-mail:* jwilmot@nacs.org
Dir of Expositions: Mary Adler-Kozak *Tel:* 800-622-7498 ext 2265 *E-mail:* madler-kozak@nacs.org
Conference & trade show dedicated exclusively to the more than $10 billion collegiate retailing industry.
Location: Henry B Gonzalez Convention Center, San Antonio, TX, USA
Feb 22-26, 2019

MARCH

Adelaide Festival
Sponsored by Adelaide Festival Corp
Level 9, 33 King William St, Adelaide, SA 5000, Australia
Mailing Address: PO Box 8221, Station Arcade, Adelaide, SA 5000, Australia
Tel: (08) 8216 4444 *Fax:* (08) 8216 4455
E-mail: info@adelaidefestival.com.au
Web Site: www.adelaidefestival.com.au
Key Personnel
Artistic Dir: Neil Armfield; Rachel Healy
Assoc Prodr: Anne Wiberg
Prog Dir: Lesley Newton
Prodn Mgr: Adam Hornhardt
Annual event highlighting the arts, including literature. Adelaide Writers' Week is one of the high-profile events held during the festival.
Location: Adelaide's Central Business District, Adelaide, SA, Australia
March 1-17, 2019

AWP Annual Conference & Bookfair
Sponsored by Association of Writers & Writing Programs (AWP)
George Mason University, 4400 University Dr, MSN 1E3, Fairfax, VA 22030
Tel: 703-993-4301 *Fax:* 703-993-4302
E-mail: awp@awpwriter.org
Web Site: www.awpwriter.org/awp_conference/; www.awpwriter.org
Key Personnel
Exec Dir: David W Fenza
Dir, Conferences: Christian Teresi
Assoc Dir, Conferences: Cynthia Sherman
Location: Oregon Convention Center, Portland, OR, USA
March 27-30, 2019

Leipzig Book Fair (Leipziger Buchmesse)
Sponsored by Leipziger Messe GmbH
Messe-Allee 1, 04356 Leipzig, Germany
Mailing Address: Postfach 10 07 20, 04007 Leipzig, Germany
Tel: (0341) 678-0 *Fax:* (0341) 678-8762
E-mail: info@leipziger-buchmesse.de
Web Site: www.leipziger-buchmesse.de
Key Personnel
Dir: Oliver Zille *Tel:* (0341) 678-8240
Held annually in conjunction with The Leipzig Antiquarian Book Fair.
Location: Leipzig Exhibition Centre, Messe-Allee 1, Leipzig, Germany
March 21-24, 2019

Virginia Festival of the Book
Sponsored by Virginia Foundation for the Humanities
145 Ednam Dr, Charlottesville, VA 22903
Tel: 434-924-3296 *Fax:* 434-296-4714
E-mail: vabook@virginia.edu
Web Site: www.vabook.org
Key Personnel
Prog Dir: Jane Kulow *Tel:* 434-924-7548
Annual public festival for children & adults featuring authors, illustrators, publishers, publicists, agents & other book professionals in panel discussions & readings. Most events are free. Hundreds of authors invited annually.
Location: Charlottesville, VA, USA
March 20-24, 2019

APRIL

Alberta Library Conference
Sponsored by Library Association of Alberta (LAA)
80 Baker Crescent NW, Calgary, AB T2L 1R4, Canada
Tel: 403-284-5818 *Toll Free Tel:* 877-522-5550 *Fax:* 403-284-5818
E-mail: info@laa.ca
Web Site: www.albertalibraryconference.com; www.laa.ca
Key Personnel
Exec Dir/Conference Coord: Christine Sheppard
Co-hosted by Alberta Library Trustees Association (ALTA).

Location: Fairmont Jasper Park Lodge, Jasper, AB, CN
April 25-28, 2019

International Children's Book Day
Sponsored by International Board on Books for Young People (IBBY)
Nonnenweg 12, Postfach, 4009 Basel, Switzerland
Tel: (061) 272 29 17 *Fax:* (061) 272 27 57
E-mail: ibby@ibby.org
Web Site: www.ibby.org
Key Personnel
Exec Dir: Liz Page *E-mail:* liz.page@ibby.org
Admin Asst: Luzmaria Stauffenegger-Lobato *E-mail:* luzmaria.stauffenegger@ibby.org
On Hans Christian Andersen's birthday, April 2nd, International Children's Book Day (ICBD) is celebrated to inspire a love of reading & to call attention to children's books. Each year a different national section has the opportunity to be the international sponsor. It decides upon a theme & invites a prominent author to write a message to the children of the world & a well-known illustrator to design a poster. These materials are used in different ways to promote books & reading around the world.
April 2, 2019

NAAJ Annual Meeting
Sponsored by North American Agricultural Journalists (NAAJ)
6434 Hurta Lane, Bryan, TX 77808
Tel: 979-845-2872 *Fax:* 979-862-1202
Web Site: www.naaj.net
Key Personnel
Exec Secy & Treas: Kathleen Phillips *E-mail:* kaphillips@tamu.edu
Annual meeting, writing awards & scholarship benefit dance.
Location: Washington, DC, USA
April 2019

National Library Week
Sponsored by The American Library Association (ALA)
50 E Huron St, Chicago, IL 60611
Tel: 312-944-6780 *Toll Free Tel:* 800-545-2433 *Fax:* 312-440-9374
E-mail: ala@ala.org
Web Site: www.ala.org/nlw
Location: Nationwide throughout the USA
April 7-13, 2019

Texas Library Association Annual Conference
Sponsored by Texas Library Association (TLA)
3355 Bee Cave Rd, Suite 401, Austin, TX 78746-6763
Tel: 512-328-1518 *Toll Free Tel:* 800-580-2852 *Fax:* 512-328-8852
E-mail: tla@txla.org
Web Site: www.txla.org
Key Personnel
Conference Mgr: Elise Walker *Tel:* 512-328-1518 x145 *E-mail:* elisew@txla.org
Location: Austin, TX, USA
April 15-18, 2019

MAY

Children's Book Week
Sponsored by The Children's Book Council (CBC)
54 W 39 St, 14th fl, New York, NY 10018
Tel: 212-966-1990
E-mail: cbc.info@cbcbooks.org
Web Site: www.bookweekonline.com; www.cbcbooks.org
Key Personnel
Exec Dir: Carl Lennertz *E-mail:* carl.lennertz@cbcbooks.org
Dir, Programming: Shaina Birkhead *E-mail:* shaina.birkhead@cbcbooks.org
Location: Nationwide across the USA
May 6-12, 2019

PrintEx 2019
Sponsored by Visual Connections Australia Ltd
Shop 4, 123 Midson Rd, Epping, NSW 2121, Australia
Mailing Address: PO Box 3723, Marsfield, NSW 2122, Australia
Tel: (02) 9868 1577
E-mail: exhibitions@visualconnections.org.au
Web Site: www.printex.net.au
PrintEx brings the latest printing & graphic communications technologies to the industry. Presented by Visual Connections Australia Ltd & the Printing Industries Association of Australia (PIAA), this event is held every 4 years in Sydney, NSW, Australia.
Location: Sydney Showground, Sydney Olympic Park, Sydney, NSW, Australia
May 2019

SSP Annual Meeting
Sponsored by Society for Scholarly Publishing (SSP)
10200 W 44 Ave, Suite 304, Wheat Ridge, CO 80033-2840
Tel: 303-422-3914 *Fax:* 720-881-6101
E-mail: info@sspnet.org
Web Site: www.sspnet.org
Key Personnel
Exec/Meetings Asst: Jennifer Lanphere
Location: Marriott Marquis San Diego Marina, San Diego, CA, USA
May 29-May 31, 2019

JUNE

AAUP Annual Meeting
Sponsored by Association of American University Presses (AAUP)
1412 Broadway, Suite 2135, New York, NY 10018
Tel: 212-989-1010 *Fax:* 212-989-0275
E-mail: annualmeeting@aaup.org; info@aaupnet.org
Web Site: www.aaupnet.org
Key Personnel
Exec Dir: Peter Berkery *Tel:* 917-288-5594 *E-mail:* pberkery@aaupnet.org
Asst Dir & Cont: Tim Muench *Tel:* 917-244-1463 *E-mail:* tmuench@aaupnet.org
Dir, Mktg & Communs: Brenna McLaughlin *Tel:* 917-244-2051 *E-mail:* bmclaughlin@aaupnet.org
Off Mgr & Prog Admin: Kim Miller *Tel:* 917-244-1264 *E-mail:* kmiller@aaupnet.org
Location: Detroit Marriott at the Renaissance Center, Detroit, MI, USA
June 11-13, 2019

American Library Association Annual Conference
Sponsored by The American Library Association (ALA)
50 E Huron St, Chicago, IL 60611
Tel: 312-944-6780 *Toll Free Tel:* 800-545-2433 (ext 3223, conference servs) *Fax:* 312-440-9374
E-mail: ala@ala.org
Web Site: www.ala.org
Key Personnel
Registration & Housing Specialist: Alicia Babcock *Tel:* 800-545-2433 ext 3229 *E-mail:* ababcock@ala.org
Conference Dir: Paul Graller *Tel:* 800-545-2433 ext 3219 *E-mail:* pgraller@ala.org
Conference Mgr: Amy McGuigan *Tel:* 800-545-2433 ext 3226 *E-mail:* amcguigan@ala.org
Meetings, AV & Catering Coord: Yvonne McLean *Tel:* 800-545-2433 ext 3222 *E-mail:* ymclean@ala.org
Conference Coord: Lina Zabaneh *Tel:* 800-545-2433 ext 3227 *E-mail:* lzabaneh@ala.org
Meeting Coord: Alicia (Alee) Navarro *Tel:* 800-545-2433 ext 3216 *E-mail:* anavarro@ala.org
Location: Washington, DC, USA
June 20-25, 2019

Jerusalem International Book Fair
Sponsored by Ariel Municipal Co Ltd
PO Box 26280, Jerusalem 9126201, Israel
Tel: (02) 546 8171; (02) 546 8170 *Fax:* (02) 546 8170
E-mail: jerfair@jerusalem.muni.il
Web Site: www.jbookfair.com; www.jbookfair.com/en/ (English)
Biennial event.
Location: Jerusalem International Convention Center, Jerusalem, Israel
June 2019

JULY

IAML Annual Conference
Sponsored by International Association of Music Libraries, Archives & Documentation Centres Inc (IAML)
c/o Gothenburg University Library, Music & Drama Library, Box 210, 405 30 Gothenburg, Sweden
Tel: (031) 786 40 57 *Fax:* (031) 786 40 59
E-mail: contact@iaml.info
Web Site: www.iaml.info
Key Personnel
Secy Gen: Pia Shekhter *E-mail:* secretary@iaml.info
Location: Krakow, Poland
July 14-19, 2019

Romance Writers of America Annual Conference
Sponsored by Romance Writers of America®
14615 Benfer Rd, Houston, TX 77069
Tel: 832-717-5200 *Fax:* 832-717-5201
E-mail: info@rwa.org
Web Site: www.rwa.org
Key Personnel
Exec Dir: Allison Kelley *Tel:* 832-717-5200 ext 124 *E-mail:* allison.kelley@rwa.org
Location: New York Marriott® Marquis, 1535 Broadway, New York, NY, USA
July 24-27, 2019

AUGUST

Edinburgh International Book Festival
5 Charlotte Sq, Edinburgh EH2 4DR, United Kingdom
Tel: (0131) 718 5666
E-mail: admin@edbookfest.co.uk
Web Site: www.edbookfest.co.uk
Each year we welcome over 800 international authors & over 200,000 visitors to the biggest book festival in the world, turning Edinburgh's Charlotte Square Gardens into a literary village for 18 days every August.

Location: Charlotte Square Gardens, Edinburgh, UK
Aug 2019

IFLA World Library & Information Congress
Sponsored by International Federation of Library Associations & Institutions (IFLA) (Federation internationale des associations de bibliothecaires et des bibliotheques)
Prins Willem-Alexanderhof 5, 2595 BE The Hague, Netherlands
Mailing Address: Postbus 95312, 2509 CH The Hague, Netherlands
Tel: (70) 314 08 84 *Fax:* (70) 383 48 27
E-mail: ifla@ifla.org
Web Site: conference.ifla.org; www.ifla.org
Key Personnel
Secy Gen: Gerald Leitner
Mgr, Conferences & Busn Rel: Josche Ouwerkerk *E-mail:* josche.ouwerkerk@ifla.org
Held simultaneously with IFLA General Conference & Assembly.
Location: Worldwide
Aug 2019

SEPTEMBER

Christian Resources Retailers & Suppliers Retreat
Sponsored by Christian Resources Together
Cedar Tree, 4 Ditchingham Close, Aylesbury, Bucks HP19 7SA, United Kingdom
Tel: (01296) 489860
Web Site: www.christianresourcestogether.co.uk
Location: The Hayes Conference Centre, Swanwick, Alfreton, Derbyshire, UK
Sept 17-18, 2019

Excellence in Journalism
Sponsored by The Society of Professional Journalists (SPJ)
Eugene S Pulliam National Journalism Ctr, 3909 N Meridian St, Indianapolis, IN 46208
Tel: 317-927-8000 *Fax:* 317-920-4789
E-mail: convention@spj.org
Web Site: excellenceinjournalism.org; www.spj.org
Key Personnel
Assoc Exec Dir: Chris Vachon *Tel:* 317-927-8000 ext 207 *E-mail:* cvachon@spj.org
Events Coord: Abbi Martzall *Tel:* 319-920-4791 *E-mail:* amartzall@spj.org
Annual conference co-organized by The Native American Journalists Association (NAJA) & Radio Television Digital News Association (RTDNA).
Location: Grand Hyatt San Antonio, 600 E Market St, San Antonio, TX, USA
Sept 5-7, 2019

Goteborg Book Fair
Sponsored by Bok & Bibliotek i Norden AB
Maessans Gata 20, 412 94 Gothenburg, Sweden
Tel: (031) 708 84 00 *Fax:* (031) 20 91 03
E-mail: info@goteborg-bookfair.com; info@bokmassan.se
Web Site: www.bokmassan.se
Key Personnel
CEO: Maria Kaellsson *E-mail:* maka@goteborg-bookfair.com
Sr Advisor: Anna Falck *E-mail:* af@goteborg-bookfair.com
Prog Coord: Anneli Jonasson *Tel:* (031) 708 84 03 *E-mail:* aj@goteborg-bookfair.com
Location: Gothenburg, Sweden
Sept 26-29, 2019

Graph Expo®
Sponsored by Graphic Arts Show Company (GASC)
1899 Preston White Dr, Reston, VA 20191
Tel: 703-264-7200 *Fax:* 703-620-9187
E-mail: info@gasc.org
Web Site: www.graphexpo.com; www.gasc.org
Key Personnel
VP, Meetings & Events: Kelly Kilga *Tel:* 703-264-7200 ext 213 *E-mail:* kkilga@gasc.org
Dir, Meetings & Events: Deedee (Diana) Tinkham *Tel:* 703-264-7200 ext 245 *E-mail:* dtinkham@gasc.org
Produced for NPES The Association for Suppliers of Printing, Publishing & Converting Technologies.
Location: Orange County Convention Center, North Hall, Orlando, FL, USA
Sept 22-25, 2019

PACK EXPO Las Vegas
Sponsored by PMMI: The Association for Packaging and Processing Technologies
11911 Freedom Dr, Suite 600, Reston, VA 20190
Tel: 571-612-3200 *Toll Free Tel:* 888-ASK-PMMI (275-7664) *Fax:* 703-243-8556
E-mail: expo@pmmi.org
Web Site: www.packexpolasvegas.com; www.packexpo.com; www.pmmi.org
Key Personnel
VP, Meetings & Events: Patti Fee *Tel:* 571-612-3193
Dir, Tradeshow Opers: Laura Thompson *Tel:* 571-612-3217
Dir, Tradeshow Mktg: Tina Scott *Tel:* 571-612-3203
Events Mgr: Anna Hudson *Tel:* 571-612-3198
Exhibitor Servs Sr Mgr: Merideth Newman *Tel:* 703-243-8555 *E-mail:* mnewman@pmmi.org
Exhibitor Servs & Sales Mgr: Beth Murray *Tel:* 571-612-3186 *E-mail:* bmurray@pmmi.org
Tradeshow Asst: Nina Sader *Tel:* 571-266-4409 *E-mail:* nsader@pmmi.org
Biennial event held in odd-numbered years.
Location: Las Vegas Convention Center, 3150 Paradise Rd, Las Vegas, NV, USA
Sept 23-25, 2019

OCTOBER

American Translators Association Annual Conference
Sponsored by American Translators Association (ATA)
225 Reinekers Lane, Suite 590, Alexandria, VA 22314
Tel: 703-683-6100 *Fax:* 703-683-6122
E-mail: ata@atanet.org
Web Site: www.atanet.org
Key Personnel
Exec Dir: Walter W Barak, Jr
Meetings Mgr: Teresa C Kelly *Tel:* 703-683-6100 ext 3014 *E-mail:* teresak@atanet.org
Location: Palm Springs, CA, USA
Oct 23-26, 2019

Frankfurt Book Fair
Sponsored by Frankfurter Buchmesse GmbH
Braubachstr 16, 60311 Frankfurt am Main, Germany
Mailing Address: Postfach 100116, 60001 Frankfurt am Main, Germany
Tel: (069) 21020 *Fax:* (069) 2102 277
E-mail: info@book-fair.com
Web Site: www.frankfurt-book-fair.com; www.book-fair.com
Key Personnel
CEO & Dir: Juergen Boos
Major international book & media fair attracting 7,100 exhibitors from over 100 countries & 275,000 visitors.
Location: Frankfurt Fairgrounds, Ludwig-Erhard-Anlage One, Frankfurt, Germany
Oct 16-20, 2019

Twin Cities Book Festival
Sponsored by Rain Taxi
PO Box 3840, Minneapolis, MN 55403
Tel: 612-825-1528 *Fax:* 612-825-1528
E-mail: bookfest@raintaxi.com
Web Site: www.raintaxi.com/twin-cities-book-festival
Key Personnel
Dir: Eric Lorberer
Gala celebration of books, featuring large exhibition, author readings & signings, book art activities, panel discussions, used book sale & children's events.
Location: Minnesota State Fairgrounds, 1265 Snelling Ave N, St Paul, MN, USA
Oct 2019

Utah Humanities Book Festival
Sponsored by Utah Humanities Council
Affiliate of Utah Center for the Book
202 W 300 N, Salt Lake City, UT 84103
Tel: 801-359-9670 *Fax:* 801-531-7869
Web Site: utahhumanities.org
Key Personnel
Exec Dir: Cynthia Buckingham *E-mail:* buckingham@utahhumanities.org
Lit Prog Offr: Michael McLane *E-mail:* mclane@utahhumanities.org
Communs Dir: Deena Pyle *E-mail:* pyle@utahhumanities.org
Free literary event featuring national, regional & local authors held Oct 1-31 annually (National Book Month).
Location: Statewide, UT, USA
Oct 1-31, 2019

NOVEMBER

AMWA Annual Conference
Sponsored by American Medical Writers Association (AMWA)
30 W Gude Dr, Suite 525, Rockville, MD 20850-4357
Tel: 240-238-0940 *Fax:* 301-294-9006
E-mail: amwa@amwa.org
Web Site: www.amwa.org
Key Personnel
Conference Prog Mgr & Workshop Coord: Becky Phillips *Tel:* 240-238-0940 ext 103 *E-mail:* becky@amwa.org
Location: Sheraton San Diego Hotel & Marina, San Diego, CA, USA
Nov 7-9, 2019

Jewish Book Month
Sponsored by Jewish Book Council
520 Eighth Ave, 4th fl, New York, NY 10018
Tel: 212-201-2920 *Fax:* 212-532-4952
E-mail: jbc@jewishbooks.org
Web Site: www.jewishbookcouncil.org; www.facebook.com/JewishBookCouncil; twitter.com/jewishbook
Key Personnel
Exec Dir: Naomi Firestone-Teeter
Dir: Carolyn Starman Hessel
Dedicated to the celebration of Jewish books held annually during the month leading up to Hanukkah.
Location: Nationwide throughout the USA
Nov 22-Dec 22, 2019

2020

JANUARY

American Library Association Midwinter Meeting
Sponsored by The American Library Association (ALA)
50 E Huron St, Chicago, IL 60611
Tel: 312-944-6780 *Toll Free Tel:* 800-545-2433 (ext 3223, conference servs) *Fax:* 312-440-9374
E-mail: ala@ala.org
Web Site: www.ala.org
Key Personnel
Registration & Housing Specialist: Alicia Babcock *Tel:* 800-545-2433 ext 3229 *E-mail:* ababcock@ala.org
Conference Dir: Paul Graller *Tel:* 800-545-2433 ext 3219 *E-mail:* pgraller@ala.org
Conference Mgr: Amy McGuigan *Tel:* 800-545-2433 ext 3226 *E-mail:* amcguigan@ala.org
Meetings, AV & Catering Coord: Yvonne McLean *Tel:* 800-545-2433 ext 3222 *E-mail:* ymclean@ala.org
Conference Coord: Lina Zabaneh *Tel:* 800-545-2433 ext 3227 *E-mail:* lzabaneh@ala.org
Meeting Coord: Alicia (Alee) Navarro *Tel:* 800-545-2433 ext 3216 *E-mail:* anavarro@ala.org
Location: Philadelphia, PA, USA
Jan 17-21, 2020

MLA Annual Convention
Sponsored by Modern Language Association of America (MLA)
85 Broad St, Suite 500, New York, NY 10004-2434
SAN: 202-6422
Tel: 646-576-5266 (convention); 646-576-5000 *Fax:* 646-458-0030
E-mail: convention@mla.org
Web Site: www.mla.org/convention
Key Personnel
Assoc Dir of Convention Progs: Karin L Bagnall *E-mail:* kbagnall@mla.org
Location: Seattle, WA, USA
Jan 9-12, 2020

MARCH

AWP Annual Conference & Bookfair
Sponsored by Association of Writers & Writing Programs (AWP)
George Mason University, 4400 University Dr, MSN 1E3, Fairfax, VA 22030
Tel: 703-993-4301 *Fax:* 703-993-4302
E-mail: awp@awpwriter.org
Web Site: www.awpwriter.org/awp_conference/; www.awpwriter.org
Key Personnel
Exec Dir: David W Fenza
Dir, Conferences: Christian Teresi
Assoc Dir, Conferences: Cynthia Sherman
Location: Henry B Gonzalez Convention Center, San Antonio, TX, USA
March 4-7, 2020

Texas Library Association Annual Conference
Sponsored by Texas Library Association (TLA)
3355 Bee Cave Rd, Suite 401, Austin, TX 78746-6763
Tel: 512-328-1518 *Toll Free Tel:* 800-580-2852 *Fax:* 512-328-8852
E-mail: tla@txla.org
Web Site: www.txla.org
Key Personnel
Conference Mgr: Elise Walker *Tel:* 512-328-1518 x145 *E-mail:* elisew@txla.org
Location: Houston, TX, USA
March 24-27, 2020

Virginia Festival of the Book
Sponsored by Virginia Foundation for the Humanities
145 Ednam Dr, Charlottesville, VA 22903
Tel: 434-924-3296 *Fax:* 434-296-4714
E-mail: vabook@virginia.edu
Web Site: www.vabook.org
Key Personnel
Prog Dir: Jane Kulow *Tel:* 434-924-7548
Annual public festival for children & adults featuring authors, illustrators, publishers, publicists, agents & other book professionals in panel discussions & readings. Most events are free. Hundreds of authors invited annually.
Location: Charlottesville, VA, USA
March 18-22, 2020

APRIL

Alberta Library Conference
Sponsored by Library Association of Alberta (LAA)
80 Baker Crescent NW, Calgary, AB T2L 1R4, Canada
Tel: 403-284-5818 *Toll Free Tel:* 877-522-5550 *Fax:* 403-284-5818
E-mail: info@laa.ca
Web Site: www.albertalibraryconference.com; www.laa.ca
Key Personnel
Exec Dir/Conference Coord: Christine Sheppard
Co-hosted by Alberta Library Trustees Association (ALTA).
Location: Fairmont Jasper Park Lodge, Jasper, AB, CN
April 30-May 3, 2020

International Children's Book Day
Sponsored by International Board on Books for Young People (IBBY)
Nonnenweg 12, Postfach, 4009 Basel, Switzerland
Tel: (061) 272 29 17 *Fax:* (061) 272 27 57
E-mail: ibby@ibby.org
Web Site: www.ibby.org
Key Personnel
Exec Dir: Liz Page *E-mail:* liz.page@ibby.org
Admin Asst: Luzmaria Stauffenegger-Lobato *E-mail:* luzmaria.stauffenegger@ibby.org
On Hans Christian Andersen's birthday, April 2nd, International Children's Book Day (ICBD) is celebrated to inspire a love of reading & to call attention to children's books. Each year a different national section has the opportunity to be the international sponsor. It decides upon a theme & invites a prominent author to write a message to the children of the world & a well-known illustrator to design a poster. These materials are used in different ways to promote books & reading around the world.
April 2, 2020

NAAJ Annual Meeting
Sponsored by North American Agricultural Journalists (NAAJ)
6434 Hurta Lane, Bryan, TX 77808
Tel: 979-845-2872 *Fax:* 979-862-1202
Web Site: www.naaj.net
Key Personnel
Exec Secy & Treas: Kathleen Phillips *E-mail:* kaphillips@tamu.edu
Annual meeting, writing awards & scholarship benefit dance.
Location: Washington, DC, USA
April 2020

National Library Week
Sponsored by The American Library Association (ALA)
50 E Huron St, Chicago, IL 60611
Tel: 312-944-6780 *Toll Free Tel:* 800-545-2433 *Fax:* 312-440-9374
E-mail: ala@ala.org
Web Site: www.ala.org/nlw
Location: Nationwide throughout the USA
April 19-25, 2020

MAY

Children's Book Week
Sponsored by The Children's Book Council (CBC)
54 W 39 St, 14th fl, New York, NY 10018
Tel: 212-966-1990
E-mail: cbc.info@cbcbooks.org
Web Site: www.bookweekonline.com; www.cbcbooks.org
Key Personnel
Exec Dir: Carl Lennertz *E-mail:* carl.lennertz@cbcbooks.org
Dir, Programming: Shaina Birkhead *E-mail:* shaina.birkhead@cbcbooks.org
Location: Nationwide across the USA
May 4-10, 2020

SSP Annual Meeting
Sponsored by Society for Scholarly Publishing (SSP)
10200 W 44 Ave, Suite 304, Wheat Ridge, CO 80033-2840
Tel: 303-422-3914 *Fax:* 720-881-6101
E-mail: info@sspnet.org
Web Site: www.sspnet.org
Key Personnel
Exec/Meetings Asst: Jennifer Lanphere
Location: Westin Waterfront, Boston, MA, USA
May 27-May 29, 2020

JUNE

American Library Association Annual Conference
Sponsored by The American Library Association (ALA)
50 E Huron St, Chicago, IL 60611
Tel: 312-944-6780 *Toll Free Tel:* 800-545-2433 (ext 3223, conference servs) *Fax:* 312-440-9374
E-mail: ala@ala.org
Web Site: www.ala.org
Key Personnel
Registration & Housing Specialist: Alicia Babcock *Tel:* 800-545-2433 ext 3229 *E-mail:* ababcock@ala.org
Conference Dir: Paul Graller *Tel:* 800-545-2433 ext 3219 *E-mail:* pgraller@ala.org
Conference Mgr: Amy McGuigan *Tel:* 800-545-2433 ext 3226 *E-mail:* amcguigan@ala.org
Meetings, AV & Catering Coord: Yvonne McLean *Tel:* 800-545-2433 ext 3222 *E-mail:* ymclean@ala.org
Conference Coord: Lina Zabaneh *Tel:* 800-545-2433 ext 3227 *E-mail:* lzabaneh@ala.org
Meeting Coord: Alicia (Alee) Navarro *Tel:* 800-545-2433 ext 3216 *E-mail:* anavarro@ala.org
Location: Chicago, IL, USA
June 23-28, 2020

JULY

Romance Writers of America Annual Conference
Sponsored by Romance Writers of America®
14615 Benfer Rd, Houston, TX 77069
Tel: 832-717-5200 *Fax:* 832-717-5201
E-mail: info@rwa.org
Web Site: www.rwa.org
Key Personnel
Exec Dir: Allison Kelley *Tel:* 832-717-5200 ext 124 *E-mail:* allison.kelley@rwa.org
Location: San Francisco Marriott Marquis, 780 Mission St, San Francisco, CA, USA
July 29-Aug 1, 2020

AUGUST

Edinburgh International Book Festival
5 Charlotte Sq, Edinburgh EH2 4DR, United Kingdom
Tel: (0131) 718 5666
E-mail: admin@edbookfest.co.uk
Web Site: www.edbookfest.co.uk
Each year we welcome over 800 international authors & over 200,000 visitors to the biggest book festival in the world, turning Edinburgh's Charlotte Square Gardens into a literary village for 18 days every August.
Location: Charlotte Square Gardens, Edinburgh, UK
Aug 2020

IFLA World Library & Information Congress
Sponsored by International Federation of Library Associations & Institutions (IFLA) (Federation internationale des associations de bibliothecaires et des bibliotheques)
Prins Willem-Alexanderhof 5, 2595 BE The Hague, Netherlands
Mailing Address: Postbus 95312, 2509 CH The Hague, Netherlands
Tel: (70) 314 08 84 *Fax:* (70) 383 48 27
E-mail: ifla@ifla.org
Web Site: conference.ifla.org; www.ifla.org
Key Personnel
Secy Gen: Gerald Leitner
Mgr, Conferences & Busn Rel: Josche Ouwerkerk *E-mail:* josche.ouwerkerk@ifla.org
Held simultaneously with IFLA General Conference & Assembly.
Location: Asia Oceania
Aug 2020

SEPTEMBER

Excellence in Journalism
Sponsored by The Society of Professional Journalists (SPJ)
Eugene S Pulliam National Journalism Ctr, 3909 N Meridian St, Indianapolis, IN 46208
Tel: 317-927-8000 *Fax:* 317-920-4789
E-mail: convention@spj.org
Web Site: excellenceinjournalism.org; www.spj.org
Key Personnel
Assoc Exec Dir: Chris Vachon *Tel:* 317-927-8000 ext 207 *E-mail:* cvachon@spj.org
Events Coord: Abbi Martzall *Tel:* 319-920-4791 *E-mail:* amartzall@spj.org
Annual conference co-organized by The Native American Journalists Association (NAJA) & Radio Television Digital News Association (RTDNA).
Location: Washington Hilton, 1919 Connecticut Ave NW, Washington, DC, USA
Sept 10-12, 2020

TAPPI/AICC SuperCorrExpo® 2020
Sponsored by Technical Association of the Pulp & Paper Industry (TAPPI)
15 Technology Pkwy S, Suite 115, Peachtree Corners, GA 30092
Tel: 770-446-1400 *Toll Free Tel:* 800-332-8686 (US); 800-446-9431 (CN) *Fax:* 770-446-6947
E-mail: memberconnection@tappi.org
Web Site: www.tappi.org
Key Personnel
Dir of Mktg: Simona Marcellus *Tel:* 770-209-7293 *E-mail:* smarcellus@tappi.org
Location: Orange County Convention Center, Orlando, FL, USA
Sept 14-17, 2020

OCTOBER

American Translators Association Annual Conference
Sponsored by American Translators Association (ATA)
225 Reinekers Lane, Suite 590, Alexandria, VA 22314
Tel: 703-683-6100 *Fax:* 703-683-6122
E-mail: ata@atanet.org
Web Site: www.atanet.org
Key Personnel
Exec Dir: Walter W Barak, Jr
Meetings Mgr: Teresa C Kelly *Tel:* 703-683-6100 ext 3014 *E-mail:* teresak@atanet.org
Location: Boston, MA, USA
Oct 21-24, 2020

AMWA Annual Conference
Sponsored by American Medical Writers Association (AMWA)
30 W Gude Dr, Suite 525, Rockville, MD 20850-4357
Tel: 240-238-0940 *Fax:* 301-294-9006
E-mail: amwa@amwa.org
Web Site: www.amwa.org
Key Personnel
Conference Prog Mgr & Workshop Coord: Becky Phillips *Tel:* 240-238-0940 ext 103 *E-mail:* becky@amwa.org
Location: Baltimore Marriott Waterfront Hotel, Baltimore, MD, USA
Oct 12-14, 2020

Frankfurt Book Fair
Sponsored by Frankfurter Buchmesse GmbH
Braubachstr 16, 60311 Frankfurt am Main, Germany
Mailing Address: Postfach 100116, 60001 Frankfurt am Main, Germany
Tel: (069) 21020 *Fax:* (069) 2102 277
E-mail: info@book-fair.com
Web Site: www.frankfurt-book-fair.com; www.book-fair.com
Key Personnel
CEO & Dir: Juergen Boos
Major international book & media fair attracting 7,100 exhibitors from over 100 countries & 275,000 visitors.
Location: Frankfurt Fairgrounds, Ludwig-Erhard-Anlage One, Frankfurt, Germany
Oct 14-18, 2020

Twin Cities Book Festival
Sponsored by Rain Taxi
PO Box 3840, Minneapolis, MN 55403
Tel: 612-825-1528 *Fax:* 612-825-1528
E-mail: bookfest@raintaxi.com
Web Site: www.raintaxi.com/twin-cities-book-festival
Key Personnel
Dir: Eric Lorberer
Gala celebration of books, featuring large exhibition, author readings & signings, book art activities, panel discussions, used book sale & children's events.
Location: Minnesota State Fairgrounds, 1265 Snelling Ave N, St Paul, MN, USA
Oct 2020

Utah Humanities Book Festival
Sponsored by Utah Humanities Council
Affiliate of Utah Center for the Book
202 W 300 N, Salt Lake City, UT 84103
Tel: 801-359-9670 *Fax:* 801-531-7869
Web Site: utahhumanities.org
Key Personnel
Exec Dir: Cynthia Buckingham *E-mail:* buckingham@utahhumanities.org
Lit Prog Offr: Michael McLane *E-mail:* mclane@utahhumanities.org
Communs Dir: Deena Pyle *E-mail:* pyle@utahhumanities.org
Free literary event featuring national, regional & local authors held Oct 1-31 annually (National Book Month).
Location: Statewide, UT, USA
Oct 1-31, 2020

NOVEMBER

Jewish Book Month
Sponsored by Jewish Book Council
520 Eighth Ave, 4th fl, New York, NY 10018
Tel: 212-201-2920 *Fax:* 212-532-4952
E-mail: jbc@jewishbooks.org
Web Site: www.jewishbookcouncil.org; www.facebook.com/JewishBookCouncil; twitter.com/jewishbook
Key Personnel
Exec Dir: Naomi Firestone-Teeter
Dir: Carolyn Starman Hessel
Dedicated to the celebration of Jewish books held annually during the month leading up to Hanukkah.
Location: Nationwide throughout the USA
Nov 10-Dec 10, 2020

2021

JANUARY

American Library Association Midwinter Meeting
Sponsored by The American Library Association (ALA)
50 E Huron St, Chicago, IL 60611
Tel: 312-944-6780 *Toll Free Tel:* 800-545-2433 (ext 3223, conference servs) *Fax:* 312-440-9374
E-mail: ala@ala.org
Web Site: www.ala.org
Key Personnel
Registration & Housing Specialist: Alicia Babcock *Tel:* 800-545-2433 ext 3229 *E-mail:* ababcock@ala.org
Conference Dir: Paul Graller *Tel:* 800-545-2433 ext 3219 *E-mail:* pgraller@ala.org
Conference Mgr: Amy McGuigan *Tel:* 800-545-2433 ext 3226 *E-mail:* amcguigan@ala.org
Meetings, AV & Catering Coord: Yvonne McLean *Tel:* 800-545-2433 ext 3222 *E-mail:* ymclean@ala.org

Conference Coord: Lina Zabaneh *Tel:* 800-545-2433 ext 3227 *E-mail:* lzabaneh@ala.org
Meeting Coord: Alicia (Alee) Navarro *Tel:* 800-545-2433 ext 3216 *E-mail:* anavarro@ala.org
Location: Indianapolis, IN, USA
Jan 22-26, 2021

MARCH

AWP Annual Conference & Bookfair
Sponsored by Association of Writers & Writing Programs (AWP)
George Mason University, 4400 University Dr, MSN 1E3, Fairfax, VA 22030
Tel: 703-993-4301 *Fax:* 703-993-4302
E-mail: awp@awpwriter.org
Web Site: www.awpwriter.org/awp_conference/; www.awpwriter.org
Key Personnel
Exec Dir: David W Fenza
Dir, Conferences: Christian Teresi
Assoc Dir, Conferences: Cynthia Sherman
Location: Kansas City Convention Center, Kansas City, MO, USA
March 3-6, 2021

Virginia Festival of the Book
Sponsored by Virginia Foundation for the Humanities
145 Ednam Dr, Charlottesville, VA 22903
Tel: 434-924-3296 *Fax:* 434-296-4714
E-mail: vabook@virginia.edu
Web Site: www.vabook.org
Key Personnel
Prog Dir: Jane Kulow *Tel:* 434-924-7548
Annual public festival for children & adults featuring authors, illustrators, publishers, publicists, agents & other book professionals in panel discussions & readings. Most events are free. Hundreds of authors invited annually.
Location: Charlottesville, VA, USA
March 17-21, 2021

APRIL

International Children's Book Day
Sponsored by International Board on Books for Young People (IBBY)
Nonnenweg 12, Postfach, 4009 Basel, Switzerland
Tel: (061) 272 29 17 *Fax:* (061) 272 27 57
E-mail: ibby@ibby.org
Web Site: www.ibby.org
Key Personnel
Exec Dir: Liz Page *E-mail:* liz.page@ibby.org
Admin Asst: Luzmaria Stauffenegger-Lobato *E-mail:* luzmaria.stauffenegger@ibby.org
On Hans Christian Andersen's birthday, April 2nd, International Children's Book Day (ICBD) is celebrated to inspire a love of reading & to call attention to children's books. Each year a different national section has the opportunity to be the international sponsor. It decides upon a theme & invites a prominent author to write a message to the children of the world & a well-known illustrator to design a poster. These materials are used in different ways to promote books & reading around the world.
April 2, 2021

NAAJ Annual Meeting
Sponsored by North American Agricultural Journalists (NAAJ)
6434 Hurta Lane, Bryan, TX 77808
Tel: 979-845-2872 *Fax:* 979-862-1202
Web Site: www.naaj.net
Key Personnel
Exec Secy & Treas: Kathleen Phillips *E-mail:* ka-phillips@tamu.edu
Annual meeting, writing awards & scholarship benefit dance.
Location: Washington, DC, USA
April 2021

Texas Library Association Annual Conference
Sponsored by Texas Library Association (TLA)
3355 Bee Cave Rd, Suite 401, Austin, TX 78746-6763
Tel: 512-328-1518 *Toll Free Tel:* 800-580-2852 *Fax:* 512-328-8852
E-mail: tla@txla.org
Web Site: www.txla.org
Key Personnel
Conference Mgr: Elise Walker *Tel:* 512-328-1518 x145 *E-mail:* elisew@txla.org
Location: San Antonio, TX, USA
April 20-23, 2021

MAY

Children's Book Week
Sponsored by The Children's Book Council (CBC)
54 W 39 St, 14th fl, New York, NY 10018
Tel: 212-966-1990
E-mail: cbc.info@cbcbooks.org
Web Site: www.bookweekonline.com; www.cbcbooks.org
Key Personnel
Exec Dir: Carl Lennertz *E-mail:* carl.lennertz@cbcbooks.org
Dir, Programming: Shaina Birkhead *E-mail:* shaina.birkhead@cbcbooks.org
Location: Nationwide across the USA
May 3-9, 2021

PacPrint 2021
Sponsored by Visual Connections Australia Ltd
Shop 4, 123 Midson Rd, Epping, NSW 2121, Australia
Mailing Address: PO Box 3723, Marsfield, NSW 2122, Australia
Tel: (02) 9868 1577
E-mail: exhibitions@visualconnections.org.au
Web Site: www.pacprint.com.au
Key Personnel
Gen Mgr: Peter Harper *E-mail:* peterh@visualconnections.org.au
Event Mgr: Jenny Harris *E-mail:* jennyh@visualconnections.org.au; Sarah Moore *E-mail:* sarahm@visualconnections.org.au
Presented by Visual Connections Australia Ltd & the Printing Industries Association of Australia (PIAA), this event is held every 4 years.
Location: Melbourne Convention & Exhibitions Centre (MCEC), South Wharf, Victoria, Australia
May 2021

SSP Annual Meeting
Sponsored by Society for Scholarly Publishing (SSP)
10200 W 44 Ave, Suite 304, Wheat Ridge, CO 80033-2840
Tel: 303-422-3914 *Fax:* 720-881-6101
E-mail: info@sspnet.org
Web Site: www.sspnet.org
Key Personnel
Exec/Meetings Asst: Jennifer Lanphere
Location: Gaylord National Resort, National Harbor, MD, USA
May 26-May 28, 2021

JUNE

American Library Association Annual Conference
Sponsored by The American Library Association (ALA)
50 E Huron St, Chicago, IL 60611
Tel: 312-944-6780 *Toll Free Tel:* 800-545-2433 (ext 3223, conference servs) *Fax:* 312-440-9374
E-mail: ala@ala.org
Web Site: www.ala.org
Key Personnel
Registration & Housing Specialist: Alicia Babcock *Tel:* 800-545-2433 ext 3229 *E-mail:* ababcock@ala.org
Conference Dir: Paul Graller *Tel:* 800-545-2433 ext 3219 *E-mail:* pgraller@ala.org
Conference Mgr: Amy McGuigan *Tel:* 800-545-2433 ext 3226 *E-mail:* amcguigan@ala.org
Meetings, AV & Catering Coord: Yvonne McLean *Tel:* 800-545-2433 ext 3222 *E-mail:* ymclean@ala.org
Conference Coord: Lina Zabaneh *Tel:* 800-545-2433 ext 3227 *E-mail:* lzabaneh@ala.org
Meeting Coord: Alicia (Alee) Navarro *Tel:* 800-545-2433 ext 3216 *E-mail:* anavarro@ala.org
Location: Chicago, IL, USA
June 24-29, 2021

JULY

Romance Writers of America Annual Conference
Sponsored by Romance Writers of America®
14615 Benfer Rd, Houston, TX 77069
Tel: 832-717-5200 *Fax:* 832-717-5201
E-mail: info@rwa.org
Web Site: www.rwa.org
Key Personnel
Exec Dir: Allison Kelley *Tel:* 832-717-5200 ext 124 *E-mail:* allison.kelley@rwa.org
Location: Gaylord Opryland Resort & Convention Center, 2800 Opryland Dr, Nashville, TN, USA
July 14-17, 2021

AUGUST

Edinburgh International Book Festival
5 Charlotte Sq, Edinburgh EH2 4DR, United Kingdom
Tel: (0131) 718 5666
E-mail: admin@edbookfest.co.uk
Web Site: www.edbookfest.co.uk
Each year we welcome over 800 international authors & over 200,000 visitors to the biggest book festival in the world, turning Edinburgh's Charlotte Square Gardens into a literary village for 18 days every August.
Location: Charlotte Square Gardens, Edinburgh, UK
Aug 2021

AUTUMN

PRINT®
Sponsored by Graphic Arts Show Company (GASC)
1899 Preston White Dr, Reston, VA 20191
Tel: 703-264-7200 *Fax:* 703-620-9187

E-mail: info@gasc.org
Web Site: www.gasc.org
Key Personnel
VP, Meetings & Events: Kelly Kilga *Tel:* 703-264-7200 ext 213 *E-mail:* kkilga@gasc.org
Dir, Meetings & Events: Deedee (Diana) Tinkham *Tel:* 703-264-7200 ext 245 *E-mail:* dtinkham@gasc.org
Quadrennial event produced for NPES The Association for Suppliers of Printing, Publishing & Converting Technologies.
Location: McCormick Place, South Hall, 2301 S Lake Shore Dr, Chicago, IL, USA
Autumn 2021

OCTOBER

American Translators Association Annual Conference
Sponsored by American Translators Association (ATA)
225 Reinekers Lane, Suite 590, Alexandria, VA 22314
Tel: 703-683-6100 *Fax:* 703-683-6122
E-mail: ata@atanet.org
Web Site: www.atanet.org
Key Personnel
Exec Dir: Walter W Barak, Jr
Meetings Mgr: Teresa C Kelly *Tel:* 703-683-6100 ext 3014 *E-mail:* teresak@atanet.org
Location: Minneapolis, MN, USA
Oct 27-30, 2021

Frankfurt Book Fair
Sponsored by Frankfurter Buchmesse GmbH
Braubachstr 16, 60311 Frankfurt am Main, Germany
Mailing Address: Postfach 100116, 60001 Frankfurt am Main, Germany
Tel: (069) 21020 *Fax:* (069) 2102 277
E-mail: info@book-fair.com
Web Site: www.frankfurt-book-fair.com; www.book-fair.com
Key Personnel
CEO & Dir: Juergen Boos
Major international book & media fair attracting 7,100 exhibitors from over 100 countries & 275,000 visitors.
Location: Frankfurt Fairgrounds, Ludwig-Erhard-Anlage One, Frankfurt, Germany
Oct 20-24, 2021

Jewish Book Month
Sponsored by Jewish Book Council
520 Eighth Ave, 4th fl, New York, NY 10018
Tel: 212-201-2920 *Fax:* 212-532-4952
E-mail: jbc@jewishbooks.org
Web Site: www.jewishbookcouncil.org; www.facebook.com/JewishBookCouncil; twitter.com/jewishbook
Key Personnel
Exec Dir: Naomi Firestone-Teeter
Dir: Carolyn Starman Hessel
Dedicated to the celebration of Jewish books held annually during the month leading up to Hanukkah.
Location: Nationwide throughout the USA
Oct 28-Nov 28, 2021

Utah Humanities Book Festival
Sponsored by Utah Humanities Council
Affiliate of Utah Center for the Book
202 W 300 N, Salt Lake City, UT 84103
Tel: 801-359-9670 *Fax:* 801-531-7869
Web Site: utahhumanities.org
Key Personnel
Exec Dir: Cynthia Buckingham *E-mail:* buckingham@utahhumanities.org
Lit Prog Offr: Michael McLane *E-mail:* mclane@utahhumanities.org
Communs Dir: Deena Pyle *E-mail:* pyle@utahhumanities.org
Free literary event featuring national, regional & local authors held Oct 1-31 annually (National Book Month).
Location: Statewide, UT, USA
Oct 1-31, 2021

2022

JANUARY

American Library Association Midwinter Meeting
Sponsored by The American Library Association (ALA)
50 E Huron St, Chicago, IL 60611
Tel: 312-944-6780 *Toll Free Tel:* 800-545-2433 (ext 3223, conference servs) *Fax:* 312-440-9374
E-mail: ala@ala.org
Web Site: www.ala.org
Key Personnel
Registration & Housing Specialist: Alicia Babcock *Tel:* 800-545-2433 ext 3229 *E-mail:* ababcock@ala.org
Conference Dir: Paul Graller *Tel:* 800-545-2433 ext 3219 *E-mail:* pgraller@ala.org
Conference Mgr: Amy McGuigan *Tel:* 800-545-2433 ext 3226 *E-mail:* amcguigan@ala.org
Meetings, AV & Catering Coord: Yvonne McLean *Tel:* 800-545-2433 ext 3222 *E-mail:* ymclean@ala.org
Conference Coord: Lina Zabaneh *Tel:* 800-545-2433 ext 3227 *E-mail:* lzabaneh@ala.org
Meeting Coord: Alicia (Alee) Navarro *Tel:* 800-545-2433 ext 3216 *E-mail:* anavarro@ala.org
Location: San Antonio, TX, USA
Jan 21-25, 2022

MARCH

AWP Annual Conference & Bookfair
Sponsored by Association of Writers & Writing Programs (AWP)
George Mason University, 4400 University Dr, MSN 1E3, Fairfax, VA 22030
Tel: 703-993-4301 *Fax:* 703-993-4302
E-mail: awp@awpwriter.org
Web Site: www.awpwriter.org/awp_conference/; www.awpwriter.org
Key Personnel
Exec Dir: David W Fenza
Dir, Conferences: Christian Teresi
Assoc Dir, Conferences: Cynthia Sherman
Location: Pennsylvania Convention Center, Philadelphia, PA, USA
March 23-26, 2022

APRIL

International Children's Book Day
Sponsored by International Board on Books for Young People (IBBY)
Nonnenweg 12, Postfach, 4009 Basel, Switzerland
Tel: (061) 272 29 17 *Fax:* (061) 272 27 57
E-mail: ibby@ibby.org
Web Site: www.ibby.org
Key Personnel
Exec Dir: Liz Page *E-mail:* liz.page@ibby.org
Admin Asst: Luzmaria Stauffenegger-Lobato *E-mail:* luzmaria.stauffenegger@ibby.org
On Hans Christian Andersen's birthday, April 2nd, International Children's Book Day (ICBD) is celebrated to inspire a love of reading & to call attention to children's books. Each year a different national section has the opportunity to be the international sponsor. It decides upon a theme & invites a prominent author to write a message to the children of the world & a well-known illustrator to design a poster. These materials are used in different ways to promote books & reading around the world.
April 2, 2022

NAAJ Annual Meeting
Sponsored by North American Agricultural Journalists (NAAJ)
6434 Hurta Lane, Bryan, TX 77808
Tel: 979-845-2872 *Fax:* 979-862-1202
Web Site: www.naaj.net
Key Personnel
Exec Secy & Treas: Kathleen Phillips *E-mail:* ka-phillips@tamu.edu
Annual meeting, writing awards & scholarship benefit dance.
Location: Washington, DC, USA
April 2022

Texas Library Association Annual Conference
Sponsored by Texas Library Association (TLA)
3355 Bee Cave Rd, Suite 401, Austin, TX 78746-6763
Tel: 512-328-1518 *Toll Free Tel:* 800-580-2852 *Fax:* 512-328-8852
E-mail: tla@txla.org
Web Site: www.txla.org
Key Personnel
Conference Mgr: Elise Walker *Tel:* 512-328-1518 x145 *E-mail:* elisew@txla.org
Location: Fort Worth, TX, USA
April 5-8, 2022

MAY

Children's Book Week
Sponsored by The Children's Book Council (CBC)
54 W 39 St, 14th fl, New York, NY 10018
Tel: 212-966-1990
E-mail: cbc.info@cbcbooks.org
Web Site: www.bookweekonline.com; www.cbcbooks.org
Key Personnel
Exec Dir: Carl Lennertz *E-mail:* carl.lennertz@cbcbooks.org
Dir, Programming: Shaina Birkhead *E-mail:* shaina.birkhead@cbcbooks.org
Location: Nationwide across the USA
May 2-8, 2022

JUNE

American Library Association Annual Conference
Sponsored by The American Library Association (ALA)
50 E Huron St, Chicago, IL 60611
Tel: 312-944-6780 *Toll Free Tel:* 800-545-2433 (ext 3223, conference servs) *Fax:* 312-440-9374
E-mail: ala@ala.org
Web Site: www.ala.org

Key Personnel
Registration & Housing Specialist: Alicia Babcock *Tel:* 800-545-2433 ext 3229 *E-mail:* ababcock@ala.org
Conference Dir: Paul Graller *Tel:* 800-545-2433 ext 3219 *E-mail:* pgraller@ala.org
Conference Mgr: Amy McGuigan *Tel:* 800-545-2433 ext 3226 *E-mail:* amcguigan@ala.org
Meetings, AV & Catering Coord: Yvonne McLean *Tel:* 800-545-2433 ext 3222 *E-mail:* ymclean@ala.org
Conference Coord: Lina Zabaneh *Tel:* 800-545-2433 ext 3227 *E-mail:* lzabaneh@ala.org
Meeting Coord: Alicia (Alee) Navarro *Tel:* 800-545-2433 ext 3216 *E-mail:* anavarro@ala.org
Location: Washington, DC, USA
June 23-28, 2022

SSP Annual Meeting
Sponsored by Society for Scholarly Publishing (SSP)
10200 W 44 Ave, Suite 304, Wheat Ridge, CO 80033-2840
Tel: 303-422-3914 *Fax:* 720-881-6101
E-mail: info@sspnet.org
Web Site: www.sspnet.org
Key Personnel
Exec/Meetings Asst: Jennifer Lanphere
Location: Sheraton Chicago Hotel & Towers, Chicago, IL, USA
June 1-June 3, 2022

AUGUST

Edinburgh International Book Festival
5 Charlotte Sq, Edinburgh EH2 4DR, United Kingdom
Tel: (0131) 718 5666
E-mail: admin@edbookfest.co.uk
Web Site: www.edbookfest.co.uk
Each year we welcome over 800 international authors & over 200,000 visitors to the biggest book festival in the world, turning Edinburgh's Charlotte Square Gardens into a literary village for 18 days every August.
Location: Charlotte Square Gardens, Edinburgh, UK
Aug 2022

OCTOBER

Frankfurt Book Fair
Sponsored by Frankfurter Buchmesse GmbH
Braubachstr 16, 60311 Frankfurt am Main, Germany
Mailing Address: Postfach 100116, 60001 Frankfurt am Main, Germany
Tel: (069) 21020 *Fax:* (069) 2102 277
E-mail: info@book-fair.com
Web Site: www.frankfurt-book-fair.com; www.book-fair.com
Key Personnel
CEO & Dir: Juergen Boos
Major international book & media fair attracting 7,100 exhibitors from over 100 countries & 275,000 visitors.
Location: Frankfurt Fairgrounds, Ludwig-Erhard-Anlage One, Frankfurt, Germany
Oct 19-23, 2022

Utah Humanities Book Festival
Sponsored by Utah Humanities Council
Affiliate of Utah Center for the Book
202 W 300 N, Salt Lake City, UT 84103
Tel: 801-359-9670 *Fax:* 801-531-7869
Web Site: utahhumanities.org
Key Personnel
Exec Dir: Cynthia Buckingham *E-mail:* buckingham@utahhumanities.org
Lit Prog Offr: Michael McLane *E-mail:* mclane@utahhumanities.org
Communs Dir: Deena Pyle *E-mail:* pyle@utahhumanities.org
Free literary event featuring national, regional & local authors held Oct 1-31 annually (National Book Month).
Location: Statewide, UT, USA
Oct 1-31, 2022

NOVEMBER

Jewish Book Month
Sponsored by Jewish Book Council
520 Eighth Ave, 4th fl, New York, NY 10018
Tel: 212-201-2920 *Fax:* 212-532-4952
E-mail: jbc@jewishbooks.org
Web Site: www.jewishbookcouncil.org; www.facebook.com/JewishBookCouncil; twitter.com/jewishbook
Key Personnel
Exec Dir: Naomi Firestone-Teeter
Dir: Carolyn Starman Hessel
Dedicated to the celebration of Jewish books held annually during the month leading up to Hanukkah.
Location: Nationwide throughout the USA
Nov 18-Dec 18, 2022

Writers' Conferences & Workshops

The following lists workshops and seminars dealing with various aspects of the book trade. See **Courses for the Book Trade** for a list of college level programs and courses.

Alice B Acheson's Workshops for Writers, Illustrators & Photographers
Alice B Acheson
Unit of Acheson-Greub Inc
PO Box 735, Friday Harbor, WA 98250
Tel: 360-378-2815
E-mail: aliceba7@gmail.com
Key Personnel
Pres: Alice B Acheson
One- or two-day workshops on making a ms succeed in the market place. Writers utilize a pre-class assignment to determine techniques for finding & impressing an agent +/or publisher while class discussion includes discovering what's to come once the ms is under contract. Extensive written materials provided. Instructor shares 30 years of book publishing expertise in negotiating contracts, editing books & achieving award-winning book publicity.
The Greatest Marketing Tool of All, on verbal pitch (Spring & Fall)
Publishing Choices: Print-on-Demand, Self-Publishing, Traditional Publisher, pros/cons of each (Spring & Fall)
Your Book: What's Next?, how to find an agent & publisher, how to influence the publisher's marketing of your book (Spring & Fall)
Bound-for-Success Book Proposals (Spring & Fall).
Location: Richard Hugo House, Seattle, WA
Date: Spring 2018 (see hugohouse.org for exact dates)
Location: Book Passage, Corte Madera, CA
Date: March 2-4, 2018
Location: Richard Hugo House, Seattle, WA
Date: Fall 2018 (see hugohouse.org for exact dates)
Location: Book Passage, Corte Madera, CA
Date: Sept 21-23, 2018

American Society of Journalists and Authors Annual Writers Conference
American Society of Journalists and Authors (ASJA)
355 Lexington Ave, 15th fl, New York, NY 10017-6603
Tel: 212-997-0947
Web Site: asja.org
Key Personnel
Exec Dir: Alexandra Owens *E-mail:* director@asja.org
Inside information from editors, agents & publishers, find inspiration & gain income-boosting ideas. Open to all, the conference features topics for newer & more experienced pros. New panels & workshops will enrich you no matter where you are in your writing career.

AMWA Annual Conference
American Medical Writers Association (AMWA)
30 W Gude Dr, Suite 525, Rockville, MD 20850-4357
Tel: 240-238-0940 *Fax:* 301-294-9006
E-mail: amwa@amwa.org
Web Site: www.amwa.org
Key Personnel
Educ Mgr: Becky Philips
Annual conference includes workshops, open sessions & networking opportunities.
Location: Renaissance DC Downtown Hotel, Washington, DC
Date: Nov 1-3, 2018

Antioch Writers' Workshop
Antioch University Midwest
300 College Park Ave, Suite 200A, Dayton, OH 45469-0001
Tel: 937-567-2399
E-mail: info@antiochwritersworkshop.com
Web Site: www.antiochwritersworkshop.com
Key Personnel
Pres: T J Turner
Exec Dir: Sharon Short
A weeklong summer workshop featuring morning classes, midday presentations on writing profession, afternoon intensive seminars in a genre or type, evening faculty talks & readings. Non-refundable registration fee $125.

Appalachian Writers' Workshop
Hindman Settlement School
56 Education Lane, Hindman, KY 41822
Mailing Address: PO Box 844, Hindman, KY 41822-0844
Tel: 606-785-5475
E-mail: info@hindmansettlement.org
Web Site: www.hindmansettlement.org
Key Personnel
Exec Dir, Hindman Settlement School: Brent D Hutchinson *E-mail:* bdhutchinson@hindmansettlement.org
Poetry, nonfiction, short story, novel, dramatic writing & children's writing.

Arkansas Writers' Conference
National League of American Pen Women, Arkansas Pioneer Branch
Division of National League of American Pen Women
PO Box 24662, Little Rock, AR 72221
Tel: 501-833-2756
Web Site: www.arkansaswritersconference.org
Key Personnel
Dir: Brenda Iannacone *E-mail:* breannacone1@yahoo.com
Location: Crowne Plaza Hotel, Little Rock, AR
Date: Annually in June

Artists & Writers Summer Fellowships
The Constance Saltonstall Foundation for the Arts
435 Ellis Hollow Creek Rd, Ithaca, NY 14850
Tel: 607-539-3146
E-mail: artscolony@saltonstall.org
Web Site: www.saltonstall.org
Key Personnel
Exec Dir: Lesley Williamson
Provide month long summer fellowships for New York State artists & writers May-Sept.

The Association for Women in Communications
1717 E Republic Rd, Suite A, Springfield, MO 65804
Tel: 417-886-8606 *Fax:* 417-886-3685
E-mail: info@womcom.org
Web Site: www.womcom.org
Key Personnel
Chair: Kristin E Van Nort *E-mail:* chair@womcom.org
Exec Dir: Jean Harmison
Acct Mgr: Becky Lucas *E-mail:* members@womcom.org
Professional development workshops & exposition in various areas of the communications field. Ongoing webinars available.

Association pour l'Avancement des Sciences et des Techniques de la Documentation
2065 rue Parthenais, Bureau 387, Montreal, QC H2K 3T1, Canada
Tel: 514-281-5012 *Fax:* 514-281-8219
E-mail: info@asted.org
Web Site: www.asted.org
Key Personnel
Exec Dir: Lionel Villalonga *E-mail:* lvillalonga@asted.org

Atlantic Center for the Arts Artists-in-Residence Program
Atlantic Center for the Arts (ACA)
1414 Art Center Ave, New Smyrna Beach, FL 32168
Tel: 386-427-6975 *Toll Free Tel:* 800-393-6975 *Fax:* 386-427-5669
E-mail: program@atlanticcenterforthearts.org
Web Site: atlanticcenterforthearts.org
Key Personnel
Co-Exec Dir: Jim Frost *E-mail:* jfrost@atlanticcenterforthearts.org; Nancy Lowden Norman *E-mail:* nlowden@atlanticcenterforthearts.org
Dir, Fin & Acctg: Kevin Miller *E-mail:* kmiller@atlanticcenterforthearts.org
Residency Dir: Nick Conroy *E-mail:* nconroy@atlanticcenterforthearts.org
Mktg & Membership Mgr: Kathryn Peterson *E-mail:* kpeterson@atlanticcenterforthearts.org
Admin Asst: Kelly Timmons
Since 1982, Atlantic Center's residency program has provided artists from all artistic disciplines with spaces to live, work & collaborate during 3 week residencies. Each residency session includes 3 master artists of different disciplines. The master artists each personally select a group of associates - talented, emerging artists - through an application process administered by ACA. During the residency, artists participate in informal sessions with their group, collaborate on projects & work independently on their own projects. The relaxed atmosphere & unstructured program provide considerable time for artistic regeneration & creation.

Bard Society Fiction Writing Workshop
Bard Society
3113 Crosby Lane, Jacksonville, FL 32216
Tel: 904-250-6045
E-mail: frankgrn@comcast.net
Key Personnel
Dir: Frank Green
Fiction writing workshop in existence for more than 35 years. Schedule: One workshop a week, Tuesday evening, 3 hours; more than 40 books published by members. No fee but contributions welcome. All lovers of the written word welcome. A tribute to workshop leader Frank Green was published, Wednesdays with Frank.

Beyond the Book
Copyright Clearance Center Inc (CCC)

222 Rosewood Dr, Danvers, MA 01923
Tel: 978-750-8400 (sales)
E-mail: beyondthebook@copyright.com
Web Site: www.copyright.com; beyondthebookcast.com
Key Personnel
VP, HR: Michele R Nivens
Programs also include online seminars & telephone conference calls with distinguished experts. Created with authors in mind, Beyond the Book seeks to provide information on the latest business issues facing the creative professions - from initial research to final publication & beyond. Your connection to leading editors, publishing analysts & information technology experts, as well as innovative authors.

Big Apple Conference
The International Women's Writing Guild (IWWG)
5 Penn Plaza, 19th fl, PMB 19059, New York, NY 10001
Tel: 917-720-6959
E-mail: iwwgquestions@iwwg.org
Web Site: www.iwwg.org
Key Personnel
Exec Dir: Dixie King, PhD
Interim Opers Dir: Marj Hahne
Held twice annually.
Location: New York, NY
Date: April
Location: New York, NY
Date: Oct

Bread Loaf Writers' Conference
Middlebury College
5525 Middlebury College, 14 Old Chapel Rd, Middlebury, VT 05753
Tel: 802-443-5286 *Fax:* 802-443-2087
E-mail: blwc@middlebury.edu
Web Site: www.middlebury.edu/blwc
Key Personnel
Dir: Jennifer Grotz
Admin Dir: Noreen Cargill
Coord: Jason Lamb
Ten day conference for writers of poetry, fiction & nonfiction. Fellowship covers tuition, room & board. Work-study scholarship covers tuition, with pay to offset room & board. Tuition scholarship covers tuition.

Bucknell Seminar for Undergraduate Poets
Stadler Center for Poetry
Bucknell University, Bucknell Hall, Moore Ave, Lewisburg, PA 17837
Tel: 570-577-1853
E-mail: stadlercenter@bucknell.edu
Web Site: www.bucknell.edu/stadlercenter
Key Personnel
Prog Mgr: Andrew Ciotola
Ten applicants are accepted to participate in a 3 week residence in writing for undergraduate poets. Applications should include an academic transcript, 2 supporting recommendations (at least one from a poetry-writing instructor) & a 10-12 page portfolio. A letter of self-presentation (letter of intro stressing commitment to poetry writing, experience & any publications) should accompany the application. Applications must be submitted online or postmarked by Jan 31. See web site for details.
Location: Stadler Center for Poetry, Bucknell University, Lewisburg, PA
Date: June 9-July 30, 2018

Cape Cod Writers' Center Conference
Cape Cod Writers Center
919 Main St, Osterville, MA 02655
Mailing Address: PO Box 408, Osterville, MA 02655
Tel: 508-420-0200
E-mail: writers@capecodwriterscenter.org
Web Site: capecodwriterscenter.org
Key Personnel
Pres: Barbara Struna
Exec Dir: Nancy Rubin Stuart
Annual conference to improve your literary skills as you learn from top professionals. Open to beginning & published authors. In addition to classes in fiction, nonfiction, mystery, poetry, children's, young adult, social media & promotion & other genres, the conference offers agent query & ms mentoring sessions to participants. Participant readings. Keynote luncheon with prominent author.

Chautauqua Writers' Workshop
The Writers' Center at Chautauqua
One Ames Ave, Chautauqua, NY 14722
Mailing Address: PO Box 28, Chautauqua, NY 14722-0408
Tel: 716-357-6316; 716-357-6250
Toll Free Tel: 800-836-ARTS (836-2787)
Fax: 716-357-9014
Web Site: ciweb.org
Key Personnel
VP: Sherra Babcock
Prog Dir, Writer's Ctr: Clara Silverstein
E-mail: clrsilver@gmail.com
Dept Coord: Emily Carpenter
Writing workshop in poetry & prose at 137 year-old Chautauqua Institution, international center for the arts, education, religion & recreation.
Location: Chautauqua Institution, Chautauqua, NY
Date: Last week in June through the end of August

Chocorua Writing Workshop
World Fellowship Center
PO Box 2280, Conway, NH 03818-2280
Tel: 603-447-2280
E-mail: reservations@worldfellowship.org
Web Site: www.worldfellowship.org; www.facebook.com/World.Fellowship.Center
Key Personnel
Dir: Ellen Meeropol; Ekere Tallie
Can a letter be as powerful as a poem? Engage like good fiction? Persuade like an essay? Help the writer process like journaling? Yes! Two sessions of exploring letters & epistolary texts & writing our own.
Location: Conway (White Mountains), NH
Date: Annually in July

The Clarion Science Fiction & Fantasy Writers' Workshop
The Clarion Foundation
Arthur C Clarke Ctr for Human Imagination, UC San Diego, 9500 Gilman Dr, MC0445, La Jolla, CA 92093-0445
Tel: 858-534-2115
E-mail: clarion@ucsd.edu
Web Site: clarion.ucsd.edu; imagination.ucsd.edu
Key Personnel
Pres: Karen Joy Fowler
Prog Mgr: Patrick Coleman
Science fiction & fantasy writing workshop held for 6 weeks each summer. It is mandatory that students reside in Clarion housing.

Conference on Poetry
The Frost Place
158 Ridge Rd, Franconia, NH 03580
Mailing Address: PO Box 74, Franconia, NH 03580-0074
Tel: 603-823-5510
E-mail: frost@frostplace.org
Web Site: frostplace.org
Key Personnel
Exec Dir: Maudelle Driskell
Offers lectures, talks & craft panels by faculty in a 7-day program. See web site for details.
Date: Annually in Summer

Creative Writing Day & Workshops
Virginia Highlands Festival
PO Box 801, Abingdon, VA 24212-0801
Tel: 276-623-5266 *Fax:* 276-676-3076
E-mail: info@vahighlandsfestival.org
Web Site: vahighlandsfestival.org
Key Personnel
Chair: Steve Lindeman; Deborah Prescott
Exec Dir: Becky Caldwell
Lectures, readings & workshops in creative writing with noteworthy authors held each summer.

Djerassi Resident Artists Program
2325 Bear Gulch Rd, Woodside, CA 94062
Tel: 650-747-1250
E-mail: drap@djerassi.org
Web Site: www.djerassi.org
Key Personnel
Exec Dir: Margot Knight *Tel:* 650-747-1250 ext 14 *E-mail:* margot@djerassi.org
One month residencies for writers & other artists.

Education Writers Association Workshops
Education Writers Association (EWA)
3516 Connecticut Ave NW, Washington, DC 20008
Tel: 202-452-9830 *Fax:* 202-452-9837
E-mail: ewa@ewa.org
Web Site: www.ewa.org
Key Personnel
Exec Dir: Caroline W Hendrie *E-mail:* chendrie@ewa.org
Multimedia & Web Mgr: Michael Marriott
E-mail: mmarriott@ewa.org
National seminar, regional meetings.

Florida Writers Association Conference
Florida Writers Association Inc
PO Box 66069, St Pete Beach, FL 33736-6069
Web Site: www.floridawriters.net
Key Personnel
Pres: Cheyenne Williams *E-mail:* ckwilliams@onlinebinding.com
EVP: Jade Kerrion
VP, Admin & Fin: Larry Kokko
VP, Fin: Robyn Weinbaum
Assortment of workshops, networking, interviews with agents & editors, literary contest & banquet.
Date: Annually in Oct

Fun in the Sun Writer's Cruise Conference
Florida Romance Writers Inc (FRW)
Affiliate of Romance Writers of America®
PO Box 823414, Pembroke Pines, FL 33082
E-mail: frwfuninthesun@yahoo.com
Web Site: frwfuninthesunmain.blogspot.com/; www.frwriters.org
Key Personnel
Pres: Heidi Lynn Anderson
VP, Progs: Marcia King-Gamble
VP, Communs: Kimberly Gonzales
Secy: Aleka Nakis
Treas: Tina Stitzer
Highlights include 2 days of workshops on the art, craft & business of writing that will appeal to writers in all genres. Exclusive Q&A with our keynote speaker, editor/agent appointments, Floridian Idol (live readings), write-in, & more. Registration fees from $180-$220. Workshop speakers entitled to discounted registration fee. Group rates available for groups of 5 or more; special hotel rates for conference attendees also available. Use the mailing address for all conference correspondence.

Gell: A Finger Lakes Creative Retreat
Writers & Books
740 University Ave, Rochester, NY 14607-1259
Tel: 585-473-2590 *Fax:* 585-442-9333
Web Site: www.wab.org

Key Personnel
Dir, Opers & Programming: Kathy Pottetti *Tel:* 585-473-2590 ext 103 *E-mail:* kathyp@wab.org
Meeting center that hosts classes, workshops, conferences, etc for groups of up to 50 people.

The Glen Workshop
Image Journal
3307 Third Ave W, Seattle, WA 98119
Tel: 206-281-2988 *Fax:* 206-281-2979
E-mail: glenworkshop@imagejournal.org
Web Site: www.imagejournal.org
Key Personnel
Dir, Progs: Paul Anderson
A weeklong arts workshop for writers & visual artists that combines an intensive learning experience with a lively festival of the arts.

Gotham Writers' Workshop
555 Eighth Ave, Suite 1402, New York, NY 10018-4358
Tel: 212-974-8377
E-mail: contact@gothamwriters.com
Web Site: www.gothamwriters.com
Key Personnel
Pres: Alex Steele *E-mail:* alex@gothamwriters.com
Professional writers teach acclaimed creative writing classes online & in New York City throughout the year.

Harvard Summer Writing Program
Harvard University, Division of Continuing Education
51 Brattle St, Dept S760, Cambridge, MA 02138-3722
Tel: 617-495-4024 *Fax:* 617-495-9176
E-mail: summer@harvard.edu
Web Site: www.summer.harvard.edu
Key Personnel
Dir & Prog Contact: Dr Patricia Bellanca
Eight week program starting at the end of June; full semester college credit workshop courses in creative, professional & expository writing. These include: beginning fiction, poetry, journalism & screenwriting; advanced creative nonfiction; writing grant proposals, effective business communication, legal writing & principles of editing; cross-cultural expository writing, writing about social & ethical issues & writing about literature.

Hedgebrook Master Class Retreat Series
Hedgebrook
PO Box 1231, Freeland, WA 98249
Tel: 360-321-4786 *Fax:* 360-321-2171
E-mail: hedgebrook@hedgebrook.org
Web Site: www.hedgebrook.org; www.facebook.com/hedgebrook
Key Personnel
Prog Dir: Vito Zingarelli *E-mail:* vitoz@hedgebrook.org
Prog Assoc: Julie O'Brien *E-mail:* julieo@hedgebrook.org
Craft-focused writing workshops, where participants have the unique opportunity to be in residence & study with a celebrated teacher. Weeklong Master Classes include 6-7 participants, each housed in her own cottage. Participants receive 5 days of writing workshops, instructor-led constructive group feedback sessions, one-on-one sessions with the instructor & an additional day of retreat time. Meals featuring produce harvested from our organic garden are prepared by Hedgebrook's chefs, Writers at all levels of experience, published or not, are accepted into Hedgebrook's Master Classes. Cost is $2,500-$3,500, which covers lodging, meals & workshops; all taxes included. A portion is tax-deductible.

Hedgebrook VORTEXT
Hedgebrook
PO Box 1231, Freeland, WA 98249
Tel: 360-321-4786 *Fax:* 360-321-2171
E-mail: hedgebrook@hedgebrook.org
Web Site: www.hedgebrook.org; www.facebook.com/hedgebrook
Key Personnel
Prog Dir: Vito Zingarelli *E-mail:* vitoz@hedgebrook.org
Prog Assoc: Julie O'Brien *E-mail:* julieo@hedgebrook.org
Weekend salon led by 6 established women writers. Connect & hone your craft in diverse & powerful small group workshops. Enjoy dynamic keynotes & discussions about opportunities & challenges for women who write. Engage in dynamic discussions on hot topics specific to women who write. Share meals, open mics, conversation & community in a stunningly beautiful setting. Held at the Whidbey Institute at Chinook on Whidbey Island, WA in late May, a registration fee of $950 includes all keynotes & 3 workshops of your choice, group sessions & free time to write as well as breakfast, lunch & daily reception.

Hedgebrook Winter Salon
Hedgebrook
PO Box 1231, Freeland, WA 98249
Tel: 360-321-4786 *Fax:* 360-321-2171
E-mail: hedgebrook@hedgebrook.org
Web Site: www.hedgebrook.org; www.facebook.com/hedgebrook
Key Personnel
Prog Dir: Vito Zingarelli *E-mail:* vitoz@hedgebrook.org
Prog Assoc: Julie O'Brien *E-mail:* julieo@hedgebrook.org
Creative workshops, held early December, are led by & for women writers. Enjoy a day filled with lively conversation & delicious food, culminating in a party with an open mic. Write, learn, share stories & leave freshly inspired.

Hedgebrook Writers in Residence Program
Hedgebrook
PO Box 1231, Freeland, WA 98249
Tel: 360-321-4786 *Fax:* 360-321-2171
E-mail: hedgebrook@hedgebrook.org
Web Site: www.hedgebrook.org; www.facebook.com/hedgebrook
Key Personnel
Prog Dir: Vito Zingarelli *E-mail:* vitoz@hedgebrook.org
Prog Assoc: Julie O'Brien *E-mail:* julieo@hedgebrook.org
Program supporting fully-funded residencies of approximately 40 women writers (6 or 7 at a time) at a retreat each year on Whidbey Island, WA. Hedgebrook is one of the few writer's colonies in the world exclusively dedicated to supporting women writers & bringing their work to the world through innovative public programs. Emerging & established writers (all genres) worldwide attend. Each writer is housed in her own cottage. Residents share a home-cooked evening meal prepared by Hedgebrook's chefs. The community formed around the kitchen table is growing as Hedgebrook hosts alumnae gatherings, events & professional development workshops around the country. Applications for the upcoming residency season are available via our web site by mid-June, with a deadline in late July.

Highland Summer Writers' Conference
The Appalachian Regional Studies Center (ARSC)
Division of Radford University
PO Box 7014, Radford University, Cook Hall, Radford, VA 24142
Fax: 540-831-5951
Web Site: www.radford.edu/content/cehd/home/appalachian-studies.html
Key Personnel
Dir, ARSC: Dr Theresa Burriss *Tel:* 540-831-6857 *E-mail:* tburriss@radford.edu
Instructor & ARSC Assoc: Ruth Derrick *Tel:* 540-831-6152 *E-mail:* rbderrick@radford.edu
Annual program based on Appalachian culture & writing; directed for 2 weeks by a fiction writer/poet/dramatist. Elective seminar-workshop combination offers the opportunity to study & practice creative & expository writing & earn 3 hours graduate/undergraduate credit.
Location: Radford University, Radford, VA

Historical Novel Society North American Conference
Historical Novel Society
400 Dark Star Ct, Fairbanks, AK 99709
Tel: 217-581-7538 *Fax:* 217-581-7534
Web Site: historicalnovelsociety.org
Key Personnel
US Membership Secy: Georgine Olson *E-mail:* georgine@mosquitonet.com
Conference Prog Chair: Vanitha Sankaran *E-mail:* info@vanithasankaran.com
Held biennially, in odd-numbered years.
Date: June 2019

Hurston/Wright Writers Week
The Zora Neale Hurston/Richard Wright Foundation
840 First St NE, 3rd fl, Washington, DC 20002
Tel: 202-248-5051
E-mail: info@hurstonwright.org
Web Site: www.hurstonwright.org
Key Personnel
Co-Founder: Marita Golden; Clyde McElvane
Exec Dir: Deborah Heard
The Zora Neale Hurston/Richard Wright Foundation was founded in 1990 in Washington, DC & is dedicated to discovering, mentoring & honoring black writers. Through workshops, master classes & readings, the organization preserves the voices of black writers in the world literary canon, serves as a community for writers & continues a tradition of literary excellence in storytelling established by its namesakes. The Foundation is a 501(c)(3) nonprofit.

Idyllwild Arts Summer Workshops
Idyllwild Arts Summer Program
52500 Temecula Dr, Idyllwild, CA 92549-0038
Mailing Address: PO Box 38, Idyllwild, CA 92549-0038
Tel: 951-659-2171 *Fax:* 951-659-4552
E-mail: summer@idyllwildarts.org
Web Site: www.idyllwildarts.org/writersweek
Key Personnel
Summer Prog Registrar: Diane Dennis *Tel:* 951-659-2171 ext 2365 *E-mail:* dianed@idyllwildarts.org
Five-day writing workshops for adults in creative nonfiction, fiction, chapbooks, poetry, screenwriting & more. Two-week writing workshops for high school students in fiction, poetry & much more.

Indiana University Writers' Conference
Indiana University
464 Ballantine Hall, 1020 E Kirkwood Ave, Bloomington, IN 47405-7103
Tel: 812-855-1877 *Fax:* 812-855-9535
E-mail: writecon@indiana.edu
Web Site: www.iuwc.indiana.edu
Key Personnel
Dir: Bob Bledsoe
Weeklong, annual conference in June for writers of poetry, fiction, nonfiction & script writing.

Second oldest such conference in the US. Past staff includes Raymond Carver, Allen Tate & Katherine Anne Porter.

Intimate & Inspiring Workshops for Children's Authors & Illustrators
Highlights Foundation
814 Court St, Honesdale, PA 18431
Tel: 570-253-1192 *Fax:* 570-253-0179
E-mail: jolloyd@highlightsfoundation.org
Web Site: www.highlightsfoundation.org
Key Personnel
Exec Dir: Kent L Brown, Jr *E-mail:* klbrown@highlightsfoundation.org
For children's writers & illustrators seeking to sharpen their focus. Helps to improve your craft with the help of a master, finding the time & space in which to work & marketing yourself & your books. Cost of workshops range from $495 & up which includes tuition, meals, conference supplies & housing.

Iowa Summer Writing Festival
Division of University of Iowa
250 Continuing Educ Facility, University of Iowa, Iowa City, IA 52242
Tel: 319-335-4160
E-mail: iswfestival@uiowa.edu
Web Site: iowasummerwritingfestival.org
Key Personnel
Dir: Amy Margolis *E-mail:* amy-margolis@uiowa.edu
Annual weeklong & weekend non-credit, intensive writing workshops in all genres, all levels (for adults).

IWWG Annual Summer Conference
Formerly ReIMAGINE the MAGIC Annual Summer Conference
The International Women's Writing Guild (IWWG)
5 Penn Plaza, 19th fl, PMB 19059, New York, NY 10001
Tel: 917-720-6959
E-mail: iwwgquestions@iwwg.org
Web Site: www.iwwg.org
Key Personnel
Exec Dir: Dixie King, PhD
Interim Opers Dir: Marj Hahne
Each summer, the Guild brings together women for 7 full days of writing, crafting & connecting. Offer over 30 workshops to explore the spiritual, emotional, creative & technical side of writing.

Jentel Artist Residency Program
Jentel Foundation
130 Lower Piney Rd, Banner, WY 82832
Tel: 307-737-2311 *Fax:* 307-737-2305
E-mail: jentel@jentelarts.org
Web Site: www.jentelarts.org
Key Personnel
Exec Dir: Mary Jane Edwards
Prog Mgr: Lynn Reeves
Offers one month residencies throughout the year to visual artists in all media & writers in fiction, creative nonfiction & poetry. Located on a working cattle ranch in the foothills of the Big Horn Moutains, 20 miles from Sheridan, WY. The award includes comfortable accommodations, a separate private studio & a stipend. Residents are invited to share their work through various outreach opportunities in the community. For more info or an application, see web site. Deadline is Sept 15 & Jan 15 each year.

Juniper Summer Writing Institute
Juniper Institute
Affiliate of UMass Amherst MFA for Poets & Writers
c/o University Conference Services, 810 Campus Center, One Campus Center Way, Amherst, MA 01003
Tel: 413-545-5503
E-mail: juniperinstitute@hfa.umass.edu
Web Site: www.umass.edu/juniperinstitute
Key Personnel
Dir: Betsy Wheeler
Seven days of intensive writing workshops, craft sessions, readings & ms consultation in the beautiful Pioneer Valley. Scholarships available.

Kentucky Women Writers Conference
University of Kentucky
232 E Maxwell St, Lexington, KY 40506-0344
Tel: 859-257-2874
E-mail: kentuckywomenwriters@gmail.com
Web Site: www.kentuckywomenwriters.org
Key Personnel
Dir: Julie Kuzneski Wrinn
Founded in 1979, this is the oldest conference of its kind in the country featuring invited women writers offering workshops, reading & panel discussions.
Location: Lexington, KY
Date: Annually in Sept

Kentucky Writers Conference
Southern Kentucky Book Fest
1906 College Heights Blvd, Suite 11067, Bowling Green, KY 42101-1067
Tel: 270-745-4502
E-mail: sokybookfest@wku.edu
Web Site: www.sokybookfest.org
Key Personnel
Literary Outreach Coord: Sara Volpi *E-mail:* sara.volpi@wku.edu
Teaching craft workshops about everything from plotting techniques to employing poetic language to getting published. Free to the public. Limited seating.
Location: Knicely Conference Center, 645 Campbell Lane, Bowling Green, KY
Date: April 21, 2018

Key West Literary Seminar
717 Love Lane, Key West, FL 33040
Tel: 305-293-9291 *Toll Free Tel:* 888-293-9291
E-mail: mail@kwls.org
Web Site: www.kwls.org/seminar; www.kwls.org
Key Personnel
Exec Dir: Arlo Haskell
A 4-day readers' event that explores a unique literary theme each January. The 2018 theme is "Writers of the Caribbean".
Location: Key West, FL
Date: Jan 11-14, 2018

Key West Literary Seminar's Writers' Workshop Program
Key West Literary Seminar
717 Love Lane, Key West, FL 33040
Tel: 305-293-9291 *Toll Free Tel:* 888-293-9291
E-mail: mail@kwls.org
Web Site: www.kwls.org; www.kwls.org/writers_workshops
Key Personnel
Exec Dir: Arlo Haskell
Provides writers at any stage of development with opportunities to explore the craft of writing. Multiple workshops each with their own focus & application requirements. Enrollment for each workshop is limited to 12 participants.
Location: Key West, FL
Date: Jan 15-19, 2018

Lost Lake Writers Retreat
Springfed Arts
PO Box 304, Royal Oak, MI 48068-0304
Tel: 248-589-3913
Web Site: www.springfed.org
Key Personnel
Dir: John D Lamb *E-mail:* johndlamb@ameritech.net
Poets & writers conference, good writers, food & accomodations.

Maine Writers Conference at Ocean Park
Affiliate of Ocean Park Association
14 Temple Ave, Ocean Park, ME 04063
Mailing Address: PO Box 7206, Ocean Park, ME 04063
Tel: 401-598-1424
E-mail: www.opa@oceanpark.org
Web Site: oceanpark.org
Key Personnel
Dir: Dr Jim Brosnan *E-mail:* jbrosnan@jwu.edu
An eclectic, economical & intensive annual conference in the Summer for writers of both poetry & prose of varying abilities & accomplishments.

McHugh's Rights/Permissions Workshop™
John B McHugh Publishing Consultant
PO Box 170665, Milwaukee, WI 53217-8056
Tel: 414-351-3056
E-mail: jack@johnbmchugh.com
Web Site: www.johnbmchugh.com
Key Personnel
Principal & Consultant: John B McHugh
Provide on-site customized workshops in all aspects of publishing management.

Mississippi River Creative Writing Workshop
St Cloud State University, English Department
720 Fourth Ave S, B-151, Rm 100, St Cloud, MN 56301-4498
Tel: 320-308-4947 *Fax:* 320-308-5524
Web Site: www.stcloudstate.edu
Key Personnel
Dir, Poet, Fiction Writer & Novelist & Instructor: Bill Meissner *E-mail:* wjmeissner@stcloudstate.edu
Four-day workshop in poetry & fiction. Participants will develop creative writing skills & learn writing techniques & ideas. Includes presentation by professional published authors.

Mount Hermon Christian Writers Conference
Mount Hermon Christian Camps & Conference Center
c/o Mount Hermon Association Inc, 37 Conference Dr, Felton, CA 95018
Mailing Address: c/o Mount Hermon Association Inc, PO Box 413, Mount Hermon, CA 95041
Tel: 831-335-4466 *Toll Free Tel:* 888-MH-CAMPS (642-2677, registration) *Fax:* 831-335-9335
E-mail: info@mounthermon.org
Web Site: www.mounthermon.org/writers
Key Personnel
Adult Prog Specialist: Kathy Ide *E-mail:* kathy.ide@mounthermon.org
Two-day Head Start Mentoring Clinic for beginning writers; 5-day writers conference for all abilities, including beginning to professional. Held the weekend of Palm Sunday.

Mountain Writers Series
2804 SE 27 Ave, Suite 2, Portland, OR 97202
Tel: 503-232-4517 *Fax:* 503-232-4517
E-mail: programs@mountainwriters.org; support@mountainwriters.org
Web Site: www.mountainwriters.org
Key Personnel
Artistic Dir: Sandra Williams
Work with nationally recognized poets, fiction writers, nonfiction writers, screenwriters & agents.

MWG Writer Workshops & State Conference
Mississippi Writers Guild (MWG)

9 Janice Circle, Natchez, MS 39120
Tel: 601-442-0980
E-mail: mississippi.writersguild@outlook.com
Web Site: www.mississippiwritersguild.com
Key Personnel
Pres: G Mark Lafrances
Events Coord: Richelle Putnam
For information about this workshop or conference, please send an e-mail.
Date: Annually in Aug

Napa Valley Writers' Conference
Napa Valley College
1088 College Ave, St Helena, CA 94574
Tel: 707-967-2900 (ext 4) *Fax:* 707-967-2909
E-mail: info@napawritersconference.org; media@napawritersconference.org; fiction@napawritersconference.org; poetry@napawritersconference.org
Web Site: www.napawritersconference.org
Key Personnel
Exec Dir: Angela Pneuman
Mng Dir: Catherine Thorpe
Poetry Prog Dir: Nan Cohen
Fiction Dir: Ms Lakin Khan
Poetry & fiction sessions each year, offering small workshops, lectures & readings. Begins last Sunday in July & runs for one week.

National Society of Newspaper Columnists Annual Conference
National Society of Newspaper Columnists (NSNC)
PO Box 411532, San Francisco, CA 94141
Tel: 415-488-NCNC (488-6762) *Fax:* 484-297-0336
E-mail: director@columnists.com
Web Site: www.columnists.com
Key Personnel
Offr, Admin: Luenna Kim
Contest Chair: Cathy Turney
Conference & column writing contest; occasional newsletter; networking with staff, syndicated columnists & regular freelance columnists.
Date: Annually in June

New York State Writers Institute
State University of New York
Division of University at Albany/SUNY
University at Albany, Science Library 320, 1400 Washington Ave, Albany, NY 12222
Tel: 518-442-5620 *Fax:* 518-442-5621
E-mail: writers@albany.edu
Web Site: www.albany.edu/writers-inst
Key Personnel
Exec Dir: William Kennedy
Asst Dir: Suzanne Lance
Literary program organization featuring year-round visiting writers, classic film, special literary events & conferences, writing courses & workshops. Write or see web site for dates & locations.

North Carolina Writers' Network Annual Fall Conference
North Carolina Writers' Network
PO Box 21591, Winston-Salem, NC 27120-1591
Tel: 336-293-8844
E-mail: mail@ncwriters.org
Web Site: www.ncwriters.org
Key Personnel
Exec Dir: Ed Southern *E-mail:* ed@ncwriters.org
Workshops, readings, conferences, critiquing service & round table discussions, panels & meetings with agents, publishing workshops.

Odyssey: The Summer Fantasy Writing Workshop
PO Box 75, Mont Vernon, NH 03057
Tel: 603-673-6234 *Fax:* 603-673-6234
Web Site: www.odysseyworkshop.org
Key Personnel
Dir: Jeanne Cavelos *E-mail:* jcavelos@comcast.net
Intensive 6-week workshop for writers of fantasy, science fiction & horror. Dir Jeanne Cavelos is a former Sr Ed at Bantam Doubleday Dell Publishing & winner of the World Fantasy Award. Guest lecturers include some of the top writers in the field. College credit available. Application deadline: April 7.
Location: Saint Anselm College, Manchester, NH
Date: June 4-July 13, 2018

Oregon Christian Writers Coaching Conference
Oregon Christian Writers (OCW)
1075 Willow Lake Rd N, Keizer, OR 97303
Tel: 503-393-3356
E-mail: contact@oregonchristianwriters.org
Web Site: www.oregonchristianwriters.org
Key Personnel
Summer Conference Dir: Lindy Jacobs *E-mail:* summerconf@oregonchristianwriters.org
Registrar & Busn Mgr: Sue Miholer
Seven hours of hands-on help from well-published professionals, many specialized workshops, consultations with editors & networking with successful writers.
Location: Jantzen Beach Red Lion Hotel, Portland, OR
Date: Aug 20-23, 2018

Oregon Christian Writers Seminar
Oregon Christian Writers (OCW)
1075 Willow Lake Rd N, Keizer, OR 97303
Tel: 503-393-3356
E-mail: contact@oregonchristianwriters.org
Web Site: www.oregonchristianwriters.org
Key Personnel
Pres: Marilyn Rhoades
Prog Chmn: Don White
Registrar & Busn Mgr: Sue Miholer
Writers' workshops.
Location: Winter Conference, Chemeketa Community College, Salem, OR
Date: Feb 24, 2018
Location: Spring Conference, Eugene, OR
Date: May 19, 2018
Location: Summer Conference, Red Lion Hotel on the River-Jantzen Beach, Portland, OR
Date: Aug 20-23, 2018
Location: Fall Conference, Portland, OR
Date: Oct 2018

Orientation to the Graphic Arts
Printing Industries of America
301 Brush Creek Rd, Warrendale, PA 15086-7529
Tel: 412-741-6860 *Toll Free Tel:* 800-910-4283 *Fax:* 412-741-2311
E-mail: printingind@comm.printing.org
Web Site: www.printing.org
Key Personnel
Pres & CEO: Michael F Makin *Tel:* 412-259-1777 *E-mail:* mmakin@printing.org
VP, Technol & Res: Jim Workman *Tel:* 412-259-1710 *E-mail:* jworkman@printing.org
Sr Mktg Mgr: Jenn Strang *Tel:* 412-259-1810 *E-mail:* jstrang@printing.org
Ongoing online workshops & courses.

Outdoor Writers Association of America Annual Conference
Outdoor Writers Association of America (OWAA)
615 Oak St, Suite 201, Missoula, MT 59801
Tel: 406-728-7434 *Fax:* 406-728-7445
E-mail: info@owaa.org
Web Site: www.owaa.org
Key Personnel
Exec Dir: Brandon Shuler *E-mail:* brandon@owaa.org
Seminars & writing workshops; photography & outdoor news & conversation.
Location: Grand Wayne Convention Center, Fort Wayne, IN
Date: June 2-4, 2018
Location: Robinson Center, Little Rock, AR
Date: June 22-24, 2019

Ozark Creative Writers Inc Annual Conference
Ozark Creative Writers Inc
512 Walnut St, Mount Vernon, IN 47620
E-mail: ozarkcreativewriters@ozarkcreativewriters.com
Web Site: www.ozarkcreativewriters.com
Key Personnel
Pres: Clarissa Willis *E-mail:* clarissa@clarisawillis.com
Writers' conference for beginners & professionals. Contest information on web site.
Location: Ozarks Convention Center, Eureka Springs, AR
Date: Annually in Oct

Pennwriters Conference
Pennwriters Inc
PO Box 685, Dalton, PA 18414
E-mail: conferencecoordinator@pennwriters.org; info@pennwriters.org
Web Site: pennwriters.org
Key Personnel
Pres: Hilary Hauck *E-mail:* president@pennwriters.org
Conference Coord: Heather Desuta; Carol Silvis
Multi-genre conference with 40+ hours of workshops, panels & sessions with authors, agents & editors. Read & critique sessions. Agent/editor appointments.
Date: Annually in May

Philadelphia Writers' Conference
PO Box 7171, Elkins Park, PA 19027-0171
E-mail: info@pwcwriters.org
Web Site: pwcwriters.org
Educational conferences for writers, workshops, critiques, contests, featured speakers, agents, editors. Random free forums in Philadelphia in addition to annual 3-day event.
Location: Philadelphia, PA
Date: Annual 3-day event; 2nd full weekend of June

Poetry Flash Reading Series
Poetry Flash
1450 Fourth St, Suite 4, Berkeley, CA 94710
Tel: 510-525-5476 *Fax:* 510-525-6752
E-mail: editor@poetryflash.org
Web Site: poetryflash.org
Key Personnel
Ed, Publr & Exec Dir: Joyce Jenkins
Assoc Ed: Richard Silburg
Publication; conducts a reading & poetry series in conjunction with Moe's Books in Berkeley, CA & Diesel, A Bookstore in Oakland, CA. Host poets from all around the US.

Port Townsend Writers' Conference
Centrum Foundation
223 Battery Way, Port Townsend, WA 98368
Mailing Address: PO Box 1158, Port Townsend, WA 98368
Tel: 360-385-3102 *Toll Free Tel:* 800-733-3608 (ticket off) *Fax:* 360-385-2470
E-mail: info@centrum.org
Web Site: centrum.org
Key Personnel
Artistic Dir: Sam Ligon
Prog Mgr: Jordan Hartt *Tel:* 360-385-3102 ext 131 *E-mail:* jhartt@centrum.org
Workshops, lectures & readings.
Location: Port Townsend, WA
Date: Annually in July

The Publishing Game
Peanut Butter & Jelly Press LLC
PO Box 590239, Newton, MA 02459-0002
SAN: 299-7444
Tel: 617-630-0945 *Fax:* 617-630-0945 (call first)
E-mail: info@publishinggame.com; workshops@publishinggame.com
Web Site: www.publishinggame.com
Key Personnel
Publicist: Alyza Harris *E-mail:* alyza@publishinggame.com
All-day workshop covers how to find a literary agent, how to self-publish & how to successfully promote your book. Offered in 12 cities: New York, Boston, Philadelphia, DC, Boca Raton, Chicago, San Francisco, Los Angeles, Seattle, Phoenix, Dallas & several "floating cities" each year. $195 includes workshop course binder. See web site for latest locations, dates & details.

PNWA Writers Conference
PNWA - a writer's resource
1420 NW Gilman Blvd, Suite 8, PMB 2717, Issaquah, WA 98027
Tel: 425-673-2665
E-mail: pnwa@pnwa.org
Web Site: www.pnwa.org
Key Personnel
Pres: Pam Binder

Robert Quackenbush's Children's Book Writing & Illustration Workshops
Robert Quackenbush Studios
223 E 78 St, New York, NY 10075
Mailing Address: 460 E 79 St, New York, NY 10075
Tel: 212-744-3822
E-mail: rqstudios@aol.com
Web Site: www.rquackenbush.com
Workshops at author/artists' studio; focus on planning children's books from concept to completion.
Location: New York, NY
Date: 2nd week in July annually (4-day intensive workshop)

ReIMAGINE the MAGIC Annual Summer Conference, see IWWG Annual Summer Conference

Romance Writers of America Annual Conference
Romance Writers of America®
14615 Benfer Rd, Houston, TX 77069
Tel: 832-717-5200 *Fax:* 832-717-5201
E-mail: info@rwa.org
Web Site: www.rwa.org
Key Personnel
Exec Dir: Allison Kelley *Tel:* 832-717-5200 ext 124 *E-mail:* allison.kelley@rwa.org
Promote recognition of the genre of romance writing as a serious book form. Conduct workshops, sponsor national & regional conferences & awards for members.
Location: Sheraton Denver Downtown Hotel, 1550 Court Place, Denver, CO
Date: July 25-28, 2018
Location: New York Marriott® Marquis, 1525 Broadway, New York, NY
Date: July 24-27, 2019
Location: San Francisco Marriott Marquis, 780 Mission St, San Francisco, CA
Date: July 29-Aug 1, 2020
Location: Gaylord Opryland Resort & Convention Center, Nashville, TN
Date: July 14-17, 2021

San Diego Christian Writers' Guild Conference
San Diego Christian Writers' Guild
PO Box 270403, San Diego, CA 92198
Tel: 760-294-3269; 858-254-1402 *Fax:* 760-294-3269
E-mail: info@sandiegocwg.org
Web Site: www.sandiegocwg.org
Key Personnel
Pres: Jennie Gillespie; Robert Gillespie
One-day seminar & workshops; personal consultations with editors. Journalism, magazine writing, fiction. Seminar is always the 4th Saturday in Sept.

San Francisco Writers Conference
1029 Jones St, San Francisco, CA 94109
Tel: 415-673-0939
E-mail: sfwriterscon@aol.com
Web Site: www.sfwriters.org
Key Personnel
Co-Dir: Michael Larsen; Laurie McLean
Craft & market oriented writers' conference covering fiction, nonfiction, children's books, poetry, self-publishing, promotion with name authors.
Location: Mark Hopkins Hotel, San Francisco, CA
Date: Feb 15-18, 2018

Sandhills Writers' Series
Augusta State University
Dept of English & Foreign Languages, 1120 15 St, Augusta, GA 30912
Tel: 706-729-2417
Key Personnel
Asst Professor: James Minick *E-mail:* jminick@augusta.edu
Fiction, nonfiction, creative nonfiction & poetry craft-directed readings; participants meet in consultations with literary agents that represent commercial & literary fiction, nonfiction & children's books. Enrollment limited. Ms deadline Feb.

SCBWI-FL Florida Regional Conference
Society of Children's Book Writers & Illustrators, Florida Region (SCBWI-FL)
125 E Merritt Island Causeway, Suite 209, Merritt Island, FL 32952
Tel: 321-338-7208
E-mail: florida@scbwi.org
Web Site: florida.scbwi.org
Key Personnel
Co-Regl Advisor: Linda Rodriguez Bernfeld *E-mail:* florida-ra@scbwi.org; Dorian Cirrone *E-mail:* florida-ra2@scbwi.org
Location: Sheraton Miami Airport Hotel, 3900 NW 21 St, Miami, FL
Date: Jan 12-14, 2018

SCBWI-FL Mid-Year Workshops
Society of Children's Book Writers & Illustrators, Florida Region (SCBWI-FL)
125 E Merritt Island Causeway, Suite 209, Merritt Island, FL 32952
Tel: 321-338-7208
E-mail: florida@scbwi.org
Web Site: florida.scbwi.org
Key Personnel
Co-Regl Advisor: Linda Rodriguez Bernfeld *E-mail:* florida-ra@scbwi.org; Dorian Cirrone *E-mail:* florida-ra2@scbwi.org
Workshops in writing & illustrating picture books, juvenile & young adult fiction & nonfiction, children's magazines & marketing, given by published authors, illustrators, editors & agents. Also offer 5-7 writing boot camps across the state of Florida the last 2 weeks in Sept.

Science Fiction Writers Workshop
Center for the Study of Science Fiction
Division of University of Kansas
University of Kansas, Wescoe Hall, Rm 3001, Dept of English, 1445 Jayhawk Blvd, Lawrence, KS 66045
Tel: 785-864-2518 *Fax:* 785-864-1159
Web Site: www.sfcenter.ku.edu; www.sfcenter.ku.edu/sfworkshop; www.sfcenter.ku.edu/novel-workshop
Key Personnel
Founding Dir: James Gunn *E-mail:* jgunn@ku.edu
Dir: Christopher McKitterick *E-mail:* cmckit@ku.edu
Assoc Dir: Kij Johnson *E-mail:* kijjo@ku.edu
A noncredit, 2-week intensive workshop offered in association with the Campbell Conference on Science Fiction by the Center for the Study of Science Fiction.
Location: University of Kansas, Lawrence, KS
Date: Summer

SDSU Writers' Conference
San Diego State University College of Extended Studies
5250 Campanile Dr, Rm 2503, San Diego, CA 92182-1920
Tel: 619-594-5821 *Fax:* 619-594-8566
E-mail: sdsuwritersconference@mail.sdsu.edu
Web Site: www.neverstoplearning.net/writers
Key Personnel
Sr Prog Dir: Becky Ryan *E-mail:* rjryan@mail.sdsu.edu
Annual weekend writers' conference. Topics include fiction, nonfiction, genre novels & children's writing. Personal editor & agent appointments available.

See-More's Workshop Arts & Education Workshops
The Shadow Box Theatre
325 West End Ave, Suite 12-B, New York, NY 10023
Tel: 212-724-0677 *Fax:* 212-724-0767
E-mail: sbt@shadowboxtheatre.org
Web Site: www.shadowboxtheatre.org
Key Personnel
Exec/Artistic Dir: Sandra Robbins *E-mail:* srobbins@shadowboxtheatre.org
Mng Arts & Educ Dir: Carol Prud'homme Davis *E-mail:* cpdavis@shadowboxtheatre.org
Resident Workshops: Early learning through elementary grades, SBT's teaching artists guide students in the art of storytelling & curriculum exploration through puppetry, dramatics, dance & music. Professional Development Workshops: Hands-on staff development workshops provide classroom teachers with theatre & storytelling techniques. Author Workshops: Includes a trip or in-school SBT musical puppet show, our own storybooks with accompanying audio tapes/CDs & a meeting with playwright & author, Sandra Robbins. For more information contact us, as dates, times & locations change often.

Sewanee Writers' Conference
Stamler Ctr, 119 Gailor Hall, 735 University Ave, Sewanee, TN 37383
Tel: 931-598-1141; 931-598-1654
E-mail: swc@sewanee.edu
Web Site: www.sewaneewriters.org
Key Personnel
Dir: Wyatt Prunty *E-mail:* wprunty@sewanee.edu
Assoc Dir, Mktg & Admissions: Adam Latham *E-mail:* allatham@sewanee.edu
Assoc Dir, Progs & Fin: Megan Roberts *E-mail:* mgroberts@sewanee.edu
Workshops in poetry, fiction & playwriting.
Location: The University of the South, Sewanee, TN
Date: Annually the last 2 weeks in July

Society for Technical Communication's Annual Conference
Society for Technical Communication
9401 Lee Hwy, Suite 300, Fairfax, VA 22031
Tel: 703-522-4114 *Fax:* 703-522-2075
E-mail: stc@stc.org; summit@stc.org
Web Site: summit.stc.org; www.stc.org
Key Personnel
Dir, Meetings & Educ: Molly Jin *Tel:* 571-366-1904 *E-mail:* molly.jin@stc.org
Educational conference for technical communicators.
Date: Annually in May

Southampton Writers' Conference
Stony Brook Southampton
239 Montauk Hwy, Southampton, NY 11968
Tel: 631-632-5007
E-mail: southamptonwriters@notes.cc.sunysb.edu; southamptonarts@stonybrook.edu
Web Site: www.stonybrook.edu/southampton/mfa/summer/cwl_home.html
Key Personnel
Conference Coord: Christian McLean *E-mail:* christian.mclean@stonybrook.edu
Five & 12-day workshops including novel, short story, poetry, memoir & creative nonfiction, playwriting & screenwriting; also evening readings, performances & panels.

Southern California Writers' Conference (SCWC)
Division of Random Cove, ie
18160 Cottonwood Rd, Suite 260, Sunriver, OR 97707
Tel: 619-303-8185 *Fax:* 619-906-7462
E-mail: msg@writersconference.com
Web Site: www.writersconference.com
Key Personnel
Exec Dir: Michael Steven Gregory
Dir: Wes Albers *E-mail:* wes@writersconference.com
Asst Dir: Chrissie A Barnett *E-mail:* chrissie@writersconference.com
Annual writers' conference. Fiction, nonfiction & scriptwriting mss eligible for advance critique submission before the conference, followed by one-on-one consultation; awards given. Major speakers; banquet; workshops in fiction, nonfiction, legacy & indie publishing; conference emphasis on fiction & nonfiction; one agent panel, multiple read & critique, craft, & troubleshooting workshops.
Location: San Diego, CA
Date: Feb 16-18, 2018

SouthWest Writers Conference Series
SouthWest Writers
3200 Carlisle Blvd NE, Suite 114, Albuquerque, NM 87110-1663
Tel: 505-830-6034
E-mail: swwriters@juno.com
Web Site: www.southwestwriters.com
Key Personnel
Pres: Sarah Baker
Series of one-day conferences, twice-monthly programs, workshops & writing classes.

Spring Time Writers Creative Writing & Journaling Workshop
Spring Time Writers
PO Box 512, Lyons, CO 80540-0512
Tel: 303-823-0997
E-mail: writers@springtimewriters.com
Web Site: www.springtimewriters.com
Key Personnel
Dir: Kathleen Spring
Creative writing & self discovery journaling workshops. Four days, including lodging, small classes, professional warm instruction in the Rocky Mountains in Colorado. Conferences held 2nd & 4th weekends June-Sept. See web site for details.

Squaw Valley Community of Writers Summer Workshops
Community of Writers at Squaw Valley
PO Box 1416, Nevada City, CA 95959
Tel: 530-470-8440
E-mail: info@communityofwriters.org
Web Site: www.communityofwriters.org
Key Personnel
Exec Dir: Ms Brett Hall Jones
Dir, Fiction: Lisa Alvarez; Louis B Jones
Dir, Poetry Workshop: Robert Hass
Dir, Screenwriting: Diana Fuller
Summer writing workshops; each workshop is one week long.
Membership(s): Association of Writers & Writing Programs.
Location: Poetry Workshop
Date: June 23-30, 2018
Location: Writers Workshops
Date: July 8-15, 2018

The Summer Experience
Sage Hill Writing Experience Inc
1831 College Ave, Suite 324, Regina, SK S4P 4V5, Canada
Tel: 306-537-7243
E-mail: sage.hill@sasktel.net
Web Site: www.sagehillwriting.ca
Key Personnel
Exec Dir: Tara Solheim
Prog Mgr: Caitlin Terfloth
Offers a special working & learning opportunity to writers at different stages of development. Top quality instruction, a low instructor-writer ratio & the rural Saskatchewan setting offer conditions ideal for the pursuit of excellence in the arts of fiction & poetry. Application to The Summer Experience is open to writers 19 years of age & older, regardless of city, province or country of residence.

Summer Words Writing Conference & Literary Festival
Aspen Words
110 E Hallam St, Suite 116, Aspen, CO 81611
Tel: 970-925-3122 *Fax:* 970-920-5700
E-mail: aspenwords@aspeninstitute.org
Web Site: www.aspenwords.org
Key Personnel
Exec Dir: Adrienne Brodeur *Tel:* 646-461-3554 *E-mail:* adrienne.brodeur@aspeninstitute.org
Mng Dir: Jamie Kravitz *Tel:* 970-925-3122 ext 2 *E-mail:* jamie.kravitz@aspeninstitute.org
Sr Prog Assoc, Mktg & Communs: Caroline Tory *Tel:* 970-925-3122 ext 3 *E-mail:* caroline.tory@aspeninstitute.org
A 5-day writing retreat with morning workshops in fiction, poetry, memoir & essay complimented by a 5-day literary festival in the afternoons & evenings, featuring 20 events for readers & writers.
Location: Aspen, CO
Date: Annually in June

Summer Writing Seminar
Martha's Vineyard Institute of Creative Writing
7 E Pasture Rd, Aquinnah, MA 02535
Tel: 954-242-2903
Web Site: mvicw.com
Key Personnel
Dir/Prog Coord: Alexander Weinstein *E-mail:* mvicwdirector@gmail.com
Annual comprehensive weeklong writing program, providing writers with the necessary time to devote to their art, on the island of Martha's Vineyard. Program fee is $975, which covers participation in all workshops, evening readings, editing/ms consultation with one of the visiting poets or authors & Friday night dinner with visiting writers. Fee does not include travel or accommodations.
Location: MVICW Seminar House, 324 Main St, Vineyard Haven, MA
Date: Annually in July

Taos Summer Writers' Conference
University of New Mexico Press
One University of New Mexico, Albuquerque, NM 87131-0001
SAN: 213-9588
Mailing Address: Dept of English Language & Literature, One University of New Mexico, MSC03 2170, Albuquerque, NM 81313-0001
Tel: 505-277-5572
E-mail: taosconf@unm.edu
Web Site: taosconf.unm.edu
Key Personnel
Founding Dir: Sharon Oard Warner
Writing workshops & special events. All events associated with the conference - panels, presentations & readings, are free & open to the public.
Location: Sagebrush Inn & Conference Center, Taos, NM

Unicorn Writers' Conference
Unicorn Writers' Conference Inc
17 Church Hill Rd, Redding, CT 06896
Tel: 203-938-7405 *Fax:* 203-938-7405
E-mail: unicornwritersconference@gmail.com
Web Site: unicornwritersconference.com
Key Personnel
Chmn & Sessions Dir: Jan L Kardys *E-mail:* jan.kardys@gmail.com
Mktg Dir: Barbara Ellis
Following the keynote address, delivered by a best-selling author or celebrity. Offers 36 different sessions including fiction, nonfiction, memoir, mystery, poetry, screenwriting, writing for the children's market & other major genres. How-to tutorials from publishing professionals educating writers on all aspects of publishing including contracts, copyrights, permissions, special sales, subsidiary rights, media training, promotion & platform, social media, self-publishing, book distribution & more. Features 4 agent panels & 2 editorial panels. One-to-one ms reviews available with editors, agents & faculty for an additional fee. Price $400, breakfast, lunch & dinner included. Welcome gift for all attendees. One-to-one sessions: $150 for a 30-minute session in-person private ms consultation with the faculty member, agent, editor of your choice. Query letter & book synopses reviews also available. Conference held 7:30am-8pm.
Location: Reid Castle, Purchase, NY
Date: Sept 15, 2018

Visiting Writers Series
University of Alaska Fairbanks
English Dept, PO Box 755720, Fairbanks, AK 99775-5720
Tel: 907-474-7193 *Fax:* 907-474-5247
E-mail: faengl@uaf.edu
Web Site: www.alaska.edu/english
Key Personnel
Asst Professor: Daryl Farmer *E-mail:* dlfarmer@alaska.edu
Readings from & discussion of own writings; poetry, fiction, nonfiction. Other sponsors include: University of Alaska Foundation, Alaska State Council on the Arts, The National Endowment for the Arts, UAF College of Liberal Arts & UA President's Special Project Fund.
Location: Fairbanks, AK
Date: Contact for schedule

VONA Voices Summer Writing Workshop
Voices of Our Nations Art Foundation (VONA)

Affiliate of University of Pennsylvania
3720 Spruce St, Suite 442, Philadelphia, PA 19104
Tel: 732-842-3932; 510-421-3913
E-mail: info@vonacommunity.org
Web Site: www.vonacommunity.org
Key Personnel
Exec Dir: Diem Jones *E-mail:* diem@vonacommunity.org
VONA now makes its home at the University of Pennsylvania & offers workshops in fiction, poetry, memoir, essay writing, speculative fiction, genre writing, political content in poetry-fiction-prose, LGBTQ narrative, travel writing, playwriting & residencies in prose & poetry.
Location: University of Pennsylvania, Philadelphia, PA
Date: Annually, June-July

Wesleyan Writers Conference
Wesleyan University
c/o Wesleyan University, Downey House, 294 High St, Rm 207, Middletown, CT 06459
Tel: 860-685-3604
Web Site: www.wesleyan.edu/writing/conference
Key Personnel
Dir: Anne Greene *E-mail:* agreene@wesleyan.edu
Seminars, readings, ms consultations & talks focused on novels, short stories, film, poetry, nonfiction, journalism, multimedia work, publishing; scholarships & fellowships. Participants are welcome to attend seminars in all genres; visits from editors & agents. Award-winning writers as faculty & guest speakers.
Location: Wesleyan University, Middletown, CT
Date: Annually in June

Willamette Writers' Conference
Willamette Writers
5331 SW Macadam Ave, Suite 258, PMB 215, Portland, OR 97239
Tel: 901-200-5385
E-mail: wilwrite@willamettewriters.org
Web Site: willamettewriters.org
Key Personnel
VP & Secy: Gail Pasternack *E-mail:* secretary@willamettewriters.org
Annual summer 3-day conference: consultations with over 50 national agents, editors, film agents & producers; workshops (fiction, nonfiction, children's, screen/TV, genres, craft of writing); editing room available. Year-round: monthly meetings, writing contest, workshops, newsletter.

Windbreak House Writing Retreat
Windbreak House
PO Box 169, Hermosa, SD 57744-0169
Tel: 605-255-4064
E-mail: info@windbreakhouse.com
Web Site: www.windbreakhouse.com
Key Personnel
Owner & Writer in Residence: Linda M Hasselstrom *E-mail:* lindamhasselstrom@windbreakhouse.com
Asst: Tamara Rogers
Retreats scheduled to suit applicants.

Winter Words Author Series
Aspen Words
110 E Hallam St, Suite 116, Aspen, CO 81611
Tel: 970-925-3122 *Fax:* 970-920-5700
E-mail: aspenwords@aspeninstitute.org
Web Site: www.aspenwords.org
Key Personnel
Exec Dir: Adrienne Brodeur *Tel:* 646-461-3554 *E-mail:* adrienne.brodeur@aspeninstitute.org
Mng Dir: Jamie Kravitz *Tel:* 970-925-3122 ext 2 *E-mail:* jamie.kravitz@aspeninstitute.org
Sr Prog Assoc, Mktg & Communs: Caroline Tory *Tel:* 970-925-3122 ext 3 *E-mail:* caroline.tory@aspeninstitute.org
Series of readings with remarkable writers. Also includes book signings.
Location: Paepcke Auditorium, 1000 N Third St, Aspen, CO
Date: Annually, Jan-April

Wisconsin Annual Fall Conference
Society of Children's Book Writers and Illustrators, Wisconsin Chapter
PO Box 1463, Green Bay, WI 54305-1463
Tel: 323-782-1010 (corp off)
E-mail: wisconsin@scbwi.org
Web Site: www.scbwi.org; www.facebook.com/SCBWIWisconsin
Key Personnel
Co-Regl Advisor: Andrea Skyberg; Miranda Paul
Workshop on writing & illustrating for children. Includes ms or portfolio critique. Guest faculty includes award-winning writers & illustrators.

Write on the Sound Writers' Conference
City of Edmonds Art Commission
700 Main St, Edmonds, WA 98020
Tel: 425-771-0228 *Fax:* 425-771-0253
E-mail: wots@edmondswa.gov
Web Site: www.writeonthesound.com
Key Personnel
City of Edmonds Arts & Culture Mgr: Frances Chapin
Annual event, presented the 1st weekend in October, with over 30 workshops by noted authors, educators & trade professionals. Features a keynote address, on-site book shop, ms critique appointments & a themed writing contest.

The Writers' Colony at Dairy Hollow
515 Spring St, Eureka Springs, AR 72632
Tel: 479-253-7444
E-mail: director@writerscolony.org
Web Site: www.writerscolony.org
Key Personnel
Dir: Linda Caldwell
See web site for upcoming events & fellowships.

Writers' League of Texas (WLT)
611 S Congress Ave, Suite 200 A-3, Austin, TX 78704
Tel: 512-499-8914
E-mail: wlt@writersleague.org
Web Site: www.writersleague.org
Key Personnel
Exec Dir: Becka Oliver *E-mail:* becka@writersleague.org
Prog Dir: Michael Noll *E-mail:* michael@writersleague.org
Conferences, workshops, seminars, classes, e-mail classes.
Location: Writer's League of Texas Resource Center/Library & other locations, ongoing programs throughout Texas
Date: Throughout year

Writers Mentoring Retreat
American Christian Writers
PO Box 110390, Nashville, TN 37222-0390
Tel: 615-331-8668 *Toll Free Tel:* 800-21-WRITE (219-7483)
E-mail: acwriters@aol.com
Web Site: regaforder.wordpress.com/mentoring; regaforder.wordpress.com
Key Personnel
Pres: Reg A Forder
Correspondence courses; 36 conferences annually, approximately 3 per month in major cities throughout the US. Monthly magazine by subscription.
Location: Nashville, TN Mentoring Retreat
Date: April 20-21, 2018
Location: Grands Rapids, MI Mentoring Retreat
Date: June 8-9, 2018
Location: Atlanta, GA Mentoring Retreat
Date: July 6-7, 2018
Location: Minneapolis, MN Mentoring Retreat
Date: Aug 3-4, 2018
Location: Phoenix, AZ Mentoring Retreat
Date: Sept 7-8, 2018
Location: Nashville, TN Mentoring Retreat
Date: Oct 12-13, 2018
Location: Orlando, FL Mentoring Retreat
Date: Nov 16-17, 2018

Writers Retreat Workshop (WRW)
PO Box 170657, Austin, TX 78717
E-mail: info@writersretreatworkshop.com
Web Site: www.writersretreatworkshop.com
Key Personnel
Co-Founder: Gail Provost Stockwell
Dir: Jason Sitzes
Ed-in-Residence: Carol Doughtery
Coord: Lisa Willars-Pirc
Intensive workshop for writers of novels-in-progress, including private writing time & space, guest speakers & consultation with New York agent or editor, author instructor, as well as diagnostic sessions of participants' mss & daily assignments. Other retreats available, see web site for details.
Location: Nazareth Retreat Center, Boise, ID
Date: May 22-31, 2018

The Writers Workshop
The Kenyon Review
Finn House, 102 W Wiggin St, Gambier, OH 43022
Tel: 740-427-5207 *Fax:* 740-427-5417
E-mail: kenyonreview@kenyon.edu
Web Site: www.kenyonreview.org
Key Personnel
Progs Dir, The Kenyon Review: Anna Duke Reach
Intensive writing workshops for adults & teens, June & July annually.

Writers Workshop in Children's Literature, see SCBWI-FL Mid-Year Workshops

The Writing Center
601 E Palisade Ave, Suite 4, Englewood Cliffs, NJ 07632
Tel: 201-567-4017 *Fax:* 201-567-7202
E-mail: writingcenter@optonline.net
Web Site: www.writingcenternj.com
Key Personnel
Dir: Barry Sheinkopf *E-mail:* bsheinkopf@optonline.net
Writing seminars, editorial services, book design & publishing services.
Location: 601 Palisade Ave, Englewood Cliffs, NJ
Date: Year-round, 12 week writing seminars; Fall seminars begin Sept; Winter seminars begin Jan; Spring seminars begin April. Five week Summer session

Writing Workshops
UC Davis Extension
Affiliate of University of California, Davis
1333 Research Park Dr, Davis, CA 95618
Tel: 510-642-6362
E-mail: extension@ucdavis.edu
Web Site: extension.ucdavis.edu; writing.ucdavis.edu
Key Personnel
Dir, Univ Writing Prog: Carl Whithaus *Tel:* 530-752-0369 *E-mail:* cwwhithaus@ucdavis.edu
Workshops, courses & writing institutes.
Location: University of California, Davis & Sacramento, CA
Date: Year-round, call for dates

Yaddo Artists Residency
Yaddo
312 Union Ave, Saratoga Springs, NY 12866

Mailing Address: PO Box 395, Saratoga Springs, NY 12866-0395
Tel: 518-584-0746 *Fax:* 518-584-1312
E-mail: yaddo@yaddo.org
Web Site: www.yaddo.org
Key Personnel
Pres: Elaina Richardson *E-mail:* erichardson@yaddo.org
Prog Dir: Candace Wait *E-mail:* chwait@yaddo.org
An artists' community established in Saratoga Springs, NY in 1900 by the financier Spencer Trask & his poet wife, Katrina, to offer creative artists the rare gift of a supportive environment with uninterrupted time to think, experiment & create. Over the years, Yaddo has welcomed more than 6,000 artists working in one or more of the following media: choreography, film, literature, musical composition, painting, performance art, photography, printmaking, sculpture & video. About 220 artists are invited each year for residencies lasting up to 2 months. Application deadlines are Jan 1 & Aug 1.

Young Writers' Workshop
Cape Cod Writers Center
919 Main St, Osterville, MA 02655
Mailing Address: PO Box 408, Osterville, MA 02655
Tel: 508-420-0200
E-mail: writers@capecodwriterscenter.org
Web Site: capecodwriterscenter.org
Key Personnel
Pres: Barbara Struna
Exec Dir: Nancy Rubin Stuart
This program offers unique learning opportunities to young writers ages 12-18.
Date: Feb 2018

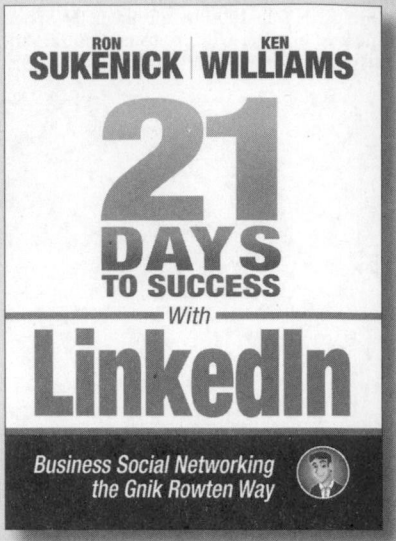

Courses for the Book Trade

Various courses covering different phases of the book trade are given each year. Detailed information on any of these courses can be obtained by writing directly to the sponsoring organization. For related information see **Writers' Conferences & Workshops**.

Arizona State University, Creative Writing Program
851 S Cady Mall, Rm 542, Tempe, AZ 85287-0302
Mailing Address: Dept of English, Box 870302, Tempe, AZ 85287-0302
Tel: 480-965-3528 *Fax:* 480-965-3451
Web Site: www.asu.edu/clas/english/creativewriting
Key Personnel
Prog Dir: Tara Ison *E-mail:* tara.ison@asu.edu
Prog Mgr, Creative Writing: Corey Campbell *E-mail:* corey.campbell@asu.edu
Undergraduate & graduate courses in creative writing: workshops, theory & special topics.

Arkansas State University Graphic Communications Program
PO Box 1930, Dept of Media, State University, AR 72467-1930
Tel: 870-972-3114 *Fax:* 870-972-3321
Web Site: www.astate.edu
Key Personnel
Dept Chair: Dr Osa Amienyi *E-mail:* osami@astate.edu
Instructor, Graphic Commun: Pradeep C Mishra *E-mail:* pmishra@astate.edu
Courses include Desktop Publishing
Digital Pre-Press Workflow & File Creation
Graphic Communications - Estimating & Schedules
Graphic Production Systems
Internet Communications
Internship
Intro to Digital Publishing
Intro to Visual Communication
Mass Communication in Modern Society
Multi-Media Production Techniques
News Design Publication
Photography

Baylor University, Professional Writing Program
One Bear Place, Unit 97404, Waco, TX 76798-7404
Tel: 254-710-1768 *Fax:* 254-710-3894
Web Site: www.baylor.edu
Key Personnel
Dept Chair: Dr Kevin J Gardner *E-mail:* kevin_gardner@baylor.edu
Prog Contact: Dr Kara Poe Alexander *E-mail:* kara_alexander@baylor.edu
Comprehensive writing program.
Courses include Argumentative & Persuasive Writing
Creative Nonfiction
Internship in Professional Writing
Literacy Studies
New Media Writing & Rhetoric
Professional & Workplace Writing
Research in Writing & Rhetoric
Rhetoric of Race
Special Topics in Writing Workshop
Special Topics Lecture in Writing & Rhetoric
Spiritual Writing
Studies in Public & Civic Writing
Style & Editing
Technical Writing
Women's Writing & Rhetoric
Writing for Social Change

Binghamton University Creative Writing Program
Division of State University of New York at Binghamton
c/o Dept of English, PO Box 6000, Binghamton, NY 13902-6000
Tel: 607-777-2168 *Fax:* 607-777-2408
E-mail: cwpro@binghamton.edu
Web Site: english.binghamton.edu/cwpro
Key Personnel
Dir, Prog: Maria Gillan
Assoc Dir, Creative Writing: Christine Gelineau
Professor: Jaimee Wriston Colbert; Thomas Glave; Leslie Heywood; Liz Rosenberg
Asst Professor: Joe Weil; Alexi Zentner
Asst to Chmn, Eng: Colleen Burke
Undergraduate & graduate courses.
Courses include Advanced Workshops in Creative Writing
Fiction Workshop
Fundamentals of Creative Writing
Independent Study in Creative Writing
Intermediate Creative Writing
Poetry Workshop
Studies for Writers

Boston University Creative Writing Program
236 Bay State Rd, Boston, MA 02215
Tel: 617-353-2510 *Fax:* 617-353-3653
E-mail: crwr@bu.edu
Web Site: www.bu.edu/creativewriting
Key Personnel
Prog Dir: Ha Jin *E-mail:* xjin@bu.edu
Prog Coord: Catherine Con
Contact: Prof Robert Pinsky *E-mail:* rpinsky@bu.edu
Workshops. Offer one-year Master's degree MSA in creative writing.
Courses include Fiction
Poetry

Bowling Green State University, Creative Writing Program
Dept of English, 409 East Hall, Bowling Green, OH 43403
Tel: 419-372-2576 *Fax:* 419-372-0333
Web Site: www.bgsu.edu/departments/creative-writing
Key Personnel
Dir & Advisor: Sharona Muir *E-mail:* smuir@bgsu.edu
Providers of comprehensive & rigorous education in professional writing, editing & marketing of poetry & fiction, since 1967.
Courses include Advanced Fiction Writing Workshop
Advanced Poetry Writing Workshop
Assistant Editing, Mid-American Review
Graduate Writers' Workshop in Poetry, Fiction
Studies in Contemporary Poetry, Fiction
Techniques of Fiction
Techniques of Poetry

The Center for Book Arts
28 W 27 St, 3rd fl, New York, NY 10001
Tel: 212-481-0295 *Toll Free Fax:* 866-708-8994
E-mail: info@centerforbookarts.org
Web Site: www.centerforbookarts.org
Key Personnel
Exec Dir: Alexander Campos *E-mail:* acampos@centerforbookarts.org
Offers classes & workshops year-round.
Courses include Hand Bookbinding
Hand Papermaking
Letterpress Printing

College of Liberal & Professional Studies, University of Pennsylvania
3440 Market St, Suite 100, Philadelphia, PA 19104-3335
Tel: 215-898-7326 *Fax:* 215-573-2053
E-mail: lps@sas.upenn.edu
Web Site: www.sas.upenn.edu/lps
Key Personnel
Vice Dean & Assoc Dir: Nora Lewis *E-mail:* nlewis@sas.upenn.edu
Dir, Mktg & Communs: Tomea Knight *E-mail:* knightt@sas.upenn.edu
Writing courses, beginning through advanced, taught by published authors; non-residential; fees vary; program catalog available for writing courses Sept-July.

Columbia Publishing Course at Columbia University
2950 Broadway, MC 3801, New York, NY 10027
Tel: 212-854-1898 *Fax:* 212-854-7618
E-mail: publishing@jrn.columbia.edu
Web Site: www.journalism.columbia.edu/publishing
Key Personnel
Dir: Shaye Areheart *E-mail:* sea2148@columbia.edu
Asst Dir: Stephanie Chan *Tel:* 212-854-9775 *E-mail:* swc37@columbia.edu
Provides an intensive introduction to book, magazine & digital publishing. Students learn the entire publishing process from established publishing professionals & gain hands-on experience from evaluations of original mss to the sales & marketing of finished products.
Courses include Book, Magazine & Digital Publishing

Columbia University School of the Arts, Creative Writing Program
Division of Columbia University
609 Kent Hall, New York, NY 10027
Tel: 212-854-3774 *Fax:* 212-854-7704
E-mail: writingprogram@columbia.edu
Web Site: www.columbia.edu/cu/writing
Key Personnel
Chair: Timothy Donnelly
Dir, Creative Writing: Heidi Julavits
Prog Asst, Creative Writing: Dorla McIntosh
Courses include Fiction
Nonfiction
Poetry

The Lisa Ekus Group LLC
57 North St, Hatfield, MA 01038
Tel: 413-247-9325 *Fax:* 413-247-9873
E-mail: info@lisaekus.com
Web Site: lisaekus.com
Key Personnel
Principal & Pres: Lisa Ekus *E-mail:* lisaekus@lisaekus.com
Mgr & Literary Assoc: Sally Ekus *E-mail:* sally@lisaekus.com
Comprehensive 1- or 2-day media training programs designed for cookbook authors, chefs, product spokespeople, show hosts & food pro-

fessionals. Participants will spend their day(s) under the lights & in front of the camera, taping & critiquing actual television demonstrations of varying lengths. Courses are typically held in the professional kitchen of our Hatfield, MA, offices but off-site training is available. Visit culinarymediatraining.com to learn more.
Courses include Cookbook Publishing 101
Honing Your Edge: Media Training for Culinary Professionals
One-On-One Media Training

Emerson College Department of Writing, Literature & Publishing
180 Tremont St, 10th fl, Boston, MA 02116
Mailing Address: 120 Boylston St, Boston, MA 02116-4624
Tel: 617-824-8750 *Fax:* 617-824-7856
Web Site: www.emerson.edu
Key Personnel
Chair: Jerald Walker
Graduate Prog Dir, MA in Publg & Writing: Lisa Diercks *E-mail:* lisa_diercks@emerson.edu
Offers BA, MA, BFA & MFA degrees in publishing & writing.
Courses include Applications for Publishing
Book Design & Production
Book Editing
Book Marketing & Sales
Book Publicity
Book Publishing Overview
Column Writing
Copyediting
Creating Electronic Publications
Digital Publishing for Tablets & Handheld Devices
Editor-Writer Relationship
Electronic Publishing Overview
Magazine Design & Production
Magazine Editing
Magazine Publishing Overview
Magazine Writing
Principles of Management for Publishing
Web Development for Electronic Publishing

Fordham University, Graduate School of Business Administration
Gabelli School of Business, 441 E Fordham Rd, Hughes Hall, Rm 516, Bronx, NY 10458
Tel: 718-817-1894
Web Site: www.bnet.fordham.edu
Key Personnel
Assoc Dean, Graduate Studies: Dawn Lerman
Mktg Professor: Albert N Greco *E-mail:* agreco@fordham.edu
Offers MBA degree with a major in Communications & Media Management. MBA Graduate courses & additional MBA course work.
Courses include Accounting
Marketing with Public Relations
The Book Publishing Industry
Broadcast & Cable Marketing & Advertising Sales Business & Legal Aspects of Cable TV
Broadcast Management
Business & the Mass Media
Consumer Behavior
Coping with Global Corporate Crisis
Corporate Power & the Public
Direct Marketing
Economics
Executive Communications
Finance
Information & Communications Systems
International Marketing
Legal & Ethical Studies
Magazine Management
Managing Newspapers & Their Electronic Ventures
Marketing Management, Advertising & Media Planning
Mass Media in America
New Media & Mass Communications
Persuasion in Public Relations
Public Relations & Broadcasting
Public Relations as a Management Tool
Sales Management
Special Topics in Communications & Media Management: Book Publishing
The Press, the Law & the Corporation

Gaylord College of Journalism & Mass Communication, Professional Writing Program
Division of University of Oklahoma
c/o University of Oklahoma, 395 W Lindsey St, Rm 3534, Norman, OK 73019-0270
Tel: 405-325-2721 *Fax:* 405-325-7565
Web Site: www.ou.edu/gaylord
Key Personnel
Professor, Prof Writing: J Madison Davis *Tel:* 405-325-4171 *E-mail:* jmadisondavis@ou.edu
Coursework on writing for commercial publication.
Courses include Analyzing Category Fiction
Film Script Writing
Magazine Article Writing
Short Story Writing
Writing The Novel

The Graphic Artists Guild Inc
31 W 34 St, 8th fl, New York, NY 10001
Tel: 212-791-3400 *Fax:* 212-791-0333
E-mail: admin@graphicartistsguild.org; membership@graphicartistsguild.org
Web Site: www.graphicartistsguild.org
Key Personnel
Pres: Lara Kisielewska *E-mail:* president@graphicartistsguild.org
Business workshops & seminars for professional graphic artists.
Eastern, Midwestern, New England, Southern & Western regional chapters.

Graphic Arts Association
1210 Northbrook Dr, Suite 200, Trevose, PA 19053
Tel: 215-396-2300 *Fax:* 215-396-9890
E-mail: gaa@gaaonline.org
Web Site: www.gaa1900.com; www.graphicartsassociation.org
Key Personnel
Pres & Dir, Membership: Melissa Jones *E-mail:* mjones@gaaonline.org
Regional trade association for the printing industry serving PA, southern NJ & DE.
Courses include Computer Laptop Training
Estimating
Graphic Arts Fundamentals
Industrial Relations Training
Production
Sales & Management

Hamilton College, English/Creative Writing
English/Creative Writing Dept, 198 College Hill Rd, Clinton, NY 13323
Tel: 315-859-4370 *Fax:* 315-859-4390
Web Site: www.hamilton.edu
Key Personnel
Chair: Margaret Thickstun *E-mail:* mthickst@hamilton.edu
Professor, Eng & Creative Writing: Naomi Guttman *E-mail:* nguttman@hamilton.edu
Professor, Eng: Doran Larson *E-mail:* dlarson@hamilton.edu
Professor, Lit & Creative Writing: Onno Oerlemans *Tel:* 315-859-4378 *E-mail:* ooerlema@hamilton.edu
Assoc Professor, Eng: Tina Hall *E-mail:* thall@hamilton.edu
Academic program; students may concentrate on creative writing.

Hofstra University, English Department
203 Mason Hall, Hempstead, NY 11549
Tel: 516-463-5454 *Fax:* 516-463-6395
Web Site: www.hofstra.edu
Key Personnel
Professor, Eng: Joseph Fichtelberg, PhD *E-mail:* joseph.fichtelberg@hofstra.edu
Assoc Prof: Erik A Brogger *E-mail:* erik.a.brogger@hofstra.edu
Undergraduate courses in all phases of publishing & creative writing, leading to a BA in English. MA in English Literature & an MFA in creative writing.

Hollins University-Jackson Center for Creative Writing
PO Box 9677, Roanoke, VA 24020
Tel: 540-362-6317 *Fax:* 540-362-6097
E-mail: creative.writing@hollins.edu
Web Site: www.hollins.edu
Key Personnel
Dir: Prof Thorpe Moeckel
BA degree in English with concentration in creative writing - 4 academic years; MFA in creative writing - 2-year program in residency.

Louisiana State University Creative Writing Program MFA
English Dept, 260 Allen Hall, Baton Rouge, LA 70803
Tel: 225-578-5922 *Fax:* 225-578-4129
Web Site: www.lsu.edu; www.english.lsu.edu/dept/programs/grad/creative_writing
Key Personnel
Dir, Creative Writing: Laura Mullen *Tel:* 225-578-3049 *E-mail:* lmullen@lsu.edu
Asst Dir: Randolph Thomas *Tel:* 225-578-2830 *E-mail:* rndlpht@aol.com
A graduate program leading to a MFA degree in creative writing.
Courses include Drama Workship, ENGL 7008
Fiction Workshop, ENGL 7006
Poetry Workshop, ENGL 7007
Screenwriting Workshop, ENGL 7009

Manhattanville College Master of Fine Arts in Creative Writing Program
2900 Purchase St, Purchase, NY 10577
Tel: 914-323-5239 *Fax:* 914-323-3122
Web Site: www.mville.edu/writing
Key Personnel
Asst Dir: Erika Stanley *E-mail:* stanleye@mville.edu
Offers courses with faculty who are well-known published writers & poets, all of whom are dedicated to helping writers explore their craft, sharpen their skills & take their writing to the next level, all within a thriving literary community. In addition, students can build on the skills gained in the editing & production course through work on our award-winning journal *Inkwell*, which gives them the editorial & production experience to succeed in publishing.
Courses include Editing & Production Workshop
Fiction Workshop
Nonfiction Workshop
Poetry Workshop
Writing for Children & Young Adults
Writing the Contemporary Novel

Massachusetts College of Art & Design Writing Children's Literature
Affiliate of Massachusetts College of Art and Design Continuing Education Dept
621 Huntington Ave, Boston, MA 02115
Tel: 617-879-7200 *Fax:* 617-879-7171
E-mail: ce@massart.edu
Web Site: www.massart.edu/ce
Key Personnel
Dean, Prof & Continuing Educ: Anne Marie Stein
Courses include Book Design
Computer Graphics
Design
Fine Arts

Illustrating Children's Books
Typography

McNeese State University, Writing Program
PO Box 92655, Lake Charles, LA 70609-0001
Tel: 337-475-5325; 337-475-5327
Web Site: www.mcneese.edu.com; www.mfa.mcneese.edu
Key Personnel
Professor & Dir, MFA Prog: Amy Fleury *E-mail:* afleury@mcneese.edu
Asst Professor, Fiction & Ed, McNeese Review: John Griswold *E-mail:* wgriswold@mcneese.edu
MFA program in creative writing - 60 hour program.
Courses include Contemporary Novel
Contemporary Poetry
Creative Writing Workshop-Fiction
Creative Writing Workshop-Poetry
Form & Theory of Fiction I
Form & Theory of Fiction II
Form & Theory of Poetry I
Form & Theory of Poetry II

Mississippi Review/University of Southern Mississippi, Center for Writers
Affiliate of University of Southern Mississippi, Dept of English
118 College Dr 5144, Hattiesburg, MS 39406-0001
Tel: 601-266-5600 *Fax:* 601-266-5757
Web Site: www.usm.edu/english/c4w.html; www.usm.edu/english/mississippireview.html
Key Personnel
Ed-in-Chief: Andrew Milward
Graduate & undergraduate courses in fiction & poetry writing.
Mississippi Review.

New York City College of Technology
Division of City University of New York
300 Jay St, Brooklyn, NY 11201
Tel: 718-260-5500 *Fax:* 718-260-5198
E-mail: connect@citytech.cuny.edu
Web Site: www.citytech.cuny.edu
Key Personnel
Pres: Russell K Hotzler, PhD *Tel:* 718-260-5400 *E-mail:* rhotzler@citytech.cuny.edu
Dir, Graphic Arts Dept: Lloyd Carr *Tel:* 718-260-5822 *E-mail:* lcarr@citytech.cuny.edu
2- or 4-year degree in graphic arts, certificates, associates or baccalaureate.
Courses include Advertising
Printing & Publishing

New York University, Center for Publishing
Affiliate of School of Continuing Education
Midtown Ctr, Rm 429, 11 W 42 St, New York, NY 10036
Tel: 212-992-3232 *Fax:* 212-992-3233
E-mail: pub.center@nyu.edu
Web Site: www.scps.nyu.edu/publishing
Key Personnel
Academic Prog Dir & Clinical Asst Professor: Andrea L Chambers
Asst Dir: Lindsey Allen *E-mail:* lindsey.allen@nyu.edu
Offers a certificate in publishing, consisting of 5 courses. Individual courses may be taken. A total of 13 book, 14 magazine & 7 online publishing courses. Also offers a certificate in editing with 10 courses each year. The Summer Publishing Institute is an intensive residential program for recent college graduates, planning to enter the publishing industry. Consists of 3-week module in book publishing & 3-week module in magazine publishing, each including an overview of the industry, lectures, workshops, field trips & professional simulations, job fair & placement assistance. Application deadline April 1 for MS in publishing. Program consists of 42 graduate credits chosen from a required core of courses in the functional areas of publishing & a concentration in either book or magazine publishing. Courses are all offered in the evening.
Courses include Advanced Copyediting
Advanced Magazine Editing
Advanced Special Project in Publishing
Advertising in Magazines
Advertising Sales & Integrated Marketing for Business-to-Business Publishers
The Basics of the Book Publishing Industry: Today & Tomorrow
Book Design Strategies
Book Editing
Book Marketing
Book Packaging
Book Production & Manufacturing
Book Publicity, Promotion
Books from Writer to Reader: An Overview of the Publishing Process
Bookselling: From Publisher to Reader
The Business of Book Publishing: Financial Management in a Creative Environment
The Business of Business-to-Business Publishing
The Business of Online Publishing
The Business of Publishing for US Hispanic Markets
Children's Book Publishing
The Circulation Challenge: Newsstand, Retail & Speciality Outlets
Controlled Circulation
Cookbook Copyediting
Copyediting & Proofreading Fundamentals
Cross-Media Programs: The Future of Magazine Advertising Sales
Developmental Editing
Disk & Online Editing
The Economics of Magazine Publishing
Economics of Publishing
Editing Periodicals
Effective Marketing in Publishing Via the Digital Channels
Electronic Content Development
Electronic Publishing for Print & Online Part 1: Survey
Electronic Publishing for Print & Online Part II: Portfolio
E-mail Newsletters
The Evolving Business of Custom Publishing
Fact Checking
Financial Analysis I: Introduction to Financial Statement Analysis in Publishing
Financial Copyediting
Freelance Book Indexing
Fundamentals of Copyediting
Fundamentals of Proofreading
Globalization & the Web
Grammar for Publishing Professionals
How to Develop Your Career in Publishing
How to Market Your Freelance Editorial Services
How to Self-Publish Successfully & Profitably in Today's Market–An Intensive Two-Day Seminar
The Independent Publisher: How to Start, Sustain & Build a Small Press
Information Technology Management in Publishing
International Magazine Publishing
International Publishing
Internship
Journal Copyediting & Production
The Laws of Book Publishing: A Practical Guide to Contracts, Copyright & More
Legal Proofreading
Magazine Advertising Sales & Marketing
Magazine Branding & Franchise Development
Magazine Circulation
Magazine Copyediting
Magazine Editorial Planning & Management
Magazine Financial Management
Magazine Production & Manufacturing
Magazine Promotion, Events & Public Relations
Magazine Research: New Techniques to Accelerate Recovery Growth
Magazines from Mission to Magic & More: An Overview
Managing the Publishing Enterprise
Manuscript Editing
Marketing for Publishing
Media Ethics for Publishing Professionals
Mentored Academic Study
Multi-Channel Sales Promotion for Books
Multimedia Marketing & Product Development
ONIX: How Good Product Information Improves Sales
Online Publishing: Business, Technology & Strategy
Principles & Applications of Publishing on the Internet
Principles of Profitability in Book Publishing
Print Technology for Publishing
Production Editing
Professional Book & Information Publishing
Publishing: Books, Magazines & Multimedia
Publishing in Cyberspace: Legal & Practical Problems of Internet & Electronic Publishing
Publishing Law: Issues in Intellectual Property
Publishing On-Line
The Role of the Literary Agent in Book Publishing
Scientific, Technical & Medical Journal Copyediting
Scientific, Technical & Medical Journal Copyediting & Production
Scientific, Technical, Professional Publishing on the Internet
Secrets to Success in Magazine Freelance Writing & Editing
Special Sales, Licensing & Merchandising for Books
Starting a Small Book Publishing Co
Summer Institute in Book & Magazine Publishing
Trade & General Book Publishing
Usability: Information Architecture & the User Experience in Publishing
Web Marketing & E-Commerce
Web Page Development With HTML

Ohio University, English Department, Creative Writing Program
Ohio University, English Dept, Ellis Hall, Athens, OH 45701
Tel: 740-593-2838 (English Dept) *Fax:* 740-593-2832
E-mail: english.department@ohio.edu
Web Site: www.ohio.edu/cas/english
Key Personnel
Dir: Dinty W Moore *E-mail:* moored4@ohio.edu
Offer PhD degree with creative writing emphasis.
Courses include Fiction
Form & Theory
Nonfiction
Novels
Poetry
Short Stories

Pace University, Master of Science in Publishing
Dept of Publishing, Rm 805-E, 551 Fifth Ave, New York, NY 10176
Tel: 212-346-1431 *Toll Free Tel:* 877-284-7670 *Fax:* 212-346-1165
Web Site: www.pace.edu/dyson/mspub
Key Personnel
Chmn & Dir, Publg Progs: Sherman Raskin *E-mail:* sraskin@pace.edu
Program educates its students in all pertinent aspects of the publishing business: books, magazines & digital publishing. Our graduates are equipped for the challenges facing the industry today.
Courses include Book Production & Design, PUB 606
Children's Book Publishing, PUB 634
Digital Issues in Publishing

Ebooks: Technology, Workflow & Business Model, PUB 621
Editorial Principles & Practices, PUB 634
Electronic Publishing for Publishers, PUB 636
Financial Aspects of Publishing, PUB 608
The Future of Publishing: Transmedia, PUB 613
General Interest Books, PUB 610
Information Systems in Publishing, PUB 612
Legal Aspects of Publishing, PUB 618
Magazine Production & Design, PUB 607
Marketing Principles & Practices in Publishing, PUB 628
Modern Technology in Publishing, PUB 620
Publishing Comics & Graphic Novels, PUB 610
Subsidiary Rights, Acquisitions & the Function of the Literary Agent, PUB 610

Parsons School of Design, Continuing Education
Division of New School University
2 W 13 St, 5th fl, Rm 504, New York, NY 10003
Tel: 212-229-5150 *Fax:* 212-229-5970
E-mail: ceinformation@newschool.edu; academy@newschool.edu
Web Site: www.newschool.edu/parsons
Comprehensive courses & advanced courses appropriate for book, magazine & advertising design.
Courses include Graphic & Advertising Design

Publishing Certificate Program at City College of New York
Division of Humanities NAC 5225, City College of New York, New York, NY 10031
Tel: 212-650-7925 *Fax:* 212-650-7912
E-mail: ccnypub@aol.com
Web Site: www.ccny.cuny.edu/publishing_certificate/index.html
Key Personnel
Dir: David Unger
Asst Dir: Retha Powers
Program for undergraduates. Take 4 of 20 courses offered & then qualify for a paid internship in a publishing house of your interest.
Courses include Books for Young Readers
Copyediting & Proofreading, etc
Ebooks & Digital Publishing
The Editorial Process
Introduction to Publishing I & II
Legal Issues in Publishing

Rochester Institute of Technology, School of Media, Arts & Technology
69 Lomb Memorial Dr, Rochester, NY 14623-5603
Tel: 585-475-2728; 585-475-5336 *Fax:* 585-475-5336
E-mail: spmofc@rit.edu
Web Site: cias.rit.edu/printmedia
Key Personnel
Chmn, School of Printing: Gregory S D'Amico *E-mail:* gsdppr@rit.edu
Classes in books & magazine production, typography, printing design, computer use, desktop prepress production, management, sales, finishing & bindery, quality control, marketing, finance & legal problems of publishing.
Courses include Computer Use
Desktop Prepress Production
Finance & Legal Problems of Publishing
Finishing & Bindery
Management
Marketing
Printing Design
Quality Control
Sales
Typography

Rosemont College
Graduate Publg Prog, 1400 Montgomery Ave, Rosemont, PA 19010
Tel: 610-527-0200 (ext 2336) *Fax:* 610-526-2964
Web Site: www.rosemont.edu
Key Personnel
Dir, Graduate Publg Progs: Anne Converse-Willkomm
Offers MA degree in publishing.
Courses include Business of Publishing
Children's & Young Adult
Design
Editorial

School of Visual Arts
209 E 23 St, New York, NY 10010-3994
Tel: 212-592-2100 *Fax:* 212-592-2116
Web Site: www.sva.edu
Key Personnel
Exec Dir, Admissions & Student Aff: Javier Vega
Non-degree programs beginning in Sept, Jan & June, including intensive 2-week workshops.
Courses include Advertising & Graphic Design
Artists' Books
BFA Programs in Advertising & Graphic Design
Book Cover Design & Illustration Book Design
Book Illustration & Children's Book Writing & Illustration
Cartooning
Computer Art & Photography
Computer Graphics
Copywriting
Editorial Design
Fine Arts
Illustration & Cartooning
Interior Design & Photography
MAT in Art Education
MFA Programs in Fine Arts Illustration
Photographic Printing Processes
Type & Design Agency Skills
Video Recording & Editing

Susquehanna University, Department of English and Creative Writing
514 University Ave, Selinsgrove, PA 17870
Tel: 570-372-0101
Key Personnel
Professor, Eng: Laurence Roth
Assoc Professor, Eng: Randy Robertson
Assoc Professor, Communs: Katherine Hastings
Assoc Professor, Creating Writing: Catherine Dent-Zobal
Assoc Professor, Creative Writing: Karla Kelsey
The English - Publishing & Editing major prepares students for careers in a digitally mediated publishing industry & for related careers in marketing, public relations, arts journalism, library & information science & media management. Courses focus on both the intellectual & practical uses of literary study, especially the technologies of writing & reading, the businesses of literature & craft.
Courses include Aesthetics & Interpretation, ENGL:290
Book Reviewing, ENGL:298
Editing, COMM:331 Intermediate focused subject course that focuses on the challenges & issues confronted in editing for journalism & teaches the process of editing a newspaper
English Grammar & the Writing Process, ENGL:269
History of the Book, ENGL:375
Internship, ENGL:540 Working with internships available in publishing or editing either on or off campus
Introduction to Modern Publishing, ENGL:190 Introduces students to the history of modern publishing, to the process, art & business of producing books
Marketing, MGMT:280
Professional Writing, ENGL:299
Public Relations, COMM:211
Publishing: Ethics, Entertainment, Art, Politics, ENGL:388 Analyzes changes & continuities in the cultural role of publishing from the beginning of mass printing to the current day
Small Press Publishing & Editing, WRIT:270 Intermediate focused subject course that focuses on the challenges & issues faced by small literary presses. Students learn to edit fiction, poetry, nonfiction & memoirs
Surveys in Forms of Writing, ENGL:265
Writing for New Media, COMM:182

Syracuse University Creative Writing Program
401 Hall of Languages, Syracuse, NY 13244-1170
Tel: 315-443-2173 *Fax:* 315-443-3660
Web Site: english.syr.edu/creative_writing; www.syr.edu
Key Personnel
Dir: Christopher Kennedy *E-mail:* ckennedy@syr.edu
Assoc Dir: Sarah C Harwell *Tel:* 315-443-9480 *E-mail:* scharwel@syr.edu
Courses include Eastern European Poetry/Translation
The Essay
Fiction Workshop
The Forms of Fiction
The Forms of Poetry
Open Workshop - Fiction
Open Workshop - Poetry
Poetry Workshop
Prose Writing
Writing of Fiction
Writing of Poetry
Writing the Novella

Syracuse University, SI Newhouse School of Public Communications
215 University Place, Syracuse, NY 13244-2100
Tel: 315-443-3627 *Fax:* 315-443-3946
E-mail: newhouse@syr.edu
Web Site: newhouse.syr.edu
Key Personnel
Dean: Lorraine Branham
Undergraduate degrees in advertising; broadcast & arts journalism, magazine, newspaper & online journalism; public relations; television, radio, film; visual & interactive communications; photography & graphics; Master's degrees in advertising; magazine; newspaper; media administration; visual & interactive communications; public relations; television-radio & film. PhD degrees in mass communications.
Courses include Advertising
Broadcast, Magazine & Newspaper Journalism
Film
Media Administration
Photography
Public Relations
Radio
Television

University of Alabama Program in Creative Writing
Affiliate of University of Alabama, Department of English
PO Box 870244, Tuscaloosa, AL 35487-0244
Tel: 205-348-5065 *Fax:* 205-348-1388
E-mail: english@ua.edu
Web Site: www.as.ua.edu/english
Key Personnel
Poet & Professor: Robin Behn *Tel:* 205-348-8488 *E-mail:* rbehn@ua.edu
Poet & Assoc Professor: Joel Brouwer *Tel:* 205-348-9524 *E-mail:* joel.brouwer@ua.edu
Fiction Writer & Professor: Michael Martone *Tel:* 205-348-5526 *E-mail:* mmartone@ua.edu
Fiction Writer & Assoc Professor: Wendy Rawlings *Tel:* 205-348-4507 *E-mail:* wendy.rawlings@ua.edu
Graduate Prog Coord: Jennifer Fuqua *Tel:* 205-348-9493 *E-mail:* jfuqua@as.ua.edu
Three-year MFA degree program & creative writing course for undergraduates, minor in creative writing. See web site for details.

University of Baltimore - Yale Gordon College of Arts & Sciences, Ampersand Institute for Words & Images
Division of Klein Family School of Communications Design
1420 N Charles St, Baltimore, MD 21201-5779
Tel: 410-837-6022 *Fax:* 410-837-6029
E-mail: scd@ubalt.edu
Web Site: www.ubalt.edu
Key Personnel
Dir: Dr Cheryl Wilson *E-mail:* cwilson2@ubalt.edu
Academic Prog Specialist: Jaye Crooks
Sponsors Fall & Spring lecture series, conducts advanced seminars, workshops, mini-courses & conferences on publishing topics including writing, design; also supports through the School of Communications Design, a MA program in Publications Design, an MFA in Integrated Design & an MFA in Creative Writing & Publishing Arts.

University of California Extension Professional Sequence in Copyediting & Courses in Publishing
1995 University Ave, Suite 110, Berkeley, CA 94720-7000
Tel: 510-642-6362 *Fax:* 510-643-0216
E-mail: letters@unex.berkeley.edu
Web Site: www.unex.berkeley.edu
Key Personnel
Prog Dir: Liz McDonough *Tel:* 510-643-1637
Certificate program in editing; evening/weekend courses & one-day seminars.
Courses include Editing
Management
Screenwriting
Writing (fiction, poetry, nonfiction)

University of Chicago, Graham School of General Studies
Division of Professional Programs
1427 E 60 St, Chicago, IL 60637
Tel: 773-702-1722 *Fax:* 773-702-6814
Web Site: www.grahamschool.uchicago.edu
Key Personnel
Prog Dir: Lisa Malvin *Tel:* 773-702-1720 *E-mail:* lmalvin@uchicago.edu
Noncredit courses.
Courses include Basic Creative Writing
Elements of Novel Writing
Getting the Story: Freelance Journalism Workshop
Intensive Short Story Workshop
Introduction to Freelance Journalism
Memoir Writing
Poetry Workshop: Outside the Self
Screenwriting Workshop
Writing Novels for Children & Young Adults
Writing the Novel 1
Writing the Novel 2
Writing the Personal Essay

University of Denver Publishing Institute
2000 E Asbury Ave, Denver, CO 80208
Tel: 303-871-2570 *Fax:* 303-871-2501
Web Site: www.du.edu/publishinginstitute
Key Personnel
Dir: Jill Smith *E-mail:* jill.smith@du.edu
Four-week graduate program in book publishing held July-Aug each year. Provides hands on workshops, lecture-teaching sessions on every phase of book publishing. Faculty consists of leading executives from publishing houses across the country. Emphasis on career counseling & job placement. Offers 6 quarter hours of graduate credit.
Courses include Children's Books
College Textbooks
E-Books
Economics of Publishing
Editing Workshop
Foreign Rights
Independent Presses
International Publishing
Marketing on the Internet
Marketing Workshop
Production & Design
Publicity & Promotion
Publishing & the Law
Scholarly Books
Trade & Scholarly Books
University Presses

University of Houston Creative Writing Program
229 Roy Cullen Bldg, Houston, TX 77204-5008
Tel: 713-743-2255 *Fax:* 713-743-3697
E-mail: cwp@uh.edu
Web Site: www.uh.edu/cwp
Key Personnel
Dir: Jay Kastely *E-mail:* jkastely@uh.edu
Asst Dir: Giuseppe Taurino *E-mail:* gtaurino@uh.edu
Offers MA, MFA & PhD in creative writing.

University of Illinois at Chicago, Program for Writers
Affiliate of University of Illinois, Dept of English
College of Liberal Arts & Sciences, 2027 University Hall, 601 S Morgan St, Chicago, IL 60607-7120
Tel: 312-413-2200 (Eng dept) *Fax:* 312-413-1005
Web Site: www.uic.edu
Key Personnel
Dir, Prog for Writers: Cris Mazza *Tel:* 312-413-2795 *E-mail:* cmazza@uic.edu
Graduate program for writers. Students in this program take literature classes as well as writing workshops. Offers MA & PhD in writing. Undergraduates seeking a BA in English may also specialize in writing.
Courses include Experimental Writing Workshop
Fiction Workshop
Nonfiction Workshop
Novel Workshop
Poetry Workshop
Publication Workshop
Translation Practicum

University of Illinois, Department of Journalism
Unit of College of Communications, University of Illinois
Gregory Hall, Rm 120-A, 810 S Wright St, Urbana, IL 61801
Tel: 217-333-0709 *Fax:* 217-333-7931
E-mail: journ@uiuc.edu
Web Site: www.comm.uiuc.edu
Key Personnel
Dept Head: Prof Brian Johnson *Tel:* 217-333-2103 *E-mail:* bjohn@illinois.edu
Master's degree program.
Courses include Graphics
Magazine Article Writing
News Editing
Photojournalism
Reporting I & II

University of Iowa, Writers' Workshop, Graduate Creative Writing Program
102 Dey House, 507 N Clinton St, Iowa City, IA 52242-1000
Tel: 319-335-0416 *Fax:* 319-335-0420
Web Site: writersworkshop.uiowa.edu
Key Personnel
Dir: Lan Samantha Chang
Graduate: fiction & poetry workshops & seminars. Undergraduate: creative, fiction & poetry writing.

University of Montana, Environmental Writing Institute
Subsidiary of Environmental Studies Program
Environmental Studies, University of Montana, Missoula, MT 59812
Tel: 406-243-2904 *Fax:* 406-243-6090
Web Site: www.umt.edu/ewi
Key Personnel
Prog Mgr & Dir: Phil Condon *E-mail:* phil.condon@mso.umt.edu
Writing workshop for environmental & nature subjects.

University of Southern California, Master of Professional Writing Program
Mark Taper Hall, THH 355, 3501 Trousedale Pkwy, Los Angeles, CA 90089-0355
Tel: 213-740-3252 *Fax:* 213-740-5002
E-mail: mpw@college.usc.edu
Web Site: college.usc.edu/mpw
Key Personnel
Dir: Brighde Mullins
Prog Specialist: Howard Ho
Student Servs Advisor: Natalie Inouye
Multidisciplinary Creative Writing Master's program & Master's of Arts degree in Professional Writing.
Courses include Creative Nonfiction
Fiction
New Media
Poetry
Writing for Stage & Screen

University of Texas at Austin, New Writers Project
Dept of English, Calhoun Hall, Rm 226, 204 W 21 St, B-5000, Austin, TX 78712
Tel: 512-471-5132; 512-471-4991 *Fax:* 512-471-4909
Web Site: newwritersproject.org
Key Personnel
Chair: Elizabeth Cullingford *E-mail:* cullingford@austin.utexas.edu
Chair, Poetry: Dean Young *E-mail:* deanyoung@mail.utexas.edu
Dir, New Writers Proj: Lisa Olstein *E-mail:* lisaolstein@gmail.com
Assoc Dir, New Writers Proj: Elizabeth McCracken *E-mail:* elizmccrack@utexas.edu
Professor: Don Graham *E-mail:* dgbb@mail.utexas.edu; Kurt Heinzelman *E-mail:* kheinz@mail.utexas.edu; Rolando Hinojosa-Smith *E-mail:* rorro@mail.utexas.edu; Lisa Moore *E-mail:* llmoore@austin.utexas.edu
Susan Taylor McDaniel Regents Professor in Creative Writing: Peter La Salle *E-mail:* pnl315@yahoo.com
Assoc Professor: Edward Carey *E-mail:* edcarey256@aol.com; Oscar Casares *E-mail:* ohcasares@utexas.edu; Deborah Paredez *E-mail:* paredez@austin.utexas.edu; Deb Unferth *E-mail:* debou@utexas.edu
Graduate Prog Coord I: Cassandra Shulter *E-mail:* cshulter@austin.utexas.edu
Graduate Prog Coord II: Patricia Schaub *E-mail:* pjschaub@austin.utexas.edu
Comprised of experienced teachers committed to advising young writers. Students work with established writers, gain editorial & teaching experience & develop the range of their work. Students graduate with an MFA in Creative Writing.

University of Texas at El Paso, Department of Creative Writing, MFA/Department of Creative Writing
901 EDUC, 500 W University Ave, El Paso, TX 79968-9991
Tel: 915-747-5713 *Fax:* 915-747-5523
E-mail: creativewriting@utep.edu
Web Site: www.utep.edu/cw
Key Personnel
Chair, Bilingual MFA: Lex Williford *Tel:* 915-747-5721 *E-mail:* lex@utep.edu

Dir, Online MFA & Assoc Professor: Daniel Chacon *Tel:* 915-747-6255 *E-mail:* danchacon@utep.edu
Graduate Dir & Assoc Professor: Jose de Pierola *Tel:* 915-747-6322 *E-mail:* jdepierola@utep.edu
Professor: Luis Arturo Ramos *Tel:* 915-747-6511 *E-mail:* laramos@utep.edu
Assoc Professor: Rosa Alcala *Tel:* 915-747-7020 *E-mail:* ralcala1@utep.edu
Asst Professor: Andrea Cote-Botero *E-mail:* acbotero@utep.edu; Tim Z Hernandez *E-mail:* tzhernandez@utep.edu; Sasha Pimentel *Tel:* 915-747-6810 *E-mail:* srpimentel@utep.edu; Jeff Sirkin *Tel:* 915-747-5529 *E-mail:* jsirkin@utep.edu
Monolingual & bilingual workshops in fiction, poetry, playwriting, screenwriting, nonfiction & literary translation.

University of Wisconsin-Madison Continuing Studies
21 N Park St, 7th fl, Madison, WI 53715
Tel: 608-262-3447
Web Site: continuingstudies.wisc.edu
Key Personnel
Faculty Assoc: Christine DeSmet *Tel:* 608-262-3447 *E-mail:* christine.desmet@wisc.edu
Writing book trade & online writing courses offered, in-person retreats & conferences.
Courses include Critique Services
Weekend With Your Novel Retreat
Write-by-the-Lake Writer's Retreat
Writers' Institute Conference

Vermont College of Fine Arts MFA in Writing for Children & Young Adults Program
36 College St, Montpelier, VT 05602
Tel: 802-828-8637; 802-828-8696
Toll Free Tel: 866-934-VCFA (934-8232)
Fax: 802-828-8649
Web Site: www.vcfa.edu
Key Personnel
Prog Dir: Melissa Fisher *E-mail:* melissa.fisher@vcfa.edu
Asst Prog Dir: Susan Sarlo *E-mail:* susan.sarlo@vcfa.edu
Writing for children & young adults. Intensive 10-day residencies & nonresident 6-month writing projects.

Vermont College of Fine Arts, MFA in Writing Program
36 College St, Montpelier, VT 05602
Tel: 802-828-8840; 802-828-8839
Toll Free Tel: 866-934-VCFA (934-8232)
Fax: 802-828-8649
Web Site: www.vcfa.edu
Key Personnel
Prog Dir: Louise Crowley *E-mail:* louise.crowley@vcfa.edu
Asst Prog Dir: Jericho Parms *E-mail:* jericho.parms@vcfa.edu
Degree work in poetry, fiction, creative nonfiction.

Warren Wilson College, MFA Program for Writers
701 Warren Wilson Rd, Swannanoa, NC 28778
Mailing Address: PO Box 9000, Asheville, NC 28815-9000
Tel: 828-771-3717 *Fax:* 828-771-7005
E-mail: mfa@warren-wilson.edu
Web Site: www.warren-wilson.edu/~mfa
Key Personnel
Dir, MFA Prog: Debra Allberry *Tel:* 828-771-3716
Full-time 2-year program with winter & summer semesters. Ten-day residency of classes, workshops & lectures on campus. The 6-month project that follows is supervised through correspondence, with detailed ms criticism by faculty who are both accomplished writers & committed teachers.
Courses include Fiction
Poetry

Writer's Digest University
Division of F+W Media Inc
10151 Carver Rd, Suite 200, Blue Ash, OH 45242-4760
Tel: 513-531-2690 *Toll Free Tel:* 800-759-0963 *Fax:* 513-531-0798
E-mail: contact_us@fwmedia.com
Web Site: www.writersonlineworkshops.com
Key Personnel
Online Prodn Mgr: Kevin Quinn
Course workshops are taught by active, published writers in the appropriate area, such as fiction & nonfiction. Students participate online, via the Internet. Workshops range in length from 4 to 28 weeks. Correspondence; student has up to 2 years to complete; tuition installment plans available for most courses.
Courses include Advanced Poetry Writing, Specialty Workshops
Blogging 101, Marking and Building a Platform
Breaking into Copywriting, Freelance/Copywriting
Business Writing, Specialty Workshops
Character Development, Fiction Writing Workshops
Conflict and Suspense, Fiction Writing Workshops
Creativity & Expression, Getting Started
Description and Setting, Fiction Writing Workshops
Dialogue, Fiction Writing Workshops
Fiction Writing 101: Fundamentals, Fiction Writing Workshops
Fiction Writing 102: Building Your Novel, Fiction Writing Workshops
Fiction Writing 103: 12 Weeks to Your First Draft, Fiction Writing Workshops
Fiction Writing 104: Advanced Novel Writing, Fiction Writing Workshops
Fitting Writing Into Your Life, Getting Started
Focus on the Short Story, Short Story/Memoir
Form and Composition, Getting Started
Freelance Writing for Stay at Home Moms, Freelance/Copywriting
Fundamentals of Poetry Writing, Specialty Workshops
Getting Started in Writing
Ghostwriting, Freelance/Copywriting
Grammar and Mechanics, Getting Started
Magazine Article Writing, Freelance/Copywriting
Marketing Your Magazine Articles, Nonfiction Writing
Master in Fine Arts Creative Writing) Application Preparation Course
Outlining Your Novel, Getting Started
Plot and Structure, Fiction Writing Workshops
Revision & Self Editing, Preparing for Publication
Social Media 101, Nonfiction Writing
Successful Self-Publishing, Preparing for Publication
Technical Writing, Specialty Workshops
The Art of Storytelling 101: Storymapping and Pacing, Fiction Writing Workshops
Travel Writing, Specialty Workshops
Turning Your Personal Essays into a Memoir, Short Story/Memoir
28 Days to Your First WordPress Site, Nonfiction Writing
Voice and Viewpoint, Fiction Writing Workshops
Writing a Memoir 101, Short Story/Memoir
Writing a Memoir 102, Short Story/Memoir
Writing a Religious Book, Specialty Workshops
Writing Nonfiction 101: Fundamentals, Nonfiction Writing
Writing Nonfiction 102: Advanced, Nonfiction Writing
Writing Nonfiction for Children, Graduate Preparation Workshops
Writing the Middle Grade Book, Specialty Workshops
Writing the Mystery Novel, Specialty Workshops
Writing the Nonfiction Book Proposal, Preparing for Publication
Writing the Novel Proposal, Preparing for Publication
Writing the Paranormal Novel, Specialty Workshops
Writing the Personal Essay 101: Fundamentals, Short Story/Memoir
Writing the Picture Book, Specialty Workshops
Writing the Query Letter, Preparing for Publication
Writing the Romance Novel, Specialty Workshops
Writing the Science Fiction & Fantasy Novel, Specialty Workshops
Writing the Young Adult Novel, Specialty Workshops

Awards, Prize Contests, Fellowships & Grants

Major awards given to books, authors and publishers by various organizations are, for the most part, not open for application. However, many prize contests may be applied for by writing to the sponsor (for prompt response, always include a self-addressed, stamped envelope). Also included in this section is information relating to fellowships and grants that are primarily available to authors and students who are pursuing publishing related studies.

For more complete information about scholarships, fellowships and grants-in-aid, see *The Annual Register of Grant Support* (Information Today, Inc., 121 Chanlon Road, Suite G-20, New Providence, NJ 07974-2195).

AAUP Book, Jacket & Journal Design Show
Association of American University Presses (AAUP)
1412 Broadway, Suite 2135, New York, NY 10018
Tel: 212-989-1010 *Fax:* 212-989-0275
E-mail: info@aaupnet.org
Web Site: www.aaupnet.org
Key Personnel
Off Mgr & Prog Admin: Kim Miller *Tel:* 917-244-1264 *E-mail:* kmiller@aaupnet.org
Prog Asst: Bailey Bretz *Tel:* 917-244-2665 *E-mail:* bbretz@aaupnet.org
Established: 1965
Excellence in design; competition limited to member presses in AAUP.
Award: Certificate, winning entries are displayed in a traveling exhibit
Presented: AAUP Annual Meeting, Annually in June

J M Abraham Poetry Award
Formerly Atlantic Poetry Prize
Writers' Federation of Nova Scotia
1113 Marginal Rd, Halifax, NS B3H 4P7, Canada
Tel: 902-423-8116 *Fax:* 902-422-0881
E-mail: contact@writers.ns.ca
Web Site: writers.ns.ca
Key Personnel
Exec Dir: Jonathan Meakin *E-mail:* director@writers.ns.ca
Established: 1998
Presented annually to the best full-length book of poetry by an Atlantic Canadian writer who has lived in one or a combination of these provinces for at least 2 concurrent years immediately prior to the submission deadline date. Non-refundable $20 administrative fee per entry.
Award: $2,000
Closing Date: Nov 1
Presented: Halifax, NS, Canada, Annually in Spring

Acclaim Film Script Competition
Acclaim Film
300 Central Ave, Suite 501, St Petersburg, FL 33701
Web Site: acclaimscripts.com
Key Personnel
Contest Coord: Frank Drouzas
Open to all writers 18 & over.
Award: $1,000 (1st place)
Closing Date: Ongoing

Acclaim TV Script Competition
Acclaim Film
300 Central Ave, Suite 501, St Petersburg, FL 33701
Web Site: acclaimscripts.com
Key Personnel
Contest Coord: Frank Drouzas
Open to all writers 18 & over. Must be original material of the author. Categories are Spec Scripts (for an existing show), Pilots & Movie of the Week.
Award: $500 for each category
Closing Date: Ongoing

The Accolades, see Cordon d' Or - Gold Ribbon International Culinary Academy Awards

Milton Acorn Poetry Awards
Prince Edward Island Writers' Guild
81 Prince St, Charlottetown, PE C1A 4R3, Canada
E-mail: peiliteraryawards@gmail.com
Web Site: www.peiwritersguild.com
Minimum 8 pages, maximum 10 pages per entry. Maximum 2 entries. Work must be original & unpublished. Entry fee for each submission is $25. Prince Edward Island residents only. See web site for complete entry requirements.
Award: Cash prizes for 1st, 2nd & 3rd place
Closing Date: Jan 31
Presented: Cox & Palmer Island Literary Awards Gala, Annually in Spring

Herbert Baxter Adams Prize
American Historical Association (AHA)
400 "A" St SE, Washington, DC 20003
Tel: 202-544-2422 *Fax:* 202-544-8307
E-mail: awards@historians.org
Web Site: www.historians.org
Established: 1905
For a distinguished book by an American author in the field of European history, from 1815 through the 20th century. Entry must be the author's first substantial book; must have been published in 2016 or 2017; must be citizen or permanent resident of the US or Canada. Submission of an entry may be made by an author or by a third party as well as by a publisher. Publishers may submit as many entries as they wish. Along with an application form, applicants must mail a copy of their book to each of the prize committee members who will be posted on our web site as the prize deadline approaches. All updated info on web site.
Award: Cash prize
Closing Date: May 15, 2018
Presented: AHA Annual Meeting, Chicago, IL, Jan 2019

Jane Addams Children's Book Award
Jane Addams Peace Association
777 United Nations Plaza, 6th fl, New York, NY 10017
Tel: 212-682-8830
E-mail: info@janeaddamspeace.org
Web Site: www.janeaddamspeace.org
Key Personnel
Award Comm Chair: Heather Palmer
Bd Pres: Tura Campanella Cook *E-mail:* president@janeaddamspeace.org
Established: 1953
Awarded to children's books published in the US the previous year with themes stressing peace, social justice, world community & the equality of the sexes & all races. Those applying must submit 1 copy to the committee chair: Heather Palmer, Valley View Middle School, 6750 Valley View Rd, Edina, MN 55439.
Award: Certificate; Cash
Closing Date: Annually, Dec 31
Presented: Winners announced April 28; ceremony held 3rd Friday in Oct annually

AFCP's Awards
Association of Free Community Papers (AFCP)
135 Old Cove Rd, Suite 210, Liverpool, NY 13090
Toll Free Tel: 877-203-2327 *Fax:* 781-459-7770
E-mail: afcp@afcp.org
Web Site: www.afcp.org
Key Personnel
Exec Dir: Loren Colburn *E-mail:* loren@afcp.org
Established: 1970
Awards for excellence revolving around the theme of free community papers.
Award: Plaques
Closing Date: Jan 23
Presented: AFCP's Annual Conference

Agatha Awards
Malice Domestic Ltd
PO Box 8007, Gaithersburg, MD 20898-8007
E-mail: malicedomesticpr@gmail.com
Web Site: www.malicedomestic.org
Key Personnel
Malice Dom Chair: Verena Rose *E-mail:* malicechair@comcast.net
Agatha Awards Comm Memb: Tonya Spratt-Williams *Tel:* 301-730-1675 *E-mail:* mdagathas@gmail.com
Established: 1989
Awards for best traditional mysteries of the calendar year. Awards given for best novel, best first novel, best nonfiction work, best short story, best children's/young adult novel. Those registered for Malice by December 31 each year receive a ballot to nominate.
Closing Date: Annually, Dec 31
Presented: Malice Domestic Convention, Agatha Awards Banquet, Annually in May

Aggiornamento Award
Catholic Library Association
8550 United Plaza Blvd, Suite 1001, Baton Rouge, LA 70809
Tel: 225-408-4417
E-mail: cla2@cathla.org
Web Site: cathla.org
Key Personnel
Pres: N Curtis LeMay
Established: 1980
To recognize contributions made by an individual or an organization for the renewal of parish & community life in the spirit of Pope John XXIII.
Award: Plaque
Closing Date: None; in-house votes
Presented: CLA Annual Convention, April

AIGA 50 Books|50 Covers
AIGA, the professional association for design
233 Broadway, Suite 1740, New York, NY 10279
Tel: 212-807-1990 *Fax:* 212-807-1799
E-mail: competitions@aiga.org
Web Site: www.aiga.org

Key Personnel
Archives Dir: Heather Strelecki
E-mail: heather_strelecki@aiga.org
Established: 1923
This annual competition aims to identify the 50 best-designed books & book covers. The selections from the 50 Books|50 Covers competition exemplify the best current work in book & book cover design. See web site for complete rules & eligibility.
Past selections from AIGA's book design competitions have been added to the online AIGA Design Archives as well as the physical archives at the Denver Art Museum & the Rare Book & Manuscript Library at Columbia University's Butler Library in New York City. Books selected this year will be housed at both the Robert B Haas Family Arts Library at Yale University & at the Rare Book & Manuscript Library at Columbia University's Butler Library.
Closing Date: Feb
Presented: Summer

AJL Judaica Bibliography Award
Association of Jewish Libraries (AJL) Inc
Affiliate of American Library Association (ALA)
PO Box 1118, Teaneck, NJ 07666
Tel: 201-371-3255
E-mail: info@jewishlibraries.org
Web Site: jewishlibraries.org
Key Personnel
Pres: Amalia Warshenbrot
Ref & Bibliography Awards Comm Chair: Sharon Benamou *E-mail:* benamou@library.ucla.edu
Established: 1984
Presented annually for best Judaica bibliography book published in previous calendar year.
Award: The seal of the Association
Closing Date: March
Presented: AJL Annual Convention, June

AJL Judaica Reference Award
Association of Jewish Libraries (AJL) Inc
Affiliate of American Library Association (ALA)
PO Box 1118, Teaneck, NJ 07666
Tel: 201-371-3255
E-mail: info@jewishlibraries.org
Web Site: jewishlibraries.org
Key Personnel
Pres: Amalia Warshenbrot
Ref & Bibliography Awards Comm Chair: Sharon Benamou *E-mail:* benamou@library.ucla.edu
Established: 1984
Annual award for outstanding Judaica reference book published during previous calendar year.
Award: The seal of the Association
Closing Date: March
Presented: AJL Annual Convention, June

AJL Scholarship
Association of Jewish Libraries (AJL) Inc
Affiliate of American Library Association (ALA)
PO Box 1118, Teaneck, NJ 07666
Tel: 201-371-3255
E-mail: scholarship@jewishlibraries.org; info@jewishlibraries.org
Web Site: jewishlibraries.org
In order to encourage students to train for & enter the field of Judaica librarianship, the Association of Jewish Libraries awards a scholarship to a student attending or planning to attend a graduate school of library & information science. Prospective candidates should have an interest in & demonstrate a potential for pursuing a career in Judaica librarianship. In addition, applicants must provide documentation showing participation in Judaica studies at an academic or less formal level +/or experience working in Judaica libraries.
Award: $1,000 per academic year
Closing Date: March 15-April 15 (varies by year)
Presented: AJL Annual Convention, June

Akron Poetry Prize
The University of Akron Press
120 E Mill St, Suite 415, Akron, OH 44308
Tel: 330-972-6960 *Fax:* 330-972-8364
E-mail: uapress@uakron.edu
Web Site: www.uakron.edu/uapress/akron-poetry-prize
Key Personnel
Poetry Ed: Mary Biddinger *E-mail:* marybid@uakron.edu
Established: 1995
Open to all poets writing in English. Mss must be at least 48 pages. Entry fee: $25.
Award: $1,500 & publication
Closing Date: Annually April 15-June 15 (postmark)
Presented: Winner announced online Sept 30

Alabama Artists Fellowship Awards
Alabama State Council on the Arts
201 Monroe St, Suite 110, Montgomery, AL 36130-1800
Tel: 334-242-4076 *Fax:* 334-240-3269
Key Personnel
Exec Dir: Albert B Head
Lit Prog Mgr: Anne Kimzey *Tel:* 334-242-4076 ext 236 *E-mail:* anne.kimzey@arts.alabama.gov
Awarded based on quality of work +/or career status, achievement & potential; two-year residency required & service to the state.
Award: Cash; Two $5,000 fellowships
Closing Date: March 1
Presented: Annually, Oct 1

Alberta Book Awards
The Book Publishers Association of Alberta (BPAA)
10523 100 Ave, Edmonton, AB T5J 0A8, Canada
Tel: 780-424-5060
E-mail: info@bookpublishers.ab.ca
Web Site: www.bookpublishers.ab.ca
Key Personnel
Exec Dir: Kieran Leblanc *E-mail:* kleblanc@bookpublishers.ab.ca
Established: 1989
Awarded annually for excellence in writing & publishing within the province of Alberta.
Award: Sculpture, certificate
Closing Date: Jan
Presented: May

Alcuin Society Awards for Excellence in Book Design in Canada
Alcuin Society
PO Box 3216, Sta Terminal, Vancouver, BC V6B 3X8, Canada
Tel: 604-732-5403
E-mail: awards@alcuinsociety.com
Web Site: alcuinsociety.com
Key Personnel
Chair, Book Design Competition: Leah Gordon
Established: 1981
Annual awards recognizing the work of Canadian book designers & publishers through the Alcuin Citations awarded for excellence in book design & production. Must fulfill the following criteria: titles published in Canada or titles copublished with a publisher in another country but representing a book by a Canadian book designer. Categories are: children, limited editions, pictorial, poetry, prose fiction, prose nonfiction, prose nonfiction illustrated, reference & comics.
Award: Certificate
Closing Date: March 1
Presented: Awards ceremonies in Toronto & Vancouver, Oct

Alex Awards
Young Adult Library Services Association (YALSA)
Division of The American Library Association (ALA)
50 E Huron St, Chicago, IL 60611
Tel: 312-280-4390 *Toll Free Tel:* 800-545-2433 *Fax:* 312-280-5276
E-mail: yalsa@ala.org
Web Site: www.ala.org/yalsa/alex-awards
Key Personnel
Chair: Mara Cota *E-mail:* maracotalib@gmail.com
Exec Dir: Beth Yoke *Tel:* 800-545-2433 ext 4391 *E-mail:* byoke@ala.org
Prog Offr, Continuing Educ: Nicole Gibby-Munguia *Tel:* 800-545-2433 ext 5293 *E-mail:* nmunguia@ala.org
Communs Specialist: Anna Lam *Tel:* 800-545-2433 ext 5849 *E-mail:* alam@ala.org
Established: 1998
Awarded annually to 10 books written for adults that have special appeal to young adults, ages 12-18. The winning titles are selected from the previous year's publishing.
Other Sponsor(s): Margaret A Edwards Trust

Nelson Algren Awards
Chicago Tribune
Subsidiary of Tribune Publishing Co
Chicago Tribune, TT200, 435 N Michigan Ave, Chicago, IL 60611
Toll Free Tel: 800-874-2863 (classifieds) *Fax:* 312-222-5816
Web Site: www.chicagotribune.com/about; algren.submittable.com
Key Personnel
Exec Ed: Terrance Noland
Established: 1981
Given for an outstanding unpublished short fiction, double-spaced & no more than 8,000 words in length, by an American writer. No entry form or fee required. Entry online via Submittable.
Award: One winner ($3,500), 4 finalists ($1,000) & 5 runners-up ($500) each & all stories will be considered for publication in *Printer's Row*
Closing Date: Jan 31
Presented: Chicago, IL, July

The Aliant Creative Writing Award for Young People, see Rotary Club of Charlottetown Royalty Creative Writing Awards for Young People

Alligator Juniper's National Writing Contest
Prescott College, Alligator Juniper
220 Grove Ave, Prescott, AZ 86301
Tel: 928-350-2012
E-mail: alligatorjuniper@prescott.edu
Web Site: alligatorjuniper.wordpress.com
Established: 1995
Annual prizes for fiction, creative nonfiction & poetry. Stories have a 30 page limit per entry or up to 5 poems. Entry fee: $18; no e-mail submissions. See web site for additional submission information.
Award: $1,000 plus publication & copy of spring issue for each of the 3 genres
Closing Date: Aug 15-Oct 15 (postmark)
Presented: Jan

ALSC Baker & Taylor Summer Reading Grant
Formerly ALSC BWI/Summer Reading Program Grant
Association for Library Service to Children (ALSC)
Division of The American Library Association (ALA)
50 E Huron St, Chicago, IL 60611-2795

Tel: 312-280-2163 *Toll Free Tel:* 800-545-2433
Fax: 312-440-9374; 312-280-5271
E-mail: alsc@ala.org
Web Site: www.ala.org/alsc
Key Personnel
Exec Dir: Aimee Strittmatter *Tel:* 312-280-2162
E-mail: astrittmatter@ala.org
Awards Coord: Courtney Jones
E-mail: alscawards@ala.org
Prog Coord: Marsha P Burgess *Tel:* 312-280-2166
E-mail: mburgess@ala.org
Encourages reading programs for children in a public library. Applicant must plan & present an outline for a theme-based summer reading program in a public library.
Award: $3,000
Closing Date: Annually, Nov 1
Presented: The ALA Midwinter Meeting, Press release announced in Dec

ALSC BWI/Summer Reading Program Grant, see ALSC Baker & Taylor Summer Reading Grant

The Ambassador Richard C Holbrooke Distinguished Achievement Award
Dayton Literary Peace Prize Foundation
PO Box 461, Wright Brothers Branch, Dayton, OH 45409-0461
Tel: 937-298-5072
E-mail: sharon.rab@daytonliterarypeaceprize.org
Web Site: www.daytonliterarypeaceprize.org/holbrooke.htm
Key Personnel
Founder & Co-Chair: Sharon Rab *E-mail:* sharon.rab@woh.rr.com
Co-Chair: Mark Meister
Literary award for a body of work that focuses on a central message of peace. Nominated works must have significant & enduring literary value, appeal to a variety of audiences & be in English or translated into English.
Award: $10,000 & sculpture

American Association of University Women Award for Juvenile Literature
AAUW, North Carolina Division
Affiliate of North Carolina Literary & Historical Association
4610 Mail Service Ctr, Raleigh, NC 27699-4610
Tel: 919-807-7290 *Fax:* 919-733-8807
Key Personnel
Awards Coord: Michael Hill *E-mail:* michael.hill@ncdcr.gov
Established: 1953
For a published work of juvenile fiction or nonfiction by a legal or actual resident of North Carolina for at least three years prior to the end of the contest period.
Other Sponsor(s): AAUW
Award: Cup
Closing Date: Annually, July 15
Presented: Raleigh, NC, Annually in Nov

American Book Award
Before Columbus Foundation
The Raymond House, 655 13 St, Suite 302, Oakland, CA 94612
SAN: 159-2955
Tel: 916-425-7916
E-mail: info@beforecolumbusfoundation.com
Web Site: www.beforecolumbusfoundation.com
Key Personnel
Founder: Ishmael Reed
Established: 1978
To recognize outstanding literary achievement by contemporary American authors without restriction for race, sex, ethnic background or genre. The purpose is to acknowledge the excellence & multicultural diversity of American writing. The awards are nonprofit. There are no categories & all winners are accorded equal status. Award is given for books published within the current year. No application forms or fees. Must submit two copies of each entry.
Award: Plaque
Closing Date: Annually, Dec 31
Presented: San Francisco, CA, Annually in Oct

American Illustration/American Photography
Amilus Inc
Subsidiary of Fadner Media
15 E 32 St, 7th fl, New York, NY 10016
Tel: 212-470-0302 *Fax:* 212-532-2064
E-mail: info@ai-ap.com
Web Site: www.ai-ap.com
Key Personnel
Dir: Mark Heflin *E-mail:* mark@ai-ap.com
Established: 1985
For the finest illustrative work by students & professionals. Categories include: editorial, advertising & books, as well as unpublished work. Work will be published in the American Illustration annual & will include the artist's name, address & telephone. Also, similar competition & annual for photography called American Photography. Both books are published in November.
Closing Date: Annually, Jan 23 (photography), Feb 20 (illustration)
Presented: The Party, New York City, Nov, Annually in Nov

American Printing History Association Award
American Printing History Association
PO Box 4519, Grand Central Sta, New York, NY 10163
Tel: 202-544-2422
E-mail: secretary@printinghistory.org
Web Site: printinghistory.org
Key Personnel
Pres: Nina Schneider
VP, Membership: Charles Cuykendall Carter
VP, Progs: Sara T Sauers
VP, Pubns: Katherine McCanless Ruffin
Established: 1976
For a distinguished contribution to the study, recording, preservation or dissemination of printing history, in any specific area or in general terms.
Award: 2 framed award certificates, one for an individual & one for an institution
Presented: APHA meeting, New York, NY, Annually in Jan

The Amy Award
Poets & Writers Inc
90 Broad St, Suite 2100, New York, NY 10004
Tel: 212-226-3586 *Fax:* 212-226-3963
E-mail: admin@pw.org
Web Site: www.pw.org
Presented to women poets age 30 & under living in the New York metropolitan area or on Long Island.
Award: Honorarium & reading in New York City

The Anisfield-Wolf Book Awards
The Cleveland Foundation
1422 Euclid Ave, Suite 1300, Cleveland, OH 44115
Tel: 216-861-3810 *Fax:* 216-861-1729
E-mail: awinfo@clevefdn.org
Web Site: www.anisfield-wolf.org; www.clevelandfoundation.org
Key Personnel
CEO & Pres, Cleveland Foundation: Ronald B Richard
Jury Chmn: Henry Louis Gates, Jr
Mgr: Karen R Long
Established: 1935
Recognizes books that have made important contributions to our understanding of racism or our appreciation of the diversity of human cultures.
Award: $10,000 each (fiction, nonfiction, poetry & Lifetime Achievement)
Closing Date: Dec 31
Presented: Ohio Theatre, Playhouse Square, Cleveland, OH, Annually in Sept

R Ross Annett Award for Children's Literature
Writers' Guild of Alberta
11759 Groat Rd, Edmonton, AB T5M 3K6, Canada
Tel: 780-422-8174 *Toll Free Tel:* 800-665-5354 (AB only) *Fax:* 780-422-2663 (attn WGA)
E-mail: mail@writersguild.ca
Web Site: writersguild.ca
Key Personnel
Exec Dir: Carol Holmes *E-mail:* carol.holmes@writersguild.ca
Communs & Partnerships Coord: Ellen Kartz
E-mail: ellen.kartz@writersguild.ca
Memb Servs Coord: Giorgia Severini
Progs Coord: Natalie Cook *E-mail:* natalie.cook@writersguild.ca; Julie Robinson *E-mail:* julie.robinson@writersguild.ca
Established: 1982
Alternates yearly between picture & chapter books.
Award: $1,500
Closing Date: Annually, Dec 31
Presented: Alberta Literary Awards Gala
Branch Office(s)
505 21 Ave SW, Calgary, AB T2S 0G9, Canada, Prog Coord: Samantha Warwick *Tel:* 403-265-2226 *E-mail:* samantha.warwick@writersguild.ca

Annual & Rolling Grants for Artists
Formerly Vermont Arts Council Grants
Vermont Arts Council
136 State St, Montpelier, VT 05602
Tel: 802-828-5425 *Fax:* 802-828-3363
E-mail: info@vermontartscouncil.org
Web Site: www.vermontartscouncil.org
Key Personnel
Artist & Community Progs Mgr: Sarah Mutrux
Tel: 802-828-5425 *E-mail:* smutrux@vermontartscouncil.org
Established: 1965
Individual grants are given to Vermont residents annually. Artist Development Grants open in July. Creation Grants open in February.
Award: $250-$1,000 Artist Development Grant; $3,000 Creation Grants
Closing Date: Artist Development Grant: rolling deadline; Creation Grant: 1st round March, 2nd round by invitation in April
Presented: Award notifications sent to applicants in Aug

The Applegate/Jackson/Parks Future Teacher Scholarship
National Institute for Labor Relations Research
5211 Port Royal Rd, Suite 510, Springfield, VA 22151
Tel: 703-321-9606 *Fax:* 703-321-7143
Web Site: www.nilrr.org
Key Personnel
Scholarship Admin: Cathy Jones *E-mail:* clj@nrtw.org
Based solely on scholastic ability demonstrating an understanding of compulsory unionism in education. Can submit application online.
Award: $1,000
Closing Date: Annually, Dec 31 (postmark or electronic submission)
Presented: Annually in April-May

The May Hill Arbuthnot Honor Lecture Award
Association for Library Service to Children (ALSC)

Division of The American Library Association (ALA)
50 E Huron St, Chicago, IL 60611-2795
Tel: 312-280-2163 *Toll Free Tel:* 800-545-2433 *Fax:* 312-440-9374; 312-280-5271
E-mail: alsc@ala.org
Web Site: www.ala.org/alsc
Key Personnel
Exec Dir: Aimee Strittmatter *Tel:* 312-280-2162 *E-mail:* astrittmatter@ala.org
Awards Coord: Courtney Jones *E-mail:* alscawards@ala.org
Prog Coord: Marsha P Burgess *Tel:* 312-280-2166 *E-mail:* mburgess@ala.org
Person appointed prepares a paper of significant contribution to the field of children's literature & delivers a lecture based on the paper in April. Libraries & other institutions apply to host the lecture. The paper is also published in the ALSC journal "Children & Libraries".
Award: $5,000
Closing Date: Dec 31
Presented: ALA Midwinter Meeting, Annually in Jan/Feb

Arkansas Diamond Primary Book Award
Arkansas State Library
Arkansas State Library, Suite 100, 900 W Capitol Ave, Little Rock, AR 72201-3108
Tel: 501-682-2860 *Fax:* 501-682-1693
Web Site: www.library.arkansas.gov; www.library.arkansas.gov
Key Personnel
Coord, Children's Progs: Cathy Howser *E-mail:* cathy@library.arkansas.gov
Established: 1999
To encourage reading for students in grades K-3. The Arkansas Department of Education & the Arkansas State Library support selected books that students all over Arkansas read or have read to them. The students vote for the one book they most enjoyed & the winning title recieves the award.
Other Sponsor(s): Arkansas Reading Association
Award: Medallion for 1st place, plaque for Honor Book
Closing Date: Annual vote in April
Presented: Little Rock, AR, Annually in Nov

Artist Grants
South Dakota Arts Council
Affiliate of Department of Tourism
711 E Wells Ave, Pierre, SD 57501-3369
Tel: 605-773-3301 *Fax:* 605-773-5977
E-mail: sdac@state.sd.us
Web Site: www.artscouncil.sd.gov/grants
Key Personnel
Dir: Patrick Baker
Awards made to residents of South Dakota, based on the quality of art work.
Award: $1,000-$5,000
Closing Date: Annually, March 1

Artist-in-Residence Program
New Brunswick Arts Board (Conseil des arts du Nouveau-Brunswick)
225 King St, Suite 201, Fredericton, NB E3B 1E1, Canada
Tel: 506-444-4444 *Toll Free Tel:* 866-460-ARTS (460-2787) *Fax:* 506-444-5543
Web Site: www.artsnb.ca
Key Personnel
Exec Dir: Joss Richer *Tel:* 506-478-4610 *E-mail:* execdirgen@artsnb.ca
Prog Offr: Sarah Beth Shiplett *Tel:* 506-440-0037 *E-mail:* sarahbeth@artsnb.ca
Opers Mgr: Tilly Jackson *Tel:* 506-478-4422 *E-mail:* tjackson@artsnb.ca
Intended for New Brunswick public or private institutions & organizations that wish to host professional artists in order to enable them to pursue specific projects relating to their creative work. This program is also open to individual professionals who seek to advance their creative work through participation in residency opportunities at home or outside the province. The artists in residence are to contribute to the promotion & understanding of the arts by means of the artists' contact with the clientele of the establishments.
Closing Date: Feb 1

Artist Projects Grants, see Artist Research & Development Grants

Artist Research & Development Grants
Formerly Artist Projects Grants
Arizona Commission on the Arts
417 W Roosevelt St, Phoenix, AZ 85003-1326
Tel: 602-771-6501 *Fax:* 602-256-0282
E-mail: info@azarts.gov
Web Site: www.azarts.gov
Key Personnel
Artists Servs Mgr: Gabriela Munoz *E-mail:* gmunoz@azarts.gov
Designed to support individual artists from all disciplines. The purpose of this grant is to aid in the development of artistic work, support the advancement of artistic research & recognize the contributions individual artists make to Arizona's communities.
The Bill Desmond Writing Award provides support to excelling nonfiction writers for specific project-related costs. This award offers funding support in the amount of $1,000 to one nonfiction writer applying for the Artist Research & Development Grant & can be offered independent of, or in addition to, the ARDG award. Funding for the Bill Desmond Writing Award is generously provided by the Bill & Kathy Desmond Endowment.
Award: $3,000-$5,000
Closing Date: Aug/Sept

Artists' Fellowships
New York Foundation for the Arts
20 Jay St, 7th fl, Brooklyn, NY 11201
Tel: 212-366-6900 *Fax:* 212-366-1778
E-mail: info@nyfa.org
Web Site: www.nyfa.org
Key Personnel
Exec Dir: Michael Royce *E-mail:* mroyce@nyfa.org
Dir, Progs: David Perry *E-mail:* dperry@nyfa.org
Exec Asst: Lauren Hilger *E-mail:* lhilger@nyfa.org
Fellowship applications limited to New York State residents. Applications will be open Fall 2017. Grants awarded in 15 artistic disciplines over a 3-year period.
Award: $7,000
Closing Date: Annually in Dec
Presented: New York, NY

Arts & Letters Awards
American Academy of Arts & Letters
633 W 155 St, New York, NY 10032
Tel: 212-368-5900 *Fax:* 212-491-4615
E-mail: academy@artsandletters.org
Web Site: www.artsandletters.org
Key Personnel
Exec Dir: Cody Upton
Given annually to artists, writers, composers & architects to encourage creative work in the arts.
Award: $10,000 each (8 awards to writers)

Arts Scholarships
New Brunswick Arts Board (Conseil des arts du Nouveau-Brunswick)
225 King St, Suite 201, Fredericton, NB E3B 1E1, Canada
Tel: 506-444-4444 *Toll Free Tel:* 866-460-ARTS (460-2787) *Fax:* 506-444-5543
Web Site: www.artsnb.ca
Key Personnel
Exec Dir: Joss Richer *Tel:* 506-478-4610 *E-mail:* execdirgen@artsnb.ca
Prog Offr: Sarah Beth Shiplett *Tel:* 506-440-0037 *E-mail:* sarahbeth@artsnb.ca
Opers Mgr: Tilly Jackson *Tel:* 506-478-4422 *E-mail:* tjackson@artsnb.ca
Designed to recognize & encourage New Brunswick students who have demonstrated exceptional artistic talent & potential & who are pursuing a career in the arts. This program awards scholarships for full-time, part-time or short-term studies.
Closing Date: Feb 1

ASF Translation Awards
American-Scandinavian Foundation (ASF)
Scandinavia House, 58 Park Ave, New York, NY 10016
Tel: 212-879-9779; 212-779-3587 *Fax:* 212-686-2115
E-mail: grants@amscan.org
Web Site: www.amscan.org
Key Personnel
Fellowships & Grant Offr: Carl Fritscher
Established: 1980
For translations of contemporary poetry or fiction by Danish, Finnish, Icelandic, Norwegian or Swedish authors born after 1800. Write to ASF or visit the ASF web site for full copy of rules.
Award: $2,500 Nadia Christensen Prize & $2,000 Inger Sjoberg Prize (given to an individual whose literature translations have not previously been published). Both prizes include a publication of excerpt in an issue of *Scandinavian Review* & a commemorative bronze medallion
Closing Date: Annually, June 15
Presented: Varies

ASI/EIS Publishing Award for Excellence in Indexing
Formerly H W Wilson Co Indexing Award
American Society for Indexing Inc (ASI)
1628 E Southern Ave, Suite 9-223, Tempe, AZ 85282
Tel: 480-245-6750
E-mail: info@asindexing.org
Web Site: www.asindexing.org
Key Personnel
Exec Dir: Gwen Henson *E-mail:* gwen@asindexing.org
Established: 1978
Awarded to the indexer & the publisher of year's best index.
Award: $1,000 & citation (indexer), citation (publisher)
Closing Date: Annually in Feb
Presented: Annual Conference

Asian American Literary Awards
Asian American Writers' Workshop
112 W 27 St, Suite 600, New York, NY 10001
Tel: 212-494-0061
E-mail: aala@aaww.org
Web Site: aaww.org/aala
Honors Asian American writers for excellence in three categories: fiction, poetry & nonfiction. Entry fee: $100.
Closing Date: Annually in Spring
Presented: AAWW Food & Books Festival

Aspen Words Literary Prize
Aspen Words
110 E Hallam St, Suite 116, Aspen, CO 81611
Tel: 970-925-3122 *Fax:* 970-920-5700
E-mail: literary.prize@aspeninstitute.org
Web Site: www.aspenwords.org

Key Personnel
Exec Dir: Adrienne Brodeur *Tel:* 646-461-3554 *E-mail:* adrienne.brodeur@aspeninstitute.org
Mng Dir: Jamie Kravitz *Tel:* 970-925-3122 ext 2 *E-mail:* jamie.kravitz@aspeninstitute.org
Sr Prog Assoc, Mktg & Communs: Caroline Tory *Tel:* 970-925-3122 ext 3 *E-mail:* caroline.tory@aspeninstitute.org
Established: 2017
Award for an influential work of fiction that focuses on vital issues - social, political, economic, environmental or otherwise - thus demonstrating the transformative power that literature has on thought & culture. Submissions accepted from publishers only. Book must be work of fiction published by a US trade publisher in the prior calendar year. Inaugural award will be conferred for books published January 1, 2017 to December 31, 2017. Submission process opens February 1. $30 entry fee for each title submitted. See web site for online submission form & full details.
Award: $35,000
Closing Date: Aug 1
Presented: Annually in Spring

Athenaeum of Philadelphia Literary Award
Athenaeum of Philadelphia
219 S Sixth St, Philadelphia, PA 19106
Tel: 215-925-2688 *Fax:* 215-925-3755
Web Site: www.philaathenaeum.org/literary.html
Key Personnel
Libn: Jill LeMin Lee *E-mail:* jilly@philaathenaeum.org
Established: 1950
In recognition & encouragement of outstanding literary achievement in Philadelphia & the vicinity.
Award: Citation
Closing Date: Annually, Dec 1
Presented: Annually in Spring

Atlantic Poetry Prize, see J M Abraham Poetry Award

Atlantic Public Art Funders (APAF) Creative Residency
New Brunswick Arts Board (Conseil des arts du Nouveau-Brunswick)
225 King St, Suite 201, Fredericton, NB E3B 1E1, Canada
Tel: 506-444-4444 *Toll Free Tel:* 866-460-ARTS (460-2787) *Fax:* 506-444-5543
Web Site: www.artsnb.ca
Key Personnel
Exec Dir: Joss Richer *Tel:* 506-478-4610 *E-mail:* execdirgen@artsnb.ca
Prog Offr: Sarah Beth Shiplett *Tel:* 506-440-0037 *E-mail:* sarahbeth@artsnb.ca
Opers Mgr: Tilly Jackson *Tel:* 506-478-4422 *E-mail:* tjackson@artsnb.ca
Artists from New Brunswick, Nova Scotia, PEI or Newfoundland & Labrador can apply. Covers a 1- to 3-month residency for a creation-based or professional development project in the province that isn't their own. The agreement establishes an annual exchange program that provides professional artists with opportunities for creation & professional development residencies in the participating provinces. Artists participating in this program enjoy complete autonomy & define the objectives of their period of residence & elaborate the parameters & conditions governing its realization in collaboration with an arts community organization in the territory where the period of residence is to take place.
Other Sponsor(s): Arts Nova Scotia; Newfoundland & Labrador Arts Council; Prince Edward Island Council of the Arts
Award: Up to $10,000
Closing Date: Feb 1

The Audies®
Audio Publishers Association (APA)
333 Hudson St, Suite 503, New York, NY 10013
Tel: 646-688-3044
E-mail: audies@audiopub.org; info@audiopub.org
Web Site: www.audiopub.org/members/audies
Key Personnel
Exec Dir: Michele Cobb *E-mail:* mcobb@audiopub.org
Premier awards program in the US recognizing distinction in audiobooks & spoken word entertainment. Publishers & rights holders enter titles in various categories for recognition of achievement. Finalists are selected & announced in February. From that group of finalists, one winner is awarded. Qualifying audiobooks contain at least 51% spoken word content & are available for sale in the US as CDs +/or in digital format. Entry fee: $100 members, $200 nonmembers.
Award: Medallions
Presented: Audies Awards Gala, Annually in May/June

Autumn House Poetry, Fiction & Nonfiction Contests
Autumn House Press
5530 Penn Ave, Pittsburgh, PA 15206
Mailing Address: PO Box 5486, Pittsburgh, PA 15206
Tel: 412-362-2665
E-mail: info@autumnhouse.org
Web Site: www.autumnhouse.org
Poetry Prize: All full-length collections of poetry 50-80 pages in length are eligible.
Fiction Contest: Submissions should be approximately 200-300 pages. All fiction sub-genres or any combination of sub-genres are eligible.
Nonfiction Contest: Submissions should be approximately 200-300 pages. All nonfiction subjects are eligible.
Enclose $30 handling fee for each prize. See web site for complete guidelines.
Award: $1,000, book publication, advance against royalties & $1,500 travel grant
Closing Date: Annually, June 30

Award of Merit
American Academy of Arts & Letters
633 W 155 St, New York, NY 10032
Tel: 212-368-5900 *Fax:* 212-491-4615
E-mail: academy@artsandletters.org
Web Site: www.artsandletters.org
Key Personnel
Exec Dir: Cody Upton
Established: 1942
Given annually, in rotation, to an outstanding person in America representing one of the following arts: Painting, the Short Story, Sculpture, the Novel, Poetry & Drama.
Award: $25,000 & medal

AWP Award Series
Association of Writers & Writing Programs (AWP)
George Mason University, 4400 University Dr, MSN 1E3, Fairfax, VA 22030
Tel: 703-993-4301 *Fax:* 703-993-4302
E-mail: awp@awpwriter.org
Web Site: www.awpwriter.org
Key Personnel
Exec Dir: David W Fenza
Dir, Conferences: Christian Teresi
Dir, Devt: Pamela Mills
Dir, Membership Servs: Diane Zinna
Dir, Pubns: Supriya Bhatnagar
Assoc Ed: Jason Gray
Established: 1967
An open competition for book-length mss in 4 categories: poetry, short fiction, novel & creative (nonfiction). Send business-size SASE after November 1 for submission guidelines.
Award: Publication by a major university press & an honorarium of $2,500 for nonfiction & novel. Donald Hall Prize in poetry-honorarium $5,500. Grace Paley Prize for short fiction-honorarium $5,500. One winner in each category
Closing Date: Annually, Feb 28 (postmark)

Axiom Business Book Awards
Independent Publisher Online
Division of Jenkins Group Inc
1129 Woodmere Ave, Suite B, Traverse City, MI 49686
Tel: 231-933-0445 *Toll Free Tel:* 800-706-4636 *Fax:* 231-933-0448
E-mail: info@axiomawards.com
Web Site: www.axiomawards.com
Key Personnel
CEO: Jerrold R Jenkins *E-mail:* jrj@bookpublishing.com
Pres: James Kalajian *Tel:* 800-706-4636 ext 1006 *E-mail:* jjk@bookpublishing.com
Mng Ed & Awards Dir: Jim Barnes *Tel:* 800-706-4636 ext 1011 *E-mail:* jimb@bookpublishing.com
Awards Coord: Amy Shamroe
Established: 2006
US based award contest focused solely on business books. The goal of the awards is to celebrate the innovative, intelligent & creative aspects of the books that make us think, see & work differently every day. The awards offer no global boundaries, giving participants from every continent the opportunity to earn further recognition for their English language titles. All publishers are eligible, ranging from large multi-title publishing houses to small one title publishers. Publishers can be throughout North America & overseas publishers who publish English language books intended for the American market. Print-on-demand & other independent authors are welcome to enter their books themselves.
Other Sponsor(s): Books Are Marketing Tools; Independent Publisher; Jenkins Group
Award: Gold medal (1st place), silver medal (2nd place) & bronze medal (3rd place)
Closing Date: Annually in Jan
Presented: BookExpo, Annually in May

Marilyn Baillie Picture Book Award
Canadian Children's Book Centre
40 Orchard View Blvd, Suite 217, Toronto, ON M4R 1B9, Canada
Tel: 416-975-0010 *Fax:* 416-975-8970
E-mail: info@bookcentre.ca
Web Site: www.bookcentre.ca
Key Personnel
Exec Dir: Charlotte Teeple *E-mail:* charlotte@bookcentre.ca
Lib Coord: Meghan Howe *E-mail:* meghan@bookcentre.ca
Mktg & Web Site Coord: Camilia Kahrizi *E-mail:* camilia@bookcentre.ca
Prog Coord: Shannon Howe Barnes *E-mail:* shannon@bookcentre.ca
Established: 2006
Awarded to a Canadian author & illustrator for excellence in the illustrated picture book format for children ages 3-8.
Other Sponsor(s): Charles Baillie
Award: $20,000 cash
Closing Date: Annually in mid-Dec

Baker & Taylor/YALSA Conference Grants
Young Adult Library Services Association (YALSA)
Division of The American Library Association (ALA)
50 E Huron St, Chicago, IL 60611
Tel: 312-280-4390 *Toll Free Tel:* 800-545-2433 *Fax:* 312-280-5276; 312-664-7459
E-mail: yalsa@ala.org

Web Site: www.ala.org/yalsa
Key Personnel
Exec Dir: Beth Yoke *Tel:* 800-545-2433 ext 4391 *E-mail:* byoke@ala.org
Prog Offr, Events & Conferences: Nichole O'Connor *Tel:* 800-545-2433 ext 4387 *E-mail:* noconnor@ala.org
Communs Specialist: Anna Lam *Tel:* 800-545-2433 ext 5849 *E-mail:* alam@ala.org
Established: 1983
Awarded to librarians who work directly with young adults to enable them to attend the Annual Conference for the first time. Two grants given annually, one to a school librarian & one to a public librarian.
Other Sponsor(s): Baker & Taylor
Award: $1,000 each
Closing Date: Annually, Dec 1
Presented: ALA's Midwinter Meeting

Nona Balakian Citation for Excellence in Reviewing
National Book Critics Circle
160 Varick St, 11th fl, New York, NY 10013
E-mail: info@bookcritics.org
Web Site: bookcritics.org
Key Personnel
Comm Chair: Gregg Barrios *E-mail:* greggbarr@outlook.com
Awarded annually to recognize outstanding work by a member of NBCC. Send up to five book reviews (all published during the year of the award) of no more than 5,000 words collectively. For e-mail submissions, include a note listing the venue along with title & word count of each piece submitted. Send links to your reviews as published online. For submissions in hard copy via mail, include brief cover letter listing the title & word count of each piece submitted.
Award: $1,000

The Balcones Fiction Prize
The Balcones Center for Creative Writing
Subsidiary of Austin Community College
1212 Rio Grande St, Austin, TX 78701
Tel: 512-828-9368
E-mail: balcones@austincc.edu
Web Site: sites.austincc.edu/crw/balcones-prizes
Key Personnel
Assoc Dir: John Herndon *E-mail:* jherndon@austincc.edu
Recognizes an outstanding book of fiction published during the year. Books of prose may be submitted by author or publisher. Send 3 copies. Books must bear a publication date within the calendar year prior to the year of the award. Reading fee: $30.
Award: $1,500
Closing Date: Jan 31

The Balcones Poetry Prize
The Balcones Center for Creative Writing
Subsidiary of Austin Community College
1212 Rio Grande St, Austin, TX 78701
Tel: 512-828-9368
E-mail: balcones@austincc.edu
Web Site: www.austincc.edu/crw/html/balconescenter.html
Key Personnel
Assoc Dir: John Herndon *E-mail:* jherndon@austincc.edu
Established: 1994
Recognizes an outstanding book of poetry published during the year. Books of poetry of 42 pages or more may be submitted by author or publisher. Send 3 copies. Must bear a publication date of the previous calendar year. $25 reading fee.
Award: $1,500
Closing Date: Jan 31

Bancroft Prizes
Columbia University
517 Butler Library, Mail Code 1101, 535 W 114 St, New York, NY 10027
Tel: 212-854-4746 *Fax:* 212-854-9099
Web Site: www.columbia.edu/about/awards/bancroft.html
Key Personnel
Communs & Devt Assoc: Matt Hampel
Established: 1948
Two awards presented annually for distinguished books in the fields of American history (including biography) & diplomacy. Award confined to books originally published in English or those with a published English translation. Books published in year preceding that in which award is made are eligible. Submit four copies & nominating letter.
Award: $10,000 each
Closing Date: Nov 1, page-proof copy may be submitted after Nov 1, provided the work will be published after that date & before Dec 31
Presented: Columbia University, Spring

Barnes & Noble Writers for Writers Award
Poets & Writers Inc
90 Broad St, Suite 2100, New York, NY 10004
Tel: 212-226-3586 *Fax:* 212-226-3963
E-mail: admin@pw.org
Web Site: www.pw.org
Established: 1996
Celebrates authors who have given generously to other writers or to the broader literary community.

Baskerville Publishers Poetry Award
Texas Christian University
Dept of English, TCU Box 298300, Fort Worth, TX 76129
Tel: 817-257-5907 *Fax:* 817-257-5905
E-mail: descant@tcu.edu
Web Site: www.descant.tcu.edu
Key Personnel
Mng Ed: Dan Williams *E-mail:* d.e.williams@tcu.edu
Established: 2003
Annual award for an outstanding poem or poems by a single author in an issue. All published submissions are eligible for prize consideration. There is no application process.
Other Sponsor(s): descant (publication), Dept of English, TCU
Award: $250
Closing Date: Sept 1-April 1
Presented: Winner announced in journal in Summer

The Mildred L Batchelder Award
Association for Library Service to Children (ALSC)
Division of The American Library Association (ALA)
50 E Huron St, Chicago, IL 60611-2795
Tel: 312-280-2163 *Toll Free Tel:* 800-545-2433 *Fax:* 312-440-9374; 312-280-5271
E-mail: alsc@ala.org
Web Site: www.ala.org/alsc
Key Personnel
Exec Dir: Aimee Strittmatter *Tel:* 312-280-2162 *E-mail:* astrittmatter@ala.org
Awards Coord: Courtney Jones *E-mail:* alscawards@ala.org
Prog Coord: Marsha P Burgess *Tel:* 312-280-2166 *E-mail:* mburgess@ala.org
Established: 1966
Awarded annually to an American publisher for an outstanding book originally published in a foreign language in a foreign country & subsequently translated to English & published in the US during the previous year.
Award: Citation
Closing Date: Dec 31
Presented: ALA Midwinter Meeting, Jan/Feb

The BC Book Prizes
West Coast Book Prize Society
207 W Hastings St, Suite 901, Vancouver, BC V6B 1H7, Canada
Fax: 604-687-2435
E-mail: info@bcbookprizes.ca
Web Site: www.bcbookprizes.ca
Key Personnel
Exec Dir: Bryan Pike *E-mail:* bryan@rebuscreative.com
Gen Mgr: Val Mason *E-mail:* val@rebuscreative.com
Creative Publicity: Karen Green *E-mail:* karen@rebuscreative.com
Proj Coord: Kristie Poole *E-mail:* kristie@rebuscreative.com
Established: 1985
The following BC Book Prizes are awarded to a resident of BC or one who has lived in BC for 3 of the past 5 years: to the author of the best work of fiction; best book written for children 16 years & younger; best original nonfiction literary work; author of the best work of poetry. The following BC Book Prizes are also offered: originating publisher of the best book judged in terms of public appeal, initiative, design, production & content (publisher must have their head office in BC); author of the book which contributes most to the appreciation & understanding of BC (published anywhere & the author may reside outside BC); author & illustrator of the best picture book written for children (author/illustrator must be a BC/Yukon resident or have lived in BC or the Yukon for 3 of the past 5 years).
Other Sponsor(s): Ampersand Inc; BC Teachers' Federation; British Columbia Booksellers Association; British Columbia Library Association; Canadian Manda Group; First Choice Books; Friends of Sheila Egoff; Friesens; Victoria Bindery; Kate Walke; WBRA
Award: $2,000 & certificate
Closing Date: Annually, Dec 1, with exceptions made for books published in Dec
Presented: The British Columbia Book Prizes Banquet, Spring

BCHF Historical Writing Competition
British Columbia Historical Federation
PO Box 5254, Sta B, Victoria, BC V8R 6N4, Canada
E-mail: writing@bchistory.ca
Web Site: www.bchistory.ca
Key Personnel
Dir: Maurice Guibord
Top prize is presented annually to the author whose book makes the most significant contribution to the historical literature of British Columbia. The book must be published within the competition year. Additional prizes also given.
Award: $2,500 & The BC Lieutenant-Governor's Medal for Historical Writing (1st place), $1,500 (2nd place), $500 (3rd place), Certificates of Honourable Mention, $500 Community History Award
Closing Date: Dec 31
Presented: BCHF Annual Awards Banquet, May/June

James Beard Foundation Book Awards
James Beard Foundation
Office of Awards, 6 W 18 St, 10th fl, New York, NY 10011
Tel: 212-627-1111 (ext 563)
Web Site: www.jamesbeard.org/awards
Established: 1991
Book, broadcast & journalism awards in the food & beverage industry. Begins October 15 annually.

Award: Certificate, silver colored medallion & complimentary 1-year foundation membership
Presented: Annually in Spring

George Louis Beer Prize
American Historical Association (AHA)
400 "A" St SE, Washington, DC 20003
Tel: 202-544-2422 *Fax:* 202-544-8307
E-mail: awards@historians.org
Web Site: www.historians.org
Established: 1923
Recognition of outstanding historical writing in European international history since 1895 that is submitted by a scholar who is a US citizen or permanent resident. Books published in 2017 are eligible. Only books of a high scholarly historical nature should be submitted. Along with an application form, applicants must mail a copy of their book to each of the prize committee members who will be posted on our web site as the prize deadline approaches. All updated info on web site.
Award: Cash prize
Closing Date: May 15, 2018
Presented: AHA Annual Meeting, Chicago, IL, Jan 2019

The Pura Belpre Award
Association for Library Service to Children (ALSC)
Division of The American Library Association (ALA)
50 E Huron St, Chicago, IL 60611-2795
Tel: 312-280-2163 *Toll Free Tel:* 800-545-2433 *Fax:* 312-440-9374; 312-280-5271
E-mail: alsc@ala.org
Web Site: www.ala.org/alsc
Key Personnel
Exec Dir: Aimee Strittmatter *Tel:* 312-280-2162 *E-mail:* astrittmatter@ala.org
Awards Coord: Courtney Jones *E-mail:* alscawards@ala.org
Prog Coord: Marsha P Burgess *Tel:* 312-280-2166 *E-mail:* mburgess@ala.org
Established: 1996
Annual award presented to a Latino/Latina writer & illustrator whose children's work best celebrates the Latino cultural experience.
Other Sponsor(s): National Association to Promote Library & Information Services to Latinos & the Spanish Speaking (REFORMA)
Award: Medal
Closing Date: Annually, Dec 31
Presented: ALA Midwinter Meeting, Jan/Feb

Benjamin Franklin Awards™
The Independent Book Publishers Association (IBPA)
1020 Manhattan Beach Blvd, Suite 204, Manhattan Beach, CA 90266
Tel: 310-546-1818 *Fax:* 310-546-3939
E-mail: info@ibpa-online.org
Web Site: www.ibpa-online.org; ibpabenjaminfranklinawards.com
Key Personnel
COO: Terry Nathan *E-mail:* terry@ibpa-online.org
Established: 1987
Excellence in independent publishing in specific genre & design (books, audio & video). Trophies are presented to the publishers during a gala awards ceremony on the last evening of the Publishing University. Entry fee: membs $95/title/category; nonmembs $225/first title (includes 1 yr membership); $95/additional titles.
Award: Gold winners: Engraved crystal trophy & award certificates with gold stickers. Silver winners: Award certificates with silver stickers
Closing Date: Sept 30 (1st call) & Dec 15 (2nd call)
Presented: May

George Bennett Fellowship
Phillips Exeter Academy
Phillips Exeter Academy, Off of the Dean of Faculty, 20 Main St, Exeter, NH 03833-2460
Tel: 603-772-4311 *Fax:* 603-777-4384
E-mail: teaching_opportunities@exeter.edu
Web Site: www.exeter.edu
Established: 1968
Established to provide support for 1 academic year for an individual contemplating or pursuing a career as a professional writer. Selection is based on the literary promise of the ms submitted. The committee favors applicants who have not yet published a book-length work with a major publisher. Send SASE for application or obtain from the Academy web site. Telephone inquiries strongly discouraged. Application fee: $15. Applications accepted beginning October 1.
Award: $15,260, housing & board at the Academy for the academic year & health insurance
Closing Date: Nov 30
Presented: Annually in April

Naomi Berber Memorial Award
Printing Industries of America
301 Brush Creek Rd, Warrendale, PA 15086-7529
Tel: 412-741-6860 *Toll Free Tel:* 800-910-4283 *Fax:* 412-741-2311
E-mail: printingind@comm.printing.org
Web Site: www.printing.org/berberaward
Key Personnel
Pres & CEO: Michael F Makin *Tel:* 412-259-1777 *E-mail:* mmakin@printing.org
VP, Educ & Mktg Strategies: Julie Schaffer
Sr Mktg Mgr: Jenn Strang *Tel:* 412-259-1810 *E-mail:* jstrang@printing.org
Mktg Mgr: Kayleigh Smith *E-mail:* ksmith@printing.org
Established: 1976
Honors a woman who has made a major contribution to the development of the printing industry. A nominee must have worked in the printing industry for 10 years or more. See web site for more information.
Other Sponsor(s): Printing Industries of America's Ben Franklin Society
Award: Engraved plaque
Closing Date: June
Presented: Printing Industries of America Fall Administrative Meetings
Branch Office(s)
1001 "G" St NW, Suite 800, Washington, DC 20001 *Tel:* 202-627-6924

Jessie Bernard Award
American Sociological Association (ASA)
c/o Governance Off, 1430 "K" St NW, Suite 600, Washington, DC 20005
Tel: 202-383-9005 *Fax:* 202-638-0882
E-mail: governance@asanet.org
Web Site: www.asanet.org
Key Personnel
Dir, Admin & Governance: Michael Murphy *Tel:* 202-383-9005 ext 327
Prog Coord: Jordan Robison *Tel:* 202-383-9005 ext 334
For scholarly contributions that enlarge the horizons of sociology to encompass fully the role of women in society. Winner announced in *Footnotes* newsletter, an ASA publication. See web site for future awards.
Award: Plaque
Closing Date: Jan 31
Presented: ASA Annual Meeting, Montreal, QC, CN, Annually in Aug

The Charles Bernheimer Prize
American Comparative Literature Association (ACLA)
University of South Carolina, Dept of Languages, Literature & Cultures, 1620 College St, Rm 813-A, Columbia, SC 29208
Tel: 803-777-3021
E-mail: info@acla.org
Web Site: www.acla.org/prize-awards
Key Personnel
Nominations Comm Chair: Antonio Barrenechea *E-mail:* abarrene@umw.edu
Admin Coord: Andy Anderson
An outstanding dissertation in comparative literature defended in the year prior to July 1. See web site for application details.
Award: $1,000 & a certificate, complimentary registration, airfare & hotel accommodations (not including food), to facilitate the recipient attending the ACLA annual meeting
Closing Date: Oct 1
Presented: ACLA Annual Meeting, July

Best Translated Book Award
Three Percent
c/o Open Letter, University of Rochester, Dewey Hall 1-219, Box 278968, Rochester, NY 14627
Tel: 585-276-5305
E-mail: msc@rochester.edu
Web Site: besttranslatedbook.org
Key Personnel
Founder & Publr: Chad Post *E-mail:* chad.post@rochester.edu
Established: 2007
Recognizes the previous year's best original translation of a work of fiction & a work of poetry into English. Long & short lists announced leading up to the award. Original translations must have been published in the previous calendar year. Reprints & retranslation are ineligible. No entry fee. Mail one copy or send e-version of publication to each of the appropriate panelists (see web site for list of judges or contact Chad Post).
Other Sponsor(s): Amazon Literary Partnership
Award: $5,000 to both author(s) & translator(s)
Presented: May

Doris Betts Fiction Prize
North Carolina Writers' Network
PO Box 21591, Winston-Salem, NC 27120-1591
Tel: 336-293-8844
E-mail: mail@ncwriters.org; nclrsubmissions@ecu.edu
Web Site: www.ncwriters.org
Key Personnel
Exec Dir: Ed Southern *E-mail:* ed@ncwriters.org
Open to any writer who is a legal resident of North Carolina or a amember of the NCWN. *North Carolina Literary Review* subscribers with North Carolina connections (lives or has lived in NC) are also eligible. The competition is for previously unpublished short stories up to 6,000 words. Multiple entries ok, but each requires a separate entry fee. No novel excerpts. Submit previously unpublished stories online at https://nclr.submittable.com/submit. Entry fee: $10 NCWN members or NCLR subscribers, $20 nonmembs/non-subscribers. Documents must be Microsoft Word or .rtf files. Stories should be double-spaced. Author's name should not appear on mss.
If submitting by mail, send story ms with cover sheet providing name, address, e-mail address, word count & ms title to: NCLR, ECU Mailstop, 555 English, Greenville, NC 27858-4353 (but mail payment per instructions on web site).
Award: $250 1st prize & publication in the *North Carolina Literary Review*. Finalists also considered for publication
Closing Date: Annually, Feb 15
Presented: May 1

Beullah Rose Poetry Prize
Smartish Pace

PO Box 22161, Baltimore, MD 21203
E-mail: smartishpace@gmail.com
Web Site: www.smartishpace.com
Key Personnel
Assoc Ed: Clare Banks *E-mail:* cbsmartishpace@gmail.com
Established: 2005
Prize for exceptional poetry by women. All poems submitted for the prize will be considered for publication in *Smartish Pace*. Online submissions at www.smartishpace.com. Postal submissions: submit 3 poems along with a $10 entry fee. Additional poems may be submitted for $1 per poem. No more than 20 poems may be submitted. All entries must include a bio. Include SASE with entry. Include name, address, e-mail & telephone number on each page of poetry submitted. Write or print "Beullah Rose Poetry Prize" on top of each poem submitted.
Award: $200 & publication of winning poem in *Smartish Pace* (1st prize). All finalists will be published in *Smartish Pace*
Closing Date: Annually, Nov 15
Presented: Baltimore, MD

Albert J Beveridge Award in American History
American Historical Association (AHA)
400 "A" St SE, Washington, DC 20003
Tel: 202-544-2422 *Fax:* 202-544-8307
E-mail: awards@historians.org
Web Site: www.historians.org
Established: 1939
To promote & honor outstanding historical writing. The award is given for a distinguished book in English on the history of the US, Latin America, or Canada, from 1492 to the present. Books that employ new methodological or conceptual tools or that constitute significant reexaminations of important interpretive problems will be given preference. Literary merit is also an important criterion. Biographies, monographs & works of synthesis & interpretation are eligible; translations, anthologies & collections of documents are not. Books published in 2017 are eligible for the award; limited to 5 titles from any one publisher & must be submitted by sending a copy to each member of the committee, along with an application form. All updated info on web site.
Award: Cash prize
Closing Date: May 15, 2018
Presented: AHA Annual Meeting, Chicago, IL, Jan 2019

Albert J Beveridge Grant for Research in the History of the Western Hemisphere
American Historical Association (AHA)
400 "A" St SE, Washington, DC 20003
Tel: 202-544-2422 *Fax:* 202-544-8307
E-mail: awards@historians.org
Web Site: www.historians.org
Established: 1939
To support research in the history of the Western hemisphere (US, CN & Latin America). Only members of the Association are eligible. The grants are intended to further research in progress & may be used for travel to a library or archive, for microfilms, photographs or photocopying - a list of purposes that is meant to be merely illustrative not exhaustive. Preference will be given to those with specific research needs, such as the completion of a project or completion of a discrete segment thereof; preference will be given to PhD candidates & junior scholars. Application forms available on web site. Applications must include application form with estimated budget, curriculum vita & statement of no more than 750 words. A one-page bibliography of the most recent relevant, secondary works on the topic. Mailed & faxed submissions are not accepted.
Award: Individual grants will not exceed $1,000
Closing Date: Annually, Feb 15

BHTG - Julie Harris Playwright Award Competition
The Beverly Hills Theatre Guild
PO Box 148, Beverly Hills, CA 90213
Tel: 310-273-3390
Web Site: www.beverlyhillstheatreguild.com
Key Personnel
Pres: Carolyn Fried
Competition Coord: Candace Coster
Established: 1978
For playwrights. Application & guidelines available upon request with SASE.
Award: $3,500, $2,500 & $1,500
Closing Date: Annually, Jan 1-April 1
Presented: Los Angeles, CA, Annually, June 30 (announcement)

BHTG - Michael J Libow Youth Theatre Award
Formerly Marilyn Hall Awards
The Beverly Hills Theatre Guild
PO Box 148, Beverly Hills, CA 90213
Tel: 310-273-3390
Web Site: www.beverlyhillstheatreguild.com
Key Personnel
Pres: Carolyn Fried
Competition Coord: Candace Coster
Established: 1999
Playwright, children's theatre grade 6th-8th, 9th-12th grade.
Award: $1,200, $600
Closing Date: Annually, Jan 15 through last day of Feb (postmark)
Presented: Los Angeles, CA, Annually, June 30

The Geoffrey Bilson Award for Historical Fiction for Young People
Canadian Children's Book Centre
40 Orchard View Blvd, Suite 217, Toronto, ON M4R 1B9, Canada
Tel: 416-975-0010 *Fax:* 416-975-8970
E-mail: info@bookcentre.ca
Web Site: www.bookcentre.ca
Key Personnel
Exec Dir: Charlotte Teeple *E-mail:* charlotte@bookcentre.ca
Lib Coord: Meghan Howe *E-mail:* meghan@bookcentre.ca
Mktg & Web Site Coord: Camilia Kahrizi *E-mail:* camilia@bookcentre.ca
Prog Coord: Shannon Howe Barnes *E-mail:* shannon@bookcentre.ca
Established: 1988
Awarded to a Canadian author for an outstanding work of historical fiction for young people.
Award: $5,000
Closing Date: Annually in mid-Dec

Robert Bingham Prize for Debut Fiction, see PEN/Robert Bingham Prize for Debut Fiction

Binghamton University John Gardner Fiction Book Award
The Binghamton Center for Writers-State University of New York
Dept of English, General Literature & Rhetoric, Library N, Rm 1149, Vestal Pkwy E, Binghamton, NY 13902
Mailing Address: PO Box 6000, Binghamton, NY 13902-6000
Tel: 607-777-2713
Web Site: www2.binghamton.edu/english/creative-writing
Key Personnel
Dir: Maria Mazziotti Gillan *Tel:* 973-684-5904 *E-mail:* mgillan@binghamton.edu
Established: 2002
Selected by judges as the strongest novel or collection of fiction published in the previous year. Minimum press run of 500 copies. Each book submitted must be accompanied by an application form; publishers may submit more than one book for prize consideration. Submit only two copies of a submitted title. Winners will be announced in *Poets & Writers*.
Award: $1,000
Closing Date: March 1

Binghamton University Milt Kessler Poetry Book Award
The Binghamton Center for Writers-State University of New York
Dept of English, General Literature & Rhetoric, Library N, Rm 1149, Vestal Pkwy E, Binghamton, NY 13902
Mailing Address: PO Box 6000, Binghamton, NY 13902-6000
Tel: 607-777-2713
Web Site: www2.binghamton.edu/english/creative-writing
Key Personnel
Dir: Maria Mazziotti Gillan *Tel:* 973-684-5904 *E-mail:* mgillan@binghamton.edu
Established: 2002
For a book of poems, 48 pages or more in length, selected by our judges as the strongest collection of poems by a poet over 40 published in the previous year. Must be accompanied by an application; publishers may submit more than one book for prize consideration; minimum press run of 500 copies; submit only two copies of a title. Winner announced in *Poets & Writers*.
Award: $1,000
Closing Date: March 1

Paul Birdsall Prize
American Historical Association (AHA)
400 "A" St SE, Washington, DC 20003
Tel: 202-544-2422 *Fax:* 202-544-8307
E-mail: awards@historians.org
Web Site: www.historians.org
Established: 1985
Awarded biennially for the most important work published in English on European military or strategic history since 1870. Preference will be given to early-career academics, but established scholars & nonacademic candidates will not be excluded. Books published in English & bearing a copyright date of 2016 or 2017 are eligible for the 2018 prize. Nominators must complete an online prize submission form for each book submitted. One copy of each entry must be sent to each committee member & clearly labeled "Birdsall Prize Entry." Electronic copies may be sent only to committee members who have indicated they will accept them.
Closing Date: May 15, 2018
Presented: AHA Annual Meeting, Chicago, IL, Jan 2019

BISG Industry Awards
Book Industry Study Group Inc (BISG)
1412 Broadway, Suite 2119, New York, NY 10018
Tel: 646-336-7141
E-mail: info@bisg.org
Web Site: www.bisg.org/bisg-industry-awards
Key Personnel
Opers Mgr: Kim Graff *E-mail:* kim@bisg.org
Established: 2014
Categories: Distinguished Service Award, Industry Champion Award, Industry Innovator Award, BISG Industry Connector Award, BISG Standards Bearer Award, Explorer Award, BISG Community Builder Award.
Presented: BISG Annual Meeting of Members, Annually in Sept

Irma S & James H Black Award
Bank Street College of Education
610 W 112 St, New York, NY 10025

Tel: 212-875-4458
E-mail: ccl@bankstreet.edu
Web Site: www.bankstreet.edu/center-childrens-literature
Key Personnel
Dir, Lib Servs: Kristin Freda *E-mail:* kfreda@bankstreet.edu
Established: 1972
For unified excellence of story line, language & illustration in a work for young children published during the previous year.
Award: Scroll & Gold Seals
Closing Date: Annually in Dec
Presented: Bank Street College of Education, Annually in May

Black Warrior Review Fiction, Nonfiction & Poetry Contest
Black Warrior Review
Off of Student Media, University of Alabama, Tuscaloosa, AL 35486-0027
Mailing Address: PO Box 870170, Tuscaloosa, AL 35487-0170
Tel: 205-348-4518
Web Site: www.bwr.ua.edu
Key Personnel
Mng Ed: Gail Aronson *E-mail:* managingeditor.bwr@gmail.com
Ed: Bronwyn Valentine
Fiction Ed: Reem Abu-Baker
Nonfiction Ed: Kayla Rae Candrilli
Poetry Ed: Shelley Feller
Established: 2005
Awards given to best nonfiction piece, short story & best poem entered. Submit 1 story (up to 7,500 words) or 3 poems. Entry fee: $20 (includes 1-year subscription). Submit online at bwr.ua.edu/submit/contest.
Award: $1,000 & publication (one for each category - poetry, nonfiction & fiction). Finalists noted & considered for publication
Closing Date: Annually, Sept 1

Neltje Blanchan Memorial Award
Wyoming Arts Council
Division of Wyoming Department of Parks & Cultural Resources
Barrett Bldg, 2nd fl, 2301 Central Ave, Cheyenne, WY 82002
Tel: 307-777-7742
Web Site: wyoarts.state.wy.us
Key Personnel
Public Art & Creative Sector Indivs Supv: Rachel Clifton *Tel:* 307-777-5305 *E-mail:* rachel.clifton@state.wy.us
Established: 1988
Best writing in any genre inspired by a relationship with nature. Open to Wyoming residents only. Blind judges, single juror.
Award: $1,000
Closing Date: Varies, see web site
Presented: Announced in the Fall

Theodore C Blegen Award
The Forest History Society Inc
701 William Vickers Ave, Durham, NC 27701-3162
Tel: 919-682-9319 *Fax:* 919-682-2349
Web Site: www.foresthistory.org
Key Personnel
Admin Asst: Andrea Anderson *E-mail:* andrea.anderson@foresthistory.org
Established: 1972
Recognizes the best scholarship in forest & conservation history published in a journal other than *Environmental History*.
Award: $500 & plaque
Closing Date: Early Spring (specific date varies)

Susan P Bloom Children's Book Discovery Award
PEN New England
Unit of PEN American Center
MIT, 14N-221A, 77 Massachusetts Ave, Cambridge, MA 02139
Tel: 617-324-1729
E-mail: pen-newengland@mit.edu
Web Site: www.pen-ne.org/susan-p-bloom-award
Annual awards to honor emerging writers & writers/illustrators.

The James Boatwright III Prize for Poetry
Shenandoah: The Washington & Lee University Review
Washington & Lee University, Mattingly House, 204 W Washington St, Lexington, VA 24450-2116
Tel: 540-458-8908
E-mail: shenandoah@wlu.edu
Web Site: shenandoahliterary.org
Key Personnel
Ed: R T Smith *E-mail:* rodsmith@wlu.edu
Asst Ed: William Wright
Annual award for the best poem published in *Shenandoah* during a volume year.
Award: $1,000

Rebekah Johnson Bobbitt National Prize for Poetry
The Poetry & Literature Center, Library of Congress
101 Independence Ave SE, Washington, DC 20540-4861
Tel: 202-707-5394
Web Site: www.loc.gov/poetry
Biennial prize recognizes the most distinguished book of poetry written by an American & published during the preceding 2 years.
Other Sponsor(s): Family of Rebekah Johnson Bobbitt
Award: $10,000

Frederick Bock Prize
Poetry Magazine
61 W Superior St, Chicago, IL 60654
Tel: 312-787-7070 *Fax:* 312-787-6650
E-mail: editors@poetrymagazine.org
Web Site: www.poetryfoundation.org
Key Personnel
Edit Asst: Holly Amos *E-mail:* hamos@poetrymagazine.org
Established: 1981
For poetry published during the preceding 2 volumes of *Poetry* magazine. No application necessary.
Award: $500
Presented: Annually in Dec

George Bogin Memorial Award
Poetry Society of America (PSA)
15 Gramercy Park, New York, NY 10003
Tel: 212-254-9628
Web Site: www.poetrysociety.org
Key Personnel
Pres: Kimiko Hahn
Exec Dir: Alice Quinn
Deputy Dir: Brett Fletcher Lauer *E-mail:* brett@poetrysociety.org
Prog Dir: Laurin Macios *E-mail:* laurin@poetrysociety.org
Established by the family & friends of George Bogin, for a selection of 4 or 5 poems that reflects the encounter of the ordinary & the extraordinary, uses language in an original way & takes a stand against oppression in any of its forms. See web site for more information.
Award: $500
Closing Date: Annually, Oct-Dec
Presented: Annual Awards Ceremony, New York, NY, Annually in Spring

Bogle International Library Travel Fund
International Relations Committee
Unit of The American Library Association (ALA)
50 E Huron St, Chicago, IL 60611-2795
Tel: 312-280-3201 *Toll Free Tel:* 800-545-2433 (ext 3201) *Fax:* 312-280-4392
E-mail: intl@ala.org
Web Site: www.ala.org
Key Personnel
Dir, Off of Chapter & Intl Rel: Michael Dowling
Prog Offr: Delin Guerra *E-mail:* dguerra@ala.org
To enable librarians to travel abroad to study +/or attend first international conferences.
Award: $1,000
Closing Date: Annually, Jan 1
Presented: ALA Conference, Annually in June

Laura Day Boggs Bolling Memorial
The Poetry Society of Virginia
900 Timber Creek Place, Virginia Beach, VA 23464
E-mail: poetryinva@aol.com
Web Site: poetrysocietyofvirginia.org
Key Personnel
Pres: Robert P Arthur *E-mail:* robert.peebles.arthur@gmail.com
Exec Dir: Guy Terrell *E-mail:* guy.terrell@earthlink.net
Adult Contest Chair: Steven Blythe *E-mail:* stevenblythepoetry@gmail.com
All entries must be in English, original & unpublished. Submit 2 copies, both copies must have the category name & number on top left of page. Entries will not be returned. Poem written by an adult for older school-age children (10-12 yrs); any rhymed or unrhymed form; 20 line limit. Entry fee: $4 nonmembs.
Other Sponsor(s): Children of Laura Day Boggs Bolling: Alma, Flora & Glade
Award: $50 (1st prize), $30 (2nd prize), $20 (3rd prize)
Closing Date: Jan
Presented: Annual PSV Awards Ceremony, April

Books for a Better Life Awards
National Multiple Sclerosis Society, New York City-Southern New York Chapter
733 Third Ave, 3rd fl, New York, NY 10017
Tel: 212-463-7787 *Toll Free Tel:* 800-344-4867 *Fax:* 212-986-7981
Web Site: msnycbooks.org
Established: 1996
Recognizes self-improvement authors whose messages are aligned with the chapter's mission of inspiring people to live their best lives.
Presented: TheTimesCenter, New York, NY, Annually in April

Boston Globe-Horn Book Award
The Boston Globe & The Horn Book Inc
c/o Book Reviews, The Horn Book Inc, Palace Road Bldg, 300 The Fenway, Suite P-311, Boston, MA 02115-5820
Tel: 617-278-0225 *Toll Free Tel:* 888-628-0225 *Fax:* 617-278-6062
E-mail: info@hbook.com
Web Site: www.hbook.com
Key Personnel
Ed-in-Chief, Horn Book Pubns: Roger Sutton *E-mail:* rsutton@hbook.com
Exec Ed: Elissa Gershowitz
Mng Ed: Katrina Hedeen *Tel:* 617-628-0225 ext 222 *E-mail:* khedeen@hbook.com
Established: 1967
Honors excellence in children's & young adult literature in 3 categories: fiction & poetry, nonfiction & picture books. Published books only. Books produced by publishers not listed in *Literary Market Place* will not be accepted.
Award: $500 each
Closing Date: Annually in May
Presented: Simmons Colloquium, Annually in Fall

Boulevard Magazine Short Fiction Contest for Emerging Writers
Boulevard Magazine
6614 Clayton Rd, PMB 325, Richmond Heights, MO 63117
E-mail: editors@boulevardmagazine.org
Web Site: www.boulevardmagazine.org
Key Personnel
Founding Ed & Publr: Richard Burgin
E-mail: richardburgin@att.net
Mng Ed: Dusty Freund
Sr Ed: Glenn Blake
Ed: Jessica Rogen *E-mail:* jessicarogen@boulevardmagazine.org
Open to writers who have not yet published a book of fiction, poetry or creative nonfiction with a nationally distributed press. Simultaneous submissions are allowed but previously accepted or published work is ineligible. Send typed, double-spaced mss & SAS postcard for acknowledgment of receipt. No mss will be returned. 8,000 word maximum length; cover sheets not necessary. Entry fee is $16 per story with no limit per author. Includes 1-year subscription.
Award: $1,500 & publication in the Spring or the Fall issue of *Boulevard*
Closing Date: Annually, Dec 31

Bound to Stay Bound Books Scholarship
Association for Library Service to Children (ALSC)
Division of The American Library Association (ALA)
50 E Huron St, Chicago, IL 60611-2795
Tel: 312-280-2163 *Toll Free Tel:* 800-545-2433 *Fax:* 312-440-9374; 312-280-5271
E-mail: alsc@ala.org
Web Site: www.ala.org/alsc
Key Personnel
Exec Dir: Aimee Strittmatter *Tel:* 312-280-2162 *E-mail:* astrittmatter@ala.org
Awards Coord: Courtney Jones
E-mail: alscawards@ala.org
Prog Coord: Marsha P Burgess *Tel:* 312-280-2166 *E-mail:* mburgess@ala.org
For study in field of library service to children toward the MLS or beyond in an ALA-accredited program.
Award: $7,500 - 4 scholarships per yr
Closing Date: Annually, March 1
Presented: ALA Annual Conference, Annually in June

Barbara Bradley Prize
New England Poetry Club
46 Wallace St, Somerville, MA 02144
Tel: 617-744-6034
E-mail: info@nepoetryclub.org
Web Site: www.nepoetryclub.org
Key Personnel
VP: Hillary Sallick
Established: 1988
Prize for a poem in lyric form, under 21 lines, written by a woman. Mark name of contest on envelope, send to address above. Send poem in duplicate with name of writer on one only. See web site for additional guidelines.
Award: $250
Closing Date: May 31
Presented: Winners announced online Aug/Sept

BrainStorm Poetry Contest for Mental Health Consumers
Northern Initiative for Social Action (NISA)
36 Elgin St, 2nd fl, Sudbury, ON P3C 5B4, Canada
Tel: 705-222-6472 (ext 303)
E-mail: openminds@nisa.on.ca
Web Site: www.openmindsquarterly.com
Key Personnel
Publr & Ed: Dinah Laprairie
Established: 2003
Contest open only to people with lived experience of mental illness internationally. It aims to eliminate the stigma associated with mental illness by showcasing the talents & creativity of individuals living with mental illness. Contest details available after December 15 online. Contest runs January to end of March each year. Call or e-mail to be added to mailing list.
Award: $250 (1st prize), $150 (2nd prize), $75 (3rd prize), plus publication in *Open Minds Quarterly*
Closing Date: Annually Jan-March

Michael Braude Award
American Academy of Arts & Letters
633 W 155 St, New York, NY 10032
Tel: 212-368-5900 *Fax:* 212-491-4615
E-mail: academy@artsandletters.org
Web Site: www.artsandletters.org
Key Personnel
Exec Dir: Cody Upton
Triennial award given for light verse written in English regardless of the writer's country of origin.
Award: $5,000

James Henry Breasted Prize
American Historical Association (AHA)
400 "A" St SE, Washington, DC 20003
Tel: 202-544-2422 *Fax:* 202-544-8307
E-mail: awards@historians.org
Web Site: www.historians.org
Established: 1985
Best book in English in any field of history prior to 1000 AD. Different geographic area will be eligible each year. Entries must be published in 2017. Along with an application form, applicants must mail a copy of their book to each of the prize committee members who will be posted on our web site as the prize deadline approaches. All updated info on web site.
Award: Cash prize
Closing Date: May 15, 2018
Presented: AHA Annual Meeting, Chicago, IL, Jan 2019

The Briar Cliff Review Fiction, Poetry & Creative Nonfiction Contest
The Briar Cliff Review-Briar Cliff University
3303 Rebecca St, Sioux City, IA 51104-2100
Tel: 712-279-1651 *Fax:* 712-279-5486
Web Site: www.bcreview.org
Key Personnel
Mktg Dir: Judy Thompson
Ed: Tricia Currans-Sheehan
Poetry, creative nonfiction & fiction contest. Submit unpublished story, essay or 3 poems with $20. Entrants receive issue. No name on mss. Include cover page with title(s), name, address, e-mail, phone. Send SASE for results only. Can also use Submittable.
Award: $1,000 each category & publication in Spring
Closing Date: Annually, Nov 1

Brick Road Poetry Book Contest
Brick Road Poetry Press
513 Broadway, Columbus, GA 31901-3117
Web Site: brickroadpoetrypress.com
Key Personnel
Ed: Keith Badowski; Ron Self
Book-length poetry mss only, original collection of 50-100 pages of poetry, excluding cover page, contents, acknowledgments, etc. Entry fee: $25. Submissions accepted starting August 1.
Award: $1,000, publication contract with Brick Road Poetry Press in both print & ebook formats & 25 copies of the printed book
Closing Date: Annually, Nov 1

Brittingham & Pollak Prizes in Poetry
University of Wisconsin Press
Dept of English, 600 N Park St, Madison, WI 53706
Web Site: www.wisc.edu/wisconsinpress
Key Personnel
Ed: Ronald Wallace
Established: 1985
Pollak & Brittingham are two prizes from one competition. For book-length mss of poetry. Mss not accepted before August 15 or after September 15; $28 reading fee required, check made payable to: University of Wisconsin Press. Mss not returned; send required business-size SASE for contest results. For guidelines check web site. Electronic submissions encouraged.
Other Sponsor(s): University of Wisconsin Creative Writing Program
Award: $1,000 & publication in University of Wisconsin Press Poetry Series for each book
Closing Date: Sept 15

The Heywood Broun Award
The NewsGuild - CWA
501 Third St NW, 6th fl, Washington, DC 20001-2797
Tel: 202-434-7177; 202-434-7162 (The Guild Reporter) *Fax:* 202-434-1472
Web Site: www.newsguild.org
Key Personnel
Ed: Sally Davidow *E-mail:* sdavidow@cwa-union.org
Established: 1941
Journalism.
Award: $5,000
Closing Date: Last Fri in Jan
Presented: Washington, DC, Annually in May

John Nicholas Brown Prize
Medieval Academy of America
17 Dunster St, Suite 202, Cambridge, MA 02138
Tel: 617-491-1622 *Fax:* 617-492-3303
E-mail: info@themedievalacademy.org
Web Site: www.medievalacademy.org
Key Personnel
Exec Dir: Lisa Fagin Davis *E-mail:* lfd@themedievalacademy.org
Established: 1978
For a first book or monograph published in the field of medieval studies judged by the selection committee to be of outstanding quality. Author must reside in North America.
Award: $1,000 & certificate
Closing Date: Annually, Oct 15
Presented: Annually in April

Georges Bugnet Award for Fiction
Writers' Guild of Alberta
11759 Groat Rd, Edmonton, AB T5M 3K6, Canada
Tel: 780-422-8174 *Toll Free Tel:* 800-665-5354 (AB only) *Fax:* 780-422-2663 (attn WGA)
E-mail: mail@writersguild.ca
Web Site: writersguild.ca
Key Personnel
Exec Dir: Carol Holmes *E-mail:* carol.holmes@writersguild.ca
Communs & Partnerships Coord: Ellen Kartz
E-mail: ellen.kartz@writersguild.ca
Memb Servs Coord: Giorgia Severini
Progs Coord: Natalie Cook *E-mail:* natalie.cook@writersguild.ca; Julie Robinson *E-mail:* julie.robinson@writersguild.ca
Established: 1982
Alberta Literary Award, author must be resident of Alberta.
Award: $1,500
Closing Date: Annually, Dec 31
Presented: Alberta Book Awards Gala
Branch Office(s)
505 21 Ave SW, Calgary, AB T2S 0G9, Canada,

Prog Coord: Samantha Warwick *Tel:* 403-265-2226 *E-mail:* samantha.warwick@writersguild.ca

The John Burroughs List of Nature Books for Young Readers, see Riverby Awards

John Burroughs Medal
John Burroughs Association Inc
261 Floyd Ackert Rd, New York, NY 12493
Mailing Address: PO Box 439, West Park, NY 12493
Tel: 212-769-5169 *Fax:* 212-313-7182
E-mail: info@johnburroughsassociation.org
Web Site: www.johnburroughsassociation.org
Key Personnel
Pres: Joan Burroughs *E-mail:* jjjburroughs@yahoo.com
Established: 1926
Awarded to the author of a distinguished book of nature writing that combines accurate scientific information with firsthand fieldwork & creative natural history writing.
Award: Medal
Closing Date: Annually in Oct
Presented: Annual Meeting, Yale Club, New York, NY, 1st Monday in April

John Burroughs Nature Essay Award
John Burroughs Association Inc
261 Floyd Ackert Rd, New York, NY 12493
Mailing Address: PO Box 439, West Park, NY 12493
Tel: 212-769-5169 *Fax:* 212-313-7182
E-mail: info@johnburroughsassociation.org
Web Site: www.johnburroughsassociation.org
Key Personnel
Pres: Joan Burroughs *E-mail:* jjjburroughs@yahoo.com
Awarded to an outstanding published natural history essay that is scientifically accurate, yet does more by using a personal point of view in vivid writing.
Award: Certificate of Recognition
Closing Date: Annually in Feb
Presented: Annual Meeting, Yale Club, New York, NY, 1st Monday in April

CAA Award for Canadian History
Canadian Authors Association (CAA)
6 West St N, Suite 203, Orillia, ON L3V 5B8, Canada
Tel: 705-325-3926
E-mail: admin@canadianauthors.org
Web Site: www.canadianauthors.org
Key Personnel
Exec Dir: Anita Purcell
Established: 1997
All entries must be historical nonfiction, on Canadian topics by Canadian authors. The books must be English language literature for adults (not "young adults"). Translations are not eligible. Fee of $40 per entry to offset a portion of administrative costs.
Award: $1,000
Closing Date: Annually, Dec 15
Presented: CAA's Annual Conference, Awards Gala & Banquet, Annually in June

CAA Award for Fiction
Canadian Authors Association (CAA)
6 West St N, Suite 203, Orillia, ON L3V 5B8, Canada
Tel: 705-325-3926
E-mail: admin@canadianauthors.org
Web Site: www.canadianauthors.org
Key Personnel
Exec Dir: Anita Purcell
Entries must be full-length English language literature for adults by Canadian authors. Reprints are not eligible. Fee at $40 per entry to offset a portion of administrative costs.
Award: $1,000
Closing Date: Annually, Dec 15
Presented: CAA's Annual Conference, Awards Gala & Banquet, Annually in June

CAA Emerging Writer Award
Canadian Authors Association (CAA)
6 West St N, Suite 203, Orillia, ON L3V 5B8, Canada
Tel: 705-325-3926
E-mail: admin@canadianauthors.org
Web Site: www.canadianauthors.org
Key Personnel
Exec Dir: Anita Purcell
Awarded to the Canadian writer under 30 yrs old deemed to show the most promise in the field of literary creation.
Award: $500 & 1 yr membership in Canadian Authors Association
Closing Date: Annually, March 31
Presented: CAA's Annual Conference, Awards Gala & Banquet, Annually in June

CAA Poetry Award
Canadian Authors Association (CAA)
6 West St N, Suite 203, Orillia, ON L3V 5B8, Canada
Tel: 705-325-3926
E-mail: admin@canadianauthors.org
Web Site: www.canadianauthors.org
Key Personnel
Exec Dir: Anita Purcell
For a volume of poetry by one poet. Entry fee $40 per title.
Award: $1,000
Closing Date: Annually, Dec 15
Presented: CAA Annual Conference, Awards Gala & Banquet, Annually in June

Gerald Cable Book Award
Silverfish Review Press
PO Box 3541, Eugene, OR 97403
Tel: 541-344-5060
E-mail: sfrpress@earthlink.net
Web Site: www.silverfishreviewpress.com
Key Personnel
Ed & Publr: Rodger Moody
Established: 1995
Poetry Book; for author who has not yet published a collection; selection by May. $25 reading fee.
Award: $1,000 & publication by Silverfish Review Press & 25 copies of the book
Closing Date: Oct 15

The Randolph Caldecott Medal
Association for Library Service to Children (ALSC)
Division of The American Library Association (ALA)
50 E Huron St, Chicago, IL 60611-2795
Tel: 312-280-2163 *Toll Free Tel:* 800-545-2433 *Fax:* 312-440-9374; 312-280-5271
E-mail: alsc@ala.org
Web Site: www.ala.org/alsc
Key Personnel
Exec Dir: Aimee Strittmatter *Tel:* 312-280-2162 *E-mail:* astrittmatter@ala.org
Awards Coord: Courtney Jones *E-mail:* alscawards@ala.org
Prog Coord: Marsha P Burgess *Tel:* 312-280-2166 *E-mail:* mburgess@ala.org
Established: 1937
Given annually to the artist who created the most distinguished American picture book for children published in the US during the previous year. The artist must be a citizen or resident of the US.
Award: Medal
Closing Date: Dec 31
Presented: ALA Midwinter Meeting, Jan/Feb

California Book Awards
Commonwealth Club of California
110 The Embarcadero, San Francisco, CA 94105
Tel: 415-597-6700 *Fax:* 415-597-6729
E-mail: bookawards@commonwealthclub.org
Web Site: www.commonwealthclub.org/bookawards
Established: 1931
Honors the exceptional literary merit of California writers & publishers. Annual awards are presented in the categories of fiction, nonfiction, poetry, first work of fiction, juvenile literature (up to age 10), adult literature (ages 11-16), Californiana, works in translation & notable contribution to publishing. To be eligible, author must be resident in California at the time of publication & books must be published under the year in consideration.
Award: Plaques with medallions for gold & silver awardees
Closing Date: Dec
Presented: 1st Thursday in June

Joe Pendleton Campbell Narrative Contest
The Poetry Society of Virginia
900 Timber Creek Place, Virginia Beach, VA 23464
E-mail: poetryinva@aol.com
Web Site: poetrysocietyofvirginia.org
Key Personnel
Pres: Robert P Arthur *E-mail:* robert.peebles.arthur@gmail.com
Exec Dir: Guy Terrell *E-mail:* guy.terrell@earthlink.net
Adult Contest Chair: Steven Blythe *E-mail:* stevenblythepoetry@gmail.com
All entries must be in English, original & unpublished. Submit 2 copies, each having the category name & number on top left of page. Any form; any subject; narrative poem; 64 line limit. Entry fee: $4 nonmembs.
Other Sponsor(s): Paula Savoy
Award: $50 (1st prize), $30 (2nd prize), $20 (3rd prize)
Closing Date: Jan
Presented: Annual PSV Awards Ceremony, April

John W Campbell Memorial Award
Center for the Study of Science Fiction
University of Kansas, Wescoe Hall, Rm 3001, Dept of English, 1445 Jayhawk Blvd, Lawrence, KS 66045
Tel: 785-864-2518 *Fax:* 785-864-1159
Web Site: www.sfcenter.ku.edu/campbell.htm
Key Personnel
Founding Dir: James Gunn *E-mail:* jgunn@ku.edu
Dir: Christopher McKitterick *E-mail:* cmckit@ku.edu
Established: 1973
Selected by jury who produces a short list & votes on that list to select a winner. Science fiction novels published in English anywhere in the world in the year of eligibility. Publishers are encouraged to submit works for consideration by the jury.
Award: Trophy & expense paid trip to the conference to receive the award
Presented: Campbell Conference Awards Banquet, University of Kansas, Lawrence, KS

Alexander Patterson Cappon Prize for Fiction
New Letters
UMKC, University House, 5101 Rockhill Rd, Kansas City, MO 64110-2499
Tel: 816-235-1169 *Fax:* 816-235-2611
E-mail: newletters@umkc.edu
Web Site: www.newletters.org
Established: 1986

Literary contest. All entries considered for publication.
Award: $1,500 & publication
Closing Date: Annually, May 18

Dorothy Churchill Cappon Prize for the Essay
New Letters
UMKC, University House, 5101 Rockhill Rd, Kansas City, MO 64110-2499
Tel: 816-235-1169 *Fax:* 816-235-2611
E-mail: newletters@umkc.edu
Web Site: www.newletters.org
Established: 1986
Literary contest. All entries considered for publication.
Award: $1,500 & publication
Closing Date: Annually, May 18

Andrew Carnegie Medals for Excellence in Fiction & Nonfiction
The American Library Association (ALA)
50 E Huron St, Chicago, IL 60611
Tel: 312-944-6780 *Toll Free Tel:* 800-545-2433 *Fax:* 312-440-9374
E-mail: ala@ala.org
Web Site: www.ala.org/awardsgrants/carnegieadult
Key Personnel
Exec Dir: Susan Hornung *E-mail:* shornung@ala.org
Mgr, Mktg & Progs: Marianne Braverman *E-mail:* mbraverman@ala.org
Membership & Awards Coord: Leighann Wood *E-mail:* lwood@ala.org
Established: 2012
To recognize the best fiction & nonfiction books for adult readers published in the US the previous year, chosen by selection committee.
Other Sponsor(s): Booklist; Carnegie Corporation of New York Grant; Reference & User Services Association (RUSA)
Award: $5,000 (winning authors, 1 in each category), $1,500 (2 finalists in each category)
Presented: ALA Annual Conference, June

Carnegie-Whitney Award
ALA Publishing Committee
Unit of The American Library Association (ALA)
50 E Huron St, Chicago, IL 60611
Tel: 312-280-5416 *Toll Free Tel:* 800-545-2433 *Fax:* 312-280-5275; 312-440-9379
Web Site: www.ala.org
Key Personnel
Grant Admin: Mary Jo Bolduc *E-mail:* mbolduc@ala.org
For the preparation of bibliographic aids for research with scholarly intent & general applicability. Decisions made at Publishing Committee Meeting, each January. Completed proposals should be sent to the Grant Administrator.
Award: Up to $5,000 annually
Closing Date: Annually in Nov

The Carter Prize For The Essay
Shenandoah: The Washington & Lee University Review
Washington & Lee University, Mattingly House, 204 W Washington St, Lexington, VA 24450-2116
Tel: 540-458-8908
E-mail: shenandoah@wlu.edu
Web Site: shenandoahliterary.org
Key Personnel
Ed: R T Smith *E-mail:* rodsmith@wlu.edu
Asst Ed: William Wright
Annual award for the best essay published in *Shenandoah* during a volume year.
Award: $1,000

Catholic Book Awards
Catholic Press Association of the United States & Canada
205 W Monroe St, Suite 470, Chicago, IL 60606
Tel: 312-380-6789 *Fax:* 312-361-0256
E-mail: cathjourn@catholicpress.org
Web Site: www.catholicpress.org
Key Personnel
Exec Dir: Timothy M Walter *E-mail:* twalter@catholicpress.org
Busn Mgr: Barbara Mastrolia
Several awards for best Catholic books in different categories.
Award: Certificate
Closing Date: Feb
Presented: Annual Convention, June

Catholic Press Association of the US & Canada Journalism Awards, see Catholic Press Awards

Catholic Press Awards
Catholic Press Association of the United States & Canada
205 W Monroe St, Suite 470, Chicago, IL 60606
Tel: 312-380-6789 *Fax:* 312-361-0256
E-mail: cathjourn@catholicpress.org
Web Site: www.catholicpress.org
Key Personnel
Exec Dir: Timothy M Walter *E-mail:* twalter@catholicpress.org
Busn Mgr: Barbara Mastrolia
Journalism entries from member publications.
Award: Certificate
Closing Date: Annually in Feb
Presented: Annual Convention, June

The Center for Fiction First Novel Prize
The Center for Fiction
17 E 47 St, New York, NY 10017
Tel: 212-755-6710 *Fax:* 212-826-0831
E-mail: info@centerforfiction.org
Web Site: centerforfiction.org/awards
Key Personnel
Exec Dir: Noreen Tomassi *E-mail:* noreen@centerforfiction.org
Writing Progs Dir: Sara Batkie *E-mail:* sara@centerforfiction.org
Established: 2006
Awarded to the best debut novel published between January 1 & December 31 of the award year.
Award: $10,000 (1st prize), $1,000 (shortlist award)
Presented: The Center for Fiction's Annual Benefit & Awards Dinner, Annually in Dec

Center for Publishing Departmental Scholarships
New York University, School of Continuing & Professional Studies
Midtown Ctr, Rm 429, 11 W 42 St, New York, NY 10036
Tel: 212-992-3232 *Fax:* 212-992-3233
E-mail: pub.center@nyu.edu
Web Site: www.scps.nyu.edu
Key Personnel
Asst Dir, MS in Publg: Lindsey Allen *E-mail:* lindsey.allen@nyu.edu
Awarded to students enrolled in at least 6 credits in Master of Science in publishing program (not available to students in first semester). Need excellent academic record. Based on financial need & merit.
Award: $500 & up
Presented: Annually in Fall & Spring

Jane Chambers Playwriting Award
Women & Theatre Program, Association for Theatre in Higher Education
Georgetown University, 108 David Performing Arts Ctr, Box 571063, 37 & "O" St, NW, Washington, DC 20057-1063
Web Site: www.athe.org/?page=Jane_Chambers
Key Personnel
Contact: Jen-Scott Mobley *E-mail:* jenscottmob@gmail.com; Maya E Roth *E-mail:* mer46@georgetown.edu
Established: 1984
Award for play or performance text by a woman which reflects a feminist perspective & contains a majority of roles for women performers. Scripts may be produced or unproduced; encourage experimentation with dramatic form. See web site for FAQ & past winners. Electronic submissions preferred. One play per playwright annually. Separate contest for student playwrights.
Award: $1,000 for reading of the winning piece at the award conference & free registration to the conference; student winner, submitted separate to WTP web site, is also recognized with $250 & selected reading of scenes
Closing Date: Feb 15
Presented: Annual ATHE National Conference

The Alfred & Fay Chandler Book Award
Business History Review
c/o Harvard Business School, Connell House 301A, Boston, MA 02163
Tel: 617-495-1003 *Fax:* 617-495-2705
E-mail: bhr@hbs.edu
Web Site: www.hbs.edu/businesshistory/fellowships
Key Personnel
Ed: Walter Friedman *E-mail:* wfriedman@hbs.edu
Established: 1964
Award given every three years for best book published in the US on the history of business. Selection by the editorial board of the Business History Review.
Award: A scroll

G S Sharat Chandra Prize for Short Fiction
BkMk Press - University of Missouri-Kansas City
University House, 5101 Rockhill Rd, Kansas City, MO 64110-2499
Tel: 816-235-2558 *Fax:* 816-235-2611
E-mail: bkmk@umkc.edu
Web Site: www.umkc.edu/bkmk
Key Personnel
Exec Ed: Robert Stewart *Tel:* 816-235-2610 *E-mail:* stewartr@umkc.edu
Mng Ed: Ben Furnish *E-mail:* furnishb@umkc.edu
Assoc Ed: Michelle Boisseau *Tel:* 816-235-2561 *E-mail:* boisseau@umkc.edu
Established: 2001
The best book-length ms of short fiction in English by a living author. Ms must be typed on standard-sized paper in English & should be 125-300 pages double-spaced. Entries must include two title pages: one with author name, address & phone number & one with no author information. Any acknowledgments should appear on a separate piece of paper. Entries must include a table of contents. Author's name must not appear anywhere on the ms. Do not submit your ms by fax or e-mail. A SASE should be included, for notification only. Note: No mss will be returned. A reading fee of $25 in US funds (check payable to BkMk Press) must accompany each ms. Entrants will receive a copy of the winning book when published. Entrants may also now submit online at www.umkc.edu/bkmk.
Award: $1,000 plus book publication of winning ms by BkMk Press
Closing Date: Annually, Jan 15
Presented: Annually in Summer

The Chautauqua Prize
Chautauqua Institution
One Ames Ave, Chautauqua, NY 14722
Mailing Address: PO Box 28, Chautauqua, NY 14722

Toll Free Tel: 800-836-ARTS (836-2787)
Web Site: www.ciweb.org/prize
Key Personnel
Contact, Educ Dept: Sara Toth *Tel:* 716-357-6376 *E-mail:* stoth@ciweb.org
Established: 2012
National prize for a book of fiction or literary/narrative nonfiction that provides a richly rewarding reading experience & honors the author for a significant contribution to the literary arts. Book must be written in English & published in the calendar year prior to the year of the award. Entries must include official entry form, 8 copies of each title entered & entry fee of $75. Each nominated eligible book is evaluated by 3 Chautauquan reviewers, after which the shortlist & winner are chosen by a 3-member independent, anonymous jury.
Award: $7,500 & travel/expenses to one-week summer residency at Chautauqua
Closing Date: Dec 15

Children's & Teen Choice Book Awards
The Children's Book Council (CBC)
54 W 39 St, 14th fl, New York, NY 10018
E-mail: cbc.info@cbcbooks.org
Web Site: everychildareader.net/choice
Key Personnel
Exec Dir: Carl Lennertz *E-mail:* carl.lennertz@cbcbooks.org
Programming & Strategic Partnerships Dir: Shaina Birkhead *E-mail:* shaina.birkhead@cbcbooks.org
Established: 2008
The only national book awards voted on only by kids & teens. Benefits ABFE & Every Child a Reader.
Closing Date: Not an open application process. Publishers submission only
Presented: The Silent Art Auction, Annually, late May/early June

Children's Literature Association Article Award
Children's Literature Association (ChLA)
1301 W 22 St, Suite 202, Oak Brook, IL 60523
Tel: 630-571-4520 *Fax:* 708-876-5598
E-mail: info@childlitassn.org
Web Site: www.childlitassn.org
Award for best literary criticism article published within a given year on the topic of children's literature. See web site for application requirements.
Award: $200 plus award certificate
Presented: ChLA Annual Conference, Annually in June

Children's Literature Association Beiter Graduate Student Research Grants
Children's Literature Association (ChLA)
1301 W 22 St, Suite 202, Oak Brook, IL 60523
Tel: 630-571-4520 *Fax:* 708-876-5598
E-mail: info@childlitassn.org
Web Site: www.childlitassn.org
Key Personnel
Grants Chair: Chris McGee
Awarded for proposals of original scholarship with the expectation that the undertaking will lead to publication or a conference presentation & contribute to the field of children's literature criticism. Winners must either be members of the Children's Literature Association or join the association before they receive any funds. Applications & supporting materials should be written in or translated into English. Encouraging new scholars to enter the field, the scholarship is intended to enable "entry-level" scholars (graduate students, instructors or assistant professors) to bring to a publishable level dissertations, theses or papers that they have written.
Award: $500-$1,500 (based on the number & needs of the winning applicants)
Closing Date: Annually, Feb 1
Presented: ChLA Annual Conference, Annually in June

Children's Literature Association Book Award
Children's Literature Association (ChLA)
1301 W 22 St, Suite 202, Oak Brook, IL 60523
Tel: 630-571-4520 *Fax:* 708-876-5598
E-mail: info@childlitassn.org
Web Site: www.childlitassn.org
Book awards given for best book on children's literature history, scholarship & criticism published as a book in a given year. See web site for application requirements.
Award: $400 plus award certificate
Presented: ChLA Annual Conference, Annually in June

Children's Sequoyah Book Award
Oklahoma Library Association
PO Box 6550, Edmond, OK 73083
Tel: 405-525-5100 *Fax:* 405-525-5103
Web Site: www.oklibs.org
Key Personnel
Exec Dir: Kay Boies *E-mail:* execdirector@oklibs.org
Established: 1959
School children's choice of a book published by a living US author from a selected list. Students grades 3-5 who have read/listened to at least 3 books from the Children's Masterlist are eligible to vote.
Award: Plaque/medal
Closing Date: Annually, March 1
Presented: OLA Annual Conference, Annually in April

The Christopher Awards
The Christophers
5 Hanover Sq, 22nd fl, New York, NY 10004-2751
Tel: 212-759-4050 *Toll Free Tel:* 888-298-4050 (orders) *Fax:* 212-838-5073
E-mail: mail@christophers.org
Web Site: www.christophers.org
Key Personnel
Prog Mgr & Event Prodr: Tony Rossi *E-mail:* t.rossi@christophers.org
Established: 1945
For adult (nonfiction only) & juvenile fiction & nonfiction published during the current calendar year. Themes must reflect "highest values of the human spirit" criteria.
Award: Bronze medallion
Closing Date: June 1 & Nov 1; books evaluated throughout the calendar year
Presented: New York, NY, Annually in May

John Ciardi Prize for Poetry
BkMk Press - University of Missouri-Kansas City
University House, 5101 Rockhill Rd, Kansas City, MO 64110-2499
Tel: 816-235-2558 *Fax:* 816-235-2611
E-mail: bkmk@umkc.edu
Web Site: www.umkc.edu/bkmk
Key Personnel
Exec Ed: Robert Stewart *Tel:* 816-235-2610 *E-mail:* stewartr@umkc.edu
Mng Ed: Ben Furnish *E-mail:* furnishb@umkc.edu
Assoc Ed: Michelle Boisseau *Tel:* 816-235-2561 *E-mail:* boisseau@umkc.edu
Established: 1998
Presented for the best full-length ms of poetry in English by a living author. Ms must be typed on standard-sized paper & should be approximately 50 pages minimum, 110 pages maximum, single-spaced. Entries must include two title pages: one with author name, address & phone & one with no author information. Any acknowledgements should appear on a separate piece of paper. Entries must include a table of contents. Author's name must not appear anywhere on the ms. Do not submit your ms by fax or e-mail. A SASE should be included, for notification only. Note: No mss will be returned. A reading fee of $25 in US funds (check made payable to BkMk Press) must accompany each ms. Entrants will receive a copy of the winning book when it is published. Entrants may also now submit online at www.umkc.edu/bkmk.
Award: $1,000 plus publication by BkMk Press
Closing Date: Annually, Jan 15
Presented: Annually in Summer

The City of Calgary W O Mitchell Book Prize
Writers' Guild of Alberta
11759 Groat Rd, Edmonton, AB T5M 3K6, Canada
Tel: 780-422-8174 *Toll Free Tel:* 800-665-5354 (AB only) *Fax:* 780-422-2663 (attn WGA)
E-mail: mail@writersguild.ca
Web Site: writersguild.ca
Key Personnel
Exec Dir: Carol Holmes *E-mail:* carol.holmes@writersguild.ca
Communs & Partnerships Coord: Ellen Kartz *E-mail:* ellen.kartz@writersguild.ca
Memb Servs Coord: Giorgia Severini
Progs Coord: Natalie Cook *E-mail:* natalie.cook@writersguild.ca; Julie Robinson *E-mail:* julie.robinson@writersguild.ca
Recognizes literary achievement by Calgary authors. Types may be fiction, poetry, nonfiction, children's literature & drama.
Award: $5,000
Closing Date: Annually, Dec 31
Presented: Calgary Awards, Spring
Branch Office(s)
505 21 Ave SW, Calgary, AB T2S 0G9, Canada, Prog Coord: Samantha Warwick *Tel:* 403-265-2226 *E-mail:* samantha.warwick@writersguild.ca

City of Vancouver Book Award
City of Vancouver, Cultural Services Department
Woodward's Heritage Bldg, Suite 501, 111 W Hastings St, Vancouver, BC V6B 1H4, Canada
Tel: 604-871-6634 *Fax:* 604-871-6005
E-mail: culture@vancouver.ca
Web Site: vancouver.ca/bookaward
Key Personnel
Cultural Planner: Marnie Rice *E-mail:* marnie.rice@vancouver.ca
Established: 1989
Annual award for authors of books - any genre - that contribute to the appreciation & understanding of Vancouver's history, unique character or achievements of its residents.
Award: $3,000
Closing Date: May
Presented: The Mayor's Arts Awards, Sept/Oct

Page Davidson Clayton Prize for Emerging Poets
Michigan Quarterly Review
University of Michigan, 0576 Rackham Bldg, 915 E Washington St, Ann Arbor, MI 48109-1070
Tel: 734-764-9265
E-mail: mqr@umich.edu
Web Site: www.umich.edu/~mqr
Key Personnel
Ed: Jonathan Freedman
Poetry Ed: Keith Taylor
Awarded annually to the best poet appearing in MQR who has not yet published a book.
Award: $500

Cleveland State University Poetry Center Prizes
Cleveland State University Poetry Center
2121 Euclid Ave, Cleveland, OH 44115

Tel: 216-687-3986 *Toll Free Tel:* 888-278-6473
Fax: 216-687-6943
E-mail: poetrycenter@csuohio.edu
Web Site: www.csupoetrycenter.com
Key Personnel
Dir: Caryl Pagel
Asst: Jessica Schantz
Established: 1986
Poetry book mss, in 2 categories, First Book or Open Competition. Minimum 48 pages of poetry (one poem per page), SASE guidelines; readers fee required; simultaneous submissions permitted; mss not returned. Open competition is limited to poets who have published a full-length collection, 48+ pp, 500+ copies. $28 reading fee.
Award: $1,000 & publication in the Cleveland State University Poetry Center series
Closing Date: March 31 (digital entry only)
Presented: July

David H Clift Scholarship
ALA Scholarship Clearinghouse
Unit of The American Library Association (ALA)
50 E Huron St, Chicago, IL 60611
Toll Free Tel: 800-545-2433 (ext 4279) *Fax:* 312-280-3256
E-mail: scholarships@ala.org
Web Site: www.ala.org/scholarships
Key Personnel
Prog Offr: Kimberly L Redd *E-mail:* klredd@ala.org
Established: 1969
Awarded annually to worthy US or Canadian citizen or permanent resident to begin an MLS degree in an ALA-accredited program.
Award: $3,000
Closing Date: Annually, March 1; applications available beginning in Sept

Coal Hill Review Poetry Chapbook Contest
Coal Hill Review
c/o Autumn House Press, PO Box 5486, Pittsburgh, PA 15206
E-mail: reviewcoalhill@gmail.com
Web Site: www.coalhillreview.com
Key Personnel
Ed: Christine Stroud
Open to all poets writing in English. Ms may be submitted by attachment to our e-mail address. Submit a ms of 12-20 pages with a $20 entry fee.
Award: $1,000 & publication by Autumn House Press & Coal Hill Review
Closing Date: Nov 1

CODiE Awards
Software & Information Industry Association (SIIA)
1090 Vermont Ave NW, 6th fl, Washington, DC 20005-4095
E-mail: info@siia.net
Web Site: www.siia.net
Key Personnel
Pres: Kenneth Wasch *Tel:* 202-789-4440
Awards Dir: Jennifer Baranowski *Tel:* 949-448-0545 *E-mail:* jbaranowski@siia.net
Established: 1986
Honors excellence in the education & business technology industries. Nomination period begins in December.
Award: Trophy
Closing Date: Annually in Feb
Presented: Annually in July

Coe College Playwriting Festival
Coe College
1220 First Ave NE, Cedar Rapids, IA 52402
Tel: 319-399-8624 *Fax:* 319-399-8557
Web Site: www.theatre.coe.edu; www.coe.edu/academics/theatrearts/theatrearts_playwritingfestival
Key Personnel
Chair, Dept of Theatre Arts: Susan Wolverton
E-mail: swolvert@coe.edu
Established: 1992
Biennial playwriting award for new, full-length, original, unproduced & unpublished play. No musicals, adaptations, translations or collaborations. Only 1 entry/indiv.
Award: Publicly staged reading by students, faculty +/or individuals from the community, $500 & room, board, travel for one week residency
Closing Date: Nov 1, even-numbered years
Presented: Coe College, Cedar Rapids, IA, April

Carla Furstenberg Cohen Literary Prize
Carla Furstenberg Cohen Literary Prize Inc
1322 Holly St NW, Washington, DC 20012
Established: 2013
Awarded annually to authors of first or second books, in both fiction & nonfiction.
Award: $5,000 to each author

Morton N Cohen Award for a Distinguished Edition of Letters
Modern Language Association of America (MLA)
85 Broad St, Suite 500, New York, NY 10004-2434
SAN: 202-6422
Tel: 646-576-5141; 646-576-5000 *Fax:* 646-458-0030
E-mail: awards@mla.org
Web Site: www.mla.org
Key Personnel
Coord, Book Prizes: Annie M Reiser
E-mail: areiser@mla.org
Established: 1989
Award for an outstanding edition of letters published in 2017 or 2018. Editions may be in single or multiple volumes. For consideration, submit 4 copies. Editors need not be members of the MLA. Presented biennially.
Award: Cash award & certificate
Closing Date: May 1, 2019
Presented: MLA Convention, Seattle, WA, Jan 2020

The Victor Cohn Prize for Excellence in Medical Science Reporting
Council for the Advancement of Science Writing (CASW)
PO Box 910, Hedgesville, WV 25427
Tel: 304-754-6786
Web Site: www.casw.org
Established: 2000
Medical science writing for the mass media within the last 5 years. Online submissions.
Award: $3,000
Closing Date: Annually, July 31
Presented: ScienceWriters Meeting, Annually in Oct/Nov

John M Collier Award for Forest History Journalism
The Forest History Society Inc
701 William Vickers Ave, Durham, NC 27701-3162
Tel: 919-682-9319 *Fax:* 919-682-2349
Web Site: www.foresthistory.org
Key Personnel
Pres: Steven Anderson *E-mail:* steven.anderson@foresthistory.org
Admin Asst: Andrea Anderson *E-mail:* andrea.anderson@foresthistory.org
Established: 1987
Recognizes contributions to forest history that are published in newspapers, trade journals & other journalistic media. Open to any newspaper, or general circulation magazine, professional or freelance journalist in North America.
Award: $1,000 & expenses for a visit to The Forest History Society Library & Archives in Durham, NC & participation in an Institutes for Journalism in Natural Resources expedition
Closing Date: Annually, Feb 28

Carr P Collins Award
Texas Institute of Letters (TIL)
c/o 7748 Hwy 290 W, Austin, TX 78736-3202
Tel: 512-683-5640
E-mail: president@texasinstituteofletters.org
Web Site: www.texasinstituteofletters.org
Key Personnel
Pres: Steve Davis
VP: Carmen Tafolla
Treas: W K Stratton
Secy: Sergio Troncoso
Recording Secy: Joe Holley
Annual award for the best nonfiction book by a Texan or about Texas. Guidelines on the web site.
Award: $5,000
Closing Date: Annually in Jan
Presented: TIL Awards Banquet, Annually in Spring

Colorado Book Awards
Colorado Humanities & Center for the Book
7935 E Prentice Ave, Suite 450, Greenwood Village, CO 80111
Tel: 303-894-7951 (ext 19) *Fax:* 303-864-9361
E-mail: info@coloradohumanities.org
Web Site: www.coloradohumanities.org
Key Personnel
Prog Coord: Bess Maher
Established: 1991
Cash prize to Colorado authors in fiction, nonfiction, young adult, children's, poetry, romance & additional categories vary from year to year.
Award: $250 (cash)
Closing Date: Annually in Jan
Presented: Colorado Book Awards Event, Annually in Spring

Betsy Colquitt Award for Poetry
Texas Christian University
Dept of English, TCU Box 298300, Fort Worth, TX 76129
Tel: 817-257-5907 *Fax:* 817-257-5905
E-mail: descant@tcu.edu
Web Site: www.descant.tcu.edu
Key Personnel
Mng Ed: Dan Williams *E-mail:* d.e.williams@tcu.edu
Established: 1996
Annual award for best poem or series of poems by a single author in a volume. No entry fee.
Other Sponsor(s): descant (publication), Dept of English, TCU
Award: $500
Closing Date: Sept 1-April 1
Presented: Winner announced in journal in Summer

Miles Conrad Memorial Lecture
National Federation of Advanced Information Services (NFAIS)
801 Compass Way, Suite 201, Annapolis, MD 21401
Tel: 443-221-2980 *Fax:* 443-221-2981
E-mail: nfais@nfais.org
Web Site: www.nfais.org
Key Personnel
Exec Dir: Marcie Granahan *Tel:* 443-221-2980 ext 101 *E-mail:* mgranahan@nfais.org
Dir, Mktg & Communs: Barbara Meyers Ford *Tel:* 443-221-2980 ext 103
E-mail: bmeyersford@nfais.org
Established: 1968
The award is presented to an individual, who, like Conrad, has made a truly significant contribution to furthering information dissemination & its role in the advancement of science & scholarship. Each year's award recipient delivers the

memorial lecture which is considered a highlight of the NFAIS Annual Conference.
Award: Plaque & honorarium
Presented: Philadelphia, PA, Annually in Feb

The Pat Conroy Southern Book Prize
Southern Independent Booksellers Alliance
3806 Yale Ave, Columbia, SC 29205
Tel: 803-994-9530 *Fax:* 309-410-0211
Web Site: www.sibaweb.com/siba-book-award
Key Personnel
Exec Dir: Wanda Jewell *E-mail:* wanda@sibaweb.com
Nominations accepted from SIBA member booksellers. Books must be Southern in nature, or by a Southern author & published in the previous calendar year.
Closing Date: Feb 14
Presented: July 4

Constance Rooke Creative Non-Fiction Prize
The Malahat Review
University of Victoria, Box 1700, Sta CSC, Victoria, BC V8W 2Y2, Canada
Tel: 250-721-8524 *Fax:* 250-472-5051
E-mail: malahat@uvic.ca
Web Site: malahatreview.ca
Key Personnel
Ed: John Barton
Established: 2007
Invite entries from Canadian, American & overseas authors. Must be between 2,000-3,000 words. No restrictions as to subject matter. Entry fees: $35 Canadian entries, $40 US entries & $45 (US) for entries from Mexico & outside North America. See web site for additional details.
Award: $1,000
Closing Date: Annually, Aug 1

James Fenimore Cooper Prize
Society of American Historians (SAH)
Affiliate of American Historical Association
2950 Broadway, New York, NY 10027
Tel: 212-854-6495
E-mail: amhistsociety@columbia.edu
Web Site: sah.columbia.edu
Key Personnel
Pres: Mary Kelley
VP: Ann Fabian
Dir, Communs: Andie Tucher
Established: 1993
For a book of historical fiction on an American subject which makes a significant contribution to historical understanding, portrays authentically the people & events of the historical past & displays skills in narrative construction & prose style. Must be published & have a copyright within 2 years prior to prize year. Awarded biennially in odd-numbered years.
Award: $2,000 & certificate
Closing Date: Dec 1, 2018
Presented: New York, NY, May 2019

Cordon d' Or - Gold Ribbon International Culinary Academy Awards
Cordon d' Or - Gold Ribbon Inc
7312 Sixth Ave N, St Petersburg, FL 33710
Tel: 727-347-2437
E-mail: cordondor@aol.com; culinaryparadise@aol.com
Web Site: www.cordondorcuisine.com; www.florida-americasculinaryparadise.com
Key Personnel
CEO & Pres: Noreen Kinney
Established: 2003
Literary Cookbook, Illustrated Cookbook & 'Potluck' Book (any genre) & 'Culinary Arts' Awards. Categories include cookbooks, photographers, food stylists, magazines, articles, web sites, recipes & menus. Full details available on the web site. Entry forms can be downloaded.
Award: $1,000 (overall winner), Crystal Globe Trophies (presented to winners in all categories)
Closing Date: Annually, Dec 31
Presented: St Petersburg, FL, Annually in May

Albert B Corey Prize
Canadian Historical Association (CHA) & American Historical Association (AHA)
c/o American Historical Association, 400 "A" St SE, Washington, DC 20003-3889
Tel: 202-544-2422 *Fax:* 202-544-8307
E-mail: cha-shc@cha-shc.ca
Web Site: www.historians.org/prizes; www.cha-shc.ca
Established: 1967
Awarded biennially for the best book dealing with Canadian/American relations; awarded jointly with the American Historical Association. Books bearing an imprint of 2016 or 2017 are eligible for the 2018 prize. No application form, applicants must simply mail a copy of their book to each of the prize committee members who will be posted on our web site as the prize deadline approaches. All updated info on web site.
Award: $1,000 CAD
Closing Date: May 15, 2018
Presented: AHA Annual Meeting, Chicago, IL, Jan 2019

Marie Coyoteblanc Award for Indigenous Writing
Prince Edward Island Writers' Guild
81 Prince St, Charlottetown, PE C1A 4R3, Canada
E-mail: peiliteraryawards@gmail.com
Web Site: www.peiwritersguild.com
Acknowledges the contribution made to PEI literary culture by Mi'kmaq writers. Indigenous stories are an important part of our culture & ultimately this category is intended to encourage more indigenous people to start writing. The prize is open to Prince Edward Island residents who are of Mi'kmaq descent, who identify as Mi'kmaq Islanders & who are accepted as such by the communities in which they live. The Prize is designed to recognize literary merit & promote works in all categories including fiction, nonfiction, poetry, writing for children & young adults, plays & scriptwriting. Maximum 2 entries. Work must be original & unpublished. Entry fee for each submission is $25. See web site for complete entry requirements.
Award: Cash prizes for 1st, 2nd & 3rd place
Closing Date: Jan 31
Presented: Cox & Palmer Island Literary Awards Gala, Annually in Spring

CPSA Prize in Comparative Politics
Canadian Political Science Association
260 rue Dalhousie St, Suite 204, Ottawa, ON K1N 7E4, Canada
Tel: 613-562-1202 *Fax:* 613-241-0019
E-mail: cpsa-acsp@cpsa-acsp.ca
Web Site: www.cpsa-acsp.ca
Key Personnel
Admin: Michelle Hopkins
Biennial prize awarded to the best book published in English or in French in the field of comparative politics. To be eligible, a book may be single or multi-authored. Single-authored: author must be a Canadian citizen or a permanent resident of Canada or a member of the CPSA in the year the book was published. Multi-authored: at least one of the authors must be a Canadian citizen or a permanent resident of Canada or a member of the CPSA in the year the book was published. For the 2018 award, a book must have a copyright date of 2016 or 2017.
Award: Commemorative plaque & receive/share the set of books submitted to the CPSA office
Closing Date: Dec 10
Presented: Annual Conference, University of Regina, Regina, SK, CN, May 26-June 1, 2018

CPSA Prize in International Relations
Canadian Political Science Association
260 rue Dalhousie St, Suite 204, Ottawa, ON K1N 7E4, Canada
Tel: 613-562-1202 *Fax:* 613-241-0019
E-mail: cpsa-acsp@cpsa-acsp.ca
Web Site: www.cpsa-acsp.ca
Key Personnel
Admin: Michelle Hopkins
This is a biennial competition. The prize was established to recognize the contribution of Canadian political scientists to the study of international relations & to encourage the best Canadian scholarship in this field. Awarded to the best book published in English or in French in the field of international relations. Book may be single-authored or multi-authored. Single-authored: must be a Canadian citizen or a permanent resident of Canada or a member of the CPSA in the year the book was published. Multi-authored: at least one of the authors must be a Canadian citizen or a permanent resident of Canada or a member of the CPSA in the year the book was published. For the 2019 award, the book must have a copyright date of 2017 or 2018.
Award: Commemorative plaque & receive/share the set of books submitted to the CPSA
Closing Date: Dec 10
Presented: Annual Conference, University of British Columbia, Vancouver, BC, CN, June 1-7, 2019

The Crazyhorse Fiction Prize
Crazyhorse
College of Charleston, Dept of English, 66 George St, Charleston, SC 29424
Tel: 843-953-4470
E-mail: crazyhorse@cofc.edu
Web Site: crazyhorse.cofc.edu/prizes
Key Personnel
Mng Ed: Jonathan Heinen
Award for best short story. Enter up to 25 pages fiction with $20 entry fee, which includes one-year subscription. Submissions accepted during the month of Jan. Nationally prominent writer judges. See web site for complete instructions.
Award: $2,000 & publication in *Crazyhorse*
Closing Date: Annually, Jan 31

Creation Grant Program
New Brunswick Arts Board (Conseil des arts du Nouveau-Brunswick)
225 King St, Suite 201, Fredericton, NB E3B 1E1, Canada
Tel: 506-444-4444 *Toll Free Tel:* 866-460-ARTS (460-2787) *Fax:* 506-444-5543
Web Site: www.artsnb.ca
Key Personnel
Exec Dir: Joss Richer *Tel:* 506-478-4610 *E-mail:* execdirgen@artsnb.ca
Prog Offr: Sarah Beth Shiplett *Tel:* 506-440-0037 *E-mail:* sarahbeth@artsnb.ca
Opers Mgr: Tilly Jackson *Tel:* 506-478-4422 *E-mail:* tjackson@artsnb.ca
Designed to provide assistance to professional New Brunswick artists for the research, development & execution of original projects in the arts. Creation Grants are intended to allow artists to devote some or most of their time to research & creative production.
Closing Date: April 1, Oct 1

Creative Nonfiction Awards
Prince Edward Island Writers' Guild
81 Prince St, Charlottetown, PE C1A 4R3, Canada

E-mail: peiliteraryawards@gmail.com
Web Site: www.peiwritersguild.com
This nonfiction category includes humour writing, memoir, biography, essay (including personal essay), travel writing & feature articles. It involves writing about real events, people, or ideas, conveying a message through the use of literary techniques such as characterization, plot, setting, dialogue, narrative & personal reflection. In works of creative nonfiction, the writer's voice & opinion are evident. The work should be accessible to a general reading audience (not written for a specialized or academic audience). Maximum length: 2,500 words. Maximum 2 entries. Work must be original & unpublished. Prince Edward Island residents only. Entry fee for each submission is $25. See web site for complete entry requirements.
Award: Cash prizes for 1st, 2nd & 3rd place
Closing Date: Jan 31
Presented: Cox & Palmer Island Literary Awards Gala, Annually in Spring

Cunningham Commission for Youth Theatre
The Theatre School, DePaul University
Lincoln Park Campus, 2350 N Racine Ave, Chicago, IL 60614-4100
Tel: 773-325-7999 *Fax:* 773-325-7920
E-mail: cunninghamcommission@depaul.edu
Web Site: theatre.depaul.edu
Key Personnel
Assoc Dean & Chair, Theatre Studies: Dean Corrin *E-mail:* dcorrin@depaul.edu
Dir, Mktg & PR: Anna Ables *E-mail:* aables@depaul.edu
Established: 1991
Playwriting commission, limited to writers whose primary residence is within 100 miles of Chicago's Loop & alumni of The Theatre School.
Award: Up to $5,000 ($2,000 paid when the commission is contracted, $1,000 paid if the script moves to a workshop, $2,000 paid as royalty if the script is produced by The Theatre School)
Closing Date: Annually in April
Presented: June

Karen & Philip Cushman Late Bloomer Award
Society of Children's Book Writers and Illustrators (SCBWI)
4727 Wilshire Blvd, Suite 301, Los Angeles, CA 90010
Tel: 323-782-1010 *Fax:* 323-782-1892
E-mail: grants@scbwi.org; scbwi@scbwi.org
Web Site: www.scbwi.org
Honors authors over the age of 50 who have not been traditionally published in the children's literature field.
Award: $500 & free tuition to any SCBWI conference anywhere in the world
Closing Date: March 1-31 (submit through the Work-In-Progress application)

Dana Awards
Literary Competition, 200 Fosseway Dr, Greensboro, NC 27455
Tel: 336-644-8028
E-mail: danaawards@gmail.com
Web Site: www.danaawards.com
Key Personnel
Chair: Mary Elizabeth Parker
Established: 1996
Three awards: for unpublished group of poems, short story, novel, (or novel-in-progress). Poetry: submit 5 poems of no more than 100 lines each with a $15 entry fee. Short story: submit up to 10,000 words with a $15 entry fee. Novel: the first 40 pages & a $30 entry fee. All types of novels accepted.
Award: $4,000 total; $1,000 each for short story & poetry, $2,000 for novel
Closing Date: Annually, Oct 31
Presented: All awards, checks & notification are presented by mail or e-mail

Robert Dana-Anhinga Prize for Poetry
Anhinga Press
PO Box 3665, Tallahassee, FL 32315
Tel: 850-577-0745
E-mail: info@anhinga.org
Web Site: www.anhingapress.org
Key Personnel
Dir: Kristine Snodgrass *E-mail:* kristine.snodgrass@gmail.com
Established: 1983
Poetry book.
Award: $2,000 & publication
Closing Date: Annually, Feb 15-May 15
Presented: Tallahassee, FL

The Danahy Fiction Prize
Tampa Review
University of Tampa Press, 401 W Kennedy Blvd, Tampa, FL 33606
Tel: 813-253-6266
E-mail: utpress@ut.edu
Web Site: tampareview.ut.edu
Key Personnel
Ed: Richard Mathews
Edit Asst: Sean Donnelly
Established: 2006
Award: $1,000 & publication in *Tampa Review*
Closing Date: Annually, Dec 31

Benjamin H Danks Award
American Academy of Arts & Letters
633 W 155 St, New York, NY 10032
Tel: 212-368-5900 *Fax:* 212-491-4615
E-mail: academy@artsandletters.org
Web Site: www.artsandletters.org
Key Personnel
Exec Dir: Cody Upton
Established: 2003
Annual prize, in rotation, awarded to a composer of ensemble works, a playwright & a writer.
Award: $20,000

Watson Davis & Helen Miles Davis Prize
History of Science Society
Affiliate of American Council of Learned Societies
440 Geddes Hall, Notre Dame, IN 46556
Tel: 574-631-1194
E-mail: info@hssonline.org
Web Site: www.hssonline.org
Key Personnel
Exec Dir: Robert Jay Malone
Established: 1985
For the best book on the history of science directed to a broad public published during the preceding three years.
Award: $1,000 & certificate
Closing Date: April 1
Presented: Awards Banquet, Nov

Dayton Literary Peace Prize
Dayton Literary Peace Prize Foundation
25 Harman Terr, Dayton, OH 45419
Mailing Address: PO Box 461, Wright Brothers Branch, Dayton, OH 45409-0461
Tel: 937-298-5072
Web Site: daytonliterarypeaceprize.org
Key Personnel
Founder & Co-Chair: Sharon Rab *E-mail:* sharon.rab@woh.rr.com
Established: 2006
First & only annual US literary award recognizing the power of the written word to promote peace. This project is the recognition of adult fiction & nonfiction books that have led readers to a better understanding of other cultures, peoples, religions & political points of view. $100 nomination fee.
Award: $10,000 each genre (fiction & nonfiction) plus $2,500 each 1st runner-up
Closing Date: Annually in March
Presented: Benjamin & Marian Schuster Performing Arts Center, Dayton, OH, Annually in Nov

Dayton Playhouse FutureFest
The Dayton Playhouse
PO Box 3017, Dayton, OH 45401-3017
Tel: 937-424-8477 *Fax:* 937-424-0062
E-mail: futurefest@thedaytonplayhouse.com
Web Site: wordpress.daytonplayhouse.com
Key Personnel
Exec Dir: Brian Sharp
FutureFest Prog Dir: Fran Pesch
Established: 1991
National Playwriting Competition. Entry must be an original work (no musicals or plays for children) that has not been published or produced where admission was charged prior to FutureFest. Send SASE or see web site for submission guidelines.
Award: $1,000 (1st place), $100 (5 runners up) - all 6 finalists are provided travel to & housing for the FutureFest weekend
Closing Date: Aug 1-Oct 31 (postmark)
Presented: The Dayton Playhouse, Annually in July

Delaware Division of the Arts Individual Artist Fellowships
Delaware Division of the Arts
Carvel State Off Bldg, 4th fl, 820 N French St, Wilmington, DE 19801
Tel: 302-577-8278 *Fax:* 302-577-6561
E-mail: delarts@state.de.us
Web Site: www.artsdel.org
Key Personnel
Art & Artist Servs Coord: Roxanne Stanulis
Individual Artist Fellowships will be awarded to beginning or established poets & other creative writers. Applicants must be Delaware residents.
Award: A Masters Fellowship of $10,000 & established Professional Fellowships of $6,000 each & Emerging Professional Fellowships of $3,000
Closing Date: Annually, Aug 1
Presented: Annually (Master's awarded every 3 years in literature); winners notified in Dec

Rick DeMarinis Short Story Award
CUTTHROAT, A Journal of the Arts
PO Box 2414, Durango, CO 81302
Tel: 970-903-7914
E-mail: cutthroatmag@gmail.com
Web Site: www.cutthroatmag.com
Key Personnel
Ed-in-Chief: Pamela Uschuk
Mng Ed: Andrew Allport
Fiction Ed: Beth Alvarado
Submit 1 unpublished short story (5,000 word limit), any subject, any style. Mss must be 12 point font & double-spaced. Reading fee: $20.
Award: $1,300 (1st place), $250 (2nd place), both include publication in *CUTTHROAT*
Closing Date: Annually in Oct
Presented: Annually in Dec

Der-Hovanessian Translation Prize
New England Poetry Club
46 Wallace St, Somerville, MA 02144
Tel: 617-744-6034
E-mail: info@nepoetryclub.org
Web Site: www.nepoetryclub.org
Key Personnel
VP: Hillary Sallick
For translation from any language. Include the poem in the original language along with the translation. See web site for additional guidelines.

Award: $250
Closing Date: Annually, May 31
Presented: Announced online Aug/Sept

Annual Design Competition
The Society of Publication Designers Inc
27 Union Sq W, Suite 207, New York, NY 10003
Tel: 212-223-3332 *Fax:* 212-223-5880
E-mail: mail@spd.org
Web Site: www.spd.org
Key Personnel
Exec Dir: Keisha Dean
Established: 1975
For continuing excellence in the field of publication design. Approximately 100 categories in Design, Photography & Illustration. Winners include: Magazine of the Year, Brand of the Year, App of the Year, Website of the Year, Video of the Year, Entire Issue, Redesign, Cover, Spread/Single Page & Story.
Closing Date: Jan
Presented: Awards Gala, May

Alice Fay Di Castagnola Award
Poetry Society of America (PSA)
15 Gramercy Park, New York, NY 10003
Tel: 212-254-9628
Web Site: www.poetrysociety.org
Key Personnel
Pres: Kimiko Hahn
Exec Dir: Alice Quinn
Deputy Dir: Brett Fletcher Lauer *E-mail:* brett@poetrysociety.org
Prog Dir: Laurin Macios *E-mail:* laurin@poetrysociety.org
Established: 1965
Offered in memory of a benefactor or friend of the society. For a ms in progress (poetry, prose or verse drama). Open to society members only. See web site for complete information.
Award: $1,000
Closing Date: Annually, Oct-Dec
Presented: Annual Awards Ceremony, New York, NY, Annually in Spring

Diagram Essay Contest
DIAGRAM
University of Arizona, ML-445, PO Box 210067, Tucson, AZ 85721
E-mail: editor@thediagram.com
Web Site: www.thediagram.com/contest.html
Key Personnel
Ed: Ander Monson
Established: 2008
For an unpublished essay, particularly one that incorporates writing in other genres or unique textual or visual elements. Submit an essay of up to 10,000 words. Entry fee $17.
Award: $1,000 & publication in *DIAGRAM*
Closing Date: Annually in Nov

Diamonstein-Spielvogel Award for the Art of the Essay, see PEN/Diamonstein-Spielvogel Award for the Art of the Essay

Philip K Dick Award
Philadelphia Science Fiction Society
PO Box 3447, Hoboken, NJ 07030
Tel: 201-876-2551
Web Site: www.philipkdickaward.org
Key Personnel
Admin: Patrick Lo Brutto; John Silbersack; Gordon Van Gelder
Established: 1983
Presented annually for distinguished science fiction in paperback original form in the US.
Other Sponsor(s): Philip K Dick Trust; NorthWest Science Fiction Society
Award: $1,000
Closing Date: Dec 1
Presented: Norwescon, SeaTac, WA, Easter weekend

Dickinson, Emily Award, see The Writer Magazine/Emily Dickinson Award

Annie Dillard Award for Creative Nonfiction
The Bellingham Review
Mail Stop 9053, Western Washington University, Bellingham, WA 98225
Tel: 360-650-4863
E-mail: bhreview@wwu.edu
Web Site: www.bhreview.org
Key Personnel
Ed-in-Chief: Suzanne Paola Antonetta
Mng Ed: Mike Oliphant
Established: 1993
Maximum length for prose is 6,000 words. No previously published works, or works accepted for publication, are eligible. Work may be under consideration elsewhere, but must be withdrawn from the competition if accepted for publication. All entries will receive a complimentary 1-issue subscription. Entry fee for the first entry (one nonfiction work) $20. Each additional essay $10.
Only accept submissions through Submittable. Mailed submissions are no longer accepted. All finalists are considered for publication. The winning piece is selected by a distinguished, outside judge. Entries accepted beginning December 1.
Award: $1,000 & publication in the *Bellingham Review* (1st prize), considered for publication (2nd, 3rd & finalists)
Closing Date: Annually, March 15
Presented: Annually in June

Gordon W Dillon/Richard C Peterson Memorial Essay Prize
American Orchid Society Inc
c/o Fairchild Tropical Botanic Garden, 10901 Old Cutler Rd, Coral Gables, FL 33156
Tel: 305-740-2010
E-mail: theaos@aos.org
Web Site: www.aos.org
Key Personnel
Chief Educ & Sci Offr: Ron McHatton, PhD *E-mail:* rmchatton@aos.org
Established: 1985
Essay contest (orchid topics only; new theme announced each year).
Award: Cash award & a certificate of recognition. Winning essay published in the June issue of *Orchids* magazine the following year
Closing Date: Annually, Nov 30

Discover Great New Writers Award
Barnes & Noble Inc
122 Fifth Ave, New York, NY 10011
Web Site: www.barnesandnoble.com
Key Personnel
Dir: Miwa Messer *Tel:* 212-633-4067 *E-mail:* mmesser@bn.com
Established: 1990
Authors cannot submit their own work to the program; self-published writers & titles published via print-on-demand or available only as NOOK books are also ineligible for submission. Literary fiction, short story collections & literary nonfiction, such as travel essays, memoirs, or other nonfiction with a strong narrative will be considered. Books should be intended for an adult or a young adult audience. Debuting authors & writers with fewer than 3 previously published books who have yet to received a major literary award are eligible for consideration. Submissions must be original publications, penned by one author.
Award: $35,000 to six young writers

Discovery/Boston Review Poetry Contest
Unterberg Poetry Center
Subsidiary of 92nd Street Y/Tisch Center for the Arts
1395 Lexington Ave, New York, NY 10128
Tel: 212-415-5760
E-mail: unterberg@92y.org
Web Site: www.92y.org/discovery
Key Personnel
Mng Dir: Ricardo Maldonado *E-mail:* rickymaldonado@92y.org
For poets who have not published a full-length poetry collection; for guidelines visit web site. $15 entry fee must accompany the submission.
Other Sponsor(s): *Boston Review*
Award: Publication in *Boston Review*, reading at The Poetry Center & $500 each to the 4 winning authors
Closing Date: Jan 12
Presented: Winner will be announced in the fall on the Boston Review web site

Distinguished Scholarly Book Award
American Sociological Association (ASA)
c/o Governance Off, 1430 "K" St NW, Suite 600, Washington, DC 20005
Tel: 202-383-9005 *Fax:* 202-638-0882
E-mail: governance@asanet.org
Web Site: www.asanet.org
Key Personnel
Dir, Admin & Governance: Michael Murphy *Tel:* 202-383-9005 ext 327
Prog Coord: Jordan Robison *Tel:* 202-383-9005 ext 334
This award is given for a single book published in the 2 calendar years preceding the award year. Any member of the ASA may nominate books for consideration for this award. Nominations should include name of author, title of book, date of publication, publisher & brief statements (of no more than 300 words) as to why the book should be considered. Nominations sent from publishers who are not active members of ASA will not be accepted. Send nominations to: ASA office at above address.
Award: Plaque
Closing Date: Jan 31
Presented: ASA Annual Meeting, Montreal, QC, CN, Annually in Aug

Documentation Grant Program
New Brunswick Arts Board (Conseil des arts du Nouveau-Brunswick)
225 King St, Suite 201, Fredericton, NB E3B 1E1, Canada
Tel: 506-444-4444 *Toll Free Tel:* 866-460-ARTS (460-2787) *Fax:* 506-444-5543
Web Site: www.artsnb.ca
Key Personnel
Exec Dir: Joss Richer *Tel:* 506-478-4610 *E-mail:* execdirgen@artsnb.ca
Prog Offr: Sarah Beth Shiplett *Tel:* 506-440-0037 *E-mail:* sarahbeth@artsnb.ca
Opers Mgr: Tilly Jackson *Tel:* 506-478-4422 *E-mail:* tjackson@artsnb.ca
Designed to provide assistance to New Brunswick arts professionals & professional artists for the research, development & execution of original documentation & contextualization (written, film, video, multimedia) of arts activities, arts products or art history. Documentation grants are intended to foster theoretical & critical discourse in the arts. Preference will be given to proposals concerning New Brunswick art or artists.
Closing Date: April 1, Oct 1

Blake Dodd Prize
American Academy of Arts & Letters
633 W 155 St, New York, NY 10032
Tel: 212-368-5900 *Fax:* 212-491-4615
E-mail: academy@artsandletters.org
Web Site: www.artsandletters.org
Key Personnel
Exec Dir: Cody Upton

Established: 2014
Triennial award for a nonfiction writer.
Award: $25,000

Dog Writers' Association of America Inc (DWAA) Annual Writing Competition
Dog Writers' Association of America Inc (DWAA)
2243 Kelmscott Ct, Westlake Village, CA 91361
Tel: 805-418-7899 *Fax:* 831-374-9231
E-mail: dogwriter@windstream.net
Web Site: www.dwaa.org
Key Personnel
Pres: Ida Estep, Esq *Tel:* 252-478-6088 *Fax:* 252-478-6089 *E-mail:* ida@dogwriters.org
VP & Contest Chair: Elaine Gerwitz *Tel:* 805-418-7899 *Fax:* 821-374-9231 *E-mail:* elaine@dogwriters.org
Treas: Marsha Pugh *E-mail:* marsha@dogwriters.org
Secy: Susan M Ewing *E-mail:* su@dogwriters.org
Established: 1935
To give recognition to an individual, club or group which has done an outstanding job in the dog writing field in numerous categories. Only original work published between September 1 & August 31 of the competition year.
Award: Over several thousand dollars in cash prizes; plaques & certificates
Closing Date: Sept 9 (postmark or submitted online)
Presented: Annual Awards Banquet, Feb, Sunday before Westminster Dog Show

The Christopher Doheny Award
The Center for Fiction
17 E 47 St, New York, NY 10017
Tel: 212-755-6710 *Fax:* 212-826-0831
E-mail: doheny@centerforfiction.org; info@centerforfiction.org
Web Site: www.centerforfiction.org/awards/the-christopher-doheny-award
Key Personnel
Writing Progs Dir: Sara Batkie *E-mail:* sara@centerforfiction.org
Annual award to recognize excellence in fiction or nonfiction on the topic of serious physical illness by a writer who has personally dealt with or is dealing with life-threatening illness, either his or her own or that of a close relative or friend.
Other Sponsor(s): Audible Inc
Award: $10,000, publication & promotion of book in print & audio

Dorothy Canfield Fisher Book Award
Vermont Department of Libraries
109 State St, Montpelier, VT 05609-0601
Tel: 802-828-2721
Web Site: libraries.vermont.gov
Key Personnel
Chpn: Hannah Peacock *E-mail:* hpeacock@colchestervt.gov
Lib Advancement Asst: Jennifer Johnson *E-mail:* jennifer.johnson@vermont.gov
Established: 1956
For a book by a living American or Canadian author published one year previous, chosen by the children of Vermont, grades 4-8, from a master list of 30 titles.
Other Sponsor(s): Friends of Dorothy Canfield Fisher
Award: Piece of artwork from a local artist
Closing Date: Annually, Dec 1
Presented: Annually in May

Dorset Prize
Tupelo Press Inc
243 Union St, Suite 305, North Adams, MA 01247
Mailing Address: PO Box 1767, North Adams, MA 01247 SAN: 254-3281
Tel: 413-664-9611 *Fax:* 413-664-9711
E-mail: info@tupelopress.org
Web Site: www.tupelopress.org
Key Personnel
Mng Ed: Jim Schley
Established: 2003
An open book competition for poetry. Full guidelines on the web site. Entries accepted beginning September 1.
Award: $3,000, publication & national distribution
Closing Date: Dec 31
Presented: Spring

John Dos Passos Prize for Literature
Longwood University
Dept of English & Modern Languages, 201 High St, Farmville, VA 23909
Tel: 434-395-2155 *Fax:* 434-395-2145
Web Site: www.longwood.edu/english/dos-passos-prize
Key Personnel
Chpn, Dos Passos Comm: Dr David Magill
Dept Chpn: Dr Wade Edwards
Established: 1980
To honor an imaginative prose writer. Preference given to those not previously honored. Winners are nominated & selected by a jury. Applications not accepted.
Award: $2,000 & medallion
Presented: Longwood University, Farmville, VA, Generally during fall semester

Frank Nelson Doubleday Memorial Award
Wyoming Arts Council
Division of Wyoming Department of Parks & Cultural Resources
Barrett Bldg, 2nd fl, 2301 Central Ave, Cheyenne, WY 82002
Tel: 307-777-7742
Web Site: wyoarts.state.wy.us
Key Personnel
Public Art & Creative Sector Indivs Supv: Rachel Clifton *Tel:* 307-777-5305 *E-mail:* rachel.clifton@state.wy.us
Established: 1988
Best poetry, fiction, nonfiction or drama written by a woman author. Wyoming residents only. Blind judges & single juror.
Award: $1,000
Closing Date: Varies, see web site
Presented: Announced in the Fall

Dragonfly Book Awards
Formerly Five Star Dragonfly Book Awards
Story Monsters LLC
4696 W Tyson St, Chandler, AZ 85226-2903
Tel: 480-940-8182 *Fax:* 480-940-8787
E-mail: info@StoryMonsters.com
Web Site: www.DragonflyBookAwards.com
Key Personnel
Pres: Linda F Radke *E-mail:* Linda@StoryMonsters.com
Established: 2009
The Royal Dragonfly Book Awards honor published authors of all types of literature—fiction & nonfiction—in 66 categories. Entry fees: $60 per category (on or before August 1), $65 per category (after August 1).
The Purple Dragonfly Book Awards honor accomplished authors in the field of children's literature. 54 subject categories. Entry fees: $60 per category (on or before March 15), $65 per category (after March 15).
The awards contests are open to books published in any calendar year & in any country as long as they are available for purchase. Books entered must be printed in English. Provided they adhere to the above criteria, we accept traditionally published, partnership published & self-published books.
Printed Books: Mail two (2) copies of each book for each category in which it is entered. Along with the books, send one (1) printed copy of the e-mail confirmation per title for each category in which the book is entered. When submitting more than one book, all entries can be sent in the same envelope. Mail entries to: Cristy Bertini, Attn: Dragonfly Book Awards, 1271 Turkey St, Hardwick, MA 01082.
Ebooks: E-mail one (1) electronic copy of the book & a copy of the e-mail confirmation to cristy@storymonsters.com with "Dragonfly Book Awards" as the subject.
Award: Grand prize winner $500, certificate & 100 seals; 1st place winners receive certificate & 25 award seals & go in drawing for $100 (1 winner); 2nd place winners receive certificate & 5 award seals; honorable mentions receive certificate & 3 award seals
Closing Date: Purple Dragonfly: Annually, March 1 (early), May 1 (final); Royal Dragonfly: Annually, Aug 1 (early), Oct 1 (final)
Presented: Award is mailed

Carleton Drewry Memorial
The Poetry Society of Virginia
900 Timber Creek Place, Virginia Beach, VA 23464
E-mail: poetryinva@aol.com
Web Site: poetrysocietyofvirginia.org
Key Personnel
Pres: Robert P Arthur *E-mail:* robert.peebles.arthur@gmail.com
Exec Dir: Guy Terrell *E-mail:* guy.terrell@earthlink.net
Adult Contest Chair: Steven Blythe *E-mail:* stevenblythepoetry@gmail.com
Lyric or sonnet. Must be in English, original & unpublished. Submit 2 copies, each having the category name & number on top left of page. Entries will not be returned. Subject: farm life or working the Earth; 48 line limit. Entry fee: $4 nonmembs.
Award: $50 (1st prize), $30 (2nd prize), $20 (3rd prize)
Closing Date: Jan
Presented: Annual PSV Awards Ceremony, April

Saint Katharine Drexel Award
Catholic Library Association
8550 United Plaza Blvd, Suite 1001, Baton Rouge, LA 70809
Tel: 225-408-4417
E-mail: cla2@cathla.org
Web Site: cathla.org
Key Personnel
Pres: N Curtis LeMay
Established: 1966
Recognizes an outstanding contribution to the growth of high school librarianship.
Award: Plaque
Closing Date: None; in-house votes
Presented: CLA Annual Convention, April

Drury University One-Act Play Competition
Drury University
900 N Benton Ave, Springfield, MO 65802-3344
Tel: 417-873-6821
Web Site: www.drury.edu
Key Personnel
Professor, Theatre: Dr Mick Sokol *E-mail:* msokol@drury.edu
Established: 1986
Biennial award for one-act plays. Open to all playwrights. Scripts are to be original, unpublished & unproduced; staged readings or workshop productions will not disqualify a script; musicals, monologues, children's plays & adaptations will not be considered; only stage plays will be judged; preference will be given to small cast, one-set shows with running times of no less than 20 & no more than 45 minutes; no more than one script per author; all scripts are to be typewritten & firmly bound; scripts

cannot be acknowledged or returned unless accompanied by a SASE.
Award: $300 plus consideration for production by Drury University (1st prize); two honorable mentions $150 each
Closing Date: Dec 1, even-numbered years
Presented: By mail no later than April 1, odd-numbered years

Dubuque Fine Arts Players Annual One Act Play Festival
Dubuque Fine Arts Players
Subsidiary of Dubuque County Fine Arts Society
PO Box 1160, Dubuque, IA 52004-1160
Tel: 563-588-3438
E-mail: contact@dbqoneacts.org
Web Site: www.dbqoneacts.org
Key Personnel
Pres: Art Roche
Established: 1977
Annual national one-act playwriting contest. Entry form & guidelines are available at the web site. Submit the entry form, two copies of the script, a synopsis of the play & entry fee. Plays may be submitted by US mail with a $15 entry fee. SASE should be enclosed if return of the reader evaluation forms +/or the scripts is desired. Plays may be submitted online for an entry fee of $20. The higher fee pays cost of printing & binding the play. Previously published or produced works, musicals & children's plays are not accepted.
Award: $600 (1st prize), $300 (2nd prize), $200 (3rd prize), production of first 3 winning plays unless production is beyond our capacity
Closing Date: Jan 31
Presented: Mindframe Theater, 555 John F Kennedy Rd, Dubuque, IA, Mid-Sept

John H Dunning Prize in United States History
American Historical Association (AHA)
400 "A" St SE, Washington, DC 20003
Tel: 202-544-2422 *Fax:* 202-544-8307
E-mail: awards@historians.org
Web Site: www.historians.org
Established: 1927
Biennial award in recognition of outstanding historical writing in US history. To be awarded to a young scholar for an outstanding monograph in ms or in print on any subject relating to US history. To be eligible for consideration, an entry must be of a scholarly historical nature. It must be the author's first or second book, published in 2017 or 2018. Research accuracy, originality & literary merit are important factors. Along with an application form, applicants must mail a copy of their book to each of the prize committee members who will be posted on our web site as the prize deadline approaches. All updated info on web site.
Award: Cash prize
Closing Date: May 15, 2019
Presented: AHA Annual Meeting, New York, NY, Jan 2020

Eaton Literary Associates Literary Awards
Eaton Literary Agency Inc
PO Box 49795, Sarasota, FL 34230-6795
Tel: 941-366-6589 *Fax:* 941-365-4679
E-mail: eatonlit@aol.com
Web Site: www.eatonliterary.com
Key Personnel
Pres: Richard Lawrence
Established: 1984
Two awards are given, one for a book-length ms & one for a short story or article. These entries should not have been previously published.
Award: $2,500 (book-length program), $500 (short story or article program)
Closing Date: Annually, March 31 (short story or article program), Aug 31 (book-length program)
Presented: Annually in April (short story or article program), Sept (book-length program)

Edgar Allan Poe Awards®
Mystery Writers of America (MWA)
1140 Broadway, Suite 1507, New York, NY 10001
Tel: 212-888-8171
E-mail: mwa@mysterywriters.org
Web Site: www.mysterywriters.org
Key Personnel
Admin Dir: Margery Flax
Established: 1945
For the best mystery novel & best first novel by an American author. Also awards for best juvenile novel & young adult, fact-crime writing, TV episode, short story, paperback original, critical/biographical work. The work must be published for the first time in the US in the calendar year prior to the award.
Award: Ceramic bust of Poe
Closing Date: Annually, Nov 30
Presented: New York, NY, Annually in late Spring

Editor's Award
Poets & Writers Inc
90 Broad St, Suite 2100, New York, NY 10004
Tel: 212-226-3586 *Fax:* 212-226-3963
Web Site: www.pw.org/about-us/sponsored-prizes
Key Personnel
Mng Dir: Melissa Ford Gradel *Tel:* 212-226-3586 ext 223
Established: 2009
Annual award to recognize a book editor who has made an outstanding contribution to the publication of poetry or literary prose over a sustained period of time.
Presented: Poets & Writers annual dinner

Education Awards of Excellence
Printing Industries of America
301 Brush Creek Rd, Warrendale, PA 15086-7529
Tel: 412-741-6860 *Toll Free Tel:* 800-910-4283 *Fax:* 412-741-2311
E-mail: printingind@comm.printing.org
Web Site: www.printing.org/educationaward
Key Personnel
Pres & CEO: Michael F Makin *Tel:* 412-259-1777 *E-mail:* mmakin@printing.org
VP, Educ & Mktg Strategies: Julie Schaffer
Sr Mktg Mgr: Jenn Strang *Tel:* 412-259-1810 *E-mail:* jstrang@printing.org
Mktg Mgr: Kayleigh Smith *E-mail:* ksmith@printing.org
Established: 1984
Honors one industry representative & one graphic arts educator who have each made outstanding contributions to graphic arts education +/or training. See web site for more information.
Award: Engraved plaque
Closing Date: Oct 31
Presented: TAGA Annual Technical Conference, March
Branch Office(s)
1001 "G" St NW, Suite 800, Washington, DC 20001 *Tel:* 202-627-6924

Educators Award
The Delta Kappa Gamma Society International
PO Box 1589, Austin, TX 78767-1589
Tel: 512-478-5748 *Toll Free Tel:* 888-762-4685 *Fax:* 512-478-3961
E-mail: societyexec@dkg.org
Web Site: www.dkg.org
Key Personnel
Membership Servs Admin: Nita Scott *Tel:* 512-478-5748 ext 113 *E-mail:* nitas@dkg.org
Annual award to the woman author(s) of a book whose work may influence the direction of thought & action necessary to meet the needs of today's complex society. The content must be of more than local interest with relationship, direct or implied, to education everywhere. The author must be a woman from Canada, Costa Rica, El Salvador, Estonia, Finland, Germany, Great Britain, Guatemala, Iceland, Mexico, Netherlands, Norway, Puerto Rico, Sweden, Japan or the US; call, e-mail or download regulations. All nominations are made by publishers or authors.
Award: $2,500
Closing Date: Feb 1 (postmark), in the year after copyright
Presented: One of five regional conferences or Society's International Convention, Summer

Margaret A Edwards Award
Young Adult Library Services Association (YALSA)
Division of The American Library Association (ALA)
50 E Huron St, Chicago, IL 60611
Tel: 312-280-4390 *Toll Free Tel:* 800-545-2433 *Fax:* 312-280-5276
E-mail: yalsa@ala.org
Web Site: www.ala.org/yalsa/edwards
Key Personnel
Exec Dir: Beth Yoke *Tel:* 800-545-2433 ext 4391 *E-mail:* byoke@ala.org
Prog Offr, Events & Conferences: Nichole O'Connor *Tel:* 800-545-2433 ext 4387 *E-mail:* noconnor@ala.org
Communs Specialist: Anna Lam *Tel:* 800-545-2433 ext 5849 *E-mail:* alam@ala.org
Established: 1988
Given to an author for lifetime achievement in helping adolescents become aware of themselves & addressing questions about their role & importance in relationships, society & in the world.
Other Sponsor(s): School Library Journal
Award: $1,000 & citation
Closing Date: Annually in June
Presented: Announced at ALA's Midwinter Meeting. Winner honored & speaks during a luncheon at ALA's Annual Conference

Edwin Markham Prize for Poetry
Reed Magazine
San Jose State University, English Dept, One Washington Sq, San Jose, CA 95192-0090
Tel: 408-924-4441
Web Site: www.reedmag.org
All submissions must be through the online system with a common file format. Writers may submit multiple entries but each must be submitted separately & accompanied by a separate entry fee of $15.
Award: $1,000 & publication in *Reed Magazine*
Closing Date: Annually, Nov 1 (submissions accepted beginning June 1)

The Maureen Egen Writers Exchange Award
Poets & Writers Inc
90 Broad St, Suite 2100, New York, NY 10004
Tel: 212-226-3586 *Fax:* 212-226-3963
E-mail: admin@pw.org
Web Site: www.pw.org
Established: 1984
Introduces emerging writers to the New York literary community & provides them with a network for professional advancement.
Award: All expenses-paid trip to New York City to meet with top literary professionals & give a public reading

Wilfrid Eggleston Award for Nonfiction
Writers' Guild of Alberta

11759 Groat Rd, Edmonton, AB T5M 3K6, Canada
Tel: 780-422-8174 *Toll Free Tel:* 800-665-5354 (AB only) *Fax:* 780-422-2663 (attn WGA)
E-mail: mail@writersguild.ca
Web Site: writersguild.ca
Key Personnel
Exec Dir: Carol Holmes *E-mail:* carol.holmes@writersguild.ca
Communs & Partnerships Coord: Ellen Kartz *E-mail:* ellen.kartz@writersguild.ca
Memb Servs Coord: Giorgia Severini
Progs Coord: Natalie Cook *E-mail:* natalie.cook@writersguild.ca; Julie Robinson *E-mail:* julie.robinson@writersguild.ca
Established: 1982
Alberta Literary Award, author must be resident of Alberta.
Award: $1,500 plus leather-bound copy of book
Closing Date: Annually, Dec 31
Presented: Alberta Book Awards Gala
Branch Office(s)
505 21 Ave SW, Calgary, AB T2S 0G9, Canada, Prog Coord: Samantha Warwick *Tel:* 403-265-2226 *E-mail:* samantha.warwick@writersguild.ca

T S Eliot Prize for Poetry
Truman State University Press
100 E Normal Ave, Kirksville, MO 63501-4221
Tel: 660-785-7336 *Toll Free Tel:* 800-916-6802 *Fax:* 660-785-4480
E-mail: tsup@truman.edu
Web Site: tsup.truman.edu
Key Personnel
Dir & Ed-in-Chief: Barbara Smith-Mandell *E-mail:* bsm@truman.edu
Established: 1997
Annual award for the best unpublished book-length collection of poetry in English. Include a non-refundable reading fee of $25 for each ms submitted.
Award: $2,000 & publication
Closing Date: Oct 31
Presented: Feb

eLit Awards
Independent Publisher Online
1129 Woodmere Ave, Suite B, Traverse City, MI 49686
Tel: 231-933-0445 *Toll Free Tel:* 800-706-4636 *Fax:* 231-933-0448
E-mail: info@elitawards.com
Web Site: www.elitawards.com
Key Personnel
CEO: Jerrold R Jenkins *E-mail:* jrj@bookpublishing.com
Pres: James Kalajian *Tel:* 800-706-4636 ext 1006 *E-mail:* jjk@bookpublishing.com
Dir: Andrew Parvel *Tel:* 800-706-4636 ext 1004 *E-mail:* aparvel@bookpublishing.com
Established: 2009
To celebrate the ever growing market of electronic publishing in the wide variety of reader formats. Publishers & authors worldwide creating electronic books written in English & created for the global marketplace are eligible for entry in 65 different categories.
Other Sponsor(s): Jenkins Group
Award: Digital seal, certificate, winners featured online
Closing Date: Annually in Jan
Presented: Online, Annually in April

Van Courtlandt Elliott Prize
Medieval Academy of America
17 Dunster St, Suite 202, Cambridge, MA 02138
Tel: 617-491-1622 *Fax:* 617-492-3303
E-mail: info@themedievalacademy.org
Web Site: www.medievalacademy.org
Key Personnel
Exec Dir: Lisa Fagin Davis *E-mail:* lfd@themedievalacademy.org
Established: 1971
For a first article published in the field of medieval studies. Author must be a resident in North America.
Award: $1,000
Closing Date: Annually, Oct 15
Presented: Annually in April

Emerging Critics Fellowship
National Book Critics Circle
c/o 38 Douglass St, Apt 3, Brooklyn, NY 11231
E-mail: info@bookcritics.org
Web Site: bookcritics.org
Key Personnel
VP, Awards: Michele Filgate *E-mail:* mfilgate@gmail.com
One-year fellowship for critics who have demonstrated a genuine interest & commitment to engaging in critical conversation about books. Each writer must submit a resume, 3 writing examples, 300-500 word statement of purpose & names/contact information for 2 references. To apply, see nbcc.submittable.com/submit.
Closing Date: Jan
Presented: Announcement early March

Emerging Playwright Award
Urban Stages
555 Eighth Ave, Suite 1800, New York, NY 10018
Tel: 212-421-1380 *Fax:* 212-421-1387
E-mail: urbanstage@aol.com
Key Personnel
Artistic Dir & Founder: Frances Hill
Literary Dir: Antoinette Mullins
Scripts not previously produced; scripts should have no more than 7 characters; well-written, imaginative situations & dialog; multicultural scripts are given special attention. Playwrights in & around NYC are given special attention. No processing fee & SASE with all submissions. Selected scripts are first given a staged reading. A select number of staged readings are given intensive workshops. A select number of workshopped plays are given full off-Broadway productions. Award given to playwrights of full productions at Urban Stages.
Award: $500
Closing Date: Year-round
Presented: New York

The Ralph Waldo Emerson Award
The Phi Beta Kappa Society
1606 New Hampshire Ave NW, Washington, DC 20009
Tel: 202-265-3808 *Fax:* 202-986-1601
E-mail: awards@pbk.org
Web Site: www.pbk.org/bookawards
Key Personnel
Prog & Event Specialist: Laura Hartnett *Tel:* 202-745-3287 *E-mail:* lhartnett@pbk.org
Established: 1960
For scholarly studies that contribute to interpretations of the intellectual & cultural condition of humanity. To be eligible, must have been published in US by American author. Works in history, philosophy, religion & related fields such as social sciences & anthropology are eligible. Nomination must come from publisher & be submitted online.
Award: $10,000
Closing Date: Annually in Jan
Presented: Washington, DC, Annually in Dec

Empire State Award for Excellence in Literature for Young People
New York Library Association
6021 State Farm Rd, Guilderland, NY 12084
Tel: 518-432-6952 *Toll Free Tel:* 800-252-6952 *Fax:* 518-427-1697
E-mail: info@nyla.org
Web Site: www.nyla.org
Key Personnel
Exec Dir: Jeremy Johannesen *Tel:* 518-432-6952 ext 101 *E-mail:* director@nyla.org
Communs & Mktg Mgr: Kelsey Dorado *Tel:* 518-432-6952 ext 105 *E-mail:* marketing@nyla.org
Established: 1990
One-time award presented to a living author or illustrator currently residing in New York State. The award honors excellence in children's or young adult literature & a body of work that has made a significant contribution to literature for young people.
Award: Engraved medallion
Presented: Annual Conference, Annually in Oct or Nov

Norma Epstein Foundation Awards in Creative Writing
University of Toronto - University College
15 King's College Circle, UC 165, Toronto, ON M5S 3H7, Canada
Tel: 416-978-8083 *Fax:* 416-978-8854
E-mail: uc.programs@utoronto.ca
Web Site: www.uc.utoronto.ca/writing-centre
Key Personnel
Registrar: Shelley Cornack
Academic Liaison & Asst to Vice Principal: Khamla Sengthavy *E-mail:* khamla.sengthavy@utoronto.ca
Biennial literary competition. Five categories: poetry, drama, novel, short story & other prose.
Award: Up to a total of $2,000
Closing Date: May 1, odd-numbered years
Presented: Toronto, Nov, odd-numbered years

The Ernest Sandeen & Richard Sullivan Prizes in Fiction & Poetry
University of Notre Dame Press/ND Creative Writing Program, Dept of English
356 O'Shaughnessy Hall, Notre Dame, IN 46556
Tel: 574-631-7526 *Fax:* 574-631-4795
E-mail: creativewriting@nd.edu
Web Site: creativewriting.nd.edu
Key Personnel
Dir: Prof Joyelle McSweeney
Awarded to authors who have published at least one volume of short fiction or one volume of poetry. Include a photocopy of the copyright & the title page of your previous volume. Vanity press publications do not fulfill this requirement. Please include a vita +/or a biographical statement which includes your publishing history. We will be glad to see a selection of reviews of the earlier collection. Submit two copies of your ms & inform us if the ms is available on computer disk. Include a SASE for acknowledgment of receipt of your submission. If you would like your ms returned, send a SASE. A $15 administrative fee should accompany submissions.
Both prizes are awarded biannually, Ernest Sandeen Prize in even-numbered years & Richard Sullivan Prize in odd-numbered years.
Award: $1,000 prize, $500 award & $500 advance against royalties from the Notre Dame Press
Closing Date: May 1-Sept 1, 2019 (Richard Sullivan Prize), May 1-Sept 1, 2020 (Ernest Sandeen Prize)
Presented: Spring following submission period

Erskine J Poetry Prize
Smartish Pace
PO Box 22161, Baltimore, MD 21203
E-mail: smartishpace@gmail.com
Web Site: www.smartishpace.com

Key Personnel
Founder & Ed: Stephen Reichert
E-mail: sreichert@smartishpace.com
Established: 2001
All poems submitted for the prize will be considered for publication in *Smartish Pace*. Online submissions at www.smartishpace.com. Postal submissions: submit 3 poems along with a $10 entry fee. Additional poems may be submitted for $1 per poem. No more than 20 poems may be submitted. All entries must include bio. Include a SASE with entry. Include name, address, e-mail & telephone number on each page of poetry submitted. Write or print "Erskine J" on the top of each poem submitted.
Award: $200 & publication of winning poem in *Smartish Pace* (1st prize). All finalists will be published in *Smartish Pace*
Closing Date: Annually, Nov 1
Presented: Baltimore, MD

ESPN Award for Literary Sports Writing, see PEN/ESPN Award for Literary Sports Writing

ESPN Lifetime Achievement Award for Literary Sports Writing, see PEN/ESPN Lifetime Achievement Award for Literary Sports Writing

David W & Beatrice C Evans Biography & Handcart Awards
Mountain West Center for Regional Studies
Division of College of Humanities & Social Sciences-Utah State University
0735 Old Main Hill, Logan, UT 84322-0735
Tel: 435-797-0299 *Fax:* 435-797-1092
E-mail: mwc@usu.edu
Web Site: mountainwest.usu.edu
Key Personnel
Prog Dir: Evelyn I Funda
Established: 1983
For the best published biography, autobiography or memoir with a significant biographical content of an individual associated with "Mormon Country" (a geographical, not religious, concept) published in 2017.
Award: $10,000 (The Evans Biography Award); $2,500 (The Evans Handcart Award)
Closing Date: Feb 22, 2018
Presented: Utah State University, Annually in the Fall

EXCEL Awards
Association Media & Publishing (AM&P)
529 14 St, Suite 750, Washington, DC 20045
Tel: 202-591-2457
E-mail: awards@associationmediaandpublishing.org; info@associationmediaandpublishing.org
Web Site: associationmediaandpublishing.org; kellencompany.com
Key Personnel
Exec Dir: Meredith Taylor
Proj Mgr: Nate Bell *E-mail:* nbell@kellencompany.com
Service excellence awards program for association publishers. The EXCEL program judges over 1,200 magazines, newsletters, scholarly journals, electronic publications & web sites in the areas of editorial quality, design, general excellence, most improved & more.
Award: Gold Award (1st prize) brass statues; Silver & Bronze (2nd & 3rd prizes) framed certificates; EXTRA! Award, best of the gold, silver & bronze winners
Closing Date: Annually in Jan
Presented: Excel Awards Gala, Annual Meeting

John K Fairbank Prize in East Asian History
American Historical Association (AHA)
400 "A" St SE, Washington, DC 20003
Tel: 202-544-2422 *Fax:* 202-544-8307
E-mail: awards@historians.org
Web Site: www.historians.org
Established: 1968
Outstanding book on the history of China proper, Vietnam, Chinese Central Asia, Mongolia, Manchuria, Korea or Japan substantially after 1800; books published in 2017 will be eligible; anthologies, edited works & pamphlets are ineligible for the competition. Along with an application form, applicants must mail a copy of their book to each of the prize committee members who will be posted on our web site as the prize deadline approaches. All updated info on web site.
Award: Cash prize
Closing Date: May 15, 2018
Presented: AHA Annual Meeting, Chicago, IL, Jan 2019

Tom Fairley Award for Editorial Excellence
Editors' Association of Canada (Association canadienne des reviseurs)
27 Carlton St, Suite 505, Toronto, ON M5B 1L2, Canada
Tel: 416-975-1379 *Toll Free Tel:* 866-CAN-EDIT (226-3348) *Fax:* 416-975-1637
E-mail: fairley_award@editors.ca; info@editors.ca
Web Site: www.editors.ca; www.reviseurs.ca
Key Personnel
Exec Dir: John Yip-Chuck
E-mail: executivedirector@editors.ca
Sr Communs Mgr: Michelle Ou
E-mail: communications@editors.ca
Membership & Conference Coord: Caitlin Stewart
Established: 1983
Recognizes the editor's often invisible contribution to written communication. $100 admission fee.
Other Sponsor(s): Breakwater Books; HarperCollins; The C D Howe Institute; New Society Publishers; Orca Book Publishers; Random House of Canada; UBC Press, Madison; University of Calgary Press
Award: $2,000 cash
Closing Date: Jan of the year after the work took place for letter of nomination & supporting material must be received by the second week in Feb
Presented: National Annual Conference, June of the year after the work took place

Family Matters
Glimmer Train Press Inc
PO Box 80430, Portland, OR 97280-1430
Tel: 503-221-0836 *Fax:* 503-221-0837
E-mail: editors@glimmertrain.org
Web Site: www.glimmertrain.org
Key Personnel
Co-Ed: Susan Burmeister-Brown *E-mail:* susan@glimmertrain.org
Established: 2007
Open to all writers, family theme, 500-12,000 word count range. Winner notification takes place 2 months after the close of each competition.
Award: $2,500, publication & 20 copies of that issue (1st place), $500 (2nd place), $300 (3rd place)
Closing Date: Annually in Nov & Dec

Far Horizons Award for Poetry
The Malahat Review
University of Victoria, Box 1700, Sta CSC, Victoria, BC V8W 2Y2, Canada
Tel: 250-721-8524 *Fax:* 250-472-5051
E-mail: malahat@uvic.ca
Web Site: www.malahatreview.ca
Key Personnel
Ed: John Barton
Established: 2006
Open to writers whose poetry has yet to be published in book form. Awarded in alternate years. See web site for details.
Award: $1,000
Closing Date: May 1, even-numbered years

Far Horizons Award for Short Fiction
The Malahat Review
University of Victoria, Box 1700, Sta CSC, Victoria, BC V8W 2Y2, Canada
Tel: 250-721-8524 *Fax:* 250-472-5051
E-mail: malahat@uvic.ca
Web Site: www.malahatreview.ca
Key Personnel
Ed: John Barton
Established: 2005
Open to writers whose fiction has yet to be published in a book of their own. Limited to 3,500 words. Awarded in alternate years. See web site for details.
Award: $1,000
Closing Date: May 1, odd-numbered years

Norma Farber First Book Award
Poetry Society of America (PSA)
15 Gramercy Park, New York, NY 10003
Tel: 212-254-9628
Web Site: www.poetrysociety.org
Key Personnel
Pres: Kimiko Hahn
Exec Dir: Alice Quinn
Deputy Dir: Brett Fletcher Lauer *E-mail:* brett@poetrysociety.org
Prog Dir: Laurin Macios *E-mail:* laurin@poetrysociety.org
For a first book of original poetry written by an American poet & published in either a hard or soft cover in a standard edition.
Award: $500
Closing Date: Annually, Oct-Dec
Presented: Annual Awards Ceremony, New York, NY, Annually in Spring

The FC2 Catherine Doctorow Innovative Fiction Prize
Fiction Collective Two Inc (FC2)
c/o Dept of English, Languages & Communications Bldg, 255 S Central Campus Dr, Rm 3500, Salt Lake City, UT 84112-0494
Tel: 773-702-7000
Web Site: www.fc2.org/prizes.html
Key Personnel
Chair, Bd of Dirs: Lance Olsen
Open to any US writer in English with at least 3 books of fiction published. Submissions may include a collection of short stories, one or more novellas or a novel of any length. Works that have previously appeared in magazines or in anthologies may be included.
Award: $15,000 & publication by FC2
Closing Date: Annually, Nov 1
Presented: Annually in May

Fellowship Program
Rhode Island State Council on the Arts
Affiliate of Department of Rhode Island State Government
One Capital Hill, 3rd fl, Providence, RI 02908
Tel: 401-222-3880 *Fax:* 401-222-3018
Web Site: www.arts.ri.gov
Key Personnel
Dir, Indiv Artists Progs: Cristina DiChiera
E-mail: cristina.dichiera@arts.ri.gov
Established: 1967
Applicants must be Rhode Island residents who are over 18 & not students in an arts discipline. Fellowship recipients are selected by a regional panel of writers. Categories include fiction, poetry, playwriting/screenwriting. Guidelines & applications on web site.
Award: $5,000 recipient, $1,000 merit award
Closing Date: Annually, April 1

Fellowship, Tuition Scholarship & Work Study Programs for Writers
Bread Loaf Writers' Conference
Middlebury College, 204 College St, Middlebury, VT 05753
Tel: 802-443-5286 *Fax:* 802-443-2087
E-mail: blwc@middlebury.edu
Web Site: www.middlebury.edu/blwc
Key Personnel
Dir: Michael Collier
Admin Dir: Noreen Cargill
Asst Dir: Jennifer Grotz
Coord: Jason Lamb *E-mail:* jlamb@middlebury.edu
Work study scholarship to be used during conference in August.
Award: Fellowship provides tuition, room & board during 10-day conference; Scholarship provides tuition during conference
Closing Date: Annually, Feb 15
Presented: Ripton, VT, Annually in Aug, 10-day event

Fellowships for Creative & Performing Artists & Writers
American Antiquarian Society (AAS)
185 Salisbury St, Worcester, MA 01609-1634
Tel: 508-755-5221 *Fax:* 508-753-3311
Web Site: www.americanantiquarian.org
Key Personnel
Dir, Outreach: James David Moran *Tel:* 508-471-2131 *E-mail:* jmoran@mwa.org
Established: 1994
Award: $1,350 stipend for fellows residing on campus (rent-free) in the Society's Scholars' housing, $1,850 stipend for fellows residing off campus (no travel allowance)
Closing Date: Annually in Oct

Fellowships for Historical Research
American Antiquarian Society (AAS)
185 Salisbury St, Worcester, MA 01609-1634
Tel: 508-471-2131 *Fax:* 508-754-9069
Web Site: www.americanantiquarian.org
Key Personnel
Dir, Outreach: James David Moran *Tel:* 508-471-2131 *E-mail:* jmoran@mwa.org
Given to poets, fiction writers & creative nonfiction writers for month long residencies at the American Antiquarian Society in Worchester, MA, to research pre-twentieth century American history & culture. Submit 10 copies of up to 25 pages of poetry, fiction or creative nonfiction, a resume, 2 letters of recommendation & a 5 page project proposal.
Award: $1,350 stipend & on-campus housing provided; fellows residing off-campus receive $1,850
Closing Date: Annually, Oct 5

Fence Modern Poets Series
Fence Books
University at Albany, Science Library 320, 1400 Washington Ave, Albany, NY 12222
Tel: 518-591-8162
E-mail: fence.fencebooks@gmail.com
Web Site: www.fenceportal.org
Key Personnel
Publr & Ed: Rebecca Wolff *E-mail:* rebeccafence@gmail.com
Mng Ed: Jess Puglisi *E-mail:* jessp.fence@gmail.com
Established: 2001
For a poet writing in English at any stage of his or her publishing career.
Award: $1,000 & publication
Closing Date: Annually, Feb 28

Shubert Fendrich Memorial Playwriting Contest
Pioneer Drama Service Inc
PO Box 4267, Englewood, CO 80155-4267
Tel: 303-779-4035 *Toll Free Tel:* 800-333-7262 *Fax:* 303-779-4315
Web Site: www.pioneerdrama.com/playwrights/contest.asp
Key Personnel
Submissions Ed: Lori Conary
Established: 1990
Presented for plays suitable for publication by Pioneer Drama Service Inc. Submission must include 100-200 word synopsis, cast list, running time, CD +/or score, set design(s), proof of production or staged reading, age of intended audience, SASE for returned materials, cover letter +/or resume. See web site for detailed guidelines.
Award: $1,000 royalty advance & publication
Closing Date: Annually, Dec 31
Presented: Annually, June 1

Fiction Open
Glimmer Train Press Inc
PO Box 80430, Portland, OR 97280-1430
Tel: 503-221-0836 *Fax:* 503-221-0837
E-mail: editors@glimmertrain.org
Web Site: www.glimmertrain.org
Key Personnel
Co-Ed: Susan Burmeister-Brown *E-mail:* susan@glimmertrain.org
Established: 1999
Open to all themes & all writers, 3,000-24,000 word count range. Winner notification takes place 2 months after the close of each competition.
Award: $3,000, publication & 20 copies of that issue (1st place), $1,000 (2nd place), $600 (3rd place)
Closing Date: Annually in March/April & July/Aug

The Field Poetry Prize
Oberlin College Press
Subsidiary of Oberlin College
50 N Professor St, Oberlin, OH 44074-1091
SAN: 212-1883
Tel: 440-775-8408 *Fax:* 440-775-8124
E-mail: oc.press@oberlin.edu
Web Site: www.oberlin.edu/ocpress; www.oberlin.edu/ocpress/prize.htm (guidelines)
Key Personnel
Mng Ed: Marco Wilkinson
Ed: David Walker; David Young
Established: 1996
Original poetry ms of 50-80 pages. Open to all poets whether or not they have previously published in book form. Reading fee: $28. Includes 1-year subscription to *Field*.
Award: $1,000 & publication in the Field Poetry Series
Closing Date: Annually, May 31
Presented: Announced in Aug (on web site)

Findley Prize, see Writers' Trust Engel/Findley Prize

Fine Arts Work Center in Provincetown
24 Pearl St, Provincetown, MA 02657
Tel: 508-487-9960 *Fax:* 508-487-8873
E-mail: general@fawc.org
Web Site: www.fawc.org
Key Personnel
Visual Art Fellowship Coord: James Stanley *Tel:* 508-487-9960 ext 105 *E-mail:* jstanley@fawc.org
Writing Fellowship Coord: Sophia Starmack *Tel:* 508-487-9960 ext 113 *E-mail:* sstarmack@fawc.org
Established: 1968
Offer 7-month fellowships to 10 artists & 10 writers, October 1-May 1. The Center aims to aid emerging artists & writers at a critical stage of their careers. See web site for application & information.
Award: Monthly stipends of up to $650 plus free rent for writers living at the Center; same for artists. Families welcome; no pets
Closing Date: Visual Arts: Feb 1; Writers: Dec 1

Firecracker Awards
Community of Literary Magazines & Presses (CLMP)
154 Christopher St, Suite 3C, New York, NY 10014-9110
Tel: 212-741-9110 *Fax:* 212-741-9112
E-mail: info@clmp.org
Web Site: www.clmp.org/firecracker
Key Personnel
Progs Dir: Kathy Daneman *E-mail:* kdaneman@clmp.org
Celebrate & promote great literary works from independent literary publishers & self-published authors. Categories: Fiction, Creative Nonfiction, Poetry, Graphic Novel & Young Adult. Awards also in three magazine/periodical categories: Poetry, Best Debut & General Excellence.
Other Sponsor(s): American Booksellers Association
Presented: At public event held in conjunction with BookExpo, May

Five Star Dragonfly Book Awards, see Dragonfly Book Awards

Norma Fleck Award for Canadian Children's Non-Fiction
Canadian Children's Book Centre
40 Orchard View Blvd, Suite 217, Toronto, ON M4R 1B9, Canada
Tel: 416-975-0010 *Fax:* 416-975-8970
E-mail: info@bookcentre.ca
Web Site: www.bookcentre.ca
Key Personnel
Exec Dir: Charlotte Teeple *E-mail:* charlotte@bookcentre.ca
Lib Coord: Meghan Howe *E-mail:* meghan@bookcentre.ca
Mktg & Web Site Coord: Camilia Kahrizi *E-mail:* camilia@bookcentre.ca
Prog Coord: Shannon Howe Barnes *E-mail:* shannon@bookcentre.ca
Established: 1999
Awarded to a Canadian author/illustrator for an outstanding work of nonfiction for young people.
Other Sponsor(s): Fleck Family Foundation
Award: $10,000
Closing Date: Annually in mid-Dec

Florida Individual Artist Fellowships, see Individual Artist Project Grant

Fordham University, Graduate School of Business Administration
113 W 60 St, New York, NY 10023
Web Site: www.fordham.edu
Key Personnel
Professor, Communs & Media Mgmt: Philip M Napoli *E-mail:* pnapoli@fordham.edu
Established: 1969
Offers MBA degree with a major in Communications & Media Management & Master of Science (MS) in Communications & Media Management for media & entertainment industries. Its mission is to educate business professionals who can manage effectively in a range of leadership roles & who are equipped for continuous growth in a changing global environment. A variety of assistantships, fellowships & scholarships are available to highly qualified MBA candidates, such as Graduate Assistantships; New York Times Foundation Scholarship; Hitachi Fellowship; Xerox Fellowship; National Black MBA Association Scholarships; Minor-

ity Business Students Alliance Scholarship & Alexis Welsh Memorial Scholarship.
Closing Date: Ongoing
Presented: Each trimester

Foreword's INDIES Awards
Foreword Reviews
425 Boardman Ave, Suite B, Traverse City, MI 49684
Tel: 231-933-3699
Web Site: www.forewordreviews.com
Key Personnel
Publr: Victoria Sutherland *E-mail:* victoria@forewordreviews.com
Any independently published book, including those from self-published authors & university presses, published in the current year & available for purchase in print or ebook formats. Revised editions of previously issued books are eligible for entry only with newly issued ISBNs. Reissued editions are not eligible for entry.
Award: $1,500 each given to best book in fiction & nonfiction
Closing Date: Annually, Jan 15 for books published in previous calendar year
Presented: ALA Annual Conference

Morris D Forkosch Prize
American Historical Association (AHA)
400 "A" St SE, Washington, DC 20003
Tel: 202-544-2422 *Fax:* 202-544-8307
E-mail: awards@historians.org
Web Site: www.historians.org
In recognition of the best in English in the field of British, British Imperial or British Commonwealth history since 1485. Submissions of books relating to the shared common law heritage of the English-speaking world are particularly encouraged. Books on British, British Imperial or British Commonwealth history published in 2017 are eligible. Along with an application form, applicants must mail a copy of their book to each of the prize committee members who will be posted on our web site as the prize deadline approaches. All updated info on web site.
Closing Date: May 15, 2018
Presented: AHA Annual Meeting, Chicago, IL, Jan 2019

E M Forster Award
American Academy of Arts & Letters
633 W 155 St, New York, NY 10032
Tel: 212-368-5900 *Fax:* 212-491-4615
E-mail: academy@artsandletters.org
Web Site: www.artsandletters.org
Key Personnel
Exec Dir: Cody Upton
Given to a young English writer toward a stay in the US.
Award: $20,000

49th Parallel Poetry Award
The Bellingham Review
Mail Stop 9053, Western Washington University, Bellingham, WA 98225
Tel: 360-650-4863
E-mail: bhreview@wwu.edu
Web Site: www.bhreview.org
Key Personnel
Ed-in-Chief: Suzanne Paola Antonetta
Mng Ed: Mike Oliphant
Established: 1983
Maximum of up to 3 poems per entry. Poems within a series of poems will each be treated as a separate entry. No previously published works, or works accepted for publication, are eligible. Work may be under consideration elsewhere, but must be withdrawn from the competition if accepted for publication. All entries will receive a complimentary 1-issue subscription. Entry fee for the first entry (up to 3 poems) $20, additional entries $10.
Only accept submissions through Submittable. Mailed submissions are no longer accepted. All finalists are considered for publication. The winning piece is selected by a distinguished, outside judge. Entries accepted beginning December 1.
Award: $1,000 & publication in the *Bellingham Review* (1st prize), considered for publication (2nd, 3rd & finalists)
Closing Date: Annually, March 15
Presented: Annually in June

Foster City International Writers Contest
Foster City Parks & Recreation Department
650 Shell Blvd, Foster City, CA 94404
Tel: 650-286-3380
E-mail: fostercity_writers@yahoo.com
Web Site: www.fostercity.org
Key Personnel
Comm Chair: Ilene Shaine
Contact: Tiffany Oren
Established: 1974
For fiction, humor, poetry & personal essay, rhymed verse, blank verse. Entries must be original, previously unpublished & in English. Fiction must be no more than 3,000 words; poetry not to exceed two double-spaced typed pages in length. Open to all writers, no age or geographic limit. Send SASE for contest flyer. Non-refundable entry fee: $20.
Award: $250 in each category (1st prize); $100 (2nd prize): nonfiction, fiction, humor, poetry

Dixon Ryan Fox Manuscript Prize
Fenimore Art Museum
5798 State Hwy 80, Cooperstown, NY 13326
Mailing Address: PO Box 800, Cooperstown, NY 13326-0800
Tel: 607-547-1416
Established: 1974
Encourage original scholarship in the history of New York State. Award granted to the best unpublished ms on the history of New York State. Electronic submissions only.
Award: $3,000
Closing Date: Annually, March 1
Presented: Fenimore Art Museum Board of Trustees Annual Meeting, Cooperstown, NY, Annually in July

Frances Henne YALSA/VOYA Research Grant
Young Adult Library Services Association (YALSA)
Division of The American Library Association (ALA)
50 E Huron St, Chicago, IL 60611
Tel: 312-280-4390 *Toll Free Tel:* 800-545-2433 *Fax:* 312-280-5276
E-mail: yalsa@ala.org
Web Site: www.ala.org/yalsa/awardsandgrants/franceshenne
Key Personnel
Exec Dir: Beth Yoke *Tel:* 800-545-2433 ext 4391 *E-mail:* byoke@ala.org
Prog Offr, Events & Conferences: Nichole O'Connor *Tel:* 800-545-2433 ext 4387 *E-mail:* noconnor@ala.org
Communs Specialist: Anna Lam *Tel:* 800-545-2433 ext 5849 *E-mail:* alam@ala.org
Established: 1986
Annually recognizes a school library media specialist with 5 years or less experience who demonstrates leadership qualities with students, teachers & administrators to attend an AASL conference or ALA Annual Conference for the first time. Applicants must be AASL personal members.
Other Sponsor(s): Voice of Youth Advocates (VOYA)
Award: $1,000
Closing Date: Dec 1
Presented: ALA Midwinter Meeting, Jan/Feb

H E Francis Award Short Story Competition
University of Alabama Department of English
UAH Huntsville Dept of English, Morton Hall 222, Huntsville, AL 35899
Web Site: www.uah.edu/la/departments/english
Key Personnel
Registrar: Patricia Sammon
Established: 1990
Mss must be unpublished & may not exceed 5,000 words in length. Multiple submissions are acceptable so long as we are notified immediately in the event that a ms is selected by another competition or publication. Submission must include $15 entry fee, cover sheet & three copies of ms. May submit story line & pay fee with Pay Pal.
Other Sponsor(s): Ruth Hindman Foundation
Award: $2,000
Closing Date: Jan 15 (postmark)
Presented: Annually in April

Prix Francophone de l'ACSP
Canadian Political Science Association
260 rue Dalhousie St, Suite 204, Ottawa, ON K1N 7E4, Canada
Tel: 613-562-1202 *Fax:* 613-241-0019
E-mail: cpsa-acsp@cpsa-acsp.ca
Web Site: www.cpsa-acsp.ca
Key Personnel
Admin: Michelle Hopkins
Established: 2014
Biennial prize awarded to the best book published in French in the field of political science. To be eligible, a book may be single-authored or multi-authored. Single-authored: author must be a member of the CPSA in the year the book was published. Multi-authored: at least one of the authors must be a member of the CPSA in the year the book was published. For the 2018 award, a book must have a copyright date of 2016 or 2017.
Award: Commemorative plaque & receive/share the set of books submitted to the CPSA office
Closing Date: Dec 10
Presented: Annual Conference, University of Regina, Regina, SK, CN, May 26-June 1, 2018

Soeurette Diehl Fraser Translation Award
Texas Institute of Letters (TIL)
c/o 7748 Hwy 290 W, Austin, TX 78736-3202
Tel: 512-683-5640
E-mail: president@texasinstituteofletters.org
Web Site: www.texasinstituteofletters.org
Key Personnel
Pres: Steve Davis
VP: Carmen Tafolla
Treas: W K Stratton
Secy: Sergio Troncoso
Recording Secy: Joe Holley
Established: 1990
Biennial award given for the best book of translation by a Texan. Guidelines available on the web site.
Award: $1,000
Closing Date: Jan, odd-numbered years
Presented: TIL Awards Banquet, Spring, odd-numbered years

George Freedley Memorial Award
Theatre Library Association (TLA)
c/o The New York Public Library for the Performing Arts, 111 Amsterdam Ave, New York, NY 10023
E-mail: TLABookAwards@gmail.com; TheatreLibraryAssociation@gmail.com
Web Site: www.tla-online.org/awards/bookawards
Key Personnel
Co-Chair, Book Awards Comm: Diana Bertolini; Annemarie van Roessel
Established: 1968

To the author of a book in the field of theatre, published in the US, on the basis of scholarship, readability & general contribution to knowledge. Only books related to live performance (including vaudeville, puppetry, pantomime & circus) will be considered.
Award: $500 (1st prize), $250 (Special Jury Prize); certificate
Closing Date: Feb 28
Presented: New York City, NY, Oct

The Don Freeman Memorial Grant-In-Aid
Society of Children's Book Writers and Illustrators (SCBWI)
4727 Wilshire Blvd, Suite 301, Los Angeles, CA 90010
Tel: 323-782-1010; 310-403-0675 (cell) *Fax:* 323-782-1892
E-mail: grants@scbwi.org; scbwi@scbwi.org
Web Site: www.scbwi.org
Key Personnel
Pres: Stephen Mooser *E-mail:* stephenmooser@scbwi.org
Exec Dir: Lin Oliver *E-mail:* linoliver@scbwi.org
Established: 1977
To enable picture-book artists to further their understanding, training +/or work in any aspect of the picture-book genre. Grant may be used for the purchase of necessary materials, enrollment in illustrators' or writers' workshops or conferences, courses in advanced illustrating or writing techniques & travel for research or to expose work to publishers/art directors. Open to Society members only.
Award: Winning works shown to editors & agents
Closing Date: Annually in March
Presented: Annually in Aug

The French-American Foundation & Florence Gould Foundation Annual Translation Prize
The French-American Foundation
28 W 44 St, Suite 1420, New York, NY 10036
Tel: 212-829-8800 *Fax:* 212-829-8810
Web Site: www.frenchamerican.org
Key Personnel
VP & CEO: Dana Arifi
Prog Offr: Katie Demallie *E-mail:* kdemallie@frenchamerican.org
Established: 1986
Award for outstanding translations of fiction & nonfiction from French into English which have been published in the US. Translations must be submitted by the US publisher. Technical, poetry, scientific, reference works & children's literature are not accepted. Works must have been published in the previous calendar year.
Other Sponsor(s): Florence Gould Foundation
Award: 2 awards of $10,000 (1 each for fiction & nonfiction)
Closing Date: Jan 15
Presented: New York, NY, Spring

Fresh Fish Award for Emerging Writers
Writers' Alliance of Newfoundland and Labrador (WANL)/Literary Arts Foundation of Newfoundland and Labrador
Haymarket Sq, 223 Duckworth St, St John's, NL A1C 6N1, Canada
Tel: 709-739-5215 *Toll Free Tel:* 866-739-5215
E-mail: wanl@nf.aibn.com
Web Site: wanl.ca
Key Personnel
Exec Dir: Wendi Smallwood
Memb Servs Coord: Samantha Fitzpatrick
Established: 2006
Intended to serve as an incentive for emerging writers in Newfoundland & Labrador by providing them with financial support, recognition & professional editing services for a book-length ms in any genre. Must be registered members of WANL; writers may join WANL at the time of submission.
Award: $5,200, $1,000 toward professional editing services for the winning ms & miniature sculpture; $1,200 each to runners-up
Closing Date: Sept, odd-numbered years

Friends of American Writers Awards
Friends of American Writers
506 Rose Ave, Des Plaines, IL 60016
Tel: 847-827-8339
Web Site: www.fawchicago.org
Key Personnel
Pres: Roberta Gates *E-mail:* robmicgates73@gmail.com
Adult Lit Awards: Tammie Bob
E-mail: bobtam410@gmail.com
Established: 1922
For literary fiction & nonfiction books published in the current year. Book must be author's first, second or third work. Author must have lived for 5 years in the Midwest, currently living in the Midwest, or book's setting must be Midwestern. No poetry or mss. See web site for full details.
Award: Two cash prizes totaling $4,000
Closing Date: Annually, Dec 20
Presented: The Fortnightly, Chicago, IL, Annually in May

Fulbright Scholar Program
Council for International Exchange of Scholars
Division of The Institute of International Education
1400 "K" St NW, Washington, DC 20005
Tel: 202-686-4000
E-mail: scholars@iie.org
Web Site: www.cies.org; www.iie.org
Key Personnel
Dir, US Scholar Progs: Jordanna Enrich *Tel:* 202-686-6233 *E-mail:* jenrich@iie.org
Dir, Outreach: Peter Van Derwater *Tel:* 202-686-4014 *E-mail:* pvanderwater@iie.org
Established: 1946
CIES cooperates with the US Dept of State, Bureau of Educational & Cultural Affairs, in the administration of the Fulbright scholar program, which offers approximately 800 grants annually to US faculty & professionals for university teaching +/or advanced research in more than 140 countries.
Award: Grant benefits, which vary by country, generally include a stipend & round-trip travel for the grantee
Closing Date: Aug 1

Gabriele Rico Creative Nonfiction Challenge
Reed Magazine
San Jose State University, English Dept, One Washington Sq, San Jose, CA 95192-0090
Tel: 408-924-4441
Web Site: www.reedmag.org
All submissions must be through the online system with a common file format. Writers may submit multiple entries but each must be submitted separately & accompanied by a separate entry fee of $15.
Award: $1,333 & publication in *Reed Magazine*
Closing Date: Annually, Nov 1 (submissions accepted beginning June 1)

Lewis Galantiere Translation Award
American Translators Association (ATA)
225 Reinekers Lane, Suite 590, Alexandria, VA 22314
Tel: 703-683-6100 *Fax:* 703-683-6122
E-mail: honors_awards@atanet.org
Web Site: www.atanet.org
Key Personnel
Chair, ATA Honors & Awards Comm: Lois Feuerle
Established: 1984
Awarded in even years for a distinguished book-length literary translation from any language, except German into English, published in the US.
Award: $1,000, a certificate of recognition & up to $500 toward expenses to attend the ATA Annual Conference
Closing Date: March 1 (even years)
Presented: ATA Annual Conference

Gannon University's High School Poetry Contest
Gannon University English Dept
Gannon University, 109 University Sq, Erie, PA 16541
Tel: 814-871-7504
Web Site: www.gannon.edu/departmental/english/poetry.asp
Key Personnel
Professor of Eng: Berwyn Moore
E-mail: moore001@gannon.edu
Established: 1985
High School students in grades 9-12 are invited to participate; must be original poetry.
Award: $100 (1st place), $75 (2nd place), $50 (3rd place), certificate (honorable mention)
Closing Date: Annually, Feb 1 (postmark)
Presented: Gannon University, Waldron Campus Center, Erie, PA, April

Francois-Xavier Garneau Medal
Canadian Historical Association
130 Albert St, Suite 1201, Ottawa, ON K1P 5G4, Canada
Tel: 613-233-7885 *Fax:* 613-565-5445
E-mail: cha-shc@cha-shc.ca
Web Site: www.cha-shc.ca
Key Personnel
Exec Dir: Michel Duquet *E-mail:* mduquet@cha-shc.ca
Established: 1980
Awarded every 5 years; commemorates the first Canadian Historian. Applicant should be a Canadian citizen or a legal immigrant. Given for the most outstanding scholarly book in the field of Canadian history within the previous five years.
Award: Minted medal & $2,000
Presented: 2020

Alfred C Gary Memorial
The Poetry Society of Virginia
900 Timber Creek Place, Virginia Beach, VA 23464
E-mail: poetryinva@aol.com
Web Site: poetrysocietyofvirginia.org
Key Personnel
Pres: Robert P Arthur *E-mail:* robert.peebles.arthur@gmail.com
Exec Dir: Guy Terrell *E-mail:* guy.terrell@earthlink.net
Adult Contest Chair: Steven Blythe
E-mail: stevenblythepoetry@gmail.com
All entries must be in English, original & unpublished. Submit 2 copies, each having the category name & number on top left of page. Entries will not be returned. Subject: a historic event that occurred between 1925 & 1992; iambic pentameter; 48 line limit. Entry fee: $4 nonmembs.
Other Sponsor(s): Claudia Gary
Award: $50 (1st prize), $30 (2nd prize), $20 (3rd prize)
Closing Date: Jan
Presented: Annual PSV Awards Ceremony, April

John Gassner Memorial Playwriting Award
The New England Theatre Conference Inc
215 Knob Hill Dr, Hamden, CT 06518
Tel: 617-851-8535 *Fax:* 203-288-5938
E-mail: mail@netconline.org
Web Site: www.netconline.org

Established: 1967
Playwriting contest for new full-length plays.
Closing Date: Annually, April 15
Presented: NETC Annual Convention, Annually in Nov

The Christian Gauss Award
The Phi Beta Kappa Society
1606 New Hampshire Ave NW, Washington, DC 20009
Tel: 202-265-3808 *Fax:* 202-986-1601
E-mail: awards@pbk.org
Web Site: www.pbk.org/bookawards
Key Personnel
Prog & Event Specialist: Laura Hartnett *Tel:* 202-745-3287 *E-mail:* lhartnett@pbk.org
Established: 1950
For outstanding books in the field of literary scholarship or criticism published in the US. Nominations must come from publisher & be submitted online.
Award: $10,000
Closing Date: Annually in Jan
Presented: Washington, DC, Annually in Dec

The Gaylactic Spectrum Awards
Gaylactic Spectrum Awards Foundation
1425 "S" St NW, Washington, DC 20009
Web Site: www.spectrumawards.org
Key Personnel
Exec Dir: Rob Gates
Established: 1998
Presented to outstanding works of science fiction, fantasy or horror which include significant gay, lesbian, bisexual or transgendered characters, themes, or issues. Awards are given in 3 categories: Best Novel, Best Short Fiction & Best Other Work.
Award: Statuette & & small cash stipend for Best Novel & Best Short Fiction categories
Closing Date: Open between March 15 & April 30 for works released during the previous calendar year
Presented: Varies - World Science Fiction Convention, Gaylaxicon or other, Fall

Lionel Gelber Prize
Lionel Gelber Foundation
University of Toronto, Munk School of Global Affairs, One Devonshire Place, Toronto, ON M5S 3K7, Canada
Tel: 416-946-8901 *Fax:* 416-946-8915
E-mail: events.munk@utoronto.ca
Web Site: munkschool.utoronto.ca/gelber; www.facebook.com/GelberPrize
Established: 1989
Given to the author of the year's most outstanding work of nonfiction in the field of international relations. Designed to encourage authors who write about international relations & to stimulate the audience for these books to grow. Open to authors of all nationalities. Six copies of each title must be submitted by the publisher. Books must be published between January 1 & December 31 in English or English translation.
Other Sponsor(s): Munk School of Global Affairs
Award: $15,000
Closing Date: Oct
Presented: Short list announced Jan; prize award in Spring

Leo Gershoy Award
American Historical Association (AHA)
400 "A" St SE, Washington, DC 20003
Tel: 202-544-2422 *Fax:* 202-544-8307
E-mail: awards@historians.org
Web Site: www.historians.org
Established: 1975
In recognition of outstanding historical writing in 17th & 18th century Western European history. Books published in 2017 will be eligible. Along with an application form, applicants must mail a copy of their book (limited to 3 titles from any one publisher) to each of the prize committee members who will be posted on our web site as the prize deadline approaches. All updated info on web site.
Award: Cash prize
Closing Date: May 15, 2018
Presented: AHA Annual Meeting, Chicago, IL, Jan 2019

Charles M Getchell Award, see Southeastern Theatre Conference New Play Project

Gilder Lehrman Lincoln Prize
The Gilder Lehrman Institute of American History
300 N Washington St, Campus Box 413, Gettysburg, PA 17325
Tel: 717-337-8255
E-mail: lincolnprize@gettysburg.edu
Web Site: www.gilderlehrman.org
Established: 1990
Awarded annually for the finest scholarly work in English on Abraham Lincoln, the American Civil War soldier, or the American Civil War era. Publishers, critics & authors may submit books published in the current year. No entry fee or form. Send six copies of the nominated work.
Other Sponsor(s): Gettysburg College
Award: $50,000
Closing Date: Nov 1

Giller Prize
Scotiabank
543 Logan Ave, Toronto, ON M4K 3B6, Canada
Web Site: www.scotiabankgillerprize.ca
Key Personnel
Exec Dir: Elana Rabinovitch
Submissions & Mktg Mgr: Michelle Kadarusman
Annual literary prize for fiction.
Award: $140,000
Closing Date: Aug 15

Allen Ginsberg Poetry Award
The Poetry Center at Passaic County Community College
One College Blvd, Paterson, NJ 07505-1179
Tel: 973-684-6555 *Fax:* 973-523-6085
Web Site: www.poetrycenterpccc.com
Key Personnel
Exec Dir: Maria Mazziotti Gillan *E-mail:* mgillan@pccc.edu
Mgr: Susan Balik *E-mail:* sbalik@pccc.edu
Poem should not be more than 2 ms pages. Sheets which contain the poems should not contain the poet's name. Do not submit poems that imitate Allen Ginsberg's work. Entry fee $18.
Award: $1,000 (1st prize), $200 (2nd prize), $100 (3rd prize)
Closing Date: Annually, Feb 1

Gival Press Novel Award
Gival Press
PO Box 3812, Arlington, VA 22203
SAN: 852-9787
Tel: 703-351-0079 *Fax:* 703-351-0079 (call first)
E-mail: givalpress@yahoo.com
Web Site: www.givalpress.com; givalpress.submittable.com
Key Personnel
Publr & Ed: Robert L Giron
Established: 2005
For best literary novel.
Award: $3,000 & publication
Closing Date: Annually, May 30
Presented: Annually, Oct 1

Gival Press Oscar Wilde Award
Gival Press
PO Box 3812, Arlington, VA 22203
SAN: 852-9787
Tel: 703-351-0079 *Fax:* 703-351-0079 (call first)
E-mail: givalpress@yahoo.com
Web Site: www.givalpress.com; givalpress.submittable.com
Key Personnel
Publr & Ed: Robert L Giron
Established: 2002
For best GLBT poem.
Award: $100 & online publication
Closing Date: Annually, June 27
Presented: Annually, Sept 1

Gival Press Poetry Award
Gival Press
PO Box 3812, Arlington, VA 22203
SAN: 852-9787
Tel: 703-351-0079 *Fax:* 703-351-0079 (call first)
E-mail: givalpress@yahoo.com
Web Site: www.givalpress.com; givalpress.submittable.com
Key Personnel
Publr & Ed: Robert L Giron
Established: 1999
For the best collection of poetry.
Award: $1,000 & book publication
Closing Date: Annually, Dec 15
Presented: Annually, May 1

Gival Press Short Story Award
Gival Press
PO Box 3812, Arlington, VA 22203
SAN: 852-9787
Tel: 703-351-0079 *Fax:* 703-351-0079 (call first)
E-mail: givalpress@yahoo.com
Web Site: www.givalpress.com; givalpress.submittable.com
Key Personnel
Publr & Ed: Robert L Giron
Established: 2004
For best literary short story.
Award: $1,000 & online publication
Closing Date: Annually, Aug 8
Presented: Annually, Dec 1

John Glassco Translation Prize
Literary Translators' Association of Canada
Concordia University, LB 601, 1455 De Maisonneuve W, Montreal, QC H3G 1M8, Canada
Tel: 514-848-2424 (ext 8702)
E-mail: info@attlc-ltac.org
Web Site: www.attlc-ltac.org
Key Personnel
Pres: Madeleine Stratford
Established: 1982
For a first book-length literary translation into French or English published in Canada during the previous year. Must be Canadian citizen or permanent resident.
Award: $1,000
Closing Date: Annually, July 31
Presented: Annually, Sept 30

GLCA New Writers Awards
Great Lakes Colleges Association (GLCA)
535 W William St, Suite 301, Ann Arbor, MI 48103
Tel: 734-661-2350 *Fax:* 734-661-2349
Web Site: www.glca.org
Key Personnel
Dir, Prog Devt: Gregory R Wegner
Established: 1969
For a first published work of fiction or creative nonfiction or a first book of poetry. Submissions may be made only by publishers; one entry each, poetry, fiction or creative nonfiction. Submit 4 copies of the work & an author's statement agreeing to the terms. See web site for details.

Award: Reading engagements at up to 13 colleges & universities of the GLCA; each engagement includes $500 honorarium; all travel expenses are paid
Closing Date: July 25

The Danuta Gleed Literary Award
The Writers' Union of Canada (TWUC)
600-460 Richmond St W, Toronto, ON M5V 1Y1, Canada
Tel: 416-703-8982 *Fax:* 416-504-9090
E-mail: info@writersunion.ca
Web Site: www.writersunion.ca
Key Personnel
Off Admin: Valerie Laws *Tel:* 416-703-8982 ext 224
Established: 1997
Annual award for best first collection of short fiction by a Canadian published in the calendar year prior to the closing date & available through bookstores & libraries.
Award: $10,000 (1st prize), $500 (2nd & 3rd prizes)
Closing Date: Annually, Jan 31

The Goddard Riverside Stephan Russo Book Prize
Goddard Riverside Community Center
593 Columbus Ave, New York, NY 10024
Web Site: bookprize.goddard.org
Key Personnel
Contact: Jenny Pfister *Tel:* 212-873-6600 ext 354 *E-mail:* jpfister@goddard.org
Annual literary award to recognize books that focus on housing, early childhood & secondary education, older adult life, city arts, social policy & other important aspects of community life that support & promote Goddard Riverside's mission. Books must be written in English & published in the US between October 1 of the previous year & September 30 of the award year. Six copies of each title should be submitted, along with prize entry form & $50 application fee.
Closing Date: May 15
Presented: Goddard Riverside's Book Fair Gala, Fall

Gold Medal
American Academy of Arts & Letters
633 W 155 St, New York, NY 10032
Tel: 212-368-5900 *Fax:* 212-491-4615
E-mail: academy@artsandletters.org
Web Site: www.artsandletters.org
Key Personnel
Exec Dir: Cody Upton
Rotating categories of Belles Lettres & Criticism & Painting; Biography & Music; Fiction & Sculpture; History & Architecture, including Landscape Architecture; Poetry & Music; Drama & Graphic Art.
Award: 2 medals annually

Golden Cylindar Awards
Gravure Association of the Americas Inc
8281 Pine Lake Rd, Denver, NC 28037
Tel: 201-523-6042 *Fax:* 201-523-6048
E-mail: gaa@gaa.org
Web Site: www.gaa.org
Key Personnel
Dir, Planning & Admin: Pamela W Schenk *Tel:* 585-288-2297 *E-mail:* pwschenk@gaa.org
Encourage highest quality gravure printing from design through production.
Award: Golden Cylinders on pedestals
Closing Date: Annually in April
Presented: Leadership Summit, Annually in Fall

Golden Kite Awards
Society of Children's Book Writers and Illustrators (SCBWI)
4727 Wilshire Blvd, Suite 301, Los Angeles, CA 90010
Tel: 323-782-1010; 310-403-0675 (cell) *Fax:* 323-782-1892
E-mail: grants@scbwi.org; scbwi@scbwi.org
Web Site: www.scbwi.org
Key Personnel
Pres: Stephen Mooser *E-mail:* stephenmooser@scbwi.org
Exec Dir: Lin Oliver *E-mail:* linoliver@scbwi.org
Established: 1973
Four awards, one each for fiction, nonfiction, picture book text & picture book illustration, awarded each year to the most outstanding children's books published during that year & written or illustrated by members of the Society of Children's Book Writers & Illustrators. An honor book plaque is awarded in each category.
Award: Free transportation & accomodations to summer conference
Closing Date: Annually in Dec
Presented: Annually in Aug

Golden Rose Award
New England Poetry Club
46 Wallace St, Somerville, MA 02144
Tel: 617-744-6034
E-mail: info@nepoetryclub.org
Web Site: www.nepoetryclub.org
Key Personnel
VP: Hillary Sallick
Established: 1920
The oldest literary award given annually to poet who has done the most for poetry during previous year or in a lifetime. Chosen by NEPC officers.
Award: Rose sculpture
Closing Date: Annually, May 31
Presented: Announced online Aug/Sept

Laurence Goldstein Poetry Prize
Michigan Quarterly Review
University of Michigan, 0576 Rackham Bldg, 915 E Washington St, Ann Arbor, MI 48109-1070
Tel: 734-764-9265
E-mail: mqr@umich.edu
Web Site: www.umich.edu/~mqr
Key Personnel
Ed: Jonathan Freedman
Poetry Ed: Keith Taylor
Awarded to the best poem published in MQR each year. No deadline or special application process.
Award: $500

Goodreads Choice Awards
Goodreads Inc
188 Spear St, 3rd fl, San Francisco, CA 94105
E-mail: press@goodreads.com
Web Site: www.goodreads.com/award
Key Personnel
Founder & CEO: Otis Chandler
Co-Founder & Ed-in-Chief: Elizabeth Khuri Chandler
VP, Communs: Suzanne Skyvara
15 nominees in each category. Books must be published in the US in English, including works in translation & other significant rereleases. Three rounds of voting open to all registered Goodreads members.

Governor General's Literary Awards
Canada Council for the Arts (Conseil des arts du Canada)
150 Elgin St, Ottawa, ON K1P 1L4, Canada
Mailing Address: PO Box 1047, Ottawa, NS K1P 5V8, Canada
Tel: 613-566-4414 *Toll Free Tel:* 800-263-5588 (CN only) *Fax:* 613-566-4390
E-mail: info@canadacouncil.ca
Web Site: canadacouncil.ca/en/council/prizes
Key Personnel
Prog Offr: Lori Knoll *Tel:* 613-566-4414 ext 5573 *E-mail:* lori.knoll@canadacouncil.ca
Established: 1936
Annual awards to the best English language & French language book in each of seven categories: fiction, poetry, drama, nonfiction, children's literature-text, children's literature-illustration & translation (from French to English & English to French).
Award: $25,000 each; non-winning finalists receive $1,000; publisher of each winning book receives $3,000 to promote the book

The Gracies®
Alliance for Women in Media (AWM)
2365 Harrodsburg Rd, Suite A325, Lexington, KY 40504
Tel: 202-750-3664 *Fax:* 202-750-3664
E-mail: info@allwomeninmedia.org
Web Site: allwomeninmedia.org
Key Personnel
Exec Dir: Becky Brooks
Awarded for programming in all mediums which contributes to positive & realistic portrayals of women, addresses interests of concern to women, enhances women's image, position & welfare.
Award: Statue
Presented: Annually in May

Grants for Literary Artists
New Brunswick Arts Board (Conseil des arts du Nouveau-Brunswick)
225 King St, Suite 201, Fredericton, NB E3B 1E1, Canada
Tel: 506-444-4444 *Toll Free Tel:* 866-460-ARTS (460-2787) *Fax:* 506-444-5543
Web Site: www.artsnb.ca
Key Personnel
Exec Dir: Joss Richer *Tel:* 506-478-4610 *E-mail:* execdirgen@artsnb.ca
Prog Offr: Sarah Beth Shiplett *Tel:* 506-440-0037 *E-mail:* sarahbeth@artsnb.ca
Opers Mgr: Tilly Jackson *Tel:* 506-478-4422 *E-mail:* tjackson@artsnb.ca
Program is designed to recognize & encourage arts professionals who have demonstrated exceptional artistic talent & potential & who are pursuing a career in the arts. The program is divided in three components:
Arts by Innovation is for assistance to present work by invitation in established arts events.
Artist in Residence is for assistance for participation in residency opportunities of three months & less. The artists in residence are to contribute to the promotion & understanding of the arts by means of the artists' contact with the clientele of the establishments.
Professional Development is for assistance for professional development scholarships for studies & mentorships.
Closing Date: Jan 15, March 1, April 15, June 1, July 15, Sept 1, Oct 15, Dec 1

James H Gray Award for Short Nonfiction
Writers' Guild of Alberta
11759 Groat Rd, Edmonton, AB T5M 3K6, Canada
Tel: 780-422-8174 *Toll Free Tel:* 800-665-5354 (AB only) *Fax:* 780-422-2663 (attn WGA)
E-mail: mail@writersguild.ca
Web Site: writersguild.ca
Key Personnel
Exec Dir: Carol Holmes *E-mail:* carol.holmes@writersguild.ca
Communs & Partnerships Coord: Ellen Kartz *E-mail:* ellen.kartz@writersguild.ca
Memb Servs Coord: Giorgia Severini
Progs Coord: Natalie Cook *E-mail:* natalie.cook@writersguild.ca; Julie Robinson *E-mail:* julie.robinson@writersguild.ca
Established: 2009

Open to published pieces on any topic by an Alberta author; no longer than 5,000 words.
Award: $700
Closing Date: Annually, Dec 31
Presented: Alberta Book Awards Gala
Branch Office(s)
505 21 Ave SW, Calgary, AB T2S 0G9, Canada, Prog Coord: Samantha Warwick *Tel:* 403-265-2226 *E-mail:* samantha.warwick@writersguild.ca

Graywolf Press Nonfiction Prize
Graywolf Press
250 Third Ave N, Suite 600, Minneapolis, MN 55401
Tel: 651-641-0077 *Fax:* 651-641-0036
E-mail: wolves@graywolfpress.org (no ms queries, sample chapters or proposals)
Web Site: www.graywolfpress.org/graywolf-press-nonfiction-prize
Awarded to the most promising & innovative literary nonfiction project by a writer not yet established in the genre. Awarded every other year to a ms in progress. One submission per person will be considered. Agented submissions are also welcome. Only electronic submissions are considered (upload ms file to Submittable). See web site for submission & contest guidelines.
Award: $12,000 advance & publication by Graywolf
Presented: Biennially in even-numbered years

The Green Rose Prize in Poetry
New Issues Poetry & Prose
c/o Western Michigan University, 1903 W Michigan Ave, Kalamazoo, MI 49008-5463
Tel: 269-387-8185
E-mail: new-issues@wmich.edu
Web Site: www.wmich.edu/newissues/sub-guide.html
Key Personnel
Mng Ed: Kimberly Kolbe
Ed-in-Chief: William Olsen
Poets writing in English who have published one or more full-length collections of poetry. A $25 reading fee must accompany each ms; do not bind ms. Include a brief bio & relevant publication information, cover page with name, address, phone number, e-mail address & title of ms; include table of contents; enclose SASE. The winning ms will be named in January & published in the Spring of the following year.
Other Sponsor(s): Western Michigan University
Award: $2,000 & book publication
Closing Date: Sept 30

Bess Gresham Memorial
The Poetry Society of Virginia
900 Timber Creek Place, Virginia Beach, VA 23464
E-mail: poetryinva@aol.com
Web Site: poetrysocietyofvirginia.org
Key Personnel
Pres: Robert P Arthur *E-mail:* robert.peebles.arthur@gmail.com
Exec Dir: Guy Terrell *E-mail:* guy.terrell@earthlink.net
Adult Contest Chair: Steven Blythe *E-mail:* stevenblythepoetry@gmail.com
All entries must be in English, original & unpublished. Submit 2 copies of each poem, each having the category name & number on top left of page. Only 1 poem per category; entries will not be returned. Subject: friends & friendship; 48 line limit. Entry fee: $4 nonmembs.
Award: $50 (1st place), $30 (2nd place), $20 (3rd place)
Closing Date: Jan
Presented: Annual PSV Awards Ceremony, April

Guggenheim Fellowships
John Simon Guggenheim Memorial Foundation
90 Park Ave, New York, NY 10016
Tel: 212-687-4470 *Fax:* 212-697-3248
E-mail: fellowships@gf.org
Web Site: www.gf.org/about/fellowship
Established: 1925
Grants to selected individuals for 6-12 months. Fellowships are awarded through 2 annual competitions: one open to citizens & permanent residents of the US & Canada & the other open to citizens & permanent residents of Latin America & the Caribbean. Application required. Approximately 175 Fellowships awarded each year.
Poets, playwrights, screenwriters, scholars & writers of fiction & general nonfiction should submit examples of published books; do not send journal articles or essays. Published writing not regarded as appropriate includes self-published works, publications for which the author has paid, & publications by publishers who do not engage in a process of critical review of submitted work. In addition, genre work (e.g., mysteries, romance, fantasy, etc.) is considered not competitive. We do not consider children's or young adult books. Mss will not be accepted except from playwrights. Send no more than 3 different published works (it would be helpful to have 2 copies of the most recent work). Include a list of the items submitted, giving the title, publisher, & date of each, as well as the address to which the material should be returned.
Closing Date: Sept (applications), Nov (work example submissions)
Presented: US & CN announced early April, Latin America & Caribbean announced early June

Guggenheim-Lehrman Prize in Military History
The Harry Frank Guggenheim Foundation
25 W 53 St, New York, NY 10019
Tel: 646-428-0971 *Fax:* 646-428-0981
E-mail: info@hfg.org
Web Site: www.hfg.org/prize/main.htm
Established: 2013
To recognize the most outstanding book in the field of military history published in English in the previous calendar year. Publishers must submit 8 copies of each book for consideration along with a completed submission form & entry fee of $50 or 30 GBP. Authors may not directly submit their books for consideration. Books can be written by no more than two authors. Self-published & children's books are not eligible.
Award: $50,000
Closing Date: Nov 1
Presented: March

Hackmatack Children's Choice Book Award
Canada Council for the Arts (Conseil des arts du Canada)
PO Box 1047, Ottawa, NS K1P 5V8, Canada
Tel: 902-424-3774 *Fax:* 902-424-0613
E-mail: hackmatack@hackmatack.ca
Web Site: www.hackmatack.ca
Key Personnel
Prog Coord: Kate Watson
Established: 1999
Atlantic Canadian Children's Choice Award for grades 4-6. Four categories: English fiction, English nonfiction, French fiction & French nonfiction.
Other Sponsor(s): New Brunswick Public Library Service; Nova Scotia Department of Education
Award: Plaques
Closing Date: Annually, Oct 15
Presented: Award ceremony, Annually in Spring

Hackney Literary Awards
4650 Old Looney Mill Rd, Birmingham, AL 35243
E-mail: info@hackneyliteraryawards.org
Web Site: www.hackneyliteraryawards.org
Established: 1969
Short story, poetry & novel awards. Check web site or send SASE for contest guidelines. Entry fee: novels $30, short stories $20, poetry $15. Presented in the *Birmingham Arts Journal*.
Award: $600 (1st place), $400 (2nd place), $250 (3rd place), plus a $5,000 prize sponsored by Morris Hackney for an unpublished novel
Closing Date: Annually, Sept 30 for novel entries, Nov 30 for short story & poetry entries
Presented: March 30

Sarah Josepha Hale Award
Trustees of the Richards Library
58 N Main, Newport, NH 03773
Tel: 603-863-3430
E-mail: rfl@newport.lib.nh.us
Web Site: www.newport.lib.nh.us
Key Personnel
Lib Dir & Award Admin: Andrea Thorpe *E-mail:* athorpe@newport.lib.nh.us
Established: 1956
A distinguished literary figure in some way associated with New England. Nominations or applications are not accepted.
Award: Bronze medal & $1,000
Presented: Newport, NH

Loretta Dunn Hall Memorial
The Poetry Society of Virginia
900 Timber Creek Place, Virginia Beach, VA 23464
E-mail: poetryinva@aol.com
Web Site: poetrysocietyofvirginia.org
Key Personnel
Pres: Robert P Arthur *E-mail:* robert.peebles.arthur@gmail.com
Exec Dir: Guy Terrell *E-mail:* guy.terrell@earthlink.net
Adult Contest Chair: Steven Blythe *E-mail:* stevenblythepoetry@gmail.com
All entries must be in English, original & unpublished. Submit 2 copies, each having the category name & number on top left of page. Subject: family; any form; 24 line limit. VA residents only. Entry fee: $4 nonmembs.
Other Sponsor(s): Phyllis Hall Haislip
Award: $50 (1st prize), $30 (2nd prize), $20 (3rd prize)
Closing Date: Jan
Presented: Annual PSV Awards Ceremony, April

Marilyn Hall Awards, see BHTG - Michael J Libow Youth Theatre Award

Virginia Hamilton Award for Lifetime Achievement, see Coretta Scott King - Virginia Hamilton Award for Lifetime Achievement

Handy Andy Prize
The Poetry Society of Virginia
900 Timber Creek Place, Virginia Beach, VA 23464
E-mail: poetryinva@aol.com
Web Site: poetrysocietyofvirginia.org
Key Personnel
Pres: Robert P Arthur *E-mail:* robert.peebles.arthur@gmail.com
Exec Dir: Guy Terrell *E-mail:* guy.terrell@earthlink.net
Adult Contest Chair: Steven Blythe *E-mail:* stevenblythepoetry@gmail.com
For a limerick. Must be in English, original & unpublished. Submit 2 copies, each having the category name & number on top left of page. Entry fee: $4 nonmembs.
Award: $25 (1st prize), $15 (2nd prize), $10 (3rd prize)

Closing Date: Jan
Presented: Annual PSV Awards Ceremony, April

Clarence H Haring Prize
American Historical Association (AHA)
400 "A" St SE, Washington, DC 20003
Tel: 202-544-2422 *Fax:* 202-544-8307
E-mail: awards@historians.org
Web Site: www.historians.org
For work by a Latin American in Latin American history during the preceding 5 years. Offered quinquennially. There is no language limitation on works submitted. Along with an application form, applicants must mail a copy of their book to each of the prize committee members who will be posted on our web site as the prize deadline approaches. Books published 2016 through 2020 will be considered. All updated info on web site.
Award: Cash prize
Closing Date: May 15, 2021
Presented: AHA Annual Meeting, New Orleans, LA, Jan 2022

Joy Harjo Poetry Award
CUTTHROAT, A Journal of the Arts
PO Box 2414, Durango, CO 81302
Tel: 970-903-7914
E-mail: cutthroatmag@gmail.com
Web Site: www.cutthroatmag.com
Key Personnel
Ed-in-Chief: Pamela Uschuk
Mng Ed: Andrew Allport
Fiction Ed: Beth Alvarado; William Luvaas
Poetry Ed: William Pitt Root
Established: 2005
Submit online up to 3 unpublished poems (100 line limit for each). Writers may submit as often as they wish. No poems that have been previously published or have won contests are eligible; $20 reading fee.
Award: $1,300 (1st place), $250 (2nd place), both include publication in *CUTTHROAT*
Closing Date: Annually in Oct
Presented: Annually in Dec

Aurand Harris Memorial Playwriting Award
The New England Theatre Conference Inc
215 Knob Hill Dr, Hamden, CT 06518
Tel: 617-851-8535 *Fax:* 203-288-5938
E-mail: mail@netconline.org
Web Site: www.netconline.org
Established: 1997
Competition for new plays for young audiences. Scripts must be unpublished & unproduced. For guidelines, go to web site.
Closing Date: Annually, May 1
Presented: NETC Annual Convention, Annually in Nov

Julie Harris Playwright Award Competition, see BHTG - Julie Harris Playwright Award Competition

Haskins Medal Award
Medieval Academy of America
17 Dunster St, Suite 202, Cambridge, MA 02138
Tel: 617-491-1622 *Fax:* 617-492-3303
E-mail: info@themedievalacademy.org
Web Site: www.medievalacademy.org
Key Personnel
Exec Dir: Lisa Fagin Davis *E-mail:* lfd@themedievalacademy.org
Established: 1940
For a book of outstanding importance in the medieval field.
Award: Gold medal
Closing Date: Annually, Oct 15
Presented: Annually in Spring

Friedrich Hayek Lecture & Book Prize
Manhattan Institute for Policy Research
52 Vanderbilt Ave, New York, NY 10017
Tel: 212-599-7000 *Fax:* 212-599-3494
Web Site: www.manhattan-institute.org
Key Personnel
Contact: Dean Ball *E-mail:* dball@manhattan-institute.org
Honors the book published within the past two years that best reflects political philosopher & Nobel laureate F A Hayek's vision of economic & individual liberty. The winner of the prize will deliver the annual Hayek Lecture in New York in early June.
Award: $50,000
Presented: Late Feb

Headlands Center for the Arts Residency for Writers
944 Fort Barry, Sausalito, CA 94965
Tel: 415-331-2787 *Fax:* 415-331-3857
Web Site: www.headlands.org
Key Personnel
Residency Mgr: Holly Blake *Tel:* 415-331-2787 ext 24 *E-mail:* hblake@headlands.org
Established: 1987
A 4 to 10-week residency at Headlands is granted each year to writers of the Artist in Residency Program. Call or write the HCA for deadline & other information. See web site for application & more information.
Award: 4 to 10-week stay, with optional stipend of $500/mo
Closing Date: June 2

Heartland Prize
Chicago Tribune
435 N Michigan Ave, Suite 1100, Chicago, IL 60611
Established: 1988
Awarded annually in two categories: fiction & nonfiction.

Drue Heinz Literature Prize
University of Pittsburgh Press
7500 Thomas Blvd, Pittsburgh, PA 15260
Tel: 412-383-2456 *Fax:* 412-383-2466
E-mail: info@upress.pitt.edu
Web Site: www.upress.pitt.edu
Key Personnel
Asst to Dir: Kelley H Johovic *E-mail:* kjohovic@upress.pitt.edu
Established: 1980
For a collection of short fiction 150-300 pages in length. Open to all writers who have published a book-length collection of short fiction or who have had 3 short stories or novellas published in commercial magazines or literary journals of national distribution. See web site for complete rules.
Other Sponsor(s): Drue Heinz & The Drue Heinz Trust
Award: $15,000 & publication by the University of Pittsburgh Press
Closing Date: Postmarked between May 1 & June 30
Presented: Pittsburgh, PA, Dec or Jan

The Hemingway Foundation/PEN Award
PEN New England
Unit of PEN American Center
MIT, 14N-221A, 77 Massachusetts Ave, Cambridge, MA 02139
Tel: 617-324-1729
E-mail: pen-newengland@mit.edu
Web Site: www.pen-ne.org/hemingway
Key Personnel
Exec Dir: Karen Wulf *E-mail:* kwulf@mit.edu
Award Admin: Helene Atwan
Established: 1976
Given to a novel or book of short stories by an American writer who has not previously published a book of fiction. Entry fee: $50.
Award: Winner receives $25,000, a one-week residency & $5,000 honorarium in the Distinguished Visiting Writers Series (University of Idaho's MFA Creative Writing Program). The winner also receives, along with the four finalists, an Artist Residency for one month at the Ucross Foundation in Wyoming
Closing Date: Annually in Dec
Presented: JFK Library, Boston, MA, Annually in April

Cecil Hemley Memorial Award
Poetry Society of America (PSA)
15 Gramercy Park, New York, NY 10003
Tel: 212-254-9628
Web Site: www.poetrysociety.org
Key Personnel
Pres: Kimiko Hahn
Exec Dir: Alice Quinn
Deputy Dir: Brett Fletcher Lauer *E-mail:* brett@poetrysociety.org
Prog Dir: Laurin Macios *E-mail:* laurin@poetrysociety.org
Established: 1969
For an unpublished lyric poem that addresses a philosophical or epistemological concern, not to exceed 100 lines. Open to society members only. See web site for more information.
Award: $500
Closing Date: Annually, Oct-Dec
Presented: Annual Awards Ceremony, New York, NY, Annually in Spring

Brodie Herndon Memorial
The Poetry Society of Virginia
900 Timber Creek Place, Virginia Beach, VA 23464
E-mail: poetryinva@aol.com
Web Site: poetrysocietyofvirginia.org
Key Personnel
Pres: Robert P Arthur *E-mail:* robert.peebles.arthur@gmail.com
Exec Dir: Guy Terrell *E-mail:* guy.terrell@earthlink.net
Adult Contest Chair: Steven Blythe *E-mail:* stevenblythepoetry@gmail.com
Poems in any form about heroism; 48 line limit. Must be original, unpublished & in English. Submit 2 copies, each having the category name & number on top left of page. Entry fee: $4 nonmembs.
Award: $50 (1st prize), $30 (2nd prize), $20 (3rd prize)
Closing Date: Jan
Presented: Annual PSV Awards Ceremony, April

Carl Hertzog Award for Excellence in Book Design
Friends of the University Library
Subsidiary of University of Texas at El Paso
c/o Dir of the Library, University of Texas at El Paso, El Paso, TX 79968-0582
Tel: 915-747-5683 *Fax:* 915-747-5345
Web Site: libraryweb.utep.edu/about/hertzog_call.php
Key Personnel
Assoc VP: Robert L Stakes *Tel:* 915-747-6710 *E-mail:* rlstakes@utep.edu
Biennial award for excellence in book design. There is a maximum number of 5 entries allowed & must have been printed in 2016 or 2017. While a printer, publisher or designer may submit an entry, only the designer is eligible to receive the award.
Award: $1,000, bronze medal & certificate
Closing Date: Nov 1, odd-numbered years
Presented: University of Texas, El Paso, Feb/March, even-numbered years

Hidden River Arts Playwriting Award
Hidden River™ Arts
PO Box 63927, Philadelphia, PA 19147
Tel: 610-764-0813
E-mail: hiddenriverarts@gmail.com
Web Site: www.hiddenriverarts.org; www.hiddenriverarts.com
Key Personnel
Founding Dir: Debra Leigh Scott
Established: 2002
Annual award for an unpublished, unproduced full-length play. Entry fee: $17.
Award: $1,000 (awarded by mail)
Closing Date: Annually, June 30
Presented: Annually in Dec

The High School Award
Oklahoma Library Association
PO Box 6550, Edmond, OK 73083
Tel: 405-525-5100 *Fax:* 405-525-5103
Web Site: www.oklibs.org
Key Personnel
Exec Dir: Kay Boies *E-mail:* execdirector@oklibs.org
Established: 2010
Student choice award: students in grades 9-12 who have read/listened to at least 3 titles from the High School Master list are eligible to vote.
Award: Plaque/Medal
Closing Date: Annually, March 1
Presented: OLA Annual Conference, Annually in April

Highlights for Children Fiction Contest
Highlights for Children Inc
803 Church St, Honesdale, PA 18431
Tel: 570-253-1080 *Fax:* 570-251-7847
E-mail: eds@highlights.com
Web Site: www.highlights.com
Key Personnel
Sr Ed: Joelle Dujardin
Established: 1980
Fiction for children, subject varies annually. Guidelines & contest topic available on web site under "About Us" area. Indicate word count in upper right-hand corner on the first page of ms. No crime, violence, or derogatory humor. Stories may be any length up to 750 words. Stories for beginning readers should not exceed 475 words.
Award: 3 prizes of $1,000 or tuition for any Highlights Foundation Workshop
Closing Date: Annually, Jan 1-Jan 31 (postmark)
Presented: Annually in June

The Tony Hillerman Prize
Western Writers of America Inc (WWA)
c/o St Martin's Press, 175 Fifth Ave, New York, NY 10010
E-mail: tonyhillermanprize@stmartins.com
Web Site: www.hillermanprize.com; us.macmillan.com/minotaurbooks/tonyhillermanprize
Established: 2007
Awarded annually for the best first mystery set in the Southwest. Entrants must submit entry form & ms online or by mail. Limit of 1 entry per person. See web site for full guidelines.
Other Sponsor(s): St Martin's Press
Award: $10,000 & publication by St Martin's Press
Closing Date: Jan 2

Hillman Prizes for Journalism
The Sidney Hillman Foundation
330 W 42 St, Suite 900, New York, NY 10036
Tel: 646-448-6413
Web Site: www.hillmanfoundation.org
Key Personnel
Pres: Bruce Raynor
Exec Dir: Alexandra Lescaze *E-mail:* alex@hillmanfoundation.org
Established: 1950
For investigative journalism that fosters social & economic justice. See web site for categories.
Award: $5,000 & certificate designed by New York cartoonist Edward Sorel
Closing Date: Jan 31
Presented: Award ceremony & cocktail party, New York, NY, Annually in mid-May

Eric Hoffer Award for Independent Books
www.HofferAward.com
Subsidiary of The Eric Hoffer Project
PO Box 11, Titusville, NJ 08560
Fax: 609-964-1718
E-mail: info@hofferaward.com
Web Site: www.hofferaward.com
Key Personnel
Chmn & Exec Ed: Christopher Klim
Publr & Coord: Dawn Shows
Established: 2002
Open to academic, small & self-published press books in the last 2 years. Books older than 2 years must enter the "Legacy" category. Results published in The US Review of Books (www.theusreview.com).
In addition to the 2 grand prizes, various other honors & distinctions are given for both prose & books, including the Montaigne Medal, the da Vinci Eye & the First Horizon Award.
Award: $2,000 (grand prize independent books); $250 (grand prize short prose)
Closing Date: Nominations Jan 21 (books), March 31 (prose)
Presented: Annually in May

Eric Hoffer Award for Short Prose
www.HofferAward.com
Subsidiary of The Eric Hoffer Project
PO Box 11, Titusville, NJ 08560
Fax: 609-964-1718
E-mail: info@hofferaward.com
Web Site: www.hofferaward.com
Key Personnel
Mng Ed: Brittany Fonte
Ed: Danielle Evennou; Christopher Helvey; Matt Ryan; Jamey Temple
Established: 2002
New fiction & creative nonfiction less than 10,000 words.
Award: $250 (Grand Prize); publication in *Best New Writing* (20-25 finalists)
Closing Date: Annually, March 31
Presented: Annually in Oct

Bess Hokin Prize
Poetry Magazine
61 W Superior St, Chicago, IL 60654
Tel: 312-787-7070 *Fax:* 312-787-6650
E-mail: editors@poetrymagazine.org
Web Site: www.poetryfoundation.org
Key Personnel
Edit Asst: Holly Amos *E-mail:* hamos@poetrymagazine.org
Established: 1948
For poetry published in the preceding 2 volumes of *Poetry* magazine. No application necessary.
Award: $1,000
Presented: Annually in Dec

Honickman First Book Prize
American Poetry Review
University of the Arts (UARTS), Hamilton Hall, 320 S Broad St, Rm 313, Philadelphia, PA 19102-4901
Tel: 215-717-6801 *Fax:* 215-717-6805
Web Site: www.aprweb.org
Key Personnel
Ed: David Bonanno *E-mail:* dbonanno@aprweb.org; Elizabeth Scanlon *E-mail:* escanlon@aprweb.org
Established: 1997
Awarded to any US citizen, writing in English & who has not published a book-length collection of poems with an ISBN. Poems previously published in periodicals or limited-edition chapbooks may be included in the ms, but the ms itself must not have been published as a book-length work exceeding 25 pages. No translations or multiple author entries accepted. Entry fee $25. Now accepting online submissions.
Award: $3,000
Closing Date: Oct 31 (postmark)
Presented: Winner announced in March/April issue of the *American Poetry Review*

Firman Houghton Prize
New England Poetry Club
46 Wallace St, Somerville, MA 02144
Tel: 617-744-6034
E-mail: info@nepoetryclub.org
Web Site: www.nepoetryclub.org
Key Personnel
VP: Hillary Sallick
Established: 1987
Award for a lyric poem in honor of the former president of the NEPC. $15 for 3 contest entries per poem entry & $3 for additional entries, free for members & students. $20 reading fee for nonmembs.
Award: $250
Closing Date: Annually, May 31
Presented: Winners announced online Aug/Sept

Tom Howard/John H Reid Fiction & Essay Contest
Winning Writers
351 Pleasant St, PMB 222, Northampton, MA 01060-3961
Tel: 413-320-1847 *Toll Free Tel:* 866-WINWRIT (946-9748) *Fax:* 413-280-0539
Web Site: www.winningwriters.com
Key Personnel
Pres: Adam Cohen *E-mail:* adam@winningwriters.com
VP: Jendi Reiter
Established: 1990
Submit short stories, essays or other works of prose, up to 6,000 words each. Must be your own original work. $20 reading fee per entry. Writers of all nations may enter, however, the works you submit should be in English. Both published & unpublished work accepted. Applications accepted October 15-April 30.
Award: $1,500 (each 1st prize, fiction & essay), $100 (10 honorable mention awards) & publication on web site for all winners
Closing Date: Annually, April 30 (postmark)
Presented: Winner announced Oct 15 on web site

Tom Howard/Margaret Reid Poetry Contest
Winning Writers
351 Pleasant St, PMB 222, Northampton, MA 01060-3961
Tel: 413-320-1847 *Toll Free Tel:* 866-WINWRIT (946-9748) *Fax:* 413-280-0539
Web Site: www.winningwriters.com
Key Personnel
Pres: Adam Cohen *E-mail:* adam@winningwriters.com
VP: Jendi Reiter
Established: 2002
The Tom Howard Prize is awarded for a poem in any style or genre. The Margaret Reid Prize is awarded for a poem that rhymes or has a traditional style. Entry fee is $12 per poem submitted up to 250 lines. See web site for complete submission details & contest results. Both published & unpublished work accepted. Poets of all nations may enter, however, the works you submit should be in English.
Award: $1,500 each (1st prize, Tom Howard & Margaret Reid), $100 each (10 honorable mention awards) & publication on web site for all winners

Closing Date: Annually, Sept 30 (postmark)
Presented: Winner announced April 15 on web site

Julia Ward Howe Book Awards
Boston Authors Club Inc
c/o Professor Mary Cronin, 2400 Beacon St, Unit 208, Beacon Hill, MA 02467
Mailing Address: 33 Brayton Rd, Brighton, MA 02135
Tel: 617-783-1357
E-mail: bostonauthors@aol.com
Web Site: www.bostonauthorsclub.org
Key Personnel
Pres: Alan Lawson *E-mail:* lawson@bc.edu
VP: Shirley Moskow *Tel:* 781-862-7697 *E-mail:* shirley.moskow@rtr.com
Dir, Book Award: Prof Mary Cronin
Established: 1997
Books must be published the year prior to the award. Prizes given in both adult & young reader's categories. Authors must live or have lived, worked or attended college within 100 miles of Boston the year their books are published. Submission fee of $25 per title.
Other Sponsor(s): Boston Public Library (Rare Books Div)
Award: $1,000 each for 2 books; certificates to finalists & authors of recommended books (number varies). All receive 1-year complimentary membership in the Club
Closing Date: Annually, Jan 15
Presented: Boston Public Library, Annually in Sept

The William Dean Howells Medal
American Academy of Arts & Letters
633 W 155 St, New York, NY 10032
Tel: 212-368-5900 *Fax:* 212-491-4615
E-mail: academy@artsandletters.org
Web Site: www.artsandletters.org
Key Personnel
Exec Dir: Cody Upton
Established: 1925
Given once every 5 years in recognition of the most distinguished American novel published during that period.

L Ron Hubbard's Writers of the Future Contest
Author Services Inc
7501 Hollywood Blvd, Hollywood, CA 90028
Tel: 323-466-3310 *Toll Free Tel:* 800-624-6504 *Fax:* 323-466-6474
E-mail: contests@authorservicesinc.com
Web Site: www.writersofthefuture.com
Key Personnel
Coordinating Judge: K D Wentworth
Contest Dir: Joni Labaqui
Established: 1983
Short stories & novelettes (under 17,000 words) of science fiction & fantasy for new & amateur writers. No entry fee required, entrants retain all publication rights.
Award: Annually: Trophy & $5,000 (Grand prize); Quarterly: $1,000 (1st place), $750 (2nd place), $500 (3rd place)
Closing Date: Quarterly: March 31, June 30, Sept 30, Dec 31

The Hugo Awards
The World Science Fiction Society
PO Box 64128, Sunnyvale, CA 94088
Web Site: www.wsfs.org/awards; www.thehugoawards.org
Established: 1953
Fan-voted awards for science fiction & fantasy literature. During Jan-March, members of Worldcon can nominate up to 5 people or works from the previous year in 15 categories. Shortlist of 5 finalists announced in April. Worldcon members cast their final ballots in July.
Award: Trophy
Presented: Hugo Ceremony, World Science Fiction Convention

Lynda Hull Memorial Poetry Prize
Crazyhorse
College of Charleston, Dept of English, 66 George St, Charleston, SC 29424
Tel: 843-953-4470
E-mail: crazyhorse@cofc.edu
Web Site: crazyhorse.cofc.edu/prizes
Key Personnel
Mng Ed: Jonathan Heinen
Awarded annually for best single poem. Enter 3 poems with $20 entry fee, which includes one-year subscription. Submissions accepted during the month of Jan. Nationally prominent poet judges. See web site for complete instructions.
Award: $2,000 & publication in *Crazyhorse*
Closing Date: Jan 31

Hurston/Wright Award for College Writers
The Zora Neale Hurston/Richard Wright Foundation
840 First St NE, 3rd fl, Washington, DC 20002
Tel: 202-248-5051
E-mail: info@hurstonwright.org
Web Site: www.hurstonwright.org
Key Personnel
Co-Founder: Marita Golden; Clyde McElvane
Exec Dir: Deborah Heard
Established: 1990
Literary award presented annually to honor excellence in fiction writing by African-American students enrolled as an undergraduate or graduate student in any college or university. Nonrefundable application fee of $10.
Award: $1,000 & story published in literary journal (1st prize), $500 (awarded to 2 runners-up)
Closing Date: Jan 31
Presented: April

Hurston/Wright Legacy Awards
The Zora Neale Hurston/Richard Wright Foundation
840 First St NE, 3rd fl, Washington, DC 20002
Tel: 202-248-5051
E-mail: info@hurstonwright.org
Web Site: www.hurstonwright.org
Key Personnel
Co-Founder: Marita Golden; Clyde McElvane
Exec Dir: Deborah Heard
Established: 2000
Annual national literary award for debut fiction, fiction, nonfiction & poetry for published black writers. Application fee: $30.
Award: $10,000 for winners in 3 categories, $5,000 for 6 runners-up (2 in each category)
Presented: Oct

IACP Cookbook Awards
International Association of Culinary Professionals (IACP)
45 Rockefeller Plaza, Suite 2000, New York, NY 10111
Tel: 646-358-4957 *Toll Free Tel:* 866-358-4951 *Toll Free Fax:* 866-358-2524
E-mail: info@iacp.com
Web Site: www.iacp.com; www.iacp.com/award/more/cookbook
Key Personnel
Memb Progs & Opers Mgr: Shani Phelan
Established: 1985
Open to any food or beverage book published in the English language. Allows publishers to enter books in the category of their choice. Through a strict, 2-tier system of judging & balloting, the entries are narrowed to 3 nominees in each category. See submission guidelines at www.iacp.com/award/more/cookbook.
Presented: Annual Conference, location varies, Date varies every year, usually in April

The Idaho Prize for Poetry
Lost Horse Press
105 Lost Horse Lane, Sandpoint, ID 83864
Tel: 208-255-4410 *Fax:* 208-255-1560
E-mail: losthorsepress@mindspring.com
Web Site: www.losthorsepress.org
Key Personnel
Publr: Christine Holbert
Established: 2003
A national competition for a book-length poetry ms written by an American poet. Accompany ms with $25 reading fee (check or money order only). Books distributed by the University of Washington Press. May also submit online using submittable.com.
Award: $1,000 & publication with 20 free author copies
Closing Date: Annually, May 15
Presented: Annually, Aug 15

ILA Children's & Young Adults' Book Awards
International Literacy Association (ILA)
PO Box 8139, Newark, DE 19714-8139
Tel: 302-731-1600 *Toll Free Tel:* 800-336-7323 (US & CN) *Fax:* 302-731-1057
E-mail: ilaawards@reading.org
Web Site: www.literacyworldwide.org
Key Personnel
Exec Dir: Marcie Craig Post *E-mail:* mpost@reading.org
Assoc Exec Dir: Stephen Sye *E-mail:* ssye@reading.org
Established: 1975
Awards for newly published authors who show unusual promise in the children's or young adult book field. Awards will be given for fiction & nonfiction in 3 categories: Primary (ages preschool-8), Intermediate (ages 9-13) & Young Adult (ages 14-17). Books from any country & published in English for the first time during the previous calendar year will be considered.
Award: $800 per book
Closing Date: Jan 15, 2018
Presented: Annual Conference, Orange County Convention Center, Orlando, FL, Annually in July

Illumination Book Awards
Independent Publisher Online
Division of Jenkins Group Inc
1129 Woodmere Ave, Suite B, Traverse City, MI 49686
Tel: 231-933-0445 *Toll Free Tel:* 800-706-4636 *Fax:* 231-933-0448
E-mail: awards@bookpublishing.com
Web Site: www.illuminationawards.com
Key Personnel
CEO: Jerrold R Jenkins *E-mail:* jrj@bookpublishing.com
Pres: James Kalajian *Tel:* 800-706-4636 ext 1006 *E-mail:* jjk@bookpublishing.com
Mng Ed & Awards Dir: Jim Barnes *Tel:* 800-706-4636 ext 1011 *E-mail:* jimb@bookpublishing.com
Awards Coord: Amy Shamroe
Established: 2013
With the motto "Shining a Light on Exemplary Christian Books," the Illumination Awards are designed to honor the year's best new titles written & published with a Christian worldview. The contest is for published books only, as our judging criteria include cover design, layout, etc. Books from all methods of publishing are welcome & authors of royalty-published books are welcome to enter their books themselves.
Other Sponsor(s): Jenkins Group
Award: Gold medal (1st place), silver medal (2nd place), bronze medal (3rd place), foil seals available, winners featured in *Independent Publisher Online*

Closing Date: Annually in Nov
Presented: Online, Annually in Jan

John Phillip Immroth Memorial Award
Intellectual Freedom Round Table (IFRT)
Unit of The American Library Association (ALA)
50 E Huron St, Chicago, IL 60611
Tel: 312-280-4226 *Toll Free Tel:* 800-545-2433
E-mail: oif@ala.org
Web Site: www.ala.org/ifrt
Key Personnel
Asst Dir: Kristen Pekoll *Tel:* 312-280-4220
Established: 1979
Annual award for notable contribution to intellectual freedom & demonstrations of personal courage in defense of freedom of expression.
Award: $500 & citation
Closing Date: Annually, Dec 1
Presented: ALA Annual Conference, Annually in June

The Independent Publisher Book Awards
Independent Publisher Online
Division of Jenkins Group Inc
1129 Woodmere Ave, Suite B, Traverse City, MI 49686
Tel: 231-933-0445 *Toll Free Tel:* 800-706-4636 *Fax:* 231-933-0448
E-mail: awards@bookpublishing.com
Web Site: www.independentpublisher.com/ipland/ipawards.php
Key Personnel
CEO: Jerrold R Jenkins *E-mail:* jrj@bookpublishing.com
Pres: James Kalajian *Tel:* 800-706-4636 ext 1006 *E-mail:* jjk@bookpublishing.com
Mng Ed & Awards Dir: Jim Barnes *Tel:* 800-706-4636 ext 1011 *E-mail:* jimb@bookpublishing.com
Awards Coord: Amy Shamroe
Established: 1996
Recognizes the works of independent publishers in 76 national & 22 regional categories, for excellence in literary merit, design & production, published during previous calendar year. Ebooks & audiobooks are welcome.
Other Sponsor(s): Jenkins Group
Award: Gold medal (1st place), silver medal (2nd place) & bronze medal (3rd place); foil seals available; winners featured in *Independent Publisher Magazine Online*
Closing Date: Annually in March
Presented: BookExpo, Annually in May

Indiana Review Fiction Prize
Indiana Review
Ballantine Hall 529, 1020 E Kirkwood Ave, Bloomington, IN 47405
Tel: 812-855-3439
E-mail: inreview@indiana.edu
Web Site: indianareview.org
Key Personnel
Ed: Tessa Yang
Assoc Ed: Essence London
Submit a short story of up to 8,000 words; only 1 story per entry, maximum 12 point font. Previously published works & works forthcoming elsewhere cannot be considered; $20 entry fee (which includes a subscription to *Indiana Review*). All prize entries are considered for publication.
Award: $1,000 & publication in *Indiana Review*
Closing Date: Annually in Oct

IndieReader Discovery Awards
IndieReader
PO Box 43121, Montclair, NJ 07043
E-mail: amy@indiereader.com
Web Site: indiereader.com/irda
Established: 2012
Annual awards open to indie authors who have self-published books. Entry fee: $150 per title plus additional $50 for each additional category entered. Submit three copies of your work or a shareable efile-no matter how many categories you've entered.
Other Sponsor(s): Amazon Kindle
Award: The top winners in the fiction & nonfiction categories will receive the following: Kindle Paperwhite 3G. First look consideration with an eye to representation from Dystel, Goderich & Bourret Literary Management. A free author web site for a year via Featherlight. The winners from each sub-category (addition to the top winners), will also receive the following: A professional IndiReader review. Exposure to a panel of judges who can make a difference in your book's success. An IndieReader "All About the Book" feature. Stickers pronouncing your book an "IndieReader Discovery Awards" winner
Closing Date: March
Presented: BookExpo|Book Con, Annually in late May/early June

Indies Choice Book Awards
American Booksellers Association
333 Westchester Ave, Suite S202, White Plains, NY 10604
Tel: 914-406-7500 *Toll Free Tel:* 800-637-0037 *Fax:* 914-410-6297
Web Site: www.bookweb.org
Key Personnel
CEO: Oren Teicher *Tel:* 800-637-0037 ext 7511 *E-mail:* oren@bookweb.org
Established: 1991
Book finalists will be picked by a bookseller jury, but the pool is limited to monthly +/or quarterly Indie Next list selections. Categories have been revamped & expanded, now honoring the book of the year in the following categories: adult fiction, adult nonfiction, adult debut, young adults, EB White Read Aloud Picture Book; EB White Middle Reader; Picture Book Hall of Fame & Indie Champion.
Presented: BookExpo & ABA Convention

Individual Artist Awards
Maryland State Arts Council
Affiliate of Maryland Dept of Commerce
175 W Ostend St, Suite E, Baltimore, MD 21230
Tel: 410-767-6555 *Fax:* 410-333-1062
E-mail: msac@msac.org
Web Site: www.msac.org
Key Personnel
Exec Dir: Theresa Colvin
Solely based on excellence of previous work. Must be a Maryland resident. Applications available. Award categories changed annually. Check with council for individual availability.
Award: $6,000 (1st prize), $3,000 (2nd prize) & $1,000 (3rd prize)
Closing Date: July (see web site for exact date)
Presented: Awards Reception, Early June

Individual Artist Fellowships
Maine Arts Commission
Division of State of Maine
25 State House Sta, 193 State St, Augusta, ME 04333-0025
Tel: 207-287-2726 *Fax:* 207-287-2725
Web Site: mainearts.maine.gov
Key Personnel
Sr Grants Dir: Kathy Ann Shaw *E-mail:* kathy.shaw@maine.gov
Established: 1987
Three prizes awarded annually to visual, performing & literary artists, craft, media/film, traditional arts.
Other Sponsor(s): Maine Community Foundation
Award: $5,000
Closing Date: May
Presented: Fall

Individual Artist Fellowships
Nebraska Arts Council
Division of State of Nebraska
1004 Farnam, Plaza Level, Omaha, NE 68102
Tel: 402-595-2122 *Toll Free Tel:* 800-341-4067 *Fax:* 402-595-2334
Web Site: www.nebraskaartscouncil.org
Key Personnel
Artist Servs & Communs Mgr: Launa Bacon *E-mail:* launa.bacon@nebraska.gov
Established: 1991
Fellowship for Nebraska residents only; operates on a 3-year cycle rotating with visual & performing arts & literature.
Award: $1,000-$5,000
Closing Date: Annually, Nov 15

Individual Artist Project Grant
Formerly Florida Individual Artist Fellowships
Florida Dept of State, Div of Cultural Affairs
500 S Bronough St, Tallahassee, FL 32399-0250
Tel: 850-245-6470 *Fax:* 850-245-6497
E-mail: info@dos.myflorida.com
Web Site: dos.myflorida.com/cultural
Key Personnel
Dir: Sandy Shaughnessy *E-mail:* sshaughnessy@dos.myflorida.com
Arts Consultant: Hillary Crawford *E-mail:* hcrawford@dos.myflorida.com
Established: 1976
Awarded annually, this fellowship program supports the general artistic & career advancement of individual artists & recognizes the creation of new artworks by these artists.
Award: Up to $25,000
Closing Date: June 1

Individual Artist's Fellowships
South Carolina Arts Commission (SCAC)
Division of State of South Carolina
1026 Sumter St, Suite 200, Columbia, SC 29201-3746
Tel: 803-734-8696 *Fax:* 803-734-8526
E-mail: info@arts.sc.gov
Web Site: www.southcarolinaarts.com
Key Personnel
Communs Dir: Milly Hough *Tel:* 803-734-8698 *E-mail:* mhough@arts.sc.gov
Established: 2007
Non-matching funds for South Carolina residents only. Up to 4 fellowships each year according to rotation cycle. Online submissions only. See commission's web site for details.
Award: $5,000 each
Closing Date: Annually, Nov (1st weekday)

Individual Excellence Awards
Ohio Arts Council
30 E Broad St, 33rd fl, Columbus, OH 43215
Tel: 614-466-2613 *Fax:* 614-466-4494
Web Site: www.oac.state.oh.us
Key Personnel
Exec Dir: Donna Collins *E-mail:* donna.collins@oac.ohio.gov
Prog Coord: Kathy Signorino *E-mail:* kathy.signorino@oac.ohio.gov
Indiv Prog: Ken Emerick *E-mail:* ken.emerick@oac.ohio.gov
Established: 1978
Available to creative artists who are residents of Ohio. Applicants must have lived in Ohio for 1 year prior to the September 1 deadline & must remain in the state during the grant period. Applications must be submitted online.
Odd-numbered calendar years, applications accepted in the following disciplines: choreography, criticism, fiction/nonfiction, music composition, playwriting/screenplays & poetry.
Even-numbered calendar years, applications accepted in these disciplines: crafts, design arts/illustration, interdisciplinary/performance art, media arts, photography & visual arts.

Award: $5,000 (number of awards given determined by panel)
Closing Date: Sept 1

Innis-Gerin Medal
Royal Society of Canada
Walter House, 282 Somerset W, Ottawa, ON K2P 0J6, Canada
Tel: 613-991-6990 (ext 106) *Fax:* 613-991-6996
E-mail: nominations@rsc-src.ca
Web Site: www.rsc-src.ca
Key Personnel
Mgr, Fellowship & Awards: Marie-Lyne Renaud *E-mail:* mlrenaud@rsc-src.ca
Established: 1966
Biennial award given in even-numbered years for a distinguished & sustained contribution to literature in social science, human geography & social psychology.
Award: Bronze medal
Closing Date: March 1
Presented: RSC business meeting, Nov

Institute of Puerto Rican Culture National Literary Awards
Institute of Puerto Rican Culture
PO Box 9024184, San Juan, PR 00902-4184
Tel: 787-724-0700 *Fax:* 787-724-8393
Web Site: www.icp.gobierno.pr
Key Personnel
Exec Dir: Jorge Irizarry Vizcarrondo *Tel:* 784-424-0700 ext 1002
Annual awards in the categories of poetry, short story, children's literature, novel & essay. An award in every category each year is not guaranteed.
Award: $5,000 & publication for each winner
Presented: June

Intermediate Sequoyah Book Award
Oklahoma Library Association
PO Box 6550, Edmond, OK 73083
Tel: 405-525-5100 *Fax:* 405-525-5103
Web Site: www.oklibs.org
Key Personnel
Exec Dir: Kay Boies *E-mail:* execdirector@oklibs.org
Established: 1988
Student choice award; students in grades 6-8 who have read/listened to at least 3 titles from the Intermediate Masterlist are eligible to vote.
Award: Plaque/medal
Closing Date: Annually, March 1
Presented: OLA Annual Conference, Annually in April

International Latino Book Awards
Latino Literacy Now
3445 Catalina Dr, Carlsbad, CA 92010
Tel: 760-434-1223 *Fax:* 760-434-7476
Web Site: www.award.news
Key Personnel
Awards Chair: Kirk Whisler *E-mail:* kirk@whisler.com
Established: 1998
Annual book awards celebrating books by & about Latinos. In 2016 there were 257 honorees.
Other Sponsor(s): California State University, Dominguez Hills; Entravision; Libros Publishing; Scholastic; VISA
Closing Date: April 11
Presented: California State University, Dominguez Hills, CA, Early Sept

International Latino Unpublished Book Awards
Latino Literacy Now
3445 Catalina Dr, Carlsbad, CA 92010
Tel: 760-434-1223 *Fax:* 760-434-7476
Web Site: www.award.news
Key Personnel
Awards Chair: Kirk Whisler *E-mail:* kirk@whisler.com
Awards for achievement in Latino literature in English & Spanish. Category groups: children, youth & young adult; nonfiction; fiction; best themed. Entries must be PDF of ms. Books written in English must be written by a Latino author or have a Latino theme. Books in Spanish, Portuguese, or a bilingual format may have been written by anyone. Entry fee: $65 per entry until November 21, $90 per entry up until final deadline.
Closing Date: April 11
Presented: MiraCosta College, San Diego County, CA, Sept

International Poetry Competition
Atlanta Review
686 Cherry St NW, Suite 333, Atlanta, GA 30332-0161
E-mail: atlantareview@gatech.edu
Web Site: www.atlantareview.com
Key Personnel
Mng Ed: J C Reilly
Ed: Karen J Head, PhD
Established: 1996
Online entry at atlantareview.submittable.com.
Award: $1,000 (grand prize), publication in *Atlanta Review* (20 publication prizes)
Closing Date: Annually, March 1

InterTech™ Technology Awards
Printing Industries of America
301 Brush Creek Rd, Warrendale, PA 15086-7529
Tel: 412-741-6860 *Toll Free Tel:* 800-910-4283 *Fax:* 412-741-2311
E-mail: intertech@printing.org
Web Site: www.printing.org/intertechawards
Key Personnel
Pres & CEO: Michael F Makin *Tel:* 412-259-1777 *E-mail:* mmakin@printing.org
VP, Educ & Mktg Strategies: Julie Schaffer
Sr Mktg Mgr: Jenn Strang *Tel:* 412-259-1810 *E-mail:* jstrang@printing.org
Mktg Mgr: Kayleigh Smith *E-mail:* ksmith@printing.org
Established: 1978
Honors innovative technology excellence for the graphic communications industry. The criteria for nomination stresses that the technology be recently developed, proved in industrial application, but not yet in widespread use. See web site for more information.
Award: Lucite Star
Closing Date: June
Presented: Printing Industries of America's Premier Print Awards Gala, Annually in the Fall
Branch Office(s)
1001 "G" St NW, Suite 800, Washington, DC 20001 *Tel:* 202-627-6924

IODE Jean Throop Book Award
IODE Ontario
9-45 Frid St, Hamilton, ON L8P 4M3, Canada
Tel: 905-522-9537 *Fax:* 905-522-3637
E-mail: iodeontario@bellnet.ca
Web Site: www.iodeontario.ca
Key Personnel
Convenor: Mary K Anderson
Area VP: Margo Mackinnon
Established: 1974
Children's book (Toronto area author +/or illustrator).
Award: $1,000 & certificate
Closing Date: Annually, Feb 1
Presented: Annually in April

IODE Violet Downey Book Award
The National Chapter of Canada IODE
40 Orchard View Blvd, Suite 219, Toronto, ON M4R 1B9, Canada
Tel: 416-487-4416 *Toll Free Tel:* 866-827-7428 *Fax:* 416-487-4417
E-mail: iodecanada@bellnet.ca
Web Site: www.iode.ca
Key Personnel
Natl Pres: Bonnie G Rees
Established: 1984
Children's book award. Must be a Canadian author with text in English. At least 500 words & printed in Canada during previous calendar year. Suitable for children 13 years & under.
Award: $5,000
Closing Date: Annually, Dec 31
Presented: The National Annual Meeting, Annually, late May

Iowa Poetry Prize
University of Iowa Press
119 W Park Rd, 100 Kuhl House, Iowa City, IA 52242-1000
SAN: 282-4868
Tel: 319-335-2000 *Fax:* 319-335-2055
E-mail: uipress@uiowa.edu
Web Site: www.uiowapress.org
Key Personnel
Dir: James McCoy *Tel:* 319-335-2013 *E-mail:* james-mccoy@uiowa.edu
Open to new as well as established poets for a book-length collection of poems written originally in English. Previous winners, current University of Iowa students & current & former University of Iowa Press employees are not eligible. Reading fee: $20.
Award: Publication by the University of Iowa Press under a standard royalty agreement
Closing Date: Postmarked during April

The Iowa Review Awards
University of Iowa-The Iowa Review
308 EPB, Iowa City, IA 52242-1408
E-mail: iowa-review@uiowa.edu
Web Site: www.iowareview.org
Key Personnel
Mng Ed: Lynne Nugent
Ed: Harilaos Stecopoulos
Established: 2003
Fiction, poetry & nonfiction categories. Submit up to 25 pages of prose (double-spaced) or 10 pages of poetry (1 poem or several, but no more than 1 poem per page). Work must be previously unpublished. There is a $20 entry fee; enclose an additional $10 for a 1-year subscription to the magazine (optional). Submissions between January 1-January 31.
Award: $1,500 & publication in December issue of *Iowa Review* (1st place), $750 & pubn in the December issue of *Iowa Review* (1st runners-up)
Closing Date: Annually, Jan 31

The Iowa Short Fiction Award
Writers' Workshop, The University of Iowa
102 Dey House, 507 N Clinton St, Iowa City, IA 52242-1000
Tel: 319-335-0416 *Fax:* 319-335-0420
Web Site: www.uiowapress.org/authors/iowa-short-fiction.htm
Key Personnel
Prog Assoc: Connie Brothers
Dir, Writers' Workshop: Lan Samantha Chang
Established: 1970
For a previously unpublished collection of short stories of at least 150 typewritten pages by a writer who has not previously published a volume of prose fiction. Stories previously published in periodicals are eligible for inclusion. Include SASE. Write for further information.
Other Sponsor(s): University of Iowa Press
Award: Publication by University of Iowa Press under the Press's standard contract
Closing Date: Aug 1-Sept 30

Jackie White Memorial National Children's Playwriting Contest
Columbia Entertainment Co
1400 Forum Blvd, 1C No 214, Columbia, MO 65203
E-mail: jwm@cectheatre.org
Web Site: www.cectheatre.org
Key Personnel
Pres, Community Theatre: Arron Pauley
Artistic Dir: Katie Hays
Devt Dir: Michele Curry
Established: 1988
The entry should be a full-length play or musical with speaking roles for at least 7 characters. The entry may be an unpublished original work or an adaptation; $25 entry fee, send SASE for complete rules & entry form. Each author who enters the contest may receive a letter from the contest committee discussing the strengths & weaknesses of his or her play if a SASE is enclosed.
Other Sponsor(s): City of Columbia, Office of Cultural Affairs
Award: $500, for 1st place
Closing Date: Annually, Dec 31
Presented: Annually, May 31

Joseph Henry Jackson Literary Award
The San Francisco Foundation
One Embarcadero Ctr, Suite 1400, San Francisco, CA 94111
Tel: 415-733-8500
E-mail: info@sff.org; artsinfo@sff.org
Web Site: www.sff.org
Established: 1957
Award for the author of fiction (novel or short stories), nonfictional prose, poetry. Awards are intended to encourage emerging artists not yet established in the genre who are currently residing in Alameda, Contra Costa, Marin, San Francisco or San Mateo County, for an unpublished ms-in-progress. By nomination only.
Award: $2,000
Presented: Annually in Autumn

The Jackson Poetry Prize
Poets & Writers Inc
90 Broad St, Suite 2100, New York, NY 10004
Tel: 212-226-3586 *Fax:* 212-226-3963
E-mail: admin@pw.org
Web Site: www.pw.org
Established: 2006
Honors an American poet of exceptional talent who deserves wider recognition. Eligible poets must have published at least 2 books of acknowledged literary merit.
Other Sponsor(s): Liana Foundation
Award: $60,000

The Joan Leiman Jacobson Poetry Prizes, see Discovery/Boston Review Poetry Contest

J Franklin Jameson Fellowship in American History
American Historical Association (AHA)
400 "A" St SE, Washington, DC 20003
Tel: 202-544-2422 *Fax:* 202-544-8307
E-mail: awards@historians.org
Web Site: www.historians.org
Established: 1980
To support significant scholarly research for one semester in the collections of the Library of Congress by new historians. At the time of application, applicants must hold the PhD degree or equivalent; must have received this degree within the last 5 years & must not have published or had accepted for publication a book-length historical work. The fellowship will not be awarded to permit completion of a doctoral dissertation. The applicant's project in American history must be one for which the general & special collections of the Library of Congress offer unique research support. Applicants should include a statement substantiating this relationship. Residency for at least 3 months at Library of Congress is required. Application instructions & all updated info available on web site.
Other Sponsor(s): Library of Congress
Award: Certificate & stipend of $5,000 that will be awarded for 3 months to spend in full-time residence at the Library of Congress
Closing Date: April 1

Japan-US Friendship Commission Translation Prize
Japan-US Friendship Commission
Affiliate of Donald Keene Center of Japanese Culture
Columbia University, 507 Kent Hall, MC3920, New York, NY 10027
Tel: 212-854-5036 *Fax:* 212-854-4019
Web Site: www.keenecenter.org
Key Personnel
Faculty Dir: David B Lurie
Established: 1979
The Donald Keene Center of Japanese Culture at Columbia University annually awards $6,000 in Japan-US Friendship Commission Prizes for the Translation of Japanese Literature. A prize is given for the best translation of a modern work or a classical work, or the prize is divided between equally distinguished translations.
Translations must be of book-length Japanese literary works: novels, collections of short stories, manga, literary essays, memoirs, drama, or poetry. Submissions may be unpublished mss, works in press, or books published during the 2 years prior to the prize year. Translators must be citizens or permanent residents of the US. Prior recipients of the award are eligible to submit new translations.
Award: $6,000 (either to one translator or divided between classical & modern)
Closing Date: Annually, Oct 31
Presented: Columbia University, Annually in April

Jefferson Cup Award
Youth Services Forum
Unit of Virginia Library Association (VLA)
c/o Virginia Library Association (VLA), PO Box 56312, Virginia Beach, VA 23456
Tel: 757-689-0594 *Fax:* 757-447-3478
Web Site: www.vla.org
Key Personnel
VLA Exec Dir: Lisa R Varga *E-mail:* vla.lisav@cox.net
Established: 1983
Honors a distinguished biography, historical fiction or American history book written especially for young people. Two awards given, one for books published for children & one for books published for young adults.
Award: $500 & engraved silver Jefferson Cup for each
Closing Date: Jan 31
Presented: Virginia Library Association (VLA) Annual Conference, Fall

Jerome Award
Catholic Library Association
8550 United Plaza Blvd, Suite 1001, Baton Rouge, LA 70809
Tel: 225-408-4417
E mail: cla2@cathla.org
Web Site: cathla.org
Key Personnel
Pres: N Curtis LeMay
Established: 1992
For outstanding work in Catholic scholarship; no unsol mss.
Award: Plaque
Closing Date: None; in-house votes
Presented: CLA Annual Convention, April

Jerome Fellowship
The Playwrights' Center
2301 Franklin Ave E, Minneapolis, MN 55406-1099
Tel: 612-332-7481 *Fax:* 612-332-6037
E-mail: info@pwcenter.org
Web Site: www.pwcenter.org
Key Personnel
Producing Artistic Dir: Jeremy Cohen *Tel:* 612-332-7481 ext 113 *E-mail:* jeremyc@pwcenter.org
Assoc Artistic Dir: Hayley Finn *Tel:* 612-332-7481 ext 119 *E-mail:* hayleyf@pwcenter.org
Artistic Progs Admin: Julia Brown *Tel:* 612-332-7481 ext 115 *E-mail:* juliab@pwcenter.org
Established: 1976
Fellowships awarded annually to emerging playwrights. Provides playwrights with funds & services to aid them in the development of their craft. One year in residence required, July 1-June 30. Contact above for application & guidelines, or download from web site.
Award: $18,000
Closing Date: See web site for details

Jewel Box Theatre Playwriting Competition
3700 N Walker, Oklahoma City, OK 73118-7031
Tel: 405-521-1786
Web Site: jewelboxtheatre.org
Key Personnel
Prodn Dir: Charles Tweed
Established: 1986
Original playwriting competition.
Award: $750
Closing Date: Jan 15
Presented: Banquet in Oklahoma City, OK, May

John Steinbeck Short Story Award
Reed Magazine
San Jose State University, English Dept, One Washington Sq, San Jose, CA 95192-0090
Tel: 408-924-4441
Web Site: www.reedmag.org
All submissions must be through the online system with a common file format. Writers may submit multiple entries but each must be submitted separately & accompanied by a separate entry fee of $15.
Award: $1,000 & publication in *Reed Magazine*
Closing Date: Annually, Nov 1 (submissions accepted beginning June 1)

Anson Jones MD Awards
Texas Medical Association
401 W 15 St, Austin, TX 78701
Tel: 512-370-1300 *Fax:* 512-370-1693
Web Site: www.texmed.org
Key Personnel
Outreach Coord: Tammy Wishard
Established: 1957
Annual awards in recognition of outstanding coverage of health & medical issues to the public by Texas Media.
Award: $500 cash award & plaque for winners
Closing Date: Jan 10

Jesse H Jones Award
Texas Institute of Letters (TIL)
c/o 7748 Hwy 290 W, Austin, TX 78736-3202
Tel: 512-683-5640
E-mail: president@texasinstituteofletters.org
Web Site: www.texasinstituteofletters.org
Key Personnel
Pres: Steve Davis
VP: Carmen Tafolla
Treas: W K Stratton
Secy: Sergio Troncoso
Recording Secy: Joe Holley

Annual award for the best book of fiction by a Texan or about Texas. Guidelines on the web site.
Award: $6,000
Closing Date: Annually in Jan
Presented: TIL Awards Banquet, Annually in Spring

Judah, Sarah, Grace & Tom Memorial
The Poetry Society of Virginia
900 Timber Creek Place, Virginia Beach, VA 23464
E-mail: poetryinva@aol.com; info@poetryvirginia.org
Web Site: poetrysocietyofvirginia.org
Key Personnel
Pres: Robert P Arthur *E-mail:* robert.peebles.arthur@gmail.com
Exec Dir: Guy Terrell *E-mail:* guy.terrell@earthlink.net
Adult Contest Chair: Steven Blythe *E-mail:* stevenblythepoetry@gmail.com
All entries must be in English, original & unpublished. Submit 2 copies of each poem, both copies must have the category name & number on top left of page. Only one poem per category; entries will not be returned. Subject: encouraging reflection on inter-ethnic relations; any form; 48 line limit. Entry fee: $4 nonmembs.
Award: $50 (1st place), $30 (2nd place), $20 (3rd place)
Closing Date: Jan
Presented: Annual PSV Awards Ceremony, April

Juniper Prize for Fiction
University of Massachusetts Press
East Experiment Sta, 671 N Pleasant St, Amherst, MA 01003
E-mail: info@umpress.umass.edu
Web Site: www.umass.edu/umpress; www.umass.edu/umpress/content/juniper-literary-prize-series
Key Personnel
Dir: Mary V Dougherty *Tel:* 413-545-4990 *E-mail:* mvd@umpress.umass.edu
Established: 2004
Two prizes: one novel, one story. Annual prize to honor & publish outstanding works of literary fiction. Open to all writers in English, whether or not they are US Citizens. Entry fee is $30 (must be drawn on US bank). Entries accepted beginning August 1.
Award: $1,000 upon publication
Closing Date: Sept 30 (postmark)
Presented: Winner announced on web site in April

Juniper Prize for Poetry
University of Massachusetts Press
East Experiment Sta, 671 N Pleasant St, Amherst, MA 01003
E-mail: info@umpress.umass.edu
Web Site: www.umass.edu/umpress; www.umass.edu/umpress/content/juniper-literary-prize-series
Key Personnel
Dir: Mary V Dougherty *Tel:* 413-545-4990 *E-mail:* mvd@umpress.umass.edu
Established: 1976
Two poetry prizes awarded annually for an original ms of poems. One prize for first publication, one is open to poets either with or without previously published books. Entry fee: $30.
Award: $1,000 & publication
Presented: Annually in April; publication by the following Spring

Juvenile Literary Awards/Young People's Literature Awards
Friends of American Writers
506 Rose Ave, Des Plaines, IL 60016
Tel: 847-827-8339
Web Site: www.fawchicago.org
Key Personnel
Pres: Roberta Gates *E-mail:* robmicgates73@gmail.com
Juv Lit Awards Chair: Martha Daniel *E-mail:* mcmdaniel@mac.com
Established: 1960
For books written for young people from toddler through high school age & published in the current year, can only be author's 1st, 2nd or 3rd book & the author must be from the Midwest +/or the book must be about the Midwest. See web site for full details.
Award: Two $2,000 prizes
Closing Date: Annually, Dec 20
Presented: The Fortnightly, Chicago, IL, Annually in May

Frederick D Kagy Education Award of Excellence
Printing Industries of America
301 Brush Creek Rd, Warrendale, PA 15086-7529
Tel: 412-741-6860 *Toll Free Tel:* 800-910-4283 *Fax:* 412-741-2311
E-mail: printingind@comm.printing.org
Web Site: www.printing.org
Key Personnel
Pres & CEO: Michael F Makin *Tel:* 412-259-1777 *E-mail:* mmakin@printing.org
VP, Educ & Mktg Strategies: Julie Schaffer
Sr Mktg Mgr: Jenn Strang *Tel:* 412-259-1810 *E-mail:* jstrang@printing.org
Mktg Mgr: Kayleigh Smith *E-mail:* ksmith@printing.org
Established: 1993
Honors an exemplary graphic communications program at the middle school, high school or community college graphic communications program. School must be staffed by Printing Industries of America's teacher member (membership cost $49). See web site for more information.
Other Sponsor(s): Printing Industries of America's Ben Franklin Society
Award: A commemorative award & selection of up to $1,000 worth of textbooks published by Printing Industries Press
Closing Date: Oct 31
Presented: TAGA Annual Technical Conference, March
Branch Office(s)
1001 "G" St NW, Suite 800, Washington, DC 20001 *Tel:* 202-627-6924

Sue Kaufman Prize for First Fiction
American Academy of Arts & Letters
633 W 155 St, New York, NY 10032
Tel: 212-368-5900 *Fax:* 212-491-4615
E-mail: academy@artsandletters.org
Web Site: www.artsandletters.org
Key Personnel
Exec Dir: Cody Upton
Established: 1979
For the best published first novel or collection of short stories of the preceding year.
Award: $5,000

Ezra Jack Keats/Kerlan Memorial Fellowship
Ezra Jack Keats Foundation
University of Minnesota, 113 Andersen Library, 222 21 Ave S, Minneapolis, MN 55455
Tel: 612-624-4576
E-mail: asc-clrc@umn.edu
Web Site: www.lib.umn.edu/clrc
Key Personnel
Curator Kerlan Collection: Lisa Von Drasek
Awarded to a talented writer +/or illustrator of children's books who wish to use the Kerlan Collection to further his or her artistic development.
Award: $1,500
Closing Date: Jan 30

Joan Kelly Memorial Prize in Women's History
American Historical Association (AHA)
400 "A" St SE, Washington, DC 20003
Tel: 202-544-2422 *Fax:* 202-544-8307
E-mail: awards@historians.org
Web Site: www.historians.org
Established: 1984
For the book in women's history +/or feminist theory that best reflects the high intellectual & scholarly ideals exemplified by the life & work of Joan Kelly. Submissions shall be books in any chronological period, any geographical location, or in any area of feminist theory that incorporates an historical perspective. Books should demonstrate originality of research, creativity of insight, graceful stylistic presentation, analytical skills & a recognition of the important role of sex & gender in the historical process. The inter-relationship between women & the historical process should be addressed. Books published in 2017 are eligible. Along with an application form, one copy of each entry must be received by each of the 5 committee members. The Association will announce the recipients of prizes & awards at its annual meeting during the 1st week in Jan. All updated info on web site.
Award: Cash prize
Closing Date: May 15, 2018
Presented: AHA Annual Meeting, Chicago, IL, Jan 2019

Robert F Kennedy Book Awards
Robert F Kennedy Center for Justice & Human Rights
1300 19 St NW, Suite 750, Washington, DC 20036
Tel: 202-463-7575 *Fax:* 202-463-6606
E-mail: info@rfkhumanrights.org
Web Site: rfkhumanrights.org
Key Personnel
Contact: Jae Regala *E-mail:* regala@rfkhumanrights.org
Established: 1980
For a book of fiction or nonfiction that most faithfully & forcefully reflects Robert Kennedy's interests & concerns. Publishers or authors should mail 6 copies of the book published in the previous year. Submit entry form, press release, review, or descriptive letter & $75 entry fee through online submission portal. See web site for further details.
Award: $2,500 & bust of Robert Kennedy
Closing Date: Feb 1
Presented: May

Coretta Scott King Book Awards
The American Library Association (ALA)
50 E Huron St, Chicago, IL 60611
Toll Free Tel: 800-545-2433
E-mail: olos@ala.org
Web Site: www.ala.org/emiert/cskbookawards
Key Personnel
Interim Dir, OLOS: Gwendolyn Prellwitz *E-mail:* gprellwitz@ala.org
Literacy Offr: Kristin Lahurd *E-mail:* klahurd@ala.org
Prog Offr: John Amundsen *E-mail:* jamundsen@ala.org
Prog Coord: Zina Clark *E-mail:* zclark@ala.org
Established: 1970
Awarded annually to outstanding African-American authors & illustrators of books for children & young adults that demonstrate an appreciation of African-American culture & universal human values. Administered by the Ethnic Multicultural Information Exchange Round Table (EMIERT).
Other Sponsor(s): Book Wholesalers Inc; Encyclopaedia Britannica; Johnson Publications; World Book

Award: Bronze award seal & $1,000 to both author & illustrator
Closing Date: Dec 1
Presented: Coretta Scott King Awards Breakfast, ALA Annual Conference, June

Coretta Scott King - Virginia Hamilton Award for Lifetime Achievement
The American Library Association (ALA)
50 E Huron St, Chicago, IL 60611
Toll Free Tel: 800-545-2433
E-mail: diversity@ala.org
Web Site: www.ala.org/emiert/virginia-hamilton-award-lifetime-achievement
Key Personnel
Prog Offr: John Amundsen *E-mail:* jamundsen@ala.org
Established: 2010
Annual award is presented in even years to an African-American author, illustrator or author/illustrator for a body of his or her published books for children +/or young adults & who has made a significant & lasting literary contribution.
In odd years, the award is presented to a practitioner for substantial contributions through active engagement with youth using award-winning African-American literature for children +/or young adults, via implementation of reading & reading related activities/programs. See web site for specific selection criteria.
Award: Medal & $1,500
Presented: Coretta Scott King Awards Breakfast, ALA Annual Conference, June

The Knight-Risser Prize for Western Environmental Journalism
John S Knight Journalism Fellowships
Stanford University, 450 Serra Mall, Bldg 120, Rm 424, Stanford, CA 94305-2050
Tel: 650-723-4937 *Fax:* 650-725-6154
E-mail: knightrisserprize@lists.stanford.edu
Web Site: knightrisser.stanford.edu
Key Personnel
Dir: Dawn E Garcia *E-mail:* degarcia@stanford.edu
Admin Mgr: Erika Bartholomew *Tel:* 650-725-1192
Established: 2006
Recognizes the best environmental reporting on the North American West, from Canada through the US to Mexico. Open to print, broadcast & online journalists, staffers & freelancers. For more information, see web site.
Other Sponsor(s): Bill Lane Center for the American West at Stanford University
Award: $5,000 cash
Closing Date: Annually in March
Presented: Annual Knight-Risser Prize Symposium, Stanford University, Stanford, CA, Summer

Knightville Poetry Contest
The New Guard
PO Box 5101, Hanover, NH 03755
E-mail: info@newguardreview.com
Web Site: www.newguardreview.com
Key Personnel
Founding Ed & Publr: Shanna McNair
Established: 2009
Submit up to 3 poems of up to 150 lines. Submit all 3 poems in a single document. Online submissions only.
Award: $1,500 & publication in *The New Guard*
Closing Date: Aug

Katherine Singer Kovacs Prize
Modern Language Association of America (MLA)
85 Broad St, Suite 500, New York, NY 10004-2434
SAN: 202-6422
Tel: 646-576-5141; 646-576-5000 *Fax:* 646-458-0030
E-mail: awards@mla.org
Web Site: www.mla.org
Key Personnel
Coord, Book Prizes: Annie M Reiser
E-mail: areiser@mla.org
Established: 1990
Prize for an outstanding book published in 2017 in English or Spanish in the field of Latin American & Spanish literatures & cultures. Authors need not be members of MLA. For consideration, submit 6 copies. Presented annually.
Award: Cash award & certificate
Closing Date: May 1, 2018
Presented: MLA Convention, Chicago, IL, Jan 2019

Michael Kraus Research Grant in American Colonial History
American Historical Association (AHA)
400 "A" St SE, Washington, DC 20003
Tel: 202-544-2422 *Fax:* 202-544-8307
E-mail: awards@historians.org
Web Site: www.historians.org
Grant given to a member of the association to recognize the most deserving proposal relating to works in progress on a research project in American colonial history, with particular reference to the intercultural aspects of American & European relations. The grants are intended to further research in progress & may be used for travel to a library or archive, for microfilms, photographs, or photocopying. Preference will be given to those with specific research needs, such as the completion of a project or completion of a discrete segment thereof. Only members of the association are eligible to apply. See web site for additional submission guidelines & eligibility.
Award: Individual grants will not exceed $800
Closing Date: Annually, Feb 15

The Robert Kroetsch City of Edmonton Book Prize
Writers' Guild of Alberta
11759 Groat Rd, Edmonton, AB T5M 3K6, Canada
Tel: 780-422-8174 *Toll Free Tel:* 800-665-5354 (AB only) *Fax:* 780-422-2663 (attn WGA)
E-mail: mail@writersguild.ca
Web Site: writersguild.ca
Key Personnel
Exec Dir: Carol Holmes *E-mail:* carol.holmes@writersguild.ca
Communs & Partnerships Coord: Ellen Kartz
E-mail: ellen.kartz@writersguild.ca
Memb Servs Coord: Giorgia Severini
Progs Coord: Natalie Cook *E-mail:* natalie.cook@writersguild.ca; Julie Robinson *E-mail:* julie.robinson@writersguild.ca
Entries must deal with some aspect of the City of Edmonton: history, geography, current affairs, its arts or its people or be written by an Edmonton author.
Award: $10,000 & leather-bound copy of book
Closing Date: Annually, Dec 31
Presented: Mayor's Evening for the Arts, Annually in Spring
Branch Office(s)
505 21 Ave SW, Calgary, AB T2S 0G9, Canada, Prog Coord: Samantha Warwick *Tel:* 403-265-2226 *E-mail:* samantha.warwick@writersguild.ca

Kumu Kahua/UHM Theatre & Dance Department Playwriting Contest
Kumu Kahua/UHM Theatre & Dance Department
46 Merchant St, Honolulu, HI 96813
Tel: 808-536-4441 (box off); 808-536-4222 *Fax:* 808-536-4226
E-mail: kumukahuatheatre@hawaiiantel.net
Web Site: www.kumukahua.org
Key Personnel
Artistic Dir: Harry L Wong, III
Hawaii Prize: Open to residents of Hawaii & non-residents; full-length (50 pages or more); play must be set in Hawaii +/or deal with the Hawaii experience.
Pacific Rim Prize: Open to residents of Hawaii & non-residents; full-length (50 pages or more); play must be set in +/or dealing with the Pacific Islands, Pacific Rim, or the Pacific/Asian-American experience.
Resident Prize: Only open to residents of Hawaii; full-length (50 pages or more) or one-acts; play can be on any topic.
Award: $600 (Hawaii Prize), $450 (Pacific Rim Prize), $250 (Resident Prize)
Closing Date: Annually, Jan 2
Presented: May

W Kaye Lamb Award
British Columbia Historical Federation
PO Box 5254, Sta B, Victoria, BC V8R 6N4, Canada
E-mail: essays@bchistory.ca
Web Site: www.bchistory.ca
Key Personnel
Contact: Marie Elliot
Scholarship offered for essays written by students in British Columbia colleges or universities on a topic relating to British Columbia history.
Award: $750 (1st or 2nd yr student), $1,000 (3rd or 4th yr student)
Closing Date: Annually, May 15
Presented: BCHF Annual Awards Banquet, Annually in May/June

Lambda Literary Awards (Lammys)
Lambda Literary
5482 Wilshire Blvd, No 1595, Los Angeles, CA 90036
Tel: 323-643-4281
E-mail: admin@lambdaliterary.org
Web Site: www.lambdaliterary.org
Key Personnel
Exec Dir: Tony Valenzuela
Awards Admin: Ella Boureau
Established: 1989
Annual award recognizing excellence in LGBT literature. Entry fee required. Guidelines on the web site.
Award: Trophy
Closing Date: Annually, Dec 1
Presented: New York, NY, Annually in June

Gerald Lampert Memorial Award
The League of Canadian Poets
192 Spadina Ave, Suite 312, Toronto, ON M5T 2C2, Canada
Tel: 416-504-1657 *Fax:* 416-504-0096
E-mail: admin@poets.ca
Web Site: poets.ca
Key Personnel
Exec Dir: Lesley Fletcher *E-mail:* lesley@poets.ca
Annual award intended to recognize the work of a Canadian writer early in his or her career. Awarded for a first book of poetry published in the preceding year. $25 handling fee.
Award: $1,000
Closing Date: Nov 1
Presented: Annual Conference, June

Langum Prize in American Historical Fiction
The Langum Charitable Trust
2809 Berkeley Dr, Birmingham, AL 35242
Tel: 360-809-0465
E-mail: langumtrust@gmail.com
Web Site: www.langumtrust.org

Key Personnel
Dir: David J Langum, Sr *E-mail:* djlangum@samford.edu
Established: 2001
Awarded to a book published by any non-subsidy press for American historical fiction set in the colonial or national periods that is both excellent fiction & excellent history.
Award: $1,000
Closing Date: Annually, Dec 1
Presented: Annually in March

Langum Prize in American Legal History or Biography
The Langum Charitable Trust
2809 Berkeley Dr, Birmingham, AL 35242
Tel: 360-809-0465
E-mail: langumtrust@gmail.com
Web Site: www.langumtrust.org
Key Personnel
Dir: David J Langum, Sr *E-mail:* djlangum@samford.edu
Established: 2001
Awarded annually to a book in the area of American legal history or American legal biography that is accessible to the educated general public, rooted in sound scholarship & with themes that touch upon matters of general concern to the American public, past or present.
Award: $1,000
Closing Date: Dec 1
Presented: March

Lannan Literary Awards & Fellowships
Lannan Foundation
313 Read St, Santa Fe, NM 87501-2628
Tel: 505-986-8160
E-mail: info@lannan.org
Web Site: www.lannan.org
Established: 1989
The awards recognize writers who have made significant contributions to English language literature. The fellowships recognize writers of distinctive literary merit who demonstrate potential for continued outstanding work.

Larew, Christian, Memorial Scholarship in Library & Information Technology, see LITA/Christian Larew Memorial Scholarship in Library & Information Technology

Latino Books Into Movies Awards
Latino Literacy Now
3445 Catalina Dr, Carlsbad, CA 92010
Tel: 760-434-1223 *Fax:* 760-434-7476
Web Site: www.award.news
Key Personnel
Awards Chair: Kirk Whisler *E-mail:* kirk@whisler.com
Accept books, movie screenplays, plays & television scripts. Send 5 copies of each book or script being nominated. In the movie & television categories, the author or co-author of the book or screenplay must be Latino, Latin American, or Spanish. Categories under Latino themes by non-Latino authors or screenwriters are open only to non-Latino writers, but must be Latino themed. Books & screenplays must be in English language. If in Spanish, must be accompanied by a PDF of English translation. Entry fee: $80 per each individual entry until November 21, $100 each after that until the final deadline.
Award: Winning books distributed to pertinent motion picture studios, television networks, producers & agents, depending on genre
Closing Date: April 11
Presented: Early Sept

Lawrence Foundation Prize
Michigan Quarterly Review
University of Michigan, 0576 Rackham Bldg, 915 E Washington St, Ann Arbor, MI 48109-1070
Tel: 734-764-9265
E-mail: mqr@umich.edu
Web Site: www.umich.edu/~mqr
Key Personnel
Ed: Jonathan Freedman
Awarded to the best work of fiction published in MQR each year. No deadline or special application process.
Award: $1,000

Stephen Leacock Memorial Medal for Humour
The Leacock Associates
149 Peter St N, Orillia, ON L3V 4Z4, Canada
Tel: 705-326-9286
Web Site: www.leacock.ca
Key Personnel
Chair, Award Comm: Bette Walker *E-mail:* bettewalkerca@gmail.com
Pres: Nathan Taylor
Contact: Don Reid *E-mail:* don_reid@sympatico.ca
Established: 1946
Humorous writing by Canadian authors. All entries must have been published in the year prior to the year the award is given. Ten copies of each book to be submitted should be sent along with $150 fee, authors bio & a 5x7 or larger B&W photograph. No ebooks accepted. Winner announced late April. Books are non-returnable.
Other Sponsor(s): TD Bank Group
Award: $15,000 TD Bank Group cash award & silver medal, each of 4 finalists receive $1,500
Closing Date: Dec 31
Presented: Gala Award Dinner, Geneva Park, Orillia, ON, Annually, early June

Harper Lee Prize for Legal Fiction
The University of Alabama School of Law
101 Paul Bryant Dr, Tuscaloosa, AL 35487
Tel: 205-348-5195
Web Site: www.law.ua.edu/programs/harper-lee-prize-for-legal-fiction
Key Personnel
Contact: Monique Fields *E-mail:* mfields@law.ua.edu
Established: 2011
Awarded annually to a published work of fiction that best illuminates the role of lawyers in society & their power to effect change.
Other Sponsor(s): ABA Journal
Closing Date: March 31
Presented: Prize ceremony, Sept in conjunction with National Book Festival, Washington, DC

Waldo G Leland Prize
American Historical Association (AHA)
400 "A" St SE, Washington, DC 20003
Tel: 202-544-2422 *Fax:* 202-544-8307
E-mail: awards@historians.org
Web Site: www.historians.org
Established: 1981
Honorific award offered every 5 years for the most outstanding reference tool in the field of history. Reference tool encompasses bibliographies, indexes, encyclopedias & other scholarly apparatus. Books with a copyright between 2016 & 2020 will be eligible for the prize in 2021. No application form, applicant must send a copy of their book to each of the prize committee members who will be posted on our web site as the prize deadline approaches. All updated info on web site.
Closing Date: May 15, 2021
Presented: AHA Annual Meeting, New Orleans, LA, Jan 2022

Vincent Lemieux Prize
Canadian Political Science Association
260 rue Dalhousie St, Suite 204, Ottawa, ON K1N 7E4, Canada
Tel: 613-562-1202 *Fax:* 613-241-0019
E-mail: cpsa-acsp@cpsa-acsp.ca
Web Site: www.cpsa-acsp.ca
Key Personnel
Admin: Michelle Hopkins
Established: 1997
This is a biennial competition awarded to the best thesis in any sub-field of political science submitted at a Canadian University, written in English or French, judged eminently worthy of publication in the form of a book or articles. A thesis is eligible only after nomination by the department of political science in which it was defended. For the 2019 award, a thesis must have been defended in 2017 or 2018.
Award: $1,000 & commemorative certificate
Presented: Annual Conference, University of British Columbia, Vancouver, BC, CN, June 1-7, 2019

Leopold-Hidy Award
The Forest History Society Inc
701 William Vickers Ave, Durham, NC 27701-3162
Tel: 919-682-9319 *Fax:* 919-682-2349
Web Site: www.foresthistory.org
Key Personnel
Admin Asst: Andrea Anderson *E-mail:* andrea.anderson@foresthistory.org
Established: 1996
To honor the best article in the journal they co-publish, "Environmental History".
Other Sponsor(s): American Society for Environmental History

Fenia & Yaakov Leviant Memorial Prize in Yiddish Studies
Modern Language Association of America (MLA)
85 Broad St, Suite 500, New York, NY 10004-2434
SAN: 202-6422
Tel: 646-576-5141; 646-576-5000 *Fax:* 646-458-0030
E-mail: awards@mla.org
Web Site: www.mla.org
Key Personnel
Coord, Book Prizes: Annie M Reiser *E-mail:* areiser@mla.org
Established: 2000
Awarded alternately to an outstanding scholarly or translation work in the field of Yiddish. The 2018 prize will be awarded to an English translation of a Yiddish literary work published between 2014 & 2017. Authors need not be members of the MLA. For consideration, submit 4 copies.
Award: Cash award & certificate
Closing Date: May 1, 2018
Presented: MLA Convention, Chicago, IL, Jan 2019

Harry Levin Prize
American Comparative Literature Association (ACLA)
University of South Carolina, Dept of Languages, Literature & Cultures, 1620 College St, Rm 813-A, Columbia, SC 29208
Tel: 803-777-3021
E-mail: info@acla.org
Web Site: www.acla.org/prize-awards
Key Personnel
Nominations Comm Chair: Antonio Barrenechea *E-mail:* abarrene@umw.edu
Admin Coord: Andy Anderson
Established: 1968
Prize recognizing an outstanding first book in the discipline of comparative literature published during the previous 2 calendar years as the author's 1st book-length publication. Awarded annually. See web site for nomination process.

Award: Complimentary registration for the annual meeting, as well as hotel & airfare accommodations (not including food)
Closing Date: Oct 1
Presented: ACLA Annual Meeting, July

Levinson Prize
Poetry Magazine
61 W Superior St, Chicago, IL 60654
Tel: 312-787-7070 *Fax:* 312-787-6650
E-mail: editors@poetrymagazine.org
Web Site: www.poetryfoundation.org
Key Personnel
Edit Asst: Holly Amos *E-mail:* hamos@poetrymagazine.org
Established: 1914
For poetry published in the preceding 2 volumes of *Poetry* magazine. No application necessary.
Award: $500
Presented: Annually in Dec

Levis Reading Prize
Virginia Commonwealth University, Dept of English
PO Box 842005, Richmond, VA 23284-2005
Tel: 804-828-1331 *Fax:* 804-828-8684
Web Site: english.vcu.edu/mfa/levis/
Established: 1997
In memory of Larry Levis, awarded annually for best first or second book of poetry (not for self-published or chapbooks).
Award: $5,000
Closing Date: Feb 1
Presented: VCU Cabell Library, Richmond, VA, Sept/Oct

Michael J Libow Youth Theatre Award, see BHTG - Michael J Libow Youth Theatre Award

Library of Congress Literacy Awards
Library of Congress
101 Independence Ave SE, Washington, DC 20540-1400
Tel: 202-707-5221 (Center for the Book)
Fax: 202-707-0269
Web Site: www.read.gov/literacyawards
Awards to 3 organizations that have made outstanding contributions to increasing literacy in the US or abroad.
Award: Rubenstein Prize $150,000, American Prize $50,000, International Prize $50,000

Library of Congress Prize for American Fiction
Library of Congress
101 Independence Ave SE, Washington, DC 20540-1400
Tel: 202-707-5221 (Center for the Book)
Fax: 202-707-0269
Web Site: www.loc.gov
Key Personnel
Communs Offr: Guy Lamolinara
Prog Offr: Anne Boni
Established: 2013
Annual award to honor an American literary writer whose body of work is distinguished not only for its mastery of the art but for its originality of thought & imagination. The award seeks to commend strong, unique, enduring voices that, throughout long, consistently accomplished careers, have told us something about the American experience.
Presented: Library of Congress National Book Festival

The Lieutenant-Governor's Awards for High Achievement in the Arts
New Brunswick Arts Board (Conseil des arts du Nouveau-Brunswick)
225 King St, Suite 201, Fredericton, NB E3B 1E1, Canada
Tel: 506-444-4444 *Toll Free Tel:* 866-460-ARTS (460-2787) *Fax:* 506-444-5543
Web Site: www.artsnb.ca
Key Personnel
Exec Dir: Joss Richer *Tel:* 506-478-4610
E-mail: execdirgen@artsnb.ca
Prog Offr: Sarah Beth Shiplett *Tel:* 506-440-0037
E-mail: sarahbeth@artsnb.ca
Opers Mgr: Tilly Jackson *Tel:* 506-478-4422
E-mail: tjackson@artsnb.ca
Established: 1989
To recognize the outstanding contribution of artists to the arts in New Brunswick.
Award: $20,000/yr
Closing Date: June 15
Presented: Fredericton, NB

Ruth Lilly & Dorothy Sargent Rosenberg Poetry Fellowships
Poetry Foundation
61 W Superior St, Chicago, IL 60654
Tel: 312-787-7070 *Fax:* 312-787-6650
E-mail: info@poetryfoundation.org; media@poetryfoundation.org
Web Site: www.poetryfoundation.org
Established: 1989
Awarded to young US poets to encourage the further study & writing of poetry. Five fellowships are awarded annually.
Award: $25,800 each

Ruth Lilly Poetry Prize
Poetry Foundation
61 W Superior St, Chicago, IL 60654
Tel: 312-787-7070 *Fax:* 312-787-6650
E-mail: editors@poetrymagazine.org
Web Site: poetrymagazine.org
Key Personnel
Ed: Don Share
Edit Asst: Holly Amos *E-mail:* hamos@poetrymagazine.org
Established: 1986
Awarded to a living US poet, to recognize extraordinary artistic accomplishment.
Award: $100,000
Presented: Annually in May

Abraham Lincoln Institute Book Award
Abraham Lincoln Institute Inc
105 Mount Olive Lane, Ephrata, PA 17522
E-mail: secretary@lincoln-institute.org
Web Site: www.lincoln-institute.org
Key Personnel
Chmn of the Bd: Paul Pascal
Pres: Michelle Krowl
VP: Jonathan W White
Gen Secy: Clark Evans
Established: 1998
Given for the previous year's most noteworthy book on the subject of Abraham Lincoln. Prize committee members must each receive one copy of the nominated book, accompanied by a brief letter stating its merits.
Award: $1,000
Closing Date: Nov 1
Presented: ALI Symposium, Ford's Theatre, Washington, DC, Annually in March

Lindquist & Vennum Prize for Poetry
Milkweed Editions
1011 Washington Ave S, Suite 300, Minneapolis, MN 55415-1246
Tel: 612-332-3192 *Toll Free Tel:* 800-520-6455
Fax: 612-215-2550
Web Site: www.milkweed.org
Key Personnel
Publg Asst: Connor Lane
Established: 2011
Annual regional prize to support outstanding poets & bring their work to a national stage. Submissions accepted in hard copy only from poets currently residing in North Dakota, South Dakota, Minnesota, Iowa, or Wisconsin. No entry fee.
Other Sponsor(s): Lindquist & Vennum Foundation
Award: $10,000 & publication contract
Presented: Annually in April

Joseph W Lippincott Award
The American Library Association (ALA)
50 E Huron St, Chicago, IL 60611
Tel: 312-280-3247 *Toll Free Tel:* 800-545-2433 (ext 3247) *Fax:* 312-944-3897
E-mail: awards@ala.org
Web Site: www.ala.org
Key Personnel
Prog Offr: Cheryl M Malden *E-mail:* cmalden@ala.org
Established: 1938
Annual award presented to a librarian for distinguished service to the profession of librarianship, such service to include outstanding participation in the activities of professional library association, notable published professional writing or other significant activity on behalf of the profession & its aims.
Other Sponsor(s): Joseph W Lippincott III
Award: $1,000 & Citation
Closing Date: Dec 1
Presented: ALA Annual Conference, June

LITA/Christian Larew Memorial Scholarship in Library & Information Technology
Library & Information Technology Association (LITA)
Division of American Library Association (ALA)
c/o American Library Association, 50 E Huron St, Chicago, IL 60611-2795
Toll Free Tel: 800-545-2433
E-mail: scholarships@ala.org
Web Site: www.ala.org/lita
Key Personnel
Prog Offr, Educ Scholarships (ALA): Kimberly Redd
Established: 1999
Awarded jointly on an annual basis. The scholarship is designed to encourage the entry of qualified persons into the library & information technology field, who plan to follow a career in that field & who demonstrate academic excellence, leadership & a vision in pursuit of library & information technology. This scholarship is for study in an ALA Accredited Master of Library Science (MLS) program.
Other Sponsor(s): Baker & Taylor
Award: $3,000
Closing Date: Annually, March 1
Presented: LITA President's program held at the American Library Association Annual Conference, Annually in June

LITA/LSSI Minority Scholarship in Library & Information Technology
Library & Information Technology Association (LITA)
Division of American Library Association (ALA)
c/o American Library Association, 50 E Huron St, Chicago, IL 60611-2795
Toll Free Tel: 800-545-2433
E-mail: scholarships@ala.org
Web Site: www.ala.org/lita
Key Personnel
Prog Offr, Educ Scholarships (ALA): Kimberly Redd
Established: 1994
Scholarship is designed to encourage the entry of qualified minorities into the library & automation field who plan to follow a career in that field & who demonstrate potential in & have a strong commitment to the use of automated systems in libraries. Applicants must be qual-

ified members of a principal minority group (American Indian or Alaskan native, Asian or Pacific Islander, African-American or Hispanic). The recipient must be a US or Canadian citizen. The scholarship is for study in an ALA Accredited Master of Library Science (MLS) program.
Other Sponsor(s): LSSI
Award: $2,500
Closing Date: Annually, March 1
Presented: LITA President's Program held at the American Library Association Annual Conference, Annually in June

LITA/OCLC Minority Scholarship in Library & Information Technology
Library & Information Technology Association (LITA)
Division of American Library Association (ALA)
c/o American Library Association, 50 E Huron St, Chicago, IL 60611-2795
Toll Free Tel: 800-545-2433
E-mail: scholarships@ala.org
Web Site: www.ala.org/lita
Key Personnel
Prog Offr, Educ Scholarships (ALA): Kimberly Redd
Established: 1991
For qualified members of a minority group. Must be US or Canadian citizen. For applicants who plan to enter a career in the library & automation field.
Other Sponsor(s): OCLC Inc
Award: $3,000
Closing Date: Annually, March 1
Presented: LITA President's Program at the American Library Association Annual Conference, Annually in June

Literary Translation Projects, see Translation Projects

Literature Fellowship
Idaho Commission on the Arts
2410 N Old Penitentiary Rd, Boise, ID 83712
Mailing Address: PO Box 83720, Boise, ID 83720-0008
Tel: 208-334-2119
E-mail: info@arts.idaho.gov
Web Site: www.arts.idaho.gov
Key Personnel
Lit Dir: Jocelyn Robertson *Tel:* 208-334-2119 ext 108 *E-mail:* jocelyn.robertson@arts.idaho.gov
Five fellowships awarded triennially for literary excellence. For Idaho residents only.
Award: $5,000
Closing Date: Jan
Presented: Triennially in July

Littleton-Griswold Prize in American Law & Society
American Historical Association (AHA)
400 "A" St SE, Washington, DC 20003
Tel: 202-544-2422 *Fax:* 202-544-8307
E-mail: awards@historians.org
Web Site: www.historians.org
Established: 1985
Best book in any subject on the history of American law & society. Only books of high scholarly & literary merit published in 2017 will be eligible for consideration. Along with an application form, applicants must mail a copy of their book to each of the prize committee members who will be posted on our web site as the prize deadline approaches. All updated info on web site.
Award: Cash prize
Closing Date: May 15, 2018
Presented: AHA Annual Meeting, Chicago, IL, Jan 2019

Littleton-Griswold Research Grants
American Historical Association (AHA)
400 "A" St SE, Washington, DC 20003
Tel: 202-544-2422 *Fax:* 202-544-8307
E-mail: awards@historians.org
Web Site: www.historians.org
For research in American legal history & the field of law & society. Only members of the Association are eligible. Applications must include application form with estimated budget, curriculum vitae & statement of no more than 750 words & a one-page bibliography of the most recent, relevant, secondary works on the topic. Application form & all updated info on web site. Preference will be given to junior scholars, PhD candidates & those without access to institutional funds.
Award: Individual grants will not exceed $1,500
Closing Date: Feb 15

Living Now Book Awards
Independent Publisher Online
Division of Jenkins Group Inc
1129 Woodmere Ave, Suite B, Traverse City, MI 49686
Tel: 231-933-0445 *Toll Free Tel:* 800-706-4636 *Fax:* 231-933-0448
E-mail: awards@bookpublishing.com
Web Site: www.livingnowawards.com
Key Personnel
CEO: Jerrold R Jenkins *E-mail:* jrj@bookpublishing.com
Pres: James Kalajian *Tel:* 800-706-4636 ext 1006 *E-mail:* jjk@bookpublishing.com
Mng Ed & Awards Dir: Jim Barnes *Tel:* 800-706-4636 ext 1011 *E-mail:* jimb@bookpublishing.com
Awards Coord: Amy Shamroe
Established: 2008
Annual award to celebrate the innovation & creativity of newly published books that can help us improve the quality of our lives, from cooking & entertaining to fitness & travel. The awards are open to all books written in English & intended for the North American market.
Other Sponsor(s): Jenkins Group
Award: Gold medal (1st place), silver medal (2nd place), bronze medal (3rd place), foil seals available, winners featured in *Independent Publisher Online*
Closing Date: July
Presented: Winner announced online in Sept

Locus Awards
Locus Science Fiction Foundation Inc
Division of Locus Publications
PO Box 13305, Oakland, CA 94661-0305
Tel: 510-339-9196 *Fax:* 510-339-9198
E-mail: locus@locusmag.com
Web Site: www.locusmag.com
Key Personnel
Ed-in-Chief: Liza Groen Trombi
Mng Ed: Kirsten Gong-Wong
Established: 1971
Presented for the best science fiction novel, best fantasy novel, best first novel, best young adult novel, best novella, best novelette, best short fiction, science fiction anthology, best nonfiction, art & artist, editor, magazine, best publisher & collection of the year.
Other Sponsor(s): Arisia; Norwescon
Award: Trophy & free subn
Presented: Seattle Center, Annually in June

The Gerald Loeb Awards
Anderson School of Management at UCLA
Gold Hall, Suite B-305, 110 Westwood Plaza, Los Angeles, CA 90095-1481
Tel: 310-825-4478 *Fax:* 310-825-4479
E-mail: loeb@anderson.ucla.edu
Web Site: www.anderson.ucla.edu/gerald-loeb-awards
Key Personnel
Exec Dir: Jonathan Daillak
Established: 1957
Distinguished business & finance journalism in print & broadcast media. See web site for a complete list of categories, eligibility & rules. $100 per entry.
Award: The winning entry in each category receives a $2,000 honorarium. Honorable mentions in each category receive $500. Under certain special circumstances, established by the final judges, a writer or entry may receive a special award
Closing Date: Annually in Feb
Presented: New York, NY, Last week in June

Loft-Mentor Series in Poetry & Creative Prose
The Loft Literary Center
Open Book, Suite 200, 1011 Washington Ave S, Minneapolis, MN 55415
Tel: 612-215-2575 *Fax:* 612-215-2576
E-mail: loft@loft.org
Web Site: www.loft.org
Key Personnel
Prog Mgr: Sherrie Fernandez-Williams *Tel:* 612-215-2586 *E-mail:* sfernandezwilliams@loft.org
Established: 1980
Annual award for poetry, nonfiction & fiction mss. Must be Minnesota State resident. Six different residencies scheduled throughout the year. Winners announced on web site. Open to poets, fiction writers & nonfiction writers.
Award: Stipend to defray costs of participating in the program & opportunity to study with six nationally known writer-mentors in brief residence during the course of the year
Closing Date: Mid-Spring
Presented: The Loft

The Jack London Award
Titan Press
Box 17897, Encino, CA 91416-7897
E-mail: cwcsfv@gmail.com
Key Personnel
Mng Ed: Stefanya Wilson
Three quarterly competitions: fiction, poetry & nonfiction. Monthly nominations are made for publication & honorable mention. Of those, one is chosen for the annual Grand Prize. Published & unpublished mss are eligible. $65 annual dues are allowed; one free submission per quarter; nonmembers; $15 reading fee per entry, up to 4 entries per quarter.
Award: Invitation to attend the Biannual Writer's Conference, plaque commemorating winner as guest of honor (give a public reading of his work) & publication
Closing Date: Submissions accepted throughout the year
Presented: Biannual Writer's Conference

Judy Lopez Memorial Award For Children's Literature
Women's National Book Association/Los Angeles Chapter
1225 Selby Ave, Los Angeles, CA 90024
Tel: 310-474-9917 *Fax:* 310-474-6436
Web Site: www.wnba-books.org/la; www.judylopezbookaward.org
Key Personnel
Chair, Lopez Comm: Margaret Flanders
Pres: Rachelle Yousef
Chair, Selection Comm: Gail Kim
Established: 1986
For best books for young readers 9-12 years of age, submitted by publishers, written by US citizen/US resident in year that precedes the award.
Award: Bronze medal & cash honorarium
Closing Date: Annually, Feb 1
Presented: Dinner, UCLA Faculty Center, Los Angeles, CA, 3rd Friday in Sept

Los Angeles Times Book Prizes
Los Angeles Times
Subsidiary of Tronc Inc
202 W First St, Los Angeles, CA 90012
Tel: 213-237-5775 *Toll Free Tel:* 800-528-4637 (ext 75775)
Web Site: www.latimesbookprizes.com
Key Personnel
Publr & CEO: Davan Maharaj
Admin: Ann Binney *E-mail:* ann.binney@latimes.com
Established: 1980
Annual prizes to authors in the categories of fiction, first fiction, autobiographical prose, young adult literature, graphic novels, comics, mystery/thriller, biography, current interest, history, poetry, science & technology. No submissions accepted; nominations are done by committees of appointed judges. There is also an award for lifetime achievement (Robert Kirsch Award) & Innovation in Storytelling (The Innovator's Award).
Other Sponsor(s): The Christopher I Sherwood Foundation
Award: $500 & citation (in 10 different categories). Robert Kirsch Award & Innovator's Award at $1,000 each, Christopher Isherwood Prize for Autobiographical prose $2,500 & a citation
Presented: The Los Angeles Times Book Prize Ceremony at Bovard Auditorium, USC Campus, Annually in April

Louise Louis/Emily F Bourne Student Poetry Award
Poetry Society of America (PSA)
15 Gramercy Park, New York, NY 10003
Tel: 212-254-9628
Web Site: www.poetrysociety.org
Key Personnel
Pres: Kimiko Hahn
Exec Dir: Alice Quinn
Deputy Dir: Brett Fletcher Lauer *E-mail:* brett@poetrysociety.org
Prog Dir: Laurin Macios *E-mail:* laurin@poetrysociety.org
Established: 1971
For the best unpublished poem by a student in grades 9-12 from the US. See web site for further guidelines.
Award: $250
Closing Date: Annually, Oct-Dec
Presented: Annual Awards Ceremony, New York, NY, Annually in Spring

Louisville Grawemeyer Award in Religion
Louisville Presbyterian Theological Seminary & University of Louisville
1044 Alta Vista Rd, Louisville, KY 40205-1798
Tel: 502-895-3411 *Toll Free Tel:* 800-264-1839 *Fax:* 502-894-2286
E-mail: grawemeyer@lpts.edu
Web Site: www.grawemeyer.org
Key Personnel
Dir: Tyler Mayfield
Established: 1990
Given for a work presented or published in the 8 years preceding the year of the award. Nominations are invited from religious organizations, appropriate academic associations, religious leaders & scholars, presidents of universities or schools of religion & publishers & editors of scholarly journals. Personal nominations accepted, self-nominations not accepted.
Award: $100,000 one-time payment
Closing Date: Nominations by Jan 15
Presented: Annually in Spring

Love Creek Annual Short Play Festival
Love Creek Productions
2144 45 Ave, Long Island City, NY 11101
Tel: 646-765-6542
E-mail: submissionslcp@gmail.com
Key Personnel
Mng Artistic Dir: Steven Barrett
Literary Mgr: Amanda Barrett
Established: 1988
Produce 5 7 evenings of one-act plays each year. Submissions must include a character breakdown, preferably 2—one basic (i.e. 2 men, 1 woman) & one detailed (including breakdown of gender, age range & other information vital to the character).
Writers should keep in mind there are mostly women ages 17-27 in the company.
Award: Cash (1st prize), mini-showcase production (finalists)
Closing Date: Revolving
Presented: New York, NY, various midtown venues, Ongoing

James Russell Lowell Prize
Modern Language Association of America (MLA)
85 Broad St, Suite 500, New York, NY 10004-2434
SAN: 202-6422
Tel: 646-576-5141; 646-576-5000 *Fax:* 646-458-0030
E-mail: awards@mla.org
Web Site: www.mla.org
Key Personnel
Coord, Book Prizes: Annie M Reiser *E-mail:* areiser@mla.org
Established: 1969
Annual prize for an outstanding literary or linguistic study, a critical edition of an important work, or critical biography by a current MLA member published in 2017. Authors or publishers should submit 6 copies & confirmation of the author's membership in the MLA.
Award: Cash award & certificate
Closing Date: March 1, 2018
Presented: MLA Convention, Chicago, IL, Jan 2019

Pat Lowther Memorial Award
The League of Canadian Poets
192 Spadina Ave, Suite 312, Toronto, ON M5T 2C2, Canada
Tel: 416-504-1657 *Fax:* 416-504-0096
E-mail: admin@poets.ca
Web Site: poets.ca
Key Personnel
Exec Dir: Lesley Fletcher *E-mail:* lesley@poets.ca
Annual award for the best book of poetry written by a Canadian woman & published in the preceding year. $25 handling fee.
Award: $1,000
Closing Date: Nov 1
Presented: June

Jeremiah Ludington Award
Educational Book & Media Association (EBMA)
11 Main St, Suite D, Warrenton, VA 20186
Mailing Address: PO Box 3363, Warrenton, VA 20188
Tel: 540-318-7770 *Fax:* 202-962-3939
E-mail: info@edupaperback.org
Web Site: www.edupaperback.org
Key Personnel
Exec Dir: Brian Gorg
Meeting Mgr: Maureen Gelwicks
Established: 1979
Presented annually to an individual who has made a significant contribution to the educational book & media business.
Award: Framed certificate & EBMA presents a $2,500 check to the charity of their choice
Presented: Annually at EBMA meeting, Annually in Jan

J Anthony Lukas Book Prize
Columbia University Graduate School of Journalism
2950 Broadway, New York, NY 10027
Tel: 212-854-6468
Web Site: www.journalism.columbia.edu
Key Personnel
Prog Mgr, Prof Prizes: Caroline L Martinet *E-mail:* cm3443@columbia.edu
Established: 1998
Awarded annually to a book-length work of narrative nonfiction on a topic of American political or social concern that exemplifies the literary grace, commitment to serious research & social concern that characterized the distinguished work of the award's namesake. Submissions must include 4 copies of each book. Entry fee: $75 non-refundable.
Award: $10,000
Closing Date: Dec 11

J Anthony Lukas Work-in-Progress Award
Columbia University Graduate School of Journalism
2950 Broadway, New York, NY 10027
Tel: 212-854-6468
Web Site: www.journalism.columbia.edu
Key Personnel
Prog Mgr, Prof Prizes: Caroline L Martinet *E-mail:* cm3443@columbia.edu
Established: 1998
Awarded annually to aid in the completion of a significant work of nonfiction on a topic of American political or social concern. Applicants should send copy of their original book proposal, sample chapter from book, photocopy of contract with US-based publisher & explanation of how award will advance progress of the book. No entry fee.
Award: $30,000
Closing Date: Dec 11

Lush Triumphant Literary Awards
subTerrain Magazine
PO Box 3008, MPO, Vancouver, BC V6B 3X5, Canada
Tel: 604-876-8710 *Fax:* 604-879-2667
E-mail: subter@portal.ca
Web Site: www.subterrain.ca
Established: 2003
Annual literary award in 3 categories: fiction, poetry & nonfiction. Entry fee: $27.50.
Award: Awarding $3,000 in cash prizes, plus publication. The winner in each category receives a $1,000 prize plus publication in the Winter issue (plus contributor's payment). The runners-up entries are published in the Spring issue of the following year (& they receive contributor's payment)
Closing Date: May 15
Presented: Vancouver, BC, Aug 15

Mark Lynton History Prize
Columbia University Graduate School of Journalism
2950 Broadway, New York, NY 10027
Tel: 212-854-6468
Web Site: www.journalism.columbia.edu
Key Personnel
Prog Mgr, Prof Prizes: Caroline L Martinet *E-mail:* cm3443@columbia.edu
Established: 1998
Awarded to a book-length work of history on any topic that best combines intellectual distinction with felicity of expression. Submissions must include 4 copies of each book. Entry fee: $75 non-refundable.
Award: $10,000
Closing Date: Dec 11

Thomas J Lyon Book Award in Western American Literary and Cultural Studies
Western Literature Association
PO Box 6815, Logan, UT 84341
Web Site: www.westernlit.org/thomas-j-lyon-book-award-in-western-american-literary-and-cultural-studies; www.westernlit.org
Key Personnel
Dir, Opers: Sabine Barcatta
E-mail: WLAoperations@gmail.com
Established: 1997
Honors outstanding single-author scholarly book on the literature & culture of the American West published in the previous year. Must submit a statement of support & 3 copies of the book.
Award: Certificate
Closing Date: June 15
Presented: Annual Conference

Lyric Poetry Award
Poetry Society of America (PSA)
15 Gramercy Park, New York, NY 10003
Tel: 212-254-9628
Web Site: www.poetrysociety.org
Key Personnel
Pres: Kimiko Hahn
Exec Dir: Alice Quinn
Deputy Dir: Brett Fletcher Lauer *E-mail:* brett@poetrysociety.org
Prog Dir: Laurin Macios *E-mail:* laurin@poetrysociety.org
Established: 1972
For a lyric poem on any subject, not to exceed 50 lines. Open to society members only. See web site for further information.
Award: $500
Closing Date: Annually, Oct-Dec
Presented: Annual Awards Ceremony, New York, NY, Annually in Spring

Lyric Poetry Prizes
The Lyric Foundation
PO Box 110, Jericho, VT 05465
Tel: 802-899-3993 *Fax:* 802-899-3993
E-mail: themuse@thelyricmagazine.com
Web Site: thelyricmagazine.com
Key Personnel
Ed: Jean Mellichamp Milliken
Assoc Ed: Nancy Mellichamp Savo
Collegiate Contest Coord: Tanya Cimonetti
Established: 1921
The Collegiate contest prize is awarded to undergraduates enrolled full-time in an American or Canadian college. The annual & quarterly prizes are awarded to poems published in *The Lyric*. Winners of annual awards are announced in the winter issue each year. Send SASE or provide e-mail address for guidelines. Sample copy of *The Lyric* $5, subscription $15/yr, $28/2 yrs, $38/3 yrs, $2/yr extra foreign or Canadian.
Award: Quarterly prize: $50. Annual awards: Lyric College Poetry Contest/Scholarship: $500, Lyric Memorial, Leslie Mellichamp & Roberts Memorial Prizes: $100 each, New England & Fluvanna Prizes: $50 each. Honorable mentions get one-year subn to *The Lyric*. Checks are mailed to recipients
Closing Date: Dec 1 (postmark)
Presented: Quarterly prizes awarded in the following issue, annual prizes in the winter issue

MacArthur Fellows Program
John D & Catherine T MacArthur Foundation
Office of Grants Management, 140 S Dearborn St, Chicago, IL 60603-5285
Tel: 312-726-8000 *Fax:* 312-920-6528
E-mail: 4answers@macfound.org
Web Site: www.macfound.org/programs/fellows
Key Personnel
Mng Dir: Cecilia A Conrad
Prog Dir: Marlies A Carruth
Awards unrestricted fellowships to talented individuals who have shown extraordinary originality & dedication in their creative pursuits & a marked capacity for self-direction. Recipients may be writers, scientists, artists, social scientists, humanists, teachers, entrepreneurs or those in other fields, with or without institutional affiliations.
The Fellows Program does not accept applications or unsol nominations.
Award: $625,000 stipend paid in equal quarterly installments over 5 years

Macavity Award
Mystery Readers International
7155 Marlborough Terr, Berkeley, CA 94705
Tel: 510-845-3600
Web Site: www.mysteryreaders.org
Key Personnel
Dir: Janet Rudolph *E-mail:* janet@mysteryreaders.org
Established: 1986
Annually awarded for works nominated by & voted on by members of Mystery Readers International in categories: Best Novel, Best First Novel, Best Short Story, Best Nonfiction/Critical; Sue Feder Award for the Historical Mystery (all published in the US the previous year).
Award: Statue
Presented: Bouchercon, the World Mystery Convention, Oct

Sir John A Macdonald Prize
Canadian Historical Association
130 Albert St, Suite 1201, Ottawa, ON K1P 5G4, Canada
Tel: 613-233-7885 *Fax:* 613-565-5445
E-mail: cha-shc@cha-shc.ca
Web Site: www.cha-shc.ca
Key Personnel
Exec Dir: Michel Duquet *E-mail:* mduquet@cha-shc.ca
Established: 1976
Awarded for the best book on Canadian history. See web site for application details.
Award: $5,000
Closing Date: Annually, Dec 1
Presented: Annual meeting, Canadian Historical Association, May

MacDowell Fellowships
The MacDowell Colony
100 High St, Peterborough, NH 03458
Tel: 603-924-3886 *Fax:* 603-924-9142
E-mail: info@macdowellcolony.org; admissions@macdowellcolony.org
Web Site: www.macdowellcolony.org
Key Personnel
Exec Dir: Cheryl Young
Admissions Dir: Courtney Bethel
Communs Mgr: Jonathan Gourlay *Tel:* 603-924-3886 ext 114 *E-mail:* jgourlay@macdowellcolony.org
Established: 1907
Fellowships of up to 8 weeks are available for writers, composers, film/video artists, theatre artists, visual artists, architects & interdisciplinary artists. Artists-in-residence receive room, board & exclusive use of a studio. The average length of stay is 6 weeks. Talent is the sole criterion for acceptance to the Colony. Established artists as well as emerging artists are encouraged to apply. Committees of distinguished professionals donate their time to judge applications, which include work samples, references & a brief project description. There are no residency fees. Grants for travel to & from the Colony are available based on need. Financial aid for all artists is available through special grants from various foundations. An aid application will be mailed following acceptance. The Edward MacDowell medal is awarded for a career of outstanding contributions to the arts, including musical composition, visual arts or literature, architecture, film & video & interdisciplinary arts.
Closing Date: For fellowships: Jan 15, April 15 & Sept 15, see application form & guidelines online for details
Presented: Peterborough, NH
Branch Office(s)
163 E 81 St, New York, NY 10028 *Tel:* 212-535-9690 *Fax:* 212-737-3803

Machigonne Fiction Contest
The New Guard
PO Box 5101, Hanover, NH 03755
E-mail: info@newguardreview.com
Web Site: www.newguardreview.com
Key Personnel
Founding Ed & Publr: Shanna McNair
Established: 2009
Submit a short story or novel excerpt up to 5,000 words. Online submissions only.
Award: $1,500 & publication in *The New Guard*
Closing Date: Aug

C B MacPherson Prize
Canadian Political Science Association
260 rue Dalhousie St, Suite 204, Ottawa, ON K1N 7E4, Canada
Tel: 613-562-1202 *Fax:* 613-241-0019
E-mail: cpsa-acsp@cpsa-acsp.ca
Web Site: www.cpsa-acsp.ca
Key Personnel
Admin: Michelle Hopkins
Established: 1992
This is a biennial competition. Awarded to the best book published in English or in French in a field relating to the study of political theory. A book may be single-authored or multi-authored. Single-authored book: must be a Canadian citizen or a permanent resident of Canada or a member of the CPSA in the year the book was published. Multi-authored book: at least one of the authors must be a Canadian citizen or a permanent resident of Canada or a member of the CPSA in the year the book was published. For the 2018 award, a book must have a copyright date of 2016 or 2017.
Award: Commemorative plaque & receive/share the set of books submitted to the CPSA office
Presented: Annual Conference, University of Regina, Regina, SK, CN, May 26-June 1, 2018

Magazine Merit Awards
Society of Children's Book Writers and Illustrators (SCBWI)
4727 Wilshire Blvd, Suite 301, Los Angeles, CA 90010
Tel: 323-782-1010; 310-403-0675 (cell) *Fax:* 323-782-1892
E-mail: grants@scbwi.org; scbwi@scbwi.org
Web Site: www.scbwi.org
Key Personnel
Pres: Stephen Mooser *E-mail:* stephenmooser@scbwi.org
Exec Dir: Lin Oliver *E-mail:* linoliver@scbwi.org
Established: 1988
For outstanding original magazine work for young people published during the calendar year & having been written or illustrated by SCBWI members.
Award: 4 plaques (fiction, nonfiction, illustration, poetry), 4 honor certificates
Closing Date: Annually in Dec
Presented: Annually in April

Mailer Prize
Norman Mailer Center
1841 Broadway, Suite 322, New York, NY 10023
Tel: 646-374-3940
Web Site: nmcenter.org

Key Personnel
Pres: Lawrence Schiller *E-mail:* lschiller@nmcenter.org
Established: 2009
Given to writers whose work over the years has challenged readers' perspectives on the world around them.

J Russell Major Prize
American Historical Association (AHA)
400 "A" St SE, Washington, DC 20003
Tel: 202-544-2422 *Fax:* 202-544-8307
E-mail: awards@historians.org
Web Site: www.historians.org
Established: 2001
Awarded for the best work in English on any aspect of French history. Books published in 2017 are eligible. Along with an application form, applicants must mail a copy of their book to each of the prize committee members who will be posted on our web site as the prize deadline approaches. All updated info on web site.
Award: Cash prize
Closing Date: May 15, 2018
Presented: AHA Annual Meeting, Chicago, IL, Jan 2019

Malahat Review Long Poem Prize
The Malahat Review
University of Victoria, Box 1700, Sta CSC, Victoria, BC V8W 2Y2, Canada
Tel: 250-721-8524 *Fax:* 250-472-5051
E-mail: malahat@uvic.ca
Web Site: www.malahatreview.ca
Key Personnel
Ed: John Barton
Established: 1988
Two awards for best long poem(s). See web site for details & entry fee. Contest runs every other year (odd-numbered years). Alternates with Novella Prize (even-numbered years).
Award: $1,000 (2 prizes)
Closing Date: Feb 1, odd-numbered years

Gene E & Adele R Malott Prize for Recording Community Activism
The Langum Charitable Trust
2809 Berkeley Dr, Birmingham, AL 35242
Tel: 360-809-0465
E-mail: langumtrust@gmail.com
Web Site: www.langumtrust.org
Key Personnel
Dir: David J Langum, Sr *E-mail:* djlangum@samford.edu
Established: 2007
Biennial prize that recognizes the best literary depiction of an individual or small group of individuals whose efforts resulted in a significant improvement of their local community. Although the work of community improvement must be significant, the basis of the prize will be the skill & power of the literary or film depiction. Must have been published or released within the past 2 years of a prize cycle.
Award: $1,000 for the writer. If film, divided between the director & screenwriter
Closing Date: Dec 1 for materials published or released the previous 2 calendar years

Ralph Manheim Medal for Translation, see PEN/Ralph Manheim Medal for Translation

Margaret Mann Citation
Association for Library Collections & Technical Services (ALCTS)
Division of The American Library Association (ALA)
50 E Huron St, Chicago, IL 60611
SAN: 201-0062
Tel: 312-280-5037 *Toll Free Tel:* 800-545-2433 *Fax:* 312-280-5033
E-mail: alcts@ala.org
Web Site: www.ala.org/alcts
Key Personnel
Exec Dir: Keri Cascio *Tel:* 312-280-5030 *E-mail:* kcascio@ala.org
Established: 1951
Award for outstanding professional achievement in cataloging or classification in a significant publication or by participation in a professional organization. Candidates are nominated. Citation recipient selected by jury.
Other Sponsor(s): OCLC
Award: Citation & $2,000 scholarship to the US or Canadian library school of winner's choice
Closing Date: Annually, Dec 1
Presented: ALA Annual Conference, Annually in June

Many Voices Fellowships
The Playwrights' Center
2301 Franklin Ave E, Minneapolis, MN 55406-1099
Tel: 612-332-7481 *Fax:* 612-332-6037
E-mail: info@pwcenter.org
Web Site: www.pwcenter.org
Key Personnel
Producing Artistic Dir: Jeremy Cohen *Tel:* 612-332-7481 ext 113 *E-mail:* jeremyc@pwcenter.org
Assoc Artistic Dir: Hayley Finn *Tel:* 612-332-7481 ext 119 *E-mail:* hayleyf@pwcenter.org
Artistic Progs Admin: Julia Brown *Tel:* 612-332-7481 ext 115 *E-mail:* juliab@pwcenter.org
Many Voices Fellowship Coord: Christina Ham *Tel:* 612-332-7481 ext 124 *E-mail:* christinah@pwcenter.org
For writers of color. Two distinct programs to serve writers of varying skill/experience levels both locally & nationally.
Award: Many Voices Mentorship: 1 Minnesota playwright with little or no playwriting experience, $2,000 stipend; Many Voices Fellowship: 2 emerging playwrights receive $18,000 stipend, $2,000 in play development funds & dramaturgical support. One must reside in Minnesota, the other may be a resident of any US state
Closing Date: See web site for details

Marfield Prize
Arts Club of Washington
2017 "I" St NW, Washington, DC 20006-1804
E-mail: award@artsclubofwashington.org
Web Site: artsclubofwashington.org
Key Personnel
Award Admin: Blake Stenning
Established: 2006
Given annually to nonfiction books about the visual, literary or performing arts written for a broad audience. Works published in the US during the previous calendar year are eligible for consideration. Publishers, agents, or authors may submit books. No entry fee. Submit 3 copies of the book with prize submission form.
Award: $10,000
Closing Date: Oct 31

Marian Library Medal
University of Dayton, Marian Library
300 College Park, Dayton, OH 45469-1390
Tel: 937-229-4214 *Fax:* 937-229-4258
Web Site: campus.udayton.edu/mary/mlmedal.html
Key Personnel
Lib Dir: Sarah Cahalan
Established: 1953
To scholars in any country for outstanding achievement in Marian research.
Award: Medal

Marick Press Poetry Prize Competition
Marick Press
PO Box 36253, Grosse Pointe Farms, MI 48236
Tel: 313-407-9236
Web Site: www.marickpress.com
Established: 2010
Submit a ms of 48-80 pages, 2 separate title pages, one with just the title & the other with full author info. Open competition for a poetry ms; submissions are accepted from anyone writing in the English language, whether living in the US or abroad (translations are not eligible). Entry fee: $15.
Award: $1,000 & publication by Marick Press
Closing Date: Annually in Oct
Presented: Annually in March

Maritime Electric Short Story Awards
Prince Edward Island Writers' Guild
81 Prince St, Charlottetown, PE C1A 4R3, Canada
E-mail: peiliteraryawards@gmail.com
Web Site: www.peiwritersguild.com
One short story, maximum 2,500 words, constitutes an entry. Maximum 2 entries. Entry fee for each submission is $25. Work must be original & unpublished. Prince Edward Island residents only. See web site for complete entry requirements.
Award: Cash prizes for 1st, 2nd & 3rd place
Closing Date: Jan 31
Presented: Cox & Palmer Island Literary Awards Gala, Annually in Spring

Morton Marr Poetry Prize
Southwest Review
PO Box 750374, Dallas, TX 75275-0374
Fax: 214-768-1408
E-mail: swr@mail.smu.edu
Web Site: www.smu.edu/southwestreview
Key Personnel
Ed-in-Chief: Greg Brownderville
Mng Ed: Preston Hutcherson *Tel:* 214-768-1036
Open to writers who have not published a book of poetry. Contestants may submit no more than 6 previously unpublished poems in a "traditional" form (e.g. sonnet, sestina, villanelle, rhymed stanzas, blank verse, etc). There is a $5 per poem entry/handling fee.
Award: $1,000 (1st prize), $500 (2nd prize) & publication in *Southwest Review*
Closing Date: Annually, Sept 30
Presented: Annually in Dec

Helen & Howard R Marraro Prize in Italian History
American Historical Association (AHA)
400 "A" St SE, Washington, DC 20003
Tel: 202-544-2422 *Fax:* 202-544-8307
E-mail: awards@historians.org
Web Site: www.historians.org
Established: 1973
Each award will be given for the book or article deemed best by the committee which treats Italian history in any epoch, Italian cultural history, or Italian-American relations. Each book must be published in 2017. Entries must first have been published in English by a historian whose usual residence is North America. Along with an application form, applicants must mail a copy of their book together with a curriculum vitae & bibliography of the author to each of the prize committee members who will be posted on our web site as the prize deadline approaches. All updated info on web site.
Other Sponsor(s): American Catholic Historical Association; Society for Italian Historical Studies
Award: Cash prize
Closing Date: May 15, 2018
Presented: AHA Annual Meeting, Chicago, IL, Jan 2019

Howard R Marraro Prize
Modern Language Association of America (MLA)
85 Broad St, Suite 500, New York, NY 10004-2434
SAN: 202-6422
Tel: 646-576-5141; 646-576-5000 *Fax:* 646-458-0030
E-mail: awards@mla.org
Web Site: www.mla.org
Key Personnel
Coord, Book Prizes: Annie M Reiser *E-mail:* areiser@mla.org
Established: 1973
Presented for an outstanding scholarly work on any phase of Italian literature or comparative literature involving Italian by an MLA member. The prize is awarded each even-numbered year. The committee solicits submissions of works published in 2017 by current members. Submit 4 copies of the work & confirm author's membership in the MLA.
Award: Cash award & certificate
Closing Date: May 1, 2018
Presented: MLA Convention, Chicago, IL, Jan 2019

Massachusetts Book Awards
Massachusetts Center for the Book
Simons College - GSLIS, 300 The Fenway, Boston, MA 02115
Tel: 617-521-2719
E-mail: bookawards@massbook.org
Web Site: www.massbook.org
Key Personnel
Exec Dir: Sharon Shaloo *E-mail:* shaloo@massbook.org
Established: 2000
The MassBooks recognize significant achievements by Massachusetts writers in fiction, nonfiction, poetry & children's literature for the previous publishing year. Also awarded, the MA Book medal for creative publishing, programming or lifetime achievement in the Massachusetts book community. Visit web site for details.
Other Sponsor(s): Massachusetts Board of Library Commissioners; Massachusetts Cultural Council; Massachusetts Library Association; Massachusetts Library System; Simmons College Graduate School of Library & Information Science

Masters Literary Awards
Titan Press
PO Box 17897, Encino, CA 91416-7897
Tel: 818-377-4006
E-mail: titan91416@yahoo.com
Key Personnel
Mng Ed: Stefanya Wilson
Established: 1981
Annual awards (including 4 quarterly prizes) for fiction, poetry & song lyrics & nonfiction. All quality published & unpublished mss are eligible, submitted from double-spaced photocopies or tearsheets. Guidelines available with No 10 SASE.
Award: $1,000 Grand Prize, 4 quarterly prizes of Honorable Mention
Closing Date: Submissions received prior to any award date are eligible for the subsequent award
Presented: Titan Press, March 15, June 15, Aug 15, Dec 15

Amy Mathers Teen Book Award
Canadian Children's Book Centre
40 Orchard View Blvd, Suite 217, Toronto, ON M4R 1B9, Canada
Tel: 416-975-0010 *Fax:* 416-975-8970
E-mail: info@bookcentre.ca
Web Site: www.bookcentre.ca
Key Personnel
Exec Dir: Charlotte Teeple *E-mail:* charlotte@bookcentre.ca
Lib Coord: Meghan Howe *E-mail:* meghan@bookcentre.ca
Mktg & Web Site Coord: Camilia Kahrizi *E-mail:* camilia@bookcentre.ca
Prog Coord: Shannon Howe Barnes *E-mail:* shannon@bookcentre.ca
Established: 2014
Awarded to a Canadian author for excellence in teen/young adult fiction.
Other Sponsor(s): Sylvan Learning
Award: $5,000
Closing Date: Annually in mid-Dec

Matt Cohen Prize: In Celebration of a Writing Life
The Writers' Trust of Canada
460 Richmond St W, Suite 600, Toronto, ON M5V 1Y1, Canada
Tel: 416-504-8222 *Toll Free Tel:* 877-906-6548 *Fax:* 416-504-9090
E-mail: info@writerstrust.com
Web Site: www.writerstrust.com
Key Personnel
Exec Dir: Mary Osborne *Tel:* 416-504-8222 ext 244 *E-mail:* mosborne@writerstrust.com
Established: 2001
Recognizes a lifetime of distinguished work by a Canadian writer, working in either poetry or prose, in either French or English. Generously sponsored by anonymous donors.
Award: $20,000
Presented: The Writers' Trust Awards, Toronto, ON, CN, Annually in Nov

Mature Women Scholarship Grant - Art/Letters/Music
National League of American Pen Women Inc
The Pen Arts Bldg & Arts Museum, 1300 17 St NW, Washington, DC 20036-1973
Tel: 202-785-1997 *Fax:* 202-452-8868
E-mail: contact@nlapw.org
Web Site: www.nlapw.org
Key Personnel
Pres: Virginia Franklin Campbell
Established: 1976
Awarded biennially (even-numbered years). Judges in each category (art, letters, music) change for each award every award year. Must send SASE with inquiry for requirements. Include an $8 fee payable to NLAPW with entry.
Award: $1,000 (1st place), $750 (2nd place), $500 (3rd place); $150 (Photography Award), $150 (Water Media Award), $100 (Jean Baber Memorial Art Fund)
Closing Date: Oct 1, odd-numbered years
Presented: NLAPW Convention, Biennially in April, even-numbered years; mail notification March 15

Maxim Mazumdar New Play Competition
Alleyway Theatre
One Curtain Up Alley, Buffalo, NY 14202-1911
Tel: 716-852-2600
E-mail: publicrelations@alleyway.com
Web Site: alleyway.com
Key Personnel
Founder, Alleyway Theatre: Neal Radice
Literary Mgr: Joyce Stilson *Tel:* 716-852-2600 ext 202 *E-mail:* jstilson@alleyway.com
Contest limited to one submission per author, per year, per category. Entry must be a previously unproduced full-length (not less than 90 minutes) play or musical of any style, requiring no more than 8 performers & able to be presented on a unit or simple set, musicals must include CD, sheet music not necessary. One acts must be less than 20 minutes & no more than five actors. Entries will not be returned without SASE. Entry fee: $25.
Award: Cash & premiere production of entry at Alleyway Theatre
Closing Date: Annually, July 1

Janet B McCabe Poetry Prize
Ruminate Magazine
1041 N Taft Hill Rd, Fort Collins, CO 80521
Tel: 970-449-2726
E-mail: editor@ruminatemagazine.org
Web Site: www.ruminatemagazine.com
Key Personnel
Ed-in-Chief: Brianna Van Dyke
Sr Ed: Amy Lowe
Assoc Ed: Kristin George Bagdanov; Stefani Rossi
All submissions must be previously unpublished & submitted via online submission form. Up to 2 poems per entry, no longer than 40 lines each. Entry fee $20.
Award: $1,500 & publication in the prize issue (1st place), $200 & publication (2nd place)
Closing Date: Annually, May 15
Presented: Dec 15

John H McGinnis Memorial Award
Southwest Review
PO Box 750374, Dallas, TX 75275-0374
Fax: 214-768-1408
E-mail: swr@mail.smu.edu
Web Site: www.smu.edu/southwestreview
Key Personnel
Ed-in-Chief: Greg Brownderville
Mng Ed: Preston Hutcherson *Tel:* 214-768-1036
Established: 1960
For the best essay & story appearing in the *Southwest Review* during the preceding year.
Award: $500 (2-4 awards)
Presented: Annually in Jan

Harold W McGraw Jr Prize in Education
McGraw-Hill Education
2 Penn Plaza, New York, NY 10121-2298
Tel: 646-766-2000
E-mail: info@mcgrawprize.com
Web Site: www.mcgrawprize.com
Key Personnel
Dir, Communs: Tyler Reed *E-mail:* tyler.reed@mheducation.com
Established: 1988
Honors 3 individuals whose accomplishments, programs & ideas can serve as effective models for the education of future generations. Categories: K-12, Higher Education, International Education.
Other Sponsor(s): Arizona State University
Award: $50,000 & bronze sculpture
Closing Date: Oct 31
Presented: ASU GSV Education Innovation Summit, Annually in May

William Holmes McGuffey Longevity Award
Textbook & Academic Authors Association (TAA)
PO Box 367, Fountain City, WI 54629
E-mail: info@taaonline.net
Web Site: www.taaonline.net/mcguffey-longevity-award
Key Personnel
Exec Dir: Michael Spinella *Tel:* 973-943-0501 *E-mail:* michael.spinella@taaonline.net
Dir, Publg & Opers: Kim Pawlak *Tel:* 608-687-3106 *E-mail:* kim.pawlak@taaonline.net
Dir, Instl Memberships & Meetings: Maureen Foerster *Tel:* 608-687-3106 *E-mail:* maureen.foerster@taaonline.net
Membership Coord: Bekky Murphy *Tel:* 608-567-9060 *E-mail:* bekky.murphy@taaonline.net
Recognizes textbooks & learning materials whose excellence has been demonstrated over time. To be nominated, a work must have been in print 15 years & still be selling. Works are judged for merit in 4 areas: pedagogy; con-

tent/scholarship; writing; appearance & design. Nomination fee: $350 (non-refundable). See web site for nomination form & entry guidelines.
Closing Date: Dec 15
Presented: TAA Annual Conference, Annually in June

McKnight Artist Fellowship for Writers
The Loft Literary Center
Open Book, Suite 200, 1011 Washington Ave S, Minneapolis, MN 55415
Tel: 612-215-2575 *Fax:* 612-215-2576
E-mail: loft@loft.org
Web Site: www.loft.org
Key Personnel
Prog Dir: Bao Phi *Tel:* 612-215-2585 *E-mail:* bphi@loft.org
Established: 1982
Contest for Minnesota residents only.
Award: Four $25,000 awards which alternate annually between poetry & creative prose; one $25,000 award in children's literature which alternates annually between writing for children 8 & under & older children
Closing Date: Annually in late Fall
Presented: The Loft, Annually in Spring

McKnight Fellowships in Playwriting
The Playwrights' Center
2301 Franklin Ave E, Minneapolis, MN 55406-1099
Tel: 612-332-7481 *Fax:* 612-332-6037
E-mail: info@pwcenter.org
Web Site: www.pwcenter.org
Key Personnel
Producing Artistic Dir: Jeremy Cohen *Tel:* 612-332-7481 ext 113 *E-mail:* jeremyc@pwcenter.org
Assoc Artistic Dir: Hayley Finn *Tel:* 612-332-7481 ext 119 *E-mail:* hayleyf@pwcenter.org
Artistic Progs Admin: Julia Brown *Tel:* 612-332-7481 ext 115 *E-mail:* juliab@pwcenter.org
Established: 1990
Grants to recognize mid-career playwrights whose work demonstrates exceptional artistic merit & potential. Playwright's primary residence must be in the state of Minnesota. Applicant must have had a minimum of one work fully produced by a professional theater at the time of application.
Award: Grants of $25,000 each

McKnight National Residency & Commission
The Playwrights' Center
2301 Franklin Ave E, Minneapolis, MN 55406-1099
Tel: 612-332-7481 *Fax:* 612-332-6037
E-mail: info@pwcenter.org
Web Site: www.pwcenter.org
Key Personnel
Producing Artistic Dir: Jeremy Cohen *Tel:* 612-332-7481 ext 113 *E-mail:* jeremyc@pwcenter.org
Assoc Artistic Dir: Hayley Finn *Tel:* 612-332-7481 ext 119 *E-mail:* hayleyf@pwcenter.org
Artistic Progs Admin: Julia Brown *Tel:* 612-332-7481 ext 115 *E-mail:* juliab@pwcenter.org
Established: 1982
Playwrights whose work has made a significant impact on the contemporary theater. Applicant must be a US citizen or permanent resident & must have had a minimum of 2 different works fully produced by professional theaters. Call or check web site for application information & deadline guidelines. Minnesota-based playwrights are not eligible for the award. Proposals for the Residency & Commission must be agent/professional only. Send writers resume, a 2- or 3-page proposal & a full-length play script.
Award: $15,000
Closing Date: See web site for details

McLaren Memorial Comedy Play Writing Competition
Midland Community Theatre
2000 W Wadley Ave, Midland, TX 79705
Tel: 432-682-2544
E-mail: tracy@mctmidland.org
Web Site: www.mctmidland.org
Key Personnel
Prodn Mgr: Tracy Alexander *E-mail:* tracy@mctmidland.org
Established: 1990
All entries must be comedies for adults, teens, or children; musical comedies no longer accepted. Requirements: full-length play (70-90 minutes); one-act plays no longer accepted. See web site for competition guidelines & required brochure with entry form. Submissions accepted beginning December 1. Attn: McLaren Competition Chairman.
Closing Date: Annually, Jan 31
Presented: McLaren Festival, Annually in early Fall

McLemore Prize
Mississippi Historical Society
Affiliate of Mississippi Dept of Archives & History
William F Winter Archives & History Bldg, 200 North St, Jackson, MS 39201
Mailing Address: PO Box 571, Jackson, MS 39205-0571
Tel: 601-576-6850 *Fax:* 601-576-6975
E-mail: mhs@mdah.ms.gov
Web Site: www.mdah.ms.gov
Key Personnel
Pres: Susannah J Ural
VP: Page Ogden
Secy-Treas, Historical Society: Elbert Hilliard
Public Info: Timothy Davis *E-mail:* tdavis@mdah.ms.gov
Established: 1980
For distinguished scholarly book published during the previous year on a subject related to Mississippi history or biography. Prize recipient is invited to be the Friday evening banquet speaker at the Society's annual meeting.
Award: $700 cash award plus $300 honorarium & reimbursement of travel expenses as banquet speaker
Closing Date: Annually, Nov 1
Presented: Annual meeting, 1st weekend in March

John McMenemy Prize
Canadian Political Science Association
260 rue Dalhousie St, Suite 204, Ottawa, ON K1N 7E4, Canada
Tel: 613-562-1202 *Fax:* 613-241-0019
E-mail: cpsa-acsp@cpsa-acsp.ca
Web Site: www.cpsa-acsp.ca
Key Personnel
Admin: Michelle Hopkins
Established: 2000
To the author or authors of the best article in English or French, published in volume 47 of the *Canadian Journal of Political Science.*
Other Sponsor(s): Societe Quebecoise de Science Politique
Award: Certificate of Award & memberships in the Canadian Political Science Association & the Societe Quebecoise de Science Politique
Presented: Annual Conference, University of British Columbia, Vancouver, BC, CN, June 1-7, 2019

Medal of Honor for Literature
National Arts Club
15 Gramercy Park S, New York, NY 10003
E-mail: literary@thenationalartsclub.org
Web Site: www.nationalartsclub.org
Key Personnel
Chair, Literary Comm: Cherry Provost
Established: 1967
Presented for a body of work of literary excellence; nominations within the committee only & awarded by the Board of Governors.
Award: Gold medal
Presented: Gala Black Tie Dinner, at discretion of recipient

Lucille Medwick Memorial Award
Poetry Society of America (PSA)
15 Gramercy Park, New York, NY 10003
Tel: 212-254-9628
Web Site: www.poetrysociety.org
Key Personnel
Pres: Kimiko Hahn
Exec Dir: Alice Quinn
Deputy Dir: Brett Fletcher Lauer *E-mail:* brett@poetrysociety.org
Prog Dir: Laurin Macios *E-mail:* laurin@poetrysociety.org
Established: 1974
For an original poem in any form on a humanitarian theme, not to exceed 100 lines. Translations are ineligible. Open to society members only. See web site for more information.
Award: $500
Closing Date: Annually, Oct-Dec
Presented: Annual Awards Ceremony, New York, NY, Annually in Spring

Frederic G Melcher Scholarship
Association for Library Service to Children (ALSC)
Division of The American Library Association (ALA)
50 E Huron St, Chicago, IL 60611-2795
Tel: 312-280-2163 *Toll Free Tel:* 800-545-2433 *Fax:* 312-440-9374; 312-280-5271
E-mail: alsc@ala.org
Web Site: www.ala.org/alsc
Key Personnel
Exec Dir: Aimee Strittmatter *Tel:* 312-280-2162 *E-mail:* astrittmatter@ala.org
Awards Coord: Courtney Jones *E-mail:* alscawards@ala.org
Prog Coord: Marsha P Burgess *Tel:* 312-280-2166 *E-mail:* mburgess@ala.org
Established: 1956
Provides financial assistance for the professional education of men & women who intend to pursue an MLS degree & who plan to work in children's librarianship. This work may be serving children up to & including the age of 14 in any type of library.
Award: $7,500 - 2 scholarships per yr
Closing Date: Annually, March 1
Presented: ALA Annual Conference, Annually in June

Addison M Metcalf Award in Literature
American Academy of Arts & Letters
633 W 155 St, New York, NY 10032
Tel: 212-368-5900 *Fax:* 212-491-4615
E-mail: academy@artsandletters.org
Web Site: www.artsandletters.org
Key Personnel
Exec Dir: Cody Upton
Established: 1986
Biennial award to honor young writers.
Award: $10,000

The David Nathan Meyerson Prize for Fiction
Southwest Review
PO Box 750374, Dallas, TX 75275-0374
Fax: 214-768-1408
E-mail: swr@mail.smu.edu
Web Site: www.smu.edu/southwestreview
Key Personnel
Ed-in-Chief: Greg Brownderville
Mng Ed: Preston Hutcherson *Tel:* 214-768-1036

Open to writers who have not published a book of fiction. Submissions must be no longer than 8,000 words. A $25 reading fee must accompany each submission.
Award: $1,000 & publication in *Southwest Review*
Closing Date: Annually, May 1
Presented: Annually in Fall

Kenneth W Mildenberger Prize
Modern Language Association of America (MLA)
85 Broad St, Suite 500, New York, NY 10004-2434
SAN: 202-6422
Tel: 646-576-5141; 646-576-5000 *Fax:* 646-458-0030
E-mail: awards@mla.org
Web Site: www.mla.org
Key Personnel
Coord, Book Prizes: Annie M Reiser
E-mail: areiser@mla.org
Established: 1980
Award for a work in the field of language, culture, literacy or literature with strong application to the teaching of languages other than English. Authors need not be members of the MLA. Awarded for a book published in 2017 or 2018. For consideration, submit 4 copies. Presented biennially.
Award: Cash award & certificate
Closing Date: May 1, 2019
Presented: MLA Convention, Seattle, WA, Jan 2020

Milkweed National Fiction Prize
Milkweed Editions
1011 Washington Ave S, Suite 300, Minneapolis, MN 55415-1246
Tel: 612-332-3192 *Toll Free Tel:* 800-520-6455 *Fax:* 612-215-2550
E-mail: submissions@milkweed.org
Web Site: www.milkweed.org
Key Personnel
CEO & Publr: Daniel Slager
Mng Dir: Patrick Thomas
E-mail: patrick_thomas@milkweed.org
Engagement Coord: Abby Travis
Established: 1988
Annual award for an unpublished novel or collection of short stories +/or one or more novellas. Awarded to the best work of fiction Milkweed accepts for publication during each calendar year by a writer not previously published by Milkweed Editions. Writers must request complete guidelines before submitting ms (send SASE or visit www.milkweed.org). Open year-round.
Award: $5,000 advance against royalties
Closing Date: Annually, Jan-March, July & Sept

Milner Award
Friends of the Atlanta-Fulton Public Library
One Margaret Mitchell Sq NW, Atlanta, GA 30303
Tel: 404-730-1865
E-mail: info@themilneraward.org
Web Site: www.themilneraward.org
Key Personnel
Exec Dir: Kelly Robinson
Established: 1983
For living American authors of children's books voted on by the children of Atlanta. No application process.
Other Sponsor(s): Milner Award Committee
Award: An honorarium & a glass sculpture (inkwell & pen) by Hans Frabel
Closing Date: 2nd week of Nov
Presented: Atlanta, GA

Minnesota Book Awards
The Friends of the Saint Paul Public Library
1080 Montreal Ave, Suite 2, St Paul, MN 55116
Tel: 651-222-3242 *Fax:* 651-222-1988
E-mail: friends@thefriends.org
Web Site: thefriends.org/events/mnba
Key Personnel
Dir: Alayne Hopkins *Tel:* 651-366-6488
E-mail: alayne@thefriends.org
Books created by writers, illustrators, or book artists who are Minnesotans are eligible for the awards through nominations. Awards are given each year for books published in the previous year.
Presented: Minnesota Book Awards Gala, annually in April

Minotaur Books/Mystery Writers of America First Crime Novel Competition
Mystery Writers of America (MWA)
1140 Broadway, Suite 1507, New York, NY 10001
Tel: 212-888-8171 *Fax:* 212-888-8107
E-mail: mb-mwafirstcrimenovelcompetition@stmartins.com
Web Site: mysterywriters.org/about-mwa/st-martins; us.macmillan.com/minotaurbooks/submit-manuscript
Open to any writer, regardless of nationality, aged 18 or older, who has never been the author of any published novel (in any genre) & is not under contract with a publisher for publication of a novel. Only one ms entry is permitted per writer. Must submit online entry form & upload electronic file of ms; do not mail or e-mail ms submission to Minotaur Books.
Other Sponsor(s): Minotaur Books
Closing Date: Dec 12
Presented: Edgar Awards Banquet

Mississippi Review Prize
University of Southern Mississippi Department of English
118 College Dr, Box 5144, Hattiesburg, MS 39406-0001
E-mail: msreview@usm.edu
Web Site: www.usm.edu/mississippi-review/contest.html
Key Personnel
Ed-in-Chief: Adam Clay
Fiction & poetry prize open to all writers in English except current or former students or employees of the University of Southern Mississippi. Entry fee $16 & $15 by post.
Award: Fiction & Poetry: $1,000 each & publication in the print issue of *Mississippi Review* next Spring
Closing Date: Annually, Jan 1
Presented: Annually in May

W O Mitchell Book Prize, see The City of Calgary W O Mitchell Book Prize

MLA Prize for a Bibliography, Archive or Digital Project
Modern Language Association of America (MLA)
85 Broad St, Suite 500, New York, NY 10004-2434
SAN: 202-6422
Tel: 646-576-5141; 646-576-5000 *Fax:* 646-458-0030
E-mail: awards@mla.org
Web Site: www.mla.org
Key Personnel
Coord, Book Prizes: Annie M Reiser
E-mail: areiser@mla.org
Established: 1998
Awarded biennually for enumerative & descriptive bibliography, archive or digital project. A multivolume bibliography is eligible if at least one volume was published in 2016 or 2017. Criteria for determining excellence include evidence of analytical rigor, meticulous scholarship, intellectual creativity & subject range & depth. Editors need not be members of MLA. For consideration, submit 4 copies.
Award: Cash award & certificate
Closing Date: May 1, 2018
Presented: MLA Convention, Chicago, IL, Jan 2019

MLA Prize for a First Book
Modern Language Association of America (MLA)
85 Broad St, Suite 500, New York, NY 10004-2434
SAN: 202-6422
Tel: 646-576-5141; 646-576-5000 *Fax:* 646-458-0030
E-mail: awards@mla.org
Web Site: www.mla.org
Key Personnel
Coord, Book Prizes: Annie M Reiser
E-mail: areiser@mla.org
Established: 1993
Awarded annually for an outstanding scholarly work published in year prior to competition as the first book-length publication by a current member of the MLA. For consideration, submit 6 copies.
Award: Cash award & certificate
Closing Date: March 1, 2018
Presented: MLA Convention, Chicago, IL, Jan 2019

MLA Prize for a Scholarly Edition
Modern Language Association of America (MLA)
85 Broad St, Suite 500, New York, NY 10004-2434
SAN: 202-6422
Tel: 646-576-5141; 646-576-5000 *Fax:* 646-458-0030
E-mail: awards@mla.org
Web Site: www.mla.org
Key Personnel
Coord, Book Prizes: Annie M Reiser
E-mail: areiser@mla.org
Established: 1995
Biennial prize offered in odd-numbered years. Committee solicits submissions of editions published in 2017 or 2018. A multivolume edition is eligible if at least one volume has been published during that period. The editor need not be a member of the MLA. Edition should be based on an examination of all available relevant textual sources. The source texts & the edited text's deviation from them should be fully described. The edition should exhibit the highest standards of accuracy in the presentation of its text & apparatus, which should be presented as accessibly & elegantly as possible. For consideration, submit 4 copies with letter.
Award: Cash award & certificate
Closing Date: May 1, 2019
Presented: MLA Convention, Seattle, WA, Jan 2020

MLA Prize for Independent Scholars
Modern Language Association of America (MLA)
85 Broad St, Suite 500, New York, NY 10004-2434
SAN: 202-6422
Tel: 646-576-5141; 646-576-5000 *Fax:* 646-458-0030
E-mail: awards@mla.org
Web Site: www.mla.org
Key Personnel
Coord, Book Prizes: Annie M Reiser
E-mail: areiser@mla.org
Established: 1983
Offered as a biennial prize with competitions in even-numbered years for a distinguished scholarly book published in 2016 or 2017 in the field of English or another modern language or literature. Author enrolled in a program leading to an academic degree & did not hold a tenured, tenure-accruing, or tenure-track position in post-secondary education at the time of publication is eligible. For consideration, submit 6 copies & a completed entry form.

Award: Cash award & certificate
Closing Date: May 1, 2018
Presented: MLA Convention, Chicago, IL, Jan 2019

MLA Prize for Studies in Native American Literatures, Cultures & Languages
Modern Language Association of America (MLA)
85 Broad St, Suite 500, New York, NY 10004-2434
SAN: 202-6422
Tel: 646-576-5141; 646-576-5000 *Fax:* 646-458-0030
E-mail: awards@mla.org
Web Site: www.mla.org
Key Personnel
Coord, Book Prizes: Annie M Reiser
E-mail: areiser@mla.org
Established: 2012
Awarded to a current MLA member for an outstanding scholarly work in the field of Native American literatures, cultures & languages published in 2016 or 2017. Selection committee is seeking works that examine & broaden understanding of the cultural expressions of first peoples or nations in the US, CN & Mexico. For consideration, submit 4 copies & a letter identifying the work.
Closing Date: May 1, 2018
Presented: MLA Convention, Chicago, IL, Jan 2019

MLA Prize in United States Latina & Latino & Chicano & Chicano Literary & Cultural Studies
Modern Language Association of America (MLA)
85 Broad St, Suite 500, New York, NY 10004-2434
SAN: 202-6422
Tel: 646-576-5141; 646-576-5000 *Fax:* 646-458-0030
E-mail: awards@mla.org
Web Site: www.mla.org
Key Personnel
Coord, Book Prizes: Annie M Reiser
E-mail: areiser@mla.org
Established: 2002
Biennial prize offered in odd-numbered years to a current member of the association for an outstanding scholarly study in any language of United States Latina & Latino or Chicana & Chicano literature or culture published in 2017 or 2018. Books that are primarily translations will not be considered. For consideration the author or publisher should send 4 copies.
Award: Cash award, certificate & 1 year association membership
Closing Date: May 1, 2019
Presented: MLA Convention, Seattle, WA, Jan 2020

Lucy Maud Montgomery PEI Literature for Children Awards
Prince Edward Island Writers' Guild
81 Prince St, Charlottetown, PE C1A 4R3, Canada
E-mail: peiliteraryawards@gmail.com
Web Site: www.peiwritersguild.com
The ms must be a story written for children. Maximum length 5,000 words. Maximum 2 entries. Entry fee for each submission is $25. Work must be original & unpublished. Illustration may be submitted with the story, but are not necessary. Prince Edward Island residents only. See web site for complete entry requirements.
Award: Cash prizes for 1st, 2nd & 3rd place
Closing Date: Jan 31
Presented: Cox & Palmer Island Literary Awards Gala, Annually in Spring

Cenie H Moon Prize
The Poetry Society of Virginia
900 Timber Creek Place, Virginia Beach, VA 23464
E-mail: poetryinva@aol.com
Web Site: poetrysocietyofvirginia.org
Key Personnel
Pres: Robert P Arthur *E-mail:* robert.peebles.arthur@gmail.com
Exec Dir: Guy Terrell *E-mail:* guy.terrell@earthlink.net
Adult Contest Chair: Steven Blythe
E-mail: stevenblythepoetry@gmail.com
All entries must be in English, original & unpublished. Submit 2 copies of each poem, each having the category name & number on top left of page. Only one poem per category; entries will not be returned. Subject: woman or women; 48 line limit; any form. Entry fee: $4 nonmembs.
Award: $50 (1st prize), $30 (2nd prize), $20 (3rd prize)
Closing Date: Jan
Presented: Annual PSV Awards Ceremony, April

Moonbeam Children's Book Awards
Independent Publisher Online
Division of Jenkins Group Inc
1129 Woodmere Ave, Suite B, Traverse City, MI 49686
Tel: 231-933-0445 *Toll Free Tel:* 800-706-4636
Fax: 231-933-0448
E-mail: info@moonbeamawards.com
Web Site: www.moonbeamawards.com
Key Personnel
CEO: Jerrold R Jenkins *E-mail:* jrj@bookpublishing.com
Pres: James Kalajian *Tel:* 800-706-4636 ext 1006
E-mail: jjk@bookpublishing.com
Mng Ed & Awards Dir: Jim Barnes *Tel:* 800-706-4636 ext 1011 *E-mail:* jimb@bookpublishing.com
Awards Coord: Amy Shamroe
Established: 2007
Annual award celebrating youthful curiosity, discovery & learning through books & reading. Recognizes the best children's books published each year for the North American market. Authors, illustrators, publishers & self-publishers of children's books intended for the North American market may enter.
Other Sponsor(s): Jenkins Group Inc
Award: Gold medal (1st place), silver medal (2nd place) & bronze medal (3rd place)
Closing Date: Aug
Presented: Traverse City Children's Book Festival, Nov

Jenny McKean Moore Writer-in-Washington
George Washington University
English Dept, Rome Hall, 801 22 St NW, Suite 643, Washington, DC 20052
Tel: 202-994-6180
E-mail: engldept@gwu.edu
Web Site: english.columbian.gwu.edu
Key Personnel
Dir, Creative Writing: Lisa Page
E-mail: lpageinc@aol.com
Established: 1976
To be considered, applications must be made by letter indicating publications, teaching experience & a selection of published work. Genre alternates from year to year. Consult AWP job list for advertisement specifying genre.
Award: One-year teaching position for approximately $60,000 plus benefits
Closing Date: Annually in Dec

Ottoline Morrell Prize
Fence Books
University at Albany, Science Library 320, 1400 Washington Ave, Albany, NY 12222
Tel: 518-591-8162
E-mail: fence.fencebooks@gmail.com
Web Site: www.fenceportal.org
Key Personnel
Publr & Ed: Rebecca Wolff
E-mail: rebeccafence@gmail.com
Mng Ed: Jess Puglisi *E-mail:* jessp.fence@gmail.com
Established: 2013
For a book of poems by a woman writing in English who has previously published one or more books of poetry.
Award: Cash prize & publication

The William C Morris YA Debut Award
The American Library Association (ALA)
50 E Huron St, Chicago, IL 60611
Tel: 312-280-4390 *Toll Free Tel:* 800-545-2433 (ext 4390) *Fax:* 312-280-5276
E-mail: yalsa@ala.org
Web Site: www.ala.org/yalsa/morris
Established: 2009
Honors a debut book published by a first-time author writing for teens & celebrating impressive new voices in young adult literature. Books must have been published November 1-October 31 of the year preceding the award. Nominations by committee.
Presented: ALA Midwinter Youth Media Awards, Annually in Winter

William Morris Society in the United States Fellowships
William Morris Society in the United States
PO Box 53263, Washington, DC 20009
E-mail: us@morrissociety.org
Web Site: www.morrissociety.org
Key Personnel
Pres: Jason Martinek
Established: 1996
For scholarly or creative projects related to William Morris (1834-96); given to US citizens or permanent residents.
Award: Up to $1,000
Closing Date: Annually, Dec 1

George L Mosse Prize
American Historical Association (AHA)
400 "A" St SE, Washington, DC 20003
Tel: 202-544-2422 *Fax:* 202-544-8307
E-mail: awards@historians.org
Web Site: www.historians.org
Established: 2001
For an outstanding major work of extraordinary scholarly distinction, creativity & originality in the intellectual & cultural history of Europe since the Renaissance. Only books of a high scholarly distinction should be submitted. Research accuracy, originality & literary merit are important selection factors. Books published in 2017 are eligible. Along with an application form, applicants must mail a copy of their book to each of the prize committee members who will be posted on our web site as the prize deadline approaches. All updated info on web site.
Award: Cash prize
Closing Date: May 15, 2018
Presented: AHA Annual Meeting, Chicago, IL, Jan 2019

Most Promising New Textbook Award
Textbook & Academic Authors Association (TAA)
PO Box 367, Fountain City, WI 54629
E-mail: info@taaonline.net
Web Site: www.taaonline.net/promising-new-textbook-award
Key Personnel
Exec Dir: Michael Spinella *Tel:* 973-943-0501
E-mail: michael.spinella@taaonline.net
Dir, Publg & Opers: Kim Pawlak *Tel:* 608-687-3106 *E-mail:* kim.pawlak@taaonline.net

Dir, Instl Memberships & Meetings: Maureen Foerster *Tel:* 608-687-3106 *E-mail:* maureen.foerster@taaonline.net
Membership Coord: Bekky Murphy *Tel:* 608-567-9060 *E-mail:* bekky.murphy@taaonline.net
Recognizes excellence in 1st edition textbooks & learning materials. Works are judged for merit in 4 areas: pedagogy; content/scholarship; writing; appearance & design. Nomination fee: $350 (non-refundable). See web site for nomination form & entry guidelines.
Closing Date: Dec 15
Presented: TAA Annual Conference, Annually in June

Most Significant Scholarly Book Award, see Ramirez Family Award

Frank Luther Mott-Kappa Tau Alpha Research Award
Kappa Tau Alpha
University of Missouri, School of Journalism, 76 Gannett Hall, Columbia, MO 65211-1200
Tel: 573-882-7685 *Fax:* 573-884-1720
E-mail: umcjourkta@missouri.edu
Web Site: www.kappataualpha.org
Key Personnel
Exec Dir: Keith P Sanders, PhD
Established: 1944
For the best research for books in journalism & mass communication, exclusive of textbooks, published in the previous year.
Award: $1,000 & plaque (1st prize)
Closing Date: Dec (see web site)
Presented: Annually in Aug

Sheila Margaret Motton Prize
New England Poetry Club
46 Wallace St, Somerville, MA 02144
Tel: 617-744-6034
E-mail: info@nepoetryclub.org
Web Site: www.nepoetryclub.org
Key Personnel
VP: Hillary Sallick
Prize presented annually for a book of poems published in the last 2 years. Send 2 copies of the book with $5 handling fee for nonmembs. See web site for additional guidelines.
Award: $250
Closing Date: May 31
Presented: Winners announced online Aug/Sept

Erika Mumford Prize
New England Poetry Club
46 Wallace St, Somerville, MA 02144
Tel: 617-744-6034
E-mail: info@nepoetryclub.org
Web Site: www.nepoetryclub.org
Key Personnel
VP: Hillary Sallick
Established: 1988
Annual contest for a poem about foreign culture or travel. See web site for additional guidelines.
Award: $250
Closing Date: May 31
Presented: Winners announced online Aug/Sept

Walter Dean Myers Grant
We Need Diverse Books™
10318 Westlake Dr, No 104, Bethesda, MD 20817
E-mail: waltergrantwndb@gmail.com
Web Site: weneeddiversebooks.org
Key Personnel
COO & SVP, Libn Servs: Dhonielle Clayton *E-mail:* dhonielleclayton@diversebooks.org
Applicants must identify as diverse, defined as one or more of the following: person of color; Native American; LGBTQIA+; person with a disability; marginalized religious & cultural minority. Applicants must be unpublished illustrators +/or authors & working toward a career as a children's author +/or illustrator. Submit application via e-mail, including cover letter, 2 essays & work sample. See web site for submission guidelines. Grant is limited to US residents only. Five winners will be selected.
Award: $2,000
Closing Date: June 21

Mythopoeic Awards
Mythopoeic Society
Friends University, 2100 W University Ave, Wichita, KS 67213
Tel: 316-295-5563
E-mail: awards@mythsoc.org
Web Site: www.mythsoc.org
Key Personnel
Awards Admin: Vicki Ronn *E-mail:* ronn@friends.edu
Established: 1967
Awards (2) honor scholarship in the Inklings (JRR Tolkien, CS Lewis, Charles Williams) & the general fields of myth & fantasy studies; each is given to the author of a book published in the previous 3 years. The Fantasy Awards (2) for adult & children's literature honor novels or single-author collections in the spirit of the Inklings; each is given to the author of a book published in the previous year.
Award: Statuette
Closing Date: Members make nominations Jan-Feb, winners picked by late July
Presented: Mythcon 43, University of Berkeley, Berkeley, CA, Annually in Aug

National Award for Arts Writing, see Marfield Prize

National Awards for Education Reporting
Education Writers Association (EWA)
3516 Connecticut Ave NW, Washington, DC 20008
Tel: 202-452-9830 *Fax:* 202-452-9837
E-mail: ewa@ewa.org
Web Site: www.ewa.org
Key Personnel
Exec Dir: Caroline W Hendrie *E-mail:* chendrie@ewa.org
Asst Dir: Lori Crouch *E-mail:* lcrouch@ewa.org
Multimedia & Web Mgr: Michael Marriott *E-mail:* mmarriott@ewa.org
Established: 1960
Best education reporting in print & broadcast media.
Award: Grand prize, 1st prize, 2nd prize, special citation, in 19 categories; plaques & certificates
Presented: EWA National Seminar

National Book Awards
National Book Foundation
90 Broad St, Suite 604, New York, NY 10004
Tel: 212-685-0261 *Fax:* 212-213-6570
E-mail: nationalbook@nationalbook.org
Web Site: www.nationalbook.org
Key Personnel
Exec Dir: Lisa Lucas
Asst Dir: Leslie Shipman
Dir, Technol: Meredith Andrews
Prog Mgr, Community Educ: Amy Gall
Prog Mgr, Community Engagement: Benjamin Samuel
Awards Coord: Courtney Gillette
Established: 1950
Living American authors for books in the US, for fiction, nonfiction, poetry; young people's literature.
Award: $10,000 cash & bronze sculpture for winner in each genre
Closing Date: Annually in May
Presented: New York City, NY, Annually in Nov

National Book Critics Circle Award
National Book Critics Circle
c/o 38 Douglass St, Apt 3, Brooklyn, NY 11231
E-mail: info@bookcritics.org
Web Site: bookcritics.org/awards
Key Personnel
VP, Awards: Michele Filgate *E-mail:* mfilgate@gmail.com
Awards to honor the best literature published in the US in 6 categories: autobiography, biography, criticism, fiction, nonfiction & poetry. Books published in English (including translations) in the US with pubn dates in the calendar year of the award are considered.
Closing Date: Dec 1
Presented: NBCC Awards Ceremony, Annually in March

The National Business Book Award
PwC
c/o Freedman & Associates Inc, 121 Richmond St W, Suite 605, Toronto, ON M5H 2K1, Canada
Tel: 416-868-1500
Web Site: www.nbbaward.com
Key Personnel
Contact: Mary Ann Freedman *E-mail:* mafreedman@freedmanandassociates.com
Established: 1985
Excellence in business writing.
Other Sponsor(s): BMO Financial Group; Globe & Mail; The Walrus Magazine
Award: $30,000
Closing Date: Annually in Dec
Presented: Spring/early Summer

National Federation of State Poetry Societies Annual Poetry Contest
National Federation of State Poetry Societies (NFSPS)
c/o PO Box 263, Huttig, AR 71747
E-mail: contestchair@nfsps.com
Web Site: www.nfsps.com
Established: 1959
Fifty poetry contests, one for students only; rules & categories change, must have current rules provided on web site.
Other Sponsor(s): Individual states' poetry society as host society
Award: $10-$1,500
Closing Date: March 15 (must not be postmarked before Jan 1)

The National Humanities Medal
National Endowment for the Humanities
400 Seventh St SW, Washington, DC 20506
Tel: 202-606-8400 *Toll Free Tel:* 800-NEH-1121 (634-1121)
E-mail: info@neh.gov
Web Site: www.neh.gov/about/awards
Key Personnel
Dir, Communs: Theola DeBose *E-mail:* tdebose@neh.gov
Established: 1997
Honors individuals or groups whose work has deepened the nation's understanding of the humanities & broadened out citizens' engagement with history, literature, languages, philosophy & other humanities subjects. Up to 12 medals awarded annually.

National Jewish Book Award-Children's Literature
Formerly National Jewish Book Award-Illustrated Children's Book
Jewish Book Council
520 Eighth Ave, 4th fl, New York, NY 10018
Tel: 212-201-2920 *Fax:* 212-532-4952
E-mail: jbc@jewishbooks.org
Web Site: www.jewishbookcouncil.org
Key Personnel
Exec Dir: Naomi Firestone-Teeter

Prog Mgr, JBC Network & National Jewish Book Awards: Evie Saphire-Bernstein *E-mail:* evie@jewishbooks.org
Award: Certificate & publication
Closing Date: Annually in Sept
Presented: Center for Jewish History, Annually in March

National Jewish Book Award-Illustrated Children's Book, see National Jewish Book Award-Children's Literature

National Jewish Book Award-Natan Book Award
Jewish Book Council
520 Eighth Ave, 4th fl, New York, NY 10018
Tel: 212-201-2920 *Fax:* 212-532-4952
E-mail: jbc@jewishbooks.org; natanbookawards@jewishbooks.org
Web Site: www.jewishbookcouncil.org
Key Personnel
Exec Dir: Naomi Firestone-Teeter
Prog Mgr, JBC Network & National Jewish Book Awards: Evie Saphire-Bernstein *E-mail:* evie@jewishbooks.org
This award brings Natan's values of infusing Jewish life with creativity & meaning into the intellectual arena by supporting & promoting a breakthrough book intended for mainstream audiences that will catalyze conversations around the issues that Natan grapples within its grantmaking.
Award: Two-stage award, offering at most a total of $25,000, to be divided as follows: a cash award to the author of $10,000 to be used during the writing process; & customized support for the marketing & publicity strategy for the book, up to $15,000. This is a pre-publication award & the prize winner will be announced prior to the book's publication date
Closing Date: Annually in March
Presented: Center for Jewish History, Status update on finalists by May

National Jewish Book Award-Young Adult Literature
Jewish Book Council
520 Eighth Ave, 4th fl, New York, NY 10018
Tel: 212-201-2920 *Fax:* 212-532-4952
E-mail: jbc@jewishbooks.org
Web Site: www.jewishbookcouncil.org
Key Personnel
Exec Dir: Naomi Firestone-Teeter
Prog Mgr, JBC Network & National Jewish Book Awards: Evie Saphire-Bernstein *E-mail:* evie@jewishbooks.org
Award: Certificate & publication
Closing Date: Annually in Sept
Presented: Center for Jewish History, Annually in March

National Jewish Book Awards
Jewish Book Council
520 Eighth Ave, 4th fl, New York, NY 10018
Tel: 212-201-2920 *Fax:* 212-532-4952
E-mail: jbc@jewishbooks.org
Web Site: www.jewishbookcouncil.org
Key Personnel
Exec Dir: Naomi Firestone-Teeter
Prog Mgr, JBC Network & National Jewish Book Awards: Evie Saphire-Bernstein *E-mail:* evie@jewishbooks.org
Established: 1950
Twenty annual awards to authors & translators of books of outstanding scholarship & literary merit on Jewish themes for the general, no specialist reader. Writing based on archival material, visual arts, poetry, Jewish family via illustrated children's. Categories: Children's Literature, Holocaust, Jewish History, (Gerrard & Ella Berman Award), Modern Jewish Thought & Experience (Dorot Foundation Award), Sephardic Culture (Mimi Frank Award), Jewish Education (Anonymous Donor), General Nonfiction, Fiction & Children's Awards, Eastern European Studies (Ronald Lauder Award), Children's & Young Adult's Books, American Jewish Studies (Celebrate 350), Women's Studies (Barbara Dobkin Award), Jewish Book of the Year Award (Everett Family Foundation Award), Biography, Autobiography & Memoir (The Krauss Family Award), Book Club Award (The Debby & Ken Miller Award), Contemporary Jewish Life & Practice (Myra H Kraft Memorial Award), Debut Fiction (Goldberg Prize), Education-Jewish Identity (In Memory of Dorothy Kripke), Fiction (J J Greenberg Memorial Award), Poetry (Berru Award), Scholarship (Nahum Sarna Memorial Award), Writing Based on Archival Material (The JDC-Herbert Katzki Award).
Award: Certificate & publication
Closing Date: Sept
Presented: Center for Jewish History, March

National Magazine Awards
National Magazine Awards Foundation
2300 Yonge St, Suite 1600, Toronto, ON M4P 1E4, Canada
Tel: 416-939-6200
E-mail: staff@magazine-awards.com
Web Site: www.magazine-awards.com; twitter.com/magawards
Key Personnel
Mng Dir: Barbara Gould *E-mail:* staff@magazine-awards.com
Established: 1977
Annual award honoring excellence in Canadian magazine journalism with awards in 45 categories.
Award: $1000 Gold Award (1st place), $500 Silver Award (2nd place) in each category
Closing Date: Mid-Jan
Presented: Early June

The National Medal of Arts
National Endowment for the Arts
400 Seventh St SW, Washington, DC 20506-0001
Tel: 202-682-5434
Web Site: www.arts.gov/honors/medals
Key Personnel
Chmn: Jane Chu *Tel:* 202-682-5414 *E-mail:* chairman@arts.gov
Dir, Pub Aff: Jessamyn Sarmiento *Tel:* 202-682-5759 *E-mail:* sarmientoj@arts.gov
Established: 1984
Highest award given to artists & arts patrons by the US government. Awarded annually by the President of the US.

National One-Act Playwriting Competition
Little Theatre of Alexandria
600 Wolfe St, Alexandria, VA 22314
Tel: 703-683-5778 (ext 2) *Fax:* 703-683-1378
E-mail: asklta@thelittletheatre.com
Web Site: www.thelittletheatre.com/info
Key Personnel
Chmn, One-Act: Bonnie Jourdan *Tel:* 703-960-5711 *E-mail:* bonniejourdan@gmail.com
Established: 1978
Open to all playwrights. Scripts must be original, unpublished & unproduced stage plays. Film & TV scripts are ineligible. Entry fee: $20 per play (limit 2 plays per person). Accept plays July 1-October 31. Prize awarded by mail by March 15.
Award: $350 (1st prize), $250 (2nd prize), $150 (3rd prize), usually stage readings of top plays
Closing Date: Annually, Oct 31

National Outdoor Book Awards
National Outdoor Book Awards Foundation Inc
921 S Eighth Ave, Stop 8128, Pocatello, ID 83209-8128
Tel: 208-282-3912 *Fax:* 208-282-2127
Web Site: www.noba-web.org
Key Personnel
Chair: Ron Watters *E-mail:* wattron@isu.edu
Established: 1995
Award recognizing the work of outstanding writers & publishers of outdoor books. Categories include history/biography, outdoor literature, instructional texts, outdoor adventure guides, nature guides, children's books, design/artistic merit & nature & environment. Guidelines on the web site.
Other Sponsor(s): Association of Outdoor Recreation & Education; National Outdoor Book Awards Foundation
Closing Date: Annually in Aug
Presented: International Conference on Outdoor Recreation & Education (depending on the year, held in different locations in the US & CN), Annually in early Nov

National Poetry Series Open Competition
National Poetry Series
57 Mountain Ave, Princeton, NJ 08540
Tel: 609-430-0999 *Fax:* 609-430-9933
Web Site: nationalpoetryseries.org
Key Personnel
Founder/Dir: Daniel Halpern
Coord: Beth Dial *E-mail:* bethdial@nationalpoetryseries.org
Established: 1978
For book-length typed ms of poetry, previously unpublished in book form; online only via Submittable with $30 entrance fee per ms. See web site for guidelines.
Award: Five books to be published by trade publishers, small presses & university publishers. $10,000 cash award for each winner
Closing Date: Feb 28
Presented: Annually in Summer

National Ten-Minute Play Contest
Actors Theatre of Louisville
316 W Main St, Louisville, KY 40202-4218
Tel: 502-584-1265
Web Site: actorstheatre.org/national-ten-minute-play-contest/
Key Personnel
Literary Mgr: Jenni Page-White *Tel:* 502-584-1265 ext 3033 *E-mail:* jpage-white@actorstheatre.org
Established: 1989
Scripts should be submitted between September 1 & November 1. Accept the first 500 plays submitted.
Award: $1,000 & possible production at Actors Theatre of Louisville
Closing Date: Annually, Nov 1
Presented: Feb

National Translation Award
American Literary Translators Association (ALTA)
900 E Seventh St, PMB 266, Bloomington, IN 47405-3201
Web Site: www.literarytranslators.org
Key Personnel
Pres: Russell Valentino *E-mail:* russell.v@indiana.edu
Established: 1991
Publishers are invited to nominate one book in each category: contemporary fiction, contemporary poetry, contemporary nonfiction & literature of the past. Must be a full-length book or anthology translated from another language into English & must have been published in the previous year. Send 4 copies of each book; $25 per entry.
Other Sponsor(s): University of Texas at Dallas
Award: $5,000
Closing Date: Annually, March 31
Presented: ALTA Conference, Philadelphia, PA, Annually in Nov

National Writers Association Novel Contest
National Writers Association
10940 S Parker Rd, Suite 508, Parker, CO 80134
Tel: 303-841-0246
E-mail: natlwritersassn@hotmail.com
Web Site: www.nationalwriters.com
Key Personnel
Exec Dir & Ed: Sandy Whelchel
E-mail: authorsandy@hotmail.com
Established: 1937
Novel contest for unpublished works. Entry fee: $35.
Award: $500 (1st prize), $250 (2nd prize), $150 (3rd prize)
Closing Date: Annually, April 1

Nautilus Book Awards
Lifethread Institute LLC
PO Box 2285, Vashon, WA 98070
Tel: 206-604-2250
Web Site: www.nautilusbookawards.com
Key Personnel
Owner & Dir: Mary Belknap, PhD
E-mail: mbelknap@nautilusbookawards.com
Established: 1997
To recognize authors & titles as *Better Books for a Better World*, books that make excellent literary contributions to any of 4 themes, spiritual growth, health & wholeness, conscious living & sustainability & positive social change.
See Book Entry procedure on the web site.
Award: Winners have option for "Author Spotlight" video interview
Closing Date: Annually in Feb
Presented: Annually in May (option for exhibit at BookExpo & American Library Association Convention in June)

Phyllis Naylor Working Writer Fellowship, see PEN/Phyllis Naylor Working Writer Fellowship

NEA Creative Writing Fellowships
Formerly NEA Literature Fellowships
National Endowment for the Arts
400 Seventh St SW, Washington, DC 20506-0001
Tel: 202-682-5400; 202-682-5496 (Voice/TTY); 202-682-5034 (lit fellowships hotline)
Fax: 202-682-5609; 202-682-5610
E-mail: litfellowships@arts.gov
Web Site: www.arts.gov
Key Personnel
Grants Dir & Contracts Offr: Nicki Jacobs
Tel: 202-682-5546 *E-mail:* jacobsn@arts.gov
Established: 1967
Given to published writers of prose (fiction & creative nonfiction) & poetry. Variable number of fellowships, based on available program funds. Applications accepted by genre (prose-even years & poetry-odd years). Applicants are restricted to applying in one fellowship category only in the same year. Guidelines available on web site.
Award: $25,000
Closing Date: Annually in March
Presented: Notifications to be sent by e-mail in Dec

NEA Literature Fellowships, see NEA Creative Writing Fellowships

Nelligan Prize for Short Fiction
Colorado Review
Unit of Colorado State University
Colorado State University, Dept of English, Center for Literary Publishing, 9105 Campus Delivery, Fort Collins, CO 80523-9105
Tel: 970-491-5449
E-mail: creview@colostate.edu
Web Site: nelliganprize.colostate.edu
Key Personnel
Dir & Ed: Stephanie G'Schwind
Established: 2004
Awarded annually to the author of an outstanding short story, previously unpublished. Entry fee $15 per story with no limit on number of entries. Stories must be at least 10, but under 50 pages. Online entry fee $17.
Award: $2,000 & publication in Fall/Winter issue of *Colorado Review*
Closing Date: March 14

Howard Nemerov Sonnet Award
The Formalist
21 Osborne Terr, Wayne, NJ 07470
Web Site: theformalist.evansville.edu/home.htm
Key Personnel
Dir: William Baer
Annual award given for the best unpublished sonnet (no translations).
Award: $1,000 & publication in *Measure: A Review of Formal Poetry*
Closing Date: Annually, Nov 15

The Pablo Neruda Prize for Poetry
Nimrod, The University of Tulsa
Subsidiary of The Nimrod Literary Awards
Nimrod International Journal, 800 S Tucker Dr, Tulsa, OK 74104
Tel: 918-631-3080 *Fax:* 918-631-3033
E-mail: nimrod@utulsa.edu
Web Site: www.utulsa.edu/nimrod
Key Personnel
Ed-in-Chief: Eilis O'Neal
Assoc Ed: Diane Burton; Cassidy McCants
Established: 1978
No previously published works. Omit author's name on mss. Must have a US address by October to enter. Works must be in English or translated by the original author. Include a cover sheet containing major title & subtitles of the work, author's name, address & phone along with 3-10 pages of poetry: 1 long poem or several short poems. Mss will not be returned. Retain the rights to publish any contest submission. Works not accepted will be released. Winners & selected finalists will be published. Include SASE & a check for $20 (includes a 1-year subscription & processing). Online submissions: nimrodjournal.submittable.com.
Award: $2,000 (1st prize), $1,000 (2nd prize); published writers receive 2 copies of the journal; winners will be flown to Tulsa for a conference & banquet
Closing Date: Annually, April 30
Presented: University of Tulsa, Annually in Oct

Neustadt International Prize for Literature
World Literature Today
Affiliate of University of Oklahoma
c/o University of Oklahoma, 630 Parrington Oval, Suite 110, Norman, OK 73019-4033
Tel: 405-325-4531
Web Site: www.worldliteraturetoday.org; www.worldlit.org
Key Personnel
Exec Dir: Robert Con Davis-Undiano
E-mail: rcdavis@ou.edu
Asst Dir & Ed-in-Chief: Daniel Simon
E-mail: dsimon@ou.edu
Art Dir: Merleyn Bell *E-mail:* merleyn@ou.edu
Mng Ed: Michelle Johnson *E-mail:* lmjohnson@ou.edu
Book Reviews Ed: Robert Vollmar
E-mail: rvollmar@ou.edu
Mktg Dir, Progs & Devt: Terri Stubblefield
E-mail: tdstubb@ou.edu
Circ & Accts Specialist: Kay Blunck
E-mail: kblunck@ou.edu
Established: 1969
To a living writer for outstanding literary achievement; prize may honor a single major work or an entire oeuvre; writer's work must be available in a representative sample in English, Spanish or French; writer must accept the award in person in ceremonies at the University of Oklahoma; a special issue of *World Literature Today* is devoted to the laureate; Candidates must be nominated by a jury member.
Award: $50,000 & an eagle feather cast in silver
Presented: University of Oklahoma, Biennially, even-numbered years

Allan Nevins Prize
Society of American Historians (SAH)
Affiliate of American Historical Association
2950 Broadway, New York, NY 10027
Tel: 212-854-6495
E-mail: amhistsociety@columbia.edu
Web Site: sah.columbia.edu
Key Personnel
Pres: Mary Kelley
VP: Ann Fabian
Dir, Communs: Andie Tucher
Established: 1961
For the best written doctoral dissertation on an American subject. The dissertation must have been defended or the PhD degree received in the calendar year preceding the award presentation & must not have already been submitted for publication.
Award: $2,000, certificate & publication by an award sponsoring publication house
Closing Date: Annually, Dec 31
Presented: New York, NY, Annually in May

New England Book Awards
New England Independent Booksellers Association Inc (NEIBA)
1955 Massachusetts Ave, Cambridge, MA 02140
Web Site: www.newenglandbooks.org/bookawards
Key Personnel
Exec Dir: Steven Fischer *E-mail:* steve@neba.org
Admin Coord: Nan Sorensen *E-mail:* nan@neba.org
Established: 1990
Annual awards for fiction, nonfiction, children's & publishing are chosen by booksellers. Fiction, nonfiction & children's awards are awarded to specific titles either about New England, set in New England or by an author residing in New England, published between September 1 & August 31.
Award: $250 donation to charity or literary group chosen by each author
Closing Date: July
Presented: Fall trade show & conference, Sept/Oct

New Hampshire Literary Awards
New Hampshire Writers' Project
2500 N River Rd, Manchester, NH 03106
Tel: 603-314-7980 *Fax:* 603-314-7981
E-mail: info@nhwritersproject.org; awards@nhwritersproject.org
Web Site: www.nhwritersproject.org
Key Personnel
Bd Chair: Rob Greene
Comm Chair: Mary Russell
Off Mgr: Nicole Escobar
Pubns Asst: Dawn Coutu *E-mail:* dcoutu@nhwritersproject.com
Established: 1992
Biennial award given in odd-numbered years. Nominees must live in New Hampshire, be a native or deal with subject matter that is deemed by judges to be inherently connected with New Hampshire.
Closing Date: Varies. Typically in Spring
Presented: Nov

New Issues Poetry Prize
New Issues Poetry & Prose

c/o Western Michigan University, 1903 W Michigan Ave, Kalamazoo, MI 49008-5463
Tel: 269-387-8185
E-mail: new-issues@wmich.edu
Web Site: www.wmich.edu/newissues
Key Personnel
Mng Ed: Kimberly Kolbe
Poets writing in English who have not previously published a full-length collection of poems. Submit ms minimum 40 pages, typed on one side, single-spaced; do not bind ms. Include brief bio & relevant publication information; cover page with name, address, phone & title of ms; include table of contents. A $20 reading fee for each ms; enclose SASE.
Other Sponsor(s): Western Michigan University
Award: $2,000 & book publication
Closing Date: Nov 30

New Letters Literary Awards
New Letters
UMKC, University House, 5101 Rockhill Rd, Kansas City, MO 64110-2499
Tel: 816-235-1169 *Fax:* 816-235-2611
E-mail: newletters@umkc.edu
Web Site: www.newletters.org
Established: 1986
Annual literary contest.
Award: $1,500 & publication for each category - fiction, poetry & essay (1st prize). All entries considered for publication
Closing Date: Annually, May 18

New Letters Prize for Poetry
New Letters
UMKC, University House, 5101 Rockhill Rd, Kansas City, MO 64110-2499
Tel: 816-235-1169 *Fax:* 816-235-2611
E-mail: newletters@umkc.edu
Web Site: www.newletters.org
Established: 1986
Annual literary contest. All entries considered for publication.
Award: $1,500 & publication
Closing Date: Annually, May 18

New Millennium Awards for Fiction, Poetry & Nonfiction
New Millennium Writings
4021 Garden Dr, Knoxville, TN 37918
Tel: 865-254-4880
E-mail: hello@newmillenniumwritings.org
Web Site: www.newmillenniumwritings.org
Key Personnel
Publr & Ed: Alexis Williams Carr *E-mail:* alexis.williams@hotmail.com
Each fiction or nonfiction prize should total no more than 6,000 words (short-short fiction no more than 1,000 words). Each poetry entry may include up to 3 poems. $17 reading fee required for each entry. See web site for further information.
Award: $1,000 each for Poem, Fiction, Nonfiction & Short Short Fiction plus publication
Closing Date: Annually in Jan

New Women's Voices Chapbook Competition
Finishing Line Press
PO Box 1626, Georgetown, KY 40324
Tel: 502-603-0670
E-mail: finishingbooks@aol.com; flpbookstore@aol.com
Web Site: www.finishinglinepress.com
Key Personnel
Publr: Leah Maines
Mng Ed: Kevin Murphy Maines
Sr Ed: Christen Kincaid
Established: 1998
Cash & publication of a chapbook of poems for women who have not yet published a full-length collection. Winner announced on web site & in *Poets & Writers Magazine*.
Award: $1,000 & publication
Closing Date: Annually, April 15
Presented: Finishing Line Press, Aug 30

New York City Book Awards
The New York Society Library
53 E 79 St, New York, NY 10075
Tel: 212-288-6900 *Fax:* 212-744-5832
E-mail: events@nysoclib.org
Web Site: www.nysoclib.org
Key Personnel
Head of Events: Sara Holliday *Tel:* 212-288-6900 ext 222
Established: 1996
Given annually to the authors of the best books about New York City. Must submit copy of nominated book the same year of publication. $40 per book fee. Make check out to The New York Society Library.
Award: Plaque & varied monetary amount
Closing Date: Dec
Presented: The New York Society Library, Early May

The New York Public Library Helen Bernstein Book Award for Excellence in Journalism
The New York Public Library
Stephen A Schwarzman Bldg, Fifth Ave at 42 St, South Court Bldg, 3rd fl, New York, NY 10018-2788
Tel: 212-930-0876
Web Site: www.nypl.org
Key Personnel
Helen Bernstein Libn, Periodicals: Karen Gisonny *E-mail:* kgisonny@nypl.org
Established: 1987
Requires overall journalistic excellence & a published book that stems from the author's reportage & exemplifies outstanding work. Note: nominations are for books published during the calendar year & are solicited only from publishers & editors-in-chief of major newspapers, news magazines & book publishers nationwide.
Award: $15,000
Closing Date: Oct 1 for books published in calendar year
Presented: The New York Public Library, Annually in April/May

New York State Edith Wharton Citation of Merit for Fiction Writers
New York State Writers Institute
Subsidiary of University at Albany
University at Albany, SL 320, Albany, NY 12222
Tel: 518-442-5620 *Fax:* 518-442-5621
E-mail: writers@albany.edu
Web Site: www.albany.edu/writers-inst
Key Personnel
Founder & Exec Dir: William Kennedy
Dir: Donald W Faulkner
Asst Dir: Suzanne Lance *E-mail:* slance@uamail.albany.edu
Established: 1985
State author designation for a New York State fiction writer. Applications not accepted. Nominations by advisory panel only.
Award: $10,000
Presented: Albany, NY, Biennially, even-numbered years

New York State Walt Whitman Citation of Merit for Poets
New York State Writers Institute
Subsidiary of University at Albany
University at Albany, SL 320, Albany, NY 12222
Tel: 518-442-5620 *Fax:* 518-442-5621
E-mail: writers@albany.edu
Web Site: www.albany.edu/writers-inst
Key Personnel
Founder & Exec Dir: William Kennedy
Dir: Donald W Faulkner
Asst Dir: Suzanne Lance *E-mail:* slance@uamail.albany.edu
Established: 1985
State author designation for a New York State poet. Applications not accepted. Nominations by advisory panel only.
Award: $10,000
Presented: Albany, NY, Biennially, even-numbered years

John Newbery Medal
Association for Library Service to Children (ALSC)
Division of The American Library Association (ALA)
50 E Huron St, Chicago, IL 60611-2795
Tel: 312-280-2163 *Toll Free Tel:* 800-545-2433 *Fax:* 312-440-9374; 312-280-5271
E-mail: alsc@ala.org
Web Site: www.ala.org/alsc
Key Personnel
Exec Dir: Aimee Strittmatter *Tel:* 312-280-2162 *E-mail:* astrittmatter@ala.org
Awards Coord: Courtney Jones *E-mail:* alscawards@ala.org
Prog Coord: Marsha P Burgess *Tel:* 312-280-2166 *E-mail:* mburgess@ala.org
Established: 1922
Awarded annually to the author of the most distinguished writing in a children's book published during the preceding year. Restricted to authors who are citizens or residents of the US.
Award: Medal
Closing Date: Dec 31
Presented: ALA Midwinter Meeting, Jan/Feb

Newfoundland and Labrador Book Awards
Writers' Alliance of Newfoundland and Labrador (WANL)/Literary Arts Foundation of Newfoundland and Labrador
Haymarket Sq, 223 Duckworth St, St John's, NL A1C 6N1, Canada
Tel: 709-739-5215 *Toll Free Tel:* 866-739-5215
E-mail: wanl@nf.aibn.com
Web Site: wanl.ca
Key Personnel
Exec Dir: Wendi Smallwood
Memb Servs Coord: Samantha Fitzpatrick
Established: 1997
Honor excellence in Newfoundland & Labrador writing in 4 categories: fiction & children's/young adult literature (in even years), nonfiction & poetry (in odd years).
Other Sponsor(s): The Bruneau Family (children's/young adult literature); Downhome Inc (fiction); Historic Sites Association (Heritage & History Book Award); Le Grow's Travel (poetry); Rogers Cable (nonfiction)
Award: $1,500 (1st prize), $500 each to runners-up
Closing Date: Jan
Presented: May

Don & Gee Nicholl Fellowships in Screenwriting
Academy of Motion Picture Arts & Sciences (AMPAS)
1313 Vine St, Hollywood, CA 90028
Tel: 310-247-3010 *Fax:* 310-247-3794
E-mail: nicholl@oscars.org
Web Site: www.oscars.org/nicholl
Key Personnel
Dir: Greg Beal
Established: 1986
Screenwriting; for information visit web site.
Award: Up to 5 awards of $35,000 each
Closing Date: Annually, May 1
Presented: Beverly Hills, CA, Annually in Nov

John Frederick Nims Memorial Prize
Poetry Magazine
61 W Superior St, Chicago, IL 60654

Tel: 312-787-7070 *Fax:* 312-787-6650
E-mail: editors@poetrymagazine.org
Web Site: www.poetryfoundation.org
Key Personnel
Edit Asst: Holly Amos *E-mail:* hamos@poetrymagazine.org
Established: 1999
For poetry published in the preceding 2 volumes of *Poetry* magazine. No application necessary.
Award: $500
Presented: Annually in Dec

North Carolina Arts Council Writers Fellowships
North Carolina Arts Council
Division of North Carolina State Government
109 E Jones St, Raleigh, NC 27601
Mailing Address: Dept of Cultural Resources, Mail Service Ctr 4632, Raleigh, NC 27699-4632
Tel: 919-807-6500 *Fax:* 919-807-6532
E-mail: ncarts@ncdcr.gov
Web Site: www.ncarts.org
Key Personnel
Exec Dir: Wayne Martin *Tel:* 919-807-6525 *E-mail:* wayne.martin@ncdcr.gov
Prog Dir, Lit: David Potorti *Tel:* 919-807-6512 *E-mail:* david.potorti@ncdcr.gov
Established: 1980
Fellowships are given every 2 years to poets & writers of fiction, literary nonfiction, literary translation playwrights & screenwriters. Writers who have lived in the state for at least 1 year as of application deadline & who intend to remain instate during the fellowship year are eligible.
Award: $10,000
Closing Date: Nov 1 of even-numbered years
Presented: Summer of odd-numbered years

North Street Book Prize
Winning Writers
351 Pleasant St, PMB 222, Northampton, MA 01060-3961
Tel: 413-320-1847 *Toll Free Tel:* 866-WINWRIT (946-9748) *Fax:* 413-280-0539
Web Site: www.winningwriters.com
Key Personnel
Pres: Adam Cohen *E-mail:* adam@winningwriters.com
VP: Jendi Reiter
Submit self-published books, any year of publication, in the following categories: mainstream/literary fiction; genre fiction; creative nonfiction, memoir & poetry. Up to 150,000 words in length. Applications accepted February 15-June 30, $60 entry fee per book.
Award: $3,000 (grand prize), $1,000 (1st prize, mainstream/literary fiction, genre fiction, creative nonfiction, memoir & poetry), $250 (4 honorable mentions)
Closing Date: June 30
Presented: Winner announced Feb 15 on web site

Northern California Book Awards
Northern California Book Reviewers (NCBR)
c/o Poetry Flash, 1450 Fourth St, Suite 4, Berkeley, CA 94710
Tel: 510-525-5476 *Fax:* 510-525-6752
E-mail: editor@poetryflash.org; ncbr@poetryflash.org
Web Site: poetryflash.org
Key Personnel
Chmn: Joyce Jenkins
Contact: Frances Phillips *E-mail:* frances@haassr.org
Established: 1981
Awarded annually by category (fiction, poetry, nonfiction, children's literature & translation) for best book in category by a Northern California writer. Publishers Award given occasionally for special achievement by a Northern California publisher or a literary organization. Send 3 copies of book; no application or fee necessary.
Other Sponsor(s): Friends of the San Francisco Public Library; Mechanics' Institute Library & Chess Room; PEN West; Poetry Flash; San Francisco Public Library; Women's National Book Assn (SF Chapter)
Award: Cash & certificate
Closing Date: Dec 1
Presented: Koret Auditorium, San Francisco Main Public Library, San Francisco, CA, Spring

Notable Wisconsin Authors
Wisconsin Library Association Inc
4610 S Biltmore Lane, Suite 100, Madison, WI 53718-2153
Tel: 608-245-3640 *Fax:* 608-245-3646
Web Site: wla.wisconsinlibraries.org
Key Personnel
Exec Dir: Mr Plumer Lovelace *E-mail:* lovelace@wisconsinlibraries.org
Events & Conferences: Brigitte Rupp Vacha *E-mail:* ruppvacha@wisconsinlibraries.org
Established: 1973
Annual award honoring Wisconsin authors, past & present, for their literary contributions.
Award: Printed brochure with biographical information on the notable author, including a list of authors' works
Closing Date: April 15
Presented: WLA Annual Conference, Oct-Nov

Novella Prize
The Malahat Review
University of Victoria, Box 1700, Sta CSC, Victoria, BC V8W 2Y2, Canada
Tel: 250-721-8524 *Fax:* 250-472-5051
E-mail: malahat@uvic.ca
Web Site: www.malahatreview.ca
Key Personnel
Ed: John Barton
Established: 1995
Awarded biennially (even-numbered years) alternating with Long Poem Prize (odd-numbered years). See web site for details & entry fee.
Award: $1,500
Closing Date: Feb 1, even-numbered years

NSK Neustadt Prize for Children's Literature
World Literature Today
c/o University of Oklahoma, 630 Parrington Oval, Suite 110, Norman, OK 73019-4033
Tel: 405-325-4531
Web Site: www.worldliteraturetoday.org; www.worldlit.org
Key Personnel
Exec Dir: Robert Con Davis-Undiano *E-mail:* rcdavis@ou.edu
Asst Dir & Ed-in-Chief: Daniel Simon *E-mail:* dsimon@ou.edu
Art Dir: Merleyn Bell *E-mail:* merleyn@ou.edu
Mktg Dir, Progs & Devt: Terri Stubblefield *E-mail:* tdstubb@ou.edu
Mng Ed: Michelle Johnson *E-mail:* lmjohnson@ou.edu
Book Reviews Ed: Robert Vollmar *E-mail:* rvollmar@ou.edu
Circ & Accts Specialist: Kay Blunck *E-mail:* kblunck@ou.edu
Established: 2003
A biennial award intended to enhance the quality of children's literature by promoting writing that contributes to the quality of their lives. Awarded to a living writer with significant achievement, either over a lifetime or in a particular publication. The essential criterion for awarding this prize is that the writer's work is having a positive impact on the quality of children's literature.
Other Sponsor(s): Nancy Barcelo; Kathy Neustadt; Susan Neustadt Schwartz; The University of Oklahoma
Award: $25,000, medal & certificate
Closing Date: No outside nominations accepted, nominations by jury member only
Presented: The University of Oklahoma, Norman, OK, Oct, odd-numbered years

Nuestras Voces National Playwriting Competition
MetLife Foundation
138 E 27 St, New York, NY 10016
Tel: 212-225-9950 *Fax:* 212-225-9085
Web Site: www.repertorio.org
Key Personnel
Spec Projs Mgr: Allison Astor Vargas *E-mail:* aav@repertorio.org
Established: 2000
Award: $3,000 & full production (winner), cash awards of $500-$3,000 (top 5), stage reading (top 10)
Closing Date: Annually in June

NYC Emerging Writers Fellowships
The Center for Fiction
17 E 47 St, New York, NY 10017
Tel: 212-755-6710
E-mail: info@centerforfiction.org
Web Site: centerforfiction.org
Key Personnel
Writing Progs Dir: Sara Batkie *E-mail:* sara@centerforfiction.org
Supports emerging writers living in New York City whose work shows promise of excellence.
Other Sponsor(s): Jerome Foundation
Award: $5,000 grant

The O. Henry Prize Stories
Anchor Books
Imprint of Knopf Doubleday Publishing Group
c/o University of Texas at Austin, One University Sta, English Dept, B5000, Austin, TX 78712
Web Site: www.randomhouse.com/anchor/ohenry
Key Personnel
Series Ed: Laura Furman
Established: 1919
Annual collection of the 20 best English language short stories published in American & Canadian magazines & written in the English language during the calendar year 2 years prior to the year presented. No submissions; selections made by the series editor from those published in the approximately 260 magazines with print editions submitted to the series.
Closing Date: May 1

Eli M Oboler Memorial Award
Intellectual Freedom Round Table (IFRT)
Unit of The American Library Association (ALA)
50 E Huron St, Chicago, IL 60611
Tel: 312-280-4226 *Toll Free Tel:* 800-545-2433
E-mail: oif@ala.org
Web Site: www.ala.org/ifrt
Key Personnel
Asst Dir: Kristen Pekoll *Tel:* 312-280-4220
Established: 1986
Biennial award given to an author of a published work in English, or an English translation dealing with issues, events, questions or controversies in the area of intellectual freedom. Must have been published within previous 2 calendar years prior to the ALA annual conference at which it is granted.
Award: $500 & certificate
Closing Date: Dec 1, odd-numbered years
Presented: ALA Annual Conference, June, even-numbered years

The Flannery O'Connor Award for Short Fiction
University of Georgia Press

Main Library, 3rd fl, 320 S Jackson St, Athens, GA 30602
Fax: 706-542-2558
Web Site: www.ugapress.org
Key Personnel
Series Ed: Lee K Abbott
Asst Acqs Ed: Beth Snead *Tel:* 706-542-7613 *E-mail:* bsnead@uga.edu
Established: 1981
Collections of original short fiction. Ms should be 40,000-75,000 words & should be accompanied by a $30 submission fee; ms will not be returned. Submissions accepted between April 1 & May 31. Open to both published & unpublished writers. Applicants should visit the press web site for guidelines. No phone calls regarding the award will be accepted. Accepting electronic submissions at georgiapress.submishmash.com.
Award: $1,000 & publication by the University of Georgia Press under a standard publishing contract
Closing Date: Annually, May 31

Frank O'Connor Prize for Fiction
Texas Christian University
Dept of English, TCU Box 298300, Fort Worth, TX 76129
Tel: 817-257-5907 *Fax:* 817-257-5905
E-mail: descant@tcu.edu
Web Site: www.descant.tcu.edu
Key Personnel
Mng Ed: Dan Williams *E-mail:* d.e.williams@tcu.edu
Established: 1957
Best published fiction in each volume of descant. No entry fee. Winners announced in journal.
Other Sponsor(s): descant (publication), Dept of English, TCU
Award: $500
Closing Date: Annually, Sept 1-April 1
Presented: Annually in Summer

Scott O'Dell Award for Historical Fiction
c/o Horn Book Inc, 300 The Fenway, Suite P-311, Palace Road Bldg, Boston, MA 02215
Tel: 617-278-0225 *Toll Free Tel:* 888-628-0225 *Fax:* 617-278-6062
Web Site: www.scottodell.com/Pages/ScottO'DellAwardforHistoricalFiction.aspx
Key Personnel
Chair: Roger Sutton
Asst to Chair: Deborah Stevenson; Ann Carlson
Established: 1982
Presented for a work of historical fiction published in the previous year for children or young adults, by a US publisher & set in the New World. Winner is selected by O'Dell Award Committee.
Award: $5,000
Closing Date: Annually, Dec 31

Annual Off Off Broadway Short Play Festival
Samuel French Inc
235 Park Ave S, 5th fl, New York, NY 10003
Tel: 212-206-8990 *Toll Free Tel:* 866-598-8449 *Fax:* 212-206-1429
E-mail: oobfestival@samuelfrench.com
Web Site: oob.samuelfrench.com; www.samuelfrench.com
Key Personnel
Festival Coord: Casey McLain *E-mail:* cmclain@samuelfrench.com
Artistic Coord: Amy Rose Marsh *E-mail:* amarsh@samuelfrench.com
Festival Mktg & Outreach: Ryan Pointer *E-mail:* rpointer@samuelfrench.com
Established: 1975
Selected plays are presented on the final day of the festival.
Award: Publication of top 6 plays
Closing Date: Jan-late Feb
Presented: July/Aug

Dayne Ogilvie Prize
The Writers' Trust of Canada
460 Richmond St W, Suite 600, Toronto, ON M5V 1Y1, Canada
Tel: 416-504-8222 *Toll Free Tel:* 877-906-6548 *Fax:* 416-504-9090
E-mail: info@writerstrust.com
Web Site: www.writerstrust.com
Key Personnel
Exec Dir: Mary Osborne *Tel:* 416-504-8222 ext 244 *E-mail:* mosborne@writerstrust.com
Established: 2007
Awarded to an emerging LGBT writer.
Other Sponsor(s): Robin Pacific
Award: $4,000
Presented: Pride Week, Toronto, ON, CN, Annually, early Summer

Howard O'Hagan Award for Short Story
Writers' Guild of Alberta
11759 Groat Rd, Edmonton, AB T5M 3K6, Canada
Tel: 780-422-8174 *Toll Free Tel:* 800-665-5354 (AB only) *Fax:* 780-422-2663 (attn WGA)
E-mail: mail@writersguild.ca
Web Site: writersguild.ca
Key Personnel
Exec Dir: Carol Holmes *E-mail:* carol.holmes@writersguild.ca
Communs & Partnerships Coord: Ellen Kartz *E-mail:* ellen.kartz@writersguild.ca
Memb Servs Coord: Giorgia Severini
Progs Coord: Natalie Cook *E-mail:* natalie.cook@writersguild.ca; Julie Robinson *E-mail:* julie.robinson@writersguild.ca
Established: 1982
Alberta literary award for published short stories only, author must be resident of Alberta; no longer than 5,000 words.
Award: $700
Closing Date: Annually, Dec 31
Presented: Alberta Book Awards Gala
Branch Office(s)
505 21 Ave SW, Calgary, AB T2S 0G9, Canada, Prog Coord: Samantha Warwick *Tel:* 403-265-2226 *E-mail:* samantha.warwick@writersguild.ca

Ohioana Book Awards
Ohioana Library Association
274 E First Ave, Suite 300, Columbus, OH 43201
Tel: 614-466-3831 *Fax:* 614-728-6974
E-mail: ohioana@ohioana.org
Web Site: www.ohioana.org
Key Personnel
Exec Dir, Ohioana Library Association: David E Weaver *E-mail:* dweaver@ohioana.org
Established: 1942
For the best books by Ohio authors in various fields of writing or books about Ohio or Ohioans. Submit 2 copies of a nominated book on or before its publication date.
Award: $1,500 cash prize for winning book in each category: fiction, poetry, juvenile literature, middle grade/young adult literature, nonfiction about Ohio/Ohioan
Closing Date: Dec 31
Presented: Ohioana Awards Ceremony, Oct

Ohioana Walter Rumsey Marvin Grant
Ohioana Library Association
274 E First Ave, Suite 300, Columbus, OH 43201
Tel: 614-466-3831 *Fax:* 614-728-6974
E-mail: ohioana@ohioana.org
Web Site: www.ohioana.org
Key Personnel
Exec Dir, Ohioana Library Association: David E Weaver *E-mail:* dweaver@ohioana.org
Established: 1982
Writing competition; awarded to young (30 yrs of age or younger), unpublished Ohio authors who were born or have lived in Ohio 5 years or more.
Award: $1,000 cash prize & publication of winning submission in the *Ohioana Quarterly*
Closing Date: Jan 31
Presented: Ohioana Awards Ceremony, Oct

Chris O'Malley Fiction Prize
The Madison Review
University of Wisconsin, 6193 Helen C White Hall, English Dept, 600 N Park St, Madison, WI 53706
E-mail: madisonrevw@gmail.com
Web Site: www.themadisonreview.com
Key Personnel
Chmn Dept: Russ Castronovo
Faculty Advisor & Prog Coord: Ronald Kuka *Tel:* 608-263-3374 *E-mail:* rfkuka@wisc.edu
Size limit 30-page maximum. Only 1 submission is allowed per person per contest. Ms must be previously unpublished & should be double-spaced with stardard 1-inch margins & 12-pt font. Entry fee $10.
Award: $1,000 & publication in Spring issue of *The Madison Review*
Closing Date: Annually, Nov 1
Presented: Announcement in March

Open Chapbook Competition
Finishing Line Press
PO Box 1626, Georgetown, KY 40324
Tel: 502-603-0670
E-mail: finishingbooks@aol.com; flpbookstore@aol.com
Web Site: www.finishinglinepress.com
Key Personnel
Publr: Leah Maines
Mng Ed: Kevin Murphy Maines
Sr Ed: Christen Kincaid
Established: 2002
Award for an unpublished chapbook of poems. Winner announced on web site & in *Poets & Writers Magazine*.
Award: $1,000 & publication
Closing Date: Oct 31
Presented: Finishing Line Press

Open Season Awards
The Malahat Review
University of Victoria, Box 1700, Sta CSC, Victoria, BC V8W 2Y2, Canada
Tel: 250-721-8524 *Fax:* 250-472-5051
E-mail: malahat@uvic.ca
Web Site: malahatreview.ca
Key Personnel
Ed: John Barton
Established: 2009
Awards in 3 categories: poetry, short fiction & creative nonfiction. See web site for additional details.
Award: $1,500 in each of 3 categories
Closing Date: Annually, Nov 1

Opie Prize
American Folklore Society/Children's Folklore Section
Indiana University, Classroom-Off Bldg, 800 E Third St, Bloomington, IN 47405
Tel: 812-856-2379 *Fax:* 812-856-2483
Web Site: www.afsnet.org
Key Personnel
Exec Dir: Timothy Lloyd *E-mail:* timlloyd@indiana.edu
Assoc Dir: Lorraine Walsh Cashman *E-mail:* lcashman@indiana.edu
Annual award for the best book-length treatment of children's folklore. Edited volumes, collections of folklore & authored studies published in English during previous 2 years are eligible.

Authors or publishers should submit 2 copies of the book.
Award: $200
Closing Date: Varies
Presented: Oct

Oregon Book Awards
Literary Arts
925 SW Washington St, Portland, OR 97205
Tel: 503-227-2583 *Fax:* 503-241-4256
E-mail: la@literary-arts.org
Web Site: www.literary-arts.org
Key Personnel
Dir, Progs for Writers: Susan Moore *Tel:* 503-227-2583 ext 107 *E-mail:* susan@literary-arts.org
Established: 1988
Available for original work published or produced in the following categories: poetry, novel, general nonfiction, creative nonfiction, children's literature, young adult literature, drama & graphic literature.
Closing Date: Annually in Sept
Presented: Jan

George Orwell Award
National Council of Teachers of English (NCTE)
1111 W Kenyon Rd, Urbana, IL 61801-1096
Tel: 217-328-3870 *Toll Free Tel:* 877-369-6283 (cust serv) *Fax:* 217-328-0977
E-mail: publiclangawards@ncte.org
Web Site: www.ncte.org
Key Personnel
Admin Liaison & Awards Contact: Linda Walters-Moore
Established: 1975
Recognizes writers for distinguished contributions to the critical analysis of public discourse.
Other Sponsor(s): NCTE Committee on Public Doublespeak
Award: Certificate
Closing Date: Annually, Sept 15
Presented: NCTE Annual Convention, Late Nov

Joyce Osterweil Award for Poetry, see PEN/Joyce Osterweil Award for Poetry

Frank L & Harriet C Owsley Award
Southern Historical Association
University of Georgia, Dept of History, Athens, GA 30602-1602
Tel: 706-542-8848 *Fax:* 706-542-2455
Web Site: thesha.org
Key Personnel
Admin Asst: Frances Berry *E-mail:* manager@thesha.org
Established: 1985
Awarded for most distinguished book in Southern history published in even-numbered years. Awarded in odd-numbered years.
Award: Cash
Closing Date: March 1
Presented: Annual meeting, odd-numbered years, Fall

Pacific Northwest Book Awards
Pacific Northwest Booksellers Association (PNBA)
338 W 11 Ave, Unit 108, Eugene, OR 97401
Tel: 541-683-4363 *Fax:* 541-683-3910
E-mail: info@pnba.org; awards@pnba.org
Web Site: www.pnba.org
Key Personnel
Exec Dir: Brian Juenemann *E-mail:* brian@pnba.org
Established: 1965
Annual awards for authors who live in Washington, Oregon, Idaho, Alaska & Montana who have published exceptional books during the calendar year.
Award: Plaque & marketing to independent bookstores of the Pacific Northwest
Closing Date: Sept 30
Presented: Early Jan

Pacific Northwest Young Reader's Choice Award
Pacific Northwest Library Association (PNLA)
Vancouver Mall Community Library, 8700 NE Vancouver Mall Dr, Suite 285, Vancouver, WA 98662
Web Site: www.pnla.org/yrca
Key Personnel
Coord: Jocie Wilson *Tel:* 780-962-2003 ext 223
Established: 1940
Nominations taken only from children, teachers, parents & librarians of the Pacific Northwest (WA, OR, AK, ID, MT, BC & AB) for titles published 3 years previously in the US or CN. Only 4th-12th graders in the Pacific Northwest vote on a selected list of titles. The categories are junior grades 4-6, intermediate grades 7-9 & senior grades 10-12. Awarded to the author of a book most popular with children. Send SASE or see web site for information.
Award: Silver Medal
Closing Date: Annually, Feb 1
Presented: Pacific Northwest Library Association's Annual Conference, Annually in Aug

The Pacific Spirit Poetry Prize
PRISM international
University of British Columbia, Buch E462, 1866 Main Mall, Vancouver, BC V6T 1Z1, Canada
Tel: 778-822-2514 *Fax:* 778-822-3616
E-mail: prismwritingcontest@gmail.com
Web Site: www.prismmagazine.ca
Key Personnel
Exec Ed: Jennifer Lori; Claire Matthews
Poetry Ed: Dominique Bernier Cormier
Prose Ed: Christopher Evans
Established: 1986
Awarded for the best original, unpublished poem (3 poems, up to 25 pages). Works of translation are eligible. Entry fee: $35 for 3 poems plus $5 for each additional entry.
Award: $1,500 grand prize, $600 (1st runner up), $400 (2nd runner up); all entries receive 1-year subn to *PRISM international*
Closing Date: Annually in Jan

PAGE International Screenwriting Awards
Production Arts Group
7190 Sunset Blvd, Suite 610, Hollywood, CA 90046
E-mail: info@pageawards.com
Web Site: www.pageawards.com
Key Personnel
Admin Dir: Jennifer Berg
Contest Coord: Zoe Simmons
Established: 2003
Each year the judges present a total of 31 awards in 10 different categories.
Award: $25,000 (grand prize) plus gold, silver & bronze prizes in all 10 categories
Closing Date: Annually in May
Presented: Hollywood, CA, Annually in Oct

Dobie Paisano Fellowship Program
University of Texas at Austin, Texas Institute of Letters
Graduate School, 110 Inner Campus Dr, Stop G0400, Austin, TX 78712-0710
Fax: 512-471-7620
Web Site: www.utexas.edu/ogs/Paisano
Key Personnel
Dir: Dr Michael Adams *E-mail:* adameve@mail.utexas.edu
Established: 1967
Provides an opportunity for creative or nonfiction writers to live & write for an extended period in an environment that offers isolation & tranquility. At the time of application, the applicant must: be a native Texan; have lived in Texas at some time for at least 3 years; or have published significant work with a Texas subject. Criteria for making the awards include quality of work, character of the proposed project & suitability of the applicant for life at Paisano, the late J Frank Dobie's ranch near Austin, TX. Applications are available at the above web site or write for more information. Application fee: $20/1 fellowship, $30/both fellowships.
Award: Ralph A Johnston Memorial Fellowship: $25,000 over four months; Jesse H Jones Writing Fellowship: $18,000 over 6 months.
Closing Date: Annually, Dec 15
Presented: Annually in May

Mildred & Albert Panowski Playwriting Award
Northern Michigan University
Forest Roberts Theatre, 1401 Presque Isle Ave, Marquette, MI 49855-5364
Tel: 906-227-2553 *Fax:* 906-227-2567
E-mail: theatre@nmu.edu
Web Site: www.nmu.edu/theatre
Key Personnel
Dir: Ansley Valentine *Tel:* 906-227-1645 *E-mail:* avalenti@nmu.edu
Established: 1977
Provides students & faculty the unique opportunity to mount & produce an original work on the university stage. The playwright will benefit from seeing the work on its feet in front of an audience & from professional adjudication by guest critics. Please check the web site for theme or genre. Play must be unproduced. Only one play per playwright may be entered. Electronic submission only.
Award: $2,000 cash, airline fare, room & board for the week of production
Closing Date: Sept 1 of odd-numbered years (receipt not postmark)
Presented: Forest Roberts Theatre, Northern Michigan Univ, In upcoming season

Francis Parkman Prize
Society of American Historians (SAH)
Affiliate of American Historical Association
2950 Broadway, New York, NY 10027
Tel: 212-854-6495
E-mail: amhistsociety@columbia.edu
Web Site: sah.columbia.edu
Key Personnel
Pres: Mary Kelley
VP: Ann Fabian
Dir, Communs: Andie Tucher
Established: 1957
For a nonfiction book, including biography, that is distinguished by its literary merit & makes an important contribution to the history of what is now the US. The author need not be a citizen or resident of the US & the book need not be published in the US although must be published & copyrighted in the year preceding the award.
Award: $2,000 & certificate
Closing Date: Annually, Dec 1
Presented: New York, NY, Annually in May

The Paterson Poetry Prize
The Poetry Center at Passaic County Community College
One College Blvd, Paterson, NJ 07505-1179
Tel: 973-684-6555 *Fax:* 973-523-6085
Web Site: www.poetrycenterpccc.com
Key Personnel
Exec Dir: Maria Mazziotti Gillan *E-mail:* mgillan@pccc.edu
Mgr: Susan Balik *E-mail:* sbalik@pccc.edu
For a book of poems, 48 pages or more in length, selected by our judges as the strongest collection of poems published in the previous year.

The poet will be asked to participate in an awards ceremony & to give a reading at the Poetry Center. Publisher may submit more than one book for prize consideration.
Award: $1,000
Closing Date: Annually, Feb 1

The Paterson Prize for Books for Young People
The Poetry Center at Passaic County Community College
One College Blvd, Paterson, NJ 07505-1179
Tel: 973-684-6555 *Fax:* 973-523-6085
Web Site: www.poetrycenterpccc.com
Key Personnel
Exec Dir: Maria Mazziotti Gillan
E-mail: mgillan@pccc.edu
Mgr: Susan Balik *E-mail:* sbalik@pccc.edu
One book in each category will be selected for the most outstanding book for young people published in the previous year.
Award: $500 in each category: PreK-Grade 3, Grades 4-6, Grades 7-12
Closing Date: Annually, Feb 1

The Alicia Patterson Foundation Fellowship Program
The Alicia Patterson Foundation
1100 Vermont Ave, Suite 900, Washington, DC 20005
Tel: 202-393-5995 *Fax:* 301-951-8512
E-mail: info@aliciapatterson.org
Web Site: www.aliciapatterson.org
Key Personnel
Exec Dir: Margaret Engel
Established: 1963
Stipend (12 or 6 months), not for academic study, for professional print journalist with 5 years experience & must write/photograph for English language medium. One additional fellowship for science & environmental topics.
Award: $40,000 over 12 months, $20,000 over 6 months. Applicants choose whether they want 6 or 12 month grants
Closing Date: Annually, Oct 1
Presented: 2nd week of Dec

William Peden Prize in Fiction
The Missouri Review
357 McReynolds Hall, Columbia, MO 65211
Tel: 573-882-4474 *Toll Free Tel:* 800-949-2505
Fax: 573-884-4671
E-mail: question@moreview.com
Web Site: www.missourireview.com
Key Personnel
Assoc Ed: Evelyn Somers *Tel:* 573-884-7839
E-mail: rogerses@missouri.edu
Awarded annually to the best story to appear in the magazine the previous volume year. Winner is selected by an outside judge. It is not a contest that writers can enter, since the winner is selected from stories already published in the magazine.
Award: $1,000
Presented: Columbia, MO

The PEN Award for Poetry in Translation
PEN American Center
Affiliate of PEN International
588 Broadway, Suite 303, New York, NY 10012
Tel: 212-334-1660 *Fax:* 212-334-2181
E-mail: awards@pen.org
Web Site: pen.org/press/grants-awards-database
Key Personnel
Exec Dir: Suzanne Nossel *Tel:* 212-334-1600 ext 4811 *E-mail:* snossel@pen.org
Pres: Andrew Solomon
Dir, Literary Progs: Paul Morris *Tel:* 212-334-1660 ext 4824 *E-mail:* paul@pen.org
Sr Mgr, Literary Awards: Nadxieli Nieto
Tel: 212-334-1660 ext 4813 *E-mail:* nnieto@pen.org
Recognizes book-length translations of poetry from any language into English, published during the current calendar year & is judged by a single translator of poetry appointed by the PEN Translation Committee. All books must have been published in the US, although translators may be of any nationality (US residency or citizenship is not required). Only publishers & literary agents may submit. Submitters must complete online submission form. Entry fee: $75 (fee may be waived for small presses).
Award: $3,000
Closing Date: Annually in Aug
Presented: PEN Literary Awards Ceremony, New York, NY, Annually in Spring

PEN/Bellwether Prize for Socially Engaged Fiction
PEN American Center
588 Broadway, Suite 303, New York, NY 10012
Tel: 212-334-1660
E-mail: awards@pen.org
Web Site: pen.org/press/grants-awards-database
Key Personnel
Dir, Literary Progs: Paul Morris *Tel:* 212-334-1660 ext 4824 *E-mail:* paul@pen.org
Sr Mgr, Literary Awards: Nadxieli Nieto
Tel: 212-334-1660 ext 4813 *E-mail:* nnieto@pen.org
Awarded biennially to the author of a previously unpublished novel of high literary caliber that promotes fiction that addresses issues of social justice & the impact of culture & politics on human relationships. Entry fee: $25.
Award: $25,000 & publishing contract with Algonquin Books

PEN Center USA Emerging Voices Fellowship
PEN Center USA
PO Box 6037, Beverly Hills, CA 90212
Tel: 323-424-4939 *Fax:* 323-424-4944
E-mail: ev@penusa.org
Web Site: penusa.org/programs/emerging-voices
Key Personnel
Prog Coord: Amanda Fletcher *Tel:* 323-424-4939 ext 1002 *E-mail:* amanda@penusa.org
Established: 1996
Literary mentorship that aims to provide new writers who are isolated from the literary establishment with the tools, skills & knowledge they need to launch a professional writing career. Fellowship is directed toward poets & writers of fiction & creative nonfiction with clear ideas of what they hope to accomplish through their writing. Application period begins May 1.
Award: Seven-month fellowship & $1,000 stipend
Closing Date: Aug 1

PEN Center USA Literary Awards
PEN Center USA
Affiliate of PEN International
8549 Wilshire Blvd, Suite 355, Beverly Hills, CA 90211
Mailing Address: PO Box 6037, Beverly Hills, CA 90212
Tel: 323-424-4939 *Fax:* 323-424-4944
E-mail: awards@penusa.org; pen@penusa.org
Web Site: penusa.org/awards
Key Personnel
Exec Dir: Michelle Franke *Tel:* 323-424-4939 ext 1 *E-mail:* michelle@penusa.org
Dir, Literary Progs: Libby Flores *Tel:* 323-424-4939 ext 5 *E-mail:* libby@penusa.org
Literary Awards: Stacy Valis *Tel:* 323-424-4939 ext 3 *E-mail:* stacy_valis@penusa.org
Established: 1982
Literary awards for: fiction, creative nonfiction, poetry, translation, children's/young adult, graphic literature, drama, research nonfiction, screenplay, teleplay, journalism (print & online). Author must live west of Mississippi River. Work must have been published/produced in the year in which submissions are accepted. Annual call for submissions opens each summer. Forms must be submitted via submittable (penawards.submittable.com). Entry fee $35 (Journalism $15).
Award: Cash awards $1,000
Closing Date: Dec 31, book categories; Jan 15, journalism; Dec 31, drama; Aug 15, screenplay; July 15, teleplay
Presented: Literary Awards Festival, Fall

PEN/Diamonstein-Spielvogel Award for the Art of the Essay
PEN American Center
588 Broadway, Suite 303, New York, NY 10012
Tel: 212-334-1660
E-mail: awards@pen.org
Web Site: pen.org/literary-awards
Key Personnel
Dir, Literary Progs: Paul Morris *Tel:* 212-334-1660 ext 4824 *E-mail:* paul@pen.org
Sr Mgr, Literary Awards: Nadxieli Nieto
Tel: 212-334-1660 ext 4813 *E-mail:* nnieto@pen.org
Nonfiction award which aims to preserve the dignity & esteem that the essay form imparts to literature. Submissions accepted only from publishers or literary agents.
Award: $10,000

PEN/E O Wilson Literary Science Writing Award
PEN American Center
588 Broadway, Suite 303, New York, NY 10012
Tel: 212-334-1660
E-mail: awards@pen.org
Web Site: pen.org/literary-awards
Key Personnel
Dir, Literary Progs: Paul Morris *Tel:* 212-334-1660 ext 4824 *E-mail:* paul@pen.org
Sr Mgr, Literary Awards: Nadxieli Nieto
Tel: 212-334-1660 ext 4813 *E-mail:* nnieto@pen.org
Nonfiction award which celebrates writing that exemplifies literary excellence on the subject of physical & biological sciences.
Award: $10,000

PEN/ESPN Award for Literary Sports Writing
PEN American Center
588 Broadway, Suite 303, New York, NY 10012
Tel: 212-334-1660
E-mail: awards@pen.org
Web Site: pen.org/literary-awards
Key Personnel
Dir, Literary Progs: Paul Morris *Tel:* 212-334-1660 ext 4824 *E-mail:* paul@pen.org
Sr Mgr, Literary Awards: Nadxieli Nieto
Tel: 212-334-1660 ext 4813 *E-mail:* nnieto@pen.org
Award to an author of a nonfiction book about sports.
Award: $5,000

PEN/ESPN Lifetime Achievement Award for Literary Sports Writing
PEN American Center
588 Broadway, Suite 303, New York, NY 10012
Tel: 212-334-1660
E-mail: awards@pen.org
Web Site: pen.org/literary-awards
Key Personnel
Dir, Literary Progs: Paul Morris *Tel:* 212-334-1660 ext 4824 *E-mail:* paul@pen.org
Sr Mgr, Literary Awards: Nadxieli Nieto
Tel: 212-334-1660 ext 4813 *E-mail:* nnieto@pen.org
Nonfiction award to a writer for their long-time contributions to the field of literary sports writing.
Award: $5,000

PEN/Faulkner Award for Fiction
PEN/Faulkner Foundation
Folger Shakespeare Library, 201 E Capitol St SE, Washington, DC 20003
Tel: 202-898-9063 *Fax:* 202-675-0360
Web Site: www.penfaulkner.org
Key Personnel
Exec Dir: Darlene Taylor
Established: 1980
Annual award for the best work of fiction published by an American citizen writer (for published work only) in a single calendar year. Send 4 copies of each book or 4 bound gallies for those being published in November & December.
Award: $15,000 (1st prize), $5,000 to each of 4 finalists
Closing Date: Oct 31
Presented: Awards Ceremony, Washington, DC, May

PEN/Fusion Emerging Writers Prize
PEN American Center
588 Broadway, Suite 303, New York, NY 10012
Tel: 212-334-1660
E-mail: awards@pen.org
Web Site: pen.org/literary-awards
Key Personnel
Dir, Literary Progs: Paul Morris *Tel:* 212-334-1660 ext 4824 *E-mail:* paul@pen.org
Sr Mgr, Literary Awards: Nadxieli Nieto *Tel:* 212-334-1660 ext 4813 *E-mail:* nnieto@pen.org
Annual award that recognizes a promising young writer (35 & under) of an unpublished work of nonfiction that addresses a global +/or multicultural issue. Ms submission must be an original, previously unpublished work of nonfiction written by one person, in English, 8,000-80,000 words in length. Entry fee: $35.
Award: $10,000

PEN/Jacqueline Bograd Weld Award for Biography
PEN American Center
588 Broadway, Suite 303, New York, NY 10012
Tel: 212-334-1660
E-mail: awards@pen.org
Web Site: pen.org/literary-awards
Key Personnel
Dir, Literary Progs: Paul Morris *Tel:* 212-334-1660 ext 4824 *E-mail:* paul@pen.org
Sr Mgr, Literary Awards: Nadxieli Nieto *Tel:* 212-334-1660 ext 4813 *E-mail:* nnieto@pen.org
Nonfiction award for excellence in the art of biography.
Award: $5,000

PEN/Jean Stein Book Award
PEN American Center
588 Broadway, Suite 303, New York, NY 10012
Tel: 212-334-1660
E-mail: info@pen.org
Web Site: pen.org/press/grants-awards-database
Key Personnel
Dir, Literary Progs: Paul Morris *Tel:* 212-334-1660 ext 4824 *E-mail:* paul@pen.org
Sr Mgr, Literary Awards: Nadxieli Nieto *Tel:* 212-334-1660 ext 4813 *E-mail:* nnieto@pen.org
Deputy Dir, Communs: Sarah Edkins *Tel:* 212-334-1600 ext 4830 *E-mail:* sedkins@pen.org
Established: 2017
Annual award which recognizes a book-length work of any genre for its originality, merit & impact. Judging panel will serve anonymously & will nominate candidates internally & without submissions from the public.
Award: $75,000
Presented: PEN Literary Awards Ceremony, New York, NY, Annually in Feb

PEN/Joyce Osterweil Award for Poetry
PEN American Center
588 Broadway, Suite 303, New York, NY 10012
Tel: 212-334-1660
E-mail: awards@pen.org
Web Site: pen.org/press/grants-awards-database
Key Personnel
Dir, Literary Progs: Paul Morris *Tel:* 212-334-1660 ext 4824 *E-mail:* paul@pen.org
Sr Mgr, Literary Awards: Nadxieli Nieto *Tel:* 212-334-1660 ext 4813 *E-mail:* nnieto@pen.org
Awarded in odd-numbered years (alternates with PEN/Voelcker Award for Poetry). Recognizes the high literary character of the published work to date of a new & emerging American poet of any age & the promise of further literary achievement.
Award: $5,000

PEN/Nabokov Award for Achievement in International Literature
PEN American Center
588 Broadway, Suite 303, New York, NY 10012
Tel: 212-334-1660 *Fax:* 212-334-2181
E-mail: awards@pen.org
Web Site: pen.org/literary-awards
Key Personnel
Sr Mgr, Literary Awards: Nadxieli Nieto *Tel:* 212-334-1660 ext 4813 *E-mail:* nnieto@pen.org
Dir, Literary Progs: Paul Morris *Tel:* 212-334-1660 ext 4824 *E-mail:* paul@pen.org
Deputy Dir, Communs: Sarah Edkins *Tel:* 212-334-1600 ext 4830 *E-mail:* sedkins@pen.org
Award to honor an international writer whose work, either written in or translated into English, represents the highest level of achievement in fiction, nonfiction, poetry, +/or drama & is of enduring originality & consummate craftsmanship.
Other Sponsor(s): Vladimir Nabokov Literary Foundation
Award: $50,000
Presented: PEN America Literary Awards Ceremony, NY, Feb 2018

PEN/New England Awards
Formerly The Laurence L & Thomas Winship/PEN New England Award
Boston Globe & PEN New England
MIT, 14N-221A, 77 Massachusetts Ave, Cambridge, MA 02139
Tel: 617-324-1729
E-mail: pen-newengland@mit.edu; pen-ne@lesley.edu
Web Site: www.pen-ne.org
Key Personnel
Exec Dir: Karen Wulf *E-mail:* kwulf@mit.edu
Established: 1975
To recognize the writing of New England's best in fiction, poetry & nonfiction. Eligible books must be written by New England authors or have a New England topic or setting & must have been published by a US publisher in the previous calendar year. Submit 3 copies. Entry fee is $50 for each title.
Award: 3 $1,000 awards
Closing Date: Annually in Dec
Presented: John F Kennedy Library, Boston, MA, Annually in April

PEN Open Book Award
PEN American Center
588 Broadway, Suite 303, New York, NY 10012
Tel: 212-334-1660
E-mail: awards@pen.org
Web Site: pen.org/literary-awards
Key Personnel
Dir, Literary Progs: Paul Morris *Tel:* 212-334-1660 ext 4824 *E-mail:* paul@pen.org
Sr Mgr, Literary Awards: Nadxieli Nieto *Tel:* 212-334-1660 ext 4813 *E-mail:* nnieto@pen.org
For a book-length work by an author of color.
Award: $5,000

PEN/Phyllis Naylor Working Writer Fellowship
PEN American Center
Affiliate of PEN International
588 Broadway, Suite 303, New York, NY 10012
Tel: 212-334-1660 *Fax:* 212-334-2181
E-mail: awards@pen.org
Web Site: pen.org/press/grants-awards-database
Key Personnel
Exec Dir: Suzanne Nossel *Tel:* 212-334-1600 ext 4811 *E-mail:* snossel@pen.org
Pres: Andrew Solomon
Dir, Literary Progs: Paul Morris *Tel:* 212-334-1660 ext 4824 *E-mail:* paul@pen.org
Sr Mgr, Literary Awards: Nadxieli Nieto *Tel:* 212-334-1660 ext 4813 *E-mail:* nnieto@pen.org
Established: 2001
Annual award presented to an author of children's or young adult fiction. Provides a writer with a measure of financial sustenance in order to make possible an extended period of time to complete a book-length work-in-progress & to assist a writer at a crucial moment in his or her career when monetary support is particularly needed.
Award: $5,000
Closing Date: Summer
Presented: PEN Literary Awards Ceremony, New York, NY, Spring

PEN/Ralph Manheim Medal for Translation
PEN American Center
Affiliate of PEN International
588 Broadway, Suite 303, New York, NY 10012
Tel: 212-334-1660 *Fax:* 212-334-2181
E-mail: awards@pen.org
Web Site: pen.org/press/grants-awards-database
Key Personnel
Exec Dir: Suzanne Nossel *Tel:* 212-334-1600 ext 4811 *E-mail:* snossel@pen.org
Pres: Andrew Solomon
Dir, Literary Progs: Paul Morris *Tel:* 212-334-1660 ext 4824 *E-mail:* paul@pen.org
Sr Mgr, Literary Awards: Nadxieli Nieto *Tel:* 212-334-1660 ext 4813 *E-mail:* nnieto@pen.org
Established: 1982
Given every 3 years to a translator who has demonstrated exceptional commitment to excellence throughout the body of his work. Candidates nominated by the PEN Translation Committee; internal nomination only. See web site for more information.
Award: Medal
Closing Date: None
Presented: PEN Literary Awards Ceremony, New York, NY, Every 3 years in Summer

PEN/Robert Bingham Prize for Debut Fiction
PEN American Center
Affiliate of PEN International
588 Broadway, Suite 303, New York, NY 10012
Tel: 212-334-1660 *Fax:* 212-334-2181
E-mail: awards@pen.org
Web Site: pen.org/press/grants-awards-database
Key Personnel
Exec Dir: Suzanne Nossel *Tel:* 212-334-1600 ext 4811 *E-mail:* snossel@pen.org
Pres: Andrew Solomon
Dir, Literary Progs: Paul Morris *Tel:* 212-334-1660 ext 4824 *E-mail:* paul@pen.org
Sr Mgr, Literary Awards: Nadxieli Nieto *Tel:* 212-334-1660 ext 4813 *E-mail:* nnieto@pen.org

Honor an exceptionally talented fiction writer whose debut work–a first fiction novel or collection of short stories–represents distinguished literary achievement & suggests great promise. Nominations are welcome from any source. Candidates must be US residents but American citizenship is not required. Self-published authors are not eligible. Only publishers & literary agents may apply. Entry fee: $75. (Entry fee may be waived for small presses).
Award: $25,000
Closing Date: Annually in Summer
Presented: PEN Literary Awards Ceremony, New York, NY, Annually in Spring

PEN/Saul Bellow Award for Achievement in American Fiction
PEN American Center
588 Broadway, Suite 303, New York, NY 10012
Tel: 212-334-1660 *Fax:* 212-334-2181
E-mail: awards@pen.org
Web Site: pen.org/press/grants-awards-database
Key Personnel
Dir, Literary Progs: Paul Morris *Tel:* 212-334-1660 ext 4824 *E-mail:* paul@pen.org
Sr Mgr, Literary Awards: Nadxieli Nieto *Tel:* 212-334-1660 ext 4813 *E-mail:* nnieto@pen.org
Established: 2007
Award to a living American author whose scale of achievement in fiction, over a sustained career, places him or her in the highest rank of American literature. Administered by internal nomination only.
Award: $25,000

PEN Translation Prize
PEN American Center
Affiliate of PEN International
588 Broadway, Suite 303, New York, NY 10012
Tel: 212-334-1660 *Fax:* 212-334-2181
E-mail: awards@pen.org
Web Site: pen.org/press/grants-awards-database
Key Personnel
Exec Dir: Suzanne Nossel *Tel:* 212-334-1600 ext 4811 *E-mail:* snossel@pen.org
Pres: Andrew Solomon
Dir, Literary Progs: Paul Morris *Tel:* 212-334-1660 ext 4824 *E-mail:* paul@pen.org
Sr Mgr, Literary Awards: Nadxieli Nieto *Tel:* 212-334-1660 ext 4813 *E-mail:* nnieto@pen.org
Established: 1963
For the best book-length translation into English from any language published in the US during the previous year. Technical, scientific or reference works are not eligible. See web site for more information. Entry fee: $75 (fee may be waived for small presses). Only publishers & literary agents may submit.
Award: $3,000
Closing Date: Annually in Summer
Presented: PEN Literary Awards Ceremony, New York, NY, Annually in Spring

PEN/Voelcker Award
PEN American Center
588 Broadway, Suite 303, New York, NY 10012
Tel: 212-334-1660
E-mail: awards@pen.org
Web Site: pen.org/literary-awards
Key Personnel
Dir, Literary Progs: Paul Morris *Tel:* 212-334-1660 ext 4824 *E-mail:* paul@pen.org
Sr Mgr, Literary Awards: Nadxieli Nieto *Tel:* 212-334-1660 ext 4813 *E-mail:* nnieto@pen.org
Awarded to a poet whose distinguished & growing body of work to date represents a notable & accomplished presence in American literature. Only professional members of PEN may nominate a poet.
Award: $5,000

PEN Writers' Emergency Fund
PEN American Center
Affiliate of PEN International
588 Broadway, Suite 303, New York, NY 10012
Tel: 212-334-1660 *Fax:* 212-334-2181
Web Site: pen.org/press/grants-awards-database
Key Personnel
Exec Dir: Suzanne Nossel *Tel:* 212-334-1600 ext 4811 *E-mail:* snossel@pen.org
Pres: Andrew Solomon
Dir, Literary Progs: Paul Morris *Tel:* 212-334-1660 ext 4824 *E-mail:* paul@pen.org
Writer's Fund Coord: Arielle Anema *Tel:* 212-334-1660 ext 4813 *E-mail:* arielle@pen.org
Established: 1921
Grants for professional published writers & produced playwrights in financial emergencies due to personal circumstances. These are not literary awards. Application form available online.
Award: Up to $2,000
Closing Date: Annually, Jan 15, March 15, June 15, Sept 15

Maxwell E Perkins Award
The Center for Fiction
17 E 47 St, New York, NY 10017
Tel: 212-755-6710 *Fax:* 212-826-0831
E-mail: info@centerforfiction.org
Web Site: www.centerforfiction.org/awards/perkins
Key Personnel
Writing Progs Dir: Sara Batkie *E-mail:* sara@centerforfiction.org
Established: 2005
To honor the work of an editor, publisher, or agent who over the course of his or her career has discovered, nurtured & championed writers of fiction in the US.

Perugia Press Prize for a First or Second Book by a Woman
Perugia Press
PO Box 60364, Florence, MA 01062
Web Site: www.perugiapress.com; perugiapress.org
Key Personnel
Dir: Rebecca Olander
Established: 1997
For a first or second book of poetry by a woman.
Award: $1,000 & publication
Closing Date: Annually, Nov 15
Presented: Winner announced annually by April 15

Pfizer Award
History of Science Society
Affiliate of American Council of Learned Societies
440 Geddes Hall, Notre Dame, IN 46556
Tel: 574-631-1194
E-mail: info@hssonline.org
Web Site: www.hssonline.org
Key Personnel
Exec Dir: Robert Jay Malone
Established: 1958
Award given annually for an outstanding book in English, published during the preceding 3 years, on a topic related to the history of science.
Award: $2,500 & a medal
Closing Date: April 1
Presented: Oct or Nov

James D Phelan Literary Award
The San Francisco Foundation
One Embarcadero Ctr, Suite 1400, San Francisco, CA 94111
Tel: 415-733-8500
E-mail: info@sff.org; artsinfo@sff.org
Web Site: www.sff.org
Established: 1935
Award for the author of fiction (novel or short stories), nonfictional prose, poetry, spoken word. Awards are intended to encourage emerging artists not yet established in the genre who are California-born & currently residing in Alameda, Contra Costa, Marin, San Francisco or San Mateo County, for an unpublished ms-in-progress. By nomination only.
Award: $2,000
Presented: Annually in Autumn

Phi Beta Kappa Award in Science
The Phi Beta Kappa Society
1606 New Hampshire Ave NW, Washington, DC 20009
Tel: 202-265-3808 *Fax:* 202-986-1601
E-mail: awards@pbk.org
Web Site: www.pbk.org/bookawards
Key Personnel
Prog & Event Specialist: Laura Hartnett *Tel:* 202-745-3287 *E-mail:* lhartnett@pbk.org
Established: 1959
For an outstanding interpretation of science written by a scientist & published in the US during the previous year. Works in the physical & biological sciences & mathematics are eligible for the award. Highly technical works, monographs & reports on research are not eligible. Nominations must come from publisher & be submitted online.
Award: $10,000
Closing Date: Annually in Jan
Presented: Washington, DC, Annually in Dec

Robert J Pickering Award for Playwriting Excellence
Branch County Community Theatre
89 Division, Coldwater, MI 49036
Tel: 517-279-7963 *Fax:* 517-279-8095
E-mail: j7eden@aol.com
Web Site: www.branchcct.org
Key Personnel
Pres & Comm Chmn: J Richard Colbeck
Contact: Jennifer Colbeck
Established: 1984
Playwriting, must be unproduced full-length plays +/or musicals.
Award: $200 & production (1st prize), $50 (2nd prize), $25 (3rd prize)
Closing Date: Annually, Dec 31 (entries ongoing)
Presented: Tibbits Opera House, Coldwater, MI, Annually, Feb or March

Lorne Pierce Medal
Royal Society of Canada
Walter House, 282 Somerset W, Ottawa, ON K2P 0J6, Canada
Tel: 613-991-6990 (ext 106) *Fax:* 613-991-6996
E-mail: nominations@rsc-src.ca
Web Site: www.rsc-src.ca
Key Personnel
Mgr, Fellowship & Awards: Marie-Lyne Renaud *E-mail:* mlrenaud@rsc-src.ca
Established: 1926
Biennial award given in even-numbered years for an achievement of significance & conspicuous merit in imaginative or critical literature.
Award: Medal
Closing Date: March 1
Presented: RSC business meeting, Nov

The Pinch Writing Awards in Fiction
The Pinch Literary Journal
University of Memphis, English Dept, 435 Patterson Hall, Memphis, TN 38152
Tel: 901-678-2651 *Fax:* 901-678-2226
E-mail: editor@pinchjournal.com
Web Site: www.pinchjournal.com

Key Personnel
Ed-in-Chief: Courtney Miller Santo
Mng Ed: Severin Allgood
Asst Mng Ed: Kendra Vanderlip
Established: 1987
Awarded annually. Submit 1 previously unpublished story not to exceed 5,000 words accompanied by a $3 reading fee. No longer accepting paper submissions. Submit through online portal beginning August 15.
Award: $200 & publication in the following Spring issue of *The Pinch* (1st prize), 2nd & 3rd place winners may also be published. All entrants receive 2 free copies of the journal in which the work appears
Closing Date: March 15
Presented: Mid-Sept

The Pinch Writing Awards in Poetry
The Pinch Literary Journal
University of Memphis, English Dept, 435 Patterson Hall, Memphis, TN 38152
Tel: 901-678-2651 *Fax:* 901-678-2226
E-mail: editor@pinchjournal.com
Web Site: www.pinchjournal.com
Key Personnel
Ed-in-Chief: Courtney Miller Santo
Mng Ed: Severin Allgood
Asst Mng Ed: Kendra Vanderlip
Established: 1987
Annual award. Submit up to a max of 5 unpublished poems accompanied by a $3 reading fee. No longer accepting paper submissions. Submit through online portal beginning August 5.
Award: $200 & publication in the subsequent issue of *The Pinch* will be awarded to the 1st place winner, 2nd & 3rd place winners may also be published. All entrants receive 2 free copies of the journal in which the work appears
Closing Date: March 15
Presented: Mid-Sept

Pinnacle Book Achievement Awards
National Association of Book Entrepreneurs (NABE)
PO Box 606, Cottage Grove, OR 97424
Tel: 541-942-7455 *Fax:* 541-942-7455
E-mail: nabe@bookmarketingprofits.com
Web Site: www.bookmarketingprofits.com
Key Personnel
Exec Dir: Al Galasso
Annual awards to recognize the finest books published by NABE members based on book content, quality, writing style, presentation & cover design. One free entry form for one book for NABE members. Additional books or additional categories can be entered for $50 per book or category for members. All printed books written in English & published in the previous 2 years or in the year of the awards are eligible.
Award: Honor & mention in upcoming issue of *Book Dealers World*, Award Winners web page, press releases, book stickers & certificates for their web site
Closing Date: Sept 5 (1st round)

Playwright Discovery Award, see The Jean Kennedy Smith VSA Playwright Discovery Award

Playwrights Project
3675 Ruffin Rd, Suite 330, San Diego, CA 92123
Tel: 858-384-2970 *Fax:* 858-384-2974
E-mail: write@playwrightsproject.org
Web Site: www.playwrightsproject.org
Key Personnel
Exec Dir: Cecelia Kouma
Devt Mgr: Linnea Searle
Established: 1985
Annual playwriting contest for Californians under 19 years of age.
Award: Professional production (location to be announced), royalty
Closing Date: June 1
Presented: Jan-Feb following application

The Plimpton Prize
The Paris Review Foundation
544 W 27 St, New York, NY 10001
Tel: 212-343-1333 *Fax:* 212-343-1988
E-mail: queries@theparisreview.org
Web Site: www.theparisreview.org
Key Personnel
Mng Ed: Nicole Rudick
Sr Ed: Dierdre Foley-Mendelssohn
Awarded annually to the best work of fiction publishing in *The Paris Review* that year by an emerging or previously unpublished writer.
Award: $10,000
Presented: April

Plutarch Award
Biographers International Organization
PO Box 33020, Santa Fe, NM 87594
Tel: 505-983-4671
Web Site: biographersinternational.org
Key Personnel
Admin: Lori Izykowski *E-mail:* lori@biographersinternational.org
Established: 2013
Awarded by a committee of distinguished biographers for the best biographical work of the calendar year.
Closing Date: Dec 1
Presented: BIO Conference, Annually in May

PNWA Literary Contest
PNWA - a writer's resource
1420 NW Gilman Blvd, Suite 8, PMB 2717, Issaquah, WA 98027
Tel: 425-673-2665
E-mail: pnwa@pnwa.org
Web Site: www.pnwa.org
Key Personnel
Pres: Pam Binder
Multiple categories by genre.
Closing Date: Annually in Feb
Presented: Annual Summer Conference

Edgar Allan Poe Memorial
The Poetry Society of Virginia
900 Timber Creek Place, Virginia Beach, VA 23464
E-mail: poetryinva@aol.com
Web Site: poetrysocietyofvirginia.org
Key Personnel
Pres: Robert P Arthur *E-mail:* robert.peebles.arthur@gmail.com
Exec Dir: Guy Terrell *E-mail:* guy.terrell@earthlink.net
Adult Contest Chair: Steven Blythe
E-mail: stevenblythepoetry@gmail.com
All entries must be in English, original & unpublished. Submit 2 copies of each poem, each having the category name & number on top left of page. Only 1 poem per category; any form; any subject; 48 line limit. Entries will not be returned. Entry fee: $4 nonmembs.
Award: $100
Closing Date: Jan
Presented: Annual PSV Awards Ceremony, April

Poetry Book Contest
Accents Publishing
PO Box 910456, Lexington, KY 40591-0456
Web Site: www.accents-publishing.com/contest.html
Key Personnel
Founder & Sr Ed: Katerina Stoykova-Klemer
Established: 2010
Include submission form, ms, biography or CV & check or confirmation of payment. Ms should be 20-30 pages of poetry & single spaced. Entry fee $10.
Award: $250 cash, publication & 25 perfect-bound copies
Closing Date: Annually, Feb 1-June 30
Presented: Annually in July

Poetry Center Book Award
Poetry Center & American Poetry Archives at San Francisco State University
1600 Holloway Ave, San Francisco, CA 94132
Tel: 415-338-2227 *Fax:* 415-338-0966
E-mail: poetry@sfsu.edu
Web Site: www.sfsu.edu/~poetry
Key Personnel
Assoc Dir: Elise Ficarra
Established: 1980
For an outstanding book of poetry published in the year of the award. Volumes by individual authors only; anthologies & translations not accepted. Poets or publishers should send 1 copy of each book & a $10 fee. Include a cover letter noting author name, book title(s), name of person issuing check & check number.
Award: $500 & an invitation to read in the Poetry Center's series
Closing Date: Jan 31
Presented: Fall

Poetry Chapbook Contest
Palettes & Quills
1935 Penfield Rd, Penfield, NY 14526
Tel: 585-383-0812
E-mail: palettesnquills@gmail.com
Web Site: www.palettesnquills.com
Key Personnel
Owner, Ed & Publr: Donna M Marbach
E-mail: dmmarbach@gmail.com
Complete submission should include ms 14-48 pages, cover sheet, statement that all poems are your own original work, title page, acknowledgements page & complete Table of Contents. Submissions may be mailed or submitted online. $20 non-refundable entry fee per submission. Hard copy submissions are preferred, but e-mailed submissions will be accepted. Simultaneous submissions are accepted as are multiple submissions (but they must be submitted individually). See web site for complete submission guidelines.
Award: Cash ($200) plus 50 copies of the published book
Closing Date: Sept, even-numbered years
Presented: Winners announced online in Dec

The George Polk Awards
Long Island University
The Brooklyn Campus, One University Plaza, Brooklyn, NY 11201-5372
Tel: 718-488-1009
Web Site: www.liu.edu/polk
Key Personnel
Curator: John Darnton
Coord: Ralph Engelman *E-mail:* ralph.engelman@liu.edu
Established: 1949
For outstanding discernment & reporting of a news or feature story on the Internet, in newspapers, radio or television. Entries originating from publication offices, newsrooms or individual reporters are considered. In 2015, we established the George Polk Award for Documentary Film within the George Polk Awards. Only online submissions are accepted at liu.edu/polk. See web site for entry fee information & submission guidelines.
Award: Plaque & cash award
Closing Date: End of 1st week in Jan for the previous calendar year
Presented: Luncheon in New York, NY, Annually in Spring

Katherine Anne Porter Award
American Academy of Arts & Letters
633 W 155 St, New York, NY 10032
Tel: 212-368-5900 *Fax:* 212-491-4615
E-mail: academy@artsandletters.org
Web Site: www.artsandletters.org
Key Personnel
Exec Dir: Cody Upton
Established: 2001
Biennial award to honor a prose writer whose achievements & dedication to the literary profession have been demonstrated.
Award: $20,000

Katherine Anne Porter Prize for Fiction
Nimrod, The University of Tulsa
Subsidiary of The Nimrod Literary Awards
Nimrod International Journal, 800 S Tucker Dr, Tulsa, OK 74104
Tel: 918-631-3080 *Fax:* 918-631-3033
E-mail: nimrod@utulsa.edu
Web Site: www.utulsa.edu/nimrod
Key Personnel
Ed-in-Chief: Eilis O'Neal
Assoc Ed: Diane Burton; Cassidy McCants
Established: 1978
Annual prize. 7,500 words maximum. No previously published works or works accepted for publication elsewhere. Must have a US address by October to enter. Works must be in English or translated by original author. Author's name must not appear on ms. Include a cover sheet containing major title & subtitles, author's name, address, phone number & e-mail address. "Contest Entry" must be on envelope. Mss will not be returned. Nimrod retains the right to publish any submission. Works not accepted will be released; SASE for results only. $20 entry fee includes processing & 1-year subscription. Online submissions: nimrodjournal.submittable.com.
Award: $2,000 (1st prize), $1,000 (2nd prize); plus each published writer receives 2 copies of the journal; winners are flown to Tulsa for a conference & banquet
Closing Date: April 30
Presented: Tulsa, OK, Oct

Prairie Schooner Annual Strousse Award
Prairie Schooner
University of Nebraska, 123 Andrews Hall, 625 N 14 St, Lincoln, NE 68508
Mailing Address: PO Box 880334, Lincoln, NE 68588-0334
Tel: 402-472-0911 *Fax:* 402-472-9771
E-mail: prairieschooner@unl.edu
Web Site: prairieschooner.unl.edu
Key Personnel
Mng Ed: Ashley Strosnider
Ed: Kwame Dawes
Established: 1975
For best poetry published in the magazine each year.
Other Sponsor(s): Friends & famliy of Fora Strousse
Award: $500
Presented: Prairie Schooner, March

Prairie Schooner Bernice Slote Award
Prairie Schooner
University of Nebraska, 123 Andrews Hall, 625 N 14 St, Lincoln, NE 68508
Mailing Address: PO Box 880334, Lincoln, NE 68588-0334
Tel: 402-472-0911
E-mail: prairieschooner@unl.edu
Web Site: prairieschooner.unl.edu
Key Personnel
Mng Ed: Ashley Strosnider
Ed: Kwame Dawes
Established: 1985
Annual writing prize for best work by a beginning writer published in *Prairie Schooner* in the previous year.
Award: $500
Presented: Winners announced in Spring issue of *Prairie Schooner* magazine

Prairie Schooner Book Prize Contest in Fiction
Prairie Schooner
University of Nebraska, 123 Andrews Hall, 625 N 14 St, Lincoln, NE 68508
Mailing Address: PO Box 880334, Lincoln, NE 68588-0334
Tel: 402-472-0911 *Fax:* 402-472-9771
E-mail: psbookprize@unl.edu
Web Site: prairieschooner.unl.edu
Key Personnel
Mng Ed: Ashley Strosnider
Ed: Kwame Dawes
Welcomes mss from all living writers, including non-US citizens, writing in English. Mss previously published will not be considered. Writers may enter both fiction & poetry contests. For fiction mss, at least 150 pages in length is preferred. Entry fee: $25 per submission. Mss accepted by electronic or hard copy submission beginning January 15.
Award: $3,000 & publication through the University of Nebraska Press
Closing Date: March 15, annually

Prairie Schooner Book Prize Contest in Poetry
Prairie Schooner
University of Nebraska, 123 Andrews Hall, 625 N 14 St, Lincoln, NE 68508
Mailing Address: PO Box 880334, Lincoln, NE 68588-0334
Tel: 402-472-0911 *Fax:* 402-472-9771
E-mail: psbookprize@unl.edu
Web Site: prairieschooner.unl.edu
Key Personnel
Mng Ed: Ashley Strosnider
Ed: Kwame Dawes
Welcomes mss from all living writers, including non-US citizens, writing in English. Mss previously published will not be considered. Writers may enter both fiction & poetry contests. For poetry mss, at least 50 pages in length is preferred. Entry fee: $25 per submission. Mss accepted by electronic or hard copy submission beginning January 15.
Award: $3,000 & publication through the University of Nebraska Press
Closing Date: March 15, annually

Prairie Schooner Edward Stanley Award
Prairie Schooner
University of Nebraska, 123 Andrews Hall, 625 N 14 St, Lincoln, NE 68508
Mailing Address: PO Box 880334, Lincoln, NE 68588-0334
Tel: 402-472-0911 *Fax:* 402-472-9771
E-mail: prairieschooner@unl.edu
Web Site: prairieschooner.unl.edu
Key Personnel
Mng Ed: Ashley Strosnider
Ed: Kwame Dawes
Established: 1992
Annual writing prize for best poem or group of poems in the volume. Only contributors to the magazine are eligible.
Other Sponsor(s): Friends & family of Marion Edward Stanley (in memorium)
Award: $1,000
Presented: Winners announced in Spring issue of *Prairie Schooner* magazine

Prairie Schooner Glenna Luschei Award
Prairie Schooner
University of Nebraska, 123 Andrews Hall, 625 N 14 St, Lincoln, NE 68508
Mailing Address: PO Box 880334, Lincoln, NE 68588-0334
Tel: 402-472-0911 *Fax:* 402-472-9771
E-mail: prairieschooner@unl.edu
Web Site: prairieschooner.unl.edu
Key Personnel
Mng Ed: Ashley Strosnider
Ed: Kwame Dawes
Established: 1989
Annual writing prizes for best work published in the magazine. Only work published in *Prairie Schooner* in the previous year is considered.
Other Sponsor(s): Glenna Luschei
Award: $1,500 (first place), $250 (10 runners up)
Presented: Winners announced in Spring issue of *Prairie Schooner* magazine

Prairie Schooner Hugh J Luke Award
Prairie Schooner
University of Nebraska, 123 Andrews Hall, 625 N 14 St, Lincoln, NE 68508
Mailing Address: PO Box 880334, Lincoln, NE 68588-0334
Tel: 402-472-0911 *Fax:* 402-472-9771
E-mail: prairieschooner@unl.edu
Web Site: prairieschooner.unl.edu
Key Personnel
Mng Ed: Ashley Strosnider
Ed: Kwame Dawes
Established: 1989
Annual writing prize for best work published in the *Prairie Schooner* magazine in the previous year.
Other Sponsor(s): Friends & family of Hugh J Luke (in memoriam)
Award: $250
Presented: Winners announced in Spring issue of *Prairie Schooner* magazine

Prairie Schooner Jane Geske Award
Prairie Schooner
University of Nebraska, 123 Andrews Hall, 625 N 14 St, Lincoln, NE 68508
Mailing Address: PO Box 880334, Lincoln, NE 68588-0334
Tel: 402-472-0911 *Fax:* 402-472-9771
E-mail: prairieschooner@unl.edu
Web Site: prairieschooner.unl.edu
Key Personnel
Mng Ed: Ashley Strosnider
Ed: Kwame Dawes
Established: 2000
Annual award for work in any genre published in *Prairie Schooner* in the previous year.
Other Sponsor(s): Family of Jane Geske
Award: $250
Presented: Winners announced in Spring issue of *Prairie Schooner* magazine

Prairie Schooner Lawrence Foundation Award
Prairie Schooner
University of Nebraska, 123 Andrews Hall, 625 N 14 St, Lincoln, NE 68508
Mailing Address: PO Box 880334, Lincoln, NE 68588-0334
Tel: 402-472-0911 *Fax:* 402-472-9771
E-mail: prairieschooner@unl.edu
Web Site: prairieschooner.unl.edu
Key Personnel
Mng Ed: Ashley Strosnider
Ed: Kwame Dawes
Established: 1978
Annual writing prize for the best short story published in *Prairie Schooner* magazine; only work published in the previous year will be considered.
Other Sponsor(s): The Lawrence Foundation of New York City
Award: $1,000
Presented: Winners announced in Spring issue of *Prairie Schooner* magazine

Prairie Schooner Virginia Faulkner Award for Excellence in Writing
Prairie Schooner
University of Nebraska, 123 Andrews Hall, 625 N 14 St, Lincoln, NE 68508
Mailing Address: PO Box 880334, Lincoln, NE 68588-0334
Tel: 402-472-0911 *Fax:* 402-472-9771
E-mail: prairieschooner@unl.edu
Web Site: prairieschooner.unl.edu
Key Personnel
Mng Ed: Ashley Strosnider
Ed: Kwame Dawes
Established: 1987
Annual writing prize for work published in *Prairie Schooner* magazine. Only work published in the previous year is considered.
Other Sponsor(s): Friends & family of Virginia Faulkner
Award: $1,000
Presented: Winners announced in Spring issue of *Prairie Schooner* magazine

Premier Print Awards
Printing Industries of America
301 Brush Creek Rd, Warrendale, PA 15086-7529
Tel: 412-741-6860 *Toll Free Tel:* 800-910-4283 *Fax:* 412-741-2311
E-mail: printingind@comm.printing.org
Web Site: www.printing.org/premierprint
Key Personnel
Pres & CEO: Michael F Makin *Tel:* 412-259-1777 *E-mail:* mmakin@printing.org
VP, Educ & Mktg Strategies: Julie Schaffer
VP, Mktg: Lisa Rawa *E-mail:* lrawa@printing.org
Sponsorship Mgr: Mike Packard *E-mail:* mpackard@printing.org
Established: 1950
Recognizes the highest quality printed pieces in various categories from around the world. See web site for more information.
Other Sponsor(s): Domtar
Award: Certificates of Merit & the highest honor; the Benny Statue
Closing Date: Annually in May
Presented: Premier Print Awards Gala, Annually in Sept
Branch Office(s)
1001 "G" St NW, Suite 800, Washington, DC 20001 *Tel:* 202-627-6924

Derek Price/Rod Webster Prize Award
History of Science Society
Affiliate of American Council of Learned Societies
440 Geddes Hall, Notre Dame, IN 46556
Tel: 574-631-1194
E-mail: info@hssonline.org
Web Site: www.hssonline.org
Key Personnel
Exec Dir: Robert Jay Malone
Established: 1978
For article appearing in Isis during the preceding 3 years.
Award: $1,000
Closing Date: Annually, April 1
Presented: Annual meeting, Late Oct or early Nov

Michael L Printz Award
Young Adult Library Services Association (YALSA)
Division of The American Library Association (ALA)
50 E Huron St, Chicago, IL 60611
Tel: 312-280-4390 *Toll Free Tel:* 800-545-2433 *Fax:* 312-280-5276
E-mail: yalsa@ala.org
Web Site: www.ala.org/yalsa/printz
Key Personnel
Exec Dir: Beth Yoke *Tel:* 800-545-2433 ext 4391 *E-mail:* byoke@ala.org
Prog Offr, Events & Conferences: Nichole O'Connor *Tel:* 800-545-2433 ext 4387 *E-mail:* noconnor@ala.org
Communs Specialist: Anna Lam *Tel:* 800-545-2433 ext 5849 *E-mail:* alam@ala.org
Established: 1999
Honors excellence in literature written for young adults. May be fiction, nonfiction, poetry or an anthology & must have been published during the preceding year & designated as young adult book or ages 12-18.
Other Sponsor(s): Booklist
Closing Date: Annually, Dec 1
Presented: YALSA Printz Reception during ALA Annual Conference

PRISM international Literary Non-Fiction Contest
PRISM international
University of British Columbia, Buch E462, 1866 Main Mall, Vancouver, BC V6T 1Z1, Canada
Tel: 778-822-2514 *Fax:* 778-822-3616
E-mail: prismwritingcontest@gmail.com
Web Site: www.prismmagazine.ca
Key Personnel
Exec Ed: Jennifer Lori; Claire Matthews
Poetry Ed: Dominique Bernier Cormier
Prose Ed: Christopher Evans
Entry fee: $35 (includes a 1-year subscription); additional entries: $5.
Other Sponsor(s): University of British Columbia Bookstore
Award: $1,500 (grand prize), $600 (1st runner up), $400 (2nd runner up)
Closing Date: Annually in Nov (check web site for exact date)

Pritzker Military Museum & Library Literature Award for Lifetime Achievement in Military Writing
Pritzker Military Museum & Library
104 S Michigan Ave, Suite 400, Chicago, IL 60603
Tel: 312-374-9390 *Fax:* 312-374-9394
E-mail: info@pritzkermilitary.org
Web Site: www.pritzkermilitary.org
Established: 2007
To recognize a living author who has made a significant contribution to the understanding of American military history, including military affairs.
Other Sponsor(s): Pritzker Military Foundation
Award: $100,000, citation & gold medallion
Closing Date: Annually in March
Presented: The Pritzker Military Museum & Library Liberty Gala, Annually in Nov

Prix Alvine-Belisle
Association pour l'Avancement des Sciences et des Techniques de la Documentation
2065 rue Parthenais, Bureau 387, Montreal, QC H2K 3T1, Canada
Tel: 514-281-5012 *Fax:* 514-281-8219
E-mail: info@asted.org
Web Site: www.asted.org
Key Personnel
Exec Dir: Lionel Villalonga *E-mail:* lvillalonga@asted.org
To the best books for young people published in French in Canada during the previous year.
Closing Date: Annually, end of June
Presented: Mount Royal Centre, Montreal, QC, CN, Annually in Nov

Prix Emile-Nelligan
La Fondation Emile Nelligan
100, rue Sherbrooke, Suite 202, Montreal, QC H2X 1C3, Canada
Tel: 514-278-4657 *Toll Free Tel:* 888-849-8540 *Fax:* 514-278-1943
E-mail: info@fondation-nelligan.org
Web Site: www.fondation-nelligan.org
Key Personnel
CEO: Manon Gagnon
Pres: Michel Dallaire
VP: Marie-Andree Beaudet
Treas/Secy: Michel Gonneville
Established: 1979
Collection must be published between January 1-December 31 of the preceding year.
Award: $7,500 & a bronze medal
Presented: Annually in May

Prize for the Translation of Japanese Literature, see Japan-US Friendship Commission Translation Prize

Prometheus Awards
Libertarian Futurist Society
650 Castro St, Suite 120-433, Mountain View, CA 94041
Tel: 650-968-6319
Web Site: www.lfs.org
Key Personnel
Bd Pres: Bill Stoddard
VP: Charles Morrison
Established: 1979
Recognize works of fiction that champion individual freedom. The Best Novel category is limited to novels published during the previous year or so. The Hall of Fame category (for Best Classic Fiction) is broadly inclusive: Novels, novellas, short stories, poems, plays, films, TV shows (individual episodes or entire series), series & trilogies are all eligible for nomination. Works are eligible 5 years after first publication or broadcast. Best Novel & Best Classic Fiction categories are presented annually. Special Awards are occasional & focus on outstanding pro-freedom achievements that fall outside the realm of the Best Novel category.
Award: One ounce gold coin mounted on an engraved plaque for both the Prometheus Best Novel Award & the Hall of Fame Award
Closing Date: Annually, Feb 1 (Special Awards), March 1st (Best Novel), Oct 1 (Best Classic Fiction)
Presented: World Science Fiction Convention or NASFIC, Labor Day weekend

PROSE Awards
Association of American Publishers (AAP)
455 Massachusetts Ave NW, Suite 700, Washington, DC 20001-2777
Tel: 212-255-0200
Web Site: www.proseawards.com; publishers.org
Key Personnel
Proj Mgr, Prof & Scholarly Publg: Kate Kolendo *Tel:* 212-255-0326 *E-mail:* kkolendo@publishers.org
Established: 1976
The PROSE Awards honor the very best in professional & scholarly publishing. With awards in over 60 catergories, PROSE is unique in its breath & depth. AAP, PSP & AAUP members are eligible.
Award: Plaque & glass cubes
Closing Date: Annually, Nov 1
Presented: Annually in Feb

Public Scholar Program
National Endowment for the Humanities, Division of Research Programs
400 Seventh St SW, Washington, DC 20506
Tel: 202-606-8200
E-mail: publicscholar@neh.gov
Web Site: www.neh.gov/grants/research
Key Personnel
NEH Chmn: William Adams
Supports well-researched books in the humanities intended to reach a broad readership. Fellowship periods last from 6-12 months & must be full-time & continuous. Open to both individuals affiliated with scholarly institutions & independent scholars. All applications to this

program must be submitted via Grants.gov. Applications receive peer review & NEH Chairman makes all funding decisions.
Award: $4,200 monthly stipend (maximum $50,400 for 12-month period)
Closing Date: Feb 7, 2018 for projects beginning Sept 2018
Presented: Aug 2018

The Publishing Triangle Literary Awards
The Publishing Triangle
332 Bleecker St, Suite D-36, New York, NY 10014
E-mail: publishingtriangle@gmail.com
Web Site: www.publishingtriangle.org
Established: 1997
Contests for poetry, debut fiction, nonfiction & trans/gender-variant literature. Books must be published in the US or CN between January 1 & December 31. Entries are accepted only between October 1 & December 1. General instructions, specific guidelines, for each award & submission form are available on web site starting October 1. For hard copy, send your mailing address to publishingtriangle@gmail.com. Entry fee: $40.
Award: $1,000 for debut fiction, nonfiction, trans/gender-variant & poetry
Closing Date: Dec 1
Presented: Ceremony in New York City, Late April/early May

PubWest Book Design Awards
Publishers Association of the West Inc (PubWest)
17501 Hill Way, Lake Oswego, OR 97035
Tel: 503-901-9865
Web Site: pubwest.org
Key Personnel
Pres: Katie Burke
Exec Dir: Kent Watson
E-mail: executivedirector@pubwest.org
Established: 1977
Gold, silver & bronze awards are given in 24 categories. Adult trade book (illustrated), adult trade book (non-illustrated), children's/young adult (illustrated), children's/young adult (non-illustrated), artist's book, academic book/non-trade, guide/travel book, how-to book/crafts, cookbook, art/photography book, sports/fitness/recreation book, reference book, short stories/poetry/anthologies, gift/holiday/specialty book, historical/biographical book, graphic album-new material & previously published, jacket/cover special edition, ebook fixed layout, ebook standard, book apps, fixed layout children's ebook. Entry fee $75 (PubWest membs), $100 (non-membs).
Award: Medallions & glass award for best of show
Closing Date: April

Pulitzer Prizes
709 Journalism Bldg, Columbia University, 2950 Broadway, New York, NY 10027
Tel: 212-854-3841 *Fax:* 212-854-3342
E-mail: pulitzer@pulitzer.org
Web Site: www.pulitzer.org
Key Personnel
Admin: Dana Canedy
Established: 1917
Given to American authors for a distinguished book of fiction, performed play, history of the US, biography or autobiography, verse or general nonfiction, as well as journalism prizes for newspaper work in US dailies or weeklies. Books must be first published in the calendar year.
Award: Gold medal for public service journalism category; $10,000 & certificate in all other categories

Closing Date: June 15 for bks published Jan 1-June 14, Oct 15 for bks published June 15-Dec 31; literary prizes, Jan 15 (music), Feb 1 (journalism), Dec 31 (drama)
Presented: Annually in Spring

Pushcart Prize: Best of the Small Presses
Pushcart Press
PO Box 380, Wainscott, NY 11975-0380
SAN: 202-9871
Tel: 631-324-9300
Key Personnel
Pres: Bill Henderson
Established: 1976
Awarded for works previously published by a small press or literary journal.
Award: Copies of the book *The Pushcart Prize: Best of the Small Presses*
Closing Date: Annually, Dec 1
Presented: Annually in Spring

Ron Pynn Award
Textbook & Academic Authors Association (TAA)
PO Box 367, Fountain City, WI 54629
E-mail: info@taaonline.net
Web Site: www.taaonline.net/ron-pynn-award
Key Personnel
Exec Dir: Michael Spinella *Tel:* 973-943-0501 *E-mail:* michael.spinella@taaonline.net
Dir, Publg & Opers: Kim Pawlak *Tel:* 608-687-3106 *E-mail:* kim.pawlak@taaonline.net
Dir, Instl Memberships & Meetings: Maureen Foerster *Tel:* 608-687-3106 *E-mail:* maureen.foerster@taaonline.net
Membership Coord: Bekky Murphy *Tel:* 608-567-9060 *E-mail:* bekky.murphy@taaonline.net
Open to TAA members who have authored, co-authored, or co-edited at least 5 textbooks, at least 2 of which are authored or edited solely by the nominee. The nominee's textbooks must be published in more than 1 discipline or more than 1 area of discipline. Any TAA member may nominate him or herself or another TAA member. One recipient is selected by the TAA Council via ballot. Submit nominee & documentation via e-mail.
Closing Date: Jan 15
Presented: TAA Annual Conference, Annually in June

QWF Literary Awards
Quebec Writers' Federation (QWF)
1200 Atwater Ave, Rm 3, Westmount, QC H3Z 1X4, Canada
Tel: 514-933-0878
E-mail: info@qwf.org
Web Site: www.qwf.org
Key Personnel
Exec Dir: Lori Schubert *E-mail:* admin@qwf.org
Established: 1988
Literary awards for Quebec, English language authors. Request submission details.
Awards: A M Klein Prize for Poetry; Paragraphe Hugh MacLennan Prize for Fiction; Mavis Gallant Prize for Nonfiction; Concordia University First Book Prize; Cole Foundation Prize for Translation; QWF Prize for Children's & Young Adult Literature.
Award: $2,000 each
Closing Date: Annually, June 1
Presented: Annually in Nov

Miriam Rachimi Memorial
The Poetry Society of Virginia
900 Timber Creek Place, Virginia Beach, VA 23464
E-mail: poetryinva@aol.com
Web Site: poetrysocietyofvirginia.org
Key Personnel
Pres: Robert P Arthur *E-mail:* robert.peebles.arthur@gmail.com

Exec Dir: Guy Terrell *E-mail:* guy.terrell@earthlink.net
Adult Contest Chair: Steven Blythe
E-mail: stevenblythepoetry@gmail.com
All entries must be in English, original & unpublished. Submit 2 copies, each having the category name & number on top left of page. Subject: the spiritual impact of losing (or almost losing) a loved one; any form; 48 line limit. Entry fee: $4 nonmembs.
Other Sponsor(s): Ben Mahgerefteh; Michal Mahgerefteh
Award: $50 (1st prize), $30 (2nd prize), $20 (3rd prize)
Closing Date: Jan
Presented: Annual PSV Awards Ceremony, April

Radcliffe Fellowship
The Radcliffe Institute for Advanced Study
8 Garden St, Cambridge, MA 02138
Tel: 617-496-1324 (application off) *Fax:* 617-495-8136
Web Site: www.radcliffe.harvard.edu
Key Personnel
Admin, Fellowships: Alison Ney
Radcliffe Institute fellowships are designed to support scholars, scientists, artists & writers of exceptional promise & demonstrated accomplishments who wish to pursue work in academic & professional fields & in the creative arts.
Award: Stipend & office space
Closing Date: Sept 15 for Creative Arts & Humanities & Social Sciences; Oct 6 for Natural Sciences & Mathematics

Thomas Raddall Atlantic Fiction Award
Writers' Federation of Nova Scotia
1113 Marginal Rd, Halifax, NS B3H 4P7, Canada
Tel: 902-423-8116 *Fax:* 902-422-0881
E-mail: contact@writers.ns.ca
Web Site: writers.ns.ca
Key Personnel
Exec Dir: Jonathan Meakin *E-mail:* director@writers.ns.ca
Established: 1991
Awarded for a novel or book of short fiction, published by an Atlantic Canadian writer who has lived in one or a combination of these provinces for at least 2 concurrent years immediately prior to the submission deadline date. Non-refundable $20 administrative fee per entry.
Award: $25,000
Closing Date: Nov 1
Presented: Halifax, NS, CN, Annually in Spring

The Ragan Old North State Award Cup for Nonfiction
North Carolina Literary & Historical Association
Affiliate of Historical Book Club of North Carolina
4610 Mail Service Ctr, Raleigh, NC 27699-4610
Tel: 919-807-7290 *Fax:* 919-733-8807
Web Site: www.history.ncdcr.gov/affiliates/lit-hist/awards/awards.htm
Key Personnel
Awards Coord: Michael Hill *E-mail:* michael.hill@ncdcr.gov
Established: 2003
For published book of nonfiction, not technical or scientific, by a legal or actual resident of North Carolina for at least 3 years prior to end of contest.
Award: Cup
Closing Date: Annually, July 15
Presented: Raleigh, NC, Annually in Nov

Raiziss/de Palchi Fellowship
The Academy of American Poets Inc
75 Maiden Lane, Suite 901, New York, NY 10038

Tel: 212-274-0343 *Fax:* 212-274-9427
E-mail: academy@poets.org
Web Site: www.poets.org
Key Personnel
Exec Dir: Jennifer Benka
Prog Coord: Nikay Paredes *Tel:* 212-274-0343 ext 13 *E-mail:* nparedes@poets.org
Sr Content Ed: Alex Dimitrov *Tel:* 212-274-0343 ext 15 *E-mail:* adimitrov@poets.org
Established: 1995
Award to recognize outstanding translations into English of modern Italian poetry. Given to enable an American translator of 20th century Italian poetry to travel, study, or otherwise advance a significant work-in-progress. Book prize is awarded in even-numbered years & fellowship awarded in odd-numbered years.
Award: $10,000 book prize & a $25,000 fellowship
Closing Date: Sept 15-Feb 15
Presented: Sept

Sir Walter Raleigh Award for Fiction
Historical Book Club of North Carolina
Affiliate of North Carolina Literary & Historical Association
4610 Mail Service Ctr, Raleigh, NC 27699-4610
Tel: 919-807-7290 *Fax:* 919-733-8807
Key Personnel
Awards Coord: Michael Hill *E-mail:* michael.hill@ncdcr.gov
Award for the best book of fiction by an author who has been a legal or actual resident of North Carolina for at least 3 years prior to the end of the contest.

Ramirez Family Award
Formerly Most Significant Scholarly Book Award
Texas Institute of Letters (TIL)
c/o 7748 Hwy 290 W, Austin, TX 78736-3202
Tel: 512-683-5640
E-mail: president@texasinstituteofletters.org
Web Site: www.texasinstituteofletters.org
Key Personnel
Pres: Steve Davis
VP: Carmen Tafolla
Treas: W K Stratton
Secy: Sergio Troncoso
Recording Secy: Joe Holley
Annual award for the most useful & informative scholarly book contributing to general knowledge, by a Texan or about Texas. See web site for guidelines.
Award: $2,500
Closing Date: Annually in Jan
Presented: TIL Awards Banquet, Annually in Spring

RBC Bronwen Wallace Award for Emerging Writers
The Writers' Trust of Canada
460 Richmond St W, Suite 600, Toronto, ON M5V 1Y1, Canada
Tel: 416-504-8222 *Toll Free Tel:* 877-906-6548 *Fax:* 416-504-9090
E-mail: info@writerstrust.com
Web Site: www.writerstrust.com
Key Personnel
Exec Dir: Mary Osborne *Tel:* 416-504-8222 ext 244 *E-mail:* mosborne@writerstrust.com
Established: 1994
Awarded to a young author, 35 years of age & under, who has not been previously published in book form. The award alternates each year between short fiction & poetry.
Other Sponsor(s): RBC Foundation
Award: $10,000 (winner), $2,500 (finalists)
Presented: Annually in Spring

The Rea Award for the Short Story
Dungannon Foundation
53 W Church Hill Rd, Washington, CT 06794
Web Site: reaaward.org
Key Personnel
Pres: Elizabeth R Rea
Established: 1986
Established by Michael M Rea to honor a living US or Canadian writer who has made a significant contribution to the short story form. No submissions accepted. The recipient is nominated & selected by a jury.
Award: $30,000

Robert F Reed Technology Medal
Printing Industries of America
301 Brush Creek Rd, Warrendale, PA 15086-7529
Tel: 412-741-6860 *Toll Free Tel:* 800-910-4283 *Fax:* 412-741-2311
E-mail: printingind@comm.printing.org
Web Site: www.printing.org/reedaward
Key Personnel
Pres & CEO: Michael F Makin *Tel:* 412-259-1777 *E-mail:* mmakin@printing.org
Sr Mktg Mgr: Jenn Strang *Tel:* 412-259-1810 *E-mail:* jstrang@printing.org
VP, Educ & Mktg Strategies: Julie Schaffer
Mktg Mgr: Kayleigh Smith *E-mail:* ksmith@printing.org
Established: 1974
Acknowledges an individual who has made a major career contribution to the technical & scientific development of the graphic communications industry. See web site for more information.
Other Sponsor(s): Printing Industries of America's Ben Franklin Society
Award: Engraved medal
Closing Date: Oct 31
Presented: TAGA Annual Technical Conference, March
Branch Office(s)
1001 "G" St NW, Suite 800, Washington, DC 20001 *Tel:* 202-627-6924

Regina Medal Award
Catholic Library Association
8550 United Plaza Blvd, Suite 1001, Baton Rouge, LA 70809
Tel: 225-408-4417
E-mail: cla2@cathla.org
Web Site: cathla.org
Key Personnel
Pres: N Curtis LeMay
Established: 1959
For continued distinguished lifetime contribution to children's literature; no unsol mss.
Award: Sterling silver medal
Closing Date: None; in-house votes
Presented: CLA Annual Convention, April

Nathan Reingold Prize
History of Science Society
Affiliate of American Council of Learned Societies
440 Geddes Hall, Notre Dame, IN 46556
Tel: 574-631-1194
E-mail: info@hssonline.org
Web Site: www.hssonline.org
Key Personnel
Exec Dir: Robert Jay Malone
Established: 1955
For an original essay, not to exceed 8,000 words, in history of science & its cultural influences. Open to graduate students only. Must send in 3 copies of essay with a detachable author/title page.
Award: $500 (& up to $500 travel reimbursement)
Closing Date: Annually, June 1
Presented: Annually in Oct or Nov

Arthur Rense Prize
American Academy of Arts & Letters
633 W 155 St, New York, NY 10032
Tel: 212-368-5900 *Fax:* 212-491-4615
E-mail: academy@artsandletters.org
Web Site: www.artsandletters.org
Key Personnel
Exec Dir: Cody Upton
Established: 1998
Given triennially to an exceptional poet.
Award: $20,000

Residency
Millay Colony for the Arts
454 E Hill Rd, Austerlitz, NY 12017
Mailing Address: PO Box 3, Austerlitz, NY 12017-0003
Tel: 518-392-3103; 518-392-4144
E-mail: apply@millaycolony.org
Web Site: www.millaycolony.org
Key Personnel
Exec Dir: Caroline Crumpacker *E-mail:* director@millaycolony.org
Residency Dir: Calliope Nicholas *E-mail:* residency@millaycolony.org
Residencies for writers, composers & visual artists. Information & applications available by e-mail or on web site.
Award: One-month residencies offered including room, studio & meals; no cash award
Closing Date: Oct 1 & March 1

The Harold U Ribalow Prize
Hadassah Magazine
40 Wall St, 8th fl, New York, NY 10005-1387
Tel: 212-451-6286 *Fax:* 212-451-6257
E-mail: magtemp3@hadassah.org
Web Site: www.hadassah.org/magazine
Key Personnel
Exec Ed: Alan M Tigay
Established: 1983
Annual award for an outstanding English-language work of fiction on a Jewish theme by an author deserving of recognition.
Other Sponsor(s): Harold U Ribalow family
Award: $3,000
Closing Date: April of the year following publication
Presented: Autumn

Evelyn Richardson Nonfiction Award
Writers' Federation of Nova Scotia
1113 Marginal Rd, Halifax, NS B3H 4P7, Canada
Tel: 902-423-8116 *Fax:* 902-422-0881
E-mail: contact@writers.ns.ca
Web Site: writers.ns.ca
Key Personnel
Exec Dir: Jonathan Meakin *E-mail:* director@writers.ns.ca
Established: 1978
Presented to the best nonfiction book, published by a native or resident Nova Scotian who has lived in the province for at least 2 concurrent years immediately prior to the submission deadline date. Non-refundable $20 administrative fee per entry.
Award: $2,000
Closing Date: Nov 1
Presented: Halifax, NS, CN, Annually in Spring

The Ridenhour Book Prize
The Nation Institute
116 E 16 St, 8th fl, New York, NY 10003
Tel: 212-822-0250 *Fax:* 212-253-5356
E-mail: ridenhour@nationinstitute.org
Web Site: www.ridenhour.org
Key Personnel
Exec Dir & CEO: Taya Kitman *Tel:* 212-822-0252 *E-mail:* taya@nationinstitute.org
Established: 2003
Honors an outstanding work of social significance from the prior publishing year. The prize also recognizes investigative & reportorial distinction.
Other Sponsor(s): The Fertel Foundation
Award: $10,000 stipend

The Ridenhour Courage Prize
The Nation Institute
116 E 16 St, 8th fl, New York, NY 10003
Tel: 212-822-0250 *Fax:* 212-253-5356
E-mail: ridenhour@nationinstitute.org
Web Site: www.ridenhour.org
Key Personnel
Exec Dir & CEO: Taya Kitman *Tel:* 212-822-0252 *E-mail:* taya@nationinstitute.org
Established: 2003
Presented to an individual in recognition of his or her courageous & life-long defense of the public interest & passionate commitment to social justice.
Other Sponsor(s): The Fertel Foundation
Award: $10,000 stipend

The Ridenhour Prize for Truth-Telling
The Nation Institute
116 E 16 St, 8th fl, New York, NY 10003
Tel: 212-822-0250 *Fax:* 212-253-5356
E-mail: ridenhour@nationinstitute.org
Web Site: www.ridenhour.org
Key Personnel
Exec Dir & CEO: Taya Kitman *Tel:* 212-822-0252 *E-mail:* taya@nationinstitute.org
Established: 2003
Presented to a citizen, corporate or government whistleblower, investigative journalist, or organization for bringing a specific issue of social importance to the public's attention.
Other Sponsor(s): The Fertel Foundation
Award: $10,000 stipend

Gwen Pharis Ringwood Award for Drama
Writers' Guild of Alberta
11759 Groat Rd, Edmonton, AB T5M 3K6, Canada
Tel: 780-422-8174 *Toll Free Tel:* 800-665-5354 (AB only) *Fax:* 780-422-2663 (attn WGA)
E-mail: mail@writersguild.ca
Web Site: writersguild.ca
Key Personnel
Exec Dir: Carol Holmes *E-mail:* carol.holmes@writersguild.ca
Communs & Partnerships Coord: Ellen Kartz *E-mail:* ellen.kartz@writersguild.ca
Memb Servs Coord: Giorgia Severini
Progs Coord: Natalie Cook *E-mail:* natalie.cook@writersguild.ca; Julie Robinson *E-mail:* julie.robinson@writersguild.ca
Established: 1982
Alberta literary award, author must be resident of Alberta, CN.
Award: $1,500 plus leather-bound copy of book
Closing Date: Annually, Dec 31
Presented: Alberta Book Awards Gala
Branch Office(s)
505 21 Ave SW, Calgary, AB T2S 0G9, Canada, Prog Coord: Samantha Warwick *Tel:* 403-265-2226 *E-mail:* samantha.warwick@writersguild.ca

Jack D Rittenhouse Award
Publishers Association of the West Inc (PubWest)
17501 Hill Way, Lake Oswego, OR 97035
Tel: 503-901-9865
Web Site: pubwest.org
Key Personnel
Exec Dir: Kent Watson *E-mail:* executivedirector@pubwest.org
Honors individuals who have made outstanding contributions to the book community in the West.
Presented: PubWest Annual Conference

Riverby Awards
Formerly The John Burroughs List of Nature Books for Young Readers
John Burroughs Association Inc
261 Floyd Ackert Rd, New York, NY 12493
Mailing Address: PO Box 439, West Park, NY 12493
Tel: 212-769-5169 *Fax:* 212-313-7182
E-mail: info@johnburroughsassociation.org
Web Site: www.johnburroughsassociation.org
Key Personnel
Pres: Joan Burroughs *E-mail:* jjjburroughs@yahoo.com
To recognize writers, artists & publishers who produce outstanding nature literature for young readers that contains perceptive & artistic accounts of direct experiences in the world of nature.
Award: John Burroughs Certificate of Recognition to authors, illustrators & publishers of each selected book
Closing Date: Annually in Dec
Presented: Annual Meeting, Yale Club, New York, NY, 1st Monday in April

Roanoke-Chowan Award for Poetry
North Carolina Literary & Historical Association
Affiliate of Historical Book Club of North Carolina
4610 Mail Service Ctr, Raleigh, NC 27699-4610
Tel: 919-807-7290 *Fax:* 919-733-8807
Web Site: www.history.ncdcr.gov/affiliates/lit-hist/awards/awards.htm
Key Personnel
Awards Coord: Michael Hill *E-mail:* michael.hill@ncdcr.gov
Established: 1953
Award for the best published book of poetry by a legal or actual resident of North Carolina for at least 3 years prior to the end of the contest period.
Award: Cup
Closing Date: Annually, July 15
Presented: Raleigh, NC, Annually in Nov

Rocky Mountain Book Award
PO Box 42, Lethbridge, AB T1J 3Y3, Canada
Tel: 403-381-7164
E-mail: rockymountainbookaward@shaw.ca
Web Site: www.rmba.info
Key Personnel
Contact: Michelle Dimnik
Established: 2001
Alberta children's choice book award, grades 4-7.
Closing Date: Jan 15
Presented: Winner announced electronically on April 22

Rogers Writers' Trust Fiction Prize
The Writers' Trust of Canada
460 Richmond St W, Suite 600, Toronto, ON M5V 1Y1, Canada
Tel: 416-504-8222 *Toll Free Tel:* 877-906-6548 *Fax:* 416-504-9090
E-mail: info@writerstrust.com
Web Site: www.writerstrust.com
Key Personnel
Exec Dir: Mary Osborne *Tel:* 416-504-8222 ext 244 *E-mail:* mosborne@writerstrust.com
Established: 1997
Awarded to the year's best novel or collection of short stories.
Other Sponsor(s): Rogers Communications
Award: $25,000 (winner), $2,500 (finalists)
Presented: The Writers' Trust Awards, Toronto, ON, CN, Annually in Nov

Sami Rohr Prize for Jewish Literature
Jewish Book Council
520 Eighth Ave, 4th fl, New York, NY 10018
Tel: 212-201-2920 *Fax:* 212-532-4952
E-mail: jbc@jewishbooks.org
Web Site: www.jewishbookcouncil.org
Key Personnel
Exec Dir: Naomi Firestone-Teeter
Prog Mgr, JBC Network & National Jewish Book Awards: Evie Saphire-Bernstein *E-mail:* evie@jewishbooks.org
Established: 2006
Annual award which recognizes the unique role of contemporary writers in the transmission & examination of Jewish values & is intended to encourage & promote outstanding writing of Jewish interest. Rewards an emerging writer whose work has demonstrated a fresh vision & evidence of future potential. Recipients must have written a book of exceptional literary merit that stimulates an interest in themes of Jewish concern. Fiction & nonfiction books will be considered in alternate years.
Award: $100,000
Presented: Center for Jewish History, March

Romance Writers of America Awards
Romance Writers of America®
14615 Benfer Rd, Houston, TX 77069
Tel: 832-717-5200 *Fax:* 832-717-5201
E-mail: info@rwa.org
Web Site: www.rwa.org
Key Personnel
Exec Dir: Allison Kelley *Tel:* 832-717-5200 ext 124 *E-mail:* allison.kelley@rwa.org
Deputy Exec Dir: Carol Ritter *Tel:* 832-717-5200 ext 127 *E-mail:* carol.ritter@rwa.org
Established: 1981
Golden Heart: for unpublished romance fiction mss; RITA Award: best romance fiction mss published; for publication dated in 2017.
Award: Heart necklace for Golden Heart, statue for RITA Award
Closing Date: Nov
Presented: Annual National Conference, Denver, CO, July

Rosenthal Family Foundation Awards
American Academy of Arts & Letters
633 W 155 St, New York, NY 10032
Tel: 212-368-5900 *Fax:* 212-491-4615
E-mail: academy@artsandletters.org
Web Site: www.artsandletters.org
Key Personnel
Exec Dir: Cody Upton
Award for a work of fiction published during the preceding year that is a considerable literary achievement. Second award is given for a young painter of distinction.
Other Sponsor(s): The Rosenthal Foundation
Award: $10,000 each

Margaret W Rossiter History of Women in Science Prize
History of Science Society
Affiliate of American Council of Learned Societies
440 Geddes Hall, Notre Dame, IN 46556
Tel: 574-631-1194
E-mail: info@hssonline.org
Web Site: www.hssonline.org
Key Personnel
Exec Dir: Robert Jay Malone
Recognition of an outstanding book (or, in even-numbered years, article) on the history of women in science. Books & articles published in the preceding 4 years are eligible.
Award: $1,000
Closing Date: April 1

Rotary Club of Charlottetown Royalty Creative Writing Awards for Young People
Prince Edward Island Writers' Guild
81 Prince St, Charlottetown, PE C1A 4R3, Canada
E-mail: peiliteraryawards@gmail.com
Web Site: www.peiwritersguild.com
Elementary, junior & high school students may write on the topic of their choice & submit in 1 of 4 categories: Early Elementary (grades 1-

3), Late Elementary (grades 4-6), Junior High (grades 7-9) & Senior High (grades 10-12). A maximum of 5 pages of poetry or 10 page short story will constitute an entry. No entry fee. Prince Edward Island residents only. See web site for complete entry requirements.
Award: Cash prizes for 1st, 2nd & 3rd place
Closing Date: Jan 31
Presented: Cox & Palmer Island Literary Awards Gala, Annually in Spring

Lois Roth Award
Modern Language Association of America (MLA)
85 Broad St, Suite 500, New York, NY 10004-2434
SAN: 202-6422
Tel: 646-576-5141; 646-576-5000 *Fax:* 646-458-0030
E-mail: awards@mla.org
Web Site: www.mla.org
Key Personnel
Coord, Book Prizes: Annie M Reiser
E-mail: areiser@mla.org
Established: 1999
Committee solicits submissions of outstanding translations into English of a book-length literary work. Translations published in 2017 are eligible. For consideration, submit 6 copies & 12-15 pages of original text in its original language taken from the beginning, middle & end of the work & a letter identifying the translator & the date of publication. Translators need not be members of the association.
Award: Cash award & certificate
Closing Date: April 1, 2018
Presented: MLA Convention, Chicago, IL, Jan 2019

Lexi Rudnitsky First Book Prize in Poetry
Persea Books
277 Broadway, Suite 708, New York, NY 10007
SAN: 212-8233
Tel: 212-260-9256 *Fax:* 212-267-3165
E-mail: info@perseabooks.com
Web Site: www.perseabooks.com
Key Personnel
Pres & Publr: Michael Braziller
VP & Edit Dir: Karen Braziller
Established: 2006
First book by an American woman poet.
Award: $1,000, publication & expenses paid residency at the Civitella Ranieri Foundation in Italy
Closing Date: Oct 31

William B Ruggles Journalism Scholarship
National Institute for Labor Relations Research
5211 Port Royal Rd, Suite 510, Springfield, VA 22151
Tel: 703-321-9606 *Fax:* 703-321-7143
Web Site: www.nilrr.org
Key Personnel
Scholarship Admin: Cathy Jones *E-mail:* clj@nrtw.org
Established: 1974
Scholarship grant for students majoring in journalism or related majors. Based on scholastic ability demonstrating an understanding of the economic, political & social implications of compulsory unionism.
Award: $2,000
Closing Date: Annually, Dec 31 (postmark or electronic submission)
Presented: Annually in April-May

Stephan Russo Book Prize, see The Goddard Riverside Stephan Russo Book Prize

The Cornelius Ryan Award
Overseas Press Club of America (OPC)
40 W 45 St, New York, NY 10036
Tel: 212-626-9220 *Fax:* 212-626-9210
E-mail: info@opcofamerica.org
Web Site: www.opcofamerica.org
Key Personnel
Exec Dir: Patricia Kranz
Awarded for best nonfiction book on international affairs.
Award: Certificate & cash award
Closing Date: Annually, last week of Jan
Presented: New York City, Annually in late April

Saint Louis Literary Award
Saint Louis University Library Associates
Pius XII Memorial Library, 3650 Lindell Blvd, St Louis, MO 63108
Tel: 314-977-3100; 314-977-3087 *Fax:* 314-977-3108
E-mail: slula@slu.edu
Web Site: lib.slu.edu/about/associates/literary-award
Key Personnel
Pres: Lana Pepper
VP: Ted Ibur
Off Admin: Donna Neeley
Established: 1967
For body of author's work. No applications; awardee chosen by committee.
Award: Honorarium, Citation
Presented: Award Ceremony, Sheldon Concert Hall, Autumn

San Francisco Writing Contest (SFWC)
San Francisco Writers Conference
1029 Jones St, San Francisco, CA 94109
Tel: 415-673-0939
E-mail: sfwriterscon@aol.com
Web Site: www.sfwriters.org
Key Personnel
Contest Dir: Laurie McLean
All entries must be original, unpublished work not submitted to this contest in previous years & be in English. Complete an official entry form & attach to the entry. Entry fee: $40. Four categories: adult fiction, nonfiction/memoir & children's/young adult. Register online at www.sfwriters.org.
Award: $500 (grand prize), $100 (1st prize in each category)
Closing Date: Dec
Presented: Annual Conference, InterContinental Mark Hopkins Hotel, San Francisco, CA

The Carl Sandburg Literary Awards
The Chicago Public Library Foundation & Chicago Public Library
20 N Michigan Ave, Suite 520, Chicago, IL 60602
Tel: 312-201-9830 *Fax:* 312-201-9833
Web Site: www.cplfoundation.org
Key Personnel
CEO & Pres: Rhona Frazin *E-mail:* rfrazin@cplfoundation.org
Established: 2000
Honors a significant work or a body of work that has enhanced the public's awareness of the written word & reflects the library's commitment to the freedom of all people reading, discovery & creativity.
Award: $10,000
Presented: The Forum, University of Illinois at Chicago, Annually in Oct

Ada Sanderson Memorial
The Poetry Society of Virginia
900 Timber Creek Place, Virginia Beach, VA 23464
E-mail: poetryinva@aol.com
Web Site: poetrysocietyofvirginia.org
Key Personnel
Pres: Robert P Arthur *E-mail:* robert.peebles.arthur@gmail.com
Exec Dir: Guy Terrell *E-mail:* guy.terrell@earthlink.net
Adult Contest Chair: Steven Blythe
E-mail: stevenblythepoetry@gmail.com
All entries must be in English, orginal & unpublished. Submit 2 copies, each having the category name & number on top left of page. Only one poem per category; entries will not be returned. Subject: nature; any form; 48 line limit. Entry fee: $4 nonmembs.
Award: $100
Closing Date: Jan
Presented: Annual PSV Awards Ceremony, April

Mari Sandoz Award
Nebraska Library Association
PO Box 21756, Lincoln, NE 68542-1756
E-mail: nebraskalibraries@gmail.com
Web Site: www.nebraskalibraries.org
Key Personnel
Exec Dir: Nicole Zink
E-mail: nlaexecutivedirector@gmail.com
Established: 1971
Given annually to a distinguished Nebraska author.
Award: Plaque
Closing Date: May 30
Presented: NLA/NSLA Fall Convention, Late Oct

Ivan Sandrof Lifetime Achievement Award
National Book Critics Circle
160 Varick St, 11th fl, New York, NY 10013
E-mail: info@bookcritics.org
Web Site: bookcritics.org
Key Personnel
Contact: Steven Kellman
Awarded annually to a person or institution who has, over time, made significant contributions to book culture. Nominations from members only.

Dorothy Sargent Rosenberg Poetry Prizes, see Ruth Lilly & Dorothy Sargent Rosenberg Poetry Fellowships

William Saroyan International Prize for Writing
William Saroyan Foundation
Admin, Saroyan Prize Committee, Stanford University Libraries, 557 Escondido Mall, Stanford, CA 94305-6004
Tel: 650-736-9538
Web Site: library.stanford.edu/saroyan
Key Personnel
Contact: Sonia Lee *E-mail:* sonialee@stanford.edu
Established: 2002
Biennial competition for newly published books. Entry form & 5 copies of publication required. Entry fee: $50.
Other Sponsor(s): The Stanford University Libraries
Award: $5,000 each in fiction & nonfiction
Closing Date: Jan 31, 2018

May Sarton Award
New England Poetry Club
46 Wallace St, Somerville, MA 02144
Tel: 617-744-6034
E-mail: info@nepoetryclub.org
Web Site: www.nepoetryclub.org
Key Personnel
VP: Hillary Sallick
Honorary awards for work that inspires other poets. Chosen by board of directors.
Award: $250 & publication of poem on NEPC web site
Closing Date: Annually, May 31
Presented: Announced online Aug/Sept

Saturnalia Books Poetry Prize
Saturnalia Books
105 Woodside Rd, Ardmore, PA 19003
Tel: 267-278-9541
E-mail: info@saturnaliabooks.com
Web Site: www.saturnaliabooks.org
Key Personnel
Publr: Henry Israeli
Established: 2003
Recognizes a poetry ms of high merit.
Award: $2,000 & publication
Closing Date: Annually, April 1

SATW Foundation Lowell Thomas Travel Journalism Competition
Society of American Travel Writers Foundation
306 Summer Hill Dr, Fredericksburg, TX 78654
Tel: 281-217-2872
E-mail: awards@satwf.com
Web Site: www.satwfoundation.org
Key Personnel
Pres: David G Molyneaux
Established: 1985
Premier awards for the best work in travel journalism. Competition is open to all North American journalists & is judged by leading schools of journalism. There are 20-plus categories, including individual & publication awards. Among them: Grand Award for Travel Journalist of the Year for a portfolio of work, Best Newspaper Travel Coverage, Best Travel Magazine, Best Travel Coverage in Other Magazines, Best Guidebook, Best Travel Book, Best Online Travel Journalism Site & categories for writing, photography, audio broadcast, video broadcast, multimedia work & apps. For entry details & forms, see web site. New materials usually updated early February annually.
Award: Nearly $20,000 total in prize money: $1,500 (top prize), $500 (1st place)
Closing Date: April 1 (subject to change)
Presented: Location varies

Aldo & Jeanne Scaglione Prize for a Translation of a Literary Work
Modern Language Association of America (MLA)
85 Broad St, Suite 500, New York, NY 10004-2434
SAN: 202-6422
Tel: 646-576-5141; 646-576-5000 *Fax:* 646-458-0030
E-mail: awards@mla.org
Web Site: www.mla.org
Key Personnel
Coord, Book Prizes: Annie M Reiser
E-mail: areiser@mla.org
Awarded annually for an outstanding translation into English of a book-length literary work; books must have been published in 2017. Translators need not be members of the MLA. For consideration, submit 6 copies & 12-15 pages of the text in its original language taken from the beginning, middle & end of the work.
Award: Cash award & certificate
Closing Date: April 1, 2018
Presented: MLA Convention, Chicago, IL, Jan 2019

Aldo & Jeanne Scaglione Prize for a Translation of a Scholarly Study of Literature
Modern Language Association of America (MLA)
85 Broad St, Suite 500, New York, NY 10004-2434
SAN: 202-6422
Tel: 646-576-5141; 646-576-5000 *Fax:* 646-458-0030
E-mail: awards@mla.org
Web Site: www.mla.org
Key Personnel
Coord, Book Prizes: Annie M Reiser
E-mail: areiser@mla.org
Established: 1993
Awarded biennially for an outstanding translation into English of a book-length work of literary history, literary criticism, philology or literary theory published in 2017 or 2018. For consideration, submit 4 copies.
Award: Cash award & certificate
Closing Date: May 1, 2019
Presented: MLA Convention, Seattle, WA, Jan 2020

Aldo & Jeanne Scaglione Prize for Comparative Literary Studies
Modern Language Association of America (MLA)
85 Broad St, Suite 500, New York, NY 10004-2434
SAN: 202-6422
Tel: 646-576-5141; 646-576-5000 *Fax:* 646-458-0030
E-mail: awards@mla.org
Web Site: www.mla.org
Key Personnel
Coord, Book Prizes: Annie M Reiser
E-mail: areiser@mla.org
Established: 1992
Prize awarded annually for an outstanding scholarly work by a current member of the MLA in the field of comparative literary studies involving at least 2 literatures, published in 2017. For consideration, submit 4 copies.
Award: Cash award & certificate
Closing Date: May 1, 2018
Presented: MLA Convention, Chicago, IL, Jan 2019

Aldo & Jeanne Scaglione Prize for French & Francophone Studies
Modern Language Association of America (MLA)
85 Broad St, Suite 500, New York, NY 10004-2434
SAN: 202-6422
Tel: 646-576-5141; 646-576-5000 *Fax:* 646-458-0030
E-mail: awards@mla.org
Web Site: www.mla.org
Key Personnel
Coord, Book Prizes: Annie M Reiser
E-mail: areiser@mla.org
Established: 1992
Awarded annually for an outstanding scholarly work by a current member of the MLA in the field of French or Francophone linguistic or literary studies published in 2017. Books that are primarily translations will not be considered. For consideration, submit 4 copies.
Award: Cash award & certificate
Closing Date: May 1, 2018
Presented: MLA Convention, Chicago, IL, Jan 2019

Aldo & Jeanne Scaglione Prize for Italian Studies
Modern Language Association of America (MLA)
85 Broad St, Suite 500, New York, NY 10004-2434
SAN: 202-6422
Tel: 646-576-5141; 646-576-5000 *Fax:* 646-458-0030
E-mail: awards@mla.org
Web Site: www.mla.org
Key Personnel
Coord, Book Prizes: Annie M Reiser
E-mail: areiser@mla.org
Established: 2000
Awarded each odd-numbered year to the author of an outstanding scholarly book on any phase of Italian literature or culture or comparative literature involving Italian by a current MLA member for books published in 2018. For consideration, submit 4 copies.
Award: Cash award & certificate
Closing Date: May 1, 2019
Presented: MLA Convention, Seattle, WA, Jan 2020

Aldo & Jeanne Scaglione Prize for Studies in Germanic Languages & Literatures
Modern Language Association of America (MLA)
85 Broad St, Suite 500, New York, NY 10004-2434
SAN: 202-6422
Tel: 646-576-5141; 646-576-5000 *Fax:* 646-458-0030
E-mail: awards@mla.org
Web Site: www.mla.org
Key Personnel
Coord, Book Prizes: Annie M Reiser
E-mail: areiser@mla.org
Established: 1992
Awarded biennially in even-numbered years to a current MLA member for an outstanding scholarly work on the linguistics or literatures of the Germanic languages including Danish, Dutch, German, Icelandic, Norwegian, Swedish & Yiddish & published 2016 or 2017. For consideration, submit 4 copies, a letter identifying the work & confirming the author's membership.
Award: Cash award & certificate
Closing Date: May 1, 2018
Presented: MLA Convention, Chicago, IL, Jan 2019

Aldo & Jeanne Scaglione Prize for Studies in Slavic Languages & Literatures
Modern Language Association of America (MLA)
85 Broad St, Suite 500, New York, NY 10004-2434
SAN: 202-6422
Tel: 646-576-5141; 646-576-5000 *Fax:* 646-458-0030
E-mail: awards@mla.org
Web Site: www.mla.org
Key Personnel
Coord, Book Prizes: Annie M Reiser
E-mail: areiser@mla.org
Established: 1993
Awarded biennially in odd-numbered years for an outstanding scholarly work on the linguistics or literatures of the Slavic languages published in 2017 or 2018. Works of literary history, literary criticism, philology & literary theory are eligible. Books that are primarily translations will not be considered. Authors need not be members of the MLA. For consideration, submit 4 copies.
Award: Cash award & certificate
Closing Date: May 1, 2019
Presented: MLA Convention, Seattle, WA, Jan 2020

Aldo & Jeanne Scaglione Publication Award for a Manuscript in Italian Literary Studies
Modern Language Association of America (MLA)
85 Broad St, Suite 500, New York, NY 10004-2434
SAN: 202-6422
Tel: 646-576-5141; 646-576-5000 *Fax:* 646-458-0030
E-mail: awards@mla.org
Web Site: www.mla.org
Key Personnel
Coord, Book Prizes: Annie M Reiser
E-mail: areiser@mla.org
Established: 1998
Awarded annually to the author of an outstanding ms dealing with any aspect of the languages & literatures of Italy, including medieval Latin & comparative studies or intellectual history of the work's main point is related to the humanities. Ms must be under consideration or accepted for publication by a not-for-profit member of the AAUP before the award deadline;

authors must be current members of the MLA residing in the US or CN. For consideration, submit 4 copies, plus contact & biographical information.
Award: Cash award & certificate
Closing Date: June 1, 2018
Presented: MLA Convention, Chicago, IL, Jan 2019

William Sanders Scarborough Prize
Modern Language Association of America (MLA)
85 Broad St, Suite 500, New York, NY 10004-2434
SAN: 202-6422
Tel: 646-576-5141; 646-576-5000 *Fax:* 646-458-0030
E-mail: awards@mla.org
Web Site: www.mla.org
Key Personnel
Coord, Book Prizes: Annie M Reiser
E-mail: areiser@mla.org
Established: 2001
Annual prize for an outstanding scholarly study of Black American literature or culture published the previous calendar year. Author need not be a member of the MLA. For consideration, submit 4 copies.
Award: Cash award & certificate
Closing Date: May 1, 2018
Presented: MLA Convention, Chicago, IL, Jan 2019

SCBWI Work-In-Progress Grants
Society of Children's Book Writers and Illustrators (SCBWI)
4727 Wilshire Blvd, Suite 301, Los Angeles, CA 90010
Tel: 323-782-1010; 310-403-0675 (cell) *Fax:* 323-782-1892
E-mail: grants@scbwi.org; scbwi@scbwi.org
Web Site: www.scbwi.org
Key Personnel
Pres: Stephen Mooser *E-mail:* stephenmooser@scbwi.org
Exec Dir: Lin Oliver *E-mail:* linoliver@scbwi.org
Established: 1978
The General Work-In-Progress Grant, the Work-In-Progress Grant for Nonfiction Research, the Work-In-Progress Grant for a Contemporary Novel for Young People & the Grant for a Work by an Author Who Has Never Been Published have been established to assist children's book writers in the completion of a specific project. Must be SCBWI member to qualify.
Award: Winning works shown to editors & agents
Closing Date: Annually in March
Presented: Annually in Aug

William D Schaeffer Environmental Award
Printing Industries of America
301 Brush Creek Rd, Warrendale, PA 15086-7529
Tel: 412-741-6860 *Toll Free Tel:* 800-910-4283 *Fax:* 412-741-2311
E-mail: printingind@comm.printing.org
Web Site: www.printing.org/schaefferaward
Key Personnel
Pres & CEO: Michael F Makin *Tel:* 412-259-1777 *E-mail:* mmakin@printing.org
VP, Educ & Mktg Strategies: Julie Schaffer
Sr Mktg Mgr: Jenn Strang *Tel:* 412-259-1810 *E-mail:* jstrang@printing.org
Mktg Mgr: Kayleigh Smith *E-mail:* ksmith@printing.org
Established: 1990
Honors significant contributions to environmental awareness by an individual in the printing industry. See web site for more information.
Award: Engraved plaque
Closing Date: Jan 31
Presented: Printing Industries of America Spring Administrative Meeting, April-June
Branch Office(s)
1001 "G" St NW, Suite 800, Washington, DC 20001 *Tel:* 202-627-6924

Bernadotte E Schmitt Grants
American Historical Association (AHA)
400 "A" St SE, Washington, DC 20003
Tel: 202-544-2422 *Fax:* 202-544-8307
E-mail: awards@historians.org
Web Site: www.historians.org
Awarded to support research in the history of Europe, Africa & Asia. Only members of the Association are eligible. The grants are intended to further research in progress & may be used for travel to a library or archive, for microfilms, photographs, or photocopying. Preference will be given to those with specific research needs, such as the completion of a project or completion of a discrete segment thereof. Preference will be given to advanced doctoral students, non-tenured faculty & unaffiliated scholars. All updated info on web site. Winners notified by e-mail mid-May.
Award: Individual grants will not exceed $1,500
Closing Date: Annually, Feb 15
Presented: June

Ruth & Sylvia Schwartz Children's Book Awards
Ruth Schwartz Foundation
c/o Ontario Arts Council, 121 Bloor St E, 7th fl, Toronto, ON M4W 3M5, Canada
Tel: 416-961-1660 *Toll Free Tel:* 800-387-0058 (ON) *Fax:* 416-961-7796 (Ontario Arts Council); 416-969-7450 (Ontario Arts Foundation)
E-mail: info@arts.on.ca; foundation@arts.on.ca
Web Site: www.arts.on.ca; ontarioartsfoundation.on.ca/pages/ruth-sylvia-schwartz-awards
Key Personnel
Exec Dir, Ontario Arts Foundation: Alan F Walker *Tel:* 416-969-7413 *E-mail:* awalker@arts.on.ca
Dir of Admin, Ontario Arts Foundation: Ann Boyd *Tel:* 416-969-7411 *E-mail:* aboyd@arts.on.ca
Assoc Awards Offr, Ontario Arts Council: Carolyn Gloude *Tel:* 416-969-7423 *E-mail:* cgloude@arts.on.ca
Established: 1976
Annual awards to recognize artistic excellence in writing & illustration in Canadian children's literature.
Other Sponsor(s): Ontario Arts Council; Ontario Arts Foundation
Award: $6,000 each for picture book & young adult/middle reader
Presented: An Ontario, CN public school, May

Science in Society Journalism Awards
National Association of Science Writers (NASW)
PO Box 7905, Berkeley, CA 94707
Tel: 510-647-9500
Web Site: www.nasw.org
Key Personnel
Exec Dir: Tinsley Davis *E-mail:* director@nasw.org
Established: 1972
Awarded annually to provide recognition for investigative reporting about the sciences & their impact on society, for material published or broadcast between the period of January 1-December 31. Publishers & broadcasters will also receive certificates of recognition.
Award: $2,500, Certificate of Recognition in each category, travel to awards presentation for 1 author or representative
Closing Date: Feb 1 (postmark)
Presented: Annual Meeting, Oct

The Robert S Sergeant Memorial
The Poetry Society of Virginia
900 Timber Creek Place, Virginia Beach, VA 23464
E-mail: poetryinva@aol.com
Web Site: poetrysocietyofvirginia.org
Key Personnel
Pres: Robert P Arthur *E-mail:* robert.peebles.arthur@gmail.com
Exec Dir: Guy Terrell *E-mail:* guy.terrell@earthlink.net
Adult Contest Chair: Steven Blythe *E-mail:* stevenblythepoetry@gmail.com
All entries must be in English, original & unpublished. Submit 2 copies, each having the category name & number on top left of page. Subject: birds; any form; 48 line limit. Entry fee: $4 nonmembs.
Award: $50
Closing Date: Jan
Presented: Annual PSV Awards Ceremony, April

SFWA Nebula Awards
Science Fiction & Fantasy Writers of America Inc (SFWA)
PO Box 3238, Enfield, CT 06083-3238
E-mail: office@sfwa.org
Web Site: www.sfwa.org
Key Personnel
Pres: Cat Rambo *E-mail:* cat.rambo@sfwa.org
VP: Erin M Hartshorn *E-mail:* erin.hortshorn@sfwa.org
Treas & CFO: Bud Sparhawk *E-mail:* bud.sparhawk@sfwa.org
Secy: Susan Forest *E-mail:* susan.forest@sfwa.org
Nebula Awards Comm: Dawn Bonanno *E-mail:* nac@sfwa.org
Established: 1965
Winners are selected by the members of the SFWA in the categories of novel, novella, novelette & short story. Andre Norton award for Outstanding Young Adult Fantasy or Science Fiction first presented in 2006. Also Grand Master for lifetime achievement in science fiction & fantasy, not necessarily awarded annually. Ray Bradbury Award for outstanding dramatic presentation first presented in April 2009.
Award: Lucite trophy for Grand Master & Norton; bronze sculpture for Ray Bradbury Award

Shaughnessy Cohen Prize for Political Writing
The Writers' Trust of Canada
460 Richmond St W, Suite 600, Toronto, ON M5V 1Y1, Canada
Tel: 416-504-8222 *Toll Free Tel:* 877-906-6548 *Fax:* 416-504-9090
E-mail: info@writerstrust.com
Web Site: www.writerstrust.com
Key Personnel
Exec Dir: Mary Osborne *Tel:* 416-504-8222 ext 244 *E-mail:* mosborne@writerstrust.com
Established: 2000
Awarded for a nonfiction book that captures a political subject of relevance to the Canadian reader & enhances understanding of the issue. The winning work combines compelling new insights with depth of research & is of significant literary merit.
Other Sponsor(s): CTV
Award: $25,000 (winner), $2,500 (finalists)
Presented: Politics & the Pen, Ottawa, ON, CN, Annually in Spring

Mina P Shaughnessy Prize
Modern Language Association of America (MLA)
85 Broad St, Suite 500, New York, NY 10004-2434
SAN: 202-6422
Tel: 646-576-5141; 646-576-5000 *Fax:* 646-458-0030
E-mail: awards@mla.org

Web Site: www.mla.org
Key Personnel
Coord, Book Prizes: Annie M Reiser
E-mail: areiser@mla.org
Established: 1980
Biennial prize awarded in even-numbered years for an outstanding scholarly book in the fields of language, culture, literacy & literature with strong application to the teaching of English, published in 2016 or 2017. Authors need not be a member of the MLA. For consideration, submit 4 copies.
Award: Cash award & certificate
Closing Date: May 1, 2018
Presented: MLA Convention, Chicago, IL, Jan 2019

Charlotte Sheedy Fellowship
The MacDowell Colony
100 High St, Peterborough, NH 03458
Tel: 603-924-3886 *Fax:* 603-924-9142
E-mail: admissions@macdowellcolony.org
Web Site: www.macdowellcolony.org
Key Personnel
Chmn: Michael Chabon
Communs Mgr: Jonathan Gourlay *Tel:* 603-924-3886 ext 114 *E-mail:* jgourlay@macdowellcolony.org
Established: 2015
Awarded to writers representing populations across racial & cultural boundaries. Funds an annual residency of up to 2 months at The MacDowell Colony, the nation's first artist residency program. All artists are encouraged to apply at www.macdowellcolony.org/apply.html.
Closing Date: Sept 15

Short Prose Competition for Developing Writers
The Writers' Union of Canada (TWUC)
600-460 Richmond St W, Toronto, ON M5V 1Y1, Canada
Tel: 416-703-8982 *Fax:* 416-504-9090
E-mail: info@writersunion.ca
Web Site: www.writersunion.ca
Key Personnel
Competitions Coord: Nancy MacLeod *Tel:* 416-703-8982 ext 226 *E-mail:* nmacleod@writersunion.ca
Off Admin: Valerie Laws *Tel:* 416-703-8982 ext 224
Short prose up to 2,500 words by an unpublished Canadian writer.
Award: $2,500
Closing Date: Annually, March 1

Short Story Award for New Writers
Glimmer Train Press Inc
PO Box 80430, Portland, OR 97280-1430
Tel: 503-221-0836 *Fax:* 503-221-0837
E-mail: editors@glimmertrain.org
Web Site: www.glimmertrain.org
Key Personnel
Co-Ed: Susan Burmeister-Brown *E-mail:* susan@glimmertrain.org
Established: 1993
Open to writers whose fiction has not appeared in a print publication with a circulation over 5,000, with a 500-12,000 word count range. Winner notification takes place 2 months after the close of each competition.
Award: $2,500, publication & 20 copies of that issue (1st place), $500 (2nd place), $300 (3rd place)
Closing Date: Annually in Jan/Feb, May/June & Sept/Oct

Edwin "Bud" Shrake Award for Best Short Nonfiction
Texas Institute of Letters (TIL)
c/o 7748 Hwy 290 W, Austin, TX 78736-3202
Tel: 512-683-5640
E-mail: president@texasinstituteofletters.org
Web Site: www.texasinstituteofletters.org
Key Personnel
Pres: Steve Davis
VP: Carmen Tafolla
Treas: W K Stratton
Secy: Sergio Troncoso
Recording Secy: Joe Holley
Annual award for best nonfiction writing appearing in a magazine, journal or other periodical or in a newspaper Sunday supplement. Only one story per entrant. Guidelines on the web site.
Award: $1,000
Closing Date: Annually in Jan
Presented: TIL Awards Banquet, Annually in Spring

Robert F Sibert Informational Book Award
Association for Library Service to Children (ALSC)
Division of The American Library Association (ALA)
50 E Huron St, Chicago, IL 60611-2795
Tel: 312-280-2163 *Toll Free Tel:* 800-545-2433 *Fax:* 312-440-9374; 312-280-5271
E-mail: alsc@ala.org
Web Site: www.ala.org/alsc
Key Personnel
Exec Dir: Aimee Strittmatter *Tel:* 312-280-2162 *E-mail:* astrittmatter@ala.org
Awards Coord: Courtney Jones
E-mail: alscawards@ala.org
Prog Coord: Marsha P Burgess *Tel:* 312-280-2166 *E-mail:* mburgess@ala.org
Presented annually to the author of the most distinguished informational book published in English during the previous year for its significant contribution to children's literature.
Award: Medal
Closing Date: Dec 31
Presented: ALA Midwinter Meeting, Jan/Feb

Silver Gavel Awards
American Bar Association
321 N Clark St, Chicago, IL 60654
Tel: 312-988-5719 *Toll Free Tel:* 800-285-2221 (orders) *Fax:* 312-988-5494
Web Site: www.ambar.org/gavelawards
Key Personnel
Staff Liaison: Howard Kaplan
E-mail: howardkaplan@americanbar.org
Div Coord & Contact: Christina Cerveny
E-mail: christina.cerveny@americanbar.org
Prog Specialist & Contact: Pamela Hollins
E-mail: pamela.hollins@americanbar.org
Established: 1958
Media & arts awards competition to recognize communications media that have been exemplary in fostering public understanding of the law & the legal system during the previous calendar year.
Award: Silver Gavel, Honorable Mentions
Closing Date: Jan
Presented: July

Francis B Simkins Award
Southern Historical Association
University of Georgia, Dept of History, Athens, GA 30602-1602
Tel: 706-542-8848 *Fax:* 706-542-2455
Web Site: thesha.org
Key Personnel
Admin Asst: Frances Berry *E-mail:* manager@thesha.org
Established: 1977
Awarded for the most distinguished first book by an author in Southern history over a 2-year period. Awarded in odd-numbered years for book published in 2 previous calendar years.
Award: Cash
Closing Date: March 1
Presented: Annual meeting, odd-numbered years, Fall

The John Simmons Short Fiction Award
Writers' Workshop, The University of Iowa
102 Dey House, 507 N Clinton St, Iowa City, IA 52242-1000
Tel: 319-335-0416 *Fax:* 319-335-0420
Open to any writer who has not previously published a volume of prose fiction. Revised mss which have been previously entered may be resubmitted as well as writers who have published a volume of poetry are eligible. Mss must be a collection of short stories of at least 150 typewritten pages. Photo copies are acceptable; SASE return packaging must accompany the mss or these will not be returned. No cash, checks, or money orders accepted.
Other Sponsor(s): University of Iowa Press
Award: Publication by University of Iowa Press under the Press's standard contract
Closing Date: Annually, Aug 1-Sept 30
Presented: Annually in Autumn

Charlie May Simon Children's Book Award
Arkansas State Library
Arkansas State Library, Suite 100, 900 W Capitol Ave, Little Rock, AR 72201-3108
Tel: 501-682-2860 *Fax:* 501-682-1693
Web Site: www.library.arkansas.gov
Key Personnel
Coord, Children's Progs: Cathy Howser
E-mail: cathy@library.arkansas.gov
Established: 1970
State of Arkansas upper elementary students read books selected by the award committee throughout the year & vote on favorite choice. Most popular book wins award (medallion) & 2nd place award rewarded as Honor Book (plaque).
Other Sponsor(s): Arkansas Department of Education; Arkansas Reading Association
Award: CMS Medallion for 1st place, plaque for Honor Book
Closing Date: Annual vote in April
Presented: Little Rock, AR, Nov

The Simpson Family Literary Prize
Simpson Family Literary Project
Lafayette Lib & Learning Ctr Foundation, 3491 Mount Diablo Blvd, Suite 214, Lafayette, CA 94549
Tel: 925-283-6513
E-mail: sflpweb@gmail.com
Web Site: www.simpsonliteraryproject.org/programs
Key Personnel
Chair, Literary Proj: Joe Di Prisco
Established: 2017
Annual award to a writer who has earned a distinguished reputation & the approbation of gratitude of readers. There is no application process. An anonymous jury selects the recipient. The winner will give a public reading, make a limited number of public appearances & be in brief residence at the Lafayette Library & the University of California, Berkeley.
Award: $50,000
Presented: Spring

Skipping Stones Honor Awards
Skipping Stones Inc
166 W 12 Ave, Eugene, OR 97401
Mailing Address: PO Box 3939, Eugene, OR 97403
Tel: 541-342-4956
E-mail: info@skippingstones.org
Web Site: www.skippingstones.org
Key Personnel
Exec Ed: Arun N Toke *E-mail:* editor@skippingstones.org
Established: 1993

Honors exceptional multicultural & international awareness books, nature/ecology books, bilingual books, teaching resources & educational videos/DVDs. A panel of parents, teachers, librarians, students & editors of *Skipping Stones* select the honors list in the above categories. Entry fee: $50. Winners announced in the Summer issue of *Skipping Stones* & on our web site.
Award: Honor award certificates, award seals, reviews, press releases, e-releases, web site hyperlinks. Also displayed at NAME (National Association for Multicultural Education) Conference in November annually. Publicity in many educational journals
Closing Date: Annually, Feb 1
Presented: Annually in May

The Skipping Stones Youth Honor Awards
Skipping Stones Inc
166 W 12 Ave, Eugene, OR 97401
Mailing Address: PO Box 3939, Eugene, OR 97403
Tel: 541-342-4956
E-mail: info@skippingstones.org
Web Site: www.skippingstones.org
Key Personnel
Exec Ed: Arun N Toke *E-mail:* editor@skippingstones.org
Established: 1993
Recognizes 10 creative & artistic works (writing, art, photo, essays, etc) by young people that promote multicultural & nature awareness. Entry fee: $5. Everyone who enters the awards program receives the Autumn issue with 10 winners & a few noteworthy entries.
Award: Honor award certificate, subn to *Skipping Stones* & 5 nature +/or multicultural books
Closing Date: Annually, June 25
Presented: Winners announced in Autumn issue of *Skipping Stones*

Slipstream Annual Poetry Chapbook Contest
Slipstream Press
PO Box 2071, Dept W-1, Niagara Falls, NY 14301
Web Site: www.slipstreampress.org
Key Personnel
Co-Ed: Dan Sicoli
Established: 1986
Prize awarded to best 40-page ms of poetry. $20 entry fee.
Award: $1,000 & 50 copies of book
Closing Date: Dec 1

Donald Smiley Prize
Canadian Political Science Association
260 rue Dalhousie St, Suite 204, Ottawa, ON K1N 7E4, Canada
Tel: 613-562-1202 *Fax:* 613-241-0019
E-mail: cpsa-acsp@cpsa-acsp.ca
Web Site: www.cpsa-acsp.ca
Key Personnel
Admin: Michelle Hopkins
Established: 1995
Awarded to the best book published in French & the best book published in English in a field relating to the study of government & politics in Canada. To be eligible, a book may be single-authored or multi-authored. Single-authored: author must be a Canadian citizen or a permanent resident of Canada or a member of the CPSA in the year the book was published. Multi-authored: at least one of the authors must be a Canadian citizen or a permanent resident of Canada or a member of the CPSA in the year the book was published.
Award: Commemorative plaque & receive/share the set of books submitted in the language of their own book
Closing Date: Annually, Dec 10
Presented: Annual Conference, University of Regina, SK, CN, May 26-June 1, 2018

Helen C Smith Memorial Award
Texas Institute of Letters (TIL)
c/o 7748 Hwy 290 W, Austin, TX 78736-3202
Tel: 512-683-5640
E-mail: president@texasinstituteofletters.org
Web Site: www.texasinstituteofletters.org
Key Personnel
Pres: Steve Davis
VP: Carmen Tafolla
Treas: W K Stratton
Secy: Sergio Troncoso
Recording Secy: Joe Holley
Annual award for the first best book of poetry by a poet with a Texas association. Guidelines on the web site.
Award: $1,200
Closing Date: Annually in Jan
Presented: TIL Awards Banquet, Annually in Spring

The Jean Kennedy Smith VSA Playwright Discovery Award
VSA
Affiliate of The John F Kennedy Center for the Performing Arts
2700 "F" St NW, Washington, DC 20566
Tel: 202-416-8898 *Fax:* 202-416-4840
E-mail: vsainfo@kennedy-center.org
Web Site: www.kennedy-center.org/pdp
Key Personnel
Admin Asst, VSA Progs: Megan Bailey *Tel:* 202-416-8822 *E-mail:* mebailey@kennedy-center.org
Established: 1984
Open to writers with disabilities & groups that include students with disabilities (ages 14-22). High school students are invited to explore the disability experience through the art of script writing. Young writers with disabilities & collaborative groups that include students with disabilities are encouraged to submit 10-minute scripts of any genre. Selected winners will receive exclusive access to participate in the Kennedy Center American College Theater Festival in Washington, DC in April with the opportunity to perform & workshop alongside the nation's premier collegiate playwrights as well as participate in the festival's award ceremony. See web site for more information & details on how to enter.
Award: Attend performance of their script at JFK Center, scholarship funds
Closing Date: Feb 1
Presented: The John F Kennedy Center for Performing Arts, Washington, DC

The Jeffrey E Smith Editors' Prize
The Missouri Review
357 McReynolds Hall, Columbia, MO 65211
Tel: 573-882-4474 *Toll Free Tel:* 800-949-2505 *Fax:* 573-884-4671
Web Site: www.missourireview.com
Key Personnel
Mng Ed: Kate McIntyre *Tel:* 573-882-7127 *E-mail:* mcintyrekl@missouri.edu
Established: 1991
Awarded annually in fiction, essay & poetry. Entry fee entitles entrant to 1-year subscription. Writers should consult web site or send a SASE for guidelines.
Award: $5,000 each (short fiction, essay & poetry) & publication in the Spring issue
Closing Date: Annually, Oct 1
Presented: Spring

Kay Snow Writing Contest
Willamette Writers
5331 SW Macadam Ave, Suite 258, PMB 215, Portland, OR 97239
Tel: 901-200-5385
E-mail: wilwrite@willamettewriters.org
Web Site: willamettewriters.org
Key Personnel
VP & Secy: Gail Pasternack *E-mail:* secretary@willamettewriters.org
Awards Dir: Blythe Ayne *E-mail:* awards@willamettewriters.org
Established: 1971
Annual writing competition in 6 categories: fiction, nonfiction, YA/MG, poetry, screenplay & college student. Entry fee: $10 members, $15 general public, $10 college students, free for el-hi students. Winners listed on Willamette Writers web site.
Award: $100 (1st prize) & 1-day admission to the Willamette Writers Conference, $25 (2nd prize) & 1-day admission to the Willamette Writers Conference, $50 (3rd prize)
Presented: Annual Conference, Aug

The Society of Midland Authors Awards
The Society of Midland Authors (SMA)
PO Box 10419, Chicago, IL 60610
E-mail: info@midlandauthors.com
Web Site: www.midlandauthors.com
Key Personnel
Awards Coord: Marlene Targ Brill
Established: 1915
Juried award offers prizes in each of 6 literary categories: children's fiction, children's nonfiction, adult fiction & nonfiction, biography & poetry. Awarded annually to authors in any of the Midland states: Illinois, Indiana, Iowa, Kansas, Michigan, Minnesota, Missouri, Nebraska, North Dakota, Ohio, South Dakota & Wisconsin.
Award: Monetary award $500 & plaque
Closing Date: Jan
Presented: Chicago, IL, 2nd Tuesday in May

The Society of Southwestern Authors Writing Contest
The Society of Southwestern Authors (SSA)
PO Box 30355, Tucson, AZ 85751-0355
E-mail: info@ssa-az.org
Web Site: www.ssa-az.org
Established: 1972
Annual awards for short fiction, 2,500 words max; personal essays & memoirs, 2,500 words max; poetry, 40 lines max.
Award: $200 (1st prize), $100 (2nd prize), $50 (3rd prize)
Closing Date: Sept 30
Presented: Awards Forum, Nov

Sophie Kerr Prize
Washington College
c/o College Relations Off, 300 Washington Ave, Chestertown, MD 21620
Tel: 410-778-2800 *Toll Free Tel:* 800-422-1782 *Fax:* 410-810-7150
Web Site: www.washcoll.edu
Key Personnel
Dir, Communs: Marcia Landskroener *Tel:* 410-778-7797 *E-mail:* mlandskroener2@washcoll.edu
Established: 1968
Annual literary award to graduating senior. Only open to undergraduates of Washington College.
Award: $65,000
Closing Date: April
Presented: Washington College Commencement, Chestertown, MD, May

Southeast Review Narrative Nonfiction Contest
The Southeast Review
Florida State University, Dept of English, Tallahassee, FL 32306
E-mail: southeastreview@gmail.com

Web Site: www.southeastreview.org
Key Personnel
Ed: Alex Quinlan
Established: 1986
Best previously unpublished 6,000 word (maximum) nonfiction essay. Include a brief (100 word) bio. All entries will be considered for publication. $16 entry fee per nonfiction entry.
Other Sponsor(s): Florida State University English Department Creative Writing Program
Award: $500
Closing Date: March

Southeast Review's Gearhart Poetry Contest
The Southeast Review
Florida State University, Dept of English, Tallahassee, FL 32306
E-mail: southeastreview@gmail.com
Web Site: www.southeastreview.org
Key Personnel
Ed: Alex Quinlan
Established: 1996
Award for best poem. All entries will be considered for publication. $16 entry fee for up to 3 poems, no more than 10 pages total.
Other Sponsor(s): Florida State University English Department Creative Writing Program
Award: $500
Closing Date: Annually in March

Southeastern Theatre Conference New Play Project
Southeastern Theatre Conference (SETC)
1175 Revolution Mill Dr, Suite 14, Greensboro, NC 27405
Tel: 336-272-3645 *Fax:* 336-272-8810
E-mail: info@setc.org
Web Site: www.setc.org
Key Personnel
Chair, New Play Proj: Todd Ristau
New play contest. Submission begins March 1.
Award: $1,000, travel & expenses to annual convention
Closing Date: Annually, June 1
Presented: Southeastern Theatre Conference Convention, March of the year following the closing date

Southern Books Competition
Southeastern Library Association
PO Box 950, Rex, GA 30273
Tel: 678-466-4334 *Fax:* 678-466-4349
Web Site: selaonline.org
Key Personnel
Chmn: Camille McCutcheon
Admin Servs: Dr Gordon N Baker
E-mail: gordonbaker@clayton.edu
Established: 1952
Recognition for excellence in bookmaking awarded biennially in even-numbered years for a title published during the previous 2 years. Trade publishers, university presses, specialty publishers & private presses located in Alabama, Arkansas, Florida, Georgia, Kentucky, Louisiana, Mississippi, North Carolina, South Carolina, Tennessee, Virginia, West Virginia or Puerto Rico are eligible to enter the competition. Awards are given based on design, typography & quality of production. Winners are displayed at SELA Conference & in a traveling exhibit available to institutions & organizations. It has been borrowed throughout the South, Canada, Scandinavia, Russia & South Africa.
Award: Published recognition list. Rotating & permanent display of winning books
Presented: SELA Conference, even-numbered years, Oct

Southern Playwrights Competition
Jacksonville State University, Dept of English
700 Pelham Rd N, Jacksonville, AL 36265-1602
Tel: 256-782-5412
Web Site: www.jsu.edu/english/southpla.html
Key Personnel
Coord: Joy Maloney *E-mail:* jmaloney@jsu.edu
Established: 1988
Identify & encourage the best of Southern play writing. Entries accepted beginning Sept 1.
Award: $1,000 honorarium & possible production of winning entry
Closing Date: Annually, Jan 15

Terry Southern Prize
The Paris Review Foundation
544 W 27 St, New York, NY 10001
Tel: 212-343-1333 *Fax:* 212-343-1988
E-mail: queries@theparisreview.org
Web Site: www.theparisreview.org
Honors "humor, wit & sprezzatura" in work from either *The Paris Review* or the *Daily*.
Award: $5,000

Sovereign Award for Outstanding Writing
The Jockey Club of Canada
Woodbine Sales Pavilion, 555 Rexdale Blvd, Toronto, ON M9W 5L2, Canada
Mailing Address: PO Box 66, Sta B, Toronto, ON M9W 5K9, Canada
Tel: 416-675-7756 *Fax:* 416-675-6378
E-mail: jockeyclub@bellnet.ca
Web Site: www.jockeyclubcanada.com; www.sovereignawards.ca
Key Personnel
Exec Dir: Melanie O'Sullivan
Established: 1975
Submissions must be of Canadian Thoroughbred Racing content. See guidelines on web site.
Award: Bronze statue of Saint Simon
Closing Date: Annually, Dec 31
Presented: Ontario, CN, Annually, date TBD upon confirmation of the first day of racing for that calendar year

The Sow's Ear Poetry Prize & The Sow's Ear Chapbook Prize
The Sow's Ear Poetry Review
Division of The Word Process Inc
1748 Cave Ridge Rd, Mount Jackson, VA 22842
Tel: 540-477-3257
E-mail: sepoetryreview@gmail.com
Web Site: sowsearpoetry.org
Key Personnel
Mng Ed: Sarah Kohrs
Ed: Kristin Zimet
Established: 1988
Single poem & chapbook.
Award: $1,000 each (poem & chapbook), plus 25 copies for chapbook winner
Closing Date: Annually, May 1 (chapbook), Nov 1 (poem)

Spark Award
Society of Children's Book Writers and Illustrators (SCBWI)
4727 Wilshire Blvd, Suite 301, Los Angeles, CA 90010
Tel: 323-782-1010 *Fax:* 323-782-1892
E-mail: grants@scbwi.org; scbwi@scbwi.org
Web Site: www.scbwi.org
Key Personnel
COO: Sara Rutenberg *E-mail:* sararutenberg@scbwi.org
Established: 2013
Annual award that recognizes excellence in a children's book published through a non-traditional publishing route.
Closing Date: Dec 15
Presented: March 31

John Spray Mystery Award
Canadian Children's Book Centre
40 Orchard View Blvd, Suite 217, Toronto, ON M4R 1B9, Canada
Tel: 416-975-0010 *Fax:* 416-975-8970
E-mail: info@bookcentre.ca
Web Site: www.bookcentre.ca
Key Personnel
Exec Dir: Charlotte Teeple *E-mail:* charlotte@bookcentre.ca
Lib Coord: Meghan Howe *E-mail:* meghan@bookcentre.ca
Mktg & Web Site Coord: Camilia Kahrizi
E-mail: camilia@bookcentre.ca
Prog Coord: Shannon Howe Barnes
E-mail: shannon@bookcentre.ca
Established: 2011
Awarded to a Canadian author for excellence in mystery writing for children & adolescents.
Other Sponsor(s): John Spray
Award: $5,000
Closing Date: Annually in mid-Dec

Spur Awards
Western Writers of America Inc (WWA)
271 CR 219, Encampment, WY 82325
Tel: 307-329-8942
E-mail: wwa.moulton@gmail.com
Web Site: westernwriters.org
Key Personnel
Pres: Kirk Ellis *E-mail:* president@westernwriters.org
Exec Dir & Secy-Treas: Candy Moulton
E-mail: wwa.moulton@gmail.com
Established: 1953
Western fiction/nonfiction (various categories).
Award: Plaques & recognition
Closing Date: Jan 4 of year following publication
Presented: Annual Convention, June

The Edna Staebler Award for Creative Non-Fiction
Wilfrid Laurier University
Office of the Dean, Faculty of Arts, 75 University Ave W, Waterloo, ON N2L 3C5, Canada
Tel: 519-884-1970 (ext 3361)
E-mail: staebleraward@wlu.ca
Web Site: wlu.ca/staebleraward
Key Personnel
Dir, Communs & Pub Aff: Kevin Crowley *Tel:* 519-884-0710 ext 3070
E-mail: kcrowley@wlu.ca
Admin Asst to Dean of Arts: Cathy Mahler
Tel: 519-884-0710 ext 3361 *E-mail:* cmahler@wlu.ca
Established: 1991
Annual literary award for a first or second published book of creative nonfiction with a Canadian locale +/or significance published in the previous calendar year. Open to works & distinguished by first-hand research, well-crafted interpretive writing & creative use of language or approach to the subject matter. Writer must be Canadian. Award is open to print books & ebooks.
Award: $10,000
Closing Date: See web site
Presented: Wilfrid Laurier University, Nov, announcement in Sept

Stanley Drama Award
Wagner College
One Campus Rd, Staten Island, NY 10301
Tel: 718-390-3223 *Fax:* 718-390-3323
Web Site: wagner.edu/theatre/stanley-drama
Key Personnel
Assoc Professor: Todd Alan Price *E-mail:* todd.price@wagner.edu
Established: 1957
Award given for original full-length play or musical which has not been professionally produced or received trade book publication. Writers of musicals are urged to submit music on tape or CD as well as books & lyrics. Consideration will also be given to a series of 2 or 3 thematically related one-act plays. Scripts must be

accompanied by a SASE. Former winners are not eligible to compete. Applications are obtained by sending SASE or online. A reading fee of $30 must accompany submission.
Award: $2,000
Closing Date: Oct 31
Presented: Annually in April

Agnes Lynch Starrett Poetry Prize
University of Pittsburgh Press
7500 Thomas Blvd, Pittsburgh, PA 15260
Tel: 412-383-2456 *Fax:* 412-383-2466
E-mail: info@upress.pitt.edu
Web Site: www.upress.pitt.edu
Key Personnel
Asst to Dir: Kelley H Johovic *E-mail:* kjohovic@upress.pitt.edu
Established: 1981
Open to any poet who has not had a full-length book previously published. Submit typed 48-100 page poetry mss on white paper with SASE & check or money order of $25 for each ms submitted. See web site for complete rules.
Award: $5,000 & publication
Closing Date: March 1-April 30 (postmark)
Presented: Pittsburgh, PA, Autumn

Stegner Fellowship
Stanford University Creative Writing Program
Stanford University, Dept of English, Stanford, CA 94305-2087
Tel: 650-723-0011 *Fax:* 650-723-3679
E-mail: stegnerfellowship@stanford.edu
Web Site: creativewriting.stanford.edu
Key Personnel
Prog Asst: Katherine Batanero
Fellowship; residence required for 2 years at Stanford beginning Autumn quarter each year.
Award: $26,000, required tuition & health insurance
Closing Date: Dec 1

Jean Stein Book Award, see PEN/Jean Stein Book Award

Stephan G Stephansson Award for Poetry
Writers' Guild of Alberta
11759 Groat Rd, Edmonton, AB T5M 3K6, Canada
Tel: 780-422-8174 *Toll Free Tel:* 800-665-5354 (AB only) *Fax:* 780-422-2663 (attn WGA)
E-mail: mail@writersguild.ca
Web Site: writersguild.ca
Key Personnel
Exec Dir: Carol Holmes *E-mail:* carol.holmes@writersguild.ca
Communs & Partnerships Coord: Ellen Kartz *E-mail:* ellen.kartz@writersguild.ca
Memb Servs Coord: Giorgia Severini
Progs Coord: Natalie Cook *E-mail:* natalie.cook@writersguild.ca; Julie Robinson *E-mail:* julie.robinson@writersguild.ca
Established: 1982
Alberta literary award, author must be resident of Alberta.
Award: $1,500 plus leather-bound copy of book
Closing Date: Annually, Dec 31
Presented: Alberta Book Awards Gala, AB, CN
Branch Office(s)
505 21 Ave SW, Calgary, AB T2S 0G9, Canada, Prog Coord: Samantha Warwick *Tel:* 403-265-2226 *Fax:* 403-234-9532 (attn: WGA) *E-mail:* samantha.warwick@writersguild.ca

Wallace Stevens Award
The Academy of American Poets Inc
75 Maiden Lane, Suite 901, New York, NY 10038
Tel: 212-274-0343 *Fax:* 212-274-9427
E-mail: awards@poets.org
Web Site: www.poets.org
Key Personnel
Exec Dir: Jennifer Benka
Prog Coord: Nikay Paredes *Tel:* 212-274-0343 ext 13 *E-mail:* nparedes@poets.org
Established: 1994
Awarded annually to recognize outstanding & proven mastery in the art of poetry. Recipients are chosen by the Academy of American Poets Board of Chancellors. No applications are accepted.

Bram Stoker Awards®
Horror Writers Association (HWA)
c/o Horror Writers Association, PO Box 56687, Sherman Oaks, CA 91413
Tel: 818-220-3965
E-mail: hwa@horror.org
Web Site: horror.org/awards/stokers.htm
Key Personnel
Co-Chmn: Ron Breznay; Rena Mason
Established: 1988
11 award categories: novel, first novel, short fiction, long fiction, young adult, fiction collection, poetry collection, anthology, screenplay, graphic novel & nonfiction.

Story Monsters Approved! Program
Story Monsters LLC
4696 W Tyson St, Chandler, AZ 85226-2903
Tel: 480-940-8182 *Fax:* 480-940-8787
Web Site: www.StoryMonstersApproved.com
Key Personnel
Pres: Linda F Radke *E-mail:* Linda@StoryMonsters.com
Designation to recognize & honor accomplished authors in the field of children's literature, as well as children's products that inspire, inform, teach, or entertain. Each honoree gains permission to use the seal on collateral material, web site & on reprints of book or product cover, a fill-in-the-blank news release to send to their own local media contacts, book or product listing on Story Monster LLC's web site & social media pages & a book or product listing in *Story Monsters Ink®* magazine.
Program is open to printed children's books published in any calendar year or any products for children. Books entered must be printed in English. Authors age 17 & younger must have parent or guardian permission to enter. Nonrefundable entry fee $85 for one title in one category, $99 for one product in one category.
Award: Certificate, 50 seals & iron-on patch

The Story Prize
41 Watchung Plaza, No 384, Montclair, NJ 07042
Tel: 973-932-0324
E-mail: info@thestoryprize.org
Web Site: www.thestoryprize.org
Key Personnel
Dir: Larry Dark *E-mail:* ldark@thestoryprize.org
Established: 2004
Annual book award honoring the author of an outstanding collection of short fiction.
Award: $20,000, $5,000 (runners up)
Closing Date: July 15 (books published Jan-June), Nov 15 (books published July-Dec)
Presented: The New School, 66 W 12 St, New York, NY, March

Elizabeth Matchett Stover Memorial Award
Southwest Review
PO Box 750374, Dallas, TX 75275-0374
Fax: 214-768-1408
E-mail: swr@mail.smu.edu
Web Site: www.smu.edu/southwestreview
Key Personnel
Ed-in-Chief: Greg Brownderville
Mng Ed: Preston Hutcherson *Tel:* 214-768-1036
Established: 1978
Awarded annually to the author of the best poem or group of poems published in the *Southwest Review*" during the preceding year.
Award: $300

Jessamy Stursberg Poetry Contest for Youth
The League of Canadian Poets
192 Spadina Ave, Suite 312, Toronto, ON M5T 2C2, Canada
Tel: 416-504-1657 *Fax:* 416-504-0096
E-mail: admin@poets.ca
Web Site: poets.ca
Key Personnel
Exec Dir: Lesley Fletcher *E-mail:* lesley@poets.ca
Established: 1995
Seeking poems by young poets across the country. Two age categories with 3 prizes awarded in both: Junior (grades 7-9) & Senior (grades 10-12). All winning poems will be published in the e-zine. Submission open August 1.
Award: $400 cash (1st place), $350 cash (2nd place), $300 cash (3rd place); all winners will be featured on the League of Canadian Poets' web site
Closing Date: Annually, Dec 1
Presented: Annually, last week of April

Sudden Fiction Contest
Berkeley Fiction Review
c/o ASUC Publications, Univ of California, 10-B Eshleman Hall, Berkeley, CA 94720-4500
E-mail: bfictionreview@yahoo.com
Web Site: www.ocf.berkeley.edu/~bfr/
Key Personnel
Mng Ed: Jennifer Brown; Brighton Early
All entries must be 1,000 words or less; typed, double-spaced, with a 12 pt font; include cover letter & e-mail only. Entry fee $6 ($4 each additional story).
Award: $200 (1st place); 1st, 2nd & 3rd place are published in upcoming newsletter

The Sugarman Family Award for Jewish Children's Literature
Washington DC Jewish Community Center
Irwin P Edlavitch Bldg, 1529 16 St NW, Washington, DC 20036
Tel: 202-518-9400 *Fax:* 202-518-9420
Web Site: www.washingtondcjcc.org
Key Personnel
Chief Programming Offr, Jewish Life & Learning: Sara Shalva *Tel:* 202-777-3249 *E-mail:* saras@edcjcc.org
Established: 1994
Award for the best Jewish children's book published between March 1, 2017 & March 1, 2018. Submissions accepted starting August 1. Presented biennially; contact office for dates.
Award: Fluctuates year to year. Approximately $300-$500
Closing Date: Jan 30
Presented: Washington Jewish Literary Festival, Spring

Ronald Sukenick American Book Review Innovative Fiction Prize
Fiction Collective Two Inc (FC2)
c/o Dept of English, Languages & Communincations Bldg, 255 S Central Campus Dr, Rm 3500, Salt Lake City, UT 84112-0494
Tel: 773-702-7000
Web Site: www.fc2.org/prizes.html
Key Personnel
Chair, Bd of Dirs: Lance Olsen
Open to any US writer in English who has not previously published with Fiction Collective Two. Submissions may include a collection of short stories, one or more novellas or a novel of any length. Works that have previously appeared in magazines or in anthologies may be included.

Award: $1,500 & publication by FC2
Closing Date: Annually, Nov 1
Presented: Annually in May

Hollis Summers Poetry Prize
Ohio University Press
31 S Court St, Suite 143, Athens, OH 45701-2979
Web Site: www.ohioswallow.com/poetry_prize
Key Personnel
Dir & Ed-in-Chief: Gillian Berchowitz *Tel:* 740-593-1159 *E-mail:* berchowi@ohio.edu
This competition invites writers to submit unpublished collections of original poems. Individual collections must be the work of a single author. Translations are not accepted. Submit a ms of 60-95 pages of a poetry collection & a $30 entry fee.
Award: $1,000 & publication
Closing Date: Annually in Oct

Sydney Taylor Book Awards
Association of Jewish Libraries (AJL) Inc
Affiliate of American Library Association (ALA)
PO Box 1118, Teaneck, NJ 07666
Tel: 201-371-3255
E-mail: chair@sydneytaylorbookaward.org; info@jewishlibraries.org
Web Site: www.sydneytaylorbookaward.org
Key Personnel
Pres: Amalia Warshenbrot
Established: 1968
Literary content for outstanding children's books in field of Jewish literature. Three categories of prizes: younger readers, older readers, teen readers.
Award: $500 prize for each category; $500 award to illustrator of Young Readers Award book
Closing Date: Dec 1
Presented: AJL Annual Convention, June

Sydney Taylor Manuscript Award
Association of Jewish Libraries (AJL) Inc
Affiliate of American Library Association (ALA)
204 Park St, Montclair, NJ 07042
Tel: 201-371-3255
E-mail: info@jewishlibraries.org
Web Site: jewishlibraries.org
Key Personnel
Chpn: Aileen Grossberg *E-mail:* stmacajl@aol.com
Annual award to encourage outstanding Jewish themed fiction written by an unpublished author. Story will appeal to all children ages 8-13 & to help launch new children's writers in their careers.
Award: $1,000
Closing Date: Sept 30
Presented: AJL Annual Convention, June

Charles S Sydnor Award
Southern Historical Association
University of Georgia, Dept of History, Athens, GA 30602-1602
Tel: 706-542-8848 *Fax:* 706-542-2455
Web Site: thesha.org
Key Personnel
Admin Asst: Frances Berry *E-mail:* manager@thesha.org
Established: 1956
Awarded for the most distinguished book in Southern history published in odd-numbered years. Awarded in even-numbered years.
Award: Cash
Closing Date: March 1
Presented: Annual meeting, even-numbered years, Fall

TAA Council of Fellows
Textbook & Academic Authors Association (TAA)
PO Box 367, Fountain City, WI 54629
E-mail: info@taaonline.net
Web Site: www.taaonline.net/council-of-fellows
Key Personnel
Exec Dir: Michael Spinella *Tel:* 973-943-0501 *E-mail:* michael.spinella@taaonline.net
Dir, Publg & Opers: Kim Pawlak *Tel:* 608-687-3106 *E-mail:* kim.pawlak@taaonline.net
Dir, Instl Memberships & Meetings: Maureen Foerster *Tel:* 608-687-3106 *E-mail:* maureen.foerster@taaonline.net
Membership Coord: Bekky Murphy *Tel:* 608-567-9060 *E-mail:* bekky.murphy@taaonline.net
Honors distinguished authors who have a long record of successful publishing. Any author whose textbook or other instructional materials have established his/her presence in the market place over time, who has been innovative in the presentation of material, is qualified for nomination. Members are chosen by a TAA Selection Committee based on a set of criteria which includes their: level of participation in TAA activities; teaching excellence; quality & quantity of textbooks (if textbook authors); quality & quantity of professional journal articles, monographs & edited books (if academic authors).
Closing Date: Jan 15

The Tampa Review Prize for Poetry
Tampa Review
University of Tampa Press, 401 W Kennedy Blvd, Tampa, FL 33606
Tel: 813-253-6266
E-mail: utpress@ut.edu
Web Site: tampareview.ut.edu
Key Personnel
Ed: Richard Mathews
Edit Asst: Sean Donnelly
Established: 2001
Award: $2,000 & book publication in hardcover & paperback
Closing Date: Dec 31

The Charles Taylor Prize
Charles Taylor Foundation
14-20 Brockton Ave, Toronto, ON M6K 1S5, Canada
E-mail: rbctaylorprize@gmail.com
Web Site: rbctaylorprize.ca
Key Personnel
Admin: Su Hutchinson
Established: 2000
To enhance public appreciation for literary nonfiction.
Award: $25,000 for winner, $5,000 for each runner up
Presented: Toronto, Ontario, CN, Annually, early Spring

Rennie Taylor & Alton Blakeslee Fellowships in Science Writing
Council for the Advancement of Science Writing (CASW)
PO Box 910, Hedgesville, WV 25427
Tel: 304-754-6786
Web Site: www.casw.org
Key Personnel
Exec Dir: Rosalind Reid *E-mail:* rosreid@gmail.com
Established: 1975
For tuition & books for graduate study only. Online submissions.
Award: $5,000
Closing Date: Annually in March
Presented: ScienceWriters Meeting, Annually in Oct/Nov

TD Canadian Children's Literature Award
Canadian Children's Book Centre
40 Orchard View Blvd, Suite 217, Toronto, ON M4R 1B9, Canada
Tel: 416-975-0010 *Fax:* 416-975-8970
E-mail: info@bookcentre.ca
Web Site: www.bookcentre.ca
Key Personnel
Exec Dir: Charlotte Teeple *E-mail:* charlotte@bookcentre.ca
Lib Coord: Meghan Howe *E-mail:* meghan@bookcentre.ca
Mktg & Web Site Coord: Camilia Kahrizi *E-mail:* camilia@bookcentre.ca
Prog Coord: Shannon Howe Barnes *E-mail:* shannon@bookcentre.ca
Established: 2004
Awarded to a Canadian author/illustrator for the most distinguished book of the year.
Other Sponsor(s): TD Bank Group
Award: $30,000 cash each to one English language & one French language book, $10,000 to an English language honour book (maximum of 4), $10,000 to a French language honour book (maximum of 4), $2,500 to the publishers of the grand prize winning books for promotion & publicity purposes
Closing Date: Annually in mid-Dec

Tennessee Arts Commission Fellowships
Tennessee Arts Commission
401 Charlotte Ave, Nashville, TN 37243-0780
Tel: 615-741-1701 *Fax:* 615-741-8559
Web Site: www.tnartscommission.org
Key Personnel
Dir, Literary Arts & Grants Analyst: Lee Baird *Tel:* 615-532-0493 *E-mail:* lee.baird@tn.gov
Annual literary fellowships given to Tennessee writers of every genre. Tennessee residents only.
Award: $5,000
Closing Date: Annually in Jan

The Tenth Gate Prize
The Word Works
Mailing Address: PO Box 42164, Washington, DC 20015
Tel: 301-581-9439 *Fax:* 301-581-9443
E-mail: editor@wordworksbooks.org
Web Site: www.wordworksbooks.org
Key Personnel
Pres: Nancy White *E-mail:* nancywhitepoetry@gmail.com
Series Ed: Leslie McGrath
Established: 2014
Annual prize for an unpublished ms of poetry written in English, by a poet who has previously published at least 2 full-length collections. Online submissions only; please visit web site for guidelines. Submissions should be 48-80 pages in length. A reading fee of $25 is required.
Award: $1,000 & publication
Closing Date: July 15

The Texas Bluebonnet Award
Texas Library Association (TLA)
3355 Bee Cave Rd, Suite 401, Austin, TX 78746-6763
Tel: 512-328-1518 *Toll Free Tel:* 800-580-2852 *Fax:* 512-328-8852
E-mail: tla@txla.org
Web Site: www.txla.org
Key Personnel
Progs & Events Asst: Julie Serafini *E-mail:* julies@txla.org
Established: 1979
Awarded to favorite title on annual list, voted on by 200,000 children, grades 3-6.
Other Sponsor(s): Children's Round Table; Texas Association of School Librarians
Award: Medallion in desk mount
Closing Date: Aug 1
Presented: April

Texas Institute of Letters Awards
Texas Institute of Letters (TIL)

c/o 7748 Hwy 290 W, Austin, TX 78736-3202
Tel: 512-683-5640
E-mail: president@texasinstituteofletters.org
Web Site: www.texasinstituteofletters.org
Key Personnel
Pres: Steve Davis
VP: Carmen Tafolla
Treas: W K Stratton
Secy: Sergio Troncoso
Recording Secy: Joe Holley
Established: 1936
Annual award for books published by Texas residents or on Texas-related subjects. Guidelines on the web site.
Award: Eleven cash awards, totalling $22,000
Closing Date: Jan
Presented: TIL Awards Banquet, Spring

Textbook Excellence Award
Textbook & Academic Authors Association (TAA)
PO Box 367, Fountain City, WI 54629
E-mail: info@taaonline.net
Web Site: www.taaonline.net/textbook-excellence-award
Key Personnel
Exec Dir: Michael Spinella *Tel:* 973-943-0501 *E-mail:* michael.spinella@taaonline.net
Dir, Publg & Opers: Kim Pawlak *Tel:* 608-687-3106 *E-mail:* kim.pawlak@taaonline.net
Dir, Instl Memberships & Meetings: Maureen Foerster *Tel:* 608-687-3106 *E-mail:* maureen.foerster@taaonline.net
Membership Coord: Bekky Murphy *Tel:* 608-567-9060 *E-mail:* bekky.murphy@taaonline.net
Recognizes excellence in current textbooks & learning materials. Works are judged for merit in 4 areas: pedagogy; content/scholarship; writing; appearance & design. Nomination fee: $350 (non-refundable). See web site for nomination form & entry guidelines.
Closing Date: Dec 15
Presented: TAA Annual Conference, Annually in June

Third Coast Poetry & Fiction Contest
Third Coast Magazine
Western Michigan University English Dept, 1903 W Michigan Ave, Kalamazoo, MI 49008-5331
E-mail: editors@thirdcoastmagazine.com
Web Site: www.thirdcoastmagazine.com/contests
Two awards given annually for a poem & a short story. Submit up to 3 poems or a short story of up to 9,000 words with a $16 entry fee, which includes a subscription to *Third Coast.*
Award: $1,000 & publication in *Third Coast*
Closing Date: Jan 15

3-Day Novel Contest
The Geist Foundation
201-111 W Hastings St, Vancouver, BC V6B 1H4, Canada
Tel: 604-681-9161
E-mail: info@3daynovel.com
Web Site: www.3daynovel.com
Established: 1977
Annual international novel writing competition. Entry fee: $50 ($35 early bird) for US & CN entries; may be postmarked up until 1 day before contest.
Award: Publication (1st prize), $500 (2nd prize), $100 (3rd prize)
Closing Date: Friday before Labor Day (postmark)
Presented: Labor Day weekend

Thurber Prize for American Humor
Thurber House
77 Jefferson Ave, Columbus, OH 43215
Tel: 614-464-1032 *Fax:* 614-280-3645
E-mail: thurberhouse@thurberhouse.org
Web Site: www.thurberhouse.org
Key Personnel
Exec Dir: Laurie Lathan
Deputy Dir: Anne Touvell *Tel:* 614-464-1032 ext 10
Annual award for the most outstanding book of humor writing published in the US. The award is presented by Thurber House, a nonprofit literary center in Columbus, OH & the former home of American humorist, author & New Yorker cartoonist James Thurber.
Award: $5,000, commemorative plaque & a nationwide media campaign
Closing Date: April 1
Presented: Caroline's Comedy Club on Broadway, New York, NY, Fall

James Tiptree Jr Award
James Tiptree Jr Literary Award Council
680 66 St, Oakland, CA 94609
Tel: 510-658-7176
E-mail: info@tiptree.org
Web Site: tiptree.org
Key Personnel
Founder: Karen Joy Fowler; Pat Murphy
Established: 1991
Annual literary prize for science fiction or fantasy that expands or explores our understanding of gender.
Presented: WisCon, Madison, WI

Toronto Book Awards
Toronto Cultural Partnerships
Division of City of Toronto
c/o Toronto Arts & Culture, City Hall, 9E, 100 Queen St W, Toronto, ON M5H 2N2, Canada
Web Site: www.toronto.ca/book_awards
Key Personnel
Cultural Devt Offr: Christopher Jones *Tel:* 416-392-6832 *E-mail:* cjones2@toronto.ca
Established: 1974
To honor authors of books of literary or artistic merit that are evocative of Toronto published between January 1 & May 31 the preceding year.
Other Sponsor(s): Toronto Public Library (in partnership)
Award: $15,000 annually, $1,000 to each short listed book, usually 4 books, remainder to winner
Closing Date: Last weekday in April
Presented: Toronto, ON, CN, Shortlist announced in Aug & winner in Oct

Towson University Prize for Literature
Towson University
English Dept, 8000 York Rd, Towson, MD 21252
Tel: 410-704-2000 *Fax:* 410-704-3999
Web Site: www.towson.edu/english
Key Personnel
Chair: Dr H George Hahn
Established: 1979
Annual award for a single book or book-length ms of fiction, poetry, drama or imaginative nonfiction by a Maryland writer. Applicant must have resided in Maryland at least 3 years prior to applying & must be a Maryland resident when the prize is awarded.
Award: $1,000
Closing Date: June 15
Presented: Spring

Translation Projects
Formerly Literary Translation Projects
National Endowment for the Arts
400 Seventh St SW, Washington, DC 20506-0001
Tel: 202-682-5400; 202-682-5496 (Voice/TTY); 202-682-5034 (lit fellowships hotline)
Fax: 202-682-5609; 202-682-5610
E-mail: litfellowships@arts.gov
Web Site: www.arts.gov
Key Personnel
Grants Dir & Contracts Offr: Nicki Jacobs *Tel:* 202-682-5546 *E-mail:* jacobsn@arts.gov
Fellowships for published translators: for translations of published literary material into English. Applications accepted by genre. Guidelines available on web site.
Award: $12,500 or $25,000, depending on the artistic excellence & merit of the project
Closing Date: Annually in Dec
Presented: Notification by mail, Annually in Aug

Trillium Book Award/Prix Trillium
Ontario Media Development Corp (OMDC)
Division of Ministry of Culture, Ontario Government
South Tower, Suite 501, 175 Bloor St E, Toronto, ON M4W 3R8, Canada
Tel: 416-314-6858 (ext 698) *Fax:* 416-314-6876
Web Site: www.omdc.on.ca
Key Personnel
Consultant, Indus Initiatives: Janet Hawkins *Tel:* 416-642-6698 *E-mail:* jhawkins@omdc.on.ca
Established: 1987
Open to books in any genre; fiction, nonfiction, drama & children's books. There are no restrictions regarding the previous works of the author.
Award: $20,000 to winning authors in English & French; $2,500 to publishers of winning book in English & French
Closing Date: Jan
Presented: Award ceremony, Late Spring

Harry S Truman Book Award
Truman Library Institute
500 W US Hwy 24, Independence, MO 64050
Tel: 816-268-8245 *Toll Free Tel:* 800-833-1225
Web Site: trumanlibraryinstitute.org
Key Personnel
Book Award Admin: Mary McMurray, PhD *E-mail:* mary.mcmurray@gmail.com
Established: 1963
Presented biennially in even-numbered years for the best book published on the presidency of Harry S Truman. The book must deal with some aspect of the political, economic or social development of the US, principally between April 12, 1945 & January 20, 1953 or with the life or career of Truman. Submit 6 copies of the nominated book to Mary McMurray, Book Award Administrator. Book must have been published between January 1, 2016 & December 31, 2017.
Award: $2,500
Closing Date: Before Jan 20, 2018
Presented: No later than May 8 (Truman's birthday), 2018

Trustus Playwrights' Festival
Trustus Theatre
520 Lady St, Columbia, SC 29201
Tel: 803-254-9732
Web Site: www.trustus.org
Key Personnel
Artistic Dir: Chad Henderson *E-mail:* chad@trustus.org
Established: 1988
Experimental, hard-hitting, off-the-wall comedies or dramas suitable for open-minded audiences. No topic taboo, no musicals or plays for young audiences. Two copies of synopsis, resume & completed application. Send SASE for application & guidelines. Applications available on our web site.
Award: Selected play receives public staged reading & $250, followed by a 1-year development period, full production, additional $500, plus travel/accommodations for festival opening
Closing Date: Dec 1-Feb 1
Presented: Trustus, Aug, full production

Kate Tufts Discovery Award
Claremont Graduate University
Harper East, Unit B-7, 160 E Tenth St, Claremont, CA 91711-6165
Tel: 909-621-8974
E-mail: tufts@cgu.edu
Web Site: www.cgu.edu/tufts
Key Personnel
Poetry Awards Coord: Genevieve Kaplan
Established: 1993
Most worthy 1st book of poetry published between July 1 & June 30. Award presented annually for a 1st book by a poet of genuine promise.
Award: $10,000 cash
Closing Date: July 1
Presented: Claremont Graduate University, Claremont, CA, April

Kingsley Tufts Poetry Award
Claremont Graduate University
Harper East, Unit B-7, 160 E Tenth St, Claremont, CA 91711-6165
Tel: 909-621-8974
E-mail: tufts@cgu.edu
Web Site: www.cgu.edu/tufts
Key Personnel
Poetry Awards Coord: Genevieve Kaplan
Established: 1992
Most worthy book of poetry published between July 1 & June 30. Mss, CDs & chapbooks not accepted. This annual award honors a poet who is past the very beginning, but has not yet reached the acknowledged pinnacle of his or her career.
Award: $100,000 cash
Closing Date: July 1
Presented: Claremont Graduate University, Claremont, CA, April

Tupelo Press Berkshire Prize for a First or Second Book of Poetry
Formerly Tupelo Press Poetry Contest for First or Second Books of Poetry
Tupelo Press Inc
243 Union St, Suite 305, North Adams, MA 01247
Mailing Address: PO Box 1767, North Adams, MA 01247 SAN: 254-3281
Tel: 413-664-9611 *Fax:* 413-664-9711
E-mail: info@tupelopress.org
Web Site: www.tupelopress.org
Key Personnel
Mng Ed: Jim Schley
Established: 2000
An annual competition for 1st or 2nd books of poetry. Full guidelines on the web site. Entries accepted beginning January 1.
Award: $3,000 & publication & distribution
Closing Date: April 30
Presented: Summer

Tupelo Press Poetry Contest for First or Second Books of Poetry, see Tupelo Press Berkshire Prize for a First or Second Book of Poetry

Tupelo Press Snowbound Series Chapbook Award
Tupelo Press Inc
243 Union St, Suite 305, North Adams, MA 01247
Mailing Address: PO Box 1767, North Adams, MA 01247 SAN: 254-3281
Tel: 413-664-9611 *Fax:* 413-664-9711
E-mail: info@tupelopress.org
Web Site: www.tupelopress.org
Key Personnel
Mng Ed: Jim Schley
Established: 2004
An annual open poetry chapbook competition. Full guidelines on the web site. Entries accepted beginning December 1.
Award: $1,000 & publication
Closing Date: Feb 28
Presented: Spring

The Tusculum Review Prize for Fiction
The Tusculum Review
60 Shiloh Rd, PO Box 5113, Greeneville, TN 37743
Web Site: www.tusculum.edu/tusculumreview
Established: 2005
Award: $1,000 & publication in *The Tusculum Review*
Closing Date: March 15

The 25 Most "Censored" Stories Annual
Project Censored - Media Freedom Foundation
PO Box 750940, Petaluma, CA 94975
Tel: 707-241-4596
Web Site: www.projectcensored.org
Key Personnel
Pres, Media Freedom Foundation & Dir, Project Censored: Mickey Huff *E-mail:* mickey@projectcensored.org
Established: 1976
Investigative journalism.
Award: Certificate
Presented: Oct 1

Ucross Foundation Residency Program
Ucross Foundation
30 Big Red Lane, Clearmont, WY 82835
Tel: 307-737-2291 *Fax:* 307-737-2322
E-mail: info@ucross.org
Web Site: www.ucrossfoundation.org
Key Personnel
Pres, Ucross Foundation: Sharon Dynak *E-mail:* sdynak@ucross.org
Residency Mgr: Ruth Salvatore *E-mail:* rsalvatore@ucross.org
Established: 1983
Artist & writer residency program. Approximately 100 individuals per year for 2-6 week lengths of time. Application fee: $40.
Award: Room, studio & board
Closing Date: Annually, March 1 (Fall session) & Oct 1 (Spring session)

John Updike Award
American Academy of Arts & Letters
633 W 155 St, New York, NY 10032
Tel: 212-368-5900 *Fax:* 212-491-4615
E-mail: academy@artsandletters.org
Web Site: www.artsandletters.org
Key Personnel
Exec Dir: Cody Upton
Biennial award to recognize a writer in mid-career who has demonstrated consistent excellence.
Award: $20,000

Utah Original Writing Competition
Utah Division of Arts & Museums
Subsidiary of Utah State Department of Heritage & Arts
617 E South Temple, Salt Lake City, UT 84102
Tel: 801-236-7555 *Fax:* 801-236-7556
Web Site: arts.utah.gov
Key Personnel
Literary Arts Specialist: Alyssa Hickman Grove *Tel:* 801-236-7548 *E-mail:* agrove@utah.gov
Established: 1958
Applicants must be Utah residents. Guidelines & forms posted on web site by April 1.
Award: $8,450 in prizes in 7 categories
Closing Date: Last Friday in June
Presented: Salt Lake City, UT, Annually in Oct

William Van Dyke Short Story Prize
Ruminate Magazine
1041 N Taft Hill Rd, Fort Collins, CO 80521
Tel: 970-449-2726
E-mail: editor@ruminatemagazine.org
Web Site: www.ruminatemagazine.com
Key Personnel
Ed-in-Chief: Brianna Van Dyke
Sr Ed: Amy Lowe
Assoc Ed: Kristin George Bagdanov; Stefani Rossi
Established: 2009
All submissions must be previously unpublished & submitted via online submission form. One short story per contest entry, 5,500 words or less. No limit on number of entries per person. Entry fee: $20.
Award: $1,500 & publication in Spring issue (1st place), $200 & publication (2nd place)
Closing Date: Annually, Feb 15
Presented: Aug 15

The William Van Wert Memorial Fiction Award
Hidden River™ Arts
PO Box 63927, Philadelphia, PA 19147
Tel: 610-764-0813
E-mail: hiddenriverarts@gmail.com
Web Site: www.hiddenriverarts.org; www.hiddenriverarts.com
Key Personnel
Founding Dir: Debra Leigh Scott
Established: 2002
Annual award for a work of unpublished short story or novel excerpt of 25 pages or less. Entry fee: $17.
Award: $1,000 (awarded by mail)
Closing Date: June 30
Presented: Dec

VanderMey Nonfiction Prize
Ruminate Magazine
1041 N Taft Hill Rd, Fort Collins, CO 80521
Tel: 970-449-2726
E-mail: editor@ruminatemagazine.org
Web Site: www.ruminatemagazine.com
Key Personnel
Ed-in-Chief: Brianna Van Dyke
Sr Ed: Amy Lowe
Assoc Ed: Kristin George Bagdanov; Stefani Rossi
Established: 2011
One nonfiction piece per entry, 5,500 words or less & must be previously unpublished. No limit on number of entries per person. Entry fee $20.
Award: $1,500 & publication in prize issue (1st place), $200 & publication (2nd place)
Closing Date: Annually, Nov 15
Presented: May 15

Daniel Varoujan Award
New England Poetry Club
46 Wallace St, Somerville, MA 02144
Tel: 617-744-6034
E-mail: info@nepoetryclub.org
Web Site: www.nepoetryclub.org
Key Personnel
VP: Hillary Sallick
Established: 1979
Award for an unpublished poem in English (not a translation) worthy of the Armenian poet, Daniel Varoujan, executed by the Turks in 1915 at the onset of the genocide of the Armenian population; $15 for up to 3 entries & $3 for each additional poem for nonmembs. Send poem in duplicate, name of writer on one only. Previous winners may not enter again. See web site for additional guidelines.
Award: $500 & publication of poem on NEPC web site

Closing Date: Annually, May 31
Presented: Winners announced online Aug/Sept

Vermont Arts Council Grants, see Annual & Rolling Grants for Artists

Vermont Studio Center Writer's Program Fellowships
Vermont Studio Center
80 Pearl St, Johnson, VT 05656
Mailing Address: PO Box 613, Johnson, VT 05656
Tel: 802-635-2727 *Fax:* 802-635-2730
E-mail: writing@vermontstudiocenter.org; info@vermontstudiocenter.org
Web Site: www.vermontstudiocenter.org
Key Personnel
Writing Prog Dir: Jody Gladding *E-mail:* jody@vermontstudiocenter.org
Prog Dir: Kathy Black *E-mail:* kblack@vermontstudiocenter.org
Accepts 16 writers per month year-round. Fellowship awards are given as funds are available through VSC Fellowships.
Award: Four-week residency
Closing Date: Feb 15, June 15, Oct 1, apply 6 months prior to residency date

Very Short Fiction Award
Glimmer Train Press Inc
PO Box 80430, Portland, OR 97280-1430
Tel: 503-221-0836 *Fax:* 503-221-0837
E-mail: editors@glimmertrain.org
Web Site: www.glimmertrain.org
Key Personnel
Co-Ed: Susan Burmeister-Brown *E-mail:* susan@glimmertrain.org
Established: 1997
Open to short stories under 3,000 words. Winner notification takes place 2 months after the close of each competition.
Award: $2,000, publication & 20 copies of that issue (1st place), $500 (2nd place), $300 (3rd place)
Closing Date: Annually in March/April & July/Aug

Jill Vickers Prize
Canadian Political Science Association
260 rue Dalhousie St, Suite 204, Ottawa, ON K1N 7E4, Canada
Tel: 613-562-1202 *Fax:* 613-241-0019
E-mail: cpsa-acsp@cpsa-acsp.ca
Web Site: www.cpsa-acsp.ca
Key Personnel
Admin: Michelle Hopkins
Awarded to the author or authors of the best paper presented in English or French on the topic of gender & politics.
Award: Commemorative certificate
Presented: University of Regina, SK, CN, May 26-June 1, 2018

Vicky Metcalf Award for Literature for Young People
The Writers' Trust of Canada
460 Richmond St W, Suite 600, Toronto, ON M5V 1Y1, Canada
Tel: 416-504-8222 *Toll Free Tel:* 877-906-6548 *Fax:* 416-504-9090
E-mail: info@writerstrust.com
Web Site: www.writerstrust.com
Key Personnel
Exec Dir: Mary Osborne *Tel:* 416-504-8222 ext 244 *E-mail:* mosborne@writerstrust.com
Awarded to a Canadian writer of young people's literature for a body of work.
Other Sponsor(s): George Cedric Metcalf Charitable Foundation
Award: $20,000
Presented: The Writers' Trust Awards, Toronto, ON, CN, Annually in Nov

Voelcker Award, see PEN/Voelcker Award

Harold D Vursell Memorial Award
American Academy of Arts & Letters
633 W 155 St, New York, NY 10032
Tel: 212-368-5900 *Fax:* 212-491-4615
E-mail: academy@artsandletters.org
Web Site: www.artsandletters.org
Key Personnel
Exec Dir: Cody Upton
Given annually to single out recent prose that merits recognition for the quality of its style.
Award: $20,000

Richard Wall Memorial Award
Theatre Library Association (TLA)
c/o The New York Public Library for the Performing Arts, 111 Amsterdam Ave, New York, NY 10023
E-mail: TheatreLibraryAssociation@gmail.com; TLABookAwards@gmail.com
Web Site: www.tla-online.org/awards/bookawards
Key Personnel
Co-Chair, Book Awards Comm: Diana Bertolini; Annemarie van Roessel
Established: 1973
Honors books published in US in the field of recorded performance including motion picture, TV & radio. Ineligible books are: directories, collections from previously published sources & reprints.
Award: $500 (1st prize), $250 (Special Jury prize); certificate
Closing Date: Feb 28
Presented: New York, NY, Oct

Edward Lewis Wallant Book Award
Dr & Mrs Irving Waltman
3 Brighton Rd, West Hartford, CT 06117
Tel: 860-232-1421
Key Personnel
Sponsor of Award: Fran Waltman; Irving Waltman
Established: 1963
Awarded annually for a creative work of fiction (novel or collection of short stories) significant to American Jews. The author must be American & the book must have been published during the current year.
Award: $500 & scroll
Closing Date: Dec 31

George Washington Book Prize
Washington College, CV Starr Center for the Study of the American Experience
101 S Water St, Chestertown, MD 21620
Tel: 410-810-7165 *Fax:* 410-810-7175
Web Site: starrcenter.washcoll.edu/centers/starr/george-washington-book-prize.php
Key Personnel
Book Prize Coord: Jean Wortman *E-mail:* jwortman2@washcoll.edu
Established: 2005
Created to recognize outstanding published works that contribute to a greater understanding of America's Founding era. Books must be published in the year prior to the year prize is awarded. Announcement of finalists on George Washington's Birthday, February 22. Announcement of winner at Mount Vernon, VA in May.
Other Sponsor(s): George Washington's Mount Vernon; Gilder Lehrman Institute of American History
Award: $50,000
Closing Date: Dec 1
Presented: Mount Vernon Estate & Gardens, 3200 Mount Vernon Memorial Hwy, Mount Vernon, VA, Spring

The Robert Watson Literary Prizes in Fiction & Poetry
The Greensboro Review
MFA Writing Program, The Greensboro Review, UNC-Greensboro, 3302 MHRA Bldg, Greensboro, NC 27402-6170
Tel: 336-334-5459 *Fax:* 336-256-1470
Web Site: www.greensbororeview.org
Key Personnel
Ed: Jim Clark *E-mail:* jlclark@uncg.edu
Assoc Ed: Terry Kennedy *E-mail:* tlkenned@uncg.edu
Established: 1984
Short story & poetry.
Other Sponsor(s): MFA Writing Program at UNC Greensboro
Award: $1,000 (each category)
Closing Date: Annually, Sept 15

Jacqueline Bograd Weld Award for Biography, see PEN/Jacqueline Bograd Weld Award for Biography

Rene Wellek Prize
American Comparative Literature Association (ACLA)
University of South Carolina, Dept of Languages, Literature & Cultures, 1620 College St, Rm 813-A, Columbia, SC 29208
Tel: 803-777-3021
E-mail: info@acla.org
Web Site: www.acla.org/prize-awards
Key Personnel
Nominations Comm Chair: Antonio Barrenechea *E-mail:* abarrene@umw.edu
Admin Coord: Andy Anderson
Established: 1968
To recognize the best book published in the field of comparative literature published in the 2 calendar years prior to presentation. See web site for nomination process.
Award: Complimentary registration for the annual meeting as well as hotel & airfare accommodations (not including food)
Closing Date: Oct 1
Presented: ACLA Annual Meeting, July

Wergle Flomp Humor Poetry Contest
Winning Writers
351 Pleasant St, PMB 222, Northampton, MA 01060-3961
Tel: 413-320-1847 *Toll Free Tel:* 866-WINWRIT (946-9748) *Fax:* 413-280-0539
Web Site: www.winningwriters.com
Key Personnel
Pres: Adam Cohen *E-mail:* adam@winningwriters.com
VP: Jendi Reiter
Established: 2001
Seeks best humor poems. Both published & unpublished works are welcome. Submit poems in English or inspired gibberish. No entry fee. Contestants may enter one poem per year up to 250 lines. Poets from all nations welcome.
Award: $1,000 (1st prize), $250 (2nd prize), $100 (10 honorable mentions), plus publication on web site for all winners
Closing Date: Annually, April 1
Presented: Winners announced Aug 15 on web site

Wesley-Logan Prize
American Historical Association (AHA)
400 "A" St SE, Washington, DC 20003
Tel: 202-544-2422 *Fax:* 202-544-8307
E-mail: awards@historians.org
Web Site: www.historians.org
Established: 1992
For an outstanding book in African diaspora history. The prize is offered on some aspect of the history of the dispersion, settlement & adjustment +/or return of peoples originally from

Africa. Eligible for consideration are books in any chronological period & any geological location. Only books of high scholarly & literary merit will be considered. Along with an application form, applicants must mail a copy of their book to each of the prize committee members who will be posted on our web site as the prize deadline approaches. All updated info on web site. Books published in 2017 will be considered.
Other Sponsor(s): Association for the Study of Afro-American Life & History
Award: Cash
Closing Date: May 15, 2018
Presented: AHA Annual Meeting, Chicago, IL, Jan 2019

Western Heritage Awards (Wrangler Award)
National Cowboy & Western Heritage Museum®
1700 NE 63 St, Oklahoma City, OK 73111
Tel: 405-478-2250 *Fax:* 405-478-4714
E-mail: info@nationalcowboymuseum.org
Web Site: nationalcowboymuseum.org
Key Personnel
McCaslend Chair of Cowboy Culture & Exhibit Curator: Don Reeves *E-mail:* donreeves@nationalcowboymuseum.org
Established: 1961
Awarded annually honoring works in TV, film, literary & music which preserve the spirit of the American West.
Award: Bronze sculpture of a cowboy on horseback
Closing Date: Dec 31 (TV, film & literary)
Presented: Banquet & Awards Ceremonies, National Cowboy & Western Heritage Museum, April (must be in attendance to receive bronze sculpture)

Hilary Weston Writers' Trust Prize for Nonfiction
The Writers' Trust of Canada
460 Richmond St W, Suite 600, Toronto, ON M5V 1Y1, Canada
Tel: 416-504-8222 *Toll Free Tel:* 877-906-6548 *Fax:* 416-504-9090
E-mail: info@writerstrust.com
Web Site: www.writerstrust.com
Key Personnel
Exec Dir: Mary Osborne *Tel:* 416-504-8222 ext 244 *E-mail:* mosborne@writerstrust.com
Established: 1997
Awarded for literary exellence in nonfiction, which includes personal or journalistic essays, history, biography, memoirs, commentary & criticism, both social & political.
Award: $60,000 (1st prize), $5,000 (finalists)
Presented: Annually in Nov

Charles A Weyerhauser Book Award
The Forest History Society Inc
701 William Vickers Ave, Durham, NC 27701-3162
Tel: 919-682-9319 *Fax:* 919-682-2349
Web Site: www.foresthistory.org
Key Personnel
Admin Asst: Andrea Anderson *E-mail:* andrea.anderson@foresthistory.org
Established: 1977
Rewards superior scholarship in forest & conservation history. Annual award goes to an author who has exhibited fresh insight into a topic & whose narrative analysis is clear, inventive & thought-provoking. Books are selected by award giver to avoid receipt of too many ineligible books.

E B White Award
American Academy of Arts & Letters
633 W 155 St, New York, NY 10032
Tel: 212-368-5900 *Fax:* 212-491-4615
E-mail: academy@artsandletters.org
Web Site: www.artsandletters.org
Key Personnel
Exec Dir: Cody Upton
Established: 2013
Given to a writer for achievement in children's literature.
Award: $10,000

White, Jackie, Memorial National Children's Playwriting Contest, see Jackie White Memorial National Children's Playwriting Contest

William Allen White Children's Book Awards
Emporia State University, William Allen White Library
One Kellogg Circle, Emporia, KS 66801-5092
Mailing Address: Emporia State University, Campus Box 4051, Emporia, KS 66801-5092
Tel: 620-341-5208 *Toll Free Tel:* 877-613-7323 *Fax:* 620-341-6208
E-mail: wawbookaward@emporia.edu
Web Site: waw.emporia.edu/libsv/wawbookaward
Key Personnel
Exec Dir: Michelle Hammond *E-mail:* mhammon2@emporia.edu
Established: 1952
Two children's books are selected by the children of Kansas, grades 3-5 & 6-8, from 2 master lists of books chosen by a selection committee. When a student has read 2 books from either of the master lists, he or she is eligible to vote at their school (homeschooled vote at their local public library) for the annual White Award winners. Votes are recorded by each school, district or public library & submitted to the William Allen White Children Book Awards Program.
Other Sponsor(s): Trusler Foundation
Award: Two bronze medals, one for each grade level & a $2,500 check for each winner
Closing Date: Votes must be received by April 15
Presented: Emporia State University, Albert Taylor Hall, Winners announced late April & awards presented in Autumn

Whiting Awards
Mrs Giles Whiting Foundation
16 Court St, Suite 2308, Brooklyn, NY 11241
Tel: 718-701-5962
E-mail: info@whiting.org
Web Site: www.whiting.org
Key Personnel
Exec Dir: Daniel Reid
Foundation Bd Pres: Peter Pennoyer
Dir, Writers' Progs: Courtney Hodell
Prog Asst: Adina Applebaum
Res & Web Asst: Katy Einerson
Established: 1985
For creative writing in fiction, nonfiction, poetry & plays. Applications not accepted by the foundation; confidential nominators propose candidates for selection committee consideration.
Award: Ten awards of $50,000 each
Presented: Annually in March

Whiting Creative Nonfiction Grant
Mrs Giles Whiting Foundation
16 Court St, Suite 2308, Brooklyn, NY 11241
Tel: 718-701-5962
E-mail: nonfiction@whiting.org; info@whiting.org
Web Site: www.whiting.org
Key Personnel
Exec Dir: Daniel Reid
Foundation Bd Pres: Peter Pennoyer
Dir, Writers' Progs: Courtney Hodell
Prog Asst: Adina Applebaum
Res & Web Asst: Katy Einerson
Established: 2016
Program offers allocations to as many as 6 works in progress to enable authors to complete their books. To be eligible, writers must be under contract with a publisher & at least 2 years into their contract. Submissions welcome for nonfiction works of history, cultural or political reportage, biography, memoir, the sciences, philosophy, criticism, food or travel writing & personal essays, among other categories, for a general, not academic, readership. To apply, writers should submit their original proposal that led to the contract, as many as 3 sample chapters, a budget & schedule for completion, a letter of support from their publisher & 2 other letters of support (not to come from their agent). Writers can submit applications online at www.whiting.org/nonfiction/application.
Award: $40,000
Closing Date: May 1
Presented: Annually in Dec

Walt Whitman Award
The Academy of American Poets Inc
75 Maiden Lane, Suite 901, New York, NY 10038
Tel: 212-274-0343 *Fax:* 212-274-9427
E-mail: academy@poets.org
Web Site: www.poets.org
Key Personnel
Exec Dir: Jennifer Benka
Prog Coord: Nikay Paredes *Tel:* 212-274-0343 ext 13 *E-mail:* nparedes@poets.org
Established: 1975
Annual award for a book-length ms of poetry by a living American poet who has not published a book of poetry. Visit academy web site for entry form & guidelines.
Award: First book publication $5,000, publication by Graywolf Press, an all-expenses-paid 6-week residency at the Civitella Ranieri Center in Italy & distribution of the winning book to thousands of Academy of American Poet members
Closing Date: Sept 15-Nov 15
Presented: April

Jon Whyte Memorial Essay Prize
Writers' Guild of Alberta
11759 Groat Rd, Edmonton, AB T5M 3K6, Canada
Tel: 780-422-8174 *Toll Free Tel:* 800-665-5354 (AB only) *Fax:* 780-422-2663 (attn WGA)
E-mail: mail@writersguild.ca
Web Site: writersguild.ca
Key Personnel
Exec Dir: Carol Holmes *E-mail:* carol.holmes@writersguild.ca
Communs & Partnerships Coord: Ellen Kartz *E-mail:* ellen.kartz@writersguild.ca
Memb Servs Coord: Giorgia Severini
Progs Coord: Natalie Cook *E-mail:* natalie.cook@writersguild.ca; Julie Robinson *E-mail:* julie.robinson@writersguild.ca
Established: 1992
Awarded to an outstanding unpublished essay by an Alberta author; no longer than 3,000 words.
Award: $700
Closing Date: Annually, Dec 31
Presented: Alberta Book Awards Gala
Branch Office(s)
505 21 Ave SW, Calgary, AB T2S 0G9, Canada, Prog Coord: Samantha Warwick *Tel:* 403-265-2226 *E-mail:* samantha.warwick@writersguild.ca

Wichita State University Playwriting Contest
School of Performing Arts
Division of Wichita State University
1845 Fairmount St, Box 153, Wichita, KS 67260-0153
Tel: 316-978-3360 *Fax:* 316-978-3202
Web Site: www.wichita.edu

Key Personnel
Admin Specialist: Renea Goforth *Tel:* 316-978-6634
For college students only (graduate or undergraduate).
Award: Production of play, transportation & housing for playwright to attend performance
Closing Date: Annually, Jan 15
Presented: Welsbacher Theatre, Wichita State University, Wichita, KS, Annually in Spring

The Laura Ingalls Wilder Medal
Association for Library Service to Children (ALSC)
Division of The American Library Association (ALA)
50 E Huron St, Chicago, IL 60611-2795
Tel: 312-280-2163 *Toll Free Tel:* 800-545-2433 *Fax:* 312-440-9374; 312-280-5271
E-mail: alsc@ala.org
Web Site: www.ala.org/alsc
Key Personnel
Exec Dir: Aimee Strittmatter *Tel:* 312-280-2162 *E-mail:* astrittmatter@ala.org
Awards Coord: Courtney Jones *E-mail:* alscawards@ala.org
Prog Coord: Marsha P Burgess *Tel:* 312-280-2166 *E-mail:* mburgess@ala.org
Established: 1954
Annual award presented to an author or illustrator whose books have made a substantial & lasting contribution to children's literature. The books must have been published in the US.
Award: Medal
Closing Date: Dec 31
Presented: ALA Midwinter Meeting, Jan/Feb

Thornton Wilder Prize for Translation
American Academy of Arts & Letters
633 W 155 St, New York, NY 10032
Tel: 212-368-5900 *Fax:* 212-491-4615
E-mail: academy@artsandletters.org
Web Site: www.artsandletters.org
Key Personnel
Exec Dir: Cody Upton
Established: 2009
Recognizes a practitioner, scholar, or patron who has made a significant contribution to the art of literary translation.
Award: $20,000

William Flanagan Memorial Creative Persons Center
Edward F Albee Foundation
14 Harrison St, New York, NY 10013
Tel: 212-226-2020 *Fax:* 212-226-5551
E-mail: info@albeefoundation.org
Web Site: www.albeefoundation.org
Key Personnel
Founder & Pres: Edward Albee
Exec Dir: Jakob Holder
Annual residency program for writers & visual artists. The only requirements are talent & need.
Award: Room (writers)/Room & Studio (visual artists)
Closing Date: Jan 1-March 1 for Summer season
Presented: The Barn, Montauk, Long Island, NY, Mid-May through mid-Oct, every writer or artist can choose 4 or 6 weeks, depending on availability

Oscar Williams/Gene Derwood Award
NY Community Trust
909 Third Ave, New York, NY 10022
Tel: 212-686-0010 *Fax:* 212-532-8528
E-mail: info@nycommunitytrust.org
Web Site: www.nycommunitytrust.org
Key Personnel
Pres: Lorie Slutsky *Tel:* 212-686-2565
VP, Communs: David Marcus *Tel:* 212-889-3963
VP, Grants: Pat Jenny *Tel:* 212-686-0010 ext 201
Dir, Grants Budgeting: Liza Lagunoff *Tel:* 212-686-7196 *E-mail:* ll@nyct-cfi.org
Asst to Pres: Barbara Wybraniec *Tel:* 212-686-0010 ext 229
Established: 1971
Annual award intended to help needy or worthy poets & artists who have had long & distinguished careers. Nominations or applications are not accepted in any form.
Award: Cash varies in amount

William Carlos Williams Award
Poetry Society of America (PSA)
15 Gramercy Park, New York, NY 10003
Tel: 212-254-9628
Web Site: www.poetrysociety.org
Key Personnel
Pres: Kimiko Hahn
Exec Dir: Alice Quinn
Deputy Dir: Brett Fletcher Lauer *E-mail:* brett@poetrysociety.org
Prog Dir: Laurin Macios *E-mail:* laurin@poetrysociety.org
For a book of poetry published by a small press or a nonprofit or university press. Submissions, accompanied by an entry form, from publishers only. See web site for complete guidelines.
Award: Purchase prize between $500 & $1,000
Closing Date: Annually, Oct-Dec
Presented: Announced on web site early April

E O Wilson Literary Science Writing Award, see PEN/E O Wilson Literary Science Writing Award

Gary Wilson Award for Short Fiction
Texas Christian University
Dept of English, TCU Box 298300, Fort Worth, TX 76129
Tel: 817-257-5907 *Fax:* 817-257-5905
E-mail: descant@tcu.edu
Web Site: www.descant.tcu.edu
Key Personnel
Mng Ed: Dan Williams *E-mail:* d.e.williams@tcu.edu
Established: 2005
For an outstanding story in an issue. No application process, no entry fee; all published submissions are eligible for prize consideration. Submit work with a SASE.
Other Sponsor(s): descant (publication), Dept of English, TCU
Award: $250 cash
Closing Date: Annually, Sept 1-April 1
Presented: Winners announced in the Summer in *descant*

H W Wilson Co Indexing Award, see ASI/EIS Publishing Award for Excellence in Indexing

The H W Wilson Library Staff Development Grant
ALA Awards Program
Affiliate of The American Library Association (ALA)
50 E Huron St, Chicago, IL 60611
Tel: 312-280-3247 *Toll Free Tel:* 800-545-2433 (ext 3247) *Fax:* 312-944-3897; 312-440-9379
E-mail: awards@ala.org
Web Site: www.ala.org
Key Personnel
Prog Off: Cheryl Malden *E-mail:* cmalden@ala.org
To a library organization for a program to further its staff development goals & objectives.
Award: $3,500 & 24k gold-framed citation
Closing Date: Annually, Dec 1
Presented: ALA Annual Conference

Herbert Warren Wind Book Award
USGA Museum & Archives
77 Liberty Corner Rd, Far Hills, NJ 07931-0708
Tel: 908-234-2300
Web Site: www.usga.org
Key Personnel
Libn: Nancy Stulack *Tel:* 908-781-1107 *E-mail:* nstulack@usga.org
Established: 1987
Recognizes & honors outstanding contributions to golf literature. Named in honor of the famed golf writer, the annual award acknowledges & encourages outstanding research, writing & publishing about golf. The award attempts to broaden the public's interest & knowledge in the game of golf. Presented by the USGA Museum & Archives, the Book Award is the top literary prize awarded by the USGA.
Award: Silver inkwell with feather
Closing Date: Oct 31
Presented: USGA Annual Meeting, Feb

Windham-Campbell Prizes
Yale University, Windham-Campbell Prizes Endowment
Beinecke Library, 121 Whitney Ave, Suite 102, New Haven, CT 06510-1242
Fax: 203-432-9033
Web Site: windhamcampbell.org
Key Personnel
Prog Dir: Michael Kelleher *Tel:* 203-432-2956
Prog Asst: Jennifer Castellon *Tel:* 203-432-7325
Global English language awards that call attention to literary achievement & provide writers with the opportunity to focus on their work independent of financial concerns. Nomination only. Nine prizes available each year. Categories: fiction, nonfiction, drama.
Award: $150,000 unrestricted grant
Presented: Annually in Spring

The Laurence L & Thomas Winship/PEN New England Award, see PEN/New England Awards

Justin Winsor Prize for Library History Essay
The Library History Round Table of the American Library Association
50 E Huron St, Chicago, IL 60611
Tel: 312-280-4283 *Toll Free Tel:* 800-545-2433 (ext 4283) *Fax:* 312-280-4392
E-mail: ors@ala.org
Web Site: www.ala.org; ala.org/lhrt
Key Personnel
Prog Offr & LHRT Liaison: Kelsey Henke *E-mail:* khenke@ala.org
To author of an outstanding essay embodying original historical research on a significant subject of library history.
Award: $500 & invitation to have paper considered for publication in *Libraries & the Cultural Record*
Closing Date: Jan

The Wisconsin Writers Awards
Council for Wisconsin Writers
c/o 450 E Beaumont Ave, No 1005, Whitefish Bay, WI 53217-4805
E-mail: wiswriters@gmail.com
Web Site: wiswriters.org/awards
Key Personnel
Pres & Awards Co-Chair: Geoff Gilpin *E-mail:* geoff@geoffgilpin.com
VP & Awards Co-Chair: Carolyn Kott Washburne *Tel:* 414-961-1779 *E-mail:* ckw44@wi.rr.com
Secy & Awards Co-Chair: Karla Huston *E-mail:* karlahuston@gmail.com
Awards Co-Chair: Jerrianne Hayslett *E-mail:* jfarhsi@aol.com
Eight annual awards for deserving writers throughout the state & 2 biennial awards to individuals or organizations who have made significant contributions to literature in the state. Submissions accepted November 1-January 31 for work published in the year prior to the

close of the contest. Entry fee: $25 for nonmembers (exc Essay Award for Young Writers). Two biennial awards are offered in alternating years - Major Achievement Award & Christopher Latham Sholes Award.
Award: $500 each, $250 Essay Award for Young Writers, $1,000 for Major Achievement Award
Closing Date: Feb 1 (postmark)
Presented: CWW Annual Banquet, May

WLA Literary Award
Wisconsin Library Association Inc
4610 S Biltmore Lane, Suite 100, Madison, WI 53718-2153
Tel: 608-245-3640 *Fax:* 608-245-3646
Web Site: wla.wisconsinlibraries.org
Key Personnel
Exec Dir: Mr Plumer Lovelace *E-mail:* lovelace@wisconsinlibraries.org
Events & Conferences: Brigitte Rupp Vacha *E-mail:* ruppvacha@wisconsinlibraries.org
Established: 1974
To honor a work by a Wisconsin author for a book published in the preceding year that contributes to the world of literature & ideas.
Award: Monetary award
Closing Date: April 15
Presented: WLA Annual Conference, Oct-Nov

WNBA Pannell Award for Excellence in Children's Bookselling
Women's National Book Association Inc
PO Box 237, FDR Sta, New York, NY 10150-0231
Toll Free Tel: 866-610-9622
E-mail: WNBAPannell@gmail.com
Web Site: www.wnba-books.org; www.NationalReadingGroupMonth.org; www.wnba-books.org/awards
Key Personnel
Chair: Susan Knopf *E-mail:* susan@scoutbooksandmedia.com
Established: 1981
Recognizes retail bookstores that excel at creatively bringing books & children together & inspiring children's interest in books & reading. Nominations come from customers, sales & marketing people & other book industry professionals & stores themselves. One general book store with a children's section & one children's specialty store are selected each year by a jury of 5 book industry professionals based on creativity, responsiveness to community needs, passion & understanding of children's books & young readers.
Other Sponsor(s): Estate of Lucille Micheels Pannell; Penguin Young Readers Group
Award: $2,000 (2 at $1,000 each) plus 1 piece of original art for each recipient
Closing Date: Feb
Presented: BookExpo, June

Thomas Wolfe Fiction Prize
North Carolina Writers' Network
PO Box 21591, Winston-Salem, NC 27120-1591
E-mail: mail@ncwriters.org
Web Site: www.ncwriters.org
Key Personnel
Exec Dir: Ed Southern *E-mail:* ed@ncwriters.org
Competition is open to all writers regardless of geographical location or prior publication. Submit 2 copies of an unpublished fiction ms not to exceed 12 double-spaced pages. Entry fee: $15 membs, $25 nonmembs. Submissions accepted December 1-January 30. Send submissions to Thomas Wolfe Fiction Prize, Great Smokies Writing Program, UNCA, One University Heights, Asheville, NC 28804.
Award: $1,000 & possible publication in *The Thomas Wolfe Review*
Closing Date: Annually, Jan 30

Tobias Wolff Award for Fiction
The Bellingham Review
Mail Stop 9053, Western Washington University, Bellingham, WA 98225
Tel: 360-650-4863
E-mail: bhreview@wwu.edu
Web Site: www.bhreview.org
Key Personnel
Ed-in-Chief: Suzanne Paola Antonetta
Mng Ed: Mike Oliphant
Established: 1993
Maximum length for prose is 6,000 words. Novel excerpts up to 6,000 words are accepted. No previously published works, or works accepted for publication, are eligible. Work may be under consideration elsewhere, but must be withdrawn from the competition if accepted for publication. All entries will receive a complimentary 1-issue subscription. Entry fee for the first entry (1 short story, or novel excerpt up to 6,000 words) $20. Each additional entry $10.
Only accept submissions through Submittable. Mailed submissions are no longer accepted. All finalists are considered for publication. The winning piece is selected by a distinguished, outside judge. Entries accepted beginning December 1.
Award: $1,000 & publication in *The Bellingham Review* (1st prize); considered for publication (2nd, 3rd & finalists)
Closing Date: Annually, March 15
Presented: Annually in June

Women's National Book Association Award
Women's National Book Association Inc
PO Box 237, FDR Sta, New York, NY 10150-0231
Tel: 212-208-4629 (headquarters)
Toll Free Tel: 866-610-9622 *Fax:* 212-208-4629
Web Site: www.wnba-books.org; www.NationalReadingGroupMonth.org
Key Personnel
Natl Pres: Jane Kinney Denning *E-mail:* nationalpresidentwnba@gmail.com
Natl Treas: Nicole Pilo *E-mail:* npilo@cplanning.com
NYC Pres: Hannah Bennett *E-mail:* h.bennett42@gmail.com
Secy: Celine Keating
Established: 1940
Presented to a living American woman who derives part or all of her income from books & allied arts & who has done meritorious work in the world of books beyond the duties or responsibilities of her profession or occupation. Offered biennially in even-numbered years.
Award: Citation
Presented: Varies

The J Howard & Barbara M J Wood Prize
Poetry Magazine
61 W Superior St, Chicago, IL 60654
Tel: 312-787-7070 *Fax:* 312-787-6650
E-mail: editors@poetrymagazine.org
Web Site: www.poetryfoundation.org
Key Personnel
Edit Asst: Holly Amos *E-mail:* hamos@poetrymagazine.org
Established: 1994
For poetry published in the preceding 2 volumes of *Poetry* magazine. No application necessary.
Award: $5,000
Presented: Annually in Dec

Carter G Woodson Book Awards
National Council for the Social Studies
8555 16 St, Suite 500, Silver Spring, MD 20910
Tel: 301-588-1800 *Toll Free Tel:* 800-296-7840 *Fax:* 301-588-2049
E-mail: excellence@ncss.org; publications@ncss.org
Web Site: www.socialstudies.org
Key Personnel
Exec Dir: Lawrence Paska *E-mail:* lpaska@ncss.org
Dir, Meetings & Exhibits: David Bailor *Tel:* 301-588-1800 ext 109 *E-mail:* dbailor@ncss.org
Dir, Pubns: Michael Simpson *Tel:* 301-588-1800 ext 105 *E-mail:* msimpson@ncss.org
Dir, External Rel & Council Communs: Ana Post *Tel:* 301-588-1800 ext 114 *E-mail:* apost@ncss.org
Prog Mgr, External Rel & Council Communs: Victoria Nayiga *Tel:* 301-588-1800 ext 107 *E-mail:* victoria@ncss.org
Established: 1974
Annual award to recognize the most distinguished nonfiction books for young readers which depict ethnicity in the US. Eligible books deal with the experiences of one or more racial/ethnic minority groups in the US. Publisher must provide copy of each title for submission requirements.
Award: One elementary (K-6) & one middle level (5-8), one secondary (7-12) annual award, 3 runner-up books designated Woodson Honor Books, seals are now available to publishers $.25 each for less than 1,000 & less for larger quantities
Closing Date: Annually, Sept 30
Presented: Awards Reception, NCSS Annual Conference

Word Works Washington Prize
The Word Works
Adirondack Community College, Dearlove Hall, 640 Bay Rd, Queensbury, NY 12804
Mailing Address: PO Box 42164, Washington, DC 20015
Tel: 301-581-9439 *Fax:* 301-581-9443
E-mail: editor@wordworksbooks.org
Web Site: www.wordworksbooks.org
Key Personnel
Chpn, Bd of Dirs: Karren L Alenier
Pres: Nancy White *E-mail:* nancywhitepoetry@gmail.com
Established: 1981
Annual prize for an unpublished ms of poetry. Submission may be made by any living American or Canadian writer. Include 2 title pages, one with & one without name, address, telephone number & e-mail. No entry form is required. Online submissions available. Submissions should be 48-80 pages in English; please attach $25 entry fee, acknowledgment page & brief bio. Business sized SASE mandatory with entry. Visit web site for guidelines.
Award: $1,500 & publication
Closing Date: March 15

World Fantasy Awards
World Fantasy Awards Association
PO Box 43, Mukilteo, WA 98275-0043
Web Site: www.worldfantasy.org
Key Personnel
Pres: Peter Dennis Pautz *E-mail:* sfexecsec@gmail.com
To acknowledge excellence in fantasy writing & art.
Award: Trophy
Closing Date: June 1
Presented: World Fantasy Convention, Halloween weekend

World's Best Short-Short Story Contest
The Southeast Review
Florida State University, Dept of English, Tallahassee, FL 32306
E-mail: southeastreview@gmail.com
Web Site: www.southeastreview.org
Key Personnel
Ed: Alex Quinlan
Established: 1986
Best 500 word (maximum) previously unpublished short-short story. All entries will be con-

sidered for publication. $16 entry fee for up to 3 stories.
Other Sponsor(s): Florida State University English Department Creative Writing Program
Award: $500
Closing Date: Annually in March

Write Now
Indiana Repertory Theatre Inc
140 W Washington St, Indianapolis, IN 46204-3465
Tel: 317-635-5277 *Fax:* 317-236-0767
E-mail: info@writenow.co
Web Site: www.writenow.co
Key Personnel
Founder: Dorothy Webb *E-mail:* dwebb@irtlive.com
Artistic Dir: Janet Allen *Tel:* 317-635-5277 ext 4800
Established: 1988
Biennial workshop to encourage writers to create artistic theatrical scripts for young audiences. A collaboration between Childsplay & Indiana Repertory Theatre.
Other Sponsor(s): Doris Duke Charitable Foundation
Award: $1,000, development workshop & rehearsed reading (up to 4 winners); certificates for semi-finalists & excerpts read at symposium
Closing Date: July 31, 2018
Presented: Spring 2019

Writer in Residence
Idaho Commission on the Arts
2410 N Old Penitentiary Rd, Boise, ID 83712
Mailing Address: PO Box 83720, Boise, ID 83720-0008
Tel: 208-334-2119
E-mail: info@arts.idaho.gov
Web Site: www.arts.idaho.gov
Key Personnel
Lit Dir: Jocelyn Robertson *Tel:* 208-334-2119 ext 108 *E-mail:* jocelyn.robertson@arts.idaho.gov
Open only to residents of Idaho; must have resided in Idaho at least 1 year. Triennial award for artistic excellence. Recipient serves a 3-year term, tours the state & gives at least 4 annual readings (8 of 12 in rural communities).
Award: $15,000 ($5,000 annually) plus allowable travel expenses
Closing Date: Jan 31, 2019
Presented: Trienially in July

The Writer Magazine/Emily Dickinson Award
Poetry Society of America (PSA)
15 Gramercy Park, New York, NY 10003
Tel: 212-254-9628
Web Site: www.poetrysociety.org
Key Personnel
Pres: Kimiko Hahn
Exec Dir: Alice Quinn
Deputy Dir: Brett Fletcher Lauer *E-mail:* brett@poetrysociety.org
Prog Dir: Laurin Macios *E-mail:* laurin@poetrysociety.org
Established: 1971
For a poem inspired by Dickinson (though not necessarily in her style), not to exceed 30 lines. Open to society members only. See web site for more information.
Award: $250
Closing Date: Annually, Oct-Dec
Presented: Annual Awards Ceremony, New York, NY, Annually in Spring

Writer's Digest Annual Writing Competition
Writer's Digest
Imprint of F+W Media Inc
10151 Carver Rd, Suite 200, Blue Ash, OH 45242
Tel: 715-445-4612 (ext 13430) *Fax:* 920-744-1760
E-mail: writersdigestwritingcompetition@fwmedia.com
Web Site: www.writersdigest.com
Key Personnel
Cust Serv: Nicole Howard
Original, unpublished mss in 10 categories: inspirational writing (spiritual/religious); memoirs/personal essay; magazine feature article; genre short story (mystery, romance, etc); mainstream/literary short story; rhyming poetry; non-rhyming poetry; scripts (stage play or television/movie script) & children's young adult fiction. Poems are $15 for the first entry; $10 for each additional poem submitted in the same online session. All other entries are $25 for the first entry; $15 for each additional ms submitted in the same online session. Refer to web site for current information.
Award: Trip to New York for the Writer's Digest Conference with (grand prize) $5,000 in cash & more, interview in *Writer's Digest*, one-on-one attention from 4 editors or agent, one year subscription to Writer's Digest Tutorials, a 30-minute platform strategy consultation with Chuck Sambuchino. Refer to web site for additional prizes for 1st-10th place & honorable mention
Presented: Annually in Oct

Writers-Editors Network International Writing Competition
Florida Freelance Writers Association
Affiliate of Writers-Editors Network
45 Main St, North Stratford, NH 03590
Mailing Address: PO Box A, North Stratford, NH 03590
Tel: 603-922-8338 *Fax:* 603-922-8339
E-mail: contest@writers-editors.com
Web Site: www.writers-editors.com; www.ffwamembers.com
Key Personnel
Exec Dir: Dana K Cassell *E-mail:* dana@writers-editors.com
Established: 1984
Fiction, nonfiction, juvenile & poetry.
Award: Cash & certificate, critiques for most promising
Closing Date: Annually, March 15
Presented: Annually, May 31

Writers Guild of America Awards
Writers Guild of America, West (WGAW)
7000 W Third St, Los Angeles, CA 90048
Tel: 323-951-4000; 323-782-4569 *Fax:* 323-782-4800
Web Site: www.wga.org
Key Personnel
Pres: Howard Rodman
VP: David Goodman
Secy & Treas: Aaron Mendelsohn
Awards: Jennifer Burt
Established: 1948
Annual awards. Any eligible film exhibited for 1 week during calendar year; original screenplay; adapted screenplay. TV & radio awards. Only members can enter.
Award: Statuette
Presented: Annual Writer's Guild Award Show, Feb

Writers' League of Texas Book Awards
Writers' League of Texas (WLT)
611 S Congress Ave, Suite 200 A-3, Austin, TX 78704
Tel: 512-499-8914
E-mail: wlt@writersleague.org
Web Site: www.writersleague.org
Key Personnel
Prog Dir: Michael Noll *E-mail:* michael@writersleague.org
Established: 1991
Members of the Writers' League of Texas annually recognize outstanding books (fiction, nonfiction, poetry & literary prose, children's long & children's short) published in the year prior to presentation. Membership is not required. See web site for complete submission details.
Other Sponsor(s): University Co-op
Award: $1,000 each award, commemorative award & appearance at the Texas Book Festival
Closing Date: Late Feb
Presented: Autumn

Writers' Trust Engel/Findley Prize
The Writers' Trust of Canada
460 Richmond St W, Suite 600, Toronto, ON M5V 1Y1, Canada
Tel: 416-504-8222 *Toll Free Tel:* 877-906-6548 *Fax:* 416-504-9090
E-mail: info@writerstrust.com
Web Site: www.writerstrust.com
Key Personnel
Exec Dir: Mary Osborne *Tel:* 416-504-8222 ext 244 *E-mail:* mosborne@writerstrust.com
Established: 1986
Presented to a Canadian writer in mid-career. Writers are judged on their body of work—no less than 3 works of literary merit which are predominantly fiction rather than a single book. All Canadian writers are considered.
Award: $25,000
Presented: The Writers' Trust Awards, Toronto, ON, CN, Annually in Nov

The Writers Trust/McClelland & Stewart Journey Prize
The Writers' Trust of Canada
460 Richmond St W, Suite 600, Toronto, ON M5V 1Y1, Canada
Tel: 416-504-8222 *Toll Free Tel:* 877-906-6548 *Fax:* 416-504-9090
E-mail: info@writerstrust.com
Web Site: www.writerstrust.com
Key Personnel
Exec Dir: Mary Osborne *Tel:* 416-504-8222 ext 244 *E-mail:* mosborne@writerstrust.com
Established: 1988
Awarded to a new & developing writer of distinction for a short story published in a Canadian literary publication.
Other Sponsor(s): James A Michener (donation of his Canadian royalty earnings from his novel *Journey*)
Award: $10,000 (winner), $2,500 (finalists)
Presented: The Writers' Trust Awards, Toronto, ON, CN, Annually in Nov

WritersWeekly.com's 24-Hour Short Story Contest
WritersWeekly
5726 Cortez Rd, Suite 349, Bradenton, FL 34210
Fax: 305-768-0261
Web Site: www.writersweekly.com
Key Personnel
Publr: Angela Hoy *E-mail:* angela@writersweekly.com
Held quarterly & limited to 500 entrants. You must be entered in the contest before the topic is posted in order to submit your story. Late stories are disqualified. Entry fee $5.
Award: $300 (1st prize), $250 (2nd place), $200 (3rd place); all winners will receive publication of their story on WritersWeekly.com & 1 Freelance Income Kit. There will be 30 honorable mentions
Closing Date: 24 hours after contest start

Wyoming Arts Council Creative Writing Fellowships
Formerly Wyoming Arts Council Literature Fellowships
Wyoming Arts Council
Division of Wyoming Department of Parks & Cultural Resources

Barrett Bldg, 2nd fl, 2301 Central Ave, Cheyenne, WY 82002
Tel: 307-777-7742
Web Site: wyoarts.state.wy.us
Key Personnel
Public Art & Creative Sector Indivs Supv: Rachel Clifton *Tel:* 307-777-5305 *E-mail:* rachel.clifton@state.wy.us
Established: 1986
Awarded annually for the most exciting new creative writing by Wyoming residents. The 3 categories are: poetry, fiction & nonfiction. Blind judges & one juror.
Award: $3,000 each
Closing Date: Varies, see web site
Presented: Announced in the Fall

Wyoming Arts Council Literature Fellowships, see Wyoming Arts Council Creative Writing Fellowships

Yale Series of Younger Poets
Yale University Press
302 Temple St, New Haven, CT 06511
Mailing Address: PO Box 209040, New Haven, CT 06520-9040
Tel: 203-432-0960 *Fax:* 203-432-0948
Web Site: www.yalebooks.com
Key Personnel
Ed: Sarah Miller
Edit Asst: Eva Skewes
Established: 1919
Awarded annually for poetry mss, 48-64 pages, by early-career American poets who have not previously had a volume of verse published. Submission fee: $25. Mss accepted October 1-November 15. See web site for further details.
Award: Publication & royalties
Closing Date: Nov 15

YALSA/VOYA Research Grant, see Frances Henne YALSA/VOYA Research Grant

Anne & Philip Yandle Best Article Award
British Columbia Historical Federation
PO Box 5254, Sta B, Victoria, BC V8R 6N4, Canada
E-mail: info@bchistory.ca; recognition@bchistory.ca
Web Site: www.bchistory.ca
Key Personnel
Pres: Gary Mitchell *E-mail:* president@bchistory.ca
Dir: Shannon Bettles
Awarded annually to the author of an article published in *British Columbia History* that best enhances knowledge of the history of British Columbia & provides enjoyable reading. Judging is based upon subject development, writing skill, freshness of material & its appeal to a general readership interested in all aspects of the history of the province.
Award: $250 cash prize & certificate
Closing Date: Dec 31
Presented: Annual Awards Banquet

YES New Play Festival
Northern Kentucky University
205 FA Theatre Dept, Nunn Dr, Highland Heights, KY 41099-1007
Tel: 859-572-6362 *Fax:* 859-572-6057
Key Personnel
Proj Dir: Corrie Danieley *E-mail:* daneileyc1@nku.edu; Michael King *E-mail:* mking@nku.edu
Established: 1983
New play contest (biennial).
Award: $500 honoraria, travel & housing for 2-3 different playwrights to attend fully produced premiers of their plays
Closing Date: Plays accepted May 1-Sept 30 in even-numbered year prior to year of presentation
Presented: April 2019

Young Lions Fiction Award
New York Public Library
445 Fifth Ave, 4th fl, New York, NY 10016
Tel: 212-930-0887 *Fax:* 212-930-0983
E-mail: younglions@nypl.org
Web Site: www.nypl.org
Key Personnel
Assoc Mgr, Young Lions Fiction Award: Kayla Ponturo *E-mail:* kaylaponturo@nypl.org
Established: 2001
Given annually to an American writer age 35 or younger for either a novel or collection of short stories.
Award: $10,000
Closing Date: Aug
Presented: The New York Public Library, June

Phyllis Smart-Young Poetry Prize
The Madison Review
University of Wisconsin, 6193 Helen C White Hall, English Dept, 600 N Park St, Madison, WI 53706
E-mail: madisonrevw@gmail.com
Web Site: www.themadisonreview.com
Key Personnel
Chmn Dept: Russ Castronovo
Faculty Advisor & Prog Coord: Ronald Kuka *Tel:* 608-263-3374 *E-mail:* rfkuka@wisc.edu
Ed: Kiyoko Reidy
Mss must be previously unpublished & should be double-spaced with standard 1-inch margins. There is a maximum of 15 pages for combined 3 poems. Only 1 submission (3 poems) is allowed per person per contest. Entry fee $10.
Award: $1,000 & publication in Spring issue of *The Madison Review*
Closing Date: Annually, Nov 1
Presented: Announcement in March

YoungArts
National YoungArts Foundation
2100 Biscayne Blvd, Miami, FL 33137
Tel: 305-377-1140 *Toll Free Tel:* 800-970-ARTS (970-2787)
E-mail: info@youngarts.org; apply@youngarts.org
Web Site: www.youngarts.org
Key Personnel
Media: Dejha Carrington *E-mail:* dcarrington@youngarts.org
Established: 1981
Annual cash award & scholarship opportunities for 15-18 year old artists with demonstrated talent in dance, jazz, cinematic arts, classical music, photography, theater, visual arts, voice & writing. Registration fee: $35. Applicants must be US citizens or have permanent resident status.
Other Sponsor(s): Carnival Foundation
Award: Up to $10,000 in individual awards with potential for Presidential Scholar in the Arts Award
Closing Date: Oct 14
Presented: Alumni Performance & Awards Ceremony, New World Center, Miami, FL, Jan

Morton Dauwen Zabel Award
American Academy of Arts & Letters
633 W 155 St, New York, NY 10032
Tel: 212-368-5900 *Fax:* 212-491-4615
E-mail: academy@artsandletters.org
Web Site: www.artsandletters.org
Key Personnel
Exec Dir: Cody Upton
Biennial award presented in even-numbered years in rotation to a poet, writer of fiction, or critic, of progressive, original & experimental tendencies.
Award: $10,000

The Jacob Zilber Prize for Short Fiction
PRISM international
University of British Columbia, Buch E462, 1866 Main Mall, Vancouver, BC V6T 1Z1, Canada
Tel: 778-822-2514 *Fax:* 778-822-3616
E-mail: prismwritingcontest@gmail.com
Web Site: www.prismmagazine.ca
Key Personnel
Exec Ed: Jennifer Lori; Claire Matthews
Poetry Ed: Dominique Bernier Cormier
Prose Ed: Christopher Evans
Established: 1986
Short fiction. Entry fee: $35 (CN), $40 (US), $45 (intl).
Award: $1,500 (grand prize), $600 (1st runner up), $400 (2nd runner up)
Closing Date: Annually in Jan (check web site for exact date)

Anna Zornio Memorial Children's Theatre Playwriting Award
University of New Hampshire Department of Theatre & Dance
D22 Paul Creative Arts Center, 30 Academic Way, Durham, NH 03824
Tel: 603-862-2919 *Fax:* 603-862-0298
Web Site: cola.unh.edu/theatre-dance/resource/zornio
Key Personnel
Admin Mgr: Michael Wood *Tel:* 603-862-3038 *E-mail:* mike.wood@unh.edu
Chair, Dept of Theatre & Dance: David Kaye
Established: 1980
Award for well written play or musical appropriate for young audiences, PreK-12.
Award: Cash award, up to $500 & play underwritten & produced by the UNH Theatre Department
Closing Date: March 1, 2021
Presented: University of New Hampshire, Durham, NH, Winner announced Nov 2021

Books & Magazines for the Trade

Reference Books for the Trade

All-in-One Media Contacts Directory
Published by Gebbie Press Inc
PO Box 1000, New Paltz, NY 12561-0017
Tel: 845-255-7560 *Toll Free Fax:* 888-345-2790
E-mail: gebbie@gebbiepress.com
Web Site: www.gebbieinc.com
Key Personnel
Pres: Mark Gebbie
Published in 3 sections. The Daily & Weekly Newspaper Directory section lists contact information for all US daily & weekly newspapers, including Black & Spanish language papers. The Radio & Television Directory section includes, radio & TV stations including Black & Spanish language stations & the Trade & Consumer Directory section includes a comprehensive listing of magazines available in various formats.
Annual (print version).
46th ed, 2017: 462 pp, $165 paper, $395 online application or text files
ISBN(s): 978-0-692-80154-3

Almanac of Famous People
Published by Gale
Division of Cengage Learning
27500 Drake Rd, Farmington Hills, MI 48331-3535
SAN: 213-4373
Tel: 248-699-4253 *Toll Free Tel:* 800-877-4253 *Fax:* 248-699-8070 *Toll Free Fax:* 800-414-5043 (orders)
E-mail: gale.galeord@cengage.com
Web Site: www.gale.com
A guide to sources of biographical information on more than 30,000 famous individuals & groups. Entries provide: Subject's best-known name, complete name, nickname, name of group, dates & places of birth & death (when appropriate), nationality & occupation. Most entries include citations to sources that provide additional biographical information. Four indexes: geographic, occupation, chronological index by date & chronological index by year.
10th ed, 2011, $340 hardcover
First published 2001
ISBN(s): 978-1-4144-4548-9

American Book Prices Current
Published by Bancroft Parkman Inc
PO Box 1236, Washington, CT 06793-0236
Tel: 860 868-7408
E-mail: abpc@snet.net
Web Site: www.bookpricescurrent.com
Key Personnel
Publr: Daniel J Leab
Exec Ed: Katharine Kyes Leab
Research price guide detailing prices realized at auction in the US & abroad in the world of books, mss, autographs, maps, broadsides & charts. Now online only, continually updated.
Online price: libr or dealer $595, others $800, update $198.90
First published 1895

American Book Publishing Record® Annual
Published by Grey House Publishing Inc™
4919 Rte 22, Amenia, NY 12501
Mailing Address: PO Box 56, Amenia, NY 12501-0056
Tel: 518-789-8700 *Toll Free Tel:* 800-562-2139 *Fax:* 518-789-0556
E-mail: books@greyhouse.com
Web Site: www.greyhouse.com
Provides immediate access to the 73,000 cataloging records for the entire previous year, for books published or distributed in the US.
Annual.
2017: 3,800 pp, $805/2 vol set
ISBN(s): 978-1-68217-483-8 (2 vol set)

American Book Trade Directory
Published by Information Today, Inc
121 Chanlon Rd, Suite G-20, New Providence, NJ 07974-2195
Toll Free Tel: 800-824-2470 *Fax:* 813-855-2309
E-mail: custserv@infotoday.com
Key Personnel
Mgr, Tampa Edit Opers: Debra James *Tel:* 800-824-2470 ext 222 *E-mail:* djames@infotoday.com
Comprehensive directory of over 14,300 booksellers & wholesalers in the US & Canada, arranged by state/province & city; includes information on sidelines, appraisers, auctioneers & dealers in foreign language books.
Annual.
63rd ed, 2017-2018: 1,222 pp, $399
ISBN(s): 978-1-57387-534-9

American Ethnic Writers
Published by Grey House Publishing Inc™
2 University Plaza, Suite 310, Hackensack, NJ 07601
SAN: 208-838X
Tel: 201-968-0500 *Toll Free Tel:* 800-221-1592 *Fax:* 201-968-0511
E-mail: csr@salempress.com
Web Site: salempress.com
Coverage of 225 ethnic writers, including summary descriptions of the writer's significance, associated ethnicities, birth/death dates, biography & thorough analysis of the writer's works.
Aug 2008: 1,000 pp, $217/3 vol set
ISBN(s): 978-1-58765-462-6

American Library Directory
Published by Information Today, Inc
121 Chanlon Rd, Suite G-20, New Providence, NJ 07974-2195
Toll Free Tel: 800-300-9868 (cust serv); 800-409-4929 (press 4)
E-mail: custserv@infotoday.com
Web Site: www.americanlibrarydirectory.com
Key Personnel
Mng Ed: Stephen L Torpie *Tel:* 908-219-0278 *E-mail:* storpie@infotoday.com
Comprehensive directory of over 30,000 libraries (public, academic & special) throughout the US & CN. Also includes listings of library schools, networks & systems, consortia & state library agencies. Automation information, as well as URLs for libraries & e-mails for library personnel included. Entries arranged geographically. Personnel Index section arranged alphabetically.
Annual.
70th ed, 2017-2018: 3,922 pp, $399/2 vol set cloth
ISBN(s): 978-1-57387-535-6 (2 vol set)

American Reference Books Annual
Published by Libraries Unlimited
Imprint of ABC-CLIO
130 Cremona Dr, Santa Barbara, CA 93117
Mailing Address: PO Box 1911, Santa Barbara, CA 93116-1911
Tel: 805-968-1911 *Toll Free Tel:* 800-368-6868 *Fax:* 805-685-9685 *Toll Free Fax:* 866-270-3856
E-mail: customerservice@abc-clio.com
Web Site: www.abc-clio.com
Key Personnel
Assoc Ed: Juneal M Chenoweth
The premier sources of information for the library & information community for more than 3 decades. Includes descriptive & evaluative entries for recent reference publications. Reviews by subject experts of materials from more than 300 publishers & in nearly 500 subject areas. ARBA assists in answering everyday reference questions & in building a reference collection. Also available online.
Annual.
Vol 48, 2017: 600 pp, $140
ISBN(s): 978-1-4408-5660-0

The Art & Science of Book Publishing
Published by Ohio University Press
31 S Court St, Suite 143, Athens, OH 45701-2979
Tel: 740-593-1154 *Fax:* 740-593-4536
Web Site: www.ohioswallow.com
Key Personnel
Dir & Ed-in-Chief: Gillian Berchowitz *Tel:* 740-593-1159 *E-mail:* berchowi@ohio.edu
Author: Herbert S Bailey, Jr
Introduction to basics of book publishing.

1993 ed: 234 pp, $18.95 paper
First published 1970
ISBN(s): 978-0-8214-0970-1

The Association of American University Presses Directory
Published by Association of American University Presses (AAUP)
1412 Broadway, Suite 2135, New York, NY 10018
Tel: 212-989-1010 *Toll Free Tel:* 800-621-2736 (orders) *Fax:* 773-702-7212 (orders); 212-989-0275
E-mail: info@aaupnet.org
Web Site: www.aaupnet.org
A detailed introduction to the structure & staff of the AAUP & to the publishing programs & personnel of member presses.
Annual.
2017: 295 pp, $30 print, $30 full-access digital, $7 30-day access digital
ISBN(s): 978-0-945103-37-0 (print); 978-0-945103-38-7 (digital)

Author in Progress
Published by Writer's Digest
Imprint of F+W Media Inc
10151 Carver Rd, Suite 200, Blue Ash, OH 45242
Tel: 513-531-2690 *Toll Free Tel:* 800-289-0963 *Fax:* 513-531-0798
E-mail: writersdigest@fwmedia.com (edit)
Web Site: www.writersdigest.com; www.writersdigestshop.com; www.fwmedia.com
Key Personnel
Gen Mgr: David Pyle *E-mail:* david.pyle@fwmedia.com
Content Strategist: Rachel Randall *E-mail:* rachel.randall@fwmedia.com
No-nonsense guide for excelling at every step of the novel writing process, from setting goals, researching & drafting to giving a receiving critiques, polishing prose & seeking publication.
352 pp, $19.99 paper & ebook (retail)
ISBN(s): 978-1-4403-4671-2 (paper); 978-1-4403-4672-9 (ebook)

Authors, Copyright, and Publishing in the Digital Era
Published by IGI Global
701 E Chocolate Ave, Hershey, PA 17033
Tel: 717-533-8845 (ext 100) *Toll Free Tel:* 866-342-6657 *Fax:* 717-533-8661; 717-533-7115
E-mail: cust@igi-global.com
Web Site: www.igi-global.com
2014: 262 pp, $195
ISBN(s): 978-1-4666-5214-9; 978-1-4666-5215-6 (ebook)

AV Market Place (AVMP)
Published by Information Today, Inc
121 Chanlon Rd, Suite G-20, New Providence, NJ 07974-2195
Tel: 908-795-3755 *Toll Free Tel:* 800-409-4929 (press 3); 800-300-9868 (cust serv)
E-mail: custserv@infotoday.com
Key Personnel
Mng Ed: Karen Hallard *Tel:* 908-219-0277 *E-mail:* khallard@infotoday.com
A comprehensive directory of the AV market, listing the activities of almost 5,000 manufacturers, distributors & production service companies & over 1,250 products & services. Heavily indexed. Also contains information on related associations, state & local film & television commissions, awards & festivals, periodicals, reference books & AV-oriented conferences & exhibits. Covers all 50 states plus Canada.
Annual.
45th ed, 2017: 1,480 pp, $359 paper
ISBN(s): 978-1-57387-533-2

Awards & Prizes Online
Published by The Children's Book Council (CBC)
54 W 39 St, 14th fl, New York, NY 10018
Tel: 212-966-1990
E-mail: cbc.info@cbcbooks.org
Web Site: www.cbcbooks.org
Key Personnel
Exec Dir: Carl Lennertz *E-mail:* carl.lennertz@cbcbooks.org
Lists over 300 major US, British Commonwealth & international children's & young adult book awards; for teachers, librarians & universities with English, library or education schools teaching children's literature or creative writing. Includes indices, appendix & a list of information resources.
$150 online

Banned in the USA: A Reference Guide to Book Censorship in Schools & Public Libraries Revised & Expanded Edition
Published by Greenwood Press
Imprint of ABC-CLIO
130 Cremona Dr, Suite C, Santa Barbara, CA 93117
Mailing Address: PO Box 1911, Santa Barbara, CA 93116-1911
Tel: 805-968-1911 *Toll Free Tel:* 800-368-6868 *Fax:* 805-685-9685 *Toll Free Fax:* 866-270-3856
E-mail: customerservice@abc-clio.com
Web Site: www.abc-clio.com
Key Personnel
Dir, Edit-Print: Anthony Chiffolo
Author: Herbert N Foerstel
Foerstel's book is the perfect book to hand to students writing papers on censorship or anyone doing research on the subject.
2002: 328 pp, $72 hardcover
ISBN(s): 978-0-313-31166-6

Be the Media
Published by Natural E Creative Group LLC
1110 Jericho Tpke, 2nd fl, New Hyde Park, NY 11040
Tel: 516-488-1143 *Fax:* 516-488-4111
E-mail: info@bethemedia.com
Web Site: www.bethemedia.com
1st ed: 536 pp, $34.95 US
First published 2008
ISBN(s): 978-0-9760814-5-6

Biography and Genealogy Master Index (BGMI)
Published by Gale
Division of Cengage Learning
27500 Drake Rd, Farmington Hills, MI 48331-3535
SAN: 213-4373
Tel: 248-699-4253 *Toll Free Tel:* 800-877-4253 *Fax:* 248-699-8075 *Toll Free Fax:* 800-414-5043 (orders)
E-mail: gale.galeord@cengage.com
Web Site: www.gale.com
Provides more than 17 million citations compiled from more than 2,000 publications, covering over 5 million people. Available online, updated twice annually.

Book Blitz, Getting Your Book in the News
Published by Best Sellers
7456 Evergreen Dr, Goleta, CA 93117
Tel: 805-968-8567 *Fax:* 805-968-8567
Key Personnel
Author: Barbara Gaughen *E-mail:* bgaughenmu@aol.com; Ernest Weckbaugh
A hands-on publicity guide for authors; 60 steps for instant book success.
1996: 268 pp, $12.95
ISBN(s): 978-1-881474-02-9

Book Review Digest
Published by Grey House Publishing Inc™
4919 Rte 22, Amenia, NY 12501
Mailing Address: PO Box 56, Amenia, NY 12501-0056
Tel: 518-789-8700 *Toll Free Tel:* 800-562-2139 *Fax:* 518-789-0556
E-mail: books@greyhouse.com
Web Site: www.greyhouse.com
Concise critical evaluations, including citations & excerpts from book reviews, from more than 100 selected American, British & Canadian periodicals.
Annual.
2017 (2016 annual cumulation): 2,200 pp, $695
ISBN(s): 978-1-68217-205-6

Book Review Index
Published by Gale
Division of Cengage Learning
27500 Drake Rd, Farmington Hills, MI 48331-3535
SAN: 213-4373
Tel: 248-699-4253 *Toll Free Tel:* 800-877-4253 *Fax:* 248-699-8075 *Toll Free Fax:* 800-414-5043 (orders)
E-mail: gale.galeord@cengage.com
Web Site: www.gale.com
Provides quick access to reviews of books, periodicals, books on tape & electronic media representing a wide range of popular, academic & professional interests. More than 400 publications are indexed, including journals & national general interest publications & newspapers. Available as 3 issue subscription or as an annual cumulation.
2017 ed: 1,100 pp, $652 paper
ISBN(s): 978-1-41032-808-3

Bookbinding Materials & Techniques 1700-1920
Published by Canadian Bookbinders and Book Artists Guild (CBBAG)
80 Ward St, Suite 207, Toronto, ON M6H 4A6, Canada
Tel: 416-581-1071
E-mail: cbbag@cbbag.ca
Web Site: www.cbbag.ca
Key Personnel
Author: Margaret Lock
160 pp, $20
First published 2003
ISBN(s): 978-0-9695091-9-6

Bookman's Price Index: A Guide to the Values of Rare & Other Out-of-Print Books
Published by Gale
Unit of Cengage Learning
27500 Drake Rd, Farmington Hills, MI 48331-3535
SAN: 213-4373
Tel: 248-699-4253 *Toll Free Tel:* 800-877-4253 *Fax:* 248-699-8075 *Toll Free Fax:* 800-414-5043 (orders)
E-mail: gale.galeord@cengage.com
Web Site: www.gale.com
Gathers the most recent listings in the antiquarian book world in order to create a catalog of recent trends & pricing in the field of collectible books. Volumes do not supersede previous volumes. Each volume covers catalogs from the previous 4-6 months. Each entry includes title, author, edition, year published, physical description (size, binding, illustrations), condition of the book & price.
Vol 103, 2016: 1,184 pp, $814 hardcover
First published 1964
ISBN(s): 978-1-4103-1794-0

Books in Print®
Published by Grey House Publishing Inc™

4919 Rte 22, Amenia, NY 12501
Mailing Address: PO Box 56, Amenia, NY 12501-0056
Tel: 518-789-8700 *Toll Free Tel:* 800-562-2139 *Fax:* 518-789-0556
E-mail: books@greyhouse.com
Web Site: www.greyhouse.com
Serves the library & book trade communities as the definitive bibliographic resource. Features more than 2.5 million titles from more than 75,000 US publishers, to offer unparalleled coverage of the full range of books currently published or distributed in the US.
Annual.
2017-2018: 18,000 pp, $1,525/7 vol set
ISBN(s): 978-1-68217-498-2 (7 vol set)

Books in Print® Supplement
Published by Grey House Publishing Inc™
4919 Rte 22, Amenia, NY 12501
Mailing Address: PO Box 56, Amenia, NY 12501-0056
Tel: 518-789-8700 *Toll Free Tel:* 800-562-2139 *Fax:* 518-789-0556
E-mail: books@greyhouse.com
Web Site: www.greyhouse.com
This essential mid-year supplement to *Books In Print®* provides the latest book publishing updates for the past 6 months. This resource is crucial in ensuring that libraries & bookstores have access to the most accurate information throughout the year.
Annual.
2016-2017: 8,400 pp, $875/3 vol set
ISBN(s): 978-1-68217-476-0 (3 vol set)

Books Out Loud™: Bowker's Guide to Audiobooks
Published by Grey House Publishing Inc™
4919 Rte 22, Amenia, NY 12501
Mailing Address: PO Box 56, Amenia, NY 12501-0056
Tel: 518-789-8700 *Toll Free Tel:* 800-562-2139 *Fax:* 518-789-0556
E-mail: books@greyhouse.com
Web Site: www.greyhouse.com
Must-have collection development & reference tool for your library or bookstore. Offers bibliographic information on over 154,000 audiobooks from over 6,000 producers & 1,200 distributors & wholesalers.
Annual.
2017: 5,800 pp, $555/2 vol set
ISBN(s): 978-1-68217-448-7 (2 vol set)

Business & Legal Forms for Authors & Self-Publishers
Published by Allworth Press
Imprint of Skyhorse Publishing Inc
307 W 36 St, 11th fl, New York, NY 10018
Tel: 212-643-6816 *Fax:* 212-643-6819
Web Site: www.allworth.com
Key Personnel
Founder & Publr: Tad Crawford *E-mail:* crawford@allworth.com
Busn Mgr: Marrissa Jones *E-mail:* mjones@skyhorsepublishing.com
Contains 32 ready-to-use forms, negotiation checklist & extra tear-out forms; digital forms available online.
4th ed, 2015: 176 pp, $24.99
ISBN(s): 978-1-62153-464-2

Cabell's Directory of Publishing Opportunities in Accounting
Published by Cabell Publishing Co
PO Box 5428, Beaumont, TX 77726-5428
Tel: 409-898-0575 *Fax:* 409-866-9554
E-mail: orders@cabells.com
Web Site: www.cabells.com
Key Personnel
Founder & Pres: David Cabell *E-mail:* dave@cabells.com
VP, Busn Devt: Lacey E Earle *E-mail:* lacey@cabells.com
VP, Global Mktg: Sheree Crosby *E-mail:* sheree@cabells.com
Online directory of information on over 517 journals in accounting.
First published 1978
ISBN(s): 978-0-911753-49-3

Cabell's Directory of Publishing Opportunities in All Directories
Published by Cabell Publishing Co
PO Box 5428, Beaumont, TX 77726-5428
Tel: 409-898-0575 *Fax:* 409-866-9554
E-mail: orders@cabells.com
Web Site: www.cabells.com
Key Personnel
Founder & Pres: David Cabell *E-mail:* dave@cabells.com
VP, Busn Devt: Lacey E Earle *E-mail:* lacey@cabells.com
VP, Global Mktg: Sheree Crosby *E-mail:* sheree@cabells.com

Cabell's Directory of Publishing Opportunities in Astronomy
Published by Cabell Publishing Co
PO Box 5428, Beaumont, TX 77726-5428
Tel: 409-898-0575 *Fax:* 409-866-9554
E-mail: orders@cabells.com
Web Site: www.cabells.com
Key Personnel
Founder & Pres: David Cabell *E-mail:* dave@cabells.com
VP, Busn Devt: Lacey E Earle *E-mail:* lacey@cabells.com
VP, Global Mktg: Sheree Crosby *E-mail:* sheree@cabells.com

Cabell's Directory of Publishing Opportunities in Biological Sciences
Published by Cabell Publishing Co
PO Box 5428, Beaumont, TX 77726-5428
Tel: 409-898-0575 *Fax:* 409-866-9554
E-mail: orders@cabells.com
Web Site: www.cabells.com
Key Personnel
Founder & Pres: David Cabell *E-mail:* dave@cabells.com
VP, Busn Devt: Lacey E Earle *E-mail:* lacey@cabells.com
VP, Global Mktg: Sheree Crosby *E-mail:* sheree@cabells.com
First published 2016
ISBN(s): 978-0-911753-76-9

Cabell's Directory of Publishing Opportunities in Business - College/Library Set
Published by Cabell Publishing Co
PO Box 5428, Beaumont, TX 77726-5428
Tel: 409-898-0575 *Fax:* 409-866-9554
E-mail: orders@cabells.com
Web Site: www.cabells.com
Key Personnel
Founder & Pres: David Cabell *E-mail:* dave@cabells.com
VP, Busn Devt: Lacey E Earle *E-mail:* lacey@cabells.com
VP, Global Mktg: Sheree Crosby *E-mail:* sheree@cabells.com
Online directory of information on over 4,617 academic journals in business.
First published 1978
ISBN(s): 978-0-911753-65-3

Cabell's Directory of Publishing Opportunities in Chemistry
Published by Cabell Publishing Co
PO Box 5428, Beaumont, TX 77726-5428
Tel: 409-898-0575 *Fax:* 409-866-9554
E-mail: orders@cabells.com
Web Site: www.cabells.com
Key Personnel
Founder & Pres: David Cabell *E-mail:* dave@cabells.com
VP, Busn Devt: Lacey E Earle *E-mail:* lacey@cabells.com
VP, Global Mktg: Sheree Crosby *E-mail:* sheree@cabells.com

Cabell's Directory of Publishing Opportunities in Computer Science-Business Information Systems
Published by Cabell Publishing Co
PO Box 5428, Beaumont, TX 77726-5428
Tel: 409-898-0575 *Fax:* 409-866-9554
E-mail: orders@cabells.com
Web Site: www.cabells.com
Key Personnel
Founder & Pres: David Cabell *E-mail:* dave@cabells.com
VP, Busn Devt: Lacey E Earle *E-mail:* lacey@cabells.com
VP, Global Mktg: Sheree Crosby *E-mail:* sheree@cabells.com
Information on over 1,618 journals in computer science & business information systems.
First published 2010
ISBN(s): 978-0-911753-70-7

Cabell's Directory of Publishing Opportunities in Economics & Finance
Published by Cabell Publishing Co
PO Box 5428, Beaumont, TX 77726-5428
Tel: 409-898-0575 *Fax:* 409-866-9554
E-mail: orders@cabells.com
Web Site: www.cabells.com
Key Personnel
Founder & Pres: David Cabell *E-mail:* dave@cabells.com
VP, Busn Devt: Lacey E Earle *E-mail:* lacey@cabells.com
VP, Global Mktg: Sheree Crosby *E-mail:* sheree@cabells.com
Online directory of information on over 1,362 journals in economics & finance.
First published 1978
ISBN(s): 978-0-911753-50-9

Cabell's Directory of Publishing Opportunities in Education, Curriculum & Methods
Published by Cabell Publishing Co
PO Box 5428, Beaumont, TX 77726-5428
Tel: 409-898-0575 *Fax:* 409-866-9554
E-mail: orders@cabells.com
Web Site: www.cabells.com
Key Personnel
Founder & Pres: David Cabell *E-mail:* dave@cabells.com
VP, Busn Devt: Lacey E Earle *E-mail:* lacey@cabells.com
VP, Global Mktg: Sheree Crosby *E-mail:* sheree@cabells.com
Online indexes of over 906 journals on 28 different topic areas related to educational curriculum & methods.
First published 1981
ISBN(s): 978-0-911753-66-0

Cabell's Directory of Publishing Opportunities in Education Set
Published by Cabell Publishing Co
PO Box 5428, Beaumont, TX 77726-5428
Tel: 409-898-0575 *Fax:* 409-866-9554
E-mail: orders@cabells.com
Web Site: www.cabells.com
Key Personnel
Founder & Pres: David Cabell *E-mail:* dave@cabells.com

VP, Busn Devt: Lacey E Earle *E-mail:* lacey@cabells.com
VP, Global Mktg: Sheree Crosby *E-mail:* sheree@cabells.com
Information on over 2,119 journals in education. Electronic version only.
First published 2009
ISBN(s): 978-0-911753-69-1

Cabell's Directory of Publishing Opportunities in Educational Psychology & Administration
Published by Cabell Publishing Co
PO Box 5428, Beaumont, TX 77726-5428
Tel: 409-898-0575 *Fax:* 409-866-9554
E-mail: orders@cabells.com
Web Site: www.cabells.com
Key Personnel
Founder & Pres: David Cabell *E-mail:* dave@cabells.com
VP, Busn Devt: Lacey E Earle *E-mail:* lacey@cabells.com
VP, Global Mktg: Sheree Crosby *E-mail:* sheree@cabells.com
Online indexes of over 718 journals on 28 different topic areas related to educational psychology & administration.
First published 1981
ISBN(s): 978-0-911753-67-7

Cabell's Directory of Publishing Opportunities in Educational Technology & Library Science
Published by Cabell Publishing Co
PO Box 5428, Beaumont, TX 77726-5428
Tel: 409-898-0575 *Fax:* 409-866-9554
E-mail: orders@cabells.com
Web Site: www.cabells.com
Key Personnel
Founder & Pres: David Cabell *E-mail:* dave@cabells.com
VP, Busn Devt: Lacey E Earle *E-mail:* lacey@cabells.com
VP, Global Mktg: Sheree Crosby *E-mail:* sheree@cabells.com
Online directory of information on over 495 journals in educational technology & library science.
First published 2007
ISBN(s): 978-0-911753-68-4

Cabell's Directory of Publishing Opportunities in Geology
Published by Cabell Publishing Co
PO Box 5428, Beaumont, TX 77726-5428
Tel: 409-898-0575 *Fax:* 409-866-9554
E-mail: orders@cabells.com
Web Site: www.cabells.com
Key Personnel
Founder & Pres: David Cabell *E-mail:* dave@cabells.com
VP, Busn Devt: Lacey E Earle *E-mail:* lacey@cabells.com
VP, Global Mktg: Sheree Crosby *E-mail:* sheree@cabells.com
First published 2016
ISBN(s): 978-0-911753-78-3

Cabell's Directory of Publishing Opportunities in Health Administration
Published by Cabell Publishing Co
PO Box 5428, Beaumont, TX 77726-5428
Tel: 409-898-0575 *Fax:* 409-866-9554
E-mail: orders@cabells.com
Web Site: www.cabells.com
Key Personnel
Founder & Pres: David Cabell *E-mail:* dave@cabells.com
VP, Busn Devt: Lacey E Earle *E-mail:* lacey@cabells.com
VP, Global Mktg: Sheree Crosby *E-mail:* sheree@cabells.com
Information on 788 journals listed in health administration.
First published 2010
ISBN(s): 978-0-911753-71-4

Cabell's Directory of Publishing Opportunities in Management
Published by Cabell Publishing Co
PO Box 5428, Beaumont, TX 77726-5428
Tel: 409-898-0575 *Fax:* 409-866-9554
E-mail: orders@cabells.com
Web Site: www.cabells.com
Key Personnel
Founder & Pres: David Cabell *E-mail:* dave@cabells.com
VP, Busn Devt: Lacey E Earle *E-mail:* lacey@cabells.com
VP, Global Mktg: Sheree Crosby *E-mail:* sheree@cabells.com
Online directory of information on over 2,080 journals in management.
First published 1978
ISBN(s): 978-0-911753-51-6

Cabell's Directory of Publishing Opportunities in Marketing
Published by Cabell Publishing Co
PO Box 5428, Beaumont, TX 77726-5428
Tel: 409-898-0575 *Fax:* 409-866-9554
E-mail: orders@cabells.com
Web Site: www.cabells.com
Key Personnel
Founder & Pres: David Cabell *E-mail:* dave@cabells.com
VP, Busn Devt: Lacey E Earle *E-mail:* lacey@cabells.com
VP, Global Mktg: Sheree Crosby *E-mail:* sheree@cabells.com
Online directory of information on over 658 journals in marketing.
First published 1978
ISBN(s): 978-0-911753-64-6

Cabell's Directory of Publishing Opportunities in Mathematics
Published by Cabell Publishing Co
PO Box 5428, Beaumont, TX 77726-5428
Tel: 409-898-0575 *Fax:* 409-866-9554
E-mail: orders@cabells.com
Web Site: www.cabells.com
Key Personnel
Founder & Pres: David Cabell *E-mail:* dave@cabells.com
VP, Busn Devt: Lacey E Earle *E-mail:* lacey@cabells.com
VP, Global Mktg: Sheree Crosby *E-mail:* sheree@cabells.com

Cabell's Directory of Publishing Opportunities in Nursing
Published by Cabell Publishing Co
PO Box 5428, Beaumont, TX 77726-5428
Tel: 409-898-0575 *Fax:* 409-866-9554
E-mail: orders@cabells.com
Web Site: www.cabells.com
Key Personnel
Founder & Pres: David Cabell *E-mail:* dave@cabells.com
VP, Busn Devt: Lacey E Earle *E-mail:* lacey@cabells.com
VP, Global Mktg: Sheree Crosby *E-mail:* sheree@cabells.com
Information on over 571 academic journals in nursing. Electronic version only.
First published 2010
ISBN(s): 978-0-911753-72-1

Cabell's Directory of Publishing Opportunities in Oceanography
Published by Cabell Publishing Co
PO Box 5428, Beaumont, TX 77726-5428
Tel: 409-898-0575 *Fax:* 409-866-9554
E-mail: orders@cabells.com
Web Site: www.cabells.com
Key Personnel
Founder & Pres: David Cabell *E-mail:* dave@cabells.com
VP, Busn Devt: Lacey E Earle *E-mail:* lacey@cabells.com
VP, Global Mktg: Sheree Crosby *E-mail:* sheree@cabells.com
First published 2016
ISBN(s): 978-0-911753-79-0

Cabell's Directory of Publishing Opportunities in Physics
Published by Cabell Publishing Co
PO Box 5428, Beaumont, TX 77726-5428
Tel: 409-898-0575 *Fax:* 409-866-9554
E-mail: orders@cabells.com
Web Site: www.cabells.com
Key Personnel
Founder & Pres: David Cabell *E-mail:* dave@cabells.com
VP, Busn Devt: Lacey E Earle *E-mail:* lacey@cabells.com
VP, Global Mktg: Sheree Crosby *E-mail:* sheree@cabells.com
First published 2016
ISBN(s): 978-0-911753-80-6

Cabell's Directory of Publishing Opportunities in Psychology & Psychiatry
Published by Cabell Publishing Co
PO Box 5428, Beaumont, TX 77726-5428
Tel: 409-898-0575 *Fax:* 409-866-9554
E-mail: orders@cabells.com
Web Site: www.cabells.com
Key Personnel
Founder & Pres: David Cabell *E-mail:* dave@cabells.com
VP, Busn Devt: Lacey E Earle *E-mail:* lacey@cabells.com
VP, Global Mktg: Sheree Crosby *E-mail:* sheree@cabells.com
Online directory of information on 1,841 journals listed in psychology & psychiatry.
First published 2002
ISBN(s): 978-0-911753-73-8

Careers in Communications & Media
Published by Grey House Publishing Inc™
2 University Plaza, Suite 310, Hackensack, NJ 07601
SAN: 208-838X
Tel: 201-968-0500 *Toll Free Tel:* 800-221-1592 *Fax:* 201-968-0511
E-mail: csr@salempress.com
Web Site: salempress.com
Provides a current overview & future outlook of occupations in this high-growth industry. Companies in this field are involved in television & radio broadcasting, motion picture/video production, publishing, advertising & telecommunications.
Nov 2013: 300 pp, $125 (includes online access with print purchase)
ISBN(s): 978-1-61925-230-1; 978-1-61925-231-8 (ebook)

Catholic Press Directory
Published by Catholic Press Association of the United States & Canada
205 W Monroe St, Suite 470, Chicago, IL 60606
Tel: 312-380-6789 *Fax:* 312-361-0256
E-mail: cathjourn@catholicpress.org
Web Site: www.catholicpress.org
Key Personnel
Exec Dir: Timothy M Walter *E-mail:* twalter@catholicpress.org
Busn Mgr: Barbara Mastrolia
Proj Coord: Elise Freed-Brown
Proj Asst: Carol Arnold

Complete listings of more than 600 Catholic newspapers, magazines, newsletters & foreign language publications in the US & CN. Also includes Catholic book & general publishers; Diocesan directories & media services.
Annual.
2018: 132 pp, Free to membs, $80 for nonmembs

CCOD, see Consultants & Consulting Organizations Directory (CCOD)

The Chicago Guide to Fact-Checking
Published by University of Chicago Press
1427 E 60 St, Chicago, IL 60637-2954
SAN: 202-5280
E-mail: custserv@press.uchicago.edu; marketing@press.uchicago.edu
Web Site: www.press.uchicago.edu
Key Personnel
Sr Ed: Mary E Laur *E-mail:* mlaur@uchicago.edu
This book is an accessible, one-stop guide to the why, what & how of contemporary fact-checking. Brooke Borel covers best practices for fact-checking in a variety of media—from magazine articles, both print & online, to books & documentaries—& from the perspective of both in-house & freelance checkers. She also offers advice on navigating relationships with writers, editors & sources; considers the realities of fact-checking on a budget & checking one's own work; & reflects on the place of fact-checking in today's media landscape.
1st ed: 192 pp, $55 cloth, $17 paper, $15 ebook
First published 2016
ISBN(s): 978-0-226-29076-8 (cloth); 978-0-226-29093-5 (paper); 978-0-226-29109-3 (ebook)

The Chicago Manual of Style
Published by University of Chicago Press
1427 E 60 St, Chicago, IL 60637-2954
SAN: 202-5280
Tel: 773-702-7700; 773-702-7000 (cust serv, print); 773-753-3347 (cust serv, online, outside US & CN) *Toll Free Tel:* 800-621-2736 (orders); 877-705-1878 (cust serv, online) *Fax:* 773-702-9756
E-mail: custserv@press.uchicago.edu; marketing@press.uchicago.edu; cmoshelpdesk@press.uchicago.edu
Web Site: www.press.uchicago.edu; www.chicagomanualofstyle.org
Key Personnel
Sr Ed: Mary E Laur *E-mail:* mlaur@uchicago.edu
Style manual for authors, editors & copywriters. Also available as an online subscription.
Revised every 7-10 yrs.
17th ed, 2017: 1,184 pp, $70
ISBN(s): 978-0-226-28705-8

Children's Books in Print®
Published by Grey House Publishing Inc™
4919 Rte 22, Amenia, NY 12501
Mailing Address: PO Box 56, Amenia, NY 12501-0056
Tel: 518-789-8700 *Toll Free Tel:* 800-562-2139 *Fax:* 518-789-0556
E-mail: books@greyhouse.com
Web Site: www.greyhouse.com
Vital resource for locating children's & young adult titles in the US, offering immediate access to over 250,000 children's books from 18,000 US publishers.
Annual.
2017: 3,500 pp, $665/2 vol set
ISBN(s): 978-1-61925-058-8 (2 vol set)

Children's Core Collection
Published by Grey House Publishing Inc™
4919 Rte 22, Amenia, NY 12501
Mailing Address: PO Box 56, Amenia, NY 12501-0056
Tel: 518-789-8700 *Toll Free Tel:* 800-562-2139 *Fax:* 518-789-0556
E-mail: books@greyhouse.com
Web Site: www.greyhouse.com
Guide to approximately 15,000 books, covering fiction & nonfiction works, story collections, picture books, graphic novels & magazines recommended for readers from preschool through grade 6.
23rd ed, 2017: 3,400 pp, $240/2 vol set
ISBN(s): 978-1-68217-235-3 (2 vol set)

Children's Literature Review
Published by Gale
Unit of Cengage Learning
27500 Drake Rd, Farmington Hills, MI 48331-3535
SAN: 213-4373
Tel: 248-699-4253 *Toll Free Tel:* 800-877-4253 *Fax:* 248-699-8070 *Toll Free Fax:* 800-414-5043 (orders)
E-mail: gale.galeord@cengage.com
Web Site: www.gale.com
Provides full texts from criticism on authors & illustrators of books for children & young adults. Includes indexes to titles, authors & nationality. A cumulative title index to the entire series is published seperately (included in subscription). Illustrations & photographs are included. Also available as an ebook.

Children's Writer's Word Book
Published by Writer's Digest
Imprint of F+W Media Inc
10151 Carver Rd, Suite 200, Blue Ash, OH 45242
Tel: 513-531-2690 *Toll Free Tel:* 800-289-0963 *Fax:* 513-531-0798
E-mail: writersdigest@fwmedia.com (edit)
Web Site: www.writersdigest.com; www.writersdigestshop.com
Key Personnel
Gen Mgr: David Pyle *E-mail:* david.pyle@fwmedia.com
Content Strategist: Rachel Randall *E-mail:* rachel.randall@fwmedia.com
Handy reference book to be used along with your dictionary or thesaurus. Gives guidelines for sentence length, word usage & theme at each reading level.
2nd ed: 352 pp, $19.99 paper (retail)
First published 1999
ISBN(s): 978-1-58297-413-2

Communicating Ideas: The Politics of Scholarly Publishing
Published by Transaction Publishers Inc
10 Corporate Place S, Suite 102, Piscataway, NJ 08854
Mailing Address: 1247 State Rd, Princeton, NJ 08540
Tel: 732-445-2280 *Fax:* 732-445-3138
Web Site: www.transactionpub.com
View of publishing in America & abroad. Addresses the political implications of scholarly communication in the era of the new computerized technology. This title was originally published by Oxford University Press.
2nd ed: 356 pp, $30.95 paper
First published 1991
ISBN(s): 978-0-88738-898-9

The Complete Directory of Large Print Books & Serials™
Published by Grey House Publishing Inc™
4919 Rte 22, Amenia, NY 12501
Mailing Address: PO Box 56, Amenia, NY 12501-0056
Tel: 518-789-8700 *Toll Free Tel:* 800-562-2139 *Fax:* 518-789-0556
E-mail: books@greyhouse.com
Web Site: www.greyhouse.com
Important resource for building or managing a large print books or serials collection containing detailed data on over 32,000 large print active titles.
2013: 2,600 pp, $475
ISBN(s): 978-1-61925-053-4

The Complete Guide to Book Marketing
Published by Allworth Press
Imprint of Skyhorse Publishing Inc
307 W 36 St, 11th fl, New York, NY 10018
Tel: 212-643-6816 *Fax:* 212-643-6819
Web Site: www.allworth.com
Key Personnel
Founder & Publr: Tad Crawford *E-mail:* crawford@allworth.com
Busn Mgr: Marrissa Jones *E-mail:* mjones@skyhorsepublishing.com
Author: David Cole
Comprehensive resource book covering all aspects of book marketing.
2004 (revised): 256 pp, $19.95
ISBN(s): 978-1-58115-322-4

The Complete Guide to Book Publicity
Published by Allworth Press
Imprint of Skyhorse Publishing Inc
307 W 36 St, 11th fl, New York, NY 10018
Tel: 212-643-6816 *Fax:* 212-643-6819
Web Site: www.allworth.com
Key Personnel
Founder & Publr: Tad Crawford *E-mail:* crawford@allworth.com
Busn Mgr: Marrissa Jones *E-mail:* mjones@skyhorsepublishing.com
Author: Jodee Blanco
A comprehensive resource book covering all aspects of book publicity.
2nd ed, 2004: 304 pp, $19.95
ISBN(s): 978-1-58115-349-1

The Complete Guide to Self-Publishing
Published by Writer's Digest
Imprint of F+W Media Inc
10151 Carver Rd, Suite 200, Blue Ash, OH 45242
Tel: 513-531-2690 *Toll Free Tel:* 800-289-0963 *Fax:* 513-531-0798
E-mail: writersdigest@fwmedia.com (edit)
Web Site: www.writersdigest.com; www.writersdigestshop.com
Key Personnel
Gen Mgr: David Pyle *E-mail:* david.pyle@fwmedia.com
Content Strategist: Rachel Randall *E-mail:* rachel.randall@fwmedia.com
Everything you need to write, publish, promote & sell your book.
5th ed: 576 pp, $24.99 paper & ebook (retail)
First published 1991
ISBN(s): 978-1-58297-718-8 (paper); 978-1-59963-184-4 (ebook)

The Complete Guide to Successful Publishing
Published by Cardoza Publishing
808 S Main St, Las Vegas, NV 89101
Tel: 702-870-7200 *Fax:* 702-822-6500
E-mail: info@cardozabooks.com
Web Site: www.cardozabooks.com
Key Personnel
Publr & Author: Avery Cardoza
This step-by-step guide shows beginning & established publishers how to successfully produce professional-looking books that not only look good, but sell in the open market; readers learn how to find & develop ideas; set up the business from the ground up; design & layout a book; find authors, work contracts & negotiate deals; get distribution; expand a publishing company into a large enterprise & more.
3rd ed, April 2003: 416 pp, $12.97
First published 1995
ISBN(s): 978-1-58042-097-6

The Complete Handbook of Novel Writing
Published by Writer's Digest
Imprint of F+W Media Inc
10151 Carver Rd, Suite 200, Blue Ash, OH 45242
Tel: 513-531-2690 *Toll Free Tel:* 800-289-0963 *Fax:* 513-531-0798
E-mail: writersdigest@fwmedia.com (edit)
Web Site: www.writersdigest.com; www.writersdigestshop.com
Key Personnel
Gen Mgr: David Pyle *E-mail:* david.pyle@fwmedia.com
Content Strategist: Rachel Randall *E-mail:* rachel.randall@fwmedia.com
Everything you need to know about creating & selling your work.
3rd ed: 528 pp, $19.99 paper & ebook (retail)
First published 2002
ISBN(s): 978-1-4403-4839-6 (paper); 978-1-4403-4842-6 (ebook)

Complete Television, Radio & Cable Industry Directory
Published by Grey House Publishing Inc™
4919 Rte 22, Amenia, NY 12501
Mailing Address: PO Box 56, Amenia, NY 12501-0056
Tel: 518-789-8700 *Toll Free Tel:* 800-562-2139 *Fax:* 518-789-0556
E-mail: books@greyhouse.com
Web Site: www.greyhouse.com
Data & industry contacts on over 20,000 US & Canadian stations & organizations in the field: Television, Radio & Cable Stations, Programming Services & Technological Solutions, Brokers & Professional Services, Associations, Events, Education, Awards, Law & Regulation & Government Agencies.
2017: 2,000 pp, $350
ISBN(s): 978-1-61925-938-6

Complete Video Directory™
Published by Grey House Publishing Inc™
4919 Rte 22, Amenia, NY 12501
Mailing Address: PO Box 56, Amenia, NY 12501-0056
Tel: 518-789-8700 *Toll Free Tel:* 800-562-2139 *Fax:* 518-789-0556
E-mail: books@greyhouse.com
Web Site: www.greyhouse.com
Extensive listing of currently available entertainment titles along with education & special interest videos for home, school & business.
Annual.
2017: 7,900 pp, $830/4 vol set
ISBN(s): 978-1-68217-486-9 (4 vol set)

Concise Dictionary of American Literary Biography
Published by Gale
Unit of Cengage Learning
27500 Drake Rd, Farmington Hills, MI 48331-3535
SAN: 213-4373
Tel: 248-699-4253 *Toll Free Tel:* 800-877-4253 *Fax:* 248-699-8070 *Toll Free Fax:* 800-414-5043 (orders)
E-mail: gale.galeord@cengage.com
Web Site: www.gale.com
Organized chronologically, this set covers only the American authors most frequently studied in high school & college literature courses, extracts & fully updates essays in their entirety from the much larger Dictionary of Literary Biography series. A one volume supplement highlighting Modern American Writers is available seperately.
Volumes include: *Colonization to the American Renaissance, 1640-1865*
Realism, Naturalism & Local Color, 1865-1917
The Twenties, 1917-1929
The Age of Maturity, 1929-1941
The New Consciousness, 1941-1968
Broadening Views, 1968-1988
Supplement: Modern American Writers.
2,506 pp, $799/6 vol set
First published 1987
ISBN(s): 978-0-8103-1818-2 (6 vol set)

Concise Dictionary of British Literary Biography
Published by Gale
Unit of Cengage Learning
27500 Drake Rd, Farmington Hills, MI 48331-3535
SAN: 213-4373
Tel: 248-699-4253 *Toll Free Tel:* 800-877-4253 *Fax:* 248-699-8070 *Toll Free Fax:* 800-414-5043 (orders)
E-mail: gale.galeord@cengage.com
Web Site: www.gale.com
Key Personnel
Ed: Matthew J Bruccoli; Richard Layman
Illustrated set provides thorough coverage of major British literary figures of all eras. Each volume covers 20-30 writers from all genres who were active during a single historical period.
Vol 1: *Writers of the Middle Ages and Renaissance Before 1660*
Vol 2: *Writers of the Restoration and 18th Century 1660-1789*
Vol 3: *Writers of the Romantic Period, 1789-1832*
Vol 4: *Victorian Writers, 1832-1890*
Vol 5: *Late Victorian and Edwardian Writers, 1890-1914*
Vol 6: *Modern Writers, 1914-1945*
Vol 7: *Writers After World War II, 1945-1960*
Vol 8: *Contemporary Writers, 1960-Present.*
1st ed, 1992: 24,000 pp, $1,380/8-vol set hardcover
ISBN(s): 978-0-8103-7980-0

Concise Major 21st-Century Writers
Published by Gale
Division of Cengage Learning
27500 Drake Rd, Farmington Hills, MI 48331-3535
SAN: 213-4373
Tel: 248-699-4253 *Toll Free Tel:* 800-877-4253 *Fax:* 248-699-8070 *Toll Free Fax:* 800-414-5043 (orders)
E-mail: gale.galeord@cengage.com
Web Site: www.gale.com
Detailed biographical & bibliographical information on approxiately 700 authors who are most often studied in college & high school. Sketches typically include personal information, addresses, career history, writings, works in progress, biographical/critical sources & authors' comments +/or informative essays about their lives & work.
3rd ed, 2006: 3,890 pp, $803/5-vol set hardcover, $883.30 ebook
ISBN(s): 978-0-7876-7539-4 (hardcover/5-vol set); 978-1-4144-1048-7 (ebook)

Consultants & Consulting Organizations Directory (CCOD)
Published by Gale
Unit of Cengage Learning
27500 Drake Rd, Farmington Hills, MI 48331-3535
SAN: 213-4373
Tel: 248-699-4253 *Toll Free Tel:* 800-877-4253 *Fax:* 248-699-8069 *Toll Free Fax:* 800-414-5043 (orders)
E-mail: gale.galeord@cengage.com; businessproducts@cengage.com
Web Site: www.gale.com
Key Personnel
Ed: Julie A Gough *E-mail:* julie.gough@cengage.com
Important details, including services offered, full contact information, date founded & principal business executives. More than 26,000 firms & individuals listed are arranged in subject sections under 14 general fields of consulting activity ranging from agriculture to marketing. More than 400 specialties are represented, including finance, computers, fund raising & others. Also available as an ebook.
41st ed, 2016: 3,586 pp, $1,605 paper, $1,765.50 ebook
ISBN(s): 978-1-4103-1219-8 (paper); 978-1-4103-1723-0 (ebook)

Contemporary Authors
Published by Gale
Unit of Cengage Learning
27500 Drake Rd, Farmington Hills, MI 48331-3535
SAN: 213-4373
Tel: 248-699-4253 *Toll Free Tel:* 800-877-4253 *Fax:* 248-699-8070 *Toll Free Fax:* 800-414-5043 (orders)
E-mail: gale.galeord@cengage.com
Web Site: www.gale.com
Find biographical information on more than 156,000 modern novelists, poets, playwrights, nonfiction writers, journalists & scriptwriters. Also available as an ebook.
Vol 399, 2017: 450 pp, $362 hardcover, $398.20 ebook
ISBN(s): 978-1-4103-2250-0 (hardcover); 978-1-4103-2275-3 (ebook)

Contemporary Literary Criticism
Published by Gale
Unit of Cengage Learning
27500 Drake Rd, Farmington Hills, MI 48331-3535
SAN: 213-4373
Tel: 248-699-4253 *Toll Free Tel:* 800-877-4253 *Fax:* 248-699-8070 *Toll Free Fax:* 800-414-5043 (orders)
E-mail: gale.galeord@cengage.com
Web Site: www.gale.com
Key Personnel
Ed: Jeffrey Hunter
Covers authors who are currently active or who died after Dec 31, 1959. Each print volume profiles approximately 6-8 novelists, poets, playwrights & other creative & nonfiction writers by providing full-text or excerpted criticism taken from books, magazines, literary reviews, newspapers & scholarly journals. Most critical essays are full text. Each of the approximately 200 essays per volume is prefaced by a full citation & annotation & most entries in the print series include an author portrait. Each volume includes cumulative author name, topic & nationality indexes, as well as a volume-specific title index. A cumulative title index to the entire series is available separately. Also available online.
$397 hardcover

Copy Editing
Published by Cambridge University Press
1 Liberty Plaza, 20th fl, New York, NY 10006
SAN: 200-206X
Tel: 212-337-5000
E-mail: newyork@cambridge.org
Web Site: www.cambridge.org/us
Key Personnel
Author: Judith Butcher
Copy Editing covers all aspects of the editorial process involved in converting an author's ms to the printed page. It covers the basics from how to mark a ms for the designer & typesetter, through the ground rules of house style & consistency, to how to read & correct proofs.
4th ed, 2006: 558 pp, $120
ISBN(s): 978-521-84713-1

Critical Approaches to Literature
Published by Grey House Publishing Inc™
2 University Plaza, Suite 310, Hackensack, NJ 07601
SAN: 208-838X
Tel: 201-968-0500 *Toll Free Tel:* 800-221-1592 *Fax:* 201-968-0511
E-mail: csr@salempress.com
Web Site: salempress.com
Each volume contains 300 pages & provides literature students with the tools necessary to study each approach to literary criticism using a unique combination of critical contexts & analysis of several works. Also includes in-depth critical readings of popular works.
Individual volumes: *Feminist*, published Feb 2017
Moral, published April 2017
Multicultural, published Nov 2017
Psychological, published Nov 2017.
$125/vol (includes online access)
ISBN(s): 978-1-68217-272-8 (Psychological); 978-1-68217-274-2 (Moral); 978-1-68217-575-0 (Multicultural); 978-1-68217-577-4 (Feminist)

Critical Insights: Authors
Published by Grey House Publishing Inc™
2 University Plaza, Suite 310, Hackensack, NJ 07601
SAN: 208-838X
Tel: 201-968-0500 *Toll Free Tel:* 800-221-1592 *Fax:* 201-968-0511
E-mail: csr@salempress.com
Web Site: salempress.com
Key Personnel
Ed, Maya Angelou: Mildred R Mickle
Ed, Isaac Asimov: M Keith Booker
Ed, Mary Shelley: Virginia Brackett
Ed, Geoffrey Chaucer: James M Dean
Ed, Joseph Conrad: Jeremiah J Garsha
Ed, Neil Gaiman: Joseph M Sommers
Each volume contains 300 pages & includes: General bibliography, chronology of author's life, complete list of author's works, publication dates of works, detailed bio of the editor & general subject index.
Volumes published Oct-Dec 2016:
Maya Angelou
Joseph Conrad
Neil Gaiman
Mary Shelley.
Volumes published Jan-Dec 2017:
Isaac Asimov
Ray Bradbury
Geoffrey Chaucer
Leo Tolstoy
Edith Wharton.
$105/vol (includes online access)
ISBN(s): 978-1-68217-112-7 (Maya Angelou); 978-1-68217-113-4 (Maya Angelou ebook); 978-1-68217-114-1 (Joseph Conrad); 978-1-68217-115-8 (Joseph Conrad ebook); 978-1-68217-116-5 (Mary Shelley); 978-1-68217-117-2 (Mary Shelley ebook); 978-1-68217-254-4 (Isaac Asimov); 978-1-68217-255-1 (Isaac Asimov ebook); 978-1-68217-256-8 (Geoffrey Chaucer); 978-1-68217-257-5 (Geoffrey Chaucer ebook); 978-1-68217-260-5 (Neil Gaiman); 978-1-68217-261-2 (Neil Gaiman ebook); 978-1-68217-571-2 (Ray Bradbury); 978-1-68217-572-9 (Ray Bradbury ebook); 978-1-68217-573-6 (Edith Wharton); 978-1-68217-574-3 (Edith Wharton ebook); 978-1-68217-611-5 (Leo Tolstoy); 978-1-68217-612-2 (Leo Tolstoy ebook)

Critical Insights: Themes
Published by Grey House Publishing Inc™
2 University Plaza, Suite 310, Hackensack, NJ 07601
SAN: 208-838X
Tel: 201-968-0500 *Toll Free Tel:* 800-221-1592 *Fax:* 201-968-0511
E-mail: csr@salempress.com
Web Site: salempress.com
Key Personnel
Ed, Civil Rights Literature: Christopher A Varlack
Ed, Flash Fiction: Michael Cocchiarale; Scott Emmert
Ed, Holocaust Literature: Dorian Stuber
Ed, Modern Japanese Literature: Frank Jacob
Ed, Paranoia, Fear & Alienation: Kimberly Drake
Each volume contains 300 pages & explores a popular literary theme.
Volumes published Oct-Dec 2016:
Holocaust Literature
Paranoia, Fear & Alienation.
Volumes published Jan-Dec 2017:
Civil Rights Literature
Flash Fiction
Latin American Fiction
Modern Japanese Literature
Post-Colonial Literature
Rebellion
Social Justice and American Literature.
300 pp, $105/vol (includes online access)
ISBN(s): 978-1-61925-527-2 (Holocaust Literature); 978-1-61925-528-9 (Holocaust Literature ebook); 978-1-68217-126-4 (Paranoia, Fear & Alienation); 978-1-68217-127-1 (Paranoia, Fear & Alienation ebook); 978-1-68217-258-2 (Modern Japanese Literature); 978-1-68217-259-9 (Modern Japanese Literature ebook); 978-1-68217-268-1 (Civil Rights Literature); 978-1-68217-269-8 (Civil Rights Literature ebook); 978-1-68217-270-4 (Flash Fiction); 978-1-68217-271-1 (Flash Fiction ebook); 978-1-68217-557-6 (Rebellion); 978-1-68217-558-3 (Rebellion ebook); 978-1-68217-559-0 (Post-Colonial Literature); 978-1-68217-560-6 (Post-Colonial Literature ebook); 978-1-68217-561-3 (Latin American Fiction); 978-1-68217-562-0 (Latin American Fiction ebook); 978-1-68217-565-1 (Social Justice and American Literature); 978-1-68217-566-8 (Social Justice and American Literature ebook)

Critical Insights: Works
Published by Grey House Publishing Inc™
2 University Plaza, Suite 310, Hackensack, NJ 07601
SAN: 208-838X
Tel: 201-968-0500 *Toll Free Tel:* 800-221-1592 *Fax:* 201-968-0511
E-mail: csr@salempress.com
Web Site: salempress.com
Key Personnel
Ed, The Adventures of Huckleberry Finn: R Kent Rasmussen
Ed, The Diary of a Young Girl: Ruth Amir; Pnina Rosenberg
Ed, Nineteen Eighty-Four: Thomas Horan
Ed, Of Mice and Men: Barbara Heavilin
Ed, Romeo and Juliet: Robert Evans
Ed, The Woman Warrior: Linda Trinh Moser; Kathryn West
Each essay is 5,000 words in length & offers comprehensive, in-depth coverage of a single work. Each volume is 300 pages & contains 16-18 essays that break down the work from several different perspectives & includes a brief biography of the author.
Volumes published Oct-Dec 2016:
Nineteen Eighty-Four by George Orwell
The Woman Warrior by Maxine Hong Kingston.
Volumes published Jan-Nov 2017:
The Adventures of Huckleberry Finn by Mark Twain
Billy Budd, Sailor by Herman Melville
The Diary of a Young Girl by Anne Frank
Lord of the Flies by William Golding
Macbeth by William Shakespeare
Of Mice and Men by John Steinbeck
Romeo and Juliet by William Shakespeare.
$105/vol (includes online access)
ISBN(s): 978-1-68217-118-9 (Nineteen Eighty-Four); 978-1-68217-119-6 (Nineteen Eighty-Four ebook); 978-1-68217-122-6 (The Adventures of Huckleberry Finn); 978-1-68217-123-3 (The Adventures of Huckleberry Finn ebook); 978-1-68217-262-9 (The Diary of a Young Girl); 978-1-68217-263-6 (The Diary of a Young Girl ebook); 978-1-68217-264-3 (Romeo and Juliet); 978-1-68217-265-0 (Romeo and Juliet ebook); 978-1-68217-266-7 (Of Mice and Men); 978-1-68217-267-4 (Of Mice and Men ebook); 978-1-68217-394-7 (The Woman Warrior); 978-1-68217-395-4 (The Woman Warrior ebook); 978-1-68217-563-7 (Macbeth); 978-1-68217-564-4 (Macbeth ebook); 978-1-68217-567-5 (Lord of the Flies); 978-1-68217-568-2 (Lord of the Flies ebook); 978-1-68217-569-9 (Billy Budd, Sailor); 978-1-68217-570-5 (Billy Budd, Sailor ebook)

Critical Survey of American Literature
Published by Grey House Publishing Inc™
2 University Plaza, Suite 310, Hackensack, NJ 07601
SAN: 208-838X
Tel: 201-968-0500 *Toll Free Tel:* 800-221-1592 *Fax:* 201-968-0511
E-mail: csr@salempress.com
Web Site: salempress.com
Detailed profiles of over 400 major American authors of fiction, drama & poetry, each with sections on biography, general analysis & analysis of the author's most important works. Originally published as *Magill's Survey of American Literature*.
Dec 2016: 3,000 pp, $499/6 vol set (includes online access)
First published 2006
ISBN(s): 978-1-68217-128-8 (6 vol set)

Critical Survey of Drama
Published by Grey House Publishing Inc™
2 University Plaza, Suite 310, Hackensack, NJ 07601
SAN: 208-838X
Tel: 201-968-0500 *Toll Free Tel:* 800-221-1592 *Fax:* 201-968-0511
E-mail: csr@salempress.com
Web Site: salempress.com
Contains 650 essays that discuss both individual dramatists & overview topics. Also contains a listing of major dramatic awards, time line of drama history, glossary & bibliography.
4th ed, 2017: 4,800 pp, $599/8 vol set
ISBN(s): 978-1-68217-622-1 (8 vol set)

Critical Survey of Graphic Novels: Heroes & Superheroes
Published by Grey House Publishing Inc™
2 University Plaza, Suite 310, Hackensack, NJ 07601
SAN: 208-838X
Tel: 201-968-0500 *Toll Free Tel:* 800-221-1592 *Fax:* 201-968-0511
E-mail: csr@salempress.com
Web Site: salempress.com
Key Personnel
Ed: Bart H Beaty; Stephen Weiner
Provides in-depth insight into over 130 of the most popular & studied graphic novels. Arranged alphabetically.
April 2012: 800 pp, $295 (includes online access with print purchase)
ISBN(s): 978-1-58765-865-5 (2 vol set); 978-1-58765-869-3 (ebook set)

Critical Survey of Graphic Novels: History, Theme & Technique
Published by Grey House Publishing Inc™
2 University Plaza, Suite 310, Hackensack, NJ 07601
SAN: 208-838X

Tel: 201-968-0500 *Toll Free Tel:* 800-221-1592
Fax: 201-968-0511
E-mail: csr@salempress.com
Web Site: salempress.com
Key Personnel
Ed: Bart H Beaty; Stephen Weiner
Contains over 70 essays covering themes & concepts of graphic novels, including genres, time periods, foreign language traditions, social relevance & craftsmanship such as penciling & inking.
Oct 2012: 475 pp, $195 (includes online access with print purchase)
ISBN(s): 978-1-58765-957-7; 978-1-58765-958-4 (ebook)

Critical Survey of Graphic Novels: Independents & Underground Classics
Published by Grey House Publishing Inc™
2 University Plaza, Suite 310, Hackensack, NJ 07601
SAN: 208-838X
Tel: 201-968-0500 *Toll Free Tel:* 800-221-1592
Fax: 201-968-0511
E-mail: csr@salempress.com
Web Site: salempress.com
Key Personnel
Ed: Bart H Beaty; Stephen Weiner
215 essays covering graphic novels & core comics series, focusing on the independents & underground genre.
May 2012: 1,088 pp, $395 (includes online access with print purchase)
ISBN(s): 978-1-58765-950-8 (3 vol set); 978-1-58765-954-6 (ebook set)

Critical Survey of Graphic Novels: Manga
Published by Grey House Publishing Inc™
2 University Plaza, Suite 310, Hackensack, NJ 07601
SAN: 208-838X
Tel: 201-968-0500 *Toll Free Tel:* 800-221-1592
Fax: 201-968-0511
E-mail: csr@salempress.com
Web Site: salempress.com
Key Personnel
Ed: Bart H Beaty; Stephen Weiner
Provides in-depth insight for over 65 of the most popular manga graphic novels, ranging from metaseries to stand-alone books.
Sept 2012: 400 pp, $195 (includes online access with print purchase)
ISBN(s): 978-1-58765-955-3; 978-1-58765-956-0 (ebook)

Critical Survey of Long Fiction
Published by Grey House Publishing Inc™
2 University Plaza, Suite 310, Hackensack, NJ 07601
SAN: 208-838X
Tel: 201-968-0500 *Toll Free Tel:* 800-221-1592
Fax: 201-968-0511
E-mail: csr@salempress.com
Web Site: salempress.com
Set offers 678 profiles of major writers of long fiction throughout history & the world, including critical analyses of their significant novels & novellas. Single hardcover volumes with the most popular content also available, each profiling authors & works in a particular genre or geography. Each volume covers about 22 authors & each essay is 5,000-7,500 words in length.
6,056 pp, $995/10 vol set, $105/vol (includes online access with print purchase)
First published 1983
ISBN(s): 978-1-58765-535-7 (10 vol set); 978-1-58765-546-3 (ebook set); 978-1-58765-929-4 (Gothic Novelists ebook); 978-1-58765-930-0 (Naturalist Novelists ebook); 978-1-58765-934-8 (Science Fiction Novelists ebook); 978-1-58765-935-5 (Novelists with Feminist Themes ebook); 978-1-58765-938-6 (African American Culture ebook); 978-1-58765-939-3 (Asian Novelists ebook); 978-1-58765-940-9 (English Novelists ebook); 978-1-58765-943-0 (Irish Novelists ebook); 978-1-58765-946-1 (Latin American Novelists ebook); 978-1-58765-947-8 (Native American Novelists ebook); 978-1-58765-948-5 (Russian Novelists ebook); 978-1-61925-717-7 (African American Culture); 978-1-61925-718-4 (Asian Novelists); 978-1-61925-719-1 (English Novelists); 978-1-61925-720-7 (French Novelists); 978-1-61925-721-4 (Gothic Novelists); 978-1-61925-722-1 (Irish Novelists); 978-1-61925-723-8 (Latin American Novelists); 978-1-61925-724-5 (Native American Novelists); 978-1-61925-725-2 (Naturalist Novelists); 978-1-61925-726-9 (Novelists with Feminist Themes); 978-1-61925-727-6 (Russian Novelists); 978-1-61925-728-3 (Science Fiction Novelists)

Critical Survey of Mystery & Detective Fiction
Published by Grey House Publishing Inc™
2 University Plaza, Suite 310, Hackensack, NJ 07601
SAN: 208-838X
Tel: 201-968-0500 *Toll Free Tel:* 800-221-1592
Fax: 201-968-0511
E-mail: csr@salempress.com
Web Site: salempress.com
Key Personnel
Ed: Carl Rollyson, PhD
Provides detailed analyses of the lives & writings of major contributors to mystery & detective fiction.
Jan 2008 (revised): 2,388 pp, $399/5 vol set
ISBN(s): 978-1-58765-397-1 (5 vol set); 978-1-58765-444-2 (ebook set)

Critical Survey of Mythology & Folklore: Heroes & Heroines
Published by Grey House Publishing Inc™
2 University Plaza, Suite 310, Hackensack, NJ 07601
SAN: 208-838X
Tel: 201-968-0500 *Toll Free Tel:* 800-221-1592
Fax: 201-968-0511
E-mail: csr@salempress.com
Web Site: salempress.com
Covers a diverse range of countries & cultures, as well as important retellings in the modern tradition. Articles cover: *Birth & Prophecy*, *The Host of Heroines*, *The Culture Hero*, *Trial & Quest*, *Myth & Monstrosity*, *Survey of Myth & Folklore*.
Oct 2013: 516 pp, $175 (includes online access)
ISBN(s): 978-1-61925-181-6

Critical Survey of Mythology & Folklore: Love, Sexuality & Desire
Published by Grey House Publishing Inc™
2 University Plaza, Suite 310, Hackensack, NJ 07601
SAN: 208-838X
Tel: 201-968-0500 *Toll Free Tel:* 800-221-1592
Fax: 201-968-0511
E-mail: csr@salempress.com
Web Site: salempress.com
Each title examines familiar & unfamiliar myths, from a diverse range of countries & cultures, as well as important retellings in the modern tradition. Topics covered include *Gods & Mortals in Love*, *The Myth of the Second Half*, *Animal Wives & Husbands*, *Modern Tales & Myths*, *Forbidden Love*, *Love Unrequited*, *The Lover's Quest*.
Jan 2013: 984 pp, $295/2 vol set (includes online access with print purchase)
ISBN(s): 978-1-4298-3765-1 (2 vol set); 978-1-4298-3768-2 (ebook set)

Critical Survey of Mythology & Folklore: World Mythology
Published by Grey House Publishing Inc™
2 University Plaza, Suite 310, Hackensack, NJ 07601
SAN: 208-838X
Tel: 201-968-0500 *Toll Free Tel:* 800-221-1592
Fax: 201-968-0511
E-mail: csr@salempress.com
Web Site: salempress.com
Presents articles on myths, folktales, legends & other traditional literature. Covers a diverse range of authors, countries & cultures that spans the globe. Articles begin with a summary that offers readers the major actions & characters in the tale followed by an analysis of the important cultural & social interpretations of the author & myth.
Dec 2013: 326 pp, $175 (includes online access)
ISBN(s): 978-1-61925-182-3

Critical Survey of Poetry
Published by Grey House Publishing Inc™
2 University Plaza, Suite 310, Hackensack, NJ 07601
SAN: 208-838X
Tel: 201-968-0500 *Toll Free Tel:* 800-221-1592
Fax: 201-968-0511
E-mail: csr@salempress.com
Web Site: salempress.com
An in-depth resource covering 843 poets throughout history & the world. Organized into 5 subsets by geography & essay type.
American Poets, 4 vol set, 2,414 pp, $495.
British, Irish & Commonwealth Poets, 3 vol set, 1,470 pp, $395.
European Poets, 3 vol set, 1,262 pp, $395.
World Poets, 1 vol, 442 pp, $150.
Topical Essays, 2 vol set, 924 pp, $295.
Cumulative Indexes, 1 vol, 266 pp, free with purchase of more than one subset.
4th ed, Jan 2011: 6,778 pp, $1,295/14 vol set (includes online access with print purchase)
First published 2002
ISBN(s): 978-1-58765-582-1 (14 vol set); 978-1-58765-583-8 (American Poets set); 978-1-58765-588-3 (British, Irish & Commonwealth Poets set); 978-1-58765-592-0 (American Poets ebook set); 978-1-58765-593-7 (14 vol ebook set); 978-1-58765-755-9 (British, Irish & Commonwealth Poets ebook set); 978-1-58765-756-6 (European Poets set); 978-1-58765-760-3 (European Poets ebook set); 978-1-58765-761-0 (World Poets); 978-1-58765-762-7 (World Poets ebook); 978-1-58765-763-4 (Topical Essays set); 978-1-58765-766-5 (Topical Essays ebook set); 978-1-58765-767-2 (Cumulative Indexes)

Critical Survey of Science Fiction & Fantasy Literature
Published by Grey House Publishing Inc™
2 University Plaza, Suite 310, Hackensack, NJ 07601
SAN: 208-838X
Tel: 201-968-0500 *Toll Free Tel:* 800-221-1592
Fax: 201-968-0511
E-mail: csr@salempress.com
Web Site: salempress.com
Key Personnel
Ed: Paul DiFilippo
Provides descriptions of hundreds of important works of science fiction & fantasy, summarizing plots & analyzing the works in terms of their contributions to literature.
2nd ed, March 2017: 1,400 pp, $295/3 vol set (includes online access)
ISBN(s): 978-1-68217-278-0 (3 vol set)

Critical Survey of Shakespeare's Sonnets
Published by Grey House Publishing Inc™
2 University Plaza, Suite 310, Hackensack, NJ 07601

SAN: 208-838X
Tel: 201-968-0500 *Toll Free Tel:* 800-221-1592
Fax: 201-968-0511
E-mail: csr@salempress.com
Web Site: salempress.com
Collection of 25 essays on the sonnets written by William Shakespeare, each providing an in-depth analysis of its historical significance, literary technique & discusses its meaning to a contemporary audience.
July 2014: 355 pp, $125 (includes online access)
ISBN(s): 978-1-61925-499-2

Critical Survey of Short Fiction
Published by Grey House Publishing Inc™
2 University Plaza, Suite 310, Hackensack, NJ 07601
SAN: 208-838X
Tel: 201-968-0500 *Toll Free Tel:* 800-221-1592
Fax: 201-968-0511
E-mail: csr@salempress.com
Web Site: salempress.com
Key Personnel
Ed: Charles E May
625 essays providing in-depth overviews of short story writers throughout history & the world. Organized into 5 subsets by geography & essay type.
American Writers, 4 vol set, 1,600 pp, $495.
British, Irish & Commonwealth Writers, 2 vol set, 800 pp, $295.
European Writers, 1 vol, 400 pp, $175.
World Writers, 1 vol, 400 pp, $175.
Topical Essays, 1 vol, 400 pp, $175.
Cumulative Indexes, 1 vol, 400 pp, free with purchase of more than one subset.
4th ed, Jan 2012: 4,000 pp, $995/10 vol set (includes online access with print purchase)
ISBN(s): 978-1-58765-789-4 (10 vol set); 978-1-58765-790-0 (American Writers set); 978-1-58765-795-5 (British, Irish & Commonwealth Writers set); 978-1-58765-798-6 (European Writers); 978-1-58765-799-3 (World Writers); 978-1-58765-800-6 (Topical Essays); 978-1-58765-803-7 (Cumulative Indexes); 978-1-58765-804-4 (10 vol ebook set); 978-1-58765-805-1 (American Writers ebook set); 978-1-58765-806-8 (British, Irish & Commonwealth Writers ebook set); 978-1-58765-807-5 (European Writers ebook); 978-1-58765-808-2 (World Writers ebook); 978-1-58765-809-9 (Topical Essays ebook)

Critical Survey of World Literature
Published by Grey House Publishing Inc™
2 University Plaza, Suite 310, Hackensack, NJ 07601
SAN: 208-838X
Tel: 201-968-0500 *Toll Free Tel:* 800-221-1592
Fax: 201-968-0511
E-mail: csr@salempress.com
Web Site: salempress.com
Key Personnel
Ed: Dr Christopher Gonzalez, PhD
Each volume contains 500 pages & covers major writers from outside the US & their significant works in fiction, drama, poetry & nonfiction.
Individual regional volumes: *Africa*
The Americas
Asia
Eastern Europe
Middle East
Western Europe.
3rd ed, Dec 2017: 3,000 pp, $499/6 vol set, $125/vol (includes online access)
ISBN(s): 978-1-68217-615-3 (6 vol set); 978-1-68217-616-0 (Africa); 978-1-68217-617-7 (The Americas); 978-1-68217-618-4 (Asia); 978-1-68217-619-1 (Eastern Europe); 978-1-68217-620-7 (Western Europe); 978-1-68217-621-4 (Middle East)

Critical Survey of Young Adult Literature
Published by Grey House Publishing Inc™
2 University Plaza, Suite 310, Hackensack, NJ 07601
SAN: 208-838X
Tel: 201 968 0500 *Toll Free Tel:* 800-221-1592
Fax: 201-968-0511
E-mail: csr@salempress.com
Web Site: salempress.com
Author biographies, genre overviews, plot summaries, theme overviews & film analysis for the young adult genre.
April 2016: 400 pp, $185 (includes online access)
ISBN(s): 978-1-61925-971-3

Current Biography Cumulative Index 1946-2013
Published by Grey House Publishing Inc™
4919 Rte 22, Amenia, NY 12501
Mailing Address: PO Box 56, Amenia, NY 12501-0056
Tel: 518-789-8700 *Toll Free Tel:* 800-562-2139
Fax: 518-789-0556
E-mail: books@greyhouse.com
Web Site: www.greyhouse.com
Name & profession indexes to late issues in which biographies appear in *Current Biography Yearbook*.
2014: 800 pp, $199
ISBN(s): 978-1-61925-472-5

Current Biography Yearbook
Published by Grey House Publishing Inc™
4919 Rte 22, Amenia, NY 12501
Mailing Address: PO Box 56, Amenia, NY 12501-0056
Tel: 518-789-8700 *Toll Free Tel:* 800-562-2139
Fax: 518-789-0556
E-mail: books@greyhouse.com
Web Site: www.greyhouse.com
Compilation of 175 up-to-date, contemporary profiles of accomplished & rising stars of politics, industry, entertainment & the arts from the US & around the world.
Annual.
2017: 750 pp, $199
ISBN(s): 978-1-61925-848-8

Cyclopedia of Literary Characters
Published by Grey House Publishing Inc™
2 University Plaza, Suite 310, Hackensack, NJ 07601
SAN: 208-838X
Tel: 201-968-0500 *Toll Free Tel:* 800-221-1592
Fax: 201-968-0511
E-mail: csr@salempress.com
Web Site: salempress.com
Provides critical descriptions of more than 29,000 major characters that appear in 3,500 important works of literature. New to this edition are 245 characters published in popular works of fiction from 2000 to 2013.
4th ed, Feb 2015: 2,700 pp, $455/5 vol set (includes online access)
ISBN(s): 978-1-61925-497-8 (5 vol set)

Cyclopedia of Literary Places
Published by Grey House Publishing Inc™
2 University Plaza, Suite 310, Hackensack, NJ 07601
SAN: 208-838X
Tel: 201-968-0500 *Toll Free Tel:* 800-221-1592
Fax: 201-968-0511
E-mail: csr@salempress.com
Web Site: salempress.com
In-depth discussion of the use of place in over 1,400 popular literary works. Each article provides the full title of the work, author's name & vital dates, type of work, type of plot, time of plot & date of original publication.
2nd ed, April 2016: 1,500 pp, $395/3 vol set (includes online access)
ISBN(s): 978-1-61925-884-6

Developmental Editing: A Handbook for Freelancers, Authors, and Publishers
Published by University of Chicago Press
1427 E 60 St, Chicago, IL 60637-2954
SAN: 202-5280
E-mail: custserv@press.uchicago.edu; marketing@press.uchicago.edu
Web Site: www.press.uchicago.edu
Key Personnel
Sr Ed: Mary E Laur *E-mail:* mlaur@uchicago.edu
Transforming a mss into a book that edifies, inspires & sells is the job of the developmental editor. Author Scott Norton starts with the core tasks of shaping the proposal, finding the hook & building the narrative or argument & then turns to the hard work of executing the plan & establishing a style. The book also includes detailed case studies featuring a variety of nonfiction books & authors ranging from first-timer to veteran, journalist to scholar.
1st ed: 252 pp, $50 cloth, $28 paper or ebook
First published 2009
ISBN(s): 978-0-226-59514-6 (cloth); 978-0-226-59515-3 (paper); 978-0-226-59516-0 (ebook)

Dictionary of Literary Biography
Published by Gale
Unit of Cengage Learning
27500 Drake Rd, Farmington Hills, MI 48331-3535
SAN: 213-4373
Tel: 248-699-4253 *Toll Free Tel:* 800-877-4253
Fax: 248-699-8070 *Toll Free Fax:* 800-414-5043 (orders)
E-mail: gale.galeord@cengage.com
Web Site: www.gale.com
Multivolume series; each volume focuses on a specific literary movement or period. Series aims to encompass all who have contributed to literary history from the Elizabethan Era to 20th century English, American, Canadian, French & German literature, drama & history. Major biographical & critical essays are presented for the most important figures of each era. Each essay includes a career chronology, list of publications & a bibliography of works by & about the subject. Also available online.
$381 hardcover

Dictionary of Modern English Usage
Published by Oxford University Press USA
198 Madison Ave, New York, NY 10016
SAN: 202-5892
Toll Free Tel: 800-451-7556 (orders) *Fax:* 212-726-6453
E-mail: orders.us@oup.com
Web Site: www.oup.com/us
Key Personnel
Author: H W Fowler
2010 (Dec): 832 pp, $17.95
First published 2009
ISBN(s): 978-0-19-958589-2

Direct Marketing Market Place® (DMMP)
Published by NRP Direct
430 Mountain Ave, Suite 403, New Providence, NJ 07974
Tel: 908-517-0780 *Toll Free Tel:* 844-592-4197
Fax: 908-608-3012 (cust serv)
E-mail: sales@nrpdirect.com
Web Site: www.dirmktgplace.com; www.nrpdirect.com
A comprehensive source of direct marketing, listing over 17,500 key personnel & over 8,800 leading direct marketing companies, suppliers & creative sources.
Annual.
2017 ed

Directories in Print (DIP)
Published by Gale
Unit of Cengage Learning
27500 Drake Rd, Farmington Hills, MI 48331-3535
SAN: 213-4373
Tel: 248-699-4253 *Toll Free Tel:* 800-877-4253 *Fax:* 248-699-8075 *Toll Free Fax:* 800-414-5043 (orders)
E-mail: gale.galeord@cengage.com
Web Site: www.gale.com
Profiles of more than 15,000 directories, guides & other print or non-print address listings in the US & around the world. Details both active & archived publications, including directories no longer published. Each listing offers up to 29 points of key information for the details to make informed choices. Also available as an ebook.
Annual.
39th ed, 2017: 2,258 pp, $1,223 paper, $1,345.30 ebook
ISBN(s): 978-1-4103-1858-9 (paper); 978-1-4103-1926-5 (ebook)

A Directory of American Poets & Writers
Published by Poets & Writers Inc
90 Broad St, Suite 2100, New York, NY 10004
Tel: 212-226-3586 *Fax:* 212-226-3963
E-mail: directory@pw.org
Web Site: www.pw.org/directory
Key Personnel
Exec Dir: Elliot Figman
Mng Dir: Melissa Ford Gradel *Tel:* 212-226-3586 ext 223
Names, addresses, telephone numbers & e-mail addresses of over 10,000 contemporary American writers & poets. Available online only.
Free

The Directory of Business Information Resources
Published by Grey House Publishing Inc™
4919 Rte 22, Amenia, NY 12501
Mailing Address: PO Box 56, Amenia, NY 12501-0056
Tel: 518-789-8700 *Toll Free Tel:* 800-562-2139 *Fax:* 518-789-0556
E-mail: books@greyhouse.com
Web Site: www.greyhouse.com
Source for contacts in 101 business areas. The over 20,000 detailed, informative entries include contact names, phone & fax numbers, web sites & e-mail addresses along with descriptions, membership information, ordering details & more.
Annual.
2017: 2,500 pp, $495 busn, $195 academic & lib (includes online access)
ISBN(s): 978-1-68217-341-1

The Directory of Mail Order Catalogs
Published by Grey House Publishing Inc™
4919 Rte 22, Amenia, NY 12501
Mailing Address: PO Box 56, Amenia, NY 12501-0056
Tel: 518-789-8700 *Toll Free Tel:* 800-562-2139 *Fax:* 518-789-0556
E-mail: books@greyhouse.com
Web Site: www.greyhouse.com
Complete listing of direct-to-consumer & business-to-business mail order catalogs, including detailed contact information.
Annual.
2017: 900 pp, $450, $250 academic & lib (includes online access)
First published 1981
ISBN(s): 978-1-61925-936-2

Directory of Mailing List Companies
Published by Todd Publications
920 Dogwood Dr, No 461, Delray Beach, FL 33483
SAN: 207-0804
Tel: 561-910-0440 *Fax:* 561-910-0440
E-mail: toddpub@yahoo.com
Key Personnel
Ed/Publr: Barry Klein
Provides alphabetically, with addresses, phone numbers & zip codes, the names of more than 1100 list companies, specialists & brokers, together with their managers' names & telephones & other pertinent information.
18th ed, 2014: 150 pp, $95 paper
ISBN(s): 978-0-87340-024-4

Directory of Poetry Publishers
Published by Dustbooks
PO Box 100, Paradise, CA 95967-0100
SAN: 204-1871
Tel: 530-877-6110 *Fax:* 530-877-0222
E-mail: publisher@dustbooks.com; info@dustbooks.com
Web Site: www.dustbooks.com
Key Personnel
Publr: Kathleen Glanville
Ed: Neil McIntyre
Information on more than 1,900 book & magazine publishers of poetry worldwide, including university presses & e-zines.
Annual (CD-ROM), continuously (online).
32nd ed, 2016-2017, $21 CD-ROM, $65 CD-ROM (3 directories), $49.95 online (4 directories)
ISBN(s): 978-1-935742-42-5 (CD-ROM)

Directory of Small Press/Magazine Editors & Publishers
Published by Dustbooks
PO Box 100, Paradise, CA 95967-0100
SAN: 204-1871
Tel: 530-877-6110 *Fax:* 530-877-0222
E-mail: publisher@dustbooks.com; info@dustbooks.com
Web Site: www.dustbooks.com
Key Personnel
Publr: Kathleen Glanville
Ed: Neil McIntyre
Names & numbers guide to the small press & magazine industry.
Annual (CD-ROM), continuously (online).
47th ed, 2016-2017, $21 CD-ROM, $65 CD-ROM (3 directories), $49.95 online (4 directories)
ISBN(s): 978-1-935742-40-1 (CD-ROM)

Directory of Special Libraries and Information Centers (DSL)
Published by Gale
Unit of Cengage Learning
27500 Drake Rd, Farmington Hills, MI 48331-3535
SAN: 213-4373
Tel: 248-699-4253 *Toll Free Tel:* 800-877-4253 *Fax:* 248-699-8075 *Toll Free Fax:* 800-414-5043 (orders)
E-mail: gale.galeord@cengage.com
Web Site: www.gale.com
Key Personnel
Content Proj Ed: Matthew Miskelly *E-mail:* matthew.miskelly@cengage.com
Vol 1, in 3 parts, provides detailed contact & descriptive info on subject-specific resource collections maintained by various government agencies, businesses, publishers, educational & nonprofit organizations & associations around the world. Vol 2 contains geographical & personnel indexes. Available as ebook only.
44th ed: 2,937 pp, $2,374 ebook
ISBN(s): 978-1-4144-8789-2

Do-It-Yourself Book Publicity Kit
Published by Open Horizons Publishing Co
PO Box 2887, Taos, NM 87571
Tel: 575-751-3398
E-mail: info@bookmarket.com
Web Site: www.bookmarket.com
Key Personnel
Publr & Ed: John Kremer *E-mail:* johnkremer@bookmarket.com
How to write a news release, put together a media kit, get reviews, schedule interviews & get on-going national publicity.
2017: 256 pp, $30

Drama Criticism
Published by Gale
Unit of Cengage Learning
27500 Drake Rd, Farmington Hills, MI 48331-3535
SAN: 213-4373
Tel: 248-699-4253 *Toll Free Tel:* 800-877-4253 *Fax:* 248-699-8070 *Toll Free Fax:* 800-414-5043 (orders)
E-mail: gale.galeord@cengage.com
Web Site: www.gale.com
Each volume covers 4-8 significant dramatists or plays. For each play or playwright featured, a full range of critical opinion is presented, along with a biographical sketch, a chronological list of the writer's major works & more. Most critical essays are full text.
$271 hardcover

E-Publishing and Digital Libraries: Legal and Organizational Issues
Published by IGI Global
701 E Chocolate Ave, Hershey, PA 17033
Tel: 717-533-8845 (ext 100) *Toll Free Tel:* 866-342-6657 *Fax:* 717-533-8661; 717-533-7115
E-mail: cust@igi-global.com
Web Site: www.igi-global.com
2011: 552 pp, $180
ISBN(s): 978-1-60960-031-0; 978-1-60960-033-4 (ebook)

EFA Online Directory
Published by Editorial Freelancers Association (EFA)
71 W 23 St, 4th fl, New York, NY 10010-4102
Tel: 212-929-5400 *Toll Free Tel:* 866-929-5425 *Fax:* 212-929-5439 *Toll Free Fax:* 866-929-5439
E-mail: info@the-efa.org; office@the-efa.org
Web Site: www.the-efa.org
Key Personnel
Exec: William P Keenan, Jr; J P Partland
National, nonprofit professional organization comprising editors, writers, indexers, proofreaders, researchers, translators & other self-employed workers in the publishing industry. Online directory searchable by skills, subject matter, expertise & location. Members may post descriptions of services, resumes & contact information. Clients can directly hire the freelance help they need.
2,300 pp, free (online)
ISBN(s): 978-1-880407-13-4

El-Hi Textbooks & Serials in Print®
Published by Grey House Publishing Inc™
4919 Rte 22, Amenia, NY 12501
Mailing Address: PO Box 56, Amenia, NY 12501-0056
Tel: 518-789-8700 *Toll Free Tel:* 800-562-2139 *Fax:* 518-789-0556
E-mail: books@greyhouse.com
Web Site: www.greyhouse.com
Includes the in-print titles of publishers of textbooks & related materials. Coverage includes over 195,000 elementary, junior high & high school textbooks from over 17,000 publishers nationwide.
Annual.
2017: 4,000 pp, $620/2 vol set
ISBN(s): 978-1-68217-480-7 (2 vol set)

The Elements of Style
Published by Pearson Arts & Sciences
Division of Pearson Education Ltd
330 Hudson St, 9th fl, New York, NY 10013-1048
Tel: 917-981-2200
Web Site: www.pearsonhighered.com
Key Personnel
Author: William Strunk; E B White
50th Anniversary, 2008: 105 pp, $19.95
ISBN(s): 978-0-205-63264-0 (cloth)

The Emotional Craft of Fiction
Published by Writer's Digest
Imprint of F+W Media Inc
10151 Carver Rd, Suite 200, Blue Ash, OH 45242
Tel: 513-531-2690 *Toll Free Tel:* 800-289-0963 *Fax:* 513-531-0798
E-mail: writersdigest@fwmedia.com (edit)
Web Site: www.writersdigest.com; www.fwmedia.com; www.writersdigestshop.com
Key Personnel
Gen Mgr: David Pyle *E-mail:* david.pyle@fwmedia.com
Content Strategist: Rachel Randall *E-mail:* rachel.randall@fwmedia.com
Veteran literary agent & expert fiction instructor Donald Maass shows you how to use story to provoke a visceral & emotional experience in readers.
224 pp, $16.99 paper & ebook (retail)
ISBN(s): 978-1-4403-4837-2 (paper); 978-1-4403-4840-2 (ebook)

Encyclopedia of African American Writing
Published by Grey House Publishing Inc™
4919 Rte 22, Amenia, NY 12501
Mailing Address: PO Box 56, Amenia, NY 12501-0056
Tel: 518-789-8700 *Toll Free Tel:* 800-562-2139 *Fax:* 518-789-0556
E-mail: books@greyhouse.com; customerservice@greyhouse.com
Web Site: www.greyhouse.com
Highlights the role & influence of African-American authors from the 18th century to the present. Over 500 author biographies, with illustrations, cover the important events in each writer's life, education, major works, awards, family & important associates.
2nd ed, Oct 2009: 800 pp, $165 hardcover
ISBN(s): 978-1-59237-291-1

Encyclopedia of Associations: National Organizations
Published by Gale
Unit of Cengage Learning
27500 Drake Rd, Farmington Hills, MI 48331-3535
SAN: 213-4373
Tel: 248-699-4253 *Toll Free Tel:* 800-877-4253 *Fax:* 248-699-8075 *Toll Free Fax:* 800-414-5043 (orders)
E-mail: gale.galeord@cengage.com
Web Site: www.gale.com
Key Personnel
Ed: Kristy Swartout *E-mail:* kristy.swartout@cengage.com
A guide to more than 24,000 nonprofit American membership organizations of national & international scope. Detailed entries furnish association name & complete contact information. This information is not duplicated anywhere in Encyclopedia of Associations. Name & keyword indexes accompany each volume. Two companion volumes: Vol 2: *Geographic & Executive Indexes* & Vol 3: *Supplement*.
55th ed, 2017: 4,000 pp, $1,771 ebook
ISBN(s): 978-1-4144-8785-4 (ebook)

Fiction Core Collection
Published by Grey House Publishing Inc™
4919 Rte 22, Amenia, NY 12501
Mailing Address: PO Box 56, Amenia, NY 12501-0056
Tel: 518-789-8700 *Toll Free Tel:* 800-562-2139 *Fax:* 518-789-0556
E-mail: books@greyhouse.com
Web Site: www.greyhouse.com
Recommends novels, novellas & story collections for the general adult audience. Guide to over 8,500 books plus review sources & other professional aids for librarians.
18th ed, 2016: 1,643 pp, $295
ISBN(s): 978-1-61925-736-8

Fierce on the Page
Published by Writer's Digest
Imprint of F+W Media Inc
10151 Carver Rd, Suite 200, Blue Ash, OH 45242
Tel: 513-531-2690 *Toll Free Tel:* 800-289-0963 *Fax:* 513-531-0798
E-mail: writersdigest@fwmedia.com (edit)
Web Site: www.writersdigest.com; www.fwmedia.com; www.writersdigestshop.com
Key Personnel
Gen Mgr: David Pyle *E-mail:* david.pyle@fwmedia.com
Content Strategist: Rachel Randall *E-mail:* rachel.randall@fwmedia.com
Craft your best writing & your best life with this collection of contemplative & inspiring essays.
240 pp, $16.99 paper & ebook (retail)
ISBN(s): 978-1-59963-993-2 (paper); 978-1-59963-994-9 (ebook)

45 Master Characters
Published by Writer's Digest
Imprint of F+W Media Inc
10151 Carver Rd, Suite 200, Blue Ash, OH 45242
Tel: 513-531-2690 *Toll Free Tel:* 800-289-0963 *Fax:* 513-531-0798
E-mail: writersdigest@fwmedia.com (edit)
Web Site: www.writersdigest.com; www.writersdigestshop.com
Key Personnel
Gen Mgr: David Pyle *E-mail:* david.pyle@fwmedia.com
Content Strategist: Rachel Randall *E-mail:* rachel.randall@fwmedia.com
Gives all the information you need to develop believable characters that resonate with every reader.
288 pp, $17.99 paper & ebook (retail)
First published 2001
ISBN(s): 978-1-59963-534-7 (paper); 978-1-59963-535-4 (ebook)

Gale Directory of Databases (GDD)
Published by Gale
Unit of Cengage Learning
27500 Drake Rd, Farmington Hills, MI 48331-3535
SAN: 213-4373
Tel: 248-699-4253 *Toll Free Tel:* 800-877-4253 *Fax:* 248-699-8070 *Toll Free Fax:* 800-414-5043 (orders)
E-mail: gale.galeord@cengage.com
Web Site: www.gale.com
Current information about more than 14,000 databases & more than 3,000 producers, online services & vendors/distributors available worldwide in a variety of formats. Also available as an ebook.
40th ed, 2017: 2,556 pp, $1,001 paper, $1,101.10 ebook
ISBN(s): 978-1-4103-2675-1 (paper); 978-1-4103-2682-9 (ebook)

Gale Directory of Publications and Broadcast Media (GDPBM)
Published by Gale
Unit of Cengage Learning
27500 Drake Rd, Farmington Hills, MI 48331-3535
SAN: 213-4373
Tel: 248-699-4253 *Toll Free Tel:* 800-877-4253 *Fax:* 248-699-8075 *Toll Free Fax:* 800-414-5043 (orders)
E-mail: gale.galeord@cengage.com
Web Site: www.gale.com
Each edition contains approximately 53,000 listings for radio & television stations, cable companies & print/online companies as well as more than 13,500 international entries. Includes phone & fax number, e-mail addresses & web site URLs, listing of key personnel & more. Also available as an ebook.
152nd ed, 2016: 5,851 pp, $1,569 hardcover, $1,725.90 ebook
First published 1869
ISBN(s): 978-1-4144-8781-6 (ebook); 978-1-4144-8802-8 (hardcover)

General Issues in Literacy/Illiteracy in the World: A Bibliography
Published by Greenwood Press
Imprint of ABC-CLIO
130 Cremona Dr, Suite C, Santa Barbara, CA 93117
Mailing Address: PO Box 1911, Santa Barbara, CA 93116-1911
Tel: 805-968-1911 *Toll Free Tel:* 800-368-6868 *Fax:* 805-685-9685 *Toll Free Fax:* 866-270-3856
E-mail: customerservice@abc-clio.com
Web Site: www.abc-clio.com
Key Personnel
Dir, Edit-Print: Anthony Chiffolo
Author: William Eller; John Hladczuk; Sharon Hladczuk
Literacy-illiteracy; bibliography.
1st ed, 1990: 435 pp, $106.95 hardbound
ISBN(s): 978-0-313-27327-8

Getting It Published: A Guide for Scholars & Anyone Else Serious About Serious Books
Published by University of Chicago Press
1427 E 60 St, Chicago, IL 60637-2954
SAN: 202-5280
E-mail: custserv@press.uchicago.edu; marketing@press.uchicago.edu
Web Site: www.press.uchicago.edu
Key Personnel
Edit Dir: Alan G Thomas
A professor, author & 30-year veteran of the book industry, William Germano, knows what editors want & what writers need to know to get their work published. This 3rd edition of *Getting It Published* offers clear, practicable guidance on developing a compelling book proposal, finding the right publisher, evaluating a contract, negotiating the production process & emerging as a published author.
Revised every 5-7 yrs.
3rd ed: 304 pp, $60 cloth, $20 paper, $18 ebook
First published 2001
ISBN(s): 978-0-226-28137-7 (cloth); 978-0-226-28140-7 (paper); 978-0-226-28154-4 (ebook)

Gordon's Radio List
Published by North Ridge Books
PO Box 2832, Rancho Mirage, CA 92270
Tel: 949-533-5106 (cell) *Toll Free Fax:* 800-763-9881
E-mail: nrbooks@aol.com
Web Site: www.radiopublicity.net
Key Personnel
Ed: William A Gordon
Book-length database of over 900 radio shows that interview authors, updated on a day-to-day

basis. Available in both Excel & Word versions.
$369 includes free e-mailed updates for 3 months with the option to purchase additional updates

Grammatically Correct
Published by Writer's Digest
Imprint of F+W Media Inc
10151 Carver Rd, Suite 200, Blue Ash, OH 45242
Tel: 513-531-2690 *Toll Free Tel:* 800-289-0963 *Fax:* 513-531-0798
E-mail: writersdigest@fwmedia.com (edit)
Web Site: www.writersdigest.com; www.writersdigestshop.com
Key Personnel
Gen Mgr: David Pyle *E-mail:* david.pyle@fwmedia.com
Content Strategist: Rachel Randall *E-mail:* rachel.randall@fwmedia.com
Easy to use, quick reference & most of all, comprehensive.
2nd ed: 352 pp, $19.99 paper & ebook (retail)
First published 1997
ISBN(s): 978-1-58297-616-7 (paper); 978-1-59963-160-8 (ebook)

Grants & Awards
Published by PEN American Center
Affiliate of PEN International
588 Broadway, Suite 303, New York, NY 10012
Tel: 212-334-1660 *Fax:* 212-334-2181
E-mail: info@pen.org
Web Site: pen.org/press/grants-awards-database
Key Personnel
Exec Dir: Suzanne Nossel *Tel:* 212-334-1600 ext 4811 *E-mail:* snossel@pen.org
Pres: Andrew Solomon
Website Ed: Antonio Aiello *Tel:* 212-334-1660 ext 114 *E-mail:* antonio@pen.org
Database with nearly 1,500 domestic & foreign grants, literary awards, fellowships & residencies.
Online annual subn: free for membs; $12 nonmembs, $200 instns

Graphic Novels Core Collection
Published by Grey House Publishing Inc™
4919 Rte 22, Amenia, NY 12501
Mailing Address: PO Box 56, Amenia, NY 12501-0056
Tel: 518-789-8700 *Toll Free Tel:* 800-562-2139 *Fax:* 518-789-0556
E-mail: books@greyhouse.com
Web Site: www.greyhouse.com
Essential resource for library & media specialists looking to energize, enhance & enrich their collection with 3,500 important & highly recommended fiction & nonfiction graphic novel titles.
1st ed, June 2016: 1,391 pp, $295
ISBN(s): 978-1-68217-070-0

A Guide to Academic Writing
Published by Praeger
Imprint of ABC-CLIO
130 Cremona Dr, Suite C, Santa Barbara, CA 93117
Mailing Address: PO Box 1911, Santa Barbara, CA 93116-1911
Tel: 805-968-1911 *Toll Free Tel:* 800-368-6868 *Fax:* 805-685-9685 *Toll Free Fax:* 866-270-3856
E-mail: custserv@abc-clio.com
Web Site: www.abc-clio.com
Key Personnel
Dir, Edit-Print: Anthony Chiffolo
Author: Jeffery A Cantor
A comprehensive guide to academic writing & publishing.
200 pp, $26.95 paper, $64 hardcover
ISBN(s): 978-0-275-94660-9 (paper); 978-0-313-29017-6 (hardcover)

Guide to American & International Directories
Published by Todd Publications
920 Dogwood Dr, No 461, Delray Beach, FL 33483
SAN: 207-0804
Tel: 561-910-0440 *Fax:* 561-910-0440
E-mail: toddpub@yahoo.com
Key Personnel
Ed/Publr: Barry Klein
Complete information on more than 12,000 directories, covering more than 300 trade, educational & professional categories. Index.
Annual.
27th ed, 2018: 660 pp, $195.00
ISBN(s): 978-0-873400-466

Guide to Literary Agents
Published by Writer's Digest
Imprint of F+W Media Inc
10151 Carver Rd, Suite 200, Blue Ash, OH 45242
Tel: 513-531-2690 *Toll Free Tel:* 800-289-0963 *Fax:* 513-531-0798
E-mail: writersdigest@fwmedia.com (edit)
Web Site: www.writersdigest.com; www.writersdigestshop.com
Key Personnel
Gen Mgr: David Pyle *E-mail:* david.pyle@fwmedia.com
Content Strategist: Rachel Randall *E-mail:* rachel.randall@fwmedia.com
Annual.
26th ed, 2017: 336 pp, $29.99 paper & ebook (retail)
ISBN(s): 978-1-4403-4776-4 (paper); 978-1-4403-4783-2 (ebook)

Guide to Writers Conferences & Writing Workshops
Published by ShawGuides
PO Box 61569, Staten Island, NY 10306-7569
Tel: 718-874-3311
E-mail: support@shawguides.com
Web Site: shawguides.com
Key Personnel
Pres: Ron Janorkar
Online directory of conferences, seminars, workshops & retreats. Includes information about dates, facilities, faculty, writing specialties, daily activities, tuition, accommodations, refund policies, handicapped accessibility, nearby attractions. Includes information on organizations (dues, benefits, activities). Contents indexed by location (covers 50 states & 11 countries); specialties (9 genres); availability of college credit, continuing education credit & scholarships; writing contests, college writing programs. Available at writing.shawguides.com.

How to Get Your Book Published Free in Minutes & Marketed Worldwide in Days
Published by Communication Unlimited
185 Shevelin Rd, Novato, CA 94947
Tel: 415-884-2941 *Toll Free Tel:* 800-563-1454 *Fax:* 415-883-5707
E-mail: gordon@gordonburgett.com
Web Site: www.gordonburgett.com
Key Personnel
Pres: Gordon Burgett *E-mail:* glburgett@aol.com
How-to information, step-by-step process & detailed examples of "ancillary" publishing.
1st ed, 2010: 208 pp, $15 paper, $10 digital download
ISBN(s): 978-0-9826635-0-9 (digital download); 978-0-9826635-1-6 (print)

How to Publish & Market Your Own Book as an Independent African Heritage Book Publisher
Published by ECA Associates Press
PO Box 15004, Chesapeake, VA 23328-0004
Tel: 757-547-5542 *Fax:* 757-547-5542 (call first)
E-mail: embracinghistory2@gmail.com
Key Personnel
Pres: Dr E Curtis Alexander
Ed: Dr Mwalimu I Mwadilifu
1st ed: 140 pp, $15.95
ISBN(s): 978-0-938818-09-0

How to Write a Book Proposal
Published by Writer's Digest
Imprint of F+W Media Inc
10151 Carver Rd, Suite 200, Blue Ash, OH 45242
Tel: 513-531-2690 *Toll Free Tel:* 800-289-0963 *Fax:* 513-531-0798
E-mail: writersdigest@fwmedia.com (edit)
Web Site: www.writersdigest.com; www.writersdigestshop.com
Key Personnel
Gen Mgr: David Pyle *E-mail:* david.pyle@fwmedia.com
Content Strategist: Rachel Randall *E-mail:* rachel.randall@fwmedia.com
Details how the industry works, where it's headed & how you can be part of it.
4th ed: 336 pp, $19.99 paper & ebook (retail)
First published 2003
ISBN(s): 978-1-58297-702-7 (paper); 978-1-59963-307-7 (ebook)

Hudson's Washington News Media Contacts Directory
Published by Grey House Publishing Inc™
4919 Rte 22, Amenia, NY 12501
Mailing Address: PO Box 56, Amenia, NY 12501-0056
Tel: 518-789-8700 *Toll Free Tel:* 800-562-2139 *Fax:* 518-789-0556
E-mail: books@greyhouse.com
Web Site: www.greyhouse.com
Comprehensive listing of 4,000 news media sources in Washington, DC.
Annual.
2017: 400 pp, $289, online database available (see web site for quote)
ISBN(s): 978-1-68217-344-2

Index to Legal Periodicals & Books
Published by Grey House Publishing Inc™
4919 Rte 22, Amenia, NY 12501
Mailing Address: PO Box 56, Amenia, NY 12501-0056
Tel: 518-789-8700 *Toll Free Tel:* 800-562-2139 *Fax:* 518-789-0556
E-mail: books@greyhouse.com
Web Site: www.greyhouse.com
A cumulative author-subject index to legal publications with a table of cases & statutes & listing of book reviews.
2017 ed (2016 annual cumulation): 3,000 pp, $695
ISBN(s): 978-1-68217-204-9

Indexing from A to Z
Published by Grey House Publishing Inc™
4919 Rte 22, Amenia, NY 12501
Mailing Address: PO Box 56, Amenia, NY 12501-0056
Tel: 518-789-8700 *Toll Free Tel:* 800-562-2139 *Fax:* 518-789-0556
E-mail: books@greyhouse.com
Web Site: www.greyhouse.com
Includes the latest national & international standards & recommended practices pertaining to indexes & indexing.
Available for purchase at www.hwwilsoninprint.com/index_AZ.php.

2nd ed, 1996: 569 pp, $80
First published 1991
ISBN(s): 978-0-8242-0882-0

International Directory of Little Magazines & Small Presses
Published by Dustbooks
PO Box 100, Paradise, CA 95967-0100
SAN: 204-1871
Tel: 530-877-6110 *Fax:* 530-877-0222
E-mail: publisher@dustbooks.com; info@dustbooks.com
Web Site: www.dustbooks.com
Key Personnel
Publr: Kathleen Glanville
Ed: Neil McIntyre
For libraries & writers; 4,000 small book & magazine publishers with full data.
Annual (CD-ROM), continuously (online).
52nd ed, 2016-2017, $30 CD-ROM, $65 CD-ROM (3 directories), $49.95 online (4 directories)
ISBN(s): 978-1-935742-39-5 (CD-ROM)

International Literary Market Place (ILMP)
Published by Information Today, Inc
121 Chanlon Rd, Suite G-20, New Providence, NJ 07974-2195
Tel: 908-795-3755 *Toll Free Tel:* 800-409-4929 (press 3); 800-300-9868 (cust serv)
E-mail: custserv@infotoday.com
Web Site: www.literarymarketplace.com
Key Personnel
Mng Ed: Karen Hallard *Tel:* 908-219-0277 *E-mail:* khallard@infotoday.com
A comprehensive directory of data on the book trade industry in over 175 countries outside the US & Canada, with over 9,400 publishers & over 3,300 book organizations, including agents, booksellers & library associations. Includes information basic to conducting business in each country. The US & Canada are covered by *Literary Market Place*. Web version, which includes *Literary Market Place*, also available.
Annual.
51st ed, 2018: 1,890 pp, $339.50 paper, $429.50 online subn
ISBN(s): 978-1-57387-538-7

Introduction to Literary Context
Published by Grey House Publishing Inc™
2 University Plaza, Suite 310, Hackensack, NJ 07601
SAN: 208-838X
Tel: 201-968-0500 *Toll Free Tel:* 800-221-1592 *Fax:* 201-968-0511
E-mail: csr@salempress.com
Web Site: salempress.com
Each volume contains 300 pages & explores literary content. Each essay examines works through the following categories: content synopsis, religious context, historical context, societal context, biographic context, scientific & technological context. Includes discussion questions, essay ideas, works cited, bibliography & general index.
Volumes published Oct 2013:
American Post-Modernist Novels
American Short Fiction.
Volumes published April-Dec 2014:
American Poetry of the 20th Century
English Literature
Plays
World Literature.
$165/vol (includes online access)
ISBN(s): 978-1-61925-210-3 (American Post-Modernist Novels); 978-1-61925-212-7 (American Short Fiction); 978-1-61925-483-1 (World Literature); 978-1-61925-485-5 (English Literature); 978-1-61925-713-9 (American Poetry of the 20th Century); 978-1-61925-715-3 (Plays)

Jeff Herman's Guide to Book Publishers, Editors and Literary Agents: Who They Are, What They Want, How to Win Them Over
Published by New World Library
Division of Whatever Publishing Inc
14 Pamaron Way, Novato, CA 94949
SAN: 211-8777
Tel: 415-884-2100 *Toll Free Tel:* 800-972-6657; 800-227-3900 (ext 52, retail orders) *Fax:* 415-884-2199
Web Site: www.newworldlibrary.com
Key Personnel
Author: Jeff Herman
Writing/reference book. Directory of publishers (US, University, CN) & US literary agents. Includes interviews with editors & agents as well as additional information on submitting material to the publishing industry.
Annual.
27th ed, 2017: 672 pp, $29.95 paper
First published 1990
ISBN(s): 978-1-6086-84052

The Joy of Publishing!
Published by Open Horizons Publishing Co
PO Box 2887, Taos, NM 87571
Tel: 575-751-3398
E-mail: info@bookmarket.com
Web Site: www.bookmarket.com
Key Personnel
Publr & Ed: John Kremer *E-mail:* johnkremer@bookmarket.com
Fascinating facts, anecdotes, curiosities & historic origins about books & authors, editors & publishers, bookmaking & bookselling.
2000: 256 pp, $29.99 (hardcover), $19.95 (Internet special)
First published 1996
ISBN(s): 978-0-912411-47-7

Keys to Great Writing
Published by Writer's Digest
Imprint of F+W Media Inc
10151 Carver Rd, Suite 200, Blue Ash, OH 45242
Tel: 513-531-2690 *Toll Free Tel:* 800-289-0963 *Fax:* 513-531-0798
E-mail: writersdigest@fwmedia.com (edit)
Web Site: www.writersdigest.com; www.writersdigestshop.com
Key Personnel
Gen Mgr: David Pyle *E-mail:* david.pyle@fwmedia.com
Content Strategist: Rachel Randall *E-mail:* rachel.randall@fwmedia.com
From grammar to revision strategies.
1st ed: 240 pp, $14.99 (retail)
ISBN(s): 978-1-58297-492-7

Law Books & Serials in Print™
Published by Grey House Publishing Inc™
4919 Rte 22, Amenia, NY 12501
Mailing Address: PO Box 56, Amenia, NY 12501-0056
Tel: 518-789-8700 *Toll Free Tel:* 800-562-2139 *Fax:* 518-789-0556
E-mail: books@greyhouse.com
Web Site: www.greyhouse.com
Provides immediate access to current legal books, serials & multimedia publications. Offers data on 90,000 titles, including print & non-print materials & over 20,000 serials entries from domestic & international publishers.
Annual.
2017: 3,900 pp, $1,615/3 vol set
ISBN(s): 978-1-68217-494-4 (3 vol set)

The Library & Book Trade Almanac
Published by Information Today, Inc
121 Chanlon Rd, Suite G-20, New Providence, NJ 07974-2195
Tel: 908-219-0279 *Toll Free Tel:* 800-300-9868 (cust serv)
E-mail: custserv@infotoday.com
Almanac of US library & book trade statistics, standards, programs & major events of the year, as well as international statistics & developments. Includes lists of library & literary awards & prizes, notable books, library schools, scholarship sources; directory of book trade & library associations at state, regional, national & international levels; employment sources; calendar of events.
Annual.
62nd ed, 2017: 590 pp, $299.00 hardbound
ISBN(s): 978-1-57387-536-3

Literary Market Place (LMP)
Published by Information Today, Inc
121 Chanlon Rd, Suite G-20, New Providence, NJ 07974-2195
Tel: 908-795-3755 *Toll Free Tel:* 800-409-4929 (press 3); 800-300-9868 (cust serv)
E-mail: custserv@infotoday.com
Web Site: www.literarymarketplace.com
Key Personnel
Mng Ed: Karen Hallard *Tel:* 908-219-0277 *E-mail:* khallard@infotoday.com
Directory of over 26,000 companies & individuals in US & Canadian publishing. Areas covered include book publishers; associations; book trade events; courses, conferences & contests; agents & agencies; services & suppliers; direct-mail promotion; review, selection & reference; radio & television; wholesale, export & import & book manufacturing. A 2 volume set, each containing 2 alphabetical names & numbers indexes, one for key companies listed & one for individuals. The rest of the world is covered by *International Literary Market Place*. Web version, which also includes *International Literary Market Place*, also available.
Annual.
78th ed, 2018: 1,630 pp, $429.50/2 vol set paper, $429.50 online subn
ISBN(s): 978-1-57387-540-0 (2 vol set)

Magazines for Libraries
Published by ProQuest LLC
Subsidiary of Cambridge Information Group Inc
630 Central Ave, New Providence, NJ 07974
E-mail: info@proquest.com
Web Site: www.proquest.com
Key Personnel
Gen Ed: Cheryl LaGuardia
Creator: Bill Katz
A critically annotated guide to magazine selection for public, college, school & special libraries, with approximately 6,000 periodicals critically evaluated by more than 200 subject specialists & classified under more than 160 subject headings. Includes journals (print & electronic) & newspapers.
Annual.
26th ed, 2018, $1,318 cloth
First published 1969
ISBN(s): 978-1-60030-669-3

Magill's Choice: Holocaust Literature
Published by Grey House Publishing Inc™
2 University Plaza, Suite 310, Hackensack, NJ 07601
SAN: 208-838X
Tel: 201-968-0500 *Toll Free Tel:* 800-221-1592 *Fax:* 201-968-0511
E-mail: csr@salempress.com
Web Site: salempress.com
Key Personnel
Ed: John K Roth; Edward J Sexton
More than 100 in-depth reviews of the classics of Holocaust literature, including histories, biographies, memoirs, diaries, testimonials, philosophy, social criticism, novels, short fiction, poetry & plays.

March 2008: 960 pp, $130/2 vol set
ISBN(s): 978-1-58765-375-9 (2 vol set); 978-1-58765-443-5 (ebook set)

Magill's Literary Annual
Published by Grey House Publishing Inc™
2 University Plaza, Suite 310, Hackensack, NJ 07601
SAN: 208-838X
Tel: 201-968-0500 *Toll Free Tel:* 800-221-1592 *Fax:* 201-968-0511
E-mail: csr@salempress.com
Web Site: salempress.com
Offers over 150 major examples of serious literature published during the previous calendar year, covering the best of the best in fiction & nonfiction.
Annual.
2017: 700 pp, $195/2 vol set (includes online access)
First published 1954
ISBN(s): 978-1-68217-276-6 (2 vol set)

Magill's Survey of American Literature
Published by Grey House Publishing Inc™
2 University Plaza, Suite 310, Hackensack, NJ 07601
SAN: 208-838X
Tel: 201-968-0500 *Toll Free Tel:* 800-221-1592 *Fax:* 201-968-0511
E-mail: csr@salempress.com
Web Site: salempress.com
Key Personnel
Ed: Steven G Kellman
Profiles of 339 major US & Canadian authors of fiction, drama & poetry, accompanied by analysis of their significant works.
Available for purchase at www.salempress.com/press_titles.html?book=343.
Sept 2006: 2,904 pp, $499/6 vol set
First published 1991
ISBN(s): 978-1-58765-285-1 (6 vol set)

Magill's Survey of World Literature
Published by Grey House Publishing Inc™
2 University Plaza, Suite 310, Hackensack, NJ 07601
SAN: 208-838X
Tel: 201-968-0500 *Toll Free Tel:* 800-221-1592 *Fax:* 201-968-0511
E-mail: csr@salempress.com
Web Site: salempress.com
Key Personnel
Ed: Steven G Kellman
Profiles of 380 major authors of fiction, drama, poetry & essays, each with sections on biography, general analysis & analysis of the author's most important works-novels, short stories, poems & works of nonfiction.
Jan 2009: 3,032 pp, $499/6 vol set
ISBN(s): 978-1-58765-431-2 (6 vol set); 978-1-58765-446-6 (ebook set)

Mail Order Business Directory
Published by Todd Publications
920 Dogwood Dr, No 461, Delray Beach, FL 33483
SAN: 207-0804
Tel: 561-910-0440 *Fax:* 561-910-0440
E-mail: toddpub@yahoo.com
Key Personnel
Ed/Publr: Barry Klein
Contains the names of the 5,500 most active mail order catalogs, listed by 40 product categories with Alphabetical Index & Merchandise Category Index.
35th ed, 2016: 470 pp, $195 paper
ISBN(s): 978-0-873400-374

Managing the Publishing Process: An Annotated Bibliography
Published by Greenwood Press
Imprint of ABC-CLIO
130 Cremona Dr, Suite C, Santa Barbara, CA 93117
Mailing Address: PO Box 1911, Santa Barbara, CA 93116-1911
Tel: 805-968-1911 *Toll Free Tel:* 800-368-6868 *Fax:* 805-685-9685 *Toll Free Fax:* 866-270-3856
E-mail: customerservice@abc-clio.com
Web Site: www.abc-clio.com
Key Personnel
Dir, Edit-Print: Anthony Chiffolo
Author: Bruce Speck
Cites & annotates more than 1,200 books & articles on how to manage the publishing process.
1995: 360 pp, $75 hardcover
ISBN(s): 978-0-313-27956-0

Manufacturing Standards & Specifications for (El-Hi) Textbooks (MSST)
Published by State Instructional Materials Review Administrators (SIMRA)
PO Box 731388, Ormond Beach, FL 32173
Tel: 386-986-4552 *Fax:* 386-986-4553
E-mail: info@bmibook.com
Web Site: www.bmibook.org
Key Personnel
EVP & ACTS Coord: Daniel N Bach
The official Advisory Commission on Textbook Specifications (ACTS) publication detailing the approved guidelines for the manufacture of elementary & high school textbooks.
Sept 2012: 92 pp, $35 per copy looseleaf bound, adhesive bound or CD

Masterplots
Published by Grey House Publishing Inc™
2 University Plaza, Suite 310, Hackensack, NJ 07601
SAN: 208-838X
Tel: 201-968-0500 *Toll Free Tel:* 800-221-1592 *Fax:* 201-968-0511
E-mail: csr@salempress.com
Web Site: salempress.com
Fundamental reference data, plot synopses & critical evaluations of the most important works in all genres throughout history & around the world.
4th ed, Nov 2010: 7,316 pp, $1,200/12 vol set (includes online access)
First published 1976
ISBN(s): 978-1-58765-568-5 (12 vol set)

Masterplots II: African American Literature
Published by Grey House Publishing Inc™
2 University Plaza, Suite 310, Hackensack, NJ 07601
SAN: 208-838X
Tel: 201-968-0500 *Toll Free Tel:* 800-221-1592 *Fax:* 201-968-0511
E-mail: csr@salempress.com
Web Site: salempress.com
Key Personnel
Ed: Tyrone Williams
Essays on individual titles by great novelists, playwrights, memoirists, historians, critics, major poets, short story writers, essayists & orators.
Dec 2008 (revised): 2,160 pp, $404/4 vol set
ISBN(s): 978-1-58765-438-1 (4 vol set); 978-1-58765-447-3 (ebook set)

Masterplots II: Christian Literature
Published by Grey House Publishing Inc™
2 University Plaza, Suite 310, Hackensack, NJ 07601
SAN: 208-838X
Tel: 201-968-0500 *Toll Free Tel:* 800-221-1592 *Fax:* 201-968-0511
E-mail: csr@salempress.com
Web Site: salempress.com
Key Personnel
Ed: John K Roth
Covers over 500 classic & contemporary works of Christian fiction, nonfiction, poetry & drama, providing a plot summary, analysis of Christian themes & an annotated bibliography for each title.
Sept 2007: 2,126 pp, $385/4 vol set
ISBN(s): 978-1-58765-379-7 (4 vol set); 978-1-58765-413-8 (ebook set)

Masterplots II: Drama Series
Published by Grey House Publishing Inc™
2 University Plaza, Suite 310, Hackensack, NJ 07601
SAN: 208-838X
Tel: 201-968-0500 *Toll Free Tel:* 800-221-1592 *Fax:* 201-968-0511
E-mail: csr@salempress.com
Web Site: salempress.com
Key Personnel
Ed: Christian H Moe
Covers plays by important 20th century playwrights. No other *Masterplots* covers these 345 plays.
Sept 2003 (revised): 1,850 pp, $404/4 vol set
ISBN(s): 978-1-58765-116-8 (4 vol set)

Masterplots II: Short Story Series
Published by Grey House Publishing Inc™
2 University Plaza, Suite 310, Hackensack, NJ 07601
SAN: 208-838X
Tel: 201-968-0500 *Toll Free Tel:* 800-221-1592 *Fax:* 201-968-0511
E-mail: csr@salempress.com
Web Site: salempress.com
Key Personnel
Ed: Charles E May
Penetrating discussions of the content, themes, structure & techniques of 1,490 stories by writers from around the world.
2nd ed (revised), Jan 2004: 4,944 pp, $599/8 vol set
ISBN(s): 978-1-58765-140-3 (8 vol set)

Medical & Health Care Books & Serials in Print™
Published by Grey House Publishing Inc™
4919 Rte 22, Amenia, NY 12501
Mailing Address: PO Box 56, Amenia, NY 12501-0056
Tel: 518-789-8700 *Toll Free Tel:* 800-562-2139 *Fax:* 518-789-0556
E-mail: books@greyhouse.com
Web Site: www.greyhouse.com
Provides immediate access to the highly specialized publishing activity in the health sciences & allied health fields.
Annual.
2017: 6,300 pp, $785/2 vol set
ISBN(s): 978-1-68217-491-3 (2 vol set)

Middle & Junior High Core Collection
Published by Grey House Publishing Inc™
4919 Rte 22, Amenia, NY 12501
Mailing Address: PO Box 56, Amenia, NY 12501-0056
Tel: 518-789-8700 *Toll Free Tel:* 800-562-2139 *Fax:* 518-789-0556
E-mail: books@greyhouse.com
Web Site: www.greyhouse.com
Guide to over 11,000 fiction & nonfiction books recommended for children & young adolescents, grades 5-9.
13th ed, 2017: 2,500 pp, $295
ISBN(s): 978-1-68217-238-4

MLRC 50-State Survey: Employment Libel & Privacy Law
Published by Media Law Resource Center Inc
North Tower, 20th fl, 520 Eighth Ave, New York, NY 10018

Tel: 212-337-0200 *Fax:* 212-337-9893
E-mail: medialaw@medialaw.org
Web Site: www.medialaw.org
Key Personnel
Exec Dir: George Freeman
Easy-to-use compendiums of the law in all US jurisdictions, state & federal, used by journalists, lawyers, judges & law schools nationwide. Each state's chapter, prepared by experts in that jurisdiction, is presented in a uniform outline format. Also available as an ebook.
Annual.
2017, $205
ISBN(s): 978-1-63283-8599 (paper); 978-1-63283-8605 (ebook)

MLRC 50-State Survey: Media Libel Law
Published by Media Law Resource Center Inc
North Tower, 20th fl, 520 Eighth Ave, New York, NY 10018
Tel: 212-337-0200 *Fax:* 212-337-9893
E-mail: medialaw@medialaw.org
Web Site: www.medialaw.org
Key Personnel
Exec Dir: George Freeman
Easy-to-use compendiums of the law in all US jurisdictions, state & federal, used by journalists, lawyers, judges & law schools nationwide. Each state's chapter, prepared by experts in that jurisdiction, is presented in a uniform outline format. Also available as an ebook.
Annual.
2016-2017, $205
ISBN(s): 978-1-63283-8551 (paper); 978-1-63283-8568 (ebook)

MLRC 50-State Survey: Media Privacy & Related Law
Published by Media Law Resource Center Inc
North Tower, 20th fl, 520 Eighth Ave, New York, NY 10018
Tel: 212-337-0200 *Fax:* 212-337-9893
E-mail: medialaw@medialaw.org
Web Site: www.medialaw.org
Key Personnel
Exec Dir: George Freeman
Easy-to-use compendiums of the law in all US jurisdictions, state & federal, used by journalists, lawyers, judges & law schools nationwide. Each state's chapter, prepared by experts in that jurisdiction, is presented in a uniform outline format. Also available as an ebook.
Annual.
2016-2017, $205
ISBN(s): 978-1-63283-8575 (paper); 978-1-63283-8582 (ebook)

National Trade and Professional Associations of the United States
Published by Columbia Books & Information Services (CBIS)
4340 East-West Hwy, Suite 300, Bethesda, MD 20814
Tel: 202-464-1662 *Toll Free Tel:* 888-265-0600 (cust serv) *Fax:* 301-664-9600
E-mail: info@columbiabooks.com
Web Site: www.columbiabooks.com
Key Personnel
Sr Mktg Mgr: Jamie Herring *Tel:* 240-235-0271 *E-mail:* jherring@columbiabooks.com
Covers over 8,000 trade associations, professional societies & labor unions with national memberships with such data as chief executive, size of membership & staff, budget, telephone, facsimile number, e-mail address, publications, meeting data & historical background. Includes indexes by subject, geography, budget, acronym, chief executive officer & annual meeting location. Also available online at www.associationexecs.com.
Annual.
52nd ed, 2017, $299
First published 1965
ISBN(s): 978-1-938939-48-8 (paper)

The New York Times Manual of Style & Usage
Published by Three Rivers Press
Division of Penguin Random House Inc
1745 Broadway, New York, NY 10019
Tel: 212-782-9000 *Toll Free Tel:* 800-733-3000 (cust serv)
Web Site: www.penguinrandomhouse.com
Key Personnel
Author: William G Connolly; Allan M Siegal
5th ed, 2015, $18 paper, $12.99 ebook
ISBN(s): 978-1-10190-322-3 (ebook); 978-1-10190-544-9 (paper)

Niche Publishing: Publish Profitably Every Time
Published by Communication Unlimited
185 Shevelin Rd, Novato, CA 94947
Tel: 415-884-2941 *Toll Free Tel:* 800-563-1454 *Fax:* 415-883-5707
E-mail: gordon@gordonburgett.com
Web Site: www.gordonburgett.com
Key Personnel
Pres & Ed: Gordon Burgett *E-mail:* glburgett@aol.com
How-to information, step-by-step process & detailed example of niche publishing.
2008: 208 pp, $15 paper, $10 digital download
First published 2008
ISBN(s): 978-0-979629-525

Nineteenth-Century Literature Criticism
Published by Gale
Unit of Cengage Learning
27500 Drake Rd, Farmington Hills, MI 48331-3535
SAN: 213-4373
Tel: 248-699-4253 *Toll Free Tel:* 800-877-4253 *Fax:* 248-699-8070 *Toll Free Fax:* 800-414-5043 (orders)
E-mail: gale.galeord@cengage.com
Web Site: www.gale.com
Profiles 4-8 literary figures by providing full-text or excerpted criticism taken from books, magazines, literary reviews, newspapers & scholarly journals.
$397 hardcover

Notable African American Writers
Published by Grey House Publishing Inc™
2 University Plaza, Suite 310, Hackensack, NJ 07601
SAN: 208-838X
Tel: 201-968-0500 *Toll Free Tel:* 800-221-1592 *Fax:* 201-968-0511
E-mail: csr@salempress.com
Web Site: salempress.com
Contains 80 essays on important African American writers in all genres.
April 2006: 1,350 pp, $217/3 vol set
ISBN(s): 978-1-58765-272-1 (3 vol set)

Notable American Novelists
Published by Grey House Publishing Inc™
2 University Plaza, Suite 310, Hackensack, NJ 07601
SAN: 208-838X
Tel: 201-968-0500 *Toll Free Tel:* 800-221-1592 *Fax:* 201-968-0511
E-mail: csr@salempress.com
Web Site: salempress.com
Presents biographical sketches & analytical overviews of 145 of the best known American writers of long fiction that are studied in the core curricula of high school & undergraduate literature studies.
Aug 2007 (revised): 1,536 pp, $217/3 vol set
ISBN(s): 978-1-58765-393-3 (3 vol set)

Notable Playwrights
Published by Grey House Publishing Inc™
2 University Plaza, Suite 310, Hackensack, NJ 07601
SAN: 208-838X
Tel: 201-968-0500 *Toll Free Tel:* 800-221-1592 *Fax:* 201-968-0511
E-mail: csr@salempress.com
Web Site: salempress.com
Biographical sketches & critical studies of 106 of the best known dramatists, from the development of drama in ancient Greece & Rome to European, American, Asian & African writers of today.
Aug 2004: 1,131 pp, $217/3 vol set
ISBN(s): 978-1-58765-195-3 (3 vol set); 978-1-58765-316-2 (ebook set)

O'Dwyer's Directory of Public Relations Firms
Published by J R O'Dwyer Co Inc
271 Madison Ave, Rm 600, New York, NY 10016
Tel: 212-679-2471 *Toll Free Tel:* 866-395-7710 *Fax:* 212-683-2750
Web Site: www.odwyerpr.com
Key Personnel
Ed-in-Chief & Publr: Jack O'Dwyer *E-mail:* jack@odwyerpr.com
Assoc Publr & Ed: Jane Landers *E-mail:* jane@odwyerpr.com; John O'Dwyer *E-mail:* john@odwyerpr.com
Dir, Mktg: Christine O'Dwyer *E-mail:* christine@odwyerpr.com
Sr Ed: Fraser P Seitel *E-mail:* yusake@aol.com
Directory Ed-in-Chief: Melissa Werbell *E-mail:* melissa@odwyerpr.com
A listing of more than 1,200 PR firms in the US & abroad. Also available on web site as PDF download.
Annual.
47th ed, 2017: 330 pp, $95
First published 1970
ISBN(s): 978-0-9976910-1-6

100 Things Every Writer Needs to Know
Published by TarcherPerigee
Imprint of Penguin Group USA, A Penguin Random House Company
375 Hudson St, New York, NY 10014
Tel: 212-366-2000 *Fax:* 212-366-2365
Web Site: www.penguin.com
Key Personnel
Edit Dir: Marian Lizzi
Author: Scott Edelstein
256 pp, $14.95
First published 1996
ISBN(s): 978-0-399-52508-7

1001 Ways to Market Your Books
Published by Open Horizons Publishing Co
PO Box 2887, Taos, NM 87571
Tel: 575-751-3398
E-mail: info@bookmarket.com
Web Site: www.bookmarket.com
Key Personnel
Publr & Ed: John Kremer *E-mail:* johnkremer@bookmarket.com
Outlines more than 1,000 different ways to market books. Uses many real-life examples describing how other publishers market their books. Includes planning & design, advertising & distribution, subsidiary rights & spinoffs.
7th ed, 2016: 704 pp, $27.95 paper

1,001 Tips for Writers: Words of Wisdom About Writing, Getting Published, and Living the Literary Life
Published by North Ridge Books
PO Box 2832, Rancho Mirage, CA 92270
Tel: 949-533-5106 (cell) *Toll Free Fax:* 800-763-9881
E-mail: nrbooks@aol.com
Web Site: www.1001tipsforwriters.com

Key Personnel
Ed: William A Gordon
1,001 Tips for Writers is a quotation book offering "Words of Wisdom About Writing, Getting Published, and Living the Literary Life." The book quotes literary greats; working writers, publishers, editors on subjects such as "How to Get Traditionally Published", "Self-Publishing", "Book Publicity" & writing history, humor, novels, & journalism.
1st ed, 2014, $16.95 paper, $8.95 ebook
ISBN(s): 978-0-937813-09-6 (ebook); 978-0-937813-10-2 (paper)

Photographer's Market
Published by F+W Media Inc
10151 Carver Rd, Suite 200, Blue Ash, OH 45242
Tel: 513-531-2690 *Toll Free Tel:* 855-842-5267 (cust serv) *Fax:* 513-891-7153
E-mail: photomarket@fwmedia.com
Web Site: www.artistsmarketonline.com (online ed)
Key Personnel
Sr Content Developer: Mary Burzlaff Bostic
More than 1,500 listings of photo buyers with complete contact information; for freelance & stock photographers.
Annual.
40th ed, 2017: 688 pp, $34.99
ISBN(s): 978-1-4403-4658-3

The Pocket Muse 2
Published by Writer's Digest
Imprint of F+W Media Inc
10151 Carver Rd, Suite 200, Blue Ash, OH 45242
Tel: 513-531-2690 *Toll Free Tel:* 800-289-0963 *Fax:* 513-531-0798
E-mail: writersdigest@fwmedia.com (edit)
Web Site: www.writersdigest.com; www.writersdigestshop.com
Key Personnel
Gen Mgr: David Pyle *E-mail:* david.pyle@fwmedia.com
Content Strategist: Rachel Randall *E-mail:* rachel.randall@fwmedia.com
Unique ideas for overcoming writer's block, creativity boosters, revision tips & more. Available as ebook only.
2nd ed, $12.99 ebook (retail)

Poetry Criticism
Published by Gale
Unit of Cengage Learning
27500 Drake Rd, Farmington Hills, MI 48331-3535
SAN: 213-4373
Tel: 248-699-4253 *Toll Free Tel:* 800-877-4253 *Fax:* 248-699-8070 *Toll Free Fax:* 800-414-5043 (orders)
E-mail: gale.galeord@cengage.com
Web Site: www.gale.com
Each volume of this reference provides substantial critical essays & biographical information on 4-8 major poets from all eras. Entries provide an introductory biographical sketch, an author portrait, a primary bibliography, annotated full-text & excerpted criticism of the poets' works & sources for additional reading. When available, comments from the poets themselves are included. Also available online.
$297 hardcover

Poet's Market
Published by Writer's Digest
Imprint of F+W Media Inc
10151 Carver Rd, Suite 200, Blue Ash, OH 45242
Tel: 513-531-2690 *Toll Free Tel:* 800-289-0963 *Fax:* 513-531-0798
E-mail: writersdigest@fwmedia.com (edit)
Web Site: www.writersdigest.com; www.writersdigestshop.com
Key Personnel
Gen Mgr: David Pyle *E-mail:* david.pyle@fwmedia.com
Content Strategist: Rachel Randall *E-mail:* rachel.randall@fwmedia.com
Where & how to get poetry published; 1,800 US & international publisher listings, also includes contests & awards, writing colonies, organizations, conferences, workshops & publications useful to poets. Also available as an ebook.
Annual.
30th ed, 2017: 480 pp, $29.99 paper & ebook (retail)
ISBN(s): 978-1-4403-4778-8 (paper); 978-1-4403-4785-6 (ebook)

Professional Writing: Processes, Strategies & Tips for Publishing in Education Journals
Published by Krieger Publishing Co
1725 Krieger Dr, Malabar, FL 32950
SAN: 202-6562
Tel: 321-724-9542 *Fax:* 321-951-3671
E-mail: info@krieger-publishing.com
Web Site: www.krieger-publishing.com
Key Personnel
Author: Roger Hiemstra
Provides insights, tips, strategies & recommendations for publishing in educational periodicals.
1994: 152 pp, $27.50 cloth
First published 1993
ISBN(s): 978-0-89464-660-7

Public Library Core Collection: Nonfiction
Published by Grey House Publishing Inc™
4919 Rte 22, Amenia, NY 12501
Mailing Address: PO Box 56, Amenia, NY 12501-0056
Tel: 518-789-8700 *Toll Free Tel:* 800-562-2139 *Fax:* 518-789-0556
E-mail: books@greyhouse.com
Web Site: www.greyhouse.com
Recommends reference & nonfiction books for the general adult audience. Guide to over 12,000 books, plus review sources & other professional aids for librarians & media specialists.
16th ed, 2017: 2,700 pp, $420
ISBN(s): 978-1-68217-071-7

Publish, Don't Perish: The Scholar's Guide to Academic Writing & Publishing
Published by Praeger
Imprint of ABC-CLIO
130 Cremona Dr, Suite C, Santa Barbara, CA 93117
Mailing Address: PO Box 1911, Santa Barbara, CA 93116-1911
Tel: 805-968-1911 *Toll Free Tel:* 800-368-6868 *Fax:* 805-685-9685 *Toll Free Fax:* 866-270-3856
E-mail: custserv@abc-clio.com
Web Site: www.abc-clio.com
Key Personnel
Dir, Edit-Print: Anthony Chiffolo
Author: Joseph M Moxley
Expressing a strongly positive view of the value of academic publishing that reaches far beyond what is implied by the book title, Moxley offers informed suggestions to faculty members for conceiving, developing & publishing scholarly documents as books or journal articles.
224 pp, $27.95 paper, $40 hardcover
First published 1992
ISBN(s): 978-0-275-94453-7 (paper); 978-0-313-27735-1 (hardcover)

Publishers Directory (PD)
Published by Gale
Unit of Cengage Learning
27500 Drake Rd, Farmington Hills, MI 48331-3535
SAN: 213-4373
Tel: 248-699-4253 *Toll Free Tel:* 800-877-4253 *Fax:* 248-699-8070 *Toll Free Fax:* 800-414-5043 (orders)
E-mail: gale.galeord@cengage.com; businessproducts@cengage.com
Web Site: www.gale.com
Contains over 20,000 US & Canadian publishers & distributors. Entries contain full organization contact information, including corporate e-mails & web sites when provided. In addition, most entries feature a wealth of descriptive (when available), including principal officers with personal e-mails; year founded; annual sales; number of titles per year, including an estimate for current year; total title count; discount policy; percentage of sales. Also available as an ebook.
Annual.
42nd ed, 2017: 2,106 pp, $916/3 vol set paper, $1,007.60 ebook
ISBN(s): 978-1-4103-2740-6 (3 vol set paper); 978-1-4103-2744-4 (ebook)

Publishers, Distributors & Wholesalers of the United States™
Published by Grey House Publishing Inc™
4919 Rte 22, Amenia, NY 12501
Mailing Address: PO Box 56, Amenia, NY 12501-0056
Tel: 518-789-8700 *Toll Free Tel:* 800-562-2139 *Fax:* 518-789-0556
E-mail: books@greyhouse.com
Web Site: www.greyhouse.com
Two information-packed volumes offering detailed data on 186,000 active US publishers, distributors, associations, software, video & audio producers & more.
Annual.
2017: 5,400 pp, $705/2 vol set hardcover
ISBN(s): 978-1-68217-055-7 (2 vol set)

Publishers' International ISBN Directory
Published by De Gruyter Saur
Imprint of Walter de Gruyter GmbH & Co KG
Genthiner Str 13, 10785 Berlin, Germany
Tel: (030) 260 05-0 *Fax:* (030) 260 05-251
E-mail: service@degruyter.com
Web Site: www.degruyter.com
Seven volume set containing the names of more than 1,000,000 active publishing houses & more than 1,100,000 ISBN prefixes from 221 countries & territories.
41st ed, 2015: 9,217 pp, $2,366 hardcover, $3,346 print & ebook
ISBN(s): 978-3-11-033619-1 (hardcover/7-vol set); 978-3-11-033735-8 (eBookPLUS); 978-3-11-033736-5 (print & ebook)

Publishing as a Vocation: Studies of an Old Occupation in a New Technological Era
Published by Transaction Publishers Inc
10 Corporate Place S, Suite 102, Piscataway, NJ 08854
Mailing Address: 1247 State Rd, Princeton, NJ 08540
Tel: 732-445-2280 *Fax:* 732-445-3138
Web Site: www.transactionpub.com
Places publishing in America in its political & commercial setting. Addresses the political implications of scholary communication in the era of new computerized technology. Examines problems of political theory in the context of property rights versus the presumed right to know & the special strains involved in publishing as commerce versus information as a public trust.
1st ed, 2010: 167 pp, $40.95 paper
First published 2010
ISBN(s): 978-1-4128-1110-1

Publishing for the PreK-12 Market
Published by Simba Information
Division of Market Research.com
1266 E Main St, Suite 700, Stamford, CT 06902
SAN: 210-2021
Tel: 203-325-8193 *Toll Free Tel:* 888-297-4622 (cust serv)
E-mail: customerservice@simbainformation.com
Web Site: www.simbainformation.com
Key Personnel
Sr Analyst/Mng Ed: Kathy Mickey
Sr Analyst/Ed: Karen Meaney
Prodn Coord: Farah Pierre
Up-to-date descriptions & statistics on enrollments, demographic trends, in several categories; publishers' sales, forecasts, expenditures & profiles of the leading publishers in the K-12 market place.
Annual.
2016-2017: 160 pp, $3,250 online download

Publishing in the Information Age: A New Management Framework for the Digital Era
Published by Praeger
Imprint of ABC-CLIO
130 Cremona Dr, Suite C, Santa Barbara, CA 93117
Mailing Address: PO Box 1911, Santa Barbara, CA 93116-1911
Tel: 805-968-1911 *Toll Free Tel:* 800-368-6868 *Fax:* 805-685-9685 *Toll Free Fax:* 866-270-3856
E-mail: custserv@abc-clio.com
Web Site: www.abc-clio.com
Key Personnel
Dir, Edit-Print: Anthony Chiffolo
Author: Douglas M Eisenhart
A comprehensive single-volume study of the transformations underway in the publishing industry attributable to the penetration of digital information technologies & how publishers can benefit from them.
$39.95 paper, $84 hardcover
First published 1999
ISBN(s): 978-0-275-95696-7 (paper); 978-0-89930-847-0 (hardcover)

Recommended Reading: 600 Classics Reviewed
Published by Grey House Publishing Inc™
2 University Plaza, Suite 310, Hackensack, NJ 07601
SAN: 208-838X
Tel: 201-968-0500 *Toll Free Tel:* 800-221-1592 *Fax:* 201-968-0511
E-mail: csr@salempress.com
Web Site: salempress.com
Covers 600 noteworthy works of literature (fiction, nonfiction, poetry or drama) & introduces brief, ready-reference data for the user's convenience: title, author, date of first publication, type of work & brief extract of book's content or impact.
2nd ed, Oct 2015: 400 pp, $125 (includes online access with print purchase)
First published 1995
ISBN(s): 978-1-61925-867-9; 978-1-61925-868-6 (ebook)

The Reference Shelf: Graphic Novels and Comic Books
Published by Grey House Publishing Inc™
4919 Rte 22, Amenia, NY 12501
Mailing Address: PO Box 56, Amenia, NY 12501-0056
Tel: 518-789-8700 *Toll Free Tel:* 800-562-2139 *Fax:* 518-789-0556
E-mail: books@greyhouse.com
Web Site: www.greyhouse.com
Explores the origins, development & future of comic books & graphic novels.
Available for purchase at www.hwwilsoninprint.com/ref_graphic.php.
Nov 2010: 200 pp, $60
ISBN(s): 978-0-8242-1100-4

Research Centers Directory (RCD)
Published by Gale
Unit of Cengage Learning
27500 Drake Rd, Farmington Hills, MI 48331-3535
SAN: 213-4373
Tel: 248-699-4253 *Toll Free Tel:* 800-877-4253 *Fax:* 248-699-8075 *Toll Free Fax:* 800-414-5043 (orders)
E-mail: gale.galeord@cengage.com
Web Site: www.gale.com
Directory describes university affiliated & other nonprofit research institutes in North America. Indexes: subject, geographic, personal name & master. Also available as an ebook.
46th ed, 2016: 3,157 pp, $1,296/5 vol set paper, $1,425.60 ebook
ISBN(s): 978-1-5730-2885-1 (5 vol set paper); 978-1-5730-2891-2 (ebook)

Sears List of Subject Headings
Published by Grey House Publishing Inc™
4919 Rte 22, Amenia, NY 12501
Mailing Address: PO Box 56, Amenia, NY 12501-0056
Tel: 518-789-8700 *Toll Free Tel:* 800-562-2139 *Fax:* 518-789-0556
E-mail: books@greyhouse.com
Web Site: www.greyhouse.com
Standard thesaurus of subject terminology for small & medium-sized libraries. Also includes "Principles of the Sears List," a 23-page insert outlining theoretical foundations of the *Sears List* & the general principles of subject cataloging.
21st ed, April 2014: 850 pp, $165
First published 1923
ISBN(s): 978-1-61925-190-8

Sears: Lista de Encabezamientos de Materia
Published by Grey House Publishing Inc™
4919 Rte 22, Amenia, NY 12501
Mailing Address: PO Box 56, Amenia, NY 12501-0056
Tel: 518-789-8700 *Toll Free Tel:* 800-562-2139 *Fax:* 518-789-0556
E-mail: books@greyhouse.com
Web Site: www.greyhouse.com
Sears List of Subject Headings adapted for the Spanish language.
June 2010: 800 pp, $150
ISBN(s): 978-0-8242-1058-8

The Secrets of Story
Published by Writer's Digest
Imprint of F+W Media Inc
10151 Carver Rd, Suite 200, Blue Ash, OH 45242
Tel: 513-531-2690 *Toll Free Tel:* 800-289-0963 *Fax:* 513-531-0798
E-mail: writersdigest@fwmedia.com (edit)
Web Site: www.writersdigest.com; www.fwmedia.com; www.writersdigestshop.com
Key Personnel
Gen Mgr: David Pyle *E-mail:* david.pyle@fwmedia.com
Content Strategist: Rachel Randall *E-mail:* rachel.randall@fwmedia.com
Provides comprehensive, audience-focused strategies for becoming a master storyteller.
368 pp, $19.99 paper & ebook (retail)
ISBN(s): 978-1-4403-4823-5 (paper); 978-1-4403-4826-6 (ebook)

Senior High Core Collection
Published by Grey House Publishing Inc™
4919 Rte 22, Amenia, NY 12501
Mailing Address: PO Box 56, Amenia, NY 12501-0056
Tel: 518-789-8700 *Toll Free Tel:* 800-562-2139 *Fax:* 518-789-0556
E-mail: books@greyhouse.com
Web Site: www.greyhouse.com
Guide to over 8,500 fiction & nonfiction books recommended for adolescents & young adults, grades 9-12.
20th ed, 2016: 2,005 pp, $295
ISBN(s): 978-1-68217-069-4

Shakespearean Criticism
Published by Gale
Unit of Cengage Learning
27500 Drake Rd, Farmington Hills, MI 48331-3535
SAN: 213-4373
Tel: 248-699-4253 *Toll Free Tel:* 800-877-4253 *Fax:* 248-699-8070 *Toll Free Fax:* 800-414-5043 (orders)
E-mail: gale.galeord@cengage.com
Web Site: www.gale.com
Thematically arranged essays from 1960 to the present of commentary on Shakespeare's plays & poems. Illustrated series provides support to students & teachers at high school & college levels. Beginning with Vol 60, presents topical entries comprised of essays that analyze various topics or themes of Shakespeare's works. Each volume has a cumulative character index, a topic index & a topic index arranged by play title. Also available online.
Vol 175, 2017: 416 pp, $397 hardcover
ISBN(s): 978-1-4103-2946-2

Short Story Criticism: Excerpts from Criticism of the Works of Short Fiction Writers
Published by Gale
Unit of Cengage Learning
27500 Drake Rd, Farmington Hills, MI 48331-3535
SAN: 213-4373
Tel: 248-699-4253 *Toll Free Tel:* 800-877-4253 *Fax:* 248-699-8070 *Toll Free Fax:* 800-414-5043 (orders)
E-mail: gale.galeord@cengage.com
Web Site: www.gale.com
Series presenting critical views on the most widely studied writers of short fiction. Each volume includes overview of 3-6 short story writers, works, or topics & historical survey of the critical response. Most critical essays are full text. Also available online.
$297 hardcover

Short Story Index
Published by Grey House Publishing Inc™
4919 Rte 22, Amenia, NY 12501
Mailing Address: PO Box 56, Amenia, NY 12501-0056
Tel: 518-789-8700 *Toll Free Tel:* 800-562-2139 *Fax:* 518-789-0556
E-mail: books@greyhouse.com
Web Site: www.greyhouse.com
Indexing coverage of short stories written in or translated into English & published in collections, covering all styles & genres, from classics to experimental fiction.
Annual.
2017 ed (2016 annual cumulation): 260 pp, $295
ISBN(s): 978-1-61925-850-1

Short Story Writers
Published by Grey House Publishing Inc™
2 University Plaza, Suite 310, Hackensack, NJ 07601
SAN: 208-838X
Tel: 201-968-0500 *Toll Free Tel:* 800-221-1592 *Fax:* 201-968-0511
E-mail: csr@salempress.com
Web Site: salempress.com

Key Personnel
Ed: Charles May
Covers 146 of the most frequently taught, read & researched short fiction writers studied in schools & colleges.
Oct 2007 (revised): 1,164 pp, $217/3 vol set
ISBN(s): 978-1-58765-389-6 (3 vol set); 978-1-58765-411-4 (ebook set)

The Small Press Record of Books in Print
Published by Dustbooks
PO Box 100, Paradise, CA 95967-0100
SAN: 204-1871
Tel: 530-877-6110 *Fax:* 530-877-0222
E-mail: publisher@dustbooks.com; info@dustbooks.com
Web Site: www.dustbooks.com
Key Personnel
Publr: Kathleen Glanville
Ed: Neil McIntyre
More than 43,400 titles from more than 5,000 small, independent, educational & self-publishers worldwide.
41st ed, $37.95 CD-ROM, $49.95 online (4 directories)
ISBN(s): 978-1-935742-36-4 (CD-ROM)

Software and Intellectual Property Protection: Copyright and Patent Issues for Computer and Legal Professionals
Published by Praeger
Imprint of ABC-CLIO
130 Cremona Dr, Suite C, Santa Barbara, CA 93117
Mailing Address: PO Box 1911, Santa Barbara, CA 93116-1911
Tel: 805-968-1911 *Toll Free Tel:* 800-368-6868 *Fax:* 805-685-9685 *Toll Free Fax:* 866-270-3856
E-mail: custserv@abc-clio.com
Web Site: www.abc-clio.com
Key Personnel
Dir, Edit-Print: Anthony Chiffolo
Author: Bernard A Galler
A succinct, readable survey of the critical issues & cases in copyright & patent law applied to computer software, intended for computer professionals, academics & lawyers.
224 pp, $84 hardcover
ISBN(s): 978-0-89930-974-3

Something About the Author
Published by Gale
Unit of Cengage Learning
27500 Drake Rd, Farmington Hills, MI 48331-3535
SAN: 213-4373
Tel: 248-699-4253 *Toll Free Tel:* 800-877-4253 *Fax:* 248-699-8070 *Toll Free Fax:* 800-414-5043 (orders)
E-mail: gale.galeord@cengage.com
Web Site: www.gale.com
Provides illustrated biographical articles on approximately 75 children's authors & artists. The series covers more than 15,000 individuals, ranging from established award-winners to authors & illustrators who are just beginning their careers. Entries cover: personal life, career, writings, adaptation, additional sources, photographs & illustrations. Also available as an ebook.
Vol 306, 2017: 434 pp, $246 hardcover, $247 ebook
ISBN(s): 978-1-4103-2426-9 (hardcover); 978-1-4103-2449-8 (ebook)

The Standard Periodical Directory
Published by Oxbridge® Communications Inc
388 Second Ave, Suite 503, New York, NY 10010
Tel: 212-741-0231 *Toll Free Tel:* 800-955-0231 *Fax:* 212-633-2938
E-mail: info@oxbridge.com
Web Site: www.oxbridge.com; www.mediafinder.com
Key Personnel
CEO: Louis Hagood
Pres: Patricia Hagood
Over 63,000 US & Canadian periodicals arranged by subject matter into 262 classifications & indexed by title. Listings include publishing company, address, telephone number; names of editor, publisher, ad director; annotations; frequency, circulation, advertising & subscription rates; year established; trim size, print method, page count.
Annually in Jan.
40th ed, 2017: 2,150 pp, $1,995 hardcover, $995 digital, $1,995 single user CD-ROM, $2,995 print & CD-ROM
First published 1964
ISBN(s): 978-1-891783-66-1 (hardcover)

Subject Guide to Books in Print®
Published by Grey House Publishing Inc™
4919 Rte 22, Amenia, NY 12501
Mailing Address: PO Box 56, Amenia, NY 12501-0056
Tel: 518-789-8700 *Toll Free Tel:* 800-562-2139 *Fax:* 518-789-0556
E-mail: books@greyhouse.com
Web Site: www.greyhouse.com
Master subject reference to titles, authors, publishers & distributors in the US.
Annual.
2017-2018: 15,500 pp, $1,115/6 vol set
ISBN(s): 978-1-68217-506-4 (6 vol set)

Subject Guide to Children's Books in Print®
Published by Grey House Publishing Inc™
4919 Rte 22, Amenia, NY 12501
Mailing Address: PO Box 56, Amenia, NY 12501-0056
Tel: 518-789-8700 *Toll Free Tel:* 800-562-2139 *Fax:* 518-789-0556
E-mail: books@greyhouse.com
Web Site: www.greyhouse.com
A natural complement to *Children's Books in Print*® & valuable tool when expanding children's literature collections & new curriculum areas. Coverage includes over 350,000 titles classified under 9,500 Library of Congress subject headings.
Annual.
2017: 2,900 pp, $505
ISBN(s): 978-1-68217-061-8

The Subversive Copy Editor: Advice from Chicago (Or, How to Negotiate Good Relationships with Your Writers, Your Colleagues, and Yourself)
Published by University of Chicago Press
1427 E 60 St, Chicago, IL 60637-2954
SAN: 202-5280
E-mail: custserv@press.uchicago.edu; marketing@press.uchicago.edu
Web Site: www.press.uchicago.edu
Key Personnel
Sr Ed: Mary E Laur *E-mail:* mlaur@uchicago.edu
Longtime mss editor & *Chicago Manual of Style* guru Carol Fisher Saller brings a refreshingly levelheaded approach to the classic battle between writers & editors. The 2nd edition reflects today's publishing practices while retaining the self-deprecating tone & sharp humor that helped make the 1st edition so popular. Saller's sage advice will prove useful & entertaining to anyone charged with the sometimes perilous task of improving the writing of others.
Revised every 5-7 yrs.
2nd ed: 200 pp, $45 cloth, $15 paper or ebook
First published 2009
ISBN(s): 978-0-226-23990-3 (cloth); 978-0-226-24007-7 (paper); 978-0-226-24010-7 (ebook)

Survey of Compensation & Personnel Practices in the Publishing Industry
Published by Association of American Publishers (AAP)
455 Massachusetts Ave NW, Suite 700, Washington, DC 20001-2777
Tel: 212-255-0200 *Fax:* 212-255-7007
Web Site: publishers.org
Key Personnel
Pres & CEO: Maria Pallante
VP: Tina Jordan *Tel:* 212-255-0275 *E-mail:* tjordan@publishers.org
VP & Exec Dir, Prof & Scholarly Publg: John Tagler *Tel:* 212-255-1407 *E-mail:* jtagler@publishers.org
Gen Coun & VP, Govt Aff: Allan R Adler *Tel:* 202-220-4544 *E-mail:* adler@publishers.org
Exec Dir, PreK-12 Learning Group: Jay Diskey *Tel:* 202-220-4549 *E-mail:* jdiskey@publishers.org
Survey report contains salary & personnel practices information for more than 120 benchmark jobs in the publishing industry.
Annual.
220 pp, Varies based on participation, company site & AAP membership status

Training Guide to Frontline Bookselling
Published by Paz & Associates
1417 Sadler Rd, PMB 274, Fernandina Beach, FL 32034
Tel: 904-277-2664 *Fax:* 904-261-6742
E-mail: mkaufman@pazbookbiz.com
Web Site: www.pazbookbiz.com
Key Personnel
Partner: Donna Paz Kaufman *E-mail:* dpaz@pazbookbiz.com
12 chapters on all aspects of bookstore operations, includes trainers outline.
4th ed, Jan 2014: 125 pp, $189 plus shipping

Travel Writer's Guide
Published by Communication Unlimited
185 Shevelin Rd, Novato, CA 94947
Tel: 415-884-2941 *Toll Free Tel:* 800-563-1454 *Fax:* 415-883-5707
E-mail: gordon@gordonburgett.com
Web Site: www.gordonburgett.com
Key Personnel
Pres: Gordon Burgett *E-mail:* glburgett@aol.com
Writing/reference.
3rd ed (revised), updated 2005: 376 pp, $15 paper, $10 digital download
ISBN(s): 978-0-9708621-1-3

Troubleshooting Your Novel
Published by Writer's Digest
Imprint of F+W Media Inc
10151 Carver Rd, Suite 200, Blue Ash, OH 45242
Tel: 513-531-2690 *Toll Free Tel:* 800-289-0963 *Fax:* 513-531-0798
E-mail: writersdigest@fwmedia.com (edit)
Web Site: www.writersdigest.com; www.fwmedia.com; www.writersdigestshop.com
Key Personnel
Gen Mgr: David Pyle *E-mail:* david.pyle@fwmedia.com
Content Strategist: Rachel Randall *E-mail:* rachel.randall@fwmedia.com
Helpful techniques & checklists, timesaving tricks of the trade & hundreds of questions for ms analysis & revision.
368 pp, $19.99 paper & ebook (retail)
ISBN(s): 978-1-59963-980-2 (paper); 978-1-59963-982-6 (ebook)

TRUMATCH Colorfinder
Published by TRUMATCH Inc
122 Mill Pond Lane, Water Mill, NY 11976
Mailing Address: PO Box 501, Water Mill, NY 11976-0501
Tel: 631-204-9100 *Toll Free Tel:* 800-TRU-9100 (878-9100, US & CN)
E-mail: info@trumatch.com
Web Site: www.trumatch.com
Key Personnel
Pres: Steven J Abramson
VP: Jane E Nichols *E-mail:* janen@trumatch.com
Digital guides for 4-color printing.
$85 paper for coated ed or uncoated ed

Twentieth-Century Literary Criticism
Published by Gale
Unit of Cengage Learning
27500 Drake Rd, Farmington Hills, MI 48331-3535
SAN: 213-4373
Tel: 248-699-4253 *Toll Free Tel:* 800-877-4253 *Fax:* 248-699-8070 *Toll Free Fax:* 800-414-5043 (orders)
E-mail: gale.galeord@cengage.com
Web Site: www.gale.com
Key Personnel
Ed: Linda Pavlovski
Presents overviews of authors & furnishes full texts from representative criticism on the great novelists, poets, playwrights & literary theorists of the period 1900-1999. Each volume presents overviews of 4-8 authors. Every fourth volume covers literary topics including major literary movements, trends & other topics related to 20th century literature.
$397 hardcover

20 Master Plots
Published by Writer's Digest
Imprint of F+W Media Inc
10151 Carver Rd, Suite 200, Blue Ash, OH 45242
Tel: 513-531-2690 *Toll Free Tel:* 800-289-0963 *Fax:* 513-531-0798
E-mail: writersdigest@fwmedia.com (edit)
Web Site: www.writersdigest.com; www.writersdigestshop.com
Key Personnel
Gen Mgr: David Pyle *E-mail:* david.pyle@fwmedia.com
Content Strategist: Rachel Randall *E-mail:* rachel.randall@fwmedia.com
How to take timeless storytelling structures & make them immediate, now, for fiction that's universal in how it speaks to the reader's heart.
1st ed: 288 pp, $16.99 paper, $14.99 ebook (retail)
First published 2003
ISBN(s): 978-1-59963-537-8 (paper); 978-1-59963-538-5 (ebook)

Ulrich's Periodicals Directory
Published by ProQuest LLC
Subsidiary of Cambridge Information Group Inc
630 Central Ave, New Providence, NJ 07974
Tel: 908-795-3659 (edit) *Toll Free Tel:* 800-346-6049 (Ulrich's hotline, US only)
E-mail: ulrichs@proquest.com; core_service@proquest.com (orders)
Web Site: www.ulrichsweb.com; www.proquest.com
Four-volume set, arranged by subject classification, includes periodicals, newsletters, newspapers, annuals & irregular serials published worldwide. Also available online.
Annual.
56th ed, 2018: 12,192 pp, $3,189/4 vol set
First published 1932
ISBN(s): 978-1-60030-668-6 (4 vol set)

Walden's Paper Catalog
Published by Walden-Mott Corp
225 N Franklin Tpke, Ramsey, NJ 07446-1600
Tel: 201-818-8630 *Fax:* 201-818-8720
Web Site: www.waldenmott.com
Key Personnel
Ed: Alfred F Walden *Tel:* 201-818-8630 ext 11
National directory of fine printing & writing papers. Alphabetical listing of brand names, their characteristics along with merchants that carry those manufacturers' grades. Sections: "Brand Name Index", "Paper Distributors", "Papers by Grade" & "How to Buy Paper".
2 issues/yr.
$85/yr
First published 1914

Walden's Paper Handbook
Published by Walden-Mott Corp
225 N Franklin Tpke, Ramsey, NJ 07446-1600
Tel: 201-818-8630 *Fax:* 201-818-8720
Web Site: www.waldenmott.com
Key Personnel
Ed: Alfred F Walden *Tel:* 201-818-8630 ext 11
Pulp & paper industry pocket guide.
5th ed: 277 pp, $25

What Editors Do: The Art, Craft, and Business of Book Editing
Published by University of Chicago Press
1427 E 60 St, Chicago, IL 60637-2954
SAN: 202-5280
E-mail: custserv@press.uchicago.edu; marketing@press.uchicago.edu
Web Site: www.press.uchicago.edu
Key Personnel
Sr Ed: Mary E Laur *E-mail:* mlaur@uchicago.edu
In this volume, Peter Ginna gathers essays from 27 leading editors in book publishing about their work. Representing both large houses & small & encompassing trade, textbook, academic & children's publishing, the contributors shed light on such issues as how editors acquire books, what constitutes a strong author-editor relationship & the editor's vital role at each stage of the publishing process. The book serves as a resource both for those entering the profession (or already in it) & for those outside publishing who seek an understanding of it.
1st ed: 320 pp, $75 cloth, $25 paper, $18 ebook
First published 2017
ISBN(s): 978-0-226-29983-9 (cloth); 978-0-226-29997-6 (paper); 978-0-226-30003-0 (ebook)

Word Painting
Published by Writer's Digest
Imprint of F+W Media Inc
10151 Carver Rd, Suite 200, Blue Ash, OH 45242
Tel: 513-531-2690 *Toll Free Tel:* 800-289-0963 *Fax:* 513-531-0798
E-mail: writersdigest@fwmedia.com (edit)
Web Site: www.writersdigest.com; www.writersdigestshop.com
Key Personnel
Gen Mgr: David Pyle *E-mail:* david.pyle@fwmedia.com
Content Strategist: Rachel Randall *E-mail:* rachel.randall@fwmedia.com
Combines direct instruction with intriguing word exercises to teach you how to "paint" evocative descriptions that capture the images of your mind's eye & improve your writing.
Revised ed: 272 pp, $18.99 paper & ebook (retail)
First published 2000
ISBN(s): 978-1-59963-868-3 (paper); 978-1-59963-870-6 (ebook)

World Authors 2000-2005
Published by Grey House Publishing Inc™
4919 Rte 22, Amenia, NY 12501
Mailing Address: PO Box 56, Amenia, NY 12501-0056
Tel: 518-789-8700 *Toll Free Tel:* 800-562-2139 *Fax:* 518-789-0556
E-mail: books@greyhouse.com
Web Site: www.greyhouse.com
Covers some 300 novelists, poets, dramatists, essayists, scientists, biographers & other authors whose books, published 2000 through 2005, represent the dawn of a new millenium of great literature.
Available for purchase at www.hwwilsoninprint.com/world_authors05.php.
Jan 2007: 800 pp, $170
ISBN(s): 978-0-8242-1077-9

World Literature Criticism: A Selection of Major Authors from Gale's Literary Criticism - Supplement
Published by Gale
Unit of Cengage Learning
27500 Drake Rd, Farmington Hills, MI 48331-3535
SAN: 213-4373
Tel: 248-699-4253 *Toll Free Tel:* 800-877-4253 *Fax:* 248-699-8070 *Toll Free Fax:* 800-414-5043 (orders)
E-mail: gale.galeord@cengage.com
Web Site: www.gale.com
Updated supplement listing 20th Century authors collection of their biographical data, criticisms, list of principal works, historical survey of critical response to the author's works & sources for further study. Three indexes consist of authors, nationality & titles.
1997 supplement still in print.
961 pp, $231/2 vol set
ISBN(s): 978-07876-1696-0

Write Naked
Published by Writer's Digest
Imprint of F+W Media Inc
10151 Carver Rd, Suite 200, Blue Ash, OH 45242
Tel: 513-531-2690 *Toll Free Tel:* 800-289-0963 *Fax:* 513-531-0798
E-mail: writersdigest@fwmedia.com (edit)
Web Site: www.writersdigest.com; www.fwmedia.com; www.writersdigestshop.com
Key Personnel
Gen Mgr: David Pyle *E-mail:* david.pyle@fwmedia.com
Content Strategist: Rachel Randall *E-mail:* rachel.randall@fwmedia.com
Lessons & craft advice every writer needs in order to carve out a rewarding career in the romance genre.
240 pp, $16.99 paper & ebook (retail)
ISBN(s): 978-1-4403-4734-4 (paper); 978-1-4403-4740-5 (ebook)

Writer's Guide to Character Traits
Published by Writer's Digest
Imprint of F+W Media Inc
10151 Carver Rd, Suite 200, Blue Ash, OH 45242
Tel: 513-531-2690 *Toll Free Tel:* 800-289-0963 *Fax:* 513-531-0798
E-mail: writersdigest@fwmedia.com (edit)
Web Site: www.writersdigest.com; www.writersdigestshop.com
Key Personnel
Gen Mgr: David Pyle *E-mail:* david.pyle@fwmedia.com
Content Strategist: Rachel Randall *E-mail:* rachel.randall@fwmedia.com
Profiles the mental, emotional & physical qualities of dozens of different personality types.
384 pp, $17.99 paper (retail)
First published 1999
ISBN(s): 978-1-58297-390-6

The Writer's Guide to Crafting Stories for Children
Published by Writer's Digest
Imprint of F+W Media Inc
10151 Carver Rd, Suite 200, Blue Ash, OH 45242
Tel: 513-531-2690 *Toll Free Tel:* 800-289-0963 *Fax:* 513-531-0798
E-mail: writersdigest@fwmedia.com (edit)
Web Site: www.writersdigest.com; www.writersdigestshop.com
Key Personnel
Gen Mgr: David Pyle *E-mail:* david.pyle@fwmedia.com
Content Strategist: Rachel Randall *E-mail:* rachel.randall@fwmedia.com
Insightful advice for mastering storytelling basics with dozens of examples that illustrate a variety of plot-building techniques.
1st ed: 192 pp, $16.99 paper (retail)
First published 2001
ISBN(s): 978-1-58297-052-3

The Writer's Idea Book 10th Anniversary Edition
Published by Writer's Digest
Imprint of F+W Media Inc
10151 Carver Rd, Suite 200, Blue Ash, OH 45242
Tel: 513-531-2690 *Toll Free Tel:* 800-289-0963 *Fax:* 513-531-0798
E-mail: writersdigest@fwmedia.com (edit)
Web Site: www.writersdigest.com; www.writersdigestshop.com
Key Personnel
Gen Mgr: David Pyle *E-mail:* david.pyle@fwmedia.com
Content Strategist: Rachel Randall *E-mail:* rachel.randall@fwmedia.com
Helps you to jump-start your creativity & develop original ideas.
352 pp, $19.99 paper & ebook (retail)
First published 2002
ISBN(s): 978-1-59963-386-2 (paper); 978-1-59963-387-9 (ebook)

Writer's Market
Published by Writer's Digest
Imprint of F+W Media Inc
10151 Carver Rd, Suite 200, Blue Ash, OH 45242
Tel: 513-531-2690 *Toll Free Tel:* 800-289-0963 *Fax:* 513-531-0798
E-mail: writersdigest@fwmedia.com (edit)
Web Site: www.writersmarket.com; www.fwmedia.com; www.writersdigestshop.com
Key Personnel
Gen Mgr: David Pyle *E-mail:* david.pyle@fwmedia.com
Content Strategist: Rachel Randall *E-mail:* rachel.randall@fwmedia.com
Lists more than 4,000 places where freelance writers can sell articles, books, novels, stories, fillers & scripts.
Annual.
97th ed, 2018: 896 pp, $29.99 paper regular ed, $49.99 paper deluxe ed (retail, includes online)
ISBN(s): 978-1-4403-5263-8 (regular ed); 978-1-4403-5264-5 (deluxe ed)

The Writer's Market Guide to Getting Published
Published by Writer's Digest
Imprint of F+W Media Inc
10151 Carver Rd, Suite 200, Blue Ash, OH 45242
Tel: 513-531-2690 *Toll Free Tel:* 800-289-0963 *Fax:* 513-531-0798
E-mail: writersdigest@fwmedia.com (edit)
Web Site: www.writersdigest.com; www.writersdigestshop.com
Key Personnel
Gen Mgr: David Pyle *E-mail:* david.pyle@fwmedia.com
Content Strategist: Rachel Randall *E-mail:* rachel.randall@fwmedia.com
Sound information on professional writing issues, focusing on everything from contracts to creativity. Available as an ebook only.
$19.99 ebook (retail)
First published 2004
ISBN(s): 978-1-59963-151-6

Writer's Yearbook
Published by F+W Media Inc
10151 Carver Rd, Suite 200, Blue Ash, OH 45242
Tel: 513-531-2690
E-mail: writersdigest@fwmedia.com
Web Site: www.writersdigest.com
Key Personnel
Ed: Jessica Strawser *E-mail:* jessica.strawser@fwcommunity.com
Includes lists of book & magazine article markets & how-to articles on writing & publishing.
Annual.
72 pp, $6.99 paper
First published 1990

Writing Creative Nonfiction
Published by Writer's Digest
Imprint of F+W Media Inc
10151 Carver Rd, Suite 200, Blue Ash, OH 45242
Tel: 513-531-2690 *Toll Free Tel:* 800-289-0963 *Fax:* 513-531-0798
E-mail: writersdigest@fwmedia.com (edit)
Web Site: www.writersdigest.com; www.writersdigestshop.com
Key Personnel
Gen Mgr: David Pyle *E-mail:* david.pyle@fwmedia.com
Content Strategist: Rachel Randall *E-mail:* rachel.randall@fwmedia.com
More than thirty essays examining every key element of the craft, from researching ideas & structuring the story, to reportage & personal reflection.
400 pp, $18.99 paper (retail)
First published 2001
ISBN(s): 978-1-884910-50-0

Writing Down the Bones: Freeing the Writer Within
Published by Shambhala Publications Inc
4720 Walnut St, No 106, Boulder, CO 80301
Tel: 303-222-9598; 978-829-2599 (intl callers) *Toll Free Tel:* 888-424-2329 (cust serv); 866-424-0030 (off) *Fax:* 617-236-1563
E-mail: editorialdept@shambhala.com
Web Site: www.shambhala.com
Key Personnel
Owner & EVP: Sara Bercholz
Pres: Nikko Odiseos
Publr: Steven Pomije
Mng Ed: Liz Shaw
Author: Natalie Goldberg
Brings together Zen meditation & writing.
224 pp, $14 paper, $18.95 hardcover
First published 2005
ISBN(s): 978-1-59030-261-3 (paper); 978-1-59030-794-6 (hardcover); 987-0-8348-2113-2 (ebook)

Writing Life Stories
Published by Writer's Digest
Imprint of F+W Media Inc
10151 Carver Rd, Suite 200, Blue Ash, OH 45242
Tel: 513-531-2690 *Toll Free Tel:* 800-289-0963 *Fax:* 513-531-0798
E-mail: writersdigest@fwmedia.com (edit)
Web Site: www.writersdigest.com; www.writersdigestshop.com
Key Personnel
Gen Mgr: David Pyle *E-mail:* david.pyle@fwmedia.com
Content Strategist: Rachel Randall *E-mail:* rachel.randall@fwmedia.com
How to capture your own experiences & turn them into personal essays & book-length memoirs.
304 pp, $16.99 paper & ebook (retail)
First published 1998
ISBN(s): 978-1-58297-527-6 (paper); 978-1-58297-707-2 (ebook)

Writing the Breakout Novel
Published by Writer's Digest
Imprint of F+W Media Inc
10151 Carver Rd, Suite 200, Blue Ash, OH 45242
Tel: 513-531-2690 *Toll Free Tel:* 800-289-0963 *Fax:* 513-531-0798
E-mail: writersdigest@fwmedia.com (edit)
Web Site: www.writersdigest.com; www.writersdigestshop.com
Key Personnel
Gen Mgr: David Pyle *E-mail:* david.pyle@fwmedia.com
Content Strategist: Rachel Randall *E-mail:* rachel.randall@fwmedia.com
How to take your prose to the next level & write a breakout novel.
1st ed: 256 pp, $17.99 paper (retail)
First published 2001
ISBN(s): 978-1-58297-182-7

The Yearbook of Experts®
Published by Broadcast Interview Source Inc
2500 Wisconsin Ave NW, Suite 949, Washington, DC 20007-4132
Tel: 202-333-5000 *Fax:* 202-342-5411
E-mail: expertclick@gmail.com
Web Site: www.expertclick.com
Key Personnel
Publr & Ed: Mitchell P Davis *Tel:* 203-333-4904 *E-mail:* mitchell@yearbookofexperts.com
Listings of contacts at publishers, trade associations & public interest groups that welcome media contacts; for both print & broadcast journalist use. Also available online.
Annual.
34th ed: 248 pp, $39.95 print ed
First published 1984
ISBN(s): 978-0-934333-97-1

The Yearbook of Experts, Authorities & Spokespersons®, see The Yearbook of Experts®

You Can Write Children's Books Workbook
Published by Writer's Digest
Imprint of F+W Media Inc
10151 Carver Rd, Suite 200, Blue Ash, OH 45242
Tel: 513-531-2690 *Toll Free Tel:* 800-289-0963 *Fax:* 513-531-0798
E-mail: writersdigest@fwmedia.com (edit)
Web Site: www.writersdigest.com; www.writersdigestshop.com
Key Personnel
Gen Mgr: David Pyle *E-mail:* david.pyle@fwmedia.com
Content Strategist: Rachel Randall *E-mail:* rachel.randall@fwmedia.com
Provides hands-on instruction for finishing a ms, preparing it for publication & getting it published. Available as ebook only.
2nd ed, $14.99 ebook (retail)
First published 2004

Young Adult Fiction Core Collection
Published by Grey House Publishing Inc™

4919 Rte 22, Amenia, NY 12501
Mailing Address: PO Box 56, Amenia, NY 12501-0056
Tel: 518-789-8700 *Toll Free Tel:* 800-562-2139
Fax: 518-789-0556
E-mail: books@greyhouse.com
Web Site: www.greyhouse.com

Essential resource for library & media specialists looking to enhance & enrich their collection with more than 2,500 important & highly recommended titles for young adult readers.

2nd ed, July 2017: 750 pp, $255
ISBN(s): 978-1-68217-239-1

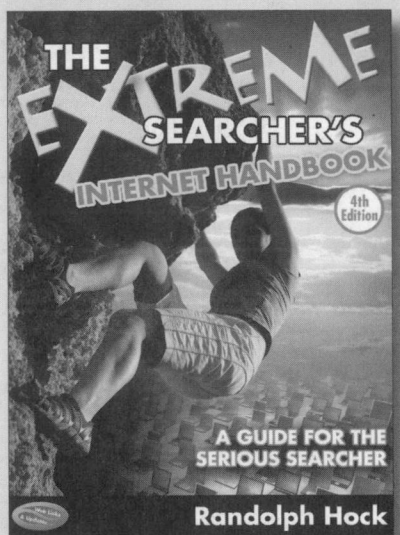

Magazines for the Trade

The magazines listed have been selected because they are published specifically for the book trade industry (apart from book review and index journals, which are listed in **Book Review & Index Journals & Services** in volume 2) or because they are widely used in the industry for reference. Also included in this section are literary journals.

For a comprehensive international directory of periodicals, see *Ulrich's Periodicals Directory* (ProQuest LLC, 630 Central Avenue, New Providence, NJ 07974), which lists magazines by subject and includes notations indicating those that carry book reviews.

Advertising Age
Published by Crain Communications Inc
685 Third Ave, New York, NY 10017-4024
Tel: 212-210-0100 *Fax:* 212-210-0200 (NY)
E-mail: AdAgeEditor@adage.com
Web Site: adage.com
Subscription Address: 1155 Gratiot Ave, Detroit, MI 48207-2732 *Tel:* 313-446-1665 *Fax:* 313-446-6777 *E-mail:* AdAgeSubscriptions@adage.com
Key Personnel
Publr: Josh Golden *Tel:* 212-210-0794 *E-mail:* jgolden@adage.com
Ed-in-Chief, NY: Rance Crain *E-mail:* rcrain@crain.com
Ed: Ken Wheaton *Tel:* 212-210-0761 *E-mail:* kwheaton@adage.com
Deputy Ed: Judann Pollack *Tel:* 212-210-0458 *E-mail:* jpollack@adage.com
Covers advertising in business, media, trade newspapers & magazines. Also available on-line.
First published 1930
Frequency: Weekly
Circulation: 58,000
$4.99/issue
ISSN: 0001-8899 (print); 1557-7414 (online)
Trim Size: 10 x 13
Ad Rates: 4-color full page (1-5x) $35,190; B&W full page (1-5x) $27,060

Adweek
Published by Mediabistro Holdings LLC
Subsidiary of Prometheus Global Media LLC
825 Eighth Ave, 29th fl, New York, NY 10019
Tel: 212-493-4100 *Fax:* 646-654-5637
E-mail: info@adweek.com
Web Site: www.adweek.com
Subscription Address: PO Box 15, Congers, NY 10920 *Toll Free Tel:* 877-496-5246 *E-mail:* subscriptions@adweek.com
Key Personnel
Edit Dir: James Cooper
Exec Ed: Tony Case
Mng Ed: Lisa Granastein
Creative Ed: Tim Nudd
First published 1978
Frequency: 45 issues/yr
$69/yr print or digital
ISSN: 1549-9553
Trim Size: 9 x 10 3/4
Ad Rates: Full page $29,400 (1x), 1/2 page $17,600 (1x)

American Poetry Review
University of the Arts (UARTS), Hamilton Hall, 320 S Broad St, Rm 313, Philadelphia, PA 19102-4901
Tel: 215-717-6801 *Fax:* 215-717-6805
Web Site: www.aprweb.org
Key Personnel
Busn Mgr: Michael Duffy
Ed: David Bonanno *E-mail:* dbonanno@aprweb.org; Elizabeth Scanlon *E-mail:* escanlon@aprweb.org
Poetry, general essays, fiction, translations, columns & interviews.
First published 1972
Book Use: Excerpts & serial rights, reviews
Frequency: 6 issues/yr
Avg pages per issue: 44
Circulation: 7,000
$4.50/issue, $25/yr
ISSN: 0360-3709
Ad Rates: Full page $950
Ad Closing Date(s): 45 days prior

The American Spectator
Subsidiary of The American Spectator Foundation
933 N Kenmore St, Suite 405, Arlington, VA 22201
Tel: 703-807-2011 *Toll Free Tel:* 800-524-3469
E-mail: editor@spectator.org; amspec@spectator.org
Web Site: spectator.org
Key Personnel
Exec Dir: Donald Rieck *E-mail:* rieckd@spectator.org
Ed-in-Chief: R Emmett Tyrrell, Jr
Edit Dir: Wladyslaw Pleszczynski
Occasional book reviews & articles featuring books. Online only.
First published 1924

ANQ: A Quarterly Journal of Short Articles, Notes & Reviews
Published by Taylor & Francis Inc
530 Walnut St, Suite 850, Philadelphia, PA 19106
Tel: 215-625-8900 (ext 4) *Toll Free Tel:* 800-354-1420 *Fax:* 215-207-0050; 215-207-0046 (cust serv)
E-mail: support@tandfonline.com
Web Site: www.tandfonline.com; www.routledge.com
Key Personnel
Global Publg Dir, Journals: Leon Heward-Mills
Mng Ed II: Sarah Sidoti
English & American literature for an academic & library audience.
First published 1987
Book Use: Reviews
Frequency: Quarterly
Avg pages per issue: 64
Circulation: 500
$92/yr indivs (print only or print & online), $236/yr instns (online only), $270/yr instns (print & online)
ISSN: 0895-769X (print); 1940-3364 (online)
Trim Size: 6 x 9
Ad Rates: Full page $550, 1/2 page $350
Ad Closing Date(s): Winter, Dec 1; Spring, March 21; Summer, June 18; Fall, Sept 19

The Artist's Magazine
Published by F+W Media Inc
10151 Carver Rd, Suite 200, Blue Ash, OH 45242
Tel: 513-531-2222 *Fax:* 513-891-7153
E-mail: tamedit@fwmedia.com
Web Site: www.theartistsnetwork.com; www.artistsnetwork.com
Subscription Address: PO Box 421751, Palm Coast, FL 32142-1751 *Toll Free Tel:* 800-333-0444 (US & CN)
Key Personnel
Mng Ed: Brian Riley
Ed: Maureen Bloomfield
Art instruction & advice for the working artist.
First published 1984
Book Use: Occasional book reviews (art-related titles only)
Frequency: 10 issues/yr
Avg pages per issue: 100
Circulation: 80,000
$17.99/yr (digital), $21.99/yr (print), $23.99/yr US (print & digital), $40.96/yr CN, $45.96/yr foreign
ISSN: 0741-3351
Trim Size: 7 3/4 x 10 1/2

AudioFile®
Published by AudioFile® Publications Inc
37 Silver St, Portland, ME 04101
Mailing Address: PO Box 109, Portland, ME 04112-0109
Tel: 207-774-7563 *Toll Free Tel:* 800-506-1212 *Fax:* 207-775-3744
E-mail: info@audiofilemagazine.com; editorial@audiofilemagazine.com
Web Site: www.audiofilemagazine.com
Key Personnel
Founder & Ed: Robin F Whitten *E-mail:* robin@audiofilemagazine.com
Publr: Michele L Cobb *E-mail:* michele@audiofilemagazine.com
Art Dir: Jennifer Steele
Mng Ed: Jennifer M Dowell *E-mail:* jennifer@audiofilemagazine.com
Review Ed: Elizabeth K Dodge *E-mail:* edodge@maine.edu
Assoc Ed: Leslie N Dillon *E-mail:* leslie@audiofilemagazine.com
Edit Asst: Alisha Langerman; Joanne Simonean
Cust Serv: Cheryl Gray *E-mail:* csr@audiofilemagazine.com
For people who love audiobooks, is indispensable for anyone who enjoys spoken-word audio. We review nearly 400 audiobooks every 60 days, feature narrator & author profiles & award exceptional performances with AudioFile's Earphone Awards.
First published 1992
Frequency: 6 issues/yr
Avg pages per issue: 72
Circulation: 15,000
$19.95/yr, $26.95/2 yrs
ISSN: 1063-0244
Avg reviews per issue: 400
Trim Size: 8 3/8 x 10 7/8
Ad Rates: Full page $3,250

Authorship
Published by National Writers Association
10940 S Parker Rd, Suite 508, Parker, CO 80134
Tel: 303-841-0246
E-mail: natlwritersassn@hotmail.com
Web Site: www.nationalwriters.com
Key Personnel
Exec Dir & Ed: Sandy Whelchel *E-mail:* authorsandy@hotmail.com
Only take submissions dealing with writing. Also available online.

Book Use: Review books for writers (in-house staff)
Frequency: Quarterly
Avg pages per issue: 28
Circulation: 8,000
$20/yr
ISSN: 1092-9347

Book Dealers World
Published by National Association of Book Entrepreneurs (NABE)
PO Box 606, Cottage Grove, OR 97424
Tel: 541-942-7455
E-mail: bookdealersworld@bookmarketingprofits.com
Key Personnel
Exec Dir: Al Galasso
Book marketing, self-publishing, mail order.
First published 1980
Book Use: From NABE members
Frequency: Quarterly
Avg pages per issue: 32
Circulation: 10,000
$50/yr, sample $5
ISSN: 1098-8521

BookPage
Published by ProMotion Inc
2143 Belcourt Ave, Nashville, TN 37212
Tel: 615-292-8926 *Fax:* 615-292-8249
Web Site: bookpage.com
Key Personnel
Pres & Publr: Michael A Zibart
Assoc Publr: Julia Steele *E-mail:* julia@bookpage.com
Subn Mgr: Elizabeth Grace Herbert *Tel:* 615-292-8926 ext 34 *E-mail:* elizabeth@bookpage.com
Book reviews, author interviews; focus on general interest new releases. Columns on romance, mystery, audio & paperback, plus individual reviews on books in all categories. Focus is completely on new releases; no backlist reviewed. Hardcover & paperback titles reviewed.
First published 1988
Book Use: Reviews
Frequency: Monthly
Avg pages per issue: 32
Circulation: 400,000
Trim Size: 9 x 10.9
Ad Rates: Full page color $9,650, 1/2 page $5,600

Bookselling This Week
Published by American Booksellers Association
333 Westchester Ave, Suite S202, White Plains, NY 10604
Tel: 914-406-7500 *Toll Free Tel:* 800-637-0037 *Fax:* 914-410-6297
E-mail: info@bookweb.org
Web Site: www.bookweb.org
Key Personnel
Dir, Content Devt: Rosemary Hawkins *Tel:* 914-406-7500 ext 7561 *E-mail:* rosemary@bookweb.org
Book industry news; ABA membership news. Available online only; no print edition.
Frequency: Weekly
Circulation: 10,000

Canadian Children's Book News
Published by Canadian Children's Book Centre
40 Orchard View Blvd, Suite 217, Toronto, ON M4R 1B9, Canada
Tel: 416-975-0010 *Fax:* 416-975-8970
E-mail: info@bookcentre.ca
Web Site: www.bookcentre.ca
Key Personnel
Ed: Sandra O'Brien *E-mail:* sandra@bookcentre.ca
News, book reviews (only reviews books by Canadian authors & illustrators), author & illustrator profiles & information about the world of children's books in Canada. Visit web site for media kit. CCBN is available with membership to the Canadian Children's Book Centre; also available in bulk subns & on newsstands across Canada.
First published 1977
Frequency: Quarterly
Avg pages per issue: 40
Circulation: 8,000
ISSN: 1705-7809
Trim Size: 8 1/8 x 10 7/8

Catholic Library World
Published by Catholic Library Association
8550 United Plaza Blvd, Suite 1001, Baton Rouge, LA 70809
Tel: 225-408-4417
E-mail: cla2@cathla.org
Web Site: cathla.org
Key Personnel
Pres: N Curtis LeMay
Gen Ed: Sigrid Kelsey *E-mail:* skelsey@lsu.edu
Articles, book & media reviews for library information professionals.
First published 1929
Book Use: Regularly publish reviews of books & other media
Frequency: Quarterly
Avg pages per issue: 90
Circulation: 1,100
Free to CLA membs, $100/yr nonmembs US, $125/yr + postage, back issues & single copies $25 + postage
ISSN: 0008-820X
Ad Rates: Full page $425, 2/3 page $360, 1/2 page $295, 1/3 page $230, 1/6 page $185; preferred space also available, color additional
Ad Closing Date(s): March issue, Jan 2; June issue, April 1; Sept issue, July 1; Dec issue, Oct 1

CBA Retailers+Resources
Published by CBA: The Association for Christian Retail
1365 Garden of the Gods Rd, Suite 105, Colorado Springs, CO 80907
Tel: 719-265-9895 *Toll Free Tel:* 800-252-1950 *Fax:* 719-272-3508
E-mail: info@cbaonline.org
Web Site: cbaonline.org
Key Personnel
Pres: Curtis Riskey *E-mail:* criskey@cbaonline.org
Trade publication for the Christian retail industry; official publication of Christian Booksellers Association.
First published 1968
Book Use: Review, bestseller lists
Frequency: Monthly
Circulation: 6,700
$7.50/issue membs, $9.50/issue nonmembs, $49.95/yr membs, $59.95/yr nonmembs
ISSN: 0006-7563

The Bulletin of the Center for Children's Books
Published by The Johns Hopkins University Press
2715 N Charles St, Baltimore, MD 21218-4363
SAN: 202-7348
Tel: 410-516-6900; 410-516-6987 (journal orders outside US & CN); 217-244-0324 *Toll Free Tel:* 800-548-1784 (journal orders) *Fax:* 410-516-6968; 410-516-3866 (journal orders)
E-mail: bccb@illinois.edu; jlorder@jhupress.jhu.edu
Web Site: bccb.lis.illinois.edu
Subscription Address: PO Box 19966, Baltimore, MD 21211-0966
Key Personnel
Ed: Deborah Stevenson
For teachers, librarians, parents & booksellers.
First published 1947
Book Use: Reviews of children's & young adult books for teachers, librarians, parents & booksellers
Frequency: 11 issues/yr
Avg pages per issue: 40
Circulation: 6,500
$20/yr students, $55/yr indivs, $108/yr instns (print or online)
ISSN: 0008-9036

Christian Retailing
Published by Charisma Media
600 Rinehart Rd, Lake Mary, FL 32746
Tel: 407-333-0600 *Fax:* 407-333-7133
E-mail: christian.retailing@charismamedia.com
Web Site: www.christianretailing.com; www.charismamedia.com
Key Personnel
Ed: Christine D Johnson *E-mail:* chris.johnson@charismamedia.com
Trade publication for the Christian retail market including industry news, books, music, inspirational gifts & other market news, new releases & marketing & industry trends. Includes one supplement: Inspirational Gift Mart.
First published 1955
Book Use: News & reviews of new releases
Frequency: Monthly
Avg pages per issue: 60
Circulation: 12,000
$40/yr, $65/yr CN, $80/yr foreign, free to qualified readers
ISSN: 0892-0281

The Chronicle of Higher Education
1255 23 St NW, Suite 700, Washington, DC 20037
Tel: 202-466-1000 *Fax:* 202-452-1033
E-mail: editor@chronicle.com
Web Site: chronicle.com
Key Personnel
Ed: Liz McMillan *E-mail:* liz.mcmillan@chronicle.com
Books Ed: Nina Ayoub *Tel:* 202-466-1020 *E-mail:* nina.ayoub@chronicle.com
Weekly newspaper covering higher education, including scholarly & publishing news.
First published 1966
Book Use: Articles on books of interest to an academic audience & on academic aspects of the publishing industry. Lists new books on higher education & new scholarly books; short- & medium-length excerpts from books on academic & literary issues
Frequency: Weekly (except for 2 issues in Dec & 1 in Aug)
Avg pages per issue: 100
Circulation: 350,000
$7.75/mo print, $6.65/mo digital
ISSN: 0009-5982

College & Research Libraries Journal
Published by Association of College & Research Libraries (ACRL)
Division of The American Library Association (ALA)
50 E Huron St, Chicago, IL 60611
Tel: 312-280-2516 *Toll Free Tel:* 800-545-2433 (ext 2516) *Fax:* 312-280-2520
E-mail: acrl@ala.org
Web Site: www.ala.org/acrl
Subscription Address: PO Box 141, Annapolis Junction, MD 20701 *Tel:* 240-646-7027 *Fax:* 240-757-7223 *E-mail:* choicesubscriptions@brightkey.net
Key Personnel
Sr Prodn Ed: Dawn Mueller
Ed: Wendi Arant Kaspar
Theory & research relevant to academic & research librarians. Check web site for submission information.

First published 1939
Book Use: Reviews
Frequency: 6 issues/yr
$15/issue, free online
ISSN: 0010-0870

Columbia Journalism Review
Published by Columbia Graduate School of Journalism
Affiliate of Columbia University
Journalism Bldg, 801 Pulitzer Hall, 2950 Broadway, New York, NY 10027
Tel: 212-854-1881; 212-854-2718 (busn)
Toll Free Tel: 888-425-7782 (US subns)
Fax: 212-854-8367
E-mail: editors@cjr.org
Web Site: www.cjr.org
Key Personnel
Ed-in-Chief & Publr: Elizabeth Spayd
Mng Ed: Vanessa M Gezari
Sr Ed: Christie Chisholm
Assoc Ed: Liz Cox Barrett; Greg Marx
Monitors & assesses the performance of journalism in all forms.
First published 1961
Frequency: 2 issues/yr
Circulation: 30,000
Free to membs
ISSN: 0010-194X

Connections
Published by Printing Industries of New England
5 Crystal Pond Rd, Southborough, MA 01772-1758
Tel: 508-804-4171 *Toll Free Tel:* 800-365-7463
Fax: 508-804-4119
Web Site: www.pine.org
Key Personnel
Pres & Publr: Tad Parker
Members only trade magazine for printing & graphic communication companies in New England.
First published 1938
Frequency: 6 issues/yr
Avg pages per issue: 48
Circulation: 1,200
Free to membs
ISSN: 0162-8771
Trim Size: 8 1/2 x 11
Ad Closing Date(s): 10th of the month preceding publication

Editors' Association of Canada - Online Directory of Editors
Published by Editors' Association of Canada (Association canadienne des reviseurs)
27 Carlton St, Suite 505, Toronto, ON M5B 1L2, Canada
Tel: 416-975-1379 *Toll Free Tel:* 866-CAN-EDIT (226-3348) *Fax:* 416-975-1637
E-mail: info@editors.ca
Web Site: www.editors.ca
Key Personnel
Exec Dir: John Yip-Chuck
E-mail: executivedirector@editors.ca
Sr Communs Mgr: Michelle Ou
E-mail: communications@editors.ca
Prof Standards Mgr: Sebastian Koch
E-mail: professionalstandards@editors.ca
Membership & Conference Coord: Caitlin Stewart
Online directory of descriptive listings of current association members indexed by specialty.
$90.40/yr CN

Educational Marketer
Published by Simba Information
Division of Market Research.com
1266 E Main St, Suite 700, Stamford, CT 06902
SAN: 210-2021
Tel: 203-325-8193 *Toll Free Tel:* 888-297-4622 (cust serv)
E-mail: customerservice@simbainformation.com
Web Site: www.simbainformation.com
Key Personnel
Sr Analyst/Mng Ed: Kathy Mickey
Sr Analyst/Ed: Karen Meaney
Prodn Coord: Farah Pierre
Newsletter; reports on educational publishing field (el-hi & college): enrollments, demographics, funding, mergers & acquisitions, new product developments & personnel changes. For publishers, suppliers & dealers in the educational market.
First published 1968
Frequency: 24 issues/yr
Avg pages per issue: 8
$695/yr
ISSN: 1013-1806
Ad Rates: 4-color full page $1,650; 4-color 1/2 page $1,320; B&W full page $1,150; B&W 1/2 page $1,150
Ad Closing Date(s): 12 days before publication date

Electronic Education Report
Published by Simba Information
Division of Market Research.com
1266 E Main St, Suite 700, Stamford, CT 06902
SAN: 210-2021
Tel: 203-325-8193 *Toll Free Tel:* 888-297-4622 (cust serv)
E-mail: customerservice@simbainformation.com
Web Site: www.simbainformation.com
Key Personnel
Sr Analyst/Mng Ed: Kathy Mickey
Sr Analyst/Ed: Karen Meaney
Prodn Coord: Farah Pierre
Published twice each month to provide industry decision-makers with the problem-solving information they need to make prudent business decisions in a rapidly evolving, multi-billion dollar market. Technologies covered include hardware, software, multimedia/CD-ROM, integrated learning systems, video, distance learning, online services & educational videocassettes News coverage includes sales & distribution trends, company rankings & financial profiles, trademark & rights issues, strategic alliances & mergers, site licensing & networks, etc. Analyzes K-12. Readers are upper & middle management textbook & software publishers, software distributors, online service providers, video publishers & computer hardware manufacturers.
First published 1994
Frequency: 24 issues/yr
$650/yr PDF download
ISSN: 1077-9949
Trim Size: 8 1/2 x 11
Ad Rates: 4-color full page $1,320; 4-color 1/2 page $1,060; B&W full page $1,120; B&W 1/2 page $920

Event
Published by Douglas College
700 Royal Ave, New Westminster, BC V3M 5Z5, Canada
Mailing Address: PO Box 2503, New Westminster, BC V3L 5B2, Canada
Tel: 604-527-5293 *Fax:* 604-527-5095
E-mail: event@douglascollege.ca
Web Site: www.eventmagazine.ca
Key Personnel
Mng Ed: Ian Cockfield
Ed: Shashi Bhat
Fiction Ed: Christine Dewar
Poetry Ed: Joann Arnott
Reviews Ed: Susan Wasserman
Literary journal. Occasionally publish unsol reviews but should query first. Publish mostly Canadian writers, but are open to anyone writing in English. Do not read mss in Jan, July, Aug & Dec. Buy fiction, poetry, creative non-fiction.
First published 1971
Frequency: 3 issues/yr
Avg pages per issue: 128
Circulation: 1,100
$19/issue, $29.95/yr
ISSN: 0315-3770
Trim Size: 6 x 9
Ad Rates: Full page $200, 1/2 page $100
Ad Closing Date(s): March 15 (Summer), July 15 (Fall/Winter), Nov 15 (Spring)

Facilities & Destinations
Published by Bedrock Communications Inc
152 Madison Ave, Suite 802, New York, NY 10016
Tel: 212-532-4150 *Fax:* 212-213-6382
Web Site: www.facilitiesonline.com
Key Personnel
Assoc Publr: Michael Caffin *E-mail:* mcaffin@facilitiesonline.com
Edit Dir: George Seli *E-mail:* gseli@facilitiesonline.com
Trade magazine chronicling the facility, event & convention marketplace.
First published 1991
Frequency: Quarterly
Avg pages per issue: 48
Circulation: 30,303
Free to qualified readers

Facilities & Event Management
Published by Bedrock Communications Inc
152 Madison Ave, Suite 802, New York, NY 10016
Tel: 212-532-4150 *Fax:* 212-213-6382
Web Site: www.facilitiesonline.com
Key Personnel
Assoc Publr: Michael Caffin *E-mail:* mcaffin@facilitiesonline.com
Edit Dir: George Seli *E-mail:* gseli@facilitiesonline.com
Trade magazine chronicling the facility, event & convention marketplace.
First published 1991
Frequency: 2 issues/yr
Free to qualified readers

Folio: The Magazine for Magazine Management
Published by Access Intelligence
10 Norden Place, Norwalk, CT 06855
Tel: 203-854-6730; 203-899-8433 *Fax:* 203-854-6735
E-mail: folioedit@foliomag.com
Web Site: www.foliomag.com
Key Personnel
Pres & CEO: Jay Lauf
VP: Tony Silber *E-mail:* tsilber@accessintel.com
News & articles for the magazine publishing executive.
First published 1972
Book Use: Excerpts & condensations
Frequency: Monthly
Avg pages per issue: 60
Circulation: 8,500
$96/yr, $106/yr CN & Mexico, $116/yr elsewhere, $8/issue newsstand
ISSN: 0046-4333

Forecast
Published by Baker & Taylor Inc
2550 W Tyvola Rd, Suite 300, Charlotte, NC 28217
Mailing Address: PO Box 6885, Bridgewater, NJ 08807-0855
Tel: 704-998-3100 *Toll Free Tel:* 800-775-1800 (info servs) *Fax:* 704-998-3319
E-mail: btinfo@baker-taylor.com
Web Site: www.baker-taylor.com
Key Personnel
Mktg Specialist: Donna Heffner
Prepublication announcements for booksellers & librarians containing bibliographic data & descriptions of forthcoming adult hardcover

future bestsellers, noteworthy midlist titles, university & independent press releases; includes spoken-word audio. Online only.
Free

Foreword Reviews
Division of Foreword Magazine Inc
425 Boardman Ave, Suite B, Traverse City, MI 49684
Tel: 231-933-3699
E-mail: sales@forewordreviews.com
Web Site: www.forewordreviews.com
Key Personnel
Publr: Victoria Sutherland *E-mail:* victoria@forewordreviews.com
Dir, Circ & Audience Devt: Seth Dellon
Exec Ed: Howard Lovy *E-mail:* howard@forewordreviews.com
Mng Ed: Matt Sutherland *E-mail:* matt@forewordreviews.com
Assoc Ed: Michelle Anne Schingler
Ad Sales: Stacy Price *E-mail:* stacy@forewordreviews.com
Review journal of books from independent presses, university presses & self-publishers. Distributed to librarians & booksellers for collection development.
First published 1998
Frequency: Quarterly
Avg pages per issue: 64
Circulation: 15,000
$19.95/yr US, $39.95/yr CN, $59.95/yr foreign (print), $9.99/yr (online)
ISSN: 1099-2642
Trim Size: 8 1/2 x 11
Ad Rates: B&W full page $2,257, 1/2 page $1,349
Ad Closing Date(s): 3 weeks prior to issue date

Gateway Journalism Review/St Louis Journalism Review
Published by St Louis Journalism Review (SJR)
Communications Bldg, 1100 Lincoln Dr, Mail Code 6601, Carbondale, IL 62901
Tel: 618-536-3361; 618-453-3262
E-mail: gatewayjr@siu.edu
Web Site: gatewayjr.org
Key Personnel
Publr: William Freivogel
Media critic of press & broadcasting - particularly of St Louis region & the Midwest, but also nationally.
First published 1970
Book Use: Book review & excerpts
Frequency: Quarterly
Avg pages per issue: 36
Circulation: 1,250
$32/yr, $50/2 yrs
ISSN: 0036-2972
Trim Size: 8 1/2 x 11
Ad Closing Date(s): 20th of each month

Geist
Published by The Geist Foundation
201-111 W Hastings St, Vancouver, BC V6B 1H4, Canada
Tel: 604-681-9161 *Toll Free Tel:* 888-GEIST-EH (434-7834) *Fax:* 604-677-6319
E-mail: geist@geist.com
Web Site: www.geist.com
Key Personnel
Publr: Michal Kozlowski
Assoc Publr: AnnMarie MacKinnon
Canadian ideas & culture with a strong literary focus. The 'Geist' tone is intelligent, plain-talking, inclusive & offbeat. Submissions must have a Canadian angle content or author. Mail-in submissions only (except for contests).
First published 1990
Frequency: Quarterly
Avg pages per issue: 72
Circulation: 7,000
$21/yr CN, $27/yr US & foreign, $35 2/yrs CN, $47 2/yrs US & foreign, $44 3/yrs CN, $62 3/yrs US & foreign
ISSN: 1181-6554
Ad Rates: Full page $970; 2/3 page $735; 1/2 page $685; 1/3 page $425; 1/6 page $270; ad rates decrease with frequent advertisement

Graphic Monthly
Published by North Island Publishing Ltd
1606 Sedlescomb Dr, Suite 8, Mississauga, ON L4X 1M6, Canada
Tel: 905-625-7070 *Toll Free Tel:* 800-331-7408 (US only) *Fax:* 905-625-4856
Web Site: www.graphicmonthly.ca
Key Personnel
Publr: Alexander Donald *Tel:* 905-625-7070 ext 230 *E-mail:* s.donald@northisland.ca
Mng Ed & Online Ed: Leslie Emmons *Tel:* 905-625-7070 ext 234 *E-mail:* leslie@graphicmonthly.ca
Graphic, printing info.
First published 1980
Frequency: 6 issues/yr
Avg pages per issue: 60
Circulation: 10,500
Free to qualified Canadian businesses
ISSN: 0227-2806
Trim Size: 8 1/4 x 11
Ad Rates: 4-color full page $4,532 (1x), $4,120 (3x), $3,900 (6x)

Guild of Book Workers Newsletter
Published by Guild of Book Workers
521 Fifth Ave, New York, NY 10175
Tel: 212-292-4444
E-mail: communications@guildofbookworkers.org
Web Site: www.guildofbookworkers.org
Key Personnel
Pres: Mark Andersson *Tel:* 520-682-7241 *E-mail:* president@guildofbookworkers.org
VP: Bexx Caswell *E-mail:* vicepresident@guildofbookworkers.org
Newsletter Ed: Cindy Haller *E-mail:* newsletter@guildofbookworkers.org
Secy: Katy Baum *Tel:* 214-363-7946 *E-mail:* secretary@guildofbookworkers.org
Treas: Laura Bedford *E-mail:* treasurer@guildofbookworkers.org
Articles, calendar of activities related to the book arts.
Frequency: 6 issues/yr
Avg pages per issue: 15
Circulation: 900
Free with membership

The Horn Book Guide
Published by Horn Book Inc
300 The Fenway, Suite P-311, Palace Road Bldg, Boston, MA 02115
Tel: 617-278-0225 *Toll Free Tel:* 888-628-0225 *Fax:* 617-278-6062
E-mail: info@hbook.com
Web Site: www.hbook.com
Subscription Address: 7585 Industrial Pkwy, Plain City, OH 43064 *Tel:* 614-873-7954 *Fax:* 614-873-7135
Key Personnel
Publr: David Greenough *Tel:* 917-886-0718 *E-mail:* dgreenough@mediasourceinc.com
Creative Dir: Lolly Robinson *Tel:* 617-628-0225 ext 226 *E-mail:* lrobinson@hbook.com
Ed-in-Chief: Roger Sutton
Mng Ed: Katrina Hedeen *E-mail:* khedeen@hbook.com
Brief, critical reviews of nearly every hardcover trade children's & young adult book published in the US.
First published 1990
Book Use: Subject, series, reissues, new editions, author/illustrator & title indexes
Frequency: Semiannual
Avg pages per issue: 288
Circulation: 2,600
$35/issue, $60/yr
ISSN: 1044-405X
Trim Size: 8 3/8 x 11 1/16
Ad Rates: Color covers 2 & 3 $1,690/each; color cover 4 $1,740; B&W full page $1,690
Ad Closing Date(s): Feb 1 for Spring issue, Aug 1 for Fall issue

The Horn Book Magazine
Published by Horn Book Inc
300 The Fenway, Suite P-311, Palace Road Bldg, Boston, MA 02115
Tel: 617-278-0225 *Toll Free Tel:* 888-628-0225 *Fax:* 617-278-6062
E-mail: info@hbook.com
Web Site: www.hbook.com
Subscription Address: 7585 Industrial Pkwy, Plain City, OH 43064 *Tel:* 614-873-7954 *Fax:* 614-873-7135
Key Personnel
Publr: David Greenough *Tel:* 917-886-0718 *E-mail:* dgreenough@mediasourceinc.com
Creative Dir: Lolly Robinson *Tel:* 617-628-0225 ext 226 *E-mail:* lrobinson@hbook.com
Ed-in-Chief: Roger Sutton
Book Review Ed: Martha V Parravano *E-mail:* mvp@hbook.com
Exec Ed: Elissa Gershowitz *E-mail:* egershowitz@hbook.com
Asst Ed: Shoshana Flax *E-mail:* sflax@hbook.com
Children's literature journal featuring reviews, articles, essays, columns, interviews with children's book authors & illustrators, current announcements.
First published 1924
Book Use: Reviews & occasional excerpts
Frequency: 6 issues/yr
Avg pages per issue: 128
Circulation: 8,500
$72/yr
ISSN: 0018-5078
Trim Size: 6 x 9
Ad Rates: Color covers 2, 3 & 4 $2,577/each; full page interior $2,150
Ad Closing Date(s): 2 months before pubn date

Independent Publisher
Published by Jenkins Group Inc
1129 Woodmere Ave, Suite B, Traverse City, MI 49686
Tel: 231-933-0445 *Toll Free Tel:* 800-706-4636 *Fax:* 231-933-0448
Web Site: www.independentpublisher.com
Key Personnel
CEO: Jerrold R Jenkins *Tel:* 231-933-0445 ext 1008 *E-mail:* jrj@bookpublishing.com
Pres & COO: James Kalajian *Tel:* 231-933-0445 ext 1006 *E-mail:* jjk@bookpublishing.com
Mng Ed, Independent Publisher Online: Jim Barnes *E-mail:* jimb@bookpublishing.com
Article topics relevant to the business of independent book publishing & retailing, including marketing, book awards, promotion & distribution. Available online since 2000.
First published 1983
Book Use: Featured reviews & individual reviews from independently published works of the current year
Frequency: Monthly
Avg pages per issue: 80
Circulation: 10,000
Free online; sent monthly via e-mail
ISSN: 1098-5735
Avg reviews per issue: 40

Information Today
Published by Information Today, Inc
143 Old Marlton Pike, Medford, NJ 08055-8750

Tel: 609-654-6266 *Toll Free Tel:* 800-300-9868 (cust serv) *Fax:* 609-654-4309
E-mail: custserv@infotoday.com
Web Site: www.infotoday.com/IT/default.asp
Key Personnel
Publr/Pres & CEO: Thomas H Hogan, Sr
Ed: Brandi Scardilli *E-mail:* bscardilli@infotoday.com
The newspaper for users & producers of digital information services.
First published 1983
Frequency: 10 issues/yr
Avg pages per issue: 32
Circulation: 8,000
$99.95/yr, $188/2yrs, $288/3yrs US; $128/yr, $241/2 yrs, $369/3 yrs CN & Mexico; $143/yr, $269/2 yrs, $412/3 yrs other; agencies $2 less
ISSN: 8755-6286
Trim Size: 9 1/2 x 11 3/4
Ad Rates: See web site for complete details

Journal of International Marketing
Published by American Marketing Association
130 E Randolph St, 22nd fl, Chicago, IL 60601
Tel: 312-542-9000 *Toll Free Tel:* 800-AMA-1150 (262-1150) *Fax:* 312-542-9001
E-mail: info@ama.org
Web Site: www.ama.org
Key Personnel
CEO: Russ Klein *E-mail:* ceo@ama.org
Dir, Digital Content: Christopher Bartone *Tel:* 312-542-9029 *E-mail:* cbartone@ama.org
Ed-in-Chief: Constantine S Katsikeas *E-mail:* csk@lubs.leeds.ac.uk
Sr Mng Ed, Integrated Academic Content: Marilyn Stone *E-mail:* mstone@ama.org
Timely insights from executives along with reports on new trends & tactics. Each issue also features analysis of the latest marketing theories, in-depth articles by practitioners & coverage of new methods.
Frequency: Quarterly
Avg pages per issue: 144
Circulation: 1,300
$55/yr AMA membs, $130/yr indivs US & CN, $160/yr indivs foreign, $250/yr instns US; print/online combo rates available (see web site for more options)
ISSN: 1069-031X

Journal of Marketing
Published by American Marketing Association
130 E Randolph St, 22nd fl, Chicago, IL 60601
Tel: 312-542-9000 *Toll Free Tel:* 800-AMA-1150 (262-1150) *Fax:* 312-542-9001
E-mail: info@ama.org
Web Site: www.ama.org
Key Personnel
CEO: Russ Klein *E-mail:* ceo@ama.org
Ad Sales: Bob Lorber *E-mail:* rlorber@yourmembership.com
Ed-in-Chief: V Kumar *E-mail:* vkjm@gsu.edu
Thought-provoking, in-depth articles covering vital aspects of the marketing industry. You'll find original research on all aspects of marketing & you'll appreciate how the journal bridges the gap between theory & application.
First published 1936
Book Use: Some reviews & excerpts
Frequency: 6 times/yr
Avg pages per issue: 144
Circulation: 8,200
$145/yr indivs US, $385/yr instns US; online & print/online combo rates available
ISSN: 0022-2429

Journal of Marketing Research
Published by American Marketing Association
130 E Randolph St, 22nd fl, Chicago, IL 60601
Tel: 312-542-9000 *Toll Free Tel:* 800-AMA-1150 (262-1150) *Fax:* 312-542-9001
E-mail: info@ama.org
Web Site: www.ama.org
Key Personnel
CEO: Russ Klein *E-mail:* ceo@ama.org
Ed-in-Chief: Rajdeep Grewal *E-mail:* Rajdeep_Grewal@kenan-flagler.unc.edu
Sr Mng Ed, Integrated Academic Content: Marilyn Stone *E-mail:* mstone@ama.org
Ad Sales: Bob Lorber *E-mail:* rlorber@yourmembership.com
For the latest thinking in marketing research. The journal covers a wide range of marketing-research concepts, methods & applications. You'll read about new techniques; contributions to knowledge based on experimental methods; & developments in related fields that have a bearing on marketing research.
First published 1963
Book Use: Some reviews
Frequency: 6 times/yr
Avg pages per issue: 128
Circulation: 4,400
$145/yr indivs US, $175/yr indivs foreign, $385/yr instns US, $415/yr instns foreign; online & print/online combo rates available
ISSN: 0022-2437 (print); 1547-7193 (online)

Journal of Scholarly Publishing
Published by University of Toronto Press Journals Division
Division of University of Toronto Press Inc
5201 Dufferin St, Toronto, ON M3H 5T8, Canada
Tel: 416-667-7810 *Toll Free Tel:* 800-221-9985 (CN) *Fax:* 416-667-7881
E-mail: journals@utpress.utoronto.ca
Web Site: www.utpjournals.com
Key Personnel
Ed-in-Chief: Robert Brown; Alex Holzman
Sr Mgr, Journals: Antonia Pop *Tel:* 416-667-7777 ext 7838 *E-mail:* apop@utpress.utoronto.ca
Ad & Mktg Coord: Audrey Greenwood *Tel:* 416-667-7777 ext 7766 *E-mail:* agreenwood@utpress.utoronto.ca
Articles on the writing, publication & use of serious nonfiction addressed to scholars, authors, publishers, reviewers, editors & librarians.
First published 1969
Book Use: Reviews of books relating to publishing
Frequency: Quarterly
Avg pages per issue: 64
Circulation: 800
$150/yr instns, $46/yr indivs, $40/yr membs; online version $129/yr instns, $36/yr indivs, $30/yr membs
ISSN: 1198-9742
Trim Size: 6 x 9
Ad Rates: Full page $395, 1/2 page $295, inside back cover $435, outside back cover $500; frequency discount; 30% 4 consecutive insertions, 20% for 3 & 10% for 2 inserts

Journalism & Mass Communication Quarterly
Published by SAGE Publishing
2455 Teller Rd, Thousand Oaks, CA 91320
Toll Free Tel: 800-818-7243 *Toll Free Fax:* 800-583-2665
E-mail: journals@sagepub.com
Web Site: www.sagepub.com
Key Personnel
VP & Edit Dir: Michele Sordi
Book Review Ed: Daniel C Hallin
Ed: Louisa Ha
Research in journalism & mass communication.
First published 1924
Frequency: Quarterly
Avg pages per issue: 1,000
Circulation: 5,000
Indivs: $170 (print only); Instns: $316 (electronic only), $344 (print only), $351 (print & electronic)
ISSN: 1077-6990 (print); 2161-430X (online)

The Kenyon Review
Subsidiary of Kenyon College
Finn House, 102 W Wiggin St, Gambier, OH 43022
Tel: 740-427-5208 *Fax:* 740-427-5417
E-mail: kenyonreview@kenyon.edu
Web Site: www.kenyonreview.org
Key Personnel
Mng Ed: Abigail Wadsworth Serfass *Tel:* 740-427-5389 *E-mail:* serfassam@kenyon.edu
Ed: David Lynn
Assoc Ed: Kristen Reach
Fiction, poetry, essays, book reviews, drama. See web site for details.
First published 1939
Book Use: Reviews of 12 books
Frequency: 6 issues/yr
Avg pages per issue: 120
Circulation: 7,500
$10/issue, $30/yr, $50/2 yrs, $70/3 yrs
ISSN: 0163-075X
Trim Size: 6 1/8 x 10
Ad Rates: Full page $375
Ad Closing Date(s): Nov 10, Jan 10, March 10, May 10, July 10, Sept 10

Knowledge Quest
Published by American Association of School Librarians
Division of The American Library Association (ALA)
50 E Huron St, Chicago, IL 60611
Tel: 312-944-6780 *Toll Free Tel:* 800-545-2433 *Fax:* 312-280-5276
E-mail: aasl@ala.org
Web Site: www.ala.org/aasl/kq
Key Personnel
Mng Ed, Knowledge Quest: Meg Featheringham *Tel:* 312-280-1396
Devoted to offering substantive information to assist in building-level library media specialists, supervisors, library educators & other decision makers concerned with the development of school library media programs & services. Articles address the integration of theory & practice in school librarianship & new developments in education, learning theory & relevant disciplines.
First published 1997
Frequency: 5 issues/yr
Avg pages per issue: 80
Circulation: 10,000
$12/issue, $50/yr nonmembs US, $60/yr nonmembs foreign
ISSN: 1094-9046

Library Journal
Published by Media Source Inc
123 William St, Suite 802, New York, NY 10038
Tel: 646-380-0752 *Toll Free Tel:* 800-588-1030 *Fax:* 646-380-0756
E-mail: ljinfo@mediasourceinc.com
Web Site: lj.libraryjournal.com
Key Personnel
CEO & Publr: Randall J Asmo *Tel:* 614-873-7635 *E-mail:* rasmo@mediasourceinc.com
Ed-in-Chief: Rebecca T Miller *Tel:* 646-380-0738 *E-mail:* rmiller@mediasourceinc.com
Exec Ed: Meredith Schwartz *Tel:* 646-380-0745 *E-mail:* mschwartz@mediasourceinc.com
Mng Ed: Bette-Lee Fox *Tel:* 646-380-0717 *E-mail:* blfox@mediasourceinc.com
Ed-at-Large: John N Berry, III *Tel:* 646-380-0760 *E-mail:* jberry@mediasourceinc.com
Reviews are written & edited specifically to assess the value of a book for the library collection. Also review videotapes, DVDs, audiobooks, ebooks, CD-ROMs, magazines, databases & web sites.
First published 1876
Book Use: Reviews, news
Frequency: Semimonthly (exc monthly during Jan, July, Aug & Dec)

Avg pages per issue: 144
Circulation: 12,000
$157.99/yr US, $199.99/yr CN & Mexico, $259.99/yr foreign
ISSN: 0363-0277

The Library Quarterly
Published by The University of Chicago Press, Journals Division
University of Maryland, College of Information Studies, 4105 Hornbake Bldg, South Wing, College Park, MD 20742
Tel: 310-405-3267 *Fax:* 301-405-3267
E-mail: lq@press.uchicago.edu
Web Site: www.journals.uchicago.edu
Subscription Address: PO Box 37005, Chicago, IL 60637
Key Personnel
Mng Ed: Karen Kettnich *E-mail:* kkettnich@umd.edu
Ed: Paul Jaeger
Reviews Ed: Lindsay C Sarin
Library & information science & related subjects.
First published 1931
Book Use: Reviews
Frequency: Quarterly
Avg pages per issue: 128
Circulation: 1,018
$17/issue indivs, $73/issue instns, $54/yr indivs combined print & online
ISSN: 0024-2519
Ad Rates: Full page $724

Locus: The Magazine of the Science Fiction & Fantasy Field
Published by Locus Science Fiction Foundation Inc
PO Box 13305, Oakland, CA 94661-0305
Tel: 510-339-9196 *Fax:* 510-339-9198
E-mail: locus@locusmag.com
Web Site: www.locusmag.com
Key Personnel
Ed-in-Chief: Liza Groen Trombi
Mng Ed: Kirsten Gong-Wong
Includes news, awards, interviews & annual analysis of the science fiction field, monthly bestseller list & a complete monthly listing of new publications. Primarily a trade magazine for science fiction professionals, booksellers & libraries.
First published 1968
Book Use: Reviews
Frequency: Monthly
Avg pages per issue: 88
Circulation: 6,000
$7.50/issue + $3 S&H, $63/yr indivs (print), $75/yr (print & digital)
ISSN: 0047-4959
Trim Size: 8 3/8 x 10 7/8
Ad Rates: B&W full page $1,075

Los Angeles Review of Books
6671 Sunset Blvd, Suite 1521, Los Angeles, CA 90028
E-mail: info@lareviewofbooks.org; editorial@lareviewofbooks.org
Web Site: lareviewofbooks.org
Key Personnel
Publr & Ed-in-Chief: Tom Lutz *E-mail:* tom@lareviewofbooks.org
Exec Ed: Boris Dralyuk *E-mail:* boris@lareviewofbooks.org
Mng Ed: Medaya Ocher *E-mail:* medaya@lareviewofbooks.org
Publicity: Jessica Kubinec *E-mail:* jessica@lareviewofbooks.org
Multimedia literary & cultural arts magazine.
Frequency: Monthly (print ed quarterly)
$10/mo or $100/yr (LARB membership)

Marketing Insights
Published by American Marketing Association
130 E Randolph St, 22nd fl, Chicago, IL 60601
Tel: 312-542-9000 *Toll Free Tel:* 800-AMA-1150 (262-1150) *Fax:* 312-542-9001
E-mail: info@ama.org
Web Site: www.ama.org
Each issue offers thought-provoking analyses of the latest trends & methodologies in marketing research applications & management. Written in clear, concise language with a focus on practical application, *Marketing Insights* clearly shows how marketing research strategies affect real-world businesses.
First published 1989
Book Use: Book & software reviews in each issue
$110/indivs, $145/instns (digital only)
ISSN: 1040-8460
Ad Rates: Contact Ad Sales Dir for more information

Marketing News
Published by American Marketing Association
130 E Randolph St, 22nd fl, Chicago, IL 60601
Tel: 312-542-9000 *Toll Free Tel:* 800-AMA-1150 (262-1150) *Fax:* 312-542-9001
E-mail: info@ama.org
Web Site: www.ama.org
Key Personnel
CEO: Russ Klein *E-mail:* ceo@ama.org
Dir, Digital Content: Christopher Bartone *Tel:* 312-542-9029 *E-mail:* cbartone@ama.org
Ed-in-Chief: Molly Soat *Tel:* 312-542-9036 *E-mail:* msoat@ama.org
Focuses on strategic issues that marketing managers face every day. Covers brand management, CRM, product innovation, ROI, marketing effectiveness & B2B – to help managers keep pace with this rapidly changing field.
Frequency: Monthly
Circulation: 20,000
$60/yr membs, $80/yr indivs US & CN, $110/yr indivs foreign, $110/yr instns US & CN, $140/yr instns foreign
ISSN: 1061-3846
Trim Size: 8 x 10 1/2

Medical Reference Services Quarterly
Published by Routledge
Member of Taylor & Francis Group, an Informa Business
530 Walnut St, Suite 850, Philadelphia, PA 19106
Tel: 215-625-8900 *Toll Free Tel:* 800-354-1420 *Fax:* 215-207-0050
Web Site: www.tandfonline.com
Key Personnel
Ed: M Sandra Wood
Working tool journal for medical & health sciences librarians. Regularly publishes practice-oriented articles relating to medical reference services with an emphasis on user education, database searching & electronic information.
First published 1982
Book Use: Reviews
Frequency: Quarterly
Avg pages per issue: 116
Indiv: print & online $174, online only $152; Instns: print & online $635, online only $555
ISSN: 0276-3869 (print); 1540-9597 (online)

Mergers & Acquisitions
Published by Source Media
One State Street Plaza, 27th fl, New York, NY 10004
Tel: 212-803-6051 *Toll Free Tel:* 888-807-8667
E-mail: custserv@sourcemedia.com
Web Site: www.themiddlemarket.com
Key Personnel
Ed-in-Chief: Mary Kathleen Flynn *Tel:* 212-803-8708 *E-mail:* marykathleen.flynn@sourcemedia.com
Professional journal; covers the latest trends & influences impacting the buying & selling of businesses. Articles cover how to make money, save money & avoid disaster in the constantly changing merger & acquisition environment.
First published 1965
Frequency: Monthly
Avg pages per issue: 56
Circulation: 20,000
$995/yr, free 2 week trial available
ISSN: 0026-0010

MLQ (Modern Language Quarterly): A Journal of Literary History
Published by Duke University Press
University of Washington, English Dept, Box 354330, Seattle, WA 98195-4430
Tel: 206-543-6827; 919-688-5134 *Toll Free Tel:* 888-651-0122 (US) *Fax:* 206-685-2673; 919-688-2615 *Toll Free Fax:* 888-651-0124
E-mail: mlq@u.washington.edu
Web Site: www.mlq.washington.edu/journals; www.dukeupress.edu; www.dukeupress.edu/journals
Subscription Address: Duke University Press, Box 90660, Durham, NC 27708-0660 *Tel:* 919-687-3653 *E-mail:* subscriptions@dukeupress.edu
Key Personnel
Journals Dir: Rob Dilworth
Academic Ed: Marshall Brown
Journals Acqs Ed: Erich Staib *Tel:* 919-687-3664 *E-mail:* erich.staib@dukeupress.edu
Asst Ed: Sam Hushagen
Scholarly articles on literary history.
First published 1940
Book Use: Reviews
Frequency: Quarterly
Avg pages per issue: 130
Circulation: 1,350
$259/yr instns (print only); $226/yr instns (electronic); $266/yr instns (print & electronic); $35/yr indivs; $18/yr students; add $12 postage & 7% GST for CN; $16 postage for outside US & CN
ISSN: 0026-7929 (print); 1527-1943 (online)
Ad Rates: B&W full page $250; B&W 1/2 page $200

Network
Published by The International Women's Writing Guild (IWWG)
5 Penn Plaza, 19th fl, PMB 19059, New York, NY 10001
Tel: 917-720-6959
E-mail: iwwgquestions@iwwg.org
Web Site: www.iwwg.org
Key Personnel
Exec Dir: Dixie King, PhD
Interim Opers Dir: Marj Hahne
Member news, regional clusters, correspondence corner, letters to the editor, environmental, special offerings, profile of guild members. Several hundred opportunities for publication & submission in every issue.
First published 1978
Frequency: Quarterly
Avg pages per issue: 32
Circulation: 3,000
$25; digital version free to membs

New Millennium Writings
4021 Garden Dr, Knoxville, TN 37918
Tel: 865-254-4880
E-mail: npf@nationalpress.org
Web Site: www.newmillenniumwritings.org
Key Personnel
Publr & Ed: Alexis Williams Carr *E-mail:* alexis.williams@hotmail.com
Contains fiction, poetry & creative nonfiction by both emerging & well known writers. Regularly features profiles, interviews & essay on famous writers. Also includes writing tips & commentary by the editor.
First published 1996

News & Tech, see Newspapers & Technology

Newspapers & Technology
Published by Conley Magazines LLC
PO Box 478, Beaver Dam, WI 53916
Tel: 303-575-9595 *Fax:* 303-575-9555
E-mail: letters@newsandtech.com
Web Site: www.newsandtech.com
Key Personnel
Publr & Editor-in-Chief: Mary Van Meter *E-mail:* vanmeternt@aol.com
Mng Ed: Sarah Zook *E-mail:* szook@newsandtech.com
Trade publication for newspaper publishers & department managers involved in applying & integrating technology. Written by industry experts who provide regular coverage of the following departments: prepress, press, postpress & new media.
First published 1988
Frequency: 6 issues/yr
Avg pages per issue: 48
Circulation: 15,000
Free to qualified personnel
ISSN: 1052-5572

North Carolina Literary Review (NCLR)
Published by East Carolina University & North Carolina Literary & Historical Association
East Carolina University, English Dept, ECU Mailstop 555 English, Greenville, NC 27858-4353
Tel: 252-328-1537 *Fax:* 252-328-4889
E-mail: ncluser@ecu.edu
Web Site: www.nclr.ecu.edu
Key Personnel
Ed: Margaret Bauer *E-mail:* bauerm@ecu.edu
Articles, essays, interviews, fiction/poetry by & about North Carolina writers & literature, culture & history.
First published 1992
Book Use: Excerpts from forthcoming books; essay reviews only - 2 or more books treated thematically
Frequency: Annual
Avg pages per issue: 200
Circulation: 650 + bookstore sales
$15/yr indiv, $25/2 yrs indiv, $25/yr instn & foreign instn/indiv
ISSN: 1063-0724
Ad Rates: Full page $250, 1/2 page $150, 1/4 page $100
Ad Closing Date(s): Feb 1

Poetics Today
Published by Duke University Press
Ohio State University, Dept of English, 164 W 17 Ave, Columbus, OH 43210
Mailing Address: PO Box 90660, Durham, NC 27708-0660
Tel: 919-687-3686 *Toll Free Tel:* 888-651-0122 (US) *Fax:* 919-688-2615 *Toll Free Fax:* 888-651-0124
E-mail: subscriptions@dukeupress.edu
Web Site: www.dukeupress.edu
Key Personnel
Journals Dir: Rob Dilworth
Dir, Mktg & Sales: Cason Lynley *E-mail:* cason.lynley@dukeupress.edu
Academic Ed: Brian McHale
Book Review Ed: Eyal Segal
Academic Exhibits & Publicity Coord: Katie Smart
Book Use: Book reviews
Frequency: Quarterly
Avg pages per issue: 200
Circulation: 800
$40/yr indiv, $20/yr students (with photocopy of ID), $462/yr instns print only, $372/yr electronic only, $490/yr instns print & electronic
ISSN: 0333-5372 (print); 1527-5507 (online)
Ad Rates: B&W full page $250, 1/2 page $200

Poetry
Published by Poetry Foundation
61 W Superior St, Chicago, IL 60654
Tel: 312-787-7070 *Fax:* 312-787-6650
E-mail: editors@poetrymagazine.org
Web Site: www.poetryfoundation.org/poetrymagazine
Subscription Address: PO Box 421141, Palm Coast, FL 32142-1141
Key Personnel
Ed: Don Share
Poetry, essays & book reviews. Complete submission guidelines can be found on the web site.
First published 1912
Frequency: Monthly
Avg pages per issue: 90
Circulation: 26,000
US: $3.75/issue, $35/yr indivs, $38/yr instns; Foreign: $47/yr indivs, $50/yr instns
ISSN: 0032-2032
Trim Size: 5 1/2 x 9
Ad Rates: Full page $800, 1/2 page $500, 1/4 page $375
Ad Closing Date(s): 15th of the 3rd month before issue date

Poets & Writers Magazine
Published by Poets & Writers Inc
90 Broad St, Suite 2100, New York, NY 10004
Tel: 212-226-3586 *Fax:* 212-226-3963
E-mail: editor@pw.org
Web Site: www.pw.org
Key Personnel
Ed-in-Chief: Kevin Larimer
Prodn Ed: Bill Smyth
News for & about the contemporary literary community in the US. Pertinent articles, grants & awards, publishing opportunities, essays, interviews with writers.
First published 1973
Book Use: First serial, excerpts, author interviews
Frequency: 6 issues/yr
Avg pages per issue: 132
Circulation: 60,000
$5.95/issue, $12.95/yr, $19.95/2 yrs
ISSN: 0891-6136

Print
Published by F+W Media Inc
10151 Carver Rd, Suite 200, Blue Ash, OH 45242
Tel: 212-447-1400 *Fax:* 212-447-5231
E-mail: info@printmag.com
Web Site: www.printmag.com
Subscription Address: PO Box 420235, Palm Coast, FL 32142-0235 *Tel:* 386-246-3361 *Toll Free Tel:* 877-860-9145 *E-mail:* print@palmcoastd.com
Key Personnel
Ed-in-Chief: Zachary Petit
Art Dir: Adam Ladd
Sales Dir: Elayne Recupero *Tel:* 267-247-5874 *E-mail:* elayne.recupero@gmail.com
Graphic design & visual communication for the creators of this material.
First published 1940
Book Use: Reviews
Frequency: 4 issues/yr
Avg pages per issue: 112
Circulation: 50,000
$40/yr US, 55/yr CN, $81/yr foreign; $19.95/yr digital
ISSN: 445-120

PRISM international
Published by University of British Columbia
Creative Writing Program UBC, 1866 Main Mall, Buch E-462, Vancouver, BC V6T 1Z1, Canada
Tel: 778-822-2514 *Fax:* 778-822-3616
E-mail: prismcirculation@gmail.com
Web Site: www.prismmagazine.ca
Key Personnel
Exec Ed, Circ: Selina Boan
Exec Ed, Promos: Curtis LeBlanc
First published 1959
Frequency: Quarterly
Avg pages per issue: 90
Circulation: 1,200
$13/issue at newsstand; indivs: $35/yr, $55/2 yrs
Trim Size: 6 x 9
Ad Rates: Full page interior $220 (1 issue), $700 (1 yr, 4 issues); 1/2 page interior $160 (1 issue), $500 (1 yr, 4 issues); pre-printed inserts $50/100

Professional Photographer
Published by PPA Publications & Events Inc
229 Peachtree St NE, Suite 2200, Atlanta, GA 30303
Tel: 404-522-8600 *Toll Free Tel:* 800-786-6277 *Fax:* 404-614-6406
Web Site: www.ppa.com; www.ppmag.com
Key Personnel
Dir, Pubns: Jane Gaboury *E-mail:* jgaboury@ppa.com
Dir, Sales & Strategic Alliances: Wayne Jones *E-mail:* wjones@ppa.com
Illustrated feature articles about photographers, business & photographic techniques & trends; for practicing professional photographers (portrait, wedding, commercial, illustration, freelance, industrial, biomedical & scientific).
First published 1907
Frequency: Monthly
Avg pages per issue: 80
Circulation: 31,000 paid
$19.95/yr (digital), $29.95/yr US (digital & print combo), $45.95/yr CN (digital & print combo), $35.95/yr CN (print)

ProtoView
Published by Ringgold Inc
7515 NE Ambassador Place, Suite A, Portland, OR 97220
Tel: 503-281-9230 *Fax:* 503-287-4485
E-mail: info@protoview.com
Web Site: www.protoview.com
Key Personnel
Ed: Eithne O'Leyne *E-mail:* eithne.oleyne@ringgold.com
Subscription database incorporating reference & research & *SciTech Book News*. Abstracts, bibliographic & expanded metadata on scholary works in all media. ProtoView content licensed to Discovery channels, including vendors & related products owned by Baker & Taylor, ProQuest, Gale/Cengage, Powells & others.
ISSN: 2372-3424

Publishers Weekly
Published by PWxyz LLC
71 W 23 St, Suite 1608, New York, NY 10010
Tel: 212-377-5500 *Fax:* 212-377-2733
Web Site: www.publishersweekly.com
Key Personnel
Pres: George Slowik, Jr *E-mail:* george@publishersweekly.com
Publr: Cevin Bryerman *Tel:* 212-377-5703 *E-mail:* cbryerman@publishersweekly.com
VP, Busn Devt: Carl Pritzkat *E-mail:* cpritzkat@publishersweekly.com
VP, Opers: Patrick Turner *E-mail:* patrick@publishersweekly.com
Art Dir: Clive Chiu *E-mail:* cchiu@publishersweekly.com
Dir, Digital Opers: Craig Teicher *E-mail:* cteicher@publishersweekly.com
Edit Dir: Jim Milliot *Tel:* 212-377-5705 *E-mail:* jmilliot@publishersweekly.com
News Dir: Rachel Deahl *E-mail:* rdeahl@publishersweekly.com
Reviews Dir: Louisa Ermelino *E-mail:* lermelino@publishersweekly.com

Exec Ed: Jonathan Segura *E-mail:* jsegura@publishersweekly.com
Mng Ed: Dan Berchenko *E-mail:* dberchenko@publishersweekly.com
Sr Writer: Andrew R Albanese *E-mail:* aalbanese@publishersweekly.com
Sr Ed: Mark Rotella *E-mail:* mrotella@publishersweekly.com
Sr News Ed: Calvin Reid *E-mail:* creid@publishersweekly.com
News Ed: John Maher *E-mail:* jmaher@publishersweekly.com
Children's Book Ed: Diane Roback *E-mail:* roback@publishersweekly.com
Children's Reviews Ed: John A Sellers *E-mail:* jsellers@publishersweekly.com
Assoc Ed, Children's Books: Emma Kantor *E-mail:* ekantor@publishersweekly.com
Asst Ed, Children's Books: Matia Burnett *E-mail:* mburnett@publishersweekly.com
Features Ed: Carolyn Juris *E-mail:* cjuris@publishersweekly.com
Religion News Ed: Emma Koonse *E-mail:* ekoonse@publishersweekly.com
Religion Reviews Ed: Seth Satterlee *E-mail:* ssatterlee@publishersweekly.com
Sr Religion Ed: Lynn Garrett *E-mail:* lgarrett@publishersweekly.com
Sr Reviews Ed: Peter Cannon; Rose Fox
Deputy Reviews Ed: Gabe Habash
Reviews Ed: Alex Crowley; Annie Coreno; Everett Jones
BookLife Ed: Adam Boretz *E-mail:* aboretz@publishersweekly.com
Bookselling Ed: Ed Nawotka *E-mail:* enawotka@publishersweekly.com
Copy Ed: Hannah Kushnick *E-mail:* hkushnick@publishersweekly.com
Mktg/Licensing Mgr: Christi Cassidy *E-mail:* ccassidy@publishersweekly.com
News for the book trade.
First published 1872
Book Use: Reviews, excerpts, news, features & statistics
Frequency: Weekly (51 issues/yr)
Avg pages per issue: 112
Circulation: 16,000+ subscribers
$8/issue, $249.99/yr US, $299.99/yr CN, $399.99 yr/foreign, $209/yr digital
ISSN: 0000-0019 (print); 2150-4000 (digital)
Trim Size: 7 7/8 x 10 1/2

Publishing Perspectives
17 Battery Place, Suite 906, New York, NY 10004
Tel: 212-794-2851
Web Site: publishingperspectives.com
Key Personnel
Publr: Hannah Johnson *E-mail:* hannah@publishingperspectives.com
Ed-in-Chief: Porter Anderson *E-mail:* porter@publishingperspectives.com
Busn Devt Dir: Erin Cox *E-mail:* erin@publishingperspectives.com
Online trade magazine for the international publishing industry.
First published 2009
Frequency: Daily (Mon-Fri)
Free

Quill & Quire
Published by St Joseph Communications
111 Queen St E, Suite 320, Toronto, ON M5C 1S2, Canada
Tel: 416-364-3333 *Fax:* 416-595-5415
Web Site: www.quillandquire.com
Key Personnel
Publr: Alison Jones *Tel:* 416-364-3333 ext 3119 *E-mail:* ajones@quillandquire.com
Ed: Sue Carter
Articles & features on book selling, publishing & Canadian libraries for writers, booksellers, publishers & librarians. Includes section, *Books for Young People*, with news & reviews of children's books & authors; review section for books for adults.
First published 1935
Book Use: Reviews
Frequency: 10 issues/yr
Avg pages per issue: 56
Circulation: 4,500
$79.50/yr CN, $130/2 yrs CN, $125/yr outside CN
ISSN: 0033-6491

Quill & Scroll
Published by Quill and Scroll Society
University of Iowa, School of Journalism, E346 Adler Journalism Bldg, Iowa City, IA 52242
Tel: 319-335-3457 *Fax:* 319-335-3989
E-mail: quill-scroll@uiowa.edu
Web Site: quillandscroll.org
Key Personnel
Exec Dir: Vanessa Shelton *E-mail:* vanessa-shelton@uiowa.edu
Off Mgr: Judy M Hauge
Scholastic journalism publishing, editing, writing, design, legal, ethics, broadcast & multimedia production.
First published 1926
Frequency: Semiannual during school yr
Avg pages per issue: 24
Circulation: 9,300
$17/yr, $30/2 yrs
ISSN: 0033-6505

Quill Magazine
Published by The Society of Professional Journalists (SPJ)
Eugene S Pulliam National Journalism Ctr, 3909 N Meridian St, Indianapolis, IN 46208
Tel: 317-927-8000 *Fax:* 317-920-4789
E-mail: spj@spj.org
Web Site: www.spj.org/quill.asp; www.spj.org
Key Personnel
Dir, Educ: Scott Leadingham *Tel:* 317-640-9304 (cell) *E-mail:* sleadingham@spj.org
Examines the issues, changes & trends that influence the journalism profession.
Book Use: Book reviews
Frequency: 6 issues/yr
Circulation: 10,500
$75/yr, free for membs
ISSN: 0033-6475

Radio-TV Interview Report
Published by Bradley Communications Corp
390 Reed Rd, Broomall, PA 19008
Tel: 484-477-4220 *Toll Free Tel:* 800-989-1400 (ext 408)
E-mail: info@rtir.com
Web Site: www.rtir.com; www.rtironline.com
Key Personnel
Publr: Steve Harrison
Lists authors, experts, celebrities, entrepreneurs & others available for radio & TV appearances.
Frequency: 26 issues/yr
Circulation: 4,000
Free to qualified personnel

Reference & User Services Quarterly (RUSQ)
Published by Reference & User Services Association
Division of The American Library Association (ALA)
50 E Huron St, Chicago, IL 60611
SAN: 201-0062
Tel: 312-280-4395 *Toll Free Tel:* 800-545-2433 *Fax:* 312-280-5273
E-mail: rusa@ala.org
Web Site: www.ala.org/rusa
Key Personnel
Contact: Leighann Wood
First published 1960
Frequency: Quarterly
Circulation: 3,825
$25/issue, $65/yr CN & Mexico, $75/yr all other foreign
ISSN: 2163-5242
Avg reviews per issue: 35-40

Reference Desk
Published by International Encyclopedia Society
3689 Campbell Ct, Yorktown Heights, NY 10598
Tel: 914-962-3287
Key Personnel
Pres & Ed: George Thomas Kurian *E-mail:* gtkurian@aol.com
Articles on reference book publishing; reviews; quarterly record of reference books; publisher profiles.
First published 1991
Book Use: Book reviews; Index of publications
Frequency: Quarterly
Avg pages per issue: 32
Circulation: 902
$29/yr
ISSN: 1055-4777
Trim Size: 8 1/2 x 11
Ad Rates: Full page $300; 1/2 page $175
Ad Closing Date(s): March 30, June 30, Sept 30, Dec 30

Rosebud Magazine
Published by Rosebud Inc
PO Box 459, Cambridge, WI 53523
Tel: 608-423-9780
Web Site: www.rsbd.net
Key Personnel
Publr & Mng Ed: Roderick Clark *E-mail:* jrodclark@rsbd.net
Short story, poetry & nonfiction.
First published 1993
Book Use: Excerpts
Frequency: 3 issues/yr
Avg pages per issue: 136
Circulation: 6,000
$6.95/issue, $20/yr, $35/2yrs
ISSN: 1072-1681

Sales & Marketing Management Magazine
Published by Mach1 Business Media LLC
27020 Noble Rd, Excelsior, MN 55331
Mailing Address: PO Box 247, Excelsior, MN 55331-0247
Tel: 952-401-1283 *Fax:* 952-401-7899
Web Site: www.salesandmarketing.com
Key Personnel
Pres & Publr: Mike Murrell *Tel:* 952-401-1283 *E-mail:* mike@salesandmarketing.com
Ed-in-Chief: Paul Nolan *Tel:* 763-350-3411 *E-mail:* paul@salesandmarketing.com
Mktg Mgr: Vicki Blomquist *E-mail:* vicki@salesandmarketing.com
Print & online magazine providing information on major marketing, sales & management trends.
First published 1918
Book Use: Reviews
Frequency: Updated 2-3 times a week
Avg pages per issue: 36
Circulation: 25,000 print
Free online. Print free to qualified recipients. Otherwise $48 US; $67 CN; $146 other countries
ISSN: 0163-7517
Trim Size: 8 x 10 3/4
Ad Rates: 2-page spread: $13,995 (1x), $13,695 (3x), $13,265 (6x); full page: $8,995 (1x), $8,695 (3x), $8,265 (6x); 1/2 page $6,075 (1x), $5,765 (3x), $5,460 (6x)
Ad Closing Date(s): See media kit online

School Library Connection
Published by Libraries Unlimited
130 Cremona Dr, Suite C, Santa Barbara, CA 93117
Mailing Address: PO Box 1911, Santa Barbara, CA 93116-1911

Toll Free Tel: 800-368-6868 *Toll Free Fax:* 866-270-3856
E-mail: customerservice@abc-clio.com
Web Site: slc.librariesunlimited.com
Key Personnel
Publr: Kathryn C Suarez
Mng Ed: David Paige
K-12 school librarians & educators. See blog for information regarding ad rates & ad closing dates as well as submission & reviewer information: blog.schoollibraryconnection.com.
First published 1982
Book Use: Reviews; articles written by school librarians
Frequency: 6 print issues/school yr plus 4 online issues
Avg pages per issue: 80
$150/yr
ISSN: 1542-4715

School Library Journal
Published by Media Source Inc
123 William St, Suite 802, New York, NY 10038
Tel: 646-380-0752 *Toll Free Tel:* 800-588-1030 *Fax:* 646-380-0756
E-mail: slj@mediasourceinc.com; sljsubs@pcspublink.com
Web Site: www.slj.com; www.facebook.com/schoollibraryjournal; twitter.com/sljournal
Subscription Address: PO Box 461119, Escondido, CA 92046
Key Personnel
Ed-in-Chief: Rebecca T Miller *Tel:* 646-380-0738 *E-mail:* rmiller@mediasourceinc.com
Mng Ed: Luann Toth *Tel:* 646-380-0749 *E-mail:* ltoth@mediasourceinc.com
Articles about library service to children & young adults; reviews of new books & multimedia products for children & young adults by school & public librarians.
First published 1954
Book Use: Reviews
Frequency: 15 issues/yr
Avg pages per issue: 115
Circulation: 38,000
$11/issue newsstand, $136.99/yr US, $179.99/yr CN, $209.99/yr foreign
ISSN: 0362-8930

School Selection Guide
Published by Baker & Taylor Inc
2550 W Tyvola Rd, Suite 300, Charlotte, NC 28217
Mailing Address: PO Box 6885, Bridgewater, NJ 08807-0855
Tel: 704-998-3100 *Toll Free Tel:* 800-775-1800 (info servs) *Fax:* 704-998-3319
E-mail: btinfo@baker-taylor.com
Web Site: www.baker-taylor.com
Key Personnel
Mktg Specialist: Donna Heffner
Recommended & high-demand titles for school libraries. Online only.
Book Use: Selection for recommendation
Free

Science & Technology Libraries
Published by Routledge
Member of Taylor & Francis Group, an Informa Business
530 Walnut St, Suite 850, Philadelphia, PA 19106
Tel: 215-625-8900 *Toll Free Tel:* 800-354-1420 *Fax:* 215-207-0050
Web Site: www.tandfonline.com
Key Personnel
Ed-in-Chief: Tony Stankus
Topics relevant to management, operations, collections, services & staffing of specialized libraries in science & technology fields.
First published 1980
Book Use: Reviews
Frequency: Quarterly
Avg pages per issue: 105
Circulation: 343
Indivs: $180 print & online or print only, $158 online only; Instns: $730 print & online, $638 online only
ISSN: 0194-262X (print); 1541-1109 (online)

Scroll Original Artist Magazine
Published by Scroll Publications Inc
646 Saint Vrain Ave, Las Animas, CO 81054
Tel: 719-469-4847
E-mail: scrollpubl@outlook.com
Web Site: twitter.com/scrollpublinc
Key Personnel
Pres & Publr: Cherylann Gray
Original works by original people from all over the world.
First published 2000
Frequency: 6 issues/yr
Circulation: 3,700
$9.95/issue, $54.50/yr
Ad Rates: $3 per CR inch
Ad Closing Date(s): 15th of every month

The Serials Librarian
Published by Routledge
Member of Taylor & Francis Group, an Informa Business
530 Walnut St, Suite 850, Philadelphia, PA 19106
Tel: 215-625-8900 *Toll Free Tel:* 800-354-1420 *Fax:* 215-207-0050
Web Site: www.tandfonline.com
Key Personnel
Ed: Andrew Shroyer
Serials librarianship in academic, public, medical, law & other special libraries.
First published 1976
Book Use: Reviews
Frequency: Quarterly
Avg pages per issue: 154
Circulation: 712
Indivs: $341 print & online, $298 online only; Instns: $1,235 print & online, $1,080 online only
ISSN: 0361-526X (print); 1541-1095 (online)

Story Monsters Ink®
Published by Story Monsters Press
Imprint of Story Monsters LLC
4696 W Tyson St, Chandler, AZ 85226-2903
Tel: 480-940-8182 *Fax:* 480-940-8787
Web Site: www.StoryMonsters.com
Key Personnel
Pres: Linda F Radke *E-mail:* Linda@StoryMonsters.com
Ed-in-Chief: Cristy Bertini *Tel:* 413-477-1105 *E-mail:* cristy@storymonsters.com
E-mail article submissions to cristy@storymonsters.com.
First published 2014
Frequency: Monthly
Avg pages per issue: 64
Circulation: 130,000
$7.95/issue, $39/yr
ISSN: 2374-4413
Trim Size: 8.375 x 10.875
Ad Rates: $95-$1,600
Ad Closing Date(s): 1st of each month

subTerrain Magazine
Published by subTERRAIN Literary Collective Society
PO Box 3008, MPO, Vancouver, BC V6B 3X5, Canada
Tel: 604-876-8710 *Fax:* 604-879-2667
E-mail: subter@portal.ca
Web Site: www.subterrain.ca
Key Personnel
Ed-in-Chief: Brian Kaufman
Literary magazine with the motto "Strong Words for a Polite Nation".
First published 1988
Frequency: 3 issues/yr
Avg pages per issue: 80
Circulation: 4,000
$7/issue US, $8 issue/CN; $18/yr, $32/2 yrs (US & CN)
ISSN: 0840-7533
Trim Size: 8 1/2 x 11
Ad Rates: Back cover-color $900; inside front/back cover $800; inside full page color $847; 1/2 page color $575. Prices in Canadian dollars. For other sizes & B&W rates, visit www.subterrain.ca
Ad Closing Date(s): Feb 13, May 30, Oct 15

The Wordsworth Circle
Published by The Editorial Institute at Boston University
143 Bay St Rd, Rm 212, Boston, MA 02215
Web Site: www.bu.edu/editinst/about/the-wordsworth-circle
Key Personnel
Ed: Marilyn Gaull *E-mail:* mgaull@bu.edu
Peer-reviewed essays on all areas of British Romanticism.
First published 1970
Frequency: Quarterly
Avg pages per issue: 64
Circulation: 2,200
$35/yr US, $40/yr CN & foreign
ISSN: 0043-8006

World Literature Today
Published by University of Oklahoma
630 Parrington Oval, Suite 110, Norman, OK 73019-4033
Tel: 405-325-4531
E-mail: wlt@ou.edu
Web Site: www.worldliteraturetoday.org
Key Personnel
Exec Dir: Robert Con Davis-Undiano
Asst Dir & Ed-in-Chief: Daniel Simon *E-mail:* dsimon@ou.edu
Art Dir: Jennifer Blair
Mktg Dir, Progs & Devt: Terry D Stubblefield *E-mail:* tdstubb@ou.edu
Mng Ed: Michelle Johnson *E-mail:* lmjohnson@ou.edu
Book Reviews Ed: Robert Vollmar
Circ & Accts Specialist: Kay Blunck *E-mail:* kblunck@ou.edu
Critical essays & reviews covering all the major & most of the smaller languages & literatures of the world. Also available online.
First published 1927
Frequency: 6 issues/yr
Avg pages per issue: 96
Circulation: 300,000
$8.95/issue, $35/yr indivs, $60/yr foreign indivs, $135/yr instns, $205/yr foreign instns
ISSN: 0196-3570 (print); 1945-8134 (online)
Ad Rates: Full page $500; 1/2 page $350; inside cover (front or back) $700; back cover $1,000

The Writer
Published by Madavor Media LLC
25 Braintree Hill Office Park, Suite 404, Braintree, MA 02184
Tel: 617-706-9110 (cust serv) *Toll Free Tel:* 800-437-5828 (cust serv) *Fax:* 617-536-0102
E-mail: info@madavor.com
Web Site: www.writermag.com
Key Personnel
Editor-in-Chief: Alicia Anstead *Tel:* 617-315-9153 *E-mail:* aanstead@writermag.com
Mng Ed: Aubrey Everett *Tel:* 617-706-9077 *E-mail:* aeverett@madavor.com
Instructional articles on fiction, nonfiction & freelance writing, plus markets for ms sales. See guidelines on web site. Accept unsol mss.
First published 1887
Book Use: Regular book review section
Frequency: Monthly

Avg pages per issue: 60
Circulation: 30,000
$6.95/issue, $32.95/yr US, $42.95/yr CN, $44.95/yr elsewhere
ISSN: 0043-9517 (print); 2163-0046 (online)

Writer's Digest Magazine
Published by F+W Media Inc
10151 Carver Rd, Suite 200, Blue Ash, OH 45242
Tel: 513-531-2690 *Fax:* 513-891-7153
E-mail: writersdigest@fwmedia.com
Web Site: www.writersdigest.com
Subscription Address: PO Box 421365, Palm Coast, FL 32142-7104
Key Personnel
Ed: Jessica Strawser *E-mail:* jessica.strawser@fwcommunity.com

A publication focused on the craft & business of writing. No mail or phone queries. Submit full ms or pitch to writersdigest@fwmedia.com. No attachments.

First published 1920
Book Use: Excerpts, profiles of authors, tips & techniques
Frequency: 8 issues/yr
Avg pages per issue: 72
Circulation: 100,000
$19.96/yr US, $29.96/yr CN, $31.96/yr foreign
ISSN: 0043-9525
Trim Size: 7 3/4 x 10 1/2

Company Index

Included in this index are the names, addresses, telecommunication numbers and electronic addresses of the organizations included in this volume of *LMP*. Entries also include the page number(s) on which the listings appear.

Sections not represented in this index are **Imprints, Subsidiaries & Distributors; Calendar of Book Trade & Promotional Events; Reference Books for the Trade** and **Magazines for the Trade.**

A+ English LLC/Book-Editing.com/Book Editing Associates, PO Box 1369, Mansfield, TX 76063 *Tel:* 469-789-3030 *E-mail:* editingnetwork@gmail.com *Web Site:* www.editing-writing.com; www.book-editing.com; www.helpwithstatistics.com; www.apawriting.com; childrensbookeditors.com; www.christianeditorsnetwork.com; dissertationwriting.com; statisticstutors.com, pg 487

A-R Editions Inc, 1600 Aspen Commons, Suite 100, Middleton, WI 53562 *Tel:* 608-836-9000 *Toll Free Tel:* 800-736-0070 (North America book orders only) *Fax:* 608-831-8200 *E-mail:* info@areditions.com; orders@areditions.com *Web Site:* www.areditions.com, pg 1

A 2 Z Press LLC, 445 Cortez Ave, Deleon Springs, FL 32130 *Tel:* 386-681-7402 *Web Site:* www.a2zpress.com; www.terriesizemorestoryteller.com, pg 1

A Westport Wordsmith, 101 Winfield St, Norwalk, CT 06855 *Tel:* 203-939-9484 *E-mail:* pj104daily@aol.com, pg 487

AAA Books Unlimited, 3060 Blackthorn Rd, Riverwoods, IL 60015 *Tel:* 847-444-1220 *Fax:* 847-607-8335 *Web Site:* www.aaabooksunlimited.com, pg 505

AAA Photos, 401 Ocean Dr, Unit 804, Miami Beach, FL 33139 *Tel:* 305-534-0804 *Web Site:* www.photosphotos.net, pg 487

AAAI Press, 2275 E Bayshore Rd, Suite 160, Palo Alto, CA 94303 *Tel:* 650-328-3123 *Fax:* 650-321-4457 *E-mail:* publications17@aaai.org *Web Site:* www.aaaipress.org; www.aaai.org, pg 1

AACC International, 3340 Pilot Knob Rd, St Paul, MN 55121 *Tel:* 651-454-7250 *Fax:* 651-454-0766 *E-mail:* aacc@scisoc.org *Web Site:* www.aaccnet.org, pg 1

AAH Graphics Inc, 9293 Fort Valley Rd, Fort Valley, VA 22652-2020 *Tel:* 540-933-6211 *Fax:* 540-933-6523 *E-mail:* srhunter@aahgraphics.com *Web Site:* www.aahgraphics.com, pg 487

The Aaland Agency, PO Box 849, Inyokern, CA 93527-0849 *Tel:* 760-384-3910 *Web Site:* www.the-aaland-agency.com, pg 505

AAP PreK-12 Learning Group, 455 Massachusetts Ave NW, Suite 700, Washington, DC 20001 *Tel:* 267-351-4310 *Fax:* 267-351-4317 *E-mail:* prek12learning@publishers.org *Web Site:* www.aepweb.org, pg 553

AAPG (American Association of Petroleum Geologists), 1444 S Boulder Ave, Tulsa, OK 74119 *Tel:* 918-584-2555 *Toll Free Tel:* 800-364-AAPG (364-2274) *Fax:* 918-580-2665 *E-mail:* info@aapg.org *Web Site:* www.aapg.org, pg 1

Aaron-Spear, PO Box 42, Brooksville, ME 04617 *Tel:* 207-326-8764, pg 487

AAUP Book, Jacket & Journal Design Show, 1412 Broadway, Suite 2135, New York, NY 10018 *Tel:* 212-989-1010 *Fax:* 212-989-0275 *E-mail:* info@aaupnet.org *Web Site:* www.aaupnet.org, pg 625

ABAC/ALAC, 368 Dalhousie St, Suite 301, Ottawa, ON K1N 7G3, Canada *Tel:* 416-364-2376 *E-mail:* info@abac.org *Web Site:* www.abac.org, pg 553

Abaris Books, 70 New Canaan Ave, Norwalk, CT 06850 *Tel:* 203-838-8402 *Fax:* 203-857-0730 *E-mail:* abaris@abarisbooks.com *Web Site:* abarisbooks.com, pg 2

Abbeville Press, 116 W 23 St, 5th fl, New York, NY 10011 *Tel:* 212-366-5585 *Toll Free Tel:* 800-ART-BOOK (278-2665); 800-343-4499 (orders) *Fax:* 646-375-2359 *Toll Free Fax:* 800-351-5073 (orders) *E-mail:* abbeville@abbeville.com; sales@abbeville.com; marketing@abbeville.com; rights@abbeville.com *Web Site:* www.abbeville.com, pg 2

Abbeville Publishing Group, 137 Varick St, Suite 504, New York, NY 10013-1105 *Tel:* 212-366-5585 *Toll Free Tel:* 800-ART-BOOK (278-2665) *Fax:* 212-366-6966 *E-mail:* abbeville@abbeville.com; marketing@abbeville.com; sales@abbeville.com; rights@abbeville.com *Web Site:* www.abbeville.com, pg 2

ABC-CLIO, 130 Cremona Dr, Santa Barbara, CA 93117 *Tel:* 805-968-1911 *Toll Free Tel:* 800-368-6868 *Fax:* 805-685-9685 *Toll Free Fax:* 866-270-3856 *E-mail:* customerservice@abc-clio.com *Web Site:* www.abc-clio.com, pg 2

ABDO Publishing Group, 8000 W 78 St, Suite 310, Edina, MN 55439 *Tel:* 952-831-2120 *Toll Free Tel:* 800-800-1312 *Toll Free Fax:* 800-862-3480 *E-mail:* customerservice@abdopublishing.com *Web Site:* abdopublishing.com, pg 2

Dominick Abel Literary Agency Inc, 146 W 82 St, Suite 1-A, New York, NY 10024 *Tel:* 212-877-0710 *Fax:* 212-595-3133 *E-mail:* agency@dalainc.com *Web Site:* www.dalainc.com, pg 505

Aberdeen Bay, 3848 Dominion Mill Dr, Alexandria, VA 22304 *Tel:* 703-473-1392 *Web Site:* aberdeenbay.azurewebsites.net, pg 2

Abingdon Press, 201 Eighth Ave S, Nashville, TN 37203-3919 *Tel:* 615-749-6000 (academic books) *Toll Free Tel:* 800-251-3320 *Fax:* 615-749-6056 (academic books) *Toll Free Fax:* 800-836-7802 (orders) *E-mail:* orders@abingdonpress.com *Web Site:* www.abingdonpress.com, pg 2

About Books Inc, 1001 Taurus Dr, Colorado Springs, CO 80906 *Tel:* 719-445-8875 *Fax:* 719-213-2602 *Web Site:* www.about-books.com, pg 487

J M Abraham Poetry Award, 1113 Marginal Rd, Halifax, NS B3H 4P7, Canada *Tel:* 902-423-8116 *Fax:* 902-422-0881 *E-mail:* contact@writers.ns.ca *Web Site:* writers.ns.ca, pg 625

Abrams Artists Agency, 275 Seventh Ave, 26th fl, New York, NY 10001 *Tel:* 646-486-4600 *Fax:* 646-486-0100 *E-mail:* literary@abramsartny.com *Web Site:* www.abramsartists.com, pg 505

Harry N Abrams Inc, 195 Broadway, 9th fl, New York, NY 10007 *Tel:* 212-206-7715 *Toll Free Tel:* 800-345-1359 *Fax:* 212-519-1210 *E-mail:* abrams@abramsbooks.com *Web Site:* www.abramsbooks.com, pg 2

Abrams Learning Trends, 16310 Bratton Lane, Suite 250, Austin, TX 78728-2403 *Toll Free Tel:* 800-227-9120 *Toll Free Fax:* 800-737-3322 *E-mail:* customerservice@abramslearningtrends.com (orders, cust serv); contactus@abramslearningtrends.com *Web Site:* www.abramslearningtrends.com (orders, cust serv), pg 3

Acacia House Publishing Services Ltd, 51 Chestnut Ave, Brantford, ON N3T 4C3, Canada *Tel:* 519-752-0978 *Fax:* 519-752-0978, pg 505

Academic Press, 50 Hampshire St, 5th fl, Cambridge, MA 02139 *Tel:* 781-663-5200 *Fax:* 937-247-0808 *Web Site:* store.elsevier.com/Academic-Press, pg 3

Academica Press, 1727 Massachusetts Ave NW, Suite 507, Washington, DC 20036 *Tel:* 978-829-2577 *E-mail:* editorial@academicapress.com *Web Site:* www.academicapress.com, pg 3

Academy Chicago, 814 N Franklin St, Chicago, IL 60610 *Tel:* 312-337-0747 *Toll Free Tel:* 800-888-4741 (orders) *Fax:* 312-337-5110 *E-mail:* frontdesk@chicagoreviewpress.com *Web Site:* www.chicagoreviewpress.com, pg 3

The Academy of American Poets Inc, 75 Maiden Lane, Suite 901, New York, NY 10038 *Tel:* 212-274-0343 *Fax:* 212-274-9427 *E-mail:* academy@poets.org *Web Site:* www.poets.org, pg 553

Academy of Motion Picture Arts & Sciences (AMPAS), 8949 Wilshire Blvd, Beverly Hills, CA 90211 *Tel:* 310-247-3000 *Fax:* 310-859-9619 *E-mail:* ampas@oscars.org *Web Site:* www.oscars.org, pg 553

Academy of Nutrition & Dietetics, 120 S Riverside Plaza, Suite 2000, Chicago, IL 60606-6995 *Tel:* 312-899-0040 (ext 5000) *Toll Free Tel:* 800-877-1600 *E-mail:* sales@eatright.org *Web Site:* www.eatright.org, pg 3

Access Copyright, The Canadian Copyright Licensing Agency, 56 Wellesley St W, Suite 401A, Toronto, ON M5S 2S3, Canada *Tel:* 416-868-1620 *Toll Free Tel:* 800-893-5777 *Fax:* 416-868-1621 *E-mail:* info@accesscopyright.ca *Web Site:* www.accesscopyright.ca, pg 553

Access Editorial Services, 1133 Broadway, Suite 528, New York, NY 10010 *Tel:* 212-255-7306 *E-mail:* wiseword@juno.com, pg 487

Acclaim Film Script Competition, 300 Central Ave, Suite 501, St Petersburg, FL 33701 *Web Site:* acclaimscripts.com, pg 625

Acclaim TV Script Competition, 300 Central Ave, Suite 501, St Petersburg, FL 33701 *Web Site:* acclaimscripts.com, pg 625

Accuity, 4709 W Golf Rd, Skokie, IL 60076 *Tel:* 847-676-9600 *Toll Free Tel:* 800-321-3373 *Fax:* 847-933-8101 *E-mail:* custserv@accuity.com; sales@accuity.com *Web Site:* www.accuity.com, pg 3

Accurate Writing & More, 16 Barstow Lane, Hadley, MA 01035 *Tel:* 413-586-2388 *Web Site:* www.accuratewriting.com; www.frugalmarketing.com; www.goingbeyondsustainability.com; www.transformpreneur.com; www.greenandprofitable.com; www.twitter.com/shelhorowitz, pg 487

Alice B Acheson's Workshops for Writers, Illustrators & Photographers, PO Box 735, Friday Harbor, WA 98250 *Tel:* 360-378-2815 *E-mail:* aliceba7@gmail.com, pg 609

Milton Acorn Poetry Awards, 81 Prince St, Charlottetown, PE C1A 4R3, Canada *E-mail:* peiliteraryawards@gmail.com *Web Site:* www.peiwritersguild.com, pg 625

Acres USA, 501 Eighth Ave, Greenley, CO 80631 *Tel:* 512-892-4400 *Toll Free Tel:* 800-355-5313 *E-mail:* orders@acresusa.com; editor@acresusa.com; info@acresusa.com *Web Site:* www.acresusa.com, pg 4

Acroterion Books, 5305 Harvard Rd, Lawrence, KS 66049-4781 *Tel:* 785-917-0773 *E-mail:* info@acroterionbooks.com *Web Site:* www.acroterionbooks.com, pg 477

ACTA Press, 2451 Dieppe Ave SW, Bldg B1, Suite 230, Calgary, AB T3E 7K1, Canada *Tel:* 403-288-1195 *Fax:* 403-247-6851 *E-mail:* journals@actapress.com; publish@actapress.com; sales@actapress.com *Web Site:* www.actapress.com, pg 445

ACTA Publications, 4848 N Clark St, Chicago, IL 60640 *Tel:* 773-271-1030 *Toll Free Tel:* 800-397-2282 *Fax:* 773-271-7399 *Toll Free Fax:* 800-397-0079 *E-mail:* info@actapublications.com *Web Site:* www.actapublications.com, pg 4

ACU Press, 1648 Campus Ct, Abilene, TX 79601 *Tel:* 325-674-2720 *Toll Free Tel:* 877-816-4455 *Web Site:* www.acupressbooks.com; www.leafwoodpublishers.com, pg 4

Adams & Ambrose Publishing, PO Box 259684, Madison, WI 53725-9684 *Tel:* 608-977-1825 *E-mail:* info@adamsambrose.com, pg 4

Herbert Baxter Adams Prize, 400 "A" St SE, Washington, DC 20003 *Tel:* 202-544-2422 *Fax:* 202-544-8307 *E-mail:* awards@historians.org *Web Site:* www.historians.org, pg 625

Adams Media, 57 Littlefield St, Avon, MA 02322 *Tel:* 508-427-7100 *Web Site:* www.simonandschuster.com, pg 4

Adams-Pomeroy Press, 103 N Jackson St, Albany, WI 53502 *Tel:* 608-862-3645 *Toll Free Tel:* 877-862-3645 *Fax:* 608-862-3647 *E-mail:* adamspomeroy@tds.net, pg 477

ADASI Publishing Co, 13 Riverdale Ave, Dover, NH 03820-4698 *Tel:* 603-866-9426 *E-mail:* info@adasi.com *Web Site:* www.adasi.com, pg 4

Jane Addams Children's Book Award, 777 United Nations Plaza, 6th fl, New York, NY 10017 *Tel:* 212-682-8830 *E-mail:* info@janeaddamspeace.org *Web Site:* www.janeaddamspeace.org, pg 625

Addicus Books Inc, PO Box 45327, Omaha, NE 68145 *Tel:* 402-330-7493 *Fax:* 402-330-1707 *E-mail:* info@addicusbooks.com; addicusbks@aol.com *Web Site:* www.addicusbooks.com, pg 4

J Adel Art & Design, 586 Ramapo Rd, Teaneck, NJ 07666 *Tel:* 201-836-2606 *E-mail:* jadelnj@aol.com, pg 487

Adirondack Mountain Club (ADK), 814 Goggins Rd, Lake George, NY 12845-4117 *Tel:* 518-668-4447 *Toll Free Tel:* 800-395-8080 *Fax:* 518-668-3746 *E-mail:* info@adk.org *Web Site:* www.adk.org, pg 4

Adler Publishing Inc, 46937 Monarch Dr, Parker, CO 80138 *Tel:* 303-660-2158 *Toll Free Tel:* 800-660-5107 (sales & orders) *E-mail:* customerservice@adlerpublishing.com; orders@4wdbooks.com *Web Site:* www.adlerpublishing.com, pg 4

Advance Publishing Inc, 6950 Fulton St, Houston, TX 77022 *Tel:* 713-695-0600 *Toll Free Tel:* 800-917-9630 *Fax:* 713-695-8585 *E-mail:* info@advancepublishing.com *Web Site:* www.advancepublishing.com, pg 4

Adventure House, 914 Laredo Rd, Silver Spring, MD 20901 *Tel:* 301-754-1589 *Web Site:* www.adventurehouse.com, pg 5

AdventureKEEN, 2204 First Ave S, Suite 102, Birmingham, AL 35233 *Tel:* 763-689-9800 *Toll Free Tel:* 800-678-7006 *Fax:* 763-689-9039 *Toll Free Fax:* 877-374-9016 *E-mail:* info@adventurewithkeen.com *Web Site:* adventurewithkeen.com, pg 5

Adventures Unlimited Press (AUP), One Adventure Place, Kempton, IL 60946 *Tel:* 815-253-6390 *Fax:* 815-253-6300 *E-mail:* auphq@frontiernet.net; info@adventuresunlimitedpress.com *Web Site:* www.adventuresunlimitedpress.com, pg 5

Advertising Research Foundation (ARF), 432 Park Ave S, 4th fl, New York, NY 10016-8013 *Tel:* 212-751-5656 *Fax:* 212-319-5265 *E-mail:* info@thearf.org; jar@thearf.org (edit) *Web Site:* www.thearf.org, pg 553

Aegean Publishing Co, PO Box 6790, Santa Barbara, CA 93160 *Tel:* 805-964-6669 *Fax:* 805-683-4798 *E-mail:* info@aegeanpublishing.com *Web Site:* aegeanpublishing.com, pg 5

The AEI Press, 1789 Massachusetts Ave NW, Washington, DC 20036 *Tel:* 202-862-5800 *Fax:* 202-862-7177 *Web Site:* www.aei.org, pg 5

AEIOU Inc, 894 Piermont Ave, Piermont, NY 10968 *Tel:* 845-680-5380, pg 487

Aevitas Creative Management, 19 W 21 St, Suite 501, New York, NY 10010 *Tel:* 212-765-6900 *Web Site:* aevitascreative.com, pg 506

AFB Press, 1401 S Clark St, Suite 730, Arlington, VA 22202 *Tel:* 304-710-3043 *Toll Free Tel:* 800-232-3044 (orders) *Fax:* 917-210-3979 (orders) *E-mail:* afbpress@afb.net *Web Site:* www.afb.org, pg 5

AFCP's Awards, 135 Old Cove Rd, Suite 210, Liverpool, NY 13090 *Toll Free Tel:* 877-203-2327 *Fax:* 781-459-7770 *E-mail:* afcp@afcp.org *Web Site:* www.afcp.org, pg 625

Africa World Press Inc, 541 W Ingham Ave, Suite B, Trenton, NJ 08638 *Tel:* 609-695-3200 *Fax:* 609-695-6466 *E-mail:* customerservice@africaworldpressbooks.com *Web Site:* www.africaworldpressbooks.com, pg 5

African American Images, PO Box 1799, Chicago Heights, IL 60412 *Tel:* 708-672-4909 (cust serv) *Fax:* 708-672-0466 *E-mail:* customersvc@africanamericanimages.com *Web Site:* www.africanamericanimages.com, pg 5

Africana Homestead Legacy Publishers Inc, 926 Haddonfield Rd, Suite E, No 329, Cherry Hill, NJ 08002 *Tel:* 856-673-0363 *Fax:* 856-486-1135 *E-mail:* customer-service@ahlpub.com; sales@ahlpub.com; editors@ahlpub.com *Web Site:* www.ahlpub.com, pg 5

Agatha Awards, PO Box 8007, Gaithersburg, MD 20898-8007 *E-mail:* malicedomesticpr@gmail.com *Web Site:* www.malicedomestic.org, pg 625

Ageless Press, 3759 Collins St, Sarasota, FL 34232 *Tel:* 941-365-1367 *Fax:* 941-365-1367 *E-mail:* irishope@comcast.net, pg 5

Agency Chicago, 332 S Michigan Ave, Suite 1032, No A600, Chicago, IL 60604 *E-mail:* ernsant@aol.com, pg 506

Agent's Ink, PO Box 4956, Fresno, CA 93744-4956 *Tel:* 559-438-1883 *Fax:* 559-438-8289 *Web Site:* agents-ink.com, pg 506

Aggiornamento Award, 8550 United Plaza Blvd, Suite 1001, Baton Rouge, LA 70809 *Tel:* 225-408-4417 *E-mail:* cla2@cathla.org *Web Site:* cathla.org, pg 625

The Ahearn Agency Inc, 2021 Pine St, New Orleans, LA 70118 *Tel:* 504-861-8395 *Fax:* 504-866-6434 *Web Site:* www.ahearnagency.com, pg 506

Ahsahta Press, Boise State University, Mail Stop 1525, 1910 University Dr, Boise, ID 83725-1525 *Tel:* 208-426-3134 *E-mail:* ahsahta@boisestate.edu *Web Site:* ahsahtapress.org, pg 6

AIC Publications, PO Box 181467, Arlington, TX 76002-1467 *E-mail:* submissions@aicpublications.com *Web Site:* aicpublications.com, pg 477

AICPA Professional Publications, 220 Leigh Farm Rd, Durham, NC 27707 *Tel:* 919-402-4500 *Toll Free Tel:* 888-777-7077 (memb serv ctr) *Fax:* 919-402-4505 *Toll Free Fax:* 800-362-5066 (memb serv ctr) *E-mail:* acquisitions@aicpa.org; service@aicpa.org *Web Site:* www.aicpa.org, pg 6

AIGA 50 Books|50 Covers, 233 Broadway, Suite 1740, New York, NY 10279 *Tel:* 212-807-1990 *Fax:* 212-807-1799 *E-mail:* competitions@aiga.org *Web Site:* www.aiga.org, pg 625

AIGA, the professional association for design, 233 Broadway, Suite 1740, New York, NY 10279 *Tel:* 212-807-1990 *Fax:* 212-807-1799 *E-mail:* general@aiga.org *Web Site:* www.aiga.org, pg 553

Aitken Alexander Associates LLC, 30 Vandam St, Suite 5A, New York, NY 10013 *Web Site:* www.aitkenalexander.co.uk, pg 506

AJL Judaica Bibliography Award, PO Box 1118, Teaneck, NJ 07666 *Tel:* 201-371-3255 *E-mail:* info@jewishlibraries.org *Web Site:* jewishlibraries.org, pg 626

AJL Judaica Reference Award, PO Box 1118, Teaneck, NJ 07666 *Tel:* 201-371-3255 *E-mail:* info@jewishlibraries.org *Web Site:* jewishlibraries.org, pg 626

AJL Scholarship, PO Box 1118, Teaneck, NJ 07666 *Tel:* 201-371-3255 *E-mail:* scholarship@jewishlibraries.org; info@jewishlibraries.org *Web Site:* jewishlibraries.org, pg 626

AK Press Distribution, 370 Ryan Ave, Unit 100, Chico, CA 95973 *Tel:* 510-208-1700 *Fax:* 510-208-1701 *E-mail:* info@akpress.org *Web Site:* www.akpress.org, pg 6

Akashic Books, 232 Third St, Suite A-115, Brooklyn, NY 11215 *Tel:* 718-643-9193 *Fax:* 718-643-9195 *E-mail:* info@akashicbooks.com *Web Site:* www.akashicbooks.com, pg 6

Akron Poetry Prize, 120 E Mill St, Suite 415, Akron, OH 44308 *Tel:* 330-972-6960 *Fax:* 330-972-8364 *E-mail:* uapress@uakron.edu *Web Site:* www.uakron.edu/uapress/akron-poetry-prize, pg 626

ALA Neal-Schuman, 50 E Huron St, Chicago, IL 60611 *Toll Free Tel:* 800-545-2433 *Fax:* 312-280-5275 *E-mail:* editionsmarketing@ala.org *Web Site:* www.alastore.ala.org, pg 6

Alabama Artists Fellowship Awards, 201 Monroe St, Suite 110, Montgomery, AL 36130-1800 *Tel:* 334-242-4076 *Fax:* 334-240-3269, pg 626

Alaska Native Language Center, PO Box 757680, Fairbanks, AK 99775-7680 *Fax:* 907-474-6586 *E-mail:* uaf-anlc@alaska.edu (orders) *Web Site:* www.uaf.edu/anlc, pg 6

Alazar Press, 201 Orchard Lane, Carrboro, NC 27510 *Tel:* 919-274-0653 *E-mail:* alazar.press@gmail.com *Web Site:* www.alazar-press.com, pg 477

Albert Whitman & Co, 250 S Northwest Hwy, Suite 320, Park Ridge, IL 60068 *Tel:* 847-232-2800 *Toll Free Tel:* 800-255-7675 *Fax:* 847-581-0039 *E-mail:* mail@albertwhitman.com *Web Site:* www.albertwhitman.com, pg 6

Alberta Book Awards, 10523 100 Ave, Edmonton, AB T5J 0A8, Canada *Tel:* 780-424-5060 *E-mail:* info@bookpublishers.ab.ca *Web Site:* www.bookpublishers.ab.ca, pg 626

Rodelinde Albrecht, PO Box 444, Lenox Dale, MA 01242-0444 *Tel:* 413-243-4350 *E-mail:* rodelinde@gmail.com, pg 487

Alcuin Society, PO Box 3216, Sta Terminal, Vancouver, BC V6B 3X8, Canada *Tel:* 604-732-5403 *E-mail:* info@alcuinsociety.com; awards@alcuinsociety.com *Web Site:* alcuinsociety.com, pg 553

Alcuin Society Awards for Excellence in Book Design in Canada, PO Box 3216, Sta Terminal, Vancouver, BC V6B 3X8, Canada *Tel:* 604-732-5403 *E-mail:* awards@alcuinsociety.com *Web Site:* alcuinsociety.com, pg 626

Alex Awards, 50 E Huron St, Chicago, IL 60611 *Tel:* 312-280-4390 *Toll Free Tel:* 800-545-2433 *Fax:* 312-280-5276 *E-mail:* yalsa@ala.org *Web Site:* www.ala.org/yalsa/alex-awards, pg 626

The Alexander Graham Bell Association for the Deaf & Hard of Hearing, 3417 Volta Place NW, Washington, DC 20007 *Tel:* 202-337-5220 *Toll Free Tel:* 866-337-5220 (orders) *Fax:* 202-337-8314 *E-mail:* info@agbell.org; publications@agbell.org *Web Site:* www.agbell.org, pg 6

Alexander Street, a ProQuest Company, 3212 Duke St, Alexandria, VA 22314 *Tel:* 703-212-8520 *Toll Free Tel:* 800-889-5937 *Fax:* 703-940-6584 *E-mail:* sales@alexanderstreet.com; marketing@alexanderstreet.com; info@alexanderstreet.com *Web Site:* alexanderstreet.com, pg 7

Alfred Music Publishing, PO Box 10003, Van Nuys, CA 91410 *Tel:* 818-891-5999 (dealer sales, intl); 818-891-2452 (cust serv) *Toll Free Tel:* 800-292-6122 (dealer sales, US & CN) *Fax:* 818-893-5560 (dealer sales);

818-830-6252 (cust serv) *Toll Free Fax:* 800-632-1928 (dealer sales) *E-mail:* customerservice@alfred.com; sales@alfred.com *Web Site:* www.alfred.com, pg 7

Algonquin Books, 400 Silver Cedar Ct, Suite 300, Chapel Hill, NC 27514-1585 *Tel:* 919-967-0108 *Fax:* 919-933-0272 *E-mail:* inquiry@algonquin.com *Web Site:* www.workman.com/algonquin, pg 7

Algora Publishing, 1732 First Ave, No 20330, New York, NY 10128 *Tel:* 212-678-0232 *Fax:* 212-666-3682 *E-mail:* editors@algora.com *Web Site:* www.algora.com, pg 7

Nelson Algren Awards, Chicago Tribune, TT200, 435 N Michigan Ave, Chicago, IL 60611 *Toll Free Tel:* 800-874-2863 (classifieds) *Fax:* 312-222-5816 *Web Site:* www.chicagotribune.com/about; algren.submittable.com, pg 626

Alice James Books, 114 Prescott St, Farmington, ME 04938 *Tel:* 207-778-7071 *Fax:* 207-778-7766 *E-mail:* info@alicejamesbooks.org *Web Site:* alicejamesbooks.org, pg 7

All About Kids Publishing, PO Box 159, Gilroy, CA 95021 *Tel:* 408-337-1152 *E-mail:* info@allaboutkidspub.com *Web Site:* www.allaboutkidspub.com, pg 7

All Things That Matter Press, 79 Jones Rd, Somerville, ME 04348 *E-mail:* allthingsthatmatterpress@gmail.com *Web Site:* www.allthingsthatmatterpress.com, pg 7

Alliance for Audited Media (AAM), 48 W Seegers Rd, Arlington Heights, IL 60005 *Tel:* 224-366-6939 *Fax:* 224-366-6949 *Web Site:* www.auditedmedia.com, pg 553

Alliance for Audited Media (AAM), Canadian Office, 151 Bloor St W, Suite 850, Toronto, ON M5S 1S4, Canada *Tel:* 416-962-5840 *Fax:* 416-962-5844 *Web Site:* auditedmedia.com, pg 554

Alliance for Women in Media (AWM), 1250 24 St NW, Suite 300, Washington, DC 20037 *Tel:* 202-750-3664 *Fax:* 202-750-3664 *E-mail:* info@allwomeninmedia.org *Web Site:* allwomeninmedia.org, pg 554

Alligator Juniper's National Writing Contest, 220 Grove Ave, Prescott, AZ 86301 *Tel:* 928-350-2012 *E-mail:* alligatorjuniper@prescott.edu *Web Site:* alligatorjuniper.wordpress.com, pg 626

Allium Press of Chicago, 1530 Elgin Ave, Forest Park, IL 60130 *Tel:* 708-689-9323 *E-mail:* info@alliumpress.com *Web Site:* www.alliumpress.com, pg 7

Alloy Entertainment LLC, 1325 Avenue of the Americas, 29th fl, New York, NY 10019 *E-mail:* collaborative@alloyentertainment.com, pg 8

Allworth Press, 307 W 36 St, 11th fl, New York, NY 10018 *Tel:* 212-643-6816 *Fax:* 212-643-6819 *Web Site:* www.allworth.com, pg 8

AllWrite Advertising & Publishing, 241 Peachtree St NE, Suite 400, Atlanta, GA 30303 *Tel:* 404-221-0703 *Fax:* 770-284-8986 *E-mail:* questions@allwritepublishing.com; support@allwritepublishing.com (orders & returns) *Web Site:* allwritepublishing.com, pg 8

AllWrite Advertising & Publishing, 241 Peachtree St NE, Suite 400, Atlanta, GA 30303 *Tel:* 404-221-0703 *Fax:* 770-284-8986 *E-mail:* questions@allwritepublishing.com *Web Site:* www.e-allwrite.com, pg 487

Jeanette Almada, 452 W Aldine, Unit 215, Chicago, IL 60657 *Tel:* 773-404-9350 *E-mail:* jmalmada@sbcglobal.net, pg 487

Alpha Books, 6081 E 82 St, 4th fl, Indianapolis, IN 46250 *Tel:* 212-366-2000 *E-mail:* ecommerce@us.penguingroup.com *Web Site:* www.dk.com; www.idiotguides.com, pg 8

Alpha II LLC, 7480 Halcyon Pointe Dr, Suite 204, Montgomery, AL 36117 *Tel:* 334-260-8150 *Toll Free Tel:* 800-825-7421 *Toll Free Fax:* 800-305-8030 *E-mail:* sales@alphaii.com *Web Site:* www.alphaii.com, pg 8

Alpine Publications Inc, PO Box 188, Crawford, CO 81415 *Tel:* 970-921-5005 *Toll Free Tel:* 800-777-7257 *E-mail:* alpinepublishing@aol.com; customerservice@alpinepub.com *Web Site:* www.alpinepub.com, pg 8

ALSC Baker & Taylor Summer Reading Grant, 50 E Huron St, Chicago, IL 60611-2795 *Tel:* 312-280-2163 *Toll Free Tel:* 800-545-2433 *Fax:* 312-440-9374; 312-280-5271 *E-mail:* alsc@ala.org *Web Site:* www.ala.org/alsc, pg 626

AltaMira Press, 4501 Forbes Blvd, Suite 200, Lanham, MD 20706 *Tel:* 301-459-3366 *Toll Free Tel:* 800-462-6420 (cust serv) *Fax:* 301-429-5748 *E-mail:* custserv@rowman.com *Web Site:* www.altamirapress.com, pg 8

AMACOM Books, 1601 Broadway, New York, NY 10019-7420 *Tel:* 212-586-8100 *Toll Free Tel:* 800-250-5308 (cust serv) *Fax:* 212-903-8083; 518-891-2372 (orders) *E-mail:* pubs_cust_serv@amanet.org *Web Site:* www.amacombooks.org, pg 8

Amadeus Press/Hal Leonard Performing Arts Publishing Group, 33 Plymouth St, Suite 302, Montclair, NJ 07042 *Tel:* 973-337-5034 *Toll Free Tel:* 800-524-4425 *E-mail:* info@halleonardbooks.com *Web Site:* www.amadeuspress.com; www.halleonardbooks.com, pg 8

Amakella Publishing, PO Box 9445, Arlington, VA 22219 *Tel:* 202-239-8381 *E-mail:* info@amakella.com *Web Site:* www.amakella.com, pg 9

Frank Amato Publications Inc, 4040 SE Wister St, Milwaukie, OR 97222 *Tel:* 503-653-8108 *Toll Free Tel:* 800-541-9498 *Fax:* 503-653-2766 *E-mail:* customerservice@amatobooks.com; info@amatobooks.com *Web Site:* www.amatobooks.com, pg 9

Ambassador International, 411 University Ridge, Suite B14, Greenville, SC 29601 *Tel:* 864-751-4844 *E-mail:* info@emeraldhouse.com; publisher@emeraldhouse.com (ms submissions); sales@emeraldhouse.com (orders/order inquiries) *Web Site:* ambassador-international.com; www.facebook.com/AmbassadorIntl; twitter.com/ambassadorintl, pg 9

The Ambassador Richard C Holbrooke Distinguished Achievement Award, PO Box 461, Wright Brothers Branch, Dayton, OH 45409-0461 *Tel:* 937-298-5072 *E-mail:* sharon.rab@daytonliterarypeaceprize.org *Web Site:* www.daytonliterarypeaceprize.org/holbrooke.htm, pg 627

Amber Lotus Publishing, PO Box 11329, Portland, OR 97211 *Tel:* 503-284-6400 *Toll Free Tel:* 800-326-2375 (orders only) *Fax:* 503-284-6417 *E-mail:* info@amberlotus.com *Web Site:* www.amberlotus.com, pg 9

America West Publishers, 5872 Government Way, Unit 1-10, Dalton Gardens, ID 83814 *Tel:* 208-762-0633 *Toll Free Tel:* 800-729-4131 *Web Site:* www.nohoax.com, pg 9

American Academy of Arts & Sciences (AAAS), Norton's Woods, 136 Irving St, Cambridge, MA 02138 *Tel:* 617-576-5000 *Fax:* 617-576-5050 *E-mail:* aaas@amacad.org *Web Site:* www.amacad.org, pg 554

American Academy of Environmental Engineers & Scientists™, 147 Old Solomons Island Rd, Suite 303, Annapolis, MD 21401 *Tel:* 410-266-3311 *Fax:* 410-266-7653 *E-mail:* info@aaees.org *Web Site:* www.aaees.org, pg 9

American Academy of Orthopaedic Surgeons (AAOS), 9400 W Higgins Rd, Rosemont, IL 60018-4976 *Tel:* 847-823-7186 *Toll Free Tel:* 800-346-2267 *E-mail:* custserv@aaos.org *Web Site:* www.aaos.org, pg 9

American Academy of Pediatrics, 141 NW Point Blvd, Elk Grove Village, IL 60007-1098 *Tel:* 847-434-4000 *Toll Free Tel:* 888-227-1770 *Fax:* 847-434-8000 *E-mail:* pubs@aap.org *Web Site:* www.aap.org, pg 9

American Academy of Political & Social Science, 202 S 36 St, Philadelphia, PA 19104-3806 *Tel:* 215-746-6500 *Fax:* 215-573-2667 *Web Site:* www.aapss.org, pg 554

The American Alpine Club Press, 710 Tenth St, Suite 100, Golden, CO 80401 *Tel:* 303-384-0110 *Fax:* 303-384-0111 *E-mail:* info@americanalpineclub.org *Web Site:* americanalpineclub.org, pg 9

American Anthropological Association (AAA), 2300 Clarendon Blvd, Suite 1301, Arlington, VA 22201 *Tel:* 703-528-1902 *Fax:* 703-528-3546 *E-mail:* pubs@americananthro.org *Web Site:* www.americananthro.org, pg 10

American Antiquarian Society (AAS), 185 Salisbury St, Worcester, MA 01609-1634 *Tel:* 508-755-5221 *Fax:* 508-753-3311 *E-mail:* library@americanantiquarian.org *Web Site:* www.americanantiquarian.org, pg 554

American Association for the Advancement of Science (AAAS), 1200 New York Ave NW, Washington, DC 20005 *Tel:* 202-326-6400 *Web Site:* www.aaas.org, pg 554

American Association for Vocational Instructional Materials, 220 Smithonia Rd, Winterville, GA 30683 *Tel:* 706-742-5355 *Fax:* 706-742-7005 *E-mail:* sales@aavim.com *Web Site:* www.aavim.com, pg 10

American Association of Blood Banks, North Tower, 4550 Montgomery Ave, Suite 700, Bethesda, MD 20814 *Tel:* 301-907-6977 *Toll Free Tel:* 866-222-2498 (sales) *Fax:* 301-907-6895 *E-mail:* aabb@aabb.org; sales@aabb.org (ordering); publications1@aabb.org (catalog) *Web Site:* www.aabb.org, pg 10

American Association of Collegiate Registrars & Admissions Officers (AACRAO), One Dupont Circle NW, Suite 520, Washington, DC 20036 *Tel:* 202-293-9161 *Fax:* 202-872-8857 *Web Site:* www.aacrao.org, pg 10

American Association of University Women Award for Juvenile Literature, 4610 Mail Service Ctr, Raleigh, NC 27699-4610 *Tel:* 919-807-7290 *Fax:* 919-733-8807, pg 627

American Auto Racing Writers & Broadcasters, 922 N Pass Ave, Burbank, CA 91505 *Tel:* 818-842-7005 *Fax:* 818-842-7020, pg 554

American Bar Association, 321 N Clark St, Chicago, IL 60654 *Tel:* 312-988-5000 *Toll Free Tel:* 800-285-2221 (orders) *Fax:* 312-988-6281 *E-mail:* orders@abanet.org *Web Site:* www.americanbar.org, pg 10

American Bible Society, 101 N Independence Mall E, 8th fl, Philadelphia, PA 19106-2112 *Tel:* 215-309-0900 *Toll Free Tel:* 800-322-4253 (cust serv); 888-596-6296 *E-mail:* info@americanbible.org *Web Site:* www.americanbible.org, pg 10

American Book Award, The Raymond House, 655 13 St, Suite 302, Oakland, CA 94612 *Tel:* 916-425-7916 *E-mail:* info@beforecolumbusfoundation.com *Web Site:* www.beforecolumbusfoundation.com, pg 627

American Book Producers Association (ABPA), 31 W Eighth St, 2nd fl, New York, NY 10011 *Tel:* 212-675-1363 *Fax:* 212-675-1364 *E-mail:* office@abpaonline.org *Web Site:* www.abpaonline.org, pg 554

American Booksellers Association, 333 Westchester Ave, Suite S202, White Plains, NY 10604 *Tel:* 914-406-7500 *Toll Free Tel:* 800-637-0037 *Fax:* 914-410-6297 *E-mail:* info@bookweb.org *Web Site:* www.bookweb.org, pg 554

American Carriage House Publishing, 400 Idaho Maryland Rd, Grass Valley, CA 95945 *Tel:* 530-432-8860 *Toll Free Tel:* 866-986-2665 *E-mail:* editor@carriagehousepublishing.com *Web Site:* www.americancarriagehousepublishing.com, pg 10

American Catholic Press (ACP), 16565 S State St, South Holland, IL 60473 *Tel:* 708-331-5485 *Fax:* 708-331-5484 *E-mail:* acp@acpress.org *Web Site:* www.acpress.org, pg 10

The American Ceramic Society, 600 N Cleveland Ave, Suite 210, Westerville, OH 43082 *Tel:* 240-646-7054 *Toll Free Tel:* 866-721-3322 *Fax:* 240-396-5637 *E-mail:* customerservice@ceramics.org *Web Site:* ceramics.org, pg 10

The American Chemical Society, 1155 16 St NW, Washington, DC 20036 *Tel:* 202-872-4600 *Toll Free Tel:* 800-227-5558 (US) *Fax:* 202-872-6067 *E-mail:* help@acs.org *Web Site:* www.acs.org, pg 10

American Christian Writers, PO Box 110390, Nashville, TN 37222-0390 *Tel:* 615-331-8668 *Toll Free Tel:* 800-21-WRITE (219-7483) *E-mail:* acwriters@aol.com *Web Site:* regaforder.wordpress.com, pg 554

American Civil Liberties Union, 125 Broad St, 18th fl, New York, NY 10004 *Tel:* 212-549-2500 *E-mail:* media@aclu.org *Web Site:* www.aclu.org, pg 554

American College, 270 S Bryn Mawr Ave, Bryn Mawr, PA 19010 *Tel:* 610-526-1000 *Toll Free Tel:* 888-263-7265 *Fax:* 610-526-1310 *Web Site:* www.theamericancollege.edu, pg 11

American College of Surgeons, 633 N Saint Clair St, Chicago, IL 60611-3211 *Tel:* 312-202-5000 *Fax:* 312-202-5001 *E-mail:* postmaster@facs.org *Web Site:* www.facs.org, pg 11

American Correctional Association, 206 N Washington St, Suite 200, Alexandria, VA 22314 *Tel:* 703-224-0000 *Toll Free Tel:* 800-222-5646 *Fax:* 703-224-0179 *E-mail:* publications@aca.org *Web Site:* www.aca.org, pg 11

American Council on Education, One Dupont Circle NW, Washington, DC 20036 *Tel:* 202-939-9300; 202-939-9452 (publg dept); 301-632-6757 (orders) *E-mail:* pubs@acenet.edu *Web Site:* www.acenet.edu, pg 11

American Council on Education, One Dupont Circle NW, Washington, DC 20036 *Tel:* 202-939-9300 *Web Site:* www.acenet.edu, pg 554

American Counseling Association, 6101 Stevenson Ave, Suite 600, Alexandria, VA 22304 *Tel:* 703-823-9800 (ext 222, book orders) *Toll Free Tel:* 800-347-6647 (ext 222, book orders) *Fax:* 703-823-0252 *Toll Free Fax:* 800-473-2329 *E-mail:* membership@counseling.org (book orders) *Web Site:* www.counseling.org, pg 11

American Diabetes Association, 1701 N Beauregard St, Alexandria, VA 22311 *Toll Free Tel:* 800-342-2383 *E-mail:* booksinfo@diabetes.org *Web Site:* www.diabetes.org, pg 11

American Federation of Arts, 305 E 47 St, 10th fl, New York, NY 10017 *Tel:* 212-988-7700 *Toll Free Tel:* 800-232-0270 *Fax:* 212-861-2487 *E-mail:* pubinfo@amfedarts.org *Web Site:* www.amfedarts.org, pg 11

American Federation of Astrologers Inc, 6535 S Rural Rd, Tempe, AZ 85283-3746 *Tel:* 480-838-1751 *Toll Free Tel:* 888-301-7630 *Fax:* 480-838-8293 *Web Site:* www.astrologers.com, pg 11

American Fisheries Society, 425 Barlow Place, Suite 110, Bethesda, MD 20814-2144 *Tel:* 301-897-8616; 703-661-1570 (book orders) *Fax:* 301-897-8096; 703-996-1010 (book orders) *E-mail:* main@fisheries.org *Web Site:* www.fisheries.org, pg 11

American Forest & Paper Association (AF&PA), 1101 "K" St NW, Suite 700, Washington, DC 20005 *Tel:* 202-463-2700 *E-mail:* info@afandpa.org *Web Site:* www.afandpa.org, pg 554

American Geophysical Union (AGU), 2000 Florida Ave NW, Washington, DC 20009 *Tel:* 202-462-6900 *Toll Free Tel:* 800-966-2481 (North America) *Fax:* 202-328-0566 *E-mail:* service@agu.org (cust serv); earthspacescience@agu.org *Web Site:* www.agu.org, pg 11

American Geosciences Institute (AGI), 4220 King St, Alexandria, VA 22302-1502 *Tel:* 703-379-2480 (ext 246) *Fax:* 703-379-7563 *E-mail:* pubs@agiweb.org *Web Site:* www.agiweb.org, pg 11

American Girl Publishing, 8400 Fairway Place, Middleton, WI 53562 *Tel:* 608-836-4848; 608-831-5210 (outside US & CN) *Toll Free Tel:* 800-233-0264; 800-360-1861; 800-845-0005 (US & CN) *Fax:* 608-836-1999 *Web Site:* www.americangirl.com, pg 12

American Historical Association (AHA), 400 "A" St SE, Washington, DC 20003 *Tel:* 202-544-2422 *Fax:* 202-544-8307 *E-mail:* aha@historians.org; awards@historians.org *Web Site:* www.historians.org, pg 12

American Illustration/American Photography, 15 E 32 St, 7th fl, New York, NY 10016 *Tel:* 212-470-0302 *Fax:* 212-532-2064 *E-mail:* info@ai-ap.com *Web Site:* www.ai-ap.com, pg 627

American Industrial Hygiene Association - AIHA, 3141 Fairview Park Dr, Suite 777, Falls Church, VA 22042 *Tel:* 703-849-8888 *Fax:* 703-207-3561 *E-mail:* infonet@aiha.org *Web Site:* www.aiha.org, pg 12

American Institute for Economic Research (AIER), 250 Division St, Great Barrington, MA 01230 *Tel:* 413-528-1216 *Toll Free Tel:* 888-528-1216 (orders) *E-mail:* info@aier.org *Web Site:* www.aier.org, pg 12

American Institute of Aeronautics & Astronautics (AIAA), 1801 Alexander Bell Dr, Suite 500, Reston, VA 20191-4344 *Tel:* 703-264-7500 *Toll Free Tel:* 800-639-AIAA (639-2422) *Fax:* 703-264-7551 *E-mail:* custserv@aiaa.org *Web Site:* www.aiaa.org, pg 12

American Institute of Chemical Engineers (AIChE), 120 Wall St, 23rd fl, New York, NY 10005-4020 *Tel:* 203-702-7660 *Toll Free Tel:* 800-242-4363 *Fax:* 203-775-5177 *E-mail:* customerservice@aiche.org *Web Site:* www.aiche.org, pg 12

American Institute of Physics, One Physics Ellipse, College Park, MD 20740-3843 *Tel:* 516-576-2200; 301-209-3165 (orders) *Fax:* 301-209-0882 (orders) *E-mail:* aipinfo@aip.org *Web Site:* www.aip.org, pg 12

American Jewish Committee (AJC), Jacob Blaustein Bldg, 165 E 56 St, New York, NY 10022 *Tel:* 212-751-4000; 212-891-1456 (membership) *Fax:* 212-891-1450 *Web Site:* www.ajc.org, pg 555

American Law Institute, 4025 Chestnut St, Philadelphia, PA 19104-3099 *Tel:* 215-243-1600 *Toll Free Tel:* 800-253-6397 *Fax:* 215-243-1664 *Web Site:* www.ali.org, pg 12

American Law Institute Continuing Legal Education (ALI CLE), 4025 Chestnut St, Philadelphia, PA 19104 *Tel:* 215-243-1600 *Toll Free Tel:* 800-CLE-NEWS (253-6397) *Fax:* 215-243-1664; 215-243-1608 *Web Site:* www.ali-cle.org, pg 12

The American Library Association (ALA), 50 E Huron St, Chicago, IL 60611 *Tel:* 312-944-6780 *Toll Free Tel:* 800-545-2433 *Fax:* 312-280-5275 *E-mail:* editionsmarketing@ala.org *Web Site:* www.alastore.ala.org, pg 12

The American Library Association (ALA), 50 E Huron St, Chicago, IL 60611 *Tel:* 312-944-6780; 312-280-4299 (memb & cust serv) *Toll Free Tel:* 800-545-2433 *Fax:* 312-440-9374 *E-mail:* ala@ala.org; customerservice@ala.org *Web Site:* www.ala.org, pg 555

American Literacy Council, 1441 Mariposa Ave, Boulder, CO 80302 *Tel:* 303-440-7385 *Web Site:* www.americanliteracy.com, pg 555

American Literary Translators Association (ALTA), 900 E Seventh St, PMB 266, Bloomington, IN 47405-3201 *Tel:* 972-883-2093 *Fax:* 972-883-6303 *Web Site:* www.literarytranslators.org, pg 555

American Management Association (AMA), 1601 Broadway, New York, NY 10019 *Tel:* 212-586-8100 *Toll Free Tel:* 877-566-9441 *Fax:* 212-903-8168; 518-891-0368 *E-mail:* customerservice@amanet.org *Web Site:* www.amanet.org, pg 555

American Map Corp, 36-36 33 St, 4th fl, Long Island City, NY 11106 *Tel:* 718-784-0055 *Toll Free Tel:* 888-774-7979 *Fax:* 718-784-0640 (admin); 718-784-1216 (sales & orders) *E-mail:* info@kappamapgroup.com *Web Site:* www.kappamapgroup.com, pg 13

American Marketing Association, 130 E Randolph St, 22nd fl, Chicago, IL 60601 *Tel:* 312-542-9000 *Toll Free Tel:* 800-AMA-1150 (262-1150) *Fax:* 312-542-9001 *E-mail:* info@ama.org *Web Site:* www.ama.org, pg 555

American Mathematical Society, 201 Charles St, Providence, RI 02904-2294 *Tel:* 401-455-4000 *Toll Free Tel:* 800-321-4267 *Fax:* 401-331-3842; 401-455-4046 (cust serv) *E-mail:* ams@ams.org; cust-serv@ams.org *Web Site:* www.ams.org, pg 13

American Medical Association, AMA Plaza, 330 N Wabash, Suite 39300, Chicago, IL 60611-5885 *Tel:* 312-464-5000 *Toll Free Tel:* 800-621-8335 *Fax:* 312-464-4184 *Web Site:* www.ama-assn.org, pg 13, 555

American Medical Writers Association (AMWA), 30 W Gude Dr, Suite 525, Rockville, MD 20850-4357 *Tel:* 240-238-0940 *Fax:* 301-294-9006 *E-mail:* amwa@amwa.org *Web Site:* www.amwa.org, pg 555

American Numismatic Society, 75 Varick St, 11th fl, New York, NY 10013 *Tel:* 212-571-4470 *Fax:* 212-571-4479 *E-mail:* ans@numismatics.org; orders@numismatics.org *Web Site:* www.numismatics.org, pg 13

The American Occupational Therapy Association Inc (AOTA), 4720 Montgomery Lane, Suite 200, Bethesda, MD 20814-3449 *Tel:* 301-652-6611 *Toll Free Tel:* 800-377-8555 (TDD); 877-404-AOTA (404-2682, orders) *Fax:* 301-652-7711; 770-238-0414 (orders) *E-mail:* aotacustomerservice@pbd.com *Web Site:* www.aota.org; store.aota.org, pg 13

American Philosophical Society, 104 S Fifth St, Philadelphia, PA 19106 *Tel:* 215-440-3425 *Fax:* 215-440-3450 *E-mail:* orders@dianepublishing.net *Web Site:* www.amphilsoc.org, pg 13

American Political Science Association, 1527 New Hampshire Ave NW, Washington, DC 20036-1203 *Tel:* 202-483-2512 *Fax:* 202-483-2657 *E-mail:* apsa@apsanet.org *Web Site:* www.apsanet.org, pg 555

American Press, 60 State St, Suite 700, Boston, MA 02109 *Tel:* 617-247-0022 *E-mail:* americanpress@flash.net *Web Site:* www.americanpresspublishers.com, pg 13

American Printing History Association, PO Box 4519, Grand Central Sta, New York, NY 10163 *Tel:* 202-544-2422 *E-mail:* secretary@printinghistory.org *Web Site:* printinghistory.org, pg 556

American Printing History Association Award, PO Box 4519, Grand Central Sta, New York, NY 10163 *Tel:* 202-544-2422 *E-mail:* secretary@printinghistory.org *Web Site:* printinghistory.org, pg 627

American Printing House for the Blind Inc, 1839 Frankfort Ave, Louisville, KY 40206 *Tel:* 502-895-2405 *Toll Free Tel:* 800-223-1839 (cust serv) *Fax:* 502-899-2274 *E-mail:* info@aph.org *Web Site:* www.aph.org; shop.aph.org, pg 13

American Products Publishing Co, 8260 SW Nimbus Ave, Beaverton, OR 97008 *Tel:* 503-672-7502 *Toll Free Tel:* 800-668-8181 *Fax:* 503-672-7104 *E-mail:* info@american-products.com *Web Site:* www.american-products.com, pg 14

American Program Bureau Inc, One Gateway Center, Suite 751, Newton, MA 02458 *Tel:* 617-614-1600 *Fax:* 617-965-6610 *E-mail:* apb@apbspeakers.com *Web Site:* www.apbspeakers.com, pg 547

American Psychiatric Association Publishing, 1000 Wilson Blvd, Suite 1825, Arlington, VA 22209 *Tel:* 703-907-7322 *Toll Free Tel:* 800-368-5777 *Fax:* 703-907-1091 *E-mail:* appi@psych.org *Web Site:* www.appi.org; www.psychiatryonline.org, pg 14

American Psychological Association, 750 First St NE, Washington, DC 20002-4242 *Tel:* 202-336-5510 *Toll Free Tel:* 800-374-2721 *Fax:* 202-336-5502 *E-mail:* order@apa.org *Web Site:* www.apa.org/books, pg 14

American Psychological Association, 750 First St NE, Washington, DC 20002-4242 *Tel:* 202-336-5500 *Toll Free Tel:* 800-374-2721 *E-mail:* order@apa.org *Web Site:* www.apa.org, pg 556

American Public Human Services Association, 1133 19 St NW, Suite 400, Washington, DC 20036 *Tel:* 202-682-0100 *Fax:* 202-289-6555 *Web Site:* www.aphsa.org, pg 556

American Public Works Association (APWA), 2345 Grand Blvd, Suite 700, Kansas City, MO 64108-2625 *Tel:* 816-472-6100 *Toll Free Tel:* 800-848-APWA (848-2792) *Fax:* 816-472-1610 *Web Site:* www.apwa.net, pg 14

American Quilter's Society, 5801 Kentucky Dam Rd, Paducah, KY 42003-9323 *Tel:* 270-898-7903 *Toll Free Tel:* 800-626-5420 (orders) *Fax:* 270-898-1173 *E-mail:* orders@americanquilter.com *Web Site:* www.americanquilter.com, pg 14

American Society for Indexing Inc (ASI), 1628 E Southern Ave, Suite 9-223, Tempe, AZ 85282 *Tel:* 480-245-6750 *E-mail:* info@asindexing.org *Web Site:* www.asindexing.org, pg 556

American Society for Nondestructive Testing, 1711 Arlingate Lane, Columbus, OH 43228-0518 *Tel:* 614-274-6003 *Toll Free Tel:* 800-222-2768 *Fax:* 614-274-6899 *Web Site:* www.asnt.org, pg 14

American Society for Quality (ASQ), 600 N Plankinton Ave, Milwaukee, WI 53203 *Tel:* 414-272-8575 *Toll Free Tel:* 800-248-1946 (US & CN); 800-514-1564 (Mexico) *Fax:* 414-272-1734 *E-mail:* help@asq.org *Web Site:* www.asq.org, pg 14

American Society of Agricultural & Biological Engineers (ASABE), 2950 Niles Rd, St Joseph, MI 49085-9659 *Tel:* 269-429-0300 *Toll Free Tel:* 800-371-2723 *Fax:* 269-429-3852 *E-mail:* hq@asabe.org *Web Site:* www.asabe.org, pg 14

American Society of Agronomy, 5585 Guilford Rd, Madison, WI 53711-5801 *Tel:* 608-273-8080 *Fax:* 608-273-2021 *E-mail:* headquarters@sciencesocieties.org *Web Site:* www.agronomy.org, pg 15

American Society of Civil Engineers (ASCE), 1801 Alexander Bell Dr, Reston, VA 20191-4400 *Tel:* 703-295-6300 *Toll Free Tel:* 800-548-2723 *Fax:* 703-295-6278 *E-mail:* ascelibrary@asce.org *Web Site:* www.asce.org, pg 15

American Society of Composers, Authors & Publishers (ASCAP), 1900 Broadway, New York City, NY 10023 *Tel:* 212-621-6000 *Toll Free Tel:* 800-952-7227 *Fax:* 212-612-8453 *E-mail:* info@ascap.com *Web Site:* www.ascap.com, pg 556

American Society of Health-System Pharmacists (ASHP), 4500 East-West Hwy, Suite 900, Bethesda, MD 20814 *Tel:* 301-657-3000; 301-664-8700 *Toll Free Tel:* 866-279-0681 (orders) *Fax:* 301-657-1251 (orders) *E-mail:* custserv@ashp.org *Web Site:* www.ashp.org, pg 15

American Society of Journalists and Authors (ASJA), 355 Lexington Ave, 15th fl, New York, NY 10017-6603 *Tel:* 212-997-0947 *Web Site:* asja.org, pg 556

American Society of Journalists and Authors Annual Writers Conference, 355 Lexington Ave, 15th fl, New York, NY 10017-6603 *Tel:* 212-997-0947 *Web Site:* asja.org, pg 609

American Society of Magazine Editors (ASME), 757 Third Ave, 11th fl, New York, NY 10017 *Tel:* 212-872-3700 *Fax:* 212-906-0128 *E-mail:* asme@magazine.org *Web Site:* www.magazine.org/asme, pg 556

American Society of Mechanical Engineers (ASME), 2 Park Ave, New York, NY 10016-5990 *Tel:* 212-591-7000 *Toll Free Tel:* 800-843-2763 (cust serv-US, CN & Mexico) *Fax:* 212-591-7674; 973-882-8113 (cust serv); 973-882-1717 (orders & inquiries) *E-mail:* infocentral@asme.org *Web Site:* www.asme.org, pg 15

American Society of Media Photographers (ASMP), PO Box 31207, Bethesda, MD 20804 *Toll Free Tel:* 877-771-2767 *Fax:* 231-946-6180 *E-mail:* info@asmp.org *Web Site:* asmp.org, pg 556

American Society of News Editors (ASNE), 209 Reynolds Journalism Institute, Missouri School of Journalism, Columbia, MO 65211 *Tel:* 573-882-2430 *Fax:* 573-884-3824 *Web Site:* asne.org, pg 556

American Society of Plant Taxonomists, University of Wyoming, Dept of Botany 3165, 1000 E University Ave, Laramie, WY 82071 *Tel:* 307-766-2556 *Fax:* 307-766-2851 *E-mail:* aspt@uwyo.edu *Web Site:* www.aspt.net, pg 15

American Sociological Association (ASA), 1430 "K" St NW, Suite 600, Washington, DC 20005-4701 *Tel:* 202-383-9005 *Fax:* 202-638-0882 *E-mail:* customer@asanet.org *Web Site:* www.asanet.org, pg 556

American Speech-Language-Hearing Association (ASHA), 2200 Research Blvd, Rockville, MD 20850-3289 *Tel:* 301-296-5700 *Toll Free Tel:* 800-638-8255 (nonmembs); 800-498-2071 (membs) *Fax:* 301-296-5777; 301-296-8580 *E-mail:* actioncenter@asha.org *Web Site:* www.asha.org, pg 557

American Technical Publishers Inc, 10100 Orland Pkwy, Suite 200, Orland Park, IL 60467-5756 *Toll Free Tel:* 800-323-3471 *Fax:* 708-957-1101 *E-mail:* service@atplearning.com; order@atplearning.com *Web Site:* www.atplearning.com, pg 15

American Translators Association (ATA), 225 Reinekers Lane, Suite 590, Alexandria, VA 22314 *Tel:* 703-683-6100 *Fax:* 703-683-6122 *E-mail:* ata@atanet.org *Web Site:* www.atanet.org, pg 557

American Water Works Association (AWWA), 6666 W Quincy Ave, Denver, CO 80235 *Tel:* 303-794-7711 *Toll Free Tel:* 800-926-7337 *Fax:* 303-347-0804 *E-mail:* service@awwa.org (cust serv) *Web Site:* www.awwa.org, pg 15

Amherst Media Inc, PO Box 538, Buffalo, NY 14213 *Tel:* 716-874-4450 *E-mail:* marketing@amherstmedia.com *Web Site:* www.amherstmedia.com, pg 15

Amicus, PO Box 1329, Mankato, MN 56002 *Tel:* 507-388-9357 *Fax:* 507-388-1779 *E-mail:* info@amicuspublishing.us; orders@amicuspublishing.us *Web Site:* www.amicuspublishing.us, pg 16

AMMO Books LLC, 5022 N Eagle Rock Blvd, Los Angeles, CA 90041 *Tel:* 323-223-AMMO (223-2666) *Fax:* 323-978-4200 *E-mail:* weborders@ammobooks.com; orders@ammobooks.com *Web Site:* ammobooks.com, pg 16

Ampersand Group, 12 Morenz Terr, Kanata, ON K2K 3G9, Canada *Tel:* 613-435-5066, pg 487

Ampersand Inc/Professional Publishing Services, 515 Madison St, New Orleans, LA 70116 *Tel:* 312-280-8905 *Fax:* 312-944-1582 *E-mail:* info@ampersandworks.com *Web Site:* www.ampersandworks.com, pg 16

Betsy Amster Literary Enterprises, 6312 SW Capitol Hwy, No 503, Portland, OR 97239 *Tel:* 503-496-4007 *E-mail:* rights@amsterlit.com (rts inquiries); b.amster.assistant@gmail.com (adult book queries); b.amster.kidsbooks@gmail.com (children & young adult book queries) *Web Site:* www.amsterlit.com, pg 506

AMWA Annual Conference, 30 W Gude Dr, Suite 525, Rockville, MD 20850-4357 *Tel:* 240-238-0940 *Fax:* 301-294-9006 *E-mail:* amwa@amwa.org *Web Site:* www.amwa.org, pg 609

The Amy Award, 90 Broad St, Suite 2100, New York, NY 10004 *Tel:* 212-226-3586 *Fax:* 212-226-3963 *E-mail:* admin@pw.org *Web Site:* www.pw.org, pg 627

Joyce L Ananian, 25 Forest Circle, Waltham, MA 02452-4719 *Tel:* 781-894-4330 *E-mail:* jlananian@hotmail.com, pg 487

Anaphora Literary Press, 1898 Athens St, Brownsville, TX 78520 *Tel:* 470-289-6395 *Web Site:* anaphoraliterary.com, pg 16

Anchor Books, c/o Penguin Random House Inc, 1745 Broadway, New York, NY 10019 *Tel:* 212-572-2420 *E-mail:* vintageanchorpublicity@randomhouse.com *Web Site:* knopfdoubleday.com/imprint/anchor, pg 16

Anchor Group Publishing, PO Box 551, Flushing, MI 48433 *E-mail:* anchorgrouppublishing@gmail.com *Web Site:* anchorgrouppublishing.com, pg 16

Ancient Faith Publishing, 2747 Bond St, University Park, IL 60484 *Tel:* 219-728-2216 *Toll Free Tel:* 800-967-7377 *Toll Free Fax:* 866-599-5208 *E-mail:* info@ancientfaith.com; orders@ancientfaith.com *Web Site:* www.ancientfaith.com/publishing, pg 16

Barbara S Anderson, 706 W Davis Ave, Ann Arbor, MI 48103-4855 *Tel:* 734-995-0125 *E-mail:* bsa@watercolorbarbara.com, pg 488

Denice A Anderson, 210 E Church St, Clinton, MI 49236 *Tel:* 517-456-4990 *Fax:* 517-456-4990 *E-mail:* deniceanderson@frontier.com, pg 488

Jim Anderson, 77 S Second St, Brooklyn, NY 11249 *Tel:* 718-388-1083 *E-mail:* jim.and@att.net, pg 488

Anderson Literary Management LLC, 244 Fifth Ave, 11th fl, New York, NY 10001 *Tel:* 212-645-6045 *Fax:* 212-741-1936 *E-mail:* info@andersonliterary.com *Web Site:* www.andersonliterary.com, pg 506

Patricia Anderson, PhD, Editor & Literary Consultant, 1489 Marine Dr, Suite 515, West Vancouver, BC V7T 1B8, Canada *Tel:* 604-740-0805 *E-mail:* query@helpingyougetpublished.com; patriciaanderson@helpingyougetpublished.com *Web Site:* www.helpingyougetpublished.com, pg 488

Sara Anderson Children's Books, PO Box 47182, Seattle, WA 98146 *Tel:* 206-285-1520 *Web Site:* www.saranderson.com, pg 16

Andrews McMeel Publishing LLC, 1130 Walnut St, Kansas City, MO 64106-2109 *Toll Free Tel:* 800-851-8923; 800-943-9839 (cust serv) *Toll Free Fax:* 800-943-9831 (orders) *Web Site:* www.andrewsmcmeel.com, pg 16

Andrews University Press, Sutherland House, 8360 W Campus Circle Dr, Berrien Springs, MI 49104-1700 *Tel:* 269-471-6134 *Toll Free Tel:* 800-467-6369 (Visa, MC & American Express orders only) *Fax:* 269-471-6224 *E-mail:* aupo@andrews.edu; aup@andrews.edu; aupress@andrews.edu *Web Site:* www.universitypress.andrews.edu, pg 17

Andy Ross Literary Agency, 767 Santa Ray Ave, Oakland, CA 94610 *Tel:* 510-238-8965 *E-mail:* andyrossagency@hotmail.com *Web Site:* www.andyrossagency.com, pg 506

Angel City Press, 2118 Wilshire Blvd, Suite 880, Santa Monica, CA 90403 *Tel:* 310-395-9982 *Toll Free Tel:* 800-949-8039 *Fax:* 310-395-3353 *E-mail:* info@angelcitypress.com *Web Site:* www.angelcitypress.com, pg 17

Angel Editing Services, PO Box 752, Mountain Ranch, CA 95246 *Tel:* 209-728-8364 *E-mail:* info@stephaniemarohn.com *Web Site:* www.stephaniemarohn.com, pg 488

Angels Editorial Services, 1630 Main St, Suite 41, Coventry, CT 06238 *Tel:* 860-742-5279 *E-mail:* angelsus@aol.com, pg 488

Angelus Press, 2915 Forest Ave, Kansas City, MO 64109 *Tel:* 816-753-3150 *Toll Free Tel:* 800-966-7337 *Fax:* 816-753-3557 *E-mail:* support@angeluspress.org *Web Site:* www.angeluspress.org, pg 17

Anhinga Press, PO Box 3665, Tallahassee, FL 32315 *Tel:* 850-577-0745 *E-mail:* info@anhinga.org *Web Site:* www.anhingapress.org; www.facebook.com/anhingapress, pg 17

Animal Media Group LLC, 100 First Ave, Suite 1100, Pittsburgh, PA 15222-1519 *Tel:* 412-566-5656 *Fax:* 412-566-5656 *E-mail:* info@animalmediagroup.com *Web Site:* www.animalmediagroup.com, pg 17

The Anisfield-Wolf Book Awards, 1422 Euclid Ave, Suite 1300, Cleveland, OH 44115 *Tel:* 216-861-3810 *Fax:* 216-861-1729 *E-mail:* awinfo@clevefdn.org *Web Site:* www.anisfield-wolf.org; www.clevelandfoundation.org, pg 627

R Ross Annett Award for Children's Literature, 11759 Groat Rd, Edmonton, AB T5M 3K6, Canada *Tel:* 780-422-8174 *Toll Free Tel:* 800-665-5354 (AB only) *Fax:* 780-422-2663 (attn WGA) *E-mail:* mail@writersguild.ca *Web Site:* writersguild.ca, pg 627

Annick Press Ltd, 15 Patricia Ave, Toronto, ON M2M 1H9, Canada *Tel:* 416-221-4802 *Fax:* 416-221-8400 *E-mail:* annickpress@annickpress.com *Web Site:* www.annickpress.com, pg 445

Annual & Rolling Grants for Artists, 136 State St, Montpelier, VT 05602 *Tel:* 802-828-5425 *Fax:* 802-828-3363 *E-mail:* info@vermontartscouncil.org *Web Site:* www.vermontartscouncil.org, pg 627

Annual Reviews, 4139 El Camino Way, Palo Alto, CA 94306 *Tel:* 650-493-4400 *Toll Free Tel:* 800-523-8635 *Fax:* 650-424-0910; 650-855-9815 *E-mail:* service@annualreviews.org *Web Site:* www.annualreviews.org, pg 17

ANR Publications University of California, 1301 S 46 St, Bldg 478 - MC 3580, Richmond, CA 94804 *Tel:* 510-665-2195 (cust serv) *Toll Free Tel:* 800-994-8849 *Fax:* 510-665-3427 *E-mail:* anrcatalog@ucdavis.edu *Web Site:* anrcatalog.ucanr.edu, pg 17

Antioch Writers' Workshop, 300 College Park Ave, Suite 200A, Dayton, OH 45469-0001 *Tel:* 937-567-2399 *E-mail:* info@antiochwritersworkshop.com *Web Site:* www.antiochwritersworkshop.com, pg 609

Antiquarian Booksellers' Association of America (ABAA), 20 W 44 St, Suite 507, New York, NY 10036 *Tel:* 212-944-8291 *Fax:* 212-944-8293 *E-mail:* hq@abaa.org *Web Site:* www.abaa.org, pg 557

Antique Collectors' Club Ltd, 6 W 18 St, Suite 4B, New York, NY 10011 *Tel:* 212-645-1111 *Toll Free Tel:* 800-252-5231 *Fax:* 212-989-3205 *E-mail:* ussales@accpublishinggroup.com *Web Site:* www.accdistribution.com, pg 17

Antique Trader, c/o Krause Publications, 700 E State St, Iola, WI 54990-0001 *Tel:* 715-445-2214 *Toll Free Tel:* 888-457-2873 *Fax:* 715-445-4087 *Web Site:* www.krausebooks.com, pg 18

Antrim House, 21 Goodrich Rd, Simsbury, CT 06070-1804 *Tel:* 860-217-0023 *E-mail:* eds@antrimhousebooks.com *Web Site:* www.antrimhousebooks.com, pg 18

Anvil Press Publishers, 278 E First Ave, Vancouver, BC V5T 1A6, Canada *Tel:* 604-876-8710 *Fax:* 604-879-2667 *E-mail:* info@anvilpress.com *Web Site:* www.anvilpress.com, pg 445

AOCS Press, 2710 S Boulder Dr, Urbana, IL 61802-6996 *Tel:* 217-693-4838 *Fax:* 217-351-8091 *E-mail:* general@aocs.org *Web Site:* www.aocs.org, pg 18

APA Planners Press, 205 N Michigan Ave, Suite 1200, Chicago, IL 60601 *Tel:* 312-431-9100 *Fax:* 312-786-6700 *E-mail:* customerservice@planning.org *Web Site:* www.planning.org, pg 18

APA Talent & Literary Agency, 405 S Beverly Dr, Beverly Hills, CA 90212 *Tel:* 310-888-4200 *Fax:* 310-888-4242 *Web Site:* www.apa-agency.com, pg 507

Aperture Books, 547 W 27 St, 4th fl, New York, NY 10001 *Tel:* 212-505-5555 *Toll Free Tel:* 800-929-2323 *Fax:* 212-979-7759 *E-mail:* info@aperture.org *Web Site:* www.aperture.org, pg 18

The Apex Press, 4501 Forbes Blvd, Suite 200, Lanham, MD 20706 *Tel:* 301-459-3366 *Toll Free Tel:* 800-462-6420 (orders) *Toll Free Fax:* 800-388-4450 *E-mail:* customercare@rowman.com *Web Site:* rowman.com/page/apex, pg 18

The Apocryphile Press, 1700 Shattuck Ave, Suite 81, Berkeley, CA 94709 *Tel:* 510-290-4349 *E-mail:* apocryphile@me.com *Web Site:* www.apocryphilepress.com, pg 18

Apogee Press, 2308 Sixth St, Berkeley, CA 94710 *E-mail:* editors.apogee@gmail.com *Web Site:* www.apogeepress.com, pg 18

Apollo Managed Care Inc, 1100 Town & Country Rd, Suite 1250, Orange, CA 92868 *Toll Free Tel:* 888-276-5563 *E-mail:* info@apollomanagedcare.com *Web Site:* www.apollomanagedcare.com, pg 18

APPA: The Association of Higher Education Facilities Officers, 1643 Prince St, Alexandria, VA 22314-2818 *Tel:* 703-684-1446 *Fax:* 703-549-2772 *Web Site:* www.appa.org, pg 18

Appalachian Mountain Club Books, 5 Joy St, Boston, MA 02108 *Tel:* 617-523-0655 *Toll Free Tel:* 800-262-4455 (orders) *Fax:* 617-523-0722 *E-mail:* amcbooks@outdoors.org *Web Site:* www.outdoors.org, pg 19

Appalachian Trail Conservancy, 799 Washington St, Harpers Ferry, WV 25425 *Tel:* 304-535-6331 *Toll Free Tel:* 888-287-8673 (orders only) *Fax:* 304-535-2667 *E-mail:* publisher@appalachiantrail.org *Web Site:* www.appalachiantrail.org; www.atctrailstore.org, pg 19

Appalachian Writers' Workshop, 56 Education Lane, Hindman, KY 41822 *Tel:* 606-785-5475 *E-mail:* info@hindmansettlement.org *Web Site:* www.hindmansettlement.org, pg 609

Applause Theatre & Cinema Books, 33 Plymouth St, Suite 302, Montclair, NJ 07042 *Tel:* 973-337-5034 *Toll Free Tel:* 800-637-2852 *Fax:* 973-337-5227 *E-mail:* info@applausepub.com *Web Site:* www.applausepub.com, pg 19

The Applegate/Jackson/Parks Future Teacher Scholarship, 5211 Port Royal Rd, Suite 510, Springfield, VA 22151 *Tel:* 703-321-9606 *Fax:* 703-321-7143 *Web Site:* www.nilrr.org, pg 627

Appletree Press Inc, 151 Good Counsel Dr, Suite 125, Mankato, MN 56001 *Tel:* 507-345-4848 *Fax:* 507-345-3002 *E-mail:* eatwell@hickorytech.net *Web Site:* www.appletreepress.com; www.letscookhealthymeals.com, pg 19

Applewood Books Inc, One River Rd, Carlisle, MA 01741 *Tel:* 781-271-0055 *Toll Free Tel:* 800-277-5312 (orders) *Fax:* 781-271-0056 *E-mail:* bookorder@awb.com; customercare@awb.com *Web Site:* www.awb.com, pg 19

Appraisal Institute, 200 W Madison, Suite 1500, Chicago, IL 60606 *Tel:* 312-335-4100 *Toll Free Tel:* 888-756-4624 *Fax:* 312-335-4400 *Web Site:* www.appraisalinstitute.org, pg 19

Apress Media LLC, 233 Spring St, New York, NY 10013 *Tel:* 212-460-1500 *E-mail:* editorial@apress.com *Web Site:* www.apress.com, pg 19

APS PRESS, 3340 Pilot Knob Rd, St Paul, MN 55121 *Tel:* 651-454-7250 *Toll Free Tel:* 800-328-7560 *Fax:* 651-454-0766 *E-mail:* aps@scisoc.org *Web Site:* www.shopapspress.org, pg 19

Aptara Inc, 3110 Fairview Park Dr, Suite 900, Falls Church, VA 22042 *Tel:* 703-352-0001 *E-mail:* moreinfo@aptaracorp.com *Web Site:* www.aptaracorp.com, pg 488

Aqua Quest Publications Inc, 486 Bayville Rd, Locust Valley, NY 11560-1209 *Tel:* 516-759-0476 *E-mail:* info@aquaquest.com *Web Site:* www.aquaquest.com, pg 19

Aquila Communications Inc, 281 rue Alice-Carriere St, Beaconsville, QC H9W 6E6, Canada *Toll Free Tel:* 800-667-7071 *Fax:* 514-505-4579 *Toll Free Fax:* 866-338-1948 *Web Site:* www.aquilacommunications.com, pg 445

Arbordale Publishing, 612 Johnnie Dodds Blvd, Suite A2, Mount Pleasant, SC 29464 *Tel:* 843-971-6722 *Toll Free Tel:* 877-243-3457 *Fax:* 843-216-3804 *E-mail:* customerservice@arbordalepublishing.com; info@arbordalepublishing.com *Web Site:* www.arbordalepublishing.com, pg 19

The May Hill Arbuthnot Honor Lecture Award, 50 E Huron St, Chicago, IL 60611-2795 *Tel:* 312-280-2163 *Toll Free Tel:* 800-545-2433 *Fax:* 312-440-9374; 312-280-5271 *E-mail:* alsc@ala.org *Web Site:* www.ala.org/alsc, pg 627

Arbutus Press, 2364 Pinehurst Trail, Traverse City, MI 49696 *Tel:* 231-946-7240 *E-mail:* info@arbutuspress.com *Web Site:* www.arbutuspress.com, pg 20

Arcade Publishing Inc, 307 W 36 St, 11th fl, New York, NY 10018 *Tel:* 212-643-6816 *Fax:* 212-643-6819 *E-mail:* info@skyhorsepublishing.com (subs & foreign rts) *Web Site:* www.arcadepub.com, pg 20

Arcadia, 31 Lake Place N, Danbury, CT 06810 *Tel:* 203-797-0993 *E-mail:* arcadialit@sbcglobal.net, pg 507

Arcadia Publishing Inc, 420 Wando Park Blvd, Mount Pleasant, SC 29464 *Tel:* 843-853-2070 *Toll Free Tel:* 888-313-2665 (orders only) *Fax:* 843-853-0044 *E-mail:* sales@arcadiapublishing.com *Web Site:* www.arcadiapublishing.com, pg 20

Archon Editorial LLC, 815 King St, Suite 204, Alexandria, VA 22314 *Tel:* 703-838-1650 *E-mail:* stoddardbc@gmail.com *Web Site:* www.archoneditorial.com, pg 488

ARE Press, 215 67 St, Virginia Beach, VA 23451 *Tel:* 757-428-3588 *Toll Free Tel:* 800-333-4499 *Fax:* 757-491-0689 *Web Site:* www.edgarcayce.org, pg 20

Ariadne Press, 270 Goins Ct, Riverside, CA 92507 *Tel:* 951-684-9202 *Fax:* 951-779-0449 *E-mail:* ariadnepress@aol.com *Web Site:* www.ariadnebooks.com, pg 20

Ariel Press, 2317 Quail Cove Dr, Jasper, GA 30143 *Tel:* 770-894-4226 *E-mail:* lig201@lightariel.com *Web Site:* www.lightariel.com, pg 20

Ariel Starr Productions Inc, PO Box 575, Woodstock, NY 12498 *Tel:* 201-784-9148 *E-mail:* arielstarrprod@aol.com *Web Site:* arielstarrprod.wix.com/arielstarr, pg 20

The Arion Press, The Presidio, 1802 Hays St, San Francisco, CA 94129 *Tel:* 415-668-2542 *Fax:* 415-668-2550 *E-mail:* arionpress@arionpress.com *Web Site:* www.arionpress.com, pg 20

Arizona State University, Creative Writing Program, 851 S Cady Mall, Rm 542, Tempe, AZ 85287-0302 *Tel:* 480-965-3528 *Fax:* 480-965-3451 *Web Site:* www.asu.edu/clas/english/creativewriting, pg 619

Arkansas Diamond Primary Book Award, Arkansas State Library, Suite 100, 900 W Capitol Ave, Little Rock, AR 72201-3108 *Tel:* 501-682-2860 *Fax:* 501-682-1693 *Web Site:* www.library.arkansas.gov; www.library.arkansas.gov, pg 628

Arkansas State University Graphic Communications Program, PO Box 1930, Dept of Media, State University, AR 72467-1930 *Tel:* 870-972-3114 *Fax:* 870-972-3321 *Web Site:* www.astate.edu, pg 619

Arkansas Writers' Conference, PO Box 24662, Little Rock, AR 72221 *Tel:* 501-833-2756 *Web Site:* www.arkansaswritersconference.org, pg 609

Arkham House Publishers Inc, PO Box 546, Sauk City, WI 53583 *Tel:* 608-643-4500 *Fax:* 608-643-5043 *E-mail:* sales@arkhamhouse.com *Web Site:* www.arkhamhouse.com, pg 21

Aro Book Publishing Co, 130 S 800 W, Salt Lake City, UT 84104-1120 *Tel:* 801-637-9115 *Fax:* 801-419-0125 *E-mail:* arobook@yahoo.com *Web Site:* www.arobookpublishing.com, pg 21

Jason Aronson Inc, 4501 Forbes Blvd, Suite 200, Lanham, MD 20706 *Tel:* 301-459-3366 *Toll Free Tel:* 800-462-6420 (orders) *Fax:* 301-429-5748 *Web Site:* www.rowman.com, pg 21

Arsenal Pulp Press, 211 E Georgia St, No 202, Vancouver, BC V6A 1Z6, Canada *Tel:* 604-687-4233 *Toll Free Tel:* 888-600-PULP (600-7857) *Fax:* 604-687-4283 *E-mail:* info@arsenalpulp.com *Web Site:* www.arsenalpulp.com, pg 445

Art Image Publications, PO Box 160, Derby Line, VT 05830 *Toll Free Tel:* 800-361-2598 *Toll Free Fax:* 800-559-2598 *E-mail:* info@artimagepublications.com; customer.service@artimagepublications.com *Web Site:* www.artimagepublications.com, pg 21

The Art Institute of Chicago, 111 S Michigan Ave, Chicago, IL 60603-6404 *Tel:* 312-443-3600; 312-443-3540 (pubns) *Fax:* 312-443-1334 (pubns) *Web Site:* www.artic.edu; www.artinstituteshop.org, pg 21

Art of Living, PrimaMedia Inc, 1250 Bethlehem Pike, Suite 241, Hatfield, PA 19440 *Tel:* 215-660-5045 *E-mail:* primamedia4@yahoo.com, pg 21

ArtAge Publications, PO Box 19955, Portland, OR 97280 *Tel:* 503-246-3000 *Toll Free Tel:* 800-858-4998 *Web Site:* www.seniortheatre.com, pg 21

Arte Publico Press, University of Houston, Bldg 19, Rm 100, 4902 Gulf Fwy, Houston, TX 77204-2004 *Tel:* 713-743-2998 (sales) *Toll Free Tel:* 800-633-2783 *Fax:* 713-743-2847 (sales) *E-mail:* appinfo@uh.edu; bkorders@uh.edu *Web Site:* artepublicopress.com, pg 21

Artech House Inc, 685 Canton St, Norwood, MA 02062 *Tel:* 781-769-9750 *Toll Free Tel:* 800-225-9977 *Fax:* 781-769-6334 *E-mail:* artech@artechhouse.com *Web Site:* www.artechhouse.com, pg 21

Artisan Books, 225 Varick St, New York, NY 10014-4381 *Tel:* 212-254-5900 *Toll Free Tel:* 800-722-7202 *Fax:* 212-677-6692 *E-mail:* artisaninfo@artisanbooks.com *Web Site:* www.workman.com/artisanbooks, pg 22

Artisan Bookworks, 921 S Third Ave, No 8, Sequim, WA 98382 *Tel:* 425-954-5277 *E-mail:* books@artisanbookworks.com *Web Site:* www.artisanbookworks.com, pg 22

Artist Grants, 711 E Wells Ave, Pierre, SD 57501-3369 *Tel:* 605-773-3301 *Fax:* 605-773-5977 *E-mail:* sdac@state.sd.us *Web Site:* www.artscouncil.sd.gov/grants, pg 628

Artist-in-Residence Program, 225 King St, Suite 201, Fredericton, NB E3B 1E1, Canada *Tel:* 506-444-4444 *Toll Free Tel:* 866-460-ARTS (460-2787) *Fax:* 506-444-5543 *Web Site:* www.artsnb.ca, pg 628

Artist Research & Development Grants, 417 W Roosevelt St, Phoenix, AZ 85003-1326 *Tel:* 602-771-6501 *Fax:* 602-256-0282 *E-mail:* info@azarts.gov *Web Site:* www.azarts.gov, pg 628

Artists & Writers Summer Fellowships, 435 Ellis Hollow Creek Rd, Ithaca, NY 14850 *Tel:* 607-539-3146 *E-mail:* artscolony@saltonstall.org *Web Site:* www.saltonstall.org, pg 609

Artists Associates, 4416 La Jolla Dr, Bradenton, FL 34210-3927 *Tel:* 941-756-8445, pg 543

Artists' Fellowships, 20 Jay St, 7th fl, Brooklyn, NY 11201 *Tel:* 212-366-6900 *Fax:* 212-366-1778 *E-mail:* info@nyfa.org *Web Site:* www.nyfa.org, pg 628

Arts & Letters Awards, 633 W 155 St, New York, NY 10032 *Tel:* 212-368-5900 *Fax:* 212-491-4615 *E-mail:* academy@artsandletters.org *Web Site:* www.artsandletters.org, pg 628

Arts Scholarships, 225 King St, Suite 201, Fredericton, NB E3B 1E1, Canada *Tel:* 506-444-4444 *Toll Free Tel:* 866-460-ARTS (460-2787) *Fax:* 506-444-5543 *Web Site:* www.artsnb.ca, pg 628

Artworks Illustration, PO Box 453, New York, NY 10156 *Tel:* 212-239-4946 *E-mail:* artworksillustration@earthlink.net *Web Site:* www.artworksillustration.com, pg 543

ArtWrite Productions, 1555 Gardena Ave NE, Minneapolis, MN 55432-5848 *Tel:* 612-803-0436 *E-mail:* artwriteprod@gmail.com *Web Site:* artwriteproductions.com; adaptedclassics.com, pg 22

ASCD, 1703 N Beauregard St, Alexandria, VA 22311-1714 *Tel:* 703-578-9600 *Toll Free Tel:* 800-933-2723 *Fax:* 703-575-5400 *E-mail:* member@ascd.org *Web Site:* www.ascd.org, pg 22

Ascend Books LLC, 12710 Pflumm Rd, Suite 200, Olathe, KS 66062 *Tel:* 913-948-5500 *Web Site:* www.ascendbooks.com, pg 22

Ascension Press, PO Box 1990, West Chester, PA 19380 *Tel:* 610-696-7795; 484-875-4550 (admin) *Toll Free Tel:* 800-376-0520 (sales & cust serv) *Web Site:* ascensionpress.com, pg 22

ASCP Press, 33 W Monroe St, Suite 1600, Chicago, IL 60603 *Tel:* 312-541-4999 *Toll Free Tel:* 800-267-2727 *Fax:* 312-541-4998 *Web Site:* www.ascp.org, pg 22

ASCSA Publications, 6-8 Charlton St, Princeton, NJ 08540-5232 *Tel:* 609-683-0800 *Fax:* 609-924-0578 *Web Site:* www.ascsa.edu.gr/publications, pg 23

ASET - The Neurodiagnostic Society, 402 E Bannister Rd, Suite A, Kansas City, KS 64131-3019 *Tel:* 816-931-1120 *Fax:* 816-931-1145 *E-mail:* info@aset.org *Web Site:* www.aset.org, pg 23

ASF Translation Awards, Scandinavia House, 58 Park Ave, New York, NY 10016 *Tel:* 212-879-9779; 212-779-3587 *Fax:* 212-686-2115 *E-mail:* grants@amscan.org *Web Site:* www.amscan.org, pg 628

Ash Tree Publishing, PO Box 64, Woodstock, NY 12498 *Tel:* 845-246-8081 *Fax:* 845-246-8081 *Web Site:* www.ashtreepublishing.com, pg 23

Ashland Creek Press, 2305 Ashland St, Suite C417, Ashland, OR 97520 *Tel:* 760-300-3620 *E-mail:* editors@ashlandcreekpress.com *Web Site:* www.ashlandcreekpress.com, pg 23

ASI/EIS Publishing Award for Excellence in Indexing, 1628 E Southern Ave, Suite 9-223, Tempe, AZ 85282 *Tel:* 480-245-6750 *E-mail:* info@asindexing.org *Web Site:* www.asindexing.org, pg 628

Asian American Literary Awards, 112 W 27 St, Suite 600, New York, NY 10001 *Tel:* 212-494-0061 *E-mail:* aala@aaww.org *Web Site:* aaww.org/aala, pg 628

Asian American Writers' Workshop, 110-112 W 27 St, Suite 600, New York, NY 10001 *Tel:* 212-494-0061 *E-mail:* desk@aaww.org *Web Site:* aaww.org, pg 557

ASIS International, 1625 Prince St, Alexandria, VA 22314 *Tel:* 703-519-6200 *Fax:* 703-519-6299 *E-mail:* asis@asisonline.org *Web Site:* www.asisonline.org, pg 23

ASJA Freelance Writer Search, 355 Lexington Ave, 15th fl, New York, NY 10017 *Tel:* 212-997-0947 *E-mail:* asjaoffice@asja.org *Web Site:* www.freelancewritersearch.com, pg 488

Aslan Publishing, 857 Post Rd, Suite 302, Fairfield, CT 06824 *Tel:* 203-372-0300; 203-374-6224 *Fax:* 203-374-4766 *E-mail:* information@aslanpublishing.com *Web Site:* www.aslanpublishing.com, pg 23

ASM International, 9639 Kinsman Rd, Materials Park, OH 44073-0002 *Tel:* 440-338-5151 *Toll Free Tel:* 800-336-5152; 800-368-9800 (Europe) *Fax:* 440-338-4634 *E-mail:* memberservicecenter@asminternational.org *Web Site:* www.asminternational.org, pg 23

ASM Press, 1752 "N" St NW, Washington, DC 20036-2904 *Tel:* 202-737-3600 *Fax:* 202-942-9342 *E-mail:* books@asmusa.org *Web Site:* www.asmscience.org, pg 23

Aspatore Books, 610 Opperman Dr, Eagan, MN 55123 *Tel:* 651-687-7000 *Toll Free Tel:* 866-ASPATORE (277-2867); 888-728-7677; 800-328-4880 *E-mail:* customerservice@thomsonreuters.com *Web Site:* legalsolutions.thomsonreuters.com; www.aspatore.com, pg 23

Aspen Words, 110 E Hallam St, Suite 116, Aspen, CO 81611 *Tel:* 970-925-3122 *Fax:* 970-920-5700 *E-mail:* aspenwords@aspeninstitute.org *Web Site:* www.aspenwords.org, pg 557

Aspen Words Literary Prize, 110 E Hallam St, Suite 116, Aspen, CO 81611 *Tel:* 970-925-3122 *Fax:* 970-920-5700 *E-mail:* literary.prize@aspeninstitute.org *Web Site:* www.aspenwords.org, pg 628

Associated Business Writers of America Inc, 10940 S Parker Rd, Suite 508, Parker, CO 80134 *Tel:* 303-841-0246 *E-mail:* natlwritersassn@hotmail.com *Web Site:* www.nationalwriters.com, pg 557

Associated Editors, 27 W 96 St, New York, NY 10025 *Tel:* 212-662-9703 *Fax:* 212-662-9703, pg 488

Associated Press Broadcast, 1100 13 St NW, Suite 700, Washington, DC 20005 *Tel:* 202-641-9000 *Toll Free Tel:* 800-821-4747 *Fax:* 202-370-2710 *E-mail:* info@ap.org *Web Site:* www.ap.org, pg 557

Associated University Presses, 10 Schalks Crossing Rd, Suite 501-330, Plainsboro, NJ 08536 *Tel:* 609-269-8094 *Fax:* 609-269-8096 *E-mail:* aup440@aol.com, pg 24

Association des Libraires du Quebec (ALQ), 407 St-Laurent, bureau 801, Montreal, QC H2Y 2Y5, Canada *Tel:* 514-526-3349 *Fax:* 514-526-3340 *E-mail:* info@alq.qc.ca *Web Site:* www.alq.qc.ca, pg 557

Association for Computing Machinery, 2 Penn Plaza, Suite 701, New York, NY 10121-0701 *Tel:* 212-869-7440 *Toll Free Tel:* 800-342-6626 *Fax:* 212-944-1318 (memb servs) *E-mail:* acmhelp@acm.org *Web Site:* www.acm.org, pg 24

Association for Information & Image Management International (AIIM), 1100 Wayne Ave, Suite 1100, Silver Spring, MD 20910 *Tel:* 301-587-8202 *Toll Free Tel:* 800-477-2446 *Fax:* 301-587-2711 *E-mail:* aiim@aiim.org; info@aiim.org *Web Site:* www.aiim.org, pg 557

Association for Information Science & Technology (ASIS&T), 8555 16 St, Suite 850, Silver Spring, MD 20910 *Tel:* 301-495-0900 *Fax:* 301-495-0810 *E-mail:* asist@asist.org *Web Site:* www.asist.org, pg 24, 557

Association for Talent Development (ATD) Press, 1640 King St, Box 1443, Alexandria, VA 22313-1443 *Tel:* 703-683-8100 *Toll Free Tel:* 800-628-2783 *Fax:* 703-299-8723; 703-683-1523 (cust care) *E-mail:* customercare@td.org *Web Site:* www.astd.org; www.td.org, pg 24

The Association for Women in Communications, 1717 E Republic Rd, Suite A, Springfield, MO 65804 *Tel:* 417-886-8606 *Fax:* 417-886-3685 *E-mail:* info@womcom.org *Web Site:* www.womcom.org, pg 609

Association Media & Publishing (AM&P), 529 14 St, Suite 750, Washington, DC 20045 *Tel:* 202-591-2457 *E-mail:* info@associationmediaandpublishing.org *Web Site:* associationmediaandpublishing.org, pg 558

Association Nationale des Editeurs de Livres, 2514, blvd Rosemont, Montreal, QC H1Y 1K4, Canada *Tel:* 514-273-8130 *Toll Free Tel:* 866-900-ANEL (900-2635) *E-mail:* info@anel.qc.ca *Web Site:* www.anel.qc.ca, pg 558

Association of American Editorial Cartoonists, PO Box 460673, Fort Lauderdale, FL 33346 *Tel:* 954-356-4945 *Web Site:* www.editorialcartoonists.com, pg 558

Association of American Publishers (AAP), 455 Massachusetts Ave NW, Suite 700, Washington, DC 20001-2777 *Tel:* 212-255-0200 *Fax:* 212-255-7007 *E-mail:* info@publishers.org *Web Site:* publishers.org, pg 558

Association of American University Presses (AAUP), 1412 Broadway, Suite 2135, New York, NY 10018 *Tel:* 212-989-1010 *Fax:* 212-989-0275 *E-mail:* info@aaupnet.org *Web Site:* www.aaupnet.org, pg 558

Association of Authors' Representatives Inc, 302A W 12 St, No 122, New York, NY 10014 *Tel:* 212-840-5770 *E-mail:* administrator@aaronline.org *Web Site:* www.aaronline.org, pg 558

Association of Book Publishers of British Columbia, 600-402 W Pender St, Vancouver, BC V6B 1T6, Canada *Tel:* 604-684-0228 *Fax:* 604-684-5788 *E-mail:* admin@books.bc.ca *Web Site:* www.books.bc.ca, pg 558

Association of Canadian Publishers (ACP), 174 Spadina Ave, Suite 306, Toronto, ON M5T 2C2, Canada *Tel:* 416-487-6116 *Fax:* 416-487-8815 *E-mail:* admin@canbook.org *Web Site:* publishers.ca, pg 558

Association of Canadian University Presses, 10 Saint Mary St, Suite 700, Toronto, ON M4Y 2W8, Canada *Tel:* 416-978-2239 ext 237 *Fax:* 416-978-4738 *Web Site:* www.acup.ca, pg 558

Association of Catholic Publishers Inc, 4725 Dorsey Hall Dr, Suite A, PMB 709, Elliott City, MD 21042 *Tel:* 410-988-2926 *Fax:* 410-571-4946 *Web Site:* www.catholicsread.org; www.catholicpublishers.org; www.midatlanticcongress.org, pg 558

Association of College & Research Libraries (ACRL), 50 E Huron St, Chicago, IL 60611 *Tel:* 312-280-2523 *Toll Free Tel:* 800-545-2433 (ext 2523) *Fax:* 312-280-2520 *E-mail:* acrl@ala.org *Web Site:* www.ala.org/acrl, pg 24

Association of College & University Printers (ACUP), PO Box 285, Carrabelle, FL 32322 *Tel:* 850-570-5241 *Web Site:* www.acup-edu.org, pg 559

The Association of English-Language Publishers of Quebec-AELAQ (Association des Editeurs de Langue Anglaise du Quebec), Atwater Library, 1200 Atwater Ave, Suite 3, Westmount, QC H3Z 1X4, Canada *Tel:* 514-932-5633 *E-mail:* admin@aelaq.org *Web Site:* aelaq.org, pg 559

Association of Free Community Papers (AFCP), 135 Old Cove Rd, Suite 210, Liverpool, NY 13090 *Toll Free Tel:* 877-203-2327 *Fax:* 781-459-7770 *E-mail:* afcp@afcp.org *Web Site:* www.afcp.org, pg 559

Association of Jewish Libraries (AJL) Inc, PO Box 1118, Teaneck, NJ 07666 *Tel:* 201-371-3255 *E-mail:* info@jewishlibraries.org *Web Site:* jewishlibraries.org, pg 559

Association of Manitoba Book Publishers, 100 Arthur St, Suite 404, Winnipeg, MB R3B 1H3, Canada *Tel:* 204-947-3335 *Fax:* 204-956-4689 *E-mail:* ambp@mts.net *Web Site:* ambp.ca, pg 559

The Association of Medical Illustrators (AMI), 201 E Main St, Suite 1405, Lexington, KY 40507 *Toll Free Tel:* 866-393-4264 *Fax:* 859-514-9166 *E-mail:* hq@ami.org *Web Site:* www.ami.org, pg 559

Association of Publishers for Special Sales (APSS), PO Box 715, Avon, CT 06001-0715 *Tel:* 860-675-1344 *Web Site:* www.spannet.org, pg 559

Association of Research Libraries, 21 Dupont Circle NW, Suite 800, Washington, DC 20036 *Tel:* 202-296-2296 *Fax:* 202-872-0884 *E-mail:* arlhq@arl.org *Web Site:* www.arl.org, pg 24

Association of School Business Officials International, 11401 N Shore Dr, Reston, VA 20190 *Tel:* 703-478-0405 *Toll Free Tel:* 866-682-2729 *Fax:* 703-708-7060 *E-mail:* asboreq@asbointl.org; asbosba@asbointl.org *Web Site:* www.asbointl.org, pg 24

Association of Writers & Writing Programs (AWP), George Mason University, 4400 University Dr, MSN 1E3, Fairfax, VA 22030 *Tel:* 703-993-4301 *Fax:* 703-993-4302 *E-mail:* awp@awpwriter.org *Web Site:* www.awpwriter.org, pg 559

Association pour l'Avancement des Sciences et des Techniques de la Documentation, 2065 rue Parthenais, Bureau 387, Montreal, QC H2K 3T1, Canada *Tel:* 514-281-5012 *Fax:* 514-281-8219 *E-mail:* info@asted.org *Web Site:* www.asted.org, pg 559, 609

Asta Publications LLC, 275 W Clarkstown Rd, New City, NY 10956 *Tel:* 678-814-1320 *Toll Free Tel:* 800-482-4190 *Fax:* 678-814-1370 *E-mail:* info@astapublications.com *Web Site:* www.astapublications.com, pg 24

Editions ASTED, 2065 rue Parthenais, Bureau 387, Montreal, QC H2K 3T1, Canada *Tel:* 514-281-5012 *Fax:* 514-281-8219 *E-mail:* editions@asted.org; info@asted.org *Web Site:* www.asted.org, pg 445

ASTM International, 100 Barr Harbor Dr, West Conshohocken, PA 19428-2959 *Tel:* 610-832-9500; 610-832-9585 (intl) *Toll Free Tel:* 877-909-2786 (sales & cust support) *Fax:* 610-832-9555 *E-mail:* service@astm.org *Web Site:* www.astm.org, pg 24

Astor Indexers, 22 S Commons, Kent, CT 06757 *Tel:* 860-592-0225; 570-534-8951 (cell), pg 488

Astragal Press, 5995 149 St W, Suite 105, Apple Valley, MN 55124 *Tel:* 952-469-6699 *Toll Free Tel:* 866-543-3045 *Fax:* 952-469-1968 *Toll Free Fax:* 800-330-6232 *E-mail:* info@finneyco.com *Web Site:* www.astragalpress.com, pg 25

The Astronomical Society of the Pacific, 390 Ashton Ave, San Francisco, CA 94112 *Tel:* 415-337-1100 *Toll Free Tel:* 800-335-2624 *Fax:* 415-337-5205 *Web Site:* www.astrosociety.org, pg 25

Athabasca University Press, Edmonton Learning Ctr, Peace Hills Trust Tower, 1200, 10011-109 St, Edmonton, AB T5J 3S8, Canada *Tel:* 780-497-3412 *Fax:* 780-421-3298 *E-mail:* aupress@athabascau.ca *Web Site:* www.aupress.ca, pg 446

Athenaeum of Philadelphia Literary Award, 219 S Sixth St, Philadelphia, PA 19106 *Tel:* 215-925-2688 *Fax:* 215-925-3755 *Web Site:* www.philaathenaeum.org/literary.html, pg 629

Athletic Guide Publishing, PO Box 1050, Flagler Beach, FL 32136 *Tel:* 386-439-2050 *Toll Free Tel:* 800-255-1050 *E-mail:* flaglernet@gmail.com *Web Site:* www.athleticguidepublishing.com, pg 25

Atlantic Center for the Arts Artists-in-Residence Program, 1414 Art Center Ave, New Smyrna Beach, FL 32168 *Tel:* 386-427-6975 *Toll Free Tel:* 800-393-6975 *Fax:* 386-427-5669 *E-mail:* program@atlanticcenterforthearts.org *Web Site:* atlanticcenterforthearts.org, pg 609

Atlantic Law Book Co, 22 Grassmere Ave, West Hartford, CT 06110-1215 *Tel:* 860-231-9300 *Toll Free Tel:* 800-259-5534 *Fax:* 860-231-9242 *E-mail:* atlanticlawbooks@aol.com *Web Site:* www.atlanticlawbooks.com, pg 25

Atlantic Public Art Funders (APAF) Creative Residency, 225 King St, Suite 201, Fredericton, NB E3B 1E1, Canada *Tel:* 506-444-4444 *Toll Free Tel:* 866-460-ARTS (460-2787) *Fax:* 506-444-5543 *Web Site:* www.artsnb.ca, pg 629

Atlantic Publishing Group Inc, 1405 SW Sixth Ave, Ocala, FL 34471 *Tel:* 352-622-1825 *Toll Free Tel:* 800-814-1132 *Fax:* 352-622-1875 *E-mail:* sales@atlantic-pub.com *Web Site:* www.atlantic-pub.com, pg 25

Atlas Publishing, 25185 Madison Ave, Suite A, Murrieta, CA 92562 *Tel:* 858-222-3747 *E-mail:* permissions@atlaspublishing.biz *Web Site:* www.atlaspublishing.biz, pg 25

Atria Books, 1230 Avenue of the Americas, New York, NY 10020 *Tel:* 212-698-7000 *Fax:* 212-698-7007 *Web Site:* www.simonandschuster.com, pg 25

Atwood Publishing, PO Box 3185, Madison, WI 53704 *Tel:* 608-242-7101 *Toll Free Tel:* 888-242-7101 *Fax:* 608-242-7102 *E-mail:* customerservice@atwoodpublishing.com *Web Site:* www.atwoodpublishing.com, pg 25

The Audies®, 333 Hudson St, Suite 503, New York, NY 10013 *Tel:* 646-688-3044 *E-mail:* audies@audiopub.org; info@audiopub.org *Web Site:* www.audiopub.org/members/audies, pg 629

Audrey Owen, 494 Eaglecrest Dr, Gibsons, BC V0N 1V8, Canada *E-mail:* editor@writershelper.com *Web Site:* www.writershelper.com, pg 488

Augsburg Fortress Publishers, Publishing House of the Evangelical Lutheran Church in America, 510 Marquette Ave S, Minneapolis, MN 55402 *Tel:* 612-330-3300 *Toll Free Tel:* 800-426-0115 (ext 639, subns); 800-328-4648 (orders) *Fax:* 612-330-3455 *E-mail:* info@augsburgfortress.org; copyright@augsburgfortress.org (reprint permission requests); customercare@augsburgfortress.org *Web Site:* www.augsburgfortress.org, pg 25

August House Inc, 3500 Piedmont Rd NE, Suite 310, Atlanta, GA 30305 *Tel:* 404-442-4420 *Toll Free Tel:* 800-284-8784 *Fax:* 404-442-4435 *E-mail:* ahinfo@augusthouse.com *Web Site:* www.augusthouse.com, pg 26

Aum Publications, 86-10 Parsons Blvd, Jamaica, NY 11432-3314 *Tel:* 347-744-3199, pg 26

Aurous Inc, PO Box 20490, New York, NY 10017 *Tel:* 212-628-9729 *Fax:* 212-535-7861, pg 507

AuthorHouse, 1663 Liberty Dr, Bloomington, IN 47403 *Tel:* 812-339-6000 (outside US) *Toll Free Tel:* 888-519-5121 *E-mail:* authorsupport@authorhouse.com *Web Site:* www.authorhouse.com, pg 26

Authorlink Press, 103 Guadalupe Dr, Irving, TX 75039-3334 *Tel:* 972-402-0101 *E-mail:* admin@authorlink.com *Web Site:* www.authorlink.com, pg 26

Authors Alliance, 2705 Webster St, No 5805, Berkeley, CA 94705 *E-mail:* info@authorsalliance.org *Web Site:* www.authorsalliance.org, pg 559

The Author's Friend, 548 Ocean Blvd, No 12, Long Branch, NJ 07740 *Tel:* 732-571-8051, pg 488

The Authors Guild, 31 E 32 St, 7th fl, New York, NY 10016 *Tel:* 212-563-5904 *Fax:* 212-564-5363 *E-mail:* staff@authorsguild.org *Web Site:* www.authorsguild.org, pg 559

The Authors League Fund, 31 E 32 St, 7th fl, New York, NY 10016 *Tel:* 212-268-1208 *Fax:* 212-564-5363 *E-mail:* staff@authorsleaguefund.org *Web Site:* www.authorsleaguefund.org, pg 559

The Authors Registry Inc, 31 E 32 St, 7th fl, New York, NY 10016 *Tel:* 212-563-6920 *Fax:* 212-564-5363 *E-mail:* staff@authorsregistry.org *Web Site:* www.authorsregistry.org, pg 559

Autism Asperger Publishing Co, 11209 Strang Line Rd, Lenexa, KS 66215 *Tel:* 913-897-1004 *Toll Free Tel:* 877-277-8254 *Fax:* 913-681-9473 *E-mail:* info@aapcpublishing.net *Web Site:* www.aapcpublishing.net, pg 26

Autumn House Poetry, Fiction & Nonfiction Contests, 5530 Penn Ave, Pittsburgh, PA 15206 *Tel:* 412-362-2665 *E-mail:* info@autumnhouse.org *Web Site:* www.autumnhouse.org, pg 629

Autumn House Press, 5530 Penn Ave, Pittsburgh, PA 15206 *Tel:* 412-362-2665 *E-mail:* info@autumnhouse.org *Web Site:* www.autumnhouse.org, pg 26

Ave Maria Press, PO Box 428, Notre Dame, IN 46556 *Tel:* 574-287-2831 *Toll Free Tel:* 800-282-1865 *Fax:* 574-239-2904 *Toll Free Fax:* 800-282-5681 *E-mail:* avemariapress.1@nd.edu *Web Site:* www.avemariapress.com, pg 26

Avention Inc, 300 Baker Ave, Concord, MA 01742 *Tel:* 978-318-4300 *Toll Free Tel:* 866-354-6936 *Fax:* 978-318-4690 *E-mail:* sales@avention.com *Web Site:* www.avention.com, pg 27

Avery, 375 Hudson St, New York, NY 10014 *Tel:* 212-366-2000 *Fax:* 212-366-2643 *Web Site:* www.penguin.com; www.penguinrandomhouse.com, pg 27

Avery Color Studios, 511 "D" Ave, Gwinn, MI 49841 *Tel:* 906-346-3908 *Toll Free Tel:* 800-722-9925 *Fax:* 906-346-3015 *E-mail:* averycolor@averycolorstudios.com *Web Site:* www.averycolorstudios.com, pg 27

AVKO Educational Research Foundation Inc, 3084 Willard Rd, Birch Run, MI 48415-9404 *Tel:* 810-686-9283 (orders & billing) *Fax:* 810-686-1101 *E-mail:* info@avko.org (gen inquiry) *Web Site:* www.avko.org; www.avko.blogspot.org, pg 27

Avotaynu Inc, 794 Edgewood Ave, New Haven, CT 06515 *Tel:* 475-202-6575 *Toll Free Tel:* 800-AVOTAYNU (286-8296) *E-mail:* info@avotaynu.com *Web Site:* www.avotaynu.com, pg 27

Award of Merit, 633 W 155 St, New York, NY 10032 *Tel:* 212-368-5900 *Fax:* 212-491-4615 *E-mail:* academy@artsandletters.org *Web Site:* www.artsandletters.org, pg 629

Awe-Struck Publishing, 6457 Glenway Ave, Suite 109, Cincinnati, OH 45211-5222 *Toll Free Tel:* 888-402-6657 *Toll Free Fax:* 888-460-4752 *E-mail:* inquiry@mundania.com; orders@mundania.com; submissions@awe-struck.net; books@mundania.com *Web Site:* www.awe-struck.net; www.mundania.com, pg 27

AWP Award Series, George Mason University, 4400 University Dr, MSN 1E3, Fairfax, VA 22030 *Tel:* 703-993-4301 *Fax:* 703-993-4302 *E-mail:* awp@awpwriter.org *Web Site:* www.awpwriter.org, pg 629

The Axelrod Agency, 55 Main St, Chatham, NY 12037 *Tel:* 518-392-2100, pg 507

Axiom Business Book Awards, 1129 Woodmere Ave, Suite B, Traverse City, MI 49686 *Tel:* 231-933-0445 *Toll Free Tel:* 800-706-4636 *Fax:* 231-933-0448 *E-mail:* info@axiomawards.com *Web Site:* www.axiomawards.com, pg 629

AZ Books LLC, 320 Fifth Ave, New York, NY 10001 *Toll Free Tel:* 888-945-7723 *Toll Free Fax:* 888-945-7724 *Web Site:* www.azbooksusa.com, pg 27

Azro Press, 1704 Llano St B, PMB 342, Santa Fe, NM 87505 *Tel:* 505-989-3272 *Fax:* 505-989-3832 *E-mail:* books@azropress.com *Web Site:* www.azropress.com, pg 27

B & B Publishing, 4823 Sherbrooke St W, Off 275, Westmount, QC H3Z 1G7, Canada *Tel:* 514-932-9466 *Fax:* 514-932-5929 *E-mail:* editions@ebbp.ca, pg 446

Babalu Inc, PO Box 23026, Santa Barbara, CA 93121 *Toll Free Tel:* 877-522-2258 *E-mail:* morefun@babaluinc.com *Web Site:* www.babaluinc.com, pg 27

Baby Tattoo Books, 6045 Longridge Ave, Van Nuys, CA 91401 *Tel:* 818-416-5314 *E-mail:* info@babytattoo.com *Web Site:* www.babytattoo.com, pg 27

Backbeat Books, 33 Plymouth St, Suite 302, Montclair, NJ 07042 *Tel:* 973-337-5034 *Toll Free Tel:* 800-637-2852 (Music Dispatch) *Fax:* 973-337-5227 *Web Site:* www.backbeatbooks.com, pg 28

Elizabeth H Backman, 86 Johnnycake Hollow Rd, Pine Plains, NY 12567 *Tel:* 518-398-9344 *Fax:* 518-398-6368 *E-mail:* bethcountry@fairpoint.net, pg 507

Backman Writing & Communications, 32 Hillview Ave, Rensselaer, NY 12144 *Tel:* 518-449-4985 *Web Site:* www.backwrite.com, pg 489

The Backwaters Press, 1124 Pacific St, Suite 8392, Omaha, NE 68108 *Tel:* 402-451-4052 *E-mail:* thebackwaterspress@gmail.com *Web Site:* www.thebackwaterspress.org, pg 28

Baen Publishing Enterprises, PO Box 1188, Wake Forest, NC 27588 *Tel:* 919-570-1640 *Fax:* 919-570-1644 *E-mail:* info@baen.com *Web Site:* www.baen.com, pg 28

Bagwyn Books, Lattie F Coor Hall, 4th fl, Rms 4426-4442, 975 S Myrtle Ave, Tempe, AZ 85281 *Tel:* 480-965-5900 *Fax:* 480-965-1681 *E-mail:* bagwynbooks@acmrs.org *Web Site:* acmrs.org/publications/bagwyn, pg 28

Baha'i Publishing, 401 Greenleaf Ave, Wilmette, IL 60091 *Tel:* 847-425-7950 *Toll Free Tel:* 800-999-9019 (orders) *Fax:* 847-425-7951 *E-mail:* bds@usbnc.org *Web Site:* books.bahai.us; www.bahaibookstore.com, pg 28

Marilyn Baillie Picture Book Award, 40 Orchard View Blvd, Suite 217, Toronto, ON M4R 1B9, Canada *Tel:* 416-975-0010 *Fax:* 416-975-8970 *E-mail:* info@bookcentre.ca *Web Site:* www.bookcentre.ca, pg 629

Baker & Taylor/YALSA Conference Grants, 50 E Huron St, Chicago, IL 60611 *Tel:* 312-280-4390 *Toll Free Tel:* 800-545-2433 *Fax:* 312-280-5276; 312-664-7459 *E-mail:* yalsa@ala.org *Web Site:* www.ala.org/yalsa, pg 629

Baker Books, PO Box 6287, Grand Rapids, MI 49516-6287 *Tel:* 616-676-9185 *Toll Free Tel:* 800-877-2665; 800-679-1957 *Fax:* 616-676-9573 *Toll Free Fax:* 800-398-3111 *Web Site:* www.bakerpublishinggroup.com, pg 28

The Baker Street Irregulars (BSI), 7938 Mill Stream Circle, Indianapolis, IN 46278 *Tel:* 317-293-2212; 317-956-6666 (cell) *Web Site:* bakerstreetjournal.com, pg 560

Nona Balakian Citation for Excellence in Reviewing, 160 Varick St, 11th fl, New York, NY 10013 *E-mail:* info@bookcritics.org *Web Site:* bookcritics.org, pg 630

Balance Sports Publishing LLC, 195 Lucero Way, Portola Valley, CA 94028 *Tel:* 650-561-9586 *Fax:* 650-391-9850 *E-mail:* info@balancesportspublishing.com *Web Site:* www.balancesportspublishing.com, pg 28

The Balcones Fiction Prize, 1212 Rio Grande St, Austin, TX 78701 *Tel:* 512-828-9368 *E-mail:* balcones@austincc.edu *Web Site:* sites.austincc.edu/crw/balcones-prizes, pg 630

The Balcones Poetry Prize, 1212 Rio Grande St, Austin, TX 78701 *Tel:* 512-828-9368 *E-mail:* balcones@austincc.edu *Web Site:* www.austincc.edu/crw/html/balconescenter.html, pg 630

Malaga Baldi Literary Agency, 233 W 99, Suite 19C, New York, NY 10025 *Tel:* 212-222-3213 *E-mail:* baldibooks@gmail.com *Web Site:* www.baldibooks.com, pg 507

Baldwin Literary Services, 935 Hayes St, Baldwin, NY 11510-4834 *Tel:* 516-546-8338 *Fax:* 516-546-8338, pg 489

Ball-Stick-Bird Publications Inc, PO Box 429, Williamstown, MA 01267-0429 *Tel:* 413-664-0002 *Fax:* 413-664-0002 *E-mail:* info@ballstickbird.com, pg 28

Ballinger Publishing, 314 N Spring St, Suite A, Pensacola, FL 32501 *Tel:* 850-433-1166 *Fax:* 850-435-9174 *E-mail:* info@ballingerpublishing.com *Web Site:* www.ballingerpublishing.com, pg 28

Carol Bancroft & Friends, PO Box 2030, Danbury, CT 06813 *Tel:* 203-730-8270 *Fax:* 203-730-8275 *E-mail:* cbfriends@sbcglobal.net *Web Site:* www.carolbancroft.com, pg 543

Bancroft Press, 3209 Bancroft Rd, Baltimore, MD 21215 *Tel:* 410-358-0658 *Fax:* 410-764-1967 *Web Site:* www.bancroftpress.com, pg 29

Bancroft Prizes, 517 Butler Library, Mail Code 1101, 535 W 114 St, New York, NY 10027 *Tel:* 212-854-4746 *Fax:* 212-854-9099 *Web Site:* www.columbia.edu/about/awards/bancroft.html, pg 630

Bandanna Books, 1212 Punta Gorda St, No 13, Santa Barbara, CA 93103 *E-mail:* bandanna@cox.net *Web Site:* www.bandannabooks.com; www.mudbornpress.us; www.betabooks.us; www.shakespeareplaybook.com; www.bookdoc.us; catandbirdiebooks.com, pg 29

B&H Publishing Group, One LifeWay Plaza, Nashville, TN 37234 *Tel:* 615-251-2520 *Fax:* 615-251-5004 *Web Site:* www.bhpublishinggroup.com, pg 29

Banff Centre Press, 107 Tunnel Mountain Dr, Banff, AB T1L 1H5, Canada *Tel:* 403-762-6408 *E-mail:* press@banffcentre.ca *Web Site:* www.banffcentre.ca/press, pg 446

Banner of Truth, 63 E Louther St, Carlisle, PA 17013 *Tel:* 717-249-5747 *Toll Free Tel:* 800-263-8085 (orders) *Fax:* 717-249-0604 *E-mail:* info@banneroftruth.org *Web Site:* www.banneroftruth.co.uk; www.banneroftruth.org, pg 29

A Richard Barber/Peter Berinstein & Associates, 60 E Eighth St, Suite 21-N, New York, NY 10003 *Tel:* 212-737-7266 *Fax:* 860-927-3942 *E-mail:* barberrich@aol.com, pg 507

Barbour Publishing Inc, 1810 Barbour Dr, Uhrichsville, OH 44683 *Tel:* 740-922-6045 *Fax:* 740-922-5948 *E-mail:* info@barbourbooks.com *Web Site:* www.barbourbooks.com, pg 29

Barcelona Publishers, 27602 Bogen Rd, New Braunfels, TX 78132-3873 *Tel:* 830-980-6422 *E-mail:* barcelonapublishers@gvtc.com; barcelonapublishers@ware-pak.com (orders) *Web Site:* www.barcelonapublishers.com, pg 29

Bard Society Fiction Writing Workshop, 3113 Crosby Lane, Jacksonville, FL 32216 *Tel:* 904-250-6045 *E-mail:* frankgrn@comcast.net, pg 609

Barefoot Books, 2067 Massachusetts Ave, 5th fl, Cambridge, MA 02140 *Tel:* 617-576-0660 *Toll Free Tel:* 866-215-1756 (cust serv); 866-417-2369 (orders) *Fax:* 617-576-0049 *E-mail:* help@barefootbooks.com *Web Site:* www.barefootbooks.com, pg 29

The Barnabas Agency, PO Box 3113, Corsicana, TX 75151-3113 *Toll Free Tel:* 800-927-0517 *E-mail:* info@barnabasagency.com *Web Site:* www.barnabasagency.com, pg 547

Barnes & Noble Writers for Writers Award, 90 Broad St, Suite 2100, New York, NY 10004 *Tel:* 212-226-3586 *Fax:* 212-226-3963 *E-mail:* admin@pw.org *Web Site:* www.pw.org, pg 630

Kathleen Barnes, 238 W Fourth St, Suite 3-C, New York, NY 10014 *Tel:* 212-924-8084 *E-mail:* kbarnes@compasscommunications.org, pg 489

Barnhardt & Ashe Publishing Inc, 444 Brickell Ave, Suite 51, PMB 432, Miami, FL 33131 *Toll Free Tel:* 800-283-6360 (orders) *E-mail:* barnhardtashe@aol.com *Web Site:* barnhardtashepublishing.com, pg 29

Baror International Inc, PO Box 868, Armonk, NY 10504-0868 *Tel:* 914-273-9199 *Fax:* 914-273-5058 *Web Site:* www.barorint.com, pg 507

Barranca Press, 1450 Couse St, No 10, Taos, NM 87571 *Tel:* 575-613-1026 *E-mail:* editor@barrancapress.com *Web Site:* www.barrancapress.com, pg 29

Loretta Barrett Books Inc, 220 E 23 St, 11th fl, New York, NY 10010 *Tel:* 212-242-3420 *E-mail:* lbbquery@gmail.com *Web Site:* www.lorettabarrettbooks.com, pg 507

Melinda Barrett, 37915 Sundance Dr, Coarsegold, CA 93614 *Tel:* 559-641-0944 *E-mail:* mbarrett_3@netzero.net, pg 489

Barricade Books Inc, 2037 LeMoine Ave, Fort Lee, NJ 07024 *Tel:* 201-944-7600 *E-mail:* customerservice@barricadebooks.com *Web Site:* www.barricadebooks.com, pg 29

Barringer Publishing, 3259 Sundance Circle, Naples, FL 34109 *Tel:* 239-514-7364 *E-mail:* schlesadv@gmail.com *Web Site:* www.barringerpublishing.com, pg 30

Barron's Educational Series Inc, 250 Wireless Blvd, Hauppauge, NY 11788 *Tel:* 631-434-3311 *Toll Free Tel:* 800-645-3476 *Fax:* 631-434-3723 *E-mail:* barrons@barronseduc.com *Web Site:* www.barronseduc.com, pg 30

Barrytown/Station Hill Press, 120 Station Hill Rd, Barrytown, NY 12507 *Tel:* 845-758-5293 *E-mail:* publishers@stationhill.org *Web Site:* www.stationhill.org, pg 30

Diana Barth, 535 W 51 St, Suite 3-A, New York, NY 10019 *Tel:* 212-307-5465 *E-mail:* diabarth@juno.com, pg 489

Anita Bartholomew, 16650 SE Sunridge Lane, Portland, OR 97267 *Tel:* 941-358-0495 *E-mail:* anita@anitabartholomew.com *Web Site:* www.anitabartholomew.com, pg 489

Bartleby Press, 8926 Baltimore St, No 858, Savage, MD 20763 *Tel:* 301-589-5831 *Toll Free Tel:* 800-953-9929 *E-mail:* inquiries@bartlebythepublisher.com *Web Site:* www.bartlebythepublisher.com, pg 30

Basic Health Publications, 4507 Charlotte Ave, Suite 100, Nashville, TN 37209 *Tel:* 615-255-2665, pg 30

Baskerville Publishers Poetry Award, Dept of English, TCU Box 298300, Fort Worth, TX 76129 *Tel:* 817-257-5907 *Fax:* 817-257-5905 *E-mail:* descant@tcu.edu *Web Site:* www.descant.tcu.edu, pg 630

The Mildred L Batchelder Award, 50 E Huron St, Chicago, IL 60611-2795 *Tel:* 312-280-2163 *Toll Free Tel:* 800-545-2433 *Fax:* 312-440-9374; 312-280-5271 *E-mail:* alsc@ala.org *Web Site:* www.ala.org/alsc, pg 630

Mark E Battersby, PO Box 527, Ardmore, PA 19003 *Tel:* 610-924-9157 *Fax:* 610-924-9159 *E-mail:* mebatt12@earthlink.net *Web Site:* www.thetaxscribe.com, pg 489

Bay Tree Publishing LLC, 1400 Pinnacle Ct, Suite 406, Point Richmond, CA 94801 *Tel:* 510-236-1475 *Toll Free Fax:* 866-552-7329 *Web Site:* www.baytreepublish.com, pg 30

Bayeux Arts Inc, 119 Stratton Crescent SW, Calgary, AB T3H 1T7, Canada *E-mail:* mail@bayeux.com *Web Site:* bayeux.com, pg 446

Baylor University Press, Baylor University, One Bear Place, Waco, TX 76798-7363 *Tel:* 254-710-3164 *Fax:* 254-710-3440 *Web Site:* www.baylorpress.com, pg 30

Baylor University, Professional Writing Program, One Bear Place, Unit 97404, Waco, TX 76798-7404 *Tel:* 254-710-1768 *Fax:* 254-710-3894 *Web Site:* www.baylor.edu, pg 619

The BC Book Prizes, 207 W Hastings St, Suite 901, Vancouver, BC V6B 1H7, Canada *Fax:* 604-687-2435 *E-mail:* info@bcbookprizes.ca *Web Site:* www.bcbookprizes.ca, pg 630

BCHF Historial Writing Competition, PO Box 5254, Sta B, Victoria, BC V8R 6N4, Canada *E-mail:* writing@bchistory.ca *Web Site:* www.bchistory.ca, pg 630

Beach Lloyd Publishers LLC, 40 Cabot Dr, Wayne, PA 19087-5619 *Tel:* 610-407-9107 *Fax:* 775-254-0633 *E-mail:* beachlloyd@erols.com *Web Site:* www.beachlloyd.com, pg 30

Beacon Hill Press of Kansas City, PO Box 419527, Kansas City, MO 64141 *Tel:* 816-931-1900 *Toll Free Tel:* 800-877-0700 (cust serv) *Fax:* 816-753-4071 *Web Site:* www.nph.com, pg 30

Beacon Press, 24 Farnsworth St, Boston, MA 02210-1409 *Tel:* 617-742-2110 *Fax:* 617-723-3097; 617-742-2290 *Web Site:* www.beacon.org, pg 31

Bear & Co Inc, One Park St, Rochester, VT 05767 *Tel:* 802-767-3174 *Toll Free Tel:* 800-932-3277 *Fax:* 802-767-3726 *E-mail:* customerservice@InnerTraditions.com *Web Site:* InnerTraditions.com, pg 31

James Beard Foundation Book Awards, Office of Awards, 6 W 18 St, 10th fl, New York, NY 10011 *Tel:* 212-627-1111 (ext 563) *Web Site:* www.jamesbeard.org/awards, pg 630

BearManor Media, PO Box 71426, Albany, GA 31708 *Tel:* 580-252-3547 *E-mail:* orders@benohmart.com; books@benohmart.com *Web Site:* www.bearmanormedia.com, pg 31

Bearport Publishing Co Inc, 45 W 21 St, Suite 3B, New York, NY 10010 *Tel:* 212-337-8577 *Toll Free Tel:* 877-337-8577 *Fax:* 212-337-8557 *Toll Free Fax:* 866-337-8557 *E-mail:* service@bearportpublishing.com; info@bearportpublishing.com *Web Site:* www.bearportpublishing.com, pg 31

Beaver Wood Associates, 655 Alstead Center Rd, Alstead, NH 03602 *Tel:* 603-835-7900 *Web Site:* www.beaverwood.com, pg 489

Beaver's Pond Press Inc, 7108 Ohms Lane, Edina, MN 55439 *Tel:* 952-829-8818 *E-mail:* info@beaverspondpress.com *Web Site:* www.beaverspondpress.com, pg 31

Bedford/St Martin's, 75 Arlington St, Boston, MA 02116 *Tel:* 617-399-4000 *Toll Free Tel:* 800-779-7440 *Fax:* 617-426-8582 *Web Site:* www.bedfordstmartins.com, pg 31

Beekman Books Inc, 300 Old All Angels Hill Rd, Wappingers Falls, NY 12590 *Tel:* 845-297-2690 *Fax:* 845-297-1002 *E-mail:* beekmanbooks@yahoo.com *Web Site:* www.beekmanbooks.com, pg 32

George Louis Beer Prize, 400 "A" St SE, Washington, DC 20003 *Tel:* 202-544-2422 *Fax:* 202-544-8307 *E-mail:* awards@historians.org *Web Site:* www.historians.org, pg 631

Before Columbus Foundation, The Raymond House, 655 13 St, Suite 302, Oakland, CA 94612 *Tel:* 916-425-7916 *E-mail:* info@beforecolumbusfoundation.com *Web Site:* www.beforecolumbusfoundation.com, pg 560

Begell House Inc Publishers, 50 North St, Danbury, CT 06810 *Tel:* 203-456-6161 *Fax:* 203-456-6167 *E-mail:* orders@begellhouse.com *Web Site:* www.begellhouse.com, pg 32

Behrman House Inc, 11 Edison Place, Springfield, NJ 07081 *Tel:* 973-379-7200 *Toll Free Tel:* 800-221-2755 *Fax:* 973-379-7280 *E-mail:* customersupport@behrmanhouse.com *Web Site:* www.behrmanhouse.com, pg 32

Frederic C Beil Publisher Inc, 609 Whitaker St, Savannah, GA 31401 *Tel:* 912-233-2446 *E-mail:* editor@beil.com; order@beil.com *Web Site:* www.beil.com, pg 32

Beliveau Editeur, 567 rue Bienville, Boucherville, QC J4B 2Z5, Canada *Tel:* 450-679-1933 *Web Site:* www.beliveauediteur.com, pg 446

Bell Springs Publishing, PO Box 1240, Willits, CA 95490-1240 *Tel:* 707-272-3472 *E-mail:* publisher@bellsprings.com *Web Site:* bellsprings.com; aboutpinball.com, pg 32

Bella Books, PO Box 10543, Tallahassee, FL 32302 *Tel:* 850-576-2370 *Toll Free Tel:* 800-729-4992 *Fax:* 850-576-3498 *E-mail:* info@bellabooks.com; orders@bellabooks.com; ebooks@bellabooks.com *Web Site:* www.bellabooks.com, pg 32

BelleBooks, PO Box 300921, Memphis, TN 38130 *Tel:* 901-344-9024 *Fax:* 901-344-9068 *E-mail:* bellebooks@bellebooks.com *Web Site:* www.bellebooks.com, pg 32

Bellerophon Books, PO Box 21307, Santa Barbara, CA 93121-1307 *Tel:* 805-965-7034 *Toll Free Tel:* 800-253-9943 *Fax:* 805-965-8286 *E-mail:* sales.bellerophon@gmail.com *Web Site:* www.bellerophonbooks.com, pg 32

Belltown Media, PO Box 980985, Houston, TX 77098 *Tel:* 713-344-1956 *Fax:* 713-583-7956 *E-mail:* subs@linuxjournal.com *Web Site:* www.belltownmedia.com, pg 32

The Pura Belpre Award, 50 E Huron St, Chicago, IL 60611-2795 *Tel:* 312-280-2163 *Toll Free Tel:* 800-545-2433 *Fax:* 312-440-9374; 312-280-5271 *E-mail:* alsc@ala.org *Web Site:* www.ala.org/alsc, pg 631

Ben Yehuda Press, 122 Ayers Ct, No 1B, Teaneck, NJ 07666 *Tel:* 201-836-0180 *Fax:* 201-917-1278 *E-mail:* orders@benyehudapress.com; yudel@benyehudapress.com *Web Site:* www.benyehudapress.com, pg 32

BenBella Books Inc, 10300 N Central Expwy, Suite 400, Dallas, TX 75231 *Tel:* 214-750-3600 *Fax:* 214-750-3645 *E-mail:* feedback@benbellabooks.com *Web Site:* www.benbellabooks.com; www.smartpopbooks.com, pg 32

R James Bender Publishing, PO Box 23456, San Jose, CA 95153-3456 *Tel:* 408-225-5777 *Fax:* 408-225-4739 *Web Site:* www.bender-publishing.com, pg 33

Benjamin Franklin Awards™, 1020 Manhattan Beach Blvd, Suite 204, Manhattan Beach, CA 90266 *Tel:* 310-546-1818 *Fax:* 310-546-3939 *E-mail:* info@ibpa-online.org *Web Site:* www.ibpa-online.org; ibpabenjaminfranklinawards.com, pg 631

John Benjamins Publishing Co, 763 N 24 St, Philadelphia, PA 19130 *Tel:* 207-725-7250 *Toll Free Tel:* 800-562-5666 (orders) *Fax:* 207-725-7252 *E-mail:* service@benjamins.com *Web Site:* www.benjamins.com, pg 33

George Bennett Fellowship, Phillips Exeter Academy, Off of the Dean of Faculty, 20 Main St, Exeter, NH 03833-2460 *Tel:* 603-772-4311 *Fax:* 603-777-4384 *E-mail:* teaching_opportunities@exeter.edu *Web Site:* www.exeter.edu, pg 631

Benoit & Associates, 279 S Schuyler Ave, Kankakee, IL 60901 *Tel:* 815-932-2582 *Fax:* 815-932-2582 *Web Site:* www.benoit-associates.com, pg 543

Bentley Publishers, 1734 Massachusetts Ave, Cambridge, MA 02138-1804 *Tel:* 617-547-4170 *Toll Free Tel:* 800-423-4595 *Fax:* 617-876-9235 *E-mail:* sales@bentleypublishers.com *Web Site:* www.bentleypublishers.com, pg 33

BePuzzled, 2030 Harrison St, San Francisco, CA 94110 *Tel:* 415-503-1600 *Toll Free Tel:* 800-347-4818 *Fax:* 415-503-0085 *E-mail:* info@ugames.com *Web Site:* www.ugames.com, pg 33

Naomi Berber Memorial Award, 301 Brush Creek Rd, Warrendale, PA 15086-7529 *Tel:* 412-741-6860 *Toll Free Tel:* 800-910-4283 *Fax:* 412-741-2311 *E-mail:* printingind@comm.printing.org *Web Site:* www.printing.org/berberaward, pg 631

Berghahn Books, 20 Jay St, Suite 512, Brooklyn, NY 11201 *Tel:* 212-233-6004 *Fax:* 212-233-6007 *E-mail:* info@berghahnbooks.com; salesus@berghahnbooks.com; editorial@journals.berghahnbooks.com *Web Site:* www.berghahnbooks.com, pg 33

Barbara Bergstrom MA LLC, 13 Stockton Way, Howell, NJ 07731 *Tel:* 732-363-8372, pg 489

Berkeley Slavic Specialties, PO Box 3034, Oakland, CA 94609-0034 *Tel:* 510-653-8048 *Fax:* 510-653-6313 *E-mail:* 71034.456@compuserve.com *Web Site:* www.berkslav.com, pg 33

Berkley Publishing Group, 375 Hudson St, New York, NY 10014 *Tel:* 212-366-2000 *Fax:* 212-366-2385 *Web Site:* www.penguin.com, pg 33

Berkshire Publishing Group LLC, PO Box 177, Great Barrington, MA 01230 *E-mail:* info@berkshirepublishing.com *Web Site:* www.berkshirepublishing.com, pg 33

Bernan, 4501 Forbes Blvd, Suite 200, Lanham, MD 20706 *Tel:* 301-459-7666 (cust serv & orders) *Fax:* 301-459-6988 *E-mail:* customercare@bernan.com *Web Site:* www.bernan.com, pg 33

Jean Brodsky Bernard, 4609 Chevy Chase Blvd, Chevy Chase, MD 20815-5343 *Tel:* 301-654-8914 *E-mail:* dranreb@starpower.net, pg 489

Jessie Bernard Award, c/o Governance Off, 1430 "K" St NW, Suite 600, Washington, DC 20005 *Tel:* 202-383-9005 *Fax:* 202-638-0882 *E-mail:* governance@asanet.org *Web Site:* www.asanet.org, pg 631

The Charles Bernheimer Prize, University of South Carolina, Dept of Languages, Literature & Cultures, 1620 College St, Rm 813-A, Columbia, SC 29208 *Tel:* 803-777-3021 *E-mail:* info@acla.org *Web Site:* www.acla.org/prize-awards, pg 631

Bernstein & Andriulli Inc, 190 Bowery, 3rd fl, New York, NY 10012 *Tel:* 212-682-1490 *Fax:* 212-286-1890 *E-mail:* info@ba-reps.com *Web Site:* www.ba-reps.com, pg 543

Meredith Bernstein Literary Agency Inc, 2095 Broadway, Suite 505, New York, NY 10023 *Tel:* 212-799-1007 *Fax:* 212-799-1145 *E-mail:* MGoodBern@aol.com *Web Site:* www.meredithbernsteinliteraryagency.com, pg 507

Berrett-Koehler Publishers Inc, 1333 Broadway, Suite 1000, Oakland, CA 94612 *Tel:* 510-817-2277 *Fax:* 510-817-2278 *E-mail:* bkpub@bkpub.com *Web Site:* www.bkconnection.com, pg 34

Bess Press, 3565 Harding Ave, Honolulu, HI 96816 *Tel:* 808-734-7159 *Fax:* 808-732-3627 *E-mail:* customerservice@besspress.com *Web Site:* www.besspress.com, pg 34

A M Best Co, One Ambest Rd, Oldwick, NJ 08858 *Tel:* 908-439-2200 (ext 5311, sales); 908-439-2200 *Fax:* 908-439-3385 *E-mail:* customer_service@ambest.com; sales@ambest.com *Web Site:* www.ambest.com, pg 34

Best Translated Book Award, c/o Open Letter, University of Rochester, Dewey Hall 1-219, Box 278968, Rochester, NY 14627 *Tel:* 585-276-5305 *E-mail:* msc@rochester.edu *Web Site:* besttranslatedbook.org, pg 631

Bethany House Publishers, 11400 Hampshire Ave S, Bloomington, MN 55438 *Tel:* 952-829-2500 *Toll Free Tel:* 800-877-2665 (orders) *Fax:* 952-829-2568 *Toll Free Fax:* 800-398-3111 (orders) *Web Site:* www.bethanyhouse.com; www.bakerpublishinggroup.com, pg 34

The Bethel Agency, PO Box 21043, Park West Sta, New York, NY 10025 *Tel:* 212-864-4510 *E-mail:* bethelagcy@aol.com, pg 507

Bethlehem Books, 10194 Garfield St S, Bathgate, ND 58216 *Toll Free Tel:* 800-757-6831 *Fax:* 701-265-3716 *E-mail:* contact@bethlehembooks.com *Web Site:* www.bethlehembooks.com, pg 34

Betterway Books, 10151 Carver Rd, Suite 200, Blue Ash, OH 45242 *Tel:* 513-531-2690 *Toll Free Tel:* 800-666-0963 *Fax:* 513-891-7185 *Toll Free Fax:* 888-590-4082 *Web Site:* www.fwmedia.com, pg 34

Doris Betts Fiction Prize, PO Box 21591, Winston-Salem, NC 27120-1591 *Tel:* 336-293-8844 *E-mail:* mail@ncwriters.org; nclrsubmissions@ecu.edu *Web Site:* www.ncwriters.org, pg 631

Between the Lines, 401 Richmond St W, No 277, Toronto, ON M5V 3A8, Canada *Tel:* 416-535-9914 *Toll Free Tel:* 800-718-7201 *Fax:* 416-535-1484 *E-mail:* info@btlbooks.com *Web Site:* btlbooks.com, pg 446

Beullah Rose Poetry Prize, PO Box 22161, Baltimore, MD 21203 *E-mail:* smartishpace@gmail.com *Web Site:* www.smartishpace.com, pg 631

Blue Apple Books, 515 Valley St, Suite 170, Maplewood, NJ 07040 *Tel:* 973-763-8191 *Toll Free Tel:* 800-283-3572 (orders) *Fax:* 973-763-5944 *E-mail:* info@blueapplebooks.com *Web Site:* blueapplebooks.com, pg 38

Blue Bike Books, 58 Lodgepole Crescent, St Albert, AB T8N 2R7, Canada *Tel:* 780-435-2376 *E-mail:* info@bluebikebooks.com *Web Site:* www.bluebikebooks.com, pg 446

Blue Book Publications Inc, 8009 34 Ave S, Suite 250, Minneapolis, MN 55425 *Tel:* 952-854-5229 *Toll Free Tel:* 800-877-4867 *Fax:* 952-853-1486 *E-mail:* support@bluebookinc.com *Web Site:* www.bluebookofgunvalues.com; www.bluebookofguitarvalues.com, pg 38

Blue Crane Books Inc, 36 Hazel St, Watertown, MA 02472 *Tel:* 617-926-8989, pg 38

Blue Mountain Arts Inc, 2905 Wilderness Place, Suite 100, Boulder, CO 80301 *Tel:* 303-449-0536 *Toll Free Tel:* 800-525-0642 *Fax:* 303-417-6472 *Toll Free Fax:* 800-545-8573 *E-mail:* info@sps.com *Web Site:* www.sps.com, pg 38

Blue Note Publications Inc, *Tel:* 321-799-2583 *Toll Free Tel:* 800-624-0401 (orders) *Fax:* 321-799-1942 *E-mail:* bluenotepress@gmail.com *Web Site:* www.bluenotebooks.com, pg 38

Blue Poppy Press, 1990 57 Ct, Unit A, Boulder, CO 80301 *Tel:* 303-447-8372 *Toll Free Tel:* 800-487-9296 *Fax:* 303-245-8362 *E-mail:* info@bluepoppy.com *Web Site:* www.bluepoppy.com, pg 38

BlueBridge, PO Box 601, Katonah, NY 10536 *Tel:* 914-301-5901 *Web Site:* www.bluebridgebooks.com, pg 38

Bluestocking Press, 3045 Sacramento St, No 1014, Placerville, CA 95667-1014 *Tel:* 530-622-8586 *Toll Free Tel:* 800-959-8586 *Fax:* 530-642-9222 *E-mail:* customerservice@bluestockingpress.com; orders@bluestockingpress.com *Web Site:* www.bluestockingpress.com, pg 38

BMI®, 7 World Trade Ctr, 250 Greenwich St, New York, NY 10007-0030 *Tel:* 212-586-2000; 212-220-3000 *Toll Free Tel:* 888-689-5264 (sales); 800-925-8451 (cust rel) *Fax:* 212-246-2163 *E-mail:* foundation@bmi.com *Web Site:* www.bmi.com, pg 560

BNi Building News, 990 Park Center Dr, Suite E, Vista, CA 92081-8352 *Tel:* 760-734-1113 *Toll Free Tel:* 888-BNI-BOOK (264-2665) *Web Site:* www.bnibooks.com, pg 39

BOA Editions Ltd, 250 N Goodman St, Suite 306, Rochester, NY 14607 *Tel:* 585-546-3410 *Fax:* 585-546-3913 *E-mail:* contact@boaeditions.org *Web Site:* www.boaeditions.org, pg 39

BoardSource, 750 Ninth St NW, Suite 650, Washington, DC 20001-4793 *Tel:* 202-349-2500 *Toll Free Tel:* 877-892-6273 *Fax:* 202-349-2599 *E-mail:* members@boardsource.org *Web Site:* www.boardsource.org, pg 39

Reid Boates Literary Agency, 69 Cooks Crossroad, Pittstown, NJ 08867-0328 *Tel:* 908-797-8087 *E-mail:* reid.boates@gmail.com, pg 508

The James Boatwright III Prize for Poetry, Washington & Lee University, Mattingly House, 204 W Washington St, Lexington, VA 24450-2116 *Tel:* 540-458-8908 *E-mail:* shenandoah@wlu.edu *Web Site:* shenandoahliterary.org, pg 633

Rebekah Johnson Bobbitt National Prize for Poetry, 101 Independence Ave SE, Washington, DC 20540-4861 *Tel:* 202-707-5394 *Web Site:* www.loc.gov/poetry, pg 633

Frederick Bock Prize, 61 W Superior St, Chicago, IL 60654 *Tel:* 312-787-7070 *Fax:* 312-787-6650 *E-mail:* editors@poetrymagazine.org *Web Site:* www.poetryfoundation.org, pg 633

George Bogin Memorial Award, 15 Gramercy Park, New York, NY 10003 *Tel:* 212-254-9628 *Web Site:* www.poetrysociety.org, pg 633

Bogle International Library Travel Fund, 50 E Huron St, Chicago, IL 60611-2795 *Tel:* 312-280-3201 *Toll Free Tel:* 800-545-2433 (ext 3201) *Fax:* 312-280-4392 *E-mail:* intl@ala.org *Web Site:* www.ala.org, pg 633

Editions du Bois-de-Coulonge, 1140 Ave de Montigny, Sillery, QC G1S 3T7, Canada *Tel:* 418-683-6332 *Web Site:* www.ebc.qc.ca, pg 447

Bolchazy-Carducci Publishers Inc, 1570 Baskin Rd, Mundelein, IL 60060 *Tel:* 847-526-4344 *Toll Free Tel:* 800-392-6453 *Fax:* 847-526-2867 *E-mail:* info@bolchazy.com; orders@bolchazy.com *Web Site:* www.bolchazy.com, pg 39

Bold Strokes Books Inc, PO Box 249, Valley Falls, NY 12185 *Tel:* 518-677-5127 *Fax:* 518-677-5291 *E-mail:* bsb@boldstrokesbooks.com *Web Site:* www.boldstrokesbooks.com, pg 39

Laura Day Boggs Bolling Memorial, 900 Timber Creek Place, Virginia Beach, VA 23464 *E-mail:* poetryinva@aol.com *Web Site:* poetrysocietyofvirginia.org, pg 633

Bonasa Press, PO Box 340, Crosby, ND 58730 *Tel:* 701-965-3974 *E-mail:* new@bonasapress.com (inquiries) *Web Site:* www.bonasapress.com, pg 39

Alison Bond Literary Agency, 171 W 79 St, No 143, New York, NY 10024, pg 508

Bond Literary Agency, 4340 E Kentucky Ave, Suite 471, Denver, CO 80246 *Tel:* 303-781-9305 *E-mail:* queries@bondliteraryagency.com *Web Site:* bondliteraryagency.com, pg 508

Bondfire Books, 7680 Goddard St, Suite 220, Colorado Springs, CO 80920 *Tel:* 719-260-7080 *Web Site:* www.bondfirebooks.com, pg 39

Book & Periodical Council (BPC), 192 Spadina Ave, Suite 107, Toronto, ON M5T 2C2, Canada *Tel:* 416-975-9366 *Fax:* 416-975-1839 *E-mail:* info@thebpc.ca *Web Site:* www.thebpc.ca, pg 560

Book Industry Guild of New York, PO Box 2001, New York, NY 10113-2001 *E-mail:* admin@bookindustryguildofny.org *Web Site:* www.bookindustryguildofny.org, pg 560

Book Industry Study Group Inc (BISG), 1412 Broadway, Suite 2119, New York, NY 10018 *Tel:* 646-336-7141 *E-mail:* info@bisg.org *Web Site:* bisg.org, pg 560

Book Manufacturers' Institute Inc (BMI), PO Box 731388, Ormond Beach, FL 32173 *Tel:* 386-986-4552 *Fax:* 386-986-4553 *E-mail:* info@bmibook.com *Web Site:* www.bmibook.org, pg 560

Book Marketing Works LLC, 50 Lovely St (Rte 177), Avon, CT 06001 *Tel:* 860-675-1344 *Web Site:* www.bookmarketingworks.com, pg 39

Book Peddlers, 18330 Minnetonka Blvd, Deephaven, MN 55391 *Tel:* 952-544-1154 *Fax:* 206-339-6913 *E-mail:* bookpeddlers@aol.com *Web Site:* www.bookpeddlers.com, pg 39

Book Publicists of Southern California, 714 Crescent Dr, Beverly Hills, CA 90210 *Tel:* 323-461-3921 *Fax:* 323-461-0917 *Web Site:* www.bookpublicists.org, pg 560

The Book Publishers Association of Alberta (BPAA), 10523 100 Ave, Edmonton, AB T5J 0A8, Canada *Tel:* 780-424-5060 *E-mail:* info@bookpublishers.ab.ca *Web Site:* www.bookpublishers.ab.ca, pg 561

Book Publishing Co, 415 Farm Rd, Summertown, TN 38483 *Tel:* 931-964-3571 *Fax:* 931-964-3518 *E-mail:* info@bookpubco.com *Web Site:* www.bookpubco.com, pg 39

Book Sales, 142 W 36 St, 4th fl, New York, NY 10018 *Tel:* 212-779-4972; 212-779-4971 *Fax:* 212-779-6058 *E-mail:* booksales@quarto.com; customerservice@quarto.com *Web Site:* www.quartoknows.com, pg 40

The Book Tree, 3316 Adams Ave, Suite A, San Diego, CA 92116 *Tel:* 619-280-1263 *Toll Free Tel:* 800-700-8733 (orders) *Fax:* 619-280-1285 *E-mail:* orders@thebooktree.com; titles@thebooktree.com; info@thebooktree.com *Web Site:* thebooktree.com, pg 40

Bookbuilders of Boston, 115 Webster Woods Lane, North Andover, MA 01845 *Tel:* 781-378-1361 *Fax:* 419-821-2171 *E-mail:* office@bbboston.org *Web Site:* www.bbboston.org, pg 561

BookCrafters LLC, Box C, Convent Station, NJ 07961 *Tel:* 973-984-7880 *Web Site:* bookcraftersllc.com, pg 489

BookEnds Literary Agency, 136 Long Hill Rd, Gillette, NJ 07933 *Web Site:* www.bookendsliterary.com, pg 508

Bookhaven Press LLC, 302 Scenic Ct, Moon Township, PA 15108 *Tel:* 412-494-6926 *E-mail:* info@bookhavenpress.com; orders@bookhavenpress.com *Web Site:* bookhavenpress.com, pg 40

BookLogix, 1264 Old Alpharetta Rd, Alpharetta, GA 30005 *Tel:* 470-239-8547 *Toll Free Fax:* 888-564-7890 *E-mail:* sales@booklogix.com *Web Site:* www.booklogix.com, pg 40

The Bookmill, 501 Palisades Dr, No 315, Pacific Palisades, CA 90272-2848 *Tel:* 310-459-0190 *E-mail:* thebookmill1@verizon.net *Web Site:* www.thebookmill.us, pg 490

Books & Such, 52 Mission Circle, Suite 122, PMB 170, Santa Rosa, CA 95409-5370 *Tel:* 707-538-4184 *Web Site:* booksandsuch.com, pg 509

Books for a Better Life Awards, 733 Third Ave, 3rd fl, New York, NY 10017 *Tel:* 212-463-7787 *Toll Free Tel:* 800-344-4867 *Fax:* 212-986-7981 *Web Site:* msnycbooks.org, pg 633

Books for Everybody, 111 Queen St E, Suite 320, Toronto, ON M5C 1S2, Canada *Tel:* 416-364-3333 *Toll Free Tel:* 888-360-6658 *Fax:* 416-595-5415, pg 561

Books In Motion, 9922 E Montgomery, Suite 31, Spokane Valley, WA 99206 *Tel:* 509-922-1646 *Toll Free Tel:* 800-752-3199 *Fax:* 509-922-1445 *E-mail:* info@booksinmotion.com *Web Site:* www.booksinmotion.com, pg 40

Books on Tape®, 1745 Broadway, New York, NY 10019 *Toll Free Tel:* 800-733-3000 (cust serv) *Toll Free Fax:* 800-940-7046 *Web Site:* www.booksontape.com, pg 40

Books We Love Ltd, 100 Chinook Winds Place SW, Unit 4407, Airdrie, AB T4B 4B4, Canada *Tel:* 403-710-4869 *E-mail:* bookswelove@telus.net *Web Site:* bookswelove.net; www.facebook.com/Books.We.Love.Ltd, pg 447

BookStop Literary Agency LLC, 67 Meadow View Rd, Orinda, CA 94563 *E-mail:* info@bookstopliterary.com *Web Site:* www.bookstopliterary.com, pg 509

Boom! Studios, 5670 Wilshire Blvd, Suite 450, Los Angeles, CA 90036 *Web Site:* www.boom-studios.com, pg 40

Georges Borchardt Inc, 136 E 57 St, New York, NY 10022 *Tel:* 212-753-5785 *E-mail:* georges@gbagency.com *Web Site:* www.gbagency.com, pg 509

Borealis Press Ltd, 8 Mohawk Crescent, Nepean, ON K2H 7G6, Canada *Tel:* 613-829-0150 *Toll Free Tel:* 877-696-2585 *Fax:* 613-829-7783 *E-mail:* drt@borealispress.com *Web Site:* www.borealispress.com, pg 447

Boson Books, 1262 Sunnyoaks Circle, Altadena, CA 91001 *Tel:* 626-507-8033; 626-395-2405 *Web Site:* www.bosonbooks.com; bitingduckpress.com, pg 40

Boston Authors Club Inc, 33 Brayton Rd, Brighton, MA 02135 *Tel:* 617-783-1357 *E-mail:* bostonauthors@aol.com *Web Site:* www.bostonauthorsclub.org, pg 561

Boston Globe-Horn Book Award, c/o Book Reviews, The Horn Book Inc, Palace Road Bldg, 300 The Fenway, Suite P-311, Boston, MA 02115-5820 *Tel:* 617-278-0225 *Toll Free Tel:* 888-628-0225 *Fax:* 617-278-6062 *E-mail:* info@hbook.com *Web Site:* www.hbook.com, pg 633

Boston Informatics, 35 Byard Lane, Westborough, MA 01581 *Tel:* 508-366-8176 *Web Site:* www.bostoninformatics.com, pg 490

The Boston Mills Press, 50 Staples Ave, Unit 1, Richmond Hill, ON L4B 0A7, Canada *Tel:* 416-499-8412 *Toll Free Tel:* 800-387-6192 *Fax:* 416-499-8313 *Toll Free Fax:* 800-450-0391 *E-mail:* service@fireflybooks.com *Web Site:* www.fireflybooks.com, pg 447

Boston Road Communications, 227 Boston Rd, Groton, MA 01450-1959 *Tel:* 978-448-8133 *Web Site:* www.bostonrdcom.com, pg 490

Boston University Creative Writing Program, 236 Bay State Rd, Boston, MA 02215 *Tel:* 617-353-2510 *Fax:* 617-353-3653 *E-mail:* crwr@bu.edu *Web Site:* www.bu.edu/creativewriting, pg 619

Bottom Dog Press, 813 Seneca Ave, Huron, OH 44839 *Tel:* 419-433-3573 *Fax:* 419-616-3966 *Web Site:* smithdocs.net, pg 41

Boulevard Magazine Short Fiction Contest for Emerging Writers, 6614 Clayton Rd, PMB 325, Richmond Heights, MO 63117 *E-mail:* editors@boulevardmagazine.org *Web Site:* www.boulevardmagazine.org, pg 634

Bound to Stay Bound Books Scholarship, 50 E Huron St, Chicago, IL 60611-2795 *Tel:* 312-280-2163 *Toll Free Tel:* 800-545-2433 *Fax:* 312-440-9374; 312-280-5271 *E-mail:* alsc@ala.org *Web Site:* www.ala.org/alsc, pg 634

R R Bowker LLC, 789 E Eisenhower Pkwy, Ann Arbor, MI 48106 *Tel:* 908-286-1090 *Toll Free Tel:* 888-269-5372 (edit & cust serv, press 2 for returns) *Fax:* 908-219-0098; (020) 7832 1710 (UK for intl) *Toll Free Fax:* 877-337-7015 (US & CN) *E-mail:* orders@proquest.com (dom orders); isbn-san@bowker.com *Web Site:* www.bowker.com, pg 41

Bowling Green State University, Creative Writing Program, Dept of English, 409 East Hall, Bowling Green, OH 43403 *Tel:* 419-372-2576 *Fax:* 419-372-0333 *Web Site:* www.bgsu.edu/departments/creative-writing, pg 619

Boydell & Brewer Inc, 668 Mount Hope Ave, Rochester, NY 14620-2731 *Tel:* 585-275-0419 *Fax:* 585-271-8778 *E-mail:* boydell@boydellusa.net *Web Site:* www.boydellandbrewer.com, pg 41

Boyds Mills Press, 815 Church St, Honesdale, PA 18431 *Tel:* 570-253-1164 *Toll Free Tel:* 800-490-5111 *Fax:* 570-253-0179 *E-mail:* contact@boydsmillspress.com *Web Site:* www.boydsmillspress.com, pg 41

Boynton/Cook Publishers, 361 Hanover St, Portsmouth, NH 03801-3912 *Tel:* 603-431-7894 *Toll Free Tel:* 800-225-5800 *Fax:* 603-431-2214 *Toll Free Fax:* 877-231-6980 *E-mail:* custserv@heinemann.com *Web Site:* www.heinemann.com/boyntoncook, pg 41

Boys Town Press, 13603 Flanagan Blvd, 2nd fl, Boys Town, NE 68010 *Tel:* 402-498-1320 *Toll Free Tel:* 800-282-6657 *Fax:* 402-498-1310 *E-mail:* btpress@boystown.org *Web Site:* www.boystownpress.org, pg 41

BPA Worldwide, 100 Beard Sawmill Rd, 6th fl, Shelton, CT 06484 *Tel:* 203-447-2800 *Fax:* 203-447-2900 *E-mail:* info@bpaww.com *Web Site:* www.bpaww.com, pg 561

BPS Books, 47 Anderson Ave, Toronto, ON M5P 1H6, Canada *Tel:* 416-609-2004 *Web Site:* www.bpsbooks.com, pg 447

Bradford Literary Agency, 5694 Mission Center Rd, Suite 347, San Diego, CA 92108 *Tel:* 619-521-1201 *E-mail:* queries@bradfordlit.com *Web Site:* www.bradfordlit.com, pg 509

Bradford Publishing Co, 1743 Wazee St, Denver, CO 80202 *Tel:* 303-292-2590 *Toll Free Tel:* 800-446-2831 *Fax:* 303-298-5014 *E-mail:* marketing@bradfordpublishing.com; customerservice@bradfordpublishing.com *Web Site:* www.bradfordpublishing.com, pg 41

Barbara Bradley Prize, 46 Wallace St, Somerville, MA 02144 *Tel:* 617-744-6034 *E-mail:* info@nepoetryclub.org *Web Site:* www.nepoetryclub.org, pg 634

bradylit, 81 Town Farm Hill, Hartland Four Corners, VT 05049 *Tel:* 802-436-2455, pg 490

BrainStorm Poetry Contest for Mental Health Consumers, 36 Elgin St, 2nd fl, Sudbury, ON P3C 5B4, Canada *Tel:* 705-222-6472 (ext 303) *E-mail:* openminds@nisa.on.ca *Web Site:* www.openmindsquarterly.com, pg 634

Branden Books, PO Box 812094, Wellesley, MA 02482-0013 *Tel:* 781-235-3347 *E-mail:* branden@brandenbooks.com *Web Site:* www.brandenbooks.com, pg 42

Brandt & Hochman Literary Agents Inc, 1501 Broadway, Suite 2310, New York, NY 10036 *Tel:* 212-840-5760 *Fax:* 212-840-5776 *Web Site:* brandthochman.com, pg 509

The Joan Brandt Agency, 788 Wesley Dr NW, Atlanta, GA 30305 *Tel:* 404-351-8877 *Fax:* 404-351-0068, pg 510

Brandylane Publishers Inc, 5 S First St, Richmond, VA 23219 *Tel:* 804-644-3090 *Fax:* 804-644-3092 *Web Site:* brandylanepublishers.com, pg 42

Michael Braude Award, 633 W 155 St, New York, NY 10032 *Tel:* 212-368-5900 *Fax:* 212-491-4615 *E-mail:* academy@artsandletters.org *Web Site:* www.artsandletters.org, pg 634

Brault & Bouthillier, 700 ave Beaumont, Montreal, QC H3N 1V5, Canada *Tel:* 514-273-9186 *Toll Free Tel:* 800-361-0378 *Fax:* 514-273-8627 *Toll Free Fax:* 800-361-0378 *E-mail:* ventes@bb.ca *Web Site:* bb.ca, pg 447

Barbara Braun Associates Inc, 7 E 14 St, Suite 19F, New York, NY 10003 *Tel:* 212-604-9023 *Web Site:* www.barbarabraunagency.com, pg 510

George Braziller Inc, 277 Broadway, Suite 708, New York, NY 10007 *Tel:* 212-260-9256 *Fax:* 212-267-3165 *E-mail:* editorial@georgebraziller.com *Web Site:* www.georgebraziller.com, pg 42

Bread Loaf Writers' Conference, 5525 Middlebury College, 14 Old Chapel Rd, Middlebury, VT 05753 *Tel:* 802-443-5286 *Fax:* 802-443-2087 *E-mail:* blwc@middlebury.edu *Web Site:* www.middlebury.edu/blwc, pg 610

Breakaway Books, PO Box 24, Halcottsville, NY 12438-0024 *Tel:* 607-326-4805 *E-mail:* breakawaybooks@gmail.com *Web Site:* www.breakawaybooks.com, pg 42

Breakthrough Publications Inc, 3 Iroquois St, Barn, Emmaus, PA 18049 *Toll Free Tel:* 800-824-5001 (ext 12) *Fax:* 610-928-4064 *E-mail:* dot@booksonhorses.com; ruth@booksonhorses.com *Web Site:* www.booksonhorses.com, pg 42

Breakwater Books Ltd, One Stamp's Lane, St John's, NL A1C 6E6, Canada *Tel:* 709-722-6680 *Toll Free Tel:* 800-563-3333 (orders) *Fax:* 709-753-0708 *E-mail:* info@breakwaterbooks.com; orders@breakwaterbooks.com *Web Site:* www.breakwaterbooks.com, pg 447

Nicholas Brealey Publishing, 53 State St, 9th fl, Boston, MA 02109 *Tel:* 617-523-3801 *E-mail:* info@nicholasbrealey.com; sales-us@nicholasbrealey.com *Web Site:* www.nicholasbrealey.com, pg 42

James Henry Breasted Prize, 400 "A" St SE, Washington, DC 20003 *Tel:* 202-544-2422 *Fax:* 202-544-8307 *E-mail:* awards@historians.org *Web Site:* www.historians.org, pg 634

Brentwood Christian Press, 4000 Beallwood Ave, Columbus, GA 31904 *Toll Free Tel:* 800-334-8861 *E-mail:* brentwood@aol.com *Web Site:* www.brentwoodbooks.com, pg 42

Brethren Press, 1451 Dundee Ave, Elgin, IL 60120 *Tel:* 847-742-5100 *Toll Free Tel:* 800-323-8039 *Toll Free Fax:* 800-667-8188 *E-mail:* brethrenpress@brethren.org *Web Site:* www.brethrenpress.com, pg 42

Brewers Publications, 1372 Spruce St, Boulder, CO 80302 *Tel:* 303-447-0816 *Toll Free Tel:* 888-822-6273 (CN & US) *Fax:* 303-447-2825 *E-mail:* info@brewersassociation.org *Web Site:* www.brewersassociation.org, pg 42

The Briar Cliff Review Fiction, Poetry & Creative Nonfiction Contest, 3303 Rebecca St, Sioux City, IA 51104-2100 *Tel:* 712-279-1651 *Fax:* 712-279-5486 *Web Site:* www.bcreview.org, pg 634

Brick Books, Box 20081, 431 Boler Rd, London, ON N6K 4G6, Canada *Tel:* 519-657-8579 *E-mail:* brick.books@sympatico.ca *Web Site:* www.brickbooks.ca, pg 447

Brick Mantel Books, 4735 S State Rd 446, Bloomington, IN 47401 *Tel:* 314-827-6567; 812-837-9226 *E-mail:* info@brickmantelbooks.com *Web Site:* brickmantelbooks.com, pg 42

Brick Road Poetry Book Contest, 513 Broadway, Columbus, GA 31901-3117 *Web Site:* brickroadpoetrypress.com, pg 634

Brick Tower Press, Manhanset House, PO Box 342, Shelter Island Heights, NY 11965-0342 *Tel:* 212-427-7139 *E-mail:* bricktower@aol.com *Web Site:* www.bricktowerpress.com, pg 43

BrickHouse Books Inc, 306 Suffolk Rd, Baltimore, MD 21218 *Fax:* 410-235-7690 *Web Site:* brickhousebooks.wordpress.com, pg 43

Bridge-Logos, 1426W Newberry Rd, No 409, Newberry, FL 32669-2765 *Toll Free Tel:* 800-320-4108 *Web Site:* www.bridgelogos.com, pg 43

Bridge Publications Inc, 5600 E Olympic Blvd, Commerce, CA 90022 *Tel:* 323-888-6200 *Toll Free Tel:* 800-722-1733 *Fax:* 323-888-6202 *E-mail:* info@bridgepub.com *Web Site:* www.bridgepub.com, pg 43

Bridge to Asia, 1505 Juanita Way, Berkeley, CA 94702-1103 *Tel:* 510-665-3998 *E-mail:* asianet@bridge.org *Web Site:* www.bridge.org, pg 583

Brigantine Media, 211 North Ave, St Johnsbury, VT 05819 *Tel:* 802-751-8802 *Fax:* 802-751-8804 *Web Site:* brigantinemedia.com, pg 43

M Courtney Briggs Esq, Authors Representative, Chase Tower, 28th fl, 100 N Broadway Ave, Oklahoma City, OK 73102, pg 510

Bright Connections Media, A World Book Encyclopedia Company, 180 N LaSalle St, Suite 900, Chicago, IL 60601 *Tel:* 312-729-5800 *Web Site:* www.brightconnectionsmedia.com, pg 43

Brill Inc, 2 Liberty Sq, 11th fl, Boston, MA 02109 *Tel:* 617-263-2323 *Toll Free Tel:* 800-962-4406 *Fax:* 617-263-2324 *E-mail:* cs@brillusa.com *Web Site:* www.brill.com, pg 43

Brilliance Audio, 1704 Eaton Dr, Grand Haven, MI 49417 *Tel:* 616-846-5256 *Toll Free Tel:* 800-648-2312 (orders only) *Fax:* 616-846-0630 *E-mail:* customerservice@brillianceaudio.com *Web Site:* www.brillianceaudio.com, pg 43

Brindle & Glass Publishing Ltd, 1075 Pendergast St, Suite 103, Victoria, BC V8V 0A1, Canada *Tel:* 250-360-0829 *Fax:* 250-386-0829 *E-mail:* info@brindleandglass.com *Web Site:* www.brindleandglass.com, pg 447

Bristol Park Books, 252 W 38 St, Suite 206, New York, NY 10018 *Tel:* 212-842-0700 *Fax:* 212-842-1771 *E-mail:* info@bristolparkbooks.com *Web Site:* bristolparkbooks.com, pg 44

Brittingham & Pollak Prizes in Poetry, Dept of English, 600 N Park St, Madison, WI 53706 *Web Site:* www.wisc.edu/wisconsinpress, pg 634

Broadview Press, 280 Perry St, Unit 5, Peterborough, ON K9J 2J4, Canada *Tel:* 705-743-8990 *Fax:* 705-743-8353 *E-mail:* customerservice@broadviewpress.com *Web Site:* www.broadviewpress.com, pg 447

Brockman Inc, 260 Fifth Ave, 10th fl, New York, NY 10001 *Tel:* 212-935-8900 *Fax:* 212-935-5535 *E-mail:* rights@brockman.com *Web Site:* www.brockman.com, pg 510

Broden Books LLC, 3824 Sunset Dr, Spring Park, MN 55384 *Tel:* 952-471-1066 *E-mail:* media@brodenbooks.com *Web Site:* www.brodenbooks.com, pg 44

Brookes Publishing Co Inc, PO Box 10624, Baltimore, MD 21285-0624 *Tel:* 410-337-9580 (outside US & CN) *Toll Free Tel:* 800-638-3775 (US & CN) *Fax:* 410-337-8539 *E-mail:* custserv@brookespublishing.com *Web Site:* www.brookespublishing.com, pg 44

The Brookings Institution Press, 1775 Massachusetts Ave NW, Washington, DC 20036-2188 *Tel:* 202-536-3600 *Toll Free Tel:* 800-537-5487 *Fax:* 202-536-3623 *E-mail:* permissions@brookings.edu *Web Site:* www.brookings.edu, pg 44

Brookline Books, 8 Trumbull Rd, Suite B-001, Northampton, MA 01060 *Tel:* 603-669-7032 (orders) *Toll Free Tel:* 800-666-2665 (orders) *Fax:* 413-584-6184 *E-mail:* brbooks@yahoo.com, pg 44

Brooklyn Publishers LLC, PO Box 248, Cedar Rapids, IA 52406 *Tel:* 319-368-8012 *Toll Free Tel:* 888-473-8521 *Fax:* 319-368-8011 *E-mail:* customerservice@brookpub.com; editor@brookpub.com *Web Site:* www.brookpub.com, pg 44

Broquet Inc, 97-B, Montee des Bouleaux, St-Constant, QC J5A 1A9, Canada *Tel:* 450-638-3338 *Fax:* 450-638-4338 *E-mail:* info@broquet.qc.ca *Web Site:* www.broquet.qc.ca, pg 448

The Heywood Broun Award, 501 Third St NW, 6th fl, Washington, DC 20001-2797 *Tel:* 202-434-7177; 202-434-7162 (The Guild Reporter) *Fax:* 202-434-1472 *Web Site:* www.newsguild.org, pg 634

Brown Books Publishing Group, 16250 Knoll Trail, Suite 205, Dallas, TX 75248 *Tel:* 972-381-0009 *Fax:* 972-248-4336 *E-mail:* publishing@brownbooks.com *Web Site:* www.brownbooks.com, pg 44

Curtis Brown Ltd, 10 Astor Place, New York, NY 10003 *Tel:* 212-473-5400 *Web Site:* www.curtisbrown.com, pg 510

John Nicholas Brown Prize, 17 Dunster St, Suite 202, Cambridge, MA 02138 *Tel:* 617-491-1622 *Fax:* 617-492-3303 *E-mail:* info@themedievalacademy.org *Web Site:* www.medievalacademy.org, pg 634

Karen Brown's Guides Inc, 16 E Third Ave, Suite 9, San Mateo, CA 94401 *Tel:* 650-342-9117 *Fax:* 650-342-9153 *Web Site:* www.karenbrown.com, pg 44

Marie Brown Associates, 412 W 154 St, New York, NY 10032 *Tel:* 212-939-9725 *E-mail:* submissions.mbrownlit@gmail.com, pg 510

Browne & Miller Literary Associates, 410 S Michigan Ave, Suite 460, Chicago, IL 60605 *Tel:* 312-922-3063 *E-mail:* mail@browneandmiller.com *Web Site:* www.browneandmiller.com, pg 510

Brush Education Inc, 6531-111 St, Edmonton, AB T6H 4R5, Canada *Tel:* 780-989-0910 *Toll Free Tel:* 855-283-0900 *Fax:* 780-989-0930 *Toll Free Fax:* 855-283-6947 *E-mail:* contact@brusheducation.ca *Web Site:* www.brusheducation.ca, pg 448

J B Bryans Literary, 7 Meetinghouse Ct, Indian Mills, NJ 08088 *Tel:* 609-922-0369 *E-mail:* info@brylit.com *Web Site:* brylit.com, pg 510

Don Buchwald & Associates Inc, 10 E 44 St, New York, NY 10017 *Tel:* 212-867-1200 *Fax:* 212-867-2434 *E-mail:* info@buchwald.com *Web Site:* www.buchwald.com, pg 510

Bucknell Seminar for Undergraduate Poets, Bucknell University, Bucknell Hall, Moore Ave, Lewisburg, PA 17837 *Tel:* 570-577-1853 *E-mail:* stadlercenter@bucknell.edu *Web Site:* www.bucknell.edu/stadlercenter, pg 610

Bucknell University Press, 6 Taylor Hall, Bucknell University, Lewisburg, PA 17837 *Tel:* 570-577-3674 *E-mail:* universitypress@bucknell.edu *Web Site:* www.bucknell.edu/universitypress, pg 45

Judith Buckner Literary Agency, 12721 Hart St, North Hollywood, CA 91605 *Tel:* 818-982-8202 *Fax:* 818-764-6844, pg 510

Georges Bugnet Award for Fiction, 11759 Groat Rd, Edmonton, AB T5M 3K6, Canada *Tel:* 780-422-8174 *Toll Free Tel:* 800-665-5354 (AB only) *Fax:* 780-422-2663 (attn WGA) *E-mail:* mail@writersguild.ca *Web Site:* writersguild.ca, pg 634

BuilderBooks.com, 1201 15 St NW, Washington, DC 20005 *Tel:* 202-822-0200 *Toll Free Tel:* 800-223-2665 *Fax:* 202-266-8096 (edit) *E-mail:* builderbooks@nahb.com *Web Site:* www.builderbooks.com, pg 45

The Bukowski Agency Ltd, 14 Prince Arthur Ave, Suite 202, Toronto, ON M5R 1A9, Canada *Tel:* 416-928-6728 *Fax:* 416-963-9978 *E-mail:* info@bukowskiagency.com *Web Site:* www.bukowskiagency.com, pg 510

Bull Publishing Co, PO Box 1377, Boulder, CO 80306 *Tel:* 303-545-6350 *Toll Free Tel:* 800-676-2855 *Fax:* 303-545-6354 *E-mail:* bullpublishing@msn.com *Web Site:* www.bullpub.com, pg 45

Bureau of Economic Geology, University of Texas at Austin, 10100 Burnet Rd, Bldg 130, Austin, TX 78758 *Tel:* 512-471-1534 *Fax:* 512-471-0140 *E-mail:* pubsales@beg.utexas.edu *Web Site:* www.beg.utexas.edu, pg 45

Burford Books, 101 E State St, No 301, Ithaca, NY 14850 *Tel:* 607-319-4373 *Fax:* 607-319-4373 *Toll Free Fax:* 866-212-7750 *E-mail:* info@burfordbooks.com *Web Site:* www.burfordbooks.com, pg 45

Hilary R Burke, 59 Sparks St, Ottawa, ON K1P 6C3, Canada *Tel:* 613-237-4658 *E-mail:* hburke99@yahoo.com, pg 490

Burns Archive Press, 140 E 38 St, New York, NY 10016 *Tel:* 212-889-1938 *Fax:* 212-481-9113 *E-mail:* info@burnsarchive.com *Web Site:* www.burnsarchive.com, pg 45

Burns Entertainment & Sports Marketing, 820 Davis St, Suite 222, Evanston, IL 60201 *Tel:* 847-866-9400 *Fax:* 847-491-9778 *E-mail:* burnsl@burnsent.com *Web Site:* burnsent.com, pg 547

John Burroughs Medal, 261 Floyd Ackert Rd, New York, NY 12493 *Tel:* 212-769-5169 *Fax:* 212-313-7182 *E-mail:* info@johnburroughsassociation.org *Web Site:* www.johnburroughsassociation.org, pg 635

John Burroughs Nature Essay Award, 261 Floyd Ackert Rd, New York, NY 12493 *Tel:* 212-769-5169 *Fax:* 212-313-7182 *E-mail:* info@johnburroughsassociation.org *Web Site:* www.johnburroughsassociation.org, pg 635

Business & Legal Resources Inc, 100 Winners Circle, Suite 300, Brentwood, TN 37027 *Tel:* 860-510-0100 *Toll Free Tel:* 800-727-5257 *E-mail:* service@blr.com *Web Site:* www.blr.com, pg 45

Business Expert Press, 222 E 46 St, New York, NY 10017-2906 *Tel:* 630-207-5927 *E-mail:* charlene.kronstadt@businessexpertpress.com *Web Site:* www.businessexpertpress.com, pg 45

Business Forms Management Association (BFMA), 1147 Fleetwood Ave, Madison, WI 53716 *Toll Free Tel:* 888-367-3078 *E-mail:* bfma@bfma.org *Web Site:* www.bfma.org, pg 561

Business Marketing Association (BMA), 708 Third Ave, New York, NY 10017 *Tel:* 212-697-5950 *Fax:* 212-687-7310 *E-mail:* info@marketing.org *Web Site:* www.marketing.org, pg 561

Business Research Services Inc, 4641 Montgomery Ave, Suite 208, Bethesda, MD 20814 *Tel:* 301-229-5561 *Toll Free Tel:* 800-845-8420 *Toll Free Fax:* 877-516-0818 *E-mail:* brspubs@sba8a.com *Web Site:* www.sba8a.com; www.setasidealert.com, pg 45

Butte Publications Inc, PO Box 1328, Hillsboro, OR 97123-1328 *Toll Free Tel:* 866-312-8883 *Toll Free Fax:* 866-412-8883 (orders only) *E-mail:* service@buttepublications.com *Web Site:* www.buttepublications.com, pg 45

Byer-Sprinzeles Agency, 5800 Arlington Ave, Suite 16-C, Riverdale, NY 10471 *Tel:* 718-543-9399 *Web Site:* www.maggiebyersprinzeles.com, pg 543

Sheree Bykofsky Associates Inc, PO Box 706, Brigantine, NJ 08203 *E-mail:* submitbee@aol.com *Web Site:* www.shereebee.com, pg 511

Bywater Books, PO Box 3671, Ann Arbor, MI 48106-3671 *Tel:* 734-662-8815 *Web Site:* bywaterbooks.com, pg 46

BZ/Rights & Permissions Inc, 145 W 86 St, New York, NY 10024 *Tel:* 212-924-3000 *Fax:* 212-924-2525 *E-mail:* info@bzrights.com *Web Site:* www.bzrights.com, pg 490

CAA Award for Canadian History, 6 West St N, Suite 203, Orillia, ON L3V 5B8, Canada *Tel:* 705-325-3926 *E-mail:* admin@canadianauthors.org *Web Site:* www.canadianauthors.org, pg 635

CAA Award for Fiction, 6 West St N, Suite 203, Orillia, ON L3V 5B8, Canada *Tel:* 705-325-3926 *E-mail:* admin@canadianauthors.org *Web Site:* www.canadianauthors.org, pg 635

CAA Emerging Writer Award, 6 West St N, Suite 203, Orillia, ON L3V 5B8, Canada *Tel:* 705-325-3926 *E-mail:* admin@canadianauthors.org *Web Site:* www.canadianauthors.org, pg 635

CAA Poetry Award, 6 West St N, Suite 203, Orillia, ON L3V 5B8, Canada *Tel:* 705-325-3926 *E-mail:* admin@canadianauthors.org *Web Site:* www.canadianauthors.org, pg 635

Gerald Cable Book Award, PO Box 3541, Eugene, OR 97403 *Tel:* 541-344-5060 *E-mail:* sfrpress@earthlink.net *Web Site:* www.silverfishreviewpress.com, pg 635

Caissa Editions, PO Box 151, Yorklyn, DE 19736-0151 *Tel:* 302-239-4608 *Web Site:* www.chessbookstore.com, pg 46

The Randolph Caldecott Medal, 50 E Huron St, Chicago, IL 60611-2795 *Tel:* 312-280-2163 *Toll Free Tel:* 800-545-2433 *Fax:* 312-440-9374; 312-280-5271 *E-mail:* alsc@ala.org *Web Site:* www.ala.org/alsc, pg 635

California Book Awards, 110 The Embarcadero, San Francisco, CA 94105 *Tel:* 415-597-6700 *Fax:* 415-597-6729 *E-mail:* bookawards@commonwealthclub.org *Web Site:* www.commonwealthclub.org/bookawards, pg 635

Callawind Publications Inc, 3551 St Charles Blvd, Suite 179, Kirkland, QC H9H 3C4, Canada *Tel:* 514-685-9109 *E-mail:* info@callawind.com *Web Site:* www.callawind.com, pg 448

Cambridge Educational, 132 W 31 St, 17th fl, New York, NY 10001 *Toll Free Tel:* 800-322-8755 *Fax:* 609-671-0266 *Toll Free Fax:* 800-329-6687 *E-mail:* custserve@infobaselearning.com *Web Site:* www.infobasepublishing.com, pg 46

Cambridge Literary Associates, 135 Beach Rd, Unit C-3, Salisbury, MA 01952 *Tel:* 978-499-0374 *Fax:* 978-499-9774 *Web Site:* www.cambridgeliterary.com, pg 511

Cambridge University Press, 1 Liberty Plaza, 20th fl, New York, NY 10006 *Tel:* 212-924-3900; 212-337-5000 *Fax:* 212-691-3239 *E-mail:* newyork@cambridge.org *Web Site:* www.cambridge.org/us, pg 46

Kimberley Cameron & Associates LLC, 1550 Tiburon Blvd, Suite 704, Tiburon, CA 94920 *Tel:* 415-789-9191 *Fax:* 415-789-9177 *Web Site:* www.kimberleycameron.com, pg 511

Camino Books Inc, PO Box 59026, Philadelphia, PA 19102-9026 *Tel:* 215-413-1917 *Fax:* 215-413-3255 *E-mail:* camino@caminobooks.com *Web Site:* www.caminobooks.com, pg 46

Joe Pendleton Campbell Narrative Contest, 900 Timber Creek Place, Virginia Beach, VA 23464 *E-mail:* poetryinva@aol.com *Web Site:* poetrysocietyofvirginia.org, pg 635

John W Campbell Memorial Award, University of Kansas, Wescoe Hall, Rm 3001, Dept of English, 1445 Jayhawk Blvd, Lawrence, KS 66045 *Tel:* 785-864-2518 *Fax:* 785-864-1159 *Web Site:* www.sfcenter.ku.edu/campbell.htm, pg 635

Campfield & Campfield Publishing LLC, 6521 Cutler St, Philadelphia, PA 19126 *Toll Free Tel:* 888-518-2440 *Fax:* 215-224-6696 *E-mail:* info@campfieldspublishing.com *Web Site:* www.campfieldspublishing.com, pg 46

Canada Council for the Arts (Conseil des arts du Canada), 150 Elgin St, Ottawa, ON K1P 1L4, Canada *Tel:* 613-566-4414 *Toll Free Tel:* 800-263-5588 (CN only) *Fax:* 613-566-4390 *E-mail:* info@canadacouncil.ca *Web Site:* www.canadacouncil.ca, pg 561

Canada Law Book®, One Corporate Plaza, 2075 Kennedy Rd, Toronto, ON M1T 3V4, Canada *Tel:* 416-609-3800 (cust rel & orders) *Toll Free Tel:* 800-387-5351 (cust rel, CN & US only); 800-347-5164 (cust rel & orders, CN & US) *Fax:* 416-298-5082 (cust rel & orders, Toronto) *Toll Free Fax:* 877-750-9041 (cust rel & orders, CN only) *E-mail:* customersupport.legaltaxcanada@thomsonreuters.com; printorders.legaltaxcanada@thomsonreuters.com *Web Site:* www.carswell.com, pg 448

Canadian Authors Association (CAA), 6 West St N, Suite 203, Orillia, ON L3V 5B8, Canada *Tel:* 705-325-3926 *E-mail:* admin@canadianauthors.org *Web Site:* www.canadianauthors.org, pg 561

Canadian Bible Society, 10 Carnforth Rd, Toronto, ON M4A 2S4, Canada *Tel:* 416-757-4171 *Toll Free Tel:* 800-465-2425 *Fax:* 416-757-3376 *E-mail:* custserv@biblesociety.ca *Web Site:* www.biblescanada.com; www.biblesociety.ca, pg 448

Canadian Bookbinders and Book Artists Guild (CBBAG), 80 Ward St, Suite 207, Toronto, ON M6H 4A6, Canada *Tel:* 416-581-1071 *E-mail:* cbbag@cbbag.ca *Web Site:* www.cbbag.ca, pg 561

Canadian Cataloguing in Publication Program, Library & Archives Canada, 395 Wellington St, Ottawa, ON K1A 0N4, Canada *Tel:* 819-994-6881 *Toll Free Tel:* 866-578-7777 (CN) *Fax:* 819-934-6777 *E-mail:* cip@lac-bac.gc.ca *Web Site:* www.collectionscanada.gc.ca/cip/index-e.html, pg 561

Canadian Children's Book Centre, 40 Orchard View Blvd, Suite 217, Toronto, ON M4R 1B9, Canada *Tel:* 416-975-0010 *Fax:* 416-975-8970 *E-mail:* info@bookcentre.ca *Web Site:* www.bookcentre.ca, pg 561

Canadian Circumpolar Institute (CCI) Press, University of Alberta, Ring House 2, Edmonton, AB T6G 2E1, Canada *Tel:* 780-492-3662 *Fax:* 780-492-0719 *Web Site:* www.uap.ualberta.ca, pg 448

Canadian Council on Social Development (Conseil canadien de developpement social), 190 O'Connor St, Suite 100, Ottawa, ON K2P 2R3, Canada *Tel:* 613-236-8977 *Fax:* 613-236-2750 *E-mail:* info@ccsd.ca *Web Site:* www.ccsd.ca, pg 448

Canadian Energy Research Institute, 3512 33 St NW, Suite 150, Calgary, AB T2L 2A6, Canada *Tel:* 403-282-1231 *Fax:* 403-284-4181 *E-mail:* info@ceri.ca *Web Site:* www.ceri.ca, pg 448

Canadian Institute for Studies in Publishing, Simon Fraser University at Harbour Centre, 515 W Hastings St, Suite 3576, Vancouver, BC V6B 5K3, Canada *Tel:* 778-782-5242 *E-mail:* pub-info@sfu.ca *Web Site:* publishing.sfu.ca, pg 562

Canadian Institute of Resources Law (L'Institut canadien du droit des ressources), Faculty of Law, University of Calgary, 2500 University Dr NW, MFH 3353, Calgary, AB T2N 1N4, Canada *Tel:* 403-220-3200 *Fax:* 403-282 6182 *E-mail:* cirl@ucalgary.ca *Web Site:* www.cirl.ca, pg 449

Canadian Institute of Ukrainian Studies Press, University of Toronto, 256 McCaul St, Rm 308, Toronto, ON M5T 1W5, Canada *Tel:* 416-946-7326 *Fax:* 416-978-2672 *E-mail:* cius@ualberta.ca *Web Site:* www.ciuspress.com, pg 449

Canadian ISBN Agency, Library & Archives Canada, 395 Wellington St, Ottawa, ON K1A 0N4, Canada *Tel:* 613-996-5115 *Toll Free Tel:* 866-578-7777 (CN & US) *Fax:* 613-995-6274 *E-mail:* isbn@lac-bac.gc.ca *Web Site:* www.collectionscanada.gc.ca/ciss-ssci/index-e.html, pg 562

Canadian Museum of History (Musee canadien de l'histoire), 100 Laurier St, Gatineau, QC K1A 0M8, Canada *Tel:* 819-776-7000 *Toll Free Tel:* 800-555-5621 (North American orders only) *Fax:* 819-776-7187 *Web Site:* www.historymuseum.ca, pg 449

Canadian Newspaper Association, 890 Yonge St, Suite 200, Toronto, ON M4W 3P4, Canada *Tel:* 416-923-3567; 416-482-1090 *Toll Free Tel:* 877-305-2262 *Fax:* 416-923-7206; 416-482-1908 *E-mail:* info@newspaperscanada.ca *Web Site:* www.newspaperscanada.ca, pg 562

Canadian Poetry Press, Dept of English, University of Western Ontario, London, ON N6A 3K7, Canada *Tel:* 519-661-2111 (ext 85813); 519-661-2111 (ext 85834) *Fax:* 519-661-3776 *E-mail:* canadianpoetry@uwo.ca *Web Site:* canadianpoetry.org, pg 449

Canadian Publishers' Council (CPC), 250 Merton St, Suite 203, Toronto, ON M4S 1B1, Canada *Tel:* 416-322-7011 *Fax:* 416-322-6999 *Web Site:* www.pubcouncil.ca, pg 562

Canadian Scholars' Press Inc, 425 Adelaide St W, Suite 200, Toronto, ON M5V 3C1, Canada *Tel:* 416-929-2774 *Toll Free Tel:* 800-463-1998 *Fax:* 416-929-1926 *E-mail:* info@cspi.org; info@canadianscholars.ca; editorial@canadianscholars.ca; orders@canadianscholars.ca *Web Site:* www.canadianscholars.ca; www.womenspress.ca, pg 449

Canadian Society of Children's Authors, Illustrators & Performers (CANSCAIP), 720 Bathurst St, Suite 503, Toronto, ON M5S 2R4, Canada *Tel:* 416-515-1559 *E-mail:* office@canscaip.org *Web Site:* www.canscaip.org, pg 562

The Canadian Writers' Foundation Inc (La Fondation des Ecrivains Canadiens), PO Box 13281, Kanata Sta, Ottawa, ON K2K 1X4, Canada *Tel:* 613-256-6937 *Fax:* 613-256-5457 *E-mail:* info@canadianwritersfoundation.org *Web Site:* www.canadianwritersfoundation.org, pg 583

Candied Plums, 7548 Ravenna Ave NE, Seattle, WA 98115 *E-mail:* candiedplums@gmail.com *Web Site:* www.candiedplums.com, pg 46

Candlewick Press, 99 Dover St, Somerville, MA 02144-2825 *Tel:* 617-661-3330 *Fax:* 617-661-0565 *E-mail:* bigbear@candlewick.com; salesinfo@candlewick.com *Web Site:* www.candlewick.com, pg 46

C&T Publishing Inc, 1651 Challenge Dr, Concord, CA 94520-5206 *Tel:* 925-677-0377 *Toll Free Tel:* 800-284-1114 *Fax:* 925-677-0373 *E-mail:* support@ctpub.com *Web Site:* www.ctpub.com, pg 46

Canon Law Society of America, Hecker Ctr, Suite 111, 3025 Fourth St NE, Washington, DC 20017-1102 *Tel:* 202-832-2350 *Fax:* 202-832-2331 *E-mail:* coordinator@clsa.org; info@clsa.org *Web Site:* www.clsa.org, pg 47

Cantos Para Todos, 4749 Hillcrest St, Bel Aire, KS 67220 *Tel:* 316-239 6477 *E-mail:* cantos@cantos.org *Web Site:* www.cantos.org, pg 47

Cape Cod Writers' Center Conference, 919 Main St, Osterville, MA 02655 *Tel:* 508-420-0200 *E-mail:* writers@capecodwriterscenter.org *Web Site:* capecodwriterscenter.org, pg 610

Capital Enquiry Inc, 1034 Emerald Bay Rd, No 435, South Lake Tahoe, CA 96150 *Tel:* 916-442-1434 *Toll Free Tel:* 800-922-7486 *Fax:* 916-244-2704 *E-mail:* info@capenq.com *Web Site:* www.govbuddy.com, pg 47

Alexander Patterson Cappon Prize for Fiction, UMKC, University House, 5101 Rockhill Rd, Kansas City, MO 64110-2499 *Tel:* 816-235-1169 *Fax:* 816-235-2611 *E-mail:* newletters@umkc.edu *Web Site:* www.newletters.org, pg 635

Dorothy Churchill Cappon Prize for the Essay, UMKC, University House, 5101 Rockhill Rd, Kansas City, MO 64110-2499 *Tel:* 816-235-1169 *Fax:* 816-235-2611 *E-mail:* newletters@umkc.edu *Web Site:* www.newletters.org, pg 636

Capstone Publishers™, 1710 Roe Crest Dr, North Mankato, MN 56003 *Toll Free Tel:* 800-747-4992 (cust serv) *Toll Free Fax:* 888-262-0705 *Web Site:* www.capstonepress.com, pg 47

Captain Fiddle Music & Publications, 94 Wiswall Rd, Lee, NH 03861 *Tel:* 603-659-2658 *E-mail:* cfiddle@tiac.net *Web Site:* captainfiddle.com, pg 47

Captus Press Inc, 1600 Steeles Ave W, Units 14 & 15, Concord, ON L4K 4M2, Canada *Tel:* 416-736-5537 *Fax:* 416-736-5793 *E-mail:* info@captus.com *Web Site:* www.captus.com, pg 449

Cardiotext Publishing, 3405 W 44 St, Minneapolis, MN 55410 *Tel:* 612-925-2053 *Fax:* 612-922-7556 *E-mail:* info@cardiotextpublishing.com *Web Site:* www.cardiotextpublishing.com, pg 47

Cardoza Publishing, 808 S Main St, Las Vegas, NV 89101 *Tel:* 702-870-7200 *Toll Free Tel:* 800-577-WINS (577-9467) *Fax:* 702-822-6500 *E-mail:* info@cardozabooks.com *Web Site:* www.cardozabooks.com, pg 47

The Career Press Inc, 12 Parish Dr, Wayne, NJ 07470 *Tel:* 201-848-0310 *Toll Free Tel:* 800-CAREER-1 (227-3371) *Fax:* 201-848-1727 *E-mail:* sales@careerpress.com *Web Site:* www.careerpress.com, pg 47

Caribe Betania Editores, PO Box 141000, Nashville, TN 37214-1000 *Tel:* 615-902-1893 *Fax:* 615-883-9376 *Web Site:* www.caribebetania.com, pg 47

Carlisle Press - Walnut Creek, 2673 Township Rd 421, Sugarcreek, OH 44681 *Tel:* 330-852-1900 *Toll Free Tel:* 800-852-4482 *Fax:* 330-852-3285, pg 47

Andrew Carnegie Medals for Excellence in Fiction & Nonfiction, 50 E Huron St, Chicago, IL 60611 *Tel:* 312-944-6780 *Toll Free Tel:* 800-545-2433 *Fax:* 312-440-9374 *E-mail:* ala@ala.org *Web Site:* www.ala.org/awardsgrants/carnegieadult, pg 636

Carnegie Mellon University Press, 5032 Forbes Ave, Pittsburgh, PA 15289-1021 *Tel:* 412-268-2861 *Fax:* 412-268-8706 *E-mail:* carnegiemellonuniversitypress@gmail.com *Web Site:* www.cmu.edu/universitypress, pg 48

Carnegie-Whitney Award, 50 E Huron St, Chicago, IL 60611 *Tel:* 312-280-5416 *Toll Free Tel:* 800-545-2433 *Fax:* 312-280-5275; 312-440-9379 *Web Site:* www.ala.org, pg 636

Carolina Academic Press, 700 Kent St, Durham, NC 27701 *Tel:* 919-489-7486 *Toll Free Tel:* 800-489-7486 *Fax:* 919-493-5668 *E-mail:* cap@cap-press.com *Web Site:* www.cap-press.com; www.caplaw.com, pg 48

Carolrhoda Books, 241 First Ave N, Minneapolis, MN 55401 *Tel:* 612-332-3344 *Toll Free Tel:* 800-328-4929 *Fax:* 612-332-7615 *Toll Free Fax:* 800-332-1132 *E-mail:* info@lernerbooks.com; custserve@lernerbooks.com *Web Site:* www.lernerbooks.com; www.facebook.com/lernerbooks, pg 48

Carolrhoda Lab™, 241 First Ave N, Minneapolis, MN 55401 *Tel:* 612-332-3344 *Toll Free Tel:* 800-328-4929 *Fax:* 612-332-7615 *Toll Free Fax:* 800-332-1132 (US) *E-mail:* info@lernerbooks.com; custserve@lernerbooks.com *Web Site:* www.lernerbooks.com; www.facebook.com/lernerbooks, pg 48

Carpe Indexum, 1960 Deer Run Rd, LaFayette, NY 13084 *Tel:* 315-677-3030 *E-mail:* info@carpeindexum.com *Web Site:* www.carpeindexum.com, pg 490

Carroll Publishing, 4701 Sangamore Rd, Suite S-155, Bethesda, MD 20816 *Tel:* 301-263-9800 *Toll Free Tel:* 800-336-4240 *Fax:* 301-263 9801 *E-mail:* info@carrollpub.com; customersvc@carrollpub.com *Web Site:* www.carrollpublishing.com, pg 48

R E Carsch, MS-Consultant, 1453 Rhode Island St, San Francisco, CA 94107-3248 *Tel:* 415-641-1095 *Fax:* 415-641-1095 *E-mail:* recarsch@mzinfo.com, pg 490

Anne Carson Associates, 3323 Nebraska Ave NW, Washington, DC 20016 *Tel:* 202-244-6679, pg 490

Carson-Dellosa Publishing LLC, PO Box 35665, Greensboro, NC 27425-5665 *Tel:* 336-632-0084 *Toll Free Tel:* 800-321-0943 *Fax:* 336-632-0087 *Toll Free Fax:* 800-535-2669 *E-mail:* custsvc@carsondellosa.com *Web Site:* www.carsondellosa.com, pg 48

Carswell, One Corporate Plaza, 2075 Kennedy Rd, Toronto, ON M1T 3V4, Canada *Tel:* 416-298-5141; 416-609-3800 *Toll Free Tel:* 800-387-5164 (CN & US) *Fax:* 416-298-5094; 416-298-5082 *Toll Free Fax:* 877-750-9041 (CN only) *E-mail:* carswell.customerrelations@thomsonreuters.com; carswell.orders@thomsonreuters.com *Web Site:* www.carswell.com, pg 449

Carol Cartaino, 2000 Flat Run Rd, Seaman, OH 45679 *Tel:* 937-764-1303 *Fax:* 937-764-1303 *E-mail:* cartaino@aol.com, pg 490

CarTech Inc, 39966 Grand Ave, North Branch, MN 55056 *Tel:* 651-277-1200 *Toll Free Tel:* 800-551-4754 *Fax:* 651-277-1203 *E-mail:* info@cartechbooks.com *Web Site:* www.cartechbooks.com, pg 48

The Carter Prize For The Essay, Washington & Lee University, Mattingly House, 204 W Washington St, Lexington, VA 24450-2116 *Tel:* 540-458-8908 *E-mail:* shenandoah@wlu.edu *Web Site:* shenandoahliterary.org, pg 636

Claudia Caruana, PO Box 654, Murray Hill Sta, New York, NY 10016 *Tel:* 516-488-5815 *E-mail:* ccaruana29@hotmail.com, pg 490

Maria Carvainis Agency Inc, Rockefeller Center, 1270 Avenue of the Americas, Suite 2320, New York, NY 10020 *Tel:* 212-245-6365 *Fax:* 212-245-7196 *E-mail:* mca@mariacarvainisagency.com *Web Site:* mariacarvainisagency.com, pg 511

Casa Bautista de Publicaciones, 7000 Alabama Ave, El Paso, TX 79904 *Tel:* 915-566-9656 *Toll Free Tel:* 800-755-5958 (cust serv & orders) *Fax:* 915-562-6502; 915-565-9008 (orders) *E-mail:* orders@editorialmh.org *Web Site:* www.editorialmh.org, pg 48

Cascade Pass Inc, 4223 Glencoe Ave, Suite C-105, Marina del Rey, CA 90292-8801 *Tel:* 310-305-0210 *Toll Free Tel:* 888-837-0704 *Fax:* 310-305-7850 *Web Site:* www.cascadepass.com, pg 49

Casemate | publishers, 1950 Lawrence Rd, Havertown, PA 19083 *Tel:* 610-853-9131 *Fax:* 610-853-9146 *E-mail:* casemate@casematepublishers.com *Web Site:* www.casematepublishers.com, pg 49

Angela M Casey, 42 Nathaniel Blvd, Delmar, NY 12054 *Tel:* 518-729-2693 *E-mail:* casey.angela.m@gmail.com, pg 490

Castle Connolly Medical Ltd, 42 W 24 St, 2nd fl, New York, NY 10010 *Tel:* 212-367-8400 *Fax:* 212-367-0964 *Web Site:* www.castleconnolly.com, pg 49

Catalyst Communication Arts, 94 Chuparrosa Dr, San Luis Obispo, CA 93401 *Tel:* 805-235-2351 *Fax:* 805-543-7140 *Web Site:* www.sonsieconroy.com, pg 490

Catalyst Creative Services, 619 Marion Plaza, Palo Alto, CA 94301-4251 *Tel:* 650-325-1500 *E-mail:* afriendlyghostwriter@gmail.com *Web Site:* www.catalystcreative.us, pg 490

Catholic Book Awards, 205 W Monroe St, Suite 470, Chicago, IL 60606 *Tel:* 312-380-6789 *Fax:* 312-361-0256 *E-mail:* cathjourn@catholicpress.org *Web Site:* www.catholicpress.org, pg 636

Catholic Book Publishing Corp, 77 West End Rd, Totowa, NJ 07512 *Tel:* 973-890-2400 *Toll Free Tel:* 877-228-2665 *Fax:* 973-890-2410 *E-mail:* info@catholicbookpublishing.com *Web Site:* www.catholicbookpublishing.com, pg 49

The Catholic Health Association of the United States, 4455 Woodson Rd, St Louis, MO 63134-3797 *Tel:* 314-427-2500 *Fax:* 314-427-0029 *E-mail:* servicecenter@chausa.org *Web Site:* www.chausa.org, pg 49

Catholic Library Association, 8550 United Plaza Blvd, Suite 1001, Baton Rouge, LA 70809 *Tel:* 225-408-4417 *E-mail:* cla2@cathla.org *Web Site:* cathla.org, pg 562

Catholic Press Association of the United States & Canada, 205 W Monroe St, Suite 470, Chicago, IL 60606 *Tel:* 312-380-6789 *Fax:* 312-361-0256 *E-mail:* journalist@catholicpress.org *Web Site:* www.catholicpress.org, pg 562

Catholic Press Awards, 205 W Monroe St, Suite 470, Chicago, IL 60606 *Tel:* 312-380-6789 *Fax:* 312-361-0256 *E-mail:* cathjourn@catholicpress.org *Web Site:* www.catholicpress.org, pg 636

The Catholic University of America Press, 240 Leahy Hall, 620 Michigan Ave NE, Washington, DC 20064 *Tel:* 202-319-5052 *Toll Free Tel:* 800-537-5487 (orders only) *Fax:* 202-319-4985 *E-mail:* cua-press@cua.edu *Web Site:* cuapress.cua.edu, pg 49

Cato Institute, 1000 Massachusetts Ave NW, Washington, DC 20001-5403 *Tel:* 202-842-0200 *Toll Free Tel:* 800-767-1241 *Fax:* 202-842-3490 *E-mail:* catostore@cato.org *Web Site:* www.cato.org, pg 49

Jeanne Cavelos Editorial Services, PO Box 75, Mont Vernon, NH 03057 *Tel:* 603-673-6234 *Web Site:* jeannecavelos.com, pg 490

Caxton Press, 312 Main St, Caldwell, ID 83605-3299 *Tel:* 208-459-7421 *Toll Free Tel:* 800-657-6465 *Fax:* 208-459-7450 *E-mail:* publish@caxtonpress.com *Web Site:* www.caxtonpress.com, pg 49

CBA: The Association for Christian Retail, 1365 Garden of the Gods Rd, Suite 105, Colorado Springs, CO 80907 *Tel:* 719-265-9895 *Toll Free Tel:* 800-252-1950 *Fax:* 719-272-3508 *E-mail:* info@cbaonline.org *Web Site:* cbaonline.org, pg 562

CCAB Inc, One Concorde Gate, Suite 800, Toronto, ON M3C 3N6, Canada *Tel:* 416-487-2418 *Fax:* 416-487-6405 *E-mail:* info@bpaww.com *Web Site:* www.bpaww.com, pg 562

CCH, a Wolters Kluwer business, 2700 Lake Cook Rd, Riverwoods, IL 60015 *Tel:* 847-267-7000 *Web Site:* www.cch.com, pg 49

CDL Press, PO Box 34454, Bethesda, MD 20827 *Tel:* 301-762-2066 *Fax:* 253-484-5542 *E-mail:* cdlpress@erols.com *Web Site:* www.cdlpress.com, pg 50

CeciBooks Editorial & Publishing Consultation, 7057 26 Ave NW, Seattle, WA 98117 *Tel:* 206-706-9565 *E-mail:* cecibooks@gmail.com *Web Site:* www.cecibooks.com, pg 490

Cedar Fort Inc, 2373 W 700 S, Springville, UT 84663 *Tel:* 801-489-4084 *Toll Free Tel:* 800-SKY-BOOK (759-2665) *Fax:* 801-489-1097 *Toll Free Fax:* 800-388-3727 *Web Site:* cedarfort.com, pg 50

Cedar Grove Books, 2215 High Point Dr, Carrollton, TX 75007 *Tel:* 415-364-8292 *Fax:* 415-276-9858 *E-mail:* queries@cedargrovebooks.com *Web Site:* www.cedargrovebooks.com, pg 50

Cedar Tree Books, PO Box 4256, Wilmington, DE 19807 *Tel:* 302-998-4171 *Fax:* 302-998-4185 *E-mail:* books@ctpress.com *Web Site:* www.cedartreebooks.com, pg 50

CEF Press, 17482 State Hwy M, Warrenton, MO 63383-0348 *Tel:* 636-456-4321 *Toll Free Tel:* 800-748-7710 (cust serv); 800-300-4033 (USA ministries) *Fax:* 636-456-2078 (cust serv) *E-mail:* custserv@cefonline.com *Web Site:* www.cefonline.com, pg 50

Celebra, 375 Hudson St, New York, NY 10014 *Tel:* 212-366-2000 *E-mail:* ecommerce@us.penguingroup.com *Web Site:* www.penguin.com, pg 50

Celebrity Profiles Publishing, PO Box 344, Stony Brook, NY 11790 *Tel:* 631-862-8555 *Fax:* 631-862-0139 *E-mail:* celebpro4@aol.com *Web Site:* www.richardgrudens.com; richardgrudensblog.blogspot.com, pg 50

Cengage Learning, 20 Channel Center St, Boston, MA 02210 *Tel:* 617-289-7700 *Toll Free Tel:* 800-354-9706 *Fax:* 617-289-7844 *Toll Free Fax:* 800-487-8488 *E-mail:* esales@cengage.com *Web Site:* www.cengage.com, pg 50

The Center for Book Arts, 28 W 27 St, 3rd fl, New York, NY 10001 *Tel:* 212-481-0295 *E-mail:* info@centerforbookarts.org *Web Site:* www.centerforbookarts.org, pg 562

The Center for Book Arts, 28 W 27 St, 3rd fl, New York, NY 10001 *Tel:* 212-481-0295 *Toll Free Fax:* 866-708-8994 *E-mail:* info@centerforbookarts.org *Web Site:* www.centerforbookarts.org, pg 619

Center for Creative Leadership LLC, One Leadership Place, Greensboro, NC 27410-9427 *Tel:* 336-545-2810; 336-288-7210 *Fax:* 336-282-3284 *E-mail:* info@ccl.org *Web Site:* www.ccl.org/publications, pg 50

Center for East Asian Studies (CEAS), Western Washington University, 516 High St, Bellingham, WA 98225 *Tel:* 360-650-3339 *Fax:* 360-650-6110 *E-mail:* easpress@wwu.edu *Web Site:* www.wwu.edu/eas, pg 51

The Center for Exhibition Industry Research (CEIR), 12700 Park Central Dr, Suite 308, Dallas, TX 75251 *Tel:* 972-687-9242 *Fax:* 972-692-6020 *E-mail:* info@ceir.org *Web Site:* www.ceir.org, pg 562

The Center for Fiction, 17 E 47 St, New York, NY 10017 *Tel:* 212-755-6710 *Fax:* 212-826-0831 *E-mail:* info@centerforfiction.org *Web Site:* centerforfiction.org/awards, pg 563

The Center for Fiction First Novel Prize, 17 E 47 St, New York, NY 10017 *Tel:* 212-755-6710 *Fax:* 212-826-0831 *E-mail:* info@centerforfiction.org *Web Site:* centerforfiction.org/awards, pg 636

Center for Futures Education Inc, 345 Erie St, Grove City, PA 16127 *Tel:* 724-458-5860 *Fax:* 724-458-5962 *E-mail:* info@thectr.com *Web Site:* www.thectr.com, pg 51

The Center for Learning, 10200 Jefferson Blvd, Culver City, CA 90232 *Tel:* 310-839-2436 *Toll Free Tel:* 800-421-4246 *Fax:* 310-839-2249 *Toll Free Fax:* 800-944-5432 *E-mail:* customerservice@centerforlearning.org *Web Site:* www.centerforlearning.org, pg 51

Center for Publishing Departmental Scholarships, Midtown Ctr, Rm 429, 11 W 42 St, New York, NY 10036 *Tel:* 212-992-3232 *Fax:* 212-992-3233 *E-mail:* pub.center@nyu.edu *Web Site:* www.scps.nyu.edu, pg 636

The Center for the Book in the Library of Congress, The Library of Congress, 101 Independence Ave SE, Washington, DC 20540-4920 *Tel:* 202-707-5221 *Fax:* 202-707-0269 *E-mail:* cfbook@loc.gov *Web Site:* www.read.gov; www.read.gov/cfb, pg 563

Center for the Collaborative Classroom, 1250 53 St, Suite 3, Emeryville, CA 94608 *Tel:* 510-533-0213 *Toll Free Tel:* 800-666-7270 *Fax:* 510-464-3670 *E-mail:* info@collaborativeclassroom.org; clientsupport@collaborativeclassroom.org *Web Site:* www.collaborativeclassroom.org, pg 51

Center for Women Policy Studies, 4620 N Park Ave, Suite 302W, Chevy Chase, MD 20815 *Tel:* 301-986-0795 *E-mail:* cwps@centerwomenpolicy.org *Web Site:* www.centerwomenpolicy.org, pg 51

Centering Corp, 7230 Maple St, Omaha, NE 68134 *Tel:* 402-553-1200 *Toll Free Tel:* 866-218-0101 *Fax:* 402-553-0507 *E-mail:* orders@centering.org *Web Site:* www.centering.org, pg 51

Centerstream Publishing LLC, PO Box 17878, Anaheim Hills, CA 92817-7878 *Tel:* 714-779-9390 *E-mail:* centerstrm@aol.com *Web Site:* www.centerstream-usa.com, pg 51

Central Conference of American Rabbis/CCAR Press, 355 Lexington Ave, 18th fl, New York, NY 10017 *Tel:* 212-972-3636 *E-mail:* info@ccarnet.org *Web Site:* www.ccarpress.org, pg 51

Central European University Press, 224 W 57 St, New York, NY 10019 *Web Site:* www.ceupress.com, pg 51

Central Recovery Press (CRP), 3321 N Buffalo Dr, Suite 275, Las Vegas, NV 89129 *Tel:* 702-868-5830 *Fax:* 702-868-5831 *E-mail:* info@centralrecovery.com *Web Site:* centralrecoverypress.com, pg 52

Centre for Reformation & Renaissance Studies (CRRS), 71 Queen's Park Crescent E, Toronto, ON M5S 1K7, Canada *Tel:* 416-585-4465 *Fax:* 416-585-4430 (attn: CRRS) *E-mail:* crrs.publications@utoronto.ca *Web Site:* crrs.ca, pg 450

Centre Franco-Ontarien de Ressources en Alphabetisation (Centre FORA), PO Box 56, Hanmer, ON P3P 1S9, Canada *Tel:* 705-524-3672 *Toll Free Tel:* 888-814-4422 (orders, CN only) *Fax:* 705-524-8535 *E-mail:* info@centrefora.on.ca *Web Site:* www.centrefora.on.ca, pg 450

The Century Foundation Press, One Whitehall St, 15th fl, New York, NY 10004 *Tel:* 212-452-7700 *Fax:* 212-535-7534 *E-mail:* info@tcf.org *Web Site:* www.tcf.org, pg 52

Cenveo Publisher Services, 555 Virginia Dr, Fort Washington, PA 19034 *Tel:* 215-591-9125 *E-mail:* info.psg@cenveo.com *Web Site:* cenveopublisherservices.com, pg 491

Chain Store Guide (CSG), 10117 Princess Palm Ave, Suite 375, Tampa, FL 33610 *Tel:* 813-627-6957 *Toll Free Tel:* 800-927-9292 (orders) *Fax:* 813-627-6888 *E-mail:* info@csgis.com *Web Site:* www.csgis.com, pg 52

Chalice Press, 483 E Lockwood Ave, Suite 100, St Louis, MO 63119 *Tel:* 314-231-8500 *Toll Free Tel:* 800-366-3383 *Fax:* 314-231-8524; 770-280-4039 (orders) *E-mail:* customerservice@chalicepress.com *Web Site:* www.chalicepress.com, pg 52

Jane Chambers Playwriting Award, Georgetown University, 108 David Performing Arts Ctr, Box 571063, 37 & "O" St, NW, Washington, DC 20057-1063 *Web Site:* www.athe.org/?page=Jane_Chambers, pg 636

The Alfred & Fay Chandler Book Award, c/o Harvard Business School, Connell House 301A, Boston, MA 02163 *Tel:* 617-495-1003 *Fax:* 617-495-2705 *E-mail:* bhr@hbs.edu *Web Site:* www.hbs.edu/businesshistory/fellowships, pg 636

G S Sharat Chandra Prize for Short Fiction, University House, 5101 Rockhill Rd, Kansas City, MO 64110-2499 *Tel:* 816-235-2558 *Fax:* 816-235-2611 *E-mail:* bkmk@umkc.edu *Web Site:* www.umkc.edu/bkmk, pg 636

Channel Photographics, 980 Lincoln Ave, Suite 200-B, San Rafael, CA 94901 *Tel:* 415-456-2934 *Fax:* 415-456-4124 *Web Site:* www.channelphotographics.com, pg 52

Chaosium Inc, 3450 Wooddale Ct, Ann Arbor, MI 48104 *Tel:* 734-972-9551 *E-mail:* customerservice@chaosium.com *Web Site:* www.chaosium.com, pg 52

Character Publishing, PO Box 322, Pass Christian, MS 39571, pg 52

Charisma Media, 600 Rinehart Rd, Lake Mary, FL 32746 *Tel:* 407-333-0600 (all imprints) *Toll Free Tel:* 800-283-8494 (Charisma Media, Siloam Press, Creation House); 800-665-1468 *Fax:* 407-333-7100 (all imprints) *E-mail:* charisma@charismamedia.com *Web Site:* www.charismamedia.com, pg 52

CharismaLife Publishers, 600 Rinehart Rd, Lake Mary, FL 32746 *Tel:* 407-333-0600 *Toll Free Tel:* 800-451-4598 *Fax:* 407-333-7100 *E-mail:* charismalife@charismamedia.com *Web Site:* www.charismamedia.com, pg 52

The Charles Press, Publishers, 230 N 21 St, Suite 312, Philadelphia, PA 19103 *Tel:* 215-561-2786 *Fax:* 215-600-1248 *E-mail:* mail@charlespresspub.com *Web Site:* www.charlespresspub.com, pg 53

Charles River Media, 20 Channel Center St, Boston, MA 02210 *Toll Free Tel:* 800-354-9706 *Toll Free Fax:* 800-487-8488 *E-mail:* crminfo@cengage.com *Web Site:* www.cengage.com; www.delmarlearning.com/charlesriver, pg 53

Charles Scribner's Sons®, 27500 Drake Rd, Farmington Hills, MI 48331-3535 *Toll Free Tel:* 800-877-4253 *Toll Free Fax:* 800-414-5043 *E-mail:* gale.galeord@cengage.com *Web Site:* www.gale.com/scribners, pg 53

Charlesbridge Publishing Inc, 85 Main St, Watertown, MA 02472 *Tel:* 617-926-0329 *Toll Free Tel:* 800-225-3214 *Fax:* 617-926-5720 *Toll Free Fax:* 800-926-5775 *E-mail:* books@charlesbridge.com *Web Site:* www.charlesbridge.com, pg 53

The Charlton Press Corp, 991 Victoria St N, Kitchener, ON N2B 3C7, Canada *Tel:* 416-962-2665 *Toll Free Tel:* 866-663-8827 *Fax:* 519-579-0532 *E-mail:* chpress@charltonpress.com *Web Site:* www.charltonpress.com, pg 450

Chartered Professional Accountants of Canada (CPA Canada), 277 Wellington St W, Toronto, ON M5V 3H2, Canada *Tel:* 416-977-3222 *Toll Free Tel:* 800-268-3793 *Fax:* 416-977-8585 *E-mail:* member.services@cpacanada.ca *Web Site:* www.cpacanada.ca; www.facebook.com/CPACanada/, pg 450

The Chautauqua Prize, One Ames Ave, Chautauqua, NY 14722 *Toll Free Tel:* 800-836-ARTS (836-2787) *Web Site:* www.ciweb.org/prize, pg 636

Chautauqua Writers' Workshop, One Ames Ave, Chautauqua, NY 14722 *Tel:* 716-357-6316; 716-357-6250 *Toll Free Tel:* 800-836-ARTS (836-2787) *Fax:* 716-357-9014 *Web Site:* ciweb.org, pg 610

Margaret Cheasebro, 246 Rd 2900, Aztec, NM 87410 *Tel:* 505-334-2869 *E-mail:* mwriter4571@yahoo.com *Web Site:* www.wordsandwellness.com, pg 491

Chelsea Green Publishing Co, 85 N Main St, Suite 120, White River Junction, VT 05001 *Tel:* 802-295-6300 *Toll Free Tel:* 800-639-4099 (cust serv, consumer & trade orders) *Fax:* 802-295-6444 *Web Site:* www.chelseagreen.com, pg 53

Chelsea House Publishers, 132 W 31 St, 17th fl, New York, NY 10001 *Tel:* 212-967-8800 *Toll Free Tel:* 800-322-8755 *Fax:* 917-339-0325 *Toll Free Fax:* 800-678-3633 *E-mail:* custserv@factsonfile.com *Web Site:* www.infobasepublishing.com; www.infobaselearning.com, pg 53

ChemTec Publishing, 38 Earswick Dr, Toronto, ON M1E 1C6, Canada *Tel:* 416-265-2603 *Fax:* 416-265-1399 *E-mail:* orderdesk@chemtec.org *Web Site:* www.chemtec.org, pg 450

Cheneliere Education Inc, 5800, rue St Denis, bureau 900, Montreal, QC H2S 3L5, Canada *Tel:* 514-273-1066 *Toll Free Tel:* 800-565-5531 *Fax:* 514-276-0324 *Toll Free Fax:* 800-814-0324 *E-mail:* info@cheneliere.ca *Web Site:* www.cheneliere.ca, pg 450

Cheng & Tsui Co Inc, 25 West St, 2nd fl, Boston, MA 02111-1213 *Tel:* 617-988-2401 *Toll Free Tel:* 800-554-1963 *Fax:* 617-426-3669; 617-556-8964 *E-mail:* service@cheng-tsui.com; orders@cheng-tsui.com *Web Site:* www.cheng-tsui.com, pg 53

Ruth Chernia, 198 Victor Ave, Toronto, ON M4K 1B2, Canada *Tel:* 416-466-0164 *E-mail:* rchernia@editors.ca; rchernia@sympatico.ca *Web Site:* www.editors.ca/profile/444/ruth-chernia, pg 491

Cherry Hill Publishing LLC, 24344 Del Amo Rd, Ramona, CA 92065 *Tel:* 858-829-5550 *Toll Free Tel:* 800-407-1072 *Fax:* 760-203-1200 *E-mail:* operations@cherryhillpublishing.com; sales@cherryhillpublishing.com *Web Site:* www.cherryhillpublishing.com, pg 54

Linda Chester Literary Agency, 630 Fifth Ave, Suite 2000, New York, NY 10111 *Tel:* 212-218-3350 *E-mail:* submissions@lindachester.com *Web Site:* www.lindachester.com, pg 511

Chestnut Publishing Group Inc, 44 Stubbs Dr, Suite 207, Toronto, ON M2L 2R3, Canada *Tel:* 416-224-5824 *Fax:* 416-224-0595 *Web Site:* www.chestnutpublishing.com, pg 450

Chicago Review Press, 814 N Franklin St, Chicago, IL 60610 *Tel:* 312-337-0747 *Toll Free Tel:* 800-888-4741 *Fax:* 312-337-5110 *E-mail:* frontdesk@chicagoreviewpress.com *Web Site:* www.chicagoreviewpress.com, pg 54

Chicago Women in Publishing, PO Box 268107, Chicago, IL 60626 *Tel:* 773-508-0351 *Fax:* 303-942-7164 *E-mail:* info@cwip.org *Web Site:* www.cwip.org, pg 563

Child Welfare League of America (CWLA), 1726 "M" St, Suite 500, Washington, DC 20036 *Tel:* 202-688-4200 *Fax:* 202-833-1689 *E-mail:* cwla@cwla.org *Web Site:* www.cwla.org/publications, pg 54

Children's & Teen Choice Book Awards, 54 W 39 St, 14th fl, New York, NY 10018 *E-mail:* cbc.info@cbcbooks.org *Web Site:* everychildareader.net/choice, pg 637

The Children's Book Council (CBC), 54 W 39 St, 14th fl, New York, NY 10018 *Tel:* 212-966-1990 *E-mail:* cbc.info@cbcbooks.org *Web Site:* www.cbcbooks.org, pg 563

Children's Book Press, 95 Madison Ave, Suite 1205, New York, NY 10016 *Tel:* 212-779-4400 *Fax:* 212-683-1894 *E-mail:* general@leeandlow.com; orders@leeandlow.com; sales@leeandlow.com *Web Site:* www.leeandlow.com, pg 54

Children's Literature Association Article Award, 1301 W 22 St, Suite 202, Oak Brook, IL 60523 *Tel:* 630-571-4520 *Fax:* 708-876-5598 *E-mail:* info@childlitassn.org *Web Site:* www.childlitassn.org, pg 637

Children's Literature Association Beiter Graduate Student Research Grants, 1301 W 22 St, Suite 202, Oak Brook, IL 60523 *Tel:* 630-571-4520 *Fax:* 708-876-5598 *E-mail:* info@childlitassn.org *Web Site:* www.childlitassn.org, pg 637

Children's Literature Association Book Award, 1301 W 22 St, Suite 202, Oak Brook, IL 60523 *Tel:* 630-571-4520 *Fax:* 708-876-5598 *E-mail:* info@childlitassn.org *Web Site:* www.childlitassn.org, pg 637

Children's Sequoyah Book Award, PO Box 6550, Edmond, OK 73083 *Tel:* 405-525-5100 *Fax:* 405-525-5103 *Web Site:* www.oklibs.org, pg 637

Faith Childs Literary Agency Inc, 111 John St, Suite 1620, New York, NY 10038 *Tel:* 212-995-9600 *Web Site:* faithchildsliteraryagency.com, pg 511

Child's Play®, 250 Minot Ave, Auburn, ME 04210 *Tel:* 207-784-7252 *Toll Free Tel:* 800-639-6404 *Fax:* 207-784-7358 *Toll Free Fax:* 800-854-6989 *E-mail:* chpmaine@aol.com; cplay@earthlink.net *Web Site:* www.childs-play.com, pg 54

The Child's World Inc, 1980 Lookout Dr, North Mankato, MN 56003-1705 *Tel:* 507-385-1044 *Toll Free Tel:* 800-599-READ (599-7323) *Toll Free Fax:* 888-320-2329 *E-mail:* sales@childsworld.com *Web Site:* childsworld.com, pg 54

China Books, 360 Swift Ave, Suite 48, South San Francisco, CA 94080 *Tel:* 650-872-7076 *Toll Free Tel:* 800-818-2017 (US only) *Fax:* 650-872-7808 *E-mail:* info@chinabooks.com *Web Site:* www.chinabooks.com, pg 54

Chinese Connection Agency, 67 Banksville Rd, Armonk, NY 10504 *Tel:* 914-765-0296 *Fax:* 914-765-0297 *Web Site:* www.yaollc.com, pg 511

Chocorua Writing Workshop, PO Box 2280, Conway, NH 03818-2280 *Tel:* 603-447-2280 *E-mail:* reservations@worldfellowship.org *Web Site:* www.worldfellowship.org; www.facebook.com/World.Fellowship.Center, pg 610

Chosen Books, 11400 Hampshire Ave S, Bloomington, MN 55438-2852 *Tel:* 616-676-9185 *Toll Free Tel:* 800-877-2665 (orders only) *Fax:* 616-676-9573 *Toll Free Fax:* 800-398-3111 (orders only) *Web Site:* www.chosenbooks.com, pg 54

Chouette Publishing, 1001 Lenoir St, Suite B-238, Montreal, QC H4C 2Z6, Canada *Tel:* 514-925-3325 *Fax:* 514-925-3323 *E-mail:* info@editions-chouette.com *Web Site:* www.chouette-publishing.com, pg 450

Christian Liberty Press, 502 W Euclid Ave, Arlington Heights, IL 60004-5402 *Tel:* 847-259-4444 *Toll Free Tel:* 800-832-2741 (cust serv) *Fax:* 847-259-2941 *E-mail:* custserv@christianlibertypress.com *Web Site:* www.shopchristianliberty.com, pg 55

Christian Light Publications Inc, 1051 Mount Clinton Pike, Harrisonburg, VA 22802 *Tel:* 540-434-1003 *Toll Free Tel:* 800-776-0478 *Fax:* 540-433-8896 *E-mail:* info@clp.org; orders@clp.org *Web Site:* www.clp.org, pg 55

Christian Schools International, 3350 E Paris Ave SE, Grand Rapids, MI 49512-3054 *Tel:* 616-957-1070 *Toll Free Tel:* 800-635-8288 *Fax:* 616-957-5022 *E-mail:* info@csionline.org *Web Site:* www.csionline.org, pg 55

The Christian Science Publishing Society, 210 Massachusetts Ave, Boston, MA 02115 *Tel:* 617-450-2000 *Toll Free Tel:* 800-288-7090 *Fax:* 617-450-7334 *E-mail:* contact@csps.com *Web Site:* christianscience.com, pg 55

The Christopher Awards, 5 Hanover Sq, 22nd fl, New York, NY 10004-2751 *Tel:* 212-759-4050 *Toll Free Tel:* 888-298-4050 (orders) *Fax:* 212-838-5073 *E-mail:* mail@christophers.org *Web Site:* www.christophers.org, pg 637

Chronicle Books LLC, 680 Second St, San Francisco, CA 94107 *Tel:* 415-537-4200 *Toll Free Tel:* 800-759-0190 (cust serv) *Fax:* 415-537-4460 *Toll Free Fax:* 800-858-7787 (orders); 800-286-9471 (cust serv) *E-mail:* frontdesk@chroniclebooks.com *Web Site:* www.chroniclebooks.com, pg 55

John Ciardi Prize for Poetry, University House, 5101 Rockhill Rd, Kansas City, MO 64110-2499 *Tel:* 816-235-2558 *Fax:* 816-235-2611 *E-mail:* bkmk@umkc.edu *Web Site:* www.umkc.edu/bkmk, pg 637

Cider Mill Press Book Publishers LLC, 12 Spring St, Kennebunkport, ME 04046 *Tel:* 207-967-8232 *Fax:* 207-967-8233 *Web Site:* www.cidermillpress.com, pg 56

Cinco Puntos Press, 701 Texas Ave, El Paso, TX 79901 *Tel:* 915-838-1625 *Toll Free Tel:* 800-566-9072 *Fax:* 915-838-1635 *E-mail:* info@cincopuntos.com *Web Site:* www.cincopuntos.com, pg 56

Cine/Lit Representation, PO Box 802918, Santa Clarita, CA 91380-2918 *Tel:* 661-513-0268 *E-mail:* cinelit@att.net, pg 511

Circlet Press Inc, 39 Hurlbut St, Cambridge, MA 02138 *Toll Free Tel:* 800-729-6423 *E-mail:* circletintern@gmail.com *Web Site:* www.circlet.com, pg 56

Cistercian Publications, Saint John's Abbey, PO Box 7500, Collegeville, MN 56321 *Tel:* 320-363-2213 *Toll Free Tel:* 800-436-8431 *Fax:* 320-363-3299 *Toll Free Fax:* 800-445-5899 *E-mail:* sales@litpress.org *Web Site:* www.cistercianpublications.org, pg 56

City & Regional Magazine Association, 2512 Artesia Blvd, Suite 200, Redondo Beach, CA 90278 *Tel:* 310-379-8261 *Fax:* 310-379-8283 *E-mail:* admin@citymag.org *Web Site:* www.citymag.org, pg 563

City Lights Publishers, 261 Columbus Ave, San Francisco, CA 94133 *Tel:* 415-362-8193 *Fax:* 415-362-4921 *E-mail:* staff@citylights.com *Web Site:* www.citylights.com, pg 56

The City of Calgary W O Mitchell Book Prize, 11759 Groat Rd, Edmonton, AB T5M 3K6, Canada *Tel:* 780-422-8174 *Toll Free Tel:* 800-665-5354 (AB only) *Fax:* 780-422-2663 (attn WGA) *E-mail:* mail@writersguild.ca *Web Site:* writersguild.ca, pg 637

City of Vancouver Book Award, Woodward's Heritage Bldg, Suite 501, 111 W Hastings St, Vancouver, BC V6B 1H4, Canada *Tel:* 604-871-6634 *Fax:* 604-871-6005 *E-mail:* culture@vancouver.ca *Web Site:* vancouver.ca/bookaward, pg 637

Clarion Books, 3 Park Ave, New York, NY 10016 *Tel:* 212-420-5800 *Toll Free Tel:* 800-225-3362 (orders) *Fax:* 212-420-5855 *Toll Free Fax:* 800-634-7568 (orders) *Web Site:* www.hmhco.com, pg 56

The Clarion Science Fiction & Fantasy Writers' Workshop, Arthur C Clarke Ctr for Human Imagination, UC San Diego, 9500 Gilman Dr, MC0445, La Jolla, CA 92093-0445 *Tel:* 858-534-2115 *E-mail:* clarion@ucsd.edu *Web Site:* clarion.ucsd.edu; imagination.ucsd.edu, pg 610

Clarity Press Inc, 2625 Piedmont Rd NE, Suite 56, Atlanta, GA 30324 *Toll Free Tel:* 877-613-1495 (edit) *Toll Free Fax:* 877-613-7868 *E-mail:* claritypress@usa.net (foreign rts & perms) *Web Site:* www.claritypress.com, pg 56

Wm Clark Associates, 186 Fifth Ave, 2nd fl, New York, NY 10010 *Tel:* 212-675-2784 *E-mail:* general@wmclark.com *Web Site:* www.wmclark.com, pg 511

Class Action Ink, 1300 NE 16 Ave, Suite 712, Portland, OR 97232-1483 *Tel:* 503-280-2448 *E-mail:* pamg0822@gmail.com *Web Site:* www.classactionink.com, pg 477

Classical Academic Press, 2151 Market St, Camp Hill, PA 17011 *Tel:* 717-730-0711 *Fax:* 717-730-0721 *E-mail:* office@classicalsubjects.com *Web Site:* classicalacademicpress.com, pg 57

Page Davidson Clayton Prize for Emerging Poets, University of Michigan, 0576 Rackham Bldg, 915 E Washington St, Ann Arbor, MI 48109-1070 *Tel:* 734-764-9265 *E-mail:* mqr@umich.edu *Web Site:* www.umich.edu/~mqr, pg 637

Clear Concepts, 1329 Federal Ave, Suite 6, Los Angeles, CA 90025 *Tel:* 323-285-0325, pg 491

Clear Light Publishers, 823 Don Diego Ave, Santa Fe, NM 87505 *Tel:* 505-989-9590 *Toll Free Tel:* 800-253-2747 (orders) *Fax:* 505-989-9519 *E-mail:* market@clearlightbooks.com *Web Site:* www.clearlightbooks.com, pg 57

Clearfield Co Inc, 3600 Clipper Mill Rd, Suite 260, Baltimore, MD 21211 *Tel:* 410-837-8271 *Toll Free Tel:* 800-296-6687 (orders & cust serv) *Fax:* 410-752-8492 *E-mail:* sales@genealogical.com *Web Site:* www.genealogical.com, pg 57

Cleis Press, 2246 Sixth St, Berkeley, CA 94710 *Tel:* 510-845-8000 *Toll Free Tel:* 800-780-2279 (US) *Fax:* 510-845-8001 *E-mail:* orders@cleispress.com *Web Site:* www.cleispress.com; www.vivaeditions.com, pg 57

Clerical Plus, 97 Blueberry Lane, Shelton, CT 06484 *Tel:* 203-225-0879 *Fax:* 203-225-0879 *E-mail:* clericalplus@aol.com *Web Site:* www.clericalplus.net, pg 491

Clerisy Press, 306 Greenup St, Covington, KY 41011 *Tel:* 859-815-7200 *Toll Free Tel:* 888-604-4537 *Fax:* 859-291-9111 *E-mail:* info@clerisypress.com *Web Site:* www.clerisypress.com, pg 57

Cleveland State University Poetry Center Prizes, 2121 Euclid Ave, Cleveland, OH 44115 *Tel:* 216-687-3986 *Toll Free Tel:* 888-278-6473 *Fax:* 216-687-6943 *E-mail:* poetrycenter@csuohio.edu *Web Site:* www.csupoetrycenter.com, pg 637

David H Clift Scholarship, 50 E Huron St, Chicago, IL 60611 *Toll Free Tel:* 800-545-2433 (ext 4279) *Fax:* 312-280-3256 *E-mail:* scholarships@ala.org *Web Site:* www.ala.org/scholarships, pg 638

Clinical Laboratory & Standards Institute (CLSI), 950 W Valley Rd, Suite 2500, Wayne, PA 19087 *Tel:* 610-688-0100 *Toll Free Tel:* 877-447-1888 (orders) *Fax:* 610-688-0700 *E-mail:* customerservice@clsi.org *Web Site:* www.clsi.org, pg 57

Close Up Publishing, 1330 Braddock Place, Suite 400, Alexandria, VA 22314 *Tel:* 703-706-3300 *Toll Free Tel:* 800-CLOSE-UP (256-7387) *Fax:* 703-706-3564 *E-mail:* info@closeup.org *Web Site:* www.closeup.org, pg 57

Closson Press, 257 Delilah St, Apollo, PA 15613-1933 *Tel:* 724-337-4482 *Fax:* 724-337-9484 *E-mail:* clossonpress@comcast.net *Web Site:* www.clossonpress.com, pg 57

Clotilde's Secretarial & Management Services, PO Box 871926, New Orleans, LA 70187 *Tel:* 504-242-2912; 504-800-4853 (cell) *E-mail:* elcsy58@aol.com; elcsy58@att.net, pg 491

Dwight Clough, 311 W Main St, Sun Prairie, WI 53590 *Tel:* 608-834-8291 *E-mail:* lmp@dwightclough.com *Web Site:* dwightclough.com, pg 491

CN Times Books, 501 Fifth Ave, Suite 1708, New York, NY 10017 *Tel:* 212-867-8666 *Web Site:* cntimesbooks.com, pg 57

Coach House Books, 80 bpNichol Lane, Toronto, ON M5S 3J4, Canada *Tel:* 416-979-2217 *Toll Free Tel:* 800-367-6360 (outside Toronto) *Fax:* 416-977-1158 *E-mail:* mail@chbooks.com *Web Site:* www.chbooks.com, pg 450

Coaches Choice, 514 Airport Way, Monterey, CA 93940 *Toll Free Tel:* 888-229-5745 *Fax:* 831-372-6075 *E-mail:* info@coacheschoice.com *Web Site:* www.coacheschoice.com, pg 57

Coachlight Press LLC, 1704 Craig's Store Rd, Afton, VA 22920-2017 *Tel:* 434-823-1692 *E-mail:* sales@coachlightpress.com *Web Site:* www.coachlightpress.com, pg 58

Coal Hill Review Poetry Chapbook Contest, c/o Autumn House Press, PO Box 5486, Pittsburgh, PA 15206 *E-mail:* reviewcoalhill@gmail.com *Web Site:* www.coalhillreview.com, pg 638

Coastside Editorial, PO Box 181, Moss Beach, CA 94038 *E-mail:* bevjoe@pacific.net, pg 491

Codhill Press, One Arden Lane, New Paltz, NY 12561 *E-mail:* codhillpress@aol.com *Web Site:* www.codhill.com, pg 58

CODiE Awards, 1090 Vermont Ave NW, 6th fl, Washington, DC 20005-4095 *E-mail:* info@siia.net *Web Site:* www.siia.net, pg 638

Coe College Playwriting Festival, 1220 First Ave NE, Cedar Rapids, IA 52402 *Tel:* 319-399-8624 *Fax:* 319-399-8557 *Web Site:* www.theatre.coe.edu; www.coe.edu/academics/theatrearts/theatrearts_playwritingfestival, pg 638

Coffee House Press, 79 13 Ave NE, Suite 110, Minneapolis, MN 55413 *Tel:* 612-338-0125 *Fax:* 612-338-4004 *E-mail:* info@coffeehousepress.org *Web Site:* coffeehousepress.org, pg 58

Cognizant Communication Corp, 18 Peekskill Hollow Rd, Putnam Valley, NY 10579-0037 *Tel:* 845-603-6440; 845-603-6441 (warehouse & orders) *Fax:* 845-603-6442 *E-mail:* inquiries@cognizantcommunication.com; sales@cognizantcommunication.com *Web Site:* www.cognizantcommunication.com, pg 58

Carla Furstenberg Cohen Literary Prize, 1322 Holly St NW, Washington, DC 20012, pg 638

Morton N Cohen Award for a Distinguished Edition of Letters, 85 Broad St, Suite 500, New York, NY 10004-2434 *Tel:* 646-576-5141; 646-576-5000 *Fax:* 646-458-0030 *E-mail:* awards@mla.org *Web Site:* www.mla.org, pg 638

Robert L Cohen, 182-12 Horace Harding Expwy, Suite 2M, Fresh Meadows, NY 11365 *Tel:* 718-762-1195 *Toll Free Tel:* 866-EDITING (334-8464) *E-mail:* wordsmith@sterlingmp.com *Web Site:* www.rlcwordsandmusic.com; www.linkedin.com/in/robertcohen17, pg 491

Cohesion®, 511 W Bay St, Suite 480, Tampa, FL 33606 *Tel:* 813-999-3111 *Toll Free Tel:* 877-774-3000 *E-mail:* info@cohesion.com *Web Site:* www.cohesion.com, pg 491

The Victor Cohn Prize for Excellence in Medical Science Reporting, PO Box 910, Hedgesville, WV 25427 *Tel:* 304-754-6786 *Web Site:* www.casw.org, pg 638

Cold Spring Harbor Laboratory Press, 500 Sunnyside Blvd, Woodbury, NY 11797-2924 *Tel:* 516-422-4100 *Toll Free Tel:* 800-843-4388 *Fax:* 516-422-4097; 516-422-4092 (submissions) *E-mail:* cshpress@cshl.edu *Web Site:* www.cshlpress.com, pg 58

Collector Grade Publications Inc, PO Box 1046, Cobourg, ON K9A 4W5, Canada *Tel:* 905-342-3434 *Fax:* 905-342-3688 *E-mail:* info@collectorgrade.com *Web Site:* www.collectorgrade.com, pg 451

College & University Professional Association for Human Resources (CUPA-HR), 1811 Commons Point Dr, Knoxville, TN 37932 *Tel:* 865-637-7673 *Toll Free Tel:* 877-CUPA-HR4 (287-2474) *Fax:* 865-637-7674 *E-mail:* communications@cupahr.org *Web Site:* www.cupahr.org/publications, pg 58

The College Board, 250 Vesey St, New York, NY 10281 *Tel:* 212-713-8000 *Web Site:* www.collegeboard.com, pg 58

College of Liberal & Professional Studies, University of Pennsylvania, 3440 Market St, Suite 100, Philadelphia, PA 19104-3335 *Tel:* 215-898-7326 *Fax:* 215-573-2053 *E-mail:* lps@sas.upenn.edu *Web Site:* www.sas.upenn.edu/lps, pg 619

College Publishing, 12309 Lynwood Dr, Glen Allen, VA 23059 *Tel:* 804-364-8410 *Toll Free Tel:* 800-827-0723 *Fax:* 804-364-8408 *E-mail:* collegepub@mindspring.com *Web Site:* www.collegepublishing.us, pg 58

Collier Associates, 37 Marina Gardens Dr, Palm Beach Gardens, FL 33410 *Tel:* 561-514-6548 *E-mail:* dmccabooks@gmail.com, pg 512

John M Collier Award for Forest History Journalism, 701 William Vickers Ave, Durham, NC 27701-3162 *Tel:* 919-682-9319 *Fax:* 919-682-2349 *Web Site:* www.foresthistory.org, pg 638

Frances Collin Literary Agency, PO Box 33, Wayne, PA 19087 *Tel:* 610-254-0555 *E-mail:* queries@francescollin.com *Web Site:* www.francescollin.com, pg 512

Carr P Collins Award, c/o 7748 Hwy 290 W, Austin, TX 78736-3202 *Tel:* 512-683-5640 *E-mail:* president@texasinstituteofletters.org *Web Site:* www.texasinstituteofletters.org, pg 638

The Colonial Williamsburg Foundation, PO Box 1776, Williamsburg, VA 23187-1776 *Tel:* 757-229-1000 *Toll Free Tel:* 800-HISTORY (447-8679) *E-mail:* geninfo@cwf.org *Web Site:* www.colonialwilliamsburg.org, pg 58

Colorado Authors' League, PO Box 24905, Denver, CO 80224 *Web Site:* coloradoauthors.org, pg 563

Colorado Book Awards, 7935 E Prentice Ave, Suite 450, Greenwood Village, CO 80111 *Tel:* 303-894-7951 (ext 19) *Fax:* 303-864-9361 *E-mail:* info@coloradohumanities.org *Web Site:* www.coloradohumanities.org, pg 638

Betsy Colquitt Award for Poetry, Dept of English, TCU Box 298300, Fort Worth, TX 76129 *Tel:* 817-257-5907 *Fax:* 817-257-5905 *E-mail:* descant@tcu.edu *Web Site:* www.descant.tcu.edu, pg 638

Columbia Books & Information Services (CBIS), 4340 East-West Hwy, Suite 300, Bethesda, MD 20814 *Tel:* 202-464-1662 *Fax:* 301-664-9600 *E-mail:* info@columbiabooks.com *Web Site:* www.columbiabooks.com; www.lobbyists.info; www.associationexecs.com, pg 58

Columbia Publishing Course at Columbia University, 2950 Broadway, MC 3801, New York, NY 10027 *Tel:* 212-854-1898 *Fax:* 212-854-7618 *E-mail:* publishing@jrn.columbia.edu *Web Site:* www.journalism.columbia.edu/publishing, pg 619

Columbia University Press, 61 W 62 St, New York, NY 10023 *Tel:* 212-459-0600 *Toll Free Tel:* 800-944-8648 *Fax:* 212-459-3678 *E-mail:* cup_book@columbia.edu (orders & cust serv) *Web Site:* cup.columbia.edu, pg 59

Columbia University School of the Arts, Creative Writing Program, 609 Kent Hall, New York, NY 10027 *Tel:* 212-854-3774 *Fax:* 212-854-7704 *E-mail:* writingprogram@columbia.edu *Web Site:* www.columbia.edu/cu/writing, pg 619

Comex Systems Inc, 101 Pleasant Hill Rd, Chester, NJ 07930 *Tel:* 908-881-6301 *Toll Free Tel:* 800-543-6959 *Fax:* 908-879-0070 *E-mail:* mail@comexsystems.com *Web Site:* www.comexsystems.com, pg 59

Committee On Scholarly Editions, c/o Modern Language Association of America, 26 Broadway, 3rd fl, New York, NY 10004-1789 *Tel:* 646-576-5044 *Fax:* 646-458-0030 *Web Site:* www.mla.org, pg 563

Common Courage Press, One Red Barn Rd, Monroe, ME 04951 *Tel:* 207-525-0900 *Toll Free Tel:* 800-497-3207 *Fax:* 207-525-3068 *Web Site:* www.commoncouragepress.com, pg 59

Commonwealth Editions, One River Rd, Carlisle, MA 01741 *Tel:* 781-271-0055 *Toll Free Tel:* 800-277-5312 *Fax:* 781-271-0056 *E-mail:* customercare@awb.com *Web Site:* www.awb.com, pg 59

Community of Literary Magazines & Presses (CLMP), 154 Christopher St, Suite 3C, New York, NY 10014-9110 *Tel:* 212-741-9110 *Fax:* 212-741-9112 *E-mail:* info@clmp.org *Web Site:* www.clmp.org, pg 563

Company's Coming Publishing Ltd, 87 E Pender St, Vancouver, BC V6A 1S9, Canada *Tel:* 780-450-6223 (orders & inquiries) *Toll Free Tel:* 800-661-9017 (CN); 800-518-3541 (US) *Fax:* 780-450-1857 *E-mail:* info@companyscoming.com *Web Site:* www.companyscoming.com, pg 451

Concordia Publishing House, 3558 S Jefferson Ave, St Louis, MO 63118-3968 *Tel:* 314-268-1000; 314-268-1268 (bookshop) *Toll Free Tel:* 800-325-3040 (cust serv) *Toll Free Fax:* 800-490-9889 (cust serv) *E-mail:* order@cph.org *Web Site:* www.cph.org, pg 59

The Conference Board Inc, 845 Third Ave, New York, NY 10022-6600 *Tel:* 212-759-0900; 212-339-0345 (cust serv) *Fax:* 212-980-7014; 212-836-9740 (cust serv) *E-mail:* customer.service@conferenceboard.org; membership@conferenceboard.org *Web Site:* www.conference-board.org; www.linkedin.com/company/the-conference-board, pg 59

Conference on Poetry, 158 Ridge Rd, Franconia, NH 03580 *Tel:* 603-823-5510 *E-mail:* frost@frostplace.org *Web Site:* frostplace.org, pg 610

Don Congdon Associates Inc, 110 William St, Suite 2202, New York, NY 10038-3914 *Tel:* 212-645-1229 *Fax:* 212-727-2688 *E-mail:* dca@doncongdon.com *Web Site:* www.doncongdon.com, pg 512

Connecticut Authors & Publishers Association (CAPA), PO Box 715, Avon, CT 06001-0715 *Tel:* 860-675-1344 *Fax:* 860-673-7650 *Web Site:* www.aboutcapa.com, pg 563

The Connecticut Law Tribune, 201 Ann Uccello St, 4th fl, Hartford, CT 06103 *Tel:* 860-527-7900 *Toll Free Tel:* 877-256-2472 *Web Site:* www.ctlawtribune.com/book-center; www.lawcatalog.com, pg 60

Miles Conrad Memorial Lecture, 801 Compass Way, Suite 201, Annapolis, MD 21401 *Tel:* 443-221-2980 *Fax:* 443-221-2981 *E-mail:* nfais@nfais.org *Web Site:* www.nfais.org, pg 638

The Pat Conroy Southern Book Prize, 3806 Yale Ave, Columbia, SC 29205 *Tel:* 803-994-9530 *Fax:* 309-410-0211 *Web Site:* www.sibaweb.com/siba-book-award, pg 639

Constance Rooke Creative Non-Fiction Prize, University of Victoria, Box 1700, Sta CSC, Victoria, BC V8W 2Y2, Canada *Tel:* 250-721-8524 *Fax:* 250-472-5051 *E-mail:* malahat@uvic.ca *Web Site:* malahatreview.ca, pg 639

Consumer Press, 13326 SW 28 St, Suite 102, Fort Lauderdale, FL 33330-1102 *Tel:* 954-370-9153 *Fax:* 954-472-1008 *E-mail:* info@consumerpress.com *Web Site:* www.consumerpress.com, pg 60

Consumertronics, PO Box 23097, Albuquerque, NM 87192 *Tel:* 505-321-1034 *E-mail:* wizguru@consumertronics.net *Web Site:* www.consumertronics.net, pg 60

Contemporary Publishing Co of Raleigh Inc, 5849 Lease Lane, Raleigh, NC 27617 *Tel:* 919-851-8221 *Fax:* 919-851-6666 *E-mail:* questions@contemporarypublishing.com *Web Site:* www.contemporarypublishing.com, pg 60

Continental AfrikaPublishers, 182 Stribling Circle, Spartanburg, SC 29301 *Tel:* 864-576-7992 *Fax:* 864-576-7992 *E-mail:* afrikalion@aol.com; profafrikadzatadeku@facebook.com; profafrikadzatadeku@yahoo.com; afrikapharaoh@gmail.com *Web Site:* www.afrikacentricity.com, pg 60

The Continuing Legal Education Society of British Columbia (CLEBC), 500-1155 W Pender St, Vancouver, BC V6E 2P4, Canada *Tel:* 604-669-3544; 604-893-2121 (cust serv) *Toll Free Tel:* 800-663-0437 (CN) *Fax:* 604-669-9260 *E-mail:* custserv@cle.bc.ca *Web Site:* www.cle.bc.ca, pg 451

David C Cook, 4050 Lee Vance View, Colorado Springs, CO 80918 *Tel:* 719-536-0100 *Toll Free Tel:* 800-708-5550; 800-323-7543 (orders & cust serv) *Toll Free Fax:* 800-430-0726 (cust serv) *Web Site:* www.davidccook.com, pg 60

James Fenimore Cooper Prize, 2950 Broadway, New York, NY 10027 *Tel:* 212-854-6495 *E-mail:* amhistsociety@columbia.edu *Web Site:* sah.columbia.edu, pg 639

The Doe Coover Agency, PO Box 668, Winchester, MA 01890 *Tel:* 781-721-6000 *Fax:* 781-721-6727 *E-mail:* info@doecooveragency.com *Web Site:* www.doecooveragency.com, pg 512

Copley Custom Textbooks, 530 Great Rd, Acton, MA 01720 *Tel:* 978-263-9090 *Toll Free Tel:* 800-562-2147 *Fax:* 978-263-9190 *E-mail:* textbookorders@xanedu.com; publish@copleycustom.com *Web Site:* www.xanedu.com, pg 60

Copper Canyon Press, Fort Worden State Park, Bldg 313, Port Townsend, WA 98368 *Tel:* 360-385-4925 *Toll Free Tel:* 877-501-1393 (orders) *Fax:* 360-385-4985 *E-mail:* poetry@coppercanyonpress.org *Web Site:* www.coppercanyonpress.org, pg 60

Copywriter's Council of America™ (CCA), CCA Bldg, 7 Putter Lane, Middle Island, NY 11953-1920 *Tel:* 631-924-3888; 631-775-6075 *Fax:* 631-924-8555 *E-mail:* cca4dmcopy@gmail.com *Web Site:* www.andrewlinickdirectmarketing.com/Copywriters-Council.html; www.newworldpressbooks.com, pg 61, 491, 563

Corbett Gordon Co, 6 Fort Rachel Place, Mystic, CT 06355 *Tel:* 860-536-4108 *Fax:* 860-536-3732 *E-mail:* corbettgordon@comcast.net, pg 492

Cordon d' Or - Gold Ribbon International Culinary Academy Awards, 7312 Sixth Ave N, St Petersburg, FL 33710 *Tel:* 727-347-2437 *E-mail:* cordondor@aol.com; culinaryparadise@aol.com *Web Site:* www.cordondorcuisine.com; www.florida-americasculinaryparadise.com, pg 639

Albert B Corey Prize, c/o American Historical Association, 400 "A" St SE, Washington, DC 20003-3889 *Tel:* 202-544-2422 *Fax:* 202-544-8307 *E-mail:* cha-shc@cha-shc.ca *Web Site:* www.historians.org/prizes; www.cha-shc.ca, pg 639

Cormorant Books Inc, 10 St Mary St, Suite 615, Toronto, ON M4Y 1P9, Canada *Tel:* 416-925-8887 *E-mail:* info@cormorantbooks.com *Web Site:* www.cormorantbooks.com, pg 451

Cornell & McCarthy LLC, 2-D Cross Hwy, Westport, CT 06880 *Tel:* 203-454-4210 *E-mail:* contact@cmartreps.com *Web Site:* www.cmartreps.com, pg 543

Cornell Maritime Press Inc, 4880 Lower Valley Rd, Atglen, PA 19310 *Tel:* 610-593-1777 *Fax:* 610-593-2002 *E-mail:* info@schifferbooks.com *Web Site:* www.cmptp.com, pg 61

Cornell University Press, Sage House, 512 E State St, Ithaca, NY 14850 *Tel:* 607-277-2338 *Fax:* 607-277-2374 *E-mail:* cupressinfo@cornell.edu; cupress-sales@cornell.edu *Web Site:* www.cornellpress.cornell.edu, pg 61

Cornerstone Book Publishers, PO Box 24652, New Orleans, LA 70184 *E-mail:* info@cornerstonepublishers.com *Web Site:* www.cornerstonepublishers.com, pg 61

Corporation for Public Broadcasting (CPB), 401 Ninth St NW, Washington, DC 20004-2129 *Tel:* 202-879-9600 *Web Site:* www.cpb.org, pg 563

Corporation of Professional Librarians of Quebec, 1453, rue Beaubien Est, Bureau 215, Montreal, QC H2G 3C6, Canada *Tel:* 514-845-3327 *Fax:* 514-845-1618 *E-mail:* info@cbpq.qc.ca *Web Site:* www.cbpq.qc.ca, pg 564

Cortina Institute of Languages, 9 Hollyhock Rd, Wilton, CT 06897 *Tel:* 203-762-2510 *Toll Free Tel:* 800-245-2145 *Web Site:* www.cortina-languages.com, pg 61

Cortina Learning International Inc, 9 Hollyhock Rd, Wilton, CT 06897 *Tel:* 203-762-2510 *Toll Free Tel:* 800-245-2145 *Fax:* 203-762-2514 *Web Site:* www.cortinalearning.com, pg 61

Corwin, a Sage Co, 2455 Teller Rd, Thousand Oaks, CA 91320 *Tel:* 805-499-9734 *Toll Free Tel:* 800-233-9936 *Fax:* 805-499-5323 *Toll Free Fax:* 800-417-2466 *E-mail:* info@corwin.com; order@corwin.com *Web Site:* www.corwin.com, pg 61

Cosimo Inc, Old Chelsea Sta, PO Box 416, New York, NY 10011-0416 *Tel:* 212-989-3616 *Fax:* 212-989-3662 *E-mail:* info@cosimobooks.com *Web Site:* www.cosimobooks.com, pg 62

Coteau Books, 2517 Victoria Ave, Regina, SK S4P 0T2, Canada *Tel:* 306-777-0170 *Toll Free Tel:* 800-440-4471 (CN only) *Fax:* 306-522-5152 *E-mail:* coteau@coteaubooks.com *Web Site:* www.coteaubooks.com, pg 451

Cotsen Institute of Archaeology Press, 308 Charles E Young Dr N, Fowler A163, Box 951510, Los Angeles, CA 90095 *Tel:* 310-206-9384 *Fax:* 310-206-4723 *E-mail:* cioapress@ioa.ucla.edu *Web Site:* www.ioa.ucla.edu, pg 62

Cottonwood Press, University of Kansas, Kansas Union, Rm 400, 1301 Jayhawk Blvd, Lawrence, KS 66045 *Tel:* 785-864-4520 *Web Site:* www.englishcw.ku.edu/cottonwood, pg 62

Council for Advancement & Support of Education (CASE), 1307 New York Ave NW, Suite 1000, Washington, DC 20005-4701 *Tel:* 202-328-CASE (328-2273) *Fax:* 202-387-4973 *E-mail:* membersupportcenter@case.org *Web Site:* www.case.org, pg 564

Council for Exceptional Children (CEC), 2900 Crystal Dr, Suite 100, Arlington, VA 22202 *Toll Free Tel:* 888-232-7733; 866-915-5000 (TTY) *E-mail:* service@cec.sped.org *Web Site:* www.cec.sped.org, pg 62

Council for Research in Values & Philosophy (RVP), The Catholic University of America, Gibbons Hall, Rm B-12, 620 Michigan Ave NE, Washington, DC 20064 *Tel:* 202-319-6089 *Fax:* 202-319-6089 *E-mail:* cua-rvp@cua.edu *Web Site:* www.crvp.org, pg 62

Council for the Advancement of Science Writing (CASW), PO Box 910, Hedgesville, WV 25427 *Tel:* 304-754-6786 *Web Site:* www.casw.org, pg 564

Council Oak Books LLC, 2822 Van Ness Ave, San Francisco, CA 94109 *Tel:* 415-931-7700 *Toll Free Tel:* 888-275-2596 *E-mail:* marketing@counciloakbooks.com *Web Site:* www.counciloakbooks.com, pg 62

Council of State Governments, 2760 Research Park Dr, Lexington, KY 40511 *Tel:* 859-244-8000 *Toll Free Tel:* 800-800-1910 *Fax:* 859-244-8001 *E-mail:* sales@csg.org *Web Site:* www.csg.org; www.csgstore.org, pg 62

Council on Foreign Relations Press, The Harold Pratt House, 58 E 68 St, New York, NY 10065 *Tel:* 212-434-9400 *Fax:* 212-434-9800 *E-mail:* publications@cfr.org *Web Site:* www.cfr.org, pg 62

Counterpath Press, 613 22 St, Denver, CO 80205 *E-mail:* counterpath@counterpathpress.org; editors@counterpathpress.org *Web Site:* www.counterpathpress.org, pg 62

Counterpoint Press LLC, 1919 Fifth St, Berkeley, CA 94710 *Tel:* 510-704-0230 *Fax:* 510-704-0268 *E-mail:* info@counterpointpress.com *Web Site:* counterpointpress.com; www.sierraclub.org/books; softskull.com, pg 63

Country Music Foundation Press, 222 Fifth Ave S, Nashville, TN 37203 *Tel:* 615-416-2001 *Fax:* 615-255-2245 *E-mail:* info@countrymusichalloffame.com *Web Site:* www.countrymusichalloffame.com, pg 63

The Countryman Press, c/o W W Norton & Company Inc, 500 Fifth Ave, New York, NY 10110 *Tel:* 212-354-5500 *Fax:* 212-869-0856 *E-mail:* countrymanpress@wwnorton.com *Web Site:* www.countrymanpress.com, pg 63

Course Crafters Inc, PO Box 100, Amesbury, MA 01913 *Tel:* 978-372-3446 *E-mail:* info@coursecrafters.com *Web Site:* www.coursecrafters.com, pg 492

La Courte Echelle, 4388, rue Saint-Denis, Suite 315, Montreal, QC H2J 2L1, Canada *Tel:* 514-312-6950 *E-mail:* info@courteechelle.com *Web Site:* courteechelle.groupecourteechelle.com, pg 451

Covenant Communications Inc, 920 E State Rd, Suite F, American Fork, UT 84003-0416 *Tel:* 801-756-1041 *E-mail:* info@covenant-lds.com *Web Site:* www.covenant-lds.com, pg 63

Coyote Press, PO Box 3377, Salinas, CA 93912-3377 *Tel:* 831-422-4912 *Fax:* 831-422-4913 *E-mail:* orders@coyotepress.com *Web Site:* www.coyotepress.com, pg 63

Marie Coyoteblanc Award for Indigenous Writing, 81 Prince St, Charlottetown, PE C1A 4R3, Canada *E-mail:* peiliteraryawards@gmail.com *Web Site:* www.peiwritersguild.com, pg 639

CPSA Prize in Comparative Politics, 260 rue Dalhousie St, Suite 204, Ottawa, ON K1N 7E4, Canada *Tel:* 613-562-1202 *Fax:* 613-241-0019 *E-mail:* cpsa-acsp@cpsa-acsp.ca *Web Site:* www.cpsa-acsp.ca, pg 639

CPSA Prize in International Relations, 260 rue Dalhousie St, Suite 204, Ottawa, ON K1N 7E4, Canada *Tel:* 613-562-1202 *Fax:* 613-241-0019 *E-mail:* cpsa-acsp@cpsa-acsp.ca *Web Site:* www.cpsa-acsp.ca, pg 639

CQ Press, 2300 "N" St NW, Suite 800, Washington, DC 20037 *Tel:* 202-729-1900 *Toll Free Tel:* 866-4CQ-PRESS (427-7737) *Fax:* 202-729-1923 *Toll Free Fax:* 800-380-3810 *E-mail:* customerservice@cqpress.com; librarysales@cqpress.com *Web Site:* www.cqpress.com, pg 63

Crabtree Publishing Co, 350 Fifth Ave, 59th fl, PMB 59051, New York, NY 10118 *Tel:* 212-496-5040 *Toll Free Tel:* 800-387-7650 *Toll Free Fax:* 800-355-7166 *E-mail:* custserv@crabtreebooks.com *Web Site:* www.crabtreebooks.com, pg 63

Crabtree Publishing Co Ltd, 616 Welland Ave, St Catharines, ON L2M 5V6, Canada *Tel:* 905-682-5221 *Toll Free Tel:* 800-387-7650 *Fax:* 905-682-7166 *Toll Free Fax:* 800-355-7166 *E-mail:* custserv@crabtreebooks.com; sales@crabtreebooks.com; orders@crabtreebooks.com *Web Site:* www.crabtreebooks.com, pg 451

Craftsman Book Co, 6058 Corte Del Cedro, Carlsbad, CA 92011 *Tel:* 760-438-7828 *Toll Free Tel:* 800-829-8123 *Fax:* 760-438-0398 *Web Site:* www.craftsman-book.com, pg 63

Craven Design Inc, 229 E 85 St, New York, NY 10028 *Tel:* 212-288-1022 *Fax:* 212-249-9910 *E-mail:* cravendesign@mac.com *Web Site:* www.cravendesignstudios.com, pg 543

The Crazyhorse Fiction Prize, College of Charleston, Dept of English, 66 George St, Charleston, SC 29424 *Tel:* 843-953-4470 *E-mail:* crazyhorse@cofc.edu *Web Site:* crazyhorse.cofc.edu/prizes, pg 639

CRC Press, 6000 Broken Sound Pkwy NW, Suite 300, Boca Raton, FL 33487 *Tel:* 561-994-0555 *Toll Free Tel:* 800-272-7737 (orders) *Toll Free Fax:* 800-643-9428 (sales); 800-374-3401 (orders) *E-mail:* orders@crcpress.com; orders@taylorandfrancis.com *Web Site:* www.crcpress.com, pg 64

Creation Grant Program, 225 King St, Suite 201, Fredericton, NB E3B 1E1, Canada *Tel:* 506-444-4444 *Toll Free Tel:* 866-460-ARTS (460-2787) *Fax:* 506-444-5543 *Web Site:* www.artsnb.ca, pg 639

The Creative Co, PO Box 227, Mankato, MN 56002 *Tel:* 507-388-6273 *Toll Free Tel:* 800-445-6209 *Fax:* 507-388-2746 *E-mail:* info@thecreativecompany.us; orders@thecreativecompany.us *Web Site:* www.thecreativecompany.us, pg 64

Creative Freelancers Inc, PO Box 366, Tallevast, FL 34270 *Toll Free Tel:* 800-398-9544 *Web Site:* www.freelancers1.com, pg 492

Creative Homeowner, 1970 Broad St, East Petersburg, PA 17520 *Tel:* 717-560-4703 *Toll Free Tel:* 800-475-9112 *Fax:* 717-560-4702 *Toll Free Fax:* 888-369-2885 *E-mail:* customerservice@foxchapelpublishing.com; sales@foxchapelpublishing.com *Web Site:* www.foxchapelpublishing.com/home-and-garden/creative-homeowner, pg 64

Creative Inspirations Inc, 6203 Old Springville Rd, Pinson, AL 35126 *Web Site:* www.manuscriptcritique.com, pg 492

Creative Nonfiction Awards, 81 Prince St, Charlottetown, PE C1A 4R3, Canada *E-mail:* peiliteraryawards@gmail.com *Web Site:* www.peiwritersguild.com, pg 639

Creative Writing Day & Workshops, PO Box 801, Abingdon, VA 24212-0801 *Tel:* 276-623-5266 *Fax:* 276-676-3076 *E-mail:* info@vahighlandsfestival.org *Web Site:* vahighlandsfestival.org, pg 610

CreativeWell Inc, PO Box 3130, Memorial Sta, Upper Montclair, NJ 07043 *Tel:* 973-783-7575 *Fax:* 973-783-7530 *E-mail:* info@creativewell.com *Web Site:* www.creativewell.com, pg 512

CreativeWell Inc, PO Box 3130, Memorial Sta, Upper Montclair, NJ 07043 *Tel:* 973-783-7575 *Toll Free Tel:* 800-743-9182 *Fax:* 973-783-7530 *E-mail:* info@creativewell.com *Web Site:* www.creativewell.com, pg 547

Crichton & Associates Inc, 6940 Carroll Ave, Takoma Park, MD 20912 *Tel:* 301-495-9663 *E-mail:* crichtl@aol.com *Web Site:* www.crichton-associates.com, pg 512

Cricket Cottage Publishing LLC, 1500 Beville Rd, Suite 606-346, Daytona Beach, FL 32114 *Tel:* 585-687-7291 *E-mail:* cricketcottage@att.net *Web Site:* thecricketpublishing.com, pg 64

Crickhollow Books, 3147 S Pennsylvania Ave, Milwaukee, WI 53207 *Tel:* 414-294-4319 *E-mail:* info@crickhollowbooks.com *Web Site:* www.crickhollowbooks.com, pg 64

Cross-Cultural Communications, 239 Wynsum Ave, Merrick, NY 11566-4725 *Tel:* 516-868-5635 *Fax:* 516-379-1901 *E-mail:* info@cross-culturalcommunications.com; cccbarkan@optonline.net; cccpoetry@aol.com *Web Site:* www.cross-culturalcommunications.com, pg 64

Crossquarter Publishing Group, PO Box 23749, Santa Fe, NM 87502 *Tel:* 505-690-3923 *Fax:* 214-975-9715 *E-mail:* sales@crossquarter.com; info@crossquarter.com *Web Site:* www.crossquarter.com, pg 64

The Crossroad Publishing Co, 831 Chestnut Ridge Rd, Chestnut Ridge, NY 10977 *Tel:* 845-517-0180 *Toll Free Tel:* 800-888-4741 (orders) *Fax:* 845-517-0181 *E-mail:* office@crossroadpublishing.com *Web Site:* www.CrossroadPublishing.com, pg 65

Crossway, 1300 Crescent St, Wheaton, IL 60187 *Tel:* 630-682-4300 *Toll Free Tel:* 800-635-7993 (orders); 800-543-1659 (cust serv) *Fax:* 630-682-4785 *E-mail:* info@crossway.org *Web Site:* www.crossway.org, pg 65

Crown House Publishing Co LLC, 81 Brook Hills Circle, White Plains, NY 10605 *Tel:* 914-946-3517 *Toll Free Tel:* 877-925-1213 (cust serv) *Fax:* 914-946-1160 *E-mail:* info@chpus.com *Web Site:* www.crownhousepublishing.com, pg 65

Crown Publishing Group, 1745 Broadway, New York, NY 10019 *Tel:* 212-782-9000 *Toll Free Tel:* 888-264-1745 *Fax:* 212-940-7408 *E-mail:* crownosm@penguinrandomhouse.com *Web Site:* crownpublishing.com, pg 65

Crumb Elbow Publishing, PO Box 294, Rhododendron, OR 97049-0294 *Tel:* 503-622-4798, pg 65

Crystal Clarity Publishers, 14618 Tyler Foote Rd, Nevada City, CA 95959 *Tel:* 530-478-7600 *Toll Free Tel:* 800-424-1055 *Fax:* 530-478-7610 *E-mail:* clarity@crystalclarity.com *Web Site:* www.crystalclarity.com, pg 65

Crystal Productions, 5320 Carpinteria Ave, Suite K, Carpinteria, CA 93013-2107 *Tel:* 847-657-8144 *Toll Free Tel:* 800-255-8629 *Fax:* 847-657-8149 *Toll Free Fax:* 800-657-8149 *E-mail:* custserv@crystalproductions.com *Web Site:* www.crystalproductions.com, pg 65

Crystal Publishers Inc, 3460 Lost Hills Dr, Las Vegas, NV 89122 *Tel:* 702-434-3037 *Fax:* 702-434-3037 *Web Site:* www.crystalpub.com, pg 65

CS International Literary Agency, 43 W 39 St, New York, NY 10018 *Tel:* 212-921-1610; 212-391-9208 *E-mail:* query@csliterary.com; csliterary08@gmail.com *Web Site:* www.csliterary.com, pg 492

The CSIS Press, 1616 Rhode Island Ave NW, Washington, DC 20036 *Tel:* 202-887-0200 *Fax:* 202-775-3199 *E-mail:* books@csis.org *Web Site:* www.csis.org, pg 65

CSLI Publications, Stanford University, Cordura Hall, 220 Panama St, Stanford, CA 94305-4115 *Tel:* 650-723-1839 *Fax:* 650-725-2166 *E-mail:* pubs@csli.stanford.edu *Web Site:* cslipublications.stanford.edu, pg 66

CSWE Press, 1701 Duke St, Suite 200, Alexandria, VA 22314-3457 *Tel:* 703-683-8080 *Fax:* 703-683-8493 *E-mail:* publications@cswe.org; info@cswe.org *Web Site:* www.cswe.org, pg 66

Cultural Studies & Analysis, 1123 Montrose St, Philadelphia, PA 19147-3721 *Tel:* 215-592-8544 *E-mail:* info@culturalanalysis.com *Web Site:* www.culturalanalysis.com, pg 492

Cumberland House, 1935 Brookdale Rd, Suite 139, Naperville, IL 60563 *Tel:* 630-961-3900 *Toll Free Tel:* 800-43-BRIGHT (432-7444) *Fax:* 630-961-2168 *E-mail:* info@sourcebooks.com *Web Site:* www.sourcebooks.com, pg 66

Cummings & Hathaway Publishers, 395 Atlantic Ave, East Rockaway, NY 11518 *Tel:* 516-593-3607 *Fax:* 516-593-1401, pg 66

Cunningham Commission for Youth Theatre, Lincoln Park Campus, 2350 N Racine Ave, Chicago, IL 60614-4100 *Tel:* 773-325-7999 *Fax:* 773-325-7920 *E-mail:* cunninghamcommission@depaul.edu *Web Site:* theatre.depaul.edu, pg 640

CUNY Journalism Press, 219 W 40 St, New York, NY 10018 *Tel:* 646-758-7824 *Fax:* 646-758-7809 *Web Site:* www.journalism.cuny.edu; press.journalism.cuny.edu, pg 66

Cup of Tea Books, PO Box 21133, Columbus, OH 43221 *Tel:* 614-264-5588 *E-mail:* sales@pagespringpublishing.com *Web Site:* www.cupofteabooks.com, pg 66

Richard Curtis Associates Inc, 200 E 72 St, Suite 28J, New York, NY 10021 *Tel:* 212-772-7363 *Fax:* 212-772-7393 *E-mail:* info@curtisagency.com *Web Site:* www.curtisagency.com, pg 512

Karen & Philip Cushman Late Bloomer Award, 4727 Wilshire Blvd, Suite 301, Los Angeles, CA 90010 *Tel:* 323-782-1010 *Fax:* 323-782-1892 *E-mail:* grants@scbwi.org; scbwi@scbwi.org *Web Site:* www.scbwi.org, pg 640

CWA/SCA Canada, 2200 Prince of Wales Dr, Suite 301, Ottawa, ON K2E 6Z9, Canada *Tel:* 613-820-9777 *Toll Free Tel:* 877-486-4292 *Fax:* 613-820-8188 *E-mail:* info@cwa-scacanada.ca *Web Site:* www.cwa-scacanada.ca, pg 564

Cycle Publishing LLC, 1282 Seventh Ave, San Francisco, CA 94122-2526 *Tel:* 415-665-8214 *Fax:* 415-753-8572 *Web Site:* www.cyclepublishing.com, pg 66

Cyclotour Guide Books, 160 Harvard St, Rochester, NY 14607-3174 *Tel:* 585-244-6157 *E-mail:* cyclotour@cyclotour.com *Web Site:* www.cyclotour.com, pg 66

Cypress House, 155 Cypress St, Fort Bragg, CA 95437 *Tel:* 707-964-9520 *Toll Free Tel:* 800-773-7782 *Fax:* 707-964-7531 *E-mail:* cypresshouse@cypresshouse.com *Web Site:* www.cypresshouse.com, pg 66, 492

Dalkey Archive Press, University of Houston-Victoria, 3402 N Ben Wilson, Victoria, TX 77901 *E-mail:* contact@dalkeyarchive.com *Web Site:* www.dalkeyarchive.com, pg 66

Damron Co, PO Box 422458, San Francisco, CA 94142-2458 *Tel:* 415-255-0404 *Toll Free Tel:* 800-462-6654 *Fax:* 415-703-9049 *E-mail:* info@damron.com *Web Site:* www.damron.com, pg 66

Dana Awards, Literary Competition, 200 Fosseway Dr, Greensboro, NC 27455 *Tel:* 336-644-8028 *E-mail:* danaawards@gmail.com *Web Site:* www.danaawards.com, pg 640

Robert Dana-Anhinga Prize for Poetry, PO Box 3665, Tallahassee, FL 32315 *Tel:* 850-577-0745 *E-mail:* info@anhinga.org *Web Site:* www.anhingapress.org, pg 640

The Danahy Fiction Prize, University of Tampa Press, 401 W Kennedy Blvd, Tampa, FL 33606 *Tel:* 813-253-6266 *E-mail:* utpress@ut.edu *Web Site:* tampareview.ut.edu, pg 640

Dancing Dakini Press, 77 Morning Sun Dr, Sedona, AZ 86336 *Tel:* 928-852-0129 *E-mail:* editor@dancingdakinipress.com *Web Site:* www.dancingdakinipress.com, pg 66

Dancing Lemur Press LLC, PO Box 383, Pikeville, NC 27863-0383 *E-mail:* inquiries@dancinglemurpressllc.com *Web Site:* www.dancinglemurpressllc.com, pg 67

John Daniel & Co, PO Box 2790, McKinleyville, CA 95519-2790 *Tel:* 707-839-3495 *Toll Free Tel:* 800-662-8351 *Fax:* 707-839-3242 *E-mail:* dandd@danielpublishing.com *Web Site:* www.danielpublishing.com, pg 67

John M Daniel Literary Services, PO Box 2790, McKinleyville, CA 95519 *Tel:* 707-839-3495 *Fax:* 707-839-3242 *E-mail:* jmd@danielpublishing.com *Web Site:* www.danielpublishing.com/litserv.htm, pg 492

Benjamin H Danks Award, 633 W 155 St, New York, NY 10032 *Tel:* 212-368-5900 *Fax:* 212-491-4615 *E-mail:* academy@artsandletters.org *Web Site:* www.artsandletters.org, pg 640

Dante University Press, PO Box 812158, Wellesley, MA 02482-0014 *Tel:* 781-235-3634 *Web Site:* www.danteuniversity.org/books, pg 67

Darhansoff & Verrill, 133 W 72 St, Rm 304, New York, NY 10023 *Tel:* 917-305-1300 *E-mail:* permissions@dvagency.com *Web Site:* www.dvagency.com, pg 512

Dark Horse Comics, 10956 SE Main St, Milwaukie, OR 97222 *Tel:* 503-652-8815 *Fax:* 503-654-9440 *E-mail:* dhcomics@darkhorse.com *Web Site:* www.darkhorse.com, pg 67

Darla Bruno Writing Coach, Developmental Editor, PO Box 243, Madison, NJ 07940 *E-mail:* editor@darlabruno.com *Web Site:* www.darlabruno.com, pg 492

The Dartnell Corporation, 2222 Sedwick Dr, Durham, NC 27713 *Toll Free Tel:* 800-223-8720; 800-472-0148 (cust serv) *Toll Free Fax:* 800-508-2592 *E-mail:* customerservice@dartnellcorp.com *Web Site:* www.dartnellcorp.com, pg 67

The Darwin Press Inc, PO Box 2202, Princeton, NJ 08543 *Tel:* 609-737-1349 *Fax:* 609-737-0929 *E-mail:* books@darwinpress.com *Web Site:* www.darwinpress.com, pg 67

Data & Marketing Association (DMA), 1333 Broadway, Suite 301, New York, NY 10018 *Tel:* 212-768-7277 *Fax:* 212-302-6714 *E-mail:* memberservices@thedma.org *Web Site:* thedma.org, pg 67, 564

Data Trace Publishing Co (DTP), 110 West Rd, Suite 227, Towson, MD 21204-2316 *Tel:* 410-494-4994 *Toll Free Tel:* 800-342-0454 (orders only) *Fax:* 410-494-0515 *E-mail:* info@datatrace.com; salesandmarketing@datatrace.com; editorial@datatrace.com; info@datatrace.com *Web Site:* www.datatrace.com, pg 67

Database Directories, 588 Dufferin Ave, London, ON N6B 2A4, Canada *Tel:* 519-433-1666 *Fax:* 519-430-1131 *E-mail:* mail@databasedirectory.com *Web Site:* www.databasedirectory.com, pg 451

May Davenport Publishers, 26313 Purissima Rd, Los Altos Hills, CA 94022 *Tel:* 650-947-6499 *E-mail:* mdbooks@earthlink.net *Web Site:* www.maydavenportpublishers.org, pg 67

Suzanne B Davidson, 8084 N 44 St, Brown Deer, WI 53223 *Tel:* 414-355-6640 *E-mail:* davidson@milwpc.com, pg 492

Davies-Black Publishing, 53 State St, Boston, MA 02109 *Tel:* 617-523-3801 *Fax:* 617-523-3708 *E-mail:* info@nicholasbrealey.com *Web Site:* www.nicholasbrealey.com, pg 67

The Davies Group Publishers, PO Box 440140, Aurora, CO 80044-0140 *Tel:* 303-750-8374 *Fax:* 303-337-0952 *E-mail:* info@thedaviesgrouppublishers.com; daviesgroup@msn.com (orders) *Web Site:* www.thedaviesgrouppublishers.com, pg 68

Davies Publishing Inc, 32 S Raymond Ave, Suites 4 & 5, Pasadena, CA 91105-1961 *Tel:* 626-792-3046 *Toll Free Tel:* 877-792-0005 *Fax:* 626-792-5308 *E-mail:* info@daviespublishing.com *Web Site:* daviespublishing.com, pg 68

F A Davis Co, 1915 Arch St, Philadelphia, PA 19103 *Tel:* 215-568-2270; 215-440-3001 *Toll Free Tel:* 800-523-4049 *Fax:* 215-568-5065; 215-440-3016 *E-mail:* info@fadavis.com; orders@fadavis.com *Web Site:* www.fadavis.com, pg 68

Watson Davis & Helen Miles Davis Prize, 440 Geddes Hall, Notre Dame, IN 46556 *Tel:* 574-631-1194 *E-mail:* info@hssonline.org *Web Site:* www.hssonline.org, pg 640

DAW Books Inc, 375 Hudson St, New York, NY 10014 *Tel:* 212-366-2096 *Fax:* 212-366-2090 *E-mail:* daw@penguinrandomhouse.com *Web Site:* www.dawbooks.com; www.penguin.com; www.penguinrandomhouse.com, pg 68

The Dawn Horse Press, 10336 Loch Lomond Rd, No 305, Middletown, CA 95461 *Tel:* 707-928-6590 *Toll Free Tel:* 877-770-0772 *Fax:* 707-928-6590 *E-mail:* dhp@adidam.org *Web Site:* www.dawnhorsepress.com, pg 68

Dawn Publications Inc, 12402 Bitney Springs Rd, Nevada City, CA 95959 *Tel:* 530-274-7775 *Toll Free Tel:* 800-545-7475 *Fax:* 530-274-7778 *E-mail:* nature@dawnpub.com; orders@dawnpub.com *Web Site:* www.dawnpub.com, pg 68

DawnSignPress, 6130 Nancy Ridge Dr, San Diego, CA 92121-3223 *Tel:* 858-625-0600 *Toll Free Tel:* 800-549-5350 *Fax:* 858-625-2336 *E-mail:* contactus@dawnsign.com *Web Site:* www.dawnsign.com, pg 68

Liza Dawson Associates, 350 Seventh Ave, Suite 2003, New York, NY 10001 *Tel:* 212-465-9071 *Fax:* 212-947-0460 *Web Site:* www.lizadawsonassociates.com, pg 513

Day Owl Press Corp, 201 W Ocean Ave, Unit 3574, Lantana, FL 33465 *Toll Free Tel:* 888-806-6981 *Toll Free Fax:* 866-854-4375 *E-mail:* info@dayowl.net *Web Site:* www.dayowl.net, pg 68

Dayton Literary Peace Prize, 25 Harman Terr, Dayton, OH 45419 *Tel:* 937-298-5072 *Web Site:* daytonliterarypeaceprize.org, pg 640

Dayton Playhouse FutureFest, PO Box 3017, Dayton, OH 45401-3017 *Tel:* 937-424-8477 *Fax:* 937-424-0062 *E-mail:* futurefest@thedaytonplayhouse.com *Web Site:* wordpress.daytonplayhouse.com, pg 640

dbS Productions, PO Box 94, Charlottesville, VA 22902 *Tel:* 434-293-5502 *Toll Free Tel:* 800-745-1581 *Fax:* 434-293-5502 *E-mail:* info@dbs-sar.com *Web Site:* www.dbs-sar.com, pg 68

DC Canada Education Publishing (DCCED), 180 Metcalfe St, Suite 204, Ottawa, ON K2P 1P5, Canada *Tel:* 613-565-8885 *Toll Free Tel:* 888-565-0262 *Fax:* 613-565-8881 *E-mail:* info@dc-canada.ca *Web Site:* www.dc-canada.ca, pg 452

DC Entertainment, 2900 Alameda, Burbank, CA 91505 *Toll Free Tel:* 800-887-6789 *E-mail:* dccomics@cambeywest.com *Web Site:* www.dcentertainment.com; www.dccomics.com; www.madmag.com, pg 69

Walter De Gruyter Inc, 125 Pearl St, 3rd fl, Boston, MA 02110 *Tel:* 857-284-7073 *Fax:* 857-284-7358 *E-mail:* service@degruyter.com *Web Site:* www.degruyter.com, pg 69

J de S Associates Inc, 9 Shagbark Rd, South Norwalk, CT 06854 *Tel:* 203-838-7571 *Fax:* 203-866-2713 *Web Site:* www.jdesassociates.com, pg 513

Deadline Club, c/o Salmagundi Club, 47 Fifth Ave, New York, NY 10003 *Tel:* 646-481-7584 *E-mail:* info@deadlineclub.org *Web Site:* www.deadlineclub.org, pg 564

Deborah Wolfe Ltd, 731 N 24 St, Philadelphia, PA 19130 *Tel:* 215-232-6666 *Fax:* 215-232-6585 *E-mail:* info@illustrationonline.com *Web Site:* www.illustrationonline.com, pg 543

The Jennifer DeChiara Literary Agency, 299 Park Ave, 6th fl, New York, NY 10171 *Tel:* 212-739-0803 *Web Site:* www.jdlit.com, pg 513

Deep River Books LLC, PO Box 310, Sisters, OR 97759 *Tel:* 541-549-1139 *E-mail:* info@deepriverbooks.com *Web Site:* deepriverbooks.com, pg 69

DeFiore and Company Literary Management Inc, 47 E 19 St, 3rd fl, New York, NY 10003 *Tel:* 212-925-7744 *Fax:* 212-925-9803 *E-mail:* info@defliterary.com; submissions@defliterary.com *Web Site:* www.defliterary.com, pg 513

Delaware Division of the Arts Individual Artist Fellowships, Carvel State Off Bldg, 4th fl, 820 N French St, Wilmington, DE 19801 *Tel:* 302-577-8278 *Fax:* 302-577-6561 *E-mail:* delarts@state.de.us *Web Site:* www.artsdel.org, pg 640

Joelle Delbourgo Associates Inc, 101 Park St, Montclair, NJ 07042 *Tel:* 973-773-0836 (call only during standard business hours) *Web Site:* www.delbourgo.com, pg 513

Delphinium Books, PO Box 703, Harrison, NY 10528 *Tel:* 917-301-7496 (e-mail first) *E-mail:* contactform@delphiniumbooks.com *Web Site:* www.delphiniumbooks.com, pg 69

Rick DeMarinis Short Story Award, PO Box 2414, Durango, CO 81302 *Tel:* 970-903-7914 *E-mail:* cutthroatmag@gmail.com *Web Site:* www.cutthroatmag.com, pg 640

Demos Medical Publishing, 11 W 42 St, 15th fl, New York, NY 10036 *Tel:* 212-683-0072 *E-mail:* info@demosmedpub.com; orderdept@demosmedical.com; editorial@demosmedical.com *Web Site:* www.demosmedical.com, pg 69

Der-Hovanessian Translation Prize, 46 Wallace St, Somerville, MA 02144 *Tel:* 617-744-6034 *E-mail:* info@nepoetryclub.org *Web Site:* www.nepoetryclub.org, pg 640

Deseret Book Co, 57 W South Temple, Salt Lake City, UT 84101-1511 *Tel:* 801-517-3369 *Toll Free Tel:* 800-453-4532 (orders); 888-846-7302 (orders) *Fax:* 801-517-3126 *E-mail:* service@deseretbook.com *Web Site:* www.deseretbook.com, pg 69

Annual Design Competition, 27 Union Sq W, Suite 207, New York, NY 10003 *Tel:* 212-223-3332 *Fax:* 212-223-5880 *E-mail:* mail@spd.org *Web Site:* www.spd.org, pg 641

DEStech Publications Inc, 439 N Duke St, Lancaster, PA 17602-4967 *Tel:* 717-290-1660 *Toll Free Tel:* 877-500-4337 *Fax:* 717-509-6100 *E-mail:* info@destechpub.com *Web Site:* www.destechpub.com, pg 69

Destiny Image Inc, 167 Walnut Bottom Rd, Shippensburg, PA 17257-0310 *Tel:* 717-532-3040 *Toll Free Tel:* 800-722-6774 (orders only) *Fax:* 717-532-9291 *Web Site:* www.destinyimage.com, pg 69

DeVorss & Co, 553 Constitution Ave, Camarillo, CA 93012-8510 *Tel:* 805-322-9010 *Toll Free Tel:* 800-843-5743 *Fax:* 805-322-9011 *E-mail:* service@devorss.com *Web Site:* www.devorss.com, pg 70

Dewey Publications Inc, 1840 Wilson Blvd, Suite 203, Arlington, VA 22201 *Tel:* 703-524-1355 *Fax:* 703-524-1463 *E-mail:* deweypublications@gmail.com *Web Site:* www.deweypub.com, pg 70

Dharma Publishing, 35788 Hauser Bridge Rd, Cazadero, CA 95421 *Tel:* 707-847-3717 *Toll Free Tel:* 800-873-4276 *Fax:* 707-847-3380 *E-mail:* contact@dharmapublishing.com; customerservice@dharmapublishing.com *Web Site:* www.dharmapublishing.com, pg 70

Alice Fay Di Castagnola Award, 15 Gramercy Park, New York, NY 10003 *Tel:* 212-254-9628 *Web Site:* www.poetrysociety.org, pg 641

Christina Di Martino Literary Services, 139 Sandpiper Ave, Royal Palm Beach, FL 33411 *Tel:* 212-996-9086 *E-mail:* writealotmail@gmail.com, pg 492

Diagram Essay Contest, University of Arizona, ML-445, PO Box 210067, Tucson, AZ 85721 *E-mail:* editor@thediagram.com *Web Site:* www.thediagram.com/contest.html, pg 641

Dial Books for Young Readers, 345 Hudson St, New York, NY 10014 *Tel:* 212-366-2000 *Toll Free Tel:* 800-733-3000 (orders) *Fax:* 212-414-3396 *Web Site:* www.penguin.com, pg 70

Diane Publishing Co, 330 Pusey Ave, Suite 3 (rear), Collingdale, PA 19023-0617 *Tel:* 610-461-6200 *Toll Free Tel:* 800-782-3833 *Fax:* 610-461-6130 *Web Site:* www.dianepublishing.net, pg 70

Philip K Dick Award, PO Box 3447, Hoboken, NJ 07030 *Tel:* 201-876-2551 *Web Site:* www.philipkdickaward.org, pg 641

D4EO Literary Agency, 7 Indian Valley Rd, Weston, CT 06883 *Tel:* 203-544-7180 *Fax:* 203-544-7160 *Web Site:* www.d4eoliteraryagency.com; www.publishersmarketplace.com/members/d4eo/; twitter.com/d4eo, pg 514

Sandra Dijkstra Literary Agency, 1155 Camino del Mar, PMB 515, Del Mar, CA 92014-2605 *E-mail:* queries@dijkstraagency.com *Web Site:* dijkstraagency.com, pg 514

Annie Dillard Award for Creative Nonfiction, Mail Stop 9053, Western Washington University, Bellingham, WA 98225 *Tel:* 360-650-4863 *E-mail:* bhreview@wwu.edu *Web Site:* www.bhreview.org, pg 641

Gordon W Dillon/Richard C Peterson Memorial Essay Prize, c/o Fairchild Tropical Botanic Garden, 10901 Old Cutler Rd, Coral Gables, FL 33156 *Tel:* 305-740-2010 *E-mail:* theaos@aos.org *Web Site:* www.aos.org, pg 641

Discover Great New Writers Award, 122 Fifth Ave, New York, NY 10011 *Web Site:* www.barnesandnoble.com, pg 641

DiscoverNet Publishing, 2474 Walnut St, Suite 105, Cary, NC 27518 *Tel:* 919-301-0109 *Fax:* 919-557-2261 *E-mail:* info@discovernet.com *Web Site:* www.discovernet.com, pg 70

Discovery/Boston Review Poetry Contest, 1395 Lexington Ave, New York, NY 10128 *Tel:* 212-415-5760 *E-mail:* unterberg@92y.org *Web Site:* www.92y.org/discovery, pg 641

Discovery House Publishers, 3000 Kraft Ave SE, Grand Rapids, MI 49512 *Tel:* 616-942-2803 *Toll Free Tel:* 800-653-8333 (cust serv) *E-mail:* support@dhp.org *Web Site:* www.dhp.org, pg 70

Disney-Hyperion Books, 1101 Flower St, Glendale, CA 91201 *Web Site:* books.disney.com, pg 70

Disney Press, 1101 Flower St, Glendale, CA 91201 *Web Site:* books.disney.com, pg 70

Disney Publishing Worldwide, 1101 Flower St, Glendale, CA 91201 *Web Site:* books.disney.com, pg 71

Dissertation.com, 23331 Water Circle, Boca Raton, FL 33486-8540 *Tel:* 561-750-4344 *Toll Free Tel:* 800-636-8329 *Fax:* 561-750-6797 *Web Site:* www.dissertation.com, pg 71

Distinguished Scholarly Book Award, c/o Governance Off, 1430 "K" St NW, Suite 600, Washington, DC 20005 *Tel:* 202-383-9005 *Fax:* 202-638-0882 *E-mail:* governance@asanet.org *Web Site:* www.asanet.org, pg 641

Diversion Books, 443 Park Ave S, Suite 1008, New York, NY 10016 *Tel:* 212-961-6390 *E-mail:* info@diversionbooks.com *Web Site:* www.diversionbooks.com, pg 71

Djerassi Resident Artists Program, 2325 Bear Gulch Rd, Woodside, CA 94062 *Tel:* 650-747-1250 *E-mail:* drap@djerassi.org *Web Site:* www.djerassi.org, pg 610

DK Publishing, 345 Hudson St, 2nd fl, New York, NY 10014 *Tel:* 646-674-4000 *Toll Free Tel:* 877-342-5357 (cust serv); 800-733-3000 *Web Site:* www.dk.com; www.penguin.com, pg 71

DK Research Inc, 14 Mohegan Lane, Commack, NY 11725 *Tel:* 631-543-5537 *Fax:* 631-543-5549 *E-mail:* dkresearch@optimum.net *Web Site:* www.dkresearchinc.com, pg 492

Do It Now Foundation, PO Box 27568, Tempe, AZ 85285-7568 *Tel:* 480-736-0599 *Fax:* 480-736-0771 *E-mail:* e-mail@doitnow.org; orders@doitnow.org *Web Site:* www.doitnow.org, pg 71

Documentation Grant Program, 225 King St, Suite 201, Fredericton, NB E3B 1E1, Canada *Tel:* 506-444-4444 *Toll Free Tel:* 866-460-ARTS (460-2787) *Fax:* 506-444-5543 *Web Site:* www.artsnb.ca, pg 641

Blake Dodd Prize, 633 W 155 St, New York, NY 10032 *Tel:* 212-368-5900 *Fax:* 212-491-4615 *E-mail:* academy@artsandletters.org *Web Site:* www.artsandletters.org, pg 641

Dog Writers' Association of America Inc (DWAA), 66 Adams St, Jamestown, NY 14701 *Tel:* 716-484-6155 *E-mail:* dogwriter@windstream.net *Web Site:* www.dwaa.org, pg 564

Dog Writers' Association of America Inc (DWAA) Annual Writing Competition, 2243 Kelmscott Ct, Westlake Village, CA 91361 *Tel:* 805-418-7899 *Fax:* 831-374-9231 *E-mail:* dogwriter@windstream.net *Web Site:* www.dwaa.org, pg 642

Dogwise Publishing, 403 S Mission St, Wenatchee, WA 98801 *Tel:* 509-663-9115 *Toll Free Tel:* 800-776-2665 *E-mail:* mail@dogwise.com *Web Site:* www.dogwise.com, pg 71

The Christopher Doheny Award, 17 E 47 St, New York, NY 10017 *Tel:* 212-755-6710 *Fax:* 212-826-0831 *E-mail:* doheny@centerforfiction.org; info@centerforfiction.org *Web Site:* www.centerforfiction.org/awards/the-christopher-doheny-award, pg 642

Tom Doherty Associates, LLC, 175 Fifth Ave, 14th fl, New York, NY 10010 *Tel:* 646-307-5511 *Toll Free Tel:* 800-455-0340 *Web Site:* www.tor-forge.com, pg 71

Donadio & Olson Inc, 40 W 27 St, 5th fl, New York, NY 10001 *Tel:* 212-691-8077 *Fax:* 212-633-2837 *E-mail:* mail@donadio.com *Web Site:* donadio.com, pg 514

Janis A Donnaud & Associates Inc, 77 Bleecker St, No C1-25, New York, NY 10012 *Tel:* 212-431-2663 *Fax:* 212-431-2667 *E-mail:* jdonnaud@aol.com, pg 514

The Donning Company Publishers, 184 Business Park Dr, Suite 206, Virginia Beach, VA 23462 *Tel:* 757-497-1789 *Toll Free Tel:* 800-296-8572 *Fax:* 757-497-2542 *Web Site:* www.donning.com, pg 71

Jim Donovan Literary, 5635 SMU Blvd, Suite 201, Dallas, TX 75206 *Tel:* 214-696-9411 *E-mail:* jdlqueries@sbcglobal.net, pg 514

Doodle and Peck Publishing, 413 Cedarburg Ct, Yukon, OK 73099 *Tel:* 405-354-7422 *E-mail:* contact@doodleandpeck.com *Web Site:* www.doodleandpeck.com, pg 72

Dordt College Press, 498 Fourth Ave NE, Sioux Center, IA 51250-1606 *Tel:* 712-722-6420 *Toll Free Tel:* 800-343-6738 *Fax:* 712-722-6035 *E-mail:* dordtpress@dordt.edu; bookstore@dordt.edu *Web Site:* www.dordt.edu/about-dordt/publications/dordt-press-catalog, pg 72

Dorland Health, 4 Choke Cherry Rd, 2nd fl, Rockville, MD 20850 *Tel:* 301-354-2000 *Toll Free Tel:* 855-225-5341 *Fax:* 301-287-2535 *E-mail:* customer@decisionhealth.com *Web Site:* www.dorlandhealth.com, pg 72

Dorothy Canfield Fisher Book Award, 109 State St, Montpelier, VT 05609-0601 *Tel:* 802-828-2721 *Web Site:* libraries.vermont.gov, pg 642

Dorrance Publishing Co Inc, 585 Alpha Dr, Suite 103, Pittsburgh, PA 15238 *Toll Free Tel:* 800-695-9599; 800-788-7654 (gen cust orders) *Fax:* 412-288-1786 *E-mail:* dorrinfo@dorrancepublishing.com; redleadbookorders@dorrancepublishing.com; bookorders@rosedogbooks.com *Web Site:* www.dorrancepublishing.com, pg 72

Dorset Prize, 243 Union St, Suite 305, North Adams, MA 01247 *Tel:* 413-664-9611 *Fax:* 413-664-9711 *E-mail:* info@tupelopress.org *Web Site:* www.tupelopress.org, pg 642

John Dos Passos Prize for Literature, Dept of English & Modern Languages, 201 High St, Farmville, VA 23909 *Tel:* 434-395-2155 *Fax:* 434-395-2145 *Web Site:* www.longwood.edu/english/dos-passos-prize, pg 642

Double Dragon Publishing Inc, 1-5762 Hwy 7 E, Markham, ON L3P 7Y4, Canada *E-mail:* sales@double-dragon-ebooks.com *Web Site:* www.double-dragon-ebooks.com, pg 452

Double Play, 303 Hillcrest Rd, Belton, MO 64012-1852 *Tel:* 816-651-7118 *E-mail:* wlloydj@lyahoo.com, pg 492

Doubleday Canada, 320 Front St W, Suite 1400, Toronto, ON M5V 3B6, Canada *Tel:* 416-364-4449 *Fax:* 416-598-7764 *Web Site:* www.penguinrandomhouse.ca, pg 452

Frank Nelson Doubleday Memorial Award, Barrett Bldg, 2nd fl, 2301 Central Ave, Cheyenne, WY 82002 *Tel:* 307-777-7742 *Web Site:* wyoarts.state.wy.us, pg 642

Doubleday/Nan A Talese, c/o Penguin Random House Inc, 1745 Broadway, New York, NY 10019 *Tel:* 212-751-2600 *Fax:* 212-572-2662 *E-mail:* ddaypub@randomhouse.com *Web Site:* knopfdoubleday.com, pg 72

Douglas & McIntyre (2013) Ltd, 4437 Rondeview Rd, Madeira Park, BC V0N 2H1, Canada *Toll Free Tel:* 800-667-2988 *E-mail:* info@douglas-mcintyre.com *Web Site:* www.douglas-mcintyre.com, pg 452

Dover Publications Inc, 31 E Second St, Mineola, NY 11501-3852 *Tel:* 516-294-7000 *Toll Free Tel:* 800-223-3130 (orders) *Fax:* 516-742-6953 *E-mail:* rights@doverpublications.com; service@doverpublications.com *Web Site:* store.doverdirect.com; www.doverpublications.com, pg 72

Down East Books, 680 Commercial St (US Rte 1), Rockport, ME 04856 *Tel:* 207-594-9544 *Toll Free Tel:* 800-685-7962 (US orders, cust serv); 800-766-1670 *E-mail:* support@downeast.com *Web Site:* secure.downeast.com/books/maine/books.html, pg 72

Down The Shore Publishing Corp, 106 Stafford Forge Rd, West Creek, NJ 08092 *Tel:* 609-812-5076 *Fax:* 609-812-5098 *E-mail:* dtsbooks@comcast.net; info@down-the-shore.com *Web Site:* www.down-the-shore.com, pg 72

Dragon Door Publications, 5 E Country Rd B, Suite 3, Little Canada, MN 55117 *Tel:* 651-487-2180 *Toll Free Tel:* 800-899-5111 (orders & cust serv) *E-mail:* support@dragondoor.com *Web Site:* www.dragondoor.com, pg 72

Dragonfairy Press, 2107 N Decatur Rd, Suite 211, Decatur, GA 30033 *Tel:* 404-955-8150 *E-mail:* info@dragonfairypress.com *Web Site:* www.dragonfairypress.com, pg 73

Dragonfly Book Awards, 4696 W Tyson St, Chandler, AZ 85226-2903 *Tel:* 480-940-8182 *Fax:* 480-940-8787 *E-mail:* info@StoryMonsters.com *Web Site:* www.DragonflyBookAwards.com, pg 642

Dramatic Publishing Co, 311 Washington St, Woodstock, IL 60098-3308 *Tel:* 815-338-7170 *Toll Free Tel:* 800-448-7469 *Fax:* 815-338-8981 *Toll Free Fax:* 800-334-5302 *E-mail:* plays@dramaticpublishing.com; customerservice@dpcplays.com *Web Site:* www.dramaticpublishing.com, pg 73

Dramatists Play Service Inc, 440 Park Ave S, New York, NY 10016 *Tel:* 212-683-8960 *Fax:* 212-213-1539 *E-mail:* postmaster@dramatists.com; orders@dramatists.com; publications@dramatists.com *Web Site:* www.dramatists.com, pg 73

Dreaming Publications LLC, 1126 Bel Air Dr, Santa Barbara, CA 93103 *Tel:* 661-776-5152; 310-560-4732 *E-mail:* dreamingpublications@gmail.com *Web Site:* dreamingpublications.com, pg 477

Dreaming Robot Press, 1214 San Francisco Ave, Las Vegas, NM 87701 *Tel:* 505-264-3830 *E-mail:* books@dreamingrobotpress.com *Web Site:* dreamingrobotpress.com, pg 73

Dreamscape Media LLC, 6940 Hall St, Holland, OH 43528 *Tel:* 419-867-6965 *Toll Free Tel:* 877-983-7326 *E-mail:* info@dreamscapeab.com *Web Site:* www.dreamscapeab.com, pg 73

Drennan Communications, 6 Robin Lane, East Kingston, NH 03827 *Tel:* 603-642-8002 *Fax:* 603-642-8002, pg 492

Drennan Literary Agency, 6 Robin Lane, East Kingston, NH 03827 *Tel:* 603-642-8002 *Fax:* 603-642-8002, pg 514

Carleton Drewry Memorial, 900 Timber Creek Place, Virginia Beach, VA 23464 *E-mail:* poetryinva@aol.com *Web Site:* poetrysocietyofvirginia.org, pg 642

Saint Katharine Drexel Award, 8550 United Plaza Blvd, Suite 1001, Baton Rouge, LA 70809 *Tel:* 225-408-4417 *E-mail:* cla2@cathla.org *Web Site:* cathla.org, pg 642

Drummond Books, 2111 Cleveland St, Evanston, IL 60202 *Tel:* 847-302-2534 *E-mail:* drummondbooks@gmail.com, pg 492

Drury University One-Act Play Competition, 900 N Benton Ave, Springfield, MO 65802-3344 *Tel:* 417-873-6821 *Web Site:* www.drury.edu, pg 642

Dubuque Fine Arts Players Annual One Act Play Festival, PO Box 1160, Dubuque, IA 52004-1160 *Tel:* 563-588-3438 *E-mail:* contact@dbqoneacts.org *Web Site:* www.dbqoneacts.org, pg 643

Dufour Editions Inc, PO Box 7, Chester Springs, PA 19425 *Tel:* 610-458-5005 *Fax:* 610-458-7103 *E-mail:* info@dufoureditions.com *Web Site:* www.dufoureditions.com, pg 73

Duke University Press, 905 W Main St, Suite 18B, Durham, NC 27701 *Tel:* 919-688-5134 *Toll Free Tel:* 888-651-0122 (US) *Fax:* 919-688-2615 *Toll Free Fax:* 888-651-0124 *E-mail:* orders@dukeupress.edu *Web Site:* www.dukeupress.edu, pg 73

Dumbarton Oaks, 1703 32 St NW, Washington, DC 20007 *Tel:* 202-339-6400 *Fax:* 202-339-6401; 202-298-8407 *E-mail:* doaksbooks@doaks.org *Web Site:* www.doaks.org, pg 73

Dun & Bradstreet, 103 JFK Pkwy, Short Hills, NJ 07078 *Tel:* 973-921-5500 *Toll Free Tel:* 800-526-0651; 800-234-3867 (cust serv) *E-mail:* custserv@dnb.com *Web Site:* www.dnb.com, pg 73

Dundurn Press Ltd, 3 Church St, Suite 500, Toronto, ON M5E 1M2, Canada *Tel:* 416-214-5544 *Fax:* 416-214-5556 *E-mail:* info@dundurn.com *Web Site:* www.dundurn.com, pg 452

Dunham Literary Inc, 110 William St, Suite 2202, New York, NY 10038 *Tel:* 212-929-0994 *Web Site:* dunhamlit.com, pg 514

John H Dunning Prize in United States History, 400 "A" St SE, Washington, DC 20003 *Tel:* 202-544-2422 *Fax:* 202-544-8307 *E-mail:* awards@historians.org *Web Site:* www.historians.org, pg 643

Dunow, Carlson & Lerner Literary Agency Inc, 27 W 20 St, Suite 1107, New York, NY 10011 *Tel:* 212-645-7606 *E-mail:* mail@dclagency.com *Web Site:* www.dclagency.com, pg 514

Dupree, Miller & Associates Inc, 100 Highland Park Village, Suite 350, Dallas, TX 75205 *Tel:* 214-559-2665 *Fax:* 214-559-7243 *E-mail:* editorial@dupreemiller.com *Web Site:* www.dupreemiller.com, pg 515

Duquesne University Press, 600 Forbes Ave, Pittsburgh, PA 15282 *Tel:* 412-396-6610 *Fax:* 412-396-5984 *E-mail:* dupress@duq.edu *Web Site:* www.dupress.duq.edu, pg 74

Dustbooks, PO Box 100, Paradise, CA 95967-0100 *Tel:* 530-877-6110 *Fax:* 530-877-0222 *E-mail:* publisher@dustbooks.com; info@dustbooks.com *Web Site:* www.dustbooks.com, pg 74

Dutton, 375 Hudson St, New York, NY 10014 *Tel:* 212-366-2000 *Fax:* 212-366-2262 *Web Site:* www.penguin.com, pg 74

Dutton Children's Books, 345 Hudson St, New York, NY 10014 *Tel:* 212-366-2000 *Web Site:* www.penguin.com, pg 74

DWJ BOOKS LLC, 46 Cliff Dr, Sag Harbor, NY 11963 *Tel:* 631-899-4500 *E-mail:* info@dwjbooks.com *Web Site:* www.dwjbooks.com, pg 492

Dystel, Goderich & Bourret LLC, One Union Sq W, Suite 904, New York, NY 10003 *Tel:* 212-627-9100 *Fax:* 212-627-9313 *Web Site:* www.dystel.com, pg 515

Eagan Press, 3340 Pilot Knob Rd, St Paul, MN 55121 *Tel:* 651-454-7250 *Toll Free Tel:* 800-328-7560 *Fax:* 651-454-0766 *E-mail:* aacc@scisoc.org *Web Site:* www.aaccnet.org, pg 74

Eagle's View Publishing, 6756 North Fork Rd, Liberty, UT 84310 *Tel:* 801-393-4555; 801-745-0905 (edit) *Fax:* 801-745-0903 (edit); 801-393-4647 *E-mail:* sales@eaglefeathertrading.com *Web Site:* www.eaglefeathertrading.com, pg 74

Eakin Press, PO Box 331779, Fort Worth, TX 76163 *Tel:* 817-344-7036 *Toll Free Tel:* 888-982-8270 *Fax:* 817-344-7036 *Web Site:* www.eakinpress.com, pg 74

Earth Edit, PO Box 114, Maiden Rock, WI 54750 *Tel:* 715-448-3009, pg 493

East Asian Legal Studies Program (EALSP), 500 W Baltimore St, Suite 411, Baltimore, MD 21201-1786 *Tel:* 410-706-3870 *Fax:* 410-706-1516 *E-mail:* eastasia@law.umaryland.edu *Web Site:* www.law.umaryland.edu/programs/international/eastasia, pg 74

East Mountain Editing Services, PO Box 1895, Tijeras, NM 87059-1895 *Tel:* 505-281-8422 *Web Site:* www.spanishindexing.com, pg 493

East West Discovery Press, PO Box 3585, Manhattan Beach, CA 90266 *Tel:* 310-545-3730 *Fax:* 310-545-3731 *E-mail:* info@eastwestdiscovery.com *Web Site:* www.eastwestdiscovery.com, pg 74

EastBridge, 70 New Canaan Ave, Norwalk, CT 06850 *Tel:* 203-855-9125 *Fax:* 203-857-0730 *E-mail:* asia@eastbridgebooks.org; ask@eastbridgebooks.org *Web Site:* www.eastbridgebooks.org, pg 74

Eastland Press, 1240 Activity Dr, Suite D, Vista, CA 92081 *Tel:* 206-217-0204 (edit); 760-598-9695 (orders) *Toll Free Tel:* 800-453-3278 (orders) *Fax:* 760-598-6083 (orders) *Toll Free Fax:* 800-241-3329 (orders) *E-mail:* info@eastlandpress.com; orders@eastlandpress.com (credit card orders only) *Web Site:* www.eastlandpress.com, pg 74

Easy Money Press, 5419 87 St, Lubbock, TX 79424 *Tel:* 806-543-5215 *E-mail:* easymoneypress@yahoo.com, pg 75

Eaton Literary Associates Literary Awards, PO Box 49795, Sarasota, FL 34230-6795 *Tel:* 941-366-6589 *Fax:* 941-365-4679 *E-mail:* eatonlit@aol.com *Web Site:* www.eatonliterary.com, pg 643

Eclectic Book Press, 11 Larchdell Way, Mountain Lakes, NJ 07046 *Tel:* 862-251-2296 *E-mail:* info@eclecticbookpress.com *Web Site:* eclecticbookpress.com, pg 75

Ecopress, 5995 149 St W, Suite 105, Apple Valley, MN 55124 *Tel:* 952-469-6699 *Toll Free Tel:* 800-846-7027 *Fax:* 952-469-1968 *Toll Free Fax:* 800-330-6232 *E-mail:* info@finneyco.com *Web Site:* www.ecopress.com, pg 75

Ecrits des Forges, 992-A rue Royale, Trois-Rivieres, QC G9A 4H9, Canada *Tel:* 819-840-8492 *E-mail:* ecritsdesforges@gmail.com *Web Site:* www.ecritsdesforges.com, pg 452

ECS Publishing Corp, 1727 Larkin Williams Rd, Fenton, MO 63026 *Tel:* 636-305-0100 *Toll Free Tel:* 800-647-2117 *Web Site:* ecspublishing.com; www.facebook.com/ecspublishing, pg 75

ECW Press, 665 Gerrard St E, Toronto, ON M4M 1Y2, Canada *Tel:* 416-694-3348 *E-mail:* info@ecwpress.com *Web Site:* www.ecwpress.com, pg 452

EDC Publishing, 10302 E 55 Place, Tulsa, OK 74146-6515 *Tel:* 918-622-4522 *Toll Free Tel:* 800-475-4522 *Fax:* 918-665-7919 *Toll Free Fax:* 800-743-5660 *E-mail:* edc@edcpub.com *Web Site:* www.edcpub.com, pg 75

EdCan Network, 60 St Clair Ave E, Suite 703, Toronto, ON M4T 1N5, Canada *Tel:* 416-591-6300 *Toll Free Tel:* 866-803-9549 *Fax:* 416-591-5345 *Toll Free Fax:* 866-803-9549 *E-mail:* info@edcan.ca *Web Site:* www.edcan.ca, pg 564

Edda USA, 373 Park Ave S, 6th fl, New York, NY 10016 *Tel:* 646-755-9210 *Web Site:* eddausa.com, pg 75

Anne Edelstein Literary Agency LLC, 404 Riverside Dr, New York, NY 10025 *Tel:* 212-414-4923 *E-mail:* info@aeliterary.com; rights@aeliterary.com *Web Site:* www.aeliterary.com, pg 515

Edgar Allan Poe Awards®, 1140 Broadway, Suite 1507, New York, NY 10001 *Tel:* 212-888-8171 *E-mail:* mwa@mysterywriters.org *Web Site:* www.mysterywriters.org, pg 643

EDGE Science Fiction & Fantasy Publishing Inc, PO Box 1714, Calgary, AB T2P 2L7, Canada *Tel:* 403-254-0160 *Fax:* 403-254-0456 *E-mail:* admin@hadespublications.com *Web Site:* www.edgewebsite.com, pg 452

Edgewise Press Inc, 24 Fifth Ave, Suite 224, New York, NY 10011 *Tel:* 212-982-4818 *Fax:* 212-982-1364 *E-mail:* epinc@mindspring.com *Web Site:* www.edgewisepress.org, pg 75

ediciones Lerner, 241 First Ave N, Minneapolis, MN 55401 *Tel:* 612-332-3344 *Toll Free Tel:* 800-328-4929 *Fax:* 612-332-7615 *Toll Free Fax:* 800-332-1132 *E-mail:* info@lernerbooks.com; custserve@lernerbooks.com *Web Site:* www.lernerbooks.com; www.facebook.com/lernerbooks, pg 75

EditAndPublishYourBook.com, PO Box 2965, Nantucket, MA 02584-2965 *E-mail:* michaeltheauthor@yahoo.com *Web Site:* www.editandpublishyourbook.com, pg 493

Edit Etc, 26 Country Lane, Brunswick, ME 04011 *Tel:* 914-715-5849 *E-mail:* atkedit@cs.com *Web Site:* www.anntkeene.com, pg 493

Edit Resource LLC, 19265 Lincoln Green Lane, Monument, CO 80132 *Tel:* 719-290-0757 *E-mail:* info@editresource.com *Web Site:* www.editresource.com, pg 493

EditAmerica, 115 Jacobs Creek Rd, Ewing, NJ 08628 *Tel:* 609-882-5852 *Web Site:* www.editamerica.com; www.linkedin.com/in/PaulaPlantier, pg 493

Editcetera, 2034 Blake St, Suite 5, Berkeley, CA 94704 *Tel:* 510-849-1110 *Fax:* 510-900-6141 *E-mail:* info@editcetera.com *Web Site:* www.editcetera.com, pg 493

EditCraft Editorial Services, 422 Pine St, Grass Valley, CA 95945 *Tel:* 530-273-3934 *Web Site:* www.editcraft.com, pg 493

Les Editions Alire, 120 cote du Passage, Levis, QC G6V 5S9, Canada *Tel:* 418-835-4441 *Fax:* 418-838-4443 *E-mail:* info@alire.com *Web Site:* www.alire.com, pg 452

Les Editions Caractere, 5800, rue St-Denis, bureau 900, Montreal, QC H2S 3L5, Canada *Tel:* 514-273-1066 *Fax:* 514-276-0324 *E-mail:* caractere@tc.tc *Web Site:* www.editionscaractere.com, pg 453

Editions de la Pleine Lune, 223 34 Ave, Lachine, QC H8T 1Z4, Canada *Tel:* 514-634-7954 *E-mail:* editpllune@videotron.ca *Web Site:* www.pleinelune.qc.ca, pg 453

Les Editions de l'Hexagone, 1055, blvd Rene Levesque Est, Bureau 300, Montreal, QC H2L 4S5, Canada *Tel:* 514-523-7993 *Fax:* 514-849-1388 *Web Site:* www.edhexagone.com, pg 453

Les Editions de Mortagne, CP 116, Boucherville, QC J4B 5E6, Canada *Tel:* 450-641-2387 *Fax:* 450-655-6092 *E-mail:* info@editionsdemortagne.com *Web Site:* www.editionsdemortagne.com, pg 453

Les Editions du Ble, 340, blvd Provencher, St Boniface, MB R2H 0G7, Canada *Tel:* 204-237-8200 *Fax:* 204-233-8182 *E-mail:* direction@editionsduble.ca *Web Site:* ble.avoslivres.ca, pg 453

Les Editions du Boreal, 4447, rue St-Denis, Montreal, QC H2J 2L2, Canada *Tel:* 514-287-7401 *Fax:* 514-287-7664 *E-mail:* boreal@editionsboreal.qc.ca *Web Site:* www.editionsboreal.qc.ca, pg 453

Editions du CHU Sainte-Justine, 3175, chemin de la Cote-Sainte-Catherine, Montreal, QC H3T 1C5, Canada *Tel:* 514-345-4671 *Fax:* 514-345-4631 *E-mail:* edition.hsj@ssss.gouv.qc.ca *Web Site:* www.editions-chu-sainte-justine.org, pg 453

Les Editions du Noroit, 4609, rue D'Iberville, espace 202, Montreal, QC H2H 2L9, Canada *Tel:* 514-727-0005 *E-mail:* lenoroit@lenoroit.com *Web Site:* www.lenoroit.com, pg 453

Les Editions du Remue-Menage, La Maison Parent-Roback, 110 rue Sainte-Therese, bureau 303, Montreal, QC H2Y 1E6, Canada *Tel:* 514-876-0097 *Fax:* 514-876-7951 *E-mail:* info@editions-rm.ca *Web Site:* www.editions-rm.ca, pg 453

Les Editions du Septentrion, 835 Turnbull Ave, Quebec City, QC G1R 2X4, Canada *Tel:* 418-688-3556 *Fax:* 418-527-4978 *E-mail:* info@septentrion.qc.ca *Web Site:* www.septentrion.qc.ca, pg 454

Les Editions du Vermillon, 305, rue St-Patrick, Ottawa, ON K1N 5K4, Canada *Tel:* 613-241-4032 *Fax:* 613-241-3109 *E-mail:* leseditionsduvermillon@rogers.com *Web Site:* www.leseditionsduvermillon.ca, pg 454

Les Editions Fides, 7333 place des Roseraies, bureau 100, Anjou, QC H1M 2X6, Canada *Tel:* 514-745-4290 *Fax:* 514-745-4299 *E-mail:* editions@groupefides.com *Web Site:* www.editionsfides.com, pg 454

Editions FouLire, 4339, rue des Becassines, Quebec, QC G1G 1V5, Canada *Tel:* 418-628-4029 *Toll Free Tel:* 877-628-4029 (CN & US) *Fax:* 418-628-4801 *E-mail:* info@foulire.com; edition@foulire.com *Web Site:* www.foulire.com, pg 454

Les Editions Ganesha Inc, CP 484, succursale d'Youville, Montreal, QC H2P 2W1, Canada *Tel:* 450-641-2395 *E-mail:* courriel@editions-ganesha.qc.ca *Web Site:* www.editions-ganesha.qc.ca, pg 454

Les Editions Goelette Inc, 1350 Marie-Victorin, St-Bruno-de-Montarville, Quebec, QC J3V 6B9, Canada *Tel:* 450-653-1337 *Toll Free Tel:* 800-463-4961 *Fax:* 450-653-9924 *E-mail:* info@boutiquegoelette.com *Web Site:* www.boutiquegoelette.com, pg 454

Les Editions Heritage Inc, 1101, ave Victoria, St-Lambert, QC J4R 1P8, Canada *Tel:* 514-875-0327, pg 454

Editions Hurtubise, 1815, ave De Lorimier, Montreal, QC H2K 3W6, Canada *Tel:* 514-523-1523 *Toll Free Tel:* 800-361-1664 *Fax:* 514-523-9969 *Web Site:* www.editionshurtubise.com, pg 454

Les Editions JCL, 688, rue St-Joseph, Marieville, QC J3M 1H1, Canada *Tel:* 450-460-4438 *E-mail:* info@jcl.qc.ca *Web Site:* www.jcl.qc.ca, pg 454

Editions Le Dauphin Blanc Inc, 825, blvd Lebourgneuf, Suite 125, Quebec, QC G2J 0B9, Canada *Tel:* 418-845-4045 *Fax:* 418-845-1933 *E-mail:* info@dauphinblanc.com *Web Site:* www.dauphinblanc.com, pg 455

Editions Marie-France, CP 32263 BP Waverly, Montreal, QC H3L 3X1, Canada *Tel:* 514-329-3700 *Toll Free Tel:* 800-563-6644 (CN) *Fax:* 514-329-0630 *E-mail:* editions@marie-france.qc.ca *Web Site:* www.marie-france.qc.ca, pg 455

Editions Mediaspaul, 3965, blvd Henri-Bourassa E, Montreal, QC H1H 1L1, Canada *Tel:* 514-322-7341 *Fax:* 514-322-4281 *E-mail:* editeur@mediaspaul.ca *Web Site:* mediaspaul.ca, pg 455

Editions Michel Quintin, 2259 Papineau Ave, Suite 104, Montreal, QC H2K 4J5, Canada *Tel:* 514-379-3774 *E-mail:* info@editionsmichelquintin.ca *Web Site:* www.editionsmichelquintin.ca, pg 455

Editions MultiMondes, 1815, Avenue de Lorimier, Montreal, QC H2K 3W6, Canada *Tel:* 514-523-1523 *Toll Free Tel:* 800-361-1664 *Fax:* 514-523-9969 *Web Site:* www.multim.com, pg 455

Editions Orphee Inc, 1240 Clubview Blvd N, Columbus, OH 43235-1226 *Tel:* 614-846-9517 *Fax:* 614-846-9794 *E-mail:* sales@editionsorphee.com *Web Site:* www.editionsorphee.com, pg 75

Les Editions Phidal Inc, 5740 Ferrier, Montreal, QC H4P 1M7, Canada *Tel:* 514-738-0202 *Toll Free Tel:* 800-738-7349 *Fax:* 514-738-5102 *E-mail:* info@phidal.com; customer@phidal.com (sales & export) *Web Site:* www.phidal.com, pg 455

Les Editions Pierre Tisseyre, 155, rue Maurice, Rosemere, QC J7A 2S8, Canada *Tel:* 514-335-0777 *Fax:* 514-335-6723 *E-mail:* info@edtisseyre.ca *Web Site:* www.tisseyre.ca, pg 455

Editions Trecarre, La Tourelle, 1055, blvd Rene-Levesque E, Bureau 300, Montreal, QC H2L 4S5, Canada *Tel:* 514-849-5259 *Fax:* 514-849-1388 *Web Site:* www.editions-trecarre.com, pg 455

Les Editions Un Monde Different, 3905 Isabelle, bureau 101, Brossard, QC J4Y 2R2, Canada *Tel:* 450-656-2660 *Toll Free Tel:* 800-443-2582 *Fax:* 450-659-9328 *E-mail:* info@umd.ca *Web Site:* www.umd.ca, pg 455

Les Editions Vents d'Ouest, 109, rue Wright, bureau 202, Gatineau, QC J8X 2G7, Canada *Tel:* 819-770-6377 *E-mail:* info@ventsdouest.ca *Web Site:* www.ventsdouest.ca, pg 455

Les Editions XYZ inc, 1815, ave De Lorimier, Montreal, QC H2K 3W6, Canada *Tel:* 514-525-2170 *Fax:* 514-525-7537 *E-mail:* info@editionsxyz.com *Web Site:* www.editionsxyz.com, pg 456

Editions Yvon Blais, 75 rue Queen, Bureau 4700, Montreal, QC H3C 2N6, Canada *Toll Free Tel:* 800-363-3047 *Fax:* 450-263-9256 *E-mail:* editionsyvonblais.commandes@thomsonreuters.com (cust serv) *Web Site:* www.editionsyvonblais.com, pg 456

Editorial Bautista Independiente, 3417 Kenilworth Blvd, Sebring, FL 33870-4469 *Tel:* 863-382-6350 *Toll Free Tel:* 800-398-7187 (US) *Fax:* 863-382-8650 *E-mail:* info@ebi-bmm.org; ebiweb@ebi-bmm.org *Web Site:* www.ebi-bmm.org, pg 75

The Editorial Department LLC, 7650 E Broadway, Suite 308, Tucson, AZ 85710 *Tel:* 520-546-9992 *Fax:* 520-979-3408 *E-mail:* admin@editorialdepartment.com *Web Site:* www.editorialdepartment.com, pg 493

Editorial Freelancers Association (EFA), 71 W 23 St, 4th fl, New York, NY 10010-4102 *Tel:* 212-929-5400 *Toll Free Tel:* 866-929-5425 *Fax:* 212-929-5439 *Toll Free Fax:* 866-929-5439 *E-mail:* office@the-efa.org *Web Site:* www.the-efa.org, pg 564

Editorial Portavoz, 2450 Oak Industrial Dr NE, Grand Rapids, MI 49505 *Toll Free Tel:* 877-733-2607 (ext 206) *Fax:* 616-493-1790 *E-mail:* portavoz@portavoz.com *Web Site:* www.portavoz.com, pg 75

Editors' Association of Canada (Association canadienne des reviseurs), 27 Carlton St, Suite 505, Toronto, ON M5B 1L2, Canada *Tel:* 416-975-1379 *Toll Free Tel:* 866-CAN-EDIT (226-3348) *Fax:* 416-975-1637 *E-mail:* info@editors.ca; info@reviseurs.ca *Web Site:* www.editors.ca; www.reviseurs.ca, pg 564

Editor's Award, 90 Broad St, Suite 2100, New York, NY 10004 *Tel:* 212-226-3586 *Fax:* 212-226-3963 *Web Site:* www.pw.org/about-us/sponsored-prizes, pg 643

The Editors Circle, 462 Grove St, Montclair, NJ 07043 *Tel:* 862-596-9709 *E-mail:* query@theeditorscircle.com *Web Site:* www.theeditorscircle.com, pg 493

Education Awards of Excellence, 301 Brush Creek Rd, Warrendale, PA 15086-7529 *Tel:* 412-741-6860 *Toll Free Tel:* 800-910-4283 *Fax:* 412-741-2311 *E-mail:* printingind@comm.printing.org *Web Site:* www.printing.org/educationaward, pg 643

Education Writers Association (EWA), 3516 Connecticut Ave NW, Washington, DC 20008 *Tel:* 202-452-9830 *Fax:* 202-452-9837 *E-mail:* ewa@ewa.org *Web Site:* www.ewa.org, pg 565

Education Writers Association Workshops, 3516 Connecticut Ave NW, Washington, DC 20008 *Tel:* 202-452-9830 *Fax:* 202-452-9837 *E-mail:* ewa@ewa.org *Web Site:* www.ewa.org, pg 610

Educational Book & Media Association (EBMA), 11 Main St, Suite D, Warrenton, VA 20186 *Tel:* 540-318-7770 *Fax:* 202-962-3939 *E-mail:* info@edupaperback.org *Web Site:* www.edupaperback.org, pg 565

Educational Design Services LLC, 5750 Bou Ave, Suite 1508, North Bethesda, MD 20852 *Tel:* 301-881-8611 *Web Site:* www.educationaldesignservices.com, pg 515

Educational Directories Inc (EDI), 1025 W Wise Rd, Suite 101, Schaumburg, IL 60193 *Tel:* 847-891-1250 *Toll Free Tel:* 800-357-6183 *Fax:* 847-891-0945 *E-mail:* info@ediusa.com *Web Site:* www.ediusa.com, pg 76

Educational Impressions Inc, 785 Franklin Ave, Franklin Lakes, NJ 07417 *Tel:* 201-644-0908 *Toll Free Tel:* 800-451-7450 *Fax:* 201-644-0907 *Web Site:* www.edimpressions.com; www.awpeller.com, pg 76

Educational Insights, 152 W Walnut St, Suite 201, Gardena, CA 90248 *Toll Free Tel:* 800-995-4436 *Toll Free Fax:* 888-892-8731 *E-mail:* cs@educationalinsights.com *Web Site:* www.educationalinsights.com, pg 76

Educators Award, PO Box 1589, Austin, TX 78767-1589 *Tel:* 512-478-5748 *Toll Free Tel:* 888-762-4685 *Fax:* 512-478-3961 *E-mail:* societyexec@dkg.org *Web Site:* www.dkg.org, pg 643

Educator's International Press Inc (EIP), 84 Hardenburgh Ave, Haworth, NJ 07641 *Tel:* 518-334-0276 *Fax:* 703-661-1547 *E-mail:* info@edint.com *Web Site:* edint.presswarehouse.com, pg 76

Educators Progress Service Inc, 214 Center St, Randolph, WI 53956 *Tel:* 920-326-3126 *Toll Free Tel:* 888-951-4469 *Fax:* 920-326-3127 *E-mail:* epsinc@centurytel.net, pg 76

Edupress Inc, 4810 Forest Run Rd, Madison, WI 53704 *Toll Free Tel:* 800-835-7978 *Toll Free Fax:* 800-558-9332 *E-mail:* edupressdealers@edupress.com *Web Site:* www.edupress.com, pg 76

Margaret A Edwards Award, 50 E Huron St, Chicago, IL 60611 *Tel:* 312-280-4390 *Toll Free Tel:* 800-545-2433 *Fax:* 312-280-5276 *E-mail:* yalsa@ala.org *Web Site:* www.ala.org/yalsa/edwards, pg 643

Edwin Markham Prize for Poetry, San Jose State University, English Dept, One Washington Sq, San Jose, CA 95192-0090 *Tel:* 408-924-4441 *Web Site:* www.reedmag.org, pg 643

Wm B Eerdmans Publishing Co, 2140 Oak Industrial Dr NE, Grand Rapids, MI 49505 *Tel:* 616-459-4591 *Toll Free Tel:* 800-253-7521 *Fax:* 616-459-6540 *E-mail:* customerservice@eerdmans.com; sales@eerdmans.com *Web Site:* www.eerdmans.com, pg 76

The Maureen Egen Writers Exchange Award, 90 Broad St, Suite 2100, New York, NY 10004 *Tel:* 212-226-3586 *Fax:* 212-226-3963 *E-mail:* admin@pw.org *Web Site:* www.pw.org, pg 643

Wilfrid Eggleston Award for Nonfiction, 11759 Groat Rd, Edmonton, AB T5M 3K6, Canada *Tel:* 780-422-8174 *Toll Free Tel:* 800-665-5354 (AB only) *Fax:* 780-422-2663 (attn WGA) *E-mail:* mail@writersguild.ca *Web Site:* writersguild.ca, pg 643

Diane Eickhoff, 3808 Genessee St, Kansas City, MO 64111 *Tel:* 816-561-6693 *E-mail:* diane.eickhoff@gmail.com, pg 493

Eifrig Publishing LLC, PO Box 66, Lemont, PA 16851 *Toll Free Tel:* 888-340-6543 *E-mail:* info@eifrigpublishing.com *Web Site:* www.eifrigpublishing.com, pg 76

Eisenbrauns, PO Box 275, Winona Lake, IN 46590-0275 *Tel:* 574 269 2011 *Fax:* 574-269-6788 *E-mail:* customer_service@eisenbrauns.com; publisher@eisenbrauns.com *Web Site:* www.eisenbrauns.com, pg 76

The Lisa Ekus Group LLC, 57 North St, Hatfield, MA 01038 *Tel:* 413-247-9325 *Fax:* 413-247-9873 *E-mail:* info@lisaekus.com *Web Site:* lisaekus.com, pg 515, 619

Elderberry Press Inc, 1393 Old Homestead Dr, Oakland, OR 97462-9690 *Tel:* 541-459-6043 *Web Site:* www.elderberrypress.com, pg 76

The Electrochemical Society (ECS), 65 S Main St, Bldg D, Pennington, NJ 08534-2839 *Tel:* 609-737-1902 *Fax:* 609-737-2743 *E-mail:* publications@electrochem.org; customerservice@electrochem.org *Web Site:* www.electrochem.org, pg 77

Edward Elgar Publishing Inc, The William Pratt House, 9 Dewey Ct, Northampton, MA 01060-3815 *Tel:* 413-584-5551 *Toll Free Tel:* 800-390-3149 (orders) *Fax:* 413-584-9933 *E-mail:* elgarinfo@e-elgar.com; elgarsales@e-elgar.com; elgarsubmissions@e-elgar.com (edit) *Web Site:* www.e-elgar.com; www.elgaronline.com (ebooks & journals), pg 77

T S Eliot Prize for Poetry, 100 E Normal Ave, Kirksville, MO 63501-4221 *Tel:* 660-785-7336 *Toll Free Tel:* 800-916-6802 *Fax:* 660-785-4480 *E-mail:* tsup@truman.edu *Web Site:* tsup.truman.edu, pg 644

eLit Awards, 1129 Woodmere Ave, Suite B, Traverse City, MI 49686 *Tel:* 231-933-0445 *Toll Free Tel:* 800-706-4636 *Fax:* 231-933-0448 *E-mail:* info@elitawards.com *Web Site:* www.elitawards.com, pg 644

Elite Books, PO Box 442, Fulton, CA 95439 *Tel:* 707-525-9292 *Toll Free Fax:* 800-330-9798 *E-mail:* support@eftuniverse.com *Web Site:* www.elitebooksonline.com, pg 77

Ethan Ellenberg Literary Agency, 155 Suffolk St, Suite 2R, New York, NY 10002 *Tel:* 212-431-4554 *E-mail:* agent@ethanellenberg.com *Web Site:* www.ethanellenberg.com, pg 516

Van Courtlandt Elliott Prize, 17 Dunster St, Suite 202, Cambridge, MA 02138 *Tel:* 617-491-1622 *Fax:* 617-492-3303 *E-mail:* info@themedievalacademy.org *Web Site:* www.medievalacademy.org, pg 644

Nicholas Ellison Agency, 469 W 147 St, Apt 1, New York, NY 10031 *Web Site:* www.thenicholasellisonagency.com, pg 516

Irene Elmer, 2806 Cherry St, Berkeley, CA 94705-2310 *Tel:* 510-841-0466 *E-mail:* ielmer@earthlink.net, pg 493

Elsevier Engineering Information (Ei), 230 Park Ave, 8th fl, New York, NY 10169-0123 *Tel:* 212-989-5800 *Fax:* 212-633-3990 *E-mail:* eicustomersupport@elsevier.com *Web Site:* www.ei.org, pg 77

Elsevier, Health Sciences Division, 1600 John F Kennedy Blvd, Suite 1800, Philadelphia, PA 19103-2899 *Tel:* 215-239-3900 *Toll Free Tel:* 800-523-1649 *Fax:* 215-239-3990 *Web Site:* www.us.elsevierhealth.com, pg 77

Elsevier Inc, 50 Hampshire St, 5th fl, Cambridge, MA 02139 *Toll Free Tel:* 866-607-1414 *Fax:* 617-661-7061 *E-mail:* usbkinfo@elsevier.com *Web Site:* www.elsevier.com, pg 77

Elva Resa Publishing, 8362 Tamarack Village, Suite 119-106, St Paul, MN 55125 *Tel:* 651-357-8770 *Fax:* 501-641-0777 *E-mail:* staff@elvaresa.com *Web Site:* www.elvaresa.com; www.militaryfamilybooks.com, pg 77

Catherine C Elverston ELS, 9 Red Bay Lane, Kitty Hawk, NC 27949-3307 *Tel:* 352-222-0625 (cell) *E-mail:* celverston@gmail.com, pg 493

R Elwell Indexing, 193 Main St, Cold Spring, NY 10516 *Tel:* 845-667-1036 *E-mail:* r.elwell.indexing@gmail.com, pg 493

EMC Publishing LLC, 875 Montreal Way, St Paul, MN 55102 *Tel:* 651-290-2800 (corp) *Toll Free Tel:* 800-328-1452 *Toll Free Fax:* 800-328-4564 *E-mail:* educate@emcp.com *Web Site:* www.emcp.com, pg 77

Emerald Books, PO Box 55787, Seattle, WA 98155 *Tel:* 425-771-1153 *Toll Free Tel:* 800-922-2143 *Fax:* 425-775-2383 *E-mail:* books@ywampublishing.com *Web Site:* www.ywampublishing.com, pg 78

Emerging Critics Fellowship, c/o 38 Douglass St, Apt 3, Brooklyn, NY 11231 *E-mail:* info@bookcritics.org *Web Site:* bookcritics.org, pg 644

Emerging Playwright Award, 555 Eighth Ave, Suite 1800, New York, NY 10018 *Tel:* 212-421-1380 *Fax:* 212-421-1387 *E-mail:* urbanstage@aol.com, pg 644

Emerson College Department of Writing, Literature & Publishing, 180 Tremont St, 10th fl, Boston, MA 02116 *Tel:* 617-824-8750 *Fax:* 617-824-7856 *Web Site:* www.emerson.edu, pg 620

The Ralph Waldo Emerson Award, 1606 New Hampshire Ave NW, Washington, DC 20009 *Tel:* 202-265-3808 *Fax:* 202-986-1601 *E-mail:* awards@pbk.org *Web Site:* www.pbk.org/bookawards, pg 644

Emmaus Road Publishing Inc, 1468 Parkview Circle, Steubenville, OH 43952 *Tel:* 740-283-2880 (outside US) *Toll Free Tel:* 800-398-5470 (orders) *Fax:* 740-283-4011 (orders) *E-mail:* questions@emmausroad.org *Web Site:* www.emmausroad.org, pg 78

Emond Montgomery Publications Ltd, 60 Shaftesbury Ave, Toronto, ON M4T 1A3, Canada *Tel:* 416-975-3925 *Toll Free Tel:* 888-837-0815 *Fax:* 416-975-3924 *E-mail:* orders@emp.ca *Web Site:* www.emp.ca, pg 456

Empire Press Media/Avant-Guide, 244 Fifth Ave, Suite 2053, New York, NY 10001-7604 *Tel:* 917-512-3881 *Fax:* 212-202-7757 *E-mail:* info@avantguide.com; communications@avantguide.com; editor@avantguide.com *Web Site:* www.avantguide.com, pg 78

Empire Publishing Service, PO Box 1344, Studio City, CA 91614-0344 *Tel:* 818-784-8918 *E-mail:* empirepubsvc@att.net, pg 78

Empire State Award for Excellence in Literature for Young People, 6021 State Farm Rd, Guilderland, NY 12084 *Tel:* 518-432-6952 *Toll Free Tel:* 800-252-6952 *Fax:* 518-427-1697 *E-mail:* info@nyla.org *Web Site:* www.nyla.org, pg 644

Enchanted Lion Books, 351 Van Brunt St, Ground fl-Gallery, Brooklyn, NY 11231 *Tel:* 646-785-9272 *E-mail:* enchantedlion@gmail.com *Web Site:* www.enchantedlionbooks.com, pg 78

Encounter Books, 900 Broadway, Suite 601, New York, NY 10003 *Tel:* 212-871-6310 *Toll Free Tel:* 800-786-3839 *Fax:* 212-871-6311 *E-mail:* publicity@encounterbooks.com *Web Site:* www.encounterbooks.com, pg 78

Encyclopaedia Britannica Inc, 325 N La Salle St, Chicago, IL 60654 *Tel:* 312 347 7159 (all other countries) *Toll Free Tel:* 800-323-1229 (US & CN) *Fax:* 312-294-2104 *E-mail:* contact@eb.com *Web Site:* www.eb.com; www.britannica.com, pg 78

Energy Information Administration (EIA), 1000 Independence Ave SW, Washington, DC 20585 *Tel:* 202-586-8800 *Fax:* 202-586-0727 *E-mail:* infoctr@eia.doe.gov *Web Site:* www.eia.doe.gov, pg 78

Energy Psychology Press, 1490 Mark West Springs Rd, Santa Rosa, CA 95404 *Tel:* 707-525-9292 *Toll Free Fax:* 800-330-9798 *E-mail:* support@eftuniverse.com *Web Site:* www.energypsychologypress.com; www.elitebooksonline.com, pg 79

Enfield Publishing & Distribution Co, 234 May St, Enfield, NH 03748 *Tel:* 603-632-7377 *Fax:* 603-632-5611 *E-mail:* info@enfieldbooks.com *Web Site:* www.enfieldbooks.com, pg 79

Enough Said, 3959 NW 29 Lane, Gainesville, FL 32606 *Tel:* 352-262-2971 *Fax:* 352-372-5747 (call first) *E-mail:* enoughsaid@cox.net *Web Site:* users.navi.net/~heathlynn, pg 493

Enslow Publishing LLC, 101 W 23 St, Suite 240, New York, NY 10011 *Tel:* 908-771-9400 *Toll Free Tel:* 800-398-2504 *Fax:* 908-771-0925 *Toll Free Fax:* 877-980-4454 *E-mail:* customerservice@enslow.com *Web Site:* www.enslow.com, pg 79

Entangled Publishing, 2614 S Timberline Rd, Suite 109, Fort Collins, CO 80525 *Toll Free Tel:* 877-677-9451 *E-mail:* publisher@entangledpublishing.com *Web Site:* www.entangledpublishing.com, pg 79

Entomological Society of America, 3 Park Place, Suite 307, Annapolis, MD 21401-3722 *Tel:* 301-731-4535 *Fax:* 301-731-4538 *E-mail:* esa@entsoc.org *Web Site:* www.entsoc.org, pg 79

Environmental Law Institute, 1730 "M" St NW, Suite 700, Washington, DC 20036 *Tel:* 202-939-3800 *Toll Free Tel:* 800-433-5120 *Fax:* 202-939-3868 *E-mail:* law@eli.org *Web Site:* www.eli.org, pg 79

Epicenter Press Inc, 6524 NE 181 St, Suite 2, Kenmore, WA 98028 *Tel:* 425-485-6822 (edit, mktg, busn off) *Fax:* 425-481-8253 *E-mail:* info@epicenterpress.com *Web Site:* www.epicenterpress.com, pg 79

Epicomm, 1800 Diagonal Rd, Suite 320, Alexandria, VA 22314-2862 *Tel:* 703-836-9200 *E-mail:* webmaster@epicomm.org *Web Site:* epicomm.org, pg 565

EPS/School Specialty Literacy & Intervention, 625 Mount Auburn St, 3rd fl, Cambridge, MA 02138-3039 *Toll Free Tel:* 800-225-5750 *Toll Free Fax:* 888-440-2665 *E-mail:* customerservice.eps@schoolspecialty.com *Web Site:* eps.schoolspecialty.com, pg 79

Norma Epstein Foundation Awards in Creative Writing, 15 King's College Circle, UC 165, Toronto, ON M5S 3H7, Canada *Tel:* 416-978-8083 *Fax:* 416-978-8854 *E-mail:* uc.programs@utoronto.ca *Web Site:* www.uc.utoronto.ca/writing-centre, pg 644

Ericson Books, 1614 Redbud St, Nacogdoches, TX 75965-2936 *Tel:* 936-564-3625 *Fax:* 936-552-8999, pg 79

The Ernest Sandeen & Richard Sullivan Prizes in Fiction & Poetry, 356 O'Shaughnessy Hall, Notre Dame, IN 46556 *Tel:* 574-631-7526 *Fax:* 574-631-4795 *E-mail:* creativewriting@nd.edu *Web Site:* creativewriting.nd.edu, pg 644

Erskine J Poetry Prize, PO Box 22161, Baltimore, MD 21203 *E-mail:* smartishpace@gmail.com *Web Site:* www.smartishpace.com, pg 644

Felicia Eth Literary Representation, 555 Bryant St, Suite 350, Palo Alto, CA 94301 *Tel:* 415-970-9717 *E-mail:* feliciaeth.literary@gmail.com *Web Site:* www.ethliterary.com, pg 516

Etruscan Press, Wilkes University, 84 W South St, Wilkes-Barre, PA 18766 *Tel:* 570-408-4546 *Fax:* 570-408-3333 *E-mail:* books@etruscanpress.org *Web Site:* www.etruscanpress.org, pg 80

Europa Editions, 214 W 29 St, Suite 1003, New York, NY 10001 *Tel:* 212-868-6844 *Fax:* 212-868-6845 *E-mail:* info@europaeditions.com *Web Site:* www.europaeditions.com, pg 80

Evan-Moor Educational Publishers, 18 Lower Ragsdale Dr, Monterey, CA 93940-5746 *Tel:* 831-649-5901 *Toll Free Tel:* 800-777-4362 (orders) *Fax:* 831-649-6256 *Toll Free Fax:* 800-777-4332 (orders) *E-mail:* sales@evan-moor.com; marketing@evan-moor.com *Web Site:* www.evan-moor.com, pg 80

Evangelical Christian Publishers Association (ECPA), 5801 S McClintock Dr, Suite 104, Tempe, AZ 85283 *Tel:* 480-966-3998 *Fax:* 480-966-1944 *E-mail:* info@ecpa.org *Web Site:* www.ecpa.org, pg 565

Evangelical Press Association (EPA), PO Box 1787, Queen Creek, AZ 85142 *Toll Free Tel:* 888-311-1731 *E-mail:* info@evangelicalpress.com *Web Site:* www.evangelicalpress.com, pg 565

David W & Beatrice C Evans Biography & Handcart Awards, 0735 Old Main Hill, Logan, UT 84322-0735 *Tel:* 435-797-0299 *Fax:* 435-797-1092 *E-mail:* mwc@usu.edu *Web Site:* mountainwest.usu.edu, pg 645

M Evans & Company, c/o Rowman & Littlefield Publishing Group, 4501 Forbes Blvd, Suite 200, Lanham, MD 20706 *Tel:* 301-459-3366 *Fax:* 301-429-5748 *Web Site:* rowman.com, pg 80

Mary Evans Inc, 242 E Fifth St, New York, NY 10003-8501 *Tel:* 212-979-0880 *Fax:* 212-979-5344 *E-mail:* info@maryevansinc.com *Web Site:* www.maryevansinc.com, pg 516

Evergreen Pacific Publishing Ltd, 4204 Russell Rd, Suite M, Mukilteo, WA 98275-5424 *Tel:* 425-493-1451 *Fax:* 425-493-1453 *E-mail:* sales@evergreenpacific.com *Web Site:* www.evergreenpacific.com, pg 80

Everything Goes Media LLC, PO Box 1524, Milwaukee, WI 53201 *Tel:* 312-226-8400 *E-mail:* info@everythinggoesmedia.com *Web Site:* www.everythinggoesmedia.com, pg 80

Excalibur Publications, PO Box 89667, Tucson, AZ 85752-9667 *Tel:* 520-575-9057 *E-mail:* excaliburpublications@centurylink.net, pg 80

EXCEL Awards, 529 14 St, Suite 750, Washington, DC 20045 *Tel:* 202-591-2457 *E-mail:* awards@associationmediaandpublishing.org; info@associationmediaandpublishing.org *Web Site:* associationmediaandpublishing.org; kellencompany.com, pg 645

Excelsior Editions, 10 N Pearl St, 4th fl, Albany, NY 12207 *Tel:* 518-944-2800 *Toll Free Tel:* 866-430-7869 *Fax:* 518-320-1592 *E-mail:* info@sunypress.edu *Web Site:* www.sunypress.edu, pg 80

The Experiment, 220 E 23 St, Suite 301, New York, NY 10010-4674 *Tel:* 212-889-1659 *E-mail:* info@theexperimentpublishing.com *Web Site:* www.theexperimentpublishing.com, pg 80

Eye in the Ear Children's Audio, 5 Crescent St, Portland, ME 04102 *Toll Free Tel:* 855-99-STORY (997-8679) *Fax:* 207-699-1380 (attn: Laurence Kelly) *E-mail:* info@eyeintheear.com *Web Site:* www.eyeintheear.com, pg 81

Facts On File, 132 W 31 St, 17th fl, New York, NY 10001 *Tel:* 212-967-8800 *Toll Free Tel:* 800-322-8755 *Toll Free Fax:* 800-678-3633 *E-mail:* custserv@factsonfile.com *Web Site:* infobasepublishing.com, pg 81

Fair Winds Press, 100 Cummings Ctr, Suite 406-L, Beverly, MA 01915 *Tel:* 978-282-9590 *Fax:* 978-282-7765 *E-mail:* sales@quarto.com *Web Site:* www.quartoknows.com, pg 81

John K Fairbank Prize in East Asian History, 400 "A" St SE, Washington, DC 20003 *Tel:* 202-544-2422 *Fax:* 202-544-8307 *E-mail:* awards@historians.org *Web Site:* www.historians.org, pg 645

Fairchild Books, 1385 Broadway, 5th fl, New York, NY 10018 *Tel:* 212-419-5300 *Toll Free Tel:* 800-932-4724; 888-330-8477 (orders) *Fax:* 212-704-5975 *Web Site:* bloomsbury.com/us/academic/fairchildbooks, pg 81

Fairleigh Dickinson University Press, M-GH2-01, 285 Madison Ave, Madison, NJ 07940 *Tel:* 973-443-8564 *Fax:* 974-443-8364 *E-mail:* fdupress@fdu.edu *Web Site:* www.fdupress.org, pg 81

Tom Fairley Award for Editorial Excellence, 27 Carlton St, Suite 505, Toronto, ON M5B 1L2, Canada *Tel:* 416-975-1379 *Toll Free Tel:* 866-CAN-EDIT (226-3348) *Fax:* 416-975-1637 *E-mail:* fairley_award@editors.ca; info@editors.ca *Web Site:* www.editors.ca; www.reviseurs.ca, pg 645

The Fairmont Press Inc, 700 Indian Trail, Lilburn, GA 30047 *Tel:* 770-925-9388 *Fax:* 770-381-9865 *Web Site:* www.fairmontpress.com, pg 81

Fairwinds Press, PO Box 668, Lions Bay, BC V0N 2E0, Canada *Tel:* 604-913-0649 *E-mail:* orders@fairwinds-press.com *Web Site:* www.fairwinds-press.com, pg 456

Faith Alive Christian Resources, 1700 28 St SE, Grand Rapids, MI 49508-1407 *Tel:* 616-224-0728 *Toll Free Tel:* 800-333-8300 *Toll Free Fax:* 888-642-8606 *E-mail:* info@faithaliveresources.org; sales@faithaliveresources.org; orders@faithaliveresources.org *Web Site:* www.faithaliveresources.org, pg 81

Faith & Fellowship Publishing, 1020 W Alcott Ave, Fergus Falls, MN 56537 *Tel:* 218-736-7357 *Toll Free Tel:* 800-332-9232 *E-mail:* clb@clba.org *Web Site:* www.clba.org, pg 82

Faith Library Publications, PO Box 50126, Tulsa, OK 74150-0126 *Tel:* 918-258-1588 (ext 2218) *Toll Free Tel:* 888-258-0999 (orders) *Fax:* 918-872-7710 (orders) *E-mail:* flp@rhema.org *Web Site:* www.rhema.org/store, pg 82

Faithlife Corp, 1313 Commercial St, Bellingham, WA 98225 *Tel:* 360-527-1700 *Toll Free Tel:* 800-875-6467 *Fax:* 360-527-1707 *E-mail:* sales@faithlife.com; customerservice@faithlife.com *Web Site:* faithlife.com, pg 82

FaithWalk Publishing, 5450 N Dixie Hwy, Lima, OH 45807 *Tel:* 419-227-1818 *Toll Free Tel:* 800-537-1030 (orders: non-bookstore mkts) *Fax:* 419-224-9184 *E-mail:* orders@csspub.com *Web Site:* www.faithwalkpub.com, pg 82

Familius, 1254 Commerce Way, Sanger, CA 93657 *Tel:* 559-876-2170 *Fax:* 559-876-2180 *E-mail:* orders@familius.com *Web Site:* www.familius.com, pg 82

Family Matters, PO Box 80430, Portland, OR 97280-1430 *Tel:* 503-221-0836 *Fax:* 503-221-0837 *E-mail:* editors@glimmertrain.org *Web Site:* www.glimmertrain.org, pg 645

F+W Media Inc, 10151 Carver Rd, Suite 200, Blue Ash, OH 45242 *Tel:* 513-531-2690 *Toll Free Tel:* 800-289-0963 (trade accts); 800-258-0929 (cust serv) *E-mail:* contact_us@fwmedia.com *Web Site:* www.fwcommunity.com, pg 82

Far Horizons Award for Poetry, University of Victoria, Box 1700, Sta CSC, Victoria, BC V8W 2Y2, Canada *Tel:* 250-721-8524 *Fax:* 250-472-5051 *E-mail:* malahat@uvic.ca *Web Site:* www.malahatreview.ca, pg 645

Far Horizons Award for Short Fiction, University of Victoria, Box 1700, Sta CSC, Victoria, BC V8W 2Y2, Canada *Tel:* 250-721-8524 *Fax:* 250-472-5051 *E-mail:* malahat@uvic.ca *Web Site:* www.malahatreview.ca, pg 645

Norma Farber First Book Award, 15 Gramercy Park, New York, NY 10003 *Tel:* 212-254-9628 *Web Site:* www.poetrysociety.org, pg 645

Farcountry Press, 2750 Broadwater Ave, Helena, MT 59602-9202 *Tel:* 406-422-1263 *Toll Free Tel:* 800-821-3874 (sales off) *Fax:* 406-443-5480 *E-mail:* books@farcountrypress.com; sales@farcountrypress.com *Web Site:* www.farcountrypress.com, pg 82

Farrar, Straus & Giroux Books for Young Readers, 175 Fifth Ave, 7th fl, New York, NY 10010 *Tel:* 212-741-6900 *Toll Free Tel:* 888-330-8477 (orders) *Fax:* 212-633-9385 *Web Site:* us.macmillan.com/mackids; www.mackidsbooks.com, pg 82

Farrar, Straus & Giroux, LLC, 18 W 18 St, New York, NY 10011 *Tel:* 212-741-6900 *E-mail:* fsg.publicity@fsgbooks.com *Web Site:* us.macmillan.com/fsg.aspx, pg 82

Farrar Writing & Editing, 4638 Manchester Rd, Mound, MN 55364 *Tel:* 952-472-6874 *Fax:* 952-472-6874 (call first) *Web Site:* www.writeandedit.net, pg 493

Father & Son Publishing Inc, 4909 N Monroe St, Tallahassee, FL 32303-7015 *Tel:* 850-562-2612 *Toll Free Tel:* 800-741-2712 (orders only) *Fax:* 850-562-0916 *Web Site:* www.fatherson.com, pg 83

Favorable Impressions, 51910 Shoreview Dr, Shelby Township, MI 48316 *Tel:* 248-635-2957 *Web Site:* www.favimp.com, pg 83

The FC2 Catherine Doctorow Innovative Fiction Prize, c/o Dept of English, Languages & Communincations Bldg, 255 S Central Campus Dr, Rm 3500, Salt Lake City, UT 84112-0494 *Tel:* 773-702-7000 *Web Site:* www.fc2.org/prizes.html, pg 645

FC&A Publishing, 103 Clover Green, Peachtree City, GA 30269 *Tel:* 770-487-6307 *Toll Free Tel:* 800-226-8024 *Fax:* 770-631-4357 *E-mail:* customer_service@fca.com *Web Site:* www.fca.com, pg 83

Federal Bar Association, 1220 N Filmore St, Suite 444, Arlington, VA 22201 *Tel:* 571-481-9100 *Fax:* 571-481-9090 *E-mail:* fba@fedbar.org *Web Site:* www.fedbar.org, pg 83

Federal Street Press, 25-13 Old Kings Hwy N, No 277, Darien, CT 06820 *Tel:* 203-852-1280 *Toll Free Tel:* 877-886-2830 *Fax:* 203-852-1389 *E-mail:* info@federalstreetpress.com; sales@federalstreetpress.com; customerservice@federalstreetpress.com; orders@federalstreetpress.com *Web Site:* federalstreetpress.com, pg 83

Federation of BC Writers, PO Box 16028, 617 Belmont St, New Westminster, BC V3M 6W6, Canada *E-mail:* info@bcwriters.ca *Web Site:* bcwriters.ca, pg 565

Feigenbaum Publishing Consultants Inc, 61 Bounty Lane, Jericho, NY 11753 *Tel:* 516-647-8314 (cell), pg 516

Betsy Feist Resources, 140 E 81 St, Unit 7-E, New York, NY 10028-1875 *Tel:* 212-861-2014 *E-mail:* bfresources@rcn.com, pg 494

Feldheim Publishers, 208 Airport Executive Park, Nanuet, NY 10954 *Tel:* 845-356-2282 *Toll Free Tel:* 800-237-7149 (orders) *Fax:* 845-425-1908 *E-mail:* sales@feldheim.com *Web Site:* www.feldheim.com, pg 83

Fellowship Program, One Capital Hill, 3rd fl, Providence, RI 02908 *Tel:* 401-222-3880 *Fax:* 401-222-3018 *Web Site:* www.arts.ri.gov, pg 645

Fellowship, Tuition Scholarship & Work Study Programs for Writers, Middlebury College, 204 College St, Middlebury, VT 05753 *Tel:* 802-443-5286 *Fax:* 802-443-2087 *E-mail:* blwc@middlebury.edu *Web Site:* www.middlebury.edu/blwc, pg 646

Fellowships for Creative & Performing Artists & Writers, 185 Salisbury St, Worcester, MA 01609-1634 *Tel:* 508-755-5221 *Fax:* 508-753-3311 *Web Site:* www.americanantiquarian.org, pg 646

Fellowships for Historical Research, 185 Salisbury St, Worcester, MA 01609-1634 *Tel:* 508-471-2131 *Fax:* 508-754-9069 *Web Site:* www.americanantiquarian.org, pg 646

Jerry Felsen, 3960 NW 196 St, Miami Gardens, FL 33055-1869 *Tel:* 305-625-5012 *E-mail:* jfelsen0@att.net *Web Site:* beatthemarket.org, pg 494

The Feminist Press at The City University of New York, 365 Fifth Ave, Suite 5406, New York, NY 10016 *Tel:* 212-817-7915 *Fax:* 212-817-1593 *E-mail:* info@feministpress.org *Web Site:* www.feministpress.org, pg 83

Fence Books, University at Albany, Science Library 320, 1400 Washington Ave, Albany, NY 12222 *Tel:* 518-591-8162 *E-mail:* fence.fencebooks@gmail.com *Web Site:* www.fenceportal.org, pg 84

Fence Modern Poets Series, University at Albany, Science Library 320, 1400 Washington Ave, Albany, NY 12222 *Tel:* 518-591-8162 *E-mail:* fence.fencebooks@gmail.com *Web Site:* www.fenceportal.org, pg 646

Shubert Fendrich Memorial Playwriting Contest, PO Box 4267, Englewood, CO 80155-4267 *Tel:* 303-779-4035 *Toll Free Tel:* 800-333-7262 *Fax:* 303-779-4315 *Web Site:* www.pioneerdrama.com/playwrights/contest.asp, pg 646

Robert L Fenton, PO Box 300885, Waterford, MI 48330 *Tel:* 248-855-8780, pg 516

Feral House, 1240 W Sims Way, Suite 124, Port Townsend, WA 98368 *Tel:* 323-666-3311 *Fax:* 323-297-4331 *E-mail:* info@feralhouse.com *Web Site:* feralhouse.com, pg 84

Ferguson Publishing, 132 W 31 St, 17th fl, New York, NY 10001 *Tel:* 212-967-8800 *Toll Free Tel:* 800-322-8755 *Fax:* 917-339-0323 *Toll Free Fax:* 800-678-3633 *E-mail:* custserv@factsonfile.com *Web Site:* infobasepublishing.com, pg 84

Fernwood Publishing, 32 Oceanvista Lane, Black Point, NS B0J 1B0, Canada *Tel:* 902-857-1388 *Fax:* 902-857-1328 *E-mail:* info@fernpub.ca; roseway@fernpub.ca *Web Site:* fernwoodpublishing.ca, pg 456

Howard Fertig, Publisher, 80 E 11 St, New York, NY 10003 *Tel:* 212 982 7922 *Fax:* 212 982 1099 *E-mail:* enquiries@hfertigbooks.com; orders@hfertigbooks.com *Web Site:* www.hfertigbooks.com, pg 84

Fiction Collective Two Inc (FC2), c/o Dept of English, Languages & Communincations Bldg, 255 S Central Campus Dr, Rm 3500, Salt Lake City, UT 84112-0494 *Tel:* 773-702-7000 *E-mail:* fc2.cmu@gmail.com *Web Site:* www.fc2.org/prizes.html, pg 84

Fiction Open, PO Box 80430, Portland, OR 97280-1430 *Tel:* 503-221-0836 *Fax:* 503-221-0837 *E-mail:* editors@glimmertrain.org *Web Site:* www.glimmertrain.org, pg 646

The Field Poetry Prize, 50 N Professor St, Oberlin, OH 44074-1091 *Tel:* 440-775-8408 *Fax:* 440-775-8124 *E-mail:* oc.press@oberlin.edu *Web Site:* www.oberlin.edu/ocpress; www.oberlin.edu/ocpress/prize.htm (guidelines), pg 646

Fifth Estate Publishing, 2795 County Hwy 57, Blounstville, AL 35031 *Toll Free Tel:* 855-299-2160 *E-mail:* fifth-estate@hotmail.com *Web Site:* fifthestatepub.com, pg 84

Fifth House Publishers, 195 Allstate Pkwy, Markham, ON L3R 4T8, Canada *Tel:* 905-477-9700 *Toll Free Tel:* 800-387-9776 *Toll Free Fax:* 800-260-9777 *E-mail:* godwit@fitzhenry.ca; bookinfo@fitzhenry.ca (cust serv) *Web Site:* www.fitzhenry.ca/fifthhouse.aspx, pg 456

Filsinger & Company Ltd, 288 W 12 St, Suite 2R, New York, NY 10014 *Tel:* 212-243-7421 (by appt) *E-mail:* filsingercompany@gmail.com *Web Site:* www.filsingerco.com, pg 477

Filter Press LLC, PO Box 95, Palmer Lake, CO 80133 *Tel:* 719-481-2420 *Toll Free Tel:* 888-570-2663 *Fax:* 719-481-2420 *E-mail:* info@filterpressbooks.com; orders@filterpressbooks.com *Web Site:* filterpressbooks.com, pg 84

Financial Executives Research Foundation Inc (FERF), West Tower, 7th fl, 1250 Headquarters Plaza, Morristown, NJ 07960-6837 *Tel:* 973-765-1000 *Fax:* 973-765-1023 *Web Site:* www.financialexecutives.org, pg 84

Financial Times Press, 800 E 96 St, Indianapolis, IN 46240 *Web Site:* www.informit.com/ftpress, pg 84

Finding My Way Books, 3512 SW Huntoon St, Topeka, KS 66604 *Tel:* 785-273-6239 *E-mail:* info@findingmywaybooks.com; findingmywaybooks@gmail.com *Web Site:* www.findingmywaybooks.net, pg 84

Fine Arts Work Center in Provincetown, 24 Pearl St, Provincetown, MA 02657 *Tel:* 508-487-9960 *Fax:* 508-487-8873 *E-mail:* general@fawc.org *Web Site:* www.fawc.org, pg 646

Fine Creative Media, Inc, 322 Eighth Ave, 15th fl, New York, NY 10001 *Tel:* 212-595-3500 *Fax:* 212-595-3779, pg 85

Fine Wordworking, PO Box 3041, Monterey, CA 93942-3041 *Tel:* 831-375-6278 *E-mail:* info@finewordworking.com *Web Site:* marilynch.com, pg 494

FineEdge.com LLC, 14004 Biz Point Lane, Anacortes, WA 98221 *Tel:* 360-299-8500 *Fax:* 360-299-0535 *E-mail:* pub@fineedge.com; orders@fineedge.com *Web Site:* www.fineedge.com, pg 85

FinePrint Literary Management, 207 W 106 St, Suite 1D, New York, NY 10025 *Tel:* 212-279-6214 *E-mail:* assist@fineprint.com *Web Site:* www.fineprintlit.com, pg 516

Finney Company Inc, 5995 149 St W, Suite 105, Apple Valley, MN 55124 *Tel:* 952-469-6699 *Toll Free Tel:* 800-846-7027 *Fax:* 952-469-1968 *Toll Free Fax:* 800-330-6232 *E-mail:* info@finneyco.com *Web Site:* www.finneyco.com, pg 85

Fire Engineering Books & Videos, 1421 S Sheridan Rd, Tulsa, OK 74112 *Tel:* 918-831-9421 *Toll Free Tel:* 800-752-9764 *Fax:* 918-832-0319 *E-mail:* sales@pennwell.com *Web Site:* www.pennwellbooks.com, pg 85

Firecracker Awards, 154 Christopher St, Suite 3C, New York, NY 10014-9110 *Tel:* 212-741-9110 *Fax:* 212-741-9112 *E-mail:* info@clmp.org *Web Site:* www.clmp.org/firecracker, pg 646

Firefall Editions, 4905 Tunlaw St, Alexandria, VA 22312 *Tel:* 510-549-2461 *E-mail:* literary@att.net *Web Site:* www.firefallmedia.com, pg 85

Firefly Books Ltd, 50 Staples Ave, Unit 1, Richmond Hill, ON L4B 0A7, Canada *Tel:* 416-499-8412 *Toll Free Tel:* 800-387-6192 (CN); 800-387-5085 (US) *Fax:* 416-499-8313 *Toll Free Fax:* 800-450-0391 (CN); 800-565-6034 (US) *E-mail:* info@fireflybooks.com *Web Site:* www.fireflybooks.com, pg 456

First Avenue Editions, 241 First Ave N, Minneapolis, MN 55401 *Tel:* 612-332-3344 *Toll Free Tel:* 800-328-4929 *Fax:* 612-332-7615 *Toll Free Fax:* 800-332-1132 *E-mail:* info@lernerbooks.com; custserve@lernerbooks.com *Web Site:* www.lernerbooks.com; www.facebook.com/lernerbooks, pg 85

The Fischer-Harbage Agency Inc, 540 President St, 3rd fl, Brooklyn, NY 11215 *Tel:* 212-695-7105 *E-mail:* info@fischerharbage.com *Web Site:* www.fischerharbage.com, pg 517

The Fischer Ross Group Inc, 75 Holly Hill Lane, Suite 100, Greenwich, CT 06830 *Tel:* 203-622-4950 *Fax:* 203-531-4132 *E-mail:* frgstaff@frg-speakers.com *Web Site:* www.frg-speakers.com, pg 547

Fitzhenry & Whiteside Limited, 195 Allstate Pkwy, Markham, ON L3R 4T8, Canada *Tel:* 905-477-9700 *Toll Free Tel:* 800-387-9776 *Fax:* 905-477-2834 *Toll Free Fax:* 800-260-9777 *E-mail:* bookinfo@fitzhenry.ca; godwit@fitzhenry.ca *Web Site:* www.fitzhenry.ca, pg 457

FJH Music Co Inc, 2525 Davie Rd, Suite 360, Fort Lauderdale, FL 33317-7424 *Tel:* 954-382-6061 *Toll Free Tel:* 800-262-8744 *Fax:* 954-382-3073 *E-mail:* custserv@fjhmusic.com; sales@fjhmusic.com *Web Site:* www.fjhmusic.com, pg 85

Flammarion Quebec, 375 Ave Laurier W, Montreal, QC H2V 2K3, Canada *Tel:* 514-277-8807 *Fax:* 514-278-2085 *E-mail:* info@flammarion.qc.ca *Web Site:* www.flammarion.qc.ca, pg 457

Flanker Press Ltd, 1243 Kenmount Rd, Unit 1, Paradise, NL A1L 0V8, Canada *Tel:* 709-739-4477 *Toll Free Tel:* 866-739-4420 *Fax:* 709-739-4420 *E-mail:* info@flankerpress.com; sales@flankerpress.com *Web Site:* www.flankerpress.com, pg 457

Flannery Literary, 1140 Wickfield Ct, Naperville, IL 60563 *Web Site:* flanneryliterary.com, pg 517

Flashlight Press, 527 Empire Blvd, Brooklyn, NY 11225 *Tel:* 718-288-8300 *Fax:* 718-972-6307 *Web Site:* www.flashlightpress.com, pg 85

Norma Fleck Award for Canadian Children's Non-Fiction, 40 Orchard View Blvd, Suite 217, Toronto, ON M4R 1B9, Canada *Tel:* 416-975-0010 *Fax:* 416-975-8970 *E-mail:* info@bookcentre.ca *Web Site:* www.bookcentre.ca, pg 646

FleetSeek, 6190 Powers Ferry Rd, Suite 320, Atlanta, GA 30339 *Tel:* 540-899-9872 *Toll Free Tel:* 888-ONLY-TTS (665-9887) *Fax:* 540-899-1948 *E-mail:* fleetseek@fleetseek.com *Web Site:* www.fleetseek.com, pg 85

Peter Fleming Agency, PO Box 458, Pacific Palisades, CA 90272 *Tel:* 310-454-1373 *E-mail:* peterfleming@earthlink.net, pg 517

Fleur Publishing Inc, 4 Embarcadero Ctr, 14th fl, San Francisco, CA 94111 *Tel:* 415-766-3512 *Fax:* 415-789-4525 *Web Site:* fleurpublishing.com, pg 86

Florida Academic Press, PO Box 357425, Gainesville, FL 32635 *Tel:* 352-332-5104 *E-mail:* fapress@gmail.com *Web Site:* www.florida-academic-press.com, pg 86

Florida Authors & Publishers Association Inc (FAPA), 1702 N Woodland Blvd, Suite 116, Box 145, Deland, FL 32720 *E-mail:* member.services@floridapublishersassociation.com *Web Site:* www.floridapublishersassociation.com, pg 565

Florida Freelance Writers Association, 45 Main St, North Stratford, NH 03590 *Tel:* 603-922-8338 *Fax:* 603-922-8339 *E-mail:* ffwa@writers-editors.com; info@writers-editors.com *Web Site:* www.writers-editors.com; www.ffwamembers.com, pg 565

Florida Outdoor Writers Association Inc, 24 NW 33 Ct, Suite A, Gainesville, FL 32607 *Tel:* 352-284-1763 *E-mail:* info@fowa.org *Web Site:* www.fowa.org, pg 565

Florida Writers Association Conference, PO Box 66069, St Pete Beach, FL 33736-6069 *Web Site:* www.floridawriters.net, pg 610

Florida Writers Association Inc, PO Box 66069, St Pete Beach, FL 33736-6069 *Web Site:* www.floridawriters.net, pg 565

Flowerpot Press, 2160 S Service Rd W, Oakville, ON L6L 5N1, Canada *Tel:* 416-479-0695 *Toll Free Tel:* 866-927-5001 *E-mail:* info@flowerpotpress.com; order@flowerpotpress.com *Web Site:* www.flowerpotpress.com, pg 457

Flying Pen Press LLC, 1416 S Newport St, Denver, CO 80224 *Tel:* 303-375-0499 *Fax:* 303-375-0499 *Web Site:* www.flyingpenpress.com, pg 86

Focus, PO Box 44937, Indianapolis, IN 46244-0937 *Tel:* 317-635-9250 *Fax:* 317-635-9292 *E-mail:* customer@hackettpublishing.com; editorial@hackettpublishing.com *Web Site:* focusbookstore.com, pg 86

Focus on the Family, 8605 Explorer Dr, Colorado Springs, CO 80920-1051 *Tel:* 719-531-5181 *Toll Free Tel:* 800-A-FAMILY (232-6459) *Fax:* 719-531-3424 *Web Site:* www.focusonthefamily.com; www.facebook.com/focusonthefamily, pg 86

Focus Strategic Communications Inc, 2474 Waterford St, Oakville, ON L6L 5E6, Canada *Tel:* 905-825-8757 *Toll Free Tel:* 866-263-6287 *Fax:* 905-825-5724 *Toll Free Fax:* 866-613-6287 *E-mail:* info@focussc.com *Web Site:* www.focussc.com, pg 494

Fodor's Travel Publications, 1745 Broadway, 15th fl, New York, NY 10019 *Toll Free Tel:* 800-733-3000 *E-mail:* publicity@fodors.com; editors@fodors.com *Web Site:* www.fodors.com, pg 86

Sheldon Fogelman Agency Inc, 420 E 72 St, New York, NY 10021 *Tel:* 212-532-7250 *Fax:* 212-685-8939 *E-mail:* info@sheldonfogelmanagency.com *Web Site:* sheldonfogelmanagency.com, pg 517

Foil & Specialty Effects Association (FSEA), 2150 SW Westport Dr, Suite 101, Topeka, KS 66614 *Tel:* 785-271-5816 *Fax:* 785-271-6404 *E-mail:* info@fsea.com; fseamail@fsea.com *Web Site:* www.fsea.com, pg 566

The Foley Literary Agency, 34 E 38 St, Suite 1B, New York, NY 10016 *Tel:* 212-686-6930, pg 517

Folio Literary Management, The Film Center Bldg, 630 Ninth Ave, Suite 1101, New York, NY 10036 *Tel:* 212-400-1494 *Fax:* 212-967-0977 *Web Site:* www.foliolit.com, pg 517

Folklore Publishing, 11717-9B Ave NW, Unit 2, Edmonton, AB T6J 7B7, Canada *Tel:* 780-435-2376 *E-mail:* submissions@folklorepublishing.com (ms submissions) *Web Site:* www.folklorepublishing.com, pg 457

La Fondation Emile Nelligan, 100, rue Sherbrooke, Suite 202, Montreal, QC H2X 1C3, Canada *Tel:* 514-278-4657 *Fax:* 514-278-1943 *E-mail:* info@fondation-nelligan.org *Web Site:* www.fondation-nelligan.org, pg 566

Fons Vitae, 49 Mockingbird Valley Dr, Louisville, KY 40207-1366 *Tel:* 502-897-3641 *Fax:* 502-893-7373 *E-mail:* fonsvitaeky@aol.com *Web Site:* www.fonsvitae.com, pg 86

Fordham University, Graduate School of Business Administration, Gabelli School of Business, 441 E Fordham Rd, Hughes Hall, Rm 516, Bronx, NY 10458 *Tel:* 718-817-1894 *Web Site:* www.bnet.fordham.edu, pg 620

Fordham University, Graduate School of Business Administration, 113 W 60 St, New York, NY 10023 *Web Site:* www.fordham.edu, pg 646

Fordham University Press, Joseph A Martino Hall, 45 Columbus Ave, New York, NY 10023 *Fax:* 347-842-3083 *Web Site:* www.fordhampress.com, pg 86

Foreword's INDIES Awards, 425 Boardman Ave, Suite B, Traverse City, MI 49684 *Tel:* 231-933-3699 *Web Site:* www.forewordreviews.com, pg 647

Morris D Forkosch Prize, 400 "A" St SE, Washington, DC 20003 *Tel:* 202-544-2422 *Fax:* 202-544-8307 *E-mail:* awards@historians.org *Web Site:* www.historians.org, pg 647

E M Forster Award, 633 W 155 St, New York, NY 10032 *Tel:* 212-368-5900 *Fax:* 212-491-4615 *E-mail:* academy@artsandletters.org *Web Site:* www.artsandletters.org, pg 647

Fort Ross Inc - International Representation for Artists, 26 Arthur Place, Yonkers, NY 10701 *Tel:* 914-375-6448 *Web Site:* www.fortrossinc.com, pg 517

Fort Ross Inc - International Representation for Artists, 26 Arthur Place, Yonkers, NY 10701 *Tel:* 914-375-6448; 718-775-8340 *Web Site:* www.fortrossinc.com, pg 543

49th Parallel Poetry Award, Mail Stop 9053, Western Washington University, Bellingham, WA 98225 *Tel:* 360-650-4863 *E-mail:* bhreview@wwu.edu *Web Site:* www.bhreview.org, pg 647

Forum Publishing Co, 383 E Main St, Centerport, NY 11721 *Tel:* 631-754-5000 *Toll Free Tel:* 800-635-7654 *Fax:* 631-754-0630 *E-mail:* forumpublishing@aol.com *Web Site:* www.forum123.com, pg 87

Forward Movement, 412 Sycamore St, Cincinnati, OH 45202-4110 *Tel:* 513-721-6659 *Toll Free Tel:* 800-543-1813 *Fax:* 513-721-0729 (orders) *E-mail:* orders@forwardmovement.org (orders & cust serv) *Web Site:* www.forwardmovement.org, pg 87

Foster City International Writers Contest, 650 Shell Blvd, Foster City, CA 94404 *Tel:* 650-286-3380 *E-mail:* fostercity_writers@yahoo.com *Web Site:* www.fostercity.org, pg 647

Foster Travel Publishing, 1623 Martin Luther King, Berkeley, CA 94709 *Tel:* 510-549-2202 *Web Site:* www.fostertravel.com, pg 494

Walter Foster Publishing Inc, 6 Orchard Rd, Suite 100, Lake Forest, CA 92630 *Tel:* 949-380-7510 *Toll Free Tel:* 800-426-0099; 800-759-0190 (orders) *Fax:* 949-380-7575 *E-mail:* walterfoster@quartous.com *Web Site:* www.quartous.com, pg 87

The Foundation Center, 32 Old Slip, 24th fl, New York, NY 10005-3500 *Tel:* 212-620-4230 *Toll Free Tel:* 800-424-9836 *Fax:* 212-807-3677 *E-mail:* customerservice@foundationcenter.org *Web Site:* foundationcenter.org, pg 87

Foundation Press, c/o West Academic Publishing, 444 Cedar St, Suite 700, St Paul, MN 55101 *Toll Free Tel:* 877-888-1330 *E-mail:* customerservice@westacademic.com *Web Site:* www.westacademic.com, pg 87

Foundation Publications, 900 S Euclid St, La Habra, CA 90631 *Tel:* 714-879-2286 *Toll Free Tel:* 800-257-6272 *Fax:* 714-535-2164 *E-mail:* info@foundationpublications.com *Web Site:* www.foundationpublications.com, pg 87

4A's (American Association of Advertising Agencies), 1065 Avenue of the Americas, 16th fl, New York, NY 10018 *Tel:* 212-682-2500 *Web Site:* www.aaaa.org, pg 566

4Kidz Publishing, 265 El Dorado Blvd, No 1712, Webster, TX 77598 *Tel:* 601-467-2743 *E-mail:* info@4kidzpublishing.com *Web Site:* www.facebook.com/4kidzpublishing/, pg 477

Fowler Museum at UCLA, PO Box 951549, Los Angeles, CA 90095-1549 *Tel:* 310-825-4361 *Fax:* 310-206-7007 *E-mail:* fowlerws@arts.ucla.edu *Web Site:* www.fowler.ucla.edu, pg 87

Fox Chapel Publishing Co Inc, 1970 Broad St, East Petersburg, PA 17520 *Tel:* 717-560-4703 *Toll Free Tel:* 800-457-9112 *Fax:* 717-560-4702 *E-mail:* customerservice@foxchapelpublishing.com *Web Site:* www.foxchapelpublishing.com, pg 87

Dixon Ryan Fox Manuscript Prize, 5798 State Hwy 80, Cooperstown, NY 13326 *Tel:* 607-547-1416, pg 647

FPMI Solutions Inc, 689 Discovery Dr, Suite 300, Huntsville, AL 35806 *Toll Free Tel:* 888-644-3764 *E-mail:* info@fpmi.com *Web Site:* www.fpmisolutions.com; www.fpmi.com, pg 87

Frances Henne YALSA/VOYA Research Grant, 50 E Huron St, Chicago, IL 60611 *Tel:* 312-280-4390 *Toll Free Tel:* 800-545-2433 *Fax:* 312-280-5276 *E-mail:* yalsa@ala.org *Web Site:* www.ala.org/yalsa/awardsandgrants/franceshenne, pg 647

H E Francis Award Short Story Competition, UAH Huntsville Dept of English, Morton Hall 222, Huntsville, AL 35899 *Web Site:* www.uah.edu/la/departments/english, pg 647

Franciscan Media, 28 W Liberty St, Cincinnati, OH 45202 *Tel:* 513-241-5615 *Toll Free Tel:* 800-488-0488 *Fax:* 513-241-0399 *E-mail:* books@americancatholic.org *Web Site:* www.americancatholic.org; www.franciscanmedia.org, pg 87

Prix Francophone de l'ACSP, 260 rue Dalhousie St, Suite 204, Ottawa, ON K1N 7E4, Canada *Tel:* 613-562-1202 *Fax:* 613-241-0019 *E-mail:* cpsa-acsp@cpsa-acsp.ca *Web Site:* www.cpsa-acsp.ca, pg 647

Sandi Frank, 8 Fieldcrest Ct, Cortlandt Manor, NY 10567 *Tel:* 914-739-7088 *E-mail:* sfrankmail@aol.com, pg 494

Franklin, Beedle & Associates Inc, 2154 NE Broadway, Suite 100, Portland, OR 97232 *Tel:* 503-284-6348 *Toll Free Tel:* 800-322-2665 *Fax:* 503-625-4434 *Web Site:* www.fbeedle.com, pg 88

Lynn C Franklin Associates Ltd, 1350 Broadway, Suite 2015, New York, NY 10018 *Tel:* 212-868-6311 *Fax:* 212-868-6312 *E-mail:* agency@franklinandsiegal.com, pg 517

Soeurette Diehl Fraser Translation Award, c/o 7748 Hwy 290 W, Austin, TX 78736-3202 *Tel:* 512-683-5640 *E-mail:* president@texasinstituteofletters.org *Web Site:* www.texasinstituteofletters.org, pg 647

Frederick Fell Publishers Inc, 2131 Hollywood Blvd, Suite 305, Hollywood, FL 33020 *Tel:* 954-925-5242 *E-mail:* fellpub@aol.com (admin only) *Web Site:* www.fellpub.com, pg 88

Jeanne Fredericks Literary Agency Inc, 221 Benedict Hill Rd, New Canaan, CT 06840 *Tel:* 203-972-3011 *Fax:* 203-972-3011 *E-mail:* jeanne.fredericks@gmail.com (no unsol attachments) *Web Site:* jeannefredericks.com, pg 517

Free Spirit Publishing Inc, 217 Fifth Ave N, Suite 200, Minneapolis, MN 55401-1299 *Tel:* 612-338-2068 *Toll Free Tel:* 800-735-7323 *Fax:* 612-337-5050 *Toll Free Fax:* 866-419-5199 *E-mail:* help4kids@freespirit.com *Web Site:* www.freespirit.com, pg 88

George Freedley Memorial Award, c/o The New York Public Library for the Performing Arts, 111 Amsterdam Ave, New York, NY 10023 *E-mail:* TLABookAwards@gmail.com; TheatreLibraryAssociation@gmail.com *Web Site:* www.tla-online.org/awards/bookawards, pg 647

Robert A Freedman Dramatic Agency Inc, 1501 Broadway, Suite 2310, New York, NY 10036 *Tel:* 212-840-5760 *Fax:* 212-840-5776, pg 518

The Don Freeman Memorial Grant-In-Aid, 4727 Wilshire Blvd, Suite 301, Los Angeles, CA 90010 *Tel:* 323-782-1010; 310-403-0675 (cell) *Fax:* 323-782-1892 *E-mail:* grants@scbwi.org; scbwi@scbwi.org *Web Site:* www.scbwi.org, pg 648

W H Freeman, 41 Madison Ave, New York, NY 10010 *Tel:* 212-576-9400 *Fax:* 212-689-2383 *Web Site:* www.macmillanlearning.com, pg 88

The French-American Foundation & Florence Gould Foundation Annual Translation Prize, 28 W 44 St, Suite 1420, New York, NY 10036 *Tel:* 212-829-8800 *Fax:* 212-829-8810 *Web Site:* www.frenchamerican.org, pg 648

Samuel French Inc, 235 Park Ave S, 5th fl, New York, NY 10003 *Tel:* 212-206-8990 *Toll Free Tel:* 866-598-8449 *Fax:* 212-206-1429 *E-mail:* info@samuelfrench.com; publications@samuelfrench.com *Web Site:* www.samuelfrench.com, pg 88

Samuel French Inc, 235 Park Ave S, 5th fl, New York, NY 10003 *Tel:* 212-206-8990 *Toll Free Tel:* 866-598-8449 *Fax:* 212-206-1429 *E-mail:* info@samuelfrench.com *Web Site:* www.samuelfrench.com, pg 518

Fresh Air Books, 1908 Grand Ave, Nashville, TN 37212 *Tel:* 615-340-7200 *Toll Free Tel:* 800-972-0433 (orders) *Web Site:* books.upperroom.org, pg 88

Fresh Fish Award for Emerging Writers, Haymarket Sq, 223 Duckworth St, St John's, NL A1C 6N1, Canada *Tel:* 709-739-5215 *Toll Free Tel:* 866-739-5215 *E-mail:* wanl@nf.aibn.com *Web Site:* wanl.ca, pg 648

Sarah Jane Freymann Literary Agency LLC, 59 W 71 St, Suite 9-B, New York, NY 10023 *Tel:* 212-362-9277 *E-mail:* submissions@sarahjanefreymann.com *Web Site:* www.sarahjanefreymann.com, pg 518

Fredrica S Friedman & Co Inc, 136 E 57 St, 14th fl, New York, NY 10022 *Tel:* 212-829-9600 *Fax:* 212-829-9669 *E-mail:* info@fredricafriedman.com; submissions@fredricafriedman.com *Web Site:* www.fredricafriedman.com, pg 518

Friends of American Writers Awards, 506 Rose Ave, Des Plaines, IL 60016 *Tel:* 847-827-8339 *Web Site:* www.fawchicago.org, pg 648

Friends United Press, 101 Quaker Hill Dr, Richmond, IN 47374 *Tel:* 765-962-7573 *Fax:* 765-966-1293 *E-mail:* friendspress@fum.org; orders@fum.org *Web Site:* shop.fum.org, pg 89

Fromer Editorial Services, 1606 Noyes Dr, Silver Spring, MD 20910-2224 *Tel:* 301-585-8827, pg 494

Candice Fuhrman Literary Agency, 10 Cypress Hollow Dr, Tiburon, CA 94920 *Tel:* 415-383-1014 *E-mail:* fuhrmancandice@gmail.com, pg 518

Fulbright Scholar Program, 1400 "K" St NW, Washington, DC 20005 *Tel:* 202-686-4000 *E-mail:* scholars@iie.org *Web Site:* www.cies.org; www.iie.org, pg 648

Fulcrum Publishing Inc, 4690 Table Mountain Dr, Suite 100, Golden, CO 80403 *Tel:* 303-277-1623 *Toll Free Tel:* 800-992-2908 *Fax:* 303-279-7111 *Toll Free Fax:* 800-726-7112 *E-mail:* info@fulcrumbooks.com; orders@fulcrumbooks.com *Web Site:* www.fulcrumbooks.com, pg 89

Fun in the Sun Writer's Cruise Conference, PO Box 823414, Pembroke Pines, FL 33082 *E-mail:* frwfuninthesun@yahoo.com *Web Site:* frwfuninthesunmain.blogspot.com/; www.frwriters.org, pg 610

FurnitureCore, 1389 Peachtree St NE, Suite 310, Atlanta, GA 30309 *Tel:* 404-961-3734 *Toll Free Tel:* 800-826-8868 *Fax:* 404-961-3749 *E-mail:* info@furniturecore.com *Web Site:* www.furniturecore.com, pg 89

Future Horizons Inc, 721 W Abram St, Arlington, TX 76013 *Tel:* 817-277-0727 *Toll Free Tel:* 800-489-0727 *Fax:* 817-277-2270 *E-mail:* info@fhautism.com *Web Site:* www.fhautism.com, pg 89

Gabriele Rico Creative Nonfiction Challenge, San Jose State University, English Dept, One Washington Sq, San Jose, CA 95192-0090 *Tel:* 408-924-4441 *Web Site:* www.reedmag.org, pg 648

Gaetan Morin Editeur, 5800, rue St-Denis, bureau 900, Montreal, QC H2S 3L5, Canada *Tel:* 514-273-1066 *Toll Free Tel:* 800-565-5531 *Fax:* 514-276-0324 *Toll Free Fax:* 800-814-0324 *E-mail:* info@cheneliere.ca *Web Site:* www.cheneliere.ca, pg 457

Gagosian Gallery, 980 Madison Ave, New York, NY 10075 *Tel:* 212-744-2313 *Fax:* 212-772-7962 *E-mail:* newyork@gagosian.com *Web Site:* www.gagosian.com, pg 89

Lewis Galantiere Translation Award, 225 Reinekers Lane, Suite 590, Alexandria, VA 22314 *Tel:* 703-683-6100 *Fax:* 703-683-6122 *E-mail:* honors_awards@atanet.org *Web Site:* www.atanet.org, pg 648

Galaxy Press, 7051 Hollywood Blvd, Suite 200, Hollywood, CA 90028 *Tel:* 323-466-7815 *Toll Free Tel:* 877-8GALAXY (842-5299) *E-mail:* info@galaxypress.com; customers@galaxypress.com *Web Site:* www.galaxypress.com, pg 89

Galde Press Inc, PO Box 460, Lakeville, MN 55044 *Tel:* 952-891-5991 *Toll Free Tel:* 800-777-3454 *Web Site:* www.galdepress.com, pg 89

Gale, 27500 Drake Rd, Farmington Hills, MI 48331-3535 *Tel:* 248-699-4253 *Toll Free Tel:* 800-877-4253 *Toll Free Fax:* 800-414-5043 (orders) *E-mail:* gale.customercare@cengage.com *Web Site:* www.gale.com, pg 89

Galen Press Ltd, PO Box 64400-WB, Tucson, AZ 85728-4400 *Tel:* 520-577-8363 *Fax:* 520-529-6459 *E-mail:* sales@galenpress.com *Web Site:* www.galenpress.com, pg 89

Gallaudet University Press, 800 Florida Ave NE, Washington, DC 20002-3695 *Tel:* 202-651-5488 *Fax:* 202-651-5489 *E-mail:* gupress@gallaudet.edu *Web Site:* gupress.gallaudet.edu, pg 89

Gallery Books, 1230 Avenue of the Americas, New York, NY 10020 *Toll Free Tel:* 800-456-6798 *Fax:* 212-698-7284 *E-mail:* consumer.customerservice@simonandschuster.com *Web Site:* www.simonsays.com, pg 90

Diane Gallo, 49 Hilton St, Gilbertsville, NY 13776 *Tel:* 607-783-2386 *Fax:* 607-783-2386 *E-mail:* dgallo@stny.rr.com *Web Site:* www.dianegallo.com, pg 494

Gallopade International Inc, 611 Hwy 74 S, Suite 2000, Peachtree City, GA 30269 *Tel:* 770-631-4222 *Toll Free Tel:* 800-536-2GET (536-2438) *Fax:* 770-631-4810 *Toll Free Fax:* 800-871-2979 *E-mail:* customerservice@gallopade.com *Web Site:* www.gallopade.com, pg 90

Gannon University's High School Poetry Contest, Gannon University, 109 University Sq, Erie, PA 16541 *Tel:* 814-871-7504 *Web Site:* www.gannon.edu/departmental/english/poetry.asp, pg 648

The Garamond Agency Inc, 12 Horton St, Newburyport, MA 01950 *E-mail:* query@garamondagency.com *Web Site:* www.garamondagency.com, pg 518

Gareth Stevens Publishing, 111 E 14 St, Suite 349, New York, NY 10003 *Toll Free Tel:* 800-542-2595 *Toll Free Fax:* 877-542-2596 (cust serv) *E-mail:* customerservice@gspub.com *Web Site:* garethstevens.com, pg 90

Garland Science Publishing, 711 Third Ave, 8th fl, New York, NY 10017 *Tel:* 212-216-7800; 212-281-4487 *Fax:* 212-947-3027 *E-mail:* science@garland.com *Web Site:* www.garlandscience.com, pg 90

Francois-Xavier Garneau Medal, 130 Albert St, Suite 1201, Ottawa, ON K1P 5G4, Canada *Tel:* 613-233-7885 *Fax:* 613-565-5445 *E-mail:* cha-shc@cha-shc.ca *Web Site:* www.cha-shc.ca, pg 648

Max Gartenberg Literary Agency, 912 N Pennsylvania Ave, Yardley, PA 19067 *Tel:* 215-295-9230 *Web Site:* www.maxgartenberg.com, pg 518

Alfred C Gary Memorial, 900 Timber Creek Place, Virginia Beach, VA 23464 *E-mail:* poetryinva@aol.com *Web Site:* poetrysocietyofvirginia.org, pg 648

The Gary-Paul Agency, 1549 Main St, Stratford, CT 06615 *Tel:* 203-345-6167 *Web Site:* www.thegarypaulagency.com; www.nutmegpictures.com, pg 494

John Gassner Memorial Playwriting Award, 215 Knob Hill Dr, Hamden, CT 06518 *Tel:* 617-851-8535 *Fax:* 203-288-5938 *E-mail:* mail@netconline.org *Web Site:* www.netconline.org, pg 648

Gatekeeper Press, 3971 Hoover Rd, Suite 77, Columbus, OH 43123-2839 *Toll Free Tel:* 866-535-0913 *Fax:* 216-803-0350 *E-mail:* info@gatekeeperpress.com *Web Site:* www.gatekeeperpress.com, pg 90

Gateways Books & Tapes, PO Box 370, Nevada City, CA 95959 *Tel:* 530-271-2239 *Toll Free Tel:* 800-869-0658 *Fax:* 530-272-0184 *E-mail:* info@gatewaysbooksandtapes.com *Web Site:* www.gatewaysbooksandtapes.com; www.retrosf.com (Retro Science Fiction imprint), pg 90

Gault Millau Inc/Gayot Publications, 4311 Wilshire Blvd, Suite 405, Los Angeles, CA 90010 *Tel:* 323-965-3529 *Fax:* 323-936-2883 *E-mail:* info@gayot.com *Web Site:* www.gayot.com, pg 90

The Christian Gauss Award, 1606 New Hampshire Ave NW, Washington, DC 20009 *Tel:* 202-265-3808 *Fax:* 202-986-1601 *E-mail:* awards@pbk.org *Web Site:* www.pbk.org/bookawards, pg 649

Gauthier Publications Inc, PO Box 806241, St Clair Shores, MI 48080 *Tel:* 313-458-7141 *Fax:* 586-279-1515 *E-mail:* info@gauthierpublications.com *Web Site:* www.gauthierpublications.com, pg 91

The Gaylactic Spectrum Awards, 1425 "S" St NW, Washington, DC 20009 *Web Site:* www.spectrumawards.org, pg 649

Gaylord College of Journalism & Mass Communication, Professional Writing Program, c/o University of Oklahoma, 395 W Lindsey St, Rm 3534, Norman, OK 73019-0270 *Tel:* 405-325-2721 *Fax:* 405-325-7565 *Web Site:* www.ou.edu/gaylord, pg 620

Fred Gebhart, PO Box 111, Gold Hill, OR 97525 *Tel:* 541-855-8975 *E-mail:* fgebhart@pobox.com *Web Site:* www.fredgebhart.com, pg 494

Gefen Books, c/o Storch, 255 Central Ave, B-206, Lawrence, NY 11559 *Tel:* 516-593-1234 *Toll Free Tel:* 800-477-5257 *Fax:* 516-295-2739 *E-mail:* gefenny@gefenpublishing.com; info@gefenpublishing.com *Web Site:* www.gefenpublishing.com, pg 91

Lionel Gelber Prize, University of Toronto, Munk School of Global Affairs, One Devonshire Place, Toronto, ON M5S 3K7, Canada *Tel:* 416-946-8901 *Fax:* 416-946-8915 *E-mail:* events.munk@utoronto.ca *Web Site:* munkschool.utoronto.ca/gelber; www.facebook.com/GelberPrize, pg 649

Gelfman Schneider/ICM Partners, 850 Seventh Ave, Suite 903, New York, NY 10019 *Tel:* 212-245-1993 *Fax:* 212-245-8678 *E-mail:* mail@gelfmanschneider.com *Web Site:* gelfmanschneider.com, pg 518

Gell: A Finger Lakes Creative Retreat, 740 University Ave, Rochester, NY 14607-1259 *Tel:* 585-473-2590 *Fax:* 585-442-9333 *Web Site:* www.wab.org, pg 610

Gelles-Cole Literary Enterprises, 135 John Joy Rd, Woodstock, NY 12498-0341 *Web Site:* www.literaryenterprises.com, pg 494

Gem Guides Book Co, 1275 W Ninth St, Upland, CA 91786 *Tel:* 626-855-1611 *Toll Free Tel:* 800-824-5118 (orders) *Fax:* 626-855-1610 *E-mail:* info@gemguidesbooks.com *Web Site:* www.gemguidesbooks.com, pg 91

GemStone Press, 4507 Charlotte Ave, Suite 100, Nashville, TN 37209 *Tel:* 615-255-BOOK (255-2665) *Fax:* 615-255-5081 *E-mail:* marketing@turnerpublishing.com *Web Site:* gemstonepress.com; www.turnerpublishing.com, pg 91

Genealogical Publishing Co, 3600 Clipper Mill Rd, Suite 260, Baltimore, MD 21211 *Tel:* 410-837-8271 *Toll Free Tel:* 800-296-6687 *Fax:* 410-752-8492 *Toll Free*

Fax: 800-599-9561 *E-mail:* info@genealogical.com; web@genealogical.com *Web Site:* www.genealogical.com, pg 91

Genesis Press Inc, PO Box 101, Columbus, MS 39701 *Toll Free Tel:* 888-463-4461 (orders only) *E-mail:* customerservice@genesis-press.com *Web Site:* www.genesis-press.com, pg 91

Geological Society of America (GSA), 3300 Penrose Place, Boulder, CO 80301-1806 *Tel:* 303-357-1000 *Fax:* 303-357-1070 *E-mail:* pubs@geosociety.org (prodn); editing@geosociety.org (edit) *Web Site:* www.geosociety.org, pg 91

GeoLytics Inc, 3322 Rte 22, Suite 806, Branchburg, NJ 08876 *Tel:* 908-707-1505 *Toll Free Tel:* 800-577-6717 *Fax:* 908-707-1595 *E-mail:* support@geolytics.com; questions@geolytics.com *Web Site:* www.geolytics.com, pg 91

Georgetown University Press, 3240 Prospect St NW, Suite 250, Washington, DC 20007 *Tel:* 202-687-5889 (busn) *Fax:* 202-687-6340 (edit) *E-mail:* gupress@georgetown.edu *Web Site:* press.georgetown.edu, pg 91

The Gersh Agency (TGA), 41 Madison Ave, 33rd fl, New York, NY 10010 *Tel:* 212-997-1818 *Web Site:* gershbooks.com, pg 518

Leo Gershoy Award, 400 "A" St SE, Washington, DC 20003 *Tel:* 202-544-2422 *Fax:* 202-544-8307 *E-mail:* awards@historians.org *Web Site:* www.historians.org, pg 649

Nancy C Gerth PhD, 1431 Harlan's Trail, Sagle, ID 83860 *Tel:* 208-304-9066 *E-mail:* docnangee@nancygerth.com *Web Site:* www.nancygerth.com, pg 494

Gestalt Journal Press, PO Box 278, Gouldsboro, ME 04607-0278 *Tel:* 207-404-9954 *Fax:* 207-510-4889 *E-mail:* press@gestalt.org *Web Site:* gestalt.org, pg 92

Getty Publications, 1200 Getty Center Dr, Suite 500, Los Angeles, CA 90049-1682 *Tel:* 310-440-7365 *Toll Free Tel:* 800-223-3431 (orders) *Fax:* 310-440-7758 *E-mail:* pubsinfo@getty.edu *Web Site:* www.getty.edu/publications, pg 92

GGP Publishing Inc, 105 Calvert St, Suite 201, Harrison, NY 10528-3138 *Tel:* 914-834-8896 *Fax:* 914-834-7566 *Web Site:* www.GGPPublishing.com, pg 494, 518

GIA Publications Inc, 7404 S Mason Ave, Chicago, IL 60638 *Tel:* 708-496-3800 *Toll Free Tel:* 800-GIA-1358 (442-1358) *Fax:* 708-496-3828 *E-mail:* custserv@giamusic.com *Web Site:* www.giamusic.com, pg 92

Gibbs Smith Publisher, 1877 E Gentile St, Layton, UT 84041 *Tel:* 801-544-9800 *Toll Free Tel:* 800-748-5439; 800-835-4993 (orders) *Fax:* 801-544-5582 *Toll Free Fax:* 800-213-3023 (orders only) *E-mail:* info@gibbs-smith.com; tradeorders@gibbs-smith.com *Web Site:* www.gibbs-smith.com, pg 92

Gifted Education Press, 10201 Yuma Ct, Manassas, VA 20109 *Tel:* 703-369-5017 *Web Site:* www.giftededpress.com, pg 92

Sheri Gilbert, 123 Van Voorhis Ave, Rochester, NY 14617 *Tel:* 585-342-0331 *E-mail:* shergilb@aol.com *Web Site:* www.permissionseditor.com, pg 495

Gilder Lehrman Lincoln Prize, 300 N Washington St, Campus Box 413, Gettysburg, PA 17325 *Tel:* 717-337-8255 *E-mail:* lincolnprize@gettysburg.edu *Web Site:* www.gilderlehrman.org, pg 649

Giller Prize, 543 Logan Ave, Toronto, ON M4K 3B6, Canada *Web Site:* www.scotiabankgillerprize.ca, pg 649

Gingko Press Inc, 1321 Fifth St, Berkeley, CA 94710 *Tel:* 510-898-1195 *Fax:* 510-898-1196 *E-mail:* books@gingkopress.com *Web Site:* www.gingkopress.com, pg 92

Allen Ginsberg Poetry Award, One College Blvd, Paterson, NJ 07505-1179 *Tel:* 973-684-6555 *Fax:* 973-523-6085 *Web Site:* www.poetrycenterpccc.com, pg 649

Gival Press, 5200 N First St, Arlington, VA 22203 *Tel:* 703-351-0079 *Fax:* 703-351-0079 (call first) *E-mail:* givalpress@yahoo.com *Web Site:* www.givalpress.com, pg 92

Gival Press Novel Award, PO Box 3812, Arlington, VA 22203 *Tel:* 703-351-0079 *Fax:* 703-351-0079 (call first) *E-mail:* givalpress@yahoo.com *Web Site:* www.givalpress.com; givalpress.submittable.com, pg 649

Gival Press Oscar Wilde Award, PO Box 3812, Arlington, VA 22203 *Tel:* 703-351-0079 *Fax:* 703-351-0079 (call first) *E-mail:* givalpress@yahoo.com *Web Site:* www.givalpress.com; givalpress.submittable.com, pg 649

Gival Press Poetry Award, PO Box 3812, Arlington, VA 22203 *Tel:* 703-351-0079 *Fax:* 703-351-0079 (call first) *E-mail:* givalpress@yahoo.com *Web Site:* www.givalpress.com; givalpress.submittable.com, pg 649

Gival Press Short Story Award, PO Box 3812, Arlington, VA 22203 *Tel:* 703-351-0079 *Fax:* 703-351-0079 (call first) *E-mail:* givalpress@yahoo.com *Web Site:* www.givalpress.com; givalpress.submittable.com, pg 649

John Glassco Translation Prize, Concordia University, LB 601, 1455 De Maisonneuve W, Montreal, QC H3G 1M8, Canada *Tel:* 514-848-2424 (ext 8702) *E-mail:* info@attlc-ltac.org *Web Site:* www.attlc-ltac.org, pg 649

GLCA New Writers Awards, 535 W William St, Suite 301, Ann Arbor, MI 48103 *Tel:* 734-661-2350 *Fax:* 734-661-2349 *Web Site:* www.glca.org, pg 649

Susan Gleason, 325 Riverside Dr, Suite 41, New York, NY 10025 *Tel:* 212-662-3876 *Fax:* 212-864-3298 *E-mail:* sgleasonliteraryagent@gmail.com, pg 519

The Danuta Gleed Literary Award, 600-460 Richmond St W, Toronto, ON M5V 1Y1, Canada *Tel:* 416-703-8982 *Fax:* 416-504-9090 *E-mail:* info@writersunion.ca *Web Site:* www.writersunion.ca, pg 650

The Glen Workshop, 3307 Third Ave W, Seattle, WA 98119 *Tel:* 206-281-2988 *Fax:* 206-281-2979 *E-mail:* glenworkshop@imagejournal.org *Web Site:* www.imagejournal.org, pg 611

Glenbridge Publishing Ltd, 19923 E Long Ave, Centennial, CO 80016-1969 *Tel:* 720-870-8381 *Toll Free Tel:* 800-986-4135 (orders) *Fax:* 720-230-1209 *E-mail:* glenbridge10@gmail.com *Web Site:* www.glenbridgepublishing.com, pg 93

Peter Glenn Publications, 306 NE Second St, 2nd fl, Delray Beach, FL 33483 *Tel:* 561-404-4290 *Fax:* 561-892-5786 *Web Site:* pgdirect.com, pg 93

Glimmer Train Press Inc, PO Box 80430, Portland, OR 97280-1430 *Tel:* 503-221-0836 *Fax:* 503-221-0837 *E-mail:* editors@glimmertrain.org *Web Site:* www.glimmertrain.org, pg 93

Glitterati Inc, 630 Ninth Ave, Suite 603, New York, NY 10036 *Tel:* 212-362-9119 *Fax:* 646-607-4433 *E-mail:* info@glitteratiincorporated.com *Web Site:* glitteratiincorporated.com, pg 93

Global Authors Publications (GAP), 38 Bluegrass, Middleberg, FL 32068 *Tel:* 904-425-1608 *E-mail:* gapbook@yahoo.com *Web Site:* www.globalauthorspublications.com, pg 93

Global Lion Intellectual Property Management Inc, PO Box 669238, Pompano Beach, FL 33066 *Tel:* 754-222-6948 *Fax:* 754-222-6948 *E-mail:* queriesgloballionmgt@gmail.com *Web Site:* www.globallionmanagement.com, pg 519

Global Publishing, Sales & Distribution, 980 Lincoln Ave, Suite 200 B, San Rafael, CA 94901 *Tel:* 415-456-2934 *Fax:* 415-456-4124 *Web Site:* www.globalpsd.com, pg 93

Global Training Center Inc, 550 S Mesa Hills Dr, Suite E4, El Paso, TX 79912 *Tel:* 915-534-7900 *Toll Free Tel:* 800-860-5030 *Fax:* 915-534-7903 *E-mail:* contact@globaltrainingcenter.com *Web Site:* www.globaltrainingcenter.com, pg 93

The Globe Pequot Press, 246 Goose Lane, Guilford, CT 06437 *Tel:* 203-458-4500 *Toll Free Tel:* 800-243-0495 (orders only); 888-249-7586 (cust serv) *Fax:* 203-458-4601 *Toll Free Fax:* 800-820-2329 (orders & cust serv) *E-mail:* editorial@globepequot.com; info@rowman.com; orders@rowman.com *Web Site:* rowman.com, pg 93

Globo Libros Literary Agency, 450 E 63 St, New York, NY 10065 *Web Site:* www.globo-libros.com; www.publishersmarketplace.com/members/dstockwell, pg 519

The Goddard Riverside Stephan Russo Book Prize, 593 Columbus Ave, New York, NY 10024 *Web Site:* bookprize.goddard.org, pg 650

David R Godine Publisher Inc, 15 Court Sq, Suite 320, Boston, MA 02108-4715 *Tel:* 617-451-9600 *Fax:* 617-350-0250 *E-mail:* info@godine.com *Web Site:* www.godine.com, pg 93

Gold Leaf Press, 3670 Morrissey Ave, Warren, MI 48091 *Tel:* 313-331-3571 *Web Site:* www.goldleafpress.com, pg 495

Gold Medal, 633 W 155 St, New York, NY 10032 *Tel:* 212-368-5900 *Fax:* 212-491-4615 *E-mail:* academy@artsandletters.org *Web Site:* www.artsandletters.org, pg 650

Golden Cylindar Awards, 8281 Pine Lake Rd, Denver, NC 28037 *Tel:* 201-523-6042 *Fax:* 201-523-6048 *E-mail:* gaa@gaa.org *Web Site:* www.gaa.org, pg 650

Golden Kite Awards, 4727 Wilshire Blvd, Suite 301, Los Angeles, CA 90010 *Tel:* 323-782-1010; 310-403-0675 (cell) *Fax:* 323-782-1892 *E-mail:* grants@scbwi.org; scbwi@scbwi.org *Web Site:* www.scbwi.org, pg 650

Golden Meteorite Press, 11919 82 St NW, Suite 103, Edmonton, AB T5B 2W4, Canada *Tel:* 780-378-0063 *Fax:* 780-378-0063, pg 458

Golden Rose Award, 46 Wallace St, Somerville, MA 02144 *Tel:* 617-744-6034 *E-mail:* info@nepoetryclub.org *Web Site:* www.nepoetryclub.org, pg 650

Golden West Cookbooks, 5738 N Central Ave, Phoenix, AZ 85012-1316 *Tel:* 602-234-1574 *Toll Free Tel:* 800-521-9221 *Fax:* 602-234-3062 *E-mail:* info@americantravelerpress.com *Web Site:* www.americantravelerpress.com, pg 94

Goldfarb & Associates, 721 Gibbon St, Alexandria, VA 22314 *Tel:* 202-466-3030 *Fax:* 703-836-5644 *E-mail:* rlglawlit@gmail.com *Web Site:* www.ronaldgoldfarb.com, pg 519

Frances Goldin Literary Agency, Inc, 214 W 29 St, Suite 410, New York, NY 10001 *Tel:* 212-777-0047 *Fax:* 212-228-1660 *E-mail:* agency@goldinlit.com *Web Site:* www.goldinlit.com, pg 519

Donald Goldstein, 1500 E 17 St, Brooklyn, NY 11230 *Tel:* 718-375-9346 *E-mail:* dgoldsbkyn@aol.com, pg 495

Laurence Goldstein Poetry Prize, University of Michigan, 0576 Rackham Bldg, 915 E Washington St, Ann Arbor, MI 48109-1070 *Tel:* 734-764-9265 *E-mail:* mqr@umich.edu *Web Site:* www.umich.edu/~mqr, pg 650

Gollehon Press Inc, 3655 Glenn Dr SE, Grand Rapids, MI 49546 *Tel:* 616-949-3515 *Fax:* 616-949-8674 *E-mail:* sales@gollehonbooks.com; editorial@gollehonbooks.com *Web Site:* www.gollehonbooks.com, pg 94

Goodheart-Willcox Publisher, 18604 W Creek Dr, Tinley Park, IL 60477-6243 *Tel:* 708-687-5000 *Toll Free Tel:* 800-323-0440 *Fax:* 708-468-8692 *Toll Free Fax:* 888-409-3900 *E-mail:* custserv@g-w.com; orders@g-w.com *Web Site:* www.g-w.com, pg 94

Goodman Associates, 500 West End Ave, New York, NY 10024 *Tel:* 212-873-4806, pg 519

Irene Goodman Literary Agency, 27 W 24 St, Suite 700B, New York, NY 10010 *Tel:* 212-604-0330 *E-mail:* queries@irenegoodman.com *Web Site:* www.irenegoodman.com, pg 519

Robert M Goodman, 140 West End Ave, Unit 11-J, New York, NY 10023 *Tel:* 917-439-1097 *E-mail:* bobbybgood@gmail.com, pg 495

Goodreads Choice Awards, 188 Spear St, 3rd fl, San Francisco, CA 94105 *E-mail:* press@goodreads.com *Web Site:* www.goodreads.com/award, pg 650

Goose Lane Editions, 500 Beaverbrook Ct, Suite 330, Fredericton, NB E3B 5X4, Canada *Tel:* 506-450-4251 *Toll Free Tel:* 888-926-8377 *Fax:* 506-459-4991 *E-mail:* info@gooselane.com; customerservice@gooselane.com *Web Site:* www.gooselane.com, pg 458

Goose River Press, 3400 Friendship Rd, Waldoboro, ME 04572-6337 *Tel:* 207-832-6665 *E-mail:* gooseriverpress@roadrunner.com *Web Site:* gooseriverpress.com, pg 94

Goosebottom Books, 543 Trinidad Lane, Foster City, CA 94404 *Tel:* 650-556-3782 *Toll Free Fax:* 888-407-5286 *E-mail:* info@goosebottombooks.com *Web Site:* goosebottombooks.com, pg 94

P M Gordon Associates Inc, 2115 Wallace St, Philadelphia, PA 19130 *Tel:* 215-769-2525 *E-mail:* pmga@pond1.net *Web Site:* www.pmgordonassociates.com, pg 495

Gorgias Press LLC, PO Box 6939, Piscataway, NJ 08854-6939 *Tel:* 732-885-8900 *Fax:* 732-885-8908 *E-mail:* helpdesk@gorgiaspress.com *Web Site:* www.gorgiaspress.com, pg 94

Gospel Publishing House (GPH), 1445 Boonville Ave, Springfield, MO 65802 *Tel:* 417-862-2781; 417-831-8000 (outside US) *Toll Free Tel:* 800-641-4310 *Fax:* 417-863-1874; 417-862-5881 *Toll Free Fax:* 800-328-0294 *E-mail:* custsrvreps@ag.org *Web Site:* www.gospelpublishing.com, pg 94

Gotham Writers' Workshop, 555 Eighth Ave, Suite 1402, New York, NY 10018-4358 *Tel:* 212-974-8377 *E-mail:* contact@gothamwriters.com *Web Site:* www.gothamwriters.com, pg 611

Sherry Gottlieb, 4900 Dunes St, Oxnard, CA 93035 *Tel:* 805-382-3425 *E-mail:* writer@wordservices.com *Web Site:* www.wordservices.com, pg 495

Governor General's Literary Awards, 150 Elgin St, Ottawa, ON K1P 1L4, Canada *Tel:* 613-566-4414 *Toll Free Tel:* 800-263-5588 (CN only) *Fax:* 613-566-4390 *E-mail:* info@canadacouncil.ca *Web Site:* canadacouncil.ca/en/council/prizes, pg 650

The Gracies®, 2365 Harrodsburg Rd, Suite A325, Lexington, KY 40504 *Tel:* 202-750-3664 *Fax:* 202-750-3664 *E-mail:* info@allwomeninmedia.org *Web Site:* allwomeninmedia.org, pg 650

Doug Grad Literary Agency Inc, 68 Jay St, Suite W11, Brooklyn, NY 11201-1189 *Tel:* 718-788-6067 *E-mail:* query@dgliterary.com *Web Site:* www.dgliterary.com, pg 519

The Graduate Group/Booksellers, 86 Norwood Rd, West Hartford, CT 06117-2236 *Tel:* 860-233-2330 *E-mail:* graduategroup@hotmail.com *Web Site:* www.graduategroup.com, pg 94

Graham Agency, 115 W 45 St, Suite 505, New York, NY 10036 *Tel:* 212-489-7730, pg 519

Grand & Archer Publishing, 611 S Palm Canyon Dr, Suite 7451, Palm Springs, CA 92264 *Tel:* 323-493-2785 *E-mail:* grandandarcher@gmail.com, pg 94

Grand Central Publishing, 1290 Avenue of the Americas, New York, NY 10019 *Tel:* 212-364-1100 *Web Site:* www.hachettebookgroup.com, pg 95

Granite Peak Publications, 5131 NE 201 Place, Lake Forest Park, WA 98155 *Tel:* 206-417-2861 *E-mail:* publicity@yellowstonetreasures.com *Web Site:* www.yellowstonetreasures.com, pg 478

Donald M Grant Publisher Inc, PO Box 187, Hampton Falls, NH 03844-0187 *Tel:* 603-778-7191 *Fax:* 603-778-7191 *E-mail:* office@grantbooks.com *Web Site:* secure.grantbooks.com, pg 95

Grants for Literary Artists, 225 King St, Suite 201, Fredericton, NB E3B 1E1, Canada *Tel:* 506-444-4444 *Toll Free Tel:* 866-460-ARTS (460-2787) *Fax:* 506-444-5543 *Web Site:* www.artsnb.ca, pg 650

The Graphic Artists Guild Inc, 31 W 34 St, 8th fl, New York, NY 10001 *Tel:* 212-791-3400 *Fax:* 212-791-0333 *E-mail:* admin@graphicartistsguild.org; membership@graphicartistsguild.org *Web Site:* www.graphicartistsguild.org, pg 566, 620

Graphic Arts Association, 1210 Northbrook Dr, Suite 200, Trevose, PA 19053 *Tel:* 215-396-2300 *Fax:* 215-396-9890 *E-mail:* gaa@gaaonline.org *Web Site:* www.gaa1900.com; www.graphicartsassociation.org, pg 620

Graphic Arts Books, 7820 NE Holman St, Suite B-9, Portland, OR 97218 *Tel:* 503-254-5591 *Fax:* 503-254-5609 *E-mail:* info-ga@graphicartsbooks.com *Web Site:* www.graphicartsbooks.com, pg 95

Graphic Arts Education & Research Foundation (GAERF), 1899 Preston White Dr, Reston, VA 20191 *Tel:* 703-264-7200 *Toll Free Tel:* 844-381-9839 *Fax:* 703-620-3165 *E-mail:* gaerf@npes.org *Web Site:* www.gaerf.org, pg 583

Graphic Arts Show Company (GASC), 1899 Preston White Dr, Reston, VA 20191 *Tel:* 703-264-7200 *Fax:* 703-620-9187 *E-mail:* info@gasc.org *Web Site:* www.gasc.org, pg 566

Graphic Universe™, 241 First Ave N, Minneapolis, MN 55401 *Tel:* 612-332-3344 *Toll Free Tel:* 800-328-4929 *Fax:* 612-332-7615 *Toll Free Fax:* 800-332-1132 *E-mail:* info@lernerbooks.com; custserve@lernerbooks.com *Web Site:* www.lernerbooks.com; www.facebook.com/lernerbooks, pg 95

Graphic World Publishing Services, 11687 Adie Rd, St Louis, MO 63043 *Tel:* 314-567-9854 *Fax:* 314-567-7178 *E-mail:* quote@gwinc.com *Web Site:* www.gwinc.com, pg 495

Gravure Association of the Americas Inc, 8281 Pine Lake Rd, Denver, NC 28037 *Tel:* 201-523-6042 *Fax:* 201-523-6048 *E-mail:* gaa@gaa.org *Web Site:* www.gaa.org, pg 566

Gray & Company Publishers, 1588 E 40 St, Suite 3A, Cleveland, OH 44103 *Tel:* 216-431-2665 *Toll Free Tel:* 800-915-3609 *E-mail:* sales@grayco.com; editorial@grayco.com; support@grayco.com; publicity@grayco.com *Web Site:* www.grayco.com, pg 95

James H Gray Award for Short Nonfiction, 11759 Groat Rd, Edmonton, AB T5M 3K6, Canada *Tel:* 780-422-8174 *Toll Free Tel:* 800-665-5354 (AB only) *Fax:* 780-422-2663 (attn WGA) *E-mail:* mail@writersguild.ca *Web Site:* writersguild.ca, pg 650

Graywolf Press, 250 Third Ave N, Suite 600, Minneapolis, MN 55401 *Tel:* 651-641-0077 *Fax:* 651-641-0036 *E-mail:* wolves@graywolfpress.org (no ms queries, sample chapters or proposals) *Web Site:* www.graywolfpress.org, pg 95

Graywolf Press Nonfiction Prize, 250 Third Ave N, Suite 600, Minneapolis, MN 55401 *Tel:* 651-641-0077 *Fax:* 651-641-0036 *E-mail:* wolves@graywolfpress.org (no ms queries, sample chapters or proposals) *Web Site:* www.graywolfpress.org/graywolf-press-nonfiction-prize, pg 651

Great Lakes Graphics Association, W232 N2950 Roundy Circle E, Pewaukee, WI 53072 *Tel:* 262-522-2210 *Toll Free Tel:* 855-522-2210 *Fax:* 262-522-2211 *E-mail:* admin@piw.org *Web Site:* www.piw.org, pg 566

Great Potential Press Inc, 1650 N Kolb Rd, Suite 200, Tucson, AZ 85715 *Tel:* 520-777-6161 *Fax:* 520-777-6217 *Web Site:* www.greatpotentialpress.com, pg 95

Great Quotations Inc, 1410 Brook Dr, Downers Grove, IL 60515 *Tel:* 630-985-2628 *Toll Free Tel:* 800-830-3020 *Fax:* 630-985-2610 *E-mail:* info@greatquotationsinc.com *Web Site:* www.greatquotationsinc.com, pg 96

Greater Talent Network Inc, 437 Fifth Ave, New York, NY 10016 *Tel:* 212-645-4200 *Toll Free Tel:* 800-326-4211 *Fax:* 212-627-1471 *E-mail:* info@greatertalent.com *Web Site:* www.greatertalent.com, pg 547

Green Dragon Books, 2875 S Ocean Blvd, Suite 200, Palm Beach, FL 33480 *Tel:* 561-533-6231 *Toll Free Tel:* 800-874-8844 *Fax:* 561-533-6233 *Toll Free Fax:* 888-874-8844 *E-mail:* info@greendragonbooks.com *Web Site:* greendragonbooks.com, pg 96

Green Integer, 6210 Wilshire Blvd, Suite 211, Los Angeles, CA 90048 *Tel:* 323-857-1115 *Fax:* 323-857-0143 *Web Site:* www.greeninteger.com, pg 96

The Green Rose Prize in Poetry, c/o Western Michigan University, 1903 W Michigan Ave, Kalamazoo, MI 49008-5463 *Tel:* 269-387-8185 *E-mail:* new-issues@wmich.edu *Web Site:* www.wmich.edu/newissues/sub-guide.html, pg 651

Sanford J Greenburger Associates Inc, 55 Fifth Ave, New York, NY 10003 *Tel:* 212-206-5600 *Fax:* 212-463-8718 *Web Site:* greenburger.com; www.sjga.com, pg 520

Greenhaven Press®, 29 E 21 St, New York, NY 10010 *Toll Free Tel:* 800-237-9932 *Toll Free Fax:* 888-436-4643 *Web Site:* www.rosenpublishing.com, pg 96

Paul Greenland Communications Inc, 9184 Longfellow Lane, Machesney Park, IL 61115 *Tel:* 815-240-4108 *Toll Free Tel:* 888-798-7786 *Web Site:* www.paulgreenland.com, pg 495

Greenleaf Book Group LLC, 3 Park Place, 4005 Banister Lane, Suite B, Austin, TX 78704 *Tel:* 512-891-6100 *Fax:* 512-891-6150 *E-mail:* contact@greenleafbookgroup.com *Web Site:* www.greenleafbookgroup.com, pg 96

Greenwood Research Books & Software, PO Box 12102, Wichita, KS 67277-2102 *Tel:* 316-272-2937 *Web Site:* greenray4ever.com (ordering), pg 96

Bess Gresham Memorial, 900 Timber Creek Place, Virginia Beach, VA 23464 *E-mail:* poetryinva@aol.com *Web Site:* poetrysocietyofvirginia.org, pg 651

Rosemary F Gretton, 1029 El Capitan Dr, Danville, CA 94526 *Tel:* 925-336-0003 *Fax:* 925-336-0003 *E-mail:* rgretton@lyricism.ca *Web Site:* www.lyricism.ca, pg 495

Grey House Publishing Inc™, 4919 Rte 22, Amenia, NY 12501 *Tel:* 518-789-8700 *Toll Free Tel:* 800-562-2139 *Fax:* 518-789-0556 *E-mail:* books@greyhouse.com; customerservice@greyhouse.com *Web Site:* www.greyhouse.com, pg 96

Greystone Books Ltd, 343 Railway St, Suite 201, Vancouver, BC V6A 1A4, Canada *Tel:* 604-875-1550 *Fax:* 604-875-1556 *E-mail:* info@greystonebooks.com *Web Site:* www.greystonebooks.com, pg 458

Joan K Griffitts Indexing, 3909 W 71 St, Indianapolis, IN 46268-2257 *Tel:* 317-297-7312 *E-mail:* jkgriffitts@gmail.com *Web Site:* www.joankgriffittsindexing.com, pg 495

Jill Grinberg Literary Management LLC, 392 Vanderbilt Ave, Brooklyn, NY 11238 *Tel:* 212-620-5883 *E-mail:* info@jillgrinbergliterary.com *Web Site:* www.jillgrinbergliterary.com, pg 520

Jill Grosjean Literary Agency, 1390 Millstone Rd, Sag Harbor, NY 11963 *Tel:* 631-725-7419 *Fax:* 631-725-8632 *E-mail:* JillLit310@aol.com, pg 520

Laura Gross Literary Agency Ltd, PO Box 610326, Newton Highlands, MA 02461 *Tel:* 617-964-2977 *Fax:* 617-964-3023 *E-mail:* query@lg-la.com *Web Site:* www.lg-la.com, pg 520

Grosset & Dunlap, 345 Hudson St, New York, NY 10014 *Tel:* 212-366-2000 *Web Site:* www.penguinrandomhouse.com, pg 96

Groundwood Books, 128 Sterling Rd, Lower Level, Toronto, ON M6R 2B7, Canada *Tel:* 416-363-4343 *Fax:* 416-363-1017 *E-mail:* genmail@groundwoodbooks.com *Web Site:* www.houseofanansi.com, pg 458

Group Publishing Inc, 1515 Cascade Ave, Loveland, CO 80538 *Tel:* 970-669-3836 *Toll Free Tel:* 800-447-1070 *E-mail:* puorgbus@group.com (submissions) *Web Site:* www.group.com, pg 96

Groupe Educalivres Inc, 955, rue Bergar, Laval, QC H7L 4Z6, Canada *Tel:* 514-334-8466 *Toll Free Tel:* 800-567-3671 (info serv) *Fax:* 514-334-8387 *E-mail:* infoservice@grandduc.com *Web Site:* www.educalivres.com, pg 458

Groupe Modulo, c/o TC Media Books Inc, 5800 St Denis St, Suite 900, Montreal, QC H2S 3L5, Canada *Tel:* 514-273-1066 *Toll Free Tel:* 800-565-5531 *Fax:* 514-276-0234 *Toll Free Fax:* 800-814-0324 *Web Site:* www.groupemodulo.com, pg 458

Groupe Sogides Inc, 955 rue Amherst, Montreal, QC H2L 3K4, Canada *Tel:* 514-523-1182 *Fax:* 514-597-0370 *Web Site:* www.sogides.com, pg 458

Grove Atlantic Inc, 154 W 14 St, 12th fl, New York, NY 10011 *Tel:* 212-614-7850 *Toll Free Tel:* 800-521-0178 *Fax:* 212-614-7886 *E-mail:* info@groveatlantic.com; sales@groveatlantic.com; publicity@groveatlantic.com; rights@groveatlantic.com *Web Site:* www.groveatlantic.com, pg 97

Gryphon Editions, PO Box 241823, Omaha, NE 68124 *Tel:* 402-298-5385 (intl) *Toll Free Tel:* 888-655-0134 (US & CN) *E-mail:* customerservice@gryphoneditions.com *Web Site:* www.gryphoneditions.com, pg 97

Gryphon House Inc, 6848 Leon's Way, Lewisville, NC 27023 *Toll Free Tel:* 800-638-0928 *Toll Free Fax:* 877-638-7576 *E-mail:* info@ghbooks.com *Web Site:* www.gryphonhouse.com, pg 97

Carol Guenzi Agents Inc, 865 Delaware St, Denver, CO 80204 *Tel:* 303-820-2599 *Toll Free Tel:* 800-417-5120 *Fax:* 303-820-2598 *E-mail:* art@artagent.com *Web Site:* www.artagent.com, pg 543

Guerin Editeur Ltee, 800, Blvd Industriel, bureau 200, St-Jean-sur-Richelieu, QC J3B 8G4, Canada *Tel:* 514-842-3481 *Fax:* 514-842-4923 *Web Site:* www.guerin-editeur.qc.ca, pg 459

Guernica Editions Inc, 1569 Heritage Way, Oakville, ON L6M 2Z7, Canada *Tel:* 905-599-5304 *E-mail:* info@guernicaeditions.com *Web Site:* www.guernicaeditions.com, pg 459

Guggenheim Fellowships, 90 Park Ave, New York, NY 10016 *Tel:* 212-687-4470 *Fax:* 212-697-3248 *E-mail:* fellowships@gf.org *Web Site:* www.gf.org/about/fellowship, pg 651

John Simon Guggenheim Memorial Foundation, 90 Park Ave, New York, NY 10016 *Tel:* 212-687-4470 *Fax:* 212-697-3248 *E-mail:* fellowships@gf.org *Web Site:* www.gf.org, pg 583

Guggenheim-Lehrman Prize in Military History, 25 W 53 St, New York, NY 10019 *Tel:* 646-428-0971 *Fax:* 646-428-0981 *E-mail:* info@hfg.org *Web Site:* www.hfg.org/prize/main.htm, pg 651

Guideposts Book & Inspirational Media, 16 E 34 St, 12th fl, New York, NY 10016 *Tel:* 212-251-8100 *Toll Free Tel:* 800-431-2344 (cust serv) *Fax:* 212-684-0689 *E-mail:* gpsprod@cdsfulfillment.com *Web Site:* guideposts.org, pg 97

Guild of Book Workers, 521 Fifth Ave, New York, NY 10175 *Tel:* 212-292-4444 *E-mail:* communications@guildofbookworkers.org *Web Site:* www.guildofbookworkers.org, pg 566

The Guilford Press, 370 Seventh Ave, Suite 1200, New York, NY 10001-1020 *Tel:* 212-431-9800 *Toll Free Tel:* 800-365-7006 *Fax:* 212-966-6708 *E-mail:* info@guilford.com *Web Site:* www.guilford.com, pg 97

Gulf Publishing Co, 2 Greenway Plaza, Suite 1020, Houston, TX 77046 *Tel:* 713-529-4301 *Fax:* 713-520-4433 *E-mail:* store@gulfpub.com; customerservice@gulfpub.com *Web Site:* www.gulfpub.com, pg 98

The Charlotte Gusay Literary Agency, 10532 Blythe Ave, Los Angeles, CA 90064 *Tel:* 310-559-0831 *Fax:* 310-559-2639 *E-mail:* gusay1@ca.rr.com (queries only) *Web Site:* www.gusay.com, pg 520, 543

GWA: The Association for Garden Communicators, 355 Lexington Ave, 15th fl, New York, NY 10017 *Tel:* 806-832-1870 *Fax:* 806-832-5244 *E-mail:* info@gardenwriters.org *Web Site:* www.gardenwriters.org, pg 566

Hachai Publishing, 527 Empire Blvd, Brooklyn, NY 11225 *Tel:* 718-633-0100 *Fax:* 718-633-0103 *E-mail:* info@hachai.com *Web Site:* www.hachai.com, pg 98

Hachette Audio, 1290 Avenue of the Americas, New York, NY 10019 *Tel:* 212-364-1100 *Web Site:* www.hachetteaudio.com, pg 98

Hachette Book Group, 1290 Avenue of the Americas, New York, NY 10019 *Tel:* 212-364-1100 *Toll Free Tel:* 800-759-0190 (cust serv) *Fax:* 212-364-0933 (intl orders) *Toll Free Fax:* 800-286-9471 (cust serv) *Web Site:* www.hachettebookgroup.com, pg 98

Hachette Books, 1290 Avenue of the Americas, New York, NY 10019 *Tel:* 212-364-1100 *Web Site:* www.hachettebookgroup.com, pg 98

Hachette Nashville, 12 Cadillac Dr, Suite 480, Brentwood, TN 37027 *Tel:* 615-221-0996 *Fax:* 615-221-0962 *Web Site:* www.hachettebookgroup.com, pg 98

Hackett Publishing Co Inc, 3333 Massachusetts Ave, Indianapolis, IN 46218 *Tel:* 317-635-9250 (orders & cust serv); 617-497-6303 (edit off & sales) *Fax:* 317-635-9292; 617-661-8703 (edit off) *Toll Free Fax:* 800-783-9213 *E-mail:* customer@hackettpublishing.com; editorial@hackettpublishing.com *Web Site:* www.hackettpublishing.com, pg 98

Hackmatack Children's Choice Book Award, PO Box 1047, Ottawa, NS K1P 5V8, Canada *Tel:* 902-424-3774 *Fax:* 902-424-0613 *E-mail:* hackmatack@hackmatack.ca *Web Site:* www.hackmatack.ca, pg 651

Hackney Literary Awards, 4650 Old Looney Mill Rd, Birmingham, AL 35243 *E-mail:* info@hackneyliteraryawards.org *Web Site:* www.hackneyliteraryawards.org, pg 651

Lisa Hagan Literary, 110 Martin Dr, Bracey, VA 23919 *Tel:* 434-636-4138 *E-mail:* LisaHaganLiterary@yahoo.com *Web Site:* www.publishersmarketplace.com/members/LisaHagan/, pg 520

Hagstrom Map, 1800 Lovering Ave, Wilmington, DE 19806 *Toll Free Tel:* 800-432-MAPS (432-6277) *Toll Free Fax:* 888-210-9654, pg 99

Haights Cross Communications®, 136 Madison Ave, 8th fl, New York, NY 10016 *Tel:* 212-209-0500 *E-mail:* info@haightscross.com *Web Site:* www.haightscross.com, pg 99

Hal Leonard Books, 33 Plymouth St, Suite 302, Montclair, NJ 07042 *Toll Free Tel:* 800-637-2852 *E-mail:* info@halleonardbooks.com; custserv@halleonardbooks.com *Web Site:* www.halleonardbooks.com, pg 99

Hal Leonard Corp, 7777 W Bluemound Rd, Milwaukee, WI 53213 *Tel:* 414-774-3630 *Fax:* 414-774-3259 *E-mail:* halinfo@halleonard.com; info@halleonard.com *Web Site:* www.halleonard.com, pg 99

Sarah Josepha Hale Award, 58 N Main, Newport, NH 03773 *Tel:* 603-863-3430 *E-mail:* rfl@newport.lib.nh.us *Web Site:* www.newport.lib.nh.us, pg 651

Loretta Dunn Hall Memorial, 900 Timber Creek Place, Virginia Beach, VA 23464 *E-mail:* poetryinva@aol.com *Web Site:* poetrysocietyofvirginia.org, pg 651

Hamilton Books, 4501 Forbes Blvd, Suite 200, Lanham, MD 20706 *Tel:* 301-459-3366 *Toll Free Tel:* 800-462-6420 (cust serv) *Fax:* 301-429-5748 *Toll Free Fax:* 800-388-4550 (cust serv), pg 99

Hamilton College, English/Creative Writing, English/Creative Writing Dept, 198 College Hill Rd, Clinton, NY 13323 *Tel:* 315-859-4370 *Fax:* 315-859-4390 *Web Site:* www.hamilton.edu, pg 620

Hamilton Stone Editions, PO Box 43, Maplewood, NJ 07040 *Tel:* 973-378-8361 *E-mail:* hstone@hamiltonstone.org *Web Site:* www.hamiltonstone.org, pg 99

Hampton Press Inc, 307 Seventh Ave, Suite 506, New York, NY 10001 *Tel:* 646-638-3800 *Toll Free Tel:* 800-894-8955 *Fax:* 646-638-3802 *E-mail:* hamptonpr1@aol.com *Web Site:* www.hamptonpress.com, pg 100

Hampton Roads Publishing Co, 65 Parker St, Suite 7, Newburyport, MA 01950-4600 *Tel:* 978-465-0504 *Toll Free Tel:* 800-423-7087 (orders) *Fax:* 978-465-0243 *Toll Free Fax:* 877-337-3309 *E-mail:* orders@rwwbooks.com *Web Site:* redwheelweiser.com, pg 100

Hancock House Publishers, 4550 Birch Bay Lynden Rd, Suite 104, Blaine, WA 98230-9436 *Tel:* 604-538-1114 *Toll Free Tel:* 800-938-1114 *Fax:* 604-538-2262 *Toll Free Fax:* 800-983-2262 *E-mail:* sales@hancockhouse.com *Web Site:* www.hancockhouse.com, pg 100

Hancock House Publishers Ltd, 19313 Zero Ave, Surrey, BC V3S 9R9, Canada *Tel:* 604-538-1114 *Toll Free Tel:* 800-938-1114 *Fax:* 604-538-2262 *Toll Free Fax:* 800-983-2262 *E-mail:* sales@hancockhouse.com; info@hancockhouse.com *Web Site:* www.hancockhouse.com, pg 459

Handprint Books Inc, 413 Sixth Ave, Brooklyn, NY 11215-3310 *Tel:* 718-768-3696 *Toll Free Tel:* 800-722-6657 (orders) *Fax:* 718-369-0844 *Toll Free Fax:* 800-858-7787 (orders) *E-mail:* info@handprintbooks.com *Web Site:* www.handprintbooks.com, pg 100

Handy Andy Prize, 900 Timber Creek Place, Virginia Beach, VA 23464 *E-mail:* poetryinva@aol.com *Web Site:* poetrysocietyofvirginia.org, pg 651

Hanging Loose Press, 231 Wyckoff St, Brooklyn, NY 11217 *Tel:* 347-529-4738 *Fax:* 347-227-8215 *E-mail:* print225@aol.com *Web Site:* www.hangingloosepress.com, pg 100

Hannacroix Creek Books Inc, 1127 High Ridge Rd, No 110-B, Stamford, CT 06905-1203 *Tel:* 203-968-8098 *Web Site:* www.hannacroixcreekbooks.com, pg 100

Hanser Publications LLC, 6915 Valley Ave, Cincinnati, OH 45244-3029 *Toll Free Tel:* 800-950-8977; 877-751-5052 (orders) *Fax:* 513-527-8801 *E-mail:* info@hanserpublications.com *Web Site:* www.hanserpublications.com, pg 100

Harbour Publishing Co Ltd, 4437 Rondeview Rd, Madeira Park, BC V0N 2H0, Canada *Tel:* 604-883-2730 *Toll Free Tel:* 800-667-2988 *Fax:* 604-883-9451 *E-mail:* info@harbourpublishing.com *Web Site:* www.harbourpublishing.com, pg 459

Hard Shell Word Factory, 6457 Glenway Ave, No 109, Cincinnati, OH 45211 *Toll Free Tel:* 888-232-0808 *Toll Free Fax:* 888-460-4752 *E-mail:* inquiry@mundania.com *Web Site:* www.mundania.com, pg 100

Clarence H Haring Prize, 400 "A" St SE, Washington, DC 20003 *Tel:* 202-544-2422 *Fax:* 202-544-8307 *E-mail:* awards@historians.org *Web Site:* www.historians.org, pg 652

Joy Harjo Poetry Award, PO Box 2414, Durango, CO 81302 *Tel:* 970-903-7914 *E-mail:* cutthroatmag@gmail.com *Web Site:* www.cutthroatmag.com, pg 652

Harlequin Enterprises Ltd, 233 Broadway, Suite 1001, New York, NY 10279 *Tel:* 212-553-4200 *Fax:* 212-227-8969 *E-mail:* customerservice@harlequin.com *Web Site:* www.harlequin.com, pg 100

Harlequin Enterprises Ltd, 225 Duncan Mill Rd, Don Mills, ON M3B 3K9, Canada *Tel:* 416-445-5860 *Toll Free Tel:* 888-432-4879; 800-370-5838 (ebook inquiries) *E-mail:* customerservice@harlequin.com *Web Site:* www.harlequin.com, pg 459

HarperCollins Canada Ltd, 2 Bloor St E, 20th fl, Toronto, ON M4W 1A8, Canada *Tel:* 416-975-9334 *Fax:* 416-975-5223 *E-mail:* hcorder@harpercollins.com *Web Site:* www.harpercollins.ca, pg 459

HarperCollins Children's Books, 195 Broadway, New York, NY 10007 *Tel:* 212-207-7000 *Web Site:* www.harpercollins.com/childrens, pg 101

HarperCollins General Books Group, 195 Broadway, New York, NY 10007 *Tel:* 212-207-7000 *Web Site:* www.harpercollins.com, pg 101

HarperCollins Publishers, 195 Broadway, New York, NY 10007 *Tel:* 212-207-7000 *Fax:* 212-207-7145 *Web Site:* www.harpercollins.com, pg 101

Harper's Magazine Foundation, 666 Broadway, 11th fl, New York, NY 10012 *Tel:* 212-420-5720 *Toll Free Tel:* 800-444-4653 *Fax:* 212-228-5889 *E-mail:* harpers@harpers.org *Web Site:* www.harpers.org, pg 102

Aurand Harris Memorial Playwriting Award, 215 Knob Hill Dr, Hamden, CT 06518 *Tel:* 617-851-8535 *Fax:* 203-288-5938 *E-mail:* mail@netconline.org *Web Site:* www.netconline.org, pg 652

The Joy Harris Literary Agency Inc, 1501 Broadway, Suite 2310, New York, NY 10036 *Tel:* 212-924-6269 *Fax:* 212-840-5776 *E-mail:* contact@joyharrisliterary.com *Web Site:* www.joyharrisliterary.com, pg 520

Harrison House Publishers, 7498 E 46 Place, Tulsa, OK 74145 *Tel:* 918-523-5700 *Toll Free Tel:* 800-888-4126 *Toll Free Fax:* 800-830-5688 *Web Site:* www.harrisonhouse.com, pg 102

Hartline Literary Agency LLC, 123 Queenston Dr, Pittsburgh, PA 15235 *Web Site:* www.hartlineliterary.com, pg 520

Hartman Publishing Inc, 1313 Iron Ave SW, Albuquerque, NM 87102 *Tel:* 505-291-1274 *Toll Free Tel:* 800-999-9534 *Fax:* 505-291-1284 *Toll Free Fax:* 800-474-6106 *E-mail:* orders@hartmanonline.com; help@hartmanonline.com *Web Site:* www.hartmanonline.com, pg 102

Harvard Art Museums, 32 Quincy St, Cambridge, MA 02138 *Tel:* 617-495-1440; 617-496-6529 (edit) *Fax:* 617-495-9985 *Web Site:* www.harvardartmuseums.org, pg 102

Harvard Business Review Press, 300 N Beacon St, Watertown, MA 02472 *Tel:* 617-783-7400 *Fax:* 617-783-7489 *E-mail:* custserv@hbsp.harvard.edu *Web Site:* www.harvardbusiness.org, pg 102

The Harvard Common Press, 100 Cummings Ctr, Suite 265-D, Beverly, MA 01915 *Tel:* 978-282-9590 *Fax:* 978-282-7765 *Web Site:* www.quartoknows.com/harvard-common-press, pg 102

Harvard Education Publishing Group, 8 Story St, 1st fl, Cambridge, MA 02138 *Tel:* 617-495-3432 *Toll Free Tel:* 800-513-0763 (subns); 888-437-1437 (orders) *Fax:* 617-496-3584; 978-348-1233 (orders) *E-mail:* hepg@harvard.edu *Web Site:* www.hepg.org, pg 102

Harvard Square Editions, 2152 Beachwood Terr, Hollywood, CA 90068 *Tel:* 323-203-0233 *E-mail:* submissions@harvardsquareeditions.org *Web Site:* harvardsquareeditions.org, pg 102

Harvard Summer Writing Program, 51 Brattle St, Dept S760, Cambridge, MA 02138-3722 *Tel:* 617-495-4024 *Fax:* 617-495-9176 *E-mail:* summer@harvard.edu *Web Site:* www.summer.harvard.edu, pg 611

Harvard Ukrainian Research Institute, 34 Kirkland St, Cambridge, MA 02138 *Tel:* 617-495-4053 *Fax:* 617-495-8097 *E-mail:* huri@fas.harvard.edu *Web Site:* www.huri.harvard.edu, pg 103

Harvard University Press, 79 Garden St, Cambridge, MA 02138-1499 *Tel:* 617-495-2600; 401-531-2800 (intl orders) *Toll Free Tel:* 800-405-1619 (orders) *Fax:* 617-495-5898 (general); 617-496-4677 (edit & rts); 401-531-2801 (intl orders) *Toll Free Fax:* 800-406-9145 (orders) *E-mail:* contact_hup@harvard.edu *Web Site:* www.hup.harvard.edu, pg 103

Harvest Hill Press, PO Box 55, Salisbury Cove, ME 04672-0055 *Tel:* 207-288-8900 *E-mail:* shop@harvesthillpress.com *Web Site:* www.harvesthillpress.com, pg 103

Harvest House Publishers Inc, 990 Owen Loop N, Eugene, OR 97402-9173 *Tel:* 541-343-0123 *Toll Free Tel:* 888-501-6991 *Fax:* 541-342-6410 *E-mail:* admin@harvesthousepublishers.com *Web Site:* harvesthousepublishers.com, pg 103

Haskins Medal Award, 17 Dunster St, Suite 202, Cambridge, MA 02138 *Tel:* 617-491-1622 *Fax:* 617-492-3303 *E-mail:* info@themedievalacademy.org *Web Site:* www.medievalacademy.org, pg 652

Hatherleigh Press Ltd, 62545 State Hwy 10, Hobart, NY 13788 *E-mail:* info@hatherleighpress.com; publicity@hatherleighpress.com *Web Site:* www.hatherleighpress.com, pg 103

John Hawkins and Associates Inc, 80 Maiden Lane, Suite 1503, New York, NY 10038 *Tel:* 212-807-7040 *E-mail:* jha@jhalit.com *Web Site:* jhalit.com, pg 521

Hay House Inc, 2776 Loker Ave W, Carlsbad, CA 92010 *Tel:* 760-431-7695 (ext 2, intl) *Toll Free Tel:* 800-654-5126 (ext 2, US) *Toll Free Fax:* 800-650-5115 *E-mail:* info@hayhouse.com; editorial@hayhouse.com *Web Site:* www.hayhouse.com, pg 103

Friedrich Hayek Lecture & Book Prize, 52 Vanderbilt Ave, New York, NY 10017 *Tel:* 212-599-7000 *Fax:* 212-599-3494 *Web Site:* www.manhattan-institute.org, pg 652

Haynes Manuals Inc, 859 Lawrence Dr, Newbury Park, CA 91320-2232 *Tel:* 805-498-6703 *Toll Free Tel:* 800-4-HAYNES (442-9637) *Fax:* 805-498-2867 *E-mail:* cstn@haynes.com *Web Site:* www.haynes.com, pg 104

Hazelden Publishing, 15251 Pleasant Valley Rd, Center City, MN 55012-0011 *Tel:* 651-213-4200 *Toll Free Tel:* 800-257-7810 *Fax:* 651-213-4590 *E-mail:* info@hazelden.org *Web Site:* www.hazelden.org, pg 104

HCPro Inc, 75 Sylvan St, Suite A-101, Danvers, MA 01923 *Toll Free Tel:* 800-650-6787 *Toll Free Fax:* 800-785-9212 *E-mail:* customerservice@hcpro.com *Web Site:* www.hcpro.com, pg 104

Headlands Center for the Arts Residency for Writers, 944 Fort Barry, Sausalito, CA 94965 *Tel:* 415-331-2787 *Fax:* 415-331-3857 *Web Site:* www.headlands.org, pg 652

Health Administration Press, One N Franklin St, Suite 1700, Chicago, IL 60606-3491 *Tel:* 312-424-2800 *Fax:* 312-424-0014 *E-mail:* hap1@ache.org *Web Site:* www.ache.org/publications (orders), pg 104

Health Communications Inc, 3201 SW 15 St, Deerfield Beach, FL 33442 *Tel:* 954-360-0909 *Toll Free Tel:* 800-851-9100; 800-441-5569 (cust serv & orders) *Fax:* 954-360-0034 *Toll Free Fax:* 800-424-7652 (cust serv & orders) *E-mail:* customerservice2@hcibooks.com *Web Site:* www.hcibooks.com, pg 104

Health Forum Inc, 155 N Wacker Dr, Suite 400, Chicago, IL 60606 *Tel:* 312-893-6800 *Toll Free Tel:* 800-242-2626 *Fax:* 312-422-4500 *E-mail:* hfcustsvc@healthforum.com *Web Site:* www.ahaonlinestore.com; www.healthforum.com, pg 104

Health Professions Press, 409 Washington Ave, Suite 500, Towson, MD 21204 *Tel:* 410-337-9585 *Toll Free Tel:* 888-337-8808 *Fax:* 410-337-8539 *E-mail:* custserv@healthpropress.com *Web Site:* www.healthpropress.com, pg 104

Health Research Books, 62 Seventh St, Pomeroy, WA 99347 *Tel:* 509-843-2385 *Toll Free Tel:* 888-844-2386 *Fax:* 509-843-2387 *E-mail:* publish@pomeroy-wa.com *Web Site:* www.healthresearchbooks.com, pg 105

Heartland Prize, 435 N Michigan Ave, Suite 1100, Chicago, IL 60611, pg 652

HeartMath LLC, 14700 W Park Ave, Boulder Creek, CA 95006 *Tel:* 831-338-8700 *Toll Free Tel:* 800-450-9111 *Fax:* 831-338-9861 *E-mail:* info@heartmath.com; inquiry@heartmath.com *Web Site:* www.heartmath.com, pg 105

Hearts 'n Tummies Cookbook Co, 3544 Blakslee St, Wever, IA 52658 *Tel:* 319-372-7480 *Toll Free Tel:* 800-571-2665 *Fax:* 319-372-7485 *E-mail:* quixotepress@gmail.com; heartsntummies@gmail.com *Web Site:* www.heartsntummies.com, pg 105

Anne Hebenstreit, 20 Tip Top Way, Berkeley Heights, NJ 07922 *Tel:* 908-665-0536, pg 495

Hebrew Union College Press, 3101 Clifton Ave, Cincinnati, OH 45220 *Tel:* 513-221-1875 *Fax:* 513-221-0321 *Web Site:* press.huc.edu, pg 105

Hedgebrook Master Class Retreat Series, PO Box 1231, Freeland, WA 98249 *Tel:* 360-321-4786 *Fax:* 360-321-2171 *E-mail:* hedgebrook@hedgebrook.org *Web Site:* www.hedgebrook.org; www.facebook.com/hedgebrook, pg 611

Hedgebrook VORTEXT, PO Box 1231, Freeland, WA 98249 *Tel:* 360-321-4786 *Fax:* 360-321-2171 *E-mail:* hedgebrook@hedgebrook.org *Web Site:* www.hedgebrook.org; www.facebook.com/hedgebrook, pg 611

Hedgebrook Winter Salon, PO Box 1231, Freeland, WA 98249 *Tel:* 360-321-4786 *Fax:* 360-321-2171 *E-mail:* hedgebrook@hedgebrook.org *Web Site:* www.hedgebrook.org; www.facebook.com/hedgebrook, pg 611

Hedgebrook Writers in Residence Program, PO Box 1231, Freeland, WA 98249 *Tel:* 360-321-4786 *Fax:* 360-321-2171 *E-mail:* hedgebrook@hedgebrook.org *Web Site:* www.hedgebrook.org; www.facebook.com/hedgebrook, pg 611

Heian, 1393 Solono Ave, Albany, CA 94706 *Tel:* 510-524-8732 *Toll Free Fax:* 888-411-8527 *E-mail:* sbp@stonebridge.com *Web Site:* www.stonebridge.com, pg 105

Heimburger House Publishing Co, 7236 W Madison St, Forest Park, IL 60130 *Tel:* 708-366-1973 *Fax:* 708-366-1973 *E-mail:* info@heimburgerhouse.com *Web Site:* www.heimburgerhouse.com, pg 105

William S Hein & Co Inc, 2350 N Forest Rd, Getzville, NY 14068 *Tel:* 716-882-2600 *Toll Free Tel:* 800-828-7571 *Fax:* 716-883-8100 *E-mail:* mail@wshein.com; marketing@wshein.com *Web Site:* www.wshein.com, pg 105

Heinemann, 361 Hanover St, Portsmouth, NH 03801-3912 *Tel:* 603-431-7894 *Toll Free Tel:* 800-225-5800 (US) *Fax:* 603-431-2214 *Toll Free Fax:* 877-231-6980 (US) *E-mail:* custserv@heinemann.com *Web Site:* www.heinemann.com, pg 105

Drue Heinz Literature Prize, 7500 Thomas Blvd, Pittsburgh, PA 15260 *Tel:* 412-383-2456 *Fax:* 412-383-2466 *E-mail:* info@upress.pitt.edu *Web Site:* www.upress.pitt.edu, pg 652

Hellgate Press, PO Box 3531, Ashland, OR 97520 *Tel:* 541-973-5154 *Toll Free Tel:* 800-795-4059 *E-mail:* sales@hellgatepress.com *Web Site:* www.hellgatepress.com, pg 105

Helm Book Publishing, 3437 Huntington Place Dr, Sarasota, FL 34237 *Tel:* 727-623-5014 *Web Site:* www.helmbookpublishing.com, pg 106

Helm Editorial Services, 707 SW Eighth Way, Fort Lauderdale, FL 33315 *Tel:* 954-525-5626 *E-mail:* lynnehelm12@aol.com, pg 495

The Hemingway Foundation/PEN Award, MIT, 14N-221A, 77 Massachusetts Ave, Cambridge, MA 02139 *Tel:* 617-324-1729 *E-mail:* pen-newengland@mit.edu *Web Site:* www.pen-ne.org/hemingway, pg 652

Cecil Hemley Memorial Award, 15 Gramercy Park, New York, NY 10003 *Tel:* 212-254-9628 *Web Site:* www.poetrysociety.org, pg 652

Hendrickson Publishers Inc, PO Box 3473, Peabody, MA 01961-3473 *Tel:* 978-532-6546 *Toll Free Tel:* 800-358-3111 *Fax:* 978-573-8111 *E-mail:* orders@hendrickson.com *Web Site:* www.hendrickson.com, pg 106

Her Own Words LLC, PO Box 5264, Madison, WI 53705-0264 *Tel:* 608-271-7083 *Fax:* 608-271-0209 *Web Site:* www.herownwords.com; www.nontraditionalcareers.com, pg 106

Herald Press, 1251 Virginia Ave, Harrisonburg, VA 22802-2434 *Toll Free Tel:* 800-245-7894 (orders) *Toll Free Fax:* 877-271-0760 *E-mail:* info@MennoMedia.org *Web Site:* www.heraldpress.com; store.mennomedia.org, pg 106

Herald Publishing House, 1001 W Walnut St, Independence, MO 64051 *Tel:* 816-521-3015 *Toll Free Tel:* 800-767-8181 *Fax:* 816-521-3066 *E-mail:* sales@heraldhouse.org *Web Site:* www.heraldhouse.org, pg 106

Heritage Books Inc, 5810 Ruatan St, Berwyn Heights, MD 20740 *Toll Free Tel:* 800-876-6103 *Toll Free Fax:* 800-876-6103 *E-mail:* orders@heritagebooks.com; submissions@heritagebooks.com *Web Site:* www.heritagebooks.com, pg 106

The Heritage Foundation, 214 Massachusetts Ave NE, Washington, DC 20002-4999 *Tel:* 202-546-4400 *Toll Free Tel:* 800-544-4843 *Fax:* 202-546-8328 *E-mail:* info@heritage.org *Web Site:* www.heritage.org, pg 106

Heritage House Publishing Co Ltd, 1075 Pendergast St, No 103, Victoria, BC V8V 0A1, Canada *Tel:* 250-360-0829 *Fax:* 250-386-0829 *E-mail:* heritage@heritagehouse.ca *Web Site:* www.heritagehouse.ca, pg 459

Herman Agency, 350 Central Park W, Apt 4I, New York, NY 10025 *Tel:* 212-749-4907 *Web Site:* www.hermanagencyinc.com, pg 543

The Jeff Herman Agency LLC, 29 Park St, Stockbridge, MA 01262 *Tel:* 413-298-0077 *Fax:* 413-298-8188 *E-mail:* submissions@jeffherman.com *Web Site:* www.jeffherman.com, pg 521

Brodie Herndon Memorial, 900 Timber Creek Place, Virginia Beach, VA 23464 *E-mail:* poetryinva@aol.com *Web Site:* poetrysocietyofvirginia.org, pg 652

Susan Herner Rights Agency Inc, 10 Upper Shad Rd, Pound Ridge, NY 10576 *Tel:* 914-234-2864 *Fax:* 914-234-2866 *E-mail:* sherneragency@optonline.net, pg 521

Herr's Indexing Service, 76-340 Kealoha St, Kailua Kona, HI 96740 *Tel:* 808-365-4348 *E-mail:* lindahallinger@gmail.com *Web Site:* www.herrsindexing.com, pg 495

Carl Hertzog Award for Excellence in Book Design, c/o Dir of the Library, University of Texas at El Paso, El Paso, TX 79968-0582 *Tel:* 915-747-5683 *Fax:* 915-747-5345 *Web Site:* libraryweb.utep.edu/about/hertzog_call.php, pg 652

Heuer Publishing LLC, PO Box 248, Cedar Rapids, IA 52406 *Tel:* 319-368-8008 *Toll Free Tel:* 800-950-7529 *Fax:* 319-368-8011 *E-mail:* editor@heuerpub.com; customerservice@heuerpub.com *Web Site:* www.hitplays.com, pg 106

Les Heures bleues, 560, rue Mercier, St-Lambert, QC J4P 1Z5, Canada *Tel:* 450-671-7718 *Fax:* 450-671-7718 *E-mail:* info@heuresbleues.com *Web Site:* www.heuresbleues.com, pg 460

Hewitt Homeschooling Resources, 3140 Evergreen Way, Washougal, WA 98671 *Tel:* 360-835-8708 *Toll Free Tel:* 800-348-1750 *Fax:* 360-835-8697 *E-mail:* sales@hewitthomeschooling.com *Web Site:* hewitthomeschooling.com, pg 106

Heyday Books, 1633 University Ave, Berkeley, CA 94703 *Tel:* 510-549-3564 *Fax:* 510-549-1889 *E-mail:* heyday@heydaybooks.com; orders@heydaybooks.com *Web Site:* heydaybooks.com, pg 106

Hi Willow Research & Publishing, 123 E Second Ave, Suite 1106, Salt Lake City, UT 84103 *Tel:* 801-755-1122 *E-mail:* lmcsourcesales@gmail.com *Web Site:* www.lmcsource.com; www.davidvl.org, pg 106

Hidden River Arts Playwriting Award, PO Box 63927, Philadelphia, PA 19147 *Tel:* 610-764-0813 *E-mail:* hiddenriverarts@gmail.com *Web Site:* www.hiddenriverarts.org; www.hiddenriverarts.com, pg 653

Higginson Book Co, 10 Colonial Rd, Salem, MA 01970 *Tel:* 978-745-7170 *Fax:* 978-745-8025 *Web Site:* www.higginsonbooks.com, pg 107

High Plains Press, PO Box 123, Glendo, WY 82213 *Tel:* 307-735-4370 *Toll Free Tel:* 800-552-7819 *Fax:* 307-735-4590 *E-mail:* editor@highplainspress.com *Web Site:* highplainspress.com, pg 107

The High School Award, PO Box 6550, Edmond, OK 73083 *Tel:* 405-525-5100 *Fax:* 405-525-5103 *Web Site:* www.oklibs.org, pg 653

High Tide Press, 301 Veterans Pkwy, New Lenox, IL 60451 *Web Site:* cherryhillhightide.com/high-tide-press/, pg 107

Highland Summer Writers' Conference, PO Box 7014, Radford University, Cook Hall, Radford, VA 24142 *Fax:* 540-831-5951 *Web Site:* www.radford.edu/content/cehd/home/appalachian-studies.html, pg 611

Highlights for Children, 1800 Watermark Dr, Columbus, OH 43215 *Tel:* 614-486-0631 *Toll Free Tel:* 800-962-3661 (Highlights Club cust serv); 800-255-9517 (Highlights Magazine cust serv) *Web Site:* www.highlights.com; www.facebook.com/HighlightsforChildren, pg 107

Highlights for Children Fiction Contest, 803 Church St, Honesdale, PA 18431 *Tel:* 570-253-1080 *Fax:* 570-251-7847 *E-mail:* eds@highlights.com *Web Site:* www.highlights.com, pg 653

Hill & Wang, 18 W 18 St, New York, NY 10011 *Tel:* 212-741-6900 *Fax:* 212-633-9385 *E-mail:* fsg.publicity@fsgbooks.com; fsg.editorial@fsgbooks.com; sales@fsgbooks.com *Web Site:* us.macmillan.com/hillandwang.aspx, pg 107

Hill Nadell Literary Agency, 6442 Santa Monica Blvd, Suite 201, Los Angeles, CA 90038 *Tel:* 310-860-9605 *Fax:* 323-380-5206 *E-mail:* queries@hillnadell.com; rights@hillnadell.com (rts & perms) *Web Site:* www.hillnadell.com, pg 521

The Tony Hillerman Prize, c/o St Martin's Press, 175 Fifth Ave, New York, NY 10010 *E-mail:* tonyhillermanprize@stmartins.com *Web Site:* www.hillermanprize.com; us.macmillan.com/minotaurbooks/tonyhillermanprize, pg 653

Hillman Prizes for Journalism, 330 W 42 St, Suite 900, New York, NY 10036 *Tel:* 646-448-6413 *Web Site:* www.hillmanfoundation.org, pg 653

Hillsdale College Press, 33 E College St, Hillsdale, MI 49242 *Tel:* 517-437-7341 *Toll Free Tel:* 800-437-2268 *Fax:* 517-607-2658 *E-mail:* news@hillsdale.edu *Web Site:* www.hillsdale.edu, pg 107

Hillsdale Educational Publishers Inc, 39 North St, Hillsdale, MI 49242 *Tel:* 517-437-3179 *Fax:* 517-437-0531 *E-mail:* davestory@aol.com *Web Site:* www.hillsdalepublishers.com; michbooks.com, pg 107

Hilton Publishing, 1630 45 St, Suite 103, Munster, IN 46321 *Tel:* 219-922-4868 *Fax:* 219-924-6811 *E-mail:* info@hiltonpub.com; orders@hiltonpub.com *Web Site:* www.hiltonpub.com, pg 107

Himalayan Institute Press, 952 Bethany Tpke, Honesdale, PA 18431 *Tel:* 570-253-5551 *Toll Free Tel:* 800-822-4547 *E-mail:* info@himalayaninstitute.org *Web Site:* www.himalayaninstitute.org, pg 107

Hippocrene Books Inc, 171 Madison Ave, New York, NY 10016 *Tel:* 212-685-4373 *Fax:* 212-779-9338 *E-mail:* info@hippocrenebooks.com; orderdept@hippocrenebooks.com (orders) *Web Site:* www.hippocrenebooks.com, pg 108

L Anne Hirschel DDS, 5990 Highgate Ave, East Lansing, MI 48823 *Tel:* 517-333-1748 *E-mail:* alicerichard@comcast.net, pg 495

The Historic New Orleans Collection, 533 Royal St, New Orleans, LA 70130 *Tel:* 504-523-4662 *Fax:* 504-598-7108 *E-mail:* wrc@hnoc.org *Web Site:* www.hnoc.org, pg 108

Historical Novel Society North American Conference, 400 Dark Star Ct, Fairbanks, AK 99709 *Tel:* 217-581-7538 *Fax:* 217-581-7534 *Web Site:* historicalnovelsociety.org, pg 611

History Publishing Co LLC, PO Box 700, Palisades, NY 10964 *Tel:* 845-359-1765 *Fax:* 845-818-3730 (sales) *E-mail:* info@historypublishingco.com *Web Site:* www.historypublishingco.com, pg 108

W D Hoard & Sons Co, 28 W Milwaukee Ave, Fort Atkinson, WI 53538 *Tel:* 920-563-5551 *Fax:* 920-563-7298 *E-mail:* hdbooks@hoards.com; editors@hoards.com *Web Site:* www.hoards.com; www.hoardprinting.com, pg 108

Hobar Publications, 5995 149 St W, Suite 105, Apple Valley, MN 55124 *Tel:* 952-469-6699 *Toll Free Tel:* 800-846-7027 *Fax:* 952-469-1968 *Toll Free Fax:* 800-330-6232 *E-mail:* info@finneyco.com *Web Site:* www.finney-hobar.com, pg 108

Hobbes End Publishing LLC, PO Box 193, Aubrey, TX 76227 *Web Site:* hobbesendpublishing.com, pg 108

Hobblebush Books, 17-A Old Milford Rd, Brookline, NH 03033 *Tel:* 603-672-4317 *Fax:* 603-672-4317 *E-mail:* hobblebush@charter.net; info@hobblebush.com *Web Site:* www.hobblebush.com, pg 108

Eric Hoffer Award for Independent Books, PO Box 11, Titusville, NJ 08560 *Fax:* 609-964-1718 *E-mail:* info@hofferaward.com *Web Site:* www.hofferaward.com, pg 653

Eric Hoffer Award for Short Prose, PO Box 11, Titusville, NJ 08560 *Fax:* 609-964-1718 *E-mail:* info@hofferaward.com *Web Site:* www.hofferaward.com, pg 653

Hofstra University, English Department, 203 Mason Hall, Hempstead, NY 11549 *Tel:* 516-463-5454 *Fax:* 516-463-6395 *Web Site:* www.hofstra.edu, pg 620

The Barbara Hogenson Agency Inc, 165 West End Ave, Suite 19-C, New York, NY 10023 *Tel:* 212-874-8084 *Fax:* 212-595-6748 *E-mail:* bhogenson@aol.com, pg 521

Hogrefe Publishing Corp, 7 Bulfinch Place, Suite 202, Boston, MA 02114 *Toll Free Tel:* 866-823-4726 *Fax:* 617-354-6875 *E-mail:* publishing@hogrefe.com; customerservice@hogrefe-publishing.com *Web Site:* us.hogrefe.com, pg 108

Hohm Press, PO Box 4410, Chino Valley, AZ 86323 *Tel:* 928-636-3331 *Toll Free Tel:* 800-381-2700 *Fax:* 928-636-7519 *E-mail:* hppublisher@cableone.net; hohmpresseditor@gmail.com *Web Site:* www.hohmpress.com, pg 108

Bess Hokin Prize, 61 W Superior St, Chicago, IL 60654 *Tel:* 312-787-7070 *Fax:* 312-787-6650 *E-mail:* editors@poetrymagazine.org *Web Site:* www.poetryfoundation.org, pg 653

Holiday House Inc, 425 Madison Ave, New York, NY 10017 *Tel:* 212-688-0085 *Fax:* 212-421-6134 *E-mail:* info@holidayhouse.com *Web Site:* www.holidayhouse.com, pg 109

Hollins University-Jackson Center for Creative Writing, PO Box 9677, Roanoke, VA 24020 *Tel:* 540-362-6317 *Fax:* 540-362-6097 *E-mail:* creative.writing@hollins.edu *Web Site:* www.hollins.edu, pg 620

Hollym International Corp, 18 Donald Place, Elizabeth, NJ 07208 *Tel:* 908-353-1655 *Fax:* 908-353-0255 *E-mail:* contact@hollym.com *Web Site:* www.hollym.com, pg 109

Hollywood Film Archive, 8391 Beverly Blvd, Los Angeles, CA 90048 *Tel:* 323-655-4968 *Web Site:* hfarchive.com, pg 109

Burnham Holmes, 182 Lakeview Hill Rd, Poultney, VT 05764-9179 *Tel:* 802-287-9707 *Fax:* 802-287-9707 (computer fax/modem) *E-mail:* burnham.holmes@castleton.edu, pg 495

Henry Holmes Literary Agent/Book Publicist/Marketing Consultant, Mitchell Heights, Apt 205, 2100 S Main St, Fall River, MA 02724 *Tel:* 508-672-2258, pg 495, 521

Holmes Publishing Group LLC, PO Box 2370, Sequim, WA 98382 *Tel:* 360-681-2900 *E-mail:* holmespub@fastmail.fm *Web Site:* www.jdholmes.com, pg 109

Henry Holt and Company, LLC, 175 Fifth Ave, New York, NY 10010 *Tel:* 646-307-5151 *Toll Free Tel:* 888-330-8477 (orders) *Fax:* 646-307-5285 *E-mail:* firstname.lastname@hholt.com *Web Site:* www.henryholt.com, pg 109

Holy Cow! Press, PO Box 3170, Mount Royal Sta, Duluth, MN 55803 *Tel:* 218-724-1653 *E-mail:* holycow@holycowpress.org *Web Site:* www.holycowpress.org, pg 109

Holy Cross Orthodox Press, 50 Goddard Ave, Brookline, MA 02445 *Tel:* 617-731-3500; 617-850-1200 *Fax:* 617-850-1460 *E-mail:* info@hchc.edu *Web Site:* www.hchc.edu, pg 109

Homa & Sekey Books, 140 E Ridgewood Ave, Paramus, NJ 07652 *Tel:* 201-261-8810 *Toll Free Tel:* 800-870-HOMA (870-4662 orders) *Fax:* 201-261-8890 *E-mail:* info@homabooks.com *Web Site:* www.homabooks.com, pg 110

Homestead Publishing, Box 193, Moose, WY 83012-0193 *Tel:* 307-733-6248 *Fax:* 307-733-6248 *E-mail:* orders@homesteadpublishing.net *Web Site:* www.homesteadpublishing.net, pg 110

Honickman First Book Prize, University of the Arts (UARTS), Hamilton Hall, 320 S Broad St, Rm 313, Philadelphia, PA 19102-4901 *Tel:* 215-717-6801 *Fax:* 215-717-6805 *Web Site:* www.aprweb.org, pg 653

Hoover Institution Press, Stanford University, 434 Galvez Mall, Stanford, CA 94305-6003 *Tel:* 650-725-7146; 650-723-3373 *Toll Free Tel:* 800-935-2882 *Fax:* 650-723-8626 *E-mail:* hooverpress@stanford.edu *Web Site:* www.hooverpress.org; www.hoover.org, pg 110

Hoover's Inc, 7700 W Parmer Lane, Bldg A, Austin, TX 78729 *Tel:* 512-374-4500 *Toll Free Tel:* 844-201-0407; 888-234-4567 (sales) *Fax:* 512-374-4501 *Web Site:* www.hoovers.com, pg 110

Hope Publishing Co, 380 S Main Place, Carol Stream, IL 60188 *Tel:* 630-665-3200 *Toll Free Tel:* 800-323-1049 *Fax:* 630-665-2552 *E-mail:* hope@hopepublishing.com *Web Site:* www.hopepublishing.com, pg 110

Hope Street Publishing, PO Box 2705, Philadelphia, PA 19120 *E-mail:* contact@hopestreetpublishing.com *Web Site:* www.hopestreetpublishing.com, pg 110

Horizon Publishers & Distributors Inc, 191 N 650 E, Bountiful, UT 84010-3628 *Tel:* 801-292-7102 *E-mail:* ldshorizonpublishers1@gmail.com *Web Site:* www.ldshorizonpublishers.com, pg 110

Hornfischer Literary Management LP, PO Box 50544, Austin, TX 78763 *Tel:* 512-472-0011 *E-mail:* queries@hornfischerlit.com *Web Site:* www.hornfischerlit.com, pg 521

Horror Writers Association (HWA), c/o Horror Writers Association, PO Box 56687, Sherman Oaks, CA 91413 *E-mail:* hwa@horror.org *Web Site:* horror.org, pg 566

Hospital & Healthcare Compensation Service, 3 Post Rd, Suite 3, Oakland, NJ 07436 *Tel:* 201-405-0075 *Fax:* 201-405-2110 *E-mail:* allinfo@hhcsinc.com *Web Site:* www.hhcsinc.com, pg 110

Host Publications, 3408 West Ave, Austin, TX 78705 *Tel:* 512-236-1290 *Fax:* 512-236-1208 *Web Site:* www.hostpublications.com, pg 110

Firman Houghton Prize, 46 Wallace St, Somerville, MA 02144 *Tel:* 617-744-6034 *E-mail:* info@nepoetryclub.org *Web Site:* www.nepoetryclub.org, pg 653

Houghton Mifflin Harcourt, 125 High St, Boston, MA 02110 *Tel:* 617-351-5000 *Toll Free Tel:* 855-969-4642; 800-225-5425 (K-12 educ materials); 800-323-9540 (assessment materials); 877-219-1537 (SkillsTutor); 888-242-6747 (Innovation in Educ Group); 800-225-3362 (Trade & Ref Div) *Toll Free Fax:* 800-269-5232 *E-mail:* myhmhco@hmhco.com *Web Site:* www.hmhco.com, pg 110

Houghton Mifflin Harcourt Assessments, 900 Pierce Place, Suite 900, Itasca, IL 60143 *Tel:* 630-467-7000 *Toll Free Tel:* 800-323-9540 *Fax:* 630-467-7192 (cust serv) *E-mail:* rpc_customer_service@hmhpub.com (cust serv) *Web Site:* www.riversidepublishing.com, pg 111

Houghton Mifflin Harcourt K-12 Publishers, 125 High St, Boston, MA 02110 *Tel:* 617-351-5000 *Toll Free Tel:* 800-225-5425 (cust serv) *Web Site:* www.hmhco.com/classroom; www.hmhco.com, pg 111

Houghton Mifflin Harcourt Trade & Reference Division, 125 High St, Boston, MA 02110 *Tel:* 617-351-5000 *Toll Free Tel:* 800-225-3362 *Web Site:* www.hmhco.com, pg 111

House of Anansi Press Inc, 128 Sterling Rd, Lower Level, Toronto, ON M6R 2B7, Canada *Tel:* 416-363-4343 *Fax:* 416-363-1017 *E-mail:* customerservice@houseofanansi.com *Web Site:* www.houseofanansi.com, pg 460

House of Collectibles, 1745 Broadway, New York, NY 10019 *Tel:* 212-782-9000 *Web Site:* www.penguinrandomhouse.com, pg 112

House to House Publications, 11 Toll Gate Rd, Lititz, PA 17543 *Tel:* 717-627-1996 *Toll Free Tel:* 800-848-5892 *Fax:* 717-627-4004 *E-mail:* h2hp@dcfi.org *Web Site:* www.h2hp.com, pg 112

Housing Assistance Council, 1025 Vermont Ave NW, Suite 606, Washington, DC 20005 *Tel:* 202-842-8600 *Fax:* 202-347-3441 *E-mail:* hac@ruralhome.org *Web Site:* www.ruralhome.org, pg 112

Howard Books, c/o Simon & Schuster, Inc, 1230 Avenue of the Americas, New York, NY 10020 *E-mail:* howardbooks@simonandschuster.com (info) *Web Site:* simonandschusterpublishing.com/howard-books/, pg 112

Tom Howard/John H Reid Fiction & Essay Contest, 351 Pleasant St, PMB 222, Northampton, MA 01060-3961 *Tel:* 413-320-1847 *Toll Free Tel:* 866-WINWRIT (946-9748) *Fax:* 413-280-0539 *Web Site:* www.winningwriters.com, pg 653

Tom Howard/Margaret Reid Poetry Contest, 351 Pleasant St, PMB 222, Northampton, MA 01060-3961 *Tel:* 413-320-1847 *Toll Free Tel:* 866-WINWRIT (946-9748) *Fax:* 413-280-0539 *Web Site:* www.winningwriters.com, pg 653

C D Howe Institute, 67 Yonge St, Suite 300, Toronto, ON M5E 1J8, Canada *Tel:* 416-865-1904 *Fax:* 416-865-1866 *E-mail:* cdhowe@cdhowe.org *Web Site:* www.cdhowe.org, pg 460

Julia Ward Howe Book Awards, c/o Professor Mary Cronin, 2400 Beacon St, Unit 208, Beacon Hill, MA 02467 *Tel:* 617-783-1357 *E-mail:* bostonauthors@aol.com *Web Site:* www.bostonauthorsclub.org, pg 654

The William Dean Howells Medal, 633 W 155 St, New York, NY 10032 *Tel:* 212-368-5900 *Fax:* 212-491-4615 *E-mail:* academy@artsandletters.org *Web Site:* www.artsandletters.org, pg 654

HPBooks, 375 Hudson St, New York, NY 10014 *Tel:* 212-366-2000 *E-mail:* online@penguinputnam.com *Web Site:* www.penguinputnam.com; www.penguin.com, pg 112

HRD Press, 22 Amherst Rd, Amherst, MA 01002-9709 *Tel:* 413-253-3488 *Toll Free Tel:* 800-822-2801 *Fax:* 413-253-3490 *E-mail:* info@hrdpress.com; customerservice@hrdpress.com *Web Site:* www.hrdpress.com, pg 112

L Ron Hubbard's Writers of the Future Contest, 7501 Hollywood Blvd, Hollywood, CA 90028 *Tel:* 323-466-3310 *Toll Free Tel:* 800-624-6504 *Fax:* 323-466-6474 *E-mail:* contests@authorservicesinc.com *Web Site:* www.writersofthefuture.com, pg 654

Hudson Institute, 1015 15 St NW, 6th fl, Washington, DC 20005 *Tel:* 202-974-2400 *Fax:* 202-974-2410 *E-mail:* info@hudson.org *Web Site:* www.hudson.org, pg 112

The Hugo Awards, PO Box 64128, Sunnyvale, CA 94088 *Web Site:* www.wsfs.org/awards; www.thehugoawards.org, pg 654

Lynda Hull Memorial Poetry Prize, College of Charleston, Dept of English, 66 George St, Charleston, SC 29424 *Tel:* 843-953-4470 *E-mail:* crazyhorse@cofc.edu *Web Site:* crazyhorse.cofc.edu/prizes, pg 654

Human Kinetics Inc, 1607 N Market St, Champaign, IL 61820 *Tel:* 217-351-5076 *Toll Free Tel:* 800-747-4457 *Fax:* 217-351-1549 (orders/cust serv) *E-mail:* info@hkusa.com *Web Site:* www.humankinetics.com, pg 112

Human Rights Watch, 350 Fifth Ave, 34th fl, New York, NY 10118-3299 *Tel:* 212-290-4700 *Fax:* 212-736-1300 *E-mail:* hrwnyc@hrw.org *Web Site:* www.hrw.org, pg 113

Humanix Books LLC, 8 W 40 St, 20th fl, New York, NY 10804 *Toll Free Tel:* 855-371-7810 *E-mail:* info@humanixbooks.com *Web Site:* www.humanixbooks.com, pg 113

Hunter Publishing Inc, 222 Clematis St, West Palm Beach, FL 33401 *Tel:* 561-835-2022 *Web Site:* guidestotheworld.com, pg 113

Huntington Press Publishing, 3665 Procyon St, Las Vegas, NV 89103-1907 *Tel:* 702-252-0655 *Toll Free Tel:* 800-244-2224 *Fax:* 702-252-0675 *E-mail:* sales@huntingtonpress.com *Web Site:* www.huntingtonpress.com, pg 113

Hurston/Wright Award for College Writers, 840 First St NE, 3rd fl, Washington, DC 20002 *Tel:* 202-248-5051 *E-mail:* info@hurstonwright.org *Web Site:* www.hurstonwright.org, pg 654

Hurston/Wright Legacy Awards, 840 First St NE, 3rd fl, Washington, DC 20002 *Tel:* 202-248-5051 *E-mail:* info@hurstonwright.org *Web Site:* www.hurstonwright.org, pg 654

Hurston/Wright Writers Week, 840 First St NE, 3rd fl, Washington, DC 20002 *Tel:* 202-248-5051 *E-mail:* info@hurstonwright.org *Web Site:* www.hurstonwright.org, pg 611

The Zora Neale Hurston/Richard Wright Foundation, 840 First St NE, 3rd fl, Washington, DC 20002 *Tel:* 202-248-5051 *E-mail:* info@hurstonwright.org *Web Site:* www.hurstonwright.org, pg 583

Hutton Publishing, 140D Heritage Village, Southbury, CT 06488 *Tel:* 203-405-6227 *E-mail:* huttonbooks@hotmail.com *Web Site:* www.huttonpublishing.com, pg 113

I-5 Publishing LLC, 3 Burroughs, Irvine, CA 92618 *Tel:* 949-855-8822 *Toll Free Tel:* 888-738-2665 *Fax:* 949-458-3856 *Web Site:* www.i5publishing.com, pg 113

IACP Cookbook Awards, 45 Rockefeller Plaza, Suite 2000, New York, NY 10111 *Tel:* 646-358-4957 *Toll Free Tel:* 866-358-4951 *Toll Free Fax:* 866-358-2524 *E-mail:* info@iacp.com *Web Site:* www.iacp.com; www.iacp.com/award/more/cookbook, pg 654

Ibex Publishers, PO Box 30087, Bethesda, MD 20824 *Tel:* 301-718-8188 *Toll Free Tel:* 888-718-8188 *Fax:* 301-907-8707 *E-mail:* info@ibexpub.com *Web Site:* ibexpub.com, pg 113

IBFD North America Inc (International Bureau of Fiscal Documentation), 8300 Boone Blvd, Suite 380, Vienna, VA 22182 *Tel:* 703-442-7757 *E-mail:* info@ibfd.org *Web Site:* www.ibfd.org, pg 113

The Ibsen Society of America, University of California, Dept of Scandinavian, 6303 Dwinelle Hall, No 2690, Berkeley, CA 94720-2690 *Tel:* 510-642-4484 *Fax:* 510-642-6220 *Web Site:* www.ibsensociety.liu.edu, pg 566

ICM Lecture Division, 730 Fifth Ave, New York, NY 10019 *Tel:* 212-556-5600 *Fax:* 212-556-5665 *Web Site:* www.icmtalent.com, pg 547

ICM Partners, 65 E 55 St, New York, NY 10022 *Tel:* 212-556-5600 *Web Site:* www.icmtalent.com, pg 521

ICM/Sagalyn, 2 Wisconsin Circle, Suite 650, Chevy Chase, MD 20815-7045 *Tel:* 240-802-2760 *E-mail:* info@sagalyn.com *Web Site:* www.sagalyn.com, pg 521

The Idaho Prize for Poetry, 105 Lost Horse Lane, Sandpoint, ID 83864 *Tel:* 208-255-4410 *Fax:* 208-255-1560 *E-mail:* losthorsepress@mindspring.com *Web Site:* www.losthorsepress.org, pg 654

IDEAlliance®, 1800 Diagonal Rd, Suite 320, Alexandria, VA 22314-2862 *Tel:* 703-837-1070 *Fax:* 703-837-1072 *E-mail:* registrar@idealliance.org *Web Site:* www.idealliance.org, pg 566

Idyll Arbor Inc, 39129 264 Ave SE, Enumclaw, WA 98022 *Tel:* 360-825-7797 *Fax:* 360-825-5670 *E-mail:* sales@idyllarbor.com *Web Site:* www.idyllarbor.com, pg 113

Idyllwild Arts Summer Workshops, 52500 Temecula Dr, Idyllwild, CA 92549-0038 *Tel:* 951-659-2171 *Fax:* 951-659-4552 *E-mail:* summer@idyllwildarts.org *Web Site:* www.idyllwildarts.org/writersweek, pg 611

IEEE Computer Society, 2001 "L" St NW, Suite 700, Washington, DC 20036-4928 *Tel:* 202-371-0101 *Toll Free Tel:* 800-272-6657 (memb info) *Fax:* 202-728-9614 *E-mail:* help@computer.org *Web Site:* www.computer.org, pg 113

IEEE Press, 445 Hoes Lane, Piscataway, NJ 08854 *Tel:* 732-981-0060 *Fax:* 732-867-9946 *E-mail:* pressbooks@ieee.org (proposals & info) *Web Site:* www.ieee.org/press, pg 114

IET USA Inc, 379 Thornall St, Edison, NJ 08837 *Tel:* 732-321-5575 *Fax:* 732-321-5702 *E-mail:* ietusa@theiet.org *Web Site:* www.theiet.org, pg 114

Ignatius Press, 1348 Tenth Ave, San Francisco, CA 94122-2304 *Toll Free Tel:* 800-651-1531 (orders); 888-615-3186 (cust serv) *E-mail:* info@ignatius.com *Web Site:* www.ignatius.com, pg 114

IHS Jane's, 110 N Royal St, Suite 200, Alexandria, VA 22314-1651 *Tel:* 703-683-3700 *Toll Free Tel:* 800-824-0768 (sales) *Fax:* 703-836-0297 *Toll Free Fax:* 800-836-0297 *E-mail:* customercare@ihsmarkit.com *Web Site:* www.ihs.com; ihsmarkit.com, pg 114

IHS Press, 222 W 21 St, Suite F-122, Norfolk, VA 23517 *Toll Free Tel:* 877-447-7737 *Toll Free Fax:* 877-447-7737 *E-mail:* info@ihspress.com; tradesales@ihspress.com (wholesale sales); order@ihspress.com *Web Site:* www.ihspress.com, pg 114

ILA Children's & Young Adults' Book Awards, PO Box 8139, Newark, DE 19714-8139 *Tel:* 302-731-1600 *Toll Free Tel:* 800-336-7323 (US & CN) *Fax:* 302-731-1057 *E-mail:* ilaawards@reading.org *Web Site:* www.literacyworldwide.org, pg 654

Illinois State Museum Society, 502 S Spring St, Springfield, IL 62706-5000 *Tel:* 217-782-7386 *Fax:* 217-782-1254 *E-mail:* editor@museum.state.il.us *Web Site:* www.museum.state.il.us, pg 114

Illuminating Engineering Society of North America (IES), 120 Wall St, 17th fl, New York, NY 10005-4001 *Tel:* 212-248-5000 *Fax:* 212-248-5017; 212-248-5018 *E-mail:* ies@ies.org *Web Site:* www.ies.org, pg 114

Illumination Book Awards, 1129 Woodmere Ave, Suite B, Traverse City, MI 49686 *Tel:* 231-933-0445 *Toll Free Tel:* 800-706-4636 *Fax:* 231-933-0448 *E-mail:* awards@bookpublishing.com *Web Site:* www.illuminationawards.com, pg 654

Imagefinders Inc, 6101 Utah Ave NW, Washington, DC 20015 *Fax:* 202-244-3237, pg 495

Imagination Publishing Group, PO Box 1304, Dunedin, FL 34697 *Toll Free Tel:* 888-701-6481 *Fax:* 727-361-0584 *E-mail:* info@imaginationpublishinggroup.com *Web Site:* www.imaginationpublishinggroup.com, pg 114

Imago Press, 3710 E Edison St, Tucson, AZ 85716 *Tel:* 520-444-2265 *Web Site:* www.oasisjournal.org, pg 114

ImaJinn Books, PO Box 74274, Phoenix, AZ 85087-4274 *Tel:* 623-236-3361 *Toll Free Tel:* 877-625-3592 (US & CN) *E-mail:* orders@imajinnbooks.com; editors@imajinnbooks.com *Web Site:* www.imajinnbooks.com, pg 115

Immedium, 535 Rockdale Dr, San Francisco, CA 94127 *Tel:* 415-452-8546 *Fax:* 360-937-6272 *E-mail:* orders@immedium.com; sales@immedium.com *Web Site:* www.immedium.com, pg 115

John Phillip Immroth Memorial Award, 50 E Huron St, Chicago, IL 60611 *Tel:* 312-280-4226 *Toll Free Tel:* 800-545-2433 *E-mail:* oif@ala.org *Web Site:* www.ala.org/ifrt, pg 655

Impact Publications/Development Concepts Inc, 9104 Manassas Dr, Suite N, Manassas Park, VA 20111-5211 *Tel:* 703-361-7300 *Toll Free Tel:* 800-361-1055 (cust serv) *Fax:* 703-335-9486 *E-mail:* query@impactpublications.com *Web Site:* www.impactpublications.com; www.veteransworld.com, pg 115

In-Plant Printing & Mailing Association (IPMA), 455 S Sam Barr Dr, Suite 203, Kearney, MO 64060 *Tel:* 816-919-1691 *E-mail:* ipmainfo@ipma.org *Web Site:* www.ipma.org, pg 567

In the Garden Publishing, 7525 Paragon Rd, No 752252, Dayton, OH 45459 *Tel:* 937-317-0859 *E-mail:* editor@inthegardenpublishing.com *Web Site:* www.inthegardenpublishing.com, pg 115

Incentive Publications by World Book, 180 N LaSalle St, Suite 900, Chicago, IL 60101 *Toll Free Tel:* 800-967-5325; 800-975-3250; 888-482-9764 (trade dept) *Toll Free Fax:* 888-922-3766 *E-mail:* tradeorders@worldbook.com *Web Site:* www.incentivepublications.com, pg 115

Inclusion Press International, 47 Indian Trail, Toronto, ON M6R 1Z8, Canada *Tel:* 416-658-5363 *Fax:* 416-658-5067 *E-mail:* inclusionpress@inclusion.com *Web Site:* www.inclusion.com, pg 460

The Independent Book Publishers Association (IBPA), 1020 Manhattan Beach Blvd, Suite 204, Manhattan Beach, CA 90266 *Tel:* 310-546-1818 *Fax:* 310-546-3939 *E-mail:* info@ibpa-online.org *Web Site:* www.ibpa-online.org, pg 567

Independent Information Publications, 3357 21 St, San Francisco, CA 94110 *Tel:* 415-643-8600 *E-mail:* sharisteiner@gmail.com *Web Site:* www.movedoc.com, pg 115

Independent Institute, 100 Swan Way, Suite 200, Oakland, CA 94621-1428 *Tel:* 510-632-1366 *Toll Free Tel:* 800-927-8733 *Fax:* 510-568-6040 *E-mail:* orders@independent.org *Web Site:* www.independent.org, pg 115

The Independent Publisher Book Awards, 1129 Woodmere Ave, Suite B, Traverse City, MI 49686 *Tel:* 231-933-0445 *Toll Free Tel:* 800-706-4636 *Fax:* 231-933-0448 *E-mail:* awards@bookpublishing.com *Web Site:* www.independentpublisher.com/ipland/ipawards.php, pg 655

Independent Writers of Chicago (IWOC), 332 S Michigan Ave, Suite 1032, Chicago, IL 60604 *Toll Free Tel:* 800-804-IWOC (804-4962) *E-mail:* info@iwoc.org *Web Site:* www.iwoc.org, pg 567

IndexEmpire Indexing Services, 16740 Orville Wright Dr, Riverside, CA 92518 *Tel:* 951-697-2819 *E-mail:* indexempire@gmail.com *Web Site:* www.indexempire.com, pg 496

Indexing by the Book, PO Box 12513, Tucson, AZ 85732-2513 *Tel:* 520-750-8439 *E-mail:* indextran@cox.net *Web Site:* www.indexingbythebook.com, pg 496

Indiana Historical Society Press (IHS Press), 450 W Ohio St, Indianapolis, IN 46202-3269 *Tel:* 317-232-1882; 317-234-0026 (orders); 317-234-2716 (edit) *Toll Free Tel:* 800-447-1830 (orders) *Fax:* 317-234-0562 (orders); 317-233-0857 (edit) *E-mail:* ihspress@indianahistory.org; orders@indianahistory.org (orders) *Web Site:* www.indianahistory.org; shop.indianahistory.org (orders), pg 115

Indiana Review Fiction Prize, Ballantine Hall 529, 1020 E Kirkwood Ave, Bloomington, IN 47405 *Tel:* 812-855-3439 *E-mail:* inreview@indiana.edu *Web Site:* indianareview.org, pg 655

Indiana University African Studies Program, Indiana University, 221 Woodburn Hall, Bloomington, IN 47405 *Tel:* 812-855-8284 *Fax:* 812-855-6734 *E-mail:* afrist@indiana.edu *Web Site:* www.indiana.edu/~afrist, pg 115

Indiana University Press, Herman B Wells Library 350, 1320 E Tenth St, Bloomington, IN 47405-3907 *Tel:* 812-855-8817 *Toll Free Tel:* 800-842-6796 (orders only) *Fax:* 812-855-7931; 812-855-8507 *E-mail:* iupress@indiana.edu; iuporder@indiana.edu (orders) *Web Site:* www.iupress.indiana.edu, pg 116

Indiana University Writers' Conference, 464 Ballantine Hall, 1020 E Kirkwood Ave, Bloomington, IN 47405-7103 *Tel:* 812-855-1877 *Fax:* 812-855-9535 *E-mail:* writecon@indiana.edu *Web Site:* www.iuwc.indiana.edu, pg 611

IndieReader Discovery Awards, PO Box 43121, Montclair, NJ 07043 *E-mail:* amy@indiereader.com *Web Site:* indiereader.com/irda, pg 655

Indies Choice Book Awards, 333 Westchester Ave, Suite S202, White Plains, NY 10604 *Tel:* 914-406-7500 *Toll Free Tel:* 800-637-0037 *Fax:* 914-410-6297 *Web Site:* www.bookweb.org, pg 655

Individual Artist Awards, 175 W Ostend St, Suite E, Baltimore, MD 21230 *Tel:* 410-767-6555 *Fax:* 410-333-1062 *E-mail:* msac@msac.org *Web Site:* www.msac.org, pg 655

Individual Artist Fellowships, 1004 Farnam, Plaza Level, Omaha, NE 68102 *Tel:* 402-595-2122 *Toll Free Tel:* 800-341-4067 *Fax:* 402-595-2334 *Web Site:* www.nebraskaartscouncil.org, pg 655

Individual Artist Fellowships, 25 State House Sta, 193 State St, Augusta, ME 04333-0025 *Tel:* 207-287-2726 *Fax:* 207-287-2725 *Web Site:* mainearts.maine.gov, pg 655

Individual Artist Project Grant, 500 S Bronough St, Tallahassee, FL 32399-0250 *Tel:* 850-245-6470 *Fax:* 850-245-6497 *E-mail:* info@dos.myflorida.com *Web Site:* dos.myflorida.com/cultural, pg 655

Individual Artist's Fellowships, 1026 Sumter St, Suite 200, Columbia, SC 29201-3746 *Tel:* 803-734-8696 *Fax:* 803-734-8526 *E-mail:* info@arts.sc.gov *Web Site:* www.southcarolinaarts.com, pg 655

Individual Excellence Awards, 30 E Broad St, 33rd fl, Columbus, OH 43215 *Tel:* 614-466-2613 *Fax:* 614-466-4494 *Web Site:* www.oac.state.oh.us, pg 655

Industrial Press Inc, 32 Haviland St, Suite 3, Norwalk, CT 06854 *Tel:* 203-956-5593 ext 0 (cust serv) *Toll Free Tel:* 888-528-7852 ext 0 (cust serv) *Fax:* 203-354-9391 (cust serv) *E-mail:* info@industrialpress.com (cust serv) *Web Site:* new.industrialpress.com, pg 116

Information Age Publishing Inc, PO Box 79049, Charlotte, NC 28271-7047 *Tel:* 704-752-9125 *Fax:* 704-752-9113 *E-mail:* infoage@infoagepub.com *Web Site:* www.infoagepub.com, pg 116

Information Gatekeepers Inc (IGI), 1340 Soldiers Field Rd, Suite 2, Boston, MA 02135 *Tel:* 617-782-5033 *Fax:* 617-507-8338 *E-mail:* info@igigroup.com *Web Site:* www.igigroup.com, pg 116

Information Today, Inc, 143 Old Marlton Pike, Medford, NJ 08055-8750 *Tel:* 609-654-6266 *Toll Free Tel:* 800-300-9868 (cust serv) *Fax:* 609-654-4309 *E-mail:* custserv@infotoday.com *Web Site:* www.infotoday.com, pg 116

Infosources Publishing, 140 Norma Rd, Teaneck, NJ 07666 *Tel:* 201-836-7072 *Web Site:* www.infosourcespub.com, pg 117

Ink Smith Publishing, 710 S Myrtle Ave, Suite 209, Monrovia, CA 91016 *Tel:* 626-415-7179 *E-mail:* contact@ink-smith.com *Web Site:* ink-smith.com, pg 117

Inkwater Press, 6750 SW Franklin St, Suite A, Portland, OR 97223 *Tel:* 503-968-6777 *Fax:* 503-968-6779 *E-mail:* orders@inkwaterbooks.com *Web Site:* www.inkwater.com, pg 117

InkWell Management, 521 Fifth Ave, 26th fl, New York, NY 10175 *Tel:* 212-922-3500 *Fax:* 212-922-0535 *E-mail:* info@inkwellmanagement.com *Web Site:* inkwellmanagement.com, pg 522

Inner Traditions International Ltd, One Park St, Rochester, VT 05767 *Tel:* 802-767-3174 *Toll Free Tel:* 800-246-8648 *Fax:* 802-767-3726 *E-mail:* customerservice@InnerTraditions.com *Web Site:* www.InnerTraditions.com, pg 117

Innis-Gerin Medal, Walter House, 282 Somerset W, Ottawa, ON K2P 0J6, Canada *Tel:* 613-991-6990 (ext 106) *Fax:* 613-991-6996 *E-mail:* nominations@rsc-src.ca *Web Site:* www.rsc-src.ca, pg 656

The Innovation Press, 1001 Fourth Ave, Suite 3200, Seattle, WA 98154 *Tel:* 360-870-9988 *E-mail:* info@theinnovationpress.com *Web Site:* www.theinnovationpress.com, pg 117

innovativeKids®, 50 Washington St, Suite 201, Norwalk, CT 06854 *Tel:* 203-838-6400 *E-mail:* info@innovativekids.com *Web Site:* www.innovativekids.com, pg 117

InScribe Christian Writers' Fellowship (ICWF), PO Box 6201, Wetaskiwin, AB T9A 2E9, Canada *E-mail:* inscribe.mail@gmail.com *Web Site:* inscribe.org, pg 567

Insight Editions, 800 "A" St, San Rafael, CA 94901 *Tel:* 415-526-1370 *Toll Free Tel:* 800-809-3792 *Toll Free Fax:* 866-509-0515 *E-mail:* info@insighteditions.com *Web Site:* www.insighteditions.com, pg 117

Insomniac Press, 520 Princess Ave, London, ON N6B 2B8, Canada *Tel:* 519-266-3556 *Web Site:* www.insomniacpress.com, pg 460

The Institute for Cooperation on Adult Education (Institut de Cooperation pour l'Education des Adultes-ICEA), 4321, ave Papineau, Montreal, QC H2H 1T3, Canada *Tel:* 514-948-2044 *Fax:* 514-948-2046 *E-mail:* icae@icea.qc.ca *Web Site:* www.icea.qc.ca, pg 567

Institute for Research on Public Policy (IRPP), 1470 Peel St, No 200, Montreal, QC H3A 1T1, Canada *Tel:* 514-985-2461 *Fax:* 514-985-2559 *E-mail:* irpp@irpp.org *Web Site:* irpp.org, pg 460

Institute of Continuing Legal Education, 1020 Greene St, Ann Arbor, MI 48109-1444 *Tel:* 734-764-0533 *Toll Free Tel:* 877-229-4350 *Fax:* 734-763-2412 *Toll Free Fax:* 877-229-4351 *E-mail:* icle@umich.edu *Web Site:* www.icle.org, pg 117

Institute of Environmental Sciences & Technology - IEST, 2340 S Arlington Heights Rd, Suite 620, Arlington Heights, IL 60005-4510 *Tel:* 847-981-0100 *Fax:* 847-981-4130 *E-mail:* information@iest.org *Web Site:* www.iest.org, pg 118

Institute of Governmental Studies, 109 Moses Hall, No 2370, Berkeley, CA 94720-2370 *Tel:* 510-642-1428 *Fax:* 510-642-3020; 510-642-5537 (orders) *E-mail:* igspress@berkeley.edu *Web Site:* www.igs.berkeley.edu, pg 118

Institute of Intergovernmental Relations, Queen's University, Robert Sutherland Hall, Rm 301, Kingston, ON K7L 3N6, Canada *Tel:* 613-533-2080 *Fax:* 613-533-6868 *E-mail:* iigr@queensu.ca *Web Site:* www.queensu.ca/iigr, pg 460

Institute of Jesuit Sources (IJS), Boston College, Institute for Advanced Jesuit Studies, 140 Commonwealth Ave, Chestnut, MA 02467 *Tel:* 617-552-2568 *Fax:* 617-552-2575 *E-mail:* jesuitsources@bc.edu *Web Site:* jesuitsources.bc.edu, pg 118

Institute of Mathematical Geography, 1964 Boulder Dr, Ann Arbor, MI 48104 *Tel:* 734-975-0246 *E-mail:* image@imagenet.org *Web Site:* www.imagenet.org, pg 118

Institute of Police Technology & Management, 12000 Alumni Dr, Jacksonville, FL 32224-2678 *Tel:* 904-620-4786 *Fax:* 904-620-2453 *E-mail:* info@iptm.org *Web Site:* www.iptm.org, pg 118

Institute of Psychological Research, Inc., 76 Ave, Mozart W, Montreal, QC H2S 1C4, Canada *Tel:* 514-382-3000 *Toll Free Tel:* 800-363-7800 *Fax:* 514-382-3007 *Toll Free Fax:* 888-382-3007 *E-mail:* info@irpcanada.com *Web Site:* www.irpcanada.com, pg 460

Institute of Public Administration of Canada, 1075 Bay St, Suite 401, Toronto, ON M5S 2B1, Canada *Tel:* 416-924-8787 *Fax:* 416-924-4992 *E-mail:* ntl@ipac.ca *Web Site:* www.ipac.ca, pg 461

Institute of Puerto Rican Culture National Literary Awards, PO Box 9024184, San Juan, PR 00902-4184 *Tel:* 787-724-0700 *Fax:* 787-724-8393 *Web Site:* www.icp.gobierno.pr, pg 656

The Institutes™, 720 Providence Rd, Suite 100, Malvern, PA 19355-3433 *Tel:* 610-644-2100 *Toll Free Tel:* 800-644-2101 *Fax:* 610-640-9576 *E-mail:* customerservice@theinstitutes.org *Web Site:* www.theinstitutes.org, pg 118

Integra Software Services Inc, 1110 Jorie Blvd, Suite 200, Oak Brook, IL 60523 *Tel:* 630-586-2579 *Fax:* 630-586-2599 *E-mail:* marketing@integra.co.in *Web Site:* www.integra.co.in, pg 496

Inter-American Development Bank, 1300 New York Ave NW, Washington, DC 20577 *Tel:* 202-623-1000 *Fax:* 202-623-3096 *E-mail:* pic@iadb.org *Web Site:* www.iadb.org/pub, pg 118

Inter American Press Association (IAPA), 3511 NW 91 Ave, Miami, FL 33172 *Tel:* 305-634-2465 *Fax:* 305-635-2272 *E-mail:* info@sipiapa.org *Web Site:* www.sipiapa.org, pg 567

Inter-University Consortium for Political & Social Research (ICPSR), 330 Packard St, Ann Arbor, MI 48104 *Tel:* 734-647-5000 *Fax:* 734-647-8200 *E-mail:* netmail@icpsr.umich.edu *Web Site:* www.icpsr.umich.edu, pg 118

Intercultural Development Research Association (IDRA), 5815 Callaghan Rd, Suite 101, San Antonio, TX 78228 *Tel:* 210-444-1710 *Fax:* 210-444-1714 *E-mail:* contact@idra.org *Web Site:* www.idra.org, pg 118

Intercultural Press Inc, 53 State St, Boston, MA 02109 *Tel:* 617-523-3801 *Toll Free Tel:* 888-273-2539 *Fax:* 617-523-3708 *E-mail:* info@interculturalpress.com *Web Site:* nicholasbrealey.com, pg 118

InterLicense Ltd, 110 Country Club Dr, Suite A, Mill Valley, CA 94941 *Tel:* 415-381-9780 *Fax:* 415-381-6485 *E-mail:* interlicense@interlicense.net *Web Site:* interlicense.net, pg 522

Interlink Publishing Group Inc, 46 Crosby St, Northampton, MA 01060 *Tel:* 413-582-7054 *Toll Free Tel:* 800-238-LINK (238-5465) *Fax:* 413-582-7057 *E-mail:* info@interlinkbooks.com *Web Site:* www.interlinkbooks.com, pg 118

Intermediate Sequoyah Book Award, PO Box 6550, Edmond, OK 73083 *Tel:* 405-525-5100 *Fax:* 405-525-5103 *Web Site:* www.oklibs.org, pg 656

International Association of Business Communicators (IABC), 155 Montgomery St, Suite 1210, San Francisco, CA 94104 *Tel:* 415-544-4700 *Toll Free Tel:* 800-776-4222 (US & CN) *Fax:* 415-544-4747 *E-mail:* leader_centre@iabc.com *Web Site:* www.iabc.com, pg 567

International Association of Crime Writers Inc, North American Branch, 243 Fifth Ave, Suite 537, New York, NY 10016 *Tel:* 212-243-8966 *Fax:* 815-361-1477 *E-mail:* info@crimewritersna.org *Web Site:* www.crimewritersna.org, pg 567

International Book Centre Inc, 2391 Auburn Rd, Shelby Township, MI 48317 *Tel:* 586-254-7230 *Fax:* 586-254-7230 *E-mail:* ibc@ibcbooks.com *Web Site:* www.ibcbooks.com, pg 119

International City/County Management Association (ICMA), 777 N Capitol St NE, Suite 500, Washington, DC 20002-4201 *Tel:* 202-289-4262 *Toll Free Tel:* 800-745-8780 *Fax:* 202-962-3500 *E-mail:* customerservices@icma.org *Web Site:* icma.org, pg 119

International Code Council Inc, 3060 Saturn St, Suite 100, Brea, CA 92821 *Tel:* 562-699-0541 *Toll Free Tel:* 888-422-7233 *Fax:* 562-908-5524; 562-699-8031 *E-mail:* es@icc-es.org; order@icc-es.org *Web Site:* www.iccsafe.org, pg 119

International Council of Shopping Centers (ICSC), 1221 Avenue of the Americas, 41st fl, New York, NY 10020-1099 *Tel:* 646-728-3800 *Fax:* 732-694-1755 *E-mail:* icsc@icsc.org *Web Site:* www.icsc.org, pg 119

International Encyclopedia Society, 3689 Campbell Ct, Yorktown Heights, NY 10598 *Tel:* 914-962-3287 *Fax:* 914-962-3287, pg 567

International Entertainment Bureau, 3612 N Washington Blvd, Indianapolis, IN 46205-3592 *Tel:* 317-926-7566 *E-mail:* ieb@prodigy.net, pg 547

International Food Policy Research Institute, 2033 "K" St NW, Washington, DC 20006-1002 *Tel:* 202-862-5600 *Fax:* 202-467-4439 *E-mail:* ifpri@cgiar.org *Web Site:* www.ifpri.org, pg 119

International Foundation of Employee Benefit Plans, 18700 W Bluemound Rd, Brookfield, WI 53045 *Tel:* 262-786-6700 *Toll Free Tel:* 888-334-3327 *Fax:* 262-786-8780 *E-mail:* editor@ifebp.org *Web Site:* www.ifebp.org, pg 119

The International Institute of Islamic Thought, 500 Grove St, Suite 200, Herndon, VA 20170 *Tel:* 703-471-1133 *Fax:* 703-471-3922 *E-mail:* iiit@iiit.org *Web Site:* www.iiit.org, pg 119

International Latino Book Awards, 3445 Catalina Dr, Carlsbad, CA 92010 *Tel:* 760-434-1223 *Fax:* 760-434-7476 *Web Site:* www.award.news, pg 656

International Latino Unpublished Book Awards, 3445 Catalina Dr, Carlsbad, CA 92010 *Tel:* 760-434-1223 *Fax:* 760-434-7476 *Web Site:* www.award.news, pg 656

International Linguistics Corp, 12220 Blue Ridge Blvd, Suite G, Kansas City, MO 64030 *Tel:* 816-765-8855 *Toll Free Tel:* 800-237-1830 (orders) *Fax:* 816-765-2855 *E-mail:* learnables@sbcglobal.net *Web Site:* www.learnables.com, pg 119

International Literacy Association (ILA), 800 Barksdale Rd, Newark, DE 19711-3204 *Tel:* 302-731-1600 *Toll Free Tel:* 800-336-7323 (US & CN) *Fax:* 302-731-1057 *E-mail:* customerservice@reading.org *Web Site:* www.literacyworldwide.org; www.reading.org, pg 119, 567

International Monetary Fund (IMF), Editorial & Publications Division, 700 19 St NW, HQ1-7-124, Washington, DC 20431 *Tel:* 202-623-7430 *Fax:* 202-623-7201 *E-mail:* publications@imf.org *Web Site:* bookstore.imf.org; elibrary.imf.org (online collection), pg 119

International Poetry Competition, 686 Cherry St NW, Suite 333, Atlanta, GA 30332-0161 *E-mail:* atlantareview@gatech.edu *Web Site:* www.atlantareview.com, pg 656

International Press of Boston Inc, 387 Somerville Ave, Somerville, MA 02143 *Tel:* 617-623-3016 *Fax:* 617-623-3101 *E-mail:* ipb-info@intlpress.com; ipb-orders@intlpress.com *Web Site:* www.intlpress.com, pg 120

International Publishers Co Inc, 235 W 23 St, New York, NY 10011 *Tel:* 212-366-9816 *Fax:* 212-366-9820 *E-mail:* service@intpubnyc.com *Web Site:* www.intpubnyc.com, pg 120

International Research Center for Energy & Economic Development, 850 Willowbrook Rd, Boulder, CO 80302 *Tel:* 303-442-4014 *Fax:* 303-442-5042 *E-mail:* info@iceed.org *Web Site:* www.iceed.org, pg 120

International Risk Management Institute Inc, 12222 Merit Dr, Suite 1600, Dallas, TX 75251-2266 *Tel:* 972-960-7693 *Fax:* 972-371-5120 *E-mail:* info27@irmi.com *Web Site:* www.irmi.com, pg 120

International Society for Technology in Education, 1530 Wilson Blvd, Suite 730, Arlington, VA 22209 *Tel:* 503-342-2848 (intl) *Toll Free Tel:* 800-336-5191 (US & CN) *E-mail:* iste@iste.org *Web Site:* www.iste.org; www.isteconference.org, pg 120

International Society of Automation (ISA), 67 T W Alexander Dr, Research Triangle Park, NC 27709-0185 *Tel:* 919-549-8411 *Fax:* 919-549-8288 *E-mail:* info@isa.org *Web Site:* www.isa.org, pg 120

International Society of Latino Authors, c/o Latino Literacy Now, 3445 Catalina Dr, Carlsbad, CA 92010 *Tel:* 760-434-1223 *Fax:* 760-434-7476, pg 567

International Society of Weekly Newspaper Editors, Missouri Southern State University, 3950 E Newman Rd, Joplin, MO 64801-1595 *Tel:* 417-625-9736 *Fax:* 417-659-4445 *Web Site:* www.iswne.org, pg 567

International Standard Book Numbering (ISBN) US Agency, A Cambridge Information Group Co, 630 Central Ave, New Providence, NJ 07974 *Toll Free Tel:* 877-310-7333 *Fax:* 908-219-0188 *E-mail:* isbn-san@bowker.com *Web Site:* www.isbn.org, pg 568

International Titles, 931 E 56 St, Austin, TX 78751-1724 *Tel:* 512-909-2447 *Web Site:* www.internationaltitles.com, pg 522

International Transactions Inc, 28 Alope Way, Gila, NM 88038 *Tel:* 845-373-9696 *Fax:* 480-393-5162 *E-mail:* info@intltrans.com *Web Site:* www.intltrans.com, pg 522

International Wealth Success Inc, PO Box 186, Merrick, NY 11566-0186 *Tel:* 516-766-5850 *Toll Free Tel:* 800-323-0548 *Fax:* 516-766-5919 *E-mail:* admin@iwsmoney.com *Web Site:* www.iwsmoney.com, pg 120

The International Women's Writing Guild (IWWG), 5 Penn Plaza, 19th fl, PMB 19059, New York, NY 10001 *Tel:* 917-720-6959 *E-mail:* iwwgquestions@iwwg.org *Web Site:* www.iwwg.org, pg 568

InterTech™ Technology Awards, 301 Brush Creek Rd, Warrendale, PA 15086-7529 *Tel:* 412-741-6860 *Toll Free Tel:* 800-910-4283 *Fax:* 412-741-2311 *E-mail:* intertech@printing.org *Web Site:* www.printing.org/intertechawards, pg 656

InterVarsity Press, 430 Plaza Dr, Westmont, IL 60559-1234 *Tel:* 630-734-4000 *Toll Free Tel:* 800-843-9487 *Fax:* 630-734-4200 *E-mail:* email@ivpress.com *Web Site:* www.ivpress.com, pg 120

Interweave Press LLC, 201 E Fourth St, Loveland, CO 80537 *Toll Free Tel:* 800-272-2193; 800-289-0963 *Fax:* 970-613-4656 *Toll Free Fax:* 888-590-4082 *Web Site:* www.interweave.com, pg 120

Intimate & Inspiring Workshops for Children's Authors & Illustrators, 814 Court St, Honesdale, PA 18431 *Tel:* 570-253-1192 *Fax:* 570-253-0179 *E-mail:* jolloyd@highlightsfoundation.org *Web Site:* www.highlightsfoundation.org, pg 612

The Intrepid Traveler, 152 Staltonstall Pkwy (rear entrance), East Haven, CT 06512 *Tel:* 203-469-0214 *E-mail:* admin@intrepidtraveler.com *Web Site:* www.intrepidtraveler.com, pg 121

Investigative Reporters & Editors, Missouri School of Journalism, 141 Neff Annex, Columbia, MO 65211 *Tel:* 573-882-2042 *Fax:* 573-882-5431 *E-mail:* info@ire.org *Web Site:* www.ire.org, pg 568

IODE Jean Throop Book Award, 9-45 Frid St, Hamilton, ON L8P 4M3, Canada *Tel:* 905-522-9537 *Fax:* 905-522-3637 *E-mail:* iodeontario@bellnet.ca *Web Site:* www.iodeontario.ca, pg 656

IODE Violet Downey Book Award, 40 Orchard View Blvd, Suite 219, Toronto, ON M4R 1B9, Canada *Tel:* 416-487-4416 *Toll Free Tel:* 866-827-7428 *Fax:* 416-487-4417 *E-mail:* iodecanada@bellnet.ca *Web Site:* www.iode.ca, pg 656

Iowa Poetry Prize, 119 W Park Rd, 100 Kuhl House, Iowa City, IA 52242-1000 *Tel:* 319-335-2000 *Fax:* 319-335-2055 *E-mail:* uipress@uiowa.edu *Web Site:* www.uiowapress.org, pg 656

The Iowa Review Awards, 308 EPB, Iowa City, IA 52242-1408 *E-mail:* iowa-review@uiowa.edu *Web Site:* www.iowareview.org, pg 656

The Iowa Short Fiction Award, 102 Dey House, 507 N Clinton St, Iowa City, IA 52242-1000 *Tel:* 319-335-0416 *Fax:* 319-335-0420 *Web Site:* www.uiowapress.org/authors/iowa-short-fiction.htm, pg 656

Iowa Summer Writing Festival, 250 Continuing Educ Facility, University of Iowa, Iowa City, IA 52242 *Tel:* 319-335-4160 *E-mail:* iswfestival@uiowa.edu *Web Site:* iowasummerwritingfestival.org, pg 612

Iris Press, 969 Oak Ridge Tpke, No 328, Oak Ridge, TN 37830 *Web Site:* www.irisbooks.com, pg 121

Iron Gate Publishing, PO Box 999, Niwot, CO 80544 *Tel:* 303-530-2551 *Fax:* 303-530-5273 *E-mail:* editor@irongate.com *Web Site:* www.irongate.com, pg 121

Irwin Law Inc, 14 Duncan St, Suite 206, Toronto, ON M5H 3G8, Canada *Tel:* 416-862-7690 *Toll Free Tel:* 888-314-9014 *Fax:* 416-862-9236 *Web Site:* www.irwinlaw.com, pg 461

ISI Books, 3901 Centerville Rd, Wilmington, DE 19807-1938 *Tel:* 302-652-4600 *Toll Free Tel:* 800-526-7022 *Fax:* 302-652-1760 *E-mail:* info@isi.org; isibooks@isi.org *Web Site:* www.isibooks.org, pg 121

Island Press, 2000 "M" St NW, Suite 650, Washington, DC 20036 *Tel:* 202-232-7933 *Toll Free Tel:* 800-828-1302 *Fax:* 202-234-1328 *E-mail:* info@islandpress.org *Web Site:* www.islandpress.org, pg 121

Italica Press, 595 Main St, Suite 605, New York, NY 10044 *Tel:* 917-371-0563 *E-mail:* inquiries@italicapress.com *Web Site:* www.italicapress.com, pg 121

ITMB Publishing Ltd, 12300 Bridgeport Rd, Richmond, BC V6V 1J5, Canada *Tel:* 604-273-1400 *Fax:* 604-273-1488 *E-mail:* itmb@itmb.com *Web Site:* www.itmb.com, pg 461

iUniverse, 1663 Liberty Dr, Bloomington, IN 47403 *Toll Free Tel:* 800-AUTHORS (288-4677) *Fax:* 812-355-4085 *Web Site:* www.iuniverse.com, pg 121

Richard Ivey School of Business, Ivey Business School at Western University, 1255 Western Rd, London, ON N6G 0N1, Canada *Tel:* 519-661-3206; 519-661-3208 *Toll Free Tel:* 800-649-6355 *Fax:* 519-661-3485; 519-661-3882 *E-mail:* cases@ivey.uwo.ca *Web Site:* www.iveycases.com; www.ivey.uwo.ca, pg 461

The Ivy League of Artists Inc, 18 Edgemere Rd, Livingston, NJ 07039 *Tel:* 973-992-4048 *Fax:* 973-992-4049 *E-mail:* ilartists2@gmail.com, pg 543

IWWG Annual Summer Conference, 5 Penn Plaza, 19th fl, PMB 19059, New York, NY 10001 *Tel:* 917-720-6959 *E-mail:* iwwgquestions@iwwg.org *Web Site:* www.iwwg.org, pg 612

JABberwocky Literary Agency Inc, 49 W 45 St, 12th fl, New York, NY 10036 *Tel:* 917-388-3010 *Fax:* 917-388-2998 *Web Site:* www.awfulagent.com, pg 522

Jackie White Memorial National Children's Playwriting Contest, 1400 Forum Blvd, 1C No 214, Columbia, MO 65203 *E-mail:* jwm@cectheatre.org *Web Site:* www.cectheatre.org, pg 657

Joseph Henry Jackson Literary Award, One Embarcadero Ctr, Suite 1400, San Francisco, CA 94111 *Tel:* 415-733-8500 *E-mail:* info@sff.org; artsinfo@sff.org *Web Site:* www.sff.org, pg 657

Melanie Jackson Agency LLC, 41 W 72 St, Suite 3F, New York, NY 10023 *Tel:* 212-873-3373, pg 522

The Jackson Poetry Prize, 90 Broad St, Suite 2100, New York, NY 10004 *Tel:* 212-226-3586 *Fax:* 212-226-3963 *E-mail:* admin@pw.org *Web Site:* www.pw.org, pg 657

Jain Publishing Co, PO Box 3523, Fremont, CA 94539 *Tel:* 510-659-8272 *Fax:* 510-659-0501 *E-mail:* mail@jainpub.com *Web Site:* www.jainpub.com, pg 121

James Peter Associates Inc, PO Box 358, New Canaan, CT 06840 *Tel:* 203-972-1070 *Web Site:* www.jamespeterassociates.com, pg 522

J Franklin Jameson Fellowship in American History, 400 "A" St SE, Washington, DC 20003 *Tel:* 202-544-2422 *Fax:* 202-544-8307 *E-mail:* awards@historians.org *Web Site:* www.historians.org, pg 657

Jan Williams Indexing Services, 300 Dartmouth College Hwy, Lyme, NH 03768-3207 *Tel:* 603-795-4924 *Web Site:* www.janwilliamsindexing.com, pg 496

Janklow & Nesbit Associates, 285 Madison Ave, 21st fl, New York, NY 10017 *Tel:* 212-421-1700 *Fax:* 212-355-1403 *E-mail:* info@janklow.com *Web Site:* www.janklowandnesbit.com, pg 522

Janus Literary Agency, PO Box 837, Methuen, MA 01844 *Tel:* 978-273-4227 *E-mail:* janusliteraryagency@gmail.com *Web Site:* janusliteraryagency.com, pg 522

Japan-US Friendship Commission Translation Prize, Columbia University, 507 Kent Hall, MC3920, New York, NY 10027 *Tel:* 212-854-5036 *Fax:* 212-854-4019 *Web Site:* www.keenecenter.org, pg 657

JayJo Books LLC, One Huntington Quadrangle, Suite 1N03, Melville, NY 11747 *Tel:* 516-496-4863 *Toll Free Tel:* 800-999-6884 *Fax:* 516-496-4050 *Toll Free Fax:* 800-262-1886 *E-mail:* jayjobooks@guidance-group.com *Web Site:* www.guidance-group.com; www.jayjo.com, pg 121

Jefferson Cup Award, c/o Virginia Library Association (VLA), PO Box 56312, Virginia Beach, VA 23456 *Tel:* 757-689-0594 *Fax:* 757-447-3478 *Web Site:* www.vla.org, pg 657

Jellinek & Murray Literary Agency, 47-231 Kamakoi Rd, Kaneohe, HI 96744 *Tel:* 808-239-8451, pg 522

Jenkins Group Inc, 1129 Woodmere Ave, Suite B, Traverse City, MI 49686 *Tel:* 231-933-0445 *Toll Free Tel:* 800-706-4636 *Fax:* 231-933-0448 *E-mail:* info@bookpublishing.com *Web Site:* www.bookpublishing.com, pg 496

Carolyn Jenks Agency, 30 Cambridge Park Dr, Suite 3140, Cambridge, MA 02140 *Tel:* 617-233-9130 *E-mail:* queries@carolynjenksagency.com (submissions) *Web Site:* www.carolynjenksagency.com, pg 522

Jentel Artist Residency Program, 130 Lower Piney Rd, Banner, WY 82832 *Tel:* 307-737-2311 *Fax:* 307-737-2305 *E-mail:* jentel@jentelarts.org *Web Site:* www.jentelarts.org, pg 612

Jerome Award, 8550 United Plaza Blvd, Suite 1001, Baton Rouge, LA 70809 *Tel:* 225-408-4417 *E-mail:* cla2@cathla.org *Web Site:* cathla.org, pg 657

Jerome Fellowship, 2301 Franklin Ave E, Minneapolis, MN 55406-1099 *Tel:* 612-332-7481 *Fax:* 612-332-6037 *E-mail:* info@pwcenter.org *Web Site:* www.pwcenter.org, pg 657

JET Literary Associates Inc, 941 Calle Mejia, Suite 507, Santa Fe, NM 87501 *Tel:* 505-780-0721 *E-mail:* etp@jetliterary.com *Web Site:* www.jetliterary.wordpress.com, pg 523

Jewel Box Theatre Playwriting Competition, 3700 N Walker, Oklahoma City, OK 73118-7031 *Tel:* 405-521-1786 *Web Site:* jewelboxtheatre.org, pg 657

Jewish Book Council, 520 Eighth Ave, 4th fl, New York, NY 10018 *Tel:* 212-201-2920 *Fax:* 212-532-4952 *E-mail:* jbc@jewishbooks.org *Web Site:* www.jewishbookcouncil.org, pg 568

Jewish Lights, 4507 Charlotte Ave, Suite 100, Nashville, TN 37209 *Tel:* 615-255-BOOK (255-2665) *Fax:* 615-255-5081 *E-mail:* marketing@turnerpublishing.com *Web Site:* jewishlights.com; www.turnerpublishing.com, pg 121

Jewish Publication Society, 2100 Arch St, Philadelphia, PA 19103 *Tel:* 215-832-0600 *Toll Free Tel:* 800-234-3151 *Fax:* 215-568-2017 *Web Site:* www.jps.org, pg 122

JFE Editorial, 8425 Doreen Ave, Fort Worth, TX 76116-4922 *Tel:* 817-560-7018, pg 496

Jhpiego, 1615 Thames St, Baltimore, MD 21231-3492 *Tel:* 410-537-1800 *Fax:* 410-537-1473 *E-mail:* info@jhpiego.net *Web Site:* www.jhpiego.org, pg 122

JIST Publishing, 875 Montreal Way, St Paul, MN 55102 *Toll Free Tel:* 800-328-1452 *Toll Free Fax:* 800-328-4564 *E-mail:* educate@emcp.com *Web Site:* jist.emcp.com, pg 122

JL Communications, 10205 Green Holly Terr, Silver Spring, MD 20902 *Tel:* 301-593-0640, pg 496

JMW Group Inc, 347 Rte 6, No 867, Mahopac, NY 10541 *Tel:* 914-841-7105 *Fax:* 914-248-8861 *E-mail:* jmwgroup@jmwgroup.net *Web Site:* jmwgroup.net, pg 523

The JOC Group Inc, 2 Penn Plaza E, Newark, NJ 07105 *Tel:* 973-776-8660 *Web Site:* www.joc.com, pg 122

Jody Rein Books Inc, 7741 S Ash Ct, Centennial, CO 80122 *Tel:* 303-694-9386 *Web Site:* www.jodyreinbooks.com, pg 523

John Deere Publishing, 5440 Corporate Park Dr, Davenport, IA 52807 *Toll Free Tel:* 800-522-7448 (orders) *Fax:* 563-355-3690 *E-mail:* johndeerepublishing@johndeere.com *Web Site:* www.johndeere.com/publications, pg 122

John Steinbeck Short Story Award, San Jose State University, English Dept, One Washington Sq, San Jose, CA 95192-0090 *Tel:* 408-924-4441 *Web Site:* www.reedmag.org, pg 657

The Johns Hopkins University Press, 2715 N Charles St, Baltimore, MD 21218-4363 *Tel:* 410-516-6900; 410-516-6987 (journal orders outside US & CN) *Toll Free Tel:* 800-537-5487 (book orders & cust serv); 800-548-1784 (journal orders) *Fax:* 410-516-6968; 410-516-3866 (journal orders) *E-mail:* hfscustserv@press.

jhu.edu (cust serv); jrnlcirc@press.jhu.edu (journal orders) *Web Site:* www.press.jhu.edu; muse.jhu.edu, pg 122

Cliff Johnson & Associates, 10867 Fruitland Dr, Studio City, CA 91604 *Tel:* 818-761-5665 *Fax:* 818-761-9501 *E-mail:* quest543@yahoo.com, pg 496

Jones & Bartlett Learning LLC, 5 Wall St, Burlington, MA 01803 *Tel:* 978-443-5000 *Toll Free Tel:* 800-832-0034 *Fax:* 978-443-8000 *E-mail:* info@jblearning.com *Web Site:* www.jblearning.com, pg 123

Anson Jones MD Awards, 401 W 15 St, Austin, TX 78701 *Tel:* 512-370-1300 *Fax:* 512-370-1693 *Web Site:* www.texmed.org, pg 657

Jones Hutton Literary Associates, 140D Heritage Village, Southbury, CT 06488 *Tel:* 203-558-4478 *E-mail:* huttonbooks@hotmail.com, pg 523

Jesse H Jones Award, c/o 7748 Hwy 290 W, Austin, TX 78736-3202 *Tel:* 512-683-5640 *E-mail:* president@texasinstituteofletters.org *Web Site:* www.texasinstituteofletters.org, pg 657

Jones McClure Publishing, 3131 Eastside St, Suite 300, Houston, TX 77098 *Tel:* 713-335-8200 *Toll Free Tel:* 800-626-6667 *Fax:* 713-335-8201 *E-mail:* comments@jonesmcclure.com *Web Site:* www.jonesmcclure.com, pg 123

Joshua Tree Publishing, 3 Golf Ctr, Suite 201, Hoffman Estates, IL 60169 *Tel:* 312-893-7525 *E-mail:* info@joshuatreepublishing.com *Web Site:* www.joshuatreepublishing.com; www.centaurbooks.com (imprint); www.chiralhouse.com (imprint), pg 123

Journal of Roman Archaeology LLC, 95 Peleg Rd, Portsmouth, RI 02871 *Tel:* 401-683-1955 *Fax:* 401-683-1975 *E-mail:* jra@journalofromanarch.com *Web Site:* www.journalofromanarch.com, pg 123

Joy Publishing Co, PO Box 9901, Fountain Valley, CA 92708 *Tel:* 714-545-4321 *Toll Free Tel:* 800-454-8228 (orders) *Fax:* 714-708-2099 *Web Site:* www.joypublishing.com; kit-cat.com, pg 123

Joyce Media Inc, 3413 Soledad Canyon Rd, Acton, CA 93510-1974 *Tel:* 661-269-1169 *Fax:* 661-269-2139 *E-mail:* help@joycemediainc.com *Web Site:* www.joycemediainc.com, pg 123

Judah, Sarah, Grace & Tom Memorial, 900 Timber Creek Place, Virginia Beach, VA 23464 *E-mail:* poetryinva@aol.com; info@poetryvirginia.org *Web Site:* poetrysocietyofvirginia.org, pg 658

Judaica Press Inc, 123 Ditmas Ave, Brooklyn, NY 11218 *Tel:* 718-972-6200 *Toll Free Tel:* 800-972-6201 *Fax:* 718-972-6204 *E-mail:* info@judaicapress.com; orders@judaicapress.com *Web Site:* www.judaicapress.com, pg 123

Judson Press, 588 N Gulph Rd, King of Prussia, PA 19406 *Toll Free Tel:* 800-458-3766 *Fax:* 610-768-2107 *Web Site:* www.judsonpress.com, pg 123

Jump!, 5357 Penn Ave, Minneapolis, MN 55419 *Toll Free Tel:* 888-799-1860 *Toll Free Fax:* 800-675-6679 *E-mail:* customercare@jumplibrary.com *Web Site:* www.jumplibrary.com, pg 123

Jump at the Sun, 125 West End Ave, 3rd fl, New York, NY 10023 *Web Site:* books.disney.com, pg 124

Jungle Wagon Press, 5116 Didier Ave, Rockford, IL 61101 *Tel:* 815-988-9048 *E-mail:* junglewagonpress@gmail.com *Web Site:* www.junglewagonpress.com, pg 124

Juniper Prize for Fiction, East Experiment Sta, 671 N Pleasant St, Amherst, MA 01003 *E-mail:* info@umpress.umass.edu *Web Site:* www.umass.edu/umpress; www.umass.edu/umpress/content/juniper-literary-prize-series, pg 658

Juniper Prize for Poetry, East Experiment Sta, 671 N Pleasant St, Amherst, MA 01003 *E-mail:* info@umpress.umass.edu *Web Site:* www.umass.edu/umpress; www.umass.edu/umpress/content/juniper-literary-prize-series, pg 658

Juniper Summer Writing Institute, c/o University Conference Services, 810 Campus Center, One Campus Center Way, Amherst, MA 01003 *Tel:* 413-545-5503 *E-mail:* juniperinstitute@hfa.umass.edu *Web Site:* www.umass.edu/juniperinstitute, pg 612

Just Creative Writing & Indexing Services (JCR), 301 Wood Duck Dr, Greensboro, MD 21639 *Tel:* 410-482-6337 *E-mail:* support@justcreativewriting.com *Web Site:* www.justcreativewriting.com, pg 496

Just World Books LLC, PO Box 5484, Charlottesville, VA 22905 *Toll Free Tel:* 888-506-3769 *E-mail:* sales@justworldbooks.com *Web Site:* justworldbooks.com, pg 124

Juvenile Literary Awards/Young People's Literature Awards, 506 Rose Ave, Des Plaines, IL 60016 *Tel:* 847-827-8339 *Web Site:* www.fawchicago.org, pg 658

Kabbalah Publishing, 1100 S Robertson Blvd, Los Angeles, CA 90035 *Tel:* 310-601-1039 *Fax:* 310-657-7957 *E-mail:* customerservice@kabbalahpublishing.com; kcla@kabbalah.com *Web Site:* publishing.kabbalah.com; www.kabbalah.com, pg 124

Kaeden Corp, PO Box 16190, Rocky River, OH 44116-0190 *Tel:* 440-617-1400 *Toll Free Tel:* 800-890-7323 *Fax:* 440-617-1403 *E-mail:* info@kaeden.com *Web Site:* www.kaeden.com, pg 124

Frederick D Kagy Education Award of Excellence, 301 Brush Creek Rd, Warrendale, PA 15086-7529 *Tel:* 412-741-6860 *Toll Free Tel:* 800-910-4283 *Fax:* 412-741-2311 *E-mail:* printingind@comm.printing.org *Web Site:* www.printing.org, pg 658

Kalmbach Publishing Co, 21027 Crossroads Circle, Waukesha, WI 53186 *Tel:* 262-796-8776 *Toll Free Tel:* 800-533-6644 (cust serv & orders); 800-558-1544 *Fax:* 262-798-6592 *E-mail:* customerservice@kalmbach.com *Web Site:* www.kalmbach.com, pg 124

Kamehameha Publishing, 567 S King St, Suite 118, Honolulu, HI 96813 *Tel:* 808-534-8205 *Fax:* 808-541-5305 *E-mail:* publishing@ksbe.edu *Web Site:* kamehamehapublishing.org, pg 124

Kane Miller Books, 4901 Morena Blvd, Suite 213, San Diego, CA 92117 *E-mail:* submissions@kanemiller.com; info@kanemiller.com *Web Site:* www.kanemiller.com, pg 124

Kane Press Inc, 225 E 46 St, Suite 4D, New York, NY 10017-2924 *Tel:* 212-935-0246 *Web Site:* www.kanepress.com, pg 124

Sharon Kapnick, 185 West End Ave, New York, NY 10023-5547 *Tel:* 212-787-7231 *Web Site:* sharonswineline.wordpress.com, pg 496

Kapp Books LLC, 3602 Rocky Meadow Ct, Fairfax, VA 22033 *Tel:* 703-261-9171 *Fax:* 703-621-7162 *E-mail:* info@kappbooks.com *Web Site:* www.kappbooks.com, pg 124

Kar-Ben Publishing, 241 First Ave N, Minneapolis, MN 55401 *Tel:* 612-332-3344 *Toll Free Tel:* 800-4-KARBEN (452-7236) *Fax:* 612-332-7615 *Toll Free Fax:* 800-332-1132 *Web Site:* www.karben.com, pg 124

The Karpfinger Agency, 357 W 20 St, New York, NY 10011-3379 *Tel:* 212-691-2690 *Fax:* 212-691-7129 *E-mail:* info@karpfinger.com (no queries or submissions) *Web Site:* karpfinger.com, pg 523

Sue Kaufman Prize for First Fiction, 633 W 155 St, New York, NY 10032 *Tel:* 212-368-5900 *Fax:* 212-491-4615 *E-mail:* academy@artsandletters.org *Web Site:* www.artsandletters.org, pg 658

Kazi Publications Inc, 3023 W Belmont Ave, Chicago, IL 60618 *Tel:* 773-267-7001 *Fax:* 773-267-7002 *E-mail:* info@kazi.org *Web Site:* www.kazi.org, pg 125

Ezra Jack Keats/Kerlan Memorial Fellowship, University of Minnesota, 113 Andersen Library, 222 21 Ave S, Minneapolis, MN 55455 *Tel:* 612-624-4576 *E-mail:* asc-clrc@umn.edu *Web Site:* www.lib.umn.edu/clrc, pg 658

Keim Publishing, 66 Main St, Suite 807, Yonkers, NY 10701 *Tel:* 917-655-7190, pg 496

J J Keller & Associates, Inc, 3003 Breezewood Lane, Neenah, WI 54957 *Tel:* 920-722-2848 *Toll Free Tel:* 877-564-2333 *Toll Free Fax:* 800-727-7516 *E-mail:* contactus@jjkeller.com; customerservice@jjkeller.com *Web Site:* www.jjkeller.com, pg 125

Keller Media Inc, 578 Washington Blvd, No 745, Marina del Rey, CA 90292 *Toll Free Tel:* 800-278-8706 *E-mail:* query@kellermedia.com *Web Site:* kellermedia.com/query, pg 523

Joan Kelly Memorial Prize in Women's History, 400 "A" St SE, Washington, DC 20003 *Tel:* 202-544-2422 *Fax:* 202-544-8307 *E-mail:* awards@historians.org *Web Site:* www.historians.org, pg 658

Kelsey Street Press, 2824 Kelsey St, Berkeley, CA 94705 *E-mail:* info@kelseyst.com *Web Site:* www.kelseyst.com, pg 125

Kendall Hunt Publishing Co, 4050 Westmark Dr, Dubuque, IA 52002-2624 *Tel:* 563-589-1000 *Toll Free Tel:* 800-228-0810 (orders) *Fax:* 563-589-1046 *Toll Free Fax:* 800-772-9165 *E-mail:* orders@kendallhunt.com *Web Site:* www.kendallhunt.com, pg 125

Kennedy Information Inc, 24 Railroad St, Keene, NH 03431 *Tel:* 603-924-0900 *Toll Free Tel:* 800-531-0140 *Fax:* 603-357-8112 *E-mail:* customerservice@kennedyinfo.com *Web Site:* www.kennedyinfo.com, pg 125

Robert F Kennedy Book Awards, 1300 19 St NW, Suite 750, Washington, DC 20036 *Tel:* 202-463-7575 *Fax:* 202-463-6606 *E-mail:* info@rfkhumanrights.org *Web Site:* rfkhumanrights.org, pg 658

Kensington Publishing Corp, 119 W 40 St, New York, NY 10018 *Tel:* 212-407-1500 *Toll Free Tel:* 800-221-2647 *Fax:* 212-935-0699 *Web Site:* www.kensingtonbooks.com, pg 125

Kent State University Press, 1118 University Library Bldg, 1125 Risman Dr, Kent, OH 44242 *Tel:* 330-672-7913 *Fax:* 330-672-3104 *E-mail:* ksupress@kent.edu *Web Site:* www.kentstateuniversitypress.com, pg 126

Kentucky Women Writers Conference, 232 E Maxwell St, Lexington, KY 40506-0344 *Tel:* 859-257-2874 *E-mail:* kentuckywomenwriters@gmail.com *Web Site:* www.kentuckywomenwriters.org, pg 612

Kentucky Writers Conference, 1906 College Heights Blvd, Suite 11067, Bowling Green, KY 42101-1067 *Tel:* 270-745-4502 *E-mail:* sokybookfest@wku.edu *Web Site:* www.sokybookfest.org, pg 612

Natasha Kern Literary Agency Inc, PO Box 1069, White Salmon, WA 98672 *Tel:* 509-493-3803 *E-mail:* agent@natashakern.com *Web Site:* www.natashakern.com, pg 523

Kessinger Publishing LLC, PO Box 1404, Whitefish, MT 59937 *Web Site:* www.kessinger.net, pg 126

Jascha Kessler, 218 16 St, Santa Monica, CA 90402-2216 *Tel:* 310-393-7968 *Fax:* 310-393-7968 (by request only) *E-mail:* urim.urim@gmail.com *Web Site:* www.jfkessler.com; www.xlibris.com, pg 496

Louise B Ketz Agency, 414 E 78 St, Suite 1-B, New York, NY 10075 *Tel:* 212-249-0668 *E-mail:* ketzagency@aol.com, pg 523

Key West Literary Seminar, 717 Love Lane, Key West, FL 33040 *Tel:* 305-293-9291 *Toll Free Tel:* 888-293-9291 *E-mail:* mail@kwls.org *Web Site:* www.kwls.org/seminar; www.kwls.org, pg 612

Key West Literary Seminar's Writers' Workshop Program, 717 Love Lane, Key West, FL 33040 *Tel:* 305-293-9291 *Toll Free Tel:* 888-293-9291 *E-mail:* mail@kwls.org *Web Site:* www.kwls.org; www.kwls.org/writers_workshops, pg 612

Virginia Kidd Agency Inc, 538 E Harford St, PO Box 278, Milford, PA 18337 *Tel:* 570-296-6205 *Web Site:* vk-agency.com, pg 524

Kids Can Press Ltd, 25 Dockside Dr, Toronto, ON M5A 0B5, Canada *Tel:* 416-479-7000 *Toll Free Tel:* 800-265-0884 *Fax:* 416-960-5437 *E-mail:* info@kidscan.com; customerservice@kidscan.com *Web Site:* www.kidscanpress.com; www.kidscanpress.ca, pg 461

Kidsbooks LLC, 3535 W Peterson Ave, Chicago, IL 60659 *Tel:* 773-509-0707 *Fax:* 773-509-0404 *E-mail:* sales@kidsbooks.com; customerservice@kidsbooks.com *Web Site:* www.kidsbooks.com, pg 126

Kindred Productions, 1310 Taylor Ave, Winnipeg, MB R3M 3Z6, Canada *Tel:* 204-669-6575 *Toll Free Tel:* 800-545-7322 *Fax:* 204-654-1865 *E-mail:* kindred@mbchurches.ca *Web Site:* www.kindredproductions.com, pg 461

Kinesiology Books Publisher, 212 Robert St (side basement door), Toronto, ON M5S 2K7, Canada *Tel:* 416-323-9438 *Fax:* 416-966-9022 *E-mail:* sbp@sportbookspub.com; kbp@kinesiology101.com *Web Site:* www.sportbookspub.com, pg 461

Coretta Scott King Book Awards, 50 E Huron St, Chicago, IL 60611 *Toll Free Tel:* 800-545-2433 *E-mail:* olos@ala.org *Web Site:* www.ala.org/emiert/cskbookawards, pg 658

Coretta Scott King - Virginia Hamilton Award for Lifetime Achievement, 50 E Huron St, Chicago, IL 60611 *Toll Free Tel:* 800-545-2433 *E-mail:* diversity@ala.org *Web Site:* www.ala.org/emiert/virginia-hamilton-award-lifetime-achievement, pg 659

Jessica Kingsley Publishers Inc, 400 Market St, Suite 400, Philadelphia, PA 19106 *Tel:* 215-922-1161 *Toll Free Tel:* 866-416-1078 (cust serv) *Fax:* 215-922-1474 *E-mail:* orders@jkp.com; hello.usa@jkp.com *Web Site:* www.jkp.com, pg 126

Kinship Books, 305 Cedar Heights Rd, Rhinebeck, NY 12572 *Tel:* 845-876-4592 (orders) *E-mail:* kinship@hvc.rr.com *Web Site:* www.kinshipny.com, pg 126

Kirchoff/Wohlberg Inc, 897 Boston Post Rd, Madison, CT 06443 *Tel:* 203-245-7308 *Fax:* 203-245-3218 *Web Site:* www.kirchoffwohlberg.com, pg 524

Kirk House Publishers, PO Box 390759, Minneapolis, MN 55439 *Tel:* 952-835-1828 *Toll Free Tel:* 888-696-1828 *Fax:* 952-835-2613 *E-mail:* publisher@kirkhouse.com *Web Site:* www.kirkhouse.com, pg 126

Kirkbride Bible Co Inc, 1102 Deloss St, Indianapolis, IN 46203 *Tel:* 317-633-1900 *Toll Free Tel:* 800-428-4385 *Fax:* 317-633-1444 *E-mail:* sales@kirkbride.com; info@kirkbride.com *Web Site:* www.kirkbride.com, pg 126

Kiva Publishing Inc, 10 Bella Loma, Santa Fe, NM 87506 *Tel:* 909-896-0518 *E-mail:* kivapub@aol.com *Web Site:* www.kivapub.com, pg 126

Harvey Klinger Inc, 300 W 55 St, Suite 11V, New York, NY 10019 *Tel:* 212-581-7068 *Fax:* 212-315-3823 *E-mail:* queries@harveyklinger.com *Web Site:* www.harveyklinger.com, pg 524

Klutz, 568 Broadway, Suite 503, New York, NY 10012 *Tel:* 212-343-6360 *Fax:* 212-343-6366 *E-mail:* sales@klutz.com *Web Site:* store.scholastic.com, pg 126

Wolters Kluwer Law & Business, 76 Ninth Ave, 7th fl, New York, NY 10011-5201 *Tel:* 212-771-0600; 301-698-7100 (cust serv outside US) *Toll Free Tel:* 800-234-1660 (cust serv) *E-mail:* customer.service@wolterskluwer.com; sales@kluwerlaw.com *Web Site:* www.wklawbusiness.com, pg 127

Kneerim & Williams Agency, 90 Canal St, Boston, MA 02114 *Tel:* 617-303-1650 *Web Site:* www.kwlit.com, pg 524

The Knight Agency Inc, 570 East Ave, Madison, GA 30650 *E-mail:* submissions@knightagency.net *Web Site:* www.knightagency.net, pg 524

The Knight-Risser Prize for Western Environmental Journalism, Stanford University, 450 Serra Mall, Bldg 120, Rm 424, Stanford, CA 94305-2050 *Tel:* 650-723-4937 *Fax:* 650-725-6154 *E-mail:* knightrisserprize@lists.stanford.edu *Web Site:* knightrisser.stanford.edu, pg 659

Theodore Knight PhD, RockCliff Farm, 40 Old Louisquisset Pike, Unit 101A, North Smithfield, RI 02896 *Tel:* 401-597-6982 *E-mail:* tedknight1@cox.net, pg 496

Knightville Poetry Contest, PO Box 5101, Hanover, NH 03755 *E-mail:* info@newguardreview.com *Web Site:* www.newguardreview.com, pg 659

Allen A Knoll Publishers, 200 W Victoria St, Santa Barbara, CA 93101-3627 *Tel:* 805-564-3377 *Toll Free Tel:* 800-777-7623 *Fax:* 805-966-6657 *E-mail:* bookinfo@knollpublishers.com *Web Site:* www.knollpublishers.com, pg 127

Alfred A Knopf/Everyman's Library, c/o Penguin Random House Inc, 1745 Broadway, New York, NY 10019 *Tel:* 212-751-2600 *Toll Free Tel:* 800-638-6460 *Fax:* 212-572-2593 *Web Site:* www.knopfdoubleday.com, pg 127

Knopf Canada, 320 Front St W, Suite 1400, Toronto, ON M5V 3B6, Canada *Tel:* 416-364-4449 *Toll Free Tel:* 888-523-9292 *Fax:* 416-598-7764 *Web Site:* www.penguinrandomhouse.ca, pg 462

Kodansha USA Inc, 451 Park Ave S, 7th fl, New York, NY 10016 *Tel:* 917-322-6200 *Fax:* 212-935-6929 *E-mail:* info@kodansha-usa.com *Web Site:* www.kodanshausa.com, pg 127

Bill Koehnlein, 236 E Fifth St, New York, NY 10003-8545 *Tel:* 212-674-9145 *E-mail:* koehnlein.bill@gmail.com, pg 496

Barry R Koffler, Featherside, 14 Ginger Rd, High Falls, NY 12440 *Tel:* 845-687-9851 *E-mail:* barkof@feathersite.com, pg 496

Kogan Page Publishers, 1518 Walnut St, Suite 900, Philadelphia, PA 19102 *Tel:* 215-928-9112 *Fax:* 215-928-9113 *E-mail:* info@koganpage.com *Web Site:* www.koganpageusa.com, pg 127

Paul Kohner Agency, 9300 Wilshire Blvd, Suite 555, Beverly Hills, CA 90212 *Tel:* 310-550-1060 *Fax:* 310-276-1083, pg 525

Koho Pono LLC, 15024 SE Pinegrove Loop, Clackamas, OR 97015 *Tel:* 503-723-7392 *Toll Free Tel:* 800-937-8000 (orders) *Toll Free Fax:* 800-876-0186 (orders) *E-mail:* info@kohopono.com; orders@ingrambook.com *Web Site:* kohopono.com, pg 127

KOK Edit, 15 Hare Lane, East Setauket, NY 11733-3606 *Tel:* 631-997-8191 *Fax:* 631-474-9849 *E-mail:* editor@kokedit.com *Web Site:* www.kokedit.com; twitter.com/kokedit; www.facebook.com/K.OmooreKlopf; www.linkedin.com/in/kokedit; www.editor-mom.blogspot.com, pg 496

Konecky & Konecky LLC, 72 Ayers Point Rd, Old Saybrook, CT 06475 *Tel:* 860-388-0878 *Fax:* 860-388-0273 *Web Site:* www.koneckyandkonecky.com, pg 128

Linda Konner Literary Agency, 10 W 15 St, Suite 1918, New York, NY 10011 *Tel:* 212-691-3419 *Fax:* 212-691-0935 *Web Site:* www.lindakonnerliteraryagency.com, pg 525

Barbara S Kouts Literary Agency LLC, PO Box 560, Bellport, NY 11713 *Tel:* 631-286-1278 *Fax:* 631-286-1538 *E-mail:* bkouts@aol.com, pg 525

Katherine Singer Kovacs Prize, 85 Broad St, Suite 500, New York, NY 10004-2434 *Tel:* 646-576-5141; 646-576-5000 *Fax:* 646-458-0030 *E-mail:* awards@mla.org *Web Site:* www.mla.org, pg 659

Kraft & Kraft, 40 Memorial Hwy, Apt 23-C, New Rochelle, NY 10801 *Tel:* 914-319-3320 *Web Site:* www.erickraft.com, pg 497

Eileen Kramer, 336 Great Rd, Stow, MA 01775 *Tel:* 978-897-4121 *E-mail:* kramer@tiac.net, pg 497

HJ Kramer Inc, PO Box 1082, Tiburon, CA 94920 *Tel:* 415-884-2100 (ext 10) *Toll Free Tel:* 800-972-6657 *Fax:* 415-435-5364 *E-mail:* hjkramer@jps.net *Web Site:* www.hjkramer.com; www.newworldlibrary.com, pg 128

Michael Kraus Research Grant in American Colonial History, 400 "A" St SE, Washington, DC 20003 *Tel:* 202-544-2422 *Fax:* 202-544-8307 *E-mail:* awards@historians.org *Web Site:* www.historians.org, pg 659

Krause Publications Inc, 700 E State St, Iola, WI 54990 *Tel:* 715-445-2214 *Toll Free Tel:* 800-258-0929 (cust serv); 888-457-2873 (orders) *Fax:* 715-445-4087 *E-mail:* bookorders@krause.com *Web Site:* www.krausebooks.com, pg 128

Kregel Publications, 2450 Oak Industrial Dr NE, Grand Rapids, MI 49505 *Tel:* 616-451-4775 *Toll Free Tel:* 800-733-2607 *Fax:* 616-451-9330 *E-mail:* kregelbooks@kregel.com *Web Site:* www.kregel.com, pg 128

Stuart Krichevsky Literary Agency Inc, 6 E 39 St, Suite 500, New York, NY 10016 *Tel:* 212-725-5288 *Fax:* 212-725-5275 *E-mail:* query@skagency.com *Web Site:* skagency.com, pg 525

Krieger Publishing Co, 1725 Krieger Lane, Malabar, FL 32950 *Tel:* 321-724-9542 *Fax:* 321-951-3671 *E-mail:* info@krieger-publishing.com *Web Site:* www.krieger-publishing.com, pg 128

The Robert Kroetsch City of Edmonton Book Prize, 11759 Groat Rd, Edmonton, AB T5M 3K6, Canada *Tel:* 780-422-8174 *Toll Free Tel:* 800-665-5354 (AB only) *Fax:* 780-422-2663 (attn WGA) *E-mail:* mail@writersguild.ca *Web Site:* writersguild.ca, pg 659

Edite Kroll Literary Agency Inc, 20 Cross St, Saco, ME 04072 *Tel:* 207-283-8797 *Fax:* 207-283-8799, pg 525

Lynn C Kronzek & Richard A Flom, 145 S Glenoaks Blvd, Suite 240, Burbank, CA 91502 *Tel:* 818-768-7688 *Fax:* 818-768-7648, pg 497

KTAV Publishing House Inc, 888 Newark Ave, Jersey City, NJ 07306 *Tel:* 201-963-9524 *Fax:* 201-963-0102 *E-mail:* orders@ktav.com *Web Site:* www.ktav.com, pg 128

Kumarian Press, 1800 30 St, Suite 314, Boulder, CO 80301 *Tel:* 303-444-6684 *Fax:* 303-444-0824 *E-mail:* questions@rienner.com *Web Site:* www.rienner.com, pg 128

Polly Kummel LLC, 624 Boardman Rd, Aiken, SC 29803 *Tel:* 803-641-6831 *E-mail:* editor@amazinphrasin.com; pollyk1@msn.com *Web Site:* www.amazinphrasin.com, pg 497

Kumon Publishing North America, 300 Frank Burr Blvd, Suite 6, Teaneck, NJ 07666 *Tel:* 201-836-2105 *Fax:* 201-836-1559 *E-mail:* books@kumon.com *Web Site:* www.kumonbooks.com, pg 128

Kumu Kahua/UHM Theatre & Dance Department Playwriting Contest, 46 Merchant St, Honolulu, HI 96813 *Tel:* 808-536-4441 (box off); 808-536-4222 *Fax:* 808-536-4226 *E-mail:* kumukahuatheatre@hawaiiantel.net *Web Site:* www.kumukahua.org, pg 659

George Kurian Reference Books, 3689 Campbell Ct, Yorktown Heights, NY 10598 *Tel:* 914-962-3287 *Fax:* 914-962-3287, pg 128

The LA Literary Agency, PO Box 46370, Los Angeles, CA 90046 *Tel:* 323-654-5288 *E-mail:* laliteraryagency@mac.com; mail@laliteraryagency.com *Web Site:* www.laliteraryagency.com, pg 525

Lachina Publishing Services Inc, 3791 S Green Rd, Cleveland, OH 44122 *Tel:* 216-292-7959 *E-mail:* info@lachina.com *Web Site:* www.lachina.com, pg 497

Lynne Lackenbach Editorial Services, 31 Pillsbury Rd, East Hampstead, NH 03826 *Tel:* 603-329-8133 *E-mail:* lynnelack@gmail.com, pg 497

Lake Claremont Press, PO Box 711, Chicago, IL 60690 *Tel:* 312-226-8400 *Fax:* 312-226-8420 *Web Site:* www.lakeclaremont.com, pg 129

Lake Superior Port Cities Inc, 310 E Superior St, Suite 125, Duluth, MN 55802 *Tel:* 218-722-5002 *Toll Free Tel:* 888-BIG-LAKE (244-5253) *Fax:* 218-722-4096 *E-mail:* reader@lakesuperior.com *Web Site:* www.lakesuperior.com, pg 129

LAMA Books, 2381 Sleepy Hollow Ave, Hayward, CA 94545-3429 *Tel:* 510-785-1091 *Toll Free Tel:* 888-452-6244 *Fax:* 510-785-1099 *Web Site:* www.lamabooks.com, pg 129

W Kaye Lamb Award, PO Box 5254, Sta B, Victoria, BC V8R 6N4, Canada *E-mail:* essays@bchistory.ca *Web Site:* www.bchistory.ca, pg 659

Lambda Literary Awards (Lammys), 5482 Wilshire Blvd, No 1595, Los Angeles, CA 90036 *Tel:* 323-643-4281 *E-mail:* admin@lambdaliterary.org *Web Site:* www.lambdaliterary.org, pg 659

Peter Lampack Agency Inc, 350 Fifth Ave, Suite 5300, New York, NY 10118 *Tel:* 212-687-9106 *Fax:* 212-687-9109 *Web Site:* www.peterlampackagency.com, pg 525

Gerald Lampert Memorial Award, 192 Spadina Ave, Suite 312, Toronto, ON M5T 2C2, Canada *Tel:* 416-504-1657 *Fax:* 416-504-0096 *E-mail:* admin@poets.ca *Web Site:* poets.ca, pg 659

Lanahan Publishers Inc, 324 Hawthorne Rd, Baltimore, MD 21210-2303 *Tel:* 410-366-2434 *Toll Free Tel:* 866-345-1949 *Fax:* 410-366-8798 *E-mail:* lanahan@aol.com *Web Site:* www.lanahanpublishers.com, pg 129

Land on Demand, 20 Long Crescent Dr, Bristol, VA 24201 *Tel:* 423-366-0513 *E-mail:* landondemand@gmail.com *Web Site:* boblandedits.blogspot.com, pg 497

Landauer Corp, 3100 101 St, Suite A, Urbandale, IA 50322 *Tel:* 515-287-2144 *Toll Free Tel:* 800-557-2144 *Fax:* 515-276-5102 *E-mail:* info@landauercorp.com *Web Site:* www.landauercorp.com, pg 129

Peter Lang Publishing Inc, 29 Broadway, 18th fl, New York, NY 10006-3223 *Tel:* 212-647-7706 *Toll Free Tel:* 800-770-5264 (cust serv) *Fax:* 212-647-7707 *Web Site:* www.peterlang.com, pg 129

LangMarc Publishing, 7500 Shadowridge Run, No 28, Austin, TX 78749 *Tel:* 512-394-0989 *Toll Free Tel:* 800-864-1648 (orders) *Fax:* 512-394-0829 *E-mail:* langmarc@booksails.com *Web Site:* www.langmarc.com, pg 129

Langum Prize in American Historical Fiction, 2809 Berkeley Dr, Birmingham, AL 35242 *Tel:* 360-809-0465 *E-mail:* langumtrust@gmail.com *Web Site:* www.langumtrust.org, pg 659

Langum Prize in American Legal History or Biography, 2809 Berkeley Dr, Birmingham, AL 35242 *Tel:* 360-809-0465 *E-mail:* langumtrust@gmail.com *Web Site:* www.langumtrust.org, pg 660

Lannan Literary Awards & Fellowships, 313 Read St, Santa Fe, NM 87501-2628 *Tel:* 505-986-8160 *E-mail:* info@lannan.org *Web Site:* www.lannan.org, pg 660

Lantern Books, 128 Second Place, Garden Suite, Brooklyn, NY 11231 *Tel:* 212-414-2275 *E-mail:* editorial@lanternbooks.com; info@lanternmedia.net *Web Site:* lanternbooks.presswarehouse.com/Home/home.aspx, pg 129

Laredo Publishing Co Inc, 465 Westview Ave, Englewood, NJ 07631 *Tel:* 201-408-4048 *E-mail:* info@laredopublishing.com *Web Site:* www.laredopublishing.com, pg 129

Lark Crafts, 1166 Avenue of the Americas, 17th fl, New York, NY 10036 *Tel:* 212-532-7160 *E-mail:* larkeditorial@sterlingpublishing.com; customerservice@sterlingpublishing.com *Web Site:* larkcrafts.com; www.facebook.com/LarkCrafts; www.sterlingpublishing.com, pg 129

Larson Publications, 4936 State Rte 414, Burdett, NY 14818 *Tel:* 607-546-9342 *Toll Free Tel:* 800-828-2197 *Fax:* 607-546-9344 *E-mail:* custserv@larsonpublications.com *Web Site:* www.larsonpublications.com, pg 129

Lasaria Creative Publishing, 4094 Majestic Lane, Suite 352, Fairfax, VA 22033 *E-mail:* info@lasariacreative.com *Web Site:* www.lasariacreative.com, pg 130

Latin American Literary Review Press, PO Box 7530, Pittsburgh, PA 15213 *Tel:* 412-824-7903 *E-mail:* lalrp.editor@gmail.com *Web Site:* www.lalrp.org, pg 130

Latino Books Into Movies Awards, 3445 Catalina Dr, Carlsbad, CA 92010 *Tel:* 760-434-1223 *Fax:* 760-434-7476 *Web Site:* www.award.news, pg 660

Laughing Elephant, 3645 Interlake N, Seattle, WA 98103 *Tel:* 206-447-9229 *Toll Free Tel:* 800-354-0400 *Fax:* 206-447-9189 *E-mail:* support@laughingelephant.com *Web Site:* www.laughingelephant.com, pg 130

LaurelTech, 4 S Market St, 4th fl, Boston, MA 02109-6201 *Tel:* 617-600-3366 *Fax:* 617-848-2938 *Web Site:* www.diacritech.com, pg 497

Laurier Books Ltd, PO Box 8493, Ottawa, ON K1G 3H9, Canada *Tel:* 613-738-2163 *Toll Free Fax:* 855-736-9160 *E-mail:* laurierbooks@yahoo.com, pg 462

Law School Admission Council, 662 Penn St, Newtown, PA 18940 *Tel:* 215-968-1101 *E-mail:* lsacaccounts@lsac.org *Web Site:* www.lsac.org, pg 130

The Lawbook Exchange Ltd, 33 Terminal Ave, Clark, NJ 07066-1321 *Tel:* 732-382-1800 *Toll Free Tel:* 800-422-6686 *Fax:* 732-382-1887 *E-mail:* law@lawbookexchange.com *Web Site:* www.lawbookexchange.com, pg 130

Lawrence Foundation Prize, University of Michigan, 0576 Rackham Bldg, 915 E Washington St, Ann Arbor, MI 48109-1070 *Tel:* 734-764-9265 *E-mail:* mqr@umich.edu *Web Site:* www.umich.edu/~mqr, pg 660

Merloyd Lawrence Inc, 102 Chestnut St, Boston, MA 02108 *Tel:* 617-523-5895 *Fax:* 617-263-2749, pg 130

Lawyers & Judges Publishing Co Inc, 917 N Swan Rd, Suite 300, Tucson, AZ 85711 *Tel:* 520-323-1500 *Toll Free Tel:* 800-209-7109 *Fax:* 520-323-0055 *Toll Free Fax:* 800-330-8795 *E-mail:* sales@lawyersandjudges.com *Web Site:* www.lawyersandjudges.com, pg 130

Sarah Lazin Books, 19 W 21 St, Suite 501, New York, NY 10010 *Tel:* 212-989-5757 *Fax:* 212-989-1393, pg 525

Stephen Leacock Memorial Medal for Humour, 149 Peter St N, Orillia, ON L3V 4Z4, Canada *Tel:* 705-326-9286 *Web Site:* www.leacock.ca, pg 660

Leadership Directories, 1407 Broadway, Suite 318, New York, NY 10018 *Tel:* 212-627-4140 *Toll Free Tel:* 800-627-0311 *Fax:* 212-645-0931 *E-mail:* info@leadershipdirectories.com *Web Site:* www.leadershipdirectories.com, pg 130

Leadership Ministries Worldwide/OBR, 3755 Pilot Point, Chattanooga, TN 37416 *Tel:* 423-855-2181 *Toll Free Tel:* 800-987-8790 *Fax:* 423-855-8616 *E-mail:* info@outlinebible.org *Web Site:* www.outlinebible.org, pg 130

Leaf Storm Press, PO Box 4670, Santa Fe, NM 87502-4670 *Tel:* 505-216-6155 *E-mail:* leafstormpress@gmail.com *Web Site:* leafstormpress.com, pg 131

The League of Canadian Poets, 192 Spadina Ave, Suite 312, Toronto, ON M5T 2C2, Canada *Tel:* 416-504-1657 *Fax:* 416-504-0096 *Web Site:* poets.ca, pg 568

League of Vermont Writers, PO Box 5046, Burlington, VT 05402 *Tel:* 802-349-7475 *E-mail:* lvw@leaguevtwriters.org *Web Site:* www.leagueofvermontwriters.org, pg 568

THE Learning Connection®, 4100 Silverstar Rd, Suite D, Orlando, FL 32808 *Toll Free Tel:* 800-218-8489 *Fax:* 407-292-2123 *E-mail:* tlc@tlconnection.com *Web Site:* www.tlconnection.com, pg 131

Learning Links Inc, PO Box 326, Cranbury, NJ 08512 *Tel:* 516-437-9071 *Toll Free Tel:* 888-960-2508 *Fax:* 516-437-5392 *E-mail:* info@learninglinks.com *Web Site:* www.learninglinks.com, pg 131

The Learning Source Ltd, 644 Tenth St, Brooklyn, NY 11215 *Tel:* 718-768-0231 (ext 10) *Fax:* 718-369-3467 *E-mail:* info@learningsourceltd.com *Web Site:* www.learningsourceltd.com, pg 497

LearningExpress LLC, 80 Broad St, 4th fl, New York, NY 10004 *Toll Free Tel:* 800-295-9556 (ext 2) *E-mail:* marketing@learningexpressllc.com (cust serv) *Web Site:* www.learningexpressllc.com, pg 131

The Ned Leavitt Agency, 70 Wooster St, Suite 4-F, New York, NY 10012 *Tel:* 212-334-0999 *Web Site:* www.nedleavittagency.com, pg 525

Lectorum Publications Inc, 205 Chubb Ave, Lyndhurst, NJ 07071 *Toll Free Tel:* 800-345-5946 *Fax:* 201-559-2201 *Toll Free Fax:* 877-532-8676 *E-mail:* lectorum@lectorum.com *Web Site:* www.lectorum.com, pg 131

Lederer Books, 6120 Day Long Lane, Clarksville, MD 21029 *Tel:* 410-531-6644 *Toll Free Tel:* 800-410-7367 (orders) *Fax:* 410-531-9440 *E-mail:* lederer@messianicjewish.net; customerservice@messianicjewish.net *Web Site:* www.messianicjewish.net, pg 131

Lee & Low Books Inc, 95 Madison Ave, New York, NY 10016 *Tel:* 212-779-4400 *Toll Free Tel:* 888-320-3190 (ext 28, orders only) *Fax:* 212-683-1894 (orders only); 212-532-6035 *E-mail:* general@leeandlow.com *Web Site:* www.leeandlow.com, pg 131

Harper Lee Prize for Legal Fiction, 101 Paul Bryant Dr, Tuscaloosa, AL 35487 *Tel:* 205-348-5195 *Web Site:* www.law.ua.edu/programs/harper-lee-prize-for-legal-fiction, pg 660

Lehigh University Press, B-040 Christmas-Saucon Hall, 14 E Packer Ave, Bethlehem, PA 18015 *Tel:* 610-758-3933 *Fax:* 610-758-6331 *E-mail:* inlup@lehigh.edu *Web Site:* inpress.sites.lehigh.edu, pg 131

Leilah Publications, 510 E University Dr, No 3413, Tempe, AZ 85281 *Tel:* 847-275-1657 *E-mail:* leilah@leilahpublications.com *Web Site:* facebook.com/leilahpublications, pg 131

Leisure Arts Inc, 104 Champs Blvd, Suite 100, Maumelle, AR 72113 *Tel:* 501-868-8800 *Toll Free Tel:* 800-643-8030 *E-mail:* customer_service@leisurearts.com *Web Site:* www.leisurearts.com, pg 132

Waldo G Leland Prize, 400 "A" St SE, Washington, DC 20003 *Tel:* 202-544-2422 *Fax:* 202-544-8307 *E-mail:* awards@historians.org *Web Site:* www.historians.org, pg 660

Vincent Lemieux Prize, 260 rue Dalhousie St, Suite 204, Ottawa, ON K1N 7E4, Canada *Tel:* 613-562-1202 *Fax:* 613-241-0019 *E-mail:* cpsa-acsp@cpsa-acsp.ca *Web Site:* www.cpsa-acsp.ca, pg 660

Debra Lemonds, PO Box 5516, Pasadena, CA 91117-0516 *Tel:* 626-844-9363 *E-mail:* dlemonds@zoho.com, pg 497

The Lentz Leadership Institute LLC, 7124 Glyndon Trail NW, Albuquerque, NM 87114 *Tel:* 702-719-9214 *E-mail:* orders@lentzleadership.com *Web Site:* www.lentzleadership.com; www.refractivethinker.com, pg 132

Leopold-Hidy Award, 701 William Vickers Ave, Durham, NC 27701-3162 *Tel:* 919-682-9319 *Fax:* 919-682-2349 *Web Site:* www.foresthistory.org, pg 660

Lerner Publications, 241 First Ave N, Minneapolis, MN 55401 *Tel:* 612-332-3344 *Toll Free Tel:* 800-328-4929 *Fax:* 612-332-7615 *Toll Free Fax:* 800-332-1132 *E-mail:* info@lernerbooks.com; custserve@lernerbooks.com *Web Site:* www.lernerbooks.com; www.facebook.com/lernerbooks, pg 132

Lerner Publishing Group Inc, 241 First Ave N, Minneapolis, MN 55401 *Tel:* 612-332-3344 *Toll Free Tel:* 800-328-4929 *Fax:* 612-332-7615 *Toll Free Fax:* 800-332-1132 *E-mail:* info@lernerbooks.com; custserve@lernerbooks.com *Web Site:* www.lernerbooks.com; www.facebook.com/lernerbooks, pg 132

LernerClassroom, 241 First Ave N, Minneapolis, MN 55401 *Tel:* 612-332-3344 *Toll Free Tel:* 800-328-4929 *Fax:* 612-332-7615 *Toll Free Fax:* 800-332-1132 *E-mail:* info@lernerbooks.com; custserve@lernerbooks.com *Web Site:* www.lernerbooks.com; www.facebook.com/lernerbooks, pg 132

Lessiter Media, 16655 W Wisconsin Ave, Brookfield, WI 53005 *Tel:* 262-782-4480 *Toll Free Tel:* 800-645-8455 *Fax:* 262-782-1252; 262-786-5564 *E-mail:* info@lessitermedia.com *Web Site:* www.lesspub.com; lessitermedia.com, pg 132

Letterbox/Papyrus of London Publishers USA, 10501 Broom Hill Dr, Suite 1-F, Las Vegas, NV 89134-7339 *Tel:* 702-256-3838 *E-mail:* lb27383@cox.net, pg 132

Lucky Marble Books, 2671 Bristol Rd, Columbus, OH 43221 *Tel:* 614-264-5588 *E-mail:* sales@pagespringpublishing.com *Web Site:* www.luckymarblebooks.com, pg 139

Jeremiah Ludington Award, 11 Main St, Suite D, Warrenton, VA 20186 *Tel:* 540-318-7770 *Fax:* 202-962-3939 *E-mail:* info@edupaperback.org *Web Site:* www.edupaperback.org, pg 663

Lugus Publications, 28 Industrial St, Studio 203, Toronto, ON M4G 1Y9, Canada *Tel:* 416-467-0924 *Web Site:* www.thestudio203.com, pg 462

J Anthony Lukas Book Prize, 2950 Broadway, New York, NY 10027 *Tel:* 212-854-6468 *Web Site:* www.journalism.columbia.edu, pg 663

J Anthony Lukas Work-in-Progress Award, 2950 Broadway, New York, NY 10027 *Tel:* 212-854-6468 *Web Site:* www.journalism.columbia.edu, pg 663

Lumina Datamatics Inc, 4 Collins Ave, Plymouth, MA 02360 *Tel:* 508-746-0300 *Fax:* 508-746-3233 *Web Site:* luminadatamatics.com, pg 497

Luminis Books Inc, 1950 E Greyhound Pass, Suite 18, PMB 280, Carmel, IN 46033 *Tel:* 317-840-5838 *E-mail:* editor@luminisbooks.com *Web Site:* www.luminisbooks.com, pg 139

Luna Bisonte Prods, 137 Leland Ave, Columbus, OH 43214 *Tel:* 614-846-4126 *Web Site:* www.johnmbennett.net; www.lulu.com/spotlight/lunabisonteprods, pg 139

Lush Triumphant Literary Awards, PO Box 3008, MPO, Vancouver, BC V6B 3X5, Canada *Tel:* 604-876-8710 *Fax:* 604-879-2667 *E-mail:* subter@portal.ca *Web Site:* www.subterrain.ca, pg 663

Lutheran Braille Workers Inc, 13471 California St, Yucaipa, CA 92399 *Tel:* 909-795-8977 *Toll Free Tel:* 800-925-6092 *Fax:* 909-795-8970 *E-mail:* lbw@lbwinc.org *Web Site:* www.lbwinc.org, pg 139

Lyndon B Johnson School of Public Affairs, University of Texas at Austin, 2315 Red River St, Austin, TX 78712-1536 *Tel:* 512-471-3200 *Fax:* 512-471-4697 *E-mail:* lbjdeansoffice@austin.utexas.edu *Web Site:* www.utexas.edu/lbj, pg 139

Mark Lynton History Prize, 2950 Broadway, New York, NY 10027 *Tel:* 212-854-6468 *Web Site:* www.journalism.columbia.edu, pg 663

Lynx House Press, 420 W 24 St, Spokane, WA 99203 *Tel:* 509-624-4894 *E-mail:* lynxhousepress@gmail.com *Web Site:* www.lynxhousepress.org, pg 139

Elizabeth Lyon, 3530 E Game Farm Rd, No 39, Springfield, OR 97477 *Tel:* 541-357-4181 *E-mail:* elyon123@comcast.net *Web Site:* www.elizabethlyon.com, pg 498

Thomas J Lyon Book Award in Western American Literary and Cultural Studies, PO Box 6815, Logan, UT 84341 *Web Site:* www.westernlit.org/thomas-j-lyon-book-award-in-western-american-literary-and-cultural-studies; www.westernlit.org, pg 664

The Lyons Press, 246 Goose Lane, Guilford, CT 06437 *Tel:* 203-458-4500 *Fax:* 203-458-4668 *E-mail:* info@rowman.com *Web Site:* rowman.com/page/lyonspress, pg 139

Lyric Poetry Award, 15 Gramercy Park, New York, NY 10003 *Tel:* 212-254-9628 *Web Site:* www.poetrysociety.org, pg 664

Lyric Poetry Prizes, PO Box 110, Jericho, VT 05465 *Tel:* 802-899-3993 *Fax:* 802-899-3993 *E-mail:* themuse@thelyricmagazine.com *Web Site:* thelyricmagazine.com, pg 664

Donald Maass Literary Agency, 1000 Dean St, Suite 252, Brooklyn, NY 11238 *Tel:* 212-727-8383 *Fax:* 212-727-3271 *E-mail:* info@maassagency.com *Web Site:* www.maassagency.com, pg 526

MacArthur Fellows Program, Office of Grants Management, 140 S Dearborn St, Chicago, IL 60603-5285 *Tel:* 312-726-8000 *Fax:* 312-920-6528 *E-mail:* 4answers@macfound.org *Web Site:* www.macfound.org/programs/fellows, pg 664

Macavity Award, 7155 Marlborough Terr, Berkeley, CA 94705 *Tel:* 510-845-3600 *Web Site:* www.mysteryreaders.org, pg 664

Gina Maccoby Literary Agency, PO Box 60, Chappaqua, NY 10514-0060 *Tel:* 914-238-5630 *E-mail:* query@maccobylit.com *Web Site:* www.publishersmarketplace.com/members/GinaMaccoby, pg 526

Sir John A Macdonald Prize, 130 Albert St, Suite 1201, Ottawa, ON K1P 5G4, Canada *Tel:* 613-233-7885 *Fax:* 613-565-5445 *E-mail:* cha-shc@cha-shc.ca *Web Site:* www.cha-shc.ca, pg 664

MacDowell Fellowships, 100 High St, Peterborough, NH 03458 *Tel:* 603-924-3886 *Fax:* 603-924-9142 *E-mail:* info@macdowellcolony.org; admissions@macdowellcolony.org *Web Site:* www.macdowellcolony.org, pg 664

Machigonne Fiction Contest, PO Box 5101, Hanover, NH 03755 *E-mail:* info@newguardreview.com *Web Site:* www.newguardreview.com, pg 664

Macmillan, 175 Fifth Ave, New York, NY 10010 *Tel:* 646-307-5151 *E-mail:* press.inquiries@macmillan.com *Web Site:* www.macmillan.com, pg 139

Macmillan Audio, 175 Fifth Ave, New York, NY 10010 *Tel:* 646-307-5151 *Toll Free Tel:* 888-330-8477 (cust serv) *Fax:* 917-534-0980 *Web Site:* www.macmillanaudio.com, pg 140

Macmillan Learning, 41 Madison Ave, New York, NY 10010 *Tel:* 212-576-9400 *Fax:* 212-689-2383 *Web Site:* www.macmillanlearning.com, pg 140

Macmillan Reference USA™, 27500 Drake Rd, Farmington Hills, MI 48331-3535 *Tel:* 248-699-4253 *Toll Free Tel:* 800-877-4253 *Toll Free Fax:* 877-363-4253 *E-mail:* gale.customercare@cengage.com *Web Site:* www.gale.cengage.com/macmillan, pg 140

C B MacPherson Prize, 260 rue Dalhousie St, Suite 204, Ottawa, ON K1N 7E4, Canada *Tel:* 613-562-1202 *Fax:* 613-241-0019 *E-mail:* cpsa-acsp@cpsa-acsp.ca *Web Site:* www.cpsa-acsp.ca, pg 664

Madison Press Books, 155 Edward St, Suite 1, Aurora, ON L4G 1W3, Canada *E-mail:* info@madisonpressbooks.com *Web Site:* www.madisonpressbooks.com, pg 462

Madonna House Publications, 2888 Dafoe Rd, Combermere, ON K0J 1L0, Canada *Tel:* 613-756-3728 *Toll Free Tel:* 888-703-7110 *Fax:* 613-756-0103 *Toll Free Fax:* 877-717-2888 *E-mail:* publications@madonnahouse.org *Web Site:* www.madonnahouse.org/publications, pg 462

Magazine Merit Awards, 4727 Wilshire Blvd, Suite 301, Los Angeles, CA 90010 *Tel:* 323-782-1010; 310-403-0675 (cell) *Fax:* 323-782-1892 *E-mail:* grants@scbwi.org; scbwi@scbwi.org *Web Site:* www.scbwi.org, pg 664

Magazines Canada (MC), 425 Adelaide St W, Suite 700, Toronto, ON M5V 3C1, Canada *Tel:* 416-504-0274 *Fax:* 416-504-0437 *E-mail:* info@magazinescanada.ca *Web Site:* www.magazinescanada.ca/development/magnet, pg 569

Mage Publishers Inc, 1408 35 St NW, Washington, DC 20007 *Tel:* 202-342-1642 *Web Site:* www.mage.com, pg 140

The Magni Co, 7106 Wellington Point Rd, McKinney, TX 75070 *Tel:* 972-540-2050 *Fax:* 972-540-1057 *E-mail:* sales@magnico.com; info@magnico.com *Web Site:* www.magnico.com, pg 140

Maharishi University of Management Press, 1000 N Fourth St, Dept 1155, Fairfield, IA 52557-1155 *Tel:* 641-472-1101 *Toll Free Tel:* 800-831-6523 *Fax:* 641-472-1122 *E-mail:* mumpress@mum.edu *Web Site:* www.mumpress.com, pg 140

Mailer Prize, 1841 Broadway, Suite 322, New York, NY 10023 *Tel:* 646-374-3940 *Web Site:* nmcenter.org, pg 664

Maine Writers & Publishers Alliance, 314 Forest Ave, Rm 318, Portland, ME 04101 *Tel:* 207-228-8263 *Fax:* 207-228-8150 *E-mail:* info@mainewriters.org *Web Site:* mainewriters.org, pg 569

Maine Writers Conference at Ocean Park, 14 Temple Ave, Ocean Park, ME 04063 *Tel:* 401-598-1424 *E-mail:* www.opa@oceanpark.org *Web Site:* oceanpark.org, pg 612

J Russell Major Prize, 400 "A" St SE, Washington, DC 20003 *Tel:* 202-544-2422 *Fax:* 202-544-8307 *E-mail:* awards@historians.org *Web Site:* www.historians.org, pg 665

Malahat Review Long Poem Prize, University of Victoria, Box 1700, Sta CSC, Victoria, BC V8W 2Y2, Canada *Tel:* 250-721-8524 *Fax:* 250-472-5051 *E-mail:* malahat@uvic.ca *Web Site:* www.malahatreview.ca, pg 665

Gene E & Adele R Malott Prize for Recording Community Activism, 2809 Berkeley Dr, Birmingham, AL 35242 *Tel:* 360-809-0465 *E-mail:* langumtrust@gmail.com *Web Site:* www.langumtrust.org, pg 665

Management Advisory Services & Publications (MASP), PO Box 81151, Wellesley Hills, MA 02481-0001 *Tel:* 781-235-2895 *Fax:* 781-235-5446 *E-mail:* info@masp.com *Web Site:* www.masp.com, pg 140

Management Sciences for Health, 200 Rivers Edge Dr, Medford, MA 02155 *Tel:* 617-250-9500 *Fax:* 617-250-9090 *E-mail:* bookstore@msh.org *Web Site:* www.msh.org, pg 140

Mandala Earth, 800 "A" St, San Rafael, CA 94901 *Tel:* 415-526-1370 *Toll Free Fax:* 866-509-0515 *E-mail:* info@mandalapublishing.com *Web Site:* www.mandalaeartheditions.com, pg 141

Manhattan Publishing Co, 670 White Plains Rd, Scarsdale, NY 10583 *Tel:* 914-472-4650 *Fax:* 914-472-4316 *E-mail:* coe@manhattanpublishing.com *Web Site:* www.manhattanpublishing.com, pg 141

Manhattanville College Master of Fine Arts in Creative Writing Program, 2900 Purchase St, Purchase, NY 10577 *Tel:* 914-323-5239 *Fax:* 914-323-3122 *Web Site:* www.mville.edu/writing, pg 620

Manic D Press Inc, 250 Banks St, San Francisco, CA 94110 *Tel:* 415-648-8288 *E-mail:* info@manicdpress.com *Web Site:* www.manicdpress.com, pg 141

Manitoba Arts Council, 525-93 Lombard Ave, Winnipeg, MB R3B 3B1, Canada *Tel:* 204-945-2237 *Toll Free Tel:* 866-994-2787 *Fax:* 204-945-5925 *E-mail:* info@artscouncil.mb.ca *Web Site:* artscouncil.mb.ca, pg 569

The Manitoba Writers' Guild Inc, 218-100 Arthur St, Winnipeg, MB R3B 1H3, Canada *Tel:* 204-944-8013 *E-mail:* info@mbwriter.mb.ca *Web Site:* www.mbwriter.mb.ca, pg 569

Carol Mann Agency, 55 Fifth Ave, New York, NY 10003 *Tel:* 212-206-5635 *Fax:* 212-675-4809 *E-mail:* submissions@carolmannagency.com *Web Site:* www.carolmannagency.com, pg 527

Margaret Mann Citation, 50 E Huron St, Chicago, IL 60611 *Tel:* 312-280-5037 *Toll Free Tel:* 800-545-2433 *Fax:* 312-280-5033 *E-mail:* alcts@ala.org *Web Site:* www.ala.org/alcts, pg 665

Phyllis Manner, 17 Springdale Rd, New Rochelle, NY 10804 *Tel:* 914-834-4707 *Fax:* 914-834-4707 *E-mail:* pmanner@aol.com; manneredit@gmail.com, pg 498

Manning Publications Co, PO Box 761, Shelter Island, NY 11964 *Tel:* 203-626-1510 *E-mail:* sales@manning.com; support@manning.com (cust serv) *Web Site:* www.manning.com, pg 141

Freya Manston Associates Inc, 145 W 58 St, New York, NY 10019 *Tel:* 212-247-3075, pg 527

Many Voices Fellowships, 2301 Franklin Ave E, Minneapolis, MN 55406-1099 *Tel:* 612-332-7481 *Fax:* 612-332-6037 *E-mail:* info@pwcenter.org *Web Site:* www.pwcenter.org, pg 665

MapEasy Inc, PO Box 80, Wainscott, NY 11975-0080 *Tel:* 631-537-6213 *Fax:* 631-537-4541 *E-mail:* info@mapeasy.com *Web Site:* www.mapeasy.com, pg 141

MB Artists, 775 Sixth Ave, Suite 6, New York, NY 10001 *Tel:* 212-689-7830 *Fax:* 212-689-7829 *Web Site:* www.mbartists.com, pg 544

McBooks Press Inc, ID Booth Bldg, 520 N Meadow St, Ithaca, NY 14850 *Tel:* 607-272-2114 *E-mail:* mcbooks@mcbooks.com *Web Site:* www.mcbooks.com, pg 144

Margret McBride Literary Agency, PO Box 9128, La Jolla, CA 92038 *Tel:* 858-454-1550 *E-mail:* staff@mcbridelit.com *Web Site:* www.mcbrideliterary.com, pg 528

Janet B McCabe Poetry Prize, 1041 N Taft Hill Rd, Fort Collins, CO 80521 *Tel:* 970-449-2726 *E-mail:* editor@ruminatemagazine.org *Web Site:* www.ruminatemagazine.com, pg 666

E J McCarthy Agency, 405 Maple St, Suite A, Mill Valley, CA 94941 *Tel:* 415-383-6639 *Fax:* 415-383-6639 *E-mail:* ejmagency@gmail.com *Web Site:* www.publishersmarketplace.com/members/ejmccarthy, pg 529

Gerard McCauley Agency Inc, PO Box 844, Katonah, NY 10536-0844 *Tel:* 914-232-5700, pg 529

McClanahan Publishing House Inc, 107 W Main, Princeton, KY 42445 *Tel:* 270-963-9005 *E-mail:* books@kybooks.com *Web Site:* kybooks.com, pg 145

Anita D McClellan Associates, 464 Common St, Suite 142, Belmont, MA 02478-2704 *Tel:* 617-575-9203 *E-mail:* adm@anitamcclellan.com *Web Site:* www.anitamcclellan.com, pg 498, 529

McClelland & Stewart Ltd, 320 Front St W, Suite 1400, Toronto, ON M5V 3B6, Canada *Tel:* 416-364-4449 *Fax:* 416-598-7764 *E-mail:* customerservicescanada@penguinrandomhouse.com; publicity@ca.penguingroup.com *Web Site:* penguinrandomhouse.ca/imprints/mcclelland-stewart, pg 463

McCutchan Publishing Corp, 2694 Ohart Rd, Richmond, CA 94806 *Tel:* 510-758-5510 *Toll Free Tel:* 800-227-1540 *Fax:* 510-758-6078 *E-mail:* mccutchanpublish@sbcglobal.net *Web Site:* www.mccutchanpublishing.com, pg 145

The McDonald & Woodward Publishing Co, 695 Tall Oaks Dr, Newark, OH 43055 *Tel:* 740-641-2691 *Toll Free Tel:* 800-233-8787 *Fax:* 740-641-2692 *E-mail:* mwpubco@mwpubco.com *Web Site:* www.mwpubco.com, pg 145

McFarland, 960 NC Hwy 88 W, Jefferson, NC 28640 *Tel:* 336-246-4460 *Toll Free Tel:* 800-253-2187 (orders) *Fax:* 336-246-5018; 336-246-4403 (orders) *E-mail:* info@mcfarlandpub.com *Web Site:* www.mcfarlandpub.com, pg 145

McGill-Queen's University Press, 1010 Sherbrooke W, Suite 1720, Montreal, QC H3A 2R7, Canada *Tel:* 514-398-3750 *Fax:* 514-398-4333 *E-mail:* mqup@mqup.ca *Web Site:* www.mqup.ca, pg 463

John H McGinnis Memorial Award, PO Box 750374, Dallas, TX 75275-0374 *Fax:* 214-768-1408 *E-mail:* swr@mail.smu.edu *Web Site:* www.smu.edu/southwestreview, pg 666

Harold W McGraw Jr Prize in Education, 2 Penn Plaza, New York, NY 10121-2298 *Tel:* 646-766-2000 *E-mail:* info@mcgrawprize.com *Web Site:* www.mcgrawprize.com, pg 666

McGraw-Hill Career Education, 1333 Burr Ridge Pkwy, Burr Ridge, IL 60527 *Tel:* 630-789-4000 *Toll Free Tel:* 800-338-3987 (cust serv) *Fax:* 630-789-5523; 614-755-5645 (cust serv) *Web Site:* www.mhhe.com, pg 145

McGraw-Hill Contemporary Learning Series, 501 Bell St, Dubuque, IA 52001 *Toll Free Tel:* 800-243-6532 *Web Site:* www.mhcls.com, pg 145

McGraw-Hill Create, 2 Penn Plaza, New York, NY 10121 *Toll Free Tel:* 800-962-9342 *E-mail:* mhhe.create@mheducation.com *Web Site:* create.mheducation.com; shop.mheducation.com, pg 145

McGraw-Hill Education, 2 Penn Plaza, New York, NY 10121-2298 *Tel:* 212-904-2000 *E-mail:* customer.service@mheducation.com; international_cs@mheducation.com *Web Site:* www.mheducation.com, pg 145

McGraw-Hill Higher Education, 1333 Burr Ridge Pkwy, Burr Ridge, IL 60527 *Tel:* 630-789-4000 *Toll Free Tel:* 800-338-3987 (cust serv) *Fax:* 614-755-5645 (cust serv) *Web Site:* www.mhhe.com, pg 146

McGraw-Hill Humanities, Social Sciences, Languages, 2 Penn Plaza, 21st fl, New York, NY 10121 *Tel:* 212-904-2000 *Toll Free Tel:* 800-338-3987 (cust serv) *Fax:* 614-755-5645 (cust serv) *Web Site:* www.mhhe.com, pg 146

McGraw-Hill International & Professional Publishing Group, 2 Penn Plaza, New York, NY 10121 *Tel:* 646-766-2000 *Web Site:* www.mheducation.com, pg 146

McGraw-Hill/Irwin, 1333 Burr Ridge Pkwy, Burr Ridge, IL 60527 *Tel:* 630-789-4000 *Toll Free Tel:* 800-338-3987 (cust serv) *Fax:* 630-789-6942; 614-755-5645 (cust serv) *Web Site:* www.mhhe.com, pg 146

McGraw-Hill Ryerson Limited, 300 Water St, Whitby, ON L1N 9B6, Canada *Tel:* 905-430-5000 *Toll Free Tel:* 800-565-5758 (cust serv) *Fax:* 905-430-5020 *Toll Free Fax:* 800-463-5885 *Web Site:* www.mheducation.ca, pg 463

McGraw-Hill School Education Group, 8787 Orion Place, Columbus, OH 43240 *Tel:* 614-430-4000 *Toll Free Tel:* 800-848-1567 *Web Site:* www.mheducation.com, pg 146

McGraw-Hill Science, Engineering, Mathematics, 501 Bell St, Dubuque, IA 52001 *Tel:* 563-584-6000 *Toll Free Tel:* 800-338-3987 (cust serv) *Fax:* 614-755-5645 (cust serv) *Web Site:* www.mhhe.com, pg 146

William Holmes McGuffey Longevity Award, PO Box 367, Fountain City, WI 54629 *E-mail:* info@taaonline.net *Web Site:* www.taaonline.net/mcguffey-longevity-award, pg 666

McHugh's Rights/Permissions Workshop™, PO Box 170665, Milwaukee, WI 53217-8056 *Tel:* 414-351-3056 *E-mail:* jack@johnbmchugh.com *Web Site:* www.johnbmchugh.com, pg 612

McIntosh & Otis Inc, 353 Lexington Ave, New York, NY 10016-0900 *Tel:* 212-687-7400 *Fax:* 212-687-6894 *E-mail:* info@mcintoshandotis.com *Web Site:* www.mcintoshandotis.com, pg 529

McKnight Artist Fellowship for Writers, Open Book, Suite 200, 1011 Washington Ave S, Minneapolis, MN 55415 *Tel:* 612-215-2575 *Fax:* 612-215-2576 *E-mail:* loft@loft.org *Web Site:* www.loft.org, pg 667

McKnight Fellowships in Playwriting, 2301 Franklin Ave E, Minneapolis, MN 55406-1099 *Tel:* 612-332-7481 *Fax:* 612-332-6037 *E-mail:* info@pwcenter.org *Web Site:* www.pwcenter.org, pg 667

McKnight National Residency & Commission, 2301 Franklin Ave E, Minneapolis, MN 55406-1099 *Tel:* 612-332-7481 *Fax:* 612-332-6037 *E-mail:* info@pwcenter.org *Web Site:* www.pwcenter.org, pg 667

Pamela Dittmer McKuen, 87 Tanglewood Dr, Glen Ellyn, IL 60137 *Tel:* 630-545-0867 *Fax:* 630-545-0868 *E-mail:* pmckuen@gmail.com *Web Site:* www.pamelamckuen.com; www.allthewriteplaces.com, pg 498

McLaren Memorial Comedy Play Writing Competition, 2000 W Wadley Ave, Midland, TX 79705 *Tel:* 432-682-2544 *E-mail:* tracy@mctmidland.org *Web Site:* www.mctmidland.org, pg 667

McLemore Prize, William F Winter Archives & History Bldg, 200 North St, Jackson, MS 39201 *Tel:* 601-576-6850 *Fax:* 601-576-6975 *E-mail:* mhs@mdah.ms.gov *Web Site:* www.mdah.ms.gov, pg 667

John McMenemy Prize, 260 rue Dalhousie St, Suite 204, Ottawa, ON K1N 7E4, Canada *Tel:* 613-562-1202 *Fax:* 613-241-0019 *E-mail:* cpsa-acsp@cpsa-acsp.ca *Web Site:* www.cpsa-acsp.ca, pg 667

Sally Hill McMillan LLC, 429 E Kingston Ave, Charlotte, NC 28203 *Tel:* 704-334-0897 *E-mail:* mcmagency@aol.com, pg 529

Pat McNees, 10643 Weymouth St, Suite 204, Bethesda, MD 20814 *Tel:* 301-897-8557 *E-mail:* patmcnees@gmail.com *Web Site:* www.patmcnees.com; www.writersandeditors.com, pg 498

McNeese State University, Writing Program, PO Box 92655, Lake Charles, LA 70609-0001 *Tel:* 337-475-5325; 337-475-5327 *Web Site:* www.mcneese.edu.com; www.mfa.mcneese.edu, pg 621

McPherson & Co, 148 Smith Ave, Kingston, NY 12401 *Tel:* 845-331-5807 *Fax:* 845-331-5807 *E-mail:* bmcphersonco@gmail.com *Web Site:* www.mcphersonco.com, pg 146

McSweeney's Publishing, 849 Valencia St, San Francisco, CA 94110 *Tel:* 415-642-5609 (cust serv) *Web Site:* www.mcsweeneys.net, pg 147

MC2 Solutions LLC, 5101 Violet Lane, Madison, WI 53714 *Tel:* 608-240-4959, pg 498

MDR, A D&B Co, 6 Armstrong Rd, Suite 301, Shelton, CT 06484 *Tel:* 203-926-4800 *Toll Free Tel:* 800-333-8802 *Fax:* 203-225-4603 *Toll Free Fax:* 866-532-7097 *E-mail:* mdrinfo@dnb.com *Web Site:* www.schooldata.com, pg 147

Meadowbrook Press, 6110 Blue Circle Dr, Suite 237, Minnetonka, MN 55343 *Toll Free Tel:* 800-338-2232 *Fax:* 952-930-1940 *E-mail:* info@meadowbrookpress.com *Web Site:* www.meadowbrookpress.com, pg 147

me+mi publishing inc, 400 S Knoll St, Suite B, Wheaton, IL 60187 *Toll Free Tel:* 888-251-1444 *Fax:* 630-588-9804 *E-mail:* rw@rosawesley.com *Web Site:* www.memima.com, pg 147

R S Means from The Gordian Group, 1099 Hingham St, Suite 201, Rockland, MA 02370 *Tel:* 781-422-5000 *Toll Free Tel:* 800-448-8182 *Fax:* 781-585-8814 *Toll Free Fax:* 800-632-6701 *Web Site:* www.rsmeans.com, pg 147

Medal of Honor for Literature, 15 Gramercy Park S, New York, NY 10003 *E-mail:* literary@thenationalartsclub.org *Web Site:* www.nationalartsclub.org, pg 667

MedBooks, 101 W Buckingham Rd, Richardson, TX 75081-4802 *Tel:* 972-643-1809 *Fax:* 972-643-1859 *E-mail:* medbooks@medbooks.com *Web Site:* www.medbooks.com, pg 147

Media Alliance, 2830 20 St, Suite 102, San Francisco, CA 94110 *Tel:* 415-746-9475 *E-mail:* information@media-alliance.org *Web Site:* www.media-alliance.org, pg 569

Media Coalition Inc, 19 Fulton St, Suite 407, New York, NY 10038 *Tel:* 212-587-4025 *Fax:* 212-587-2436 *E-mail:* info@mediacoalition.org *Web Site:* mediacoalition.org, pg 569

Medical Group Management Association (MGMA), 104 Inverness Terr E, Englewood, CO 80112-5306 *Tel:* 303-799-1111; 303-799-1111 (ext 1888, book orders) *Toll Free Tel:* 877-275-6462 *E-mail:* support@mgma.com; infocenter@mgma.com *Web Site:* www.mgma.com, pg 147

Medical Physics Publishing Corp (MPP), 4555 Helgesen Dr, Madison, WI 53718 *Tel:* 608-262-4021; 608-224-4508 *Toll Free Tel:* 800-442-5778 (cust serv) *Fax:* 608-224-5016 *E-mail:* mpp@medicalphysics.org *Web Site:* www.medicalphysics.org, pg 147

Medieval Institute Publications, WMU East Campus, 100-E Walwood Hall, Kalamazoo, MI 49008 *Tel:* 269-387-8754 *Fax:* 269-387-8750 *Web Site:* www.wmich.edu/medievalpublications, pg 147

MedMaster Inc, 3337 Hollywood Oaks Dr, Fort Lauderdale, FL 33312 *Tel:* 954-962-8414 *Toll Free Tel:* 800-335-3480 *Fax:* 954-962-4508 *E-mail:* mmbks@aol.com *Web Site:* www.medmaster.net, pg 148

Lucille Medwick Memorial Award, 15 Gramercy Park, New York, NY 10003 *Tel:* 212-254-9628 *Web Site:* www.poetrysociety.org, pg 667

The Russell Meerdink Co Ltd, 1555 S Park Ave, Neenah, WI 54956 *Tel:* 920-725-0955 *Toll Free Tel:* 800-635-6499 *Fax:* 920-725-0709 *E-mail:* questions@horseinfo.com *Web Site:* www.horseinfo.com, pg 148

Mel Bay Publications Inc, 4 Industrial Dr, Pacific, MO 63069-0066 *Tel:* 636-257-3970 *Toll Free Tel:* 800-863-5229 *Fax:* 636-257-5062 *Toll Free Fax:* 800-660-9818 *E-mail:* email@melbay.com *Web Site:* www.melbay.com, pg 148

Frederic G Melcher Scholarship, 50 E Huron St, Chicago, IL 60611-2795 *Tel:* 312-280-2163 *Toll Free Tel:* 800-545-2433 *Fax:* 312-440-9374; 312-280-5271 *E-mail:* alsc@ala.org *Web Site:* www.ala.org/alsc, pg 667

Barbara A Mele, 2525 Holland Ave, New York, NY 10467-8703 *Tel:* 718-654-8047 *Fax:* 718-654-8047 *E-mail:* bannmele@aol.com, pg 498

Melissa Turk & the Artist Network, 9 Babbling Brook Lane, Suffern, NY 10901 *Tel:* 845-368-8606 *E-mail:* melissa@melissaturk.com *Web Site:* www.melissaturk.com, pg 544

The Edwin Mellen Press, 415 Ridge St, Lewiston, NY 14092 *Tel:* 716-754-2266; 716-754-1400 (mktg); 716-754-2788 (order fulfillment) *Fax:* 716-754-4056 *E-mail:* editor@mellenpress.com *Web Site:* www.mellenpress.com, pg 148

Tom Mellers Publishing Services (TMPS), 60 Second Ave, New York, NY 10003 *Tel:* 212-254-4958 *E-mail:* tmps71@yahoo.com, pg 498

The Melville Society, Johns Hopkins University Press, PO Box 19966, Baltimore, MD 21211-0966 *Web Site:* melvillesociety.org, pg 569

Menasha Ridge Press Inc, 2204 First Ave S, Suite 102, Birmingham, AL 35233 *Toll Free Tel:* 888-604-4537 *Fax:* 205-326-1012 *E-mail:* info@adventurewithkeen.com *Web Site:* www.menasharidge.com, pg 148

Fred C Mench Professor of Classics Emeritus, 207 Saint Martins Lane, Smyrna, TN 37167 *Tel:* 615-459-0765 *E-mail:* fmench@earthlink.net, pg 498

Mendel Media Group LLC, 115 W 30 St, Suite 800, New York, NY 10001 *Tel:* 646-239-9896 *Fax:* 212-685-4717 *Web Site:* www.mendelmedia.com, pg 529

MennoMedia, 1251 Virginia Ave, Harrisonburg, VA 22802-2434 *Toll Free Tel:* 800-245-7894 (orders & cust serv US) *Toll Free Fax:* 877-271-0760 *E-mail:* info@mennomedia.org *Web Site:* www.mennomedia.org, pg 148

Mercer University Press, 368 Orange St, Macon, GA 31201 *Tel:* 478-301-2880 *Toll Free Tel:* 866-895-1472 *Fax:* 478-301-2585 *E-mail:* mupressorders@mercer.edu *Web Site:* www.mupress.org, pg 148

Scott Meredith Literary Agency LP, Exchange Plaza, 55 Broadway, Suite 2002, New York, NY 10006 *Tel:* 646-218-9240 *Fax:* 212-977-5997 *E-mail:* info@scottmeredith.com *Web Site:* www.scottmeredith.com, pg 529

Merit Publishing International Inc, 6839 Villas Dr S, Boca Raton, FL 33433 *Tel:* 561-350-0329 *E-mail:* merituk@aol.com *Web Site:* www.meritpublishing.com, pg 148

Meriwether Publishing, c/o Pioneer Drama Service, 9707-A E Easter Lane, Englewood, CO 80112 *Tel:* 303-779-4035 *Toll Free Tel:* 800-333-7262 *Fax:* 303-779-4315 *E-mail:* books@pioneerdrama.com *Web Site:* www.pioneerdrama.com, pg 149

Merriam Press, 133 Elm St, Suite 3R, Bennington, VT 05201-2250 *Tel:* 802-447-0313 *Web Site:* www.merriam-press.com, pg 149

Merriam-Webster Inc, 47 Federal St, Springfield, MA 01102 *Tel:* 413-734-3134 *Toll Free Tel:* 800-828-1880 (orders & cust serv) *Fax:* 413-731-5979 (sales) *E-mail:* support@merriam-webster.com *Web Site:* www.merriam-webster.com, pg 149

Mesorah Publications Ltd, 4401 Second Ave, Brooklyn, NY 11232 *Tel:* 718-921-9000 *Toll Free Tel:* 800-637-6724 *Fax:* 718-680-1875 *E-mail:* info@artscroll.com; orders@artscroll.com *Web Site:* www.artscroll.com, pg 149

Messianic Jewish Publishers, 6120 Day Long Lane, Clarksville, MD 21029 *Tel:* 410-531-6644 *Toll Free Tel:* 800-410-7367 (orders) *Fax:* 410-531-9440; 717-761-7273 (orders) *Toll Free Fax:* 800-327-0048 (orders) *E-mail:* editor@messianicjewish.net; customerservice@messianicjewish.net; permissions@messianicjewish.net (rights & perms) *Web Site:* messianicjewish.net/publish, pg 149

Metamorphosis Literary Agency, 12837 S Seminole Dr, Olathe, KS 66062 *Tel:* 646-397-1640 *E-mail:* info@metamorphosisliteraryagency.com *Web Site:* www.metamorphosisliteraryagency.com, pg 529

Addison M Metcalf Award in Literature, 633 W 155 St, New York, NY 10032 *Tel:* 212-368-5900 *Fax:* 212-491-4615 *E-mail:* academy@artsandletters.org *Web Site:* www.artsandletters.org, pg 667

Metropolitan Classics, 26 Arthur Place, Yonkers, NY 10701 *Tel:* 914-375-6448 *Web Site:* www.fortrossinc.com, pg 149

Metropolitan Editorial & Writing Service, 4455 Douglas Ave, Riverdale, NY 10471 *Tel:* 718-549-5518, pg 498

Metropolitan Lithographers Association Inc, c/o Pictorial Offset, 111 Amor Ave, Carlstadt, NJ 07072 *Tel:* 201-935-7100, pg 569

The Metropolitan Museum of Art, 1000 Fifth Ave, New York, NY 10028 *Tel:* 212-879-5500; 212-570-3725 (edit) *Fax:* 212-396-5062 *E-mail:* editorial@metmuseum.org *Web Site:* www.metmuseum.org, pg 149

The David Nathan Meyerson Prize for Fiction, PO Box 750374, Dallas, TX 75275-0374 *Fax:* 214-768-1408 *E-mail:* swr@mail.smu.edu *Web Site:* www.smu.edu/southwestreview, pg 667

MFA Publications, 465 Huntington Ave, Boston, MA 02115 *Tel:* 617-369-4233 *Fax:* 617-369-3459 *E-mail:* publications@mfa.org *Web Site:* www.mfa.org/publications, pg 149

MGI Management Institute Inc, 12 Skyline Dr, Hawthorne, NY 10532 *Tel:* 914-428-6500 *Toll Free Tel:* 800-932-0191 *Fax:* 914-428-0773 *E-mail:* mgiusa@aol.com *Web Site:* www.mgi.org, pg 149

Michelin Maps & Guides, One Parkway S, Greenville, SC 29615-5022 *Tel:* 864-458-5565 *Fax:* 864-458-5665 *Toll Free Fax:* 866-297-0914; 888-773-7979 *E-mail:* orders@americanmap.com (orders) *Web Site:* www.michelintravel.com; www.michelinguide.com, pg 149

Michigan Municipal League, 1675 Green Rd, Ann Arbor, MI 48105 *Tel:* 734-662-3246 *Toll Free Tel:* 800-653-2483 *E-mail:* contact@mml.org *Web Site:* www.mml.org, pg 150

Michigan State University Press (MSU Press), Manly Miles Bldg, Suite 25, 1405 S Harrison Rd, East Lansing, MI 48823-5245 *Tel:* 517-355-9543 *Fax:* 517-432-2611 *Web Site:* msupress.org, pg 150

Susan T Middleton, 366-A Norton Hill Rd, Ashfield, MA 01330-9601 *Tel:* 413-628-4039 *E-mail:* smiddle@crocker.com, pg 499

Midmarch Arts Press, 300 Riverside Dr, New York, NY 10025-5239 *Tel:* 212-666-6990 *Web Site:* midmarchartspress.org, pg 150

Midnight Marquee Press Inc, 9721 Britinay Lane, Baltimore, MD 21234 *Tel:* 410-665-1198 *E-mail:* mmarquee@aol.com *Web Site:* www.midmar.com, pg 150

Midwest Independent Booksellers Association (MIBA), 2355 Louisiana Ave N, Suite A, Golden Valley, MN 55427-3646 *Tel:* 763-544-2993 *Toll Free Tel:* 800-784-7522 *Fax:* 612-354-5728 *E-mail:* info@midwestbooksellers.org *Web Site:* midwestbooksellers.org, pg 569

Midwest Travel Writers Association, 902 S Randall Rd, Suite C311, St Charles, IL 60174 *Toll Free Tel:* 888-551-8184 *E-mail:* admin@mtwa.org *Web Site:* www.mtwa.org, pg 569

Mighty Media Press, 1201 Currie Ave, Minneapolis, MN 55403 *Tel:* 612-455-0252 *Fax:* 612-338-4817 *Web Site:* www.mightymediapress.com, pg 150

Mike Murach & Associates Inc, 4340 N Knoll Ave, Fresno, CA 93722 *Tel:* 559-440-9071 *Toll Free Tel:* 800-221-5528 *Fax:* 559-440-0963 *E-mail:* murachbooks@murach.com *Web Site:* www.murach.com, pg 150

Milady, Executive Woods, 5 Maxwell Dr, Clifton Park, NY 12065-2919 *Tel:* 518-348-2300 *Toll Free Tel:* 800-998-7498 *Fax:* 518-373-6309 *E-mail:* info@milady.com *Web Site:* milady.cengage.com, pg 150

Kenneth W Mildenberger Prize, 85 Broad St, Suite 500, New York, NY 10004-2434 *Tel:* 646-576-5141; 646-576-5000 *Fax:* 646-458-0030 *E-mail:* awards@mla.org *Web Site:* www.mla.org, pg 668

Military Info Publishing, PO Box 41211, Plymouth, MN 55442 *Tel:* 763-533-8627 *Fax:* 763-533-8627 *E-mail:* publisher@military-info.com *Web Site:* www.military-info.com, pg 150

Military Living Publications, 333 Maple Ave E, Suite 3130, Vienna, VA 22180-4717 *Tel:* 703-237-0203 *Fax:* 703-552-7552 *E-mail:* customerservice@militaryliving.com *Web Site:* www.militaryliving.com, pg 150

Milkweed Editions, 1011 Washington Ave S, Suite 300, Minneapolis, MN 55415-1246 *Tel:* 612-332-3192 *Toll Free Tel:* 800-520-6455 *Fax:* 612-215-2550 *Web Site:* milkweed.org, pg 151

Milkweed National Fiction Prize, 1011 Washington Ave S, Suite 300, Minneapolis, MN 55415-1246 *Tel:* 612-332-3192 *Toll Free Tel:* 800-520-6455 *Fax:* 612-215-2550 *E-mail:* submissions@milkweed.org *Web Site:* www.milkweed.org, pg 668

Millbrook Press, 241 First Ave N, Minneapolis, MN 55401 *Tel:* 612-332-3344 *Toll Free Tel:* 800-328-4929 (US only) *Fax:* 612-332-7615 *Toll Free Fax:* 800-332-1132 *E-mail:* info@lernerbooks.com; custserve@lernerbooks.com *Web Site:* www.lernerbooks.com; www.facebook.com/millbrookpress, pg 151

The Miller Agency Inc, 630 Ninth Ave, Suite 1102, New York, NY 10036 *Tel:* 212-206-0913 *Fax:* 212-206-1473, pg 530

Richard K Miller Associates, 4132 Atlanta Hwy, Suite 110, Loganville, GA 30052 *Toll Free Tel:* 888-928-RKMA (928-7562) *Toll Free Fax:* 877-928-7562 *Web Site:* rkma.com, pg 151

Robert Miller Gallery, 524 W 26 St, New York, NY 10001 *Tel:* 212-366-4774 *Fax:* 212-366-4454 *E-mail:* rmg@robertmillergallery.com *Web Site:* www.robertmillergallery.com, pg 151

Stephen M Miller Inc, 15727 S Madison Dr, Olathe, KS 66062 *Tel:* 913-768-7997 *Web Site:* www.stephenmillerbooks.com, pg 499

Milliken Publishing Co, 501 E Third St, Dayton, OH 45402 *Tel:* 937-228-6118 *Toll Free Tel:* 800-444-1144 *Fax:* 937-223-2042 *E-mail:* order@lorenz.com *Web Site:* www.lorenzeducationalpress.com, pg 151

Kathleen Mills Editorial Services, 327 E King St, Chardon, OH 44024 *Tel:* 440-285-4347 *E-mail:* mills_edit@yahoo.com, pg 499

Milner Award, One Margaret Mitchell Sq NW, Atlanta, GA 30303 *Tel:* 404-730-1865 *E-mail:* info@themilneraward.org *Web Site:* www.themilneraward.org, pg 668

The Minerals, Metals & Materials Society (TMS), 5700 Corporate Dr, Suite 750, Pittsburgh, PA 15237 *Tel:* 724-776-9000 *Toll Free Tel:* 800-759-4867 *Fax:* 724-776-3770 *E-mail:* publications@tms.org (orders) *Web Site:* www.tms.org/bookstore (orders); www.tms.org, pg 151

Miniature Book Society Inc, 702 Rosecrans St, San Diego, CA 92106-3013 *Tel:* 619-226-4441 *Fax:* 619-226-4441 *E-mail:* minibook@cox.net *Web Site:* www.mbs.org, pg 569

Minnesota Book Awards, 1080 Montreal Ave, Suite 2, St Paul, MN 55116 *Tel:* 651-222-3242 *Fax:* 651-222-1988 *E-mail:* friends@thefriends.org *Web Site:* thefriends.org/events/mnba, pg 668

Minnesota Historical Society Press, 345 Kellogg Blvd W, St Paul, MN 55102-1906 *Tel:* 651-259-3205 *Toll Free Tel:* 800-621-2736 (warehouse) *Fax:* 651-297-1345 *Toll Free Fax:* 800-621-8476 (warehouse) *E-mail:* info-mnhspress@mnhs.org *Web Site:* www.mnhs.org/mnhspress, pg 151

Minotaur Books/Mystery Writers of America First Crime Novel Competition, 1140 Broadway, Suite 1507, New York, NY 10001 *Tel:* 212-888-8171 *Fax:* 212-888-8107 *E-mail:* mb-mwafirstcrimenovelcompetition@stmartins.com *Web Site:* mysterywriters.org/about-mwa/st-martins; us.macmillan.com/minotaurbooks/submit-manuscript, pg 668

Mississippi Review Prize, 118 College Dr, Box 5144, Hattiesburg, MS 39406-0001 *E-mail:* msreview@usm.edu *Web Site:* www.usm.edu/mississippi-review/contest.html, pg 668

Mississippi Review/University of Southern Mississippi, Center for Writers, 118 College Dr 5144, Hattiesburg, MS 39406-0001 *Tel:* 601-266-5600 *Fax:* 601-266-5757 *Web Site:* www.usm.edu/english/c4w.html; www.usm.edu/english/mississippireview.html, pg 621

Mississippi River Creative Writing Workshop, 720 Fourth Ave S, B-151, Rm 100, St Cloud, MN 56301-4498 *Tel:* 320-308-4947 *Fax:* 320-308-5524 *Web Site:* www.stcloudstate.edu, pg 612

MIT List Visual Arts Center, MIT E 15-109, 20 Ames St, Cambridge, MA 02139 *Tel:* 617-253-4400; 617-253-4680 *Fax:* 617-258-7265 *E-mail:* mlinga@mit.edu *Web Site:* listart.mit.edu, pg 151

The MIT Press, One Rogers St, Cambridge, MA 02142 *Tel:* 617-253-5255 *Toll Free Tel:* 800-207-8354 (orders) *Fax:* 617-258-6779; 617-577-1545 (orders) *Web Site:* mitpress.mit.edu, pg 151

Mitchell Lane Publishers Inc, PO Box 196, Hockessin, DE 19707 *Tel:* 302-234-9426 *Toll Free Tel:* 800-814-5484 *Fax:* 302-234-4742 *Toll Free Fax:* 866-834-4164 *E-mail:* orders@mitchelllane.com *Web Site:* www.mitchelllane.com, pg 152

MLA Prize for a Bibliography, Archive or Digital Project, 85 Broad St, Suite 500, New York, NY 10004-2434 *Tel:* 646-576-5141; 646-576-5000 *Fax:* 646-458-0030 *E-mail:* awards@mla.org *Web Site:* www.mla.org, pg 668

MLA Prize for a First Book, 85 Broad St, Suite 500, New York, NY 10004-2434 *Tel:* 646-576-5141; 646-576-5000 *Fax:* 646-458-0030 *E-mail:* awards@mla.org *Web Site:* www.mla.org, pg 668

MLA Prize for a Scholarly Edition, 85 Broad St, Suite 500, New York, NY 10004-2434 *Tel:* 646-576-5141; 646-576-5000 *Fax:* 646-458-0030 *E-mail:* awards@mla.org *Web Site:* www.mla.org, pg 668

MLA Prize for Independent Scholars, 85 Broad St, Suite 500, New York, NY 10004-2434 *Tel:* 646-576-5141; 646-576-5000 *Fax:* 646-458-0030 *E-mail:* awards@mla.org *Web Site:* www.mla.org, pg 668

MLA Prize for Studies in Native American Literatures, Cultures & Languages, 85 Broad St, Suite 500, New York, NY 10004-2434 *Tel:* 646-576-5141; 646-576-5000 *Fax:* 646-458-0030 *E-mail:* awards@mla.org *Web Site:* www.mla.org, pg 669

MLA Prize in United States Latina & Latino & Chicano & Chicano Literary & Cultural Studies, 85 Broad St, Suite 500, New York, NY 10004-2434 *Tel:* 646-576-5141; 646-576-5000 *Fax:* 646-458-0030 *E-mail:* awards@mla.org *Web Site:* www.mla.org, pg 669

Mobility International USA, 132 E Broadway, Suite 343, Eugene, OR 97401 *Tel:* 541-343-1284 *Fax:* 541-343-6812 *E-mail:* info@miusa.org *Web Site:* www.miusa.org, pg 152

Sondra Mochson, 18 Overlook Dr, Port Washington, NY 11050 *Tel:* 516-883-0961, pg 499

Modern Language Association of America (MLA), 85 Broad St, Suite 500, New York, NY 10004-2434 *Tel:* 646-576-5000 *Fax:* 646-458-0030 *Web Site:* www.mla.org, pg 152

Modern Language Association of America (MLA), 85 Broad St, Suite 500, New York, NY 10004-2434 *Tel:* 646-576-5000 *Fax:* 646-458-0030 *E-mail:* convention@mla.org *Web Site:* www.mla.org, pg 570

Modern Memoirs, 34 Main St, No 6, Amherst, MA 01002-2367 *Tel:* 413-253-2353 *Web Site:* www.modernmemoirs.com; www.whitepoppypress.com, pg 152

Modern Publishing, 6198 Butler Pike, Suite 200, Blue Bell, PA 19422 *Tel:* 215-643-6385 *Fax:* 215-628-3571 *Web Site:* www.modernpublishing.com, pg 152

Modus Vivendi Publishing Inc, 55, rue Jean-Talon Ouest, 2e etage, Montreal, QC H2R 2W8, Canada *Tel:* 514-272-0433 *Fax:* 514-272-7234 *E-mail:* info@groupemodus.com *Web Site:* www.groupemodus.com, pg 463

The Monacelli Press, 236 W 27 St, 4th fl, New York, NY 10001 *Tel:* 212-229-9925 (ext 25) *E-mail:* contact@monacellipress.com *Web Site:* www.monacellipress.com, pg 152

Mondial, 203 W 107 St, Suite 6-C, New York, NY 10025 *Tel:* 646-807-8031 *Fax:* 208-361-2863 *E-mail:* contact@mondialbooks.com *Web Site:* www.mondialbooks.com, pg 153

Mondo Publishing, 980 Avenue of the Americas, New York, NY 10018 *Tel:* 212-268-3560 *Toll Free Tel:* 888-88-MONDO (886-6636) *Toll Free Fax:* 888-532-4492 *E-mail:* info@mondopub.com *Web Site:* www.mondopub.com, pg 153

Money Market Directories, 401 E Market St, Charlottesville, VA 22902 *Tel:* 434-977-1450 *Toll Free Tel:* 800-446-2810 *Fax:* 434-979-9962 *E-mail:* mmdsales@spcapitaliq.com *Web Site:* www.mmdwebaccess.com, pg 153

The Mongolia Society Inc, Indiana University, 322 Goodbody Hall, 1011 E Third St, Bloomington, IN 47405-7005 *Tel:* 812-855-4078 *Fax:* 812-855-4078 *E-mail:* monsoc@indiana.edu *Web Site:* www.mongoliasociety.org, pg 153

Monkfish Book Publishing Co, 22 E Market St, Suite 304, Rhinebeck, NY 12572 *Tel:* 845-876-4861 *E-mail:* monkfish@monkfishpublishing.com *Web Site:* www.monkfishpublishing.com, pg 153

Montana Historical Society Press, Capitol Complex, 225 N Roberts St, Helena, MT 59620 *Tel:* 406-444-0090 (edit); 406-444-2890 (orders/mktg); 406-444-2694 *Toll Free Tel:* 800-243-9900 *Fax:* 406-444-2696 (orders/mktg) *Web Site:* mhs.mt.gov/pubs, pg 153

Montemayor Press, 663 Hyland Hill Rd, Washington, VT 05675 *Tel:* 802-552-0750 *E-mail:* mail@montemayorpress.com *Web Site:* www.montemayorpress.com, pg 153

Lucy Maud Montgomery PEI Literature for Children Awards, 81 Prince St, Charlottetown, PE C1A 4R3, Canada *E-mail:* peiliteraryawards@gmail.com *Web Site:* www.peiwritersguild.com, pg 669

Monthly Review Press, 146 W 29 St, Suite 6W, New York, NY 10001 *Tel:* 212-691-2555 *Toll Free Tel:* 800-670-9499 *Fax:* 212-727-3676 *E-mail:* mreview@igc.org *Web Site:* monthlyreview.org, pg 153

Montreal-Contacts/The Rights Agency, 1350 Sherbrooke St E, Suite 1, Montreal, QC H2L 1M4, Canada *Tel:* 514-400-7075 *Fax:* 514-400-1045 *Web Site:* www.montreal-contacts.com/?lang=en, pg 530

Moody Publishers, 820 N La Salle Blvd, Chicago, IL 60610 *Tel:* 312-329-4000 *Toll Free Tel:* 800-678-8812 (cust serv) *Fax:* 312-329-2019 *E-mail:* mpcustomerservice@moody.edu *Web Site:* www.moodypublishers.com, pg 153

Cenie H Moon Prize, 900 Timber Creek Place, Virginia Beach, VA 23464 *E-mail:* poetryinva@aol.com *Web Site:* poetrysocietyofvirginia.org, pg 669

Moonbeam Children's Book Awards, 1129 Woodmere Ave, Suite B, Traverse City, MI 49686 *Tel:* 231-933-0445 *Toll Free Tel:* 800-706-4636 *Fax:* 231-933-0448 *E-mail:* info@moonbeamawards.com *Web Site:* www.moonbeamawards.com, pg 669

Moonstone Press LLC, 4816 Carrington Circle, Sarasota, FL 34243 *Tel:* 301-765-1081 *Fax:* 301-765-0510 *E-mail:* mazeprod@erols.com *Web Site:* www.moonstonepress.net, pg 478

Jenny McKean Moore Writer-in-Washington, English Dept, Rome Hall, 801 22 St NW, Suite 643, Washington, DC 20052 *Tel:* 202-994-6180 *E-mail:* engldept@gwu.edu *Web Site:* english.columbian.gwu.edu, pg 669

Moose Hide Books, 684 Walls Rd, Prince Township, ON P6A 6K4, Canada *Tel:* 705-779-3331 *Fax:* 705-779-3331 *E-mail:* mooseenterprises@on.aibn.com *Web Site:* www.moosehidebooks.com, pg 464

Morehouse Publishing, 19 E 34 St, New York, NY 10016 *Tel:* 212-592-1800 *Toll Free Tel:* 800-672-1789 (retail orders only); 800-251-3320 (wholesale orders only) *Web Site:* www.morehousepublishing.com; www.churchpublishing.org, pg 154

Morgan Gaynin Inc, 149 Madison Ave, Suite 1140, New York, NY 10016 *Tel:* 212-475-0440 *E-mail:* info@morgangaynin.com *Web Site:* www.morgangaynin.com, pg 544

Morgan James Publishing, 5 Penn Plaza, 23rd fl, New York, NY 10001 *Tel:* 212-655-5470 *Toll Free Tel:* 800-485-4943 *Fax:* 516-908-4496 *E-mail:* csauer@morganjamespublishing.com *Web Site:* www.morganjamespublishing.com, pg 154

Morgan Kaufmann, 50 Hampshire St, 5th fl, Cambridge, MA 02139 *Toll Free Tel:* 866-607-1417 *Fax:* 617-661-7061 *Web Site:* www.mkp.com; www.elsevier.com, pg 154

Morgan Reynolds Publishing, 620 S Elm St, Suite 387, Greensboro, NC 27406 *Tel:* 336-275-1311 *Toll Free Tel:* 800-535-1504 *Fax:* 336-275-1152 *Toll Free Fax:* 800-535-5725 *E-mail:* editorial@morganreynolds.com; sales@morganreynolds.com *Web Site:* www.morganreynolds.com, pg 154

Howard Morhaim Literary Agency Inc, 30 Pierrepont St, Brooklyn, NY 11201-3371 *Tel:* 718-222-8400 *Fax:* 718-222-5056 *E-mail:* info@morhaimliterary.com *Web Site:* www.morhaimliterary.com, pg 530

Moriah Books, PO Box 1094, Casper, WY 82602 *Web Site:* moriahbook.com, pg 154

Morning Sun Books Inc, 1200 County Rd 523, Flemington, NJ 08822 *Tel:* 908-806-6216 *Fax:* 908-237-2407 *E-mail:* sales.morningsunbooks@gmail.com *Web Site:* morningsunbooks.com, pg 154

Ottoline Morrell Prize, University at Albany, Science Library 320, 1400 Washington Ave, Albany, NY 12222 *Tel:* 518-591-8162 *E-mail:* fence.fencebooks@gmail.com *Web Site:* www.fenceportal.org, pg 669

The William C Morris YA Debut Award, 50 E Huron St, Chicago, IL 60611 *Tel:* 312-280-4390 *Toll Free Tel:* 800-545-2433 (ext 4390) *Fax:* 312-280-5276 *E-mail:* yalsa@ala.org *Web Site:* www.ala.org/yalsa/morris, pg 669

William Morris Society in the United States Fellowships, PO Box 53263, Washington, DC 20009 *E-mail:* us@morrissociety.org *Web Site:* www.morrissociety.org, pg 669

Henry Morrison Inc, PO Box 235, Bedford Hills, NY 10507-0235 *Tel:* 914-666-3500 *Fax:* 914-241-7846 *E-mail:* hmorrison1@aol.com, pg 530

Morton Publishing Co, 925 W Kenyon Ave, Unit 12, Englewood, CO 80110 *Tel:* 303-761-4805 *Fax:* 303-762-9923 *E-mail:* contact@morton-pub.com; returns@morton-pub.com *Web Site:* www.morton-pub.com, pg 154

Mosaic Press, 1252 Speers Rd, Units 1 & 2, Oakville, ON L6L 5N9, Canada *Tel:* 905-825-2130 *E-mail:* info@mosaic-press.com *Web Site:* www.mosaic-press.com, pg 464

George L Mosse Prize, 400 "A" St SE, Washington, DC 20003 *Tel:* 202-544-2422 *Fax:* 202-544-8307 *E-mail:* awards@historians.org *Web Site:* www.historians.org, pg 669

Most Promising New Textbook Award, PO Box 367, Fountain City, WI 54629 *E-mail:* info@taaonline.net *Web Site:* www.taaonline.net/promising-new-textbook-award, pg 669

Motion Picture Association of America Inc (MPAA), 1600 "I" St NW, Washington, DC 20006 *Tel:* 202-293-1966 *Fax:* 202-296-7410 *E-mail:* contactus@mpaa.org *Web Site:* www.mpaa.org, pg 570

Frank Luther Mott-Kappa Tau Alpha Research Award, University of Missouri, School of Journalism, 76 Gannett Hall, Columbia, MO 65211-1200 *Tel:* 573-882-7685 *Fax:* 573-884-1720 *E-mail:* umcjourkta@missouri.edu *Web Site:* www.kappataualpha.org, pg 670

Sheila Margaret Motton Prize, 46 Wallace St, Somerville, MA 02144 *Tel:* 617-744-6034 *E-mail:* info@nepoetryclub.org *Web Site:* www.nepoetryclub.org, pg 670

Mount Hermon Christian Writers Conference, c/o Mount Hermon Association Inc, 37 Conference Dr, Felton, CA 95018 *Tel:* 831-335-4466 *Toll Free Tel:* 888-MH-CAMPS (642-2677, registration) *Fax:* 831-335-9335 *E-mail:* info@mounthermon.org *Web Site:* www.mounthermon.org/writers, pg 612

Mount Olive College Press, 634 Henderson St, Mount Olive, NC 28365 *Tel:* 919-658-2502 *Fax:* 919-658-7180 *Web Site:* www.umo.edu, pg 154

Mountain n' Air Books, 2947-A Honolulu Ave, La Crescenta, CA 91214 *Tel:* 818-248-9345 *Toll Free Tel:* 800-446-9696 *Toll Free Fax:* 800-303-5578 *Web Site:* www.mountain-n-air.com, pg 154

Mountain Press Publishing Co, 1301 S Third W, Missoula, MT 59801 *Tel:* 406-728-1900 *Toll Free Tel:* 800-234-5308 *Fax:* 406-728-1635 *E-mail:* info@mtnpress.com *Web Site:* www.mountain-press.com, pg 154

Mountain Writers Series, 2804 SE 27 Ave, Suite 2, Portland, OR 97202 *Tel:* 503-232-4517 *Fax:* 503-232-4517 *E-mail:* programs@mountainwriters.org; support@mountainwriters.org *Web Site:* www.mountainwriters.org, pg 612

The Mountaineers Books, 1001 SW Klickitat Way, Suite 201, Seattle, WA 98134 *Tel:* 206-223-6303 *Toll Free Tel:* 800-553-4453 *Fax:* 206-223-6306 *Toll Free Fax:* 800-568-7604 *E-mail:* mbooks@mountaineersbooks.org; customerservice@mountaineersbooks.org *Web Site:* www.mountaineersbooks.org, pg 154

De Gruyter Mouton, 125 Pearl St, Boston, MA 02110 *Tel:* 857-284-7073 *Fax:* 857-284-7358 *E-mail:* service@degruyter.com *Web Site:* www.degruyter.com, pg 155

Moveable Type Management, 244 Madison Ave, Suite 334, New York, NY 10016 *Web Site:* www.movabletm.com, pg 530

Moznaim Publishing Corp, 4304 12 Ave, Brooklyn, NY 11219 *Tel:* 718-438-7680 *Fax:* 718-438-1305 *E-mail:* sales@moznaim.com *Web Site:* www.moznaim.com, pg 155

MPA - The Association of Magazine Media, 757 Third Ave, 11th fl, New York, NY 10012 *Tel:* 212-872-3700 *Fax:* 212-888-4217 *Web Site:* www.magazine.org, pg 570

MRTS, PO Box 874402, Tempe, AZ 85287-4402 *Tel:* 480-727-6503 *Toll Free Tel:* 800-621-2736 (orders) *Fax:* 480-965-1681 *Toll Free Fax:* 800-621-8476 (orders) *E-mail:* mrts@asu.edu *Web Site:* acmrs.org/publications/mrts, pg 155

Mary Mueller, 516 Bartram Rd, Moorestown, NJ 08057 *Tel:* 856-778-4769 *E-mail:* mamam49@aol.com, pg 499

Multicultural Publications Inc, 1939 Manchester Rd, Akron, OH 44314 *Tel:* 330-865-9578 *Fax:* 330-865-9578 *E-mail:* multiculturalpub@prodigy.net *Web Site:* www.multiculturalpub.net, pg 155

Multnomah, 10807 New Allegiance Dr, Suite 500, Colorado Springs, CO 80921 *Tel:* 719-590-4999 *Toll Free Tel:* 800-603-7051 (orders) *Fax:* 719-590-8977 *Toll Free Fax:* 800-294-5686 (orders) *E-mail:* info@waterbrookmultnomah.com *Web Site:* waterbrookmultnomah.com, pg 155

Erika Mumford Prize, 46 Wallace St, Somerville, MA 02144 *Tel:* 617-744-6034 *E-mail:* info@nepoetryclub.org *Web Site:* www.nepoetryclub.org, pg 670

Mundania Press LLC, 6457 Glenway Ave, Suite 109, Cincinnati, OH 45211 *Tel:* 513-404-7357 *Fax:* 513-598-9220 *Toll Free Fax:* 888-460-4752 *E-mail:* books@mundania.com; inquiry@mundania.com *Web Site:* www.mundania.com, pg 155

Municipal Analysis Services Inc, PO Box 13453, Austin, TX 78711-3453 *Tel:* 512-704-7194 *E-mail:* munilysis@gmail.com *Web Site:* sites.google.com/site/gregmichels/home, pg 155

The Museum of Modern Art (MoMA), 11 W 53 St, New York, NY 10019 *Tel:* 212-708-9443 *Fax:* 212-333-6575 *E-mail:* moma_publications@moma.org *Web Site:* www.moma.org, pg 155

Museum of New Mexico Press, 725 Camino Lejo, Suite C, Santa Fe, NM 87505 *Tel:* 505-476-1155; 505-272-7777 (orders); 505-277-4810 *Toll Free Tel:* 800-249-7737 (orders) *Fax:* 505-476-1156 *Toll Free Fax:* 800-622-8667 (orders) *Web Site:* www.mnmpress.org, pg 156

Music Publishers Association (MPA), 243 Fifth Ave, Suite 236, New York, NY 10016 *Tel:* 212-327-4044 *E-mail:* admin@mpa.org *Web Site:* www.mpa.org, pg 570

Mutual Publishing LLC, 1215 Center St, Suite 210, Honolulu, HI 96816 *Tel:* 808-732-1709 *Fax:* 808-734-4094 *E-mail:* info@mutualpublishing.com *Web Site:* www.mutualpublishing.com, pg 156

MWG Writer Workshops & State Conference, 9 Janice Circle, Natchez, MS 39120 *Tel:* 601-442-0980 *E-mail:* mississippi.writersguild@outlook.com *Web Site:* www.mississippiwritersguild.com, pg 612

Walter Dean Myers Grant, 10318 Westlake Dr, No 104, Bethesda, MD 20817 *E-mail:* waltergrantwndb@gmail.com *Web Site:* weneeddiversebooks.org, pg 670

Mystery Writers of America (MWA), 1140 Broadway, Suite 1507, New York, NY 10001 *Tel:* 212-888-8171 *E-mail:* mwa@mysterywriters.org *Web Site:* www.mysterywriters.org, pg 570

Mystic Seaport Museum Inc, PO Box 6000, Mystic, CT 06355-0990 *Tel:* 860-572-5302; 860-572-0711 (visitor serv) *Toll Free Tel:* 800-248-1066 (wholesale orders only); 800-331-2665 (retail orders only) *Fax:* 860-572-5321 *E-mail:* info@mysticseaport.org *Web Site:* www.mysticseaport.org, pg 156

Mythopoeic Awards, Friends University, 2100 W University Ave, Wichita, KS 67213 *Tel:* 316-295-5563 *E-mail:* awards@mythsoc.org *Web Site:* www.mythsoc.org, pg 670

NACE International, 15835 Park Ten Place, Houston, TX 77084 *Tel:* 281-228-6200; 281-228-6223 *Toll Free Tel:* 800-797-NACE (797-6223) *Fax:* 281-228-6300 *E-mail:* firstservice@nace.org *Web Site:* www.nace.org, pg 156

Jean V Naggar Literary Agency Inc (JVNLA), 216 E 75 St, Suite 1-E, New York, NY 10021 *Tel:* 212-794-1082 *E-mail:* jvnla@jvnla.com *Web Site:* www.jvnla.com, pg 530

Napa Valley Writers' Conference, 1088 College Ave, St Helena, CA 94574 *Tel:* 707-967-2900 (ext 4) *Fax:* 707-967-2909 *E-mail:* info@napawritersconference.org; media@napawritersconference.org; fiction@napawritersconference.org; poetry@napawritersconference.org *Web Site:* www.napawritersconference.org, pg 613

Narada Press, 3165-133 Weber St N, Waterloo, ON N2J 3G9, Canada *Tel:* 519-886-1969, pg 464

NASW Press, 750 First St NE, Suite 800, Washington, DC 20002 *Tel:* 202-408-8600 *Fax:* 203-336-8312 *E-mail:* press@naswdc.org *Web Site:* www.naswpress.org, pg 156

Nataraj Books, 7967 Twist Lane, Springfield, VA 22153 *Tel:* 703-455-4996 *Fax:* 703-455-4001 *E-mail:* nataraj@erols.com; orders@natarajbooks.com; natarajbooks@gmail.com *Web Site:* www.natarajbooks.com, pg 156

National Academies Press (NAP), Lockbox 285, 500 Fifth St NW, Washington, DC 20001 *Tel:* 202-334-3313 *Fax:* 202-334-2451 (cust serv); 202-334-2793 (mktg dept) *E-mail:* customer_service@nap.edu *Web Site:* www.nap.edu, pg 156

The National Alliance Research Academy, 3630 N Hills Dr, Austin, TX 78755 *Tel:* 512-345-7932 *Toll Free Tel:* 800-633-2165 *Fax:* 512-349-6194 *E-mail:* alliance@scic.com *Web Site:* www.scic.com/academy, pg 157

National Association for Music Education (NAfME), 1806 Robert Fulton Dr, Reston, VA 20191 *Tel:* 703-860-4000 *Toll Free Tel:* 800-462-6420 (orders & returns); 800-336-3768 *Fax:* 703-860-1531 *Web Site:* www.menc.org; www.nafme.org, pg 157

National Association of Black Journalists (NABJ), 1100 Knight Hall, Suite 3100, College Park, MD 20742 *Tel:* 301-405-0248 *Fax:* 301-314-1714 *E-mail:* nabj@nabj.org *Web Site:* www.nabj.org, pg 570

National Association of Book Entrepreneurs (NABE), PO Box 606, Cottage Grove, OR 97424 *Tel:* 541-942-7455 *E-mail:* nabe@bookmarketingprofits.com *Web Site:* www.bookmarketingprofits.com, pg 570

National Association of Broadcasters (NAB), 1771 "N" St NW, Washington, DC 20036 *Tel:* 202-429-5300 *E-mail:* nab@nab.org *Web Site:* www.nab.org, pg 157, 570

National Association of College Stores (NACS), 500 E Lorain St, Oberlin, OH 44074 *Tel:* 440-775-7777 *Toll Free Tel:* 800-622-7498 *Fax:* 440-775-4769 *Web Site:* www.nacs.org, pg 570

National Association of Hispanic Publications Inc (NAHP), 529 14 St NW, Suite 1126, Washington, DC 20045 *Tel:* 202-662-7250 *Web Site:* www.nahp.org, pg 571

National Association of Independent Publishers Representatives, 111 E 14 St, PMB 157, New York, NY 10003 *Tel:* 267-546-6561 *Toll Free Tel:* 888-624-7779 *Web Site:* naipr.org, pg 571

National Association of Insurance Commissioners, 1100 Walnut St, Suite 1500, Kansas City, MO 64106-2197 *Tel:* 816-842-3600; 816-783-8300 (cust serv) *Fax:* 816-783-8175; 816-460-7593 (cust serv) *E-mail:* prodserv@naic.org *Web Site:* www.naic.org, pg 157

National Association of Printing Ink Manufacturers (NAPIM), 15 Technology Pkwy S, Peachtree Corners, GA 30092 *Tel:* 770-209-7289 *Fax:* 678-680-4920; 770-209-7217 *E-mail:* napim@napim.org *Web Site:* www.napim.org, pg 571

National Association of Real Estate Editors (NAREE), 1003 NW Sixth Terr, Boca Raton, FL 33486-3455 *Tel:* 561-391-3599 *Fax:* 561-391-0099 *Web Site:* www.naree.org, pg 571

National Association of Science Writers (NASW), PO Box 7905, Berkeley, CA 94707 *Tel:* 510-647-9500 *Web Site:* www.nasw.org, pg 571

National Association of Secondary School Principals (NASSP), 1904 Association Dr, Reston, VA 20191-1537 *Tel:* 703-860-0200 *Toll Free Tel:* 800-253-7746 *E-mail:* sales@nassp.org; publications2@nassp.org (communs & devt); membership@nassp.org *Web Site:* www.nassp.org, pg 157

National Awards for Education Reporting, 3516 Connecticut Ave NW, Washington, DC 20008 *Tel:* 202-452-9830 *Fax:* 202-452-9837 *E-mail:* ewa@ewa.org *Web Site:* www.ewa.org, pg 670

National Book Awards, 90 Broad St, Suite 604, New York, NY 10004 *Tel:* 212-685-0261 *Fax:* 212-213-6570 *E-mail:* nationalbook@nationalbook.org *Web Site:* www.nationalbook.org, pg 670

National Book Co, PO Box 19069, Portland, OR 97280-0069 *Tel:* 503-228-6345 *Fax:* 810-885-5811 *E-mail:* info@eralearning.com *Web Site:* www.eralearning.com, pg 157

National Book Critics Circle Award, c/o 38 Douglass St, Apt 3, Brooklyn, NY 11231 *E-mail:* info@bookcritics.org *Web Site:* bookcritics.org/awards, pg 670

National Braille Press, 88 Saint Stephen St, Boston, MA 02115-4302 *Tel:* 617-266-6160 *Toll Free Tel:* 800-548-7323 (cust serv); 888-965-8965 *Fax:* 617-437-0456 *E-mail:* orders@nbp.org; contact@nbp.org *Web Site:* www.nbp.org, pg 157

The National Business Book Award, c/o Freedman & Associates Inc, 121 Richmond St W, Suite 605, Toronto, ON M5H 2K1, Canada *Tel:* 416-868-1500 *Web Site:* www.nbbaward.com, pg 670

National Cartoonists Society (NCS), PO Box 592927, Orlando, FL 32859-2927 *Tel:* 407-994-6703 *Fax:* 407-442-0786 *E-mail:* info@reuben.org *Web Site:* www.reuben.org, pg 571

National Catholic Educational Association, 1005 N Glebe Rd, Suite 525, Arlington, VA 22201 *Tel:* 571-257-0010 *Toll Free Tel:* 800-711-6232 *Fax:* 703-243-0025 *E-mail:* nceaadmin@ncea.org *Web Site:* www.ncea.org, pg 157

National Center for Children in Poverty, 215 W 125 St, 3rd fl, New York, NY 10027 *Tel:* 646-284-9600 *Fax:* 646-284-9623 *E-mail:* info@nccp.org *Web Site:* www.nccp.org, pg 157

National Center For Employee Ownership (NCEO), 1629 Telegraph Ave, Suite 200, Oakland, CA 94612 *Tel:* 510-208-1300 *Fax:* 510-272-9510 *E-mail:* customerservice@nceo.org *Web Site:* www.nceo.org, pg 157

National Coalition Against Censorship (NCAC), 19 Fulton St, Suite 407, New York, NY 10038 *Tel:* 212-807-6222 *Fax:* 212-807-6245 *E-mail:* ncac@ncac.org *Web Site:* www.ncac.org, pg 571

National Coalition for Literacy (NCL), PO Box 2932, Washington, DC 20013-2932 *E-mail:* ncl@ncladvocacy.org *Web Site:* www.national-coalition-literacy.org, pg 571

National Communication Association, 1765 "N" St NW, Washington, DC 20036 *Tel:* 202-464-4622 *Fax:* 202-464-4600 *E-mail:* inbox@natcom.org *Web Site:* www.natcom.org, pg 571

National Conference of State Legislatures (NCSL), 7700 E First Place, Denver, CO 80230 *Tel:* 303-364-7700 *Fax:* 303-364-7800 *E-mail:* books@ncsl.org *Web Site:* www.ncsl.org, pg 157

National Council of Teachers of English (NCTE), 1111 W Kenyon Rd, Urbana, IL 61801-1096 *Tel:* 217-328-3870 *Toll Free Tel:* 877-369-6283 (cust serv) *Fax:* 217-328-9645 *E-mail:* orders@ncte.org *Web Site:* www.ncte.org, pg 158

National Council of Teachers of English (NCTE), 1111 W Kenyon Rd, Urbana, IL 61801-1096 *Tel:* 217-328-3870 *Toll Free Tel:* 877-369-6283 (cust serv) *Fax:* 217-328-9645 *E-mail:* public_info@ncte.org *Web Site:* www.ncte.org, pg 571

National Council of Teachers of Mathematics (NCTM), 1906 Association Dr, Reston, VA 20191-1502 *Tel:* 703-620-9840 *Toll Free Tel:* 800-235-7566 *Fax:* 703-476-2970 *E-mail:* nctm@nctm.org *Web Site:* www.nctm.org, pg 158

National Education Association (NEA), 1201 16 St NW, Washington, DC 20036-3290 *Tel:* 202-833-4000 *Fax:* 202-822-7974 *Web Site:* www.nea.org, pg 158, 572

National Endowment for the Arts, 400 Seventh St SW, Washington, DC 20506-0001 *Tel:* 202-682-5400 *Web Site:* www.arts.gov, pg 583

National Federation of Advanced Information Services (NFAIS), 801 Compass Way, Suite 201, Annapolis, MD 21401 *Tel:* 443-221-2980 *Fax:* 443-221-2981 *E-mail:* nfais@nfais.org *Web Site:* www.nfais.org, pg 572

National Federation of Press Women Inc (NFPW), PO Box 3007, Mechanicsville, VA 23116-0026 *Tel:* 703-237-9804 *Fax:* 703-237-9808 *E-mail:* presswomen@aol.com *Web Site:* www.nfpw.org, pg 572

National Federation of State Poetry Societies Annual Poetry Contest, c/o PO Box 263, Huttig, AR 71747 *E-mail:* contestchair@nfsps.com *Web Site:* www.nfsps.com, pg 670

National Freedom of Information Coalition (NFOIC), 101C Reynolds Journalism Institute, Columbia, MO 65211 *Tel:* 573-882-4856 *Web Site:* nfoic.org, pg 572

National Gallery of Art, Sixth & Constitution Ave NW, Washington, DC 20565 *Tel:* 202-737-4215; 202-842-6480 *Fax:* 202-842-6733 *E-mail:* casva@nga.gov *Web Site:* www.nga.gov, pg 158

National Gallery of Canada Boutique, 380 Sussex Dr, Ottawa, ON K1N 9N4, Canada *Tel:* 613-990-0962 (mail order sales) *E-mail:* ngcbook@gallery.ca *Web Site:* www.gallery.ca, pg 464

National Geographic Books, 1145 17 St NW, Washington, DC 20036-4688 *Tel:* 202-857-7000 *Toll Free Tel:* 877-866-6486 *E-mail:* ngbooks@cdsfulfillment.com *Web Site:* www.nationalgeographic.com/books/; ngbooks.buysub.com, pg 158

National Geographic Learning, 20 Channel Center St, Boston, MA 02210 *Tel:* 617-289-7796 *E-mail:* schoolcustomerservice@cengage.com *Web Site:* www.ngl.cengage.com/school, pg 158

National Golf Foundation, 501 N Hwy A1A, Jupiter, FL 33477-4577 *Tel:* 561-744-6006 *Toll Free Tel:* 888-275-4643 *Fax:* 561-744-6107 *E-mail:* general@ngf.org *Web Site:* www.ngf.org, pg 158

The National Humanities Medal, 400 Seventh St SW, Washington, DC 20506 *Tel:* 202-606-8400 *Toll Free Tel:* 800-NEH-1121 (634-1121) *E-mail:* info@neh.gov *Web Site:* www.neh.gov/about/awards, pg 670

National Information Standards Organization (NISO), 3600 Clipper Mill Rd, Suite 302, Baltimore, MD 21211 *Tel:* 301-654-2512 *Fax:* 410-685-5278 *E-mail:* nisohq@niso.org *Web Site:* www.niso.org, pg 158, 572

National Institute for Trial Advocacy (NITA), 1685 38 St, Suite 200, Boulder, CO 80301-2735 *Tel:* 720-890-4860 *Toll Free Tel:* 877-648-2632; 800-225-6482 (orders & returns) *Fax:* 720-890-7069 *E-mail:* info@nita.org *Web Site:* www.nita.org, pg 158

National Jewish Book Award-Children's Literature, 520 Eighth Ave, 4th fl, New York, NY 10018 *Tel:* 212-201-2920 *Fax:* 212-532-4952 *E-mail:* jbc@jewishbooks.org *Web Site:* www.jewishbookcouncil.org, pg 670

National Jewish Book Award-Natan Book Award, 520 Eighth Ave, 4th fl, New York, NY 10018 *Tel:* 212-201-2920 *Fax:* 212-532-4952 *E-mail:* jbc@jewishbooks.org; natanbookawards@jewishbooks.org *Web Site:* www.jewishbookcouncil.org, pg 671

National Jewish Book Award-Young Adult Literature, 520 Eighth Ave, 4th fl, New York, NY 10018 *Tel:* 212-201-2920 *Fax:* 212-532-4952 *E-mail:* jbc@jewishbooks.org *Web Site:* www.jewishbookcouncil.org, pg 671

National Jewish Book Awards, 520 Eighth Ave, 4th fl, New York, NY 10018 *Tel:* 212-201-2920 *Fax:* 212-532-4952 *E-mail:* jbc@jewishbooks.org *Web Site:* www.jewishbookcouncil.org, pg 671

National League of American Pen Women Inc, The Pen Arts Bldg & Arts Museum, 1300 17 St NW, Washington, DC 20036-1973 *Tel:* 202-785-1997 *Fax:* 202-452-8868 *E-mail:* contact@nlapw.org *Web Site:* www.nlapw.org, pg 572

National Learning Corp, 212 Michael Dr, Syosset, NY 11791 *Tel:* 516-921-8888 *Toll Free Tel:* 800-632-8888 *Fax:* 516-921-8743 *E-mail:* info@passbooks.com *Web Site:* www.passbooks.com, pg 159

National Magazine Awards, 2300 Yonge St, Suite 1600, Toronto, ON M4P 1E4, Canada *Tel:* 416-939-6200 *E-mail:* staff@magazine-awards.com *Web Site:* www.magazine-awards.com; twitter.com/magawards, pg 671

The National Medal of Arts, 400 Seventh St SW, Washington, DC 20506-0001 *Tel:* 202-682-5434 *Web Site:* www.arts.gov/honors/medals, pg 671

National Music Publishers' Association (NMPA), 975 "F" St NW, Suite 315, Washington, DC 20004 *Tel:* 202-393-6672 *Fax:* 202-393-6673 *E-mail:* pr@nmpa.org *Web Site:* www.nmpa.org, pg 572

National Newspaper Association, 900 Community Dr, Springfield, IL 62703-5180 *Tel:* 217-241-1400 *Fax:* 217-241-1301 *E-mail:* nna@nna.org *Web Site:* nnaweb.org, pg 572

National Newspaper Publishers Association (NNPA), 1816 12 St NW, Washington, DC 20009 *Tel:* 202-588-8764 *Fax:* 202-588-8960 *E-mail:* info@nnpa.org *Web Site:* www.nnpa.org; www.blackpressusa.com, pg 572

National Notary Association (NNA), 9350 De Soto Ave, Chatsworth, CA 91311-4926 *Tel:* 818-739-4000 *Toll Free Tel:* 800-876-6827 *Toll Free Fax:* 800-833-1211 *E-mail:* nna@nationalnotary.org *Web Site:* www.nationalnotary.org, pg 159

National One-Act Playwriting Competition, 600 Wolfe St, Alexandria, VA 22314 *Tel:* 703-683-5778 (ext 2) *Fax:* 703-683-1378 *E-mail:* asklta@thelittletheatre.com *Web Site:* www.thelittletheatre.com/info, pg 671

National Outdoor Book Awards, 921 S Eighth Ave, Stop 8128, Pocatello, ID 83209-8128 *Tel:* 208-282-3912 *Fax:* 208-282-2127 *Web Site:* www.noba-web.org, pg 671

National Poetry Series Open Competition, 57 Mountain Ave, Princeton, NJ 08540 *Tel:* 609-430-0999 *Fax:* 609-430-9933 *Web Site:* nationalpoetryseries.org, pg 671

National Press Club (NPC), 529 14 St NW, 13th fl, Washington, DC 20045 *Tel:* 202-662-7500 *Fax:* 202-662-7569 *E-mail:* infocenter@npcpress.org *Web Site:* www.press.org, pg 572

National Press Club of Canada Foundation Inc, 17 York St, Suite 201, Ottawa, ON K1N 9J6, Canada *E-mail:* info@pressclubcanada.ca *Web Site:* pressclubcanada.ca, pg 572

National Press Foundation, 1211 Connecticut Ave NW, Suite 310, Washington, DC 20036 *Tel:* 202-663-7280 *Web Site:* nationalpress.org, pg 572

National Press Photographers Association Inc (NPPA), 3200 Croasdaile Dr, Suite 306, Durham, NC 27705 *Tel:* 919-383-7246 *Fax:* 919-383-7261 *E-mail:* info@nppa.org *Web Site:* www.nppa.org, pg 573

National Resource Center for Youth Services (NRCYS), Schusterman Ctr, Bldg 4W, 4502 E 41 St, Tulsa, OK 74135-2512 *Tel:* 918-660-3700 *Toll Free Tel:* 800-274-2687 *Fax:* 918-660-3737 *Web Site:* www.nrcys.ou.edu, pg 159

National Science Teachers Association (NSTA), 1840 Wilson Blvd, Arlington, VA 22201-3000 *Tel:* 703-312-9205 *Toll Free Tel:* 800-277-5300 (orders) *Toll Free Fax:* 888-433-0526 (orders) *E-mail:* publisher@nsta.org (gen info); orders@nsta.org *Web Site:* www.nsta.org/store, pg 159

National Society of Newspaper Columnists (NSNC), PO Box 411532, San Francisco, CA 94141 *Tel:* 415-488-NCNC (488-6762) *Fax:* 484-297-0336 *E-mail:* director@columnists.com *Web Site:* www.columnists.com, pg 573

National Society of Newspaper Columnists Annual Conference, PO Box 411532, San Francisco, CA 94141 *Tel:* 415-488-NCNC (488-6762) *Fax:* 484-297-0336 *E-mail:* director@columnists.com *Web Site:* www.columnists.com, pg 613

National Ten-Minute Play Contest, 316 W Main St, Louisville, KY 40202-4218 *Tel:* 502-584-1265 *Web Site:* actorstheatre.org/national-ten-minute-play-contest/, pg 671

New York City Book Awards, 53 E 79 St, New York, NY 10075 *Tel:* 212-288-6900 *Fax:* 212-744-5832 *E-mail:* events@nysoclib.org *Web Site:* www.nysoclib.org, pg 673

New York City College of Technology, 300 Jay St, Brooklyn, NY 11201 *Tel:* 718-260-5500 *Fax:* 718-260-5198 *E-mail:* connect@citytech.cuny.edu *Web Site:* www.citytech.cuny.edu, pg 621

The New York Public Library Helen Bernstein Book Award for Excellence in Journalism, Stephen A Schwarzman Bldg, Fifth Ave at 42 St, South Court Bldg, 3rd fl, New York, NY 10018-2788 *Tel:* 212-930-0876 *Web Site:* www.nypl.org, pg 673

New York State Bar Association, One Elk St, Albany, NY 12207 *Tel:* 518-463-3200 *Toll Free Tel:* 800-582-2452 *Fax:* 518-487-5517 *E-mail:* mrc@nysba.org *Web Site:* www.nysba.org, pg 162

New York State Edith Wharton Citation of Merit for Fiction Writers, University at Albany, SL 320, Albany, NY 12222 *Tel:* 518-442-5620 *Fax:* 518-442-5621 *E-mail:* writers@albany.edu *Web Site:* www.albany.edu/writers-inst, pg 673

New York State Walt Whitman Citation of Merit for Poets, University at Albany, SL 320, Albany, NY 12222 *Tel:* 518-442-5620 *Fax:* 518-442-5621 *E-mail:* writers@albany.edu *Web Site:* www.albany.edu/writers-inst, pg 673

New York State Writers Institute, University at Albany, Science Library 320, 1400 Washington Ave, Albany, NY 12222 *Tel:* 518-442-5620 *Fax:* 518-442-5621 *E-mail:* writers@albany.edu *Web Site:* www.albany.edu/writers-inst, pg 613

New York University, Center for Publishing, Midtown Ctr, Rm 429, 11 W 42 St, New York, NY 10036 *Tel:* 212-992-3232 *Fax:* 212-992-3233 *E-mail:* pub.center@nyu.edu *Web Site:* www.scps.nyu.edu/publishing, pg 621

New York University Press, 838 Broadway, 3rd fl, New York, NY 10003-4812 *Tel:* 212-998-2575 (edit) *Toll Free Tel:* 800-996-6987 (orders) *Fax:* 212-995-4798 (orders) *E-mail:* information@nyupress.org; nyupressinfo@nyu.edu; orders@nyupress.org *Web Site:* www.nyupress.org, pg 162

John Newbery Medal, 50 E Huron St, Chicago, IL 60611-2795 *Tel:* 312-280-2163 *Toll Free Tel:* 800-545-2433 *Fax:* 312-440-9374; 312-280-5271 *E-mail:* alsc@ala.org *Web Site:* www.ala.org/alsc, pg 673

Newbury Street Press, 99-101 Newbury St, Boston, MA 02116 *Tel:* 617-536-5740 *Toll Free Tel:* 888-296-3447 (NEHGS membership) *Fax:* 617-536-7307 *E-mail:* sales@nehgs.org *Web Site:* www.americanancestors.org, pg 162

NeWest Press, 8540 109 St, No 201, Edmonton, AB T6G 1E6, Canada *Tel:* 780-432-9427 *Fax:* 780-433-3179 *E-mail:* info@newestpress.com; orders@newestpress.com *Web Site:* www.newestpress.com, pg 464

Newfoundland and Labrador Book Awards, Haymarket Sq, 223 Duckworth St, St John's, NL A1C 6N1, Canada *Tel:* 709-739-5215 *Toll Free Tel:* 866-739-5215 *E-mail:* wanl@nf.aibn.com *Web Site:* wanl.ca, pg 673

Newgen North America Inc, 2714 Bee Cave Rd, Suite 201, Austin, TX 78746 *Tel:* 512-478-5341 *Fax:* 512-476-4756 *Web Site:* www.newgen.co, pg 499

News Media Alliance, 4401 N Fairfax Dr, Suite 300, Arlington, VA 22203 *Tel:* 571-366-1000 *E-mail:* info@newsmediaalliance.org *Web Site:* www.newsmediaalliance.org, pg 573

The NewsGuild - CWA, 501 Third St NW, 6th fl, Washington, DC 20001-2797 *Tel:* 202-434-7177; 202-434-7162 (The Guild Reporter) *Fax:* 202-434-1472 *E-mail:* guild@cwa-union.org *Web Site:* www.newsguild.org, pg 573

NewSouth Books, 105 S Court St, Montgomery, AL 36104 *Tel:* 334-834-3556 *Fax:* 334-834-3557 *E-mail:* info@newsouthbooks.com *Web Site:* www.newsouthbooks.com, pg 162

Sue Newton, 1385 Cypress Point Lane, Suite 202, Ventura, CA 93003 *Tel:* 805-765-4412; 805-827-1961 *E-mail:* sue.edit@gmail.com, pg 499

Don & Gee Nicholl Fellowships in Screenwriting, 1313 Vine St, Hollywood, CA 90028 *Tel:* 310-247-3010 *Fax:* 310-247-3794 *E-mail:* nicholl@oscars.org *Web Site:* www.oscars.org/nicholl, pg 673

Donald Nicholson-Smith, 50 Plaza St E, Apt 1D, Brooklyn, NY 11238 *Tel:* 718-636-4732 *E-mail:* mnr.dns@verizon.net, pg 499

Nightingale-Conant, Bldg 300, Suite 103, 1400 S Wolf Rd, Wheeling, IL 60090 *Tel:* 847-647-0306 *Toll Free Tel:* 800-557-1660 (sales); 800-560-6081 (cust serv) *Web Site:* www.nightingale.com, pg 162

Nilgiri Press, 3600 Tomales Rd, Tomales, CA 94971 *Tel:* 707-878-2369 *E-mail:* info@easwaran.org *Web Site:* www.easwaran.org, pg 162

Nimbus Publishing Ltd, 3731 Mackintosh St, Halifax, NS B3K 5A5, Canada *Tel:* 902-455-4286 *Toll Free Tel:* 800-NIMBUS9 (646-2879) *Fax:* 902-455-5440 *Toll Free Fax:* 888-253-3133 *E-mail:* customerservice@nimbus.ca *Web Site:* www.nimbus.ca, pg 465

John Frederick Nims Memorial Prize, 61 W Superior St, Chicago, IL 60654 *Tel:* 312-787-7070 *Fax:* 312-787-6650 *E-mail:* editors@poetrymagazine.org *Web Site:* www.poetryfoundation.org, pg 673

No Frills Buffalo, 119 Dorchester Rd, Buffalo, NY 14213 *Tel:* 716-510-0520 *E-mail:* contact@nofrillsbuffalo.com; submissions@nofrillsbuffalo.com *Web Site:* www.nofrillsbuffalo.com, pg 162

No Starch Press, 245 Eighth St, San Francisco, CA 94103 *Tel:* 415-863-9900 *Toll Free Tel:* 800-420-7240 *Fax:* 415-863-9950 *E-mail:* info@nostarch.com; sales@nostarch.com *Web Site:* www.nostarch.com, pg 162

Regula Noetzli Literary Agent, 2344 County Rte 83, Pine Plains, NY 12567 *Tel:* 518-398-6260 *E-mail:* regula@taconic.net; regula@sheedylit.com, pg 531

The Betsy Nolan Literary Agency, 112 E 17 St, Suite 1W, New York, NY 10003 *Tel:* 212-967-8200 *Fax:* 212-967-7292 *E-mail:* dblehr@cs.com, pg 531

NOLO, 7031 Koll Center Pkwy, Suite 100, Pleasanton, CA 94566 *Web Site:* www.nolo.com, pg 162

The Noontide Press, PO Box 2719, Newport Beach, CA 92659-1319 *Tel:* 714-593-9725 *E-mail:* orders@noontidepress.com *Web Site:* www.noontidepress.com, pg 163

Norilana Books, PO Box 209, Highgate Center, VT 05459-0209 *E-mail:* service@norilana.com *Web Site:* www.norilana.com, pg 163

North American Agricultural Journalists (NAAJ), 6434 Hurta Lane, Bryan, TX 77808 *Tel:* 979-845-2872 *Web Site:* www.naaj.net, pg 573

North American Snowsports Journalists Association (NASJA), 11728 SE Madison St, Portland, OR 97216-3849 *Tel:* 503-255-3771 *Fax:* 503-255-3771 *Web Site:* www.nasja.org, pg 574

North Atlantic Books, 2526 Martin Luther King Jr Way, Berkeley, CA 94704 *Tel:* 510-549-4270 *Fax:* 510-549-4276 *Web Site:* www.northatlanticbooks.com, pg 163

North Carolina Arts Council Writers Fellowships, 109 E Jones St, Raleigh, NC 27601 *Tel:* 919-807-6500 *Fax:* 919-807-6532 *E-mail:* ncarts@ncdcr.gov *Web Site:* www.ncarts.org, pg 674

North Carolina Office of Archives & History, Historical Publications Branch, 4610 Mail Service Ctr, Raleigh, NC 27699-4610 *Tel:* 919-807-7290 *E-mail:* historical.publications@ncdcr.gov *Web Site:* www.ncdcr.gov, pg 163

North Carolina Writers' Network, PO Box 21591, Winston-Salem, NC 27120-1591 *Tel:* 336-293-8844 *Web Site:* www.ncwriters.org, pg 574

North Carolina Writers' Network Annual Fall Conference, PO Box 21591, Winston-Salem, NC 27120-1591 *Tel:* 336-293-8844 *E-mail:* mail@ncwriters.org *Web Site:* www.ncwriters.org, pg 613

North Country Books Inc, 220 Lafayette St, Utica, NY 13502-4312 *Tel:* 315-735-4877 *Toll Free Tel:* 800-342-7409 (orders) *Fax:* 315-738-4342 *E-mail:* ncbooks@verizon.net *Web Site:* www.northcountrybooks.com, pg 163

North Country Press, 126 Main St, Unity, ME 04988 *Tel:* 207-948-2208 *Fax:* 207-948-9000 *E-mail:* info@northcountrypress.com *Web Site:* www.northcountrypress.com, pg 163

North Point Press, 18 W 18 St, 8th fl, New York, NY 10011 *Tel:* 212-741-6900 *Toll Free Tel:* 888-330-8477 *Fax:* 212-633-9385 *Web Site:* www.fsgbooks.com, pg 163

North River Press Publishing Corp, 27 Rosseter St, Great Barrington, MA 01230 *Tel:* 413-528-0034 *Toll Free Tel:* 800-486-2665 *Fax:* 413-528-3163 *Toll Free Fax:* 800-BOOK-FAX (266-5329) *E-mail:* info@northriverpress.com *Web Site:* www.northriverpress.com, pg 163

North Star Editions Inc, 2297 Waters Dr, Mendota Heights, MN 55120 *Tel:* 651-204-3515 *Toll Free Tel:* 888-417-0195 *Fax:* 952-582-1000 *E-mail:* sales@northstareditions.com *Web Site:* www.northstareditions.com, pg 163

North Star Press of Saint Cloud Inc, PO Box 451, St Cloud, MN 56302-0451 *Tel:* 320-558-9062 *E-mail:* info@northstarpress.com *Web Site:* www.northstarpress.com, pg 164

North Street Book Prize, 351 Pleasant St, PMB 222, Northampton, MA 01060-3961 *Tel:* 413-320-1847 *Toll Free Tel:* 866-WINWRIT (946-9748) *Fax:* 413-280-0539 *Web Site:* www.winningwriters.com, pg 674

Northeast-Midwest Institute, 50 "F" St NW, Suite 950, Washington, DC 20001 *Tel:* 202-544-5200 *Fax:* 202-544-0043 *E-mail:* info@nemw.org *Web Site:* www.nemw.org, pg 164

Northern California Book Awards, c/o Poetry Flash, 1450 Fourth St, Suite 4, Berkeley, CA 94710 *Tel:* 510-525-5476 *Fax:* 510-525-6752 *E-mail:* editor@poetryflash.org; ncbr@poetryflash.org *Web Site:* poetryflash.org, pg 674

Northern California Independent Booksellers Association (NCIBA), 651 Broadway, Sonoma, CA 95476 *Tel:* 415-561-7686 *Fax:* 415-561-7685 *E-mail:* info@nciba.com *Web Site:* www.nciba.com, pg 574

Northern California Translators Association, 2261 Market St, Suite 160, San Francisco, CA 94114-1600 *Tel:* 510-845-8712 *E-mail:* administrator@ncta.org *Web Site:* www.ncta.org, pg 574

Northern Illinois University Press, 2280 Bethany Rd, DeKalb, IL 60115 *Tel:* 815-753-1075 *Fax:* 815-753-1845 *Web Site:* www.niupress.niu.edu, pg 164

Northwest Independent Editors Guild, 7511 Greenwood Ave N, No 307, Seattle, WA 98103 *E-mail:* info@edsguild.org *Web Site:* www.edsguild.org, pg 574

Northwest Territories Public Library Services, 75 Woodland Dr, Hay River, NT X0E 1G1, Canada *Tel:* 867-874-6531 *Toll Free Tel:* 866-297-0232 (CN) *Fax:* 867-874-3321 *Web Site:* www.nwtpls.gov.nt.ca, pg 574

Northwestern University Press, 629 Noyes St, Evanston, IL 60208-4210 *Tel:* 847-491-2046 *Toll Free Tel:* 800-621-2736 (orders only) *Fax:* 847-491-8150 *E-mail:* nupress@northwestern.edu *Web Site:* www.nupress.northwestern.edu, pg 164

W W Norton & Company Inc, 500 Fifth Ave, New York, NY 10110-0017 *Tel:* 212-354-5500 *Toll Free Tel:* 800-233-4830 (orders & cust serv) *Fax:* 212-869-0856 *Toll Free Fax:* 800-458-6515 *E-mail:* orders@wwnorton.com *Web Site:* books.wwnorton.com, pg 164

Norwood House Press, PO Box 316598, Chicago, IL 60631 *Tel:* 773-467-0837 *Toll Free Tel:* 866-565-2900 *Fax:* 773-467-9686 *Toll Free Fax:* 866-565-2901 *E-mail:* customerservice@norwoodhousepress.com *Web Site:* www.norwoodhousepress.com, pg 165

Notable Wisconsin Authors, 4610 S Biltmore Lane, Suite 100, Madison, WI 53718-2153 *Tel:* 608-245-3640 *Fax:* 608-245-3646 *Web Site:* wla.wisconsinlibraries.org, pg 674

Nova Press, 9058 Lloyd Place, West Hollywood, CA 90069 *Tel:* 310-275-3513 *Fax:* 310-281-5629 *E-mail:* novapress@aol.com *Web Site:* www.novapress.net, pg 165

Nova Science Publishers Inc, 400 Oser Ave, Suite 1600, Hauppauge, NY 11788-3619 *Tel:* 631-231-7269 *Fax:* 631-231-8175 *E-mail:* main@novapublishers.com *Web Site:* www.novapublishers.com, pg 165

Novalis Publishing, 10 Lower Spadina Ave, Suite 400, Toronto, ON M5V 2Z2, Canada *Tel:* 416-363-3303 *Toll Free Tel:* 877-702-7773 *Fax:* 416-363-9409 *Toll Free Fax:* 877-702-7775 *E-mail:* books@novalis.ca *Web Site:* www.novalis.ca, pg 465

Novella Prize, University of Victoria, Box 1700, Sta CSC, Victoria, BC V8W 2Y2, Canada *Tel:* 250-721-8524 *Fax:* 250-472-5051 *E-mail:* malahat@uvic.ca *Web Site:* www.malahatreview.ca, pg 674

Wanda Nowak Creative Illustrators Agency, 231 E 76 St, Suite 5-D, New York, NY 10021 *Tel:* 212-535-0438 *E-mail:* wanda@wandanow.com *Web Site:* www.wandanow.com, pg 544

NPES The Association for Suppliers of Printing, Publishing & Converting Technologies, 1899 Preston White Dr, Reston, VA 20191 *Tel:* 703-264-7200 *Fax:* 703-620-0994 *E-mail:* npes@npes.org *Web Site:* www.npes.org, pg 574

NPTA Alliance, 330 N Wabash Ave, Suite 2000, Chicago, IL 60611 *Tel:* 312-321-4092 *Toll Free Tel:* 800-355-NPTA (355-6782) *Fax:* 312-673-6736 *Web Site:* www.gonpta.com, pg 574

NRP Direct, 430 Mountain Ave, Suite 403, New Providence, NJ 07974 *Tel:* 908-517-0780 *Toll Free Tel:* 844-592-4197 *Fax:* 908-608-3012 (cust serv) *E-mail:* sales@nrpdirect.com *Web Site:* www.nrpdirect.com, pg 165

NSK Neustadt Prize for Children's Literature, c/o University of Oklahoma, 630 Parrington Oval, Suite 110, Norman, OK 73019-4033 *Tel:* 405-325-4531 *Web Site:* www.worldliteraturetoday.org; www.worldlit.org, pg 674

Nuestras Voces National Playwriting Competition, 138 E 27 St, New York, NY 10016 *Tel:* 212-225-9950 *Fax:* 212-225-9085 *Web Site:* www.repertorio.org, pg 674

Nursesbooks.org, The Publishing Program of ANA, 8515 Georgia Ave, Suite 400, Silver Spring, MD 20910-3492 *Tel:* 301-628-5000 *Toll Free Tel:* 800-274-4262; 800-637-0323 (orders) *Fax:* 301-628-5342 *E-mail:* anp@ana.org *Web Site:* www.Nursesbooks.org; www.NursingWorld.org, pg 165

NYC Emerging Writers Fellowships, 17 E 47 St, New York, NY 10017 *Tel:* 212-755-6710 *E-mail:* info@centerforfiction.org *Web Site:* centerforfiction.org, pg 674

Nystrom Education, 10200 Jefferson Blvd, Culver City, CA 90232 *Tel:* 310-839-2436 *Toll Free Tel:* 800 421-4246 *Fax:* 310-839-2249 *Toll Free Fax:* 800-944-5432 *E-mail:* access@nystromeducation.com; customerservice@nystromeducation.com *Web Site:* www.nystromeducation.com, pg 165

The O. Henry Prize Stories, c/o University of Texas at Austin, One University Sta, English Dept, B5000, Austin, TX 78712 *Web Site:* www.randomhouse.com/anchor/ohenry, pg 674

OAG Worldwide, 3025 Highland Pkwy, Suite 200, Downers Grove, IL 60515-5561 *Tel:* 630-515-5300 *Toll Free Tel:* 800-342-5624 (cust serv) *E-mail:* contactus@oag.com *Web Site:* www.oag.com, pg 165

Oak Knoll Press, 310 Delaware St, New Castle, DE 19720 *Tel:* 302-328-7232 *Toll Free Tel:* 800-996-2556 *Fax:* 302-328-7274 *E-mail:* oakknoll@oakknoll.com; publishing@oakknoll.com *Web Site:* www.oakknoll.com, pg 166

Oak Tree Press, 1700 Dairy Ave, No 149, Corcoran, CA 93212 *Tel:* 217-824-6500 *E-mail:* publisher@oaktreebooks.com; info@oaktreebooks.com; query@oaktreebooks.com; pressdept@oaktreebooks.com; bookorders@oaktreebooks.com *Web Site:* www.oaktreebooks.com; www.otpblog.blogspot.com, pg 166

The Oaklea Press, 41 Old Mill Rd, Richmond, VA 23226-3111 *Tel:* 804-218-2394 *Web Site:* oakleapress.com, pg 166

Harold Ober Associates Inc, 425 Madison Ave, New York, NY 10017 *Tel:* 212-759-8600 *Fax:* 212-759-9428 *Web Site:* www.haroldober.com, pg 531

Oberlin College Press, 50 N Professor St, Oberlin, OH 44074-1091 *Tel:* 440-775-8408 *Fax:* 440-775-8124 *E-mail:* oc.press@oberlin.edu *Web Site:* www.oberlin.edu/ocpress, pg 166

Oberon Press, 145 Spruce St, Suite 205, Ottawa, ON K1R 6P1, Canada *Tel:* 613-238-3275 *Fax:* 613-238-3275 *E-mail:* oberon@sympatico.ca *Web Site:* www.oberonpress.ca, pg 465

Objective Entertainment, 609 Greenwich St, 6th fl, New York, NY 10014 *Tel:* 212-431-5454 *Fax:* 917-464-6394 *Web Site:* www.objectiveent.com, pg 531

Eli M Oboler Memorial Award, 50 E Huron St, Chicago, IL 60611 *Tel:* 312-280-4226 *Toll Free Tel:* 800-545-2433 *E-mail:* oif@ala.org *Web Site:* www.ala.org/ifrt, pg 674

Ocean Press, c/o CBSD The Keg House, 34 13 Ave NE, Suite 101, Minneapolis, MN 55413-1007 *E-mail:* info@oceanbooks.com.au; orders@oceanbooks.com.au (orders only); rights@oceanbooks.com.au *Web Site:* www.oceanbooks.com.au, pg 166

Ocean Tree Books, 1325 Cerro Gordo Rd, Santa Fe, NM 87501 *Tel:* 505-983-1412 *Fax:* 505-983-0899 *Web Site:* www.oceantree.com, pg 166

Oceanview Publishing, CEO Center at Mediterranean Plaza, Suite 120-G, 595 Bay Isles Rd, Longboat Key, FL 34228 *Tel:* 941-387-8500 *Web Site:* oceanviewpub.com, pg 166

The Flannery O'Connor Award for Short Fiction, Main Library, 3rd fl, 320 S Jackson St, Athens, GA 30602 *Fax:* 706-542-2558 *Web Site:* www.ugapress.org, pg 674

Frank O'Connor Prize for Fiction, Dept of English, TCU Box 298300, Fort Worth, TX 76129 *Tel:* 817-257-5907 *Fax:* 817-257-5905 *E-mail:* descant@tcu.edu *Web Site:* www.descant.tcu.edu, pg 675

OCP, 5536 NE Hassalo St, Portland, OR 97213 *Tel:* 503-281-1191 *Toll Free Tel:* 800-548-8749 *Fax:* 503-282-3486 *Toll Free Fax:* 800-843-8181 *E-mail:* liturgy@ocp.org *Web Site:* www.ocp.org, pg 166

Octane Press, 809 S Lamar Blvd, Suite H, Austin, TX 78704 *Tel:* 512-334-9441 *Fax:* 512-852-4737 *E-mail:* info@octanepress.com; orders@octanepress.com; sales@octanepress.com *Web Site:* octanepress.com, pg 166

Scott O'Dell Award for Historical Fiction, c/o Horn Book Inc, 300 The Fenway, Suite P-311, Palace Road Bldg, Boston, MA 02215 *Tel:* 617-278-0225 *Toll Free Tel:* 888-628-0225 *Fax:* 617-278-6062 *Web Site:* www.scottodell.com/Pages/ScottO'DellAwardforHistoricalFiction.aspx, pg 675

Odyssey Books, 2421 Redwood Ct, Longmont, CO 80503-8155 *Tel:* 720-494-1473 *Fax:* 720-494-1471 *E-mail:* books@odysseybooks.net, pg 167

Odyssey: The Summer Fantasy Writing Workshop, PO Box 75, Mont Vernon, NH 03057 *Tel:* 603-673-6234 *Fax:* 603-673-6234 *Web Site:* www.odysseyworkshop.org, pg 613

OECD Washington Center, 1776 "I" St NW, Suite 450, Washington, DC 20006 *Tel:* 202-785-6323 *Toll Free Tel:* 800-456-6323 (dist ctr/pubns orders) *Fax:* 202-785-0350 *E-mail:* washington.contact@oecd.org *Web Site:* www.oecd-ilibrary.org, pg 167

Annual Off Off Broadway Short Play Festival, 235 Park Ave S, 5th fl, New York, NY 10003 *Tel:* 212-206-8990 *Toll Free Tel:* 866-598-8449 *Fax:* 212-206-1429 *E-mail:* oobfestival@samuelfrench.com *Web Site:* oob.samuelfrench.com; www.samuelfrench.com, pg 675

Dayne Ogilvie Prize, 460 Richmond St W, Suite 600, Toronto, ON M5V 1Y1, Canada *Tel:* 416-504-8222 *Toll Free Tel:* 877-906-6548 *Fax:* 416-504-9090 *E-mail:* info@writerstrust.com *Web Site:* www.writerstrust.com, pg 675

Howard O'Hagan Award for Short Story, 11759 Groat Rd, Edmonton, AB T5M 3K6, Canada *Tel:* 780-422-8174 *Toll Free Tel:* 800-665-5354 (AB only) *Fax:* 780-422-2663 (attn WGA) *E-mail:* mail@writersguild.ca *Web Site:* writersguild.ca, pg 675

Ohio Genealogical Society, 611 State Rte 97 W, Bellville, OH 44813-8813 *Tel:* 419-886-1903 *Fax:* 419-886-0092 *E-mail:* ogs@ogs.org *Web Site:* www.ogs.org, pg 167

Ohio State University Foreign Language Publications, 198 Hagerty Hall, 1775 College Rd, Columbus, OH 43210-1309 *Tel:* 614-292-3838 *Toll Free Tel:* 800-678-6999 *E-mail:* flpubs@osu.edu *Web Site:* flpubs.osu.edu, pg 167

The Ohio State University Press, 180 Pressey Hall, 1070 Carmack Rd, Columbus, OH 43210-1002 *Tel:* 614-292-6930 *Fax:* 614-292-2065 *Toll Free Fax:* 800-621-8476 *E-mail:* info@osupress.org *Web Site:* ohiostatepress.org, pg 167

Ohio University, English Department, Creative Writing Program, Ohio University, English Dept, Ellis Hall, Athens, OH 45701 *Tel:* 740-593-2838 (English Dept) *Fax:* 740-593-2832 *E-mail:* english.department@ohio.edu *Web Site:* www.ohio.edu/cas/english, pg 621

Ohio University Press, 31 S Court St, Suite 143, Athens, OH 45701-2979 *Fax:* 740-593-4536 *Web Site:* www.ohioswallow.com, pg 167

Ohioana Book Awards, 274 E First Ave, Suite 300, Columbus, OH 43201 *Tel:* 614-466-3831 *Fax:* 614-728-6974 *E-mail:* ohioana@ohioana.org *Web Site:* www.ohioana.org, pg 675

Ohioana Walter Rumsey Marvin Grant, 274 E First Ave, Suite 300, Columbus, OH 43201 *Tel:* 614-466-3831 *Fax:* 614-728-6974 *E-mail:* ohioana@ohioana.org *Web Site:* www.ohioana.org, pg 675

Olde & Oppenheim Publishers, 3219 N Margate Place, Chandler, AZ 85224 *E-mail:* olde_oppenheim@hotmail.com, pg 167

Veronica Oliva, 304 Lily St, San Francisco, CA 94102-5608 *Tel:* 415-337-7707 *E-mail:* veronicaoliva@sbcglobal.net, pg 499

The Oliver Press Inc, Charlotte Sq, 5707 W 36 St, Minneapolis, MN 55416-2510 *Tel:* 952-926-8981 *Toll Free Tel:* 800-8-OLIVER (865-4837) *Fax:* 952-926-8965 *E-mail:* orders@oliverpress.com *Web Site:* www.oliverpress.com, pg 167

Chris O'Malley Fiction Prize, University of Wisconsin, 6193 Helen C White Hall, English Dept, 600 N Park St, Madison, WI 53706 *E-mail:* madisonrevw@gmail.com *Web Site:* www.themadisonreview.com, pg 675

OMNI Publishers Inc, PO Box 408, Bulverde, TX 78163 *Tel:* 210-778-4437 *Fax:* 830-438-4645 *Web Site:* www.omnipublishers.com; educatorsethicsseries.com, pg 167

Omnibus Press, 257 Park Ave S, 20th fl, New York, NY 10010 *Tel:* 212-254-2100 *Toll Free Tel:* 800-431-7187 *Fax:* 212-254-2013 *Toll Free Fax:* 800-345-6842 *E-mail:* info@omnibuspress.com *Web Site:* www.omnibuspress.com; www.musicsales.com, pg 167

Omnidawn Publishing, 1632 Elm Ave, Richmond, CA 94805-1614 *Tel:* 510-237-5472 *Toll Free Tel:* 800-792-4957 *Fax:* 510-232-8525 *E-mail:* manager@omnidawn.com *Web Site:* www.omnidawn.com, pg 168

Omnigraphics Inc, 615 Griswold, Suite 901, Detroit, MI 48226 *Tel:* 610-461-3548 *Toll Free Tel:* 800-234-1340 (cust serv) *Fax:* 610-532-9001 *Toll Free Fax:* 800-875-1340 (cust serv) *E-mail:* contact@omnigraphics.com; customerservice@omnigraphics.com *Web Site:* omnigraphics.com, pg 168

Pace University, Master of Science in Publishing, Dept of Publishing, Rm 805-E, 551 Fifth Ave, New York, NY 10176 *Tel:* 212-346-1431 *Toll Free Tel:* 877-284-7670 *Fax:* 212-346-1165 *Web Site:* www.pace.edu/dyson/mspub, pg 621

Pace University Press, Dept of Publishing, Rm 805-E, 551 Fifth Ave, New York, NY 10176 *Tel:* 212-346-1417 *Fax:* 212-346-1165 *Web Site:* www.pace.edu/press, pg 172

Pacific Educational Press, c/o UBC Press, 2029 West Mall, Vancouver, BC V6T 1Z2, Canada *Tel:* 604-822-5959; 604-827-2232 (cust serv) *Toll Free Tel:* 855-827-2232 *E-mail:* pep.admin@ubc.ca; pep.sales@ubc.ca *Web Site:* pacificedpress.ca, pg 465

Pacific Northwest Book Awards, 338 W 11 Ave, Unit 108, Eugene, OR 97401 *Tel:* 541-683-4363 *Fax:* 541-683-3910 *E-mail:* info@pnba.org; awards@pnba.org *Web Site:* www.pnba.org, pg 676

Pacific Northwest Booksellers Association (PNBA), 338 W 11 Ave, Unit 108, Eugene, OR 97401 *Tel:* 541-683-4363 *Toll Free Tel:* 800-353-6764 *Fax:* 541-683-3910 *E-mail:* info@pnba.org *Web Site:* www.pnba.org, pg 575

Pacific Northwest Young Reader's Choice Award, Vancouver Mall Community Library, 8700 NE Vancouver Mall Dr, Suite 285, Vancouver, WA 98662 *Web Site:* www.pnla.org/yrca, pg 676

Pacific Press Publishing Association, 1350 N Kings Rd, Nampa, ID 83687-3193 *Tel:* 208-465-2500 *Toll Free Tel:* 800-447-7377 *Fax:* 208-465-2531 *Web Site:* www.pacificpress.com, pg 172

Pacific Printing Industries Association, 6825 SW Sandburg St, Portland, OR 97223 *Tel:* 503-221-3944 *Toll Free Tel:* 877-762-7742 *Fax:* 503-221-5691 *E-mail:* info@ppiassociation.org *Web Site:* www.ppiassociation.org, pg 575

Pacific Publishing Services, PO Box 1150, Capitola, CA 95010-1150 *Tel:* 831-476-8284 *Fax:* 831-476-8294 *E-mail:* pacpubs@attglobal.net, pg 499

The Pacific Spirit Poetry Prize, University of British Columbia, Buch E462, 1866 Main Mall, Vancouver, BC V6T 1Z1, Canada *Tel:* 778-822-2514 *Fax:* 778-822-3616 *E-mail:* prismwritingcontest@gmail.com *Web Site:* www.prismmagazine.ca, pg 676

PAGE International Screenwriting Awards, 7190 Sunset Blvd, Suite 610, Hollywood, CA 90046 *E-mail:* info@pageawards.com *Web Site:* www.pageawards.com, pg 676

Paintbox Press, 275 Madison Ave, Suite 600, New York, NY 10016 *Tel:* 212-878-6610 *E-mail:* info@paintboxpress.com *Web Site:* www.paintboxpress.com, pg 172

Painted Hills Publishing, 16500 Dakota Ridge Rd, Longmont, CO 80503 *Tel:* 303-823-6642 *E-mail:* cw@livingimagescjw.com *Web Site:* www.wildhoofbeats.com; www.livingimagescjw.com, pg 478

Painted-Words Inc, 310 W 97 St, Suite 24, New York, NY 10025 *Tel:* 212-663-2311 *Fax:* 212-663-2891 *E-mail:* info@painted-words.com *Web Site:* painted-words.com, pg 544

Dobie Paisano Fellowship Program, Graduate School, 110 Inner Campus Dr, Stop G0400, Austin, TX 78712-0710 *Fax:* 512-471-7620 *Web Site:* www.utexas.edu/ogs/Paisano, pg 676

Paladin Press, 5540 Central Ave, Suite 200, Boulder, CO 80301 *Tel:* 303-443-7250 *Toll Free Tel:* 800-392-2400 *Fax:* 303-442-8741 *E-mail:* service@paladin-press.com *Web Site:* www.paladin-press.com, pg 172

Palgrave Macmillan, One New York Plaza, Suite 4500, New York, NY 10004-1562 *Tel:* 212-726-9200 *E-mail:* sales-ny@springernature.com; sales@palgrave-usa.com *Web Site:* www.palgrave.com, pg 172

Palimpsest Press, 1171 Eastlawn Ave, Windsor, ON N8S 3J1, Canada *Tel:* 519-259-2112 *E-mail:* info@palimpsestpress.ca *Web Site:* www.palimpsestpress.ca, pg 465

Palladium Books Inc, 39074 Webb Ct, Westland, MI 48185 *Tel:* 734-721-2903 (orders) *Fax:* 734-721-1238 *Web Site:* www.palladiumbooks.com, pg 172

Palm Island Press, 411 Truman Ave, Key West, FL 33040 *Tel:* 305-296-3102 *E-mail:* pipress2@gmail.com, pg 173

Palm Springs Writers Guild, PO Box 947, Rancho Mirage, CA 92270-0947 *Web Site:* www.palmspringswritersguild.org, pg 575

Palmetto Bug Books, 121 N Hibiscus Dr, Miami Beach, FL 33139 *Tel:* 305-531-9813 *Fax:* 305-604-1516 *E-mail:* palmettobugbooks@gmail.com, pg 173

Pangaea Publications, 402 Church St, Wisconsin Dells, WI 53965 *Tel:* 651-226-2032 *Fax:* 651-226-2032 *E-mail:* info@pangaea.org *Web Site:* pangaea.org, pg 173

Karen L Pangallo, 27 Buffum St, Salem, MA 01970 *Tel:* 978-744-8796 *E-mail:* pangallo@noblenet.org, pg 499

Mildred & Albert Panowski Playwriting Award, Forest Roberts Theatre, 1401 Presque Isle Ave, Marquette, MI 49855-5364 *Tel:* 906-227-2553 *Fax:* 906-227-2567 *E-mail:* theatre@nmu.edu *Web Site:* www.nmu.edu/theatre, pg 676

Pantheon Books/Schocken Books, c/o Penguin Random House Inc, 1745 Broadway, New York, NY 10019 *Tel:* 212-751-2600 *Web Site:* knopfdoubleday.com/imprint/pantheon, pg 173

Pants On Fire Press, 2062 Harbor Cove Way, Winter Garden, FL 34787 *Tel:* 863-546-0760 *E-mail:* submission@pantsonfirepress.com *Web Site:* www.pantsonfirepress.com, pg 173

Papercutz, 160 Broadway, E Wing, Suite 700, New York, NY 10038 *Tel:* 646-559-4681 *Toll Free Tel:* 800-886-1223 *Fax:* 212-643-1545 *E-mail:* papercutz@papercutz.com *Web Site:* www.papercutz.com, pg 173

Parachute Publishing LLC, 157 Columbus Ave, Suite 518, New York, NY 10023 *Tel:* 212-691-1421 *Web Site:* www.parachutepublishing.com, pg 173

Paraclete Press Inc, 36 Southern Eagle Cartway, Brewster, MA 02631 *Tel:* 508-255-4685 *Toll Free Tel:* 800-451-5006 *Fax:* 508-255-5705 *E-mail:* mail@paracletepress.com *Web Site:* www.paracletepress.com, pg 173

Paradigm Publications, 202 Bendix Dr, Taos, NM 87571 *Tel:* 575-758-7758 *Toll Free Tel:* 800-873-3946 (US); 888-873-3947 (CN) *Fax:* 575-758-7768 *E-mail:* info@paradigm-pubs.com *Web Site:* www.paradigm-pubs.com; www.redwingbooks.com, pg 173

Paradise Cay Publications Inc, 120 Monda Way, Blue Lake, CA 95525 *Tel:* 707-822-9063 *Toll Free Tel:* 800-736-4509 *Fax:* 707-822-9163 *E-mail:* info@paracay.com *Web Site:* www.paracay.com, pg 173

Paragon House, 3600 Labore Rd, Suite 1, St Paul, MN 55110-4144 *Tel:* 651-644-3087 *Toll Free Tel:* 800-447-3709 *Fax:* 651-644-0997 *E-mail:* paragon@paragonhouse.com *Web Site:* www.paragonhouse.com, pg 174

Parallax Press, 2236-B Sixth St, Berkeley, CA 94710 *Tel:* 510-540-6411 *Toll Free Tel:* 800-863-5290 (orders) *Fax:* 510-981-1157 *Web Site:* www.parallax.org, pg 174

Paramount Market Publishing Inc, 950 Danby Rd, Suite 136, Ithaca, NY 14850 *Tel:* 607-275-8100 *E-mail:* editors@paramountbooks.com *Web Site:* www.paramountbooks.com, pg 174

Parenting Press Inc, 13751 Lake City Way NE, Suite 110, Seattle, WA 98125 *Tel:* 206-364-2900 *Toll Free Tel:* 800 99 BOOKS (992 6657) *Fax:* 206 364 0702 *E-mail:* office@parentingpress.com; marketing@parentingpress.com *Web Site:* www.parentingpress.com, pg 174

Park Place Publications, 591 Lighthouse Ave, Suite 10, Pacific Grove, CA 93950 *Tel:* 831-649-6640 *E-mail:* publishingbiz@sbcglobal.net *Web Site:* www.parkplacepublications.com, pg 174

Francis Parkman Prize, 2950 Broadway, New York, NY 10027 *Tel:* 212-854-6495 *E-mail:* amhistsociety@columbia.edu *Web Site:* sah.columbia.edu, pg 676

Parmenides Publishing, 3753 Howard Hughes Pkwy, Suite 200, Las Vegas, NV 89169 *Tel:* 702-892-3934 *Fax:* 702-892-3939 *E-mail:* info@parmenides.com *Web Site:* www.parmenides.com, pg 174

Parsons School of Design, Continuing Education, 2 W 13 St, 5th fl, Rm 504, New York, NY 10003 *Tel:* 212-229-5150 *Fax:* 212-229-5970 *E-mail:* ceinformation@newschool.edu; academy@newschool.edu *Web Site:* www.newschool.edu/parsons, pg 622

The Paterson Poetry Prize, One College Blvd, Paterson, NJ 07505-1179 *Tel:* 973-684-6555 *Fax:* 973-523-6085 *Web Site:* www.poetrycenterpccc.com, pg 676

The Paterson Prize for Books for Young People, One College Blvd, Paterson, NJ 07505-1179 *Tel:* 973-684-6555 *Fax:* 973-523-6085 *Web Site:* www.poetrycenterpccc.com, pg 677

Path Press Inc, 708 Washington St, Evanston, IL 60202 *Tel:* 847-492-0177 *E-mail:* pathpressinc@aol.com, pg 174

Pathfinder Publishing Inc, 120 S Houghton Rd, Suite 138, Tucson, AZ 85748 *Tel:* 520-647-0158 *Web Site:* www.pathfinderpublishing.com, pg 175

Kathi J Paton Literary Agency, Box 2236, Radio City Sta, New York, NY 10101-2236 *Tel:* 212-265-6586 *E-mail:* kjplitbiz@optonline.net *Web Site:* www.patonliterary.com, pg 531

Patria Press Inc, PO Box 752, Carmel, IN 46082 *Tel:* 317-577-1321 *Toll Free Tel:* 888-859-8221 *Fax:* 413-215-8030 *E-mail:* moreinfo@patriapress.com *Web Site:* www.patriapress.com; www.facebook.com/YoungPatriotsBooks; twitter.com/kidsbios, pg 175

Diane Patrick, 140 Carver Loop, No 21A, Bronx, NY 10475-2954 *E-mail:* dpatrickediting@aol.com *Web Site:* www.dianepatrick.net, pg 499

The Alicia Patterson Foundation Fellowship Program, 1100 Vermont Ave, Suite 900, Washington, DC 20005 *Tel:* 202-393-5995 *Fax:* 301-951-8512 *E-mail:* info@aliciapatterson.org *Web Site:* www.aliciapatterson.org, pg 677

Paul Dry Books, 1700 Sansom St, Suite 700, Philadelphia, PA 19103 *Tel:* 215-231-9939 *Fax:* 215-231-9942 *E-mail:* editor@pauldrybooks.com *Web Site:* www.pauldrybooks.com, pg 175

Pauline Books & Media, 50 Saint Paul's Ave, Boston, MA 02130 *Tel:* 617-522-8911 *Toll Free Tel:* 800-876-4463 (orders); 800-836-9723 (cust serv) *Fax:* 617-541-9805 *E-mail:* editorial@paulinemedia.com (ms submissions); orderentry@pauline.org (cust serv) *Web Site:* www.pauline.org/publishing; www.pauline.org/PBMPublishing, pg 175

Paulines Editions, 5610 rue Beaubien est, Montreal, QC H1T 1X5, Canada *Tel:* 514-253-5610 *Fax:* 514-253-1907 *E-mail:* fsp-paulines@videotron.ca *Web Site:* www.editions.paulines.qc.ca, pg 466

Paulist Press, 997 Macarthur Blvd, Mahwah, NJ 07430-9990 *Tel:* 201-825-7300 *Toll Free Tel:* 800-218-1903 *Fax:* 201-825-6921 *Toll Free Fax:* 800-836-3161 *E-mail:* info@paulistpress.com; publicity@paulistpress.com *Web Site:* www.paulistpress.com, pg 175

Peabody Museum Press, 11 Divinity Ave, Cambridge, MA 02138 *Tel:* 617-495-4255; 617-495-3938 (edit) *Fax:* 617-495-7535 *E-mail:* peapub@fas.harvard.edu *Web Site:* www.peabody.harvard.edu/publications, pg 175

Peace Hill Press, 18021 The Glebe Lane, Charles City, VA 23030 *Tel:* 804 829 5043 *Toll Free Tel:* 877-322-3445 (orders) *Fax:* 804-829-5704 *E-mail:* info@peacehillpress.com *Web Site:* www.peacehillpress.com, pg 175

Peachpit Press, 1301 Sansome St, San Francisco, CA 94111 *Toll Free Tel:* 800-283-9444 *E-mail:* info@peachpit.com; ask@peachpit.com *Web Site:* www.peachpit.com, pg 175

Peachtree Publishers, 1700 Chattahoochee Ave, Atlanta, GA 30318-2112 *Tel:* 404-876-8761 *Toll Free Tel:* 800-241-0113 *Fax:* 404-875-2578 *Toll Free Fax:* 800-875-8909 *E-mail:* hello@peachtree-online.com *Web Site:* www.peachtree-online.com, pg 176

PearlCo Literary Agency, LLC, 6596 Heronswood Cove, Memphis, TN 38119 *Tel:* 901-754-5276, pg 531

Pearson, 1900 E Lake Ave, Glenview, IL 60025 *Tel:* 847-729-3000 *Toll Free Tel:* 800-535-4391 (Midwest) *Fax:* 847-729-8910 *Web Site:* www.pearsonschool.com, pg 176

Pearson Allyn & Bacon, 501 Boylston St, Boston, MA 02116 *Tel:* 617-848-6000 *Toll Free Tel:* 800-428-4466 *Fax:* 617-848-6016 *Web Site:* home.pearsonhighered.com, pg 176

Pearson Arts & Sciences, 221 River St, Hoboken, NJ 07030 *Tel:* 917-981-2200 *Web Site:* www.pearsonhighered.com, pg 176

Pearson Benjamin Cummings, 1301 Sansome St, San Francisco, CA 94111-1122 *Tel:* 415-402-2500 *Toll Free Tel:* 800-922-0579 (orders) *Toll Free Fax:* 800-445-6991 (orders) *E-mail:* question@aol.com *Web Site:* home.pearsonhighered.com, pg 176

Pearson Business Publishing, 225 River St, Hoboken, NJ 07030-4772 *Tel:* 201-236-7000 *Web Site:* www.pearsonhighered.com, pg 176

Pearson Career, Health, Education & Technology, 225 River St, Hoboken, NJ 07030-4772 *Tel:* 201-236-7000 *Toll Free Tel:* 800-848-9500 *Fax:* 201-236-7755, pg 176

Pearson Education Canada, 26 Prince Andrew Place, North York, ON M3C 2H4, Canada *Tel:* 416-447-5101 *Toll Free Tel:* 800-263-9965 *Fax:* 416-443-0948 *Toll Free Fax:* 800-263-7733; 888-465-0536 *Web Site:* www.pearsoncanada.ca, pg 466

Pearson Education International Group, 225 River St, Hoboken, NJ 07030-4772 *Tel:* 201-236-7000, pg 176

Pearson Education Ltd, 225 River St, Hoboken, NJ 07030-4772 *Tel:* 201-236-7000 *Fax:* 201-236-6549 *E-mail:* communications@pearsoned.com *Web Site:* www.pearsoned.com, pg 176

Pearson ELT, 221 River St, Hoboken, NJ 07030 *Toll Free Tel:* 877-202-4572 *Toll Free Fax:* 800-445-6991 *E-mail:* english@pearson.com *Web Site:* www.pearsonelt.com, pg 176

Pearson ERPI, 1611 Cremazie Blvd E, 10th fl, Montreal, QC H2M 2P2, Canada *Tel:* 514-334-2690 *Toll Free Tel:* 800-263-3678 *Fax:* 514-334-4720 *Toll Free Fax:* 800-643-4720 *E-mail:* erpidlm@erpi.com *Web Site:* www.erpi.com; pearsonplc.ca, pg 466

Pearson Higher Education, 225 River St, Hoboken, NJ 07030-4772 *Tel:* 201-236-7000 *Web Site:* www.pearson.com/us/higher-education.html, pg 176

Pearson Humanities & Social Sciences, 225 River St, Hoboken, NJ 07030-4772 *Tel:* 201-236-7000, pg 176

Pearson Learning Solutions, 501 Boyleston St, Suite 900, Boston, MA 02116 *Toll Free Tel:* 800-428-4466 (orders); 800-635-1579 *Fax:* 201-784-6131 *Web Site:* www.pearsoned.com, pg 176

Pearson School, 221 River St, Hoboken, NJ 07030 *Tel:* 201-236-7000 *Toll Free Tel:* 800-848-9500 (K-12 prods) *Web Site:* www.pearsonschool.com, pg 176

William Peden Prize in Fiction, 357 McReynolds Hall, Columbia, MO 65211 *Tel:* 573-882-4474 *Toll Free Tel:* 800-949-2505 *Fax:* 573-884-4671 *E-mail:* question@moreview.com *Web Site:* www.missourireview.com, pg 677

T H Peek Publisher, PO Box 7406, Ann Arbor, MI 48107 *Tel:* 734-222-8205 *Fax:* 734-661-0136 *E-mail:* info@thpeekpublisher.com *Web Site:* www.thpeekpublisher.com, pg 176

Pelican Publishing Co, 1000 Burmaster St, Gretna, LA 70053-2246 *Tel:* 504-368-1175 *Toll Free Tel:* 800-843-1724 *Fax:* 504-368-1195 *E-mail:* sales@pelicanpub.com (sales); office@pelicanpub.com (permission); promo@pelicanpub.com (publicity) *Web Site:* www.pelicanpub.com, pg 176

Pembroke Publishers Ltd, 538 Hood Rd, Markham, ON L3R 3K9, Canada *Tel:* 905-477-0650 *Toll Free Tel:* 800-997-9807 *Fax:* 905-477-3691 *Toll Free Fax:* 800-339-5568 *Web Site:* www.pembrokepublishers.com, pg 466

Pemmican Publications Inc, 150 Henry Ave, Winnipeg, MB R3B 0J7, Canada *Tel:* 204-589-6346 *Fax:* 204-589-2063 *E-mail:* pemmican@pemmican.mb.ca *Web Site:* www.pemmicanpublications.ca, pg 466

PEN American Center, 588 Broadway, Suite 303, New York, NY 10012 *Tel:* 212-334-1660 *Fax:* 212-334-2181 *E-mail:* info@pen.org *Web Site:* pen.org, pg 575

Pen & Publish Inc, 4735 S State Rd 446, Bloomington, IN 47401 *Tel:* 314-827-6567 *E-mail:* info@penandpublish.com *Web Site:* www.penandpublish.com, pg 176

The PEN Award for Poetry in Translation, 588 Broadway, Suite 303, New York, NY 10012 *Tel:* 212-334-1660 *Fax:* 212-334-2181 *E-mail:* awards@pen.org *Web Site:* pen.org/press/grants-awards-database, pg 677

PEN/Bellwether Prize for Socially Engaged Fiction, 588 Broadway, Suite 303, New York, NY 10012 *Tel:* 212-334-1660 *E-mail:* awards@pen.org *Web Site:* pen.org/press/grants-awards-database, pg 677

PEN Canada, 24 Ryerson Ave, Suite 301, Toronto, ON M5T 2P3, Canada *Tel:* 416-703-8448 *Fax:* 416-703-3870 *E-mail:* queries@pencanada.ca *Web Site:* www.pencanada.ca, pg 575

PEN Center USA, PO Box 6037, Beverly Hills, CA 90212 *Tel:* 323-424-4939 *Fax:* 323-424-4944 *E-mail:* pen@penusa.org *Web Site:* penusa.org, pg 575

PEN Center USA Emerging Voices Fellowship, PO Box 6037, Beverly Hills, CA 90212 *Tel:* 323-424-4939 *Fax:* 323-424-4944 *E-mail:* ev@penusa.org *Web Site:* penusa.org/programs/emerging-voices, pg 677

PEN Center USA Literary Awards, 8549 Wilshire Blvd, Suite 355, Beverly Hills, CA 90211 *Tel:* 323-424-4939 *Fax:* 323-424-4944 *E-mail:* awards@penusa.org; pen@penusa.org *Web Site:* penusa.org/awards, pg 677

PEN/Diamonstein-Spielvogel Award for the Art of the Essay, 588 Broadway, Suite 303, New York, NY 10012 *Tel:* 212-334-1660 *E-mail:* awards@pen.org *Web Site:* pen.org/literary-awards, pg 677

PEN/E O Wilson Literary Science Writing Award, 588 Broadway, Suite 303, New York, NY 10012 *Tel:* 212-334-1660 *E-mail:* awards@pen.org *Web Site:* pen.org/literary-awards, pg 677

PEN/ESPN Award for Literary Sports Writing, 588 Broadway, Suite 303, New York, NY 10012 *Tel:* 212-334-1660 *E-mail:* awards@pen.org *Web Site:* pen.org/literary-awards, pg 677

PEN/ESPN Lifetime Achievement Award for Literary Sports Writing, 588 Broadway, Suite 303, New York, NY 10012 *Tel:* 212-334-1660 *E-mail:* awards@pen.org *Web Site:* pen.org/literary-awards, pg 677

PEN/Faulkner Award for Fiction, Folger Shakespeare Library, 201 E Capitol St SE, Washington, DC 20003 *Tel:* 202-898-9063 *Fax:* 202-675-0360 *Web Site:* www.penfaulkner.org, pg 678

PEN/Fusion Emerging Writers Prize, 588 Broadway, Suite 303, New York, NY 10012 *Tel:* 212-334-1660 *E-mail:* awards@pen.org *Web Site:* pen.org/literary-awards, pg 678

PEN/Jacqueline Bograd Weld Award for Biography, 588 Broadway, Suite 303, New York, NY 10012 *Tel:* 212-334-1660 *E-mail:* awards@pen.org *Web Site:* pen.org/literary-awards, pg 678

PEN/Jean Stein Book Award, 588 Broadway, Suite 303, New York, NY 10012 *Tel:* 212-334-1660 *E-mail:* info@pen.org *Web Site:* pen.org/press/grants-awards-database, pg 678

PEN/Joyce Osterweil Award for Poetry, 588 Broadway, Suite 303, New York, NY 10012 *Tel:* 212-334-1660 *E-mail:* awards@pen.org *Web Site:* pen.org/press/grants-awards-database, pg 678

Pen-L Publishing, 12 W Dickson St, No 4455, Fayetteville, AR 72702 *Web Site:* www.pen-l.com, pg 177

PEN/Nabokov Award for Achievement in International Literature, 588 Broadway, Suite 303, New York, NY 10012 *Tel:* 212-334-1660 *Fax:* 212-334-2181 *E-mail:* awards@pen.org *Web Site:* pen.org/literary-awards, pg 678

PEN New England, MIT, 14N-221A, 77 Massachusetts Ave, Cambridge, MA 02139 *Tel:* 617-324-1729 *E-mail:* pen-newengland@mit.edu *Web Site:* www.pen-ne.org/hemingway, pg 575

PEN/New England Awards, MIT, 14N-221A, 77 Massachusetts Ave, Cambridge, MA 02139 *Tel:* 617-324-1729 *E-mail:* pen-newengland@mit.edu; pen-ne@lesley.edu *Web Site:* www.pen-ne.org, pg 678

PEN Open Book Award, 588 Broadway, Suite 303, New York, NY 10012 *Tel:* 212-334-1660 *E-mail:* awards@pen.org *Web Site:* pen.org/literary-awards, pg 678

PEN/Phyllis Naylor Working Writer Fellowship, 588 Broadway, Suite 303, New York, NY 10012 *Tel:* 212-334-1660 *Fax:* 212-334-2181 *E-mail:* awards@pen.org *Web Site:* pen.org/press/grants-awards-database, pg 678

PEN/Ralph Manheim Medal for Translation, 588 Broadway, Suite 303, New York, NY 10012 *Tel:* 212-334-1660 *Fax:* 212-334-2181 *E-mail:* awards@pen.org *Web Site:* pen.org/press/grants-awards-database, pg 678

PEN/Robert Bingham Prize for Debut Fiction, 588 Broadway, Suite 303, New York, NY 10012 *Tel:* 212-334-1660 *Fax:* 212-334-2181 *E-mail:* awards@pen.org *Web Site:* pen.org/press/grants-awards-database, pg 678

PEN/Saul Bellow Award for Achievement in American Fiction, 588 Broadway, Suite 303, New York, NY 10012 *Tel:* 212-334-1660 *Fax:* 212-334-2181 *E-mail:* awards@pen.org *Web Site:* pen.org/press/grants-awards-database, pg 679

PEN Translation Prize, 588 Broadway, Suite 303, New York, NY 10012 *Tel:* 212-334-1660 *Fax:* 212-334-2181 *E-mail:* awards@pen.org *Web Site:* pen.org/press/grants-awards-database, pg 679

PEN/Voelcker Award, 588 Broadway, Suite 303, New York, NY 10012 *Tel:* 212-334-1660 *E-mail:* awards@pen.org *Web Site:* pen.org/literary-awards, pg 679

PEN Writers' Emergency Fund, 588 Broadway, Suite 303, New York, NY 10012 *Tel:* 212-334-1660 *Fax:* 212-334-2181 *Web Site:* pen.org/press/grants-awards-database, pg 679

Pendragon Press, 52 White Hill Rd, Hillsdale, NY 12529-5839 *Tel:* 518-325-6100 *Toll Free Tel:* 877-656-6381 (orders) *E-mail:* editor@pendragonpress.com *Web Site:* www.pendragonpress.com, pg 177

Penfield Books, 215 Brown St, Iowa City, IA 52245 *Tel:* 319-337-9998 *Toll Free Tel:* 800-728-9998 *Fax:* 319-351-6846 *E-mail:* penfield@penfieldbooks.com *Web Site:* www.penfieldbooks.com, pg 177

Penguin Books, 375 Hudson St, New York, NY 10014 *Tel:* 212-366-2000 *E-mail:* penguinpublicity@us.penguingroup.com *Web Site:* www.penguinclassics.com; www.penguin.com, pg 177

Penguin Group (Canada), 320 Front St W, Suite 1400, Toronto, ON M5V 3B6, Canada *Tel:* 416-364-4449 *Fax:* 416-598-7764 *E-mail:* customerservicescanada@penguinrandomhouse.com; publicity@ca.penguingroup.com *Web Site:* penguinrandomhouse.ca/imprints/penguin-canada, pg 466

Penguin Group USA, A Penguin Random House Company, 375 Hudson St, New York, NY 10014 *Tel:* 212-366-2000 *Toll Free Tel:* 800-847-5515 (inside sales); 800-631-8571 (cust serv) *Fax:* 212-366-2666; 607-775-4829 (inside sales) *E-mail:* online@us.penguingroup.com *Web Site:* www.penguin.com, pg 177

The Penguin Press, 375 Hudson St, New York, NY 10014 *Web Site:* thepenguinpress.com, pg 178

Penguin Random House Audio Publishing, 1745 Broadway, New York, NY 10019 *E-mail:* audio@penguinrandomhouse.com *Web Site:* www.penguinrandomhouseaudio.com, pg 178

Penguin Random House Canada, 320 Front St W, Suite 1400, Toronto, ON M5V 3B6, Canada *Tel:* 416-364-4449 *Toll Free Tel:* 888-523-9292 (cust serv) *Fax:* 416-598-7764 *Web Site:* www.penguinrandomhouse.ca, pg 467

Penguin Random House Inc, 1745 Broadway, New York, NY 10019 *Tel:* 212-782-9000 *Toll Free Tel:* 800-726-0600 *Web Site:* www.penguinrandomhouse.com, pg 178

Penguin Random House Large Print, 1745 Broadway, New York, NY 10019 *Tel:* 212-782-9000 *Web Site:* www.penguinrandomhouse.com, pg 179

Penguin Random House Speakers Bureau, A Penguin Random House Company, 1745 Broadway, Mail Drop 13-1, New York, NY 10019 *Tel:* 212-572-2013 *E-mail:* speakers@penguinrandomhouse.com *Web Site:* www.prhspeakers.com, pg 547

Penguin Young Readers Group, 345 Hudson St, New York, NY 10014 *Tel:* 212-366-2000; 212-414-3553 *Fax:* 212-414-3340 *Web Site:* www.penguin.com/children, pg 179

Peninsula Publishing, 1630 Post Rd E, Unit 312, Westport, CT 06880 *E-mail:* sales@peninsulapublishing.com *Web Site:* www.peninsulapublishing.com, pg 179

Pennsylvania Historical & Museum Commission, Commonwealth Keystone Bldg, 400 North St, Harrisburg, PA 17120-0053 *Tel:* 717-783-8946; 717-787-5526 (orders) *E-mail:* ra-shoppaheritage@pa.gov *Web Site:* www.shoppaheritage.com; www.phmc.pa.gov, pg 179

Pennsylvania State Data Center, Penn State Harrisburg, 777 W Harrisburg Pike, Middletown, PA 17057-4898 *Tel:* 717-948-6336 *Fax:* 717-948-6754 *E-mail:* pasdc@psu.edu *Web Site:* pasdc.hbg.psu.edu, pg 179

The Pennsylvania State University Press, University Support Bldg 1, Suite C, 820 N University Dr, University Park, PA 16802-1003 *Tel:* 814-865-1327 *Toll Free Tel:* 800-326-9180 *Fax:* 814-863-1408 *Toll Free Fax:* 877-778-2665 *E-mail:* info@psupress.org *Web Site:* www.psupress.org, pg 179

PennWell Books, 1421 S Sheridan Rd, Tulsa, OK 74112 *Tel:* 918-831-9421 *Toll Free Tel:* 800-752-9764 *Fax:* 918-831-9555 *Toll Free Fax:* 877-218-1348 *E-mail:* sales@pennwell.com *Web Site:* www.pennwellbooks.com, pg 179

Pennwriters Conference, PO Box 685, Dalton, PA 18414 *E-mail:* conferencecoordinator@pennwriters.org; info@pennwriters.org *Web Site:* pennwriters.org, pg 613

Pentecostal Publishing House, 8855 Dunn Rd, Hazelwood, MO 63042 *Tel:* 314-837-7300 *Toll Free Tel:* 866-819-7667 *Fax:* 314-837-6574 (orders) *Web Site:* www.pentecostalpublishing.com; wordaflamepress.com, pg 180

Penton Media Inc, 9800 Metcalf Ave, Overland Park, KS 66212 *Tel:* 913-967-1719; 913-341-1300 *Toll Free Tel:* 800-262-1954 (cust serv) *Toll Free Fax:* 800-633-6219 *E-mail:* bookorders@penton.com *Web Site:* www.penton.com, pg 180

PeopleSpeak, 25401 Alicia Pkwy, Suite L-512, Laguna Hills, CA 92653 *Tel:* 949-581-6190 *Fax:* 949-581-4958 *E-mail:* pplspeak@att.net *Web Site:* www.detailsplease.com/peoplespeak, pg 499

Rebecca Pepper, 434 NE Floral Place, Portland, OR 97232 *Tel:* 503-236-5802 *E-mail:* rpepper@rpepper.net *Web Site:* pepperedit.com, pg 499

Peradam Press, PO Box 6, North San Juan, CA 95960-0006 *Tel:* 530-277-9324 *Fax:* 530-559-0754 *E-mail:* peradam@earthlink.net, pg 180

Dan Peragine Literary Agency, 227 Beechwood Ave, Bogota, NJ 07603 *Tel:* 201-390-0468 *Fax:* 201-390-0468 *E-mail:* dpliterary@aol.com, pg 531

Perfection Learning Corp, 1000 N Second Ave, Logan, IA 51546 *Tel:* 712-644-2831 *Toll Free Tel:* 800-831-4190 *Toll Free Fax:* 800-543-2745 *E-mail:* orders@perfectionlearning.com *Web Site:* perfectionlearning.com, pg 180

Periodical & Book Association of America Inc (PBAA), 481 Eighth Ave, Suite 526, New York, NY 10001 *Tel:* 212-563-6502 *Fax:* 212-563-4098 *Web Site:* www.pbaa.net, pg 575

Maxwell E Perkins Award, 17 E 47 St, New York, NY 10017 *Tel:* 212-755-6710 *Fax:* 212-826-0831 *E-mail:* info@centerforfiction.org *Web Site:* www.centerforfiction.org/awards/perkins, pg 679

The Permanent Press, 4170 Noyac Rd, Sag Harbor, NY 11963 *Tel:* 631-725-1101 *E-mail:* info@thepermanentpress.com *Web Site:* www.thepermanentpress.com, pg 180

The Permissions Group Inc, 401 S Milwaukee Ave, Suite 180, Wheeling, IL 60090 *Tel:* 847-635-6550 *Toll Free Tel:* 800-374-7985 *Fax:* 847-635-6968 *E-mail:* info@permissionsgroup.com *Web Site:* www.permissionsgroup.com, pg 499

Persea Books, 277 Broadway, Suite 708, New York, NY 10007 *Tel:* 212-260-9256 *Fax:* 212-267-3165 *E-mail:* info@perseabooks.com *Web Site:* www.perseabooks.com, pg 180

Perseus Books, 250 W 57 St, 15th fl, New York, NY 10107 *Tel:* 212-340-8100 *Toll Free Tel:* 800-343-4499 (cust serv) *Fax:* 212-340-8105 *Web Site:* www.perseusbooks.com, pg 180

Perugia Press Prize for a First or Second Book by a Woman, PO Box 60364, Florence, MA 01062 *Web Site:* www.perugiapress.com; perugiapress.org, pg 679

Peter Pauper Press, Inc, 202 Mamaroneck Ave, Suite 400, White Plains, NY 10601-5376 *Tel:* 914-681-0144 *Fax:* 914-681-0389 *E-mail:* customerservice@peterpauper.com; orders@peterpauper.com; marketing@peterpauper.com *Web Site:* www.peterpauper.com, pg 181

Elsa Peterson Ltd, 41 East Ave, Norwalk, CT 06851-3919 *Tel:* 203-846-8331 *E-mail:* epltd@earthlink.net, pg 499

Peterson Institute for International Economics (PIIE), 1750 Massachusetts Ave NW, Washington, DC 20036-1903 *Tel:* 202-328-9000 *Fax:* 202-328-5432; 202-659-3225 *E-mail:* orders@petersoninstitute.org; media@piie.com *Web Site:* www.petersoninstitute.org, pg 181

Peterson's, a Nelnet Company, 3 Columbia Circle, Suite 205, Albany, NY 12203-5158 *Tel:* 609-896-1800 (ext 53277) *Toll Free Tel:* 800-338-3282 *E-mail:* pubmarketing@petersons.com *Web Site:* www.petersonspublishing.com, pg 181

Petroleum Extension Service (PETEX), JJ Pickle Research Campus, 10100 Burnet Rd, Bldg 2, Austin, TX 78758-4445 *Tel:* 512-471-5940 *Toll Free Tel:* 800-687-4132 *Fax:* 512-471-9410 *Toll Free Fax:* 800-687-7839 *E-mail:* info@petex.utexas.edu *Web Site:* cee.utexas.edu/ce/petex/, pg 181

Evelyn Walters Pettit, 114 S Park Ave, Suite E, Winter Park, FL 32789-7012 *Tel:* 407-620-0131 (cell); 407-644-1711 *Fax:* 407-644-1711 *E-mail:* bookseller@brandywinebooks.com, pg 499

Pfizer Award, 440 Geddes Hall, Notre Dame, IN 46556 *Tel:* 574-631-1194 *E-mail:* info@hssonline.org *Web Site:* www.hssonline.org, pg 679

Pflaum Publishing Group, 2621 Dryden Rd, Suite 300, Dayton, OH 45439 *Tel:* 937-293-1415 *Toll Free Tel:* 800-543-4383 (sales) *Fax:* 937-293-1310 *Toll Free Fax:* 800-370-4450 *E-mail:* service@pflaum.com *Web Site:* pflaum.com, pg 181

Phaidon, 65 Bleecker St, 8th fl, New York, NY 10012 *Tel:* 212-652-5400 *Toll Free Tel:* 800-759-0190 (cust serv) *Fax:* 212-652-5410 *Toll Free Fax:* 800-286-9471 (cust serv) *E-mail:* ussales@phaidon.com *Web Site:* www.phaidon.com, pg 182

James D Phelan Literary Award, One Embarcadero Ctr, Suite 1400, San Francisco, CA 94111 *Tel:* 415-733-8500 *E-mail:* info@sff.org; artsinfo@sff.org *Web Site:* www.sff.org, pg 679

Phi Beta Kappa Award in Science, 1606 New Hampshire Ave NW, Washington, DC 20009 *Tel:* 202 265-3808 *Fax:* 202-986-1601 *E-mail:* awards@pbk.org *Web Site:* www.pbk.org/bookawards, pg 679

Phi Delta Kappa International®, 1525 Wilson Blvd, Suite 705, Arlington, VA 22209 *Tel:* 812-339-1156 *Toll Free Tel:* 800-766-1156 *Fax:* 812-339-0018 *E-mail:* memberservices@pdkintl.org *Web Site:* www.pdkintl.org, pg 182

Philadelphia Museum of Art, 2525 Pennsylvania Ave, Philadelphia, PA 19130 *Tel:* 215-684-7250 *Fax:* 215-235-8715 *Web Site:* www.philamuseum.org, pg 182

Philadelphia Writers' Conference, PO Box 7171, Elkins Park, PA 19027-0171 *E-mail:* info@pwcwriters.org *Web Site:* pwcwriters.org, pg 613

Meredith Phillips, 4127 Old Adobe Rd, Palo Alto, CA 94306 *Tel:* 650-857-9555 *E-mail:* mphillips0743@comcast.net, pg 500

Philomel, 345 Hudson St, New York, NY 10014 *Tel:* 212-366-2000, pg 182

Philosophical Library Inc, 275 Central Park W, Suite 12D, New York, NY 10024 *Tel:* 212-886-1873 *Fax:* 212-873-6070 *E-mail:* editors@philosophicallibrary.com *Web Site:* philosophicallibrary.com, pg 182

Philosophy Documentation Center, PO Box 7147, Charlottesville, VA 22906-7147 *Tel:* 434-220-3300 *Toll Free Tel:* 800-444-2419 *Fax:* 434-220-3301 *E-mail:* order@pdcnet.org *Web Site:* www.pdcnet.org, pg 182

Phoenix Society for Burn Survivors, 1835 R W Berends Dr SW, Grand Rapids, MI 49519-4955 *Tel:* 616-458-2773 *Toll Free Tel:* 800-888-BURN (888-2876) *E-mail:* info@phoenix-society.org *Web Site:* www.phoenix-society.org, pg 182

PhotoEdit Inc, 3505 Cadillac Ave, Suite P-101, Costa Mesa, CA 92626 *Toll Free Tel:* 888-450-0946 *Fax:* 714-434-5937 *Toll Free Fax:* 800-804-3707 *E-mail:* sales@photoeditinc.com *Web Site:* www.photoeditinc.com, pg 500

Photographic Society of America® (PSA®), 8241 S Walker Ave, Suite 104, Oklahoma City, OK 73139 *Tel:* 405-843-1437 *Toll Free Tel:* 855-PSA-INFO (772-4636) *Fax:* 405-843-1438 *E-mail:* hq@psa-photo.org *Web Site:* www.psa-photo.org, pg 575

Piano Press, 1425 Ocean Ave, Suite 5, Del Mar, CA 92014 *Tel:* 619-884-1401 *Fax:* 858-755-1104 *E-mail:* pianopress@pianopress.com *Web Site:* www.pianopress.com, pg 182

Picador, 175 Fifth Ave, 19th fl, New York, NY 10010 *Tel:* 646-307-5151 *Fax:* 212-253-9627 *Web Site:* www.picadorusa.com, pg 182

Alison Picard Literary Agent, PO Box 2000, Cotuit, MA 02635 *Tel:* 508-477-7192 *Fax:* 508-477-7192 (call first) *E-mail:* ajpicard@aol.com, pg 531

Picasso Project, 1109 Geary Blvd, San Francisco, CA 94109 *Tel:* 415-292-6500 *Fax:* 415-292-6594 *E-mail:* editeur@earthlink.net (edit); picasso@art-books.com (orders) *Web Site:* www.art-books.com, pg 183

Piccadilly Books Ltd, PO Box 25203, Colorado Springs, CO 80936-5203 *Tel:* 719-550-9887 *E-mail:* orders@piccadillybooks.com *Web Site:* www.piccadillybooks.com, pg 183

Robert J Pickering Award for Playwriting Excellence, 89 Division, Coldwater, MI 49036 *Tel:* 517-279-7963 *Fax:* 517-279-8095 *E-mail:* j7eden@aol.com *Web Site:* www.branchcct.org, pg 679

Picton Press, 814 E Elkcam Circle, Marco Island, FL 34145-2558 *Tel:* 239-970-2442 *E-mail:* sales@pictonpress.com (orders) *Web Site:* www.pictonpress.com, pg 183

Pictures & Words Editorial Services, 3100 "B" Ave, Anacortes, WA 98221 *Tel:* 360-293-8476 *E-mail:* editor@picturesandwords.com *Web Site:* www.picturesandwords.com/words, pg 500

Pie in the Sky Publishing LLC, 8031 E Phillips Circle, Centennial, CO 80112 *Tel:* 303-773-0851 *Fax:* 303-773-0851 *E-mail:* pieintheskypublishing@msn.com *Web Site:* www.pieintheskypublishing.com, pg 183

Pieces of Learning Inc, 1990 Market Rd, Marion, IL 62959-8976 *Tel:* 618-964-9426 *Toll Free Tel:* 800-729-5137 *Toll Free Fax:* 800-844-0455 *E-mail:* info@piecesoflearning.com *Web Site:* www.piecesoflearning.com, pg 183

Lorne Pierce Medal, Walter House, 282 Somerset W, Ottawa, ON K2P 0J6, Canada *Tel:* 613-991-6990 (ext 106) *Fax:* 613-991-6996 *E-mail:* nominations@rsc-src.ca *Web Site:* www.rsc-src.ca, pg 679

The Pilgrim Press/United Church Press, 700 Prospect Ave, Cleveland, OH 44115-1100 *Tel:* 216-736-2100 *Toll Free Tel:* 800-537-3394 (orders) *Fax:* 216-736-2207 (orders) *E-mail:* permissions@thepilgrimpress.com; store@ucc.org *Web Site:* www.thepilgrimpress.com; www.uccresources.com, pg 183

The Pinch Writing Awards in Fiction, University of Memphis, English Dept, 435 Patterson Hall, Memphis, TN 38152 *Tel:* 901-678-2651 *Fax:* 901-678-2226 *E-mail:* editor@pinchjournal.com *Web Site:* www.pinchjournal.com, pg 679

The Pinch Writing Awards in Poetry, University of Memphis, English Dept, 435 Patterson Hall, Memphis, TN 38152 *Tel:* 901-678-2651 *Fax:* 901-678-2226 *E-mail:* editor@pinchjournal.com *Web Site:* www.pinchjournal.com, pg 680

Caroline Pincus Book Midwife, 101 Wool St, San Francisco, CA 94110 *Tel:* 415-516-6206 *E-mail:* caroline@carolinepincus.com *Web Site:* carolinepincus.com, pg 500

Pinder Lane & Garon-Brooke Associates Ltd, 159 W 53 St, New York, NY 10019 *Tel:* 212-489-0880 *Fax:* 212-489-7104 *E-mail:* pinderlanegaronbrooke@gmail.com *Web Site:* www.pinderlaneandgaronbrooke.com, pg 531

Pineapple Press Inc, PO Box 3889, Sarasota, FL 34230-3889 *Tel:* 941-706-2507 *Toll Free Tel:* 866-766-3850 (orders) *Fax:* 941-706-2509 *Toll Free Fax:* 800-838-1149 (orders) *E-mail:* info@pineapplepress.com; customer.service@ingrampublisherservices.com *Web Site:* www.pineapplepress.com, pg 183

Pinnacle Book Achievement Awards, PO Box 606, Cottage Grove, OR 97424 *Tel:* 541-942-7455 *Fax:* 541-942-7455 *E-mail:* nabe@bookmarketingprofits.com *Web Site:* www.bookmarketingprofits.com, pg 680

Pippin Press, 229 E 85 St, New York, NY 10028 *Tel:* 212-288-4920 *Fax:* 908-237-2407, pg 183

Pippin Properties Inc, 110 W 40 St, Suite 1704, New York, NY 10018 *Tel:* 212-338-9310 *Fax:* 212-338-9579 *E-mail:* info@pippinproperties.com *Web Site:* www.pippinproperties.com; www.facebook.com/pippinproperties, pg 531

Pippin Publishing, 5201 Dufferin St, Toronto, ON M3H 5T8, Canada *Tel:* 416-667-8731; 426-667-7791 (CN warehouse) *Toll Free Tel:* 800-565-9523 (CN warehouse) *Fax:* 416-667-7832 *Toll Free Fax:* 800-221-9985 (CN warehouse) *E-mail:* utpbooks@utpress.utoronto.ca (CN warehouse) *Web Site:* www.utpguidancecentre.com, pg 467

Planert Creek Press, E4843 395 Ave, Menomonie, WI 54751 *Tel:* 715-235-4110 *E-mail:* publisher@planertcreekpress.com *Web Site:* www.planertcreekpress.com, pg 183

Platinum Press LLC, 281 Hicks St, Brooklyn, NY 11201 *Tel:* 718-875-4092 *Fax:* 718-875-5065, pg 183

Platypus Media LLC, 725 Eighth St SE, Washington, DC 20003 *Tel:* 202-546-1674 *Toll Free Tel:* 877-PLATYPS (752-8977) *Fax:* 202-546-2356 *E-mail:* info@platypusmedia.com *Web Site:* www.platypusmedia.com, pg 183

Players Press Inc, PO Box 1132, Studio City, CA 91614-0132 *Tel:* 818-789-4980 *E-mail:* playerspress@att.net, pg 184

Playwrights Guild of Canada, 401 Richmond St W, Suite 350, Toronto, ON M5V 3A8, Canada *Tel:* 416-703-0201 *Fax:* 416-703-0059 *E-mail:* info@playwrightsguild.ca *Web Site:* www.playwrightsguild.ca, pg 575

Playwrights Project, 3675 Ruffin Rd, Suite 330, San Diego, CA 92123 *Tel:* 858-384-2970 *Fax:* 858-384-2974 *E-mail:* write@playwrightsproject.org *Web Site:* www.playwrightsproject.org, pg 680

Pleasure Boat Studio: A Literary Press, 201 W 89 St, New York, NY 10024 *Tel:* 212-362-8563; 413-337-5346 *Fax:* 413-677-0085 *E-mail:* pleasboat@nyc.rr.com *Web Site:* www.pleasureboatstudio.com, pg 184

Plexus Publishing, Inc, 143 Old Marlton Pike, Medford, NJ 08055 *Tel:* 609-654-6500 *Fax:* 609-654-4309 *E-mail:* info@plexuspublishing.com *Web Site:* www.plexuspublishing.com, pg 184

The Plimpton Prize, 544 W 27 St, New York, NY 10001 *Tel:* 212-343-1333 *Fax:* 212-343-1988 *E-mail:* queries@theparisreview.org *Web Site:* www.theparisreview.org, pg 680

Plough Publishing House, 151 Bowne Dr, Walden, NY 12586-2832 *Tel:* 845-572-3455 *Toll Free Tel:* 800-521-8011 *Fax:* 845-572-3472 *E-mail:* info@plough.com *Web Site:* www.plough.com, pg 184

Ploughshares, Emerson College, 120 Boylston St, Boston, MA 02116 *Tel:* 617-824-3757 *E-mail:* pshares@pshares.org *Web Site:* www.pshares.org, pg 184

Plowshare Media, 405 Vincente Way, La Jolla, CA 92037 *E-mail:* sales@plowsharemedia.com *Web Site:* plowsharemedia.com, pg 184

Plum Tree Books, 2151 Market St, Camp Hill, PA 17011 *Tel:* 717-730-0711 *Fax:* 717-730-0721 *E-mail:* info@classicalsubjects.com *Web Site:* www.plumtreebooks.com, pg 184

Plume, 375 Hudson St, New York, NY 10014 *Tel:* 212-366-2000 *Fax:* 212-243-6002 *Web Site:* www.penguin.com/publishers/plume, pg 184

Plunkett Research Ltd, PO Drawer 541737, Houston, TX 77254-1737 *Tel:* 713-932-0000 *Fax:* 713-932-7080 *E-mail:* customersupport@plunkettresearch.com *Web Site:* www.plunkettresearch.com, pg 184

Plutarch Award, PO Box 33020, Santa Fe, NM 87594 *Tel:* 505-983-4671 *Web Site:* biographersinternational.org, pg 680

PNWA Literary Contest, 1420 NW Gilman Blvd, Suite 8, PMB 2717, Issaquah, WA 98027 *Tel:* 425-673-2665 *E-mail:* pnwa@pnwa.org *Web Site:* www.pnwa.org, pg 680

PNWA - a writer's resource, 1420 NW Gilman Blvd, Suite 8, PMB 2717, Issaquah, WA 98027 *Tel:* 425-673-2665 *Fax:* 425-961-0768 *E-mail:* pnwa@pnwa.org *Web Site:* www.pnwa.org, pg 575

J P Pochron Writer for Hire, 830 Lake Orchid Circle, No 203, Vero Beach, FL 32962 *Tel:* 772-569-2967 *E-mail:* hotwriter15@hotmail.com, pg 500

Pocket Press Inc, PO Box 25124, Portland, OR 97298-0124 *Toll Free Tel:* 888-237-2110 *Toll Free Fax:* 877-643-3732 *E-mail:* sales@pocketpressinc.com *Web Site:* www.pocketpressinc.com, pg 185

Pocol Press, 6023 Pocol Dr, Clifton, VA 20124-1333 *Tel:* 703-830-5862 *E-mail:* info@pocolpress.com *Web Site:* www.pocolpress.com, pg 185

Edgar Allan Poe Memorial, 900 Timber Creek Place, Virginia Beach, VA 23464 *E-mail:* poetryinva@aol.com *Web Site:* poetrysocietyofvirginia.org, pg 680

Poetry Book Contest, PO Box 910456, Lexington, KY 40591-0456 *Web Site:* www.accents-publishing.com/contest.html, pg 680

Poetry Center Book Award, 1600 Holloway Ave, San Francisco, CA 94132 *Tel:* 415-338-2227 *Fax:* 415-338-0966 *E-mail:* poetry@sfsu.edu *Web Site:* www.sfsu.edu/~poetry, pg 680

Poetry Chapbook Contest, 1935 Penfield Rd, Penfield, NY 14526 *Tel:* 585-383-0812 *E-mail:* palettesnquills@gmail.com *Web Site:* www.palettesnquills.com, pg 680

Poetry Flash Reading Series, 1450 Fourth St, Suite 4, Berkeley, CA 94710 *Tel:* 510-525-5476 *Fax:* 510-525-6752 *E-mail:* editor@poetryflash.org *Web Site:* poetryflash.org, pg 613

Poetry Society of America (PSA), 15 Gramercy Park, New York, NY 10003 *Tel:* 212-254-9628 *Web Site:* www.poetrysociety.org, pg 575

Poets & Writers Inc, 90 Broad St, Suite 2100, New York, NY 10004 *Tel:* 212-226-3586 *Fax:* 212-226-3963 *E-mail:* admin@pw.org *Web Site:* www.pw.org, pg 575

Pointed Leaf Press, 136 Baxter St, New York, NY 10013 *Tel:* 212-941-1800 *Fax:* 212-941-1822 *E-mail:* info@pointedleafpress.com *Web Site:* www.pointedleafpress.com, pg 185

Poisoned Pen Press, 6962 E First Ave, Suite 103, Scottsdale, AZ 85251 *Tel:* 480-945-3375 *Toll Free Tel:* 800-421-3976 *Fax:* 480-949-1707 *E-mail:* info@poisonedpenpress.com *Web Site:* www.poisonedpenpress.com, pg 185

Polar Bear & Company, PO Box 311, Solon, ME 04979-0311 *Tel:* 207-643-2795 *Web Site:* www.polarbearandco.com, pg 185

Polebridge Press, PO Box 346, Farmington, MN 55024 *Tel:* 651-200-2372 *E-mail:* orders@westarinstitute.org *Web Site:* www.westarinstitute.org, pg 185

Wendy Polhemus-Annibell, PO Box 464, Peconic, NY 11958 *Tel:* 631-276-0684 *E-mail:* wannibell@gmail.com, pg 500

Police Executive Research Forum, 1120 Connecticut Ave NW, Suite 930, Washington, DC 20036 *Tel:* 202-466-7820 *Web Site:* www.policeforum.org, pg 185

Polis Books, 1201 Hudson St, No 211S, Hoboken, NJ 07030 *E-mail:* info@polisbooks.com; submissions@polisbooks.com *Web Site:* www.polisbooks.com; facebook.com/PolisBooks; twitter.com/PolisBooks, pg 185

The George Polk Awards, The Brooklyn Campus, One University Plaza, Brooklyn, NY 11201-5372 *Tel:* 718-488-1009 *Web Site:* www.liu.edu/polk, pg 680

Pom Inc, 18-15 215 St, Bayside, NY 11360 *Tel:* 516-487-3441, pg 531

Pomegranate Communications Inc, 19018 NE Portal Way, Portland, OR 97230 *Tel:* 503-328-6500 *Toll Free Tel:* 800-227-1428 *Fax:* 503-328-9330 *Toll Free Fax:* 800-848-4376 *E-mail:* contactus@pomegranate.com *Web Site:* www.pomegranate.com, pg 185

Pontifical Institute of Mediaeval Studies, Department of Publications, 59 Queen's Park Crescent E, Toronto, ON M5S 2C4, Canada *Tel:* 416-926-7142 *Fax:* 416-926-7258 *Web Site:* www.pims.ca, pg 467

Porcupine's Quill Inc, 68 Main St, Erin, ON N0B 1T0, Canada *Tel:* 519-833-9158 *E-mail:* pql@sentex.net *Web Site:* porcupinesquill.ca, pg 467

Port Townsend Writers' Conference, 223 Battery Way, Port Townsend, WA 98368 *Tel:* 360-385-3102 *Toll Free Tel:* 800-733-3608 (ticket off) *Fax:* 360-385-2470 *E-mail:* info@centrum.org *Web Site:* centrum.org, pg 613

Portage & Main Press, 318 McDermot, Suite 100, Winnipeg, MB R3A 0A2, Canada *Tel:* 204-987-3500 *Toll Free Tel:* 800-667-9673 *Fax:* 204-947-0080 *Toll Free Fax:* 866-734-8477 *E-mail:* books@portageandmainpress.com *Web Site:* www.portageandmainpress.com, pg 467

Katherine Anne Porter Award, 633 W 155 St, New York, NY 10032 *Tel:* 212-368-5900 *Fax:* 212-491-4615 *E-mail:* academy@artsandletters.org *Web Site:* www.artsandletters.org, pg 681

Privacy Journal, PO Box 28577, Providence, RI 02908 *Tel:* 401-274-7861 *E-mail:* orders@privacyjournal.net *Web Site:* www.privacyjournal.net, pg 189

Prix Alvine-Belisle, 2065 rue Parthenais, Bureau 387, Montreal, QC H2K 3T1, Canada *Tel:* 514-281-5012 *Fax:* 514-281-8219 *E-mail:* info@asted.org *Web Site:* www.asted.org, pg 682

Prix Emile-Nelligan, 100, rue Sherbrooke, Suite 202, Montreal, QC H2X 1C3, Canada *Tel:* 514-278-4657 *Toll Free Tel:* 888-849-8540 *Fax:* 514-278-1943 *E-mail:* info@fondation-nelligan.org *Web Site:* www.fondation-nelligan.org, pg 682

PRO-ED Inc, 8700 Shoal Creek Blvd, Austin, TX 78757-6897 *Tel:* 512-451-3246 *Toll Free Tel:* 800-897-3202 *Fax:* 512-451-8542 *Toll Free Fax:* 800-397-7633 *E-mail:* general@proedinc.com; info@proedinc.com *Web Site:* www.proedinc.com, pg 189

Pro Lingua Associates Inc, 74 Cotton Mill Hill, Suite A-315, Brattleboro, VT 05301 *Tel:* 802-257-7779 *Toll Free Tel:* 800-366-4775 *Fax:* 802-257-5117 *E-mail:* info@prolinguaassociates.com *Web Site:* www.prolinguaassociates.com, pg 189

Productive Publications, 7-B Pleasant Blvd, Unit 1210, Toronto, ON M4T 1K2, Canada *Tel:* 416-483-0634 *Toll Free Tel:* 877-879-2669 (orders) *Fax:* 416-322-7434 *E-mail:* productivepublications@rogers.com *Web Site:* www.productivepublications.ca, pg 468

Productivity Press, 711 Third Ave, 8th fl, New York, NY 10017 *Tel:* 212-216-7800 *Toll Free Tel:* 800-634-7064 (orders); 800-797-3803 *E-mail:* orders@taylorandfrancis.com *Web Site:* www.productivitypress.com, pg 189

Professional Communications Inc, 1223 W Main, Suite 1427, Caddo, OK 74702-1427 *Tel:* 580-745-9838 *Toll Free Tel:* 800-337-9838 *Fax:* 580-745-9837 *E-mail:* info@pcibooks.com *Web Site:* www.pcibooks.com, pg 189

The Professional Education Group LLC (PEG), 700 Twelve Oaks Center Dr, Suite 716, Wayzata, MN 55391 *Tel:* 952-933-9990 *Toll Free Tel:* 800-229-2531 *Fax:* 952-933-7784 *E-mail:* orders@proedgroup.com *Web Site:* www.proedgroup.com, pg 189

Professional Publications Inc (PPI), 1250 Fifth Ave, Belmont, CA 94002 *Tel:* 650-593-9119 *Fax:* 650-592-4519 *E-mail:* acquisitions@ppi2pass.com *Web Site:* ppi2pass.com; feprep.com, pg 189

Professional Resource Press, 1958 Barber Rd, Sarasota, FL 34240 *Tel:* 941-343-9601 *Toll Free Tel:* 800-443-3364 (orders & cust serv) *Fax:* 941-343-9201 *Toll Free Fax:* 866-804-4843 (orders only) *E-mail:* cs.prpress@gmail.com *Web Site:* www.prpress.com, pg 189

The Professional Writer, 175 W 12 St, Suite 6D, New York, NY 10011 *Tel:* 212-414-0188; 917-658-1946 (cell) *E-mail:* paul@theprofessionalwriter.com *Web Site:* www.theprofessionalwriter.com, pg 500

Professional Writers Association of Canada (PWAC), c/o Canadian Brownfields Network (CBN), 2800 14 Ave, Suite 210, Markham, ON L3R 0E4, Canada *Tel:* 416-504-1645 *E-mail:* info@pwac.ca *Web Site:* pwac.ca; www.writers.ca, pg 576

Progressive Press, 3716 37 St, San Diego, CA 92105-2409 *Tel:* 619-892-7781 *Fax:* 619-892-7781 *E-mail:* info@progressivepress.com *Web Site:* www.progressivepress.com, pg 189

Prometheus Awards, 650 Castro St, Suite 120-433, Mountain View, CA 94041 *Tel:* 650-968-6319 *Web Site:* www.lfs.org, pg 682

Prometheus Books, 59 John Glenn Dr, Amherst, NY 14228-2119 *Tel:* 716-691-0133 *Fax:* 716-691-0137 *E-mail:* marketing@prometheusbooks.com; editorial@prometheusbooks.com; rights@prometheusmail.com *Web Site:* www.prometheusbooks.com, pg 190

Pronk Media Inc, PO Box 340, Beaverton, ON L0K 1A0, Canada *Tel:* 416-441-3760 *E-mail:* info@pronk.com *Web Site:* www.pronk.com, pg 500

Proofed to Perfection Editing Services, 6519 Sherrill Baggett Rd, Godwin, NC 28344 *Tel:* 919-908-1912 *E-mail:* inquiries@proofedtoperfection.com *Web Site:* www.proofedtoperfection.com, pg 500

ProQuest LLC, 789 E Eisenhower Pkwy, Ann Arbor, MI 48108 *Tel:* 734-761-4700 *Toll Free Tel:* 800-521-0600 *Web Site:* www.proquest.com, pg 190

PROSE Awards, 455 Massachusetts Ave NW, Suite 700, Washington, DC 20001-2777 *Tel:* 212-255-0200 *Web Site:* www.proseawards.com; publishers.org, pg 682

Prospect Agency, 285 Fifth Ave, PMB 445, Brooklyn, NY 11215 *Tel:* 718-788-3217 *Fax:* 718-360-9582 *Web Site:* www.prospectagency.com, pg 532

Prospect Park Books, 2359 Lincoln Ave, Altadena, CA 91001 *Tel:* 626-793-9796 *E-mail:* info@prospectparkbooks.com *Web Site:* www.prospectparkbooks.com, pg 190

ProStar Publications Inc, 3 Church Circle, Suite 109, Annapolis, MD 21401 *Toll Free Tel:* 800-481-6277 *Toll Free Fax:* 800-487-6277 *E-mail:* editor@prostarpublications.com *Web Site:* www.prostarpublications.com, pg 190

Protestant Church-Owned Publishers Association, 6631 Westbury Oaks Ct, Springfield, VA 22152 *Tel:* 703-220-5989 *Web Site:* www.pcpaonline.org, pg 576

The PRS Group Inc, 5800 Heritage Landing Dr, Suite E, East Syracuse, NY 13057-9358 *Tel:* 315-431-0511 *Fax:* 315-431-0200 *E-mail:* custserv@prsgroup.com *Web Site:* www.prsgroup.com, pg 190

Prufrock Press, PO Box 8813, Waco, TX 76714-8813 *Tel:* 254-756-3337 *Toll Free Tel:* 800-998-2208 *Fax:* 254-756-3339 *Toll Free Fax:* 800-240-0333 *E-mail:* info@prufrock.com *Web Site:* www.prufrock.com, pg 191

PSMJ Resources Inc, 10 Midland Ave, Newton, MA 02458 *Tel:* 617-965-0055 *Toll Free Tel:* 800-537-7765 *Fax:* 617-965-5152 *E-mail:* info@psmj.com *Web Site:* www.psmj.com, pg 191

Psychological Assessment Resources Inc (PAR), 16204 N Florida Ave, Lutz, FL 33549 *Tel:* 813-968-3003; 813-449-4065 *Toll Free Tel:* 800-331-8378 *Fax:* 813-968-2598; 813-961-2196 *Toll Free Fax:* 800-727-9329 *E-mail:* custsup@parinc.com *Web Site:* www4.parinc.com, pg 191

Public Citizen, 1600 20 St NW, Washington, DC 20009 *Tel:* 202-588-1000 *Fax:* 202-588-7798 *E-mail:* public_citizen@citizen.org *Web Site:* www.citizen.org, pg 191

Public Relations Society of America, 33 Maiden Lane, 11th fl, New York, NY 10038-5150 *Tel:* 212-460-1400 *Fax:* 212-995-0757 *Web Site:* www.prsa.org, pg 576

Public Scholar Program, 400 Seventh St SW, Washington, DC 20506 *Tel:* 202-606-8200 *E-mail:* publicscholar@neh.gov *Web Site:* www.neh.gov/grants/research, pg 682

Publication Consultants, 8370 Eleusis Dr, Anchorage, AK 99502 *Tel:* 907-349-2424 *Fax:* 907-349-2426 *E-mail:* books@publicationconsultants.com *Web Site:* www.publicationconsultants.com, pg 191

Les Publications du Quebec, 1000, rte de l'Eqalise, Bureau 500, Quebec, QC G1V 3V9, Canada *Tel:* 418-643-5150 *Toll Free Tel:* 800-463-2100 (Quebec province only) *Fax:* 418-643-6177 *Toll Free Fax:* 800-561-3479 *E-mail:* publicationsduquebec@cspq.gouv.qc.ca *Web Site:* www.publicationsduquebec.gouv.qc.ca, pg 468

Publications International Ltd (PIL), 7373 N Cicero Ave, Lincolnwood, IL 60712 *Tel:* 847-676-3470 *Fax:* 847-676-3671 *E-mail:* customer_service@pubint.com *Web Site:* pilbooks.com, pg 191

Publishers Association of the West Inc (PubWest), 17501 Hill Way, Lake Oswego, OR 97035 *Tel:* 503-901-9865 *Web Site:* pubwest.org, pg 576

Publishers Information Bureau (PIB)®, 757 Third Ave, 11th fl, New York, NY 10017 *Tel:* 212-872-3745; 212-872-3700 (MPA) *E-mail:* infocenter@magazine.org *Web Site:* www.magazine.org, pg 576

Publishing Certificate Program at City College of New York, Division of Humanities NAC 5225, City College of New York, New York, NY 10031 *Tel:* 212-650-7925 *Fax:* 212-650-7912 *E-mail:* ccnypub@aol.com *Web Site:* www.ccny.cuny.edu/publishing_certificate/index.html, pg 622

The Publishing Game, PO Box 590239, Newton, MA 02459-0002 *Tel:* 617-630-0945 *Fax:* 617-630-0945 (call first) *E-mail:* info@publishinggame.com; workshops@publishinggame.com *Web Site:* www.publishinggame.com, pg 614

Publishing Professionals Network, c/o Postal Annex, 274 Redwood Shores Pkwy, Box 129, Redwood City, CA 94065-1173 *E-mail:* operations@pubpronetwork.org *Web Site:* www.pubpronetwork.org, pg 577

Publishing Resources Inc, 425 Carr 693, PMB 160, Dorado, PR 00646 *Tel:* 787-647-9342 *E-mail:* pri@chevako.net, pg 500

Publishing Synthesis Ltd, 39 Crosby St, New York, NY 10013 *Tel:* 212-219-0135 *Fax:* 212-219-0136 *E-mail:* mainmail@pubsyn.com *Web Site:* www.pubsyn.com, pg 500

The Publishing Triangle Literary Awards, 332 Bleecker St, Suite D-36, New York, NY 10014 *E-mail:* publishingtriangle@gmail.com *Web Site:* www.publishingtriangle.org, pg 683

PubWest Book Design Awards, 17501 Hill Way, Lake Oswego, OR 97035 *Tel:* 503-901-9865 *Web Site:* pubwest.org, pg 683

Puddingstone Literary, Authors' Agents, 11 Mabro Dr, Denville, NJ 07834-9607 *Tel:* 973-366-3622, pg 532

Puffin Books, 345 Hudson St, New York, NY 10014 *Tel:* 212-366-2000 *Web Site:* www.penguin.com/publishers/puffin, pg 191

Pulitzer Prizes, 709 Journalism Bldg, Columbia University, 2950 Broadway, New York, NY 10027 *Tel:* 212-854-3841 *Fax:* 212-854-3342 *E-mail:* pulitzer@pulitzer.org *Web Site:* www.pulitzer.org, pg 683

Purdue University Press, Stewart Ctr 190, 504 W State St, West Lafayette, IN 47907-2058 *Tel:* 765-494-2038 *Fax:* 765-496-2442 *E-mail:* pupress@purdue.edu *Web Site:* www.thepress.purdue.edu, pg 191

Purple House Press, 8100 US Hwy 62 E, Cynthiana, KY 41031 *Tel:* 859-235-9970 *Web Site:* www.purplehousepress.com, pg 191

Purple Mountain Press Ltd, 1060 Main St, Fleischmanns, NY 12430 *Tel:* 845-254-4062 *Toll Free Tel:* 800-325-2665 (orders) *Fax:* 845-254-4476 *E-mail:* purple@catskill.net *Web Site:* www.catskill.net/purple, pg 191

Pushcart Press, PO Box 380, Wainscott, NY 11975-0380 *Tel:* 631-324-9300, pg 192

Pushcart Prize: Best of the Small Presses, PO Box 380, Wainscott, NY 11975-0380 *Tel:* 631-324-9300, pg 683

GP Putnam's Sons (Children's), 345 Hudson St, New York, NY 10014 *Tel:* 212-366-2000 *Fax:* 212-414-3393 *Web Site:* www.penguin.com/publishers/gpputnamssonsbooksforyoungread, pg 192

GP Putnam's Sons (Hardcover), 375 Hudson St, New York, NY 10014 *Tel:* 212-366-2000 *Fax:* 212-366-2643 *E-mail:* online@penguinputnam.com *Web Site:* www.penguin.com/publishers/gpputnamssons, pg 192

PNWA Writers Conference, 1420 NW Gilman Blvd, Suite 8, PMB 2717, Issaquah, WA 98027 *Tel:* 425-673-2665 *E-mail:* pnwa@pnwa.org *Web Site:* www.pnwa.org, pg 614

Pyncheon House, 6 University Dr, Suite 105, Amherst, MA 01002, pg 192

Ron Pynn Award, PO Box 367, Fountain City, WI 54629 *E-mail:* info@taaonline.net *Web Site:* www.taaonline.net/ron-pynn-award, pg 683

QA International (QAI), 329 De la Commune W, 3rd fl, Montreal, QC H2Y 2E1, Canada *Tel:* 514-499-3000 *Fax:* 514-499-3010 *Web Site:* www.qa-international.com, pg 468

Robert Quackenbush's Children's Book Writing & Illustration Workshops, 223 E 78 St, New York, NY 10075 *Tel:* 212-744-3822 *E-mail:* rqstudios@aol.com *Web Site:* www.rquackenbush.com, pg 614

Quail Ridge Press, 101 Brooks Dr, Brandon, MS 39042 *Tel:* 601-825-2063 *Toll Free Tel:* 800-343-1583 *Fax:* 601-825-3091 *Toll Free Fax:* 800-864-1082 *E-mail:* info@quailridge.com *Web Site:* quailridge.com, pg 192

Quality Medical Publishing Inc, 2248 Welsch Industrial Ct, St Louis, MO 63146-4222 *Tel:* 314-878-7808 *Toll Free Tel:* 800-348-7808 *Fax:* 314-878-9937 *E-mail:* qmp@qmp.com; customerservice@qmp.com *Web Site:* www.qmp.com, pg 192

Quarto Publishing Group USA Inc, 400 First Ave N, Suite 400, Minneapolis, MN 55401 *Tel:* 612-344-8100 *Toll Free Tel:* 800-328-0590 (sales); 800-458-0454 *Fax:* 612-344-8691 *E-mail:* sales@quartous.com *Web Site:* www.quartoknows.com, pg 192

Quattro Books Inc, 12 Concord Ave, 2nd fl, Toronto, ON M6H 2P1, Canada *Tel:* 647-748-7484 *E-mail:* info@quattrobooks.ca *Web Site:* www.quattrobooks.ca, pg 468

Quebec Dans Le Monde, 335, rue Saint-Joseph E, bureau 600, Quebec, QC G1K 3B4, Canada *Fax:* 418-659-4143 *E-mail:* info@quebecmonde.com *Web Site:* www.quebecmonde.com, pg 468

Quebec Writers' Federation (QWF), 1200 Atwater Ave, Rm 3, Westmount, QC H3Z 1X4, Canada *Tel:* 514-933-0878 *E-mail:* info@qwf.org *Web Site:* www.qwf.org; www.hireawriter.ca, pg 577

Quicksilver Productions, PO Box 340, Ashland, OR 97520-0012 *Tel:* 541-482-5343 *Toll Free Fax:* 888-974-6462 *E-mail:* celestialcalendars@email.com *Web Site:* www.quicksilverproductions.com, pg 192

Quincannon Publishing Group, PO Box 8100, Glen Ridge, NJ 07028-8100 *Tel:* 973-380-9942 *E-mail:* editors@quincannongroup.com *Web Site:* www.quincannongroup.com, pg 192

Quintessence Publishing Co Inc, 4350 Chandler Dr, Hanover Park, IL 60133 *Tel:* 630-736-3600 *Toll Free Tel:* 800-621-0387 *Fax:* 630-736-3633 *E-mail:* contact@quintbook.com; service@quintbook.com *Web Site:* www.quintpub.com, pg 193

Quirk Books, 215 Church St, Philadelphia, PA 19106 *Tel:* 215-627-3581 *Fax:* 215-627-5220 *E-mail:* general@quirkbooks.com *Web Site:* www.quirkbooks.com, pg 193

Quite Specific Media Group Ltd, 141 N Clark Dr, Unit 1, West Hollywood, CA 90048 *Tel:* 310-205-0665 *E-mail:* info@silmanjamespress.com *Web Site:* www.quitespecificmedia.com; www.silmanjamespress.com, pg 193

Quixote Press, 3544 Blakslee St, Wever, IA 52658 *Tel:* 319-372-7480 *Toll Free Tel:* 800-571-2665 *Fax:* 319-372-7485 *E-mail:* heartsntummies@gmail.com, pg 193

QWF Literary Awards, 1200 Atwater Ave, Rm 3, Westmount, QC H3Z 1X4, Canada *Tel:* 514-933-0878 *E-mail:* info@qwf.org *Web Site:* www.qwf.org, pg 683

Miriam Rachimi Memorial, 900 Timber Creek Place, Virginia Beach, VA 23464 *E-mail:* poetryinva@aol.com *Web Site:* poetrysocietyofvirginia.org, pg 683

Radcliffe Fellowship, 8 Garden St, Cambridge, MA 02138 *Tel:* 617-496-1324 (application off) *Fax:* 617-495-8136 *Web Site:* www.radcliffe.harvard.edu, pg 683

Thomas Raddall Atlantic Fiction Award, 1113 Marginal Rd, Halifax, NS B3H 4P7, Canada *Tel:* 902-423-8116 *Fax:* 902-422-0881 *E-mail:* contact@writers.ns.ca *Web Site:* writers.ns.ca, pg 683

Radix Press, 11715 Bandlon Dr, Houston, TX 77072 *Tel:* 281-879-5688 *Web Site:* www.vvfh.org; www.specialforcesbooks.com, pg 193

The Ragan Old North State Award Cup for Nonfiction, 4610 Mail Service Ctr, Raleigh, NC 27699-4610 *Tel:* 919-807-7290 *Fax:* 919-733-8807 *Web Site:* www.history.ncdcr.gov/affiliates/lit-hist/awards/awards.htm, pg 683

Rainbow Books Inc, PO Box 430, Highland City, FL 33846 *Tel:* 863-648-4420 *Fax:* 863-647-5951 *E-mail:* info@rainbowbooksinc.com; rbibooks@aol.com *Web Site:* www.rainbowbooksinc.com, pg 193

Rainbow Publishers, 4733 Torrance Blvd, No 259, Torrance, CA 90503 *Tel:* 858-277-1167 *Toll Free Tel:* 800-323-7337; 800-532-4278 *Fax:* 310-353-2116 *Toll Free Fax:* 800-331-0297 *E-mail:* info@rainbowpublishers.com; editor@rainbowpublishers.com (edit dept); orders@rainbowpublishers.com *Web Site:* www.rainbowpublishers.com, pg 193

Raines & Raines, 103 Kenyon Rd, Medusa, NY 12120 *Tel:* 518-239-8311 *Fax:* 518-239-6029, pg 532

Raiziss/de Palchi Fellowship, 75 Maiden Lane, Suite 901, New York, NY 10038 *Tel:* 212-274-0343 *Fax:* 212-274-9427 *E-mail:* academy@poets.org *Web Site:* www.poets.org, pg 683

Sir Walter Raleigh Award for Fiction, 4610 Mail Service Ctr, Raleigh, NC 27699-4610 *Tel:* 919-807-7290 *Fax:* 919-733-8807, pg 684

Jerry Ralya, 7909 Vt Rte 14, Craftsbury Common, VT 05827 *Tel:* 802-586-7514 *E-mail:* jerryralya@gmail.com, pg 500

Ram Publishing Co, 1881 W State St, Garland, TX 75042 *Tel:* 972-494-6151 *Toll Free Tel:* 800-527-4011 *Fax:* 972-494-1881 *E-mail:* sales@garrett.com *Web Site:* www.garrett.com, pg 193

Ramirez Family Award, c/o 7748 Hwy 290 W, Austin, TX 78736-3202 *Tel:* 512-683-5640 *E-mail:* president@texasinstituteofletters.org *Web Site:* www.texasinstituteofletters.org, pg 684

RAND Corp, 1776 Main St, Santa Monica, CA 90407-2138 *Tel:* 310-393-0411 *Fax:* 310-393-4818 *Web Site:* www.rand.org, pg 193

Rand McNally, 9855 Woods Dr, Skokie, IL 60077 *Tel:* 847-329-8100 *E-mail:* ctsales@randmcnally.com; mediarelations@randmcnally.com *Web Site:* www.randmcnally.com, pg 194

Peter E Randall Publisher, 5 Greenleaf Woods Dr, Suite 102, Portsmouth, NH 03801 *Tel:* 603-431-5667 *Fax:* 603-431-3566 *E-mail:* media@perpublisher.com *Web Site:* www.perpublisher.com, pg 194

Random House Children's Books, 1745 Broadway, 10th fl, New York, NY 10019 *Tel:* 212-782-9000 *Web Site:* www.randomhousekids.com, pg 194

Random House Publishing Group, 1745 Broadway, New York, NY 10019 *Toll Free Tel:* 800-200-3552 *Web Site:* atrandom.com, pg 195

Random House Reference/Random House Puzzles & Games, c/o Penguin Random House Inc, 1745 Broadway, New York, NY 10019 *Tel:* 212-782-9000 *Web Site:* www.penguinrandomhouse.com, pg 195

Ransom Note Press, 143 E Ridgewood Ave, Box 419, Ridgewood, NJ 07451 *Tel:* 201-835-2790 *E-mail:* editorial@ransomnotepress.com *Web Site:* www.ransomnotepress.com, pg 478

Gerald & Cullen Rapp, 420 Lexington Ave, New York, NY 10170 *Tel:* 212-889-3337 *Fax:* 212-889-3341 *E-mail:* info@rappart.com *Web Site:* www.rappart.com, pg 544

Rational Island Publishers, 719 Second Ave N, Seattle, WA 98109 *Tel:* 206-284-0311 *Fax:* 206-284-8429 *E-mail:* ircc@rc.org *Web Site:* www.rc.org, pg 195

Rattapallax Press, 217 Thompson St, Suite 353, New York, NY 10012 *E-mail:* info@rattapallax.com *Web Site:* www.rattapallax.com, pg 195

Raven Productions Inc, 34 S Second Ave, Suite 204, Ely, MN 55731 *Tel:* 218-365-3375 *E-mail:* raven@ravenwords.com; order@ravenwords.com *Web Site:* www.ravenwords.com, pg 195

Raven Publishing Inc, 125 Cherry Creek Rd, Norris, MT 59745 *Tel:* 406-685-3545 *Toll Free Tel:* 866-685-3545 *E-mail:* info@ravenpublishing.net *Web Site:* www.ravenpublishing.net, pg 196

Ravenhawk™ Books, 8364 E Balfour Place, Tucson, AZ 85710 *Tel:* 520-296-4491 *Fax:* 520-296-4491 *E-mail:* the6dofcompany@gmail.com, pg 196

Charlotte Cecil Raymond, Literary Agent, 32 Bradlee Rd, Marblehead, MA 01945 *Tel:* 781-631-6722 *Fax:* 781-631-6722 *E-mail:* raymondliterary@gmail.com, pg 532

Razorbill, 345 Hudson St, New York, NY 10014 *Tel:* 212-366-2000 *Web Site:* www.penguin.com/meet/publishers/razorbill, pg 196

RBC Bronwen Wallace Award for Emerging Writers, 460 Richmond St W, Suite 600, Toronto, ON M5V 1Y1, Canada *Tel:* 416-504-8222 *Toll Free Tel:* 877-906-6548 *Fax:* 416-504-9090 *E-mail:* info@writerstrust.com *Web Site:* www.writerstrust.com, pg 684

The Rea Award for the Short Story, 53 W Church Hill Rd, Washington, CT 06794 *Web Site:* reaaward.org, pg 684

Reader's Digest Association Canada ULC (Selection du Reader's Digest Canada SRI), 1100 Rene Levesque Blvd W, 8th fl, Suite 822, Montreal, QC H3B 5H5, Canada *Tel:* 514-940-0751 *Toll Free Tel:* 888-459-3333 (cust serv) *Fax:* 514-940-3637 *E-mail:* erdcustserv@cdsfulfillment.com *Web Site:* www.readersdigest.ca, pg 468

Reader's Digest Trade Publishing, 44 S Broadway, White Plains, NY 10601 *Tel:* 914-238-1000 *Web Site:* www.rdtradepublishing.com, pg 196

Reader's Digest USA Select Editions, 44 S Broadway, 7th fl, White Plains, NY 10601 *Tel:* 914-238-1000 *Toll Free Tel:* 800-304-2807 (cust serv) *Fax:* 914-831-1560, pg 196

The Reading Component, 3900 Parkview Lane, 3B, Irvine, CA 92612-2003 *Tel:* 949-387-6330, pg 500

Recorded Books Inc, an RBmedia company, 270 Skipjack Rd, Prince Frederick, MD 20678 *Tel:* 410-535-5590 *Toll Free Tel:* 877-732-2898 *Fax:* 410-535-5499 *E-mail:* customerservice@recordedbooks.com *Web Site:* www.recordedbooks.com, pg 196

Red Chair Press, PO Box 333, South Egremont, MA 01258-0333 *Tel:* 413-528-2398 (edit off) *Toll Free Tel:* 800-328-4929 (orders & cust serv) *Toll Free Fax:* 800-332-1132 *E-mail:* info@redchairpress.com *Web Site:* www.redchairpress.com, pg 196

Red Deer Press Inc, 195 Allstate Pkwy, Markham, ON L3R 4T8, Canada *Tel:* 905-477-9700 *Toll Free Tel:* 800-387-9776 (orders) *E-mail:* rdp@reddeerpress.com; bookinfo@fitzhenry.ca *Web Site:* www.reddeerpress.com, pg 468

Red Dust Inc, 1148 Fifth Ave, New York, NY 10128 *Tel:* 212-348-4388 *Web Site:* www.reddustbooks.com, pg 196

Red Hen Press, 1335 N Lake Ave, Suite 200, Pasadena, CA 91104 *Tel:* 626-356-4760 *Fax:* 626-356-9974 *Web Site:* www.redhen.org, pg 196

Red Moon Press, PO Box 2461, Winchester, VA 22604-1661 *Tel:* 540-722-2156 *Web Site:* www.redmoonpress.com, pg 197

Red Rock Press, 205 W 57 St, Suite 8B, New York, NY 10019 *Tel:* 212-362-8304 *Fax:* 212-362-6216 *E-mail:* info@redrockpress.com; sales@redrockpress.com; rights@redrockpress.com *Web Site:* www.redrockpress.com, pg 197

Red Sea Press Inc, 541 W Ingham Ave, Suite B, Trenton, NJ 08638 *Tel:* 609-695-3200 *Fax:* 609-695-6466 *E-mail:* customerservice@africaworldpressbooks.com *Web Site:* www.africaworldpressbooks.com, pg 197

Red Wheel/Weiser/Conari, 65 Parker St, Suite 7, Newburyport, MA 01950 *Tel:* 978-465-0504 *Toll Free Tel:* 800-423-7087 (orders) *Fax:* 978-465-0243 *E-mail:* info@rwwbooks.com *Web Site:* www.redwheelweiser.com, pg 197

Redleaf Press, 10 Yorkton Ct, St Paul, MN 55117 *Tel:* 651-641-0508 *Toll Free Tel:* 800-423-8309 *Toll Free Fax:* 800-641-0115 *E-mail:* customerservice@redleafpress.org *Web Site:* www.redleafpress.org, pg 197

Robert D Reed Publishers, PO Box 1992, Bandon, OR 97411-1192 *Tel:* 541-347-9882 *Fax:* 541-347-9883 *E-mail:* 4bobreed@msn.com *Web Site:* rdrpublishers.com, pg 197

Robert F Reed Technology Medal, 301 Brush Creek Rd, Warrendale, PA 15086-7529 *Tel:* 412-741-6860 *Toll Free Tel:* 800-910-4283 *Fax:* 412-741-2311 *E-mail:* printingind@comm.printing.org *Web Site:* www.printing.org/reedaward, pg 684

Reedswain Inc, 88 Wells Rd, Spring City, PA 19475 *Tel:* 610-495-9578 *Toll Free Tel:* 800-331-5191 *Fax:* 610-495-6632 *E-mail:* orders@reedswain.com *Web Site:* www.reedswain.com, pg 197

Rees Literary Agency, 14 Beacon St, Suite 710, Boston, MA 02108 *Tel:* 617-227-9014 *Fax:* 617-227-8762 *Web Site:* www.reesagency.com, pg 532

Referee Books, 2017 Lathrop Ave, Racine, WI 53405 *Tel:* 262-632-8855 *Toll Free Tel:* 800-733-6100 *Fax:* 262-632-5460 *E-mail:* questions@referee.com *Web Site:* www.referee.com, pg 197

Reference Publications Inc, 218 Saint Clair River Dr, Algonac, MI 48001 *Tel:* 810-794-5722 *E-mail:* referencepub@sbcglobal.net, pg 197

ReferencePoint Press Inc, 17150 Via del Campo, Suite 205, San Diego, CA 92127 *Tel:* 858-618-1314 *Toll Free Tel:* 888-479-6436 *Fax:* 858-618-1730 *E-mail:* info@referencepointpress.com *Web Site:* www.referencepointpress.com, pg 197

Reformation Heritage Books, 2965 Leonard St NE, Grand Rapids, MI 49525 *Tel:* 616-977-0889 *Fax:* 616-285-3246 *E-mail:* orders@heritagebooks.org *Web Site:* www.heritagebooks.org, pg 197

Regal Crest Enterprises, 1042 Mount Lebanon Rd, Maryville, TN 37804 *Tel:* 409-527-1188 *Toll Free Fax:* 866-294-9628 *E-mail:* info@regalcrestbooks.biz *Web Site:* www.regalcrest.biz, pg 198

Regal House Publishing, 1723 Hickory Overlook Trail, No 110, Raleigh, NC 27607 *Tel:* 305-360-5969 *E-mail:* info@regalhousepublishing.com *Web Site:* regalhousepublishing.com, pg 198

Regina Medal Award, 8550 United Plaza Blvd, Suite 1001, Baton Rouge, LA 70809 *Tel:* 225-408-4417 *E-mail:* cla2@cathla.org *Web Site:* cathla.org, pg 684

Regnery Publishing, 300 New Jersey Ave NW, Washington, DC 20001 *Tel:* 202-216-0600 *Toll Free Tel:* 888-219-4747 *Fax:* 202-393-1795 *Web Site:* www.regnery.com, pg 198

Regular Baptist Press, 3715 N Ventura Dr, Arlington Heights, IL 60004 *Tel:* 847-843-1600 *Toll Free Tel:* 800-727-4440; 800-727-4440 (cust serv) *Fax:* 847-843-3757 *E-mail:* rbp@garbc.org *Web Site:* regularbaptistpress.org, pg 198

Kerry Reilly: Representatives, 1826 Asheville Place, Charlotte, NC 28203 *Tel:* 704-372-6007 *E-mail:* kerry@reillyreps.com *Web Site:* www.reillyreps.com, pg 544

Marian Reiner, 71 Disbrow Lane, New Rochelle, NY 10804 *Tel:* 914-235-7808 *Fax:* 914-576-1432 *E-mail:* mreinerlit@aol.com, pg 532

Nathan Reingold Prize, 440 Geddes Hall, Notre Dame, IN 46556 *Tel:* 574-631-1194 *E-mail:* info@hssonline.org *Web Site:* www.hssonline.org, pg 684

Renaissance House, 465 Westview Ave, Englewood, NJ 07631 *Tel:* 201-408-4048 *E-mail:* info@renaissancehouse.net *Web Site:* www.renaissancehouse.net, pg 198

Renaissance House, 465 Westview Ave, Englewood, NJ 07631 *Tel:* 201-408-4048 *E-mail:* laredo@renaissancehouse.net; contact@renaissancehouse.net *Web Site:* www.renaissancehouse.net, pg 544

Renaissance Literary & Talent, PO Box 17379, Beverly Hills, CA 90209 *Tel:* 323-848-8305 *Fax:* 424-298-2588 *E-mail:* query@renaissancemgmt.net *Web Site:* renaissancemgmt.net, pg 532

The Amy Rennert Agency Inc, 1550 Tiburon Blvd, Suite 302, Tiburon, CA 94920 *Tel:* 415-789-8955 *E-mail:* queries@amyrennert.com *Web Site:* amyrennert.com, pg 532

Arthur Rense Prize, 633 W 155 St, New York, NY 10032 *Tel:* 212-368-5900 *Fax:* 212-491-4615 *E-mail:* academy@artsandletters.org *Web Site:* www.artsandletters.org, pg 684

Reporters Committee for Freedom of the Press, 1156 15 St NW, Suite 1250, Washington, DC 20005-1779 *Tel:* 202-795-9300 *Toll Free Tel:* 800-336-4243 *E-mail:* info@rcfp.org *Web Site:* www.rcfp.org, pg 577

Research & Education Association (REA), 61 Ethel Rd W, Piscataway, NJ 08854 *Tel:* 732-819-8880 *Fax:* 732-819-8808 (orders) *E-mail:* info@rea.com *Web Site:* www.rea.com, pg 198

Research Press, 2612 N Mattis Ave, Champaign, IL 61822 *Tel:* 217-352-3273 *Toll Free Tel:* 800-519-2707 *Fax:* 217-352-1221 *E-mail:* rp@researchpress.com; orders@researchpress.com *Web Site:* www.researchpress.com, pg 198

Research Research, 240 E 27 St, Suite 20-K, New York, NY 10016-9238 *Tel:* 212-779-9540 *Fax:* 212-779-9540 *E-mail:* ehtac@msn.com, pg 500

Residency, 454 E Hill Rd, Austerlitz, NY 12017 *Tel:* 518-392-3103; 518-392-4144 *E-mail:* apply@millaycolony.org *Web Site:* www.millaycolony.org, pg 684

Resilient Publishing, 406 S Third St, Boise, ID 83702 *Tel:* 208-258-9544 *E-mail:* submissions@resilientpublishing.com *Web Site:* www.resilientpublishing.com; www.facebook.com/ResilientPub, pg 198

Revell, PO Box 6287, Grand Rapids, MI 49516-6287 *Tel:* 616-676-9185 *Toll Free Tel:* 800-877-2665; 800-679-1957 *Fax:* 616-676-9573 *Web Site:* www.bakerpublishinggroup.com, pg 198

Review & Herald Publishing Association, 55 W Oak Ridge Dr, Hagerstown, MD 21740 *Tel:* 301-393-3000 *Toll Free Tel:* 800-234-7630; 800-456-3991 *Fax:* 301-393-3222 (book div) *Web Site:* www.reviewandherald.com; www.rhpa.org, pg 199

The Harold U Ribalow Prize, 40 Wall St, 8th fl, New York, NY 10005-1387 *Tel:* 212-451-6286 *Fax:* 212-451-6257 *E-mail:* magtemp3@hadassah.org *Web Site:* www.hadassah.org/magazine, pg 684

Evelyn Richardson Nonfiction Award, 1113 Marginal Rd, Halifax, NS B3H 4P7, Canada *Tel:* 902-423-8116 *Fax:* 902-422-0881 *E-mail:* contact@writers.ns.ca *Web Site:* writers.ns.ca, pg 684

The Ridenhour Book Prize, 116 E 16 St, 8th fl, New York, NY 10003 *Tel:* 212-822-0250 *Fax:* 212-253-5356 *E-mail:* ridenhour@nationinstitute.org *Web Site:* www.ridenhour.org, pg 684

The Ridenhour Courage Prize, 116 E 16 St, 8th fl, New York, NY 10003 *Tel:* 212-822-0250 *Fax:* 212-253-5356 *E-mail:* ridenhour@nationinstitute.org *Web Site:* www.ridenhour.org, pg 685

The Ridenhour Prize for Truth-Telling, 116 E 16 St, 8th fl, New York, NY 10003 *Tel:* 212-822-0250 *Fax:* 212-253-5356 *E-mail:* ridenhour@nationinstitute.org *Web Site:* www.ridenhour.org, pg 685

Lynne Rienner Publishers Inc, 1800 30 St, Suite 314, Boulder, CO 80301 *Tel:* 303-444-6684 *Fax:* 303-444-0824 *E-mail:* questions@rienner.com; cservice@rienner.com *Web Site:* www.rienner.com, pg 199

Gwen Pharis Ringwood Award for Drama, 11759 Groat Rd, Edmonton, AB T5M 3K6, Canada *Tel:* 780-422-8174 *Toll Free Tel:* 800-665-5354 (AB only) *Fax:* 780-422-2663 (attn WGA) *E-mail:* mail@writersguild.ca *Web Site:* writersguild.ca, pg 685

Rio Nuevo Publishers, 451 N Bonita Ave, Tucson, AZ 85745 *Tel:* 520-623-9558 *Toll Free Tel:* 800-969-9558 *Fax:* 520-624-5888 *Toll Free Fax:* 800-715-5888 *E-mail:* info@rionuevo.com (cust serv) *Web Site:* www.rionuevo.com, pg 199

Rising Sun Publishing, PO Box 70906, Marietta, GA 30007-0906 *Tel:* 770-518-0369 *Toll Free Tel:* 800-524-2813 *Fax:* 770-587-0862 *E-mail:* info@rspublishing.com *Web Site:* www.rspublishing.com, pg 199

Ann Rittenberg Literary Agency Inc, 15 Maiden Lane, Suite 206, New York, NY 10038 *Tel:* 212-684-6936 *Fax:* 212-684-6929 *E-mail:* info@rittlit.com *Web Site:* www.rittlit.com, pg 532

Jack D Rittenhouse Award, 17501 Hill Way, Lake Oswego, OR 97035 *Tel:* 503-901-9865 *Web Site:* pubwest.org, pg 685

Judith Riven Literary Agent LLC, 250 W 16 St, Suite 4F, New York, NY 10011 *Tel:* 212-255-1009 *Fax:* 212-255-8547 *E-mail:* rivenlitqueries@gmail.com *Web Site:* rivenlit.com, pg 500, 533

Rivendell Books, PO Box 29348, St Louis, MO 63126-0348 *Tel:* 314-609-6534 *E-mail:* butch@rivendellbooks.com *Web Site:* www.rivendellbooks.com, pg 478

River City Publishing LLC, 1719 Mulberry St, Montgomery, AL 36106 *Tel:* 334-265-6753 *Fax:* 334-265-8880 *E-mail:* sales@rivercitypublishing.com *Web Site:* rivercitypublishing.com, pg 199

River Road Press LLC, 9 Dakin, New Orleans, LA 70121 *Tel:* 504-722-8139 *Web Site:* riverroadpress.com, pg 199

Riverby Awards, 261 Floyd Ackert Rd, New York, NY 12493 *Tel:* 212-769-5169 *Fax:* 212-313-7182 *E-mail:* info@johnburroughsassociation.org *Web Site:* www.johnburroughsassociation.org, pg 685

Riverdale Avenue Books (RAB), 5676 Riverdale Ave, Bronx, NY 10471 *Tel:* 212-279-6418 *E-mail:* customerservice@riverdaleavebooks.com *Web Site:* www.riverdaleavebooks.com, pg 199

Riverhead Books, 375 Hudson St, New York, NY 10014 *Tel:* 212-366-2000 *Web Site:* www.penguin.com/publishers/riverhead, pg 199

Riverside Literary Agency, 41 Simon Keets Rd, Leyden, MA 01337 *Tel:* 413-772-0067 *Fax:* 413-772-0969 *E-mail:* rivlit@sover.net *Web Site:* www.riversideliteraryagency.com, pg 533

Rizzoli International Publications Inc, 300 Park Ave S, 4th fl, New York, NY 10010-5399 *Tel:* 212-387-3400 *Toll Free Tel:* 800-522-6657 (orders only) *Fax:* 212-387-3535 *E-mail:* publicity@rizzoliusa.com *Web Site:* www.rizzoliusa.com, pg 199

RLR Associates Ltd, 7 W 51 St, New York, NY 10019 *Tel:* 212-541-8641 *Fax:* 212-262-7084 *Web Site:* www.rlrassociates.net, pg 533

RMA, 85 Lincoln St, 1st fl, Meriden, CT 06451 *Tel:* 718-434-1893 *Fax:* 203-440-1013 *Web Site:* www.ricia.com, pg 533

The RoadRunner Press, 124 NW 32 St, Oklahoma City, OK 73118 *Tel:* 405-524-6205 *Fax:* 405-524-6312 *E-mail:* info@theroadrunnerpress.com; orders@theroadrunnerpress.com *Web Site:* www.theroadrunnerpress.com, pg 200

Roam Agency, 45 Main St, Suite 727, Brooklyn, NY 11201-1076 *E-mail:* roam@roamagency.com *Web Site:* www.roamagency.com, pg 533

Roanoke-Chowan Award for Poetry, 4610 Mail Service Ctr, Raleigh, NC 27699-4610 *Tel:* 919-807-7290 *Fax:* 919-733-8807 *Web Site:* www.history.ncdcr.gov/affiliates/lit-hist/awards/awards.htm, pg 685

Roaring Brook Press, 175 Fifth Ave, New York, NY 10010 *Tel:* 646-307-5151 *Web Site:* us.macmillan.com/publishers/roaring-brook-press, pg 200

Roaring Forties Press, 1053 Santa Fe Ave, Berkeley, CA 94706 *Tel:* 510-527-5461 *E-mail:* info@roaringfortiespress.com *Web Site:* www.roaringfortiespress.com, pg 200

BJ Robbins Literary Agency, 5130 Bellaire Ave, North Hollywood, CA 91607 *E-mail:* robbinsliterary@gmail.com, pg 533

The Roberts Group, 12803 Eastview Curve, Apple Valley, MN 55124 *Tel:* 952-322-4005 *E-mail:* info@editorialservice.com *Web Site:* www.editorialservice.com, pg 500

Rochester Institute of Technology, School of Media, Arts & Technology, 69 Lomb Memorial Dr, Rochester, NY 14623-5603 *Tel:* 585-475-2728; 585-475-5336 *Fax:* 585-475-5336 *E-mail:* spmofc@rit.edu *Web Site:* cias.rit.edu/printmedia, pg 622

RockBench Publishing Corp, 6101 Stillmeadow Dr, Nashville, TN 37211-6518 *Tel:* 615-831-2277 *Fax:* 615-831-2212 *E-mail:* info@rockbench.com, pg 200

The Rockefeller University Press, 950 Third Ave, 2nd fl, New York, NY 10022 *Tel:* 212-327-7938 *Fax:* 212-319-1081 *E-mail:* rupress@rockefeller.edu *Web Site:* www.rupress.org, pg 200

RockHill Publishing LLC, PO Box 62241, Virginia Beach, VA 23466-2241 *Tel:* 757-692-2021 *E-mail:* jlh@rockhillpublishing.com *Web Site:* rockhillpublishing.com, pg 200

Rocky Mountain Book Award, PO Box 42, Lethbridge, AB T1J 3Y3, Canada *Tel:* 403-381-7164 *E-mail:* rockymountainbookaward@shaw.ca *Web Site:* www.rmba.info, pg 685

Rocky Mountain Books Ltd (RMB), 103-1075 Pendergast St, Victoria, BC V8V 0A1, Canada *Tel:* 250-360-0829 *Fax:* 250-386-0829 *Web Site:* www.rmbooks.com, pg 469

Rocky Mountain Mineral Law Foundation, 9191 Sheridan Blvd, Suite 203, Westminster, CO 80031 *Tel:* 303-321-8100 *Fax:* 303-321-7657 *E-mail:* info@rmmlf.org *Web Site:* www.rmmlf.org, pg 200

Rod & Staff Publishers Inc, Hwy 172, Crockett, KY 41413 *Tel:* 606-522-4348 *Fax:* 606-522-4896 *Toll Free Fax:* 800-643-1244 (US orders), pg 200

Rodale Inc, 400 S Tenth St, Emmaus, PA 18049 *Tel:* 610-967-5171 *Toll Free Tel:* 866-387-0509 *E-mail:* bookmarketing@rodale.com; bookpublicity@rodale.com *Web Site:* www.rodale.com, pg 200

Roger Williams Agency, 17 Paddock Dr, Lawrence Twp, NJ 08648 *Tel:* 860-973-2439 *E-mail:* roger@rogerwilliamsagency.com *Web Site:* www.rogerwilliamsagency.com, pg 533

Rogers Writers' Trust Fiction Prize, 460 Richmond St W, Suite 600, Toronto, ON M5V 1Y1, Canada *Tel:* 416-504-8222 *Toll Free Tel:* 877-906-6548 *Fax:* 416-504-9090 *E-mail:* info@writerstrust.com *Web Site:* www.writerstrust.com, pg 685

Linda Roghaar Literary Agency LLC, 133 High Point Dr, Amherst, MA 01002 *Tel:* 413-256-1921 *E-mail:* contact@lindaroghaar.com *Web Site:* www.lindaroghaar.com, pg 533

Sami Rohr Prize for Jewish Literature, 520 Eighth Ave, 4th fl, New York, NY 10018 *Tel:* 212-201-2920 *Fax:* 212-532-4952 *E-mail:* jbc@jewishbooks.org *Web Site:* www.jewishbookcouncil.org, pg 685

The Roistacher Literary Agency, 545 W 111 St, Suite 7-J, New York, NY 10025 *Tel:* 212-222-1405, pg 533

Roman Catholic Books, PO Box 2286, Fort Collins, CO 80522-2286 *Tel:* 970-490-2735 *Fax:* 904-493-8781 *Web Site:* www.booksforcatholics.com, pg 201

Romance Writers of America®, 14615 Benfer Rd, Houston, TX 77069 *Tel:* 832-717-5200 *Fax:* 832-717-5201 *E-mail:* info@rwa.org *Web Site:* www.rwa.org, pg 577

Romance Writers of America Annual Conference, 14615 Benfer Rd, Houston, TX 77069 *Tel:* 832-717-5200 *Fax:* 832-717-5201 *E-mail:* info@rwa.org *Web Site:* www.rwa.org, pg 614

Romance Writers of America Awards, 14615 Benfer Rd, Houston, TX 77069 *Tel:* 832-717-5200 *Fax:* 832-717-5201 *E-mail:* info@rwa.org *Web Site:* www.rwa.org, pg 685

Roncorp Music, PO Box 517, Glenmoore, PA 19343 *Tel:* 610-942-2370 *Toll Free Tel:* 866-385-8446 *Fax:* 610-942-0660 *E-mail:* info@nemusicpub.com *Web Site:* www.nemusicpub.com, pg 201

Ronin Publishing Inc, PO Box 3436, Oakland, CA 94609 *Tel:* 510-420-3669 *Fax:* 510-420-3672 *E-mail:* ronin@roninpub.com *Web Site:* www.roninpub.com, pg 201

Ronsdale Press Ltd, 3350 W 21 Ave, Vancouver, BC V6S 1G7, Canada *Tel:* 604-738-4688 *Fax:* 604-731-4548 *E-mail:* ronsdale@shaw.ca *Web Site:* ronsdalepress.com, pg 469

Peter Rooney, 332 Bleecker St, PMB X-6, New York, NY 10014-2980 *Tel:* 917-376-1792 *Fax:* 212-226-8047 *E-mail:* magnetix@ix.netcom.com *Web Site:* www.magneticreports.com, pg 500

Robert Rose Inc, 120 Eglinton Ave E, Suite 800, Toronto, ON M4P 1E2, Canada *Tel:* 416-322-6552 *Fax:* 416-322-6936 *Web Site:* www.robertrose.ca, pg 469

Rosemont College, Graduate Publg Prog, 1400 Montgomery Ave, Rosemont, PA 19010 *Tel:* 610-527-0200 (ext 2336) *Fax:* 610-526-2964 *Web Site:* www.rosemont.edu, pg 622

The Rosen Publishing Group Inc, 29 E 21 St, New York, NY 10010 *Toll Free Tel:* 800-237-9932 *Toll Free Fax:* 888-436-4643 *E-mail:* info@rosenpub.com *Web Site:* www.rosenpublishing.com, pg 201

The Rosenberg Group, 23 Lincoln Ave, Marblehead, MA 01945 *Tel:* 781-990-1341 *Fax:* 781-990-1344 *E-mail:* rosenberglitsubmit@icloud.com *Web Site:* www.rosenberggroup.com, pg 533

Rita Rosenkranz Literary Agency, 440 West End Ave, Suite 15D, New York, NY 10024-5358 *Tel:* 212-873-6333 *Fax:* 212-873-5225 *Web Site:* www.ritarosenkranzliteraryagency.com, pg 533

Rosenthal Family Foundation Awards, 633 W 155 St, New York, NY 10032 *Tel:* 212-368-5900 *Fax:* 212-491-4615 *E-mail:* academy@artsandletters.org *Web Site:* www.artsandletters.org, pg 685

Rosenthal Represents, 23725 Hartland St, West Hills, CA 91307 *Tel:* 818-222-5445 *E-mail:* eliselicenses@earthlink.net, pg 544

RosettaBooks, 55 Broadway, Suite 2002, New York, NY 10006 *Tel:* 646-274-1970 *Fax:* 212-977-5997 (e-fax) *E-mail:* rights@rosettabooks.com; production@rosettabooks.com *Web Site:* www.rosettabooks.com, pg 201

Ross Books, PO Box 4340, Berkeley, CA 94704-0340 *Tel:* 510-841-2474 *Fax:* 510-295-2531 *E-mail:* sales@rossbooks.com *Web Site:* www.rossbooks.com, pg 201

Margaret W Rossiter History of Women in Science Prize, 440 Geddes Hall, Notre Dame, IN 46556 *Tel:* 574-631-1194 *E-mail:* info@hssonline.org *Web Site:* www.hssonline.org, pg 685

Rotary Club of Charlottetown Royalty Creative Writing Awards for Young People, 81 Prince St, Charlottetown, PE C1A 4R3, Canada *E-mail:* peiliteraryawards@gmail.com *Web Site:* www.peiwritersguild.com, pg 685

Lois Roth Award, 85 Broad St, Suite 500, New York, NY 10004-2434 *Tel:* 646-576-5141; 646-576-5000 *Fax:* 646-458-0030 *E-mail:* awards@mla.org *Web Site:* www.mla.org, pg 686

Rothstein Associates Inc, 4 Arapaho Rd, Brookfield, CT 06804-3104 *Tel:* 203-740-7400 *Toll Free Tel:* 888-768-4783 *Fax:* 203-740-7401 *E-mail:* info@rothstein.com *Web Site:* www.rothstein.com; www.rothsteinpublishing.com, pg 201

Jane Rotrosen Agency LLC, 85 Broad St, 28th fl, New York, NY 10004 *Tel:* 212-593-4330 *Fax:* 212-935-6985 *Web Site:* janerotrosen.com, pg 533

The Rough Notes Co Inc, 11690 Technology Dr, Carmel, IN 46032-5600 *Tel:* 317-582-1600 *Toll Free Tel:* 800-428-4384 (cust serv) *Fax:* 317-816-1000 *Toll Free Fax:* 800-321-1909 *E-mail:* rnc@roughnotes.com *Web Site:* www.roughnotes.com, pg 201

Round Table Companies, 1027 Kenton Rd, Deerfield, IL 60015 *Tel:* 949-375-1006 *Fax:* 815-346-2398 *Web Site:* www.roundtablecompanies.com, pg 201

Routledge, 711 Third Ave, New York, NY 10017 *Tel:* 212-216-7800 *Toll Free Tel:* 800-634-7064 (order enquiries, cust servs) *Fax:* 212-564-7854 *Web Site:* www.routledge.com, pg 202

Rowman & Littlefield Publishers Inc, 4501 Forbes Blvd, Suite 200, Lanham, MD 20706 *Tel:* 301-459-3366 *Toll Free Tel:* 800-462-6420 (cust serv) *Fax:* 301-429-5748 *Web Site:* rowman.com, pg 202

Dick Rowson, 4701 Connecticut Ave NW, Suite 503, Washington, DC 20008 *Tel:* 202-244-8104 *E-mail:* rcrowson2@aol.com, pg 501

Royal Fireworks Press, PO Box 399, Unionville, NY 10988 *Tel:* 845-726-4444 *Fax:* 845-726-3824 *E-mail:* mail@rfwp.com *Web Site:* www.rfwp.com, pg 202

Royal Ontario Museum Press, 100 Queen's Park, Toronto, ON M5S 2C6, Canada *Tel:* 416-586-8000 *Fax:* 416-586-5642 *E-mail:* info@rom.on.ca *Web Site:* www.rom.on.ca, pg 469

Royce Carlton Inc, 866 United Nations Plaza, Suite 587, New York, NY 10017-1880 *Tel:* 212-355-7700 *Toll Free Tel:* 800-LECTURE (532-8873) *Fax:* 212-888-8659 *E-mail:* info@roycecarlton.com *Web Site:* www.roycecarlton.com, pg 547

Lexi Rudnitsky First Book Prize in Poetry, 277 Broadway, Suite 708, New York, NY 10007 *Tel:* 212-260-9256 *Fax:* 212-267-3165 *E-mail:* info@perseabooks.com *Web Site:* www.perseabooks.com, pg 686

William B Ruggles Journalism Scholarship, 5211 Port Royal Rd, Suite 510, Springfield, VA 22151 *Tel:* 703-321-9606 *Fax:* 703-321-7143 *Web Site:* www.nilrr.org, pg 686

Russell Sage Foundation, 112 E 64 St, New York, NY 10065 *Tel:* 212-750-6000 *Toll Free Tel:* 800-524-6401 *Fax:* 212-371-4761 *E-mail:* info@rsage.org *Web Site:* www.russellsage.org, pg 202

Russian Information Services Inc, PO Box 567, Montpelier, VT 05601 *Tel:* 802-223-4955 *Toll Free Tel:* 800-639-4301 *E-mail:* orders@russianlife.com *Web Site:* www.russianlife.com, pg 202

Rutgers University Press, 106 Somerset St, 3rd fl, New Brunswick, NJ 08901 *Tel:* 848-445-7762 *Toll Free Tel:* 800-848-6224 (orders only) *Fax:* 732-745-4935 (acqs, edit, mktg, perms & prodn) *Toll Free Fax:* 800-272-6817 (fulfillment) *Web Site:* rutgerspress.rutgers.edu, pg 202

The Cornelius Ryan Award, 40 W 45 St, New York, NY 10036 *Tel:* 212-626-9220 *Fax:* 212-626-9210 *E-mail:* info@opcofamerica.org *Web Site:* www.opcofamerica.org, pg 686

Regina Ryan Books, 251 Central Park W, Suite 7-D, New York, NY 10024 *Tel:* 212-787-5589 *E-mail:* queries@reginaryanbooks.com *Web Site:* www.reginaryanbooks.com, pg 534

Sachem Publishing Associates Inc, 402 W Lyon Farm Dr, Greenwich, CT 06831 *Tel:* 203-813-3077 *E-mail:* sachempub@optonline.net, pg 501

Saddleback Educational Publishing, 3120-A Pullman St, Costa Mesa, CA 92626 *Tel:* 714-640-5200 *Toll Free Tel:* 888-SDLBACK (735-2225); 800-637-8715 *Fax:* 714-640-5297 *Toll Free Fax:* 888-734-4010 *E-mail:* contact@sdlback.com *Web Site:* www.sdlback.com, pg 203

William H Sadlier Inc, 9 Pine St, New York, NY 10005 *Tel:* 212-227-2120 *Toll Free Tel:* 800-221-5175 (cust serv) *Fax:* 212-312-6080 *E-mail:* customerservice@sadlier.com *Web Site:* www.sadlier.com, pg 203

SAE (Society of Automotive Engineers International), 400 Commonwealth Dr, Warrendale, PA 15096-0001 *Tel:* 724-776-4841; 724-776-4970 (outside US & CN) *Toll Free Tel:* 877-606-7323 (cust serv) *Fax:* 724-776-0790 (cust serv) *E-mail:* publications@sae.org; customerservice@sae.org *Web Site:* www.sae.org, pg 203

Aldo & Jeanne Scaglione Prize for Studies in Slavic Languages & Literatures, 85 Broad St, Suite 500, New York, NY 10004-2434 *Tel:* 646-576-5141; 646-576-5000 *Fax:* 646-458-0030 *E-mail:* awards@mla.org *Web Site:* www.mla.org, pg 687

Aldo & Jeanne Scaglione Publication Award for a Manuscript in Italian Literary Studies, 85 Broad St, Suite 500, New York, NY 10004-2434 *Tel:* 646-576-5141; 646-576-5000 *Fax:* 646-458-0030 *E-mail:* awards@mla.org *Web Site:* www.mla.org, pg 687

Jack Scagnetti Talent & Literary Agency, 5136 Vineland Ave, North Hollywood, CA 91601 *Tel:* 818-762-3871 *Web Site:* www.jackscagnettiagency.com; www.facebook.com/jackscagnettiagency/, pg 534

William Sanders Scarborough Prize, 85 Broad St, Suite 500, New York, NY 10004-2434 *Tel:* 646-576-5141; 646-576-5000 *Fax:* 646-458-0030 *E-mail:* awards@mla.org *Web Site:* www.mla.org, pg 688

Scarecrow Press Inc, 4501 Forbes Blvd, Suite 200, Lanham, MD 20706 *Tel:* 301-459-3366 *Fax:* 301-429-5748 *Web Site:* www.scarecrowpress.com, pg 207

SCBWI-FL Florida Regional Conference, 125 E Merritt Island Causeway, Suite 209, Merritt Island, FL 32952 *Tel:* 321-338-7208 *E-mail:* florida@scbwi.org *Web Site:* florida.scbwi.org, pg 614

SCBWI-FL Mid-Year Workshops, 125 E Merritt Island Causeway, Suite 209, Merritt Island, FL 32952 *Tel:* 321-338-7208 *E-mail:* florida@scbwi.org *Web Site:* florida.scbwi.org, pg 614

SCBWI Work-In-Progress Grants, 4727 Wilshire Blvd, Suite 301, Los Angeles, CA 90010 *Tel:* 323-782-1010; 310-403-0675 (cell) *Fax:* 323-782-1892 *E-mail:* grants@scbwi.org; scbwi@scbwi.org *Web Site:* www.scbwi.org, pg 688

Scepter Publishers, PO Box 360694, Strongsville, OH 44149 *Tel:* 212-354-0670 *Toll Free Tel:* 800-322-8773 *Fax:* 212-354-0736 *Web Site:* www.scepterpublishers.org, pg 207

William D Schaeffer Environmental Award, 301 Brush Creek Rd, Warrendale, PA 15086-7529 *Tel:* 412-741-6860 *Toll Free Tel:* 800-910-4283 *Fax:* 412-741-2311 *E-mail:* printingind@comm.printing.org *Web Site:* www.printing.org/schaefferaward, pg 688

Schaffner Press, PO Box 41567, Tucson, AZ 85717 *E-mail:* tim@schaffnerpress.com *Web Site:* www.schaffnerpress.com, pg 207

C J Scheiner Books, PO Box 96, Brooklyn, NY 11226-0096 *Tel:* 718-469-1089, pg 501

Schiavone Literary Agency Inc, 236 Trails End, West Palm Beach, FL 33413-2135 *Tel:* 561-966-9294 *Fax:* 561-966-9294 *E-mail:* profschia@aol.com *Web Site:* www.publishersmarketplace.com/members/profschia, pg 534

Schiffer Publishing Ltd, 4880 Lower Valley Rd, Atglen, PA 19310 *Tel:* 610-593-1777 *Fax:* 610-593-2002 *E-mail:* info@schifferbooks.com *Web Site:* www.schifferbooks.com, pg 207

G Schirmer Inc/Associated Music Publishers Inc, 180 Madison Ave, 24th fl, New York, NY 10016 *Tel:* 212-254-2100 *Fax:* 212-254-2013 *E-mail:* schirmer@schirmer.com; info@musicsales.com *Web Site:* www.musicsalesclassical.com, pg 207

Schlager Group Inc, 325 N Saint Paul, Suite 3425, Dallas, TX 75201 *Toll Free Tel:* 888-416-5727 *Fax:* 214-347-9469 *E-mail:* info@schlagergroup.com *Web Site:* www.schlagergroup.com, pg 207

Wendy Schmalz Agency, 402 Union St, Unit 831, Hudson, NY 12534 *Tel:* 518-672-7697 *E-mail:* wendy@schmalzagency.com *Web Site:* www.schmalzagency.com, pg 534

Harold Schmidt Literary Agency, 415 W 23 St, Suite 6-F, New York, NY 10011 *Tel:* 212-727-7473, pg 534

Bernadotte E Schmitt Grants, 400 "A" St SE, Washington, DC 20003 *Tel:* 202-544-2422 *Fax:* 202-544-8307 *E-mail:* awards@historians.org *Web Site:* www.historians.org, pg 688

Scholastic Canada Ltd, 604 King St W, Toronto, ON M5V 1E1, Canada *Tel:* 905-887-7323 *Toll Free Tel:* 800-268-3860 (CN) *Toll Free Fax:* 866-387-4944 *E-mail:* custserve@scholastic.ca *Web Site:* www.scholastic.ca, pg 469

Scholastic Education, 557 Broadway, New York, NY 10012 *Tel:* 212-343-6100 *Fax:* 212-343-6189 *Web Site:* www.scholastic.com, pg 207

Scholastic Inc, 557 Broadway, New York, NY 10012 *Tel:* 212-343-6100 *Toll Free Tel:* 800-SCHOLASTIC (724-6527) *Web Site:* www.scholastic.com, pg 208

Scholastic International, 557 Broadway, New York, NY 10012 *Tel:* 212-343-6100; 646-330-5288 (intl cust serv) *Toll Free Tel:* 800-SCHOLASTIC (724-6527) *Fax:* 646-837-7878 *E-mail:* international@scholastic.com, pg 208

Scholastic Trade Division, 557 Broadway, New York, NY 10012 *Tel:* 212-343-6100; 212-343-4685 (export sales) *Fax:* 212-343-4714 (export sales) *Web Site:* www.scholastic.com, pg 208

Schonfeld & Associates Inc, 1931 Lynn Circle, Libertyville, IL 60048 *Tel:* 847-816-4870 *Toll Free Tel:* 800-205-0030 *Fax:* 847-816-4872 *E-mail:* saiinfo@saibooks.com *Web Site:* www.saibooks.com, pg 208

School for Advanced Research Press, 660 Garcia St, Santa Fe, NM 87505 *Tel:* 505-954-7206 *Toll Free Tel:* 888-390-6070 *E-mail:* press@sarsf.org *Web Site:* sarweb.org, pg 208

School Guide Publications, 606 Halstead Ave, Mamaroneck, NY 10543 *Tel:* 914-632-1220 *Toll Free Tel:* 800-433-7771 *Fax:* 914-632-3412 *E-mail:* info@religiousministries.com *Web Site:* www.graduateguide.com; www.schoolguides.com; www.religiousministries.com, pg 208

School of Government, University of North Carolina, CB 3330, Chapel Hill, NC 27599-3330 *Tel:* 919-966-4119 *Fax:* 919-962-2709 *Web Site:* www.sog.unc.edu, pg 208

School of Visual Arts, 209 E 23 St, New York, NY 10010-3994 *Tel:* 212-592-2100 *Fax:* 212-592-2116 *Web Site:* www.sva.edu, pg 622

School Zone Publishing Co, 1819 Industrial Dr, Grand Haven, MI 49417 *Tel:* 616-846-5030 *Toll Free Tel:* 800-253-0564 *Fax:* 616-846-6181 *Toll Free Fax:* 800-550-4618 (orders only) *Web Site:* www.schoolzone.com, pg 208

Schoolhouse Indexing, 10-B Parade Ground Rd, Etna, NH 03750 *Tel:* 603-643-1617 *Web Site:* schoolhouseindexing.com, pg 501

Schoolhouse Network, PO Box 1518, Northampton, MA 01061 *Tel:* 480-427-4836 *E-mail:* schoolhousenetwork@gmail.com, pg 501

Schreiber Publishing, PO Box 4193, Rockville, MD 20849 *Tel:* 301-589-5831 *Toll Free Tel:* 800-296-1961 (sales) *Fax:* 667-309-6993 *E-mail:* publisher@schreiberpublishing.net *Web Site:* schreiberlanguage.com; shengold.com, pg 209

Schroeder Indexing Services, 23 Camilla Pink Ct, Bluffton, SC 29909 *Tel:* 843-705-9779 *E-mail:* sanindex@schroederindexing.com *Web Site:* www.schroederindexing.com, pg 501

Franklin L Schulaner, PO Box 507, Kealakekua, HI 96750-0507 *Tel:* 808-322-3785 *E-mail:* fschulaner@hawaii.rr.com, pg 501

Susan Schulman Literary Agency LLC, 454 W 44 St, New York, NY 10036 *Tel:* 212-713-1633 *E-mail:* queries@schulmanagency.com; linda@schulmanagency.com (translation & audio rts), pg 534

Sherri Schultz/Words with Grace, 1631 16 Ave, Seattle, WA 98122 *Tel:* 206-323-3348 *E-mail:* WordsWithGraceEditorial@gmail.com, pg 501

The Schuna Group Inc, 1503 Briarknoll Dr, Arden Hills, MN 55112 *Tel:* 651-631-8480 *Web Site:* www.schunagroup.com, pg 544

Laurens R Schwartz, Esquire, 5 E 22 St, Suite 15-D, New York, NY 10010-5325 *Tel:* 212-228-2614, pg 535

Ruth & Sylvia Schwartz Children's Book Awards, c/o Ontario Arts Council, 121 Bloor St E, 7th fl, Toronto, ON M4W 3M5, Canada *Tel:* 416-961-1660 *Toll Free Tel:* 800-387-0058 (ON) *Fax:* 416-961-7796 (Ontario Arts Council); 416-969-7450 (Ontario Arts Foundation) *E-mail:* info@arts.on.ca; foundation@arts.on.ca *Web Site:* www.arts.on.ca; ontarioartsfoundation.on.ca/pages/ruth-sylvia-schwartz-awards, pg 688

Science & Humanities Press, 63 Summit Point, St Charles, MO 63301-0571 *Tel:* 636-394-4950 *Web Site:* sciencehumanitiespress.com; beachhousebooks.com; macroprintbooks.com; earlyeditionsbooks.com; heuristicsbooks.com, pg 209

Science Fiction & Fantasy Writers of America Inc (SFWA), PO Box 3238, Enfield, CT 06083-3238 *E-mail:* office@sfwa.org *Web Site:* www.sfwa.org, pg 577

Science Fiction Writers Workshop, University of Kansas, Wescoe Hall, Rm 3001, Dept of English, 1445 Jayhawk Blvd, Lawrence, KS 66045 *Tel:* 785-864-2518 *Fax:* 785-864-1159 *Web Site:* www.sfcenter.ku.edu; www.sfcenter.ku.edu/sfworkshop; www.sfcenter.ku.edu/novel-workshop, pg 614

Science in Society Journalism Awards, PO Box 7905, Berkeley, CA 94707 *Tel:* 510-647-9500 *Web Site:* www.nasw.org, pg 688

Science, Naturally, 725 Eighth St SE, Washington, DC 20003 *Tel:* 202-465-4798 *Toll Free Tel:* 866-724-9876 *Fax:* 202-558-2132 *E-mail:* info@sciencenaturally.com *Web Site:* www.sciencenaturally.com, pg 209

ScienceThrillers Media, PO Box 601392, Sacramento, CA 95860-1392 *Tel:* 916-712-3334 *E-mail:* query@sciencethrillersmedia.com *Web Site:* www.sciencethrillersmedia.com, pg 209

Scobre Press Corp, 2255 Calle Clara, La Jolla, CA 92037 *Fax:* 858-551-1232 *E-mail:* info@scobre.com *Web Site:* www.scobre.com; scobre.bookbuddyaudio.com, pg 209

S©ott Treimel NY, 434 Lafayette St, New York, NY 10003-6943 *Tel:* 212-505-8353 *E-mail:* general@scotttreimelny.com *Web Site:* scotttreimelny.com; scotttreimelny.blogspot.com, pg 535

Scovil Galen Ghosh Literary Agency Inc, 276 Fifth Ave, Suite 708, New York, NY 10001 *Tel:* 212-679-8686 *Fax:* 212-679-6710 *E-mail:* info@sgglit.com *Web Site:* www.sgglit.com, pg 535

Scribendi Inc, 405 Riverview Dr, Chatham, ON N7M 0N3, Canada *Tel:* 519-351-1626 (cust serv) *Fax:* 519-354-0192 *E-mail:* customerservice@scribendi.com *Web Site:* www.scribendi.com, pg 501

Scribner, 1230 Avenue of the Americas, New York, NY 10020, pg 209

Scripta Humanistica Publishing International, 1383 Kersey Lane, Potomac, MD 20854 *Tel:* 301-294-7949 *Fax:* 301-424-9584 *E-mail:* info@scriptahumanistica.com *Web Site:* www.scriptahumanistica.com, pg 209

The Scriptural Research & Publishing Co Inc, 344 E Johnson Ave, Cheshire, CT 06410 *Tel:* 203-272-1780 *Fax:* 203-272-2296 *E-mail:* src1@srpublish.org *Web Site:* www.scripturalresearch.com, pg 210

SDP Publishing Solutions LLC, 36 Captain's Way, East Bridgewater, MA 02333 *Tel:* 617-775-0656 *Web Site:* www.sdppublishingsolutions.com, pg 501

SDSU Writers' Conference, 5250 Campanile Dr, Rm 2503, San Diego, CA 92182-1920 *Tel:* 619-594-5821 *Fax:* 619-594-8566 *E-mail:* sdsuwritersconference@mail.sdsu.edu *Web Site:* www.neverstoplearning.net/writers, pg 614

Seal Books, 320 Front St W, Suite 1400, Toronto, ON M5V 3B6, Canada *Tel:* 416-364-4449 *Toll Free Tel:* 888-523-9292 (order desk) *Fax:* 416-598-7764 *Web Site:* www.penguinrandomhouse.ca, pg 470

Search Institute Press®, The Banks Bldg, Suite 125, 615 First Ave NE, Minneapolis, MN 55413 *Tel:* 612-376-8955; 612-692-5520 *Toll Free Tel:* 800-888-7828 *Fax:* 612-692-5553 *E-mail:* si@search-institute.org *Web Site:* www.search-institute.org, pg 210

Second Chance Press, 4170 Noyac Rd, Sag Harbor, NY 11963 *Tel:* 631-725-1101 *E-mail:* info@thepermanentpress.com *Web Site:* www.thepermanentpress.com, pg 210

Second Story Press, 20 Maud St, Suite 401, Toronto, ON M5V 2M5, Canada *Tel:* 416-537-7850 *Fax:* 416-537-0588 *E-mail:* info@secondstorypress.ca *Web Site:* secondstorypress.ca, pg 470

See-More's Workshop Arts & Education Workshops, 325 West End Ave, Suite 12-B, New York, NY 10023 *Tel:* 212-724-0677 *Fax:* 212-724-0767 *E-mail:* sbt@shadowboxtheatre.org *Web Site:* www.shadowboxtheatre.org, pg 614

Seedling Publications Inc, 520 E Bainbridge St, Elizabethtown, PA 17022 *Toll Free Tel:* 800-233-0759 *Toll Free Fax:* 888-834-1303 *E-mail:* info@continentalpress.com *Web Site:* www.continentalpress.com, pg 210

SelectBooks Inc, 87 Walker St, Suite B1, New York, NY 10013 *Tel:* 212-206-1997 *Fax:* 212-206-3815 *E-mail:* info@selectbooks.com *Web Site:* www.selectbooks.com, pg 210

Self-Counsel Press Inc, 1481 Charlotte Rd, North Vancouver, BC V7J 1H1, Canada *Tel:* 604-986-3366 *Toll Free Tel:* 800-663-3007 *E-mail:* orders@self-counsel.com; sales@self-counsel.com *Web Site:* www.self-counsel.com, pg 470

Self-Realization Fellowship Publishers, 3208 Humboldt St, Los Angeles, CA 90031 *Tel:* 323-276-6002 *Toll Free Tel:* 888-773-8680 *Fax:* 323-927-1624 *E-mail:* sales@yogananda-srf.org *Web Site:* www.yogananda-srf.org; bookstore.yogananda-srf.org/ (orders), pg 210

Lynn Seligman, 400 Highland Ave, Upper Montclair, NJ 07043 *Tel:* 973-783-3631 *Fax:* 973-783-3691 *E-mail:* seliglit@aol.com, pg 535

Edythea Ginis Selman Literary Agency Inc, 14 Washington Place, New York, NY 10003 *Tel:* 212-473-1874 *Fax:* 212-473-1875, pg 535

Richard Selman, 14 Washington Place, New York, NY 10003 *Tel:* 212-473-1874 *Fax:* 212-473-1875, pg 501

Alexa Selph, 4300 McClatchey Circle, Atlanta, GA 30342 *Tel:* 404-256-3717 *E-mail:* lexa101@aol.com, pg 501

Sentient Publications LLC, PO Box 7204, Boulder, CO 80306 *Tel:* 303-443-2188 *Fax:* 303-381-2538 *E-mail:* contact@sentientpublications.com *Web Site:* www.sentientpublications.com, pg 210

The Robert S Sergeant Memorial, 900 Timber Creek Place, Virginia Beach, VA 23464 *E-mail:* poetryinva@aol.com *Web Site:* poetrysocietyofvirginia.org, pg 688

Serindia Publications, PO Box 10335, Chicago, IL 60610-0335 *Fax:* 312-664-4389 *E-mail:* info@serindia.com *Web Site:* www.serindia.com, pg 210

Seven Stories Press, 140 Watts St, New York, NY 10013 *Tel:* 212-226-8760 *Toll Free Tel:* 800-733-3000 (orders) *Fax:* 212-226-1411 *E-mail:* info@sevenstories.com *Web Site:* www.sevenstories.com, pg 211

1765 Productions, PO Box 4151, Fairfax, VA 22124-8151 *Tel:* 202-813-9421 *E-mail:* 1765productions@gmail.com, pg 211

Seventh Avenue Literary Agency, 2052 124 St, South Surrey, BC V4A 9K3, Canada *Tel:* 604-538-7252 *Fax:* 604-538-7252 *E-mail:* info@seventhavenuelit.com *Web Site:* www.seventhavenuelit.com, pg 535

Sewanee Writers' Conference, Stamler Ctr, 119 Gailor Hall, 735 University Ave, Sewanee, TN 37383 *Tel:* 931-598-1141; 931-598-1654 *E-mail:* swc@sewanee.edu *Web Site:* www.sewaneewriters.org, pg 614

The Seymour Agency, 475 Miner Street Rd, Canton, NY 13617 *Tel:* 315-386-1831 *Web Site:* www.theseymouragency.com, pg 535

SF Canada, c/o Judy McCrosky, Secy-Treas, 516 Ninth St E, Saskatoon, SK S7N 0B1, Canada *Web Site:* www.sfcanada.org, pg 577

SFWA Nebula Awards, PO Box 3238, Enfield, CT 06083-3238 *E-mail:* office@sfwa.org *Web Site:* www.sfwa.org, pg 688

Shadow Mountain, PO Box 30178, Salt Lake City, UT 84130-0178 *Tel:* 801-534-1515 *Toll Free Tel:* 800-453-3876 *Fax:* 801-517-3119 *E-mail:* submissions@shadowmountain.com *Web Site:* shadowmountain.com, pg 211

Shambhala Publications Inc, 4720 Walnut St, Boulder, CO 80301 *Tel:* 303-222-9598 *Toll Free Tel:* 866-424-0030 (off); 888-424-2329 (cust serv) *Fax:* 303-200-9406 *E-mail:* customercare@shambhala.com *Web Site:* www.shambhala.com, pg 211

Shaughnessy Cohen Prize for Political Writing, 460 Richmond St W, Suite 600, Toronto, ON M5V 1Y1, Canada *Tel:* 416-504-8222 *Toll Free Tel:* 877-906-6548 *Fax:* 416-504-9090 *E-mail:* info@writerstrust.com *Web Site:* www.writerstrust.com, pg 688

Mina P Shaughnessy Prize, 85 Broad St, Suite 500, New York, NY 10004-2434 *Tel:* 646-576-5141; 646-576-5000 *Fax:* 646-458-0030 *E-mail:* awards@mla.org *Web Site:* www.mla.org, pg 688

Charlotte Sheedy Fellowship, 100 High St, Peterborough, NH 03458 *Tel:* 603-924-3886 *Fax:* 603-924-9142 *E-mail:* admissions@macdowellcolony.org *Web Site:* www.macdowellcolony.org, pg 689

Charlotte Sheedy Literary Agency Inc, 928 Broadway, Suite 901, New York, NY 10010 *Tel:* 212-780-9800 *Web Site:* www.sheedylit.com, pg 535

Barry Sheinkopf, c/o The Writing Ctr, 601 Palisade Ave, Englewood Cliffs, NJ 07632 *Tel:* 201-567-4017 *Fax:* 201-567-7202 *E-mail:* bsheinkopf@optonline.net, pg 501

Shenanigan Books, 84 River Rd, Summit, NJ 07901 *Tel:* 908-219-4275 *Fax:* 908-219-4485 *Web Site:* www.shenaniganbooks.com, pg 211

Shen's Books, 95 Madison Ave, Suite 1205, New York, NY 10016 *Tel:* 212-779-4400 *Fax:* 212-683-1894 *E-mail:* general@leeandlow.com *Web Site:* www.leeandlow.com, pg 211

Shepard Publications, PO Box 280, Friday Harbor, WA 98250 *Web Site:* www.shepardpub.com, pg 211

The Robert E Shepard Agency, 4804 Laurel Canyon Blvd, Box 592, Valley Village, CA 91607-3717 *Web Site:* www.shepardagency.com, pg 535

Sherman Asher Publishing, 126 Candelario St, Santa Fe, NM 87501 *Tel:* 505-988-7214 *E-mail:* westernedge@santa-fe.net *Web Site:* www.shermanasher.com; www.westernedgepress.com, pg 211

Ken Sherman & Associates, 1275 N Hayworth, Suite 103, Los Angeles, CA 90046 *Tel:* 310-273-8840 *E-mail:* kenshermanassociates@gmail.com *Web Site:* www.kenshermanassociates.com, pg 535

Wendy Sherman Associates Inc, 27 W 24 St, Suite 700-B, New York, NY 10010 *Tel:* 212-279-9027 *E-mail:* submissions@wsherman.com *Web Site:* www.wsherman.com, pg 536

Sheron Enterprises Inc, 1035 S Carley Ct, North Bellmore, NY 11710 *Tel:* 516-783-5885 *E-mail:* sheronent1@msn.com *Web Site:* www.longislandbookpublisher.com, pg 211

J Gordon Shillingford Publishing Inc, PO Box 86, RPO Corydon Ave, Winnipeg, MB R3M 3S3, Canada *Tel:* 204-779-6967 *Web Site:* www.jgshillingford.com, pg 470

Monika Shoffman-Graves, 70 Transylvania Ave, Key Largo, FL 33037 *Tel:* 305-451-1462 *Fax:* 305-451-1462 *E-mail:* keysmobill@earthlink.net; mograv@gmail.com, pg 501

Shoreline Press, 23 Rue Sainte-Anne, Ste-Anne-de-Bellevue, QC H9X 1L1, Canada *Tel:* 514-457-5733 *E-mail:* info@shorelinepress.ca *Web Site:* shorelinepress.ca, pg 470

Short Prose Competition for Developing Writers, 600-460 Richmond St W, Toronto, ON M5V 1Y1, Canada *Tel:* 416-703-8982 *Fax:* 416-504-9090 *E-mail:* info@writersunion.ca *Web Site:* www.writersunion.ca, pg 689

Short Story Award for New Writers, PO Box 80430, Portland, OR 97280-1430 *Tel:* 503-221-0836 *Fax:* 503-221-0837 *E-mail:* editors@glimmertrain.org *Web Site:* www.glimmertrain.org, pg 689

Show What You Know® Publishing, A Lorenz Company, c/o The Lorenz Corp, 501 E Third St, Dayton, OH 45402 *Tel:* 614-764-1211; 937-228-6118 *Toll Free Tel:* 877-PASSING (727-7464) *Fax:* 937-233-2042 *E-mail:* info@lorenz.com *Web Site:* www.lorenzeducationalpress.com, pg 211

Edwin "Bud" Shrake Award for Best Short Nonfiction, c/o 7748 Hwy 290 W, Austin, TX 78736-3202 *Tel:* 512-683-5640 *E-mail:* president@texasinstituteofletters.org *Web Site:* www.texasinstituteofletters.org, pg 689

Robert F Sibert Informational Book Award, 50 E Huron St, Chicago, IL 60611-2795 *Tel:* 312-280-2163 *Toll Free Tel:* 800-545-2433 *Fax:* 312-440-9374; 312-280-5271 *E-mail:* alsc@ala.org *Web Site:* www.ala.org/alsc, pg 689

Side by Side Literary Productions Inc, 145 E 35 St, Suite 7FE, New York, NY 10016 *Tel:* 212-685-6831 *Web Site:* sidebysidelit.com, pg 536

Siglio, PO Box 111, Catskill, NY 12414 *Tel:* 310-857-6935 *E-mail:* publisher@sigliopress.com *Web Site:* sigliopress.com, pg 212

Signalman Publishing, 3700 Commerce Blvd, Kissimmee, FL 34741 *Tel:* 407-504-4103 *Toll Free Tel:* 888-907-4423 *E-mail:* info@signalmanpublishing.com *Web Site:* www.signalmanpublishing.com, pg 212

Signature Books Publishing LLC, 564 W 400 N, Salt Lake City, UT 84116-3411 *Tel:* 801-531-1483 *Fax:* 801-531-1488 *E-mail:* people@signaturebooks.com *Web Site:* www.signaturebooks.com; www.signaturebookslibrary.org, pg 212

Signature Editions, PO Box 206, RPO Corydon, Winnipeg, MB R3M 3S7, Canada *Tel:* 204-779-7803 *E-mail:* submissions@signature-editions.com; orders@signature-editions.com *Web Site:* www.signature-editions.com, pg 470

SIL International, 7500 W Camp Wisdom Rd, Dallas, TX 75236-5629 *Tel:* 972-708-7400; 972-708-7404 *Fax:* 972-708-7350; 972-708-7363 *E-mail:* publications_intl@sil.org *Web Site:* www.sil.org; www.ethnologue.com, pg 212

Silicon Press, 25 Beverly Rd, Summit, NJ 07901 *Tel:* 908-273-8919 *Fax:* 908-273-6149 *E-mail:* info@silicon-press.com *Web Site:* www.silicon-press.com, pg 212

Silman-James Press Inc, 141 N Clark Dr, Unit 1, West Hollywood, CA 90048 *Tel:* 310-205-0665 *Fax:* 323 214-7943 *E-mail:* info@silmanjamespress.com *Web Site:* www.silmanjamespress.com, pg 212

Silver Gavel Awards, 321 N Clark St, Chicago, IL 60654 *Tel:* 312-988-5719 *Toll Free Tel:* 800-285-2221 (orders) *Fax:* 312-988-5494 *Web Site:* www.ambar.org/gavelawards, pg 689

Silver Leaf Books LLC, 13 Temi Rd, Holliston, MA 01746 *E-mail:* sales@silverleafbooks.com; editor@silverleafbooks.com; customerservice@silverleafbooks.com *Web Site:* www.silverleafbooks.com, pg 212

Simcha Press, 3201 SW 15 St, Deerfield Beach, FL 33442-8190 *Tel:* 954-360-0909 ext 212 *Toll Free Tel:* 800-851-9100 ext 212 *Toll Free Fax:* 800-424-7652 *E-mail:* simchapress@hcibooks.com *Web Site:* www.hcibooks.com, pg 212

Francis B Simkins Award, University of Georgia, Dept of History, Athens, GA 30602-1602 *Tel:* 706-542-8848 *Fax:* 706-542-2455 *Web Site:* thesha.org, pg 689

The John Simmons Short Fiction Award, 102 Dey House, 507 N Clinton St, Iowa City, IA 52242-1000 *Tel:* 319-335-0416 *Fax:* 319-335-0420, pg 689

Simon & Pierre Publishing Co Ltd, 3 Church St, Suite 500, Toronto, ON M5E 1M2, Canada *Tel:* 416-214-5544 *E-mail:* info@dundurn.com *Web Site:* www.dundurn.com, pg 471

Simon & Schuster, 1230 Avenue of the Americas, New York, NY 10020 *Tel:* 212-698-7000 *Toll Free Tel:* 800-223-2348 (cust serv); 800-223-2336 (orders) *Toll Free Fax:* 800-943-9831 (orders) *Web Site:* www.simonandschuster.com, pg 212

Simon & Schuster Audio, 1230 Avenue of the Americas, New York, NY 10020 *Web Site:* audio.simonandschuster.com, pg 213

Simon & Schuster Canada, 166 King St E, Suite 300, Toronto, ON M5A 1J3, Canada *Tel:* 647-427-8882 *Toll Free Tel:* 800-387-0446; 800-268-3216 (orders) *Fax:* 647-430-9446 *Toll Free Fax:* 888-849-8151 (orders) *E-mail:* info@simonandschuster.ca *Web Site:* www.simonandschuster.ca, pg 471

Simon & Schuster Children's Publishing, 1230 Avenue of the Americas, New York, NY 10020 *Tel:* 212-698-7000 *Web Site:* www.simonandschuster.com/kids; www.simonandschuster.com/teen; simonandschuster.net; simonandschuster.biz, pg 213

Simon & Schuster, Inc, 1230 Avenue of the Americas, New York, NY 10020 *Tel:* 212-698-7000 *Fax:* 212-698-7007 *E-mail:* firstname.lastname@simonandschuster.com *Web Site:* www.simonandschuster.com, pg 213

Simon & Schuster Sales Division, 1230 Avenue of the Americas, New York, NY 10020 *Tel:* 212-698-7000, pg 214

Charlie May Simon Children's Book Award, Arkansas State Library, Suite 100, 900 W Capitol Ave, Little Rock, AR 72201-3108 *Tel:* 501-682-2860 *Fax:* 501-682-1693 *Web Site:* www.library.arkansas.gov, pg 689

Simply Read Books, 501-5525 West Blvd, Vancouver, BC V6M 3W6, Canada *Tel:* 604-727-2960 *E-mail:* go@simplyreadbooks.com *Web Site:* www.simplyreadbooks.com, pg 471

The Simpson Family Literary Prize, Lafayette Lib & Learning Ctr Foundation, 3491 Mount Diablo Blvd, Suite 214, Lafayette, CA 94549 *Tel:* 925-283-6513 *E-mail:* sflpweb@gmail.com *Web Site:* www.simpsonliteraryproject.org/programs, pg 689

Sinauer Associates Inc, 23 Plumtree Rd, Sunderland, MA 01375 *Tel:* 413-549-4300 *Fax:* 413-549-1118 *E-mail:* publish@sinauer.com; orders@sinauer.com *Web Site:* sinauer.com, pg 214

Six Gallery Press, PO Box 90145, Pittsburgh, PA 15224-0545 *Web Site:* www.sixgallerypress.com, pg 214

SkillPath Publications, 6900 Squibb Rd, Mission, KS 66202 *Tel:* 913-362-3900 *Toll Free Tel:* 800-873-7545 *Fax:* 913-362-4241 *E-mail:* customercare@skillpath.com; products@skillpath.com *Web Site:* www.skillpath.com, pg 214

Skinner House Books, c/o Unitarian Universalist Assn, 24 Farnsworth St, Boston, MA 02210-1409 *Tel:* 617-742-2100 *Fax:* 617-948-6466 *E-mail:* skinnerhouse@uua.org *Web Site:* www.skinnerhouse.org, pg 214

Skipping Stones Honor Awards, 166 W 12 Ave, Eugene, OR 97401 *Tel:* 541-342-4956 *E-mail:* info@skippingstones.org *Web Site:* www.skippingstones.org, pg 689

The Skipping Stones Youth Honor Awards, 166 W 12 Ave, Eugene, OR 97401 *Tel:* 541-342-4956 *E-mail:* info@skippingstones.org *Web Site:* www.skippingstones.org, pg 690

Irene Skolnick Literary Agency, 27 W 20 St, Suite 305, New York, NY 10011 *Tel:* 212-727-3648 *Fax:* 212-352-2059 *E-mail:* office@skolnickliterary.com (queries) *Web Site:* www.skolnickagency.com, pg 536

Sky Pony Press, 307 W 36 St, 11th fl, New York, NY 10018 *Tel:* 212-643-6816 *Fax:* 212-643-6819 *E-mail:* skypony@skyhorsepublishing.com; info@skyhorsepublishing.com; submissions@skyhorsepublishing.com *Web Site:* www.skyponypress.com, pg 214

SkyLight Paths, 4507 Charlotte Ave, Suite 100, Nashville, TN 37209 *Tel:* 615-255-BOOK (255-2665) *Fax:* 615-255-5081 *E-mail:* marketing@turnerpublishing.com *Web Site:* www.skylightpaths.com; www.turnerpublishing.com, pg 214

SLACK® Incorporated, A Wyanoke Group Company, 6900 Grove Rd, Thorofare, NJ 08086-9447 *Tel:* 856-848-1000 *Toll Free Tel:* 800-257-8290 *Fax:* 856-848-6091 *E-mail:* sales@slackinc.com; editor@slackinc.com; customerservice@slackinc.com *Web Site:* www.healio.com/books, pg 215

Sleeping Bear Press™, 2395 S Huron Pkwy, Suite 200, Ann Arbor, MI 48104 *Toll Free Tel:* 800-487-2323 *Fax:* 734-929-2649 *E-mail:* customerservice@sleepingbearpress.com *Web Site:* www.sleepingbearpress.com, pg 215

Slipstream Annual Poetry Chapbook Contest, PO Box 2071, Dept W-1, Niagara Falls, NY 14301 *Web Site:* www.slipstreampress.org, pg 690

Beverley Slopen Literary Agency, 131 Bloor St W, Suite 711, Toronto, ON M5S 1S3, Canada *Tel:* 416-964-9598 *Fax:* 416-921-7726 *Web Site:* www.slopenagency.com, pg 536

Small Beer Press, 150 Pleasant St, No 306, Easthampton, MA 01027 *Tel:* 413-203-1636 *Fax:* 413-203-1636 *E-mail:* info@smallbeerpress.com *Web Site:* smallbeerpress.com, pg 215

Small Business Advisors Inc, 11 Franklin Ave, Hewlett, NY 11557 *Tel:* 516-374-1387 *Fax:* 516-374-1175 *Web Site:* www.smallbusinessadvice.com, pg 215

Small Publishers, Artists & Writers Network (SPAWN), 323 E Matilija St, Suite 110, PMB 123, Ojai, CA 93023 *Tel:* 805-646-3045 *Fax:* 805-640-8213 *E-mail:* execdir@spawn.org *Web Site:* www.spawn.org, pg 577

Donald Smiley Prize, 260 rue Dalhousie St, Suite 204, Ottawa, ON K1N 7E4, Canada *Tel:* 613-562-1202 *Fax:* 613-241-0019 *E-mail:* cpsa-acsp@cpsa-acsp.ca *Web Site:* www.cpsa-acsp.ca, pg 690

Smith & Kraus Publishers Inc, 40 Walch Dr, Portland, ME 04103 *Tel:* 207-523-2585 *Toll Free Tel:* 877-668-8680 *Fax:* 207-699-3698 *E-mail:* editor@smithandkraus.com *Web Site:* www.smithandkraus.com, pg 215

Helen C Smith Memorial Award, c/o 7748 Hwy 290 W, Austin, TX 78736-3202 *Tel:* 512-683-5640 *E-mail:* president@texasinstituteofletters.org *Web Site:* www.texasinstituteofletters.org, pg 690

The Jean Kennedy Smith VSA Playwright Discovery Award, 2700 "F" St NW, Washington, DC 20566 *Tel:* 202-416-8898 *Fax:* 202-416-4840 *E-mail:* vsainfo@kennedy-center.org *Web Site:* www.kennedy-center.org/pdp, pg 690

The Jeffrey E Smith Editors' Prize, 357 McReynolds Hall, Columbia, MO 65211 *Tel:* 573-882-4474 *Toll Free Tel:* 800-949-2505 *Fax:* 573-884-4671 *Web Site:* www.missourireview.com, pg 690

M Lee Smith Publishers, 100 Winners Circle, Suite 300, Brentwood, TN 37027 *Tel:* 615-373-7517 *Toll Free Tel:* 800-274-6774; 800-727-5257 *E-mail:* custserv@mleesmith.com; service@blr.com *Web Site:* www.mleesmith.com; www.blr.com, pg 215

Roger W Smith, 59 67 58 Rd, Maspeth, NY 11378-3211 *Tel:* 718-416-1334 *E-mail:* brandeis106@gmail.com, pg 501

Steve Smith Autosports, PO Box 11631, Santa Ana, CA 92711-1631 *Tel:* 714-639-7681 *Fax:* 714-639-9741 *Web Site:* www.stevesmithautosports.com, pg 215

Valerie Smith, Literary Agent, 1746 Rte 44-55, Modena, NY 12548 *Tel:* 845-883-5848, pg 536

Smithsonian Scholarly Press, Aerospace Bldg, 704-A, MRC 957, Washington, DC 20013 *Tel:* 202-633-3017 *Fax:* 202-633-6877 *E-mail:* scholarlypress@si.edu *Web Site:* www.scholarlypress.si.edu, pg 215

Smyth & Helwys Publishing Inc, 6316 Peake Rd, Macon, GA 31210-3960 *Tel:* 478-757-0564 *Toll Free Tel:* 800-747-3016 (orders only); 800-568-1248 (orders only) *Fax:* 478-757-1305 *E-mail:* information@helwys.com *Web Site:* www.helwys.com, pg 215

Michael Snell Literary Agency, PO Box 1206, Truro, MA 02666-1206 *Tel:* 508-349-3718 *Web Site:* www.michaelsnellagency.com, pg 536

Kay Snow Writing Contest, 5331 SW Macadam Ave, Suite 258, PMB 215, Portland, OR 97239 *Tel:* 901-200-5385 *E-mail:* wilwrite@willamettewriters.org *Web Site:* willamettewriters.org, pg 690

Snow Lion, 4720 Walnut St, Boulder, CO 80301 *Tel:* 617-236-0030 *Fax:* 303-200-9406 *E-mail:* customercare@shambhala.com *Web Site:* www.shambhala.com/snowlion, pg 215

Sobel Weber Associates Inc, 146 E 19 St, New York, NY 10003-2404 *Tel:* 212-420-8585 *E-mail:* info@sobelweber.com *Web Site:* www.sobelweber.com, pg 536

Social Sciences & Humanities Research Council of Canada (SSHRC), 350 Albert St, Ottawa, ON K1P 6G4, Canada *Tel:* 613-992-0691 *E-mail:* research@sshrc-crsh.gc.ca *Web Site:* www.sshrc.ca, pg 577

Society for Features Journalism (SFJ), University of Maryland, Philip Merrill College of Journalism, 1100 Knight Hall, College Park, MD 20742 *Tel:* 301-314-2631 *Fax:* 301-314-9166 *Web Site:* featuresjournalism.org, pg 578

Society for Human Resource Management (SHRM), 1800 Duke St, Alexandria, VA 22314 *Tel:* 703-548-3440 *Toll Free Tel:* 800-444-5006 (orders) *Fax:* 703-535-6490 *E-mail:* shrm@shrm.org; shrmstore@shrm.org *Web Site:* www.shrm.org, pg 216

Society for Industrial & Applied Mathematics, 3600 Market St, 6th fl, Philadelphia, PA 19104-2688 *Tel:* 215-382-9800 *Toll Free Tel:* 800-447-7426 *Fax:* 215-386-7999 *E-mail:* siambooks@siam.org *Web Site:* www.siam.org, pg 216

Society for Mining, Metallurgy & Exploration, 12999 E Adam Aircraft Circle, Englewood, CO 80112 *Tel:* 303-948-4200 *Toll Free Tel:* 800-763-3132 *Fax:* 303-973-3845 *E-mail:* cs@smenet.org; books@smenet.org *Web Site:* www.smenet.org, pg 216

Society for Scholarly Publishing (SSP), 10200 W 44 Ave, Suite 304, Wheat Ridge, CO 80033-2840 *Tel:* 303-422-3914 *Fax:* 720-881-6101 *E-mail:* info@sspnet.org *Web Site:* www.sspnet.org, pg 578

Society for Technical Communication, 9401 Lee Hwy, Suite 300, Fairfax, VA 22031 *Tel:* 703-522-4114 *Fax:* 703-522-2075 *E-mail:* stc@stc.org *Web Site:* www.stc.org, pg 578

Society for Technical Communication's Annual Conference, 9401 Lee Hwy, Suite 300, Fairfax, VA 22031 *Tel:* 703-522-4114 *Fax:* 703-522-2075 *E-mail:* stc@stc.org; summit@stc.org *Web Site:* summit.stc.org; www.stc.org, pg 615

Society for the History of Authorship, Reading & Publishing Inc (SHARP), c/o The Johns Hopkins University Press, Journals Publishing Div, PO Box 19966, Baltimore, MD 21211-0966 *Tel:* 410-516-6987 *Toll Free Tel:* 800-548-1784 *Fax:* 410-516-3866 *E-mail:* members@sharpweb.org *Web Site:* www.sharpweb.org, pg 578

Society of American Archivists, 17 N State St, Suite 1425, Chicago, IL 60602-4061 *Tel:* 312-606-0722 *Toll Free Tel:* 866-722-7858 *Fax:* 312-606-0728 *Web Site:* www.archivists.org, pg 216

Society of American Business Editors & Writers Inc (SABEW), Walter Cronkite School of Journalism & Mass Communication, Arizona State University, 555 N Central Ave, Suite 406E, Phoenix, AZ 85004-1248 *Tel:* 602-496-7862 *Fax:* 602-496-7041 *E-mail:* sabew@sabew.org *Web Site:* sabew.org, pg 578

Society of American Travel Writers (SATW), One Parkview Plaza, Suite 800, Oakbrook Terrace, IL 60181 *Tel:* 202-591-2476 *E-mail:* info@satw.org *Web Site:* www.satw.org, pg 578

Society of Children's Book Writers and Illustrators (SCBWI), 4727 Wilshire Blvd, Suite 301, Los Angeles, CA 90010 *Tel:* 323-782-1010 *Fax:* 323-782-1892 *E-mail:* scbwi@scbwi.org; membership@scbwi.org *Web Site:* www.scbwi.org, pg 578

Society of Environmental Toxicology & Chemistry (SETAC), 229 S Baylen St, 2nd fl, Pensacola, FL 32502 *Tel:* 850-469-1500 *Toll Free Fax:* 888-296-4136 *E-mail:* setac@setac.org; etc@setac.org (edit) *Web Site:* www.setac.org, pg 216

Society of Exploration Geophysicists, 8801 S Yale Ave, Tulsa, OK 74137 *Tel:* 918-497-5500 *Fax:* 918-497-5557 *E-mail:* web@seg.org *Web Site:* www.seg.org, pg 216

Society of Illustrators (SI), 128 E 63 St, New York, NY 10065 *Tel:* 212-838-2560 *Fax:* 212-838-2561 *E-mail:* info@societyillustrators.org *Web Site:* www.societyillustrators.org, pg 578

Society of Manufacturing Engineers, One SME Dr, Dearborn, MI 48121 *Tel:* 313-425-3000 *Toll Free Tel:* 800-733-4763 (cust serv) *Fax:* 313-425-3400 *E-mail:* publications@sme.org *Web Site:* www.sme.org, pg 216

The Society of Midland Authors (SMA), PO Box 10419, Chicago, IL 60610 *E-mail:* info@midlandauthors.com *Web Site:* www.midlandauthors.com, pg 578

The Society of Midland Authors Awards, PO Box 10419, Chicago, IL 60610 *E-mail:* info@midlandauthors.com *Web Site:* www.midlandauthors.com, pg 690

Society of Motion Picture & Television Engineers® (SMPTE®), 3 Barker Ave, 5th fl, White Plains, NY 10601 *Tel:* 914-761-1100 *Fax:* 914-761-3115 *Web Site:* www.smpte.org, pg 578

The Society of Naval Architects & Marine Engineers (SNAME), 99 Canal Center Plaza, Suite 310, Alexandria, VA 22314 *Tel:* 703-997-6701 *Toll Free Tel:* 800-798-2188 *Fax:* 703-997-6702 *Web Site:* www.sname.org, pg 216

The Society of Southwestern Authors (SSA), PO Box 30355, Tucson, AZ 85751-0355 *E-mail:* info@ssa-az.org *Web Site:* www.ssa-az.org, pg 579

The Society of Southwestern Authors Writing Contest, PO Box 30355, Tucson, AZ 85751-0355 *E-mail:* info@ssa-az.org *Web Site:* www.ssa-az.org, pg 690

Software & Information Industry Association (SIIA), 1090 Vermont Ave NW, 6th fl, Washington, DC 20005-4095 *Tel:* 202-289-7442 *Fax:* 202-289-7097 *Web Site:* www.siia.net, pg 579

Soho Press Inc, 853 Broadway, New York, NY 10003 *Tel:* 212-260-1900 *E-mail:* soho@sohopress.com; publicity@sohopress.com; contact@sohopress.com *Web Site:* www.sohopress.com, pg 216

Soil Science Society of America, 5585 Guilford Rd, Madison, WI 53711-5801 *Tel:* 608-273-8080 *Web Site:* www.soils.org, pg 217

Solano Press Books, PO Box 773, Point Arena, CA 95468 *Tel:* 707-884-4508 *Toll Free Tel:* 800-931-9373 *Fax:* 707-884-4109 *E-mail:* spbooks@solano.com *Web Site:* www.solano.com, pg 217

Jodi Solomon Speakers Bureau, 295 Huntington Ave, Suite 211, Boston, MA 02115 *Tel:* 617-266-3450 *Fax:* 617-266-5660 *E-mail:* inquiries@jodisolomonspeakers.com *Web Site:* www.jodisolomonspeakers.com, pg 548

Solution Tree, 555 N Morton St, Bloomington, IN 47404 *Tel:* 812-336-7700 *Toll Free Tel:* 800-733-6786 *Fax:* 812-336-7790 *E-mail:* pubs@solution-tree.com *Web Site:* www.solution-tree.com, pg 217

SOM Publishing, 163 Moon Valley Rd, Windyville, MO 65783 *Tel:* 417-345-8411 *Fax:* 417-345-6668 *E-mail:* som@som.org; dreams@dreamschool.org *Web Site:* www.som.org; www.dreamschool.org, pg 217

Somerset Hall Press, 416 Commonwealth Ave, Suite 612, Boston, MA 02215 *Tel:* 617-236-5126 *E-mail:* info@somersethallpress.com *Web Site:* www.somersethallpress.com, pg 217

Soncino Press Ltd, 123 Ditmas Ave, Brooklyn, NY 11218 *Tel:* 718-972-6200 *Toll Free Tel:* 800-972-6201 *Fax:* 718-972-6204 *E-mail:* info@soncino.com *Web Site:* www.soncino.com, pg 217

Sophia Institute Press®, 522 Donald St, Unit 3, Bedford, NH 03110 *Tel:* 603-836-5505 *Toll Free Tel:* 800-888-9344 *Fax:* 603-641-8108 *Toll Free Fax:* 888-288-2259 *E-mail:* orders@sophiainstitute.com *Web Site:* www.sophiainstitute.com, pg 217

Sophie Kerr Prize, c/o College Relations Off, 300 Washington Ave, Chestertown, MD 21620 *Tel:* 410-778-2800 *Toll Free Tel:* 800-422-1782 *Fax:* 410-810-7150 *Web Site:* www.washcoll.edu, pg 690

Soul Mate Publishing, 3210 Sherwood Dr, Walworth, NY 14568 *Tel:* 585-598-4791 *E-mail:* submissions@soulmatepublishing.com *Web Site:* www.soulmatepublishing.com, pg 217

Gordon Soules Book Publishers Ltd, 2372 Haywood Ave, West Vancouver, BC V7V 1X7, Canada *Tel:* 604-922-6588 *Fax:* 604-922-6574 *E-mail:* books@gordonsoules.com *Web Site:* www.gordonsoules.com, pg 471

Sound Feelings Publishing, 18375 Ventura Blvd, No 8000, Tarzana, CA 91356 *Tel:* 818-757-0600 *E-mail:* information@soundfeelings.com *Web Site:* www.soundfeelings.com, pg 217

Sounds True Inc, 413 S Arthur Ave, Louisville, CO 80027 *Tel:* 303-665-3151 *Toll Free Tel:* 800-333-9185 *E-mail:* customerservice@soundstrue.com; sales@soundstrue.com *Web Site:* www.soundstrue.com, pg 217

Sourcebooks Inc, 1935 Brookdale Rd, Suite 139, Naperville, IL 60563 *Tel:* 630-961-3900 *Toll Free Tel:* 800-432-7444 *Fax:* 630-961-2168 *E-mail:* info@sourcebooks.com; customersupport@sourcebooks.com *Web Site:* www.sourcebooks.com, pg 217

Sourced Media Books, 15 Via Picato, San Clemente, CA 92673 *Tel:* 949-813-0182 *E-mail:* editor@sourcedmediabooks.com *Web Site:* sourcedmediabooks.com, pg 218

South Carolina Bar, Continuing Legal Education Div, 950 Taylor St, Columbia, SC 29201 *Tel:* 803-799-6653 *Toll Free Tel:* 800-768-7787 *Fax:* 803-799-4118 *E-mail:* scbar-info@scbar.org *Web Site:* www.scbar.org, pg 218

South Dakota Historical Society Press, 900 Governors Dr, Pierre, SD 57501 *Tel:* 605-773-6009 *Fax:* 605-773-6041 *E-mail:* info@sdshspress.com; orders@sdshspress.com *Web Site:* sdshspress.com, pg 218

South Platte Press, PO Box 163, David City, NE 68632-0163 *Tel:* 402-367-3554 *E-mail:* railroads@windstream.net *Web Site:* www.southplattepress.net, pg 218

Southampton Writers' Conference, 239 Montauk Hwy, Southampton, NY 11968 *Tel:* 631-632-5007 *E-mail:* southamptonwriters@notes.cc.sunysb.edu; southamptonarts@stonybrook.edu *Web Site:* www.stonybrook.edu/southampton/mfa/summer/cwl_home.html, pg 615

Southeast Review Narrative Nonfiction Contest, Florida State University, Dept of English, Tallahassee, FL 32306 *E-mail:* southeastreview@gmail.com *Web Site:* www.southeastreview.org, pg 690

Southeast Review's Gearhart Poetry Contest, Florida State University, Dept of English, Tallahassee, FL 32306 *E-mail:* southeastreview@gmail.com *Web Site:* www.southeastreview.org, pg 691

Southeastern Theatre Conference New Play Project, 1175 Revolution Mill Dr, Suite 14, Greensboro, NC 27405 *Tel:* 336-272-3645 *Fax:* 336-272-8810 *E-mail:* info@setc.org *Web Site:* www.setc.org, pg 691

Southern Books Competition, PO Box 950, Rex, GA 30273 *Tel:* 678-466-4334 *Fax:* 678-466-4349 *Web Site:* selaonline.org, pg 691

Southern California Writers' Conference (SCWC), 18160 Cottonwood Rd, Suite 260, Sunriver, OR 97707 *Tel:* 619-303-8185 *Fax:* 619-906-7462 *E-mail:* msg@writersconference.com *Web Site:* www.writersconference.com, pg 615

Southern Historical Press Inc, 375 W Broad St, Greenville, SC 29601 *Tel:* 864-233-2346 *Toll Free Tel:* 800-233-0152 *E-mail:* southernhistoricalpress@gmail.com *Web Site:* www.southernhistoricalpress.com, pg 218

Southern Illinois University Press, 1915 University Press Dr, SIUC Mail Code 6806, Carbondale, IL 62901-4323 *Tel:* 618-453-2281 *Fax:* 618-453-1221 *E-mail:* custserv@press.uchicago.edu; rights@siu.edu *Web Site:* www.siupress.com, pg 218

Southern Independent Booksellers Alliance, 3806 Yale Ave, Columbia, SC 29205 *Tel:* 803-994-9530 *Fax:* 309-410-0211 *E-mail:* info@sibaweb.com *Web Site:* www.sibaweb.com, pg 579

Southern Playwrights Competition, 700 Pelham Rd N, Jacksonville, AL 36265-1602 *Tel:* 256-782-5412 *Web Site:* www.jsu.edu/english/southpla.html, pg 691

Terry Southern Prize, 544 W 27 St, New York, NY 10001 *Tel:* 212-343-1333 *Fax:* 212-343-1988 *E-mail:* queries@theparisreview.org *Web Site:* www.theparisreview.org, pg 691

SouthWest Writers Conference Series, 3200 Carlisle Blvd NE, Suite 114, Albuquerque, NM 87110-1663 *Tel:* 505-830-6034 *E-mail:* swwriters@juno.com *Web Site:* www.southwestwriters.com, pg 615

Sovereign Award for Outstanding Writing, Woodbine Sales Pavilion, 555 Rexdale Blvd, Toronto, ON M9W 5L2, Canada *Tel:* 416-675-7756 *Fax:* 416-675-6378 *E-mail:* jockeyclub@bellnet.ca *Web Site:* www.jockeyclubcanada.com; www.sovereignawards.ca, pg 691

The Sow's Ear Poetry Prize & The Sow's Ear Chapbook Prize, 1748 Cave Ridge Rd, Mount Jackson, VA 22842 *Tel:* 540-477-3257 *E-mail:* sepoetryreview@gmail.com *Web Site:* sowsearpoetry.org, pg 691

Soyinfo Center, PO Box 234, Lafayette, CA 94549-0234 *Tel:* 925-283-2991 *Web Site:* www.soyinfocenter.com, pg 219

Spark Award, 4727 Wilshire Blvd, Suite 301, Los Angeles, CA 90010 *Tel:* 323-782-1010 *Fax:* 323-782-1892 *E-mail:* grants@scbwi.org; scbwi@scbwi.org *Web Site:* www.scbwi.org, pg 691

Special Libraries Association (SLA), 7918 Jones Branch Dr, Suite 300, McLean, VA 22102 *Tel:* 703-647-4900 *Fax:* 703-506-3266 *Web Site:* www.sla.org, pg 579

Specialized Information Publishers Association (SIPA), 1090 Vermont Ave NW, 6th fl, Washington, DC 20005-4095 *Web Site:* www.sipaonline.com, pg 579

Specialty Graphic Imaging Association (SGIA), 10015 Main St, Fairfax, VA 22031-3489 *Tel:* 703-385-1335 *Toll Free Tel:* 888-385-3588 *Fax:* 703-273-0456 *E-mail:* sgia@sgia.org *Web Site:* www.sgia.org, pg 579

Specialty Press Inc, 300 NW 70 Ave, Suite 102, Plantation, FL 33317 *Tel:* 954-792-8100 *Toll Free Tel:* 800-233-9273 *Fax:* 954-792-8545 *E-mail:* websales@addwarehouse.com *Web Site:* addwarehouse.com, pg 219

Spectrum Literary Agency, 320 Central Park W, Suite 1-D, New York, NY 10025 *Tel:* 212-362-4323 *Fax:* 212-362-4562 *Web Site:* www.spectrumliteraryagency.com, pg 536

SPIE, 1000 20 St, Bellingham, WA 98225-6705 *Tel:* 360-676-3290 *Toll Free Tel:* 888-504-8171 (orders) *Fax:* 360-647-1445 *E-mail:* help@spie.org; customerservice@spie.org (orders) *Web Site:* www.spie.org, pg 219

The Spieler Agency, 27 W 20 St, Suite 302, New York, NY 10011 *Tel:* 212-757-4439 *Fax:* 212-333-2019 *E-mail:* spieleragency@spieleragency.com, pg 537

Spinsters Ink, PO Box 10543, Tallahassee, FL 32302 *Tel:* 850-576-2370 *Toll Free Tel:* 800-729-4992 *E-mail:* info@bellabooks.com *Web Site:* www.bellabooks.com/Publisher-spinsters-ink-cat.html, pg 219

Philip G Spitzer Literary Agency Inc, 50 Talmage Farm Lane, East Hampton, NY 11937 *Tel:* 631-329-3650 *Fax:* 631-329-3651 *Web Site:* www.spitzeragency.com, pg 537

Spizzirri Publishing Inc, PO Box 9397, Rapid City, SD 57709-9397 *Tel:* 605-348-2749 *Toll Free Tel:* 800-325-9819 *Fax:* 605-348-6251 *Toll Free Fax:* 800-322-9819 *E-mail:* spizzpub@aol.com *Web Site:* www.spizzirri.com, pg 219

John Spray Mystery Award, 40 Orchard View Blvd, Suite 217, Toronto, ON M4R 1B9, Canada *Tel:* 416-975-0010 *Fax:* 416-975-8970 *E-mail:* info@bookcentre.ca *Web Site:* www.bookcentre.ca, pg 691

Spring Time Writers Creative Writing & Journaling Workshop, PO Box 512, Lyons, CO 80540-0512 *Tel:* 303-823-0997 *E-mail:* writers@springtimewriters.com *Web Site:* www.springtimewriters.com, pg 615

Springer, 233 Spring St, New York, NY 10013-1578 *Tel:* 212-460-1500 *Toll Free Tel:* 800-SPRINGER (777-4643) *Fax:* 212-460-1700 *E-mail:* customerservice@springer.com *Web Site:* www.springer.com, pg 219

Springer Publishing Co, 11 W 42 St, 15th fl, New York, NY 10036-8002 *Tel:* 212-431-4370 *Toll Free Tel:* 877-687-7476 *Fax:* 212-941-7842 *E-mail:* marketing@springerpub.com; cs@springerpub.com (orders); editorial@springerpub.com *Web Site:* www.springerpub.com, pg 219

Spry Publishing, 315 E Eisenhower Pkwy, Suite 2, Ann Arbor, MI 48108 *Tel:* 734-531-7600 *Toll Free Tel:* 877-722-2264 *E-mail:* info@sprypub.com *Web Site:* www.sprypub.com, pg 219

Spur Awards, 271 CR 219, Encampment, WY 82325 *Tel:* 307-329-8942 *E-mail:* wwa.moulton@gmail.com *Web Site:* westernwriters.org, pg 691

Square One Publishers Inc, 115 Herricks Rd, Garden City Park, NY 11040 *Tel:* 516-535-2010 *Toll Free Tel:* 877-900-BOOK (900-2665) *Fax:* 516-535-2014 *E-mail:* sq1publish@aol.com *Web Site:* www.squareonepublishers.com, pg 220

Squaw Valley Community of Writers Summer Workshops, PO Box 1416, Nevada City, CA 95959 *Tel:* 530-470-8440 *E-mail:* info@communityofwriters.org *Web Site:* www.communityofwriters.org, pg 615

SSPC: The Society for Protective Coatings, 800 Trumbull Dr, Pittsburgh, PA 15220-4365 *Tel:* 412-281-2331 *Toll Free Tel:* 877-281-7772 (US only) *Fax:* 412-281-9992 *E-mail:* info@sspc.org *Web Site:* www.sspc.org, pg 220

ST Media Group Book Division, 11262 Cornell Park Dr, Cincinnati, OH 45242 *Tel:* 513-421-2050 *Toll Free Tel:* 866-265-0954 *Fax:* 513-263-6999 *E-mail:* books@stmediagroup.com *Web Site:* www.stmediagroup.com, pg 220

Stackler Editorial Agency, 200 Woodland Ave, Summit, NJ 07901 *Tel:* 510-912-9187 *E-mail:* ed.stackler@gmail.com *Web Site:* www.fictioneditor.com, pg 501

Stackpole Books, 5067 Ritter Rd, Mechanicsburg, PA 17055 *Tel:* 717-796-0411 *Toll Free Tel:* 800-732-3669 *Fax:* 717-796-0412 *Web Site:* www.stackpolebooks.com, pg 220

The Edna Staebler Award for Creative Non-Fiction, Office of the Dean, Faculty of Arts, 75 University Ave W, Waterloo, ON N2L 3C5, Canada *Tel:* 519-884-1970 (ext 3361) *E-mail:* staebleraward@wlu.ca *Web Site:* wlu.ca/staebleraward, pg 691

Standard International Media Holdings, 568 Ninth St S, Suite 201, Naples, FL 34102-7336 *Tel:* 239-248-5550 *Fax:* 239-649-5832 *Toll Free Fax:* 866-948-7883 *E-mail:* sales@standardinternationalmedia.com *Web Site:* www.standardinternationalmedia.com, pg 220

Standard Publishing, 4050 Lee Vance View, Colorado Springs, CO 80918 *Tel:* 513-931-4050 *Toll Free Tel:* 800-323-7543 *Fax:* 513-931-0950 *Toll Free Fax:* 800-323-0726 *E-mail:* customerservice@standardpub.com *Web Site:* www.standardpub.com, pg 220

Standard Publishing Corp, 10 High St, Boston, MA 02110 *Tel:* 617-457-0600 *Toll Free Tel:* 800-682-5759 *Fax:* 617-457-0608 *Web Site:* www.spcpub.com, pg 220

Stanford University Press, 425 Broadway St, Redwood City, CA 94063-3126 *Tel:* 650-723-9434 *Fax:* 650-725-3457 *E-mail:* info@www.sup.org; publicity@www.sup.org *Web Site:* www.sup.org, pg 220

Stanley Drama Award, One Campus Rd, Staten Island, NY 10301 *Tel:* 718-390-3223 *Fax:* 718-390-3323 *Web Site:* wagner.edu/theatre/stanley-drama, pg 691

Star Bright Books Inc, 13 Landsdowne St, Cambridge, MA 02139 *Tel:* 617-354-1300 *Fax:* 617-354-1399 *E-mail:* info@starbrightbooks.com; orders@starbrightbooks.com *Web Site:* www.starbrightbooks.org, pg 221

Star Publishing Co Inc, PO Box 5165, Belmont, CA 94002-5165 *Tel:* 650-591-3505 *Fax:* 650-752-9212 *Web Site:* www.starpublishing.com, pg 221

STARbooks Press, PO Box 711612, Herndon, VA 20171 *E-mail:* publish@starbookspress.com *Web Site:* www.starbookspress.com, pg 221

Starcrafts LLC, 334-A Calef Hwy, Epping, NH 03042 *Tel:* 603-734-4300 *Toll Free Tel:* 866-953-8458 (24/7 message ctr) *Fax:* 603-734-4311 *E-mail:* astrosales@astrocom.com *Web Site:* acspublications.com; www.starcraftseast.com; www.astrocom.com, pg 221

Stargazer Publishing Co, 958 Stanislaus Dr, Corona, CA 92881 *Tel:* 951-898-4619 *Toll Free Tel:* 800-606-7895 (orders) *Fax:* 951-898-4633 *E-mail:* stargazer@stargazerpub.com; orders@stargazerpub.com *Web Site:* www.stargazerpub.com, pg 221

StarGroup International Inc, 1194 Old Dixie Hwy, Suite 201, West Palm Beach, FL 33413 *Tel:* 561-547-0667 *Fax:* 561-843-8530 *E-mail:* info@stargroupinternational.com *Web Site:* stargroupinternational.com, pg 221

Agnes Lynch Starrett Poetry Prize, 7500 Thomas Blvd, Pittsburgh, PA 15260 *Tel:* 412-383-2456 *Fax:* 412-383-2466 *E-mail:* info@upress.pitt.edu *Web Site:* www.upress.pitt.edu, pg 692

State University of New York Press, 10 N Pearl St, 4th fl, Albany, NY 12207 *Tel:* 518-944-2800 *Toll Free Tel:* 877-204-6073 (orders) *Fax:* 518-320-1592 *Toll Free Fax:* 877-204-6074 (orders) *E-mail:* info@sunypress.edu (edit off); suny@presswarehouse.com (orders) *Web Site:* www.sunypress.edu, pg 221

Nancy Stauffer Associates, 30 Corbin Dr, Suite 1203, Darien, CT 06820 *Tel:* 203-202-2500 *Web Site:* staufferliterary.com; publishersmarketplace.com/members/nstauffer, pg 537

Nancy Steele, 2210 Pine St, Philadelphia, PA 19103-6516 *Tel:* 215-732-5175 *E-mail:* Nancy.Steele.Edits@gmail.com, pg 502

Steerforth Press, 45 Lyme Rd, Suite 208, Hanover, NH 03755-1222 *Tel:* 603-643-4787 *Fax:* 603-643-4788 *E-mail:* info@steerforth.com *Web Site:* www.steerforth.com, pg 221

Stegner Fellowship, Stanford University, Dept of English, Stanford, CA 94305-2087 *Tel:* 650-723-0011 *Fax:* 650-723-3679 *E-mail:* stegnerfellowship@stanford.edu *Web Site:* creativewriting.stanford.edu, pg 692

Michael Steinberg Literary Agent, PO Box 274, Glencoe, IL 60022-0274 *Tel:* 847-626-1000 *Fax:* 847-626-1002 *E-mail:* michael14steinberg@comcast.net, pg 537

SteinerBooks, 610 Main St, Great Barrington, MA 01230 *Tel:* 413-528-8233 *Fax:* 413-528-8826 *E-mail:* friends@steinerbooks.org *Web Site:* steiner.presswarehouse.com, pg 221

Stellar Publishing, 2114 S Live Oak Pkwy, Wilmington, NC 28403 *Tel:* 910-269-7444 *Web Site:* www.stellar-publishing.com, pg 222

Stemmer House Publishers Inc, 4 White Brook Rd, Gilsum, NH 03448 *Tel:* 603-357-0236 *Toll Free Tel:* 800-345-6665 *Fax:* 603-965-2181 *E-mail:* pbs@pathwaybook.com *Web Site:* www.stemmer.com, pg 222

Stenhouse Publishers, 480 Congress St, Portland, ME 04101-3451 *Tel:* 207-253-1600 *Toll Free Tel:* 888-363-0566 *Fax:* 207-253-5121 *Toll Free Fax:* 800-833-9164 *E-mail:* customerservice@stenhouse.com *Web Site:* www.stenhouse.com, pg 222

Stephan G Stephansson Award for Poetry, 11759 Groat Rd, Edmonton, AB T5M 3K6, Canada *Tel:* 780-422-8174 *Toll Free Tel:* 800-665-5354 (AB only) *Fax:* 780-422-2663 (attn WGA) *E-mail:* mail@writersguild.ca *Web Site:* writersguild.ca, pg 692

Sterling Lord Literistic Inc, 115 Broadway, Suite 1602, New York, NY 10006 *Tel:* 212-780-6050 *Fax:* 212-780-6095 *E-mail:* info@sll.com *Web Site:* www.sll.com, pg 537

Sterling Publishing Co Inc, 1166 Avenue of the Americas, 17th fl, New York, NY 10036 *Tel:* 212-532-7160 *Toll Free Tel:* 800-367-9692 *Fax:* 212-213-2495 *Web Site:* www.sterlingpublishing.com, pg 222

Miriam Stern, Entertainment Attorney/Literary Agent, 303 E 83 St, 20th fl, New York, NY 10028 *Tel:* 212-794-1289, pg 537

Wallace Stevens Award, 75 Maiden Lane, Suite 901, New York, NY 10038 *Tel:* 212-274-0343 *Fax:* 212-274-9427 *E-mail:* awards@poets.org *Web Site:* www.poets.org, pg 692

Stewart, Tabori & Chang, 115 W 18 St, 6th fl, New York, NY 10011 *Tel:* 212-519-1200; 212-206-7715 *Fax:* 212-519-1210 *E-mail:* abrams@abramsbooks.com *Web Site:* www.abramsbooks.com/imprints/stc, pg 222

Stimola Literary Studio Inc, 308 Livingston Ct, Edgewater, NJ 07020 *Tel:* 201-945-9353 *Fax:* 201-945-9353; 201-490-5920 *E-mail:* info@stimolaliterarystudio.com *Web Site:* www.stimolaliterarystudio.com, pg 537

Stipes Publishing LLC, 204 W University Ave, Champaign, IL 61820 *Tel:* 217-356-8391 *Fax:* 217-356-5753 *E-mail:* stipes01@sbcglobal.net *Web Site:* www.stipes.com, pg 222

STM Learning Inc, 1220 Paddock Dr, Florissant, MO 63033 *Tel:* 314-434-2424 *E-mail:* info@stmlearning.com; orders@stmlearning.com *Web Site:* www.stmlearning.com, pg 222

STOCKCERO Inc, 3785 NW 82 Ave, Suite 302, Doral, FL 33166 *Tel:* 305-722-7628 *Fax:* 305-477-5794 *E-mail:* academicservices@stockcero.com; sales@stockcero.com *Web Site:* www.stockcero.com, pg 223

Bram Stoker Awards®, c/o Horror Writers Association, PO Box 56687, Sherman Oaks, CA 91413 *Tel:* 818-220-3965 *E-mail:* hwa@horror.org *Web Site:* horror.org/awards/stokers.htm, pg 692

Jeri L Stolk, 8 Rush Vine Ct, Owings Mills, MD 21117 *Tel:* 410-864-8109 *E-mail:* jeristolk@gmail.com, pg 502

Stone Bridge Press Inc, 1393 Solano Ave, Suite C, Albany, CA 94706 *Tel:* 510-524-8732 *E-mail:* sbp@stonebridge.com; sbpedit@stonebridge.com *Web Site:* www.stonebridge.com, pg 223

Stone Pier Press, PO Box 170572, San Francisco, CA 94117 *Tel:* 415-484-2821 *E-mail:* hello@stonepierpress.org *Web Site:* www.stonepierpress.org, pg 223

The Stonesong Press LLC, 270 W 39 St, No 201, New York, NY 10018 *Tel:* 212-929-4600 *E-mail:* editors@stonesong.com *Web Site:* www.stonesong.com, pg 538

Stoneydale Press Publishing Co, 523 Main St, Stevensville, MT 59870-2839 *Tel:* 406-777-2729 *Toll Free Tel:* 800-735-7006 *Fax:* 406-777-2521 *E-mail:* stoneydale@stoneydale.com *Web Site:* www.stoneydale.com, pg 223

Storey Publishing LLC, 210 MASS MoCA Way, North Adams, MA 01247 *Tel:* 413-346-2100 *Toll Free Tel:* 800-441-5700 (orders); 800-793-9396 (edit) *Fax:* 413-346-2199; 413-346-2196 (edit) *E-mail:* sales@storey.com *Web Site:* www.storey.com, pg 223

Story Monsters Approved! Program, 4696 W Tyson St, Chandler, AZ 85226-2903 *Tel:* 480-940-8182 *Fax:* 480-940-8787 *Web Site:* www.StoryMonstersApproved.com, pg 692

Story Monsters LLC, 4696 W Tyson St, Chandler, AZ 85226-2903 *Tel:* 480-940-8182 *Fax:* 480-940-8787 *Web Site:* www.StoryMonsters.com; www.DragonflyBookAwards.com; www.AuthorsandExperts.com; www.SchoolBookings.com, pg 223

The Story Plant, PO Box 4331, Stamford, CT 06907 *Tel:* 203-722-7920 *E-mail:* thestoryplant@thestoryplant.com *Web Site:* www.thestoryplant.com, pg 223

The Story Prize, 41 Watchung Plaza, No 384, Montclair, NJ 07042 *Tel:* 973-932-0324 *E-mail:* info@thestoryprize.org *Web Site:* www.thestoryprize.org, pg 692

Storybook Arts Inc, 414 Poplar Hill Rd, Dover Plains, NY 12522 *Tel:* 845-877-3305 *Web Site:* www.storybookartsinc.com, pg 544

Elizabeth Matchett Stover Memorial Award, PO Box 750374, Dallas, TX 75275-0374 *Fax:* 214-768-1408 *E-mail:* swr@mail.smu.edu *Web Site:* www.smu.edu/southwestreview, pg 692

Strata Publishing Inc, PO Box 1303, State College, PA 16804 *Tel:* 814-234-8545 *Web Site:* www.stratapub.com, pg 223

Strategic Book Publishing & Rights Agency (SBPRA), 12620 FM W 1960, Suite A-4507, Houston, TX 77065 *Tel:* 703-637-6006 *Web Site:* sbpra.net; www.facebook.com/sbpra.us, pg 224

Strategic Media Books LLC, 782 Wofford St, Rock Hill, SC 29730 *Tel:* 803-366-5440 *E-mail:* contact@strategicmediabooks.com *Web Site:* strategicmediabooks.com, pg 224

Straus Literary, 319 Lafayette St, Suite 220, New York, NY 10012 *Tel:* 646-843-9950 *Fax:* 646-390-3320 *Web Site:* www.strausliterary.com, pg 538

Robin Straus Agency Inc, 229 E 79 St, Suite 5A, New York, NY 10075 *Tel:* 212-472-3282 *Fax:* 212-472-3833 *E-mail:* info@robinstrausagency.com *Web Site:* www.robinstrausagency.com, pg 538

Stress Free Kids®, 2561 Chimney Springs Dr, Marietta, GA 30062 *Tel:* 678-642-9555 *Toll Free Fax:* 866-302-2759 *E-mail:* media@stressfreekids.com *Web Site:* www.stressfreekids.com, pg 224

Marianne Strong Literary Agency, 65 E 96 St, New York, NY 10128 *Tel:* 212-249-1000 *Fax:* 212-831-3241 *Web Site:* stronglit.com, pg 538

Strothman Agency LLC, 63 E Ninth St, 10X, New York, NY 10003 *E-mail:* info@strothmanagency.com *Web Site:* www.strothmanagency.com, pg 538

The Jesse Stuart Foundation (JSF), 4440 13 St, Ashland, KY 41102 *Tel:* 606-326-1667 *Fax:* 606-325-2519 *E-mail:* jsf@jsfbooks.com *Web Site:* www.jsfbooks.com, pg 224

Jessamy Stursberg Poetry Contest for Youth, 192 Spadina Ave, Suite 312, Toronto, ON M5T 2C2, Canada *Tel:* 416-504-1657 *Fax:* 416-504-0096 *E-mail:* admin@poets.ca *Web Site:* poets.ca, pg 692

Stylus Publishing LLC, 22883 Quicksilver Dr, Sterling, VA 20166-2012 *Tel:* 703-661-1504 (edit & sales) *Toll Free Tel:* 800-232-0223 (orders & cust serv) *Fax:* 703-661-1547 *E-mail:* stylusmail@presswarehouse.com (orders & cust serv); stylusinfo@styluspub.com *Web Site:* www.styluspub.com, pg 224

Success Advertising & Publishing, 3419 Dunham Rd, Warsaw, NY 14569 *Tel:* 585-786-5663, pg 224

Sudden Fiction Contest, c/o ASUC Publications, Univ of California, 10-B Eshleman Hall, Berkeley, CA 94720-4500 *E-mail:* bfictionreview@yahoo.com *Web Site:* www.ocf.berkeley.edu/~bfr/, pg 692

Vivian Sudhalter, 1202 Loma Dr, No 117, Ojai, CA 93023 *Tel:* 805-640-9737 *E-mail:* vivians09@att.net, pg 502

The Sugarman Family Award for Jewish Children's Literature, Irwin P Edlavitch Bldg, 1529 16 St NW, Washington, DC 20036 *Tel:* 202-518-9400 *Fax:* 202-518-9420 *Web Site:* www.washingtondcjcc.org, pg 692

Ronald Sukenick American Book Review Innovative Fiction Prize, c/o Dept of English, Languages & Communincations Bldg, 255 S Central Campus Dr, Rm 3500, Salt Lake City, UT 84112-0494 *Tel:* 773-702-7000 *Web Site:* www.fc2.org/prizes.html, pg 692

The Summer Experience, 1831 College Ave, Suite 324, Regina, SK S4P 4V5, Canada *Tel:* 306-537-7243 *E-mail:* sage.hill@sasktel.net *Web Site:* www.sagehillwriting.ca, pg 615

Summer Words Writing Conference & Literary Festival, 110 E Hallam St, Suite 116, Aspen, CO 81611 *Tel:* 970-925-3122 *Fax:* 970-920-5700 *E-mail:* aspenwords@aspeninstitute.org *Web Site:* www.aspenwords.org, pg 615

Summer Writing Seminar, 7 E Pasture Rd, Aquinnah, MA 02535 *Tel:* 954-242-2903 *Web Site:* mvicw.com, pg 615

Hollis Summers Poetry Prize, 31 S Court St, Suite 143, Athens, OH 45701-2979 *Web Site:* www.ohioswallow.com/poetry_prize, pg 693

Summerthought Publishing, PO Box 2309, Banff, AB T1L 1C1, Canada *Tel:* 403-762-0535 *Fax:* 403-762-3095 *Toll Free Fax:* 800-762-3095 (orders) *E-mail:* info@summerthought.com; sales@summerthought.com *Web Site:* summerthought.com, pg 471

Summertime Publications Inc, 4115 E Palo Verde Dr, Phoenix, AZ 85018 *Tel:* 480-409-1554 *E-mail:* handell@summertimepublications.com *Web Site:* www.summertimepublications.com, pg 224

Summit University Press, 63 Summit Way, Gardiner, MT 59030-9314 *Tel:* 406-848-9742; 406-848-9500 (retail orders) *Toll Free Tel:* 800-245-5445 (retail orders) *Fax:* 406-848-9744 *E-mail:* info@summituniversitypress.com; marketing@summituniversitypress.com; production@summituniversitypress.com; rights@summituniversitypress.com *Web Site:* www.summituniversitypress.com, pg 224

Sun Publishing Company, PO Box 5588, Santa Fe, NM 87502-5588 *Tel:* 505-471-5177; 505-473-4161 *Toll Free Tel:* 877-849-0051 *E-mail:* info@sunbooks.com *Web Site:* www.sunbooks.com, pg 224

Sunbelt Publications Inc, 1250 Fayette St, El Cajon, CA 92020-1511 *Tel:* 619-258-4911 *Toll Free Tel:* 800-626-6579 (cust serv) *Fax:* 619-258-4916 *E-mail:* service@sunbeltpub.com; info@sunbeltpub.com *Web Site:* www.sunbeltbooks.com, pg 225

Sundance/Newbridge Publishing, 33 Boston Post Rd W, Suite 440, Marlborough, MA 01752 *Toll Free Tel:* 888-200-2720; 800-343-8204 (Sundance cust serv & orders); 800-867-0307 (Newbridge cust serv & orders) *Toll Free Fax:* 800-456-2419 (orders) *E-mail:* info@sundancepub.com; info@newbridgeonline.com *Web Site:* www.sundancepub.com; www.newbridgeonline.com, pg 225

Sunrise River Press, 838 Lake St S, Forrest Lake, MN 55025 *Tel:* 651-277-1400 *Toll Free Tel:* 800-895-4585 *Fax:* 651-277-1203 *E-mail:* info@sunriseriverpress.com; sales@sunriseriverpress.com *Web Site:* www.sunriseriverpress.com, pg 225

Sunstone Press, PO Box 2321, Santa Fe, NM 87504-2321 *Tel:* 505-988-4418 *Toll Free Tel:* 800-243-5644 *Fax:* 505-988-1025 (orders only) *Web Site:* www.sunstonepress.com, pg 225

Surrey Books, 1328 Greenleaf St, Evanston, IL 60202 *Tel:* 847-475-4457 *Toll Free Tel:* 800-326-4430 *Web Site:* agatepublishing.com/surrey, pg 225

Susquehanna University, Department of English and Creative Writing, 514 University Ave, Selinsgrove, PA 17870 *Tel:* 570-372-0101, pg 622

Fraser Sutherland, 39 Helena Ave, Toronto, ON M6G 2H3, Canada *Tel:* 416-652-5735 *E-mail:* rodfrasers@gmail.com, pg 502

Swagger Literary Agency, 601 Shenandoah Valley Dr, Front Royal, VA 22630 *Tel:* 540-636-7076 *E-mail:* swaggerlit@gmail.com *Web Site:* www.swaggerliterary.com, pg 538

Swallow Press, 31 S Court St, Suite 143, Athens, OH 45701 *Tel:* 740-593-1155 *Toll Free Tel:* 800-621-2736 *Fax:* 740-593-4536 *Web Site:* www.ohioswallow.com, pg 225

Swan Isle Press, 11030 S Langley Ave, Chicago, IL 60628 *Tel:* 773-728-3780 (edit); 773-702-7000 (cust serv) *Toll Free Tel:* 800-621-2736 (cust serv) *Fax:* 773-702-7212 (cust serv) *Toll Free Fax:* 800-621-8476 (cust serv) *E-mail:* info@swanislepress.com *Web Site:* www.swanislepress.com, pg 225

Carolyn Swayze Literary Agency Ltd, 7360 137 St, Suite 319, Surrey, BC V3W 1A3, Canada *Tel:* 604-503-3895 *E-mail:* reception@swayzeagency.com *Web Site:* www.swayzeagency.com, pg 539

Swedenborg Foundation, 320 N Church St, West Chester, PA 19380 *Tel:* 610-430-3222 *Toll Free Tel:* 800-355-3222 (cust serv) *Fax:* 610-430-7982 *E-mail:* info@swedenborg.com *Web Site:* www.swedenborg.com, pg 225

SYBEX Inc, 111 River St, Hoboken, NJ 07030-5774 *Tel:* 201-748-6000 *Fax:* 201-748-6088 *E-mail:* info@wiley.com *Web Site:* www.sybex.com; www.wiley.com, pg 226

Sydney Taylor Book Awards, PO Box 1118, Teaneck, NJ 07666 *Tel:* 201-371-3255 *E-mail:* chair@sydneytaylorbookaward.org; info@jewishlibraries.org *Web Site:* www.sydneytaylorbookaward.org, pg 693

Sydney Taylor Manuscript Award, 204 Park St, Montclair, NJ 07042 *Tel:* 201-371-3255 *E-mail:* info@jewishlibraries.org *Web Site:* jewishlibraries.org, pg 693

Charles S Sydnor Award, University of Georgia, Dept of History, Athens, GA 30602-1602 *Tel:* 706-542-8848 *Fax:* 706-542-2455 *Web Site:* thesha.org, pg 693

Synapse Information Resources Inc, 1247 Taft Ave, Endicott, NY 13760 *Tel:* 607-748-4145 *Toll Free Tel:* 888-SYN-CHEM (796-2436) *Fax:* 607-786-3966 *E-mail:* salesinfo@synapseinfo.com *Web Site:* www.synapseinfo.com, pg 226

Synaxis Press, 37323 Hawkins Rd, Dewdney, BC V0M 1H0, Canada *Tel:* 604-826-9336 *E-mail:* synaxis@new-ostrog.org *Web Site:* synaxispress.ca, pg 471

SynergEbooks, 948 New Hwy 7, Columbia, TN 38401 *Tel:* 931-548-2494 *E-mail:* synergebooks@aol.com *Web Site:* www.synergebooks.com, pg 226

Syracuse University Creative Writing Program, 401 Hall of Languages, Syracuse, NY 13244-1170 *Tel:* 315-443-2173 *Fax:* 315-443-3660 *Web Site:* english.syr.edu/creative_writing; www.syr.edu, pg 622

Syracuse University Press, 621 Skytop Rd, Suite 110, Syracuse, NY 13244-5290 *Tel:* 315-443-5534 *Toll Free Tel:* 800-365-8929 (cust serv) *Fax:* 315-443-5545 *E-mail:* supress@syr.edu *Web Site:* syracuseuniversitypress.syr.edu, pg 226

Syracuse University, SI Newhouse School of Public Communications, 215 University Place, Syracuse, NY 13244-2100 *Tel:* 315-443-3627 *Fax:* 315-443-3946 *E-mail:* newhouse@syr.edu *Web Site:* newhouse.syr.edu, pg 622

TAA Council of Fellows, PO Box 367, Fountain City, WI 54629 *E-mail:* info@taaonline.net *Web Site:* www.taaonline.net/council-of-fellows, pg 693

Tachyon Publications LLC, 1459 18 St, No 139, San Francisco, CA 94107 *Tel:* 415-285-5615 *E-mail:* tachyon@tachyonpublications.com *Web Site:* www.tachyonpublications.com, pg 226

Tahrike Tarsile Qur'an Inc, 80-08 51 Ave, Elmhurst, NY 11373 *Tel:* 718-446-6472 *Fax:* 718-446-4370 *E-mail:* read@koranusa.org *Web Site:* www.koranusa.org, pg 226

The Tampa Review Prize for Poetry, University of Tampa Press, 401 W Kennedy Blvd, Tampa, FL 33606 *Tel:* 813-253-6266 *E-mail:* utpress@ut.edu *Web Site:* tampareview.ut.edu, pg 693

TAN Books, PO Box 410487, Charlotte, NC 28241 *Tel:* 704-731-0651 *Toll Free Tel:* 800-437-5876 *Fax:* 815-226-7770 *E-mail:* customerservice@tanbooks.com *Web Site:* www.tanbooks.com, pg 226

T&T Clark International, 1385 Broadway, 5th fl, New York, NY 10018, pg 227

Tanglewood Publishing, 1060 N Capitol Ave, Suite E-395, Indianapolis, IN 46204 *Tel:* 812-877-9488 *Toll Free Tel:* 800-788-3123 (orders) *E-mail:* info@tanglewoodbooks.com; orders@tanglewoodbooks.com *Web Site:* www.tanglewoodbooks.com, pg 227

Tantor Media Inc, 6 Business Park, Old Saybrook, CT 06475 *Toll Free Tel:* 877-782-6867 *Toll Free Fax:* 888-782-7821 *Web Site:* www.tantor.com, pg 227

Taos Summer Writers' Conference, One University of New Mexico, Albuquerque, NM 87131-0001 *Tel:* 505-277-5572 *E-mail:* taosconf@unm.edu *Web Site:* taosconf.unm.edu, pg 615

Tapestry Press Ltd, 19 Nashoba Rd, Littleton, MA 01460 *Tel:* 978-486-0200 *Toll Free Tel:* 800-535-2007 *Fax:* 978-486-0244 *E-mail:* publish@tapestrypress.com *Web Site:* www.tapestrypress.com, pg 227

Taplinger Publishing Co Inc, PO Box 175, Marlboro, NJ 07746-0175 *Tel:* 305-256-7880 *Fax:* 305-256-7816 *E-mail:* taplingerpub@yahoo.com (rts & perms, edit, corp only), pg 227

TarcherPerigee, 375 Hudson St, New York, NY 10014 *Tel:* 212-366-2000 *Fax:* 212-366-2643 *E-mail:* customerservice@penguinrandomhouse.com (cust serv); TarcherPerigeePublicity@penguinrandomhouse.com (media queries) *Web Site:* www.tarcherbooks.com; www.facebook.com/TarcherPerigee/; www.penguin.com/publishers/tarcherperigee, pg 227

Taschen America, 6671 Sunset Blvd, Suite 1508, Los Angeles, CA 90028 *Tel:* 323-463-4441 *Toll Free Tel:* 888-TASCHEN (827-2436) *Fax:* 323-463-4442 *E-mail:* contact-us@taschen.com *Web Site:* www.taschen.com, pg 227

The Taunton Press Inc, 63 S Main St, Newtown, CT 06470 *Tel:* 203-426-8171 *Toll Free Tel:* 800-477-8727 (cust serv); 800-888-8286 (orders) *Fax:* 203-426-3434 *E-mail:* booksales@taunton.com *Web Site:* www.taunton.com, pg 227

Taylor & Francis Inc, 530 Walnut St, Suite 850, Philadelphia, PA 19106 *Tel:* 215-625-8900 *Toll Free Tel:* 800-354-1420 *Fax:* 215-207-0050; 215-207-0046 (cust serv) *E-mail:* support@tandfonline.com *Web Site:* www.taylorandfrancis.com, pg 227

The Charles Taylor Prize, 14-20 Brockton Ave, Toronto, ON M6K 1S5, Canada *E-mail:* rbctaylorprize@gmail.com *Web Site:* rbctaylorprize.ca, pg 693

Taylor-Dth Publishing, 108 Caribe Isle, Novato, CA 94949 *Tel:* 415-299-1087 *Web Site:* www.taylor-dth.com, pg 228

Rennie Taylor & Alton Blakeslee Fellowships in Science Writing, PO Box 910, Hedgesville, WV 25427 *Tel:* 304-754-6786 *Web Site:* www.casw.org, pg 693

TCP Press, 20200 Marsh Hill Rd, Uxbridge, ON L9P 1R3, Canada *Tel:* 905-852-3777 *Toll Free Tel:* 800-772-7765 *E-mail:* tcp@tcpnow.com *Web Site:* www.tcppress.com, pg 471

TCU Press, 3000 Sandage Ave, Fort Worth, TX 76109 *Tel:* 817-257-7822 *Toll Free Tel:* 800-826-8911 (orders) *Fax:* 817-257-5075 *Web Site:* www.prs.tcu.edu, pg 228

TD Canadian Children's Literature Award, 40 Orchard View Blvd, Suite 217, Toronto, ON M4R 1B9, Canada *Tel:* 416-975-0010 *Fax:* 416-975-8970 *E-mail:* info@bookcentre.ca *Web Site:* www.bookcentre.ca, pg 693

Teach Me Tapes Inc, 10400 N Enterprise Dr, Mequon, WI 53092 *Toll Free Tel:* 800-456-4656 *E-mail:* marie@teachmetapes.com *Web Site:* www.teachmetapes.com, pg 228

Teacher Created Resources Inc, 12621 Western Ave, Garden Grove, CA 92481 *Tel:* 714-891-7895 *Toll Free Tel:* 800-662-4321; 888-343-4335 *Toll Free Fax:* 800-525-1254 *E-mail:* custserv@teachercreated.com *Web Site:* www.teachercreated.com, pg 228

Teachers & Writers Collaborative, 520 Eighth Ave, Suite 2020, New York, NY 10018-4165 *Tel:* 212-691-6590 *Toll Free Tel:* 888-BOOKS-TW (266-5789) *Fax:* 212-675-0171 *E-mail:* info@twc.org *Web Site:* www.twc.org, pg 579

Teachers College Press, 1234 Amsterdam Ave, New York, NY 10027 *Tel:* 212-678-3929 *Toll Free Tel:* 800-575-6566 *Fax:* 212-678-4149; 802-864-7626 *E-mail:* tcpress@tc.columbia.edu; tcp.orders@aidcvt.com (orders) *Web Site:* www.teacherscollegepress.com, pg 228

Teacher's Discovery, 2741 Paldan Dr, Auburn Hills, MI 48326 *Toll Free Tel:* 800-832-2437 *Toll Free Fax:* 800-287-4509 *E-mail:* help@teachersdiscovery.com *Web Site:* www.teachersdiscovery.com, pg 228

Teaching & Learning Co, 501 E Third St, Dayton, OH 45402 *Tel:* 937-228-6118 *Toll Free Tel:* 800-444-1144 *Fax:* 937-223-2042 *E-mail:* info@lorenz.com *Web Site:* www.lorenzeducationalpress.com, pg 228

Teaching Strategies LLC, 4500 East-West Hwy, Suite 300, Bethesda, MD 20814 *Tel:* 301-634-0818 *Toll Free Tel:* 800-637-3652 *Fax:* 301-657-0250; 301-634-0833 *E-mail:* info@teachingstrategies.com *Web Site:* www.teachingstrategies.com, pg 228

Technical Association of the Pulp & Paper Industry (TAPPI), 15 Technology Pkwy S, Suite 115, Peachtree Corners, GA 30092 *Tel:* 770-446-1400 *Toll Free Tel:* 800-332-8686 (US); 800-446-9431 (CN) *Fax:* 770-446-6947 *E-mail:* memberconnection@tappi.org *Web Site:* www.tappi.org, pg 579

Television Academy, 5220 Lankershim Blvd, North Hollywood, CA 91601-3109 *Tel:* 818-754-2800 *Fax:* 818-761-2827 *Web Site:* www.emmys.com, pg 579

Temple University Press, 1852 N Tenth St, Philadelphia, PA 19122-6099 *Tel:* 215-926-2140 *Toll Free Tel:* 800-621-2736 *Fax:* 215-926-2141 *E-mail:* tempress@temple.edu *Web Site:* www.temple.edu/tempress, pg 228

Templegate Publishers, 302 E Adams St, Springfield, IL 62701 *Tel:* 217-522-3353 (edit & sales) *Toll Free Tel:* 800-367-4844 (orders only) *E-mail:* wisdom@templegate.com; orders@templegate.com (sales) *Web Site:* www.templegate.com, pg 229

Templeton Press, 300 Conshohocken State Rd, Suite 665, West Conshohocken, PA 19428 *Tel:* 484-531-8380 *Fax:* 484-531-8382 *E-mail:* tpinfo@templetonpress.org *Web Site:* www.templetonpress.org, pg 229

Temporal Mechanical Press, 6760 Hwy 7, Estes Park, CO 80517-6404 *Tel:* 970-586-4706 *E-mail:* info@enosmills.com *Web Site:* www.enosmills.com, pg 229

Ten Speed Press, 6001 Shellmound St, Suite 600, Emeryville, CA 94608 *Tel:* 510-285-3000 *Toll Free Tel:* 800-841-BOOK (841-2665) *Web Site:* crownpublishing.com/imprint/ten-speed-press, pg 229

Tennessee Arts Commission Fellowships, 401 Charlotte Ave, Nashville, TN 37243-0780 *Tel:* 615-741-1701 *Fax:* 615-741-8559 *Web Site:* www.tnartscommission.org, pg 693

The Tenth Gate Prize, *Tel:* 301-581-9439 *Fax:* 301-581-9443 *E-mail:* editor@wordworksbooks.org *Web Site:* www.wordworksbooks.org, pg 693

Teora USA LLC, 505 Hampton Park Blvd, Unit G, Capitol Heights, MD 20743 *Tel:* 301-986-6990 *Fax:* 301-350-5480 *E-mail:* 2010@teora.com *Web Site:* www.teora.com, pg 229

Terra Nova Books, 33 Alondra Rd, Santa Fe, NM 87508 *Tel:* 505-670-9319 *Fax:* 509-461-9333 *E-mail:* publisher@terranovabooks.com; marketing@terranovabooks.com *Web Site:* www.terranovabooks.com, pg 229

TESOL International Association, 1925 Ballenger Ave, Alexandria, VA 22314-6820 *Tel:* 703-836-0774 *Fax:* 703-836-7864; 703-836-6447 *E-mail:* publications@tesol.org; info@tesol.org; members@tesol.org *Web Site:* www.tesol.org, pg 229

Tessler Literary Agency LLC, 27 W 20 St, Suite 1003, New York, NY 10011 *Tel:* 212-242-0466 *Web Site:* www.tessleragency.com, pg 539

Teton NewMedia Inc, 90 E Simpson, Suite 110, Jackson, WY 83001 *Tel:* 307-732-0028 *Toll Free Tel:* 877-306-9793 *Fax:* 307-734-0841 *E-mail:* sales@tetonnm.com *Web Site:* www.tetonnm.com, pg 229

Texas A&M University Press, John H Lindsey Bldg, Lewis St, 4354 TAMU, College Station, TX 77843-4354 *Tel:* 979-845-1436 *Toll Free Tel:* 800-826-8911 (orders) *Fax:* 979-847-8752 *Toll Free Fax:* 888-617-2421 (orders) *E-mail:* bookorders@tamu.edu *Web Site:* www.tamupress.com, pg 230

The Texas Bluebonnet Award, 3355 Bee Cave Rd, Suite 401, Austin, TX 78746-6763 *Tel:* 512-328-1518 *Toll Free Tel:* 800-580-2852 *Fax:* 512-328-8852 *E-mail:* tla@txla.org *Web Site:* www.txla.org, pg 693

Texas Institute of Letters (TIL), c/o 7748 Hwy 290 W, Austin, TX 78736-3202 *E-mail:* president@texasinstituteofletters.org; secretary@texasinstituteofletters.org *Web Site:* www.texasinstituteofletters.org, pg 579

Texas Institute of Letters Awards, c/o 7748 Hwy 290 W, Austin, TX 78736-3202 *Tel:* 512-683-5640 *E-mail:* president@texasinstituteofletters.org *Web Site:* www.texasinstituteofletters.org, pg 693

Texas Library Association (TLA), 3355 Bee Cave Rd, Suite 401, Austin, TX 78746-6763 *Tel:* 512-328-1518 *Toll Free Tel:* 800-580-2852 *Fax:* 512-328-8852 *E-mail:* tla@txla.org *Web Site:* www.txla.org, pg 579

Texas State Historical Association, 3001 Lake Austin Blvd, Suite 3.116, Austin, TX 78703 *Tel:* 512-471-2600 *Fax:* 512-473-8691 *Web Site:* www.tshaonline.org, pg 230

Texas Tech University Press, 1120 Main St, 2nd fl, Lubbock, TX 79401 *Tel:* 806-742-2982 *Toll Free Tel:* 800-832-4042 *Fax:* 806-742-2979 *E-mail:* ttup@ttu.edu *Web Site:* www.ttupress.org, pg 230

University of Texas Press, 3001 Lake Austin Blvd, 2.200, Austin, TX 78703 *Tel:* 512-471-7233 *Fax:* 512-232-7178 *E-mail:* utpress@uts.cc.utexas.edu; info@utpress.utexas.edu *Web Site:* www.utexaspress.com, pg 230

Texas Western Press, c/o University of Texas at El Paso, 500 W University Ave, El Paso, TX 79968-0633 *Tel:* 915-747-5688 *Toll Free Tel:* 800-488-3798 (orders only) *Fax:* 915-747-7515 *E-mail:* twpress@utep.edu *Web Site:* twp.utep.edu, pg 230

Textbook Excellence Award, PO Box 367, Fountain City, WI 54629 *E-mail:* info@taaonline.net *Web Site:* www.taaonline.net/textbook-excellence-award, pg 694

TFH Publications Inc, PO Box 427, Neptune, NJ 07754 *Toll Free Tel:* 855-273-7527 (cust serv) *Fax:* 732-988-5466 (cust serv); 732-776-8763 (sales) *E-mail:* info@tfh.com (cust serv); sales@tfh.com *Web Site:* www.tfhpublications.com; www.tfh.com; www.facebook.com/TfhPetBooks, pg 230

Thames & Hudson, 500 Fifth Ave, New York, NY 10110 *Tel:* 212-354-3763 *Toll Free Tel:* 800-233-4830 *Fax:* 212-398-1252 *E-mail:* bookinfo@thames.wwnorton.com *Web Site:* www.thamesandhudsonusa.com, pg 230

The Society of Professional Journalists (SPJ), Eugene S Pulliam National Journalism Ctr, 3909 N Meridian St, Indianapolis, IN 46208 *Tel:* 317-927-8000 *Fax:* 317-920-4789 *E-mail:* spj@spj.org *Web Site:* www.spj.org, pg 580

Theatre Communications Group, 520 Eighth Ave, 24th fl, New York, NY 10018-4156 *Tel:* 212-609-5900 *Fax:* 212-609-5901 *E-mail:* tcg@tcg.org *Web Site:* www.tcg.org, pg 231

Theatre Library Association (TLA), c/o The New York Public Library for the Performing Arts, 40 Lincoln Center Plaza, New York, NY 10023 *E-mail:* TheatreLibraryAssociation@gmail.com *Web Site:* www.tla-online.org/awards/bookawards, pg 580

Theosophical University Press, PO Box C, Pasadena, CA 91109-7107 *Tel:* 626-798-3378 *E-mail:* tupress@theosociety.org *Web Site:* www.theosociety.org, pg 231

Theytus Books Ltd, RR 2, Green Mountain Rd, Site 50, Comp 8, Lot 45, Penticton, BC V2A 6J7, Canada *Tel:* 250-493-7181 *Fax:* 250-493-5302 *E-mail:* order@theytus.com *Web Site:* www.theytus.com, pg 471

Thieme Medical Publishers Inc, 333 Seventh Ave, 18th fl, New York, NY 10001 *Tel:* 212-760-0888 *Toll Free Tel:* 800-782-3488 *Fax:* 212-947-1112 *E-mail:* customerservice@thieme.com *Web Site:* www.thieme.com, pg 231

Third Coast Poetry & Fiction Contest, Western Michigan University English Dept, 1903 W Michigan Ave, Kalamazoo, MI 49008-5331 *E-mail:* editors@thirdcoastmagazine.com *Web Site:* www.thirdcoastmagazine.com/contests, pg 694

Third World Press, 7822 S Dobson Ave, Chicago, IL 60619 *Tel:* 773-651-0700 *Fax:* 773-651-7286 *E-mail:* twpress3@aol.com *Web Site:* www.thirdworldpressfoundation.com, pg 231

Thistledown Press, 410 Second Ave, Saskatoon, SK S7K 2C3, Canada *Tel:* 306-244-1722 *Fax:* 306-244-1762 *E-mail:* tdpress@thistledownpress.com; editorial@thistledownpress.com; marketing@thistledownpress.com *Web Site:* www.thistledownpress.com, pg 472

Thodestool Fiction Editing, 40 McDougall Rd, Waterloo, ON N2L 2W5, Canada *Web Site:* www.thodestool.com, pg 502

Charles C Thomas Publisher Ltd, 2600 S First St, Springfield, IL 62704 *Tel:* 217-789-8980 *Toll Free Tel:* 800-258-8980 *Fax:* 217-789-9130 *E-mail:* books@ccthomas.com *Web Site:* www.ccthomas.com, pg 231

Thomas Nelson, 501 Nelson Place, Nashville, TN 37214 *Tel:* 615-889-9000 *Toll Free Tel:* 800-251-4000 *Fax:* 615-902-1548 *Web Site:* www.thomasnelson.com, pg 231

Thompson Educational Publishing Inc, 20 Ripley Ave, Toronto, ON M6S 3N9, Canada *Tel:* 416-766-2763 (admin & orders) *Toll Free Tel:* 877-366-2763 *Fax:* 416-766-0398 (admin & orders) *E-mail:* info@thompsonbooks.com *Web Site:* www.thompsonbooks.com, pg 472

Thompson Mill Press LLC, 2110 S Eagle Rd, No 368, Newtown, PA 18940 *Tel:* 215-431-1424 *E-mail:* bob.regan@thompsonmillpress.com *Web Site:* www.thompsonmillpress.com; www.KobeeManatee.com, pg 478

Thomson Reuters Westlaw™, 610 Opperman Dr, Eagan, MN 55123 *Tel:* 651-687-7000 *Toll Free Tel:* 888-728-7677 (sales); 800-328-4880 (cust serv) *E-mail:* legalsolutions@thomsonreuters.com *Web Site:* legalsolutions.thomsonreuters.com, pg 231

Thorndike Press, 10 Water St, Suite 310, Waterville, ME 04901 *Toll Free Tel:* 800-223-1244 (ext 4, cust serv/orders) *Toll Free Fax:* 800-558-4676 (orders) *E-mail:* gale.printorders@cengage.com; international@cengage.com (cust orders outside US & CN) *Web Site:* www.gale.com/thorndike, pg 231

Susan Thornton, 6090 Liberty Ave, Vermilion, OH 44089 *Tel:* 440-967-1757 *E-mail:* allenthornton@earthlink.net, pg 502

3-Day Novel Contest, 201-111 W Hastings St, Vancouver, BC V6B 1H4, Canada *Tel:* 604-681-9161 *E-mail:* info@3daynovel.com *Web Site:* www.3daynovel.com, pg 694

3 Seas Literary Agency, PO Box 444, Sun Prairie, WI 53590 *Tel:* 608-834-9317 *E-mail:* threeseaslit@aol.com *Web Site:* threeseasagency.com, pg 539

Three Wishes Publishing Company, 26500 W Agoura Rd, Suite 102-754, Calabasas, CA 91302 *Tel:* 818-878-0902 *Fax:* 818-878-1805 *E-mail:* Alva710@aol.com *Web Site:* www.threewishespublishing.com, pg 478

ThunderStone Books, 6575 Horse Dr, Las Vegas, NV 89131 *E-mail:* info@thunderstonebooks.com *Web Site:* www.thunderstonebooks.com, pg 232

Thurber Prize for American Humor, 77 Jefferson Ave, Columbus, OH 43215 *Tel:* 614-464-1032 *Fax:* 614-280-3645 *E-mail:* thurberhouse@thurberhouse.org *Web Site:* www.thurberhouse.org, pg 694

Tide-mark Press, 22 Prestige Park Circle, East Hartford, CT 06108-1917 *Tel:* 860-310-3370 *Toll Free Tel:* 800-338-2508 *Fax:* 860-310-3654 *E-mail:* customerservice@tide-mark.com *Web Site:* www.tidemarkpress.com, pg 232

Tiger Tales, 5 River Rd, Suite 128, Wilton, CT 06897-4069 *Tel:* 920-387-2333 *Fax:* 920-387-9994 *Web Site:* www.tigertalesbooks.com, pg 232

Tilbury House Publishers, 12 Starr St, Thomaston, ME 04861 *Tel:* 207-582-1899 *Toll Free Tel:* 800-582-1899 (orders) *Fax:* 207-582-8227 *E-mail:* tilbury@tilburyhouse.com *Web Site:* www.tilburyhouse.com, pg 232

Timber Press Inc, 133 SW Second Ave, Suite 450, Portland, OR 97204 *Tel:* 503-227-2878 *Toll Free Tel:* 800-327-5680 *Fax:* 503-227-3070 *E-mail:* info@timberpress.com *Web Site:* www.timberpress.com, pg 232

James Tiptree Jr Award, 680 66 St, Oakland, CA 94609 *Tel:* 510-658-7176 *E-mail:* info@tiptree.org *Web Site:* tiptree.org, pg 694

TJ Publishers Inc, PO Box 702701, Dallas, TX 75370 *Toll Free Tel:* 800-999-1168 *Fax:* 972-416-0944 *E-mail:* TJPubinc@aol.com, pg 478

The Toby Press LLC, PO Box 8531, New Milford, CT 06776-8531 *Tel:* 203-830-8508 *Fax:* 203-830-8512 *E-mail:* toby@tobypress.com; sales@korenpub.com *Web Site:* www.tobypress.com; www.korenpub.com, pg 232

Todd Publications, 920 Dogwood Dr, No 461, Delray Beach, FL 33483 *Tel:* 561-910-0440 *Fax:* 561-910-0440 *E-mail:* toddpub@yahoo.com, pg 232

The Tomasino Agency Inc, 70 Chestnut St, Dobbs Ferry, NY 10522 *Tel:* 914-674-9659 *Fax:* 914-693-0381 *E-mail:* info@tomasinoagency.com *Web Site:* www.tomasinoagency.com, pg 539

Tommy Nelson, 501 Nelson Place, Nashville, TN 37214 *Tel:* 615-889-9000; 615-902-1485 (cust serv) *Toll Free Tel:* 800-251-4000 *Fax:* 615-391-5225 *Web Site:* www.tommynelson.com, pg 233

Top of the Mountain Publishing, 4837 62 St N, St Petersburg, FL 33709 *Tel:* 727-391-3958 *Web Site:* www.topofthemountain.com, pg 233

Top Publications Ltd, 2745 Dallas Pkwy, Suite 420, Plano, TX 75093 *Tel:* 972-628-6414 *Fax:* 972-233-0713 *E-mail:* info@toppub.com *Web Site:* topfiction.net, pg 233

Torah Aura Productions, 4423 Fruitland Ave, Los Angeles, CA 90058 *Tel:* 323-585-7312 *Toll Free Tel:* 800-238-6724 *Fax:* 323-585-0327 *E-mail:* misrad@torahaura.com; orders@torahaura.com *Web Site:* www.torahaura.com, pg 233

Torah Umesorah Publications, 620 Foster Ave, Brooklyn, NY 11230 *Tel:* 718-259-1223 *Fax:* 718-259-1795 *E-mail:* publications@torah-umesorah.org, pg 233

Toronto Book Awards, c/o Toronto Arts & Culture, City Hall, 9E, 100 Queen St W, Toronto, ON M5H 2N2, Canada *Web Site:* www.toronto.ca/book_awards, pg 694

Tortuga Press, 2777 Yulupa Ave, PMB 181, Santa Rosa, CA 95405 *Tel:* 707-544-4720 *Fax:* 707-595-5331 *E-mail:* info@tortugapress.com *Web Site:* www.tortugapress.com, pg 233

TotalRecall Publications Inc, 1103 Middlecreek, Friendswood, TX 77546 *Tel:* 281-992-3131 *E-mail:* sales@totalrecallpress.com *Web Site:* www.totalrecallpress.com, pg 233

Touchstone, 1230 Avenue of the Americas, New York, NY 10020, pg 233

TouchWood Editions, 103-1075 Pendergast St, Victoria, BC V8V 0A1, Canada *Tel:* 250-360-0829 *Fax:* 250-386-0829 *E-mail:* info@touchwoodeditions.com *Web Site:* www.touchwoodeditions.com, pg 472

Tower Publishing Co, 588 Saco Rd, Standish, ME 04084 *Tel:* 207-642-5400 *Toll Free Tel:* 800-969-8693 *Fax:* 207-264-3870 *E-mail:* info@towerpub.com *Web Site:* www.towerpub.com, pg 233

Townson Publishing Co Ltd, PO Box 1404, Sta A, Vancouver, BC V6C 2P7, Canada *Tel:* 604-886-0594 *E-mail:* townsonpublishing@gmail.com *Web Site:* generalpublishing.co.uk, pg 472

Towson University Prize for Literature, English Dept, 8000 York Rd, Towson, MD 21252 *Tel:* 410-704-2000 *Fax:* 410-704-3999 *Web Site:* www.towson.edu/english, pg 694

Tracks Publishing, 140 Brightwood Ave, Chula Vista, CA 91910 *Tel:* 619-476-7125 *Toll Free Tel:* 800-443-3570 *Fax:* 619-476-8173 *E-mail:* tracks@cox.net *Web Site:* www.startupsports.com, pg 233

Tradewind Books, 202-1807 Maritime Mews, Vancouver, BC V6H 3W7, Canada *Tel:* 604-662-4405 *E-mail:* tradewindbooks@yahoo.com; tradewindbooks@gmail.com *Web Site:* www.tradewindbooks.com, pg 472

Trafalgar Square Books, 388 Howe Hill Rd, North Pomfret, VT 05053 *Tel:* 802-457-1911 *Toll Free Tel:* 800-423-4525 *Fax:* 802-457-1913 *E-mail:* contact@trafalgarbooks.com *Web Site:* www.trafalgarbooks.com; www.horseandriderbooks.com, pg 234

Trafford, 1663 Liberty Dr, Bloomington, IN 47403 *Toll Free Tel:* 888-232-4444 *E-mail:* customersupport@trafford.com; sales@trafford.com *Web Site:* www.trafford.com, pg 234

Tralco-Lingo Fun, PO Box 79008, RPO Garth, Hamilton, ON L9C 7N6, Canada *Tel:* 905-575-5717 *Toll Free Tel:* 888-487-2526 *E-mail:* contact_tralco@tralco.com; sales@tralco.com *Web Site:* www.tralco.com, pg 472

Trans-Atlantic Publications Inc, 311 Bainbridge St, Philadelphia, PA 19147 *Tel:* 215-925-5083 *Fax:* 215-925-1912 *Web Site:* www.transatlanticpub.com; www.businesstitles.com, pg 234

Trans Tech Publications Inc, c/o Enfield Distribution Co, 234 May St, Enfield, NH 03748 *Tel:* 603-632-7377 *Fax:* 603-632-5611 *E-mail:* info@enfieldbooks.com *Web Site:* www.ttp.net, pg 234

Transaction Publishers Inc, 10 Corporate Place S, Suite 102, Piscataway, NJ 08854 *Tel:* 732-445-2280; 703-661-1589 (orders) *Toll Free Tel:* 888-999-6778 (dist ctr) *Fax:* 732-445-3138 *E-mail:* trans@transactionpub.com; orders@transactionpub.om *Web Site:* www.transactionpub.com, pg 234

Transatlantic Agency, 2 Bloor St E, Suite 3500, Toronto, ON M4W 1A8, Canada *Tel:* 416-488-9214 *E-mail:* info@transatlanticagency.com *Web Site:* www.transatlanticagency.com, pg 539

Transcontinental Music Publications (TMP), 1375 Remington Rd, Suite M, Schaumburg, IL 60173-4844 *Tel:* 847-781-7800 *Fax:* 847-781-7801 *E-mail:* tmp@accantors.org *Web Site:* www.transcontinentalmusic.com, pg 234

Translation Projects, 400 Seventh St SW, Washington, DC 20506-0001 *Tel:* 202-682-5400; 202-682-5496 (Voice/TTY); 202-682-5034 (lit fellowships hotline) *Fax:* 202-682-5609; 202-682-5610 *E-mail:* litfellowships@arts.gov *Web Site:* www.arts.gov, pg 694

Transportation Research Board (TRB), 500 Fifth St NW, Washington, DC 20001 *Tel:* 202-334-3213 (orders); 202-334-3072 (subns) *Fax:* 202-334-2519 *E-mail:* trbsales@nas.edu *Web Site:* trb.org, pg 234

Travel Keys, PO Box 160691, Sacramento, CA 95816-0691 *Tel:* 916-452-5200 *Fax:* 916-452-5200, pg 234

Travelers' Tales, 2320 Bowdoin St, Palo Alto, CA 94306 *Tel:* 650-462-2110 *Fax:* 650-462-6305 *E-mail:* ttales@travelerstales.com *Web Site:* travelerstales.com, pg 234

Treasure Bay Inc, PO Box 119, Novato, CA 94948 *Tel:* 415-884-2888 *Fax:* 415-884-2840 *E-mail:* webothread@comcast.net *Web Site:* www.webothread.com, pg 235

Treehaus Communications Inc, PO Box 249, Loveland, OH 45140-0249 *Tel:* 513-683-5716 *Toll Free Tel:* 800-638-4287 (orders) *Fax:* 513-683-2882 (orders) *E-mail:* treehaus@treehaus1.com *Web Site:* www.treehaus1.com, pg 235

Triad Publishing Co, PO Box 13355, Gainesville, FL 32604 *Fax:* 304-727-9345 *Toll Free Fax:* 800-854-4947 *E-mail:* orders@triadpublishing.com *Web Site:* www.triadpublishing.com, pg 235

TriadaUS Literary Agency, PO Box 561, Sewickley, PA 15143 *Tel:* 412-401-3376 *Web Site:* www.triadaus.com, pg 540

Trident Media Group LLC, 41 Madison Ave, 36th fl, New York, NY 10010 *Tel:* 212-333-1511 *E-mail:* info@tridentmediagroup.com; press@tridentmediagroup.com *Web Site:* www.tridentmediagroup.com, pg 540

Trillium Book Award/Prix Trillium, South Tower, Suite 501, 175 Bloor St E, Toronto, ON M4W 3R8, Canada *Tel:* 416-314-6858 (ext 698) *Fax:* 416-314-6876 *Web Site:* www.omdc.on.ca, pg 694

The Trinity Foundation, PO Box 68, Unicoi, TN 37692-0068 *Tel:* 423-743-0199 *Fax:* 423-743-2005 *Web Site:* www.trinityfoundation.org, pg 235

Trinity University Press, One Trinity Place, San Antonio, TX 78212-7200 *Tel:* 210-999-8884 *Fax:* 210-999-8838 *E-mail:* books@trinity.edu *Web Site:* www.tupress.org, pg 235

TripBuilder Media Inc, 180 Post Rd E, Suite 200, Westport, CT 06880 *Tel:* 203-227-1255 *Toll Free Tel:* 800-525-9745 *Fax:* 203-227-1257 *E-mail:* info@tripbuildermedia.com *Web Site:* www.tripbuildermedia.com, pg 235

TriQuarterly Books, 629 Noyes St, Evanston, IL 60208 *Tel:* 847-491-7420 *Toll Free Tel:* 800-621-2736 (orders only) *Fax:* 847-491-8150 *E-mail:* nupress@northwestern.edu *Web Site:* www.nupress.northwestern.edu, pg 235

TRISTAN Publishing, 2355 Louisiana Ave N, Minneapolis, MN 55427 *Tel:* 763-545-1383 *Toll Free Tel:* 866-545-1383 *Fax:* 763-545-1387 *E-mail:* info@tristanpublishing.com *Web Site:* www.tristanpublishing.com, pg 235

Triumph Books, 814 N Franklin St, Chicago, IL 60610 *Tel:* 312-337-0747 *Toll Free Tel:* 800-888-4741 (cust serv) *Fax:* 312-280-5470; 312-337-5985 *Web Site:* www.triumphbooks.com, pg 235

Triumph Learning LLC, 136 Madison Ave, 7th fl, New York, NY 10016 *Tel:* 212-652-0200 *Toll Free Tel:* 800-338-6519 (cust serv) *Toll Free Fax:* 866-805-5723 *E-mail:* info@triumphlearning.com; customerservice@triumphlearning.com *Web Site:* www.triumphlearning.com, pg 235

Harry S Truman Book Award, 500 W US Hwy 24, Independence, MO 64050 *Tel:* 816-268-8245 *Toll Free Tel:* 800-833-1225 *Web Site:* trumanlibraryinstitute.org, pg 694

Truman State University Press, 100 E Normal Ave, Kirksville, MO 63501-4221 *Tel:* 660-785-7336 *Toll Free Tel:* 800-916-6802 *Fax:* 660-785-4480 *E-mail:* tsup@truman.edu *Web Site:* tsup.truman.edu, pg 236

Trusted Media Brands Inc, 750 Third Ave, 3rd fl, New York, NY 10017 *Toll Free Tel:* 800-310-6261 (cust serv) *E-mail:* customercare@tmbi.com *Web Site:* www.tmbi.com; www.rd.com, pg 236

Trustus Playwrights' Festival, 520 Lady St, Columbia, SC 29201 *Tel:* 803-254-9732 *Web Site:* www.trustus.org, pg 694

TSG Publishing Foundation Inc, 28641 N 63 Place, Cave Creek, AZ 85331 *Tel:* 480-502-1909 *Fax:* 480-502-0713 *E-mail:* info@tsgfoundation.org *Web Site:* www.tsgfoundation.org, pg 236

Tudor Publishers Inc, 3109 Shady Lawn Dr, Greensboro, NC 27408 *Tel:* 336-288-5395 *E-mail:* tudorpublishers@triad.rr.com, pg 236

The Tuesday Agency, 132 1/2 E Washington St, Iowa City, IA 52240 *Tel:* 319-338-7080 *E-mail:* trinity@tuesdayagency.com *Web Site:* tuesdayagency.com, pg 548

Kate Tufts Discovery Award, Harper East, Unit B-7, 160 E Tenth St, Claremont, CA 91711-6165 *Tel:* 909-621-8974 *E-mail:* tufts@cgu.edu *Web Site:* www.cgu.edu/tufts, pg 695

Kingsley Tufts Poetry Award, Harper East, Unit B-7, 160 E Tenth St, Claremont, CA 91711-6165 *Tel:* 909-621-8974 *E-mail:* tufts@cgu.edu *Web Site:* www.cgu.edu/tufts, pg 695

Christina A Tugeau Artist Agency LLC, 29 Newman Place, Fairfield, CT 06825 *Tel:* 917-434-3141 *E-mail:* chris@catugeau.com *Web Site:* www.catugeau.com, pg 544

Tugeau 2 Inc, 2231 Grandview Ave, Cleveland Heights, OH 44106 *Tel:* 216-707-0854 *Web Site:* www.tugeau2.com, pg 544

Tughra Books, 335 Clifton Ave, Clifton, NJ 07011 *Tel:* 973-777-2704 *Fax:* 973-457-7334 *E-mail:* info@tughrabooks.com *Web Site:* www.tughrabooks.com, pg 236

Tumblehome Learning Inc, 201 Newbury St, Suite 201, Boston, MA 02116 *E-mail:* info@tumblehomelearning.com *Web Site:* www.tumblehomelearning.com, pg 236

Tundra Books, 320 Front St W, Suite 1400, Toronto, ON M5V 3B6, Canada *Tel:* 416-364-4449 *Toll Free Tel:* 888-523-9292 (orders); 800-588-1074 *Fax:* 416-598-7764 *Toll Free Fax:* 888-562-9924 (orders) *E-mail:* tundra@mcclelland.com *Web Site:* tundrabooks.wordpress.com, pg 472

Tupelo Press Berkshire Prize for a First or Second Book of Poetry, 243 Union St, Suite 305, North Adams, MA 01247 *Tel:* 413-664-9611 *Fax:* 413-664-9711 *E-mail:* info@tupelopress.org *Web Site:* www.tupelopress.org, pg 695

Tupelo Press Inc, 243 Union St, Suite 305, North Adams, MA 01247 *Tel:* 413-664-9611 *Fax:* 413-664-9711 *E-mail:* info@tupelopress.org *Web Site:* www.tupelopress.org, pg 236

Tupelo Press Snowbound Series Chapbook Award, 243 Union St, Suite 305, North Adams, MA 01247 *Tel:* 413-664-9611 *Fax:* 413-664-9711 *E-mail:* info@tupelopress.org *Web Site:* www.tupelopress.org, pg 695

Turner Publishing Co, 4507 Charlotte Ave, Suite 100, Nashville, TN 37209 *Tel:* 615-255-BOOK (255-2665) *Fax:* 615-255-5081 *E-mail:* marketing@turnerpublishing.com; submissions@turnerpublishing.com *Web Site:* www.turnerpublishing.com; www.facebook.com/turner.publishing, pg 236

Turnstone Press, Artspace Bldg, 206-100 Arthur St, Winnipeg, MB R3B 1H3, Canada *Tel:* 204-947-1555 *Toll Free Tel:* 888-363-7718 *Fax:* 204-942-1556 *E-mail:* info@turnstonepress.com *Web Site:* www.turnstonepress.com, pg 473

Turtle Point Press, 208 Java St, 5th fl, Brooklyn, NY 11222-5748 *Tel:* 212-741-1393 *E-mail:* info@turtlepointpress.com *Web Site:* www.turtlepointpress.com, pg 236

The Tusculum Review Prize for Fiction, 60 Shiloh Rd, PO Box 5113, Greeneville, TN 37743 *Web Site:* www.tusculum.edu/tusculumreview, pg 695

Tuttle Publishing, Airport Business Park, 364 Innovation Dr, North Clarendon, VT 05759-9436 *Tel:* 802-773-8930 *Toll Free Tel:* 800-526-2778 *Fax:* 802-773-6993 *Toll Free Fax:* 800-FAX-TUTL (329-8885) *E-mail:* info@tuttlepublishing.com; orders@tuttlepublishing.com *Web Site:* www.tuttlepublishing.com, pg 236

Tuxedo Press, 546 E Springville Rd, Carlisle, PA 17015 *Tel:* 717-258-9733 *Fax:* 717-243-0074 *E-mail:* info@tuxedo-press.com *Web Site:* tuxedo-press.com, pg 237

Twenty-First Century Books, 241 First Ave N, Minneapolis, MN 55401 *Tel:* 612-332-3344 *Toll Free Tel:* 800-328-4929 *Fax:* 612-332-7615 *Toll Free Fax:* 800-332-1132 *E-mail:* info@lernerbooks.com; custserve@lernerbooks.com *Web Site:* www.lernerbooks.com; www.facebook.com/lernerbooks, pg 237

The 25 Most "Censored" Stories Annual, PO Box 750940, Petaluma, CA 94975 *Tel:* 707-241-4596 *Web Site:* www.projectcensored.org, pg 695

Twenty-Third Publications, One Montauk Ave, Suite 200, New London, CT 06320 *Tel:* 860-437-3012 *Toll Free Tel:* 800-321-0411 (orders) *Toll Free Fax:* 800-572-0788 *E-mail:* resources@twentythirdpublications.com *Web Site:* www.twentythirdpublications.com, pg 237

Twilight Times Books, PO Box 3340, Kingsport, TN 37664-0340 *Tel:* 423-323-0183 *Fax:* 423-323-0183 *E-mail:* publisher@twilighttimes.com *Web Site:* www.twilighttimesbooks.com, pg 237

Twin Oaks Indexing, 138 Twin Oaks Rd, Suite W, Louisa, VA 23093 *Tel:* 540-894-5126 *Web Site:* www.twinoakscommunity.org, pg 502

Two Thousand Three Associates, 135 Chilean Ave, Palm Beach, FL 33480 *Tel:* 386-690-2503 *E-mail:* ttta1@att.net *Web Site:* www.twothousandthree.com, pg 237

2M Communications Ltd, 19 W 21 St, Suite 501, New York, NY 10010 *Tel:* 212-741-1509 *Fax:* 212-691-4460 *Web Site:* www.2mcommunications.com, pg 540

Tyndale House Publishers Inc, 351 Executive Dr, Carol Stream, IL 60188 *Tel:* 630-668-8300 *Toll Free Tel:* 800-323-9400 *Toll Free Fax:* 800-684-0247 *Web Site:* www.tyndale.com, pg 237

UCLA Latin American Center Publications, UCLA Latin American Institute, 10343 Bunche Hall, Los Angeles, CA 90095 *Tel:* 310-825-4571 *Fax:* 310-206-6859 *E-mail:* latinamctr@international.ucla.edu *Web Site:* www.international.ucla.edu/lai, pg 238

Ucross Foundation Residency Program, 30 Big Red Lane, Clearmont, WY 82835 *Tel:* 307-737-2291 *Fax:* 307-737-2322 *E-mail:* info@ucross.org *Web Site:* www.ucrossfoundation.org, pg 695

Ugly Duckling Presse, The Old American Can Factory, 232 Third St, Suite E303, Brooklyn, NY 11215 *Tel:* 347-948-5170 *E-mail:* info@uglyducklingpresse.org *Web Site:* www.uglyducklingpresse.org, pg 238

Ulysses Press, PO Box 3440, Berkeley, CA 94703-0440 *Tel:* 510-601-8301 *Toll Free Tel:* 800-377-2542 *Fax:* 510-601-8307 *E-mail:* ulysses@ulyssespress.com *Web Site:* www.ulyssespress.com, pg 238

Ulysses Travel Guides, 4176, rue Saint-Denis, Montreal, QC H2W 2M5, Canada *Tel:* 514-843-9882 (ext 2232); 514-843-9447 (bookstore) *Toll Free Tel:* 800-748-9171 *Fax:* 514-843-9448 *E-mail:* info@ulysses.ca; st-denis@ulysses.ca *Web Site:* www.ulyssesguides.com, pg 473

Unarius Academy of Science Publications, 145 S Magnolia Ave, El Cajon, CA 92020-4522 *Tel:* 619-444-7062 *Toll Free Tel:* 800-475-7062 *Fax:* 619-444-9637 *E-mail:* uriel@unarius.org *Web Site:* www.unarius.org, pg 238

Unicorn Writers' Conference, 17 Church Hill Rd, Redding, CT 06896 *Tel:* 203-938-7405 *Fax:* 203-938-7405 *E-mail:* unicornwritersconference@gmail.com *Web Site:* unicornwritersconference.com, pg 615

Editorial Unilit, 8167 NW 84 St, Medley, FL 33166 *Tel:* 305-592-6136 *Toll Free Tel:* 800-767-7726 *Fax:* 305-592-0087 *E-mail:* info@editorialunilit.com; customerservice@editorialunilit.com *Web Site:* www.editorialunilit.com, pg 238

The United Educators Inc, 900 W North Shore Dr, Suite 276, Lake Bluff, IL 60044 *Tel:* 847-234-3700 *Toll Free Tel:* 800-323-5875 *Fax:* 847-234-8705, pg 238

United for Libraries, 859 W Lancaster Ave, Suite 2-1, Bryn Mawr, PA 19010 *Tel:* 312-280-2161 *Toll Free Tel:* 800-545-2433 (ext 2161) *Fax:* 484-698-7868 *E-mail:* united@ala.org *Web Site:* www.ala.org/united, pg 580

United Nations Association of the United States of America, 1750 Pennsylvania Ave NW, Suite 300, Washington, DC 20006 *Tel:* 202-887-9040 *Fax:* 202-887-9021 *Web Site:* www.unausa.org, pg 580

United Nations Publications, 300 E 42 St, 9th fl, New York, NY 10017 *Tel:* 703-661-1571 *Fax:* 703-996-1010 *E-mail:* publications@un.org *Web Site:* shop.un.org, pg 238

United States Holocaust Memorial Museum, 100 Raoul Wallenberg Place SW, Washington, DC 20024-2126 *Tel:* 202-314-7837; 202-488-6144 (orders) *Toll Free Tel:* 800-259-9998 (orders) *Fax:* 202-479-9726; 202-488-0438 (orders) *E-mail:* cahs_publications@ushmm.org *Web Site:* www.ushmm.org, pg 238

United States Institute of Peace Press, 2301 Constitution Ave NW, Washington, DC 20037 *Tel:* 202-457-1700 (edit); 703-661-1590 (cust serv) *Toll Free Tel:* 800-868-8064 (cust serv) *Fax:* 202-429-6063; 703-661-1501 (cust serv) *E-mail:* usipmail@presswarehouse.com (orders) *Web Site:* bookstore.usip.org, pg 239

United States Pharmacopeia, 12601 Twinbrook Pkwy, Rockville, MD 20852-1790 *Tel:* 301-881-0666 *Toll Free Tel:* 800-227-8772 *Fax:* 301-816-8237 (mktg) *E-mail:* marketing@usp.org *Web Site:* www.usp.org, pg 239

United States Tennis Association, 70 W Red Oak Lane, White Plains, NY 10604 *Tel:* 914-696-7000 *Fax:* 914-696-7027 *Web Site:* www.usta.com, pg 239

United Talent Agency, 9336 Civic Center Dr, Beverly Hills, CA 90210 *Tel:* 310-273-6700 *Fax:* 310-247-1111 *Web Site:* www.unitedtalent.com, pg 540

Univelt Inc, 740 Metcalf St, No 13, Escondido, CA 92025 *Tel:* 760-746-4005 *Fax:* 760-746-3139 *E-mail:* sales@univelt.com *Web Site:* www.univelt.com; www.astronautical.org, pg 239

Universal-Publishers Inc, 23331 Water Circle, Boca Raton, FL 33486-8540 *Tel:* 561-750-4344 *Toll Free Tel:* 800-636-8329 (US only) *Fax:* 561-750-6797 *Web Site:* www.universal-publishers.com, pg 239

Universe Publishing, 300 Park Ave S, 4th fl, New York, NY 10010 *Tel:* 212-387-3400 *Fax:* 212-387-3535, pg 239

University Council for Educational Administration, University of Virginia, Curry School of Education, 405 Emmet St S, Ruffner Hall, Rm 400287, Charlottesville, VA 22903-2424 *Tel:* 434-243-1041 *E-mail:* ucea.org@gmail.com *Web Site:* www.ucea.org, pg 239

University of Alabama Press, 200 Hackberry Lane, 2nd fl, Tuscaloosa, AL 35487 *Tel:* 205-348-5180 *Fax:* 205-348-9201 *Web Site:* www.uapress.ua.edu, pg 239

University of Alabama Program in Creative Writing, PO Box 870244, Tuscaloosa, AL 35487-0244 *Tel:* 205-348-5065 *Fax:* 205-348-1388 *E-mail:* english@ua.edu *Web Site:* www.as.ua.edu/english, pg 622

University of Alaska Press, 1760 Westwood Way, Fairbanks, AK 99709 *Tel:* 907-474-5831 *Toll Free Tel:* 888-252-6657 (US only) *Fax:* 907-474-5502 *Web Site:* www.alaska.edu/uapress, pg 239

University of Alberta Press, Ring House 2, Edmonton, AB T6G 2E1, Canada *Tel:* 780-492-3662 *Fax:* 780-492-0719 *Web Site:* www.uap.ualberta.ca, pg 473

The University of Arizona Press, 1510 E University Blvd, Tucson, AZ 85721 *Tel:* 520-621-1441 *Toll Free Tel:* 800-426-3797 (orders) *Fax:* 520-621-8899 *Toll Free Fax:* 800-426-3797 *E-mail:* uap@uapress.arizona.edu *Web Site:* www.uapress.arizona.edu, pg 240

The University of Arkansas Press, McIlroy House, 105 N McIlroy Ave, Fayetteville, AR 72701 *Tel:* 479-575-3246 *Toll Free Tel:* 800-626-0090 *Fax:* 479-575-6044 *E-mail:* info@uapress.com *Web Site:* www.uapress.com, pg 240

University of Baltimore - Yale Gordon College of Arts & Sciences, Ampersand Institute for Words & Images, 1420 N Charles St, Baltimore, MD 21201-5779 *Tel:* 410-837-6022 *Fax:* 410-837-6029 *E-mail:* scd@ubalt.edu *Web Site:* www.ubalt.edu, pg 623

University of British Columbia Press, 2029 West Mall, Vancouver, BC V6T 1Z2, Canada *Tel:* 604-822-5959 *Toll Free Tel:* 877-377-9378 *Fax:* 604-822-6083 *Toll Free Fax:* 800-668-0821 *E-mail:* frontdesk@ubcpress.ca *Web Site:* www.ubcpress.ca, pg 473

University of Calgary Press, 2500 University Dr NW, Calgary, AB T2N 1N4, Canada *Tel:* 403-220-7578 *Fax:* 403-282-0085 *E-mail:* ucpress@ucalgary.ca *Web Site:* press.ucalgary.ca, pg 474

University of California Extension Professional Sequence in Copyediting & Courses in Publishing, 1995 University Ave, Suite 110, Berkeley, CA 94720-7000 *Tel:* 510-642-6362 *Fax:* 510-643-0216 *E-mail:* letters@unex.berkeley.edu *Web Site:* www.unex.berkeley.edu, pg 623

University of California Institute on Global Conflict & Cooperation, 9500 Gilman Dr, MC 0518, La Jolla, CA 92093-0518 *Tel:* 858-534-6106 *Fax:* 858-534-7655 *E-mail:* igcc-communications@ucsd.edu *Web Site:* igcc.ucsd.edu, pg 240

University of California Press, 155 Grand Ave, Suite 400, Oakland, CA 94612-3758 *Tel:* 510-883-8232 *Fax:* 510-836-8910 *E-mail:* customerservice@ucpressjournals.com *Web Site:* www.ucpress.edu, pg 240

University of Chicago, Graham School of General Studies, 1427 E 60 St, Chicago, IL 60637 *Tel:* 773-702-1722 *Fax:* 773-702-6814 *Web Site:* www.grahamschool.uchicago.edu, pg 623

University of Chicago Press, 1427 E 60 St, Chicago, IL 60637-2954 *Tel:* 773-702-7700; 773-702-7600 *Toll Free Tel:* 800-621-2736 (orders) *Fax:* 773-702-9756; 773-660-2235 (orders); 773-702-2708 *E-mail:* custserv@press.uchicago.edu; marketing@press.uchicago.edu *Web Site:* www.press.uchicago.edu, pg 240

University of Delaware Press, 200A Morris Library, 181 S College Ave, Newark, DE 19717-5267 *Tel:* 302-831-1149 *Fax:* 302-831-6549 *E-mail:* ud-press@udel.edu *Web Site:* library.udel.edu/udpress, pg 241

University of Denver Publishing Institute, 2000 E Asbury Ave, Denver, CO 80208 *Tel:* 303-871-2570 *Fax:* 303-871-2501 *Web Site:* www.du.edu/publishinginstitute, pg 623

University of Georgia Press, Main Library, 3rd fl, 320 S Jackson St, Athens, GA 30602 *Fax:* 706-542-2558; 706-542-6770 *Web Site:* www.ugapress.org, pg 241

University of Hawaii Press, 2840 Kolowalu St, Honolulu, HI 96822 *Tel:* 808-956-8255 *Toll Free Tel:* 888-UHPRESS (847-7377) *Fax:* 808-988-6052 *Toll Free Fax:* 800-650-7811 *E-mail:* uhpbooks@hawaii.edu *Web Site:* www.uhpress.hawaii.edu, pg 241

University of Houston Creative Writing Program, 229 Roy Cullen Bldg, Houston, TX 77204-5008 *Tel:* 713-743-2255 *Fax:* 713-743-3697 *E-mail:* cwp@uh.edu *Web Site:* www.uh.edu/cwp, pg 623

University of Illinois at Chicago, Program for Writers, College of Liberal Arts & Sciences, 2027 University Hall, 601 S Morgan St, Chicago, IL 60607-7120 *Tel:* 312-413-2200 (Eng dept) *Fax:* 312-413-1005 *Web Site:* www.uic.edu, pg 623

University of Illinois, Department of Journalism, Gregory Hall, Rm 120-A, 810 S Wright St, Urbana, IL 61801 *Tel:* 217-333-0709 *Fax:* 217-333-7931 *E-mail:* journ@uiuc.edu *Web Site:* www.comm.uiuc.edu, pg 623

University of Illinois Press, 1325 S Oak St, MC-566, Champaign, IL 61820-6903 *Tel:* 217-333-0950 *Fax:* 217-244-8082 *E-mail:* uipress@uillinois.edu; journals@uillinois.edu *Web Site:* www.press.uillinois.edu, pg 241

University of Iowa Press, 119 W Park Rd, 100 Kuhl House, Iowa City, IA 52242-1000 *Tel:* 319-335-2000 *Toll Free Tel:* 800-621-2736 (orders only) *Fax:* 319-335-2055 *Toll Free Fax:* 800-621-8476 (orders only) *E-mail:* uipress@uiowa.edu *Web Site:* www.uiowapress.org, pg 242

University of Iowa, Writers' Workshop, Graduate Creative Writing Program, 102 Dey House, 507 N Clinton St, Iowa City, IA 52242-1000 *Tel:* 319-335-0416 *Fax:* 319-335-0420 *Web Site:* writersworkshop.uiowa.edu, pg 623

University of Louisiana at Lafayette Press, PO Box 43558, Lafayette, LA 70504-3558 *Tel:* 337-482-6027 *Fax:* 337-482-6028 *E-mail:* ulpress@louisiana.edu *Web Site:* www.ulpress.org, pg 242

University of Manitoba Press, University of Manitoba, 301 St Johns College, 92 Dysart Rd, Winnipeg, MB R3T 2M5, Canada *Tel:* 204-474-9495 *Fax:* 204-474-7566 *E-mail:* uofmpress@umanitoba.ca *Web Site:* uofmpress.ca, pg 474

University of Massachusetts Press, East Experiment Sta, 671 N Pleasant St, Amherst, MA 01003 *Tel:* 413-545-2217 *Fax:* 413-545-1226 *E-mail:* info@umpress.umass.edu *Web Site:* www.umass.edu/umpress, pg 242

University of Michigan Press, 839 Greene St, Ann Arbor, MI 48104-3209 *Tel:* 734-764-4388 *Fax:* 734-615-1540 *E-mail:* esladmin@umich.edu *Web Site:* www.press.umich.edu, pg 242

University of Minnesota Press, 111 Third Ave S, Suite 290, Minneapolis, MN 55401-2520 *Tel:* 612-301-1990 *Fax:* 612-301-1980 *E-mail:* ump@umn.edu *Web Site:* www.upress.umn.edu, pg 242

University of Missouri Press, 113 Heinkel Bldg, 201 S Seventh St, Columbia, MO 65211 *Tel:* 573-882-7641 *Toll Free Tel:* 800-621-2736 (orders) *Fax:* 573-884-4498 *Toll Free Fax:* 800-621-8476 (orders) *E-mail:* upress@missouri.edu *Web Site:* upress.missouri.edu; press.umsystem.edu, pg 242

University of Montana, Environmental Writing Institute, Environmental Studies, University of Montana, Missoula, MT 59812 *Tel:* 406-243-2904 *Fax:* 406-243-6090 *Web Site:* www.umt.edu/ewi, pg 623

University of Nebraska Press, 1111 Lincoln Mall, Lincoln, NE 68588-0630 *Tel:* 402-472-3581; 919-966-7449 (cust serv & foreign orders) *Toll Free Tel:* 800-848-6224 (cust serv & US orders) *Fax:* 402-472-6214; 919-962-2704 (cust serv & foreign orders) *Toll Free Fax:* 800-526-2617 (cust serv & US orders) *E-mail:* pressmail@unl.edu *Web Site:* www.nebraskapress.unl.edu, pg 243

University of Nevada Press, c/o University of Nevada, Continuing Educ Bldg, MS 0166, Reno, NV 89557-0166 *Tel:* 775-784-6573 *Fax:* 775-784-6200 *Web Site:* www.unpress.nevada.edu, pg 243

University of New Mexico Press, One University of New Mexico, Albuquerque, NM 87131-0001 *Tel:* 505-272-7777 *Fax:* 505-277-3343; 505-272-7778 (cust serv) *Toll Free Fax:* 800-622-8667 (orders only) *E-mail:* unmpress@unm.edu; custserv@unm.edu (order dept) *Web Site:* unmpress.com, pg 243

The University of North Carolina Press, 116 S Boundary St, Chapel Hill, NC 27514-3808 *Tel:* 919-966-3561 *Fax:* 919-966-3829 *E-mail:* uncpress@unc.edu *Web Site:* www.uncpress.unc.edu, pg 243

University of North Texas Press, Willis Library, Rm 251, 1506 Highland St, Denton, TX 76203-5017 *Tel:* 940-565-2142 *Fax:* 940-565-4590 *Web Site:* untpress.unt.edu, pg 243

University of Notre Dame Press, 310 Flanner Hall, Notre Dame, IN 46556 *Tel:* 574-631-6346 *Fax:* 574-631-8148 *E-mail:* undpress@nd.edu *Web Site:* www.undpress.nd.edu, pg 244

University of Oklahoma Press, 2800 Venture Dr, Norman, OK 73069-8216 *Tel:* 405-325-2000 *Toll Free Tel:* 800-627-7377 (orders) *Fax:* 405-364-5798 (orders) *Toll Free Fax:* 800-735-0476 (orders) *E-mail:* presscs@ou.edu *Web Site:* www.oupress.com, pg 244

University of Ottawa Press (Presses de l'Université d'Ottawa), 542 King Edward Ave, Ottawa, ON K1N 6N5, Canada *Tel:* 613-562-5246 *Fax:* 613-562-5247 *E-mail:* puo-oup@uottawa.ca *Web Site:* press.uottawa.ca, pg 474

University of Pennsylvania Museum of Archaeology & Anthropology, 3260 South St, Philadelphia, PA 19104-6324 *Tel:* 215-898-6322; 215-898-4119 *E-mail:* publications@pennmuseum.org; info@pennmuseum.org *Web Site:* www.penn.museum, pg 244

University of Pennsylvania Press, 3905 Spruce St, Philadelphia, PA 19104 *Tel:* 215-898-6261 *Fax:* 215-898-0404 *E-mail:* custserv@pobox.upenn.edu *Web Site:* www.pennpress.org, pg 244

University of Pittsburgh Press, 7500 Thomas Blvd, Pittsburgh, PA 15260 *Tel:* 412-383-2456 *Fax:* 412-383-2466 *E-mail:* info@upress.pitt.edu *Web Site:* www.upress.pitt.edu, pg 244

University of Puerto Rico Press, Edificio La Editorial (level 2), Carr No 1, KM 12.0, Jardin Botanico Norte, San Juan, PR 00927 *Tel:* 787-250-0435; 787-250-0550 *Toll Free Tel:* 877-338-7788 *Fax:* 787-753-9116 *E-mail:* info@laeditorialupr.com *Web Site:* www.laeditorialupr.com, pg 244

University of Regina Press, 2 Research Dr, Suite 246, Regina, SK S4S 7H9, Canada *Tel:* 306-585-4758 *Fax:* 306-585-4699 *E-mail:* uofrpress@uregina.ca *Web Site:* uofrpress.ca, pg 474

University of Rochester Press, 668 Mount Hope Ave, Rochester, NY 14620-2731 *Tel:* 585-275-0419 *Fax:* 585-271-8778 *E-mail:* boydell@boydellusa.net *Web Site:* www.urpress.com, pg 245

University of South Carolina Press, 1600 Hampton St, Suite 544, Columbia, SC 29208 *Tel:* 803-777-5245 *Toll Free Tel:* 800-768-2500 (orders) *Fax:* 803-777-0160 *Toll Free Fax:* 800-868-0740 (orders) *Web Site:* www.sc.edu/uscpress, pg 245

University of Southern California, Master of Professional Writing Program, Mark Taper Hall, THH 355, 3501 Trousedale Pkwy, Los Angeles, CA 90089-0355 *Tel:* 213-740-3252 *Fax:* 213-740-5002 *E-mail:* mpw@college.usc.edu *Web Site:* college.usc.edu/mpw, pg 623

University of Tennessee Press, 110 Conference Center Bldg, 600 Henley St, Knoxville, TN 37996-4108 *Tel:* 865-974-3321 *Toll Free Tel:* 800-621-2736 (orders) *Fax:* 865-974-3724 *Toll Free Fax:* 800-621-8476 (orders) *E-mail:* custserv@utpress.org *Web Site:* www.utpress.org, pg 245

University of Texas at Arlington College of Architecture, Planning & Public Affairs, 601 S Nedderman Dr, Suite 203, Arlington, TX 76019 *Fax:* 817-272-5008 *E-mail:* cappa@uta.edu *Web Site:* www.uta.edu/cappa, pg 245

University of Texas at Austin, New Writers Project, Dept of English, Calhoun Hall, Rm 226, 204 W 21 St, B-5000, Austin, TX 78712 *Tel.* 512-471-5132, 512-471-4991 *Fax:* 512-471-4909 *Web Site:* newwritersproject.org, pg 623

University of Texas at El Paso, Department of Creative Writing, MFA/Department of Creative Writing, 901 EDUC, 500 W University Ave, El Paso, TX 79968-9991 *Tel:* 915-747-5713 *Fax:* 915-747-5523 *E-mail:* creativewriting@utep.edu *Web Site:* www.utep.edu/cw, pg 623

University of Toronto Press, 10 St Mary St, Suite 700, Toronto, ON M4Y 2W8, Canada *Tel:* 416-978-2239 *Fax:* 416-978-4738 *E mail:* info@utpress.utoronto.ca *Web Site:* www.utpress.utoronto.ca; www.utppublishing.com, pg 474

The University of Utah Press, J Willard Marriott Library, Suite 5400, 295 S 1500 E, Salt Lake City, UT 84112-0860 *Tel:* 801-585-9786 *Fax:* 801-581-3365 *E-mail:* hannah.new@utah.edu *Web Site:* www.uofupress.com, pg 245

The University of Virginia Press, PO Box 400318, Charlottesville, VA 22904-4318 *Tel:* 434-924-3468 (cust serv); 434-924-3469 (cust serv) *Toll Free Tel:* 800-831-3406 (orders) *Fax:* 434-982-2655 *Toll Free Fax:* 877-288-6400 *E-mail:* vapress@virginia.edu *Web Site:* www.upress.virginia.edu, pg 245

University of Washington Press, 4333 Brooklyn Ave NE, Seattle, WA 98105-9570 *Tel:* 206-543-4050 *Toll Free Tel:* 800-537-5487 (orders) *Fax:* 206-543-3932; 410-516-6998 (orders) *E-mail:* uwapress@uw.edu *Web Site:* www.washington.edu/uwpress, pg 246

University of Wisconsin-Madison Continuing Studies, 21 N Park St, 7th fl, Madison, WI 53715 *Tel:* 608-262-3447 *Web Site:* continuingstudies.wisc.edu, pg 624

University of Wisconsin Press, 1930 Monroe St, 3rd fl, Madison, WI 53711-2059 *Tel:* 608-263-0668 *Toll Free Tel:* 800-621-2736 (orders) *Fax:* 608-263-1173 *Toll Free Fax:* 800-621-2736 (orders) *E-mail:* uwiscpress@uwpress.wisc.edu (main off); publicity@uwpress.wisc.edu *Web Site:* uwpress.wisc.edu, pg 246

University Press of America Inc, 4501 Forbes Blvd, Suite 200, Lanham, MD 20706 *Tel:* 301-459-3366 *Toll Free Tel:* 800-462-6420 *Fax:* 301-429-5748 *Toll Free Fax:* 800-338-4550 *Web Site:* www.univpress.com, pg 246

University Press of Colorado, 5589 Arapahoe Ave, Suite 206-C, Boulder, CO 80303 *Tel:* 720-406-8849 *Toll Free Tel:* 800-621-2736 (orders) *Fax:* 720-406-3443 *Web Site:* www.upcolorado.com, pg 246

University Press of Florida, 15 NW 15 St, Gainesville, FL 32603-2079 *Tel:* 352-392-1351 *Toll Free Tel:* 800-226-3822 (orders only) *Fax:* 352-392-0590 *Toll Free Fax:* 800-680-1955 (orders only) *E-mail:* press@upress.ufl.edu; orders@upress.ufl.edu *Web Site:* www.upf.com, pg 246

University Press of Kansas, 2502 Westbrooke Circle, Lawrence, KS 66045-4444 *Tel:* 785-864-4154; 785-864-4155 (orders) *Fax:* 785-864-4586 *E-mail:* upress@ku.edu; upkorders@ku.edu (orders) *Web Site:* www.kansaspress.ku.edu, pg 246

The University Press of Kentucky, 663 S Limestone St, Lexington, KY 40508-4008 *Tel:* 859-257-8400 *Fax:* 859-257-8481 *Web Site:* www.kentuckypress.com, pg 247

University Press of Mississippi, 3825 Ridgewood Rd, Jackson, MS 39211-6492 *Tel:* 601-432-6205 *Toll Free Tel:* 800-737-7788 (orders & cust serv) *Fax:* 601-432-6217 *E-mail:* press@mississippi.edu *Web Site:* www.upress.state.ms.us, pg 247

University Press of New England, One Court St, Suite 250, Lebanon, NH 03766 *Tel:* 603-448-1533 *Toll Free Tel:* 800-421-1561 (orders only) *Fax:* 603-448-7006; 603-448-9429 (orders only) *E-mail:* university.press@dartmouth.edu *Web Site:* www.upne.com, pg 247

University Publishing Group, 6 W Washington St, Suite 302, Hagerstown, MD 21740 *Tel:* 240-420-0036 *Fax:* 240-718-7100 *E-mail:* orders@upgbooks.com, pg 247

University Publishing House, PO Box 1664, Mannford, OK 74044 *Tel:* 918-865-4726 *E-mail:* upub5@outlook.com *Web Site:* www.universitypublishinghouse.net, pg 247

University Science Books, 20 Edgeshill Rd, Mill Valley, CA 94941 *Tel:* 703-661-1572 (cust serv, orders) *Fax:* 703-661-1572 (cust serv, orders) *E-mail:* usbmail@presswarehouse.com (cust serv, orders) *Web Site:* www.uscibooks.com, pg 247

UnKnownTruths.com Publishing Co, 8815 Conroy Windermere Rd, Suite 190, Orlando, FL 32835 *Tel:* 407-929-9207 *E-mail:* info@unknowntruths.com *Web Site:* unknowntruths.com, pg 248

Unlimited Publishing LLC, PO Box 99, Nashville, IN 47448 *Tel:* 206-666-5484 *E-mail:* acquisitions@unlimitedpublishing.com *Web Site:* www.unlimitedpublishing.com, pg 248

UNO Press, University of New Orleans Metro College, 2000 Lakeshore Dr, New Orleans, LA 70148 *Tel:* 504-280-7457 *E-mail:* unopress@uno.edu *Web Site:* unopress.org, pg 248

Unveiled Media LLC, PO Box 930463, Verona, WI 53593 *Tel:* 707-986-8345 *Web Site:* www.unveiledmedia.com, pg 248

John Updike Award, 633 W 155 St, New York, NY 10032 *Tel:* 212-368-5900 *Fax:* 212-491-4615 *E-mail:* academy@artsandletters.org *Web Site:* www.artsandletters.org, pg 695

W E Upjohn Institute for Employment Research, 300 S Westnedge Ave, Kalamazoo, MI 49007-4686 *Tel:* 269-343-5541; 269-343-4330 (pubns) *Toll Free Tel:* 888-227-8569 *Fax:* 269-343-7310 *E-mail:* publications@upjohn.org; communications@upjohn.org *Web Site:* www.upjohn.org, pg 248

Upper Access Inc, 87 Upper Access Rd, Hinesburg, VT 05461 *Tel:* 802-482-2988 *Toll Free Tel:* 800-310-8320 (orders) *Fax:* 802-417-3002 *E-mail:* info@upperaccess.com *Web Site:* www.upperaccess.com, pg 248

Upper Room Books, 1908 Grand Ave, Nashville, TN 37212 *Tel:* 615-340-7200 *Toll Free Tel:* 800-972-0433 *Fax:* 615-340-7266 *Web Site:* books.upperroom.org, pg 248

Upstart Books™, 4810 Forest Run Rd, Madison, WI 53704 *Tel:* 608-241-1201 *Toll Free Tel:* 800-448-4887 (orders) *Toll Free Fax:* 800-448-5828 *E-mail:* custsvc@upstartpromotions.com *Web Site:* www.demco.com/category/upstart-promotions, pg 248

The Urban Institute, 2100 "M" St NW, Washington, DC 20037 *Tel:* 202-833-7200 *Web Site:* www.urban.org, pg 249

Urim Publications, 527 Empire Blvd, Brooklyn, NY 11225-3121 *Tel:* 718-972-5449 *Fax:* 718-972-6307 *E-mail:* publisher@urimpublications.com; editor@urimpublications.com *Web Site:* urimpublications.com, pg 249

US Board on Books For Young People (USBBY), c/o V Ellis Vance, 5503 N El Adobe Dr, Fresno, CA 93711-2363 *Tel:* 559-351-6119 *Web Site:* www.usbby.org, pg 580

US Conference of Catholic Bishops, USCCB Publishing, 3211 Fourth St NE, Washington, DC 20017 *Tel:* 202-541-3090 *Toll Free Tel:* 800-235-8722 *Fax:* 202-722-8709 (orders) *E-mail:* css@usccb.org; publications@usccb.org *Web Site:* store.usccb.org, pg 249

US Games Systems Inc, 179 Ludlow St, Stamford, CT 06902 *Tel:* 203-353-8400 *Toll Free Tel:* 800-54-GAMES (544-2637) *Fax:* 203-353-8431 *E-mail:* info@usgamesinc.com *Web Site:* www.usgamesinc.com, pg 249

US Government Publishing Office (GPO), Superintendent of Documents, 732 N Capitol St NW, Washington, DC 20401 *Tel:* 202-512-1800 *Toll Free Tel:* 866-512-1800 (orders) *Fax:* 202-512-2104 *E-mail:* contactcenter@gpo.gov *Web Site:* www.gpo.gov; bookstore.gpo.gov (sales), pg 249

USBE: United States Book Exchange, 2969 W 25 St, Cleveland, OH 44113 *Tel:* 216 241 6960 *Fax:* 216 241-6966 *E-mail:* usbe@usbe.com *Web Site:* www.usbe.com, pg 580

Utah Geological Survey, 1594 W North Temple, Suite 3110, Salt Lake City, UT 84116-3154 *Tel:* 801-537-3300 *Toll Free Tel:* 888-UTAH-MAP (882-4627 bookstore) *Fax:* 801-537-3400 *E-mail:* geostore@utah.gov *Web Site:* geology.utah.gov, pg 249

Utah Original Writing Competition, 617 E South Temple, Salt Lake City, UT 84102 *Tel:* 801-236-7555 *Fax:* 801-236-7556 *Web Site:* arts.utah.gov, pg 695

Utah State University Press, 3078 Old Main Hill, Logan, UT 84322-3078 *Tel:* 435-797-1362 *Web Site:* www.usupress.com, pg 249

Janis Vallely Literary Agency, 111 Raup Rd, Chatham, NY 12037 *Tel:* 518-392-0897 *E-mail:* janvall@aol.com *Web Site:* www.janisvallely.com, pg 540

William Van Dyke Short Story Prize, 1041 N Taft Hill Rd, Fort Collins, CO 80521 *Tel:* 970-449-2726 *E-mail:* editor@ruminatemagazine.org *Web Site:* www.ruminatemagazine.com, pg 695

The William Van Wert Memorial Fiction Award, PO Box 63927, Philadelphia, PA 19147 *Tel:* 610-764-0813 *E-mail:* hiddenriverarts@gmail.com *Web Site:* www.hiddenriverarts.org; www.hiddenriverarts.com, pg 695

VanDam Inc, The VanDam Bldg, 121 W 27 St, New York, NY 10001 *Tel:* 212-929-0416 *Toll Free Tel:* 800-UNFOLDS (863-6537) *Fax:* 212-929-0426 *E-mail:* info@vandam.com *Web Site:* www.vandam.com, pg 249

Vandamere Press, 3580 Morris St N, St Petersburg, FL 33713 *Tel:* 727-556-0950 *Toll Free Tel:* 800-551-7776 *Fax:* 727-556-2560 *E-mail:* orders@vandamere.com *Web Site:* www.vandamere.com, pg 249

Vanderbilt University Press, 2014 Broadway, Suite 320, Nashville, TN 37203 *Tel:* 615-322-3585 *Toll Free Tel:* 800-627-7377 (orders only) *Fax:* 615-343-8823 *Toll Free Fax:* 800-735-0476 (orders only) *E-mail:* vupress@vanderbilt.edu *Web Site:* www.vanderbiltuniversitypress.com, pg 249

VanderMey Nonfiction Prize, 1041 N Taft Hill Rd, Fort Collins, CO 80521 *Tel:* 970-449-2726 *E-mail:* editor@ruminatemagazine.org *Web Site:* www.ruminatemagazine.com, pg 695

Daniel Varoujan Award, 46 Wallace St, Somerville, MA 02144 *Tel:* 617-744-6034 *E-mail:* info@nepoetryclub.org *Web Site:* www.nepoetryclub.org, pg 695

Vault.com Inc, 132 W 31 St, 16th fl, New York, NY 10001 *Tel:* 212-366-4212 *Toll Free Tel:* 800-535-2074 *Fax:* 212-366-6117 (cust serv) *E-mail:* editors@vault.com; customerservice@vault.com *Web Site:* www.vault.com, pg 250

Vedanta Press, 1946 Vedanta Place, Hollywood, CA 90068 *Tel:* 323-960-1327 *Toll Free Tel:* 800-816-2242 (catalog) *Fax:* 323-465-9568 *E-mail:* vpress@vedanta.org *Web Site:* www.vedanta.com, pg 250

Vehicule Press, PO Box 42094, CP Roy, Montreal, QC H2W-2T3, Canada *Tel:* 514-844-6073 *Fax:* 514-844-7543 *E-mail:* vp@vehiculepress.com; admin@vehiculepress.com *Web Site:* www.vehiculepress.com, pg 475

Velazquez Press, 9682 Telstar Ave, Suite 110, El Monte, CA 91731 *Tel:* 626-448-3448 *Fax:* 626-602-3817 *E-mail:* info@academiclearningcompany.com *Web Site:* www.velazquezpress.com, pg 250

The Vendome Press, 244 Fifth Ave, Suite 2043, New York, NY 10001 *Tel:* 212-737-1857 *E-mail:* info@vendomepress.com *Web Site:* www.vendomepress.com, pg 250

Venture Publishing Inc, 1999 Cato Ave, State College, PA 16801 *Tel:* 814-234-4561 *Fax:* 814-234-1651 *E-mail:* vpublish@venturepublish.com *Web Site:* www.venturepublish.com, pg 250

Vermont College of Fine Arts MFA in Writing for Children & Young Adults Program, 36 College St, Montpelier, VT 05602 *Tel:* 802-828-8637; 802-828-8696 *Toll Free Tel:* 866-934-VCFA (934-8232) *Fax:* 802-828-8649 *Web Site:* www.vcfa.edu, pg 624

Vermont College of Fine Arts, MFA in Writing Program, 36 College St, Montpelier, VT 05602 *Tel:* 802-828-8840; 802-828-8839 *Toll Free Tel:* 866-934-VCFA (934-8232) *Fax:* 802-828-8649 *Web Site:* www.vcfa.edu, pg 624

Vermont Studio Center Writer's Program Fellowships, 80 Pearl St, Johnson, VT 05656 *Tel:* 802-635-2727 *Fax:* 802-635-2730 *E-mail:* writing@vermontstudiocenter.org; info@vermontstudiocenter.org *Web Site:* www.vermontstudiocenter.org, pg 696

Vernon Press, 1000 N West St, Suite 1200, Wilmington, DE 19801 *Tel:* 302-250-4440 *E-mail:* info@vernonpress.com *Web Site:* www.vernonpress.com, pg 250

Verso, 20 Jay St, Suite 1010, Brooklyn, NY 11201 *Tel:* 718-246-8160 *Fax:* 718-246-8165 *E-mail:* verso@versobooks.com *Web Site:* www.versobooks.com, pg 250

Very Short Fiction Award, PO Box 80430, Portland, OR 97280-1430 *Tel:* 503-221-0836 *Fax:* 503-221-0837 *E-mail:* editors@glimmertrain.org *Web Site:* www.glimmertrain.org, pg 696

Vesuvian Books, 2817 West End Ave, Nashville, TN 37203 *E-mail:* info@vesuvianmedia.com *Web Site:* www.vesuvianbooks.com, pg 250

Jill Vickers Prize, 260 rue Dalhousie St, Suite 204, Ottawa, ON K1N 7E4, Canada *Tel:* 613-562-1202 *Fax:* 613-241-0019 *E-mail:* cpsa-acsp@cpsa-acsp.ca *Web Site:* www.cpsa-acsp.ca, pg 696

Vicky Metcalf Award for Literature for Young People, 460 Richmond St W, Suite 600, Toronto, ON M5V 1Y1, Canada *Tel:* 416-504-8222 *Toll Free Tel:* 877-906-6548 *Fax:* 416-504-9090 *E-mail:* info@writerstrust.com *Web Site:* www.writerstrust.com, pg 696

Victory in Grace Press, 60 Quentin Rd, Lake Zurich, IL 60047 *Tel:* 847-438-4494 *Toll Free Tel:* 800-78-GRACE (784-7223) *Fax:* 847-438-4232 *E-mail:* feedback@victoryingrace.org *Web Site:* www.victoryingrace.org, pg 250

Viking, 375 Hudson St, New York, NY 10014 *Tel:* 212-366-2000 *Fax:* 212-243-6002 *Web Site:* www.penguin.com/publishers/vikingbooks, pg 250

Viking Children's Books, 345 Hudson St, New York, NY 10014 *Fax:* 212-414-3393 *E-mail:* youngreaderspublicity@us.penguingroup.com *Web Site:* www.penguin.com/publishers/vikingchildrensbooks, pg 251

Viking Studio, 375 Hudson St, New York, NY 10014 *Tel:* 212-366-2000 *Fax:* 212-366-2636 *E-mail:* averystudiopublicity@us.penguingroup.com *Web Site:* www.penguin.com, pg 251

Carl Vinson Institute of Government, University of Georgia, 201 N Milledge Ave, Athens, GA 30602 *Tel:* 706-542-2736 *Fax:* 706-542-9301 *Web Site:* www.cviog.uga.edu, pg 251

Vintage Books, c/o Penguin Random House Inc, 1745 Broadway, New York, NY 10019 *Tel:* 212-572-2420 *E-mail:* vintageanchorpublicity@randomhouse.com *Web Site:* knopfdoubleday.com/imprint/vintage, pg 251

Visible Ink Press®, 43311 Joy Rd, Suite 414, Canton, MI 48187-2075 *Tel:* 734-667-3211 *Fax:* 734-667-4311 *E-mail:* info@visibleinkpress.com *Web Site:* www.visibleinkpress.com, pg 251

Visiting Writers Series, English Dept, PO Box 755720, Fairbanks, AK 99775-5720 *Tel:* 907-474-7193 *Fax:* 907-474-5247 *E-mail:* faengl@uaf.edu *Web Site:* www.alaska.edu/english, pg 615

Visual Artists & Galleries Association Inc (VAGA), 111 Broadway, Suite 1006, New York, NY 10006 *Tel:* 212-736-6666 *Fax:* 212-736-6767 *E-mail:* info@vagarights.com *Web Site:* vagarights.com, pg 580

Visual Media Alliance (VMA), 665 Third St, Suite 500, San Francisco, CA 94107-1956 *Tel:* 415-489-7601 *Toll Free Tel:* 800-659-3363 *Toll Free Fax:* 800-824-1911 *E-mail:* info@vma.bz *Web Site:* main.vma.bz, pg 580

Visual Profile Books Inc, 389 Fifth Ave, Suite 1105, New York, NY 10016 *Tel:* 212-279-7000 *Web Site:* www.visualprofilebooks.com, pg 251

Visuals Unlimited Inc, 27 Meadow Dr, Hollis, NH 03049 *Tel:* 603-465-3340 *Fax:* 603-465-3360 *E-mail:* staff@visualsunlimited.com *Web Site:* www.visualsunlimited.com, pg 502

VLB Editeur Inc, 1055, boul Rene-Levesque Est, bureau 300, Montréal, QC H2L 4S5, Canada *Tel:* 514-849-5259 *Fax:* 514-849-1388 *Web Site:* www.edvlb.com, pg 475

Volcano Press, 21496 National St, Volcano, CA 95689 *Tel:* 209-296-7989 *E-mail:* sales@volcanopress.com *Web Site:* www.volcanopress.com, pg 251

Ludwig von Mises Institute, 518 W Magnolia Ave, Auburn, AL 36832 *Tel:* 334-321-2100 *Fax:* 334-321-2119 *E-mail:* info@mises.org *Web Site:* www.mises.org, pg 251

VONA Voices Summer Writing Workshop, 3720 Spruce St, Suite 442, Philadelphia, PA 19104 *Tel:* 732-842-3932; 510-421-3913 *E-mail:* info@vonacommunity.org *Web Site:* www.vonacommunity.org, pg 615

Voyager Sopris Learning Inc, 17855 Dallas Pkwy, Suite 400, Dallas, TX 75287 *Tel:* 303-651-2829 *Toll Free Tel:* 800-547-6747 *Fax:* 303-776-5934 *Toll Free Fax:* 888-819-7767 *E-mail:* customerservice@voyagersopris.com *Web Site:* www.voyagersopris.com, pg 251

Harold D Vursell Memorial Award, 633 W 155 St, New York, NY 10032 *Tel:* 212-368-5900 *Fax:* 212-491-4615 *E-mail:* academy@artsandletters.org *Web Site:* www.artsandletters.org, pg 696

Wake Forest University Press, A5 Tribble Hall, Wake Forest University, Winston-Salem, NC 27109 *Tel:* 336-758-5448 *Fax:* 336-758-5636 *E-mail:* wfupress@wfu.edu *Web Site:* wfupress.wfu.edu, pg 251

Walch Education, 40 Walch Dr, Portland, ME 04103-1286 *Tel:* 207-772-2846 *Toll Free Tel:* 800-558-2846 *Fax:* 207-772-3105 *Toll Free Fax:* 888-991-5755 *E-mail:* customerservice@walch.com *Web Site:* www.walch.com, pg 251

Waldorf Publishing, 2140 Hall Johnson Rd, No 102-345, Grapevine, TX 76051 *Tel:* 972-674-3131 *E-mail:* info@waldorfpublishing.com *Web Site:* www.waldorfpublishing.com, pg 252

Wales Literary Agency Inc, 1508 Tenth Ave E, No 401, Seattle, WA 98102 *Tel:* 206-284-7114 *E-mail:* waleslit@waleslit.com *Web Site:* www.waleslit.com, pg 540

Richard Wall Memorial Award, c/o The New York Public Library for the Performing Arts, 111 Amsterdam Ave, New York, NY 10023 *E-mail:* TheatreLibraryAssociation@gmail.com; TLABookAwards@gmail.com *Web Site:* www.tla-online.org/awards/bookawards, pg 696

The Wallace Literary Agency, 229 E 79 St, No 5A, New York, NY 10075 *Tel:* 212-472-3282 *Fax:* 212-472-3833 *E-mail:* info@wallaceliteraryagency.com, pg 541

Edward Lewis Wallant Book Award, 3 Brighton Rd, West Hartford, CT 06117 *Tel:* 860-232-1421, pg 696

Wambtac Communications, 1512 E Santa Clara Ave, Santa Ana, CA 92705 *Tel:* 714-954-0580 *Toll Free Tel:* 800-641-3936 *E-mail:* wambtac@wambtac.com *Web Site:* www.wambtac.com; claudiasuzanne.com (prof servs), pg 502

Frederick Warne, 375 Hudson St, New York, NY 10014 *Tel:* 212-366-2000 *Web Site:* www.penguin.com, pg 252

Warner Press, 1201 E Fifth St, Anderson, IN 46018 *Tel:* 765-644-7721 *Toll Free Tel:* 800-741-7721 (orders) *Fax:* 765-640-8005 *Toll Free Fax:* 800-347-6411 *E-mail:* wporders@warnerpress.org *Web Site:* www.warnerpress.org, pg 252

Warren Communications News Inc, 2115 Ward Ct NW, Washington, DC 20037 *Tel:* 202-872-9200 *Toll Free Tel:* 800-771-9202 *Fax:* 202-293-3435; 202-318-8350 *E-mail:* info@warren-news.com; newsroom@warren-news.com *Web Site:* www.warren-news.com, pg 252

Warren Wilson College, MFA Program for Writers, 701 Warren Wilson Rd, Swannanoa, NC 28778 *Tel:* 828-771-3717 *Fax:* 828-771-7005 *E-mail:* mfa@warren-wilson.edu *Web Site:* www.warren-wilson.edu/~mfa, pg 624

Warwick Associates, 18340 Sonoma Hwy, Sonoma, CA 95476 *Tel:* 707-939-9212 *Fax:* 707-938-3515 *E-mail:* warwick@vom.com *Web Site:* www.warwickassociates.com, pg 541

George Washington Book Prize, 101 S Water St, Chestertown, MD 21620 *Tel:* 410-810-7165 *Fax:* 410-810-7175 *Web Site:* starrcenter.washcoll.edu/centers/starr/george-washington-book-prize.php, pg 696

Washington State University Press, Cooper Publications Bldg, Grimes Way, Pullman, WA 99164-5910 *Tel:* 509-335-3518; 509-335-7880 (order fulfillment)

Toll Free Tel: 800-354-7360 (orders) *Fax:* 509-335-8568 *E-mail:* wsupress@wsu.edu *Web Site:* wsupress.wsu.edu, pg 252

Water Environment Federation, 601 Wythe St, Alexandria, VA 22314-1994 *Tel:* 703-684-2400 *Toll Free Tel:* 800 666 0206 (cust serv) *Fax:* 703 684-2492 *E-mail:* inquiry@wef.org *Web Site:* www.wef.org, pg 252

Water Resources Publications LLC, PO Box 630026, Highlands Ranch, CO 80163-0026 *Tel:* 720-873-0171 *Toll Free Tel:* 800-736-2405 *Fax:* 720-873-0173 *Toll Free Fax:* 800-616-1971 *E-mail:* info@wrpllc.com *Web Site:* www.wrpllc.com, pg 252

WaterBrook, 10807 New Allegiance Dr, Suite 500, Colorado Springs, CO 80921 *Tel:* 719-590-4999 *Toll Free Tel:* 800-603-7051 (orders) *Fax:* 719-590-8977 *Toll Free Fax:* 800-294-5686 (orders) *E-mail:* info@waterbrookmultnomah.com *Web Site:* waterbrookmultnomah.com, pg 252

Watermark Publishing, 1000 Bishop St, Suite 806, Honolulu, HI 96813 *Tel:* 808-587-7766 *Toll Free Tel:* 866-900-BOOK (900-2665) *Fax:* 808-521-3461 *E-mail:* info@bookshawaii.net *Web Site:* www.bookshawaii.net, pg 252

Waterside Productions Inc, 2055 Oxford Ave, Cardiff, CA 92007 *Tel:* 760-632-9190 *Fax:* 760-632-9295 *E-mail:* admin@waterside.com *Web Site:* www.waterside.com, pg 541

Watkins/Loomis Agency Inc, PO Box 20925, New York, NY 10025 *Tel:* 212-532-0080 *Fax:* 646-383-2449 *E-mail:* assistant@watkinsloomis.com *Web Site:* www.watkinsloomis.com, pg 541

Watson-Guptill Publications, c/o Ten Speed Press, 6001 Shellmount St, Suite 600, Emeryville, CA 94608 *Web Site:* crownpublishing.com/imprint/watson-guptill, pg 252

Watson Publishing International LLC, PO Box 1240, Sagamore Beach, MA 02562-1240 *Tel:* 508-888-9113 *E-mail:* orders@watsonpublishing.com; orders@shpusa.com *Web Site:* www.shpusa.com; www.watsonpublishing.com, pg 253

The Robert Watson Literary Prizes in Fiction & Poetry, MFA Writing Program, The Greensboro Review, UNC-Greensboro, 3302 MHRA Bldg, Greensboro, NC 27402-6170 *Tel:* 336-334-5459 *Fax:* 336-256-1470 *Web Site:* www.greensbororeview.org, pg 696

Waveland Press Inc, 4180 IL Rte 83, Suite 101, Long Grove, IL 60047-9580 *Tel:* 847-634-0081 *Fax:* 847-634-9501 *E-mail:* info@waveland.com *Web Site:* www.waveland.com, pg 253

Waverly Place Literary Agency, 124 E 84 St, No 2D, New York, NY 10028-0918 *Tel:* 212-925-3721 *E-mail:* waverlyplaceliterary@aol.com *Web Site:* www.waverlyplaceliterary.com; twitter.com/waverlyplacelit, pg 541

Waxman Leavell Literary Agency, 443 Park Ave S, No 1004, New York, NY 10016 *Tel:* 212-675-5556 *Fax:* 212-675-1381 *Web Site:* www.waxmanleavell.com, pg 541

Wayne State University Press, Leonard N Simons Bldg, 4809 Woodward Ave, Detroit, MI 48201-1309 *Tel:* 313-577-6120 *Toll Free Tel:* 800-978-7323 *Fax:* 313-577-6131 *E-mail:* bookorders@wayne.edu *Web Site:* www.wsupress.wayne.edu, pg 253

Wayside Publishing, 262 US Route 1, Suite 2, Freeport, ME 04032 *Toll Free Tel:* 888-302-2519 *E-mail:* sales@waysidepublishing.com *Web Site:* www.waysidepublishing.com, pg 253

Weigl Educational Publishers Ltd, 6325 Tenth St SE, Calgary, AB T2H 2Z9, Canada *Tel:* 403-233-7747 *Toll Free Tel:* 800-668-0766 *Fax:* 403-233-7769 *Toll Free Fax:* 866-449-3445 *E-mail:* orders@weigl.com *Web Site:* www.weigl.ca; av2books.com, pg 475

Cherry Weiner Literary Agency, 925 Oak Bluff Ct, Dacula, GA 30019-6660 *Tel:* 732-446-2096 *Fax:* 732-792-0506 *E-mail:* cherry8486@aol.com, pg 541

The Weingel-Fidel Agency, 310 E 46 St, Suite 21-E, New York, NY 10017 *Tel:* 212-599-2959 *Fax:* 212-286-1986 *E-mail:* queries@theweingel-fidelagency.com, pg 541

Welcome Enterprises Inc, 300 Park Ave S, New York, NY 10010 *Tel:* 212 387 3400 *Web Site:* www.rizzoliusa.com, pg 253

Welcome Rain Publishers LLC, 217 Thompson St, Suite 473, New York, NY 10012 *Tel:* 212-686-1909 *Web Site:* welcomerain.com, pg 253

Rene Wellek Prize, University of South Carolina, Dept of Languages, Literature & Cultures, 1620 College St, Rm 813-A, Columbia, SC 29208 *Tel:* 803-777-3021 *E-mail:* info@acla.org *Web Site:* www.acla.org/prize-awards, pg 696

Wellington Press, 9601-30 Miccosukee Rd, Tallahassee, FL 32309 *E-mail:* peacegames@aol.com *Web Site:* www.peacegames.com, pg 253

WendyLynn & Co, 504 Wilson Rd, Annapolis, MD 21401 *Tel:* 410-224-2729; 410-507-1059 *Web Site:* wendylynn.com, pg 544

Wergle Flomp Humor Poetry Contest, 351 Pleasant St, PMB 222, Northampton, MA 01060-3961 *Tel:* 413-320-1847 *Toll Free Tel:* 866-WINWRIT (946-9748) *Fax:* 413-280-0539 *Web Site:* www.winningwriters.com, pg 696

Eliot Werner Publications Inc, 31 Willow Lane, Clinton Corners, NY 12514 *Tel:* 845-266-4241 *Fax:* 845-266-3317 *E-mail:* eliotwerner@optonline.net *Web Site:* www.eliotwerner.com, pg 253

Toby Wertheim, 240 E 76 St, New York, NY 10021 *Tel:* 212-472-8587 *E-mail:* tobywertheim@yahoo.com, pg 502

Wesley-Logan Prize, 400 "A" St SE, Washington, DC 20003 *Tel:* 202-544-2422 *Fax:* 202-544-8307 *E-mail:* awards@historians.org *Web Site:* www.historians.org, pg 696

Wesleyan Publishing House, 13300 Olio Rd, Fishers, IN 46037 *Tel:* 317-774-3853 *Toll Free Tel:* 800-493-7539 *Fax:* 317-774-3865 *Toll Free Fax:* 800-788-3535 *E-mail:* wph@wesleyan.org *Web Site:* www.wesleyan.org/books, pg 253

Wesleyan University Press, 215 Long Lane, Middletown, CT 06459-0433 *Tel:* 860-685-7711 *Fax:* 860-685-7712 *Web Site:* www.wesleyan.edu/wespress, pg 253

Wesleyan Writers Conference, c/o Wesleyan University, Downey House, 294 High St, Rm 207, Middletown, CT 06459 *Tel:* 860-685-3604 *Web Site:* www.wesleyan.edu/writing/conference, pg 616

West Academic Publishing, 444 Cedar St, Suite 700, St Paul, MN 55101 *Toll Free Tel:* 877-888-1330 *E-mail:* customerservice@westacademic.com; support@westacademic.com; media@westacademic.com *Web Site:* www.westacademic.com, pg 254

West Virginia University Press, West Virginia University, PO Box 6295, Morgantown, WV 26506-6295 *Tel:* 304-293-8400 *Fax:* 304-293-6585 *Web Site:* www.wvupress.com, pg 254

Western Edge Press, 126 Candelario St, Santa Fe, NM 87501 *Tel:* 505-988-7214 *E-mail:* westernedge@santa-fe.net *Web Site:* www.westernedgepress.com, pg 254

Western Heritage Awards (Wrangler Award), 1700 NE 63 St, Oklahoma City, OK 73111 *Tel:* 405-478-2250 *Fax:* 405-478-4714 *E-mail:* info@nationalcowboymuseum.org *Web Site:* nationalcowboymuseum.org, pg 697

Western Pennsylvania Genealogical Society, 4400 Forbes Ave, Pittsburgh, PA 15213-4080 *Tel:* 412-687-6811 (answering machine) *E-mail:* info@wpgs.org *Web Site:* www.wpgs.org, pg 254

Western Reflections Publishing Co, 951B N Hwy 149, Lake City, CO 81235 *Tel:* 970-944-0110 *E-mail:* publisher@westernreflectionspublishing.com *Web Site:* www.westernreflectionspublishing.com, pg 254

Western States Arts Federation, 1743 Wazee St, Suite 300, Denver, CO 80202 *Tel:* 303-629-1166 *Toll Free Tel:* 888-562-7232 *Fax:* 303-629-9717 *E-mail:* staff@westaf.org *Web Site:* www.westaf.org, pg 583

Western Writers of America Inc (WWA), 271 CR 219, Encampment, WY 82325 *Tel:* 307-329-8942 *Web Site:* westernwriters.org, pg 580

Westernlore Press, PO Box 35305, Tucson, AZ 85740-5305 *Tel:* 520-297-5491, pg 254

Westminster John Knox Press (WJK), 100 Witherspoon St, Louisville, KY 40202-1396 *Toll Free Tel:* 800-523-1631 (US only) *Fax:* 502-569-5113 *Toll Free Fax:* 800-541-5113 (US & CN) *E-mail:* wjk@wjkbooks.com; customer_service@wjkbooks.com *Web Site:* www.wjkbooks.com, pg 254

Hilary Weston Writers' Trust Prize for Nonfiction, 460 Richmond St W, Suite 600, Toronto, ON M5V 1Y1, Canada *Tel:* 416-504-8222 *Toll Free Tel:* 877-906-6548 *Fax:* 416-504-9090 *E-mail:* info@writerstrust.com *Web Site:* www.writerstrust.com, pg 697

Westwood Creative Artists Ltd, 138 Sussex Mews, Toronto, ON M5S-2K1, Canada *Tel:* 416-964-3302 *Fax:* 416-964-3302 *E-mail:* wca_office@wcaltd.com *Web Site:* www.wcaltd.com, pg 541

Rosemary Wetherold, 4507 Cliffstone Cove, Austin, TX 78735 *Tel:* 512-892-1606 *E-mail:* roses@ix.netcom.com, pg 502

Charles A Weyerhauser Book Award, 701 William Vickers Ave, Durham, NC 27701-3162 *Tel:* 919-682-9319 *Fax:* 919-682-2349 *Web Site:* www.foresthistory.org, pg 697

Wheatherstone Press, 11595 SW Butner Rd, No 22, Portland, OR 97225 *Tel:* 503-244-8929 *E-mail:* relocntr@nwlink.com *Web Site:* www.wheatherstonepress.com, pg 254

Helen Rippier Wheeler, 1909 Cedar St, Suite 212, Berkeley, CA 94709-2037 *Tel:* 510-549-2970 *E-mail:* pen136@dslextreme.com, pg 502

Barbara Mlotek Whelehan, 7064 SE Cricket Ct, Stuart, FL 34997 *Tel:* 954-554-0765 (cell); 772-463-0818 (home) *E-mail:* barbarawhelehan@bellsouth.net, pg 502

Whiskey Creek Press, c/o Start Publishing LLC, 101 Hudson St, 37th fl, Suite 3705, Jersey City, NJ 07302 *Tel:* 212-431-5455 *Fax:* 917-464-6394 *E-mail:* publisher@whiskeycreekpress.com *Web Site:* whiskeycreekpress.com, pg 254

Whitaker House, 1030 Hunt Valley Circle, New Kensington, PA 15068 *Tel:* 724-334-7000 *Fax:* 724-334-1200 *E-mail:* publisher@whitakerhouse.com *Web Site:* www.whitakerhouse.com, pg 254

White Cloud Press, 300 E Hersey St, Suite 11, Ashland, OR 97520 *Tel:* 541-488-6415 *Fax:* 541-482-7708 *E-mail:* info@whitecloudpress.com *Web Site:* www.whitecloudpress.com, pg 254

E B White Award, 633 W 155 St, New York, NY 10032 *Tel:* 212-368-5900 *Fax:* 212-491-4615 *E-mail:* academy@artsandletters.org *Web Site:* www.artsandletters.org, pg 697

Martin L White, 10511 Preston St, Westchester, IL 60154-5311 *Tel:* 708-492-1253 *Fax:* 708-492-1253 *E-mail:* mlw@mlwindexing.com *Web Site:* www.mlwindexing.com, pg 502

White Pine Press, PO Box 236, Buffalo, NY 14201 *Tel:* 716-627-4665 *Fax:* 716-627-4665 *E-mail:* wpine@whitepine.org *Web Site:* www.whitepine.org, pg 255

William Allen White Children's Book Awards, One Kellogg Circle, Emporia, KS 66801-5092 *Tel:* 620-341-5208 *Toll Free Tel:* 877-613-7323 *Fax:* 620-341-6208 *E-mail:* wawbookaward@emporia.edu *Web Site:* waw.emporia.edu/libsv/wawbookaward, pg 697

Whitecap Books, 314 W Cordova St, Suite 209, Vancouver, BC V6B 1E8, Canada *Tel:* 604-681-6181 *Toll Free Tel:* 800-387-9776 *Toll Free Fax:* 800-260-9777 *Web Site:* www.whitecap.ca, pg 475

Whiting Awards, 16 Court St, Suite 2308, Brooklyn, NY 11241 *Tel:* 718-701-5962 *E-mail:* info@whiting.org *Web Site:* www.whiting.org, pg 697

Wizards of the Coast LLC, 1600 Lind Ave SW, Suite 400, Renton, WA 98057-3305 *Tel:* 425-226-6500 *E-mail:* press@wizards.com *Web Site:* company.wizards.com; www.wizards.com, pg 258

WLA Literary Award, 4610 S Biltmore Lane, Suite 100, Madison, WI 53718-2153 *Tel:* 608-245-3640 *Fax:* 608-245-3646 *Web Site:* wla.wisconsinlibraries.org, pg 699

WME, 11 Madison Ave, 18th fl, New York, NY 10010 *Tel:* 212-586-5100 *Web Site:* www.wmeentertainment.com, pg 542

WNBA Pannell Award for Excellence in Children's Bookselling, PO Box 237, FDR Sta, New York, NY 10150-0231 *Toll Free Tel:* 866-610-9622 *E-mail:* WNBAPannell@gmail.com *Web Site:* www.wnba-books.org; www.NationalReadingGroupMonth.org; www.wnba-books.org/awards, pg 699

Alan Wofsy Fine Arts, 1109 Geary Blvd, San Francisco, CA 94109 *Tel:* 415-292-6500 *Toll Free Tel:* 800-660-6403 *Fax:* 415-292-6594 (off & cust serv); 510-251-1840 (acctg) *E-mail:* order@art-books.com (orders); editeur@earthlink.net (edit); beauxarts@earthlink.net (cust serv) *Web Site:* www.art-books.com, pg 258

Wolf Pirate Project Inc, 337 Lost Lake Dr, Divide, CO 80814 *Tel:* 305-333-3186 *E-mail:* contact@wolfpiratebooks.com; workshop@wolfpiratebooks.com *Web Site:* www.wolf-pirate.com, pg 502

Thomas Wolfe Fiction Prize, PO Box 21591, Winston-Salem, NC 27120-1591 *E-mail:* mail@ncwriters.org *Web Site:* www.ncwriters.org, pg 699

Tobias Wolff Award for Fiction, Mail Stop 9053, Western Washington University, Bellingham, WA 98225 *Tel:* 360-650-4863 *E-mail:* bhreview@wwu.edu *Web Site:* www.bhreview.org, pg 699

Wolters Kluwer US Corp, 2700 Lake Cook Rd, Riverwoods, IL 60015 *Tel:* 847-267-7000 *Fax:* 847-580-5192 *E-mail:* info@wolterskluwer.com *Web Site:* www.wolterskluwer.com, pg 258

Women Who Write Inc, PO Box 652, Madison, NJ 07940-0652 *E-mail:* info@womenwhowrite.org *Web Site:* womenwhowrite.org, pg 580

Women's National Book Association Award, PO Box 237, FDR Sta, New York, NY 10150-0231 *Tel:* 212-208-4629 (headquarters) *Toll Free Tel:* 866-610-9622 *Fax:* 212-208-4629 *Web Site:* www.wnba-books.org; www.NationalReadingGroupMonth.org, pg 699

Women's National Book Association Inc, PO Box 237, FDR Sta, New York, NY 10150-0231 *Tel:* 212-208-4629 (headquarters) *Fax:* 212-208-4629 *E-mail:* publicity@bookbuzz.com; info@wnba-books.org *Web Site:* www.wnba-books.org; www.NationalReadingGroupMonth.org, pg 580

The J Howard & Barbara M J Wood Prize, 61 W Superior St, Chicago, IL 60654 *Tel:* 312-787-7070 *Fax:* 312-787-6650 *E-mail:* editors@poetrymagazine.org *Web Site:* www.poetryfoundation.org, pg 699

Wood Lake Publishing Inc, 485 Beaver Lake Rd, Kelowna, BC V4V 1S5, Canada *Tel:* 250-766-2778 *Toll Free Tel:* 800-663-2775 (orders & cust serv) *Fax:* 250-766-2736 *Toll Free Fax:* 888-841-9991 (orders & cust serv) *E-mail:* info@woodlake.com; customerservice@woodlake.com *Web Site:* www.woodlakebooks.com, pg 476

Woodbine House, 6510 Bells Mill Rd, Bethesda, MD 20817 *Tel:* 301-897-3570 *Toll Free Tel:* 800-843-7323 *Fax:* 301-897-5838 *E-mail:* info@woodbinehouse.com *Web Site:* www.woodbinehouse.com, pg 258

Woodland Publishing Inc, 515 S 700 E, Suite 2D, Salt Lake City, UT 84102 *Toll Free Tel:* 800-277-3243 *E-mail:* info@woodlandpublishing.com *Web Site:* www.woodlandpublishing.com, pg 258

Woodrow Wilson Center Press, One Woodrow Wilson Plaza, 1300 Pennsylvania Ave NW, Washington, DC 20004-3027 *Tel:* 202-691-4000 *Fax:* 202-691-4001 *Web Site:* wilsoncenter.org, pg 258

Carter G Woodson Book Awards, 8555 16 St, Suite 500, Silver Spring, MD 20910 *Tel:* 301-588-1800 *Toll Free Tel:* 800-296-7840 *Fax:* 301-588-2049 *E-mail:* excellence@ncss.org; publications@ncss.org *Web Site:* www.socialstudies.org, pg 699

WoodstockArts, PO Box 1342, Woodstock, NY 12498 *Tel:* 845-679-8111 *Fax:* 419-793-3452 *E-mail:* info@woodstockarts.com *Web Site:* woodstockarts.com, pg 258

Word Works Washington Prize, Adirondack Community College, Dearlove Hall, 640 Bay Rd, Queensbury, NY 12804 *Tel:* 301-581-9439 *Fax:* 301-581-9443 *E-mail:* editor@wordworksbooks.org *Web Site:* www.wordworksbooks.org, pg 699

WordCo Indexing Services Inc, 49 Church St, Norwich, CT 06360 *Tel:* 860-886-2532 *Toll Free Tel:* 877-WORDCO-3 (967-3263) *Fax:* 860-886-1155 *E-mail:* office@wordco.com *Web Site:* www.wordco.com, pg 502

WordForce Communications, 35 Ormskirk Ave, Suite 805, Toronto, ON M6S 1A8, Canada *Tel:* 416-534-9881 *E-mail:* info@wordforce.ca *Web Site:* www.wordforce.ca, pg 503

Words into Print, 208 Java St, 6th fl, Brooklyn, NY 11222 *E-mail:* query@wordsintoprint.org *Web Site:* wordsintoprint.org, pg 503

WordWitlox, 1261 Ashland Dr, Cobourg, ON K9A 5S5, Canada *Tel:* 647-505-9673 *Web Site:* www.wordwitlox.com, pg 503

Workers Compensation Research Institute, 955 Massachusetts Ave, Cambridge, MA 02139 *Tel:* 617-661-9274 *Fax:* 617-661-9284 *E-mail:* wcri@wcrinet.org *Web Site:* www.wcrinet.org, pg 258

Working With Words, 5320 SW Mayfair Ct, Beaverton, OR 97005 *Tel:* 503-644-4317 *E-mail:* editor@zzz.com, pg 503

Workman Publishing Co Inc, 225 Varick St, 9th fl, New York, NY 10014-4381 *Tel:* 212-254-5900 *Toll Free Tel:* 800-722-7202 *Fax:* 212-254-8098 *E-mail:* info@workman.com *Web Site:* www.workman.com, pg 258

World Almanac®, 132 W 31 St, New York, NY 10001 *Toll Free Tel:* 800-322-8755 *E-mail:* almanac@infobaselearning.com *Web Site:* www.worldalmanac.com, pg 259

World Bank Publications, Office of the Publisher, 1818 "H" St NW, U-11-1104, Washington, DC 20433 *Tel:* 202-458-4497; 202-473-1000 *Toll Free Tel:* 800-645-7247 (cust serv) *Fax:* 202-522-2631 *E-mail:* books@worldbank.org; pubrights@worldbank.org (foreign rts) *Web Site:* www.worldbank.org/en/publication/reference, pg 259

World Book Inc, 180 N LaSalle, Suite 900, Chicago, IL 60601 *Tel:* 312-729-5800 *Toll Free Tel:* 800-967-5325 (consumer sales, US); 800-463-8845 (consumer sales, CN); 800-975-3250 (school & lib sales, US); 800-837-5365 (school & lib sales, CN); 866-866-5200 (web sales) *Fax:* 312-729-5600; 312-729-5606 *Toll Free Fax:* 800-433-9330 (school & lib sales, US); 888-690-4002 (school lib sales, CN) *E-mail:* customercare@worldbook.com *Web Site:* www.worldbook.com, pg 259

World Citizens, PO Box 131, Mill Valley, CA 94942-0131 *Tel:* 415-380-8020 *Toll Free Tel:* 800-247-6553 (orders only), pg 259

World Class Speakers & Entertainers, 5200 Kanan Rd, Suite 210, Agoura Hills, CA 91301 *Tel:* 818-991-5400 *E-mail:* wcse@wcspeakers.com *Web Site:* www.wcspeakers.com, pg 548

World Fantasy Awards, PO Box 43, Mukilteo, WA 98275-0043 *Web Site:* www.worldfantasy.org, pg 699

World Resources Institute, 10 "G" St NE, Suite 800, Washington, DC 20002 *Tel:* 202-729-7600 *Fax:* 202-729-7610 *Web Site:* www.wri.org, pg 259

World Scientific Publishing Co Inc, 27 Warren St, Suite 401-402, Hackensack, NJ 07601 *Tel:* 201-487-9655 *Fax:* 201-487-9656 *E-mail:* wspc_us@wspc.com; sales@wspc.com; mkt@wspc.com; editor@wspc.com *Web Site:* www.worldscientific.com, pg 259

World Trade Press, 800 Lindberg Lane, Suite 190, Petaluma, CA 94952 *Tel:* 707-778-1124 *Toll Free Tel:* 800-833-8586 *Fax:* 707-778-1329 *Web Site:* www.worldtradepress.com, pg 260

World's Best Short-Short Story Contest, Florida State University, Dept of English, Tallahassee, FL 32306 *E-mail:* southeastreview@gmail.com *Web Site:* www.southeastreview.org, pg 699

WorldTariff, 220 Montgomery St, Suite 448, San Francisco, CA 94104-3410 *Tel:* 415-391-7501 *Toll Free Tel:* 866-268-7602 *Web Site:* ftn.fedex.com/wtonline, pg 260

Worldwide Library, 225 Duncan Mill Rd, Don Mills, ON M3B 3K9, Canada *Tel:* 416-445-5860 *Toll Free Tel:* 888-432-4879 *E-mail:* customerservice@harlequin.com *Web Site:* www.harlequin.com, pg 476

Worth Publishers, 41 Madison Ave, 37th fl, New York, NY 10010 *Tel:* 212-576-9400; 212-375-7000 *Fax:* 212-561-8281 *E-mail:* press.inquiries@macmillan.com *Web Site:* www.macmillanlearning.com, pg 260

Worthy & James Publishing, PO Box 362015, Milpitas, CA 95036 *Tel:* 408-945-3963 *E-mail:* worthy1234@sbcglobal.net; mail@worthyjames.com *Web Site:* www.worthyjames.com, pg 478

WorthyKids/Ideals, 6100 Tower Circle, Suite 210, Franklin, TN 37067 *Tel:* 615-932-7600 *E-mail:* idealsinfo@worthypublishing.com *Web Site:* www.idealsbooks.com, pg 260

Wright Information Indexing Services, PO Box 658, Sandia Park, NM 87047 *Tel:* 505-281-2600 *Web Site:* www.wrightinformation.com, pg 503

Write for Success Editing Services, PO Box 292153, Los Angeles, CA 90029-8653 *Tel:* 323-356-8833 *E-mail:* writeforsuccess@yahoo.com *Web Site:* www.write-for-success.com, pg 503

Write Now, 140 W Washington St, Indianapolis, IN 46204-3465 *Tel:* 317-635-5277 *Fax:* 317-236-0767 *E-mail:* info@writenow.co *Web Site:* www.writenow.co, pg 700

Write on the Sound Writers' Conference, 700 Main St, Edmonds, WA 98020 *Tel:* 425-771-0228 *Fax:* 425-771-0253 *E-mail:* wots@edmondswa.gov *Web Site:* www.writeonthesound.com, pg 616

Write Stuff Enterprises LLC, 1001 S Andrews Ave, Suite 120, Fort Lauderdale, FL 33316 *Tel:* 954-462-6657 *Toll Free Tel:* 800-900-2665 *Fax:* 954-462-6023 *E-mail:* legends@writestuffbooks.com *Web Site:* www.writestuffbooks.com, pg 260

The Write Way, 3048 Horizon Lane, Suite 1102, Naples, FL 34109 *Tel:* 239-273-9145 *E-mail:* darekane@gmail.com, pg 503

WriteLife LLC, 2323 S 171 St, Suite 202, Omaha, NE 68130 *Tel:* 402-934-1412 *Toll Free Tel:* 877-974-8354 *E-mail:* info@writelife.com *Web Site:* www.writelife.com; www.facebook.com/WriteLife, pg 260

Writer in Residence, 2410 N Old Penitentiary Rd, Boise, ID 83712 *Tel:* 208-334-2119 *E-mail:* info@arts.idaho.gov *Web Site:* www.arts.idaho.gov, pg 700

The Writer Magazine/Emily Dickinson Award, 15 Gramercy Park, New York, NY 10003 *Tel:* 212-254-9628 *Web Site:* www.poetrysociety.org, pg 700

Writers' Alliance of Newfoundland & Labrador, Haymarket Sq, 223 Duckworth St, Suite 208, St John's, NL A1C 6N1, Canada *Tel:* 709-739-5215 *Toll Free Tel:* 866-739-5215 *E-mail:* wanl@nf.aibn.com *Web Site:* wanl.ca, pg 580

Writers Anonymous Inc, 1302 E Coronado Rd, Phoenix, AZ 85006 *Tel:* 602-256-2830 *Fax:* 602-256-2830 *Web Site:* writersanonymousinc.blogspot.com, pg 503

Writer's AudioShop, 1316 Overland Stage Rd, Dripping Springs, TX 78620 *Tel:* 512-476-1616 *E-mail:* wrtaudshop@aol.com *Web Site:* www.writersaudio.com, pg 260

The Writers' Colony at Dairy Hollow, 515 Spring St, Eureka Springs, AR 72632 *Tel:* 479-253-7444 *E-mail:* director@writerscolony.org *Web Site:* www.writerscolony.org, pg 616

Barbara J Zitwer Agency, 525 West End Ave, Unit 11-H, New York, NY 10024 *Tel:* 212-501-8423 *E-mail:* zitwer@gmail.com, pg 542

Robert Zolnerzak, 101 Clark St, Unit 20 K, Brooklyn, NY 11201 *Tel:* 718-522-0591 *E-mail:* rzolnerzak@gmail.com, pg 503

Zondervan, 3900 Sparks Dr, Grand Rapids, MI 49546 *Tel:* 616-698-6900 *Toll Free Tel:* 800-226-1122; 800-727-1309 (retail orders) *Fax:* 616-698-3350 *Toll Free Fax:* 800-698-3256 (retail orders) *E-mail:* zinfo@zondervan.com *Web Site:* www.zondervan.com, pg 263

Zone Books, 633 Vanderbilt St, Brooklyn, NY 11218 *Tel:* 718-686-0048 *Toll Free Tel:* 800-405-1619 (orders & cust serv) *Fax:* 718-686-9045 *E-mail:* orders@triliteral.org *Web Site:* www.zonebooks.org, pg 263

Anna Zornio Memorial Children's Theatre Playwriting Award, D22 Paul Creative Arts Center, 30 Academic Way, Durham, NH 03824 *Tel:* 603-862-2919 *Fax:* 603-862-0298 *Web Site:* cola.unh.edu/theatre-dance/resource/zornio, pg 701

Zumaya Publications LLC, 3209 S IH 35, Suite 1086, Austin, TX 78741 *Tel:* 512-537-3145 *Fax:* 512-276-6745 *E-mail:* acquisitions@zumayapublications.com *Web Site:* www.zumayapublications.com, pg 263

Personnel Index

Included in this index are the personnel included in the entries in this volume of *LMP*, along with the page number(s) on which they appear. Not included in this index are those individuals associated with listings in the **Calendar of Book Trade & Promotional Events; Reference Books for the Trade** and **Magazines for the Trade** sections. Also, personnel associated with secondary addresses within listings (such as branch offices, sales offices, editorial offices, etc.) are not included.

Aalto, Helena, Canadian Society of Children's Authors, Illustrators & Performers (CANSCAIP), 720 Bathurst St, Suite 503, Toronto, ON M5S 2R4, Canada *Tel:* 416-515-1559 *E-mail:* office@canscaip.org *Web Site:* www.canscaip.org, pg 562

Aardema, John, Sourcebooks Inc, 1935 Brookdale Rd, Suite 139, Naperville, IL 60563 *Tel:* 630-961-3900 *Toll Free Tel:* 800-432-7444 *Fax:* 630-961-2168 *E-mail:* info@sourcebooks.com; customersupport@sourcebooks.com *Web Site:* www.sourcebooks.com, pg 218

Aaron, David H, Hebrew Union College Press, 3101 Clifton Ave, Cincinnati, OH 45220 *Tel:* 513-221-1875 *Fax:* 513-221-0321 *Web Site:* press.huc.edu, pg 105

Aaronson, Deborah, Phaidon, 65 Bleecker St, 8th fl, New York, NY 10012 *Tel:* 212-652-5400 *Toll Free Tel:* 800-759-0190 (cust serv) *Fax:* 212-652-5410 *Toll Free Fax:* 800-286-9471 (cust serv) *E-mail:* ussales@phaidon.com *Web Site:* www.phaidon.com, pg 182

Aballe, Sabrina, Holiday House Inc, 425 Madison Ave, New York, NY 10017 *Tel:* 212-688-0085 *Fax:* 212-421-6134 *E-mail:* info@holidayhouse.com *Web Site:* www.holidayhouse.com, pg 109

Abbots, Jennifer, Harlequin Enterprises Ltd, 233 Broadway, Suite 1001, New York, NY 10279 *Tel:* 212-553-4200 *Fax:* 212-227-8969 *E-mail:* customerservice@harlequin.com *Web Site:* www.harlequin.com, pg 101

Abbott, George, AFB Press, 1401 S Clark St, Suite 730, Arlington, VA 22202 *Tel:* 304-710-3043 *Toll Free Tel:* 800-232-3044 (orders) *Fax:* 917-210-3979 (orders) *E-mail:* afbpress@afb.net *Web Site:* www.afb.org, pg 5

Abbott, Joseph P Jr, Houghton Mifflin Harcourt, 125 High St, Boston, MA 02110 *Tel:* 617-351-5000 *Toll Free Tel:* 855-969-4642; 800-225-5425 (K-12 educ materials); 800-323-9540 (assessment materials); 877-219-1537 (SkillsTutor); 888-242-6747 (Innovation in Educ Group); 800-225-3362 (Trade & Ref Div) *Toll Free Fax:* 800-269-5232 *E-mail:* myhmhco@hmhco.com *Web Site:* www.hmhco.com, pg 110

Abbott, Lee K, The Flannery O'Connor Award for Short Fiction, Main Library, 3rd fl, 320 S Jackson St, Athens, GA 30602 *Fax:* 706-542-2558 *Web Site:* www.ugapress.org, pg 675

Abbott, Stephen E, Maine Writers & Publishers Alliance, 314 Forest Ave, Rm 318, Portland, ME 04101 *Tel:* 207-228-8263 *Fax:* 207-228-8150 *E-mail:* info@mainewriters.org *Web Site:* mainewriters.org, pg 569

Abdo, Jim, ABDO Publishing Group, 8000 W 78 St, Suite 310, Edina, MN 55439 *Tel:* 952-831-2120 *Toll Free Tel:* 800-800-1312 *Toll Free Fax:* 800-862-3480 *E-mail:* customerservice@abdopublishing.com *Web Site:* abdopublishing.com, pg 2

Abdo, Paul, ABDO Publishing Group, 8000 W 78 St, Suite 310, Edina, MN 55439 *Tel:* 952-831-2120 *Toll Free Tel:* 800-800-1312 *Toll Free Fax:* 800-862-3480 *E-mail:* customerservice@abdopublishing.com *Web Site:* abdopublishing.com, pg 2

Abdulhamid, Abusolayman, The International Institute of Islamic Thought, 500 Grove St, Suite 200, Herndon, VA 20170 *Tel:* 703-471-1133 *Fax:* 703-471-3922 *E-mail:* iiit@iiit.org *Web Site:* www.iiit.org, pg 119

Abe, Carol, University of Hawaii Press, 2840 Kolowalu St, Honolulu, HI 96822 *Tel:* 808-956-8255 *Toll Free Tel:* 888-UHPRESS (847-7377) *Fax:* 808-988-6052 *Toll Free Fax:* 800-650-7811 *E-mail:* uhpbooks@hawaii.edu *Web Site:* www.uhpress.hawaii.edu, pg 241

Abel, Dominick, Dominick Abel Literary Agency Inc, 146 W 82 St, Suite 1-A, New York, NY 10024 *Tel:* 212-877-0710 *Fax:* 212-595-3133 *E-mail:* agency@dalainc.com *Web Site:* www.dalainc.com, pg 505

Abellera, Lisa, Kimberley Cameron & Associates LLC, 1550 Tiburon Blvd, Suite 704, Tiburon, CA 94920 *Tel:* 415-789-9191 *Fax:* 415-789-9177 *Web Site:* www.kimberleycameron.com, pg 511

Abfier, Mel, StarGroup International Inc, 1194 Old Dixie Hwy, Suite 201, West Palm Beach, FL 33413 *Tel:* 561-547-0667 *Fax:* 561-843-8530 *E-mail:* info@stargroupinternational.com *Web Site:* stargroupinternational.com, pg 221

Abkemeier, Laurie, DeFiore and Company Literary Management Inc, 47 E 19 St, 3rd fl, New York, NY 10003 *Tel:* 212-925-7744 *Fax:* 212-925-9803 *E-mail:* info@defliterary.com; submissions@defliterary.com *Web Site:* www.defliterary.com, pg 513

Ableman, Brian, The Learning Source Ltd, 644 Tenth St, Brooklyn, NY 11215 *Tel:* 718-768-0231 (ext 10) *Fax:* 718-369-3467 *E-mail:* info@learningsourceltd.com *Web Site:* www.learningsourceltd.com, pg 497

Ables, Anna, Cunningham Commission for Youth Theatre, Lincoln Park Campus, 2350 N Racine Ave, Chicago, IL 60614-4100 *Tel:* 773-325-7999 *Fax:* 773-325-7920 *E-mail:* cunninghamcommission@depaul.edu *Web Site:* theatre.depaul.edu, pg 640

Abramo, Lauren E, Dystel, Goderich & Bourret LLC, One Union Sq W, Suite 904, New York, NY 10003 *Tel:* 212-627-9100 *Fax:* 212-627-9313 *Web Site:* www.dystel.com, pg 515

Abrams, Joanne, Square One Publishers Inc, 115 Herricks Rd, Garden City Park, NY 11040 *Tel:* 516-535-2010 *Toll Free Tel:* 877-900-BOOK (900-2665) *Fax:* 516-535-2014 *E-mail:* sq1publish@aol.com *Web Site:* www.squareonepublishers.com, pg 220

Abrams, Liesa, Simon & Schuster Children's Publishing, 1230 Avenue of the Americas, New York, NY 10020 *Tel:* 212-698-7000 *Web Site:* www.simonandschuster.com/kids; www.simonandschuster.com/teen; simonandschuster.net; simonandschuster.biz, pg 213

Abrams, Robert, Columbia University Press, 61 W 62 St, New York, NY 10023 *Tel:* 212-459-0600 *Toll Free Tel:* 800-944-8648 *Fax:* 212-459-3678 *E-mail:* cup_book@columbia.edu (orders & cust serv) *Web Site:* cup.columbia.edu, pg 59

Abrams, Robert E, Abbeville Publishing Group, 137 Varick St, Suite 504, New York, NY 10013 1105 *Tel:* 212-366-5585 *Toll Free Tel:* 800-ART-BOOK (278-2665) *Fax:* 212-366-6966 *E-mail:* abbeville@abbeville.com; marketing@abbeville.com; sales@abbeville.com; rights@abbeville.com *Web Site:* www.abbeville.com, pg 2

Abu-Baker, Reem, Black Warrior Review Fiction, Nonfiction & Poetry Contest, Off of Student Media, University of Alabama, Tuscaloosa, AL 35486-0027 *Tel:* 205-348-4518 *Web Site:* www.bwr.ua.edu, pg 633

Acebo, Caroline, Diversion Books, 443 Park Ave S, Suite 1008, New York, NY 10016 *Tel:* 212-961-6390 *E-mail:* info@diversionbooks.com *Web Site:* www.diversionbooks.com, pg 71

Acevedo, Amanda, Houghton Mifflin Harcourt Trade & Reference Division, 125 High St, Boston, MA 02110 *Tel:* 617-351-5000 *Toll Free Tel:* 800-225-3362 *Web Site:* www.hmhco.com, pg 111

Acheson, Alice B, Alice B Acheson's Workshops for Writers, Illustrators & Photographers, PO Box 735, Friday Harbor, WA 98250 *Tel:* 360-378-2815 *E-mail:* aliceba7@gmail.com, pg 609

Acland, Marigold, Cambridge University Press, 1 Liberty Plaza, 20th fl, New York, NY 10006 *Tel:* 212-924-3900; 212-337-5000 *Fax:* 212-691-3239 *E-mail:* newyork@cambridge.org *Web Site:* www.cambridge.org/us, pg 46

Acocella, Amy, Gryphon House Inc, 6848 Leon's Way, Lewisville, NC 27023 *Toll Free Tel:* 800-638-0928 *Toll Free Fax:* 877-638-7576 *E-mail:* info@ghbooks.com *Web Site:* www.gryphonhouse.com, pg 97

Acquarola, Amy, Swedenborg Foundation, 320 N Church St, West Chester, PA 19380 *Tel:* 610-430-3222 *Toll Free Tel:* 800-355-3222 (cust serv) *Fax:* 610-430-7982 *E-mail:* info@swedenborg.com *Web Site:* www.swedenborg.com, pg 225

Acton, Amy, Phoenix Society for Burn Survivors, 1835 R W Berends Dr SW, Grand Rapids, MI 49519-4955 *Tel:* 616-458-2773 *Toll Free Tel:* 800-888-BURN (888-2876) *E-mail:* info@phoenix-society.org *Web Site:* www.phoenix-society.org, pg 182

Adamo, John, Random House Children's Books, 1745 Broadway, 10th fl, New York, NY 10019 *Tel:* 212-782-9000 *Web Site:* www.randomhousekids.com, pg 194

Adams, Benjamin, Perseus Books, 250 W 57 St, 15th fl, New York, NY 10107 *Tel:* 212-340-8100 *Toll Free Tel:* 800-343-4499 (cust serv) *Fax:* 212-340-8105 *Web Site:* www.perseusbooks.com, pg 181

Adams, Beth, Howard Books, c/o Simon & Schuster, Inc, 1230 Avenue of the Americas, New York, NY 10020 *E-mail:* howardbooks@simonandschuster.com (info) *Web Site:* simonandschusterpublishing.com/howard-books/, pg 112

Adams, Bill, HarperCollins Publishers, 195 Broadway, New York, NY 10007 *Tel:* 212-207-7000 *Fax:* 212-207-7145 *Web Site:* www.harpercollins.com, pg 101

Adams, Chuck, Algonquin Books, 400 Silver Cedar Ct, Suite 300, Chapel Hill, NC 27514-1585 *Tel:* 919-967-0108 *Fax:* 919-933-0272 *E-mail:* inquiry@algonquin.com *Web Site:* www.workman.com/algonquin, pg 7

Adams, Jen, Sounds True Inc, 413 S Arthur Ave, Louisville, CO 80027 *Tel:* 303-665-3151 *Toll Free Tel:* 800-333-9185 *E-mail:* customerservice@soundstrue.com; sales@soundstrue.com *Web Site:* www.soundstrue.com, pg 217

Adams, Jennifer, Clinical Laboratory & Standards Institute (CLSI), 950 W Valley Rd, Suite 2500, Wayne, PA 19087 *Tel:* 610-688-0100 *Toll Free Tel:* 877-447-1888 (orders) *Fax:* 610-688-0700 *E-mail:* customerservice@clsi.org *Web Site:* www.clsi.org, pg 57

Adams, Katie Henderson, W W Norton & Company Inc, 500 Fifth Ave, New York, NY 10110-0017 *Tel:* 212-354-5500 *Toll Free Tel:* 800-233-4830 (orders & cust serv) *Fax:* 212-869-0856 *Toll Free Fax:* 800-458-6515 *E-mail:* orders@wwnorton.com *Web Site:* books.wwnorton.com, pg 164

Adams, Kelli, Counterpoint Press LLC, 1919 Fifth St, Berkeley, CA 94710 *Tel:* 510-704-0230 *Fax:* 510-704-0268 *E-mail:* info@counterpointpress.com *Web Site:* counterpointpress.com; www.sierraclub.org/books; softskull.com, pg 63

Adams, Lauren, Random House Children's Books, 1745 Broadway, 10th fl, New York, NY 10019 *Tel:* 212-782-9000 *Web Site:* www.randomhousekids.com, pg 194

Adams, Lisa, The Garamond Agency Inc, 12 Horton St, Newburyport, MA 01950 *E-mail:* query@garamondagency.com *Web Site:* www.garamondagency.com, pg 518

Adams, Martha, Leisure Arts Inc, 104 Champs Blvd, Suite 100, Maumelle, AR 72113 *Tel:* 501-868-8800 *Toll Free Tel:* 800-643-8030 *E-mail:* customer_service@leisurearts.com *Web Site:* www.leisurearts.com, pg 132

Adams, Matthew, Between the Lines, 401 Richmond St W, No 277, Toronto, ON M5V 3A8, Canada *Tel:* 416-535-9914 *Toll Free Tel:* 800-718-7201 *Fax:* 416-535-1484 *E-mail:* info@btlbooks.com *Web Site:* btlbooks.com, pg 446

Adams, Dr Michael, Dobie Paisano Fellowship Program, Graduate School, 110 Inner Campus Dr, Stop G0400, Austin, TX 78712-0710 *Fax:* 512-471-7620 *Web Site:* www.utexas.edu/ogs/Paisano, pg 676

Adams, Michele, 4A's (American Association of Advertising Agencies), 1065 Avenue of the Americas, 16th fl, New York, NY 10018 *Tel:* 212-682-2500 *Web Site:* www.aaaa.org, pg 566

Adams, Sandra, National Academies Press (NAP), Lockbox 285, 500 Fifth St NW, Washington, DC 20001 *Tel:* 202-334-3313 *Fax:* 202-334-2451 (cust serv); 202-334-2793 (mktg dept) *E-mail:* customer_service@nap.edu *Web Site:* www.nap.edu, pg 156

Adams, Stephanie, Stanford University Press, 425 Broadway St, Redwood City, CA 94063-3126 *Tel:* 650-723-9434 *Fax:* 650-725-3457 *E-mail:* info@www.sup.org; publicity@www.sup.org *Web Site:* www.sup.org, pg 220

Adams, Terry, Little, Brown and Company, 1290 Avenue of the Americas, New York, NY 10019 *Tel:* 212-364-1100 *Fax:* 212-364-0952 *E-mail:* firstname.lastname@hbgusa.com *Web Site:* www.littlebrown.com; www.HachetteBookGroup.com, pg 135

Adams, Wesley, Farrar, Straus & Giroux Books for Young Readers, 175 Fifth Ave, 7th fl, New York, NY 10010 *Tel:* 212-741-6900 *Toll Free Tel:* 888-330-8477 (orders) *Fax:* 212-633-9385 *Web Site:* us.macmillan.com/mackids; www.mackidsbooks.com, pg 82

Adams, William, Public Scholar Program, 400 Seventh St SW, Washington, DC 20506 *Tel:* 202-606-8200 *E-mail:* publicscholar@neh.gov *Web Site:* www.neh.gov/grants/research, pg 682

Adams, William, University of South Carolina Press, 1600 Hampton St, Suite 544, Columbia, SC 29208 *Tel:* 803-777-5245 *Toll Free Tel:* 800-768-2500 (orders) *Fax:* 803-777-0160 *Toll Free Fax:* 800-868-0740 (orders) *Web Site:* www.sc.edu/uscpress, pg 245

Addo, Stephan, Association for Information Science & Technology (ASIS&T), 8555 16 St, Suite 850, Silver Spring, MD 20910 *Tel:* 301-495-0900 *Fax:* 301-495-0810 *E-mail:* asist@asist.org *Web Site:* www.asist.org, pg 557

Adel, Judith, J Adel Art & Design, 586 Ramapo Rd, Teaneck, NJ 07666 *Tel:* 201-836-2606 *E-mail:* jadelnj@aol.com, pg 487

Adelsberger, Ann, Massachusetts Institute of Technology Libraries, 77 Massachusetts Ave, Bldg 14-S, Rm 0551, Cambridge, MA 02139-4307 *Tel:* 617-253-5671 *E-mail:* docs@mit.edu *Web Site:* libraries.mit.edu/docs, pg 144

Aders-Weremczuk, Coco, Federation of BC Writers, PO Box 16028, 617 Belmont St, New Westminster, BC V3M 6W6, Canada *E-mail:* info@bcwriters.ca *Web Site:* bcwriters.ca, pg 565

Adjemian, Robert, Vedanta Press, 1946 Vedanta Place, Hollywood, CA 90068 *Tel:* 323-960-1327 *Toll Free Tel:* 800-816-2242 (catalog) *Fax:* 323-465-9568 *E-mail:* vpress@vedanta.org *Web Site:* www.vedanta.com, pg 250

Adkins, David, Council of State Governments, 2760 Research Park Dr, Lexington, KY 40511 *Tel:* 859-244-8000 *Toll Free Tel:* 800-800-1910 *Fax:* 859-244-8001 *E-mail:* sales@csg.org *Web Site:* www.csg.org; www.csgstore.org, pg 62

Adler, Allan R, Association of American Publishers (AAP), 455 Massachusetts Ave NW, Suite 700, Washington, DC 20001-2777 *Tel:* 212-255-0200 *Fax:* 212-255-7007 *E-mail:* info@publishers.org *Web Site:* publishers.org, pg 558

Adler, Allison, Andrews McMeel Publishing LLC, 1130 Walnut St, Kansas City, MO 64106-2109 *Toll Free Tel:* 800-851-8923; 800-943-9839 (cust serv) *Toll Free Fax:* 800-943-9831 (orders) *Web Site:* www.andrewsmcmeel.com, pg 17

Adler, Ellen, The New Press, 38 Greene St, 4th fl, New York, NY 10013 *Tel:* 212-629-8802 *Toll Free Tel:* 800-343-4489 (orders) *Fax:* 212-629-8617 *Toll Free Fax:* 800-351-5073 (orders) *E-mail:* newpress@thenewpress.com *Web Site:* www.thenewpress.com, pg 161

Adler, Laina, HarperCollins General Books Group, 195 Broadway, New York, NY 10007 *Tel:* 212-207-7000 *Web Site:* www.harpercollins.com, pg 101

Adler-Kozak, Mary, National Association of College Stores (NACS), 500 E Lorain St, Oberlin, OH 44074 *Tel:* 440-775-7777 *Toll Free Tel:* 800-622-7498 *Fax:* 440-775-4769 *Web Site:* www.nacs.org, pg 570

Agnew, John, Coteau Books, 2517 Victoria Ave, Regina, SK S4P 0T2, Canada *Tel:* 306-777-0170 *Toll Free Tel:* 800-440-4471 (CN only) *Fax:* 306-522-5152 *E-mail:* coteau@coteaubooks.com *Web Site:* www.coteaubooks.com, pg 451

Agnew, Tim, Concordia Publishing House, 3558 S Jefferson Ave, St Louis, MO 63118-3968 *Tel:* 314-268-1000; 314-268-1268 (bookshop) *Toll Free Tel:* 800-325-3040 (cust serv) *Toll Free Fax:* 800-490-9889 (cust serv) *E-mail:* order@cph.org *Web Site:* www.cph.org, pg 59

Agree, Peter A, University of Pennsylvania Press, 3905 Spruce St, Philadelphia, PA 19104 *Tel:* 215-898-6261 *Fax:* 215-898-0404 *E-mail:* custserv@pobox.upenn.edu *Web Site:* www.pennpress.org, pg 244

Aguilo, Maria Jesus, Berrett-Koehler Publishers Inc, 1333 Broadway, Suite 1000, Oakland, CA 94612 *Tel:* 510-817-2277 *Fax:* 510-817-2278 *E-mail:* bkpub@bkpub.com *Web Site:* www.bkconnection.com, pg 34

Ahearn, Pamela G, The Ahearn Agency Inc, 2021 Pine St, New Orleans, LA 70118 *Tel:* 504-861-8395 *Fax:* 504-866-6434 *Web Site:* www.ahearnagency.com, pg 506

Ahern, G Thomas, Capstone Publishers™, 1710 Roe Crest Dr, North Mankato, MN 56003 *Toll Free Tel:* 800-747-4992 (cust serv) *Toll Free Fax:* 888-262-0705 *Web Site:* www.capstonepress.com, pg 47

Ahlquist, Susan, Second Chance Press, 4170 Noyac Rd, Sag Harbor, NY 11963 *Tel:* 631-725-1101 *E-mail:* info@thepermanentpress.com *Web Site:* www.thepermanentpress.com, pg 210

Ahmad, Ibrahim, Akashic Books, 232 Third St, Suite A-115, Brooklyn, NY 11215 *Tel:* 718-643-9193 *Fax:* 718-643-9195 *E-mail:* info@akashicbooks.com *Web Site:* www.akashicbooks.com, pg 6

Ahuja, Parveen, Kapp Books LLC, 3602 Rocky Meadow Ct, Fairfax, VA 22033 *Tel:* 703-261-9171 *Fax:* 703-621-7162 *E-mail:* info@kappbooks.com *Web Site:* www.kappbooks.com, pg 124

Aielli, Michelle, Hachette Books, 1290 Avenue of the Americas, New York, NY 10019 *Tel:* 212-364-1100 *Web Site:* www.hachettebookgroup.com, pg 98

Ainsley, Martin, Goose Lane Editions, 500 Beaverbrook Ct, Suite 330, Fredericton, NB E3B 5X4, Canada *Tel:* 506-450-4251 *Toll Free Tel:* 888-926-8377 *Fax:* 506-459-4991 *E-mail:* info@gooselane.com; customerservice@gooselane.com *Web Site:* www.gooselane.com, pg 458

Aippersbach, Kim, Tradewind Books, 202-1807 Maritime Mews, Vancouver, BC V6H 3W7, Canada *Tel:* 604-662-4405 *E-mail:* tradewindbooks@yahoo.com; tradewindbooks@gmail.com *Web Site:* www.tradewindbooks.com, pg 472

Aitken, Daniel, Wisdom Publications Inc, 199 Elm St, Somerville, MA 02144 *Tel:* 617-776-7416 *Toll Free Tel:* 800-272-4050 (orders) *Fax:* 617-776-7841 *E-mail:* info@wisdompubs.org; submission@wisdompubs.org *Web Site:* www.wisdompubs.org, pg 257

Akers, Terrie, Other Press, 267 Fifth Ave, 6th fl, New York, NY 10016 *Tel:* 212-414-0054 *Toll Free Tel:* 877-843-6843 *Fax:* 212-414-0939 *E-mail:* editor@otherpress.com; marketing@otherpress.com; publicity@otherpress.com *Web Site:* www.otherpress.com, pg 170

Akoury-Ross, Lisa, SDP Publishing Solutions LLC, 36 Captain's Way, East Bridgewater, MA 02333 *Tel:* 617-775-0656 *Web Site:* www.sdppublishingsolutions.com, pg 501

Al-Hillal, Semareh, Kids Can Press Ltd, 25 Dockside Dr, Toronto, ON M5A 0B5, Canada *Tel:* 416-479-7000 *Toll Free Tel:* 800-265-0884 *Fax:* 416-960-5437 *E-mail:* info@kidscan.com; customerservice@kidscan.com *Web Site:* www.kidscanpress.com; www.kidscanpress.ca, pg 461

Alain, Louise, Les Editions Alire, 120 cote du Passage, Levis, QC G6V 5S9, Canada *Tel:* 418-835-4441 *Fax:* 418-838-4443 *E-mail:* info@alire.com *Web Site:* www.alire.com, pg 452

Alain, Marc, Modus Vivendi Publishing Inc, 55, rue Jean-Talon Ouest, 2e etage, Montreal, QC H2R 2W8, Canada *Tel:* 514-272-0433 *Fax:* 514-272-7234 *E-mail:* info@groupemodus.com *Web Site:* www.groupemodus.com, pg 463

Alan, Yusuf, Tughra Books, 335 Clifton Ave, Clifton, NJ 07011 *Tel:* 973-777-2704 *Fax:* 973-457-7334 *E-mail:* info@tughrabooks.com *Web Site:* www.tughrabooks.com, pg 236

Albanese, Frank, HarperCollins Publishers, 195 Broadway, New York, NY 10007 *Tel:* 212-207-7000 *Fax:* 212-207-7145 *Web Site:* www.harpercollins.com, pg 101

Albee, Edward, William Flanagan Memorial Creative Persons Center, 14 Harrison St, New York, NY 10013 *Tel:* 212-226-2020 *Fax:* 212-226-5551 *E-mail:* info@albeefoundation.org *Web Site:* www.albeefoundation.org, pg 698

Albers, Wes, Southern California Writers' Conference (SCWC), 18160 Cottonwood Rd, Suite 260, Sunriver, OR 97707 *Tel:* 619-303-8185 *Fax:* 619-906-7462 *E-mail:* msg@writersconference.com *Web Site:* www.writersconference.com, pg 615

Albert, M Jean-Pierre, Les Editions Fides, 7333 place des Roseraies, bureau 100, Anjou, QC H1M 2X6, Canada *Tel:* 514-745-4290 *Fax:* 514-745-4299 *E-mail:* editions@groupefides.com *Web Site:* www.editionsfides.com, pg 454

Alberti, Milena, Random House Publishing Group, 1745 Broadway, New York, NY 10019 *Toll Free Tel:* 800-200-3552 *Web Site:* atrandom.com, pg 195

Albiniak, Mike, Teton NewMedia Inc, 90 E Simpson, Suite 110, Jackson, WY 83001 *Tel:* 307-732-0028 *Toll Free Tel:* 877-306-9793 *Fax:* 307-734-0841 *E-mail:* sales@tetonnm.com *Web Site:* www.tetonnm.com, pg 230

Albrecht, Ms Geri, Heuer Publishing LLC, PO Box 248, Cedar Rapids, IA 52406 *Tel:* 319-368-8008 *Toll Free Tel:* 800-950-7529 *Fax:* 319-368-8011 *E-mail:* editor@heuerpub.com; customerservice@heuerpub.com *Web Site:* www.hitplays.com, pg 106

Alcala, Rosa, University of Texas at El Paso, Department of Creative Writing, MFA/Department of Creative Writing, 901 EDUC, 500 W University Ave, El Paso, TX 79968-9991 *Tel:* 915-747-5713 *Fax:* 915-747-5523 *E-mail:* creativewriting@utep.edu *Web Site:* www.utep.edu/cw, pg 624

Alcid, Edmond, Moose Hide Books, 684 Walls Rd, Prince Township, ON P6A 6K4, Canada *Tel:* 705-779-3331 *Fax:* 705-779-3331 *E-mail:* mooseenterprises@on.aibn.com *Web Site:* www.moosehidebooks.com, pg 464

Alden, Laura, Judson Press, 588 N Gulph Rd, King of Prussia, PA 19406 *Toll Free Tel:* 800-458-3766 *Fax:* 610-768-2107 *Web Site:* www.judsonpress.com, pg 123

Aldis, Sherri, United Nations Publications, 300 E 42 St, 9th fl, New York, NY 10017 *Tel:* 703-661-1571 *Fax:* 703-996-1010 *E-mail:* publications@un.org *Web Site:* shop.un.org, pg 238

Alenier, Karren L, Word Works Washington Prize, Adirondack Community College, Dearlove Hall, 640 Bay Rd, Queensbury, NY 12804 *Tel:* 301-581-9439 *Fax:* 301-581-9443 *E-mail:* editor@wordworksbooks.org *Web Site:* www.wordworksbooks.org, pg 699

Alesse, Craig, Amherst Media Inc, PO Box 538, Buffalo, NY 14213 *Tel:* 716-874-4450 *E-mail:* marketing@amherstmedia.com *Web Site:* www.amherstmedia.com, pg 15

Alessi, Darren, Perseus Books, 250 W 57 St, 15th fl, New York, NY 10107 *Tel:* 212-340-8100 *Toll Free Tel:* 800-343-4499 (cust serv) *Fax:* 212-340-8105 *Web Site:* www.perseusbooks.com, pg 180

Alewel, Rex, Marathon Press, 1500 Square Turn Blvd, Norfolk, NE 68701 *Tel:* 402-371-5040 *Toll Free Tel:* 800-228-0629 *Fax:* 402-371-9382 *Web Site:* www.marathonpress.com, pg 141

Alexander, Britta, The Ned Leavitt Agency, 70 Wooster St, Suite 4-F, New York, NY 10012 *Tel:* 212-334-0999 *Web Site:* www.nedleavittagency.com, pg 525

Alexander, Heather, Pippin Properties Inc, 110 W 40 St, Suite 1704, New York, NY 10018 *Tel:* 212-338-9310 *Fax:* 212-338-9579 *E-mail:* info@pippinproperties.com *Web Site:* www.pippinproperties.com; www.facebook.com/pippinproperties, pg 531

Alexander, Jeff, Words into Print, 208 Java St, 6th fl, Brooklyn, NY 11222 *E-mail:* query@wordsintoprint.org *Web Site:* wordsintoprint.org, pg 503

Alexander, Dr Kara Poe, Baylor University, Professional Writing Program, One Bear Place, Unit 97404, Waco, TX 76798-7404 *Tel:* 254-710-1768 *Fax:* 254-710-3894 *Web Site:* www.baylor.edu, pg 619

Alexander, Lee Ann, Pentecostal Publishing House, 8855 Dunn Rd, Hazelwood, MO 63042 *Tel:* 314-837-7300 *Toll Free Tel:* 866-819-7667 *Fax:* 314-837-6574 (orders) *Web Site:* www.pentecostalpublishing.com; wordaflamepress.com, pg 180

Alexander, Neil M, Abingdon Press, 201 Eighth Ave S, Nashville, TN 37203-3919 *Tel:* 615-749-6000 (academic books) *Toll Free Tel:* 800-251-3320 *Fax:* 615-749-6056 (academic books) *Toll Free Fax:* 800-836-7802 (orders) *E-mail:* orders@abingdonpress.com *Web Site:* www.abingdonpress.com, pg 2

Alexander, Pamela, Oberlin College Press, 50 N Professor St, Oberlin, OH 44074-1091 *Tel:* 440-775-8408 *Fax:* 440-775-8124 *E-mail:* oc.press@oberlin.edu *Web Site:* www.oberlin.edu/ocpress, pg 166

Alexander, Patrick, The Pennsylvania State University Press, University Support Bldg 1, Suite C, 820 N University Dr, University Park, PA 16802-1003 *Tel:* 814-865-1327 *Toll Free Tel:* 800-326-9180 *Fax:* 814-863-1408 *Toll Free Fax:* 877-778-2665 *E-mail:* info@psupress.org *Web Site:* www.psupress.org, pg 179

Alexander, Richard, Bristol Park Books, 252 W 38 St, Suite 206, New York, NY 10018 *Tel:* 212-842-0700 *Fax:* 212-842-1771 *E-mail:* info@bristolparkbooks.com *Web Site:* bristolparkbooks.com, pg 44

Alexander, Sandy, University Press of Mississippi, 3825 Ridgewood Rd, Jackson, MS 39211-6492 *Tel:* 601-432-6205 *Toll Free Tel:* 800-737-7788 (orders & cust serv) *Fax:* 601-432-6217 *E-mail:* press@mississippi.edu *Web Site:* www.upress.state.ms.us, pg 247

Alexander, Shara, Harlequin Enterprises Ltd, 233 Broadway, Suite 1001, New York, NY 10279 *Tel:* 212-553-4200 *Fax:* 212-227-8969 *E-mail:* customerservice@harlequin.com *Web Site:* www.harlequin.com, pg 101

Alexander, Susanne, Goose Lane Editions, 500 Beaverbrook Ct, Suite 330, Fredericton, NB E3B 5X4, Canada *Tel:* 506-450-4251 *Toll Free Tel:* 888-926-8377 *Fax:* 506-459-4991 *E-mail:* info@gooselane.com; customerservice@gooselane.com *Web Site:* www.gooselane.com, pg 458

Alexander, Susanne M, Marriage Transformation LLC, PO Box 249, Harrison, TN 37341 *Tel:* 423-599-0153 *Web Site:* www.marriagetransformation.com, pg 142

Alexander, Tracy, McLaren Memorial Comedy Play Writing Competition, 2000 W Wadley Ave, Midland, TX 79705 *Tel:* 432-682-2544 *E-mail:* tracy@mctmidland.org *Web Site:* www.mctmidland.org, pg 667

Algar, Liza, Chronicle Books LLC, 680 Second St, San Francisco, CA 94107 *Tel:* 415-537-4200 *Toll Free Tel:* 800-759-0190 (cust serv) *Fax:* 415-537-4460 *Toll Free Fax:* 800-858-7787 (orders); 800-286-9471 (cust serv) *E-mail:* frontdesk@chroniclebooks.com *Web Site:* www.chroniclebooks.com, pg 55

Alguire, Julie, Crabtree Publishing Co, 350 Fifth Ave, 59th fl, PMB 59051, New York, NY 10118 *Tel:* 212-496-5040 *Toll Free Tel:* 800-387-7650 *Toll Free Fax:* 800-355-7166 *E-mail:* custserv@crabtreebooks.com *Web Site:* www.crabtreebooks.com, pg 63

Alguire, Julie, Crabtree Publishing Co Ltd, 616 Welland Ave, St Catharines, ON L2M 5V6, Canada *Tel:* 905-682-5221 *Toll Free Tel:* 800-387-7650 *Fax:* 905-682-7166 *Toll Free Fax:* 800-355-7166 *E-mail:* custserv@crabtreebooks.com; sales@crabtreebooks.com; orders@crabtreebooks.com *Web Site:* www.crabtreebooks.com, pg 451

Ali, Kazim, Oberlin College Press, 50 N Professor St, Oberlin, OH 44074-1091 *Tel:* 440-775-8408 *Fax:* 440-775-8124 *E-mail:* oc.press@oberlin.edu *Web Site:* www.oberlin.edu/ocpress, pg 166

Ali, Liaquat, Kazi Publications Inc, 3023 W Belmont Ave, Chicago, IL 60618 *Tel:* 773-267-7001 *Fax:* 773-267-7002 *E-mail:* info@kazi.org *Web Site:* www.kazi.org, pg 125

Alighieri, Christian, Ransom Note Press, 143 E Ridgewood Ave, Box 419, Ridgewood, NJ 07451 *Tel:* 201-835-2790 *E-mail:* editorial@ransomnotepress.com *Web Site:* www.ransomnotepress.com, pg 478

Alimonti, Isabella, Picador, 175 Fifth Ave, 19th fl, New York, NY 10010 *Tel:* 646-307-5151 *Fax:* 212-253-9627 *Web Site:* www.picadorusa.com, pg 182

Aliotti, Tracee, International Society for Technology in Education, 1530 Wilson Blvd, Suite 730, Arlington, VA 22209 *Tel:* 503-342-2848 (intl) *Toll Free Tel:* 800-336-5191 (US & CN) *E-mail:* iste@iste.org *Web Site:* www.iste.org; www.isteconference.org, pg 120

Allaman, Hannah, Disney-Hyperion Books, 1101 Flower St, Glendale, CA 91201 *Web Site:* books.disney.com, pg 70

Allan, Alex, DK Publishing, 345 Hudson St, 2nd fl, New York, NY 10014 *Tel:* 646-674-4000 *Toll Free Tel:* 877-342-5357 (cust serv); 800-733-3000 *Web Site:* www.dk.com; www.penguin.com, pg 71

Allan, Richard, The Aaland Agency, PO Box 849, Inyokern, CA 93527-0849 *Tel:* 760-384-3910 *Web Site:* www.the-aaland-agency.com, pg 505

Allannic, Rica, David Black Agency, 335 Adams St, 27th fl, Suite 2707, Brooklyn, NY 11201 *Tel:* 718-852-5500 *Fax:* 718-852-5539 *Web Site:* www.davidblackagency.com, pg 508

Allberry, Debra, Warren Wilson College, MFA Program for Writers, 701 Warren Wilson Rd, Swannanoa, NC 28778 *Tel:* 828-771-3717 *Fax:* 828-771-7005 *E-mail:* mfa@warren-wilson.edu *Web Site:* www.warren-wilson.edu/~mfa, pg 624

Allday, Liana, Stewart, Tabori & Chang, 115 W 18 St, 6th fl, New York, NY 10011 *Tel:* 212-519-1200; 212-206-7715 *Fax:* 212-519-1210 *E-mail:* abrams@abramsbooks.com *Web Site:* www.abramsbooks.com/imprints/stc, pg 222

Allen, Christopher, Summit University Press, 63 Summit Way, Gardiner, MT 59030-9314 *Tel:* 406-848-9742; 406-848-9500 (retail orders) *Toll Free Tel:* 800-245-5445 (retail orders) *Fax:* 406-848-9744 *E-mail:* info@summituniversitypress.com; marketing@summituniversitypress.com; production@summituniversitypress.com; rights@summituniversitypress.com *Web Site:* www.summituniversitypress.com, pg 224

Allen, Inge, Crystal Publishers Inc, 3460 Lost Hills Dr, Las Vegas, NV 89122 *Tel:* 702-434-3037 *Fax:* 702-434-3037 *Web Site:* www.crystalpub.com, pg 65

Allen, Janet, Write Now, 140 W Washington St, Indianapolis, IN 46204-3465 *Tel:* 317-635-5277 *Fax:* 317-236-0767 *E-mail:* info@writenow.co *Web Site:* www.writenow.co, pg 700

Allen, Lenny, Bloomsbury Publishing Inc, 1385 Broadway, 5th fl, New York, NY 10018 *Tel:* 212-419-5300 *E-mail:* marketingusa@bloomsbury.com; adultpublicityusa@bloomsbury.com; askacademic@bloomsbury.com *Web Site:* www.bloomsbury.com, pg 38

Allen, Lindsey, Center for Publishing Departmental Scholarships, Midtown Ctr, Rm 429, 11 W 42 St, New York, NY 10036 *Tel:* 212-992-3232 *Fax:* 212-992-3233 *E-mail:* pub.center@nyu.edu *Web Site:* www.scps.nyu.edu, pg 636

Allen, Lindsey, New York University, Center for Publishing, Midtown Ctr, Rm 429, 11 W 42 St, New York, NY 10036 *Tel:* 212-992-3232 *Fax:* 212-992-3233 *E-mail:* pub.center@nyu.edu *Web Site:* www.scps.nyu.edu/publishing, pg 621

Allen, Marc, New World Library, 14 Pamaron Way, Novato, CA 94949 *Tel:* 415-884-2100 *Toll Free Tel:* 800-227-3900 (ext 52, retail orders); 800-972-6657 *Fax:* 415-884-2199 *E-mail:* escort@newworldlibrary.com *Web Site:* www.newworldlibrary.com, pg 161

Allen, Pete, JMW Group Inc, 347 Rte 6, No 867, Mahopac, NY 10541 *Tel:* 914-841-7105 *Fax:* 914-248-8861 *E-mail:* jmwgroup@jmwgroup.net *Web Site:* jmwgroup.net, pg 523

Allen, Rebecca, TCU Press, 3000 Sandage Ave, Fort Worth, TX 76109 *Tel:* 817-257-7822 *Toll Free Tel:* 800-826-8911 (orders) *Fax:* 817-257-5075 *Web Site:* www.prs.tcu.edu, pg 228

Allen, Robert, Macmillan Audio, 175 Fifth Ave, New York, NY 10010 *Tel:* 646-307-5151 *Toll Free Tel:* 888-330-8477 (cust serv) *Fax:* 917-534-0980 *Web Site:* www.macmillanaudio.com, pg 140

Allen, Ron, International Risk Management Institute Inc, 12222 Merit Dr, Suite 1600, Dallas, TX 75251-2266 *Tel:* 972-960-7693 *Fax:* 972-371-5120 *E-mail:* info27@irmi.com *Web Site:* www.irmi.com, pg 120

Allen, Tom, Sterling Publishing Co Inc, 1166 Avenue of the Americas, 17th fl, New York, NY 10036 *Tel:* 212-532-7160 *Toll Free Tel:* 800-367-9692 *Fax:* 212-213-2495 *Web Site:* www.sterlingpublishing.com, pg 222

Aller, Gary, Gallaudet University Press, 800 Florida Ave NE, Washington, DC 20002-3695 *Tel:* 202-651-5488 *Fax:* 202-651-5489 *E-mail:* gupress@gallaudet.edu *Web Site:* gupress.gallaudet.edu, pg 89

Allgood, Severin, The Pinch Writing Awards in Fiction, University of Memphis, English Dept, 435 Patterson Hall, Memphis, TN 38152 *Tel:* 901-678-2651 *Fax:* 901-678-2226 *E-mail:* editor@pinchjournal.com *Web Site:* www.pinchjournal.com, pg 680

Allgood, Severin, The Pinch Writing Awards in Poetry, University of Memphis, English Dept, 435 Patterson Hall, Memphis, TN 38152 *Tel:* 901-678-2651 *Fax:* 901 678 2226 *E-mail:* editor@pinchjournal.com *Web Site:* www.pinchjournal.com, pg 680

Allison, Kevin, Oxford University Press USA, 198 Madison Ave, New York, NY 10016 *Tel:* 212-726-6000 *Toll Free Tel:* 800-451-7556 (orders); 800-445-9714 (cust serv) *Fax:* 919-677-1303 *E-mail:* custserv.us@oup.com *Web Site:* www.oup.com/us, pg 171

Allison, Mark, Stackpole Books, 5067 Ritter Rd, Mechanicsburg, PA 17055 *Tel:* 717-796-0411 *Toll Free Tel:* 800-732-3669 *Fax:* 717-796-0412 *Web Site:* www.stackpolebooks.com, pg 220

Allport, Andrew, Rick DeMarinis Short Story Award, PO Box 2414, Durango, CO 81302 *Tel:* 970-903-7914 *E-mail:* cutthroatmag@gmail.com *Web Site:* www.cutthroatmag.com, pg 640

Allport, Andrew, Joy Harjo Poetry Award, PO Box 2414, Durango, CO 81302 *Tel:* 970-903-7914 *E-mail:* cutthroatmag@gmail.com *Web Site:* www.cutthroatmag.com, pg 652

Ally, Shameiza, Random House Children's Books, 1745 Broadway, 10th fl, New York, NY 10019 *Tel:* 212-782-9000 *Web Site:* www.randomhousekids.com, pg 194

Almeida, Alia, Houghton Mifflin Harcourt Trade & Reference Division, 125 High St, Boston, MA 02110 *Tel:* 617-351-5000 *Toll Free Tel:* 800-225-3362 *Web Site:* www.hmhco.com, pg 111

Almqvist, Johan, Chronicle Books LLC, 680 Second St, San Francisco, CA 94107 *Tel:* 415-537-4200 *Toll Free Tel:* 800-759-0190 (cust serv) *Fax:* 415-537-4460 *Toll Free Fax:* 800-858-7787 (orders); 800-286-9471 (cust serv) *E-mail:* frontdesk@chroniclebooks.com *Web Site:* www.chroniclebooks.com, pg 55

Alonso-Mendoza, Emilio, The Alexander Graham Bell Association for the Deaf & Hard of Hearing, 3417 Volta Place NW, Washington, DC 20007 *Tel:* 202-337-5220 *Toll Free Tel:* 866-337-5220 (orders) *Fax:* 202-337-8314 *E-mail:* info@agbell.org; publications@agbell.org *Web Site:* www.agbell.org, pg 6

Alperen, Jennifer, The Betsy Nolan Literary Agency, 112 E 17 St, Suite 1W, New York, NY 10003 *Tel:* 212-967-8200 *Fax:* 212-967-7292 *E-mail:* dblehr@cs.com, pg 531

Alps, Marisa, Harbour Publishing Co Ltd, 4437 Rondeview Rd, Madeira Park, BC V0N 2H0, Canada *Tel:* 604-883-2730 *Toll Free Tel:* 800-667-2988 *Fax:* 604-883-9451 *E-mail:* info@harbourpublishing.com *Web Site:* www.harbourpublishing.com, pg 459

Alter, George, Inter-University Consortium for Political & Social Research (ICPSR), 330 Packard St, Ann Arbor, MI 48104 *Tel:* 734-647-5000 *Fax:* 734-647-8200 *E-mail:* netmail@icpsr.umich.edu *Web Site:* www.icpsr.umich.edu, pg 118

Altman, David G, Center for Creative Leadership LLC, One Leadership Place, Greensboro, NC 27410-9427 *Tel:* 336-545-2810; 336-288-7210 *Fax:* 336-282-3284 *E-mail:* info@ccl.org *Web Site:* www.ccl.org/publications, pg 51

Altman, Elias, Aevitas Creative Management, 19 W 21 St, Suite 501, New York, NY 10010 *Tel:* 212-765-6900 *Web Site:* aevitascreative.com, pg 506

Altschuler, Miriam, DeFiore and Company Literary Management Inc, 47 E 19 St, 3rd fl, New York, NY 10003 *Tel:* 212-925-7744 *Fax:* 212-925-9803 *E-mail:* info@defliterary.com; submissions@defliterary.com *Web Site:* www.defliterary.com, pg 513

Alvarado, Beth, Rick DeMarinis Short Story Award, PO Box 2414, Durango, CO 81302 *Tel:* 970-903-7914 *E-mail:* cutthroatmag@gmail.com *Web Site:* www.cutthroatmag.com, pg 640

Alvarado, Beth, Joy Harjo Poetry Award, PO Box 2414, Durango, CO 81302 *Tel:* 970-903-7914 *E-mail:* cutthroatmag@gmail.com *Web Site:* www.cutthroatmag.com, pg 652

Alvarez, Awilda, Hippocrene Books Inc, 171 Madison Ave, New York, NY 10016 *Tel:* 212-685-4373 *Fax:* 212-779-9338 *E-mail:* info@hippocrenebooks.com; orderdept@hippocrenebooks.com (orders) *Web Site:* www.hippocrenebooks.com, pg 108

Alvarez, Jessica, BookEnds Literary Agency, 136 Long Hill Rd, Gillette, NJ 07933 *Web Site:* www.bookendsliterary.com, pg 508

Alvarez, Lisa, Squaw Valley Community of Writers Summer Workshops, PO Box 1416, Nevada City, CA 95959 *Tel:* 530-470-8440 *E-mail:* info@communityofwriters.org *Web Site:* www.communityofwriters.org, pg 615

Alvaro, David PhD, New York Academy of Sciences (NYAS), 7 World Trade, 40th fl, 250 Greenwich St, New York, NY 10007-2157 *Tel:* 212-298-8600 *Toll Free Tel:* 800-843-6927 *Fax:* 212-298-3668 *E-mail:* nyas@nyas.org; annals@nyas.org; customerservice@nyas.org *Web Site:* www.nyas.org, pg 161

Alward, Kathy, Piano Press, 1425 Ocean Ave, Suite 5, Del Mar, CA 92014 *Tel:* 619-884-1401 *Fax:* 858-755-1104 *E-mail:* pianopress@pianopress.com *Web Site:* www.pianopress.com, pg 182

Amato, Frank W, Frank Amato Publications Inc, 4040 SE Wister St, Milwaukie, OR 97222 *Tel:* 503-653-8108 *Toll Free Tel:* 800-541-9498 *Fax:* 503-653-2766 *E-mail:* customerservice@amatobooks.com; info@amatobooks.com *Web Site:* www.amatobooks.com, pg 9

Amato, Nick S, Frank Amato Publications Inc, 4040 SE Wister St, Milwaukie, OR 97222 *Tel:* 503-653-8108 *Toll Free Tel:* 800-541-9498 *Fax:* 503-653-2766 *E-mail:* customerservice@amatobooks.com; info@amatobooks.com *Web Site:* www.amatobooks.com, pg 9

Amato, Tony F, Frank Amato Publications Inc, 4040 SE Wister St, Milwaukie, OR 97222 *Tel:* 503-653-8108 *Toll Free Tel:* 800-541-9498 *Fax:* 503-653-2766 *E-mail:* customerservice@amatobooks.com; info@amatobooks.com *Web Site:* www.amatobooks.com, pg 9

Ambrosio, Dan, Perseus Books, 250 W 57 St, 15th fl, New York, NY 10107 *Tel:* 212-340-8100 *Toll Free Tel:* 800-343-4499 (cust serv) *Fax:* 212-340-8105 *Web Site:* www.perseusbooks.com, pg 181

Amendolara, Paula, Simon & Schuster Sales Division, 1230 Avenue of the Americas, New York, NY 10020 *Tel:* 212-698-7000, pg 214

Amer, Morgan, Chronicle Books LLC, 680 Second St, San Francisco, CA 94107 *Tel:* 415-537-4200 *Toll Free Tel:* 800-759-0190 (cust serv) *Fax:* 415-537-4460 *Toll Free Fax:* 800-858-7787 (orders); 800-286-9471 (cust serv) *E-mail:* frontdesk@chroniclebooks.com *Web Site:* www.chroniclebooks.com, pg 55

Ames, Joanna, Canadian Publishers' Council (CPC), 250 Merton St, Suite 203, Toronto, ON M4S 1B1, Canada *Tel:* 416-322-7011 *Fax:* 416-322-6999 *Web Site:* www.pubcouncil.ca, pg 562

Ames, Michael, Vanderbilt University Press, 2014 Broadway, Suite 320, Nashville, TN 37203 *Tel:* 615-322-3585 *Toll Free Tel:* 800-627-7377 (orders only) *Fax:* 615-343-8823 *Toll Free Fax:* 800-735-0476 (orders only) *E-mail:* vupress@vanderbilt.edu *Web Site:* www.vanderbiltuniversitypress.com, pg 249

Ames, Steve, World Citizens, PO Box 131, Mill Valley, CA 94942-0131 *Tel:* 415-380-8020 *Toll Free Tel:* 800-247-6553 (orders only), pg 259

Amienyi, Dr Osa, Arkansas State University Graphic Communications Program, PO Box 1930, Dept of Media, State University, AR 72467-1930 *Tel:* 870-972-3114 *Fax:* 870-972-3321 *Web Site:* www.astate.edu, pg 619

Amini, Christina, Chronicle Books LLC, 680 Second St, San Francisco, CA 94107 *Tel:* 415-537-4200 *Toll Free Tel:* 800-759-0190 (cust serv) *Fax:* 415-537-4460 *Toll Free Fax:* 800-858-7787 (orders); 800-286-9471 (cust serv) *E-mail:* frontdesk@chroniclebooks.com *Web Site:* www.chroniclebooks.com, pg 55

Amirault, Jillian, Orbit, 1290 Avenue of the Americas, New York, NY 10019 *Tel:* 212-364-1100 *Toll Free Tel:* 800-759-0190 *Web Site:* www.orbitbooks.net, pg 169

Amling, Eric, Darhansoff & Verrill, 133 W 72 St, Rm 304, New York, NY 10023 *Tel:* 917-305-1300 *E-mail:* permissions@dvagency.com *Web Site:* www.dvagency.com, pg 512

Ammons-Longtin, Cheryl, Oxford University Press USA, 198 Madison Ave, New York, NY 10016 *Tel:* 212-726-6000 *Toll Free Tel:* 800-451-7556 (orders); 800-445-9714 (cust serv) *Fax:* 919-677-1303 *E-mail:* custserv.us@oup.com *Web Site:* www.oup.com/us, pg 171

Amoroso, Connie, Carnegie Mellon University Press, 5032 Forbes Ave, Pittsburgh, PA 15289-1021 *Tel:* 412-268-2861 *Fax:* 412-268-8706 *E-mail:* carnegiemellonuniversitypress@gmail.com *Web Site:* www.cmu.edu/universitypress, pg 48

Amos, Holly, Frederick Bock Prize, 61 W Superior St, Chicago, IL 60654 *Tel:* 312-787-7070 *Fax:* 312-787-6650 *E-mail:* editors@poetrymagazine.org *Web Site:* www.poetryfoundation.org, pg 633

Amos, Holly, Bess Hokin Prize, 61 W Superior St, Chicago, IL 60654 *Tel:* 312-787-7070 *Fax:* 312-787-6650 *E-mail:* editors@poetrymagazine.org *Web Site:* www.poetryfoundation.org, pg 653

Amos, Holly, Levinson Prize, 61 W Superior St, Chicago, IL 60654 *Tel:* 312-787-7070 *Fax:* 312-787-6650 *E-mail:* editors@poetrymagazine.org *Web Site:* www.poetryfoundation.org, pg 661

Amos, Holly, Ruth Lilly Poetry Prize, 61 W Superior St, Chicago, IL 60654 *Tel:* 312-787-7070 *Fax:* 312-787-6650 *E-mail:* editors@poetrymagazine.org *Web Site:* poetrymagazine.org, pg 661

Amos, Holly, John Frederick Nims Memorial Prize, 61 W Superior St, Chicago, IL 60654 *Tel:* 312-787-7070 *Fax:* 312-787-6650 *E-mail:* editors@poetrymagazine.org *Web Site:* www.poetryfoundation.org, pg 674

Amos, Holly, The J Howard & Barbara M J Wood Prize, 61 W Superior St, Chicago, IL 60654 *Tel:* 312-787-7070 *Fax:* 312-787-6650 *E-mail:* editors@poetrymagazine.org *Web Site:* www.poetryfoundation.org, pg 699

Amour, Lucie, Visual Artists & Galleries Association Inc (VAGA), 111 Broadway, Suite 1006, New York, NY 10006 *Tel:* 212-736-6666 *Fax:* 212-736-6767 *E-mail:* info@vagarights.com *Web Site:* vagarights.com, pg 580

Amper, Julie, Holiday House Inc, 425 Madison Ave, New York, NY 10017 *Tel:* 212-688-0085 *Fax:* 212-421-6134 *E-mail:* info@holidayhouse.com *Web Site:* www.holidayhouse.com, pg 109

Amphlett, Nick, HarperCollins General Books Group, 195 Broadway, New York, NY 10007 *Tel:* 212-207-7000 *Web Site:* www.harpercollins.com, pg 101

Amster, Betsy, Betsy Amster Literary Enterprises, 6312 SW Capitol Hwy, No 503, Portland, OR 97239 *Tel:* 503-496-4007 *E-mail:* rights@amsterlit.com (rts inquiries); b.amster.assistant@gmail.com (adult book queries); b.amster.kidsbooks@gmail.com (children & young adult book queries) *Web Site:* www.amsterlit.com, pg 506

Amundsen, John, Coretta Scott King Book Awards, 50 E Huron St, Chicago, IL 60611 *Toll Free Tel:* 800-545-2433 *E-mail:* olos@ala.org *Web Site:* www.ala.org/emiert/cskbookawards, pg 658

Amundsen, John, Coretta Scott King - Virginia Hamilton Award for Lifetime Achievement, 50 E Huron St, Chicago, IL 60611 *Toll Free Tel:* 800-545-2433 *E-mail:* diversity@ala.org *Web Site:* www.ala.org/emiert/virginia-hamilton-award-lifetime-achievement, pg 659

Amundson, Sandy, Augsburg Fortress Publishers, Publishing House of the Evangelical Lutheran Church in America, 510 Marquette Ave S, Minneapolis, MN 55402 *Tel:* 612-330-3300 *Toll Free Tel:* 800-426-0115 (ext 639, subns); 800-328-4648 (orders) *Fax:* 612-330-3455 *E-mail:* info@augsburgfortress.org; copyright@augsburgfortress.org (reprint permission requests); customercare@augsburgfortress.org *Web Site:* www.augsburgfortress.org, pg 26

Anastas, Mara, Simon & Schuster Children's Publishing, 1230 Avenue of the Americas, New York, NY 10020 *Tel:* 212-698-7000 *Web Site:* www.simonandschuster.com/kids; www.simonandschuster.com/teen; simonandschuster.net; simonandschuster.biz, pg 213

Anders, Tim, FC&A Publishing, 103 Clover Green, Peachtree City, GA 30269 *Tel:* 770-487-6307 *Toll Free Tel:* 800-226-8024 *Fax:* 770-631-4357 *E-mail:* customer_service@fca.com *Web Site:* www.fca.com, pg 83

Andersen, Peter, Doubleday/Nan A Talese, c/o Penguin Random House Inc, 1745 Broadway, New York, NY 10019 *Tel:* 212-751-2600 *Fax:* 212-572-2662 *E-mail:* ddaypub@randomhouse.com *Web Site:* knopfdoubleday.com, pg 72

Andersen, Peter, Alfred A Knopf/Everyman's Library, c/o Penguin Random House Inc, 1745 Broadway, New York, NY 10019 *Tel:* 212-751-2600 *Toll Free Tel:* 800-638-6460 *Fax:* 212-572-2593 *Web Site:* www.knopfdoubleday.com, pg 127

Andersen, Vicki, North American Snowsports Journalists Association (NASJA), 11728 SE Madison St, Portland, OR 97216-3849 *Tel:* 503-255-3771 *Fax:* 503-255-3771 *Web Site:* www.nasja.org, pg 574

Andersen-Zantop, Ashley, Capstone Publishers™, 1710 Roe Crest Dr, North Mankato, MN 56003 *Toll Free Tel:* 800-747-4992 (cust serv) *Toll Free Fax:* 888-262-0705 *Web Site:* www.capstonepress.com, pg 47

Anderson, Andrea, Theodore C Blegen Award, 701 William Vickers Ave, Durham, NC 27701-3162 *Tel:* 919-682-9319 *Fax:* 919-682-2349 *Web Site:* www.foresthistory.org, pg 633

Anderson, Andrea, John M Collier Award for Forest History Journalism, 701 William Vickers Ave, Durham, NC 27701-3162 *Tel:* 919-682-9319 *Fax:* 919-682-2349 *Web Site:* www.foresthistory.org, pg 638

Anderson, Andrea, Leopold-Hidy Award, 701 William Vickers Ave, Durham, NC 27701-3162 *Tel:* 919-682-9319 *Fax:* 919-682-2349 *Web Site:* www.foresthistory.org, pg 660

Anderson, Andrea, Charles A Weyerhauser Book Award, 701 William Vickers Ave, Durham, NC 27701-3162 *Tel:* 919-682-9319 *Fax:* 919-682-2349 *Web Site:* www.foresthistory.org, pg 697

Anderson, Andy, The Charles Bernheimer Prize, University of South Carolina, Dept of Languages, Literature & Cultures, 1620 College St, Rm 813-A, Columbia, SC 29208 *Tel:* 803-777-3021 *E-mail:* info@acla.org *Web Site:* www.acla.org/prize-awards, pg 631

Anderson, Andy, Harry Levin Prize, University of South Carolina, Dept of Languages, Literature & Cultures, 1620 College St, Rm 813-A, Columbia, SC 29208 *Tel:* 803-777-3021 *E-mail:* info@acla.org *Web Site:* www.acla.org/prize-awards, pg 660

Anderson, Andy, Rene Wellek Prize, University of South Carolina, Dept of Languages, Literature & Cultures, 1620 College St, Rm 813-A, Columbia, SC 29208 *Tel:* 803-777-3021 *E-mail:* info@acla.org *Web Site:* www.acla.org/prize-awards, pg 696

Anderson, Ann-Marie, Temple University Press, 1852 N Tenth St, Philadelphia, PA 19122-6099 *Tel:* 215-926-2140 *Toll Free Tel:* 800-621-2736 *Fax:* 215-926-2141 *E-mail:* tempress@temple.edu *Web Site:* www.temple.edu/tempress, pg 228

Anderson, Aubrey, Epicenter Press Inc, 6524 NE 181 St, Suite 2, Kenmore, WA 98028 *Tel:* 425-485-6822 (edit, mktg, busn off) *Fax:* 425-481-8253 *E-mail:* info@epicenterpress.com *Web Site:* www.epicenterpress.com, pg 79

Anderson, Becky, Gollehon Press Inc, 3655 Glenn Dr SE, Grand Rapids, MI 49546 *Tel:* 616-949-3515 *Fax:* 616-949-8674 *E-mail:* sales@gollehonbooks.com; editorial@gollehonbooks.com *Web Site:* www.gollehonbooks.com, pg 94

Anderson, Colleen, Balance Sports Publishing LLC, 195 Lucero Way, Portola Valley, CA 94028 *Tel:* 650-561-9586 *Fax:* 650-391-9850 *E-mail:* info@balancesportspublishing.com *Web Site:* www.balancesportspublishing.com, pg 28

Anderson, Don, Pelican Publishing Co, 1000 Burmaster St, Gretna, LA 70053-2246 *Tel:* 504-368-1175 *Toll Free Tel:* 800-843-1724 *Fax:* 504-368-1195 *E-mail:* sales@pelicanpub.com (sales); office@pelicanpub.com (permission); promo@pelicanpub.com (publicity) *Web Site:* www.pelicanpub.com, pg 176

Anderson, Duane, ACU Press, 1648 Campus Ct, Abilene, TX 79601 *Tel:* 325-674-2720 *Toll Free Tel:* 877-816-4455 *Web Site:* www.acupressbooks.com; www.leafwoodpublishers.com, pg 4

Anderson, Elizabeth, Houghton Mifflin Harcourt, 125 High St, Boston, MA 02110 *Tel:* 617-351-5000 *Toll Free Tel:* 855-969-4642; 800-225-5425 (K-12 educ materials); 800-323-9540 (assessment materials); 877-219-1537 (SkillsTutor); 888-242-6747 (Innovation in Educ Group); 800-225-3362 (Trade & Ref Div) *Toll Free Fax:* 800-269-5232 *E-mail:* myhmhco@hmhco.com *Web Site:* www.hmhco.com, pg 110

Anderson, Erik, University of Minnesota Press, 111 Third Ave S, Suite 290, Minneapolis, MN 55401-2520 *Tel:* 612-301-1990 *Fax:* 612-301-1980 *E-mail:* ump@umn.edu *Web Site:* www.upress.umn.edu, pg 242

Anderson, Gordon L, Paragon House, 3600 Labore Rd, Suite 1, St Paul, MN 55110-4144 *Tel:* 651-644-3087 *Toll Free Tel:* 800-447-3709 *Fax:* 651-644-0997 *E-mail:* paragon@paragonhouse.com *Web Site:* www.paragonhouse.com, pg 174

Anderson, Heidi Lynn, Fun in the Sun Writer's Cruise Conference, PO Box 823414, Pembroke Pines, FL 33082 *E-mail:* frwfuninthesun@yahoo.com *Web Site:* frwfuninthesunmain.blogspot.com/; www.frwriters.org, pg 610

Anderson, Jon, Simon & Schuster Children's Publishing, 1230 Avenue of the Americas, New York, NY 10020 *Tel:* 212-698-7000 *Web Site:* www.simonandschuster.com/kids; www.simonandschuster.com/teen; simonandschuster.net; simonandschuster.biz, pg 213

Anderson, Jon, Simon & Schuster, Inc, 1230 Avenue of the Americas, New York, NY 10020 *Tel:* 212-698-7000 *Fax:* 212-698-7007 *E-mail:* firstname.lastname@simonandschuster.com *Web Site:* www.simonandschuster.com, pg 213

Anderson, Kathleen, Anderson Literary Management LLC, 244 Fifth Ave, 11th fl, New York, NY 10001 *Tel:* 212-645-6045 *Fax:* 212-741-1936 *E-mail:* info@andersonliterary.com *Web Site:* www.andersonliterary.com, pg 506

Anderson, Krista, Perseus Books, 250 W 57 St, 15th fl, New York, NY 10107 *Tel:* 212-340-8100 *Toll Free Tel:* 800-343-4499 (cust serv) *Fax:* 212-340-8105 *Web Site:* www.perseusbooks.com, pg 180

Anderson, Kristin, Corwin, a Sage Co, 2455 Teller Rd, Thousand Oaks, CA 91320 *Tel:* 805-499-9734 *Toll Free Tel:* 800-233-9936 *Fax:* 805-499-5323 *Toll Free Fax:* 800-417-2466 *E-mail:* info@corwin.com; order@corwin.com *Web Site:* www.corwin.com, pg 61

Anderson, Kristine, Quarto Publishing Group USA Inc, 400 First Ave N, Suite 400, Minneapolis, MN 55401 *Tel:* 612-344-8100 *Toll Free Tel:* 800-328-0590 (sales); 800-458-0454 *Fax:* 612-344-8691 *E-mail:* sales@quartous.com *Web Site:* www.quartoknows.com, pg 192

Anderson, Liz, Houghton Mifflin Harcourt, 125 High St, Boston, MA 02110 *Tel:* 617-351-5000 *Toll Free Tel:* 855-969-4642; 800-225-5425 (K-12 educ materials); 800-323-9540 (assessment materials); 877-219-1537 (SkillsTutor); 888-242-6747 (Innovation in Educ Group); 800-225-3362 (Trade & Ref Div) *Toll Free Fax:* 800-269-5232 *E-mail:* myhmhco@hmhco.com *Web Site:* www.hmhco.com, pg 110

Anderson, Lydia, Wisdom Publications Inc, 199 Elm St, Somerville, MA 02144 *Tel:* 617-776-7416 *Toll Free Tel:* 800-272-4050 (orders) *Fax:* 617-776-7841 *E-mail:* info@wisdompubs.org; submission@wisdompubs.org *Web Site:* www.wisdompubs.org, pg 257

Anderson, Mary K, IODE Jean Throop Book Award, 9-45 Frid St, Hamilton, ON L8P 4M3, Canada *Tel:* 905-522-9537 *Fax:* 905-522-3637 *E-mail:* iodeontario@bellnet.ca *Web Site:* www.iodeontario.ca, pg 656

Anderson, Monty, Presbyterian Publishing Corp (PPC), 100 Witherspoon St, Louisville, KY 40202 *Tel:* 502-569-5000 *Toll Free Tel:* 800-523-1631 (US only) *Fax:* 502-569-5113 *E-mail:* ppcmail@presbypub.com *Web Site:* www.ppcbooks.com, pg 187

Anderson, Monty, Westminster John Knox Press (WJK), 100 Witherspoon St, Louisville, KY 40202-1396 *Toll Free Tel:* 800-523-1631 (US only) *Fax:* 502-569-5113 *Toll Free Fax:* 800-541-5113 (US & CN) *E-mail:* wjk@wjkbooks.com; customer_service@wjkbooks.com *Web Site:* www.wjkbooks.com, pg 254

Anderson, Dr Patricia PhD, Patricia Anderson, PhD, Editor & Literary Consultant, 1489 Marine Dr, Suite 515, West Vancouver, BC V7T 1B8, Canada *Tel:* 604-740-0805 *E-mail:* query@helpingyougetpublished.com; patriciaanderson@helpingyougetpublished.com *Web Site:* www.helpingyougetpublished.com, pg 488

Anderson, Patricia PhD, Maryland Historical Society, 201 W Monument St, Baltimore, MD 21201 *Tel:* 410-685-3750 *Fax:* 410-385-2105 *Web Site:* www.mdhs.org, pg 143

Anderson, Paul, The Glen Workshop, 3307 Third Ave W, Seattle, WA 98119 *Tel:* 206-281-2988 *Fax:* 206-281-2979 *E-mail:* glenworkshop@imagejournal.org *Web Site:* www.imagejournal.org, pg 611

Anderson, Robert, Bloomberg BNA Books, 1801 S Bell St, Arlington, VA 22202 *Tel:* 732-476-6397 *Toll Free Tel:* 800-960-1220 *Fax:* 732-346-1624 *E-mail:* books@bna.com *Web Site:* www.bna.com/bnabooks, pg 37

Anderson, Samara, Robert A Freedman Dramatic Agency Inc, 1501 Broadway, Suite 2310, New York, NY 10036 *Tel:* 212-840-5760 *Fax:* 212-840-5776, pg 518

Anderson, Sara, Sara Anderson Children's Books, PO Box 47182, Seattle, WA 98146 *Tel:* 206-285-1520 *Web Site:* www.saranderson.com, pg 16

Anderson, Steven, John M Collier Award for Forest History Journalism, 701 William Vickers Ave, Durham, NC 27701-3162 *Tel:* 919-682-9319 *Fax:* 919-682-2349 *Web Site:* www.foresthistory.org, pg 638

Andersson, Mark, Guild of Book Workers, 521 Fifth Ave, New York, NY 10175 *Tel:* 212-292-4444 *E-mail:* communications@guildofbookworkers.org *Web Site:* www.guildofbookworkers.org, pg 566

Andonian, Mr Aramais, Blue Crane Books Inc, 36 Hazel St, Watertown, MA 02472 *Tel:* 617-926-8989, pg 38

Andrade, Jamie, Perseus Books, 250 W 57 St, 15th fl, New York, NY 10107 *Tel:* 212-340-8100 *Toll Free Tel:* 800-343-4499 (cust serv) *Fax:* 212-340-8105 *Web Site:* www.perseusbooks.com, pg 180

Andreadis, Tina, HarperCollins General Books Group, 195 Broadway, New York, NY 10007 *Tel:* 212-207-7000 *Web Site:* www.harpercollins.com, pg 101

Andree, Courtney, Yale University Press, 302 Temple St, New Haven, CT 06511-8909 *Tel:* 203-432-0960; 203-432-0966 (sales); 401-531-2800 (cust serv) *Toll Free Tel:* 800-405-1619 (cust serv) *Fax:* 203-432-0948; 203-432-8485 (sales); 401-531-2801 (cust serv) *Toll Free Fax:* 800-406-9145 (cust serv) *E-mail:* sales.press@yale.edu (sales); customer.care@triliteral.org (cust serv) *Web Site:* www.yalebooks.com; yalepress.yale.edu/yupbooks, pg 261

Andree, Courtney J, University of Massachusetts Press, East Experiment Sta, 671 N Pleasant St, Amherst, MA 01003 *Tel:* 413-545-2217 *Fax:* 413-545-1226 *E-mail:* info@umpress.umass.edu *Web Site:* www.umass.edu/umpress, pg 242

Andreou, George, Harvard University Press, 79 Garden St, Cambridge, MA 02138-1499 *Tel:* 617-495-2600; 401-531-2800 (intl orders) *Toll Free Tel:* 800-405-1619 (orders) *Fax:* 617-495-5898 (general); 617-496-4677 (edit & rts); 401-531-2801 (intl orders) *Toll Free Fax:* 800-406-9145 (orders) *E-mail:* contact_hup@harvard.edu *Web Site:* www.hup.harvard.edu, pg 103

Andrewes, Lancelot, Wittenborn Art Books, 1109 Geary Blvd, San Francisco, CA 94109 *Tel:* 415-292-6500 *Toll Free Tel:* 800-660-6403 *Fax:* 415-292-6594 *E-mail:* wittenborn@art-books.com *Web Site:* www.art-books.com, pg 258

Andrews, Gaylen, Copywriter's Council of America™ (CCA), CCA Bldg, 7 Putter Lane, Middle Island, NY 11953-1920 *Tel:* 631-924-3888; 631-775-6075 *Fax:* 631-924-8555 *E-mail:* cca4dmcopy@gmail.com *Web Site:* www.andrewlinickdirectmarketing.com/Copywriters-Council.html; www.newworldpressbooks.com, pg 563

Andrews, Hugh, Andrews McMeel Publishing LLC, 1130 Walnut St, Kansas City, MO 64106-2109 *Toll Free Tel:* 800-851-8923; 800-943-9839 (cust serv) *Toll Free Fax:* 800-943-9831 (orders) *Web Site:* www.andrewsmcmeel.com, pg 17

Andrews, Meredith, National Book Awards, 90 Broad St, Suite 604, New York, NY 10004 *Tel:* 212-685-0261 *Fax:* 212-213-6570 *E-mail:* nationalbook@nationalbook.org *Web Site:* www.nationalbook.org, pg 670

Andrews, Vaughn, Workman Publishing Co Inc, 225 Varick St, 9th fl, New York, NY 10014-4381 *Tel:* 212-254-5900 *Toll Free Tel:* 800-722-7202 *Fax:* 212-254-8098 *E-mail:* info@workman.com *Web Site:* www.workman.com, pg 259

Andrikanich, Chris, Gray & Company Publishers, 1588 E 40 St, Suite 3A, Cleveland, OH 44103 *Tel:* 216-431-2665 *Toll Free Tel:* 800-915-3609 *E-mail:* sales@grayco.com; editorial@grayco.com; support@grayco.com; publicity@grayco.com *Web Site:* www.grayco.com, pg 95

Anema, Arielle, PEN Writers' Emergency Fund, 588 Broadway, Suite 303, New York, NY 10012 *Tel:* 212-334-1660 *Fax:* 212-334-2181 *Web Site:* pen.org/press/grants-awards-database, pg 679

Angelilli, Chris, Random House Children's Books, 1745 Broadway, 10th fl, New York, NY 10019 *Tel:* 212-782-9000 *Web Site:* www.randomhousekids.com, pg 194

Angelo, Jim, The Mathematical Association of America, 1529 18 St NW, Washington, DC 20036-1358 *Tel:* 202-387-5200 *Toll Free Tel:* 800-741-9415 *Fax:* 202-265-2384 *E-mail:* maahq@maa.org; advertising@maa.org (pubns) *Web Site:* www.maa.org, pg 144

Angeloro, Nicole, Houghton Mifflin Harcourt Trade & Reference Division, 125 High St, Boston, MA 02110 *Tel:* 617-351-5000 *Toll Free Tel:* 800-225-3362 *Web Site:* www.hmhco.com, pg 111

Angulo, Albert, Perseus Books, 250 W 57 St, 15th fl, New York, NY 10107 *Tel:* 212-340-8100 *Toll Free Tel:* 800-343-4499 (cust serv) *Fax:* 212-340-8105 *Web Site:* www.perseusbooks.com, pg 181

Anixter, Julie, AIGA, the professional association for design, 233 Broadway, Suite 1740, New York, NY 10279 *Tel:* 212-807-1990 *Fax:* 212-807-1799 *E-mail:* general@aiga.org *Web Site:* www.aiga.org, pg 553

Annis, Amanda O'Connor, Trident Media Group LLC, 41 Madison Ave, 36th fl, New York, NY 10010 *Tel:* 212-333-1511 *E-mail:* info@tridentmediagroup.com; press@tridentmediagroup.com *Web Site:* www.tridentmediagroup.com, pg 540

Anthony, Graham, August House Inc, 3500 Piedmont Rd NE, Suite 310, Atlanta, GA 30305 *Tel:* 404-442-4420 *Toll Free Tel:* 800-284-8784 *Fax:* 404-442-4435 *E-mail:* ahinfo@augusthouse.com *Web Site:* www.augusthouse.com, pg 26

Anthony, Joya, Chronicle Books LLC, 680 Second St, San Francisco, CA 94107 *Tel:* 415-537-4200 *Toll Free Tel:* 800-759-0190 (cust serv) *Fax:* 415-537-4460 *Toll Free Fax:* 800-858-7787 (orders); 800-286-9471 (cust serv) *E-mail:* frontdesk@chroniclebooks.com *Web Site:* www.chroniclebooks.com, pg 55

Anthony, Dr Michelle, David C Cook, 4050 Lee Vance View, Colorado Springs, CO 80918 *Tel:* 719-536-0100 *Toll Free Tel:* 800-708-5550; 800-323-7543 (orders & cust serv) *Toll Free Fax:* 800-430-0726 (cust serv) *Web Site:* www.davidccook.com, pg 60

Antoine, Marie-Claire, Lynne Rienner Publishers Inc, 1800 30 St, Suite 314, Boulder, CO 80301 *Tel:* 303-444-6684 *Fax:* 303-444-0824 *E-mail:* questions@rienner.com; cservice@rienner.com *Web Site:* www.rienner.com, pg 199

Antonacci, Laura, Chronicle Books LLC, 680 Second St, San Francisco, CA 94107 *Tel:* 415-537-4200 *Toll Free Tel:* 800-759-0190 (cust serv) *Fax:* 415-537-4460 *Toll Free Fax:* 800-858-7787 (orders); 800-286-9471 (cust serv) *E-mail:* frontdesk@chroniclebooks.com *Web Site:* www.chroniclebooks.com, pg 55

Antonetta, Suzanne Paola, Annie Dillard Award for Creative Nonfiction, Mail Stop 9053, Western Washington University, Bellingham, WA 98225 *Tel:* 360-650-4863 *E-mail:* bhreview@wwu.edu *Web Site:* www.bhreview.org, pg 641

Antonetta, Suzanne Paola, 49th Parallel Poetry Award, Mail Stop 9053, Western Washington University, Bellingham, WA 98225 *Tel:* 360-650-4863 *E-mail:* bhreview@wwu.edu *Web Site:* www.bhreview.org, pg 647

Antonetta, Suzanne Paola, Tobias Wolff Award for Fiction, Mail Stop 9053, Western Washington University, Bellingham, WA 98225 *Tel:* 360-650-4863 *E-mail:* bhreview@wwu.edu *Web Site:* www.bhreview.org, pg 699

Antonetti, Martin, Bibliographical Society of America, PO Box 1537, Lenox Hill Sta, New York, NY 10021-0043 *Tel:* 212-452-2710 *Fax:* 212-452-2710 *E-mail:* bsa@bibsocamer.org *Web Site:* www.bibsocamer.org, pg 560

Antonson, Lori, The Axelrod Agency, 55 Main St, Chatham, NY 12037 *Tel:* 518-392-2100, pg 507

Antony, Peter, The Metropolitan Museum of Art, 1000 Fifth Ave, New York, NY 10028 *Tel:* 212-879-5500; 212-570-3725 (edit) *Fax:* 212-396-5062 *E-mail:* editorial@metmuseum.org *Web Site:* www.metmuseum.org, pg 149

Antony, Wayne, Fernwood Publishing, 32 Oceanvista Lane, Black Point, NS B0J 1B0, Canada *Tel:* 902-857-1388 *Fax:* 902-857-1328 *E-mail:* info@fernpub.ca; roseway@fernpub.ca *Web Site:* fernwoodpublishing.ca, pg 456

Apelian, Bill, BJU Press, 1430 Wade Hampton Blvd, Greenville, SC 29609-5046 *Tel:* 864-770-1317; 864-546-4600 *Toll Free Tel:* 800-845-5731 *E-mail:* bjupinfo@bju.edu *Web Site:* www.bjupress.com, pg 36

Appel, Celeste, Unarius Academy of Science Publications, 145 S Magnolia Ave, El Cajon, CA 92020-4522 *Tel:* 619-444-7062 *Toll Free Tel:* 800-475-7062 *Fax:* 619-444-9637 *E-mail:* uriel@unarius.org *Web Site:* www.unarius.org, pg 238

Appel, Fred, Princeton University Press, 41 William St, Princeton, NJ 08540-5237 *Tel:* 609-258-4900 *Fax:* 609-258-6305 *Web Site:* press.princeton.edu, pg 188

Appelbaum, David, Codhill Press, One Arden Lane, New Paltz, NY 12561 *E-mail:* codhillpress@aol.com *Web Site:* www.codhill.com, pg 58

Applebaum, Adina, Whiting Awards, 16 Court St, Suite 2308, Brooklyn, NY 11241 *Tel:* 718-701-5962 *E-mail:* info@whiting.org *Web Site:* www.whiting.org, pg 697

Applebaum, Adina, Whiting Creative Nonfiction Grant, 16 Court St, Suite 2308, Brooklyn, NY 11241 *Tel:* 718-701-5962 *E-mail:* nonfiction@whiting.org; info@whiting.org *Web Site:* www.whiting.org, pg 697

Applebee, Jessica, The Art Institute of Chicago, 111 S Michigan Ave, Chicago, IL 60603-6404 *Tel:* 312-443-3600; 312-443-3540 (pubns) *Fax:* 312-443-1334 (pubns) *Web Site:* www.artic.edu; www.artinstituteshop.org, pg 21

Appleton, Lauren, TarcherPerigee, 375 Hudson St, New York, NY 10014 *Tel:* 212-366-2000 *Fax:* 212-366-2643 *E-mail:* customerservice@penguinrandomhouse.com (cust serv); TarcherPerigeePublicity@penguinrandomhouse.com (media queries) *Web Site:* www.tarcherbooks.com; www.facebook.com/TarcherPerigee/; www.penguin.com/publishers/tarcherperigee, pg 227

Appoloni, Simon, Novalis Publishing, 10 Lower Spadina Ave, Suite 400, Toronto, ON M5V 2Z2, Canada *Tel:* 416-363-3303 *Toll Free Tel:* 877-702-7773 *Fax:* 416-363-9409 *Toll Free Fax:* 877-702-7775 *E-mail:* books@novalis.ca *Web Site:* www.novalis.ca, pg 465

Arca, Deborah, Chalice Press, 483 E Lockwood Ave, Suite 100, St Louis, MO 63119 *Tel:* 314-231-8500 *Toll Free Tel:* 800-366-3383 *Fax:* 314-231-8524; 770-280-4039 (orders) *E-mail:* customerservice@chalicepress.com *Web Site:* www.chalicepress.com, pg 52

Archer, Ellen, Houghton Mifflin Harcourt, 125 High St, Boston, MA 02110 *Tel:* 617-351-5000 *Toll Free Tel:* 855-969-4642; 800-225-5425 (K-12 educ materials); 800-323-9540 (assessment materials); 877-219-1537 (SkillsTutor); 888-242-6747 (Innovation in Educ Group); 800-225-3362 (Trade & Ref Div) *Toll Free Fax:* 800-269-5232 *E-mail:* myhmhco@hmhco.com *Web Site:* www.hmhco.com, pg 110

Archer, Ellen, Houghton Mifflin Harcourt Trade & Reference Division, 125 High St, Boston, MA 02110 *Tel:* 617-351-5000 *Toll Free Tel:* 800-225-3362 *Web Site:* www.hmhco.com, pg 111

Archer, Peter, Adams Media, 57 Littlefield St, Avon, MA 02322 *Tel:* 508-427-7100 *Web Site:* www.simonandschuster.com, pg 4

Areheart, Shaye, Columbia Publishing Course at Columbia University, 2950 Broadway, MC 3801, New York, NY 10027 *Tel:* 212-854-1898 *Fax:* 212-854-7618 *E-mail:* publishing@jrn.columbia.edu *Web Site:* www.journalism.columbia.edu/publishing, pg 619

Arellano, Susan, Templeton Press, 300 Conshohocken State Rd, Suite 665, West Conshohocken, PA 19428 *Tel:* 484-531-8380 *Fax:* 484-531-8382 *E-mail:* tpinfo@templetonpress.org *Web Site:* www.templetonpress.org, pg 229

Arena, Michael, Deadline Club, c/o Salmagundi Club, 47 Fifth Ave, New York, NY 10003 *Tel:* 646-481-7584 *E-mail:* info@deadlineclub.org *Web Site:* www.deadlineclub.org, pg 564

Argentine, Jan, Cold Spring Harbor Laboratory Press, 500 Sunnyside Blvd, Woodbury, NY 11797-2924 *Tel:* 516-422-4100 *Toll Free Tel:* 800-843-4388 *Fax:* 516-422-4097; 516-422-4092 (submissions) *E-mail:* cshpress@cshl.edu *Web Site:* www.cshlpress.com, pg 58

Arifi, Dana, The French-American Foundation & Florence Gould Foundation Annual Translation Prize, 28 W 44 St, Suite 1420, New York, NY 10036 *Tel:* 212-829-8800 *Fax:* 212-829-8810 *Web Site:* www.frenchamerican.org, pg 648

Arlinghaus, Sandra Lach, Institute of Mathematical Geography, 1964 Boulder Dr, Ann Arbor, MI 48104 *Tel:* 734-975-0246 *E-mail:* image@imagenet.org *Web Site:* www.imagenet.org, pg 118

Armato, Doug, University of Minnesota Press, 111 Third Ave S, Suite 290, Minneapolis, MN 55401-2520 *Tel:* 612-301-1990 *Fax:* 612-301-1980 *E-mail:* ump@umn.edu *Web Site:* www.upress.umn.edu, pg 242

Armbruster, Bruce, University Science Books, 20 Edgeshill Rd, Mill Valley, CA 94941 *Tel:* 703-661-1572 (cust serv, orders) *Fax:* 703-661-1572 (cust serv, orders) *E-mail:* usbmail@presswarehouse.com (cust serv, orders) *Web Site:* www.uscibooks.com, pg 248

Armbruster, Kathy, University Science Books, 20 Edgeshill Rd, Mill Valley, CA 94941 *Tel:* 703-661-1572 (cust serv, orders) *Fax:* 703-661-1572 (cust serv, orders) *E-mail:* usbmail@presswarehouse.com (cust serv, orders) *Web Site:* www.uscibooks.com, pg 248

Armengol, Norma C, Casa Bautista de Publicaciones, 7000 Alabama Ave, El Paso, TX 79904 *Tel:* 915-566-9656 *Toll Free Tel:* 800-755-5958 (cust serv & orders) *Fax:* 915-562-6502; 915-565-9008 (orders) *E-mail:* orders@editorialmh.org *Web Site:* www.editorialmh.org, pg 48

Armstrong, Gail Paul, Saskatchewan Arts Board, 1355 Broad St, Regina, SK S4R 7V1, Canada *Tel:* 306-787-4056 *Toll Free Tel:* 800-667-7526 (CN) *Fax:* 306-787-4199 *E-mail:* info@saskartsboard.ca *Web Site:* www.saskartsboard.ca, pg 577

Armstrong, Kevin, Chronicle Books LLC, 680 Second St, San Francisco, CA 94107 *Tel:* 415-537-4200 *Toll Free Tel:* 800-759-0190 (cust serv) *Fax:* 415-537-4460 *Toll Free Fax:* 800-858-7787 (orders); 800-286-9471 (cust serv) *E-mail:* frontdesk@chroniclebooks.com *Web Site:* www.chroniclebooks.com, pg 55

Arnold, Carol, American Marketing Association, 130 E Randolph St, 22nd fl, Chicago, IL 60601 *Tel:* 312-542-9000 *Toll Free Tel:* 800-AMA-1150 (262-1150) *Fax:* 312-542-9001 *E-mail:* info@ama.org *Web Site:* www.ama.org, pg 555

Arnold, David, CarTech Inc, 39966 Grand Ave, North Branch, MN 55056 *Tel:* 651-277-1200 *Toll Free Tel:* 800-551-4754 *Fax:* 651-277-1203 *E-mail:* info@cartechbooks.com *Web Site:* www.cartechbooks.com, pg 48

Arnove, Anthony, Roam Agency, 45 Main St, Suite 727, Brooklyn, NY 11201-1076 *E-mail:* roam@roamagency.com *Web Site:* www.roamagency.com, pg 533

Arnovitz, Benton M, United States Holocaust Memorial Museum, 100 Raoul Wallenberg Place SW, Washington, DC 20024-2126 *Tel:* 202-314-7837; 202-488-6144 (orders) *Toll Free Tel:* 800-259-9998 (orders) *Fax:* 202-479-9726; 202-488-0438 (orders) *E-mail:* cahs_publications@ushmm.org *Web Site:* www.ushmm.org, pg 238

Arnow, Ann, Bridge Publications Inc, 5600 E Olympic Blvd, Commerce, CA 90022 *Tel:* 323-888-6200 *Toll Free Tel:* 800-722-1733 *Fax:* 323-888-6202 *E-mail:* info@bridgepub.com *Web Site:* www.bridgepub.com, pg 43

Arnow, Don, Bridge Publications Inc, 5600 E Olympic Blvd, Commerce, CA 90022 *Tel:* 323-888-6200 *Toll Free Tel:* 800-722-1733 *Fax:* 323-888-6202 *E-mail:* info@bridgepub.com *Web Site:* www.bridgepub.com, pg 43

Aron, Paul, The Colonial Williamsburg Foundation, PO Box 1776, Williamsburg, VA 23187-1776 *Tel:* 757-229-1000 *Toll Free Tel:* 800-HISTORY (447-8679) *E-mail:* geninfo@cwf.org *Web Site:* www.colonialwilliamsburg.org, pg 58

Aronica, Lou, The Story Plant, PO Box 4331, Stamford, CT 06907 *Tel:* 203-722-7920 *E-mail:* thestoryplant@thestoryplant.com *Web Site:* www.thestoryplant.com, pg 223

Aronson, Gail, Black Warrior Review Fiction, Nonfiction & Poetry Contest, Off of Student Media, University of Alabama, Tuscaloosa, AL 35486-0027 *Tel:* 205-348-4518 *Web Site:* www.bwr.ua.edu, pg 633

Aronson, Rosa PhD, TESOL International Association, 1925 Ballenger Ave, Alexandria, VA 22314-6820 *Tel:* 703-836-0774 *Fax:* 703-836-7864; 703-836-6447 *E-mail:* publications@tesol.org; info@tesol.org; members@tesol.org *Web Site:* www.tesol.org, pg 229

Arriaza, David, UCLA Latin American Center Publications, UCLA Latin American Institute, 10343 Bunche Hall, Los Angeles, CA 90095 *Tel:* 310-825-4571 *Fax:* 310-206-6859 *E-mail:* latinamctr@international.ucla.edu *Web Site:* www.international.ucla.edu/lai, pg 238

Arrington, Jay, The Little Entrepreneur, c/o Harper Arrington Media, 18701 Grand River, Suite 105, Detroit, MI 48223 *Toll Free Tel:* 888-435-9234 *Fax:* 248-281-0373 *E-mail:* info@harperarringtonmedia.com *Web Site:* www.thelittlee.com, pg 136

Arrow, Kevin P, Graphic World Publishing Services, 11687 Adie Rd, St Louis, MO 63043 *Tel:* 314-567-9854 *Fax:* 314-567-7178 *E-mail:* quote@gwinc.com *Web Site:* www.gwinc.com, pg 495

Arsenault, Jessica, Bear & Co Inc, One Park St, Rochester, VT 05767 *Tel:* 802-767-3174 *Toll Free Tel:* 800-932-3277 *Fax:* 802-767-3726 *E-mail:* customerservice@InnerTraditions.com *Web Site:* InnerTraditions.com, pg 31

Arsenault, Jessica, Inner Traditions International Ltd, One Park St, Rochester, VT 05767 *Tel:* 802-767-3174 *Toll Free Tel:* 800-246-8648 *Fax:* 802-767-3726 *E-mail:* customerservice@InnerTraditions.com *Web Site:* www.InnerTraditions.com, pg 117

Arthur, Michael, Beekman Books Inc, 300 Old All Angels Hill Rd, Wappingers Falls, NY 12590 *Tel:* 845-297-2690 *Fax:* 845-297-1002 *E-mail:* beekmanbooks@yahoo.com *Web Site:* www.beekmanbooks.com, pg 32

Arthur, Reagan, Hachette Book Group, 1290 Avenue of the Americas, New York, NY 10019 *Tel:* 212-364-1100 *Toll Free Tel:* 800-759-0190 (cust serv) *Fax:* 212-364-0933 (intl orders) *Toll Free Fax:* 800-286-9471 (cust serv) *Web Site:* www.hachettebookgroup.com, pg 98

Arthur, Reagan, Little, Brown and Company, 1290 Avenue of the Americas, New York, NY 10019 *Tel:* 212-364-1100 *Fax:* 212-364-0952 *E-mail:* firstname.lastname@hbgusa.com *Web Site:* www.littlebrown.com; www.HachetteBookGroup.com, pg 135

Arthur, Robert P, Laura Day Boggs Bolling Memorial, 900 Timber Creek Place, Virginia Beach, VA 23464 *E-mail:* poetryinva@aol.com *Web Site:* poetrysocietyofvirginia.org, pg 633

Arthur, Robert P, Joe Pendleton Campbell Narrative Contest, 900 Timber Creek Place, Virginia Beach, VA 23464 *E-mail:* poetryinva@aol.com *Web Site:* poetrysocietyofvirginia.org, pg 635

Arthur, Robert P, Carleton Drewry Memorial, 900 Timber Creek Place, Virginia Beach, VA 23464 *E-mail:* poetryinva@aol.com *Web Site:* poetrysocietyofvirginia.org, pg 642

Arthur, Robert P, Alfred C Gary Memorial, 900 Timber Creek Place, Virginia Beach, VA 23464 *E-mail:* poetryinva@aol.com *Web Site:* poetrysocietyofvirginia.org, pg 648

Arthur, Robert P, Bess Gresham Memorial, 900 Timber Creek Place, Virginia Beach, VA 23464 *E-mail:* poetryinva@aol.com *Web Site:* poetrysocietyofvirginia.org, pg 651

Arthur, Robert P, Loretta Dunn Hall Memorial, 900 Timber Creek Place, Virginia Beach, VA 23464 *E-mail:* poetryinva@aol.com *Web Site:* poetrysocietyofvirginia.org, pg 651

Arthur, Robert P, Handy Andy Prize, 900 Timber Creek Place, Virginia Beach, VA 23464 *E-mail:* poetryinva@aol.com *Web Site:* poetrysocietyofvirginia.org, pg 651

Arthur, Robert P, Brodie Herndon Memorial, 900 Timber Creek Place, Virginia Beach, VA 23464 *E-mail:* poetryinva@aol.com *Web Site:* poetrysocietyofvirginia.org, pg 652

Arthur, Robert P, Judah, Sarah, Grace & Tom Memorial, 900 Timber Creek Place, Virginia Beach, VA 23464 *E-mail:* poetryinva@aol.com; info@poetryvirginia.org *Web Site:* poetrysocietyofvirginia.org, pg 658

Arthur, Robert P, Cenie H Moon Prize, 900 Timber Creek Place, Virginia Beach, VA 23464 *E-mail:* poetryinva@aol.com *Web Site:* poetrysocietyofvirginia.org, pg 669

Arthur, Robert P, Edgar Allan Poe Memorial, 900 Timber Creek Place, Virginia Beach, VA 23464 *E-mail:* poetryinva@aol.com *Web Site:* poetrysocietyofvirginia.org, pg 680

Arthur, Robert P, Miriam Rachimi Memorial, 900 Timber Creek Place, Virginia Beach, VA 23464 *E-mail:* poetryinva@aol.com *Web Site:* poetrysocietyofvirginia.org, pg 683

Arthur, Robert P, Ada Sanderson Memorial, 900 Timber Creek Place, Virginia Beach, VA 23464 *E-mail:* poetryinva@aol.com *Web Site:* poetrysocietyofvirginia.org, pg 686

Arthur, Robert P, The Robert S Sergeant Memorial, 900 Timber Creek Place, Virginia Beach, VA 23464 *E-mail:* poetryinva@aol.com *Web Site:* poetrysocietyofvirginia.org, pg 688

Asbury, Julie, Prima Games, 3000 Lava Ridge Ct, Roseville, CA 95661 *Tel:* 916-787-7000 *Web Site:* www.primagames.com, pg 187

Ascher, David, Scholastic Trade Division, 557 Broadway, New York, NY 10012 *Tel:* 212-343-6100; 212-343-4685 (export sales) *Fax:* 212-343-4714 (export sales) *Web Site:* www.scholastic.com, pg 208

Ash, Irene, Synapse Information Resources Inc, 1247 Taft Ave, Endicott, NY 13760 *Tel:* 607-748-4145 *Toll Free Tel:* 888-SYN-CHEM (796-2436) *Fax:* 607-786-3966 *E-mail:* salesinfo@synapseinfo.com *Web Site:* www.synapseinfo.com, pg 226

Ash, Michael, Synapse Information Resources Inc, 1247 Taft Ave, Endicott, NY 13760 *Tel:* 607-748-4145 *Toll Free Tel:* 888-SYN-CHEM (796-2436) *Fax:* 607-786-3966 *E-mail:* salesinfo@synapseinfo.com *Web Site:* www.synapseinfo.com, pg 226

Ashe, Rosann, Oxford University Press USA, 198 Madison Ave, New York, NY 10016 *Tel:* 212-726-6000 *Toll Free Tel:* 800-451-7556 (orders); 800-445-9714 (cust serv) *Fax:* 919-677-1303 *E-mail:* custserv.us@oup.com *Web Site:* www.oup.com/us, pg 171

Ashfield, Keith, Kogan Page Publishers, 1518 Walnut St, Suite 900, Philadelphia, PA 19102 *Tel:* 215-928-9112 *Fax:* 215-928-9113 *E-mail:* info@koganpage.com *Web Site:* www.koganpageusa.com, pg 127

Ashwood-Viala, Shana, LearningExpress LLC, 80 Broad St, 4th fl, New York, NY 10004 *Toll Free Tel:* 800-295-9556 (ext 2) *E-mail:* marketing@learningexpressllc.com (cust serv) *Web Site:* www.learningexpressllc.com, pg 131

Asiaghi, Anthony, American Society of Mechanical Engineers (ASME), 2 Park Ave, New York, NY 10016-5990 *Tel:* 212-591-7000 *Toll Free Tel:* 800-843-2763 (cust serv-US, CN & Mexico) *Fax:* 212-591-7674; 973-882-8113 (cust serv); 973-882-1717 (orders & inquiries) *E-mail:* infocentral@asme.org *Web Site:* www.asme.org, pg 15

Aspey, Susan, Cengage Learning, 20 Channel Center St, Boston, MA 02210 *Tel:* 617-289-7700 *Toll Free Tel:* 800-354-9706 *Fax:* 617-289-7844 *Toll Free Fax:* 800-487-8488 *E-mail:* esales@cengage.com *Web Site:* www.cengage.com, pg 50

Assathiany, Pascal, Les Editions du Boreal, 4447, rue St-Denis, Montreal, QC H2J 2L2, Canada *Tel:* 514-287-7401 *Fax:* 514-287-7664 *E-mail:* boreal@editionsboreal.qc.ca *Web Site:* www.editionsboreal.qc.ca, pg 453

Assouad, Maya, Vehicule Press, PO Box 42094, CP Roy, Montreal, QC H2W-2T3, Canada *Tel:* 514-844-6073 *Fax:* 514-844-7543 *E-mail:* vp@vehiculepress.com; admin@vehiculepress.com *Web Site:* www.vehiculepress.com, pg 475

Aster, Howard, Mosaic Press, 1252 Speers Rd, Units 1 & 2, Oakville, ON L6L 5N9, Canada *Tel:* 905-825-2130 *E-mail:* info@mosaic-press.com *Web Site:* www.mosaic-press.com, pg 464

Asteriou, Michael, The Apocryphile Press, 1700 Shattuck Ave, Suite 81, Berkeley, CA 94709 *Tel:* 510-290-4349 *E-mail:* apocryphile@me.com *Web Site:* www.apocryphilepress.com, pg 18

Atchity, Kenneth PhD, The Writer's Lifeline Inc, 400 S Burnside Ave, Suite 11B, Los Angeles, CA 90036 *Tel:* 323-932-1685 *Fax:* 323-932-1220 *Web Site:* www.thewriterslifeline.com, pg 503

Athens, Phil, Resilient Publishing, 406 S Third St, Boise, ID 83702 *Tel:* 208-258-9544 *E-mail:* submissions@resilientpublishing.com *Web Site:* www.resilientpublishing.com; www.facebook.com/ResilientPub, pg 198

Atkinson, Marisa, Graywolf Press, 250 Third Ave N, Suite 600, Minneapolis, MN 55401 *Tel:* 651-641-0077 *Fax:* 651-641-0036 *E-mail:* wolves@graywolfpress.org (no ms queries, sample chapters or proposals) *Web Site:* www.graywolfpress.org, pg 95

Atkocaitis, John, Sundance/Newbridge Publishing, 33 Boston Post Rd W, Suite 440, Marlborough, MA 01752 *Toll Free Tel:* 888-200-2720; 800-343-8204 (Sundance cust serv & orders); 800-867-0307 (Newbridge cust serv & orders) *Toll Free Fax:* 800-456-2419 (orders) *E-mail:* info@sundancepub.com; info@newbridgeonline.com *Web Site:* www.sundancepub.com; www.newbridgeonline.com, pg 225

Atlas, Amelia "Molly", ICM Partners, 65 E 55 St, New York, NY 10022 *Tel:* 212-556-5600 *Web Site:* www.icmtalent.com, pg 521

Atsma, Helen, Houghton Mifflin Harcourt Trade & Reference Division, 125 High St, Boston, MA 02110 *Tel:* 617-351-5000 *Toll Free Tel:* 800-225-3362 *Web Site:* www.hmhco.com, pg 111

Attebery, Gerilyn, Lonely Planet, 150 Linden St, Oakland, CA 94607 *Tel:* 510-893-8555; 510-250-6400 *Toll Free Tel:* 800-275-8555 (orders) *Fax:* 510-893-8572 *E-mail:* info@lonelyplanet.com *Web Site:* www.lonelyplanet.com, pg 137

Attlee, James, University of Chicago Press, 1427 E 60 St, Chicago, IL 60637-2954 *Tel:* 773-702-7700; 773-702-7600 *Toll Free Tel:* 800-621-2736 (orders) *Fax:* 773-702-9756; 773-660-2235 (orders); 773-702-2708 *E-mail:* custserv@press.uchicago.edu; marketing@press.uchicago.edu *Web Site:* www.press.uchicago.edu, pg 241

Attwood, Beth, Harlequin Enterprises Ltd, 233 Broadway, Suite 1001, New York, NY 10279 *Tel:* 212-553-4200 *Fax:* 212-227-8969 *E-mail:* customerservice@harlequin.com *Web Site:* www.harlequin.com, pg 100

Attwood, Beth, Harlequin Enterprises Ltd, 225 Duncan Mill Rd, Don Mills, ON M3B 3K9, Canada *Tel:* 416-445-5860 *Toll Free Tel:* 888-432-4879; 800-370-5838 (ebook inquiries) *E-mail:* customerservice@harlequin.com *Web Site:* www.harlequin.com, pg 459

Atwan, Helene, Beacon Press, 24 Farnsworth St, Boston, MA 02210-1409 *Tel:* 617-742-2110 *Fax:* 617-723-3097; 617-742-2290 *Web Site:* www.beacon.org, pg 31

Atwan, Helene, The Hemingway Foundation/PEN Award, MIT, 14N-221A, 77 Massachusetts Ave, Cambridge, MA 02139 *Tel:* 617-324-1729 *E-mail:* pen-newengland@mit.edu *Web Site:* www.pen-ne.org/hemingway, pg 652

Atwood, Dr Christopher, The Mongolia Society Inc, Indiana University, 322 Goodbody Hall, 1011 E Third St, Bloomington, IN 47405-7005 *Tel:* 812-855-4078 *Fax:* 812-855-4078 *E-mail:* monsoc@indiana.edu *Web Site:* www.mongoliasociety.org, pg 153

Aubert, Stephen, Nelson Education Ltd, 1120 Birchmount Rd, Scarborough, ON M1K 5G4, Canada *Tel:* 416-752-9100 *Toll Free Tel:* 800-268-2222 (cust serv) *Fax:* 416-752-8101 *Toll Free Fax:* 800-430-4445 *E-mail:* peopleandengagement@nelson.com *Web Site:* www.nelson.com, pg 464

Audet, Janice, Harvard University Press, 79 Garden St, Cambridge, MA 02138-1499 *Tel:* 617-495-2600; 401-531-2800 (intl orders) *Toll Free Tel:* 800-405-1619 (orders) *Fax:* 617-495-5898 (general); 617-496-4677 (edit & rts); 401-531-2801 (intl orders) *Toll Free Fax:* 800-406-9145 (orders) *E-mail:* contact_hup@harvard.edu *Web Site:* www.hup.harvard.edu, pg 103

Auerbach, Karen, Kensington Publishing Corp, 119 W 40 St, New York, NY 10018 *Tel:* 212-407-1500 *Toll Free Tel:* 800-221-2647 *Fax:* 212-935-0699 *Web Site:* www.kensingtonbooks.com, pg 125

Aufmuth, Christopher, Michelin Maps & Guides, One Parkway S, Greenville, SC 29615-5022 *Tel:* 864-458-5565 *Fax:* 864-458-5665 *Toll Free Fax:* 866-297-0914; 888-773-7979 *E-mail:* orders@americanmap.com (orders) *Web Site:* www.michelintravel.com; www.michelinguide.com, pg 149

August, Scott, Haights Cross Communications®, 136 Madison Ave, 8th fl, New York, NY 10016 *Tel:* 212-209-0500 *E-mail:* info@haightscross.com *Web Site:* www.haightscross.com, pg 99

Auh, Jin, The Wylie Agency LLC, 250 W 57 St, Suite 2114, New York, NY 10107 *Tel:* 212-246-0069 *Fax:* 212-586-8953 *E-mail:* mail@wylieagency.com *Web Site:* www.wylieagency.com, pg 542

Aujla, Simmi, Houghton Mifflin Harcourt Trade & Reference Division, 125 High St, Boston, MA 02110 *Tel:* 617-351-5000 *Toll Free Tel:* 800-225-3362 *Web Site:* www.hmhco.com, pg 111

Aulisio, Michael, Thomas Nelson, 501 Nelson Place, Nashville, TN 37214 *Tel:* 615-889-9000 *Toll Free Tel:* 800-251-4000 *Fax:* 615-902-1548 *Web Site:* www.thomasnelson.com, pg 231

Aulisio, Michael, Zondervan, 3900 Sparks Dr, Grand Rapids, MI 49546 *Tel:* 616-698-6900 *Toll Free Tel:* 800-226-1122; 800-727-1309 (retail orders) *Fax:* 616-698-3350 *Toll Free Fax:* 800-698-3256 (retail orders) *E-mail:* zinfo@zondervan.com *Web Site:* www.zondervan.com, pg 263

Aument, Glenn, Evan-Moor Educational Publishers, 18 Lower Ragsdale Dr, Monterey, CA 93940-5746 *Tel:* 831-649-5901 *Toll Free Tel:* 800-777-4362 (orders) *Fax:* 831-649-6256 *Toll Free Fax:* 800-777-4332 (orders) *E-mail:* sales@evan-moor.com; marketing@evan-moor.com *Web Site:* www.evan-moor.com, pg 80

Austin, Kurt, National Council of Teachers of English (NCTE), 1111 W Kenyon Rd, Urbana, IL 61801-1096 *Tel:* 217-328-3870 *Toll Free Tel:* 877-369-6283 (cust serv) *Fax:* 217-328-9645 *E-mail:* orders@ncte.org *Web Site:* www.ncte.org, pg 158

Austin, Kurt, National Council of Teachers of English (NCTE), 1111 W Kenyon Rd, Urbana, IL 61801-1096 *Tel:* 217-328-3870 *Toll Free Tel:* 877-369-6283 (cust serv) *Fax:* 217-328-9645 *E-mail:* public_info@ncte.org *Web Site:* www.ncte.org, pg 571

Avery, Gayley, Little Bee Books, 853 Broadway, Suite 2014, New York, NY 10003 *E-mail:* info@littlebeebooks.com *Web Site:* www.littlebeebooks.com, pg 135

Avery, Laurie, The Ohio State University Press, 180 Pressey Hall, 1070 Carmack Rd, Columbus, OH 43210-1002 *Tel:* 614-292-6930 *Fax:* 614-292-2065 *Toll Free Fax:* 800-621-8476 *E-mail:* info@osupress.org *Web Site:* ohiostatepress.org, pg 167

Awalt, Barbe, LPD Press, 925 Salamanca NW, Los Ranchos de Albuquerque, NM 87107-5647 *Tel:* 505-344-9382 *Fax:* 505-345-5129 *E-mail:* lpdpress@q.com *Web Site:* nmsantos.com, pg 138

Axelrod, Glen, TFH Publications Inc, PO Box 427, Neptune, NJ 07754 *Toll Free Tel:* 855-273-7527 (cust serv) *Fax:* 732-988-5466 (cust serv); 732-776-8763 (sales) *E-mail:* info@tfh.com (cust serv); sales@tfh.com *Web Site:* www.tfhpublications.com; www.tfh.com; www.facebook.com/TfhPetBooks, pg 230

Axelrod, Steven, The Axelrod Agency, 55 Main St, Chatham, NY 12037 *Tel:* 518-392-2100, pg 507

Axelson-Berry, Kitty, Modern Memoirs, 34 Main St, No 6, Amherst, MA 01002-2367 *Tel:* 413-253-2353 *Web Site:* www.modernmemoirs.com; www.whitepoppypress.com, pg 152

Axford, Elizabeth C, Piano Press, 1425 Ocean Ave, Suite 5, Del Mar, CA 92014 *Tel:* 619-884-1401 *Fax:* 858-755-1104 *E-mail:* pianopress@pianopress.com *Web Site:* www.pianopress.com, pg 182

Ayne, Blythe, Kay Snow Writing Contest, 5331 SW Macadam Ave, Suite 258, PMB 215, Portland, OR 97239 *Tel:* 901-200-5385 *E-mail:* wilwrite@willamettewriters.org *Web Site:* willamettewriters.org, pg 690

Azar, Phyllis, Tom Doherty Associates, LLC, 175 Fifth Ave, 14th fl, New York, NY 10010 *Tel:* 646-307-5511 *Toll Free Tel:* 800-455-0340 *Web Site:* www.tor-forge.com, pg 71

Aziz, Ms Nurjehan, Mawenzi House Publishers Ltd, 39 Woburn Ave (B), Toronto, ON M5W 1K5, Canada *Tel:* 416-483-7191 *E-mail:* info@mawenzihouse.com *Web Site:* www.mawenzihouse.com, pg 463

Aziz, Omar, Ohio University Press, 31 S Court St, Suite 143, Athens, OH 45701-2979 *Fax:* 740-593-4536 *Web Site:* www.ohioswallow.com, pg 167

Aziz, Omar, Swallow Press, 31 S Court St, Suite 143, Athens, OH 45701 *Tel:* 740-593-1155 *Toll Free Tel:* 800-621-2736 *Fax:* 740-593-4536 *Web Site:* www.ohioswallow.com, pg 225

B, Vanna, Hope Street Publishing, PO Box 2705, Philadelphia, PA 19120 *E-mail:* contact@hopestreetpublishing.com *Web Site:* www.hopestreetpublishing.com, pg 110

Baake, Mike, Self-Realization Fellowship Publishers, 3208 Humboldt St, Los Angeles, CA 90031 *Tel:* 323-276-6002 *Toll Free Tel:* 888-773-8680 *Fax:* 323-927-1624 *E-mail:* sales@yogananda-srf.org *Web Site:* www.yogananda-srf.org; bookstore.yogananda-srf.org/ (orders), pg 210

Baar, Emily, Oceanview Publishing, CEO Center at Mediterranean Plaza, Suite 120-G, 595 Bay Isles Rd, Longboat Key, FL 34228 *Tel:* 941-387-8500 *Web Site:* oceanviewpub.com, pg 166

Babb, Billy, Pentecostal Publishing House, 8855 Dunn Rd, Hazelwood, MO 63042 *Tel:* 314-837-7300 *Toll Free Tel:* 866-819-7667 *Fax:* 314-837-6574 (orders) *Web Site:* www.pentecostalpublishing.com; wordaflamepress.com, pg 180

Babcock, Sherra, Chautauqua Writers' Workshop, One Ames Ave, Chautauqua, NY 14722 *Tel:* 716-357-6316; 716-357-6250 *Toll Free Tel:* 800-836-ARTS (836-2787) *Fax:* 716-357-9014 *Web Site:* ciweb.org, pg 610

Baber, Meredith, Dumbarton Oaks, 1703 32 St NW, Washington, DC 20007 *Tel:* 202-339-6400 *Fax:* 202-339-6401; 202-298-8407 *E-mail:* doaksbooks@doaks.org *Web Site:* www.doaks.org, pg 73

Babler, Linda, Atwood Publishing, PO Box 3185, Madison, WI 53704 *Tel:* 608-242-7101 *Toll Free Tel:* 888-242-7101 *Fax:* 608-242-7102 *E-mail:* customerservice@atwoodpublishing.com *Web Site:* www.atwoodpublishing.com, pg 25

Baca, Michelle, Western States Arts Federation, 1743 Wazee St, Suite 300, Denver, CO 80202 *Tel:* 303-629-1166 *Toll Free Tel:* 888-562-7232 *Fax:* 303-629-9717 *E-mail:* staff@westaf.org *Web Site:* www.westaf.org, pg 583

Bace, Marjan, Manning Publications Co, PO Box 761, Shelter Island, NY 11964 *Tel:* 203-626-1510 *E-mail:* sales@manning.com; support@manning.com (cust serv) *Web Site:* www.manning.com, pg 141

Bach, Daniel N, Book Manufacturers' Institute Inc (BMI), PO Box 731388, Ormond Beach, FL 32173 *Tel:* 386-986-4552 *Fax:* 386-986-4553 *E-mail:* info@bmibook.com *Web Site:* www.bmibook.org, pg 560

Bach, Lisa, Chronicle Books LLC, 680 Second St, San Francisco, CA 94107 *Tel:* 415-537-4200 *Toll Free Tel:* 800-759-0190 (cust serv) *Fax:* 415-537-4460 *Toll Free Fax:* 800-858-7787 (orders); 800-286-9471 (cust serv) *E-mail:* frontdesk@chroniclebooks.com *Web Site:* www.chroniclebooks.com, pg 55

Bacha, Diane M, Kalmbach Publishing Co, 21027 Crossroads Circle, Waukesha, WI 53186 *Tel:* 262-796-8776 *Toll Free Tel:* 800-533-6644 (cust serv & orders); 800-558-1544 *Fax:* 262-798-6592 *E-mail:* customerservice@kalmbach.com *Web Site:* www.kalmbach.com, pg 124

Bachman, Margie K, University of Pittsburgh Press, 7500 Thomas Blvd, Pittsburgh, PA 15260 *Tel:* 412-383-2456 *Fax:* 412-383-2466 *E-mail:* info@upress.pitt.edu *Web Site:* www.upress.pitt.edu, pg 244

Bachofen, Andrea, Penguin Random House Inc, 1745 Broadway, New York, NY 10019 *Tel:* 212-782-9000 *Toll Free Tel:* 800-726-0600 *Web Site:* www.penguinrandomhouse.com, pg 178

Bacigalupi, John, The Taunton Press Inc, 63 S Main St, Newtown, CT 06470 *Tel:* 203-426-8171 *Toll Free Tel:* 800-477-8727 (cust serv); 800-888-8286 (orders) *Fax:* 203-426-3434 *E-mail:* booksales@taunton.com *Web Site:* www.taunton.com, pg 227

Backing, Janis, Moody Publishers, 820 N La Salle Blvd, Chicago, IL 60610 *Tel:* 312-329-4000 *Toll Free Tel:* 800-678-8812 (cust serv) *Fax:* 312-329-2019 *E-mail:* mpcustomerservice@moody.edu *Web Site:* www.moodypublishers.com, pg 153

Backman, Devorah, The Countryman Press, c/o W W Norton & Company Inc, 500 Fifth Ave, New York, NY 10110 *Tel:* 212-354-5500 *Fax:* 212-869-0856 *E-mail:* countrymanpress@wwnorton.com *Web Site:* www.countrymanpress.com, pg 63

Backman, Elizabeth H, Elizabeth H Backman, 86 Johnnycake Hollow Rd, Pine Plains, NY 12567 *Tel:* 518-398-9344 *Fax:* 518-398-6368 *E-mail:* bethcountry@fairpoint.net, pg 507

Backman, John, Backman Writing & Communications, 32 Hillview Ave, Rensselaer, NY 12144 *Tel:* 518-449-4985 *Web Site:* www.backwrite.com, pg 489

Bacon, Launa, Individual Artist Fellowships, 1004 Farnam, Plaza Level, Omaha, NE 68102 *Tel:* 402-595-2122 *Toll Free Tel:* 800-341-4067 *Fax:* 402-595-2334 *Web Site:* www.nebraskaartscouncil.org, pg 655

Badalian, Alvart, Blue Crane Books Inc, 36 Hazel St, Watertown, MA 02472 *Tel:* 617-926-8989, pg 38

Badalov, Anar, The MIT Press, One Rogers St, Cambridge, MA 02142 *Tel:* 617-253-5255 *Toll Free Tel:* 800-207-8354 (orders) *Fax:* 617-258-6779; 617-577-1545 (orders) *Web Site:* mitpress.mit.edu, pg 152

Bade, David, The Mongolia Society Inc, Indiana University, 322 Goodbody Hall, 1011 E Third St, Bloomington, IN 47405-7005 *Tel:* 812-855-4078 *Fax:* 812-855-4078 *E-mail:* monsoc@indiana.edu *Web Site:* www.mongoliasociety.org, pg 153

Bader, Bonnie, Grosset & Dunlap, 345 Hudson St, New York, NY 10014 *Tel:* 212-366-2000 *Web Site:* www.penguinrandomhouse.com, pg 96

Bader, Rachel, Random House Children's Books, 1745 Broadway, 10th fl, New York, NY 10019 *Tel:* 212-782-9000 *Web Site:* www.randomhousekids.com, pg 194

Badowski, Keith, Brick Road Poetry Book Contest, 513 Broadway, Columbus, GA 31901-3117 *Web Site:* brickroadpoetrypress.com, pg 634

Baehrecke, Astrid, The MIT Press, One Rogers St, Cambridge, MA 02142 *Tel:* 617-253-5255 *Toll Free Tel:* 800-207-8354 (orders) *Fax:* 617-258-6779; 617-577-1545 (orders) *Web Site:* mitpress.mit.edu, pg 152

Baer, D Richard, Hollywood Film Archive, 8391 Beverly Blvd, Los Angeles, CA 90048 *Tel:* 323-655-4968 *Web Site:* hfarchive.com, pg 109

Baer, Rebbecca, Fodor's Travel Publications, 1745 Broadway, 15th fl, New York, NY 10019 *Toll Free Tel:* 800-733-3000 *E-mail:* publicity@fodors.com; editors@fodors.com *Web Site:* www.fodors.com, pg 86

Baer, William, Howard Nemerov Sonnet Award, 21 Osborne Terr, Wayne, NJ 07470 *Web Site:* theformalist.evansville.edu/home.htm, pg 672

Baffa, Grace, Mason Crest Publishers, 450 Parkway Dr, Suite D, Broomall, PA 19008 *Tel:* 610-543-6200 *Toll Free Tel:* 866-MCP-BOOK (627-2665) *Fax:* 610-543-3878 *Web Site:* www.masoncrest.com, pg 143

Bagatella, Andrew, Whitecap Books, 314 W Cordova St, Suite 209, Vancouver, BC V6B 1E8, Canada *Tel:* 604-681-6181 *Toll Free Tel:* 800-387-9776 *Toll Free Fax:* 800-260-9777 *Web Site:* www.whitecap.ca, pg 475

Bagdanov, Kristin George, Janet B McCabe Poetry Prize, 1041 N Taft Hill Rd, Fort Collins, CO 80521 *Tel:* 970-449-2726 *E-mail:* editor@ruminatemagazine.org *Web Site:* www.ruminatemagazine.com, pg 666

Bagdanov, Kristin George, William Van Dyke Short Story Prize, 1041 N Taft Hill Rd, Fort Collins, CO 80521 *Tel:* 970-449-2726 *E-mail:* editor@ruminatemagazine.org *Web Site:* www.ruminatemagazine.com, pg 695

Bagdanov, Kristin George, VanderMey Nonfiction Prize, 1041 N Taft Hill Rd, Fort Collins, CO 80521 *Tel:* 970-449-2726 *E-mail:* editor@ruminatemagazine.org *Web Site:* www.ruminatemagazine.com, pg 695

Bagnato, Laura, Chronicle Books LLC, 680 Second St, San Francisco, CA 94107 *Tel:* 415-537-4200 *Toll Free Tel:* 800-759-0190 (cust serv) *Fax:* 415-537-4460 *Toll Free Fax:* 800-858-7787 (orders); 800-286-9471 (cust serv) *E-mail:* frontdesk@chroniclebooks.com *Web Site:* www.chroniclebooks.com, pg 55

Bagshaw, Sean, The Optical Society (OSA), 2010 Massachusetts Ave NW, Washington, DC 20036-1023 *Tel:* 202-223-8130 *Toll Free Tel:* 800-766-4672 *E-mail:* custserv@osa.org *Web Site:* www.osa.org, pg 169

Bahador, Gee Cee Addison, Society of Children's Book Writers and Illustrators (SCBWI), 4727 Wilshire Blvd, Suite 301, Los Angeles, CA 90010 *Tel:* 323-782-1010 *Fax:* 323-782-1892 *E-mail:* scbwi@scbwi.org; membership@scbwi.org *Web Site:* www.scbwi.org, pg 578

Bahr, Ed, Pacific Press Publishing Association, 1350 N Kings Rd, Nampa, ID 83687-3193 *Tel:* 208-465-2500 *Toll Free Tel:* 800-447-7377 *Fax:* 208-465-2531 *Web Site:* www.pacificpress.com, pg 172

Baida, Laura, The Brookings Institution Press, 1775 Massachusetts Ave NW, Washington, DC 20036-2188 *Tel:* 202-536-3600 *Toll Free Tel:* 800-537-5487 *Fax:* 202-536-3623 *E-mail:* permissions@brookings.edu *Web Site:* www.brookings.edu, pg 44

Bailey, Anne G, Westernlore Press, PO Box 35305, Tucson, AZ 85740-5305 *Tel:* 520-297-5491, pg 254

Bailey, Diane, HarperCollins Publishers, 195 Broadway, New York, NY 10007 *Tel:* 212-207-7000 *Fax:* 212-207-7145 *Web Site:* www.harpercollins.com, pg 101

Bailey, Lynn R, Westernlore Press, PO Box 35305, Tucson, AZ 85740-5305 *Tel:* 520-297-5491, pg 254

Bailey, Megan, The Jean Kennedy Smith VSA Playwright Discovery Award, 2700 "F" St NW, Washington, DC 20566 *Tel:* 202-416-8898 *Fax:* 202-416-4840 *E-mail:* vsainfo@kennedy-center.org *Web Site:* www.kennedy-center.org/pdp, pg 690

Bailey, Simon, Standard International Media Holdings, 568 Ninth St S, Suite 201, Naples, FL 34102-7336 *Tel:* 239-248-5550 *Fax:* 239-649-5832 *Toll Free Fax:* 866-948-7883 *E-mail:* sales@standardinternationalmedia.com *Web Site:* www.standardinternationalmedia.com, pg 220

Bailor, David, Carter G Woodson Book Awards, 8555 16 St, Suite 500, Silver Spring, MD 20910 *Tel:* 301-588-1800 *Toll Free Tel:* 800-296-7840 *Fax:* 301-588-2049 *E-mail:* excellence@ncss.org; publications@ncss.org *Web Site:* www.socialstudies.org, pg 699

Baines, Jennika, Indiana University Press, Herman B Wells Library 350, 1320 E Tenth St, Bloomington, IN 47405-3907 *Tel:* 812-855-8817 *Toll Free Tel:* 800-842-6796 (orders only) *Fax:* 812-855-7931; 812-855-8507 *E-mail:* iupress@indiana.edu; iuporder@indiana.edu (orders) *Web Site:* www.iupress.indiana.edu, pg 116

Baird, Lee, Tennessee Arts Commission Fellowships, 401 Charlotte Ave, Nashville, TN 37243-0780 *Tel:* 615-741-1701 *Fax:* 615-741-8559 *Web Site:* www.tnartscommission.org, pg 693

Bakamjian, Ted, Society of Exploration Geophysicists, 8801 S Yale Ave, Tulsa, OK 74137 *Tel:* 918-497-5500 *Fax:* 918-497-5557 *E-mail:* web@seg.org *Web Site:* www.seg.org, pg 216

Bakeman, Karl, W W Norton & Company Inc, 500 Fifth Ave, New York, NY 10110-0017 *Tel:* 212-354-5500 *Toll Free Tel:* 800-233-4830 (orders & cust serv) *Fax:* 212-869-0856 *Toll Free Fax:* 800-458-6515 *E-mail:* orders@wwnorton.com *Web Site:* books.wwnorton.com, pg 164

Baker, Amy, HarperCollins General Books Group, 195 Broadway, New York, NY 10007 *Tel:* 212-207-7000 *Web Site:* www.harpercollins.com, pg 101

Baker, Carolyn C, American Counseling Association, 6101 Stevenson Ave, Suite 600, Alexandria, VA 22304 *Tel:* 703-823-9800 (ext 222, book orders) *Toll Free Tel:* 800-347-6647 (ext 222, book orders) *Fax:* 703-823-0252 *Toll Free Fax:* 800-473-2329 *E-mail:* membership@counseling.org (book orders) *Web Site:* www.counseling.org, pg 11

Baker, Daniel W, The Library of America, 14 E 60 St, New York, NY 10022-1006 *Tel:* 212-308-3360 *Fax:* 212-750-8352 *E-mail:* info@loa.org *Web Site:* www.loa.org, pg 133

Baker, David C, RockBench Publishing Corp, 6101 Stillmeadow Dr, Nashville, TN 37211-6518 *Tel:* 615-831-2277 *Fax:* 615-831-2212 *E-mail:* info@rockbench.com, pg 200

Baker, Doris, Filter Press LLC, PO Box 95, Palmer Lake, CO 80133 *Tel:* 719-481-2420 *Toll Free Tel:* 888-570-2663 *Fax:* 719-481-2420 *E-mail:* info@filterpressbooks.com; orders@filterpressbooks.com *Web Site:* filterpressbooks.com, pg 84

Baker, Dwight, Baker Books, PO Box 6287, Grand Rapids, MI 49516-6287 *Tel:* 616-676-9185 *Toll Free Tel:* 800-877-2665; 800-679-1957 *Fax:* 616-676-9573 *Toll Free Fax:* 800-398-3111 *Web Site:* www.bakerpublishinggroup.com, pg 28

Baker, Dwight, Bethany House Publishers, 11400 Hampshire Ave S, Bloomington, MN 55438 *Tel:* 952-829-2500 *Toll Free Tel:* 800-877-2665 (orders) *Fax:* 952-829-2568 *Toll Free Fax:* 800-398-3111 (orders) *Web Site:* www.bethanyhouse.com; www.bakerpublishinggroup.com, pg 34

Baker, Dwight, Chosen Books, 11400 Hampshire Ave S, Bloomington, MN 55438-2852 *Tel:* 616-676-9185 *Toll Free Tel:* 800-877-2665 (orders only) *Fax:* 616-676-9573 *Toll Free Fax:* 800-398-3111 (orders only) *Web Site:* www.chosenbooks.com, pg 54

Baker, Dwight, Revell, PO Box 6287, Grand Rapids, MI 49516-6287 *Tel:* 616-676-9185 *Toll Free Tel:* 800-877-2665; 800-679-1957 *Fax:* 616-676-9573 *Web Site:* www.bakerpublishinggroup.com, pg 198

Baker, Dr Gordon N, Southern Books Competition, PO Box 950, Rex, GA 30273 *Tel:* 678-466-4334 *Fax:* 678-466-4349 *Web Site:* selaonline.org, pg 691

Baker, John F, Barbara Braun Associates Inc, 7 E 14 St, Suite 19F, New York, NY 10003 *Tel:* 212-604-9023 *Web Site:* www.barbarabraunagency.com, pg 510

Baker, Karen, Temple University Press, 1852 N Tenth St, Philadelphia, PA 19122-6099 *Tel:* 215-926-2140 *Toll Free Tel:* 800-621-2736 *Fax:* 215-926-2141 *E-mail:* tempress@temple.edu *Web Site:* www.temple.edu/tempress, pg 228

Baker, Kate, Science Fiction & Fantasy Writers of America Inc (SFWA), PO Box 3238, Enfield, CT 06083-3238 *E-mail:* office@sfwa.org *Web Site:* www.sfwa.org, pg 577

Baker, Lucy Childs, The Aaron M Priest Literary Agency Inc, 200 W 41 St, 21st fl, New York, NY 10036 *Tel:* 212-818-0344 *Fax:* 212-573-9417 *E-mail:* info@aaronpriest.com *Web Site:* www.aaronpriest.com, pg 532

Baker, Matt, The Minerals, Metals & Materials Society (TMS), 5700 Corporate Dr, Suite 750, Pittsburgh, PA 15237 *Tel:* 724-776-9000 *Toll Free Tel:* 800-759-4867 *Fax:* 724-776-3770 *E-mail:* publications@tms.org (orders) *Web Site:* www.tms.org/bookstore (orders); www.tms.org, pg 151

Baker, Patrick, Artist Grants, 711 E Wells Ave, Pierre, SD 57501-3369 *Tel:* 605-773-3301 *Fax:* 605-773-5977 *E-mail:* sdac@state.sd.us *Web Site:* www.artscouncil.sd.gov/grants, pg 628

Baker, Richard, Baker Books, PO Box 6287, Grand Rapids, MI 49516-6287 *Tel:* 616-676-9185 *Toll Free Tel:* 800-877-2665; 800-679-1957 *Fax:* 616-676-9573 *Toll Free Fax:* 800-398-3111 *Web Site:* www.bakerpublishinggroup.com, pg 28

Baker, Sarah, SouthWest Writers Conference Series, 3200 Carlisle Blvd NE, Suite 114, Albuquerque, NM 87110-1663 *Tel:* 505-830-6034 *E-mail:* swwriters@juno.com *Web Site:* www.southwestwriters.com, pg 615

Baker, Scottie, Andrews University Press, Sutherland House, 8360 W Campus Circle Dr, Berrien Springs, MI 49104-1700 *Tel:* 269-471-6134 *Toll Free Tel:* 800-467-6369 (Visa, MC & American Express orders only) *Fax:* 269-471-6224 *E-mail:* aupo@andrews.edu; aup@andrews.edu; aupress@andrews.edu *Web Site:* www.universitypress.andrews.edu, pg 17

Baker, Steven, University of Oklahoma Press, 2800 Venture Dr, Norman, OK 73069-8216 *Tel:* 405-325-2000 *Toll Free Tel:* 800-627-7377 (orders) *Fax:* 405-364-5798 (orders) *Toll Free Fax:* 800-735-0476 (orders) *E-mail:* presscs@ou.edu *Web Site:* www.oupress.com, pg 244

Baker-Baughman, Bernadette, Victoria Sanders & Associates LLC, 241 Avenue of the Americas, Suite 11-H, New York, NY 10014 *Tel:* 212-633-8811 *Fax:* 212-633-0525 *E-mail:* queriesvsa@gmail.com *Web Site:* www.victoriasanders.com, pg 534

Bakhtiar, Mary, Kazi Publications Inc, 3023 W Belmont Ave, Chicago, IL 60618 *Tel:* 773-267-7001 *Fax:* 773-267-7002 *E-mail:* info@kazi.org *Web Site:* www.kazi.org, pg 125

Baldi, Malaga, Malaga Baldi Literary Agency, 233 W 99, Suite 19C, New York, NY 10025 *Tel:* 212-222-3213 *E-mail:* baldibooks@gmail.com *Web Site:* www.baldibooks.com, pg 507

Baldwin, Margo, Chelsea Green Publishing Co, 85 N Main St, Suite 120, White River Junction, VT 05001 *Tel:* 802-295-6300 *Toll Free Tel:* 800-639-4099 (cust serv, consumer & trade orders) *Fax:* 802-295-6444 *Web Site:* www.chelseagreen.com, pg 53

Balik, Susan, Allen Ginsberg Poetry Award, One College Blvd, Paterson, NJ 07505-1179 *Tel:* 973-684-6555 *Fax:* 973-523-6085 *Web Site:* www.poetrycenterpccc.com, pg 649

Balik, Susan, The Paterson Poetry Prize, One College Blvd, Paterson, NJ 07505-1179 *Tel:* 973-684-6555 *Fax:* 973-523-6085 *Web Site:* www.poetrycenterpccc.com, pg 676

Balik, Susan, The Paterson Prize for Books for Young People, One College Blvd, Paterson, NJ 07505-1179 *Tel:* 973-684-6555 *Fax:* 973-523-6085 *Web Site:* www.poetrycenterpccc.com, pg 677

Balin, Sandy, C&T Publishing Inc, 1651 Challenge Dr, Concord, CA 94520-5206 *Tel:* 925-677-0377 *Toll Free Tel:* 800-284-1114 *Fax:* 925-677-0373 *E-mail:* support@ctpub.com *Web Site:* www.ctpub.com, pg 47

Baline, Sarah, Counterpoint Press LLC, 1919 Fifth St, Berkeley, CA 94710 *Tel:* 510-704-0230 *Fax:* 510-704-0268 *E-mail:* info@counterpointpress.com *Web Site:* counterpointpress.com; www.sierraclub.org/books; softskull.com, pg 63

Ball, Christine, Berkley Publishing Group, 375 Hudson St, New York, NY 10014 *Tel:* 212-366-2000 *Fax:* 212-366-2385 *Web Site:* www.penguin.com, pg 33

Ball, Christine, Dutton, 375 Hudson St, New York, NY 10014 *Tel:* 212-366-2000 *Fax:* 212-366-2262 *Web Site:* www.penguin.com, pg 74

Ball, Christine, GP Putnam's Sons (Hardcover), 375 Hudson St, New York, NY 10014 *Tel:* 212-366-2000 *Fax:* 212-366-2643 *E-mail:* online@penguinputnam.com *Web Site:* www.penguin.com/publishers/gpputnamssons, pg 192

Ball, Dean, Friedrich Hayek Lecture & Book Prize, 52 Vanderbilt Ave, New York, NY 10017 *Tel:* 212-599-7000 *Fax:* 212-599-3494 *Web Site:* www.manhattan-institute.org, pg 652

Ball, Don, National Endowment for the Arts, 400 Seventh St SW, Washington, DC 20506-0001 *Tel:* 202-682-5400 *Web Site:* www.arts.gov, pg 583

Ballantyne, Robert, Arsenal Pulp Press, 211 E Georgia St, No 202, Vancouver, BC V6A 1Z6, Canada *Tel:* 604-687-4233 *Toll Free Tel:* 888-600-PULP (600-7857) *Fax:* 604-687-4283 *E-mail:* info@arsenalpulp.com *Web Site:* www.arsenalpulp.com, pg 445

Ballard, Holly, Data Trace Publishing Co (DTP), 110 West Rd, Suite 227, Towson, MD 21204-2316 *Tel:* 410-494-4994 *Toll Free Tel:* 800-342-0454 (orders only) *Fax:* 410-494-0515 *E-mail:* info@datatrace.com; salesandmarketing@datatrace.com; editorial@datatrace.com; info@datatrace.com *Web Site:* www.datatrace.com, pg 67

Ballard, John, World Citizens, PO Box 131, Mill Valley, CA 94942-0131 *Tel:* 415-380-8020 *Toll Free Tel:* 800-247-6553 (orders only), pg 259

Ballard, Noah, Curtis Brown Ltd, 10 Astor Place, New York, NY 10003 *Tel:* 212-473-5400 *Web Site:* www.curtisbrown.com, pg 510

Ballast, Matthew, Grand Central Publishing, 1290 Avenue of the Americas, New York, NY 10019 *Tel:* 212-364-1100 *Web Site:* www.hachettebookgroup.com, pg 95

Ballenger, Seale, Disney Publishing Worldwide, 1101 Flower St, Glendale, CA 91201 *Web Site:* books.disney.com, pg 71

Balliett, Will, Thames & Hudson, 500 Fifth Ave, New York, NY 10110 *Tel:* 212-354-3763 *Toll Free Tel:* 800-233-4830 *Fax:* 212-398-1252 *E-mail:* bookinfo@thames.wwnorton.com *Web Site:* www.thamesandhudsonusa.com, pg 230

Ballinger, Glenys, Ballinger Publishing, 314 N Spring St, Suite A, Pensacola, FL 32501 *Tel:* 850-433-1166 *Fax:* 850-435-9174 *E-mail:* info@ballingerpublishing.com *Web Site:* www.ballingerpublishing.com, pg 28

Ballinger, Malcolm, Ballinger Publishing, 314 N Spring St, Suite A, Pensacola, FL 32501 *Tel:* 850-433-1166 *Fax:* 850-435-9174 *E-mail:* info@ballingerpublishing.com *Web Site:* www.ballingerpublishing.com, pg 28

Ballinger, Peter R, PRB Productions, 963 Peralta Ave, Albany, CA 94706-2144 *Tel:* 510-526-0722 *Fax:* 510-527-4763 *E-mail:* prbprdns@aol.com *Web Site:* www.prbmusic.com, pg 186

Balmuth, Deborah, Storey Publishing LLC, 210 MASS MoCA Way, North Adams, MA 01247 *Tel:* 413-346-2100 *Toll Free Tel:* 800-441-5700 (orders); 800-793-9396 (edit) *Fax:* 413-346-2199; 413-346-2196 (edit) *E-mail:* sales@storey.com *Web Site:* www.storey.com, pg 223

Balotro, April, I-5 Publishing LLC, 3 Burroughs, Irvine, CA 92618 *Tel:* 949-855-8822 *Toll Free Tel:* 888-738-2665 *Fax:* 949-458-3856 *Web Site:* www.i5publishing.com, pg 113

Balser, Frank, IDEAlliance®, 1800 Diagonal Rd, Suite 320, Alexandria, VA 22314-2862 *Tel:* 703-837-1070 *Fax:* 703-837-1072 *E-mail:* registrar@idealliance.org *Web Site:* www.idealliance.org, pg 567

Balthazar, Martin, Les Editions de l'Hexagone, 1055, blvd Rene Levesque Est, Bureau 300, Montreal, QC H2L 4S5, Canada *Tel:* 514-523-7993 *Fax:* 514-849-1388 *Web Site:* www.edhexagone.com, pg 453

Balthazar, Martin, VLB Editeur Inc, 1055, boul Rene-Levesque Est, bureau 300, Montréal, QC H2L 4S5, Canada *Tel:* 514-849-5259 *Fax:* 514-849-1388 *Web Site:* www.edvlb.com, pg 475

Baltzer, Keren, Hachette Nashville, 12 Cadillac Dr, Suite 480, Brentwood, TN 37027 *Tel:* 615-221-0996 *Fax:* 615-221-0962 *Web Site:* www.hachettebookgroup.com, pg 98

Balvenie, K, One Act Play Depot, 618 Memorial Dr, PO Box 335, Spiritwood, SK S0J 2M0, Canada *E-mail:* plays@oneactplays.net; orders@oneactplays.net *Web Site:* oneactplays.net, pg 465

Bamford, Christopher, Lindisfarne Books, 610 Main St, Great Barrington, MA 01230 *Tel:* 413-528-8233 *Fax:* 413-528-8826 *E-mail:* service@steinerbooks.org *Web Site:* www.steinerbooks.org, pg 134

Bamford, Christopher, SteinerBooks, 610 Main St, Great Barrington, MA 01230 *Tel:* 413-528-8233 *Fax:* 413-528-8826 *E-mail:* friends@steinerbooks.org *Web Site:* steiner.presswarehouse.com, pg 222

Bamford, Emily, Random House Children's Books, 1745 Broadway, 10th fl, New York, NY 10019 *Tel:* 212-782-9000 *Web Site:* www.randomhousekids.com, pg 194

Ban, Ana, The Experiment, 220 E 23 St, Suite 301, New York, NY 10010-4674 *Tel:* 212-889-1659 *E-mail:* info@theexperimentpublishing.com *Web Site:* www.theexperimentpublishing.com, pg 81

Bandini, Lisa Kent, Center for the Collaborative Classroom, 1250 53 St, Suite 3, Emeryville, CA 94608 *Tel:* 510-533-0213 *Toll Free Tel:* 800-666-7270 *Fax:* 510-464-3670 *E-mail:* info@collaborativeclassroom.org; clientsupport@collaborativeclassroom.org *Web Site:* www.collaborativeclassroom.org, pg 51

Bandos, Kate, Bookhaven Press LLC, 302 Scenic Ct, Moon Township, PA 15108 *Tel:* 412-494-6926 *E-mail:* info@bookhavenpress.com; orders@bookhavenpress.com *Web Site:* bookhavenpress.com, pg 40

Banducci, JoAnne, University of Nevada Press, c/o University of Nevada, Continuing Educ Bldg, MS 0166, Reno, NV 89557-0166 *Tel:* 775-784-6573 *Fax:* 775-784-6200 *Web Site:* www.unpress.nevada.edu, pg 243

Bandy, Emily, University Press of Mississippi, 3825 Ridgewood Rd, Jackson, MS 39211-6492 *Tel:* 601-432-6205 *Toll Free Tel:* 800-737-7788 (orders & cust serv) *Fax:* 601-432-6217 *E-mail:* press@mississippi.edu *Web Site:* www.upress.state.ms.us, pg 247

Banis, Robert J, Science & Humanities Press, 63 Summit Point, St Charles, MO 63301-0571 *Tel:* 636-394-4950 *Web Site:* sciencehumanitiespress.com; beachhousebooks.com; macroprintbooks.com; earlyeditionsbooks.com; heuristicsbooks.com, pg 209

Bank, Josh, Alloy Entertainment LLC, 1325 Avenue of the Americas, 29th fl, New York, NY 10019 *E-mail:* collaborative@alloyentertainment.com, pg 8

Banks, Clare, Beullah Rose Poetry Prize, PO Box 22161, Baltimore, MD 21203 *E-mail:* smartishpace@gmail.com *Web Site:* www.smartishpace.com, pg 632

Banks, Jennifer, Yale University Press, 302 Temple St, New Haven, CT 06511-8909 *Tel:* 203-432-0960; 203-432-0966 (sales); 401-531-2800 (cust serv) *Toll Free Tel:* 800-405-1619 (cust serv) *Fax:* 203-432-0948; 203-432-8485 (sales); 401-531-2801 (cust serv) *Toll Free Fax:* 800-406-9145 (cust serv) *E-mail:* sales.press@yale.edu (sales); customer.care@triliteral.org (cust serv) *Web Site:* www.yalebooks.com; yalepress.yale.edu/yupbooks, pg 261

Bannon, Dr Joseph J Sr, Sagamore Publishing LLC, 1807 N Federal Dr, Urbana, IL 61801 *Tel:* 217-359-5940 *Toll Free Tel:* 800-327-5557 (orders) *Fax:* 217-359-5975 *E-mail:* web@sagamorepub.com *Web Site:* www.sagamorepub.com, pg 203

Bannon, Peter L, Sagamore Publishing LLC, 1807 N Federal Dr, Urbana, IL 61801 *Tel:* 217-359-5940 *Toll Free Tel:* 800-327-5557 (orders) *Fax:* 217-359-5975 *E-mail:* web@sagamorepub.com *Web Site:* www.sagamorepub.com, pg 203

Barak, Walter W Jr, American Translators Association (ATA), 225 Reinekers Lane, Suite 590, Alexandria, VA 22314 *Tel:* 703-683-6100 *Fax:* 703-683-6122 *E-mail:* ata@atanet.org *Web Site:* www.atanet.org, pg 557

Baranowski, Jennifer, CODiE Awards, 1090 Vermont Ave NW, 6th fl, Washington, DC 20005-4095 *E-mail:* info@siia.net *Web Site:* www.siia.net, pg 638

Barathon, Marie-Pierre, Les Editions XYZ inc, 1815, ave De Lorimier, Montreal, QC H2K 3W6, Canada *Tel:* 514-525-2170 *Fax:* 514-525-7537 *E-mail:* info@editionsxyz.com *Web Site:* www.editionsxyz.com, pg 456

Barbasa, Santos, University of Hawaii Press, 2840 Kolowalu St, Honolulu, HI 96822 *Tel:* 808-956-8255 *Toll Free Tel:* 888-UHPRESS (847-7377) *Fax:* 808-988-6052 *Toll Free Fax:* 800-650-7811 *E-mail:* uhpbooks@hawaii.edu *Web Site:* www.uhpress.hawaii.edu, pg 241

Barber, A Richard, A Richard Barber/Peter Berinstein & Associates, 60 E Eighth St, Suite 21-N, New York, NY 10003 *Tel:* 212-737-7266 *Fax:* 860-927-3942 *E-mail:* barberrich@aol.com, pg 507

Barber, Terry, Parallax Press, 2236-B Sixth St, Berkeley, CA 94710 *Tel:* 510-540-6411 *Toll Free Tel:* 800-863-5290 (orders) *Fax:* 510-981-1157 *Web Site:* www.parallax.org, pg 174

Barbour, Bruce R, Literary Management Group LLC, 521 Oakley Dr, Nashville, TN 37220 *Tel:* 615-812-4445 *Web Site:* www.literarymanagementgroup.com, pg 526

Barbour, Wanda, American Industrial Hygiene Association - AIHA, 3141 Fairview Park Dr, Suite 777, Falls Church, VA 22042 *Tel:* 703-849-8888 *Fax:* 703-207-3561 *E-mail:* infonet@aiha.org *Web Site:* www.aiha.org, pg 12

Barcatta, Sabine, Thomas J Lyon Book Award in Western American Literary and Cultural Studies, PO Box 6815, Logan, UT 84341 *Web Site:* www.westernlit.org/thomas-j-lyon-book-award-in-western-american-literary-and-cultural-studies; www.westernlit.org, pg 664

Barich, Steven, Alan Wofsy Fine Arts, 1109 Geary Blvd, San Francisco, CA 94109 *Tel:* 415-292-6500 *Toll Free Tel:* 800-660-6403 *Fax:* 415-292-6594 (off & cust serv); 510-251-1840 (acctg) *E-mail:* order@art-books.com (orders); editeur@earthlink.net (edit); beauxarts@earthlink.net (cust serv) *Web Site:* www.art-books.com, pg 258

Baril, Andre, Les Presses de l'Universite Laval, 2180, Chemin Sainte-Foy, 1st fl, Quebec, QC G1V 0A6, Canada *Tel:* 418-656-2803 *Fax:* 418-656-3305 *E-mail:* presses@pul.ulaval.ca *Web Site:* www.pulaval.com, pg 468

Baril, Daniel, The Institute for Cooperation on Adult Education (Institut de Cooperation pour l'Education des Adultes-ICEA), 4321, ave Papineau, Montreal, QC H2H 1T3, Canada *Tel:* 514-948-2044 *Fax:* 514-948-2046 *E-mail:* icae@icea.qc.ca *Web Site:* www.icea.qc.ca, pg 567

Barkan, Bebe, Cross-Cultural Communications, 239 Wynsum Ave, Merrick, NY 11566-4725 *Tel:* 516-868-5635 *Fax:* 516-379-1901 *E-mail:* info@cross-culturalcommunications.com; cccbarkan@optonline.net; cccpoetry@aol.com *Web Site:* www.cross-culturalcommunications.com, pg 64

Barkan, Stanley H, Cross-Cultural Communications, 239 Wynsum Ave, Merrick, NY 11566-4725 *Tel:* 516-868-5635 *Fax:* 516-379-1901 *E-mail:* info@cross-culturalcommunications.com; cccbarkan@optonline.net; cccpoetry@aol.com *Web Site:* www.cross-culturalcommunications.com, pg 64

Barker, Clyde F, American Philosophical Society, 104 S Fifth St, Philadelphia, PA 19106 *Tel:* 215-440-3425 *Fax:* 215-440-3450 *E-mail:* orders@dianepublishing.net *Web Site:* www.amphilsoc.org, pg 13

Barker, Leah, Dramatists Play Service Inc, 440 Park Ave S, New York, NY 10016 *Tel:* 212-683-8960 *Fax:* 212-213-1539 *E-mail:* postmaster@dramatists.com; orders@dramatists.com; publications@dramatists.com *Web Site:* www.dramatists.com, pg 73

Barks, Daniel, Beacon Press, 24 Farnsworth St, Boston, MA 02210-1409 *Tel:* 617-742-2110 *Fax:* 617-723-3097; 617-742-2290 *Web Site:* www.beacon.org, pg 31

Barmash, Erica, Bloomsbury Publishing Inc, 1385 Broadway, 5th fl, New York, NY 10018 *Tel:* 212-419-5300 *E-mail:* marketingusa@bloomsbury.com; adultpublicityusa@bloomsbury.com; askacademic@bloomsbury.com *Web Site:* www.bloomsbury.com, pg 38

Barnes, Jacqueline, BuilderBooks.com, 1201 15 St NW, Washington, DC 20005 *Tel:* 202-822-0200 *Toll Free Tel:* 800-223-2665 *Fax:* 202-266-8096 (edit) *E-mail:* builderbooks@nahb.com *Web Site:* www.builderbooks.com, pg 45

Barnes, Janet, Bentley Publishers, 1734 Massachusetts Ave, Cambridge, MA 02138-1804 *Tel:* 617-547-4170 *Toll Free Tel:* 800-423-4595 *Fax:* 617-876-9235 *E-mail:* sales@bentleypublishers.com *Web Site:* www.bentleypublishers.com, pg 33

Barnes, Jim, Axiom Business Book Awards, 1129 Woodmere Ave, Suite B, Traverse City, MI 49686 *Tel:* 231-933-0445 *Toll Free Tel:* 800-706-4636 *Fax:* 231-933-0448 *E-mail:* info@axiomawards.com *Web Site:* www.axiomawards.com, pg 629

Barnes, Jim, Illumination Book Awards, 1129 Woodmere Ave, Suite B, Traverse City, MI 49686 *Tel:* 231-933-0445 *Toll Free Tel:* 800-706-4636 *Fax:* 231-933-0448 *E-mail:* awards@bookpublishing.com *Web Site:* www.illuminationawards.com, pg 654

Barnes, Jim, The Independent Publisher Book Awards, 1129 Woodmere Ave, Suite B, Traverse City, MI 49686 *Tel:* 231-933-0445 *Toll Free Tel:* 800-706-4636 *Fax:* 231-933-0448 *E-mail:* awards@bookpublishing.com *Web Site:* www.independentpublisher.com/ipland/ipawards.php, pg 655

Barnes, Jim, Jenkins Group Inc, 1129 Woodmere Ave, Suite B, Traverse City, MI 49686 *Tel:* 231-933-0445 *Toll Free Tel:* 800-706-4636 *Fax:* 231-933-0448 *E-mail:* info@bookpublishing.com *Web Site:* www.bookpublishing.com, pg 496

Barnes, Jim, Living Now Book Awards, 1129 Woodmere Ave, Suite B, Traverse City, MI 49686 *Tel:* 231-933-0445 *Toll Free Tel:* 800-706-4636 *Fax:* 231-933-0448 *E-mail:* awards@bookpublishing.com *Web Site:* www.livingnowawards.com, pg 662

Barnes, Jim, Moonbeam Children's Book Awards, 1129 Woodmere Ave, Suite B, Traverse City, MI 49686 *Tel:* 231-933-0445 *Toll Free Tel:* 800-706-4636 *Fax:* 231-933-0448 *E-mail:* info@moonbeamawards.com *Web Site:* www.moonbeamawards.com, pg 669

Barnes, Lisa, Penguin Random House Speakers Bureau, A Penguin Random House Company, 1745 Broadway, Mail Drop 13-1, New York, NY 10019 *Tel:* 212-572-2013 *E-mail:* speakers@penguinrandomhouse.com *Web Site:* www.prhspeakers.com, pg 547

Barnes, Marcy, Beacon Press, 24 Farnsworth St, Boston, MA 02210-1409 *Tel:* 617-742-2110 *Fax:* 617-723-3097; 617-742-2290 *Web Site:* www.beacon.org, pg 31

Barnes, Meredith, Harlequin Enterprises Ltd, 233 Broadway, Suite 1001, New York, NY 10279 *Tel:* 212-553-4200 *Fax:* 212-227-8969 *E-mail:* customerservice@harlequin.com *Web Site:* www.harlequin.com, pg 101

Barnes, Shannon Howe, Marilyn Baillie Picture Book Award, 40 Orchard View Blvd, Suite 217, Toronto, ON M4R 1B9, Canada *Tel:* 416-975-0010 *Fax:* 416-975-8970 *E-mail:* info@bookcentre.ca *Web Site:* www.bookcentre.ca, pg 629

Barnes, Shannon Howe, The Geoffrey Bilson Award for Historical Fiction for Young People, 40 Orchard View Blvd, Suite 217, Toronto, ON M4R 1B9, Canada *Tel:* 416-975-0010 *Fax:* 416-975-8970 *E-mail:* info@bookcentre.ca *Web Site:* www.bookcentre.ca, pg 632

Barnes, Shannon Howe, Canadian Children's Book Centre, 40 Orchard View Blvd, Suite 217, Toronto, ON M4R 1B9, Canada *Tel:* 416-975-0010 *Fax:* 416-975-8970 *E-mail:* info@bookcentre.ca *Web Site:* www.bookcentre.ca, pg 562

Barnes, Shannon Howe, Norma Fleck Award for Canadian Children's Non-Fiction, 40 Orchard View Blvd, Suite 217, Toronto, ON M4R 1B9, Canada *Tel:* 416-975-0010 *Fax:* 416-975-8970 *E-mail:* info@bookcentre.ca *Web Site:* www.bookcentre.ca, pg 646

Barnes, Shannon Howe, Amy Mathers Teen Book Award, 40 Orchard View Blvd, Suite 217, Toronto, ON M4R 1B9, Canada *Tel:* 416-975-0010 *Fax:* 416-975-8970 *E-mail:* info@bookcentre.ca *Web Site:* www.bookcentre.ca, pg 666

Barnes, Shannon Howe, John Spray Mystery Award, 40 Orchard View Blvd, Suite 217, Toronto, ON M4R 1B9, Canada *Tel:* 416-975-0010 *Fax:* 416-975-8970 *E-mail:* info@bookcentre.ca *Web Site:* www.bookcentre.ca, pg 691

Barnes, Shannon Howe, TD Canadian Children's Literature Award, 40 Orchard View Blvd, Suite 217, Toronto, ON M4R 1B9, Canada *Tel:* 416-975-0010 *Fax:* 416-975-8970 *E-mail:* info@bookcentre.ca *Web Site:* www.bookcentre.ca, pg 693

Barnett, Chrissie A, Southern California Writers' Conference (SCWC), 18160 Cottonwood Rd, Suite 260, Sunriver, OR 97707 *Tel:* 619-303-8185 *Fax:* 619-906-7462 *E-mail:* msg@writersconference.com *Web Site:* www.writersconference.com, pg 615

Barnett, Katie, Clinical Laboratory & Standards Institute (CLSI), 950 W Valley Rd, Suite 2500, Wayne, PA 19087 *Tel:* 610-688-0100 *Toll Free Tel:* 877-447-1888 (orders) *Fax:* 610-688-0700 *E-mail:* customerservice@clsi.org *Web Site:* www.clsi.org, pg 57

Barnett, Marilyn, Workman Publishing Co Inc, 225 Varick St, 9th fl, New York, NY 10014-4381 *Tel:* 212-254-5900 *Toll Free Tel:* 800-722-7202 *Fax:* 212-254-8098 *E-mail:* info@workman.com *Web Site:* www.workman.com, pg 259

Barnett, Robin, Zondervan, 3900 Sparks Dr, Grand Rapids, MI 49546 *Tel:* 616-698-6900 *Toll Free Tel:* 800-226-1122; 800-727-1309 (retail orders) *Fax:* 616-698-3350 *Toll Free Fax:* 800-698-3256 (retail orders) *E-mail:* zinfo@zondervan.com *Web Site:* www.zondervan.com, pg 263

Barney, Jenny, Publications International Ltd (PIL), 7373 N Cicero Ave, Lincolnwood, IL 60712 *Tel:* 847-676-3470 *Fax:* 847-676-3671 *E-mail:* customer_service@pubint.com *Web Site:* pilbooks.com, pg 191

Barney, Stacey, GP Putnam's Sons (Children's), 345 Hudson St, New York, NY 10014 *Tel:* 212-366-2000 *Fax:* 212-414-3393 *Web Site:* www.penguin.com/publishers/gpputnamssonsbooksforyoungread, pg 192

Baron, Carole, Alfred A Knopf/Everyman's Library, c/o Penguin Random House Inc, 1745 Broadway, New York, NY 10019 *Tel:* 212-751-2600 *Toll Free Tel:* 800-638-6460 *Fax:* 212-572-2593 *Web Site:* www.knopfdoubleday.com, pg 127

Baron, Herman, Diane Publishing Co, 330 Pusey Ave, Suite 3 (rear), Collingdale, PA 19023-0617 *Tel:* 610-461-6200 *Toll Free Tel:* 800-782-3833 *Fax:* 610-461-6130 *Web Site:* www.dianepublishing.net, pg 70

Baror, Danny, Baror International Inc, PO Box 868, Armonk, NY 10504-0868 *Tel:* 914-273-9199 *Fax:* 914-273-5058 *Web Site:* www.barorint.com, pg 507

Baror-Shapiro, Heather, Baror International Inc, PO Box 868, Armonk, NY 10504-0868 *Tel:* 914-273-9199 *Fax:* 914-273-5058 *Web Site:* www.barorint.com, pg 507

Barot, Len, Bold Strokes Books Inc, PO Box 249, Valley Falls, NY 12185 *Tel:* 518-677-5127 *Fax:* 518-677-5291 *E-mail:* bsb@boldstrokesbooks.com *Web Site:* www.boldstrokesbooks.com, pg 39

Barr, Stephen, Writers House, 21 W 26 St, New York, NY 10010 *Tel:* 212-685-2400 *Fax:* 212-685-1781 *Web Site:* www.writershouse.com, pg 542

Barr, Wayne, Barron's Educational Series Inc, 250 Wireless Blvd, Hauppauge, NY 11788 *Tel:* 631-434-3311 *Toll Free Tel:* 800-645-3476 *Fax:* 631-434-3723 *E-mail:* barrons@barronseduc.com *Web Site:* www.barronseduc.com, pg 30

Barrales-Saylor, Kelly, Sourcebooks Inc, 1935 Brookdale Rd, Suite 139, Naperville, IL 60563 *Tel:* 630-961-3900 *Toll Free Tel:* 800-432-7444 *Fax:* 630-961-2168 *E-mail:* info@sourcebooks.com; customersupport@sourcebooks.com *Web Site:* www.sourcebooks.com, pg 218

Barras, Lise, Pearson ERPI, 1611 Cremazie Blvd E, 10th fl, Montreal, QC H2M 2P2, Canada *Tel:* 514-334-2690 *Toll Free Tel:* 800-263-3678 *Fax:* 514-334-4720 *Toll Free Fax:* 800-643-4720 *E-mail:* erpidlm@erpi.com *Web Site:* www.erpi.com; pearsonplc.ca, pg 466

Barrenechea, Antonio, The Charles Bernheimer Prize, University of South Carolina, Dept of Languages, Literature & Cultures, 1620 College St, Rm 813-A, Columbia, SC 29208 *Tel:* 803-777-3021 *E-mail:* info@acla.org *Web Site:* www.acla.org/prize-awards, pg 631

Barrenechea, Antonio, Harry Levin Prize, University of South Carolina, Dept of Languages, Literature & Cultures, 1620 College St, Rm 813-A, Columbia, SC 29208 *Tel:* 803-777-3021 *E-mail:* info@acla.org *Web Site:* www.acla.org/prize-awards, pg 660

Bates, Colleen Dunn, Prospect Park Books, 2359 Lincoln Ave, Altadena, CA 91001 *Tel:* 626-793-9796 *E-mail:* info@prospectparkbooks.com *Web Site:* www.prospectparkbooks.com, pg 190

Bates, Greg, Common Courage Press, One Red Barn Rd, Monroe, ME 04951 *Tel:* 207-525-0900 *Toll Free Tel:* 800-497-3207 *Fax:* 207-525-3068 *Web Site:* www.commoncouragepress.com, pg 59

Bates, Vicki, University of South Carolina Press, 1600 Hampton St, Suite 544, Columbia, SC 29208 *Tel:* 803-777-5245 *Toll Free Tel:* 800-768-2500 (orders) *Fax:* 803-777-0160 *Toll Free Fax:* 800-868-0740 (orders) *Web Site:* www.sc.edu/uscpress, pg 245

Bathgate, Linda, University Press of Florida, 15 NW 15 St, Gainesville, FL 32603-2079 *Tel:* 352-392-1351 *Toll Free Tel:* 800-226-3822 (orders only) *Fax:* 352-392-0590 *Toll Free Fax:* 800-680-1955 (orders only) *E-mail:* press@upress.ufl.edu; orders@upress.ufl.edu *Web Site:* www.upf.com, pg 246

Batiz-Benet, Mercedes, Bayeux Arts Inc, 119 Stratton Crescent SW, Calgary, AB T3H 1T7, Canada *E-mail:* mail@bayeux.com *Web Site:* bayeux.com, pg 446

Batkie, Sara, The Center for Fiction First Novel Prize, 17 E 47 St, New York, NY 10017 *Tel:* 212-755-6710 *Fax:* 212-826-0831 *E-mail:* info@centerforfiction.org *Web Site:* centerforfiction.org/awards, pg 636

Batkie, Sara, The Christopher Doheny Award, 17 E 47 St, New York, NY 10017 *Tel:* 212-755-6710 *Fax:* 212-826-0831 *E-mail:* doheny@centerforfiction.org; info@centerforfiction.org *Web Site:* www.centerforfiction.org/awards/the-christopher-doheny-award, pg 642

Batkie, Sara, NYC Emerging Writers Fellowships, 17 E 47 St, New York, NY 10017 *Tel:* 212-755-6710 *E-mail:* info@centerforfiction.org *Web Site:* centerforfiction.org, pg 674

Batkie, Sara, Maxwell E Perkins Award, 17 E 47 St, New York, NY 10017 *Tel:* 212-755-6710 *Fax:* 212-826-0831 *E-mail:* info@centerforfiction.org *Web Site:* www.centerforfiction.org/awards/perkins, pg 679

Batmanglij, Mohammad, Mage Publishers Inc, 1408 35 St NW, Washington, DC 20007 *Tel:* 202-342-1642 *Web Site:* www.mage.com, pg 140

Batmanglij, Najmieh, Mage Publishers Inc, 1408 35 St NW, Washington, DC 20007 *Tel:* 202-342-1642 *Web Site:* www.mage.com, pg 140

Battista, Dino, The University of North Carolina Press, 116 S Boundary St, Chapel Hill, NC 27514-3808 *Tel:* 919-966-3561 *Fax:* 919-966-3829 *E-mail:* uncpress@unc.edu *Web Site:* www.uncpress.unc.edu, pg 243

Battista, Garth, Breakaway Books, PO Box 24, Halcottsville, NY 12438-0024 *Tel:* 607-326-4805 *E-mail:* breakawaybooks@gmail.com *Web Site:* www.breakawaybooks.com, pg 42

Batura, Paul, Focus on the Family, 8605 Explorer Dr, Colorado Springs, CO 80920-1051 *Tel:* 719-531-5181 *Toll Free Tel:* 800-A-FAMILY (232-6459) *Fax:* 719-531-3424 *Web Site:* www.focusonthefamily.com; www.facebook.com/focusonthefamily, pg 86

Bauchner, Howard C MD, American Medical Association, AMA Plaza, 330 N Wabash, Suite 39300, Chicago, IL 60611-5885 *Tel:* 312-464-5000 *Toll Free Tel:* 800-621-8335 *Fax:* 312-464-4184 *Web Site:* www.ama-assn.org, pg 13

Bauer, Susan Wise, Peace Hill Press, 18021 The Glebe Lane, Charles City, VA 23030 *Tel:* 804-829-5043 *Toll Free Tel:* 877-322-3445 (orders) *Fax:* 804-829-5704 *E-mail:* info@peacehillpress.com *Web Site:* www.peacehillpress.com, pg 175

Bauerle, Chris, Sourcebooks Inc, 1935 Brookdale Rd, Suite 139, Naperville, IL 60563 *Tel:* 630-961-3900 *Toll Free Tel:* 800-432-7444 *Fax:* 630-961-2168 *E-mail:* info@sourcebooks.com; customersupport@sourcebooks.com *Web Site:* www.sourcebooks.com, pg 218

Baugher, Matt, Thomas Nelson, 501 Nelson Place, Nashville, TN 37214 *Tel:* 615-889-9000 *Toll Free Tel:* 800-251-4000 *Fax:* 615-902-1548 *Web Site:* www.thomasnelson.com, pg 231

Baule, Deirdre, Hachette Nashville, 12 Cadillac Dr, Suite 480, Brentwood, TN 37027 *Tel:* 615-221-0996 *Fax:* 615-221-0962 *Web Site:* www.hachettebookgroup.com, pg 98

Baum, Katy, Guild of Book Workers, 521 Fifth Ave, New York, NY 10175 *Tel:* 212-292-4444 *E-mail:* communications@guildofbookworkers.org *Web Site:* www.guildofbookworkers.org, pg 566

Baumann, David, University of Pittsburgh Press, 7500 Thomas Blvd, Pittsburgh, PA 15260 *Tel:* 412-383-2456 *Fax:* 412-383-2466 *E-mail:* info@upress.pitt.edu *Web Site:* www.upress.pitt.edu, pg 244

Baumann, Rebecca, Montana Historical Society Press, Capitol Complex, 225 N Roberts St, Helena, MT 59620 *Tel:* 406-444-0090 (edit); 406-444-2890 (orders/mktg); 406-444-2694 *Toll Free Tel:* 800-243-9900 *Fax:* 406-444-2696 (orders/mktg) *Web Site:* mhs.mt.gov/pubs, pg 153

Baumstein, Hali, Bloomsbury Publishing Inc, 1385 Broadway, 5th fl, New York, NY 10018 *Tel:* 212-419-5300 *E-mail:* marketingusa@bloomsbury.com; adultpublicityusa@bloomsbury.com; askacademic@bloomsbury.com *Web Site:* www.bloomsbury.com, pg 38

Bautista, Fr Tony, St Pauls, 2187 Victory Blvd, Staten Island, NY 10314-6603 *Tel:* 718-761-0047 (edit & prodn); 718-698-2759 (mktg & billing) *Toll Free Tel:* 800-343-2522 *Fax:* 718-761-0057 *E-mail:* sales@stpauls.us; marketing@stpauls.us *Web Site:* www.stpauls.us, pg 205

Baxter, Carol, The Mathematical Association of America, 1529 18 St NW, Washington, DC 20036-1358 *Tel:* 202-387-5200 *Toll Free Tel:* 800-741-9415 *Fax:* 202-265-2384 *E-mail:* maahq@maa.org; advertising@maa.org (pubns) *Web Site:* www.maa.org, pg 144

Baxter, James, National Press Club of Canada Foundation Inc, 17 York St, Suite 201, Ottawa, ON K1N 9J6, Canada *E-mail:* info@pressclubcanada.ca *Web Site:* pressclubcanada.ca, pg 572

Bay, Bill, Mel Bay Publications Inc, 4 Industrial Dr, Pacific, MO 63069-0066 *Tel:* 636-257-3970 *Toll Free Tel:* 800-863-5229 *Fax:* 636-257-5062 *Toll Free Fax:* 800-660-9818 *E-mail:* email@melbay.com *Web Site:* www.melbay.com, pg 148

Bay, Linda, Penguin Group USA, A Penguin Random House Company, 375 Hudson St, New York, NY 10014 *Tel:* 212-366-2000 *Toll Free Tel:* 800-847-5515 (inside sales); 800-631-8571 (cust serv) *Fax:* 212-366-2666; 607-775-4829 (inside sales) *E-mail:* online@us.penguingroup.com *Web Site:* www.penguin.com, pg 177

Bay, Stephanie, Random House Children's Books, 1745 Broadway, 10th fl, New York, NY 10019 *Tel:* 212-782-9000 *Web Site:* www.randomhousekids.com, pg 194

Bayer, Lisa, University of Georgia Press, Main Library, 3rd fl, 320 S Jackson St, Athens, GA 30602 *Fax:* 706-542-2558; 706-542-6770 *Web Site:* www.ugapress.org, pg 241

Bayers, William, Houghton Mifflin Harcourt, 125 High St, Boston, MA 02110 *Tel:* 617-351-5000 *Toll Free Tel:* 855-969-4642; 800-225-5425 (K-12 educ materials); 800-323-9540 (assessment materials); 877-219-1537 (SkillsTutor); 888-242-6747 (Innovation in Educ Group); 800-225-3362 (Trade & Ref Div) *Toll Free Fax:* 800-269-5232 *E-mail:* myhmhco@hmhco.com *Web Site:* www.hmhco.com, pg 110

Bays, Susan, Arbutus Press, 2364 Pinehurst Trail, Traverse City, MI 49696 *Tel:* 231-946-7240 *E-mail:* info@arbutuspress.com *Web Site:* www.arbutuspress.com, pg 20

Bayuk, Michelle, Quarto Publishing Group USA Inc, 400 First Ave N, Suite 400, Minneapolis, MN 55401 *Tel:* 612-344-8100 *Toll Free Tel:* 800-328-0590 (sales); 800-458-0454 *Fax:* 612-344-8691 *E-mail:* sales@quartous.com *Web Site:* www.quartoknows.com, pg 192

Bazzy, William M, Artech House Inc, 685 Canton St, Norwood, MA 02062 *Tel:* 781-769-9750 *Toll Free Tel:* 800-225-9977 *Fax:* 781-769-6334 *E-mail:* artech@artechhouse.com *Web Site:* www.artechhouse.com, pg 21

Beacom, David, National Science Teachers Association (NSTA), 1840 Wilson Blvd, Arlington, VA 22201-3000 *Tel:* 703-312-9205 *Toll Free Tel:* 800-277-5300 (orders) *Toll Free Fax:* 888-433-0526 (orders) *E-mail:* publisher@nsta.org (gen info); orders@nsta.org *Web Site:* www.nsta.org/store, pg 159

Beal, Greg, Don & Gee Nicholl Fellowships in Screenwriting, 1313 Vine St, Hollywood, CA 90028 *Tel:* 310-247-3010 *Fax:* 310-247-3794 *E-mail:* nicholl@oscars.org *Web Site:* www.oscars.org/nicholl, pg 673

Beale, Sarah, Woodland Publishing Inc, 515 S 700 E, Suite 2D, Salt Lake City, UT 84102 *Toll Free Tel:* 800-277-3243 *E-mail:* info@woodlandpublishing.com *Web Site:* www.woodlandpublishing.com, pg 258

Bean, Joy, Little Bee Books, 853 Broadway, Suite 2014, New York, NY 10003 *E-mail:* info@littlebeebooks.com *Web Site:* www.littlebeebooks.com, pg 135

Beard, Morgan, Swedenborg Foundation, 320 N Church St, West Chester, PA 19380 *Tel:* 610-430-3222 *Toll Free Tel:* 800-355-3222 (cust serv) *Fax:* 610-430-7982 *E-mail:* info@swedenborg.com *Web Site:* www.swedenborg.com, pg 225

Beard, Stephanie, Turner Publishing Co, 4507 Charlotte Ave, Suite 100, Nashville, TN 37209 *Tel:* 615-255-BOOK (255-2665) *Fax:* 615-255-5081 *E-mail:* marketing@turnerpublishing.com; submissions@turnerpublishing.com *Web Site:* www.turnerpublishing.com; www.facebook.com/turner.publishing, pg 236

Beasley, Barbara, Paladin Press, 5540 Central Ave, Suite 200, Boulder, CO 80301 *Tel:* 303-443-7250 *Toll Free Tel:* 800-392-2400 *Fax:* 303-442-8741 *E-mail:* service@paladin-press.com *Web Site:* www.paladin-press.com, pg 172

Beasley, Crystal, Society of American Business Editors & Writers Inc (SABEW), Walter Cronkite School of Journalism & Mass Communication, Arizona State University, 555 N Central Ave, Suite 406E, Phoenix, AZ 85004-1248 *Tel:* 602-496-7862 *Fax:* 602-496-7041 *E-mail:* sabew@sabew.org *Web Site:* sabew.org, pg 578

Beasley, J Malcolm, Professional Communications Inc, 1223 W Main, Suite 1427, Caddo, OK 74702-1427 *Tel:* 580-745-9838 *Toll Free Tel:* 800-337-9838 *Fax:* 580-745-9837 *E-mail:* info@pcibooks.com *Web Site:* www.pcibooks.com, pg 189

Beaudet, Marie-Andree, La Fondation Emile Nelligan, 100, rue Sherbrooke, Suite 202, Montreal, QC H2X 1C3, Canada *Tel:* 514-278-4657 *Fax:* 514-278-1943 *E-mail:* info@fondation-nelligan.org *Web Site:* www.fondation-nelligan.org, pg 566

Beaudet, Marie-Andree, Prix Emile-Nelligan, 100, rue Sherbrooke, Suite 202, Montreal, QC H2X 1C3, Canada *Tel:* 514-278-4657 *Toll Free Tel:* 888-849-8540 *Fax:* 514-278-1943 *E-mail:* info@fondation-nelligan.org *Web Site:* www.fondation-nelligan.org, pg 682

Beaudoin, Andre, Les Editions Ganesha Inc, CP 484, succursale d'Youville, Montreal, QC H2P 2W1, Canada *Tel:* 450-641-2395 *E-mail:* courriel@editions-ganesha.qc.ca *Web Site:* www.editions-ganesha.qc.ca, pg 454

Becerra, Nannette, Gem Guides Book Co, 1275 W Ninth St, Upland, CA 91786 *Tel:* 626-855-1611 *Toll Free Tel:* 800-824-5118 (orders) *Fax:* 626-855-1610 *E-mail:* info@gemguidesbooks.com *Web Site:* www.gemguidesbooks.com, pg 91

Becher, Bill, AuthorHouse, 1663 Liberty Dr, Bloomington, IN 47403 *Tel:* 812-339-6000 (outside US) *Toll Free Tel:* 888-519-5121 *E-mail:* authorsupport@authorhouse.com *Web Site:* www.authorhouse.com, pg 26

Becher, Bill, iUniverse, 1663 Liberty Dr, Bloomington, IN 47403 *Toll Free Tel:* 800-AUTHORS (288-4677) *Fax:* 812-355-4085 *Web Site:* www.iuniverse.com, pg 121

Becher, Bill, Trafford, 1663 Liberty Dr, Bloomington, IN 47403 *Toll Free Tel:* 888-232-4444 *E-mail:* customersupport@trafford.com; sales@trafford.com *Web Site:* www.trafford.com, pg 234

Becher, Bill, Xlibris Corp, 1663 Liberty Dr, Suite 200, Bloomington, IN 47403 *Toll Free Tel:* 888-795-4274 *Fax:* 610-915-0294 *E-mail:* info@xlibris.com *Web Site:* www.xlibris.com, pg 261

Bechthold, Mike, Wilfrid Laurier University Press, 75 University Ave W, Waterloo, ON N2L 3C5, Canada *Tel:* 519-884-0710 *Toll Free Tel:* 866-836-5551 (CN & US) *Fax:* 519-725-1399 *E-mail:* press@wlu.ca *Web Site:* www.wlupress.wlu.ca, pg 476

Beck, Eric, Seedling Publications Inc, 520 E Bainbridge St, Elizabethtown, PA 17022 *Toll Free Tel:* 800-233-0759 *Toll Free Fax:* 888-834-1303 *E-mail:* info@continentalpress.com *Web Site:* www.continentalpress.com, pg 210

Beck, Robyn, Meadowbrook Press, 6110 Blue Circle Dr, Suite 237, Minnetonka, MN 55343 *Toll Free Tel:* 800-338-2232 *Fax:* 952-930-1940 *E-mail:* info@meadowbrookpress.com *Web Site:* www.meadowbrookpress.com, pg 147

Becker, Amy, Eisenbrauns, PO Box 275, Winona Lake, IN 46590-0275 *Tel:* 574-269-2011 *Fax:* 574-269-6788 *E-mail:* customer_service@eisenbrauns.com; publisher@eisenbrauns.com *Web Site:* www.eisenbrauns.com, pg 76

Becker, Matt, University of Massachusetts Press, East Experiment Sta, 671 N Pleasant St, Amherst, MA 01003 *Tel:* 413-545-2217 *Fax:* 413-545-1226 *E-mail:* info@umpress.umass.edu *Web Site:* www.umass.edu/umpress, pg 242

Becker, Ulrich, Mondial, 203 W 107 St, Suite 6-C, New York, NY 10025 *Tel:* 646-807-8031 *Fax:* 208-361-2863 *E-mail:* contact@mondialbooks.com *Web Site:* www.mondialbooks.com, pg 153

Beckerman, Chad, Harry N Abrams Inc, 195 Broadway, 9th fl, New York, NY 10007 *Tel:* 212-206-7715 *Toll Free Tel:* 800-345-1359 *Fax:* 212-519-1210 *E-mail:* abrams@abramsbooks.com *Web Site:* www.abramsbooks.com, pg 3

Beckman, Andrew, Timber Press Inc, 133 SW Second Ave, Suite 450, Portland, OR 97204 *Tel:* 503-227-2878 *Toll Free Tel:* 800-327-5680 *Fax:* 503-227-3070 *E-mail:* info@timberpress.com *Web Site:* www.timberpress.com, pg 232

Bedard, Rachel, Les Editions du Remue-Menage, La Maison Parent-Roback, 110 rue Sainte-Therese, bureau 303, Montreal, QC H2Y 1E6, Canada *Tel:* 514-876-0097 *Fax:* 514-876-7951 *E-mail:* info@editions-rm.ca *Web Site:* www.editions-rm.ca, pg 453

Bedford, Laura, Guild of Book Workers, 521 Fifth Ave, New York, NY 10175 *Tel:* 212-292-4444 *E-mail:* communications@guildofbookworkers.org *Web Site:* www.guildofbookworkers.org, pg 566

Bedford, Stephen, Simon & Schuster, 1230 Avenue of the Americas, New York, NY 10020 *Tel:* 212-698-7000 *Toll Free Tel:* 800-223-2348 (cust serv); 800-223-2336 (orders) *Toll Free Fax:* 800-943-9831 (orders) *Web Site:* www.simonandschuster.com, pg 212

Bedick, Cara, Touchstone, 1230 Avenue of the Americas, New York, NY 10020, pg 233

Bedingfield, Kate, Motion Picture Association of America Inc (MPAA), 1600 "I" St NW, Washington, DC 20006 *Tel:* 202-293-1966 *Fax:* 202-296-7410 *E-mail:* contactus@mpaa.org *Web Site:* www.mpaa.org, pg 570

Bedingfield, Sarah, Levine|Greenberg|Rostan Literary Agency, 307 Seventh Ave, Suite 2407, New York, NY 10001 *Tel:* 212-337-0934 *Fax:* 212-337-0948 *Web Site:* lgrliterary.com, pg 525

Beditz, Dr Joseph, National Golf Foundation, 501 N Hwy A1A, Jupiter, FL 33477-4577 *Tel:* 561-744-6006 *Toll Free Tel:* 888-275-4643 *Fax:* 561-744-6107 *E-mail:* general@ngf.org *Web Site:* www.ngf.org, pg 158

Bednarik, Joseph, Copper Canyon Press, Fort Worden State Park, Bldg 313, Port Townsend, WA 98368 *Tel:* 360-385-4925 *Toll Free Tel:* 877-501-1393 (orders) *Fax:* 360-385-4985 *E-mail:* poetry@coppercanyonpress.org *Web Site:* www.coppercanyonpress.org, pg 60

Bedney, Steve, Book Industry Guild of New York, PO Box 2001, New York, NY 10113-2001 *E-mail:* admin@bookindustryguildofny.org *Web Site:* www.bookindustryguildofny.org, pg 560

Bedrick, Claudia, Enchanted Lion Books, 351 Van Brunt St, Ground fl-Gallery, Brooklyn, NY 11231 *Tel:* 646-785-9272 *E-mail:* enchantedlion@gmail.com *Web Site:* www.enchantedlionbooks.com, pg 78

Beeke, Joel R, Reformation Heritage Books, 2965 Leonard St NE, Grand Rapids, MI 49525 *Tel:* 616-977-0889 *Fax:* 616-285-3246 *E-mail:* orders@heritagebooks.org *Web Site:* www.heritagebooks.org, pg 198

Beers, Ron, Tyndale House Publishers Inc, 351 Executive Dr, Carol Stream, IL 60188 *Tel:* 630-668-8300 *Toll Free Tel:* 800-323-9400 *Toll Free Fax:* 800-684-0247 *Web Site:* www.tyndale.com, pg 237

Beetham, Christopher, Zondervan, 3900 Sparks Dr, Grand Rapids, MI 49546 *Tel:* 616-698-6900 *Toll Free Tel:* 800-226-1122; 800-727-1309 (retail orders) *Fax:* 616-698-3350 *Toll Free Fax:* 800-698-3256 (retail orders) *E-mail:* zinfo@zondervan.com *Web Site:* www.zondervan.com, pg 263

Behar, Ann, Scovil Galen Ghosh Literary Agency Inc, 276 Fifth Ave, Suite 708, New York, NY 10001 *Tel:* 212-679-8686 *Fax:* 212-679-6710 *E-mail:* info@sgglit.com *Web Site:* www.sgglit.com, pg 535

Behm, Melissa A, Brookes Publishing Co Inc, PO Box 10624, Baltimore, MD 21285-0624 *Tel:* 410-337-9580 (outside US & CN) *Toll Free Tel:* 800-638-3775 (US & CN) *Fax:* 410-337-8539 *E-mail:* custserv@brookespublishing.com *Web Site:* www.brookespublishing.com, pg 44

Behm, Melissa A, Health Professions Press, 409 Washington Ave, Suite 500, Towson, MD 21204 *Tel:* 410-337-9585 *Toll Free Tel:* 888-337-8808 *Fax:* 410-337-8539 *E-mail:* custserv@healthpropress.com *Web Site:* www.healthpropress.com, pg 105

Behn, Robin, University of Alabama Program in Creative Writing, PO Box 870244, Tuscaloosa, AL 35487-0244 *Tel:* 205-348-5065 *Fax:* 205-348-1388 *E-mail:* english@ua.edu *Web Site:* www.as.ua.edu/english, pg 622

Behning, Janet, Princeton Architectural Press, 37 E Seventh St, New York, NY 10003 *Tel:* 212-995-9620 *Toll Free Tel:* 800-722-6657 (dist); 800-759-0190 (sales) *Fax:* 212-995-9454 *E-mail:* sales@papress.com *Web Site:* www.papress.com, pg 188

Behrman, David, Behrman House Inc, 11 Edison Place, Springfield, NJ 07081 *Tel:* 973-379-7200 *Toll Free Tel:* 800-221-2755 *Fax:* 973-379-7280 *E-mail:* customersupport@behrmanhouse.com *Web Site:* www.behrmanhouse.com, pg 32

Behroozi, Cyrus, The Brookings Institution Press, 1775 Massachusetts Ave NW, Washington, DC 20036-2188 *Tel:* 202-536-3600 *Toll Free Tel:* 800-537-5487 *Fax:* 202-536-3623 *E-mail:* permissions@brookings.edu *Web Site:* www.brookings.edu, pg 44

Beier, Elizabeth, St Martin's Press, LLC, 175 Fifth Ave, New York, NY 10010 *Tel:* 646-307-5151 *Web Site:* us.macmillan.com/smp, pg 204

Beil, Frederic C, Frederic C Beil Publisher Inc, 609 Whitaker St, Savannah, GA 31401 *Tel:* 912-233-2446 *E-mail:* editor@beil.com; order@beil.com *Web Site:* www.beil.com, pg 32

Beilenson, Esther, Peter Pauper Press, Inc, 202 Mamaroneck Ave, Suite 400, White Plains, NY 10601-5376 *Tel:* 914-681-0144 *Fax:* 914-681-0389 *E-mail:* customerservice@peterpauper.com; orders@peterpauper.com; marketing@peterpauper.com *Web Site:* www.peterpauper.com, pg 181

Beilenson, Evelyn L, Peter Pauper Press, Inc, 202 Mamaroneck Ave, Suite 400, White Plains, NY 10601-5376 *Tel:* 914-681-0144 *Fax:* 914-681-0389 *E-mail:* customerservice@peterpauper.com; orders@peterpauper.com; marketing@peterpauper.com *Web Site:* www.peterpauper.com, pg 181

Beilenson, Laurence, Peter Pauper Press, Inc, 202 Mamaroneck Ave, Suite 400, White Plains, NY 10601-5376 *Tel:* 914-681-0144 *Fax:* 914-681-0389 *E-mail:* customerservice@peterpauper.com; orders@peterpauper.com; marketing@peterpauper.com *Web Site:* www.peterpauper.com, pg 181

Beitzel, Tim, Kendall Hunt Publishing Co, 4050 Westmark Dr, Dubuque, IA 52002-2624 *Tel:* 563-589-1000 *Toll Free Tel:* 800-228-0810 (orders) *Fax:* 563-589-1046 *Toll Free Fax:* 800-772-9165 *E-mail:* orders@kendallhunt.com *Web Site:* www.kendallhunt.com, pg 125

Bejarano, Laura, Lectorum Publications Inc, 205 Chubb Ave, Lyndhurst, NJ 07071 *Toll Free Tel:* 800-345-5946 *Fax:* 201-559-2201 *Toll Free Fax:* 877-532-8676 *E-mail:* lectorum@lectorum.com *Web Site:* www.lectorum.com, pg 131

Belanger, Paul, Les Editions du Noroit, 4609, rue D'Iberville, espace 202, Montreal, QC H2H 2L9, Canada *Tel:* 514-727-0005 *E-mail:* lenoroit@lenoroit.com *Web Site:* www.lenoroit.com, pg 453

Belanger, Rich, ProQuest LLC, 789 E Eisenhower Pkwy, Ann Arbor, MI 48108 *Tel:* 734-761-4700 *Toll Free Tel:* 800-521-0600 *Web Site:* www.proquest.com, pg 190

Belden, Kathryn, Scribner, 1230 Avenue of the Americas, New York, NY 10020, pg 209

Belderis, Ina, Theosophical University Press, PO Box C, Pasadena, CA 91109-7107 *Tel:* 626-798-3378 *E-mail:* tupress@theosociety.org *Web Site:* www.theosociety.org, pg 231

Belfiglio, Brian, Scribner, 1230 Avenue of the Americas, New York, NY 10020, pg 209

Belfiglio, Brian, Touchstone, 1230 Avenue of the Americas, New York, NY 10020, pg 233

Belfus, Linda, Elsevier, Health Sciences Division, 1600 John F Kennedy Blvd, Suite 1800, Philadelphia, PA 19103-2899 *Tel:* 215-239-3900 *Toll Free Tel:* 800-523-1649 *Fax:* 215-239-3990 *Web Site:* www.us.elsevierhealth.com, pg 77

Beliveau, Mathieu, Beliveau Editeur, 567 rue Bienville, Boucherville, QC J4B 2Z5, Canada *Tel:* 450-679-1933 *Web Site:* www.beliveauediteur.com, pg 446

Belkind, Myron, National Press Club (NPC), 529 14 St NW, 13th fl, Washington, DC 20045 *Tel:* 202-662-7500 *Fax:* 202-662-7569 *E-mail:* infocenter@npcpress.org *Web Site:* www.press.org, pg 572

Belknap, Mary PhD, Nautilus Book Awards, PO Box 2285, Vashon, WA 98070 *Tel:* 206-604-2250 *Web Site:* www.nautilusbookawards.com, pg 672

Bell, Duncan, Columbia Books & Information Services (CBIS), 4340 East-West Hwy, Suite 300, Bethesda, MD 20814 *Tel:* 202-464-1662 *Fax:* 301-664-9600 *E-mail:* info@columbiabooks.com *Web Site:* www.columbiabooks.com; www.lobbyists.info; www.associationexecs.com, pg 59

Bell, Emily, Farrar, Straus & Giroux, LLC, 18 W 18 St, New York, NY 10011 *Tel:* 212-741-6900 *E-mail:* fsg.publicity@fsgbooks.com *Web Site:* us.macmillan.com/fsg.aspx, pg 83

Bell, Justin, Spectrum Literary Agency, 320 Central Park W, Suite 1-D, New York, NY 10025 *Tel:* 212-362-4323 *Fax:* 212-362-4562 *Web Site:* www.spectrumliteraryagency.com, pg 537

Bell, Merleyn, Neustadt International Prize for Literature, c/o University of Oklahoma, 630 Parrington Oval, Suite 110, Norman, OK 73019-4033 *Tel:* 405-325-4531 *Web Site:* www.worldliteraturetoday.org; www.worldlit.org, pg 672

Bell, Merleyn, NSK Neustadt Prize for Children's Literature, c/o University of Oklahoma, 630 Parrington Oval, Suite 110, Norman, OK 73019-4033 *Tel:* 405-325-4531 *Web Site:* www.worldliteraturetoday.org; www.worldlit.org, pg 674

Bell, Nate, Association Media & Publishing (AM&P), 529 14 St, Suite 750, Washington, DC 20045 *Tel:* 202-591-2457 *E-mail:* info@associationmediaandpublishing.org *Web Site:* associationmediaandpublishing.org, pg 558

Bell, Nate, EXCEL Awards, 529 14 St, Suite 750, Washington, DC 20045 *Tel:* 202-591-2457 *E-mail:* awards@associationmediaandpublishing.org; info@associationmediaandpublishing.org *Web Site:* associationmediaandpublishing.org; kellencompany.com, pg 645

Bellanca, Dr Patricia, Harvard Summer Writing Program, 51 Brattle St, Dept S760, Cambridge, MA 02138-3722 *Tel:* 617-495-4024 *Fax:* 617-495-9176 *E-mail:* summer@harvard.edu *Web Site:* www.summer.harvard.edu, pg 611

Bellani, Kaushik, McGraw-Hill International & Professional Publishing Group, 2 Penn Plaza, New York, NY 10121 *Tel:* 646-766-2000 *Web Site:* www.mheducation.com, pg 146

Bellitto, Christopher, Paulist Press, 997 Macarthur Blvd, Mahwah, NJ 07430-9990 *Tel:* 201-825-7300 *Toll Free Tel:* 800-218-1903 *Fax:* 201-825-6921 *Toll Free Fax:* 800-836-3161 *E-mail:* info@paulistpress.com; publicity@paulistpress.com *Web Site:* www.paulistpress.com, pg 175

Bellow, Adam, St Martin's Press, LLC, 175 Fifth Ave, New York, NY 10010 *Tel:* 646-307-5151 *Web Site:* us.macmillan.com/smp, pg 204

Bellows, Melinda Gerosa, National Geographic Books, 1145 17 St NW, Washington, DC 20036-4688 *Tel:* 202-857-7000 *Toll Free Tel:* 877-866-6486 *E-mail:* ngbooks@cdsfulfillment.com *Web Site:* www.nationalgeographic.com/books/; ngbooks.buysub.com, pg 158

Bemis, Carol Stiles, W W Norton & Company Inc, 500 Fifth Ave, New York, NY 10110-0017 *Tel:* 212-354-5500 *Toll Free Tel:* 800-233-4830 (orders & cust serv) *Fax:* 212-869-0856 *Toll Free Fax:* 800-458-6515 *E-mail:* orders@wwnorton.com *Web Site:* books.wwnorton.com, pg 164

Ben, Crystal, Orbit, 1290 Avenue of the Americas, New York, NY 10019 *Tel:* 212-364-1100 *Toll Free Tel:* 800-759-0190 *Web Site:* www.orbitbooks.net, pg 169

Benamou, Sharon, AJL Judaica Bibliography Award, PO Box 1118, Teaneck, NJ 07666 *Tel:* 201-371-3255 *E-mail:* info@jewishlibraries.org *Web Site:* jewishlibraries.org, pg 626

Benamou, Sharon, AJL Judaica Reference Award, PO Box 1118, Teaneck, NJ 07666 *Tel:* 201-371-3255 *E-mail:* info@jewishlibraries.org *Web Site:* jewishlibraries.org, pg 626

Benard, Mary, Skinner House Books, c/o Unitarian Universalist Assn, 24 Farnsworth St, Boston, MA 02210-1409 *Tel:* 617-742-2100 *Fax:* 617-948-6466 *E-mail:* skinnerhouse@uua.org *Web Site:* www.skinnerhouse.org, pg 214

Benatar, Raquel, Laredo Publishing Co Inc, 465 Westview Ave, Englewood, NJ 07631 *Tel:* 201-408-4048 *E-mail:* info@laredopublishing.com *Web Site:* www.laredopublishing.com, pg 129

Benatar, Raquel, Renaissance House, 465 Westview Ave, Englewood, NJ 07631 *Tel:* 201-408-4048 *E-mail:* info@renaissancehouse.net *Web Site:* www.renaissancehouse.net, pg 198

Bendell, Amy, HarperCollins General Books Group, 195 Broadway, New York, NY 10007 *Tel:* 212-207-7000 *Web Site:* www.harpercollins.com, pg 101

Bender, Robert, Simon & Schuster, 1230 Avenue of the Americas, New York, NY 10020 *Tel:* 212-698-7000 *Toll Free Tel:* 800-223-2348 (cust serv); 800-223-2336 (orders) *Toll Free Fax:* 800-943-9831 (orders) *Web Site:* www.simonandschuster.com, pg 212

Bender, Roger J, R James Bender Publishing, PO Box 23456, San Jose, CA 95153-3456 *Tel:* 408-225-5777 *Fax:* 408-225-4739 *Web Site:* www.bender-publishing.com, pg 33

Benedict, Holly, Quincannon Publishing Group, PO Box 8100, Glen Ridge, NJ 07028-8100 *Tel:* 973-380-9942 *E-mail:* editors@quincannongroup.com *Web Site:* www.quincannongroup.com, pg 192

Benezra, Mark, Original Publications, PO Box 236, Old Beth Page, NY 11804 *Tel:* 516-605-0547 *Toll Free Tel:* 888-622-8581 *Fax:* 516-605-0549 *E-mail:* originalpub@aol.com *Web Site:* www.occult1.com, pg 170

Benjamin, Matthew, Touchstone, 1230 Avenue of the Americas, New York, NY 10020, pg 233

Benjey, Thomas R, Tuxedo Press, 546 E Springville Rd, Carlisle, PA 17015 *Tel:* 717-258-9733 *Fax:* 717-243-0074 *E-mail:* info@tuxedo-press.com *Web Site:* tuxedo-press.com, pg 237

Benka, Jennifer, The Academy of American Poets Inc, 75 Maiden Lane, Suite 901, New York, NY 10038 *Tel:* 212-274-0343 *Fax:* 212-274-9427 *E-mail:* academy@poets.org *Web Site:* www.poets.org, pg 553

Benka, Jennifer, Raiziss/de Palchi Fellowship, 75 Maiden Lane, Suite 901, New York, NY 10038 *Tel:* 212-274-0343 *Fax:* 212-274-9427 *E-mail:* academy@poets.org *Web Site:* www.poets.org, pg 684

Benka, Jennifer, Wallace Stevens Award, 75 Maiden Lane, Suite 901, New York, NY 10038 *Tel:* 212-274-0343 *Fax:* 212-274-9427 *E-mail:* awards@poets.org *Web Site:* www.poets.org, pg 692

Benka, Jennifer, Walt Whitman Award, 75 Maiden Lane, Suite 901, New York, NY 10038 *Tel:* 212-274-0343 *Fax:* 212-274-9427 *E-mail:* academy@poets.org *Web Site:* www.poets.org, pg 697

Benne, Susan, Antiquarian Booksellers' Association of America (ABAA), 20 W 44 St, Suite 507, New York, NY 10036 *Tel:* 212-944-8291 *Fax:* 212-944-8293 *E-mail:* hq@abaa.org *Web Site:* www.abaa.org, pg 557

Benner, Deborah J, Goose River Press, 3400 Friendship Rd, Waldoboro, ME 04572-6337 *Tel:* 207-832-6665 *E-mail:* gooseriverpress@roadrunner.com *Web Site:* gooseriverpress.com, pg 94

Bennett, Barbara, Kensington Publishing Corp, 119 W 40 St, New York, NY 10018 *Tel:* 212-407-1500 *Toll Free Tel:* 800-221-2647 *Fax:* 212-935-0699 *Web Site:* www.kensingtonbooks.com, pg 125

Bennett, David, Transatlantic Agency, 2 Bloor St E, Suite 3500, Toronto, ON M4W 1A8, Canada *Tel:* 416-488-9214 *E-mail:* info@transatlanticagency.com *Web Site:* www.transatlanticagency.com, pg 539

Bennett, Elizabeth, Houghton Mifflin Harcourt Trade & Reference Division, 125 High St, Boston, MA 02110 *Tel:* 617-351-5000 *Toll Free Tel:* 800-225-3362 *Web Site:* www.hmhco.com, pg 111

Bennett, Hannah, Women's National Book Association Award, PO Box 237, FDR Sta, New York, NY 10150-0231 *Tel:* 212-208-4629 (headquarters) *Toll Free Tel:* 866-610-9622 *Fax:* 212-208-4629 *Web Site:* www.wnba-books.org; www.NationalReadingGroupMonth.org, pg 699

Bennett, Jed, Penguin Young Readers Group, 345 Hudson St, New York, NY 10014 *Tel:* 212-366-2000; 212-414-3553 *Fax:* 212-414-3340 *Web Site:* www.penguin.com/children, pg 179

Bennett, John M, Luna Bisonte Prods, 137 Leland Ave, Columbus, OH 43214 *Tel:* 614-846-4126 *Web Site:* www.johnmbennett.net; www.lulu.com/spotlight/lunabisonteprods, pg 139

Bennett, Katherine, Perseus Books, 250 W 57 St, 15th fl, New York, NY 10107 *Tel:* 212-340-8100 *Toll Free Tel:* 800-343-4499 (cust serv) *Fax:* 212-340-8105 *Web Site:* www.perseusbooks.com, pg 181

Bennett, Lori, Nelson Literary Agency LLC, 1732 Wazee St, Suite 207, Denver, CO 80202-1284 *Tel:* 303-292-2805 *E-mail:* query@nelsonagency.com *Web Site:* www.nelsonagency.com, pg 530

Bennett, Lynn, Transatlantic Agency, 2 Bloor St E, Suite 3500, Toronto, ON M4W 1A8, Canada *Tel:* 416-488-9214 *E-mail:* info@transatlanticagency.com *Web Site:* www.transatlanticagency.com, pg 539

Bennett, Meagan, Phaidon, 65 Bleecker St, 8th fl, New York, NY 10012 *Tel:* 212-652-5400 *Toll Free Tel:* 800-759-0190 (cust serv) *Fax:* 212-652-5410 *Toll Free Fax:* 800-286-9471 (cust serv) *E-mail:* ussales@phaidon.com *Web Site:* www.phaidon.com, pg 182

Bennett, Tina, WME, 11 Madison Ave, 18th fl, New York, NY 10010 *Tel:* 212-586-5100 *Web Site:* www.wmeentertainment.com, pg 542

Bennett, Zelina, Workman Publishing Co Inc, 225 Varick St, 9th fl, New York, NY 10014-4381 *Tel:* 212-254-5900 *Toll Free Tel:* 800-722-7202 *Fax:* 212-254-8098 *E-mail:* info@workman.com *Web Site:* www.workman.com, pg 259

Bennie, Dale, University of Oklahoma Press, 2800 Venture Dr, Norman, OK 73069-8216 *Tel:* 405-325-2000 *Toll Free Tel:* 800-627-7377 (orders) *Fax:* 405-364-5798 (orders) *Toll Free Fax:* 800-735-0476 (orders) *E-mail:* presscs@ou.edu *Web Site:* www.oupress.com, pg 244

Bennion, Greta, Northwestern University Press, 629 Noyes St, Evanston, IL 60208-4210 *Tel:* 847-491-2046 *Toll Free Tel:* 800-621-2736 (orders only) *Fax:* 847-491-8150 *E-mail:* nupress@northwestern.edu *Web Site:* www.nupress.northwestern.edu, pg 164

Benoit, Michael J, Benoit & Associates, 279 S Schuyler Ave, Kankakee, IL 60901 *Tel:* 815-932-2582 *Fax:* 815-932-2582 *Web Site:* www.benoit-associates.com, pg 543

Bensaid, Barbara, US Games Systems Inc, 179 Ludlow St, Stamford, CT 06902 *Tel:* 203-353-8400 *Toll Free Tel:* 800-54-GAMES (544-2637) *Fax:* 203-353-8431 *E-mail:* info@usgamesinc.com *Web Site:* www.usgamesinc.com, pg 249

Bensky, Dan, Eastland Press, 1240 Activity Dr, Suite D, Vista, CA 92081 *Tel:* 206-217-0204 (edit); 760-598-9695 (orders) *Toll Free Tel:* 800-453-3278 (orders) *Fax:* 760-598-6083 (orders) *Toll Free Fax:* 800-241-3329 (orders) *E-mail:* info@eastlandpress.com; orders@eastlandpress.com (credit card orders only) *Web Site:* www.eastlandpress.com, pg 74

Benson, Ms Frances, Cornell University Press, Sage House, 512 E State St, Ithaca, NY 14850 *Tel:* 607-277-2338 *Fax:* 607-277-2374 *E-mail:* cupressinfo@cornell.edu; cupress-sales@cornell.edu *Web Site:* www.cornellpress.cornell.edu, pg 61

Benson, Ingrid, Integra Software Services Inc, 1110 Jorie Blvd, Suite 200, Oak Brook, IL 60523 *Tel:* 630-586-2579 *Fax:* 630-586-2599 *E-mail:* marketing@integra.co.in *Web Site:* www.integra.co.in, pg 496

Benson, John W, BK Nelson Inc Lecture Bureau, 6726 Moonriver St, Mira Loma, CA 91752-3428 *Tel:* 760-902-1868 *Fax:* 760-778-6242 *E-mail:* bknelson4@cs.com, pg 547

Benson, John W, BK Nelson Inc Literary Agency, 6726 Moonriver St, Mira Loma, CA 91752-3428 *Tel:* 760-902-1868 *Fax:* 760-778-6242 *E-mail:* bknelson4@cs.com, pg 530

Benson, Stephanae, The Center for Learning, 10200 Jefferson Blvd, Culver City, CA 90232 *Tel:* 310-839-2436 *Toll Free Tel:* 800-421-4246 *Fax:* 310-839-2249 *Toll Free Fax:* 800-944-5432 *E-mail:* customerservice@centerforlearning.org *Web Site:* www.centerforlearning.org, pg 51

Bentley, D M R, Canadian Poetry Press, Dept of English, University of Western Ontario, London, ON N6A 3K7, Canada *Tel:* 519-661-2111 (ext 85813); 519-661-2111 (ext 85834) *Fax:* 519-661-3776 *E-mail:* canadianpoetry@uwo.ca *Web Site:* canadianpoetry.org, pg 449

Bentley, Michael, Bentley Publishers, 1734 Massachusetts Ave, Cambridge, MA 02138-1804 *Tel:* 617-547-4170 *Toll Free Tel:* 800-423-4595 *Fax:* 617-876-9235 *E-mail:* sales@bentleypublishers.com *Web Site:* www.bentleypublishers.com, pg 33

Bentley, Susan, Canadian Poetry Press, Dept of English, University of Western Ontario, London, ON N6A 3K7, Canada *Tel:* 519-661-2111 (ext 85813); 519-661-2111 (ext 85834) *Fax:* 519-661-3776 *E-mail:* canadianpoetry@uwo.ca *Web Site:* canadianpoetry.org, pg 449

Benton, Lori, Scholastic Trade Division, 557 Broadway, New York, NY 10012 *Tel:* 212-343-6100; 212-343-4685 (export sales) *Fax:* 212-343-4714 (export sales) *Web Site:* www.scholastic.com, pg 208

Benton, Thomas J, Data & Marketing Association (DMA), 1333 Broadway, Suite 301, New York, NY 10018 *Tel:* 212-768-7277 *Fax:* 212-302-6714 *E-mail:* memberservices@the-dma.org *Web Site:* thedma.org, pg 67, 564

Benvenuto, Kerri, Random House Children's Books, 1745 Broadway, 10th fl, New York, NY 10019 *Tel:* 212-782-9000 *Web Site:* www.randomhousekids.com, pg 194

Berbary, Don, Practising Law Institute, 1177 Avenue of the Americas, New York, NY 10036 *Tel:* 212-824-5700 *Toll Free Tel:* 800-260-4PLI (260-4754, cust serv) *Fax:* 212-265-4742 (intl) *Toll Free Fax:* 800-321-0093 (local) *E-mail:* info@pli.edu (cust serv) *Web Site:* www.pli.edu, pg 186

Bercholz, Ivan, Shambhala Publications Inc, 4720 Walnut St, Boulder, CO 80301 *Tel:* 303-222-9598 *Toll Free Tel:* 866-424-0030 (off); 888-424-2329 (cust serv) *Fax:* 303-200-9406 *E-mail:* customercare@shambhala.com *Web Site:* www.shambhala.com, pg 211

Bercholz, Samuel, Shambhala Publications Inc, 4720 Walnut St, Boulder, CO 80301 *Tel:* 303-222-9598 *Toll Free Tel:* 866-424-0030 (off); 888-424-2329 (cust serv) *Fax:* 303-200-9406 *E-mail:* customercare@shambhala.com *Web Site:* www.shambhala.com, pg 211

Bercholz, Sara, Shambhala Publications Inc, 4720 Walnut St, Boulder, CO 80301 *Tel:* 303-222-9598 *Toll Free Tel:* 866-424-0030 (off); 888-424-2329 (cust serv) *Fax:* 303-200-9406 *E-mail:* customercare@shambhala.com *Web Site:* www.shambhala.com, pg 211

Berchowitz, Gillian, Ohio University Press, 31 S Court St, Suite 143, Athens, OH 45701-2979 *Fax:* 740-593-4536 *Web Site:* www.ohioswallow.com, pg 167

Berchowitz, Gillian, Hollis Summers Poetry Prize, 31 S Court St, Suite 143, Athens, OH 45701-2979 *Web Site:* www.ohioswallow.com/poetry_prize, pg 693

Berchowitz, Gillian, Swallow Press, 31 S Court St, Suite 143, Athens, OH 45701 *Tel:* 740-593-1155 *Toll Free Tel:* 800-621-2736 *Fax:* 740-593-4536 *Web Site:* www.ohioswallow.com, pg 225

Beresford, Lea, Bloomsbury Publishing Inc, 1385 Broadway, 5th fl, New York, NY 10018 *Tel:* 212-419-5300 *E-mail:* marketingusa@bloomsbury.com; adultpublicityusa@bloomsbury.com; askacademic@bloomsbury.com *Web Site:* www.bloomsbury.com, pg 38

Berg, Betsy, ICM Lecture Division, 730 Fifth Ave, New York, NY 10019 *Tel:* 212-556-5600 *Fax:* 212-556-5665 *Web Site:* www.icmtalent.com, pg 547

Berg, Jennifer, PAGE International Screenwriting Awards, 7190 Sunset Blvd, Suite 610, Hollywood, CA 90046 *E-mail:* info@pageawards.com *Web Site:* www.pageawards.com, pg 676

Berge, Pablo Agrest, STOCKCERO Inc, 3785 NW 82 Ave, Suite 302, Doral, FL 33166 *Tel:* 305-722-7628 *Fax:* 305-477-5794 *E-mail:* academicservices@stockcero.com; sales@stockcero.com *Web Site:* www.stockcero.com, pg 223

Bergen, Glenn, University of Manitoba Press, University of Manitoba, 301 St Johns College, 92 Dysart Rd, Winnipeg, MB R3T 2M5, Canada *Tel:* 204-474-9495 *Fax:* 204-474-7566 *E-mail:* uofmpress@umanitoba.ca *Web Site:* uofmpress.ca, pg 474

Berger, Andrew, Quality Medical Publishing Inc, 2248 Welsch Industrial Ct, St Louis, MO 63146-4222 *Tel:* 314-878-7808 *Toll Free Tel:* 800-348-7808 *Fax:* 314-878-9937 *E-mail:* qmp@qmp.com; customerservice@qmp.com *Web Site:* www.qmp.com, pg 192

Berger, Ellie, Scholastic Inc, 557 Broadway, New York, NY 10012 *Tel:* 212-343-6100 *Toll Free Tel:* 800-SCHOLASTIC (724-6527) *Web Site:* www.scholastic.com, pg 208

Berger, Ellie, Scholastic Trade Division, 557 Broadway, New York, NY 10012 *Tel:* 212-343-6100; 212-343-4685 (export sales) *Fax:* 212-343-4714 (export sales) *Web Site:* www.scholastic.com, pg 208

Berger, Erin, Penguin Young Readers Group, 345 Hudson St, New York, NY 10014 *Tel:* 212-366-2000; 212-414-3553 *Fax:* 212-414-3340 *Web Site:* www.penguin.com/children, pg 179

Berger, Dr John, Cambridge University Press, 1 Liberty Plaza, 20th fl, New York, NY 10006 *Tel:* 212-924-3900; 212-337-5000 *Fax:* 212-691-3239 *E-mail:* newyork@cambridge.org *Web Site:* www.cambridge.org/us, pg 46

Berger, Karen, Dark Horse Comics, 10956 SE Main St, Milwaukie, OR 97222 *Tel:* 503-652-8815 *Fax:* 503-654-9440 *E-mail:* dhcomics@darkhorse.com *Web Site:* www.darkhorse.com, pg 67

Berger, Mel, WME, 11 Madison Ave, 18th fl, New York, NY 10010 *Tel:* 212-586-5100 *Web Site:* www.wmeentertainment.com, pg 542

Bergeron, Amanda, Berkley Publishing Group, 375 Hudson St, New York, NY 10014 *Tel:* 212-366-2000 *Fax:* 212-366-2385 *Web Site:* www.penguin.com, pg 33

Bergeron, Catherine, The Johns Hopkins University Press, 2715 N Charles St, Baltimore, MD 21218-4363 *Tel:* 410-516-6900; 410-516-6987 (journal orders outside US & CN) *Toll Free Tel:* 800-537-5487 (book orders & cust serv); 800-548-1784 (journal orders) *Fax:* 410-516-6968; 410-516-3866 (journal orders) *E-mail:* hfscustserv@press.jhu.edu (cust serv); jrnlcirc@press.jhu.edu (journal orders) *Web Site:* www.press.jhu.edu; muse.jhu.edu, pg 122

Bergfeld, Ellen, American Society of Agronomy, 5585 Guilford Rd, Madison, WI 53711-5801 *Tel:* 608-273-8080 *Fax:* 608-273-2021 *E-mail:* headquarters@sciencesocieties.org *Web Site:* www.agronomy.org, pg 15

Bergfeld, Ellen, Soil Science Society of America, 5585 Guilford Rd, Madison, WI 53711-5801 *Tel:* 608-273-8080 *Web Site:* www.soils.org, pg 217

Bergh, Lily, Canadian Scholars' Press Inc, 425 Adelaide St W, Suite 200, Toronto, ON M5V 3C1, Canada *Tel:* 416-929-2774 *Toll Free Tel:* 800-463-1998 *Fax:* 416-929-1926 *E-mail:* info@cspi.org; info@canadianscholars.ca; editorial@canadianscholars.ca; orders@canadianscholars.ca *Web Site:* www.canadianscholars.ca; www.womenspress.ca, pg 449

Berghahn, Dr Marion, Berghahn Books, 20 Jay St, Suite 512, Brooklyn, NY 11201 *Tel:* 212-233-6004 *Fax:* 212-233-6007 *E-mail:* info@berghahnbooks.com; salesus@berghahnbooks.com; editorial@journals.berghahnbooks.com *Web Site:* www.berghahnbooks.com, pg 33

Berghahn, Vivian, Berghahn Books, 20 Jay St, Suite 512, Brooklyn, NY 11201 *Tel:* 212-233-6004 *Fax:* 212-233-6007 *E-mail:* info@berghahnbooks.com; salesus@berghahnbooks.com; editorial@journals.berghahnbooks.com *Web Site:* www.berghahnbooks.com, pg 33

Bergkamp, Will, Augsburg Fortress Publishers, Publishing House of the Evangelical Lutheran Church in America, 510 Marquette Ave S, Minneapolis, MN 55402 *Tel:* 612-330-3300 *Toll Free Tel:* 800-426-0115 (ext 639, subns); 800-328-4648 (orders) *Fax:* 612-330-3455 *E-mail:* info@augsburgfortress.org; copyright@augsburgfortress.org (reprint permission requests); customercare@augsburgfortress.org *Web Site:* www.augsburgfortress.org, pg 26

Bergonzi, Megan, Seedling Publications Inc, 520 E Bainbridge St, Elizabethtown, PA 17022 *Toll Free Tel:* 800-233-0759 *Toll Free Fax:* 888-834-1303 *E-mail:* info@continentalpress.com *Web Site:* www.continentalpress.com, pg 210

Bergsten, C Fred, Peterson Institute for International Economics (PIIE), 1750 Massachusetts Ave NW, Washington, DC 20036-1903 *Tel:* 202-328-9000 *Fax:* 202-328-5432; 202-659-3225 *E-mail:* orders@petersoninstitute.org; media@piie.com *Web Site:* www.petersoninstitute.org, pg 181

Bergstrom, Jennifer, Gallery Books, 1230 Avenue of the Americas, New York, NY 10020 *Toll Free Tel:* 800-456-6798 *Fax:* 212-698-7284 *E-mail:* consumer.customerservice@simonandschuster.com *Web Site:* www.simonsays.com, pg 90

Bergstrom, Jennifer, Simon & Schuster, Inc, 1230 Avenue of the Americas, New York, NY 10020 *Tel:* 212-698-7000 *Fax:* 212-698-7007 *E-mail:* firstname.lastname@simonandschuster.com *Web Site:* www.simonandschuster.com, pg 213

Berinstein, Peter, A Richard Barber/Peter Berinstein & Associates, 60 E Eighth St, Suite 21-N, New York, NY 10003 *Tel:* 212-737-7266 *Fax:* 860-927-3942 *E-mail:* barberrich@aol.com, pg 507

Berkery, Peter, Association of American University Presses (AAUP), 1412 Broadway, Suite 2135, New York, NY 10018 *Tel:* 212-989-1010 *Fax:* 212-989-0275 *E-mail:* info@aaupnet.org *Web Site:* www.aaupnet.org, pg 558

Berkey, Jane Rotrosen, Jane Rotrosen Agency LLC, 85 Broad St, 28th fl, New York, NY 10004 *Tel:* 212-593-4330 *Fax:* 212-935-6985 *Web Site:* janerotrosen.com, pg 533

Berki, Attila, Books for Everybody, 111 Queen St E, Suite 320, Toronto, ON M5C 1S2, Canada *Tel:* 416-364-3333 *Toll Free Tel:* 888-360-6658 *Fax:* 416-595-5415, pg 561

Berkman, Hilary, Candlewick Press, 99 Dover St, Somerville, MA 02144-2825 *Tel:* 617-661-3330 *Fax:* 617-661-0565 *E-mail:* bigbear@candlewick.com; salesinfo@candlewick.com *Web Site:* www.candlewick.com, pg 46

Berkower, Amy, Writers House, 21 W 26 St, New York, NY 10010 *Tel:* 212-685-2400 *Fax:* 212-685-1781 *Web Site:* www.writershouse.com, pg 542

Berkowitz, Daniel, Writers House, 21 W 26 St, New York, NY 10010 *Tel:* 212-685-2400 *Fax:* 212-685-1781 *Web Site:* www.writershouse.com, pg 542

Berman, Sam, The Rough Notes Co Inc, 11690 Technology Dr, Carmel, IN 46032-5600 *Tel:* 317-582-1600 *Toll Free Tel:* 800-428-4384 (cust serv) *Fax:* 317-816-1000 *Toll Free Fax:* 800-321-1909 *E-mail:* rnc@roughnotes.com *Web Site:* www.roughnotes.com, pg 201

Bernard, Alec, Puddingstone Literary, Authors' Agents, 11 Mabro Dr, Denville, NJ 07834-9607 *Tel:* 973-366-3622, pg 532

Bernard, Andre, John Simon Guggenheim Memorial Foundation, 90 Park Ave, New York, NY 10016 *Tel:* 212-687-4470 *Fax:* 212-697-3248 *E-mail:* fellowships@gf.org *Web Site:* www.gf.org, pg 583

Bernard, Kimberly, Paulist Press, 997 Macarthur Blvd, Mahwah, NJ 07430-9990 *Tel:* 201-825-7300 *Toll Free Tel:* 800-218-1903 *Fax:* 201-825-6921 *Toll Free Fax:* 800-836-3161 *E-mail:* info@paulistpress.com; publicity@paulistpress.com *Web Site:* www.paulistpress.com, pg 175

Berner, Mary, Publishers Information Bureau (PIB)®, 757 Third Ave, 11th fl, New York, NY 10017 *Tel:* 212-872-3745; 212-872-3700 (MPA) *E-mail:* infocenter@magazine.org *Web Site:* www.magazine.org, pg 577

Berner-Tobin, Julia, The Feminist Press at The City University of New York, 365 Fifth Ave, Suite 5406, New York, NY 10016 *Tel:* 212-817-7915 *Fax:* 212-817-1593 *E-mail:* info@feministpress.org *Web Site:* www.feministpress.org, pg 83

Bernfeld, Linda Rodriguez, SCBWI-FL Florida Regional Conference, 125 E Merritt Island Causeway, Suite 209, Merritt Island, FL 32952 *Tel:* 321-338-7208 *E-mail:* florida@scbwi.org *Web Site:* florida.scbwi.org, pg 614

Bernfeld, Linda Rodriguez, SCBWI-FL Mid-Year Workshops, 125 E Merritt Island Causeway, Suite 209, Merritt Island, FL 32952 *Tel:* 321-338-7208 *E-mail:* florida@scbwi.org *Web Site:* florida.scbwi.org, pg 614

Bernier, Jean, Les Editions du Boreal, 4447, rue St-Denis, Montreal, QC H2J 2L2, Canada *Tel:* 514-287-7401 *Fax:* 514-287-7664 *E-mail:* boreal@editionsboreal.qc.ca *Web Site:* www.editionsboreal.qc.ca, pg 453

Bernstein, Barbara, Hampton Press Inc, 307 Seventh Ave, Suite 506, New York, NY 10001 *Tel:* 646-638-3800 *Toll Free Tel:* 800-894-8955 *Fax:* 646-638-3802 *E-mail:* hamptonpr1@aol.com *Web Site:* www.hamptonpress.com, pg 100

Bernstein, Laurie, Side by Side Literary Productions Inc, 145 E 35 St, Suite 7FE, New York, NY 10016 *Tel:* 212-685-6831 *Web Site:* sidebysidelit.com, pg 536

Bernstein, Meredith, Meredith Bernstein Literary Agency Inc, 2095 Broadway, Suite 505, New York, NY 10023 *Tel:* 212-799-1007 *Fax:* 212-799-1145 *E-mail:* MGoodBern@aol.com *Web Site:* www.meredithbernsteinliteraryagency.com, pg 507

Bernstein, Rachel, Random House Publishing Group, 1745 Broadway, New York, NY 10019 *Toll Free Tel:* 800-200-3552 *Web Site:* atrandom.com, pg 195

Berrios, Frank, Random House Children's Books, 1745 Broadway, 10th fl, New York, NY 10019 *Tel:* 212-782-9000 *Web Site:* www.randomhousekids.com, pg 194

Berry, Frances, Frank L & Harriet C Owsley Award, University of Georgia, Dept of History, Athens, GA 30602-1602 *Tel:* 706-542-8848 *Fax:* 706-542-2455 *Web Site:* thesha.org, pg 676

Berry, Frances, Francis B Simkins Award, University of Georgia, Dept of History, Athens, GA 30602-1602 *Tel:* 706-542-8848 *Fax:* 706-542-2455 *Web Site:* thesha.org, pg 689

Berry, Frances, Charles S Sydnor Award, University of Georgia, Dept of History, Athens, GA 30602-1602 *Tel:* 706-542-8848 *Fax:* 706-542-2455 *Web Site:* thesha.org, pg 693

Bershtel, Sara, Henry Holt and Company, LLC, 175 Fifth Ave, New York, NY 10010 *Tel:* 646-307-5151 *Toll Free Tel:* 888-330-8477 (orders) *Fax:* 646-307-5285 *E-mail:* firstname.lastname@hholt.com *Web Site:* www.henryholt.com, pg 109

Bertin, Joan E, National Coalition Against Censorship (NCAC), 19 Fulton St, Suite 407, New York, NY 10038 *Tel:* 212-807-6222 *Fax:* 212-807-6245 *E-mail:* ncac@ncac.org *Web Site:* www.ncac.org, pg 571

Bertoli, Monique, Les Editions du Vermillon, 305, rue St-Patrick, Ottawa, ON K1N 5K4, Canada *Tel:* 613-241-4032 *Fax:* 613-241-3109 *E-mail:* leseditionsduvermillon@rogers.com *Web Site:* www.leseditionsduvermillon.ca, pg 454

Bertolini, Diana, George Freedley Memorial Award, c/o The New York Public Library for the Performing Arts, 111 Amsterdam Ave, New York, NY 10023 *E-mail:* TLABookAwards@gmail.com; TheatreLibraryAssociation@gmail.com *Web Site:* www.tla-online.org/awards/bookawards, pg 647

Bertolini, Diana, Richard Wall Memorial Award, c/o The New York Public Library for the Performing Arts, 111 Amsterdam Ave, New York, NY 10023 *E-mail:* TheatreLibraryAssociation@gmail.com; TLABookAwards@gmail.com *Web Site:* www.tla-online.org/awards/bookawards, pg 696

Bertrand, Al, Princeton University Press, 41 William St, Princeton, NJ 08540-5237 *Tel:* 609-258-4900 *Fax:* 609-258-6305 *Web Site:* press.princeton.edu, pg 188

Bertrand, Daniel, Les Editions JCL, 688, rue St-Joseph, Marieville, QC J3M 1H1, Canada *Tel:* 450-460-4438 *E-mail:* info@jcl.qc.ca *Web Site:* www.jcl.qc.ca, pg 454

Berube, Patty, Wood Lake Publishing Inc, 485 Beaver Lake Rd, Kelowna, BC V4V 1S5, Canada *Tel:* 250-766-2778 *Toll Free Tel:* 800-663-2775 (orders & cust serv) *Fax:* 250-766-2736 *Toll Free Fax:* 888-841-9991 (orders & cust serv) *E-mail:* info@woodlake.com; customerservice@woodlake.com *Web Site:* www.woodlakebooks.com, pg 476

Bess, Benjamin E, Bess Press, 3565 Harding Ave, Honolulu, HI 96816 *Tel:* 808-734-7159 *Fax:* 808-732-3627 *E-mail:* customerservice@besspress.com *Web Site:* www.besspress.com, pg 34

Besser, Jennifer, GP Putnam's Sons (Children's), 345 Hudson St, New York, NY 10014 *Tel:* 212-366-2000 *Fax:* 212-414-3393 *Web Site:* www.penguin.com/publishers/gpputnamssonsbooksforyoungread, pg 192

Bestall, May, Wolf Pirate Project Inc, 337 Lost Lake Dr, Divide, CO 80814 *Tel:* 305-333-3186 *E-mail:* contact@wolfpiratebooks.com; workshop@wolfpiratebooks.com *Web Site:* www.wolf-pirate.com, pg 502

Bestler, Emily, Atria Books, 1230 Avenue of the Americas, New York, NY 10020 *Tel:* 212-698-7000 *Fax:* 212-698-7007 *Web Site:* www.simonandschuster.com, pg 25

Betancourt, John, Wildside Press LLC, 9710 Traville Gateway Dr, Suite 234, Rockville, MD 20850 *Tel:* 301-762-1305 *Fax:* 301-762-1306 *E-mail:* wildside@wildsidepress.com; wildsidepress@yahoo.com *Web Site:* wildsidepress.com, pg 256

Betancourt, Lorraine, Oxford University Press USA, 198 Madison Ave, New York, NY 10016 *Tel:* 212-726-6000 *Toll Free Tel:* 800-451-7556 (orders); 800-445-9714 (cust serv) *Fax:* 919-677-1303 *E-mail:* custserv.us@oup.com *Web Site:* www.oup.com/us, pg 171

Bethel, Courtney, MacDowell Fellowships, 100 High St, Peterborough, NH 03458 *Tel:* 603-924-3886 *Fax:* 603-924-9142 *E-mail:* info@macdowellcolony.org; admissions@macdowellcolony.org *Web Site:* www.macdowellcolony.org, pg 664

Betita, Isabella, Touchstone, 1230 Avenue of the Americas, New York, NY 10020, pg 233

Bettles, Shannon, Anne & Philip Yandle Best Article Award, PO Box 5254, Sta B, Victoria, BC V8R 6N4, Canada *E-mail:* info@bchistory.ca; recognition@bchistory.ca *Web Site:* www.bchistory.ca, pg 701

Betz, James L, George T Bisel Co Inc, 710 S Washington Sq, Philadelphia, PA 19106-3519 *Tel:* 215-922-5760 *Toll Free Tel:* 800-247-3526 *Fax:* 215-922-2235 *E-mail:* gbisel@bisel.com *Web Site:* www.bisel.com, pg 35

Betz, Paul, The University of North Carolina Press, 116 S Boundary St, Chapel Hill, NC 27514-3808 *Tel:* 919-966-3561 *Fax:* 919-966-3829 *E-mail:* uncpress@unc.edu *Web Site:* www.uncpress.unc.edu, pg 243

Beuhler, Beth, Rodale Inc, 400 S Tenth St, Emmaus, PA 18049 *Tel:* 610-967-5171 *Toll Free Tel:* 866-387-0509 *E-mail:* bookmarketing@rodale.com; bookpublicity@rodale.com *Web Site:* www.rodale.com, pg 200

Beullac, Paul, B & B Publishing, 4823 Sherbrooke St W, Off 275, Westmount, QC H3Z 1G7, Canada *Tel:* 514-932-9466 *Fax:* 514-932-5929 *E-mail:* editions@ebbp.ca, pg 446

Beusse, Thomas, Writer's Digest, 10151 Carver Rd, Suite 200, Blue Ash, OH 45242 *Tel:* 513-531-2690 *Toll Free Tel:* 800-289-0963 *E-mail:* writersdigest@fwmedia.com (edit) *Web Site:* www.writersdigest.com, pg 260

Beusse, Tom, F+W Media Inc, 10151 Carver Rd, Suite 200, Blue Ash, OH 45242 *Tel:* 513-531-2690 *Toll Free Tel:* 800-289-0963 (trade accts); 800-258-0929 (cust serv) *E-mail:* contact_us@fwmedia.com *Web Site:* www.fwcommunity.com, pg 82

Bevens, Robert, University of Texas Press, 3001 Lake Austin Blvd, 2.200, Austin, TX 78703 *Tel:* 512-471-7233 *Fax:* 512-232-7178 *E-mail:* utpress@uts.cc.utexas.edu; info@utpress.utexas.edu *Web Site:* www.utexaspress.com, pg 230

Bevington, Stan, Coach House Books, 80 bpNichol Lane, Toronto, ON M5S 3J4, Canada *Tel:* 416-979-2217 *Toll Free Tel:* 800-367-6360 (outside Toronto) *Fax:* 416-977-1158 *E-mail:* mail@chbooks.com *Web Site:* www.chbooks.com, pg 450

Bewley, Elizabeth, Sterling Lord Literistic Inc, 115 Broadway, Suite 1602, New York, NY 10006 *Tel:* 212-780-6050 *Fax:* 212-780-6095 *E-mail:* info@sll.com *Web Site:* www.sll.com, pg 537

Bhatnagar, Supriya, Association of Writers & Writing Programs (AWP), George Mason University, 4400 University Dr, MSN 1E3, Fairfax, VA 22030 *Tel:* 703-993-4301 *Fax:* 703-993-4302 *E-mail:* awp@awpwriter.org *Web Site:* www.awpwriter.org, pg 559

Bhatnagar, Supriya, AWP Award Series, George Mason University, 4400 University Dr, MSN 1E3, Fairfax, VA 22030 *Tel:* 703-993-4301 *Fax:* 703-993-4302 *E-mail:* awp@awpwriter.org *Web Site:* www.awpwriter.org, pg 629

Bhattacharjee, Mala, Kensington Publishing Corp, 119 W 40 St, New York, NY 10018 *Tel:* 212-407-1500 *Toll Free Tel:* 800-221-2647 *Fax:* 212-935-0699 *Web Site:* www.kensingtonbooks.com, pg 125

Bial, Daniel, Daniel Bial & Associates, 41 W 83 St, Suite 5-C, New York, NY 10024 *Tel:* 212-721-1786 *E-mail:* dbialagency@msn.com *Web Site:* www.danielbialagency.com, pg 489

Bialer, Matt, Sanford J Greenburger Associates Inc, 55 Fifth Ave, New York, NY 10003 *Tel:* 212-206-5600 *Fax:* 212-463-8718 *Web Site:* greenburger.com; www.sjga.com, pg 520

Bialosky, Jill, W W Norton & Company Inc, 500 Fifth Ave, New York, NY 10110-0017 *Tel:* 212-354-5500 *Toll Free Tel:* 800-233-4830 (orders & cust serv) *Fax:* 212-869-0856 *Toll Free Fax:* 800-458-6515 *E-mail:* orders@wwnorton.com *Web Site:* books.wwnorton.com, pg 164

Bianchini, Bob, Random House Children's Books, 1745 Broadway, 10th fl, New York, NY 10019 *Tel:* 212-782-9000 *Web Site:* www.randomhousekids.com, pg 194

Bianchini, Brian, International Press of Boston Inc, 387 Somerville Ave, Somerville, MA 02143 *Tel:* 617-623-3016 *Fax:* 617-623-3101 *E-mail:* ipb-info@intlpress.com; ipb-orders@intlpress.com *Web Site:* www.intlpress.com, pg 120

Bianchini, Lori, National Council of Teachers of English (NCTE), 1111 W Kenyon Rd, Urbana, IL 61801-1096 *Tel:* 217-328-3870 *Toll Free Tel:* 877-369-6283 (cust serv) *Fax:* 217-328-9645 *E-mail:* public_info@ncte.org *Web Site:* www.ncte.org, pg 571

Bicknell, Liz, Candlewick Press, 99 Dover St, Somerville, MA 02144-2825 *Tel:* 617-661-3330 *Fax:* 617-661-0565 *E-mail:* bigbear@candlewick.com; salesinfo@candlewick.com *Web Site:* www.candlewick.com, pg 46

Biddinger, Mary, Akron Poetry Prize, 120 E Mill St, Suite 415, Akron, OH 44308 *Tel:* 330-972-6960 *Fax:* 330-972-8364 *E-mail:* uapress@uakron.edu *Web Site:* www.uakron.edu/uapress/akron-poetry-prize, pg 626

Bider, Rich, Printing Association of Florida Inc (PAF), 6250 Hazeltine National Dr, Suite 114, Orlando, FL 32822 *Tel:* 407-240-8009 *Toll Free Tel:* 800-331-0461 *Fax:* 407-240-8333 *Web Site:* www.flprint.org, pg 576

Biehl, Michael, Write for Success Editing Services, PO Box 292153, Los Angeles, CA 90029-8653 *Tel:* 323-356-8833 *E-mail:* writeforsuccess@yahoo.com *Web Site:* www.write-for-success.com, pg 503

Bieker, Lauren, FinePrint Literary Management, 207 W 106 St, Suite 1D, New York, NY 10025 *Tel:* 212-279-6214 *E-mail:* assist@fineprint.com *Web Site:* www.fineprintlit.com, pg 516

Bieker, Mike, The University of Arkansas Press, McIlroy House, 105 N McIlroy Ave, Fayetteville, AR 72701 *Tel:* 479-575-3246 *Toll Free Tel:* 800-626-0090 *Fax:* 479-575-6044 *E-mail:* info@uapress.com *Web Site:* www.uapress.com, pg 240

Bielstein, Susan, University of Chicago Press, 1427 E 60 St, Chicago, IL 60637-2954 *Tel:* 773-702-7700; 773-702-7600 *Toll Free Tel:* 800-621-2736 (orders) *Fax:* 773-702-9756; 773-660-2235 (orders); 773-702-2708 *E-mail:* custserv@press.uchicago.edu; marketing@press.uchicago.edu *Web Site:* www.press.uchicago.edu, pg 241

Bierling, Sara, Zondervan, 3900 Sparks Dr, Grand Rapids, MI 49546 *Tel:* 616-698-6900 *Toll Free Tel:* 800-226-1122; 800-727-1309 (retail orders) *Fax:* 616-698-3350 *Toll Free Fax:* 800-698-3256 (retail orders) *E-mail:* zinfo@zondervan.com *Web Site:* www.zondervan.com, pg 263

Biesel, David, Saint Johann Press, 315 Schraalenburgh Rd, Haworth, NJ 07641 *Tel:* 201-387-1529 *Fax:* 201-501-0698 *Web Site:* www.stjohannpress.com, pg 204

Biesel, Diane, Saint Johann Press, 315 Schraalenburgh Rd, Haworth, NJ 07641 *Tel:* 201-387-1529 *Fax:* 201-501-0698 *Web Site:* www.stjohannpress.com, pg 204

Bieze, Linda, Wm B Eerdmans Publishing Co, 2140 Oak Industrial Dr NE, Grand Rapids, MI 49505 *Tel:* 616-459-4591 *Toll Free Tel:* 800-253-7521 *Fax:* 616-459-6540 *E-mail:* customerservice@eerdmans.com; sales@eerdmans.com *Web Site:* www.eerdmans.com, pg 76

Bigelow, Christopher, Zarahemla Books, 869 E 2680 N, Provo, UT 84604 *Tel:* 801-368-7374 *Web Site:* www.zarahemlabooks.com, pg 262

Bijur, Vicky, Vicky Bijur Literary Agency, 27 W 20 St, Suite 1003, New York, NY 10011 *Tel:* 212-580-4108 *E-mail:* queries@vickybijuragency.com *Web Site:* www.vickybijuragency.com, pg 508

Bileak, Jerry, Minnesota Historical Society Press, 345 Kellogg Blvd W, St Paul, MN 55102-1906 *Tel:* 651-259-3205 *Toll Free Tel:* 800-621-2736 (warehouse) *Fax:* 651-297-1345 *Toll Free Fax:* 800-621-8476 (warehouse) *E-mail:* info-mnhspress@mnhs.org *Web Site:* www.mnhs.org/mnhspress, pg 151

Billings, Hyacinth, World Resources Institute, 10 "G" St NE, Suite 800, Washington, DC 20002 *Tel:* 202-729-7600 *Fax:* 202-729-7610 *Web Site:* www.wri.org, pg 259

Billingsley, Sarah, Chronicle Books LLC, 680 Second St, San Francisco, CA 94107 *Tel:* 415-537-4200 *Toll Free Tel:* 800-759-0190 (cust serv) *Fax:* 415-537-4460 *Toll Free Fax:* 800-858-7787 (orders); 800-286-9471 (cust serv) *E-mail:* frontdesk@chroniclebooks.com *Web Site:* www.chroniclebooks.com, pg 55

Binder, Pam, PNWA Literary Contest, 1420 NW Gilman Blvd, Suite 8, PMB 2717, Issaquah, WA 98027 *Tel:* 425-673-2665 *E-mail:* pnwa@pnwa.org *Web Site:* www.pnwa.org, pg 680

Binder, Pam, PNWA - a writer's resource, 1420 NW Gilman Blvd, Suite 8, PMB 2717, Issaquah, WA 98027 *Tel:* 425-673-2665 *Fax:* 425-961-0768 *E-mail:* pnwa@pnwa.org *Web Site:* www.pnwa.org, pg 575

Binder, Pam, PNWA Writers Conference, 1420 NW Gilman Blvd, Suite 8, PMB 2717, Issaquah, WA 98027 *Tel:* 425-673-2665 *E-mail:* pnwa@pnwa.org *Web Site:* www.pnwa.org, pg 614

Binford, Susan, Lyndon B Johnson School of Public Affairs, University of Texas at Austin, 2315 Red River St, Austin, TX 78712-1536 *Tel:* 512-471-3200 *Fax:* 512-471-4697 *E-mail:* lbjdeansoffice@austin.utexas.edu *Web Site:* www.utexas.edu/lbj, pg 139

Bingham, Chelsea, David R Godine Publisher Inc, 15 Court Sq, Suite 320, Boston, MA 02108-4715 *Tel:* 617-451-9600 *Fax:* 617-350-0250 *E-mail:* info@godine.com *Web Site:* www.godine.com, pg 93

Bingham, Tony, Association for Talent Development (ATD) Press, 1640 King St, Box 1443, Alexandria, VA 22313-1443 *Tel:* 703-683-8100 *Toll Free Tel:* 800-628-2783 *Fax:* 703-299-8723; 703-683-1523 (cust care) *E-mail:* customercare@td.org *Web Site:* www.astd.org; www.td.org, pg 24

Binney, Ann, Los Angeles Times Book Prizes, 202 W First St, Los Angeles, CA 90012 *Tel:* 213-237-5775 *Toll Free Tel:* 800-528-4637 (ext 75775) *Web Site:* www.latimesbookprizes.com, pg 663

Binns, Beth, Woodbine House, 6510 Bells Mill Rd, Bethesda, MD 20817 *Tel:* 301-897-3570 *Toll Free Tel:* 800-843-7323 *Fax:* 301-897-5838 *E-mail:* info@woodbinehouse.com *Web Site:* www.woodbinehouse.com, pg 258

Binyominson, Yerachmiel, Hachai Publishing, 527 Empire Blvd, Brooklyn, NY 11225 *Tel:* 718-633-0100 *Fax:* 718-633-0103 *E-mail:* info@hachai.com *Web Site:* www.hachai.com, pg 98

Birchfield, Holly, Perseus Books, 250 W 57 St, 15th fl, New York, NY 10107 *Tel:* 212-340-8100 *Toll Free Tel:* 800-343-4499 (cust serv) *Fax:* 212-340-8105 *Web Site:* www.perseusbooks.com, pg 180

Birckhead, Molly, HarperCollins General Books Group, 195 Broadway, New York, NY 10007 *Tel:* 212-207-7000 *Web Site:* www.harpercollins.com, pg 101

Birdsell, Mary, Finding My Way Books, 3512 SW Huntoon St, Topeka, KS 66604 *Tel:* 785-273-6239 *E-mail:* info@findingmywaybooks.com; findingmywaybooks@gmail.com *Web Site:* www.findingmywaybooks.net, pg 84

Birkhead, Shaina, Children's & Teen Choice Book Awards, 54 W 39 St, 14th fl, New York, NY 10018 *E-mail:* cbc.info@cbcbooks.org *Web Site:* everychildareader.net/choice, pg 637

Birkhead, Shaina, The Children's Book Council (CBC), 54 W 39 St, 14th fl, New York, NY 10018 *Tel:* 212-966-1990 *E-mail:* cbc.info@cbcbooks.org *Web Site:* www.cbcbooks.org, pg 563

Birkholz, Linda, Peradam Press, PO Box 6, North San Juan, CA 95960-0006 *Tel:* 530-277-9324 *Fax:* 530-559-0754 *E-mail:* peradam@earthlink.net, pg 180

Birnbaum, Agnes, Bleecker Street Associates Inc, 215 Thompson St, Suite 519, New York, NY 10012 *Tel:* 212-677-4492 *Fax:* 212-388-0001, pg 508

Biro, Martin, Kensington Publishing Corp, 119 W 40 St, New York, NY 10018 *Tel:* 212-407-1500 *Toll Free Tel:* 800-221-2647 *Fax:* 212-935-0699 *Web Site:* www.kensingtonbooks.com, pg 125

Birtch, Brigitte, Scholastic Canada Ltd, 604 King St W, Toronto, ON M5V 1E1, Canada *Tel:* 905-887-7323 *Toll Free Tel:* 800-268-3860 (CN) *Toll Free Fax:* 866-387-4944 *E-mail:* custserve@scholastic.ca *Web Site:* www.scholastic.ca, pg 469

Bisch, Florence, Groupe Sogides Inc, 955 rue Amherst, Montreal, QC H2L 3K4, Canada *Tel:* 514-523-1182 *Fax:* 514-597-0370 *Web Site:* www.sogides.com, pg 458

Bischel, Dr Margaret, Apollo Managed Care Inc, 1100 Town & Country Rd, Suite 1250, Orange, CA 92868 *Toll Free Tel:* 888-276-5563 *E-mail:* info@apollomanagedcare.com *Web Site:* www.apollomanagedcare.com, pg 18

Bishop, Amy Elizabeth, Dystel, Goderich & Bourret LLC, One Union Sq W, Suite 904, New York, NY 10003 *Tel:* 212-627-9100 *Fax:* 212-627-9313 *Web Site:* www.dystel.com, pg 515

Bishop, Sandra, Transatlantic Agency, 2 Bloor St E, Suite 3500, Toronto, ON M4W 1A8, Canada *Tel:* 416-488-9214 *E-mail:* info@transatlanticagency.com *Web Site:* www.transatlanticagency.com, pg 539

Bisk, Alison L, Bisk Education, 9417 Princess Palm Ave, Suite 400, Tampa, FL 33619 *Tel:* 813-621-6200 *Toll Free Tel:* 800-280-9718 (cust serv) *E-mail:* customerservice@bisk.com *Web Site:* www.bisk.com, pg 35

Bisk, Michael D, Bisk Education, 9417 Princess Palm Ave, Suite 400, Tampa, FL 33619 *Tel:* 813-621-6200 *Toll Free Tel:* 800-280-9718 (cust serv) *E-mail:* customerservice@bisk.com *Web Site:* www.bisk.com, pg 35

Bisk, Nathan M, Bisk Education, 9417 Princess Palm Ave, Suite 400, Tampa, FL 33619 *Tel:* 813-621-6200 *Toll Free Tel:* 800-280-9718 (cust serv) *E-mail:* customerservice@bisk.com *Web Site:* www.bisk.com, pg 35

Bissonnette, Melanie, Les Editions Alire, 120 cote du Passage, Levis, QC G6V 5S9, Canada *Tel:* 418-835-4441 *Fax:* 418-838-4443 *E-mail:* info@alire.com *Web Site:* www.alire.com, pg 452

Bivens, Collin, Concordia Publishing House, 3558 S Jefferson Ave, St Louis, MO 63118-3968 *Tel:* 314-268-1000; 314-268-1268 (bookshop) *Toll Free Tel:* 800-325-3040 (cust serv) *Toll Free Fax:* 800-490-9889 (cust serv) *E-mail:* order@cph.org *Web Site:* www.cph.org, pg 59

Bixler, Gina, University of Notre Dame Press, 310 Flanner Hall, Notre Dame, IN 46556 *Tel:* 574-631-6346 *Fax:* 574-631-8148 *E-mail:* undpress@nd.edu *Web Site:* www.undpress.nd.edu, pg 244

Bjerke, Paisius, Saint Herman Press, 10 Beegum Gorge Rd, Platina, CA 96076 *Tel:* 530-352-4430 *Fax:* 530-352-4432 *E-mail:* stherman@stherman.com *Web Site:* www.stherman.com, pg 204

Blachere, Natalie, McGill-Queen's University Press, 1010 Sherbrooke W, Suite 1720, Montreal, QC H3A 2R7, Canada *Tel:* 514-398-3750 *Fax:* 514-398-4333 *E-mail:* mqup@mqup.ca *Web Site:* www.mqup.ca, pg 463

Black, Dr Adam, Macmillan Learning, 41 Madison Ave, New York, NY 10010 *Tel:* 212-576-9400 *Fax:* 212-689-2383 *Web Site:* www.macmillanlearning.com, pg 140

Black, Amy, Doubleday Canada, 320 Front St W, Suite 1400, Toronto, ON M5V 3B6, Canada *Tel:* 416-364-4449 *Fax:* 416-598-7764 *Web Site:* www.penguinrandomhouse.ca, pg 452

Black, David, David Black Agency, 335 Adams St, 27th fl, Suite 2707, Brooklyn, NY 11201 *Tel:* 718-852-5500 *Fax:* 718-852-5539 *Web Site:* www.davidblackagency.com, pg 508

Black, Hannah, Random House Children's Books, 1745 Broadway, 10th fl, New York, NY 10019 *Tel:* 212-782-9000 *Web Site:* www.randomhousekids.com, pg 194

Black, Hilary, National Geographic Books, 1145 17 St NW, Washington, DC 20036-4688 *Tel:* 202-857-7000 *Toll Free Tel:* 877-866-6486 *E-mail:* ngbooks@cdsfulfillment.com *Web Site:* www.nationalgeographic.com/books/; ngbooks.buysub.com, pg 158

Black, Kathy, Vermont Studio Center Writer's Program Fellowships, 80 Pearl St, Johnson, VT 05656 *Tel:* 802-635-2727 *Fax:* 802-635-2730 *E-mail:* writing@vermontstudiocenter.org; info@vermontstudiocenter.org *Web Site:* www.vermontstudiocenter.org, pg 696

Black, Lindsay, David C Cook, 4050 Lee Vance View, Colorado Springs, CO 80918 *Tel:* 719-536-0100 *Toll Free Tel:* 800-708-5550; 800-323-7543 (orders & cust serv) *Toll Free Fax:* 800-430-0726 (cust serv) *Web Site:* www.davidccook.com, pg 60

Black, Peter D, BPA Worldwide, 100 Beard Sawmill Rd, 6th fl, Shelton, CT 06484 *Tel:* 203-447-2800 *Fax:* 203-447-2900 *E-mail:* info@bpaww.com *Web Site:* www.bpaww.com, pg 561

Black, Stephen, Simon & Schuster, Inc, 1230 Avenue of the Americas, New York, NY 10020 *Tel:* 212-698-7000 *Fax:* 212-698-7007 *E-mail:* firstname.lastname@simonandschuster.com *Web Site:* www.simonandschuster.com, pg 213

Blackburn, Celeste, Business & Legal Resources Inc, 100 Winners Circle, Suite 300, Brentwood, TN 37027 *Tel:* 860-510-0100 *Toll Free Tel:* 800-727-5257 *E-mail:* service@blr.com *Web Site:* www.blr.com, pg 45

Blackburn, Kacie, Poisoned Pen Press, 6962 E First Ave, Suite 103, Scottsdale, AZ 85251 *Tel:* 480-945-3375 *Toll Free Tel:* 800-421-3976 *Fax:* 480-949-1707 *E-mail:* info@poisonedpenpress.com *Web Site:* www.poisonedpenpress.com, pg 185

Blackman, Lara, Touchstone, 1230 Avenue of the Americas, New York, NY 10020, pg 233

Blackstock, Peter, Grove Atlantic Inc, 154 W 14 St, 12th fl, New York, NY 10011 *Tel:* 212-614-7850 *Toll Free Tel:* 800-521-0178 *Fax:* 212-614-7886 *E-mail:* info@groveatlantic.com; sales@groveatlantic.com; publicity@groveatlantic.com; rights@groveatlantic.com *Web Site:* www.groveatlantic.com, pg 97

Blain, Phyllis, Summit University Press, 63 Summit Way, Gardiner, MT 59030-9314 *Tel:* 406-848-9742; 406-848-9500 (retail orders) *Toll Free Tel:* 800-245-5445 (retail orders) *Fax:* 406-848-9744 *E-mail:* info@summituniversitypress.com; marketing@summituniversitypress.com; production@summituniversitypress.com; rights@summituniversitypress.com *Web Site:* www.summituniversitypress.com, pg 224

Blair, Diane, Genesis Press Inc, PO Box 101, Columbus, MS 39701 *Toll Free Tel:* 888-463-4461 (orders only) *E-mail:* customerservice@genesis-press.com *Web Site:* www.genesis-press.com, pg 91

Blair, Susan, National Geographic Books, 1145 17 St NW, Washington, DC 20036-4688 *Tel:* 202-857-7000 *Toll Free Tel:* 877-866-6486 *E-mail:* ngbooks@cdsfulfillment.com *Web Site:* www.nationalgeographic.com/books/; ngbooks.buysub.com, pg 158

Blair-DeLeon, Nancy, National Federation of Advanced Information Services (NFAIS), 801 Compass Way, Suite 201, Annapolis, MD 21401 *Tel:* 443-221-2980 *Fax:* 443-221-2981 *E-mail:* nfais@nfais.org *Web Site:* www.nfais.org, pg 572

Blake, Corey Michael, Round Table Companies, 1027 Kenton Rd, Deerfield, IL 60015 *Tel:* 949-375-1006 *Fax:* 815-346-2398 *Web Site:* www.roundtablecompanies.com, pg 201

Blake, Deborah, University of Pennsylvania Press, 3905 Spruce St, Philadelphia, PA 19104 *Tel:* 215-898-6261 *Fax:* 215-898-0404 *E-mail:* custserv@pobox.upenn.edu *Web Site:* www.pennpress.org, pg 244

Blake, Gillian, Henry Holt and Company, LLC, 175 Fifth Ave, New York, NY 10010 *Tel:* 646-307-5151 *Toll Free Tel:* 888-330-8477 (orders) *Fax:* 646-307-5285 *E-mail:* firstname.lastname@hholt.com *Web Site:* www.henryholt.com, pg 109

Blake, Glenn, Boulevard Magazine Short Fiction Contest for Emerging Writers, 6614 Clayton Rd, PMB 325, Richmond Heights, MO 63117 *E-mail:* editors@boulevardmagazine.org *Web Site:* www.boulevardmagazine.org, pg 634

Blake, Holly, Headlands Center for the Arts Residency for Writers, 944 Fort Barry, Sausalito, CA 94965 *Tel:* 415-331-2787 *Fax:* 415-331-3857 *Web Site:* www.headlands.org, pg 652

Blake, Stephanie, Chronicle Books LLC, 680 Second St, San Francisco, CA 94107 *Tel:* 415-537-4200 *Toll Free Tel:* 800-759-0190 (cust serv) *Fax:* 415-537-4460 *Toll Free Fax:* 800-858-7787 (orders); 800-286-9471 (cust serv) *E-mail:* frontdesk@chroniclebooks.com *Web Site:* www.chroniclebooks.com, pg 55

Blakeslee, Kristine M, Michigan State University Press (MSU Press), Manly Miles Bldg, Suite 25, 1405 S Harrison Rd, East Lansing, MI 48823-5245 *Tel:* 517-355-9543 *Fax:* 517-432-2611 *Web Site:* msupress.org, pg 150

Blanc-Tal, Jennifer, Rutgers University Press, 106 Somerset St, 3rd fl, New Brunswick, NJ 08901 *Tel:* 848-445-7762 *Toll Free Tel:* 800-848-6224 (orders only) *Fax:* 732-745-4935 (acqs, edit, mktg, perms & prodn) *Toll Free Fax:* 800-272-6817 (fulfillment) *Web Site:* rutgerspress.rutgers.edu, pg 202

Blanchard, Marshall, Hoover Institution Press, Stanford University, 434 Galvez Mall, Stanford, CA 94305-6003 *Tel:* 650-725-7146; 650-723-3373 *Toll Free Tel:* 800-935-2882 *Fax:* 650-723-8626 *E-mail:* hooverpress@stanford.edu *Web Site:* www.hooverpress.org; www.hoover.org, pg 110

Bland, Jacqueline M, Print Industries Market Information & Research Organization, 1899 Preston White Dr, Reston, VA 20191 *Tel:* 703-264-7200 *Fax:* 703-620-0994 *E-mail:* npes@npes.org *Web Site:* www.primir.org; www.npes.org/primirresearch/primir.aspx, pg 576

Bland, Jared, McClelland & Stewart Ltd, 320 Front St W, Suite 1400, Toronto, ON M5V 3B6, Canada *Tel:* 416-364-4449 *Fax:* 416-598-7764 *E-mail:* customerservicescanada@penguinrandomhouse.com; publicity@ca.penguingroup.com *Web Site:* penguinrandomhouse.ca/imprints/mcclelland-stewart, pg 463

Blank, Chris, Harry N Abrams Inc, 195 Broadway, 9th fl, New York, NY 10007 *Tel:* 212-206-7715 *Toll Free Tel:* 800-345-1359 *Fax:* 212-519-1210 *E-mail:* abrams@abramsbooks.com *Web Site:* www.abramsbooks.com, pg 3

Blaschko, Tom, Idyll Arbor Inc, 39129 264 Ave SE, Enumclaw, WA 98022 *Tel:* 360-825-7797 *Fax:* 360-825-5670 *E-mail:* sales@idyllarbor.com *Web Site:* www.idyllarbor.com, pg 113

Blasdell, Caitlin, Liza Dawson Associates, 350 Seventh Ave, Suite 2003, New York, NY 10001 *Tel:* 212-465-9071 *Fax:* 212-947-0460 *Web Site:* www.lizadawsonassociates.com, pg 513

Blau, Dan, Kidsbooks LLC, 3535 W Peterson Ave, Chicago, IL 60659 *Tel:* 773-509-0707 *Fax:* 773-509-0404 *E-mail:* sales@kidsbooks.com; customerservice@kidsbooks.com *Web Site:* www.kidsbooks.com, pg 126

Bledsoe, Bob, Indiana University Writers' Conference, 464 Ballantine Hall, 1020 E Kirkwood Ave, Bloomington, IN 47405-7103 *Tel:* 812-855-1877 *Fax:* 812-855-9535 *E-mail:* writecon@indiana.edu *Web Site:* www.iuwc.indiana.edu, pg 611

Bleichmar, Fernando, Cengage Learning, 20 Channel Center St, Boston, MA 02210 *Tel:* 617-289-7700 *Toll Free Tel:* 800-354-9706 *Fax:* 617-289-7844 *Toll Free Fax:* 800-487-8488 *E-mail:* esales@cengage.com *Web Site:* www.cengage.com, pg 50

Blelock, Julia, WoodstockArts, PO Box 1342, Woodstock, NY 12498 *Tel:* 845-679-8111 *Fax:* 419-793-3452 *E-mail:* info@woodstockarts.com *Web Site:* woodstockarts.com, pg 258

Blelock, Weston, WoodstockArts, PO Box 1342, Woodstock, NY 12498 *Tel:* 845-679-8111 *Fax:* 419-793-3452 *E-mail:* info@woodstockarts.com *Web Site:* woodstockarts.com, pg 258

Blevins, Tim, Augsburg Fortress Publishers, Publishing House of the Evangelical Lutheran Church in America, 510 Marquette Ave S, Minneapolis, MN 55402 *Tel:* 612-330-3300 *Toll Free Tel:* 800-426-0115 (ext 639, subns); 800-328-4648 (orders) *Fax:* 612-330-3455 *E-mail:* info@augsburgfortress.org; copyright@augsburgfortress.org (reprint permission requests); customercare@augsburgfortress.org *Web Site:* www.augsburgfortress.org, pg 26

Bleyer, Craig, Macmillan Learning, 41 Madison Ave, New York, NY 10010 *Tel:* 212-576-9400 *Fax:* 212-689-2383 *Web Site:* www.macmillanlearning.com, pg 140

Bliss, Anna, The Experiment, 220 E 23 St, Suite 301, New York, NY 10010-4674 *Tel:* 212-889-1659 *E-mail:* info@theexperimentpublishing.com *Web Site:* www.theexperimentpublishing.com, pg 81

Bliss, Anthony A Jr, Aqua Quest Publications Inc, 486 Bayville Rd, Locust Valley, NY 11560-1209 *Tel:* 516-759-0476 *E-mail:* info@aquaquest.com *Web Site:* www.aquaquest.com, pg 19

Blizard, Freesia, Chronicle Books LLC, 680 Second St, San Francisco, CA 94107 *Tel:* 415-537-4200 *Toll Free Tel:* 800-759-0190 (cust serv) *Fax:* 415-537-4460 *Toll Free Fax:* 800-858-7787 (orders); 800-286-9471 (cust serv) *E-mail:* frontdesk@chroniclebooks.com *Web Site:* www.chroniclebooks.com, pg 55

Bloch, Mitchell, Bloch Publishing Co, 10030 E W Pappy Rd, PMB 0015, Jacksonville, FL 32259 *Tel:* 904-880-7302 *Fax:* 904-880-7307 *E-mail:* info@blochpub.com *Web Site:* www.blochpub.com, pg 37

Block, Gwen M, Marine Education Textbooks, 124 N Van Ave, Houma, LA 70363-5895 *Tel:* 985-879-3866 *Fax:* 985-879-3911 *E-mail:* email@marineeducationtextbooks.com *Web Site:* www.marineeducationtextbooks.com, pg 142

Block, Richard A, Marine Education Textbooks, 124 N Van Ave, Houma, LA 70363-5895 *Tel:* 985-879-3866 *Fax:* 985-879-3911 *E-mail:* email@marineeducationtextbooks.com *Web Site:* www.marineeducationtextbooks.com, pg 142

Blom, Harry, Springer, 233 Spring St, New York, NY 10013-1578 *Tel:* 212-460-1500 *Toll Free Tel:* 800-SPRINGER (777-4643) *Fax:* 212-460-1700 *E-mail:* customerservice@springer.com *Web Site:* www.springer.com, pg 219

Blonshine, Christian, Health Communications Inc, 3201 SW 15 St, Deerfield Beach, FL 33442 *Tel:* 954-360-0909 *Toll Free Tel:* 800-851-9100; 800-441-5569 (cust serv & orders) *Fax:* 954-360-0034 *Toll Free Fax:* 800-424-7652 (cust serv & orders) *E-mail:* customerservice2@hcibooks.com *Web Site:* www.hcibooks.com, pg 104

Bloom, Barbara, Bloom Ink, 3497 Bennington Ct, Bloomfield Hills, MI 48301 *Tel:* 248-291-0370 *E-mail:* info@bloomwriting.com *Web Site:* www.bloomwriting.com, pg 489

Bloom, Lexy, Anchor Books, c/o Penguin Random House Inc, 1745 Broadway, New York, NY 10019 *Tel:* 212-572-2420 *E-mail:* vintageanchorpublicity@randomhouse.com *Web Site:* knopfdoubleday.com/imprint/anchor, pg 16

Bloom, Lexy, Vintage Books, c/o Penguin Random House Inc, 1745 Broadway, New York, NY 10019 *Tel:* 212-572-2420 *E-mail:* vintageanchorpublicity@randomhouse.com *Web Site:* knopfdoubleday.com/imprint/vintage, pg 251

Bloom, Patience, Harlequin Enterprises Ltd, 233 Broadway, Suite 1001, New York, NY 10279 *Tel:* 212-553-4200 *Fax:* 212-227-8969 *E-mail:* customerservice@harlequin.com *Web Site:* www.harlequin.com, pg 100

Bloomfield, Mark, Regnery Publishing, 300 New Jersey Ave NW, Washington, DC 20001 *Tel:* 202-216-0600 *Toll Free Tel:* 888-219-4747 *Fax:* 202-393-1795 *Web Site:* www.regnery.com, pg 198

Blough, Diana, Random House Children's Books, 1745 Broadway, 10th fl, New York, NY 10019 *Tel:* 212-782-9000 *Web Site:* www.randomhousekids.com, pg 194

Blough, Heidi, Heidi Blough, Book Indexer, 502 Tanager Rd, St Augustine, FL 32086 *Tel:* 904-797-6572 *E-mail:* indexing@heidiblough.com *Web Site:* www.heidiblough.com, pg 489

Blount, Gregory James, Peter Glenn Publications, 306 NE Second St, 2nd fl, Delray Beach, FL 33483 *Tel:* 561-404-4290 *Fax:* 561-892-5786 *Web Site:* pgdirect.com, pg 93

Blount, Steve, Gospel Publishing House (GPH), 1445 Boonville Ave, Springfield, MO 65802 *Tel:* 417-862-2781; 417-831-8000 (outside US) *Toll Free Tel:* 800-641-4310 *Fax:* 417-863-1874; 417-862-5881 *Toll Free Fax:* 800-328-0294 *E-mail:* custsrvreps@ag.org *Web Site:* www.gospelpublishing.com, pg 94

Blow, Nathan S PhD, BioTechniques Books, 52 Vanderbilt Ave, 11th fl, New York, NY 10017 *Tel:* 212-520-2777 *Fax:* 212-520-2705 *Web Site:* www.biotechniques.com, pg 35

Bloxson, Carrie, HarperCollins General Books Group, 195 Broadway, New York, NY 10007 *Tel:* 212-207-7000 *Web Site:* www.harpercollins.com, pg 101

Blue, Marian, Blue & Ude Writers' Services, 4249 Nuthatch Way, Clinton, WA 98236 *Tel:* 360-341-1630 *E-mail:* blueyude@whidbey.com *Web Site:* www.bluedewritersservices.com, pg 489

Blue, Zach, AK Press Distribution, 370 Ryan Ave, Unit 100, Chico, CA 95973 *Tel:* 510-208-1700 *Fax:* 510-208-1701 *E-mail:* info@akpress.org *Web Site:* www.akpress.org, pg 6

Bluey, Melissa, The Heritage Foundation, 214 Massachusetts Ave NE, Washington, DC 20002-4999 *Tel:* 202-546-4400 *Toll Free Tel:* 800-544-4843 *Fax:* 202-546-8328 *E-mail:* info@heritage.org *Web Site:* www.heritage.org, pg 106

Blum, Michele, Westminster John Knox Press (WJK), 100 Witherspoon St, Louisville, KY 40202-1396 *Toll Free Tel:* 800-523-1631 (US only) *Fax:* 502-569-5113 *Toll Free Fax:* 800-541-5113 (US & CN) *E-mail:* wjk@wjkbooks.com; customer_service@wjkbooks.com *Web Site:* www.wjkbooks.com, pg 254

Blume, Judy, The Authors Guild, 31 E 32 St, 7th fl, New York, NY 10016 *Tel:* 212-563-5904 *Fax:* 212-564-5363 *E-mail:* staff@authorsguild.org *Web Site:* www.authorsguild.org, pg 559

Blumenfeld, Josef, Cengage Learning, 20 Channel Center St, Boston, MA 02210 *Tel:* 617-289-7700 *Toll Free Tel:* 800-354-9706 *Fax:* 617-289-7844 *Toll Free Fax:* 800-487-8488 *E-mail:* esales@cengage.com *Web Site:* www.cengage.com, pg 50

Blumenthal, Scott, Scobre Press Corp, 2255 Calle Clara, La Jolla, CA 92037 *Fax:* 858-551-1232 *E-mail:* info@scobre.com *Web Site:* www.scobre.com; scobre.bookbuddyaudio.com, pg 209

Blunck, Kay, Neustadt International Prize for Literature, c/o University of Oklahoma, 630 Parrington Oval, Suite 110, Norman, OK 73019-4033 *Tel:* 405-325-4531 *Web Site:* www.worldliteraturetoday.org; www.worldlit.org, pg 672

Blunck, Kay, NSK Neustadt Prize for Children's Literature, c/o University of Oklahoma, 630 Parrington Oval, Suite 110, Norman, OK 73019-4033 *Tel:* 405-325-4531 *Web Site:* www.worldliteraturetoday.org; www.worldlit.org, pg 674

Blythe, Heather, Society for Industrial & Applied Mathematics, 3600 Market St, 6th fl, Philadelphia, PA 19104-2688 *Tel:* 215-382-9800 *Toll Free Tel:* 800-447-7426 *Fax:* 215-386-7999 *E-mail:* siambooks@siam.org *Web Site:* www.siam.org, pg 216

Blythe, Steven, Laura Day Boggs Bolling Memorial, 900 Timber Creek Place, Virginia Beach, VA 23464 *E-mail:* poetryinva@aol.com *Web Site:* poetrysocietyofvirginia.org, pg 633

Blythe, Steven, Joe Pendleton Campbell Narrative Contest, 900 Timber Creek Place, Virginia Beach, VA 23464 *E-mail:* poetryinva@aol.com *Web Site:* poetrysocietyofvirginia.org, pg 635

Blythe, Steven, Carleton Drewry Memorial, 900 Timber Creek Place, Virginia Beach, VA 23464 *E-mail:* poetryinva@aol.com *Web Site:* poetrysocietyofvirginia.org, pg 642

Blythe, Steven, Alfred C Gary Memorial, 900 Timber Creek Place, Virginia Beach, VA 23464 *E-mail:* poetryinva@aol.com *Web Site:* poetrysocietyofvirginia.org, pg 648

Blythe, Steven, Bess Gresham Memorial, 900 Timber Creek Place, Virginia Beach, VA 23464 *E-mail:* poetryinva@aol.com *Web Site:* poetrysocietyofvirginia.org, pg 651

Blythe, Steven, Loretta Dunn Hall Memorial, 900 Timber Creek Place, Virginia Beach, VA 23464 *E-mail:* poetryinva@aol.com *Web Site:* poetrysocietyofvirginia.org, pg 651

Blythe, Steven, Handy Andy Prize, 900 Timber Creek Place, Virginia Beach, VA 23464 *E-mail:* poetryinva@aol.com *Web Site:* poetrysocietyofvirginia.org, pg 651

Blythe, Steven, Brodie Herndon Memorial, 900 Timber Creek Place, Virginia Beach, VA 23464 *E-mail:* poetryinva@aol.com *Web Site:* poetrysocietyofvirginia.org, pg 652

Blythe, Steven, Judah, Sarah, Grace & Tom Memorial, 900 Timber Creek Place, Virginia Beach, VA 23464 *E-mail:* poetryinva@aol.com; info@poetryvirginia.org *Web Site:* poetrysocietyofvirginia.org, pg 658

Blythe, Steven, Cenie H Moon Prize, 900 Timber Creek Place, Virginia Beach, VA 23464 *E-mail:* poetryinva@aol.com *Web Site:* poetrysocietyofvirginia.org, pg 669

Blythe, Steven, Edgar Allan Poe Memorial, 900 Timber Creek Place, Virginia Beach, VA 23464 *E-mail:* poetryinva@aol.com *Web Site:* poetrysocietyofvirginia.org, pg 680

Blythe, Steven, Miriam Rachimi Memorial, 900 Timber Creek Place, Virginia Beach, VA 23464 *E-mail:* poetryinva@aol.com *Web Site:* poetrysocietyofvirginia.org, pg 683

Blythe, Steven, Ada Sanderson Memorial, 900 Timber Creek Place, Virginia Beach, VA 23464 *E-mail:* poetryinva@aol.com *Web Site:* poetrysocietyofvirginia.org, pg 686

Blythe, Steven, The Robert S Sergeant Memorial, 900 Timber Creek Place, Virginia Beach, VA 23464 *E-mail:* poetryinva@aol.com *Web Site:* poetrysocietyofvirginia.org, pg 688

Boardman, Ted, Indiana University Press, Herman B Wells Library 350, 1320 E Tenth St, Bloomington, IN 47405-3907 *Tel:* 812-855-8817 *Toll Free Tel:* 800-842-6796 (orders only) *Fax:* 812-855-7931; 812-855-8507 *E-mail:* iupress@indiana.edu; iuporder@indiana.edu (orders) *Web Site:* www.iupress.indiana.edu, pg 116

Boates, Reid, Reid Boates Literary Agency, 69 Cooks Crossroad, Pittstown, NJ 08867-0328 *Tel:* 908-797-8087 *E-mail:* reid.boates@gmail.com, pg 508

Boatright, Shantelle, Business Forms Management Association (BFMA), 1147 Fleetwood Ave, Madison, WI 53716 *Toll Free Tel:* 888-367-3078 *E-mail:* bfma@bfma.org *Web Site:* www.bfma.org, pg 561

Bob, Tammie, Friends of American Writers Awards, 506 Rose Ave, Des Plaines, IL 60016 *Tel:* 847-827-8339 *Web Site:* www.fawchicago.org, pg 648

Bobbitt, Michael D, Twilight Times Books, PO Box 3340, Kingsport, TN 37664-0340 *Tel:* 423-323-0183 *Fax:* 423-323-0183 *E-mail:* publisher@twilighttimes.com *Web Site:* www.twilighttimesbooks.com, pg 237

Bobco, Ann, Simon & Schuster Children's Publishing, 1230 Avenue of the Americas, New York, NY 10020 *Tel:* 212-698-7000 *Web Site:* www.simonandschuster.com/kids; www.simonandschuster.com/teen; simonandschuster.net; simonandschuster.biz, pg 213

Bobris, Seth, University of California Press, 155 Grand Ave, Suite 400, Oakland, CA 94612-3758 *Tel:* 510-883-8232 *Fax:* 510-836-8910 *E-mail:* customerservice@ucpressjournals.com *Web Site:* www.ucpress.edu, pg 240

Boccardi, Paul, Little, Brown and Company, 1290 Avenue of the Americas, New York, NY 10019 *Tel:* 212-364-1100 *Fax:* 212-364-0952 *E-mail:* firstname.lastname@hbgusa.com *Web Site:* www.littlebrown.com; www.HachetteBookGroup.com, pg 135

Bodnar, Georgia, Viking, 375 Hudson St, New York, NY 10014 *Tel:* 212-366-2000 *Fax:* 212-243-6002 *Web Site:* www.penguin.com/publishers/vikingbooks, pg 250

Bodwell, Joshua, Maine Writers & Publishers Alliance, 314 Forest Ave, Rm 318, Portland, ME 04101 *Tel:* 207-228-8263 *Fax:* 207-228-8150 *E-mail:* info@mainewriters.org *Web Site:* mainewriters.org, pg 569

Boehm, Ronald, ABC-CLIO, 130 Cremona Dr, Santa Barbara, CA 93117 *Tel:* 805-968-1911 *Toll Free Tel:* 800-368-6868 *Fax:* 805-685-9685 *Toll Free Fax:* 866-270-3856 *E-mail:* customerservice@abc-clio.com *Web Site:* www.abc-clio.com, pg 2

Boehmer, Gabriella, HeartMath LLC, 14700 W Park Ave, Boulder Creek, CA 95006 *Tel:* 831-338-8700 *Toll Free Tel:* 800-450-9111 *Fax:* 831-338-9861 *E-mail:* info@heartmath.com; inquiry@heartmath.com *Web Site:* www.heartmath.com, pg 105

Boehmer, Susan Wallace, Harvard University Press, 79 Garden St, Cambridge, MA 02138-1499 *Tel:* 617-495-2600; 401-531-2800 (intl orders) *Toll Free Tel:* 800-405-1619 (orders) *Fax:* 617-495-5898 (general); 617-496-4677 (edit & rts); 401-531-2801 (intl orders) *Toll Free Fax:* 800-406-9145 (orders) *E-mail:* contact_hup@harvard.edu *Web Site:* www.hup.harvard.edu, pg 103

Boer, Faye, Folklore Publishing, 11717-9B Ave NW, Unit 2, Edmonton, AB T6J 7B7, Canada *Tel:* 780-435-2376 *E-mail:* submissions@folklorepublishing.com (ms submissions) *Web Site:* www.folklorepublishing.com, pg 457

Boer, Peter J, Blue Bike Books, 58 Lodgepole Crescent, St Albert, AB T8N 2R7, Canada *Tel:* 780-435-2376 *E-mail:* info@bluebikebooks.com *Web Site:* www.bluebikebooks.com, pg 446

Boers, Jack, Baker Books, PO Box 6287, Grand Rapids, MI 49516-6287 *Tel:* 616-676-9185 *Toll Free Tel:* 800-877-2665; 800-679-1957 *Fax:* 616-676-9573 *Toll Free Fax:* 800-398-3111 *Web Site:* www.bakerpublishinggroup.com, pg 28

Boersma, Karen, Owlkids Books Inc, 10 Lower Spadina Ave, Suite 400, Toronto, ON M5V 2Z2, Canada *Tel:* 416-340-2700 *Fax:* 416-340-9769 *E-mail:* owlkids@owlkids.com *Web Site:* www.owlkidsbooks.com, pg 465

Bogaards, Paul, Alfred A Knopf/Everyman's Library, c/o Penguin Random House Inc, 1745 Broadway, New York, NY 10019 *Tel:* 212-751-2600 *Toll Free Tel:* 800-638-6460 *Fax:* 212-572-2593 *Web Site:* www.knopfdoubleday.com, pg 127

Bogie, Patty, MPA - The Association of Magazine Media, 757 Third Ave, 11th fl, New York, NY 10012 *Tel:* 212-872-3700 *Fax:* 212-888-4217 *Web Site:* www.magazine.org, pg 570

Boies, Kay, Children's Sequoyah Book Award, PO Box 6550, Edmond, OK 73083 *Tel:* 405-525-5100 *Fax:* 405-525-5103 *Web Site:* www.oklibs.org, pg 637

Boies, Kay, The High School Award, PO Box 6550, Edmond, OK 73083 *Tel:* 405-525-5100 *Fax:* 405-525-5103 *Web Site:* www.oklibs.org, pg 653

Boies, Kay, Intermediate Sequoyah Book Award, PO Box 6550, Edmond, OK 73083 *Tel:* 405-525-5100 *Fax:* 405-525-5103 *Web Site:* www.oklibs.org, pg 656

Boileau, Kendra, The Pennsylvania State University Press, University Support Bldg 1, Suite C, 820 N University Dr, University Park, PA 16802-1003 *Tel:* 814-865-1327 *Toll Free Tel:* 800-326-9180 *Fax:* 814-863-1408 *Toll Free Fax:* 877-778-2665 *E-mail:* info@psupress.org *Web Site:* www.psupress.org, pg 179

Boisseau, Michelle, BkMk Press - University of Missouri-Kansas City, University House, 5101 Rockhill Rd, Kansas City, MO 64110-2499 *Tel:* 816-235-2558 *Fax:* 816-235-2611 *E-mail:* bkmk@umkc.edu *Web Site:* www.umkc.edu/bkmk, pg 36

Boisseau, Michelle, G S Sharat Chandra Prize for Short Fiction, University House, 5101 Rockhill Rd, Kansas City, MO 64110-2499 *Tel:* 816-235-2558 *Fax:* 816-235-2611 *E-mail:* bkmk@umkc.edu *Web Site:* www.umkc.edu/bkmk, pg 636

Boisseau, Michelle, John Ciardi Prize for Poetry, University House, 5101 Rockhill Rd, Kansas City, MO 64110-2499 *Tel:* 816-235-2558 *Fax:* 816-235-2611 *E-mail:* bkmk@umkc.edu *Web Site:* www.umkc.edu/bkmk, pg 637

Boitnott, Sally, Pelican Publishing Co, 1000 Burmaster St, Gretna, LA 70053-2246 *Tel:* 504-368-1175 *Toll Free Tel:* 800-843-1724 *Fax:* 504-368-1195 *E-mail:* sales@pelicanpub.com (sales); office@pelicanpub.com (permission); promo@pelicanpub.com (publicity) *Web Site:* www.pelicanpub.com, pg 176

Bol, Bob, Baker Books, PO Box 6287, Grand Rapids, MI 49516-6287 *Tel:* 616-676-9185 *Toll Free Tel:* 800-877-2665; 800-679-1957 *Fax:* 616-676-9573 *Toll Free Fax:* 800-398-3111 *Web Site:* www.bakerpublishinggroup.com, pg 28

Bol, Robert, Revell, PO Box 6287, Grand Rapids, MI 49516-6287 *Tel:* 616-676-9185 *Toll Free Tel:* 800-877-2665; 800-679-1957 *Fax:* 616-676-9573 *Web Site:* www.bakerpublishinggroup.com, pg 198

Bolan, Michael, LinguaText LLC, 103 Walker Way, Newark, DE 19711 *Tel:* 302-453-8695 *E-mail:* text@linguatextbooks.com *Web Site:* www.linguatextbooks.com, pg 134

Bolchazy, Allan, Bolchazy-Carducci Publishers Inc, 1570 Baskin Rd, Mundelein, IL 60060 *Tel:* 847-526-4344 *Toll Free Tel:* 800-392-6453 *Fax:* 847-526-2867 *E-mail:* info@bolchazy.com; orders@bolchazy.com *Web Site:* www.bolchazy.com, pg 39

Bolchazy, Dr Marie Carducci PhD, Bolchazy-Carducci Publishers Inc, 1570 Baskin Rd, Mundelein, IL 60060 *Tel:* 847-526-4344 *Toll Free Tel:* 800-392-6453 *Fax:* 847-526-2867 *E-mail:* info@bolchazy.com; orders@bolchazy.com *Web Site:* www.bolchazy.com, pg 39

Boldrick, Penelope, Ignatius Press, 1348 Tenth Ave, San Francisco, CA 94122-2304 *Toll Free Tel:* 800-651-1531 (orders); 888-615-3186 (cust serv) *E-mail:* info@ignatius.com *Web Site:* www.ignatius.com, pg 114

Bolduc, Mary Jo, The American Library Association (ALA), 50 E Huron St, Chicago, IL 60611 *Tel:* 312-944-6780 *Toll Free Tel:* 800-545-2433 *Fax:* 312-280-5275 *E-mail:* editionsmarketing@ala.org *Web Site:* www.alastore.ala.org, pg 13

Bolduc, Mary Jo, Carnegie-Whitney Award, 50 E Huron St, Chicago, IL 60611 *Tel:* 312-280-5416 *Toll Free Tel:* 800-545-2433 *Fax:* 312-280-5275; 312-440-9379 *Web Site:* www.ala.org, pg 636

Bole, Angela, The Independent Book Publishers Association (IBPA), 1020 Manhattan Beach Blvd, Suite 204, Manhattan Beach, CA 90266 *Tel:* 310-546-1818 *Fax:* 310-546-3939 *E-mail:* info@ibpa-online.org *Web Site:* www.ibpa-online.org, pg 567

Bolger, Loretta, Quincannon Publishing Group, PO Box 8100, Glen Ridge, NJ 07028-8100 *Tel:* 973-380-9942 *E-mail:* editors@quincannongroup.com *Web Site:* www.quincannongroup.com, pg 192

Bolinao, Mela, MB Artists, 775 Sixth Ave, Suite 6, New York, NY 10001 *Tel:* 212-689-7830 *Fax:* 212-689-7829 *Web Site:* www.mbartists.com, pg 544

Boling, John Mark, Grove Atlantic Inc, 154 W 14 St, 12th fl, New York, NY 10011 *Tel:* 212-614-7850 *Toll Free Tel:* 800-521-0178 *Fax:* 212-614-7886 *E-mail:* info@groveatlantic.com; sales@groveatlantic.com; publicity@groveatlantic.com; rights@groveatlantic.com *Web Site:* www.groveatlantic.com, pg 97

Bolinger, Becke, Indiana Historical Society Press (IHS Press), 450 W Ohio St, Indianapolis, IN 46202-3269 *Tel:* 317-232-1882; 317-234-0026 (orders); 317-234-2716 (edit) *Toll Free Tel:* 800-447-1830 (orders) *Fax:* 317-234-0562 (orders); 317-233-0857 (edit) *E-mail:* ihspress@indianahistory.org; orders@indianahistory.org (orders) *Web Site:* www.indianahistory.org; shop.indianahistory.org (orders), pg 115

Bollas, George, Cortina Institute of Languages, 9 Hollyhock Rd, Wilton, CT 06897 *Tel:* 203-762-2510 *Toll Free Tel:* 800-245-2145 *Web Site:* www.cortina-languages.com, pg 61

Bollas, George, Cortina Learning International Inc, 9 Hollyhock Rd, Wilton, CT 06897 *Tel:* 203-762-2510 *Toll Free Tel:* 800-245-2145 *Fax:* 203-762-2514 *Web Site:* www.cortinalearning.com, pg 61

Boller, Katherine, Yale University Press, 302 Temple St, New Haven, CT 06511-8909 *Tel:* 203-432-0960; 203-432-0966 (sales); 401-531-2800 (cust serv) *Toll Free Tel:* 800-405-1619 (cust serv) *Fax:* 203-432-0948; 203-432-8485 (sales); 401-531-2801 (cust serv) *Toll Free Fax:* 800-406-9145 (cust serv) *E-mail:* sales.press@yale.edu (sales); customer.care@triliteral.org (cust serv) *Web Site:* www.yalebooks.com; yalepress.yale.edu/yupbooks, pg 261

Bolm, Jennifer, Adventures Unlimited Press (AUP), One Adventure Place, Kempton, IL 60946 *Tel:* 815-253-6390 *Fax:* 815-253-6300 *E-mail:* auphq@frontiernet.net; info@adventuresunlimitedpress.com *Web Site:* www.adventuresunlimitedpress.com, pg 5

Bolotin, Susan, Workman Publishing Co Inc, 225 Varick St, 9th fl, New York, NY 10014-4381 *Tel:* 212-254-5900 *Toll Free Tel:* 800-722-7202 *Fax:* 212-254-8098 *E-mail:* info@workman.com *Web Site:* www.workman.com, pg 259

Bomberger, Rachel, Wm B Eerdmans Publishing Co, 2140 Oak Industrial Dr NE, Grand Rapids, MI 49505 *Tel:* 616-459-4591 *Toll Free Tel:* 800-253-7521 *Fax:* 616-459-6540 *E-mail:* customerservice@eerdmans.com; sales@eerdmans.com *Web Site:* www.eerdmans.com, pg 76

Bonacum, Leslie, CCH, a Wolters Kluwer business, 2700 Lake Cook Rd, Riverwoods, IL 60015 *Tel:* 847-267-7000 *Web Site:* www.cch.com, pg 50

Bonaddio, Teresa, Perseus Books, 250 W 57 St, 15th fl, New York, NY 10107 *Tel:* 212-340-8100 *Toll Free Tel:* 800-343-4499 (cust serv) *Fax:* 212-340-8105 *Web Site:* www.perseusbooks.com, pg 181

Bonanno, David, Honickman First Book Prize, University of the Arts (UARTS), Hamilton Hall, 320 S Broad St, Rm 313, Philadelphia, PA 19102-4901 *Tel:* 215-717-6801 *Fax:* 215-717-6805 *Web Site:* www.aprweb.org, pg 653

Bonanno, Dawn, SFWA Nebula Awards, PO Box 3238, Enfield, CT 06083-3238 *E-mail:* office@sfwa.org *Web Site:* www.sfwa.org, pg 688

Bonanno, Michelle, Houghton Mifflin Harcourt Trade & Reference Division, 125 High St, Boston, MA 02110 *Tel:* 617-351-5000 *Toll Free Tel:* 800-225-3362 *Web Site:* www.hmhco.com, pg 111

Bonaventura, Philip, Public Relations Society of America, 33 Maiden Lane, 11th fl, New York, NY 10038-5150 *Tel:* 212-460-1400 *Fax:* 212-995-0757 *Web Site:* www.prsa.org, pg 576

Boncottie, John, Antique Collectors' Club Ltd, 6 W 18 St, Suite 4B, New York, NY 10011 *Tel:* 212-645-1111 *Toll Free Tel:* 800-252-5231 *Fax:* 212-989-3205 *E-mail:* ussales@accpublishinggroup.com *Web Site:* www.accdistribution.com, pg 17

Bond, Alison M, Alison Bond Literary Agency, 171 W 79 St, No 143, New York, NY 10024, pg 508

Bond, Sandra, Bond Literary Agency, 4340 E Kentucky Ave, Suite 471, Denver, CO 80246 *Tel:* 303-781-9305 *E-mail:* queries@bondliteraryagency.com *Web Site:* bondliteraryagency.com, pg 508

Bonelli, Kristen, Ave Maria Press, PO Box 428, Notre Dame, IN 46556 *Tel:* 574-287-2831 *Toll Free Tel:* 800-282-1865 *Fax:* 574-239-2904 *Toll Free Fax:* 800-282-5681 *E-mail:* avemariapress.1@nd.edu *Web Site:* www.avemariapress.com, pg 27

Bonenberger, John, William H Sadlier Inc, 9 Pine St, New York, NY 10005 *Tel:* 212-227-2120 *Toll Free Tel:* 800-221-5175 (cust serv) *Fax:* 212-312-6080 *E-mail:* customerservice@sadlier.com *Web Site:* www.sadlier.com, pg 203

Bonenfant, Rene, Les Heures bleues, 560, rue Mercier, St-Lambert, QC J4P 1Z5, Canada *Tel:* 450-671-7718 *Fax:* 450-671-7718 *E-mail:* info@heuresbleues.com *Web Site:* www.heuresbleues.com, pg 460

Boni, Anne, The Center for the Book in the Library of Congress, The Library of Congress, 101 Independence Ave SE, Washington, DC 20540-4920 *Tel:* 202-707-5221 *Fax:* 202-707-0269 *E-mail:* cfbook@loc.gov *Web Site:* www.read.gov; www.read.gov/cfb, pg 563

Boni, Anne, Library of Congress Prize for American Fiction, 101 Independence Ave SE, Washington, DC 20540-1400 *Tel:* 202-707-5221 (Center for the Book) *Fax:* 202-707-0269 *Web Site:* www.loc.gov, pg 661

Bonifacio, Kris Anne, Media Coalition Inc, 19 Fulton St, Suite 407, New York, NY 10038 *Tel:* 212-587-4025 *Fax:* 212-587-2436 *E-mail:* info@mediacoalition.org *Web Site:* mediacoalition.org, pg 569

Bonk, Rich, Philadelphia Museum of Art, 2525 Pennsylvania Ave, Philadelphia, PA 19130 *Tel:* 215-684-7250 *Fax:* 215-235-8715 *Web Site:* www.philamuseum.org, pg 182

Bonner, Pat, International Foundation of Employee Benefit Plans, 18700 W Bluemound Rd, Brookfield, WI 53045 *Tel:* 262-786-6700 *Toll Free Tel:* 888-334-3327 *Fax:* 262-786-8780 *E-mail:* editor@ifebp.org *Web Site:* www.ifebp.org, pg 119

Bonoff, Steve, IDEAlliance®, 1800 Diagonal Rd, Suite 320, Alexandria, VA 22314-2862 *Tel:* 703-837-1070 *Fax:* 703-837-1072 *E-mail:* registrar@idealliance.org *Web Site:* www.idealliance.org, pg 567

Booker, Darryl, The Mountaineers Books, 1001 SW Klickitat Way, Suite 201, Seattle, WA 98134 *Tel:* 206-223-6303 *Toll Free Tel:* 800-553-4453 *Fax:* 206-223-6306 *Toll Free Fax:* 800-568-7604 *E-mail:* mbooks@mountaineersbooks.org; customerservice@mountaineersbooks.org *Web Site:* www.mountaineersbooks.org, pg 155

Boomer, Helen, Penguin Young Readers Group, 345 Hudson St, New York, NY 10014 *Tel:* 212-366-2000; 212-414-3553 *Fax:* 212-414-3340 *Web Site:* www.penguin.com/children, pg 179

Boomhower, Ray, Indiana Historical Society Press (IHS Press), 450 W Ohio St, Indianapolis, IN 46202-3269 *Tel:* 317-232-1882; 317-234-0026 (orders); 317-234-2716 (edit) *Toll Free Tel:* 800-447-1830 (orders) *Fax:* 317-234-0562 (orders); 317-233-0857 (edit) *E-mail:* ihspress@indianahistory.org; orders@indianahistory.org (orders) *Web Site:* www.indianahistory.org; shop.indianahistory.org (orders), pg 115

Boot, Chris, Aperture Books, 547 W 27 St, 4th fl, New York, NY 10001 *Tel:* 212-505-5555 *Toll Free Tel:* 800-929-2323 *Fax:* 212-979-7759 *E-mail:* info@aperture.org *Web Site:* www.aperture.org, pg 18

Booth, Doris, Authorlink Press, 103 Guadalupe Dr, Irving, TX 75039-3334 *Tel:* 972-402-0101 *E-mail:* admin@authorlink.com *Web Site:* www.authorlink.com, pg 26

Booth, Jessica, The University of Utah Press, J Willard Marriott Library, Suite 5400, 295 S 1500 E, Salt Lake City, UT 84112-0860 *Tel:* 801-585-9786 *Fax:* 801-581-3365 *E-mail:* hannah.new@utah.edu *Web Site:* www.uofupress.com, pg 245

Booth, Tom, Oregon State University Press, 121 The Valley Library, Corvallis, OR 97331-4501 *Tel:* 541-737-3166 *Toll Free Tel:* 800-621-2736 (orders), pg 170

Borchardt, Anne, Georges Borchardt Inc, 136 E 57 St, New York, NY 10022 *Tel:* 212-753-5785 *E-mail:* georges@gbagency.com *Web Site:* www.gbagency.com, pg 509

Borchardt, Georges, Georges Borchardt Inc, 136 E 57 St, New York, NY 10022 *Tel:* 212-753-5785 *E-mail:* georges@gbagency.com *Web Site:* www.gbagency.com, pg 509

Borchardt, Valerie, Georges Borchardt Inc, 136 E 57 St, New York, NY 10022 *Tel:* 212-753-5785 *E-mail:* georges@gbagency.com *Web Site:* www.gbagency.com, pg 509

Borden, Julia, No Starch Press, 245 Eighth St, San Francisco, CA 94103 *Tel:* 415-863-9900 *Toll Free Tel:* 800-420-7240 *Fax:* 415-863-9950 *E-mail:* info@nostarch.com; sales@nostarch.com *Web Site:* www.nostarch.com, pg 162

Borgenicht, David, Quirk Books, 215 Church St, Philadelphia, PA 19106 *Tel:* 215-627-3581 *Fax:* 215-627-5220 *E-mail:* general@quirkbooks.com *Web Site:* www.quirkbooks.com, pg 193

Borland, Peter, Atria Books, 1230 Avenue of the Americas, New York, NY 10020 *Tel:* 212-698-7000 *Fax:* 212-698-7007 *Web Site:* www.simonandschuster.com, pg 25

Born, Bob, Pocket Press Inc, PO Box 25124, Portland, OR 97298-0124 *Toll Free Tel:* 888-237-2110 *Toll Free Fax:* 877-643-3732 *E-mail:* sales@pocketpressinc.com *Web Site:* www.pocketpressinc.com, pg 185

Borne, Joell Smith, Vanderbilt University Press, 2014 Broadway, Suite 320, Nashville, TN 37203 *Tel:* 615-322-3585 *Toll Free Tel:* 800-627-7377 (orders only) *Fax:* 615-343-8823 *Toll Free Fax:* 800-735-0476 (orders only) *E-mail:* vupress@vanderbilt.edu *Web Site:* www.vanderbiltuniversitypress.com, pg 249

Borodyanskaya, Yulia, Harry N Abrams Inc, 195 Broadway, 9th fl, New York, NY 10007 *Tel:* 212-206-7715 *Toll Free Tel:* 800-345-1359 *Fax:* 212-519-1210 *E-mail:* abrams@abramsbooks.com *Web Site:* www.abramsbooks.com, pg 3

Borsecnik, Mary, J J Keller & Associates, Inc, 3003 Breezewood Lane, Neenah, WI 54957 *Tel:* 920-722-2848 *Toll Free Tel:* 877-564-2333 *Toll Free Fax:* 800-727-7516 *E-mail:* contactus@jjkeller.com; customerservice@jjkeller.com *Web Site:* www.jjkeller.com, pg 125

Borski, Jill Zima, Florida Outdoor Writers Association Inc, 24 NW 33 Ct, Suite A, Gainesville, FL 32607 *Tel:* 352-284-1763 *E-mail:* info@fowa.org *Web Site:* www.fowa.org, pg 565

Bortz, Andrew, Bancroft Press, 3209 Bancroft Rd, Baltimore, MD 21215 *Tel:* 410-358-0658 *Fax:* 410-764-1967 *Web Site:* www.bancroftpress.com, pg 29

Bortz, Bruce L, Bancroft Press, 3209 Bancroft Rd, Baltimore, MD 21215 *Tel:* 410-358-0658 *Fax:* 410-764-1967 *Web Site:* www.bancroftpress.com, pg 29

Bortz, Eli, University of Notre Dame Press, 310 Flanner Hall, Notre Dame, IN 46556 *Tel:* 574-631-6346 *Fax:* 574-631-8148 *E-mail:* undpress@nd.edu *Web Site:* www.undpress.nd.edu, pg 244

Borzumato-Greenberg, Terry, Holiday House Inc, 425 Madison Ave, New York, NY 10017 *Tel:* 212-688-0085 *Fax:* 212-421-6134 *E-mail:* info@holidayhouse.com *Web Site:* www.holidayhouse.com, pg 109

Bosch, Sammy, Mighty Media Press, 1201 Currie Ave, Minneapolis, MN 55403 *Tel:* 612-455-0252 *Fax:* 612-338-4817 *Web Site:* www.mightymediapress.com, pg 150

Bostic, Amanda, Thomas Nelson, 501 Nelson Place, Nashville, TN 37214 *Tel:* 615-889-9000 *Toll Free Tel:* 800-251-4000 *Fax:* 615-902-1548 *Web Site:* www.thomasnelson.com, pg 231

Botsford, Marj, CWA/SCA Canada, 2200 Prince of Wales Dr, Suite 301, Ottawa, ON K2E 6Z9, Canada *Tel:* 613-820-9777 *Toll Free Tel:* 877-486-4292 *Fax:* 613-820-8188 *E-mail:* info@cwa-scacanada.ca *Web Site:* www.cwa-scacanada.ca, pg 564

Botton, Maury, The New Press, 38 Greene St, 4th fl, New York, NY 10013 *Tel:* 212-629-8802 *Toll Free Tel:* 800-343-4489 (orders) *Fax:* 212-629-8617 *Toll Free Fax:* 800-351-5073 (orders) *E-mail:* newpress@thenewpress.com *Web Site:* www.thenewpress.com, pg 161

Bottorff, Todd, GemStone Press, 4507 Charlotte Ave, Suite 100, Nashville, TN 37209 *Tel:* 615-255-BOOK (255-2665) *Fax:* 615-255-5081 *E-mail:* marketing@turnerpublishing.com *Web Site:* gemstonepress.com; www.turnerpublishing.com, pg 91

Bottorff, Todd, Jewish Lights, 4507 Charlotte Ave, Suite 100, Nashville, TN 37209 *Tel:* 615-255-BOOK (255-2665) *Fax:* 615-255-5081 *E-mail:* marketing@turnerpublishing.com *Web Site:* jewishlights.com; www.turnerpublishing.com, pg 122

Bottorff, Todd, SkyLight Paths, 4507 Charlotte Ave, Suite 100, Nashville, TN 37209 *Tel:* 615-255-BOOK (255-2665) *Fax:* 615-255-5081 *E-mail:* marketing@turnerpublishing.com *Web Site:* www.skylightpaths.com; www.turnerpublishing.com, pg 215

Bottorff, Todd, Turner Publishing Co, 4507 Charlotte Ave, Suite 100, Nashville, TN 37209 *Tel:* 615-255-BOOK (255-2665) *Fax:* 615-255-5081 *E-mail:* marketing@turnerpublishing.com; submissions@turnerpublishing.com *Web Site:* www.turnerpublishing.com; www.facebook.com/turner.publishing, pg 236

Botzman, Harvey, Cyclotour Guide Books, 160 Harvard St, Rochester, NY 14607-3174 *Tel:* 585-244-6157 *E-mail:* cyclotour@cyclotour.com *Web Site:* www.cyclotour.com, pg 66

Boucher, Jayme, Penguin Random House Speakers Bureau, A Penguin Random House Company, 1745 Broadway, Mail Drop 13-1, New York, NY 10019 *Tel:* 212-572-2013 *E-mail:* speakers@penguinrandomhouse.com *Web Site:* www.prhspeakers.com, pg 547

Boucher, Johanne, Ordre des traducteurs, terminologues et interpretes agrees du quebec, 2021 Union Ave, Suite 1108, Montreal, QC H3A 2S9, Canada *Tel:* 514-845-4411 *Toll Free Tel:* 800-265-4815 *Fax:* 514-845-9903 *E-mail:* info@ottiaq.org *Web Site:* www.ottiaq.org, pg 574

Boudreaux, Lee, Little, Brown and Company, 1290 Avenue of the Americas, New York, NY 10019 *Tel:* 212-364-1100 *Fax:* 212-364-0952 *E-mail:* firstname.lastname@hbgusa.com *Web Site:* www.littlebrown.com; www.HachetteBookGroup.com, pg 135

Boughton, Simon, Roaring Brook Press, 175 Fifth Ave, New York, NY 10010 *Tel:* 646-307-5151 *Web Site:* us.macmillan.com/publishers/roaring-brook-press, pg 200

Boulder, Sharon, Top of the Mountain Publishing, 4837 62 St N, St Petersburg, FL 33709 *Tel:* 727-391-3958 *Web Site:* www.topofthemountain.com, pg 233

Boulerice, Yvan, Art Image Publications, PO Box 160, Derby Line, VT 05830 *Toll Free Tel:* 800-361-2598 *Toll Free Fax:* 800-559-2598 *E-mail:* info@artimagepublications.com; customer.service@artimagepublications.com *Web Site:* www.artimagepublications.com, pg 21

Boultinghouse, Philis, Howard Books, c/o Simon & Schuster, Inc, 1230 Avenue of the Americas, New York, NY 10020 *E-mail:* howardbooks@simonandschuster.com (info) *Web Site:* simonandschusterpublishing.com/howard-books/, pg 112

Bourbon Ramirez, Melissa, Entangled Publishing, 2614 S Timberline Rd, Suite 109, Fort Collins, CO 80525 *Toll Free Tel:* 877-677-9451 *E-mail:* publisher@entangledpublishing.com *Web Site:* www.entangledpublishing.com, pg 79

Bourdon, Pierre, Groupe Sogides Inc, 955 rue Amherst, Montreal, QC H2L 3K4, Canada *Tel:* 514-523-1182 *Fax:* 514-597-0370 *Web Site:* www.sogides.com, pg 458

Boureau, Ella, Lambda Literary Awards (Lammys), 5482 Wilshire Blvd, No 1595, Los Angeles, CA 90036 *Tel:* 323-643-4281 *E-mail:* admin@lambdaliterary.org *Web Site:* www.lambdaliterary.org, pg 659

Bourg, Chris, Massachusetts Institute of Technology Libraries, 77 Massachusetts Ave, Bldg 14-S, Rm 0551, Cambridge, MA 02139-4307 *Tel:* 617-253-5671 *E-mail:* docs@mit.edu *Web Site:* libraries.mit.edu/docs, pg 144

Bourgogne, Beatrice, University of Chicago Press, 1427 E 60 St, Chicago, IL 60637-2954 *Tel:* 773-702-7700; 773-702-7600 *Toll Free Tel:* 800-621-2736 (orders) *Fax:* 773-702-9756; 773-660-2235 (orders); 773-702-2708 *E-mail:* custserv@press.uchicago.edu; marketing@press.uchicago.edu *Web Site:* www.press.uchicago.edu, pg 241

Bourma, Melinda, Zondervan, 3900 Sparks Dr, Grand Rapids, MI 49546 *Tel:* 616-698-6900 *Toll Free Tel:* 800-226-1122; 800-727-1309 (retail orders) *Fax:* 616-698-3350 *Toll Free Fax:* 800-698-3256 (retail orders) *E-mail:* zinfo@zondervan.com *Web Site:* www.zondervan.com, pg 263

Bourret, Joan Liffring-Zug, Penfield Books, 215 Brown St, Iowa City, IA 52245 *Tel:* 319-337-9998 *Toll Free Tel:* 800-728-9998 *Fax:* 319-351-6846 *E-mail:* penfield@penfieldbooks.com *Web Site:* www.penfieldbooks.com, pg 177

Bourret, Michael, Dystel, Goderich & Bourret LLC, One Union Sq W, Suite 904, New York, NY 10003 *Tel:* 212-627-9100 *Fax:* 212-627-9313 *Web Site:* www.dystel.com, pg 515

Boutillier, Katie Shea, Donald Maass Literary Agency, 1000 Dean St, Suite 252, Brooklyn, NY 11238 *Tel:* 212-727-8383 *Fax:* 212-727-3271 *E-mail:* info@maassagency.com *Web Site:* www.maassagency.com, pg 526

Boutin, Carole, Editions Trecarre, La Tourelle, 1055, blvd Rene-Levesque E, Bureau 300, Montreal, QC H2L 4S5, Canada *Tel:* 514-849-5259 *Fax:* 514-849-1388 *Web Site:* www.editions-trecarre.com, pg 455

Boutote, Claudia, HarperCollins General Books Group, 195 Broadway, New York, NY 10007 *Tel:* 212-207-7000 *Web Site:* www.harpercollins.com, pg 101

Bovay, Nicolas, United Nations Publications, 300 E 42 St, 9th fl, New York, NY 10017 *Tel:* 703-661-1571 *Fax:* 703-996-1010 *E-mail:* publications@un.org *Web Site:* shop.un.org, pg 238

Bowen, Brenda, Sanford J Greenburger Associates Inc, 55 Fifth Ave, New York, NY 10003 *Tel:* 212-206-5600 *Fax:* 212-463-8718 *Web Site:* greenburger.com; www.sjga.com, pg 520

Bowen, Deborah J, Health Administration Press, One N Franklin St, Suite 1700, Chicago, IL 60606-3491 *Tel:* 312-424-2800 *Fax:* 312-424-0014 *E-mail:* hap1@ache.org *Web Site:* www.ache.org/publications (orders), pg 104

Bowen, Kelly, Arcadia Publishing Inc, 420 Wando Park Blvd, Mount Pleasant, SC 29464 *Tel:* 843-853-2070 *Toll Free Tel:* 888-313-2665 (orders only) *Fax:* 843-853-0044 *E-mail:* sales@arcadiapublishing.com *Web Site:* www.arcadiapublishing.com, pg 20

Bowen, Stephanie, TarcherPerigee, 375 Hudson St, New York, NY 10014 *Tel:* 212-366-2000 *Fax:* 212-366-2643 *E-mail:* customerservice@penguinrandomhouse.com (cust serv); TarcherPerigeePublicity@penguinrandomhouse.com (media queries) *Web Site:* www.tarcherbooks.com; www.facebook.com/TarcherPerigee/; www.penguin.com/publishers/tarcherperigee, pg 227

Bower, Susan, Natasha Kern Literary Agency Inc, PO Box 1069, White Salmon, WA 98672 *Tel:* 509-493-3803 *E-mail:* agent@natashakern.com *Web Site:* www.natashakern.com, pg 523

Bowers, Ford, Specialty Graphic Imaging Association (SGIA), 10015 Main St, Fairfax, VA 22031-3489 *Tel:* 703-385-1335 *Toll Free Tel:* 888-385-3588 *Fax:* 703-273-0456 *E-mail:* sgia@sgia.org *Web Site:* www.sgia.org, pg 579

Bowers, Jennifer, Association of College & University Printers (ACUP), PO Box 285, Carrabelle, FL 32322 *Tel:* 850-570-5241 *Web Site:* www.acup-edu.org, pg 559

Bowers, John, Sanford J Greenburger Associates Inc, 55 Fifth Ave, New York, NY 10003 *Tel:* 212-206-5600 *Fax:* 212-463-8718 *Web Site:* greenburger.com; www.sjga.com, pg 520

Bowers, Sharon, The Miller Agency Inc, 630 Ninth Ave, Suite 1102, New York, NY 10036 *Tel:* 212-206-0913 *Fax:* 212-206-1473, pg 530

Bowes, Matt, NeWest Press, 8540 109 St, No 201, Edmonton, AB T6G 1E6, Canada *Tel:* 780-432-9427 *Fax:* 780-433-3179 *E-mail:* info@newestpress.com; orders@newestpress.com *Web Site:* www.newestpress.com, pg 464

Bowker, Scott, Houghton Mifflin Harcourt, 125 High St, Boston, MA 02110 *Tel:* 617-351-5000 *Toll Free Tel:* 855-969-4642; 800-225-5425 (K-12 educ materials); 800-323-9540 (assessment materials); 877-219-1537 (SkillsTutor); 888-242-6747 (Innovation in Educ Group); 800-225-3362 (Trade & Ref Div) *Toll Free Fax:* 800-269-5232 *E-mail:* myhmhco@hmhco.com *Web Site:* www.hmhco.com, pg 110

Bowles, Brandi, United Talent Agency, 9336 Civic Center Dr, Beverly Hills, CA 90210 *Tel:* 310-273-6700 *Fax:* 310-247-1111 *Web Site:* www.unitedtalent.com, pg 540

Bowlin, Sarah, Aevitas Creative Management, 19 W 21 St, Suite 501, New York, NY 10010 *Tel:* 212-765-6900 *Web Site:* aevitascreative.com, pg 506

Bowman, Hannah, Liza Dawson Associates, 350 Seventh Ave, Suite 2003, New York, NY 10001 *Tel:* 212-465-9071 *Fax:* 212-947-0460 *Web Site:* www.lizadawsonassociates.com, pg 513

Bowman, Ryland, Carolina Academic Press, 700 Kent St, Durham, NC 27701 *Tel:* 919-489-7486 *Toll Free Tel:* 800-489-7486 *Fax:* 919-493-5668 *E-mail:* cap@cap-press.com *Web Site:* www.cap-press.com; www.caplaw.com, pg 48

Bowyer, Clifford B, Silver Leaf Books LLC, 13 Temi Rd, Holliston, MA 01746 *E-mail:* sales@silverleafbooks.com; editor@silverleafbooks.com; customerservice@silverleafbooks.com *Web Site:* www.silverleafbooks.com, pg 212

Bowzer, Melanie, The Association of Medical Illustrators (AMI), 201 E Main St, Suite 1405, Lexington, KY 40507 *Toll Free Tel:* 866-393-4264 *Fax:* 859-514-9166 *E-mail:* hq@ami.org *Web Site:* www.ami.org, pg 559

Boyajian, Lisa, Rutgers University Press, 106 Somerset St, 3rd fl, New Brunswick, NJ 08901 *Tel:* 848-445-7762 *Toll Free Tel:* 800-848-6224 (orders only) *Fax:* 732-745-4935 (acqs, edit, mktg, perms & prodn) *Toll Free Fax:* 800-272-6817 (fulfillment) *Web Site:* rutgerspress.rutgers.edu, pg 202

Boyd, Ann, Ruth & Sylvia Schwartz Children's Book Awards, c/o Ontario Arts Council, 121 Bloor St E, 7th fl, Toronto, ON M4W 3M5, Canada *Tel:* 416-961-1660 *Toll Free Tel:* 800-387-0058 (ON) *Fax:* 416-961-7796 (Ontario Arts Council); 416-969-7450 (Ontario Arts Foundation) *E-mail:* info@arts.on.ca; foundation@arts.on.ca *Web Site:* www.arts.on.ca; ontarioartsfoundation.on.ca/pages/ruth-sylvia-schwartz-awards, pg 688

Boyd, Taryn, Brindle & Glass Publishing Ltd, 1075 Pendergast St, Suite 103, Victoria, BC V8V 0A1, Canada *Tel:* 250-360-0829 *Fax:* 250-386-0829 *E-mail:* info@brindleandglass.com *Web Site:* www.brindleandglass.com, pg 447

Boyd, Taryn, TouchWood Editions, 103-1075 Pendergast St, Victoria, BC V8V 0A1, Canada *Tel:* 250-360-0829 *Fax:* 250-386-0829 *E-mail:* info@touchwoodeditions.com *Web Site:* www.touchwoodeditions.com, pg 472

Boyd, Vicki, Boynton/Cook Publishers, 361 Hanover St, Portsmouth, NH 03801-3912 *Tel:* 603-431-7894 *Toll Free Tel:* 800-225-5800 *Fax:* 603-431-2214 *Toll Free Fax:* 877-231-6980 *E-mail:* custserv@heinemann.com *Web Site:* www.heinemann.com/boyntoncook, pg 41

Boyd, Vicki, Heinemann, 361 Hanover St, Portsmouth, NH 03801-3912 *Tel:* 603-431-7894 *Toll Free Tel:* 800-225-5800 (US) *Fax:* 603-431-2214 *Toll Free Fax:* 877-231-6980 (US) *E-mail:* custserv@heinemann.com *Web Site:* www.heinemann.com, pg 105

Boyer, Emma, Zest Books, 2443 Stillman St, Suite 340, San Francisco, CA 94115 *Tel:* 415-777-8654; 510-984-0841 *Fax:* 415-777-8653 *E-mail:* info@zestbooks.net; publicity@zestbooks.net *Web Site:* zestbooks.net, pg 263

Boyer, Heather, Island Press, 2000 "M" St NW, Suite 650, Washington, DC 20036 *Tel:* 202-232-7933 *Toll Free Tel:* 800-828-1302 *Fax:* 202-234-1328 *E-mail:* info@islandpress.org *Web Site:* www.islandpress.org, pg 121

Boyer, Jennifer, American Association of Blood Banks, North Tower, 4550 Montgomery Ave, Suite 700, Bethesda, MD 20814 *Tel:* 301-907-6977 *Toll Free Tel:* 866-222-2498 (sales) *Fax:* 301-907-6895 *E-mail:* aabb@aabb.org; sales@aabb.org (ordering); publications1@aabb.org (catalog) *Web Site:* www.aabb.org, pg 10

Boykins, Jennifer, Scholastic Education, 557 Broadway, New York, NY 10012 *Tel:* 212-343-6100 *Fax:* 212-343-6189 *Web Site:* www.scholastic.com, pg 207

Boyko, Alan, Scholastic Inc, 557 Broadway, New York, NY 10012 *Tel:* 212-343-6100 *Toll Free Tel:* 800-SCHOLASTIC (724-6527) *Web Site:* www.scholastic.com, pg 208

Boyle, Aileen, Plume, 375 Hudson St, New York, NY 10014 *Tel:* 212-366-2000 *Fax:* 212-243-6002 *Web Site:* www.penguin.com/publishers/plume, pg 184

Boyle, Candace, Bradford Publishing Co, 1743 Wazee St, Denver, CO 80202 *Tel:* 303-292-2590 *Toll Free Tel:* 800-446-2831 *Fax:* 303-298-5014 *E-mail:* marketing@bradfordpublishing.com; customerservice@bradfordpublishing.com *Web Site:* www.bradfordpublishing.com, pg 42

Boyle, Corinne, Peradam Press, PO Box 6, North San Juan, CA 95960-0006 *Tel:* 530-277-9324 *Fax:* 530-559-0754 *E-mail:* peradam@earthlink.net, pg 180

Boyle, Matt, American Society of Civil Engineers (ASCE), 1801 Alexander Bell Dr, Reston, VA 20191-4400 *Tel:* 703-295-6300 *Toll Free Tel:* 800-548-2723 *Fax:* 703-295-6278 *E-mail:* ascelibrary@asce.org *Web Site:* www.asce.org, pg 15

Boynton-Trigg, Anne, Scholastic International, 557 Broadway, New York, NY 10012 *Tel:* 212-343-6100; 646-330-5288 (intl cust serv) *Toll Free Tel:* 800-SCHOLASTIC (724-6527) *Fax:* 646-837-7878 *E-mail:* international@scholastic.com, pg 208

Boys, Christina, Hachette Nashville, 12 Cadillac Dr, Suite 480, Brentwood, TN 37027 *Tel:* 615-221-0996 *Fax:* 615-221-0962 *Web Site:* www.hachettebookgroup.com, pg 98

Bozzi, Debra, Yale University Press, 302 Temple St, New Haven, CT 06511-8909 *Tel:* 203-432-0960; 203-432-0966 (sales); 401-531-2800 (cust serv) *Toll Free Tel:* 800-405-1619 (cust serv) *Fax:* 203-432-0948; 203-432-8485 (sales); 401-531-2801 (cust serv) *Toll Free Fax:* 800-406-9145 (cust serv) *E-mail:* sales.press@yale.edu (sales); customer.care@triliteral.org (cust serv) *Web Site:* www.yalebooks.com; yalepress.yale.edu/yupbooks, pg 261

Braaten, Douglas PhD, New York Academy of Sciences (NYAS), 7 World Trade, 40th fl, 250 Greenwich St, New York, NY 10007-2157 *Tel:* 212-298-8600 *Toll Free Tel:* 800-843-6927 *Fax:* 212-298-3668 *E-mail:* nyas@nyas.org; annals@nyas.org; customerservice@nyas.org *Web Site:* www.nyas.org, pg 161

Brabec, Kimberly, Waterside Productions Inc, 2055 Oxford Ave, Cardiff, CA 92007 *Tel:* 760-632-9190 *Fax:* 760-632-9295 *E-mail:* admin@waterside.com *Web Site:* www.waterside.com, pg 541

Brach, Courtney, Touchstone, 1230 Avenue of the Americas, New York, NY 10020, pg 233

Brachfeld, Janea, Storey Publishing LLC, 210 MASS MoCA Way, North Adams, MA 01247 *Tel:* 413-346-2100 *Toll Free Tel:* 800-441-5700 (orders); 800-793-9396 (edit) *Fax:* 413-346-2199; 413-346-2196 (edit) *E-mail:* sales@storey.com *Web Site:* www.storey.com, pg 223

Brachfeld, Janea, Timber Press Inc, 133 SW Second Ave, Suite 450, Portland, OR 97204 *Tel:* 503-227-2878 *Toll Free Tel:* 800-327-5680 *Fax:* 503-227-3070 *E-mail:* info@timberpress.com *Web Site:* www.timberpress.com, pg 232

Bracken, Don, History Publishing Co LLC, PO Box 700, Palisades, NY 10964 *Tel:* 845-359-1765 *Fax:* 845-818-3730 (sales) *E-mail:* info@historypublishingco.com *Web Site:* www.historypublishingco.com, pg 108

Bradford, Laura, Bradford Literary Agency, 5694 Mission Center Rd, Suite 347, San Diego, CA 92108 *Tel:* 619-521-1201 *E-mail:* queries@bradfordlit.com *Web Site:* www.bradfordlit.com, pg 509

Bradhering, Gary, MapEasy Inc, PO Box 80, Wainscott, NY 11975-0080 *Tel:* 631-537-6213 *Fax:* 631-537-4541 *E-mail:* info@mapeasy.com *Web Site:* www.mapeasy.com, pg 141

Bradie, Ian R, Cambridge University Press, 1 Liberty Plaza, 20th fl, New York, NY 10006 *Tel:* 212-924-3900; 212-337-5000 *Fax:* 212-691-3239 *E-mail:* newyork@cambridge.org *Web Site:* www.cambridge.org/us, pg 46

Bradley, Cheryl, NASW Press, 750 First St NE, Suite 800, Washington, DC 20002 *Tel:* 202-408-8600 *Fax:* 203-336-8312 *E-mail:* press@naswdc.org *Web Site:* www.naswpress.org, pg 156

Bradley, Elizabeth, The Foundation Center, 32 Old Slip, 24th fl, New York, NY 10005-3500 *Tel:* 212-620-4230 *Toll Free Tel:* 800-424-9836 *Fax:* 212-807-3677 *E-mail:* customerservice@foundationcenter.org *Web Site:* foundationcenter.org, pg 87

Bradley, Fern Marshall, Chelsea Green Publishing Co, 85 N Main St, Suite 120, White River Junction, VT 05001 *Tel:* 802-295-6300 *Toll Free Tel:* 800-639-4099 (cust serv, consumer & trade orders) *Fax:* 802-295-6444 *Web Site:* www.chelseagreen.com, pg 53

Bradley, Joanna, Fresh Air Books, 1908 Grand Ave, Nashville, TN 37212 *Tel:* 615-340-7200 *Toll Free Tel:* 800-972-0433 (orders) *Web Site:* books.upperroom.org, pg 88

Bradley, Joanna, Upper Room Books, 1908 Grand Ave, Nashville, TN 37212 *Tel:* 615-340-7200 *Toll Free Tel:* 800-972-0433 *Fax:* 615-340-7266 *Web Site:* books.upperroom.org, pg 248

Bradley, Kevin J, Taylor & Francis Inc, 530 Walnut St, Suite 850, Philadelphia, PA 19106 *Tel:* 215-625-8900 *Toll Free Tel:* 800-354-1420 *Fax:* 215-207-0050; 215-207-0046 (cust serv) *E-mail:* support@tandfonline.com *Web Site:* www.taylorandfrancis.com, pg 227

Bradley, Shaun, Transatlantic Agency, 2 Bloor St E, Suite 3500, Toronto, ON M4W 1A8, Canada *Tel:* 416-488-9214 *E-mail:* info@transatlanticagency.com *Web Site:* www.transatlanticagency.com, pg 539

Bradshaw, Jenny, McClelland & Stewart Ltd, 320 Front St W, Suite 1400, Toronto, ON M5V 3B6, Canada *Tel:* 416-364-4449 *Fax:* 416-598-7764 *E-mail:* customerservicescanada@penguinrandomhouse.com; publicity@ca.penguingroup.com *Web Site:* penguinrandomhouse.ca/imprints/mcclelland-stewart, pg 463

Brady, Dr Philip, Etruscan Press, Wilkes University, 84 W South St, Wilkes-Barre, PA 18766 *Tel:* 570-408-4546 *Fax:* 570-408-3333 *E-mail:* books@etruscanpress.org *Web Site:* www.etruscanpress.org, pg 80

Brady, Robert L, Business & Legal Resources Inc, 100 Winners Circle, Suite 300, Brentwood, TN 37027 *Tel:* 860-510-0100 *Toll Free Tel:* 800-727-5257 *E-mail:* service@blr.com *Web Site:* www.blr.com, pg 45

Brady, Sally R, bradylit, 81 Town Farm Hill, Hartland Four Corners, VT 05049 *Tel:* 802-436-2455, pg 490

Braeckel, Maria, Random House Publishing Group, 1745 Broadway, New York, NY 10019 *Toll Free Tel:* 800-200-3552 *Web Site:* atrandom.com, pg 195

Braithwaite, Jill, Carolrhoda Books, 241 First Ave N, Minneapolis, MN 55401 *Tel:* 612-332-3344 *Toll Free Tel:* 800-328-4929 *Fax:* 612-332-7615 *Toll Free Fax:* 800-332-1132 *E-mail:* info@lernerbooks.com; custserve@lernerbooks.com *Web Site:* www.lernerbooks.com; www.facebook.com/lernerbooks, pg 48

Braithwaite, Jill, Carolrhoda Lab™, 241 First Ave N, Minneapolis, MN 55401 *Tel:* 612-332-3344 *Toll Free Tel:* 800-328-4929 *Fax:* 612-332-7615 *Toll Free Fax:* 800-332-1132 (US) *E-mail:* info@lernerbooks.com; custserve@lernerbooks.com *Web Site:* www.lernerbooks.com; www.facebook.com/lernerbooks, pg 48

Braithwaite, Jill, ediciones Lerner, 241 First Ave N, Minneapolis, MN 55401 *Tel:* 612-332-3344 *Toll Free Tel:* 800-328-4929 *Fax:* 612-332-7615 *Toll Free Fax:* 800-332-1132 *E-mail:* info@lernerbooks.com; custserve@lernerbooks.com *Web Site:* www.lernerbooks.com; www.facebook.com/lernerbooks, pg 75

Braithwaite, Jill, First Avenue Editions, 241 First Ave N, Minneapolis, MN 55401 *Tel:* 612-332-3344 *Toll Free Tel:* 800-328-4929 *Fax:* 612-332-7615 *Toll Free Fax:* 800-332-1132 *E-mail:* info@lernerbooks.com; custserve@lernerbooks.com *Web Site:* www.lernerbooks.com; www.facebook.com/lernerbooks, pg 85

Braithwaite, Jill, Graphic Universe™, 241 First Ave N, Minneapolis, MN 55401 *Tel:* 612-332-3344 *Toll Free Tel:* 800-328-4929 *Fax:* 612-332-7615 *Toll Free Fax:* 800-332-1132 *E-mail:* info@lernerbooks.com; custserve@lernerbooks.com *Web Site:* www.lernerbooks.com; www.facebook.com/lernerbooks, pg 95

Braithwaite, Jill, Lerner Publications, 241 First Ave N, Minneapolis, MN 55401 *Tel:* 612-332-3344 *Toll Free Tel:* 800-328-4929 *Fax:* 612-332-7615 *Toll Free Fax:* 800-332-1132 *E-mail:* info@lernerbooks.com; custserve@lernerbooks.com *Web Site:* www.lernerbooks.com; www.facebook.com/lernerbooks, pg 132

Braithwaite, Jill, Lerner Publishing Group Inc, 241 First Ave N, Minneapolis, MN 55401 *Tel:* 612-332-3344 *Toll Free Tel:* 800-328-4929 *Fax:* 612-332-7615 *Toll Free Fax:* 800-332-1132 *E-mail:* info@lernerbooks.com; custserve@lernerbooks.com *Web Site:* www.lernerbooks.com; www.facebook.com/lernerbooks, pg 132

Braithwaite, Jill, LernerClassroom, 241 First Ave N, Minneapolis, MN 55401 *Tel:* 612-332-3344 *Toll Free Tel:* 800-328-4929 *Fax:* 612-332-7615 *Toll Free Fax:* 800-332-1132 *E-mail:* info@lernerbooks.com; custserve@lernerbooks.com *Web Site:* www.lernerbooks.com; www.facebook.com/lernerbooks, pg 132

Braithwaite, Jill, Millbrook Press, 241 First Ave N, Minneapolis, MN 55401 *Tel:* 612-332-3344 *Toll Free Tel:* 800-328-4929 (US only) *Fax:* 612-332-7615 *Toll Free Fax:* 800-332-1132 *E-mail:* info@lernerbooks.com; custserve@lernerbooks.com *Web Site:* www.lernerbooks.com; www.facebook.com/millbrookpress, pg 151

Braithwaite, Jill, Twenty-First Century Books, 241 First Ave N, Minneapolis, MN 55401 *Tel:* 612-332-3344 *Toll Free Tel:* 800-328-4929 *Fax:* 612-332-7615 *Toll Free Fax:* 800-332-1132 *E-mail:* info@lernerbooks.com; custserve@lernerbooks.com *Web Site:* www.lernerbooks.com; www.facebook.com/lernerbooks, pg 237

Brallier, Jess, Harry N Abrams Inc, 195 Broadway, 9th fl, New York, NY 10007 *Tel:* 212-206-7715 *Toll Free Tel:* 800-345-1359 *Fax:* 212-519-1210 *E-mail:* abrams@abramsbooks.com *Web Site:* www.abramsbooks.com, pg 3

Bramson, Ann, Workman Publishing Co Inc, 225 Varick St, 9th fl, New York, NY 10014-4381 *Tel:* 212-254-5900 *Toll Free Tel:* 800-722-7202 *Fax:* 212-254-8098 *E-mail:* info@workman.com *Web Site:* www.workman.com, pg 259

Branch, Justin, Greenleaf Book Group LLC, 3 Park Place, 4005 Banister Lane, Suite B, Austin, TX 78704 *Tel:* 512-891-6100 *Fax:* 512-891-6150 *E-mail:* contact@greenleafbookgroup.com *Web Site:* www.greenleafbookgroup.com, pg 96

Brand, Amy, The MIT Press, One Rogers St, Cambridge, MA 02142 *Tel:* 617-253-5255 *Toll Free Tel:* 800-207-8354 (orders) *Fax:* 617-258-6779; 617-577-1545 (orders) *Web Site:* mitpress.mit.edu, pg 151

Brand, Dionne, McClelland & Stewart Ltd, 320 Front St W, Suite 1400, Toronto, ON M5V 3B6, Canada *Tel:* 416-364-4449 *Fax:* 416-598-7764 *E-mail:* customerservicescanada@penguinrandomhouse.com; publicity@ca.penguingroup.com *Web Site:* penguinrandomhouse.ca/imprints/mcclelland-stewart, pg 463

Brand, Megan, University of British Columbia Press, 2029 West Mall, Vancouver, BC V6T 1Z2, Canada *Tel:* 604-822-5959 *Toll Free Tel:* 877-377-9378 *Fax:* 604-822-6083 *Toll Free Fax:* 800-668-0821 *E-mail:* frontdesk@ubcpress.ca *Web Site:* www.ubcpress.ca, pg 473

Brandel, Ms Dusty, American Auto Racing Writers & Broadcasters, 922 N Pass Ave, Burbank, CA 91505 *Tel:* 818-842-7005 *Fax:* 818-842-7020, pg 554

Brandenburgh, Greg, Red Wheel/Weiser/Conari, 65 Parker St, Suite 7, Newburyport, MA 01950 *Tel:* 978-465-0504 *Toll Free Tel:* 800-423-7087 (orders) *Fax:* 978-465-0243 *E-mail:* info@rwwbooks.com *Web Site:* www.redwheelweiser.com, pg 197

Brander, Jacob, Mesorah Publications Ltd, 4401 Second Ave, Brooklyn, NY 11232 *Tel:* 718-921-9000 *Toll Free Tel:* 800-637-6724 *Fax:* 718-680-1875 *E-mail:* info@artscroll.com; orders@artscroll.com *Web Site:* www.artscroll.com, pg 149

Brandon, Leslie, Henry Holt and Company, LLC, 175 Fifth Ave, New York, NY 10010 *Tel:* 646-307-5151 *Toll Free Tel:* 888-330-8477 (orders) *Fax:* 646-307-5285 *E-mail:* firstname.lastname@hholt.com *Web Site:* www.henryholt.com, pg 109

Brandreth, Dale, Caissa Editions, PO Box 151, Yorklyn, DE 19736-0151 *Tel:* 302-239-4608 *Web Site:* www.chessbookstore.com, pg 46

Brandt, Eric, The University of Virginia Press, PO Box 400318, Charlottesville, VA 22904-4318 *Tel:* 434-924-3468 (cust serv); 434-924-3469 (cust serv) *Toll Free Tel:* 800-831-3406 (orders) *Fax:* 434-982-2655 *Toll Free Fax:* 877-288-6400 *E-mail:* vapress@virginia.edu *Web Site:* www.upress.virginia.edu, pg 245

Brandt, Joan, The Joan Brandt Agency, 788 Wesley Dr NW, Atlanta, GA 30305 *Tel:* 404-351-8877 *Fax:* 404-351-0068, pg 510

Brandt, Rosemary, The University of Arizona Press, 1510 E University Blvd, Tucson, AZ 85721 *Tel:* 520-621-1441 *Toll Free Tel:* 800-426-3797 (orders) *Fax:* 520-621-8899 *Toll Free Fax:* 800-426-3797 *E-mail:* uap@uapress.arizona.edu *Web Site:* www.uapress.arizona.edu, pg 240

Branham, Lorraine, Syracuse University, SI Newhouse School of Public Communications, 215 University Place, Syracuse, NY 13244-2100 *Tel:* 315-443-3627 *Fax:* 315-443-3946 *E-mail:* newhouse@syr.edu *Web Site:* newhouse.syr.edu, pg 622

Brants, Keith, Martingale®, 19021 120 Ave NE, Suite 102, Bothell, WA 98011 *Tel:* 425-483-3313 *Toll Free Tel:* 800-426-3126 *Fax:* 425-486-7596 *E-mail:* info@martingale-pub.com *Web Site:* www.martingale-pub.com, pg 143

Bratcher, Joe W III, Host Publications, 3408 West Ave, Austin, TX 78705 *Tel:* 512-236-1290 *Fax:* 512-236-1208 *Web Site:* www.hostpublications.com, pg 110

Bratton, Chuck, EMC Publishing LLC, 875 Montreal Way, St Paul, MN 55102 *Tel:* 651-290-2800 (corp) *Toll Free Tel:* 800-328-1452 *Toll Free Fax:* 800-328-4564 *E-mail:* educate@emcp.com *Web Site:* www.emcp.com, pg 77

Brault, Carol, Dorland Health, 4 Choke Cherry Rd, 2nd fl, Rockville, MD 20850 *Tel:* 301-354-2000 *Toll Free Tel:* 855-225-5341 *Fax:* 301-287-2535 *E-mail:* customer@decisionhealth.com *Web Site:* www.dorlandhealth.com, pg 72

Brault, Yves, Brault & Bouthillier, 700 ave Beaumont, Montreal, QC H3N 1V5, Canada *Tel:* 514-273-9186 *Toll Free Tel:* 800-361-0378 *Fax:* 514-273-8627 *Toll Free Fax:* 800-361-0378 *E-mail:* ventes@bb.ca *Web Site:* bb.ca, pg 447

Braun, Barbara, Barbara Braun Associates Inc, 7 E 14 St, Suite 19F, New York, NY 10003 *Tel:* 212-604-9023 *Web Site:* www.barbarabraunagency.com, pg 510

Braun, Mary Elizabeth, Oregon State University Press, 121 The Valley Library, Corvallis, OR 97331-4501 *Tel:* 541-737-3166 *Toll Free Tel:* 800-621-2736 (orders), pg 170

Braunstein, Bruce, Book Publicists of Southern California, 714 Crescent Dr, Beverly Hills, CA 90210 *Tel:* 323-461-3921 *Fax:* 323-461-0917 *Web Site:* www.bookpublicists.org, pg 560

Braverman, Marianne, Andrew Carnegie Medals for Excellence in Fiction & Nonfiction, 50 E Huron St, Chicago, IL 60611 *Tel:* 312-944-6780 *Toll Free Tel:* 800-545-2433 *Fax:* 312-440-9374 *E-mail:* ala@ala.org *Web Site:* www.ala.org/awardsgrants/carnegieadult, pg 636

Braziller, Karen, Persea Books, 277 Broadway, Suite 708, New York, NY 10007 *Tel:* 212-260-9256 *Fax:* 212-267-3165 *E-mail:* info@perseabooks.com *Web Site:* www.perseabooks.com, pg 180

Braziller, Karen, Lexi Rudnitsky First Book Prize in Poetry, 277 Broadway, Suite 708, New York, NY 10007 *Tel:* 212-260-9256 *Fax:* 212-267-3165 *E-mail:* info@perseabooks.com *Web Site:* www.perseabooks.com, pg 686

Braziller, Michael, George Braziller Inc, 277 Broadway, Suite 708, New York, NY 10007 *Tel:* 212-260-9256 *Fax:* 212-267-3165 *E-mail:* editorial@georgebraziller.com *Web Site:* www.georgebraziller.com, pg 42

Braziller, Michael, Persea Books, 277 Broadway, Suite 708, New York, NY 10007 *Tel:* 212-260-9256 *Fax:* 212-267-3165 *E-mail:* info@perseabooks.com *Web Site:* www.perseabooks.com, pg 180

Braziller, Michael, Lexi Rudnitsky First Book Prize in Poetry, 277 Broadway, Suite 708, New York, NY 10007 *Tel:* 212-260-9256 *Fax:* 212-267-3165 *E-mail:* info@perseabooks.com *Web Site:* www.perseabooks.com, pg 686

Brazis, Tamar, Harry N Abrams Inc, 195 Broadway, 9th fl, New York, NY 10007 *Tel:* 212-206-7715 *Toll Free Tel:* 800-345-1359 *Fax:* 212-519-1210 *E-mail:* abrams@abramsbooks.com *Web Site:* www.abramsbooks.com, pg 3

Brebner, Nicole, Harlequin Enterprises Ltd, 225 Duncan Mill Rd, Don Mills, ON M3B 3K9, Canada *Tel:* 416-445-5860 *Toll Free Tel:* 888-432-4879; 800-370-5838 (ebook inquiries) *E-mail:* customerservice@harlequin.com *Web Site:* www.harlequin.com, pg 459

Brecker, Lora, Ascension Press, PO Box 1990, West Chester, PA 19380 *Tel:* 610-696-7795; 484-875-4550 (admin) *Toll Free Tel:* 800-376-0520 (sales & cust serv) *Web Site:* ascensionpress.com, pg 22

Breden, Cathy, The Center for Exhibition Industry Research (CEIR), 12700 Park Central Dr, Suite 308, Dallas, TX 75251 *Tel:* 972-687-9242 *Fax:* 972-692-6020 *E-mail:* info@ceir.org *Web Site:* www.ceir.org, pg 562

Breeden, Elizabeth, Simon & Schuster, 1230 Avenue of the Americas, New York, NY 10020 *Tel:* 212-698-7000 *Toll Free Tel:* 800-223-2348 (cust serv); 800-223-2336 (orders) *Toll Free Fax:* 800-943-9831 (orders) *Web Site:* www.simonandschuster.com, pg 212

Brehl, Joan, Alliance for Audited Media (AAM), Canadian Office, 151 Bloor St W, Suite 850, Toronto, ON M5S 1S4, Canada *Tel:* 416-962-5840 *Fax:* 416-962-5844 *Web Site:* auditedmedia.com, pg 554

Breichner, William M, The Johns Hopkins University Press, 2715 N Charles St, Baltimore, MD 21218-4363 *Tel:* 410-516-6900; 410-516-6987 (journal orders outside US & CN) *Toll Free Tel:* 800-537-5487 (book orders & cust serv); 800-548-1784 (journal orders) *Fax:* 410-516-6968; 410-516-3866 (journal orders) *E-mail:* hfscustserv@press.jhu.edu (cust serv); jrnlcirc@press.jhu.edu (journal orders) *Web Site:* www.press.jhu.edu; muse.jhu.edu, pg 122

Breier, Davida, The Johns Hopkins University Press, 2715 N Charles St, Baltimore, MD 21218-4363 *Tel:* 410-516-6900; 410-516-6987 (journal orders outside US & CN) *Toll Free Tel:* 800-537-5487 (book orders & cust serv); 800-548-1784 (journal orders) *Fax:* 410-516-6968; 410-516-3866 (journal orders) *E-mail:* hfscustserv@press.jhu.edu (cust serv); jrnlcirc@press.jhu.edu (journal orders) *Web Site:* www.press.jhu.edu; muse.jhu.edu, pg 122

Breisacher, Ed, The Darwin Press Inc, PO Box 2202, Princeton, NJ 08543 *Tel:* 609-737-1349 *Fax:* 609-737-0929 *E-mail:* books@darwinpress.com *Web Site:* www.darwinpress.com, pg 67

Brendan, Stephen, Light Publications, Hope Artiste Village, 1005 Main St, Suite 1212, Pawtucket, RI 02806 *Tel:* 401-484-0228 *E-mail:* info@lightpublications.com *Web Site:* lightpublications.com, pg 134

Brengelman, Laura, Industrial Press Inc, 32 Haviland St, Suite 3, Norwalk, CT 06854 *Tel:* 203-956-5593 ext 0 (cust serv) *Toll Free Tel:* 888-528-7852 ext 0 (cust serv) *Fax:* 203-354-9391 (cust serv) *E-mail:* info@industrialpress.com (cust serv) *Web Site:* new.industrialpress.com, pg 116

Brennan, Linda, Phaidon, 65 Bleecker St, 8th fl, New York, NY 10012 *Tel:* 212-652-5400 *Toll Free Tel:* 800-759-0190 (cust serv) *Fax:* 212-652-5410 *Toll Free Fax:* 800-286-9471 (cust serv) *E-mail:* ussales@phaidon.com *Web Site:* www.phaidon.com, pg 182

Brent, Barbara, Two Thousand Three Associates, 135 Chilean Ave, Palm Beach, FL 33480 *Tel:* 386-690-2503 *E-mail:* ttta1@att.net *Web Site:* www.twothousandthree.com, pg 237

Brent, T David, University of Chicago Press, 1427 E 60 St, Chicago, IL 60637-2954 *Tel:* 773-702-7700; 773-702-7600 *Toll Free Tel:* 800-621-2736 (orders) *Fax:* 773-702-9756; 773-660-2235 (orders); 773-

702-2708 *E-mail:* custserv@press.uchicago.edu; marketing@press.uchicago.edu *Web Site:* www.press.uchicago.edu, pg 241

Breschini, Gary PhD, Coyote Press, PO Box 3377, Salinas, CA 93912-3377 *Tel:* 831-422-4912 *Fax:* 831-422-4913 *E-mail:* orders@coyotepress.com *Web Site:* www.coyotepress.com, pg 63

Breslin, Ramsay, Kelsey Street Press, 2824 Kelsey St, Berkeley, CA 94705 *E-mail:* info@kelseyst.com *Web Site:* www.kelseyst.com, pg 125

Bretz, Bailey, AAUP Book, Jacket & Journal Design Show, 1412 Broadway, Suite 2135, New York, NY 10018 *Tel:* 212-989-1010 *Fax:* 212-989-0275 *E-mail:* info@aaupnet.org *Web Site:* www.aaupnet.org, pg 625

Bretz, Bailey, Association of American University Presses (AAUP), 1412 Broadway, Suite 2135, New York, NY 10018 *Tel:* 212-989-1010 *Fax:* 212-989-0275 *E-mail:* info@aaupnet.org *Web Site:* www.aaupnet.org, pg 558

Breunig, Kevin, Appalachian Mountain Club Books, 5 Joy St, Boston, MA 02108 *Tel:* 617-523-0655 *Toll Free Tel:* 800-262-4455 (orders) *Fax:* 617-523-0722 *E-mail:* amcbooks@outdoors.org *Web Site:* www.outdoors.org, pg 19

Brewer, Andrew, University of California Press, 155 Grand Ave, Suite 400, Oakland, CA 94612-3758 *Tel:* 510-883-8232 *Fax:* 510-836-8910 *E-mail:* customerservice@ucpressjournals.com *Web Site:* www.ucpress.edu, pg 240

Brewer, Anne, St Martin's Press, LLC, 175 Fifth Ave, New York, NY 10010 *Tel:* 646-307-5151 *Web Site:* us.macmillan.com/smp, pg 204

Brewer, Rachel, Wm B Eerdmans Publishing Co, 2140 Oak Industrial Dr NE, Grand Rapids, MI 49505 *Tel:* 616-459-4591 *Toll Free Tel:* 800-253-7521 *Fax:* 616-459-6540 *E-mail:* customerservice@eerdmans.com; sales@eerdmans.com *Web Site:* www.eerdmans.com, pg 76

Breznay, Ron, Bram Stoker Awards®, c/o Horror Writers Association, PO Box 56687, Sherman Oaks, CA 91413 *Tel:* 818-220-3965 *E-mail:* hwa@horror.org *Web Site:* horror.org/awards/stokers.htm, pg 692

Bricsoe, Kisha, National Catholic Educational Association, 1005 N Glebe Rd, Suite 525, Arlington, VA 22201 *Tel:* 571-257-0010 *Toll Free Tel:* 800-711-6232 *Fax:* 703-243-0025 *E-mail:* nceaadmin@ncea.org *Web Site:* www.ncea.org, pg 157

Bridges, Lois, Scholastic Education, 557 Broadway, New York, NY 10012 *Tel:* 212-343-6100 *Fax:* 212-343-6189 *Web Site:* www.scholastic.com, pg 207

Bridges, Shirin Yim, Goosebottom Books, 543 Trinidad Lane, Foster City, CA 94404 *Tel:* 650-556-3782 *Toll Free Fax:* 888-407-5286 *E-mail:* info@goosebottombooks.com *Web Site:* goosebottombooks.com, pg 94

Briel, Barbara, Sourcebooks Inc, 1935 Brookdale Rd, Suite 139, Naperville, IL 60563 *Tel:* 630-961-3900 *Toll Free Tel:* 800-432-7444 *Fax:* 630-961-2168 *E-mail:* info@sourcebooks.com; customersupport@sourcebooks.com *Web Site:* www.sourcebooks.com, pg 217

Briere, Sylvie, Les Editions de l'Hexagone, 1055, blvd Rene Levesque Est, Bureau 300, Montreal, QC H2L 4S5, Canada *Tel:* 514 523 7993 *Fax:* 514 849 1388 *Web Site:* www.edhexagone.com, pg 453

Briggs, Barbara, University Press of New England, One Court St, Suite 250, Lebanon, NH 03766 *Tel:* 603-448-1533 *Toll Free Tel:* 800-421-1561 (orders only) *Fax:* 603-448-7006; 603-448-9429 (orders only) *E-mail:* university.press@dartmouth.edu *Web Site:* www.upne.com, pg 247

Briggs, David, Philomel, 345 Hudson St, New York, NY 10014 *Tel:* 212-366-2000, pg 182

Briggs, David, GP Putnam's Sons (Children's), 345 Hudson St, New York, NY 10014 *Tel:* 212-366-2000 *Fax:* 212-414-3393 *Web Site:* www.penguin.com/publishers/gpputnamssonsbooksforyoungread, pg 192

Briggs, M Courtney, M Courtney Briggs Esq, Authors Representative, Chase Tower, 28th fl, 100 N Broadway Ave, Oklahoma City, OK 73102, pg 510

Bright, Harry, Maharishi University of Management Press, 1000 N Fourth St, Dept 1155, Fairfield, IA 52557-1155 *Tel:* 641-472-1101 *Toll Free Tel:* 800 831 6523 *Fax:* 641-472-1122 *E-mail:* mumpress@mum.edu *Web Site:* www.mumpress.com, pg 140

Brill, Calista, Roaring Brook Press, 175 Fifth Ave, New York, NY 10010 *Tel:* 646-307-5151 *Web Site:* us.macmillan.com/publishers/roaring-brook-press, pg 200

Brill, L Chip, Peter Glenn Publications, 306 NE Second St, 2nd fl, Delray Beach, FL 33483 *Tel:* 561-404-4290 *Fax:* 561-892-5786 *Web Site:* pgdirect.com, pg 93

Brill, Marlene Targ, The Society of Midland Authors Awards, PO Box 10419, Chicago, IL 60610 *E-mail:* info@midlandauthors.com *Web Site:* www.midlandauthors.com, pg 690

Brill, Paula, Between the Lines, 401 Richmond St W, No 277, Toronto, ON M5V 3A8, Canada *Tel:* 416-535-9914 *Toll Free Tel:* 800-718-7201 *Fax:* 416-535-1484 *E-mail:* info@btlbooks.com *Web Site:* btlbooks.com, pg 446

Brinati, Teresa, Society of American Archivists, 17 N State St, Suite 1425, Chicago, IL 60602-4061 *Tel:* 312-606-0722 *Toll Free Tel:* 866-722-7858 *Fax:* 312-606-0728 *Web Site:* www.archivists.org, pg 216

Brinbury, Rebecca, Northwest Independent Editors Guild, 7511 Greenwood Ave N, No 307, Seattle, WA 98103 *E-mail:* info@edsguild.org *Web Site:* www.edsguild.org, pg 574

Brink, Matthew H, Butte Publications Inc, PO Box 1328, Hillsboro, OR 97123-1328 *Toll Free Tel:* 866-312-8883 *Toll Free Fax:* 866-412-8883 (orders only) *E-mail:* service@buttepublications.com *Web Site:* www.buttepublications.com, pg 46

Brinker, Spencer, Bearport Publishing Co Inc, 45 W 21 St, Suite 3B, New York, NY 10010 *Tel:* 212-337-8577 *Toll Free Tel:* 877-337-8577 *Fax:* 212-337-8557 *Toll Free Fax:* 866-337-8557 *E-mail:* service@bearportpublishing.com; info@bearportpublishing.com *Web Site:* www.bearportpublishing.com, pg 31

Briskin, Dennis Alan, Catalyst Creative Services, 619 Marion Plaza, Palo Alto, CA 94301-4251 *Tel:* 650-325-1500 *E-mail:* afriendlyghostwriter@gmail.com *Web Site:* www.catalystcreative.us, pg 490

Brissie, Gene, James Peter Associates Inc, PO Box 358, New Canaan, CT 06840 *Tel:* 203-972-1070 *Web Site:* www.jamespeterassociates.com, pg 522

Britt, Nadine, Penguin Young Readers Group, 345 Hudson St, New York, NY 10014 *Tel:* 212-366-2000; 212-414-3553 *Fax:* 212-414-3340 *Web Site:* www.penguin.com/children, pg 179

Britton, Greg, The Johns Hopkins University Press, 2715 N Charles St, Baltimore, MD 21218-4363 *Tel:* 410-516-6900; 410-516-6987 (journal orders outside US & CN) *Toll Free Tel:* 800-537-5487 (book orders & cust serv); 800-548-1784 (journal orders) *Fax:* 410-516-6968; 410-516-3866 (journal orders) *E-mail:* hfscustserv@press.jhu.edu (cust serv); jrnlcirc@press.jhu.edu (journal orders) *Web Site:* www.press.jhu.edu; muse.jhu.edu, pg 122

Broad, Molly Corbett, American Council on Education, One Dupont Circle NW, Washington, DC 20036 *Tel:* 202-939-9300; 202-939-9452 (publg dept); 301-632-6757 (orders) *E-mail:* pubs@acenet.edu *Web Site:* www.acenet.edu, pg 11

Broad, Molly Corbett, American Council on Education, One Dupont Circle NW, Washington, DC 20036 *Tel:* 202-939-9300 *Web Site:* www.acenet.edu, pg 554

Brochu, Yvon, Editions FouLire, 4339, rue des Becassines, Quebec, QC G1G 1V5, Canada *Tel:* 418-628-4029 *Toll Free Tel:* 877-628-4029 (CN & US) *Fax:* 418-628-4801 *E-mail:* info@foulire.com; edition@foulire.com *Web Site:* www.foulire.com, pg 454

Brock, Emily, Dutton, 375 Hudson St, New York, NY 10014 *Tel:* 212-366-2000 *Fax:* 212-366-2262 *Web Site:* www.penguin.com, pg 74

Brock, John, Texas Tech University Press, 1120 Main St, 2nd fl, Lubbock, TX 79401 *Tel:* 806-742-2982 *Toll Free Tel:* 800-832-4042 *Fax:* 806-742-2979 *E-mail:* ttup@ttu.edu *Web Site:* www.ttupress.org, pg 230

Brock, Sheila, PennWell Books, 1421 S Sheridan Rd, Tulsa, OK 74112 *Tel:* 918-831-9421 *Toll Free Tel:* 800-752-9764 *Fax:* 918-831-9555 *Toll Free Fax:* 877-218-1348 *E-mail:* sales@pennwell.com *Web Site:* www.pennwellbooks.com, pg 179

Brockenbrough, Gina, SLACK® Incorporated, A Wyanoke Group Company, 6900 Grove Rd, Thorofare, NJ 08086-9447 *Tel:* 856-848-1000 *Toll Free Tel:* 800-257-8290 *Fax:* 856-848-6091 *E-mail:* sales@slackinc.com; editor@slackinc.com; customerservice@slackinc.com *Web Site:* www.healio.com/books, pg 215

Brockett, Louise, W W Norton & Company Inc, 500 Fifth Ave, New York, NY 10110-0017 *Tel:* 212-354-5500 *Toll Free Tel:* 800-233-4830 (orders & cust serv) *Fax:* 212-869-0856 *Toll Free Fax:* 800-458-6515 *E-mail:* orders@wwnorton.com *Web Site:* books.wwnorton.com, pg 164

Brockman, John, Brockman Inc, 260 Fifth Ave, 10th fl, New York, NY 10001 *Tel:* 212-935-8900 *Fax:* 212-935-5535 *E-mail:* rights@brockman.com *Web Site:* www.brockman.com, pg 510

Brockman, Max, Brockman Inc, 260 Fifth Ave, 10th fl, New York, NY 10001 *Tel:* 212-935-8900 *Fax:* 212-935-5535 *E-mail:* rights@brockman.com *Web Site:* www.brockman.com, pg 510

Brodeur, Adrienne, Aspen Words, 110 E Hallam St, Suite 116, Aspen, CO 81611 *Tel:* 970-925-3122 *Fax:* 970-920-5700 *E-mail:* aspenwords@aspeninstitute.org *Web Site:* www.aspenwords.org, pg 557

Brodeur, Adrienne, Aspen Words Literary Prize, 110 E Hallam St, Suite 116, Aspen, CO 81611 *Tel:* 970-925-3122 *Fax:* 970-920-5700 *E-mail:* literary.prize@aspeninstitute.org *Web Site:* www.aspenwords.org, pg 629

Brodeur, Adrienne, Summer Words Writing Conference & Literary Festival, 110 E Hallam St, Suite 116, Aspen, CO 81611 *Tel:* 970-925-3122 *Fax:* 970-920-5700 *E-mail:* aspenwords@aspeninstitute.org *Web Site:* www.aspenwords.org, pg 615

Brodeur, Adrienne, Winter Words Author Series, 110 E Hallam St, Suite 116, Aspen, CO 81611 *Tel:* 970-925-3122 *Fax:* 970-920-5700 *E-mail:* aspenwords@aspeninstitute.org *Web Site:* www.aspenwords.org, pg 616

Brodie, Emma, HarperCollins General Books Group, 195 Broadway, New York, NY 10007 *Tel:* 212-207-7000 *Web Site:* www.harpercollins.com, pg 101

Brody, Deb, Houghton Mifflin Harcourt Trade & Reference Division, 125 High St, Boston, MA 02110 *Tel:* 617-351-5000 *Toll Free Tel:* 800-225-3362 *Web Site:* www.hmhco.com, pg 111

Brody, Samantha, Maria Carvainis Agency Inc, Rockefeller Center, 1270 Avenue of the Americas, Suite 2320, New York, NY 10020 *Tel:* 212-245-6365 *Fax:* 212-245-7196 *E-mail:* mca@mariacarvainisagency.com *Web Site:* mariacarvainisagency.com, pg 511

Brogan, Jim, Miniature Book Society Inc, 702 Rosecrans St, San Diego, CA 92106-3013 *Tel:* 619-226-4441 *Fax:* 619-226-4441 *E-mail:* minibook@cox.net *Web Site:* www.mbs.org, pg 569

Brogger, Erik A, Hofstra University, English Department, 203 Mason Hall, Hempstead, NY 11549 *Tel:* 516-463-5454 *Fax:* 516-463-6395 *Web Site:* www.hofstra.edu, pg 620

Broich, Alexander, Cengage Learning, 20 Channel Center St, Boston, MA 02210 *Tel:* 617-289-7700 *Toll Free Tel:* 800-354-9706 *Fax:* 617-289-7844 *Toll Free Fax:* 800-487-8488 *E-mail:* esales@cengage.com *Web Site:* www.cengage.com, pg 50

Broida, Peter, Dewey Publications Inc, 1840 Wilson Blvd, Suite 203, Arlington, VA 22201 *Tel:* 703-524-1355 *Fax:* 703-524-1463 *E-mail:* deweypublications@gmail.com *Web Site:* www.deweypub.com, pg 70

Bromley, Carl, The New Press, 38 Greene St, 4th fl, New York, NY 10013 *Tel:* 212-629-8802 *Toll Free Tel:* 800-343-4489 (orders) *Fax:* 212-629-8617 *Toll Free Fax:* 800-351-5073 (orders) *E-mail:* newpress@thenewpress.com *Web Site:* www.thenewpress.com, pg 161

Bromley, Lizzy, Simon & Schuster Children's Publishing, 1230 Avenue of the Americas, New York, NY 10020 *Tel:* 212-698-7000 *Web Site:* www.simonandschuster.com/kids; www.simonandschuster.com/teen; simonandschuster.net; simonandschuster.biz, pg 213

Brook, Susan Todd, Naval Institute Press, 291 Wood Rd, Annapolis, MD 21402-5034 *Tel:* 410-268-6110 *Toll Free Tel:* 800-233-8764 *Fax:* 410-295-1084; 410-571-1703 (cust serv) *E-mail:* webmaster@navalinstitute.org; customer@navalinstitute.org (cust serv) *Web Site:* www.nip.org; www.usni.org, pg 159

Brookes, Jeffrey D, Brookes Publishing Co Inc, PO Box 10624, Baltimore, MD 21285-0624 *Tel:* 410-337-9580 (outside US & CN) *Toll Free Tel:* 800-638-3775 (US & CN) *Fax:* 410-337-8539 *E-mail:* custserv@brookespublishing.com *Web Site:* www.brookespublishing.com, pg 44

Brookes, Paul H, Brookes Publishing Co Inc, PO Box 10624, Baltimore, MD 21285-0624 *Tel:* 410-337-9580 (outside US & CN) *Toll Free Tel:* 800-638-3775 (US & CN) *Fax:* 410-337-8539 *E-mail:* custserv@brookespublishing.com *Web Site:* www.brookespublishing.com, pg 44

Brooking, Denise, National Association of Black Journalists (NABJ), 1100 Knight Hall, Suite 3100, College Park, MD 20742 *Tel:* 301-405-0248 *Fax:* 301-314-1714 *E-mail:* nabj@nabj.org *Web Site:* www.nabj.org, pg 570

Brooks, Arthur, The AEI Press, 1789 Massachusetts Ave NW, Washington, DC 20036 *Tel:* 202-862-5800 *Fax:* 202-862-7177 *Web Site:* www.aei.org, pg 5

Brooks, Becky, Alliance for Women in Media (AWM), 1250 24 St NW, Suite 300, Washington, DC 20037 *Tel:* 202-750-3664 *Fax:* 202-750-3664 *E-mail:* info@allwomeninmedia.org *Web Site:* allwomeninmedia.org, pg 554

Brooks, Becky, The Gracies®, 2365 Harrodsburg Rd, Suite A325, Lexington, KY 40504 *Tel:* 202-750-3664 *Fax:* 202-750-3664 *E-mail:* info@allwomeninmedia.org *Web Site:* allwomeninmedia.org, pg 650

Brooks, Chris, The JOC Group Inc, 2 Penn Plaza E, Newark, NJ 07105 *Tel:* 973-776-8660 *Web Site:* www.joc.com, pg 122

Brooks, Gabrielle, Alfred A Knopf/Everyman's Library, c/o Penguin Random House Inc, 1745 Broadway, New York, NY 10019 *Tel:* 212-751-2600 *Toll Free Tel:* 800-638-6460 *Fax:* 212-572-2593 *Web Site:* www.knopfdoubleday.com, pg 127

Brooks, Ken, Macmillan Learning, 41 Madison Ave, New York, NY 10010 *Tel:* 212-576-9400 *Fax:* 212-689-2383 *Web Site:* www.macmillanlearning.com, pg 140

Brooks, Linda Thomas, MPA - The Association of Magazine Media, 757 Third Ave, 11th fl, New York, NY 10012 *Tel:* 212-872-3700 *Fax:* 212-888-4217 *Web Site:* www.magazine.org, pg 570

Brooks, Rachel, BookEnds Literary Agency, 136 Long Hill Rd, Gillette, NJ 07933 *Web Site:* www.bookendsliterary.com, pg 508

Brooks, Sofie, Penguin Group USA, A Penguin Random House Company, 375 Hudson St, New York, NY 10014 *Tel:* 212-366-2000 *Toll Free Tel:* 800-847-5515 (inside sales); 800-631-8571 (cust serv) *Fax:* 212-366-2666; 607-775-4829 (inside sales) *E-mail:* online@us.penguingroup.com *Web Site:* www.penguin.com, pg 177

Brophy, Philippa, Sterling Lord Literistic Inc, 115 Broadway, Suite 1602, New York, NY 10006 *Tel:* 212-780-6050 *Fax:* 212-780-6095 *E-mail:* info@sll.com *Web Site:* www.sll.com, pg 537

Broquet, Antoine, Broquet Inc, 97-B, Montee des Bouleaux, St-Constant, QC J5A 1A9, Canada *Tel:* 450-638-3338 *Fax:* 450-638-4338 *E-mail:* info@broquet.qc.ca *Web Site:* www.broquet.qc.ca, pg 448

Brosnan, Dr Jim, Maine Writers Conference at Ocean Park, 14 Temple Ave, Ocean Park, ME 04063 *Tel:* 401-598-1424 *E-mail:* www.opa@oceanpark.org *Web Site:* oceanpark.org, pg 612

Brosnan, Rosemary, HarperCollins Children's Books, 195 Broadway, New York, NY 10007 *Tel:* 212-207-7000 *Web Site:* www.harpercollins.com/childrens, pg 101

Brothers, Connie, The Iowa Short Fiction Award, 102 Dey House, 507 N Clinton St, Iowa City, IA 52242-1000 *Tel:* 319-335-0416 *Fax:* 319-335-0420 *Web Site:* www.uiowapress.org/authors/iowa-short-fiction.htm, pg 656

Broughton, Paul, Life Cycle Books, PO Box 799, Fort Collins, CO 80522 *Toll Free Tel:* 800-214-5849 *Toll Free Fax:* 888-690-8532 *E-mail:* orders@lifecyclebooks.com; support@lifecyclebooks.com *Web Site:* www.lifecyclebooks.com, pg 134

Broughton, Paul, Life Cycle Books Ltd, 11 Progress Ave, Unit 6, Toronto, ON M1P 4S7, Canada *Toll Free Tel:* 866-880-5860 *Toll Free Fax:* 866-260-8172 *E-mail:* orders@lifecyclebooks.ca; billing@lifecyclebooks.ca; support@lifecyclebooks.ca *Web Site:* www.lifecyclebooks.com, pg 462

Broussard, Linda N, Special Libraries Association (SLA), 7918 Jones Branch Dr, Suite 300, McLean, VA 22102 *Tel:* 703-647-4900 *Fax:* 703-506-3266 *Web Site:* www.sla.org, pg 579

Brouwer, Joel, University of Alabama Program in Creative Writing, PO Box 870244, Tuscaloosa, AL 35487-0244 *Tel:* 205-348-5065 *Fax:* 205-348-1388 *E-mail:* english@ua.edu *Web Site:* www.as.ua.edu/english, pg 622

Brower, Michelle, Aevitas Creative Management, 19 W 21 St, Suite 501, New York, NY 10010 *Tel:* 212-765-6900 *Web Site:* aevitascreative.com, pg 506

Brown, Alexandra, Chronicle Books LLC, 680 Second St, San Francisco, CA 94107 *Tel:* 415-537-4200 *Toll Free Tel:* 800-759-0190 (cust serv) *Fax:* 415-537-4460 *Toll Free Fax:* 800-858-7787 (orders); 800-286-9471 (cust serv) *E-mail:* frontdesk@chroniclebooks.com *Web Site:* www.chroniclebooks.com, pg 55

Brown, Arthur, Vandamere Press, 3580 Morris St N, St Petersburg, FL 33713 *Tel:* 727-556-0950 *Toll Free Tel:* 800-551-7776 *Fax:* 727-556-2560 *E-mail:* orders@vandamere.com *Web Site:* www.vandamere.com, pg 249

Brown, Barbara, Kensington Publishing Corp, 119 W 40 St, New York, NY 10018 *Tel:* 212-407-1500 *Toll Free Tel:* 800-221-2647 *Fax:* 212-935-0699 *Web Site:* www.kensingtonbooks.com, pg 125

Brown, Becky, Louisiana State University Press, 338 Johnston Hall, Baton Rouge, LA 70803 *Tel:* 225-578-6294 *Fax:* 225-578-6461 *E-mail:* lsupress@lsu.edu *Web Site:* lsupress.org, pg 138

Brown, Bruce, Reporters Committee for Freedom of the Press, 1156 15 St NW, Suite 1250, Washington, DC 20005-1779 *Tel:* 202-795-9300 *Toll Free Tel:* 800-336-4243 *E-mail:* info@rcfp.org *Web Site:* www.rcfp.org, pg 577

Brown, Carl, Aum Publications, 86-10 Parsons Blvd, Jamaica, NY 11432-3314 *Tel:* 347-744-3199, pg 26

Brown, Cheri, Hackett Publishing Co Inc, 3333 Massachusetts Ave, Indianapolis, IN 46218 *Tel:* 317-635-9250 (orders & cust serv); 617-497-6303 (edit off & sales) *Fax:* 317-635-9292; 617-661-8703 (edit off) *Toll Free Fax:* 800-783-9213 *E-mail:* customer@hackettpublishing.com; editorial@hackettpublishing.com *Web Site:* www.hackettpublishing.com, pg 99

Brown, Mr Chris, National Association of Broadcasters (NAB), 1771 "N" St NW, Washington, DC 20036 *Tel:* 202-429-5300 *E-mail:* nab@nab.org *Web Site:* www.nab.org, pg 157, 570

Brown, Christine, Texas A&M University Press, John H Lindsey Bldg, Lewis St, 4354 TAMU, College Station, TX 77843-4354 *Tel:* 979-845-1436 *Toll Free Tel:* 800-826-8911 (orders) *Fax:* 979-847-8752 *Toll Free Fax:* 888-617-2421 (orders) *E-mail:* bookorders@tamu.edu *Web Site:* www.tamupress.com, pg 230

Brown, Curtis, Dun & Bradstreet, 103 JFK Pkwy, Short Hills, NJ 07078 *Tel:* 973-921-5500 *Toll Free Tel:* 800-526-0651; 800-234-3867 (cust serv) *E-mail:* custserv@dnb.com *Web Site:* www.dnb.com, pg 73

Brown, Douglas R, Atlantic Publishing Group Inc, 1405 SW Sixth Ave, Ocala, FL 34471 *Tel:* 352-622-1825 *Toll Free Tel:* 800-814-1132 *Fax:* 352-622-1875 *E-mail:* sales@atlantic-pub.com *Web Site:* www.atlantic-pub.com, pg 25

Brown, Evan, Charlotte Sheedy Literary Agency Inc, 928 Broadway, Suite 901, New York, NY 10010 *Tel:* 212-780-9800 *Web Site:* www.sheedylit.com, pg 535

Brown, Jennifer, Pantheon Books/Schocken Books, c/o Penguin Random House Inc, 1745 Broadway, New York, NY 10019 *Tel:* 212-751-2600 *Web Site:* knopfdoubleday.com/imprint/pantheon, pg 173

Brown, Jennifer, Sudden Fiction Contest, c/o ASUC Publications, Univ of California, 10-B Eshleman Hall, Berkeley, CA 94720-4500 *E-mail:* bfictionreview@yahoo.com *Web Site:* www.ocf.berkeley.edu/~bfr/, pg 692

Brown, Jennifer M, Random House Children's Books, 1745 Broadway, 10th fl, New York, NY 10019 *Tel:* 212-782-9000 *Web Site:* www.randomhousekids.com, pg 194

Brown, Julia, Jerome Fellowship, 2301 Franklin Ave E, Minneapolis, MN 55406-1099 *Tel:* 612-332-7481 *Fax:* 612-332-6037 *E-mail:* info@pwcenter.org *Web Site:* www.pwcenter.org, pg 657

Brown, Julia, Many Voices Fellowships, 2301 Franklin Ave E, Minneapolis, MN 55406-1099 *Tel:* 612-332-7481 *Fax:* 612-332-6037 *E-mail:* info@pwcenter.org *Web Site:* www.pwcenter.org, pg 665

Brown, Julia, McKnight Fellowships in Playwriting, 2301 Franklin Ave E, Minneapolis, MN 55406-1099 *Tel:* 612-332-7481 *Fax:* 612-332-6037 *E-mail:* info@pwcenter.org *Web Site:* www.pwcenter.org, pg 667

Brown, Julia, McKnight National Residency & Commission, 2301 Franklin Ave E, Minneapolis, MN 55406-1099 *Tel:* 612-332-7481 *Fax:* 612-332-6037 *E-mail:* info@pwcenter.org *Web Site:* www.pwcenter.org, pg 667

Brown, Kate, Quirk Books, 215 Church St, Philadelphia, PA 19106 *Tel:* 215-627-3581 *Fax:* 215-627-5220 *E-mail:* general@quirkbooks.com *Web Site:* www.quirkbooks.com, pg 193

Brown, Kate, Yale University Press, 302 Temple St, New Haven, CT 06511-8909 *Tel:* 203-432-0960; 203-432-0966 (sales); 401-531-2800 (cust serv) *Toll Free Tel:* 800-405-1619 (cust serv) *Fax:* 203-432-0948; 203-432-8485 (sales); 401-531-2801 (cust serv) *Toll Free Fax:* 800-406-9145 (cust serv) *E-mail:* sales.press@yale.edu (sales); customer.care@triliteral.org (cust serv) *Web Site:* www.yalebooks.com; yalepress.yale.edu/yupbooks, pg 261

Brown, Kent, Dramatic Publishing Co, 311 Washington St, Woodstock, IL 60098-3308 *Tel:* 815-338-7170 *Toll Free Tel:* 800-448-7469 *Fax:* 815-338-8981 *Toll Free Fax:* 800-334-5302 *E-mail:* plays@dramaticpublishing.com; customerservice@dpcplays.com *Web Site:* www.dramaticpublishing.com, pg 73

Brown, Kent L Jr, Intimate & Inspiring Workshops for Children's Authors & Illustrators, 814 Court St, Honesdale, PA 18431 *Tel:* 570-253-1192 *Fax:* 570-253-0179 *E-mail:* jolloyd@highlightsfoundation.org *Web Site:* www.highlightsfoundation.org, pg 612

Brown, Linda, American Society of Plant Taxonomists, University of Wyoming, Dept of Botany 3165, 1000 E University Ave, Laramie, WY 82071 *Tel:* 307-766-2556 *Fax:* 307-766-2851 *E-mail:* aspt@uwyo.edu *Web Site:* www.aspt.net, pg 15

Brown, Lucia, The Feminist Press at The City University of New York, 365 Fifth Ave, Suite 5406, New York, NY 10016 *Tel:* 212-817-7915 *Fax:* 212-817-1593 *E-mail:* info@feministpress.org *Web Site:* www.feministpress.org, pg 83

Brown, Mallory, TriadaUS Literary Agency, PO Box 561, Sewickley, PA 15143 *Tel:* 412-401-3376 *Web Site:* www.triadaus.com, pg 540

Brown, Marian, Henry Holt and Company, LLC, 175 Fifth Ave, New York, NY 10010 *Tel:* 646-307-5151 *Toll Free Tel:* 888-330-8477 (orders) *Fax:* 646-307-5285 *E-mail:* firstname.lastname@hholt.com *Web Site:* www.henryholt.com, pg 109

Brown, Marian, Plume, 375 Hudson St, New York, NY 10014 *Tel:* 212-366-2000 *Fax:* 212-243-6002 *Web Site:* www.penguin.com/publishers/plume, pg 184

Brown, Marie D, Marie Brown Associates, 412 W 154 St, New York, NY 10032 *Tel:* 212-939-9725 *E-mail:* submissions.mbrownlit@gmail.com, pg 510

Brown, Marlena, Picador, 175 Fifth Ave, 19th fl, New York, NY 10010 *Tel:* 646-307-5151 *Fax:* 212-253-9627 *Web Site:* www.picadorusa.com, pg 182

Brown, Merle, Harry N Abrams Inc, 195 Broadway, 9th fl, New York, NY 10007 *Tel:* 212-206-7715 *Toll Free Tel:* 800-345-1359 *Fax:* 212-519-1210 *E-mail:* abrams@abramsbooks.com *Web Site:* www.abramsbooks.com, pg 3

Brown, Milli, Brown Books Publishing Group, 16250 Knoll Trail, Suite 205, Dallas, TX 75248 *Tel:* 972-381-0009 *Fax:* 972-248-4336 *E-mail:* publishing@brownbooks.com *Web Site:* www.brownbooks.com, pg 44

Brown, Richard, University of South Carolina Press, 1600 Hampton St, Suite 544, Columbia, SC 29208 *Tel:* 803-777-5245 *Toll Free Tel:* 800-768-2500 (orders) *Fax:* 803-777-0160 *Toll Free Fax:* 800-868-0740 (orders) *Web Site:* www.sc.edu/uscpress, pg 245

Brown, Robby, Random House Children's Books, 1745 Broadway, 10th fl, New York, NY 10019 *Tel:* 212-782-9000 *Web Site:* www.randomhousekids.com, pg 194

Brown, Rose, Clerical Plus, 97 Blueberry Lane, Shelton, CT 06484 *Tel:* 203-225-0879 *Fax:* 203-225-0879 *E-mail:* clericalplus@aol.com *Web Site:* www.clericalplus.net, pg 491

Brown, Shay, Random House Children's Books, 1745 Broadway, 10th fl, New York, NY 10019 *Tel:* 212-782-9000 *Web Site:* www.randomhousekids.com, pg 194

Brown, Sherri L, Atlantic Publishing Group Inc, 1405 SW Sixth Ave, Ocala, FL 34471 *Tel:* 352-622-1825 *Toll Free Tel:* 800-814-1132 *Fax:* 352-622-1875 *E-mail:* sales@atlantic-pub.com *Web Site:* www.atlantic-pub.com, pg 25

Brown, Stephanie, Vandamere Press, 3580 Morris St N, St Petersburg, FL 33713 *Tel:* 727-556-0950 *Toll Free Tel:* 800-551-7776 *Fax:* 727-556-2560 *E-mail:* orders@vandamere.com *Web Site:* www.vandamere.com, pg 249

Brown, Stephen, Random House Children's Books, 1745 Broadway, 10th fl, New York, NY 10019 *Tel:* 212-782-9000 *Web Site:* www.randomhousekids.com, pg 194

Brown, Steven, Nelson Education Ltd, 1120 Birchmount Rd, Scarborough, ON M1K 5G4, Canada *Tel:* 416-752-9100 *Toll Free Tel:* 800-268-2222 (cust serv) *Fax:* 416-752-8101 *Toll Free Fax:* 800-430-4445 *E-mail:* peopleandengagement@nelson.com *Web Site:* www.nelson.com, pg 464

Brown, Susan, Macmillan Learning, 41 Madison Ave, New York, NY 10010 *Tel:* 212-576-9400 *Fax:* 212-689-2383 *Web Site:* www.macmillanlearning.com, pg 140

Brown, Tammy, Society of Children's Book Writers and Illustrators (SCBWI), 4727 Wilshire Blvd, Suite 301, Los Angeles, CA 90010 *Tel:* 323-782-1010 *Fax:* 323-782-1892 *E-mail:* scbwi@scbwi.org; membership@scbwi.org *Web Site:* www.scbwi.org, pg 578

Brown, Therese, Association of Catholic Publishers Inc, 4725 Dorsey Hall Dr, Suite A, PMB 709, Elliott City, MD 21042 *Tel:* 410-988-2926 *Fax:* 410-571-4946 *Web Site:* www.catholicsread.org; www.catholicpublishers.org; www.midatlanticcongress.org, pg 558

Browndervillle, Greg, Morton Marr Poetry Prize, PO Box 750374, Dallas, TX 75275-0374 *Fax:* 214-768-1408 *E-mail:* swr@mail.smu.edu *Web Site:* www.smu.edu/southwestreview, pg 665

Brownderville, Greg, John H McGinnis Memorial Award, PO Box 750374, Dallas, TX 75275-0374 *Fax:* 214-768-1408 *E-mail:* swr@mail.smu.edu *Web Site:* www.smu.edu/southwestreview, pg 666

Brownderville, Greg, The David Nathan Meyerson Prize for Fiction, PO Box 750374, Dallas, TX 75275-0374 *Fax:* 214-768-1408 *E-mail:* swr@mail.smu.edu *Web Site:* www.smu.edu/southwestreview, pg 667

Brownderville, Greg, Elizabeth Matchett Stover Memorial Award, PO Box 750374, Dallas, TX 75275-0374 *Fax:* 214-768-1408 *E-mail:* swr@mail.smu.edu *Web Site:* www.smu.edu/southwestreview, pg 692

Browne, Anne, Scholastic Canada Ltd, 604 King St W, Toronto, ON M5V 1E1, Canada *Tel:* 905-887-7323 *Toll Free Tel:* 800-268-3860 (CN) *Toll Free Fax:* 866-387-4944 *E-mail:* custserve@scholastic.ca *Web Site:* www.scholastic.ca, pg 469

Browne, Renni, The Editorial Department LLC, 7650 E Broadway, Suite 308, Tucson, AZ 85710 *Tel:* 520-546-9992 *Fax:* 520-979-3408 *E-mail:* admin@editorialdepartment.com *Web Site:* www.editorialdepartment.com, pg 493

Browne, Ross, The Editorial Department LLC, 7650 E Broadway, Suite 308, Tucson, AZ 85710 *Tel:* 520-546-9992 *Fax:* 520-979-3408 *E-mail:* admin@editorialdepartment.com *Web Site:* www.editorialdepartment.com, pg 493

Browning, Niki, Mundania Press LLC, 6457 Glenway Ave, Suite 109, Cincinnati, OH 45211 *Tel:* 513-404-7357 *Fax:* 513-598-9220 *Toll Free Fax:* 888-460-4752 *E-mail:* books@mundania.com; inquiry@mundania.com *Web Site:* www.mundania.com, pg 155

Brownoff, Alan, University of Alberta Press, Ring House 2, Edmonton, AB T6G 2E1, Canada *Tel:* 780-492-3662 *Fax:* 780-492-0719 *Web Site:* www.uap.ualberta.ca, pg 473

Bruce, Elizabeth, Picador, 175 Fifth Ave, 19th fl, New York, NY 10010 *Tel:* 646-307-5151 *Fax:* 212-253-9627 *Web Site:* www.picadorusa.com, pg 182

Bruce, Sandra, Milady, Executive Woods, 5 Maxwell Dr, Clifton Park, NY 12065-2919 *Tel:* 518-348-2300 *Toll Free Tel:* 800-998-7498 *Fax:* 518-373-6309 *E-mail:* info@milady.com *Web Site:* milady.cengage.com, pg 150

Brueggeman, George, Haynes Manuals Inc, 859 Lawrence Dr, Newbury Park, CA 91320-2232 *Tel:* 805-498-6703 *Toll Free Tel:* 800-4-HAYNES (442-9637) *Fax:* 805-498-2867 *E-mail:* cstn@haynes.com *Web Site:* www.haynes.com, pg 104

Brugger, Deborah, Saint Johann Press, 315 Schraalenburgh Rd, Haworth, NJ 07641 *Tel:* 201-387-1529 *Fax:* 201-501-0698 *Web Site:* www.stjohannpress.com, pg 204

Bruins, Kathy, SDP Publishing Solutions LLC, 36 Captain's Way, East Bridgewater, MA 02333 *Tel:* 617-775-0656 *Web Site:* www.sdppublishingsolutions.com, pg 501

Brumley, Mark, Ignatius Press, 1348 Tenth Ave, San Francisco, CA 94122-2304 *Toll Free Tel:* 800-651-1531 (orders); 888-615-3186 (cust serv) *E-mail:* info@ignatius.com *Web Site:* www.ignatius.com, pg 114

Brumwell, Barbara, LexisNexis® Canada Inc, 111 Gordon Baker Rd, Suite 900, Toronto, ON M2H 3R1, Canada *Tel:* 905-479-2665 *Toll Free Tel:* 800-668-6481; 800-387-0899 (cust care); 800-255-5174 (sales) *E-mail:* service@lexisnexis.ca (cust serv); sales@lexisnexis.ca *Web Site:* www.lexisnexis.ca, pg 462

Brunette, Paul, Concordia Publishing House, 3558 S Jefferson Ave, St Louis, MO 63118-3968 *Tel:* 314-268-1000; 314-268-1268 (bookshop) *Toll Free Tel:* 800-325-3040 (cust serv) *Toll Free Fax:* 800-490-9889 (cust serv) *E-mail:* order@cph.org *Web Site:* www.cph.org, pg 59

Brunn, Jennifer, Harry N Abrams Inc, 195 Broadway, 9th fl, New York, NY 10007 *Tel:* 212-206-7715 *Toll Free Tel:* 800-345-1359 *Fax:* 212-519-1210 *E-mail:* abrams@abramsbooks.com *Web Site:* www.abramsbooks.com, pg 3

Brunsek, Judy, Owlkids Books Inc, 10 Lower Spadina Ave, Suite 400, Toronto, ON M5V 2Z2, Canada *Tel:* 416-340-2700 *Fax:* 416-340-9769 *E-mail:* owlkids@owlkids.com *Web Site:* www.owlkidsbooks.com, pg 465

Bruschi, Ally, Avery, 375 Hudson St, New York, NY 10014 *Tel:* 212-366-2000 *Fax:* 212-366-2643 *Web Site:* www.penguin.com; www.penguinrandomhouse.com, pg 27

Bruscia, Kenneth E, Barcelona Publishers, 27602 Bogen Rd, New Braunfels, TX 78132-3873 *Tel:* 830-980-6422 *E-mail:* barcelonapublishers@gvtc.com; barcelonapublishers@ware-pak.com (orders) *Web Site:* www.barcelonapublishers.com, pg 29

Brussel, Gail, The Penguin Press, 375 Hudson St, New York, NY 10014 *Web Site:* thepenguinpress.com, pg 178

Bryan, Athena, Perseus Books, 250 W 57 St, 15th fl, New York, NY 10107 *Tel:* 212-340-8100 *Toll Free Tel:* 800-343-4499 (cust serv) *Fax:* 212-340-8105 *Web Site:* www.perseusbooks.com, pg 181

Bryan, Heather, Nimbus Publishing Ltd, 3731 Mackintosh St, Halifax, NS B3K 5A5, Canada *Tel:* 902-455-4286 *Toll Free Tel:* 800-NIMBUS9 (646-2879) *Fax:* 902-455-5440 *Toll Free Fax:* 888-253-3133 *E-mail:* customerservice@nimbus.ca *Web Site:* www.nimbus.ca, pg 465

Bryan, Nancy, University of Texas Press, 3001 Lake Austin Blvd, 2.200, Austin, TX 78703 *Tel:* 512-471-7233 *Fax:* 512-232-7178 *E-mail:* utpress@uts.cc.utexas.edu; info@utpress.utexas.edu *Web Site:* www.utexaspress.com, pg 230

Bryans, John B, J B Bryans Literary, 7 Meetinghouse Ct, Indian Mills, NJ 08088 *Tel:* 609-922-0369 *E-mail:* info@brylit.com *Web Site:* brylit.com, pg 510

Bryant, Del R, BMI®, 7 World Trade Ctr, 250 Greenwich St, New York, NY 10007-0030 *Tel:* 212-586-2000; 212-220-3000 *Toll Free Tel:* 888-689-5264 (sales); 800-925-8451 (cust rel) *Fax:* 212-246-2163 *E-mail:* foundation@bmi.com *Web Site:* www.bmi.com, pg 560

Bryant, L J, Wildflower Press, c/o Oakbrook Press, 3301 S Valley Dr, Rapid City, SD 57703 *Tel:* 605-381-6385 *E-mail:* info@wildflowerpress.org *Web Site:* www.wildflowerpress.org, pg 255

Bryerose, Cathy C, Regal Crest Enterprises, 1042 Mount Lebanon Rd, Maryville, TN 37804 *Tel:* 409-527-1188 *Toll Free Fax:* 866-294-9628 *E-mail:* info@regalcrestbooks.biz *Web Site:* www.regalcrest.biz, pg 198

Bucaria, Catherine, Penguin Random House Audio Publishing, 1745 Broadway, New York, NY 10019 *E-mail:* audio@penguinrandomhouse.com *Web Site:* www.penguinrandomhouseaudio.com, pg 178

Buchanan, Holly, Hamilton Books, 4501 Forbes Blvd, Suite 200, Lanham, MD 20706 *Tel:* 301-459-3366 *Toll Free Tel:* 800-462-6420 (cust serv) *Fax:* 301-429-5748 *Toll Free Fax:* 800-388-4550 (cust serv), pg 99

Buchanan, Holly, University Press of America Inc, 4501 Forbes Blvd, Suite 200, Lanham, MD 20706 *Tel:* 301-459-3366 *Toll Free Tel:* 800-462-6420 *Fax:* 301-429-5748 *Toll Free Fax:* 800-338-4550 *Web Site:* www.univpress.com, pg 246

Buchanan, Latonya, National Association of Insurance Commissioners, 1100 Walnut St, Suite 1500, Kansas City, MO 64106-2197 *Tel:* 816-842-3600; 816-783-8300 (cust serv) *Fax:* 816-783-8175; 816-460-7593 (cust serv) *E-mail:* prodserv@naic.org *Web Site:* www.naic.org, pg 157

Buchanan, Melissa, University of Georgia Press, Main Library, 3rd fl, 320 S Jackson St, Athens, GA 30602 *Fax:* 706-542-2558; 706-542-6770 *Web Site:* www.ugapress.org, pg 241

Buchwald, Don, Don Buchwald & Associates Inc, 10 E 44 St, New York, NY 10017 *Tel:* 212-867-1200 *Fax:* 212-867-2434 *E-mail:* info@buchwald.com *Web Site:* www.buchwald.com, pg 510

Buck, Bethany, Bloomsbury Publishing Inc, 1385 Broadway, 5th fl, New York, NY 10018 *Tel:* 212-419-5300 *E-mail:* marketingusa@bloomsbury.com; adultpublicityusa@bloomsbury.com; askacademic@bloomsbury.com *Web Site:* www.bloomsbury.com, pg 38

Buck, Susan, Coteau Books, 2517 Victoria Ave, Regina, SK S4P 0T2, Canada *Tel:* 306-777-0170 *Toll Free Tel:* 800-440-4471 (CN only) *Fax:* 306-522-5152 *E-mail:* coteau@coteaubooks.com *Web Site:* www.coteaubooks.com, pg 451

Buckles, Kristen, The University of Arizona Press, 1510 E University Blvd, Tucson, AZ 85721 *Tel:* 520-621-1441 *Toll Free Tel:* 800-426-3797 (orders) *Fax:* 520-621-8899 *Toll Free Fax:* 800-426-3797 *E-mail:* uap@uapress.arizona.edu *Web Site:* www.uapress.arizona.edu, pg 240

Buckley, Carol, Piano Press, 1425 Ocean Ave, Suite 5, Del Mar, CA 92014 *Tel:* 619-884-1401 *Fax:* 858-755-1104 *E-mail:* pianopress@pianopress.com *Web Site:* www.pianopress.com, pg 182

Buckley, Cicely, Oyster River Press, 36 Oyster River Rd, Durham, NH 03824-3029 *Tel:* 603-868-5006 *E-mail:* oysterriverpress@comcast.net *Web Site:* www.facebook.com/OysterRiverPress/, pg 499

Buckley, Kerri, Harlequin Enterprises Ltd, 233 Broadway, Suite 1001, New York, NY 10279 *Tel:* 212-553-4200 *Fax:* 212-227-8969 *E-mail:* customerservice@harlequin.com *Web Site:* www.harlequin.com, pg 100

Buckley, Paul, Penguin Books, 375 Hudson St, New York, NY 10014 *Tel:* 212-366-2000 *E-mail:* penguinpublicity@us.penguingroup.com *Web Site:* www.penguinclassics.com; www.penguin.com, pg 177

Buckley, Paul, Viking, 375 Hudson St, New York, NY 10014 *Tel:* 212-366-2000 *Fax:* 212-243-6002 *Web Site:* www.penguin.com/publishers/vikingbooks, pg 250

Buckner, Judith, Judith Buckner Literary Agency, 12721 Hart St, North Hollywood, CA 91605 *Tel:* 818-982-8202 *Fax:* 818-764-6844, pg 510

Buckner, Julie Dupre, River Road Press LLC, 9 Dakin, New Orleans, LA 70121 *Tel:* 504-722-8139 *Web Site:* riverroadpress.com, pg 199

Budnick, Philip, Penguin Group USA, A Penguin Random House Company, 375 Hudson St, New York, NY 10014 *Tel:* 212-366-2000 *Toll Free Tel:* 800-847-5515 (inside sales); 800-631-8571 (cust serv) *Fax:* 212-366-2666; 607-775-4829 (inside sales) *E-mail:* online@us.penguingroup.com *Web Site:* www.penguin.com, pg 177

Buerger, Martin, Independent Institute, 100 Swan Way, Suite 200, Oakland, CA 94621-1428 *Tel:* 510-632-1366 *Toll Free Tel:* 800-927-8733 *Fax:* 510-568-6040 *E-mail:* orders@independent.org *Web Site:* www.independent.org, pg 115

Buevich, Alina, Chronicle Books LLC, 680 Second St, San Francisco, CA 94107 *Tel:* 415-537-4200 *Toll Free Tel:* 800-759-0190 (cust serv) *Fax:* 415-537-4460 *Toll Free Fax:* 800-858-7787 (orders); 800-286-9471 (cust serv) *E-mail:* frontdesk@chroniclebooks.com *Web Site:* www.chroniclebooks.com, pg 55

Buffa, Christopher, Prima Games, 3000 Lava Ridge Ct, Roseville, CA 95661 *Tel:* 916-787-7000 *Web Site:* www.primagames.com, pg 187

Bui, Francoise, Random House Children's Books, 1745 Broadway, 10th fl, New York, NY 10019 *Tel:* 212-782-9000 *Web Site:* www.randomhousekids.com, pg 194

Buis, Micah, Harvard Art Museums, 32 Quincy St, Cambridge, MA 02138 *Tel:* 617-495-1440; 617-496-6529 (edit) *Fax:* 617-495-9985 *Web Site:* www.harvardartmuseums.org, pg 102

Bukowski, Danielle, Sterling Lord Literistic Inc, 115 Broadway, Suite 1602, New York, NY 10006 *Tel:* 212-780-6050 *Fax:* 212-780-6095 *E-mail:* info@sll.com *Web Site:* www.sll.com, pg 537

Bukowski, Denise, The Bukowski Agency Ltd, 14 Prince Arthur Ave, Suite 202, Toronto, ON M5R 1A9, Canada *Tel:* 416-928-6728 *Fax:* 416-963-9978 *E-mail:* info@bukowskiagency.com *Web Site:* www.bukowskiagency.com, pg 510

Bulgarelli, Br Marco, St Pauls, 2187 Victory Blvd, Staten Island, NY 10314-6603 *Tel:* 718-761-0047 (edit & prodn); 718-698-2759 (mktg & billing) *Toll Free Tel:* 800-343-2522 *Fax:* 718-761-0057 *E-mail:* sales@stpauls.us; marketing@stpauls.us *Web Site:* www.stpauls.us, pg 205

Bulger, Joe, Simon & Schuster, Inc, 1230 Avenue of the Americas, New York, NY 10020 *Tel:* 212-698-7000 *Fax:* 212-698-7007 *E-mail:* firstname.lastname@simonandschuster.com *Web Site:* www.simonandschuster.com, pg 213

Bulger, Terrilee, Nimbus Publishing Ltd, 3731 Mackintosh St, Halifax, NS B3K 5A5, Canada *Tel:* 902-455-4286 *Toll Free Tel:* 800-NIMBUS9 (646-2879) *Fax:* 902-455-5440 *Toll Free Fax:* 888-253-3133 *E-mail:* customerservice@nimbus.ca *Web Site:* www.nimbus.ca, pg 465

Bull, James, Bull Publishing Co, PO Box 1377, Boulder, CO 80306 *Tel:* 303-545-6350 *Toll Free Tel:* 800-676-2855 *Fax:* 303-545-6354 *E-mail:* bullpublishing@msn.com *Web Site:* www.bullpub.com, pg 45

Buller, Bob, SBL Press, The Luce Ctr, Suite 350, 825 Houston Mill Rd, Atlanta, GA 30329 *Tel:* 404-727-3100 *Fax:* 404-727-3101 (corp) *E-mail:* sbl@sbl-site.org *Web Site:* www.sbl-site.org, pg 207

Bullock, Karen, Meriwether Publishing, c/o Pioneer Drama Service, 9707-A E Easter Lane, Englewood, CO 80112 *Tel:* 303-779-4035 *Toll Free Tel:* 800-333-7262 *Fax:* 303-779-4315 *E-mail:* books@pioneerdrama.com *Web Site:* www.pioneerdrama.com, pg 149

Bumps, Susan, North Atlantic Books, 2526 Martin Luther King Jr Way, Berkeley, CA 94704 *Tel:* 510-549-4270 *Fax:* 510-549-4276 *Web Site:* www.northatlanticbooks.com, pg 163

Bunch, Cindy, InterVarsity Press, 430 Plaza Dr, Westmont, IL 60559-1234 *Tel:* 630-734-4000 *Toll Free Tel:* 800-843-9487 *Fax:* 630-734-4200 *E-mail:* email@ivpress.com *Web Site:* www.ivpress.com, pg 120

Bunker, Jane, Northwestern University Press, 629 Noyes St, Evanston, IL 60208-4210 *Tel:* 847-491-2046 *Toll Free Tel:* 800-621-2736 (orders only) *Fax:* 847-491-8150 *E-mail:* nupress@northwestern.edu *Web Site:* www.nupress.northwestern.edu, pg 164

Bunker, Jane, TriQuarterly Books, 629 Noyes St, Evanston, IL 60208 *Tel:* 847-491-7420 *Toll Free Tel:* 800-621-2736 (orders only) *Fax:* 847-491-8150 *E-mail:* nupress@northwestern.edu *Web Site:* www.nupress.northwestern.edu, pg 235

Bunner, Bruce, AuthorHouse, 1663 Liberty Dr, Bloomington, IN 47403 *Tel:* 812-339-6000 (outside US) *Toll Free Tel:* 888-519-5121 *E-mail:* authorsupport@authorhouse.com *Web Site:* www.authorhouse.com, pg 26

Bunzel, Mark, FineEdge.com LLC, 14004 Biz Point Lane, Anacortes, WA 98221 *Tel:* 360-299-8500 *Fax:* 360-299-0535 *E-mail:* pub@fineedge.com; orders@fineedge.com *Web Site:* www.fineedge.com, pg 85

Burch, Martin, Ocean Tree Books, 1325 Cerro Gordo Rd, Santa Fe, NM 87501 *Tel:* 505-983-1412 *Fax:* 505-983-0899 *Web Site:* www.oceantree.com, pg 166

Burch, Renee C, Wildlife Education Ltd, 2418 Noyes St, Evanston, IL 60201 *Tel:* 859-261-2556 *Toll Free Tel:* 800-477-5034 *Fax:* 859-261-2355 *Web Site:* www.zoobooks.com; wildlife-ed.com, pg 256

Burford, Peter, Burford Books, 101 E State St, No 301, Ithaca, NY 14850 *Tel:* 607-319-4373 *Fax:* 607-319-4373 *Toll Free Fax:* 866-212-7750 *E-mail:* info@burfordbooks.com *Web Site:* www.burfordbooks.com, pg 45

Burgard, Timothy H, AMACOM Books, 1601 Broadway, New York, NY 10019-7420 *Tel:* 212-586-8100 *Toll Free Tel:* 800-250-5308 (cust serv) *Fax:* 212-903-8083; 518-891-2372 (orders) *E-mail:* pubs_cust_serv@amanet.org *Web Site:* www.amacombooks.org, pg 8

Burgess, Angela R, IEEE Computer Society, 2001 "L" St NW, Suite 700, Washington, DC 20036-4928 *Tel:* 202-371-0101 *Toll Free Tel:* 800-272-6657 (memb info) *Fax:* 202-728-9614 *E-mail:* help@computer.org *Web Site:* www.computer.org, pg 114

Burgess, Kathy, University Press of Mississippi, 3825 Ridgewood Rd, Jackson, MS 39211-6492 *Tel:* 601-432-6205 *Toll Free Tel:* 800-737-7788 (orders & cust serv) *Fax:* 601-432-6217 *E-mail:* press@mississippi.edu *Web Site:* www.upress.state.ms.us, pg 247

Burgess, Marsha P, ALSC Baker & Taylor Summer Reading Grant, 50 E Huron St, Chicago, IL 60611-2795 *Tel:* 312-280-2163 *Toll Free Tel:* 800-545-2433 *Fax:* 312-440-9374; 312-280-5271 *E-mail:* alsc@ala.org *Web Site:* www.ala.org/alsc, pg 627

Burgess, Marsha P, The May Hill Arbuthnot Honor Lecture Award, 50 E Huron St, Chicago, IL 60611-2795 *Tel:* 312-280-2163 *Toll Free Tel:* 800-545-2433 *Fax:* 312-440-9374; 312-280-5271 *E-mail:* alsc@ala.org *Web Site:* www.ala.org/alsc, pg 628

Burgess, Marsha P, The Mildred L Batchelder Award, 50 E Huron St, Chicago, IL 60611-2795 *Tel:* 312-280-2163 *Toll Free Tel:* 800-545-2433 *Fax:* 312-440-9374; 312-280-5271 *E-mail:* alsc@ala.org *Web Site:* www.ala.org/alsc, pg 630

Burgess, Marsha P, The Pura Belpre Award, 50 E Huron St, Chicago, IL 60611-2795 *Tel:* 312-280-2163 *Toll Free Tel:* 800-545-2433 *Fax:* 312-440-9374; 312-280-5271 *E-mail:* alsc@ala.org *Web Site:* www.ala.org/alsc, pg 631

Burgess, Marsha P, Bound to Stay Bound Books Scholarship, 50 E Huron St, Chicago, IL 60611-2795 *Tel:* 312-280-2163 *Toll Free Tel:* 800-545-2433 *Fax:* 312-440-9374; 312-280-5271 *E-mail:* alsc@ala.org *Web Site:* www.ala.org/alsc, pg 634

Burgess, Marsha P, The Randolph Caldecott Medal, 50 E Huron St, Chicago, IL 60611-2795 *Tel:* 312-280-2163 *Toll Free Tel:* 800-545-2433 *Fax:* 312-440-9374; 312-280-5271 *E-mail:* alsc@ala.org *Web Site:* www.ala.org/alsc, pg 635

Burgess, Marsha P, Frederic G Melcher Scholarship, 50 E Huron St, Chicago, IL 60611-2795 *Tel:* 312-280-2163 *Toll Free Tel:* 800-545-2433 *Fax:* 312-440-9374; 312-280-5271 *E-mail:* alsc@ala.org *Web Site:* www.ala.org/alsc, pg 667

Burgess, Marsha P, John Newbery Medal, 50 E Huron St, Chicago, IL 60611-2795 *Tel:* 312-280-2163 *Toll Free Tel:* 800-545-2433 *Fax:* 312-440-9374; 312-280-5271 *E-mail:* alsc@ala.org *Web Site:* www.ala.org/alsc, pg 673

Burgess, Marsha P, Robert F Sibert Informational Book Award, 50 E Huron St, Chicago, IL 60611-2795 *Tel:* 312-280-2163 *Toll Free Tel:* 800-545-2433 *Fax:* 312-440-9374; 312-280-5271 *E-mail:* alsc@ala.org *Web Site:* www.ala.org/alsc, pg 689

Burgess, Marsha P, The Laura Ingalls Wilder Medal, 50 E Huron St, Chicago, IL 60611-2795 *Tel:* 312-280-2163 *Toll Free Tel:* 800-545-2433 *Fax:* 312-440-9374; 312-280-5271 *E-mail:* alsc@ala.org *Web Site:* www.ala.org/alsc, pg 698

Burgin, Richard, Boulevard Magazine Short Fiction Contest for Emerging Writers, 6614 Clayton Rd, PMB 325, Richmond Heights, MO 63117 *E-mail:* editors@boulevardmagazine.org *Web Site:* www.boulevardmagazine.org, pg 634

Burgos, Jose, University of Puerto Rico Press, Edificio La Editorial (level 2), Carr No 1, KM 12.0, Jardin Botanico Norte, San Juan, PR 00927 *Tel:* 787-250-0435; 787-250-0550 *Toll Free Tel:* 877-338-7788 *Fax:* 787-753-9116 *E-mail:* info@laeditorialupr.com *Web Site:* www.laeditorialupr.com, pg 245

Burgos, Rachel, AAP PreK-12 Learning Group, 455 Massachusetts Ave NW, Suite 700, Washington, DC 20001 *Tel:* 267-351-4310 *Fax:* 267-351-4317 *E-mail:* prek12learning@publishers.org *Web Site:* www.aepweb.org, pg 553

Burk, Dale A, Stoneydale Press Publishing Co, 523 Main St, Stevensville, MT 59870-2839 *Tel:* 406-777-2729 *Toll Free Tel:* 800-735-7006 *Fax:* 406-777-2521 *E-mail:* stoneydale@stoneydale.com *Web Site:* www.stoneydale.com, pg 223

Burke, Amy Lestition, Special Libraries Association (SLA), 7918 Jones Branch Dr, Suite 300, McLean, VA 22102 *Tel:* 703-647-4900 *Fax:* 703-506-3266 *Web Site:* www.sla.org, pg 579

Burke, Charlie, Bentley Publishers, 1734 Massachusetts Ave, Cambridge, MA 02138-1804 *Tel:* 617-547-4170 *Toll Free Tel:* 800-423-4595 *Fax:* 617-876-9235 *E-mail:* sales@bentleypublishers.com *Web Site:* www.bentleypublishers.com, pg 33

Burke, Colleen, Binghamton University Creative Writing Program, c/o Dept of English, PO Box 6000, Binghamton, NY 13902-6000 *Tel:* 607-777-2168 *Fax:* 607-777-2408 *E-mail:* cwpro@binghamton.edu *Web Site:* english.binghamton.edu/cwpro, pg 619

Burke, Craig, Berkley Publishing Group, 375 Hudson St, New York, NY 10014 *Tel:* 212-366-2000 *Fax:* 212-366-2385 *Web Site:* www.penguin.com, pg 33

Burke, Darius, Pomegranate Communications Inc, 19018 NE Portal Way, Portland, OR 97230 *Tel:* 503-328-6500 *Toll Free Tel:* 800-227-1428 *Fax:* 503-328-9330 *Toll Free Fax:* 800-848-4376 *E-mail:* contactus@pomegranate.com *Web Site:* www.pomegranate.com, pg 185

Burke, Jackie, Algonquin Books, 400 Silver Cedar Ct, Suite 300, Chapel Hill, NC 27514-1585 *Tel:* 919-967-0108 *Fax:* 919-933-0272 *E-mail:* inquiry@algonquin.com *Web Site:* www.workman.com/algonquin, pg 7

Burke, Katie, Pomegranate Communications Inc, 19018 NE Portal Way, Portland, OR 97230 *Tel:* 503-328-6500 *Toll Free Tel:* 800-227-1428 *Fax:* 503-328-9330 *Toll Free Fax:* 800-848-4376 *E-mail:* contactus@pomegranate.com *Web Site:* www.pomegranate.com, pg 185

Burke, Katie, PubWest Book Design Awards, 17501 Hill Way, Lake Oswego, OR 97035 *Tel:* 503-901-9865 *Web Site:* pubwest.org, pg 683

Burke, Lori, Grosset & Dunlap, 345 Hudson St, New York, NY 10014 *Tel:* 212-366-2000 *Web Site:* www.penguinrandomhouse.com, pg 96

Burke, Lori, Penguin Young Readers Group, 345 Hudson St, New York, NY 10014 *Tel:* 212-366-2000; 212-414-3553 *Fax:* 212-414-3340 *Web Site:* www.penguin.com/children, pg 179

Burke, Michele, Random House Children's Books, 1745 Broadway, 10th fl, New York, NY 10019 *Tel:* 212-782-9000 *Web Site:* www.randomhousekids.com, pg 194

Burke, Penny, Rutgers University Press, 106 Somerset St, 3rd fl, New Brunswick, NJ 08901 *Tel:* 848-445-7762 *Toll Free Tel:* 800-848-6224 (orders only) *Fax:* 732-745-4935 (acqs, edit, mktg, perms & prodn) *Toll Free Fax:* 800-272-6817 (fulfillment) *Web Site:* rutgerspress.rutgers.edu, pg 202

Burke, Thomas F, Pomegranate Communications Inc, 19018 NE Portal Way, Portland, OR 97230 *Tel:* 503-328-6500 *Toll Free Tel:* 800-227-1428 *Fax:* 503-328-9330 *Toll Free Fax:* 800-848-4376 *E-mail:* contactus@pomegranate.com *Web Site:* www.pomegranate.com, pg 185

Burke, Vincent J, The Johns Hopkins University Press, 2715 N Charles St, Baltimore, MD 21218-4363 *Tel:* 410-516-6900; 410-516-6987 (journal orders outside US & CN) *Toll Free Tel:* 800-537-5487 (book orders & cust serv); 800-548-1784 (journal orders) *Fax:* 410-516-6968; 410-516-3866 (journal orders) *E-mail:* hfscustserv@press.jhu.edu (cust serv); jrnlcirc@press.jhu.edu (journal orders) *Web Site:* www.press.jhu.edu; muse.jhu.edu, pg 122

Burke, William, Cummings & Hathaway Publishers, 395 Atlantic Ave, East Rockaway, NY 11518 *Tel:* 516-593-3607 *Fax:* 516-593-1401, pg 66

Burkholder, Bruce, Editorial Bautista Independiente, 3417 Kenilworth Blvd, Sebring, FL 33870-4469 *Tel:* 863-382-6350 *Toll Free Tel:* 800-398-7187 (US) *Fax:* 863-382-8650 *E-mail:* info@ebi-bmm.org; ebiweb@ebi-bmm.org *Web Site:* www.ebi-bmm.org, pg 75

Burkholder, Courtney, Texas Tech University Press, 1120 Main St, 2nd fl, Lubbock, TX 79401 *Tel:* 806-742-2982 *Toll Free Tel:* 800-832-4042 *Fax:* 806-742-2979 *E-mail:* ttup@ttu.edu *Web Site:* www.ttupress.org, pg 230

Burkle, Sharon, Random House Children's Books, 1745 Broadway, 10th fl, New York, NY 10019 *Tel:* 212-782-9000 *Web Site:* www.randomhousekids.com, pg 194

Burkman, Sarah, News Media Alliance, 4401 N Fairfax Dr, Suite 300, Arlington, VA 22203 *Tel:* 571-366-1000 *E-mail:* info@newsmediaalliance.org *Web Site:* www.newsmediaalliance.org, pg 573

Burkot, Rachel, Harlequin Enterprises Ltd, 225 Duncan Mill Rd, Don Mills, ON M3B 3K9, Canada *Tel:* 416-445-5860 *Toll Free Tel:* 888-432-4879; 800-370-5838 (ebook inquiries) *E-mail:* customerservice@harlequin.com *Web Site:* www.harlequin.com, pg 459

Burmeister-Brown, Susan, Family Matters, PO Box 80430, Portland, OR 97280-1430 *Tel:* 503-221-0836 *Fax:* 503-221-0837 *E-mail:* editors@glimmertrain.org *Web Site:* www.glimmertrain.org, pg 645

Burmeister-Brown, Susan, Fiction Open, PO Box 80430, Portland, OR 97280-1430 *Tel:* 503-221-0836 *Fax:* 503-221-0837 *E-mail:* editors@glimmertrain.org *Web Site:* www.glimmertrain.org, pg 646

Burmeister-Brown, Susan, Glimmer Train Press Inc, PO Box 80430, Portland, OR 97280-1430 *Tel:* 503-221-0836 *Fax:* 503-221-0837 *E-mail:* editors@glimmertrain.org *Web Site:* www.glimmertrain.org, pg 93

Burmeister-Brown, Susan, Short Story Award for New Writers, PO Box 80430, Portland, OR 97280-1430 *Tel:* 503-221-0836 *Fax:* 503-221-0837 *E-mail:* editors@glimmertrain.org *Web Site:* www.glimmertrain.org, pg 689

Burmeister-Brown, Susan, Very Short Fiction Award, PO Box 80430, Portland, OR 97280-1430 *Tel:* 503-221-0836 *Fax:* 503-221-0837 *E-mail:* editors@glimmertrain.org *Web Site:* www.glimmertrain.org, pg 696

Burnett, Sheila, Scarecrow Press Inc, 4501 Forbes Blvd, Suite 200, Lanham, MD 20706 *Tel:* 301-459-3366 *Fax:* 301-429-5748 *Web Site:* www.scarecrowpress.com, pg 207

Burnett, Terry, South Carolina Bar, Continuing Legal Education Div, 950 Taylor St, Columbia, SC 29201 *Tel:* 803-799-6653 *Toll Free Tel:* 800-768-7787 *Fax:* 803-799-4118 *E-mail:* scbar-info@scbar.org *Web Site:* www.scbar.org, pg 218

Burnett, Sheila, Rowman & Littlefield Publishers Inc, 4501 Forbes Blvd, Suite 200, Lanham, MD 20706 *Tel:* 301-459-3366 *Toll Free Tel:* 800-462-6420 (cust serv) *Fax:* 301-429-5748 *Web Site:* rowman.com, pg 202

Burnham, Jonathan, HarperCollins General Books Group, 195 Broadway, New York, NY 10007 *Tel:* 212-207-7000 *Web Site:* www.harpercollins.com, pg 101

Burns, Katie, Pantheon Books/Schocken Books, c/o Penguin Random House Inc, 1745 Broadway, New York, NY 10019 *Tel:* 212-751-2600 *Web Site:* knopfdoubleday.com/imprint/pantheon, pg 173

Burns, Marilyn, Math Solutions®, One Harbor Dr, Suite 101, Sausalito, CA 94965 *Tel:* 415-332-4181 *Toll Free Tel:* 800-868-9092 *Fax:* 415-331-1931 *Toll Free Fax:* 877-942-8837 *E-mail:* info@mathsolutions.com; orders@mathsolutions.com *Web Site:* www.mathsolutions.com, pg 144

Burns, Nanette, Advertising Research Foundation (ARF), 432 Park Ave S, 4th fl, New York, NY 10016-8013 *Tel:* 212-751-5656 *Fax:* 212-319-5265 *E-mail:* info@thearf.org; jar@thearf.org (edit) *Web Site:* www.thearf.org, pg 553

Burns, Scott, Marshall Cavendish Corp, 99 White Plains Rd, Tarrytown, NY 10591-9001 *Tel:* 914-332-8888 *Toll Free Tel:* 800-821-9881 *Fax:* 914-332-8102 *E-mail:* mce@marshallcavendish.com *Web Site:* www.marshallcavendish.com; www.mceducation.us, pg 143

Burns, Shona, Chronicle Books LLC, 680 Second St, San Francisco, CA 94107 *Tel:* 415-537-4200 *Toll Free Tel:* 800-759-0190 (cust serv) *Fax:* 415-537-4460 *Toll Free Fax:* 800-858-7787 (orders); 800-286-9471 (cust serv) *E-mail:* frontdesk@chroniclebooks.com *Web Site:* www.chroniclebooks.com, pg 55

Burns, Stanley B MD, Burns Archive Press, 140 E 38 St, New York, NY 10016 *Tel:* 212-889-1938 *Fax:* 212-481-9113 *E-mail:* info@burnsarchive.com *Web Site:* www.burnsarchive.com, pg 45

Burr, Jim, University of Texas Press, 3001 Lake Austin Blvd, 2.200, Austin, TX 78703 *Tel:* 512-471-7233 *Fax:* 512-232-7178 *E-mail:* utpress@uts.cc.utexas.edu; info@utpress.utexas.edu *Web Site:* www.utexaspress.com, pg 230

Burr, Scott, Koho Pono LLC, 15024 SE Pinegrove Loop, Clackamas, OR 97015 *Tel:* 503-723-7392 *Toll Free Tel:* 800-937-8000 (orders) *Toll Free Fax:* 800-876-0186 (orders) *E-mail:* info@kohopono.com; orders@ingrambook.com *Web Site:* kohopono.com, pg 127

Burrell, Carol, Workman Publishing Co Inc, 225 Varick St, 9th fl, New York, NY 10014-4381 *Tel:* 212-254-5900 *Toll Free Tel:* 800-722-7202 *Fax:* 212-254-8098 *E-mail:* info@workman.com *Web Site:* www.workman.com, pg 259

Burri, Peter, The Experiment, 220 E 23 St, Suite 301, New York, NY 10010-4674 *Tel:* 212-889-1659 *E-mail:* info@theexperimentpublishing.com *Web Site:* www.theexperimentpublishing.com, pg 81

Burri, Peter, Industrial Press Inc, 32 Haviland St, Suite 3, Norwalk, CT 06854 *Tel:* 203-956-5593 ext 0 (cust serv) *Toll Free Tel:* 888-528-7852 ext 0 (cust serv) *Fax:* 203-354-9391 (cust serv) *E-mail:* info@industrialpress.com (cust serv) *Web Site:* new.industrialpress.com, pg 116

Burriss, Dr Theresa, Highland Summer Writers' Conference, PO Box 7014, Radford University, Cook Hall, Radford, VA 24142 *Fax:* 540-831-5951 *Web Site:* www.radford.edu/content/cehd/home/appalachian-studies.html, pg 611

Burroughs, Joan, John Burroughs Medal, 261 Floyd Ackert Rd, New York, NY 12493 *Tel:* 212-769-5169 *Fax:* 212-313-7182 *E-mail:* info@johnburroughsassociation.org *Web Site:* www.johnburroughsassociation.org, pg 635

Burroughs, Joan, John Burroughs Nature Essay Award, 261 Floyd Ackert Rd, New York, NY 12493 *Tel:* 212-769-5169 *Fax:* 212 313 7182 *E-mail:* info@johnburroughsassociation.org *Web Site:* www.johnburroughsassociation.org, pg 635

Burroughs, Joan, Riverby Awards, 261 Floyd Ackert Rd, New York, NY 12493 *Tel:* 212-769-5169 *Fax:* 212-313-7182 *E-mail:* info@johnburroughsassociation.org *Web Site:* www.johnburroughsassociation.org, pg 685

Burrows, Arthur A, Pro Lingua Associates Inc, 74 Cotton Mill Hill, Suite A-315, Brattleboro, VT 05301 *Tel:* 802-257-7779 *Toll Free Tel:* 800-366-4775 *Fax:* 802-257-5117 *E-mail:* info@prolinguaassociates.com *Web Site:* www.prolinguaassociates.com, pg 189

Burrows, Elise C, Pro Lingua Associates Inc, 74 Cotton Mill Hill, Suite A-315, Brattleboro, VT 05301 *Tel:* 802-257-7779 *Toll Free Tel:* 800-366-4775 *Fax:* 802-257-5117 *E-mail:* info@prolinguaassociates.com *Web Site:* www.prolinguaassociates.com, pg 189

Burrows, Roberta, Institute of Environmental Sciences & Technology - IEST, 2340 S Arlington Heights Rd, Suite 620, Arlington Heights, IL 60005-4510 *Tel:* 847-981-0100 *Fax:* 847-981-4130 *E-mail:* information@iest.org *Web Site:* www.iest.org, pg 118

Burson, Kayla, Workman Publishing Co Inc, 225 Varick St, 9th fl, New York, NY 10014-4381 *Tel:* 212-254-5900 *Toll Free Tel:* 800-722-7202 *Fax:* 212-254-8098 *E-mail:* info@workman.com *Web Site:* www.workman.com, pg 259

Burt, Dee, Brick Mantel Books, 4735 S State Rd 446, Bloomington, IN 47401 *Tel:* 314-827-6567; 812-837-9226 *E-mail:* info@brickmantelbooks.com *Web Site:* brickmantelbooks.com, pg 43

Burt, Dee, Open Books Press, 4735 S State Rd 446, Bloomington, IN 47401 *Tel:* 314-827-6567; 812-837-9226 *E-mail:* info@openbookspress.com *Web Site:* openbookspress.com, pg 168

Burt, Dee, Pen & Publish Inc, 4735 S State Rd 446, Bloomington, IN 47401 *Tel:* 314-827-6567 *E-mail:* info@penandpublish.com *Web Site:* www.penandpublish.com, pg 176

Burt, Jennifer, Writers Guild of America Awards, 7000 W Third St, Los Angeles, CA 90048 *Tel:* 323-951-4000; 323-782-4569 *Fax:* 323-782-4800 *Web Site:* www.wga.org, pg 700

Burt, Paul, Brick Mantel Books, 4735 S State Rd 446, Bloomington, IN 47401 *Tel:* 314-827-6567; 812-837-9226 *E-mail:* info@brickmantelbooks.com *Web Site:* brickmantelbooks.com, pg 43

Burt, Paul, Open Books Press, 4735 S State Rd 446, Bloomington, IN 47401 *Tel:* 314-827-6567; 812-837-9226 *E-mail:* info@openbookspress.com *Web Site:* openbookspress.com, pg 168

Burt, Paul, Pen & Publish Inc, 4735 S State Rd 446, Bloomington, IN 47401 *Tel:* 314-827-6567 *E-mail:* info@penandpublish.com *Web Site:* www.penandpublish.com, pg 176

Burt, Staci, St Martin's Press, LLC, 175 Fifth Ave, New York, NY 10010 *Tel:* 646-307-5151 *Web Site:* us.macmillan.com/smp, pg 204

Burton, David, Brooklyn Publishers LLC, PO Box 248, Cedar Rapids, IA 52406 *Tel:* 319-368-8012 *Toll Free Tel:* 888-473-8521 *Fax:* 319-368-8011 *E-mail:* customerservice@brookpub.com; editor@brookpub.com *Web Site:* www.brookpub.com, pg 44

Burton, Diane, The Pablo Neruda Prize for Poetry, Nimrod International Journal, 800 S Tucker Dr, Tulsa, OK 74104 *Tel:* 918-631-3080 *Fax:* 918-631-3033 *E-mail:* nimrod@utulsa.edu *Web Site:* www.utulsa.edu/nimrod, pg 672

Burton, Diane, Katherine Anne Porter Prize for Fiction, Nimrod International Journal, 800 S Tucker Dr, Tulsa, OK 74104 *Tel:* 918-631-3080 *Fax:* 918-631-3033 *E-mail:* nimrod@utulsa.edu *Web Site:* www.utulsa.edu/nimrod, pg 681

Burton, Harry, Thames & Hudson, 500 Fifth Ave, New York, NY 10110 *Tel:* 212-354-3763 *Toll Free Tel:* 800-233-4830 *Fax:* 212-398-1252 *E-mail:* bookinfo@thames.wwnorton.com *Web Site:* www.thamesandhudsonusa.com, pg 230

Burton, Julie, HarperCollins General Books Group, 195 Broadway, New York, NY 10007 *Tel:* 212-207-7000 *Web Site:* www.harpercollins.com, pg 101

Burton, Libby, Henry Holt and Company, LLC, 175 Fifth Ave, New York, NY 10010 *Tel:* 646-307-5151 *Toll Free Tel:* 888-330-8477 (orders) *Fax:* 646-307-5285 *E-mail:* firstname.lastname@hholt.com *Web Site:* www.henryholt.com, pg 109

Burton, Liz, Zumaya Publications LLC, 3209 S IH 35, Suite 1086, Austin, TX 78741 *Tel:* 512-537-3145 *Fax:* 512-276-6745 *E-mail:* acquisitions@zumayapublications.com *Web Site:* www.zumayapublications.com, pg 263

Burton, Melissa, Princeton University Press, 41 William St, Princeton, NJ 08540-5237 *Tel:* 609-258-4900 *Fax:* 609-258-6305 *Web Site:* press.princeton.edu, pg 188

Burton, Michael, University Press of New England, One Court St, Suite 250, Lebanon, NH 03766 *Tel:* 603-448-1533 *Toll Free Tel:* 800-421-1561 (orders only) *Fax:* 603-448-7006; 603-448-9429 (orders only) *E-mail:* university.press@dartmouth.edu *Web Site:* www.upne.com, pg 247

Burton, Rebecca, Playwrights Guild of Canada, 401 Richmond St W, Suite 350, Toronto, ON M5V 3A8, Canada *Tel:* 416-703-0201 *Fax:* 416-703-0059 *E-mail:* info@playwrightsguild.ca *Web Site:* www.playwrightsguild.ca, pg 575

Burwell, Robyn, Zondervan, 3900 Sparks Dr, Grand Rapids, MI 49546 *Tel:* 616-698-6900 *Toll Free Tel:* 800-226-1122; 800-727-1309 (retail orders) *Fax:* 616-698-3350 *Toll Free Fax:* 800-698-3256 (retail orders) *E-mail:* zinfo@zondervan.com *Web Site:* www.zondervan.com, pg 263

Busch, Susan, Sourcebooks Inc, 1935 Brookdale Rd, Suite 139, Naperville, IL 60563 *Tel:* 630-961-3900 *Toll Free Tel:* 800-432-7444 *Fax:* 630-961-2168 *E-mail:* info@sourcebooks.com; customersupport@sourcebooks.com *Web Site:* www.sourcebooks.com, pg 218

Buschardt, Stephanie, Houghton Mifflin Harcourt, 125 High St, Boston, MA 02110 *Tel:* 617-351-5000 *Toll Free Tel:* 855-969-4642; 800-225-5425 (K-12 educ materials); 800-323-9540 (assessment materials); 877-219-1537 (SkillsTutor); 888-242-6747 (Innovation in Educ Group); 800-225-3362 (Trade & Ref Div) *Toll Free Fax:* 800-269-5232 *E-mail:* myhmhco@hmhco.com *Web Site:* www.hmhco.com, pg 110

Bush, Lynne, University of California Institute on Global Conflict & Cooperation, 9500 Gilman Dr, MC 0518, La Jolla, CA 92093-0518 *Tel:* 858-534-6106 *Fax:* 858-534-7655 *E-mail:* igcc-communications@ucsd.edu *Web Site:* igcc.ucsd.edu, pg 240

Butler, Adios, Picasso Project, 1109 Geary Blvd, San Francisco, CA 94109 *Tel:* 415-292-6500 *Fax:* 415-292-6594 *E-mail:* editeur@earthlink.net (edit); picasso@art-books.com (orders) *Web Site:* www.art-books.com, pg 183

Butler, Adios, Alan Wofsy Fine Arts, 1109 Geary Blvd, San Francisco, CA 94109 *Tel:* 415-292-6500 *Toll Free Tel:* 800-660-6403 *Fax:* 415-292-6594 (off & cust serv); 510-251-1840 (acctg) *E-mail:* order@art-books.com (orders); editeur@earthlink.net (edit); beauxarts@earthlink.net (cust serv) *Web Site:* www.art-books.com, pg 258

Butler, Butch, StarGroup International Inc, 1194 Old Dixie Hwy, Suite 201, West Palm Beach, FL 33413 *Tel:* 561-547-0667 *Fax:* 561-843-8530 *E-mail:* info@stargroupinternational.com *Web Site:* stargroupinternational.com, pg 221

Butler, Leigh, Penguin Group USA, A Penguin Random House Company, 375 Hudson St, New York, NY 10014 *Tel:* 212-366-2000 *Toll Free Tel:* 800-847-5515 (inside sales); 800-631-8571 (cust serv) *Fax:* 212-366-2666; 607-775-4829 (inside sales) *E-mail:* online@us.penguingroup.com *Web Site:* www.penguin.com, pg 177

Byer-Sprinzeles, Maggie, Byer-Sprinzeles Agency, 5800 Arlington Ave, Suite 16-C, Riverdale, NY 10471 *Tel:* 718-543-9399 *Web Site:* www.maggiebyersprinzeles.com, pg 543

Bykofsky, Sheree, Sheree Bykofsky Associates Inc, PO Box 706, Brigantine, NJ 08203 *E-mail:* submitbee@aol.com *Web Site:* www.shereebee.com, pg 511

Byl, Craig, American Institute of Aeronautics & Astronautics (AIAA), 1801 Alexander Bell Dr, Suite 500, Reston, VA 20191-4344 *Tel:* 703-264-7500 *Toll Free Tel:* 800-639-AIAA (639-2422) *Fax:* 703-264-7551 *E-mail:* custserv@aiaa.org *Web Site:* www.aiaa.org, pg 12

Byler, Josh, Herald Press, 1251 Virginia Ave, Harrisonburg, VA 22802-2434 *Toll Free Tel:* 800-245-7894 (orders) *Toll Free Fax:* 877-271-0760 *E-mail:* info@MennoMedia.org *Web Site:* www.heraldpress.com; store.mennomedia.org, pg 106

Bynum, Robert C, Travel Keys, PO Box 160691, Sacramento, CA 95816-0691 *Tel:* 916-452-5200 *Fax:* 916-452-5200, pg 234

Byram, John W, University of New Mexico Press, One University of New Mexico, Albuquerque, NM 87131-0001 *Tel:* 505-272-7777 *Fax:* 505-277-3343; 505-272-7778 (cust serv) *Toll Free Fax:* 800-622-8667 (orders only) *E-mail:* unmpress@unm.edu; custserv@unm.edu (order dept) *Web Site:* unmpress.com, pg 243

Byrd, Bobby, Cinco Puntos Press, 701 Texas Ave, El Paso, TX 79901 *Tel:* 915-838-1625 *Toll Free Tel:* 800-566-9072 *Fax:* 915-838-1635 *E-mail:* info@cincopuntos.com *Web Site:* www.cincopuntos.com, pg 56

Byrd, John, Cinco Puntos Press, 701 Texas Ave, El Paso, TX 79901 *Tel:* 915-838-1625 *Toll Free Tel:* 800-566-9072 *Fax:* 915-838-1635 *E-mail:* info@cincopuntos.com *Web Site:* www.cincopuntos.com, pg 56

Byrd, Lee, Cinco Puntos Press, 701 Texas Ave, El Paso, TX 79901 *Tel:* 915-838-1625 *Toll Free Tel:* 800-566-9072 *Fax:* 915-838-1635 *E-mail:* info@cincopuntos.com *Web Site:* www.cincopuntos.com, pg 56

Byrd, Megan, Perseus Books, 250 W 57 St, 15th fl, New York, NY 10107 *Tel:* 212-340-8100 *Toll Free Tel:* 800-343-4499 (cust serv) *Fax:* 212-340-8105 *Web Site:* www.perseusbooks.com, pg 181

Byrne, Stephen, Miniature Book Society Inc, 702 Rosecrans St, San Diego, CA 92106-3013 *Tel:* 619-226-4441 *Fax:* 619-226-4441 *E-mail:* minibook@cox.net *Web Site:* www.mbs.org, pg 569

Byrns, Bob, Paulist Press, 997 Macarthur Blvd, Mahwah, NJ 07430-9990 *Tel:* 201-825-7300 *Toll Free Tel:* 800-218-1903 *Fax:* 201-825-6921 *Toll Free Fax:* 800-836-3161 *E-mail:* info@paulistpress.com; publicity@paulistpress.com *Web Site:* www.paulistpress.com, pg 175

Cabasin, Linda, Fodor's Travel Publications, 1745 Broadway, 15th fl, New York, NY 10019 *Toll Free Tel:* 800-733-3000 *E-mail:* publicity@fodors.com; editors@fodors.com *Web Site:* www.fodors.com, pg 86

Cabaza, Becky, Words into Print, 208 Java St, 6th fl, Brooklyn, NY 11222 *E-mail:* query@wordsintoprint.org *Web Site:* wordsintoprint.org, pg 503

Cabezas, Sue, Applewood Books Inc, One River Rd, Carlisle, MA 01741 *Tel:* 781-271-0055 *Toll Free Tel:* 800-277-5312 (orders) *Fax:* 781-271-0056 *E-mail:* bookorder@awb.com; customercare@awb.com *Web Site:* www.awb.com, pg 19

Cabin, John, Vandamere Press, 3580 Morris St N, St Petersburg, FL 33713 *Tel:* 727-556-0950 *Toll Free Tel:* 800-551-7776 *Fax:* 727-556-2560 *E-mail:* orders@vandamere.com *Web Site:* www.vandamere.com, pg 249

Cabrera, Javier, Santillana USA Publishing Co, 2023 NW 84 Ave, Doral, FL 33122 *Tel:* 305-591-9522 *Toll Free Tel:* 800-245-8584 *E-mail:* customerservice@santillanausa.com *Web Site:* www.santillanausa.com, pg 206

Caggiula, Samuel M, Casemate | publishers, 1950 Lawrence Rd, Havertown, PA 19083 *Tel:* 610-853-9131 *Fax:* 610-853-9146 *E-mail:* casemate@casematepublishers.com *Web Site:* www.casematepublishers.com, pg 49

Cahalan, Sarah, Marian Library Medal, 300 College Park, Dayton, OH 45469-1390 *Tel:* 937-229-4214 *Fax:* 937-229-4258 *Web Site:* campus.udayton.edu/mary/mlmedal.html, pg 665

Cahill, Brendan, Penguin Random House Inc, 1745 Broadway, New York, NY 10019 *Tel:* 212-782-9000 *Toll Free Tel:* 800-726-0600 *Web Site:* www.penguinrandomhouse.com, pg 178

Cahill, Kerry, The Johns Hopkins University Press, 2715 N Charles St, Baltimore, MD 21218-4363 *Tel:* 410-516-6900; 410-516-6987 (journal orders outside US & CN) *Toll Free Tel:* 800-537-5487 (book orders & cust serv); 800-548-1784 (journal orders) *Fax:* 410-516-6968; 410-516-3866 (journal orders) *E-mail:* hfscustserv@press.jhu.edu (cust serv); jrnlcirc@press.jhu.edu (journal orders) *Web Site:* www.press.jhu.edu; muse.jhu.edu, pg 122

Cahoon, Nancy Stauffer, Nancy Stauffer Associates, 30 Corbin Dr, Suite 1203, Darien, CT 06820 *Tel:* 203-202-2500 *Web Site:* staufferliterary.com; publishersmarketplace.com/members/nstauffer, pg 537

Caiati, Michael, Random House Children's Books, 1745 Broadway, 10th fl, New York, NY 10019 *Tel:* 212-782-9000 *Web Site:* www.randomhousekids.com, pg 195

Cain, Karen, Standard Publishing, 4050 Lee Vance View, Colorado Springs, CO 80918 *Tel:* 513-931-4050 *Toll Free Tel:* 800-323-7543 *Fax:* 513-931-0950 *Toll Free Fax:* 800-323-0726 *E-mail:* customerservice@standardpub.com *Web Site:* www.standardpub.com, pg 220

Calamia, Joseph, Yale University Press, 302 Temple St, New Haven, CT 06511-8909 *Tel:* 203-432-0960; 203-432-0966 (sales); 401-531-2800 (cust serv) *Toll Free Tel:* 800-405-1619 (cust serv) *Fax:* 203-432-0948; 203-432-8485 (sales); 401-531-2801 (cust serv) *Toll Free Fax:* 800-406-9145 (cust serv) *E-mail:* sales.press@yale.edu (sales); customer.care@triliteral.org (cust serv) *Web Site:* www.yalebooks.com; yalepress.yale.edu/yupbooks, pg 261

Calarco, Catherine, HeartMath LLC, 14700 W Park Ave, Boulder Creek, CA 95006 *Tel:* 831-338-8700 *Toll Free Tel:* 800-450-9111 *Fax:* 831-338-9861 *E-mail:* info@heartmath.com; inquiry@heartmath.com *Web Site:* www.heartmath.com, pg 105

Calderara, Theo, Oxford University Press USA, 198 Madison Ave, New York, NY 10016 *Tel:* 212-726-6000 *Toll Free Tel:* 800-451-7556 (orders); 800-445-9714 (cust serv) *Fax:* 919-677-1303 *E-mail:* custserv.us@oup.com *Web Site:* www.oup.com/us, pg 171

Caldwell, Amy, Beacon Press, 24 Farnsworth St, Boston, MA 02210-1409 *Tel:* 617-742-2110 *Fax:* 617-723-3097; 617-742-2290 *Web Site:* www.beacon.org, pg 31

Caldwell, Becky, Creative Writing Day & Workshops, PO Box 801, Abingdon, VA 24212-0801 *Tel:* 276-623-5266 *Fax:* 276-676-3076 *E-mail:* info@vahighlandsfestival.org *Web Site:* vahighlandsfestival.org, pg 610

Caldwell, Linda, The Writers' Colony at Dairy Hollow, 515 Spring St, Eureka Springs, AR 72632 *Tel:* 479-253-7444 *E-mail:* director@writerscolony.org *Web Site:* www.writerscolony.org, pg 616

Caldwell, Madeline, Alfred A Knopf/Everyman's Library, c/o Penguin Random House Inc, 1745 Broadway, New York, NY 10019 *Tel:* 212-751-2600 *Toll Free Tel:* 800-638-6460 *Fax:* 212-572-2593 *Web Site:* www.knopfdoubleday.com, pg 127

Calistro, Paddy, Angel City Press, 2118 Wilshire Blvd, Suite 880, Santa Monica, CA 90403 *Tel:* 310-395-9982 *Toll Free Tel:* 800-949-8039 *Fax:* 310-395-3353 *E-mail:* info@angelcitypress.com *Web Site:* www.angelcitypress.com, pg 17

Callahan, Allison, Gallery Books, 1230 Avenue of the Americas, New York, NY 10020 *Toll Free Tel:* 800-456-6798 *Fax:* 212-698-7284 *E-mail:* consumer.customerservice@simonandschuster.com *Web Site:* www.simonsays.com, pg 90

Callahan, Laurie, New Directions Publishing Corp, 80 Eighth Ave, New York, NY 10011 *Tel:* 212-255-0230 *Fax:* 212-255-0231 *E-mail:* newdirections@ndbooks.com *Web Site:* ndbooks.com, pg 160

Callahan, Pat, University of South Carolina Press, 1600 Hampton St, Suite 544, Columbia, SC 29208 *Tel:* 803-777-5245 *Toll Free Tel:* 800-768-2500 (orders) *Fax:* 803-777-0160 *Toll Free Fax:* 800-868-0740 (orders) *Web Site:* www.sc.edu/uscpress, pg 245

Callahan, Sabrina, Little, Brown and Company, 1290 Avenue of the Americas, New York, NY 10019 *Tel:* 212-364-1100 *Fax:* 212-364-0952 *E-mail:* firstname.lastname@hbgusa.com *Web Site:* www.littlebrown.com; www.HachetteBookGroup.com, pg 135

Callanan, Annie, Taylor & Francis Inc, 530 Walnut St, Suite 850, Philadelphia, PA 19106 *Tel:* 215-625-8900 *Toll Free Tel:* 800-354-1420 *Fax:* 215-207-0050; 215-207-0046 (cust serv) *E-mail:* support@tandfonline.com *Web Site:* www.taylorandfrancis.com, pg 227

Callaway, Jaimee, Perseus Books, 250 W 57 St, 15th fl, New York, NY 10107 *Tel:* 212-340-8100 *Toll Free Tel:* 800-343-4499 (cust serv) *Fax:* 212-340-8105 *Web Site:* www.perseusbooks.com, pg 180

Callaway, MaryKatherine, Louisiana State University Press, 338 Johnston Hall, Baton Rouge, LA 70803 *Tel:* 225-578-6294 *Fax:* 225-578-6461 *E-mail:* lsupress@lsu.edu *Web Site:* lsupress.org, pg 138

Callaway, Terry, River Road Press LLC, 9 Dakin, New Orleans, LA 70121 *Tel:* 504-722-8139 *Web Site:* riverroadpress.com, pg 199

Callery, Maryann, Plowshare Media, 405 Vincente Way, La Jolla, CA 92037 *E-mail:* sales@plowsharemedia.com *Web Site:* plowsharemedia.com, pg 184

Callison, Richard, Penguin Random House Inc, 1745 Broadway, New York, NY 10019 *Tel:* 212-782-9000 *Toll Free Tel:* 800-726-0600 *Web Site:* www.penguinrandomhouse.com, pg 178

Calvi, Paul, Annual Reviews, 4139 El Camino Way, Palo Alto, CA 94306 *Tel:* 650-493-4400 *Toll Free Tel:* 800-523-8635 *Fax:* 650-424-0910; 650-855-9815 *E-mail:* service@annualreviews.org *Web Site:* www.annualreviews.org, pg 17

Calvo, Roque J, The Electrochemical Society (ECS), 65 S Main St, Bldg D, Pennington, NJ 08534-2839 *Tel:* 609-737-1902 *Fax:* 609-737-2743 *E-mail:* publications@electrochem.org; customerservice@electrochem.org *Web Site:* www.electrochem.org, pg 77

Camacho, Linda, Prospect Agency, 285 Fifth Ave, PMB 445, Brooklyn, NY 11215 *Tel:* 718-788-3217 *Fax:* 718-360-9582 *Web Site:* www.prospectagency.com, pg 532

Camacho, Linda, Random House Children's Books, 1745 Broadway, 10th fl, New York, NY 10019 *Tel:* 212-782-9000 *Web Site:* www.randomhousekids.com, pg 194

Cambell, Cloves C Jr, National Newspaper Publishers Association (NNPA), 1816 12 St NW, Washington, DC 20009 *Tel:* 202-588-8764 *Fax:* 202-588-8960 *E-mail:* info@nnpa.org *Web Site:* www.nnpa.org; www.blackpressusa.com, pg 572

Cameron, Claire, Bull Publishing Co, PO Box 1377, Boulder, CO 80306 *Tel:* 303-545-6350 *Toll Free Tel:* 800-676-2855 *Fax:* 303-545-6354 *E-mail:* bullpublishing@msn.com *Web Site:* www.bullpub.com, pg 45

Cameron, Hamish, University of Toronto Press, 10 St Mary St, Suite 700, Toronto, ON M4Y 2W8, Canada *Tel:* 416-978-2239 *Fax:* 416-978-4738 *E-mail:* info@utpress.utoronto.ca *Web Site:* www.utpress.utoronto.ca; www.utppublishing.com, pg 475

Cameron, Kimberley, Kimberley Cameron & Associates LLC, 1550 Tiburon Blvd, Suite 704, Tiburon, CA 94920 *Tel:* 415-789-9191 *Fax:* 415-789-9177 *Web Site:* www.kimberleycameron.com, pg 511

Cameron, Laura, Flanker Press Ltd, 1243 Kenmount Rd, Unit 1, Paradise, NL A1L 0V8, Canada *Tel:* 709-739-4477 *Toll Free Tel:* 866-739-4420 *Fax:* 709-739-4420 *E-mail:* info@flankerpress.com; sales@flankerpress.com *Web Site:* www.flankerpress.com, pg 457

Cameron, Linda, University of Alberta Press, Ring House 2, Edmonton, AB T6G 2E1, Canada *Tel:* 780-492-3662 *Fax:* 780-492-0719 *Web Site:* www.uap.ualberta.ca, pg 473

Caminiti, Phil, Disney-Hyperion Books, 1101 Flower St, Glendale, CA 91201 *Web Site:* books.disney.com, pg 70

Camlin, Alex, Perseus Books, 250 W 57 St, 15th fl, New York, NY 10107 *Tel:* 212-340-8100 *Toll Free Tel:* 800-343-4499 (cust serv) *Fax:* 212-340-8105 *Web Site:* www.perseusbooks.com, pg 180, 181

Camma, Tina, Perseus Books, 250 W 57 St, 15th fl, New York, NY 10107 *Tel:* 212-340-8100 *Toll Free Tel:* 800-343-4499 (cust serv) *Fax:* 212-340-8105 *Web Site:* www.perseusbooks.com, pg 181

Camp, Aaron, Crossway, 1300 Crescent St, Wheaton, IL 60187 *Tel:* 630-682-4300 *Toll Free Tel:* 800-635-7993 (orders); 800-543-1659 (cust serv) *Fax:* 630-682-4785 *E-mail:* info@crossway.org *Web Site:* www.crossway.org, pg 65

Campana, Piya, Harlequin Enterprises Ltd, 225 Duncan Mill Rd, Don Mills, ON M3B 3K9, Canada *Tel:* 416-445-5860 *Toll Free Tel:* 888-432-4879; 800-370-5838 (ebook inquiries) *E-mail:* customerservice@harlequin.com *Web Site:* www.harlequin.com, pg 459

Campbell, Abigail, Association of Writers & Writing Programs (AWP), George Mason University, 4400 University Dr, MSN 1E3, Fairfax, VA 22030 *Tel:* 703-993-4301 *Fax:* 703-993-4302 *E-mail:* awp@awpwriter.org *Web Site:* www.awpwriter.org, pg 559

Campbell, Adam, Rodale Inc, 400 S Tenth St, Emmaus, PA 18049 *Tel:* 610-967-5171 *Toll Free Tel:* 866-387-0509 *E-mail:* bookmarketing@rodale.com; bookpublicity@rodale.com *Web Site:* www.rodale.com, pg 200

Campbell, Beth, BookEnds Literary Agency, 136 Long Hill Rd, Gillette, NJ 07933 *Web Site:* www.bookendsliterary.com, pg 508

Campbell, Bruce, Capital Enquiry Inc, 1034 Emerald Bay Rd, No 435, South Lake Tahoe, CA 96150 *Tel:* 916-442-1434 *Toll Free Tel:* 800-922-7486 *Fax:* 916-244-2704 *E-mail:* info@capenq.com *Web Site:* www.govbuddy.com, pg 47

Campbell, Corey, Arizona State University, Creative Writing Program, 851 S Cady Mall, Rm 542, Tempe, AZ 85287-0302 *Tel:* 480-965-3528 *Fax:* 480-965-3451 *Web Site:* www.asu.edu/clas/english/creativewriting, pg 619

Campbell, Jane, Chosen Books, 11400 Hampshire Ave S, Bloomington, MN 55438-2852 *Tel:* 616-676-9185 *Toll Free Tel:* 800-877-2665 (orders only) *Fax:* 616-676-9573 *Toll Free Fax:* 800-398-3111 (orders only) *Web Site:* www.chosenbooks.com, pg 54

Campbell, Jennie, Water Resources Publications LLC, PO Box 630026, Highlands Ranch, CO 80163-0026 *Tel:* 720-873-0171 *Toll Free Tel:* 800-736-2405 *Fax:* 720-873-0173 *Toll Free Fax:* 800-616-1971 *E-mail:* info@wrpllc.com *Web Site:* www.wrpllc.com, pg 252

Campbell, Joe, Albert Whitman & Co, 250 S Northwest Hwy, Suite 320, Park Ridge, IL 60068 *Tel:* 847-232-2800 *Toll Free Tel:* 800-255-7675 *Fax:* 847-581-0039 *E-mail:* mail@albertwhitman.com *Web Site:* www.albertwhitman.com, pg 6

Campbell, Lakisha, BuilderBooks.com, 1201 15 St NW, Washington, DC 20005 *Tel:* 202-822-0200 *Toll Free Tel:* 800-223-2665 *Fax:* 202-266-8096 (edit) *E-mail:* builderbooks@nahb.com *Web Site:* www.builderbooks.com, pg 45

Campbell, Logan, Pearson Higher Education, 225 River St, Hoboken, NJ 07030-4772 *Tel:* 201-236-7000 *Web Site:* www.pearson.com/us/higher-education.html, pg 176

Campbell, Marie, Transatlantic Agency, 2 Bloor St E, Suite 3500, Toronto, ON M4W 1A8, Canada *Tel:* 416-488-9214 *E-mail:* info@transatlanticagency.com *Web Site:* www.transatlanticagency.com, pg 539

Campbell, Marilyn A, Rutgers University Press, 106 Somerset St, 3rd fl, New Brunswick, NJ 08901 *Tel:* 848-445-7762 *Toll Free Tel:* 800-848-6224 (orders only) *Fax:* 732-745-4935 (acqs, edit, mktg, perms & prodn) *Toll Free Fax:* 800-272-6817 (fulfillment) *Web Site:* rutgerspress.rutgers.edu, pg 202

Campbell, Michael O, Lone Pine Publishing, 87 E Pender, Vancouver, BC V6A 1S9, Canada *Tel:* 780-433-9333 *Toll Free Tel:* 800-661-9017 *Fax:* 780-433-9646 *Toll Free Fax:* 800-424-7173 *E-mail:* info@lonepinepublishing.com *Web Site:* www.lonepinepublishing.com, pg 462

Campbell, Rebecca, Interweave Press LLC, 201 E Fourth St, Loveland, CO 80537 *Toll Free Tel:* 800-272-2193; 800-289-0963 *Fax:* 970-613-4656 *Toll Free Fax:* 888-590-4082 *Web Site:* www.interweave.com, pg 120

Campbell, Scott, River Road Press LLC, 9 Dakin, New Orleans, LA 70121 *Tel:* 504-722-8139 *Web Site:* riverroadpress.com, pg 199

Campbell, Thomas P, The Metropolitan Museum of Art, 1000 Fifth Ave, New York, NY 10028 *Tel:* 212-879-5500; 212-570-3725 (edit) *Fax:* 212-396-5062 *E-mail:* editorial@metmuseum.org *Web Site:* www.metmuseum.org, pg 149

Campbell, Tim, Amber Lotus Publishing, PO Box 11329, Portland, OR 97211 *Tel:* 503-284-6400 *Toll Free Tel:* 800-326-2375 (orders only) *Fax:* 503-284-6417 *E-mail:* info@amberlotus.com *Web Site:* www.amberlotus.com, pg 9

Campbell, Virginia Franklin, Mature Women Scholarship Grant - Art/Letters/Music, The Pen Arts Bldg & Arts Museum, 1300 17 St NW, Washington, DC 20036-1973 *Tel:* 202-785-1997 *Fax:* 202-452-8868 *E-mail:* contact@nlapw.org *Web Site:* www.nlapw.org, pg 666

Campbell, Virginia Franklin, National League of American Pen Women Inc, The Pen Arts Bldg & Arts Museum, 1300 17 St NW, Washington, DC 20036-1973 *Tel:* 202-785-1997 *Fax:* 202-452-8868 *E-mail:* contact@nlapw.org *Web Site:* www.nlapw.org, pg 572

Campfield, Charlene M, Campfield & Campfield Publishing LLC, 6521 Cutler St, Philadelphia, PA 19126 *Toll Free Tel:* 888-518-2440 *Fax:* 215-224-6696 *E-mail:* info@campfieldspublishing.com *Web Site:* www.campfieldspublishing.com, pg 46

Campi, Dr Alicia, The Mongolia Society Inc, Indiana University, 322 Goodbody Hall, 1011 E Third St, Bloomington, IN 47405-7005 *Tel:* 812-855-4078 *Fax:* 812-855-4078 *E-mail:* monsoc@indiana.edu *Web Site:* www.mongoliasociety.org, pg 153

Campion, Owen, Our Sunday Visitor Publishing, 200 Noll Plaza, Huntington, IN 46750 *Tel:* 260-356-8400 *Toll Free Tel:* 800-348-2440 (orders) *Fax:* 260-356-8472 *Toll Free Fax:* 800-498-6709 *E-mail:* osvbooks@osv.com (book orders) *Web Site:* www.osv.com, pg 170

Campo, Gigi, Penguin Group USA, A Penguin Random House Company, 375 Hudson St, New York, NY 10014 *Tel:* 212-366-2000 *Toll Free Tel:* 800-847-5515 (inside sales); 800-631-8571 (cust serv) *Fax:* 212-366-2666; 607-775-4829 (inside sales) *E-mail:* online@us.penguingroup.com *Web Site:* www.penguin.com, pg 177

Campo, Joan, Art of Living, PrimaMedia Inc, 1250 Bethlehem Pike, Suite 241, Hatfield, PA 19440 *Tel:* 215-660-5045 *E-mail:* primamedia4@yahoo.com, pg 21

Campoli, Leila, The Stonesong Press LLC, 270 W 39 St, No 201, New York, NY 10018 *Tel:* 212-929-4600 *E-mail:* editors@stonesong.com *Web Site:* www.stonesong.com, pg 538

Campos, Alexander, The Center for Book Arts, 28 W 27 St, 3rd fl, New York, NY 10001 *Tel:* 212-481-0295 *E-mail:* info@centerforbookarts.org *Web Site:* www.centerforbookarts.org, pg 562

Campos, Alexander, The Center for Book Arts, 28 W 27 St, 3rd fl, New York, NY 10001 *Tel:* 212-481-0295 *Toll Free Fax:* 866-708-8994 *E-mail:* info@centerforbookarts.org *Web Site:* www.centerforbookarts.org, pg 619

Canales, Michael J, Vesuvian Books, 2817 West End Ave, Nashville, TN 37203 *E-mail:* info@vesuvianmedia.com *Web Site:* www.vesuvianbooks.com, pg 250

Canavan, Susan, Houghton Mifflin Harcourt Trade & Reference Division, 125 High St, Boston, MA 02110 *Tel:* 617-351-5000 *Toll Free Tel:* 800-225-3362 *Web Site:* www.hmhco.com, pg 111

Cancio, Jose, Periodical & Book Association of America Inc (PBAA), 481 Eighth Ave, Suite 526, New York, NY 10001 *Tel:* 212-563-6502 *Fax:* 212-563-4098 *Web Site:* www.pbaa.net, pg 575

Candrilli, Kayla Rae, Black Warrior Review Fiction, Nonfiction & Poetry Contest, Off of Student Media, University of Alabama, Tuscaloosa, AL 35486-0027 *Tel:* 205-348-4518 *Web Site:* www.bwr.ua.edu, pg 633

Canedy, Dana, Pulitzer Prizes, 709 Journalism Bldg, Columbia University, 2950 Broadway, New York, NY 10027 *Tel:* 212-854-3841 *Fax:* 212-854-3342 *E-mail:* pulitzer@pulitzer.org *Web Site:* www.pulitzer.org, pg 683

Canfield, Doug, The Mountaineers Books, 1001 SW Klickitat Way, Suite 201, Seattle, WA 98134 *Tel:* 206-223-6303 *Toll Free Tel:* 800-553-4453 *Fax:* 206-223-6306 *Toll Free Fax:* 800-568-7604 *E-mail:* mbooks@mountaineersbooks.org; customerservice@mountaineersbooks.org *Web Site:* www.mountaineersbooks.org, pg 155

Canfield, Thomas, Starcrafts LLC, 334-A Calef Hwy, Epping, NH 03042 *Tel:* 603-734-4300 *Toll Free Tel:* 866-953-8458 (24/7 message ctr) *Fax:* 603-734-4311 *E-mail:* astrosales@astrocom.com *Web Site:* acspublications.com; www.starcraftseast.com; www.astrocom.com, pg 221

Cangioli, Pamela, Proofed to Perfection Editing Services, 6519 Sherrill Baggett Rd, Godwin, NC 28344 *Tel:* 919-908-1912 *E-mail:* inquiries@proofedtoperfection.com *Web Site:* www.proofedtoperfection.com, pg 500

Cann, Carroll C, Teton NewMedia Inc, 90 E Simpson, Suite 110, Jackson, WY 83001 *Tel:* 307-732-0028 *Toll Free Tel:* 877-306-9793 *Fax:* 307-734-0841 *E-mail:* sales@tetonnm.com *Web Site:* www.tetonnm.com, pg 230

Cannady, Renee, Columbia Books & Information Services (CBIS), 4340 East-West Hwy, Suite 300, Bethesda, MD 20814 *Tel:* 202-464-1662 *Fax:* 301-664-9600 *E-mail:* info@columbiabooks.com *Web Site:* www.columbiabooks.com; www.lobbyists.info; www.associationexecs.com, pg 59

Cannon, Pamela, Random House Publishing Group, 1745 Broadway, New York, NY 10019 *Toll Free Tel:* 800-200-3552 *Web Site:* atrandom.com, pg 195

Cannon, Sam, Cedar Grove Books, 2215 High Point Dr, Carrollton, TX 75007 *Tel:* 415-364-8292 *Fax:* 415-276-9858 *E-mail:* queries@cedargrovebooks.com *Web Site:* www.cedargrovebooks.com, pg 50

Cannon, Timothy L, Houghton Mifflin Harcourt, 125 High St, Boston, MA 02110 *Tel:* 617-351-5000 *Toll Free Tel:* 855-969-4642; 800-225-5425 (K-12 educ materials); 800-323-9540 (assessment materials); 877-219-1537 (SkillsTutor); 888-242-6747 (Innovation in Educ Group); 800-225-3362 (Trade & Ref Div) *Toll Free Fax:* 800-269-5232 *E-mail:* myhmhco@hmhco.com *Web Site:* www.hmhco.com, pg 110

Canonico, Amy, Yale University Press, 302 Temple St, New Haven, CT 06511-8909 *Tel:* 203-432-0960; 203-432-0966 (sales); 401-531-2800 (cust serv) *Toll Free Tel:* 800-405-1619 (cust serv) *Fax:* 203-432-0948; 203-432-8485 (sales); 401-531-2801 (cust serv) *Toll Free Fax:* 800-406-9145 (cust serv) *E-mail:* sales.press@yale.edu (sales); customer.care@triliteral.org (cust serv) *Web Site:* www.yalebooks.com; yalepress.yale.edu/yupbooks, pg 261

Cantada, Daniel, Perseus Books, 250 W 57 St, 15th fl, New York, NY 10107 *Tel:* 212-340-8100 *Toll Free Tel:* 800-343-4499 (cust serv) *Fax:* 212-340-8105 *Web Site:* www.perseusbooks.com, pg 181

Cantin, Sarah, Atria Books, 1230 Avenue of the Americas, New York, NY 10020 *Tel:* 212-698-7000 *Fax:* 212-698-7007 *Web Site:* www.simonandschuster.com, pg 25

Cantor, Carrie, Joelle Delbourgo Associates Inc, 101 Park St, Montclair, NJ 07042 *Tel:* 973-773-0836 (call only during standard business hours) *Web Site:* www.delbourgo.com, pg 513

Cantor, Jackie, Gallery Books, 1230 Avenue of the Americas, New York, NY 10020 *Toll Free Tel:* 800-456-6798 *Fax:* 212-698-7284 *E-mail:* consumer.customerservice@simonandschuster.com *Web Site:* www.simonsays.com, pg 90

Canzoneri, Jennifer, BenBella Books Inc, 10300 N Central Expwy, Suite 400, Dallas, TX 75231 *Tel:* 214-750-3600 *Fax:* 214-750-3645 *E-mail:* feedback@benbellabooks.com *Web Site:* www.benbellabooks.com; www.smartpopbooks.com, pg 32

Capik, Gloria, Paulist Press, 997 Macarthur Blvd, Mahwah, NJ 07430-9990 *Tel:* 201-825-7300 *Toll Free Tel:* 800-218-1903 *Fax:* 201-825-6921 *Toll Free Fax:* 800-836-3161 *E-mail:* info@paulistpress.com; publicity@paulistpress.com *Web Site:* www.paulistpress.com, pg 175

Caplan, David, Little, Brown Books for Young Readers, 1290 Avenue of the Americas, New York, NY 10019 *Tel:* 212-364-1100 *Toll Free Tel:* 800-759-0190 (cust serv) *Web Site:* www.HachetteBookGroup.com, pg 136

Capobiano, John, Society of Illustrators (SI), 128 E 63 St, New York, NY 10065 *Tel:* 212-838-2560 *Fax:* 212-838-2561 *E-mail:* info@societyillustrators.org *Web Site:* www.societyillustrators.org, pg 578

Capone, Connie, Perseus Books, 250 W 57 St, 15th fl, New York, NY 10107 *Tel:* 212-340-8100 *Toll Free Tel:* 800-343-4499 (cust serv) *Fax:* 212-340-8105 *Web Site:* www.perseusbooks.com, pg 181

Capps, Karen, Concordia Publishing House, 3558 S Jefferson Ave, St Louis, MO 63118-3968 *Tel:* 314-268-1000; 314-268-1268 (bookshop) *Toll Free Tel:* 800-325-3040 (cust serv) *Toll Free Fax:* 800-490-9889 (cust serv) *E-mail:* order@cph.org *Web Site:* www.cph.org, pg 59

Capron, Elise, Sandra Dijkstra Literary Agency, 1155 Camino del Mar, PMB 515, Del Mar, CA 92014-2605 *E-mail:* queries@dijkstraagency.com *Web Site:* dijkstraagency.com, pg 514

Caputo, Nicole, Counterpoint Press LLC, 1919 Fifth St, Berkeley, CA 94710 *Tel:* 510-704-0230 *Fax:* 510-704-0268 *E-mail:* info@counterpointpress.com *Web Site:* counterpointpress.com; www.sierraclub.org/books; softskull.com, pg 63

Caratozzolo, Marie, Square One Publishers Inc, 115 Herricks Rd, Garden City Park, NY 11040 *Tel:* 516-535-2010 *Toll Free Tel:* 877-900-BOOK (900-2665) *Fax:* 516-535-2014 *E-mail:* sq1publish@aol.com *Web Site:* www.squareonepublishers.com, pg 220

Carbone, Courtney, Random House Children's Books, 1745 Broadway, 10th fl, New York, NY 10019 *Tel:* 212-782-9000 *Web Site:* www.randomhousekids.com, pg 194

Carden, Gwen, StarGroup International Inc, 1194 Old Dixie Hwy, Suite 201, West Palm Beach, FL 33413 *Tel:* 561-547-0667 *Fax:* 561-843-8530 *E-mail:* info@stargroupinternational.com *Web Site:* stargroupinternational.com, pg 221

Cardenas, Yvonne, Other Press, 267 Fifth Ave, 6th fl, New York, NY 10016 *Tel:* 212-414-0054 *Toll Free Tel:* 877-843-6843 *Fax:* 212-414-0939 *E-mail:* editor@otherpress.com; marketing@otherpress.com; publicity@otherpress.com *Web Site:* www.otherpress.com, pg 170

Carder, Sara, TarcherPerigee, 375 Hudson St, New York, NY 10014 *Tel:* 212-366-2000 *Fax:* 212-366-2643 *E-mail:* customerservice@penguinrandomhouse.com (cust serv); TarcherPerigeePublicity@penguinrandomhouse.com (media queries) *Web Site:* www.tarcherbooks.com; www.facebook.com/TarcherPerigee/; www.penguin.com/publishers/tarcherperigee, pg 227

Carr, Lloyd, New York City College of Technology, 300 Jay St, Brooklyn, NY 11201 *Tel:* 718-260-5500 *Fax:* 718-260-5198 *E-mail:* connect@citytech.cuny.edu *Web Site:* www.citytech.cuny.edu, pg 621

Carr, Rosalyn, University of Alabama Press, 200 Hackberry Lane, 2nd fl, Tuscaloosa, AL 35487 *Tel:* 205-348-5180 *Fax:* 205-348-9201 *Web Site:* www.uapress.ua.edu, pg 239

Carr, Shida, Touchstone, 1230 Avenue of the Americas, New York, NY 10020, pg 233

Carrigan, Bob, Dun & Bradstreet, 103 JFK Pkwy, Short Hills, NJ 07078 *Tel:* 973-921-5500 *Toll Free Tel:* 800-526-0651; 800-234-3867 (cust serv) *E-mail:* custserv@dnb.com *Web Site:* www.dnb.com, pg 73

Carrigan, Henry L Jr, Northwestern University Press, 629 Noyes St, Evanston, IL 60208-4210 *Tel:* 847-491-2046 *Toll Free Tel:* 800-621-2736 (orders only) *Fax:* 847-491-8150 *E-mail:* nupress@northwestern.edu *Web Site:* www.nupress.northwestern.edu, pg 164

Carrillo, Nica, Coffee House Press, 79 13 Ave NE, Suite 110, Minneapolis, MN 55413 *Tel:* 612-338-0125 *Fax:* 612-338-4004 *E-mail:* info@coffeehousepress.org *Web Site:* coffeehousepress.org, pg 58

Carrington, Dejha, YoungArts, 2100 Biscayne Blvd, Miami, FL 33137 *Tel:* 305-377-1140 *Toll Free Tel:* 800-970-ARTS (970-2787) *E-mail:* info@youngarts.org; apply@youngarts.org *Web Site:* www.youngarts.org, pg 701

Carroll, Allison, Harlequin Enterprises Ltd, 233 Broadway, Suite 1001, New York, NY 10279 *Tel:* 212-553-4200 *Fax:* 212-227-8969 *E-mail:* customerservice@harlequin.com *Web Site:* www.harlequin.com, pg 100

Carroll, Katie, Franciscan Media, 28 W Liberty St, Cincinnati, OH 45202 *Tel:* 513-241-5615 *Toll Free Tel:* 800-488-0488 *Fax:* 513-241-0399 *E-mail:* books@americancatholic.org *Web Site:* www.americancatholic.org; www.franciscanmedia.org, pg 88

Carroll, Kent, Europa Editions, 214 W 29 St, Suite 1003, New York, NY 10001 *Tel:* 212-868-6844 *Fax:* 212-868-6845 *E-mail:* info@europaeditions.com *Web Site:* www.europaeditions.com, pg 80

Carroll, Lisa, Allen A Knoll Publishers, 200 W Victoria St, Santa Barbara, CA 93101-3627 *Tel:* 805-564-3377 *Toll Free Tel:* 800-777-7623 *Fax:* 805-966-6657 *E-mail:* bookinfo@knollpublishers.com *Web Site:* www.knollpublishers.com, pg 127

Carroll, Patrick, Princeton University Press, 41 William St, Princeton, NJ 08540-5237 *Tel:* 609-258-4900 *Fax:* 609-258-6305 *Web Site:* press.princeton.edu, pg 188

Carroll, Sydney, Sinauer Associates Inc, 23 Plumtree Rd, Sunderland, MA 01375 *Tel:* 413-549-4300 *Fax:* 413-549-1118 *E-mail:* publish@sinauer.com; orders@sinauer.com *Web Site:* sinauer.com, pg 214

Carruth, Marlies A, MacArthur Fellows Program, Office of Grants Management, 140 S Dearborn St, Chicago, IL 60603-5285 *Tel:* 312-726-8000 *Fax:* 312-920-6528 *E-mail:* 4answers@macfound.org *Web Site:* www.macfound.org/programs/fellows, pg 664

Carruthers, Madeline, Chronicle Books LLC, 680 Second St, San Francisco, CA 94107 *Tel:* 415-537-4200 *Toll Free Tel:* 800-759-0190 (cust serv) *Fax:* 415-537-4460 *Toll Free Fax:* 800-858-7787 (orders); 800-286-9471 (cust serv) *E-mail:* frontdesk@chroniclebooks.com *Web Site:* www.chroniclebooks.com, pg 55

Carsley, Lauren, Simon & Schuster, 1230 Avenue of the Americas, New York, NY 10020 *Tel:* 212-698-7000 *Toll Free Tel:* 800-223-2348 (cust serv); 800-223-2336 (orders) *Toll Free Fax:* 800-943-9831 (orders) *Web Site:* www.simonandschuster.com, pg 212

Carson, Anne Conover, Anne Carson Associates, 3323 Nebraska Ave NW, Washington, DC 20016 *Tel:* 202-244-6679, pg 490

Carson, Carol, Alfred A Knopf/Everyman's Library, c/o Penguin Random House Inc, 1745 Broadway, New York, NY 10019 *Tel:* 212-751-2600 *Toll Free Tel:* 800-638-6460 *Fax:* 212-572-2593 *Web Site:* www.knopfdoubleday.com, pg 127

Carson, Dina C, Iron Gate Publishing, PO Box 999, Niwot, CO 80544 *Tel:* 303-530-2551 *Fax:* 303-530-5273 *E-mail:* editor@irongate.com *Web Site:* www.irongate.com, pg 121

Carson, Ken, Cengage Learning, 20 Channel Center St, Boston, MA 02210 *Tel:* 617-289-7700 *Toll Free Tel:* 800-354-9706 *Fax:* 617-289-7844 *Toll Free Fax:* 800-487-8488 *E-mail:* esales@cengage.com *Web Site:* www.cengage.com, pg 50

Carstens, Sarah, Rizzoli International Publications Inc, 300 Park Ave S, 4th fl, New York, NY 10010-5399 *Tel:* 212-387-3400 *Toll Free Tel:* 800-522-6657 (orders only) *Fax:* 212-387-3535 *E-mail:* publicity@rizzoliusa.com *Web Site:* www.rizzoliusa.com, pg 199

Carswell, Christine, Chronicle Books LLC, 680 Second St, San Francisco, CA 94107 *Tel:* 415-537-4200 *Toll Free Tel:* 800-759-0190 (cust serv) *Fax:* 415-537-4460 *Toll Free Fax:* 800-858-7787 (orders); 800-286-9471 (cust serv) *E-mail:* frontdesk@chroniclebooks.com *Web Site:* www.chroniclebooks.com, pg 55

Carter, Dr Allyson, The University of Arizona Press, 1510 E University Blvd, Tucson, AZ 85721 *Tel:* 520-621-1441 *Toll Free Tel:* 800-426-3797 (orders) *Fax:* 520-621-8899 *Toll Free Fax:* 800-426-3797 *E-mail:* uap@uapress.arizona.edu *Web Site:* www.uapress.arizona.edu, pg 240

Carter, Brenda, American Psychological Association, 750 First St NE, Washington, DC 20002-4242 *Tel:* 202-336-5510 *Toll Free Tel:* 800-374-2721 *Fax:* 202-336-5502 *E-mail:* order@apa.org *Web Site:* www.apa.org/books, pg 14

Carter, Brenda, American Psychological Association, 750 First St NE, Washington, DC 20002-4242 *Tel:* 202-336-5500 *Toll Free Tel:* 800-374-2721 *E-mail:* order@apa.org *Web Site:* www.apa.org, pg 556

Carter, Brittany, Columbia Books & Information Services (CBIS), 4340 East-West Hwy, Suite 300, Bethesda, MD 20814 *Tel:* 202-464-1662 *Fax:* 301-664-9600 *E-mail:* info@columbiabooks.com *Web Site:* www.columbiabooks.com; www.lobbyists.info; www.associationexecs.com, pg 59

Carter, Charles Cuykendall, American Printing History Association, PO Box 4519, Grand Central Sta, New York, NY 10163 *Tel:* 202-544-2422 *E-mail:* secretary@printinghistory.org *Web Site:* printinghistory.org, pg 556

Carter, Charles Cuykendall, American Printing History Association Award, PO Box 4519, Grand Central Sta, New York, NY 10163 *Tel:* 202-544-2422 *E-mail:* secretary@printinghistory.org *Web Site:* printinghistory.org, pg 627

Carter, Deborah, Waverly Place Literary Agency, 124 E 84 St, No 2D, New York, NY 10028-0918 *Tel:* 212-925-3721 *E-mail:* waverlyplaceliterary@aol.com *Web Site:* www.waverlyplaceliterary.com; twitter.com/waverlyplacelit, pg 541

Carter, Eryn, Hampton Roads Publishing Co, 65 Parker St, Suite 7, Newburyport, MA 01950-4600 *Tel:* 978-465-0504 *Toll Free Tel:* 800-423-7087 (orders) *Fax:* 978-465-0243 *Toll Free Fax:* 877-337-3309 *E-mail:* orders@rwwbooks.com *Web Site:* redwheelweiser.com, pg 100

Carter, Jamie, Bookbuilders of Boston, 115 Webster Woods Lane, North Andover, MA 01845 *Tel:* 781-378-1361 *Fax:* 419-821-2171 *E-mail:* office@bbboston.org *Web Site:* www.bbboston.org, pg 561

Carter, Jill, Crossway, 1300 Crescent St, Wheaton, IL 60187 *Tel:* 630-682-4300 *Toll Free Tel:* 800-635-7993 (orders); 800-543-1659 (cust serv) *Fax:* 630-682-4785 *E-mail:* info@crossway.org *Web Site:* www.crossway.org, pg 65

Carvainis, Maria, Maria Carvainis Agency Inc, Rockefeller Center, 1270 Avenue of the Americas, Suite 2320, New York, NY 10020 *Tel:* 212-245-6365 *Fax:* 212-245-7196 *E-mail:* mca@mariacarvainisagency.com *Web Site:* mariacarvainisagency.com, pg 511

Carvalho, Julia, Chronicle Books LLC, 680 Second St, San Francisco, CA 94107 *Tel:* 415-537-4200 *Toll Free Tel:* 800-759-0190 (cust serv) *Fax:* 415-537-4460 *Toll Free Fax:* 800-858-7787 (orders); 800-286-9471 (cust serv) *E-mail:* frontdesk@chroniclebooks.com *Web Site:* www.chroniclebooks.com, pg 55

Carver, Peter, Red Deer Press Inc, 195 Allstate Pkwy, Markham, ON L3R 4T8, Canada *Tel:* 905-477-9700 *Toll Free Tel:* 800-387-9776 (orders) *E-mail:* rdp@reddeerpress.com; bookinfo@fitzhenry.ca *Web Site:* www.reddeerpress.com, pg 468

Cary, Ursula, The Globe Pequot Press, 246 Goose Lane, Guilford, CT 06437 *Tel:* 203-458-4500 *Toll Free Tel:* 800-243-0495 (orders only); 888-249-7586 (cust serv) *Fax:* 203-458-4601 *Toll Free Fax:* 800-820-2329 (orders & cust serv) *E-mail:* editorial@globepequot.com; info@rowman.com; orders@rowman.com *Web Site:* rowman.com, pg 93

Casares, Oscar, University of Texas at Austin, New Writers Project, Dept of English, Calhoun Hall, Rm 226, 204 W 21 St, B-5000, Austin, TX 78712 *Tel:* 512-471-5132; 512-471-4991 *Fax:* 512-471-4909 *Web Site:* newwritersproject.org, pg 623

Cascardi, Andrea, Transatlantic Agency, 2 Bloor St E, Suite 3500, Toronto, ON M4W 1A8, Canada *Tel:* 416-488-9214 *E-mail:* info@transatlanticagency.com *Web Site:* www.transatlanticagency.com, pg 539

Cascio, Keri, Margaret Mann Citation, 50 E Huron St, Chicago, IL 60611 *Tel:* 312-280-5037 *Toll Free Tel:* 800-545-2433 *Fax:* 312-280-5033 *E-mail:* alcts@ala.org *Web Site:* www.ala.org/alcts, pg 665

Casey, Adrianne, Channel Photographics, 980 Lincoln Ave, Suite 200-B, San Rafael, CA 94901 *Tel:* 415-456-2934 *Fax:* 415-456-4124 *Web Site:* www.channelphotographics.com, pg 52

Casey, Adrianne, Global Publishing, Sales & Distribution, 980 Lincoln Ave, Suite 200 B, San Rafael, CA 94901 *Tel:* 415-456-2934 *Fax:* 415-456-4124 *Web Site:* www.globalpsd.com, pg 93

Casey, Al, Strategic Media Books LLC, 782 Wofford St, Rock Hill, SC 29730 *Tel:* 803-366-5440 *E-mail:* contact@strategicmediabooks.com *Web Site:* strategicmediabooks.com, pg 224

Casey, Alec, Trusted Media Brands Inc, 750 Third Ave, 3rd fl, New York, NY 10017 *Toll Free Tel:* 800-310-6261 (cust serv) *E-mail:* customercare@tmbi.com *Web Site:* www.tmbi.com; www.rd.com, pg 236

Casey, Barbara, Strategic Media Books LLC, 782 Wofford St, Rock Hill, SC 29730 *Tel:* 803-366-5440 *E-mail:* contact@strategicmediabooks.com *Web Site:* strategicmediabooks.com, pg 224

Casey, Brian D, The Center for Exhibition Industry Research (CEIR), 12700 Park Central Dr, Suite 308, Dallas, TX 75251 *Tel:* 972-687-9242 *Fax:* 972-692-6020 *E-mail:* info@ceir.org *Web Site:* www.ceir.org, pg 562

Casey, Caitlin, Little Bee Books, 853 Broadway, Suite 2014, New York, NY 10003 *E-mail:* info@littlebeebooks.com *Web Site:* www.littlebeebooks.com, pg 135

Casey, Caroline, Coffee House Press, 79 13 Ave NE, Suite 110, Minneapolis, MN 55413 *Tel:* 612-338-0125 *Fax:* 612-338-4004 *E-mail:* info@coffeehousepress.org *Web Site:* coffeehousepress.org, pg 58

Casey, Maribeth, Storey Publishing LLC, 210 MASS MoCA Way, North Adams, MA 01247 *Tel:* 413-346-2100 *Toll Free Tel:* 800-441-5700 (orders); 800-793-9396 (edit) *Fax:* 413-346-2199; 413-346-2196 (edit) *E-mail:* sales@storey.com *Web Site:* www.storey.com, pg 223

Cash, Amy Opperman, Larson Publications, 4936 State Rte 414, Burdett, NY 14818 *Tel:* 607-546-9342 *Toll Free Tel:* 800-828-2197 *Fax:* 607-546-9344 *E-mail:* custserv@larsonpublications.com *Web Site:* www.larsonpublications.com, pg 130

Cash, Mary, Holiday House Inc, 425 Madison Ave, New York, NY 10017 *Tel:* 212-688-0085 *Fax:* 212-421-6134 *E-mail:* info@holidayhouse.com *Web Site:* www.holidayhouse.com, pg 109

Cash, Susan, Kent State University Press, 1118 University Library Bldg, 1125 Risman Dr, Kent, OH 44242 *Tel:* 330-672-7913 *Fax:* 330-672-3104 *E-mail:* ksupress@kent.edu *Web Site:* www.kentstateuniversitypress.com, pg 126

Cash, Susan L, Kent State University Press, 1118 University Library Bldg, 1125 Risman Dr, Kent, OH 44242 *Tel:* 330-672-7913 *Fax:* 330-672-3104 *E-mail:* ksupress@kent.edu *Web Site:* www.kentstateuniversitypress.com, pg 126

Cashion, David, Harry N Abrams Inc, 195 Broadway, 9th fl, New York, NY 10007 *Tel:* 212-206-7715 *Toll Free Tel:* 800-345-1359 *Fax:* 212-519-1210 *E-mail:* abrams@abramsbooks.com *Web Site:* www.abramsbooks.com, pg 3

Cashman, Ann, The LA Literary Agency, PO Box 46370, Los Angeles, CA 90046 *Tel:* 323-654-5288 *E-mail:* laliteraryagency@mac.com; mail@laliteraryagency.com *Web Site:* www.laliteraryagency.com, pg 525

Cashman, Lorraine Walsh, Opie Prize, Indiana University, Classroom-Off Bldg, 800 E Third St, Bloomington, IN 47405 *Tel:* 812-856-2379 *Fax:* 812-856-2483 *Web Site:* www.afsnet.org, pg 675

Caso, Adolph, Branden Books, PO Box 812094, Wellesley, MA 02482-0013 *Tel:* 781-235-3347 *E-mail:* branden@brandenbooks.com *Web Site:* www.brandenbooks.com, pg 42

Caso, Robert, Branden Books, PO Box 812094, Wellesley, MA 02482-0013 *Tel:* 781-235-3347 *E-mail:* branden@brandenbooks.com *Web Site:* www.brandenbooks.com, pg 42

Cason, Mary, Philadelphia Museum of Art, 2525 Pennsylvania Ave, Philadelphia, PA 19130 *Tel:* 215-684-7250 *Fax:* 215-235-8715 *Web Site:* www.philamuseum.org, pg 182

Cassell, Dana K, Florida Freelance Writers Association, 45 Main St, North Stratford, NH 03590 *Tel:* 603-922-8338 *Fax:* 603-922-8339 *E-mail:* ffwa@writers-editors.com; info@writers-editors.com *Web Site:* www.writers-editors.com; www.ffwamembers.com, pg 565

Cassell, Dana K, Writers-Editors Network International Writing Competition, 45 Main St, North Stratford, NH 03590 *Tel:* 603-922-8338 *Fax:* 603-922-8339 *E-mail:* contest@writers-editors.com *Web Site:* www.writers-editors.com; www.ffwamembers.com, pg 700

Cassidy, Kyran, HarperCollins Publishers, 195 Broadway, New York, NY 10007 *Tel:* 212-207-7000 *Fax:* 212-207-7145 *Web Site:* www.harpercollins.com, pg 101

Cassity, Liza, Dutton, 375 Hudson St, New York, NY 10014 *Tel:* 212-366-2000 *Fax:* 212-366-2262 *Web Site:* www.penguin.com, pg 74

Castaldo, John, G Schirmer Inc/Associated Music Publishers Inc, 180 Madison Ave, 24th fl, New York, NY 10016 *Tel:* 212-254-2100 *Fax:* 212-254-2013 *E-mail:* schirmer@schirmer.com; info@musicsales.com *Web Site:* www.musicsalesclassical.com, pg 207

Castellani, Mary Kate, Bloomsbury Publishing Inc, 1385 Broadway, 5th fl, New York, NY 10018 *Tel:* 212-419-5300 *E-mail:* marketingusa@bloomsbury.com; adultpublicityusa@bloomsbury.com; askacademic@bloomsbury.com *Web Site:* www.bloomsbury.com, pg 38

Castellano, Giuseppe, Grosset & Dunlap, 345 Hudson St, New York, NY 10014 *Tel:* 212-366-2000 *Web Site:* www.penguinrandomhouse.com, pg 96

Castellon, Jennifer, Windham-Campbell Prizes, Beinecke Library, 121 Whitney Ave, Suite 102, New Haven, CT 06510-1242 *Fax:* 203-432-9033 *Web Site:* windhamcampbell.org, pg 698

Castignoli, Doreen, BPA Worldwide, 100 Beard Sawmill Rd, 6th fl, Shelton, CT 06484 *Tel:* 203-447-2800 *Fax:* 203-447-2900 *E-mail:* info@bpaww.com *Web Site:* www.bpaww.com, pg 561

Castillo, Johanna, Atria Books, 1230 Avenue of the Americas, New York, NY 10020 *Tel:* 212-698-7000 *Fax:* 212-698-7007 *Web Site:* www.simonandschuster.com, pg 25

Castillon, Arturo, Santillana USA Publishing Co, 2023 NW 84 Ave, Doral, FL 33122 *Tel:* 305-591-9522 *Toll Free Tel:* 800-245-8584 *E-mail:* customerservice@santillanausa.com *Web Site:* www.santillanausa.com, pg 206

Castle, John K, Castle Connolly Medical Ltd, 42 W 24 St, 2nd fl, New York, NY 10010 *Tel:* 212-367-8400 *Fax:* 212-367-0964 *Web Site:* www.castleconnolly.com, pg 49

Castle, Sara, JMW Group Inc, 347 Rte 6, No 867, Mahopac, NY 10541 *Tel:* 914-841-7105 *Fax:* 914-248-8861 *E-mail:* jmwgroup@jmwgroup.net *Web Site:* jmwgroup.net, pg 523

Castonguay, Joanne, Institute for Research on Public Policy (IRPP), 1470 Peel St, No 200, Montreal, QC H3A 1T1, Canada *Tel:* 514-985-2461 *Fax:* 514-985-2559 *E-mail:* irpp@irpp.org *Web Site:* irpp.org, pg 460

Castro, Kylie, Babalu Inc, PO Box 23026, Santa Barbara, CA 93121 *Toll Free Tel:* 877-522-2258 *E-mail:* morefun@babaluinc.com *Web Site:* www.babaluinc.com, pg 27

Castro, Steve, Annual Reviews, 4139 El Camino Way, Palo Alto, CA 94306 *Tel:* 650-493-4400 *Toll Free Tel:* 800-523-8635 *Fax:* 650-424-0910; 650-855-9815 *E-mail:* service@annualreviews.org *Web Site:* www.annualreviews.org, pg 17

Castronovo, Russ, Chris O'Malley Fiction Prize, University of Wisconsin, 6193 Helen C White Hall, English Dept, 600 N Park St, Madison, WI 53706 *E-mail:* madisonrevw@gmail.com *Web Site:* www.themadisonreview.com, pg 675

Castronovo, Russ, Phyllis Smart-Young Poetry Prize, University of Wisconsin, 6193 Helen C White Hall, English Dept, 600 N Park St, Madison, WI 53706 *E-mail:* madisonrevw@gmail.com *Web Site:* www.themadisonreview.com, pg 701

Caswell, Bexx, Guild of Book Workers, 521 Fifth Ave, New York, NY 10175 *Tel:* 212-292-4444 *E-mail:* communications@guildofbookworkers.org *Web Site:* www.guildofbookworkers.org, pg 566

Catalano, Kim, Galaxy Press, 7051 Hollywood Blvd, Suite 200, Hollywood, CA 90028 *Tel:* 323-466-7815 *Toll Free Tel:* 877-8GALAXY (842-5299) *E-mail:* info@galaxypress.com; customers@galaxypress.com *Web Site:* www.galaxypress.com, pg 89

Catarino, Christine, St Martin's Press, LLC, 175 Fifth Ave, New York, NY 10010 *Tel:* 646-307-5151 *Web Site:* us.macmillan.com/smp, pg 204

Cathcart, Caryn, House of Anansi Press Inc, 128 Sterling Rd, Lower Level, Toronto, ON M6R 2B7, Canada *Tel:* 416-363-4343 *Fax:* 416-363-1017 *E-mail:* customerservice@houseofanansi.com *Web Site:* www.houseofanansi.com, pg 460

Catogge, Tara, Quarto Publishing Group USA Inc, 400 First Ave N, Suite 400, Minneapolis, MN 55401 *Tel:* 612-344-8100 *Toll Free Tel:* 800-328-0590 (sales); 800-458-0454 *Fax:* 612-344-8691 *E-mail:* sales@quartous.com *Web Site:* www.quartoknows.com, pg 192

Caulfield, Charlene, Wildflower Press, c/o Oakbrook Press, 3301 S Valley Dr, Rapid City, SD 57703 *Tel:* 605-381-6385 *E-mail:* info@wildflowerpress.org *Web Site:* www.wildflowerpress.org, pg 255

Cauz, Jorge, Encyclopaedia Britannica Inc, 325 N La Salle St, Chicago, IL 60654 *Tel:* 312-347-7159 (all other countries) *Toll Free Tel:* 800-323-1229 (US & CN) *Fax:* 312-294-2104 *E-mail:* contact@eb.com *Web Site:* www.eb.com; www.britannica.com, pg 78

Cavallaro, Lenny, Janus Literary Agency, PO Box 837, Methuen, MA 01844 *Tel:* 978-273-4227 *E-mail:* janusliteraryagency@gmail.com *Web Site:* janusliteraryagency.com, pg 522

Cavanah, Lex, The Donning Company Publishers, 184 Business Park Dr, Suite 206, Virginia Beach, VA 23462 *Tel:* 757-497-1789 *Toll Free Tel:* 800-296-8572 *Fax:* 757-497-2542 *Web Site:* www.donning.com, pg 71

Cavelos, Jeanne, Jeanne Cavelos Editorial Services, PO Box 75, Mont Vernon, NH 03057 *Tel:* 603-673-6234 *Web Site:* jeannecavelos.com, pg 490

Cavelos, Jeanne, Odyssey: The Summer Fantasy Writing Workshop, PO Box 75, Mont Vernon, NH 03057 *Tel:* 603-673-6234 *Fax:* 603 673 6234 *Web Site:* www.odysseyworkshop.org, pg 613

Cazares, Yolanda, Chronicle Books LLC, 680 Second St, San Francisco, CA 94107 *Tel:* 415-537-4200 *Toll Free Tel:* 800-759-0190 (cust serv) *Fax:* 415-537-4460 *Toll Free Fax:* 800-858-7787 (orders); 800-286-9471 (cust serv) *E-mail:* frontdesk@chroniclebooks.com *Web Site:* www.chroniclebooks.com, pg 55

Cebik, Stephen, Yale University Press, 302 Temple St, New Haven, CT 06511-8909 *Tel:* 203-432-0960; 203-432-0966 (sales); 401-531-2800 (cust serv) *Toll Free Tel:* 800-405-1619 (cust serv) *Fax:* 203-432-0948; 203-432-8485 (sales); 401-531-2801 (cust serv) *Toll Free Fax:* 800-406-9145 (cust serv) *E-mail:* sales.press@yale.edu (sales); customer.care@triliteral.org (cust serv) *Web Site:* www.yalebooks.com; yalepress.yale.edu/yupbooks, pg 261

Cecka, Melanie, Random House Children's Books, 1745 Broadway, 10th fl, New York, NY 10019 *Tel:* 212-782-9000 *Web Site:* www.randomhousekids.com, pg 194

Cedeno, Aaron, Ascend Books LLC, 12710 Pflumm Rd, Suite 200, Olathe, KS 66062 *Tel:* 913-948-5500 *Web Site:* www.ascendbooks.com, pg 22

Cegielski, Stephanie, Public Relations Society of America, 33 Maiden Lane, 11th fl, New York, NY 10038-5150 *Tel:* 212-460-1400 *Fax:* 212-995-0757 *Web Site:* www.prsa.org, pg 576

Cekola, Kim, Michigan Municipal League, 1675 Green Rd, Ann Arbor, MI 48105 *Tel:* 734-662-3246 *Toll Free Tel:* 800-653-2483 *E-mail:* contact@mml.org *Web Site:* www.mml.org, pg 150

Cella, Joe, Quarto Publishing Group USA Inc, 400 First Ave N, Suite 400, Minneapolis, MN 55401 *Tel:* 612-344-8100 *Toll Free Tel:* 800-328-0590 (sales); 800-458-0454 *Fax:* 612-344-8691 *E-mail:* sales@quartous.com *Web Site:* www.quartoknows.com, pg 192

Centrello, Gina, Penguin Random House Inc, 1745 Broadway, New York, NY 10019 *Tel:* 212-782-9000 *Toll Free Tel:* 800-726-0600 *Web Site:* www.penguinrandomhouse.com, pg 178

Centrello, Gina, Random House Publishing Group, 1745 Broadway, New York, NY 10019 *Toll Free Tel:* 800-200-3552 *Web Site:* atrandom.com, pg 195

Cerasoli, Lisa, The Writer's Lifeline Inc, 400 S Burnside Ave, Suite 11B, Los Angeles, CA 90036 *Tel:* 323-932-1685 *Fax:* 323-932-1220 *Web Site:* www.thewriterslifeline.com, pg 503

Cerbone, Will, Fordham University Press, Joseph A Martino Hall, 45 Columbus Ave, New York, NY 10023 *Fax:* 347-842-3083 *Web Site:* www.fordhampress.com, pg 86

Cercone, Philip, McGill-Queen's University Press, 1010 Sherbrooke W, Suite 1720, Montreal, QC H3A 2R7, Canada *Tel:* 514-398-3750 *Fax:* 514-398-4333 *E-mail:* mqup@mqup.ca *Web Site:* www.mqup.ca, pg 463

Cerullo, John, Amadeus Press/Hal Leonard Performing Arts Publishing Group, 33 Plymouth St, Suite 302, Montclair, NJ 07042 *Tel:* 973-337-5034 *Toll Free Tel:* 800-524-4425 *E-mail:* info@halleonardbooks.com *Web Site:* www.amadeuspress.com; www.halleonardbooks.com, pg 8

Cerullo, John, Hal Leonard Books, 33 Plymouth St, Suite 302, Montclair, NJ 07042 *Toll Free Tel:* 800-637-2852 *E-mail:* info@halleonardbooks.com; custserv@halleonardbooks.com *Web Site:* www.halleonardbooks.com, pg 99

Cerullo, John, Limelight Editions, 33 Plymouth St, Suite 302, Montclair, NJ 07042 *Tel:* 973-337-5034 *Fax:* 973-337-5227 *Web Site:* limelighteditions.com, pg 134

Cervantes, Miguel, Perseus Books, 250 W 57 St, 15th fl, New York, NY 10107 *Tel:* 212-340-8100 *Toll Free Tel:* 800-343-4499 (cust serv) *Fax:* 212-340-8105 *Web Site:* www.perseusbooks.com, pg 181

Cerveny, Christina, Silver Gavel Awards, 321 N Clark St, Chicago, IL 60654 *Tel:* 312-988-5719 *Toll Free Tel:* 800-285-2221 (orders) *Fax:* 312-988-5494 *Web Site:* www.ambar.org/gavelawards, pg 689

Cervone, Emily, Chronicle Books LLC, 680 Second St, San Francisco, CA 94107 *Tel:* 415-537-4200 *Toll Free Tel:* 800-759-0190 (cust serv) *Fax:* 415-537-4460 *Toll Free Fax:* 800-858-7787 (orders); 800-286-9471 (cust serv) *E-mail:* frontdesk@chroniclebooks.com *Web Site:* www.chroniclebooks.com, pg 55

Chaban, Enid, Random House Children's Books, 1745 Broadway, 10th fl, New York, NY 10019 *Tel:* 212-782-9000 *Web Site:* www.randomhousekids.com, pg 194

Chabert, Sally, Irene Skolnick Literary Agency, 27 W 20 St, Suite 305, New York, NY 10011 *Tel:* 212-727-3648 *Fax:* 212-352-2059 *E-mail:* office@skolnickliterary.com (queries) *Web Site:* www.skolnickagency.com, pg 536

Chabon, Michael, Charlotte Sheedy Fellowship, 100 High St, Peterborough, NH 03458 *Tel:* 603-924-3886 *Fax:* 603-924-9142 *E-mail:* admissions@macdowellcolony.org *Web Site:* www.macdowellcolony.org, pg 689

Chacon, Daniel, University of Texas at El Paso, Department of Creative Writing, MFA/Department of Creative Writing, 901 EDUC, 500 W University Ave, El Paso, TX 79968-9991 *Tel:* 915-747-5713 *Fax:* 915-747-5523 *E-mail:* creativewriting@utep.edu *Web Site:* www.utep.edu/cw, pg 624

Chadwell, Faye, Oregon State University Press, 121 The Valley Library, Corvallis, OR 97331-4501 *Tel:* 541-737-3166 *Toll Free Tel:* 800-621-2736 (orders), pg 170

Chagnot, Annie, Random House Publishing Group, 1745 Broadway, New York, NY 10019 *Toll Free Tel:* 800-200-3552 *Web Site:* atrandom.com, pg 195

Chait, Mark, HarperCollins General Books Group, 195 Broadway, New York, NY 10007 *Tel:* 212-207-7000 *Web Site:* www.harpercollins.com, pg 101

Chalfant, Sarah, The Wylie Agency LLC, 250 W 57 St, Suite 2114, New York, NY 10107 *Tel:* 212-246-0069 *Fax:* 212-586-8953 *E-mail:* mail@wylieagency.com *Web Site:* www.wylieagency.com, pg 542

Chalifoux, Ed, Printing Industry Association of the South (PIAS), 305 Plus Park Blvd, Nashville, TN 37217 *Tel:* 615-366-1094 *Fax:* 615-366-4192 *E-mail:* info@pias.org *Web Site:* www.pias.org, pg 576

Chalker, Bob, NACE International, 15835 Park Ten Place, Houston, TX 77084 *Tel:* 281-228-6200; 281-228-6223 *Toll Free Tel:* 800-797-NACE (797-6223) *Fax:* 281-228-6300 *E-mail:* firstservice@nace.org *Web Site:* www.nace.org, pg 156

Challender, Gary, Books In Motion, 9922 E Montgomery, Suite 31, Spokane Valley, WA 99206 *Tel:* 509-922-1646 *Toll Free Tel:* 800-752-3199 *Fax:* 509-922-1445 *E-mail:* info@booksinmotion.com *Web Site:* www.booksinmotion.com, pg 40

Challice, John, Oxford University Press USA, 198 Madison Ave, New York, NY 10016 *Tel:* 212-726-6000 *Toll Free Tel:* 800-451-7556 (orders); 800-445-9714 (cust serv) *Fax:* 919-677-1303 *E-mail:* custserv.us@oup.com *Web Site:* www.oup.com/us, pg 171

Chambers, Andrea L, New York University, Center for Publishing, Midtown Ctr, Rm 429, 11 W 42 St, New York, NY 10036 *Tel:* 212-992-3232 *Fax:* 212-992-3233 *E-mail:* pub.center@nyu.edu *Web Site:* www.scps.nyu.edu/publishing, pg 621

Chambers, Jennifer, In-Plant Printing & Mailing Association (IPMA), 455 S Sam Barr Dr, Suite 203, Kearney, MO 64060 *Tel:* 816-919-1691 *E-mail:* ipmainfo@ipma.org *Web Site:* www.ipma.org, pg 567

Chambers, Lewis R, The Bethel Agency, PO Box 21043, Park West Sta, New York, NY 10025 *Tel:* 212-864-4510 *E-mail:* bethelagcy@aol.com, pg 507

Chambers, Nathaniel, National Association of Black Journalists (NABJ), 1100 Knight Hall, Suite 3100, College Park, MD 20742 *Tel:* 301-405-0248 *Fax:* 301-314-1714 *E-mail:* nabj@nabj.org *Web Site:* www.nabj.org, pg 570

Chambliss, Jamie, Folio Literary Management, The Film Center Bldg, 630 Ninth Ave, Suite 1101, New York, NY 10036 *Tel:* 212-400-1494 *Fax:* 212-967-0977 *Web Site:* www.foliolit.com, pg 517

Chamenko, Tiffany, Information Today, Inc, 143 Old Marlton Pike, Medford, NJ 08055-8750 *Tel:* 609-654-6266 *Toll Free Tel:* 800-300-9868 (cust serv) *Fax:* 609-654-4309 *E-mail:* custserv@infotoday.com *Web Site:* www.infotoday.com, pg 116

Chan, Stephanie, Columbia Publishing Course at Columbia University, 2950 Broadway, MC 3801, New York, NY 10027 *Tel:* 212-854-1898 *Fax:* 212-854-7618 *E-mail:* publishing@jrn.columbia.edu *Web Site:* www.journalism.columbia.edu/publishing, pg 619

Chance, Rachel, The American Library Association (ALA), 50 E Huron St, Chicago, IL 60611 *Tel:* 312-944-6780 *Toll Free Tel:* 800-545-2433 *Fax:* 312-280-5275 *E-mail:* editionsmarketing@ala.org *Web Site:* www.alastore.ala.org, pg 13

Chanda, Justin, Simon & Schuster Children's Publishing, 1230 Avenue of the Americas, New York, NY 10020 *Tel:* 212-698-7000 *Web Site:* www.simonandschuster.com/kids; www.simonandschuster.com/teen; simonandschuster.net; simonandschuster.biz, pg 213

Chandlee, Chad M, Kendall Hunt Publishing Co, 4050 Westmark Dr, Dubuque, IA 52002-2624 *Tel:* 563-589-1000 *Toll Free Tel:* 800-228-0810 (orders) *Fax:* 563-589-1046 *Toll Free Fax:* 800-772-9165 *E-mail:* orders@kendallhunt.com *Web Site:* www.kendallhunt.com, pg 125

Chandler, Elizabeth Khuri, Goodreads Choice Awards, 188 Spear St, 3rd fl, San Francisco, CA 94105 *E-mail:* press@goodreads.com *Web Site:* www.goodreads.com/award, pg 650

Chandler, Otis, Goodreads Choice Awards, 188 Spear St, 3rd fl, San Francisco, CA 94105 *E-mail:* press@goodreads.com *Web Site:* www.goodreads.com/award, pg 650

Chandler, Pamela Siege, Foundation Press, c/o West Academic Publishing, 444 Cedar St, Suite 700, St Paul, MN 55101 *Toll Free Tel:* 877-888-1330 *E-mail:* customerservice@westacademic.com *Web Site:* www.westacademic.com, pg 87

Chaney, Margo, University of Illinois Press, 1325 S Oak St, MC-566, Champaign, IL 61820-6903 *Tel:* 217-333-0950 *Fax:* 217-244-8082 *E-mail:* uipress@uillinois.edu; journals@uillinois.edu *Web Site:* www.press.uillinois.edu, pg 241

Chang, Lan Samantha, The Iowa Short Fiction Award, 102 Dey House, 507 N Clinton St, Iowa City, IA 52242-1000 *Tel:* 319-335-0416 *Fax:* 319-335-0420 *Web Site:* www.uiowapress.org/authors/iowa-short-fiction.htm, pg 656

Chang, Lan Samantha, University of Iowa, Writers' Workshop, Graduate Creative Writing Program, 102 Dey House, 507 N Clinton St, Iowa City, IA 52242-1000 *Tel:* 319-335-0416 *Fax:* 319-335-0420 *Web Site:* writersworkshop.uiowa.edu, pg 623

Chang, Melanie, Harry N Abrams Inc, 195 Broadway, 9th fl, New York, NY 10007 *Tel:* 212-206-7715 *Toll Free Tel:* 800-345-1359 *Fax:* 212-519-1210 *E-mail:* abrams@abramsbooks.com *Web Site:* www.abramsbooks.com, pg 3

Chang, Melanie, Little, Brown Books for Young Readers, 1290 Avenue of the Americas, New York, NY 10019 *Tel:* 212-364-1100 *Toll Free Tel:* 800-759-0190 (cust serv) *Web Site:* www.HachetteBookGroup.com, pg 136

Chang, Ms Minju, BookStop Literary Agency LLC, 67 Meadow View Rd, Orinda, CA 94563 *E-mail:* info@bookstopliterary.com *Web Site:* www.bookstopliterary.com, pg 509

Chao, Victoria, Chronicle Books LLC, 680 Second St, San Francisco, CA 94107 *Tel:* 415-537-4200 *Toll Free Tel:* 800-759-0190 (cust serv) *Fax:* 415-537-4460 *Toll Free Fax:* 800-858-7787 (orders); 800-286-9471 (cust serv) *E-mail:* frontdesk@chroniclebooks.com *Web Site:* www.chroniclebooks.com, pg 55

Chapin, Amy, Avery Color Studios, 511 "D" Ave, Gwinn, MI 49841 *Tel:* 906-346-3908 *Toll Free Tel:* 800-722-9925 *Fax:* 906-346-3015 *E-mail:* averycolor@averycolorstudios.com *Web Site:* www.averycolorstudios.com, pg 27

Chapin, Frances, Write on the Sound Writers' Conference, 700 Main St, Edmonds, WA 98020 *Tel:* 425-771-0228 *Fax:* 425-771-0253 *E-mail:* wots@edmondswa.gov *Web Site:* www.writeonthesound.com, pg 616

Chapin, Wells, Avery Color Studios, 511 "D" Ave, Gwinn, MI 49841 *Tel:* 906-346-3908 *Toll Free Tel:* 800-722-9925 *Fax:* 906-346-3015 *E-mail:* averycolor@averycolorstudios.com *Web Site:* www.averycolorstudios.com, pg 27

Chaplin, Karen, HarperCollins Children's Books, 195 Broadway, New York, NY 10007 *Tel:* 212-207-7000 *Web Site:* www.harpercollins.com/childrens, pg 101

Chapman, Guy, Kensington Publishing Corp, 119 W 40 St, New York, NY 10018 *Tel:* 212-407-1500 *Toll Free Tel:* 800-221-2647 *Fax:* 212-935-0699 *Web Site:* www.kensingtonbooks.com, pg 125

Chapman, Ian, Simon & Schuster, Inc, 1230 Avenue of the Americas, New York, NY 10020 *Tel:* 212-698-7000 *Fax:* 212-698-7007 *E-mail:* firstname.lastname@simonandschuster.com *Web Site:* www.simonandschuster.com, pg 213

Chappell, Chris, Berghahn Books, 20 Jay St, Suite 512, Brooklyn, NY 11201 *Tel:* 212-233-6004 *Fax:* 212-233-6007 *E-mail:* info@berghahnbooks.com; salesus@berghahnbooks.com; editorial@journals.berghahnbooks.com *Web Site:* www.berghahnbooks.com, pg 33

Chappell, John, Lumina Datamatics Inc, 4 Collins Ave, Plymouth, MA 02360 *Tel:* 508-746-0300 *Fax:* 508-746-3233 *Web Site:* luminadatamatics.com, pg 498

Chapple, Beth, Granite Peak Publications, 5131 NE 201 Place, Lake Forest Park, WA 98155 *Tel:* 206-417-2861 *E-mail:* publicity@yellowstonetreasures.com *Web Site:* www.yellowstonetreasures.com, pg 478

Charbonneau, Catherine, La Courte Echelle, 4388, rue Saint-Denis, Suite 315, Montreal, QC H2J 2L1, Canada *Tel:* 514-312-6950 *E-mail:* info@courteechelle.com *Web Site:* courteechelle.groupecourteechelle.com, pg 451

Charette, Francois, Livres Canada Books, One Nicholas, Suite 504, Ottawa, ON K1N 7B7, Canada *Tel:* 613-562-2324 *Fax:* 613-562-2329 *E-mail:* info@livrescanadabooks.com *Web Site:* www.livrescanadabooks.com, pg 569

Charles, Kristi, National Resource Center for Youth Services (NRCYS), Schusterman Ctr, Bldg 4W, 4502 E 41 St, Tulsa, OK 74135-2512 *Tel:* 918-660-3700 *Toll Free Tel:* 800-274-2687 *Fax:* 918-660-3737 *Web Site:* www.nrcys.ou.edu, pg 159

Charlip, Christine, ASM Press, 1752 "N" St NW, Washington, DC 20036-2904 *Tel:* 202-737-3600 *Fax:* 202-942-9342 *E-mail:* books@asmusa.org *Web Site:* www.asmscience.org, pg 23

Chasan, Gail, Harlequin Enterprises Ltd, 233 Broadway, Suite 1001, New York, NY 10279 *Tel:* 212-553-4200 *Fax:* 212-227-8969 *E-mail:* customerservice@harlequin.com *Web Site:* www.harlequin.com, pg 100

Chasan-Taber, Jessie, Touchstone, 1230 Avenue of the Americas, New York, NY 10020, pg 233

Chatterjee, Jaya Aninda, Yale University Press, 302 Temple St, New Haven, CT 06511-8909 *Tel:* 203-432-0960; 203-432-0966 (sales); 401-531-2800 (cust serv) *Toll Free Tel:* 800-405-1619 (cust serv) *Fax:* 203-432-0948; 203-432-8485 (sales); 401-531-2801 (cust serv) *Toll Free Fax:* 800-406-9145 (cust serv) *E-mail:* sales.

press@yale.edu (sales); customer.care@triliteral.org (cust serv) *Web Site:* www.yalebooks.com; yalepress.yale.edu/yupbooks, pg 261

Chauhan, Bhavna, Doubleday Canada, 320 Front St W, Suite 1400, Toronto, ON M5V 3B6, Canada *Tel:* 416-364-4449 *Fax:* 416-598-7764 *Web Site:* www.penguinrandomhouse.ca, pg 452

Chauncey, Caroline, Harvard Education Publishing Group, 8 Story St, 1st fl, Cambridge, MA 02138 *Tel:* 617-495-3432 *Toll Free Tel:* 800-513-0763 (subns); 888-437-1437 (orders) *Fax:* 617-496-3584; 978-348-1233 (orders) *E-mail:* hepg@harvard.edu *Web Site:* www.hepg.org, pg 102

Chavern, David, News Media Alliance, 4401 N Fairfax Dr, Suite 300, Arlington, VA 22203 *Tel:* 571-366-1000 *E-mail:* info@newsmediaalliance.org *Web Site:* www.newsmediaalliance.org, pg 573

Checole, Kassahun, Africa World Press Inc, 541 W Ingham Ave, Suite B, Trenton, NJ 08638 *Tel:* 609-695-3200 *Fax:* 609-695-6466 *E-mail:* customerservice@africaworldpressbooks.com *Web Site:* www.africaworldpressbooks.com, pg 5

Checole, Kassahun, Red Sea Press Inc, 541 W Ingham Ave, Suite B, Trenton, NJ 08638 *Tel:* 609-695-3200 *Fax:* 609-695-6466 *E-mail:* customerservice@africaworldpressbooks.com *Web Site:* www.africaworldpressbooks.com, pg 197

Cheiffetz, Julia, HarperCollins General Books Group, 195 Broadway, New York, NY 10007 *Tel:* 212-207-7000 *Web Site:* www.harpercollins.com, pg 101

Chelstowski, Ray, Betterway Books, 10151 Carver Rd, Suite 200, Blue Ash, OH 45242 *Tel:* 513-531-2690 *Toll Free Tel:* 800-666-0963 *Fax:* 513-891-7185 *Toll Free Fax:* 888-590-4082 *Web Site:* www.fwmedia.com, pg 34

Chen, Ken, Asian American Writers' Workshop, 110-112 W 27 St, Suite 600, New York, NY 10001 *Tel:* 212-494-0061 *E-mail:* desk@aaww.org *Web Site:* aaww.org, pg 557

Chen, May, HarperCollins General Books Group, 195 Broadway, New York, NY 10007 *Tel:* 212-207-7000 *Web Site:* www.harpercollins.com, pg 101

Chen, Roxanne, Fodor's Travel Publications, 1745 Broadway, 15th fl, New York, NY 10019 *Toll Free Tel:* 800-733-3000 *E-mail:* publicity@fodors.com; editors@fodors.com *Web Site:* www.fodors.com, pg 86

Chenault, Earlita, Parallax Press, 2236-B Sixth St, Berkeley, CA 94710 *Tel:* 510-540-6411 *Toll Free Tel:* 800-863-5290 (orders) *Fax:* 510-981-1157 *Web Site:* www.parallax.org, pg 174

Cheney, Margaret, Ohio Genealogical Society, 611 State Rte 97 W, Bellville, OH 44813-8813 *Tel:* 419-886-1903 *Fax:* 419-886-0092 *E-mail:* ogs@ogs.org *Web Site:* www.ogs.org, pg 167

Cheng, Jill, Cheng & Tsui Co Inc, 25 West St, 2nd fl, Boston, MA 02111-1213 *Tel:* 617-988-2401 *Toll Free Tel:* 800-554-1963 *Fax:* 617-426-3669; 617-556-8964 *E-mail:* service@cheng-tsui.com; orders@cheng-tsui.com *Web Site:* www.cheng-tsui.com, pg 53

Cheng, Vivian, Marshall Cavendish Corp, 99 White Plains Rd, Tarrytown, NY 10591-9001 *Tel:* 914-332-8888 *Toll Free Tel:* 800-821-9881 *Fax:* 914-332-8102 *E-mail:* mce@marshallcavendish.com *Web Site:* www.marshallcavendish.com; www.mceducation.us, pg 143

Chenoweth, Allie, Second Story Press, 20 Maud St, Suite 401, Toronto, ON M5V 2M5, Canada *Tel:* 416-537-7850 *Fax:* 416-537-0588 *E-mail:* info@secondstorypress.ca *Web Site:* secondstorypress.ca, pg 470

Chepesiuk, Ron, Strategic Media Books LLC, 782 Wofford St, Rock Hill, SC 29730 *Tel:* 803 366 5440 *E-mail:* contact@strategicmediabooks.com *Web Site:* strategicmediabooks.com, pg 224

Chernoff, Mitch, Society for Industrial & Applied Mathematics, 3600 Market St, 6th fl, Philadelphia, PA 19104-2688 *Tel:* 215-382-9800 *Toll Free Tel:* 800-447-7426 *Fax:* 215-386-7999 *E-mail:* siambooks@siam.org *Web Site:* www.siam.org, pg 216

Cherrington, Janelle, Scholastic Education, 557 Broadway, New York, NY 10012 *Tel:* 212-343-6100 *Fax:* 212-343-6189 *Web Site:* www.scholastic.com, pg 207

Cherrix, Amy, Houghton Mifflin Harcourt Trade & Reference Division, 125 High St, Boston, MA 02110 *Tel:* 617-351-5000 *Toll Free Tel:* 800-225-3362 *Web Site:* www.hmhco.com, pg 111

Cherry, Amy, W W Norton & Company Inc, 500 Fifth Ave, New York, NY 10110-0017 *Tel:* 212-354-5500 *Toll Free Tel:* 800-233-4830 (orders & cust serv) *Fax:* 212-869-0856 *Toll Free Fax:* 800-458-6515 *E-mail:* orders@wwnorton.com *Web Site:* books.wwnorton.com, pg 164

Cherullo, Helen, The Mountaineers Books, 1001 SW Klickitat Way, Suite 201, Seattle, WA 98134 *Tel:* 206-223-6303 *Toll Free Tel:* 800-553-4453 *Fax:* 206-223-6306 *Toll Free Fax:* 800-568-7604 *E-mail:* mbooks@mountaineersbooks.org; customerservice@mountaineersbooks.org *Web Site:* www.mountaineersbooks.org, pg 155

Chesman, Andrea, Little Chicago Editorial Services, 154 Natural Tpke, Ripton, VT 05766 *Tel:* 802-388-9782 *Web Site:* andreachesman.com, pg 497

Chester, Linda, Linda Chester Literary Agency, 630 Fifth Ave, Suite 2000, New York, NY 10111 *Tel:* 212-218-3350 *E-mail:* submissions@lindachester.com *Web Site:* www.lindachester.com, pg 511

Cheuse, Sonya, HarperCollins General Books Group, 195 Broadway, New York, NY 10007 *Tel:* 212-207-7000 *Web Site:* www.harpercollins.com, pg 101

Chevako, Anne W, Publishing Resources Inc, 425 Carr 693, PMB 160, Dorado, PR 00646 *Tel:* 787-647-9342 *E-mail:* pri@chevako.net, pg 500

Chevako, Jay A, Publishing Resources Inc, 425 Carr 693, PMB 160, Dorado, PR 00646 *Tel:* 787-647-9342 *E-mail:* pri@chevako.net, pg 500

Chevako, Ronald J, Publishing Resources Inc, 425 Carr 693, PMB 160, Dorado, PR 00646 *Tel:* 787-647-9342 *E-mail:* pri@chevako.net, pg 500

Chia, Douglas, The Conference Board Inc, 845 Third Ave, New York, NY 10022-6600 *Tel:* 212-759-0900; 212-339-0345 (cust serv) *Fax:* 212-980-7014; 212-836-9740 (cust serv) *E-mail:* customer.service@conferenceboard.org; membership@conferenceboard.org *Web Site:* www.conference-board.org; www.linkedin.com/company/the-conference-board, pg 60

Childers, Kimberly B, Indiana University Press, Herman B Wells Library 350, 1320 E Tenth St, Bloomington, IN 47405-3907 *Tel:* 812-855-8817 *Toll Free Tel:* 800-842-6796 (orders only) *Fax:* 812-855-7931; 812-855-8507 *E-mail:* iupress@indiana.edu; iuporder@indiana.edu (orders) *Web Site:* www.iupress.indiana.edu, pg 116

Childress, David H, Adventures Unlimited Press (AUP), One Adventure Place, Kempton, IL 60946 *Tel:* 815-253-6390 *Fax:* 815-253-6300 *E-mail:* auphq@frontiernet.net; info@adventuresunlimitedpress.com *Web Site:* www.adventuresunlimitedpress.com, pg 5

Childs, Faith Hampton, Faith Childs Literary Agency Inc, 111 John St, Suite 1620, New York, NY 10038 *Tel:* 212-995-9600 *Web Site:* faithchildsliteraryagency.com, pg 511

Childs, Jennifer, Penguin Random House Inc, 1745 Broadway, New York, NY 10019 *Tel:* 212-782-9000 *Toll Free Tel:* 800-726-0600 *Web Site:* www.penguinrandomhouse.com, pg 178

Childs, Jim, The Globe Pequot Press, 246 Goose Lane, Guilford, CT 06437 *Tel:* 203-458-4500 *Toll Free Tel:* 800-243-0495 (orders only); 888-249-7586 (cust serv) *Fax:* 203-458-4601 *Toll Free Fax:* 800-820-2329 (orders & cust serv) *E-mail:* editorial@globepequot.com; info@rowman.com; orders@rowman.com *Web Site:* rowman.com, pg 93

Childs, Jim, Rowman & Littlefield Publishers Inc, 4501 Forbes Blvd, Suite 200, Lanham, MD 20706 *Tel:* 301-459-3366 *Toll Free Tel:* 800-462-6420 (cust serv) *Fax:* 301-429-5748 *Web Site:* rowman.com, pg 202

Chiles, Nick, Aevitas Creative Management, 19 W 21 St, Suite 501, New York, NY 10010 *Tel:* 212-765-6900 *Web Site:* aevitascreative.com, pg 506

Chin, Brenda, BelleBooks, PO Box 300921, Memphis, TN 38130 *Tel:* 901-344-9024 *Fax:* 901-344-9068 *E-mail:* bellebooks@bellebooks.com *Web Site:* www.bellebooks.com, pg 32

Chin, Brenda, Entangled Publishing, 2614 S Timberline Rd, Suite 109, Fort Collins, CO 80525 *Toll Free Tel:* 877-677-9451 *E-mail:* publisher@entangledpublishing.com *Web Site:* www.entangledpublishing.com, pg 79

Chin, Kristine, American Institute of Chemical Engineers (AIChE), 120 Wall St, 23rd fl, New York, NY 10005-4020 *Tel:* 203-702-7660 *Toll Free Tel:* 800-242-4363 *Fax:* 203-775-5177 *E-mail:* customerservice@aiche.org *Web Site:* www.aiche.org, pg 12

Chin, Oliver, Immedium, 535 Rockdale Dr, San Francisco, CA 94127 *Tel:* 415-452-8546 *Fax:* 360-937-6272 *E-mail:* orders@immedium.com; sales@immedium.com *Web Site:* www.immedium.com, pg 115

Chinski, Eric, Farrar, Straus & Giroux, LLC, 18 W 18 St, New York, NY 10011 *Tel:* 212-741-6900 *E-mail:* fsg.publicity@fsgbooks.com *Web Site:* us.macmillan.com/fsg.aspx, pg 83

Chipponeri, Kelli, Chronicle Books LLC, 680 Second St, San Francisco, CA 94107 *Tel:* 415-537-4200 *Toll Free Tel:* 800-759-0190 (cust serv) *Fax:* 415-537-4460 *Toll Free Fax:* 800-858-7787 (orders); 800-286-9471 (cust serv) *E-mail:* frontdesk@chroniclebooks.com *Web Site:* www.chroniclebooks.com, pg 55

Chirapurath, John "JG", ProQuest LLC, 789 E Eisenhower Pkwy, Ann Arbor, MI 48108 *Tel:* 734-761-4700 *Toll Free Tel:* 800-521-0600 *Web Site:* www.proquest.com, pg 190

Chirico, Anthony, Doubleday/Nan A Talese, c/o Penguin Random House Inc, 1745 Broadway, New York, NY 10019 *Tel:* 212-751-2600 *Fax:* 212-572-2662 *E-mail:* ddaypub@randomhouse.com *Web Site:* knopfdoubleday.com, pg 72

Chirico, Anthony, Alfred A Knopf/Everyman's Library, c/o Penguin Random House Inc, 1745 Broadway, New York, NY 10019 *Tel:* 212-751-2600 *Toll Free Tel:* 800-638-6460 *Fax:* 212-572-2593 *Web Site:* www.knopfdoubleday.com, pg 127

Chirico, Tony, Penguin Random House Inc, 1745 Broadway, New York, NY 10019 *Tel:* 212-782-9000 *Toll Free Tel:* 800-726-0600 *Web Site:* www.penguinrandomhouse.com, pg 178

Chittenden, Laurie, St Martin's Press, LLC, 175 Fifth Ave, New York, NY 10010 *Tel:* 646-307-5151 *Web Site:* us.macmillan.com/smp, pg 204

Chmiel, Barbara R, The Blackburn Press, PO Box 287, Caldwell, NJ 07006-0287 *Tel:* 973-228-7077 *Fax:* 973-228-7276 *Web Site:* www.blackburnpress.com, pg 36

Cho, Alino, Random House Publishing Group, 1745 Broadway, New York, NY 10019 *Toll Free Tel:* 800-200-3552 *Web Site:* atrandom.com, pg 195

Cho, Barbara, Little Bee Books, 853 Broadway, Suite 2014, New York, NY 10003 *E-mail:* info@littlebeebooks.com *Web Site:* www.littlebeebooks.com, pg 135

Cho, Tom, Princeton Architectural Press, 37 E Seventh St, New York, NY 10003 *Tel:* 212-995-9620 *Toll Free Tel:* 800-722-6657 (dist); 800-759-0190 (sales) *Fax:* 212-995-9454 *E-mail:* sales@papress.com *Web Site:* www.papress.com, pg 188

Chodosh, Ellen, New York University Press, 838 Broadway, 3rd fl, New York, NY 10003-4812 *Tel:* 212-998-2575 (edit) *Toll Free Tel:* 800-996-6987 (orders) *Fax:* 212-995-4798 (orders) *E-mail:* information@nyupress.org; nyupressinfo@nyu.edu; orders@nyupress.org *Web Site:* www.nyupress.org, pg 162

Chong, Anita, McClelland & Stewart Ltd, 320 Front St W, Suite 1400, Toronto, ON M5V 3B6, Canada *Tel:* 416-364-4449 *Fax:* 416-598-7764 *E-mail:* customerservicescanada@penguinrandomhouse.com; publicity@ca.penguingroup.com *Web Site:* penguinrandomhouse.ca/imprints/mcclelland-stewart, pg 463

Chong, Michele, Michael Wiese Productions, 12400 Ventura Blvd, No 1111, Studio City, CA 91604 *Tel:* 818-379-8799 *Toll Free Tel:* 800-833-5738 (orders) *Fax:* 818-986-3408 *E-mail:* mwpsales@mwp.com; fulfillment@portcity.com *Web Site:* www.mwp.com, pg 255

Choron, Harry, March Tenth Inc, 24 Hillside Terr, Montvale, NJ 07645 *Tel:* 201-387-6551 *Fax:* 201-387-6552 *Web Site:* www.march10th.com, pg 527

Choron, Sandra, March Tenth Inc, 24 Hillside Terr, Montvale, NJ 07645 *Tel:* 201-387-6551 *Fax:* 201-387-6552 *Web Site:* www.march10th.com, pg 527

Chorpenning, Rev Joseph F, St Joseph's University Press, 5600 City Ave, Philadelphia, PA 19131-1395 *Tel:* 610-660-3402 *Fax:* 610-660-3412 *E-mail:* sjupress@sju.edu *Web Site:* www.sjupress.com, pg 204

Chou, Arthur, New Win Publishing, 9682 Telstar Ave, Suite 110, El Monte, CA 91731 *Tel:* 626-448-3448 *Fax:* 626-602-3817 *E-mail:* info@academiclearningcompany.com *Web Site:* newwinpublishing.com; wbusinessbooks.com, pg 161

Chou, Arthur, Velazquez Press, 9682 Telstar Ave, Suite 110, El Monte, CA 91731 *Tel:* 626-448-3448 *Fax:* 626-602-3817 *E-mail:* info@academiclearningcompany.com *Web Site:* www.velazquezpress.com, pg 250

Chou, Shelly, Agency Chicago, 332 S Michigan Ave, Suite 1032, No A600, Chicago, IL 60604 *E-mail:* ernsant@aol.com, pg 506

Choyce, Lesley, Pottersfield Press, 248 Leslie Rd, East Lawrencetown, NS B2Z 1T4, Canada *Toll Free Tel:* 800-646-2879 (orders only) *Toll Free Fax:* 888-253-3133 *Web Site:* www.pottersfieldpress.com, pg 467

Chrichton, John, Bibliographical Society of America, PO Box 1537, Lenox Hill Sta, New York, NY 10021-0043 *Tel:* 212-452-2710 *Fax:* 212-452-2710 *E-mail:* bsa@bibsocamer.org *Web Site:* www.bibsocamer.org, pg 560

Chrisman, Ronald, University of North Texas Press, Willis Library, Rm 251, 1506 Highland St, Denton, TX 76203-5017 *Tel:* 940-565-2142 *Fax:* 940-565-4590 *Web Site:* untpress.unt.edu, pg 243

Christensen, Alicia, University of Nebraska Press, 1111 Lincoln Mall, Lincoln, NE 68588-0630 *Tel:* 402-472-3581; 919-966-7449 (cust serv & foreign orders) *Toll Free Tel:* 800-848-6224 (cust serv & US orders) *Fax:* 402-472-6214; 919-962-2704 (cust serv & foreign orders) *Toll Free Fax:* 800-526-2617 (cust serv & US orders) *E-mail:* pressmail@unl.edu *Web Site:* www.nebraskapress.unl.edu, pg 243

Christensen, Karen, Berkshire Publishing Group LLC, PO Box 177, Great Barrington, MA 01230 *E-mail:* info@berkshirepublishing.com *Web Site:* www.berkshirepublishing.com, pg 33

Christensen, Ulrik Juul MD, McGraw-Hill Education, 2 Penn Plaza, New York, NY 10121-2298 *Tel:* 212-904-2000 *E-mail:* customer.service@mheducation.com; international_cs@mheducation.com *Web Site:* www.mheducation.com, pg 145

Christenson, Neal, University of California Press, 155 Grand Ave, Suite 400, Oakland, CA 94612-3758 *Tel:* 510-883-8232 *Fax:* 510-836-8910 *E-mail:* customerservice@ucpressjournals.com *Web Site:* www.ucpress.edu, pg 240

Christian, Abigail, Society of American Archivists, 17 N State St, Suite 1425, Chicago, IL 60602-4061 *Tel:* 312-606-0722 *Toll Free Tel:* 866-722-7858 *Fax:* 312-606-0728 *Web Site:* www.archivists.org, pg 216

Christian, Rick, Bondfire Books, 7680 Goddard St, Suite 220, Colorado Springs, CO 80920 *Tel:* 719-260-7080 *Web Site:* www.bondfirebooks.com, pg 39

Christiansen, Gayla, Texas A&M University Press, John H Lindsey Bldg, Lewis St, 4354 TAMU, College Station, TX 77843-4354 *Tel:* 979-845-1436 *Toll Free Tel:* 800-826-8911 (orders) *Fax:* 979-847-8752 *Toll Free Fax:* 888-617-2421 (orders) *E-mail:* bookorders@tamu.edu *Web Site:* www.tamupress.com, pg 230

Christiansen, Hillary, Palm Springs Writers Guild, PO Box 947, Rancho Mirage, CA 92270-0947 *Web Site:* www.palmspringswritersguild.org, pg 575

Christmas, Bobbie, Zebra Communications, 230 Deerchase Dr, Woodstock, GA 30188-4438 *Tel:* 770-924-0528 *Web Site:* www.zebraeditor.com, pg 503

Christofferson, Andrea, University of Wisconsin Press, 1930 Monroe St, 3rd fl, Madison, WI 53711-2059 *Tel:* 608-263-0668 *Toll Free Tel:* 800-621-2736 (orders) *Fax:* 608-263-1173 *Toll Free Fax:* 800-621-2736 (orders) *E-mail:* uwiscpress@uwpress.wisc.edu (main off); publicity@uwpress.wisc.edu *Web Site:* uwpress.wisc.edu, pg 246

Christopher, Rob, ALA Neal-Schuman, 50 E Huron St, Chicago, IL 60611 *Toll Free Tel:* 800-545-2433 *Fax:* 312-280-5275 *E-mail:* editionsmarketing@ala.org *Web Site:* www.alastore.ala.org, pg 6

Christopher, Rob, The American Library Association (ALA), 50 E Huron St, Chicago, IL 60611 *Tel:* 312-944-6780 *Toll Free Tel:* 800-545-2433 *Fax:* 312-280-5275 *E-mail:* editionsmarketing@ala.org *Web Site:* www.alastore.ala.org, pg 13

Chu, Elaine, Immedium, 535 Rockdale Dr, San Francisco, CA 94127 *Tel:* 415-452-8546 *Fax:* 360-937-6272 *E-mail:* orders@immedium.com; sales@immedium.com *Web Site:* www.immedium.com, pg 115

Chu, Jane, National Endowment for the Arts, 400 Seventh St SW, Washington, DC 20506-0001 *Tel:* 202-682-5400 *Web Site:* www.arts.gov, pg 583

Chu, Jane, The National Medal of Arts, 400 Seventh St SW, Washington, DC 20506-0001 *Tel:* 202-682-5434 *Web Site:* www.arts.gov/honors/medals, pg 671

Chu, Lily, Captus Press Inc, 1600 Steeles Ave W, Units 14 & 15, Concord, ON L4K 4M2, Canada *Tel:* 416-736-5537 *Fax:* 416-736-5793 *E-mail:* info@captus.com *Web Site:* www.captus.com, pg 449

Chu, Lynn, Writers' Representatives LLC, 116 W 14 St, 11th fl, New York, NY 10011-7305 *Tel:* 212-620-9009 *Fax:* 212-620-0023 *E-mail:* transom@writersreps.com *Web Site:* www.writersreps.com, pg 542

Chun, Stephanie, University of Hawaii Press, 2840 Kolowalu St, Honolulu, HI 96822 *Tel:* 808-956-8255 *Toll Free Tel:* 888-UHPRESS (847-7377) *Fax:* 808-988-6052 *Toll Free Fax:* 800-650-7811 *E-mail:* uhpbooks@hawaii.edu *Web Site:* www.uhpress.hawaii.edu, pg 241

Church, Dawson, Energy Psychology Press, 1490 Mark West Springs Rd, Santa Rosa, CA 95404 *Tel:* 707-525-9292 *Toll Free Fax:* 800-330-9798 *E-mail:* support@eftuniverse.com *Web Site:* www.energypsychologypress.com; www.elitebooksonline.com, pg 79

Church, Doug, Pacific Press Publishing Association, 1350 N Kings Rd, Nampa, ID 83687-3193 *Tel:* 208-465-2500 *Toll Free Tel:* 800-447-7377 *Fax:* 208-465-2531 *Web Site:* www.pacificpress.com, pg 172

Churko, Helen, Royce Carlton Inc, 866 United Nations Plaza, Suite 587, New York, NY 10017-1880 *Tel:* 212-355-7700 *Toll Free Tel:* 800-LECTURE (532-8873) *Fax:* 212-888-8659 *E-mail:* info@roycecarlton.com *Web Site:* www.roycecarlton.com, pg 548

Chutjian, Lisa, The Alexander Graham Bell Association for the Deaf & Hard of Hearing, 3417 Volta Place NW, Washington, DC 20007 *Tel:* 202-337-5220 *Toll Free Tel:* 866-337-5220 (orders) *Fax:* 202-337-8314 *E-mail:* info@agbell.org; publications@agbell.org *Web Site:* www.agbell.org, pg 6

Cianfarani, Nick, New City Press, 202 Comforter Blvd, Hyde Park, NY 12538 *Tel:* 845-229-0335 *Toll Free Tel:* 800-462-5980 (orders only) *Fax:* 845-229-0351 *E-mail:* info@newcitypress.com *Web Site:* www.newcitypress.com, pg 160

Cianfrone, Amy, Perseus Books, 250 W 57 St, 15th fl, New York, NY 10107 *Tel:* 212-340-8100 *Toll Free Tel:* 800-343-4499 (cust serv) *Fax:* 212-340-8105 *Web Site:* www.perseusbooks.com, pg 181

Ciccone, Patti, Midwest Travel Writers Association, 902 S Randall Rd, Suite C311, St Charles, IL 60174 *Toll Free Tel:* 888-551-8184 *E-mail:* admin@mtwa.org *Web Site:* www.mtwa.org, pg 569

Ciecierski, Andrea, Stylus Publishing LLC, 22883 Quicksilver Dr, Sterling, VA 20166-2012 *Tel:* 703-661-1504 (edit & sales) *Toll Free Tel:* 800-232-0223 (orders & cust serv) *Fax:* 703-661-1547 *E-mail:* stylusmail@presswarehouse.com (orders & cust serv); stylusinfo@styluspub.com *Web Site:* www.styluspub.com, pg 224

Cihlar, James, The Backwaters Press, 1124 Pacific St, Suite 8392, Omaha, NE 68108 *Tel:* 402-451-4052 *E-mail:* thebackwaterspress@gmail.com *Web Site:* www.thebackwaterspress.org, pg 28

Cilberberg, Melissa, Firefly Books Ltd, 50 Staples Ave, Unit 1, Richmond Hill, ON L4B 0A7, Canada *Tel:* 416-499-8412 *Toll Free Tel:* 800-387-6192 (CN); 800-387-5085 (US) *Fax:* 416-499-8313 *Toll Free Fax:* 800-450-0391 (CN); 800-565-6034 (US) *E-mail:* info@fireflybooks.com *Web Site:* www.fireflybooks.com, pg 456

Ciletti, Barbara, Odyssey Books, 2421 Redwood Ct, Longmont, CO 80503-8155 *Tel:* 720-494-1473 *Fax:* 720-494-1471 *E-mail:* books@odysseybooks.net, pg 167

Cilurso, Ed, Taylor & Francis Inc, 530 Walnut St, Suite 850, Philadelphia, PA 19106 *Tel:* 215-625-8900 *Toll Free Tel:* 800-354-1420 *Fax:* 215-207-0050; 215-207-0046 (cust serv) *E-mail:* support@tandfonline.com *Web Site:* www.taylorandfrancis.com, pg 227

Cimina, Dominique, Random House Children's Books, 1745 Broadway, 10th fl, New York, NY 10019 *Tel:* 212-782-9000 *Web Site:* www.randomhousekids.com, pg 194

Ciminera, Siobhan, Simon & Schuster Children's Publishing, 1230 Avenue of the Americas, New York, NY 10020 *Tel:* 212-698-7000 *Web Site:* www.simonandschuster.com/kids; www.simonandschuster.com/teen; simonandschuster.net; simonandschuster.biz, pg 213

Cimino, Antoinette, Springer, 233 Spring St, New York, NY 10013-1578 *Tel:* 212-460-1500 *Toll Free Tel:* 800-SPRINGER (777-4643) *Fax:* 212-460-1700 *E-mail:* customerservice@springer.com *Web Site:* www.springer.com, pg 219

Cimonetti, Tanya, Lyric Poetry Prizes, PO Box 110, Jericho, VT 05465 *Tel:* 802-899-3993 *Fax:* 802-899-3993 *E-mail:* themuse@thelyricmagazine.com *Web Site:* thelyricmagazine.com, pg 664

Ciommo, Dave, EPS/School Specialty Literacy & Intervention, 625 Mount Auburn St, 3rd fl, Cambridge, MA 02138-3039 *Toll Free Tel:* 800-225-5750 *Toll Free Fax:* 888-440-2665 *E-mail:* customerservice.eps@schoolspecialty.com *Web Site:* eps.schoolspecialty.com, pg 79

Ciotola, Andrew, Bucknell Seminar for Undergraduate Poets, Bucknell University, Bucknell Hall, Moore Ave, Lewisburg, PA 17837 *Tel:* 570-577-1853 *E-mail:* stadlercenter@bucknell.edu *Web Site:* www.bucknell.edu/stadlercenter, pg 610

Circosta, Karey, Ave Maria Press, PO Box 428, Notre Dame, IN 46556 *Tel:* 574-287-2831 *Toll Free Tel:* 800-282-1865 *Fax:* 574-239-2904 *Toll Free Fax:* 800-282-5681 *E-mail:* avemariapress.1@nd.edu *Web Site:* www.avemariapress.com, pg 27

Cirillo, Andrea, Jane Rotrosen Agency LLC, 85 Broad St, 28th fl, New York, NY 10004 *Tel:* 212-593-4330 *Fax:* 212-935-6985 *Web Site:* janerotrosen.com, pg 533

Cirrone, Dorian, SCBWI-FL Florida Regional Conference, 125 E Merritt Island Causeway, Suite 209, Merritt Island, FL 32952 *Tel:* 321-338-7208 *E-mail:* florida@scbwi.org *Web Site:* florida.scbwi.org, pg 614

Cirrone, Dorian, SCBWI-FL Mid-Year Workshops, 125 E Merritt Island Causeway, Suite 209, Merritt Island, FL 32952 *Tel:* 321-338-7208 *E-mail:* florida@scbwi.org *Web Site:* florida.scbwi.org, pg 614

Citro, Asia, The Innovation Press, 1001 Fourth Ave, Suite 3200, Seattle, WA 98154 *Tel:* 360-870-9988 *E-mail:* info@theinnovationpress.com *Web Site:* www.theinnovationpress.com, pg 117

Cizek, Nick, The Experiment, 220 E 23 St, Suite 301, New York, NY 10010-4674 *Tel:* 212-889-1659 *E-mail:* info@theexperimentpublishing.com *Web Site:* www.theexperimentpublishing.com, pg 81

Clain, Judy, Little, Brown and Company, 1290 Avenue of the Americas, New York, NY 10019 *Tel:* 212-364-1100 *Fax:* 212-364-0952 *E-mail:* firstname.lastname@hbgusa.com *Web Site:* www.littlebrown.com; www.HachetteBookGroup.com, pg 135

Clancy, Alicia, St Martin's Press, LLC, 175 Fifth Ave, New York, NY 10010 *Tel:* 646-307-5151 *Web Site:* us.macmillan.com/smp, pg 204

Clancy, Julianne, Pantheon Books/Schocken Books, c/o Penguin Random House Inc, 1745 Broadway, New York, NY 10019 *Tel:* 212-751-2600 *Web Site:* knopfdoubleday.com/imprint/pantheon, pg 173

Clapps, Bobbi, Syracuse University Press, 621 Skytop Rd, Suite 110, Syracuse, NY 13244-5290 *Tel:* 315-443-5534 *Toll Free Tel:* 800-365-8929 (cust serv) *Fax:* 315-443-5545 *E-mail:* supress@syr.edu *Web Site:* syracuseuniversitypress.syr.edu, pg 226

Clark, Becky Brasington, The Johns Hopkins University Press, 2715 N Charles St, Baltimore, MD 21218-4363 *Tel:* 410-516-6900; 410-516-6987 (journal orders outside US & CN) *Toll Free Tel:* 800-537-5487 (book orders & cust serv); 800-548-1784 (journal orders) *Fax:* 410-516-6968; 410-516-3866 (journal orders) *E-mail:* hfscustserv@press.jhu.edu (cust serv); jrnlcirc@press.jhu.edu (journal orders) *Web Site:* www.press.jhu.edu; muse.jhu.edu, pg 122

Clark, Billy, Hachette Nashville, 12 Cadillac Dr, Suite 480, Brentwood, TN 37027 *Tel:* 615-221-0996 *Fax:* 615-221-0962 *Web Site:* www.hachettebookgroup.com, pg 98

Clark, Ginger, Curtis Brown Ltd, 10 Astor Place, New York, NY 10003 *Tel:* 212-473-5400 *Web Site:* www.curtisbrown.com, pg 510

Clark, James C, Penguin Group USA, A Penguin Random House Company, 375 Hudson St, New York, NY 10014 *Tel:* 212-366-2000 *Toll Free Tel:* 800-847-5515 (inside sales); 800-631-8571 (cust serv) *Fax:* 212-366-2666; 607-775-4829 (inside sales) *E-mail:* online@us.penguingroup.com *Web Site:* www.penguin.com, pg 177

Clark, Jim, The Robert Watson Literary Prizes in Fiction & Poetry, MFA Writing Program, The Greensboro Review, UNC-Greensboro, 3302 MHRA Bldg, Greensboro, NC 27402-6170 *Tel:* 336-334-5459 *Fax:* 336-256-1470 *Web Site:* www.greensbororeview.org, pg 696

Clark, June, FinePrint Literary Management, 207 W 106 St, Suite 1D, New York, NY 10025 *Tel:* 212-279-6214 *E-mail:* assist@fineprint.com *Web Site:* www.fineprintlit.com, pg 516

Clark, Kevin, American Public Works Association (APWA), 2345 Grand Blvd, Suite 700, Kansas City, MO 64108-2625 *Tel:* 816-472-6100 *Toll Free Tel:* 800-848-APWA (848-2792) *Fax:* 816-472-1610 *Web Site:* www.apwa.net, pg 14

Clark, Laura, St Martin's Press, LLC, 175 Fifth Ave, New York, NY 10010 *Tel:* 646-307-5151 *Web Site:* us.macmillan.com/smp, pg 204

Clark, Michiko, Pantheon Books/Schocken Books, c/o Penguin Random House Inc, 1745 Broadway, New York, NY 10019 *Tel:* 212-751-2600 *Web Site:* knopfdoubleday.com/imprint/pantheon, pg 173

Clark, Raymond C, Pro Lingua Associates Inc, 74 Cotton Mill Hill, Suite A-315, Brattleboro, VT 05301 *Tel:* 802-257-7779 *Toll Free Tel:* 800-366-4775 *Fax:* 802-257-5117 *E-mail:* info@prolinguaassociates.com *Web Site:* www.prolinguaassociates.com, pg 189

Clark, Rob, National Notary Association (NNA), 9350 De Soto Ave, Chatsworth, CA 91311-4926 *Tel:* 818-739-4000 *Toll Free Tel:* 800-876-6827 *Toll Free Fax:* 800-833-1211 *E-mail:* nna@nationalnotary.org *Web Site:* www.nationalnotary.org, pg 159

Clark, Simon, Oxford University Press USA, 198 Madison Ave, New York, NY 10016 *Tel:* 212-726-6000 *Toll Free Tel:* 800-451-7556 (orders); 800-445-9714 (cust serv) *Fax:* 919-677-1303 *E-mail:* custserv.us@oup.com *Web Site:* www.oup.com/us, pg 171

Clark, William, Wm Clark Associates, 186 Fifth Ave, 2nd fl, New York, NY 10010 *Tel:* 212-675-2784 *E-mail:* general@wmclark.com *Web Site:* www.wmclark.com, pg 511

Clark, Zina, Coretta Scott King Book Awards, 50 E Huron St, Chicago, IL 60611 *Toll Free Tel:* 800-545-2433 *E-mail:* olos@ala.org *Web Site:* www.ala.org/emiert/cskbookawards, pg 658

Clarke, Anne, Orbit, 1290 Avenue of the Americas, New York, NY 10019 *Tel:* 212-364-1100 *Toll Free Tel:* 800-759-0190 *Web Site:* www.orbitbooks.net, pg 169

Clarke, Chandra, Scribendi Inc, 405 Riverview Dr, Chatham, ON N7M 0N3, Canada *Tel:* 519-351-1626 (cust serv) *Fax:* 519-354-0192 *E-mail:* customerservice@scribendi.com *Web Site:* www.scribendi.com, pg 501

Clarke, Erin, Random House Children's Books, 1745 Broadway, 10th fl, New York, NY 10019 *Tel:* 212-782-9000 *Web Site:* www.randomhousekids.com, pg 194

Clarke, Meghan, Taschen America, 6671 Sunset Blvd, Suite 1508, Los Angeles, CA 90028 *Tel:* 323-463-4441 *Toll Free Tel:* 888-TASCHEN (827-2436) *Fax:* 323-463-4442 *E-mail:* contact-us@taschen.com *Web Site:* www.taschen.com, pg 227

Clarke, Mia Barkan, Cross-Cultural Communications, 239 Wynsum Ave, Merrick, NY 11566-4725 *Tel:* 516-868-5635 *Fax:* 516-379-1901 *E-mail:* info@cross-culturalcommunications.com; cccbarkan@optonline.net; cccpoetry@aol.com *Web Site:* www.cross-culturalcommunications.com, pg 64

Clarke, Vicky, Utah Geological Survey, 1594 W North Temple, Suite 3110, Salt Lake City, UT 84116-3154 *Tel:* 801-537-3300 *Toll Free Tel:* 888-UTAH-MAP (882-4627 bookstore) *Fax:* 801-537-3400 *E-mail:* geostore@utah.gov *Web Site:* geology.utah.gov, pg 249

Classic, Lesley, Database Directories, 588 Dufferin Ave, London, ON N6B 2A4, Canada *Tel:* 519-433-1666 *Fax:* 519-430-1131 *E-mail:* mail@databasedirectory.com *Web Site:* www.databasedirectory.com, pg 451

Clay, Adam, Mississippi Review Prize, 118 College Dr, Box 5144, Hattiesburg, MS 39406-0001 *E-mail:* msreview@usm.edu *Web Site:* www.usm.edu/mississippi-review/contest.html, pg 668

Clay, Carolyn, Day Owl Press Corp, 201 W Ocean Ave, Unit 3574, Lantana, FL 33465 *Toll Free Tel:* 888-806-6981 *Toll Free Fax:* 866-854-4375 *E-mail:* info@dayowl.net *Web Site:* www.dayowl.net, pg 68

Clayton, Cheryl, Workman Publishing Co Inc, 225 Varick St, 9th fl, New York, NY 10014-4381 *Tel:* 212-254-5900 *Toll Free Tel:* 800-722-7202 *Fax:* 212-254-8098 *E-mail:* info@workman.com *Web Site:* www.workman.com, pg 259

Clayton, Dhonielle, Walter Dean Myers Grant, 10318 Westlake Dr, No 104, Bethesda, MD 20817 *E-mail:* waltergrantwndb@gmail.com *Web Site:* weneeddiversebooks.org, pg 670

Clayton, Douglas, Harvard Education Publishing Group, 8 Story St, 1st fl, Cambridge, MA 02138 *Tel:* 617-495-3432 *Toll Free Tel:* 800-513-0763 (subns); 888-437-1437 (orders) *Fax:* 617-496-3584; 978-348-1233 (orders) *E-mail:* hepg@harvard.edu *Web Site:* www.hepg.org, pg 102

Clayton, Keith, Random House Publishing Group, 1745 Broadway, New York, NY 10019 *Toll Free Tel:* 800-200-3552 *Web Site:* atrandom.com, pg 195

Clayton, Patricia Mulrane, Peter Lang Publishing Inc, 29 Broadway, 18th fl, New York, NY 10006-3223 *Tel:* 212-647-7706 *Toll Free Tel:* 800-770-5264 (cust serv) *Fax:* 212-647-7707 *Web Site:* www.peterlang.com, pg 129

Cleary, Amy, Chronicle Books LLC, 680 Second St, San Francisco, CA 94107 *Tel:* 415-537-4200 *Toll Free Tel:* 800-759-0190 (cust serv) *Fax:* 415-537-4460 *Toll Free Fax:* 800-858-7787 (orders); 800-286-9471 (cust serv) *E-mail:* frontdesk@chroniclebooks.com *Web Site:* www.chroniclebooks.com, pg 55

Cleland, Lucy, Kneerim & Williams Agency, 90 Canal St, Boston, MA 02114 *Tel:* 617-303-1650 *Web Site:* www.kwlit.com, pg 524

Clements, Caley, Canadian Scholars' Press Inc, 425 Adelaide St W, Suite 200, Toronto, ON M5V 3C1, Canada *Tel:* 416-929-2774 *Toll Free Tel:* 800-463-1998 *Fax:* 416-929-1926 *E-mail:* info@cspi.org; info@canadianscholars.ca; editorial@canadianscholars.ca; orders@canadianscholars.ca *Web Site:* www.canadianscholars.ca; www.womenspress.ca, pg 449

Clements, Pamela, Abingdon Press, 201 Eighth Ave S, Nashville, TN 37203-3919 *Tel:* 615-749-6000 (academic books) *Toll Free Tel:* 800-251-3320 *Fax:* 615-749-6056 (academic books) *Toll Free Fax:* 800-836-7802 (orders) *E-mail:* orders@abingdonpress.com *Web Site:* www.abingdonpress.com, pg 2

Clementson, Elizabeth, W W Norton & Company Inc, 500 Fifth Ave, New York, NY 10110-0017 *Tel:* 212-354-5500 *Toll Free Tel:* 800-233-4830 (orders & cust serv) *Fax:* 212-869-0856 *Toll Free Fax:* 800-458-6515 *E-mail:* orders@wwnorton.com *Web Site:* books.wwnorton.com, pg 164

Clemons, G Scott, Bibliographical Society of America, PO Box 1537, Lenox Hill Sta, New York, NY 10021-0043 *Tel:* 212-452-2710 *Fax:* 212-452-2710 *E-mail:* bsa@bibsocamer.org *Web Site:* www.bibsocamer.org, pg 560

Cleveland, Marisa, The Seymour Agency, 475 Miner Street Rd, Canton, NY 13617 *Tel:* 315-386-1831 *Web Site:* www.theseymouragency.com, pg 535

Cleveland, Rob, August House Inc, 3500 Piedmont Rd NE, Suite 310, Atlanta, GA 30305 *Tel:* 404-442-4420 *Toll Free Tel:* 800-284-8784 *Fax:* 404-442-4435 *E-mail:* ahinfo@augusthouse.com *Web Site:* www.augusthouse.com, pg 26

Clevenger, Beth, The MIT Press, One Rogers St, Cambridge, MA 02142 *Tel:* 617-253-5255 *Toll Free Tel:* 800-207-8354 (orders) *Fax:* 617-258-6779; 617-577-1545 (orders) *Web Site:* mitpress.mit.edu, pg 152

Clifford, Christina, Harlequin Enterprises Ltd, 225 Duncan Mill Rd, Don Mills, ON M3B 3K9, Canada *Tel:* 416-445-5860 *Toll Free Tel:* 888-432-4879; 800-370-5838 (ebook inquiries) *E-mail:* customerservice@harlequin.com *Web Site:* www.harlequin.com, pg 459

Clifton, Rachel, Neltje Blanchan Memorial Award, Barrett Bldg, 2nd fl, 2301 Central Ave, Cheyenne, WY 82002 *Tel:* 307-777-7742 *Web Site:* wyoarts.state.wy.us, pg 633

Clifton, Rachel, Frank Nelson Doubleday Memorial Award, Barrett Bldg, 2nd fl, 2301 Central Ave, Cheyenne, WY 82002 *Tel:* 307-777-7742 *Web Site:* wyoarts.state.wy.us, pg 642

Clifton, Rachel, Wyoming Arts Council Creative Writing Fellowships, Barrett Bldg, 2nd fl, 2301 Central Ave, Cheyenne, WY 82002 *Tel:* 307-777-7742 *Web Site:* wyoarts.state.wy.us, pg 701

Cline, Susan, Nelson Education Ltd, 1120 Birchmount Rd, Scarborough, ON M1K 5G4, Canada *Tel:* 416-752-9100 *Toll Free Tel:* 800-268-2222 (cust serv)

Fax: 416-752-8101 *Toll Free Fax:* 800-430-4445 *E-mail:* peopleandengagement@nelson.com *Web Site:* www.nelson.com, pg 464

Clingham, Greg, Bucknell University Press, 6 Taylor Hall, Bucknell University, Lewisburg, PA 17837 *Tel:* 570-577-3674 *E-mail:* universitypress@bucknell.edu *Web Site:* www.bucknell.edu/universitypress, pg 45

Clinton, John, Penguin Random House Inc, 1745 Broadway, New York, NY 10019 *Tel:* 212-782-9000 *Toll Free Tel:* 800-726-0600 *Web Site:* www.penguinrandomhouse.com, pg 178

Clockel, William, Educator's International Press Inc (EIP), 84 Hardenburgh Ave, Haworth, NJ 07641 *Tel:* 518-334-0276 *Fax:* 703-661-1547 *E-mail:* info@edint.com *Web Site:* edint.presswarehouse.com, pg 76

Cloidt, Kim, Independent Institute, 100 Swan Way, Suite 200, Oakland, CA 94621-1428 *Tel:* 510-632-1366 *Toll Free Tel:* 800-927-8733 *Fax:* 510-568-6040 *E-mail:* orders@independent.org *Web Site:* www.independent.org, pg 115

Close, Amanda, Random House Publishing Group, 1745 Broadway, New York, NY 10019 *Toll Free Tel:* 800-200-3552 *Web Site:* atrandom.com, pg 195

Close, Ann, Alfred A Knopf/Everyman's Library, c/o Penguin Random House Inc, 1745 Broadway, New York, NY 10019 *Tel:* 212-751-2600 *Toll Free Tel:* 800-638-6460 *Fax:* 212-572-2593 *Web Site:* www.knopfdoubleday.com, pg 127

Close, Tim, David C Cook, 4050 Lee Vance View, Colorado Springs, CO 80918 *Tel:* 719-536-0100 *Toll Free Tel:* 800-708-5550; 800-323-7543 (orders & cust serv) *Toll Free Fax:* 800-430-0726 (cust serv) *Web Site:* www.davidccook.com, pg 60

Closson, Bob, Closson Press, 257 Delilah St, Apollo, PA 15613-1933 *Tel:* 724-337-4482 *Fax:* 724-337-9484 *E-mail:* clossonpress@comcast.net *Web Site:* www.clossonpress.com, pg 57

Closson, Marietta, Closson Press, 257 Delilah St, Apollo, PA 15613-1933 *Tel:* 724-337-4482 *Fax:* 724-337-9484 *E-mail:* clossonpress@comcast.net *Web Site:* www.clossonpress.com, pg 57

Cloughly, Amy, Kimberley Cameron & Associates LLC, 1550 Tiburon Blvd, Suite 704, Tiburon, CA 94920 *Tel:* 415-789-9191 *Fax:* 415-789-9177 *Web Site:* www.kimberleycameron.com, pg 511

Cloutier, Suzanne, University of Ottawa Press (Presses de l'Université d'Ottawa), 542 King Edward Ave, Ottawa, ON K1N 6N5, Canada *Tel:* 613-562-5246 *Fax:* 613-562-5247 *E-mail:* puo-oup@uottawa.ca *Web Site:* press.uottawa.ca, pg 474

Clute, Sharla, State University of New York Press, 10 N Pearl St, 4th fl, Albany, NY 12207 *Tel:* 518-944-2800 *Toll Free Tel:* 877-204-6073 (orders) *Fax:* 518-320-1592 *Toll Free Fax:* 877-204-6074 (orders) *E-mail:* info@sunypress.edu (edit off); suny@presswarehouse.com (orders) *Web Site:* www.sunypress.edu, pg 221

Clyne, Cat, Sourcebooks Inc, 1935 Brookdale Rd, Suite 139, Naperville, IL 60563 *Tel:* 630-961-3900 *Toll Free Tel:* 800-432-7444 *Fax:* 630-961-2168 *E-mail:* info@sourcebooks.com; customersupport@sourcebooks.com *Web Site:* www.sourcebooks.com, pg 218

Coalson, Lance, Father & Son Publishing Inc, 4909 N Monroe St, Tallahassee, FL 32303-7015 *Tel:* 850-562-2612 *Toll Free Tel:* 800-741-2712 (orders only) *Fax:* 850-562-0916 *Web Site:* www.fatherson.com, pg 83

Coan, Cynthia J, Indexing by the Book, PO Box 12513, Tucson, AZ 85732-2513 *Tel:* 520-750-8439 *E-mail:* indextran@cox.net *Web Site:* www.indexingbythebook.com, pg 496

Coates, Damani, Black Classic Press, 3921 Vero Rd, Suite F, Baltimore, MD 21203-3414 *Tel:* 410-242-6954 *Toll Free Tel:* 800-476-8870 *Fax:* 410-242-6959 *E-mail:* email@blackclassicbooks.com; blackclassicpress@yahoo.com *Web Site:* www.blackclassicbooks.com; www.bcpdigital.com, pg 36

Coates, Laraine, University of British Columbia Press, 2029 West Mall, Vancouver, BC V6T 1Z2, Canada *Tel:* 604-822-5959 *Toll Free Tel:* 877-377-9378 *Fax:* 604-822-6083 *Toll Free Fax:* 800-668-0821 *E-mail:* frontdesk@ubcpress.ca *Web Site:* www.ubcpress.ca, pg 473

Coates, W Paul, Black Classic Press, 3921 Vero Rd, Suite F, Baltimore, MD 21203-3414 *Tel:* 410-242-6954 *Toll Free Tel:* 800-476-8870 *Fax:* 410-242-6959 *E-mail:* email@blackclassicbooks.com; blackclassicpress@yahoo.com *Web Site:* www.blackclassicbooks.com; www.bcpdigital.com, pg 36

Cobb, Caelyn, Columbia University Press, 61 W 62 St, New York, NY 10023 *Tel:* 212-459-0600 *Toll Free Tel:* 800-944-8648 *Fax:* 212-459-3678 *E-mail:* cup_book@columbia.edu (orders & cust serv) *Web Site:* cup.columbia.edu, pg 59

Cobb, David, The University Press of Kentucky, 663 S Limestone St, Lexington, KY 40508-4008 *Tel:* 859-257-8400 *Fax:* 859-257-8481 *Web Site:* www.kentuckypress.com, pg 247

Cobb, Jennifer, Society of Exploration Geophysicists, 8801 S Yale Ave, Tulsa, OK 74137 *Tel:* 918-497-5500 *Fax:* 918-497-5557 *E-mail:* web@seg.org *Web Site:* www.seg.org, pg 216

Cobb, Kiara, Glitterati Inc, 630 Ninth Ave, Suite 603, New York, NY 10036 *Tel:* 212-362-9119 *Fax:* 646-607-4433 *E-mail:* info@glitteratiincorporated.com *Web Site:* glitteratiincorporated.com, pg 93

Cobb, Michele, The Audies®, 333 Hudson St, Suite 503, New York, NY 10013 *Tel:* 646-688-3044 *E-mail:* audies@audiopub.org; info@audiopub.org *Web Site:* www.audiopub.org/members/audies, pg 629

Cobban, Helena, Just World Books LLC, PO Box 5484, Charlottesville, VA 22905 *Toll Free Tel:* 888-506-3769 *E-mail:* sales@justworldbooks.com *Web Site:* justworldbooks.com, pg 124

Cobra, Alison, University of Calgary Press, 2500 University Dr NW, Calgary, AB T2N 1N4, Canada *Tel:* 403-220-7578 *Fax:* 403-282-0085 *E-mail:* ucpress@ucalgary.ca *Web Site:* press.ucalgary.ca, pg 474

Coburn, Tristram, Tilbury House Publishers, 12 Starr St, Thomaston, ME 04861 *Tel:* 207-582-1899 *Toll Free Tel:* 800-582-1899 (orders) *Fax:* 207-582-8227 *E-mail:* tilbury@tilburyhouse.com *Web Site:* www.tilburyhouse.com, pg 232

Cochran, Angela, American Society of Civil Engineers (ASCE), 1801 Alexander Bell Dr, Reston, VA 20191-4400 *Tel:* 703-295-6300 *Toll Free Tel:* 800-548-2723 *Fax:* 703-295-6278 *E-mail:* ascelibrary@asce.org *Web Site:* www.asce.org, pg 15

Cochran, Heather, Television Academy, 5220 Lankershim Blvd, North Hollywood, CA 91601-3109 *Tel:* 818-754-2800 *Fax:* 818-761-2827 *Web Site:* www.emmys.com, pg 579

Cochran, Marnie, Random House Publishing Group, 1745 Broadway, New York, NY 10019 *Toll Free Tel:* 800-200-3552 *Web Site:* atrandom.com, pg 195

Cochran, Nina, Frances Goldin Literary Agency, Inc, 214 W 29 St, Suite 410, New York, NY 10001 *Tel:* 212-777-0047 *Fax:* 212-228-1660 *E-mail:* agency@goldinlit.com *Web Site:* www.goldinlit.com, pg 519

Cochran, Terry, Sunbelt Publications Inc, 1250 Fayette St, El Cajon, CA 92020-1511 *Tel:* 619-258-4911 *Toll Free Tel:* 800-626-6579 (cust serv) *Fax:* 619-258-4916 *E-mail:* service@sunbeltpub.com; info@sunbeltpub.com *Web Site:* www.sunbeltbooks.com, pg 225

Cochrane, Kristin, Doubleday Canada, 320 Front St W, Suite 1400, Toronto, ON M5V 3B6, Canada *Tel:* 416-364-4449 *Fax:* 416-598-7764 *Web Site:* www.penguinrandomhouse.ca, pg 452

Cochrane, Kristin, Knopf Canada, 320 Front St W, Suite 1400, Toronto, ON M5V 3B6, Canada *Tel:* 416-364-4449 *Toll Free Tel:* 888-523-9292 *Fax:* 416-598-7764 *Web Site:* www.penguinrandomhouse.ca, pg 462

Cochrane, Kristin, Penguin Random House Canada, 320 Front St W, Suite 1400, Toronto, ON M5V 3B6, Canada *Tel:* 416-364-4449 *Toll Free Tel:* 888-523-9292 (cust serv) *Fax:* 416-598-7764 *Web Site:* www.penguinrandomhouse.ca, pg 467

Cochrane, Kristin, Seal Books, 320 Front St W, Suite 1400, Toronto, ON M5V 3B6, Canada *Tel:* 416-364-4449 *Toll Free Tel:* 888-523-9292 (order desk) *Fax:* 416-598-7764 *Web Site:* www.penguinrandomhouse.ca, pg 470

Cocks, Catherine, University of Washington Press, 4333 Brooklyn Ave NE, Seattle, WA 98105-9570 *Tel:* 206-543-4050 *Toll Free Tel:* 800-537-5487 (orders) *Fax:* 206-543-3932; 410-516-6998 (orders) *E-mail:* uwapress@uw.edu *Web Site:* www.washington.edu/uwpress, pg 246

Cocks, Pamela, Tudor Publishers Inc, 3109 Shady Lawn Dr, Greensboro, NC 27408 *Tel:* 336-288-5395 *E-mail:* tudorpublishers@triad.rr.com, pg 236

Coe, Karen, United States Holocaust Memorial Museum, 100 Raoul Wallenberg Place SW, Washington, DC 20024-2126 *Tel:* 202-314-7837; 202-488-6144 (orders) *Toll Free Tel:* 800-259-9998 (orders) *Fax:* 202-479-9726; 202-488-0438 (orders) *E-mail:* cahs_publications@ushmm.org *Web Site:* www.ushmm.org, pg 239

Coffey, Darla Spence PhD, CSWE Press, 1701 Duke St, Suite 200, Alexandria, VA 22314-3457 *Tel:* 703-683-8080 *Fax:* 703-683-8493 *E-mail:* publications@cswe.org; info@cswe.org *Web Site:* www.cswe.org, pg 66

Coffin, Christina, Yale University Press, 302 Temple St, New Haven, CT 06511-8909 *Tel:* 203-432-0960; 203-432-0966 (sales); 401-531-2800 (cust serv) *Toll Free Tel:* 800-405-1619 (cust serv) *Fax:* 203-432-0948; 203-432-8485 (sales); 401-531-2801 (cust serv) *Toll Free Fax:* 800-406-9145 (cust serv) *E-mail:* sales.press@yale.edu (sales); customer.care@triliteral.org (cust serv) *Web Site:* www.yalebooks.com; yalepress.yale.edu/yupbooks, pg 261

Coglianese, Diana, Alfred A Knopf/Everyman's Library, c/o Penguin Random House Inc, 1745 Broadway, New York, NY 10019 *Tel:* 212-751-2600 *Toll Free Tel:* 800-638-6460 *Fax:* 212-572-2593 *Web Site:* www.knopfdoubleday.com, pg 127

Cohan, Darcy, HarperCollins General Books Group, 195 Broadway, New York, NY 10007 *Tel:* 212-207-7000 *Web Site:* www.harpercollins.com, pg 101

Cohan, Darcy, Insight Editions, 800 "A" St, San Rafael, CA 94901 *Tel:* 415-526-1370 *Toll Free Tel:* 800-809-3792 *Toll Free Fax:* 866-509-0515 *E-mail:* info@insighteditions.com *Web Site:* www.insighteditions.com, pg 117

Cohen, Adam, Tom Howard/John H Reid Fiction & Essay Contest, 351 Pleasant St, PMB 222, Northampton, MA 01060-3961 *Tel:* 413-320-1847 *Toll Free Tel:* 866-WINWRIT (946-9748) *Fax:* 413-280-0539 *Web Site:* www.winningwriters.com, pg 653

Cohen, Adam, Tom Howard/Margaret Reid Poetry Contest, 351 Pleasant St, PMB 222, Northampton, MA 01060-3961 *Tel:* 413-320-1847 *Toll Free Tel:* 866-WINWRIT (946-9748) *Fax:* 413-280-0539 *Web Site:* www.winningwriters.com, pg 653

Cohen, Adam, North Street Book Prize, 351 Pleasant St, PMB 222, Northampton, MA 01060-3961 *Tel:* 413-320-1847 *Toll Free Tel:* 866-WINWRIT (946-9748) *Fax:* 413-280-0539 *Web Site:* www.winningwriters.com, pg 674

Cohen, Adam, Wergle Flomp Humor Poetry Contest, 351 Pleasant St, PMB 222, Northampton, MA 01060-3961 *Tel:* 413-320-1847 *Toll Free Tel:* 866-WINWRIT (946-9748) *Fax:* 413-280-0539 *Web Site:* www.winningwriters.com, pg 696

Cohen, Allison, The Gersh Agency (TGA), 41 Madison Ave, 33rd fl, New York, NY 10010 *Tel:* 212-997-1818 *Web Site:* gershbooks.com, pg 518

Cohen, Barbara, Oxford University Press USA, 198 Madison Ave, New York, NY 10016 *Tel:* 212-726-6000 *Toll Free Tel:* 800-451-7556 (orders); 800-445-9714 (cust serv) *Fax:* 919-677-1303 *E-mail:* custserv.us@oup.com *Web Site:* www.oup.com/us, pg 171

Cohen, Brett, Quirk Books, 215 Church St, Philadelphia, PA 19106 *Tel:* 215-627-3581 *Fax:* 215-627-5220 *E-mail:* general@quirkbooks.com *Web Site:* www.quirkbooks.com, pg 193

Cohen, Carmela, Barricade Books Inc, 2037 LeMoine Ave, Fort Lee, NJ 07024 *Tel:* 201-944-7600 *E-mail:* customerservice@barricadebooks.com *Web Site:* www.barricadebooks.com, pg 29

Cohen, Christine M, Virginia Kidd Agency Inc, 538 E Harford St, PO Box 278, Milford, PA 18337 *Tel:* 570-296-6205 *Web Site:* vk-agency.com, pg 524

Cohen, Craig, powerHouse Books, 37 Main St, Brooklyn, NY 11201 *Tel:* 212-604-9074 *E-mail:* info@powerhousebooks.com *Web Site:* www.powerhousebooks.com, pg 186

Cohen, Emily-Jane, Stanford University Press, 425 Broadway St, Redwood City, CA 94063-3126 *Tel:* 650-723-9434 *Fax:* 650-725-3457 *E-mail:* info@www.sup.org; publicity@www.sup.org *Web Site:* www.sup.org, pg 220

Cohen, Herbert J, Platinum Press LLC, 281 Hicks St, Brooklyn, NY 11201 *Tel:* 718-875-4092 *Fax:* 718-875-5065, pg 183

Cohen, Jeremy, Jerome Fellowship, 2301 Franklin Ave E, Minneapolis, MN 55406-1099 *Tel:* 612-332-7481 *Fax:* 612-332-6037 *E-mail:* info@pwcenter.org *Web Site:* www.pwcenter.org, pg 657

Cohen, Jeremy, Many Voices Fellowships, 2301 Franklin Ave E, Minneapolis, MN 55406-1099 *Tel:* 612-332-7481 *Fax:* 612-332-6037 *E-mail:* info@pwcenter.org *Web Site:* www.pwcenter.org, pg 665

Cohen, Jeremy, McKnight Fellowships in Playwriting, 2301 Franklin Ave E, Minneapolis, MN 55406-1099 *Tel:* 612-332-7481 *Fax:* 612-332-6037 *E-mail:* info@pwcenter.org *Web Site:* www.pwcenter.org, pg 667

Cohen, Jeremy, McKnight National Residency & Commission, 2301 Franklin Ave E, Minneapolis, MN 55406-1099 *Tel:* 612-332-7481 *Fax:* 612-332-6037 *E-mail:* info@pwcenter.org *Web Site:* www.pwcenter.org, pg 667

Cohen, Jonathan, Kensington Publishing Corp, 119 W 40 St, New York, NY 10018 *Tel:* 212-407-1500 *Toll Free Tel:* 800-221-2647 *Fax:* 212-935-0699 *Web Site:* www.kensingtonbooks.com, pg 125

Cohen, Judith, Cascade Pass Inc, 4223 Glencoe Ave, Suite C-105, Marina del Rey, CA 90292-8801 *Tel:* 310-305-0210 *Toll Free Tel:* 888-837-0704 *Fax:* 310-305-7850 *Web Site:* www.cascadepass.com, pg 49

Cohen, Katia Segre, GeoLytics Inc, 3322 Rte 22, Suite 806, Branchburg, NJ 08876 *Tel:* 908-707-1505 *Toll Free Tel:* 800-577-6717 *Fax:* 908-707-1595 *E-mail:* support@geolytics.com; questions@geolytics.com *Web Site:* www.geolytics.com, pg 91

Cohen, Kelly, The Optical Society (OSA), 2010 Massachusetts Ave NW, Washington, DC 20036-1023 *Tel:* 202-223-8130 *Toll Free Tel:* 800-766-4672 *E-mail:* custserv@osa.org *Web Site:* www.osa.org, pg 169

Cohen, Lord, Alan Wofsy Fine Arts, 1109 Geary Blvd, San Francisco, CA 94109 *Tel:* 415-292-6500 *Toll Free Tel:* 800-660-6403 *Fax:* 415-292-6594 (off & cust serv); 510-251-1840 (acctg) *E-mail:* order@art-books.com (orders); editeur@earthlink.net (edit); beauxarts@earthlink.net (cust serv) *Web Site:* www.art-books.com, pg 258

Cohen, Louis, Mason Crest Publishers, 450 Parkway Dr, Suite D, Broomall, PA 19008 *Tel:* 610-543-6200 *Toll Free Tel:* 866-MCP-BOOK (627-2665) *Fax:* 610-543-3878 *Web Site:* www.masoncrest.com, pg 143

Cohen, M, Players Press Inc, PO Box 1132, Studio City, CA 91614-0132 *Tel:* 818-789-4980 *E-mail:* playerspress@att.net, pg 184

Cohen, Mark E, CDL Press, PO Box 34454, Bethesda, MD 20827 *Tel:* 301-762-2066 *Fax:* 253-484-5542 *E-mail:* cdlpress@erols.com *Web Site:* www.cdlpress.com, pg 50

Cohen, Meagan, Trident Media Group LLC, 41 Madison Ave, 36th fl, New York, NY 10010 *Tel:* 212-333-1511 *E-mail:* info@tridentmediagroup.com; press@tridentmediagroup.com *Web Site:* www.tridentmediagroup.com, pg 540

Cohen, Michael R, Puddingstone Literary, Authors' Agents, 11 Mabro Dr, Denville, NJ 07834-9607 *Tel:* 973-366-3622, pg 532

Cohen, Mo, Gingko Press Inc, 1321 Fifth St, Berkeley, CA 94710 *Tel:* 510-898-1195 *Fax:* 510-898-1196 *E-mail:* books@gingkopress.com *Web Site:* www.gingkopress.com, pg 92

Cohen, Mort, Houghton Mifflin Harcourt Assessments, 900 Pierce Place, Suite 900, Itasca, IL 60143 *Tel:* 630-467-7000 *Toll Free Tel:* 800-323-9540 *Fax:* 630-467-7192 (cust serv) *E-mail:* rpc_customer_service@hmhpub.com (cust serv) *Web Site:* www.riversidepublishing.com, pg 111

Cohen, Nan, Napa Valley Writers' Conference, 1088 College Ave, St Helena, CA 94574 *Tel:* 707-967-2900 (ext 4) *Fax:* 707-967-2909 *E-mail:* info@napawritersconference.org; media@napawritersconference.org; fiction@napawritersconference.org; poetry@napawritersconference.org *Web Site:* www.napawritersconference.org, pg 613

Cohen, Paul, Monkfish Book Publishing Co, 22 E Market St, Suite 304, Rhinebeck, NY 12572 *Tel:* 845-876-4861 *E-mail:* monkfish@monkfishpublishing.com *Web Site:* www.monkfishpublishing.com, pg 153

Cohen, Peter, McGraw-Hill Education, 2 Penn Plaza, New York, NY 10121-2298 *Tel:* 212-904-2000 *E-mail:* customer.service@mheducation.com; international_cs@mheducation.com *Web Site:* www.mheducation.com, pg 145

Cohen, Peter, McGraw-Hill Higher Education, 1333 Burr Ridge Pkwy, Burr Ridge, IL 60527 *Tel:* 630-789-4000 *Toll Free Tel:* 800-338-3987 (cust serv) *Fax:* 614-755-5645 (cust serv) *Web Site:* www.mhhe.com, pg 146

Cohen, Peter, McGraw-Hill School Education Group, 8787 Orion Place, Columbus, OH 43240 *Tel:* 614-430-4000 *Toll Free Tel:* 800-848-1567 *Web Site:* www.mheducation.com, pg 146

Cohen, Samantha, Simon & Schuster, Inc, 1230 Avenue of the Americas, New York, NY 10020 *Tel:* 212-698-7000 *Fax:* 212-698-7007 *E-mail:* firstname.lastname@simonandschuster.com *Web Site:* www.simonandschuster.com, pg 213

Cohen, Sarah, Anne Edelstein Literary Agency LLC, 404 Riverside Dr, New York, NY 10025 *Tel:* 212-414-4923 *E-mail:* info@aeliterary.com; rights@aeliterary.com *Web Site:* www.aeliterary.com, pg 515

Cohen, Steve, St Martin's Press, LLC, 175 Fifth Ave, New York, NY 10010 *Tel:* 646-307-5151 *Web Site:* us.macmillan.com/smp, pg 204

Cohen, Susan, Writers House, 21 W 26 St, New York, NY 10010 *Tel:* 212-685-2400 *Fax:* 212-685-1781 *Web Site:* www.writershouse.com, pg 542

Cohen, Susan Lee, Riverside Literary Agency, 41 Simon Keets Rd, Leyden, MA 01337 *Tel:* 413-772-0067 *Fax:* 413-772-0969 *E-mail:* rivlit@sover.net *Web Site:* www.riversideliteraryagency.com, pg 533

Cohen, Susan Perlman, PearlCo Literary Agency, LLC, 6596 Heronswood Cove, Memphis, TN 38119 *Tel:* 901-754-5276, pg 531

Cohn, Anthony G, AAAI Press, 2275 E Bayshore Rd, Suite 160, Palo Alto, CA 94303 *Tel:* 650-328-3123 *Fax:* 650-321-4457 *E-mail:* publications17@aaai.org *Web Site:* www.aaaipress.org; www.aaai.org, pg 1

Colangelo, Brook, Houghton Mifflin Harcourt, 125 High St, Boston, MA 02110 *Tel:* 617-351-5000 *Toll Free Tel:* 855-969-4642; 800-225-5425 (K-12 educ materials); 800-323-9540 (assessment materials); 877-219-1537 (SkillsTutor); 888-242-6747 (Innovation in Educ Group); 800-225-3362 (Trade & Ref Div) *Toll Free Fax:* 800-269-5232 *E-mail:* myhmhco@hmhco.com *Web Site:* www.hmhco.com, pg 110

Colarusso, Paul, Harry N Abrams Inc, 195 Broadway, 9th fl, New York, NY 10007 *Tel:* 212-206-7715 *Toll Free Tel:* 800-345-1359 *Fax:* 212-519-1210 *E-mail:* abrams@abramsbooks.com *Web Site:* www.abramsbooks.com, pg 3

Colbeck, J Richard, Robert J Pickering Award for Playwriting Excellence, 89 Division, Coldwater, MI 49036 *Tel:* 517-279-7963 *Fax:* 517-279-8095 *E-mail:* j7eden@aol.com *Web Site:* www.branchcct.org, pg 679

Colbeck, Jennifer, Robert J Pickering Award for Playwriting Excellence, 89 Division, Coldwater, MI 49036 *Tel:* 517-279-7963 *Fax:* 517-279-8095 *E-mail:* j7eden@aol.com *Web Site:* www.branchcct.org, pg 679

Colbert, Jaimee Wriston, Binghamton University Creative Writing Program, c/o Dept of English, PO Box 6000, Binghamton, NY 13902-6000 *Tel:* 607-777-2168 *Fax:* 607-777-2408 *E-mail:* cwpro@binghamton.edu *Web Site:* english.binghamton.edu/cwpro, pg 619

Colburn, Loren, AFCP's Awards, 135 Old Cove Rd, Suite 210, Liverpool, NY 13090 *Toll Free Tel:* 877-203-2327 *Fax:* 781-459-7770 *E-mail:* afcp@afcp.org *Web Site:* www.afcp.org, pg 625

Colburn, Loren, Association of Free Community Papers (AFCP), 135 Old Cove Rd, Suite 210, Liverpool, NY 13090 *Toll Free Tel:* 877-203-2327 *Fax:* 781-459-7770 *E-mail:* afcp@afcp.org *Web Site:* www.afcp.org, pg 559

Colby, Clifford, Peachpit Press, 1301 Sansome St, San Francisco, CA 94111 *Toll Free Tel:* 800-283-9444 *E-mail:* info@peachpit.com; ask@peachpit.com *Web Site:* www.peachpit.com, pg 175

Colby, John T Jr, Brick Tower Press, Manhanset House, PO Box 342, Shelter Island Heights, NY 11965-0342 *Tel:* 212-427-7139 *E-mail:* bricktower@aol.com *Web Site:* www.bricktowerpress.com, pg 43

Colding, Robert, Information Today, Inc, 143 Old Marlton Pike, Medford, NJ 08055-8750 *Tel:* 609-654-6266 *Toll Free Tel:* 800-300-9868 (cust serv) *Fax:* 609-654-4309 *E-mail:* custserv@infotoday.com *Web Site:* www.infotoday.com, pg 116

Colding, Robert, Plexus Publishing, Inc, 143 Old Marlton Pike, Medford, NJ 08055 *Tel:* 609-654-6500 *Fax:* 609-654-4309 *E-mail:* info@plexuspublishing.com *Web Site:* www.plexuspublishing.com, pg 184

Cole, Becky, Plume, 375 Hudson St, New York, NY 10014 *Tel:* 212-366-2000 *Fax:* 212-243-6002 *Web Site:* www.penguin.com/publishers/plume, pg 184

Cole, David, Bay Tree Publishing LLC, 1400 Pinnacle Ct, Suite 406, Point Richmond, CA 94801 *Tel:* 510-236-1475 *Toll Free Fax:* 866-552-7329 *Web Site:* www.baytreepublish.com, pg 30

Cole, David, Empire Publishing Service, PO Box 1344, Studio City, CA 91614-0344 *Tel:* 818-784-8918 *E-mail:* empirepubsvc@att.net, pg 78

Cole, David, Players Press Inc, PO Box 1132, Studio City, CA 91614-0132 *Tel:* 818-789-4980 *E-mail:* playerspress@att.net, pg 184

Cole, John Y, The Center for the Book in the Library of Congress, The Library of Congress, 101 Independence Ave SE, Washington, DC 20540-4920 *Tel:* 202-707-5221 *Fax:* 202-707-0269 *E-mail:* cfbook@loc.gov *Web Site:* www.read.gov; www.read.gov/cfb, pg 563

Cole, Maureen, HarperCollins General Books Group, 195 Broadway, New York, NY 10007 *Tel:* 212-207-7000 *Web Site:* www.harpercollins.com, pg 101

Cole, Sue, Highlights for Children, 1800 Watermark Dr, Columbus, OH 43215 *Tel:* 614-486-0631 *Toll Free Tel:* 800-962-3661 (Highlights Club cust serv); 800-255-9517 (Highlights Magazine cust serv) *Web Site:* www.highlights.com; www.facebook.com/HighlightsforChildren, pg 107

Coleburn, Carolyn, Viking, 375 Hudson St, New York, NY 10014 *Tel:* 212-366-2000 *Fax:* 212-243-6002 *Web Site:* www.penguin.com/publishers/vikingbooks, pg 250

Coleman, Ayanna, Tanglewood Publishing, 1060 N Capitol Ave, Suite E-395, Indianapolis, IN 46204 *Tel:* 812-877-9488 *Toll Free Tel:* 800-788-3123 (orders) *E-mail:* info@tanglewoodbooks.com; orders@tanglewoodbooks.com *Web Site:* www.tanglewoodbooks.com, pg 227

Coleman, David, The College Board, 250 Vesey St, New York, NY 10281 *Tel:* 212-713-8000 *Web Site:* www.collegeboard.com, pg 58

Coleman, Jason, The University of Virginia Press, PO Box 400318, Charlottesville, VA 22904-4318 *Tel:* 434-924-3468 (cust serv); 434-924-3469 (cust serv) *Toll Free Tel:* 800-831-3406 (orders) *Fax:* 434-982-2655 *Toll Free Fax:* 877-288-6400 *E-mail:* vapress@virginia.edu *Web Site:* www.upress.virginia.edu, pg 245

Coleman, Patrick, The Clarion Science Fiction & Fantasy Writers' Workshop, Arthur C Clarke Ctr for Human Imagination, UC San Diego, 9500 Gilman Dr, MC0445, La Jolla, CA 92093-0445 *Tel:* 858-534-2115 *E-mail:* clarion@ucsd.edu *Web Site:* clarion.ucsd.edu; imagination.ucsd.edu, pg 610

Coleman, Robin W, The Johns Hopkins University Press, 2715 N Charles St, Baltimore, MD 21218-4363 *Tel:* 410-516-6900; 410-516-6987 (journal orders outside US & CN) *Toll Free Tel:* 800-537-5487 (book orders & cust serv); 800-548-1784 (journal orders) *Fax:* 410-516-6968; 410-516-3866 (journal orders) *E-mail:* hfscustserv@press.jhu.edu (cust serv); jrnlcirc@press.jhu.edu (journal orders) *Web Site:* www.press.jhu.edu; muse.jhu.edu, pg 122

Colgan, Mary, Highlights for Children, 1800 Watermark Dr, Columbus, OH 43215 *Tel:* 614-486-0631 *Toll Free Tel:* 800-962-3661 (Highlights Club cust serv); 800-255-9517 (Highlights Magazine cust serv) *Web Site:* www.highlights.com; www.facebook.com/HighlightsforChildren, pg 107

Colgan, Tom, Berkley Publishing Group, 375 Hudson St, New York, NY 10014 *Tel:* 212-366-2000 *Fax:* 212-366-2385 *Web Site:* www.penguin.com, pg 33

Collette, Ann, Rees Literary Agency, 14 Beacon St, Suite 710, Boston, MA 02108 *Tel:* 617-227-9014 *Fax:* 617-227-8762 *Web Site:* www.reesagency.com, pg 532

Collicelli, Gilles, Editions Mediaspaul, 3965, blvd Henri-Bourassa E, Montreal, QC H1H 1L1, Canada *Tel:* 514-322-7341 *Fax:* 514-322-4281 *E-mail:* editeur@mediaspaul.ca *Web Site:* mediaspaul.ca, pg 455

Collier, Diana G, Clarity Press Inc, 2625 Piedmont Rd NE, Suite 56, Atlanta, GA 30324 *Toll Free Tel:* 877-613-1495 (edit) *Toll Free Fax:* 877-613-7868 *E-mail:* claritypress@usa.net (foreign rts & perms) *Web Site:* www.claritypress.com, pg 56

Collier, Dianna, Collier Associates, 37 Marina Gardens Dr, Palm Beach Gardens, FL 33410 *Tel:* 561-514-6548 *E-mail:* dmccabooks@gmail.com, pg 512

Collier, Michael, Fellowship, Tuition Scholarship & Work Study Programs for Writers, Middlebury College, 204 College St, Middlebury, VT 05753 *Tel:* 802-443-5286 *Fax:* 802-443-2087 *E-mail:* blwc@middlebury.edu *Web Site:* www.middlebury.edu/blwc, pg 646

Collier, Theresa, Artisan Books, 225 Varick St, New York, NY 10014-4381 *Tel:* 212-254-5900 *Toll Free Tel:* 800-722-7202 *Fax:* 212-677-6692 *E-mail:* artisaninfo@artisanbooks.com *Web Site:* www.workman.com/artisanbooks, pg 22

Collignon, Kimberly, Data Trace Publishing Co (DTP), 110 West Rd, Suite 227, Towson, MD 21204-2316 *Tel:* 410-494-4994 *Toll Free Tel:* 800-342-0454 (orders only) *Fax:* 410-494-0515 *E-mail:* info@datatrace.com; salesandmarketing@datatrace.com; editorial@datatrace.com; info@datatrace.com *Web Site:* www.datatrace.com, pg 67

Collin, Frances, Frances Collin Literary Agency, PO Box 33, Wayne, PA 19087 *Tel:* 610-254-0555 *E-mail:* queries@francescollin.com *Web Site:* www.francescollin.com, pg 512

Collins, Allison Janse, Health Communications Inc, 3201 SW 15 St, Deerfield Beach, FL 33442 *Tel:* 954-360-0909 *Toll Free Tel:* 800-851-9100; 800-441-5569 (cust serv & orders) *Fax:* 954-360-0034 *Toll Free Fax:* 800-424-7652 (cust serv & orders) *E-mail:* customerservice2@hcibooks.com *Web Site:* www.hcibooks.com, pg 104

Collins, Anne, Knopf Canada, 320 Front St W, Suite 1400, Toronto, ON M5V 3B6, Canada *Tel:* 416-364-4449 *Toll Free Tel:* 888-523-9292 *Fax:* 416-598-7764 *Web Site:* www.penguinrandomhouse.ca, pg 462

Collins, Beth, Beacon Press, 24 Farnsworth St, Boston, MA 02210-1409 *Tel:* 617-742-2110 *Fax:* 617-723-3097; 617-742-2290 *Web Site:* www.beacon.org, pg 31

Collins, Christy, White Cloud Press, 300 E Hersey St, Suite 11, Ashland, OR 97520 *Tel:* 541-488-6415 *Fax:* 541-482-7708 *E-mail:* info@whitecloudpress.com *Web Site:* www.whitecloudpress.com, pg 255

Collins, Donna, Individual Excellence Awards, 30 E Broad St, 33rd fl, Columbus, OH 43215 *Tel:* 614-466-2613 *Fax:* 614-466-4494 *Web Site:* www.oac.state.oh.us, pg 655

Collins, JoAnn, International Transactions Inc, 28 Alope Way, Gila, NM 88038 *Tel:* 845-373-9696 *Fax:* 480-393-5162 *E-mail:* info@intltrans.com *Web Site:* www.intltrans.com, pg 522

Collins, Kate, Random House Publishing Group, 1745 Broadway, New York, NY 10019 *Toll Free Tel:* 800-200-3552 *Web Site:* atrandom.com, pg 195

Collins, Ken, Triumph Learning LLC, 136 Madison Ave, 7th fl, New York, NY 10016 *Tel:* 212-652-0200 *Toll Free Tel:* 800-338-6519 (cust serv) *Toll Free Fax:* 866-805-5723 *E-mail:* info@triumphlearning.com; customerservice@triumphlearning.com *Web Site:* www.triumphlearning.com, pg 235

Collins, Martha, Oberlin College Press, 50 N Professor St, Oberlin, OH 44074-1091 *Tel:* 440-775-8408 *Fax:* 440-775-8124 *E-mail:* oc.press@oberlin.edu *Web Site:* www.oberlin.edu/ocpress, pg 166

Collins, Nate, Samuel French Inc, 235 Park Ave S, 5th fl, New York, NY 10003 *Tel:* 212-206-8990 *Toll Free Tel:* 866-598-8449 *Fax:* 212-206-1429 *E-mail:* info@samuelfrench.com; publications@samuelfrench.com *Web Site:* www.samuelfrench.com, pg 88

Collins, Nate, Samuel French Inc, 235 Park Ave S, 5th fl, New York, NY 10003 *Tel:* 212-206-8990 *Toll Free Tel:* 866-598-8449 *Fax:* 212-206-1429 *E-mail:* info@samuelfrench.com *Web Site:* www.samuelfrench.com, pg 518

Collins, Teresa Wells, The University Press of Kentucky, 663 S Limestone St, Lexington, KY 40508-4008 *Tel:* 859-257-8400 *Fax:* 859-257-8481 *Web Site:* www.kentuckypress.com, pg 247

Collom, Ashley, DeFiore and Company Literary Management Inc, 47 E 19 St, 3rd fl, New York, NY 10003 *Tel:* 212-925-7744 *Fax:* 212-925-9803 *E-mail:* info@defliterary.com; submissions@defliterary.com *Web Site:* www.defliterary.com, pg 513

Colom, Wilbur O, Genesis Press Inc, PO Box 101, Columbus, MS 39701 *Toll Free Tel:* 888-463-4461 (orders only) *E-mail:* customerservice@genesis-press.com *Web Site:* www.genesis-press.com, pg 91

Columbus, Nadia, Nova Science Publishers Inc, 400 Oser Ave, Suite 1600, Hauppauge, NY 11788-3619 *Tel:* 631-231-7269 *Fax:* 631-231-8175 *E-mail:* main@novapublishers.com *Web Site:* www.novapublishers.com, pg 165

Colvin, Rod, Addicus Books Inc, PO Box 45327, Omaha, NE 68145 *Tel:* 402-330-7493 *Fax:* 402-330-1707 *E-mail:* info@addicusbooks.com; addicusbks@aol.com *Web Site:* www.addicusbooks.com, pg 4

Colvin, Theresa, Individual Artist Awards, 175 W Ostend St, Suite E, Baltimore, MD 21230 *Tel:* 410-767-6555 *Fax:* 410-333-1062 *E-mail:* msac@msac.org *Web Site:* www.msac.org, pg 655

Combs, Michele, Carpe Indexum, 1960 Deer Run Rd, LaFayette, NY 13084 *Tel:* 315-677-3030 *E-mail:* info@carpeindexum.com *Web Site:* www.carpeindexum.com, pg 490

Combs, Misty, Money Market Directories, 401 E Market St, Charlottesville, VA 22902 *Tel:* 434-977-1450 *Toll Free Tel:* 800-446-2810 *Fax:* 434-979-9962 *E-mail:* mmdsales@spcapitaliq.com *Web Site:* www.mmdwebaccess.com, pg 153

Comeau, Jennifer, University of Illinois Press, 1325 S Oak St, MC-566, Champaign, IL 61820-6903 *Tel:* 217-333-0950 *Fax:* 217-244-8082 *E-mail:* uipress@uillinois.edu; journals@uillinois.edu *Web Site:* www.press.uillinois.edu, pg 241

Comfort, Anna, Harbour Publishing Co Ltd, 4437 Rondeview Rd, Madeira Park, BC V0N 2H0, Canada *Tel:* 604-883-2730 *Toll Free Tel:* 800-667-2988 *Fax:* 604-883-9451 *E-mail:* info@harbourpublishing.com *Web Site:* www.harbourpublishing.com, pg 459

Commella, Victoria, HarperCollins General Books Group, 195 Broadway, New York, NY 10007 *Tel:* 212-207-7000 *Web Site:* www.harpercollins.com, pg 101

Compton, Lacy, Prufrock Press, PO Box 8813, Waco, TX 76714-8813 *Tel:* 254-756-3337 *Toll Free Tel:* 800-998-2208 *Fax:* 254-756-3339 *Toll Free Fax:* 800-240-0333 *E-mail:* info@prufrock.com *Web Site:* www.prufrock.com, pg 191

Comrie, Tim, YMAA Publication Center Inc, PO Box 480, Wolfeboro, NH 03894 *Tel:* 603-569-7988 *Toll Free Tel:* 800-669-8892 *Fax:* 603-569-1889 *E-mail:* info@ymaa.com *Web Site:* www.ymaa.com, pg 262

Comtois, Celine, La Courte Echelle, 4388, rue Saint-Denis, Suite 315, Montreal, QC H2J 2L1, Canada *Tel:* 514-312-6950 *E-mail:* info@courteechelle.com *Web Site:* courteechelle.groupecourteechelle.com, pg 451

Con, Catherine, Boston University Creative Writing Program, 236 Bay State Rd, Boston, MA 02215 *Tel:* 617-353-2510 *Fax:* 617-353-3653 *E-mail:* crwr@bu.edu *Web Site:* www.bu.edu/creativewriting, pg 619

Conant, Vic, Nightingale-Conant, Bldg 300, Suite 103, 1400 S Wolf Rd, Wheeling, IL 60090 *Tel:* 847-647-0306 *Toll Free Tel:* 800-557-1660 (sales); 800-560-6081 (cust serv) *Web Site:* www.nightingale.com, pg 162

Conary, Lori, Shubert Fendrich Memorial Playwriting Contest, PO Box 4267, Englewood, CO 80155-4267 *Tel:* 303-779-4035 *Toll Free Tel:* 800-333-7262 *Fax:* 303-779-4315 *Web Site:* www.pioneerdrama.com/playwrights/contest.asp, pg 646

Conaway, Dan, Writers House, 21 W 26 St, New York, NY 10010 *Tel:* 212-685-2400 *Fax:* 212-685-1781 *Web Site:* www.writershouse.com, pg 542

Concepcion, Cristina, Don Congdon Associates Inc, 110 William St, Suite 2202, New York, NY 10038-3914 *Tel:* 212-645-1229 *Fax:* 212-727-2688 *E-mail:* dca@doncongdon.com *Web Site:* www.doncongdon.com, pg 512

Conde, Sidney, St Martin's Press, LLC, 175 Fifth Ave, New York, NY 10010 *Tel:* 646-307-5151 *Web Site:* us.macmillan.com/smp, pg 204

Condit, Carl Daniel, Sunstone Press, PO Box 2321, Santa Fe, NM 87504-2321 *Tel:* 505-988-4418 *Toll Free Tel:* 800-243-5644 *Fax:* 505-988-1025 (orders only) *Web Site:* www.sunstonepress.com, pg 225

Condon, Alicia, Kensington Publishing Corp, 119 W 40 St, New York, NY 10018 *Tel:* 212-407-1500 *Toll Free Tel:* 800-221-2647 *Fax:* 212-935-0699 *Web Site:* www.kensingtonbooks.com, pg 125

Condon, Phil, University of Montana, Environmental Writing Institute, Environmental Studies, University of Montana, Missoula, MT 59812 *Tel:* 406-243-2904 *Fax:* 406-243-6090 *Web Site:* www.umt.edu/ewi, pg 623

Condron, Dr Barbara, SOM Publishing, 163 Moon Valley Rd, Windyville, MO 65783 *Tel:* 417-345-8411 *Fax:* 417-345-6668 *E-mail:* som@som.org; dreams@dreamschool.org *Web Site:* www.som.org; www.dreamschool.org, pg 217

Congdon, Michael, Don Congdon Associates Inc, 110 William St, Suite 2202, New York, NY 10038-3914 *Tel:* 212-645-1229 *Fax:* 212-727-2688 *E-mail:* dca@doncongdon.com *Web Site:* www.doncongdon.com, pg 512

Congleton, Robert, Pacific Press Publishing Association, 1350 N Kings Rd, Nampa, ID 83687-3193 *Tel:* 208-465-2500 *Toll Free Tel:* 800-447-7377 *Fax:* 208-465-2531 *Web Site:* www.pacificpress.com, pg 172

Conis, Kym, Foil & Specialty Effects Association (FSEA), 2150 SW Westport Dr, Suite 101, Topeka, KS 66614 *Tel:* 785-271-5816 *Fax:* 785-271-6404 *E-mail:* info@fsea.com; fseamail@fsea.com *Web Site:* www.fsea.com, pg 566

Conley, Tricia, The Penguin Press, 375 Hudson St, New York, NY 10014 *Web Site:* thepenguinpress.com, pg 178

Conley, Tricia, Portfolio, 375 Hudson St, New York, NY 10014 *Web Site:* www.penguin.com/meet/publishers/portfolio, pg 186

Conley, Tricia, Viking, 375 Hudson St, New York, NY 10014 *Tel:* 212-366-2000 *Fax:* 212-243-6002 *Web Site:* www.penguin.com/publishers/vikingbooks, pg 250

Conlon, Julianne, Random House Children's Books, 1745 Broadway, 10th fl, New York, NY 10019 *Tel:* 212-782-9000 *Web Site:* www.randomhousekids.com, pg 194

Conlon, Michael, Red Wheel/Weiser/Conari, 65 Parker St, Suite 7, Newburyport, MA 01950 *Tel:* 978-465-0504 *Toll Free Tel:* 800-423-7087 (orders) *Fax:* 978-465-0243 *E-mail:* info@rwwbooks.com *Web Site:* www.redwheelweiser.com, pg 197

Connelly, Prof Claire PhD, Angels Editorial Services, 1630 Main St, Suite 41, Coventry, CT 06238 *Tel:* 860-742-5279 *E-mail:* angelsus@aol.com, pg 488

Conners, Peter, BOA Editions Ltd, 250 N Goodman St, Suite 306, Rochester, NY 14607 *Tel:* 585-546-3410 *Fax:* 585-546-3913 *E-mail:* contact@boaeditions.org *Web Site:* www.boaeditions.org, pg 39

Connolly, Carolyn, Simon & Schuster, Inc, 1230 Avenue of the Americas, New York, NY 10020 *Tel:* 212-698-7000 *Fax:* 212-698-7007 *E-mail:* firstname.lastname@simonandschuster.com *Web Site:* www.simonandschuster.com, pg 213

Connolly, Claudia, Pembroke Publishers Ltd, 538 Hood Rd, Markham, ON L3R 3K9, Canada *Tel:* 905-477-0650 *Toll Free Tel:* 800-997-9807 *Fax:* 905-477-3691 *Toll Free Fax:* 800-339-5568 *Web Site:* www.pembrokepublishers.com, pg 466

Connolly, John, Swedenborg Foundation, 320 N Church St, West Chester, PA 19380 *Tel:* 610-430-3222 *Toll Free Tel:* 800-355-3222 (cust serv) *Fax:* 610-430-7982 *E-mail:* info@swedenborg.com *Web Site:* www.swedenborg.com, pg 225

Connolly, John J EdD, Castle Connolly Medical Ltd, 42 W 24 St, 2nd fl, New York, NY 10010 *Tel:* 212-367-8400 *Fax:* 212-367-0964 *Web Site:* www.castleconnolly.com, pg 49

Connor, Heather, Berkley Publishing Group, 375 Hudson St, New York, NY 10014 *Tel:* 212-366-2000 *Fax:* 212-366-2385 *Web Site:* www.penguin.com, pg 33

Connors, Dan, Twenty-Third Publications, One Montauk Ave, Suite 200, New London, CT 06320 *Tel:* 860-437-3012 *Toll Free Tel:* 800-321-0411 (orders) *Toll Free Fax:* 800-572-0788 *E-mail:* resources@twentythirdpublications.com *Web Site:* www.twentythirdpublications.com, pg 237

Connors, Katie, Hachette Nashville, 12 Cadillac Dr, Suite 480, Brentwood, TN 37027 *Tel:* 615-221-0996 *Fax:* 615-221-0962 *Web Site:* www.hachettebookgroup.com, pg 98

Connors, Shannon, Perseus Books, 250 W 57 St, 15th fl, New York, NY 10107 *Tel:* 212-340-8100 *Toll Free Tel:* 800-343-4499 (cust serv) *Fax:* 212-340-8105 *Web Site:* www.perseusbooks.com, pg 181

Conover, Roger L, The MIT Press, One Rogers St, Cambridge, MA 02142 *Tel:* 617-253-5255 *Toll Free Tel:* 800-207-8354 (orders) *Fax:* 617-258-6779; 617-577-1545 (orders) *Web Site:* mitpress.mit.edu, pg 152

Conrad, Cecilia A, MacArthur Fellows Program, Office of Grants Management, 140 S Dearborn St, Chicago, IL 60603-5285 *Tel:* 312-726-8000 *Fax:* 312-920-6528 *E-mail:* 4answers@macfound.org *Web Site:* www.macfound.org/programs/fellows, pg 664

Conrad, Joanna, Texas Tech University Press, 1120 Main St, 2nd fl, Lubbock, TX 79401 *Tel:* 806-742-2982 *Toll Free Tel:* 800-832-4042 *Fax:* 806-742-2979 *E-mail:* ttup@ttu.edu *Web Site:* www.ttupress.org, pg 230

Conrad, Kathryn, The University of Arizona Press, 1510 E University Blvd, Tucson, AZ 85721 *Tel:* 520-621-1441 *Toll Free Tel:* 800-426-3797 (orders) *Fax:* 520-621-8899 *Toll Free Fax:* 800-426-3797 *E-mail:* uap@uapress.arizona.edu *Web Site:* www.uapress.arizona.edu, pg 240

Conroy, Nick, Atlantic Center for the Arts Artists-in-Residence Program, 1414 Art Center Ave, New Smyrna Beach, FL 32168 *Tel:* 386-427-6975 *Toll Free Tel:* 800-393-6975 *Fax:* 386-427-5669 *E-mail:* program@atlanticcenterforthearts.org *Web Site:* atlanticcenterforthearts.org, pg 609

Conroy, Sonsie Carbonara, Catalyst Communication Arts, 94 Chuparrosa Dr, San Luis Obispo, CA 93401 *Tel:* 805-235-2351 *Fax:* 805-543-7140 *Web Site:* www.sonsieconroy.com, pg 490

Contardi, Bill, Brandt & Hochman Literary Agents Inc, 1501 Broadway, Suite 2310, New York, NY 10036 *Tel:* 212-840-5760 *Fax:* 212-840-5776 *Web Site:* brandthochman.com, pg 509

Conte, Beth, Random House Children's Books, 1745 Broadway, 10th fl, New York, NY 10019 *Tel:* 212-782-9000 *Web Site:* www.randomhousekids.com, pg 194

Contreras, Raquel, Casa Bautista de Publicaciones, 7000 Alabama Ave, El Paso, TX 79904 *Tel:* 915-566-9656 *Toll Free Tel:* 800-755-5958 (cust serv & orders) *Fax:* 915-562-6502; 915-565-9008 (orders) *E-mail:* orders@editorialmh.org *Web Site:* www.editorialmh.org, pg 48

Converse-Willkomm, Anne, Rosemont College, Graduate Publg Prog, 1400 Montgomery Ave, Rosemont, PA 19010 *Tel:* 610-527-0200 (ext 2336) *Fax:* 610-526-2964 *Web Site:* www.rosemont.edu, pg 622

Conway, Mike, Chronicle Books LLC, 680 Second St, San Francisco, CA 94107 *Tel:* 415-537-4200 *Toll Free Tel:* 800-759-0190 (cust serv) *Fax:* 415-537-4460 *Toll Free Fax:* 800-858-7787 (orders); 800-286-9471 (cust serv) *E-mail:* frontdesk@chroniclebooks.com *Web Site:* www.chroniclebooks.com, pg 55

Cook, Amy PhD, Sourced Media Books, 15 Via Picato, San Clemente, CA 92673 *Tel:* 949-813-0182 *E-mail:* editor@sourcedmediabooks.com *Web Site:* sourcedmediabooks.com, pg 218

Cook, Bill, Soil Science Society of America, 5585 Guilford Rd, Madison, WI 53711-5801 *Tel:* 608-273-8080 *Web Site:* www.soils.org, pg 217

Cook, Charles, Kendall Hunt Publishing Co, 4050 Westmark Dr, Dubuque, IA 52002-2624 *Tel:* 563-589-1000 *Toll Free Tel:* 800-228-0810 (orders) *Fax:* 563-589-1046 *Toll Free Fax:* 800-772-9165 *E-mail:* orders@kendallhunt.com *Web Site:* www.kendallhunt.com, pg 125

Cook, Chris, University of California Press, 155 Grand Ave, Suite 400, Oakland, CA 94612-3758 *Tel:* 510-883-8232 *Fax:* 510-836-8910 *E-mail:* customerservice@ucpressjournals.com *Web Site:* www.ucpress.edu, pg 240

Cook, Dorothy M, W W Norton & Company Inc, 500 Fifth Ave, New York, NY 10110-0017 *Tel:* 212-354-5500 *Toll Free Tel:* 800-233-4830 (orders & cust serv) *Fax:* 212-869-0856 *Toll Free Fax:* 800-458-6515 *E-mail:* orders@wwnorton.com *Web Site:* books.wwnorton.com, pg 164

Cook, Katie, Piano Press, 1425 Ocean Ave, Suite 5, Del Mar, CA 92014 *Tel:* 619-884-1401 *Fax:* 858-755-1104 *E-mail:* pianopress@pianopress.com *Web Site:* www.pianopress.com, pg 182

Cook, Kelli, Math Solutions®, One Harbor Dr, Suite 101, Sausalito, CA 94965 *Tel:* 415-332-4181 *Toll Free Tel:* 800-868-9092 *Fax:* 415-331-1931 *Toll Free Fax:* 877-942-8837 *E-mail:* info@mathsolutions.com; orders@mathsolutions.com *Web Site:* www.mathsolutions.com, pg 144

Cook, Kim, Trafalgar Square Books, 388 Howe Hill Rd, North Pomfret, VT 05053 *Tel:* 802-457-1911 *Toll Free Tel:* 800-423-4525 *Fax:* 802-457-1913 *E-mail:* contact@trafalgarbooks.com *Web Site:* www.trafalgarbooks.com; www.horseandriderbooks.com, pg 234

Cook, Martha, Trafalgar Square Books, 388 Howe Hill Rd, North Pomfret, VT 05053 *Tel:* 802-457-1911 *Toll Free Tel:* 800-423-4525 *Fax:* 802-457-1913 *E-mail:* contact@trafalgarbooks.com *Web Site:* www.trafalgarbooks.com; www.horseandriderbooks.com, pg 234

Cook, Natalie, R Ross Annett Award for Children's Literature, 11759 Groat Rd, Edmonton, AB T5M 3K6, Canada *Tel:* 780-422-8174 *Toll Free Tel:* 800-665-5354 (AB only) *Fax:* 780-422-2663 (attn WGA) *E-mail:* mail@writersguild.ca *Web Site:* writersguild.ca, pg 627

Cook, Natalie, Georges Bugnet Award for Fiction, 11759 Groat Rd, Edmonton, AB T5M 3K6, Canada *Tel:* 780-422-8174 *Toll Free Tel:* 800-665-5354 (AB only) *Fax:* 780-422-2663 (attn WGA) *E-mail:* mail@writersguild.ca *Web Site:* writersguild.ca, pg 634

Cook, Natalie, The City of Calgary W O Mitchell Book Prize, 11759 Groat Rd, Edmonton, AB T5M 3K6, Canada *Tel:* 780-422-8174 *Toll Free Tel:* 800-665-5354 (AB only) *Fax:* 780-422-2663 (attn WGA) *E-mail:* mail@writersguild.ca *Web Site:* writersguild.ca, pg 637

Cook, Natalie, Wilfrid Eggleston Award for Nonfiction, 11759 Groat Rd, Edmonton, AB T5M 3K6, Canada *Tel:* 780-422-8174 *Toll Free Tel:* 800-665-5354 (AB only) *Fax:* 780-422-2663 (attn WGA) *E-mail:* mail@writersguild.ca *Web Site:* writersguild.ca, pg 644

Cook, Natalie, James H Gray Award for Short Nonfiction, 11759 Groat Rd, Edmonton, AB T5M 3K6, Canada *Tel:* 780-422-8174 *Toll Free Tel:* 800-665-5354 (AB only) *Fax:* 780-422-2663 (attn WGA) *E-mail:* mail@writersguild.ca *Web Site:* writersguild.ca, pg 650

Cook, Natalie, The Robert Kroetsch City of Edmonton Book Prize, 11759 Groat Rd, Edmonton, AB T5M 3K6, Canada *Tel:* 780-422-8174 *Toll Free Tel:* 800-665-5354 (AB only) *Fax:* 780-422-2663 (attn WGA) *E-mail:* mail@writersguild.ca *Web Site:* writersguild.ca, pg 659

Cook, Natalie, Howard O'Hagan Award for Short Story, 11759 Groat Rd, Edmonton, AB T5M 3K6, Canada *Tel:* 780-422-8174 *Toll Free Tel:* 800-665-5354 (AB only) *Fax:* 780-422-2663 (attn WGA) *E-mail:* mail@writersguild.ca *Web Site:* writersguild.ca, pg 675

Cook, Natalie, Gwen Pharis Ringwood Award for Drama, 11759 Groat Rd, Edmonton, AB T5M 3K6, Canada *Tel:* 780-422-8174 *Toll Free Tel:* 800-665-5354 (AB only) *Fax:* 780-422-2663 (attn WGA) *E-mail:* mail@writersguild.ca *Web Site:* writersguild.ca, pg 685

Cook, Natalie, Stephan G Stephansson Award for Poetry, 11759 Groat Rd, Edmonton, AB T5M 3K6, Canada *Tel:* 780-422-8174 *Toll Free Tel:* 800-665-5354 (AB only) *Fax:* 780-422-2663 (attn WGA) *E-mail:* mail@writersguild.ca *Web Site:* writersguild.ca, pg 692

Cook, Natalie, Jon Whyte Memorial Essay Prize, 11759 Groat Rd, Edmonton, AB T5M 3K6, Canada *Tel:* 780-422-8174 *Toll Free Tel:* 800-665-5354 (AB only) *Fax:* 780-422-2663 (attn WGA) *E-mail:* mail@writersguild.ca *Web Site:* writersguild.ca, pg 697

Cook, Natalie, Writers' Guild of Alberta, 11759 Groat Rd, Edmonton, AB T5M 3K6, Canada *Tel:* 780-422-8174 *Toll Free Tel:* 800-665-5354 (AB only) *Fax:* 780-422-2663 (attn WGA) *E-mail:* mail@writersguild.ca *Web Site:* writersguild.ca, pg 581

Cook, Tonya, Cornell University Press, Sage House, 512 E State St, Ithaca, NY 14850 *Tel:* 607-277-2338 *Fax:* 607-277-2374 *E-mail:* cupressinfo@cornell.edu; cupress-sales@cornell.edu *Web Site:* www.cornellpress.cornell.edu, pg 61

Cook, Tura Campanella, Jane Addams Children's Book Award, 777 United Nations Plaza, 6th fl, New York, NY 10017 *Tel:* 212-682-8830 *E-mail:* info@janeaddamspeace.org *Web Site:* www.janeaddamspeace.org, pg 625

Cook, W Richard, University of Alabama Press, 200 Hackberry Lane, 2nd fl, Tuscaloosa, AL 35487 *Tel:* 205-348-5180 *Fax:* 205-348-9201 *Web Site:* www.uapress.ua.edu, pg 239

Cooke, Janet, Doubleday/Nan A Talese, c/o Penguin Random House Inc, 1745 Broadway, New York, NY 10019 *Tel:* 212-751-2600 *Fax:* 212-572-2662 *E-mail:* ddaypub@randomhouse.com *Web Site:* knopfdoubleday.com, pg 72

Cooke, Janet, Alfred A Knopf/Everyman's Library, c/o Penguin Random House Inc, 1745 Broadway, New York, NY 10019 *Tel:* 212-751-2600 *Toll Free Tel:* 800-638-6460 *Fax:* 212-572-2593 *Web Site:* www.knopfdoubleday.com, pg 127

Cooke, Max, EdCan Network, 60 St Clair Ave E, Suite 703, Toronto, ON M4T 1N5, Canada *Tel:* 416-591-6300 *Toll Free Tel:* 866-803-9549 *Fax:* 416-591-5345 *Toll Free Fax:* 866-803-9549 *E-mail:* info@edcan.ca *Web Site:* www.edcan.ca, pg 564

Coolman, Marie, Bloomsbury Publishing Inc, 1385 Broadway, 5th fl, New York, NY 10018 *Tel:* 212-419-5300 *E-mail:* marketingusa@bloomsbury.com; adultpublicityusa@bloomsbury.com; askacademic@bloomsbury.com *Web Site:* www.bloomsbury.com, pg 37

Cooper, Alexandra, HarperCollins Children's Books, 195 Broadway, New York, NY 10007 *Tel:* 212-207-7000 *Web Site:* www.harpercollins.com/childrens, pg 101

Cooper, Karen, Adams Media, 57 Littlefield St, Avon, MA 02322 *Tel:* 508-427-7100 *Web Site:* www.simonandschuster.com, pg 4

Cooper, Karen, F+W Media Inc, 10151 Carver Rd, Suite 200, Blue Ash, OH 45242 *Tel:* 513-531-2690 *Toll Free Tel:* 800-289-0963 (trade accts); 800-258-0929 (cust serv) *E-mail:* contact_us@fwmedia.com *Web Site:* www.fwcommunity.com, pg 82

Cooper, Kevin, New York University Press, 838 Broadway, 3rd fl, New York, NY 10003-4812 *Tel:* 212-998-2575 (edit) *Toll Free Tel:* 800-996-6987 (orders) *Fax:* 212-995-4798 (orders) *E-mail:* information@nyupress.org; nyupressinfo@nyu.edu; orders@nyupress.org *Web Site:* www.nyupress.org, pg 162

Cooper, Paul B, The Electrochemical Society (ECS), 65 S Main St, Bldg D, Pennington, NJ 08534-2839 *Tel:* 609-737-1902 *Fax:* 609-737-2743 *E-mail:* publications@electrochem.org; customerservice@electrochem.org *Web Site:* www.electrochem.org, pg 77

Cooper, Stephanie, HarperCollins Publishers, 195 Broadway, New York, NY 10007 *Tel:* 212-207-7000 *Fax:* 212-207-7145 *Web Site:* www.harpercollins.com, pg 102

Cooper, Tim, Houghton Mifflin Harcourt Assessments, 900 Pierce Place, Suite 900, Itasca, IL 60143 *Tel:* 630-467-7000 *Toll Free Tel:* 800-323-9540 *Fax:* 630-467-7192 (cust serv) *E-mail:* rpc_customer_service@hmhpub.com (cust serv) *Web Site:* www.riversidepublishing.com, pg 111

Coorpender, Bruce, Pocket Press Inc, PO Box 25124, Portland, OR 97298-0124 *Toll Free Tel:* 888-237-2110 *Toll Free Fax:* 877-643-3732 *E-mail:* sales@pocketpressinc.com *Web Site:* www.pocketpressinc.com, pg 185

Coover, Doe, The Doe Coover Agency, PO Box 668, Winchester, MA 01890 *Tel:* 781-721-6000 *Fax:* 781-721-6727 *E-mail:* info@doecooveragency.com *Web Site:* www.doecooveragency.com, pg 512

Copan, Lil, Wm B Eerdmans Publishing Co, 2140 Oak Industrial Dr NE, Grand Rapids, MI 49505 *Tel:* 616-459-4591 *Toll Free Tel:* 800-253-7521 *Fax:* 616-459-6540 *E-mail:* customerservice@eerdmans.com; sales@eerdmans.com *Web Site:* www.eerdmans.com, pg 76

Copeland, Brenda, St Martin's Press, LLC, 175 Fifth Ave, New York, NY 10010 *Tel:* 646-307-5151 *Web Site:* us.macmillan.com/smp, pg 204

Copeland, Charley, ISI Books, 3901 Centerville Rd, Wilmington, DE 19807-1938 *Tel:* 302-652-4600 *Toll Free Tel:* 800-526-7022 *Fax:* 302-652-1760 *E-mail:* info@isi.org; isibooks@isi.org *Web Site:* www.isibooks.org, pg 121

Copeland, John, National Association of Printing Ink Manufacturers (NAPIM), 15 Technology Pkwy S, Peachtree Corners, GA 30092 *Tel:* 770-209-7289 *Fax:* 678-680-4920; 770-209-7217 *E-mail:* napim@napim.org *Web Site:* www.napim.org, pg 571

Copella, Susan, Pennsylvania State Data Center, Penn State Harrisburg, 777 W Harrisburg Pike, Middletown, PA 17057-4898 *Tel:* 717-948-6336 *Fax:* 717-948-6754 *E-mail:* pasdc@psu.edu *Web Site:* pasdc.hbg.psu.edu, pg 179

Copp, Karen, University of Iowa Press, 119 W Park Rd, 100 Kuhl House, Iowa City, IA 52242-1000 *Tel:* 319-335-2000 *Toll Free Tel:* 800-621-2736 (orders only) *Fax:* 319-335-2055 *Toll Free Fax:* 800-621-8476 (orders only) *E-mail:* uipress@uiowa.edu *Web Site:* www.uiowapress.org, pg 242

Copps, Elizabeth, Maria Carvainis Agency Inc, Rockefeller Center, 1270 Avenue of the Americas, Suite 2320, New York, NY 10020 *Tel:* 212-245-6365 *Fax:* 212-245-7196 *E-mail:* mca@mariacarvainisagency.com *Web Site:* mariacarvainisagency.com, pg 511

Copty, Julie, AAP PreK-12 Learning Group, 455 Massachusetts Ave NW, Suite 700, Washington, DC 20001 *Tel:* 267-351-4310 *Fax:* 267-351-4317 *E-mail:* prek12learning@publishers.org *Web Site:* www.aepweb.org, pg 553

Corbia, Thomas, Marshall Cavendish Corp, 99 White Plains Rd, Tarrytown, NY 10591-9001 *Tel:* 914-332-8888 *Toll Free Tel:* 800-821-9881 *Fax:* 914-332-8102 *E-mail:* mce@marshallcavendish.com *Web Site:* www.marshallcavendish.com; www.mceducation.us, pg 143

Corbin, Kim, New World Library, 14 Pamaron Way, Novato, CA 94949 *Tel:* 415-884-2100 *Toll Free Tel:* 800-227-3900 (ext 52, retail orders); 800-972-6657 *Fax:* 415-884-2199 *E-mail:* escort@newworldlibrary.com *Web Site:* www.newworldlibrary.com, pg 161

Corcoran-Lytle, Katherine, Adams Media, 57 Littlefield St, Avon, MA 02322 *Tel:* 508-427-7100 *Web Site:* www.simonandschuster.com, pg 4

Cordero, Chris, Empire Publishing Service, PO Box 1344, Studio City, CA 91614-0344 *Tel:* 818-784-8918 *E-mail:* empirepubsvc@att.net, pg 78

Cordero, Chris, Players Press Inc, PO Box 1132, Studio City, CA 91614-0132 *Tel:* 818-789-4980 *E-mail:* playerspress@att.net, pg 184

Cordova, Alyssa, Regnery Publishing, 300 New Jersey Ave NW, Washington, DC 20001 *Tel:* 202-216-0600 *Toll Free Tel:* 888-219-4747 *Fax:* 202-393-1795 *Web Site:* www.regnery.com, pg 198

Corenswet, John, Paul Dry Books, 1700 Sansom St, Suite 700, Philadelphia, PA 19103 *Tel:* 215-231-9939 *Fax:* 215-231-9942 *E-mail:* editor@pauldrybooks.com *Web Site:* www.pauldrybooks.com, pg 175

Corey, Abbey, Random House Publishing Group, 1745 Broadway, New York, NY 10019 *Toll Free Tel:* 800-200-3552 *Web Site:* atrandom.com, pg 195

Corey, David, Jessica Kingsley Publishers Inc, 400 Market St, Suite 400, Philadelphia, PA 19106 *Tel:* 215-922-1161 *Toll Free Tel:* 866-416-1078 (cust serv) *Fax:* 215-922-1474 *E-mail:* orders@jkp.com; hello.usa@jkp.com *Web Site:* www.jkp.com, pg 126

Corey, Robin, Random House Children's Books, 1745 Broadway, 10th fl, New York, NY 10019 *Tel:* 212-782-9000 *Web Site:* www.randomhousekids.com, pg 194

Cormier, Dominique Bernier, The Pacific Spirit Poetry Prize, University of British Columbia, Buch E462, 1866 Main Mall, Vancouver, BC V6T 1Z1, Canada *Tel:* 778-822-2514 *Fax:* 778-822-3616 *E-mail:* prismwritingcontest@gmail.com *Web Site:* www.prismmagazine.ca, pg 676

Cormier, Dominique Bernier, PRISM international Literary Non-Fiction Contest, University of British Columbia, Buch E462, 1866 Main Mall, Vancouver, BC V6T 1Z1, Canada *Tel:* 778-822-2514 *Fax:* 778-822-3616 *E-mail:* prismwritingcontest@gmail.com *Web Site:* www.prismmagazine.ca, pg 682

Cormier, Dominique Bernier, The Jacob Zilber Prize for Short Fiction, University of British Columbia, Buch E462, 1866 Main Mall, Vancouver, BC V6T 1Z1, Canada *Tel:* 778-822-2514 *Fax:* 778-822-3616 *E-mail:* prismwritingcontest@gmail.com *Web Site:* www.prismmagazine.ca, pg 701

Cormier, Helene, Les Presses de l'Universite Laval, 2180, Chemin Sainte-Foy, 1st fl, Quebec, QC G1V 0A6, Canada *Tel:* 418-656-2803 *Fax:* 418-656-3305 *E-mail:* presses@pul.ulaval.ca *Web Site:* www.pulaval.com, pg 468

Cormier, Stephane, Prise de parole Inc, 109 Elm St, Suite 205, Sudbury, ON P3C 1T4, Canada *Tel:* 705-675-6491 *Fax:* 705-673-1817 *E-mail:* info@prisedeparole.ca *Web Site:* www.prisedeparole.ca, pg 468

Corn, Alison, Insight Editions, 800 "A" St, San Rafael, CA 94901 *Tel:* 415-526-1370 *Toll Free Tel:* 800-809-3792 *Toll Free Fax:* 866-509-0515 *E-mail:* info@insighteditions.com *Web Site:* www.insighteditions.com, pg 117

Cornack, Shelley, Norma Epstein Foundation Awards in Creative Writing, 15 King's College Circle, UC 165, Toronto, ON M5S 3H7, Canada *Tel:* 416-978-8083 *Fax:* 416-978-8854 *E-mail:* uc.programs@utoronto.ca *Web Site:* www.uc.utoronto.ca/writing-centre, pg 644

Cornelius, Vicki, Blue Mountain Arts Inc, 2905 Wilderness Place, Suite 100, Boulder, CO 80301 *Tel:* 303-449-0536 *Toll Free Tel:* 800-525-0642 *Fax:* 303-417-6472 *Toll Free Fax:* 800-545-8573 *E-mail:* info@sps.com *Web Site:* www.sps.com, pg 38

Cornell, Merial, Cornell & McCarthy LLC, 2-D Cross Hwy, Westport, CT 06880 *Tel:* 203-454-4210 *E-mail:* contact@cmartreps.com *Web Site:* www.cmartreps.com, pg 543

Corpus, Angela, Walter Foster Publishing Inc, 6 Orchard Rd, Suite 100, Lake Forest, CA 92630 *Tel:* 949-380-7510 *Toll Free Tel:* 800-426-0099; 800-759-0190 (orders) *Fax:* 949-380-7575 *E-mail:* walterfoster@quartous.com *Web Site:* www.quartous.com, pg 87

Corrado, Susan, Naval Institute Press, 291 Wood Rd, Annapolis, MD 21402-5034 *Tel:* 410-268-6110 *Toll Free Tel:* 800-233-8764 *Fax:* 410-295-1084; 410-571-1703 (cust serv) *E-mail:* webmaster@navalinstitute.org; customer@navalinstitute.org (cust serv) *Web Site:* www.nip.org; www.usni.org, pg 159

Corral, Rodrigo, Farrar, Straus & Giroux, LLC, 18 W 18 St, New York, NY 10011 *Tel:* 212-741-6900 *E-mail:* fsg.publicity@fsgbooks.com *Web Site:* us.macmillan.com/fsg.aspx, pg 83

Correa, Alex, Lectorum Publications Inc, 205 Chubb Ave, Lyndhurst, NJ 07071 *Toll Free Tel:* 800-345-5946 *Fax:* 201-559-2201 *Toll Free Fax:* 877-532-8676 *E-mail:* lectorum@lectorum.com *Web Site:* www.lectorum.com, pg 131

Correa, Nick, Cambridge University Press, 1 Liberty Plaza, 20th fl, New York, NY 10006 *Tel:* 212-924-3900; 212-337-5000 *Fax:* 212-691-3239 *E-mail:* newyork@cambridge.org *Web Site:* www.cambridge.org/us, pg 46

Correia, Peter R III, National Resource Center for Youth Services (NRCYS), Schusterman Ctr, Bldg 4W, 4502 E 41 St, Tulsa, OK 74135-2512 *Tel:* 918-660-3700 *Toll Free Tel:* 800-274-2687 *Fax:* 918-660-3737 *Web Site:* www.nrcys.ou.edu, pg 159

Crocker, Harry W III, Regnery Publishing, 300 New Jersey Ave NW, Washington, DC 20001 *Tel:* 202-216-0600 *Toll Free Tel:* 888-219-4747 *Fax:* 202-393-1795 *Web Site:* www.regnery.com, pg 198

Crockett, Janet, Davies-Black Publishing, 53 State St, Boston, MA 02109 *Tel:* 617-523-3801 *Fax:* 617-523-3708 *E-mail:* info@nicholasbrealey.com *Web Site:* www.nicholasbrealey.com, pg 67

Crockett, Janet, Intercultural Press Inc, 53 State St, Boston, MA 02109 *Tel:* 617-523-3801 *Toll Free Tel:* 888-273-2539 *Fax:* 617-523-3708 *E-mail:* info@interculturalpress.com *Web Site:* nicholasbrealey.com, pg 118

Crockett, Laura, TriadaUS Literary Agency, PO Box 561, Sewickley, PA 15143 *Tel:* 412-401-3376 *Web Site:* www.triadaus.com, pg 540

Crone, Jeanie M, EDC Publishing, 10302 E 55 Place, Tulsa, OK 74146-6515 *Tel:* 918-622-4522 *Toll Free Tel:* 800-475-4522 *Fax:* 918-665-7919 *Toll Free Fax:* 800-743-5660 *E-mail:* edc@edcpub.com *Web Site:* www.edcpub.com, pg 75

Cronin, Denise, Random House Publishing Group, 1745 Broadway, New York, NY 10019 *Toll Free Tel:* 800-200-3552 *Web Site:* atrandom.com, pg 195

Cronin, Denise, Viking Children's Books, 345 Hudson St, New York, NY 10014 *Fax:* 212-414-3393 *E-mail:* youngreaderspublicity@us.penguingroup.com *Web Site:* www.penguin.com/publishers/vikingchildrensbooks, pg 251

Cronin, John, The Johns Hopkins University Press, 2715 N Charles St, Baltimore, MD 21218-4363 *Tel:* 410-516-6900; 410-516-6987 (journal orders outside US & CN) *Toll Free Tel:* 800-537-5487 (book orders & cust serv); 800-548-1784 (journal orders) *Fax:* 410-516-6968; 410-516-3866 (journal orders) *E-mail:* hfscustserv@press.jhu.edu (cust serv); jrnlcirc@press.jhu.edu (journal orders) *Web Site:* www.press.jhu.edu; muse.jhu.edu, pg 122

Cronin, Prof Mary, Julia Ward Howe Book Awards, c/o Professor Mary Cronin, 2400 Beacon St, Unit 208, Beacon Hill, MA 02467 *Tel:* 617-783-1357 *E-mail:* bostonauthors@aol.com *Web Site:* www.bostonauthorsclub.org, pg 654

Cronin, Sam, Nelson Literary Agency LLC, 1732 Wazee St, Suite 207, Denver, CO 80202-1284 *Tel:* 303-292-2805 *E-mail:* query@nelsonagency.com *Web Site:* www.nelsonagency.com, pg 530

Cronin, Thomas, St Martin's Press, LLC, 175 Fifth Ave, New York, NY 10010 *Tel:* 646-307-5151 *Web Site:* us.macmillan.com/smp, pg 204

Cronshaw, Francine, East Mountain Editing Services, PO Box 1895, Tijeras, NM 87059-1895 *Tel:* 505-281-8422 *Web Site:* www.spanishindexing.com, pg 493

Crooks, Cathie, University of Alberta Press, Ring House 2, Edmonton, AB T6G 2E1, Canada *Tel:* 780-492-3662 *Fax:* 780-492-0719 *Web Site:* www.uap.ualberta.ca, pg 473

Crooks, Jaye, University of Baltimore - Yale Gordon College of Arts & Sciences, Ampersand Institute for Words & Images, 1420 N Charles St, Baltimore, MD 21201-5779 *Tel:* 410-837-6022 *Fax:* 410-837-6029 *E-mail:* scd@ubalt.edu *Web Site:* www.ubalt.edu, pg 623

Crooms, Sandy, University of Pittsburgh Press, 7500 Thomas Blvd, Pittsburgh, PA 15260 *Tel:* 412-383-2456 *Fax:* 412-383-2466 *E-mail:* info@upress.pitt.edu *Web Site:* www.upress.pitt.edu, pg 244

Cropsey, Marvin, Abingdon Press, 201 Eighth Ave S, Nashville, TN 37203-3919 *Tel:* 615-749-6000 (academic books) *Toll Free Tel:* 800-251-3320 *Fax:* 615-749-6056 (academic books) *Toll Free Fax:* 800-836-7802 (orders) *E-mail:* orders@abingdonpress.com *Web Site:* www.abingdonpress.com, pg 2

Crosby, Calvin, Northern California Independent Booksellers Association (NCIBA), 651 Broadway, Sonoma, CA 95476 *Tel:* 415-561-7686 *Fax:* 415-561-7685 *E-mail:* info@nciba.com *Web Site:* www.nciba.com, pg 574

Crosby, Jeff, InterVarsity Press, 430 Plaza Dr, Westmont, IL 60559-1234 *Tel:* 630-734-4000 *Toll Free Tel:* 800-843-9487 *Fax:* 630-734-4200 *E-mail:* email@ivpress.com *Web Site:* www.ivpress.com, pg 120

Crosby, Lori R, Duquesne University Press, 600 Forbes Ave, Pittsburgh, PA 15282 *Tel:* 412-396-6610 *Fax:* 412-396-5984 *E-mail:* dupress@duq.edu *Web Site:* www.dupress.duq.edu, pg 74

Cross, Claudia, Folio Literary Management, The Film Center Bldg, 630 Ninth Ave, Suite 1101, New York, NY 10036 *Tel:* 212-400-1494 *Fax:* 212-967-0977 *Web Site:* www.foliolit.com, pg 517

Cross, Jamie, Math Solutions®, One Harbor Dr, Suite 101, Sausalito, CA 94965 *Tel:* 415-332-4181 *Toll Free Tel:* 800-868-9092 *Fax:* 415-331-1931 *Toll Free Fax:* 877-942-8837 *E-mail:* info@mathsolutions.com; orders@mathsolutions.com *Web Site:* www.mathsolutions.com, pg 144

Cross, John C Esq, Standard Publishing Corp, 10 High St, Boston, MA 02110 *Tel:* 617-457-0600 *Toll Free Tel:* 800-682-5759 *Fax:* 617-457-0608 *Web Site:* www.spcpub.com, pg 220

Crosse, Ann Mehan, Society for Scholarly Publishing (SSP), 10200 W 44 Ave, Suite 304, Wheat Ridge, CO 80033-2840 *Tel:* 303-422-3914 *Fax:* 720-881-6101 *E-mail:* info@sspnet.org *Web Site:* www.sspnet.org, pg 578

Crouch, Lori, Education Writers Association (EWA), 3516 Connecticut Ave NW, Washington, DC 20008 *Tel:* 202-452-9830 *Fax:* 202-452-9837 *E-mail:* ewa@ewa.org *Web Site:* www.ewa.org, pg 565

Crouch, Lori, National Awards for Education Reporting, 3516 Connecticut Ave NW, Washington, DC 20008 *Tel:* 202-452-9830 *Fax:* 202-452-9837 *E-mail:* ewa@ewa.org *Web Site:* www.ewa.org, pg 670

Crouchet, Mike, Cardiotext Publishing, 3405 W 44 St, Minneapolis, MN 55410 *Tel:* 612-925-2053 *Fax:* 612-922-7556 *E-mail:* info@cardiotextpublishing.com *Web Site:* www.cardiotextpublishing.com, pg 47

Crowley, Kevin, The Edna Staebler Award for Creative Non-Fiction, Office of the Dean, Faculty of Arts, 75 University Ave W, Waterloo, ON N2L 3C5, Canada *Tel:* 519-884-1970 (ext 3361) *E-mail:* staebleraward@wlu.ca *Web Site:* wlu.ca/staebleraward, pg 691

Crowley, Louise, Vermont College of Fine Arts, MFA in Writing Program, 36 College St, Montpelier, VT 05602 *Tel:* 802-828-8840; 802-828-8839 *Toll Free Tel:* 866-934-VCFA (934-8232) *Fax:* 802-828-8649 *Web Site:* www.vcfa.edu, pg 624

Crowley, Michael, Berrett-Koehler Publishers Inc, 1333 Broadway, Suite 1000, Oakland, CA 94612 *Tel:* 510-817-2277 *Fax:* 510-817-2278 *E-mail:* bkpub@bkpub.com *Web Site:* www.bkconnection.com, pg 34

Crowther, Duane S, Horizon Publishers & Distributors Inc, 191 N 650 E, Bountiful, UT 84010-3628 *Tel:* 801-292-7102 *E-mail:* ldshorizonpublishers1@gmail.com *Web Site:* www.ldshorizonpublishers.com, pg 110

Crowther, Jean D, Horizon Publishers & Distributors Inc, 191 N 650 E, Bountiful, UT 84010-3628 *Tel:* 801-292-7102 *E-mail:* ldshorizonpublishers1@gmail.com *Web Site:* www.ldshorizonpublishers.com, pg 110

Crum, Erin, HarperCollins Publishers, 195 Broadway, New York, NY 10007 *Tel:* 212-207-7000 *Fax:* 212-207-7145 *Web Site:* www.harpercollins.com, pg 101

Crumpacker, Caroline, Residency, 454 E Hill Rd, Austerlitz, NY 12017 *Tel:* 518-392-3103; 518-392-4144 *E-mail:* apply@millaycolony.org *Web Site:* www.millaycolony.org, pg 684

Cruz, Ricky, US Games Systems Inc, 179 Ludlow St, Stamford, CT 06902 *Tel:* 203-353-8400 *Toll Free Tel:* 800-54-GAMES (544-2637) *Fax:* 203-353-8431 *E-mail:* info@usgamesinc.com *Web Site:* www.usgamesinc.com, pg 249

Cryer, Bruce, HeartMath LLC, 14700 W Park Ave, Boulder Creek, CA 95006 *Tel:* 831-338-8700 *Toll Free Tel:* 800-450-9111 *Fax:* 831-338-9861 *E-mail:* info@heartmath.com; inquiry@heartmath.com *Web Site:* www.heartmath.com, pg 105

Cseh, Viktoria, Tradewind Books, 202-1807 Maritime Mews, Vancouver, BC V6H 3W7, Canada *Tel:* 604-662-4405 *E-mail:* tradewindbooks@yahoo.com; tradewindbooks@gmail.com *Web Site:* www.tradewindbooks.com, pg 472

Csuka, Brooke, Algonquin Books, 400 Silver Cedar Ct, Suite 300, Chapel Hill, NC 27514-1585 *Tel:* 919-967-0108 *Fax:* 919-933-0272 *E-mail:* inquiry@algonquin.com *Web Site:* www.workman.com/algonquin, pg 7

Cubberley, William, Practising Law Institute, 1177 Avenue of the Americas, New York, NY 10036 *Tel:* 212-824-5700 *Toll Free Tel:* 800-260-4PLI (260-4754, cust serv) *Fax:* 212-265-4742 (intl) *Toll Free Fax:* 800-321-0093 (local) *E-mail:* info@pli.edu (cust serv) *Web Site:* www.pli.edu, pg 186

Culatta, Richard, International Society for Technology in Education, 1530 Wilson Blvd, Suite 730, Arlington, VA 22209 *Tel:* 503-342-2848 (intl) *Toll Free Tel:* 800-336-5191 (US & CN) *E-mail:* iste@iste.org *Web Site:* www.iste.org; www.isteconference.org, pg 120

Cull, Mark E, Red Hen Press, 1335 N Lake Ave, Suite 200, Pasadena, CA 91104 *Tel:* 626-356-4760 *Fax:* 626-356-9974 *Web Site:* www.redhen.org, pg 196

Cullen, Dan, American Booksellers Association, 333 Westchester Ave, Suite S202, White Plains, NY 10604 *Tel:* 914-406-7500 *Toll Free Tel:* 800-637-0037 *Fax:* 914-410-6297 *E-mail:* info@bookweb.org *Web Site:* www.bookweb.org, pg 554

Culliford, Craig, Crabtree Publishing Co, 350 Fifth Ave, 59th fl, PMB 59051, New York, NY 10118 *Tel:* 212-496-5040 *Toll Free Tel:* 800-387-7650 *Toll Free Fax:* 800-355-7166 *E-mail:* custserv@crabtreebooks.com *Web Site:* www.crabtreebooks.com, pg 63

Culliford, Craig, Crabtree Publishing Co Ltd, 616 Welland Ave, St Catharines, ON L2M 5V6, Canada *Tel:* 905-682-5221 *Toll Free Tel:* 800-387-7650 *Fax:* 905-682-7166 *Toll Free Fax:* 800-355-7166 *E-mail:* custserv@crabtreebooks.com; sales@crabtreebooks.com; orders@crabtreebooks.com *Web Site:* www.crabtreebooks.com, pg 451

Cullingford, Elizabeth, University of Texas at Austin, New Writers Project, Dept of English, Calhoun Hall, Rm 226, 204 W 21 St, B-5000, Austin, TX 78712 *Tel:* 512-471-5132; 512-471-4991 *Fax:* 512-471-4909 *Web Site:* newwritersproject.org, pg 623

Cullmann, Erica, New York Academy of Sciences (NYAS), 7 World Trade, 40th fl, 250 Greenwich St, New York, NY 10007-2157 *Tel:* 212-298-8600 *Toll Free Tel:* 800-843-6927 *Fax:* 212-298-3668 *E-mail:* nyas@nyas.org; annals@nyas.org; customerservice@nyas.org *Web Site:* www.nyas.org, pg 161

Cully, Christine French, Highlights for Children, 1800 Watermark Dr, Columbus, OH 43215 *Tel:* 614-486-0631 *Toll Free Tel:* 800-962-3661 (Highlights Club cust serv); 800-255-9517 (Highlights Magazine cust serv) *Web Site:* www.highlights.com; www.facebook.com/HighlightsforChildren, pg 107

Cully, Lynn, Kensington Publishing Corp, 119 W 40 St, New York, NY 10018 *Tel:* 212-407-1500 *Toll Free Tel:* 800-221-2647 *Fax:* 212-935-0699 *Web Site:* www.kensingtonbooks.com, pg 125

Culotti, Liz, Westwood Creative Artists Ltd, 138 Sussex Mews, Toronto, ON M5S-2K1, Canada *Tel:* 416-964-3302 *Fax:* 416-964-3302 *E-mail:* wca_office@wcaltd.com *Web Site:* www.wcaltd.com, pg 541

Cumberland, Brian, Faith Library Publications, PO Box 50126, Tulsa, OK 74150-0126 *Tel:* 918-258-1588 (ext 2218) *Toll Free Tel:* 888-258-0999 (orders) *Fax:* 918-872-7710 (orders) *E-mail:* flp@rhema.org *Web Site:* www.rhema.org/store, pg 82

Cumming, Beto, Iris Press, 969 Oak Ridge Tpke, No 328, Oak Ridge, TN 37830 *Web Site:* www.irisbooks.com, pg 121

Cumming, Robert, Iris Press, 969 Oak Ridge Tpke, No 328, Oak Ridge, TN 37830 *Web Site:* www.irisbooks.com, pg 121

Cumming, Willie, Iris Press, 969 Oak Ridge Tpke, No 328, Oak Ridge, TN 37830 *Web Site:* www.irisbooks.com, pg 121

Cummings, Andy, Lerner Publications, 241 First Ave N, Minneapolis, MN 55401 *Tel:* 612-332-3344 *Toll Free Tel:* 800-328-4929 *Fax:* 612-332-7615 *Toll Free Fax:* 800-332-1132 *E-mail:* info@lernerbooks.com; custserve@lernerbooks.com *Web Site:* www.lernerbooks.com; www.facebook.com/lernerbooks, pg 132

Cummings, Andy, Lerner Publishing Group Inc, 241 First Ave N, Minneapolis, MN 55401 *Tel:* 612-332-3344 *Toll Free Tel:* 800-328-4929 *Fax:* 612-332-7615 *Toll Free Fax:* 800-332-1132 *E-mail:* info@lernerbooks.com; custserve@lernerbooks.com *Web Site:* www.lernerbooks.com; www.facebook.com/lernerbooks, pg 132

Cummings, Mary, Betsy Amster Literary Enterprises, 6312 SW Capitol Hwy, No 503, Portland, OR 97239 *Tel:* 503-496-4007 *E-mail:* rights@amsterlit.com (rts inquiries); b.amster.assistant@gmail.com (adult book queries); b.amster.kidsbooks@gmail.com (children & young adult book queries) *Web Site:* www.amsterlit.com, pg 506

Cummings, Pat, The Authors League Fund, 31 E 32 St, 7th fl, New York, NY 10016 *Tel:* 212-268-1208 *Fax:* 212-564-5363 *E-mail:* staff@authorsleaguefund.org *Web Site:* www.authorsleaguefund.org, pg 559

Cunningham, David Scott, The University of Arkansas Press, McIlroy House, 105 N McIlroy Ave, Fayetteville, AR 72701 *Tel:* 479-575-3246 *Toll Free Tel:* 800-626-0090 *Fax:* 479-575-6044 *E-mail:* info@uapress.com *Web Site:* www.uapress.com, pg 240

Cunningham, Emily, The Penguin Press, 375 Hudson St, New York, NY 10014 *Web Site:* thepenguinpress.com, pg 178

Cunningham, Kay, Psychological Assessment Resources Inc (PAR), 16204 N Florida Ave, Lutz, FL 33549 *Tel:* 813-968-3003; 813-449-4065 *Toll Free Tel:* 800-331-8378 *Fax:* 813-968-2598; 813-961-2196 *Toll Free Fax:* 800-727-9329 *E-mail:* custsup@parinc.com *Web Site:* www4.parinc.com, pg 191

Cunningham, Michael, Health Administration Press, One N Franklin St, Suite 1700, Chicago, IL 60606-3491 *Tel:* 312-424-2800 *Fax:* 312-424-0014 *E-mail:* hap1@ache.org *Web Site:* www.ache.org/publications (orders), pg 104

Cunningham, Sue, Council for Advancement & Support of Education (CASE), 1307 New York Ave NW, Suite 1000, Washington, DC 20005-4701 *Tel:* 202-328-CASE (328-2273) *Fax:* 202-387-4973 *E-mail:* membersupportcenter@case.org *Web Site:* www.case.org, pg 564

Cunningham, Tammy, LearningExpress LLC, 80 Broad St, 4th fl, New York, NY 10004 *Toll Free Tel:* 800-295-9556 (ext 2) *E-mail:* marketing@learningexpressllc.com (cust serv) *Web Site:* www.learningexpressllc.com, pg 131

Cuocci, Kerri, Sterling Publishing Co Inc, 1166 Avenue of the Americas, 17th fl, New York, NY 10036 *Tel:* 212-532-7160 *Toll Free Tel:* 800-367-9692 *Fax:* 212-213-2495 *Web Site:* www.sterlingpublishing.com, pg 222

Curr, Judith, Atria Books, 1230 Avenue of the Americas, New York, NY 10020 *Tel:* 212-698-7000 *Fax:* 212-698-7007 *Web Site:* www.simonandschuster.com, pg 25

Curr, Judith, Simon & Schuster, Inc, 1230 Avenue of the Americas, New York, NY 10020 *Tel:* 212-698-7000 *Fax:* 212-698-7007 *E-mail:* firstname.lastname@simonandschuster.com *Web Site:* www.simonandschuster.com, pg 213

Curran, Katherine, American Diabetes Association, 1701 N Beauregard St, Alexandria, VA 22311 *Toll Free Tel:* 800-342-2383 *E-mail:* booksinfo@diabetes.org *Web Site:* www.diabetes.org, pg 11

Currans-Sheehan, Tricia, The Briar Cliff Review Fiction, Poetry & Creative Nonfiction Contest, 3303 Rebecca St, Sioux City, IA 51104-2100 *Tel:* 712-279-1651 *Fax:* 712-279-5486 *Web Site:* www.bcreview.org, pg 634

Curren, Vincent, Corporation for Public Broadcasting (CPB), 401 Ninth St NW, Washington, DC 20004-2129 *Tel:* 202-879-9600 *Web Site:* www.cpb.org, pg 563

Curry, Brendan, W W Norton & Company Inc, 500 Fifth Ave, New York, NY 10110-0017 *Tel:* 212-354-5500 *Toll Free Tel:* 800-233-4830 (orders & cust serv) *Fax:* 212-869-0856 *Toll Free Fax:* 800-458-6515 *E-mail:* orders@wwnorton.com *Web Site:* books.wwnorton.com, pg 164

Curry, C, Golden Meteorite Press, 11919 82 St NW, Suite 103, Edmonton, AB T5B 2W4, Canada *Tel:* 780-378-0063 *Fax:* 780-378-0063, pg 458

Curry, Michael, Donald Maass Literary Agency, 1000 Dean St, Suite 252, Brooklyn, NY 11238 *Tel:* 212-727-8383 *Fax:* 212-727-3271 *E-mail:* info@maassagency.com *Web Site:* www.maassagency.com, pg 526

Curry, Michele, Jackie White Memorial National Children's Playwriting Contest, 1400 Forum Blvd, 1C No 214, Columbia, MO 65203 *E-mail:* jwm@cectheatre.org *Web Site:* www.cectheatre.org, pg 657

Curtin, Diane, Triumph Learning LLC, 136 Madison Ave, 7th fl, New York, NY 10016 *Tel:* 212-652-0200 *Toll Free Tel:* 800-338-6519 (cust serv) *Toll Free Fax:* 866-805-5723 *E-mail:* info@triumphlearning.com; customerservice@triumphlearning.com *Web Site:* www.triumphlearning.com, pg 235

Curtin, Thomas, Waveland Press Inc, 4180 IL Rte 83, Suite 101, Long Grove, IL 60047-9580 *Tel:* 847-634-0081 *Fax:* 847-634-9501 *E-mail:* info@waveland.com *Web Site:* www.waveland.com, pg 253

Curtis, Anthony, Huntington Press Publishing, 3665 Procyon St, Las Vegas, NV 89103-1907 *Tel:* 702-252-0655 *Toll Free Tel:* 800-244-2224 *Fax:* 702-252-0675 *E-mail:* sales@huntingtonpress.com *Web Site:* www.huntingtonpress.com, pg 113

Curtis, Carolyn, Pacific Press Publishing Association, 1350 N Kings Rd, Nampa, ID 83687-3193 *Tel:* 208-465-2500 *Toll Free Tel:* 800-447-7377 *Fax:* 208-465-2531 *Web Site:* www.pacificpress.com, pg 172

Curtis, Mary E, Transaction Publishers Inc, 10 Corporate Place S, Suite 102, Piscataway, NJ 08854 *Tel:* 732-445-2280; 703-661-1589 (orders) *Toll Free Tel:* 888-999-6778 (dist ctr) *Fax:* 732-445-3138 *E-mail:* trans@transactionpub.com; orders@transactionpub.com *Web Site:* www.transactionpub.com, pg 234

Curtis, Nancy, High Plains Press, PO Box 123, Glendo, WY 82213 *Tel:* 307-735-4370 *Toll Free Tel:* 800-552-7819 *Fax:* 307-735-4590 *E-mail:* editor@highplainspress.com *Web Site:* highplainspress.com, pg 107

Curtis, Richard, Richard Curtis Associates Inc, 200 E 72 St, Suite 28J, New York, NY 10021 *Tel:* 212-772-7363 *Fax:* 212-772-7393 *E-mail:* info@curtisagency.com *Web Site:* www.curtisagency.com, pg 512

Cusack, John, St Martin's Press, LLC, 175 Fifth Ave, New York, NY 10010 *Tel:* 646-307-5151 *Web Site:* us.macmillan.com/smp, pg 204

Cusick, John, Folio Literary Management, The Film Center Bldg, 630 Ninth Ave, Suite 1101, New York, NY 10036 *Tel:* 212-400-1494 *Fax:* 212-967-0977 *Web Site:* www.foliolit.com, pg 517

Cussen, David M, Pineapple Press Inc, PO Box 3889, Sarasota, FL 34230-3889 *Tel:* 941-706-2507 *Toll Free Tel:* 866-766-3850 (orders) *Fax:* 941-706-2509 *Toll Free Fax:* 800-838-1149 (orders) *E-mail:* info@pineapplepress.com; customer.service@ingrampublisherservices.com *Web Site:* www.pineapplepress.com, pg 183

Cussen, June, Pineapple Press Inc, PO Box 3889, Sarasota, FL 34230-3889 *Tel:* 941-706-2507 *Toll Free Tel:* 866-766-3850 (orders) *Fax:* 941-706-2509 *Toll Free Fax:* 800-838-1149 (orders) *E-mail:* info@pineapplepress.com; customer.service@ingrampublisherservices.com *Web Site:* www.pineapplepress.com, pg 183

Cutler, Thomas, Naval Institute Press, 291 Wood Rd, Annapolis, MD 21402-5034 *Tel:* 410-268-6110 *Toll Free Tel:* 800-233-8764 *Fax:* 410-295-1084; 410-571-1703 (cust serv) *E-mail:* webmaster@navalinstitute.org; customer@navalinstitute.org (cust serv) *Web Site:* www.nip.org; www.usni.org, pg 159

Cyphers, Tara, The Ohio State University Press, 180 Pressey Hall, 1070 Carmack Rd, Columbus, OH 43210-1002 *Tel:* 614-292-6930 *Fax:* 614-292-2065 *Toll Free Fax:* 800-621-8476 *E-mail:* info@osupress.org *Web Site:* ohiostatepress.org, pg 167

Cywinski, David, Hal Leonard Corp, 7777 W Bluemound Rd, Milwaukee, WI 53213 *Tel:* 414-774-3630 *Fax:* 414-774-3259 *E-mail:* halinfo@halleonard.com; info@halleonard.com *Web Site:* www.halleonard.com, pg 99

D'Acierno, Amanda, Books on Tape®, 1745 Broadway, New York, NY 10019 *Toll Free Tel:* 800-733-3000 (cust serv) *Toll Free Fax:* 800-940-7046 *Web Site:* www.booksontape.com, pg 40

D'Acierno, Amanda, Fodor's Travel Publications, 1745 Broadway, 15th fl, New York, NY 10019 *Toll Free Tel:* 800-733-3000 *E-mail:* publicity@fodors.com; editors@fodors.com *Web Site:* www.fodors.com, pg 86

D'Acierno, Amanda, Living Language, c/o Penguin Random House Inc, 1745 Broadway, New York, NY 10019 *Tel:* 212-782-9000 *Toll Free Tel:* 800-733-3000 (orders) *Toll Free Fax:* 800-659-2436 *E-mail:* livinglanguage@randomhouse.com *Web Site:* www.livinglanguage.com, pg 136

D'Acierno, Amanda, Penguin Random House Audio Publishing, 1745 Broadway, New York, NY 10019 *E-mail:* audio@penguinrandomhouse.com *Web Site:* www.penguinrandomhouseaudio.com, pg 178

D'Acierno, Amanda, Random House Reference/Random House Puzzles & Games, c/o Penguin Random House Inc, 1745 Broadway, New York, NY 10019 *Tel:* 212-782-9000 *Web Site:* www.penguinrandomhouse.com, pg 195

D'Agnes, Glenn, Workman Publishing Co Inc, 225 Varick St, 9th fl, New York, NY 10014-4381 *Tel:* 212-254-5900 *Toll Free Tel:* 800-722-7202 *Fax:* 212-254-8098 *E-mail:* info@workman.com *Web Site:* www.workman.com, pg 259

D'Agostino, Kerry, Curtis Brown Ltd, 10 Astor Place, New York, NY 10003 *Tel:* 212-473-5400 *Web Site:* www.curtisbrown.com, pg 510

D'Agostino, Sonia, Quattro Books Inc, 12 Concord Ave, 2nd fl, Toronto, ON M6H 2P1, Canada *Tel:* 647-748-7484 *E-mail:* info@quattrobooks.ca *Web Site:* www.quattrobooks.ca, pg 468

D'Amato, Sally-Ann, Society of Motion Picture & Television Engineers® (SMPTE®), 3 Barker Ave, 5th fl, White Plains, NY 10601 *Tel:* 914-761-1100 *Fax:* 914-761-3115 *Web Site:* www.smpte.org, pg 578

D'Ambrosi, Dean, Epicomm, 1800 Diagonal Rd, Suite 320, Alexandria, VA 22314-2862 *Tel:* 703-836-9200 *E-mail:* webmaster@epicomm.org *Web Site:* epicomm.org, pg 565

D'Amico, Gregory S, Rochester Institute of Technology, School of Media, Arts & Technology, 69 Lomb Memorial Dr, Rochester, NY 14623-5603 *Tel:* 585-475-2728; 585-475-5336 *Fax:* 585-475-5336 *E-mail:* spmofc@rit.edu *Web Site:* cias.rit.edu/printmedia, pg 622

d'Arbonne, Jessica, University Press of Colorado, 5589 Arapahoe Ave, Suite 206-C, Boulder, CO 80303 *Tel:* 720-406-8849 *Toll Free Tel:* 800-621-2736 (orders) *Fax:* 720-406-3443 *Web Site:* www.upcolorado.com, pg 246

D'Auria, Heather, Yale University Press, 302 Temple St, New Haven, CT 06511-8909 *Tel:* 203-432-0960; 203-432-0966 (sales); 401-531-2800 (cust serv) *Toll Free Tel:* 800-405-1619 (cust serv) *Fax:* 203-432-

(inside sales); 800-631-8571 (cust serv) *Fax:* 212-366-2666; 607-775-4829 (inside sales) *E-mail:* online@us.penguingroup.com *Web Site:* www.penguin.com, pg 177

Danzinger, Sheldon, Russell Sage Foundation, 112 E 64 St, New York, NY 10065 *Tel:* 212-750-6000 *Toll Free Tel:* 800-524-6401 *Fax:* 212-371-4761 *E-mail:* info@rsage.org *Web Site:* www.russellsage.org, pg 202

Darby, George, UNO Press, University of New Orleans Metro College, 2000 Lakeshore Dr, New Orleans, LA 70148 *Tel:* 504-280-7457 *E-mail:* unopress@uno.edu *Web Site:* unopress.org, pg 248

Dardick, Simon, Vehicule Press, PO Box 42094, CP Roy, Montreal, QC H2W-2T3, Canada *Tel:* 514-844-6073 *Fax:* 514-844-7543 *E-mail:* vp@vehiculepress.com; admin@vehiculepress.com *Web Site:* www.vehiculepress.com, pg 475

Darhansoff, Liz, Darhansoff & Verrill, 133 W 72 St, Rm 304, New York, NY 10023 *Tel:* 917-305-1300 *E-mail:* permissions@dvagency.com *Web Site:* www.dvagency.com, pg 512

Dark, Larry, The Story Prize, 41 Watchung Plaza, No 384, Montclair, NJ 07042 *Tel:* 973-932-0324 *E-mail:* info@thestoryprize.org *Web Site:* www.thestoryprize.org, pg 692

Darling, Abigail, Laughing Elephant, 3645 Interlake N, Seattle, WA 98103 *Tel:* 206-447-9229 *Toll Free Tel:* 800-354-0400 *Fax:* 206-447-9189 *E-mail:* support@laughingelephant.com *Web Site:* www.laughingelephant.com, pg 130

Darling, Christina, Laughing Elephant, 3645 Interlake N, Seattle, WA 98103 *Tel:* 206-447-9229 *Toll Free Tel:* 800-354-0400 *Fax:* 206-447-9189 *E-mail:* support@laughingelephant.com *Web Site:* www.laughingelephant.com, pg 130

Darling, Harold, Laughing Elephant, 3645 Interlake N, Seattle, WA 98103 *Tel:* 206-447-9229 *Toll Free Tel:* 800-354-0400 *Fax:* 206-447-9189 *E-mail:* support@laughingelephant.com *Web Site:* www.laughingelephant.com, pg 130

Darling, Karen Merikangas, University of Chicago Press, 1427 E 60 St, Chicago, IL 60637-2954 *Tel:* 773-702-7700; 773-702-7600 *Toll Free Tel:* 800-621-2736 (orders) *Fax:* 773-702-9756; 773-660-2235 (orders); 773-702-2708 *E-mail:* custserv@press.uchicago.edu; marketing@press.uchicago.edu *Web Site:* www.press.uchicago.edu, pg 241

Darnton, John, The George Polk Awards, The Brooklyn Campus, One University Plaza, Brooklyn, NY 11201-5372 *Tel:* 718-488-1009 *Web Site:* www.liu.edu/polk, pg 680

DaSilva, Isabel, Touchstone, 1230 Avenue of the Americas, New York, NY 10020, pg 233

Daswani, Deepak, Simon & Schuster, Inc, 1230 Avenue of the Americas, New York, NY 10020 *Tel:* 212-698-7000 *Fax:* 212-698-7007 *E-mail:* firstname.lastname@simonandschuster.com *Web Site:* www.simonandschuster.com, pg 213

Dattorre, Michael, Ash Tree Publishing, PO Box 64, Woodstock, NY 12498 *Tel:* 845-246-8081 *Fax:* 845-246-8081 *Web Site:* www.ashtreepublishing.com, pg 23

Datz, Arielle, Dunow, Carlson & Lerner Literary Agency Inc, 27 W 20 St, Suite 1107, New York, NY 10011 *Tel:* 212-645-7606 *E-mail:* mail@dclagency.com *Web Site:* www.dclagency.com, pg 515

Daulton, Sue, Penguin Random House Audio Publishing, 1745 Broadway, New York, NY 10019 *E-mail:* audio@penguinrandomhouse.com *Web Site:* www.penguinrandomhouseaudio.com, pg 178

Daum, Kathy, National Endowment for the Arts, 400 Seventh St SW, Washington, DC 20506-0001 *Tel:* 202-682-5400 *Web Site:* www.arts.gov, pg 583

Dave, Rishi, Dun & Bradstreet, 103 JFK Pkwy, Short Hills, NJ 07078 *Tel:* 973-921-5500 *Toll Free Tel:* 800-526-0651; 800-234-3867 (cust serv) *E-mail:* custserv@dnb.com *Web Site:* www.dnb.com, pg 73

Davenport, Elaine, Writer's AudioShop, 1316 Overland Stage Rd, Dripping Springs, TX 78620 *Tel:* 512-476-1616 *E-mail:* wrtaudshop@aol.com *Web Site:* www.writersaudio.com, pg 260

Davenport, May, May Davenport Publishers, 26313 Purissima Rd, Los Altos Hills, CA 94022 *Tel:* 650-947-6499 *E-mail:* mdbooks@earthlink.net *Web Site:* www.maydavenportpublishers.org, pg 67

David, Jack, ECW Press, 665 Gerrard St E, Toronto, ON M4M 1Y2, Canada *Tel:* 416-694-3348 *E-mail:* info@ecwpress.com *Web Site:* www.ecwpress.com, pg 452

David, Kim, McGraw-Hill Higher Education, 1333 Burr Ridge Pkwy, Burr Ridge, IL 60527 *Tel:* 630-789-4000 *Toll Free Tel:* 800-338-3987 (cust serv) *Fax:* 614-755-5645 (cust serv) *Web Site:* www.mhhe.com, pg 146

David, Kim, McGraw-Hill Humanities, Social Sciences, Languages, 2 Penn Plaza, 21st fl, New York, NY 10121 *Tel:* 212-904-2000 *Toll Free Tel:* 800-338-3987 (cust serv) *Fax:* 614-755-5645 (cust serv) *Web Site:* www.mhhe.com, pg 146

David, Kim, McGraw-Hill/Irwin, 1333 Burr Ridge Pkwy, Burr Ridge, IL 60527 *Tel:* 630-789-4000 *Toll Free Tel:* 800-338-3987 (cust serv) *Fax:* 630-789-6942; 614-755-5645 (cust serv) *Web Site:* www.mhhe.com, pg 146

David, Kim, McGraw-Hill Science, Engineering, Mathematics, 501 Bell St, Dubuque, IA 52001 *Tel:* 563-584-6000 *Toll Free Tel:* 800-338-3987 (cust serv) *Fax:* 614-755-5645 (cust serv) *Web Site:* www.mhhe.com, pg 146

Davidow, Sally, The Heywood Broun Award, 501 Third St NW, 6th fl, Washington, DC 20001-2797 *Tel:* 202-434-7177; 202-434-7162 (The Guild Reporter) *Fax:* 202-434-1472 *Web Site:* www.newsguild.org, pg 634

Davidow, Sally, The NewsGuild - CWA, 501 Third St NW, 6th fl, Washington, DC 20001-2797 *Tel:* 202-434-7177; 202-434-7162 (The Guild Reporter) *Fax:* 202-434-1472 *E-mail:* guild@cwa-union.org *Web Site:* www.newsguild.org, pg 573

Davidson, Andrew J, University of Missouri Press, 113 Heinkel Bldg, 201 S Seventh St, Columbia, MO 65211 *Tel:* 573-882-7641 *Toll Free Tel:* 800-621-2736 (orders) *Fax:* 573-884-4498 *Toll Free Fax:* 800-621-8476 (orders) *E-mail:* upress@missouri.edu *Web Site:* upress.missouri.edu; press.umsystem.edu, pg 243

Davidson, Gary, Hachette Nashville, 12 Cadillac Dr, Suite 480, Brentwood, TN 37027 *Tel:* 615-221-0996 *Fax:* 615-221-0962 *Web Site:* www.hachettebookgroup.com, pg 98

Davidson, Scott, McGraw-Hill Career Education, 1333 Burr Ridge Pkwy, Burr Ridge, IL 60527 *Tel:* 630-789-4000 *Toll Free Tel:* 800-338-3987 (cust serv) *Fax:* 630-789-5523; 614-755-5645 (cust serv) *Web Site:* www.mhhe.com, pg 145

Davies, Mr Glyn, Rothstein Associates Inc, 4 Arapaho Rd, Brookfield, CT 06804-3104 *Tel:* 203-740-7400 *Toll Free Tel:* 888-768-4783 *Fax:* 203-740-7401 *E-mail:* info@rothstein.com *Web Site:* www.rothstein.com; www.rothsteinpublishing.com, pg 201

Davies, Jeremy, Farrar, Straus & Giroux, LLC, 18 W 18 St, New York, NY 10011 *Tel:* 212-741-6900 *E-mail:* fsg.publicity@fsgbooks.com *Web Site:* us.macmillan.com/fsg.aspx, pg 83

Davies, Jocelyn, HarperCollins Children's Books, 195 Broadway, New York, NY 10007 *Tel:* 212-207-7000 *Web Site:* www.harpercollins.com/childrens, pg 101

Davies, Jon, University of Georgia Press, Main Library, 3rd fl, 320 S Jackson St, Athens, GA 30602 *Fax:* 706-542-2558; 706-542-6770 *Web Site:* www.ugapress.org, pg 241

Davies, Michael, Davies Publishing Inc, 32 S Raymond Ave, Suites 4 & 5, Pasadena, CA 91105-1961 *Tel:* 626-792-3046 *Toll Free Tel:* 877-792-0005 *Fax:* 626-792-5308 *E-mail:* info@daviespublishing.com *Web Site:* daviespublishing.com, pg 68

Davies, Dr Shannon, Texas A&M University Press, John H Lindsey Bldg, Lewis St, 4354 TAMU, College Station, TX 77843-4354 *Tel:* 979-845-1436 *Toll Free Tel:* 800-826-8911 (orders) *Fax:* 979-847-8752 *Toll Free Fax:* 888-617-2421 (orders) *E-mail:* bookorders@tamu.edu *Web Site:* www.tamupress.com, pg 230

Davis, Aida, American Institute of Aeronautics & Astronautics (AIAA), 1801 Alexander Bell Dr, Suite 500, Reston, VA 20191-4344 *Tel:* 703-264-7500 *Toll Free Tel:* 800-639-AIAA (639-2422) *Fax:* 703-264-7551 *E-mail:* custserv@aiaa.org *Web Site:* www.aiaa.org, pg 12

Davis, Dr Alan, New Rivers Press, c/o Minnesota State University Moorhead, 1104 Seventh Ave S, Moorhead, MN 56563 *Tel:* 218-477-5870 *Fax:* 218-477-2236 *E-mail:* nrp@mnstate.edu *Web Site:* www.newriverspress.com; www.mnstate.edu/newriverspress, pg 161

Davis, Carol Prud'homme, See-More's Workshop Arts & Education Workshops, 325 West End Ave, Suite 12-B, New York, NY 10023 *Tel:* 212-724-0677 *Fax:* 212-724-0767 *E-mail:* sbt@shadowboxtheatre.org *Web Site:* www.shadowboxtheatre.org, pg 614

Davis, Chris, The American Occupational Therapy Association Inc (AOTA), 4720 Montgomery Lane, Suite 200, Bethesda, MD 20814-3449 *Tel:* 301-652-6611 *Toll Free Tel:* 800-377-8555 (TDD); 877-404-AOTA (404-2682, orders) *Fax:* 301-652-7711; 770-238-0414 (orders) *E-mail:* aotacustomerservice@pbd.com *Web Site:* www.aota.org; store.aota.org, pg 13

Davis, Dawn, Atria Books, 1230 Avenue of the Americas, New York, NY 10020 *Tel:* 212-698-7000 *Fax:* 212-698-7007 *Web Site:* www.simonandschuster.com, pg 25

Davis, Dawn, HarperCollins General Books Group, 195 Broadway, New York, NY 10007 *Tel:* 212-207-7000 *Web Site:* www.harpercollins.com, pg 101

Davis, Dina, Harlequin Enterprises Ltd, 233 Broadway, Suite 1001, New York, NY 10279 *Tel:* 212-553-4200 *Fax:* 212-227-8969 *E-mail:* customerservice@harlequin.com *Web Site:* www.harlequin.com, pg 100

Davis, Gary, The Learning Source Ltd, 644 Tenth St, Brooklyn, NY 11215 *Tel:* 718-768-0231 (ext 10) *Fax:* 718-369-3467 *E-mail:* info@learningsourceltd.com *Web Site:* www.learningsourceltd.com, pg 497

Davis, J Madison, Gaylord College of Journalism & Mass Communication, Professional Writing Program, c/o University of Oklahoma, 395 W Lindsey St, Rm 3534, Norman, OK 73019-0270 *Tel:* 405-325-2721 *Fax:* 405-325-7565 *Web Site:* www.ou.edu/gaylord, pg 620

Davis, J Madison, International Association of Crime Writers Inc, North American Branch, 243 Fifth Ave, Suite 537, New York, NY 10016 *Tel:* 212-243-8966 *Fax:* 815-361-1477 *E-mail:* info@crimewritersna.org *Web Site:* www.crimewritersna.org, pg 567

Davis, James B, Practice Management Information Corp (PMIC), 4727 Wilshire Blvd, Suite 300, Los Angeles, CA 90010 *Tel:* 323-954-0224 *Fax:* 323-954-0253 *E-mail:* customer.service@pmiconline.com *Web Site:* pmiconline.stores.yahoo.net, pg 186

Davis, Janet, Health Administration Press, One N Franklin St, Suite 1700, Chicago, IL 60606-3491 *Tel:* 312-424-2800 *Fax:* 312-424-0014 *E-mail:* hap1@ache.org *Web Site:* www.ache.org/publications (orders), pg 104

Davis, Jill, The American Library Association (ALA), 50 E Huron St, Chicago, IL 60611 *Tel:* 312-944-6780 *Toll Free Tel:* 800-545-2433 *Fax:* 312-280-5275 *E-mail:* editionsmarketing@ala.org *Web Site:* www.alastore.ala.org, pg 13

Davis, John, Central Recovery Press (CRP), 3321 N Buffalo Dr, Suite 275, Las Vegas, NV 89129 *Tel:* 702-868-5830 *Fax:* 702-868-5831 *E-mail:* info@centralrecovery.com *Web Site:* centralrecoverypress.com, pg 52

Davis, Julie, Indiana University Press, Herman B Wells Library 350, 1320 E Tenth St, Bloomington, IN 47405-3907 *Tel:* 812-855-8817 *Toll Free Tel:* 800-842-6796 (orders only) *Fax:* 812-855-7931; 812-855-8507 *E-mail:* iupress@indiana.edu; iuporder@indiana.edu (orders) *Web Site:* www.iupress.indiana.edu, pg 116

Davis, Kara, Lantern Books, 128 Second Place, Garden Suite, Brooklyn, NY 11231 *Tel:* 212-414-2275 *E-mail:* editorial@lanternbooks.com; info@lanternmedia.net *Web Site:* lanternbooks.presswarehouse.com/Home/home.aspx, pg 129

Davis, Lisa, University of Tennessee Press, 110 Conference Center Bldg, 600 Henley St, Knoxville, TN 37996-4108 *Tel:* 865-974-3321 *Toll Free Tel:* 800-621-2736 (orders) *Fax:* 865-974-3724 *Toll Free Fax:* 800-621-8476 (orders) *E-mail:* custserv@utpress.org *Web Site:* www.utpress.org, pg 245

Davis, Lisa Fagin, John Nicholas Brown Prize, 17 Dunster St, Suite 202, Cambridge, MA 02138 *Tel:* 617-491-1622 *Fax:* 617-492-3303 *E-mail:* info@themedievalacademy.org *Web Site:* www.medievalacademy.org, pg 634

Davis, Lisa Fagin, Van Courtlandt Elliott Prize, 17 Dunster St, Suite 202, Cambridge, MA 02138 *Tel:* 617-491-1622 *Fax:* 617-492-3303 *E-mail:* info@themedievalacademy.org *Web Site:* www.medievalacademy.org, pg 644

Davis, Lisa Fagin, Haskins Medal Award, 17 Dunster St, Suite 202, Cambridge, MA 02138 *Tel:* 617-491-1622 *Fax:* 617-492-3303 *E-mail:* info@themedievalacademy.org *Web Site:* www.medievalacademy.org, pg 652

Davis, Mary Ellen K, Association of College & Research Libraries (ACRL), 50 E Huron St, Chicago, IL 60611 *Tel:* 312-280-2523 *Toll Free Tel:* 800-545-2433 (ext 2523) *Fax:* 312-280-2520 *E-mail:* acrl@ala.org *Web Site:* www.ala.org/acrl, pg 24

Davis, Melodie, MennoMedia, 1251 Virginia Ave, Harrisonburg, VA 22802-2434 *Toll Free Tel:* 800-245-7894 (orders & cust serv US) *Toll Free Fax:* 877-271-0760 *E-mail:* info@mennomedia.org *Web Site:* www.mennomedia.org, pg 148

Davis, Nancy, Peachpit Press, 1301 Sansome St, San Francisco, CA 94111 *Toll Free Tel:* 800-283-9444 *E-mail:* info@peachpit.com; ask@peachpit.com *Web Site:* www.peachpit.com, pg 175

Davis, Patti, The PRS Group Inc, 5800 Heritage Landing Dr, Suite E, East Syracuse, NY 13057-9358 *Tel:* 315-431-0511 *Fax:* 315-431-0200 *E-mail:* custserv@prsgroup.com *Web Site:* www.prsgroup.com, pg 190

Davis, Randy, AuthorHouse, 1663 Liberty Dr, Bloomington, IN 47403 *Tel:* 812-339-6000 (outside US) *Toll Free Tel:* 888-519-5121 *E-mail:* authorsupport@authorhouse.com *Web Site:* www.authorhouse.com, pg 26

Davis, Rebecca, Boyds Mills Press, 815 Church St, Honesdale, PA 18431 *Tel:* 570-253-1164 *Toll Free Tel:* 800-490-5111 *Fax:* 570-253-0179 *E-mail:* contact@boydsmillspress.com *Web Site:* www.boydsmillspress.com, pg 41

Davis, Reiko, DeFiore and Company Literary Management Inc, 47 E 19 St, 3rd fl, New York, NY 10003 *Tel:* 212-925-7744 *Fax:* 212-925-9803 *E-mail:* info@defliterary.com; submissions@defliterary.com *Web Site:* www.defliterary.com, pg 513

Davis, Robert, Tom Doherty Associates, LLC, 175 Fifth Ave, 14th fl, New York, NY 10010 *Tel:* 646-307-5511 *Toll Free Tel:* 800-455-0340 *Web Site:* www.tor-forge.com, pg 71

Davis, Roisin, Roam Agency, 45 Main St, Suite 727, Brooklyn, NY 11201-1076 *E-mail:* roam@roamagency.com *Web Site:* www.roamagency.com, pg 533

Davis, Ryan, Emerald Books, PO Box 55787, Seattle, WA 98155 *Tel:* 425-771-1153 *Toll Free Tel:* 800-922-2143 *Fax:* 425-775-2383 *E-mail:* books@ywampublishing.com *Web Site:* www.ywampublishing.com, pg 78

Davis, Sara, University of Missouri Press, 113 Heinkel Bldg, 201 S Seventh St, Columbia, MO 65211 *Tel:* 573-882-7641 *Toll Free Tel:* 800-621-2736 (orders) *Fax:* 573-884-4498 *Toll Free Fax:* 800-621-8476 (orders) *E-mail:* upress@missouri.edu *Web Site:* upress.missouri.edu; press.umsystem.edu, pg 243

Davis, Steve, Carr P Collins Award, c/o 7748 Hwy 290 W, Austin, TX 78736-3202 *Tel:* 512-683-5640 *E-mail:* president@texasinstituteofletters.org *Web Site:* www.texasinstituteofletters.org, pg 638

Davis, Steve, Soeurette Diehl Fraser Translation Award, c/o 7748 Hwy 290 W, Austin, TX 78736-3202 *Tel:* 512-683-5640 *E-mail:* president@texasinstituteofletters.org *Web Site:* www.texasinstituteofletters.org, pg 647

Davis, Steve, Jesse H Jones Award, c/o 7748 Hwy 290 W, Austin, TX 78736-3202 *Tel:* 512-683-5640 *E-mail:* president@texasinstituteofletters.org *Web Site:* www.texasinstituteofletters.org, pg 657

Davis, Steve, Ramirez Family Award, c/o 7748 Hwy 290 W, Austin, TX 78736-3202 *Tel:* 512-683-5640 *E-mail:* president@texasinstituteofletters.org *Web Site:* www.texasinstituteofletters.org, pg 684

Davis, Steve, Edwin "Bud" Shrake Award for Best Short Nonfiction, c/o 7748 Hwy 290 W, Austin, TX 78736-3202 *Tel:* 512-683-5640 *E-mail:* president@texasinstituteofletters.org *Web Site:* www.texasinstituteofletters.org, pg 689

Davis, Steve, Helen C Smith Memorial Award, c/o 7748 Hwy 290 W, Austin, TX 78736-3202 *Tel:* 512-683-5640 *E-mail:* president@texasinstituteofletters.org *Web Site:* www.texasinstituteofletters.org, pg 690

Davis, Steve, Texas Institute of Letters (TIL), c/o 7748 Hwy 290 W, Austin, TX 78736-3202 *E-mail:* president@texasinstituteofletters.org; secretary@texasinstituteofletters.org *Web Site:* www.texasinstituteofletters.org, pg 579

Davis, Steve, Texas Institute of Letters Awards, c/o 7748 Hwy 290 W, Austin, TX 78736-3202 *Tel:* 512-683-5640 *E-mail:* president@texasinstituteofletters.org *Web Site:* www.texasinstituteofletters.org, pg 694

Davis, Susan M, Sagamore Publishing LLC, 1807 N Federal Dr, Urbana, IL 61801 *Tel:* 217-359-5940 *Toll Free Tel:* 800-327-5557 (orders) *Fax:* 217-359-5975 *E-mail:* web@sagamorepub.com *Web Site:* www.sagamorepub.com, pg 203

Davis, Timothy, McLemore Prize, William F Winter Archives & History Bldg, 200 North St, Jackson, MS 39201 *Tel:* 601-576-6850 *Fax:* 601-576-6975 *E-mail:* mhs@mdah.ms.gov *Web Site:* www.mdah.ms.gov, pg 667

Davis, Timothy S Esq, Close Up Publishing, 1330 Braddock Place, Suite 400, Alexandria, VA 22314 *Tel:* 703-706-3300 *Toll Free Tel:* 800-CLOSE-UP (256-7387) *Fax:* 703-706-3564 *E-mail:* info@closeup.org *Web Site:* www.closeup.org, pg 57

Davis, Tinsley, National Association of Science Writers (NASW), PO Box 7905, Berkeley, CA 94707 *Tel:* 510-647-9500 *Web Site:* www.nasw.org, pg 571

Davis, Tinsley, Science in Society Journalism Awards, PO Box 7905, Berkeley, CA 94707 *Tel:* 510-647-9500 *Web Site:* www.nasw.org, pg 688

Davis, Wendy, The Learning Source Ltd, 644 Tenth St, Brooklyn, NY 11215 *Tel:* 718-768-0231 (ext 10) *Fax:* 718-369-3467 *E-mail:* info@learningsourceltd.com *Web Site:* www.learningsourceltd.com, pg 497

Davis-Undiano, Robert Con, Neustadt International Prize for Literature, c/o University of Oklahoma, 630 Parrington Oval, Suite 110, Norman, OK 73019-4033 *Tel:* 405-325-4531 *Web Site:* www.worldliteraturetoday.org; www.worldlit.org, pg 672

Davis-Undiano, Robert Con, NSK Neustadt Prize for Children's Literature, c/o University of Oklahoma, 630 Parrington Oval, Suite 110, Norman, OK 73019-4033 *Tel:* 405-325-4531 *Web Site:* www.worldliteraturetoday.org; www.worldlit.org, pg 674

Davisson, Leslie, Pomegranate Communications Inc, 19018 NE Portal Way, Portland, OR 97230 *Tel:* 503-328-6500 *Toll Free Tel:* 800-227-1428 *Fax:* 503-328-9330 *Toll Free Fax:* 800-848-4376 *E-mail:* contactus@pomegranate.com *Web Site:* www.pomegranate.com, pg 185

Davy, Martin, Houghton Mifflin Harcourt, 125 High St, Boston, MA 02110 *Tel:* 617-351-5000 *Toll Free Tel:* 855-969-4642; 800-225-5425 (K-12 educ materials); 800-323-9540 (assessment materials); 877-219-1537 (SkillsTutor); 888-242-6747 (Innovation in Educ Group); 800-225-3362 (Trade & Ref Div) *Toll Free Fax:* 800-269-5232 *E-mail:* myhmhco@hmhco.com *Web Site:* www.hmhco.com, pg 110

Dawes, John, Piano Press, 1425 Ocean Ave, Suite 5, Del Mar, CA 92014 *Tel:* 619-884-1401 *Fax:* 858-755-1104 *E-mail:* pianopress@pianopress.com *Web Site:* www.pianopress.com, pg 182

Dawes, Kwame, Prairie Schooner Annual Strousse Award, University of Nebraska, 123 Andrews Hall, 625 N 14 St, Lincoln, NE 68508 *Tel:* 402-472-0911 *Fax:* 402-472-9771 *E-mail:* prairieschooner@unl.edu *Web Site:* prairieschooner.unl.edu, pg 681

Dawes, Kwame, Prairie Schooner Bernice Slote Award, University of Nebraska, 123 Andrews Hall, 625 N 14 St, Lincoln, NE 68508 *Tel:* 402-472-0911 *E-mail:* prairieschooner@unl.edu *Web Site:* prairieschooner.unl.edu, pg 681

Dawes, Kwame, Prairie Schooner Book Prize Contest in Fiction, University of Nebraska, 123 Andrews Hall, 625 N 14 St, Lincoln, NE 68508 *Tel:* 402-472-0911 *Fax:* 402-472-9771 *E-mail:* psbookprize@unl.edu *Web Site:* prairieschooner.unl.edu, pg 681

Dawes, Kwame, Prairie Schooner Book Prize Contest in Poetry, University of Nebraska, 123 Andrews Hall, 625 N 14 St, Lincoln, NE 68508 *Tel:* 402-472-0911 *Fax:* 402-472-9771 *E-mail:* psbookprize@unl.edu *Web Site:* prairieschooner.unl.edu, pg 681

Dawes, Kwame, Prairie Schooner Edward Stanley Award, University of Nebraska, 123 Andrews Hall, 625 N 14 St, Lincoln, NE 68508 *Tel:* 402-472-0911 *Fax:* 402-472-9771 *E-mail:* prairieschooner@unl.edu *Web Site:* prairieschooner.unl.edu, pg 681

Dawes, Kwame, Prairie Schooner Glenna Luschei Award, University of Nebraska, 123 Andrews Hall, 625 N 14 St, Lincoln, NE 68508 *Tel:* 402-472-0911 *Fax:* 402-472-9771 *E-mail:* prairieschooner@unl.edu *Web Site:* prairieschooner.unl.edu, pg 681

Dawes, Kwame, Prairie Schooner Hugh J Luke Award, University of Nebraska, 123 Andrews Hall, 625 N 14 St, Lincoln, NE 68508 *Tel:* 402-472-0911 *Fax:* 402-472-9771 *E-mail:* prairieschooner@unl.edu *Web Site:* prairieschooner.unl.edu, pg 681

Dawes, Kwame, Prairie Schooner Jane Geske Award, University of Nebraska, 123 Andrews Hall, 625 N 14 St, Lincoln, NE 68508 *Tel:* 402-472-0911 *Fax:* 402-472-9771 *E-mail:* prairieschooner@unl.edu *Web Site:* prairieschooner.unl.edu, pg 681

Dawes, Kwame, Prairie Schooner Lawrence Foundation Award, University of Nebraska, 123 Andrews Hall, 625 N 14 St, Lincoln, NE 68508 *Tel:* 402-472-0911 *Fax:* 402-472-9771 *E-mail:* prairieschooner@unl.edu *Web Site:* prairieschooner.unl.edu, pg 681

Dawes, Kwame, Prairie Schooner Virginia Faulkner Award for Excellence in Writing, University of Nebraska, 123 Andrews Hall, 625 N 14 St, Lincoln, NE 68508 *Tel:* 402-472-0911 *Fax:* 402-472-9771 *E-mail:* prairieschooner@unl.edu *Web Site:* prairieschooner.unl.edu, pg 682

Dawson, Havis, Liza Dawson Associates, 350 Seventh Ave, Suite 2003, New York, NY 10001 *Tel:* 212-465-9071 *Fax:* 212-947-0460 *Web Site:* www.lizadawsonassociates.com, pg 513

Dawson, Kathy, Dial Books for Young Readers, 345 Hudson St, New York, NY 10014 *Tel:* 212-366-2000 *Toll Free Tel:* 800-733-3000 (orders) *Fax:* 212-414-3396 *Web Site:* www.penguin.com, pg 70

Dawson, Liza, Liza Dawson Associates, 350 Seventh Ave, Suite 2003, New York, NY 10001 *Tel:* 212-465-9071 *Fax:* 212-947-0460 *Web Site:* www.lizadawsonassociates.com, pg 513

DeGenaro, Angelo T, McGraw-Hill Education, 2 Penn Plaza, New York, NY 10121-2298 *Tel:* 212-904-2000 *E-mail:* customer.service@mheducation.com; international_cs@mheducation.com *Web Site:* www.mheducation.com, pg 145

DeGennaro, Denise, Random House Children's Books, 1745 Broadway, 10th fl, New York, NY 10019 *Tel:* 212-782-9000 *Web Site:* www.randomhousekids.com, pg 194

Dehmler, Mari Lynch, Fine Wordworking, PO Box 3041, Monterey, CA 93942-3041 *Tel:* 831-375-6278 *E-mail:* info@finewordworking.com *Web Site:* marilynch.com, pg 494

Deisinger, Robert D, American Technical Publishers Inc, 10100 Orland Pkwy, Suite 200, Orland Park, IL 60467-5756 *Toll Free Tel:* 800-323-3471 *Fax:* 708-957-1101 *E-mail:* service@atplearning.com; order@atplearning.com *Web Site:* www.atplearning.com, pg 15

Deitch, Lisa, F A Davis Co, 1915 Arch St, Philadelphia, PA 19103 *Tel:* 215-568-2270; 215-440-3001 *Toll Free Tel:* 800-523-4049 *Fax:* 215-568-5065; 215-440-3016 *E-mail:* info@fadavis.com; orders@fadavis.com *Web Site:* www.fadavis.com, pg 68

DeJesu, Betsy, Perseus Books, 250 W 57 St, 15th fl, New York, NY 10107 *Tel:* 212-340-8100 *Toll Free Tel:* 800-343-4499 (cust serv) *Fax:* 212-340-8105 *Web Site:* www.perseusbooks.com, pg 180

DeKock, Meredith, Regular Baptist Press, 3715 N Ventura Dr, Arlington Heights, IL 60004 *Tel:* 847-843-1600 *Toll Free Tel:* 800-727-4440; 800-727-4440 (cust serv) *Fax:* 847-843-3757 *E-mail:* rbp@garbc.org *Web Site:* regularbaptistpress.org, pg 198

Deku, Prof Afrikadzata PhD, Continental AfrikaPublishers, 182 Stribling Circle, Spartanburg, SC 29301 *Tel:* 864-576-7992 *Fax:* 864-576-7992 *E-mail:* afrikalion@aol.com; profafrikadzatadeku@facebook.com; profafrikadzatadeku@yahoo.com; afrikapharaoh@gmail.com *Web Site:* www.afrikacentricity.com, pg 60

Del Valle, Daniel, Farrar, Straus & Giroux, LLC, 18 W 18 St, New York, NY 10011 *Tel:* 212-741-6900 *E-mail:* fsg.publicity@fsgbooks.com *Web Site:* us.macmillan.com/fsg.aspx, pg 83

del Valle, Emma, Simon & Schuster, 1230 Avenue of the Americas, New York, NY 10020 *Tel:* 212-698-7000 *Toll Free Tel:* 800-223-2348 (cust serv); 800-223-2336 (orders) *Toll Free Fax:* 800-943-9831 (orders) *Web Site:* www.simonandschuster.com, pg 212

Delaney, Ian, Chronicle Books LLC, 680 Second St, San Francisco, CA 94107 *Tel:* 415-537-4200 *Toll Free Tel:* 800-759-0190 (cust serv) *Fax:* 415-537-4460 *Toll Free Fax:* 800-858-7787 (orders); 800-286-9471 (cust serv) *E-mail:* frontdesk@chroniclebooks.com *Web Site:* www.chroniclebooks.com, pg 55

Delaney, Jennifer, Davies-Black Publishing, 53 State St, Boston, MA 02109 *Tel:* 617-523-3801 *Fax:* 617-523-3708 *E-mail:* info@nicholasbrealey.com *Web Site:* www.nicholasbrealey.com, pg 67

Delaney, Jennifer, Intercultural Press Inc, 53 State St, Boston, MA 02109 *Tel:* 617-523-3801 *Toll Free Tel:* 888-273-2539 *Fax:* 617-523-3708 *E-mail:* info@interculturalpress.com *Web Site:* nicholasbrealey.com, pg 118

Delaney, Kelly, Random House Children's Books, 1745 Broadway, 10th fl, New York, NY 10019 *Tel:* 212-782-9000 *Web Site:* www.randomhousekids.com, pg 194

DeLappe, Kathryn, Firefall Editions, 4905 Tunlaw St, Alexandria, VA 22312 *Tel:* 510-549-2461 *E-mail:* literary@att.net *Web Site:* www.firefallmedia.com, pg 85

Delbourgo, Joelle, Joelle Delbourgo Associates Inc, 101 Park St, Montclair, NJ 07042 *Tel:* 973-773-0836 (call only during standard business hours) *Web Site:* www.delbourgo.com, pg 513

Dellon, Hope, St Martin's Press, LLC, 175 Fifth Ave, New York, NY 10010 *Tel:* 646-307-5151 *Web Site:* us.macmillan.com/smp, pg 204

Delman, Scott, Association for Computing Machinery, 2 Penn Plaza, Suite 701, New York, NY 10121-0701 *Tel:* 212-869-7440 *Toll Free Tel:* 800-342-6626 *Fax:* 212-944-1318 (memb servs) *E-mail:* acmhelp@acm.org *Web Site:* www.acm.org, pg 24

Delman, Stephanie, Sanford J Greenburger Associates Inc, 55 Fifth Ave, New York, NY 10003 *Tel:* 212-206-5600 *Fax:* 212-463-8718 *Web Site:* greenburger.com; www.sjga.com, pg 520

Delorme, Alain, Les Editions Goelette Inc, 1350 Marie-Victorin, St-Bruno-de-Montarville, Quebec, QC J3V 6B9, Canada *Tel:* 450-653-1337 *Toll Free Tel:* 800-463-4961 *Fax:* 450-653-9924 *E-mail:* info@boutiquegoelette.com *Web Site:* www.boutiquegeolette.com, pg 454

DeLozier, Sara, Picador, 175 Fifth Ave, 19th fl, New York, NY 10010 *Tel:* 646-307-5151 *Fax:* 212-253-9627 *Web Site:* www.picadorusa.com, pg 182

DeLuca, David, Bess Press, 3565 Harding Ave, Honolulu, HI 96816 *Tel:* 808-734-7159 *Fax:* 808-732-3627 *E-mail:* customerservice@besspress.com *Web Site:* www.besspress.com, pg 34

Deluca, Michael J, Small Beer Press, 150 Pleasant St, No 306, Easthampton, MA 01027 *Tel:* 413-203-1636 *Fax:* 413-203-1636 *E-mail:* info@smallbeerpress.com *Web Site:* smallbeerpress.com, pg 215

Dema, Leslie, Broadview Press, 280 Perry St, Unit 5, Peterborough, ON K9J 2J4, Canada *Tel:* 705-743-8990 *Fax:* 705-743-8353 *E-mail:* customerservice@broadviewpress.com *Web Site:* www.broadviewpress.com, pg 447

DeMaiolo, James, Tachyon Publications LLC, 1459 18 St, No 139, San Francisco, CA 94107 *Tel:* 415-285-5615 *E-mail:* tachyon@tachyonpublications.com *Web Site:* www.tachyonpublications.com, pg 226

Demakos, Michael, EMC Publishing LLC, 875 Montreal Way, St Paul, MN 55102 *Tel:* 651-290-2800 (corp) *Toll Free Tel:* 800-328-1452 *Toll Free Fax:* 800-328-4564 *E-mail:* educate@emcp.com *Web Site:* www.emcp.com, pg 77

Demallie, Katie, The French-American Foundation & Florence Gould Foundation Annual Translation Prize, 28 W 44 St, Suite 1420, New York, NY 10036 *Tel:* 212-829-8800 *Fax:* 212-829-8810 *Web Site:* www.frenchamerican.org, pg 648

Demers, Elizabeth Sherburn, The Johns Hopkins University Press, 2715 N Charles St, Baltimore, MD 21218-4363 *Tel:* 410-516-6900; 410-516-6987 (journal orders outside US & CN) *Toll Free Tel:* 800-537-5487 (book orders & cust serv); 800-548-1784 (journal orders) *Fax:* 410-516-6968; 410-516-3866 (journal orders) *E-mail:* hfscustserv@press.jhu.edu (cust serv); jrnlcirc@press.jhu.edu (journal orders) *Web Site:* www.press.jhu.edu; muse.jhu.edu, pg 122

DeMier, Chrissy, Morton Publishing Co, 925 W Kenyon Ave, Unit 12, Englewood, CO 80110 *Tel:* 303-761-4805 *Fax:* 303-762-9923 *E-mail:* contact@morton-pub.com; returns@morton-pub.com *Web Site:* www.morton-pub.com, pg 154

DeMint, Jim, The Heritage Foundation, 214 Massachusetts Ave NE, Washington, DC 20002-4999 *Tel:* 202-546-4400 *Toll Free Tel:* 800-544-4843 *Fax:* 202-546-8328 *E-mail:* info@heritage.org *Web Site:* www.heritage.org, pg 106

DeMonico, Michael, Sophia Institute Press®, 522 Donald St, Unit 3, Bedford, NH 03110 *Tel:* 603-836-5505 *Toll Free Tel:* 800-888-9344 *Fax:* 603-641-8108 *Toll Free Fax:* 888-288-2259 *E-mail:* orders@sophiainstitute.com *Web Site:* www.sophiainstitute.com, pg 217

Dempsey, Aoife, Triumph Learning LLC, 136 Madison Ave, 7th fl, New York, NY 10016 *Tel:* 212-652-0200 *Toll Free Tel:* 800-338-6519 (cust serv) *Toll Free Fax:* 866-805-5723 *E-mail:* info@triumphlearning.com; customerservice@triumphlearning.com *Web Site:* www.triumphlearning.com, pg 235

Dempsey, Luke, HarperCollins General Books Group, 195 Broadway, New York, NY 10007 *Tel:* 212-207-7000 *Web Site:* www.harpercollins.com, pg 101

DeMuzio, Stephanie, Jessica Kingsley Publishers Inc, 400 Market St, Suite 400, Philadelphia, PA 19106 *Tel:* 215-922-1161 *Toll Free Tel:* 866-416-1078 (cust serv) *Fax:* 215-922-1474 *E-mail:* orders@jkp.com; hello.usa@jkp.com *Web Site:* www.jkp.com, pg 126

DeNardo, Melanie, Random House Publishing Group, 1745 Broadway, New York, NY 10019 *Toll Free Tel:* 800-200-3552 *Web Site:* atrandom.com, pg 195

Denato, Sr Maria Grace, Pauline Books & Media, 50 Saint Paul's Ave, Boston, MA 02130 *Tel:* 617-522-8911 *Toll Free Tel:* 800-876-4463 (orders); 800-836-9723 (cust serv) *Fax:* 617-541-9805 *E-mail:* editorial@paulinemedia.com (ms submissions); orderentry@pauline.org (cust serv) *Web Site:* www.pauline.org/publishing; www.pauline.org/PBMPublishing, pg 175

Denehy, Debby, Petroleum Extension Service (PETEX), JJ Pickle Research Campus, 10100 Burnet Rd, Bldg 2, Austin, TX 78758-4445 *Tel:* 512-471-5940 *Toll Free Tel:* 800-687-4132 *Fax:* 512-471-9410 *Toll Free Fax:* 800-687-7839 *E-mail:* info@petex.utexas.edu *Web Site:* cee.utexas.edu/ce/petex/, pg 181

Denekamp, Hope, Kneerim & Williams Agency, 90 Canal St, Boston, MA 02114 *Tel:* 617-303-1650 *Web Site:* www.kwlit.com, pg 524

Denning, Jane Kinney, Women's National Book Association Award, PO Box 237, FDR Sta, New York, NY 10150-0231 *Tel:* 212-208-4629 (headquarters) *Toll Free Tel:* 866-610-9622 *Fax:* 212-208-4629 *Web Site:* www.wnba-books.org; www.NationalReadingGroupMonth.org, pg 699

Dennis, Diane, Idyllwild Arts Summer Workshops, 52500 Temecula Dr, Idyllwild, CA 92549-0038 *Tel:* 951-659-2171 *Fax:* 951-659-4552 *E-mail:* summer@idyllwildarts.org *Web Site:* www.idyllwildarts.org/writersweek, pg 611

Dennis, Josh, Crossway, 1300 Crescent St, Wheaton, IL 60187 *Tel:* 630-682-4300 *Toll Free Tel:* 800-635-7993 (orders); 800-543-1659 (cust serv) *Fax:* 630-682-4785 *E-mail:* info@crossway.org *Web Site:* www.crossway.org, pg 65

Dennis, Lane T, Crossway, 1300 Crescent St, Wheaton, IL 60187 *Tel:* 630-682-4300 *Toll Free Tel:* 800-635-7993 (orders); 800-543-1659 (cust serv) *Fax:* 630-682-4785 *E-mail:* info@crossway.org *Web Site:* www.crossway.org, pg 65

Dennys, Louise, Knopf Canada, 320 Front St W, Suite 1400, Toronto, ON M5V 3B6, Canada *Tel:* 416-364-4449 *Toll Free Tel:* 888-523-9292 *Fax:* 416-598-7764 *Web Site:* www.penguinrandomhouse.ca, pg 462

Dennys, Louise, Penguin Random House Canada, 320 Front St W, Suite 1400, Toronto, ON M5V 3B6, Canada *Tel:* 416-364-4449 *Toll Free Tel:* 888-523-9292 (cust serv) *Fax:* 416-598-7764 *Web Site:* www.penguinrandomhouse.ca, pg 467

Dent-Zobal, Catherine, Susquehanna University, Department of English and Creative Writing, 514 University Ave, Selinsgrove, PA 17870 *Tel:* 570-372-0101, pg 622

Deol, Amar, Simon & Schuster, 1230 Avenue of the Americas, New York, NY 10020 *Tel.* 212-698-7000 *Toll Free Tel:* 800-223-2348 (cust serv); 800-223-2336 (orders) *Toll Free Fax:* 800-943-9831 (orders) *Web Site:* www.simonandschuster.com, pg 212

Deraco, Anthony, DEStech Publications Inc, 439 N Duke St, Lancaster, PA 17602-4967 *Tel:* 717-290-1660 *Toll Free Tel:* 877-500-4337 *Fax:* 717-509-6100 *E-mail:* info@destechpub.com *Web Site:* www.destechpub.com, pg 69

Derleth, Damon, Arkham House Publishers Inc, PO Box 546, Sauk City, WI 53583 *Tel:* 608-643-4500 *Fax:* 608-643-5043 *E-mail:* sales@arkhamhouse.com *Web Site:* www.arkhamhouse.com, pg 21

DeRobertis-Theye, Nicola, Trident Media Group LLC, 41 Madison Ave, 36th fl, New York, NY 10010 *Tel:* 212-333-1511 *E-mail:* info@tridentmediagroup.com; press@tridentmediagroup.com *Web Site:* www.tridentmediagroup.com, pg 540

Derrick, Ruth, Highland Summer Writers' Conference, PO Box 7014, Radford University, Cook Hall, Radford, VA 24142 *Fax:* 540-831-5951 *Web Site:* www.radford.edu/content/cehd/home/appalachian-studies.html, pg 611

Derviskadic, Dado, Folio Literary Management, The Film Center Bldg, 630 Ninth Ave, Suite 1101, New York, NY 10036 *Tel:* 212-400-1494 *Fax:* 212-967-0977 *Web Site:* www.foliolit.com, pg 517

Des Jardines, David E, University of Georgia Press, Main Library, 3rd fl, 320 S Jackson St, Athens, GA 30602 *Fax:* 706-542-2558; 706-542-6770 *Web Site:* www.ugapress.org, pg 241

Desai, Amit, DC Entertainment, 2900 Alameda, Burbank, CA 91505 *Toll Free Tel:* 800-887-6789 *E-mail:* dccomics@cambeywest.com *Web Site:* www.dcentertainment.com; www.dccomics.com; www.madmag.com, pg 69

DeSanti, Carole, Viking, 375 Hudson St, New York, NY 10014 *Tel:* 212-366-2000 *Fax:* 212-243-6002 *Web Site:* www.penguin.com/publishers/vikingbooks, pg 250

Desautels, Jon, Bear & Co Inc, One Park St, Rochester, VT 05767 *Tel:* 802-767-3174 *Toll Free Tel:* 800-932-3277 *Fax:* 802-767-3726 *E-mail:* customerservice@InnerTraditions.com *Web Site:* InnerTraditions.com, pg 31

Desautels, Jon, Inner Traditions International Ltd, One Park St, Rochester, VT 05767 *Tel:* 802-767-3174 *Toll Free Tel:* 800-246-8648 *Fax:* 802-767-3726 *E-mail:* customerservice@InnerTraditions.com *Web Site:* www.InnerTraditions.com, pg 117

Descombes, Eric, McGraw-Hill International & Professional Publishing Group, 2 Penn Plaza, New York, NY 10121 *Tel:* 646-766-2000 *Web Site:* www.mheducation.com, pg 146

DesHotel, Robyn, American Booksellers Association, 333 Westchester Ave, Suite S202, White Plains, NY 10604 *Tel:* 914-406-7500 *Toll Free Tel:* 800-637-0037 *Fax:* 914-410-6297 *E-mail:* info@bookweb.org *Web Site:* www.bookweb.org, pg 554

DeSio, Andrew, Princeton University Press, 41 William St, Princeton, NJ 08540-5237 *Tel:* 609-258-4900 *Fax:* 609-258-6305 *Web Site:* press.princeton.edu, pg 188

Desjardins, Daniel, Ulysses Travel Guides, 4176, rue Saint-Denis, Montreal, QC H2W 2M5, Canada *Tel:* 514-843-9882 (ext 2232); 514-843-9447 (bookstore) *Toll Free Tel:* 800-748-9171 *Fax:* 514-843-9448 *E-mail:* info@ulysses.ca; st-denis@ulysses.ca *Web Site:* www.ulyssesguides.com, pg 473

Desjardins, Francoise, Art Image Publications, PO Box 160, Derby Line, VT 05830 *Toll Free Tel:* 800-361-2598 *Toll Free Fax:* 800-559-2598 *E-mail:* info@artimagepublications.com; customer.service@artimagepublications.com *Web Site:* www.artimagepublications.com, pg 21

DeSmet, Christine, University of Wisconsin-Madison Continuing Studies, 21 N Park St, 7th fl, Madison, WI 53715 *Tel:* 608-262-3447 *Web Site:* continuingstudies.wisc.edu, pg 624

Desmond, Sean, Grand Central Publishing, 1290 Avenue of the Americas, New York, NY 10019 *Tel:* 212-364-1100 *Web Site:* www.hachettebookgroup.com, pg 95

Despain, Ashley, Chronicle Books LLC, 680 Second St, San Francisco, CA 94107 *Tel:* 415-537-4200 *Toll Free Tel:* 800-759-0190 (cust serv) *Fax:* 415-537-4460 *Toll Free Fax:* 800-858-7787 (orders); 800-286-9471 (cust serv) *E-mail:* frontdesk@chroniclebooks.com *Web Site:* www.chroniclebooks.com, pg 55

Desser, Robin, Alfred A Knopf/Everyman's Library, c/o Penguin Random House Inc, 1745 Broadway, New York, NY 10019 *Tel:* 212-751-2600 *Toll Free Tel:* 800-638-6460 *Fax:* 212-572-2593 *Web Site:* www.knopfdoubleday.com, pg 127

Desuta, Heather, Pennwriters Conference, PO Box 685, Dalton, PA 18414 *E-mail:* conferencecoordinator@pennwriters.org; info@pennwriters.org *Web Site:* pennwriters.org, pg 613

Dettman, Tracey, Fifth House Publishers, 195 Allstate Pkwy, Markham, ON L3R 4T8, Canada *Tel:* 905-477-9700 *Toll Free Tel:* 800-387-9776 *Toll Free Fax:* 800-260-9777 *E-mail:* godwit@fitzhenry.ca; bookinfo@fitzhenry.ca (cust serv) *Web Site:* www.fitzhenry.ca/fifthhouse.aspx, pg 456

Detweiler, Katelyn, Jill Grinberg Literary Management LLC, 392 Vanderbilt Ave, Brooklyn, NY 11238 *Tel:* 212-620-5883 *E-mail:* info@jillgrinbergliterary.com *Web Site:* www.jillgrinbergliterary.com, pg 520

Deutsch, Phyllis, University Press of New England, One Court St, Suite 250, Lebanon, NH 03766 *Tel:* 603-448-1533 *Toll Free Tel:* 800-421-1561 (orders only) *Fax:* 603-448-7006; 603-448-9429 (orders only) *E-mail:* university.press@dartmouth.edu *Web Site:* www.upne.com, pg 247

Devane, Christine, Rand McNally, 9855 Woods Dr, Skokie, IL 60077 *Tel:* 847-329-8100 *E-mail:* ctsales@randmcnally.com; mediarelations@randmcnally.com *Web Site:* www.randmcnally.com, pg 194

Devine, Tracy, Random House Publishing Group, 1745 Broadway, New York, NY 10019 *Toll Free Tel:* 800-200-3552 *Web Site:* atrandom.com, pg 195

Devineni, Ram, Rattapallax Press, 217 Thompson St, Suite 353, New York, NY 10012 *E-mail:* info@rattapallax.com *Web Site:* www.rattapallax.com, pg 195

DeVinney, Karen, University of North Texas Press, Willis Library, Rm 251, 1506 Highland St, Denton, TX 76203-5017 *Tel:* 940-565-2142 *Fax:* 940-565-4590 *Web Site:* untpress.unt.edu, pg 243

Devlin, Anne G, Max Gartenberg Literary Agency, 912 N Pennsylvania Ave, Yardley, PA 19067 *Tel:* 215-295-9230 *Web Site:* www.maxgartenberg.com, pg 518

Devlin, Jeanne, The RoadRunner Press, 124 NW 32 St, Oklahoma City, OK 73118 *Tel:* 405-524-6205 *Fax:* 405-524-6312 *E-mail:* info@theroadrunnerpress.com; orders@theroadrunnerpress.com *Web Site:* www.theroadrunnerpress.com, pg 200

deVries, Anna, Picador, 175 Fifth Ave, 19th fl, New York, NY 10010 *Tel:* 646-307-5151 *Fax:* 212-253-9627 *Web Site:* www.picadorusa.com, pg 182

DeVries, Catherine, David C Cook, 4050 Lee Vance View, Colorado Springs, CO 80918 *Tel:* 719-536-0100 *Toll Free Tel:* 800-708-5550; 800-323-7543 (orders & cust serv) *Toll Free Fax:* 800-430-0726 (cust serv) *Web Site:* www.davidccook.com, pg 60

DeVries, Tom, Wm B Eerdmans Publishing Co, 2140 Oak Industrial Dr NE, Grand Rapids, MI 49505 *Tel:* 616-459-4591 *Toll Free Tel:* 800-253-7521 *Fax:* 616-459-6540 *E-mail:* customerservice@eerdmans.com; sales@eerdmans.com *Web Site:* www.eerdmans.com, pg 76

Dew, Dr Jay, Texas A&M University Press, John H Lindsey Bldg, Lewis St, 4354 TAMU, College Station, TX 77843-4354 *Tel:* 979-845-1436 *Toll Free Tel:* 800-826-8911 (orders) *Fax:* 979-847-8752 *Toll Free Fax:* 888-617-2421 (orders) *E-mail:* bookorders@tamu.edu *Web Site:* www.tamupress.com, pg 230

Dew, Sheri L, Deseret Book Co, 57 W South Temple, Salt Lake City, UT 84101-1511 *Tel:* 801-517-3369 *Toll Free Tel:* 800-453-4532 (orders); 888-846-7302 (orders) *Fax:* 801-517-3126 *E-mail:* service@deseretbook.com *Web Site:* www.deseretbook.com, pg 69

DeWall, Jan, Search Institute Press®, The Banks Bldg, Suite 125, 615 First Ave NE, Minneapolis, MN 55413 *Tel:* 612-376-8955; 612-692-5520 *Toll Free Tel:* 800-888-7828 *Fax:* 612-692-5553 *E-mail:* si@search-institute.org *Web Site:* www.search-institute.org, pg 210

Dewan, John, ACTA Publications, 4848 N Clark St, Chicago, IL 60640 *Tel:* 773-271-1030 *Toll Free Tel:* 800-397-2282 *Fax:* 773-271-7399 *Toll Free Fax:* 800-397-0079 *E-mail:* info@actapublications.com *Web Site:* www.actapublications.com, pg 4

Dewerd, Andrea, Random House Publishing Group, 1745 Broadway, New York, NY 10019 *Toll Free Tel:* 800-200-3552 *Web Site:* atrandom.com, pg 195

Dewey, Arthur J, Polebridge Press, PO Box 346, Farmington, MN 55024 *Tel:* 651-200-2372 *E-mail:* orders@westarinstitute.org *Web Site:* www.westarinstitute.org, pg 185

DeWitt, David, Little Bee Books, 853 Broadway, Suite 2014, New York, NY 10003 *E-mail:* info@littlebeebooks.com *Web Site:* www.littlebeebooks.com, pg 135

Dextor, Roger, Copywriter's Council of America™ (CCA), CCA Bldg, 7 Putter Lane, Middle Island, NY 11953-1920 *Tel:* 631-924-3888; 631-775-6075 *Fax:* 631-924-8555 *E-mail:* cca4dmcopy@gmail.com *Web Site:* www.andrewlinickdirectmarketing.com/Copywriters-Council.html; www.newworldpressbooks.com, pg 61, 491, 563

Dextor, Roger, Andrew S Linick PhD, The Copyologist®, Linick Bldg, 7 Putter Lane, Middle Island, NY 11953 *Tel:* 631-924-3888; 631-775-6075 *Fax:* 631-924-8555 *E-mail:* linickgroup@gmail.com; topmarketingadvisor@gmail.com *Web Site:* www.andrewlinickdirectmarketing.com/The-Copyologist.html; www.newworldpressbooks.com, pg 497

Dextre, Natalia, Random House Children's Books, 1745 Broadway, 10th fl, New York, NY 10019 *Tel:* 212-782-9000 *Web Site:* www.randomhousekids.com, pg 194

Deyoe, Cori, 3 Seas Literary Agency, PO Box 444, Sun Prairie, WI 53590 *Tel:* 608-834-9317 *E-mail:* threeseaslit@aol.com *Web Site:* threeseasagency.com, pg 539

DeYoung, Christina, Harvard Education Publishing Group, 8 Story St, 1st fl, Cambridge, MA 02138 *Tel:* 617-495-3432 *Toll Free Tel:* 800-513-0763 (subns); 888-437-1437 (orders) *Fax:* 617-496-3584; 978-348-1233 (orders) *E-mail:* hepg@harvard.edu *Web Site:* www.hepg.org, pg 102

Dhar, Uday K, Mondial, 203 W 107 St, Suite 6-C, New York, NY 10025 *Tel:* 646-807-8031 *Fax:* 208-361-2863 *E-mail:* contact@mondialbooks.com *Web Site:* www.mondialbooks.com, pg 153

Di Gioia, Tony, George T Bisel Co Inc, 710 S Washington Sq, Philadelphia, PA 19106-3519 *Tel:* 215-922-5760 *Toll Free Tel:* 800-247-3526 *Fax:* 215-922-2235 *E-mail:* gbisel@bisel.com *Web Site:* www.bisel.com, pg 35

Di Martino, Christina, Christina Di Martino Literary Services, 139 Sandpiper Ave, Royal Palm Beach, FL 33411 *Tel:* 212-996-9086 *E-mail:* writealotmail@gmail.com, pg 492

Di Piazza, Domenica, Twenty-First Century Books, 241 First Ave N, Minneapolis, MN 55401 *Tel:* 612-332-3344 *Toll Free Tel:* 800-328-4929 *Fax:* 612-332-7615 *Toll Free Fax:* 800-332-1132 *E-mail:* info@lernerbooks.com; custserve@lernerbooks.com *Web Site:* www.lernerbooks.com; www.facebook.com/lernerbooks, pg 237

Di Prisco, Joe, The Simpson Family Literary Prize, Lafayette Lib & Learning Ctr Foundation, 3491 Mount Diablo Blvd, Suite 214, Lafayette, CA 94549 *Tel:* 925-283-6513 *E-mail:* sflpweb@gmail.com *Web Site:* www.simpsonliteraryproject.org/programs, pg 689

Di Sarro, Lisa, Houghton Mifflin Harcourt K-12 Publishers, 125 High St, Boston, MA 02110 *Tel:* 617-351-5000 *Toll Free Tel:* 800-225-5425 (cust serv) *Web Site:* www.hmhco.com/classroom; www.hmhco.com, pg 111

Dial, Beth, National Poetry Series Open Competition, 57 Mountain Ave, Princeton, NJ 08540 *Tel:* 609-430-0999 *Fax:* 609-430-9933 *Web Site:* nationalpoetryseries.org, pg 671

DiAngelo, Brianne, Magazines Canada (MC), 425 Adelaide St W, Suite 700, Toronto, ON M5V 3C1, Canada *Tel:* 416-504-0274 *Fax:* 416-504-0437 *E-mail:* info@magazinescanada.ca *Web Site:* www.magazinescanada.ca/development/magnet, pg 569

Diaz, Paula, Special Libraries Association (SLA), 7918 Jones Branch Dr, Suite 300, McLean, VA 22102 *Tel:* 703-647-4900 *Fax:* 703-506-3266 *Web Site:* www.sla.org, pg 579

Diaz, Stefanie, Sanford J Greenburger Associates Inc, 55 Fifth Ave, New York, NY 10003 *Tel:* 212-206-5600 *Fax:* 212-463-8718 *Web Site:* greenburger.com; www.sjga.com, pg 520

DiBiase, Diane, Poisoned Pen Press, 6962 E First Ave, Suite 103, Scottsdale, AZ 85251 *Tel:* 480-945-3375 *Toll Free Tel:* 800-421-3976 *Fax:* 480-949-1707 *E-mail:* info@poisonedpenpress.com *Web Site:* www.poisonedpenpress.com, pg 185

DiChiera, Cristina, Fellowship Program, One Capital Hill, 3rd fl, Providence, RI 02908 *Tel:* 401-222-3880 *Fax:* 401-222-3018 *Web Site:* www.arts.ri.gov, pg 645

Dick, Janet L, Museum of New Mexico Press, 725 Camino Lejo, Suite C, Santa Fe, NM 87505 *Tel:* 505-476-1155; 505-272-7777 (orders); 505-277-4810 *Toll Free Tel:* 800-249-7737 (orders) *Fax:* 505-476-1156 *Toll Free Fax:* 800-622-8667 (orders) *Web Site:* www.mnmpress.org, pg 156

Dickemper, Cheryl, Houghton Mifflin Harcourt Trade & Reference Division, 125 High St, Boston, MA 02110 *Tel:* 617-351-5000 *Toll Free Tel:* 800-225-3362 *Web Site:* www.hmhco.com, pg 111

Dickerson, Donna, Peabody Museum Press, 11 Divinity Ave, Cambridge, MA 02138 *Tel:* 617-495-4255; 617-495-3938 (edit) *Fax:* 617-495-7535 *E-mail:* peapub@fas.harvard.edu *Web Site:* www.peabody.harvard.edu/publications, pg 175

Dickerson, Donya, McGraw-Hill International & Professional Publishing Group, 2 Penn Plaza, New York, NY 10121 *Tel:* 646-766-2000 *Web Site:* www.mheducation.com, pg 146

Dickinson, Jan, Wheatherstone Press, 11595 SW Butner Rd, No 22, Portland, OR 97225 *Tel:* 503-244-8929 *E-mail:* relocntr@nwlink.com *Web Site:* www.wheatherstonepress.com, pg 254

Dickinson, Kimberly, Manning Publications Co, PO Box 761, Shelter Island, NY 11964 *Tel:* 203-626-1510 *E-mail:* sales@manning.com; support@manning.com (cust serv) *Web Site:* www.manning.com, pg 141

Didier, Rebecca, Trafalgar Square Books, 388 Howe Hill Rd, North Pomfret, VT 05053 *Tel:* 802-457-1911 *Toll Free Tel:* 800-423-4525 *Fax:* 802-457-1913 *E-mail:* contact@trafalgarbooks.com *Web Site:* www.trafalgarbooks.com; www.horseandriderbooks.com, pg 234

Didio, Dan, DC Entertainment, 2900 Alameda, Burbank, CA 91505 *Toll Free Tel:* 800-887-6789 *E-mail:* dccomics@cambeywest.com *Web Site:* www.dcentertainment.com; www.dccomics.com; www.madmag.com, pg 69

Diehl, Debra, University Press of Kansas, 2502 Westbrooke Circle, Lawrence, KS 66045-4444 *Tel:* 785-864-4154; 785-864-4155 (orders) *Fax:* 785-864-4586 *E-mail:* upress@ku.edu; upkorders@ku.edu (orders) *Web Site:* www.kansaspress.ku.edu, pg 247

Dienstfrey, Patricia, Kelsey Street Press, 2824 Kelsey St, Berkeley, CA 94705 *E-mail:* info@kelseyst.com *Web Site:* www.kelseyst.com, pg 125

Diercks, Lisa, Emerson College Department of Writing, Literature & Publishing, 180 Tremont St, 10th fl, Boston, MA 02116 *Tel:* 617-824-8750 *Fax:* 617-824-7856 *Web Site:* www.emerson.edu, pg 620

Dieter, George, Education Writers Association (EWA), 3516 Connecticut Ave NW, Washington, DC 20008 *Tel:* 202-452-9830 *Fax:* 202-452-9837 *E-mail:* ewa@ewa.org *Web Site:* www.ewa.org, pg 565

Diforio, Robert (Bob) G, D4EO Literary Agency, 7 Indian Valley Rd, Weston, CT 06883 *Tel:* 203-544-7180 *Fax:* 203-544-7160 *Web Site:* www.d4eoliteraryagency.com; www.publishersmarketplace.com/members/d4eo/; twitter.com/d4eo, pg 514

Dijkstra, Sandra, Sandra Dijkstra Literary Agency, 1155 Camino del Mar, PMB 515, Del Mar, CA 92014-2605 *E-mail:* queries@dijkstraagency.com *Web Site:* dijkstraagency.com, pg 514

Dilanyan, Rema, Peter Lampack Agency Inc, 350 Fifth Ave, Suite 5300, New York, NY 10118 *Tel:* 212-687-9106 *Fax:* 212-687-9109 *Web Site:* www.peterlampackagency.com, pg 525

Dilger, Lynn, Sourcebooks Inc, 1935 Brookdale Rd, Suite 139, Naperville, IL 60563 *Tel:* 630-961-3900 *Toll Free Tel:* 800-432-7444 *Fax:* 630-961-2168 *E-mail:* info@sourcebooks.com; customersupport@sourcebooks.com *Web Site:* www.sourcebooks.com, pg 217

Dillman, Susanne Edes, Standard Publishing Corp, 10 High St, Boston, MA 02110 *Tel:* 617-457-0600 *Toll Free Tel:* 800-682-5759 *Fax:* 617-457-0608 *Web Site:* www.spcpub.com, pg 220

Dillon, Sanyu, Random House Publishing Group, 1745 Broadway, New York, NY 10019 *Toll Free Tel:* 800-200-3552 *Web Site:* atrandom.com, pg 195

Dillon-Fried, Rachel, Sanford J Greenburger Associates Inc, 55 Fifth Ave, New York, NY 10003 *Tel:* 212-206-5600 *Fax:* 212-463-8718 *Web Site:* greenburger.com; www.sjga.com, pg 520

DiMattia, Nadia, Kane Press Inc, 225 E 46 St, Suite 4D, New York, NY 10017-2924 *Tel:* 212-935-0246 *Web Site:* www.kanepress.com, pg 124

Dimbleby, Robert, Hogrefe Publishing Corp, 7 Bulfinch Place, Suite 202, Boston, MA 02114 *Toll Free Tel:* 866-823-4726 *Fax:* 617-354-6875 *E-mail:* publishing@hogrefe.com; customerservice@hogrefe-publishing.com *Web Site:* us.hogrefe.com, pg 108

Dimitrov, Alex, Raiziss/de Palchi Fellowship, 75 Maiden Lane, Suite 901, New York, NY 10038 *Tel:* 212-274-0343 *Fax:* 212-274-9427 *E-mail:* academy@poets.org *Web Site:* www.poets.org, pg 684

Dimnik, Michelle, Rocky Mountain Book Award, PO Box 42, Lethbridge, AB T1J 3Y3, Canada *Tel:* 403-381-7164 *E-mail:* rockymountainbookaward@shaw.ca *Web Site:* www.rmba.info, pg 685

DiMona, Lisa, Writers House, 21 W 26 St, New York, NY 10010 *Tel:* 212-685-2400 *Fax:* 212-685-1781 *Web Site:* www.writershouse.com, pg 542

Dinardo, Jeff, Red Chair Press, PO Box 333, South Egremont, MA 01258-0333 *Tel:* 413-528-2398 (edit off) *Toll Free Tel:* 800-328-4929 (orders & cust serv) *Toll Free Fax:* 800-332-1132 *E-mail:* info@redchairpress.com *Web Site:* www.redchairpress.com, pg 196

DiNardo, Laura, Workman Publishing Co Inc, 225 Varick St, 9th fl, New York, NY 10014-4381 *Tel:* 212-254-5900 *Toll Free Tel:* 800-722-7202 *Fax:* 212-254-8098 *E-mail:* info@workman.com *Web Site:* www.workman.com, pg 259

Dinas, Jackie, Kensington Publishing Corp, 119 W 40 St, New York, NY 10018 *Tel:* 212-407-1500 *Toll Free Tel:* 800-221-2647 *Fax:* 212-935-0699 *Web Site:* www.kensingtonbooks.com, pg 125

Ding, Kristine, University of Illinois Press, 1325 S Oak St, MC-566, Champaign, IL 61820-6903 *Tel:* 217-333-0950 *Fax:* 217-244-8082 *E-mail:* uipress@uillinois.edu; journals@uillinois.edu *Web Site:* www.press.uillinois.edu, pg 242

Dinger, Angela, William H Sadlier Inc, 9 Pine St, New York, NY 10005 *Tel:* 212-227-2120 *Toll Free Tel:* 800-221-5175 (cust serv) *Fax:* 212-312-6080 *E-mail:* customerservice@sadlier.com *Web Site:* www.sadlier.com, pg 203

Dinger, Frank S, William H Sadlier Inc, 9 Pine St, New York, NY 10005 *Tel:* 212-227-2120 *Toll Free Tel:* 800-221-5175 (cust serv) *Fax:* 212-312-6080 *E-mail:* customerservice@sadlier.com *Web Site:* www.sadlier.com, pg 203

Dinger, William S, William H Sadlier Inc, 9 Pine St, New York, NY 10005 *Tel:* 212-227-2120 *Toll Free Tel:* 800-221-5175 (cust serv) *Fax:* 212-312-6080 *E-mail:* customerservice@sadlier.com *Web Site:* www.sadlier.com, pg 203

Dingledine, Kenneth, Samuel French Inc, 235 Park Ave S, 5th fl, New York, NY 10003 *Tel:* 212-206-8990 *Toll Free Tel:* 866-598-8449 *Fax:* 212-206-1429 *E-mail:* info@samuelfrench.com; publications@samuelfrench.com *Web Site:* www.samuelfrench.com, pg 88

Dingledine, Kenneth, Samuel French Inc, 235 Park Ave S, 5th fl, New York, NY 10003 *Tel:* 212-206-8990 *Toll Free Tel:* 866 598 8449 *Fax:* 212 206 1429 *E-mail:* info@samuelfrench.com *Web Site:* www.samuelfrench.com, pg 518

Dinstman, Lee, APA Talent & Literary Agency, 405 S Beverly Dr, Beverly Hills, CA 90212 *Tel:* 310-888-4200 *Fax:* 310-888-4242 *Web Site:* www.apa-agency.com, pg 507

Dion, Denis, Les Presses de l'Universite Laval, 2180, Chemin Sainte-Foy, 1st fl, Quebec, QC G1V 0A6, Canada *Tel:* 418-656-2803 *Fax:* 418-656-3305 *E-mail:* presses@pul.ulaval.ca *Web Site:* www.pulaval.com, pg 468

Dionne, Richard, Red Deer Press Inc, 195 Allstate Pkwy, Markham, ON L3R 4T8, Canada *Tel:* 905-477-9700 *Toll Free Tel:* 800-387-9776 (orders) *E-mail:* rdp@reddeerpress.com; bookinfo@fitzhenry.ca *Web Site:* www.reddeerpress.com, pg 468

DiPreta, Mauro, Hachette Book Group, 1290 Avenue of the Americas, New York, NY 10019 *Tel:* 212-364-1100 *Toll Free Tel:* 800-759-0190 (cust serv) *Fax:* 212-364-0933 (intl orders) *Toll Free Fax:* 800-286-9471 (cust serv) *Web Site:* www.hachettebookgroup.com, pg 98

DiPreta, Mauro, Hachette Books, 1290 Avenue of the Americas, New York, NY 10019 *Tel:* 212-364-1100 *Web Site:* www.hachettebookgroup.com, pg 98

DiSabatino, Nicholas, Beacon Press, 24 Farnsworth St, Boston, MA 02210-1409 *Tel:* 617-742-2110 *Fax:* 617-723-3097; 617-742-2290 *Web Site:* www.beacon.org, pg 31

DiSalvo, Julia, Liguori Publications, One Liguori Dr, Liguori, MO 63057-1000 *Tel:* 636-464-2500 *Toll Free Tel:* 866-848-2492; 800-325-9521 *Fax:* 636-464-8449 *Toll Free Fax:* 800-325-9526 (sales) *E-mail:* liguori@liguori.org (sales & cust serv) *Web Site:* www.liguori.org/contact-us.html, pg 134

Disbrow, Ethan, Amber Lotus Publishing, PO Box 11329, Portland, OR 97211 *Tel:* 503-284-6400 *Toll Free Tel:* 800-326-2375 (orders only) *Fax:* 503-284-6417 *E-mail:* info@amberlotus.com *Web Site:* www.amberlotus.com, pg 9

Diskey, Jay, AAP PreK-12 Learning Group, 455 Massachusetts Ave NW, Suite 700, Washington, DC 20001 *Tel:* 267-351-4310 *Fax:* 267-351-4317 *E-mail:* prek12learning@publishers.org *Web Site:* www.aepweb.org, pg 553

Diskey, Jay, Association of American Publishers (AAP), 455 Massachusetts Ave NW, Suite 700, Washington, DC 20001-2777 *Tel:* 212-255-0200 *Fax:* 212-255-7007 *E-mail:* info@publishers.org *Web Site:* publishers.org, pg 558

Dissen, Matthew, Melanie Jackson Agency LLC, 41 W 72 St, Suite 3F, New York, NY 10023 *Tel:* 212-873-3373, pg 522

Distelberg, Brian, Perseus Books, 250 W 57 St, 15th fl, New York, NY 10107 *Tel:* 212-340-8100 *Toll Free Tel:* 800 343 4499 (cust serv) *Fax:* 212-340-8105 *Web Site:* www.perseusbooks.com, pg 181

Ditchik, Seth, Yale University Press, 302 Temple St, New Haven, CT 06511-8909 *Tel:* 203-432-0960; 203-432-0966 (sales); 401-531-2800 (cust serv) *Toll Free Tel:* 800-405-1619 (cust serv) *Fax:* 203-432-0948; 203-432-8485 (sales); 401-531-2801 (cust serv) *Toll Free Fax:* 800-406-9145 (cust serv) *E-mail:* sales.press@yale.edu (sales); customer.care@triliteral.org (cust serv) *Web Site:* www.yalebooks.com; yalepress.yale.edu/yupbooks, pg 261

DiTella, Geri, Perseus Books, 250 W 57 St, 15th fl, New York, NY 10107 *Tel:* 212-340-8100 *Toll Free Tel:* 800-343-4499 (cust serv) *Fax:* 212-340-8105 *Web Site:* www.perseusbooks.com, pg 181

Diver, Lucienne, The Knight Agency Inc, 570 East Ave, Madison, GA 30650 *E-mail:* submissions@knightagency.net *Web Site:* www.knightagency.net, pg 524

DiVietro, Philip, American Society of Mechanical Engineers (ASME), 2 Park Ave, New York, NY 10016-5990 *Tel:* 212-591-7000 *Toll Free Tel:* 800-843-2763 (cust serv-US, CN & Mexico) *Fax:* 212-591-7674; 973-882-8113 (cust serv); 973-882-1717 (orders & inquiries) *E-mail:* infocentral@asme.org *Web Site:* www.asme.org, pg 15

Dixon, Debra, BelleBooks, PO Box 300921, Memphis, TN 38130 *Tel:* 901-344-9024 *Fax:* 901-344-9068 *E-mail:* bellebooks@bellebooks.com *Web Site:* www.bellebooks.com, pg 32

Dixon, Donna, State University of New York Press, 10 N Pearl St, 4th fl, Albany, NY 12207 *Tel:* 518-944-2800 *Toll Free Tel:* 877-204-6073 (orders) *Fax:* 518-320-1592 *Toll Free Fax:* 877-204-6074 (orders) *E-mail:* info@sunypress.edu (edit off); suny@presswarehouse.com (orders) *Web Site:* www.sunypress.edu, pg 221

Dlouhy, Caitlyn, Simon & Schuster Children's Publishing, 1230 Avenue of the Americas, New York, NY 10020 *Tel:* 212-698-7000 *Web Site:* www.simonandschuster.com/kids; www.simonandschuster.com/teen; simonandschuster.net; simonandschuster.biz, pg 213

Do, Quynh, W W Norton & Company Inc, 500 Fifth Ave, New York, NY 10110-0017 *Tel:* 212-354-5500 *Toll Free Tel:* 800-233-4830 (orders & cust serv) *Fax:* 212-869-0856 *Toll Free Fax:* 800-458-6515 *E-mail:* orders@wwnorton.com *Web Site:* books.wwnorton.com, pg 164

Dobben, Anna, Alfred A Knopf/Everyman's Library, c/o Penguin Random House Inc, 1745 Broadway, New York, NY 10019 *Tel:* 212-751-2600 *Toll Free Tel:* 800-638-6460 *Fax:* 212-572-2593 *Web Site:* www.knopfdoubleday.com, pg 127

Dobbin, Anna, Houghton Mifflin Harcourt Trade & Reference Division, 125 High St, Boston, MA 02110 *Tel:* 617-351-5000 *Toll Free Tel:* 800-225-3362 *Web Site:* www.hmhco.com, pg 111

Dobles, Gustavo, Wolters Kluwer Law & Business, 76 Ninth Ave, 7th fl, New York, NY 10011-5201 *Tel:* 212-771-0600; 301-698-7100 (cust serv outside US) *Toll Free Tel:* 800-234-1660 (cust serv) *E-mail:* customer.service@wolterskluwer.com; sales@kluwerlaw.com *Web Site:* www.wklawbusiness.com, pg 127

Dobson, Allison, Penguin Group USA, A Penguin Random House Company, 375 Hudson St, New York, NY 10014 *Tel:* 212-366-2000 *Toll Free Tel:* 800-847-5515 (inside sales); 800-631-8571 (cust serv) *Fax:* 212-366-2666; 607-775-4829 (inside sales) *E-mail:* online@us.penguingroup.com *Web Site:* www.penguin.com, pg 177

Dobson, David, Presbyterian Publishing Corp (PPC), 100 Witherspoon St, Louisville, KY 40202 *Tel:* 502-569-5000 *Toll Free Tel:* 800-523-1631 (US only) *Fax:* 502-569-5113 *E-mail:* ppcmail@presbypub.com *Web Site:* www.ppcbooks.com, pg 187

Dobson, David, Westminster John Knox Press (WJK), 100 Witherspoon St, Louisville, KY 40202-1396 *Toll Free Tel:* 800-523-1631 (US only) *Fax:* 502-569-5113 *Toll Free Fax:* 800-541-5113 (US & CN) *E-mail:* wjk@wjkbooks.com; customer_service@wjkbooks.com *Web Site:* www.wjkbooks.com, pg 254

Dobson, Megan Jayne, Thomas Nelson, 501 Nelson Place, Nashville, TN 37214 *Tel:* 615-889-9000 *Toll Free Tel:* 800-251-4000 *Fax:* 615-902-1548 *Web Site:* www.thomasnelson.com, pg 231

Dodd, Christopher, Motion Picture Association of America Inc (MPAA), 1600 "I" St NW, Washington, DC 20006 *Tel:* 202-293-1966 *Fax:* 202-296-7410 *E-mail:* contactus@mpaa.org *Web Site:* www.mpaa.org, pg 570

Dodds, Andy, Grand Central Publishing, 1290 Avenue of the Americas, New York, NY 10019 *Tel:* 212-364-1100 *Web Site:* www.hachettebookgroup.com, pg 95

Dodes, Jeff, St Martin's Press, LLC, 175 Fifth Ave, New York, NY 10010 *Tel:* 646-307-5151 *Web Site:* us.macmillan.com/smp, pg 204

Dodson, Ted, Community of Literary Magazines & Presses (CLMP), 154 Christopher St, Suite 3C, New York, NY 10014-9110 *Tel:* 212-741-9110 *Fax:* 212-741-9112 *E-mail:* info@clmp.org *Web Site:* www.clmp.org, pg 563

Dodson, Veronique, National Association of Black Journalists (NABJ), 1100 Knight Hall, Suite 3100, College Park, MD 20742 *Tel:* 301-405-0248 *Fax:* 301-314-1714 *E-mail:* nabj@nabj.org *Web Site:* www.nabj.org, pg 570

Doerr, Jennifer, Yale University Press, 302 Temple St, New Haven, CT 06511-8909 *Tel:* 203-432-0960; 203-432-0966 (sales); 401-531-2800 (cust serv) *Toll Free Tel:* 800-405-1619 (cust serv) *Fax:* 203-432-0948; 203-432-8485 (sales); 401-531-2801 (cust serv) *Toll Free Fax:* 800-406-9145 (cust serv) *E-mail:* sales.press@yale.edu (sales); customer.care@triliteral.org (cust serv) *Web Site:* www.yalebooks.com; yalepress.yale.edu/yupbooks, pg 261

Doerr, Susan, University of Minnesota Press, 111 Third Ave S, Suite 290, Minneapolis, MN 55401-2520 *Tel:* 612-301-1990 *Fax:* 612-301-1980 *E-mail:* ump@umn.edu *Web Site:* www.upress.umn.edu, pg 242

Doerrer, David, Abrams Artists Agency, 275 Seventh Ave, 26th fl, New York, NY 10001 *Tel:* 646-486-4600 *Fax:* 646-486-0100 *E-mail:* literary@abramsartny.com *Web Site:* www.abramsartists.com, pg 505

Doherty, Kathleen, Tom Doherty Associates, LLC, 175 Fifth Ave, 14th fl, New York, NY 10010 *Tel:* 646-307-5511 *Toll Free Tel:* 800-455-0340 *Web Site:* www.tor-forge.com, pg 71

Doherty, Thomas, Tom Doherty Associates, LLC, 175 Fifth Ave, 14th fl, New York, NY 10010 *Tel:* 646-307-5511 *Toll Free Tel:* 800-455-0340 *Web Site:* www.tor-forge.com, pg 71

Doherty, Thomas, Macmillan, 175 Fifth Ave, New York, NY 10010 *Tel:* 646-307-5151 *E-mail:* press.inquiries@macmillan.com *Web Site:* www.macmillan.com, pg 140

Dohle, Markus, Penguin Random House Inc, 1745 Broadway, New York, NY 10019 *Tel:* 212-782-9000 *Toll Free Tel:* 800-726-0600 *Web Site:* www.penguinrandomhouse.com, pg 178

Dolan, Deirdre F, W W Norton & Company Inc, 500 Fifth Ave, New York, NY 10110-0017 *Tel:* 212-354-5500 *Toll Free Tel:* 800-233-4830 (orders & cust serv) *Fax:* 212-869-0856 *Toll Free Fax:* 800-458-6515 *E-mail:* orders@wwnorton.com *Web Site:* books.wwnorton.com, pg 164

Dolce, Holly, Harry N Abrams Inc, 195 Broadway, 9th fl, New York, NY 10007 *Tel:* 212-206-7715 *Toll Free Tel:* 800-345-1359 *Fax:* 212-519-1210 *E-mail:* abrams@abramsbooks.com *Web Site:* www.abramsbooks.com, pg 3

Doležilek, Sarah, ASET - The Neurodiagnostic Society, 402 E Bannister Rd, Suite A, Kansas City, KS 64131-3019 *Tel:* 816-931-1120 *Fax:* 816-931-1145 *E-mail:* info@aset.org *Web Site:* www.aset.org, pg 23

Doll, Holly, Fitzhenry & Whiteside Limited, 195 Allstate Pkwy, Markham, ON L3R 4T8, Canada *Tel:* 905-477-9700 *Toll Free Tel:* 800-387-9776 *Fax:* 905-477-2834 *Toll Free Fax:* 800-260-9777 *E-mail:* bookinfo@fitzhenry.ca; godwit@fitzhenry.ca *Web Site:* www.fitzhenry.ca, pg 457

Doll, Katy, River Road Press LLC, 9 Dakin, New Orleans, LA 70121 *Tel:* 504-722-8139 *Web Site:* riverroadpress.com, pg 199

Dollar, Douglas, New Forums Press Inc, 1018 S Lewis St, Stillwater, OK 74074 *Tel:* 405-372-6158 *Toll Free Tel:* 800-606-3766 *Fax:* 405-377-2237 *E-mail:* submissions@newforums.com *Web Site:* www.newforums.com, pg 160

Dollins, Robert, Black Rose Books Ltd, CP 35788 Succ Leo Pariseau, Montreal, QC H2X 0A4, Canada *Tel:* 514-844-4076 *Toll Free Tel:* 800-565-9523 (orders) *Toll Free Fax:* 800-221-9985 (orders) *E-mail:* info@blackrosebooks.net *Web Site:* blackrosebooks.net, pg 446

Dols, Amy, The Child's World Inc, 1980 Lookout Dr, North Mankato, MN 56003-1705 *Tel:* 507-385-1044 *Toll Free Tel:* 800-599-READ (599-7323) *Toll Free Fax:* 888-320-2329 *E-mail:* sales@childsworld.com *Web Site:* childsworld.com, pg 54

Dombos, Juliet, The Pilgrim Press/United Church Press, 700 Prospect Ave, Cleveland, OH 44115-1100 *Tel:* 216-736-2100 *Toll Free Tel:* 800-537-3394 (orders) *Fax:* 216-736-2207 (orders) *E-mail:* permissions@thepilgrimpress.com; store@ucc.org *Web Site:* www.thepilgrimpress.com; www.uccresources.com, pg 183

Domenig, Kathleen, Strata Publishing Inc, PO Box 1303, State College, PA 16804 *Tel:* 814-234-8545 *Web Site:* www.stratapub.com, pg 223

Dominguez, Maria, Scholastic Trade Division, 557 Broadway, New York, NY 10012 *Tel:* 212-343-6100; 212-343-4685 (export sales) *Fax:* 212-343-4714 (export sales) *Web Site:* www.scholastic.com, pg 208

Dominguez, Sonia, DeVorss & Co, 553 Constitution Ave, Camarillo, CA 93012-8510 *Tel:* 805-322-9010 *Toll Free Tel:* 800-843-5743 *Fax:* 805-322-9011 *E-mail:* service@devorss.com *Web Site:* www.devorss.com, pg 70

Domville, Sara, Krause Publications Inc, 700 E State St, Iola, WI 54990 *Tel:* 715-445-2214 *Toll Free Tel:* 800-258-0929 (cust serv); 888-457-2873 (orders) *Fax:* 715-445-4087 *E-mail:* bookorders@krause.com *Web Site:* www.krausebooks.com, pg 128

Domville, Sara, Writer's Digest, 10151 Carver Rd, Suite 200, Blue Ash, OH 45242 *Tel:* 513-531-2690 *Toll Free Tel:* 800-289-0963 *E-mail:* writersdigest@fwmedia.com (edit) *Web Site:* www.writersdigest.com, pg 260

Donaher, Br Edward, St Pauls, 2187 Victory Blvd, Staten Island, NY 10314-6603 *Tel:* 718-761-0047 (edit & prodn); 718-698-2759 (mktg & billing) *Toll Free Tel:* 800-343-2522 *Fax:* 718-761-0057 *E-mail:* sales@stpauls.us; marketing@stpauls.us *Web Site:* www.stpauls.us, pg 205

Donahue, Jed, ISI Books, 3901 Centerville Rd, Wilmington, DE 19807-1938 *Tel:* 302-652-4600 *Toll Free Tel:* 800-526-7022 *Fax:* 302-652-1760 *E-mail:* info@isi.org; isibooks@isi.org *Web Site:* www.isibooks.org, pg 121

Donahue, Michael D, 4A's (American Association of Advertising Agencies), 1065 Avenue of the Americas, 16th fl, New York, NY 10018 *Tel:* 212-682-2500 *Web Site:* www.aaaa.org, pg 566

Donald, Brittany, American Public Human Services Association, 1133 19 St NW, Suite 400, Washington, DC 20036 *Tel:* 202-682-0100 *Fax:* 202-289-6555 *Web Site:* www.aphsa.org, pg 556

Donatelli, Michael, The University of North Carolina Press, 116 S Boundary St, Chapel Hill, NC 27514-3808 *Tel:* 919-966-3561 *Fax:* 919-966-3829 *E-mail:* uncpress@unc.edu *Web Site:* www.uncpress.unc.edu, pg 243

Donatich, John, Yale University Press, 302 Temple St, New Haven, CT 06511-8909 *Tel:* 203-432-0960; 203-432-0966 (sales); 401-531-2800 (cust serv) *Toll Free Tel:* 800-405-1619 (cust serv) *Fax:* 203-432-0948; 203-432-8485 (sales); 401-531-2801 (cust serv) *Toll Free Fax:* 800-406-9145 (cust serv) *E-mail:* sales.press@yale.edu (sales); customer.care@triliteral.org (cust serv) *Web Site:* www.yalebooks.com; yalepress.yale.edu/yupbooks, pg 261

Donnaud, Janis A, Janis A Donnaud & Associates Inc, 77 Bleecker St, No C1-25, New York, NY 10012 *Tel:* 212-431-2663 *Fax:* 212-431-2667 *E-mail:* jdonnaud@aol.com, pg 514

Donnelly, Patrick, AOCS Press, 2710 S Boulder Dr, Urbana, IL 61802-6996 *Tel:* 217-693-4838 *Fax:* 217-351-8091 *E-mail:* general@aocs.org *Web Site:* www.aocs.org, pg 18

Donnelly, Sean, The Danahy Fiction Prize, University of Tampa Press, 401 W Kennedy Blvd, Tampa, FL 33606 *Tel:* 813-253-6266 *E-mail:* utpress@ut.edu *Web Site:* tampareview.ut.edu, pg 640

Donnelly, Sean, The Tampa Review Prize for Poetry, University of Tampa Press, 401 W Kennedy Blvd, Tampa, FL 33606 *Tel:* 813-253-6266 *E-mail:* utpress@ut.edu *Web Site:* tampareview.ut.edu, pg 693

Donnelly, Susan, Harvard University Press, 79 Garden St, Cambridge, MA 02138-1499 *Tel:* 617-495-2600; 401-531-2800 (intl orders) *Toll Free Tel:* 800-405-1619 (orders) *Fax:* 617-495-5898 (general); 617-496-4677 (edit & rts); 401-531-2801 (intl orders) *Toll Free Fax:* 800-406-9145 (orders) *E-mail:* contact_hup@harvard.edu *Web Site:* www.hup.harvard.edu, pg 103

Donnelly, Timothy, Columbia University School of the Arts, Creative Writing Program, 609 Kent Hall, New York, NY 10027 *Tel:* 212-854-3774 *Fax:* 212-854-7704 *E-mail:* writingprogram@columbia.edu *Web Site:* www.columbia.edu/cu/writing, pg 619

Donohue, Jim, Cengage Learning, 20 Channel Center St, Boston, MA 02210 *Tel:* 617-289-7700 *Toll Free Tel:* 800-354-9706 *Fax:* 617-289-7844 *Toll Free Fax:* 800-487-8488 *E-mail:* esales@cengage.com *Web Site:* www.cengage.com, pg 50

Donovan, Amy, United States Holocaust Memorial Museum, 100 Raoul Wallenberg Place SW, Washington, DC 20024-2126 *Tel:* 202-314-7837; 202-488-6144 (orders) *Toll Free Tel:* 800-259-9998 (orders) *Fax:* 202-479-9726; 202-488-0438 (orders) *E-mail:* cahs_publications@ushmm.org *Web Site:* www.ushmm.org, pg 239

Donovan, Jim, Jim Donovan Literary, 5635 SMU Blvd, Suite 201, Dallas, TX 75206 *Tel:* 214-696-9411 *E-mail:* jdlqueries@sbcglobal.net, pg 514

Donovan, Lisa, Simon & Schuster Children's Publishing, 1230 Avenue of the Americas, New York, NY 10020 *Tel:* 212-698-7000 *Web Site:* www.simonandschuster.com/kids; www.simonandschuster.com/teen; simonandschuster.net; simonandschuster.biz, pg 213

Donovan, Mary Lee, Candlewick Press, 99 Dover St, Somerville, MA 02144-2825 *Tel:* 617-661-3330 *Fax:* 617-661-0565 *E-mail:* bigbear@candlewick.com; salesinfo@candlewick.com *Web Site:* www.candlewick.com, pg 46

Dooley, Tim, OCP, 5536 NE Hassalo St, Portland, OR 97213 *Tel:* 503-281-1191 *Toll Free Tel:* 800-548-8749 *Fax:* 503-282-3486 *Toll Free Fax:* 800-843-8181 *E-mail:* liturgy@ocp.org *Web Site:* www.ocp.org, pg 166

Doornbos, Cris, David C Cook, 4050 Lee Vance View, Colorado Springs, CO 80918 *Tel:* 719-536-0100 *Toll Free Tel:* 800-708-5550; 800-323-7543 (orders & cust serv) *Toll Free Fax:* 800-430-0726 (cust serv) *Web Site:* www.davidccook.com, pg 60

Dorado, Kelsey, Empire State Award for Excellence in Literature for Young People, 6021 State Farm Rd, Guilderland, NY 12084 *Tel:* 518-432-6952 *Toll Free Tel:* 800-252-6952 *Fax:* 518-427-1697 *E-mail:* info@nyla.org *Web Site:* www.nyla.org, pg 644

Dorff, Patricia, Council on Foreign Relations Press, The Harold Pratt House, 58 E 68 St, New York, NY 10065 *Tel:* 212-434-9400 *Fax:* 212-434-9800 *E-mail:* publications@cfr.org *Web Site:* www.cfr.org, pg 62

Dorfman, Debra, Scholastic Trade Division, 557 Broadway, New York, NY 10012 *Tel:* 212-343-6100; 212-343-4685 (export sales) *Fax:* 212-343-4714 (export sales) *Web Site:* www.scholastic.com, pg 208

Dorfman, Larry, Capstone Publishers™, 1710 Roe Crest Dr, North Mankato, MN 56003 *Toll Free Tel:* 800-747-4992 (cust serv) *Toll Free Fax:* 888-262-0705 *Web Site:* www.capstonepress.com, pg 47

Dorman, Dr Jessica, The Historic New Orleans Collection, 533 Royal St, New Orleans, LA 70130 *Tel:* 504-523-4662 *Fax:* 504-598-7108 *E-mail:* wrc@hnoc.org *Web Site:* www.hnoc.org, pg 108

Dorman, Mark, McGraw-Hill Education, 2 Penn Plaza, New York, NY 10121-2298 *Tel:* 212-904-2000 *E-mail:* customer.service@mheducation.com; international_cs@mheducation.com *Web Site:* www.mheducation.com, pg 145

Dorman, Mark, McGraw-Hill International & Professional Publishing Group, 2 Penn Plaza, New York, NY 10121 *Tel:* 646-766-2000 *Web Site:* www.mheducation.com, pg 146

Dorman, Pamela, Viking, 375 Hudson St, New York, NY 10014 *Tel:* 212-366-2000 *Fax:* 212-243-6002 *Web Site:* www.penguin.com/publishers/vikingbooks, pg 250

Dorning, Matthew, Ancient Faith Publishing, 2747 Bond St, University Park, IL 60484 *Tel:* 219-728-2216 *Toll Free Tel:* 800-967-7377 *Toll Free Fax:* 866-599-5208 *E-mail:* info@ancientfaith.com; orders@ancientfaith.com *Web Site:* www.ancientfaith.com/publishing, pg 16

Dorsett, Claire, Roaring Brook Press, 175 Fifth Ave, New York, NY 10010 *Tel:* 646-307-5151 *Web Site:* us.macmillan.com/publishers/roaring-brook-press, pg 200

Dosik, Anita, APPA: The Association of Higher Education Facilities Officers, 1643 Prince St, Alexandria, VA 22314-2818 *Tel:* 703-684-1446 *Fax:* 703-549-2772 *Web Site:* www.appa.org, pg 18

Doten, Mark, Soho Press Inc, 853 Broadway, New York, NY 10003 *Tel:* 212-260-1900 *E-mail:* soho@sohopress.com; publicity@sohopress.com; contact@sohopress.com *Web Site:* www.sohopress.com, pg 216

Dotson, Anne Dean, The University Press of Kentucky, 663 S Limestone St, Lexington, KY 40508-4008 *Tel:* 859-257-8400 *Fax:* 859-257-8481 *Web Site:* www.kentuckypress.com, pg 247

Dotto, Gabriel, Michigan State University Press (MSU Press), Manly Miles Bldg, Suite 25, 1405 S Harrison Rd, East Lansing, MI 48823-5245 *Tel:* 517-355-9543 *Fax:* 517-432-2611 *Web Site:* msupress.org, pg 150

Doucet, Christy, Livres Canada Books, One Nicholas, Suite 504, Ottawa, ON K1N 7B7, Canada *Tel:* 613-562-2324 *Fax:* 613-562-2329 *E-mail:* info@livrescanadabooks.com *Web Site:* www.livrescanadabooks.com, pg 569

Doucette, Bob, National Council of Teachers of Mathematics (NCTM), 1906 Association Dr, Reston, VA 20191-1502 *Tel:* 703-620-9840 *Toll Free Tel:* 800-235-7566 *Fax:* 703-476-2970 *E-mail:* nctm@nctm.org *Web Site:* www.nctm.org, pg 158

Dougherty, Adria, Sterling Publishing Co Inc, 1166 Avenue of the Americas, 17th fl, New York, NY 10036 *Tel:* 212-532-7160 *Toll Free Tel:* 800-367-9692 *Fax:* 212-213-2495 *Web Site:* www.sterlingpublishing.com, pg 222

Dougherty, Mary V, Juniper Prize for Fiction, East Experiment Sta, 671 N Pleasant St, Amherst, MA 01003 *E-mail:* info@umpress.umass.edu *Web Site:* www.umass.edu/umpress; www.umass.edu/umpress/content/juniper-literary-prize-series, pg 658

Dougherty, Mary V, Juniper Prize for Poetry, East Experiment Sta, 671 N Pleasant St, Amherst, MA 01003 *E-mail:* info@umpress.umass.edu *Web Site:* www.umass.edu/umpress; www.umass.edu/umpress/content/juniper-literary-prize-series, pg 658

Dougherty, Mary V, University of Massachusetts Press, East Experiment Sta, 671 N Pleasant St, Amherst, MA 01003 *Tel:* 413-545-2217 *Fax:* 413-545-1226 *E-mail:* info@umpress.umass.edu *Web Site:* www.umass.edu/umpress, pg 242

Doughtery, Carol, Writers Retreat Workshop (WRW), PO Box 170657, Austin, TX 78717 *E-mail:* info@writersretreatworkshop.com *Web Site:* www.writersretreatworkshop.com, pg 616

Douglas, Alecia, McIntosh & Otis Inc, 353 Lexington Ave, New York, NY 10016-0900 *Tel:* 212-687-7400 *Fax:* 212-687-6894 *E-mail:* info@mcintoshandotis.com *Web Site:* www.mcintoshandotis.com, pg 529

Douglas, Deron, Double Dragon Publishing Inc, 1-5762 Hwy 7 E, Markham, ON L3P 7Y4, Canada *E-mail:* sales@double-dragon-ebooks.com *Web Site:* www.double-dragon-ebooks.com, pg 452

Douglas, Sarah L, Abrams Artists Agency, 275 Seventh Ave, 26th fl, New York, NY 10001 *Tel:* 646-486-4600 *Fax:* 646-486-0100 *E-mail:* literary@abramsartny.com *Web Site:* www.abramsartists.com, pg 505

Douvris, Mara, Institute of Environmental Sciences & Technology - IEST, 2340 S Arlington Heights Rd, Suite 620, Arlington Heights, IL 60005-4510 *Tel:* 847-981-0100 *Fax:* 847-981-4130 *E-mail:* information@iest.org *Web Site:* www.iest.org, pg 118

Dove, Veronica, Bernan, 4501 Forbes Blvd, Suite 200, Lanham, MD 20706 *Tel:* 301-459-7666 (cust serv & orders) *Fax:* 301-459-6988 *E-mail:* customercare@bernan.com *Web Site:* www.bernan.com, pg 33

Dowden, C James, City & Regional Magazine Association, 2512 Artesia Blvd, Suite 200, Redondo Beach, CA 90278 *Tel:* 310-379-8261 *Fax:* 310-379-8283 *E-mail:* admin@citymag.org *Web Site:* www.citymag.org, pg 563

Dowen, Joyce, American Academy of Environmental Engineers & Scientists™, 147 Old Solomons Island Rd, Suite 303, Annapolis, MD 21401 *Tel:* 410-266-3311 *Fax:* 410-266-7653 *E-mail:* info@aaees.org *Web Site:* www.aaees.org, pg 9

Dowling, Michael, Bogle International Library Travel Fund, 50 E Huron St, Chicago, IL 60611-2795 *Tel:* 312-280-3201 *Toll Free Tel:* 800-545-2433 (ext 3201) *Fax:* 312-280-4392 *E-mail:* intl@ala.org *Web Site:* www.ala.org, pg 633

Downes, Terry, Disney Publishing Worldwide, 1101 Flower St, Glendale, CA 91201 *Web Site:* books.disney.com, pg 71

Downey, Floann, West Virginia University Press, West Virginia University, PO Box 6295, Morgantown, WV 26506-6295 *Tel:* 304-293-8400 *Fax:* 304-293-6585 *Web Site:* www.wvupress.com, pg 254

Downs, Larry, Thomas Nelson, 501 Nelson Place, Nashville, TN 37214 *Tel:* 615-889-9000 *Toll Free Tel:* 800-251-4000 *Fax:* 615-902-1548 *Web Site:* www.thomasnelson.com, pg 231

Doyle, Elizabeth, Pauline Books & Media, 50 Saint Paul's Ave, Boston, MA 02130 *Tel:* 617-522-8911 *Toll Free Tel:* 800-876-4463 (orders); 800-836-9723 (cust serv) *Fax:* 617-541-9805 *E-mail:* editorial@paulinemedia.com (ms submissions); orderentry@pauline.org (cust serv) *Web Site:* www.pauline.org/publishing; www.pauline.org/PBMPublishing, pg 175

Doyle, Kathy, St Martin's Press, LLC, 175 Fifth Ave, New York, NY 10010 *Tel:* 646-307-5151 *Web Site:* us.macmillan.com/smp, pg 204

Doyle, Miles, HarperCollins General Books Group, 195 Broadway, New York, NY 10007 *Tel:* 212-207-7000 *Web Site:* www.harpercollins.com, pg 101

Doyle, Patricia, Barron's Educational Series Inc, 250 Wireless Blvd, Hauppauge, NY 11788 *Tel:* 631-434-3311 *Toll Free Tel:* 800-645-3476 *Fax:* 631-434-3723 *E-mail:* barrons@barronseduc.com *Web Site:* www.barronseduc.com, pg 30

Doyle-Kimball, Mary, National Association of Real Estate Editors (NAREE), 1003 NW Sixth Terr, Boca Raton, FL 33486-3455 *Tel:* 561-391-3599 *Fax:* 561-391-0099 *Web Site:* www.naree.org, pg 571

Dozier, Laura, Harry N Abrams Inc, 195 Broadway, 9th fl, New York, NY 10007 *Tel:* 212-206-7715 *Toll Free Tel:* 800-345-1359 *Fax:* 212-519-1210 *E-mail:* abrams@abramsbooks.com *Web Site:* www.abramsbooks.com, pg 3

Drake, Marc, The Charlton Press Corp, 991 Victoria St N, Kitchener, ON N2B 3C7, Canada *Tel:* 416-962-2665 *Toll Free Tel:* 866-663-8827 *Fax:* 519-579-0532 *E-mail:* chpress@charltonpress.com *Web Site:* www.charltonpress.com, pg 450

Dreesen, Robert, Cambridge University Press, 1 Liberty Plaza, 20th fl, New York, NY 10006 *Tel:* 212-924-3900; 212-337-5000 *Fax:* 212-691-3239 *E-mail:* newyork@cambridge.org *Web Site:* www.cambridge.org/us, pg 46

Drehs, Shana, Sourcebooks Inc, 1935 Brookdale Rd, Suite 139, Naperville, IL 60563 *Tel:* 630-961-3900 *Toll Free Tel:* 800-432-7444 *Fax:* 630-961-2168 *E-mail:* info@sourcebooks.com; customersupport@sourcebooks.com *Web Site:* www.sourcebooks.com, pg 218

Dreibelbis, Dana, Rutgers University Press, 106 Somerset St, 3rd fl, New Brunswick, NJ 08901 *Tel:* 848-445-7762 *Toll Free Tel:* 800-848-6224 (orders only) *Fax:* 732-745-4935 (acqs, edit, mktg, perms & prodn) *Toll Free Fax:* 800-272-6817 (fulfillment) *Web Site:* rutgerspress.rutgers.edu, pg 202

Drennan, Christina L, Drennan Communications, 6 Robin Lane, East Kingston, NH 03827 *Tel:* 603-642-8002 *Fax:* 603-642-8002, pg 492

Drennan, Christina L, Drennan Literary Agency, 6 Robin Lane, East Kingston, NH 03827 *Tel:* 603-642-8002 *Fax:* 603-642-8002, pg 514

Drennan, William D, Drennan Communications, 6 Robin Lane, East Kingston, NH 03827 *Tel:* 603-642-8002 *Fax:* 603-642-8002, pg 492

Drennan, William D, Drennan Literary Agency, 6 Robin Lane, East Kingston, NH 03827 *Tel:* 603-642-8002 *Fax:* 603-642-8002, pg 514

Dresher, Matt, Fire Engineering Books & Videos, 1421 S Sheridan Rd, Tulsa, OK 74112 *Tel:* 918-831-9421 *Toll Free Tel:* 800-752-9764 *Fax:* 918-832-0319 *E-mail:* sales@pennwell.com *Web Site:* www.pennwellbooks.com, pg 85

Dresser, Kate, Gallery Books, 1230 Avenue of the Americas, New York, NY 10020 *Toll Free Tel:* 800-456-6798 *Fax:* 212-698-7284 *E-mail:* consumer.customerservice@simonandschuster.com *Web Site:* www.simonsays.com, pg 90

Dresser, Kate, Harlequin Enterprises Ltd, 233 Broadway, Suite 1001, New York, NY 10279 *Tel:* 212-553-4200 *Fax:* 212-227-8969 *E-mail:* customerservice@harlequin.com *Web Site:* www.harlequin.com, pg 100

Dressman, Denny, Colorado Authors' League, PO Box 24905, Denver, CO 80224 *Web Site:* coloradoauthors.org, pg 563

Drew, Courtney, Chronicle Books LLC, 680 Second St, San Francisco, CA 94107 *Tel:* 415-537-4200 *Toll Free Tel:* 800-759-0190 (cust serv) *Fax:* 415-537-4460 *Toll Free Fax:* 800-858-7787 (orders); 800-286-9471 (cust serv) *E-mail:* frontdesk@chroniclebooks.com *Web Site:* www.chroniclebooks.com, pg 55

Drew, Stephanie, Springer Publishing Co, 11 W 42 St, 15th fl, New York, NY 10036-8002 *Tel:* 212-431-4370 *Toll Free Tel:* 877-687-7476 *Fax:* 212-941-7842 *E-mail:* marketing@springerpub.com; cs@springerpub.com (orders); editorial@springerpub.com *Web Site:* www.springerpub.com, pg 219

Dreyer, Benjamin, Random House Publishing Group, 1745 Broadway, New York, NY 10019 *Toll Free Tel:* 800-200-3552 *Web Site:* atrandom.com, pg 195

Dries, Emma, HarperCollins General Books Group, 195 Broadway, New York, NY 10007 *Tel:* 212-207-7000 *Web Site:* www.harpercollins.com, pg 101

Driskell, Maudelle, Conference on Poetry, 158 Ridge Rd, Franconia, NH 03580 *Tel:* 603-823-5510 *E-mail:* frost@frostplace.org *Web Site:* frostplace.org, pg 610

Driver, Nancy, American Counseling Association, 6101 Stevenson Ave, Suite 600, Alexandria, VA 22304 *Tel:* 703-823-9800 (ext 222, book orders) *Toll Free Tel:* 800-347-6647 (ext 222, book orders) *Fax:* 703-823-0252 *Toll Free Fax:* 800-473-2329 *E-mail:* membership@counseling.org (book orders) *Web Site:* www.counseling.org, pg 11

Driver, Stephen, University Press of America Inc, 4501 Forbes Blvd, Suite 200, Lanham, MD 20706 *Tel:* 301-459-3366 *Toll Free Tel:* 800-462-6420 *Fax:* 301-429-5748 *Toll Free Fax:* 800-338-4550 *Web Site:* www.univpress.com, pg 246

Drollinger, Darrin, American Society of Agricultural & Biological Engineers (ASABE), 2950 Niles Rd, St Joseph, MI 49085-9659 *Tel:* 269-429-0300 *Toll Free Tel:* 800-371-2723 *Fax:* 269-429-3852 *E-mail:* hq@asabe.org *Web Site:* www.asabe.org, pg 14

Drost, Susie, The Mongolia Society Inc, Indiana University, 322 Goodbody Hall, 1011 E Third St, Bloomington, IN 47405-7005 *Tel:* 812-855-4078 *Fax:* 812-855-4078 *E-mail:* monsoc@indiana.edu *Web Site:* www.mongoliasociety.org, pg 153

Drouillard, Tom, Alliance for Audited Media (AAM), 48 W Seegers Rd, Arlington Heights, IL 60005 *Tel:* 224-366-6939 *Fax:* 224-366-6949 *Web Site:* www.auditedmedia.com, pg 553

Drouzas, Frank, Acclaim Film Script Competition, 300 Central Ave, Suite 501, St Petersburg, FL 33701 *Web Site:* acclaimscripts.com, pg 625

Drouzas, Frank, Acclaim TV Script Competition, 300 Central Ave, Suite 501, St Petersburg, FL 33701 *Web Site:* acclaimscripts.com, pg 625

Druding, Harry F, Cenveo Publisher Services, 555 Virginia Dr, Fort Washington, PA 19034 *Tel:* 215-591-9125 *E-mail:* info.psg@cenveo.com *Web Site:* cenveopublisherservices.com, pg 491

Drumm, Cassie, Perseus Books, 250 W 57 St, 15th fl, New York, NY 10107 *Tel:* 212-340-8100 *Toll Free Tel:* 800-343-4499 (cust serv) *Fax:* 212-340-8105 *Web Site:* www.perseusbooks.com, pg 181

Drummond, Christine, Ascend Books LLC, 12710 Pflumm Rd, Suite 200, Olathe, KS 66062 *Tel:* 913-948-5500 *Web Site:* www.ascendbooks.com, pg 22

Drummond, Siobhan, Drummond Books, 2111 Cleveland St, Evanston, IL 60202 *Tel:* 847-302-2534 *E-mail:* drummondbooks@gmail.com, pg 492

Drury, Butch, Rivendell Books, PO Box 29348, St Louis, MO 63126-0348 *Tel:* 314-609-6534 *E-mail:* butch@rivendellbooks.com *Web Site:* www.rivendellbooks.com, pg 478

Drury, Patricia, Quincannon Publishing Group, PO Box 8100, Glen Ridge, NJ 07028-8100 *Tel:* 973-380-9942 *E-mail:* editors@quincannongroup.com *Web Site:* www.quincannongroup.com, pg 192

Druskin, Julia, W W Norton & Company Inc, 500 Fifth Ave, New York, NY 10110-0017 *Tel:* 212-354-5500 *Toll Free Tel:* 800-233-4830 (orders & cust serv) *Fax:* 212-869-0856 *Toll Free Fax:* 800-458-6515 *E-mail:* orders@wwnorton.com *Web Site:* books.wwnorton.com, pg 164

Dry, Paul, Paul Dry Books, 1700 Sansom St, Suite 700, Philadelphia, PA 19103 *Tel:* 215-231-9939 *Fax:* 215-231-9942 *E-mail:* editor@pauldrybooks.com *Web Site:* www.pauldrybooks.com, pg 175

Du Cane, John, Dragon Door Publications, 5 E Country Rd B, Suite 3, Little Canada, MN 55117 *Tel:* 651-487-2180 *Toll Free Tel:* 800-899-5111 (orders & cust serv) *E-mail:* support@dragondoor.com *Web Site:* www.dragondoor.com, pg 73

du Houx, Paul Cornell, Polar Bear & Company, PO Box 311, Solon, ME 04979-0311 *Tel:* 207-643-2795 *Web Site:* www.polarbearandco.com, pg 185

du Quenoy, Dr Paul, Academica Press, 1727 Massachusetts Ave NW, Suite 507, Washington, DC 20036 *Tel:* 978-829-2577 *E-mail:* editorial@academicapress.com *Web Site:* www.academicapress.com, pg 3

Duane, Dick, Pinder Lane & Garon-Brooke Associates Ltd, 159 W 53 St, New York, NY 10019 *Tel:* 212-489-0880 *Fax:* 212-489-7104 *E-mail:* pinderlanegaronbrooke@gmail.com *Web Site:* www.pinderlaneandgaronbrooke.com, pg 531

Duane, Laura, Diversion Books, 443 Park Ave S, Suite 1008, New York, NY 10016 *Tel:* 212-961-6390 *E-mail:* info@diversionbooks.com *Web Site:* www.diversionbooks.com, pg 71

Dube, Matthew, Merriam-Webster Inc, 47 Federal St, Springfield, MA 01102 *Tel:* 413-734-3134 *Toll Free Tel:* 800-828-1880 (orders & cust serv) *Fax:* 413-731-5979 (sales) *E-mail:* support@merriam-webster.com *Web Site:* www.merriam-webster.com, pg 149

Dublinski, Katie, Graywolf Press, 250 Third Ave N, Suite 600, Minneapolis, MN 55401 *Tel:* 651-641-0077 *Fax:* 651-641-0036 *E-mail:* wolves@graywolfpress.org (no ms queries, sample chapters or proposals) *Web Site:* www.graywolfpress.org, pg 95

Duchesneau, Monique, Les Editions Un Monde Different, 3905 Isabelle, bureau 101, Brossard, QC J4Y 2R2, Canada *Tel:* 450-656-2660 *Toll Free Tel:* 800-443-2582 *Fax:* 450-659-9328 *E-mail:* info@umd.ca *Web Site:* www.umd.ca, pg 455

Duckson, Scott, West Academic Publishing, 444 Cedar St, Suite 700, St Paul, MN 55101 *Toll Free Tel:* 877-888-1330 *E-mail:* customerservice@westacademic.com; support@westacademic.com; media@westacademic.com *Web Site:* www.westacademic.com, pg 254

Duckworth, Michael, University of Hawaii Press, 2840 Kolowalu St, Honolulu, HI 96822 *Tel:* 808-956-8255 *Toll Free Tel:* 888-UHPRESS (847-7377) *Fax:* 808-988-6052 *Toll Free Fax:* 800-650-7811 *E-mail:* uhpbooks@hawaii.edu *Web Site:* www.uhpress.hawaii.edu, pg 241

Dudley, Tim, New Leaf Press, 3142 Hwy 103 N, Green Forest, AR 72638-2233 *Tel:* 870-438-5288 *Toll Free Tel:* 800-999-3777 *Fax:* 870-438-5120 *E-mail:* nlp@newleafpress.net; submissions@newleafpress.net *Web Site:* www.nlpg.com/imprint/new-leaf-press; www.nlpg.com, pg 161

Dudzik, Andy, Leaf Storm Press, PO Box 4670, Santa Fe, NM 87502-4670 *Tel:* 505-216-6155 *E-mail:* leafstormpress@gmail.com *Web Site:* leafstormpress.com, pg 131

Dufault, Christopher, Penguin Random House Inc, 1745 Broadway, New York, NY 10019 *Tel:* 212-782-9000 *Toll Free Tel:* 800-726-0600 *Web Site:* www.penguinrandomhouse.com, pg 178

Dufay, Adrianna, HarperCollins General Books Group, 195 Broadway, New York, NY 10007 *Tel:* 212-207-7000 *Web Site:* www.harpercollins.com, pg 101

Duff, John, HPBooks, 375 Hudson St, New York, NY 10014 *Tel:* 212-366-2000 *E-mail:* online@penguinputnam.com *Web Site:* www.penguinputnam.com; www.penguin.com, pg 112

Duff, John, Prentice Hall Press, 375 Hudson St, New York, NY 10014 *Tel:* 212-366-2000 *Fax:* 212-366-2666, pg 187

Duffy, Peter, Summit University Press, 63 Summit Way, Gardiner, MT 59030-9314 *Tel:* 406-848-9742; 406-848-9500 (retail orders) *Toll Free Tel:* 800-245-5445 (retail orders) *Fax:* 406-848-9744 *E-mail:* info@summituniversitypress.com; marketing@summituniversitypress.com; production@summituniversitypress.com; rights@summituniversitypress.com *Web Site:* www.summituniversitypress.com, pg 224

Dufresne, Collette, Editions Michel Quintin, 2259 Papineau Ave, Suite 104, Montreal, QC H2K 4J5, Canada *Tel:* 514-379-3774 *E-mail:* info@editionsmichelquintin.ca *Web Site:* www.editionsmichelquintin.ca, pg 455

Dufresne, Jean-Sebastien, Montreal-Contacts/The Rights Agency, 1350 Sherbrooke St E, Suite 1, Montreal, QC H2L 1M4, Canada *Tel:* 514-400-7075 *Fax:* 514-400-1045 *Web Site:* www.montreal-contacts.com/?lang=en, pg 530

Dufurrena, Caddie, University of Nevada Press, c/o University of Nevada, Continuing Educ Bldg, MS 0166, Reno, NV 89557-0166 *Tel:* 775-784-6573 *Fax:* 775-784-6200 *Web Site:* www.unpress.nevada.edu, pg 243

Duggins, Linda, Grand Central Publishing, 1290 Avenue of the Americas, New York, NY 10019 *Tel:* 212-364-1100 *Web Site:* www.hachettebookgroup.com, pg 95

Duhaime, Jeanne, Les Editions Vents d'Ouest, 109, rue Wright, bureau 202, Gatineau, QC J8X 2G7, Canada *Tel:* 819-770-6377 *E-mail:* info@ventsdouest.ca *Web Site:* www.ventsdouest.ca, pg 455

Duhe, Mary, University of Louisiana at Lafayette Press, PO Box 43558, Lafayette, LA 70504-3558 *Tel:* 337-482-6027 *Fax:* 337-482-6028 *E-mail:* ulpress@louisiana.edu *Web Site:* www.ulpress.org, pg 242

Duhon, Bryant, Association for Information & Image Management International (AIIM), 1100 Wayne Ave, Suite 1100, Silver Spring, MD 20910 *Tel:* 301-587-8202 *Toll Free Tel:* 800-477-2446 *Fax:* 301-587-2711 *E-mail:* aiim@aiim.org; info@aiim.org *Web Site:* www.aiim.org, pg 557

Dujack, Stephen, Environmental Law Institute, 1730 "M" St NW, Suite 700, Washington, DC 20036 *Tel:* 202-939-3800 *Toll Free Tel:* 800-433-5120 *Fax:* 202-939-3868 *E-mail:* law@eli.org *Web Site:* www.eli.org, pg 79

Dujan, Patricio, Math Solutions®, One Harbor Dr, Suite 101, Sausalito, CA 94965 *Tel:* 415-332-4181 *Toll Free Tel:* 800-868-9092 *Fax:* 415-331-1931 *Toll Free Fax:* 877-942-8837 *E-mail:* info@mathsolutions.com; orders@mathsolutions.com *Web Site:* www.mathsolutions.com, pg 144

Dujardin, Joelle, Highlights for Children Fiction Contest, 803 Church St, Honesdale, PA 18431 *Tel:* 570-253-1080 *Fax:* 570-251-7847 *E-mail:* eds@highlights.com *Web Site:* www.highlights.com, pg 653

Dulaney, Kristin, Little, Brown Books for Young Readers, 1290 Avenue of the Americas, New York, NY 10019 *Tel:* 212-364-1100 *Toll Free Tel:* 800-759-0190 (cust serv) *Web Site:* www.HachetteBookGroup.com, pg 136

Duncan, Michael, Cambridge University Press, 1 Liberty Plaza, 20th fl, New York, NY 10006 *Tel:* 212-924-3900; 212-337-5000 *Fax:* 212-691-3239 *E-mail:* newyork@cambridge.org *Web Site:* www.cambridge.org/us, pg 46

Dunham, C Ryan, David C Cook, 4050 Lee Vance View, Colorado Springs, CO 80918 *Tel:* 719-536-0100 *Toll Free Tel:* 800-708-5550; 800-323-7543 (orders & cust serv) *Toll Free Fax:* 800-430-0726 (cust serv) *Web Site:* www.davidccook.com, pg 60

Dunham, Gary, Indiana University Press, Herman B Wells Library 350, 1320 E Tenth St, Bloomington, IN 47405-3907 *Tel:* 812-855-8817 *Toll Free Tel:* 800-842-6796 (orders only) *Fax:* 812-855-7931; 812-855-8507 *E-mail:* iupress@indiana.edu; iuporder@indiana.edu (orders) *Web Site:* www.iupress.indiana.edu, pg 116

Dunham, Jennie, Dunham Literary Inc, 110 William St, Suite 2202, New York, NY 10038 *Tel:* 212-929-0994 *Web Site:* dunhamlit.com, pg 514

Dunigan, Erin, Chronicle Books LLC, 680 Second St, San Francisco, CA 94107 *Tel:* 415-537-4200 *Toll Free Tel:* 800-759-0190 (cust serv) *Fax:* 415-537-4460 *Toll Free Fax:* 800-858-7787 (orders); 800-286-9471 (cust serv) *E-mail:* frontdesk@chroniclebooks.com *Web Site:* www.chroniclebooks.com, pg 55

Dunlap, Chris, The Arion Press, The Presidio, 1802 Hays St, San Francisco, CA 94129 *Tel:* 415-668-2542 *Fax:* 415-668-2550 *E-mail:* arionpress@arionpress.com *Web Site:* www.arionpress.com, pg 21

Dunlap, Ellen S, American Antiquarian Society (AAS), 185 Salisbury St, Worcester, MA 01609-1634 *Tel:* 508-755-5221 *Fax:* 508-753-3311 *E-mail:* library@americanantiquarian.org *Web Site:* www.americanantiquarian.org, pg 554

Dunn, Aimee Parent, Palimpsest Press, 1171 Eastlawn Ave, Windsor, ON N8S 3J1, Canada *Tel:* 519-259-2112 *E-mail:* info@palimpsestpress.ca *Web Site:* www.palimpsestpress.ca, pg 466

Dunn, Dinah, Hachette Books, 1290 Avenue of the Americas, New York, NY 10019 *Tel:* 212-364-1100 *Web Site:* www.hachettebookgroup.com, pg 98

Dunn, Karen, Child Welfare League of America (CWLA), 1726 "M" St, Suite 500, Washington, DC 20036 *Tel:* 202-688-4200 *Fax:* 202-833-1689 *E-mail:* cwla@cwla.org *Web Site:* www.cwla.org/publications, pg 54

Dunn, Kathy, Penguin Random House Speakers Bureau, A Penguin Random House Company, 1745 Broadway, Mail Drop 13-1, New York, NY 10019 *Tel:* 212-572-2013 *E-mail:* speakers@penguinrandomhouse.com *Web Site:* www.prhspeakers.com, pg 547

Dunn, Peter, Abrams Learning Trends, 16310 Bratton Lane, Suite 250, Austin, TX 78728-2403 *Toll Free Tel:* 800-227-9120 *Toll Free Fax:* 800-737-3322 *E-mail:* customerservice@abramslearningtrends.com (orders, cust serv); contactus@abramslearningtrends.com *Web Site:* www.abramslearningtrends.com (orders, cust serv), pg 3

Dunn, Stephen P, W W Norton & Company Inc, 500 Fifth Ave, New York, NY 10110-0017 *Tel:* 212-354-5500 *Toll Free Tel:* 800-233-4830 (orders & cust serv) *Fax:* 212-869-0856 *Toll Free Fax:* 800-458-6515 *E-mail:* orders@wwnorton.com *Web Site:* books.wwnorton.com, pg 164

Dunne, Thomas, St Martin's Press, LLC, 175 Fifth Ave, New York, NY 10010 *Tel:* 646-307-5151 *Web Site:* us.macmillan.com/smp, pg 204

Dunow, Henry, Dunow, Carlson & Lerner Literary Agency Inc, 27 W 20 St, Suite 1107, New York, NY 10011 *Tel:* 212-645-7606 *E-mail:* mail@dclagency.com *Web Site:* www.dclagency.com, pg 515

Dunton, David, Harvey Klinger Inc, 300 W 55 St, Suite 11V, New York, NY 10019 *Tel:* 212-581-7068 *Fax:* 212-315-3823 *E-mail:* queries@harveyklinger.com *Web Site:* www.harveyklinger.com, pg 524

Dunton, James R, The CSIS Press, 1616 Rhode Island Ave NW, Washington, DC 20036 *Tel:* 202-887-0200 *Fax:* 202-775-3199 *E-mail:* books@csis.org *Web Site:* www.csis.org, pg 65

DuPont, Charles, Alan Wofsy Fine Arts, 1109 Geary Blvd, San Francisco, CA 94109 *Tel:* 415-292-6500 *Toll Free Tel:* 800-660-6403 *Fax:* 415-292-6594 (off & cust serv); 510-251-1840 (acctg) *E-mail:* order@art-books.com (orders); editeur@earthlink.net (edit); beauxarts@earthlink.net (cust serv) *Web Site:* www.art-books.com, pg 258

Duquet, Michel, Francois-Xavier Garneau Medal, 130 Albert St, Suite 1201, Ottawa, ON K1P 5G4, Canada *Tel:* 613-233-7885 *Fax:* 613-565-5445 *E-mail:* cha-shc@cha-shc.ca *Web Site:* www.cha-shc.ca, pg 648

Duquet, Michel, Sir John A Macdonald Prize, 130 Albert St, Suite 1201, Ottawa, ON K1P 5G4, Canada *Tel:* 613-233-7885 *Fax:* 613-565-5445 *E-mail:* cha-shc@cha-shc.ca *Web Site:* www.cha-shc.ca, pg 664

Durbin, Dean D, Trusted Media Brands Inc, 750 Third Ave, 3rd fl, New York, NY 10017 *Toll Free Tel:* 800-310-6261 (cust serv) *E-mail:* customercare@tmbi.com *Web Site:* www.tmbi.com; www.rd.com, pg 236

Durbin, Jon, W W Norton & Company Inc, 500 Fifth Ave, New York, NY 10110-0017 *Tel:* 212-354-5500 *Toll Free Tel:* 800-233-4830 (orders & cust serv) *Fax:* 212-869-0856 *Toll Free Fax:* 800-458-6515 *E-mail:* orders@wwnorton.com *Web Site:* books.wwnorton.com, pg 164

Durepos, Joseph, Loyola Press, 3441 N Ashland Ave, Chicago, IL 60657 *Tel:* 773-281-1818 *Toll Free Tel:* 800-621-1008 *Fax:* 773-281-0555 (cust serv); 773-281-4129 (edit) *E-mail:* customerservice@loyolapress.com *Web Site:* www.loyolapress.com, pg 138

Durham, Daphne, Farrar, Straus & Giroux, LLC, 18 W 18 St, New York, NY 10011 *Tel:* 212-741-6900 *E-mail:* fsg.publicity@fsgbooks.com *Web Site:* us.macmillan.com/fsg.aspx, pg 83

Durham, Judith B, Graphic Arts Education & Research Foundation (GAERF), 1899 Preston White Dr, Reston, VA 20191 *Tel:* 703-264-7200 *Toll Free Tel:* 844-381-9839 *Fax:* 703-620-3165 *E-mail:* gaerf@npes.org *Web Site:* www.gaerf.org, pg 583

Durham, Rusty, StarGroup International Inc, 1194 Old Dixie Hwy, Suite 201, West Palm Beach, FL 33413 *Tel:* 561-547-0667 *Fax:* 561-843-8530 *E-mail:* info@stargroupinternational.com *Web Site:* stargroupinternational.com, pg 221

Durrant, Jennifer, Sourced Media Books, 15 Via Picato, San Clemente, CA 92673 *Tel:* 949-813-0182 *E-mail:* editor@sourcedmediabooks.com *Web Site:* sourcedmediabooks.com, pg 218

Duval, Nathalie, Alexander Street, a ProQuest Company, 3212 Duke St, Alexandria, VA 22314 *Tel:* 703-212-8520 *Toll Free Tel:* 800-889-5937 *Fax:* 703-940-6584 *E-mail:* sales@alexanderstreet.com; marketing@alexanderstreet.com; info@alexanderstreet.com *Web Site:* alexanderstreet.com, pg 7

Duvall, Donna, Paladin Press, 5540 Central Ave, Suite 200, Boulder, CO 80301 *Tel:* 303-443-7250 *Toll Free Tel:* 800-392-2400 *Fax:* 303-442-8741 *E-mail:* service@paladin-press.com *Web Site:* www.paladin-press.com, pg 172

DuVall, Jennifer, Schiavone Literary Agency Inc, 236 Trails End, West Palm Beach, FL 33413-2135 *Tel:* 561-966-9294 *Fax:* 561-966-9294 *E-mail:* profschia@aol.com *Web Site:* www.publishersmarketplace.com/members/profschia, pg 534

Dworkin, Brooke, Disney Press, 1101 Flower St, Glendale, CA 91201 *Web Site:* books.disney.com, pg 70

Dwyer, Corinne A, North Star Press of Saint Cloud Inc, PO Box 451, St Cloud, MN 56302-0451 *Tel:* 320-558-9062 *E-mail:* info@northstarpress.com *Web Site:* www.northstarpress.com, pg 164

Dwyer, Peter, Association of Catholic Publishers Inc, 4725 Dorsey Hall Dr, Suite A, PMB 709, Elliott City, MD 21042 *Tel:* 410-988-2926 *Fax:* 410-571-4946 *Web Site:* www.catholicsread.org; www.catholicpublishers.org; www.midatlanticcongress.org, pg 558

Dwyer, Peter, Cistercian Publications, Saint John's Abbey, PO Box 7500, Collegeville, MN 56321 *Tel:* 320-363-2213 *Toll Free Tel:* 800-436-8431 *Fax:* 320-363-3299 *Toll Free Fax:* 800-445-5899 *E-mail:* sales@litpress.org *Web Site:* www.cistercianpublications.org, pg 56

Dwyer, Peter, Liturgical Press, PO Box 7500, St John's Abbey, Collegeville, MN 56321-7500 *Tel:* 320-363-2213 *Toll Free Tel:* 800-858-5450 *Fax:* 320-363-3299 *Toll Free Fax:* 800-445-5899 *E-mail:* sales@litpress.org *Web Site:* www.litpress.org, pg 136

Dye, Ann, Houghton Mifflin Harcourt Trade & Reference Division, 125 High St, Boston, MA 02110 *Tel:* 617-351-5000 *Toll Free Tel:* 800-225-3362 *Web Site:* www.hmhco.com, pg 111

Dye, Skip, Books on Tape®, 1745 Broadway, New York, NY 10019 *Toll Free Tel:* 800-733-3000 (cust serv) *Toll Free Fax:* 800-940-7046 *Web Site:* www.booksontape.com, pg 40

Dye, Skip, Penguin Random House Inc, 1745 Broadway, New York, NY 10019 *Tel:* 212-782-9000 *Toll Free Tel:* 800-726-0600 *Web Site:* www.penguinrandomhouse.com, pg 178

Dyer, Alison, Writers' Alliance of Newfoundland & Labrador, Haymarket Sq, 223 Duckworth St, Suite 208, St John's, NL A1C 6N1, Canada *Tel:* 709-739-5215 *Toll Free Tel:* 866-739-5215 *E-mail:* wanl@nf.aibn.com *Web Site:* wanl.ca, pg 581

Dyke, George, Earth Edit, PO Box 114, Maiden Rock, WI 54750 *Tel:* 715-448-3009, pg 493

Dykstra, LeeAnna, Broadview Press, 280 Perry St, Unit 5, Peterborough, ON K9J 2J4, Canada *Tel:* 705-743-8990 *Fax:* 705-743-8353 *E-mail:* customerservice@broadviewpress.com *Web Site:* www.broadviewpress.com, pg 447

Dynak, Sharon, Ucross Foundation Residency Program, 30 Big Red Lane, Clearmont, WY 82835 *Tel:* 307-737-2291 *Fax:* 307-737-2322 *E-mail:* info@ucross.org *Web Site:* www.ucrossfoundation.org, pg 695

Dyson, Elizabeth Branch, University of Chicago Press, 1427 E 60 St, Chicago, IL 60637-2954 *Tel:* 773-702-7700; 773-702-7600 *Toll Free Tel:* 800-621-2736 (orders) *Fax:* 773-702-9756; 773-660-2235 (orders); 773-702-2708 *E-mail:* custserv@press.uchicago.edu; marketing@press.uchicago.edu *Web Site:* www.press.uchicago.edu, pg 241

Dyssegaard, Elisabeth, St Martin's Press, LLC, 175 Fifth Ave, New York, NY 10010 *Tel:* 646-307-5151 *Web Site:* us.macmillan.com/smp, pg 204

Dystel, Jane, Dystel, Goderich & Bourret LLC, One Union Sq W, Suite 904, New York, NY 10003 *Tel:* 212-627-9100 *Fax:* 212-627-9313 *Web Site:* www.dystel.com, pg 515

Dzienkonski, Karen, Penguin Random House Audio Publishing, 1745 Broadway, New York, NY 10019 *E-mail:* audio@penguinrandomhouse.com *Web Site:* www.penguinrandomhouseaudio.com, pg 178

Eadicicco, John Michael, Association of American University Presses (AAUP), 1412 Broadway, Suite 2135, New York, NY 10018 *Tel:* 212-989-1010 *Fax:* 212-989-0275 *E-mail:* info@aaupnet.org *Web Site:* www.aaupnet.org, pg 558

Eagle, Sara, Alfred A Knopf/Everyman's Library, c/o Penguin Random House Inc, 1745 Broadway, New York, NY 10019 *Tel:* 212-751-2600 *Toll Free Tel:* 800-638-6460 *Fax:* 212-572-2593 *Web Site:* www.knopfdoubleday.com, pg 127

Eagle, Sara, Pantheon Books/Schocken Books, c/o Penguin Random House Inc, 1745 Broadway, New York, NY 10019 *Tel:* 212-751-2600 *Web Site:* knopfdoubleday.com/imprint/pantheon, pg 173

Eaker, Noah, Random House Publishing Group, 1745 Broadway, New York, NY 10019 *Toll Free Tel:* 800-200-3552 *Web Site:* atrandom.com, pg 195

Eanes, Russ, Herald Press, 1251 Virginia Ave, Harrisonburg, VA 22802-2434 *Toll Free Tel:* 800-245-7894 (orders) *Toll Free Fax:* 877-271-0760 *E-mail:* info@MennoMedia.org *Web Site:* www.heraldpress.com; store.mennomedia.org, pg 106

Earle, Kathryn, Bloomsbury Academic, 1385 Broadway, 5th fl, New York, NY 10018 *Tel:* 212-419-5300 *Web Site:* www.bloomsbury.com/us/academic, pg 37

Earle, Kathryn, Bloomsbury Publishing Inc, 1385 Broadway, 5th fl, New York, NY 10018 *Tel:* 212-419-5300 *E-mail:* marketingusa@bloomsbury.com; adultpublicityusa@bloomsbury.com; askacademic@bloomsbury.com *Web Site:* www.bloomsbury.com, pg 37

Early, Brighton, Sudden Fiction Contest, c/o ASUC Publications, Univ of California, 10-B Eshleman Hall, Berkeley, CA 94720-4500 *E-mail:* bfictionreview@yahoo.com *Web Site:* www.ocf.berkeley.edu/~bfr/, pg 692

Easley, Thomas J, American Medical Association, AMA Plaza, 330 N Wabash, Suite 39300, Chicago, IL 60611-5885 *Tel:* 312-464-5000 *Toll Free Tel:* 800-621-8335 *Fax:* 312-464-4184 *Web Site:* www.ama-assn.org, pg 13, 555

Eastman-Mullins, Andrea, Alexander Street, a ProQuest Company, 3212 Duke St, Alexandria, VA 22314 *Tel:* 703-212-8520 *Toll Free Tel:* 800-889-5937 *Fax:* 703-940-6584 *E-mail:* sales@alexanderstreet.com; marketing@alexanderstreet.com; info@alexanderstreet.com *Web Site:* alexanderstreet.com, pg 7

Easton, Claire, Painted-Words Inc, 310 W 97 St, Suite 24, New York, NY 10025 *Tel:* 212-663-2311 *Fax:* 212-663-2891 *E-mail:* info@painted-words.com *Web Site:* painted-words.com, pg 544

Easton, Emily, Penguin Random House Inc, 1745 Broadway, New York, NY 10019 *Tel:* 212-782-9000 *Toll Free Tel:* 800-726-0600 *Web Site:* www.penguinrandomhouse.com, pg 178

Eastwood, Hilary, Mazda Publishers Inc, One Park Plaza, Suite 600, Irvine, CA 92614 *Tel:* 714-751-5252 *Fax:* 714-751-4805 *E-mail:* mazdapub@aol.com *Web Site:* www.mazdapublishers.com, pg 144

Eaton, Brenda, Interlink Publishing Group Inc, 46 Crosby St, Northampton, MA 01060 *Tel:* 413-582-7054 *Toll Free Tel:* 800-238-LINK (238-5465) *Fax:* 413-582-7057 *E-mail:* info@interlinkbooks.com *Web Site:* www.interlinkbooks.com, pg 118

Eaton, Dena, Bitingduck Press LLC, 1262 Sunnyoaks Circle, Altadena, CA 91001 *Tel:* 626-679-2494; 626-507-8033 *E-mail:* notifications@bitingduckpress.com *Web Site:* bitingduckpress.com, pg 36

Eaton, Eryn, Red Wheel/Weiser/Conari, 65 Parker St, Suite 7, Newburyport, MA 01950 *Tel:* 978-465-0504 *Toll Free Tel:* 800-423-7087 (orders) *Fax:* 978-465-0243 *E-mail:* info@rwwbooks.com *Web Site:* www.redwheelweiser.com, pg 197

Eaton, Jonathan, Tilbury House Publishers, 12 Starr St, Thomaston, ME 04861 *Tel:* 207-582-1899 *Toll Free Tel:* 800-582-1899 (orders) *Fax:* 207-582-8227 *E-mail:* tilbury@tilburyhouse.com *Web Site:* www.tilburyhouse.com, pg 232

Eaton, Sandi, Chelsea Green Publishing Co, 85 N Main St, Suite 120, White River Junction, VT 05001 *Tel:* 802-295-6300 *Toll Free Tel:* 800-639-4099 (cust serv, consumer & trade orders) *Fax:* 802-295-6444 *Web Site:* www.chelseagreen.com, pg 53

Eberly, Chelsea, Random House Children's Books, 1745 Broadway, 10th fl, New York, NY 10019 *Tel:* 212-782-9000 *Web Site:* www.randomhousekids.com, pg 194

Echevarria, Janice, Chronicle Books LLC, 680 Second St, San Francisco, CA 94107 *Tel:* 415-537-4200 *Toll Free Tel:* 800-759-0190 (cust serv) *Fax:* 415-537-4460 *Toll Free Fax:* 800-858-7787 (orders); 800-286-9471 (cust serv) *E-mail:* frontdesk@chroniclebooks.com *Web Site:* www.chroniclebooks.com, pg 55

Eckenrode, Dr Joseph, DEStech Publications Inc, 439 N Duke St, Lancaster, PA 17602-4967 *Tel:* 717-290-1660 *Toll Free Tel:* 877-500-4337 *Fax:* 717-509-6100 *E-mail:* info@destechpub.com *Web Site:* www.destechpub.com, pg 69

Eckerle, Christy, Montana Historical Society Press, Capitol Complex, 225 N Roberts St, Helena, MT 59620 *Tel:* 406-444-0090 (edit); 406-444-2890 (orders/mktg); 406-444-2694 *Toll Free Tel:* 800-243-9900 *Fax:* 406-444-2696 (orders/mktg) *Web Site:* mhs.mt.gov/pubs, pg 153

Eckert, Carolyn, Storey Publishing LLC, 210 MASS MoCA Way, North Adams, MA 01247 *Tel:* 413-346-2100 *Toll Free Tel:* 800-441-5700 (orders); 800-793-9396 (edit) *Fax:* 413-346-2199; 413-346-2196 (edit) *E-mail:* sales@storey.com *Web Site:* www.storey.com, pg 223

Ecklebarger, David, Editorial Unilit, 8167 NW 84 St, Medley, FL 33166 *Tel:* 305-592-6136 *Toll Free Tel:* 800-767-7726 *Fax:* 305-592-0087 *E-mail:* info@editorialunilit.com; customerservice@editorialunilit.com *Web Site:* www.editorialunilit.com, pg 238

Eckmair, Leigh, Birch Brook Press, PO Box 81, Delhi, NY 13753-0081 *Tel:* 607-746-7453 (book sales & prodn) *Fax:* 607-746-7453 *E-mail:* birchbrook@copper.net *Web Site:* www.birchbrookpress.info, pg 35

Eckstut, Arielle, Levine|Greenberg|Rostan Literary Agency, 307 Seventh Ave, Suite 2407, New York, NY 10001 *Tel:* 212-337-0934 *Fax:* 212-337-0948 *Web Site:* lgrliterary.com, pg 525

Edde, Neil, Peachpit Press, 1301 Sansome St, San Francisco, CA 94111 *Toll Free Tel:* 800-283-9444 *E-mail:* info@peachpit.com; ask@peachpit.com *Web Site:* www.peachpit.com, pg 175

Edelson, Libby, HarperCollins General Books Group, 195 Broadway, New York, NY 10007 *Tel:* 212-207-7000 *Web Site:* www.harpercollins.com, pg 101

Edelson, Samantha, Macmillan Audio, 175 Fifth Ave, New York, NY 10010 *Tel:* 646-307-5151 *Toll Free Tel:* 888-330-8477 (cust serv) *Fax:* 917-534-0980 *Web Site:* www.macmillanaudio.com, pg 140

Edelstein, Anne, Anne Edelstein Literary Agency LLC, 404 Riverside Dr, New York, NY 10025 *Tel:* 212-414-4923 *E-mail:* info@aeliterary.com; rights@aeliterary.com *Web Site:* www.aeliterary.com, pg 515

Eden, Katriena, Cedar Fort Inc, 2373 W 700 S, Springville, UT 84663 *Tel:* 801-489-4084 *Toll Free Tel:* 800-SKY-BOOK (759-2665) *Fax:* 801-489-1097 *Toll Free Fax:* 800-388-3727 *Web Site:* cedarfort.com, pg 50

Eder, Elsa, Northern California Independent Booksellers Association (NCIBA), 651 Broadway, Sonoma, CA 95476 *Tel:* 415-561-7686 *Fax:* 415-561-7685 *E-mail:* info@nciba.com *Web Site:* www.nciba.com, pg 574

Edgecombe, Lindsay, Levine|Greenberg|Rostan Literary Agency, 307 Seventh Ave, Suite 2407, New York, NY 10001 *Tel:* 212-337-0934 *Fax:* 212-337-0948 *Web Site:* lgrliterary.com, pg 525

Edkins, Sarah, PEN/Jean Stein Book Award, 588 Broadway, Suite 303, New York, NY 10012 *Tel:* 212-334-1660 *E-mail:* info@pen.org *Web Site:* pen.org/press/grants-awards-database, pg 678

Edkins, Sarah, PEN/Nabokov Award for Achievement in International Literature, 588 Broadway, Suite 303, New York, NY 10012 *Tel:* 212-334-1660 *Fax:* 212-334-2181 *E-mail:* awards@pen.org *Web Site:* pen.org/literary-awards, pg 678

Edmunds, Page, Workman Publishing Co Inc, 225 Varick St, 9th fl, New York, NY 10014-4381 *Tel:* 212-254-5900 *Toll Free Tel:* 800-722-7202 *Fax:* 212-254-8098 *E-mail:* info@workman.com *Web Site:* www.workman.com, pg 259

Edsill, Rachel, The Art Institute of Chicago, 111 S Michigan Ave, Chicago, IL 60603-6404 *Tel:* 312-443-3600; 312-443-3540 (pubns) *Fax:* 312-443-1334 (pubns) *Web Site:* www.artic.edu; www.artinstituteshop.org, pg 21

Edwards, Adrianna, Focus Strategic Communications Inc, 2474 Waterford St, Oakville, ON L6L 5E6, Canada *Tel:* 905-825-8757 *Toll Free Tel:* 866-263-6287 *Fax:* 905-825-5724 *Toll Free Fax:* 866-613-6287 *E-mail:* info@focussc.com *Web Site:* www.focussc.com, pg 494

Edwards, Brittany, Houghton Mifflin Harcourt Trade & Reference Division, 125 High St, Boston, MA 02110 *Tel:* 617-351-5000 *Toll Free Tel:* 800-225-3362 *Web Site:* www.hmhco.com, pg 111

Edwards, Karen Gray, American Sociological Association (ASA), 1430 "K" St NW, Suite 600, Washington, DC 20005-4701 *Tel:* 202-383-9005 *Fax:* 202-638-0882 *E-mail:* customer@asanet.org *Web Site:* www.asanet.org, pg 556

Edwards, Kate, Association of Canadian Publishers (ACP), 174 Spadina Ave, Suite 306, Toronto, ON M5T 2C2, Canada *Tel:* 416-487-6116 *Fax:* 416-487-8815 *E-mail:* admin@canbook.org *Web Site:* publishers.ca, pg 558

Edwards, Kathy, The Ohio State University Press, 180 Pressey Hall, 1070 Carmack Rd, Columbus, OH 43210-1002 *Tel:* 614-292-6930 *Fax:* 614-292-2065 *Toll Free Fax:* 800-621-8476 *E-mail:* info@osupress.org *Web Site:* ohiostatepress.org, pg 167

Edwards, Katya, The Guilford Press, 370 Seventh Ave, Suite 1200, New York, NY 10001-1020 *Tel:* 212-431-9800 *Toll Free Tel:* 800-365-7006 *Fax:* 212-966-6708 *E-mail:* info@guilford.com *Web Site:* www.guilford.com, pg 97

Edwards, Mary Jane, Jentel Artist Residency Program, 130 Lower Piney Rd, Banner, WY 82832 *Tel:* 307-737-2311 *Fax:* 307-737-2305 *E-mail:* jentel@jentelarts.org *Web Site:* www.jentelarts.org, pg 612

Edwards, Ron, Focus Strategic Communications Inc, 2474 Waterford St, Oakville, ON L6L 5E6, Canada *Tel:* 905-825-8757 *Toll Free Tel:* 866-263-6287 *Fax:* 905-825-5724 *Toll Free Fax:* 866-613-6287 *E-mail:* info@focussc.com *Web Site:* www.focussc.com, pg 494

Edwards, Dr Wade, John Dos Passos Prize for Literature, Dept of English & Modern Languages, 201 High St, Farmville, VA 23909 *Tel:* 434-395-2155 *Fax:* 434-395-2145 *Web Site:* www.longwood.edu/english/dos-passos-prize, pg 642

Eerdmans, Anita, Wm B Eerdmans Publishing Co, 2140 Oak Industrial Dr NE, Grand Rapids, MI 49505 *Tel:* 616-459-4591 *Toll Free Tel:* 800-253-

7521 *Fax:* 616-459-6540 *E-mail:* customerservice@eerdmans.com; sales@eerdmans.com *Web Site:* www.eerdmans.com, pg 76

Eerdmans, William B Jr, Wm B Eerdmans Publishing Co, 2140 Oak Industrial Dr NE, Grand Rapids, MI 49505 *Tel:* 616-459-4591 *Toll Free Tel:* 800-253-7521 *Fax:* 616-459-6540 *E-mail:* customerservice@eerdmans.com; sales@eerdmans.com *Web Site:* www.eerdmans.com, pg 76

Efting, Brad, Paladin Press, 5540 Central Ave, Suite 200, Boulder, CO 80301 *Tel:* 303-443-7250 *Toll Free Tel:* 800-392-2400 *Fax:* 303-442-8741 *E-mail:* service@paladin-press.com *Web Site:* www.paladin-press.com, pg 172

Egan-Miller, Danielle, Browne & Miller Literary Associates, 410 S Michigan Ave, Suite 460, Chicago, IL 60605 *Tel:* 312-922-3063 *E-mail:* mail@browneandmiller.com *Web Site:* www.browneandmiller.com, pg 510

Ehart, Kimberly, Perseus Books, 250 W 57 St, 15th fl, New York, NY 10107 *Tel:* 212-340-8100 *Toll Free Tel:* 800-343-4499 (cust serv) *Fax:* 212-340-8105 *Web Site:* www.perseusbooks.com, pg 180

Ehle, Robert, Stanford University Press, 425 Broadway St, Redwood City, CA 94063-3126 *Tel:* 650-723-9434 *Fax:* 650-725-3457 *E-mail:* info@www.sup.org; publicity@www.sup.org *Web Site:* www.sup.org, pg 220

Ehrenhaft, Dan, HarperCollins Children's Books, 195 Broadway, New York, NY 10007 *Tel:* 212-207-7000 *Web Site:* www.harpercollins.com/childrens, pg 101

Eifrig, Penny Smith, Eifrig Publishing LLC, PO Box 66, Lemont, PA 16851 *Toll Free Tel:* 888-340-6543 *E-mail:* info@eifrigpublishing.com *Web Site:* www.eifrigpublishing.com, pg 76

Einerson, Katy, Whiting Awards, 16 Court St, Suite 2308, Brooklyn, NY 11241 *Tel:* 718-701-5962 *E-mail:* info@whiting.org *Web Site:* www.whiting.org, pg 697

Einerson, Katy, Whiting Creative Nonfiction Grant, 16 Court St, Suite 2308, Brooklyn, NY 11241 *Tel:* 718-701-5962 *E-mail:* nonfiction@whiting.org; info@whiting.org *Web Site:* www.whiting.org, pg 697

Eis, Arlene L, Infosources Publishing, 140 Norma Rd, Teaneck, NJ 07666 *Tel:* 201-836-7072 *Web Site:* www.infosourcespub.com, pg 117

Eisemann, Patricia, Henry Holt and Company, LLC, 175 Fifth Ave, New York, NY 10010 *Tel:* 646-307-5151 *Toll Free Tel:* 888-330-8477 (orders) *Fax:* 646-307-5285 *E-mail:* firstname.lastname@hholt.com *Web Site:* www.henryholt.com, pg 109

Eisenberg, Michael, Boyds Mills Press, 815 Church St, Honesdale, PA 18431 *Tel:* 570-253-1164 *Toll Free Tel:* 800-490-5111 *Fax:* 570-253-0179 *E-mail:* contact@boydsmillspress.com *Web Site:* www.boydsmillspress.com, pg 41

Eisenberg, Michael, Highlights for Children, 1800 Watermark Dr, Columbus, OH 43215 *Tel:* 614-486-0631 *Toll Free Tel:* 800-962-3661 (Highlights Club cust serv); 800-255-9517 (Highlights Magazine cust serv) *Web Site:* www.highlights.com; www.facebook.com/HighlightsforChildren, pg 107

Eisenbraun, James E, Eisenbrauns, PO Box 275, Winona Lake, IN 46590-0275 *Tel:* 574-269-2011 *Fax:* 574-269-6788 *E-mail:* customer_service@eisenbrauns.com; publisher@eisenbrauns.com *Web Site:* www.eisenbrauns.com, pg 76

Eisenhardt, Gae, Azro Press, 1704 Llano St B, PMB 342, Santa Fe, NM 87505 *Tel:* 505-989-3272 *Fax:* 505-989-3832 *E-mail:* books@azropress.com *Web Site:* www.azropress.com, pg 27

Eisenmann, Caroline, Frances Goldin Literary Agency, Inc, 214 W 29 St, Suite 410, New York, NY 10001 *Tel:* 212-777-0047 *Fax:* 212-228-1660 *E-mail:* agency@goldinlit.com *Web Site:* www.goldinlit.com, pg 519

Eiynck, Sandra, Liturgical Press, PO Box 7500, St John's Abbey, Collegeville, MN 56321-7500 *Tel:* 320-363-2213 *Toll Free Tel:* 800-858-5450 *Fax:* 320-363-3299 *Toll Free Fax:* 800-445-5899 *E-mail:* sales@litpress.org *Web Site:* www.litpress.org, pg 136

Ekroth, Angela, Paulist Press, 997 Macarthur Blvd, Mahwah, NJ 07430-9990 *Tel:* 201-825-7300 *Toll Free Tel:* 800-218-1903 *Fax:* 201-825-6921 *Toll Free Fax:* 800-836-3161 *E-mail:* info@paulistpress.com; publicity@paulistpress.com *Web Site:* www.paulistpress.com, pg 175

Ekstrom, Rachel, Irene Goodman Literary Agency, 27 W 24 St, Suite 700B, New York, NY 10010 *Tel:* 212-604-0330 *E-mail:* queries@irenegoodman.com *Web Site:* www.irenegoodman.com, pg 519

Ekus, Lisa, The Lisa Ekus Group LLC, 57 North St, Hatfield, MA 01038 *Tel:* 413-247-9325 *Fax:* 413-247-9873 *E-mail:* info@lisaekus.com *Web Site:* lisaekus.com, pg 515, 619

Ekus, Sally, The Lisa Ekus Group LLC, 57 North St, Hatfield, MA 01038 *Tel:* 413-247-9325 *Fax:* 413-247-9873 *E-mail:* info@lisaekus.com *Web Site:* lisaekus.com, pg 515, 619

El Mallakh, Dorothea H, International Research Center for Energy & Economic Development, 850 Willowbrook Rd, Boulder, CO 80302 *Tel:* 303-442-4014 *Fax:* 303-442-5042 *E-mail:* info@iceed.org *Web Site:* www.iceed.org, pg 120

El Mallakh, Helen, International Research Center for Energy & Economic Development, 850 Willowbrook Rd, Boulder, CO 80302 *Tel:* 303-442-4014 *Fax:* 303-442-5042 *E-mail:* info@iceed.org *Web Site:* www.iceed.org, pg 120

Elancheran, Maran, Newgen North America Inc, 2714 Bee Cave Rd, Suite 201, Austin, TX 78746 *Tel:* 512-478-5341 *Fax:* 512-476-4756 *Web Site:* www.newgen.co, pg 499

Elbe, Susan, John Wiley & Sons Inc Global Education, 111 River St, Hoboken, NJ 07030-5774 *Tel:* 201-748-6000 *Toll Free Tel:* 800-225-5945 (cust serv) *Fax:* 201-748-6008 *E-mail:* info@wiley.com *Web Site:* www.wiley.com, pg 256

Elblonk, Matthew, DeFiore and Company Literary Management Inc, 47 E 19 St, 3rd fl, New York, NY 10003 *Tel:* 212-925-7744 *Fax:* 212-925-9803 *E-mail:* info@defliterary.com; submissions@defliterary.com *Web Site:* www.defliterary.com, pg 513

Elfenbein, Reed, John Wiley & Sons Inc, 111 River St, Hoboken, NJ 07030-5774 *Tel:* 201-748-6000 *Toll Free Tel:* 800-225-5945 (cust serv) *Fax:* 201-748-6088 *E-mail:* info@wiley.com *Web Site:* www.wiley.com, pg 256

Elias, Che, Six Gallery Press, PO Box 90145, Pittsburgh, PA 15224-0545 *Web Site:* www.sixgallerypress.com, pg 214

Elias, Maria, Disney-Hyperion Books, 1101 Flower St, Glendale, CA 91201 *Web Site:* books.disney.com, pg 70

Elinsky, Rachel, HarperCollins Publishers, 195 Broadway, New York, NY 10007 *Tel:* 212-207-7000 *Fax:* 212-207-7145 *Web Site:* www.harpercollins.com, pg 102

Elizalde, Steve, Greenleaf Book Group LLC, 3 Park Place, 4005 Banister Lane, Suite B, Austin, TX 78704 *Tel:* 512-891-6100 *Fax:* 512-891-6150 *E-mail:* contact@greenleafbookgroup.com *Web Site:* www.greenleafbookgroup.com, pg 96

Ellen, Joan, World Citizens, PO Box 131, Mill Valley, CA 94942-0131 *Tel:* 415-380-8020 *Toll Free Tel:* 800-247-6553 (orders only), pg 259

Ellenberg, Ethan, Ethan Ellenberg Literary Agency, 155 Suffolk St, Suite 2R, New York, NY 10002 *Tel:* 212-431-4554 *E-mail:* agent@ethanellenberg.com *Web Site:* www.ethanellenberg.com, pg 516

Ellenson, David, Hebrew Union College Press, 3101 Clifton Ave, Cincinnati, OH 45220 *Tel:* 513-221-1875 *Fax:* 513-221-0321 *Web Site:* press.huc.edu, pg 105

Ellerbeck, Brian, Teachers College Press, 1234 Amsterdam Ave, New York, NY 10027 *Tel:* 212-678-3929 *Toll Free Tel:* 800-575-6566 *Fax:* 212-678-4149; 802-864-7626 *E-mail:* tcpress@tc.columbia.edu; tcp.orders@aidcvt.com (orders) *Web Site:* www.teacherscollegepress.com, pg 228

Elliot, Marie, W Kaye Lamb Award, PO Box 5254, Sta B, Victoria, BC V8R 6N4, Canada *E-mail:* essays@bchistory.ca *Web Site:* www.bchistory.ca, pg 659

Elliot, Nick, Random House Children's Books, 1745 Broadway, 10th fl, New York, NY 10019 *Tel:* 212-782-9000 *Web Site:* www.randomhousekids.com, pg 194

Elliott, Jennifer, International Linguistics Corp, 12220 Blue Ridge Blvd, Suite G, Kansas City, MO 64030 *Tel:* 816-765-8855 *Toll Free Tel:* 800-237-1830 (orders) *Fax:* 816-765-2855 *E-mail:* learnables@sbcglobal.net *Web Site:* www.learnables.com, pg 119

Elliott, Miranda, Dufour Editions Inc, PO Box 7, Chester Springs, PA 19425 *Tel:* 610-458-5005 *Fax:* 610-458-7103 *E-mail:* info@dufoureditions.com *Web Site:* www.dufoureditions.com, pg 73

Elliott, Stephanie, Wesleyan University Press, 215 Long Lane, Middletown, CT 06459-0433 *Tel:* 860-685-7711 *Fax:* 860-685-7712 *Web Site:* www.wesleyan.edu/wespress, pg 253

Elliott, Stephen P, Sachem Publishing Associates Inc, 402 W Lyon Farm Dr, Greenwich, CT 06831 *Tel:* 203-813-3077 *E-mail:* sachempub@optonline.net, pg 501

Ellis, Barbara, Unicorn Writers' Conference, 17 Church Hill Rd, Redding, CT 06896 *Tel:* 203-938-7405 *Fax:* 203-938-7405 *E-mail:* unicornwritersconference@gmail.com *Web Site:* unicornwritersconference.com, pg 615

Ellis, Clare, Stone Pier Press, PO Box 170572, San Francisco, CA 94117 *Tel:* 415-484-2821 *E-mail:* hello@stonepierpress.org *Web Site:* www.stonepierpress.org, pg 223

Ellis, Elaina, Copper Canyon Press, Fort Worden State Park, Bldg 313, Port Townsend, WA 98368 *Tel:* 360-385-4925 *Toll Free Tel:* 877-501-1393 (orders) *Fax:* 360-385-4985 *E-mail:* poetry@coppercanyonpress.org *Web Site:* www.coppercanyonpress.org, pg 60

Ellis, Jane, University Science Books, 20 Edgeshill Rd, Mill Valley, CA 94941 *Tel:* 703-661-1572 (cust serv, orders) *Fax:* 703-661-1572 (cust serv, orders) *E-mail:* usbmail@presswarehouse.com (cust serv, orders) *Web Site:* www.uscibooks.com, pg 248

Ellis, Kirk, Spur Awards, 271 CR 219, Encampment, WY 82325 *Tel:* 307-329-8942 *E-mail:* wwa.moulton@gmail.com *Web Site:* westernwriters.org, pg 691

Ellis, Kirk, Western Writers of America Inc (WWA), 271 CR 219, Encampment, WY 82325 *Tel:* 307-329-8942 *Web Site:* westernwriters.org, pg 580

Ellis, Mercury, Chronicle Books LLC, 680 Second St, San Francisco, CA 94107 *Tel:* 415-537-4200 *Toll Free Tel:* 800-759-0190 (cust serv) *Fax:* 415-537-4460 *Toll Free Fax:* 800-858-7787 (orders); 800-286-9471 (cust serv) *E-mail:* frontdesk@chroniclebooks.com *Web Site:* www.chroniclebooks.com, pg 55

Ellison, Nicholas, Nicholas Ellison Agency, 469 W 147 St, Apt 1, New York, NY 10031 *Web Site:* www.thenicholasellisonagency.com, pg 516

Ellsberg, Robert, Orbis Books, Price Bldg, Box 302, Maryknoll, NY 10545-0302 *Tel:* 914-941-7636 *Toll Free Tel:* 800-258-5838 (orders) *Fax:* 914-941-7005 *E-mail:* orbisbooks@maryknoll.org *Web Site:* orbisbooks.com, pg 169

Ellsworth, Sherri, Sinauer Associates Inc, 23 Plumtree Rd, Sunderland, MA 01375 *Tel:* 413-549-4300 *Fax:* 413-549-1118 *E-mail:* publish@sinauer.com; orders@sinauer.com *Web Site:* sinauer.com, pg 214

Ellsworth, Thomas N, Vesuvian Books, 2817 West End Ave, Nashville, TN 37203 *E-mail:* info@vesuvianmedia.com *Web Site:* www.vesuvianbooks.com, pg 250

Ellwood, Nancy, DK Publishing, 345 Hudson St, 2nd fl, New York, NY 10014 *Tel:* 646-674-4000 *Toll Free Tel:* 877-342-5357 (cust serv); 800-733-3000 *Web Site:* www.dk.com; www.penguin.com, pg 71

Elmer, Derek, Random House Children's Books, 1745 Broadway, 10th fl, New York, NY 10019 *Tel:* 212-782-9000 *Web Site:* www.randomhousekids.com, pg 194

Elnan, Hannah, Sasquatch Books, 1904 S Third Ave, Suite 710, Seattle, WA 98101 *Tel:* 206-467-4300 *Toll Free Tel:* 800-775-0817 *Fax:* 206-467-4301 *E-mail:* custserv@sasquatchbooks.com *Web Site:* www.sasquatchbooks.com, pg 206

Else-Mitchell, Rose, Houghton Mifflin Harcourt, 125 High St, Boston, MA 02110 *Tel:* 617-351-5000 *Toll Free Tel:* 855-969-4642; 800-225-5425 (K-12 educ materials); 800-323-9540 (assessment materials); 877-219-1537 (SkillsTutor); 888-242-6747 (Innovation in Educ Group); 800-225-3362 (Trade & Ref Div) *Toll Free Fax:* 800-269-5232 *E-mail:* myhmhco@hmhco.com *Web Site:* www.hmhco.com, pg 110

Eltman, Kerry, Fox Chapel Publishing Co Inc, 1970 Broad St, East Petersburg, PA 17520 *Tel:* 717-560-4703 *Toll Free Tel:* 800-457-9112 *Fax:* 717-560-4702 *E-mail:* customerservice@foxchapelpublishing.com *Web Site:* www.foxchapelpublishing.com, pg 87

Elwell, James, Tyndale House Publishers Inc, 351 Executive Dr, Carol Stream, IL 60188 *Tel:* 630-668-8300 *Toll Free Tel:* 800-323-9400 *Toll Free Fax:* 800-684-0247 *Web Site:* www.tyndale.com, pg 237

Elwell, Morgan, Kensington Publishing Corp, 119 W 40 St, New York, NY 10018 *Tel:* 212-407-1500 *Toll Free Tel:* 800-221-2647 *Fax:* 212-935-0699 *Web Site:* www.kensingtonbooks.com, pg 125

Emerick, Ken, Individual Excellence Awards, 30 E Broad St, 33rd fl, Columbus, OH 43215 *Tel:* 614-466-2613 *Fax:* 614-466-4494 *Web Site:* www.oac.state.oh.us, pg 655

Emmrich, Terry, University of Wisconsin Press, 1930 Monroe St, 3rd fl, Madison, WI 53711-2059 *Tel:* 608-263-0668 *Toll Free Tel:* 800-621-2736 (orders) *Fax:* 608-263-1173 *Toll Free Fax:* 800-621-2736 (orders) *E-mail:* uwiscpress@uwpress.wisc.edu (main off); publicity@uwpress.wisc.edu *Web Site:* uwpress.wisc.edu, pg 246

Emond, D Paul, Emond Montgomery Publications Ltd, 60 Shaftesbury Ave, Toronto, ON M4T 1A3, Canada *Tel:* 416-975-3925 *Toll Free Tel:* 888-837-0815 *Fax:* 416-975-3924 *E-mail:* orders@emp.ca *Web Site:* www.emp.ca, pg 456

Enderlin, Jennifer, St Martin's Press, LLC, 175 Fifth Ave, New York, NY 10010 *Tel:* 646-307-5151 *Web Site:* us.macmillan.com/smp, pg 204

Eng, Dave, Frank Amato Publications Inc, 4040 SE Wister St, Milwaukie, OR 97222 *Tel:* 503-653-8108 *Toll Free Tel:* 800-541-9498 *Fax:* 503-653-2766 *E-mail:* customerservice@amatobooks.com; info@amatobooks.com *Web Site:* www.amatobooks.com, pg 9

Eng, Kenneth, Macmillan, 175 Fifth Ave, New York, NY 10010 *Tel:* 646-307-5151 *E-mail:* press.inquiries@macmillan.com *Web Site:* www.macmillan.com, pg 140

Engel, Carrie, The Brookings Institution Press, 1775 Massachusetts Ave NW, Washington, DC 20036-2188 *Tel:* 202-536-3600 *Toll Free Tel:* 800-537-5487 *Fax:* 202-536-3623 *E-mail:* permissions@brookings.edu *Web Site:* www.brookings.edu, pg 44

Engel, Deborah, Houghton Mifflin Harcourt Trade & Reference Division, 125 High St, Boston, MA 02110 *Tel:* 617-351-5000 *Toll Free Tel:* 800-225-3362 *Web Site:* www.hmhco.com, pg 111

Engel, Margaret, The Alicia Patterson Foundation Fellowship Program, 1100 Vermont Ave, Suite 900, Washington, DC 20005 *Tel:* 202-393-5995 *Fax:* 301-951-8512 *E-mail:* info@aliciapatterson.org *Web Site:* www.aliciapatterson.org, pg 677

Engelman, Ralph, The George Polk Awards, The Brooklyn Campus, One University Plaza, Brooklyn, NY 11201-5372 *Tel:* 718-488-1009 *Web Site:* www.liu.edu/polk, pg 680

Engelmann, Sarah, Doubleday/Nan A Talese, c/o Penguin Random House Inc, 1745 Broadway, New York, NY 10019 *Tel:* 212-751-2600 *Fax:* 212-572-2662 *E-mail:* ddaypub@randomhouse.com *Web Site:* knopfdoubleday.com, pg 72

Engelsma, Jonathan, Reformation Heritage Books, 2965 Leonard St NE, Grand Rapids, MI 49525 *Tel:* 616-977-0889 *Fax:* 616-285-3246 *E-mail:* orders@heritagebooks.org *Web Site:* www.heritagebooks.org, pg 198

Engles, Eric W PhD, EditCraft Editorial Services, 422 Pine St, Grass Valley, CA 95945 *Tel:* 530-273-3934 *Web Site:* www.editcraft.com, pg 493

English, Bridget, National Geographic Books, 1145 17 St NW, Washington, DC 20036-4688 *Tel:* 202-857-7000 *Toll Free Tel:* 877-866-6486 *E-mail:* ngbooks@cdsfulfillment.com *Web Site:* www.nationalgeographic.com/books/; ngbooks.buysub.com, pg 158

Engstrand, Vida, Kensington Publishing Corp, 119 W 40 St, New York, NY 10018 *Tel:* 212-407-1500 *Toll Free Tel:* 800-221-2647 *Fax:* 212-935-0699 *Web Site:* www.kensingtonbooks.com, pg 125

Engstrom, Krister, Random House Children's Books, 1745 Broadway, 10th fl, New York, NY 10019 *Tel:* 212-782-9000 *Web Site:* www.randomhousekids.com, pg 194

Enockson, Abi, ECS Publishing Corp, 1727 Larkin Williams Rd, Fenton, MO 63026 *Tel:* 636-305-0100 *Toll Free Tel:* 800-647-2117 *Web Site:* ecspublishing.com; www.facebook.com/ecspublishing, pg 75

Enrich, Jordanna, Fulbright Scholar Program, 1400 "K" St NW, Washington, DC 20005 *Tel:* 202-686-4000 *E-mail:* scholars@iie.org *Web Site:* www.cies.org; www.iie.org, pg 648

Ensign, Rebecca J, Gold Leaf Press, 3670 Morrissey Ave, Warren, MI 48091 *Tel:* 313-331-3571 *Web Site:* www.goldleafpress.com, pg 495

Enslow, Brian D, Enslow Publishing LLC, 101 W 23 St, Suite 240, New York, NY 10011 *Tel:* 908-771-9400 *Toll Free Tel:* 800-398-2504 *Fax:* 908-771-0925 *Toll Free Fax:* 877-980-4454 *E-mail:* customerservice@enslow.com *Web Site:* www.enslow.com, pg 79

Enslow, Mark, Enslow Publishing LLC, 101 W 23 St, Suite 240, New York, NY 10011 *Tel:* 908-771-9400 *Toll Free Tel:* 800-398-2504 *Fax:* 908-771-0925 *Toll Free Fax:* 877-980-4454 *E-mail:* customerservice@enslow.com *Web Site:* www.enslow.com, pg 79

Ensor, Kendra, Rand McNally, 9855 Woods Dr, Skokie, IL 60077 *Tel:* 847-329-8100 *E-mail:* ctsales@randmcnally.com; mediarelations@randmcnally.com *Web Site:* www.randmcnally.com, pg 194

Entrekin, Morgan, Grove Atlantic Inc, 154 W 14 St, 12th fl, New York, NY 10011 *Tel:* 212-614-7850 *Toll Free Tel:* 800-521-0178 *Fax:* 212-614-7886 *E-mail:* info@groveatlantic.com; sales@groveatlantic.com; publicity@groveatlantic.com; rights@groveatlantic.com *Web Site:* www.groveatlantic.com, pg 97

Entricken, Kevin, Wolters Kluwer US Corp, 2700 Lake Cook Rd, Riverwoods, IL 60015 *Tel:* 847-267-7000 *Fax:* 847-580-5192 *E-mail:* info@wolterskluwer.com *Web Site:* www.wolterskluwer.com, pg 258

Epler, Barbara, New Directions Publishing Corp, 80 Eighth Ave, New York, NY 10011 *Tel:* 212-255-0230 *Fax:* 212-255-0231 *E-mail:* newdirections@ndbooks.com *Web Site:* ndbooks.com, pg 160

Epstein, Don R, Greater Talent Network Inc, 437 Fifth Ave, New York, NY 10016 *Tel:* 212-645-4200 *Toll Free Tel:* 800-326-4211 *Fax:* 212-627-1471 *E-mail:* info@greatertalent.com *Web Site:* www.greatertalent.com, pg 547

Epstein, Richard, Atlantic Law Book Co, 22 Grassmere Ave, West Hartford, CT 06110-1215 *Tel:* 860-231-9300 *Toll Free Tel:* 800-259-5534 *Fax:* 860-231-9242 *E-mail:* atlanticlawbooks@aol.com *Web Site:* www.atlanticlawbooks.com, pg 25

Erickson, Leslie, University of British Columbia Press, 2029 West Mall, Vancouver, BC V6T 1Z2, Canada *Tel:* 604-822-5959 *Toll Free Tel:* 877-377-9378 *Fax:* 604-822-6083 *Toll Free Fax:* 800-668-0821 *E-mail:* frontdesk@ubcpress.ca *Web Site:* www.ubcpress.ca, pg 473

Erickson, Tim, RAND Corp, 1776 Main St, Santa Monica, CA 90407-2138 *Tel:* 310-393-0411 *Fax:* 310-393-4818 *Web Site:* www.rand.org, pg 193

Ericson, Carolyn Reeves, Ericson Books, 1614 Redbud St, Nacogdoches, TX 75965-2936 *Tel:* 936-564-3625 *Fax:* 936-552-8999, pg 79

Erikson, Anna, The Creative Co, PO Box 227, Mankato, MN 56002 *Tel:* 507-388-6273 *Toll Free Tel:* 800-445-6209 *Fax:* 507-388-2746 *E-mail:* info@thecreativecompany.us; orders@thecreativecompany.us *Web Site:* www.thecreativecompany.us, pg 64

Erisman, Angela Roskop, Hebrew Union College Press, 3101 Clifton Ave, Cincinnati, OH 45220 *Tel:* 513-221-1875 *Fax:* 513-221-0321 *Web Site:* press.huc.edu, pg 105

Erlacher, Bill, Artists Associates, 4416 La Jolla Dr, Bradenton, FL 34210-3927 *Tel:* 941-756-8445, pg 543

Ernest, James, Wm B Eerdmans Publishing Co, 2140 Oak Industrial Dr NE, Grand Rapids, MI 49505 *Tel:* 616-459-4591 *Toll Free Tel:* 800-253-7521 *Fax:* 616-459-6540 *E-mail:* customerservice@eerdmans.com; sales@eerdmans.com *Web Site:* www.eerdmans.com, pg 76

Ernst, Christopher R, Artech House Inc, 685 Canton St, Norwood, MA 02062 *Tel:* 781-769-9750 *Toll Free Tel:* 800-225-9977 *Fax:* 781-769-6334 *E-mail:* artech@artechhouse.com *Web Site:* www.artechhouse.com, pg 21

Ernst, Megan, Bloomsbury Publishing Inc, 1385 Broadway, 5th fl, New York, NY 10018 *Tel:* 212-419-5300 *E-mail:* marketingusa@bloomsbury.com; adultpublicityusa@bloomsbury.com; askacademic@bloomsbury.com *Web Site:* www.bloomsbury.com, pg 38

Erochina, Barbara, The League of Canadian Poets, 192 Spadina Ave, Suite 312, Toronto, ON M5T 2C2, Canada *Tel:* 416-504-1657 *Fax:* 416-504-0096 *Web Site:* poets.ca, pg 568

Errico, Kristin, Harlequin Enterprises Ltd, 233 Broadway, Suite 1001, New York, NY 10279 *Tel:* 212-553-4200 *Fax:* 212-227-8969 *E-mail:* customerservice@harlequin.com *Web Site:* www.harlequin.com, pg 100

Errico, Vincent, Trusted Media Brands Inc, 750 Third Ave, 3rd fl, New York, NY 10017 *Toll Free Tel:* 800-310-6261 (cust serv) *E-mail:* customercare@tmbi.com *Web Site:* www.tmbi.com; www.rd.com, pg 236

Esco, Melinda, TCU Press, 3000 Sandage Ave, Fort Worth, TX 76109 *Tel:* 817-257-7822 *Toll Free Tel:* 800-826-8911 (orders) *Fax:* 817-257-5075 *Web Site:* www.prs.tcu.edu, pg 228

Escobar, Nicole, New Hampshire Literary Awards, 2500 N River Rd, Manchester, NH 03106 *Tel:* 603-314-7980 *Fax:* 603-314-7981 *E-mail:* info@nhwritersproject.org; awards@nhwritersproject.org *Web Site:* www.nhwritersproject.org, pg 672

Escobedo, Eddie Jr, National Association of Hispanic Publications Inc (NAHP), 529 14 St NW, Suite 1126, Washington, DC 20045 *Tel:* 202-662-7250 *Web Site:* www.nahp.org, pg 571

Esersky, Gareth, Carol Mann Agency, 55 Fifth Ave, New York, NY 10003 *Tel:* 212-206-5635 *Fax:* 212-675-4809 *E-mail:* submissions@carolmannagency.com *Web Site:* www.carolmannagency.com, pg 527

Esparaza, Carlos, Hachette Books, 1290 Avenue of the Americas, New York, NY 10019 *Tel:* 212-364-1100 *Web Site:* www.hachettebookgroup.com, pg 98

Espinosa, Natalie, American Federation of Arts, 305 E 47 St, 10th fl, New York, NY 10017 *Tel:* 212-988-7700 *Toll Free Tel:* 800-232-0270 *Fax:* 212-861-2487 *E-mail:* pubinfo@amfedarts.org *Web Site:* www.amfedarts.org, pg 11

Esquillo, Michelle, Regal House Publishing, 1723 Hickory Overlook Trail, No 110, Raleigh, NC 27607 *Tel:* 305-360-5969 *E-mail:* info@regalhousepublishing.com *Web Site:* regalhousepublishing.com, pg 198

Essary, Loris, International Titles, 931 E 56 St, Austin, TX 78751-1724 *Tel:* 512-909-2447 *Web Site:* www.internationaltitles.com, pg 522

Estep, Ida Esq, Dog Writers' Association of America Inc (DWAA), 66 Adams St, Jamestown, NY 14701 *Tel:* 716-484-6155 *E-mail:* dogwriter@windstream.net *Web Site:* www.dwaa.org, pg 564

Estep, Ida Esq, Dog Writers' Association of America Inc (DWAA) Annual Writing Competition, 2243 Kelmscott Ct, Westlake Village, CA 91361 *Tel:* 805-418-7899 *Fax:* 831-374-9231 *E-mail:* dogwriter@windstream.net *Web Site:* www.dwaa.org, pg 642

Estremera, Estefeni, The Guilford Press, 370 Seventh Ave, Suite 1200, New York, NY 10001-1020 *Tel:* 212-431-9800 *Toll Free Tel:* 800-365-7006 *Fax:* 212-966-6708 *E-mail:* info@guilford.com *Web Site:* www.guilford.com, pg 97

Etcheson, Amy, Southern Illinois University Press, 1915 University Press Dr, SIUC Mail Code 6806, Carbondale, IL 62901-4323 *Tel:* 618-453-2281 *Fax:* 618-453-1221 *E-mail:* custserv@press.uchicago.edu; rights@siu.edu *Web Site:* www.siupress.com, pg 218

Etcheverry, Gabrielle, Livres Canada Books, One Nicholas, Suite 504, Ottawa, ON K1N 7B7, Canada *Tel:* 613-562-2324 *Fax:* 613-562-2329 *E-mail:* info@livrescanadabooks.com *Web Site:* www.livrescanadabooks.com, pg 569

Eth, Felicia, Felicia Eth Literary Representation, 555 Bryant St, Suite 350, Palo Alto, CA 94301 *Tel:* 415-970-9717 *E-mail:* feliciaeth.literary@gmail.com *Web Site:* www.ethliterary.com, pg 516

Etra, Judith, Whittier Publications Inc, 3115 Long Beach Rd, Oceanside, NY 11572 *Tel:* 516-432-8120 *Toll Free Tel:* 800-897-TEXT (897-8398) *Fax:* 516-889-0341 *E-mail:* info@whitbooks.com *Web Site:* www.whitbooks.com, pg 255

Etsch, Janet, The Conference Board Inc, 845 Third Ave, New York, NY 10022-6600 *Tel:* 212-759-0900; 212-339-0345 (cust serv) *Fax:* 212-980-7014; 212-836-9740 (cust serv) *E-mail:* customer.service@conferenceboard.org; membership@conferenceboard.org *Web Site:* www.conference-board.org; www.linkedin.com/company/the-conference-board, pg 60

Ettinger, Kathryn, Perseus Books, 250 W 57 St, 15th fl, New York, NY 10107 *Tel:* 212-340-8100 *Toll Free Tel:* 800-343-4499 (cust serv) *Fax:* 212-340-8105 *Web Site:* www.perseusbooks.com, pg 180

Eubanks, Debra, American Psychiatric Association Publishing, 1000 Wilson Blvd, Suite 1825, Arlington, VA 22209 *Tel:* 703-907-7322 *Toll Free Tel:* 800-368-5777 *Fax:* 703-907-1091 *E-mail:* appi@psych.org *Web Site:* www.appi.org; www.psychiatryonline.org, pg 14

Eulau, Dennis, Simon & Schuster, Inc, 1230 Avenue of the Americas, New York, NY 10020 *Tel:* 212-698-7000 *Fax:* 212-698-7007 *E-mail:* firstname.lastname@simonandschuster.com *Web Site:* www.simonandschuster.com, pg 213

Evans, Christopher, The Pacific Spirit Poetry Prize, University of British Columbia, Buch E462, 1866 Main Mall, Vancouver, BC V6T 1Z1, Canada *Tel:* 778-822-2514 *Fax:* 778-822-3616 *E-mail:* prismwritingcontest@gmail.com *Web Site:* www.prismmagazine.ca, pg 676

Evans, Christopher, PRISM international Literary Non-Fiction Contest, University of British Columbia, Buch E462, 1866 Main Mall, Vancouver, BC V6T 1Z1, Canada *Tel:* 778-822-2514 *Fax:* 778-822-3616 *E-mail:* prismwritingcontest@gmail.com *Web Site:* www.prismmagazine.ca, pg 682

Evans, Christopher, The Jacob Zilber Prize for Short Fiction, University of British Columbia, Buch E462, 1866 Main Mall, Vancouver, BC V6T 1Z1, Canada *Tel:* 778-822-2514 *Fax:* 778-822-3616 *E-mail:* prismwritingcontest@gmail.com *Web Site:* www.prismmagazine.ca, pg 701

Evans, Claire Lewis, University of Alabama Press, 200 Hackberry Lane, 2nd fl, Tuscaloosa, AL 35487 *Tel:* 205-348-5180 *Fax:* 205-348-9201 *Web Site:* www.uapress.ua.edu, pg 239

Evans, Clark, Abraham Lincoln Institute Book Award, 105 Mount Olive Lane, Ephrata, PA 17522 *E-mail:* secretary@lincoln-institute.org *Web Site:* www.lincoln-institute.org, pg 661

Evans, Elaine, Standard International Media Holdings, 568 Ninth St S, Suite 201, Naples, FL 34102-7336 *Tel:* 239-248-5550 *Fax:* 239-649-5832 *Toll Free Fax:* 866-948-7883 *E-mail:* sales@standardinternationalmedia.com *Web Site:* www.standardinternationalmedia.com, pg 220

Evans, Gene, Merit Publishing International Inc, 6839 Villas Dr S, Boca Raton, FL 33433 *Tel:* 561-350-0329 *E-mail:* merituk@aol.com *Web Site:* www.meritpublishing.com, pg 148

Evans, Jennifer, Springer, 233 Spring St, New York, NY 10013-1578 *Tel:* 212-460-1500 *Toll Free Tel:* 800-SPRINGER (777-4643) *Fax:* 212-460-1700 *E-mail:* customerservice@springer.com *Web Site:* www.springer.com, pg 219

Evans, Mary, Mary Evans Inc, 242 E Fifth St, New York, NY 10003-8501 *Tel:* 212-979-0880 *Fax:* 212-979-5344 *E-mail:* info@maryevansinc.com *Web Site:* www.maryevansinc.com, pg 516

Evans, Nivia, Orbit, 1290 Avenue of the Americas, New York, NY 10019 *Tel:* 212-364-1100 *Toll Free Tel:* 800-759-0190 *Web Site:* www.orbitbooks.net, pg 169

Evans, Suzy, Sandra Dijkstra Literary Agency, 1155 Camino del Mar, PMB 515, Del Mar, CA 92014-2605 *E-mail:* queries@dijkstraagency.com *Web Site:* dijkstraagency.com, pg 514

Evans, William, Evan-Moor Educational Publishers, 18 Lower Ragsdale Dr, Monterey, CA 93940-5746 *Tel:* 831-649-5901 *Toll Free Tel:* 800-777-4362 (orders) *Fax:* 831-649-6256 *Toll Free Fax:* 800-777-4332 (orders) *E-mail:* sales@evan-moor.com; marketing@evan-moor.com *Web Site:* www.evan-moor.com, pg 80

Eveleigh, Douglas, Encyclopaedia Britannica Inc, 325 N La Salle St, Chicago, IL 60654 *Tel:* 312-347-7159 (all other countries) *Toll Free Tel:* 800-323-1229 (US & CN) *Fax:* 312-294-2104 *E-mail:* contact@eb.com *Web Site:* www.eb.com; www.britannica.com, pg 78

Evennou, Danielle, Eric Hoffer Award for Short Prose, PO Box 11, Titusville, NJ 08560 *Fax:* 609-964-1718 *E-mail:* info@hofferaward.com *Web Site:* www.hofferaward.com, pg 653

Everett, Blair, Babalu Inc, PO Box 23026, Santa Barbara, CA 93121 *Toll Free Tel:* 877-522-2258 *E-mail:* morefun@babaluinc.com *Web Site:* www.babaluinc.com, pg 27

Everhart, Deborah L, Andrews University Press, Sutherland House, 8360 W Campus Circle Dr, Berrien Springs, MI 49104-1700 *Tel:* 269-471-6134 *Toll Free Tel:* 800-467-6369 (Visa, MC & American Express orders only) *Fax:* 269-471-6224 *E-mail:* aupo@andrews.edu; aup@andrews.edu; aupress@andrews.edu *Web Site:* www.universitypress.andrews.edu, pg 17

Everhart, Sean, David C Cook, 4050 Lee Vance View, Colorado Springs, CO 80918 *Tel:* 719-536-0100 *Toll Free Tel:* 800-708-5550; 800-323-7543 (orders & cust serv) *Toll Free Fax:* 800-430-0726 (cust serv) *Web Site:* www.davidccook.com, pg 60

Everingham, Kate, Arcadia Publishing Inc, 420 Wando Park Blvd, Mount Pleasant, SC 29464 *Tel:* 843-853-2070 *Toll Free Tel:* 888-313-2665 (orders only) *Fax:* 843-853-0044 *E-mail:* sales@arcadiapublishing.com *Web Site:* www.arcadiapublishing.com, pg 20

Evers, Tony PhD, Wisconsin Department of Public Instruction, 125 S Webster St, Madison, WI 53703 *Tel:* 608-266-2188 *Toll Free Tel:* 800-441-4563 *Fax:* 608-267-9110 *Web Site:* pubsales.dpi.wi.gov, pg 257

Everson, Laney, Houghton Mifflin Harcourt Trade & Reference Division, 125 High St, Boston, MA 02110 *Tel:* 617-351-5000 *Toll Free Tel:* 800-225-3362 *Web Site:* www.hmhco.com, pg 111

Ewen, Laura, Bloomsbury Academic, 1385 Broadway, 5th fl, New York, NY 10018 *Tel:* 212-419-5300 *Web Site:* www.bloomsbury.com/us/academic, pg 37

Ewers, Christy, Christina A Tugeau Artist Agency LLC, 29 Newman Place, Fairfield, CT 06825 *Tel:* 917-434-3141 *E-mail:* chris@catugeau.com *Web Site:* www.catugeau.com, pg 544

Ewing, Christine, The United Educators Inc, 900 W North Shore Dr, Suite 276, Lake Bluff, IL 60044 *Tel:* 847-234-3700 *Toll Free Tel:* 800-323-5875 *Fax:* 847-234-8705, pg 238

Ewing, Peter, The United Educators Inc, 900 W North Shore Dr, Suite 276, Lake Bluff, IL 60044 *Tel:* 847-234-3700 *Toll Free Tel:* 800-323-5875 *Fax:* 847-234-8705, pg 238

Ewing, Susan M, Dog Writers' Association of America Inc (DWAA), 66 Adams St, Jamestown, NY 14701 *Tel:* 716-484-6155 *E-mail:* dogwriter@windstream.net *Web Site:* www.dwaa.org, pg 564

Ewing, Susan M, Dog Writers' Association of America Inc (DWAA) Annual Writing Competition, 2243 Kelmscott Ct, Westlake Village, CA 91361 *Tel:* 805-418-7899 *Fax:* 831-374-9231 *E-mail:* dogwriter@windstream.net *Web Site:* www.dwaa.org, pg 642

Eykemans, Tom, University of Washington Press, 4333 Brooklyn Ave NE, Seattle, WA 98105-9570 *Tel:* 206-543-4050 *Toll Free Tel:* 800-537-5487 (orders) *Fax:* 206-543-3932; 410-516-6998 (orders) *E-mail:* uwapress@uw.edu *Web Site:* www.washington.edu/uwpress, pg 246

Ezernack, Kristi, University Press of Mississippi, 3825 Ridgewood Rd, Jackson, MS 39211-6492 *Tel:* 601-432-6205 *Toll Free Tel:* 800-737-7788 (orders & cust serv) *Fax:* 601-432-6217 *E-mail:* press@mississippi.edu *Web Site:* www.upress.state.ms.us, pg 247

Fabian, Ann, James Fenimore Cooper Prize, 2950 Broadway, New York, NY 10027 *Tel:* 212-854-6495 *E-mail:* amhistsociety@columbia.edu *Web Site:* sah.columbia.edu, pg 639

Fabian, Ann, Allan Nevins Prize, 2950 Broadway, New York, NY 10027 *Tel:* 212-854-6495 *E-mail:* amhistsociety@columbia.edu *Web Site:* sah.columbia.edu, pg 672

Fabian, Ann, Francis Parkman Prize, 2950 Broadway, New York, NY 10027 *Tel:* 212-854-6495 *E-mail:* amhistsociety@columbia.edu *Web Site:* sah.columbia.edu, pg 676

Fabian, Elizabeth, Random House Publishing Group, 1745 Broadway, New York, NY 10019 *Toll Free Tel:* 800-200-3552 *Web Site:* atrandom.com, pg 195

Fabiny, Sarah, Grosset & Dunlap, 345 Hudson St, New York, NY 10014 *Tel:* 212-366-2000 *Web Site:* www.penguinrandomhouse.com, pg 96

Fabricant, David, Abbeville Press, 116 W 23 St, 5th fl, New York, NY 10011 *Tel:* 212-366-5585 *Toll Free Tel:* 800-ART-BOOK (278-2665); 800-343-4499 (orders) *Fax:* 646-375-2359 *Toll Free Fax:* 800-351-5073 (orders) *E-mail:* abbeville@abbeville.com; sales@abbeville.com; marketing@abbeville.com; rights@abbeville.com *Web Site:* www.abbeville.com, pg 2

Fabricant, David, Abbeville Publishing Group, 137 Varick St, Suite 504, New York, NY 10013-1105 *Tel:* 212-366-5585 *Toll Free Tel:* 800-ART-BOOK (278-2665) *Fax:* 212-366-6966 *E-mail:* abbeville@abbeville.com; marketing@abbeville.com; sales@abbeville.com; rights@abbeville.com *Web Site:* www.abbeville.com, pg 2

Faderin, Kemi, Dystel, Goderich & Bourret LLC, One Union Sq W, Suite 904, New York, NY 10003 *Tel:* 212-627-9100 *Fax:* 212-627-9313 *Web Site:* www.dystel.com, pg 515

Fafard, Katherine, Association des Libraires du Quebec (ALQ), 407 St-Laurent, bureau 801, Montreal, QC H2Y 2Y5, Canada *Tel:* 514-526-3349 *Fax:* 514-526-3340 *E-mail:* info@alq.qc.ca *Web Site:* www.alq.qc.ca, pg 557

Fagan, Jo, Fine Creative Media, Inc, 322 Eighth Ave, 15th fl, New York, NY 10001 *Tel:* 212-595-3500 *Fax:* 212-595-3779, pg 85

Fagan, John, Penguin Books, 375 Hudson St, New York, NY 10014 *Tel:* 212-366-2000 *E-mail:* penguinpublicity@us.penguingroup.com *Web Site:* www.penguinclassics.com; www.penguin.com, pg 177

Faherty, Jill, Educational Book & Media Association (EBMA), 11 Main St, Suite D, Warrenton, VA 20186 *Tel:* 540-318-7770 *Fax:* 202-962-3939 *E-mail:* info@edupaperback.org *Web Site:* www.edupaperback.org, pg 565

Fahlgren, Erik, W W Norton & Company Inc, 500 Fifth Ave, New York, NY 10110-0017 *Tel:* 212-354-5500 *Toll Free Tel:* 800-233-4830 (orders & cust serv) *Fax:* 212-869-0856 *Toll Free Fax:* 800-458-6515 *E-mail:* orders@wwnorton.com *Web Site:* books.wwnorton.com, pg 164

Fain, Heather, Hachette Book Group, 1290 Avenue of the Americas, New York, NY 10019 *Tel:* 212-364-1100 *Toll Free Tel:* 800-759-0190 (cust serv) *Fax:* 212-364-0933 (intl orders) *Toll Free Fax:* 800-286-9471 (cust serv) *Web Site:* www.hachettebookgroup.com, pg 98

Fairchild, Andrew, 4Kidz Publishing, 265 El Dorado Blvd, No 1712, Webster, TX 77598 *Tel:* 601-467-2743 *E-mail:* info@4kidzpublishing.com *Web Site:* www.facebook.com/4kidzpublishing/, pg 477

Fairchild, Carlie, Belltown Media, PO Box 980985, Houston, TX 77098 *Tel:* 713-344-1956 *Fax:* 713-583-7956 *E-mail:* subs@linuxjournal.com *Web Site:* www.belltownmedia.com, pg 32

Faktorovich, Dr Anna, Anaphora Literary Press, 1898 Athens St, Brownsville, TX 78520 *Tel:* 470-289-6395 *Web Site:* anaphoraliterary.com, pg 16

Falb, Mark C, Kendall Hunt Publishing Co, 4050 Westmark Dr, Dubuque, IA 52002-2624 *Tel:* 563-589-1000 *Toll Free Tel:* 800-228-0810 (orders) *Fax:* 563-589-1046 *Toll Free Fax:* 800-772-9165 *E-mail:* orders@kendallhunt.com *Web Site:* www.kendallhunt.com, pg 125

Falciani, LeeAnn, Picador, 175 Fifth Ave, 19th fl, New York, NY 10010 *Tel:* 646-307-5151 *Fax:* 212-253-9627 *Web Site:* www.picadorusa.com, pg 182

Falk, David, Touchstone, 1230 Avenue of the Americas, New York, NY 10020, pg 233

Falkenstein, Donald, Council for Advancement & Support of Education (CASE), 1307 New York Ave NW, Suite 1000, Washington, DC 20005-4701 *Tel:* 202-328-CASE (328-2273) *Fax:* 202-387-4973 *E-mail:* membersupportcenter@case.org *Web Site:* www.case.org, pg 564

Fan, Shenggen, International Food Policy Research Institute, 2033 "K" St NW, Washington, DC 20006-1002 *Tel:* 202-862-5600 *Fax:* 202-467-4439 *E-mail:* ifpri@cgiar.org *Web Site:* www.ifpri.org, pg 119

Fanning, Vicky, Wm B Eerdmans Publishing Co, 2140 Oak Industrial Dr NE, Grand Rapids, MI 49505 *Tel:* 616-459-4591 *Toll Free Tel:* 800-253-7521 *Fax:* 616-459-6540 *E-mail:* customerservice@eerdmans.com; sales@eerdmans.com *Web Site:* www.eerdmans.com, pg 76

Fanton, Jonathan, American Academy of Arts & Sciences (AAAS), Norton's Woods, 136 Irving St, Cambridge, MA 02138 *Tel:* 617-576-5000 *Fax:* 617-576-5050 *E-mail:* aaas@amacad.org *Web Site:* www.amacad.org, pg 554

Fargis, Alison, The Stonesong Press LLC, 270 W 39 St, No 201, New York, NY 10018 *Tel:* 212-929-4600 *E-mail:* editors@stonesong.com *Web Site:* www.stonesong.com, pg 538

Fariel, Quinn, Perseus Books, 250 W 57 St, 15th fl, New York, NY 10107 *Tel:* 212-340-8100 *Toll Free Tel:* 800-343-4499 (cust serv) *Fax:* 212-340-8105 *Web Site:* www.perseusbooks.com, pg 181

Faris, Curran, Fernwood Publishing, 32 Oceanvista Lane, Black Point, NS B0J 1B0, Canada *Tel:* 902-857-1388 *Fax:* 902-857-1328 *E-mail:* info@fernpub.ca; roseway@fernpub.ca *Web Site:* fernwoodpublishing.ca, pg 456

Farmer, Brad, Gibbs Smith Publisher, 1877 E Gentile St, Layton, UT 84041 *Tel:* 801-544-9800 *Toll Free Tel:* 800-748-5439; 800-835-4993 (orders) *Fax:* 801-544-5582 *Toll Free Fax:* 800-213-3023 (orders only) *E-mail:* info@gibbs-smith.com; tradeorders@gibbs-smith.com *Web Site:* www.gibbs-smith.com, pg 92

Farmer, Brent, Charlesbridge Publishing Inc, 85 Main St, Watertown, MA 02472 *Tel:* 617-926-0329 *Toll Free Tel:* 800-225-3214 *Fax:* 617-926-5720 *Toll Free Fax:* 800-926-5775 *E-mail:* books@charlesbridge.com *Web Site:* www.charlesbridge.com, pg 53

Farmer, Chris, University of Texas Press, 3001 Lake Austin Blvd, 2.200, Austin, TX 78703 *Tel:* 512-471-7233 *Fax:* 512-232-7178 *E-mail:* utpress@uts.cc.utexas.edu; info@utpress.utexas.edu *Web Site:* www.utexaspress.com, pg 230

Farmer, Daryl, Visiting Writers Series, English Dept, PO Box 755720, Fairbanks, AK 99775-5720 *Tel:* 907-474-7193 *Fax:* 907-474-5247 *E-mail:* faengl@uaf.edu *Web Site:* www.alaska.edu/english, pg 615

Farmer, Gary, American Association for Vocational Instructional Materials, 220 Smithonia Rd, Winterville, GA 30683 *Tel:* 706-742-5355 *Fax:* 706-742-7005 *E-mail:* sales@aavim.com *Web Site:* www.aavim.com, pg 10

Farnol, Jane, Astor Indexers, 22 S Commons, Kent, CT 06757 *Tel:* 860-592-0225; 570-534-8951 (cell), pg 488

Farnsworth, David, Casemate | publishers, 1950 Lawrence Rd, Havertown, PA 19083 *Tel:* 610-853-9131 *Fax:* 610-853-9146 *E-mail:* casemate@casematepublishers.com *Web Site:* www.casematepublishers.com, pg 49

Farnsworth, Sarah, Casemate | publishers, 1950 Lawrence Rd, Havertown, PA 19083 *Tel:* 610-853-9131 *Fax:* 610-853-9146 *E-mail:* casemate@casematepublishers.com *Web Site:* www.casematepublishers.com, pg 49

Farrace, Bob, National Association of Secondary School Principals (NASSP), 1904 Association Dr, Reston, VA 20191-1537 *Tel:* 703-860-0200 *Toll Free Tel:* 800-253-7746 *E-mail:* sales@nassp.org; publications2@nassp.org (communs & devt); membership@nassp.org *Web Site:* www.nassp.org, pg 157

Farranto, Amy, Northern Illinois University Press, 2280 Bethany Rd, DeKalb, IL 60115 *Tel:* 815-753-1075 *Fax:* 815-753-1845 *Web Site:* www.niupress.niu.edu, pg 164

Farrar, Amy E, Farrar Writing & Editing, 4638 Manchester Rd, Mound, MN 55364 *Tel:* 952-472-6874 *Fax:* 952-472-6874 (call first) *Web Site:* www.writeandedit.net, pg 494

Farrin, Cassandra, Polebridge Press, PO Box 346, Farmington, MN 55024 *Tel:* 651-200-2372 *E-mail:* orders@westarinstitute.org *Web Site:* www.westarinstitute.org, pg 185

Farris, Sienna, Simon & Schuster, Inc, 1230 Avenue of the Americas, New York, NY 10020 *Tel:* 212-698-7000 *Fax:* 212-698-7007 *E-mail:* firstname.lastname@simonandschuster.com *Web Site:* www.simonandschuster.com, pg 213

Fast, Steven, University of Illinois Press, 1325 S Oak St, MC-566, Champaign, IL 61820-6903 *Tel:* 217-333-0950 *Fax:* 217-244-8082 *E-mail:* uipress@uillinois.edu; journals@uillinois.edu *Web Site:* www.press.uillinois.edu, pg 242

Fastiggi, Ray, The Rockefeller University Press, 950 Third Ave, 2nd fl, New York, NY 10022 *Tel:* 212-327-7938 *Fax:* 212-319-1081 *E-mail:* rupress@rockefeller.edu *Web Site:* www.rupress.org, pg 200

Faulkner, Donald W, New York State Edith Wharton Citation of Merit for Fiction Writers, University at Albany, SL 320, Albany, NY 12222 *Tel:* 518-442-5620 *Fax:* 518-442-5621 *E-mail:* writers@albany.edu *Web Site:* www.albany.edu/writers-inst, pg 673

Faulkner, Donald W, New York State Walt Whitman Citation of Merit for Poets, University at Albany, SL 320, Albany, NY 12222 *Tel:* 518-442-5620 *Fax:* 518-442-5621 *E-mail:* writers@albany.edu *Web Site:* www.albany.edu/writers-inst, pg 673

Faulner, Melissa, Dutton Children's Books, 345 Hudson St, New York, NY 10014 *Tel:* 212-366-2000 *Web Site:* www.penguin.com, pg 74

Fausset, Katherine, Curtis Brown Ltd, 10 Astor Place, New York, NY 10003 *Tel:* 212-473-5400 *Web Site:* www.curtisbrown.com, pg 510

Faust, Harmony, Gale, 27500 Drake Rd, Farmington Hills, MI 48331-3535 *Tel:* 248-699-4253 *Toll Free Tel:* 800-877-4253 *Toll Free Fax:* 800-414-5043 (orders) *E-mail:* gale.customercare@cengage.com *Web Site:* www.gale.com, pg 89

Faust, Harmony, Macmillan Reference USA™, 27500 Drake Rd, Farmington Hills, MI 48331-3535 *Tel:* 248-699-4253 *Toll Free Tel:* 800-877-4253 *Toll Free Fax:* 877-363-4253 *E-mail:* gale.customercare@cengage.com *Web Site:* www.gale.cengage.com/macmillan, pg 140

Faust, Jessica H, BookEnds Literary Agency, 136 Long Hill Rd, Gillette, NJ 07933 *Web Site:* www.bookendsliterary.com, pg 508

Favreau, Marc, The New Press, 38 Greene St, 4th fl, New York, NY 10013 *Tel:* 212-629-8802 *Toll Free Tel:* 800-343-4489 (orders) *Fax:* 212-629-8617 *Toll Free Fax:* 800-351-5073 (orders) *E-mail:* newpress@thenewpress.com *Web Site:* www.thenewpress.com, pg 161

Faxel, Tammy, Brilliance Audio, 1704 Eaton Dr, Grand Haven, MI 49417 *Tel:* 616-846-5256 *Toll Free Tel:* 800-648-2312 (orders only) *Fax:* 616-846-0630 *E-mail:* customerservice@brillianceaudio.com *Web Site:* www.brillianceaudio.com, pg 44

Faxel, Tammy, Dreamscape Media LLC, 6940 Hall St, Holland, OH 43528 *Tel:* 419-867-6965 *Toll Free Tel:* 877-983-7326 *E-mail:* info@dreamscapeab.com *Web Site:* www.dreamscapeab.com, pg 73

Fazzalaro, Kristina, Perseus Books, 250 W 57 St, 15th fl, New York, NY 10107 *Tel:* 212-340-8100 *Toll Free Tel:* 800-343-4499 (cust serv) *Fax:* 212-340-8105 *Web Site:* www.perseusbooks.com, pg 181

Featherstone, Craig, B&H Publishing Group, One LifeWay Plaza, Nashville, TN 37234 *Tel:* 615-251-2520 *Fax:* 615-251-5004 *Web Site:* www.bhpublishinggroup.com, pg 29

Febus, Fernando, Lectorum Publications Inc, 205 Chubb Ave, Lyndhurst, NJ 07071 *Toll Free Tel:* 800-345-5946 *Fax:* 201-559-2201 *Toll Free Fax:* 877-532-8676 *E-mail:* lectorum@lectorum.com *Web Site:* www.lectorum.com, pg 131

Fedor, Ashley, SDP Publishing Solutions LLC, 36 Captain's Way, East Bridgewater, MA 02333 *Tel:* 617-775-0656 *Web Site:* www.sdppublishingsolutions.com, pg 501

Fedorko, Lauren, DWJ BOOKS LLC, 46 Cliff Dr, Sag Harbor, NY 11963 *Tel:* 631-899-4500 *E-mail:* info@dwjbooks.com *Web Site:* www.dwjbooks.com, pg 492

Fehr, Don, Trident Media Group LLC, 41 Madison Ave, 36th fl, New York, NY 10010 *Tel:* 212-333-1511 *E-mail:* info@tridentmediagroup.com; press@tridentmediagroup.com *Web Site:* www.tridentmediagroup.com, pg 540

Feiertag, Ruth, Regal House Publishing, 1723 Hickory Overlook Trail, No 110, Raleigh, NC 27607 *Tel:* 305-360-5969 *E-mail:* info@regalhousepublishing.com *Web Site:* regalhousepublishing.com, pg 198

Feigenbaum, Laurie, Feigenbaum Publishing Consultants Inc, 61 Bounty Lane, Jericho, NY 11753 *Tel:* 516-647-8314 (cell), pg 516

Fischer, Craig, Police Executive Research Forum, 1120 Connecticut Ave NW, Suite 930, Washington, DC 20036 *Tel:* 202-466-7820 *Web Site:* www.policeforum.org, pg 185

Fischer, Grada, The Fischer Ross Group Inc, 75 Holly Hill Lane, Suite 100, Greenwich, CT 06830 *Tel:* 203-622-4950 *Fax:* 203-531-4132 *E-mail:* frgstaff@frg-speakers.com *Web Site:* www.frg-speakers.com, pg 547

Fischer, Nicole, HarperCollins General Books Group, 195 Broadway, New York, NY 10007 *Tel:* 212-207-7000 *Web Site:* www.harpercollins.com, pg 101

Fischer, Steven, New England Book Awards, 1955 Massachusetts Ave, Cambridge, MA 02140 *Web Site:* www.newenglandbooks.org/bookawards, pg 672

Fischer, Steven, New England Independent Booksellers Association Inc (NEIBA), 1955 Massachusetts Ave, Cambridge, MA 02140 *Web Site:* www.newenglandbooks.org, pg 573

Fischer, Tom, Timber Press Inc, 133 SW Second Ave, Suite 450, Portland, OR 97204 *Tel:* 503-227-2878 *Toll Free Tel:* 800-327-5680 *Fax:* 503-227-3070 *E-mail:* info@timberpress.com *Web Site:* www.timberpress.com, pg 232

Fischer-Harbage, Ryan, The Fischer-Harbage Agency Inc, 540 President St, 3rd fl, Brooklyn, NY 11215 *Tel:* 212-695-7105 *E-mail:* info@fischerharbage.com *Web Site:* www.fischerharbage.com, pg 517

Fish, Nancy, Parallax Press, 2236-B Sixth St, Berkeley, CA 94710 *Tel:* 510-540-6411 *Toll Free Tel:* 800-863-5290 (orders) *Fax:* 510-981-1157 *Web Site:* www.parallax.org, pg 174

Fisher, Curtis, Diane Publishing Co, 330 Pusey Ave, Suite 3 (rear), Collingdale, PA 19023-0617 *Tel:* 610-461-6200 *Toll Free Tel:* 800-782-3833 *Fax:* 610-461-6130 *Web Site:* www.dianepublishing.net, pg 70

Fisher, Elizabeth, Levine|Greenberg|Rostan Literary Agency, 307 Seventh Ave, Suite 2407, New York, NY 10001 *Tel:* 212-337-0934 *Fax:* 212-337-0948 *Web Site:* lgrliterary.com, pg 525

Fisher, Grace, The Penguin Press, 375 Hudson St, New York, NY 10014 *Web Site:* thepenguinpress.com, pg 178

Fisher, Jenna, BOA Editions Ltd, 250 N Goodman St, Suite 306, Rochester, NY 14607 *Tel:* 585-546-3410 *Fax:* 585-546-3913 *E-mail:* contact@boaeditions.org *Web Site:* www.boaeditions.org, pg 39

Fisher, John, Templegate Publishers, 302 E Adams St, Springfield, IL 62701 *Tel:* 217-522-3353 (edit & sales) *Toll Free Tel:* 800-367-4844 (orders only) *E-mail:* wisdom@templegate.com; orders@templegate.com (sales) *Web Site:* www.templegate.com, pg 229

Fisher, Lynn, University of Toronto Press, 10 St Mary St, Suite 700, Toronto, ON M4Y 2W8, Canada *Tel:* 416-978-2239 *Fax:* 416-978-4738 *E-mail:* info@utpress.utoronto.ca *Web Site:* www.utpress.utoronto.ca; www.utppublishing.com, pg 475

Fisher, Maurice D, Gifted Education Press, 10201 Yuma Ct, Manassas, VA 20109 *Tel:* 703-369-5017 *Web Site:* www.giftededpress.com, pg 92

Fisher, Melissa, Vermont College of Fine Arts MFA in Writing for Children & Young Adults Program, 36 College St, Montpelier, VT 05602 *Tel:* 802-828-8637; 802-828-8696 *Toll Free Tel:* 866-934-VCFA (934-8232) *Fax:* 802-828-8649 *Web Site:* www.vcfa.edu, pg 624

Fisher, Stephen, Don Buchwald & Associates Inc, 10 E 44 St, New York, NY 10017 *Tel:* 212-867-1200 *Fax:* 212-867-2434 *E-mail:* info@buchwald.com *Web Site:* www.buchwald.com, pg 510

Fishmann, Megan, Counterpoint Press LLC, 1919 Fifth St, Berkeley, CA 94710 *Tel:* 510-704-0230 *Fax:* 510-704-0268 *E-mail:* info@counterpointpress.com *Web Site:* counterpointpress.com; www.sierraclub.org/books; softskull.com, pg 63

Fisk, Raymond G, Down The Shore Publishing Corp, 106 Stafford Forge Rd, West Creek, NJ 08092 *Tel:* 609-812-5076 *Fax:* 609-812-5098 *E-mail:* dtsbooks@comcast.net; info@down-the-shore.com *Web Site:* www.down-the-shore.com, pg 72

Fisketjon, Gary, Alfred A Knopf/Everyman's Library, c/o Penguin Random House Inc, 1745 Broadway, New York, NY 10019 *Tel:* 212-751-2600 *Toll Free Tel:* 800-638-6460 *Fax:* 212-572-2593 *Web Site:* www.knopfdoubleday.com, pg 127

Fitch, Ann, Tuxedo Press, 546 E Springville Rd, Carlisle, PA 17015 *Tel:* 717-258-9733 *Fax:* 717-243-0074 *E-mail:* info@tuxedo-press.com *Web Site:* tuxedo-press.com, pg 237

Fithian, Elizabeth, Harry N Abrams Inc, 195 Broadway, 9th fl, New York, NY 10007 *Tel:* 212-206-7715 *Toll Free Tel:* 800-345-1359 *Fax:* 212-519-1210 *E-mail:* abrams@abramsbooks.com *Web Site:* www.abramsbooks.com, pg 3

Fitterling, Michael Alan, Lost Classics Book Company LLC, 411 N Wales Dr, Lake Wales, FL 33853-3881 *Tel:* 863-632-1981 (edit off) *E-mail:* mgeditor@lostclassicsbooks.com *Web Site:* www.lostclassicsbooks.com, pg 138

Fitzgerald, Brenda, The University of Virginia Press, PO Box 400318, Charlottesville, VA 22904-4318 *Tel:* 434-924-3468 (cust serv); 434-924-3469 (cust serv) *Toll Free Tel:* 800-831-3406 (orders) *Fax:* 434-982-2655 *Toll Free Fax:* 877-288-6400 *E-mail:* vapress@virginia.edu *Web Site:* www.upress.virginia.edu, pg 245

Fitzgerald, Laura, Orbit, 1290 Avenue of the Americas, New York, NY 10019 *Tel:* 212-364-1100 *Toll Free Tel:* 800-759-0190 *Web Site:* www.orbitbooks.net, pg 169

Fitzgerald, Patrick, Columbia University Press, 61 W 62 St, New York, NY 10023 *Tel:* 212-459-0600 *Toll Free Tel:* 800-944-8648 *Fax:* 212-459-3678 *E-mail:* cup_book@columbia.edu (orders & cust serv) *Web Site:* cup.columbia.edu, pg 59

Fitzgerald, Susan Kelly, Kinship Books, 305 Cedar Heights Rd, Rhinebeck, NY 12572 *Tel:* 845-876-4592 (orders) *E-mail:* kinship@hvc.rr.com *Web Site:* www.kinshipny.com, pg 126

Fitzhenry, Sharon, Fitzhenry & Whiteside Limited, 195 Allstate Pkwy, Markham, ON L3R 4T8, Canada *Tel:* 905-477-9700 *Toll Free Tel:* 800-387-9776 *Fax:* 905-477-2834 *Toll Free Fax:* 800-260-9777 *E-mail:* bookinfo@fitzhenry.ca; godwit@fitzhenry.ca *Web Site:* www.fitzhenry.ca, pg 457

Fitzpatrick, Megan, Hachette Audio, 1290 Avenue of the Americas, New York, NY 10019 *Tel:* 212-364-1100 *Web Site:* www.hachetteaudio.com, pg 98

Fitzpatrick, Samantha, Fresh Fish Award for Emerging Writers, Haymarket Sq, 223 Duckworth St, St John's, NL A1C 6N1, Canada *Tel:* 709-739-5215 *Toll Free Tel:* 866-739-5215 *E-mail:* wanl@nf.aibn.com *Web Site:* wanl.ca, pg 648

Fitzpatrick, Samantha, Newfoundland and Labrador Book Awards, Haymarket Sq, 223 Duckworth St, St John's, NL A1C 6N1, Canada *Tel:* 709-739-5215 *Toll Free Tel:* 866-739-5215 *E-mail:* wanl@nf.aibn.com *Web Site:* wanl.ca, pg 673

Fiyak-Burkley, Michele, University Press of Florida, 15 NW 15 St, Gainesville, FL 32603-2079 *Tel:* 352-392-1351 *Toll Free Tel:* 800-226-3822 (orders only) *Fax:* 352-392-0590 *Toll Free Fax:* 800-680-1955 (orders only) *E-mail:* press@upress.ufl.edu; orders@upress.ufl.edu *Web Site:* www.upf.com, pg 246

Fjestad, S P, Blue Book Publications Inc, 8009 34 Ave S, Suite 250, Minneapolis, MN 55425 *Tel:* 952-854-5229 *Toll Free Tel:* 800-877-4867 *Fax:* 952-853-1486 *E-mail:* support@bluebookinc.com *Web Site:* www.bluebookofgunvalues.com; www.bluebookofguitarvalues.com, pg 38

Flach, Andrew, Hatherleigh Press Ltd, 62545 State Hwy 10, Hobart, NY 13788 *E-mail:* info@hatherleighpress.com; publicity@hatherleighpress.com *Web Site:* www.hatherleighpress.com, pg 103

Flaherty, Nora, Macmillan, 175 Fifth Ave, New York, NY 10010 *Tel:* 646-307-5151 *E-mail:* press.inquiries@macmillan.com *Web Site:* www.macmillan.com, pg 140

Flaherty, Rue, Perseus Books, 250 W 57 St, 15th fl, New York, NY 10107 *Tel:* 212-340-8100 *Toll Free Tel:* 800-343-4499 (cust serv) *Fax:* 212-340-8105 *Web Site:* www.perseusbooks.com, pg 181

Flamand, Jacques, Les Editions du Vermillon, 305, rue St-Patrick, Ottawa, ON K1N 5K4, Canada *Tel:* 613-241-4032 *Fax:* 613-241-3109 *E-mail:* leseditionsduvermillon@rogers.com *Web Site:* www.leseditionsduvermillon.ca, pg 454

Flamini, Michael, St Martin's Press, LLC, 175 Fifth Ave, New York, NY 10010 *Tel:* 646-307-5151 *Web Site:* us.macmillan.com/smp, pg 204

Flanagan, John F, Goodheart-Willcox Publisher, 18604 W Creek Dr, Tinley Park, IL 60477-6243 *Tel:* 708-687-5000 *Toll Free Tel:* 800-323-0440 *Fax:* 708-468-8692 *Toll Free Fax:* 888-409-3900 *E-mail:* custserv@g-w.com; orders@g-w.com *Web Site:* www.g-w.com, pg 94

Flanagin, Annette, American Medical Association, AMA Plaza, 330 N Wabash, Suite 39300, Chicago, IL 60611-5885 *Tel:* 312-464-5000 *Toll Free Tel:* 800-621-8335 *Fax:* 312-464-4184 *Web Site:* www.ama-assn.org, pg 13

Flanders, Margaret, Judy Lopez Memorial Award For Children's Literature, 1225 Selby Ave, Los Angeles, CA 90024 *Tel:* 310-474-9917 *Fax:* 310-474-6436 *Web Site:* www.wnba-books.org/la; www.judylopezbookaward.org, pg 662

Flannery, Carol, Applause Theatre & Cinema Books, 33 Plymouth St, Suite 302, Montclair, NJ 07042 *Tel:* 973-337-5034 *Toll Free Tel:* 800-637-2852 *Fax:* 973-337-5227 *E-mail:* info@applausepub.com *Web Site:* www.applausepub.com, pg 19

Flannery, Jennifer, Flannery Literary, 1140 Wickfield Ct, Naperville, IL 60563 *Web Site:* flanneryliterary.com, pg 517

Flannery-McCoy, Bridget, Columbia University Press, 61 W 62 St, New York, NY 10023 *Tel:* 212-459-0600 *Toll Free Tel:* 800-944-8648 *Fax:* 212-459-3678 *E-mail:* cup_book@columbia.edu (orders & cust serv) *Web Site:* cup.columbia.edu, pg 59

Flashman, Melissa, Janklow & Nesbit Associates, 285 Madison Ave, 21st fl, New York, NY 10017 *Tel:* 212-421-1700 *Fax:* 212-355-1403 *E-mail:* info@janklow.com *Web Site:* www.janklowandnesbit.com, pg 522

Flath, Regina, Random House Children's Books, 1745 Broadway, 10th fl, New York, NY 10019 *Tel:* 212-782-9000 *Web Site:* www.randomhousekids.com, pg 194

Flax, Margery, Edgar Allan Poe Awards®, 1140 Broadway, Suite 1507, New York, NY 10001 *Tel:* 212-888-8171 *E-mail:* mwa@mysterywriters.org *Web Site:* www.mysterywriters.org, pg 643

Flax, Margery, Mystery Writers of America (MWA), 1140 Broadway, Suite 1507, New York, NY 10001 *Tel:* 212-888-8171 *E-mail:* mwa@mysterywriters.org *Web Site:* www.mysterywriters.org, pg 570

Fleck, Robert III, Oak Knoll Press, 310 Delaware St, New Castle, DE 19720 *Tel:* 302-328-7232 *Toll Free Tel:* 800-996-2556 *Fax:* 302-328-7274 *E-mail:* oakknoll@oakknoll.com; publishing@oakknoll.com *Web Site:* www.oakknoll.com, pg 166

Fleck, Robert D, Oak Knoll Press, 310 Delaware St, New Castle, DE 19720 *Tel:* 302-328-7232 *Toll Free Tel:* 800-996-2556 *Fax:* 302-328-7274 *E-mail:* oakknoll@oakknoll.com; publishing@oakknoll.com *Web Site:* www.oakknoll.com, pg 166

Flegal, Diana, Hartline Literary Agency LLC, 123 Queenston Dr, Pittsburgh, PA 15235 *Web Site:* www.hartlineliterary.com, pg 520

Fleischer, Chip, Steerforth Press, 45 Lyme Rd, Suite 208, Hanover, NH 03755-1222 *Tel:* 603-643-4787 *Fax:* 603-643-4788 *E-mail:* info@steerforth.com *Web Site:* www.steerforth.com, pg 221

Fleishman, Samuel, Literary Artists Representatives, 575 West End Ave, Suite GRC, New York, NY 10024-2711 *Tel:* 212-679-7788 *E-mail:* litartists@aol.com, pg 526

Fleming, James, C D Howe Institute, 67 Yonge St, Suite 300, Toronto, ON M5E 1J8, Canada *Tel:* 416-865-1904 *Fax:* 416-865-1866 *E-mail:* cdhowe@cdhowe.org *Web Site:* www.cdhowe.org, pg 460

Fleming, Katherine, Fodor's Travel Publications, 1745 Broadway, 15th fl, New York, NY 10019 *Toll Free Tel:* 800-733-3000 *E-mail:* publicity@fodors.com; editors@fodors.com *Web Site:* www.fodors.com, pg 86

Fleming, Margo Beth, Stanford University Press, 425 Broadway St, Redwood City, CA 94063-3126 *Tel:* 650-723-9434 *Fax:* 650-725-3457 *E-mail:* info@www.sup.org; publicity@www.sup.org *Web Site:* www.sup.org, pg 220

Fleming, Odette, Hachette Books, 1290 Avenue of the Americas, New York, NY 10019 *Tel:* 212-364-1100 *Web Site:* www.hachettebookgroup.com, pg 98

Fleming, Peter, Peter Fleming Agency, PO Box 458, Pacific Palisades, CA 90272 *Tel:* 310-454-1373 *E-mail:* peterfleming@earthlink.net, pg 517

Fleming, Sonya, Mondo Publishing, 980 Avenue of the Americas, New York, NY 10018 *Tel:* 212-268-3560 *Toll Free Tel:* 888-88-MONDO (886-6636) *Toll Free Fax:* 888-532-4492 *E-mail:* info@mondopub.com *Web Site:* www.mondopub.com, pg 153

Fleming, Sue, Simon & Schuster, Inc, 1230 Avenue of the Americas, New York, NY 10020 *Tel:* 212-698-7000 *Fax:* 212-698-7007 *E-mail:* firstname.lastname@simonandschuster.com *Web Site:* www.simonandschuster.com, pg 213

Fletcher, Amanda, PEN Center USA Emerging Voices Fellowship, PO Box 6037, Beverly Hills, CA 90212 *Tel:* 323-424-4939 *Fax:* 323-424-4944 *E-mail:* ev@penusa.org *Web Site:* penusa.org/programs/emerging-voices, pg 677

Fletcher, J T, Northeast-Midwest Institute, 50 "F" St NW, Suite 950, Washington, DC 20001 *Tel:* 202-544-5200 *Fax:* 202-544-0043 *E-mail:* info@nemw.org *Web Site:* www.nemw.org, pg 164

Fletcher, Lesley, Gerald Lampert Memorial Award, 192 Spadina Ave, Suite 312, Toronto, ON M5T 2C2, Canada *Tel:* 416-504-1657 *Fax:* 416-504-0096 *E-mail:* admin@poets.ca *Web Site:* poets.ca, pg 659

Fletcher, Lesley, The League of Canadian Poets, 192 Spadina Ave, Suite 312, Toronto, ON M5T 2C2, Canada *Tel:* 416-504-1657 *Fax:* 416-504-0096 *Web Site:* poets.ca, pg 568

Fletcher, Lesley, Pat Lowther Memorial Award, 192 Spadina Ave, Suite 312, Toronto, ON M5T 2C2, Canada *Tel:* 416-504-1657 *Fax:* 416-504-0096 *E-mail:* admin@poets.ca *Web Site:* poets.ca, pg 663

Fletcher, Lesley, Jessamy Stursberg Poetry Contest for Youth, 192 Spadina Ave, Suite 312, Toronto, ON M5T 2C2, Canada *Tel:* 416-504-1657 *Fax:* 416-504-0096 *E-mail:* admin@poets.ca *Web Site:* poets.ca, pg 692

Fletcher, Molly, Sourcebooks Inc, 1935 Brookdale Rd, Suite 139, Naperville, IL 60563 *Tel:* 630-961-3900 *Toll Free Tel:* 800-432-7444 *Fax:* 630-961-2168 *E-mail:* info@sourcebooks.com; customersupport@sourcebooks.com *Web Site:* www.sourcebooks.com, pg 218

Fletcher, Stephanie, Houghton Mifflin Harcourt Trade & Reference Division, 125 High St, Boston, MA 02110 *Tel:* 617-351-5000 *Toll Free Tel:* 800-225-3362 *Web Site:* www.hmhco.com, pg 111

Fletcher, Stephen, Rand McNally, 9855 Woods Dr, Skokie, IL 60077 *Tel:* 847-329-8100 *E-mail:* ctsales@randmcnally.com; mediarelations@randmcnally.com *Web Site:* www.randmcnally.com, pg 194

Fletcher, Susan, AAP PreK-12 Learning Group, 455 Massachusetts Ave NW, Suite 700, Washington, DC 20001 *Tel:* 267-351-4310 *Fax:* 267-351-4317 *E-mail:* prek12learning@publishers.org *Web Site:* www.aepweb.org, pg 553

Fletty, Eric, Technical Association of the Pulp & Paper Industry (TAPPI), 15 Technology Pkwy S, Suite 115, Peachtree Corners, GA 30092 *Tel:* 770-446-1400 *Toll Free Tel:* 800-332-8686 (US); 800-446-9431 (CN) *Fax:* 770-446-6947 *E-mail:* memberconnection@tappi.org *Web Site:* www.tappi.org, pg 579

Fleury, Amy, McNeese State University, Writing Program, PO Box 92655, Lake Charles, LA 70609-0001 *Tel:* 337-475-5325; 337-475-5327 *Web Site:* www.mcneese.edu.com; www.mfa.mcneese.edu, pg 621

Flickinger, Mike, Ascension Press, PO Box 1990, West Chester, PA 19380 *Tel:* 610-696-7795; 484-875-4550 (admin) *Toll Free Tel:* 800-376-0520 (sales & cust serv) *Web Site:* ascensionpress.com, pg 22

Flight, Nancy, Greystone Books Ltd, 343 Railway St, Suite 201, Vancouver, BC V6A 1A4, Canada *Tel:* 604-875-1550 *Fax:* 604-875-1556 *E-mail:* info@greystonebooks.com *Web Site:* www.greystonebooks.com, pg 458

Flora, Debi, About Books Inc, 1001 Taurus Dr, Colorado Springs, CO 80906 *Tel:* 719-445-8875 *Fax:* 719-213-2602 *Web Site:* www.about-books.com, pg 487

Flora, Scott, About Books Inc, 1001 Taurus Dr, Colorado Springs, CO 80906 *Tel:* 719-445-8875 *Fax:* 719-213-2602 *Web Site:* www.about-books.com, pg 487

Florentin, Aleta, Amber Lotus Publishing, PO Box 11329, Portland, OR 97211 *Tel:* 503-284-6400 *Toll Free Tel:* 800-326-2375 (orders only) *Fax:* 503-284-6417 *E-mail:* info@amberlotus.com *Web Site:* www.amberlotus.com, pg 9

Flores, Libby, PEN Center USA Literary Awards, 8549 Wilshire Blvd, Suite 355, Beverly Hills, CA 90211 *Tel:* 323-424-4939 *Fax:* 323-424-4944 *E-mail:* awards@penusa.org; pen@penusa.org *Web Site:* penusa.org/awards, pg 677

Florio, Marie, Gallery Books, 1230 Avenue of the Americas, New York, NY 10020 *Toll Free Tel:* 800-456-6798 *Fax:* 212-698-7284 *E-mail:* consumer.customerservice@simonandschuster.com *Web Site:* www.simonsays.com, pg 90

Florio, Marie, Simon & Schuster, 1230 Avenue of the Americas, New York, NY 10020 *Tel:* 212-698-7000 *Toll Free Tel:* 800-223-2348 (cust serv); 800-223-2336 (orders) *Toll Free Fax:* 800-943-9831 (orders) *Web Site:* www.simonandschuster.com, pg 212

Flounders, Emer, Harlequin Enterprises Ltd, 233 Broadway, Suite 1001, New York, NY 10279 *Tel:* 212-553-4200 *Fax:* 212-227-8969 *E-mail:* customerservice@harlequin.com *Web Site:* www.harlequin.com, pg 101

Flower, Lauren, HarperCollins Children's Books, 195 Broadway, New York, NY 10007 *Tel:* 212-207-7000 *Web Site:* www.harpercollins.com/childrens, pg 101

Floyd, Chriscynethia, David C Cook, 4050 Lee Vance View, Colorado Springs, CO 80918 *Tel:* 719-536-0100 *Toll Free Tel:* 800-708-5550; 800-323-7543 (orders & cust serv) *Toll Free Fax:* 800-430-0726 (cust serv) *Web Site:* www.davidccook.com, pg 60

Floyd, Steve, August House Inc, 3500 Piedmont Rd NE, Suite 310, Atlanta, GA 30305 *Tel:* 404-442-4420 *Toll Free Tel:* 800-284-8784 *Fax:* 404-442-4435 *E-mail:* ahinfo@augusthouse.com *Web Site:* www.augusthouse.com, pg 26

Flum, Caitie, Liza Dawson Associates, 350 Seventh Ave, Suite 2003, New York, NY 10001 *Tel:* 212-465-9071 *Fax:* 212-947-0460 *Web Site:* www.lizadawsonassociates.com, pg 513

Flum, David, Rutgers University Press, 106 Somerset St, 3rd fl, New Brunswick, NJ 08901 *Tel:* 848-445-7762 *Toll Free Tel:* 800-848-6224 (orders only) *Fax:* 732-745-4935 (acqs, edit, mktg, perms & prodn) *Toll Free Fax:* 800-272-6817 (fulfillment) *Web Site:* rutgerspress.rutgers.edu, pg 202

Flynn, Daniel, Excelsior Editions, 10 N Pearl St, 4th fl, Albany, NY 12207 *Tel:* 518-944-2800 *Toll Free Tel:* 866-430-7869 *Fax:* 518-320-1592 *E-mail:* info@sunypress.edu *Web Site:* www.sunypress.edu, pg 80

Flynn, Daniel, State University of New York Press, 10 N Pearl St, 4th fl, Albany, NY 12207 *Tel:* 518-944-2800 *Toll Free Tel:* 877-204-6073 (orders) *Fax:* 518-320-1592 *Toll Free Fax:* 877-204-6074 (orders) *E-mail:* info@sunypress.edu (edit off); suny@presswarehouse.com (orders) *Web Site:* www.sunypress.edu, pg 221

Flynn, Jacquie, Joelle Delbourgo Associates Inc, 101 Park St, Montclair, NJ 07042 *Tel:* 973-773-0836 (call only during standard business hours) *Web Site:* www.delbourgo.com, pg 514

Flynn, Katherine, Kneerim & Williams Agency, 90 Canal St, Boston, MA 02114 *Tel:* 617-303-1650 *Web Site:* www.kwlit.com, pg 524

Foerster, Maureen, William Holmes McGuffey Longevity Award, PO Box 367, Fountain City, WI 54629 *E-mail:* info@taaonline.net *Web Site:* www.taaonline.net/mcguffey-longevity-award, pg 666

Foerster, Maureen, Most Promising New Textbook Award, PO Box 367, Fountain City, WI 54629 *E-mail:* info@taaonline.net *Web Site:* www.taaonline.net/promising-new-textbook-award, pg 670

Foerster, Maureen, Ron Pynn Award, PO Box 367, Fountain City, WI 54629 *E-mail:* info@taaonline.net *Web Site:* www.taaonline.net/ron-pynn-award, pg 683

Foerster, Maureen, TAA Council of Fellows, PO Box 367, Fountain City, WI 54629 *E-mail:* info@taaonline.net *Web Site:* www.taaonline.net/council-of-fellows, pg 693

Foerster, Maureen, Textbook Excellence Award, PO Box 367, Fountain City, WI 54629 *E-mail:* info@taaonline.net *Web Site:* www.taaonline.net/textbook-excellence-award, pg 694

Fogelman, Sheldon, Sheldon Fogelman Agency Inc, 420 E 72 St, New York, NY 10021 *Tel:* 212-532-7250 *Fax:* 212-685-8939 *E-mail:* info@sheldonfogelmanagency.com *Web Site:* sheldonfogelmanagency.com, pg 517

Fogle, Linda Haines, University of South Carolina Press, 1600 Hampton St, Suite 544, Columbia, SC 29208 *Tel:* 803-777-5245 *Toll Free Tel:* 800-768-2500 (orders) *Fax:* 803-777-0160 *Toll Free Fax:* 800-868-0740 (orders) *Web Site:* www.sc.edu/uscpress, pg 245

Fogwill, Allan, Canadian Energy Research Institute, 3512 33 St NW, Suite 150, Calgary, AB T2L 2A6, Canada *Tel:* 403-282-1231 *Fax:* 403-284-4181 *E-mail:* info@ceri.ca *Web Site:* www.ceri.ca, pg 448

Foley, Joan, The Foley Literary Agency, 34 E 38 St, Suite 1B, New York, NY 10016 *Tel:* 212-686-6930, pg 517

Foley, Leanne, Manitoba Arts Council, 525-93 Lombard Ave, Winnipeg, MB R3B 3B1, Canada *Tel:* 204-945-2237 *Toll Free Tel:* 866-994-2787 *Fax:* 204-945-5925 *E-mail:* info@artscouncil.mb.ca *Web Site:* artscouncil.mb.ca, pg 569

Foley, Margaret, Royal Fireworks Press, PO Box 399, Unionville, NY 10988 *Tel:* 845-726-4444 *Fax:* 845-726-3824 *E-mail:* mail@rfwp.com *Web Site:* www.rfwp.com, pg 202

Foley, Taylor, Houghton Mifflin Harcourt Trade & Reference Division, 125 High St, Boston, MA 02110 *Tel:* 617-351-5000 *Toll Free Tel:* 800-225-3362 *Web Site:* www.hmhco.com, pg 111

Foley-Mendelssohn, Dierdre, The Plimpton Prize, 544 W 27 St, New York, NY 10001 *Tel:* 212-343-1333 *Fax:* 212-343-1988 *E-mail:* queries@theparisreview.org *Web Site:* www.theparisreview.org, pg 680

Folino, Alison, Random House Children's Books, 1745 Broadway, 10th fl, New York, NY 10019 *Tel:* 212-782-9000 *Web Site:* www.randomhousekids.com, pg 194

Foltys, Karen, Martingale®, 19021 120 Ave NE, Suite 102, Bothell, WA 98011 *Tel:* 425-483-3313 *Toll Free Tel:* 800-426-3126 *Fax:* 425-486-7596 *E-mail:* info@martingale-pub.com *Web Site:* www.martingale-pub.com, pg 143

Folz, Robert, Visuals Unlimited Inc, 27 Meadow Dr, Hollis, NH 03049 *Tel:* 603-465-3340 *Fax:* 603-465-3360 *E-mail:* staff@visualsunlimited.com *Web Site:* www.visualsunlimited.com, pg 502

Folz, Shelly, Visuals Unlimited Inc, 27 Meadow Dr, Hollis, NH 03049 *Tel:* 603-465-3340 *Fax:* 603-465-3360 *E-mail:* staff@visualsunlimited.com *Web Site:* www.visualsunlimited.com, pg 502

Fontana, Frank, Dover Publications Inc, 31 E Second St, Mineola, NY 11501-3852 *Tel:* 516-294-7000 *Toll Free Tel:* 800-223-3130 (orders) *Fax:* 516-742-6953 *E-mail:* rights@doverpublications.com; service@doverpublications.com *Web Site:* store.doverdirect.com; www.doverpublications.com, pg 72

Fontana, John, Doubleday/Nan A Talese, c/o Penguin Random House Inc, 1745 Broadway, New York, NY 10019 *Tel:* 212-751-2600 *Fax:* 212-572-2662 *E-mail:* ddaypub@randomhouse.com *Web Site:* knopfdoubleday.com, pg 72

Fontana, Virginia, University of Nevada Press, c/o University of Nevada, Continuing Educ Bldg, MS 0166, Reno, NV 89557-0166 *Tel:* 775-784-6573 *Fax:* 775-784-6200 *Web Site:* www.unpress.nevada.edu, pg 243

Fontanarosa, Phil B MD, American Medical Association, AMA Plaza, 330 N Wabash, Suite 39300, Chicago, IL 60611-5885 *Tel:* 312-464-5000 *Toll Free Tel:* 800-621-8335 *Fax:* 312-464-4184 *Web Site:* www.ama-assn.org, pg 13

Fonte, Brittany, Eric Hoffer Award for Short Prose, PO Box 11, Titusville, NJ 08560 *Fax:* 609-964-1718 *E-mail:* info@hofferaward.com *Web Site:* www.hofferaward.com, pg 653

Fontille, Brigitte, Canada Council for the Arts (Conseil des arts du Canada), 150 Elgin St, Ottawa, ON K1P 1L4, Canada *Tel:* 613-566-4414 *Toll Free Tel:* 800-263-5588 (CN only) *Fax:* 613-566-4390 *E-mail:* info@canadacouncil.ca *Web Site:* www.canadacouncil.ca, pg 561

Foo, Bill, Other Press, 267 Fifth Ave, 6th fl, New York, NY 10016 *Tel:* 212-414-0054 *Toll Free Tel:* 877-843-6843 *Fax:* 212-414-0939 *E-mail:* editor@otherpress.com; marketing@otherpress.com; publicity@otherpress.com *Web Site:* www.otherpress.com, pg 170

Ford, Barbara Meyers, Miles Conrad Memorial Lecture, 801 Compass Way, Suite 201, Annapolis, MD 21401 *Tel:* 443-221-2980 *Fax:* 443-221-2981 *E-mail:* nfais@nfais.org *Web Site:* www.nfais.org, pg 638

Ford, Barbara Meyers, National Federation of Advanced Information Services (NFAIS), 801 Compass Way, Suite 201, Annapolis, MD 21401 *Tel:* 443-221-2980 *Fax:* 443-221-2981 *E-mail:* nfais@nfais.org *Web Site:* www.nfais.org, pg 572

Ford, Gregory L, Ugly Duckling Presse, The Old American Can Factory, 232 Third St, Suite E303, Brooklyn, NY 11215 *Tel:* 347-948-5170 *E-mail:* info@uglyducklingpresse.org *Web Site:* www.uglyducklingpresse.org, pg 238

Forde, Carolyn, Westwood Creative Artists Ltd, 138 Sussex Mews, Toronto, ON M5S 2K1, Canada *Tel:* 416-964-3302 *Fax:* 416-964-3302 *E-mail:* wca_office@wcaltd.com *Web Site:* www.wcaltd.com, pg 541

Forde, Michelle, Kensington Publishing Corp, 119 W 40 St, New York, NY 10018 *Tel:* 212-407-1500 *Toll Free Tel:* 800-221-2647 *Fax:* 212-935-0699 *Web Site:* www.kensingtonbooks.com, pg 125

Forde, Simon, Medieval Institute Publications, WMU East Campus, 100-E Walwood Hall, Kalamazoo, MI 49008 *Tel:* 269-387-8754 *Fax:* 269-387-8750 *Web Site:* www.wmich.edu/medievalpublications, pg 147

Forde, Tony, Penguin Books, 375 Hudson St, New York, NY 10014 *Tel:* 212-366-2000 *E-mail:* penguinpublicity@us.penguingroup.com *Web Site:* www.penguinclassics.com; www.penguin.com, pg 177

Forde, Tony, Penguin Group USA, A Penguin Random House Company, 375 Hudson St, New York, NY 10014 *Tel:* 212-366-2000 *Toll Free Tel:* 800-847-5515 (inside sales); 800-631-8571 (cust serv) *Fax:* 212-366-2666; 607-775-4829 (inside sales) *E-mail:* online@us.penguingroup.com *Web Site:* www.penguin.com, pg 177

Forde, Tony, Viking, 375 Hudson St, New York, NY 10014 *Tel:* 212-366-2000 *Fax:* 212-243-6002 *Web Site:* www.penguin.com/publishers/vikingbooks, pg 250

Forder, Reg A, American Christian Writers, PO Box 110390, Nashville, TN 37222-0390 *Tel:* 615-331-8668 *Toll Free Tel:* 800-21-WRITE (219-7483) *E-mail:* acwriters@aol.com *Web Site:* regaforder.wordpress.com, pg 554

Forder, Reg A, Writers Mentoring Retreat, PO Box 110390, Nashville, TN 37222-0390 *Tel:* 615-331-8668 *Toll Free Tel:* 800-21-WRITE (219-7483) *E-mail:* acwriters@aol.com *Web Site:* regaforder.wordpress.com/mentoring; regaforder.wordpress.com, pg 616

Forest, Kristina, Random House Children's Books, 1745 Broadway, 10th fl, New York, NY 10019 *Tel:* 212-782-9000 *Web Site:* www.randomhousekids.com, pg 194

Forest, Marsha, Inclusion Press International, 47 Indian Trail, Toronto, ON M6R 1Z8, Canada *Tel:* 416-658-5363 *Fax:* 416-658-5067 *E-mail:* inclusionpress@inclusion.com *Web Site:* www.inclusion.com, pg 460

Forest, Susan, Science Fiction & Fantasy Writers of America Inc (SFWA), PO Box 3238, Enfield, CT 06083-3238 *E-mail:* office@sfwa.org *Web Site:* www.sfwa.org, pg 577

Forest, Susan, SFWA Nebula Awards, PO Box 3238, Enfield, CT 06083-3238 *E-mail:* office@sfwa.org *Web Site:* www.sfwa.org, pg 688

Forland, Emily, Brandt & Hochman Literary Agents Inc, 1501 Broadway, Suite 2310, New York, NY 10036 *Tel:* 212-840-5760 *Fax:* 212-840-5776 *Web Site:* brandthochman.com, pg 509

Forman, Mark, Light-Beams Publishing, 36 Blandings Way, Biddeford, ME 04005 *Tel:* 603-659-1300 *E-mail:* info@light-beams.com *Web Site:* www.light-beams.com, pg 134

Formica, Ron, Tantor Media Inc, 6 Business Park, Old Saybrook, CT 06475 *Toll Free Tel:* 877-782-6867 *Toll Free Fax:* 888-782-7821 *Web Site:* www.tantor.com, pg 227

Forner, Alison, Simon & Schuster, 1230 Avenue of the Americas, New York, NY 10020 *Tel:* 212-698-7000 *Toll Free Tel:* 800-223-2348 (cust serv); 800-223-2336 (orders) *Toll Free Fax:* 800-943-9831 (orders) *Web Site:* www.simonandschuster.com, pg 212

Forrer, David, InkWell Management, 521 Fifth Ave, 26th fl, New York, NY 10175 *Tel:* 212-922-3500 *Fax:* 212-922-0535 *E-mail:* info@inkwellmanagement.com *Web Site:* inkwellmanagement.com, pg 522

Forrest, Iris, Ageless Press, 3759 Collins St, Sarasota, FL 34232 *Tel:* 941-365-1367 *Fax:* 941-365-1367 *E-mail:* irishope@comcast.net, pg 5

Forrie, Allan, Thistledown Press, 410 Second Ave, Saskatoon, SK S7K 2C3, Canada *Tel:* 306-244-1722 *Fax:* 306-244-1762 *E-mail:* tdpress@thistledownpress.com; editorial@thistledownpress.com; marketing@thistledownpress.com *Web Site:* www.thistledownpress.com, pg 472

Forrie, Jackie, Thistledown Press, 410 Second Ave, Saskatoon, SK S7K 2C3, Canada *Tel:* 306-244-1722 *Fax:* 306-244-1762 *E-mail:* tdpress@thistledownpress.com; editorial@thistledownpress.com; marketing@thistledownpress.com *Web Site:* www.thistledownpress.com, pg 472

Forrister, Brad, M Lee Smith Publishers, 100 Winners Circle, Suite 300, Brentwood, TN 37027 *Tel:* 615-373-7517 *Toll Free Tel:* 800-274-6774; 800-727-5257 *E-mail:* custserv@mleesmith.com; service@blr.com *Web Site:* www.mleesmith.com; www.blr.com, pg 215

Forsberg, Jennie, ABDO Publishing Group, 8000 W 78 St, Suite 310, Edina, MN 55439 *Tel:* 952-831-2120 *Toll Free Tel:* 800-800-1312 *Toll Free Fax:* 800-862-3480 *E-mail:* customerservice@abdopublishing.com *Web Site:* abdopublishing.com, pg 2

Forsythe, Kelly, Copper Canyon Press, Fort Worden State Park, Bldg 313, Port Townsend, WA 98368 *Tel:* 360-385-4925 *Toll Free Tel:* 877-501-1393 (orders) *Fax:* 360-385-4985 *E-mail:* poetry@coppercanyonpress.org *Web Site:* www.coppercanyonpress.org, pg 60

Forte, Fran, The New Press, 38 Greene St, 4th fl, New York, NY 10013 *Tel:* 212-629-8802 *Toll Free Tel:* 800-343-4489 (orders) *Fax:* 212-629-8617 *Toll Free Fax:* 800-351-5073 (orders) *E-mail:* newpress@thenewpress.com *Web Site:* www.thenewpress.com, pg 161

Fortgang, Adam, Princeton University Press, 41 William St, Princeton, NJ 08540-5237 *Tel:* 609-258-4900 *Fax:* 609-258-6305 *Web Site:* press.princeton.edu, pg 188

Fortin, Jacques, QA International (QAI), 329 De la Commune W, 3rd fl, Montreal, QC H2Y 2E1, Canada *Tel:* 514-499-3000 *Fax:* 514-499-3010 *Web Site:* www.qa-international.com, pg 468

Fortin, Ms Josee, Broquet Inc, 97-B, Montee des Bouleaux, St-Constant, QC J5A 1A9, Canada *Tel:* 450-638-3338 *Fax:* 450-638-4338 *E-mail:* info@broquet.qc.ca *Web Site:* www.broquet.qc.ca, pg 448

Fortuna, Nina, American Society of Magazine Editors (ASME), 757 Third Ave, 11th fl, New York, NY 10017 *Tel:* 212-872-3700 *Fax:* 212-906-0128 *E-mail:* asme@magazine.org *Web Site:* www.magazine.org/asme, pg 556

Foss, Vanessa, Association for Information Science & Technology (ASIS&T), 8555 16 St, Suite 850, Silver Spring, MD 20910 *Tel:* 301-495-0900 *Fax:* 301-495-0810 *E-mail:* asist@asist.org *Web Site:* www.asist.org, pg 557

Foster, Amelia, Coffee House Press, 79 13 Ave NE, Suite 110, Minneapolis, MN 55413 *Tel:* 612-338-0125 *Fax:* 612-338-4004 *E-mail:* info@coffeehousepress.org *Web Site:* coffeehousepress.org, pg 58

Foster, Corrin, Greenleaf Book Group LLC, 3 Park Place, 4005 Banister Lane, Suite B, Austin, TX 78704 *Tel:* 512-891-6100 *Fax:* 512-891-6150 *E-mail:* contact@greenleafbookgroup.com *Web Site:* www.greenleafbookgroup.com, pg 96

Foster, Cynthia, University Press of Mississippi, 3825 Ridgewood Rd, Jackson, MS 39211-6492 *Tel:* 601-432-6205 *Toll Free Tel:* 800-737-7788 (orders & cust serv) *Fax:* 601-432-6217 *E-mail:* press@mississippi.edu *Web Site:* www.upress.state.ms.us, pg 247

Foster, Dianne, Amber Lotus Publishing, PO Box 11329, Portland, OR 97211 *Tel:* 503-284-6400 *Toll Free Tel:* 800-326-2375 (orders only) *Fax:* 503-284-6417 *E-mail:* info@amberlotus.com *Web Site:* www.amberlotus.com, pg 9

Foster, Lee, Foster Travel Publishing, 1623 Martin Luther King, Berkeley, CA 94709 *Tel:* 510-549-2202 *Web Site:* www.fostertravel.com, pg 494

Foster, Roz, Sandra Dijkstra Literary Agency, 1155 Camino del Mar, PMB 515, Del Mar, CA 92014-2605 *E-mail:* queries@dijkstraagency.com *Web Site:* dijkstraagency.com, pg 514

Foster, Susan, Bitingduck Press LLC, 1262 Sunnyoaks Circle, Altadena, CA 91001 *Tel:* 626-679-2494; 626-507-8033 *E-mail:* notifications@bitingduckpress.com *Web Site:* bitingduckpress.com, pg 36

Fotinos, Joel, TarcherPerigee, 375 Hudson St, New York, NY 10014 *Tel:* 212-366-2000 *Fax:* 212-366-2643 *E-mail:* customerservice@penguinrandomhouse.com (cust serv); TarcherPerigeePublicity@penguinrandomhouse.com (media queries) *Web Site:* www.tarcherbooks.com; www.facebook.com/TarcherPerigee/; www.penguin.com/publishers/tarcherperigee, pg 227

Foulon, Alexandrine, Editions Hurtubise, 1815, ave De Lorimier, Montreal, QC H2K 3W6, Canada *Tel:* 514-523-1523 *Toll Free Tel:* 800-361-1664 *Fax:* 514-523-9969 *Web Site:* www.editionshurtubise.com, pg 454

Foulon, Arnaud, Editions Hurtubise, 1815, ave De Lorimier, Montreal, QC H2K 3W6, Canada *Tel:* 514-523-1523 *Toll Free Tel:* 800-361-1664 *Fax:* 514-523-9969 *Web Site:* www.editionshurtubise.com, pg 454

Foulon, Herve, Editions Hurtubise, 1815, ave De Lorimier, Montreal, QC H2K 3W6, Canada *Tel:* 514-523-1523 *Toll Free Tel:* 800-361-1664 *Fax:* 514-523-9969 *Web Site:* www.editionshurtubise.com, pg 454

Fournier, Holly, PennWell Books, 1421 S Sheridan Rd, Tulsa, OK 74112 *Tel:* 918-831-9421 *Toll Free Tel:* 800-752-9764 *Fax:* 918-831-9555 *Toll Free Fax:* 877-218-1348 *E-mail:* sales@pennwell.com *Web Site:* www.pennwellbooks.com, pg 179

Fowler, Karen Joy, The Clarion Science Fiction & Fantasy Writers' Workshop, Arthur C Clarke Ctr for Human Imagination, UC San Diego, 9500 Gilman Dr, MC0445, La Jolla, CA 92093-0445 *Tel:* 858-534-2115 *E-mail:* clarion@ucsd.edu *Web Site:* clarion.ucsd.edu; imagination.ucsd.edu, pg 610

Fowler, Karen Joy, James Tiptree Jr Award, 680 66 St, Oakland, CA 94609 *Tel:* 510-658-7176 *E-mail:* info@tiptree.org *Web Site:* tiptree.org, pg 694

Fox, Anna, ChemTec Publishing, 38 Earswick Dr, Toronto, ON M1E 1C6, Canada *Tel:* 416-265-2603 *Fax:* 416-265-1399 *E-mail:* orderdesk@chemtec.org *Web Site:* www.chemtec.org, pg 450

Fox, Graham, Institute for Research on Public Policy (IRPP), 1470 Peel St, No 200, Montreal, QC H3A 1T1, Canada *Tel:* 514-985-2461 *Fax:* 514-985-2559 *E-mail:* irpp@irpp.org *Web Site:* irpp.org, pg 460

Fox, Gretchen, NPTA Alliance, 330 N Wabash Ave, Suite 2000, Chicago, IL 60611 *Tel:* 312-321-4092 *Toll Free Tel:* 800-355-NPTA (355-6782) *Fax:* 312-673-6736 *Web Site:* www.gonpta.com, pg 574

Fox, Jim, Silman-James Press Inc, 141 N Clark Dr, Unit 1, West Hollywood, CA 90048 *Tel:* 310-205-0665 *Fax:* 323 214-7943 *E-mail:* info@silmanjamespress.com *Web Site:* www.silmanjamespress.com, pg 212

Fox, Keith, Phaidon, 65 Bleecker St, 8th fl, New York, NY 10012 *Tel:* 212-652-5400 *Toll Free Tel:* 800-759-0190 (cust serv) *Fax:* 212-652-5410 *Toll Free Fax:* 800-286-9471 (cust serv) *E-mail:* ussales@phaidon.com *Web Site:* www.phaidon.com, pg 182

Fox, Leisette, Wildflower Press, c/o Oakbrook Press, 3301 S Valley Dr, Rapid City, SD 57703 *Tel:* 605-381-6385 *E-mail:* info@wildflowerpress.org *Web Site:* www.wildflowerpress.org, pg 255

Fox, Nancy, Gem Guides Book Co, 1275 W Ninth St, Upland, CA 91786 *Tel:* 626-855-1611 *Toll Free Tel:* 800-824-5118 (orders) *Fax:* 626-855-1610 *E-mail:* info@gemguidesbooks.com *Web Site:* www.gemguidesbooks.com, pg 91

Fox, Patricia, Write for Success Editing Services, PO Box 292153, Los Angeles, CA 90029-8653 *Tel:* 323-356-8833 *E-mail:* writeforsuccess@yahoo.com *Web Site:* www.write-for-success.com, pg 503

Fox, R K, American Press, 60 State St, Suite 700, Boston, MA 02109 *Tel:* 617-247-0022 *E-mail:* americanpress@flash.net *Web Site:* www.americanpresspublishers.com, pg 13

Fox, Steven A, Central Conference of American Rabbis/CCAR Press, 355 Lexington Ave, 18th fl, New York, NY 10017 *Tel:* 212-972-3636 *E-mail:* info@ccarnet.org *Web Site:* www.ccarpress.org, pg 51

Foxman, Ariel, Aevitas Creative Management, 19 W 21 St, Suite 501, New York, NY 10010 *Tel:* 212-765-6900 *Web Site:* aevitascreative.com, pg 506

Foy, Fritz, Macmillan, 175 Fifth Ave, New York, NY 10010 *Tel:* 646-307-5151 *E-mail:* press.inquiries@macmillan.com *Web Site:* www.macmillan.com, pg 140

Fradkoff, Lindsay, Perseus Books, 250 W 57 St, 15th fl, New York, NY 10107 *Tel:* 212-340-8100 *Toll Free Tel:* 800-343-4499 (cust serv) *Fax:* 212-340-8105 *Web Site:* www.perseusbooks.com, pg 181

Franceschelli, Christopher, Handprint Books Inc, 413 Sixth Ave, Brooklyn, NY 11215-3310 *Tel:* 718-768-3696 *Toll Free Tel:* 800-722-6657 (orders) *Fax:* 718-369-0844 *Toll Free Fax:* 800-858-7787 (orders) *E-mail:* info@handprintbooks.com *Web Site:* www.handprintbooks.com, pg 100

Franceschelli, Joe, HarperCollins Publishers, 195 Broadway, New York, NY 10007 *Tel:* 212-207-7000 *Fax:* 212-207-7145 *Web Site:* www.harpercollins.com, pg 101

Franceschi, Adrienne, Storey Publishing LLC, 210 MASS MoCA Way, North Adams, MA 01247 *Tel:* 413-346-2100 *Toll Free Tel:* 800-441-5700 (orders); 800-793-9396 (edit) *Fax:* 413-346-2199; 413-346-2196 (edit) *E-mail:* sales@storey.com *Web Site:* www.storey.com, pg 223

Francet, Cris, Pants On Fire Press, 2062 Harbor Cove Way, Winter Garden, FL 34787 *Tel:* 863-546-0760 *E-mail:* submission@pantsonfirepress.com *Web Site:* www.pantsonfirepress.com, pg 173

Francis, Barbara, Pippin Press, 229 E 85 St, New York, NY 10028 *Tel:* 212-288-4920 *Fax:* 908-237-2407, pg 183

Francis, Chris, Sourcebooks Inc, 1935 Brookdale Rd, Suite 139, Naperville, IL 60563 *Tel:* 630-961-3900 *Toll Free Tel:* 800-432-7444 *Fax:* 630-961-2168 *E-mail:* info@sourcebooks.com; customersupport@sourcebooks.com *Web Site:* www.sourcebooks.com, pg 218

Francis, Fred, Perseus Books, 250 W 57 St, 15th fl, New York, NY 10107 *Tel:* 212-340-8100 *Toll Free Tel:* 800-343-4499 (cust serv) *Fax:* 212-340-8105 *Web Site:* www.perseusbooks.com, pg 181

Francis, Jason, Signature Books Publishing LLC, 564 W 400 N, Salt Lake City, UT 84116-3411 *Tel:* 801-531-1483 *Fax:* 801-531-1488 *E-mail:* people@signaturebooks.com *Web Site:* www.signaturebooks.com; www.signaturebookslibrary.org, pg 212

Francis, Mary, University of Michigan Press, 839 Greene St, Ann Arbor, MI 48104-3209 *Tel:* 734-764-4388 *Fax:* 734-615-1540 *E-mail:* esladmin@umich.edu *Web Site:* www.press.umich.edu, pg 242

Francis, Paul, American Society of Mechanical Engineers (ASME), 2 Park Ave, New York, NY 10016-5990 *Tel:* 212-591-7000 *Toll Free Tel:* 800-843-2763 (cust serv-US, CN & Mexico) *Fax:* 212-591-7674; 973-882-8113 (cust serv); 973-882-1717 (orders & inquiries) *E-mail:* infocentral@asme.org *Web Site:* www.asme.org, pg 15

Francis, Therese, Crossquarter Publishing Group, PO Box 23749, Santa Fe, NM 87502 *Tel:* 505-690-3923 *Fax:* 214-975-9715 *E-mail:* sales@crossquarter.com; info@crossquarter.com *Web Site:* www.crossquarter.com, pg 65

Franco, Carol, Kneerim & Williams Agency, 90 Canal St, Boston, MA 02114 *Tel:* 617-303-1650 *Web Site:* www.kwlit.com, pg 524

Franco, Diana, Berkley Publishing Group, 375 Hudson St, New York, NY 10014 *Tel:* 212-366-2000 *Fax:* 212-366-2385 *Web Site:* www.penguin.com, pg 33

Franco, Jimmy, Grand Central Publishing, 1290 Avenue of the Americas, New York, NY 10019 *Tel:* 212-364-1100 *Web Site:* www.hachettebookgroup.com, pg 95

Frank, Bill, Book Publicists of Southern California, 714 Crescent Dr, Beverly Hills, CA 90210 *Tel:* 323-461-3921 *Fax:* 323-461-0917 *Web Site:* www.bookpublicists.org, pg 560

Frank, Carol, Tradewind Books, 202-1807 Maritime Mews, Vancouver, BC V6H 3W7, Canada *Tel:* 604-662-4405 *E-mail:* tradewindbooks@yahoo.com; tradewindbooks@gmail.com *Web Site:* www.tradewindbooks.com, pg 472

Frank, Cynthia, Cypress House, 155 Cypress St, Fort Bragg, CA 95437 *Tel:* 707-964-9520 *Toll Free Tel:* 800-773-7782 *Fax:* 707-964-7531 *E-mail:* cypresshouse@cypresshouse.com *Web Site:* www.cypresshouse.com, pg 66, 492

Frank, Daniel, Pantheon Books/Schocken Books, c/o Penguin Random House Inc, 1745 Broadway, New York, NY 10019 *Tel:* 212-751-2600 *Web Site:* knopfdoubleday.com/imprint/pantheon, pg 173

Frank, Jerry, Vandamere Press, 3580 Morris St N, St Petersburg, FL 33713 *Tel:* 727-556-0950 *Toll Free Tel:* 800-551-7776 *Fax:* 727-556-2560 *E-mail:* orders@vandamere.com *Web Site:* www.vandamere.com, pg 249

Franke, Michelle, PEN Center USA, PO Box 6037, Beverly Hills, CA 90212 *Tel:* 323-424-4939 *Fax:* 323-424-4944 *E-mail:* pen@penusa.org *Web Site:* penusa.org, pg 575

Franke, Michelle, PEN Center USA Literary Awards, 8549 Wilshire Blvd, Suite 355, Beverly Hills, CA 90211 *Tel:* 323-424-4939 *Fax:* 323-424-4944 *E-mail:* awards@penusa.org; pen@penusa.org *Web Site:* penusa.org/awards, pg 677

Frankel, David, The Museum of Modern Art (MoMA), 11 W 53 St, New York, NY 10019 *Tel:* 212-708-9443 *Fax:* 212-333-6575 *E-mail:* moma_publications@moma.org *Web Site:* www.moma.org, pg 155

Frankl, Beth, Shambhala Publications Inc, 4720 Walnut St, Boulder, CO 80301 *Tel:* 303-222-9598 *Toll Free Tel:* 866-424-0030 (off); 888-424-2329 (cust serv) *Fax:* 303-200-9406 *E-mail:* customercare@shambhala.com *Web Site:* www.shambhala.com, pg 211

Franklin, Lynn C, Lynn C Franklin Associates Ltd, 1350 Broadway, Suite 2015, New York, NY 10018 *Tel:* 212-868-6311 *Fax:* 212-868-6312 *E-mail:* agency@franklinandsiegal.com, pg 517

Franklin, Robert, McFarland, 960 NC Hwy 88 W, Jefferson, NC 28640 *Tel:* 336-246-4460 *Toll Free Tel:* 800-253-2187 (orders) *Fax:* 336-246-5018; 336-246-4403 (orders) *E-mail:* info@mcfarlandpub.com *Web Site:* www.mcfarlandpub.com, pg 145

Fransson, Jane Fleming, Words into Print, 208 Java St, 6th fl, Brooklyn, NY 11222 *E-mail:* query@wordsintoprint.org *Web Site:* wordsintoprint.org, pg 503

Frantz, Kristen, Berrett-Koehler Publishers Inc, 1333 Broadway, Suite 1000, Oakland, CA 94612 *Tel:* 510-817-2277 *Fax:* 510-817-2278 *E-mail:* bkpub@bkpub.com *Web Site:* www.bkconnection.com, pg 34

Franzak, George, Rowman & Littlefield Publishers Inc, 4501 Forbes Blvd, Suite 200, Lanham, MD 20706 *Tel:* 301-459-3366 *Toll Free Tel:* 800-462-6420 (cust serv) *Fax:* 301-429-5748 *Web Site:* rowman.com, pg 202

Fraser, Caroline, Houghton Mifflin Harcourt, 125 High St, Boston, MA 02110 *Tel:* 617-351-5000 *Toll Free Tel:* 855-969-4642; 800-225-5425 (K-12 educ materials); 800-323-9540 (assessment materials); 877-219-1537 (SkillsTutor); 888-242-6747 (Innovation in Educ Group); 800-225-3362 (Trade & Ref Div) *Toll Free Fax:* 800-269-5232 *E-mail:* myhmhco@hmhco.com *Web Site:* www.hmhco.com, pg 110

Fraser, Kathleen, McGill-Queen's University Press, 1010 Sherbrooke W, Suite 1720, Montreal, QC H3A 2R7, Canada *Tel:* 514-398-3750 *Fax:* 514-398-4333 *E-mail:* mqup@mqup.ca *Web Site:* www.mqup.ca, pg 463

Fraser, Simon, DK Publishing, 345 Hudson St, 2nd fl, New York, NY 10014 *Tel:* 646-674-4000 *Toll Free Tel:* 877-342-5357 (cust serv); 800-733-3000 *Web Site:* www.dk.com; www.penguin.com, pg 71

Fraser, Stephen, The Jennifer DeChiara Literary Agency, 299 Park Ave, 6th fl, New York, NY 10171 *Tel:* 212-739-0803 *Web Site:* www.jdlit.com, pg 513

Fraser-Bub, MacKenzie, Howard Morhaim Literary Agency Inc, 30 Pierrepont St, Brooklyn, NY 11201-3371 *Tel:* 718-222-8400 *Fax:* 718-222-5056 *E-mail:* info@morhaimliterary.com *Web Site:* www.morhaimliterary.com, pg 530

Frazier, Felicia, Penguin Group USA, A Penguin Random House Company, 375 Hudson St, New York, NY 10014 *Tel:* 212-366-2000 *Toll Free Tel:* 800-847-5515 (inside sales); 800-631-8571 (cust serv) *Fax:* 212-366-2666; 607-775-4829 (inside sales) *E-mail:* online@us.penguingroup.com *Web Site:* www.penguin.com, pg 177

Frazier, Felicia, Penguin Young Readers Group, 345 Hudson St, New York, NY 10014 *Tel:* 212-366-2000; 212-414-3553 *Fax:* 212-414-3340 *Web Site:* www.penguin.com/children, pg 179

Frazier, Warren, John Hawkins and Associates Inc, 80 Maiden Lane, Suite 1503, New York, NY 10038 *Tel:* 212-807-7040 *E-mail:* jha@jhalit.com *Web Site:* jhalit.com, pg 521

Frazin, Rhona, The Carl Sandburg Literary Awards, 20 N Michigan Ave, Suite 520, Chicago, IL 60602 *Tel:* 312-201-9830 *Fax:* 312-201-9833 *Web Site:* www.cplfoundation.org, pg 686

Frechette, Jacques, Guy Saint-Jean Editeur Inc, 4490, rue Garand, Laval, QC H7L 5Z6, Canada *Tel:* 450-663-1777 *E-mail:* info@saint-jeanediteur.com *Web Site:* saint-jeanediteur.com, pg 469

Freda, Kristin, Irma S & James H Black Award, 610 W 112 St, New York, NY 10025 *Tel:* 212-875-4458 *E-mail:* ccl@bankstreet.edu *Web Site:* www.bankstreet.edu/center-childrens-literature, pg 633

Fredell, Eric, Software & Information Industry Association (SIIA), 1090 Vermont Ave NW, 6th fl, Washington, DC 20005-4095 *Tel:* 202-289-7442 *Fax:* 202-289-7097 *Web Site:* www.siia.net, pg 579

Frederick, Holly, Curtis Brown Ltd, 10 Astor Place, New York, NY 10003 *Tel:* 212-473-5400 *Web Site:* www.curtisbrown.com, pg 510

Fredericks, Jeanne, Jeanne Fredericks Literary Agency Inc, 221 Benedict Hill Rd, New Canaan, CT 06840 *Tel:* 203-972-3011 *Fax:* 203-972-3011 *E-mail:* jeanne.fredericks@gmail.com (no unsol attachments) *Web Site:* jeannefredericks.com, pg 517

Fredrickson, Jordan, Arbordale Publishing, 612 Johnnie Dodds Blvd, Suite A2, Mount Pleasant, SC 29464 *Tel:* 843-971-6722 *Toll Free Tel:* 877-243-3457 *Fax:* 843-216-3804 *E-mail:* customerservice@arbordalepublishing.com; info@arbordalepublishing.com *Web Site:* www.arbordalepublishing.com, pg 20

Freedman, Jonathan, Page Davidson Clayton Prize for Emerging Poets, University of Michigan, 0576 Rackham Bldg, 915 E Washington St, Ann Arbor, MI 48109-1070 *Tel:* 734-764-9265 *E-mail:* mqr@umich.edu *Web Site:* www.umich.edu/~mqr, pg 637

Freedman, Jonathan, Laurence Goldstein Poetry Prize, University of Michigan, 0576 Rackham Bldg, 915 E Washington St, Ann Arbor, MI 48109-1070 *Tel:* 734-764-9265 *E-mail:* mqr@umich.edu *Web Site:* www.umich.edu/~mqr, pg 650

Freedman, Jonathan, Lawrence Foundation Prize, University of Michigan, 0576 Rackham Bldg, 915 E Washington St, Ann Arbor, MI 48109-1070 *Tel:* 734-764-9265 *E-mail:* mqr@umich.edu *Web Site:* www.umich.edu/~mqr, pg 660

Freedman, Mary Ann, The National Business Book Award, c/o Freedman & Associates Inc, 121 Richmond St W, Suite 605, Toronto, ON M5H 2K1, Canada *Tel:* 416-868-1500 *Web Site:* www.nbbaward.com, pg 670

Freedman, Rana, Lonely Planet, 150 Linden St, Oakland, CA 94607 *Tel:* 510-893-8555; 510-250-6400 *Toll Free Tel:* 800-275-8555 (orders) *Fax:* 510-893-8572 *E-mail:* info@lonelyplanet.com *Web Site:* www.lonelyplanet.com, pg 137

Freedman, Robert A, Robert A Freedman Dramatic Agency Inc, 1501 Broadway, Suite 2310, New York, NY 10036 *Tel:* 212-840-5760 *Fax:* 212-840-5776, pg 518

Freeland, Abby, West Virginia University Press, West Virginia University, PO Box 6295, Morgantown, WV 26506-6295 *Tel:* 304-293-8400 *Fax:* 304-293-6585 *Web Site:* www.wvupress.com, pg 254

Freeman, Darla, Kensington Publishing Corp, 119 W 40 St, New York, NY 10018 *Tel:* 212-407-1500 *Toll Free Tel:* 800-221-2647 *Fax:* 212-935-0699 *Web Site:* www.kensingtonbooks.com, pg 125

Freeman, Gail, The Press at California State University, Fresno, 2380 E Keats, M/S MB 99, Fresno, CA 93740-8024 *Tel:* 559-278-3056 *Fax:* 559-278-6758 *E-mail:* press@csufresno.edu *Web Site:* shop.thepressatcsufresno.com; thepressatcsufresno.com, pg 187

Freeman, Katharine, Riverhead Books, 375 Hudson St, New York, NY 10014 *Tel:* 212-366-2000 *Web Site:* www.penguin.com/publishers/riverhead, pg 199

Freeny, Phyllis Jones, Professional Communications Inc, 1223 W Main, Suite 1427, Caddo, OK 74702-1427 *Tel:* 580-745-9838 *Toll Free Tel:* 800-337-9838 *Fax:* 580-745-9837 *E-mail:* info@pcibooks.com *Web Site:* www.pcibooks.com, pg 189

Freese, Rich, Recorded Books Inc, an RBmedia company, 270 Skipjack Rd, Prince Frederick, MD 20678 *Tel:* 410-535-5590 *Toll Free Tel:* 877-732-2898 *Fax:* 410-535-5499 *E-mail:* customerservice@recordedbooks.com *Web Site:* www.recordedbooks.com, pg 196

Freet, Roger, HarperCollins General Books Group, 195 Broadway, New York, NY 10007 *Tel:* 212-207-7000 *Web Site:* www.harpercollins.com, pg 101

Freiler, Ellen, Yale University Press, 302 Temple St, New Haven, CT 06511-8909 *Tel:* 203-432-0960; 203-432-0966 (sales); 401-531-2800 (cust serv) *Toll Free Tel:* 800-405-1619 (cust serv) *Fax:* 203-432-0948; 203-432-8485 (sales); 401-531-2801 (cust serv) *Toll Free Fax:* 800-406-9145 (cust serv) *E-mail:* sales.press@yale.edu (sales); customer.care@triliteral.org (cust serv) *Web Site:* www.yalebooks.com; yalepress.yale.edu/yupbooks, pg 261

French, Tiffany, The Pilgrim Press/United Church Press, 700 Prospect Ave, Cleveland, OH 44115-1100 *Tel:* 216-736-2100 *Toll Free Tel:* 800-537-3394 (orders) *Fax:* 216-736-2207 (orders) *E-mail:* permissions@thepilgrimpress.com; store@ucc.org *Web Site:* www.thepilgrimpress.com; www.uccresources.com, pg 183

Frerich, Stephanie, Penguin Group USA, A Penguin Random House Company, 375 Hudson St, New York, NY 10014 *Tel:* 212-366-2000 *Toll Free Tel:* 800-847-5515 (inside sales); 800-631-8571 (cust serv) *Fax:* 212-366-2666; 607-775-4829 (inside sales) *E-mail:* online@us.penguingroup.com *Web Site:* www.penguin.com, pg 177

Frerich, Stephanie, Portfolio, 375 Hudson St, New York, NY 10014 *Web Site:* www.penguin.com/meet/publishers/portfolio, pg 186

Frese, Alan, Pippin Press, 229 E 85 St, New York, NY 10028 *Tel:* 212-288-4920 *Fax:* 908-237-2407, pg 183

Freund, Dusty, Boulevard Magazine Short Fiction Contest for Emerging Writers, 6614 Clayton Rd, PMB 325, Richmond Heights, MO 63117 *E-mail:* editors@boulevardmagazine.org *Web Site:* www.boulevardmagazine.org, pg 634

Freymann, Sarah Jane, Sarah Jane Freymann Literary Agency LLC, 59 W 71 St, Suite 9-B, New York, NY 10023 *Tel:* 212-362-9277 *E-mail:* submissions@sarahjanefreymann.com *Web Site:* www.sarahjanefreymann.com, pg 518

Frick, Amalia, GP Putnam's Sons (Children's), 345 Hudson St, New York, NY 10014 *Tel:* 212-366-2000 *Fax:* 212-414-3393 *Web Site:* www.penguin.com/publishers/gpputnamssonsbooksforyoungread, pg 192

Fried, Brett, Silver Leaf Books LLC, 13 Temi Rd, Holliston, MA 01746 *E-mail:* sales@silverleafbooks.com; editor@silverleafbooks.com; customerservice@silverleafbooks.com *Web Site:* www.silverleafbooks.com, pg 212

Fried, Carolyn, BHTG - Julie Harris Playwright Award Competition, PO Box 148, Beverly Hills, CA 90213 *Tel:* 310-273-3390 *Web Site:* www.beverlyhillstheatreguild.com, pg 632

Fried, Carolyn, BHTG - Michael J Libow Youth Theatre Award, PO Box 148, Beverly Hills, CA 90213 *Tel:* 310-273-3390 *Web Site:* www.beverlyhillstheatreguild.com, pg 632

Fried, Gabriel, Persea Books, 277 Broadway, Suite 708, New York, NY 10007 *Tel:* 212-260-9256 *Fax:* 212-267-3165 *E-mail:* info@perseabooks.com *Web Site:* www.perseabooks.com, pg 180

Fried, Jonah, Persea Books, 277 Broadway, Suite 708, New York, NY 10007 *Tel:* 212-260-9256 *Fax:* 212-267-3165 *E-mail:* info@perseabooks.com *Web Site:* www.perseabooks.com, pg 180

Fried, Marilyn, Silver Leaf Books LLC, 13 Temi Rd, Holliston, MA 01746 *E-mail:* sales@silverleafbooks.com; editor@silverleafbooks.com; customerservice@silverleafbooks.com *Web Site:* www.silverleafbooks.com, pg 212

Fried, Melanie, Harlequin Enterprises Ltd, 225 Duncan Mill Rd, Don Mills, ON M3B 3K9, Canada *Tel:* 416-445-5860 *Toll Free Tel:* 888-432-4879; 800-370-5838 (ebook inquiries) *E-mail:* customerservice@harlequin.com *Web Site:* www.harlequin.com, pg 459

Friedland, Nancy, Theatre Library Association (TLA), c/o The New York Public Library for the Performing Arts, 40 Lincoln Center Plaza, New York, NY 10023 *E-mail:* TheatreLibraryAssociation@gmail.com *Web Site:* www.tla-online.org/awards/bookawards, pg 580

Friedman, Dina, Accurate Writing & More, 16 Barstow Lane, Hadley, MA 01035 *Tel:* 413-586-2388 *Web Site:* www.accuratewriting.com; www.frugalmarketing.com; www.goingbeyondsustainability.com; www.transformpreneur.com; www.greenandprofitable.com; www.twitter.com/shelhorowitz, pg 487

Friedman, Fredrica S, Fredrica S Friedman & Co Inc, 136 E 57 St, 14th fl, New York, NY 10022 *Tel:* 212-829-9600 *Fax:* 212-829-9669 *E-mail:* info@fredricafriedman.com; submissions@fredricafriedman.com *Web Site:* www.fredricafriedman.com, pg 518

Friedman, Jenna, Random House Publishing Group, 1745 Broadway, New York, NY 10019 *Toll Free Tel:* 800-200-3552 *Web Site:* atrandom.com, pg 195

Friedman, Tully M, The AEI Press, 1789 Massachusetts Ave NW, Washington, DC 20036 *Tel:* 202-862-5800 *Fax:* 202-862-7177 *Web Site:* www.aei.org, pg 5

Friedman, Walter, The Alfred & Fay Chandler Book Award, c/o Harvard Business School, Connell House 301A, Boston, MA 02163 *Tel:* 617-495-1003 *Fax:* 617-495-2705 *E-mail:* bhr@hbs.edu *Web Site:* www.hbs.edu/businesshistory/fellowships, pg 636

Friedman, Wendy, Quarto Publishing Group USA Inc, 400 First Ave N, Suite 400, Minneapolis, MN 55401 *Tel:* 612-344-8100 *Toll Free Tel:* 800-328-0590 (sales); 800-458-0454 *Fax:* 612-344-8691 *E-mail:* sales@quartous.com *Web Site:* www.quartoknows.com, pg 192

Friedman, Yali, Logos Press, 3909 Witmer Rd, Suite 416, Niagara Falls, NY 14305 *Fax:* 815-346-3514 *E-mail:* info@logos-press.com *Web Site:* www.logos-press.com, pg 137

Friel, Emily, Integra Software Services Inc, 1110 Jorie Blvd, Suite 200, Oak Brook, IL 60523 *Tel:* 630-586-2579 *Fax:* 630-586-2599 *E-mail:* marketing@integra.co.in *Web Site:* www.integra.co.in, pg 496

Friesen, Desirae, Tom Doherty Associates, LLC, 175 Fifth Ave, 14th fl, New York, NY 10010 *Tel:* 646-307-5511 *Toll Free Tel:* 800-455-0340 *Web Site:* www.tor-forge.com, pg 71

Friesen, Ron, The Continuing Legal Education Society of British Columbia (CLEBC), 500-1155 W Pender St, Vancouver, BC V6E 2P4, Canada *Tel:* 604-669-3544; 604-893-2121 (cust serv) *Toll Free Tel:* 800-663-0437 (CN) *Fax:* 604-669-9260 *E-mail:* custserv@cle.bc.ca *Web Site:* www.cle.bc.ca, pg 451

Frisch, Janice, Indiana University Press, Herman B Wells Library 350, 1320 E Tenth St, Bloomington, IN 47405-3907 *Tel:* 812-855-8817 *Toll Free Tel:* 800-842-6796 (orders only) *Fax:* 812-855-7931; 812-855-8507 *E-mail:* iupress@indiana.edu; iuporder@indiana.edu (orders) *Web Site:* www.iupress.indiana.edu, pg 116

Frisch, Shelley, Markus Wiener Publishers Inc, 231 Nassau St, Princeton, NJ 08542 *Tel:* 609-921-1141 *Fax:* 609-921-1140 *E-mail:* publisher@markuswiener.com *Web Site:* www.markuswiener.com, pg 255

Frisque, Mary A, International Association of Crime Writers Inc, North American Branch, 243 Fifth Ave, Suite 537, New York, NY 10016 *Tel:* 212-243-8966 *Fax:* 815-361-1477 *E-mail:* info@crimewritersna.org *Web Site:* www.crimewritersna.org, pg 567

Fritscher, Carl, ASF Translation Awards, Scandinavia House, 58 Park Ave, New York, NY 10016 *Tel:* 212-879-9779; 212-779-3587 *Fax:* 212-686-2115 *E-mail:* grants@amscan.org *Web Site:* www.amscan.org, pg 628

Fritz, Kristen, Penguin Random House Inc, 1745 Broadway, New York, NY 10019 *Tel:* 212-782-9000 *Toll Free Tel:* 800-726-0600 *Web Site:* www.penguinrandomhouse.com, pg 178

Froman, Craig, Master Books®, 3142 Hwy 103 N, Green Forest, AR 72638 *Tel:* 870-438-5288 *Fax:* 870-438-5120 *E-mail:* submissions@newleafpress.net; info@nlpg.com *Web Site:* www.nlpg.com, pg 144

Froman, Craig, New Leaf Press, 3142 Hwy 103 N, Green Forest, AR 72638-2233 *Tel:* 870-438-5288 *Toll Free Tel:* 800-999-3777 *Fax:* 870-438-5120 *E-mail:* nlp@newleafpress.net; submissions@newleafpress.net *Web Site:* www.nlpg.com/imprint/new-leaf-press; www.nlpg.com, pg 161

Fromer, Margot J, Fromer Editorial Services, 1606 Noyes Dr, Silver Spring, MD 20910-2224 *Tel:* 301-585-8827, pg 494

Fromm, Jessica, Perseus Books, 250 W 57 St, 15th fl, New York, NY 10107 *Tel:* 212-340-8100 *Toll Free Tel:* 800-343-4499 (cust serv) *Fax:* 212-340-8105 *Web Site:* www.perseusbooks.com, pg 181

Frontera, Samantha, Triumph Books, 814 N Franklin St, Chicago, IL 60610 *Tel:* 312-337-0747 *Toll Free Tel:* 800-888-4741 (cust serv) *Fax:* 312-280-5470; 312-337-5985 *Web Site:* www.triumphbooks.com, pg 235

Frost, Jim, Atlantic Center for the Arts Artists-in-Residence Program, 1414 Art Center Ave, New Smyrna Beach, FL 32168 *Tel:* 386-427-6975 *Toll Free Tel:* 800-393-6975 *Fax:* 386-427-5669 *E-mail:* program@atlanticcenterforthearts.org *Web Site:* atlanticcenterforthearts.org, pg 609

Frucht, William, Yale University Press, 302 Temple St, New Haven, CT 06511-8909 *Tel:* 203-432-0960; 203-432-0966 (sales); 401-531-2800 (cust serv) *Toll Free Tel:* 800-405-1619 (cust serv) *Fax:* 203-432-0948; 203-432-8485 (sales); 401-531-2801 (cust serv) *Toll Free Fax:* 800-406-9145 (cust serv) *E-mail:* sales.press@yale.edu (sales); customer.care@triliteral.org (cust serv) *Web Site:* www.yalebooks.com; yalepress.yale.edu/yupbooks, pg 261

Fry, David, I-5 Publishing LLC, 3 Burroughs, Irvine, CA 92618 *Tel:* 949-855-8822 *Toll Free Tel:* 888-738-2665 *Fax:* 949-458-3856 *Web Site:* www.i5publishing.com, pg 113

Fry, Erin, Romance Writers of America®, 14615 Benfer Rd, Houston, TX 77069 *Tel:* 832-717-5200 *Fax:* 832-717-5201 *E-mail:* info@rwa.org *Web Site:* www.rwa.org, pg 577

Fry, Ronald W, The Career Press Inc, 12 Parish Dr, Wayne, NJ 07470 *Tel:* 201-848-0310 *Toll Free Tel:* 800-CAREER-1 (227-3371) *Fax:* 201-848-1727 *E-mail:* sales@careerpress.com *Web Site:* www.careerpress.com, pg 47

Fry, Sonali, Little Bee Books, 853 Broadway, Suite 2014, New York, NY 10003 *E-mail:* info@littlebeebooks.com *Web Site:* www.littlebeebooks.com, pg 135

Fry, Stephani, Romance Writers of America®, 14615 Benfer Rd, Houston, TX 77069 *Tel:* 832-717-5200 *Fax:* 832-717-5201 *E-mail:* info@rwa.org *Web Site:* www.rwa.org, pg 577

Fryman, Alona, Bloomsbury Publishing Inc, 1385 Broadway, 5th fl, New York, NY 10018 *Tel:* 212-419-5300 *E-mail:* marketingusa@bloomsbury.com; adultpublicityusa@bloomsbury.com; askacademic@bloomsbury.com *Web Site:* www.bloomsbury.com, pg 38

Fuchs, George, National Association of Printing Ink Manufacturers (NAPIM), 15 Technology Pkwy S, Peachtree Corners, GA 30092 *Tel:* 770-209-7289 *Fax:* 678-680-4920; 770-209-7217 *E-mail:* napim@napim.org *Web Site:* www.napim.org, pg 571

Fuchs, Robert E, Wildflower Press, c/o Oakbrook Press, 3301 S Valley Dr, Rapid City, SD 57703 *Tel:* 605-381-6385 *E-mail:* info@wildflowerpress.org *Web Site:* www.wildflowerpress.org, pg 255

Fuersich, Larry, Visual Profile Books Inc, 389 Fifth Ave, Suite 1105, New York, NY 10016 *Tel:* 212-279-7000 *Web Site:* www.visualprofilebooks.com, pg 251

Fuguitt, Gayle, Advertising Research Foundation (ARF), 432 Park Ave S, 4th fl, New York, NY 10016-8013 *Tel:* 212-751-5656 *Fax:* 212-319-5265 *E-mail:* info@thearf.org; jar@thearf.org (edit) *Web Site:* www.thearf.org, pg 553

Fuhrman, Candice, Candice Fuhrman Literary Agency, 10 Cypress Hollow Dr, Tiburon, CA 94920 *Tel:* 415-383-1014 *E-mail:* fuhrmancandice@gmail.com, pg 518

Fujimoto, Grace, Perseus Books, 250 W 57 St, 15th fl, New York, NY 10107 *Tel:* 212-340-8100 *Toll Free Tel:* 800-343-4499 (cust serv) *Fax:* 212-340-8105 *Web Site:* www.perseusbooks.com, pg 180

Fulcher, Carlos, International Association of Business Communicators (IABC), 155 Montgomery St, Suite 1210, San Francisco, CA 94104 *Tel:* 415-544-4700 *Toll Free Tel:* 800-776-4222 (US & CN) *Fax:* 415-544-4747 *E-mail:* leader_centre@iabc.com *Web Site:* www.iabc.com, pg 567

Fuller, Barbara, Editcetera, 2034 Blake St, Suite 5, Berkeley, CA 94704 *Tel:* 510-849-1110 *Fax:* 510-900-6141 *E-mail:* info@editcetera.com *Web Site:* www.editcetera.com, pg 493

Fuller, Diana, Squaw Valley Community of Writers Summer Workshops, PO Box 1416, Nevada City, CA 95959 *Tel:* 530-470-8440 *E-mail:* info@communityofwriters.org *Web Site:* www.communityofwriters.org, pg 615

Fuller, Dr Renee PhD, Ball-Stick-Bird Publications Inc, PO Box 429, Williamstown, MA 01267-0429 *Tel:* 413-664-0002 *Fax:* 413-664-0002 *E-mail:* info@ballstickbird.com, pg 28

Fund, Ken, Quarto Publishing Group USA Inc, 400 First Ave N, Suite 400, Minneapolis, MN 55401 *Tel:* 612-344-8100 *Toll Free Tel:* 800-328-0590 (sales); 800-458-0454 *Fax:* 612-344-8691 *E-mail:* sales@quartous.com *Web Site:* www.quartoknows.com, pg 192

Funda, Evelyn I, David W & Beatrice C Evans Biography & Handcart Awards, 0735 Old Main Hill, Logan, UT 84322-0735 *Tel:* 435-797-0299 *Fax:* 435-797-1092 *E-mail:* mwc@usu.edu *Web Site:* mountainwest.usu.edu, pg 645

Fung, Ada, Perseus Books, 250 W 57 St, 15th fl, New York, NY 10107 *Tel:* 212-340-8100 *Toll Free Tel:* 800-343-4499 (cust serv) *Fax:* 212-340-8105 *Web Site:* www.perseusbooks.com, pg 180

Funk, Cameon, MAR*CO Products Inc, PO Box 686, Hatfield, PA 19440 *Tel:* 215-956-0313 *Toll Free Tel:* 800-448-2197 *Fax:* 215-956-9041 *E-mail:* help@marcoproducts.com *Web Site:* www.marcoproducts.com, pg 141

Funk, Susan, Mystic Seaport Museum Inc, PO Box 6000, Mystic, CT 06355-0990 *Tel:* 860-572-5302; 860-572-0711 (visitor serv) *Toll Free Tel:* 800-248-1066 (wholesale orders only); 800-331-2665 (retail orders only) *Fax:* 860-572-5321 *E-mail:* info@mysticseaport.org *Web Site:* www.mysticseaport.org, pg 156

Funk, Warren, MAR*CO Products Inc, PO Box 686, Hatfield, PA 19440 *Tel:* 215-956-0313 *Toll Free Tel:* 800-448-2197 *Fax:* 215-956-9041 *E-mail:* help@marcoproducts.com *Web Site:* www.marcoproducts.com, pg 141

Fuqua, Jennifer, University of Alabama Program in Creative Writing, PO Box 870244, Tuscaloosa, AL 35487-0244 *Tel:* 205-348-5065 *Fax:* 205-348-1388 *E-mail:* english@ua.edu *Web Site:* www.as.ua.edu/english, pg 622

Furman, Laura, The O. Henry Prize Stories, c/o University of Texas at Austin, One University Sta, English Dept, B5000, Austin, TX 78712 *Web Site:* www.randomhouse.com/anchor/ohenry, pg 674

Furnish, Ben, BkMk Press - University of Missouri-Kansas City, University House, 5101 Rockhill Rd, Kansas City, MO 64110-2499 *Tel:* 816-235-2558 *Fax:* 816-235-2611 *E-mail:* bkmk@umkc.edu *Web Site:* www.umkc.edu/bkmk, pg 36

Furnish, Ben, G S Sharat Chandra Prize for Short Fiction, University House, 5101 Rockhill Rd, Kansas City, MO 64110-2499 *Tel:* 816-235-2558 *Fax:* 816-235-2611 *E-mail:* bkmk@umkc.edu *Web Site:* www.umkc.edu/bkmk, pg 636

Furnish, Ben, John Ciardi Prize for Poetry, University House, 5101 Rockhill Rd, Kansas City, MO 64110-2499 *Tel:* 816-235-2558 *Fax:* 816-235-2611 *E-mail:* bkmk@umkc.edu *Web Site:* www.umkc.edu/bkmk, pg 637

Furr, Patti, FaithWalk Publishing, 5450 N Dixie Hwy, Lima, OH 45807 *Tel:* 419-227-1818 *Toll Free Tel:* 800-537-1030 (orders: non-bookstore mkts) *Fax:* 419-224-9184 *E-mail:* orders@csspub.com *Web Site:* www.faithwalkpub.com, pg 82

Furtkamp, Ryan, Stanford University Press, 425 Broadway St, Redwood City, CA 94063-3126 *Tel:* 650-723-9434 *Fax:* 650-725-3457 *E-mail:* info@www.sup.org; publicity@www.sup.org *Web Site:* www.sup.org, pg 220

Fusting, Donald W, Lanahan Publishers Inc, 324 Hawthorne Rd, Baltimore, MD 21210-2303 *Tel:* 410-366-2434 *Toll Free Tel:* 866-345-1949 *Fax:* 410-366-8798 *E-mail:* lanahan@aol.com *Web Site:* www.lanahanpublishers.com, pg 129

G'Schwind, Stephanie, Nelligan Prize for Short Fiction, Colorado State University, Dept of English, Center for Literary Publishing, 9105 Campus Delivery, Fort Collins, CO 80523-9105 *Tel:* 970-491-5449 *E-mail:* creview@colostate.edu *Web Site:* nelliganprize.colostate.edu, pg 672

Ga, Ellie, Ugly Duckling Presse, The Old American Can Factory, 232 Third St, Suite E303, Brooklyn, NY 11215 *Tel:* 347-948-5170 *E-mail:* info@uglyducklingpresse.org *Web Site:* www.uglyducklingpresse.org, pg 238

Gabel, Claudia, HarperCollins Children's Books, 195 Broadway, New York, NY 10007 *Tel:* 212-207-7000 *Web Site:* www.harpercollins.com/childrens, pg 101

Gadd, Laurence, North River Press Publishing Corp, 27 Rosseter St, Great Barrington, MA 01230 *Tel:* 413-528-0034 *Toll Free Tel:* 800-486-2665 *Fax:* 413-528-3163 *Toll Free Fax:* 800-BOOK-FAX (266-5329) *E-mail:* info@northriverpress.com *Web Site:* www.northriverpress.com, pg 163

Gadney, Alan, One On One Book Publishing/Film-Video Publications, 7944 Capistrano Ave, West Hills, CA 91304 *Tel:* 818-340-6620; 818-340-0175 *Fax:* 818-340-6620 *E-mail:* onebookpro@aol.com, pg 168

Gadney, Nancy, One On One Book Publishing/Film-Video Publications, 7944 Capistrano Ave, West Hills, CA 91304 *Tel:* 818-340-6620; 818-340-0175 *Fax:* 818-340-6620 *E-mail:* onebookpro@aol.com, pg 168

Gadow, Kathi, DK Publishing, 345 Hudson St, 2nd fl, New York, NY 10014 *Tel:* 646-674-4000 *Toll Free Tel:* 877-342-5357 (cust serv); 800-733-3000 *Web Site:* www.dk.com; www.penguin.com, pg 71

Gadsby, Oliver, Rowman & Littlefield Publishers Inc, 4501 Forbes Blvd, Suite 200, Lanham, MD 20706 *Tel:* 301-459-3366 *Toll Free Tel:* 800-462-6420 (cust serv) *Fax:* 301-429-5748 *Web Site:* rowman.com, pg 202

Gage, Michael, Kirkbride Bible Co Inc, 1102 Deloss St, Indianapolis, IN 46203 *Tel:* 317-633-1900 *Toll Free Tel:* 800-428-4385 *Fax:* 317-633-1444 *E-mail:* sales@kirkbride.com; info@kirkbride.com *Web Site:* www.kirkbride.com, pg 126

Gagnon, Andre, Editions Hurtubise, 1815, ave De Lorimier, Montreal, QC H2K 3W6, Canada *Tel:* 514-523-1523 *Toll Free Tel:* 800-361-1664 *Fax:* 514-523-9969 *Web Site:* www.editionshurtubise.com, pg 454

Gagnon, Manon, La Fondation Emile Nelligan, 100, rue Sherbrooke, Suite 202, Montreal, QC H2X 1C3, Canada *Tel:* 514-278-4657 *Fax:* 514-278-1943 *E-mail:* info@fondation-nelligan.org *Web Site:* www.fondation-nelligan.org, pg 566

Gagnon, Manon, Prix Emile-Nelligan, 100, rue Sherbrooke, Suite 202, Montreal, QC H2X 1C3, Canada *Tel:* 514-278-4657 *Toll Free Tel:* 888-849-8540 *Fax:* 514-278-1943 *E-mail:* info@fondation-nelligan.org *Web Site:* www.fondation-nelligan.org, pg 682

Gagnon, Matt, Boom! Studios, 5670 Wilshire Blvd, Suite 450, Los Angeles, CA 90036 *Web Site:* www.boom-studios.com, pg 40

Galardo, Elsa, Les Editions JCL, 688, rue St-Joseph, Marieville, QC J3M 1H1, Canada *Tel:* 450-460-4438 *E-mail:* info@jcl.qc.ca *Web Site:* www.jcl.qc.ca, pg 454

Galassi, Donna, Perseus Books, 250 W 57 St, 15th fl, New York, NY 10107 *Tel:* 212-340-8100 *Toll Free Tel:* 800-343-4499 (cust serv) *Fax:* 212-340-8105 *Web Site:* www.perseusbooks.com, pg 180

Galassi, Jonathan, Farrar, Straus & Giroux, LLC, 18 W 18 St, New York, NY 10011 *Tel:* 212-741-6900 *E-mail:* fsg.publicity@fsgbooks.com *Web Site:* us.macmillan.com/fsg.aspx, pg 82

Galassi, Jonathan, Macmillan, 175 Fifth Ave, New York, NY 10010 *Tel:* 646-307-5151 *E-mail:* press.inquiries@macmillan.com *Web Site:* www.macmillan.com, pg 140

Galasso, Al, National Association of Book Entrepreneurs (NABE), PO Box 606, Cottage Grove, OR 97424 *Tel:* 541-942-7455 *E-mail:* nabe@bookmarketingprofits.com *Web Site:* www.bookmarketingprofits.com, pg 570

Galasso, Al, Pinnacle Book Achievement Awards, PO Box 606, Cottage Grove, OR 97424 *Tel:* 541-942-7455 *Fax:* 541-942-7455 *E-mail:* nabe@bookmarketingprofits.com *Web Site:* www.bookmarketingprofits.com, pg 680

Galat, Danielle, New World Library, 14 Pamaron Way, Novato, CA 94949 *Tel:* 415-884-2100 *Toll Free Tel:* 800-227-3900 (ext 52, retail orders); 800-972-6657 *Fax:* 415-884-2199 *E-mail:* escort@newworldlibrary.com *Web Site:* www.newworldlibrary.com, pg 161

Galbraith, Judy, Free Spirit Publishing Inc, 217 Fifth Ave N, Suite 200, Minneapolis, MN 55401-1299 *Tel:* 612-338-2068 *Toll Free Tel:* 800-735-7323 *Fax:* 612-337-5050 *Toll Free Fax:* 866-419-5199 *E-mail:* help4kids@freespirit.com *Web Site:* www.freespirit.com, pg 88

Galde, Phyllis, Galde Press Inc, PO Box 460, Lakeville, MN 55044 *Tel:* 952-891-5991 *Toll Free Tel:* 800-777-3454 *Web Site:* www.galdepress.com, pg 89

Gale, David, Simon & Schuster Children's Publishing, 1230 Avenue of the Americas, New York, NY 10020 *Tel:* 212-698-7000 *Web Site:* www.simonandschuster.com/kids; www.simonandschuster.com/teen; simonandschuster.net; simonandschuster.biz, pg 213

Gale, Kate, Red Hen Press, 1335 N Lake Ave, Suite 200, Pasadena, CA 91104 *Tel:* 626-356-4760 *Fax:* 626-356-9974 *Web Site:* www.redhen.org, pg 196

Gale, Meighan, Zone Books, 633 Vanderbilt St, Brooklyn, NY 11218 *Tel:* 718-686-0048 *Toll Free Tel:* 800-405-1619 (orders & cust serv) *Fax:* 718-686-9045 *E-mail:* orders@triliteral.org *Web Site:* www.zonebooks.org, pg 263

Galen, Russell, Scovil Galen Ghosh Literary Agency Inc, 276 Fifth Ave, Suite 708, New York, NY 10001 *Tel:* 212-679-8686 *Fax:* 212-679-6710 *E-mail:* info@sgglit.com *Web Site:* www.sgglit.com, pg 535

Gall, Amy, National Book Awards, 90 Broad St, Suite 604, New York, NY 10004 *Tel:* 212-685-0261 *Fax:* 212-213-6570 *E-mail:* nationalbook@nationalbook.org *Web Site:* www.nationalbook.org, pg 670

Gall, John, Harry N Abrams Inc, 195 Broadway, 9th fl, New York, NY 10007 *Tel:* 212-206-7715 *Toll Free Tel:* 800-345-1359 *Fax:* 212-519-1210 *E-mail:* abrams@abramsbooks.com *Web Site:* www.abramsbooks.com, pg 3

Gallagher, Amy, North River Press Publishing Corp, 27 Rosseter St, Great Barrington, MA 01230 *Tel:* 413-528-0034 *Toll Free Tel:* 800-486-2665 *Fax:* 413-528-3163 *Toll Free Fax:* 800-BOOK-FAX (266-5329) *E-mail:* info@northriverpress.com *Web Site:* www.northriverpress.com, pg 163

Gallagher, Conor, TAN Books, PO Box 410487, Charlotte, NC 28241 *Tel:* 704-731-0651 *Toll Free Tel:* 800-437-5876 *Fax:* 815-226-7770 *E-mail:* customerservice@tanbooks.com *Web Site:* www.tanbooks.com, pg 227

Gallagher, Helen, Small Publishers, Artists & Writers Network (SPAWN), 323 E Matilija St, Suite 110, PMB 123, Ojai, CA 93023 *Tel:* 805-646-3045 *Fax:* 805-640-8213 *E-mail:* execdir@spawn.org *Web Site:* www.spawn.org, pg 577

Gallagher, Julia, Holiday House Inc, 425 Madison Ave, New York, NY 10017 *Tel:* 212-688-0085 *Fax:* 212-421-6134 *E-mail:* info@holidayhouse.com *Web Site:* www.holidayhouse.com, pg 109

Gallagher, Laird, Farrar, Straus & Giroux, LLC, 18 W 18 St, New York, NY 10011 *Tel:* 212-741-6900 *E-mail:* fsg.publicity@fsgbooks.com *Web Site:* us.macmillan.com/fsg.aspx, pg 83

Gallagher, Lisa, DeFiore and Company Literary Management Inc, 47 E 19 St, 3rd fl, New York, NY 10003 *Tel:* 212-925-7744 *Fax:* 212-925-9803 *E-mail:* info@defliterary.com; submissions@defliterary.com *Web Site:* www.defliterary.com, pg 513

Gallagher, Mike, Penguin Group USA, A Penguin Random House Company, 375 Hudson St, New York, NY 10014 *Tel:* 212-366-2000 *Toll Free Tel:* 800-847-5515 (inside sales); 800-631-8571 (cust serv) *Fax:* 212-366-2666; 607-775-4829 (inside sales) *E-mail:* online@us.penguingroup.com *Web Site:* www.penguin.com, pg 177

Gallagher, Patricia, Liberty Fund Inc, 8335 Allison Pointe Trail, Suite 300, Indianapolis, IN 46250-1684 *Tel:* 317-842-0880 *Toll Free Tel:* 800-955-8335; 800-866-3520; 800-368-7897 ext 6069 (cust serv) *Fax:* 317-577-9067; 317-579-6060 (cust serv); 708-534-7803 *E-mail:* books@libertyfund.org; info@libertyfund.org *Web Site:* www.libertyfund.org, pg 133

Gallagher, Richard, Annual Reviews, 4139 El Camino Way, Palo Alto, CA 94306 *Tel:* 650-493-4400 *Toll Free Tel:* 800-523-8635 *Fax:* 650-424-0910; 650-855-9815 *E-mail:* service@annualreviews.org *Web Site:* www.annualreviews.org, pg 17

Gallagher, Robert, TAN Books, PO Box 410487, Charlotte, NC 28241 *Tel:* 704-731-0651 *Toll Free Tel:* 800-437-5876 *Fax:* 815-226-7770 *E-mail:* customerservice@tanbooks.com *Web Site:* www.tanbooks.com, pg 227

Gallant, Barry, Doubleday Canada, 320 Front St W, Suite 1400, Toronto, ON M5V 3B6, Canada *Tel:* 416-364-4449 *Fax:* 416-598-7764 *Web Site:* www.penguinrandomhouse.ca, pg 452

Gallant, Barry, Knopf Canada, 320 Front St W, Suite 1400, Toronto, ON M5V 3B6, Canada *Tel:* 416-364-4449 *Toll Free Tel:* 888-523-9292 *Fax:* 416-598-7764 *Web Site:* www.penguinrandomhouse.ca, pg 462

Gallant, Barry, Penguin Group (Canada), 320 Front St W, Suite 1400, Toronto, ON M5V 3B6, Canada *Tel:* 416-364-4449 *Fax:* 416-598-7764 *E-mail:* customerservicescanada@penguinrandomhouse.com; publicity@ca.penguingroup.com *Web Site:* penguinrandomhouse.ca/imprints/penguin-canada, pg 466

Gallant, Barry, Penguin Random House Canada, 320 Front St W, Suite 1400, Toronto, ON M5V 3B6, Canada *Tel:* 416-364-4449 *Toll Free Tel:* 888-523-9292 (cust serv) *Fax:* 416-598-7764 *Web Site:* www.penguinrandomhouse.ca, pg 467

Gallant, Barry, Seal Books, 320 Front St W, Suite 1400, Toronto, ON M5V 3B6, Canada *Tel:* 416-364-4449 *Toll Free Tel:* 888-523-9292 (order desk) *Fax:* 416-598-7764 *Web Site:* www.penguinrandomhouse.ca, pg 470

Gallegos, Anna, Museum of New Mexico Press, 725 Camino Lejo, Suite C, Santa Fe, NM 87505 *Tel:* 505-476-1155; 505-272-7777 (orders); 505-277-4810 *Toll Free Tel:* 800-249-7737 (orders) *Fax:* 505-476-1156 *Toll Free Fax:* 800-622-8667 (orders) *Web Site:* www.mnmpress.org, pg 156

Gallman, Amanda, Sandlapper Publishing Inc, 1281 Amelia St NE, Orangeburg, SC 29115-5475 *Tel:* 803-531-1658 *Toll Free Tel:* 800-849-7263 (orders only) *Fax:* 803-534-5223 *Toll Free Fax:* 800-337-9420 *E-mail:* sales@sandlapperpublishing.com *Web Site:* www.sandlapperpublishing.com, pg 205

Gallo, Irene, Tom Doherty Associates, LLC, 175 Fifth Ave, 14th fl, New York, NY 10010 *Tel:* 646-307-5511 *Toll Free Tel:* 800-455-0340 *Web Site:* www.tor-forge.com, pg 71

Gallo, Vincent, William H Sadlier Inc, 9 Pine St, New York, NY 10005 *Tel:* 212-227-2120 *Toll Free Tel:* 800-221-5175 (cust serv) *Fax:* 212-312-6080 *E-mail:* customerservice@sadlier.com *Web Site:* www.sadlier.com, pg 203

Galloway, Greg, American Booksellers Association, 333 Westchester Ave, Suite S202, White Plains, NY 10604 *Tel:* 914-406-7500 *Toll Free Tel:* 800-637-0037 *Fax:* 914-410-6297 *E-mail:* info@bookweb.org *Web Site:* www.bookweb.org, pg 554

Galston, David, Polebridge Press, PO Box 346, Farmington, MN 55024 *Tel:* 651-200-2372 *E-mail:* orders@westarinstitute.org *Web Site:* www.westarinstitute.org, pg 185

Galusha, Dale, Pacific Press Publishing Association, 1350 N Kings Rd, Nampa, ID 83687-3193 *Tel:* 208-465-2500 *Toll Free Tel:* 800-447-7377 *Fax:* 208-465-2531 *Web Site:* www.pacificpress.com, pg 172

Galvin, Lori, Aevitas Creative Management, 19 W 21 St, Suite 501, New York, NY 10010 *Tel:* 212-765-6900 *Web Site:* aevitascreative.com, pg 506

Galvin, Tom, Triumph Books, 814 N Franklin St, Chicago, IL 60610 *Tel:* 312-337-0747 *Toll Free Tel:* 800-888-4741 (cust serv) *Fax:* 312-280-5470; 312-337-5985 *Web Site:* www.triumphbooks.com, pg 235

Galyan, Sheyna, Yotzeret Publishing, PO Box 18662, St Paul, MN 55118-0662 *Tel:* 651-470-3853 *Fax:* 651-224-7447 *E-mail:* info@yotzeretpublishing.com; orders@yotzeretpublishing.com *Web Site:* yotzeretpublishing.com, pg 262

Gamelli, Katie, Abrams Artists Agency, 275 Seventh Ave, 26th fl, New York, NY 10001 *Tel:* 646-486-4600 *Fax:* 646-486-0100 *E-mail:* literary@abramsartny.com *Web Site:* www.abramsartists.com, pg 505

Gammel, David, Entomological Society of America, 3 Park Place, Suite 307, Annapolis, MD 21401-3722 *Tel:* 301-731-4535 *Fax:* 301-731-4538 *E-mail:* esa@entsoc.org *Web Site:* www.entsoc.org, pg 79

Gammonley, Kevin, NPTA Alliance, 330 N Wabash Ave, Suite 2000, Chicago, IL 60611 *Tel:* 312-321-4092 *Toll Free Tel:* 800-355-NPTA (355-6782) *Fax:* 312-673-6736 *Web Site:* www.gonpta.com, pg 574

Gammons, Keith, Smyth & Helwys Publishing Inc, 6316 Peake Rd, Macon, GA 31210-3960 *Tel:* 478-757-0564 *Toll Free Tel:* 800-747-3016 (orders only); 800-568-1248 (orders only) *Fax:* 478-757-1305 *E-mail:* information@helwys.com *Web Site:* www.helwys.com, pg 215

PERSONNEL INDEX

Gandolfo, Italia, Vesuvian Books, 2817 West End Ave, Nashville, TN 37203 *E-mail:* info@vesuvianmedia.com *Web Site:* www.vesuvianbooks.com, pg 250

Gantz, Gabrielle, St Martin's Press, LLC, 175 Fifth Ave, New York, NY 10010 *Tel:* 646-307-5151 *Web Site:* us.macmillan.com/smp, pg 204

Garces, Cristina, HarperCollins General Books Group, 195 Broadway, New York, NY 10007 *Tel:* 212-207-7000 *Web Site:* www.harpercollins.com, pg 101

Garcia, Dawn E, The Knight-Risser Prize for Western Environmental Journalism, Stanford University, 450 Serra Mall, Bldg 120, Rm 424, Stanford, CA 94305-2050 *Tel:* 650-723-4937 *Fax:* 650-725-6154 *E-mail:* knightrisserprize@lists.stanford.edu *Web Site:* knightrisser.stanford.edu, pg 659

Garcia, Kathleen Sommers, Liturgy Training Publications, 3949 S Racine Ave, Chicago, IL 60609-2523 *Tel:* 773-579-4900 *Toll Free Tel:* 800-933-1800 (US & CN only orders) *Fax:* 773-579-4929 *Toll Free Fax:* 800-933-7094 (US & CN only orders) *E-mail:* orders@ltp.org *Web Site:* www.ltp.org, pg 136

Garcia, Lily Eskelsen, National Education Association (NEA), 1201 16 St NW, Washington, DC 20036-3290 *Tel:* 202-833-4000 *Fax:* 202-822-7974 *Web Site:* www.nea.org, pg 158, 572

Garcia, Patty, Tom Doherty Associates, LLC, 175 Fifth Ave, 14th fl, New York, NY 10010 *Tel:* 646-307-5511 *Toll Free Tel:* 800-455-0340 *Web Site:* www.tor-forge.com, pg 71

Garcia, Ray, Celebra, 375 Hudson St, New York, NY 10014 *Tel:* 212-366-2000 *E-mail:* ecommerce@us.penguingroup.com *Web Site:* www.penguin.com, pg 50

Garcia-Brown, Pilar, Houghton Mifflin Harcourt Trade & Reference Division, 125 High St, Boston, MA 02110 *Tel:* 617-351-5000 *Toll Free Tel:* 800-225-3362 *Web Site:* www.hmhco.com, pg 111

Gardiner, Eileen, Italica Press, 595 Main St, Suite 605, New York, NY 10044 *Tel:* 917-371-0563 *E-mail:* inquiries@italicapress.com *Web Site:* www.italicapress.com, pg 121

Gardiner, Ronan, Rodale Inc, 400 S Tenth St, Emmaus, PA 18049 *Tel:* 610-967-5171 *Toll Free Tel:* 866-387-0509 *E-mail:* bookmarketing@rodale.com; bookpublicity@rodale.com *Web Site:* www.rodale.com, pg 200

Gardner, Jason, New World Library, 14 Pamaron Way, Novato, CA 94949 *Tel:* 415-884-2100 *Toll Free Tel:* 800-227-3900 (ext 52, retail orders); 800-972-6657 *Fax:* 415-884-2199 *E-mail:* escort@newworldlibrary.com *Web Site:* www.newworldlibrary.com, pg 161

Gardner, Joseph, Child's Play®, 250 Minot Ave, Auburn, ME 04210 *Tel:* 207-784-7252 *Toll Free Tel:* 800-639-6404 *Fax:* 207-784-7358 *Toll Free Fax:* 800-854-6989 *E-mail:* chpmaine@aol.com; cplay@earthlink.net *Web Site:* www.childs-play.com, pg 54

Gardner, Dr Kevin J, Baylor University, Professional Writing Program, One Bear Place, Unit 97404, Waco, TX 76798-7404 *Tel:* 254-710-1768 *Fax:* 254-710-3894 *Web Site:* www.baylor.edu, pg 619

Gardner, Liana, Vesuvian Books, 2817 West End Ave, Nashville, TN 37203 *E-mail:* info@vesuvianmedia.com *Web Site:* www.vesuvianbooks.com, pg 250

Gardner, Rachelle, Books & Such, 52 Mission Circle, Suite 122, PMB 170, Santa Rosa, CA 95409-5370 *Tel:* 707-538-4184 *Web Site:* booksandsuch.com, pg 509

Garfield, Valerie, Simon & Schuster Children's Publishing, 1230 Avenue of the Americas, New York, NY 10020 *Tel:* 212-698-7000 *Web Site:* www.simonandschuster.com/kids; www.simonandschuster.com/teen; simonandschuster.net; simonandschuster.biz, pg 213

Garland, Ashley, HarperCollins General Books Group, 195 Broadway, New York, NY 10007 *Tel:* 212-207-7000 *Web Site:* www.harpercollins.com, pg 101

Garner, Ken, Epicomm, 1800 Diagonal Rd, Suite 320, Alexandria, VA 22314-2862 *Tel:* 703-836-9200 *E-mail:* webmaster@epicomm.org *Web Site:* epicomm.org, pg 565

Garner, Marion, Knopf Canada, 320 Front St W, Suite 1400, Toronto, ON M5V 3B6, Canada *Tel:* 416-364-4449 *Toll Free Tel:* 888-523-9292 *Fax:* 416-598-7764 *Web Site:* www.penguinrandomhouse.ca, pg 462

Garonzik, Joe, Clearfield Co Inc, 3600 Clipper Mill Rd, Suite 260, Baltimore, MD 21211 *Tel:* 410-837-8271 *Toll Free Tel:* 800-296-6687 (orders & cust serv) *Fax:* 410-752-8492 *E-mail:* sales@genealogical.com *Web Site:* www.genealogical.com, pg 57

Garonzik, Joe, Genealogical Publishing Co, 3600 Clipper Mill Rd, Suite 260, Baltimore, MD 21211 *Tel:* 410-837-8271 *Toll Free Tel:* 800-296-6687 *Fax:* 410-752-8492 *Toll Free Fax:* 800-599-9561 *E-mail:* info@genealogical.com; web@genealogical.com *Web Site:* www.genealogical.com, pg 91

Garretson, Jessie, Penguin Random House Speakers Bureau, A Penguin Random House Company, 1745 Broadway, Mail Drop 13-1, New York, NY 10019 *Tel:* 212-572-2013 *E-mail:* speakers@penguinrandomhouse.com *Web Site:* www.prhspeakers.com, pg 547

Garretson, Robin, Success Advertising & Publishing, 3419 Dunham Rd, Warsaw, NY 14569 *Tel:* 585-786-5663, pg 224

Garrett, Edward, Macmillan, 175 Fifth Ave, New York, NY 10010 *Tel:* 646-307-5151 *E-mail:* press.inquiries@macmillan.com *Web Site:* www.macmillan.com, pg 140

Garrett, Michael, Creative Inspirations Inc, 6203 Old Springville Rd, Pinson, AL 35126 *Web Site:* www.manuscriptcritique.com, pg 492

Garrett, Phil, Epicenter Press Inc, 6524 NE 181 St, Suite 2, Kenmore, WA 98028 *Tel:* 425-485-6822 (edit, mktg, busn off) *Fax:* 425-481-8253 *E-mail:* info@epicenterpress.com *Web Site:* www.epicenterpress.com, pg 79

Garrick, Kate, The Karpfinger Agency, 357 W 20 St, New York, NY 10011-3379 *Tel:* 212-691-2690 *Fax:* 212-691-7129 *E-mail:* info@karpfinger.com (no queries or submissions) *Web Site:* karpfinger.com, pg 523

Garrido, Dr Marta, Merit Publishing International Inc, 6839 Villas Dr S, Boca Raton, FL 33433 *Tel:* 561-350-0329 *E-mail:* merituk@aol.com *Web Site:* www.meritpublishing.com, pg 148

Garrison, Deborah, Alfred A Knopf/Everyman's Library, c/o Penguin Random House Inc, 1745 Broadway, New York, NY 10019 *Tel:* 212-751-2600 *Toll Free Tel:* 800-638-6460 *Fax:* 212-572-2593 *Web Site:* www.knopfdoubleday.com, pg 127

Garrison, Deborah, Pantheon Books/Schocken Books, c/o Penguin Random House Inc, 1745 Broadway, New York, NY 10019 *Tel:* 212-751-2600 *Web Site:* knopfdoubleday.com/imprint/pantheon, pg 173

Garrison, Jessica, Dial Books for Young Readers, 345 Hudson St, New York, NY 10014 *Tel:* 212-366-2000 *Toll Free Tel:* 800-733-3000 (orders) *Fax:* 212-414-3396 *Web Site:* www.penguin.com, pg 70

Garry, Peggy, Harry N Abrams Inc, 195 Broadway, 9th fl, New York, NY 10007 *Tel:* 212-206-7715 *Toll Free Tel:* 800-345-1359 *Fax:* 212-519-1210 *E-mail:* abrams@abramsbooks.com *Web Site:* www.abramsbooks.com, pg 3

Garton, Keith, Red Chair Press, PO Box 333, South Egremont, MA 01258-0333 *Tel:* 413-528-2398 (edit off) *Toll Free Tel:* 800-328-4929 (orders & cust serv) *Toll Free Fax:* 800-332-1132 *E-mail:* info@redchairpress.com *Web Site:* www.redchairpress.com, pg 196

Garvey, Elaine, Templegate Publishers, 302 E Adams St, Springfield, IL 62701 *Tel:* 217-522-3353 (edit & sales) *Toll Free Tel:* 800-367-4844 (orders only) *E-mail:* wisdom@templegate.com; orders@templegate.com (sales) *Web Site:* www.templegate.com, pg 229

Garvey, Thomas M, Templegate Publishers, 302 E Adams St, Springfield, IL 62701 *Tel:* 217-522-3353 (edit & sales) *Toll Free Tel:* 800-367-4844 (orders only) *E-mail:* wisdom@templegate.com; orders@templegate.com (sales) *Web Site:* www.templegate.com, pg 229

Garych, Leslie, Scholastic Trade Division, 557 Broadway, New York, NY 10012 *Tel:* 212-343-6100; 212-343-4685 (export sales) *Fax:* 212-343-4714 (export sales) *Web Site:* www.scholastic.com, pg 208

Garza, Jennifer, Random House Publishing Group, 1745 Broadway, New York, NY 10019 *Toll Free Tel:* 800-200-3552 *Web Site:* atrandom.com, pg 195

Gaterud, Abbey, Ooligan Press, Portland State University, 369 Neuberger Hall, 724 SW Harrison St, Portland, OR 97201 *Tel:* 503-725-9748 *Fax:* 503-725-3561 *E-mail:* ooligan@ooliganpress.pdx.edu *Web Site:* ooligan.pdx.edu, pg 168

Gates, Henry Louis Jr, The Anisfield-Wolf Book Awards, 1422 Euclid Ave, Suite 1300, Cleveland, OH 44115 *Tel:* 216-861-3810 *Fax:* 216-861-1729 *E-mail:* awinfo@clevefdn.org *Web Site:* www.anisfield-wolf.org; www.clevelandfoundation.org, pg 627

Gates, Jaym, Science Fiction & Fantasy Writers of America Inc (SFWA), PO Box 3238, Enfield, CT 06083-3238 *E-mail:* office@sfwa.org *Web Site:* www.sfwa.org, pg 577

Gates, Jennifer, Aevitas Creative Management, 19 W 21 St, Suite 501, New York, NY 10010 *Tel:* 212-765-6900 *Web Site:* aevitascreative.com, pg 506

Gates, Rob, The Gaylactic Spectrum Awards, 1425 "S" St NW, Washington, DC 20009 *Web Site:* www.spectrumawards.org, pg 649

Gates, Roberta, Friends of American Writers Awards, 506 Rose Ave, Des Plaines, IL 60016 *Tel:* 847-827-8339 *Web Site:* www.fawchicago.org, pg 648

Gates, Roberta, Juvenile Literary Awards/Young People's Literature Awards, 506 Rose Ave, Des Plaines, IL 60016 *Tel:* 847-827-8339 *Web Site:* www.fawchicago.org, pg 658

Gates, Tracy, Viking Children's Books, 345 Hudson St, New York, NY 10014 *Fax:* 212-414-3393 *E-mail:* youngreaderspublicity@us.penguingroup.com *Web Site:* www.penguin.com/publishers/vikingchildrensbooks, pg 251

Gatland, Steve, MDR, A D&B Co, 6 Armstrong Rd, Suite 301, Shelton, CT 06484 *Tel:* 203-926-4800 *Toll Free Tel:* 800-333-8802 *Fax:* 203-225-4603 *Toll Free Fax:* 866-532-7097 *E-mail:* mdrinfo@dnb.com *Web Site:* www.schooldata.com, pg 147

Gatsch, Mary E, Springer Publishing Co, 11 W 42 St, 15th fl, New York, NY 10036-8002 *Tel:* 212-431-4370 *Toll Free Tel:* 877-687-7476 *Fax:* 212-941-7842 *E-mail:* marketing@springerpub.com; cs@springerpub.com (orders); editorial@springerpub.com *Web Site:* www.springerpub.com, pg 219

Gatt, Michelle, SLACK® Incorporated, A Wyanoke Group Company, 6900 Grove Rd, Thorofare, NJ 08086-9447 *Tel:* 856-848-1000 *Toll Free Tel:* 800-257-8290 *Fax:* 856-848-6091 *E-mail:* sales@slackinc.com; editor@slackinc.com; customerservice@slackinc.com *Web Site:* www.healio.com/books, pg 215

Gatton, Dave, Pacific Press Publishing Association, 1350 N Kings Rd, Nampa, ID 83687-3193 *Tel:* 208-465-2500 *Toll Free Tel:* 800-447-7377 *Fax:* 208-465-2531 *Web Site:* www.pacificpress.com, pg 172

Gaudioso, Angela, Resilient Publishing, 406 S Third St, Boise, ID 83702 *Tel:* 208-258-9544 *E-mail:* submissions@resilientpublishing.com *Web Site:* www.resilientpublishing.com; www.facebook.com/ResilientPub, pg 198

Gauthier, Daniel J, Gauthier Publications Inc, PO Box 806241, St Clair Shores, MI 48080 *Tel:* 313-458-7141 *Fax:* 586-279-1515 *E-mail:* info@gauthierpublications.com *Web Site:* www.gauthierpublications.com, pg 91

Gauthier, Elizabeth, Gauthier Publications Inc, PO Box 806241, St Clair Shores, MI 48080 *Tel:* 313-458-7141 *Fax:* 586-279-1515 *E-mail:* info@gauthierpublications.com *Web Site:* www.gauthierpublications.com, pg 91

Gauthier, Jen, Greystone Books Ltd, 343 Railway St, Suite 201, Vancouver, BC V6A 1A4, Canada *Tel:* 604-875-1550 *Fax:* 604-875-1556 *E-mail:* info@greystonebooks.com *Web Site:* www.greystonebooks.com, pg 458

Gautier, Donna, Bloomsbury Publishing Inc, 1385 Broadway, 5th fl, New York, NY 10018 *Tel:* 212-419-5300 *E-mail:* marketingusa@bloomsbury.com; adultpublicityusa@bloomsbury.com; askacademic@bloomsbury.com *Web Site:* www.bloomsbury.com, pg 38

Gavacs, Jenny, Stanford University Press, 425 Broadway St, Redwood City, CA 94063-3126 *Tel:* 650-723-9434 *Fax:* 650-725-3457 *E-mail:* info@www.sup.org; publicity@www.sup.org *Web Site:* www.sup.org, pg 220

Gavin, Tara, Kensington Publishing Corp, 119 W 40 St, New York, NY 10018 *Tel:* 212-407-1500 *Toll Free Tel:* 800-221-2647 *Fax:* 212-935-0699 *Web Site:* www.kensingtonbooks.com, pg 125

Gawron, Br Zbigniew, St Pauls, 2187 Victory Blvd, Staten Island, NY 10314-6603 *Tel:* 718-761-0047 (edit & prodn); 718-698-2759 (mktg & billing) *Toll Free Tel:* 800-343-2522 *Fax:* 718-761-0057 *E-mail:* sales@stpauls.us; marketing@stpauls.us *Web Site:* www.stpauls.us, pg 205

Gay, Elizabeth, Simon & Schuster, 1230 Avenue of the Americas, New York, NY 10020 *Tel:* 212-698-7000 *Toll Free Tel:* 800-223-2348 (cust serv); 800-223-2336 (orders) *Toll Free Fax:* 800-943-9831 (orders) *Web Site:* www.simonandschuster.com, pg 212

Gayles, Jia, The Knight Agency Inc, 570 East Ave, Madison, GA 30650 *E-mail:* submissions@knightagency.net *Web Site:* www.knightagency.net, pg 524

Gaymon, Lee, SLACK® Incorporated, A Wyanoke Group Company, 6900 Grove Rd, Thorofare, NJ 08086-9447 *Tel:* 856-848-1000 *Toll Free Tel:* 800-257-8290 *Fax:* 856-848-6091 *E-mail:* sales@slackinc.com; editor@slackinc.com; customerservice@slackinc.com *Web Site:* www.healio.com/books, pg 215

Gaynin, Gail, Morgan Gaynin Inc, 149 Madison Ave, Suite 1140, New York, NY 10016 *Tel:* 212-475-0440 *E-mail:* info@morgangaynin.com *Web Site:* www.morgangaynin.com, pg 544

Gayot, Alain, Gault Millau Inc/Gayot Publications, 4311 Wilshire Blvd, Suite 405, Los Angeles, CA 90010 *Tel:* 323-965-3529 *Fax:* 323-936-2883 *E-mail:* info@gayot.com *Web Site:* www.gayot.com, pg 90

Gayot, Andre, Gault Millau Inc/Gayot Publications, 4311 Wilshire Blvd, Suite 405, Los Angeles, CA 90010 *Tel:* 323-965-3529 *Fax:* 323-936-2883 *E-mail:* info@gayot.com *Web Site:* www.gayot.com, pg 90

Gazlay, Laura, The Library of America, 14 E 60 St, New York, NY 10022-1006 *Tel:* 212-308-3360 *Fax:* 212-750-8352 *E-mail:* info@loa.org *Web Site:* www.loa.org, pg 133

Gazzolo, Paul, Gale, 27500 Drake Rd, Farmington Hills, MI 48331-3535 *Tel:* 248-699-4253 *Toll Free Tel:* 800-877-4253 *Toll Free Fax:* 800-414-5043 (orders) *E-mail:* gale.customercare@cengage.com *Web Site:* www.gale.com, pg 89

Gazzolo, Paul, Macmillan Reference USA™, 27500 Drake Rd, Farmington Hills, MI 48331-3535 *Tel:* 248-699-4253 *Toll Free Tel:* 800-877-4253 *Toll Free Fax:* 877-363-4253 *E-mail:* gale.customercare@cengage.com *Web Site:* www.gale.cengage.com/macmillan, pg 140

Geary, William III, Bisk Education, 9417 Princess Palm Ave, Suite 400, Tampa, FL 33619 *Tel:* 813-621-6200 *Toll Free Tel:* 800-280-9718 (cust serv) *E-mail:* customerservice@bisk.com *Web Site:* www.bisk.com, pg 35

Gebhardt, Phyllis, Trusted Media Brands Inc, 750 Third Ave, 3rd fl, New York, NY 10017 *Toll Free Tel:* 800-310-6261 (cust serv) *E-mail:* customercare@tmbi.com *Web Site:* www.tmbi.com; www.rd.com, pg 236

Geck, Steve, Sourcebooks Inc, 1935 Brookdale Rd, Suite 139, Naperville, IL 60563 *Tel:* 630-961-3900 *Toll Free Tel:* 800-432-7444 *Fax:* 630-961-2168 *E-mail:* info@sourcebooks.com; customersupport@sourcebooks.com *Web Site:* www.sourcebooks.com, pg 218

Gee, Connie, BePuzzled, 2030 Harrison St, San Francisco, CA 94110 *Tel:* 415-503-1600 *Toll Free Tel:* 800-347-4818 *Fax:* 415-503-0085 *E-mail:* info@ugames.com *Web Site:* www.ugames.com, pg 33

Gee, Jim, Leadership Directories, 1407 Broadway, Suite 318, New York, NY 10018 *Tel:* 212-627-4140 *Toll Free Tel:* 800-627-0311 *Fax:* 212-645-0931 *E-mail:* info@leadershipdirectories.com *Web Site:* www.leadershipdirectories.com, pg 130

Gee, Sage, Global Lion Intellectual Property Management Inc, PO Box 669238, Pompano Beach, FL 33066 *Tel:* 754-222-6948 *Fax:* 754-222-6948 *E-mail:* queriesgloballionmgt@gmail.com *Web Site:* www.globallionmanagement.com, pg 519

Geer, David, Samuel French Inc, 235 Park Ave S, 5th fl, New York, NY 10003 *Tel:* 212-206-8990 *Toll Free Tel:* 866-598-8449 *Fax:* 212-206-1429 *E-mail:* info@samuelfrench.com; publications@samuelfrench.com *Web Site:* www.samuelfrench.com, pg 88

Geers, Torsten, Cengage Learning, 20 Channel Center St, Boston, MA 02210 *Tel:* 617-289-7700 *Toll Free Tel:* 800-354-9706 *Fax:* 617-289-7844 *Toll Free Fax:* 800-487-8488 *E-mail:* esales@cengage.com *Web Site:* www.cengage.com, pg 50

Gehani, Indu, Silicon Press, 25 Beverly Rd, Summit, NJ 07901 *Tel:* 908-273-8919 *Fax:* 908-273-6149 *E-mail:* info@silicon-press.com *Web Site:* www.silicon-press.com, pg 212

Gehy, Farah, Peachtree Publishers, 1700 Chattahoochee Ave, Atlanta, GA 30318-2112 *Tel:* 404-876-8761 *Toll Free Tel:* 800-241-0113 *Fax:* 404-875-2578 *Toll Free Fax:* 800-875-8909 *E-mail:* hello@peachtree-online.com *Web Site:* www.peachtree-online.com, pg 176

Geiger, Ellen, Frances Goldin Literary Agency, Inc, 214 W 29 St, Suite 410, New York, NY 10001 *Tel:* 212-777-0047 *Fax:* 212-228-1660 *E-mail:* agency@goldinlit.com *Web Site:* www.goldinlit.com, pg 519

Geiger, Rachel, Chronicle Books LLC, 680 Second St, San Francisco, CA 94107 *Tel:* 415-537-4200 *Toll Free Tel:* 800-759-0190 (cust serv) *Fax:* 415-537-4460 *Toll Free Fax:* 800-858-7787 (orders); 800-286-9471 (cust serv) *E-mail:* frontdesk@chroniclebooks.com *Web Site:* www.chroniclebooks.com, pg 55

Geisler, Anna, Guernica Editions Inc, 1569 Heritage Way, Oakville, ON L6M 2Z7, Canada *Tel:* 905-599-5304 *E-mail:* info@guernicaeditions.com *Web Site:* www.guernicaeditions.com, pg 459

Geissler, Cynara, Arsenal Pulp Press, 211 E Georgia St, No 202, Vancouver, BC V6A 1Z6, Canada *Tel:* 604-687-4233 *Toll Free Tel:* 888-600-PULP (600-7857) *Fax:* 604-687-4283 *E-mail:* info@arsenalpulp.com *Web Site:* www.arsenalpulp.com, pg 445

Geist, Jennifer, Brick Mantel Books, 4735 S State Rd 446, Bloomington, IN 47401 *Tel:* 314-827-6567; 812-837-9226 *E-mail:* info@brickmantelbooks.com *Web Site:* brickmantelbooks.com, pg 42

Geist, Jennifer, Open Books Press, 4735 S State Rd 446, Bloomington, IN 47401 *Tel:* 314-827-6567; 812-837-9226 *E-mail:* info@openbookspress.com *Web Site:* openbookspress.com, pg 168

Geist, Jennifer, Pen & Publish Inc, 4735 S State Rd 446, Bloomington, IN 47401 *Tel:* 314-827-6567 *E-mail:* info@penandpublish.com *Web Site:* www.penandpublish.com, pg 176

Geist, Ken, Scholastic Trade Division, 557 Broadway, New York, NY 10012 *Tel:* 212-343-6100; 212-343-4685 (export sales) *Fax:* 212-343-4714 (export sales) *Web Site:* www.scholastic.com, pg 208

Gelb, Eric, Small Business Advisors Inc, 11 Franklin Ave, Hewlett, NY 11557 *Tel:* 516-374-1387 *Fax:* 516-374-1175 *Web Site:* www.smallbusinessadvice.com, pg 215

Gelb, Joe, Small Business Advisors Inc, 11 Franklin Ave, Hewlett, NY 11557 *Tel:* 516-374-1387 *Fax:* 516-374-1175 *Web Site:* www.smallbusinessadvice.com, pg 215

Gelbman, Leslie, Berkley Publishing Group, 375 Hudson St, New York, NY 10014 *Tel:* 212-366-2000 *Fax:* 212-366-2385 *Web Site:* www.penguin.com, pg 33

Gelbman, Leslie, St Martin's Press, LLC, 175 Fifth Ave, New York, NY 10010 *Tel:* 646-307-5151 *Web Site:* us.macmillan.com/smp, pg 204

Gelfand, Dr Sergei, American Mathematical Society, 201 Charles St, Providence, RI 02904-2294 *Tel:* 401-455-4000 *Toll Free Tel:* 800-321-4267 *Fax:* 401-331-3842; 401-455-4046 (cust serv) *E-mail:* ams@ams.org; cust-serv@ams.org *Web Site:* www.ams.org, pg 13

Gelfman, Jane, Gelfman Schneider/ICM Partners, 850 Seventh Ave, Suite 903, New York, NY 10019 *Tel:* 212-245-1993 *Fax:* 212-245-8678 *E-mail:* mail@gelfmanschneider.com *Web Site:* gelfmanschneider.com, pg 518

Gelineau, Christine, Binghamton University Creative Writing Program, c/o Dept of English, PO Box 6000, Binghamton, NY 13902-6000 *Tel:* 607-777-2168 *Fax:* 607-777-2408 *E-mail:* cwpro@binghamton.edu *Web Site:* english.binghamton.edu/cwpro, pg 619

Geller, Sandra R, Practising Law Institute, 1177 Avenue of the Americas, New York, NY 10036 *Tel:* 212-824-5700 *Toll Free Tel:* 800-260-4PLI (260-4754, cust serv) *Fax:* 212-265-4742 (intl) *Toll Free Fax:* 800-321-0093 (local) *E-mail:* info@pli.edu (cust serv) *Web Site:* www.pli.edu, pg 186

Gelles-Cole, Sandi, Gelles-Cole Literary Enterprises, 135 John Joy Rd, Woodstock, NY 12498-0341 *Web Site:* www.literaryenterprises.com, pg 494

Gellman, Rachel, American Society of Health-System Pharmacists (ASHP), 4500 East-West Hwy, Suite 900, Bethesda, MD 20814 *Tel:* 301-657-3000; 301-664-8700 *Toll Free Tel:* 866-279-0681 (orders) *Fax:* 301-657-1251 (orders) *E-mail:* custserv@ashp.org *Web Site:* www.ashp.org, pg 15

Gelsomino, Tara, Adams Media, 57 Littlefield St, Avon, MA 02322 *Tel:* 508-427-7100 *Web Site:* www.simonandschuster.com, pg 4

Gelsomino, Tara, F+W Media Inc, 10151 Carver Rd, Suite 200, Blue Ash, OH 45242 *Tel:* 513-531-2690 *Toll Free Tel:* 800-289-0963 (trade accts); 800-258-0929 (cust serv) *E-mail:* contact_us@fwmedia.com *Web Site:* www.fwcommunity.com, pg 82

Gelwicks, Maureen, Educational Book & Media Association (EBMA), 11 Main St, Suite D, Warrenton, VA 20186 *Tel:* 540-318-7770 *Fax:* 202-962-3939 *E-mail:* info@edupaperback.org *Web Site:* www.edupaperback.org, pg 565

Gelwicks, Maureen, Jeremiah Ludington Award, 11 Main St, Suite D, Warrenton, VA 20186 *Tel:* 540-318-7770 *Fax:* 202-962-3939 *E-mail:* info@edupaperback.org *Web Site:* www.edupaperback.org, pg 663

Gemignani, Nathan D, Cornell University Press, Sage House, 512 E State St, Ithaca, NY 14850 *Tel:* 607-277-2338 *Fax:* 607-277-2374 *E-mail:* cupressinfo@cornell.edu; cupress-sales@cornell.edu *Web Site:* www.cornellpress.cornell.edu, pg 61

Gendler, Anne, Northwestern University Press, 629 Noyes St, Evanston, IL 60208-4210 *Tel:* 847-491-2046 *Toll Free Tel:* 800-621-2736 (orders only) *Fax:* 847-491-8150 *E-mail:* nupress@northwestern.edu *Web Site:* www.nupress.northwestern.edu, pg 164

Geneste, Mark, Dun & Bradstreet, 103 JFK Pkwy, Short Hills, NJ 07078 *Tel:* 973-921-5500 *Toll Free Tel:* 800-526-0651; 800-234-3867 (cust serv) *E-mail:* custserv@dnb.com *Web Site:* www.dnb.com, pg 73

Genet, Pascal, Les Editions XYZ inc, 1815, ave De Lorimier, Montreal, QC H2K 3W6, Canada *Tel:* 514-525-2170 *Fax:* 514-525-7537 *E-mail:* info@editionsxyz.com *Web Site:* www.editionsxyz.com, pg 456

Genna, Victoria, Farrar, Straus & Giroux, LLC, 18 W 18 St, New York, NY 10011 *Tel:* 212-741-6900 *E-mail:* fsg.publicity@fsgbooks.com *Web Site:* us.macmillan.com/fsg.aspx, pg 83

Genna, Victoria, Hill & Wang, 18 W 18 St, New York, NY 10011 *Tel:* 212-741-6900 *Fax:* 212-633-9385 *E-mail:* fsg.publicity@fsgbooks.com; fsg.editorial@fsgbooks.com; sales@fsgbooks.com *Web Site:* us.macmillan.com/hillandwang.aspx, pg 107

Gensch, Chris, The Alexander Graham Bell Association for the Deaf & Hard of Hearing, 3417 Volta Place NW, Washington, DC 20007 *Tel:* 202-337-5220 *Toll Free Tel:* 866-337-5220 (orders) *Fax:* 202-337-8314 *E-mail:* info@agbell.org; publications@agbell.org *Web Site:* www.agbell.org, pg 6

Gentillo, Eileen, Simon & Schuster Sales Division, 1230 Avenue of the Americas, New York, NY 10020 *Tel:* 212-698-7000, pg 214

Gentry, Samantha, Random House Children's Books, 1745 Broadway, 10th fl, New York, NY 10019 *Tel:* 212-782-9000 *Web Site:* www.randomhousekids.com, pg 194

George, Bob, FurnitureCore, 1389 Peachtree St NE, Suite 310, Atlanta, GA 30309 *Tel:* 404-961-3734 *Toll Free Tel:* 800-826-8868 *Fax:* 404-961-3749 *E-mail:* info@furniturecore.com *Web Site:* www.furniturecore.com, pg 89

George, Lee Anne, Association of Research Libraries, 21 Dupont Circle NW, Suite 800, Washington, DC 20036 *Tel:* 202-296-2296 *Fax:* 202-872-0884 *E-mail:* arlhq@arl.org *Web Site:* www.arl.org, pg 24

Geraghty, Joe, Close Up Publishing, 1330 Braddock Place, Suite 400, Alexandria, VA 22314 *Tel:* 703-706-3300 *Toll Free Tel:* 800-CLOSE-UP (256-7387) *Fax:* 703-706-3564 *E-mail:* info@closeup.org *Web Site:* www.closeup.org, pg 57

Geraghty, Kate, Macmillan Learning, 41 Madison Ave, New York, NY 10010 *Tel:* 212-576-9400 *Fax:* 212-689-2383 *Web Site:* www.macmillanlearning.com, pg 140

Geraghty, Patrick, Whitecap Books, 314 W Cordova St, Suite 209, Vancouver, BC V6B 1E8, Canada *Tel:* 604-681-6181 *Toll Free Tel:* 800-387-9776 *Toll Free Fax:* 800-260-9777 *Web Site:* www.whitecap.ca, pg 475

Gerardi, Jan, Random House Children's Books, 1745 Broadway, 10th fl, New York, NY 10019 *Tel:* 212-782-9000 *Web Site:* www.randomhousekids.com, pg 194

Gerbasi, Catherine, Portage & Main Press, 318 McDermot, Suite 100, Winnipeg, MB R3A 0A2, Canada *Tel:* 204-987-3500 *Toll Free Tel:* 800-667-9673 *Fax:* 204-947-0080 *Toll Free Fax:* 866-734-8477 *E-mail:* books@portageandmainpress.com *Web Site:* www.portageandmainpress.com, pg 467

Gerber, Marty, Terra Nova Books, 33 Alondra Rd, Santa Fe, NM 87508 *Tel:* 505-670-9319 *Fax:* 509-461-9333 *E-mail:* publisher@terranovabooks.com; marketing@terranovabooks.com *Web Site:* www.terranovabooks.com, pg 229

Gerber, Scott, Terra Nova Books, 33 Alondra Rd, Santa Fe, NM 87508 *Tel:* 505-670-9319 *Fax:* 509-461-9333 *E-mail:* publisher@terranovabooks.com; marketing@terranovabooks.com *Web Site:* www.terranovabooks.com, pg 229

German, Donna, Arbordale Publishing, 612 Johnnie Dodds Blvd, Suite A2, Mount Pleasant, SC 29464 *Tel:* 843-971-6722 *Toll Free Tel:* 877-243-3457 *Fax:* 843-216-3804 *E-mail:* customerservice@arbordalepublishing.com; info@arbordalepublishing.com *Web Site:* www.arbordalepublishing.com, pg 20

German, Mr Lee, Arbordale Publishing, 612 Johnnie Dodds Blvd, Suite A2, Mount Pleasant, SC 29464 *Tel:* 843-971-6722 *Toll Free Tel:* 877-243-3457 *Fax:* 843-216-3804 *E-mail:* customerservice@arbordalepublishing.com; info@arbordalepublishing.com *Web Site:* www.arbordalepublishing.com, pg 20

Gerrell, Terri, Florida Authors & Publishers Association Inc (FAPA), 1702 N Woodland Blvd, Suite 116, Box 145, Deland, FL 32720 *E-mail:* member.services@floridapublishersassociation.com *Web Site:* www.floridapublishersassociation.com, pg 565

Gerrish, Debbie, Women Who Write Inc, PO Box 652, Madison, NJ 07940-0652 *E-mail:* info@womenwhowrite.org *Web Site:* womenwhowrite.org, pg 580

Gershowitz, Elissa, Boston Globe-Horn Book Award, c/o Book Reviews, The Horn Book Inc, Palace Road Bldg, 300 The Fenway, Suite P-311, Boston, MA 02115-5820 *Tel:* 617-278-0225 *Toll Free Tel:* 888-628-0225 *Fax:* 617-278-6062 *E-mail:* info@hbook.com *Web Site:* www.hbook.com, pg 633

Gerstle, Dan, Perseus Books, 250 W 57 St, 15th fl, New York, NY 10107 *Tel:* 212-340-8100 *Toll Free Tel:* 800-343-4499 (cust serv) *Fax:* 212-340-8105 *Web Site:* www.perseusbooks.com, pg 181

Gerth, Anne, InterVarsity Press, 430 Plaza Dr, Westmont, IL 60559-1234 *Tel:* 630-734-4000 *Toll Free Tel:* 800-843-9487 *Fax:* 630-734-4200 *E-mail:* email@ivpress.com *Web Site:* www.ivpress.com, pg 120

Gerth, Rob, The Electrochemical Society (ECS), 65 S Main St, Bldg D, Pennington, NJ 08534-2839 *Tel:* 609-737-1902 *Fax:* 609-737-2743 *E-mail:* publications@electrochem.org; customerservice@electrochem.org *Web Site:* www.electrochem.org, pg 77

Gervasio, Janet, HarperCollins Publishers, 195 Broadway, New York, NY 10007 *Tel:* 212-207-7000 *Fax:* 212-207-7145 *Web Site:* www.harpercollins.com, pg 101

Gerwin, Karen, DeFiore and Company Literary Management Inc, 47 E 19 St, 3rd fl, New York, NY 10003 *Tel:* 212-925-7744 *Fax:* 212-925-9803 *E-mail:* info@defliterary.com; submissions@defliterary.com *Web Site:* www.defliterary.com, pg 513

Gerwitz, Elaine, Dog Writers' Association of America Inc (DWAA), 66 Adams St, Jamestown, NY 14701 *Tel:* 716-484-6155 *E-mail:* dogwriter@windstream.net *Web Site:* www.dwaa.org, pg 564

Gerwitz, Elaine, Dog Writers' Association of America Inc (DWAA) Annual Writing Competition, 2243 Kelmscott Ct, Westlake Village, CA 91361 *Tel:* 805-418-7899 *Fax:* 831-374-9231 *E-mail:* dogwriter@windstream.net *Web Site:* www.dwaa.org, pg 642

Gesford, Mary, University Publishing Group, 6 W Washington St, Suite 302, Hagerstown, MD 21740 *Tel:* 240-420-0036 *Fax:* 240-718-7100 *E-mail:* orders@upgbooks.com, pg 247

Gethers, Peter, Penguin Random House Inc, 1745 Broadway, New York, NY 10019 *Tel:* 212-782-9000 *Toll Free Tel:* 800-726-0600 *Web Site:* www.penguinrandomhouse.com, pg 178

Gharib, Linda, Wolters Kluwer US Corp, 2700 Lake Cook Rd, Riverwoods, IL 60015 *Tel:* 847-267-7000 *Fax:* 847-580-5192 *E-mail:* info@wolterskluwer.com *Web Site:* www.wolterskluwer.com, pg 258

Ghavami, Parvaneh, ADASI Publishing Co, 13 Riverdale Ave, Dover, NH 03820-4698 *Tel:* 603-866-9426 *E-mail:* info@adasi.com *Web Site:* www.adasi.com, pg 4

Ghione, Yvette, Kids Can Press Ltd, 25 Dockside Dr, Toronto, ON M5A 0B5, Canada *Tel:* 416-479-7000 *Toll Free Tel:* 800-265-0884 *Fax:* 416-960-5437 *E-mail:* info@kidscan.com; customerservice@kidscan.com *Web Site:* www.kidscanpress.com; www.kidscanpress.ca, pg 461

Ghoura, Judy, Fitzhenry & Whiteside Limited, 195 Allstate Pkwy, Markham, ON L3R 4T8, Canada *Tel:* 905-477-9700 *Toll Free Tel:* 800-387-9776 *Fax:* 905-477-2834 *Toll Free Fax:* 800-260-9777 *E-mail:* bookinfo@fitzhenry.ca; godwit@fitzhenry.ca *Web Site:* www.fitzhenry.ca, pg 457

Ghoura, Judy, Red Deer Press Inc, 195 Allstate Pkwy, Markham, ON L3R 4T8, Canada *Tel:* 905-477-9700 *Toll Free Tel:* 800-387-9776 (orders) *E-mail:* rdp@reddeerpress.com; bookinfo@fitzhenry.ca *Web Site:* www.reddeerpress.com, pg 468

Giagnocavo, Alan, Fox Chapel Publishing Co Inc, 1970 Broad St, East Petersburg, PA 17520 *Tel:* 717-560-4703 *Toll Free Tel:* 800-457-9112 *Fax:* 717-560-4702 *E-mail:* customerservice@foxchapelpublishing.com *Web Site:* www.foxchapelpublishing.com, pg 87

Giangreco, Karen, The Experiment, 220 E 23 St, Suite 301, New York, NY 10010-4674 *Tel:* 212-889-1659 *E-mail:* info@theexperimentpublishing.com *Web Site:* www.theexperimentpublishing.com, pg 81

Giarratano, Matt, Penguin Books, 375 Hudson St, New York, NY 10014 *Tel:* 212-366-2000 *E-mail:* penguinpublicity@us.penguingroup.com *Web Site:* www.penguinclassics.com; www.penguin.com, pg 177

Giarratano, Matt, Plume, 375 Hudson St, New York, NY 10014 *Tel:* 212-366-2000 *Fax:* 212-243-6002 *Web Site:* www.penguin.com/publishers/plume, pg 184

Giarratano, Michael, Perseus Books, 250 W 57 St, 15th fl, New York, NY 10107 *Tel:* 212-340-8100 *Toll Free Tel:* 800-343-4499 (cust serv) *Fax:* 212-340-8105 *Web Site:* www.perseusbooks.com, pg 181

Gibbons, Melissa, William H Sadlier Inc, 9 Pine St, New York, NY 10005 *Tel:* 212-227-2120 *Toll Free Tel:* 800-221-5175 (cust serv) *Fax:* 212-312-6080 *E-mail:* customerservice@sadlier.com *Web Site:* www.sadlier.com, pg 203

Gibbs, Naomi, Houghton Mifflin Harcourt Trade & Reference Division, 125 High St, Boston, MA 02110 *Tel:* 617-351-5000 *Toll Free Tel:* 800-225-3362 *Web Site:* www.hmhco.com, pg 111

Gibby-Munguia, Nicole, Alex Awards, 50 E Huron St, Chicago, IL 60611 *Tel:* 312-280-4390 *Toll Free Tel:* 800-545-2433 *Fax:* 312-280-5276 *E-mail:* yalsa@ala.org *Web Site:* www.ala.org/yalsa/alex-awards, pg 626

Gibney, Bob, Cengage Learning, 20 Channel Center St, Boston, MA 02210 *Tel:* 617-289-7700 *Toll Free Tel:* 800-354-9706 *Fax:* 617-289-7844 *Toll Free Fax:* 800-487-8488 *E-mail:* esales@cengage.com *Web Site:* www.cengage.com, pg 50

Gibson, Angela, Modern Language Association of America (MLA), 85 Broad St, Suite 500, New York, NY 10004-2434 *Tel:* 646-576-5000 *Fax:* 646-458-0030 *Web Site:* www.mla.org, pg 152

Gibson, Bethany, Goose Lane Editions, 500 Beaverbrook Ct, Suite 330, Fredericton, NB E3B 5X4, Canada *Tel:* 506-450-4251 *Toll Free Tel:* 888-926-8377 *Fax:* 506-459-4991 *E-mail:* info@gooselane.com; customerservice@gooselane.com *Web Site:* www.gooselane.com, pg 458

Gibson, George, Grove Atlantic Inc, 154 W 14 St, 12th fl, New York, NY 10011 *Tel:* 212-614-7850 *Toll Free Tel:* 800-521-0178 *Fax:* 212-614-7886 *E-mail:* info@groveatlantic.com; sales@groveatlantic.com; publicity@groveatlantic.com; rights@groveatlantic.com *Web Site:* www.groveatlantic.com, pg 97

Gibson, Jack, International Risk Management Institute Inc, 12222 Merit Dr, Suite 1600, Dallas, TX 75251-2266 *Tel:* 972-960-7693 *Fax:* 972-371-5120 *E-mail:* info27@irmi.com *Web Site:* www.irmi.com, pg 120

Gibson, Katherine, Wm B Eerdmans Publishing Co, 2140 Oak Industrial Dr NE, Grand Rapids, MI 49505 *Tel:* 616-459-4591 *Toll Free Tel:* 800-253-7521 *Fax:* 616-459-6540 *E-mail:* customerservice@eerdmans.com; sales@eerdmans.com *Web Site:* www.eerdmans.com, pg 76

Gibson, Maggie, Random House Children's Books, 1745 Broadway, 10th fl, New York, NY 10019 *Tel:* 212-782-9000 *Web Site:* www.randomhousekids.com, pg 194

Gibson, Phil, National Press Club of Canada Foundation Inc, 17 York St, Suite 201, Ottawa, ON K1N 9J6, Canada *E-mail:* info@pressclubcanada.ca *Web Site:* pressclubcanada.ca, pg 572

Giddens, Mary, SteinerBooks, 610 Main St, Great Barrington, MA 01230 *Tel:* 413-528-8233 *Fax:* 413-528-8826 *E-mail:* friends@steinerbooks.org *Web Site:* steiner.presswarehouse.com, pg 222

Gifford, James M PhD, The Jesse Stuart Foundation (JSF), 4440 13 St, Ashland, KY 41102 *Tel:* 606-326-1667 *Fax:* 606-325-2519 *E-mail:* jsf@jsfbooks.com *Web Site:* www.jsfbooks.com, pg 224

Giffuni, Cathe, Research Research, 240 E 27 St, Suite 20-K, New York, NY 10016-9238 *Tel:* 212-779-9540 *Fax:* 212-779-9540 *E-mail:* ehtac@msn.com, pg 500

Giganti, Edward J, The Catholic Health Association of the United States, 4455 Woodson Rd, St Louis, MO 63134-3797 *Tel:* 314-427-2500 *Fax:* 314-427-0029 *E-mail:* servicecenter@chausa.org *Web Site:* www.chausa.org, pg 49

Gignilliat-Day, Leslie, Amber Lotus Publishing, PO Box 11329, Portland, OR 97211 *Tel:* 503-284-6400 *Toll Free Tel:* 800-326-2375 (orders only) *Fax:* 503-284-6417 *E-mail:* info@amberlotus.com *Web Site:* www.amberlotus.com, pg 9

Gilbert, Christina, Bloomsbury Publishing Inc, 1385 Broadway, 5th fl, New York, NY 10018 *Tel:* 212-419-5300 *E-mail:* marketingusa@bloomsbury.com; adultpublicityusa@bloomsbury.com; askacademic@bloomsbury.com *Web Site:* www.bloomsbury.com, pg 37

Gilbert, Deborah, Soul Mate Publishing, 3210 Sherwood Dr, Walworth, NY 14568 *Tel:* 585-598-4791 *E-mail:* submissions@soulmatepublishing.com *Web Site:* www.soulmatepublishing.com, pg 217

Gilbert, Jennifer G, Galen Press Ltd, PO Box 64400-WB, Tucson, AZ 85728-4400 *Tel:* 520-577-8363 *Fax:* 520-529-6459 *E-mail:* sales@galenpress.com *Web Site:* www.galenpress.com, pg 89

Gilbert, Jon, Seven Stories Press, 140 Watts St, New York, NY 10013 *Tel:* 212-226-8760 *Toll Free Tel:* 800-733-3000 (orders) *Fax:* 212-226-1411 *E-mail:* info@sevenstories.com *Web Site:* www.sevenstories.com, pg 211

Gilbert, Sheila E, DAW Books Inc, 375 Hudson St, New York, NY 10014 *Tel:* 212-366-2096 *Fax:* 212-366-2090 *E-mail:* daw@penguinrandomhouse.com *Web Site:* www.dawbooks.com; www.penguin.com; www.penguinrandomhouse.com, pg 68

Gilbride, Tara, Penguin Group USA, A Penguin Random House Company, 375 Hudson St, New York, NY 10014 *Tel:* 212-366-2000 *Toll Free Tel:* 800-847-5515 (inside sales); 800-631-8571 (cust serv) *Fax:* 212-366-2666; 607-775-4829 (inside sales) *E-mail:* online@us.penguingroup.com *Web Site:* www.penguin.com, pg 177

Gilbride, Tara, Portfolio, 375 Hudson St, New York, NY 10014 *Web Site:* www.penguin.com/meet/publishers/portfolio, pg 186

Gilewicz, John, Adirondack Mountain Club (ADK), 814 Goggins Rd, Lake George, NY 12845-4117 *Tel:* 518-668-4447 *Toll Free Tel:* 800-395-8080 *Fax:* 518-668-3746 *E-mail:* info@adk.org *Web Site:* www.adk.org, pg 4

Gill, Craig, University Press of Mississippi, 3825 Ridgewood Rd, Jackson, MS 39211-6492 *Tel:* 601-432-6205 *Toll Free Tel:* 800-737-7788 (orders & cust serv) *Fax:* 601-432-6217 *E-mail:* press@mississippi.edu *Web Site:* www.upress.state.ms.us, pg 247

Gill, Diana, Tom Doherty Associates, LLC, 175 Fifth Ave, 14th fl, New York, NY 10010 *Tel:* 646-307-5511 *Toll Free Tel:* 800-455-0340 *Web Site:* www.tor-forge.com, pg 71

Gillan, Maria, Binghamton University Creative Writing Program, c/o Dept of English, PO Box 6000, Binghamton, NY 13902-6000 *Tel:* 607-777-2168 *Fax:* 607-777-2408 *E-mail:* cwpro@binghamton.edu *Web Site:* english.binghamton.edu/cwpro, pg 619

Gillan, Maria Mazziotti, Binghamton University John Gardner Fiction Book Award, Dept of English, General Literature & Rhetoric, Library N, Rm 1149, Vestal Pkwy E, Binghamton, NY 13902 *Tel:* 607-777-2713 *Web Site:* www2.binghamton.edu/english/creative-writing, pg 632

Gillan, Maria Mazziotti, Binghamton University Milt Kessler Poetry Book Award, Dept of English, General Literature & Rhetoric, Library N, Rm 1149, Vestal Pkwy E, Binghamton, NY 13902 *Tel:* 607-777-2713 *Web Site:* www2.binghamton.edu/english/creative-writing, pg 632

Gillan, Maria Mazziotti, Allen Ginsberg Poetry Award, One College Blvd, Paterson, NJ 07505-1179 *Tel:* 973-684-6555 *Fax:* 973-523-6085 *Web Site:* www.poetrycenterpccc.com, pg 649

Gillan, Maria Mazziotti, The Paterson Poetry Prize, One College Blvd, Paterson, NJ 07505-1179 *Tel:* 973-684-6555 *Fax:* 973-523-6085 *Web Site:* www.poetrycenterpccc.com, pg 676

Gillan, Maria Mazziotti, The Paterson Prize for Books for Young People, One College Blvd, Paterson, NJ 07505-1179 *Tel:* 973-684-6555 *Fax:* 973-523-6085 *Web Site:* www.poetrycenterpccc.com, pg 677

Gillerman, Sharon, Hebrew Union College Press, 3101 Clifton Ave, Cincinnati, OH 45220 *Tel:* 513-221-1875 *Fax:* 513-221-0321 *Web Site:* press.huc.edu, pg 105

Gillespie, Christine, Alfred A Knopf/Everyman's Library, c/o Penguin Random House Inc, 1745 Broadway, New York, NY 10019 *Tel:* 212-751-2600 *Toll Free Tel:* 800-638-6460 *Fax:* 212-572-2593 *Web Site:* www.knopfdoubleday.com, pg 127

Gillespie, Christine, Pantheon Books/Schocken Books, c/o Penguin Random House Inc, 1745 Broadway, New York, NY 10019 *Tel:* 212-751-2600 *Web Site:* knopfdoubleday.com/imprint/pantheon, pg 173

Gillespie, Jennie, San Diego Christian Writers' Guild Conference, PO Box 270403, San Diego, CA 92198 *Tel:* 760-294-3269; 858-254-1402 *Fax:* 760-294-3269 *E-mail:* info@sandiegocwg.org *Web Site:* www.sandiegocwg.org, pg 614

Gillespie, Robert, San Diego Christian Writers' Guild Conference, PO Box 270403, San Diego, CA 92198 *Tel:* 760-294-3269; 858-254-1402 *Fax:* 760-294-3269 *E-mail:* info@sandiegocwg.org *Web Site:* www.sandiegocwg.org, pg 614

Gillette, Courtney, National Book Awards, 90 Broad St, Suite 604, New York, NY 10004 *Tel:* 212-685-0261 *Fax:* 212-213-6570 *E-mail:* nationalbook@nationalbook.org *Web Site:* www.nationalbook.org, pg 670

Gilliam, Ashley, Scribner, 1230 Avenue of the Americas, New York, NY 10020, pg 209

Gilligan, Rev Michael PhD, American Catholic Press (ACP), 16565 S State St, South Holland, IL 60473 *Tel:* 708-331-5485 *Fax:* 708-331-5484 *E-mail:* acp@acpress.org *Web Site:* www.acpress.org, pg 10

Gillis, Karen, St Martin's Press, LLC, 175 Fifth Ave, New York, NY 10010 *Tel:* 646-307-5151 *Web Site:* us.macmillan.com/smp, pg 204

Gilliss, Sonya, Fitzhenry & Whiteside Limited, 195 Allstate Pkwy, Markham, ON L3R 4T8, Canada *Tel:* 905-477-9700 *Toll Free Tel:* 800-387-9776 *Fax:* 905-477-2834 *Toll Free Fax:* 800-260-9777 *E-mail:* bookinfo@fitzhenry.ca; godwit@fitzhenry.ca *Web Site:* www.fitzhenry.ca, pg 457

Gilliss, Sonya, Red Deer Press Inc, 195 Allstate Pkwy, Markham, ON L3R 4T8, Canada *Tel:* 905-477-9700 *Toll Free Tel:* 800-387-9776 (orders) *E-mail:* rdp@reddeerpress.com; bookinfo@fitzhenry.ca *Web Site:* www.reddeerpress.com, pg 468

Gilly, Holly, Human Kinetics Inc, 1607 N Market St, Champaign, IL 61820 *Tel:* 217-351-5076 *Toll Free Tel:* 800-747-4457 *Fax:* 217-351-1549 (orders/cust serv) *E-mail:* info@hkusa.com *Web Site:* www.humankinetics.com, pg 112

Gilman, Dana S, J J Keller & Associates, Inc, 3003 Breezewood Lane, Neenah, WI 54957 *Tel:* 920-722-2848 *Toll Free Tel:* 877-564-2333 *Toll Free Fax:* 800-727-7516 *E-mail:* contactus@jjkeller.com; customerservice@jjkeller.com *Web Site:* www.jjkeller.com, pg 125

Gilmer, Rachel, Sourcebooks Inc, 1935 Brookdale Rd, Suite 139, Naperville, IL 60563 *Tel:* 630-961-3900 *Toll Free Tel:* 800-432-7444 *Fax:* 630-961-2168 *E-mail:* info@sourcebooks.com; customersupport@sourcebooks.com *Web Site:* www.sourcebooks.com, pg 218

Gilpin, Geoff, The Wisconsin Writers Awards, c/o 450 E Beaumont Ave, No 1005, Whitefish Bay, WI 53217-4805 *E-mail:* wiswriters@gmail.com *Web Site:* wiswriters.org/awards, pg 698

Gilpin, R Wayne, Future Horizons Inc, 721 W Abram St, Arlington, TX 76013 *Tel:* 817-277-0727 *Toll Free Tel:* 800-489-0727 *Fax:* 817-277-2270 *E-mail:* info@fhautism.com *Web Site:* www.fhautism.com, pg 89

Gingerich, Amy, Herald Press, 1251 Virginia Ave, Harrisonburg, VA 22802-2434 *Toll Free Tel:* 800-245-7894 (orders) *Toll Free Fax:* 877-271-0760 *E-mail:* info@MennoMedia.org *Web Site:* www.heraldpress.com; store.mennomedia.org, pg 106

Gingerich, Amy, MennoMedia, 1251 Virginia Ave, Harrisonburg, VA 22802-2434 *Toll Free Tel:* 800-245-7894 (orders & cust serv US) *Toll Free Fax:* 877-271-0760 *E-mail:* info@mennomedia.org *Web Site:* www.mennomedia.org, pg 148

Gingras, Dominique, Les Presses de l'Universite Laval, 2180, Chemin Sainte-Foy, 1st fl, Quebec, QC G1V 0A6, Canada *Tel:* 418-656-2803 *Fax:* 418-656-3305 *E-mail:* presses@pul.ulaval.ca *Web Site:* www.pulaval.com, pg 468

Ginna, Peter, The Center for Fiction, 17 E 47 St, New York, NY 10017 *Tel:* 212-755-6710 *Fax:* 212-826-0831 *E-mail:* info@centerforfiction.org *Web Site:* centerforfiction.org/awards, pg 563

Ginsberg, Peter L, Curtis Brown Ltd, 10 Astor Place, New York, NY 10003 *Tel:* 212-473-5400 *Web Site:* www.curtisbrown.com, pg 510

Ginsburg, Susan, Writers House, 21 W 26 St, New York, NY 10010 *Tel:* 212-685-2400 *Fax:* 212-685-1781 *Web Site:* www.writershouse.com, pg 542

Giovinazzo, Ana, DK Publishing, 345 Hudson St, 2nd fl, New York, NY 10014 *Tel:* 646-674-4000 *Toll Free Tel:* 877-342-5357 (cust serv); 800-733-3000 *Web Site:* www.dk.com; www.penguin.com, pg 71

Giovinazzo, Elena, Pippin Properties Inc, 110 W 40 St, Suite 1704, New York, NY 10018 *Tel:* 212-338-9310 *Fax:* 212-338-9579 *E-mail:* info@pippinproperties.com *Web Site:* www.pippinproperties.com; www.facebook.com/pippinproperties, pg 531

Gipson, Scott, Caxton Press, 312 Main St, Caldwell, ID 83605-3299 *Tel:* 208-459-7421 *Toll Free Tel:* 800-657-6465 *Fax:* 208-459-7450 *E-mail:* publish@caxtonpress.com *Web Site:* www.caxtonpress.com, pg 49

Giron, Robert L, Gival Press, 5200 N First St, Arlington, VA 22203 *Tel:* 703-351-0079 *Fax:* 703-351-0079 (call first) *E-mail:* givalpress@yahoo.com *Web Site:* www.givalpress.com, pg 92

Giron, Robert L, Gival Press Novel Award, PO Box 3812, Arlington, VA 22203 *Tel:* 703-351-0079 *Fax:* 703-351-0079 (call first) *E-mail:* givalpress@yahoo.com *Web Site:* www.givalpress.com; givalpress.submittable.com, pg 649

Giron, Robert L, Gival Press Oscar Wilde Award, PO Box 3812, Arlington, VA 22203 *Tel:* 703-351-0079 *Fax:* 703-351-0079 (call first) *E-mail:* givalpress@yahoo.com *Web Site:* www.givalpress.com; givalpress.submittable.com, pg 649

Giron, Robert L, Gival Press Poetry Award, PO Box 3812, Arlington, VA 22203 *Tel:* 703-351-0079 *Fax:* 703-351-0079 (call first) *E-mail:* givalpress@yahoo.com *Web Site:* www.givalpress.com; givalpress.submittable.com, pg 649

Giron, Robert L, Gival Press Short Story Award, PO Box 3812, Arlington, VA 22203 *Tel:* 703-351-0079 *Fax:* 703-351-0079 (call first) *E-mail:* givalpress@yahoo.com *Web Site:* www.givalpress.com; givalpress.submittable.com, pg 649

Giroux, Greg, Bartleby Press, 8926 Baltimore St, No 858, Savage, MD 20763 *Tel:* 301-589-5831 *Toll Free Tel:* 800-953-9929 *E-mail:* inquiries@bartlebythepublisher.com *Web Site:* www.bartlebythepublisher.com, pg 30

Giroux, Laura, United Nations Association of the United States of America, 1750 Pennsylvania Ave NW, Suite 300, Washington, DC 20006 *Tel:* 202-887-9040 *Fax:* 202-887-9021 *Web Site:* www.unausa.org, pg 580

Giroux, Steve, Teacher's Discovery, 2741 Paldan Dr, Auburn Hills, MI 48326 *Toll Free Tel:* 800-832-2437 *Toll Free Fax:* 800-287-4509 *E-mail:* help@teachersdiscovery.com *Web Site:* www.teachersdiscovery.com, pg 228

Girsch, Laurie, Professional Resource Press, 1958 Barber Rd, Sarasota, FL 34240 *Tel:* 941-343-9601 *Toll Free Tel:* 800-443-3364 (orders & cust serv) *Fax:* 941-343-9201 *Toll Free Fax:* 866-804-4843 (orders only) *E-mail:* cs.prpress@gmail.com *Web Site:* www.prpress.com, pg 189

Gisonny, Karen, The New York Public Library Helen Bernstein Book Award for Excellence in Journalism, Stephen A Schwarzman Bldg, Fifth Ave at 42 St, South Court Bldg, 3rd fl, New York, NY 10018-2788 *Tel:* 212-930-0876 *Web Site:* www.nypl.org, pg 673

Gissinger-Rivera, Beth, Adams Media, 57 Littlefield St, Avon, MA 02322 *Tel:* 508-427-7100 *Web Site:* www.simonandschuster.com, pg 4

Gladding, Jody, Vermont Studio Center Writer's Program Fellowships, 80 Pearl St, Johnson, VT 05656 *Tel:* 802-635-2727 *Fax:* 802-635-2730 *E-mail:* writing@vermontstudiocenter.org; info@vermontstudiocenter.org *Web Site:* www.vermontstudiocenter.org, pg 696

Gladney, Dave, AAP PreK-12 Learning Group, 455 Massachusetts Ave NW, Suite 700, Washington, DC 20001 *Tel:* 267-351-4310 *Fax:* 267-351-4317 *E-mail:* prek12learning@publishers.org *Web Site:* www.aepweb.org, pg 553

Gladstone, Bill, Waterside Productions Inc, 2055 Oxford Ave, Cardiff, CA 92007 *Tel:* 760-632-9190 *Fax:* 760-632-9295 *E-mail:* admin@waterside.com *Web Site:* www.waterside.com, pg 541

Glanville, Kathleen, Dustbooks, PO Box 100, Paradise, CA 95967-0100 *Tel:* 530-877-6110 *Fax:* 530-877-0222 *E-mail:* publisher@dustbooks.com; info@dustbooks.com *Web Site:* www.dustbooks.com, pg 74

Glaser, Rebecca, Amicus, PO Box 1329, Mankato, MN 56002 *Tel:* 507-388-9357 *Fax:* 507-388-1779 *E-mail:* info@amicuspublishing.us; orders@amicuspublishing.us *Web Site:* www.amicuspublishing.us, pg 16

Glasner, Lynne, Associated Editors, 27 W 96 St, New York, NY 10025 *Tel:* 212-662-9703 *Fax:* 212-662-9703, pg 488

Glass, Erica, Penguin Group USA, A Penguin Random House Company, 375 Hudson St, New York, NY 10014 *Tel:* 212-366-2000 *Toll Free Tel:* 800-847-5515 (inside sales); 800-631-8571 (cust serv) *Fax:* 212-366-2666; 607-775-4829 (inside sales) *E-mail:* online@us.penguingroup.com *Web Site:* www.penguin.com, pg 177

Glass, Joy L, Edgewise Press Inc, 24 Fifth Ave, Suite 224, New York, NY 10011 *Tel:* 212-982-4818 *Fax:* 212-982-1364 *E-mail:* epinc@mindspring.com *Web Site:* www.edgewisepress.org, pg 75

Glass, Maureen, Health Administration Press, One N Franklin St, Suite 1700, Chicago, IL 60606-3491 *Tel:* 312-424-2800 *Fax:* 312-424-0014 *E-mail:* hap1@ache.org *Web Site:* www.ache.org/publications (orders), pg 104

Glasser, Carla, The Betsy Nolan Literary Agency, 112 E 17 St, Suite 1W, New York, NY 10003 *Tel:* 212-967-8200 *Fax:* 212-967-7292 *E-mail:* dblehr@cs.com, pg 531

Glasser, Frederick, Barron's Educational Series Inc, 250 Wireless Blvd, Hauppauge, NY 11788 *Tel:* 631-434-3311 *Toll Free Tel:* 800-645-3476 *Fax:* 631-434-3723 *E-mail:* barrons@barronseduc.com *Web Site:* www.barronseduc.com, pg 30

Glasspool, Jonathan, Bloomsbury Academic, 1385 Broadway, 5th fl, New York, NY 10018 *Tel:* 212-419-5300 *Web Site:* www.bloomsbury.com/us/academic, pg 37

Glavash, Keith, Massachusetts Institute of Technology Libraries, 77 Massachusetts Ave, Bldg 14-S, Rm 0551, Cambridge, MA 02139-4307 *Tel:* 617-253-5671 *E-mail:* docs@mit.edu *Web Site:* libraries.mit.edu/docs, pg 144

Glave, Thomas, Binghamton University Creative Writing Program, c/o Dept of English, PO Box 6000, Binghamton, NY 13902-6000 *Tel:* 607-777-2168 *Fax:* 607-777-2408 *E-mail:* cwpro@binghamton.edu *Web Site:* english.binghamton.edu/cwpro, pg 619

Glaz, Linda, Hartline Literary Agency LLC, 123 Queenston Dr, Pittsburgh, PA 15235 *Web Site:* www.hartlineliterary.com, pg 520

Glazer, Lori, Houghton Mifflin Harcourt Trade & Reference Division, 125 High St, Boston, MA 02110 *Tel:* 617-351-5000 *Toll Free Tel:* 800-225-3362 *Web Site:* www.hmhco.com, pg 111

Glazner, Steve, APPA: The Association of Higher Education Facilities Officers, 1643 Prince St, Alexandria, VA 22314-2818 *Tel:* 703-684-1446 *Fax:* 703-549-2772 *Web Site:* www.appa.org, pg 18

Gleason, Bill, Society for Mining, Metallurgy & Exploration, 12999 E Adam Aircraft Circle, Englewood, CO 80112 *Tel:* 303-948-4200 *Toll Free Tel:* 800-763-3132 *Fax:* 303-973-3845 *E-mail:* cs@smenet.org; books@smenet.org *Web Site:* www.smenet.org, pg 216

Gleason, Bob, Tom Doherty Associates, LLC, 175 Fifth Ave, 14th fl, New York, NY 10010 *Tel:* 646-307-5511 *Toll Free Tel:* 800-455-0340 *Web Site:* www.tor-forge.com, pg 71

Gleason, Laura, Louisiana State University Press, 338 Johnston Hall, Baton Rouge, LA 70803 *Tel:* 225-578-6294 *Fax:* 225-578-6461 *E-mail:* lsupress@lsu.edu *Web Site:* lsupress.org, pg 138

Gleick, Betsy, Algonquin Books, 400 Silver Cedar Ct, Suite 300, Chapel Hill, NC 27514-1585 *Tel:* 919-967-0108 *Fax:* 919-933-0272 *E-mail:* inquiry@algonquin.com *Web Site:* www.workman.com/algonquin, pg 7

Glen, Annie, Friends United Press, 101 Quaker Hill Dr, Richmond, IN 47374 *Tel:* 765-962-7573 *Fax:* 765-966-1293 *E-mail:* friendspress@fum.org; orders@fum.org *Web Site:* shop.fum.org, pg 89

Glenn, Mary, Humanix Books LLC, 8 W 40 St, 20th fl, New York, NY 10804 *Toll Free Tel:* 855-371-7810 *E-mail:* info@humanixbooks.com *Web Site:* www.humanixbooks.com, pg 113

Glenn, Pam, Class Action Ink, 1300 NE 16 Ave, Suite 712, Portland, OR 97232-1483 *Tel:* 503-280-2448 *E-mail:* pamg0822@gmail.com *Web Site:* www.classactionink.com, pg 477

Glick, Stacey Kendall, Dystel, Goderich & Bourret LLC, One Union Sq W, Suite 904, New York, NY 10003 *Tel:* 212-627-9100 *Fax:* 212-627-9313 *Web Site:* www.dystel.com, pg 515

Gloeckler, Don, Advertising Research Foundation (ARF), 432 Park Ave S, 4th fl, New York, NY 10016-8013 *Tel:* 212-751-5656 *Fax:* 212-319-5265 *E-mail:* info@thearf.org; jar@thearf.org (edit) *Web Site:* www.thearf.org, pg 553

Glosband, Oliver, Shambhala Publications Inc, 4720 Walnut St, Boulder, CO 80301 *Tel:* 303-222-9598 *Toll Free Tel:* 866-424-0030 (off); 888-424-2329 (cust serv) *Fax:* 303-200-9406 *E-mail:* customercare@shambhala.com *Web Site:* www.shambhala.com, pg 211

Gloude, Carolyn, Ruth & Sylvia Schwartz Children's Book Awards, c/o Ontario Arts Council, 121 Bloor St E, 7th fl, Toronto, ON M4W 3M5, Canada *Tel:* 416-961-1660 *Toll Free Tel:* 800-387-0058 (ON) *Fax:* 416-961-7796 (Ontario Arts Council); 416-969-7450 (Ontario Arts Foundation) *E-mail:* info@arts.on.ca; foundation@arts.on.ca *Web Site:* www.arts.on.ca; ontarioartsfoundation.on.ca/pages/ruth-sylvia-schwartz-awards, pg 688

Glover, Elizabeth, University of Pennsylvania Press, 3905 Spruce St, Philadelphia, PA 19104 *Tel:* 215-898-6261 *Fax:* 215-898-0404 *E-mail:* custserv@pobox.upenn.edu *Web Site:* www.pennpress.org, pg 244

Glover, Sally, Lynne Rienner Publishers Inc, 1800 30 St, Suite 314, Boulder, CO 80301 *Tel:* 303-444-6684 *Fax:* 303-444-0824 *E-mail:* questions@rienner.com; cservice@rienner.com *Web Site:* www.rienner.com, pg 199

Gluck, Suzanne, WME, 11 Madison Ave, 18th fl, New York, NY 10010 *Tel:* 212-586-5100 *Web Site:* www.wmeentertainment.com, pg 542

Gluckman, Paul, Warren Communications News Inc, 2115 Ward Ct NW, Washington, DC 20037 *Tel:* 202-872-9200 *Toll Free Tel:* 800-771-9202 *Fax:* 202-293-3435; 202-318-8350 *E-mail:* info@warren-news.com; newsroom@warren-news.com *Web Site:* www.warren-news.com, pg 252

Glueck, Michael Wells, EditAndPublishYourBook.com, PO Box 2965, Nantucket, MA 02584-2965 *E-mail:* michaeltheauthor@yahoo.com *Web Site:* www.editandpublishyourbook.com, pg 493

Glusman, John, W W Norton & Company Inc, 500 Fifth Ave, New York, NY 10110-0017 *Tel:* 212-354-5500 *Toll Free Tel:* 800-233-4830 (orders & cust serv) *Fax:* 212-869-0856 *Toll Free Fax:* 800-458-6515 *E-mail:* orders@wwnorton.com *Web Site:* books.wwnorton.com, pg 164

Glynn, John, Harlequin Enterprises Ltd, 233 Broadway, Suite 1001, New York, NY 10279 *Tel:* 212-553-4200 *Fax:* 212-227-8969 *E-mail:* customerservice@harlequin.com *Web Site:* www.harlequin.com, pg 100

Go, Sarah Lin, Chronicle Books LLC, 680 Second St, San Francisco, CA 94107 *Tel:* 415-537-4200 *Toll Free Tel:* 800-759-0190 (cust serv) *Fax:* 415-537-4460 *Toll Free Fax:* 800-858-7787 (orders); 800-286-9471 (cust serv) *E-mail:* frontdesk@chroniclebooks.com *Web Site:* www.chroniclebooks.com, pg 55

Gobel, Ursula, Social Sciences & Humanities Research Council of Canada (SSHRC), 350 Albert St, Ottawa, ON K1P 6G4, Canada *Tel:* 613-992-0691 *E-mail:* research@sshrc-crsh.gc.ca *Web Site:* www.sshrc.ca, pg 578

Godbey, Geoffrey, Venture Publishing Inc, 1999 Cato Ave, State College, PA 16801 *Tel:* 814-234-4561 *Fax:* 814-234-1651 *E-mail:* vpublish@venturepublish.com *Web Site:* www.venturepublish.com, pg 250

Goderich, Miriam, Dystel, Goderich & Bourret LLC, One Union Sq W, Suite 904, New York, NY 10003 *Tel:* 212-627-9100 *Fax:* 212-627-9313 *Web Site:* www.dystel.com, pg 515

Godine, David R, David R Godine Publisher Inc, 15 Court Sq, Suite 320, Boston, MA 02108-4715 *Tel:* 617-451-9600 *Fax:* 617-350-0250 *E-mail:* info@godine.com *Web Site:* www.godine.com, pg 93

Godoff, Ann, Penguin Group USA, A Penguin Random House Company, 375 Hudson St, New York, NY 10014 *Tel:* 212-366-2000 *Toll Free Tel:* 800-847-5515 (inside sales); 800-631-8571 (cust serv) *Fax:* 212-366-2666; 607-775-4829 (inside sales) *E-mail:* online@us.penguingroup.com *Web Site:* www.penguin.com, pg 177

Godoff, Ann, The Penguin Press, 375 Hudson St, New York, NY 10014 *Web Site:* thepenguinpress.com, pg 178

Godwin, Laura, Henry Holt and Company, LLC, 175 Fifth Ave, New York, NY 10010 *Tel:* 646-307-5151 *Toll Free Tel:* 888-330-8477 (orders) *Fax:* 646-307-5285 *E-mail:* firstname.lastname@hholt.com *Web Site:* www.henryholt.com, pg 109

Goedkoop, Annie, The Electrochemical Society (ECS), 65 S Main St, Bldg D, Pennington, NJ 08534-2839 *Tel:* 609-737-1902 *Fax:* 609-737-2743 *E-mail:* publications@electrochem.org; customerservice@electrochem.org *Web Site:* www.electrochem.org, pg 77

Goettler, Peter, Cato Institute, 1000 Massachusetts Ave NW, Washington, DC 20001-5403 *Tel:* 202-842-0200 *Toll Free Tel:* 800-767-1241 *Fax:* 202-842-3490 *E-mail:* catostore@cato.org *Web Site:* www.cato.org, pg 49

Goetz, Adria, Martin Literary Management, 15601 32 Ave SE, Mill Creek, WA 98012 *Tel:* 206-466-1773 (no queries) *Fax:* 206-466-1774 *Web Site:* www.martinliterarymanagement.com, pg 528

Goff, Anthony, Hachette Audio, 1290 Avenue of the Americas, New York, NY 10019 *Tel:* 212-364-1100 *Web Site:* www.hachetteaudio.com, pg 98

Goff, Anthony, Hachette Book Group, 1290 Avenue of the Americas, New York, NY 10019 *Tel:* 212-364-1100 *Toll Free Tel:* 800-759-0190 (cust serv) *Fax:* 212-364-0933 (intl orders) *Toll Free Fax:* 800-286-9471 (cust serv) *Web Site:* www.hachettebookgroup.com, pg 98

Goff, Gordon, ORO editions, 31 Commercial Blvd, Suite F, Novato, CA 94949 *Tel:* 415-883-3300 *Fax:* 415-883-3309 *E-mail:* info@oroeditions.com *Web Site:* www.oroeditions.com, pg 170

Goff, Jacqui, Insight Editions, 800 "A" St, San Rafael, CA 94901 *Tel:* 415-526-1370 *Toll Free Tel:* 800-809-3792 *Toll Free Fax:* 866-509-0515 *E-mail:* info@insighteditions.com *Web Site:* www.insighteditions.com, pg 117

Goff, Jacqui, Mandala Earth, 800 "A" St, San Rafael, CA 94901 *Tel:* 415-526-1370 *Toll Free Fax:* 866-509-0515 *E-mail:* info@mandalapublishing.com *Web Site:* www.mandalaeartheditions.com, pg 141

Goff, Michael, Northeast-Midwest Institute, 50 "F" St NW, Suite 950, Washington, DC 20001 *Tel:* 202-544-5200 *Fax:* 202-544-0043 *E-mail:* info@nemw.org *Web Site:* www.nemw.org, pg 164

Goff, Raoul, Insight Editions, 800 "A" St, San Rafael, CA 94901 *Tel:* 415-526-1370 *Toll Free Tel:* 800-809-3792 *Toll Free Fax:* 866-509-0515 *E-mail:* info@insighteditions.com *Web Site:* www.insighteditions.com, pg 117

Goff, Raoul, Mandala Earth, 800 "A" St, San Rafael, CA 94901 *Tel:* 415-526-1370 *Toll Free Fax:* 866-509-0515 *E-mail:* info@mandalapublishing.com *Web Site:* www.mandalaeartheditions.com, pg 141

Goff, Steven, Channel Photographics, 980 Lincoln Ave, Suite 200-B, San Rafael, CA 94901 *Tel:* 415-456-2934 *Fax:* 415-456-4124 *Web Site:* www.channelphotographics.com, pg 52

Goff, Steven, Global Publishing, Sales & Distribution, 980 Lincoln Ave, Suite 200 B, San Rafael, CA 94901 *Tel:* 415-456-2934 *Fax:* 415-456-4124 *Web Site:* www.globalpsd.com, pg 93

Goforth, Renea, Wichita State University Playwriting Contest, 1845 Fairmount St, Box 153, Wichita, KS 67260-0153 *Tel:* 316-978-3360 *Fax:* 316-978-3202 *Web Site:* www.wichita.edu, pg 698

Goin, Carma, In-Plant Printing & Mailing Association (IPMA), 455 S Sam Barr Dr, Suite 203, Kearney, MO 64060 *Tel:* 816-919-1691 *E-mail:* ipmainfo@ipma.org *Web Site:* www.ipma.org, pg 567

Goin, Kenn, Bearport Publishing Co Inc, 45 W 21 St, Suite 3B, New York, NY 10010 *Tel:* 212-337-8577 *Toll Free Tel:* 877-337-8577 *Fax:* 212-337-8557 *Toll Free Fax:* 866-337-8557 *E-mail:* service@bearportpublishing.com; info@bearportpublishing.com *Web Site:* www.bearportpublishing.com, pg 31

Gold, Heather, Yale University Press, 302 Temple St, New Haven, CT 06511-8909 *Tel:* 203-432-0960; 203-432-0966 (sales); 401-531-2800 (cust serv) *Toll Free Tel:* 800-405-1619 (cust serv) *Fax:* 203-432-0948; 203-432-8485 (sales); 401-531-2801 (cust serv) *Toll Free Fax:* 800-406-9145 (cust serv) *E-mail:* sales.press@yale.edu (sales); customer.care@triliteral.org (cust serv) *Web Site:* www.yalebooks.com; yalepress.yale.edu/yupbooks, pg 261

Gold, Jerry, Black Heron Press, PO Box 13396, Mill Creek, WA 98082-1396 *Tel:* 425-355-4929 *Fax:* 425-355-4929 *Web Site:* blackheronpress.com, pg 36

Gold, Leslie J, PRB Productions, 963 Peralta Ave, Albany, CA 94706-2144 *Tel:* 510-526-0722 *Fax:* 510-527-4763 *E-mail:* prbprdns@aol.com *Web Site:* www.prbmusic.com, pg 186

Goldbach, Allan, Chestnut Publishing Group Inc, 44 Stubbs Dr, Suite 207, Toronto, ON M2L 2R3, Canada *Tel:* 416-224-5824 *Fax:* 416-224-0595 *Web Site:* www.chestnutpublishing.com, pg 450

Goldbaum, Milton J, Alan Wofsy Fine Arts, 1109 Geary Blvd, San Francisco, CA 94109 *Tel:* 415-292-6500 *Toll Free Tel:* 800-660-6403 *Fax:* 415-292-6594 (off & cust serv); 510-251-1840 (acctg) *E-mail:* order@art-books.com (orders); editeur@earthlink.net (edit); beauxarts@earthlink.net (cust serv) *Web Site:* www.art-books.com, pg 258

Goldberg, Arthur, Abbeville Publishing Group, 137 Varick St, Suite 504, New York, NY 10013-1105 *Tel:* 212-366-5585 *Toll Free Tel:* 800-ART-BOOK (278-2665) *Fax:* 212-366-6966 *E-mail:* abbeville@abbeville.com; marketing@abbeville.com; sales@abbeville.com; rights@abbeville.com *Web Site:* www.abbeville.com, pg 2

Goldberg, David, The MIT Press, One Rogers St, Cambridge, MA 02142 *Tel:* 617-253-5255 *Toll Free Tel:* 800-207-8354 (orders) *Fax:* 617-258-6779; 617-577-1545 (orders) *Web Site:* mitpress.mit.edu, pg 151

Goldberg, Michael, MedMaster Inc, 3337 Hollywood Oaks Dr, Fort Lauderdale, FL 33312 *Tel:* 954-962-8414 *Toll Free Tel:* 800-335-3480 *Fax:* 954-962-4508 *E-mail:* mmbks@aol.com *Web Site:* www.medmaster.net, pg 148

Goldberg, Sarah, Scribner, 1230 Avenue of the Americas, New York, NY 10020, pg 209

Goldberg, Stephen, MedMaster Inc, 3337 Hollywood Oaks Dr, Fort Lauderdale, FL 33312 *Tel:* 954-962-8414 *Toll Free Tel:* 800-335-3480 *Fax:* 954-962-4508 *E-mail:* mmbks@aol.com *Web Site:* www.medmaster.net, pg 148

Goldbetter, Larry, National Writers Union/UAW Local 1981, 256 W 38 St, Suite 703, New York, NY 10018 *Tel:* 212-254-0279 *Fax:* 212-254-0673 *E-mail:* nwu@nwu.org *Web Site:* www.nwu.org/, pg 573

Golden, Lori, Health Communications Inc, 3201 SW 15 St, Deerfield Beach, FL 33442 *Tel:* 954-360-0909 *Toll Free Tel:* 800-851-9100; 800-441-5569 (cust serv & orders) *Fax:* 954-360-0034 *Toll Free Fax:* 800-424-7652 (cust serv & orders) *E-mail:* customerservice2@hcibooks.com *Web Site:* www.hcibooks.com, pg 104

Golden, Marita, Hurston/Wright Award for College Writers, 840 First St NE, 3rd fl, Washington, DC 20002 *Tel:* 202-248-5051 *E-mail:* info@hurstonwright.org *Web Site:* www.hurstonwright.org, pg 654

Golden, Marita, Hurston/Wright Legacy Awards, 840 First St NE, 3rd fl, Washington, DC 20002 *Tel:* 202-248-5051 *E-mail:* info@hurstonwright.org *Web Site:* www.hurstonwright.org, pg 654

Golden, Marita, Hurston/Wright Writers Week, 840 First St NE, 3rd fl, Washington, DC 20002 *Tel:* 202-248-5051 *E-mail:* info@hurstonwright.org *Web Site:* www.hurstonwright.org, pg 611

Golden, Marita, The Zora Neale Hurston/Richard Wright Foundation, 840 First St NE, 3rd fl, Washington, DC 20002 *Tel:* 202-248-5051 *E-mail:* info@hurstonwright.org *Web Site:* www.hurstonwright.org, pg 583

Goldfarb, Ronald L, Goldfarb & Associates, 721 Gibbon St, Alexandria, VA 22314 *Tel:* 202-466-3030 *Fax:* 703-836-5644 *E-mail:* rlglawlit@gmail.com *Web Site:* www.ronaldgoldfarb.com, pg 519

Goldin, Camille, Ann Rittenberg Literary Agency Inc, 15 Maiden Lane, Suite 206, New York, NY 10038 *Tel:* 212-684-6936 *Fax:* 212-684-6929 *E-mail:* info@rittlit.com *Web Site:* www.rittlit.com, pg 532

Goldin, Frances, Frances Goldin Literary Agency, Inc, 214 W 29 St, Suite 410, New York, NY 10001 *Tel:* 212-777-0047 *Fax:* 212-228-1660 *E-mail:* agency@goldinlit.com *Web Site:* www.goldinlit.com, pg 519

Goldinger, Sharon, PeopleSpeak, 25401 Alicia Pkwy, Suite L-512, Laguna Hills, CA 92653 *Tel:* 949-581-6190 *Fax:* 949-581-4958 *E-mail:* pplspeak@att.net *Web Site:* www.detailsplease.com/peoplespeak, pg 499

Goldklang, Janice, Other Press, 267 Fifth Ave, 6th fl, New York, NY 10016 *Tel:* 212-414-0054 *Toll Free Tel:* 877-843-6843 *Fax:* 212-414-0939 *E-mail:* editor@otherpress.com; marketing@otherpress.com; publicity@otherpress.com *Web Site:* www.otherpress.com, pg 170

Goldman, David, Jack Scagnetti Talent & Literary Agency, 5136 Vineland Ave, North Hollywood, CA 91601 *Tel:* 818-762-3871 *Web Site:* www.jackscagnettiagency.com; www.facebook.com/jackscagnettiagency/, pg 534

Goldman, Gloria, Judaica Press Inc, 123 Ditmas Ave, Brooklyn, NY 11218 *Tel:* 718-972-6200 *Toll Free Tel:* 800-972-6201 *Fax:* 718-972-6204 *E-mail:* info@judaicapress.com; orders@judaicapress.com *Web Site:* www.judaicapress.com, pg 123

Goldman, Gloria, Soncino Press Ltd, 123 Ditmas Ave, Brooklyn, NY 11218 *Tel:* 718-972-6200 *Toll Free Tel:* 800-972-6201 *Fax:* 718-972-6204 *E-mail:* info@soncino.com *Web Site:* www.soncino.com, pg 217

Goldman, Jeff, Barron's Educational Series Inc, 250 Wireless Blvd, Hauppauge, NY 11788 *Tel:* 631-434-3311 *Toll Free Tel:* 800-645-3476 *Fax:* 631-434-3723 *E-mail:* barrons@barronseduc.com *Web Site:* www.barronseduc.com, pg 30

Goldman, Jeffrey, Santa Monica Press LLC, 215 S Hwy 101, Suite 110, Solana Beach, CA 92075 *Tel:* 858-793-1890 *Toll Free Tel:* 800-784-9553 *E-mail:* books@santamonicapress.com *Web Site:* www.santamonicapress.com, pg 206

Goldsmith, Cathy, Random House Children's Books, 1745 Broadway, 10th fl, New York, NY 10019 *Tel:* 212-782-9000 *Web Site:* www.randomhousekids.com, pg 194

Goldsmith, Michael, Doubleday/Nan A Talese, c/o Penguin Random House Inc, 1745 Broadway, New York, NY 10019 *Tel:* 212-751-2600 *Fax:* 212-572-2662 *E-mail:* ddaypub@randomhouse.com *Web Site:* knopfdoubleday.com, pg 72

Goldstein, Cary, Simon & Schuster, 1230 Avenue of the Americas, New York, NY 10020 *Tel:* 212-698-7000 *Toll Free Tel:* 800-223-2348 (cust serv); 800-223-2336 (orders) *Toll Free Fax:* 800-943-9831 (orders) *Web Site:* www.simonandschuster.com, pg 212

Goldstein, Gary, Kensington Publishing Corp, 119 W 40 St, New York, NY 10018 *Tel:* 212-407-1500 *Toll Free Tel:* 800-221-2647 *Fax:* 212-935-0699 *Web Site:* www.kensingtonbooks.com, pg 125

Goldstein, Jeff, Trans-Atlantic Publications Inc, 311 Bainbridge St, Philadelphia, PA 19147 *Tel:* 215-925-5083 *Fax:* 215-925-1912 *Web Site:* www.transatlanticpub.com; www.businesstitles.com, pg 234

Golebiewski, John, Shambhala Publications Inc, 4720 Walnut St, Boulder, CO 80301 *Tel:* 303-222-9598 *Toll Free Tel:* 866-424-0030 (off); 888-424-2329 (cust serv) *Fax:* 303-200-9406 *E-mail:* customercare@shambhala.com *Web Site:* www.shambhala.com, pg 211

Golembiewski, Joan, American Academy of Orthopaedic Surgeons (AAOS), 9400 W Higgins Rd, Rosemont, IL 60018-4976 *Tel:* 847-823-7186 *Toll Free Tel:* 800-346-2267 *E-mail:* custserv@aaos.org *Web Site:* www.aaos.org, pg 9

Golick, Jeff, Dover Publications Inc, 31 E Second St, Mineola, NY 11501-3852 *Tel:* 516-294-7000 *Toll Free Tel:* 800-223-3130 (orders) *Fax:* 516-742-6953 *E-mail:* rights@doverpublications.com; service@doverpublications.com *Web Site:* store.doverdirect.com; www.doverpublications.com, pg 72

Golikova, Maria, Groundwood Books, 128 Sterling Rd, Lower Level, Toronto, ON M6R 2B7, Canada *Tel:* 416 363-4343 *Fax:* 416-363-1017 *E-mail:* genmail@groundwoodbooks.com *Web Site:* www.houseofanansi.com, pg 458

Gollehon, John T, Gollehon Press Inc, 3655 Glenn Dr SE, Grand Rapids, MI 49546 *Tel:* 616-949-3515 *Fax:* 616-949-8674 *E-mail:* sales@gollehonbooks.com; editorial@gollehonbooks.com *Web Site:* www.gollehonbooks.com, pg 94

Gollehon, Kathy, Gollehon Press Inc, 3655 Glenn Dr SE, Grand Rapids, MI 49546 *Tel:* 616-949-3515 *Fax:* 616-949-8674 *E-mail:* sales@gollehonbooks.com; editorial@gollehonbooks.com *Web Site:* www.gollehonbooks.com, pg 94

Gollmer, Donna, American Bar Association, 321 N Clark St, Chicago, IL 60654 *Tel:* 312-988-5000 *Toll Free Tel:* 800-285-2221 (orders) *Fax:* 312-988-6281 *E-mail:* orders@abanet.org *Web Site:* www.americanbar.org, pg 10

Gollogly, Eugene, Lindisfarne Books, 610 Main St, Great Barrington, MA 01230 *Tel:* 413-528-8233 *Fax:* 413-528-8826 *E-mail:* service@steinerbooks.org *Web Site:* www.steinerbooks.org, pg 134

Gollogly, Gene, Lantern Books, 128 Second Place, Garden Suite, Brooklyn, NY 11231 *Tel:* 212-414-2275 *E-mail:* editorial@lanternbooks.com; info@lanternmedia.net *Web Site:* lanternbooks.presswarehouse.com/Home/home.aspx, pg 129

Gollogly, Gene, SteinerBooks, 610 Main St, Great Barrington, MA 01230 *Tel:* 413-528-8233 *Fax:* 413-528-8826 *E-mail:* friends@steinerbooks.org *Web Site:* steiner.presswarehouse.com, pg 222

Gollub, Matthew, Tortuga Press, 2777 Yulupa Ave, PMB 181, Santa Rosa, CA 95405 *Tel:* 707-544-4720 *Fax:* 707-595-5331 *E-mail:* info@tortugapress.com *Web Site:* www.tortugapress.com, pg 233

Golomb, Susan, Writers House, 21 W 26 St, New York, NY 10010 *Tel:* 212-685-2400 *Fax:* 212-685-1781 *Web Site:* www.writershouse.com, pg 542

Golski, Sara, Chronicle Books LLC, 680 Second St, San Francisco, CA 94107 *Tel:* 415-537-4200 *Toll Free Tel:* 800-759-0190 (cust serv) *Fax:* 415-537-4460 *Toll Free Fax:* 800-858-7787 (orders); 800-286-9471 (cust serv) *E-mail:* frontdesk@chroniclebooks.com *Web Site:* www.chroniclebooks.com, pg 55

Goncharenko, Kathy, Scholastic Canada Ltd, 604 King St W, Toronto, ON M5V 1E1, Canada *Tel:* 905-887-7323 *Toll Free Tel:* 800-268-3860 (CN) *Toll Free Fax:* 866-387-4944 *E-mail:* custserve@scholastic.ca *Web Site:* www.scholastic.ca, pg 469

Gong-Wong, Kirsten, Locus Awards, PO Box 13305, Oakland, CA 94661-0305 *Tel:* 510-339-9196 *Fax:* 510-339-9198 *E-mail:* locus@locusmag.com *Web Site:* www.locusmag.com, pg 662

Gonneville, Michel, La Fondation Emile Nelligan, 100, rue Sherbrooke, Suite 202, Montreal, QC H2X 1C3, Canada *Tel:* 514-278-4657 *Fax:* 514-278-1943 *E-mail:* info@fondation-nelligan.org *Web Site:* www.fondation-nelligan.org, pg 566

Gonneville, Michel, Prix Emile-Nelligan, 100, rue Sherbrooke, Suite 202, Montreal, QC H2X 1C3, Canada *Tel:* 514-278-4657 *Toll Free Tel:* 888-849-8540 *Fax:* 514-278-1943 *E-mail:* info@fondation-nelligan.org *Web Site:* www.fondation-nelligan.org, pg 682

Gonzales, Gail, Rodale Inc, 400 S Tenth St, Emmaus, PA 18049 *Tel:* 610-967-5171 *Toll Free Tel:* 866-387-0509 *E-mail:* bookmarketing@rodale.com; bookpublicity@rodale.com *Web Site:* www.rodale.com, pg 200

Gonzales, Kimberly, Fun in the Sun Writer's Cruise Conference, PO Box 823414, Pembroke Pines, FL 33082 *E-mail:* frwfuninthesun@yahoo.com *Web Site:* frwfuninthesunmain.blogspot.com/; www.frwriters.org, pg 610

Gonzalez, Diana, Consumer Press, 13326 SW 28 St, Suite 102, Fort Lauderdale, FL 33330-1102 *Tel:* 954-370-9153 *Fax:* 954-472-1008 *E-mail:* info@consumerpress.com *Web Site:* www.consumerpress.com, pg 60

Gonzalez, Elisa, Harry N Abrams Inc, 195 Broadway, 9th fl, New York, NY 10007 *Tel:* 212-206-7715 *Toll Free Tel:* 800-345-1359 *Fax:* 212-519-1210 *E-mail:* abrams@abramsbooks.com *Web Site:* www.abramsbooks.com, pg 3

Gonzalez, Neil, Greenleaf Book Group LLC, 3 Park Place, 4005 Banister Lane, Suite B, Austin, TX 78704 *Tel:* 512-891-6100 *Fax:* 512-891-6150 *E-mail:* contact@greenleafbookgroup.com *Web Site:* www.greenleafbookgroup.com, pg 96

Gooch, Emily, Arbordale Publishing, 612 Johnnie Dodds Blvd, Suite A2, Mount Pleasant, SC 29464 *Tel:* 843-971-6722 *Toll Free Tel:* 877-243-3457 *Fax:* 843-216-3804 *E-mail:* customerservice@arbordalepublishing.com; info@arbordalepublishing.com *Web Site:* www.arbordalepublishing.com, pg 20

Good, Kyle, Scholastic Inc, 557 Broadway, New York, NY 10012 *Tel:* 212-343-6100 *Toll Free Tel:* 800-SCHOLASTIC (724-6527) *Web Site:* www.scholastic.com, pg 208

Good, Lou Anne, House to House Publications, 11 Toll Gate Rd, Lititz, PA 17543 *Tel:* 717-627-1996 *Toll Free Tel:* 800-848-5892 *Fax:* 717-627-4004 *E-mail:* h2hp@dcfi.org *Web Site:* www.h2hp.com, pg 112

Goodfriend, Cathy, Macmillan, 175 Fifth Ave, New York, NY 10010 *Tel:* 646-307-5151 *E-mail:* press.inquiries@macmillan.com *Web Site:* www.macmillan.com, pg 140

Goodman, Arnold P, Goodman Associates, 500 West End Ave, New York, NY 10024 *Tel:* 212-873-4806, pg 519

Goodman, Christie, Intercultural Development Research Association (IDRA), 5815 Callaghan Rd, Suite 101, San Antonio, TX 78228 *Tel:* 210-444-1710 *Fax:* 210-444-1714 *E-mail:* contact@idra.org *Web Site:* www.idra.org, pg 118

Goodman, David, Writers Guild of America Awards, 7000 W Third St, Los Angeles, CA 90048 *Tel:* 323-951-4000; 323-782-4569 *Fax:* 323-782-4800 *Web Site:* www.wga.org, pg 700

Goodman, David, Writers Guild of America, West (WGAW), 7000 W Third St, Los Angeles, CA 90048 *Tel:* 323-951-4000 *Toll Free Tel:* 800-548-4532 *Fax:* 323-782-4800 *Web Site:* www.wga.org, pg 581

Goodman, Eleanor, The Pennsylvania State University Press, University Support Bldg 1, Suite C, 820 N University Dr, University Park, PA 16802-1003 *Tel:* 814-865-1327 *Toll Free Tel:* 800-326-9180 *Fax:* 814-863-1408 *Toll Free Fax:* 877-778-2665 *E-mail:* info@psupress.org *Web Site:* www.psupress.org, pg 179

Goodman, Elise Simon, Goodman Associates, 500 West End Ave, New York, NY 10024 *Tel:* 212-873-4806, pg 519

Goodman, Irene, Irene Goodman Literary Agency, 27 W 24 St, Suite 700B, New York, NY 10010 *Tel:* 212-604-0330 *E-mail:* queries@irenegoodman.com *Web Site:* www.irenegoodman.com, pg 519

Goodman, Peter, Heian, 1393 Solono Ave, Albany, CA 94706 *Tel:* 510-524-8732 *Toll Free Fax:* 888-411-8527 *E-mail:* sbp@stonebridge.com *Web Site:* www.stonebridge.com, pg 105

Goodman, Peter, Stone Bridge Press Inc, 1393 Solano Ave, Suite C, Albany, CA 94706 *Tel:* 510-524-8732 *E-mail:* sbp@stonebridge.com; sbpedit@stonebridge.com *Web Site:* www.stonebridge.com, pg 223

Goodman, Robert White, The Johns Hopkins University Press, 2715 N Charles St, Baltimore, MD 21218-4363 *Tel:* 410-516-6900; 410-516-6987 (journal orders outside US & CN) *Toll Free Tel:* 800-537-5487 (book orders & cust serv); 800-548-1784 (journal orders) *Fax:* 410-516-6968; 410-516-3866 (journal orders) *E-mail:* hfscustserv@press.jhu.edu (cust serv); jrnlcirc@press.jhu.edu (journal orders) *Web Site:* www.press.jhu.edu; muse.jhu.edu, pg 122

Goodman, Sara, St Martin's Press, LLC, 175 Fifth Ave, New York, NY 10010 *Tel:* 646-307-5151 *Web Site:* us.macmillan.com/smp, pg 204

Goodnough, Doris, Orbis Books, Price Bldg, Box 302, Maryknoll, NY 10545-0302 *Tel:* 914-941-7636 *Toll Free Tel:* 800-258-5838 (orders) *Fax:* 914-941-7005 *E-mail:* orbisbooks@maryknoll.org *Web Site:* orbisbooks.com, pg 169

Goodrich, David, American Printing History Association, PO Box 4519, Grand Central Sta, New York, NY 10163 *Tel:* 202-544-2422 *E-mail:* secretary@printinghistory.org *Web Site:* printinghistory.org, pg 556

Goodson, Kara, Photographic Society of America® (PSA®), 8241 S Walker Ave, Suite 104, Oklahoma City, OK 73139 *Tel:* 405-843-1437 *Toll Free Tel:* 855-PSA-INFO (772-4636) *Fax:* 405-843-1438 *E-mail:* hq@psa-photo.org *Web Site:* www.psa-photo.org, pg 575

Goodspeed, Brianne, Chelsea Green Publishing Co, 85 N Main St, Suite 120, White River Junction, VT 05001 *Tel:* 802-295-6300 *Toll Free Tel:* 800-639-4099 (cust serv, consumer & trade orders) *Fax:* 802-295-6444 *Web Site:* www.chelseagreen.com, pg 53

Goodwin, Bryan, Greenleaf Book Group LLC, 3 Park Place, 4005 Banister Lane, Suite B, Austin, TX 78704 *Tel:* 512-891-6100 *Fax:* 512-891-6150 *E-mail:* contact@greenleafbookgroup.com *Web Site:* www.greenleafbookgroup.com, pg 96

Goodwin, John, Galaxy Press, 7051 Hollywood Blvd, Suite 200, Hollywood, CA 90028 *Tel:* 323-466-7815 *Toll Free Tel:* 877-8GALAXY (842-5299) *E-mail:* info@galaxypress.com; customers@galaxypress.com *Web Site:* www.galaxypress.com, pg 89

Goody, Margo, Macmillan Audio, 175 Fifth Ave, New York, NY 10010 *Tel:* 646-307-5151 *Toll Free Tel:* 888-330-8477 (cust serv) *Fax:* 917-534-0980 *Web Site:* www.macmillanaudio.com, pg 140

Goodyear-Grant, Dr Elizabeth, Institute of Intergovernmental Relations, Queen's University, Robert Sutherland Hall, Rm 301, Kingston, ON K7L 3N6, Canada *Tel:* 613-533-2080 *Fax:* 613-533-6868 *E-mail:* iigr@queensu.ca *Web Site:* www.queensu.ca/iigr, pg 460

Goossen, Chad, PrairieView Press Ltd, PO Box 460, Gretna, MB R0G 0V0, Canada *Tel:* 204-327-6543 *Toll Free Tel:* 800-477-7377 *Toll Free Fax:* 866-480-0253 *Web Site:* www.prairieviewpress.com, pg 467

Goossen, Chester, PrairieView Press Ltd, PO Box 460, Gretna, MB R0G 0V0, Canada *Tel:* 204-327-6543 *Toll Free Tel:* 800-477-7377 *Toll Free Fax:* 866-480-0253 *Web Site:* www.prairieviewpress.com, pg 467

Gordon, Annette, Clarity Press Inc, 2625 Piedmont Rd NE, Suite 56, Atlanta, GA 30324 *Toll Free Tel:* 877-613-1495 (edit) *Toll Free Fax:* 877-613-7868 *E-mail:* claritypress@usa.net (foreign rts & perms) *Web Site:* www.claritypress.com, pg 56

Gordon, Ariel, University of Manitoba Press, University of Manitoba, 301 St Johns College, 92 Dysart Rd, Winnipeg, MB R3T 2M5, Canada *Tel:* 204-474-9495 *Fax:* 204-474-7566 *E-mail:* uofmpress@umanitoba.ca *Web Site:* uofmpress.ca, pg 474

Gordon, Brent, Penguin Random House Inc, 1745 Broadway, New York, NY 10019 *Tel:* 212-782-9000 *Toll Free Tel:* 800-726-0600 *Web Site:* www.penguinrandomhouse.com, pg 178

Gordon, Clayton, Illuminating Engineering Society of North America (IES), 120 Wall St, 17th fl, New York, NY 10005-4001 *Tel:* 212-248-5000 *Fax:* 212-248-5017; 212-248-5018 *E-mail:* ies@ies.org *Web Site:* www.ies.org, pg 114

Gordon, Douglas C, P M Gordon Associates Inc, 2115 Wallace St, Philadelphia, PA 19130 *Tel:* 215-769-2525 *E-mail:* pmga@pond1.net *Web Site:* www.pmgordonassociates.com, pg 495

Gordon, Jason, Writers Guild of America, East (WGAE), 250 Hudson St, Suite 700, New York, NY 10013 *Tel:* 212-767-7800 *Fax:* 212-582-1909 *Web Site:* www.wgaeast.org, pg 581

Gordon, Kathryn, HarperCollins General Books Group, 195 Broadway, New York, NY 10007 *Tel:* 212-207-7000 *Web Site:* www.harpercollins.com, pg 101

Gordon, Leah, Alcuin Society, PO Box 3216, Sta Terminal, Vancouver, BC V6B 3X8, Canada *Tel:* 604-732-5403 *E-mail:* info@alcuinsociety.com; awards@alcuinsociety.com *Web Site:* alcuinsociety.com, pg 553

Gordon, Leah, Alcuin Society Awards for Excellence in Book Design in Canada, PO Box 3216, Sta Terminal, Vancouver, BC V6B 3X8, Canada *Tel:* 604-732-5403 *E-mail:* awards@alcuinsociety.com *Web Site:* alcuinsociety.com, pg 626

Gordon, Leah, Perseus Books, 250 W 57 St, 15th fl, New York, NY 10107 *Tel:* 212-340-8100 *Toll Free Tel:* 800-343-4499 (cust serv) *Fax:* 212-340-8105 *Web Site:* www.perseusbooks.com, pg 180

Gordon, Lindsay, Avery, 375 Hudson St, New York, NY 10014 *Tel:* 212-366-2000 *Fax:* 212-366-2643 *Web Site:* www.penguin.com; www.penguinrandomhouse.com, pg 27

Gordon, Marilyn, Baker Books, PO Box 6287, Grand Rapids, MI 49516-6287 *Tel:* 616-676-9185 *Toll Free Tel:* 800-877-2665; 800-679-1957 *Fax:* 616-676-9573 *Toll Free Fax:* 800-398-3111 *Web Site:* www.bakerpublishinggroup.com, pg 28

Gordon, Marilyn, Revell, PO Box 6287, Grand Rapids, MI 49516-6287 *Tel:* 616-676-9185 *Toll Free Tel:* 800-877-2665; 800-679-1957 *Fax:* 616-676-9573 *Web Site:* www.bakerpublishinggroup.com, pg 198

Gordon, Peggy M, P M Gordon Associates Inc, 2115 Wallace St, Philadelphia, PA 19130 *Tel:* 215-769-2525 *E-mail:* pmga@pond1.net *Web Site:* www.pmgordonassociates.com, pg 495

Gordon, Peter, Cambridge University Press, 1 Liberty Plaza, 20th fl, New York, NY 10006 *Tel:* 212-924-3900; 212-337-5000 *Fax:* 212-691-3239 *E-mail:* newyork@cambridge.org *Web Site:* www.cambridge.org/us, pg 46

Gordon, Robert, Players Press Inc, PO Box 1132, Studio City, CA 91614-0132 *Tel:* 818-789-4980 *E-mail:* playerspress@att.net, pg 184

Gordon, Rose Corbett, Corbett Gordon Co, 6 Fort Rachel Place, Mystic, CT 06355 *Tel:* 860-536-4108 *Fax:* 860-536-3732 *E-mail:* corbettgordon@comcast.net, pg 492

Gordon, Russell, Simon & Schuster Children's Publishing, 1230 Avenue of the Americas, New York, NY 10020 *Tel:* 212-698-7000 *Web Site:* www.simonandschuster.com/kids; www.simonandschuster.com/teen; simonandschuster.net; simonandschuster.biz, pg 213

Gore, Clelia, Martin Literary Management, 15601 32 Ave SE, Mill Creek, WA 98012 *Tel:* 206-466-1773 (no queries) *Fax:* 206-466-1774 *Web Site:* www.martinliterarymanagement.com, pg 528

Gore, Janet, Great Potential Press Inc, 1650 N Kolb Rd, Suite 200, Tucson, AZ 85715 *Tel:* 520-777-6161 *Fax:* 520-777-6217 *Web Site:* www.greatpotentialpress.com, pg 95

Gorg, Brian, Educational Book & Media Association (EBMA), 11 Main St, Suite D, Warrenton, VA 20186 *Tel:* 540-318-7770 *Fax:* 202-962-3939 *E-mail:* info@edupaperback.org *Web Site:* www.edupaperback.org, pg 565

Gorg, Brian, Jeremiah Ludington Award, 11 Main St, Suite D, Warrenton, VA 20186 *Tel:* 540-318-7770 *Fax:* 202-962-3939 *E-mail:* info@edupaperback.org *Web Site:* www.edupaperback.org, pg 663

Gorham, Sarah, Sarabande Books Inc, 2234 Dundee Rd, Suite 200, Louisville, KY 40205 *Tel:* 502-458-4028 *Fax:* 502-458-4065 *E-mail:* info@sarabandebooks.org *Web Site:* www.sarabandebooks.org, pg 206

Gorman, Don, Rocky Mountain Books Ltd (RMB), 103-1075 Pendergast St, Victoria, BC V8V 0A1, Canada *Tel:* 250-360-0829 *Fax:* 250-386-0829 *Web Site:* www.rmbooks.com, pg 469

Gorman, Maire, Houghton Mifflin Harcourt Trade & Reference Division, 125 High St, Boston, MA 02110 *Tel:* 617-351-5000 *Toll Free Tel:* 800-225-3362 *Web Site:* www.hmhco.com, pg 111

Gorman, Roberta, Society of Motion Picture & Television Engineers® (SMPTE®), 3 Barker Ave, 5th fl, White Plains, NY 10601 *Tel:* 914-761-1100 *Fax:* 914-761-3115 *Web Site:* www.smpte.org, pg 578

Gosling, Anthony, Crossway, 1300 Crescent St, Wheaton, IL 60187 *Tel:* 630-682-4300 *Toll Free Tel:* 800-635-7993 (orders); 800-543-1659 (cust serv) *Fax:* 630-682-4785 *E-mail:* info@crossway.org *Web Site:* www.crossway.org, pg 65

Gosnell, Jason, West Virginia University Press, West Virginia University, PO Box 6295, Morgantown, WV 26506-6295 *Tel:* 304-293-8400 *Fax:* 304-293-6585 *Web Site:* www.wvupress.com, pg 254

Gosse, Jonathan F, American Technical Publishers Inc, 10100 Orland Pkwy, Suite 200, Orland Park, IL 60467-5756 *Toll Free Tel:* 800-323-3471 *Fax:* 708-957-1101 *E-mail:* service@atplearning.com; order@atplearning.com *Web Site:* www.atplearning.com, pg 15

Gossett, Bruce, American Society of Civil Engineers (ASCE), 1801 Alexander Bell Dr, Reston, VA 20191-4400 *Tel:* 703-295-6300 *Toll Free Tel:* 800-548-2723 *Fax:* 703-295-6278 *E-mail:* ascelibrary@asce.org *Web Site:* www.asce.org, pg 15

Gottier, Aaron, P & R Publishing Co, 1102 Marble Hill Rd, Phillipsburg, NJ 08865 *Tel:* 908-454-0505 *Toll Free Tel:* 800-631-0094 *Fax:* 908-859-2390 *E-mail:* sales@prpbooks.com; info@prpbooks.com *Web Site:* www.prpbooks.com, pg 172

Gottlieb, Mark, Trident Media Group LLC, 41 Madison Ave, 36th fl, New York, NY 10010 *Tel:* 212-333-1511 *E-mail:* info@tridentmediagroup.com; press@tridentmediagroup.com *Web Site:* www.tridentmediagroup.com, pg 540

Gottlieb, Richard, Grey House Publishing Inc™, 4919 Rte 22, Amenia, NY 12501 *Tel:* 518-789-8700 *Toll Free Tel:* 800-562-2139 *Fax:* 518-789-0556 *E-mail:* books@greyhouse.com; customerservice@greyhouse.com *Web Site:* www.greyhouse.com, pg 96

Gottlieb, Robert, Trident Media Group LLC, 41 Madison Ave, 36th fl, New York, NY 10010 *Tel:* 212-333-1511 *E-mail:* info@tridentmediagroup.com; press@tridentmediagroup.com *Web Site:* www.tridentmediagroup.com, pg 540

Gottstein, Adam, Volcano Press, 21496 National St, Volcano, CA 95689 *Tel:* 209-296-7989 *E-mail:* sales@volcanopress.com *Web Site:* www.volcanopress.com, pg 251

Gougeon, Emma, Georges Borchardt Inc, 136 E 57 St, New York, NY 10022 *Tel:* 212-753-5785 *E-mail:* georges@gbagency.com *Web Site:* www.gbagency.com, pg 509

Gougeon, Guy, Flammarion Quebec, 375 Ave Laurier W, Montreal, QC H2V 2K3, Canada *Tel:* 514-277-8807 *Fax:* 514-278-2085 *E-mail:* info@flammarion.qc.ca *Web Site:* www.flammarion.qc.ca, pg 457

Gouhin, Patrick, International Society of Automation (ISA), 67 T W Alexander Dr, Research Triangle Park, NC 27709-0185 *Tel:* 919-549-8411 *Fax:* 919-549-8288 *E-mail:* info@isa.org *Web Site:* www.isa.org, pg 120

Gould, Barbara, National Magazine Awards, 2300 Yonge St, Suite 1600, Toronto, ON M4P 1E4, Canada *Tel:* 416-939-6200 *E-mail:* staff@magazine-awards.com *Web Site:* www.magazine-awards.com; twitter.com/magawards, pg 671

Gould, Morgan, Houghton Mifflin Harcourt, 125 High St, Boston, MA 02110 *Tel:* 617-351-5000 *Toll Free Tel:* 855-969-4642; 800-225-5425 (K-12 educ materials); 800-323-9540 (assessment materials); 877-219-1537 (SkillsTutor); 888-242-6747 (Innovation in Educ Group); 800-225-3362 (Trade & Ref Div) *Toll Free Fax:* 800-269-5232 *E-mail:* myhmhco@hmhco.com *Web Site:* www.hmhco.com, pg 110

Gould, Robert, Big Guy Books Inc, 1042 N El Camino Real, Suite B-231, Encinitas, CA 92024 *Tel:* 760-652-5360 *Toll Free Tel:* 800-536-3030 (booksellers' cust serv) *Fax:* 760-652-5362 *E-mail:* info@bigguybooks.com *Web Site:* www.bigguybooks.com, pg 35

Gould, Scott, RLR Associates Ltd, 7 W 51 St, New York, NY 10019 *Tel:* 212-541-8641 *Fax:* 212-262-7084 *Web Site:* www.rlrassociates.net, pg 533

Gourlay, Jonathan, MacDowell Fellowships, 100 High St, Peterborough, NH 03458 *Tel:* 603-924-3886 *Fax:* 603-924-9142 *E-mail:* info@macdowellcolony.org; admissions@macdowellcolony.org *Web Site:* www.macdowellcolony.org, pg 664

Gourlay, Jonathan, Charlotte Sheedy Fellowship, 100 High St, Peterborough, NH 03458 *Tel:* 603-924-3886 *Fax:* 603-924-9142 *E-mail:* admissions@macdowellcolony.org *Web Site:* www.macdowellcolony.org, pg 689

Gouzoules, Leon, Firefly Books Ltd, 50 Staples Ave, Unit 1, Richmond Hill, ON L4B 0A7, Canada *Tel:* 416-499-8412 *Toll Free Tel:* 800-387-6192 (CN); 800-387-5085 (US) *Fax:* 416-499-8313 *Toll Free Fax:* 800-450-0391 (CN); 800-565-6034 (US) *E-mail:* info@fireflybooks.com *Web Site:* www.fireflybooks.com, pg 456

Governa, Mark, Perseus Books, 250 W 57 St, 15th fl, New York, NY 10107 *Tel:* 212-340-8100 *Toll Free Tel:* 800-343-4499 (cust serv) *Fax:* 212-340-8105 *Web Site:* www.perseusbooks.com, pg 181

Goyette, Sue, Writers' Federation of Nova Scotia, 1113 Marginal Rd, Halifax, NS B3H 4P7, Canada *Tel:* 902-423-8116 *Fax:* 902-422-0881 *E-mail:* contact@writers.ns.ca *Web Site:* writers.ns.ca, pg 581

Grace, Mina, American Correctional Association, 206 N Washington St, Suite 200, Alexandria, VA 22314 *Tel:* 703-224-0000 *Toll Free Tel:* 800-222-5646 *Fax:* 703-224-0179 *E-mail:* publications@aca.org *Web Site:* www.aca.org, pg 11

Grad, Doug, Doug Grad Literary Agency Inc, 68 Jay St, Suite W11, Brooklyn, NY 11201-1189 *Tel:* 718-788-6067 *E-mail:* query@dgliterary.com *Web Site:* www.dgliterary.com, pg 519

Gradel, Melissa Ford, Editor's Award, 90 Broad St, Suite 2100, New York, NY 10004 *Tel:* 212-226-3586 *Fax:* 212-226-3963 *Web Site:* www.pw.org/about-us/sponsored-prizes, pg 643

Gradel, Melissa Ford, Poets & Writers Inc, 90 Broad St, Suite 2100, New York, NY 10004 *Tel:* 212-226-3586 *Fax:* 212-226-3963 *E-mail:* admin@pw.org *Web Site:* www.pw.org, pg 576

Grady, Cindy, WriteLife LLC, 2323 S 171 St, Suite 202, Omaha, NE 68130 *Tel:* 402-934-1412 *Toll Free Tel:* 877-974-8354 *E-mail:* info@writelife.com *Web Site:* www.writelife.com; www.facebook.com/WriteLife, pg 260

Grady, Lynn, HarperCollins General Books Group, 195 Broadway, New York, NY 10007 *Tel:* 212-207-7000 *Web Site:* www.harpercollins.com, pg 101

Grady, Thomas, Ave Maria Press, PO Box 428, Notre Dame, IN 46556 *Tel:* 574-287-2831 *Toll Free Tel:* 800-282-1865 *Fax:* 574-239-2904 *Toll Free Fax:* 800-282-5681 *E-mail:* avemariapress.1@nd.edu *Web Site:* www.avemariapress.com, pg 26

Graff, Emily, Simon & Schuster, 1230 Avenue of the Americas, New York, NY 10020 *Tel:* 212-698-7000 *Toll Free Tel:* 800-223-2348 (cust serv); 800-223-2336 (orders) *Toll Free Fax:* 800-943-9831 (orders) *Web Site:* www.simonandschuster.com, pg 212

Graff, Kim, BISG Industry Awards, 1412 Broadway, Suite 2119, New York, NY 10018 *Tel:* 646-336-7141 *E-mail:* info@bisg.org *Web Site:* www.bisg.org/bisg-industry-awards, pg 632

Graff, Kim, Book Industry Study Group Inc (BISG), 1412 Broadway, Suite 2119, New York, NY 10018 *Tel:* 646-336-7141 *E-mail:* info@bisg.org *Web Site:* bisg.org, pg 560

Grafton, John, Dover Publications Inc, 31 E Second St, Mineola, NY 11501-3852 *Tel:* 516-294-7000 *Toll Free Tel:* 800-223-3130 (orders) *Fax:* 516-742-6953 *E-mail:* rights@doverpublications.com; service@doverpublications.com *Web Site:* store.doverdirect.com; www.doverpublications.com, pg 72

Graham, Alexander T, Council for Exceptional Children (CEC), 2900 Crystal Dr, Suite 100, Arlington, VA 22202 *Toll Free Tel:* 888-232-7733; 866-915-5000 (TTY) *E-mail:* service@cec.sped.org *Web Site:* www.cec.sped.org, pg 62

Graham, Bonny, National Council of Teachers of English (NCTE), 1111 W Kenyon Rd, Urbana, IL 61801-1096 *Tel:* 217-328-3870 *Toll Free Tel:* 877-369-6283 (cust serv) *Fax:* 217-328-9645 *E-mail:* orders@ncte.org *Web Site:* www.ncte.org, pg 158

Graham, Don, University of Texas at Austin, New Writers Project, Dept of English, Calhoun Hall, Rm 226, 204 W 21 St, B-5000, Austin, TX 78712 *Tel:* 512-471-5132; 512-471-4991 *Fax:* 512-471-4909 *Web Site:* newwritersproject.org, pg 623

Graham, Earl, Graham Agency, 115 W 45 St, Suite 505, New York, NY 10036 *Tel:* 212-489-7730, pg 519

Graham, Jon, Bear & Co Inc, One Park St, Rochester, VT 05767 *Tel:* 802-767-3174 *Toll Free Tel:* 800-932-3277 *Fax:* 802-767-3726 *E-mail:* customerservice@InnerTraditions.com *Web Site:* InnerTraditions.com, pg 31

Graham, Jon, Inner Traditions International Ltd, One Park St, Rochester, VT 05767 *Tel:* 802-767-3174 *Toll Free Tel:* 800-246-8648 *Fax:* 802-767-3726 *E-mail:* customerservice@InnerTraditions.com *Web Site:* www.InnerTraditions.com, pg 117

Graham, Joseph, The American Chemical Society, 1155 16 St NW, Washington, DC 20036 *Tel:* 202-872-4600 *Toll Free Tel:* 800-227-5558 (US) *Fax:* 202-872-6067 *E-mail:* help@acs.org *Web Site:* www.acs.org, pg 10

Graham, Kathleen, Society of American Business Editors & Writers Inc (SABEW), Walter Cronkite School of Journalism & Mass Communication, Arizona State University, 555 N Central Ave, Suite 406E, Phoenix, AZ 85004-1248 *Tel:* 602-496-7862 *Fax:* 602-496-7041 *E-mail:* sabew@sabew.org *Web Site:* sabew.org, pg 578

Graham, Nan, Scribner, 1230 Avenue of the Americas, New York, NY 10020, pg 209

Graham, Phil, F+W Media Inc, 10151 Carver Rd, Suite 200, Blue Ash, OH 45242 *Tel:* 513-531-2690 *Toll Free Tel:* 800-289-0963 (trade accts); 800-258-0929 (cust serv) *E-mail:* contact_us@fwmedia.com *Web Site:* www.fwcommunity.com, pg 82

Graham, Phil, Writer's Digest, 10151 Carver Rd, Suite 200, Blue Ash, OH 45242 *Tel:* 513-531-2690 *Toll Free Tel:* 800-289-0963 *E-mail:* writersdigest@fwmedia.com (edit) *Web Site:* www.writersdigest.com, pg 260

Graham, Rachel, National Geographic Books, 1145 17 St NW, Washington, DC 20036-4688 *Tel:* 202-857-7000 *Toll Free Tel:* 877-866-6486 *E-mail:* ngbooks@cdsfulfillment.com *Web Site:* www.nationalgeographic.com/books/; ngbooks.buysub.com, pg 158

Graham, Stephanie, Sourcebooks Inc, 1935 Brookdale Rd, Suite 139, Naperville, IL 60563 *Tel:* 630-961-3900 *Toll Free Tel:* 800-432-7444 *Fax:* 630-961-2168 *E-mail:* info@sourcebooks.com; customersupport@sourcebooks.com *Web Site:* www.sourcebooks.com, pg 218

Graham, Wendy, Scholastic Canada Ltd, 604 King St W, Toronto, ON M5V 1E1, Canada *Tel:* 905-887-7323 *Toll Free Tel:* 800-268-3860 (CN) *Toll Free Fax:* 866-387-4944 *E-mail:* custserve@scholastic.ca *Web Site:* www.scholastic.ca, pg 469

Grahek, Greg, AACC International, 3340 Pilot Knob Rd, St Paul, MN 55121 *Tel:* 651-454-7250 *Fax:* 651-454-0766 *E-mail:* aacc@scisoc.org *Web Site:* www.aaccnet.org, pg 1

Grahek, Greg, APS PRESS, 3340 Pilot Knob Rd, St Paul, MN 55121 *Tel:* 651-454-7250 *Toll Free Tel:* 800-328-7560 *Fax:* 651-454-0766 *E-mail:* aps@scisoc.org *Web Site:* www.shopapspress.org, pg 19

Grahek, Greg, Eagan Press, 3340 Pilot Knob Rd, St Paul, MN 55121 *Tel:* 651-454-7250 *Toll Free Tel:* 800-328-7560 *Fax:* 651-454-0766 *E-mail:* aacc@scisoc.org *Web Site:* www.aaccnet.org, pg 74

Grain, Tim, Birch Brook Press, PO Box 81, Delhi, NY 13753-0081 *Tel:* 607-746-7453 (book sales & prodn) *Fax:* 607-746-7453 *E-mail:* birchbrook@copper.net *Web Site:* www.birchbrookpress.info, pg 35

Grainger, Jeremy, Rutgers University Press, 106 Somerset St, 3rd fl, New Brunswick, NJ 08901 *Tel:* 848-445-7762 *Toll Free Tel:* 800-848-6224 (orders only) *Fax:* 732-745-4935 (acqs, edit, mktg, perms & prodn) *Toll Free Fax:* 800-272-6817 (fulfillment) *Web Site:* rutgerspress.rutgers.edu, pg 202

Grajkowski, Michelle, 3 Seas Literary Agency, PO Box 444, Sun Prairie, WI 53590 *Tel:* 608-834-9317 *E-mail:* threeseaslit@aol.com *Web Site:* threeseasagency.com, pg 539

Gramaglia, Maria Pia, Rizzoli International Publications Inc, 300 Park Ave S, 4th fl, New York, NY 10010-5399 *Tel:* 212-387-3400 *Toll Free Tel:* 800-522-6657 (orders only) *Fax:* 212-387-3535 *E-mail:* publicity@rizzoliusa.com *Web Site:* www.rizzoliusa.com, pg 199

Grames, Juliet, Soho Press Inc, 853 Broadway, New York, NY 10003 *Tel:* 212-260-1900 *E-mail:* soho@sohopress.com; publicity@sohopress.com; contact@sohopress.com *Web Site:* www.sohopress.com, pg 216

Granada, Lina, Brandt & Hochman Literary Agents Inc, 1501 Broadway, Suite 2310, New York, NY 10036 *Tel:* 212-840-5760 *Fax:* 212-840-5776 *Web Site:* brandthochman.com, pg 509

Granahan, Marcie, Miles Conrad Memorial Lecture, 801 Compass Way, Suite 201, Annapolis, MD 21401 *Tel:* 443-221-2980 *Fax:* 443-221-2981 *E-mail:* nfais@nfais.org *Web Site:* www.nfais.org, pg 638

Granahan, Marcie, National Federation of Advanced Information Services (NFAIS), 801 Compass Way, Suite 201, Annapolis, MD 21401 *Tel:* 443-221-2980 *Fax:* 443-221-2981 *E-mail:* nfais@nfais.org *Web Site:* www.nfais.org, pg 572

Grandstaff, Emily, The University of Virginia Press, PO Box 400318, Charlottesville, VA 22904-4318 *Tel:* 434-924-3468 (cust serv); 434-924-3469 (cust serv) *Toll Free Tel:* 800-831-3406 (orders) *Fax:* 434-982-2655 *Toll Free Fax:* 877-288-6400 *E-mail:* vapress@virginia.edu *Web Site:* www.upress.virginia.edu, pg 245

Granger, David, Aevitas Creative Management, 19 W 21 St, Suite 501, New York, NY 10010 *Tel:* 212-765-6900 *Web Site:* aevitascreative.com, pg 506

Granger, Heather, The Connecticut Law Tribune, 201 Ann Uccello St, 4th fl, Hartford, CT 06103 *Tel:* 860-527-7900 *Toll Free Tel:* 877-256-2472 *Web Site:* www.ctlawtribune.com/book-center; www.lawcatalog.com, pg 60

Grant, Donna, University of Regina Press, 2 Research Dr, Suite 246, Regina, SK S4S 7H9, Canada *Tel:* 306-585-4758 *Fax:* 306-585-4699 *E-mail:* uofrpress@uregina.ca *Web Site:* uofrpress.ca, pg 474

Grant, Gavin J, Small Beer Press, 150 Pleasant St, No 306, Easthampton, MA 01027 *Tel:* 413-203-1636 *Fax:* 413-203-1636 *E-mail:* info@smallbeerpress.com *Web Site:* smallbeerpress.com, pg 215

Grant, Janet Kobobel, Books & Such, 52 Mission Circle, Suite 122, PMB 170, Santa Rosa, CA 95409-5370 *Tel:* 707-538-4184 *Web Site:* booksandsuch.com, pg 509

Grantham, Charles E, Contemporary Publishing Co of Raleigh Inc, 5849 Lease Lane, Raleigh, NC 27617 *Tel:* 919-851-8221 *Fax:* 919-851-6666 *E-mail:* questions@contemporarypublishing.com *Web Site:* www.contemporarypublishing.com, pg 60

Grathwohl, Casper, Oxford University Press USA, 198 Madison Ave, New York, NY 10016 *Tel:* 212-726-6000 *Toll Free Tel:* 800-451-7556 (orders); 800-445-9714 (cust serv) *Fax:* 919-677-1303 *E-mail:* custserv.us@oup.com *Web Site:* www.oup.com/us, pg 171

Gratz, Mike, Olde & Oppenheim Publishers, 3219 N Margate Place, Chandler, AZ 85224 *E-mail:* olde_oppenheim@hotmail.com, pg 167

Grau, Julie, Random House Publishing Group, 1745 Broadway, New York, NY 10019 *Toll Free Tel:* 800-200-3552 *Web Site:* atrandom.com, pg 195

Grauman, Judith, The Guilford Press, 370 Seventh Ave, Suite 1200, New York, NY 10001-1020 *Tel:* 212-431-9800 *Toll Free Tel:* 800-365-7006 *Fax:* 212-966-6708 *E-mail:* info@guilford.com *Web Site:* www.guilford.com, pg 97

Gray, Alyssa, Hebrew Union College Press, 3101 Clifton Ave, Cincinnati, OH 45220 *Tel:* 513-221-1875 *Fax:* 513-221-0321 *Web Site:* press.huc.edu, pg 105

Gray, Carolyn, The Manitoba Writers' Guild Inc, 218-100 Arthur St, Winnipeg, MB R3B 1H3, Canada *Tel:* 204-944-8013 *E-mail:* info@mbwriter.mb.ca *Web Site:* www.mbwriter.mb.ca, pg 569

Gray, Catherine Moreton, Business & Legal Resources Inc, 100 Winners Circle, Suite 300, Brentwood, TN 37027 *Tel:* 860-510-0100 *Toll Free Tel:* 800-727-5257 *E-mail:* service@blr.com *Web Site:* www.blr.com, pg 45

Gray, David, Gray & Company Publishers, 1588 E 40 St, Suite 3A, Cleveland, OH 44103 *Tel:* 216-431-2665 *Toll Free Tel:* 800-915-3609 *E-mail:* sales@grayco.com; editorial@grayco.com; support@grayco.com; publicity@grayco.com *Web Site:* www.grayco.com, pg 95

Gray, Jason, Association of Writers & Writing Programs (AWP), George Mason University, 4400 University Dr, MSN 1E3, Fairfax, VA 22030 *Tel:* 703-993-4301 *Fax:* 703-993-4302 *E-mail:* awp@awpwriter.org *Web Site:* www.awpwriter.org, pg 559

Gray, Jason, AWP Award Series, George Mason University, 4400 University Dr, MSN 1E3, Fairfax, VA 22030 *Tel:* 703-993-4301 *Fax:* 703-993-4302 *E-mail:* awp@awpwriter.org *Web Site:* www.awpwriter.org, pg 629

Gray, Phil, Self-Realization Fellowship Publishers, 3208 Humboldt St, Los Angeles, CA 90031 *Tel:* 323-276-6002 *Toll Free Tel:* 888-773-8680 *Fax:* 323-927-1624 *E-mail:* sales@yogananda-srf.org *Web Site:* www.yogananda-srf.org; bookstore.yogananda-srf.org/ (orders), pg 210

Gray, Thomas, Upper Access Inc, 87 Upper Access Rd, Hinesburg, VT 05461 *Tel:* 802-482-2988 *Toll Free Tel:* 800-310-8320 (orders) *Fax:* 802-417-3002 *E-mail:* info@upperaccess.com *Web Site:* www.upperaccess.com, pg 248

Graziani, Mike, SLACK® Incorporated, A Wyanoke Group Company, 6900 Grove Rd, Thorofare, NJ 08086-9447 *Tel:* 856-848-1000 *Toll Free Tel:* 800-257-8290 *Fax:* 856-848-6091 *E-mail:* sales@slackinc.com; editor@slackinc.com; customerservice@slackinc.com *Web Site:* www.healio.com/books, pg 215

Grebenar, Sandy, Houghton Mifflin Harcourt Trade & Reference Division, 125 High St, Boston, MA 02110 *Tel:* 617-351-5000 *Toll Free Tel:* 800-225-3362 *Web Site:* www.hmhco.com, pg 111

Greber, Erika, Random House Publishing Group, 1745 Broadway, New York, NY 10019 *Toll Free Tel:* 800-200-3552 *Web Site:* atrandom.com, pg 195

Grecco, Melissa, Chronicle Books LLC, 680 Second St, San Francisco, CA 94107 *Tel:* 415-537-4200 *Toll Free Tel:* 800-759-0190 (cust serv) *Fax:* 415-537-4460 *Toll Free Fax:* 800-858-7787 (orders); 800-286-9471 (cust serv) *E-mail:* frontdesk@chroniclebooks.com *Web Site:* www.chroniclebooks.com, pg 55

Greco, Al, Carson-Dellosa Publishing LLC, PO Box 35665, Greensboro, NC 27425-5665 *Tel:* 336-632-0084 *Toll Free Tel:* 800-321-0943 *Fax:* 336-632-0087 *Toll Free Fax:* 800-535-2669 *E-mail:* custsvc@carsondellosa.com *Web Site:* www.carsondellosa.com, pg 48

Greco, Albert N, Fordham University, Graduate School of Business Administration, Gabelli School of Business, 441 E Fordham Rd, Hughes Hall, Rm 516, Bronx, NY 10458 *Tel:* 718-817-1894 *Web Site:* www.bnet.fordham.edu, pg 620

Greco, John, American Bible Society, 101 N Independence Mall E, 8th fl, Philadelphia, PA 19106-2112 *Tel:* 215-309-0900 *Toll Free Tel:* 800-322-4253 (cust serv); 888-596-6296 *E-mail:* info@americanbible.org *Web Site:* www.americanbible.org, pg 10

Greco, Marilyn, Schoolhouse Network, PO Box 1518, Northampton, MA 01061 *Tel:* 480-427-4836 *E-mail:* schoolhousenetwork@gmail.com, pg 501

Greeman, Amy, Storey Publishing LLC, 210 MASS MoCA Way, North Adams, MA 01247 *Tel:* 413-346-2100 *Toll Free Tel:* 800-441-5700 (orders); 800-793-9396 (edit) *Fax:* 413-346-2199; 413-346-2196 (edit) *E-mail:* sales@storey.com *Web Site:* www.storey.com, pg 223

Green, Becky, Random House Children's Books, 1745 Broadway, 10th fl, New York, NY 10019 *Tel:* 212-782-9000 *Web Site:* www.randomhousekids.com, pg 194

Green, Dan, Pom Inc, 18-15 215 St, Bayside, NY 11360 *Tel:* 516-487-3441, pg 531

Green, Frank, Bard Society Fiction Writing Workshop, 3113 Crosby Lane, Jacksonville, FL 32216 *Tel:* 904-250-6045 *E-mail:* frankgrn@comcast.net, pg 609

Green, George, America West Publishers, 5872 Government Way, Unit 1-10, Dalton Gardens, ID 83814 *Tel:* 208-762-0633 *Toll Free Tel:* 800-729-4131 *Web Site:* www.nohoax.com, pg 9

Green, J T, Workman Publishing Co Inc, 225 Varick St, 9th fl, New York, NY 10014-4381 *Tel:* 212-254-5900 *Toll Free Tel:* 800-722-7202 *Fax:* 212-254-8098 *E-mail:* info@workman.com *Web Site:* www.workman.com, pg 259

Green, James A, Greenwood Research Books & Software, PO Box 12102, Wichita, KS 67277-2102 *Tel:* 316-272-2937 *Web Site:* greenray4ever.com (ordering), pg 96

Green, Jane, PennWell Books, 1421 S Sheridan Rd, Tulsa, OK 74112 *Tel:* 918-831-9421 *Toll Free Tel:* 800-752-9764 *Fax:* 918-831-9555 *Toll Free Fax:* 877-218-1348 *E-mail:* sales@pennwell.com *Web Site:* www.pennwellbooks.com, pg 179

Green, Joanna, Beacon Press, 24 Farnsworth St, Boston, MA 02210-1409 *Tel:* 617-742-2110 *Fax:* 617-723-3097; 617-742-2290 *Web Site:* www.beacon.org, pg 31

Green, Jonathan, Shambhala Publications Inc, 4720 Walnut St, Boulder, CO 80301 *Tel:* 303-222-9598 *Toll Free Tel:* 866-424-0030 (off); 888-424-2329 (cust serv) *Fax:* 303-200-9406 *E-mail:* customercare@shambhala.com *Web Site:* www.shambhala.com, pg 211

Green, Karen, Anvil Press Publishers, 278 E First Ave, Vancouver, BC V5T 1A6, Canada *Tel:* 604-876-8710 *Fax:* 604-879-2667 *E-mail:* info@anvilpress.com *Web Site:* www.anvilpress.com, pg 445

Green, Karen, The BC Book Prizes, 207 W Hastings St, Suite 901, Vancouver, BC V6B 1H7, Canada *Fax:* 604-687-2435 *E-mail:* info@bcbookprizes.ca *Web Site:* www.bcbookprizes.ca, pg 630

Green, Michael, Philomel, 345 Hudson St, New York, NY 10014 *Tel:* 212-366-2000, pg 182

Green, Nancy, The Monacelli Press, 236 W 27 St, 4th fl, New York, NY 10001 *Tel:* 212-229-9925 (ext 25) *E-mail:* contact@monacellipress.com *Web Site:* www.monacellipress.com, pg 153

Green, Novella, Nursesbooks.org, The Publishing Program of ANA, 8515 Georgia Ave, Suite 400, Silver Spring, MD 20910-3492 *Tel:* 301-628-5000 *Toll Free Tel:* 800-274-4262; 800-637-0323 (orders) *Fax:* 301-628-5342 *E-mail:* anp@ana.org *Web Site:* www.Nursesbooks.org; www.NursingWorld.org, pg 165

Greenberg, Annalee, Portage & Main Press, 318 McDermot, Suite 100, Winnipeg, MB R3A 0A2, Canada *Tel:* 204-987-3500 *Toll Free Tel:* 800-667-9673 *Fax:* 204-947-0080 *Toll Free Fax:* 866-734-8477 *E-mail:* books@portageandmainpress.com *Web Site:* www.portageandmainpress.com, pg 467

Greenberg, Ben, Random House Publishing Group, 1745 Broadway, New York, NY 10019 *Toll Free Tel:* 800-200-3552 *Web Site:* atrandom.com, pg 195

Greenberg, Daniel, Levine|Greenberg|Rostan Literary Agency, 307 Seventh Ave, Suite 2407, New York, NY 10001 *Tel:* 212-337-0934 *Fax:* 212-337-0948 *Web Site:* lgrliterary.com, pg 525

Greenberg, Jeff, AAA Photos, 401 Ocean Dr, Unit 804, Miami Beach, FL 33139 *Tel:* 305-534-0804 *Web Site:* www.photosphotos.net, pg 487

Greenberg, Karen, Penguin Random House Inc, 1745 Broadway, New York, NY 10019 *Tel:* 212-782-9000 *Toll Free Tel:* 800-726-0600 *Web Site:* www.penguinrandomhouse.com, pg 178

Greenberg, Karen Matsu, American Book Producers Association (ABPA), 31 W Eighth St, 2nd fl, New York, NY 10011 *Tel:* 212-675-1363 *Fax:* 212-675-1364 *E-mail:* office@abpaonline.org *Web Site:* www.abpaonline.org, pg 554

Greenberg, Susannah, Women's National Book Association Inc, PO Box 237, FDR Sta, New York, NY 10150-0231 *Tel:* 212-208-4629 (headquarters) *Fax:* 212-208-4629 *E-mail:* publicity@bookbuzz.com; info@wnba-books.org *Web Site:* www.wnba-books.org; www.NationalReadingGroupMonth.org, pg 580

Greenberg, Zeke, Alan Wofsy Fine Arts, 1109 Geary Blvd, San Francisco, CA 94109 *Tel:* 415-292-6500 *Toll Free Tel:* 800-660-6403 *Fax:* 415-292-6594 (off & cust serv); 510-251-1840 (acctg) *E-mail:* order@art-books.com (orders); editeur@earthlink.net (edit); beauxarts@earthlink.net (cust serv) *Web Site:* www.art-books.com, pg 258

Greene, Anne, Wesleyan Writers Conference, c/o Wesleyan University, Downey House, 294 High St, Rm 207, Middletown, CT 06459 *Tel:* 860-685-3604 *Web Site:* www.wesleyan.edu/writing/conference, pg 616

Greene, Deirdre, Roaring Forties Press, 1053 Santa Fe Ave, Berkeley, CA 94706 *Tel:* 510-527-5461 *E-mail:* info@roaringfortiespress.com *Web Site:* www.roaringfortiespress.com, pg 200

Greene, Jennifer, Clarion Books, 3 Park Ave, New York, NY 10016 *Tel:* 212-420-5800 *Toll Free Tel:* 800-225-3362 (orders) *Fax:* 212-420-5855 *Toll Free Fax:* 800-634-7568 (orders) *Web Site:* www.hmhco.com, pg 56

Greene, Rob, New Hampshire Literary Awards, 2500 N River Rd, Manchester, NH 03106 *Tel:* 603-314-7980 *Fax:* 603-314-7981 *E-mail:* info@nhwritersproject.org; awards@nhwritersproject.org *Web Site:* www.nhwritersproject.org, pg 672

Greenfield, George M, CreativeWell Inc, PO Box 3130, Memorial Sta, Upper Montclair, NJ 07043 *Tel:* 973-783-7575 *Fax:* 973-783-7530 *E-mail:* info@creativewell.com *Web Site:* www.creativewell.com, pg 512

Greenfield, George M, CreativeWell Inc, PO Box 3130, Memorial Sta, Upper Montclair, NJ 07043 *Tel:* 973-783-7575 *Toll Free Tel:* 800-743-9182 *Fax:* 973-783-7530 *E-mail:* info@creativewell.com *Web Site:* www.creativewell.com, pg 547

Greenhut, Carol, Schonfeld & Associates Inc, 1931 Lynn Circle, Libertyville, IL 60048 *Tel:* 847-816-4870 *Toll Free Tel:* 800-205-0030 *Fax:* 847-816-4872 *E-mail:* saiinfo@saibooks.com *Web Site:* www.saibooks.com, pg 208

Greenland, Paul R, Paul Greenland Communications Inc, 9184 Longfellow Lane, Machesney Park, IL 61115 *Tel:* 815-240-4108 *Toll Free Tel:* 888-798-7786 *Web Site:* www.paulgreenland.com, pg 495

Greenleaf, Clint, Greenleaf Book Group LLC, 3 Park Place, 4005 Banister Lane, Suite B, Austin, TX 78704 *Tel:* 512-891-6100 *Fax:* 512-891-6150 *E-mail:* contact@greenleafbookgroup.com *Web Site:* www.greenleafbookgroup.com, pg 96

Greenspan, Elizabeth, Society for Industrial & Applied Mathematics, 3600 Market St, 6th fl, Philadelphia, PA 19104-2688 *Tel:* 215-382-9800 *Toll Free Tel:* 800-447-7426 *Fax:* 215-386-7999 *E-mail:* siambooks@siam.org *Web Site:* www.siam.org, pg 216

Greenspan, Shari Dash, Flashlight Press, 527 Empire Blvd, Brooklyn, NY 11225 *Tel:* 718-288-8300 *Fax:* 718-972-6307 *Web Site:* www.flashlightpress.com, pg 85

Greenspan, Shari Dash, Urim Publications, 527 Empire Blvd, Brooklyn, NY 11225-3121 *Tel:* 718-972-5449 *Fax:* 718-972-6307 *E-mail:* publisher@urimpublications.com; editor@urimpublications.com *Web Site:* urimpublications.com, pg 249

Greenstein, Ruth, Turtle Point Press, 208 Java St, 5th fl, Brooklyn, NY 11222-5748 *Tel:* 212-741-1393 *E-mail:* info@turtlepointpress.com *Web Site:* www.turtlepointpress.com, pg 236

Greenstein, Ruth, Words into Print, 208 Java St, 6th fl, Brooklyn, NY 11222 *E-mail:* query@wordsintoprint.org *Web Site:* wordsintoprint.org, pg 503

Greenwald, Emily, Scribner, 1230 Avenue of the Americas, New York, NY 10020, pg 209

Greenwald, Zachary, Artisan Books, 225 Varick St, New York, NY 10014-4381 *Tel:* 212-254-5900 *Toll Free Tel:* 800-722-7202 *Fax:* 212-677-6692 *E-mail:* artisaninfo@artisanbooks.com *Web Site:* www.workman.com/artisanbooks, pg 22

Greenwood, Daphne, The Optical Society (OSA), 2010 Massachusetts Ave NW, Washington, DC 20036-1023 *Tel:* 202-223-8130 *Toll Free Tel:* 800-766-4672 *E-mail:* custserv@osa.org *Web Site:* www.osa.org, pg 169

Greer, Jessica, Other Press, 267 Fifth Ave, 6th fl, New York, NY 10016 *Tel:* 212-414-0054 *Toll Free Tel:* 877-843-6843 *Fax:* 212-414-0939 *E-mail:* editor@otherpress.com; marketing@otherpress.com; publicity@otherpress.com *Web Site:* www.otherpress.com, pg 170

Gregg, Richard, Aperture Books, 547 W 27 St, 4th fl, New York, NY 10001 *Tel:* 212-505-5555 *Toll Free Tel:* 800-929-2323 *Fax:* 212-979-7759 *E-mail:* info@aperture.org *Web Site:* www.aperture.org, pg 18

Gregoire, Pierre, Les Editions Vents d'Ouest, 109, rue Wright, bureau 202, Gatineau, QC J8X 2G7, Canada *Tel:* 819-770-6377 *E-mail:* info@ventsdouest.ca *Web Site:* www.ventsdouest.ca, pg 455

Gregory, Alexis, The Vendome Press, 244 Fifth Ave, Suite 2043, New York, NY 10001 *Tel:* 212-737-1857 *E-mail:* info@vendomepress.com *Web Site:* www.vendomepress.com, pg 250

Gregory, Debbie, Upper Room Books, 1908 Grand Ave, Nashville, TN 37212 *Tel:* 615-340-7200 *Toll Free Tel:* 800-972-0433 *Fax:* 615-340-7266 *Web Site:* books.upperroom.org, pg 248

Gregory, Evan, Ethan Ellenberg Literary Agency, 155 Suffolk St, Suite 2R, New York, NY 10002 *Tel:* 212-431-4554 *E-mail:* agent@ethanellenberg.com *Web Site:* www.ethanellenberg.com, pg 516

Gregory, Kevin G, AuthorHouse, 1663 Liberty Dr, Bloomington, IN 47403 *Tel:* 812-339-6000 (outside US) *Toll Free Tel:* 888-519-5121 *E-mail:* authorsupport@authorhouse.com *Web Site:* www.authorhouse.com, pg 26

Gregory, Kevin G, Xlibris Corp, 1663 Liberty Dr, Suite 200, Bloomington, IN 47403 *Toll Free Tel:* 888-795-4274 *Fax:* 610-915-0294 *E-mail:* info@xlibris.com *Web Site:* www.xlibris.com, pg 261

Gregory, Michael Steven, Southern California Writers' Conference (SCWC), 18160 Cottonwood Rd, Suite 260, Sunriver, OR 97707 *Tel:* 619-303-8185 *Fax:* 619-906-7462 *E-mail:* msg@writersconference.com *Web Site:* www.writersconference.com, pg 615

Greico, Tara, Random House Children's Books, 1745 Broadway, 10th fl, New York, NY 10019 *Tel:* 212-782-9000 *Web Site:* www.randomhousekids.com, pg 194

Grench, Charles, The University of North Carolina Press, 116 S Boundary St, Chapel Hill, NC 27514-3808 *Tel:* 919-966-3561 *Fax:* 919-966-3829 *E-mail:* uncpress@unc.edu *Web Site:* www.uncpress.unc.edu, pg 243

Grennan, Karen, SDP Publishing Solutions LLC, 36 Captain's Way, East Bridgewater, MA 02333 *Tel:* 617-775-0656 *Web Site:* www.sdppublishingsolutions.com, pg 501

Gress, Priti Chitnis, Hippocrene Books Inc, 171 Madison Ave, New York, NY 10016 *Tel:* 212-685-4373 *Fax:* 212-779-9338 *E-mail:* info@hippocrenebooks.com; orderdept@hippocrenebooks.com (orders) *Web Site:* www.hippocrenebooks.com, pg 108

Greuel, Greg, Wayside Publishing, 262 US Route 1, Suite 2, Freeport, ME 04032 *Toll Free Tel:* 888-302-2519 *E-mail:* sales@waysidepublishing.com *Web Site:* www.waysidepublishing.com, pg 253

Griffes, Peter L, ProStar Publications Inc, 3 Church Circle, Suite 109, Annapolis, MD 21401 *Toll Free Tel:* 800-481-6277 *Toll Free Fax:* 800-487-6277 *E-mail:* editor@prostarpublications.com *Web Site:* www.prostarpublications.com, pg 190

Griffin, Courtney, Bloomsbury Publishing Inc, 1385 Broadway, 5th fl, New York, NY 10018 *Tel:* 212-419-5300 *E-mail:* marketingusa@bloomsbury.com; adultpublicityusa@bloomsbury.com; askacademic@bloomsbury.com *Web Site:* www.bloomsbury.com, pg 38

Griffin, Emily, HarperCollins General Books Group, 195 Broadway, New York, NY 10007 *Tel:* 212-207-7000 *Web Site:* www.harpercollins.com, pg 101

Griffin, Jean, Hachette Book Group, 1290 Avenue of the Americas, New York, NY 10019 *Tel:* 212-364-1100 *Toll Free Tel:* 800-759-0190 (cust serv) *Fax:* 212-364-0933 (intl orders) *Toll Free Fax:* 800-286-9471 (cust serv) *Web Site:* www.hachettebookgroup.com, pg 98

Griffin, Scott, Groundwood Books, 128 Sterling Rd, Lower Level, Toronto, ON M6R 2B7, Canada *Tel:* 416-363-4343 *Fax:* 416-363-1017 *E-mail:* genmail@groundwoodbooks.com *Web Site:* www.houseofanansi.com, pg 458

Griffiths, Jenese, AFB Press, 1401 S Clark St, Suite 730, Arlington, VA 22202 *Tel:* 304-710-3043 *Toll Free Tel:* 800-232-3044 (orders) *Fax:* 917-210-3979 (orders) *E-mail:* afbpress@afb.net *Web Site:* www.afb.org, pg 5

Griffor, Mariela, Marick Press, PO Box 36253, Grosse Pointe Farms, MI 48236 *Tel:* 313-407-9236 *E-mail:* orders@marickpress.com *Web Site:* www.marickpress.com, pg 142

Grilliot, Bob, JIST Publishing, 875 Montreal Way, St Paul, MN 55102 *Toll Free Tel:* 800-328-1452 *Toll Free Fax:* 800-328-4564 *E-mail:* educate@emcp.com *Web Site:* jist.emcp.com, pg 122

Grima, Tony, National Braille Press, 88 Saint Stephen St, Boston, MA 02115-4302 *Tel:* 617-266-6160 *Toll Free Tel:* 800-548-7323 (cust serv); 888-965-8965 *Fax:* 617-437-0456 *E-mail:* orders@nbp.org; contact@nbp.org *Web Site:* www.nbp.org, pg 157

Grimaldi, Dana, Harlequin Enterprises Ltd, 225 Duncan Mill Rd, Don Mills, ON M3B 3K9, Canada *Tel:* 416-445-5860 *Toll Free Tel:* 888-432-4879; 800-370-5838 (ebook inquiries) *E-mail:* customerservice@harlequin.com *Web Site:* www.harlequin.com, pg 459

Grimbleby, Jennifer, Kids Can Press Ltd, 25 Dockside Dr, Toronto, ON M5A 0B5, Canada *Tel:* 416-479-7000 *Toll Free Tel:* 800-265-0884 *Fax:* 416-960-5437 *E-mail:* info@kidscan.com; customerservice@kidscan.com *Web Site:* www.kidscanpress.com; www.kidscanpress.ca, pg 461

Grimes, Mark, American Academy of Pediatrics, 141 NW Point Blvd, Elk Grove Village, IL 60007-1098 *Tel:* 847-434-4000 *Toll Free Tel:* 888-227-1770 *Fax:* 847-434-8000 *E-mail:* pubs@aap.org *Web Site:* www.aap.org, pg 9

Grimm, Chris, Kensington Publishing Corp, 119 W 40 St, New York, NY 10018 *Tel:* 212-407-1500 *Toll Free Tel:* 800-221-2647 *Fax:* 212-935-0699 *Web Site:* www.kensingtonbooks.com, pg 125

Grimm, Katie, Don Congdon Associates Inc, 110 William St, Suite 2202, New York, NY 10038-3914 *Tel:* 212-645-1229 *Fax:* 212-727-2688 *E-mail:* dca@doncongdon.com *Web Site:* www.doncongdon.com, pg 512

Grimshaw, Sue, Penguin Random House Inc, 1745 Broadway, New York, NY 10019 *Tel:* 212-782-9000 *Toll Free Tel:* 800-726-0600 *Web Site:* www.penguinrandomhouse.com, pg 178

Grimshaw, Sue, Random House Publishing Group, 1745 Broadway, New York, NY 10019 *Toll Free Tel:* 800-200-3552 *Web Site:* atrandom.com, pg 195

Grinberg, Jill, Jill Grinberg Literary Management LLC, 392 Vanderbilt Ave, Brooklyn, NY 11238 *Tel:* 212-620-5883 *E-mail:* info@jillgrinbergliterary.com *Web Site:* www.jillgrinbergliterary.com, pg 520

Grisebach, Rolf, Thames & Hudson, 500 Fifth Ave, New York, NY 10110 *Tel:* 212-354-3763 *Toll Free Tel:* 800-233-4830 *Fax:* 212-398-1252 *E-mail:* bookinfo@thames.wwnorton.com *Web Site:* www.thamesandhudsonusa.com, pg 230

Griswold, John, McNeese State University, Writing Program, PO Box 92655, Lake Charles, LA 70609-0001 *Tel:* 337-475-5325; 337-475-5327 *Web Site:* www.mcneese.edu.com; www.mfa.mcneese.edu, pg 621

Groell, Anne, Random House Publishing Group, 1745 Broadway, New York, NY 10019 *Toll Free Tel:* 800-200-3552 *Web Site:* atrandom.com, pg 195

Grogan, David, American Booksellers Association, 333 Westchester Ave, Suite S202, White Plains, NY 10604 *Tel:* 914-406-7500 *Toll Free Tel:* 800-637-0037 *Fax:* 914-410-6297 *E-mail:* info@bookweb.org *Web Site:* www.bookweb.org, pg 554

Groopman, Sofia, HarperCollins General Books Group, 195 Broadway, New York, NY 10007 *Tel:* 212-207-7000 *Web Site:* www.harpercollins.com, pg 101

Grosjean, Jill, Jill Grosjean Literary Agency, 1390 Millstone Rd, Sag Harbor, NY 11963 *Tel:* 631-725-7419 *Fax:* 631-725-8632 *E-mail:* JillLit310@aol.com, pg 520

Gross, Laura, Laura Gross Literary Agency Ltd, PO Box 610326, Newton Highlands, MA 02461 *Tel:* 617-964-2977 *Fax:* 617-964-3023 *E-mail:* query@lg-la.com *Web Site:* www.lg-la.com, pg 520

Grossberg, Aileen, Sydney Taylor Manuscript Award, 204 Park St, Montclair, NJ 07042 *Tel:* 201-371-3255 *E-mail:* info@jewishlibraries.org *Web Site:* jewishlibraries.org, pg 693

Grossinger, Richard, North Atlantic Books, 2526 Martin Luther King Jr Way, Berkeley, CA 94704 *Tel:* 510-549-4270 *Fax:* 510-549-4276 *Web Site:* www.northatlanticbooks.com, pg 163

Grosskopf, Bill M, Newgen North America Inc, 2714 Bee Cave Rd, Suite 201, Austin, TX 78746 *Tel:* 512-478-5341 *Fax:* 512-476-4756 *Web Site:* www.newgen.co, pg 499

Grosskopf, Lauren, Pleasure Boat Studio: A Literary Press, 201 W 89 St, New York, NY 10024 *Tel:* 212-362-8563; 413-337-5346 *Fax:* 413-677-0085 *E-mail:* pleasboat@nyc.rr.com *Web Site:* www.pleasureboatstudio.com, pg 184

Grossman, Jim, American Historical Association (AHA), 400 "A" St SE, Washington, DC 20003 *Tel:* 202-544-2422 *Fax:* 202-544-8307 *E-mail:* aha@historians.org; awards@historians.org *Web Site:* www.historians.org, pg 12

Grossman, Lawrence, American Jewish Committee (AJC), Jacob Blaustein Bldg, 165 E 56 St, New York, NY 10022 *Tel:* 212-751-4000; 212-891-1456 (membership) *Fax:* 212-891-1450 *Web Site:* www.ajc.org, pg 555

Grossman, Maggie, Northwestern University Press, 629 Noyes St, Evanston, IL 60208-4210 *Tel:* 847-491-2046 *Toll Free Tel:* 800-621-2736 (orders only) *Fax:* 847-491-8150 *E-mail:* nupress@northwestern.edu *Web Site:* www.nupress.northwestern.edu, pg 164

Grossman, Max, Abrams Artists Agency, 275 Seventh Ave, 26th fl, New York, NY 10001 *Tel:* 646-486-4600 *Fax:* 646-486-0100 *E-mail:* literary@abramsartny.com *Web Site:* www.abramsartists.com, pg 505

Grossman, Moshe, Feldheim Publishers, 208 Airport Executive Park, Nanuet, NY 10954 *Tel:* 845-356-2282 *Toll Free Tel:* 800-237-7149 (orders) *Fax:* 845-425-1908 *E-mail:* sales@feldheim.com *Web Site:* www.feldheim.com, pg 83

Grosz-Ngate, Maria, Indiana University African Studies Program, Indiana University, 221 Woodburn Hall, Bloomington, IN 47405 *Tel:* 812-855-8284 *Fax:* 812-855-6734 *E-mail:* afrist@indiana.edu *Web Site:* www.indiana.edu/~afrist, pg 115

Grote, Bill, BNi Building News, 990 Park Center Dr, Suite E, Vista, CA 92081-8352 *Tel:* 760-734-1113 *Toll Free Tel:* 888-BNI-BOOK (264-2665) *Web Site:* www.bnibooks.com, pg 39

Groton, John, Quarto Publishing Group USA Inc, 400 First Ave N, Suite 400, Minneapolis, MN 55401 *Tel:* 612-344-8100 *Toll Free Tel:* 800-328-0590 (sales); 800-458-0454 *Fax:* 612-344-8691 *E-mail:* sales@quartous.com *Web Site:* www.quartoknows.com, pg 192

Grotz, Jennifer, Bread Loaf Writers' Conference, 5525 Middlebury College, 14 Old Chapel Rd, Middlebury, VT 05753 *Tel:* 802-443-5286 *Fax:* 802-443-2087 *E-mail:* blwc@middlebury.edu *Web Site:* www.middlebury.edu/blwc, pg 610

Grotz, Jennifer, Fellowship, Tuition Scholarship & Work Study Programs for Writers, Middlebury College, 204 College St, Middlebury, VT 05753 *Tel:* 802-443-5286 *Fax:* 802-443-2087 *E-mail:* blwc@middlebury.edu *Web Site:* www.middlebury.edu/blwc, pg 646

Grove, Alyssa Hickman, Utah Original Writing Competition, 617 E South Temple, Salt Lake City, UT 84102 *Tel:* 801-236-7555 *Fax:* 801-236-7556 *Web Site:* arts.utah.gov, pg 695

Grove, Susan Evans, The Society of Naval Architects & Marine Engineers (SNAME), 99 Canal Center Plaza, Suite 310, Alexandria, VA 22314 *Tel:* 703-997-6701 *Toll Free Tel:* 800-798-2188 *Fax:* 703-997-6702 *Web Site:* www.sname.org, pg 216

Grow, KJ, Shambhala Publications Inc, 4720 Walnut St, Boulder, CO 80301 *Tel:* 303-222-9598 *Toll Free Tel:* 866-424-0030 (off); 888-424-2329 (cust serv) *Fax:* 303-200-9406 *E-mail:* customercare@shambhala.com *Web Site:* www.shambhala.com, pg 211

Grow, KJ, Snow Lion, 4720 Walnut St, Boulder, CO 80301 *Tel:* 617-236-0030 *Fax:* 303-200-9406 *E-mail:* customercare@shambhala.com *Web Site:* www.shambhala.com/snowlion, pg 215

Grubb, Randell C, Theosophical University Press, PO Box C, Pasadena, CA 91109-7107 *Tel:* 626-798-3378 *E-mail:* tupress@theosociety.org *Web Site:* www.theosociety.org, pg 231

Grubbs, Rachell, Quicksilver Productions, PO Box 340, Ashland, OR 97520-0012 *Tel:* 541-482-5343 *Toll Free Fax:* 888-974-6462 *E-mail:* celestialcalendars@email.com *Web Site:* www.quicksilverproductions.com, pg 192

Grudens, Richard, Celebrity Profiles Publishing, PO Box 344, Stony Brook, NY 11790 *Tel:* 631-862-8555 *Fax:* 631-862-0139 *E-mail:* celebpro4@aol.com *Web Site:* www.richardgrudens.com; richardgrudensblog.blogspot.com, pg 50

Grunebaum, Jennifer, McGraw-Hill International & Professional Publishing Group, 2 Penn Plaza, New York, NY 10121 *Tel:* 646-766-2000 *Web Site:* www.mheducation.com, pg 146

Grunewald, Nancy, Washington State University Press, Cooper Publications Bldg, Grimes Way, Pullman, WA 99164-5910 *Tel:* 509-335-3518; 509-335-7880 (order fulfillment) *Toll Free Tel:* 800-354-7360 (orders) *Fax:* 509-335-8568 *E-mail:* wsupress@wsu.edu *Web Site:* wsupress.wsu.edu, pg 252

Guadagnolo, Frank, Venture Publishing Inc, 1999 Cato Ave, State College, PA 16801 *Tel:* 814-234-4561 *Fax:* 814-234-1651 *E-mail:* vpublish@venturepublish.com *Web Site:* www.venturepublish.com, pg 250

Guarin, Imelda, Marshall Cavendish Corp, 99 White Plains Rd, Tarrytown, NY 10591-9001 *Tel:* 914-332-8888 *Toll Free Tel:* 800-821-9881 *Fax:* 914-332-8102 *E-mail:* mce@marshallcavendish.com *Web Site:* www.marshallcavendish.com; www.mceducation.us, pg 143

Guay, Marie-Noelle, Editions Yvon Blais, 75 rue Queen, Bureau 4700, Montreal, QC H3C 2N6, Canada *Toll Free Tel:* 800-363-3047 *Fax:* 450-263-9256 *E-mail:* editionsyvonblais.commandes@thomsonreuters.com (cust serv) *Web Site:* www.editionsyvonblais.com, pg 456

Guenzel, Andrea L, The Electrochemical Society (ECS), 65 S Main St, Bldg D, Pennington, NJ 08534-2839 *Tel:* 609-737-1902 *Fax:* 609-737-2743 *E-mail:* publications@electrochem.org; customerservice@electrochem.org *Web Site:* www.electrochem.org, pg 77

Guenzi, Carol, Carol Guenzi Agents Inc, 865 Delaware St, Denver, CO 80204 *Tel:* 303-820-2599 *Toll Free Tel:* 800-417-5120 *Fax:* 303-820-2598 *E-mail:* art@artagent.com *Web Site:* www.artagent.com, pg 543

Guerra, Delin, Bogle International Library Travel Fund, 50 E Huron St, Chicago, IL 60611-2795 *Tel:* 312-280-3201 *Toll Free Tel:* 800-545-2433 (ext 3201) *Fax:* 312-280-4392 *E-mail:* intl@ala.org *Web Site:* www.ala.org, pg 633

Guerth, Jan-Erik, BlueBridge, PO Box 601, Katonah, NY 10536 *Tel:* 914-301-5901 *Web Site:* www.bluebridgebooks.com, pg 38

Guevara, Linda L, All About Kids Publishing, PO Box 159, Gilroy, CA 95021 *Tel:* 408-337-1152 *E-mail:* info@allaboutkidspub.com *Web Site:* www.allaboutkidspub.com, pg 7

Guevara, Mike G, All About Kids Publishing, PO Box 159, Gilroy, CA 95021 *Tel:* 408-337-1152 *E-mail:* info@allaboutkidspub.com *Web Site:* www.allaboutkidspub.com, pg 7

Guevin, John R, Biographical Publishing Co, 95 Sycamore Dr, Prospect, CT 06712-1011 *Tel:* 203-758-3661 *Fax:* 253-793-2618 *E-mail:* biopub@aol.com *Web Site:* www.biopub.us, pg 35

Guibord, Maurice, BCHF Historial Writing Competition, PO Box 5254, Sta B, Victoria, BC V8R 6N4, Canada *E-mail:* writing@bchistory.ca *Web Site:* www.bchistory.ca, pg 630

Guido, Umberto III, Peter Glenn Publications, 306 NE Second St, 2nd fl, Delray Beach, FL 33483 *Tel:* 561-404-4290 *Fax:* 561-892-5786 *Web Site:* pgdirect.com, pg 93

Guidone, Kimberly, The Jennifer DeChiara Literary Agency, 299 Park Ave, 6th fl, New York, NY 10171 *Tel:* 212-739-0803 *Web Site:* www.jdlit.com, pg 513

Guignard, Gayla, The Alexander Graham Bell Association for the Deaf & Hard of Hearing, 3417 Volta Place NW, Washington, DC 20007 *Tel:* 202-337-5220 *Toll Free Tel:* 866-337-5220 (orders) *Fax:* 202-337-8314 *E-mail:* info@agbell.org; publications@agbell.org *Web Site:* www.agbell.org, pg 6

Guilfoyle, Virginia, Federal Street Press, 25-13 Old Kings Hwy N, No 277, Darien, CT 06820 *Tel:* 203-852-1280 *Toll Free Tel:* 877-886-2830 *Fax:* 203-852-1389 *E-mail:* info@federalstreetpress.com; sales@federalstreetpress.com; customerservice@federalstreetpress.com; orders@federalstreetpress.com *Web Site:* federalstreetpress.com, pg 83

Guili, Lisa, Educational Insights, 152 W Walnut St, Suite 201, Gardena, CA 90248 *Toll Free Tel:* 800-995-4436 *Toll Free Fax:* 888-892-8731 *E-mail:* cs@educationalinsights.com *Web Site:* www.educationalinsights.com, pg 76

Guillemette-Bedard, Catherine, Ordre des traducteurs, terminologues et interpretes agrees du quebec, 2021 Union Ave, Suite 1108, Montreal, QC H3A 2S9, Canada *Tel:* 514-845-4411 *Toll Free Tel:* 800-265-4815 *Fax:* 514-845-9903 *E-mail:* info@ottiaq.org *Web Site:* www.ottiaq.org, pg 574

Guinsler, Robert, Sterling Lord Literistic Inc, 115 Broadway, Suite 1602, New York, NY 10006 *Tel:* 212-780-6050 *Fax:* 212-780-6095 *E-mail:* info@sll.com *Web Site:* www.sll.com, pg 537

Guinta, Kimberly, Rutgers University Press, 106 Somerset St, 3rd fl, New Brunswick, NJ 08901 *Tel:* 848-445-7762 *Toll Free Tel:* 800-848-6224 (orders only) *Fax:* 732-745-4935 (acqs, edit, mktg, perms & prodn) *Toll Free Fax:* 800-272-6817 (fulfillment) *Web Site:* rutgerspress.rutgers.edu, pg 202

Guiod, Suzanne, Syracuse University Press, 621 Skytop Rd, Suite 110, Syracuse, NY 13244-5290 *Tel:* 315-443-5534 *Toll Free Tel:* 800-365-8929 (cust serv) *Fax:* 315-443-5545 *E-mail:* supress@syr.edu *Web Site:* syracuseuniversitypress.syr.edu, pg 226

Gulla, Joseph, Alazar Press, 201 Orchard Lane, Carrboro, NC 27510 *Tel:* 919-274-0653 *E-mail:* alazar.press@gmail.com *Web Site:* www.alazar-press.com, pg 477

Gulla, Rosemarie, Alazar Press, 201 Orchard Lane, Carrboro, NC 27510 *Tel:* 919-274-0653 *E-mail:* alazar.press@gmail.com *Web Site:* www.alazar-press.com, pg 477

Gumm, Katie, New Leaf Press, 3142 Hwy 103 N, Green Forest, AR 72638-2233 *Tel:* 870-438-5288 *Toll Free Tel:* 800-999-3777 *Fax:* 870-438-5120 *E-mail:* nlp@newleafpress.net; submissions@newleafpress.net *Web Site:* www.nlpg.com/imprint/new-leaf-press; www.nlpg.com, pg 161

Gunderson, Joanna, Red Dust Inc, 1148 Fifth Ave, New York, NY 10128 *Tel:* 212-348-4388 *Web Site:* www.reddustbooks.com, pg 196

Gundry, Stan, Zondervan, 3900 Sparks Dr, Grand Rapids, MI 49546 *Tel:* 616-698-6900 *Toll Free Tel:* 800-226-1122; 800-727-1309 (retail orders) *Fax:* 616-698-3350 *Toll Free Fax:* 800-698-3256 (retail orders) *E-mail:* zinfo@zondervan.com *Web Site:* www.zondervan.com, pg 263

Gunn, James, John W Campbell Memorial Award, University of Kansas, Wescoe Hall, Rm 3001, Dept of English, 1445 Jayhawk Blvd, Lawrence, KS 66045 *Tel:* 785-864-2518 *Fax:* 785-864-1159 *Web Site:* www.sfcenter.ku.edu/campbell.htm, pg 635

Gunn, James, Science Fiction Writers Workshop, University of Kansas, Wescoe Hall, Rm 3001, Dept of English, 1445 Jayhawk Blvd, Lawrence, KS 66045 *Tel:* 785-864-2518 *Fax:* 785-864-1159 *Web Site:* www.sfcenter.ku.edu; www.sfcenter.ku.edu/sfworkshop; www.sfcenter.ku.edu/novel-workshop, pg 614

Gunnison, John P, Adventure House, 914 Laredo Rd, Silver Spring, MD 20901 *Tel:* 301-754-1589 *Web Site:* www.adventurehouse.com, pg 5

Gunnison, Toni, University of Wisconsin Press, 1930 Monroe St, 3rd fl, Madison, WI 53711-2059 *Tel:* 608-263-0668 *Toll Free Tel:* 800-621-2736 (orders) *Fax:* 608-263-1173 *Toll Free Fax:* 800-621-2736 (orders) *E-mail:* uwiscpress@uwpress.wisc.edu (main off); publicity@uwpress.wisc.edu *Web Site:* uwpress.wisc.edu, pg 246

Gupta, Ashis, Bayeux Arts Inc, 119 Stratton Crescent SW, Calgary, AB T3H 1T7, Canada *E-mail:* mail@bayeux.com *Web Site:* bayeux.com, pg 446

Gupta, Swapna, Bayeux Arts Inc, 119 Stratton Crescent SW, Calgary, AB T3H 1T7, Canada *E-mail:* mail@bayeux.com *Web Site:* bayeux.com, pg 446

Gurewich, Judith, Other Press, 267 Fifth Ave, 6th fl, New York, NY 10016 *Tel:* 212-414-0054 *Toll Free Tel:* 877-843-6843 *Fax:* 212-414-0939 *E-mail:* editor@otherpress.com; marketing@otherpress.com; publicity@otherpress.com *Web Site:* www.otherpress.com, pg 170

Gurley, Hezron, AIGA, the professional association for design, 233 Broadway, Suite 1740, New York, NY 10279 *Tel:* 212-807-1990 *Fax:* 212-807-1799 *E-mail:* general@aiga.org *Web Site:* www.aiga.org, pg 553

Gurney, James, Blue Mountain Arts Inc, 2905 Wilderness Place, Suite 100, Boulder, CO 80301 *Tel:* 303-449-0536 *Toll Free Tel:* 800-525-0642 *Fax:* 303-417-6472 *Toll Free Fax:* 800-545-8573 *E-mail:* info@sps.com *Web Site:* www.sps.com, pg 38

Gusinde-Duffy, Mick, University of Georgia Press, Main Library, 3rd fl, 320 S Jackson St, Athens, GA 30602 *Fax:* 706-542-2558; 706-542-6770 *Web Site:* www.ugapress.org, pg 241

Gutin, Julie, NASW Press, 750 First St NE, Suite 800, Washington, DC 20002 *Tel:* 202-408-8600 *Fax:* 203-336-8312 *E-mail:* press@naswdc.org *Web Site:* www.naswpress.org, pg 156

Gutmajer, Shoshana, Artisan Books, 225 Varick St, New York, NY 10014-4381 *Tel:* 212-254-5900 *Toll Free Tel:* 800-722-7202 *Fax:* 212-677-6692 *E-mail:* artisaninfo@artisanbooks.com *Web Site:* www.workman.com/artisanbooks, pg 22

Guttman, Joseph, University of Pennsylvania Press, 3905 Spruce St, Philadelphia, PA 19104 *Tel:* 215-898-6261 *Fax:* 215-898-0404 *E-mail:* custserv@pobox.upenn.edu *Web Site:* www.pennpress.org, pg 244

Guttman, Naomi, Hamilton College, English/Creative Writing, English/Creative Writing Dept, 198 College Hill Rd, Clinton, NY 13323 *Tel:* 315-859-4370 *Fax:* 315-859-4390 *Web Site:* www.hamilton.edu, pg 620

Guzman, Daniel, PEN American Center, 588 Broadway, Suite 303, New York, NY 10012 *Tel:* 212-334-1660 *Fax:* 212-334-2181 *E-mail:* info@pen.org *Web Site:* pen.org, pg 575

Guzman, Martha, Maria Carvainis Agency Inc, Rockefeller Center, 1270 Avenue of the Americas, Suite 2320, New York, NY 10020 *Tel:* 212-245-6365 *Fax:* 212-245-7196 *E-mail:* mca@mariacarvainisagency.com *Web Site:* mariacarvainisagency.com, pg 511

Guzzardo, Lindsay, The Editorial Department LLC, 7650 E Broadway, Suite 308, Tucson, AZ 85710 *Tel:* 520-546-9992 *Fax:* 520-979-3408 *E-mail:* admin@editorialdepartment.com *Web Site:* www.editorialdepartment.com, pg 493

Gwiazda, Ron, Abrams Artists Agency, 275 Seventh Ave, 26th fl, New York, NY 10001 *Tel:* 646-486-4600 *Fax:* 646-486-0100 *E-mail:* literary@abramsartny.com *Web Site:* www.abramsartists.com, pg 505

Ha, Paul C, MIT List Visual Arts Center, MIT E 15-109, 20 Ames St, Cambridge, MA 02139 *Tel:* 617-253-4400; 617-253-4680 *Fax:* 617-258-7265 *E-mail:* mlinga@mit.edu *Web Site:* listart.mit.edu, pg 151

Haas, Linda, StarGroup International Inc, 1194 Old Dixie Hwy, Suite 201, West Palm Beach, FL 33413 *Tel:* 561-547-0667 *Fax:* 561-843-8530 *E-mail:* info@stargroupinternational.com *Web Site:* stargroupinternational.com, pg 221

Haase, H W, Quintessence Publishing Co Inc, 4350 Chandler Dr, Hanover Park, IL 60133 *Tel:* 630-736-3600 *Toll Free Tel:* 800-621-0387 *Fax:* 630-736-3633 *E-mail:* contact@quintbook.com; service@quintbook.com *Web Site:* www.quintpub.com, pg 193

Haav, Julia, Princeton University Press, 41 William St, Princeton, NJ 08540-5237 *Tel:* 609-258-4900 *Fax:* 609-258-6305 *Web Site:* press.princeton.edu, pg 188

Habegger, Larry, Travelers' Tales, 2320 Bowdoin St, Palo Alto, CA 94306 *Tel:* 650-462-2110 *Fax:* 650-462-6305 *E-mail:* ttales@travelerstales.com *Web Site:* travelerstales.com, pg 235

Hachfeld, Linda, Appletree Press Inc, 151 Good Counsel Dr, Suite 125, Mankato, MN 56001 *Tel:* 507-345-4848 *Fax:* 507-345-3002 *E-mail:* eatwell@hickorytech.net *Web Site:* www.appletreepress.com; www.letscookhealthymeals.com, pg 19

Hackett, Danielle, Arkham House Publishers Inc, PO Box 546, Sauk City, WI 53583 *Tel:* 608-643-4500 *Fax:* 608-643-5043 *E-mail:* sales@arkhamhouse.com *Web Site:* www.arkhamhouse.com, pg 21

Hackinson, Frank J, FJH Music Co Inc, 2525 Davie Rd, Suite 360, Fort Lauderdale, FL 33317-7424 *Tel:* 954-382-6061 *Toll Free Tel:* 800-262-8744 *Fax:* 954-382-3073 *E-mail:* custserv@fjhmusic.com; sales@fjhmusic.com *Web Site:* www.fjhmusic.com, pg 85

Hackinson, Kevin, FJH Music Co Inc, 2525 Davie Rd, Suite 360, Fort Lauderdale, FL 33317-7424 *Tel:* 954-382-6061 *Toll Free Tel:* 800-262-8744 *Fax:* 954-382-3073 *E-mail:* custserv@fjhmusic.com; sales@fjhmusic.com *Web Site:* www.fjhmusic.com, pg 85

Hackinson, Kyle, FJH Music Co Inc, 2525 Davie Rd, Suite 360, Fort Lauderdale, FL 33317-7424 *Tel:* 954-382-6061 *Toll Free Tel:* 800-262-8744 *Fax:* 954-382-3073 *E-mail:* custserv@fjhmusic.com; sales@fjhmusic.com *Web Site:* www.fjhmusic.com, pg 85

Haderer, Russell, BPA Worldwide, 100 Beard Sawmill Rd, 6th fl, Shelton, CT 06484 *Tel:* 203-447-2800 *Fax:* 203-447-2900 *E-mail:* info@bpaww.com *Web Site:* www.bpaww.com, pg 561

Hades, Brian, EDGE Science Fiction & Fantasy Publishing Inc, PO Box 1714, Calgary, AB T2P 2L7, Canada *Tel:* 403-254-0160 *Fax:* 403-254-0456 *E-mail:* admin@hadespublications.com *Web Site:* www.edgewebsite.com, pg 452

Hadley, Candida, Fernwood Publishing, 32 Oceanvista Lane, Black Point, NS B0J 1B0, Canada *Tel:* 902-857-1388 *Fax:* 902-857-1328 *E-mail:* info@fernpub.ca; roseway@fernpub.ca *Web Site:* fernwoodpublishing.ca, pg 456

Hafftka, Michael, Six Gallery Press, PO Box 90145, Pittsburgh, PA 15224-0545 *Web Site:* www.sixgallerypress.com, pg 214

Hagaman, Jane, Red Wheel/Weiser/Conari, 65 Parker St, Suite 7, Newburyport, MA 01950 *Tel:* 978-465-0504 *Toll Free Tel:* 800-423-7087 (orders) *Fax:* 978-465-0243 *E-mail:* info@rwwbooks.com *Web Site:* www.redwheelweiser.com, pg 197

Hagan, Lisa, Lisa Hagan Literary, 110 Martin Dr, Bracey, VA 23919 *Tel:* 434-636-4138 *E-mail:* LisaHaganLiterary@yahoo.com *Web Site:* www.publishersmarketplace.com/members/LisaHagan/, pg 520

Hagan, Peter, Dramatists Play Service Inc, 440 Park Ave S, New York, NY 10016 *Tel:* 212-683-8960 *Fax:* 212-213-1539 *E-mail:* postmaster@dramatists.com; orders@dramatists.com; publications@dramatists.com *Web Site:* www.dramatists.com, pg 73

Hagenberg, Mark, Perfection Learning Corp, 1000 N Second Ave, Logan, IA 51546 *Tel:* 712-644-2831 *Toll Free Tel:* 800-831-4190 *Toll Free Fax:* 800-543-2745 *E-mail:* orders@perfectionlearning.com *Web Site:* perfectionlearning.com, pg 180

Hager, Louisa, Workman Publishing Co Inc, 225 Varick St, 9th fl, New York, NY 10014-4381 *Tel:* 212-254-5900 *Toll Free Tel:* 800-722-7202 *Fax:* 212-254-8098 *E-mail:* info@workman.com *Web Site:* www.workman.com, pg 259

Hagerbaumer, Samantha, HarperCollins Publishers, 195 Broadway, New York, NY 10007 *Tel:* 212-207-7000 *Fax:* 212-207-7145 *Web Site:* www.harpercollins.com, pg 102

Hagerty, Katrin, Insight Editions, 800 "A" St, San Rafael, CA 94901 *Tel:* 415-526-1370 *Toll Free Tel:* 800-809-3792 *Toll Free Fax:* 866-509-0515 *E-mail:* info@insighteditions.com *Web Site:* www.insighteditions.com, pg 117

Haggar, Darren, The Penguin Press, 375 Hudson St, New York, NY 10014 *Web Site:* thepenguinpress.com, pg 178

Haggen, Michael, Scholastic Education, 557 Broadway, New York, NY 10012 *Tel:* 212-343-6100 *Fax:* 212-343-6189 *Web Site:* www.scholastic.com, pg 207

Hagman, Lorri, University of Washington Press, 4333 Brooklyn Ave NE, Seattle, WA 98105-9570 *Tel:* 206-543-4050 *Toll Free Tel:* 800-537-5487 (orders) *Fax:* 206-543-3932; 410-516-6998 (orders) *E-mail:* uwapress@uw.edu *Web Site:* www.washington.edu/uwpress, pg 246

Hahn, Dr H George, Towson University Prize for Literature, English Dept, 8000 York Rd, Towson, MD 21252 *Tel:* 410-704-2000 *Fax:* 410-704-3999 *Web Site:* www.towson.edu/english, pg 694

Hahn, Kimiko, George Bogin Memorial Award, 15 Gramercy Park, New York, NY 10003 *Tel:* 212-254-9628 *Web Site:* www.poetrysociety.org, pg 633

Hahn, Kimiko, Alice Fay Di Castagnola Award, 15 Gramercy Park, New York, NY 10003 *Tel:* 212-254-9628 *Web Site:* www.poetrysociety.org, pg 641

Hahn, Kimiko, Norma Farber First Book Award, 15 Gramercy Park, New York, NY 10003 *Tel:* 212-254-9628 *Web Site:* www.poetrysociety.org, pg 645

Hahn, Kimiko, Cecil Hemley Memorial Award, 15 Gramercy Park, New York, NY 10003 *Tel:* 212-254-9628 *Web Site:* www.poetrysociety.org, pg 652

Hahn, Kimiko, Louise Louis/Emily F Bourne Student Poetry Award, 15 Gramercy Park, New York, NY 10003 *Tel:* 212-254-9628 *Web Site:* www.poetrysociety.org, pg 663

Hahn, Kimiko, Lyric Poetry Award, 15 Gramercy Park, New York, NY 10003 *Tel:* 212-254-9628 *Web Site:* www.poetrysociety.org, pg 664

Hahn, Kimiko, Lucille Medwick Memorial Award, 15 Gramercy Park, New York, NY 10003 *Tel:* 212-254-9628 *Web Site:* www.poetrysociety.org, pg 667

Hahn, Kimiko, Poetry Society of America (PSA), 15 Gramercy Park, New York, NY 10003 *Tel:* 212-254-9628 *Web Site:* www.poetrysociety.org, pg 575

Hahn, Kimiko, William Carlos Williams Award, 15 Gramercy Park, New York, NY 10003 *Tel:* 212-254-9628 *Web Site:* www.poetrysociety.org, pg 698

Hahn, Kimiko, The Writer Magazine/Emily Dickinson Award, 15 Gramercy Park, New York, NY 10003 *Tel:* 212-254-9628 *Web Site:* www.poetrysociety.org, pg 700

Hahne, Marj, Big Apple Conference, 5 Penn Plaza, 19th fl, PMB 19059, New York, NY 10001 *Tel:* 917-720-6959 *E-mail:* iwwgquestions@iwwg.org *Web Site:* www.iwwg.org, pg 610

Hahne, Marj, The International Women's Writing Guild (IWWG), 5 Penn Plaza, 19th fl, PMB 19059, New York, NY 10001 *Tel:* 917-720-6959 *E-mail:* iwwgquestions@iwwg.org *Web Site:* www.iwwg.org, pg 568

Hahne, Marj, IWWG Annual Summer Conference, 5 Penn Plaza, 19th fl, PMB 19059, New York, NY 10001 *Tel:* 917-720-6959 *E-mail:* iwwgquestions@iwwg.org *Web Site:* www.iwwg.org, pg 612

Haigler, Katherine, Perseus Books, 250 W 57 St, 15th fl, New York, NY 10107 *Tel:* 212-340-8100 *Toll Free Tel:* 800-343-4499 (cust serv) *Fax:* 212-340-8105 *Web Site:* www.perseusbooks.com, pg 181

Hajnoczky, Helen, University of Calgary Press, 2500 University Dr NW, Calgary, AB T2N 1N4, Canada *Tel:* 403-220-7578 *Fax:* 403-282-0085 *E-mail:* ucpress@ucalgary.ca *Web Site:* press.ucalgary.ca, pg 474

Haldoupis, Nicole, Thistledown Press, 410 Second Ave, Saskatoon, SK S7K 2C3, Canada *Tel:* 306-244-1722 *Fax:* 306-244-1762 *E-mail:* tdpress@thistledownpress.com; editorial@thistledownpress.com; marketing@thistledownpress.com *Web Site:* www.thistledownpress.com, pg 472

Hale, Charles, The MIT Press, One Rogers St, Cambridge, MA 02142 *Tel:* 617-253-5255 *Toll Free Tel:* 800-207-8354 (orders) *Fax:* 617-258-6779; 617-577-1545 (orders) *Web Site:* mitpress.mit.edu, pg 151

Hale, Nancy, Springer Publishing Co, 11 W 42 St, 15th fl, New York, NY 10036-8002 *Tel:* 212-431-4370 *Toll Free Tel:* 877-687-7476 *Fax:* 212-941-7842 *E-mail:* marketing@springerpub.com; cs@springerpub.com (orders); editorial@springerpub.com *Web Site:* www.springerpub.com, pg 219

Hales, Katelyn, Robin Straus Agency Inc, 229 E 79 St, Suite 5A, New York, NY 10075 *Tel:* 212-472-3282 *Fax:* 212-472-3833 *E-mail:* info@robinstrausagency.com *Web Site:* www.robinstrausagency.com, pg 538

Hales, Katelyn, The Wallace Literary Agency, 229 E 79 St, No 5A, New York, NY 10075 *Tel:* 212-472-3282 *Fax:* 212-472-3833 *E-mail:* info@wallaceliteraryagency.com, pg 541

Haley, Elma, Arbordale Publishing, 612 Johnnie Dodds Blvd, Suite A2, Mount Pleasant, SC 29464 *Tel:* 843-971-6722 *Toll Free Tel:* 877-243-3457 *Fax:* 843-216-3804 *E-mail:* customerservice@arbordalepublishing.com; info@arbordalepublishing.com *Web Site:* www.arbordalepublishing.com, pg 20

Hall, Andrea, Albert Whitman & Co, 250 S Northwest Hwy, Suite 320, Park Ridge, IL 60068 *Tel:* 847-232-2800 *Toll Free Tel:* 800-255-7675 *Fax:* 847-581-0039 *E-mail:* mail@albertwhitman.com *Web Site:* www.albertwhitman.com, pg 6

Hall, Cindy, Pippin Publishing, 5201 Dufferin St, Toronto, ON M3H 5T8, Canada *Tel:* 416-667-8731; 426-667-7791 (CN warehouse) *Toll Free Tel:* 800-565-9523 (CN warehouse) *Fax:* 416-667-7832 *Toll Free Fax:* 800-221-9985 (CN warehouse) *E-mail:* utpbooks@utpress.utoronto.ca (CN warehouse) *Web Site:* www.utpguidancecentre.com, pg 467

Hall, Eric, The Rough Notes Co Inc, 11690 Technology Dr, Carmel, IN 46032-5600 *Tel:* 317-582-1600 *Toll Free Tel:* 800-428-4384 (cust serv) *Fax:* 317-816-1000 *Toll Free Fax:* 800-321-1909 *E-mail:* rnc@roughnotes.com *Web Site:* www.roughnotes.com, pg 201

Hall, Heather, Sourcebooks Inc, 1935 Brookdale Rd, Suite 139, Naperville, IL 60563 *Tel:* 630-961-3900 *Toll Free Tel:* 800-432-7444 *Fax:* 630-961-2168 *E-mail:* info@sourcebooks.com; customersupport@sourcebooks.com *Web Site:* www.sourcebooks.com, pg 218

Hall, Kit, Financial Executives Research Foundation Inc (FERF), West Tower, 7th fl, 1250 Headquarters Plaza, Morristown, NJ 07960-6837 *Tel:* 973-765-1000 *Fax:* 973-765-1023 *Web Site:* www.financialexecutives.org, pg 84

Hall, Laurie, US Government Publishing Office (GPO), Superintendent of Documents, 732 N Capitol St NW, Washington, DC 20401 *Tel:* 202-512-1800 *Toll Free Tel:* 866-512-1800 (orders) *Fax:* 202-512-2104 *E-mail:* contactcenter@gpo.gov *Web Site:* www.gpo.gov; bookstore.gpo.gov (sales), pg 249

Hall, Linda, The Society of Professional Journalists (SPJ), Eugene S Pulliam National Journalism Ctr, 3909 N Meridian St, Indianapolis, IN 46208 *Tel:* 317-927-8000 *Fax:* 317-920-4789 *E-mail:* spj@spj.org *Web Site:* www.spj.org, pg 580

Hall, Lindsey, Orbit, 1290 Avenue of the Americas, New York, NY 10019 *Tel:* 212-364-1100 *Toll Free Tel:* 800-759-0190 *Web Site:* www.orbitbooks.net, pg 169

Hall, Marie, Fordham University Press, Joseph A Martino Hall, 45 Columbus Ave, New York, NY 10023 *Fax:* 347-842-3083 *Web Site:* www.fordhampress.com, pg 86

Hall, Megan, Athabasca University Press, Edmonton Learning Ctr, Peace Hills Trust Tower, 1200, 10011-109 St, Edmonton, AB T5J 3S8, Canada *Tel:* 780-497-3412 *Fax:* 780-421-3298 *E-mail:* aupress@athabascau.ca *Web Site:* www.aupress.ca, pg 446

Hall, Melissa, BOA Editions Ltd, 250 N Goodman St, Suite 306, Rochester, NY 14607 *Tel:* 585-546-3410 *Fax:* 585-546-3913 *E-mail:* contact@boaeditions.org *Web Site:* www.boaeditions.org, pg 39

Hall, Nancy, American Book Producers Association (ABPA), 31 W Eighth St, 2nd fl, New York, NY 10011 *Tel:* 212-675-1363 *Fax:* 212-675-1364 *E-mail:* office@abpaonline.org *Web Site:* www.abpaonline.org, pg 554

Hall, Mr Sidney Jr, Hobblebush Books, 17-A Old Milford Rd, Brookline, NH 03033 *Tel:* 603-672-4317 *Fax:* 603-672-4317 *E-mail:* hobblebush@charter.net; info@hobblebush.com *Web Site:* www.hobblebush.com, pg 108

Hall, Tanya, Greenleaf Book Group LLC, 3 Park Place, 4005 Banister Lane, Suite B, Austin, TX 78704 *Tel:* 512-891-6100 *Fax:* 512-891-6150 *E-mail:* contact@greenleafbookgroup.com *Web Site:* www.greenleafbookgroup.com, pg 96

Hall, Tina, Hamilton College, English/Creative Writing, English/Creative Writing Dept, 198 College Hill Rd, Clinton, NY 13323 *Tel:* 315-859-4370 *Fax:* 315-859-4390 *Web Site:* www.hamilton.edu, pg 620

Haller, Jennifer, Penguin Young Readers Group, 345 Hudson St, New York, NY 10014 *Tel:* 212-366-2000; 212-414-3553 *Fax:* 212-414-3340 *Web Site:* www.penguin.com/children, pg 179

Harpster, Kristin, Wayne State University Press, Leonard N Simons Bldg, 4809 Woodward Ave, Detroit, MI 48201-1309 *Tel:* 313-577-6120 *Toll Free Tel:* 800-978-7323 *Fax:* 313-577-6131 *E-mail:* bookorders@wayne.edu *Web Site:* www.wsupress.wayne.edu, pg 253

Harrell, Casey, Thomas Nelson, 501 Nelson Place, Nashville, TN 37214 *Tel:* 615-889-9000 *Toll Free Tel:* 800-251-4000 *Fax:* 615-902-1548 *Web Site:* www.thomasnelson.com, pg 231

Harri, Kaitlin, HarperCollins General Books Group, 195 Broadway, New York, NY 10007 *Tel:* 212-207-7000 *Web Site:* www.harpercollins.com, pg 101

Harriet, Sydney H PhD, Agent's Ink, PO Box 4956, Fresno, CA 93744-4956 *Tel:* 559-438-1883 *Fax:* 559-438-8289 *Web Site:* agents-ink.com, pg 506

Harrington, Dorota, Owl About Books Publisher Inc, 1632 Royalwood Circle, Joshua, TX 76058 *Tel:* 682-553-9078 *Fax:* 817-558-8983 *E-mail:* owlaboutbooks@gmail.com *Web Site:* www.owlaboutbooks.com, pg 171

Harrington, Joyce, Adams & Ambrose Publishing, PO Box 259684, Madison, WI 53725-9684 *Tel:* 608-977-1825 *E-mail:* info@adamsambrose.com, pg 4

Harrington, Paul, Berghahn Books, 20 Jay St, Suite 512, Brooklyn, NY 11201 *Tel:* 212-233-6004 *Fax:* 212-233-6007 *E-mail:* info@berghahnbooks.com; salesus@berghahnbooks.com; editorial@journals.berghahnbooks.com *Web Site:* www.berghahnbooks.com, pg 33

Harrington, Paul, CN Times Books, 501 Fifth Ave, Suite 1708, New York, NY 10017 *Tel:* 212-867-8666 *Web Site:* cntimesbooks.com, pg 57

Harrington, Dr Robert M, American Mathematical Society, 201 Charles St, Providence, RI 02904-2294 *Tel:* 401-455-4000 *Toll Free Tel:* 800-321-4267 *Fax:* 401-331-3842; 401-455-4046 (cust serv) *E-mail:* ams@ams.org; cust-serv@ams.org *Web Site:* www.ams.org, pg 13

Harrington, Roby, W W Norton & Company Inc, 500 Fifth Ave, New York, NY 10110-0017 *Tel:* 212-354-5500 *Toll Free Tel:* 800-233-4830 (orders & cust serv) *Fax:* 212-869-0856 *Toll Free Fax:* 800-458-6515 *E-mail:* orders@wwnorton.com *Web Site:* books.wwnorton.com, pg 164

Harriot, Michael, Folio Literary Management, The Film Center Bldg, 630 Ninth Ave, Suite 1101, New York, NY 10036 *Tel:* 212-400-1494 *Fax:* 212-967-0977 *Web Site:* www.foliolit.com, pg 517

Harris, Alec, GIA Publications Inc, 7404 S Mason Ave, Chicago, IL 60638 *Tel:* 708-496-3800 *Toll Free Tel:* 800-GIA-1358 (442-1358) *Fax:* 708-496-3828 *E-mail:* custserv@giamusic.com *Web Site:* www.giamusic.com, pg 92

Harris, Alyza, The Publishing Game, PO Box 590239, Newton, MA 02459-0002 *Tel:* 617-630-0945 *Fax:* 617-630-0945 (call first) *E-mail:* info@publishinggame.com; workshops@publishinggame.com *Web Site:* www.publishinggame.com, pg 614

Harris, Amy, The University Press of Kentucky, 663 S Limestone St, Lexington, KY 40508-4008 *Tel:* 859-257-8400 *Fax:* 859-257-8481 *Web Site:* www.kentuckypress.com, pg 247

Harris, Bill, BookEnds Literary Agency, 136 Long Hill Rd, Gillette, NJ 07933 *Web Site:* www.bookendsliterary.com, pg 508

Harris, Chris, MapEasy Inc, PO Box 80, Wainscott, NY 11975-0080 *Tel:* 631-537-6213 *Fax:* 631-537-4541 *E-mail:* info@mapeasy.com *Web Site:* www.mapeasy.com, pg 141

Harris, Dan R, Favorable Impressions, 51910 Shoreview Dr, Shelby Township, MI 48316 *Tel:* 248-635-2957 *Web Site:* www.favimp.com, pg 83

Harris, David A, American Jewish Committee (AJC), Jacob Blaustein Bldg, 165 E 56 St, New York, NY 10022 *Tel:* 212-751-4000; 212-891-1456 (membership) *Fax:* 212-891-1450 *Web Site:* www.ajc.org, pg 555

Harris, Debra, All Things That Matter Press, 79 Jones Rd, Somerville, ME 04348 *E-mail:* allthingsthatmatterpress@gmail.com *Web Site:* www.allthingsthatmatterpress.com, pg 7

Harris, Erin, Folio Literary Management, The Film Center Bldg, 630 Ninth Ave, Suite 1101, New York, NY 10036 *Tel:* 212-400-1494 *Fax:* 212-967-0977 *Web Site:* www.foliolit.com, pg 517

Harris, Joy, The Joy Harris Literary Agency Inc, 1501 Broadway, Suite 2310, New York, NY 10036 *Tel:* 212-924-6269 *Fax:* 212-840-5776 *E-mail:* contact@joyharrisliterary.com *Web Site:* www.joyharrisliterary.com, pg 520

Harris, Laurie Lanzen, Favorable Impressions, 51910 Shoreview Dr, Shelby Township, MI 48316 *Tel:* 248-635-2957 *Web Site:* www.favimp.com, pg 83

Harris, Mark, I-5 Publishing LLC, 3 Burroughs, Irvine, CA 92618 *Tel:* 949-855-8822 *Toll Free Tel:* 888-738-2665 *Fax:* 949-458-3856 *Web Site:* www.i5publishing.com, pg 113

Harris, Michelle, News Media Alliance, 4401 N Fairfax Dr, Suite 300, Arlington, VA 22203 *Tel:* 571-366-1000 *E-mail:* info@newsmediaalliance.org *Web Site:* www.newsmediaalliance.org, pg 573

Harris, Peter, Penguin Group USA, A Penguin Random House Company, 375 Hudson St, New York, NY 10014 *Tel:* 212-366-2000 *Toll Free Tel:* 800-847-5515 (inside sales); 800-631-8571 (cust serv) *Fax:* 212-366-2666; 607-775-4829 (inside sales) *E-mail:* online@us.penguingroup.com *Web Site:* www.penguin.com, pg 177

Harris, Ross, Stuart Krichevsky Literary Agency Inc, 6 E 39 St, Suite 500, New York, NY 10016 *Tel:* 212-725-5288 *Fax:* 212-725-5275 *E-mail:* query@skagency.com *Web Site:* skagency.com, pg 525

Harris, Sloan, ICM Partners, 65 E 55 St, New York, NY 10022 *Tel:* 212-556-5600 *Web Site:* www.icmtalent.com, pg 521

Harris, Steve, Concordia Publishing House, 3558 S Jefferson Ave, St Louis, MO 63118-3968 *Tel:* 314-268-1000; 314-268-1268 (bookshop) *Toll Free Tel:* 800-325-3040 (cust serv) *Toll Free Fax:* 800-490-9889 (cust serv) *E-mail:* order@cph.org *Web Site:* www.cph.org, pg 59

Harrison, Colin, Scribner, 1230 Avenue of the Americas, New York, NY 10020, pg 209

Harrison, DeSales, Oberlin College Press, 50 N Professor St, Oberlin, OH 44074-1091 *Tel:* 440-775-8408 *Fax:* 440-775-8124 *E-mail:* oc.press@oberlin.edu *Web Site:* www.oberlin.edu/ocpress, pg 166

Harrison, Heather, Parallax Press, 2236-B Sixth St, Berkeley, CA 94710 *Tel:* 510-540-6411 *Toll Free Tel:* 800-863-5290 (orders) *Fax:* 510-981-1157 *Web Site:* www.parallax.org, pg 174

Harrison, Joyce, University Press of Kansas, 2502 Westbrooke Circle, Lawrence, KS 66045-4444 *Tel:* 785-864-4154; 785-864-4155 (orders) *Fax:* 785-864-4586 *E-mail:* upress@ku.edu; upkorders@ku.edu (orders) *Web Site:* www.kansaspress.ku.edu, pg 246

Harrison, Katherine, Dial Books for Young Readers, 345 Hudson St, New York, NY 10014 *Tel:* 212-366-2000 *Toll Free Tel:* 800-733-3000 (orders) *Fax:* 212-414-3396 *Web Site:* www.penguin.com, pg 70

Harrison, Katherine, Random House Children's Books, 1745 Broadway, 10th fl, New York, NY 10019 *Tel:* 212-782-9000 *Web Site:* www.randomhousekids.com, pg 194

Harrison, Nick, Harvest House Publishers Inc, 990 Owen Loop N, Eugene, OR 97402-9173 *Tel:* 541-343-0123 *Toll Free Tel:* 888-501-6991 *Fax:* 541-342-6410 *E-mail:* admin@harvesthousepublishers.com *Web Site:* harvesthousepublishers.com, pg 103

Harrison, Patricia de Stacy, Corporation for Public Broadcasting (CPB), 401 Ninth St NW, Washington, DC 20004-2129 *Tel:* 202-879-9600 *Web Site:* www.cpb.org, pg 563

Harriss, Clarinda, BrickHouse Books Inc, 306 Suffolk Rd, Baltimore, MD 21218 *Fax:* 410-235-7690 *Web Site:* brickhousebooks.wordpress.com, pg 43

Hart, Jim, Hartline Literary Agency LLC, 123 Queenston Dr, Pittsburgh, PA 15235 *Web Site:* www.hartlineliterary.com, pg 520

Hart, Joyce, Hartline Literary Agency LLC, 123 Queenston Dr, Pittsburgh, PA 15235 *Web Site:* www.hartlineliterary.com, pg 520

Hart, Tara, Penguin Random House Audio Publishing, 1745 Broadway, New York, NY 10019 *E-mail:* audio@penguinrandomhouse.com *Web Site:* www.penguinrandomhouseaudio.com, pg 178

Harting, Laurie, Palgrave Macmillan, One New York Plaza, Suite 4500, New York, NY 10004-1562 *Tel:* 212-726-9200 *E-mail:* sales-ny@springernature.com; sales@palgrave-usa.com *Web Site:* www.palgrave.com, pg 172

Hartjens, Elisabeth M, Imagefinders Inc, 6101 Utah Ave NW, Washington, DC 20015 *Fax:* 202-244-3237, pg 496

Hartley, Glen, Writers' Representatives LLC, 116 W 14 St, 11th fl, New York, NY 10011-7305 *Tel:* 212-620-9009 *Fax:* 212-620-0023 *E-mail:* transom@writersreps.com *Web Site:* www.writersreps.com, pg 542

Hartley, John, Peter Pauper Press, Inc, 202 Mamaroneck Ave, Suite 400, White Plains, NY 10601-5376 *Tel:* 914-681-0144 *Fax:* 914-681-0389 *E-mail:* customerservice@peterpauper.com; orders@peterpauper.com; marketing@peterpauper.com *Web Site:* www.peterpauper.com, pg 181

Hartline, Connie, American Public Works Association (APWA), 2345 Grand Blvd, Suite 700, Kansas City, MO 64108-2625 *Tel:* 816-472-6100 *Toll Free Tel:* 800-848-APWA (848-2792) *Fax:* 816-472-1610 *Web Site:* www.apwa.net, pg 14

Hartman, Charles, National Council of Teachers of English (NCTE), 1111 W Kenyon Rd, Urbana, IL 61801-1096 *Tel:* 217-328-3870 *Toll Free Tel:* 877-369-6283 (cust serv) *Fax:* 217-328-9645 *E-mail:* orders@ncte.org *Web Site:* www.ncte.org, pg 158

Hartman, Erinn, Alfred A Knopf/Everyman's Library, c/o Penguin Random House Inc, 1745 Broadway, New York, NY 10019 *Tel:* 212-751-2600 *Toll Free Tel:* 800-638-6460 *Fax:* 212-572-2593 *Web Site:* www.knopfdoubleday.com, pg 127

Hartman, Mark, Hartman Publishing Inc, 1313 Iron Ave SW, Albuquerque, NM 87102 *Tel:* 505-291-1274 *Toll Free Tel:* 800-999-9534 *Fax:* 505-291-1284 *Toll Free Fax:* 800-474-6106 *E-mail:* orders@hartmanonline.com; help@hartmanonline.com *Web Site:* www.hartmanonline.com, pg 102

Hartman, William, Quintessence Publishing Co Inc, 4350 Chandler Dr, Hanover Park, IL 60133 *Tel:* 630-736-3600 *Toll Free Tel:* 800-621-0387 *Fax:* 630-736-3633 *E-mail:* contact@quintbook.com; service@quintbook.com *Web Site:* www.quintpub.com, pg 193

Hartnett, Laura, The Ralph Waldo Emerson Award, 1606 New Hampshire Ave NW, Washington, DC 20009 *Tel:* 202-265-3808 *Fax:* 202-986-1601 *E-mail:* awards@pbk.org *Web Site:* www.pbk.org/bookawards, pg 644

Hartnett, Laura, The Christian Gauss Award, 1606 New Hampshire Ave NW, Washington, DC 20009 *Tel:* 202-265-3808 *Fax:* 202-986-1601 *E-mail:* awards@pbk.org *Web Site:* www.pbk.org/bookawards, pg 649

Hartnett, Laura, Phi Beta Kappa Award in Science, 1606 New Hampshire Ave NW, Washington, DC 20009 *Tel:* 202-265-3808 *Fax:* 202-986-1601 *E-mail:* awards@pbk.org *Web Site:* www.pbk.org/bookawards, pg 679

Hartogh, Frances, Rocky Mountain Mineral Law Foundation, 9191 Sheridan Blvd, Suite 203, Westminster, CO 80031 *Tel:* 303-321-8100 *Fax:* 303-321-7657 *E-mail:* info@rmmlf.org *Web Site:* www.rmmlf.org, pg 200

Hartshorn, Erin M, Science Fiction & Fantasy Writers of America Inc (SFWA), PO Box 3238, Enfield, CT 06083-3238 *E-mail:* office@sfwa.org *Web Site:* www.sfwa.org, pg 577

Hartshorn, Erin M, SFWA Nebula Awards, PO Box 3238, Enfield, CT 06083-3238 *E-mail:* office@sfwa.org *Web Site:* www.sfwa.org, pg 688

Hartson, Kate, Hachette Nashville, 12 Cadillac Dr, Suite 480, Brentwood, TN 37027 *Tel:* 615-221-0996 *Fax:* 615-221-0962 *Web Site:* www.hachettebookgroup.com, pg 98

Hartt, Jordan, Port Townsend Writers' Conference, 223 Battery Way, Port Townsend, WA 98368 *Tel:* 360-385-3102 *Toll Free Tel:* 800-733-3608 (ticket off) *Fax:* 360-385-2470 *E-mail:* info@centrum.org *Web Site:* centrum.org, pg 613

Harty, Pamela, The Knight Agency Inc, 570 East Ave, Madison, GA 30650 *E-mail:* submissions@knightagency.net *Web Site:* www.knightagency.net, pg 524

Harvey, Dr Alan, Stanford University Press, 425 Broadway St, Redwood City, CA 94063-3126 *Tel:* 650-723-9434 *Fax:* 650-725-3457 *E-mail:* info@www.sup.org; publicity@www.sup.org *Web Site:* www.sup.org, pg 220

Harwell, Andrew, HarperCollins Children's Books, 195 Broadway, New York, NY 10007 *Tel:* 212-207-7000 *Web Site:* www.harpercollins.com/childrens, pg 101

Harwell, Sarah C, Syracuse University Creative Writing Program, 401 Hall of Languages, Syracuse, NY 13244-1170 *Tel:* 315-443-2173 *Fax:* 315-443-3660 *Web Site:* english.syr.edu/creative_writing; www.syr.edu, pg 622

Harwood, Josh, Houghton Mifflin Harcourt Trade & Reference Division, 125 High St, Boston, MA 02110 *Tel:* 617-351-5000 *Toll Free Tel:* 800-225-3362 *Web Site:* www.hmhco.com, pg 111

Hashimoto, Meika, Random House Children's Books, 1745 Broadway, 10th fl, New York, NY 10019 *Tel:* 212-782-9000 *Web Site:* www.randomhousekids.com, pg 194

Haskell, Arlo, Key West Literary Seminar, 717 Love Lane, Key West, FL 33040 *Tel:* 305-293-9291 *Toll Free Tel:* 888-293-9291 *E-mail:* mail@kwls.org *Web Site:* www.kwls.org/seminar; www.kwls.org, pg 612

Haskell, Arlo, Key West Literary Seminar's Writers' Workshop Program, 717 Love Lane, Key West, FL 33040 *Tel:* 305-293-9291 *Toll Free Tel:* 888-293-9291 *E-mail:* mail@kwls.org *Web Site:* www.kwls.org; www.kwls.org/writers_workshops, pg 612

Haskin, Jennifer, Metamorphosis Literary Agency, 12837 S Seminole Dr, Olathe, KS 66062 *Tel:* 646-397-1640 *E-mail:* info@metamorphosisliteraryagency.com *Web Site:* www.metamorphosisliteraryagency.com, pg 529

Hass, Robert, Squaw Valley Community of Writers Summer Workshops, PO Box 1416, Nevada City, CA 95959 *Tel:* 530-470-8440 *E-mail:* info@communityofwriters.org *Web Site:* www.communityofwriters.org, pg 615

Hassan, Shannon, Marsal Lyon Literary Agency LLC, 665 San Rodolfo Dr, Suite 124, PMB 121, Solana Beach, CA 92075 *Tel:* 760-814-8507 *Web Site:* www.marsallyonliteraryagency.com, pg 527

Hasselstrom, Linda M, Windbreak House Writing Retreat, PO Box 169, Hermosa, SD 57744-0169 *Tel:* 605-255-4064 *E-mail:* info@windbreakhouse.com *Web Site:* www.windbreakhouse.com, pg 616

Hassman, Chelsea, Random House Children's Books, 1745 Broadway, 10th fl, New York, NY 10019 *Tel:* 212-782-9000 *Web Site:* www.randomhousekids.com, pg 194

Hasso, M (May) H, Boston Informatics, 35 Byard Lane, Westborough, MA 01581 *Tel:* 508-366-8176 *Web Site:* www.bostoninformatics.com, pg 490

Hastings, Katherine, Susquehanna University, Department of English and Creative Writing, 514 University Ave, Selinsgrove, PA 17870 *Tel:* 570-372-0101, pg 622

Hastings, Vinsula, Modern Memoirs, 34 Main St, No 6, Amherst, MA 01002-2367 *Tel:* 413-253-2353 *Web Site:* www.modernmemoirs.com; www.whitepoppypress.com, pg 152

Hatch, Alexander, Adams Media, 57 Littlefield St, Avon, MA 02322 *Tel:* 508-427-7100 *Web Site:* www.simonandschuster.com, pg 4

Hatch, James C, Committee On Scholarly Editions, c/o Modern Language Association of America, 26 Broadway, 3rd fl, New York, NY 10004-1789 *Tel:* 646-576-5044 *Fax:* 646-458-0030 *Web Site:* www.mla.org, pg 563

Hatch, Ronald, Ronsdale Press Ltd, 3350 W 21 Ave, Vancouver, BC V6S 1G7, Canada *Tel:* 604-738-4688 *Fax:* 604-731-4548 *E-mail:* ronsdale@shaw.ca *Web Site:* ronsdalepress.com, pg 469

Hatch, Veronica, Ronsdale Press Ltd, 3350 W 21 Ave, Vancouver, BC V6S 1G7, Canada *Tel:* 604-738-4688 *Fax:* 604-731-4548 *E-mail:* ronsdale@shaw.ca *Web Site:* ronsdalepress.com, pg 469

Hatter, Richard W, John Simon Guggenheim Memorial Foundation, 90 Park Ave, New York, NY 10016 *Tel:* 212-687-4470 *Fax:* 212-697-3248 *E-mail:* fellowships@gf.org *Web Site:* www.gf.org, pg 583

Hatzakos, Jan, Association for Information Science & Technology (ASIS&T), 8555 16 St, Suite 850, Silver Spring, MD 20910 *Tel:* 301-495-0900 *Fax:* 301-495-0810 *E-mail:* asist@asist.org *Web Site:* www.asist.org, pg 557

Hauber, Janine, Sheldon Fogelman Agency Inc, 420 E 72 St, New York, NY 10021 *Tel:* 212-532-7250 *Fax:* 212-685-8939 *E-mail:* info@sheldonfogelmanagency.com *Web Site:* sheldonfogelmanagency.com, pg 517

Haubner, Julianna, Simon & Schuster, 1230 Avenue of the Americas, New York, NY 10020 *Tel:* 212-698-7000 *Toll Free Tel:* 800-223-2348 (cust serv); 800-223-2336 (orders) *Toll Free Fax:* 800-943-9831 (orders) *Web Site:* www.simonandschuster.com, pg 212

Hauck, Hilary, Pennwriters Conference, PO Box 685, Dalton, PA 18414 *E-mail:* conferencecoordinator@pennwriters.org; info@pennwriters.org *Web Site:* pennwriters.org, pg 613

Hauck, Michael T, DEStech Publications Inc, 439 N Duke St, Lancaster, PA 17602-4967 *Tel:* 717-290-1660 *Toll Free Tel:* 877-500-4337 *Fax:* 717-509-6100 *E-mail:* info@destechpub.com *Web Site:* www.destechpub.com, pg 69

Haugen, Sarah, HarperCollins General Books Group, 195 Broadway, New York, NY 10007 *Tel:* 212-207-7000 *Web Site:* www.harpercollins.com, pg 101

Haugh, Clare, Perseus Books, 250 W 57 St, 15th fl, New York, NY 10107 *Tel:* 212-340-8100 *Toll Free Tel:* 800-343-4499 (cust serv) *Fax:* 212-340-8105 *Web Site:* www.perseusbooks.com, pg 180

Haughian, Karen, Signature Editions, PO Box 206, RPO Corydon, Winnipeg, MB R3M 3S7, Canada *Tel:* 204-779-7803 *E-mail:* submissions@signature-editions.com; orders@signature-editions.com *Web Site:* www.signature-editions.com, pg 470

Haun, Sue, Teton NewMedia Inc, 90 E Simpson, Suite 110, Jackson, WY 83001 *Tel:* 307-732-0028 *Toll Free Tel:* 877-306-9793 *Fax:* 307-734-0841 *E-mail:* sales@tetonnm.com *Web Site:* www.tetonnm.com, pg 230

Haut, Judith, Random House Children's Books, 1745 Broadway, 10th fl, New York, NY 10019 *Tel:* 212-782-9000 *Web Site:* www.randomhousekids.com, pg 194

Hawkins, Anne, John Hawkins and Associates Inc, 80 Maiden Lane, Suite 1503, New York, NY 10038 *Tel:* 212-807-7040 *E-mail:* jha@jhalit.com *Web Site:* jhalit.com, pg 521

Hawkins, Bob Jr, Harvest House Publishers Inc, 990 Owen Loop N, Eugene, OR 97402-9173 *Tel:* 541-343-0123 *Toll Free Tel:* 888-501-6991 *Fax:* 541-342-6410 *E-mail:* admin@harvesthousepublishers.com *Web Site:* harvesthousepublishers.com, pg 103

Hawkins, Drew, Canadian Scholars' Press Inc, 425 Adelaide St W, Suite 200, Toronto, ON M5V 3C1, Canada *Tel:* 416-929-2774 *Toll Free Tel:* 800-463-1998 *Fax:* 416-929-1926 *E-mail:* info@cspi.org; info@canadianscholars.ca; editorial@canadianscholars.ca; orders@canadianscholars.ca *Web Site:* www.canadianscholars.ca; www.womenspress.ca, pg 449

Hawkins, Janet, Trillium Book Award/Prix Trillium, South Tower, Suite 501, 175 Bloor St E, Toronto, ON M4W 3R8, Canada *Tel:* 416-314-6858 (ext 698) *Fax:* 416-314-6876 *Web Site:* www.omdc.on.ca, pg 694

Hawley, Marcy, Orange Frazer Press Inc, 37 1/2 W Main St, Wilmington, OH 45177 *Tel:* 937-382-3196 *Toll Free Tel:* 800-852-9332 (orders) *Fax:* 937-383-3159 *E-mail:* ofrazer@erinet.com *Web Site:* www.orangefrazer.com, pg 169

Hawley, Sarah, Orange Frazer Press Inc, 37 1/2 W Main St, Wilmington, OH 45177 *Tel:* 937-382-3196 *Toll Free Tel:* 800-852-9332 (orders) *Fax:* 937-383-3159 *E-mail:* ofrazer@erinet.com *Web Site:* www.orangefrazer.com, pg 169

Hawley, Tom, Association of Catholic Publishers Inc, 4725 Dorsey Hall Dr, Suite A, PMB 709, Elliott City, MD 21042 *Tel:* 410-988-2926 *Fax:* 410-571-4946 *Web Site:* www.catholicsread.org; www.catholicpublishers.org; www.midatlanticcongress.org, pg 558

Hay, Louise, Hay House Inc, 2776 Loker Ave W, Carlsbad, CA 92010 *Tel:* 760-431-7695 (ext 2, intl) *Toll Free Tel:* 800-654-5126 (ext 2, US) *Toll Free Fax:* 800-650-5115 *E-mail:* info@hayhouse.com; editorial@hayhouse.com *Web Site:* www.hayhouse.com, pg 103

Hayden, Cynthia, Lake Superior Port Cities Inc, 310 E Superior St, Suite 125, Duluth, MN 55802 *Tel:* 218-722-5002 *Toll Free Tel:* 888-BIG-LAKE (244-5253) *Fax:* 218-722-4096 *E-mail:* reader@lakesuperior.com *Web Site:* www.lakesuperior.com, pg 129

Hayden, Jeffrey, International Monetary Fund (IMF), Editorial & Publications Division, 700 19 St NW, HQ1-7-124, Washington, DC 20431 *Tel:* 202-623-7430 *Fax:* 202-623-7201 *E-mail:* publications@imf.org *Web Site:* bookstore.imf.org; elibrary.imf.org (online collection), pg 120

Hayden, Patrick Nielsen, Tom Doherty Associates, LLC, 175 Fifth Ave, 14th fl, New York, NY 10010 *Tel:* 646-307-5511 *Toll Free Tel:* 800-455-0340 *Web Site:* www.tor-forge.com, pg 71

Hayden, Paul L, Lake Superior Port Cities Inc, 310 E Superior St, Suite 125, Duluth, MN 55802 *Tel:* 218-722-5002 *Toll Free Tel:* 888-BIG-LAKE (244-5253) *Fax:* 218-722-4096 *E-mail:* reader@lakesuperior.com *Web Site:* www.lakesuperior.com, pg 129

Hayden, Thomas K, National Notary Association (NNA), 9350 De Soto Ave, Chatsworth, CA 91311-4926 *Tel:* 818-739-4000 *Toll Free Tel:* 800-876-6827 *Toll Free Fax:* 800-833-1211 *E-mail:* nna@nationalnotary.org *Web Site:* www.nationalnotary.org, pg 159

Hayden, William, The H W Wilson Foundation, 420 Lexington Ave, Suite 2450, New York, NY 10170 *Tel:* 212-972-6490 *Web Site:* www.thwwf.org, pg 583

Haydon, Roger, Cornell University Press, Sage House, 512 E State St, Ithaca, NY 14850 *Tel:* 607-277-2338 *Fax:* 607-277-2374 *E-mail:* cupressinfo@cornell.edu; cupress-sales@cornell.edu *Web Site:* www.cornellpress.cornell.edu, pg 61

Hayes, Amy, Sourcebooks Inc, 1935 Brookdale Rd, Suite 139, Naperville, IL 60563 *Tel:* 630-961-3900 *Toll Free Tel:* 800-432-7444 *Fax:* 630-961-2168 *E-mail:* info@sourcebooks.com; customersupport@sourcebooks.com *Web Site:* www.sourcebooks.com, pg 218

Hayes, Kevin, Omnigraphics Inc, 615 Griswold, Suite 901, Detroit, MI 48226 *Tel:* 610-461-3548 *Toll Free Tel:* 800-234-1340 (cust serv) *Fax:* 610-532-9001 *Toll*

Henson, Gwen, ASI/EIS Publishing Award for Excellence in Indexing, 1628 E Southern Ave, Suite 9-223, Tempe, AZ 85282 *Tel:* 480-245-6750 *E-mail:* info@asindexing.org *Web Site:* www.asindexing.org, pg 628

Henson, Kristi, University of Alabama Press, 200 Hackberry Lane, 2nd fl, Tuscaloosa, AL 35487 *Tel:* 205-348-5180 *Fax:* 205-348-9201 *Web Site:* www.uapress.ua.edu, pg 239

Henson, Victoria, Perseus Books, 250 W 57 St, 15th fl, New York, NY 10107 *Tel:* 212-340-8100 *Toll Free Tel:* 800-343-4499 (cust serv) *Fax:* 212-340-8105 *Web Site:* www.perseusbooks.com, pg 181

Hentz, Brad, Sourcebooks Inc, 1935 Brookdale Rd, Suite 139, Naperville, IL 60563 *Tel:* 630-961-3900 *Toll Free Tel:* 800-432-7444 *Fax:* 630-961-2168 *E-mail:* info@sourcebooks.com; customersupport@sourcebooks.com *Web Site:* www.sourcebooks.com, pg 218

Herbert, Karen Brown, Karen Brown's Guides Inc, 16 E Third Ave, Suite 9, San Mateo, CA 94401 *Tel:* 650-342-9117 *Fax:* 650-342-9153 *Web Site:* www.karenbrown.com, pg 45

Herbert-Copley, Brent, Social Sciences & Humanities Research Council of Canada (SSHRC), 350 Albert St, Ottawa, ON K1P 6G4, Canada *Tel:* 613-992-0691 *E-mail:* research@sshrc-crsh.gc.ca *Web Site:* www.sshrc.ca, pg 578

Herbst, John, Indiana Historical Society Press (IHS Press), 450 W Ohio St, Indianapolis, IN 46202-3269 *Tel:* 317-232-1882; 317-234-0026 (orders); 317-234-2716 (edit) *Toll Free Tel:* 800-447-1830 (orders) *Fax:* 317-234-0562 (orders); 317-233-0857 (edit) *E-mail:* ihspress@indianahistory.org; orders@indianahistory.org (orders) *Web Site:* www.indianahistory.org; shop.indianahistory.org (orders), pg 115

Herd, Caroline, Basic Health Publications, 4507 Charlotte Ave, Suite 100, Nashville, TN 37209 *Tel:* 615-255-2665, pg 30

Herder, Dr Gwendolin, The Crossroad Publishing Co, 831 Chestnut Ridge Rd, Chestnut Ridge, NY 10977 *Tel:* 845-517-0180 *Toll Free Tel:* 800-888-4741 (orders) *Fax:* 845-517-0181 *E-mail:* office@crossroadpublishing.com *Web Site:* www.CrossroadPublishing.com, pg 65

Hergenroeder, Jennifer, The Experiment, 220 E 23 St, Suite 301, New York, NY 10010-4674 *Tel:* 212-889-1659 *E-mail:* info@theexperimentpublishing.com *Web Site:* www.theexperimentpublishing.com, pg 81

Heritage, Barbara, Bibliographical Society of America, PO Box 1537, Lenox Hill Sta, New York, NY 10021-0043 *Tel:* 212-452-2710 *Fax:* 212-452-2710 *E-mail:* bsa@bibsocamer.org *Web Site:* www.bibsocamer.org, pg 560

Herits, Noreen, Random House Children's Books, 1745 Broadway, 10th fl, New York, NY 10019 *Tel:* 212-782-9000 *Web Site:* www.randomhousekids.com, pg 194

Hermalyn, Sarah, Harlequin Enterprises Ltd, 233 Broadway, Suite 1001, New York, NY 10279 *Tel:* 212-553-4200 *Fax:* 212-227-8969 *E-mail:* customerservice@harlequin.com *Web Site:* www.harlequin.com, pg 101

Herman, Cheryl, Books on Tape®, 1745 Broadway, New York, NY 10019 *Toll Free Tel:* 800-733-3000 (cust serv) *Toll Free Fax:* 800-940-7046 *Web Site:* www.booksontape.com, pg 40

Herman, Gilles, Les Editions du Septentrion, 835 Turnbull Ave, Quebec City, QC G1R 2X4, Canada *Tel:* 418-688-3556 *Fax:* 418-527-4978 *E-mail:* info@septentrion.qc.ca *Web Site:* www.septentrion.qc.ca, pg 454

Herman, Heather, Morton Publishing Co, 925 W Kenyon Ave, Unit 12, Englewood, CO 80110 *Tel:* 303-761-4805 *Fax:* 303-762-9923 *E-mail:* contact@morton-pub.com; returns@morton-pub.com *Web Site:* www.morton-pub.com, pg 154

Herman, Jeffrey H, The Jeff Herman Agency LLC, 29 Park St, Stockbridge, MA 01262 *Tel:* 413-298-0077 *Fax:* 413-298-8188 *E-mail:* submissions@jeffherman.com *Web Site:* www.jeffherman.com, pg 521

Herman, Rhonda, McFarland, 960 NC Hwy 88 W, Jefferson, NC 28640 *Tel:* 336-246-4460 *Toll Free Tel:* 800-253-2187 (orders) *Fax:* 336-246-5018; 336-246-4403 (orders) *E-mail:* info@mcfarlandpub.com *Web Site:* www.mcfarlandpub.com, pg 145

Herman, Ronnie Ann, Herman Agency, 350 Central Park W, Apt 4I, New York, NY 10025 *Tel:* 212-749-4907 *Web Site:* www.hermanagencyinc.com, pg 543

Herman, Susan N, American Civil Liberties Union, 125 Broad St, 18th fl, New York, NY 10004 *Tel:* 212-549-2500 *E-mail:* media@aclu.org *Web Site:* www.aclu.org, pg 554

Hermann, Sara, Parmenides Publishing, 3753 Howard Hughes Pkwy, Suite 200, Las Vegas, NV 89169 *Tel:* 702-892-3934 *Fax:* 702-892-3939 *E-mail:* info@parmenides.com *Web Site:* www.parmenides.com, pg 174

Hermann, Suzanne, American Institute for Economic Research (AIER), 250 Division St, Great Barrington, MA 01230 *Tel:* 413-528-1216 *Toll Free Tel:* 888-528-1216 (orders) *E-mail:* info@aier.org *Web Site:* www.aier.org, pg 12

Hermelin, Christopher, The Fischer-Harbage Agency Inc, 540 President St, 3rd fl, Brooklyn, NY 11215 *Tel:* 212-695-7105 *E-mail:* info@fischerharbage.com *Web Site:* www.fischerharbage.com, pg 517

Hermes, Sr Kathryn James, Pauline Books & Media, 50 Saint Paul's Ave, Boston, MA 02130 *Tel:* 617-522-8911 *Toll Free Tel:* 800-876-4463 (orders); 800-836-9723 (cust serv) *Fax:* 617-541-9805 *E-mail:* editorial@paulinemedia.com (ms submissions); orderentry@pauline.org (cust serv) *Web Site:* www.pauline.org/publishing; www.pauline.org/PBMPublishing, pg 175

Hernandez, Debra Gersh, Reporters Committee for Freedom of the Press, 1156 15 St NW, Suite 1250, Washington, DC 20005-1779 *Tel:* 202-795-9300 *Toll Free Tel:* 800-336-4243 *E-mail:* info@rcfp.org *Web Site:* www.rcfp.org, pg 577

Hernandez, Tim Z, University of Texas at El Paso, Department of Creative Writing, MFA/Department of Creative Writing, 901 EDUC, 500 W University Ave, El Paso, TX 79968-9991 *Tel:* 915-747-5713 *Fax:* 915-747-5523 *E-mail:* creativewriting@utep.edu *Web Site:* www.utep.edu/cw, pg 624

Herndon, John, The Balcones Fiction Prize, 1212 Rio Grande St, Austin, TX 78701 *Tel:* 512-828-9368 *E-mail:* balcones@austincc.edu *Web Site:* sites.austincc.edu/crw/balcones-prizes, pg 630

Herndon, John, The Balcones Poetry Prize, 1212 Rio Grande St, Austin, TX 78701 *Tel:* 512-828-9368 *E-mail:* balcones@austincc.edu *Web Site:* www.austincc.edu/crw/html/balconescenter.html, pg 630

Herner, Susan N, Susan Herner Rights Agency Inc, 10 Upper Shad Rd, Pound Ridge, NY 10576 *Tel:* 914-234-2864 *Fax:* 914-234-2866 *E-mail:* sherneragency@optonline.net, pg 521

Herrera, Aida, BenBella Books Inc, 10300 N Central Expwy, Suite 400, Dallas, TX 75231 *Tel:* 214-750-3600 *Fax:* 214-750-3645 *E-mail:* feedback@benbellabooks.com *Web Site:* www.benbellabooks.com; www.smartpopbooks.com, pg 32

Herrera, Hoover, Marshall Cavendish Corp, 99 White Plains Rd, Tarrytown, NY 10591-9001 *Tel:* 914-332-8888 *Toll Free Tel:* 800-821-9881 *Fax:* 914-332-8102 *E-mail:* mce@marshallcavendish.com *Web Site:* www.marshallcavendish.com; www.mceducation.us, pg 143

Herrera, Jennifer, David Black Agency, 335 Adams St, 27th fl, Suite 2707, Brooklyn, NY 11201 *Tel:* 718-852-5500 *Fax:* 718-852-5539 *Web Site:* www.davidblackagency.com, pg 508

Herrera, Yesenia, Chronicle Books LLC, 680 Second St, San Francisco, CA 94107 *Tel:* 415-537-4200 *Toll Free Tel:* 800-759-0190 (cust serv) *Fax:* 415-537-4460 *Toll Free Fax:* 800-858-7787 (orders); 800-286-9471 (cust serv) *E-mail:* frontdesk@chroniclebooks.com *Web Site:* www.chroniclebooks.com, pg 55

Herrick, Becky, Sky Pony Press, 307 W 36 St, 11th fl, New York, NY 10018 *Tel:* 212-643-6816 *Fax:* 212-643-6819 *E-mail:* skypony@skyhorsepublishing.com; info@skyhorsepublishing.com; submissions@skyhorsepublishing.com *Web Site:* www.skyponypress.com, pg 214

Herring, Jamie, Columbia Books & Information Services (CBIS), 4340 East-West Hwy, Suite 300, Bethesda, MD 20814 *Tel:* 202-464-1662 *Fax:* 301-664-9600 *E-mail:* info@columbiabooks.com *Web Site:* www.columbiabooks.com; www.lobbyists.info; www.associationexecs.com, pg 59

Hershberg, Susan, Princeton Architectural Press, 37 E Seventh St, New York, NY 10003 *Tel:* 212-995-9620 *Toll Free Tel:* 800-722-6657 (dist); 800-759-0190 (sales) *Fax:* 212-995-9454 *E-mail:* sales@papress.com *Web Site:* www.papress.com, pg 188

Hershey, Jennifer, Random House Publishing Group, 1745 Broadway, New York, NY 10019 *Toll Free Tel:* 800-200-3552 *Web Site:* atrandom.com, pg 195

Hershon, Robert, Hanging Loose Press, 231 Wyckoff St, Brooklyn, NY 11217 *Tel:* 347-529-4738 *Fax:* 347-227-8215 *E-mail:* print225@aol.com *Web Site:* www.hangingloosepress.com, pg 100

Herz, Suzanne, Doubleday/Nan A Talese, c/o Penguin Random House Inc, 1745 Broadway, New York, NY 10019 *Tel:* 212-751-2600 *Fax:* 212-572-2662 *E-mail:* ddaypub@randomhouse.com *Web Site:* knopfdoubleday.com, pg 72

Heschke, Christa, McIntosh & Otis Inc, 353 Lexington Ave, New York, NY 10016-0900 *Tel:* 212-687-7400 *Fax:* 212-687-6894 *E-mail:* info@mcintoshandotis.com *Web Site:* www.mcintoshandotis.com, pg 529

Hess, John W, Geological Society of America (GSA), 3300 Penrose Place, Boulder, CO 80301-1806 *Tel:* 303-357-1000 *Fax:* 303-357-1070 *E-mail:* pubs@geosociety.org (prodn); editing@geosociety.org (edit) *Web Site:* www.geosociety.org, pg 91

Hess, Peter, American Society of Mechanical Engineers (ASME), 2 Park Ave, New York, NY 10016-5990 *Tel:* 212-591-7000 *Toll Free Tel:* 800-843-2763 (cust serv-US, CN & Mexico) *Fax:* 212-591-7674; 973-882-8113 (cust serv); 973-882-1717 (orders & inquiries) *E-mail:* infocentral@asme.org *Web Site:* www.asme.org, pg 15

Hetico, Bob, Wm B Eerdmans Publishing Co, 2140 Oak Industrial Dr NE, Grand Rapids, MI 49505 *Tel:* 616-459-4591 *Toll Free Tel:* 800-253-7521 *Fax:* 616-459-6540 *E-mail:* customerservice@eerdmans.com; sales@eerdmans.com *Web Site:* www.eerdmans.com, pg 76

Hetrick, J Thomas, Pocol Press, 6023 Pocol Dr, Clifton, VA 20124-1333 *Tel:* 703-830-5862 *E-mail:* info@pocolpress.com *Web Site:* www.pocolpress.com, pg 185

Heule, Melissa, Deadline Club, c/o Salmagundi Club, 47 Fifth Ave, New York, NY 10003 *Tel:* 646-481-7584 *E-mail:* info@deadlineclub.org *Web Site:* www.deadlineclub.org, pg 564

Heustess, Todd, Peter Glenn Publications, 306 NE Second St, 2nd fl, Delray Beach, FL 33483 *Tel:* 561-404-4290 *Fax:* 561-892-5786 *Web Site:* pgdirect.com, pg 93

Heward-Mills, Leon, Taylor & Francis Inc, 530 Walnut St, Suite 850, Philadelphia, PA 19106 *Tel:* 215-625-8900 *Toll Free Tel:* 800-354-1420 *Fax:* 215-207-0050; 215-207-0046 (cust serv) *E-mail:* support@tandfonline.com *Web Site:* www.taylorandfrancis.com, pg 227

Hewitt, Kristen, Chronicle Books LLC, 680 Second St, San Francisco, CA 94107 *Tel:* 415-537-4200 *Toll Free Tel:* 800-759-0190 (cust serv) *Fax:* 415-537-4460 *Toll Free Fax:* 800-858-7787 (orders); 800-286-9471 (cust serv) *E-mail:* frontdesk@chroniclebooks.com *Web Site:* www.chroniclebooks.com, pg 55

Hewitt, Ted, Social Sciences & Humanities Research Council of Canada (SSHRC), 350 Albert St, Ottawa, ON K1P 6G4, Canada *Tel:* 613-992-0691 *E-mail:* research@sshrc-crsh.gc.ca *Web Site:* www.sshrc.ca, pg 578

Hinton, Will, Orbit, 1290 Avenue of the Americas, New York, NY 10019 *Tel:* 212-364-1100 *Toll Free Tel:* 800-759-0190 *Web Site:* www.orbitbooks.net, pg 169

Hinz, Carol, Millbrook Press, 241 First Ave N, Minneapolis, MN 55401 *Tel:* 612-332-3344 *Toll Free Tel:* 800-328-4929 (US only) *Fax:* 612-332-7615 *Toll Free Fax:* 800-332-1132 *E-mail:* info@lernerbooks.com; custserve@lernerbooks.com *Web Site:* www.lernerbooks.com; www.facebook.com/millbrookpress, pg 151

Hirashima, Steve, University of Hawaii Press, 2840 Kolowalu St, Honolulu, HI 96822 *Tel:* 808-956-8255 *Toll Free Tel:* 888-UHPRESS (847-7377) *Fax:* 808-988-6052 *Toll Free Fax:* 800-650-7811 *E-mail:* uhpbooks@hawaii.edu *Web Site:* www.uhpress.hawaii.edu, pg 241

Hirsch, Edward, John Simon Guggenheim Memorial Foundation, 90 Park Ave, New York, NY 10016 *Tel:* 212-687-4470 *Fax:* 212-697-3248 *E-mail:* fellowships@gf.org *Web Site:* www.gf.org, pg 583

Hitchcock, Nelson, Scholastic Inc, 557 Broadway, New York, NY 10012 *Tel:* 212-343-6100 *Toll Free Tel:* 800-SCHOLASTIC (724-6527) *Web Site:* www.scholastic.com, pg 208

Hitchcock, Nelson, Scholastic International, 557 Broadway, New York, NY 10012 *Tel:* 212-343-6100; 646-330-5288 (intl cust serv) *Toll Free Tel:* 800-SCHOLASTIC (724-6527) *Fax:* 646-837-7878 *E-mail:* international@scholastic.com, pg 208

Hitchcock, Stephanie, HarperCollins General Books Group, 195 Broadway, New York, NY 10007 *Tel:* 212-207-7000 *Web Site:* www.harpercollins.com, pg 101

Hitchens, Clare, Wilfrid Laurier University Press, 75 University Ave W, Waterloo, ON N2L 3C5, Canada *Tel:* 519-884-0710 *Toll Free Tel:* 866-836-5551 (CN & US) *Fax:* 519-725-1399 *E-mail:* press@wlu.ca *Web Site:* www.wlupress.wlu.ca, pg 476

Hite, Robyn, Wimmer Cookbooks, 4650 Shelby Air Dr, Memphis, TN 38118 *Toll Free Tel:* 800-548-2537 *Fax:* 901-363-1771 *E-mail:* info@wimmerco.com *Web Site:* www.wimmerco.com, pg 257

Hitt, Raquel, Perseus Books, 250 W 57 St, 15th fl, New York, NY 10107 *Tel:* 212-340-8100 *Toll Free Tel:* 800-343-4499 (cust serv) *Fax:* 212-340-8105 *Web Site:* www.perseusbooks.com, pg 181

Hivnor, Maggie, University of Chicago Press, 1427 E 60 St, Chicago, IL 60637-2954 *Tel:* 773-702-7700; 773-702-7600 *Toll Free Tel:* 800-621-2736 (orders) *Fax:* 773-702-9756; 773-660-2235 (orders); 773-702-2708 *E-mail:* custserv@press.uchicago.edu; marketing@press.uchicago.edu *Web Site:* www.press.uchicago.edu, pg 241

Hixson, Karlyn, St Martin's Press, LLC, 175 Fifth Ave, New York, NY 10010 *Tel:* 646-307-5151 *Web Site:* us.macmillan.com/smp, pg 204

Ho, Howard, University of Southern California, Master of Professional Writing Program, Mark Taper Hall, THH 355, 3501 Trousedale Pkwy, Los Angeles, CA 90089-0355 *Tel:* 213-740-3252 *Fax:* 213-740-5002 *E-mail:* mpw@college.usc.edu *Web Site:* college.usc.edu/mpw, pg 623

Hoak, Michael, Yale University Press, 302 Temple St, New Haven, CT 06511-8909 *Tel:* 203-432-0960; 203-432-0966 (sales); 401-531-2800 (cust serv) *Toll Free Tel:* 800-405-1619 (cust serv) *Fax:* 203-432-0948; 203-432-8485 (sales); 401-531-2801 (cust serv) *Toll Free Fax:* 800-406-9145 (cust serv) *E-mail:* sales.press@yale.edu (sales); customer.care@triliteral.org (cust serv) *Web Site:* www.yalebooks.com; yalepress.yale.edu/yupbooks, pg 261

Hoard, Trish, The Library of America, 14 E 60 St, New York, NY 10022-1006 *Tel:* 212-308-3360 *Fax:* 212-750-8352 *E-mail:* info@loa.org *Web Site:* www.loa.org, pg 133

Hoare, Steve, Black Dome Press Corp, 649 Delaware Ave, Delmar, NY 12054 *Tel:* 518-439-6512 *Fax:* 518-439-1309 *E-mail:* blackdomep@aol.com *Web Site:* www.blackdomepress.com, pg 36

Hoban, Kathryn, Holiday House Inc, 425 Madison Ave, New York, NY 10017 *Tel:* 212-688-0085 *Fax:* 212-421-6134 *E-mail:* info@holidayhouse.com *Web Site:* www.holidayhouse.com, pg 109

Hobeika, Joelle, Alloy Entertainment LLC, 1325 Avenue of the Americas, 29th fl, New York, NY 10019 *E-mail:* collaborative@alloyentertainment.com, pg 8

Hocherman, Riva, Henry Holt and Company, LLC, 175 Fifth Ave, New York, NY 10010 *Tel:* 646-307-5151 *Toll Free Tel:* 888-330-8477 (orders) *Fax:* 646-307-5285 *E-mail:* firstname.lastname@hholt.com *Web Site:* www.henryholt.com, pg 109

Hochman, Gail, Brandt & Hochman Literary Agents Inc, 1501 Broadway, Suite 2310, New York, NY 10036 *Tel:* 212-840-5760 *Fax:* 212-840-5776 *Web Site:* brandthochman.com, pg 509

Hodapp, Angie, Nelson Literary Agency LLC, 1732 Wazee St, Suite 207, Denver, CO 80202-1284 *Tel:* 303-292-2805 *E-mail:* query@nelsonagency.com *Web Site:* www.nelsonagency.com, pg 530

Hodell, Courtney, Whiting Awards, 16 Court St, Suite 2308, Brooklyn, NY 11241 *Tel:* 718-701-5962 *E-mail:* info@whiting.org *Web Site:* www.whiting.org, pg 697

Hodell, Courtney, Whiting Creative Nonfiction Grant, 16 Court St, Suite 2308, Brooklyn, NY 11241 *Tel:* 718-701-5962 *E-mail:* nonfiction@whiting.org; info@whiting.org *Web Site:* www.whiting.org, pg 697

Hodges, Joanne, National Council of Teachers of Mathematics (NCTM), 1906 Association Dr, Reston, VA 20191-1502 *Tel:* 703-620-9840 *Toll Free Tel:* 800-235-7566 *Fax:* 703-476-2970 *E-mail:* nctm@nctm.org *Web Site:* www.nctm.org, pg 158

Hodges, Peter, EMC Publishing LLC, 875 Montreal Way, St Paul, MN 55102 *Tel:* 651-290-2800 (corp) *Toll Free Tel:* 800-328-1452 *Toll Free Fax:* 800-328-4564 *E-mail:* educate@emcp.com *Web Site:* www.emcp.com, pg 77

Hodson, Brad, Horror Writers Association (HWA), c/o Horror Writers Association, PO Box 56687, Sherman Oaks, CA 91413 *E-mail:* hwa@horror.org *Web Site:* horror.org, pg 566

Hodson, Nancy, Cold Spring Harbor Laboratory Press, 500 Sunnyside Blvd, Woodbury, NY 11797-2924 *Tel:* 516-422-4100 *Toll Free Tel:* 800-843-4388 *Fax:* 516-422-4097; 516-422-4092 (submissions) *E-mail:* cshpress@cshl.edu *Web Site:* www.cshlpress.com, pg 58

Hodus, Brett, Scobre Press Corp, 2255 Calle Clara, La Jolla, CA 92037 *Fax:* 858-551-1232 *E-mail:* info@scobre.com *Web Site:* www.scobre.com; scobre.bookbuddyaudio.com, pg 209

Hoesly, Sherry, The Permissions Group Inc, 401 S Milwaukee Ave, Suite 180, Wheeling, IL 60090 *Tel:* 847-635-6550 *Toll Free Tel:* 800-374-7985 *Fax:* 847-635-6968 *E-mail:* info@permissionsgroup.com *Web Site:* www.permissionsgroup.com, pg 499

Hofeldt, Sara E, Tapestry Press Ltd, 19 Nashoba Rd, Littleton, MA 01460 *Tel:* 978-486-0200 *Toll Free Tel:* 800-535-2007 *Fax:* 978-486-0244 *E-mail:* publish@tapestrypress.com *Web Site:* www.tapestrypress.com, pg 227

Hoffman, Jonathan, School Zone Publishing Co, 1819 Industrial Dr, Grand Haven, MI 49417 *Tel:* 616-846-5030 *Toll Free Tel:* 800-253-0564 *Fax:* 616-846-6181 *Toll Free Fax:* 800-550-4618 (orders only) *Web Site:* www.schoolzone.com, pg 208

Hoffman, Lauren, Simon & Schuster Children's Publishing, 1230 Avenue of the Americas, New York, NY 10020 *Tel:* 212-698-7000 *Web Site:* www.simonandschuster.com/kids; www.simonandschuster.com/teen; simonandschuster.net; simonandschuster.biz, pg 213

Hoffman, Mitch, The Aaron M Priest Literary Agency Inc, 200 W 41 St, 21st fl, New York, NY 10036 *Tel:* 212-818-0344 *Fax:* 212-573-9417 *E-mail:* info@aaronpriest.com *Web Site:* www.aaronpriest.com, pg 532

Hoffman, Philip, Penguin Random House Inc, 1745 Broadway, New York, NY 10019 *Tel:* 212-782-9000 *Toll Free Tel:* 800-726-0600 *Web Site:* www.penguinrandomhouse.com, pg 178

Hoffman, Randy, Captus Press Inc, 1600 Steeles Ave W, Units 14 & 15, Concord, ON L4K 4M2, Canada *Tel:* 416-736-5537 *Fax:* 416-736-5793 *E-mail:* info@captus.com *Web Site:* www.captus.com, pg 449

Hoffman, Scott, Folio Literary Management, The Film Center Bldg, 630 Ninth Ave, Suite 1101, New York, NY 10036 *Tel:* 212-400-1494 *Fax:* 212-967-0977 *Web Site:* www.foliolit.com, pg 517

Hoffman, Stuart A, Star Publishing Co Inc, PO Box 5165, Belmont, CA 94002-5165 *Tel:* 650-591-3505 *Fax:* 650-752-9212 *Web Site:* www.starpublishing.com, pg 221

Hoffnagle, Jerry, Rizzoli International Publications Inc, 300 Park Ave S, 4th fl, New York, NY 10010-5399 *Tel:* 212-387-3400 *Toll Free Tel:* 800-522-6657 (orders only) *Fax:* 212-387-3535 *E-mail:* publicity@rizzoliusa.com *Web Site:* www.rizzoliusa.com, pg 199

Hofford, Amy, Brilliance Audio, 1704 Eaton Dr, Grand Haven, MI 49417 *Tel:* 616-846-5256 *Toll Free Tel:* 800-648-2312 (orders only) *Fax:* 616-846-0630 *E-mail:* customerservice@brillianceaudio.com *Web Site:* www.brillianceaudio.com, pg 44

Hogan, Mary S, Plexus Publishing, Inc, 143 Old Marlton Pike, Medford, NJ 08055 *Tel:* 609-654-6500 *Fax:* 609-654-4309 *E-mail:* info@plexuspublishing.com *Web Site:* www.plexuspublishing.com, pg 184

Hogan, Megan, Simon & Schuster, 1230 Avenue of the Americas, New York, NY 10020 *Tel:* 212-698-7000 *Toll Free Tel:* 800-223-2348 (cust serv); 800-223-2336 (orders) *Toll Free Fax:* 800-943-9831 (orders) *Web Site:* www.simonandschuster.com, pg 212

Hogan, Michelle, Our Sunday Visitor Publishing, 200 Noll Plaza, Huntington, IN 46750 *Tel:* 260-356-8400 *Toll Free Tel:* 800-348-2440 (orders) *Fax:* 260-356-8472 *Toll Free Fax:* 800-498-6709 *E-mail:* osvbooks@osv.com (book orders) *Web Site:* www.osv.com, pg 170

Hogan, Patrick, The American Library Association (ALA), 50 E Huron St, Chicago, IL 60611 *Tel:* 312-944-6780 *Toll Free Tel:* 800-545-2433 *Fax:* 312-280-5275 *E-mail:* editionsmarketing@ala.org *Web Site:* www.alastore.ala.org, pg 12

Hogan, Robin, CBA: The Association for Christian Retail, 1365 Garden of the Gods Rd, Suite 105, Colorado Springs, CO 80907 *Tel:* 719-265-9895 *Toll Free Tel:* 800-252-1950 *Fax:* 719-272-3508 *E-mail:* info@cbaonline.org *Web Site:* cbaonline.org, pg 562

Hogan, Thomas Jr, Information Today, Inc, 143 Old Marlton Pike, Medford, NJ 08055-8750 *Tel:* 609-654-6266 *Toll Free Tel:* 800-300-9868 (cust serv) *Fax:* 609-654-4309 *E-mail:* custserv@infotoday.com *Web Site:* www.infotoday.com, pg 116

Hogan, Thomas Jr, Plexus Publishing, Inc, 143 Old Marlton Pike, Medford, NJ 08055 *Tel:* 609-654-6500 *Fax:* 609-654-4309 *E-mail:* info@plexuspublishing.com *Web Site:* www.plexuspublishing.com, pg 184

Hogan, Thomas H Sr, Information Today, Inc, 143 Old Marlton Pike, Medford, NJ 08055-8750 *Tel:* 609-654-6266 *Toll Free Tel:* 800-300-9868 (cust serv) *Fax:* 609-654-4309 *E-mail:* custserv@infotoday.com *Web Site:* www.infotoday.com, pg 116

Hogan, Thomas H Sr, Plexus Publishing, Inc, 143 Old Marlton Pike, Medford, NJ 08055 *Tel:* 609-654-6500 *Fax:* 609-654-4309 *E-mail:* info@plexuspublishing.com *Web Site:* www.plexuspublishing.com, pg 184

Hoge, Steve, W W Norton & Company Inc, 500 Fifth Ave, New York, NY 10110-0017 *Tel:* 212-354-5500 *Toll Free Tel:* 800-233-4830 (orders & cust serv) *Fax:* 212-869-0856 *Toll Free Fax:* 800-458-6515 *E-mail:* orders@wwnorton.com *Web Site:* books.wwnorton.com, pg 164

Hogeland, Kim, University Press of Kansas, 2502 Westbrooke Circle, Lawrence, KS 66045-4444 *Tel:* 785-864-4154; 785-864-4155 (orders) *Fax:* 785-864-4586 *E-mail:* upress@ku.edu; upkorders@ku.edu (orders) *Web Site:* www.kansaspress.ku.edu, pg 247

Hogenson, Barbara, The Barbara Hogenson Agency Inc, 165 West End Ave, Suite 19-C, New York, NY 10023 *Tel:* 212-874-8084 *Fax:* 212-595-6748 *E-mail:* bhogenson@aol.com, pg 521

Hoggutt, Brenda Jo, University of Texas Press, 3001 Lake Austin Blvd, 2.200, Austin, TX 78703 *Tel:* 512-471-7233 *Fax:* 512-232-7178 *E-mail:* utpress@uts.cc.utexas.edu; info@utpress.utexas.edu *Web Site:* www.utexaspress.com, pg 230

Hogrebe, Christina, Jane Rotrosen Agency LLC, 85 Broad St, 28th fl, New York, NY 10004 *Tel:* 212-593-4330 *Fax:* 212-935-6985 *Web Site:* janerotrosen.com, pg 533

Hohenadel, Liz, Riverhead Books, 375 Hudson St, New York, NY 10014 *Tel:* 212-366-2000 *Web Site:* www.penguin.com/publishers/riverhead, pg 199

Hokanson, Sarah, Random House Children's Books, 1745 Broadway, 10th fl, New York, NY 10019 *Tel:* 212-782-9000 *Web Site:* www.randomhousekids.com, pg 194

Holahan, Jessica, Yale University Press, 302 Temple St, New Haven, CT 06511-8909 *Tel:* 203-432-0960; 203-432-0966 (sales); 401-531-2800 (cust serv) *Toll Free Tel:* 800-405-1619 (cust serv) *Fax:* 203-432-0948; 203-432-8485 (sales); 401-531-2801 (cust serv) *Toll Free Fax:* 800-406-9145 (cust serv) *E-mail:* sales.press@yale.edu (sales); customer.care@triliteral.org (cust serv) *Web Site:* www.yalebooks.com; yalepress.yale.edu/yupbooks, pg 261

Holbert, Christine, The Idaho Prize for Poetry, 105 Lost Horse Lane, Sandpoint, ID 83864 *Tel:* 208-255-4410 *Fax:* 208-255-1560 *E-mail:* losthorsepress@mindspring.com *Web Site:* www.losthorsepress.org, pg 654

Holbert, Christine, Lost Horse Press, 105 Lost Horse Lane, Sandpoint, ID 83864 *Tel:* 208-255-4410 *E-mail:* losthorsepress@mindspring.com *Web Site:* www.losthorsepress.org, pg 138

Hold, William J, The National Alliance Research Academy, 3630 N Hills Dr, Austin, TX 78755 *Tel:* 512-345-7932 *Toll Free Tel:* 800-633-2165 *Fax:* 512-349-6194 *E-mail:* alliance@scic.com *Web Site:* www.scic.com/academy, pg 157

Hold, William T PhD, The National Alliance Research Academy, 3630 N Hills Dr, Austin, TX 78755 *Tel:* 512-345-7932 *Toll Free Tel:* 800-633-2165 *Fax:* 512-349-6194 *E-mail:* alliance@scic.com *Web Site:* www.scic.com/academy, pg 157

Holder, Jakob, William Flanagan Memorial Creative Persons Center, 14 Harrison St, New York, NY 10013 *Tel:* 212-226-2020 *Fax:* 212-226-5551 *E-mail:* info@albeefoundation.org *Web Site:* www.albeefoundation.org, pg 698

Holding, Brian, Human Kinetics Inc, 1607 N Market St, Champaign, IL 61820 *Tel:* 217-351-5076 *Toll Free Tel:* 800-747-4457 *Fax:* 217-351-1549 (orders/cust serv) *E-mail:* info@hkusa.com *Web Site:* www.humankinetics.com, pg 112

Holding, Hal, HPBooks, 375 Hudson St, New York, NY 10014 *Tel:* 212-366-2000 *E-mail:* online@penguinputnam.com *Web Site:* www.penguinputnam.com; www.penguin.com, pg 112

Holdridge, Jefferson, Wake Forest University Press, A5 Tribble Hall, Wake Forest University, Winston-Salem, NC 27109 *Tel:* 336-758-5448 *Fax:* 336-758-5636 *E-mail:* wfupress@wfu.edu *Web Site:* wfupress.wfu.edu, pg 251

Holland, Mark, Rocky Mountain Mineral Law Foundation, 9191 Sheridan Blvd, Suite 203, Westminster, CO 80031 *Tel:* 303-321-8100 *Fax:* 303-321-7657 *E-mail:* info@rmmlf.org *Web Site:* www.rmmlf.org, pg 200

Hollander, Elia, Feldheim Publishers, 208 Airport Executive Park, Nanuet, NY 10954 *Tel:* 845-356-2282 *Toll Free Tel:* 800-237-7149 (orders) *Fax:* 845-425-1908 *E-mail:* sales@feldheim.com *Web Site:* www.feldheim.com, pg 83

Hollander, Michelle, Women Who Write Inc, PO Box 652, Madison, NJ 07940-0652 *E-mail:* info@womenwhowrite.org *Web Site:* womenwhowrite.org, pg 580

Holley, Joe, Carr P Collins Award, c/o 7748 Hwy 290 W, Austin, TX 78736-3202 *Tel:* 512-683-5640 *E-mail:* president@texasinstituteofletters.org *Web Site:* www.texasinstituteofletters.org, pg 638

Holley, Joe, Soeurette Diehl Fraser Translation Award, c/o 7748 Hwy 290 W, Austin, TX 78736-3202 *Tel:* 512-683-5640 *E-mail:* president@texasinstituteofletters.org *Web Site:* www.texasinstituteofletters.org, pg 647

Holley, Joe, Jesse H Jones Award, c/o 7748 Hwy 290 W, Austin, TX 78736-3202 *Tel:* 512-683-5640 *E-mail:* president@texasinstituteofletters.org *Web Site:* www.texasinstituteofletters.org, pg 657

Holley, Joe, Ramirez Family Award, c/o 7748 Hwy 290 W, Austin, TX 78736-3202 *Tel:* 512-683-5640 *E-mail:* president@texasinstituteofletters.org *Web Site:* www.texasinstituteofletters.org, pg 684

Holley, Joe, Edwin "Bud" Shrake Award for Best Short Nonfiction, c/o 7748 Hwy 290 W, Austin, TX 78736-3202 *Tel:* 512-683-5640 *E-mail:* president@texasinstituteofletters.org *Web Site:* www.texasinstituteofletters.org, pg 689

Holley, Joe, Helen C Smith Memorial Award, c/o 7748 Hwy 290 W, Austin, TX 78736-3202 *Tel:* 512-683-5640 *E-mail:* president@texasinstituteofletters.org *Web Site:* www.texasinstituteofletters.org, pg 690

Holley, Joe, Texas Institute of Letters (TIL), c/o 7748 Hwy 290 W, Austin, TX 78736-3202 *E-mail:* president@texasinstituteofletters.org; secretary@texasinstituteofletters.org *Web Site:* www.texasinstituteofletters.org, pg 579

Holley, Joe, Texas Institute of Letters Awards, c/o 7748 Hwy 290 W, Austin, TX 78736-3202 *Tel:* 512-683-5640 *E-mail:* president@texasinstituteofletters.org *Web Site:* www.texasinstituteofletters.org, pg 694

Holliday, Sara, New York City Book Awards, 53 E 79 St, New York, NY 10075 *Tel:* 212-288-6900 *Fax:* 212-744-5832 *E-mail:* events@nysoclib.org *Web Site:* www.nysoclib.org, pg 673

Hollingsworth, Jonathan, Macmillan, 175 Fifth Ave, New York, NY 10010 *Tel:* 646-307-5151 *E-mail:* press.inquiries@macmillan.com *Web Site:* www.macmillan.com, pg 140

Hollins, Pamela, Silver Gavel Awards, 321 N Clark St, Chicago, IL 60654 *Tel:* 312-988-5719 *Toll Free Tel:* 800-285-2221 (orders) *Fax:* 312-988-5494 *Web Site:* www.ambar.org/gavelawards, pg 689

Hollman, Michael, The RoadRunner Press, 124 NW 32 St, Oklahoma City, OK 73118 *Tel:* 405-524-6205 *Fax:* 405-524-6312 *E-mail:* info@theroadrunnerpress.com; orders@theroadrunnerpress.com *Web Site:* www.theroadrunnerpress.com, pg 200

Holloway, J David, American Technical Publishers Inc, 10100 Orland Pkwy, Suite 200, Orland Park, IL 60467-5756 *Toll Free Tel:* 800-323-3471 *Fax:* 708-957-1101 *E-mail:* service@atplearning.com; order@atplearning.com *Web Site:* www.atplearning.com, pg 15

Holman, Tim, Hachette Book Group, 1290 Avenue of the Americas, New York, NY 10019 *Tel:* 212-364-1100 *Toll Free Tel:* 800-759-0190 (cust serv) *Fax:* 212-364-0933 (intl orders) *Toll Free Fax:* 800-286-9471 (cust serv) *Web Site:* www.hachettebookgroup.com, pg 98

Holman, Tim, Orbit, 1290 Avenue of the Americas, New York, NY 10019 *Tel:* 212-364-1100 *Toll Free Tel:* 800-759-0190 *Web Site:* www.orbitbooks.net, pg 169

Holmes, Carol, R Ross Annett Award for Children's Literature, 11759 Groat Rd, Edmonton, AB T5M 3K6, Canada *Tel:* 780-422-8174 *Toll Free Tel:* 800-665-5354 (AB only) *Fax:* 780-422-2663 (attn WGA) *E-mail:* mail@writersguild.ca *Web Site:* writersguild.ca, pg 627

Holmes, Carol, Georges Bugnet Award for Fiction, 11759 Groat Rd, Edmonton, AB T5M 3K6, Canada *Tel:* 780-422-8174 *Toll Free Tel:* 800-665-5354 (AB only) *Fax:* 780-422-2663 (attn WGA) *E-mail:* mail@writersguild.ca *Web Site:* writersguild.ca, pg 634

Holmes, Carol, The City of Calgary W O Mitchell Book Prize, 11759 Groat Rd, Edmonton, AB T5M 3K6, Canada *Tel:* 780-422-8174 *Toll Free Tel:* 800-665-5354 (AB only) *Fax:* 780-422-2663 (attn WGA) *E-mail:* mail@writersguild.ca *Web Site:* writersguild.ca, pg 637

Holmes, Carol, Wilfrid Eggleston Award for Nonfiction, 11759 Groat Rd, Edmonton, AB T5M 3K6, Canada *Tel:* 780-422-8174 *Toll Free Tel:* 800-665-5354 (AB only) *Fax:* 780-422-2663 (attn WGA) *E-mail:* mail@writersguild.ca *Web Site:* writersguild.ca, pg 644

Holmes, Carol, James H Gray Award for Short Nonfiction, 11759 Groat Rd, Edmonton, AB T5M 3K6, Canada *Tel:* 780-422-8174 *Toll Free Tel:* 800-665-5354 (AB only) *Fax:* 780-422-2663 (attn WGA) *E-mail:* mail@writersguild.ca *Web Site:* writersguild.ca, pg 650

Holmes, Carol, The Robert Kroetsch City of Edmonton Book Prize, 11759 Groat Rd, Edmonton, AB T5M 3K6, Canada *Tel:* 780-422-8174 *Toll Free Tel:* 800-665-5354 (AB only) *Fax:* 780-422-2663 (attn WGA) *E-mail:* mail@writersguild.ca *Web Site:* writersguild.ca, pg 659

Holmes, Carol, Howard O'Hagan Award for Short Story, 11759 Groat Rd, Edmonton, AB T5M 3K6, Canada *Tel:* 780-422-8174 *Toll Free Tel:* 800-665-5354 (AB only) *Fax:* 780-422-2663 (attn WGA) *E-mail:* mail@writersguild.ca *Web Site:* writersguild.ca, pg 675

Holmes, Carol, Gwen Pharis Ringwood Award for Drama, 11759 Groat Rd, Edmonton, AB T5M 3K6, Canada *Tel:* 780-422-8174 *Toll Free Tel:* 800-665-5354 (AB only) *Fax:* 780-422-2663 (attn WGA) *E-mail:* mail@writersguild.ca *Web Site:* writersguild.ca, pg 685

Holmes, Carol, Stephan G Stephansson Award for Poetry, 11759 Groat Rd, Edmonton, AB T5M 3K6, Canada *Tel:* 780-422-8174 *Toll Free Tel:* 800-665-5354 (AB only) *Fax:* 780-422-2663 (attn WGA) *E-mail:* mail@writersguild.ca *Web Site:* writersguild.ca, pg 692

Holmes, Carol, Jon Whyte Memorial Essay Prize, 11759 Groat Rd, Edmonton, AB T5M 3K6, Canada *Tel:* 780-422-8174 *Toll Free Tel:* 800-665-5354 (AB only) *Fax:* 780-422-2663 (attn WGA) *E-mail:* mail@writersguild.ca *Web Site:* writersguild.ca, pg 697

Holmes, Carol, Writers' Guild of Alberta, 11759 Groat Rd, Edmonton, AB T5M 3K6, Canada *Tel:* 780-422-8174 *Toll Free Tel:* 800-665-5354 (AB only) *Fax:* 780-422-2663 (attn WGA) *E-mail:* mail@writersguild.ca *Web Site:* writersguild.ca, pg 581

Holmes, Henry, Henry Holmes Literary Agent/Book Publicist/Marketing Consultant, Mitchell Heights, Apt 205, 2100 S Main St, Fall River, MA 02724 *Tel:* 508-672-2258, pg 495, 521

Holmes, J D, Holmes Publishing Group LLC, PO Box 2370, Sequim, WA 98382 *Tel:* 360-681-2900 *E-mail:* holmespub@fastmail.fm *Web Site:* www.jdholmes.com, pg 109

Holmes, Jack, The Johns Hopkins University Press, 2715 N Charles St, Baltimore, MD 21218-4363 *Tel:* 410-516-6900; 410-516-6987 (journal orders outside US & CN) *Toll Free Tel:* 800-537-5487 (book orders & cust serv); 800-548-1784 (journal orders) *Fax:* 410-516-6968; 410-516-3866 (journal orders) *E-mail:* hfscustserv@press.jhu.edu (cust serv); jrnlcirc@press.jhu.edu (journal orders) *Web Site:* www.press.jhu.edu; muse.jhu.edu, pg 122

Holmes, James, ProQuest LLC, 789 E Eisenhower Pkwy, Ann Arbor, MI 48108 *Tel:* 734-761-4700 *Toll Free Tel:* 800-521-0600 *Web Site:* www.proquest.com, pg 190

Holmes, Prof Janet, Ahsahta Press, Boise State University, Mail Stop 1525, 1910 University Dr, Boise, ID 83725-1525 *Tel:* 208-426-3134 *E-mail:* ahsahta@boisestate.edu *Web Site:* ahsahtapress.org, pg 6

Holmes, Nathan, Northern Illinois University Press, 2280 Bethany Rd, DeKalb, IL 60115 *Tel:* 815-753-1075 *Fax:* 815-753-1845 *Web Site:* www.niupress.niu.edu, pg 164

Holquist, Carol, Discovery House Publishers, 3000 Kraft Ave SE, Grand Rapids, MI 49512 *Tel:* 616-942-2803 *Toll Free Tel:* 800-653-8333 (cust serv) *E-mail:* support@dhp.org *Web Site:* www.dhp.org, pg 70

Holt, Karen, CN Times Books, 501 Fifth Ave, Suite 1708, New York, NY 10017 *Tel:* 212-867-8666 *Web Site:* cntimesbooks.com, pg 57

Holt, Sid, American Society of Magazine Editors (ASME), 757 Third Ave, 11th fl, New York, NY 10017 *Tel:* 212-872-3700 *Fax:* 212-906-0128 *E-mail:* asme@magazine.org *Web Site:* www.magazine.org/asme, pg 556

Holtz, Alex, Barron's Educational Series Inc, 250 Wireless Blvd, Hauppauge, NY 11788 *Tel:* 631-434-3311 *Toll Free Tel:* 800-645-3476 *Fax:* 631-434-3723 *E-mail:* barrons@barronseduc.com *Web Site:* www.barronseduc.com, pg 30

Holtzer, Mastan, Rand McNally, 9855 Woods Dr, Skokie, IL 60077 *Tel:* 847-329-8100 *E-mail:* ctsales@randmcnally.com; mediarelations@randmcnally.com *Web Site:* www.randmcnally.com, pg 194

Holung, Lindsay, House of Anansi Press Inc, 128 Sterling Rd, Lower Level, Toronto, ON M6R 2B7, Canada *Tel:* 416-363-4343 *Fax:* 416-363-1017 *E-mail:* customerservice@houseofanansi.com *Web Site:* www.houseofanansi.com, pg 460

Holway, Pamela, Athabasca University Press, Edmonton Learning Ctr, Peace Hills Trust Tower, 1200, 10011-109 St, Edmonton, AB T5J 3S8, Canada *Tel:* 780-497-3412 *Fax:* 780-421-3298 *E-mail:* aupress@athabascau.ca *Web Site:* www.aupress.ca, pg 446

Holway, Richard, The University of Virginia Press, PO Box 400318, Charlottesville, VA 22904-4318 *Tel:* 434-924-3468 (cust serv); 434-924-3469 (cust serv) *Toll Free Tel:* 800-831-3406 (orders) *Fax:* 434-982-2655 *Toll Free Fax:* 877-288-6400 *E-mail:* vapress@virginia.edu *Web Site:* www.upress.virginia.edu, pg 245

Holz, Molly, Montana Historical Society Press, Capitol Complex, 225 N Roberts St, Helena, MT 59620 *Tel:* 406-444-0090 (edit); 406-444-2890 (orders/mktg); 406-444-2694 *Toll Free Tel:* 800-243-9900 *Fax:* 406-444-2696 (orders/mktg) *Web Site:* mhs.mt.gov/pubs, pg 153

Holzapfel, Cynthia, Book Publishing Co, 415 Farm Rd, Summertown, TN 38483 *Tel:* 931-964-3571 *Fax:* 931-964-3518 *E-mail:* info@bookpubco.com *Web Site:* www.bookpubco.com, pg 39

Holzapfel, Robert, Book Publishing Co, 415 Farm Rd, Summertown, TN 38483 *Tel:* 931-964-3571 *Fax:* 931-964-3518 *E-mail:* info@bookpubco.com *Web Site:* www.bookpubco.com, pg 39

Homer, James, Jones & Bartlett Learning LLC, 5 Wall St, Burlington, MA 01803 *Tel:* 978-443-5000 *Toll Free Tel:* 800-832-0034 *Fax:* 978-443-8000 *E-mail:* info@jblearning.com *Web Site:* www.jblearning.com, pg 123

Homler, Michael, St Martin's Press, LLC, 175 Fifth Ave, New York, NY 10010 *Tel:* 646-307-5151 *Web Site:* us.macmillan.com/smp, pg 204

Honda, Helene, Bess Press, 3565 Harding Ave, Honolulu, HI 96816 *Tel:* 808-734-7159 *Fax:* 808-732-3627 *E-mail:* customerservice@besspress.com *Web Site:* www.besspress.com, pg 34

Honour, Carolyn, Springer, 233 Spring St, New York, NY 10013-1578 *Tel:* 212-460-1500 *Toll Free Tel:* 800-SPRINGER (777-4643) *Fax:* 212-460-1700 *E-mail:* customerservice@springer.com *Web Site:* www.springer.com, pg 219

Hooge, Tim, William S Hein & Co Inc, 2350 N Forest Rd, Getzville, NY 14068 *Tel:* 716-882-2600 *Toll Free Tel:* 800-828-7571 *Fax:* 716-883-8100 *E-mail:* mail@wshein.com; marketing@wshein.com *Web Site:* www.wshein.com, pg 105

Hoogland, Michael, Dystel, Goderich & Bourret LLC, One Union Sq W, Suite 904, New York, NY 10003 *Tel:* 212-627-9100 *Fax:* 212-627-9313 *Web Site:* www.dystel.com, pg 515

Hook, Lauren, The Feminist Press at The City University of New York, 365 Fifth Ave, Suite 5406, New York, NY 10016 *Tel:* 212-817-7915 *Fax:* 212-817-1593 *E-mail:* info@feministpress.org *Web Site:* www.feministpress.org, pg 83

Hooker, Lauren, Seven Stories Press, 140 Watts St, New York, NY 10013 *Tel:* 212-226-8760 *Toll Free Tel:* 800-733-3000 (orders) *Fax:* 212-226-1411 *E-mail:* info@sevenstories.com *Web Site:* www.sevenstories.com, pg 211

Hoole, Brunson, Algonquin Books, 400 Silver Cedar Ct, Suite 300, Chapel Hill, NC 27514-1585 *Tel:* 919-967-0108 *Fax:* 919-933-0272 *E-mail:* inquiry@algonquin.com *Web Site:* www.workman.com/algonquin, pg 7

Hooper, Barrett, Chronicle Books LLC, 680 Second St, San Francisco, CA 94107 *Tel:* 415-537-4200 *Toll Free Tel:* 800-759-0190 (cust serv) *Fax:* 415-537-4460 *Toll Free Fax:* 800-858-7787 (orders); 800-286-9471 (cust serv) *E-mail:* frontdesk@chroniclebooks.com *Web Site:* www.chroniclebooks.com, pg 55

Hooper, Niels, University of California Press, 155 Grand Ave, Suite 400, Oakland, CA 94612-3758 *Tel:* 510-883-8232 *Fax:* 510-836-8910 *E-mail:* customerservice@ucpressjournals.com *Web Site:* www.ucpress.edu, pg 240

Hoover, Cherlynn, Oxford University Press USA, 198 Madison Ave, New York, NY 10016 *Tel:* 212-726-6000 *Toll Free Tel:* 800-451-7556 (orders); 800-445-9714 (cust serv) *Fax:* 919-677-1303 *E-mail:* custserv.us@oup.com *Web Site:* www.oup.com/us, pg 171

Hope, Amy, APS PRESS, 3340 Pilot Knob Rd, St Paul, MN 55121 *Tel:* 651-454-7250 *Toll Free Tel:* 800-328-7560 *Fax:* 651-454-0766 *E-mail:* aps@scisoc.org *Web Site:* www.shopapspress.org, pg 19

Hope, Amy, Eagan Press, 3340 Pilot Knob Rd, St Paul, MN 55121 *Tel:* 651-454-7250 *Toll Free Tel:* 800-328-7560 *Fax:* 651-454-0766 *E-mail:* aacc@scisoc.org *Web Site:* www.aaccnet.org, pg 74

Hope, Katie, The MIT Press, One Rogers St, Cambridge, MA 02142 *Tel:* 617-253-5255 *Toll Free Tel:* 800-207-8354 (orders) *Fax:* 617-258-6779; 617-577-1545 (orders) *Web Site:* mitpress.mit.edu, pg 151

Hopkins, Alayne, Minnesota Book Awards, 1080 Montreal Ave, Suite 2, St Paul, MN 55116 *Tel:* 651-222-3242 *Fax:* 651-222-1988 *E-mail:* friends@thefriends.org *Web Site:* thefriends.org/events/mnba, pg 668

Hopkins, Alison, Northwest Territories Public Library Services, 75 Woodland Dr, Hay River, NT X0E 1G1, Canada *Tel:* 867-874-6531 *Toll Free Tel:* 866-297-0232 (CN) *Fax:* 867-874-3321 *Web Site:* www.nwtpls.gov.nt.ca, pg 574

Hopkins, Dana, Harlequin Enterprises Ltd, 225 Duncan Mill Rd, Don Mills, ON M3B 3K9, Canada *Tel:* 416-445-5860 *Toll Free Tel:* 888-432-4879; 800-370-5838 (ebook inquiries) *E-mail:* customerservice@harlequin.com *Web Site:* www.harlequin.com, pg 459

Hopkins, Michelle, CPSA Prize in Comparative Politics, 260 rue Dalhousie St, Suite 204, Ottawa, ON K1N 7E4, Canada *Tel:* 613-562-1202 *Fax:* 613-241-0019 *E-mail:* cpsa-acsp@cpsa-acsp.ca *Web Site:* www.cpsa-acsp.ca, pg 639

Hopkins, Michelle, CPSA Prize in International Relations, 260 rue Dalhousie St, Suite 204, Ottawa, ON K1N 7E4, Canada *Tel:* 613-562-1202 *Fax:* 613-241-0019 *E-mail:* cpsa-acsp@cpsa-acsp.ca *Web Site:* www.cpsa-acsp.ca, pg 639

Hopkins, Michelle, Prix Francophone de l'ACSP, 260 rue Dalhousie St, Suite 204, Ottawa, ON K1N 7E4, Canada *Tel:* 613-562-1202 *Fax:* 613-241-0019 *E-mail:* cpsa-acsp@cpsa-acsp.ca *Web Site:* www.cpsa-acsp.ca, pg 647

Hopkins, Michelle, Vincent Lemieux Prize, 260 rue Dalhousie St, Suite 204, Ottawa, ON K1N 7E4, Canada *Tel:* 613-562-1202 *Fax:* 613-241-0019 *E-mail:* cpsa-acsp@cpsa-acsp.ca *Web Site:* www.cpsa-acsp.ca, pg 660

Hopkins, Michelle, C B MacPherson Prize, 260 rue Dalhousie St, Suite 204, Ottawa, ON K1N 7E4, Canada *Tel:* 613-562-1202 *Fax:* 613-241-0019 *E-mail:* cpsa-acsp@cpsa-acsp.ca *Web Site:* www.cpsa-acsp.ca, pg 664

Hopkins, Michelle, John McMenemy Prize, 260 rue Dalhousie St, Suite 204, Ottawa, ON K1N 7E4, Canada *Tel:* 613-562-1202 *Fax:* 613-241-0019 *E-mail:* cpsa-acsp@cpsa-acsp.ca *Web Site:* www.cpsa-acsp.ca, pg 667

Hopkins, Michelle, Donald Smiley Prize, 260 rue Dalhousie St, Suite 204, Ottawa, ON K1N 7E4, Canada *Tel:* 613-562-1202 *Fax:* 613-241-0019 *E-mail:* cpsa-acsp@cpsa-acsp.ca *Web Site:* www.cpsa-acsp.ca, pg 690

Hopkins, Michelle, Jill Vickers Prize, 260 rue Dalhousie St, Suite 204, Ottawa, ON K1N 7E4, Canada *Tel:* 613-562-1202 *Fax:* 613-241-0019 *E-mail:* cpsa-acsp@cpsa-acsp.ca *Web Site:* www.cpsa-acsp.ca, pg 696

Hoppe, Anne, Clarion Books, 3 Park Ave, New York, NY 10016 *Tel:* 212-420-5800 *Toll Free Tel:* 800-225-3362 (orders) *Fax:* 212-420-5855 *Toll Free Fax:* 800-634-7568 (orders) *Web Site:* www.hmhco.com, pg 56

Hoppe, Joy, EMC Publishing LLC, 875 Montreal Way, St Paul, MN 55102 *Tel:* 651-290-2800 (corp) *Toll Free Tel:* 800-328-1452 *Toll Free Fax:* 800-328-4564 *E-mail:* educate@emcp.com *Web Site:* www.emcp.com, pg 77

Hopper, Ben, National Association of Printing Ink Manufacturers (NAPIM), 15 Technology Pkwy S, Peachtree Corners, GA 30092 *Tel:* 770-209-7289 *Fax:* 678-680-4920; 770-209-7217 *E-mail:* napim@napim.org *Web Site:* www.napim.org, pg 571

Hopwood, Gary, David C Cook, 4050 Lee Vance View, Colorado Springs, CO 80918 *Tel:* 719-536-0100 *Toll Free Tel:* 800-708-5550; 800-323-7543 (orders & cust serv) *Toll Free Fax:* 800-430-0726 (cust serv) *Web Site:* www.davidccook.com, pg 60

Horbachevsky, Natalie, Portfolio, 375 Hudson St, New York, NY 10014 *Web Site:* www.penguin.com/meet/publishers/portfolio, pg 186

Hordes, Amy, Phaidon, 65 Bleecker St, 8th fl, New York, NY 10012 *Tel:* 212-652-5400 *Toll Free Tel:* 800-759-0190 (cust serv) *Fax:* 212-652-5410 *Toll Free Fax:* 800-286-9471 (cust serv) *E-mail:* ussales@phaidon.com *Web Site:* www.phaidon.com, pg 182

Horgan, Rick, Scribner, 1230 Avenue of the Americas, New York, NY 10020, pg 209

Horinstein, Regine, Corporation of Professional Librarians of Quebec, 1453, rue Beaubien Est, Bureau 215, Montreal, QC H2G 3C6, Canada *Tel:* 514-845-3327 *Fax:* 514-845-1618 *E-mail:* info@cbpq.qc.ca *Web Site:* www.cbpq.qc.ca, pg 564

Horjus, Anne, Acroterion Books, 5305 Harvard Rd, Lawrence, KS 66049-4781 *Tel:* 785-917-0773 *E-mail:* info@acroterionbooks.com *Web Site:* www.acroterionbooks.com, pg 477

Horler, Fred, Groundwood Books, 128 Sterling Rd, Lower Level, Toronto, ON M6R 2B7, Canada *Tel:* 416-363-4343 *Fax:* 416-363-1017 *E-mail:* genmail@groundwoodbooks.com *Web Site:* www.houseofanansi.com, pg 458

Horn, Leah, Western States Arts Federation, 1743 Wazee St, Suite 300, Denver, CO 80202 *Tel:* 303-629-1166 *Toll Free Tel:* 888-562-7232 *Fax:* 303-629-9717 *E-mail:* staff@westaf.org *Web Site:* www.westaf.org, pg 583

Horner, Christine, In the Garden Publishing, 7525 Paragon Rd, No 752252, Dayton, OH 45459 *Tel:* 937-317-0859 *E-mail:* editor@inthegardenpublishing.com *Web Site:* www.inthegardenpublishing.com, pg 115

Hornfischer, Jim, Hornfischer Literary Management LP, PO Box 50544, Austin, TX 78763 *Tel:* 512-472-0011 *E-mail:* queries@hornfischerlit.com *Web Site:* www.hornfischerlit.com, pg 521

Hornik, Lauri, Dial Books for Young Readers, 345 Hudson St, New York, NY 10014 *Tel:* 212-366-2000 *Toll Free Tel:* 800-733-3000 (orders) *Fax:* 212-414-3396 *Web Site:* www.penguin.com, pg 70

Hornung, Susan, Andrew Carnegie Medals for Excellence in Fiction & Nonfiction, 50 E Huron St, Chicago, IL 60611 *Tel:* 312-944-6780 *Toll Free Tel:* 800-545-2433 *Fax:* 312-440-9374 *E-mail:* ala@ala.org *Web Site:* www.ala.org/awardsgrants/carnegieadult, pg 636

Hornyak, Kim, Jenkins Group Inc, 1129 Woodmere Ave, Suite B, Traverse City, MI 49686 *Tel:* 231-933-0445 *Toll Free Tel:* 800-706-4636 *Fax:* 231-933-0448 *E-mail:* info@bookpublishing.com *Web Site:* www.bookpublishing.com, pg 496

Horowitz, Beverly, Random House Children's Books, 1745 Broadway, 10th fl, New York, NY 10019 *Tel:* 212-782-9000 *Web Site:* www.randomhousekids.com, pg 194

Horowitz, David, Media Coalition Inc, 19 Fulton St, Suite 407, New York, NY 10038 *Tel:* 212-587-4025 *Fax:* 212-587-2436 *E-mail:* info@mediacoalition.org *Web Site:* mediacoalition.org, pg 569

Horowitz, Mitch, TarcherPerigee, 375 Hudson St, New York, NY 10014 *Tel:* 212-366-2000 *Fax:* 212-366-2643 *E-mail:* customerservice@penguinrandomhouse.com (cust serv); TarcherPerigeePublicity@penguinrandomhouse.com (media queries) *Web Site:* www.tarcherbooks.com; www.facebook.com/TarcherPerigee/; www.penguin.com/publishers/tarcherperigee, pg 227

Horowitz, Shel, Accurate Writing & More, 16 Barstow Lane, Hadley, MA 01035 *Tel:* 413-586-2388 *Web Site:* www.accuratewriting.com; www.frugalmarketing.com; www.goingbeyondsustainability.com; www.transformpreneur.com; www.greenandprofitable.com; www.twitter.com/shelhorowitz, pg 487

Horowitz, Valerie, The Lawbook Exchange Ltd, 33 Terminal Ave, Clark, NJ 07066-1321 *Tel:* 732-382-1800 *Toll Free Tel:* 800-422-6686 *Fax:* 732-382-1887 *E-mail:* law@lawbookexchange.com *Web Site:* www.lawbookexchange.com, pg 130

Horrer, Simon, Macmillan Learning, 41 Madison Ave, New York, NY 10010 *Tel:* 212-576-9400 *Fax:* 212-689-2383 *Web Site:* www.macmillanlearning.com, pg 140

Horst, Angelina, Templeton Press, 300 Conshohocken State Rd, Suite 665, West Conshohocken, PA 19428 *Tel:* 484-531-8380 *Fax:* 484-531-8382 *E-mail:* tpinfo@templetonpress.org *Web Site:* www.templetonpress.org, pg 229

Horst, Ines ter, University of Texas Press, 3001 Lake Austin Blvd, 2.200, Austin, TX 78703 *Tel:* 512-471-7233 *Fax:* 512-232-7178 *E-mail:* utpress@uts.cc.utexas.edu; info@utpress.utexas.edu *Web Site:* www.utexaspress.com, pg 230

Horton, Chelsea, American Anthropological Association (AAA), 2300 Clarendon Blvd, Suite 1301, Arlington, VA 22201 *Tel:* 703-528-1902 *Fax:* 703-528-3546 *E-mail:* pubs@americananthro.org *Web Site:* www.americananthro.org, pg 10

Horton, David, Bethany House Publishers, 11400 Hampshire Ave S, Bloomington, MN 55438 *Tel:* 952-829-2500 *Toll Free Tel:* 800-877-2665 (orders) *Fax:* 952-829-2568 *Toll Free Fax:* 800-398-3111 (orders) *Web Site:* www.bethanyhouse.com; www.bakerpublishinggroup.com, pg 34

Horton, Kelsey, Random House Children's Books, 1745 Broadway, 10th fl, New York, NY 10019 *Tel:* 212-782-9000 *Web Site:* www.randomhousekids.com, pg 194

Horvath, Dave, Jason Aronson Inc, 4501 Forbes Blvd, Suite 200, Lanham, MD 20706 *Tel:* 301-459-3366 *Toll Free Tel:* 800-462-6420 (orders) *Fax:* 301-429-5748 *Web Site:* www.rowman.com, pg 21

Horvath, Dave, Lexington Books, 4501 Forbes Blvd, Suite 200, Lanham, MD 20706 *Tel:* 301-459-3366 *Fax:* 301-429-5749 *Web Site:* www.lexingtonbooks.com, pg 133

Horvath, Dave, University Press of America Inc, 4501 Forbes Blvd, Suite 200, Lanham, MD 20706 *Tel:* 301-459-3366 *Toll Free Tel:* 800-462-6420 *Fax:* 301-429-5748 *Toll Free Fax:* 800-338-4550 *Web Site:* www.univpress.com, pg 246

Horvit, Mark, Investigative Reporters & Editors, Missouri School of Journalism, 141 Neff Annex, Columbia, MO 65211 *Tel:* 573-882-2042 *Fax:* 573-882-5431 *E-mail:* info@ire.org *Web Site:* www.ire.org, pg 568

Hosea, Beata, The Art Institute of Chicago, 111 S Michigan Ave, Chicago, IL 60603-6404 *Tel:* 312-443-3600; 312-443-3540 (pubns) *Fax:* 312-443-1334 (pubns) *Web Site:* www.artic.edu; www.artinstituteshop.org, pg 21

Hoshijo, Amara, Soho Press Inc, 853 Broadway, New York, NY 10003 *Tel:* 212-260-1900 *E-mail:* soho@sohopress.com; publicity@sohopress.com; contact@sohopress.com *Web Site:* www.sohopress.com, pg 216

Hosier, Chad, The Society of Professional Journalists (SPJ), Eugene S Pulliam National Journalism Ctr, 3909 N Meridian St, Indianapolis, IN 46208 *Tel:* 317-927-8000 *Fax:* 317-920-4789 *E-mail:* spj@spj.org *Web Site:* www.spj.org, pg 580

Hosier, Erin, Dunow, Carlson & Lerner Literary Agency Inc, 27 W 20 St, Suite 1107, New York, NY 10011 *Tel:* 212-645-7606 *E-mail:* mail@dclagency.com *Web Site:* www.dclagency.com, pg 515

Hoskin, Christine, Schoolhouse Indexing, 10-B Parade Ground Rd, Etna, NH 03750 *Tel:* 603-643-1617 *Web Site:* schoolhouseindexing.com, pg 501

Hotchkiss, Erin, Stewart, Tabori & Chang, 115 W 18 St, 6th fl, New York, NY 10011 *Tel:* 212-519-1200; 212-206-7715 *Fax:* 212-519-1210 *E-mail:* abrams@abramsbooks.com *Web Site:* www.abramsbooks.com/imprints/stc, pg 222

Hotzler, Russell K PhD, New York City College of Technology, 300 Jay St, Brooklyn, NY 11201 *Tel:* 718-260-5500 *Fax:* 718-260-5198 *E-mail:* connect@citytech.cuny.edu *Web Site:* www.citytech.cuny.edu, pg 621

Houder, Daniel, Kennedy Information Inc, 24 Railroad St, Keene, NH 03431 *Tel:* 603-924-0900 *Toll Free Tel:* 800-531-0140 *Fax:* 603-357-8112 *E-mail:* customerservice@kennedyinfo.com *Web Site:* www.kennedyinfo.com, pg 125

Hough, Milly, Individual Artist's Fellowships, 1026 Sumter St, Suite 200, Columbia, SC 29201-3746 *Tel:* 803-734-8696 *Fax:* 803-734-8526 *E-mail:* info@arts.sc.gov *Web Site:* www.southcarolinaarts.com, pg 655

Houghton, Daniel, Lonely Planet, 150 Linden St, Oakland, CA 94607 *Tel:* 510-893-8555; 510-250-6400 *Toll Free Tel:* 800-275-8555 (orders) *Fax:* 510-893-8572 *E-mail:* info@lonelyplanet.com *Web Site:* www.lonelyplanet.com, pg 137

Houghton, Harmon, Clear Light Publishers, 823 Don Diego Ave, Santa Fe, NM 87505 *Tel:* 505-989-9590 *Toll Free Tel:* 800-253-2747 (orders) *Fax:* 505-989-9519 *E-mail:* market@clearlightbooks.com *Web Site:* www.clearlightbooks.com, pg 57

Houghton, Stephen, Parallax Press, 2236-B Sixth St, Berkeley, CA 94710 *Tel:* 510-540-6411 *Toll Free Tel:* 800-863-5290 (orders) *Fax:* 510-981-1157 *Web Site:* www.parallax.org, pg 174

Hourigan, Katherine, Doubleday/Nan A Talese, c/o Penguin Random House Inc, 1745 Broadway, New York, NY 10019 *Tel:* 212-751-2600 *Fax:* 212-572-2662 *E-mail:* ddaypub@randomhouse.com *Web Site:* knopfdoubleday.com, pg 72

Hourigan, Katherine, Alfred A Knopf/Everyman's Library, c/o Penguin Random House Inc, 1745 Broadway, New York, NY 10019 *Tel:* 212-751-2600 *Toll Free Tel:* 800-638-6460 *Fax:* 212-572-2593 *Web Site:* www.knopfdoubleday.com, pg 127

House, Jackson, Townson Publishing Co Ltd, PO Box 1404, Sta A, Vancouver, BC V6C 2P7, Canada *Tel:* 604-886-0594 *E-mail:* townsonpublishing@gmail.com *Web Site:* generalpublishing.co.uk, pg 472

Householder, Stacy, National Conference of State Legislatures (NCSL), 7700 E First Place, Denver, CO 80230 *Tel:* 303-364-7700 *Fax:* 303-364-7800 *E-mail:* books@ncsl.org *Web Site:* www.ncsl.org, pg 158

Housley, Jim, Bloom's Literary Criticism, 132 W 31 St, 17th fl, New York, NY 10001 *Toll Free Tel:* 800-322-8755 *Toll Free Fax:* 800-678-3633 *E-mail:* custserv@factsonfile.com *Web Site:* www.infobasepublishing.com, pg 37

Housley, Jim, Chelsea House Publishers, 132 W 31 St, 17th fl, New York, NY 10001 *Tel:* 212-967-8800 *Toll Free Tel:* 800-322-8755 *Fax:* 917-339-0325 *Toll Free Fax:* 800-678-3633 *E-mail:* custserv@factsonfile.com *Web Site:* www.infobasepublishing.com; www.infobaselearning.com, pg 53

Housley, Jim, Facts On File, 132 W 31 St, 17th fl, New York, NY 10001 *Tel:* 212-967-8800 *Toll Free Tel:* 800-322-8755 *Toll Free Fax:* 800-678-3633 *E-mail:* custserv@factsonfile.com *Web Site:* infobasepublishing.com, pg 81

Housley, Jim, Ferguson Publishing, 132 W 31 St, 17th fl, New York, NY 10001 *Tel:* 212-967-8800 *Toll Free Tel:* 800-322-8755 *Fax:* 917-339-0323 *Toll Free Fax:* 800-678-3633 *E-mail:* custserv@factsonfile.com *Web Site:* infobasepublishing.com, pg 84

Houtz, Julie, ASCD, 1703 N Beauregard St, Alexandria, VA 22311-1714 *Tel:* 703-578-9600 *Toll Free Tel:* 800-933-2723 *Fax:* 703-575-5400 *E-mail:* member@ascd.org *Web Site:* www.ascd.org, pg 22

Hovemann, Glenn, Dawn Publications Inc, 12402 Bitney Springs Rd, Nevada City, CA 95959 *Tel:* 530-274-7775 *Toll Free Tel:* 800-545-7475 *Fax:* 530-274-7778 *E-mail:* nature@dawnpub.com; orders@dawnpub.com *Web Site:* www.dawnpub.com, pg 68

Hovey, Kim, Random House Publishing Group, 1745 Broadway, New York, NY 10019 *Toll Free Tel:* 800-200-3552 *Web Site:* atrandom.com, pg 195

Howard, Assuanta, Asta Publications LLC, 275 W Clarkstown Rd, New City, NY 10956 *Tel:* 678-814-1320 *Toll Free Tel:* 800-482-4190 *Fax:* 678-814-1370 *E-mail:* info@astapublications.com *Web Site:* www.astapublications.com, pg 24

Howard, Brent, Dutton, 375 Hudson St, New York, NY 10014 *Tel:* 212-366-2000 *Fax:* 212-366-2262 *Web Site:* www.penguin.com, pg 74

Howard, Elise, Algonquin Books, 400 Silver Cedar Ct, Suite 300, Chapel Hill, NC 27514-1585 *Tel:* 919-967-0108 *Fax:* 919-933-0272 *E-mail:* inquiry@algonquin.com *Web Site:* www.workman.com/algonquin, pg 7

Howard, Gerry, Doubleday/Nan A Talese, c/o Penguin Random House Inc, 1745 Broadway, New York, NY 10019 *Tel:* 212-751-2600 *Fax:* 212-572-2662 *E-mail:* ddaypub@randomhouse.com *Web Site:* knopfdoubleday.com, pg 72

Howard, Glenda, Harlequin Enterprises Ltd, 233 Broadway, Suite 1001, New York, NY 10279 *Tel:* 212-553-4200 *Fax:* 212-227-8969 *E-mail:* customerservice@harlequin.com *Web Site:* www.harlequin.com, pg 100

Howard, J Kirk, Simon & Pierre Publishing Co Ltd, 3 Church St, Suite 500, Toronto, ON M5E 1M2, Canada *Tel:* 416-214-5544 *E-mail:* info@dundurn.com *Web Site:* www.dundurn.com, pg 471

Howard, Kait, Perseus Books, 250 W 57 St, 15th fl, New York, NY 10107 *Tel:* 212-340-8100 *Toll Free Tel:* 800-343-4499 (cust serv) *Fax:* 212-340-8105 *Web Site:* www.perseusbooks.com, pg 181

Howard, Kathy, Graphic Arts Books, 7820 NE Holman St, Suite B-9, Portland, OR 97218 *Tel:* 503-254-5591 *Fax:* 503-254-5609 *E-mail:* info-ga@graphicartsbooks.com *Web Site:* www.graphicartsbooks.com, pg 95

Howard, Kirk, Dundurn Press Ltd, 3 Church St, Suite 500, Toronto, ON M5E 1M2, Canada *Tel:* 416-214-5544 *Fax:* 416-214-5556 *E-mail:* info@dundurn.com *Web Site:* www.dundurn.com, pg 452

Howard, MacKenzie, Thomas Nelson, 501 Nelson Place, Nashville, TN 37214 *Tel:* 615-889-9000 *Toll Free Tel:* 800-251-4000 *Fax:* 615-902-1548 *Web Site:* www.thomasnelson.com, pg 231

Howard, MacKenzie, Tommy Nelson, 501 Nelson Place, Nashville, TN 37214 *Tel:* 615-889-9000; 615-902-1485 (cust serv) *Toll Free Tel:* 800-251-4000 *Fax:* 615-391-5225 *Web Site:* www.tommynelson.com, pg 233

Howard, Marilyn, Creative Freelancers Inc, PO Box 366, Tallevast, FL 34270 *Toll Free Tel:* 800-398-9544 *Web Site:* www.freelancers1.com, pg 492

Howard, Meredith, Columbia University Press, 61 W 62 St, New York, NY 10023 *Tel:* 212-459-0600 *Toll Free Tel:* 800-944-8648 *Fax:* 212-459-3678 *E-mail:* cup_book@columbia.edu (orders & cust serv) *Web Site:* cup.columbia.edu, pg 59

Howard, Nicole, Writer's Digest Annual Writing Competition, 10151 Carver Rd, Suite 200, Blue Ash, OH 45242 *Tel:* 715-445-4612 (ext 13430) *Fax:* 920-744-1760 *E-mail:* writersdigestwritingcompetition@fwmedia.com *Web Site:* www.writersdigest.com, pg 700

Howard, Roy, Cantos Para Todos, 4749 Hillcrest St, Bel Aire, KS 67220 *Tel:* 316-239 6477 *E-mail:* cantos@cantos.org *Web Site:* www.cantos.org, pg 47

Howe, Isabel, The Authors League Fund, 31 E 32 St, 7th fl, New York, NY 10016 *Tel:* 212-268-1208 *Fax:* 212-564-5363 *E-mail:* staff@authorsleaguefund.org *Web Site:* www.authorsleaguefund.org, pg 559

Howe, Meghan, Marilyn Baillie Picture Book Award, 40 Orchard View Blvd, Suite 217, Toronto, ON M4R 1B9, Canada *Tel:* 416-975-0010 *Fax:* 416-975-8970 *E-mail:* info@bookcentre.ca *Web Site:* www.bookcentre.ca, pg 629

Howe, Meghan, The Geoffrey Bilson Award for Historical Fiction for Young People, 40 Orchard View Blvd, Suite 217, Toronto, ON M4R 1B9, Canada *Tel:* 416-975-0010 *Fax:* 416-975-8970 *E-mail:* info@bookcentre.ca *Web Site:* www.bookcentre.ca, pg 632

Howe, Meghan, Canadian Children's Book Centre, 40 Orchard View Blvd, Suite 217, Toronto, ON M4R 1B9, Canada *Tel:* 416-975-0010 *Fax:* 416-975-8970 *E-mail:* info@bookcentre.ca *Web Site:* www.bookcentre.ca, pg 562

Howe, Meghan, Norma Fleck Award for Canadian Children's Non-Fiction, 40 Orchard View Blvd, Suite 217, Toronto, ON M4R 1B9, Canada *Tel:* 416-975-0010 *Fax:* 416-975-8970 *E-mail:* info@bookcentre.ca *Web Site:* www.bookcentre.ca, pg 646

Howe, Meghan, Amy Mathers Teen Book Award, 40 Orchard View Blvd, Suite 217, Toronto, ON M4R 1B9, Canada *Tel:* 416-975-0010 *Fax:* 416-975-8970 *E-mail:* info@bookcentre.ca *Web Site:* www.bookcentre.ca, pg 666

Howe, Meghan, John Spray Mystery Award, 40 Orchard View Blvd, Suite 217, Toronto, ON M4R 1B9, Canada *Tel:* 416-975-0010 *Fax:* 416-975-8970 *E-mail:* info@bookcentre.ca *Web Site:* www.bookcentre.ca, pg 691

Howe, Meghan, TD Canadian Children's Literature Award, 40 Orchard View Blvd, Suite 217, Toronto, ON M4R 1B9, Canada *Tel:* 416-975-0010 *Fax:* 416-975-8970 *E-mail:* info@bookcentre.ca *Web Site:* www.bookcentre.ca, pg 693

Howe, Sally, Scribner, 1230 Avenue of the Americas, New York, NY 10020, pg 209

Howell, Christopher, Lynx House Press, 420 W 24 St, Spokane, WA 99203 *Tel:* 509-624-4894 *E-mail:* lynxhousepress@gmail.com *Web Site:* www.lynxhousepress.org, pg 139

Howell, Chuck, Library of American Broadcasting (LAB), University of Maryland, Hornbake Library, College Park, MD 20742 *Tel:* 301-405-9212 *Web Site:* www.lib.umd.edu/special/collections/massmedia/about-us, pg 568

Howie, Ashley, Ink Smith Publishing, 710 S Myrtle Ave, Suite 209, Monrovia, CA 91016 *Tel:* 626-415-7179 *E-mail:* contact@ink-smith.com *Web Site:* ink-smith.com, pg 117

Howlett, Valerie, Perseus Books, 250 W 57 St, 15th fl, New York, NY 10107 *Tel:* 212-340-8100 *Toll Free Tel:* 800-343-4499 (cust serv) *Fax:* 212-340-8105 *Web Site:* www.perseusbooks.com, pg 181

Howry, Michelle, Hachette Books, 1290 Avenue of the Americas, New York, NY 10019 *Tel:* 212-364-1100 *Web Site:* www.hachettebookgroup.com, pg 98

Howser, Cathy, Arkansas Diamond Primary Book Award, Arkansas State Library, Suite 100, 900 W Capitol Ave, Little Rock, AR 72201-3108 *Tel:* 501-682-2860 *Fax:* 501-682-1693 *Web Site:* www.library.arkansas.gov; www.library.arkansas.gov, pg 628

Howser, Cathy, Charlie May Simon Children's Book Award, Arkansas State Library, Suite 100, 900 W Capitol Ave, Little Rock, AR 72201-3108 *Tel:* 501-682-2860 *Fax:* 501-682-1693 *Web Site:* www.library.arkansas.gov, pg 689

Howson, Barbara, Groundwood Books, 128 Sterling Rd, Lower Level, Toronto, ON M6R 2B7, Canada *Tel:* 416-363-4343 *Fax:* 416-363-1017 *E-mail:* genmail@groundwoodbooks.com *Web Site:* www.houseofanansi.com, pg 458

Howson, Barbara, House of Anansi Press Inc, 128 Sterling Rd, Lower Level, Toronto, ON M6R 2B7, Canada *Tel:* 416-363-4343 *Fax:* 416-363-1017 *E-mail:* customerservice@houseofanansi.com *Web Site:* www.houseofanansi.com, pg 460

Howson, Christine, Marick Press, PO Box 36253, Grosse Pointe Farms, MI 48236 *Tel:* 313-407-9236 *E-mail:* orders@marickpress.com *Web Site:* www.marickpress.com, pg 142

Hoy, Angela, WritersWeekly.com's 24-Hour Short Story Contest, 5726 Cortez Rd, Suite 349, Bradenton, FL 34210 *Fax:* 305-768-0261 *Web Site:* www.writersweekly.com, pg 700

Hoyem, Andrew, The Arion Press, The Presidio, 1802 Hays St, San Francisco, CA 94129 *Tel:* 415-668-2542 *Fax:* 415-668-2550 *E-mail:* arionpress@arionpress.com *Web Site:* www.arionpress.com, pg 21

Hoyt, Christopher R, S©ott Treimel NY, 434 Lafayette St, New York, NY 10003-6943 *Tel:* 212-505-8353 *E-mail:* general@scotttreimelny.com *Web Site:* scotttreimelny.com; scotttreimelny.blogspot.com, pg 535

Hoyt, Debra Morton, W W Norton & Company Inc, 500 Fifth Ave, New York, NY 10110-0017 *Tel:* 212-354-5500 *Toll Free Tel:* 800-233-4830 (orders & cust serv) *Fax:* 212-869-0856 *Toll Free Fax:* 800-458-6515 *E-mail:* orders@wwnorton.com *Web Site:* books.wwnorton.com, pg 164

Hrab, Naseem, Kids Can Press Ltd, 25 Dockside Dr, Toronto, ON M5A 0B5, Canada *Tel:* 416-479-7000 *Toll Free Tel:* 800-265-0884 *Fax:* 416-960-5437 *E-mail:* info@kidscan.com; customerservice@kidscan.com *Web Site:* www.kidscanpress.com, www.kidscanpress.ca, pg 461

Hromjak, Jasmine, North Atlantic Books, 2526 Martin Luther King Jr Way, Berkeley, CA 94704 *Tel:* 510-549-4270 *Fax:* 510-549-4276 *Web Site:* www.northatlanticbooks.com, pg 163

Hruska, Bronwen, Soho Press Inc, 853 Broadway, New York, NY 10003 *Tel:* 212-260-1900 *E-mail:* soho@sohopress.com; publicity@sohopress.com; contact@sohopress.com *Web Site:* www.sohopress.com, pg 216

Hsu, Connie, Roaring Brook Press, 175 Fifth Ave, New York, NY 10010 *Tel:* 646-307-5151 *Web Site:* us.macmillan.com/publishers/roaring-brook-press, pg 200

Hsu, Ellen, InterVarsity Press, 430 Plaza Dr, Westmont, IL 60559-1234 *Tel:* 630-734-4000 *Toll Free Tel:* 800-843-9487 *Fax:* 630-734-4200 *E-mail:* email@ivpress.com *Web Site:* www.ivpress.com, pg 120

Huard, Ricky S, Ohio University Press, 31 S Court St, Suite 143, Athens, OH 45701-2979 *Fax:* 740-593-4536 *Web Site:* www.ohioswallow.com, pg 167

Huard, Ricky S, Swallow Press, 31 S Court St, Suite 143, Athens, OH 45701 *Tel:* 740-593-1155 *Toll Free Tel:* 800-621-2736 *Fax:* 740-593-4536 *Web Site:* www.ohioswallow.com, pg 225

Hubbard, Peter, HarperCollins General Books Group, 195 Broadway, New York, NY 10007 *Tel:* 212-207-7000 *Web Site:* www.harpercollins.com, pg 101

Hubbard, Sarah, Professional Publications Inc (PPI), 1250 Fifth Ave, Belmont, CA 94002 *Tel:* 650-593-9119 *Fax:* 650-592-4519 *E-mail:* acquisitions@ppi2pass.com *Web Site:* ppi2pass.com; feprep.com, pg 189

Hubbart, Dustin, University of Illinois Press, 1325 S Oak St, MC-566, Champaign, IL 61820-6903 *Tel:* 217-333-0950 *Fax:* 217-244-8082 *E-mail:* uipress@uillinois.edu; journals@uillinois.edu *Web Site:* www.press.uillinois.edu, pg 241

Hubbs, Roger A, Cornell University Press, Sage House, 512 E State St, Ithaca, NY 14850 *Tel:* 607-277-2338 *Fax:* 607-277-2374 *E-mail:* cupressinfo@cornell.edu; cupress-sales@cornell.edu *Web Site:* www.cornellpress.cornell.edu, pg 61

Hubenthal, Dayna, Koho Pono LLC, 15024 SE Pinegrove Loop, Clackamas, OR 97015 *Tel:* 503-723-7392 *Toll Free Tel:* 800-937-8000 (orders) *Toll Free Fax:* 800-876-0186 (orders) *E-mail:* info@kohopono.com; orders@ingrambook.com *Web Site:* kohopono.com, pg 127

Hubers, Laura Bardolph, Wm B Eerdmans Publishing Co, 2140 Oak Industrial Dr NE, Grand Rapids, MI 49505 *Tel:* 616-459-4591 *Toll Free Tel:* 800-253-7521 *Fax:* 616-459-6540 *E-mail:* customerservice@eerdmans.com; sales@eerdmans.com *Web Site:* www.eerdmans.com, pg 76

Huckaby, Billy, Eakin Press, PO Box 331779, Fort Worth, TX 76163 *Tel:* 817-344-7036 *Toll Free Tel:* 888-982-8270 *Fax:* 817-344-7036 *Web Site:* www.eakinpress.com, pg 74

Huckaby, Ronna, Eakin Press, PO Box 331779, Fort Worth, TX 76163 *Tel:* 817-344-7036 *Toll Free Tel:* 888-982-8270 *Fax:* 817-344-7036 *Web Site:* www.eakinpress.com, pg 74

Hudak, Carrie, Rutgers University Press, 106 Somerset St, 3rd fl, New Brunswick, NJ 08901 *Tel:* 848-445-7762 *Toll Free Tel:* 800-848-6224 (orders only) *Fax:* 732-745-4935 (acqs, edit, mktg, perms & prodn) *Toll Free Fax:* 800-272-6817 (fulfillment) *Web Site:* rutgerspress.rutgers.edu, pg 202

Hudon, Sylvie, Les Presses de l'Universite Laval, 2180, Chemin Sainte-Foy, 1st fl, Quebec, QC G1V 0A6, Canada *Tel:* 418-656-2803 *Fax:* 418-656-3305 *E-mail:* presses@pul.ulaval.ca *Web Site:* www.pulaval.com, pg 468

Hudson, Christopher, The Museum of Modern Art (MoMA), 11 W 53 St, New York, NY 10019 *Tel:* 212-708-9443 *Fax:* 212-333-6575 *E-mail:* moma_publications@moma.org *Web Site:* www.moma.org, pg 155

Hudson, Dawn, Academy of Motion Picture Arts & Sciences (AMPAS), 8949 Wilshire Blvd, Beverly Hills, CA 90211 *Tel:* 310-247-3000 *Fax:* 310-859-9619 *E-mail:* ampas@oscars.org *Web Site:* www.oscars.org, pg 553

Hudson, Deborah Orgel, Association for Talent Development (ATD) Press, 1640 King St, Box 1443, Alexandria, VA 22313-1443 *Tel:* 703-683-8100 *Toll Free Tel:* 800-628-2783 *Fax:* 703-299-8723; 703-683-1523 (cust care) *E-mail:* customercare@td.org *Web Site:* www.astd.org; www.td.org, pg 24

Hudson, Jeanne-Marie, Berkley Publishing Group, 375 Hudson St, New York, NY 10014 *Tel:* 212-366-2000 *Fax:* 212-366-2385 *Web Site:* www.penguin.com, pg 33

Hudson, Suzan, Herald Publishing House, 1001 W Walnut St, Independence, MO 64051 *Tel:* 816-521-3015 *Toll Free Tel:* 800-767-8181 *Fax:* 816-521-3066 *E-mail:* sales@heraldhouse.org *Web Site:* www.heraldhouse.org, pg 106

Hudson, Will, Regnery Publishing, 300 New Jersey Ave NW, Washington, DC 20001 *Tel:* 202-216-0600 *Toll Free Tel:* 888-219-4747 *Fax:* 202-393-1795 *Web Site:* www.regnery.com, pg 198

Huelsing, Kristi, Coaches Choice, 514 Airport Way, Monterey, CA 93940 *Toll Free Tel:* 888-229-5745 *Fax:* 831-372-6075 *E-mail:* info@coacheschoice.com *Web Site:* www.coacheschoice.com, pg 57

Huey-Steiner, Kim, I-5 Publishing LLC, 3 Burroughs, Irvine, CA 92618 *Tel:* 949-855-8822 *Toll Free Tel:* 888-738-2665 *Fax:* 949-458-3856 *Web Site:* www.i5publishing.com, pg 113

Huff, Mickey, The 25 Most "Censored" Stories Annual, PO Box 750940, Petaluma, CA 94975 *Tel:* 707-241-4596 *Web Site:* www.projectcensored.org, pg 695

Huggins, Allison, Workman Publishing Co Inc, 225 Varick St, 9th fl, New York, NY 10014-4381 *Tel:* 212-254-5900 *Toll Free Tel:* 800-722-7202 *Fax:* 212-254-8098 *E-mail:* info@workman.com *Web Site:* www.workman.com, pg 259

Hughes, Amy, Dunow, Carlson & Lerner Literary Agency Inc, 27 W 20 St, Suite 1107, New York, NY 10011 *Tel:* 212-645-7606 *E-mail:* mail@dclagency.com *Web Site:* www.dclagency.com, pg 515

Hughes, Andrew W, Doubleday/Nan A Talese, c/o Penguin Random House Inc, 1745 Broadway, New York, NY 10019 *Tel:* 212-751-2600 *Fax:* 212-572-2662 *E-mail:* ddaypub@randomhouse.com *Web Site:* knopfdoubleday.com, pg 72

Hughes, Andrew W, Alfred A Knopf/Everyman's Library, c/o Penguin Random House Inc, 1745 Broadway, New York, NY 10019 *Tel:* 212-751-2600 *Toll Free Tel:* 800-638-6460 *Fax:* 212-572-2593 *Web Site:* www.knopfdoubleday.com, pg 127

Hughes, Andy, Pantheon Books/Schocken Books, c/o Penguin Random House Inc, 1745 Broadway, New York, NY 10019 *Tel:* 212-751-2600 *Web Site:* knopfdoubleday.com/imprint/pantheon, pg 173

Hughes, Brigid, Graywolf Press, 250 Third Ave N, Suite 600, Minneapolis, MN 55401 *Tel:* 651-641-0077 *Fax:* 651-641-0036 *E-mail:* wolves@graywolfpress.org (no ms queries, sample chapters or proposals) *Web Site:* www.graywolfpress.org, pg 95

Hughes, Connie, Lippincott Williams & Wilkins, 333 Seventh Ave, New York, NY 10001 *Toll Free Tel:* 800-950-2035 *E-mail:* orders@lww.com *Web Site:* www.lww.com, pg 135

Hughes, Doug, McGraw-Hill Contemporary Learning Series, 501 Bell St, Dubuque, IA 52001 *Toll Free Tel:* 800-243-6532 *Web Site:* www.mhcls.com, pg 145

Hughes, Doug, McGraw-Hill Higher Education, 1333 Burr Ridge Pkwy, Burr Ridge, IL 60527 *Tel:* 630-789-4000 *Toll Free Tel:* 800-338-3987 (cust serv) *Fax:* 614-755-5645 (cust serv) *Web Site:* www.mhhe.com, pg 146

Hughes, Doug, McGraw-Hill Humanities, Social Sciences, Languages, 2 Penn Plaza, 21st fl, New York, NY 10121 *Tel:* 212-904-2000 *Toll Free Tel:* 800-338-3987 (cust serv) *Fax:* 614-755-5645 (cust serv) *Web Site:* www.mhhe.com, pg 146

Hughes, Doug, McGraw-Hill/Irwin, 1333 Burr Ridge Pkwy, Burr Ridge, IL 60527 *Tel:* 630-789-4000 *Toll Free Tel:* 800-338-3987 (cust serv) *Fax:* 630-789-6942; 614-755-5645 (cust serv) *Web Site:* www.mhhe.com, pg 146

Hughes, Doug, McGraw-Hill Science, Engineering, Mathematics, 501 Bell St, Dubuque, IA 52001 *Tel:* 563-584-6000 *Toll Free Tel:* 800-338-3987 (cust serv) *Fax:* 614-755-5645 (cust serv) *Web Site:* www.mhhe.com, pg 146

Hughes, Emily, Penguin Random House Inc, 1745 Broadway, New York, NY 10019 *Tel:* 212-782-9000 *Toll Free Tel:* 800-726-0600 *Web Site:* www.penguinrandomhouse.com, pg 178

Hughes, Georgia, New World Library, 14 Pamaron Way, Novato, CA 94949 *Tel:* 415-884-2100 *Toll Free Tel:* 800-227-3900 (ext 52, retail orders); 800-972-6657 *Fax:* 415-884-2199 *E-mail:* escort@newworldlibrary.com *Web Site:* www.newworldlibrary.com, pg 161

Hughes, Heather, Sleeping Bear Press™, 2395 S Huron Pkwy, Suite 200, Ann Arbor, MI 48104 *Toll Free Tel:* 800-487-2323 *Fax:* 734-929-2649 *E-mail:* customerservice@sleepingbearpress.com *Web Site:* www.sleepingbearpress.com, pg 215

Hughes, Larry, Simon & Schuster, 1230 Avenue of the Americas, New York, NY 10020 *Tel:* 212-698-7000 *Toll Free Tel:* 800-223-2348 (cust serv); 800-223-2336 (orders) *Toll Free Fax:* 800-943-9831 (orders) *Web Site:* www.simonandschuster.com, pg 212

Hughes, Nicki, Castle Connolly Medical Ltd, 42 W 24 St, 2nd fl, New York, NY 10010 *Tel:* 212-367-8400 *Fax:* 212-367-0964 *Web Site:* www.castleconnolly.com, pg 49

Hughes, Patrick, Central Recovery Press (CRP), 3321 N Buffalo Dr, Suite 275, Las Vegas, NV 89129 *Tel:* 702-868-5830 *Fax:* 702-868-5831 *E-mail:* info@centralrecovery.com *Web Site:* centralrecoverypress.com, pg 52

Huizenga, Alan, Tyndale House Publishers Inc, 351 Executive Dr, Carol Stream, IL 60188 *Tel:* 630-668-8300 *Toll Free Tel:* 800-323-9400 *Toll Free Fax:* 800-684-0247 *Web Site:* www.tyndale.com, pg 237

Hulburt, Stephen, Prestel Publishing, 900 Broadway, Suite 603, New York, NY 10003 *Tel:* 212-995-2720 *Fax:* 212-995-2733 *E-mail:* sales@prestel-usa.com *Web Site:* prestelpublishing.randomhouse.de, pg 187

Hull, Stephen, University Press of New England, One Court St, Suite 250, Lebanon, NH 03766 *Tel:* 603-448-1533 *Toll Free Tel:* 800-421-1561 (orders only) *Fax:* 603-448-7006; 603-448-9429 (orders only) *E-mail:* university.press@dartmouth.edu *Web Site:* www.upne.com, pg 247

Hullinger, Margret S, Bloomberg BNA Books, 1801 S Bell St, Arlington, VA 22202 *Tel:* 732-476-6397 *Toll Free Tel:* 800-960-1220 *Fax:* 732-346-1624 *E-mail:* books@bna.com *Web Site:* www.bna.com/bnabooks, pg 37

Hulsebosch, Betsy, Hachette Books, 1290 Avenue of the Americas, New York, NY 10019 *Tel:* 212-364-1100 *Web Site:* www.hachettebookgroup.com, pg 98

Hulsey, Dave, Indiana University Press, Herman B Wells Library 350, 1320 E Tenth St, Bloomington, IN 47405-3907 *Tel:* 812-855-8817 *Toll Free Tel:* 800-842-6796 (orders only) *Fax:* 812-855-7931; 812-855-8507 *E-mail:* iupress@indiana.edu; iuporder@indiana.edu (orders) *Web Site:* www.iupress.indiana.edu, pg 116

Hummel, Lauren, Hachette Books, 1290 Avenue of the Americas, New York, NY 10019 *Tel:* 212-364-1100 *Web Site:* www.hachettebookgroup.com, pg 98

Humphrey, John H, Journal of Roman Archaeology LLC, 95 Peleg Rd, Portsmouth, RI 02871 *Tel:* 401-683-1955 *Fax:* 401-683-1975 *E-mail:* jra@journalofromanarch.com *Web Site:* www.journalofromanarch.com, pg 123

Humphreys, Lindy, Harry N Abrams Inc, 195 Broadway, 9th fl, New York, NY 10007 *Tel:* 212-206-7715 *Toll Free Tel:* 800-345-1359 *Fax:* 212-519-1210 *E-mail:* abrams@abramsbooks.com *Web Site:* www.abramsbooks.com, pg 3

Hundley, Amy, Grove Atlantic Inc, 154 W 14 St, 12th fl, New York, NY 10011 *Tel:* 212-614-7850 *Toll Free Tel:* 800-521-0178 *Fax:* 212-614-7886 *E-mail:* info@groveatlantic.com; sales@groveatlantic.com; publicity@groveatlantic.com; rights@groveatlantic.com *Web Site:* www.groveatlantic.com, pg 97

Hung, Helena, Penguin Group (Canada), 320 Front St W, Suite 1400, Toronto, ON M5V 3B6, Canada *Tel:* 416-364-4449 *Fax:* 416-598-7764 *E-mail:* customerservicescanada@penguinrandomhouse.com; publicity@ca.penguingroup.com *Web Site:* penguinrandomhouse.ca/imprints/penguin-canada, pg 466

Hunt, Becca, Chronicle Books LLC, 680 Second St, San Francisco, CA 94107 *Tel:* 415-537-4200 *Toll Free Tel:* 800-759-0190 (cust serv) *Fax:* 415-537-4460 *Toll Free Fax:* 800-858-7787 (orders); 800-286-9471 (cust serv) *E-mail:* frontdesk@chroniclebooks.com *Web Site:* www.chroniclebooks.com, pg 55

Hunt, Lia, Princeton Architectural Press, 37 E Seventh St, New York, NY 10003 *Tel:* 212-995-9620 *Toll Free Tel:* 800-722-6657 (dist); 800-759-0190 (sales) *Fax:* 212-995-9454 *E-mail:* sales@papress.com *Web Site:* www.papress.com, pg 188

Hunt, Rebecca, Harlequin Enterprises Ltd, 233 Broadway, Suite 1001, New York, NY 10279 *Tel:* 212-553-4200 *Fax:* 212-227-8969 *E-mail:* customerservice@harlequin.com *Web Site:* www.harlequin.com, pg 100

Hunt, Richard, AdventureKEEN, 2204 First Ave S, Suite 102, Birmingham, AL 35233 *Tel:* 763-689-9800 *Toll Free Tel:* 800-678-7006 *Fax:* 763-689-9039 *Toll Free Fax:* 877-374-9016 *E-mail:* info@adventurewithkeen.com *Web Site:* adventurewithkeen.com, pg 5

Hunt, Richard, Clerisy Press, 306 Greenup St, Covington, KY 41011 *Tel:* 859-815-7200 *Toll Free Tel:* 888-604-4537 *Fax:* 859-291-9111 *E-mail:* info@clerisypress.com *Web Site:* www.clerisypress.com, pg 57

Hunt, Steve, Michelin Maps & Guides, One Parkway S, Greenville, SC 29615-5022 *Tel:* 864-458-5565 *Fax:* 864-458-5665 *Toll Free Fax:* 866-297-0914; 888-773-7979 *E-mail:* orders@americanmap.com (orders) *Web Site:* www.michelintravel.com; www.michelinguide.com, pg 149

Hunter, Allison, Janklow & Nesbit Associates, 285 Madison Ave, 21st fl, New York, NY 10017 *Tel:* 212-421-1700 *Fax:* 212-355-1403 *E-mail:* info@janklow.com *Web Site:* www.janklowandnesbit.com, pg 522

Hunter, Andy, Counterpoint Press LLC, 1919 Fifth St, Berkeley, CA 94710 *Tel:* 510-704-0230 *Fax:* 510-704-0268 *E-mail:* info@counterpointpress.com *Web Site:* counterpointpress.com; www.sierraclub.org/books; softskull.com, pg 63

Hunter, Ann A, AAH Graphics Inc, 9293 Fort Valley Rd, Fort Valley, VA 22652-2020 *Tel:* 540-933-6211 *Fax:* 540-933-6523 *E-mail:* srhunter@aahgraphics.com *Web Site:* www.aahgraphics.com, pg 487

Hunter, Ann A, Loft Press Inc, 9293 Fort Valley Rd, Fort Valley, VA 22652 *Tel:* 540-933-6210 *Fax:* 540-933-6523 *E-mail:* Books@LoftPress.com *Web Site:* www.loftpress.com, pg 137

Hunter, Chelsea, Perseus Books, 250 W 57 St, 15th fl, New York, NY 10107 *Tel:* 212-340-8100 *Toll Free Tel:* 800-343-4499 (cust serv) *Fax:* 212-340-8105 *Web Site:* www.perseusbooks.com, pg 181

Hunter, Kristy, The Knight Agency Inc, 570 East Ave, Madison, GA 30650 *E-mail:* submissions@knightagency.net *Web Site:* www.knightagency.net, pg 524

Hunter, Michael, Hunter Publishing Inc, 222 Clematis St, West Palm Beach, FL 33401 *Tel:* 561-835-2022 *Web Site:* guidestotheworld.com, pg 113

Hunter, Stephen R, Loft Press Inc, 9293 Fort Valley Rd, Fort Valley, VA 22652 *Tel:* 540-933-6210 *Fax:* 540-933-6523 *E-mail:* Books@LoftPress.com *Web Site:* www.loftpress.com, pg 137

Hunter, Todd, Atria Books, 1230 Avenue of the Americas, New York, NY 10020 *Tel:* 212-698-7000 *Fax:* 212-698-7007 *Web Site:* www.simonandschuster.com, pg 25

Huot, Mary, Houghton Mifflin Harcourt Trade & Reference Division, 125 High St, Boston, MA 02110 *Tel:* 617-351-5000 *Toll Free Tel:* 800-225-3362 *Web Site:* www.hmhco.com, pg 111

Hurdle, Priscilla, Cornell University Press, Sage House, 512 E State St, Ithaca, NY 14850 *Tel:* 607-277-2338 *Fax:* 607-277-2374 *E-mail:* cupressinfo@cornell.edu; cupress-sales@cornell.edu *Web Site:* www.cornellpress.cornell.edu, pg 61

Hurley, Alexis, InkWell Management, 521 Fifth Ave, 26th fl, New York, NY 10175 *Tel:* 212-922-3500 *Fax:* 212-922-0535 *E-mail:* info@inkwellmanagement.com *Web Site:* inkwellmanagement.com, pg 522

Imranyi, Erika, Harlequin Enterprises Ltd, 225 Duncan Mill Rd, Don Mills, ON M3B 3K9, Canada *Tel:* 416-445-5860 *Toll Free Tel:* 888-432-4879; 800-370-5838 (ebook inquiries) *E-mail:* customerservice@harlequin.com *Web Site:* www.harlequin.com, pg 459

Indrigo, Miranda, Harlequin Enterprises Ltd, 225 Duncan Mill Rd, Don Mills, ON M3B 3K9, Canada *Tel:* 416-445-5860 *Toll Free Tel:* 888-432-4879; 800-370-5838 (ebook inquiries) *E-mail:* customerservice@harlequin.com *Web Site:* www.harlequin.com, pg 459

Ingalls, Johanna, Akashic Books, 232 Third St, Suite A-115, Brooklyn, NY 11215 *Tel:* 718-643-9193 *Fax:* 718-643-9195 *E-mail:* info@akashicbooks.com *Web Site:* www.akashicbooks.com, pg 6

Ingenito, Kim Thornton, Penguin Random House Speakers Bureau, A Penguin Random House Company, 1745 Broadway, Mail Drop 13-1, New York, NY 10019 *Tel:* 212-572-2013 *E-mail:* speakers@penguinrandomhouse.com *Web Site:* www.prhspeakers.com, pg 547

Ingle, Stephen, WordCo Indexing Services Inc, 49 Church St, Norwich, CT 06360 *Tel:* 860-886-2532 *Toll Free Tel:* 877-WORDCO-3 (967-3263) *Fax:* 860-886-1155 *E-mail:* office@wordco.com *Web Site:* www.wordco.com, pg 502

Inglis, John, Cold Spring Harbor Laboratory Press, 500 Sunnyside Blvd, Woodbury, NY 11797-2924 *Tel:* 516-422-4100 *Toll Free Tel:* 800-843-4388 *Fax:* 516-422-4097; 516-422-4092 (submissions) *E-mail:* cshpress@cshl.edu *Web Site:* www.cshlpress.com, pg 58

Ingraham, Holly, St Martin's Press, LLC, 175 Fifth Ave, New York, NY 10010 *Tel:* 646-307-5151 *Web Site:* us.macmillan.com/smp, pg 204

Ingrum, Adrienne, Hachette Nashville, 12 Cadillac Dr, Suite 480, Brentwood, TN 37027 *Tel:* 615-221-0996 *Fax:* 615-221-0962 *Web Site:* www.hachettebookgroup.com, pg 98

Inkster, Tim, Porcupine's Quill Inc, 68 Main St, Erin, ON N0B 1T0, Canada *Tel:* 519-833-9158 *E-mail:* pql@sentex.net *Web Site:* porcupinesquill.ca, pg 467

Inouye, Natalie, University of Southern California, Master of Professional Writing Program, Mark Taper Hall, THH 355, 3501 Trousedale Pkwy, Los Angeles, CA 90089-0355 *Tel:* 213-740-3252 *Fax:* 213-740-5002 *E-mail:* mpw@college.usc.edu *Web Site:* college.usc.edu/mpw, pg 623

Inshiqaq, Shanta, Rizzoli International Publications Inc, 300 Park Ave S, 4th fl, New York, NY 10010-5399 *Tel:* 212-387-3400 *Toll Free Tel:* 800-522-6657 (orders only) *Fax:* 212-387-3535 *E-mail:* publicity@rizzoliusa.com *Web Site:* www.rizzoliusa.com, pg 199

Inteli, Nancy, HarperCollins Children's Books, 195 Broadway, New York, NY 10007 *Tel:* 212-207-7000 *Web Site:* www.harpercollins.com/childrens, pg 101

Ioakimedes, Nikki, Perseus Books, 250 W 57 St, 15th fl, New York, NY 10107 *Tel:* 212-340-8100 *Toll Free Tel:* 800-343-4499 (cust serv) *Fax:* 212-340-8105 *Web Site:* www.perseusbooks.com, pg 180

Ippolito, Marc, Burns Entertainment & Sports Marketing, 820 Davis St, Suite 222, Evanston, IL 60201 *Tel:* 847-866-9400 *Fax:* 847-491-9778 *E-mail:* burnsl@burnsent.com *Web Site:* burnsent.com, pg 547

Ireland, Pamela, BelleBooks, PO Box 300921, Memphis, TN 38130 *Tel:* 901-344-9024 *Fax:* 901-344-9068 *E-mail:* bellebooks@bellebooks.com *Web Site:* www.bellebooks.com, pg 32

Irgang, Mark, Belltown Media, PO Box 980985, Houston, TX 77098 *Tel:* 713-344-1956 *Fax:* 713-583-7956 *E-mail:* subs@linuxjournal.com *Web Site:* www.belltownmedia.com, pg 32

Irizarry Vizcarrondo, Jorge, Institute of Puerto Rican Culture National Literary Awards, PO Box 9024184, San Juan, PR 00902-4184 *Tel:* 787-724-0700 *Fax:* 787-724-8393 *Web Site:* www.icp.gobierno.pr, pg 656

Irle, Amanda, Regal House Publishing, 1723 Hickory Overlook Trail, No 110, Raleigh, NC 27607 *Tel:* 305-360-5969 *E-mail:* info@regalhousepublishing.com *Web Site:* regalhousepublishing.com, pg 198

Irvin, Margo, Stanford University Press, 425 Broadway St, Redwood City, CA 94063-3126 *Tel:* 650-723-9434 *Fax:* 650-725-3457 *E-mail:* info@www.sup.org; publicity@www.sup.org *Web Site:* www.sup.org, pg 220

Irvine, Marie Aline, Reference Publications Inc, 218 Saint Clair River Dr, Algonac, MI 48001 *Tel:* 810-794-5722 *E-mail:* referencepub@sbcglobal.net, pg 197

Irwin, Mark, Insight Editions, 800 "A" St, San Rafael, CA 94901 *Tel:* 415-526-1370 *Toll Free Tel:* 800-809-3792 *Toll Free Fax:* 866-509-0515 *E-mail:* info@insighteditions.com *Web Site:* www.insighteditions.com, pg 117

Irwin-Diehl, Rebecca, Judson Press, 588 N Gulph Rd, King of Prussia, PA 19406 *Toll Free Tel:* 800-458-3766 *Fax:* 610-768-2107 *Web Site:* www.judsonpress.com, pg 123

Isaac, Joanne, American Numismatic Society, 75 Varick St, 11th fl, New York, NY 10013 *Tel:* 212-571-4470 *Fax:* 212-571-4479 *E-mail:* ans@numismatics.org; orders@numismatics.org *Web Site:* www.numismatics.org, pg 13

Isaacs, Elizabeth, Vesuvian Books, 2817 West End Ave, Nashville, TN 37203 *E-mail:* info@vesuvianmedia.com *Web Site:* www.vesuvianbooks.com, pg 250

Isaacs, Suzanne Talbot, Ampersand Inc/Professional Publishing Services, 515 Madison St, New Orleans, LA 70116 *Tel:* 312-280-8905 *Fax:* 312-944-1582 *E-mail:* info@ampersandworks.com *Web Site:* www.ampersandworks.com, pg 16

Isaacson, Dana, Random House Publishing Group, 1745 Broadway, New York, NY 10019 *Toll Free Tel:* 800-200-3552 *Web Site:* atrandom.com, pg 195

Isayeff, Emily, Random House Publishing Group, 1745 Broadway, New York, NY 10019 *Toll Free Tel:* 800-200-3552 *Web Site:* atrandom.com, pg 195

Iserson, Mary Lou, Galen Press Ltd, PO Box 64400-WB, Tucson, AZ 85728-4400 *Tel:* 520-577-8363 *Fax:* 520-529-6459 *E-mail:* sales@galenpress.com *Web Site:* www.galenpress.com, pg 89

Ishay-Cohen, Michelle, Artisan Books, 225 Varick St, New York, NY 10014-4381 *Tel:* 212-254-5900 *Toll Free Tel:* 800-722-7202 *Fax:* 212-677-6692 *E-mail:* artisaninfo@artisanbooks.com *Web Site:* www.workman.com/artisanbooks, pg 22

Isherwood, Judith, Shoreline Press, 23 Rue Sainte-Anne, Ste-Anne-de-Bellevue, QC H9X 1L1, Canada *Tel:* 514-457-5733 *E-mail:* info@shorelinepress.ca *Web Site:* shorelinepress.ca, pg 470

Ison, Tara, Arizona State University, Creative Writing Program, 851 S Cady Mall, Rm 542, Tempe, AZ 85287-0302 *Tel:* 480-965-3528 *Fax:* 480-965-3451 *Web Site:* www.asu.edu/clas/english/creativewriting, pg 619

Israeli, Henry, Saturnalia Books Poetry Prize, 105 Woodside Rd, Ardmore, PA 19003 *Tel:* 267-278-9541 *E-mail:* info@saturnaliabooks.com *Web Site:* www.saturnaliabooks.org, pg 687

Israelite, David M, National Music Publishers' Association (NMPA), 975 "F" St NW, Suite 315, Washington, DC 20004 *Tel:* 202-393-6672 *Fax:* 202-393-6673 *E-mail:* pr@nmpa.org *Web Site:* www.nmpa.org, pg 572

Itkin, Bridget Monroe, Artisan Books, 225 Varick St, New York, NY 10014-4381 *Tel:* 212-254-5900 *Toll Free Tel:* 800-722-7202 *Fax:* 212-677-6692 *E-mail:* artisaninfo@artisanbooks.com *Web Site:* www.workman.com/artisanbooks, pg 22

Ivers, Mitchell, Gallery Books, 1230 Avenue of the Americas, New York, NY 10020 *Toll Free Tel:* 800-456-6798 *Fax:* 212-698-7284 *E-mail:* consumer.customerservice@simonandschuster.com *Web Site:* www.simonsays.com, pg 90

Iverson, Anne, Mountain Press Publishing Co, 1301 S Third W, Missoula, MT 59801 *Tel:* 406-728-1900 *Toll Free Tel:* 800-234-5308 *Fax:* 406-728-1635 *E-mail:* info@mtnpress.com *Web Site:* www.mountain-press.com, pg 154

Iwasutiak, Adria, Simon & Schuster Canada, 166 King St E, Suite 300, Toronto, ON M5A 1J3, Canada *Tel:* 647-427-8882 *Toll Free Tel:* 800-387-0446; 800-268-3216 (orders) *Fax:* 647-430-9446 *Toll Free Fax:* 888-849-8151 (orders) *E-mail:* info@simonandschuster.ca *Web Site:* www.simonandschuster.ca, pg 471

Izykowski, Lori, Plutarch Award, PO Box 33020, Santa Fe, NM 87594 *Tel:* 505-983-4671 *Web Site:* biographersinternational.org, pg 680

Izzo, Ben, Abrams Artists Agency, 275 Seventh Ave, 26th fl, New York, NY 10001 *Tel:* 646-486-4600 *Fax:* 646-486-0100 *E-mail:* literary@abramsartny.com *Web Site:* www.abramsartists.com, pg 505

Jabbari, Dr Ahmad, Mazda Publishers Inc, One Park Plaza, Suite 600, Irvine, CA 92614 *Tel:* 714-751-5252 *Fax:* 714-751-4805 *E-mail:* mazdapub@aol.com *Web Site:* www.mazdapublishers.com, pg 144

Jackson, Bill, Workman Publishing Co Inc, 225 Varick St, 9th fl, New York, NY 10014-4381 *Tel:* 212-254-5900 *Toll Free Tel:* 800-722-7202 *Fax:* 212-254-8098 *E-mail:* info@workman.com *Web Site:* www.workman.com, pg 259

Jackson, Bobby L, Multicultural Publications Inc, 1939 Manchester Rd, Akron, OH 44314 *Tel:* 330-865-9578 *Fax:* 330-865-9578 *E-mail:* multiculturalpub@prodigy.net *Web Site:* www.multiculturalpub.net, pg 155

Jackson, Christopher, Random House Publishing Group, 1745 Broadway, New York, NY 10019 *Toll Free Tel:* 800-200-3552 *Web Site:* atrandom.com, pg 195

Jackson, Eleanor, Dunow, Carlson & Lerner Literary Agency Inc, 27 W 20 St, Suite 1107, New York, NY 10011 *Tel:* 212-645-7606 *E-mail:* mail@dclagency.com *Web Site:* www.dclagency.com, pg 515

Jackson, Heather, David Black Agency, 335 Adams St, 27th fl, Suite 2707, Brooklyn, NY 11201 *Tel:* 718-852-5500 *Fax:* 718-852-5539 *Web Site:* www.davidblackagency.com, pg 508

Jackson, Jennifer, Doubleday/Nan A Talese, c/o Penguin Random House Inc, 1745 Broadway, New York, NY 10019 *Tel:* 212-751-2600 *Fax:* 212-572-2662 *E-mail:* ddaypub@randomhouse.com *Web Site:* knopfdoubleday.com, pg 72

Jackson, Jennifer, Alfred A Knopf/Everyman's Library, c/o Penguin Random House Inc, 1745 Broadway, New York, NY 10019 *Tel:* 212-751-2600 *Toll Free Tel:* 800-638-6460 *Fax:* 212-572-2593 *Web Site:* www.knopfdoubleday.com, pg 127

Jackson, Jennifer, Donald Maass Literary Agency, 1000 Dean St, Suite 252, Brooklyn, NY 11238 *Tel:* 212-727-8383 *Fax:* 212-727-3271 *E-mail:* info@maassagency.com *Web Site:* www.maassagency.com, pg 526

Jackson, Joe, Princeton University Press, 41 William St, Princeton, NJ 08540-5237 *Tel:* 609-258-4900 *Fax:* 609-258-6305 *Web Site:* press.princeton.edu, pg 188

Jackson, Karen, Thomas Nelson, 501 Nelson Place, Nashville, TN 37214 *Tel:* 615-889-9000 *Toll Free Tel:* 800-251-4000 *Fax:* 615-902-1548 *Web Site:* www.thomasnelson.com, pg 231

Jackson, Kate, HarperCollins Children's Books, 195 Broadway, New York, NY 10007 *Tel:* 212-207-7000 *Web Site:* www.harpercollins.com/childrens, pg 101

Jackson, Lauren, Harlequin Enterprises Ltd, 233 Broadway, Suite 1001, New York, NY 10279 *Tel:* 212-553-4200 *Fax:* 212-227-8969 *E-mail:* customerservice@harlequin.com *Web Site:* www.harlequin.com, pg 101

Jackson, Melanie, Melanie Jackson Agency LLC, 41 W 72 St, Suite 3F, New York, NY 10023 *Tel:* 212-873-3373, pg 522

Jackson, Regina, Warner Press, 1201 E Fifth St, Anderson, IN 46018 *Tel:* 765-644-7721 *Toll Free Tel:* 800-741-7721 (orders) *Fax:* 765-640-8005 *Toll Free Fax:* 800-347-6411 *E-mail:* wporders@warnerpress.org *Web Site:* www.warnerpress.org, pg 252

Jackson, Tilly, Artist-in-Residence Program, 225 King St, Suite 201, Fredericton, NB E3B 1E1, Canada *Tel:* 506-444-4444 *Toll Free Tel:* 866-460-ARTS (460-2787) *Fax:* 506-444-5543 *Web Site:* www.artsnb.ca, pg 628

Jackson, Tilly, Arts Scholarships, 225 King St, Suite 201, Fredericton, NB E3B 1E1, Canada *Tel:* 506-444-4444 *Toll Free Tel:* 866-460-ARTS (460-2787) *Fax:* 506-444-5543 *Web Site:* www.artsnb.ca, pg 628

Jackson, Tilly, Atlantic Public Art Funders (APAF) Creative Residency, 225 King St, Suite 201, Fredericton, NB E3B 1E1, Canada *Tel:* 506-444-4444 *Toll Free Tel:* 866-460-ARTS (460-2787) *Fax:* 506-444-5543 *Web Site:* www.artsnb.ca, pg 629

Jackson, Tilly, Creation Grant Program, 225 King St, Suite 201, Fredericton, NB E3B 1E1, Canada *Tel:* 506-444-4444 *Toll Free Tel:* 866-460-ARTS (460-2787) *Fax:* 506-444-5543 *Web Site:* www.artsnb.ca, pg 639

Jackson, Tilly, Documentation Grant Program, 225 King St, Suite 201, Fredericton, NB E3B 1E1, Canada *Tel:* 506-444-4444 *Toll Free Tel:* 866-460-ARTS (460-2787) *Fax:* 506-444-5543 *Web Site:* www.artsnb.ca, pg 641

Jackson, Tilly, Grants for Literary Artists, 225 King St, Suite 201, Fredericton, NB E3B 1E1, Canada *Tel:* 506-444-4444 *Toll Free Tel:* 866-460-ARTS (460-2787) *Fax:* 506-444-5543 *Web Site:* www.artsnb.ca, pg 650

Jackson, Tilly, The Lieutenant-Governor's Awards for High Achievement in the Arts, 225 King St, Suite 201, Fredericton, NB E3B 1E1, Canada *Tel:* 506-444-4444 *Toll Free Tel:* 866-460-ARTS (460-2787) *Fax:* 506-444-5543 *Web Site:* www.artsnb.ca, pg 661

Jacob, Chris, HeartMath LLC, 14700 W Park Ave, Boulder Creek, CA 95006 *Tel:* 831-338-8700 *Toll Free Tel:* 800-450-9111 *Fax:* 831-338-9861 *E-mail:* info@heartmath.com; inquiry@heartmath.com *Web Site:* www.heartmath.com, pg 105

Jacob, Mary Ann, Texas A&M University Press, John H Lindsey Bldg, Lewis St, 4354 TAMU, College Station, TX 77843-4354 *Tel:* 979-845-1436 *Toll Free Tel:* 800-826-8911 (orders) *Fax:* 979-847-8752 *Toll Free Fax:* 888-617-2421 (orders) *E-mail:* bookorders@tamu.edu *Web Site:* www.tamupress.com, pg 230

Jacobs, Andrea, The Globe Pequot Press, 246 Goose Lane, Guilford, CT 06437 *Tel:* 203-458-4500 *Toll Free Tel:* 800-243-0495 (orders only); 888-249-7586 (cust serv) *Fax:* 203-458-4601 *Toll Free Fax:* 800-820-2329 (orders & cust serv) *E-mail:* editorial@globepequot.com; info@rowman.com; orders@rowman.com *Web Site:* rowman.com, pg 93

Jacobs, Ben, Bloom's Literary Criticism, 132 W 31 St, 17th fl, New York, NY 10001 *Toll Free Tel:* 800-322-8755 *Toll Free Fax:* 800-678-3633 *E-mail:* custserv@factsonfile.com *Web Site:* www.infobasepublishing.com, pg 37

Jacobs, Ben, Chelsea House Publishers, 132 W 31 St, 17th fl, New York, NY 10001 *Tel:* 212-967-8800 *Toll Free Tel:* 800-322-8755 *Fax:* 917-339-0325 *Toll Free Fax:* 800-678-3633 *E-mail:* custserv@factsonfile.com *Web Site:* www.infobasepublishing.com; www.infobaselearning.com, pg 53

Jacobs, Ben, Facts On File, 132 W 31 St, 17th fl, New York, NY 10001 *Tel:* 212-967-8800 *Toll Free Tel:* 800-322-8755 *Toll Free Fax:* 800-678-3633 *E-mail:* custserv@factsonfile.com *Web Site:* infobasepublishing.com, pg 81

Jacobs, Ben, Ferguson Publishing, 132 W 31 St, 17th fl, New York, NY 10001 *Tel:* 212-967-8800 *Toll Free Tel:* 800-322-8755 *Fax:* 917-339-0323 *Toll Free Fax:* 800-678-3633 *E-mail:* custserv@factsonfile.com *Web Site:* infobasepublishing.com, pg 84

Jacobs, Ben, World Almanac®, 132 W 31 St, New York, NY 10001 *Toll Free Tel:* 800-322-8755 *E-mail:* almanac@infobaselearning.com *Web Site:* www.worldalmanac.com, pg 259

Jacobs, Donald, Georgetown University Press, 3240 Prospect St NW, Suite 250, Washington, DC 20007 *Tel:* 202-687-5889 (busn) *Fax:* 202-687-6340 (edit) *E-mail:* gupress@georgetown.edu *Web Site:* press.georgetown.edu, pg 91

Jacobs, Farrin, Little, Brown Books for Young Readers, 1290 Avenue of the Americas, New York, NY 10019 *Tel:* 212-364-1100 *Toll Free Tel:* 800-759-0190 (cust serv) *Web Site:* www.HachetteBookGroup.com, pg 136

Jacobs, Laurence, Craftsman Book Co, 6058 Corte Del Cedro, Carlsbad, CA 92011 *Tel:* 760-438-7828 *Toll Free Tel:* 800-829-8123 *Fax:* 760-438-0398 *Web Site:* www.craftsman-book.com, pg 64

Jacobs, Lindy, Oregon Christian Writers (OCW), 1075 Willow Lake Rd N, Keizer, OR 97303 *Tel:* 503-393-3356 *E-mail:* contact@oregonchristianwriters.org *Web Site:* www.oregonchristianwriters.org, pg 574

Jacobs, Lindy, Oregon Christian Writers Coaching Conference, 1075 Willow Lake Rd N, Keizer, OR 97303 *Tel:* 503-393-3356 *E-mail:* contact@oregonchristianwriters.org *Web Site:* www.oregonchristianwriters.org, pg 613

Jacobs, Michael, Harry N Abrams Inc, 195 Broadway, 9th fl, New York, NY 10007 *Tel:* 212-206-7715 *Toll Free Tel:* 800-345-1359 *Fax:* 212-519-1210 *E-mail:* abrams@abramsbooks.com *Web Site:* www.abramsbooks.com, pg 2

Jacobs, Michael, Stewart, Tabori & Chang, 115 W 18 St, 6th fl, New York, NY 10011 *Tel:* 212-519-1200; 212-206-7715 *Fax:* 212-519-1210 *E-mail:* abrams@abramsbooks.com *Web Site:* www.abramsbooks.com/imprints/stc, pg 222

Jacobs, Nicki, NEA Creative Writing Fellowships, 400 Seventh St SW, Washington, DC 20506-0001 *Tel:* 202-682-5400; 202-682-5496 (Voice/TTY); 202-682-5034 (lit fellowships hotline) *Fax:* 202-682-5609; 202-682-5610 *E-mail:* litfellowships@arts.gov *Web Site:* www.arts.gov, pg 672

Jacobs, Nicki, Translation Projects, 400 Seventh St SW, Washington, DC 20506-0001 *Tel:* 202-682-5400; 202-682-5496 (Voice/TTY); 202-682-5034 (lit fellowships hotline) *Fax:* 202-682-5609; 202-682-5610 *E-mail:* litfellowships@arts.gov *Web Site:* www.arts.gov, pg 694

Jacobs, Robert H, Univelt Inc, 740 Metcalf St, No 13, Escondido, CA 92025 *Tel:* 760-746-4005 *Fax:* 760-746-3139 *E-mail:* sales@univelt.com *Web Site:* www.univelt.com; www.astronautical.org, pg 239

Jacobson, Gretchen, NACE International, 15835 Park Ten Place, Houston, TX 77084 *Tel:* 281-228-6200; 281-228-6223 *Toll Free Tel:* 800-797-NACE (797-6223) *Fax:* 281-228-6300 *E-mail:* firstservice@nace.org *Web Site:* www.nace.org, pg 156

Jacobson, Hillary, ICM Partners, 65 E 55 St, New York, NY 10022 *Tel:* 212-556-5600 *Web Site:* www.icmtalent.com, pg 521

Jacobson, Kip, Blue Apple Books, 515 Valley St, Suite 170, Maplewood, NJ 07040 *Tel:* 973-763-8191 *Toll Free Tel:* 800-283-3572 (orders) *Fax:* 973-763-5944 *E-mail:* info@blueapplebooks.com *Web Site:* blueapplebooks.com, pg 38

Jacobson, Tina, The Barnabas Agency, PO Box 3113, Corsicana, TX 75151-3113 *Toll Free Tel:* 800-927-0517 *E-mail:* info@barnabasagency.com *Web Site:* www.barnabasagency.com, pg 547

Jacobson, Wendy, Martingale®, 19021 120 Ave NE, Suite 102, Bothell, WA 98011 *Tel:* 425-483-3313 *Toll Free Tel:* 800-426-3126 *Fax:* 425-486-7596 *E-mail:* info@martingale-pub.com *Web Site:* www.martingale-pub.com, pg 143

Jacoby, Judy, Doubleday/Nan A Talese, c/o Penguin Random House Inc, 1745 Broadway, New York, NY 10019 *Tel:* 212-751-2600 *Fax:* 212-572-2662 *E-mail:* ddaypub@randomhouse.com *Web Site:* knopfdoubleday.com, pg 72

Jacoby, Nancy, Oak Tree Press, 1700 Dairy Ave, No 149, Corcoran, CA 93212 *Tel:* 217-824-6500 *E-mail:* publisher@oaktreebooks.com; info@oaktreebooks.com; query@oaktreebooks.com; pressdept@oaktreebooks.com; bookorders@oaktreebooks.com *Web Site:* www.oaktreebooks.com; www.otpblog.blogspot.com, pg 166

Jacques, Julia, Adams Media, 57 Littlefield St, Avon, MA 02322 *Tel:* 508-427-7100 *Web Site:* www.simonandschuster.com, pg 4

Jade, Miranda, Imagination Publishing Group, PO Box 1304, Dunedin, FL 34697 *Toll Free Tel:* 888-701-6481 *Fax:* 727-361-0584 *E-mail:* info@imaginationpublishinggroup.com *Web Site:* www.imaginationpublishinggroup.com, pg 114

Jaferi, Azra PhD, New York Academy of Sciences (NYAS), 7 World Trade, 40th fl, 250 Greenwich St, New York, NY 10007-2157 *Tel:* 212-298-8600 *Toll Free Tel:* 800-843-6927 *Fax:* 212-298-3668 *E-mail:* nyas@nyas.org; annals@nyas.org; customerservice@nyas.org *Web Site:* www.nyas.org, pg 161

Jaffe, Gary, Linda Chester Literary Agency, 630 Fifth Ave, Suite 2000, New York, NY 10111 *Tel:* 212-218-3350 *E-mail:* submissions@lindachester.com *Web Site:* www.lindachester.com, pg 511

Jaffrey, Zareen, Simon & Schuster Children's Publishing, 1230 Avenue of the Americas, New York, NY 10020 *Tel:* 212-698-7000 *Web Site:* www.simonandschuster.com/kids; www.simonandschuster.com/teen; simonandschuster.net; simonandschuster.biz, pg 213

Jahns, Randy, Crossway, 1300 Crescent St, Wheaton, IL 60187 *Tel:* 630-682-4300 *Toll Free Tel:* 800-635-7993 (orders); 800-543-1659 (cust serv) *Fax:* 630-682-4785 *E-mail:* info@crossway.org *Web Site:* www.crossway.org, pg 65

Jain, Mukesh, Jain Publishing Co, PO Box 3523, Fremont, CA 94539 *Tel:* 510-659-8272 *Fax:* 510-659-0501 *E-mail:* mail@jainpub.com *Web Site:* www.jainpub.com, pg 121

Jaksah, Joel, Hazelden Publishing, 15251 Pleasant Valley Rd, Center City, MN 55012-0011 *Tel:* 651-213-4200 *Toll Free Tel:* 800-257-7810 *Fax:* 651-213-4590 *E-mail:* info@hazelden.org *Web Site:* www.hazelden.org, pg 104

Jalbert, Sarah, Editions MultiMondes, 1815, Avenue de Lorimier, Montreal, QC H2K 3W6, Canada *Tel:* 514-523-1523 *Toll Free Tel:* 800-361-1664 *Fax:* 514-523-9969 *Web Site:* www.multim.com, pg 455

James, Angela, Harlequin Enterprises Ltd, 225 Duncan Mill Rd, Don Mills, ON M3B 3K9, Canada *Tel:* 416-445-5860 *Toll Free Tel:* 888-432-4879; 800-370-5838 (ebook inquiries) *E-mail:* customerservice@harlequin.com *Web Site:* www.harlequin.com, pg 459

James, Casey Blue, Penguin Group USA, A Penguin Random House Company, 375 Hudson St, New York, NY 10014 *Tel:* 212-366-2000 *Toll Free Tel:* 800-847-5515 (inside sales); 800-631-8571 (cust serv) *Fax:* 212-366-2666; 607-775-4829 (inside sales) *E-mail:* online@us.penguingroup.com *Web Site:* www.penguin.com, pg 177

James, Diane, Worthy & James Publishing, PO Box 362015, Milpitas, CA 95036 *Tel:* 408-945-3963 *E-mail:* worthy1234@sbcglobal.net; mail@worthyjames.com *Web Site:* www.worthyjames.com, pg 478

James, Gethin, Lugus Publications, 28 Industrial St, Studio 203, Toronto, ON M4G 1Y9, Canada *Tel:* 416-467-0924 *Web Site:* www.thestudio203.com, pg 462

James, Jacqueline, Lugus Publications, 28 Industrial St, Studio 203, Toronto, ON M4G 1Y9, Canada *Tel:* 416-467-0924 *Web Site:* www.thestudio203.com, pg 462

James, Kristina, MDR, A D&B Co, 6 Armstrong Rd, Suite 301, Shelton, CT 06484 *Tel:* 203-926-4800 *Toll Free Tel:* 800-333-8802 *Fax:* 203-225-4603 *Toll Free Fax:* 866-532-7097 *E-mail:* mdrinfo@dnb.com *Web Site:* www.schooldata.com, pg 147

James, Selena, Kensington Publishing Corp, 119 W 40 St, New York, NY 10018 *Tel:* 212-407-1500 *Toll Free Tel:* 800-221-2647 *Fax:* 212-935-0699 *Web Site:* www.kensingtonbooks.com, pg 125

James, Thea, Workman Publishing Co Inc, 225 Varick St, 9th fl, New York, NY 10014-4381 *Tel:* 212-254-5900 *Toll Free Tel:* 800-722-7202 *Fax:* 212-254-8098 *E-mail:* info@workman.com *Web Site:* www.workman.com, pg 259

James, Tina, Harlequin Enterprises Ltd, 233 Broadway, Suite 1001, New York, NY 10279 *Tel:* 212-553-4200 *Fax:* 212-227-8969 *E-mail:* customerservice@harlequin.com *Web Site:* www.harlequin.com, pg 100

James, Tina, Love Inspired Books, 233 Broadway, Suite 1001, New York, NY 10279 *Tel:* 212-553-4200 *Fax:* 212-227-8969 *E-mail:* customer_service@harlequin.ca *Web Site:* www.harlequin.com, pg 138

James-Gilboe, Lynda, ProQuest LLC, 789 E Eisenhower Pkwy, Ann Arbor, MI 48108 *Tel:* 734-761-4700 *Toll Free Tel:* 800-521-0600 *Web Site:* www.proquest.com, pg 190

Jamison, Mark, Magazines Canada (MC), 425 Adelaide St W, Suite 700, Toronto, ON M5V 3C1, Canada *Tel:* 416-504-0274 *Fax:* 416-504-0437 *E-mail:* info@magazinescanada.ca *Web Site:* www.magazinescanada.ca/development/magnet, pg 569

Janaskie, Emma, HarperCollins General Books Group, 195 Broadway, New York, NY 10007 *Tel:* 212-207-7000 *Web Site:* www.harpercollins.com, pg 101

Janecke, Roger, Visible Ink Press®, 43311 Joy Rd, Suite 414, Canton, MI 48187-2075 *Tel:* 734-667-3211 *Fax:* 734-667-4311 *E-mail:* info@visibleinkpress.com *Web Site:* www.visibleinkpress.com, pg 251

Janeway, Brant, St Martin's Press, LLC, 175 Fifth Ave, New York, NY 10010 *Tel:* 646-307-5151 *Web Site:* us.macmillan.com/smp, pg 204

Janik, Daniel S, Savant Books & Publications LLC, 2630 Kapiolani Blvd, Suite 1601, Honolulu, HI 96826 *Tel:* 808-941-3927 *Fax:* 808-941-3927 *E-mail:* savantbooks@gmail.com; savantdistribution@gmail.com *Web Site:* www.savantbooksandpublications.com; www.savantdistribution.com, pg 206

Jankauskas, Monica, Highlights for Children, 1800 Watermark Dr, Columbus, OH 43215 *Tel:* 614-486-0631 *Toll Free Tel:* 800-962-3661 (Highlights Club cust serv); 800-255-9517 (Highlights Magazine cust serv) *Web Site:* www.highlights.com; www.facebook.com/HighlightsforChildren, pg 107

Janklow, Lucas W, Janklow & Nesbit Associates, 285 Madison Ave, 21st fl, New York, NY 10017 *Tel:* 212-421-1700 *Fax:* 212-355-1403 *E-mail:* info@janklow.com *Web Site:* www.janklowandnesbit.com, pg 522

Janklow, Morton L, Janklow & Nesbit Associates, 285 Madison Ave, 21st fl, New York, NY 10017 *Tel:* 212-421-1700 *Fax:* 212-355-1403 *E-mail:* info@janklow.com *Web Site:* www.janklowandnesbit.com, pg 522

Jankowski, Marianne, Northwestern University Press, 629 Noyes St, Evanston, IL 60208-4210 *Tel:* 847-491-2046 *Toll Free Tel:* 800-621-2736 (orders only) *Fax:* 847-491-8150 *E-mail:* nupress@northwestern.edu *Web Site:* www.nupress.northwestern.edu, pg 164

Jannsohn, Aimee, The Pilgrim Press/United Church Press, 700 Prospect Ave, Cleveland, OH 44115-1100 *Tel:* 216-736-2100 *Toll Free Tel:* 800-537-3394 (orders) *Fax:* 216-736-2207 (orders) *E-mail:* permissions@thepilgrimpress.com; store@ucc.org *Web Site:* www.thepilgrimpress.com; www.uccresources.com, pg 183

Janson, Karen, Barefoot Books, 2067 Massachusetts Ave, 5th fl, Cambridge, MA 02140 *Tel:* 617-576-0660 *Toll Free Tel:* 866-215-1756 (cust serv); 866-417-2369 (orders) *Fax:* 617-576-0049 *E-mail:* help@barefootbooks.com *Web Site:* www.barefootbooks.com, pg 29

Janssen, Karl, University Press of Kansas, 2502 Westbrooke Circle, Lawrence, KS 66045-4444 *Tel:* 785-864-4154; 785-864-4155 (orders) *Fax:* 785-864-4586 *E-mail:* upress@ku.edu; upkorders@ku.edu (orders) *Web Site:* www.kansaspress.ku.edu, pg 246

Janssen, Peter, Macmillan, 175 Fifth Ave, New York, NY 10010 *Tel:* 646-307-5151 *E-mail:* press.inquiries@macmillan.com *Web Site:* www.macmillan.com, pg 140

Janssen, Sarah, World Almanac®, 132 W 31 St, New York, NY 10001 *Toll Free Tel:* 800-322-8755 *E-mail:* almanac@infobaselearning.com *Web Site:* www.worldalmanac.com, pg 259

Jantz, Stan, Evangelical Christian Publishers Association (ECPA), 5801 S McClintock Dr, Suite 104, Tempe, AZ 85283 *Tel:* 480-966-3998 *Fax:* 480-966-1944 *E-mail:* info@ecpa.org *Web Site:* www.ecpa.org, pg 565

Janus, CSP, Mark-David, Paulist Press, 997 Macarthur Blvd, Mahwah, NJ 07430-9990 *Tel:* 201-825-7300 *Toll Free Tel:* 800-218-1903 *Fax:* 201-825-6921 *Toll Free Fax:* 800-836-3161 *E-mail:* info@paulistpress.com; publicity@paulistpress.com *Web Site:* www.paulistpress.com, pg 175

Jao, Jonathan, HarperCollins General Books Group, 195 Broadway, New York, NY 10007 *Tel:* 212-207-7000 *Web Site:* www.harpercollins.com, pg 101

Japikse, Carl, Ariel Press, 2317 Quail Cove Dr, Jasper, GA 30143 *Tel:* 770-894-4226 *E-mail:* lig201@lightariel.com *Web Site:* www.lightariel.com, pg 20

Jaque, Cathy, The Karpfinger Agency, 357 W 20 St, New York, NY 10011-3379 *Tel:* 212-691-2690 *Fax:* 212-691-7129 *E-mail:* info@karpfinger.com (no queries or submissions) *Web Site:* karpfinger.com, pg 523

Jaquith, George, Wind Canyon Books, PO Box 7035, Stockton, CA 95267 *Tel:* 209-956-1600 *Toll Free Tel:* 800-952-7007 *Fax:* 209-956-9424 *Toll Free Fax:* 888-289-7086 *E-mail:* books@windcanyonbooks.com *Web Site:* www.windcanyonbooks.com, pg 257

Jaramillo, Raquel, Workman Publishing Co Inc, 225 Varick St, 9th fl, New York, NY 10014-4381 *Tel:* 212-254-5900 *Toll Free Tel:* 800-722-7202 *Fax:* 212-254-8098 *E-mail:* info@workman.com *Web Site:* www.workman.com, pg 259

Jarrad, Mary Beth, New York University Press, 838 Broadway, 3rd fl, New York, NY 10003-4812 *Tel:* 212-998-2575 (edit) *Toll Free Tel:* 800-996-6987 (orders) *Fax:* 212-995-4798 (orders) *E-mail:* information@nyupress.org; nyupressinfo@nyu.edu; orders@nyupress.org *Web Site:* www.nyupress.org, pg 162

Jarvela, Allison, HarperCollins Publishers, 195 Broadway, New York, NY 10007 *Tel:* 212-207-7000 *Fax:* 212-207-7145 *Web Site:* www.harpercollins.com, pg 102

Jarvie, Craig, Health Communications Inc, 3201 SW 15 St, Deerfield Beach, FL 33442 *Tel:* 954-360-0909 *Toll Free Tel:* 800-851-9100; 800-441-5569 (cust serv & orders) *Fax:* 954-360-0034 *Toll Free Fax:* 800-424-7652 (cust serv & orders) *E-mail:* customerservice2@hcibooks.com *Web Site:* www.hcibooks.com, pg 104

Jasmine, Michelle, Random House Publishing Group, 1745 Broadway, New York, NY 10019 *Toll Free Tel:* 800-200-3552 *Web Site:* atrandom.com, pg 195

Javsicas, Aaron, Temple University Press, 1852 N Tenth St, Philadelphia, PA 19122-6099 *Tel:* 215-926-2140 *Toll Free Tel:* 800-621-2736 *Fax:* 215-926-2141 *E-mail:* tempress@temple.edu *Web Site:* www.temple.edu/tempress, pg 228

Jean, Monica, Random House Children's Books, 1745 Broadway, 10th fl, New York, NY 10019 *Tel:* 212-782-9000 *Web Site:* www.randomhousekids.com, pg 194

Jean-Francois, Jessica, National Press Foundation, 1211 Connecticut Ave NW, Suite 310, Washington, DC 20036 *Tel:* 202-663-7280 *Web Site:* nationalpress.org, pg 572

Jebb, Michaela, Storey Publishing LLC, 210 MASS MoCA Way, North Adams, MA 01247 *Tel:* 413-346-2100 *Toll Free Tel:* 800-441-5700 (orders); 800-793-9396 (edit) *Fax:* 413-346-2199; 413-346-2196 (edit) *E-mail:* sales@storey.com *Web Site:* www.storey.com, pg 223

Jeffrey, Douglas A, Hillsdale College Press, 33 E College St, Hillsdale, MI 49242 *Tel:* 517-437-7341 *Toll Free Tel:* 800-437-2268 *Fax:* 517-607-2658 *E-mail:* news@hillsdale.edu *Web Site:* www.hillsdale.edu, pg 107

Jeffries, Christina, Random House Children's Books, 1745 Broadway, 10th fl, New York, NY 10019 *Tel:* 212-782-9000 *Web Site:* www.randomhousekids.com, pg 194

Jeglinski, Melissa, The Knight Agency Inc, 570 East Ave, Madison, GA 30650 *E-mail:* submissions@knightagency.net *Web Site:* www.knightagency.net, pg 524

Jelen, Carole, Waterside Productions Inc, 2055 Oxford Ave, Cardiff, CA 92007 *Tel:* 760-632-9190 *Fax:* 760-632-9295 *E-mail:* admin@waterside.com *Web Site:* www.waterside.com, pg 541

Jellinek, Roger, Jellinek & Murray Literary Agency, 47-231 Kamakoi Rd, Kaneohe, HI 96744 *Tel:* 808-239-8451, pg 522

Jenkins, Jerrold R, Axiom Business Book Awards, 1129 Woodmere Ave, Suite B, Traverse City, MI 49686 *Tel:* 231-933-0445 *Toll Free Tel:* 800-706-4636 *Fax:* 231-933-0448 *E-mail:* info@axiomawards.com *Web Site:* www.axiomawards.com, pg 629

Jenkins, Jerrold R, eLit Awards, 1129 Woodmere Ave, Suite B, Traverse City, MI 49686 *Tel:* 231-933-0445 *Toll Free Tel:* 800-706-4636 *Fax:* 231-933-0448 *E-mail:* info@elitawards.com *Web Site:* www.elitawards.com, pg 644

Jenkins, Jerrold R, Illumination Book Awards, 1129 Woodmere Ave, Suite B, Traverse City, MI 49686 *Tel:* 231-933-0445 *Toll Free Tel:* 800-706-4636 *Fax:* 231-933-0448 *E-mail:* awards@bookpublishing.com *Web Site:* www.illuminationawards.com, pg 654

Jenkins, Jerrold R, The Independent Publisher Book Awards, 1129 Woodmere Ave, Suite B, Traverse City, MI 49686 *Tel:* 231-933-0445 *Toll Free Tel:* 800-706-4636 *Fax:* 231-933-0448 *E-mail:* awards@bookpublishing.com *Web Site:* www.independentpublisher.com/ipland/ipawards.php, pg 655

Jenkins, Jerrold R, Jenkins Group Inc, 1129 Woodmere Ave, Suite B, Traverse City, MI 49686 *Tel:* 231-933-0445 *Toll Free Tel:* 800-706-4636 *Fax:* 231-933-0448 *E-mail:* info@bookpublishing.com *Web Site:* www.bookpublishing.com, pg 496

Jenkins, Jerrold R, Living Now Book Awards, 1129 Woodmere Ave, Suite B, Traverse City, MI 49686 *Tel:* 231-933-0445 *Toll Free Tel:* 800-706-4636 *Fax:* 231-933-0448 *E-mail:* awards@bookpublishing.com *Web Site:* www.livingnowawards.com, pg 662

Jenkins, Jerrold R, Moonbeam Children's Book Awards, 1129 Woodmere Ave, Suite B, Traverse City, MI 49686 *Tel:* 231-933-0445 *Toll Free Tel:* 800-706-4636 *Fax:* 231-933-0448 *E-mail:* info@moonbeamawards.com *Web Site:* www.moonbeamawards.com, pg 669

Jenkins, John, The MIT Press, One Rogers St, Cambridge, MA 02142 *Tel:* 617-253-5255 *Toll Free Tel:* 800-207-8354 (orders) *Fax:* 617-258-6779; 617-577-1545 (orders) *Web Site:* mitpress.mit.edu, pg 152

Jenkins, Joyce, Northern California Book Awards, c/o Poetry Flash, 1450 Fourth St, Suite 4, Berkeley, CA 94710 *Tel:* 510-525-5476 *Fax:* 510-525-6752 *E-mail:* editor@poetryflash.org; ncbr@poetryflash.org *Web Site:* poetryflash.org, pg 674

Jenkins, Joyce, Poetry Flash Reading Series, 1450 Fourth St, Suite 4, Berkeley, CA 94710 *Tel:* 510-525-5476 *Fax:* 510-525-6752 *E-mail:* editor@poetryflash.org *Web Site:* poetryflash.org, pg 613

Jenkinson, John, Workman Publishing Co Inc, 225 Varick St, 9th fl, New York, NY 10014-4381 *Tel:* 212-254-5900 *Toll Free Tel:* 800-722-7202 *Fax:* 212-254-8098 *E-mail:* info@workman.com *Web Site:* www.workman.com, pg 259

Johnson, Howard, SDP Publishing Solutions LLC, 36 Captain's Way, East Bridgewater, MA 02333 *Tel:* 617-775-0656 *Web Site:* www.sdppublishingsolutions.com, pg 501

Johnson, Isadora, Perseus Books, 250 W 57 St, 15th fl, New York, NY 10107 *Tel:* 212-340-8100 *Toll Free Tel:* 800-343-4499 (cust serv) *Fax:* 212-340-8105 *Web Site:* www.perseusbooks.com, pg 181

Johnson, Jeff, Tyndale House Publishers Inc, 351 Executive Dr, Carol Stream, IL 60188 *Tel:* 630-668-8300 *Toll Free Tel:* 800-323-9400 *Toll Free Fax:* 800-684-0247 *Web Site:* www.tyndale.com, pg 237

Johnson, Jenna, Farrar, Straus & Giroux, LLC, 18 W 18 St, New York, NY 10011 *Tel:* 212-741-6900 *E-mail:* fsg.publicity@fsgbooks.com *Web Site:* us.macmillan.com/fsg.aspx, pg 83

Johnson, Jennifer, Craftsman Book Co, 6058 Corte Del Cedro, Carlsbad, CA 92011 *Tel:* 760-438-7828 *Toll Free Tel:* 800-829-8123 *Fax:* 760-438-0398 *Web Site:* www.craftsman-book.com, pg 64

Johnson, Jennifer, Dorothy Canfield Fisher Book Award, 109 State St, Montpelier, VT 05609-0601 *Tel:* 802-828-2721 *Web Site:* libraries.vermont.gov, pg 642

Johnson, John, Penfield Books, 215 Brown St, Iowa City, IA 52245 *Tel:* 319-337-9998 *Toll Free Tel:* 800-728-9998 *Fax:* 319-351-6846 *E-mail:* penfield@penfieldbooks.com *Web Site:* www.penfieldbooks.com, pg 177

Johnson, Joy, Centering Corp, 7230 Maple St, Omaha, NE 68134 *Tel:* 402-553-1200 *Toll Free Tel:* 866-218-0101 *Fax:* 402-553-0507 *E-mail:* orders@centering.org *Web Site:* www.centering.org, pg 51

Johnson, Karen, Martingale®, 19021 120 Ave NE, Suite 102, Bothell, WA 98011 *Tel:* 425-483-3313 *Toll Free Tel:* 800-426-3126 *Fax:* 425-486-7596 *E-mail:* info@martingale-pub.com *Web Site:* www.martingale-pub.com, pg 143

Johnson, Karyn, Peachpit Press, 1301 Sansome St, San Francisco, CA 94111 *Toll Free Tel:* 800-283-9444 *E-mail:* info@peachpit.com; ask@peachpit.com *Web Site:* www.peachpit.com, pg 175

Johnson, Kent S, Highlights for Children, 1800 Watermark Dr, Columbus, OH 43215 *Tel:* 614-486-0631 *Toll Free Tel:* 800-962-3661 (Highlights Club cust serv); 800-255-9517 (Highlights Magazine cust serv) *Web Site:* www.highlights.com; www.facebook.com/HighlightsforChildren, pg 107

Johnson, Kij, Science Fiction Writers Workshop, University of Kansas, Wescoe Hall, Rm 3001, Dept of English, 1445 Jayhawk Blvd, Lawrence, KS 66045 *Tel:* 785-864-2518 *Fax:* 785-864-1159 *Web Site:* www.sfcenter.ku.edu; www.sfcenter.ku.edu/sfworkshop; www.sfcenter.ku.edu/novel-workshop, pg 614

Johnson, Lars, Christian Liberty Press, 502 W Euclid Ave, Arlington Heights, IL 60004-5402 *Tel:* 847-259-4444 *Toll Free Tel:* 800-832-2741 (cust serv) *Fax:* 847-259-2941 *E-mail:* custserv@christianlibertypress.com *Web Site:* www.shopchristianliberty.com, pg 55

Johnson, Leslie, Graywolf Press, 250 Third Ave N, Suite 600, Minneapolis, MN 55401 *Tel:* 651-641-0077 *Fax:* 651-641-0036 *E-mail:* wolves@graywolfpress.org (no ms queries, sample chapters or proposals) *Web Site:* www.graywolfpress.org, pg 95

Johnson, Lloyd, Double Play, 303 Hillcrest Rd, Belton, MO 64012-1852 *Tel:* 816-651-7118 *E-mail:* wlloydj@lyahoo.com, pg 492

Johnson, Lynne, Spry Publishing, 315 E Eisenhower Pkwy, Suite 2, Ann Arbor, MI 48108 *Tel:* 734-531-7600 *Toll Free Tel:* 877-722-2264 *E-mail:* info@sprypub.com *Web Site:* www.sprypub.com, pg 219

Johnson, Mark, International Code Council Inc, 3060 Saturn St, Suite 100, Brea, CA 92821 *Tel:* 562-699-0541 *Toll Free Tel:* 888-422-7233 *Fax:* 562-908-5524; 562-699-8031 *E-mail:* es@icc-es.org; order@icc-es.org *Web Site:* www.iccsafe.org, pg 119

Johnson, Dr Marvin, Centering Corp, 7230 Maple St, Omaha, NE 68134 *Tel:* 402-553-1200 *Toll Free Tel:* 866-218-0101 *Fax:* 402-553-0507 *E-mail:* orders@centering.org *Web Site:* www.centering.org, pg 51

Johnson, Michelle, Neustadt International Prize for Literature, c/o University of Oklahoma, 630 Parrington Oval, Suite 110, Norman, OK 73019-4033 *Tel:* 405-325-4531 *Web Site:* www.worldliteraturetoday.org; www.worldlit.org, pg 672

Johnson, Michelle, NSK Neustadt Prize for Children's Literature, c/o University of Oklahoma, 630 Parrington Oval, Suite 110, Norman, OK 73019-4033 *Tel:* 405-325-4531 *Web Site:* www.worldliteraturetoday.org; www.worldlit.org, pg 674

Johnson, Patricia, Pantheon Books/Schocken Books, c/o Penguin Random House Inc, 1745 Broadway, New York, NY 10019 *Tel:* 212-751-2600 *Web Site:* knopfdoubleday.com/imprint/pantheon, pg 173

Johnson, Sue, AVKO Educational Research Foundation Inc, 3084 Willard Rd, Birch Run, MI 48415-9404 *Tel:* 810-686-9283 (orders & billing) *Fax:* 810-686-1101 *E-mail:* info@avko.org (gen inquiry) *Web Site:* www.avko.org; www.avko.blogspot.org, pg 27

Johnson, Tashauna, PhotoEdit Inc, 3505 Cadillac Ave, Suite P-101, Costa Mesa, CA 92626 *Toll Free Tel:* 888-450-0946 *Fax:* 714-434-5937 *Toll Free Fax:* 800-804-3707 *E-mail:* sales@photoeditinc.com *Web Site:* www.photoeditinc.com, pg 500

Johnson, Terence MA, Scribendi Inc, 405 Riverview Dr, Chatham, ON N7M 0N3, Canada *Tel:* 519-351-1626 (cust serv) *Fax:* 519-354-0192 *E-mail:* customerservice@scribendi.com *Web Site:* www.scribendi.com, pg 501

Johnson, Thomas, University Press of New England, One Court St, Suite 250, Lebanon, NH 03766 *Tel:* 603-448-1533 *Toll Free Tel:* 800-421-1561 (orders only) *Fax:* 603-448-7006; 603-448-9429 (orders only) *E-mail:* university.press@dartmouth.edu *Web Site:* www.upne.com, pg 247

Johnson, Thomas D, Business Research Services Inc, 4641 Montgomery Ave, Suite 208, Bethesda, MD 20814 *Tel:* 301-229-5561 *Toll Free Tel:* 800-845-8420 *Toll Free Fax:* 877-516-0818 *E-mail:* brspubs@sba8a.com *Web Site:* www.sba8a.com; www.setasidealert.com, pg 45

Johnson-Blalock, Jennifer, Liza Dawson Associates, 350 Seventh Ave, Suite 2003, New York, NY 10001 *Tel:* 212-465-9071 *Fax:* 212-947-0460 *Web Site:* www.lizadawsonassociates.com, pg 513

Johnson-LeBlanc, Linda, Judson Press, 588 N Gulph Rd, King of Prussia, PA 19406 *Toll Free Tel:* 800-458-3766 *Fax:* 610-768-2107 *Web Site:* www.judsonpress.com, pg 123

Johnston, Allyn, Simon & Schuster Children's Publishing, 1230 Avenue of the Americas, New York, NY 10020 *Tel:* 212-698-7000 *Web Site:* www.simonandschuster.com/kids; www.simonandschuster.com/teen; simonandschuster.net; simonandschuster.biz, pg 213

Johnston, Dillon, Wake Forest University Press, A5 Tribble Hall, Wake Forest University, Winston-Salem, NC 27109 *Tel:* 336-758-5448 *Fax:* 336-758-5636 *E-mail:* wfupress@wfu.edu *Web Site:* wfupress.wfu.edu, pg 251

Johnston, James, Random House Publishing Group, 1745 Broadway, New York, NY 10019 *Toll Free Tel:* 800-200-3552 *Web Site:* atrandom.com, pg 195

Johnston, Lisa Lyons, Kids Can Press Ltd, 25 Dockside Dr, Toronto, ON M5A 0B5, Canada *Tel:* 416-479-7000 *Toll Free Tel:* 800-265-0884 *Fax:* 416-960-5437 *E-mail:* info@kidscan.com; customerservice@kidscan.com *Web Site:* www.kidscanpress.com; www.kidscanpress.ca, pg 461

Johnston, Mr Robin, Pentecostal Publishing House, 8855 Dunn Rd, Hazelwood, MO 63042 *Tel:* 314-837-7300 *Toll Free Tel:* 866-819-7667 *Fax:* 314-837-6574 (orders) *Web Site:* www.pentecostalpublishing.com; wordaflamepress.com, pg 180

Johovic, Kelley H, Drue Heinz Literature Prize, 7500 Thomas Blvd, Pittsburgh, PA 15260 *Tel:* 412-383-2456 *Fax:* 412-383-2466 *E-mail:* info@upress.pitt.edu *Web Site:* www.upress.pitt.edu, pg 652

Johovic, Kelley H, Agnes Lynch Starrett Poetry Prize, 7500 Thomas Blvd, Pittsburgh, PA 15260 *Tel:* 412-383-2456 *Fax:* 412-383-2466 *E-mail:* info@upress.pitt.edu *Web Site:* www.upress.pitt.edu, pg 692

Joiner, Leila, Imago Press, 3710 E Edison St, Tucson, AZ 85716 *Tel:* 520-444-2265 *Web Site:* www.oasisjournal.org, pg 114

Jolley, Marc, Mercer University Press, 368 Orange St, Macon, GA 31201 *Tel:* 478-301-2880 *Toll Free Tel:* 866-895-1472 *Fax:* 478-301-2585 *E-mail:* mupressorders@mercer.edu *Web Site:* www.mupress.org, pg 148

Jonaitis, Alice, Random House Children's Books, 1745 Broadway, 10th fl, New York, NY 10019 *Tel:* 212-782-9000 *Web Site:* www.randomhousekids.com, pg 194

Jones, Alice, Apogee Press, 2308 Sixth St, Berkeley, CA 94710 *E-mail:* editors.apogee@gmail.com *Web Site:* www.apogeepress.com, pg 18

Jones, Allison, Fairchild Books, 1385 Broadway, 5th fl, New York, NY 10018 *Tel:* 212-419-5300 *Toll Free Tel:* 800-932-4724; 888-330-8477 (orders) *Fax:* 212-704-5975 *Web Site:* bloomsbury.com/us/academic/fairchildbooks, pg 81

Jones, Amy, Harlequin Enterprises Ltd, 225 Duncan Mill Rd, Don Mills, ON M3B 3K9, Canada *Tel:* 416-445-5860 *Toll Free Tel:* 888-432-4879; 800-370-5838 (ebook inquiries) *E-mail:* customerservice@harlequin.com *Web Site:* www.harlequin.com, pg 459

Jones, Andrew, Emmaus Road Publishing Inc, 1468 Parkview Circle, Steubenville, OH 43952 *Tel:* 740-283-2880 (outside US) *Toll Free Tel:* 800-398-5470 (orders) *Fax:* 740-283-4011 (orders) *E-mail:* questions@emmausroad.org *Web Site:* www.emmausroad.org, pg 78

Jones, Ms Brett Hall, Squaw Valley Community of Writers Summer Workshops, PO Box 1416, Nevada City, CA 95959 *Tel:* 530-470-8440 *E-mail:* info@communityofwriters.org *Web Site:* www.communityofwriters.org, pg 615

Jones, Briony, University of New Mexico Press, One University of New Mexico, Albuquerque, NM 87131-0001 *Tel:* 505-272-7777 *Fax:* 505-277-3343; 505-272-7778 (cust serv) *Toll Free Fax:* 800-622-8667 (orders only) *E-mail:* unmpress@unm.edu; custserv@unm.edu (order dept) *Web Site:* unmpress.com, pg 243

Jones, Carrie, Greenleaf Book Group LLC, 3 Park Place, 4005 Banister Lane, Suite B, Austin, TX 78704 *Tel:* 512-891-6100 *Fax:* 512-891-6150 *E-mail:* contact@greenleafbookgroup.com *Web Site:* www.greenleafbookgroup.com, pg 96

Jones, Cassie, HarperCollins General Books Group, 195 Broadway, New York, NY 10007 *Tel:* 212-207-7000 *Web Site:* www.harpercollins.com, pg 101

Jones, Cathy, The Applegate/Jackson/Parks Future Teacher Scholarship, 5211 Port Royal Rd, Suite 510, Springfield, VA 22151 *Tel:* 703-321-9606 *Fax:* 703-321-7143 *Web Site:* www.nilrr.org, pg 627

Jones, Cathy, William B Ruggles Journalism Scholarship, 5211 Port Royal Rd, Suite 510, Springfield, VA 22151 *Tel:* 703-321-9606 *Fax:* 703-321-7143 *Web Site:* www.nilrr.org, pg 686

Jones, Christopher, Toronto Book Awards, c/o Toronto Arts & Culture, City Hall, 9E, 100 Queen St W, Toronto, ON M5H 2N2, Canada *Web Site:* www.toronto.ca/book_awards, pg 694

Jones, Courtney, ALSC Baker & Taylor Summer Reading Grant, 50 E Huron St, Chicago, IL 60611-2795 *Tel:* 312-280-2163 *Toll Free Tel:* 800-545-2433 *Fax:* 312-440-9374; 312-280-5271 *E-mail:* alsc@ala.org *Web Site:* www.ala.org/alsc, pg 627

Jones, Courtney, The May Hill Arbuthnot Honor Lecture Award, 50 E Huron St, Chicago, IL 60611-2795 *Tel:* 312-280-2163 *Toll Free Tel:* 800-545-2433 *Fax:* 312-440-9374; 312-280-5271 *E-mail:* alsc@ala.org *Web Site:* www.ala.org/alsc, pg 628

Jones, Courtney, The Mildred L Batchelder Award, 50 E Huron St, Chicago, IL 60611-2795 *Tel:* 312-280-2163 *Toll Free Tel:* 800-545-2433 *Fax:* 312-440-9374; 312-280-5271 *E-mail:* alsc@ala.org *Web Site:* www.ala.org/alsc, pg 630

Jones, Courtney, The Pura Belpre Award, 50 E Huron St, Chicago, IL 60611-2795 *Tel:* 312-280-2163 *Toll Free Tel:* 800-545-2433 *Fax:* 312-440-9374; 312-280-5271 *E-mail:* alsc@ala.org *Web Site:* www.ala.org/alsc, pg 631

Jones, Courtney, Bound to Stay Bound Books Scholarship, 50 E Huron St, Chicago, IL 60611-2795 *Tel:* 312-280-2163 *Toll Free Tel:* 800-545-2433 *Fax:* 312-440-9374; 312-280-5271 *E-mail:* alsc@ala.org *Web Site:* www.ala.org/alsc, pg 634

Jones, Courtney, The Randolph Caldecott Medal, 50 E Huron St, Chicago, IL 60611-2795 *Tel:* 312-280-2163 *Toll Free Tel:* 800-545-2433 *Fax:* 312-440-9374; 312-280-5271 *E-mail:* alsc@ala.org *Web Site:* www.ala.org/alsc, pg 635

Jones, Courtney, Frederic G Melcher Scholarship, 50 E Huron St, Chicago, IL 60611-2795 *Tel:* 312-280-2163 *Toll Free Tel:* 800-545-2433 *Fax:* 312-440-9374; 312-280-5271 *E-mail:* alsc@ala.org *Web Site:* www.ala.org/alsc, pg 667

Jones, Courtney, John Newbery Medal, 50 E Huron St, Chicago, IL 60611-2795 *Tel:* 312-280-2163 *Toll Free Tel:* 800-545-2433 *Fax:* 312-440-9374; 312-280-5271 *E-mail:* alsc@ala.org *Web Site:* www.ala.org/alsc, pg 673

Jones, Courtney, Robert F Sibert Informational Book Award, 50 E Huron St, Chicago, IL 60611-2795 *Tel:* 312-280-2163 *Toll Free Tel:* 800-545-2433 *Fax:* 312-440-9374; 312-280-5271 *E-mail:* alsc@ala.org *Web Site:* www.ala.org/alsc, pg 689

Jones, Courtney, The Laura Ingalls Wilder Medal, 50 E Huron St, Chicago, IL 60611-2795 *Tel:* 312-280-2163 *Toll Free Tel:* 800-545-2433 *Fax:* 312-440-9374; 312-280-5271 *E-mail:* alsc@ala.org *Web Site:* www.ala.org/alsc, pg 698

Jones, Diane, Standard Publishing, 4050 Lee Vance View, Colorado Springs, CO 80918 *Tel:* 513-931-4050 *Toll Free Tel:* 800-323-7543 *Fax:* 513-931-0950 *Toll Free Fax:* 800-323-0726 *E-mail:* customerservice@standardpub.com *Web Site:* www.standardpub.com, pg 220

Jones, Diem, VONA Voices Summer Writing Workshop, 3720 Spruce St, Suite 442, Philadelphia, PA 19104 *Tel:* 732-842-3932; 510-421-3913 *E-mail:* info@vonacommunity.org *Web Site:* www.vonacommunity.org, pg 616

Jones, Doug, HarperCollins General Books Group, 195 Broadway, New York, NY 10007 *Tel:* 212-207-7000 *Web Site:* www.harpercollins.com, pg 101

Jones, Eddie, Lighthouse Publishing of the Carolinas, 2333 Barton Oaks Dr, Raleigh, NC 27614-7940 *Tel:* 919-562-8439 *E-mail:* lighthousepublishingcarolinas@gmail.com *Web Site:* lighthousepublishingofthecarolinas.com, pg 134

Jones, Erin, Odyssey Books, 2421 Redwood Ct, Longmont, CO 80503-8155 *Tel:* 720-494-1473 *Fax:* 720-494-1471 *E-mail:* books@odysseybooks.net, pg 167

Jones, Greg, Signature Books Publishing LLC, 564 W 400 N, Salt Lake City, UT 84116-3411 *Tel:* 801-531-1483 *Fax:* 801-531-1488 *E-mail:* people@signaturebooks.com *Web Site:* www.signaturebooks.com; www.signaturebookslibrary.org, pg 212

Jones, Hugh, Accuity, 4709 W Golf Rd, Skokie, IL 60076 *Tel:* 847-676-9600 *Toll Free Tel:* 800-321-3373 *Fax:* 847-933-8101 *E-mail:* custserv@accuity.com; sales@accuity.com *Web Site:* www.accuity.com, pg 3

Jones, James, Autism Asperger Publishing Co, 11209 Strang Line Rd, Lenexa, KS 66215 *Tel:* 913-897-1004 *Toll Free Tel:* 877-277-8254 *Fax:* 913-681-9473 *E-mail:* info@aapcpublishing.net *Web Site:* www.aapcpublishing.net, pg 26

Jones, Jennifer, Nilgiri Press, 3600 Tomales Rd, Tomales, CA 94971 *Tel:* 707-878-2369 *E-mail:* info@easwaran.org *Web Site:* www.easwaran.org, pg 162

Jones, Jill, McGraw-Hill International & Professional Publishing Group, 2 Penn Plaza, New York, NY 10121 *Tel:* 646-766-2000 *Web Site:* www.mheducation.com, pg 146

Jones, Josh, Cricket Cottage Publishing LLC, 1500 Beville Rd, Suite 606-346, Daytona Beach, FL 32114 *Tel:* 585-687-7291 *E-mail:* cricketcottage@att.net *Web Site:* thecricketpublishing.com, pg 64

Jones, Keasley, Peachpit Press, 1301 Sansome St, San Francisco, CA 94111 *Toll Free Tel:* 800-283-9444 *E-mail:* info@peachpit.com; ask@peachpit.com *Web Site:* www.peachpit.com, pg 175

Jones, Keiko, Signature Books Publishing LLC, 564 W 400 N, Salt Lake City, UT 84116-3411 *Tel:* 801-531-1483 *Fax:* 801-531-1488 *E-mail:* people@signaturebooks.com *Web Site:* www.signaturebooks.com; www.signaturebookslibrary.org, pg 212

Jones, Linda, Enfield Publishing & Distribution Co, 234 May St, Enfield, NH 03748 *Tel:* 603-632-7377 *Fax:* 603-632-5611 *E-mail:* info@enfieldbooks.com *Web Site:* www.enfieldbooks.com, pg 79

Jones, Linda, Trans Tech Publications Inc, c/o Enfield Distribution Co, 234 May St, Enfield, NH 03748 *Tel:* 603-632-7377 *Fax:* 603-632-5611 *E-mail:* info@enfieldbooks.com *Web Site:* www.ttp.net, pg 234

Jones, Ling-Yen, Solano Press Books, PO Box 773, Point Arena, CA 95468 *Tel:* 707-884-4508 *Toll Free Tel:* 800-931-9373 *Fax:* 707-884-4109 *E-mail:* spbooks@solano.com *Web Site:* www.solano.com, pg 217

Jones, Louis B, Squaw Valley Community of Writers Summer Workshops, PO Box 1416, Nevada City, CA 95959 *Tel:* 530-470-8440 *E-mail:* info@communityofwriters.org *Web Site:* www.communityofwriters.org, pg 615

Jones, Marjorie Gillette, Baldwin Literary Services, 935 Hayes St, Baldwin, NY 11510-4834 *Tel:* 516-546-8338 *Fax:* 516-546-8338, pg 489

Jones, Marla F, Doodle and Peck Publishing, 413 Cedarburg Ct, Yukon, OK 73099 *Tel:* 405-354-7422 *E-mail:* contact@doodleandpeck.com *Web Site:* www.doodleandpeck.com, pg 72

Jones, Melissa, Graphic Arts Association, 1210 Northbrook Dr, Suite 200, Trevose, PA 19053 *Tel:* 215-396-2300 *Fax:* 215-396-9890 *E-mail:* gaa@gaaonline.org *Web Site:* www.gaa1900.com; www.graphicartsassociation.org, pg 620

Jones, Meryl, Craven Design Inc, 229 E 85 St, New York, NY 10028 *Tel:* 212-288-1022 *Fax:* 212-249-9910 *E-mail:* cravendesign@mac.com *Web Site:* www.cravendesignstudios.com, pg 543

Jones, Michael, Saskatchewan Arts Board, 1355 Broad St, Regina, SK S4R 7V1, Canada *Tel:* 306-787-4056 *Toll Free Tel:* 800-667-7526 (CN) *Fax:* 306-787-4199 *E-mail:* info@saskartsboard.ca *Web Site:* www.saskartsboard.ca, pg 577

Jones, Michael P, Crumb Elbow Publishing, PO Box 294, Rhododendron, OR 97049-0294 *Tel:* 503-622-4798, pg 65

Jones, Nikki, Health Research Books, 62 Seventh St, Pomeroy, WA 99347 *Tel:* 509-843-2385 *Toll Free Tel:* 888-844-2386 *Fax:* 509-843-2387 *E-mail:* publish@pomeroy-wa.com *Web Site:* www.healthresearchbooks.com, pg 105

Jones, Parneshia, Northwestern University Press, 629 Noyes St, Evanston, IL 60208-4210 *Tel:* 847-491-2046 *Toll Free Tel:* 800-621-2736 (orders only) *Fax:* 847-491-8150 *E-mail:* nupress@northwestern.edu *Web Site:* www.nupress.northwestern.edu, pg 164

Jones, Patsy, Hachette Nashville, 12 Cadillac Dr, Suite 480, Brentwood, TN 37027 *Tel:* 615-221-0996 *Fax:* 615-221-0962 *Web Site:* www.hachettebookgroup.com, pg 98

Jones, Peter, LRS, 19146 Van Ness Ave, Torrance, CA 90501 *Tel:* 310-354-2610 *Toll Free Tel:* 800-255-5002 *Fax:* 310-354-2601 *E-mail:* largeprintsb@aol.com *Web Site:* lrs-largeprint.com, pg 139

Jones, Serena, Henry Holt and Company, LLC, 175 Fifth Ave, New York, NY 10010 *Tel:* 646-307-5151 *Toll Free Tel:* 888-330-8477 (orders) *Fax:* 646-307-5285 *E-mail:* firstname.lastname@hholt.com *Web Site:* www.henryholt.com, pg 109

Jones, Tim, American Society for Nondestructive Testing, 1711 Arlingate Lane, Columbus, OH 43228-0518 *Tel:* 614-274-6003 *Toll Free Tel:* 800-222-2768 *Fax:* 614-274-6899 *Web Site:* www.asnt.org, pg 14

Jones, Tim, Harvard University Press, 79 Garden St, Cambridge, MA 02138-1499 *Tel:* 617-495-2600; 401-531-2800 (intl orders) *Toll Free Tel:* 800-405-1619 (orders) *Fax:* 617-495-5898 (general); 617-496-4677 (edit & rts); 401-531-2801 (intl orders) *Toll Free Fax:* 800-406-9145 (orders) *E-mail:* contact_hup@harvard.edu *Web Site:* www.hup.harvard.edu, pg 103

Jones, Valerie, University Press of Mississippi, 3825 Ridgewood Rd, Jackson, MS 39211-6492 *Tel:* 601-432-6205 *Toll Free Tel:* 800-737-7788 (orders & cust serv) *Fax:* 601-432-6217 *E-mail:* press@mississippi.edu *Web Site:* www.upress.state.ms.us, pg 247

Jongsma, Jennifer, Annual Reviews, 4139 El Camino Way, Palo Alto, CA 94306 *Tel:* 650-493-4400 *Toll Free Tel:* 800-523-8635 *Fax:* 650-424-0910; 650-855-9815 *E-mail:* service@annualreviews.org *Web Site:* www.annualreviews.org, pg 17

Jonker, Rosie, Ann Rittenberg Literary Agency Inc, 15 Maiden Lane, Suite 206, New York, NY 10038 *Tel:* 212-684-6936 *Fax:* 212-684-6929 *E-mail:* info@rittlit.com *Web Site:* www.rittlit.com, pg 532

Joosten, Michael, Random House Children's Books, 1745 Broadway, 10th fl, New York, NY 10019 *Tel:* 212-782-9000 *Web Site:* www.randomhousekids.com, pg 194

Jordan, Sara, Sara Jordan Publishing, RPO Lakeport Box 28105, St Catharines, ON L2N 7P8, Canada *Tel:* 905-938-5050 *Toll Free Tel:* 800-567-7733 *Fax:* 905-938-9970 *Toll Free Fax:* 800-229-3855 *Web Site:* www.sara-jordan.com, pg 469

Jordan, Tina, Association of American Publishers (AAP), 455 Massachusetts Ave NW, Suite 700, Washington, DC 20001-2777 *Tel:* 212-255-0200 *Fax:* 212-255-7007 *E-mail:* info@publishers.org *Web Site:* publishers.org, pg 558

Jorden, Brooke, Familius, 1254 Commerce Way, Sanger, CA 93657 *Tel:* 559-876-2170 *Fax:* 559-876-2180 *E-mail:* orders@familius.com *Web Site:* www.familius.com, pg 82

Joseph, Jennifer, Manic D Press Inc, 250 Banks St, San Francisco, CA 94110 *Tel:* 415-648-8288 *E-mail:* info@manicdpress.com *Web Site:* www.manicdpress.com, pg 141

Joseph, Kelly, McClelland & Stewart Ltd, 320 Front St W, Suite 1400, Toronto, ON M5V 3B6, Canada *Tel:* 416-364-4449 *Fax:* 416-598-7764 *E-mail:* customerservicescanada@penguinrandomhouse.com; publicity@ca.penguingroup.com *Web Site:* penguinrandomhouse.ca/imprints/mcclelland-stewart, pg 463

Joseph, Peter, Harlequin Enterprises Ltd, 233 Broadway, Suite 1001, New York, NY 10279 *Tel:* 212-553-4200 *Fax:* 212-227-8969 *E-mail:* customerservice@harlequin.com *Web Site:* www.harlequin.com, pg 100

Jost, David, Houghton Mifflin Harcourt Trade & Reference Division, 125 High St, Boston, MA 02110 *Tel:* 617-351-5000 *Toll Free Tel:* 800-225-3362 *Web Site:* www.hmhco.com, pg 111

Jourdan, Bonnie, National One-Act Playwriting Competition, 600 Wolfe St, Alexandria, VA 22314 *Tel:* 703-683-5778 (ext 2) *Fax:* 703-683-1378 *E-mail:* asklta@thelittletheatre.com *Web Site:* www.thelittletheatre.com/info, pg 671

Jourdane, Tom, AZ Books LLC, 320 Fifth Ave, New York, NY 10001 *Toll Free Tel:* 888-945-7723 *Toll Free Fax:* 888-945-7724 *Web Site:* www.azbooksusa.com, pg 27

Jowett, Barry, Cormorant Books Inc, 10 St Mary St, Suite 615, Toronto, ON M4Y 1P9, Canada *Tel:* 416-925-8887 *E-mail:* info@cormorantbooks.com *Web Site:* www.cormorantbooks.com, pg 451

Joyce, Jack, ITMB Publishing Ltd, 12300 Bridgeport Rd, Richmond, BC V6V 1J5, Canada *Tel:* 604-273-1400 *Fax:* 604-273-1488 *E-mail:* itmb@itmb.com *Web Site:* www.itmb.com, pg 461

Joyce, John, Joyce Media Inc, 3413 Soledad Canyon Rd, Acton, CA 93510-1974 *Tel:* 661-269-1169 *Fax:* 661-269-2139 *E-mail:* help@joycemediainc.com *Web Site:* www.joycemediainc.com, pg 123

Joyce, Robinson, Firefall Editions, 4905 Tunlaw St, Alexandria, VA 22312 *Tel:* 510-549-2461 *E-mail:* literary@att.net *Web Site:* www.firefallmedia.com, pg 85

Juarez, Benny, Ross Books, PO Box 4340, Berkeley, CA 94704-0340 *Tel:* 510-841-2474 *Fax:* 510-295-2531 *E-mail:* sales@rossbooks.com *Web Site:* www.rossbooks.com, pg 201

Jud, Brian, Association of Publishers for Special Sales (APSS), PO Box 715, Avon, CT 06001-0715 *Tel:* 860-675-1344 *Web Site:* www.spannet.org, pg 559

Jud, Brian, Book Marketing Works LLC, 50 Lovely St (Rte 177), Avon, CT 06001 *Tel:* 860-675-1344 *Web Site:* www.bookmarketingworks.com, pg 39

Jud, Brian, Connecticut Authors & Publishers Association (CAPA), PO Box 715, Avon, CT 06001-0715 *Tel:* 860-675-1344 *Fax:* 860-673-7650 *Web Site:* www.aboutcapa.com, pg 563

Judd, Allison, Random House Children's Books, 1745 Broadway, 10th fl, New York, NY 10019 *Tel:* 212-782-9000 *Web Site:* www.randomhousekids.com, pg 194

Judd, Darrell, Artech House Inc, 685 Canton St, Norwood, MA 02062 *Tel:* 781-769-9750 *Toll Free Tel:* 800-225-9977 *Fax:* 781-769-6334 *E-mail:* artech@artechhouse.com *Web Site:* www.artechhouse.com, pg 21

Judd, Edwin J, Jhpiego, 1615 Thames St, Baltimore, MD 21231-3492 *Tel:* 410-537-1800 *Fax:* 410-537-1473 *E-mail:* info@jhpiego.net *Web Site:* www.jhpiego.org, pg 122

Judson, Nancy, TripBuilder Media Inc, 180 Post Rd E, Suite 200, Westport, CT 06880 *Tel:* 203-227-1255 *Toll Free Tel:* 800-525-9745 *Fax:* 203-227-1257 *E-mail:* info@tripbuildermedia.com *Web Site:* www.tripbuildermedia.com, pg 235

Juenemann, Brian, Pacific Northwest Book Awards, 338 W 11 Ave, Unit 108, Eugene, OR 97401 *Tel:* 541-683-4363 *Fax:* 541-683-3910 *E-mail:* info@pnba.org; awards@pnba.org *Web Site:* www.pnba.org, pg 676

Juenemann, Brian, Pacific Northwest Booksellers Association (PNBA), 338 W 11 Ave, Unit 108, Eugene, OR 97401 *Tel:* 541-683-4363 *Toll Free Tel:* 800-353-6764 *Fax:* 541-683-3910 *E-mail:* info@pnba.org *Web Site:* www.pnba.org, pg 575

Julavits, Heidi, Columbia University School of the Arts, Creative Writing Program, 609 Kent Hall, New York, NY 10027 *Tel:* 212-854-3774 *Fax:* 212-854-7704 *E-mail:* writingprogram@columbia.edu *Web Site:* www.columbia.edu/cu/writing, pg 619

Julien, Ria, Frances Goldin Literary Agency, Inc, 214 W 29 St, Suite 410, New York, NY 10001 *Tel:* 212-777-0047 *Fax:* 212-228-1660 *E-mail:* agency@goldinlit.com *Web Site:* www.goldinlit.com, pg 519

Jung, Zaneta, Chronicle Books LLC, 680 Second St, San Francisco, CA 94107 *Tel:* 415-537-4200 *Toll Free Tel:* 800-759-0190 (cust serv) *Fax:* 415-537-4460 *Toll Free Fax:* 800-858-7787 (orders); 800-286-9471 (cust serv) *E-mail:* frontdesk@chroniclebooks.com *Web Site:* www.chroniclebooks.com, pg 55

Junior, Bobbi, InScribe Christian Writers' Fellowship (ICWF), PO Box 6201, Wetaskiwin, AB T9A 2E9, Canada *E-mail:* inscribe.mail@gmail.com *Web Site:* inscribe.org, pg 567

Junker, Lisa, Entomological Society of America, 3 Park Place, Suite 307, Annapolis, MD 21401-3722 *Tel:* 301-731-4535 *Fax:* 301-731-4538 *E-mail:* esa@entsoc.org *Web Site:* www.entsoc.org, pg 79

Juodaitis, Thomas W, The Trinity Foundation, PO Box 68, Unicoi, TN 37692-0068 *Tel:* 423-743-0199 *Fax:* 423-743-2005 *Web Site:* www.trinityfoundation.org, pg 235

Jurewicz, Hannah Carlson, Bick Publishing House, 75 Mungertown Rd, Madison, CT 06443 *Tel:* 203-245-0341 *Fax:* 203-208-5253 *E-mail:* bickpubhse@aol.com *Web Site:* www.bickpubhouse.com, pg 35

Jusino, John, HarperCollins General Books Group, 195 Broadway, New York, NY 10007 *Tel:* 212-207-7000 *Web Site:* www.harpercollins.com, pg 101

Jutkowitz, Edward J, Camino Books Inc, PO Box 59026, Philadelphia, PA 19102-9026 *Tel:* 215-413-1917 *Fax:* 215-413-3255 *E-mail:* camino@caminobooks.com *Web Site:* www.caminobooks.com, pg 46

Kacian, Jim, Red Moon Press, PO Box 2461, Winchester, VA 22604-1661 *Tel:* 540-722-2156 *Web Site:* www.redmoonpress.com, pg 197

Kadarusman, Michelle, Giller Prize, 543 Logan Ave, Toronto, ON M4K 3B6, Canada *Web Site:* www.scotiabankgillerprize.ca, pg 649

Kadetz, Stuart, Bhaktivedanta Book Trust (BBT), 9701 Venice Blvd, Suite 3, Los Angeles, CA 90034 *Tel:* 310-837-5283 *Toll Free Tel:* 800-927-4152 *Fax:* 310-837-1056 *E-mail:* store@krishna.com *Web Site:* www.krishna.com, pg 34

Kadin, Ellen, AMACOM Books, 1601 Broadway, New York, NY 10019-7420 *Tel:* 212-586-8100 *Toll Free Tel:* 800-250-5308 (cust serv) *Fax:* 212-903-8083; 518-891-2372 (orders) *E-mail:* pubs_cust_serv@amanet.org *Web Site:* www.amacombooks.org, pg 8

Kadushin, Raphael, University of Wisconsin Press, 1930 Monroe St, 3rd fl, Madison, WI 53711-2059 *Tel:* 608-263-0668 *Toll Free Tel:* 800-621-2736 (orders) *Fax:* 608-263-1173 *Toll Free Fax:* 800-621-2736 (orders) *E-mail:* uwiscpress@uwpress.wisc.edu (main off); publicity@uwpress.wisc.edu *Web Site:* uwpress.wisc.edu, pg 246

Kaemmer, Beverly, University of Minnesota Press, 111 Third Ave S, Suite 290, Minneapolis, MN 55401-2520 *Tel:* 612-301-1990 *Fax:* 612-301-1980 *E-mail:* ump@umn.edu *Web Site:* www.upress.umn.edu, pg 242

Kaeser, Scott, Tide-mark Press, 22 Prestige Park Circle, East Hartford, CT 06108-1917 *Tel:* 860-310-3370 *Toll Free Tel:* 800-338-2508 *Fax:* 860-310-3654 *E-mail:* customerservice@tide-mark.com *Web Site:* www.tidemarkpress.com, pg 232

Kagan, Abby, Farrar, Straus & Giroux, LLC, 18 W 18 St, New York, NY 10011 *Tel:* 212-741-6900 *E-mail:* fsg.publicity@fsgbooks.com *Web Site:* us.macmillan.com/fsg.aspx, pg 83

Kagan, Heidi, Penguin Group USA, A Penguin Random House Company, 375 Hudson St, New York, NY 10014 *Tel:* 212-366-2000 *Toll Free Tel:* 800-847-5515 (inside sales); 800-631-8571 (cust serv) *Fax:* 212-366-2666; 607-775-4829 (inside sales) *E-mail:* online@us.penguingroup.com *Web Site:* www.penguin.com, pg 177

Kagan, Ute Wartenberg, American Numismatic Society, 75 Varick St, 11th fl, New York, NY 10013 *Tel:* 212-571-4470 *Fax:* 212-571-4479 *E-mail:* ans@numismatics.org; orders@numismatics.org *Web Site:* www.numismatics.org, pg 13

Kahan, Rachel, HarperCollins General Books Group, 195 Broadway, New York, NY 10007 *Tel:* 212-207-7000 *Web Site:* www.harpercollins.com, pg 101

Kahla, Keith, St Martin's Press, LLC, 175 Fifth Ave, New York, NY 10010 *Tel:* 646-307-5151 *Web Site:* us.macmillan.com/smp, pg 204

Kahn, Jody, Brandt & Hochman Literary Agents Inc, 1501 Broadway, Suite 2310, New York, NY 10036 *Tel:* 212-840-5760 *Fax:* 212-840-5776 *Web Site:* brandthochman.com, pg 509

Kahn, Kenneth F, LRP Publications, 360 Hiatt Dr, Palm Beach Gardens, FL 33418 *Tel:* 561-622-6520 *Toll Free Tel:* 800-341-7874 *Fax:* 561-622-2423 *E-mail:* custserve@lrp.com *Web Site:* www.lrp.com, pg 139

Kahrizi, Camilia, Marilyn Baillie Picture Book Award, 40 Orchard View Blvd, Suite 217, Toronto, ON M4R 1B9, Canada *Tel:* 416-975-0010 *Fax:* 416-975-8970 *E-mail:* info@bookcentre.ca *Web Site:* www.bookcentre.ca, pg 629

Kahrizi, Camilia, The Geoffrey Bilson Award for Historical Fiction for Young People, 40 Orchard View Blvd, Suite 217, Toronto, ON M4R 1B9, Canada *Tel:* 416-975-0010 *Fax:* 416-975-8970 *E-mail:* info@bookcentre.ca *Web Site:* www.bookcentre.ca, pg 632

Kahrizi, Camilia, Canadian Children's Book Centre, 40 Orchard View Blvd, Suite 217, Toronto, ON M4R 1B9, Canada *Tel:* 416-975-0010 *Fax:* 416-975-8970 *E-mail:* info@bookcentre.ca *Web Site:* www.bookcentre.ca, pg 562

Kahrizi, Camilia, Norma Fleck Award for Canadian Children's Non-Fiction, 40 Orchard View Blvd, Suite 217, Toronto, ON M4R 1B9, Canada *Tel:* 416-975-0010 *Fax:* 416-975-8970 *E-mail:* info@bookcentre.ca *Web Site:* www.bookcentre.ca, pg 646

Kahrizi, Camilia, Amy Mathers Teen Book Award, 40 Orchard View Blvd, Suite 217, Toronto, ON M4R 1B9, Canada *Tel:* 416-975-0010 *Fax:* 416-975-8970 *E-mail:* info@bookcentre.ca *Web Site:* www.bookcentre.ca, pg 666

Kahrizi, Camilia, John Spray Mystery Award, 40 Orchard View Blvd, Suite 217, Toronto, ON M4R 1B9, Canada *Tel:* 416-975-0010 *Fax:* 416-975-8970 *E-mail:* info@bookcentre.ca *Web Site:* www.bookcentre.ca, pg 691

Kahrizi, Camilia, TD Canadian Children's Literature Award, 40 Orchard View Blvd, Suite 217, Toronto, ON M4R 1B9, Canada *Tel:* 416-975-0010 *Fax:* 416-975-8970 *E-mail:* info@bookcentre.ca *Web Site:* www.bookcentre.ca, pg 693

Kaiman, Ken, Square One Publishers Inc, 115 Herricks Rd, Garden City Park, NY 11040 *Tel:* 516-535-2010 *Toll Free Tel:* 877-900-BOOK (900-2665) *Fax:* 516-535-2014 *E-mail:* sq1publish@aol.com *Web Site:* www.squareonepublishers.com, pg 220

Kain, Amanda, Hachette Books, 1290 Avenue of the Americas, New York, NY 10019 *Tel:* 212-364-1100 *Web Site:* www.hachettebookgroup.com, pg 98

Kaiser, Cecily, Phaidon, 65 Bleecker St, 8th fl, New York, NY 10012 *Tel:* 212-652-5400 *Toll Free Tel:* 800-759-0190 (cust serv) *Fax:* 212-652-5410 *Toll Free Fax:* 800-286-9471 (cust serv) *E-mail:* ussales@phaidon.com *Web Site:* www.phaidon.com, pg 182

Kaiser, Debra, Lorenz Educational Press, 501 E Third St, Dayton, OH 45402 *Tel:* 937-228-6118 *Toll Free Tel:* 800-444-1144 *Fax:* 937-223-2042 *E-mail:* order@lorenz.com *Web Site:* www.lorenzeducationalpress.com, pg 137

Kaiser, Debra, Milliken Publishing Co, 501 E Third St, Dayton, OH 45402 *Tel:* 937-228-6118 *Toll Free Tel:* 800-444-1144 *Fax:* 937-223-2042 *E-mail:* order@lorenz.com *Web Site:* www.lorenzeducationalpress.com, pg 151

Kaiser, Debra, Teaching & Learning Co, 501 E Third St, Dayton, OH 45402 *Tel:* 937-228-6118 *Toll Free Tel:* 800-444-1144 *Fax:* 937-223-2042 *E-mail:* info@lorenz.com *Web Site:* www.lorenzeducationalpress.com, pg 228

Kaiser, Jackie, Westwood Creative Artists Ltd, 138 Sussex Mews, Toronto, ON M5S-2K1, Canada *Tel:* 416-964-3302 *Fax:* 416-964-3302 *E-mail:* wca_office@wcaltd.com *Web Site:* www.wcaltd.com, pg 541

Kaiser, Kathleen Sexton, Small Publishers, Artists & Writers Network (SPAWN), 323 E Matilija St, Suite 110, PMB 123, Ojai, CA 93023 *Tel:* 805-646-3045 *Fax:* 805-640-8213 *E-mail:* execdir@spawn.org *Web Site:* www.spawn.org, pg 577

Kaita, Melissa, Second Story Press, 20 Maud St, Suite 401, Toronto, ON M5V 2M5, Canada *Tel:* 416-537-7850 *Fax:* 416-537-0588 *E-mail:* info@secondstorypress.ca *Web Site:* secondstorypress.ca, pg 470

Kakar, Samir, Aptara Inc, 3110 Fairview Park Dr, Suite 900, Falls Church, VA 22042 *Tel:* 703-352-0001 *E-mail:* moreinfo@aptaracorp.com *Web Site:* www.aptaracorp.com, pg 488

Kalajian, James, Axiom Business Book Awards, 1129 Woodmere Ave, Suite B, Traverse City, MI 49686 *Tel:* 231-933-0445 *Toll Free Tel:* 800-706-4636 *Fax:* 231-933-0448 *E-mail:* info@axiomawards.com *Web Site:* www.axiomawards.com, pg 629

Kalajian, James, eLit Awards, 1129 Woodmere Ave, Suite B, Traverse City, MI 49686 *Tel:* 231-933-0445 *Toll Free Tel:* 800-706-4636 *Fax:* 231-933-0448 *E-mail:* info@elitawards.com *Web Site:* www.elitawards.com, pg 644

Kalajian, James, Illumination Book Awards, 1129 Woodmere Ave, Suite B, Traverse City, MI 49686 *Tel:* 231-933-0445 *Toll Free Tel:* 800-706-4636 *Fax:* 231-933-0448 *E-mail:* awards@bookpublishing.com *Web Site:* www.illuminationawards.com, pg 654

Kalajian, James, The Independent Publisher Book Awards, 1129 Woodmere Ave, Suite B, Traverse City, MI 49686 *Tel:* 231-933-0445 *Toll Free Tel:* 800-706-4636 *Fax:* 231-933-0448 *E-mail:* awards@bookpublishing.com *Web Site:* www.independentpublisher.com/ipland/ipawards.php, pg 655

Kalajian, James, Jenkins Group Inc, 1129 Woodmere Ave, Suite B, Traverse City, MI 49686 *Tel:* 231-933-0445 *Toll Free Tel:* 800-706-4636 *Fax:* 231-933-0448 *E-mail:* info@bookpublishing.com *Web Site:* www.bookpublishing.com, pg 496

Kalajian, James, Living Now Book Awards, 1129 Woodmere Ave, Suite B, Traverse City, MI 49686 *Tel:* 231-933-0445 *Toll Free Tel:* 800-706-4636 *Fax:* 231-933-0448 *E-mail:* awards@bookpublishing.com *Web Site:* www.livingnowawards.com, pg 662

Kalajian, James, Moonbeam Children's Book Awards, 1129 Woodmere Ave, Suite B, Traverse City, MI 49686 *Tel:* 231-933-0445 *Toll Free Tel:* 800-706-4636 *Fax:* 231-933-0448 *E-mail:* info@moonbeamawards.com *Web Site:* www.moonbeamawards.com, pg 669

Kalett, Alison, Princeton University Press, 41 William St, Princeton, NJ 08540-5237 *Tel:* 609-258-4900 *Fax:* 609-258-6305 *Web Site:* press.princeton.edu, pg 188

Kalil, Maureen, Phoenix Society for Burn Survivors, 1835 R W Berends Dr SW, Grand Rapids, MI 49519-4955 *Tel:* 616-458-2773 *Toll Free Tel:* 800-888-BURN (888-2876) *E-mail:* info@phoenix-society.org *Web Site:* www.phoenix-society.org, pg 182

Kalish, Ilene, New York University Press, 838 Broadway, 3rd fl, New York, NY 10003-4812 *Tel:* 212-998-2575 (edit) *Toll Free Tel:* 800-996-6987 (orders) *Fax:* 212-995-4798 (orders) *E-mail:* information@nyupress.org; nyupressinfo@nyu.edu; orders@nyupress.org *Web Site:* www.nyupress.org, pg 162

Kalk, Valentina, The Brookings Institution Press, 1775 Massachusetts Ave NW, Washington, DC 20036-2188 *Tel:* 202-536-3600 *Toll Free Tel:* 800-537-5487 *Fax:* 202-536-3623 *E-mail:* permissions@brookings.edu *Web Site:* www.brookings.edu, pg 44

Kalman, Ms Bobbie, Crabtree Publishing Co, 350 Fifth Ave, 59th fl, PMB 59051, New York, NY 10118 *Tel:* 212-496-5040 *Toll Free Tel:* 800-387-7650 *Toll Free Fax:* 800-355-7166 *E-mail:* custserv@crabtreebooks.com *Web Site:* www.crabtreebooks.com, pg 63

Kalman, Bobbie, Crabtree Publishing Co Ltd, 616 Welland Ave, St Catharines, ON L2M 5V6, Canada *Tel:* 905-682-5221 *Toll Free Tel:* 800-387-7650 *Fax:* 905-682-7166 *Toll Free Fax:* 800-355-7166 *E-mail:* custserv@crabtreebooks.com; sales@crabtreebooks.com; orders@crabtreebooks.com *Web Site:* www.crabtreebooks.com, pg 451

Kalman, Jason, Hebrew Union College Press, 3101 Clifton Ave, Cincinnati, OH 45220 *Tel:* 513-221-1875 *Fax:* 513-221-0321 *Web Site:* press.huc.edu, pg 105

Kalogeridis, Carla, Association Media & Publishing (AM&P), 529 14 St, Suite 750, Washington, DC 20045 *Tel:* 202-591-2457 *E-mail:* info@associationmediaandpublishing.org *Web Site:* associationmediaandpublishing.org, pg 558

Kals, Josie, Alfred A Knopf/Everyman's Library, c/o Penguin Random House Inc, 1745 Broadway, New York, NY 10019 *Tel:* 212-751-2600 *Toll Free Tel:* 800-638-6460 *Fax:* 212-572-2593 *Web Site:* www.knopfdoubleday.com, pg 127

Kals, Josie, Pantheon Books/Schocken Books, c/o Penguin Random House Inc, 1745 Broadway, New York, NY 10019 *Tel:* 212-751-2600 *Web Site:* knopfdoubleday.com/imprint/pantheon, pg 173

Kalweit, Burk, American Academy of Environmental Engineers & Scientists™, 147 Old Solomons Island Rd, Suite 303, Annapolis, MD 21401 *Tel:* 410-266-3311 *Fax:* 410-266-7653 *E-mail:* info@aaees.org *Web Site:* www.aaees.org, pg 9

Kamil, Susan, Random House Publishing Group, 1745 Broadway, New York, NY 10019 *Toll Free Tel:* 800-200-3552 *Web Site:* atrandom.com, pg 195

Kamoroff, Bernard, Bell Springs Publishing, PO Box 1240, Willits, CA 95490-1240 *Tel:* 707-272-3472 *E-mail:* publisher@bellsprings.com *Web Site:* bellsprings.com; aboutpinball.com, pg 32

Kanagy, Dave, Society for Mining, Metallurgy & Exploration, 12999 E Adam Aircraft Circle, Englewood, CO 80112 *Tel:* 303-948-4200 *Toll Free Tel:* 800-763-3132 *Fax:* 303-973-3845 *E-mail:* cs@smenet.org; books@smenet.org *Web Site:* www.smenet.org, pg 216

Kane, Joanne E, Kane Press Inc, 225 E 46 St, Suite 4D, New York, NY 10017-2924 *Tel:* 212-935-0246 *Web Site:* www.kanepress.com, pg 124

Kane, Roberta, The Write Way, 3048 Horizon Lane, Suite 1102, Naples, FL 34109 *Tel:* 239-273-9145 *E-mail:* darekane@gmail.com, pg 503

Kane, Sonia, Boydell & Brewer Inc, 668 Mount Hope Ave, Rochester, NY 14620-2731 *Tel:* 585-275-0419 *Fax:* 585-271-8778 *E-mail:* boydell@boydellusa.net *Web Site:* www.boydellandbrewer.com, pg 41

Kane, Sonia, University of Rochester Press, 668 Mount Hope Ave, Rochester, NY 14620-2731 *Tel:* 585-275-0419 *Fax:* 585-271-8778 *E-mail:* boydell@boydellusa.net *Web Site:* www.urpress.com, pg 245

Kane, Tracey, Liguori Publications, One Liguori Dr, Liguori, MO 63057-1000 *Tel:* 636-464-2500 *Toll Free Tel:* 866-848-2492; 800-325-9521 *Fax:* 636-464-8449 *Toll Free Fax:* 800-325-9526 (sales) *E-mail:* liguori@liguori.org (sales & cust serv) *Web Site:* www.liguori.org/contact-us.html, pg 134

Kanellos, Nicolas, Arte Publico Press, University of Houston, Bldg 19, Rm 100, 4902 Gulf Fwy, Houston, TX 77204-2004 *Tel:* 713-743-2998 (sales) *Toll Free Tel:* 800-633-2783 *Fax:* 713-743-2847 (sales) *E-mail:* appinfo@uh.edu; bkorders@uh.edu *Web Site:* artepublicopress.com, pg 21

Kaneski, Sean, Business Expert Press, 222 E 46 St, New York, NY 10017-2906 *Tel:* 630-207-5927 *E-mail:* charlene.kronstadt@businessexpertpress.com *Web Site:* www.businessexpertpress.com, pg 45

Kantola, Andrew, PennWell Books, 1421 S Sheridan Rd, Tulsa, OK 74112 *Tel:* 918-831-9421 *Toll Free Tel:* 800-752-9764 *Fax:* 918-831-9555 *Toll Free Fax:* 877-218-1348 *E-mail:* sales@pennwell.com *Web Site:* www.pennwellbooks.com, pg 179

Kantor, Emma, The Children's Book Council (CBC), 54 W 39 St, 14th fl, New York, NY 10018 *Tel:* 212-966-1990 *E-mail:* cbc.info@cbcbooks.org *Web Site:* www.cbcbooks.org, pg 563

Kanya-Forstner, Martha, Doubleday Canada, 320 Front St W, Suite 1400, Toronto, ON M5V 3B6, Canada *Tel:* 416-364-4449 *Fax:* 416-598-7764 *Web Site:* www.penguinrandomhouse.ca, pg 452

Kanya-Forstner, Martha, McClelland & Stewart Ltd, 320 Front St W, Suite 1400, Toronto, ON M5V 3B6, Canada *Tel:* 416-364-4449 *Fax:* 416-598-7764 *E-mail:* customerservicescanada@penguinrandomhouse.com; publicity@ca.penguingroup.com *Web Site:* penguinrandomhouse.ca/imprints/mcclelland-stewart, pg 463

Kapanyko, Chrystal, Printing Industries of America, 301 Brush Creek Rd, Warrendale, PA 15086-7529 *Tel:* 412-741-6860 *Toll Free Tel:* 800-910-4283 *Fax:* 412-741-2311 *E-mail:* printingind@comm.printing.org *Web Site:* www.printing.org, pg 576

Kaplan, Deborah, Puffin Books, 345 Hudson St, New York, NY 10014 *Tel:* 212-366-2000 *Web Site:* www.penguin.com/publishers/puffin, pg 191

Kaplan, Genevieve, Kate Tufts Discovery Award, Harper East, Unit B-7, 160 E Tenth St, Claremont, CA 91711-6165 *Tel:* 909-621-8974 *E-mail:* tufts@cgu.edu *Web Site:* www.cgu.edu/tufts, pg 695

Kaplan, Genevieve, Kingsley Tufts Poetry Award, Harper East, Unit B-7, 160 E Tenth St, Claremont, CA 91711-6165 *Tel:* 909-621-8974 *E-mail:* tufts@cgu.edu *Web Site:* www.cgu.edu/tufts, pg 695

Kaplan, Howard, Silver Gavel Awards, 321 N Clark St, Chicago, IL 60654 *Tel:* 312-988-5719 *Toll Free Tel:* 800-285-2221 (orders) *Fax:* 312-988-5494 *Web Site:* www.ambar.org/gavelawards, pg 689

Kaplan, Joyce, Kensington Publishing Corp, 119 W 40 St, New York, NY 10018 *Tel:* 212-407-1500 *Toll Free Tel:* 800-221-2647 *Fax:* 212-935-0699 *Web Site:* www.kensingtonbooks.com, pg 125

Kaplan, Laura, HarperCollins Children's Books, 195 Broadway, New York, NY 10007 *Tel:* 212-207-7000 *Web Site:* www.harpercollins.com/childrens, pg 101

Kaplan, Lawrence D, Alaska Native Language Center, PO Box 757680, Fairbanks, AK 99775-7680 *Fax:* 907-474-6586 *E-mail:* uaf-anlc@alaska.edu (orders) *Web Site:* www.uaf.edu/anlc, pg 6

Kaplan, Linda, DeFiore and Company Literary Management Inc, 47 E 19 St, 3rd fl, New York, NY 10003 *Tel:* 212-925-7744 *Fax:* 212-925-9803 *E-mail:* info@defliterary.com; submissions@defliterary.com *Web Site:* www.defliterary.com, pg 513

Kaplan, Rebecca, Harry N Abrams Inc, 195 Broadway, 9th fl, New York, NY 10007 *Tel:* 212-206-7715 *Toll Free Tel:* 800-345-1359 *Fax:* 212-519-1210 *E-mail:* abrams@abramsbooks.com *Web Site:* www.abramsbooks.com, pg 3

Kaplan, Rob, The Editors Circle, 462 Grove St, Montclair, NJ 07043 *Tel:* 862-596-9709 *E-mail:* query@theeditorscircle.com *Web Site:* www.theeditorscircle.com, pg 493

Kaplan, Stuart R, US Games Systems Inc, 179 Ludlow St, Stamford, CT 06902 *Tel:* 203-353-8400 *Toll Free Tel:* 800-54-GAMES (544-2637) *Fax:* 203-353-8431 *E-mail:* info@usgamesinc.com *Web Site:* www.usgamesinc.com, pg 249

Kaplow, Margaret, National Catholic Educational Association, 1005 N Glebe Rd, Suite 525, Arlington, VA 22201 *Tel:* 571-257-0010 *Toll Free Tel:* 800-711-6232 *Fax:* 703-243-0025 *E-mail:* nceaadmin@ncea.org *Web Site:* www.ncea.org, pg 157

Kapoor, Prashant, Aptara Inc, 3110 Fairview Park Dr, Suite 900, Falls Church, VA 22042 *Tel:* 703-352-0001 *E-mail:* moreinfo@aptaracorp.com *Web Site:* www.aptaracorp.com, pg 488

Karagueuzian, Dikran, CSLI Publications, Stanford University, Cordura Hall, 220 Panama St, Stanford, CA 94305-4115 *Tel:* 650-723-1839 *Fax:* 650-725-2166 *E-mail:* pubs@csli.stanford.edu *Web Site:* cslipublications.stanford.edu, pg 66

Karalis, Vanessa, Workman Publishing Co Inc, 225 Varick St, 9th fl, New York, NY 10014-4381 *Tel:* 212-254-5900 *Toll Free Tel:* 800-722-7202 *Fax:* 212-254-8098 *E-mail:* info@workman.com *Web Site:* www.workman.com, pg 259

Karchmar, Dorian, WME, 11 Madison Ave, 18th fl, New York, NY 10010 *Tel:* 212-586-5100 *Web Site:* www.wmeentertainment.com, pg 542

Kardon, Julia, Mary Evans Inc, 242 E Fifth St, New York, NY 10003-8501 *Tel:* 212-979-0880 *Fax:* 212-979-5344 *E-mail:* info@maryevansinc.com *Web Site:* www.maryevansinc.com, pg 516

Kardys, Jan L, Unicorn Writers' Conference, 17 Church Hill Rd, Redding, CT 06896 *Tel:* 203-938-7405 *Fax:* 203-938-7405 *E-mail:* unicornwritersconference@gmail.com *Web Site:* unicornwritersconference.com, pg 615

Karl, Laraine, The Rockefeller University Press, 950 Third Ave, 2nd fl, New York, NY 10022 *Tel:* 212-327-7938 *Fax:* 212-319-1081 *E-mail:* rupress@rockefeller.edu *Web Site:* www.rupress.org, pg 200

Karle, John, St Martin's Press, LLC, 175 Fifth Ave, New York, NY 10010 *Tel:* 646-307-5151 *Web Site:* us.macmillan.com/smp, pg 204

Karp, Jonathan, Simon & Schuster, 1230 Avenue of the Americas, New York, NY 10020 *Tel:* 212-698-7000 *Toll Free Tel:* 800-223-2348 (cust serv); 800-223-2336 (orders) *Toll Free Fax:* 800-943-9831 (orders) *Web Site:* www.simonandschuster.com, pg 212

Karp, Jonathan, Simon & Schuster, Inc, 1230 Avenue of the Americas, New York, NY 10020 *Tel:* 212-698-7000 *Fax:* 212-698-7007 *E-mail:* firstname.lastname@simonandschuster.com *Web Site:* www.simonandschuster.com, pg 213

Karpas, Heather, ICM Partners, 65 E 55 St, New York, NY 10022 *Tel:* 212-556-5600 *Web Site:* www.icmtalent.com, pg 521

Karper, Altie, Pantheon Books/Schocken Books, c/o Penguin Random House Inc, 1745 Broadway, New York, NY 10019 *Tel:* 212-751-2600 *Web Site:* knopfdoubleday.com/imprint/pantheon, pg 173

Karpfinger, Barney M, The Karpfinger Agency, 357 W 20 St, New York, NY 10011-3379 *Tel:* 212-691-2690 *Fax:* 212-691-7129 *E-mail:* info@karpfinger.com (no queries or submissions) *Web Site:* karpfinger.com, pg 523

Karre, Andrew, Dutton Children's Books, 345 Hudson St, New York, NY 10014 *Tel:* 212-366-2000 *Web Site:* www.penguin.com, pg 74

Kartsev, Dr Vladimir, Metropolitan Classics, 26 Arthur Place, Yonkers, NY 10701 *Tel:* 914-375-6448 *Web Site:* www.fortrossinc.com, pg 149

Kartsev, Dr Vladimir P, Fort Ross Inc - International Representation for Artists, 26 Arthur Place, Yonkers, NY 10701 *Tel:* 914-375-6448 *Web Site:* www.fortrossinc.com, pg 517

Kartsev, Dr Vladimir P, Fort Ross Inc - International Representation for Artists, 26 Arthur Place, Yonkers, NY 10701 *Tel:* 914-375-6448; 718-775-8340 *Web Site:* www.fortrossinc.com, pg 543

Kartz, Ellen, R Ross Annett Award for Children's Literature, 11759 Groat Rd, Edmonton, AB T5M 3K6, Canada *Tel:* 780-422-8174 *Toll Free Tel:* 800-665-5354 (AB only) *Fax:* 780-422-2663 (attn WGA) *E-mail:* mail@writersguild.ca *Web Site:* writersguild.ca, pg 627

Kartz, Ellen, Georges Bugnet Award for Fiction, 11759 Groat Rd, Edmonton, AB T5M 3K6, Canada *Tel:* 780-422-8174 *Toll Free Tel:* 800-665-5354 (AB only) *Fax:* 780-422-2663 (attn WGA) *E-mail:* mail@writersguild.ca *Web Site:* writersguild.ca, pg 634

Kartz, Ellen, The City of Calgary W O Mitchell Book Prize, 11759 Groat Rd, Edmonton, AB T5M 3K6, Canada *Tel:* 780-422-8174 *Toll Free Tel:* 800-665-5354 (AB only) *Fax:* 780-422-2663 (attn WGA) *E-mail:* mail@writersguild.ca *Web Site:* writersguild.ca, pg 637

Kartz, Ellen, Wilfrid Eggleston Award for Nonfiction, 11759 Groat Rd, Edmonton, AB T5M 3K6, Canada *Tel:* 780-422-8174 *Toll Free Tel:* 800-665-5354 (AB only) *Fax:* 780-422-2663 (attn WGA) *E-mail:* mail@writersguild.ca *Web Site:* writersguild.ca, pg 644

Kartz, Ellen, James H Gray Award for Short Nonfiction, 11759 Groat Rd, Edmonton, AB T5M 3K6, Canada *Tel:* 780-422-8174 *Toll Free Tel:* 800-665-5354 (AB only) *Fax:* 780-422-2663 (attn WGA) *E-mail:* mail@writersguild.ca *Web Site:* writersguild.ca, pg 650

Kartz, Ellen, The Robert Kroetsch City of Edmonton Book Prize, 11759 Groat Rd, Edmonton, AB T5M 3K6, Canada *Tel:* 780-422-8174 *Toll Free Tel:* 800-665-5354 (AB only) *Fax:* 780-422-2663 (attn WGA) *E-mail:* mail@writersguild.ca *Web Site:* writersguild.ca, pg 659

Kartz, Ellen, Howard O'Hagan Award for Short Story, 11759 Groat Rd, Edmonton, AB T5M 3K6, Canada *Tel:* 780-422-8174 *Toll Free Tel:* 800-665-5354 (AB only) *Fax:* 780-422-2663 (attn WGA) *E-mail:* mail@writersguild.ca *Web Site:* writersguild.ca, pg 675

Kartz, Ellen, Gwen Pharis Ringwood Award for Drama, 11759 Groat Rd, Edmonton, AB T5M 3K6, Canada *Tel:* 780-422-8174 *Toll Free Tel:* 800-665-5354 (AB only) *Fax:* 780-422-2663 (attn WGA) *E-mail:* mail@writersguild.ca *Web Site:* writersguild.ca, pg 685

Kartz, Ellen, Stephan G Stephansson Award for Poetry, 11759 Groat Rd, Edmonton, AB T5M 3K6, Canada *Tel:* 780-422-8174 *Toll Free Tel:* 800-665-5354 (AB only) *Fax:* 780-422-2663 (attn WGA) *E-mail:* mail@writersguild.ca *Web Site:* writersguild.ca, pg 692

Kartz, Ellen, Jon Whyte Memorial Essay Prize, 11759 Groat Rd, Edmonton, AB T5M 3K6, Canada *Tel:* 780-422-8174 *Toll Free Tel:* 800-665-5354 (AB only) *Fax:* 780-422-2663 (attn WGA) *E-mail:* mail@writersguild.ca *Web Site:* writersguild.ca, pg 697

Kartz, Ellen, Writers' Guild of Alberta, 11759 Groat Rd, Edmonton, AB T5M 3K6, Canada *Tel:* 780-422-8174 *Toll Free Tel:* 800-665-5354 (AB only) *Fax:* 780-422-2663 (attn WGA) *E-mail:* mail@writersguild.ca *Web Site:* writersguild.ca, pg 581

Kasdorf, Helga, Kindred Productions, 1310 Taylor Ave, Winnipeg, MB R3M 3Z6, Canada *Tel:* 204-669-6575 *Toll Free Tel:* 800-545-7322 *Fax:* 204-654-1865 *E-mail:* kindred@mbchurches.ca *Web Site:* www.kindredproductions.com, pg 461

Kase, Josef, Letterbox/Papyrus of London Publishers USA, 10501 Broom Hill Dr, Suite 1-F, Las Vegas, NV 89134-7339 *Tel:* 702-256-3838 *E-mail:* lb27383@cox.net, pg 132

Kaser, Richard T, Information Today, Inc, 143 Old Marlton Pike, Medford, NJ 08055-8750 *Tel:* 609-654-6266 *Toll Free Tel:* 800-300-9868 (cust serv) *Fax:* 609-654-4309 *E-mail:* custserv@infotoday.com *Web Site:* www.infotoday.com, pg 116

Kasius, Jennifer, Perseus Books, 250 W 57 St, 15th fl, New York, NY 10107 *Tel:* 212-340-8100 *Toll Free Tel:* 800-343-4499 (cust serv) *Fax:* 212-340-8105 *Web Site:* www.perseusbooks.com, pg 181

Kasper, Karl, Crabtree Publishing Co, 350 Fifth Ave, 59th fl, PMB 59051, New York, NY 10118 *Tel:* 212-496-5040 *Toll Free Tel:* 800-387-7650 *Toll Free Fax:* 800-355-7166 *E-mail:* custserv@crabtreebooks.com *Web Site:* www.crabtreebooks.com, pg 63

Kasper, Karl, Crabtree Publishing Co Ltd, 616 Welland Ave, St Catharines, ON L2M 5V6, Canada *Tel:* 905-682-5221 *Toll Free Tel:* 800-387-7650 *Fax:* 905-682-7166 *Toll Free Fax:* 800-355-7166 *E-mail:* custserv@crabtreebooks.com; sales@crabtreebooks.com; orders@crabtreebooks.com *Web Site:* www.crabtreebooks.com, pg 451

Kass, Gary, University of Missouri Press, 113 Heinkel Bldg, 201 S Seventh St, Columbia, MO 65211 *Tel:* 573-882-7641 *Toll Free Tel:* 800-621-2736 (orders) *Fax:* 573-884-4498 *Toll Free Fax:* 800-621-8476 (orders) *E-mail:* upress@missouri.edu *Web Site:* upress.missouri.edu; press.umsystem.edu, pg 243

Kassahun, Senait, Red Sea Press Inc, 541 W Ingham Ave, Suite B, Trenton, NJ 08638 *Tel:* 609-695-3200 *Fax:* 609-695-6466 *E-mail:* customerservice@africaworldpressbooks.com *Web Site:* www.africaworldpressbooks.com, pg 197

Kastely, Jay, University of Houston Creative Writing Program, 229 Roy Cullen Bldg, Houston, TX 77204-5008 *Tel:* 713-743-2255 *Fax:* 713-743-3697 *E-mail:* cwp@uh.edu *Web Site:* www.uh.edu/cwp, pg 623

Kastenmeier, Edward, Anchor Books, c/o Penguin Random House Inc, 1745 Broadway, New York, NY 10019 *Tel:* 212-572-2420 *E-mail:* vintageanchorpublicity@randomhouse.com *Web Site:* knopfdoubleday.com/imprint/anchor, pg 16

Kastenmeier, Edward, Vintage Books, c/o Penguin Random House Inc, 1745 Broadway, New York, NY 10019 *Tel:* 212-572-2420 *E-mail:* vintageanchorpublicity@randomhouse.com *Web Site:* knopfdoubleday.com/imprint/vintage, pg 251

Kastner, Suzanne, Graphic World Publishing Services, 11687 Adie Rd, St Louis, MO 63043 *Tel:* 314-567-9854 *Fax:* 314-567-7178 *E-mail:* quote@gwinc.com *Web Site:* www.gwinc.com, pg 495

Kasuga, Mika, Random House Publishing Group, 1745 Broadway, New York, NY 10019 *Toll Free Tel:* 800-200-3552 *Web Site:* atrandom.com, pg 195

Kater, Julia, The Association of English-Language Publishers of Quebec-AELAQ (Association des Editeurs de Langue Anglaise du Quebec), Atwater Library, 1200 Atwater Ave, Suite 3, Westmount, QC H3Z 1X4, Canada *Tel:* 514-932-5633 *E-mail:* admin@aelaq.org *Web Site:* aelaq.org, pg 559

Katz, David, Cascade Pass Inc, 4223 Glencoe Ave, Suite C-105, Marina del Rey, CA 90292-8801 *Tel:* 310-305-0210 *Toll Free Tel:* 888-837-0704 *Fax:* 310-305-7850 *Web Site:* www.cascadepass.com, pg 49

Katz, Deanne, Chronicle Books LLC, 680 Second St, San Francisco, CA 94107 *Tel:* 415-537-4200 *Toll Free Tel:* 800-759-0190 (cust serv) *Fax:* 415-537-4460 *Toll Free Fax:* 800-858-7787 (orders); 800-286-9471 (cust serv) *E-mail:* frontdesk@chroniclebooks.com *Web Site:* www.chroniclebooks.com, pg 55

Katz, Laurie, Chelsea House Publishers, 132 W 31 St, 17th fl, New York, NY 10001 *Tel:* 212-967-8800 *Toll Free Tel:* 800-322-8755 *Fax:* 917-339-0325 *Toll Free Fax:* 800-678-3633 *E-mail:* custserv@factsonfile.com *Web Site:* www.infobasepublishing.com; www.infobaselearning.com, pg 53

Katz, Laurie, Facts On File, 132 W 31 St, 17th fl, New York, NY 10001 *Tel:* 212-967-8800 *Toll Free Tel:* 800-322-8755 *Toll Free Fax:* 800-678-3633 *E-mail:* custserv@factsonfile.com *Web Site:* infobasepublishing.com, pg 81

Katz, Laurie, Ferguson Publishing, 132 W 31 St, 17th fl, New York, NY 10001 *Tel:* 212-967-8800 *Toll Free Tel:* 800-322-8755 *Fax:* 917-339-0323 *Toll Free Fax:* 800-678-3633 *E-mail:* custserv@factsonfile.com *Web Site:* infobasepublishing.com, pg 84

Katz, Michael, Tradewind Books, 202-1807 Maritime Mews, Vancouver, BC V6H 3W7, Canada *Tel:* 604-662-4405 *E-mail:* tradewindbooks@yahoo.com; tradewindbooks@gmail.com *Web Site:* www.tradewindbooks.com, pg 472

Katzenberger, Elaine, City Lights Publishers, 261 Columbus Ave, San Francisco, CA 94133 *Tel:* 415-362-8193 *Fax:* 415-362-4921 *E-mail:* staff@citylights.com *Web Site:* www.citylights.com, pg 56

Katzman, Julie T, Inter-American Development Bank, 1300 New York Ave NW, Washington, DC 20577 *Tel:* 202-623-1000 *Fax:* 202-623-3096 *E-mail:* pic@iadb.org *Web Site:* www.iadb.org/pub, pg 118

Katzman, Ken, Dover Publications Inc, 31 E Second St, Mineola, NY 11501-3852 *Tel:* 516-294-7000 *Toll Free Tel:* 800-223-3130 (orders) *Fax:* 516-742-6953 *E-mail:* rights@doverpublications.com; service@doverpublications.com *Web Site:* store.doverdirect.com; www.doverpublications.com, pg 72

Kauffman, Lisa, Rational Island Publishers, 719 Second Ave N, Seattle, WA 98109 *Tel:* 206-284-0311 *Fax:* 206-284-8429 *E-mail:* ircc@rc.org *Web Site:* www.rc.org, pg 195

Kaufman, Andrew, Wayne State University Press, Leonard N Simons Bldg, 4809 Woodward Ave, Detroit, MI 48201-1309 *Tel:* 313-577-6120 *Toll Free Tel:* 800-978-7323 *Fax:* 313-577-6131 *E-mail:* bookorders@wayne.edu *Web Site:* www.wsupress.wayne.edu, pg 253

Kaufman, Brian, Anvil Press Publishers, 278 E First Ave, Vancouver, BC V5T 1A6, Canada *Tel:* 604-876-8710 *Fax:* 604-879-2667 *E-mail:* info@anvilpress.com *Web Site:* www.anvilpress.com, pg 445

Kaufman, Gabe, Jump!, 5357 Penn Ave, Minneapolis, MN 55419 *Toll Free Tel:* 888-799-1860 *Toll Free Fax:* 800-675-6679 *E-mail:* customercare@jumplibrary.com *Web Site:* www.jumplibrary.com, pg 123

Kaufman, Jason, Doubleday/Nan A Talese, c/o Penguin Random House Inc, 1745 Broadway, New York, NY 10019 *Tel:* 212-751-2600 *Fax:* 212-572-2662 *E-mail:* ddaypub@randomhouse.com *Web Site:* knopfdoubleday.com, pg 72

Kaufman, Shari, innovativeKids®, 50 Washington St, Suite 201, Norwalk, CT 06854 *Tel:* 203-838-6400 *E-mail:* info@innovativekids.com *Web Site:* www.innovativekids.com, pg 117

Kaufmann, Anne, FC&A Publishing, 103 Clover Green, Peachtree City, GA 30269 *Tel:* 770-487-6307 *Toll Free Tel:* 800-226-8024 *Fax:* 770-631-4357 *E-mail:* customer_service@fca.com *Web Site:* www.fca.com, pg 83

Kaufmann, Anthony S, Abaris Books, 70 New Canaan Ave, Norwalk, CT 06850 *Tel:* 203-838-8402 *Fax:* 203-857-0730 *E-mail:* abaris@abarisbooks.com *Web Site:* abarisbooks.com, pg 2

Kaufmann, Anthony S, EastBridge, 70 New Canaan Ave, Norwalk, CT 06850 *Tel:* 203-855-9125 *Fax:* 203-857-0730 *E-mail:* asia@eastbridgebooks.org; ask@eastbridgebooks.org *Web Site:* www.eastbridgebooks.org, pg 74

Kaune, Ryan, Autumn House Press, 5530 Penn Ave, Pittsburgh, PA 15206 *Tel:* 412-362-2665 *E-mail:* info@autumnhouse.org *Web Site:* www.autumnhouse.org, pg 26

Kavaler, Ethan Matt, Centre for Reformation & Renaissance Studies (CRRS), 71 Queen's Park Crescent E, Toronto, ON M5S 1K7, Canada *Tel:* 416-585-4465 *Fax:* 416-585-4430 (attn: CRRS) *E-mail:* crrs.publications@utoronto.ca *Web Site:* crrs.ca, pg 450

Kavonic, Melissa, Bloomsbury Publishing Inc, 1385 Broadway, 5th fl, New York, NY 10018 *Tel:* 212-419-5300 *E-mail:* marketingusa@bloomsbury.com; adultpublicityusa@bloomsbury.com; askacademic@bloomsbury.com *Web Site:* www.bloomsbury.com, pg 38

Kawai, Colins, University of Hawaii Press, 2840 Kolowalu St, Honolulu, HI 96822 *Tel:* 808-956-8255 *Toll Free Tel:* 888-UHPRESS (847-7377) *Fax:* 808-988-6052 *Toll Free Fax:* 800-650-7811 *E-mail:* uhpbooks@hawaii.edu *Web Site:* www.uhpress.hawaii.edu, pg 241

Kay, Jeremy, Bartleby Press, 8926 Baltimore St, No 858, Savage, MD 20763 *Tel:* 301-589-5831 *Toll Free Tel:* 800-953-9929 *E-mail:* inquiries@bartlebythepublisher.com *Web Site:* www.bartlebythepublisher.com, pg 30

Kay, Jeremy, Schreiber Publishing, PO Box 4193, Rockville, MD 20849 *Tel:* 301-589-5831 *Toll Free Tel:* 800-296-1961 (sales) *Fax:* 667-309-6993 *E-mail:* publisher@schreiberpublishing.net *Web Site:* schreiberlanguage.com; shengold.com, pg 209

Kaye, David, Anna Zornio Memorial Children's Theatre Playwriting Award, D22 Paul Creative Arts Center, 30 Academic Way, Durham, NH 03824 *Tel:* 603-862-2919 *Fax:* 603-862-0298 *Web Site:* cola.unh.edu/theatre-dance/resource/zornio, pg 701

Kaye, Terry, Behrman House Inc, 11 Edison Place, Springfield, NJ 07081 *Tel:* 973-379-7200 *Toll Free Tel:* 800-221-2755 *Fax:* 973-379-7280 *E-mail:* customersupport@behrmanhouse.com *Web Site:* www.behrmanhouse.com, pg 32

Kayser, Jason, Perseus Books, 250 W 57 St, 15th fl, New York, NY 10107 *Tel:* 212-340-8100 *Toll Free Tel:* 800-343-4499 (cust serv) *Fax:* 212-340-8105 *Web Site:* www.perseusbooks.com, pg 181

Kean, Carla, Seal Books, 320 Front St W, Suite 1400, Toronto, ON M5V 3B6, Canada *Tel:* 416-364-4449 *Toll Free Tel:* 888-523-9292 (order desk) *Fax:* 416-598-7764 *Web Site:* www.penguinrandomhouse.ca, pg 470

Kean, Linda Griffin, International Monetary Fund (IMF), Editorial & Publications Division, 700 19 St NW, HQ1-7-124, Washington, DC 20431 *Tel:* 202-623-7430 *Fax:* 202-623-7201 *E-mail:* publications@imf.org *Web Site:* bookstore.imf.org; elibrary.imf.org (online collection), pg 120

Keane, Christopher, American Geosciences Institute (AGI), 4220 King St, Alexandria, VA 22302-1502 *Tel:* 703-379-2480 (ext 246) *Fax:* 703-379-7563 *E-mail:* pubs@agiweb.org *Web Site:* www.agiweb.org, pg 12

Keating, Celine, Women's National Book Association Award, PO Box 237, FDR Sta, New York, NY 10150-0231 *Tel:* 212-208-4629 (headquarters) *Toll Free Tel:* 866-610-9622 *Fax:* 212-208-4629 *Web Site:* www.wnba-books.org; www.NationalReadingGroupMonth.org, pg 699

Keating, Kate, Random House Children's Books, 1745 Broadway, 10th fl, New York, NY 10019 *Tel:* 212-782-9000 *Web Site:* www.randomhousekids.com, pg 194

Kecskemethy, Tom, American Academy of Political & Social Science, 202 S 36 St, Philadelphia, PA 19104-3806 *Tel:* 215-746-6500 *Fax:* 215-573-2667 *Web Site:* www.aapss.org, pg 554

Keefe, Deanna M, Liturgy Training Publications, 3949 S Racine Ave, Chicago, IL 60609-2523 *Tel:* 773-579-4900 *Toll Free Tel:* 800-933-1800 (US & CN only orders) *Fax:* 773-579-4929 *Toll Free Fax:* 800-933-7094 (US & CN only orders) *E-mail:* orders@ltp.org *Web Site:* www.ltp.org, pg 136

Keefe, Laura, Bloomsbury Publishing Inc, 1385 Broadway, 5th fl, New York, NY 10018 *Tel:* 212-419-5300 *E-mail:* marketingusa@bloomsbury.com; adultpublicityusa@bloomsbury.com; askacademic@bloomsbury.com *Web Site:* www.bloomsbury.com, pg 38

Keegan, Kenneth, Omnidawn Publishing, 1632 Elm Ave, Richmond, CA 94805-1614 *Tel:* 510-237-5472 *Toll Free Tel:* 800-792-4957 *Fax:* 510-232-8525 *E-mail:* manager@omnidawn.com *Web Site:* www.omnidawn.com, pg 168

Keegan, Tom, Athletic Guide Publishing, PO Box 1050, Flagler Beach, FL 32136 *Tel:* 386-439-2050 *Toll Free Tel.* 800-255-1050 *E-mail:* flaglernet@gmail.com *Web Site:* www.athleticguidepublishing.com, pg 25

Keeler, Rev Roger H, Canon Law Society of America, Hecker Ctr, Suite 111, 3025 Fourth St NE, Washington, DC 20017-1102 *Tel:* 202-832-2350 *Fax:* 202-832-2331 *E-mail:* coordinator@clsa.org; info@clsa.org *Web Site:* www.clsa.org, pg 47

Keenan, William P Jr, Editorial Freelancers Association (EFA), 71 W 23 St, 4th fl, New York, NY 10010-4102 *Tel:* 212-929-5400 *Toll Free Tel:* 866-929-5425 *Fax:* 212-929-5439 *Toll Free Fax:* 866-929-5439 *E-mail:* office@the-efa.org *Web Site:* www.the-efa.org, pg 564

Keene, Ann T, Edit Etc, 26 Country Lane, Brunswick, ME 04011 *Tel:* 914-715-5849 *E-mail:* atkedit@cs.com *Web Site:* www.anntkeene.com, pg 493

Keene, Elizabeth, Thames & Hudson, 500 Fifth Ave, New York, NY 10110 *Tel:* 212-354-3763 *Toll Free Tel:* 800-233-4830 *Fax:* 212-398-1252 *E-mail:* bookinfo@thames.wwnorton.com *Web Site:* www.thamesandhudsonusa.com, pg 230

Keene, James A, Glenbridge Publishing Ltd, 19923 E Long Ave, Centennial, CO 80016-1969 *Tel:* 720-870-8381 *Toll Free Tel:* 800-986-4135 (orders) *Fax:* 720-230-1209 *E-mail:* glenbridge10@gmail.com *Web Site:* www.glenbridgepublishing.com, pg 93

Keene, Katie, University Press of Mississippi, 3825 Ridgewood Rd, Jackson, MS 39211-6492 *Tel:* 601-432-6205 *Toll Free Tel:* 800-737-7788 (orders & cust serv) *Fax:* 601-432-6217 *E-mail:* press@mississippi.edu *Web Site:* www.upress.state.ms.us, pg 247

Keene, Kristyn, ICM Partners, 65 E 55 St, New York, NY 10022 *Tel:* 212-556-5600 *Web Site:* www.icmtalent.com, pg 521

Keene, Mary B, Glenbridge Publishing Ltd, 19923 E Long Ave, Centennial, CO 80016-1969 *Tel:* 720-870-8381 *Toll Free Tel:* 800-986-4135 (orders) *Fax:* 720-230-1209 *E-mail:* glenbridge10@gmail.com *Web Site:* www.glenbridgepublishing.com, pg 93

Keener, Lamar, Evangelical Press Association (EPA), PO Box 1787, Queen Creek, AZ 85142 *Toll Free Tel:* 888-311-1731 *E-mail:* info@evangelicalpress.com *Web Site:* www.evangelicalpress.com, pg 565

Keesler, Darin, Picador, 175 Fifth Ave, 19th fl, New York, NY 10010 *Tel:* 646-307-5151 *Fax:* 212-253-9627 *Web Site:* www.picadorusa.com, pg 182

Kehoe, Bret, Sourcebooks Inc, 1935 Brookdale Rd, Suite 139, Naperville, IL 60563 *Tel:* 630-961-3900 *Toll Free Tel:* 800-432-7444 *Fax:* 630-961-2168 *E-mail:* info@sourcebooks.com; customersupport@sourcebooks.com *Web Site:* www.sourcebooks.com, pg 218

Kehoe, Jeff, Harvard Business Review Press, 300 N Beacon St, Watertown, MA 02472 *Tel:* 617-783-7400 *Fax:* 617-783-7489 *E-mail:* custserv@hbsp.harvard.edu *Web Site:* www.harvardbusiness.org, pg 102

Kehoe, Mike, University Press of Kansas, 2502 Westbrooke Circle, Lawrence, KS 66045-4444 *Tel:* 785-864-4154; 785-864-4155 (orders) *Fax:* 785-864-4586 *E-mail:* upress@ku.edu; upkorders@ku.edu (orders) *Web Site:* www.kansaspress.ku.edu, pg 247

Keil, Miriam, Chronicle Books LLC, 680 Second St, San Francisco, CA 94107 *Tel:* 415-537-4200 *Toll Free Tel:* 800-759-0190 (cust serv) *Fax:* 415-537-4460 *Toll Free Fax:* 800-858-7787 (orders); 800-286-9471 (cust serv) *E-mail:* frontdesk@chroniclebooks.com *Web Site:* www.chroniclebooks.com, pg 55

Keim, Betty, Keim Publishing, 66 Main St, Suite 807, Yonkers, NY 10701 *Tel:* 917-655-7190, pg 496

Keim, Lisa, Atria Books, 1230 Avenue of the Americas, New York, NY 10020 *Tel:* 212-698-7000 *Fax:* 212-698-7007 *Web Site:* www.simonandschuster.com, pg 25

Keim, Lisa, Howard Books, c/o Simon & Schuster, Inc, 1230 Avenue of the Americas, New York, NY 10020 *E-mail:* howardbooks@simonandschuster.com (info) *Web Site:* simonandschusterpublishing.com/howard-books/, pg 112

Keiper, Ben, Dramatists Play Service Inc, 440 Park Ave S, New York, NY 10016 *Tel:* 212-683-8960 *Fax:* 212-213-1539 *E-mail:* postmaster@dramatists.com; orders@dramatists.com; publications@dramatists.com *Web Site:* www.dramatists.com, pg 73

Keith, Amanda, Wake Forest University Press, A5 Tribble Hall, Wake Forest University, Winston-Salem, NC 27109 *Tel:* 336-758-5448 *Fax:* 336-758-5636 *E-mail:* wfupress@wfu.edu *Web Site:* wfupress.wfu.edu, pg 251

Kelada, Mike, Aquila Communications Inc, 281 rue Alice-Carriere St, Beaconsville, QC H9W 6E6, Canada *Toll Free Tel:* 800 667-7071 *Fax:* 514-505-4579 *Toll Free Fax:* 866-338-1948 *Web Site:* www.aquilacommunications.com, pg 445

Kelada, Sami, Aquila Communications Inc, 281 rue Alice-Carriere St, Beaconsville, QC H9W 6E6, Canada *Toll Free Tel:* 800-667-7071 *Fax:* 514-505-4579 *Toll Free Fax:* 866-338-1948 *Web Site:* www.aquilacommunications.com, pg 445

Kelleher, Michael, Windham-Campbell Prizes, Beinecke Library, 121 Whitney Ave, Suite 102, New Haven, CT 06510-1242 *Fax:* 203-432-9033 *Web Site:* windhamcampbell.org, pg 698

Kelleher, Roger, American Management Association (AMA), 1601 Broadway, New York, NY 10019 *Tel:* 212-586-8100 *Toll Free Tel:* 877-566-9441 *Fax:* 212-903-8168; 518-891-0368 *E-mail:* customerservice@amanet.org *Web Site:* www.amanet.org, pg 555

Kelleher, TJ, Perseus Books, 250 W 57 St, 15th fl, New York, NY 10107 *Tel:* 212-340-8100 *Toll Free Tel:* 800-343-4499 (cust serv) *Fax:* 212-340-8105 *Web Site:* www.perseusbooks.com, pg 180

Keller, Gary D, Bilingual Press/Editorial Bilingue, Arizona State Univ, Hispanic Research Ctr, Tempe, AZ 85287-2702 *Tel:* 480-965-3867 *Toll Free Tel:* 866-965-3867 *Fax:* 480-965-0315 *E-mail:* brp@asu.edu *Web Site:* www.asu.edu/brp, pg 35

Keller, Holly, University of British Columbia Press, 2029 West Mall, Vancouver, BC V6T 1Z2, Canada *Tel:* 604-822-5959 *Toll Free Tel:* 877-377-9378 *Fax:* 604-822-6083 *Toll Free Fax:* 800-668-0821 *E-mail:* frontdesk@ubcpress.ca *Web Site:* www.ubcpress.ca, pg 473

Keller, Jim, J J Keller & Associates, Inc, 3003 Breezewood Lane, Neenah, WI 54957 *Tel:* 920-722-2848 *Toll Free Tel:* 877-564-2333 *Toll Free Fax:* 800-727-7516 *E-mail:* contactus@jjkeller.com; customerservice@jjkeller.com *Web Site:* www.jjkeller.com, pg 125

Keller, Matthew A, Capstone Publishers™, 1710 Roe Crest Dr, North Mankato, MN 56003 *Toll Free Tel:* 800-747-4992 (cust serv) *Toll Free Fax:* 888-262-0705 *Web Site:* www.capstonepress.com, pg 47

Keller, Michael, Stanford University Press, 425 Broadway St, Redwood City, CA 94063-3126 *Tel:* 650-723-9434 *Fax:* 650-725-3457 *E-mail:* info@www.sup.org; publicity@www.sup.org *Web Site:* www.sup.org, pg 220

Keller, Robert L, J J Keller & Associates, Inc, 3003 Breezewood Lane, Neenah, WI 54957 *Tel:* 920-722-2848 *Toll Free Tel:* 877-564-2333 *Toll Free Fax:* 800-727-7516 *E-mail:* contactus@jjkeller.com; customerservice@jjkeller.com *Web Site:* www.jjkeller.com, pg 125

Keller, Rustin R, J J Keller & Associates, Inc, 3003 Breezewood Lane, Neenah, WI 54957 *Tel:* 920-722-2848 *Toll Free Tel:* 877-564-2333 *Toll Free Fax:* 800-727-7516 *E-mail:* contactus@jjkeller.com; customerservice@jjkeller.com *Web Site:* www.jjkeller.com, pg 125

Keller, Wendy, Keller Media Inc, 578 Washington Blvd, No 745, Marina del Rey, CA 90292 *Toll Free Tel:* 800-278-8706 *E-mail:* query@kellermedia.com *Web Site:* kellermedia.com/query, pg 523

Keller-Krikava, Marne, J J Keller & Associates, Inc, 3003 Breezewood Lane, Neenah, WI 54957 *Tel:* 920-722-2848 *Toll Free Tel:* 877-564-2333 *Toll Free Fax:* 800-727-7516 *E-mail:* contactus@jjkeller.com; customerservice@jjkeller.com *Web Site:* www.jjkeller.com, pg 125

Kelley, Allison, Romance Writers of America®, 14615 Benfer Rd, Houston, TX 77069 *Tel:* 832-717-5200 *Fax:* 832-717-5201 *E-mail:* info@rwa.org *Web Site:* www.rwa.org, pg 577

Kelley, Allison, Romance Writers of America Annual Conference, 14615 Benfer Rd, Houston, TX 77069 *Tel:* 832-717-5200 *Fax:* 832-717-5201 *E-mail:* info@rwa.org *Web Site:* www.rwa.org, pg 614

Kelley, Allison, Romance Writers of America Awards, 14615 Benfer Rd, Houston, TX 77069 *Tel:* 832-717-5200 *Fax:* 832-717-5201 *E-mail:* info@rwa.org *Web Site:* www.rwa.org, pg 685

Kelley, Annie, Random House Children's Books, 1745 Broadway, 10th fl, New York, NY 10019 *Tel:* 212-782-9000 *Web Site:* www.randomhousekids.com, pg 194

Kelley, Bruce, Trusted Media Brands Inc, 750 Third Ave, 3rd fl, New York, NY 10017 *Toll Free Tel:* 800-310-6261 (cust serv) *E-mail:* customercare@tmbi.com *Web Site:* www.tmbi.com; www.rd.com, pg 236

Kelley, Claire, Shambhala Publications Inc, 4720 Walnut St, Boulder, CO 80301 *Tel:* 303-222-9598 *Toll Free Tel:* 866-424-0030 (off); 888-424-2329 (cust serv) *Fax:* 303-200-9406 *E-mail:* customercare@shambhala.com *Web Site:* www.shambhala.com, pg 211

Kelley, Lynn, Kane Miller Books, 4901 Morena Blvd, Suite 213, San Diego, CA 92117 *E-mail:* submissions@kanemiller.com; info@kanemiller.com *Web Site:* www.kanemiller.com, pg 124

Kelley, Mary, James Fenimore Cooper Prize, 2950 Broadway, New York, NY 10027 *Tel:* 212-854-6495 *E-mail:* amhistsociety@columbia.edu *Web Site:* sah.columbia.edu, pg 639

Kelley, Mary, Allan Nevins Prize, 2950 Broadway, New York, NY 10027 *Tel:* 212-854-6495 *E-mail:* amhistsociety@columbia.edu *Web Site:* sah.columbia.edu, pg 672

Kelley, Mary, Francis Parkman Prize, 2950 Broadway, New York, NY 10027 *Tel:* 212-854-6495 *E-mail:* amhistsociety@columbia.edu *Web Site:* sah.columbia.edu, pg 676

Kelley, Pamela, University of Hawaii Press, 2840 Kolowalu St, Honolulu, HI 96822 *Tel:* 808-956-8255 *Toll Free Tel:* 888-UHPRESS (847-7377) *Fax:* 808-988-6052 *Toll Free Fax:* 800-650-7811 *E-mail:* uhpbooks@hawaii.edu *Web Site:* www.uhpress.hawaii.edu, pg 241

Kellman, Steven, Ivan Sandrof Lifetime Achievement Award, 160 Varick St, 11th fl, New York, NY 10013 *E-mail:* info@bookcritics.org *Web Site:* bookcritics.org, pg 686

Kelly, Claire, NeWest Press, 8540 109 St, No 201, Edmonton, AB T6G 1E6, Canada *Tel:* 780-432-9427 *Fax:* 780-433-3179 *E-mail:* info@newestpress.com; orders@newestpress.com *Web Site:* www.newestpress.com, pg 464

Kelly, Frances, Eye in the Ear Children's Audio, 5 Crescent St, Portland, ME 04102 *Toll Free Tel:* 855-99-STORY (997-8679) *Fax:* 207-699-1380 (attn: Laurence Kelly) *E-mail:* info@eyeintheear.com *Web Site:* www.eyeintheear.com, pg 81

Kelly, Francesca, Chronicle Books LLC, 680 Second St, San Francisco, CA 94107 *Tel:* 415-537-4200 *Toll Free Tel:* 800-759-0190 (cust serv) *Fax:* 415-537-4460 *Toll Free Fax:* 800-858-7787 (orders); 800-286-9471 (cust serv) *E-mail:* frontdesk@chroniclebooks.com *Web Site:* www.chroniclebooks.com, pg 55

Kelly, Jean Marie, HarperCollins Publishers, 195 Broadway, New York, NY 10007 *Tel:* 212-207-7000 *Fax:* 212-207-7145 *Web Site:* www.harpercollins.com, pg 101

Kelly, Kate, Morgan Gaynin Inc, 149 Madison Ave, Suite 1140, New York, NY 10016 *Tel:* 212-475-0440 *E-mail:* info@morgangaynin.com *Web Site:* www.morgangaynin.com, pg 544

Kelly, Laurence A, Eye in the Ear Children's Audio, 5 Crescent St, Portland, ME 04102 *Toll Free Tel:* 855-99-STORY (997-8679) *Fax:* 207-699-1380 (attn: Laurence Kelly) *E-mail:* info@eyeintheear.com *Web Site:* www.eyeintheear.com, pg 81

Kelly, Neil K, F A Davis Co, 1915 Arch St, Philadelphia, PA 19103 *Tel:* 215-568-2270; 215-440-3001 *Toll Free Tel:* 800-523-4049 *Fax:* 215-568-5065; 215-440-3016 *E-mail:* info@fadavis.com; orders@fadavis.com *Web Site:* www.fadavis.com, pg 68

Kelly, Patricia, Lonely Planet, 150 Linden St, Oakland, CA 94607 *Tel:* 510-893-8555; 510-250-6400 *Toll Free Tel:* 800-275-8555 (orders) *Fax:* 510-893-8572 *E-mail:* info@lonelyplanet.com *Web Site:* www.lonelyplanet.com, pg 137

Kelly, Robert, Goodheart-Willcox Publisher, 18604 W Creek Dr, Tinley Park, IL 60477-6243 *Tel:* 708-687-5000 *Toll Free Tel:* 800-323-0440 *Fax:* 708-468-8692 *Toll Free Fax:* 888-409-3900 *E-mail:* custserv@g-w.com; orders@g-w.com *Web Site:* www.g-w.com, pg 94

Kelly, Shannon, Penguin Books, 375 Hudson St, New York, NY 10014 *Tel:* 212-366-2000 *E-mail:* penguinpublicity@us.penguingroup.com *Web Site:* www.penguinclassics.com; www.penguin.com, pg 177

Kelly, Shannon, Penguin Group USA, A Penguin Random House Company, 375 Hudson St, New York, NY 10014 *Tel:* 212-366-2000 *Toll Free Tel:* 800-847-5515 (inside sales); 800-631-8571 (cust serv) *Fax:* 212-366-2666; 607-775-4829 (inside sales) *E-mail:* online@us.penguingroup.com *Web Site:* www.penguin.com, pg 177

Kelly, Stephanie, Penguin Group USA, A Penguin Random House Company, 375 Hudson St, New York, NY 10014 *Tel:* 212-366-2000 *Toll Free Tel:* 800-847-5515 (inside sales); 800-631-8571 (cust serv) *Fax:* 212-366-2666; 607-775-4829 (inside sales) *E-mail:* online@us.penguingroup.com *Web Site:* www.penguin.com, pg 177

Kelly-Pye, Laurie, The Career Press Inc, 12 Parish Dr, Wayne, NJ 07470 *Tel:* 201-848-0310 *Toll Free Tel:* 800-CAREER-1 (227-3371) *Fax:* 201-848-1727 *E-mail:* sales@careerpress.com *Web Site:* www.careerpress.com, pg 47

Kelpner, Jennifer, Martingale®, 19021 120 Ave NE, Suite 102, Bothell, WA 98011 *Tel:* 425-483-3313 *Toll Free Tel:* 800-426-3126 *Fax:* 425-486-7596 *E-mail:* info@martingale-pub.com *Web Site:* www.martingale-pub.com, pg 143

Kelsey, Karla, Susquehanna University, Department of English and Creative Writing, 514 University Ave, Selinsgrove, PA 17870 *Tel:* 570-372-0101, pg 622

Kelty, John, Copywriter's Council of America™ (CCA), CCA Bldg, 7 Putter Lane, Middle Island, NY 11953-1920 *Tel:* 631-924-3888; 631-775-6075 *Fax:* 631-924-8555 *E-mail:* cca4dmcopy@gmail.com *Web Site:* www.andrewlinickdirectmarketing.com/Copywriters-Council.html; www.newworldpressbooks.com, pg 61

Kemp, Jaemellah, Naval Institute Press, 291 Wood Rd, Annapolis, MD 21402-5034 *Tel:* 410-268-6110 *Toll Free Tel:* 800-233-8764 *Fax:* 410-295-1084; 410-571-1703 (cust serv) *E-mail:* webmaster@navalinstitute.org; customer@navalinstitute.org (cust serv) *Web Site:* www.nip.org; www.usni.org, pg 159

Kempster, Rachel, DK Publishing, 345 Hudson St, 2nd fl, New York, NY 10014 *Tel:* 646-674-4000 *Toll Free Tel:* 877-342-5357 (cust serv); 800-733-3000 *Web Site:* www.dk.com; www.penguin.com, pg 71

Kenady, Anne, Chronicle Books LLC, 680 Second St, San Francisco, CA 94107 *Tel:* 415-537-4200 *Toll Free Tel:* 800-759-0190 (cust serv) *Fax:* 415-537-4460 *Toll Free Fax:* 800-858-7787 (orders); 800-286-9471 (cust serv) *E-mail:* frontdesk@chroniclebooks.com *Web Site:* www.chroniclebooks.com, pg 55

Kendall, Josh, Little, Brown and Company, 1290 Avenue of the Americas, New York, NY 10019 *Tel:* 212-364-1100 *Fax:* 212-364-0952 *E-mail:* firstname.lastname@hbgusa.com *Web Site:* www.littlebrown.com; www.HachetteBookGroup.com, pg 135

Keneston, Fran, State University of New York Press, 10 N Pearl St, 4th fl, Albany, NY 12207 *Tel:* 518-944-2800 *Toll Free Tel:* 877-204-6073 (orders) *Fax:* 518-320-1592 *Toll Free Fax:* 877-204-6074 (orders) *E-mail:* info@sunypress.edu (edit off); suny@presswarehouse.com (orders) *Web Site:* www.sunypress.edu, pg 221

Kennedy, Christopher, Syracuse University Creative Writing Program, 401 Hall of Languages, Syracuse, NY 13244-1170 *Tel:* 315-443-2173 *Fax:* 315-443-3660 *Web Site:* english.syr.edu/creative_writing; www.syr.edu, pg 622

Kennedy, Frances, The Doe Coover Agency, PO Box 668, Winchester, MA 01890 *Tel:* 781-721-6000 *Fax:* 781-721-6727 *E-mail:* info@doecooveragency.com *Web Site:* www.doecooveragency.com, pg 512

Khalfan, Aun Ali, Tahrike Tarsile Qur'an Inc, 80-08 51 Ave, Elmhurst, NY 11373 *Tel:* 718-446-6472 *Fax:* 718-446-4370 *E-mail:* read@koranusa.org *Web Site:* www.koranusa.org, pg 226

Khan, Ms Lakin, Napa Valley Writers' Conference, 1088 College Ave, St Helena, CA 94574 *Tel:* 707-967-2900 (ext 4) *Fax:* 707-967-2909 *E-mail:* info@napawritersconference.org; media@napawritersconference.org; fiction@napawritersconference.org; poetry@napawritersconference.org *Web Site:* www.napawritersconference.org, pg 613

Kharbanda, Sanj, Beacon Press, 24 Farnsworth St, Boston, MA 02210-1409 *Tel:* 617-742-2110 *Fax:* 617-723-3097; 617-742-2290 *Web Site:* www.beacon.org, pg 31

Kheradi, Cyrus, Random House Publishing Group, 1745 Broadway, New York, NY 10019 *Toll Free Tel:* 800-200-3552 *Web Site:* atrandom.com, pg 195

Kheradi, Irene, Simon & Schuster, Inc, 1230 Avenue of the Americas, New York, NY 10020 *Tel:* 212-698-7000 *Fax:* 212-698-7007 *E-mail:* firstname.lastname@simonandschuster.com *Web Site:* www.simonandschuster.com, pg 213

Kichler, Florrie Binford, Patria Press Inc, PO Box 752, Carmel, IN 46082 *Tel:* 317-577-1321 *Toll Free Tel:* 888-859-8221 *Fax:* 413-215-8030 *E-mail:* moreinfo@patriapress.com *Web Site:* www.patriapress.com; www.facebook.com/YoungPatriotsBooks; twitter.com/kidsbios, pg 175

Kiefer, Emily, Westminster John Knox Press (WJK), 100 Witherspoon St, Louisville, KY 40202-1396 *Toll Free Tel:* 800-523-1631 (US only) *Fax:* 502-569-5113 *Toll Free Fax:* 800-541-5113 (US & CN) *E-mail:* wjk@wjkbooks.com; customer_service@wjkbooks.com *Web Site:* www.wjkbooks.com, pg 254

Kiefer, Kim, Houghton Mifflin Harcourt Trade & Reference Division, 125 High St, Boston, MA 02110 *Tel:* 617-351-5000 *Toll Free Tel:* 800-225-3362 *Web Site:* www.hmhco.com, pg 111

Kiefer, Randy, The Optical Society (OSA), 2010 Massachusetts Ave NW, Washington, DC 20036-1023 *Tel:* 202-223-8130 *Toll Free Tel:* 800-766-4672 *E-mail:* custserv@osa.org *Web Site:* www.osa.org, pg 169

Kielbicki, Eugenia, Puddingstone Literary, Authors' Agents, 11 Mabro Dr, Denville, NJ 07834-9607 *Tel:* 973-366-3622, pg 532

Kiely, Garrett P, University of Chicago Press, 1427 E 60 St, Chicago, IL 60637-2954 *Tel:* 773-702-7700; 773-702-7600 *Toll Free Tel:* 800-621-2736 (orders) *Fax:* 773-702-9756; 773-660-2235 (orders); 773-702-2708 *E-mail:* custserv@press.uchicago.edu; marketing@press.uchicago.edu *Web Site:* www.press.uchicago.edu, pg 240

Kier, Mary Alice, Cine/Lit Representation, PO Box 802918, Santa Clarita, CA 91380-2918 *Tel:* 661-513-0268 *E-mail:* cinelit@att.net, pg 511

Kietlinski, Teresa, Prospect Agency, 285 Fifth Ave, PMB 445, Brooklyn, NY 11215 *Tel:* 718-788-3217 *Fax:* 718-360-9582 *Web Site:* www.prospectagency.com, pg 532

Kilburn, Donald, Pearson Learning Solutions, 501 Boyleston St, Suite 900, Boston, MA 02116 *Toll Free Tel:* 800-428-4466 (orders); 800-635-1579 *Fax:* 201-784-6131 *Web Site:* www.pearsoned.com, pg 176

Kilcur, Patrick, Motion Picture Association of America Inc (MPAA), 1600 "I" St NW, Washington, DC 20006 *Tel:* 202-293-1966 *Fax:* 202-296-7410 *E-mail:* contactus@mpaa.org *Web Site:* www.mpaa.org, pg 570

Kiley, Eileen, Materials Research Society, 506 Keystone Dr, Warrendale, PA 15086-7537 *Tel:* 724-779-3003 *Fax:* 724-779-8313 *E-mail:* info@mrs.org *Web Site:* www.mrs.org, pg 144

Kilgras, Heidi, Random House Children's Books, 1745 Broadway, 10th fl, New York, NY 10019 *Tel:* 212-782-9000 *Web Site:* www.randomhousekids.com, pg 194

Kilkelly, Mary Beth, Random House Children's Books, 1745 Broadway, 10th fl, New York, NY 10019 *Tel:* 212-782-9000 *Web Site:* www.randomhousekids.com, pg 194

Killam, Ray, Business Forms Management Association (BFMA), 1147 Fleetwood Ave, Madison, WI 53716 *Toll Free Tel:* 888-367-3078 *E-mail:* bfma@bfma.org *Web Site:* www.bfma.org, pg 561

Killeen, Valerie, Central Recovery Press (CRP), 3321 N Buffalo Dr, Suite 275, Las Vegas, NV 89129 *Tel:* 702-868-5830 *Fax:* 702-868-5831 *E-mail:* info@centralrecovery.com *Web Site:* centralrecoverypress.com, pg 52

Kilmartin, Kerry, University of British Columbia Press, 2029 West Mall, Vancouver, BC V6T 1Z2, Canada *Tel:* 604-822-5959 *Toll Free Tel:* 877-377-9378 *Fax:* 604-822-6083 *Toll Free Fax:* 800-668-0821 *E-mail:* frontdesk@ubcpress.ca *Web Site:* www.ubcpress.ca, pg 473

Kim, Charles R, The Museum of Modern Art (MoMA), 11 W 53 St, New York, NY 10019 *Tel:* 212-708-9443 *Fax:* 212-333-6575 *E-mail:* moma_publications@moma.org *Web Site:* www.moma.org, pg 155

Kim, Emily Sylvan, Prospect Agency, 285 Fifth Ave, PMB 445, Brooklyn, NY 11215 *Tel:* 718-788-3217 *Fax:* 718-360-9582 *Web Site:* www.prospectagency.com, pg 532

Kim, Esther, Macmillan, 175 Fifth Ave, New York, NY 10010 *Tel:* 646-307-5151 *E-mail:* press.inquiries@macmillan.com *Web Site:* www.macmillan.com, pg 140

Kim, Esther, Other Press, 267 Fifth Ave, 6th fl, New York, NY 10016 *Tel:* 212-414-0054 *Toll Free Tel:* 877-843-6843 *Fax:* 212-414-0939 *E-mail:* editor@otherpress.com; marketing@otherpress.com; publicity@otherpress.com *Web Site:* www.otherpress.com, pg 170

Kim, Gail, Judy Lopez Memorial Award For Children's Literature, 1225 Selby Ave, Los Angeles, CA 90024 *Tel:* 310-474-9917 *Fax:* 310-474-6436 *Web Site:* www.wnba-books.org/la; www.judylopezbookaward.org, pg 662

Kim, Irene, Chronicle Books LLC, 680 Second St, San Francisco, CA 94107 *Tel:* 415-537-4200 *Toll Free Tel:* 800-759-0190 (cust serv) *Fax:* 415-537-4460 *Toll Free Fax:* 800-858-7787 (orders); 800-286-9471 (cust serv) *E-mail:* frontdesk@chroniclebooks.com *Web Site:* www.chroniclebooks.com, pg 55

Kim, Jean H, Stanford University Press, 425 Broadway St, Redwood City, CA 94063-3126 *Tel:* 650-723-9434 *Fax:* 650-725-3457 *E-mail:* info@www.sup.org; publicity@www.sup.org *Web Site:* www.sup.org, pg 220

Kim, Jennifer, Sandra Dijkstra Literary Agency, 1155 Camino del Mar, PMB 515, Del Mar, CA 92014-2605 *E-mail:* queries@dijkstraagency.com *Web Site:* dijkstraagency.com, pg 514

Kim, Dr Jim Yong, World Bank Publications, Office of the Publisher, 1818 "H" St NW, U-11-1104, Washington, DC 20433 *Tel:* 202-458-4497; 202-473-1000 *Toll Free Tel:* 800-645-7247 (cust serv) *Fax:* 202-522-2631 *E-mail:* books@worldbank.org; pubrights@worldbank.org (foreign rts) *Web Site:* www.worldbank.org/en/publication/reference, pg 259

Kim, Jisu, The Feminist Press at The City University of New York, 365 Fifth Ave, Suite 5406, New York, NY 10016 *Tel:* 212-817-7915 *Fax:* 212-817-1593 *E-mail:* info@feministpress.org *Web Site:* www.feministpress.org, pg 83

Kim, Kirby, Janklow & Nesbit Associates, 285 Madison Ave, 21st fl, New York, NY 10017 *Tel:* 212-421-1700 *Fax:* 212-355-1403 *E-mail:* info@janklow.com *Web Site:* www.janklowandnesbit.com, pg 522

Kim, Lilly, Penguin Random House Inc, 1745 Broadway, New York, NY 10019 *Tel:* 212-782-9000 *Toll Free Tel:* 800-726-0600 *Web Site:* www.penguinrandomhouse.com, pg 178

Kim, Linette, Bloomsbury Publishing Inc, 1385 Broadway, 5th fl, New York, NY 10018 *Tel:* 212-419-5300 *E-mail:* marketingusa@bloomsbury.com; adultpublicityusa@bloomsbury.com; askacademic@bloomsbury.com *Web Site:* www.bloomsbury.com, pg 38

Kim, Luenna, National Society of Newspaper Columnists (NSNC), PO Box 411532, San Francisco, CA 94141 *Tel:* 415-488-NCNC (488-6762) *Fax:* 484-297-0336 *E-mail:* director@columnists.com *Web Site:* www.columnists.com, pg 573

Kim, Luenna, National Society of Newspaper Columnists Annual Conference, PO Box 411532, San Francisco, CA 94141 *Tel:* 415-488-NCNC (488-6762) *Fax:* 484-297-0336 *E-mail:* director@columnists.com *Web Site:* www.columnists.com, pg 613

Kim, Sally, Chronicle Books LLC, 680 Second St, San Francisco, CA 94107 *Tel:* 415-537-4200 *Toll Free Tel:* 800-759-0190 (cust serv) *Fax:* 415-537-4460 *Toll Free Fax:* 800-858-7787 (orders); 800-286-9471 (cust serv) *E-mail:* frontdesk@chroniclebooks.com *Web Site:* www.chroniclebooks.com, pg 55

Kim, Sally, GP Putnam's Sons (Hardcover), 375 Hudson St, New York, NY 10014 *Tel:* 212-366-2000 *Fax:* 212-366-2643 *E-mail:* online@penguinputnam.com *Web Site:* www.penguin.com/publishers/gpputnamssons, pg 192

Kim, Steve, Chronicle Books LLC, 680 Second St, San Francisco, CA 94107 *Tel:* 415-537-4200 *Toll Free Tel:* 800-759-0190 (cust serv) *Fax:* 415-537-4460 *Toll Free Fax:* 800-858-7787 (orders); 800-286-9471 (cust serv) *E-mail:* frontdesk@chroniclebooks.com *Web Site:* www.chroniclebooks.com, pg 55

Kimball, David, National Association of Real Estate Editors (NAREE), 1003 NW Sixth Terr, Boca Raton, FL 33486-3455 *Tel:* 561-391-3599 *Fax:* 561-391-0099 *Web Site:* www.naree.org, pg 571

Kimball, James, Doubleday/Nan A Talese, c/o Penguin Random House Inc, 1745 Broadway, New York, NY 10019 *Tel:* 212-751-2600 *Fax:* 212-572-2662 *E-mail:* ddaypub@randomhouse.com *Web Site:* knopfdoubleday.com, pg 72

Kimball, James, Alfred A Knopf/Everyman's Library, c/o Penguin Random House Inc, 1745 Broadway, New York, NY 10019 *Tel:* 212-751-2600 *Toll Free Tel:* 800-638-6460 *Fax:* 212-572-2593 *Web Site:* www.knopfdoubleday.com, pg 127

Kimball, Roger, Encounter Books, 900 Broadway, Suite 601, New York, NY 10003 *Tel:* 212-871-6310 *Toll Free Tel:* 800-786-3839 *Fax:* 212-871-6311 *E-mail:* publicity@encounterbooks.com *Web Site:* www.encounterbooks.com, pg 78

Kimball, Tom, Signature Books Publishing LLC, 564 W 400 N, Salt Lake City, UT 84116-3411 *Tel:* 801-531-1483 *Fax:* 801-531-1488 *E-mail:* people@signaturebooks.com *Web Site:* www.signaturebooks.com; www.signaturebookslibrary.org, pg 212

Kimbel, Travis, Yale University Press, 302 Temple St, New Haven, CT 06511-8909 *Tel:* 203-432-0960; 203-432-0966 (sales); 401-531-2800 (cust serv) *Toll Free Tel:* 800-405-1619 (cust serv) *Fax:* 203-432-0948; 203-432-8485 (sales); 401-531-2801 (cust serv) *Toll Free Fax:* 800-406-9145 (cust serv) *E-mail:* sales.press@yale.edu (sales); customer.care@triliteral.org (cust serv) *Web Site:* www.yalebooks.com; yalepress.yale.edu/yupbooks, pg 261

Kimberling, Clint, University Press of Mississippi, 3825 Ridgewood Rd, Jackson, MS 39211-6492 *Tel:* 601-432-6205 *Toll Free Tel:* 800-737-7788 (orders & cust serv) *Fax:* 601-432-6217 *E-mail:* press@mississippi.edu *Web Site:* www.upress.state.ms.us, pg 247

Kimzey, Anne, Alabama Artists Fellowship Awards, 201 Monroe St, Suite 110, Montgomery, AL 36130-1800 *Tel:* 334-242-4076 *Fax:* 334-240-3269, pg 626

Kinard, Erin, Abrams Learning Trends, 16310 Bratton Lane, Suite 250, Austin, TX 78728-2403 *Toll Free Tel:* 800-227-9120 *Toll Free Fax:* 800-737-3322 *E-mail:* customerservice@abramslearningtrends.com (orders, cust serv); contactus@abramslearningtrends.com *Web Site:* www.abramslearningtrends.com (orders, cust serv), pg 3

Kincaid, Christen, New Women's Voices Chapbook Competition, PO Box 1626, Georgetown, KY 40324 *Tel:* 502-603-0670 *E-mail:* finishingbooks@aol.com; flpbookstore@aol.com *Web Site:* www.finishinglinepress.com, pg 673

Kincaid, Christen, Open Chapbook Competition, PO Box 1626, Georgetown, KY 40324 *Tel:* 502-603-0670 *E-mail:* finishingbooks@aol.com; flpbookstore@aol.com *Web Site:* www.finishinglinepress.com, pg 675

Kind, Rachel, Random House Publishing Group, 1745 Broadway, New York, NY 10019 *Toll Free Tel:* 800-200-3552 *Web Site:* atrandom.com, pg 195

Kindig, Jessie, Roam Agency, 45 Main St, Suite 727, Brooklyn, NY 11201-1076 *E-mail:* roam@roamagency.com *Web Site:* www.roamagency.com, pg 533

King, Brenda, Yale University Press, 302 Temple St, New Haven, CT 06511-8909 *Tel:* 203-432-0960; 203-432-0966 (sales); 401-531-2800 (cust serv) *Toll Free Tel:* 800-405-1619 (cust serv) *Fax:* 203-432-0948; 203-432-8485 (sales); 401-531-2801 (cust serv) *Toll Free Fax:* 800-406-9145 (cust serv) *E-mail:* sales.press@yale.edu (sales); customer.care@triliteral.org (cust serv) *Web Site:* www.yalebooks.com; yalepress.yale.edu/yupbooks, pg 261

King, Brian, The University of Arkansas Press, McIlroy House, 105 N McIlroy Ave, Fayetteville, AR 72701 *Tel:* 479-575-3246 *Toll Free Tel:* 800-626-0090 *Fax:* 479-575-6044 *E-mail:* info@uapress.com *Web Site:* www.uapress.com, pg 240

King, Brian B, Appalachian Trail Conservancy, 799 Washington St, Harpers Ferry, WV 25425 *Tel:* 304-535-6331 *Toll Free Tel:* 888-287-8673 (orders only) *Fax:* 304-535-2667 *E-mail:* publisher@appalachiantrail.org *Web Site:* www.appalachiantrail.org; www.atctrailstore.org, pg 19

King, Dixie PhD, Big Apple Conference, 5 Penn Plaza, 19th fl, PMB 19059, New York, NY 10001 *Tel:* 917-720-6959 *E-mail:* iwwgquestions@iwwg.org *Web Site:* www.iwwg.org, pg 610

King, Dixie PhD, The International Women's Writing Guild (IWWG), 5 Penn Plaza, 19th fl, PMB 19059, New York, NY 10001 *Tel:* 917-720-6959 *E-mail:* iwwgquestions@iwwg.org *Web Site:* www.iwwg.org, pg 568

King, Dixie PhD, IWWG Annual Summer Conference, 5 Penn Plaza, 19th fl, PMB 19059, New York, NY 10001 *Tel:* 917-720-6959 *E-mail:* iwwgquestions@iwwg.org *Web Site:* www.iwwg.org, pg 612

King, Eric, Warner Press, 1201 E Fifth St, Anderson, IN 46018 *Tel:* 765-644-7721 *Toll Free Tel:* 800-741-7721 (orders) *Fax:* 765-640-8005 *Toll Free Fax:* 800-347-6411 *E-mail:* wporders@warnerpress.org *Web Site:* www.warnerpress.org, pg 252

King, London, Random House Publishing Group, 1745 Broadway, New York, NY 10019 *Toll Free Tel:* 800-200-3552 *Web Site:* atrandom.com, pg 195

King, Margaret J PhD, Cultural Studies & Analysis, 1123 Montrose St, Philadelphia, PA 19147-3721 *Tel:* 215-592-8544 *E-mail:* info@culturalanalysis.com *Web Site:* www.culturalanalysis.com, pg 492

King, Margaret Riley, WME, 11 Madison Ave, 18th fl, New York, NY 10010 *Tel:* 212-586-5100 *Web Site:* www.wmeentertainment.com, pg 542

King, Melissa, The University of Arkansas Press, McIlroy House, 105 N McIlroy Ave, Fayetteville, AR 72701 *Tel:* 479-575-3246 *Toll Free Tel:* 800-626-0090 *Fax:* 479-575-6044 *E-mail:* info@uapress.com *Web Site:* www.uapress.com, pg 240

King, Michael, YES New Play Festival, 205 FA Theatre Dept, Nunn Dr, Highland Heights, KY 41099-1007 *Tel:* 859-572-6362 *Fax:* 859-572-6057, pg 701

King, Patricia, Berkley Publishing Group, 375 Hudson St, New York, NY 10014 *Tel:* 212-366-2000 *Fax:* 212-366-2385 *Web Site:* www.penguin.com, pg 33

King, Stacy, Federal Bar Association, 1220 N Filmore St, Suite 444, Arlington, VA 22201 *Tel:* 571-481-9100 *Fax:* 571-481-9090 *E-mail:* fba@fedbar.org *Web Site:* www.fedbar.org, pg 83

King, Stephen, W W Norton & Company Inc, 500 Fifth Ave, New York, NY 10110-0017 *Tel:* 212-354-5500 *Toll Free Tel:* 800-233-4830 (orders & cust serv) *Fax:* 212-869-0856 *Toll Free Fax:* 800-458-6515 *E-mail:* orders@wwnorton.com *Web Site:* books.wwnorton.com, pg 164

King, Terry, The Authors Registry Inc, 31 E 32 St, 7th fl, New York, NY 10016 *Tel:* 212-563-6920 *Fax:* 212-564-5363 *E-mail:* staff@authorsregistry.org *Web Site:* www.authorsregistry.org, pg 560

King, Vicki, Psychological Assessment Resources Inc (PAR), 16204 N Florida Ave, Lutz, FL 33549 *Tel:* 813-968-3003; 813-449-4065 *Toll Free Tel:* 800-331-8378 *Fax:* 813-968-2598; 813-961-2196 *Toll Free Fax:* 800-727-9329 *E-mail:* custsup@parinc.com *Web Site:* www4.parinc.com, pg 191

King-Gamble, Marcia, Fun in the Sun Writer's Cruise Conference, PO Box 823414, Pembroke Pines, FL 33082 *E-mail:* frwfuninthesun@yahoo.com *Web Site:* frwfuninthesunmain.blogspot.com/; www.frwriters.org, pg 610

Kingra, Mr Mahinder S, Cornell University Press, Sage House, 512 E State St, Ithaca, NY 14850 *Tel:* 607-277-2338 *Fax:* 607-277-2374 *E-mail:* cupressinfo@cornell.edu; cupress-sales@cornell.edu *Web Site:* www.cornellpress.cornell.edu, pg 61

Kingsley, Jessica, Jessica Kingsley Publishers Inc, 400 Market St, Suite 400, Philadelphia, PA 19106 *Tel:* 215-922-1161 *Toll Free Tel:* 866-416-1078 (cust serv) *Fax:* 215-922-1474 *E-mail:* orders@jkp.com; hello.usa@jkp.com *Web Site:* www.jkp.com, pg 126

Kingzette, John, Society of American Travel Writers (SATW), One Parkview Plaza, Suite 800, Oakbrook Terrace, IL 60181 *Tel:* 202-591-2476 *E-mail:* info@satw.org *Web Site:* www.satw.org, pg 578

Kinkaid, Ashley McDonald, Phi Delta Kappa International®, 1525 Wilson Blvd, Suite 705, Arlington, VA 22209 *Tel:* 812-339-1156 *Toll Free Tel:* 800-766-1156 *Fax:* 812-339-0018 *E-mail:* memberservices@pdkintl.org *Web Site:* www.pdkintl.org, pg 182

Kinney, Andrew, Harvard University Press, 79 Garden St, Cambridge, MA 02138-1499 *Tel:* 617-495-2600; 401-531-2800 (intl orders) *Toll Free Tel:* 800-405-1619 (orders) *Fax:* 617-495-5898 (general); 617-496-4677 (edit & rts); 401-531-2801 (intl orders) *Toll Free Fax:* 800-406-9145 (orders) *E-mail:* contact_hup@harvard.edu *Web Site:* www.hup.harvard.edu, pg 103

Kinney, Erika, Brookes Publishing Co Inc, PO Box 10624, Baltimore, MD 21285-0624 *Tel:* 410-337-9580 (outside US & CN) *Toll Free Tel:* 800-638-3775 (US & CN) *Fax:* 410-337-8539 *E-mail:* custserv@brookespublishing.com *Web Site:* www.brookespublishing.com, pg 44

Kinney, Jim, Baker Books, PO Box 6287, Grand Rapids, MI 49516-6287 *Tel:* 616-676-9185 *Toll Free Tel:* 800-877-2665; 800-679-1957 *Fax:* 616-676-9573 *Toll Free Fax:* 800-398-3111 *Web Site:* www.bakerpublishinggroup.com, pg 28

Kinney, Noreen, Cordon d' Or - Gold Ribbon International Culinary Academy Awards, 7312 Sixth Ave N, St Petersburg, FL 33710 *Tel:* 727-347-2437 *E-mail:* cordondor@aol.com; culinaryparadise@aol.com *Web Site:* www.cordondorcuisine.com; www.florida-americasculinaryparadise.com, pg 639

Kintigh, Cynthia, ANR Publications University of California, 1301 S 46 St, Bldg 478 - MC 3580, Richmond, CA 94804 *Tel:* 510-665-2195 (cust serv) *Toll Free Tel:* 800-994-8849 *Fax:* 510-665-3427 *E-mail:* anrcatalog@ucdavis.edu *Web Site:* anrcatalog.ucanr.edu, pg 17

Kintz, Dr Bruce G, Concordia Publishing House, 3558 S Jefferson Ave, St Louis, MO 63118-3968 *Tel:* 314-268-1000; 314-268-1268 (bookshop) *Toll Free Tel:* 800-325-3040 (cust serv) *Toll Free Fax:* 800-490-9889 (cust serv) *E-mail:* order@cph.org *Web Site:* www.cph.org, pg 59

Kintzer, Bonnie, Trusted Media Brands Inc, 750 Third Ave, 3rd fl, New York, NY 10017 *Toll Free Tel:* 800-310-6261 (cust serv) *E-mail:* customercare@tmbi.com *Web Site:* www.tmbi.com; www.rd.com, pg 236

Kiple, Cindy, InterVarsity Press, 430 Plaza Dr, Westmont, IL 60559-1234 *Tel:* 630-734-4000 *Toll Free Tel:* 800-843-9487 *Fax:* 630-734-4200 *E-mail:* email@ivpress.com *Web Site:* www.ivpress.com, pg 120

Kiraz, Christine PhD, Gorgias Press LLC, PO Box 6939, Piscataway, NJ 08854-6939 *Tel:* 732-885-8900 *Fax:* 732-885-8908 *E-mail:* helpdesk@gorgiaspress.com *Web Site:* www.gorgiaspress.com, pg 94

Kiraz, George Anton PhD, Gorgias Press LLC, PO Box 6939, Piscataway, NJ 08854-6939 *Tel:* 732-885-8900 *Fax:* 732-885-8908 *E-mail:* helpdesk@gorgiaspress.com *Web Site:* www.gorgiaspress.com, pg 94

Kirchoff, Morris A, Kirchoff/Wohlberg Inc, 897 Boston Post Rd, Madison, CT 06443 *Tel:* 203-245-7308 *Fax:* 203-245-3218 *Web Site:* www.kirchoffwohlberg.com, pg 524

Kirk, Kara, Getty Publications, 1200 Getty Center Dr, Suite 500, Los Angeles, CA 90049-1682 *Tel:* 310-440-7365 *Toll Free Tel:* 800-223-3431 (orders) *Fax:* 310-440-7758 *E-mail:* pubsinfo@getty.edu *Web Site:* www.getty.edu/publications, pg 92

Kirk, Margaret, Copper Canyon Press, Fort Worden State Park, Bldg 313, Port Townsend, WA 98368 *Tel:* 360-385-4925 *Toll Free Tel:* 877-501-1393 (orders) *Fax:* 360-385-4985 *E-mail:* poetry@coppercanyonpress.org *Web Site:* www.coppercanyonpress.org, pg 60

Kirk, Robert, Princeton University Press, 41 William St, Princeton, NJ 08540-5237 *Tel:* 609-258-4900 *Fax:* 609-258-6305 *Web Site:* press.princeton.edu, pg 188

Kirkey, Jeffrey E, Institute of Continuing Legal Education, 1020 Greene St, Ann Arbor, MI 48109-1444 *Tel:* 734-764-0533 *Toll Free Tel:* 877-229-4350 *Fax:* 734-763-2412 *Toll Free Fax:* 877-229-4351 *E-mail:* icle@umich.edu *Web Site:* www.icle.org, pg 118

Kirklin, Dan, Liberty Fund Inc, 8335 Allison Pointe Trail, Suite 300, Indianapolis, IN 46250-1684 *Tel:* 317-842-0880 *Toll Free Tel:* 800-955-8335; 800-866-3520; 800-368-7897 ext 6069 (cust serv) *Fax:* 317-577-9067; 317-579-6060 (cust serv); 708-534-7803 *E-mail:* books@libertyfund.org; info@libertyfund.org *Web Site:* www.libertyfund.org, pg 133

Kirkpatrick, Caitlin, Chronicle Books LLC, 680 Second St, San Francisco, CA 94107 *Tel:* 415-537-4200 *Toll Free Tel:* 800-759-0190 (cust serv) *Fax:* 415-537-4460 *Toll Free Fax:* 800-858-7787 (orders); 800-286-9471 (cust serv) *E-mail:* frontdesk@chroniclebooks.com *Web Site:* www.chroniclebooks.com, pg 55

Kirkpatrick, Emily, National Council of Teachers of English (NCTE), 1111 W Kenyon Rd, Urbana, IL 61801-1096 *Tel:* 217-328-3870 *Toll Free Tel:* 877-369-6283 (cust serv) *Fax:* 217-328-9645 *E-mail:* orders@ncte.org *Web Site:* www.ncte.org, pg 158

Kirkpatrick, Emily, National Council of Teachers of English (NCTE), 1111 W Kenyon Rd, Urbana, IL 61801-1096 *Tel:* 217-328-3870 *Toll Free Tel:* 877-369-6283 (cust serv) *Fax:* 217-328-9645 *E-mail:* public_info@ncte.org *Web Site:* www.ncte.org, pg 571

Kirkpatrick, Kristin, University Press of Mississippi, 3825 Ridgewood Rd, Jackson, MS 39211-6492 *Tel:* 601-432-6205 *Toll Free Tel:* 800-737-7788 (orders & cust serv) *Fax:* 601-432-6217 *E-mail:* press@mississippi.edu *Web Site:* www.upress.state.ms.us, pg 247

Kirsch, Julie, Hamilton Books, 4501 Forbes Blvd, Suite 200, Lanham, MD 20706 *Tel:* 301-459-3366 *Toll Free Tel:* 800-462-6420 (cust serv) *Fax:* 301-429-5748 *Toll Free Fax:* 800-388-4550 (cust serv), pg 99

Kirsch, Julie, Lexington Books, 4501 Forbes Blvd, Suite 200, Lanham, MD 20706 *Tel:* 301-459-3366 *Fax:* 301-429-5749 *Web Site:* www.lexingtonbooks.com, pg 133

Kirsch, Julie, University Press of America Inc, 4501 Forbes Blvd, Suite 200, Lanham, MD 20706 *Tel:* 301-459-3366 *Toll Free Tel:* 800-462-6420 *Fax:* 301-429-5748 *Toll Free Fax:* 800-338-4550 *Web Site:* www.univpress.com, pg 246

Kirschen, Dan, ICM Partners, 65 E 55 St, New York, NY 10022 *Tel:* 212-556-5600 *Web Site:* www.icmtalent.com, pg 521

Kirshbaum, Larry, Waxman Leavell Literary Agency, 443 Park Ave S, No 1004, New York, NY 10016 *Tel:* 212-675-5556 *Fax:* 212-675-1381 *Web Site:* www.waxmanleavell.com, pg 541

Kirshner, Sandi, Cengage Learning, 20 Channel Center St, Boston, MA 02210 *Tel:* 617-289-7700 *Toll Free Tel:* 800-354-9706 *Fax:* 617-289-7844 *Toll Free Fax:* 800-487-8488 *E-mail:* esales@cengage.com *Web Site:* www.cengage.com, pg 50

Kirsten, Naomi, Chronicle Books LLC, 680 Second St, San Francisco, CA 94107 *Tel:* 415-537-4200 *Toll Free Tel:* 800-759-0190 (cust serv) *Fax:* 415-537-4460 *Toll Free Fax:* 800-858-7787 (orders); 800-286-9471 (cust serv) *E-mail:* frontdesk@chroniclebooks.com *Web Site:* www.chroniclebooks.com, pg 55

Kiser, Gayle, College & University Professional Association for Human Resources (CUPA-HR), 1811 Commons Point Dr, Knoxville, TN 37932 *Tel:* 865-637-7673 *Toll Free Tel:* 877-CUPA-HR4 (287-2474) *Fax:* 865-637-7674 *E-mail:* communications@cupahr.org *Web Site:* www.cupahr.org/publications, pg 58

Kiser, Kristin, Perseus Books, 250 W 57 St, 15th fl, New York, NY 10107 *Tel:* 212-340-8100 *Toll Free Tel:* 800-343-4499 (cust serv) *Fax:* 212-340-8105 *Web Site:* www.perseusbooks.com, pg 180

Kish, Rudy, Hachette Nashville, 12 Cadillac Dr, Suite 480, Brentwood, TN 37027 *Tel:* 615-221-0996 *Fax:* 615-221-0962 *Web Site:* www.hachettebookgroup.com, pg 98

Kisielewska, Lara, The Graphic Artists Guild Inc, 31 W 34 St, 8th fl, New York, NY 10001 *Tel:* 212-791-3400 *Fax:* 212-791-0333 *E-mail:* admin@graphicartistsguild.org; membership@graphicartistsguild.org *Web Site:* www.graphicartistsguild.org, pg 566, 620

Kisiner, Andrea, Transportation Research Board (TRB), 500 Fifth St NW, Washington, DC 20001 *Tel:* 202-334-3213 (orders); 202-334-3072 (subns) *Fax:* 202-334-2519 *E-mail:* trbsales@nas.edu *Web Site:* trb.org, pg 234

Kissling, Mark, ST Media Group Book Division, 11262 Cornell Park Dr, Cincinnati, OH 45242 *Tel:* 513-421-2050 *Toll Free Tel:* 866-265-0954 *Fax:* 513-263-6999 *E-mail:* books@stmediagroup.com *Web Site:* www.stmediagroup.com, pg 220

Kissner, Matthew, John Wiley & Sons Inc, 111 River St, Hoboken, NJ 07030-5774 *Tel:* 201-748-6000 *Toll Free Tel:* 800-225-5945 (cust serv) *Fax:* 201-748-6088 *E-mail:* info@wiley.com *Web Site:* www.wiley.com, pg 256

Kistler, Steve, RAND Corp, 1776 Main St, Santa Monica, CA 90407-2138 *Tel:* 310-393-0411 *Fax:* 310-393-4818 *Web Site:* www.rand.org, pg 193

Kitchen, Sara, Bloomsbury Publishing Inc, 1385 Broadway, 5th fl, New York, NY 10018 *Tel:* 212-419-5300 *E-mail:* marketingusa@bloomsbury.com; adultpublicityusa@bloomsbury.com; askacademic@bloomsbury.com *Web Site:* www.bloomsbury.com, pg 38

Kitman, Taya, The Ridenhour Book Prize, 116 E 16 St, 8th fl, New York, NY 10003 *Tel:* 212-822-0250 *Fax:* 212-253-5356 *E-mail:* ridenhour@nationinstitute.org *Web Site:* www.ridenhour.org, pg 684

Kitman, Taya, The Ridenhour Courage Prize, 116 E 16 St, 8th fl, New York, NY 10003 *Tel:* 212-822-0250 *Fax:* 212-253-5356 *E-mail:* ridenhour@nationinstitute.org *Web Site:* www.ridenhour.org, pg 685

Kitman, Taya, The Ridenhour Prize for Truth-Telling, 116 E 16 St, 8th fl, New York, NY 10003 *Tel:* 212-822-0250 *Fax:* 212-253-5356 *E-mail:* ridenhour@nationinstitute.org *Web Site:* www.ridenhour.org, pg 685

Kittle, Barbara, Pearson Humanities & Social Sciences, 225 River St, Hoboken, NJ 07030-4772 *Tel:* 201-236-7000, pg 176

Kiu, Doreen, World Scientific Publishing Co Inc, 27 Warren St, Suite 401-402, Hackensack, NJ 07601 *Tel:* 201-487-9655 *Fax:* 201-487-9656 *E-mail:* wspc_us@wspc.com; sales@wspc.com; mkt@wspc.com; editor@wspc.com *Web Site:* www.worldscientific.com, pg 260

Kiyan, Juliana, The Penguin Press, 375 Hudson St, New York, NY 10014 *Web Site:* thepenguinpress.com, pg 178

Kjoller, Maria, Carolrhoda Books, 241 First Ave N, Minneapolis, MN 55401 *Tel:* 612-332-3344 *Toll Free Tel:* 800-328-4929 *Fax:* 612-332-7615 *Toll Free Fax:* 800-332-1132 *E-mail:* info@lernerbooks.com; custserve@lernerbooks.com *Web Site:* www.lernerbooks.com; www.facebook.com/lernerbooks, pg 48

Kjoller, Maria, Carolrhoda Lab™, 241 First Ave N, Minneapolis, MN 55401 *Tel:* 612-332-3344 *Toll Free Tel:* 800-328-4929 *Fax:* 612-332-7615 *Toll Free Fax:* 800-332-1132 (US) *E-mail:* info@lernerbooks.com; custserve@lernerbooks.com *Web Site:* www.lernerbooks.com; www.facebook.com/lernerbooks, pg 48

Kjoller, Maria, ediciones Lerner, 241 First Ave N, Minneapolis, MN 55401 *Tel:* 612-332-3344 *Toll Free Tel:* 800-328-4929 *Fax:* 612-332-7615 *Toll Free Fax:* 800-332-1132 *E-mail:* info@lernerbooks.com; custserve@lernerbooks.com *Web Site:* www.lernerbooks.com; www.facebook.com/lernerbooks, pg 75

Kjoller, Maria, First Avenue Editions, 241 First Ave N, Minneapolis, MN 55401 *Tel:* 612-332-3344 *Toll Free Tel:* 800-328-4929 *Fax:* 612-332-7615 *Toll Free Fax:* 800-332-1132 *E-mail:* info@lernerbooks.com; custserve@lernerbooks.com *Web Site:* www.lernerbooks.com; www.facebook.com/lernerbooks, pg 85

Kjoller, Maria, Graphic Universe™, 241 First Ave N, Minneapolis, MN 55401 *Tel:* 612-332-3344 *Toll Free Tel:* 800-328-4929 *Fax:* 612-332-7615 *Toll Free Fax:* 800-332-1132 *E-mail:* info@lernerbooks.com; custserve@lernerbooks.com *Web Site:* www.lernerbooks.com; www.facebook.com/lernerbooks, pg 95

Kjoller, Maria, Kar-Ben Publishing, 241 First Ave N, Minneapolis, MN 55401 *Tel:* 612-332-3344 *Toll Free Tel:* 800-4-KARBEN (452-7236) *Fax:* 612-332-7615 *Toll Free Fax:* 800-332-1132 *Web Site:* www.karben.com, pg 125

Kjoller, Maria, Lerner Publications, 241 First Ave N, Minneapolis, MN 55401 *Tel:* 612-332-3344 *Toll Free Tel:* 800-328-4929 *Fax:* 612-332-7615 *Toll Free Fax:* 800-332-1132 *E-mail:* info@lernerbooks.com; custserve@lernerbooks.com *Web Site:* www.lernerbooks.com; www.facebook.com/lernerbooks, pg 132

Kjoller, Maria, Lerner Publishing Group Inc, 241 First Ave N, Minneapolis, MN 55401 *Tel:* 612-332-3344 *Toll Free Tel:* 800-328-4929 *Fax:* 612-332-7615 *Toll Free Fax:* 800-332-1132 *E-mail:* info@lernerbooks.com; custserve@lernerbooks.com *Web Site:* www.lernerbooks.com; www.facebook.com/lernerbooks, pg 132

Kjoller, Maria, LernerClassroom, 241 First Ave N, Minneapolis, MN 55401 *Tel:* 612-332-3344 *Toll Free Tel:* 800-328-4929 *Fax:* 612-332-7615 *Toll Free Fax:* 800-332-1132 *E-mail:* info@lernerbooks.com; custserve@lernerbooks.com *Web Site:* www.lernerbooks.com; www.facebook.com/lernerbooks, pg 132

Kjoller, Maria, Millbrook Press, 241 First Ave N, Minneapolis, MN 55401 *Tel:* 612-332-3344 *Toll Free Tel:* 800-328-4929 (US only) *Fax:* 612-332-7615 *Toll Free Fax:* 800-332-1132 *E-mail:* info@lernerbooks.com; custserve@lernerbooks.com *Web Site:* www.lernerbooks.com; www.facebook.com/millbrookpress, pg 151

Kjoller, Maria, Twenty-First Century Books, 241 First Ave N, Minneapolis, MN 55401 *Tel:* 612-332-3344 *Toll Free Tel:* 800-328-4929 *Fax:* 612-332-7615 *Toll Free Fax:* 800-332-1132 *E-mail:* info@lernerbooks.com; custserve@lernerbooks.com *Web Site:* www.lernerbooks.com; www.facebook.com/lernerbooks, pg 237

Klancher, Lee, Octane Press, 809 S Lamar Blvd, Suite H, Austin, TX 78704 *Tel:* 512-334-9441 *Fax:* 512-852-4737 *E-mail:* info@octanepress.com; orders@octanepress.com; sales@octanepress.com *Web Site:* octanepress.com, pg 167

Klavora, Dr Peter, Kinesiology Books Publisher, 212 Robert St (side basement door), Toronto, ON M5S 2K7, Canada *Tel:* 416-323-9438 *Fax:* 416-966-9022 *E-mail:* sbp@sportbookspub.com; kbp@kinesiology101.com *Web Site:* www.sportbookspub.com, pg 461

Klavora, Tania, Kinesiology Books Publisher, 212 Robert St (side basement door), Toronto, ON M5S 2K7, Canada *Tel:* 416-323-9438 *Fax:* 416-966-9022 *E-mail:* sbp@sportbookspub.com; kbp@kinesiology101.com *Web Site:* www.sportbookspub.com, pg 461

Klaw, Rick, Tachyon Publications LLC, 1459 18 St, No 139, San Francisco, CA 94107 *Tel:* 415-285-5615 *E-mail:* tachyon@tachyonpublications.com *Web Site:* www.tachyonpublications.com, pg 226

Klebanoff, Arthur, RosettaBooks, 55 Broadway, Suite 2002, New York, NY 10006 *Tel:* 646-274-1970 *Fax:* 212-977-5997 (e-fax) *E-mail:* rights@rosettabooks.com; production@rosettabooks.com *Web Site:* www.rosettabooks.com, pg 201

Klebanoff, Arthur M, Scott Meredith Literary Agency LP, Exchange Plaza, 55 Broadway, Suite 2002, New York, NY 10006 *Tel:* 646-218-9240 *Fax:* 212-977-5997 *E-mail:* info@scottmeredith.com *Web Site:* www.scottmeredith.com, pg 529

Klein, Barry, Todd Publications, 920 Dogwood Dr, No 461, Delray Beach, FL 33483 *Tel:* 561-910-0440 *Fax:* 561-910-0440 *E-mail:* toddpub@yahoo.com, pg 232

Klein, Cheryl, Lee & Low Books Inc, 95 Madison Ave, New York, NY 10016 *Tel:* 212-779-4400 *Toll Free Tel:* 888-320-3190 (ext 28, orders only) *Fax:* 212-683-1894 (orders only); 212-532-6035 *E-mail:* general@leeandlow.com *Web Site:* www.leeandlow.com, pg 131

Klein, Kathie, SBL Press, The Luce Ctr, Suite 350, 825 Houston Mill Rd, Atlanta, GA 30329 *Tel:* 404-727-3100 *Fax:* 404-727-3101 (corp) *E-mail:* sbl@sbl-site.org *Web Site:* www.sbl-site.org, pg 207

Klein, Randall, Penguin Random House Inc, 1745 Broadway, New York, NY 10019 *Tel:* 212-782-9000 *Toll Free Tel:* 800-726-0600 *Web Site:* www.penguinrandomhouse.com, pg 178

Klein, Randall, Random House Publishing Group, 1745 Broadway, New York, NY 10019 *Toll Free Tel:* 800-200-3552 *Web Site:* atrandom.com, pg 195

Klein, Russ, American Marketing Association, 130 E Randolph St, 22nd fl, Chicago, IL 60601 *Tel:* 312-542-9000 *Toll Free Tel:* 800-AMA-1150 (262-1150) *Fax:* 312-542-9001 *E-mail:* info@ama.org *Web Site:* www.ama.org, pg 555

Klein, Ryan, Templeton Press, 300 Conshohocken State Rd, Suite 665, West Conshohocken, PA 19428 *Tel:* 484-531-8380 *Fax:* 484-531-8382 *E-mail:* tpinfo@templetonpress.org *Web Site:* www.templetonpress.org, pg 229

Klein, Shmuel Yaakov, Torah Umesorah Publications, 620 Foster Ave, Brooklyn, NY 11230 *Tel:* 718-259-1223 *Fax:* 718-259-1795 *E-mail:* publications@torah-umesorah.org, pg 233

Kleinberg, Naomi, Random House Children's Books, 1745 Broadway, 10th fl, New York, NY 10019 *Tel:* 212-782-9000 *Web Site:* www.randomhousekids.com, pg 194

Kleiner, Karen, Clear Concepts, 1329 Federal Ave, Suite 6, Los Angeles, CA 90025 *Tel:* 323-285-0325, pg 491

Kleinert, Ian, Objective Entertainment, 609 Greenwich St, 6th fl, New York, NY 10014 *Tel:* 212-431-5454 *Fax:* 917-464-6394 *Web Site:* www.objectiveent.com, pg 531

Kleinman, Jeff, Folio Literary Management, The Film Center Bldg, 630 Ninth Ave, Suite 1101, New York, NY 10036 *Tel:* 212-400-1494 *Fax:* 212-967-0977 *Web Site:* www.foliolit.com, pg 517

Kleinschmidt, Caitlin, Workman Publishing Co Inc, 225 Varick St, 9th fl, New York, NY 10014-4381 *Tel:* 212-254-5900 *Toll Free Tel:* 800-722-7202 *Fax:* 212-254-8098 *E-mail:* info@workman.com *Web Site:* www.workman.com, pg 259

Kleit, Micah, Rutgers University Press, 106 Somerset St, 3rd fl, New Brunswick, NJ 08901 *Tel:* 848-445-7762 *Toll Free Tel:* 800-848-6224 (orders only) *Fax:* 732-745-4935 (acqs, edit, mktg, perms & prodn) *Toll Free Fax:* 800-272-6817 (fulfillment) *Web Site:* rutgerspress.rutgers.edu, pg 202

Klim, Christopher, Eric Hoffer Award for Independent Books, PO Box 11, Titusville, NJ 08560 *Fax:* 609-964-1718 *E-mail:* info@hofferaward.com *Web Site:* www.hofferaward.com, pg 653

Kline, Michael, SSPC: The Society for Protective Coatings, 800 Trumbull Dr, Pittsburgh, PA 15220-4365 *Tel:* 412-281-2331 *Toll Free Tel:* 877-281-7772 (US only) *Fax:* 412-281-9992 *E-mail:* info@sspc.org *Web Site:* www.sspc.org, pg 220

Kline, Missy, College & University Professional Association for Human Resources (CUPA-HR), 1811 Commons Point Dr, Knoxville, TN 37932 *Tel:* 865-637-7673 *Toll Free Tel:* 877-CUPA-HR4 (287-2474) *Fax:* 865-637-7674 *E-mail:* communications@cupahr.org *Web Site:* www.cupahr.org/publications, pg 58

Klingborg, Brian, Kumon Publishing North America, 300 Frank Burr Blvd, Suite 6, Teaneck, NJ 07666 *Tel:* 201-836-2105 *Fax:* 201-836-1559 *E-mail:* books@kumon.com *Web Site:* www.kumonbooks.com, pg 128

Klinger, Harvey, Harvey Klinger Inc, 300 W 55 St, Suite 11V, New York, NY 10019 *Tel:* 212-581-7068 *Fax:* 212-315-3823 *E-mail:* queries@harveyklinger.com *Web Site:* www.harveyklinger.com, pg 524

Klinger, Leslie, Horror Writers Association (HWA), c/o Horror Writers Association, PO Box 56687, Sherman Oaks, CA 91413 *E-mail:* hwa@horror.org *Web Site:* horror.org, pg 566

Klinke, Kristi, Society for Scholarly Publishing (SSP), 10200 W 44 Ave, Suite 304, Wheat Ridge, CO 80033-2840 *Tel:* 303-422-3914 *Fax:* 720-881-6101 *E-mail:* info@sspnet.org *Web Site:* www.sspnet.org, pg 578

Klise, Matt, Penguin Books, 375 Hudson St, New York, NY 10014 *Tel:* 212-366-2000 *E-mail:* penguinpublicity@us.penguingroup.com *Web Site:* www.penguinclassics.com; www.penguin.com, pg 177

Klooster, Alison, Penguin Books, 375 Hudson St, New York, NY 10014 *Tel:* 212-366-2000 *E-mail:* penguinpublicity@us.penguingroup.com *Web Site:* www.penguinclassics.com; www.penguin.com, pg 177

Klooster, Alison, Viking, 375 Hudson St, New York, NY 10014 *Tel:* 212-366-2000 *Fax:* 212-243-6002 *Web Site:* www.penguin.com/publishers/vikingbooks, pg 250

Klopfer, Eric, Harry N Abrams Inc, 195 Broadway, 9th fl, New York, NY 10007 *Tel:* 212-206-7715 *Toll Free Tel:* 800-345-1359 *Fax:* 212-519-1210 *E-mail:* abrams@abramsbooks.com *Web Site:* www.abramsbooks.com, pg 3

Klose, Lisa, The Johns Hopkins University Press, 2715 N Charles St, Baltimore, MD 21218-4363 *Tel:* 410-516-6900; 410-516-6987 (journal orders outside US & CN) *Toll Free Tel:* 800-537-5487 (book orders & cust serv); 800-548-1784 (journal orders) *Fax:* 410-516-6968; 410-516-3866 (journal orders) *E-mail:* hfscustserv@press.jhu.edu (cust serv); jrnlcirc@press.jhu.edu (journal orders) *Web Site:* www.press.jhu.edu; muse.jhu.edu, pg 122

Klose, Tory, The Penguin Press, 375 Hudson St, New York, NY 10014 *Web Site:* thepenguinpress.com, pg 178

Klose, Tory, Portfolio, 375 Hudson St, New York, NY 10014 *Web Site:* www.penguin.com/meet/publishers/portfolio, pg 186

Klose, Tory, Viking, 375 Hudson St, New York, NY 10014 *Tel:* 212-366-2000 *Fax:* 212-243-6002 *Web Site:* www.penguin.com/publishers/vikingbooks, pg 250

Kloske, Geoffrey, Riverhead Books, 375 Hudson St, New York, NY 10014 *Tel:* 212-366-2000 *Web Site:* www.penguin.com/publishers/riverhead, pg 199

Kloss, Stephanie, Alfred A Knopf/Everyman's Library, c/o Penguin Random House Inc, 1745 Broadway, New York, NY 10019 *Tel:* 212-751-2600 *Toll Free Tel:* 800-638-6460 *Fax:* 212-572-2593 *Web Site:* www.knopfdoubleday.com, pg 127

Klosterman, Jeff, Professional Resource Press, 1958 Barber Rd, Sarasota, FL 34240 *Tel:* 941-343-9601 *Toll Free Tel:* 800-443-3364 (orders & cust serv) *Fax:* 941-343-9201 *Toll Free Fax:* 866-804-4843 (orders only) *E-mail:* cs.prpress@gmail.com *Web Site:* www.prpress.com, pg 189

Kmit, Kate, AZ Books LLC, 320 Fifth Ave, New York, NY 10001 *Toll Free Tel:* 888-945-7723 *Toll Free Fax:* 888-945-7724 *Web Site:* www.azbooksusa.com, pg 27

Knapp, Jamie, Dutton, 375 Hudson St, New York, NY 10014 *Tel:* 212-366-2000 *Fax:* 212-366-2262 *Web Site:* www.penguin.com, pg 74

Knapp, Renee, Between the Lines, 401 Richmond St W, No 277, Toronto, ON M5V 3A8, Canada *Tel:* 416-535-9914 *Toll Free Tel:* 800-718-7201 *Fax:* 416-535-1484 *E-mail:* info@btlbooks.com *Web Site:* btlbooks.com, pg 446

Knapp, Stephanie, Perseus Books, 250 W 57 St, 15th fl, New York, NY 10107 *Tel:* 212-340-8100 *Toll Free Tel:* 800-343-4499 (cust serv) *Fax:* 212-340-8105 *Web Site:* www.perseusbooks.com, pg 181

Knapton, Vicki, Graphic Arts Books, 7820 NE Holman St, Suite B-9, Portland, OR 97218 *Tel:* 503-254-5591 *Fax:* 503-254-5609 *E-mail:* info-ga@graphicartsbooks.com *Web Site:* www.graphicartsbooks.com, pg 95

Kneedler, Joel, Thomas Nelson, 501 Nelson Place, Nashville, TN 37214 *Tel:* 615-889-9000 *Toll Free Tel:* 800-251-4000 *Fax:* 615-902-1548 *Web Site:* www.thomasnelson.com, pg 231

Kneerim, Jill, Kneerim & Williams Agency, 90 Canal St, Boston, MA 02114 *Tel:* 617-303-1650 *Web Site:* www.kwlit.com, pg 524

Kniffen, Juliet Viola, Northern California Translators Association, 2261 Market St, Suite 160, San Francisco, CA 94114-1600 *Tel:* 510-845-8712 *E-mail:* administrator@ncta.org *Web Site:* www.ncta.org, pg 574

Knight, Barb, Tiger Tales, 5 River Rd, Suite 128, Wilton, CT 06897-4069 *Tel:* 920-387-2333 *Fax:* 920-387-9994 *Web Site:* www.tigertalesbooks.com, pg 232

Knight, Deidre, The Knight Agency Inc, 570 East Ave, Madison, GA 30650 *E-mail:* submissions@knightagency.net *Web Site:* www.knightagency.net, pg 524

Knight, Denise, Eagle's View Publishing, 6756 North Fork Rd, Liberty, UT 84310 *Tel:* 801-393-4555; 801-745-0905 (edit) *Fax:* 801-745-0903 (edit); 801-393-4647 *E-mail:* sales@eaglefeathertrading.com *Web Site:* www.eaglefeathertrading.com, pg 74

Knight, John, Farrar, Straus & Giroux, LLC, 18 W 18 St, New York, NY 10011 *Tel:* 212-741-6900 *E-mail:* fsg.publicity@fsgbooks.com *Web Site:* us.macmillan.com/fsg.aspx, pg 83

Knight, Judith, University Press of Florida, 15 NW 15 St, Gainesville, FL 32603-2079 *Tel:* 352-392-1351 *Toll Free Tel:* 800-226-3822 (orders only) *Fax:* 352-392-0590 *Toll Free Fax:* 800-680-1955 (orders only) *E-mail:* press@upress.ufl.edu; orders@upress.ufl.edu *Web Site:* www.upf.com, pg 246

Knight, Judson, The Knight Agency Inc, 570 East Ave, Madison, GA 30650 *E-mail:* submissions@knightagency.net *Web Site:* www.knightagency.net, pg 524

Knight, Margot, Djerassi Resident Artists Program, 2325 Bear Gulch Rd, Woodside, CA 94062 *Tel:* 650-747-1250 *E-mail:* drap@djerassi.org *Web Site:* www.djerassi.org, pg 610

Knight, Tom, Thomas Nelson, 501 Nelson Place, Nashville, TN 37214 *Tel:* 615-889-9000 *Toll Free Tel:* 800-251-4000 *Fax:* 615-902-1548 *Web Site:* www.thomasnelson.com, pg 231

Knight, Tom, Zondervan, 3900 Sparks Dr, Grand Rapids, MI 49546 *Tel:* 616-698-6900 *Toll Free Tel:* 800-226-1122; 800-727-1309 (retail orders) *Fax:* 616-698-3350 *Toll Free Fax:* 800-698-3256 (retail orders) *E-mail:* zinfo@zondervan.com *Web Site:* www.zondervan.com, pg 263

Knight, Tomea, College of Liberal & Professional Studies, University of Pennsylvania, 3440 Market St, Suite 100, Philadelphia, PA 19104-3335 *Tel:* 215-898-7326 *Fax:* 215-573-2053 *E-mail:* lps@sas.upenn.edu *Web Site:* www.sas.upenn.edu/lps, pg 619

Knill, Ellen, Bellerophon Books, PO Box 21307, Santa Barbara, CA 93121-1307 *Tel:* 805-965-7034 *Toll Free Tel:* 800-253-9943 *Fax:* 805-965-8286 *E-mail:* sales.bellerophon@gmail.com *Web Site:* www.bellerophonbooks.com, pg 32

Knobloch, Jamie, Thorndike Press, 10 Water St, Suite 310, Waterville, ME 04901 *Toll Free Tel:* 800-223-1244 (ext 4, cust serv/orders) *Toll Free Fax:* 800-558-4676 (orders) *E-mail:* gale.printorders@cengage.com; international@cengage.com (cust orders outside US & CN) *Web Site:* www.gale.com/thorndike, pg 232

Knoll, Lori, Governor General's Literary Awards, 150 Elgin St, Ottawa, ON K1P 1L4, Canada *Tel:* 613-566-4414 *Toll Free Tel:* 800-263-5588 (CN only) *Fax:* 613-566-4390 *E-mail:* info@canadacouncil.ca *Web Site:* canadacouncil.ca/en/council/prizes, pg 650

Knoll, Zach, Simon & Schuster, 1230 Avenue of the Americas, New York, NY 10020 *Tel:* 212-698-7000 *Toll Free Tel:* 800-223-2348 (cust serv); 800-223-2336 (orders) *Toll Free Fax:* 800-943-9831 (orders) *Web Site:* www.simonandschuster.com, pg 212

Knopf, Chris, The Permanent Press, 4170 Noyac Rd, Sag Harbor, NY 11963 *Tel:* 631-725-1101 *E-mail:* info@thepermanentpress.com *Web Site:* www.thepermanentpress.com, pg 180

Knopf, Susan, American Book Producers Association (ABPA), 31 W Eighth St, 2nd fl, New York, NY 10011 *Tel:* 212 675 1363 *Fax:* 212 675 1364 *E-mail:* office@abpaonline.org *Web Site:* www.abpaonline.org, pg 554

Knopf, Susan, WNBA Pannell Award for Excellence in Children's Bookselling, PO Box 237, FDR Sta, New York, NY 10150-0231 *Toll Free Tel:* 866-610-9622 *E-mail:* WNBAPannell@gmail.com *Web Site:* www.wnba-books.org; www.NationalReadingGroupMonth.org; www.wnba-books.org/awards, pg 699

Knotek, George, Copper Canyon Press, Fort Worden State Park, Bldg 313, Port Townsend, WA 98368 *Tel:* 360-385-4925 *Toll Free Tel:* 877-501-1393 (orders) *Fax:* 360-385-4985 *E-mail:* poetry@coppercanyonpress.org *Web Site:* www.coppercanyonpress.org, pg 60

Knott, Ronald, Andrews University Press, Sutherland House, 8360 W Campus Circle Dr, Berrien Springs, MI 49104-1700 *Tel:* 269-471-6134 *Toll Free Tel:* 800-467-6369 (Visa, MC & American Express orders only)

Fax: 269-471-6224 *E-mail:* aupo@andrews.edu; aup@andrews.edu; aupress@andrews.edu *Web Site:* www.universitypress.andrews.edu, pg 17

Knowlton, Ginger, Curtis Brown Ltd, 10 Astor Place, New York, NY 10003 *Tel:* 212-473-5400 *Web Site:* www.curtisbrown.com, pg 510

Knowlton, Timothy F, Curtis Brown Ltd, 10 Astor Place, New York, NY 10003 *Tel:* 212-473-5400 *Web Site:* www.curtisbrown.com, pg 510

Knutsen, Trond, University of Hawaii Press, 2840 Kolowalu St, Honolulu, HI 96822 *Tel:* 808-956-8255 *Toll Free Tel:* 888-UHPRESS (847-7377) *Fax:* 808-988-6052 *Toll Free Fax:* 800-650-7811 *E-mail:* uhpbooks@hawaii.edu *Web Site:* www.uhpress.hawaii.edu, pg 241

Kobasa, Paul, Bright Connections Media, A World Book Encyclopedia Company, 180 N LaSalle St, Suite 900, Chicago, IL 60601 *Tel:* 312-729-5800 *Web Site:* www.brightconnectionsmedia.com, pg 43

Kobasa, Paul A, World Book Inc, 180 N LaSalle, Suite 900, Chicago, IL 60601 *Tel:* 312-729-5800 *Toll Free Tel:* 800-967-5325 (consumer sales, US); 800-463-8845 (consumer sales, CN); 800-975-3250 (school & lib sales, US); 800-837-5365 (school & lib sales, CN); 866-866-5200 (web sales) *Fax:* 312-729-5600; 312-729-5606 *Toll Free Fax:* 800-433-9330 (school & lib sales, US); 888-690-4002 (school lib sales, CN) *E-mail:* customercare@worldbook.com *Web Site:* www.worldbook.com, pg 259

Kobe, Ellen, The Society of Professional Journalists (SPJ), Eugene S Pulliam National Journalism Ctr, 3909 N Meridian St, Indianapolis, IN 46208 *Tel:* 317-927-8000 *Fax:* 317-920-4789 *E-mail:* spj@spj.org *Web Site:* www.spj.org, pg 580

Kochan, Susan, GP Putnam's Sons (Children's), 345 Hudson St, New York, NY 10014 *Tel:* 212-366-2000 *Fax:* 212-414-3393 *Web Site:* www.penguin.com/publishers/gpputnamssonsbooksforyoungread, pg 192

Kochman, Charles, Harry N Abrams Inc, 195 Broadway, 9th fl, New York, NY 10007 *Tel:* 212-206-7715 *Toll Free Tel:* 800-345-1359 *Fax:* 212-519-1210 *E-mail:* abrams@abramsbooks.com *Web Site:* www.abramsbooks.com, pg 3

Koduvalil, Bobby, Hendrickson Publishers Inc, PO Box 3473, Peabody, MA 01961-3473 *Tel:* 978-532-6546 *Toll Free Tel:* 800-358-3111 *Fax:* 978-573-8111 *E-mail:* orders@hendrickson.com *Web Site:* www.hendrickson.com, pg 106

Koecher, Molly, CarTech Inc, 39966 Grand Ave, North Branch, MN 55056 *Tel:* 651-277-1200 *Toll Free Tel:* 800-551-4754 *Fax:* 651-277-1203 *E-mail:* info@cartechbooks.com *Web Site:* www.cartechbooks.com, pg 48

Koelsch, Han, American Academy of Orthopaedic Surgeons (AAOS), 9400 W Higgins Rd, Rosemont, IL 60018-4976 *Tel:* 847-823-7186 *Toll Free Tel:* 800-346-2267 *E-mail:* custserv@aaos.org *Web Site:* www.aaos.org, pg 9

Koenig, Wade, Moody Publishers, 820 N La Salle Blvd, Chicago, IL 60610 *Tel:* 312-329-4000 *Toll Free Tel:* 800-678-8812 (cust serv) *Fax:* 312-329-2019 *E-mail:* mpcustomerservice@moody.edu *Web Site:* www.moodypublishers.com, pg 153

Koerner, Darrell, Chelsea Green Publishing Co, 85 N Main St, Suite 120, White River Junction, VT 05001 *Tel:* 802-295-6300 *Toll Free Tel:* 800-639-4099 (cust serv, consumer & trade orders) *Fax:* 802-295-6444 *Web Site:* www.chelseagreen.com, pg 53

Koester, Robert J, dbS Productions, PO Box 94, Charlottesville, VA 22902 *Tel:* 434-293-5502 *Toll Free Tel:* 800-745-1581 *Fax:* 434-293-5502 *E-mail:* info@dbs-sar.com *Web Site:* www.dbs-sar.com, pg 68

Koetje, David, Christian Schools International, 3350 E Paris Ave SE, Grand Rapids, MI 49512-3054 *Tel:* 616-957-1070 *Toll Free Tel:* 800-635-8288 *Fax:* 616-957-5022 *E-mail:* info@csionline.org *Web Site:* www.csionline.org, pg 55

Koffler, Lionel, Firefly Books Ltd, 50 Staples Ave, Unit 1, Richmond Hill, ON L4B 0A7, Canada *Tel:* 416-499-8412 *Toll Free Tel:* 800-387-6192 (CN); 800-387-5085 (US) *Fax:* 416-499-8313 *Toll Free Fax:* 800-450-0391 (CN); 800-565-6034 (US) *E-mail:* info@fireflybooks.com *Web Site:* www.fireflybooks.com, pg 456

Koh, Becky, Hachette Books, 1290 Avenue of the Americas, New York, NY 10019 *Tel:* 212-364-1100 *Web Site:* www.hachettebookgroup.com, pg 98

Kohlmeier, Rob, Wilfrid Laurier University Press, 75 University Ave W, Waterloo, ON N2L 3C5, Canada *Tel:* 519-884-0710 *Toll Free Tel:* 866-836-5551 (CN & US) *Fax:* 519-725-1399 *E-mail:* press@wlu.ca *Web Site:* www.wlupress.wlu.ca, pg 476

Kohrs, Sarah, The Sow's Ear Poetry Prize & The Sow's Ear Chapbook Prize, 1748 Cave Ridge Rd, Mount Jackson, VA 22842 *Tel:* 540-477-3257 *E-mail:* sepoetryreview@gmail.com *Web Site:* sowsearpoetry.org, pg 691

Kok, John H, Dordt College Press, 498 Fourth Ave NE, Sioux Center, IA 51250-1606 *Tel:* 712-722-6420 *Toll Free Tel:* 800-343-6738 *Fax:* 712-722-6035 *E-mail:* dordtpress@dordt.edu; bookstore@dordt.edu *Web Site:* www.dordt.edu/about-dordt/publications/dordt-press-catalog, pg 72

Kokko, Larry, Florida Writers Association Conference, PO Box 66069, St Pete Beach, FL 33736-6069 *Web Site:* www.floridawriters.net, pg 610

Kokko, Larry, Florida Writers Association Inc, PO Box 66069, St Pete Beach, FL 33736-6069 *Web Site:* www.floridawriters.net, pg 565

Kolbe, Kimberly, The Green Rose Prize in Poetry, c/o Western Michigan University, 1903 W Michigan Ave, Kalamazoo, MI 49008-5463 *Tel:* 269-387-8185 *E-mail:* new-issues@wmich.edu *Web Site:* www.wmich.edu/newissues/sub-guide.html, pg 651

Kolbe, Kimberly, New Issues Poetry & Prose, c/o Western Michigan University, 1903 W Michigan Ave, Kalamazoo, MI 49008-5463 *Tel:* 269-387-8185 *E-mail:* new-issues@wmich.edu *Web Site:* www.wmich.edu/newissues, pg 160

Kolbe, Kimberly, New Issues Poetry Prize, c/o Western Michigan University, 1903 W Michigan Ave, Kalamazoo, MI 49008-5463 *Tel:* 269-387-8185 *E-mail:* new-issues@wmich.edu *Web Site:* www.wmich.edu/newissues, pg 673

Kolbeck, Casie, Chronicle Books LLC, 680 Second St, San Francisco, CA 94107 *Tel:* 415-537-4200 *Toll Free Tel:* 800-759-0190 (cust serv) *Fax:* 415-537-4460 *Toll Free Fax:* 800-858-7787 (orders); 800-286-9471 (cust serv) *E-mail:* frontdesk@chroniclebooks.com *Web Site:* www.chroniclebooks.com, pg 55

Kolby, Jeff, Nova Press, 9058 Lloyd Place, West Hollywood, CA 90069 *Tel:* 310-275-3513 *Fax:* 310-281-5629 *E-mail:* novapress@aol.com *Web Site:* www.novapress.net, pg 165

Kolen, Kerri, GP Putnam's Sons (Hardcover), 375 Hudson St, New York, NY 10014 *Tel:* 212-366-2000 *Fax:* 212-366-2643 *E-mail:* online@penguinputnam.com *Web Site:* www.penguin.com/publishers/gpputnamssons, pg 192

Kolendo, Kate, PROSE Awards, 455 Massachusetts Ave NW, Suite 700, Washington, DC 20001-2777 *Tel:* 212-255-0200 *Web Site:* www.proseawards.com; publishers.org, pg 682

Kolkman, Tammy, Covenant Communications Inc, 920 E State Rd, Suite F, American Fork, UT 84003-0416 *Tel:* 801-756-1041 *E-mail:* info@covenant-lds.com *Web Site:* www.covenant-lds.com, pg 63

Kollenbaum, Louise, The Amy Rennert Agency Inc, 1550 Tiburon Blvd, Suite 302, Tiburon, CA 94920 *Tel:* 415-789-8955 *E-mail:* queries@amyrennert.com *Web Site:* amyrennert.com, pg 532

Kolsrud, Kelli, International Foundation of Employee Benefit Plans, 18700 W Bluemound Rd, Brookfield, WI 53045 *Tel:* 262-786-6700 *Toll Free Tel:* 888-334-3327 *Fax:* 262-786-8780 *E-mail:* editor@ifebp.org *Web Site:* www.ifebp.org, pg 119

Komie, Michelle, Princeton University Press, 41 William St, Princeton, NJ 08540-5237 *Tel:* 609-258-4900 *Fax:* 609-258-6305 *Web Site:* press.princeton.edu, pg 188

Kondrick, Maureen, Marquette University Press, 1415 W Wisconsin Ave, Milwaukee, WI 53233 *Tel:* 414-288-1564 *Fax:* 414-288-7813 *Web Site:* www.marquette.edu/mupress, pg 142

Konecke, Kaitlin, Health Professions Press, 409 Washington Ave, Suite 500, Towson, MD 21204 *Tel:* 410-337-9585 *Toll Free Tel:* 888-337-8808 *Fax:* 410-337-8539 *E-mail:* custserv@healthpropress.com *Web Site:* www.healthpropress.com, pg 105

Konecky, Edith, Hamilton Stone Editions, PO Box 43, Maplewood, NJ 07040 *Tel:* 973-378-8361 *E-mail:* hstone@hamiltonstone.org *Web Site:* www.hamiltonstone.org, pg 99

Konecky, Sean, Konecky & Konecky LLC, 72 Ayers Point Rd, Old Saybrook, CT 06475 *Tel:* 860-388-0878 *Fax:* 860-388-0273 *Web Site:* www.koneckyandkonecky.com, pg 128

Kong, Molly, Disney Press, 1101 Flower St, Glendale, CA 91201 *Web Site:* books.disney.com, pg 70

Konieczny, Jennifer, Flanker Press Ltd, 1243 Kenmount Rd, Unit 1, Paradise, NL A1L 0V8, Canada *Tel:* 709-739-4477 *Toll Free Tel:* 866-739-4420 *Fax:* 709-739-4420 *E-mail:* info@flankerpress.com; sales@flankerpress.com *Web Site:* www.flankerpress.com, pg 457

Konner, Linda, Linda Konner Literary Agency, 10 W 15 St, Suite 1918, New York, NY 10011 *Tel:* 212-691-3419 *Fax:* 212-691-0935 *Web Site:* www.lindakonnerliteraryagency.com, pg 525

Konopinski, Natalie, American Anthropological Association (AAA), 2300 Clarendon Blvd, Suite 1301, Arlington, VA 22201 *Tel:* 703-528-1902 *Fax:* 703-528-3546 *E-mail:* pubs@americananthro.org *Web Site:* www.americananthro.org, pg 10

Konowitch, Paul, Sundance/Newbridge Publishing, 33 Boston Post Rd W, Suite 440, Marlborough, MA 01752 *Toll Free Tel:* 888-200-2720; 800-343-8204 (Sundance cust serv & orders); 800-867-0307 (Newbridge cust serv & orders) *Toll Free Fax:* 800-456-2419 (orders) *E-mail:* info@sundancepub.com; info@newbridgeonline.com *Web Site:* www.sundancepub.com; www.newbridgeonline.com, pg 225

Koohi-Kamali, Dr Farideh, Peter Lang Publishing Inc, 29 Broadway, 18th fl, New York, NY 10006-3223 *Tel:* 212-647-7706 *Toll Free Tel:* 800-770-5264 (cust serv) *Fax:* 212-647-7707 *Web Site:* www.peterlang.com, pg 129

Kooij, Nina, Pelican Publishing Co, 1000 Burmaster St, Gretna, LA 70053-2246 *Tel:* 504-368-1175 *Toll Free Tel:* 800-843-1724 *Fax:* 504-368-1195 *E-mail:* sales@pelicanpub.com (sales); office@pelicanpub.com (permission); promo@pelicanpub.com (publicity) *Web Site:* www.pelicanpub.com, pg 176

Kopelman, Charles, Abrams Artists Agency, 275 Seventh Ave, 26th fl, New York, NY 10001 *Tel:* 646-486-4600 *Fax:* 646-486-0100 *E-mail:* literary@abramsartny.com *Web Site:* www.abramsartists.com, pg 505

Kordic, Lara, Heritage House Publishing Co Ltd, 1075 Pendergast St, No 103, Victoria, BC V8V 0A1, Canada *Tel:* 250-360-0829 *Fax:* 250-386-0829 *E-mail:* heritage@heritagehouse.ca *Web Site:* www.heritagehouse.ca, pg 459

Korman, Keith, Raines & Raines, 103 Kenyon Rd, Medusa, NY 12120 *Tel:* 518-239-8311 *Fax:* 518-239-6029, pg 532

Korman, Tom, DK Publishing, 345 Hudson St, 2nd fl, New York, NY 10014 *Tel:* 646-674-4000 *Toll Free Tel:* 877-342-5357 (cust serv); 800-733-3000 *Web Site:* www.dk.com; www.penguin.com, pg 71

Korn, Adam, HarperCollins General Books Group, 195 Broadway, New York, NY 10007 *Tel:* 212-207-7000 *Web Site:* www.harpercollins.com, pg 101

Korn, Linda, Penguin Random House Audio Publishing, 1745 Broadway, New York, NY 10019 *E-mail:* audio@penguinrandomhouse.com *Web Site:* www.penguinrandomhouseaudio.com, pg 178

Korn, Mirabelle, Chronicle Books LLC, 680 Second St, San Francisco, CA 94107 *Tel:* 415-537-4200 *Toll Free Tel:* 800-759-0190 (cust serv) *Fax:* 415-537-4460 *Toll Free Fax:* 800-858-7787 (orders); 800-286-9471 (cust serv) *E-mail:* frontdesk@chroniclebooks.com *Web Site:* www.chroniclebooks.com, pg 55

Kornbluh, Rena, Hachette Book Group, 1290 Avenue of the Americas, New York, NY 10019 *Tel:* 212-364-1100 *Toll Free Tel:* 800-759-0190 (cust serv) *Fax:* 212-364-0933 (intl orders) *Toll Free Fax:* 800-286-9471 (cust serv) *Web Site:* www.hachettebookgroup.com, pg 98

Kornoelje, Kristin, Revell, PO Box 6287, Grand Rapids, MI 49516-6287 *Tel:* 616-676-9185 *Toll Free Tel:* 800-877-2665; 800-679-1957 *Fax:* 616-676-9573 *Web Site:* www.bakerpublishinggroup.com, pg 198

Kortekamp, Jeanne, Franciscan Media, 28 W Liberty St, Cincinnati, OH 45202 *Tel:* 513-241-5615 *Toll Free Tel:* 800-488-0488 *Fax:* 513-241-0399 *E-mail:* books@americancatholic.org *Web Site:* www.americancatholic.org; www.franciscanmedia.org, pg 88

Kosar, Amy, Chronicle Books LLC, 680 Second St, San Francisco, CA 94107 *Tel:* 415-537-4200 *Toll Free Tel:* 800-759-0190 (cust serv) *Fax:* 415-537-4460 *Toll Free Fax:* 800-858-7787 (orders); 800-286-9471 (cust serv) *E-mail:* frontdesk@chroniclebooks.com *Web Site:* www.chroniclebooks.com, pg 55

Kosiewska, Anthony, Scholastic Trade Division, 557 Broadway, New York, NY 10012 *Tel:* 212-343-6100; 212-343-4685 (export sales) *Fax:* 212-343-4714 (export sales) *Web Site:* www.scholastic.com, pg 208

Koski, Abby, Soho Press Inc, 853 Broadway, New York, NY 10003 *Tel:* 212-260-1900 *E-mail:* soho@sohopress.com; publicity@sohopress.com; contact@sohopress.com *Web Site:* www.sohopress.com, pg 216

Kosmach, Jack, Whole Person Associates Inc, 101 W Second St, Suite 203, Duluth, MN 55802 *Tel:* 218-727-0500 *Toll Free Tel:* 800-247-6789 *Fax:* 218-727-0505 *E-mail:* books@wholeperson.com *Web Site:* www.wholeperson.com, pg 255

Kosmoski, Anne, Avery, 375 Hudson St, New York, NY 10014 *Tel:* 212-366-2000 *Fax:* 212-366-2643 *Web Site:* www.penguin.com; www.penguinrandomhouse.com, pg 27

Kosowski, Mary Beth, Mercer University Press, 368 Orange St, Macon, GA 31201 *Tel:* 478-301-2880 *Toll Free Tel:* 866-895-1472 *Fax:* 478-301-2585 *E-mail:* mupressorders@mercer.edu *Web Site:* www.mupress.org, pg 148

Kost, Jordan, Albert Whitman & Co, 250 S Northwest Hwy, Suite 320, Park Ridge, IL 60068 *Tel:* 847-232-2800 *Toll Free Tel:* 800-255-7675 *Fax:* 847-581-0039 *E-mail:* mail@albertwhitman.com *Web Site:* www.albertwhitman.com, pg 6

Kostman, Lynne, Fowler Museum at UCLA, PO Box 951549, Los Angeles, CA 90095-1549 *Tel:* 310-825-4361 *Fax:* 310-206-7007 *E-mail:* fowlerws@arts.ucla.edu *Web Site:* www.fowler.ucla.edu, pg 87

Kot, Rick, Viking, 375 Hudson St, New York, NY 10014 *Tel:* 212-366-2000 *Fax:* 212-243-6002 *Web Site:* www.penguin.com/publishers/vikingbooks, pg 250

Kotchman, Katie, Don Congdon Associates Inc, 110 William St, Suite 2202, New York, NY 10038-3914 *Tel:* 212-645-1229 *Fax:* 212-727-2688 *E-mail:* dca@doncongdon.com *Web Site:* www.doncongdon.com, pg 512

Kouma, Cecelia, Playwrights Project, 3675 Ruffin Rd, Suite 330, San Diego, CA 92123 *Tel:* 858-384-2970 *Fax:* 858-384-2974 *E-mail:* write@playwrightsproject.org *Web Site:* www.playwrightsproject.org, pg 680

Koupal, Nancy Tystad, South Dakota Historical Society Press, 900 Governors Dr, Pierre, SD 57501 *Tel:* 605-773-6009 *Fax:* 605-773-6041 *E-mail:* info@sdshspress.com; orders@sdshspress.com *Web Site:* sdshspress.com, pg 218

Kouts, Barbara S, Barbara S Kouts Literary Agency LLC, PO Box 560, Bellport, NY 11713 *Tel:* 631-286-1278 *Fax:* 631-286-1538 *E-mail:* bkouts@aol.com, pg 525

Kovach, Gale, A 2 Z Press LLC, 445 Cortez Ave, Deleon Springs, FL 32130 *Tel:* 386-681-7402 *Web Site:* www.a2zpress.com; www.terriesizemorestoryteller.com, pg 1

Kovitz, Jennifer Abel, Counterpoint Press LLC, 1919 Fifth St, Berkeley, CA 94710 *Tel:* 510-704-0230 *Fax:* 510-704-0268 *E-mail:* info@counterpointpress.com *Web Site:* counterpointpress.com; www.sierraclub.org/books; softskull.com, pg 63

Kowal, Basia, University of Alberta Press, Ring House 2, Edmonton, AB T6G 2E1, Canada *Tel:* 780-492-3662 *Fax:* 780-492-0719 *Web Site:* www.uap.ualberta.ca, pg 473

Kowalchuk, Tavia, HarperCollins General Books Group, 195 Broadway, New York, NY 10007 *Tel:* 212-207-7000 *Web Site:* www.harpercollins.com, pg 101

Kowalewski, Christina, Focus, PO Box 44937, Indianapolis, IN 46244-0937 *Tel:* 317-635-9250 *Fax:* 317-635-9292 *E-mail:* customer@hackettpublishing.com; editorial@hackettpublishing.com *Web Site:* focusbookstore.com, pg 86

Kowaluk, Lucia, Black Rose Books Ltd, CP 35788 Succ Leo Pariseau, Montreal, QC H2X 0A4, Canada *Tel:* 514-844-4076 *Toll Free Tel:* 800-565-9523 (orders) *Toll Free Fax:* 800-221-9985 (orders) *E-mail:* info@blackrosebooks.net *Web Site:* blackrosebooks.net, pg 446

Kozlowski, Darrell, DWJ BOOKS LLC, 46 Cliff Dr, Sag Harbor, NY 11963 *Tel:* 631-899-4500 *E-mail:* info@dwjbooks.com *Web Site:* www.dwjbooks.com, pg 492

Krach, Elizabeth, Kimberley Cameron & Associates LLC, 1550 Tiburon Blvd, Suite 704, Tiburon, CA 94920 *Tel:* 415-789-9191 *Fax:* 415-789-9177 *Web Site:* www.kimberleycameron.com, pg 511

Kracht, Peter, University of Pittsburgh Press, 7500 Thomas Blvd, Pittsburgh, PA 15260 *Tel:* 412-383-2456 *Fax:* 412-383-2466 *E-mail:* info@upress.pitt.edu *Web Site:* www.upress.pitt.edu, pg 244

Kraft, Eric, Kraft & Kraft, 40 Memorial Hwy, Apt 23-C, New Rochelle, NY 10801 *Tel:* 914-319-3320 *Web Site:* www.erickraft.com, pg 497

Kraft, Madeline, Kraft & Kraft, 40 Memorial Hwy, Apt 23-C, New Rochelle, NY 10801 *Tel:* 914-319-3320 *Web Site:* www.erickraft.com, pg 497

Kral, Steve, Society for Mining, Metallurgy & Exploration, 12999 E Adam Aircraft Circle, Englewood, CO 80112 *Tel:* 303-948-4200 *Toll Free Tel:* 800-763-3132 *Fax:* 303-973-3845 *E-mail:* cs@smenet.org; books@smenet.org *Web Site:* www.smenet.org, pg 216

Kramer, David, United Talent Agency, 9336 Civic Center Dr, Beverly Hills, CA 90210 *Tel:* 310-273-6700 *Fax:* 310-247-1111 *Web Site:* www.unitedtalent.com, pg 540

Kramer, Gary, Temple University Press, 1852 N Tenth St, Philadelphia, PA 19122-6099 *Tel:* 215-926-2140 *Toll Free Tel:* 800-621-2736 *Fax:* 215-926-2141 *E-mail:* tempress@temple.edu *Web Site:* www.temple.edu/tempress, pg 228

Kramer, Jill, Waterside Productions Inc, 2055 Oxford Ave, Cardiff, CA 92007 *Tel:* 760-632-9190 *Fax:* 760-632-9295 *E-mail:* admin@waterside.com *Web Site:* www.waterside.com, pg 541

Kramer, Linda, HJ Kramer Inc, PO Box 1082, Tiburon, CA 94920 *Tel:* 415-884-2100 (ext 10) *Toll Free Tel:* 800-972-6657 *Fax:* 415-435-5364 *E-mail:* hjkramer@jps.net *Web Site:* www.hjkramer.com; www.newworldlibrary.com, pg 128

Kramp, John, Thomas Nelson, 501 Nelson Place, Nashville, TN 37214 *Tel:* 615-889-9000 *Toll Free Tel:* 800-251-4000 *Fax:* 615-902-1548 *Web Site:* www.thomasnelson.com, pg 231

Krannich, Ronald PhD, Impact Publications/Development Concepts Inc, 9104 Manassas Dr, Suite N, Manassas Park, VA 20111-5211 *Tel:* 703-361-7300 *Toll Free Tel:* 800-361-1055 (cust serv) *Fax:* 703-335-9486 *E-mail:* query@impactpublications.com *Web Site:* www.impactpublications.com; www.veteransworld.com, pg 115

Kranz, Deb, Plexus Publishing, Inc, 143 Old Marlton Pike, Medford, NJ 08055 *Tel:* 609-654-6500 *Fax:* 609-654-4309 *E-mail:* info@plexuspublishing.com *Web Site:* www.plexuspublishing.com, pg 184

Kranz, Patricia, Overseas Press Club of America (OPC), 40 W 45 St, New York, NY 10036 *Tel:* 212-626-9220 *Fax:* 212-626-9210 *Web Site:* www.opcofamerica.org, pg 575

Kranz, Patricia, The Cornelius Ryan Award, 40 W 45 St, New York, NY 10036 *Tel:* 212-626-9220 *Fax:* 212-626-9210 *E-mail:* info@opcofamerica.org *Web Site:* www.opcofamerica.org, pg 686

Krasner, Emily, Workman Publishing Co Inc, 225 Varick St, 9th fl, New York, NY 10014-4381 *Tel:* 212-254-5900 *Toll Free Tel:* 800-722-7202 *Fax:* 212-254-8098 *E-mail:* info@workman.com *Web Site:* www.workman.com, pg 259

Krasner, Justin, Workman Publishing Co Inc, 225 Varick St, 9th fl, New York, NY 10014-4381 *Tel:* 212-254-5900 *Toll Free Tel:* 800-722-7202 *Fax:* 212-254-8098 *E-mail:* info@workman.com *Web Site:* www.workman.com, pg 259

Krassner, Kaye, Association of Publishers for Special Sales (APSS), PO Box 715, Avon, CT 06001-0715 *Tel:* 860-675-1344 *Web Site:* www.spannet.org, pg 559

Krattenmaker, Kathleen, Philadelphia Museum of Art, 2525 Pennsylvania Ave, Philadelphia, PA 19130 *Tel:* 215-684-7250 *Fax:* 215-235-8715 *Web Site:* www.philamuseum.org, pg 182

Kraus, Marisa Smith, Smith & Kraus Publishers Inc, 40 Walch Dr, Portland, ME 04103 *Tel:* 207-523-2585 *Toll Free Tel:* 877-668-8680 *Fax:* 207-699-3698 *E-mail:* editor@smithandkraus.com *Web Site:* www.smithandkraus.com, pg 215

Krause, Amanda, The University of Arizona Press, 1510 E University Blvd, Tucson, AZ 85721 *Tel:* 520-621-1441 *Toll Free Tel:* 800-426-3797 (orders) *Fax:* 520-621-8899 *Toll Free Fax:* 800-426-3797 *E-mail:* uap@uapress.arizona.edu *Web Site:* www.uapress.arizona.edu, pg 240

Krause, Bill, Llewellyn Publications, 2143 Wooddale Dr, Woodbury, MN 55125 *Tel:* 651-291-1970 *Toll Free Tel:* 800-843-6666 *Fax:* 651-291-1908 *E-mail:* publicity@llewellyn.com; customerservice@llewellyn.com *Web Site:* www.llewellyn.com, pg 137

Krause, Chester L, Krause Publications Inc, 700 E State St, Iola, WI 54990 *Tel:* 715-445-2214 *Toll Free Tel:* 800-258-0929 (cust serv); 888-457-2873 (orders) *Fax:* 715-445-4087 *E-mail:* bookorders@krause.com *Web Site:* www.krausebooks.com, pg 128

Krause, Jeffrey, Society of Manufacturing Engineers, One SME Dr, Dearborn, MI 48121 *Tel:* 313-425-3000 *Toll Free Tel:* 800-733-4763 (cust serv) *Fax:* 313-425-3400 *E-mail:* publications@sme.org *Web Site:* www.sme.org, pg 216

Krause, Katrina, Houghton Mifflin Harcourt Trade & Reference Division, 125 High St, Boston, MA 02110 *Tel:* 617-351-5000 *Toll Free Tel:* 800-225-3362 *Web Site:* www.hmhco.com, pg 111

Krauss, Molly, Chronicle Books LLC, 680 Second St, San Francisco, CA 94107 *Tel:* 415-537-4200 *Toll Free Tel:* 800-759-0190 (cust serv) *Fax:* 415-537-4460 *Toll Free Fax:* 800-858-7787 (orders); 800-286-9471 (cust serv) *E-mail:* frontdesk@chroniclebooks.com *Web Site:* www.chroniclebooks.com, pg 55

Krauss, Pam, Avery, 375 Hudson St, New York, NY 10014 *Tel:* 212-366-2000 *Fax:* 212-366-2643 *Web Site:* www.penguin.com; www.penguinrandomhouse.com, pg 27

Kraut, Diane, DK Research Inc, 14 Mohegan Lane, Commack, NY 11725 *Tel:* 631-543-5537 *Fax:* 631-543-5549 *E-mail:* dkresearch@optimum.net *Web Site:* www.dkresearchinc.com, pg 492

Kravenas, Mary, Chicago Review Press, 814 N Franklin St, Chicago, IL 60610 *Tel:* 312-337-0747 *Toll Free Tel:* 800-888-4741 *Fax:* 312-337-5110 *E-mail:* frontdesk@chicagoreviewpress.com *Web Site:* www.chicagoreviewpress.com, pg 54

Kravitz, Jamie, Aspen Words, 110 E Hallam St, Suite 116, Aspen, CO 81611 *Tel:* 970-925-3122 *Fax:* 970-920-5700 *E-mail:* aspenwords@aspeninstitute.org *Web Site:* www.aspenwords.org, pg 557

Kravitz, Jamie, Aspen Words Literary Prize, 110 E Hallam St, Suite 116, Aspen, CO 81611 *Tel:* 970-925-3122 *Fax:* 970-920-5700 *E-mail:* literary.prize@aspeninstitute.org *Web Site:* www.aspenwords.org, pg 629

Kravitz, Jamie, Summer Words Writing Conference & Literary Festival, 110 E Hallam St, Suite 116, Aspen, CO 81611 *Tel:* 970-925-3122 *Fax:* 970-920-5700 *E-mail:* aspenwords@aspeninstitute.org *Web Site:* www.aspenwords.org, pg 615

Kravitz, Jamie, Winter Words Author Series, 110 E Hallam St, Suite 116, Aspen, CO 81611 *Tel:* 970-925-3122 *Fax:* 970-920-5700 *E-mail:* aspenwords@aspeninstitute.org *Web Site:* www.aspenwords.org, pg 616

Krawczyk, Andie, Candlewick Press, 99 Dover St, Somerville, MA 02144-2825 *Tel:* 617-661-3330 *Fax:* 617-661-0565 *E-mail:* bigbear@candlewick.com; salesinfo@candlewick.com *Web Site:* www.candlewick.com, pg 46

Krebs, Gary, Brilliance Audio, 1704 Eaton Dr, Grand Haven, MI 49417 *Tel:* 616-846-5256 *Toll Free Tel:* 800-648-2312 (orders only) *Fax:* 616-846-0630 *E-mail:* customerservice@brillianceaudio.com *Web Site:* www.brillianceaudio.com, pg 43

Krebs, Paula, Modern Language Association of America (MLA), 85 Broad St, Suite 500, New York, NY 10004-2434 *Tel:* 646-576-5000 *Fax:* 646-458-0030 *Web Site:* www.mla.org, pg 152

Krebs, Paula, Modern Language Association of America (MLA), 85 Broad St, Suite 500, New York, NY 10004-2434 *Tel:* 646-576-5000 *Fax:* 646-458-0030 *E-mail:* convention@mla.org *Web Site:* www.mla.org, pg 570

Kregel, James R, Editorial Portavoz, 2450 Oak Industrial Dr NE, Grand Rapids, MI 49505 *Toll Free Tel:* 877-733-2607 (ext 206) *Fax:* 616-493-1790 *E-mail:* portavoz@portavoz.com *Web Site:* www.portavoz.com, pg 76

Kregel, James R, Kregel Publications, 2450 Oak Industrial Dr NE, Grand Rapids, MI 49505 *Tel:* 616-451-4775 *Toll Free Tel:* 800-733-2607 *Fax:* 616-451-9330 *E-mail:* kregelbooks@kregel.com *Web Site:* www.kregel.com, pg 128

Kregel, Jerold W, Kregel Publications, 2450 Oak Industrial Dr NE, Grand Rapids, MI 49505 *Tel:* 616-451-4775 *Toll Free Tel:* 800-733-2607 *Fax:* 616-451-9330 *E-mail:* kregelbooks@kregel.com *Web Site:* www.kregel.com, pg 128

Krehbiel, Kenneth, National Council of Teachers of Mathematics (NCTM), 1906 Association Dr, Reston, VA 20191-1502 *Tel:* 703-620-9840 *Toll Free Tel:* 800-235-7566 *Fax:* 703-476-2970 *E-mail:* nctm@nctm.org *Web Site:* www.nctm.org, pg 158

Kreit, Eileen Bishop, Puffin Books, 345 Hudson St, New York, NY 10014 *Tel:* 212-366-2000 *Web Site:* www.penguin.com/publishers/puffin, pg 191

Kreiter, Lance, Boom! Studios, 5670 Wilshire Blvd, Suite 450, Los Angeles, CA 90036 *Web Site:* www.boom-studios.com, pg 40

Krell, Henry, Springer, 233 Spring St, New York, NY 10013-1578 *Tel:* 212-460-1500 *Toll Free Tel:* 800-SPRINGER (777-4643) *Fax:* 212-460-1700 *E-mail:* customerservice@springer.com *Web Site:* www.springer.com, pg 219

Kreloff, Elliot, Blue Apple Books, 515 Valley St, Suite 170, Maplewood, NJ 07040 *Tel:* 973-763-8191 *Toll Free Tel:* 800-283-3572 (orders) *Fax:* 973-763-5944 *E-mail:* info@blueapplebooks.com *Web Site:* blueapplebooks.com, pg 38

Kremer, John, Open Horizons Publishing Co, PO Box 2887, Taos, NM 87571 *Tel:* 575-751-3398 *E-mail:* info@bookmarket.com *Web Site:* www.bookmarket.com, pg 168

Kresan, Dawn, Palimpsest Press, 1171 Eastlawn Ave, Windsor, ON N8S 3J1, Canada *Tel:* 519-259-2112 *E-mail:* info@palimpsestpress.ca *Web Site:* www.palimpsestpress.ca, pg 466

Kress, Steven, The Pennsylvania State University Press, University Support Bldg 1, Suite C, 820 N University Dr, University Park, PA 16802-1003 *Tel:* 814-865-1327 *Toll Free Tel:* 800-326-9180 *Fax:* 814-863-1408 *Toll Free Fax:* 877-778-2665 *E-mail:* info@psupress.org *Web Site:* www.psupress.org, pg 179

Kretzer, Marilyn, Sterling Publishing Co Inc, 1166 Avenue of the Americas, 17th fl, New York, NY 10036 *Tel:* 212-532-7160 *Toll Free Tel:* 800-367-9692 *Fax:* 212-213-2495 *Web Site:* www.sterlingpublishing.com, pg 222

Kretzschmar, Lauren, Insight Editions, 800 "A" St, San Rafael, CA 94901 *Tel:* 415-526-1370 *Toll Free Tel:* 800-809-3792 *Toll Free Fax:* 866-509-0515 *E-mail:* info@insighteditions.com *Web Site:* www.insighteditions.com, pg 117

Kreuser, Joe, Bloomsbury Academic, 1385 Broadway, 5th fl, New York, NY 10018 *Tel:* 212-419-5300 *Web Site:* www.bloomsbury.com/us/academic, pg 37

Krichevsky, Stuart, Stuart Krichevsky Literary Agency Inc, 6 E 39 St, Suite 500, New York, NY 10016 *Tel:* 212-725-5288 *Fax:* 212-725-5275 *E-mail:* query@skagency.com *Web Site:* skagency.com, pg 525

Krieger, Donald E, Krieger Publishing Co, 1725 Krieger Lane, Malabar, FL 32950 *Tel:* 321-724-9542 *Fax:* 321-951-3671 *E-mail:* info@krieger-publishing.com *Web Site:* www.krieger-publishing.com, pg 128

Krienke, Mary, Sterling Lord Literistic Inc, 115 Broadway, Suite 1602, New York, NY 10006 *Tel:* 212-780-6050 *Fax:* 212-780-6095 *E-mail:* info@sll.com *Web Site:* www.sll.com, pg 537

Krinsky, Santosh, Lotus Press, PO Box 325, Twin Lakes, WI 53181-0325 *Tel:* 262-889-8561 *Toll Free Tel:* 800-824-6396 (orders) *Fax:* 262-889-8591 *E-mail:* lotuspress@lotuspress.com *Web Site:* www.lotuspress.com, pg 138

Krishnan, Priyanka, HarperCollins General Books Group, 195 Broadway, New York, NY 10007 *Tel:* 212-207-7000 *Web Site:* www.harpercollins.com, pg 101

Kriss, Miriam, Irene Goodman Literary Agency, 27 W 24 St, Suite 700B, New York, NY 10010 *Tel:* 212-604-0330 *E-mail:* queries@irenegoodman.com *Web Site:* www.irenegoodman.com, pg 519

Krissoff, Derek, West Virginia University Press, West Virginia University, PO Box 6295, Morgantown, WV 26506-6295 *Tel:* 304-293-8400 *Fax:* 304-293-6585 *Web Site:* www.wvupress.com, pg 254

Kritzmacher, John, John Wiley & Sons Inc, 111 River St, Hoboken, NJ 07030-5774 *Tel:* 201-748-6000 *Toll Free Tel:* 800-225-5945 (cust serv) *Fax:* 201-748-6088 *E-mail:* info@wiley.com *Web Site:* www.wiley.com, pg 256

Krivda, David, Simon & Schuster, Inc, 1230 Avenue of the Americas, New York, NY 10020 *Tel:* 212-698-7000 *Fax:* 212-698-7007 *E-mail:* firstname.lastname@simonandschuster.com *Web Site:* www.simonandschuster.com, pg 213

Kroger, Rev Dan OFM, Franciscan Media, 28 W Liberty St, Cincinnati, OH 45202 *Tel:* 513-241-5615 *Toll Free Tel:* 800-488-0488 *Fax:* 513-241-0399 *E-mail:* books@americancatholic.org *Web Site:* www.americancatholic.org; www.franciscanmedia.org, pg 88

Kroll, Edite, Edite Kroll Literary Agency Inc, 20 Cross St, Saco, ME 04072 *Tel:* 207-283-8797 *Fax:* 207-283-8799, pg 525

Kronenberg, Annie, John Hawkins and Associates Inc, 80 Maiden Lane, Suite 1503, New York, NY 10038 *Tel:* 212-807-7040 *E-mail:* jha@jhalit.com *Web Site:* jhalit.com, pg 521

Krones, Christine, Houghton Mifflin Harcourt Trade & Reference Division, 125 High St, Boston, MA 02110 *Tel:* 617-351-5000 *Toll Free Tel:* 800-225-3362 *Web Site:* www.hmhco.com, pg 111

Kronzek, Lynn C, Lynn C Kronzek & Richard A Flom, 145 S Glenoaks Blvd, Suite 240, Burbank, CA 91502 *Tel:* 818-768-7688 *Fax:* 818-768-7648, pg 497

Krovitz, Debbie, DeVorss & Co, 553 Constitution Ave, Camarillo, CA 93012-8510 *Tel:* 805-322-9010 *Toll Free Tel:* 800-843-5743 *Fax:* 805-322-9011 *E-mail:* service@devorss.com *Web Site:* www.devorss.com, pg 70

Krowl, Michelle, Abraham Lincoln Institute Book Award, 105 Mount Olive Lane, Ephrata, PA 17522 *E-mail:* secretary@lincoln-institute.org *Web Site:* www.lincoln-institute.org, pg 661

Krueger, Jo Ann, The Aaland Agency, PO Box 849, Inyokern, CA 93527-0849 *Tel:* 760-384-3910 *Web Site:* www.the-aaland-agency.com, pg 505

Krug, Susan, American Medical Writers Association (AMWA), 30 W Gude Dr, Suite 525, Rockville, MD 20850-4357 *Tel:* 240-238-0940 *Fax:* 301-294-9006 *E-mail:* amwa@amwa.org *Web Site:* www.amwa.org, pg 555

Krump, Emily, HarperCollins General Books Group, 195 Broadway, New York, NY 10007 *Tel:* 212-207-7000 *Web Site:* www.harpercollins.com, pg 101

Krumpe, Mr Kreig, Boyds Mills Press, 815 Church St, Honesdale, PA 18431 *Tel:* 570-253-1164 *Toll Free Tel:* 800-490-5111 *Fax:* 570-253-0179 *E-mail:* contact@boydsmillspress.com *Web Site:* www.boydsmillspress.com, pg 41

Krumpfer, Jorie, W W Norton & Company Inc, 500 Fifth Ave, New York, NY 10110-0017 *Tel:* 212-354-5500 *Toll Free Tel:* 800-233-4830 (orders & cust serv) *Fax:* 212-869-0856 *Toll Free Fax:* 800-458-6515 *E-mail:* orders@wwnorton.com *Web Site:* books.wwnorton.com, pg 164

Krup, Agnes, Sanford J Greenburger Associates Inc, 55 Fifth Ave, New York, NY 10003 *Tel:* 212-206-5600 *Fax:* 212-463-8718 *Web Site:* greenburger.com; www.sjga.com, pg 520

Krupin, Emily, Harlequin Enterprises Ltd, 233 Broadway, Suite 1001, New York, NY 10279 *Tel:* 212-553-4200 *Fax:* 212-227-8969 *E-mail:* customerservice@harlequin.com *Web Site:* www.harlequin.com, pg 101

Kruse, Katrina, Houghton Mifflin Harcourt, 125 High St, Boston, MA 02110 *Tel:* 617-351-5000 *Toll Free Tel:* 855-969-4642; 800-225-5425 (K-12 educ materials); 800-323-9540 (assessment materials); 877-219-1537 (SkillsTutor); 888-242-6747 (Innovation in Educ Group); 800-225-3362 (Trade & Ref Div) *Toll Free Fax:* 800-269-5232 *E-mail:* myhmhco@hmhco.com *Web Site:* www.hmhco.com, pg 110

Krusinski, Anna, Hatherleigh Press Ltd, 62545 State Hwy 10, Hobart, NY 13788 *E-mail:* info@hatherleighpress.com; publicity@hatherleighpress.com *Web Site:* www.hatherleighpress.com, pg 103

Krysan, Alan, Astragal Press, 5995 149 St W, Suite 105, Apple Valley, MN 55124 *Tel:* 952-469-6699 *Toll Free Tel:* 866-543-3045 *Fax:* 952-469-1968 *Toll Free Fax:* 800-330-6232 *E-mail:* info@finneyco.com *Web Site:* www.astragalpress.com, pg 25

Krysan, Alan E, Ecopress, 5995 149 St W, Suite 105, Apple Valley, MN 55124 *Tel:* 952-469-6699 *Toll Free Tel:* 800-846-7027 *Fax:* 952-469-1968 *Toll Free Fax:* 800-330-6232 *E-mail:* info@finneyco.com *Web Site:* www.ecopress.com, pg 75

Krysan, Alan E, Finney Company Inc, 5995 149 St W, Suite 105, Apple Valley, MN 55124 *Tel:* 952-469-6699 *Toll Free Tel:* 800-846-7027 *Fax:* 952-469-1968 *Toll Free Fax:* 800-330-6232 *E-mail:* info@finneyco.com *Web Site:* www.finneyco.com, pg 85

Krysan, Alan E, Hobar Publications, 5995 149 St W, Suite 105, Apple Valley, MN 55124 *Tel:* 952-469-6699 *Toll Free Tel:* 800-846-7027 *Fax:* 952-469-1968 *Toll Free Fax:* 800-330-6232 *E-mail:* info@finneyco.com *Web Site:* www.finney-hobar.com, pg 108

Krysan, Alan E, Windward Publishing, 5995 149 St W, Suite 105, Apple Valley, MN 55124 *Tel:* 952-469-6699 *Toll Free Tel:* 800-846-7027 *Fax:* 952-469-1968 *Toll Free Fax:* 800-330-6232 *E-mail:* info@finneyco.com *Web Site:* www.finneyco.com, pg 257

Kubie, Greg, Random House Publishing Group, 1745 Broadway, New York, NY 10019 *Toll Free Tel:* 800-200-3552 *Web Site:* atrandom.com, pg 195

Kuehl, Ashley, Lerner Publications, 241 First Ave N, Minneapolis, MN 55401 *Tel:* 612-332-3344 *Toll Free Tel:* 800-328-4929 *Fax:* 612-332-7615 *Toll Free Fax:* 800-332-1132 *E-mail:* info@lernerbooks.com; custserve@lernerbooks.com *Web Site:* www.lernerbooks.com; www.facebook.com/lernerbooks, pg 132

Kuehl, Kathy, The Guilford Press, 370 Seventh Ave, Suite 1200, New York, NY 10001-1020 *Tel:* 212-431-9800 *Toll Free Tel:* 800-365-7006 *Fax:* 212-966-6708 *E-mail:* info@guilford.com *Web Site:* www.guilford.com, pg 97

Kuerbis, Lisa, Syracuse University Press, 621 Skytop Rd, Suite 110, Syracuse, NY 13244-5290 *Tel:* 315-443-5534 *Toll Free Tel:* 800-365-8929 (cust serv) *Fax:* 315-443-5545 *E-mail:* supress@syr.edu *Web Site:* syracuseuniversitypress.syr.edu, pg 226

Kuhn, David, Aevitas Creative Management, 19 W 21 St, Suite 501, New York, NY 10010 *Tel:* 212-765-6900 *Web Site:* aevitascreative.com, pg 506

Kujichagulia, Phavia, Media Alliance, 2830 20 St, Suite 102, San Francisco, CA 94110 *Tel:* 415-746-9475 *E-mail:* information@media-alliance.org *Web Site:* www.media-alliance.org, pg 569

Kuka, Ronald, Chris O'Malley Fiction Prize, University of Wisconsin, 6193 Helen C White Hall, English Dept, 600 N Park St, Madison, WI 53706 *E-mail:* madisonrevw@gmail.com *Web Site:* www.themadisonreview.com, pg 675

Kuka, Ronald, Phyllis Smart-Young Poetry Prize, University of Wisconsin, 6193 Helen C White Hall, English Dept, 600 N Park St, Madison, WI 53706 *E-mail:* madisonrevw@gmail.com *Web Site:* www.themadisonreview.com, pg 701

Kulka, John, Perseus Books, 250 W 57 St, 15th fl, New York, NY 10107 *Tel:* 212-340-8100 *Toll Free Tel:* 800-343-4499 (cust serv) *Fax:* 212-340-8105 *Web Site:* www.perseusbooks.com, pg 181

Kull, Irene Imperio, Temple University Press, 1852 N Tenth St, Philadelphia, PA 19122-6099 *Tel:* 215-926-2140 *Toll Free Tel:* 800-621-2736 *Fax:* 215-926-2141 *E-mail:* tempress@temple.edu *Web Site:* www.temple.edu/tempress, pg 228

Kulsavage, Kristin, Glitterati Inc, 630 Ninth Ave, Suite 603, New York, NY 10036 *Tel:* 212-362-9119 *Fax:* 646-607-4433 *E-mail:* info@glitteratiincorporated.com *Web Site:* glitteratiincorporated.com, pg 93

Kundert, Beth, McGraw-Hill Create, 2 Penn Plaza, New York, NY 10121 *Toll Free Tel:* 800-962-9342 *E-mail:* mhhe.create@mheducation.com *Web Site:* create.mheducation.com; shop.mheducation.com, pg 145

Kunjufu, Dr Jawanza PhD, African American Images, PO Box 1799, Chicago Heights, IL 60412 *Tel:* 708-672-4909 (cust serv) *Fax:* 708-672-0466 *E-mail:* customersvc@africanamericanimages.com *Web Site:* www.africanamericanimages.com, pg 5

Kuny, Greg, American Psychiatric Association Publishing, 1000 Wilson Blvd, Suite 1825, Arlington, VA 22209 *Tel:* 703-907-7322 *Toll Free Tel:* 800-368-5777 *Fax:* 703-907-1091 *E-mail:* appi@psych.org *Web Site:* www.appi.org; www.psychiatryonline.org, pg 14

Kunz, Jeannine, Society of Manufacturing Engineers, One SME Dr, Dearborn, MI 48121 *Tel:* 313-425-3000 *Toll Free Tel:* 800-733-4763 (cust serv) *Fax:* 313-425-3400 *E-mail:* publications@sme.org *Web Site:* www.sme.org, pg 216

Kuong, Jay, Management Advisory Services & Publications (MASP), PO Box 81151, Wellesley Hills, MA 02481-0001 *Tel:* 781-235-2895 *Fax:* 781-235-5446 *E-mail:* info@masp.com *Web Site:* www.masp.com, pg 140

Kupihea, Jhanteigh, Atria Books, 1230 Avenue of the Americas, New York, NY 10020 *Tel:* 212-698-7000 *Fax:* 212-698-7007 *Web Site:* www.simonandschuster.com, pg 25

Kurdyla, Jennifer, The Experiment, 220 E 23 St, Suite 301, New York, NY 10010-4674 *Tel:* 212-889-1659 *E-mail:* info@theexperimentpublishing.com *Web Site:* www.theexperimentpublishing.com, pg 81

Kurian, George Thomas, International Encyclopedia Society, 3689 Campbell Ct, Yorktown Heights, NY 10598 *Tel:* 914-962-3287 *Fax:* 914-962-3287, pg 567

Kurian, George Thomas, George Kurian Reference Books, 3689 Campbell Ct, Yorktown Heights, NY 10598 *Tel:* 914-962-3287 *Fax:* 914-962-3287, pg 128

Kurtz, Dustin, Counterpoint Press LLC, 1919 Fifth St, Berkeley, CA 94710 *Tel:* 510-704-0230 *Fax:* 510-704-0268 *E-mail:* info@counterpointpress.com *Web Site:* counterpointpress.com; www.sierraclub.org/books; softskull.com, pg 63

Kurtz, Gretchen, Prometheus Books, 59 John Glenn Dr, Amherst, NY 14228-2119 *Tel:* 716-691-0133 *Fax:* 716-691-0137 *E-mail:* marketing@prometheusbooks.com; editorial@prometheusbooks.com; rights@prometheusmail.com *Web Site:* www.prometheusbooks.com, pg 190

Kurtz, Jonathan, Prometheus Books, 59 John Glenn Dr, Amherst, NY 14228-2119 *Tel:* 716-691-0133 *Fax:* 716-691-0137 *E-mail:* marketing@prometheusbooks.com; editorial@prometheusbooks.com; rights@prometheusmail.com *Web Site:* www.prometheusbooks.com, pg 190

Kuschner, Sarah, Harvard Art Museums, 32 Quincy St, Cambridge, MA 02138 *Tel:* 617-495-1440; 617-496-6529 (edit) *Fax:* 617-495-9985 *Web Site:* www.harvardartmuseums.org, pg 102

Kushin, Kelin, Optometric Extension Program Foundation, 2300 York Rd, Suite 113, Timonium, MD 21093 *Tel:* 410-561-3791 *E-mail:* oep@oep.org *Web Site:* www.oepf.org, pg 169

Kusler, Jack, Addicus Books Inc, PO Box 45327, Omaha, NE 68145 *Tel:* 402-330-7493 *Fax:* 402-330-1707 *E-mail:* info@addicusbooks.com; addicusbks@aol.com *Web Site:* www.addicusbooks.com, pg 4

Kutsko, John F, SBL Press, The Luce Ctr, Suite 350, 825 Houston Mill Rd, Atlanta, GA 30329 *Tel:* 404-727-3100 *Fax:* 404-727-3101 (corp) *E-mail:* sbl@sbl-site.org *Web Site:* www.sbl-site.org, pg 207

Kye-Casella, Maura, Don Congdon Associates Inc, 110 William St, Suite 2202, New York, NY 10038-3914 *Tel:* 212-645-1229 *Fax:* 212-727-2688 *E-mail:* dca@doncongdon.com *Web Site:* www.doncongdon.com, pg 512

La Due, Holly, Prestel Publishing, 900 Broadway, Suite 603, New York, NY 10003 *Tel:* 212-995-2720 *Fax:* 212-995-2733 *E-mail:* sales@prestel-usa.com *Web Site:* prestelpublishing.randomhouse.de, pg 187

La Fehr, Audrey, Kensington Publishing Corp, 119 W 40 St, New York, NY 10018 *Tel:* 212-407-1500 *Toll Free Tel:* 800-221-2647 *Fax:* 212-935-0699 *Web Site:* www.kensingtonbooks.com, pg 125

La Mattina, Elaine, White Pine Press, PO Box 236, Buffalo, NY 14201 *Tel:* 716-627-4665 *Fax:* 716-627-4665 *E-mail:* wpine@whitepine.org *Web Site:* www.whitepine.org, pg 255

La Norte, Gianna, University of Texas Press, 3001 Lake Austin Blvd, 2.200, Austin, TX 78703 *Tel:* 512-471-7233 *Fax:* 512-232-7178 *E-mail:* utpress@uts.cc.utexas.edu; info@utpress.utexas.edu *Web Site:* www.utexaspress.com, pg 230

La Pointe, Kathy, Broden Books LLC, 3824 Sunset Dr, Spring Park, MN 55384 *Tel:* 952-471-1066 *E-mail:* media@brodenbooks.com *Web Site:* www.brodenbooks.com, pg 44

La Rosa, Suzanne, NewSouth Books, 105 S Court St, Montgomery, AL 36104 *Tel:* 334-834-3556 *Fax:* 334-834-3557 *E-mail:* info@newsouthbooks.com *Web Site:* www.newsouthbooks.com, pg 162

La Rose, Charley, Association of Canadian University Presses, 10 Saint Mary St, Suite 700, Toronto, ON M4Y 2W8, Canada *Tel:* 416-978-2239 ext 237 *Fax:* 416-978-4738 *Web Site:* www.acup.ca, pg 558

La Salle, Peter, University of Texas at Austin, New Writers Project, Dept of English, Calhoun Hall, Rm 226, 204 W 21 St, B-5000, Austin, TX 78712 *Tel:* 512-471-5132; 512-471-4991 *Fax:* 512-471-4909 *Web Site:* newwritersproject.org, pg 623

La Via, Carmen, Fifi Oscard Agency Inc, 1440 Broadway, 23rd fl, New York, NY 10018 *Tel:* 212-764-1100 *E-mail:* agency@fifioscard.com *Web Site:* fifioscard.com, pg 531

Labaqui, Joni, L Ron Hubbard's Writers of the Future Contest, 7501 Hollywood Blvd, Hollywood, CA 90028 *Tel:* 323-466-3310 *Toll Free Tel:* 800-624-6504 *Fax:* 323-466-6474 *E-mail:* contests@authorservicesinc.com *Web Site:* www.writersofthefuture.com, pg 654

Labes, Karolyn, SPIE, 1000 20 St, Bellingham, WA 98225-6705 *Tel:* 360-676-3290 *Toll Free Tel:* 888-504-8171 (orders) *Fax:* 360-647-1445 *E-mail:* help@spie.org; customerservice@spie.org (orders) *Web Site:* www.spie.org, pg 219

LaBore, Lindsey, Free Spirit Publishing Inc, 217 Fifth Ave N, Suite 200, Minneapolis, MN 55401-1299 *Tel:* 612-338-2068 *Toll Free Tel:* 800-735-7323 *Fax:* 612-337-5050 *Toll Free Fax:* 866-419-5199 *E-mail:* help4kids@freespirit.com *Web Site:* www.freespirit.com, pg 88

Labov, Christine, Penguin Random House Speakers Bureau, A Penguin Random House Company, 1745 Broadway, Mail Drop 13-1, New York, NY 10019 *Tel:* 212-572-2013 *E-mail:* speakers@penguinrandomhouse.com *Web Site:* www.prhspeakers.com, pg 547

Labrecque, Marise, Editions du CHU Sainte-Justine, 3175, chemin de la Cote-Sainte-Catherine, Montreal, QC H3T 1C5, Canada *Tel:* 514-345-4671 *Fax:* 514-345-4631 *E-mail:* edition.hsj@ssss.gouv.qc.ca *Web Site:* www.editions-chu-sainte-justine.org, pg 453

Lach, Will, Abbeville Press, 116 W 23 St, 5th fl, New York, NY 10011 *Tel:* 212-366-5585 *Toll Free Tel:* 800-ART-BOOK (278-2665); 800-343-4499 (orders) *Fax:* 646-375-2359 *Toll Free Fax:* 800-351-5073 (orders) *E-mail:* abbeville@abbeville.com; sales@abbeville.com; marketing@abbeville.com; rights@abbeville.com *Web Site:* www.abbeville.com, pg 2

Lachapelle, Jean, Editions Marie-France, CP 32263 BP Waverly, Montreal, QC H3L 3X1, Canada *Tel:* 514-329-3700 *Toll Free Tel:* 800-563 6644 (CN) *Fax:* 514-329-0630 *E-mail:* editions@marie-france.qc.ca *Web Site:* www.marie-france.qc.ca, pg 455

Lachatanere, Diana, Faith Childs Literary Agency Inc, 111 John St, Suite 1620, New York, NY 10038 *Tel:* 212-995-9600 *Web Site:* faithchildsliteraryagency.com, pg 511

Lachina, Jeffrey A, Lachina Publishing Services Inc, 3791 S Green Rd, Cleveland, OH 44122 *Tel:* 216-292-7959 *E-mail:* info@lachina.com *Web Site:* www.lachina.com, pg 497

Lacombe, Joanne, Editions Marie-France, CP 32263 BP Waverly, Montreal, QC H3L 3X1, Canada *Tel:* 514-329-3700 *Toll Free Tel:* 800-563 6644 (CN) *Fax:* 514-329-0630 *E-mail:* editions@marie-france.qc.ca *Web Site:* www.marie-france.qc.ca, pg 455

Lacy, Linda M, Carolina Academic Press, 700 Kent St, Durham, NC 27701 *Tel:* 919-489-7486 *Toll Free Tel:* 800-489-7486 *Fax:* 919-493-5668 *E-mail:* cap@cap-press.com *Web Site:* www.cap-press.com; www.caplaw.com, pg 48

LaDelle, Ebony, Simon & Schuster, 1230 Avenue of the Americas, New York, NY 10020 *Tel:* 212-698-7000 *Toll Free Tel:* 800-223-2348 (cust serv); 800-223-2336 (orders) *Toll Free Fax:* 800-943-9831 (orders) *Web Site:* www.simonandschuster.com, pg 212

LaFleur, Sara, GP Putnam's Sons (Children's), 345 Hudson St, New York, NY 10014 *Tel:* 212-366-2000 *Fax:* 212-414-3393 *Web Site:* www.penguin.com/publishers/gpputnamssonsbooksforyoungread, pg 192

Lafrances, G Mark, MWG Writer Workshops & State Conference, 9 Janice Circle, Natchez, MS 39120 *Tel:* 601-442-0980 *E-mail:* mississippi.writersguild@outlook.com *Web Site:* www.mississippiwritersguild.com, pg 613

Lagace, Nettie, National Information Standards Organization (NISO), 3600 Clipper Mill Rd, Suite 302, Baltimore, MD 21211 *Tel:* 301-654-2512 *Fax:* 410-685-5278 *E-mail:* nisohq@niso.org *Web Site:* www.niso.org, pg 158, 572

Lagunoff, Liza, Oscar Williams/Gene Derwood Award, 909 Third Ave, New York, NY 10022 *Tel:* 212-686-0010 *Fax:* 212-532-8528 *E-mail:* info@nycommunitytrust.org *Web Site:* www.nycommunitytrust.org, pg 698

Lahurd, Kristin, Coretta Scott King Book Awards, 50 E Huron St, Chicago, IL 60611 *Toll Free Tel:* 800-545-2433 *E-mail:* olos@ala.org *Web Site:* www.ala.org/emiert/cskbookawards, pg 658

Lai, Pauline, Captus Press Inc, 1600 Steeles Ave W, Units 14 & 15, Concord, ON L4K 4M2, Canada *Tel:* 416-736-5537 *Fax:* 416-736-5793 *E-mail:* info@captus.com *Web Site:* www.captus.com, pg 449

Laing, Bonnie, Pacific Press Publishing Association, 1350 N Kings Rd, Nampa, ID 83687-3193 *Tel:* 208-465-2500 *Toll Free Tel:* 800-447-7377 *Fax:* 208-465-2531 *Web Site:* www.pacificpress.com, pg 172

Laing, Glenn, American Society of Agricultural & Biological Engineers (ASABE), 2950 Niles Rd, St Joseph, MI 49085-9659 *Tel:* 269-429-0300 *Toll Free Tel:* 800-371-2723 *Fax:* 269-429-3852 *E-mail:* hq@asabe.org *Web Site:* www.asabe.org, pg 14

Laing, Lisa, Adams Media, 57 Littlefield St, Avon, MA 02322 *Tel:* 508-427-7100 *Web Site:* www.simonandschuster.com, pg 4

Lajeunesse, Danielle, Editions FouLire, 4339, rue des Becassines, Quebec, QC G1G 1V5, Canada *Tel:* 418-628-4029 *Toll Free Tel:* 877-628-4029 (CN & US) *Fax:* 418-628-4801 *E-mail:* info@foulire.com; edition@foulire.com *Web Site:* www.foulire.com, pg 454

Lake, Henry, The Professional Education Group LLC (PEG), 700 Twelve Oaks Center Dr, Suite 716, Wayzata, MN 55391 *Tel:* 952-933-9990 *Toll Free Tel:* 800-229-2531 *Fax:* 952-933-7784 *E-mail:* orders@proedgroup.com *Web Site:* www.proedgroup.com, pg 189

Lake, Kim, University Press of Florida, 15 NW 15 St, Gainesville, FL 32603-2079 *Tel:* 352-392-1351 *Toll Free Tel:* 800-226-3822 (orders only) *Fax:* 352-392-0590 *Toll Free Fax:* 800-680-1955 (orders only) *E-mail:* press@upress.ufl.edu; orders@upress.ufl.edu *Web Site:* www.upf.com, pg 246

Lakin, Chuck, Zeig, Tucker & Theisen Inc, 2632 E Thomas Rd, Suite 200, Phoenix, AZ 85016 *Tel:* 480-389-4342 *Fax:* 602-944-8118 *E-mail:* marketing@zeigtucker.com *Web Site:* www.zeigtucker.com, pg 262

Lakosil, Natalie, Bradford Literary Agency, 5694 Mission Center Rd, Suite 347, San Diego, CA 92108 *Tel:* 619-521-1201 *E-mail:* queries@bradfordlit.com *Web Site:* www.bradfordlit.com, pg 509

Lalonde, Chantale Gravel, Scholastic Canada Ltd, 604 King St W, Toronto, ON M5V 1E1, Canada *Tel:* 905-887-7323 *Toll Free Tel:* 800-268-3860 (CN) *Toll Free Fax:* 866-387-4944 *E-mail:* custserve@scholastic.ca *Web Site:* www.scholastic.ca, pg 469

Lalwani, R, Laurier Books Ltd, PO Box 8493, Ottawa, ON K1G 3H9, Canada *Tel:* 613-738-2163 *Toll Free Fax:* 855-736-9160 *E-mail:* laurierbooks@yahoo.com, pg 462

Lam, Andrea, Viking, 375 Hudson St, New York, NY 10014 *Tel:* 212-366-2000 *Fax:* 212-243-6002 *Web Site:* www.penguin.com/publishers/vikingbooks, pg 250

Lam, Anna, Alex Awards, 50 E Huron St, Chicago, IL 60611 *Tel:* 312-280-4390 *Toll Free Tel:* 800-545-2433 *Fax:* 312-280-5276 *E-mail:* yalsa@ala.org *Web Site:* www.ala.org/yalsa/alex-awards, pg 626

Lam, Anna, Baker & Taylor/YALSA Conference Grants, 50 E Huron St, Chicago, IL 60611 *Tel:* 312-280-4390 *Toll Free Tel:* 800-545-2433 *Fax:* 312-280-5276; 312-664-7459 *E-mail:* yalsa@ala.org *Web Site:* www.ala.org/yalsa, pg 630

Lam, Anna, Margaret A Edwards Award, 50 E Huron St, Chicago, IL 60611 *Tel:* 312-280-4390 *Toll Free Tel:* 800-545-2433 *Fax:* 312-280-5276 *E-mail:* yalsa@ala.org *Web Site:* www.ala.org/yalsa/edwards, pg 643

Lam, Anna, Frances Henne YALSA/VOYA Research Grant, 50 E Huron St, Chicago, IL 60611 *Tel:* 312-280-4390 *Toll Free Tel:* 800-545-2433 *Fax:* 312-280-5276 *E-mail:* yalsa@ala.org *Web Site:* www.ala.org/yalsa/awardsandgrants/franceshenne, pg 647

Lam, Anna, Michael L Printz Award, 50 E Huron St, Chicago, IL 60611 *Tel:* 312-280-4390 *Toll Free Tel:* 800-545-2433 *Fax:* 312-280-5276 *E-mail:* yalsa@ala.org *Web Site:* www.ala.org/yalsa/printz, pg 682

Lam, Brian, Arsenal Pulp Press, 211 E Georgia St, No 202, Vancouver, BC V6A 1Z6, Canada *Tel:* 604-687-4233 *Toll Free Tel:* 888-600-PULP (600-7857) *Fax:* 604-687-4283 *E-mail:* info@arsenalpulp.com *Web Site:* www.arsenalpulp.com, pg 445

Lamb, Beth, Anchor Books, c/o Penguin Random House Inc, 1745 Broadway, New York, NY 10019 *Tel:* 212-572-2420 *E-mail:* vintageanchorpublicity@randomhouse.com *Web Site:* knopfdoubleday.com/imprint/anchor, pg 16

Lamb, Beth, Vintage Books, c/o Penguin Random House Inc, 1745 Broadway, New York, NY 10019 *Tel:* 212-572-2420 *E-mail:* vintageanchorpublicity@randomhouse.com *Web Site:* knopfdoubleday.com/imprint/vintage, pg 251

Lamb, Cynthia, Carnegie Mellon University Press, 5032 Forbes Ave, Pittsburgh, PA 15289-1021 *Tel:* 412-268-2861 *Fax:* 412-268-8706 *E-mail:* carnegiemellonuniversitypress@gmail.com *Web Site:* www.cmu.edu/universitypress, pg 48

Lamb, David, Hachette Books, 1290 Avenue of the Americas, New York, NY 10019 *Tel:* 212-364-1100 *Web Site:* www.hachettebookgroup.com, pg 98

Lamb, Jason, Bread Loaf Writers' Conference, 5525 Middlebury College, 14 Old Chapel Rd, Middlebury, VT 05753 *Tel:* 802-443-5286 *Fax:* 802-443-2087 *E-mail:* blwc@middlebury.edu *Web Site:* www.middlebury.edu/blwc, pg 610

Lamb, Jason, Fellowship, Tuition Scholarship & Work Study Programs for Writers, Middlebury College, 204 College St, Middlebury, VT 05753 *Tel:* 802-443-5286 *Fax:* 802-443-2087 *E-mail:* blwc@middlebury.edu *Web Site:* www.middlebury.edu/blwc, pg 646

Lamb, John D, Lost Lake Writers Retreat, PO Box 304, Royal Oak, MI 48068-0304 *Tel:* 248-589-3913 *Web Site:* www.springfed.org, pg 612

Lamb, Paul, HarperCollins General Books Group, 195 Broadway, New York, NY 10007 *Tel:* 212-207-7000 *Web Site:* www.harpercollins.com, pg 101

Lamb, Wendy, Random House Children's Books, 1745 Broadway, 10th fl, New York, NY 10019 *Tel:* 212-782-9000 *Web Site:* www.randomhousekids.com, pg 194

Lamba, Cari, The Jennifer DeChiara Literary Agency, 299 Park Ave, 6th fl, New York, NY 10171 *Tel:* 212-739-0803 *Web Site:* www.jdlit.com, pg 513

Lamba, Marie, The Jennifer DeChiara Literary Agency, 299 Park Ave, 6th fl, New York, NY 10171 *Tel:* 212-739-0803 *Web Site:* www.jdlit.com, pg 513

Lambeth, Pike, Foundation Publications, 900 S Euclid St, La Habra, CA 90631 *Tel:* 714-879-2286 *Toll Free Tel:* 800-257-6272 *Fax:* 714-535-2164 *E-mail:* info@foundationpublications.com *Web Site:* www.foundationpublications.com, pg 87

Lamkins, Tim, SPIE, 1000 20 St, Bellingham, WA 98225-6705 *Tel:* 360-676-3290 *Toll Free Tel:* 888-504-8171 (orders) *Fax:* 360-647-1445 *E-mail:* help@spie.org; customerservice@spie.org (orders) *Web Site:* www.spie.org, pg 219

Lamm, Gigi, University of Pennsylvania Press, 3905 Spruce St, Philadelphia, PA 19104 *Tel:* 215-898-6261 *Fax:* 215-898-0404 *E-mail:* custserv@pobox.upenn.edu *Web Site:* www.pennpress.org, pg 244

Lamolinara, Guy, The Center for the Book in the Library of Congress, The Library of Congress, 101 Independence Ave SE, Washington, DC 20540-4920 *Tel:* 202-707-5221 *Fax:* 202-707-0269 *E-mail:* cfbook@loc.gov *Web Site:* www.read.gov; www.read.gov/cfb, pg 563

Lamolinara, Guy, Library of Congress Prize for American Fiction, 101 Independence Ave SE, Washington, DC 20540-1400 *Tel:* 202-707-5221 (Center for the Book) *Fax:* 202-707-0269 *Web Site:* www.loc.gov, pg 661

Lampack, Andrew, Peter Lampack Agency Inc, 350 Fifth Ave, Suite 5300, New York, NY 10118 *Tel:* 212-687-9106 *Fax:* 212-687-9109 *Web Site:* www.peterlampackagency.com, pg 525

Lampack, Peter A, Peter Lampack Agency Inc, 350 Fifth Ave, Suite 5300, New York, NY 10118 *Tel:* 212-687-9106 *Fax:* 212-687-9109 *Web Site:* www.peterlampackagency.com, pg 525

Lampe, Betsy Wright, Rainbow Books Inc, PO Box 430, Highland City, FL 33846 *Tel:* 863-648-4420 *Fax:* 863-647-5951 *E-mail:* info@rainbowbooksinc.com; rbibooks@aol.com *Web Site:* www.rainbowbooksinc.com, pg 193

Lampe, C Marzen, Rainbow Books Inc, PO Box 430, Highland City, FL 33846 *Tel:* 863-648-4420 *Fax:* 863-647-5951 *E-mail:* info@rainbowbooksinc.com; rbibooks@aol.com *Web Site:* www.rainbowbooksinc.com, pg 193

Lampley, Tim, Quarto Publishing Group USA Inc, 400 First Ave N, Suite 400, Minneapolis, MN 55401 *Tel:* 612-344-8100 *Toll Free Tel:* 800-328-0590 (sales); 800-458-0454 *Fax:* 612-344-8691 *E-mail:* sales@quartous.com *Web Site:* www.quartoknows.com, pg 192

Lampo, David, Cato Institute, 1000 Massachusetts Ave NW, Washington, DC 20001-5403 *Tel:* 202-842-0200 *Toll Free Tel:* 800-767-1241 *Fax:* 202-842-3490 *E-mail:* catostore@cato.org *Web Site:* www.cato.org, pg 49

Lancaster, Brian, Africana Homestead Legacy Publishers Inc, 926 Haddonfield Rd, Suite E, No 329, Cherry Hill, NJ 08002 *Tel:* 856-673-0363 *Fax:* 856-486-1135 *E-mail:* customer-service@ahlpub.com; sales@ahlpub.com; editors@ahlpub.com *Web Site:* www.ahlpub.com, pg 5

Lancaster, Terri, Chronicle Books LLC, 680 Second St, San Francisco, CA 94107 *Tel:* 415-537-4200 *Toll Free Tel:* 800-759-0190 (cust serv) *Fax:* 415-537-4460 *Toll Free Fax:* 800-858-7787 (orders); 800-286-9471 (cust serv) *E-mail:* frontdesk@chroniclebooks.com *Web Site:* www.chroniclebooks.com, pg 55

Lance, Dan, Kalmbach Publishing Co, 21027 Crossroads Circle, Waukesha, WI 53186 *Tel:* 262-796-8776 *Toll Free Tel:* 800-533-6644 (cust serv & orders); 800-558-1544 *Fax:* 262-798-6592 *E-mail:* customerservice@kalmbach.com *Web Site:* www.kalmbach.com, pg 124

Lance, James, Cornell University Press, Sage House, 512 E State St, Ithaca, NY 14850 *Tel:* 607-277-2338 *Fax:* 607-277-2374 *E-mail:* cupressinfo@cornell.edu; cupress-sales@cornell.edu *Web Site:* www.cornellpress.cornell.edu, pg 61

Lance, Suzanne, New York State Edith Wharton Citation of Merit for Fiction Writers, University at Albany, SL 320, Albany, NY 12222 *Tel:* 518-442-5620 *Fax:* 518-442-5621 *E-mail:* writers@albany.edu *Web Site:* www.albany.edu/writers-inst, pg 673

Lance, Suzanne, New York State Walt Whitman Citation of Merit for Poets, University at Albany, SL 320, Albany, NY 12222 *Tel:* 518-442-5620 *Fax:* 518-442-5621 *E-mail:* writers@albany.edu *Web Site:* www.albany.edu/writers-inst, pg 673

Lance, Suzanne, New York State Writers Institute, University at Albany, Science Library 320, 1400 Washington Ave, Albany, NY 12222 *Tel:* 518-442-5620 *Fax:* 518-442-5621 *E-mail:* writers@albany.edu *Web Site:* www.albany.edu/writers-inst, pg 613

Land, Bob, Land on Demand, 20 Long Crescent Dr, Bristol, VA 24201 *Tel:* 423-366-0513 *E-mail:* landondemand@gmail.com *Web Site:* boblandedits.blogspot.com, pg 497

Landa, Anne, Walter Foster Publishing Inc, 6 Orchard Rd, Suite 100, Lake Forest, CA 92630 *Tel:* 949-380-7510 *Toll Free Tel:* 800-426-0099; 800-759-0190 (orders) *Fax:* 949-380-7575 *E-mail:* walterfoster@quartous.com *Web Site:* www.quartous.com, pg 87

Landau, David, Harvard Square Editions, 2152 Beachwood Terr, Hollywood, CA 90068 *Tel:* 323-203-0233 *E-mail:* submissions@harvardsquareeditions.org *Web Site:* harvardsquareeditions.org, pg 102

Landauer, Jeramy, Landauer Corp, 3100 101 St, Suite A, Urbandale, IA 50322 *Tel:* 515-287-2144 *Toll Free Tel:* 800-557-2144 *Fax:* 515-276-5102 *E-mail:* info@landauercorp.com *Web Site:* www.landauercorp.com, pg 129

Landesman, Cliff, W W Norton & Company Inc, 500 Fifth Ave, New York, NY 10110-0017 *Tel:* 212-354-5500 *Toll Free Tel:* 800-233-4830 (orders & cust serv) *Fax:* 212-869-0856 *Toll Free Fax:* 800-458-6515 *E-mail:* orders@wwnorton.com *Web Site:* books.wwnorton.com, pg 164

Landis, Sarah, HarperCollins Children's Books, 195 Broadway, New York, NY 10007 *Tel:* 212-207-7000 *Web Site:* www.harpercollins.com/childrens, pg 101

Landis, Sarah, Sterling Lord Literistic Inc, 115 Broadway, Suite 1602, New York, NY 10006 *Tel:* 212-780-6050 *Fax:* 212-780-6095 *E-mail:* info@sll.com *Web Site:* www.sll.com, pg 537

Landolf, Diane, Random House Children's Books, 1745 Broadway, 10th fl, New York, NY 10019 *Tel:* 212-782-9000 *Web Site:* www.randomhousekids.com, pg 194

Landskroener, Marcia, Sophie Kerr Prize, c/o College Relations Off, 300 Washington Ave, Chestertown, MD 21620 *Tel:* 410-778-2800 *Toll Free Tel:* 800-422-1782 *Fax:* 410-810-7150 *Web Site:* www.washcoll.edu, pg 690

Landwehr, Kathy, Peachtree Publishers, 1700 Chattahoochee Ave, Atlanta, GA 30318-2112 *Tel:* 404-876-8761 *Toll Free Tel:* 800-241-0113 *Fax:* 404-875-2578 *Toll Free Fax:* 800-875-8909 *E-mail:* hello@peachtree-online.com *Web Site:* www.peachtree-online.com, pg 176

Lane, Connor, Lindquist & Vennum Prize for Poetry, 1011 Washington Ave S, Suite 300, Minneapolis, MN 55415-1246 *Tel:* 612-332-3192 *Toll Free Tel:* 800-520-6455 *Fax:* 612-215-2550 *Web Site:* www.milkweed.org, pg 661

Lang, Amanda, Simon & Schuster, 1230 Avenue of the Americas, New York, NY 10020 *Tel:* 212-698-7000 *Toll Free Tel:* 800-223-2348 (cust serv); 800-223-2336 (orders) *Toll Free Fax:* 800-943-9831 (orders) *Web Site:* www.simonandschuster.com, pg 212

Lang, Amelia, Aperture Books, 547 W 27 St, 4th fl, New York, NY 10001 *Tel:* 212-505-5555 *Toll Free Tel:* 800-929-2323 *Fax:* 212-979-7759 *E-mail:* info@aperture.org *Web Site:* www.aperture.org, pg 18

Lang, Kara, Anvil Press Publishers, 278 E First Ave, Vancouver, BC V5T 1A6, Canada *Tel:* 604-876-8710 *Fax:* 604-879-2667 *E-mail:* info@anvilpress.com *Web Site:* www.anvilpress.com, pg 445

Lang, Rebecca, St Martin's Press, LLC, 175 Fifth Ave, New York, NY 10010 *Tel:* 646-307-5151 *Web Site:* us.macmillan.com/smp, pg 204

Lange, April, W W Norton & Company Inc, 500 Fifth Ave, New York, NY 10110-0017 *Tel:* 212-354-5500 *Toll Free Tel:* 800-233-4830 (orders & cust serv) *Fax:* 212-869-0856 *Toll Free Fax:* 800-458-6515 *E-mail:* orders@wwnorton.com *Web Site:* books.wwnorton.com, pg 164

Lange, Barbara, Society of Motion Picture & Television Engineers® (SMPTE®), 3 Barker Ave, 5th fl, White Plains, NY 10601 *Tel:* 914-761-1100 *Fax:* 914-761-3115 *Web Site:* www.smpte.org, pg 578

Lange, Heide, Sanford J Greenburger Associates Inc, 55 Fifth Ave, New York, NY 10003 *Tel:* 212-206-5600 *Fax:* 212-463-8718 *Web Site:* greenburger.com; www.sjga.com, pg 520

Lange, Marty, McGraw-Hill Science, Engineering, Mathematics, 501 Bell St, Dubuque, IA 52001 *Tel:* 563-584-6000 *Toll Free Tel:* 800-338-3987 (cust serv) *Fax:* 614-755-5645 (cust serv) *Web Site:* www.mhhe.com, pg 146

Langille, Donald, Palm Island Press, 411 Truman Ave, Key West, FL 33040 *Tel:* 305-296-3102 *E-mail:* pipress2@gmail.com, pg 173

Langlois, Dennis, Princeton University Press, 41 William St, Princeton, NJ 08540-5237 *Tel:* 609-258-4900 *Fax:* 609-258-6305 *Web Site:* press.princeton.edu, pg 188

Langman, Joe, Schiffer Publishing Ltd, 4880 Lower Valley Rd, Atglen, PA 19310 *Tel:* 610-593-1777 *Fax:* 610-593-2002 *E-mail:* info@schifferbooks.com *Web Site:* www.schifferbooks.com, pg 207

Langman, Lucy, Fons Vitae, 49 Mockingbird Valley Dr, Louisville, KY 40207-1366 *Tel:* 502-897-3641 *Fax:* 502-893-7373 *E-mail:* fonsvitaeky@aol.com *Web Site:* www.fonsvitae.com, pg 86

Langum, David J Sr, Langum Prize in American Historical Fiction, 2809 Berkeley Dr, Birmingham, AL 35242 *Tel:* 360-809-0465 *E-mail:* langumtrust@gmail.com *Web Site:* www.langumtrust.org, pg 660

Langum, David J Sr, Langum Prize in American Legal History or Biography, 2809 Berkeley Dr, Birmingham, AL 35242 *Tel:* 360-809-0465 *E-mail:* langumtrust@gmail.com *Web Site:* www.langumtrust.org, pg 660

Langum, David J Sr, Gene E & Adele R Malott Prize for Recording Community Activism, 2809 Berkeley Dr, Birmingham, AL 35242 *Tel:* 360-809-0465 *E-mail:* langumtrust@gmail.com *Web Site:* www.langumtrust.org, pg 665

Lanick, Colleen, The MIT Press, One Rogers St, Cambridge, MA 02142 *Tel:* 617-253-5255 *Toll Free Tel:* 800-207-8354 (orders) *Fax:* 617-258-6779; 617-577-1545 (orders) *Web Site:* mitpress.mit.edu, pg 152

Lansing, Jim, OMNI Publishers Inc, PO Box 408, Bulverde, TX 78163 *Tel:* 210-778-4437 *Fax:* 830-438-4645 *Web Site:* www.omnipublishers.com; educatorsethicsseries.com, pg 167

Lansing, Richard, Springer, 233 Spring St, New York, NY 10013-1578 *Tel:* 212-460-1500 *Toll Free Tel:* 800-SPRINGER (777-4643) *Fax:* 212-460-1700 *E-mail:* customerservice@springer.com *Web Site:* www.springer.com, pg 219

Lansing, Ruth, OMNI Publishers Inc, PO Box 408, Bulverde, TX 78163 *Tel:* 210-778-4437 *Fax:* 830-438-4645 *Web Site:* www.omnipublishers.com; educatorsethicsseries.com, pg 167

Lansky, Bruce, Meadowbrook Press, 6110 Blue Circle Dr, Suite 237, Minnetonka, MN 55343 *Toll Free Tel:* 800-338-2232 *Fax:* 952-930-1940 *E-mail:* info@meadowbrookpress.com *Web Site:* www.meadowbrookpress.com, pg 147

Lape, Todd, University Press of Mississippi, 3825 Ridgewood Rd, Jackson, MS 39211-6492 *Tel:* 601-432-6205 *Toll Free Tel:* 800-737-7788 (orders & cust serv) *Fax:* 601-432-6217 *E-mail:* press@mississippi.edu *Web Site:* www.upress.state.ms.us, pg 247

Laperriere, Ginette, Guerin Editeur Ltee, 800, Blvd Industriel, bureau 200, St-Jean-sur-Richelieu, QC J3B 8G4, Canada *Tel:* 514-842-3481 *Fax:* 514-842-4923 *Web Site:* www.guerin-editeur.qc.ca, pg 459

LaPolla, Sarah, Bradford Literary Agency, 5694 Mission Center Rd, Suite 347, San Diego, CA 92108 *Tel:* 619-521-1201 *E-mail:* queries@bradfordlit.com *Web Site:* www.bradfordlit.com, pg 509

Laporte, Janine, Doubleday Canada, 320 Front St W, Suite 1400, Toronto, ON M5V 3B6, Canada *Tel:* 416-364-4449 *Fax:* 416-598-7764 *Web Site:* www.penguinrandomhouse.ca, pg 452

Laporte, Janine, Knopf Canada, 320 Front St W, Suite 1400, Toronto, ON M5V 3B6, Canada *Tel:* 416-364-4449 *Toll Free Tel:* 888-523-9292 *Fax:* 416-598-7764 *Web Site:* www.penguinrandomhouse.ca, pg 462

Laporte, Janine, Penguin Random House Canada, 320 Front St W, Suite 1400, Toronto, ON M5V 3B6, Canada *Tel:* 416-364-4449 *Toll Free Tel:* 888-523-9292 (cust serv) *Fax:* 416-598-7764 *Web Site:* www.penguinrandomhouse.ca, pg 467

Laporte, Janine, Seal Books, 320 Front St W, Suite 1400, Toronto, ON M5V 3B6, Canada *Tel:* 416-364-4449 *Toll Free Tel:* 888-523-9292 (order desk) *Fax:* 416-598-7764 *Web Site:* www.penguinrandomhouse.ca, pg 470

Laprairie, Dinah, BrainStorm Poetry Contest for Mental Health Consumers, 36 Elgin St, 2nd fl, Sudbury, ON P3C 5B4, Canada *Tel:* 705-222-6472 (ext 303) *E-mail:* openminds@nisa.on.ca *Web Site:* www.openmindsquarterly.com, pg 634

Laramie, Ben, Chronicle Books LLC, 680 Second St, San Francisco, CA 94107 *Tel:* 415-537-4200 *Toll Free Tel:* 800-759-0190 (cust serv) *Fax:* 415-537-4460 *Toll Free Fax:* 800-858-7787 (orders); 800-286-9471 (cust serv) *E-mail:* frontdesk@chroniclebooks.com *Web Site:* www.chroniclebooks.com, pg 55

Laredo, Sam, Laredo Publishing Co Inc, 465 Westview Ave, Englewood, NJ 07631 *Tel:* 201-408-4048 *E-mail:* info@laredopublishing.com *Web Site:* www.laredopublishing.com, pg 129

Laredo, Sam, Renaissance House, 465 Westview Ave, Englewood, NJ 07631 *Tel:* 201-408-4048 *E-mail:* info@renaissancehouse.net *Web Site:* www.renaissancehouse.net, pg 198

Largent, Marilyn, David C Cook, 4050 Lee Vance View, Colorado Springs, CO 80918 *Tel:* 719-536-0100 *Toll Free Tel:* 800-708-5550; 800-323-7543 (orders & cust serv) *Toll Free Fax:* 800-430-0726 (cust serv) *Web Site:* www.davidccook.com, pg 60

Larkin, Prof Edward, University of Delaware Press, 200A Morris Library, 181 S College Ave, Newark, DE 19717-5267 *Tel:* 302-831-1149 *Fax:* 302-831-6549 *E-mail:* ud-press@udel.edu *Web Site:* library.udel.edu/udpress, pg 241

Larochelle, France, Guerin Editeur Ltee, 800, Blvd Industriel, bureau 200, St-Jean-sur-Richelieu, QC J3B 8G4, Canada *Tel:* 514-842-3481 *Fax:* 514-842-4923 *Web Site:* www.guerin-editeur.qc.ca, pg 459

Larouche, Jean-Claude, Les Editions JCL, 688, rue St-Joseph, Marieville, QC J3M 1H1, Canada *Tel:* 450-460-1438 *E-mail:* info@jcl.qc.ca *Web Site:* www.jcl.qc.ca, pg 454

Laroya, Colette, Hippocrene Books Inc, 171 Madison Ave, New York, NY 10016 *Tel:* 212-685-4373 *Fax:* 212-779-9338 *E-mail:* info@hippocrenebooks.com; orderdept@hippocrenebooks.com (orders) *Web Site:* www.hippocrenebooks.com, pg 108

Larsen, Brandi, DK Publishing, 345 Hudson St, 2nd fl, New York, NY 10014 *Tel:* 646-674-4000 *Toll Free Tel:* 877-342-5357 (cust serv); 800-733-3000 *Web Site:* www.dk.com; www.penguin.com, pg 71

Larsen, David, University of Manitoba Press, University of Manitoba, 301 St Johns College, 92 Dysart Rd, Winnipeg, MB R3T 2M5, Canada *Tel:* 204-474-9495 *Fax:* 204-474-7566 *E-mail:* uofmpress@umanitoba.ca *Web Site:* uofmpress.ca, pg 474

Larsen, Elizabeth A, Tapestry Press Ltd, 19 Nashoba Rd, Littleton, MA 01460 *Tel:* 978-486-0200 *Toll Free Tel:* 800-535-2007 *Fax:* 978-486-0244 *E-mail:* publish@tapestrypress.com *Web Site:* www.tapestrypress.com, pg 227

Larsen, Emily, Book Industry Guild of New York, PO Box 2001, New York, NY 10113-2001 *E-mail:* admin@bookindustryguildofny.org *Web Site:* www.bookindustryguildofny.org, pg 560

Larsen, Michael, San Francisco Writers Conference, 1029 Jones St, San Francisco, CA 94109 *Tel:* 415-673-0939 *E-mail:* sfwriterscon@aol.com *Web Site:* www.sfwriters.org, pg 614

Larsen, Todd, EMC Publishing LLC, 875 Montreal Way, St Paul, MN 55102 *Tel:* 651-290-2800 (corp) *Toll Free Tel:* 800-328-1452 *Toll Free Fax:* 800-328-4564 *E-mail:* educate@emcp.com *Web Site:* www.emcp.com, pg 77

Larson, Doran, Hamilton College, English/Creative Writing, English/Creative Writing Dept, 198 College Hill Rd, Clinton, NY 13323 *Tel:* 315-859-4370 *Fax:* 315-859-4390 *Web Site:* www.hamilton.edu, pg 620

Larson, Jeannette, Houghton Mifflin Harcourt Trade & Reference Division, 125 High St, Boston, MA 02110 *Tel:* 617-351-5000 *Toll Free Tel:* 800-225-3362 *Web Site:* www.hmhco.com, pg 111

Larson, John, Cohesion®, 511 W Bay St, Suite 480, Tampa, FL 33606 *Tel:* 813-999-3111 *Toll Free Tel:* 877-774-3000 *E-mail:* info@cohesion.com *Web Site:* www.cohesion.com, pg 491

LaSasso, Anthony, Bloomsbury Publishing Inc, 1385 Broadway, 5th fl, New York, NY 10018 *Tel:* 212-419-5300 *E-mail:* marketingusa@bloomsbury.com; adultpublicityusa@bloomsbury.com; askacademic@bloomsbury.com *Web Site:* www.bloomsbury.com, pg 38

Lasher, Eric, The LA Literary Agency, PO Box 46370, Los Angeles, CA 90046 *Tel:* 323-654-5288 *E-mail:* laliteraryagency@mac.com; mail@laliteraryagency.com *Web Site:* www.laliteraryagency.com, pg 525

Lasher, Maureen, The LA Literary Agency, PO Box 46370, Los Angeles, CA 90046 *Tel:* 323-654-5288 *E-mail:* laliteraryagency@mac.com; mail@laliteraryagency.com *Web Site:* www.laliteraryagency.com, pg 525

Lasky, Cynthia, Random House Publishing Group, 1745 Broadway, New York, NY 10019 *Toll Free Tel:* 800-200-3552 *Web Site:* atrandom.com, pg 195

Lasky, Karl, Ravenhawk™ Books, 8364 E Balfour Place, Tucson, AZ 85710 *Tel:* 520-296-4491 *Fax:* 520-296-4491 *E-mail:* the6dofcompany@gmail.com, pg 196

Lassiter, Steve, APA Talent & Literary Agency, 405 S Beverly Dr, Beverly Hills, CA 90212 *Tel:* 310-888-4200 *Fax:* 310-888-4242 *Web Site:* www.apa-agency.com, pg 507

Laster, Stephen, McGraw-Hill Education, 2 Penn Plaza, New York, NY 10121-2298 *Tel:* 212-904-2000 *E-mail:* customer.service@mheducation.com; international_cs@mheducation.com *Web Site:* www.mheducation.com, pg 145

Latham, Adam, Sewanee Writers' Conference, Stamler Ctr, 119 Gailor Hall, 735 University Ave, Sewanee, TN 37383 *Tel:* 931-598-1141; 931-598-1654 *E-mail:* swc@sewanee.edu *Web Site:* www.sewaneewriters.org, pg 614

Latham, Joyce Eileen, JL Communications, 10205 Green Holly Terr, Silver Spring, MD 20902 *Tel:* 301-593-0640, pg 496

Lathan, Laurie, Thurber Prize for American Humor, 77 Jefferson Ave, Columbus, OH 43215 *Tel:* 614-464-1032 *Fax:* 614-280-3645 *E-mail:* thurberhouse@thurberhouse.org *Web Site:* www.thurberhouse.org, pg 694

Lathbury, Roger, Orchises Press, PO Box 320533, Alexandria, VA 22320-4533 *Tel:* 703-683-1243 *E-mail:* orchises@gmail.com, pg 169

Latimer, Nicholas, Alfred A Knopf/Everyman's Library, c/o Penguin Random House Inc, 1745 Broadway, New York, NY 10019 *Tel:* 212-751-2600 *Toll Free Tel:* 800-638-6460 *Fax:* 212-572-2593 *Web Site:* www.knopfdoubleday.com, pg 127

Latour, Gilles, EdCan Network, 60 St Clair Ave E, Suite 703, Toronto, ON M4T 1N5, Canada *Tel:* 416-591-6300 *Toll Free Tel:* 866-803-9549 *Fax:* 416-591-5345 *Toll Free Fax:* 866-803-9549 *E-mail:* info@edcan.ca *Web Site:* www.edcan.ca, pg 564

Latshaw, Katherine, Folio Literary Management, The Film Center Bldg, 630 Ninth Ave, Suite 1101, New York, NY 10036 *Tel:* 212-400-1494 *Fax:* 212-967-0977 *Web Site:* www.foliolit.com, pg 517

Lauber, Kimberly, Random House Children's Books, 1745 Broadway, 10th fl, New York, NY 10019 *Tel:* 212-782-9000 *Web Site:* www.randomhousekids.com, pg 194

Lauer, Brett Fletcher, George Bogin Memorial Award, 15 Gramercy Park, New York, NY 10003 *Tel:* 212-254-9628 *Web Site:* www.poetrysociety.org, pg 633

Lauer, Brett Fletcher, Alice Fay Di Castagnola Award, 15 Gramercy Park, New York, NY 10003 *Tel:* 212-254-9628 *Web Site:* www.poetrysociety.org, pg 641

Lauer, Brett Fletcher, Norma Farber First Book Award, 15 Gramercy Park, New York, NY 10003 *Tel:* 212-254-9628 *Web Site:* www.poetrysociety.org, pg 645

Lauer, Brett Fletcher, Cecil Hemley Memorial Award, 15 Gramercy Park, New York, NY 10003 *Tel:* 212-254-9628 *Web Site:* www.poetrysociety.org, pg 652

Lauer, Brett Fletcher, Louise Louis/Emily F Bourne Student Poetry Award, 15 Gramercy Park, New York, NY 10003 *Tel:* 212-254-9628 *Web Site:* www.poetrysociety.org, pg 663

Lauer, Brett Fletcher, Lyric Poetry Award, 15 Gramercy Park, New York, NY 10003 *Tel:* 212-254-9628 *Web Site:* www.poetrysociety.org, pg 664

Lauer, Brett Fletcher, Lucille Medwick Memorial Award, 15 Gramercy Park, New York, NY 10003 *Tel:* 212-254-9628 *Web Site:* www.poetrysociety.org, pg 667

Lauer, Brett Fletcher, Poetry Society of America (PSA), 15 Gramercy Park, New York, NY 10003 *Tel:* 212-254-9628 *Web Site:* www.poetrysociety.org, pg 575

Lauer, Brett Fletcher, William Carlos Williams Award, 15 Gramercy Park, New York, NY 10003 *Tel:* 212-254-9628 *Web Site:* www.poetrysociety.org, pg 698

Lauer, Brett Fletcher, The Writer Magazine/Emily Dickinson Award, 15 Gramercy Park, New York, NY 10003 *Tel:* 212-254-9628 *Web Site:* www.poetrysociety.org, pg 700

Lauer, George, Venture Publishing Inc, 1999 Cato Ave, State College, PA 16801 *Tel:* 814-234-4561 *Fax:* 814-234-1651 *E-mail:* vpublish@venturepublish.com *Web Site:* www.venturepublish.com, pg 250

Lauer, Jack, Natasha Kern Literary Agency Inc, PO Box 1069, White Salmon, WA 98672 *Tel:* 509-493-3803 *E-mail:* agent@natashakern.com *Web Site:* www.natashakern.com, pg 523

Lauer, Valerie, Hanser Publications LLC, 6915 Valley Ave, Cincinnati, OH 45244-3029 *Toll Free Tel:* 800-950-8977; 877-751-5052 (orders) *Fax:* 513-527-8801 *E-mail:* info@hanserpublications.com *Web Site:* www.hanserpublications.com, pg 100

Laughlin, Phil, The MIT Press, One Rogers St, Cambridge, MA 02142 *Tel:* 617-253-5255 *Toll Free Tel:* 800-207-8354 (orders) *Fax:* 617-258-6779; 617-577-1545 (orders) *Web Site:* mitpress.mit.edu, pg 152

Laur, Mary, University of Chicago Press, 1427 E 60 St, Chicago, IL 60637-2954 *Tel:* 773-702-7700; 773-702-7600 *Toll Free Tel:* 800-621-2736 (orders) *Fax:* 773-702-9756; 773-660-2235 (orders); 773-702-2708 *E-mail:* custserv@press.uchicago.edu; marketing@press.uchicago.edu *Web Site:* www.press.uchicago.edu, pg 241

Laurenzo, Diane, American Management Association (AMA), 1601 Broadway, New York, NY 10019 *Tel:* 212-586-8100 *Toll Free Tel:* 877-566-9441 *Fax:* 212-903-8168; 518-891-0368 *E-mail:* customerservice@amanet.org *Web Site:* www.amanet.org, pg 555

Lauterbach, Ellen, Marshall Cavendish Corp, 99 White Plains Rd, Tarrytown, NY 10591-9001 *Tel:* 914-332-8888 *Toll Free Tel:* 800-821-9881 *Fax:* 914-332-8102 *E-mail:* mce@marshallcavendish.com *Web Site:* www.marshallcavendish.com; www.mceducation.us, pg 143

Lavender, John, CRC Press, 6000 Broken Sound Pkwy NW, Suite 300, Boca Raton, FL 33487 *Tel:* 561-994-0555 *Toll Free Tel:* 800-272-7737 (orders) *Toll Free Fax:* 800-643-9428 (sales); 800-374-3401 (orders) *E-mail:* orders@crcpress.com; orders@taylorandfrancis.com *Web Site:* www.crcpress.com, pg 64

Laventhall, Don, Harold Ober Associates Inc, 425 Madison Ave, New York, NY 10017 *Tel:* 212-759-8600 *Fax:* 212-759-9428 *Web Site:* www.haroldober.com, pg 531

Lavery, Brittany, Harlequin Enterprises Ltd, 225 Duncan Mill Rd, Don Mills, ON M3B 3K9, Canada *Tel:* 416-445-5860 *Toll Free Tel:* 888-432-4879; 800-370-5838 (ebook inquiries) *E-mail:* customerservice@harlequin.com *Web Site:* www.harlequin.com, pg 459

Lavoie, Michel, Les Editions Vents d'Ouest, 109, rue Wright, bureau 202, Gatineau, QC J8X 2G7, Canada *Tel:* 819-770-6377 *E-mail:* info@ventsdouest.ca *Web Site:* www.ventsdouest.ca, pg 455

Lawler, Kelly, Sourcebooks Inc, 1935 Brookdale Rd, Suite 139, Naperville, IL 60563 *Tel:* 630-961-3900 *Toll Free Tel:* 800-432-7444 *Fax:* 630-961-2168 *E-mail:* info@sourcebooks.com; customersupport@sourcebooks.com *Web Site:* www.sourcebooks.com, pg 218

Lawrence, Brittany, AAP PreK-12 Learning Group, 455 Massachusetts Ave NW, Suite 700, Washington, DC 20001 *Tel:* 267-351-4310 *Fax:* 267-351-4317 *E-mail:* prek12learning@publishers.org *Web Site:* www.aepweb.org, pg 553

Lawrence, Eileen, Alexander Street, a ProQuest Company, 3212 Duke St, Alexandria, VA 22314 *Tel:* 703-212-8520 *Toll Free Tel:* 800-889-5937 *Fax:* 703-940-6584 *E-mail:* sales@alexanderstreet.com; marketing@alexanderstreet.com; info@alexanderstreet.com *Web Site:* alexanderstreet.com, pg 7

Lawrence, Eileen, Algonquin Books, 400 Silver Cedar Ct, Suite 300, Chapel Hill, NC 27514-1585 *Tel:* 919-967-0108 *Fax:* 919-933-0272 *E-mail:* inquiry@algonquin.com *Web Site:* www.workman.com/algonquin, pg 7

Lawrence, Jane, RockBench Publishing Corp, 6101 Stillmeadow Dr, Nashville, TN 37211-6518 *Tel:* 615-831-2277 *Fax:* 615-831-2212 *E-mail:* info@rockbench.com, pg 200

Lawrence, Jessica, St Martin's Press, LLC, 175 Fifth Ave, New York, NY 10010 *Tel:* 646-307-5151 *Web Site:* us.macmillan.com/smp, pg 204

Lawrence, Justin Paul, InterVarsity Press, 430 Plaza Dr, Westmont, IL 60559-1234 *Tel:* 630-734-4000 *Toll Free Tel:* 800-843-9487 *Fax:* 630-734-4200 *E-mail:* email@ivpress.com *Web Site:* www.ivpress.com, pg 120

Lawrence, Merloyd Ludington, Merloyd Lawrence Inc, 102 Chestnut St, Boston, MA 02108 *Tel:* 617-523-5895 *Fax:* 617-263-2749, pg 130

Lawrence, Michael, Orbis Books, Price Bldg, Box 302, Maryknoll, NY 10545-0302 *Tel:* 914-941-7636 *Toll Free Tel:* 800-258-5838 (orders) *Fax:* 914-941-7005 *E-mail:* orbisbooks@maryknoll.org *Web Site:* orbisbooks.com, pg 169

Lawrence, Priscilla, The Historic New Orleans Collection, 533 Royal St, New Orleans, LA 70130 *Tel:* 504-523-4662 *Fax:* 504-598-7108 *E-mail:* wrc@hnoc.org *Web Site:* www.hnoc.org, pg 108

Lawrence, Richard, Eaton Literary Associates Literary Awards, PO Box 49795, Sarasota, FL 34230-6795 *Tel:* 941-366-6589 *Fax:* 941-365-4679 *E-mail:* eatonlit@aol.com *Web Site:* www.eatonliterary.com, pg 643

Lawrence, Ron, Upper Access Inc, 87 Upper Access Rd, Hinesburg, VT 05461 *Tel:* 802-482-2988 *Toll Free Tel:* 800-310-8320 (orders) *Fax:* 802-417-3002 *E-mail:* info@upperaccess.com *Web Site:* www.upperaccess.com, pg 248

Lawrence, Susannah, Akashic Books, 232 Third St, Suite A-115, Brooklyn, NY 11215 *Tel:* 718-643-9193 *Fax:* 718-643-9195 *E-mail:* info@akashicbooks.com *Web Site:* www.akashicbooks.com, pg 6

Lawrie, Colleen, Perseus Books, 250 W 57 St, 15th fl, New York, NY 10107 *Tel:* 212-340-8100 *Toll Free Tel:* 800-343-4499 (cust serv) *Fax:* 212-340-8105 *Web Site:* www.perseusbooks.com, pg 181

Laws, Gordon, Lumina Datamatics Inc, 4 Collins Ave, Plymouth, MA 02360 *Tel:* 508-746-0300 *Fax:* 508-746-3233 *Web Site:* luminadatamatics.com, pg 497

Laws, Valerie, The Danuta Gleed Literary Award, 600-460 Richmond St W, Toronto, ON M5V 1Y1, Canada *Tel:* 416-703-8982 *Fax:* 416-504-9090 *E-mail:* info@writersunion.ca *Web Site:* www.writersunion.ca, pg 650

Laws, Valerie, Short Prose Competition for Developing Writers, 600-460 Richmond St W, Toronto, ON M5V 1Y1, Canada *Tel:* 416-703-8982 *Fax:* 416-504-9090 *E-mail:* info@writersunion.ca *Web Site:* www.writersunion.ca, pg 689

Laws, Valerie, The Writers' Union of Canada (TWUC), 600-460 Richmond St W, Toronto, ON M5V 1Y1, Canada *Tel:* 416-703-8982 *Fax:* 416-504-9090 *E-mail:* info@writersunion.ca *Web Site:* www.writersunion.ca, pg 581

Lawson, Alan, Boston Authors Club Inc, 33 Brayton Rd, Brighton, MA 02135 *Tel:* 617-783-1357 *E-mail:* bostonauthors@aol.com *Web Site:* www.bostonauthorsclub.org, pg 561

Lawson, Alan, Julia Ward Howe Book Awards, c/o Professor Mary Cronin, 2400 Beacon St, Unit 208, Beacon Hill, MA 02467 *Tel:* 617-783-1357 *E-mail:* bostonauthors@aol.com *Web Site:* www.bostonauthorsclub.org, pg 654

Lawson, Alice, The Gersh Agency (TGA), 41 Madison Ave, 33rd fl, New York, NY 10010 *Tel:* 212-997-1818 *Web Site:* gershbooks.com, pg 518

Lawson, Anne, BoardSource, 750 Ninth St NW, Suite 650, Washington, DC 20001-4793 *Tel:* 202-349-2500 *Toll Free Tel:* 877-892-6273 *Fax:* 202-349-2599 *E-mail:* members@boardsource.org *Web Site:* www.boardsource.org, pg 39

Lawson, Hilary, HarperCollins General Books Group, 195 Broadway, New York, NY 10007 *Tel:* 212-207-7000 *Web Site:* www.harpercollins.com, pg 101

Lawson, Mark, ECS Publishing Corp, 1727 Larkin Williams Rd, Fenton, MO 63026 *Tel:* 636-305-0100 *Toll Free Tel:* 800-647-2117 *Web Site:* ecspublishing.com; www.facebook.com/ecspublishing, pg 75

Lawton, Caryn, Washington State University Press, Cooper Publications Bldg, Grimes Way, Pullman, WA 99164-5910 *Tel:* 509-335-3518; 509-335-7880 (order fulfillment) *Toll Free Tel:* 800-354-7360 (orders) *Fax:* 509-335-8568 *E-mail:* wsupress@wsu.edu *Web Site:* wsupress.wsu.edu, pg 252

Lawton, Wendy, Books & Such, 52 Mission Circle, Suite 122, PMB 170, Santa Rosa, CA 95409-5370 *Tel:* 707-538-4184 *Web Site:* booksandsuch.com, pg 509

Lay, J Stephen, Epicenter Press Inc, 6524 NE 181 St, Suite 2, Kenmore, WA 98028 *Tel:* 425-485-6822 (edit, mktg, busn off) *Fax:* 425-481-8253 *E-mail:* info@epicenterpress.com *Web Site:* www.epicenterpress.com, pg 79

Lay, Kevin, Scepter Publishers, PO Box 360694, Strongsville, OH 44149 *Tel:* 212-354-0670 *Toll Free Tel:* 800-322-8773 *Fax:* 212-354-0736 *Web Site:* www.scepterpublishers.org, pg 207

Lay, Tom, Fordham University Press, Joseph A Martino Hall, 45 Columbus Ave, New York, NY 10023 *Fax:* 347-842-3083 *Web Site:* www.fordhampress.com, pg 86

Laychur, Tina, The Pennsylvania State University Press, University Support Bldg 1, Suite C, 820 N University Dr, University Park, PA 16802-1003 *Tel:* 814-865-1327 *Toll Free Tel:* 800-326-9180 *Fax:* 814-863-1408 *Toll Free Fax:* 877-778-2665 *E-mail:* info@psupress.org *Web Site:* www.psupress.org, pg 179

Lazar, Dan, Writers House, 21 W 26 St, New York, NY 10010 *Tel:* 212-685-2400 *Fax:* 212-685-1781 *Web Site:* www.writershouse.com, pg 542

Lazarus, Alison, Macmillan, 175 Fifth Ave, New York, NY 10010 *Tel:* 646-307-5151 *E-mail:* press.inquiries@macmillan.com *Web Site:* www.macmillan.com, pg 140

Lazer, Jill, Houghton Mifflin Harcourt Trade & Reference Division, 125 High St, Boston, MA 02110 *Tel:* 617-351-5000 *Toll Free Tel:* 800-225-3362 *Web Site:* www.hmhco.com, pg 111

Lazin, Sarah, Sarah Lazin Books, 19 W 21 St, Suite 501, New York, NY 10010 *Tel:* 212-989-5757 *Fax:* 212-989-1393, pg 525

Lazure, Sandrine, Editions Hurtubise, 1815, ave De Lorimier, Montreal, QC H2K 3W6, Canada *Tel:* 514-523-1523 *Toll Free Tel:* 800-361-1664 *Fax:* 514-523-9969 *Web Site:* www.editionshurtubise.com, pg 454

Le Blanc, Ondine E, The Massachusetts Historical Society, 1154 Boylston St, Boston, MA 02215-3695 *Tel:* 617-536-1608 *Fax:* 617-859-0074 *E-mail:* publications@masshist.org *Web Site:* www.masshist.org, pg 144

Le Du, Nathalie, Workman Publishing Co Inc, 225 Varick St, 9th fl, New York, NY 10014-4381 *Tel:* 212-254-5900 *Toll Free Tel:* 800-722-7202 *Fax:* 212-254-8098 *E-mail:* info@workman.com *Web Site:* www.workman.com, pg 259

Le May, Konnie, Lake Superior Port Cities Inc, 310 E Superior St, Suite 125, Duluth, MN 55802 *Tel:* 218-722-5002 *Toll Free Tel:* 888-BIG-LAKE (244-5253) *Fax:* 218-722-4096 *E-mail:* reader@lakesuperior.com *Web Site:* www.lakesuperior.com, pg 129

Le Pan, Don, Broadview Press, 280 Perry St, Unit 5, Peterborough, ON K9J 2J4, Canada *Tel:* 705-743-8990 *Fax:* 705-743-8353 *E-mail:* customerservice@broadviewpress.com *Web Site:* www.broadviewpress.com, pg 447

Le, Thao, Sandra Dijkstra Literary Agency, 1155 Camino del Mar, PMB 515, Del Mar, CA 92014-2605 *E-mail:* queries@dijkstraagency.com *Web Site:* dijkstraagency.com, pg 514

Leach, Michael, Orbis Books, Price Bldg, Box 302, Maryknoll, NY 10545-0302 *Tel:* 914-941-7636 *Toll Free Tel:* 800-258-5838 (orders) *Fax:* 914-941-7005 *E-mail:* orbisbooks@maryknoll.org *Web Site:* orbisbooks.com, pg 169

Leader-Picone, Whitney, Houghton Mifflin Harcourt Trade & Reference Division, 125 High St, Boston, MA 02110 *Tel:* 617-351-5000 *Toll Free Tel:* 800-225-3362 *Web Site:* www.hmhco.com, pg 111

Leadingham, Scott, The Society of Professional Journalists (SPJ), Eugene S Pulliam National Journalism Ctr, 3909 N Meridian St, Indianapolis, IN 46208 *Tel:* 317-927-8000 *Fax:* 317-920-4789 *E-mail:* spj@spj.org *Web Site:* www.spj.org, pg 580

Leahy, John, Cengage Learning, 20 Channel Center St, Boston, MA 02210 *Tel:* 617-289-7700 *Toll Free Tel:* 800-354-9706 *Fax:* 617-289-7844 *Toll Free Fax:* 800-487-8488 *E-mail:* esales@cengage.com *Web Site:* www.cengage.com, pg 50

Leahy, P Patrick PhD, American Geosciences Institute (AGI), 4220 King St, Alexandria, VA 22302-1502 *Tel:* 703-379-2480 (ext 246) *Fax:* 703-379-7563 *E-mail:* pubs@agiweb.org *Web Site:* www.agiweb.org, pg 11

Leaman, George, Philosophy Documentation Center, PO Box 7147, Charlottesville, VA 22906-7147 *Tel:* 434-220-3300 *Toll Free Tel:* 800-444-2419 *Fax:* 434-220-3301 *E-mail:* order@pdcnet.org *Web Site:* www.pdcnet.org, pg 182

Leandro, Sam, Bell Springs Publishing, PO Box 1240, Willits, CA 95490-1240 *Tel:* 707-272-3472 *E-mail:* publisher@bellsprings.com *Web Site:* bellsprings.com; aboutpinball.com, pg 32

Leanza, Frank, Crystal Publishers Inc, 3460 Lost Hills Dr, Las Vegas, NV 89122 *Tel:* 702-434-3037 *Fax:* 702-434-3037 *Web Site:* www.crystalpub.com, pg 65

Leary, Sheila M, University of Wisconsin Press, 1930 Monroe St, 3rd fl, Madison, WI 53711-2059 *Tel:* 608-263-0668 *Toll Free Tel:* 800-621-2736 (orders) *Fax:* 608-263-1173 *Toll Free Fax:* 800-621-2736 (orders) *E-mail:* uwiscpress@uwpress.wisc.edu (main off); publicity@uwpress.wisc.edu *Web Site:* uwpress.wisc.edu, pg 246

Leavell, Byrd, Waxman Leavell Literary Agency, 443 Park Ave S, No 1004, New York, NY 10016 *Tel:* 212-675-5556 *Fax:* 212-675-1381 *Web Site:* www.waxmanleavell.com, pg 541

Leaver, Marcus, Quarto Publishing Group USA Inc, 400 First Ave N, Suite 400, Minneapolis, MN 55401 *Tel:* 612-344-8100 *Toll Free Tel:* 800-328-0590 (sales); 800-458-0454 *Fax:* 612-344-8691 *E-mail:* sales@quartous.com *Web Site:* www.quartoknows.com, pg 192

Leavitt, Ned, The Ned Leavitt Agency, 70 Wooster St, Suite 4-F, New York, NY 10012 *Tel:* 212-334-0999 *Web Site:* www.nedleavittagency.com, pg 525

LeBaron, Susan, Wesleyan Publishing House, 13300 Olio Rd, Fishers, IN 46037 *Tel:* 317-774-3853 *Toll Free Tel:* 800-493-7539 *Fax:* 317-774-3865 *Toll Free Fax:* 800-788-3535 *E-mail:* wph@wesleyan.org *Web Site:* www.wesleyan.org/books, pg 253

LeBien, Thomas, Harvard University Press, 79 Garden St, Cambridge, MA 02138-1499 *Tel:* 617-495-2600; 401-531-2800 (intl orders) *Toll Free Tel:* 800-405-1619 (orders) *Fax:* 617-495-5898 (general); 617-496-4677 (edit & rts); 401-531-2801 (intl orders) *Toll Free Fax:* 800-406-9145 (orders) *E-mail:* contact_hup@harvard.edu *Web Site:* www.hup.harvard.edu, pg 103

LeBlanc, Jeannine, Sinauer Associates Inc, 23 Plumtree Rd, Sunderland, MA 01375 *Tel:* 413-549-4300 *Fax:* 413-549-1118 *E-mail:* publish@sinauer.com; orders@sinauer.com *Web Site:* sinauer.com, pg 214

Leblanc, Kieran, Alberta Book Awards, 10523 100 Ave, Edmonton, AB T5J 0A8, Canada *Tel:* 780-424-5060 *E-mail:* info@bookpublishers.ab.ca *Web Site:* www.bookpublishers.ab.ca, pg 626

Leblanc, Kieran, The Book Publishers Association of Alberta (BPAA), 10523 100 Ave, Edmonton, AB T5J 0A8, Canada *Tel:* 780-424-5060 *E-mail:* info@bookpublishers.ab.ca *Web Site:* www.bookpublishers.ab.ca, pg 561

LeBlanc, Leslie, University Publishing Group, 6 W Washington St, Suite 302, Hagerstown, MD 21740 *Tel:* 240-420-0036 *Fax:* 240-718-7100 *E-mail:* orders@upgbooks.com, pg 247

LeBlond, Christine, Red Wheel/Weiser/Conari, 65 Parker St, Suite 7, Newburyport, MA 01950 *Tel:* 978-465-0504 *Toll Free Tel:* 800-423-7087 (orders) *Fax:* 978-465-0243 *E-mail:* info@rwwbooks.com *Web Site:* www.redwheelweiser.com, pg 197

LeBrun, Paul, Brault & Bouthillier, 700 ave Beaumont, Montreal, QC H3N 1V5, Canada *Tel:* 514-273-9186 *Toll Free Tel:* 800-361-0378 *Fax:* 514-273-8627 *Toll Free Fax:* 800-361-0378 *E-mail:* ventes@bb.ca *Web Site:* bb.ca, pg 447

LeCates, Justine, Doubleday/Nan A Talese, c/o Penguin Random House Inc, 1745 Broadway, New York, NY 10019 *Tel:* 212-751-2600 *Fax:* 212-572-2662 *E-mail:* ddaypub@randomhouse.com *Web Site:* knopfdoubleday.com, pg 72

LeCates, Justine, Alfred A Knopf/Everyman's Library, c/o Penguin Random House Inc, 1745 Broadway, New York, NY 10019 *Tel:* 212-751-2600 *Toll Free Tel:* 800-638-6460 *Fax:* 212-572-2593 *Web Site:* www.knopfdoubleday.com, pg 127

Leckie, Ross, Goose Lane Editions, 500 Beaverbrook Ct, Suite 330, Fredericton, NB E3B 5X4, Canada *Tel:* 506-450-4251 *Toll Free Tel:* 888-926-8377

Fax: 506-459-4991 *E-mail:* info@gooselane.com; customerservice@gooselane.com *Web Site:* www.gooselane.com, pg 458

Leclerc, Dr Richard PhD, Editions du Bois-de-Coulonge, 1140 Ave de Montigny, Sillery, QC G1S 3T7, Canada *Tel:* 418-683-6332 *Web Site:* www.ebc.qc.ca, pg 447

LeCount, Andy, HarperCollins General Books Group, 195 Broadway, New York, NY 10007 *Tel:* 212-207-7000 *Web Site:* www.harpercollins.com, pg 101

Leczkowski, Jennifer, Perseus Books, 250 W 57 St, 15th fl, New York, NY 10107 *Tel:* 212-340-8100 *Toll Free Tel:* 800-343-4499 (cust serv) *Fax:* 212-340-8105 *Web Site:* www.perseusbooks.com, pg 181

Leder, Meg, Penguin Books, 375 Hudson St, New York, NY 10014 *Tel:* 212-366-2000 *E-mail:* penguinpublicity@us.penguingroup.com *Web Site:* www.penguinclassics.com; www.penguin.com, pg 177

Ledges, Tserenchunt, The Mongolia Society Inc, Indiana University, 322 Goodbody Hall, 1011 E Third St, Bloomington, IN 47405-7005 *Tel:* 812-855-4078 *Fax:* 812-855-4078 *E-mail:* monsoc@indiana.edu *Web Site:* www.mongoliasociety.org, pg 153

Lee, Adam, Lasaria Creative Publishing, 4094 Majestic Lane, Suite 352, Fairfax, VA 22033 *E-mail:* info@lasariacreative.com *Web Site:* www.lasariacreative.com, pg 130

Lee, Albert, Aevitas Creative Management, 19 W 21 St, Suite 501, New York, NY 10010 *Tel:* 212-765-6900 *Web Site:* aevitascreative.com, pg 506

Lee, Benjamin, Dutton, 375 Hudson St, New York, NY 10014 *Tel:* 212-366-2000 *Fax:* 212-366-2262 *Web Site:* www.penguin.com, pg 74

Lee, Benjamin, Fine Creative Media, Inc, 322 Eighth Ave, 15th fl, New York, NY 10001 *Tel:* 212-595-3500 *Fax:* 212-595-3779, pg 85

Lee, Benjamin, Penguin Group USA, A Penguin Random House Company, 375 Hudson St, New York, NY 10014 *Tel:* 212-366-2000 *Toll Free Tel:* 800-847-5515 (inside sales); 800-631-8571 (cust serv) *Fax:* 212-366-2666; 607-775-4829 (inside sales) *E-mail:* online@us.penguingroup.com *Web Site:* www.penguin.com, pg 177

Lee, Benjamin, GP Putnam's Sons (Hardcover), 375 Hudson St, New York, NY 10014 *Tel:* 212-366-2000 *Fax:* 212-366-2643 *E-mail:* online@penguinputnam.com *Web Site:* www.penguin.com/publishers/gpputnamssons, pg 192

Lee, Calee, Xist Publishing, PO Box 61593, Irvine, CA 92602 *Tel:* 949-478-2568 *E-mail:* info@xistpublishing.com *Web Site:* www.xistpublishing.com, pg 261

Lee, Douglas, Kimberley Cameron & Associates LLC, 1550 Tiburon Blvd, Suite 704, Tiburon, CA 94920 *Tel:* 415-789-9191 *Fax:* 415-789-9177 *Web Site:* www.kimberleycameron.com, pg 511

Lee, Hanna, Random House Children's Books, 1745 Broadway, 10th fl, New York, NY 10019 *Tel:* 212-782-9000 *Web Site:* www.randomhousekids.com, pg 194

Lee, Helen, InterVarsity Press, 430 Plaza Dr, Westmont, IL 60559-1234 *Tel:* 630-734-4000 *Toll Free Tel:* 800-843-9487 *Fax:* 630-734-4200 *E-mail:* email@ivpress.com *Web Site:* www.ivpress.com, pg 120

Lee, Jacob, Xist Publishing, PO Box 61593, Irvine, CA 92602 *Tel:* 949-478-2568 *E-mail:* info@xistpublishing.com *Web Site:* www.xistpublishing.com, pg 261

Lee, Jay, Marshall Cavendish Corp, 99 White Plains Rd, Tarrytown, NY 10591-9001 *Tel:* 914-332-8888 *Toll Free Tel:* 800-821-9881 *Fax:* 914-332-8102 *E-mail:* mce@marshallcavendish.com *Web Site:* www.marshallcavendish.com; www.mceducation.us, pg 143

Lee, Jenny, Workman Publishing Co Inc, 225 Varick St, 9th fl, New York, NY 10014-4381 *Tel:* 212-254-5900 *Toll Free Tel:* 800-722-7202 *Fax:* 212-254-8098 *E-mail:* info@workman.com *Web Site:* www.workman.com, pg 259

Lee, Jill LeMin, Athenaeum of Philadelphia Literary Award, 219 S Sixth St, Philadelphia, PA 19106 *Tel:* 215-925-2688 *Fax:* 215-925-3755 *Web Site:* www.philaathenaeum.org/literary.html, pg 629

Lee, Jim, DC Entertainment, 2900 Alameda, Burbank, CA 91505 *Toll Free Tel:* 800-887-6789 *E-mail:* dccomics@cambeywest.com *Web Site:* www.dcentertainment.com; www.dccomics.com; www.madmag.com, pg 69

Lee, Joan, Insight Editions, 800 "A" St, San Rafael, CA 94901 *Tel:* 415-526-1370 *Toll Free Tel:* 800-809-3792 *Toll Free Fax:* 866-509-0515 *E-mail:* info@insighteditions.com *Web Site:* www.insighteditions.com, pg 117

Lee, Ken, Michael Wiese Productions, 12400 Ventura Blvd, No 1111, Studio City, CA 91604 *Tel:* 818-379-8799 *Toll Free Tel:* 800-833-5738 (orders) *Fax:* 818-986-3408 *E-mail:* mwpsales@mwp.com; fulfillment@portcity.com *Web Site:* www.mwp.com, pg 255

Lee, Linda, Master Point Press, 214 Merton St, Suite 205, Toronto, ON M4S 1A6, Canada *Tel:* 647-956-4933 *E-mail:* info@masterpointpress.com *Web Site:* www.masterpointpress.com; www.ebooksbridge.com (ebook sales), pg 463

Lee, Lisa, Candied Plums, 7548 Ravenna Ave NE, Seattle, WA 98115 *E-mail:* candiedplums@gmail.com *Web Site:* www.candiedplums.com, pg 46

Lee, Marie, The MIT Press, One Rogers St, Cambridge, MA 02142 *Tel:* 617-253-5255 *Toll Free Tel:* 800-207-8354 (orders) *Fax:* 617-258-6779; 617-577-1545 (orders) *Web Site:* mitpress.mit.edu, pg 151

Lee, Mark, Doubleday/Nan A Talese, c/o Penguin Random House Inc, 1745 Broadway, New York, NY 10019 *Tel:* 212-751-2600 *Fax:* 212-572-2662 *E-mail:* ddaypub@randomhouse.com *Web Site:* knopfdoubleday.com, pg 72

Lee, Ray, Master Point Press, 214 Merton St, Suite 205, Toronto, ON M4S 1A6, Canada *Tel:* 647-956-4933 *E-mail:* info@masterpointpress.com *Web Site:* www.masterpointpress.com; www.ebooksbridge.com (ebook sales), pg 463

Lee, Richard, Candied Plums, 7548 Ravenna Ave NE, Seattle, WA 98115 *E-mail:* candiedplums@gmail.com *Web Site:* www.candiedplums.com, pg 46

Lee, Sonia, William Saroyan International Prize for Writing, Admin, Saroyan Prize Committee, Stanford University Libraries, 557 Escondido Mall, Stanford, CA 94305-6004 *Tel:* 650-736-9538 *Web Site:* library.stanford.edu/saroyan, pg 686

Lee, Spenser, Farrar, Straus & Giroux, LLC, 18 W 18 St, New York, NY 10011 *Tel:* 212-741-6900 *E-mail:* fsg.publicity@fsgbooks.com *Web Site:* us.macmillan.com/fsg.aspx, pg 82

Lee-Pitts, Lisa, Holiday House Inc, 425 Madison Ave, New York, NY 10017 *Tel:* 212-688-0085 *Fax:* 212-421-6134 *E-mail:* info@holidayhouse.com *Web Site:* www.holidayhouse.com, pg 109

Leep, Jennifer, Baker Books, PO Box 6287, Grand Rapids, MI 49516-6287 *Tel:* 616-676-9185 *Toll Free Tel:* 800-877-2665; 800-679-1957 *Fax:* 616-676-9573 *Toll Free Fax:* 800-398-3111 *Web Site:* www.bakerpublishinggroup.com, pg 28

Leep, Jennifer, Revell, PO Box 6287, Grand Rapids, MI 49516-6287 *Tel:* 616-676-9185 *Toll Free Tel:* 800-877-2665; 800-679-1957 *Fax:* 616-676-9573 *Web Site:* www.bakerpublishinggroup.com, pg 198

Lefebvre, Marie-Eve, Editions du CHU Sainte-Justine, 3175, chemin de la Cote-Sainte-Catherine, Montreal, QC H3T 1C5, Canada *Tel:* 514-345-4671 *Fax:* 514-345-4631 *E-mail:* edition.hsj@ssss.gouv.qc.ca *Web Site:* www.editions-chu-sainte-justine.org, pg 453

Lefebvre-Faucher, Valerie, Les Editions du Remue-Menage, La Maison Parent-Roback, 110 rue Sainte-Therese, bureau 303, Montreal, QC H2Y 1E6, Canada *Tel:* 514-876-0097 *Fax:* 514-876-7951 *E-mail:* info@editions-rm.ca *Web Site:* www.editions-rm.ca, pg 453

Leffmann, Laurel, Summertime Publications Inc, 4115 E Palo Verde Dr, Phoenix, AZ 85018 *Tel:* 480-409-1554 *E-mail:* handell@summertimepublications.com *Web Site:* www.summertimepublications.com, pg 224

Lefkon, Wendy, Disney Press, 1101 Flower St, Glendale, CA 91201 *Web Site:* books.disney.com, pg 70

Legault, Claude, Guerin Editeur Ltee, 800, Blvd Industriel, bureau 200, St-Jean-sur-Richelieu, QC J3B 8G4, Canada *Tel:* 514-842-3481 *Fax:* 514-842-4923 *Web Site:* www.guerin-editeur.qc.ca, pg 459

Legault, Ms Josee, Brault & Bouthillier, 700 ave Beaumont, Montreal, QC H3N 1V5, Canada *Tel:* 514-273-9186 *Toll Free Tel:* 800-361-0378 *Fax:* 514-273-8627 *Toll Free Fax:* 800-361-0378 *E-mail:* ventes@bb.ca *Web Site:* bb.ca, pg 447

LeGro, Hope J, Georgetown University Press, 3240 Prospect St NW, Suite 250, Washington, DC 20007 *Tel:* 202-687-5889 (busn) *Fax:* 202-687-6340 (edit) *E-mail:* gupress@georgetown.edu *Web Site:* press.georgetown.edu, pg 91

Lehman, Michelle, National Association of Broadcasters (NAB), 1771 "N" St NW, Washington, DC 20036 *Tel:* 202-429-5300 *E-mail:* nab@nab.org *Web Site:* www.nab.org, pg 157, 570

Lehman, Susannah, The Optical Society (OSA), 2010 Massachusetts Ave NW, Washington, DC 20036-1023 *Tel:* 202-223-8130 *Toll Free Tel:* 800-766-4672 *E-mail:* custserv@osa.org *Web Site:* www.osa.org, pg 169

Lehr, Donald, The Betsy Nolan Literary Agency, 112 E 17 St, Suite 1W, New York, NY 10003 *Tel:* 212-967-8200 *Fax:* 212-967-7292 *E-mail:* dblehr@cs.com, pg 531

Lehto, Bill, Polebridge Press, PO Box 346, Farmington, MN 55024 *Tel:* 651-200-2372 *E-mail:* orders@westarinstitute.org *Web Site:* www.westarinstitute.org, pg 185

Leibovitch, Earl, Fitzhenry & Whiteside Limited, 195 Allstate Pkwy, Markham, ON L3R 4T8, Canada *Tel:* 905-477-9700 *Toll Free Tel:* 800-387-9776 *Fax:* 905-477-2834 *Toll Free Fax:* 800-260-9777 *E-mail:* bookinfo@fitzhenry.ca; godwit@fitzhenry.ca *Web Site:* www.fitzhenry.ca, pg 457

Leichum, Laura, University of Chicago Press, 1427 E 60 St, Chicago, IL 60637-2954 *Tel:* 773-702-7700; 773-702-7600 *Toll Free Tel:* 800-621-2736 (orders) *Fax:* 773-702-9756; 773-660-2235 (orders); 773-702-2708 *E-mail:* custserv@press.uchicago.edu; marketing@press.uchicago.edu *Web Site:* www.press.uchicago.edu, pg 240

Leifer, Jaime, Perseus Books, 250 W 57 St, 15th fl, New York, NY 10107 *Tel:* 212-340-8100 *Toll Free Tel:* 800-343-4499 (cust serv) *Fax:* 212-340-8105 *Web Site:* www.perseusbooks.com, pg 180

Leinberger, Anna, Berrett-Koehler Publishers Inc, 1333 Broadway, Suite 1000, Oakland, CA 94612 *Tel:* 510-817-2277 *Fax:* 510-817-2278 *E-mail:* bkpub@bkpub.com *Web Site:* www.bkconnection.com, pg 34

LeJeune, Becky, Bond Literary Agency, 4340 E Kentucky Ave, Suite 471, Denver, CO 80246 *Tel:* 303-781-9305 *E-mail:* queries@bondliteraryagency.com *Web Site:* bondliteraryagency.com, pg 508

Lelchuk, Alan, Steerforth Press, 45 Lyme Rd, Suite 208, Hanover, NH 03755-1222 *Tel:* 603-643-4787 *Fax:* 603-643-4788 *E-mail:* info@steerforth.com *Web Site:* www.steerforth.com, pg 221

Lellos, Stacy, Klutz, 568 Broadway, Suite 503, New York, NY 10012 *Tel:* 212-343-6360 *Fax:* 212-343-6366 *E-mail:* sales@klutz.com *Web Site:* store.scholastic.com, pg 126

Lellos, Stacy, Scholastic Trade Division, 557 Broadway, New York, NY 10012 *Tel:* 212-343-6100; 212-343-4685 (export sales) *Fax:* 212-343-4714 (export sales) *Web Site:* www.scholastic.com, pg 208

Lemay, Dominique, Editions Hurtubise, 1815, ave De Lorimier, Montreal, QC H2K 3W6, Canada *Tel:* 514-523-1523 *Toll Free Tel:* 800-361-1664 *Fax:* 514-523-9969 *Web Site:* www.editionshurtubise.com, pg 454

Lemay, Dominique, Editions MultiMondes, 1815, Avenue de Lorimier, Montreal, QC H2K 3W6, Canada *Tel:* 514-523-1523 *Toll Free Tel:* 800-361-1664 *Fax:* 514-523-9969 *Web Site:* www.multim.com, pg 455

LeMay, N Curtis, Aggiornamento Award, 8550 United Plaza Blvd, Suite 1001, Baton Rouge, LA 70809 *Tel:* 225-408-4417 *E-mail:* cla2@cathla.org *Web Site:* cathla.org, pg 625

LeMay, N Curtis, Catholic Library Association, 8550 United Plaza Blvd, Suite 1001, Baton Rouge, LA 70809 *Tel:* 225-408-4417 *E-mail:* cla2@cathla.org *Web Site:* cathla.org, pg 562

LeMay, N Curtis, Saint Katharine Drexel Award, 8550 United Plaza Blvd, Suite 1001, Baton Rouge, LA 70809 *Tel:* 225-408-4417 *E-mail:* cla2@cathla.org *Web Site:* cathla.org, pg 642

LeMay, N Curtis, Jerome Award, 8550 United Plaza Blvd, Suite 1001, Baton Rouge, LA 70809 *Tel:* 225-408-4417 *E-mail:* cla2@cathla.org *Web Site:* cathla.org, pg 657

LeMay, N Curtis, Regina Medal Award, 8550 United Plaza Blvd, Suite 1001, Baton Rouge, LA 70809 *Tel:* 225-408-4417 *E-mail:* cla2@cathla.org *Web Site:* cathla.org, pg 684

Lemieux, Raymond, Editions MultiMondes, 1815, Avenue de Lorimier, Montreal, QC H2K 3W6, Canada *Tel:* 514-523-1523 *Toll Free Tel:* 800-361-1664 *Fax:* 514-523-9969 *Web Site:* www.multim.com, pg 455

Lemire, Kristen, Simon & Schuster, 1230 Avenue of the Americas, New York, NY 10020 *Tel:* 212-698-7000 *Toll Free Tel:* 800-223-2348 (cust serv); 800-223-2336 (orders) *Toll Free Fax:* 800-943-9831 (orders) *Web Site:* www.simonandschuster.com, pg 212

Lemon, Carolyn, Ignatius Press, 1348 Tenth Ave, San Francisco, CA 94122-2304 *Toll Free Tel:* 800-651-1531 (orders); 888-615-3186 (cust serv) *E-mail:* info@ignatius.com *Web Site:* www.ignatius.com, pg 114

Lemon, Faith, Stone Pier Press, PO Box 170572, San Francisco, CA 94117 *Tel:* 415-484-2821 *E-mail:* hello@stonepierpress.org *Web Site:* www.stonepierpress.org, pg 223

Lencicki, Alex, Orbit, 1290 Avenue of the Americas, New York, NY 10019 *Tel:* 212-364-1100 *Toll Free Tel:* 800-759-0190 *Web Site:* www.orbitbooks.net, pg 169

Lengyel, Heather, Brookes Publishing Co Inc, PO Box 10624, Baltimore, MD 21285-0624 *Tel:* 410-337-9580 (outside US & CN) *Toll Free Tel:* 800-638-3775 (US & CN) *Fax:* 410-337-8539 *E-mail:* custserv@brookespublishing.com *Web Site:* www.brookespublishing.com, pg 44

Lenihan, Kelly, Artisan Bookworks, 921 S Third Ave, No 8, Sequim, WA 98382 *Tel:* 425-954-5277 *E-mail:* books@artisanbookworks.com *Web Site:* www.artisanbookworks.com, pg 22

Lennard, Jeff, Brethren Press, 1451 Dundee Ave, Elgin, IL 60120 *Tel:* 847-742-5100 *Toll Free Tel:* 800-323-8039 *Toll Free Fax:* 800-667-8188 *E-mail:* brethrenpress@brethren.org *Web Site:* www.brethrenpress.com, pg 42

Lennertz, Carl, Children's & Teen Choice Book Awards, 54 W 39 St, 14th fl, New York, NY 10018 *E-mail:* cbc.info@cbcbooks.org *Web Site:* everychildareader.net/choice, pg 637

Lennertz, Carl, The Children's Book Council (CBC), 54 W 39 St, 14th fl, New York, NY 10018 *Tel:* 212-966-1990 *E-mail:* cbc.info@cbcbooks.org *Web Site:* www.cbcbooks.org, pg 563

Lentz, Dr Cheryl, The Lentz Leadership Institute LLC, 7124 Glyndon Trail NW, Albuquerque, NM 87114 *Tel:* 702-719-9214 *E-mail:* orders@lentzleadership.com *Web Site:* www.lentzleadership.com; www.refractivethinker.com, pg 132

Leo, Jacqueline, Deadline Club, c/o Salmagundi Club, 47 Fifth Ave, New York, NY 10003 *Tel:* 646-481-7584 *E-mail:* info@deadlineclub.org *Web Site:* www.deadlineclub.org, pg 564

Leo, Michelle, Simon & Schuster Children's Publishing, 1230 Avenue of the Americas, New York, NY 10020 *Tel:* 212-698-7000 *Web Site:* www.simonandschuster.com/kids; www.simonandschuster.com/teen; simonandschuster.net; simonandschuster.biz, pg 213

Leo, Michelle, Simon & Schuster, Inc, 1230 Avenue of the Americas, New York, NY 10020 *Tel:* 212-698-7000 *Fax:* 212-698-7007 *E-mail:* firstname.lastname@simonandschuster.com *Web Site:* www.simonandschuster.com, pg 213

Leonard, John-Paul, Progressive Press, 3716 37 St, San Diego, CA 92105-2409 *Tel:* 619-892-7781 *Fax:* 619-892-7781 *E-mail:* info@progressivepress.com *Web Site:* www.progressivepress.com, pg 190

Leonard, Linda, Random House Children's Books, 1745 Broadway, 10th fl, New York, NY 10019 *Tel:* 212-782-9000 *Web Site:* www.randomhousekids.com, pg 194

Leonardo, Catherine, University of New Mexico Press, One University of New Mexico, Albuquerque, NM 87131-0001 *Tel:* 505-272-7777 *Fax:* 505-277-3343; 505-272-7778 (cust serv) *Toll Free Fax:* 800-622-8667 (orders only) *E-mail:* unmpress@unm.edu; custserv@unm.edu (order dept) *Web Site:* unmpress.com, pg 243

Leonards, David, International Entertainment Bureau, 3612 N Washington Blvd, Indianapolis, IN 46205-3592 *Tel:* 317-926-7566 *E-mail:* ieb@prodigy.net, pg 547

Leone, Dan, ReferencePoint Press Inc, 17150 Via del Campo, Suite 205, San Diego, CA 92127 *Tel:* 858-618-1314 *Toll Free Tel:* 888-479-6436 *Fax:* 858-618-1730 *E-mail:* info@referencepointpress.com *Web Site:* www.referencepointpress.com, pg 197

Leonesio, Chris, Harvard Education Publishing Group, 8 Story St, 1st fl, Cambridge, MA 02138 *Tel:* 617-495-3432 *Toll Free Tel:* 800-513-0763 (subns); 888-437-1437 (orders) *Fax:* 617-496-3584; 978-348-1233 (orders) *E-mail:* hepg@harvard.edu *Web Site:* www.hepg.org, pg 102

Lepage, Lucy, Royce Carlton Inc, 866 United Nations Plaza, Suite 587, New York, NY 10017-1880 *Tel:* 212-355-7700 *Toll Free Tel:* 800-LECTURE (532-8873) *Fax:* 212-888-8659 *E-mail:* info@roycecarlton.com *Web Site:* www.roycecarlton.com, pg 548

Lependorf, Jeffrey, Community of Literary Magazines & Presses (CLMP), 154 Christopher St, Suite 3C, New York, NY 10014-9110 *Tel:* 212-741-9110 *Fax:* 212-741-9112 *E-mail:* info@clmp.org *Web Site:* www.clmp.org, pg 563

LePera, Lauren, Insight Editions, 800 "A" St, San Rafael, CA 94901 *Tel:* 415-526-1370 *Toll Free Tel:* 800-809-3792 *Toll Free Fax:* 866-509-0515 *E-mail:* info@insighteditions.com *Web Site:* www.insighteditions.com, pg 117

Lerman, Dawn, Fordham University, Graduate School of Business Administration, Gabelli School of Business, 441 E Fordham Rd, Hughes Hall, Rm 516, Bronx, NY 10458 *Tel:* 718-817-1894 *Web Site:* www.bnet.fordham.edu, pg 620

Lerner, Aaron, American Fisheries Society, 425 Barlow Place, Suite 110, Bethesda, MD 20814-2144 *Tel:* 301-897-8616; 703-661-1570 (book orders) *Fax:* 301-897-8096; 703-996-1010 (book orders) *E-mail:* main@fisheries.org *Web Site:* www.fisheries.org, pg 11

Lerner, Adam, Carolrhoda Books, 241 First Ave N, Minneapolis, MN 55401 *Tel:* 612-332-3344 *Toll Free Tel:* 800-328-4929 *Fax:* 612-332-7615 *Toll Free Fax:* 800-332-1132 *E-mail:* info@lernerbooks.com; custserve@lernerbooks.com *Web Site:* www.lernerbooks.com; www.facebook.com/lernerbooks, pg 48

Lerner, Adam, Carolrhoda Lab™, 241 First Ave N, Minneapolis, MN 55401 *Tel:* 612-332-3344 *Toll Free Tel:* 800-328-4929 *Fax:* 612-332-7615 *Toll Free Fax:* 800-332-1132 (US) *E-mail:* info@lernerbooks.com; custserve@lernerbooks.com *Web Site:* www.lernerbooks.com; www.facebook.com/lernerbooks, pg 48

Lerner, Adam, ediciones Lerner, 241 First Ave N, Minneapolis, MN 55401 *Tel:* 612-332-3344 *Toll Free Tel:* 800-328-4929 *Fax:* 612-332-7615 *Toll Free Fax:* 800-332-1132 *E-mail:* info@lernerbooks.com; custserve@lernerbooks.com *Web Site:* www.lernerbooks.com; www.facebook.com/lernerbooks, pg 75

Lerner, Adam, First Avenue Editions, 241 First Ave N, Minneapolis, MN 55401 *Tel:* 612-332-3344 *Toll Free Tel:* 800-328-4929 *Fax:* 612-332-7615 *Toll Free Fax:* 800-332-1132 *E-mail:* info@lernerbooks.com; custserve@lernerbooks.com *Web Site:* www.lernerbooks.com; www.facebook.com/lernerbooks, pg 85

Lerner, Adam, Graphic Universe™, 241 First Ave N, Minneapolis, MN 55401 *Tel:* 612-332-3344 *Toll Free Tel:* 800-328-4929 *Fax:* 612-332-7615 *Toll Free Fax:* 800-332-1132 *E-mail:* info@lernerbooks.com; custserve@lernerbooks.com *Web Site:* www.lernerbooks.com; www.facebook.com/lernerbooks, pg 95

Lerner, Adam, Kar-Ben Publishing, 241 First Ave N, Minneapolis, MN 55401 *Tel:* 612-332-3344 *Toll Free Tel:* 800-4-KARBEN (452-7236) *Fax:* 612-332-7615 *Toll Free Fax:* 800-332-1132 *Web Site:* www.karben.com, pg 125

Lerner, Adam, Lerner Publications, 241 First Ave N, Minneapolis, MN 55401 *Tel:* 612-332-3344 *Toll Free Tel:* 800-328-4929 *Fax:* 612-332-7615 *Toll Free Fax:* 800-332-1132 *E-mail:* info@lernerbooks.com; custserve@lernerbooks.com *Web Site:* www.lernerbooks.com; www.facebook.com/lernerbooks, pg 132

Lerner, Adam, Lerner Publishing Group Inc, 241 First Ave N, Minneapolis, MN 55401 *Tel:* 612-332-3344 *Toll Free Tel:* 800-328-4929 *Fax:* 612-332-7615 *Toll Free Fax:* 800-332-1132 *E-mail:* info@lernerbooks.com; custserve@lernerbooks.com *Web Site:* www.lernerbooks.com; www.facebook.com/lernerbooks, pg 132

Lerner, Adam, LernerClassroom, 241 First Ave N, Minneapolis, MN 55401 *Tel:* 612-332-3344 *Toll Free Tel:* 800-328-4929 *Fax:* 612-332-7615 *Toll Free Fax:* 800-332-1132 *E-mail:* info@lernerbooks.com; custserve@lernerbooks.com *Web Site:* www.lernerbooks.com; www.facebook.com/lernerbooks, pg 132

Lerner, Adam, Millbrook Press, 241 First Ave N, Minneapolis, MN 55401 *Tel:* 612-332-3344 *Toll Free Tel:* 800-328-4929 (US only) *Fax:* 612-332-7615 *Toll Free Fax:* 800-332-1132 *E-mail:* info@lernerbooks.com; custserve@lernerbooks.com *Web Site:* www.lernerbooks.com; www.facebook.com/millbrookpress, pg 151

Lerner, Adam, Twenty-First Century Books, 241 First Ave N, Minneapolis, MN 55401 *Tel:* 612-332-3344 *Toll Free Tel:* 800-328-4929 *Fax:* 612-332-7615 *Toll Free Fax:* 800-332-1132 *E-mail:* info@lernerbooks.com; custserve@lernerbooks.com *Web Site:* www.lernerbooks.com; www.facebook.com/lernerbooks, pg 237

Lerner, Betsy, Dunow, Carlson & Lerner Literary Agency Inc, 27 W 20 St, Suite 1107, New York, NY 10011 *Tel:* 212-645-7606 *E-mail:* mail@dclagency.com *Web Site:* www.dclagency.com, pg 515

Lerner, Harry J, Carolrhoda Books, 241 First Ave N, Minneapolis, MN 55401 *Tel:* 612-332-3344 *Toll Free Tel:* 800-328-4929 *Fax:* 612-332-7615 *Toll Free Fax:* 800-332-1132 *E-mail:* info@lernerbooks.com; custserve@lernerbooks.com *Web Site:* www.lernerbooks.com; www.facebook.com/lernerbooks, pg 48

Lerner, Harry J, Carolrhoda Lab™, 241 First Ave N, Minneapolis, MN 55401 *Tel:* 612-332-3344 *Toll Free Tel:* 800-328-4929 *Fax:* 612-332-7615 *Toll Free Fax:* 800-332-1132 (US) *E-mail:* info@lernerbooks.com; custserve@lernerbooks.com *Web Site:* www.lernerbooks.com; www.facebook.com/lernerbooks, pg 48

Lerner, Harry J, ediciones Lerner, 241 First Ave N, Minneapolis, MN 55401 *Tel:* 612-332-3344 *Toll Free Tel:* 800-328-4929 *Fax:* 612-332-7615 *Toll Free Fax:* 800-332-1132 *E-mail:* info@lernerbooks.com; custserve@lernerbooks.com *Web Site:* www.lernerbooks.com; www.facebook.com/lernerbooks, pg 75

Lerner, Harry J, First Avenue Editions, 241 First Ave N, Minneapolis, MN 55401 *Tel:* 612-332-3344 *Toll Free Tel:* 800-328-4929 *Fax:* 612-332-7615 *Toll Free Fax:* 800-332-1132 *E-mail:* info@lernerbooks.com; custserve@lernerbooks.com *Web Site:* www.lernerbooks.com; www.facebook.com/lernerbooks, pg 85

Lerner, Harry J, Graphic Universe™, 241 First Ave N, Minneapolis, MN 55401 *Tel:* 612-332-3344 *Toll Free Tel:* 800-328-4929 *Fax:* 612-332-7615 *Toll Free Fax:* 800-332-1132 *E-mail:* info@lernerbooks.com; custserve@lernerbooks.com *Web Site:* www.lernerbooks.com; www.facebook.com/lernerbooks, pg 95

Lerner, Harry J, Kar-Ben Publishing, 241 First Ave N, Minneapolis, MN 55401 *Tel:* 612-332-3344 *Toll Free Tel:* 800-4-KARBEN (452-7236) *Fax:* 612-332-7615 *Toll Free Fax:* 800-332-1132 *Web Site:* www.karben.com, pg 125

Lerner, Harry J, Lerner Publications, 241 First Ave N, Minneapolis, MN 55401 *Tel:* 612-332-3344 *Toll Free Tel:* 800-328-4929 *Fax:* 612-332-7615 *Toll Free Fax:* 800-332-1132 *E-mail:* info@lernerbooks.com; custserve@lernerbooks.com *Web Site:* www.lernerbooks.com; www.facebook.com/lernerbooks, pg 132

Lerner, Harry J, Lerner Publishing Group Inc, 241 First Ave N, Minneapolis, MN 55401 *Tel:* 612-332-3344 *Toll Free Tel:* 800-328-4929 *Fax:* 612-332-7615 *Toll Free Fax:* 800-332-1132 *E-mail:* info@lernerbooks.com; custserve@lernerbooks.com *Web Site:* www.lernerbooks.com; www.facebook.com/lernerbooks, pg 132

Lerner, Harry J, LernerClassroom, 241 First Ave N, Minneapolis, MN 55401 *Tel:* 612-332-3344 *Toll Free Tel:* 800-328-4929 *Fax:* 612-332-7615 *Toll Free Fax:* 800-332-1132 *E-mail:* info@lernerbooks.com; custserve@lernerbooks.com *Web Site:* www.lernerbooks.com; www.facebook.com/lernerbooks, pg 132

Lerner, Harry J, Millbrook Press, 241 First Ave N, Minneapolis, MN 55401 *Tel:* 612-332-3344 *Toll Free Tel:* 800-328-4929 (US only) *Fax:* 612-332-7615 *Toll Free Fax:* 800-332-1132 *E-mail:* info@lernerbooks.com; custserve@lernerbooks.com *Web Site:* www.lernerbooks.com; www.facebook.com/millbrookpress, pg 151

Lerner, Harry J, Twenty-First Century Books, 241 First Ave N, Minneapolis, MN 55401 *Tel:* 612-332-3344 *Toll Free Tel:* 800-328-4929 *Fax:* 612-332-7615 *Toll Free Fax:* 800-332-1132 *E-mail:* info@lernerbooks.com; custserve@lernerbooks.com *Web Site:* www.lernerbooks.com; www.facebook.com/lernerbooks, pg 237

Lerner, Mark, MedBooks, 101 W Buckingham Rd, Richardson, TX 75081-4802 *Tel:* 972-643-1809 *Fax:* 972-643-1859 *E-mail:* medbooks@medbooks.com *Web Site:* www.medbooks.com, pg 147

Lerner, Mark, The Oliver Press Inc, Charlotte Sq, 5707 W 36 St, Minneapolis, MN 55416-2510 *Tel:* 952-926-8981 *Toll Free Tel:* 800-8-OLIVER (865-4837) *Fax:* 952-926-8965 *E-mail:* orders@oliverpress.com *Web Site:* www.oliverpress.com, pg 167

Lerner, Seth, Tom Doherty Associates, LLC, 175 Fifth Ave, 14th fl, New York, NY 10010 *Tel:* 646-307-5511 *Toll Free Tel:* 800-455-0340 *Web Site:* www.tor-forge.com, pg 71

Lerner, Shannon, Business Forms Management Association (BFMA), 1147 Fleetwood Ave, Madison, WI 53716 *Toll Free Tel:* 888-367-3078 *E-mail:* bfma@bfma.org *Web Site:* www.bfma.org, pg 561

Lesak, Susan, Host Publications, 3408 West Ave, Austin, TX 78705 *Tel:* 512-236-1290 *Fax:* 512-236-1208 *Web Site:* www.hostpublications.com, pg 110

Lesan, Susanna, Pearson Humanities & Social Sciences, 225 River St, Hoboken, NJ 07030-4772 *Tel:* 201-236-7000, pg 176

Lescaze, Alexandra, Hillman Prizes for Journalism, 330 W 42 St, Suite 900, New York, NY 10036 *Tel:* 646-448-6413 *Web Site:* www.hillmanfoundation.org, pg 653

Leslie, Nathan, Hamilton Stone Editions, PO Box 43, Maplewood, NJ 07040 *Tel:* 973-378-8361 *E-mail:* hstone@hamiltonstone.org *Web Site:* www.hamiltonstone.org, pg 99

Lessiter, Frank, Lessiter Media, 16655 W Wisconsin Ave, Brookfield, WI 53005 *Tel:* 262-782-4480 *Toll Free Tel:* 800-645-8455 *Fax:* 262-782-1252; 262-786-5564 *E-mail:* info@lessitermedia.com *Web Site:* www.lesspub.com; lessitermedia.com, pg 132

Lessiter, Mike, Lessiter Media, 16655 W Wisconsin Ave, Brookfield, WI 53005 *Tel:* 262-782-4480 *Toll Free Tel:* 800-645-8455 *Fax:* 262-782-1252; 262-786-5564 *E-mail:* info@lessitermedia.com *Web Site:* www.lesspub.com; lessitermedia.com, pg 132

Lessne, Donald L, Frederick Fell Publishers Inc, 2131 Hollywood Blvd, Suite 305, Hollywood, FL 33020 *Tel:* 954-925-5242 *E-mail:* fellpub@aol.com (admin only) *Web Site:* www.fellpub.com, pg 88

Letchworth, Lynne, Chalice Press, 483 E Lockwood Ave, Suite 100, St Louis, MO 63119 *Tel:* 314-231-8500 *Toll Free Tel:* 800-366-3383 *Fax:* 314-231-8524; 770-280-4039 (orders) *E-mail:* customerservice@chalicepress.com *Web Site:* www.chalicepress.com, pg 52

Letourneau, Helene, Association Nationale des Editeurs de Livres, 2514, blvd Rosemont, Montreal, QC H1Y 1K4, Canada *Tel:* 514-273-8130 *Toll Free Tel:* 866-900-ANEL (900-2635) *E-mail:* info@anel.qc.ca *Web Site:* www.anel.qc.ca, pg 558

Lettice, Jenna, Random House Children's Books, 1745 Broadway, 10th fl, New York, NY 10019 *Tel:* 212-782-9000 *Web Site:* www.randomhousekids.com, pg 194

Leung, Julie, Quirk Books, 215 Church St, Philadelphia, PA 19106 *Tel:* 215-627-3581 *Fax:* 215-627-5220 *E-mail:* general@quirkbooks.com *Web Site:* www.quirkbooks.com, pg 193

Leung, Mona, McGraw-Hill Higher Education, 1333 Burr Ridge Pkwy, Burr Ridge, IL 60527 *Tel:* 630-789-4000 *Toll Free Tel:* 800-338-3987 (cust serv) *Fax:* 614-755-5645 (cust serv) *Web Site:* www.mhhe.com, pg 146

LeVan, Katherine, Show What You Know® Publishing, A Lorenz Company, c/o The Lorenz Corp, 501 E Third St, Dayton, OH 45402 *Tel:* 614-764-1211; 937-228-6118 *Toll Free Tel:* 877-PASSING (727-7464) *Fax:* 937-233-2042 *E-mail:* info@lorenz.com *Web Site:* www.lorenzeducationalpress.com, pg 212

Levay, Rachael, University of Washington Press, 4333 Brooklyn Ave NE, Seattle, WA 98105-9570 *Tel:* 206-543-4050 *Toll Free Tel:* 800-537-5487 (orders) *Fax:* 206-543-3932; 410-516-6998 (orders) *E-mail:* uwapress@uw.edu *Web Site:* www.washington.edu/uwpress, pg 246

Leventhal, J P, Hachette Books, 1290 Avenue of the Americas, New York, NY 10019 *Tel:* 212-364-1100 *Web Site:* www.hachettebookgroup.com, pg 98

Leventhal, Josh, Minnesota Historical Society Press, 345 Kellogg Blvd W, St Paul, MN 55102-1906 *Tel:* 651-259-3205 *Toll Free Tel:* 800-621-2736 (warehouse) *Fax:* 651-297-1345 *Toll Free Fax:* 800-621-8476 (warehouse) *E-mail:* info-mnhspress@mnhs.org *Web Site:* www.mnhs.org/mnhspress, pg 151

Leventhal, Philip, Columbia University Press, 61 W 62 St, New York, NY 10023 *Tel:* 212-459-0600 *Toll Free Tel:* 800-944-8648 *Fax:* 212-459-3678 *E-mail:* cup_book@columbia.edu (orders & cust serv) *Web Site:* cup.columbia.edu, pg 59

Leverence, John, Television Academy, 5220 Lankershim Blvd, North Hollywood, CA 91601-3109 *Tel:* 818-754-2800 *Fax:* 818-761-2827 *Web Site:* www.emmys.com, pg 579

Leverton, Yossi, Hachai Publishing, 527 Empire Blvd, Brooklyn, NY 11225 *Tel:* 718-633-0100 *Fax:* 718-633-0103 *E-mail:* info@hachai.com *Web Site:* www.hachai.com, pg 98

Levesque, Brigit, Broquet Inc, 97-B, Montee des Bouleaux, St-Constant, QC J5A 1A9, Canada *Tel:* 450-638-3338 *Fax:* 450-638-4338 *E-mail:* info@broquet.qc.ca *Web Site:* www.broquet.qc.ca, pg 448

Levesque, Claudette, Canadian Museum of History (Musee canadien de l'histoire), 100 Laurier St, Gatineau, QC K1A 0M8, Canada *Tel:* 819-776-7000 *Toll Free Tel:* 800-555-5621 (North American orders only) *Fax:* 819-776-7187 *Web Site:* www.historymuseum.ca, pg 449

Levi, Katie, The Art Institute of Chicago, 111 S Michigan Ave, Chicago, IL 60603-6404 *Tel:* 312-443-3600; 312-443-3540 (pubns) *Fax:* 312-443-1334 (pubns) *Web Site:* www.artic.edu; www.artinstituteshop.org, pg 21

Levin, David, McGraw-Hill Education, 2 Penn Plaza, New York, NY 10121-2298 *Tel:* 212-904-2000 *E-mail:* customer.service@mheducation.com; international_cs@mheducation.com *Web Site:* www.mheducation.com, pg 145

Levin, Janet, North Atlantic Books, 2526 Martin Luther King Jr Way, Berkeley, CA 94704 *Tel:* 510-549-4270 *Fax:* 510-549-4276 *Web Site:* www.northatlanticbooks.com, pg 163

Levin, Kendra, Viking Children's Books, 345 Hudson St, New York, NY 10014 *Fax:* 212-414-3393 *E-mail:* youngreaderspublicity@us.penguingroup.com *Web Site:* www.penguin.com/publishers/vikingchildrensbooks, pg 251

Levine, Arthur A, Scholastic Trade Division, 557 Broadway, New York, NY 10012 *Tel:* 212-343-6100; 212-343-4685 (export sales) *Fax:* 212-343-4714 (export sales) *Web Site:* www.scholastic.com, pg 208

Levine, Deborah, The Jeff Herman Agency LLC, 29 Park St, Stockbridge, MA 01262 *Tel:* 413-298-0077 *Fax:* 413-298-8188 *E-mail:* submissions@jeffherman.com *Web Site:* www.jeffherman.com, pg 521

Levine, Ellen, Trident Media Group LLC, 41 Madison Ave, 36th fl, New York, NY 10010 *Tel:* 212-333-1511 *E-mail:* info@tridentmediagroup.com; press@tridentmediagroup.com *Web Site:* www.tridentmediagroup.com, pg 540

Levine, Harold, Aslan Publishing, 857 Post Rd, Suite 302, Fairfield, CT 06824 *Tel:* 203-372-0300; 203-374-6224 *Fax:* 203-374-4766 *E-mail:* information@aslanpublishing.com *Web Site:* www.aslanpublishing.com, pg 23

Levine, Jaime, Diversion Books, 443 Park Ave S, Suite 1008, New York, NY 10016 *Tel:* 212-961-6390 *E-mail:* info@diversionbooks.com *Web Site:* www.diversionbooks.com, pg 71

Levine, James, Levine|Greenberg|Rostan Literary Agency, 307 Seventh Ave, Suite 2407, New York, NY 10001 *Tel:* 212-337-0934 *Fax:* 212-337-0948 *Web Site:* lgrliterary.com, pg 525

Levine, Jeffrey, Tupelo Press Inc, 243 Union St, Suite 305, North Adams, MA 01247 *Tel:* 413-664-9611 *Fax:* 413-664-9711 *E-mail:* info@tupelopress.org *Web Site:* www.tupelopress.org, pg 236

Levine, Jonathan D, Prayer Book Press Inc, 221 E 48 St, New York, NY 10017 *Tel:* 212-319-6666 *Fax:* 212-688-8597 *E-mail:* mediajudaica@aol.com, pg 186

Levine, Karen, Getty Publications, 1200 Getty Center Dr, Suite 500, Los Angeles, CA 90049-1682 *Tel:* 310-440-7365 *Toll Free Tel:* 800-223-3431 (orders) *Fax:* 310-440-7758 *E-mail:* pubsinfo@getty.edu *Web Site:* www.getty.edu/publications, pg 92

Levine, Katie, HarperCollins Publishers, 195 Broadway, New York, NY 10007 *Tel:* 212-207-7000 *Fax:* 212-207-7145 *Web Site:* www.harpercollins.com, pg 102

Levine, Michael, Westwood Creative Artists Ltd, 138 Sussex Mews, Toronto, ON M5S-2K1, Canada *Tel:* 416-964-3302 *Fax:* 416-964-3302 *E-mail:* wca_office@wcaltd.com *Web Site:* www.wcaltd.com, pg 541

Levine, Reyna Abigale, National Press Foundation, 1211 Connecticut Ave NW, Suite 310, Washington, DC 20036 *Tel:* 202-663-7280 *Web Site:* nationalpress.org, pg 572

Levine, Ronn, Specialized Information Publishers Association (SIPA), 1090 Vermont Ave NW, 6th fl, Washington, DC 20005-4095 *Web Site:* www.sipaonline.com, pg 579

Levins, Michael S, innovativeKids®, 50 Washington St, Suite 201, Norwalk, CT 06854 *Tel:* 203-838-6400 *E-mail:* info@innovativekids.com *Web Site:* www.innovativekids.com, pg 117

Levinson, Diane, Chronicle Books LLC, 680 Second St, San Francisco, CA 94107 *Tel:* 415-537-4200 *Toll Free Tel:* 800-759-0190 (cust serv) *Fax:* 415-537-4460 *Toll Free Fax:* 800-858-7787 (orders); 800-286-9471 (cust serv) *E-mail:* frontdesk@chroniclebooks.com *Web Site:* www.chroniclebooks.com, pg 55

Levinson, Diane, Princeton Architectural Press, 37 E Seventh St, New York, NY 10003 *Tel:* 212-995-9620 *Toll Free Tel:* 800-722-6657 (dist); 800-759-0190 (sales) *Fax:* 212-995-9454 *E-mail:* sales@papress.com *Web Site:* www.papress.com, pg 188

Levinson, Meagan Stacey, Princeton University Press, 41 William St, Princeton, NJ 08540-5237 *Tel:* 609-258-4900 *Fax:* 609-258-6305 *Web Site:* press.princeton.edu, pg 188

Levinson, Wendy, Harvey Klinger Inc, 300 W 55 St, Suite 11V, New York, NY 10019 *Tel:* 212-581-7068 *Fax:* 212-315-3823 *E-mail:* queries@harveyklinger.com *Web Site:* www.harveyklinger.com, pg 524

Levitan, Jeanie, Bear & Co Inc, One Park St, Rochester, VT 05767 *Tel:* 802-767-3174 *Toll Free Tel:* 800-932-3277 *Fax:* 802-767-3726 *E-mail:* customerservice@InnerTraditions.com *Web Site:* InnerTraditions.com, pg 31

Levitan, Jeanie, Inner Traditions International Ltd, One Park St, Rochester, VT 05767 *Tel:* 802-767-3174 *Toll Free Tel:* 800-246-8648 *Fax:* 802-767-3726 *E-mail:* customerservice@InnerTraditions.com *Web Site:* www.InnerTraditions.com, pg 117

Levithan, David, Scholastic Trade Division, 557 Broadway, New York, NY 10012 *Tel:* 212-343-6100; 212-343-4685 (export sales) *Fax:* 212-343-4714 (export sales) *Web Site:* www.scholastic.com, pg 208

Levitt, Sarah, Aevitas Creative Management, 19 W 21 St, Suite 501, New York, NY 10010 *Tel:* 212-765-6900 *Web Site:* aevitascreative.com, pg 506

Levy, Michael, Corporation for Public Broadcasting (CPB), 401 Ninth St NW, Washington, DC 20004-2129 *Tel:* 202-879-9600 *Web Site:* www.cpb.org, pg 563

Levy, Roanie, Access Copyright, The Canadian Copyright Licensing Agency, 56 Wellesley St W, Suite 401A, Toronto, ON M5S 2S3, Canada *Tel:* 416-868-1620 *Toll Free Tel:* 800-893-5777 *Fax:* 416-868-1621 *E-mail:* info@accesscopyright.ca *Web Site:* www.accesscopyright.ca, pg 553

Lew, Cindy, Fine Creative Media, Inc, 322 Eighth Ave, 15th fl, New York, NY 10001 *Tel:* 212-595-3500 *Fax:* 212-595-3779, pg 85

Lewandoski, Joyce, University of Texas Press, 3001 Lake Austin Blvd, 2.200, Austin, TX 78703 *Tel:* 512-471-7233 *Fax:* 512-232-7178 *E-mail:* utpress@uts.cc.utexas.edu; info@utpress.utexas.edu *Web Site:* www.utexaspress.com, pg 230

Lewin, Arianne, GP Putnam's Sons (Children's), 345 Hudson St, New York, NY 10014 *Tel:* 212-366-2000 *Fax:* 212-414-3393 *Web Site:* www.penguin.com/publishers/gpputnamssonsbooksforyoungread, pg 192

Lewis, Beth A, Augsburg Fortress Publishers, Publishing House of the Evangelical Lutheran Church in America, 510 Marquette Ave S, Minneapolis, MN 55402 *Tel:* 612-330-3300 *Toll Free Tel:* 800-426-0115 (ext 639, subns); 800-328-4648 (orders) *Fax:* 612-330-3455 *E-mail:* info@augsburgfortress.org; copyright@augsburgfortress.org (reprint permission requests); customercare@augsburgfortress.org *Web Site:* www.augsburgfortress.org, pg 26

Lewis, BiBi, Ethan Ellenberg Literary Agency, 155 Suffolk St, Suite 2R, New York, NY 10002 *Tel:* 212-431-4554 *E-mail:* agent@ethanellenberg.com *Web Site:* www.ethanellenberg.com, pg 516

Lewis, Brent, Harlequin Enterprises Ltd, 225 Duncan Mill Rd, Don Mills, ON M3B 3K9, Canada *Tel:* 416-445-5860 *Toll Free Tel:* 888-432-4879; 800-370-5838 (ebook inquiries) *E-mail:* customerservice@harlequin.com *Web Site:* www.harlequin.com, pg 459

Lewis, Dave, Baker Books, PO Box 6287, Grand Rapids, MI 49516-6287 *Tel:* 616-676-9185 *Toll Free Tel:* 800-877-2665; 800-679-1957 *Fax:* 616-676-9573 *Toll Free Fax:* 800-398-3111 *Web Site:* www.bakerpublishinggroup.com, pg 28

Lewis, Dave, Bethany House Publishers, 11400 Hampshire Ave S, Bloomington, MN 55438 *Tel:* 952-829-2500 *Toll Free Tel:* 800-877-2665 (orders) *Fax:* 952-829-2568 *Toll Free Fax:* 800-398-3111 (orders) *Web Site:* www.bethanyhouse.com; www.bakerpublishinggroup.com, pg 34

Lewis, David, Don Buchwald & Associates Inc, 10 E 44 St, New York, NY 10017 *Tel:* 212-867-1200 *Fax:* 212-867-2434 *E-mail:* info@buchwald.com *Web Site:* www.buchwald.com, pg 510

Lewis, Dottie, National Academies Press (NAP), Lockbox 285, 500 Fifth St NW, Washington, DC 20001 *Tel:* 202-334-3313 *Fax:* 202-334-2451 (cust serv); 202-334-2793 (mktg dept) *E-mail:* customer_service@nap.edu *Web Site:* www.nap.edu, pg 156

Lewis, Jennifer, Gryphon House Inc, 6848 Leon's Way, Lewisville, NC 27023 *Toll Free Tel:* 800-638-0928 *Toll Free Fax:* 877-638-7576 *E-mail:* info@ghbooks.com *Web Site:* www.gryphonhouse.com, pg 97

Lewis, Kitty, Brick Books, Box 20081, 431 Boler Rd, London, ON N6K 4G6, Canada *Tel:* 519-657-8579 *E-mail:* brick.books@sympatico.ca *Web Site:* www.brickbooks.ca, pg 447

Lewis, Kristen, Upper Access Inc, 87 Upper Access Rd, Hinesburg, VT 05461 *Tel:* 802-482-2988 *Toll Free Tel:* 800-310-8320 (orders) *Fax:* 802-417-3002 *E-mail:* info@upperaccess.com *Web Site:* www.upperaccess.com, pg 248

Lewis, Leigh Zarelli, Houghton Mifflin Harcourt, 125 High St, Boston, MA 02110 *Tel:* 617-351-5000 *Toll Free Tel:* 855-969-4642; 800-225-5425 (K-12 educ materials); 800-323-9540 (assessment materials); 877-219-1537 (SkillsTutor); 888-242-6747 (Innovation in Educ Group); 800-225-3362 (Trade & Ref Div) *Toll Free Fax:* 800-269-5232 *E-mail:* myhmhco@hmhco.com *Web Site:* www.hmhco.com, pg 110

Lewis, Marc, Presbyterian Publishing Corp (PPC), 100 Witherspoon St, Louisville, KY 40202 *Tel:* 502-569-5000 *Toll Free Tel:* 800-523-1631 (US only) *Fax:* 502-569-5113 *E-mail:* ppcmail@presbypub.com *Web Site:* www.ppcbooks.com, pg 187

Lewis, Marc, Westminster John Knox Press (WJK), 100 Witherspoon St, Louisville, KY 40202-1396 *Toll Free Tel:* 800-523-1631 (US only) *Fax:* 502-569-5113 *Toll Free Fax:* 800-541-5113 (US & CN) *E-mail:* wjk@wjkbooks.com; customer_service@wjkbooks.com *Web Site:* www.wjkbooks.com, pg 254

Lewis, Nora, College of Liberal & Professional Studies, University of Pennsylvania, 3440 Market St, Suite 100, Philadelphia, PA 19104-3335 *Tel:* 215-898-7326 *Fax:* 215-573-2053 *E-mail:* lps@sas.upenn.edu *Web Site:* www.sas.upenn.edu/lps, pg 619

Lewis, Sherry, The Overmountain Press, PO Box 1261, Johnson City, TN 37605-1261 *Tel:* 423-926-2691 *Toll Free Tel:* 800-992-2691 (orders) *Fax:* 423-929-2464 *E-mail:* orders@overmtn.com; submissions@overmtn.com *Web Site:* www.overmtn.com, pg 171

Lewis, Stacey, City Lights Publishers, 261 Columbus Ave, San Francisco, CA 94133 *Tel:* 415-362-8193 *Fax:* 415-362-4921 *E-mail:* staff@citylights.com *Web Site:* www.citylights.com, pg 56

Lewiton, Ariel, Sarabande Books Inc, 2234 Dundee Rd, Suite 200, Louisville, KY 40205 *Tel:* 502-458-4028 *Fax:* 502-458-4065 *E-mail:* info@sarabandebooks.org *Web Site:* www.sarabandebooks.org, pg 206

Li, Cherlynne, Touchstone, 1230 Avenue of the Americas, New York, NY 10020, pg 233

Li, Johanna, Simon & Schuster, 1230 Avenue of the Americas, New York, NY 10020 *Tel:* 212-698-7000 *Toll Free Tel:* 800-223-2348 (cust serv); 800-223-2336 (orders) *Toll Free Fax:* 800-943-9831 (orders) *Web Site:* www.simonandschuster.com, pg 212

Li, Karen, Owlkids Books Inc, 10 Lower Spadina Ave, Suite 400, Toronto, ON M5V 2Z2, Canada *Tel:* 416-340-2700 *Fax:* 416-340-9769 *E-mail:* owlkids@owlkids.com *Web Site:* www.owlkidsbooks.com, pg 465

Li, Philip, The Century Foundation Press, One Whitehall St, 15th fl, New York, NY 10004 *Tel:* 212-452-7700 *Fax:* 212-535-7534 *E-mail:* info@tcf.org *Web Site:* www.tcf.org, pg 52

Liang, Elysia, Lark Crafts, 1166 Avenue of the Americas, 17th fl, New York, NY 10036 *Tel:* 212-532-7160 *E-mail:* larkeditorial@sterlingpublishing.com; customerservice@sterlingpublishing.com *Web Site:* larkcrafts.com; www.facebook.com/LarkCrafts; www.sterlingpublishing.com, pg 129

Liao, Tiffany, Henry Holt and Company, LLC, 175 Fifth Ave, New York, NY 10010 *Tel:* 646-307-5151 *Toll Free Tel:* 888-330-8477 (orders) *Fax:* 646-307-5285 *E-mail:* firstname.lastname@hholt.com *Web Site:* www.henryholt.com, pg 109

Libby, Lewis, Hudson Institute, 1015 15 St NW, 6th fl, Washington, DC 20005 *Tel:* 202-974-2400 *Fax:* 202-974-2410 *E-mail:* info@hudson.org *Web Site:* www.hudson.org, pg 112

Lieberman, Beth, Central Conference of American Rabbis/CCAR Press, 355 Lexington Ave, 18th fl, New York, NY 10017 *Tel:* 212-972-3636 *E-mail:* info@ccarnet.org *Web Site:* www.ccarpress.org, pg 51

Lieberman, Beth, The Editors Circle, 462 Grove St, Montclair, NJ 07043 *Tel:* 862-596-9709 *E-mail:* query@theeditorscircle.com *Web Site:* www.theeditorscircle.com, pg 493

Lieberman, Robert H, Robert Lieberman Agency, 475 Nelson Rd, Ithaca, NY 14850 *Tel:* 607-273-8801 *Web Site:* www.kewgardensmovie.com/CUPeople/users/rhl10, pg 526

Lieberman, Sarah, Simon & Schuster Audio, 1230 Avenue of the Americas, New York, NY 10020 *Web Site:* audio.simonandschuster.com, pg 213

Lieberman, Stefanie, Janklow & Nesbit Associates, 285 Madison Ave, 21st fl, New York, NY 10017 *Tel:* 212-421-1700 *Fax:* 212-355-1403 *E-mail:* info@janklow.com *Web Site:* www.janklowandnesbit.com, pg 522

Liebert, Mary Ann, Mary Ann Liebert Inc, 140 Huguenot St, 3rd fl, New Rochelle, NY 10801-5215 *Tel:* 914-740-2100 *Toll Free Tel:* 800-654-3237 *Fax:* 914-740-2101 *E-mail:* info@liebertpub.com *Web Site:* www.liebertonline.com, pg 133

Liebling, Sara, Disney-Hyperion Books, 1101 Flower St, Glendale, CA 91201 *Web Site:* books.disney.com, pg 70

Liebling, Sara, Disney Publishing Worldwide, 1101 Flower St, Glendale, CA 91201 *Web Site:* books.disney.com, pg 71

Liebmann, Nicholas, Saint Herman Press, 10 Beegum Gorge Rd, Platina, CA 96076 *Tel:* 530-352-4430 *Fax:* 530-352-4432 *E-mail:* stherman@stherman.com *Web Site:* www.stherman.com, pg 204

Light, Tan, The Literary Press Group of Canada, 425 Adelaide St W, Suite 700, Toronto, ON M5V 3C1, Canada *Tel:* 416-483-1321 *Fax:* 416-483-2510 *Web Site:* www.lpg.ca, pg 568

Ligon, Linda, Interweave Press LLC, 201 E Fourth St, Loveland, CO 80537 *Toll Free Tel:* 800-272-2193; 800-289-0963 *Fax:* 970-613-4656 *Toll Free Fax:* 888-590-4082 *Web Site:* www.interweave.com, pg 120

Ligon, Sam, Port Townsend Writers' Conference, 223 Battery Way, Port Townsend, WA 98368 *Tel:* 360-385-3102 *Toll Free Tel:* 800-733-3608 (ticket off) *Fax:* 360-385-2470 *E-mail:* info@centrum.org *Web Site:* centrum.org, pg 613

Likoff, Laurie, Bloom's Literary Criticism, 132 W 31 St, 17th fl, New York, NY 10001 *Toll Free Tel:* 800-322-8755 *Toll Free Fax:* 800-678-3633 *E-mail:* custserv@factsonfile.com *Web Site:* www.infobasepublishing.com, pg 37

Likoff, Laurie, Chelsea House Publishers, 132 W 31 St, 17th fl, New York, NY 10001 *Tel:* 212-967-8800 *Toll Free Tel:* 800-322-8755 *Fax:* 917-339-0325 *Toll Free Fax:* 800-678-3633 *E-mail:* custserv@factsonfile.com *Web Site:* www.infobasepublishing.com; www.infobaselearning.com, pg 53

Likoff, Laurie, Facts On File, 132 W 31 St, 17th fl, New York, NY 10001 *Tel:* 212-967-8800 *Toll Free Tel:* 800-322-8755 *Toll Free Fax:* 800-678-3633 *E-mail:* custserv@factsonfile.com *Web Site:* infobasepublishing.com, pg 81

Likoff, Laurie, Ferguson Publishing, 132 W 31 St, 17th fl, New York, NY 10001 *Tel:* 212-967-8800 *Toll Free Tel:* 800-322-8755 *Fax:* 917-339-0323 *Toll Free Fax:* 800-678-3633 *E-mail:* custserv@factsonfile.com *Web Site:* infobasepublishing.com, pg 84

Limb, John, OCP, 5536 NE Hassalo St, Portland, OR 97213 *Tel:* 503-281-1191 *Toll Free Tel:* 800-548-8749 *Fax:* 503-282-3486 *Toll Free Fax:* 800-843-8181 *E-mail:* liturgy@ocp.org *Web Site:* www.ocp.org, pg 166

Lin, Jean, Bright Connections Media, A World Book Encyclopedia Company, 180 N LaSalle St, Suite 900, Chicago, IL 60601 *Tel:* 312-729-5800 *Web Site:* www.brightconnectionsmedia.com, pg 43

Lindeburg, Michael, Professional Publications Inc (PPI), 1250 Fifth Ave, Belmont, CA 94002 *Tel:* 650-593-9119 *Fax:* 650-592-4519 *E-mail:* acquisitions@ppi2pass.com *Web Site:* ppi2pass.com; feprep.com, pg 189

Lindeman, Steve, Creative Writing Day & Workshops, PO Box 801, Abingdon, VA 24212-0801 *Tel:* 276-623-5266 *Fax:* 276-676-3076 *E-mail:* info@vahighlandsfestival.org *Web Site:* vahighlandsfestival.org, pg 610

Lindemer, Christine R, Boston Road Communications, 227 Boston Rd, Groton, MA 01450-1959 *Tel:* 978-448-8133 *Web Site:* www.bostonrdcom.com, pg 490

Linden, Brianna, Penguin Books, 375 Hudson St, New York, NY 10014 *Tel:* 212-366-2000 *E-mail:* penguinpublicity@us.penguingroup.com *Web Site:* www.penguinclassics.com; www.penguin.com, pg 177

Linden, Brianna, Viking, 375 Hudson St, New York, NY 10014 *Tel:* 212-366-2000 *Fax:* 212-243-6002 *Web Site:* www.penguin.com/publishers/vikingbooks, pg 250

Linden, Judy, The Stonesong Press LLC, 270 W 39 St, No 201, New York, NY 10018 *Tel:* 212-929-4600 *E-mail:* editors@stonesong.com *Web Site:* www.stonesong.com, pg 538

Lindensmith, Chris, Bitingduck Press LLC, 1262 Sunnyoaks Circle, Altadena, CA 91001 *Tel:* 626-679-2494; 626-507-8033 *E-mail:* notifications@bitingduckpress.com *Web Site:* bitingduckpress.com, pg 36

Lindensmith, Chris, Boson Books, 1262 Sunnyoaks Circle, Altadena, CA 91001 *Tel:* 626-507-8033; 626-395-2405 *Web Site:* www.bosonbooks.com; bitingduckpress.com, pg 40

Lindensmith, Gretchen, Bitingduck Press LLC, 1262 Sunnyoaks Circle, Altadena, CA 91001 *Tel:* 626-679-2494; 626-507-8033 *E-mail:* notifications@bitingduckpress.com *Web Site:* bitingduckpress.com, pg 36

Linder, Bertram L, Educational Design Services LLC, 5750 Bou Ave, Suite 1508, North Bethesda, MD 20852 *Tel:* 301-881-8611 *Web Site:* www.educationaldesignservices.com, pg 515

Lindgren, Pat, Lindgren & Smith, 888C Eighth Ave, No 329, New York, NY 10019 *Tel:* 212-397-7330 *E-mail:* info@lindgrensmith.com *Web Site:* lindgrensmith.com, pg 543

Lindquist, Evert A, Institute of Public Administration of Canada, 1075 Bay St, Suite 401, Toronto, ON M5S 2B1, Canada *Tel:* 416-924-8787 *Fax:* 416-924-4992 *E-mail:* ntl@ipac.ca *Web Site:* www.ipac.ca, pg 461

Lindquist, Gina, American Society of Civil Engineers (ASCE), 1801 Alexander Bell Dr, Reston, VA 20191-4400 *Tel:* 703-295-6300 *Toll Free Tel:* 800-548-2723 *Fax:* 703-295-6278 *E-mail:* ascelibrary@asce.org *Web Site:* www.asce.org, pg 15

Lindsay, Diana, Sunbelt Publications Inc, 1250 Fayette St, El Cajon, CA 92020-1511 *Tel:* 619-258-4911 *Toll Free Tel:* 800-626-6579 (cust serv) *Fax:* 619-258-4916 *E-mail:* service@sunbeltpub.com; info@sunbeltpub.com *Web Site:* www.sunbeltbooks.com, pg 225

Lindsay, Elizabeth, Alfred A Knopf/Everyman's Library, c/o Penguin Random House Inc, 1745 Broadway, New York, NY 10019 *Tel:* 212-751-2600 *Toll Free Tel:* 800-638-6460 *Fax:* 212-572-2593 *Web Site:* www.knopfdoubleday.com, pg 127

Lindsay, Lowell, Sunbelt Publications Inc, 1250 Fayette St, El Cajon, CA 92020-1511 *Tel:* 619-258-4911 *Toll Free Tel:* 800-626-6579 (cust serv) *Fax:* 619-258-4916 *E-mail:* service@sunbeltpub.com; info@sunbeltpub.com *Web Site:* www.sunbeltbooks.com, pg 225

Lindsay, Nick, The MIT Press, One Rogers St, Cambridge, MA 02142 *Tel:* 617-253-5255 *Toll Free Tel:* 800-207-8354 (orders) *Fax:* 617-258-6779; 617-577-1545 (orders) *Web Site:* mitpress.mit.edu, pg 151

Lindsey, Katie, Chronicle Books LLC, 680 Second St, San Francisco, CA 94107 *Tel:* 415-537-4200 *Toll Free Tel:* 800-759-0190 (cust serv) *Fax:* 415-537-4460 *Toll Free Fax:* 800-858-7787 (orders); 800-286-9471 (cust serv) *E-mail:* frontdesk@chroniclebooks.com *Web Site:* www.chroniclebooks.com, pg 55

Ling, Alvina, Little, Brown Books for Young Readers, 1290 Avenue of the Americas, New York, NY 10019 *Tel:* 212-364-1100 *Toll Free Tel:* 800-759-0190 (cust serv) *Web Site:* www.HachetteBookGroup.com, pg 136

Ling, Yuyi, Tumblehome Learning Inc, 201 Newbury St, Suite 201, Boston, MA 02116 *E-mail:* info@tumblehomelearning.com *Web Site:* www.tumblehomelearning.com, pg 236

Linick, Andrew S PhD, Copywriter's Council of America™ (CCA), CCA Bldg, 7 Putter Lane, Middle Island, NY 11953-1920 *Tel:* 631-924-3888; 631-775-6075 *Fax:* 631-924-8555 *E-mail:* cca4dmcopy@gmail.com *Web Site:* www.andrewlinickdirectmarketing.com/Copywriters-Council.html; www.newworldpressbooks.com, pg 61, 491, 563

Linick, Andrew S PhD, Andrew S Linick PhD, The Copyologist®, Linick Bldg, 7 Putter Lane, Middle Island, NY 11953 *Tel:* 631-924-3888; 631-775-6075 *Fax:* 631-924-8555 *E-mail:* linickgroup@gmail.com; topmarketingadvisor@gmail.com *Web Site:* www.andrewlinickdirectmarketing.com/The-Copyologist.html; www.newworldpressbooks.com, pg 497

Link, Kelly, Small Beer Press, 150 Pleasant St, No 306, Easthampton, MA 01027 *Tel:* 413-203-1636 *Fax:* 413-203-1636 *E-mail:* info@smallbeerpress.com *Web Site:* smallbeerpress.com, pg 215

Linker, Damon, University of Pennsylvania Press, 3905 Spruce St, Philadelphia, PA 19104 *Tel:* 215-898-6261 *Fax:* 215-898-0404 *E-mail:* custserv@pobox.upenn.edu *Web Site:* www.pennpress.org, pg 244

Linn, Debra, Algonquin Books, 400 Silver Cedar Ct, Suite 300, Chapel Hill, NC 27514-1585 *Tel:* 919-967-0108 *Fax:* 919-933-0272 *E-mail:* inquiry@algonquin.com *Web Site:* www.workman.com/algonquin, pg 7

Linsky, Melissa L, Haights Cross Communications®, 136 Madison Ave, 8th fl, New York, NY 10016 *Tel:* 212-209-0500 *E-mail:* info@haightscross.com *Web Site:* www.haightscross.com, pg 99

Lintao, Eileen, Public Relations Society of America, 33 Maiden Lane, 11th fl, New York, NY 10038-5150 *Tel:* 212-460-1400 *Fax:* 212-995-0757 *Web Site:* www.prsa.org, pg 576

Lionetti, Kim, BookEnds Literary Agency, 136 Long Hill Rd, Gillette, NJ 07933 *Web Site:* www.bookendsliterary.com, pg 508

Liota, Dan, Davies Publishing Inc, 32 S Raymond Ave, Suites 4 & 5, Pasadena, CA 91105-1961 *Tel:* 626-792-3046 *Toll Free Tel:* 877-792-0005 *Fax:* 626-792-5308 *E-mail:* info@daviespublishing.com *Web Site:* daviespublishing.com, pg 68

Lipinski, Michelle, Stanford University Press, 425 Broadway St, Redwood City, CA 94063-3126 *Tel:* 650-723-9434 *Fax:* 650-725-3457 *E-mail:* info@www.sup.org; publicity@www.sup.org *Web Site:* www.sup.org, pg 220

Lipowski, Vicky, Begell House Inc Publishers, 50 North St, Danbury, CT 06810 *Tel:* 203-456-6161 *Fax:* 203-456-6167 *E-mail:* orders@begellhouse.com *Web Site:* www.begellhouse.com, pg 32

Lippel, Roz, Scribner, 1230 Avenue of the Americas, New York, NY 10020, pg 209

Lippert, Jennifer, Princeton Architectural Press, 37 E Seventh St, New York, NY 10003 *Tel:* 212-995-9620 *Toll Free Tel:* 800-722-6657 (dist); 800-759-0190 (sales) *Fax:* 212-995-9454 *E-mail:* sales@papress.com *Web Site:* www.papress.com, pg 188

Lippert, Kevin C, Princeton Architectural Press, 37 E Seventh St, New York, NY 10003 *Tel:* 212-995-9620 *Toll Free Tel:* 800-722-6657 (dist); 800-759-0190 (sales) *Fax:* 212-995-9454 *E-mail:* sales@papress.com *Web Site:* www.papress.com, pg 188

Lippert, Megan, Hilton Publishing, 1630 45 St, Suite 103, Munster, IN 46321 *Tel:* 219-922-4868 *Fax:* 219-924-6811 *E-mail:* info@hiltonpub.com; orders@hiltonpub.com *Web Site:* www.hiltonpub.com, pg 107

Lippman, Barry, LearningExpress LLC, 80 Broad St, 4th fl, New York, NY 10004 *Toll Free Tel:* 800-295-9556 (ext 2) *E-mail:* marketing@learningexpressllc.com (cust serv) *Web Site:* www.learningexpressllc.com, pg 131

Lipschultz, Margo, Harlequin Enterprises Ltd, 225 Duncan Mill Rd, Don Mills, ON M3B 3K9, Canada *Tel:* 416-445-5860 *Toll Free Tel:* 888-432-4879; 800-370-5838 (ebook inquiries) *E-mail:* customerservice@harlequin.com *Web Site:* www.harlequin.com, pg 459

Lipscombe, Trevor C, The Catholic University of America Press, 240 Leahy Hall, 620 Michigan Ave NE, Washington, DC 20064 *Tel:* 202-319-5052 *Toll Free Tel:* 800-537-5487 (orders only) *Fax:* 202-319-4985 *E-mail:* cua-press@cua.edu *Web Site:* cuapress.cua.edu, pg 49

Lipskar, Simon, Writers House, 21 W 26 St, New York, NY 10010 *Tel:* 212-685-2400 *Fax:* 212-685-1781 *Web Site:* www.writershouse.com, pg 542

Liss, Laurie, Sterling Lord Literistic Inc, 115 Broadway, Suite 1602, New York, NY 10006 *Tel:* 212-780-6050 *Fax:* 212-780-6095 *E-mail:* info@sll.com *Web Site:* www.sll.com, pg 537

Liss-Levinson, William PhD, Castle Connolly Medical Ltd, 42 W 24 St, 2nd fl, New York, NY 10010 *Tel:* 212-367-8400 *Fax:* 212-367-0964 *Web Site:* www.castleconnolly.com, pg 49

Lite, Lori, Stress Free Kids®, 2561 Chimney Springs Dr, Marietta, GA 30062 *Tel:* 678-642-9555 *Toll Free Fax:* 866-302-2759 *E-mail:* media@stressfreekids.com *Web Site:* www.stressfreekids.com, pg 224

Lite, Rick, Stress Free Kids®, 2561 Chimney Springs Dr, Marietta, GA 30062 *Tel:* 678-642-9555 *Toll Free Fax:* 866-302-2759 *E-mail:* media@stressfreekids.com *Web Site:* www.stressfreekids.com, pg 224

Lithgow, Angie, Turner Publishing Co, 4507 Charlotte Ave, Suite 100, Nashville, TN 37209 *Tel:* 615-255-BOOK (255-2665) *Fax:* 615-255-

5081 *E-mail:* marketing@turnerpublishing.com; submissions@turnerpublishing.com *Web Site:* www.turnerpublishing.com; www.facebook.com/turner.publishing, pg 236

Littell, Amelie, St Martin's Press, LLC, 175 Fifth Ave, New York, NY 10010 *Tel:* 646-307-5151 *Web Site:* us.macmillan.com/smp, pg 204

Little, Joseph R, American Literacy Council, 1441 Mariposa Ave, Boulder, CO 80302 *Tel:* 303-440-7385 *Web Site:* www.americanliteracy.com, pg 555

Little, Nadine, University of California Press, 155 Grand Ave, Suite 400, Oakland, CA 94612-3758 *Tel:* 510-883-8232 *Fax:* 510-836-8910 *E-mail:* customerservice@ucpressjournals.com *Web Site:* www.ucpress.edu, pg 240

Little, Nadine, University of Hawaii Press, 2840 Kolowalu St, Honolulu, HI 96822 *Tel:* 808-956-8255 *Toll Free Tel:* 888-UHPRESS (847-7377) *Fax:* 808-988-6052 *Toll Free Fax:* 800-650-7811 *E-mail:* uhpbooks@hawaii.edu *Web Site:* www.uhpress.hawaii.edu, pg 241

Little, Stephen, University of Notre Dame Press, 310 Flanner Hall, Notre Dame, IN 46556 *Tel:* 574-631-6346 *Fax:* 574-631-8148 *E-mail:* undpress@nd.edu *Web Site:* www.undpress.nd.edu, pg 244

Littlefield, Alex, Houghton Mifflin Harcourt Trade & Reference Division, 125 High St, Boston, MA 02110 *Tel:* 617-351-5000 *Toll Free Tel:* 800-225-3362 *Web Site:* www.hmhco.com, pg 111

Littlefield, Barb, Thorndike Press, 10 Water St, Suite 310, Waterville, ME 04901 *Toll Free Tel:* 800-223-1244 (ext 4, cust serv/orders) *Toll Free Fax:* 800-558-4676 (orders) *E-mail:* gale.printorders@cengage.com; international@cengage.com (cust orders outside US & CN) *Web Site:* www.gale.com/thorndike, pg 232

Littler, Courtney, St Martin's Press, LLC, 175 Fifth Ave, New York, NY 10010 *Tel:* 646-307-5151 *Web Site:* us.macmillan.com/smp, pg 204

Litwack, Lisa, Gallery Books, 1230 Avenue of the Americas, New York, NY 10020 *Toll Free Tel:* 800-456-6798 *Fax:* 212-698-7284 *E-mail:* consumer.customerservice@simonandschuster.com *Web Site:* www.simonsays.com, pg 90

Liu, Ingsu, W W Norton & Company Inc, 500 Fifth Ave, New York, NY 10110-0017 *Tel:* 212-354-5500 *Toll Free Tel:* 800-233-4830 (orders & cust serv) *Fax:* 212-869-0856 *Toll Free Fax:* 800-458-6515 *E-mail:* orders@wwnorton.com *Web Site:* books.wwnorton.com, pg 164

Liu, Newton, Bridge to Asia, 1505 Juanita Way, Berkeley, CA 94702-1103 *Tel:* 510-665-3998 *E-mail:* asianet@bridge.org *Web Site:* www.bridge.org, pg 583

Liu, Veronica, Seven Stories Press, 140 Watts St, New York, NY 10013 *Tel:* 212-226-8760 *Toll Free Tel:* 800-733-3000 (orders) *Fax:* 212-226-1411 *E-mail:* info@sevenstories.com *Web Site:* www.sevenstories.com, pg 211

Livesey, Magdalen B, Cortina Institute of Languages, 9 Hollyhock Rd, Wilton, CT 06897 *Tel:* 203-762-2510 *Toll Free Tel:* 800-245-2145 *Web Site:* www.cortina-languages.com, pg 61

Livesey, Magdalen B, Cortina Learning International Inc, 9 Hollyhock Rd, Wilton, CT 06897 *Tel:* 203-762-2510 *Toll Free Tel:* 800-245-2145 *Fax:* 203-762-2514 *Web Site:* www.cortinalearning.com, pg 61

Livingston, Susan, Penguin Random House Inc, 1745 Broadway, New York, NY 10019 *Tel:* 212-782-9000 *Toll Free Tel:* 800-726-0600 *Web Site:* www.penguinrandomhouse.com, pg 178

Lizzi, Marian, TarcherPerigee, 375 Hudson St, New York, NY 10014 *Tel:* 212-366-2000 *Fax:* 212-366-2643 *E-mail:* customerservice@penguinrandomhouse.com (cust serv); TarcherPerigeePublicity@penguinrandomhouse.com (media queries) *Web Site:* www.tarcherbooks.com; www.facebook.com/TarcherPerigee/; www.penguin.com/publishers/tarcherperigee, pg 227

Llosa, Genoveva, HarperCollins General Books Group, 195 Broadway, New York, NY 10007 *Tel:* 212-207-7000 *Web Site:* www.harpercollins.com, pg 101

Lloyd, Casey, Random House Children's Books, 1745 Broadway, 10th fl, New York, NY 10019 *Tel:* 212-782-9000 *Web Site:* www.randomhousekids.com, pg 194

Lloyd, Dennis, University of Wisconsin Press, 1930 Monroe St, 3rd fl, Madison, WI 53711-2059 *Tel:* 608-263-0668 *Toll Free Tel:* 800-621-2736 (orders) *Fax:* 608-263-1173 *Toll Free Fax:* 800-621-2736 (orders) *E-mail:* uwiscpress@uwpress.wisc.edu (main off); publicity@uwpress.wisc.edu *Web Site:* uwpress.wisc.edu, pg 246

Lloyd, Kate, Scribner, 1230 Avenue of the Americas, New York, NY 10020, pg 209

Lloyd, Timothy, Opie Prize, Indiana University, Classroom-Off Bldg, 800 E Third St, Bloomington, IN 47405 *Tel:* 812-856-2379 *Fax:* 812-856-2483 *Web Site:* www.afsnet.org, pg 675

Lloyd-Sidle, Elena, Fons Vitae, 49 Mockingbird Valley Dr, Louisville, KY 40207-1366 *Tel:* 502-897-3641 *Fax:* 502-893-7373 *E-mail:* fonsvitaeky@aol.com *Web Site:* www.fonsvitae.com, pg 86

Lo Brutto, Patrick, Philip K Dick Award, PO Box 3447, Hoboken, NJ 07030 *Tel:* 201-876-2551 *Web Site:* www.philipkdickaward.org, pg 641

Lo Frumento, John, American Society of Composers, Authors & Publishers (ASCAP), 1900 Broadway, New York City, NY 10023 *Tel:* 212-621-6000 *Toll Free Tel:* 800-952-7227 *Fax:* 212-612-8453 *E-mail:* info@ascap.com *Web Site:* www.ascap.com, pg 556

Lobdell, Jim, Balance Sports Publishing LLC, 195 Lucero Way, Portola Valley, CA 94028 *Tel:* 650-561-9586 *Fax:* 650-391-9850 *E-mail:* info@balancesportspublishing.com *Web Site:* www.balancesportspublishing.com, pg 28

Lobynko, Anastasia, AZ Books LLC, 320 Fifth Ave, New York, NY 10001 *Toll Free Tel:* 888-945-7723 *Toll Free Fax:* 888-945-7724 *Web Site:* www.azbooksusa.com, pg 27

Lochner, Wendy, Columbia University Press, 61 W 62 St, New York, NY 10023 *Tel:* 212-459-0600 *Toll Free Tel:* 800-944-8648 *Fax:* 212-459-3678 *E-mail:* cup_book@columbia.edu (orders & cust serv) *Web Site:* cup.columbia.edu, pg 59

Lockard, Eric, Salina Bookshelf Inc, 3120 N Caden Ct, Suite 4, Flagstaff, AZ 86004 *Toll Free Tel:* 877-527-0070 *Fax:* 928-526-0386 *Web Site:* www.salinabookshelf.com, pg 205

Locke, Charlene, Davies Publishing Inc, 32 S Raymond Ave, Suites 4 & 5, Pasadena, CA 91105-1961 *Tel:* 626-792-3046 *Toll Free Tel:* 877-792-0005 *Fax:* 626-792-5308 *E-mail:* info@daviespublishing.com *Web Site:* daviespublishing.com, pg 68

Locke, Terry, Loyola Press, 3441 N Ashland Ave, Chicago, IL 60657 *Tel:* 773-281-1818 *Toll Free Tel:* 800-621-1008 *Fax:* 773-281-0555 (cust serv); 773-281-4129 (edit) *E-mail:* customerservice@loyolapress.com *Web Site:* www.loyolapress.com, pg 138

Locke, Tracy, HarperCollins General Books Group, 195 Broadway, New York, NY 10007 *Tel:* 212-207-7000 *Web Site:* www.harpercollins.com, pg 101

Locke, Tracy, Henry Holt and Company, LLC, 175 Fifth Ave, New York, NY 10010 *Tel:* 646-307-5151 *Toll Free Tel:* 888-330-8477 (orders) *Fax:* 646-307-5285 *E-mail:* firstname.lastname@hholt.com *Web Site:* www.henryholt.com, pg 109

Lockhart, Matthew, David C Cook, 4050 Lee Vance View, Colorado Springs, CO 80918 *Tel:* 719-536-0100 *Toll Free Tel:* 800-708-5550; 800-323-7543 (orders & cust serv) *Toll Free Fax:* 800-430-0726 (cust serv) *Web Site:* www.davidccook.com, pg 60

Lockhart, Robert, University of Pennsylvania Press, 3905 Spruce St, Philadelphia, PA 19104 *Tel:* 215-898-6261 *Fax:* 215-898-0404 *E-mail:* custserv@pobox.upenn.edu *Web Site:* www.pennpress.org, pg 244

Lockley, Beth, Penguin Random House Canada, 320 Front St W, Suite 1400, Toronto, ON M5V 3B6, Canada *Tel:* 416-364-4449 *Toll Free Tel:* 888-523-9292 (cust serv) *Fax:* 416-598-7764 *Web Site:* www.penguinrandomhouse.ca, pg 467

Locks, Sueyun, Locks Art Publications/Locks Gallery, 600 Washington Sq S, Philadelphia, PA 19106 *Tel:* 215-629-1000 *E-mail:* info@locksgallery.com *Web Site:* www.locksgallery.com, pg 137

Lockwood, Karen, National Institute for Trial Advocacy (NITA), 1685 38 St, Suite 200, Boulder, CO 80301-2735 *Tel:* 720-890-4860 *Toll Free Tel:* 877-648-2632; 800-225-6482 (orders & returns) *Fax:* 720-890-7069 *E-mail:* info@nita.org *Web Site:* www.nita.org, pg 158

Lockwood, Karen, Syracuse University Press, 621 Skytop Rd, Suite 110, Syracuse, NY 13244-5290 *Tel:* 315-443-5534 *Toll Free Tel:* 800-365-8929 (cust serv) *Fax:* 315-443-5545 *E-mail:* supress@syr.edu *Web Site:* syracuseuniversitypress.syr.edu, pg 226

Lodge, Anne, Stackpole Books, 5067 Ritter Rd, Mechanicsburg, PA 17055 *Tel:* 717-796-0411 *Toll Free Tel:* 800-732-3669 *Fax:* 717-796-0412 *Web Site:* www.stackpolebooks.com, pg 220

Lodwick, Kathleen, EastBridge, 70 New Canaan Ave, Norwalk, CT 06850 *Tel:* 203-855-9125 *Fax:* 203-857-0730 *E-mail:* asia@eastbridgebooks.org; ask@eastbridgebooks.org *Web Site:* www.eastbridgebooks.org, pg 74

Loedel, Daniel, Scribner, 1230 Avenue of the Americas, New York, NY 10020, pg 209

Loehnen, Ben, Simon & Schuster, 1230 Avenue of the Americas, New York, NY 10020 *Tel:* 212-698-7000 *Toll Free Tel:* 800-223-2348 (cust serv); 800-223-2336 (orders) *Toll Free Fax:* 800-943-9831 (orders) *Web Site:* www.simonandschuster.com, pg 212

Loehr, Julie L, Michigan State University Press (MSU Press), Manly Miles Bldg, Suite 25, 1405 S Harrison Rd, East Lansing, MI 48823-5245 *Tel:* 517-355-9543 *Fax:* 517-432-2611 *Web Site:* msupress.org, pg 150

Loehr, Mallory, Random House Children's Books, 1745 Broadway, 10th fl, New York, NY 10019 *Tel:* 212-782-9000 *Web Site:* www.randomhousekids.com, pg 194

Loertscher, David V, Hi Willow Research & Publishing, 123 E Second Ave, Suite 1106, Salt Lake City, UT 84103 *Tel:* 801-755-1122 *E-mail:* lmcsourcesales@gmail.com *Web Site:* www.lmcsource.com; www.davidvl.org, pg 107

Loewen, Darleen, PrairieView Press Ltd, PO Box 460, Gretna, MB R0G 0V0, Canada *Tel:* 204-327-6543 *Toll Free Tel:* 800-477-7377 *Toll Free Fax:* 866-480-0253 *Web Site:* www.prairieviewpress.com, pg 467

Loff, Christina, Chronicle Books LLC, 680 Second St, San Francisco, CA 94107 *Tel:* 415-537-4200 *Toll Free Tel:* 800-759-0190 (cust serv) *Fax:* 415-537-4460 *Toll Free Fax:* 800-858-7787 (orders); 800-286-9471 (cust serv) *E-mail:* frontdesk@chroniclebooks.com *Web Site:* www.chroniclebooks.com, pg 55

Loftus, Maria, Bear & Co Inc, One Park St, Rochester, VT 05767 *Tel:* 802-767-3174 *Toll Free Tel:* 800-932-3277 *Fax:* 802-767-3726 *E-mail:* customerservice@InnerTraditions.com *Web Site:* InnerTraditions.com, pg 31

Loftus, Maria, Inner Traditions International Ltd, One Park St, Rochester, VT 05767 *Tel:* 802-767-3174 *Toll Free Tel:* 800-246-8648 *Fax:* 802-767-3726 *E-mail:* customerservice@InnerTraditions.com *Web Site:* www.InnerTraditions.com, pg 117

Logan, Beverly, Pacific Press Publishing Association, 1350 N Kings Rd, Nampa, ID 83687-3193 *Tel:* 208-465-2500 *Toll Free Tel:* 800-447-7377 *Fax:* 208-465-2531 *Web Site:* www.pacificpress.com, pg 172

Logan, Emily, Houghton Mifflin Harcourt, 125 High St, Boston, MA 02110 *Tel:* 617-351-5000 *Toll Free Tel:* 855-969-4642; 800-225-5425 (K-12 educ materials); 800-323-9540 (assessment materials); 877-219-1537 (SkillsTutor); 888-242-6747 (Innovation in

Educ Group); 800-225-3362 (Trade & Ref Div) *Toll Free Fax:* 800-269-5232 *E-mail:* myhmhco@hmhco.com *Web Site:* www.hmhco.com, pg 110

Loggia, Wendy, Random House Children's Books, 1745 Broadway, 10th fl, New York, NY 10019 *Tel:* 212-782-9000 *Web Site:* www.randomhousekids.com, pg 194

Loh, Cindy, Bloomsbury Publishing Inc, 1385 Broadway, 5th fl, New York, NY 10018 *Tel:* 212-419-5300 *E-mail:* marketingusa@bloomsbury.com; adultpublicityusa@bloomsbury.com; askacademic@bloomsbury.com *Web Site:* www.bloomsbury.com, pg 37

Lohia, Shefali, Little Bee Books, 853 Broadway, Suite 2014, New York, NY 10003 *E-mail:* info@littlebeebooks.com *Web Site:* www.littlebeebooks.com, pg 135

Loiselle, Louise, Flammarion Quebec, 375 Ave Laurier W, Montreal, QC H2V 2K3, Canada *Tel:* 514-277-8807 *Fax:* 514-278-2085 *E-mail:* info@flammarion.qc.ca *Web Site:* www.flammarion.qc.ca, pg 457

Loja, Jen, Penguin Group USA, A Penguin Random House Company, 375 Hudson St, New York, NY 10014 *Tel:* 212-366-2000 *Toll Free Tel:* 800-847-5515 (inside sales); 800-631-8571 (cust serv) *Fax:* 212-366-2666; 607-775-4829 (inside sales) *E-mail:* online@us.penguingroup.com *Web Site:* www.penguin.com, pg 177

Loja, Jen, Penguin Young Readers Group, 345 Hudson St, New York, NY 10014 *Tel:* 212-366-2000; 212-414-3553 *Fax:* 212-414-3340 *Web Site:* www.penguin.com/children, pg 179

Lombardini, Kim, Philip G Spitzer Literary Agency Inc, 50 Talmage Farm Lane, East Hampton, NY 11937 *Tel:* 631-329-3650 *Fax:* 631-329-3651 *Web Site:* www.spitzeragency.com, pg 537

London, Essence, Indiana Review Fiction Prize, Ballantine Hall 529, 1020 E Kirkwood Ave, Bloomington, IN 47405 *Tel:* 812-855-3439 *E-mail:* inreview@indiana.edu *Web Site:* indianareview.org, pg 655

Long, Ben, Dancing Dakini Press, 77 Morning Sun Dr, Sedona, AZ 86336 *Tel:* 928-852-0129 *E-mail:* editor@dancingdakinipress.com *Web Site:* www.dancingdakinipress.com, pg 66

Long, Colton, Insight Editions, 800 "A" St, San Rafael, CA 94901 *Tel:* 415-526-1370 *Toll Free Tel:* 800-809-3792 *Toll Free Fax:* 866-509-0515 *E-mail:* info@insighteditions.com *Web Site:* www.insighteditions.com, pg 117

Long, Donna, HRD Press, 22 Amherst Rd, Amherst, MA 01002-9709 *Tel:* 413-253-3488 *Toll Free Tel:* 800-822-2801 *Fax:* 413-253-3490 *E-mail:* info@hrdpress.com; customerservice@hrdpress.com *Web Site:* www.hrdpress.com, pg 112

Long, Jennifer, Gallery Books, 1230 Avenue of the Americas, New York, NY 10020 *Toll Free Tel:* 800-456-6798 *Fax:* 212-698-7284 *E-mail:* consumer.customerservice@simonandschuster.com *Web Site:* www.simonsays.com, pg 90

Long, Karen R, The Anisfield-Wolf Book Awards, 1422 Euclid Ave, Suite 1300, Cleveland, OH 44115 *Tel:* 216-861-3810 *Fax:* 216-861-1729 *E-mail:* awinfo@clevefdn.org *Web Site:* www.anisfield-wolf.org; www.clevelandfoundation.org, pg 627

Long, Thayer, Graphic Arts Education & Research Foundation (GAERF), 1899 Preston White Dr, Reston, VA 20191 *Tel:* 703-264-7200 *Toll Free Tel:* 844-381-9839 *Fax:* 703-620-3165 *E-mail:* gaerf@npes.org *Web Site:* www.gaerf.org, pg 583

Long, Thayer, NPES The Association for Suppliers of Printing, Publishing & Converting Technologies, 1899 Preston White Dr, Reston, VA 20191 *Tel:* 703-264-7200 *Fax:* 703-620-0994 *E-mail:* npes@npes.org *Web Site:* www.npes.org, pg 574

Longmeyer, Michael, Gallopade International Inc, 611 Hwy 74 S, Suite 2000, Peachtree City, GA 30269 *Tel:* 770-631-4222 *Toll Free Tel:* 800-536-2GET (536-2438) *Fax:* 770-631-4810 *Toll Free Fax:* 800-871-2979 *E-mail:* customerservice@gallopade.com *Web Site:* www.gallopade.com, pg 90

Longo, Edward, Recorded Books Inc, an RBmedia company, 270 Skipjack Rd, Prince Frederick, MD 20678 *Tel:* 410-535-5590 *Toll Free Tel:* 877-732-2898 *Fax:* 410-535-5499 *E-mail:* customerservice@recordedbooks.com *Web Site:* www.recordedbooks.com, pg 196

Lonie, Tonia, University Press of Mississippi, 3825 Ridgewood Rd, Jackson, MS 39211-6492 *Tel:* 601-432-6205 *Toll Free Tel:* 800-737-7788 (orders & cust serv) *Fax:* 601-432-6217 *E-mail:* press@mississippi.edu *Web Site:* www.upress.state.ms.us, pg 247

Loomis, Gloria, Watkins/Loomis Agency Inc, PO Box 20925, New York, NY 10025 *Tel:* 212-532-0080 *Fax:* 646-383-2449 *E-mail:* assistant@watkinsloomis.com *Web Site:* www.watkinsloomis.com, pg 541

Loomis, Michael J, Graphic World Publishing Services, 11687 Adie Rd, St Louis, MO 63043 *Tel:* 314-567-9854 *Fax:* 314-567-7178 *E-mail:* quote@gwinc.com *Web Site:* www.gwinc.com, pg 495

Loose, Emily, Words into Print, 208 Java St, 6th fl, Brooklyn, NY 11222 *E-mail:* query@wordsintoprint.org *Web Site:* wordsintoprint.org, pg 503

Loosvelt, Derek, Vault.com Inc, 132 W 31 St, 16th fl, New York, NY 10001 *Tel:* 212-366-4212 *Toll Free Tel:* 800-535-2074 *Fax:* 212-366-6117 (cust serv) *E-mail:* editors@vault.com; customerservice@vault.com *Web Site:* www.vault.com, pg 250

Lopes, David, Gingko Press Inc, 1321 Fifth St, Berkeley, CA 94710 *Tel:* 510-898-1195 *Fax:* 510-898-1196 *E-mail:* books@gingkopress.com *Web Site:* www.gingkopress.com, pg 92

Lopez, Vanessa, Insight Editions, 800 "A" St, San Rafael, CA 94901 *Tel:* 415-526-1370 *Toll Free Tel:* 800-809-3792 *Toll Free Fax:* 866-509-0515 *E-mail:* info@insighteditions.com *Web Site:* www.insighteditions.com, pg 117

Lord, Allyson, Random House Publishing Group, 1745 Broadway, New York, NY 10019 *Toll Free Tel:* 800-200-3552 *Web Site:* atrandom.com, pg 195

Lord, Jacklyn, Indiana University Press, Herman B Wells Library 350, 1320 E Tenth St, Bloomington, IN 47405-3907 *Tel:* 812-855-8817 *Toll Free Tel:* 800-842-6796 (orders only) *Fax:* 812-855-7931; 812-855-8507 *E-mail:* iupress@indiana.edu; iuporder@indiana.edu (orders) *Web Site:* www.iupress.indiana.edu, pg 116

Lord, Sterling, Sterling Lord Literistic Inc, 115 Broadway, Suite 1602, New York, NY 10006 *Tel:* 212-780-6050 *Fax:* 212-780-6095 *E-mail:* info@sll.com *Web Site:* www.sll.com, pg 537

Lore, Matthew, The Experiment, 220 E 23 St, Suite 301, New York, NY 10010-4674 *Tel:* 212-889-1659 *E-mail:* info@theexperimentpublishing.com *Web Site:* www.theexperimentpublishing.com, pg 81

Lorentzen, Allison, Viking, 375 Hudson St, New York, NY 10014 *Tel:* 212-366-2000 *Fax:* 212-243-6002 *Web Site:* www.penguin.com/publishers/vikingbooks, pg 250

Lorenz, Geoff, Show What You Know® Publishing, A Lorenz Company, c/o The Lorenz Corp, 501 E Third St, Dayton, OH 45402 *Tel:* 614-764-1211; 937-228-6118 *Toll Free Tel:* 877-PASSING (727-7464) *Fax:* 937-233-2042 *E-mail:* info@lorenz.com *Web Site:* www.lorenzeducationalpress.com, pg 212

Lorenz, Ken, Standard Publishing, 4050 Lee Vance View, Colorado Springs, CO 80918 *Tel:* 513-931-4050 *Toll Free Tel:* 800-323-7543 *Fax:* 513-931-0950 *Toll Free Fax:* 800-323-0726 *E-mail:* customerservice@standardpub.com *Web Site:* www.standardpub.com, pg 220

Lorenz, Reiff, Show What You Know® Publishing, A Lorenz Company, c/o The Lorenz Corp, 501 E Third St, Dayton, OH 45402 *Tel:* 614-764-1211; 937-228-6118 *Toll Free Tel:* 877-PASSING (727-7464) *Fax:* 937-233-2042 *E-mail:* info@lorenz.com *Web Site:* www.lorenzeducationalpress.com, pg 212

Lorenz, Tom, Cottonwood Press, University of Kansas, Kansas Union, Rm 400, 1301 Jayhawk Blvd, Lawrence, KS 66045 *Tel:* 785-864-4520 *Web Site:* www.englishcw.ku.edu/cottonwood, pg 62

Lori, Jennifer, The Pacific Spirit Poetry Prize, University of British Columbia, Buch E462, 1866 Main Mall, Vancouver, BC V6T 1Z1, Canada *Tel:* 778-822-2514 *Fax:* 778-822-3616 *E-mail:* prismwritingcontest@gmail.com *Web Site:* www.prismmagazine.ca, pg 676

Lori, Jennifer, PRISM international Literary Non-Fiction Contest, University of British Columbia, Buch E462, 1866 Main Mall, Vancouver, BC V6T 1Z1, Canada *Tel:* 778-822-2514 *Fax:* 778-822-3616 *E-mail:* prismwritingcontest@gmail.com *Web Site:* www.prismmagazine.ca, pg 682

Lori, Jennifer, The Jacob Zilber Prize for Short Fiction, University of British Columbia, Buch E462, 1866 Main Mall, Vancouver, BC V6T 1Z1, Canada *Tel:* 778-822-2514 *Fax:* 778-822-3616 *E-mail:* prismwritingcontest@gmail.com *Web Site:* www.prismmagazine.ca, pg 701

Lorimer, James, James Lorimer & Co Ltd, Publishers, 117 Peter St, Suite 304, Toronto, ON M5V 0M3, Canada *Tel:* 416-362-4762 *Fax:* 416-362-3939 *Web Site:* www.lorimer.ca, pg 462

Lotman, Lynda, A+ English LLC/Book-Editing.com/Book Editing Associates, PO Box 1369, Mansfield, TX 76063 *Tel:* 469-789-3030 *E-mail:* editingnetwork@gmail.com *Web Site:* www.editing-writing.com; www.book-editing.com; www.helpwithstatistics.com; www.apawriting.com; childrensbookeditors.com; www.christianeditorsnetwork.com; dissertationwriting.com; statisticstutors.com, pg 487

Lotowycz, Randall, Workman Publishing Co Inc, 225 Varick St, 9th fl, New York, NY 10014-4381 *Tel:* 212-254-5900 *Toll Free Tel:* 800-722-7202 *Fax:* 212-254-8098 *E-mail:* info@workman.com *Web Site:* www.workman.com, pg 259

Lott, Peter, Lott Representatives Ltd, PO Box 3607, New York, NY 10163 *Tel:* 212-755-5737 *Web Site:* www.lottreps.com, pg 544

Lotto, Elizabeth, Gallery Books, 1230 Avenue of the Americas, New York, NY 10020 *Toll Free Tel:* 800-456-6798 *Fax:* 212-698-7284 *E-mail:* consumer.customerservice@simonandschuster.com *Web Site:* www.simonsays.com, pg 90

LoTurco, William, Aevitas Creative Management, 19 W 21 St, Suite 501, New York, NY 10010 *Tel:* 212-765-6900 *Web Site:* aevitascreative.com, pg 506

Lotz, Karen, Candlewick Press, 99 Dover St, Somerville, MA 02144-2825 *Tel:* 617-661-3330 *Fax:* 617-661-0565 *E-mail:* bigbear@candlewick.com; salesinfo@candlewick.com *Web Site:* www.candlewick.com, pg 46

Loudon, John, Yale University Press, 302 Temple St, New Haven, CT 06511-8909 *Tel:* 203-432-0960; 203-432-0966 (sales); 401-531-2800 (cust serv) *Toll Free Tel:* 800-405-1619 (cust serv) *Fax:* 203-432-0948; 203-432-8485 (sales); 401-531-2801 (cust serv) *Toll Free Fax:* 800-406-9145 (cust serv) *E-mail:* sales.press@yale.edu (sales); customer.care@triliteral.org (cust serv) *Web Site:* www.yalebooks.com; yalepress.yale.edu/yupbooks, pg 261

Loughlin, Thomas G, American Society of Mechanical Engineers (ASME), 2 Park Ave, New York, NY 10016-5990 *Tel:* 212-591-7000 *Toll Free Tel:* 800-843-2763 (cust serv-US, CN & Mexico) *Fax:* 212-591-7674; 973-882-8113 (cust serv); 973-882-1717 (orders & inquiries) *E-mail:* infocentral@asme.org *Web Site:* www.asme.org, pg 15

Loughman, Kelly, Holiday House Inc, 425 Madison Ave, New York, NY 10017 *Tel:* 212-688-0085 *Fax:* 212-421-6134 *E-mail:* info@holidayhouse.com *Web Site:* www.holidayhouse.com, pg 109

Loughrey, Mary, Looseleaf Law Publications Inc, 43-08 162 St, Flushing, NY 11358 *Tel:* 718-359-5559 *Toll Free Tel:* 800-647-5547 *Fax:* 718-539-0941 *E-mail:* info@looseleaf.com *Web Site:* www.looseleaflaw.com, pg 137

Loughrey, Michael L, Looseleaf Law Publications Inc, 43-08 162 St, Flushing, NY 11358 *Tel:* 718-359-5559 *Toll Free Tel:* 800-647-5547 *Fax:* 718-539-0941 *E-mail:* info@looseleaf.com *Web Site:* www.looseleaflaw.com, pg 137

Loule, Karen, Harlequin Enterprises Ltd, 225 Duncan Mill Rd, Don Mills, ON M3B 3K9, Canada *Tel:* 416-445-5860 *Toll Free Tel:* 888-432-4879; 800-370-5838 (ebook inquiries) *E-mail:* customerservice@harlequin.com *Web Site:* www.harlequin.com, pg 459

Louque, Bonnie, Triumph Learning LLC, 136 Madison Ave, 7th fl, New York, NY 10016 *Tel:* 212-652-0200 *Toll Free Tel:* 800-338-6519 (cust serv) *Toll Free Fax:* 866-805-5723 *E-mail:* info@triumphlearning.com; customerservice@triumphlearning.com *Web Site:* www.triumphlearning.com, pg 235

Lourette, Nicole, SSPC: The Society for Protective Coatings, 800 Trumbull Dr, Pittsburgh, PA 15220-4365 *Tel:* 412-281-2331 *Toll Free Tel:* 877-281-7772 (US only) *Fax:* 412-281-9992 *E-mail:* info@sspc.org *Web Site:* www.sspc.org, pg 220

Lourie, Dick, Hanging Loose Press, 231 Wyckoff St, Brooklyn, NY 11217 *Tel:* 347-529-4738 *Fax:* 347-227-8215 *E-mail:* print225@aol.com *Web Site:* www.hangingloosepress.com, pg 100

Lourie, Iven, Gateways Books & Tapes, PO Box 370, Nevada City, CA 95959 *Tel:* 530-271-2239 *Toll Free Tel:* 800-869-0658 *Fax:* 530-272-0184 *E-mail:* info@gatewaysbooksandtapes.com *Web Site:* www.gatewaysbooksandtapes.com; www.retrosf.com (Retro Science Fiction imprint), pg 90

Love, Robert, Square One Publishers Inc, 115 Herricks Rd, Garden City Park, NY 11040 *Tel:* 516-535-2010 *Toll Free Tel:* 877-900-BOOK (900-2665) *Fax:* 516-535-2014 *E-mail:* sq1publish@aol.com *Web Site:* www.squareonepublishers.com, pg 220

Love, Stanley F, Love Publishing Co, 9101 E Kenyon Ave, Suite 2200, Denver, CO 80237 *Tel:* 303-221-7333 *Toll Free Tel:* 877-240-6396 *Fax:* 303-221-7444 *E-mail:* lpc@lovepublishing.com *Web Site:* www.lovepublishing.com, pg 138

Lovelace, Mr Plumer, Notable Wisconsin Authors, 4610 S Biltmore Lane, Suite 100, Madison, WI 53718-2153 *Tel:* 608-245-3640 *Fax:* 608-245-3646 *Web Site:* wla.wisconsinlibraries.org, pg 674

Lovelace, Mr Plumer, WLA Literary Award, 4610 S Biltmore Lane, Suite 100, Madison, WI 53718-2153 *Tel:* 608-245-3640 *Fax:* 608-245-3646 *Web Site:* wla.wisconsinlibraries.org, pg 699

Lovell, Deborah, Taylor & Francis Inc, 530 Walnut St, Suite 850, Philadelphia, PA 19106 *Tel:* 215-625-8900 *Toll Free Tel:* 800-354-1420 *Fax:* 215-207-0050; 215-207-0046 (cust serv) *E-mail:* support@tandfonline.com *Web Site:* www.taylorandfrancis.com, pg 227

Lovell, Justin, Perseus Books, 250 W 57 St, 15th fl, New York, NY 10107 *Tel:* 212-340-8100 *Toll Free Tel:* 800-343-4499 (cust serv) *Fax:* 212-340-8105 *Web Site:* www.perseusbooks.com, pg 181

Lovett, Erin, W W Norton & Company Inc, 500 Fifth Ave, New York, NY 10110-0017 *Tel:* 212-354-5500 *Toll Free Tel:* 800-233-4830 (orders & cust serv) *Fax:* 212-869-0856 *Toll Free Fax:* 800-458-6515 *E-mail:* orders@wwnorton.com *Web Site:* books.wwnorton.com, pg 164

Lovig, Grant, Company's Coming Publishing Ltd, 87 E Pender St, Vancouver, BC V6A 1S9, Canada *Tel:* 780-450-6223 (orders & inquiries) *Toll Free Tel:* 800-661-9017 (CN); 800-518-3541 (US) *Fax:* 780-450-1857 *E-mail:* info@companyscoming.com *Web Site:* www.companyscoming.com, pg 451

Loving, Lindsey, News Media Alliance, 4401 N Fairfax Dr, Suite 300, Arlington, VA 22203 *Tel:* 571-366-1000 *E-mail:* info@newsmediaalliance.org *Web Site:* www.newsmediaalliance.org, pg 573

Low, Craig, Children's Book Press, 95 Madison Ave, Suite 1205, New York, NY 10016 *Tel:* 212-779-4400 *Fax:* 212-683-1894 *E-mail:* general@leeandlow.com; orders@leeandlow.com; sales@leeandlow.com *Web Site:* www.leeandlow.com, pg 54

Low, Craig, Lee & Low Books Inc, 95 Madison Ave, New York, NY 10016 *Tel:* 212-779-4400 *Toll Free Tel:* 888-320-3190 (ext 28, orders only) *Fax:* 212-683-1894 (orders only); 212-532-6035 *E-mail:* general@leeandlow.com *Web Site:* www.leeandlow.com, pg 131

Low, Jason, Lee & Low Books Inc, 95 Madison Ave, New York, NY 10016 *Tel:* 212-779-4400 *Toll Free Tel:* 888-320-3190 (ext 28, orders only) *Fax:* 212-683-1894 (orders only); 212-532-6035 *E-mail:* general@leeandlow.com *Web Site:* www.leeandlow.com, pg 131

Lowary, Nicole, Marianne Strong Literary Agency, 65 E 96 St, New York, NY 10128 *Tel:* 212-249-1000 *Fax:* 212-831-3241 *Web Site:* stronglit.com, pg 538

Lowe, Amy, Janet B McCabe Poetry Prize, 1041 N Taft Hill Rd, Fort Collins, CO 80521 *Tel:* 970-449-2726 *E-mail:* editor@ruminatemagazine.org *Web Site:* www.ruminatemagazine.com, pg 666

Lowe, Amy, William Van Dyke Short Story Prize, 1041 N Taft Hill Rd, Fort Collins, CO 80521 *Tel:* 970-449-2726 *E-mail:* editor@ruminatemagazine.org *Web Site:* www.ruminatemagazine.com, pg 695

Lowe, Amy, VanderMey Nonfiction Prize, 1041 N Taft Hill Rd, Fort Collins, CO 80521 *Tel:* 970-449-2726 *E-mail:* editor@ruminatemagazine.org *Web Site:* www.ruminatemagazine.com, pg 695

Lowenstein, Barbara, Lowenstein Associates Inc, 115 E 23 St, 4th fl, New York, NY 10010 *Tel:* 212-206-1630 *E-mail:* assistant@bookhaven.com (queries, no attachments) *Web Site:* www.lowensteinassociates.com, pg 526

Lowenstein, Carole, Random House Publishing Group, 1745 Broadway, New York, NY 10019 *Toll Free Tel:* 800-200-3552 *Web Site:* atrandom.com, pg 195

Lowes, Tara, Broadview Press, 280 Perry St, Unit 5, Peterborough, ON K9J 2J4, Canada *Tel:* 705-743-8990 *Fax:* 705-743-8353 *E-mail:* customerservice@broadviewpress.com *Web Site:* www.broadviewpress.com, pg 447

Lowman, Sarah, NASW Press, 750 First St NE, Suite 800, Washington, DC 20002 *Tel:* 202-408-8600 *Fax:* 203-336-8312 *E-mail:* press@naswdc.org *Web Site:* www.naswpress.org, pg 156

Lowry, Dr Samuel, Ambassador International, 411 University Ridge, Suite B14, Greenville, SC 29601 *Tel:* 864-751-4844 *E-mail:* info@emeraldhouse.com; publisher@emeraldhouse.com (ms submissions); sales@emeraldhouse.com (orders/order inquiries) *Web Site:* ambassador-international.com; www.facebook.com/AmbassadorIntl; twitter.com/ambassadorintl, pg 9

Lowry, Timothy, Ambassador International, 411 University Ridge, Suite B14, Greenville, SC 29601 *Tel:* 864-751-4844 *E-mail:* info@emeraldhouse.com; publisher@emeraldhouse.com (ms submissions); sales@emeraldhouse.com (orders/order inquiries) *Web Site:* ambassador-international.com; www.facebook.com/AmbassadorIntl; twitter.com/ambassadorintl, pg 9

Loyd, Lois, Reporters Committee for Freedom of the Press, 1156 15 St NW, Suite 1250, Washington, DC 20005-1779 *Tel:* 202-795-9300 *Toll Free Tel:* 800-336-4243 *E-mail:* info@rcfp.org *Web Site:* www.rcfp.org, pg 577

Lozar, Paula, New Mexico Book Association (NMBA), 1219 Luisa St, Suite 1, Santa Fe, NM 87505 *Tel:* 505-660-6357 *E-mail:* admin@nmbook.org *Web Site:* www.nmbook.org, pg 573

Lozo, Sarah, Boyds Mills Press, 815 Church St, Honesdale, PA 18431 *Tel:* 570-253-1164 *Toll Free Tel:* 800-490-5111 *Fax:* 570-253-0179 *E-mail:* contact@boydsmillspress.com *Web Site:* www.boydsmillspress.com, pg 41

Lu, Kitty, Cornell University Press, Sage House, 512 E State St, Ithaca, NY 14850 *Tel:* 607-277-2338 *Fax:* 607-277-2374 *E-mail:* cupressinfo@cornell.edu; cupress-sales@cornell.edu *Web Site:* www.cornellpress.cornell.edu, pg 61

Lubell, Lauren Grand, Chronicle Books LLC, 680 Second St, San Francisco, CA 94107 *Tel:* 415-537-4200 *Toll Free Tel:* 800-759-0190 (cust serv) *Fax:* 415-537-4460 *Toll Free Fax:* 800-858-7787 (orders); 800-286-9471 (cust serv) *E-mail:* frontdesk@chroniclebooks.com *Web Site:* www.chroniclebooks.com, pg 55

Lubrant, Trisha, Jewish Publication Society, 2100 Arch St, Philadelphia, PA 19103 *Tel:* 215-832-0600 *Toll Free Tel:* 800-234-3151 *Fax:* 215-568-2017 *Web Site:* www.jps.org, pg 122

Lucas, Becky, The Association for Women in Communications, 1717 E Republic Rd, Suite A, Springfield, MO 65804 *Tel:* 417-886-8606 *Fax:* 417-886-3685 *E-mail:* info@womcom.org *Web Site:* www.womcom.org, pg 609

Lucas, George, InkWell Management, 521 Fifth Ave, 26th fl, New York, NY 10175 *Tel:* 212-922-3500 *Fax:* 212-922-0535 *E-mail:* info@inkwellmanagement.com *Web Site:* inkwellmanagement.com, pg 522

Lucas, LaBruce M S, Southern Historical Press Inc, 375 W Broad St, Greenville, SC 29601 *Tel:* 864-233-2346 *Toll Free Tel:* 800-233-0152 *E-mail:* southernhistoricalpress@gmail.com *Web Site:* www.southernhistoricalpress.com, pg 218

Lucas, Lisa, National Book Awards, 90 Broad St, Suite 604, New York, NY 10004 *Tel:* 212-685-0261 *Fax:* 212-213-6570 *E-mail:* nationalbook@nationalbook.org *Web Site:* www.nationalbook.org, pg 670

Lucas, Paul, Janklow & Nesbit Associates, 285 Madison Ave, 21st fl, New York, NY 10017 *Tel:* 212-421-1700 *Fax:* 212-355-1403 *E-mail:* info@janklow.com *Web Site:* www.janklowandnesbit.com, pg 522

Lucas, Wade, Penguin Random House Speakers Bureau, A Penguin Random House Company, 1745 Broadway, Mail Drop 13-1, New York, NY 10019 *Tel:* 212-572-2013 *E-mail:* speakers@penguinrandomhouse.com *Web Site:* www.prhspeakers.com, pg 547

Lucchese, Iole, Scholastic Inc, 557 Broadway, New York, NY 10012 *Tel:* 212-343-6100 *Toll Free Tel:* 800-SCHOLASTIC (724-6527) *Web Site:* www.scholastic.com, pg 208

Lucero, Seyan, Western States Arts Federation, 1743 Wazee St, Suite 300, Denver, CO 80202 *Tel:* 303-629-1166 *Toll Free Tel:* 888-562-7232 *Fax:* 303-629-9717 *E-mail:* staff@westaf.org *Web Site:* www.westaf.org, pg 583

Luchars, Alex, Industrial Press Inc, 32 Haviland St, Suite 3, Norwalk, CT 06854 *Tel:* 203-956-5593 ext 0 (cust serv) *Toll Free Tel:* 888-528-7852 ext 0 (cust serv) *Fax:* 203-354-9391 (cust serv) *E-mail:* info@industrialpress.com (cust serv) *Web Site:* new.industrialpress.com, pg 116

Luciano, Jeannie, W W Norton & Company Inc, 500 Fifth Ave, New York, NY 10110-0017 *Tel:* 212-354-5500 *Toll Free Tel:* 800-233-4830 (orders & cust serv) *Fax:* 212-869-0856 *Toll Free Fax:* 800-458-6515 *E-mail:* orders@wwnorton.com *Web Site:* books.wwnorton.com, pg 164

Ludwin, Corey, Referee Books, 2017 Lathrop Ave, Racine, WI 53405 *Tel:* 262-632-8855 *Toll Free Tel:* 800-733-6100 *Fax:* 262-632-5460 *E-mail:* questions@referee.com *Web Site:* www.referee.com, pg 197

Luecker, Kristine, Association for Talent Development (ATD) Press, 1640 King St, Box 1443, Alexandria, VA 22313-1443 *Tel:* 703-683-8100 *Toll Free Tel:* 800-628-2783 *Fax:* 703-299-8723; 703-683-1523 (cust care) *E-mail:* customercare@td.org *Web Site:* www.astd.org; www.td.org, pg 24

Lugo, Ramon, University of Puerto Rico Press, Edificio La Editorial (level 2), Carr No 1, KM 12.0, Jardin Botanico Norte, San Juan, PR 00927 *Tel:* 787-250-0435; 787-250-0550 *Toll Free Tel:* 877-338-7788 *Fax:* 787-753-9116 *E-mail:* info@laeditorialupr.com *Web Site:* www.laeditorialupr.com, pg 245

Lui, Jenny, Workman Publishing Co Inc, 225 Varick St, 9th fl, New York, NY 10014-4381 *Tel:* 212-254-5900 *Toll Free Tel:* 800-722-7202 *Fax:* 212-254-8098 *E-mail:* info@workman.com *Web Site:* www.workman.com, pg 259

Luke, Gary, Sasquatch Books, 1904 S Third Ave, Suite 710, Seattle, WA 98101 *Tel:* 206-467-4300 *Toll Free Tel:* 800-775-0817 *Fax:* 206-467-4301 *E-mail:* custserv@sasquatchbooks.com *Web Site:* www.sasquatchbooks.com, pg 206

Lukk, Howard, Society of Motion Picture & Television Engineers® (SMPTE®), 3 Barker Ave, 5th fl, White Plains, NY 10601 *Tel:* 914-761-1100 *Fax:* 914-761-3115 *Web Site:* www.smpte.org, pg 578

Lum, Robert, PRO-ED Inc, 8700 Shoal Creek Blvd, Austin, TX 78757-6897 *Tel:* 512-451-3246 *Toll Free Tel:* 800-897-3202 *Fax:* 512-451-8542 *Toll Free Fax:* 800-397-7633 *E-mail:* general@proedinc.com; info@proedinc.com *Web Site:* www.proedinc.com, pg 189

Lum, Roxanne, Ignatius Press, 1348 Tenth Ave, San Francisco, CA 94122-2304 *Toll Free Tel:* 800-651-1531 (orders); 888-615-3186 (cust serv) *E-mail:* info@ignatius.com *Web Site:* www.ignatius.com, pg 114

Lumelsky, Irina, United Nations Publications, 300 E 42 St, 9th fl, New York, NY 10017 *Tel:* 703-661-1571 *Fax:* 703-996-1010 *E-mail:* publications@un.org *Web Site:* shop.un.org, pg 238

Lummis, Kristen, North American Snowsports Journalists Association (NASJA), 11728 SE Madison St, Portland, OR 97216-3849 *Tel:* 503-255-3771 *Fax:* 503-255-3771 *Web Site:* www.nasja.org, pg 574

Lumsden, Michal, Storey Publishing LLC, 210 MASS MoCA Way, North Adams, MA 01247 *Tel:* 413-346-2100 *Toll Free Tel:* 800-441-5700 (orders); 800-793-9396 (edit) *Fax:* 413-346-2199; 413-346-2196 (edit) *E-mail:* sales@storey.com *Web Site:* www.storey.com, pg 223

Luna, Andrea, Police Executive Research Forum, 1120 Connecticut Ave NW, Suite 930, Washington, DC 20036 *Tel:* 202-466-7820 *Web Site:* www.policeforum.org, pg 185

Lund, Tom, Llewellyn Publications, 2143 Wooddale Dr, Woodbury, MN 55125 *Tel:* 651-291-1970 *Toll Free Tel:* 800-843-6666 *Fax:* 651-291-1908 *E-mail:* publicity@llewellyn.com; customerservice@llewellyn.com *Web Site:* www.llewellyn.com, pg 137

Lundberg, Brita, Irene Goodman Literary Agency, 27 W 24 St, Suite 700B, New York, NY 10010 *Tel:* 212-604-0330 *E-mail:* queries@irenegoodman.com *Web Site:* www.irenegoodman.com, pg 519

Lunghi, Meghan, Merriam-Webster Inc, 47 Federal St, Springfield, MA 01102 *Tel:* 413-734-3134 *Toll Free Tel:* 800-828-1880 (orders & cust serv) *Fax:* 413-731-5979 (sales) *E-mail:* support@merriam-webster.com *Web Site:* www.merriam-webster.com, pg 149

Lunn, Jenny, American Geophysical Union (AGU), 2000 Florida Ave NW, Washington, DC 20009 *Tel:* 202-462-6900 *Toll Free Tel:* 800-966-2481 (North America) *Fax:* 202-328-0566 *E-mail:* service@agu.org (cust serv); earthspacescience@agu.org *Web Site:* www.agu.org, pg 11

Lunzer, Bernard, The NewsGuild - CWA, 501 Third St NW, 6th fl, Washington, DC 20001-2797 *Tel:* 202-434-7177; 202-434-7162 (The Guild Reporter) *Fax:* 202-434-1472 *E-mail:* guild@cwa-union.org *Web Site:* www.newsguild.org, pg 573

Luongo, Rose, Brill Inc, 2 Liberty Sq, 11th fl, Boston, MA 02109 *Tel:* 617-263-2323 *Toll Free Tel:* 800-962-4406 *Fax:* 617-263-2324 *E-mail:* cs@brillusa.com *Web Site:* www.brill.com, pg 43

Lupinatci, Craig, iUniverse, 1663 Liberty Dr, Bloomington, IN 47403 *Toll Free Tel:* 800-AUTHORS (288-4677) *Fax:* 812-355-4085 *Web Site:* www.iuniverse.com, pg 121

Lurie, David B, Japan-US Friendship Commission Translation Prize, Columbia University, 507 Kent Hall, MC3920, New York, NY 10027 *Tel:* 212-854-5036 *Fax:* 212-854-4019 *Web Site:* www.keenecenter.org, pg 657

Lurie, Stephanie Owens, Disney-Hyperion Books, 1101 Flower St, Glendale, CA 91201 *Web Site:* books.disney.com, pg 70

Lusardi, Alessandra, Rizzoli International Publications Inc, 300 Park Ave S, 4th fl, New York, NY 10010-5399 *Tel:* 212-387-3400 *Toll Free Tel:* 800-522-6657 (orders only) *Fax:* 212-387-3535 *E-mail:* publicity@rizzoliusa.com *Web Site:* www.rizzoliusa.com, pg 199

Lush, Janette, Penguin Group (Canada), 320 Front St W, Suite 1400, Toronto, ON M5V 3B6, Canada *Tel:* 416-364-4449 *Fax:* 416-598-7764 *E-mail:* customerservicescanada@penguinrandomhouse.com; publicity@ca.penguingroup.com *Web Site:* penguinrandomhouse.ca/imprints/penguin-canada, pg 466

Luther, Kay, Ave Maria Press, PO Box 428, Notre Dame, IN 46556 *Tel:* 574-287-2831 *Toll Free Tel:* 800-282-1865 *Fax:* 574-239-2904 *Toll Free Fax:* 800-282-5681 *E-mail:* avemariapress.1@nd.edu *Web Site:* www.avemariapress.com, pg 27

Luttrell, Marsha, Mercer University Press, 368 Orange St, Macon, GA 31201 *Tel:* 478-301-2880 *Toll Free Tel:* 866-895-1472 *Fax:* 478-301-2585 *E-mail:* mupressorders@mercer.edu *Web Site:* www.mupress.org, pg 148

Lutzy, Patrick, Cheneliere Education Inc, 5800, rue St Denis, bureau 900, Montreal, QC H2S 3L5, Canada *Tel:* 514-273-1066 *Toll Free Tel:* 800-565-5531 *Fax:* 514-276-0324 *Toll Free Fax:* 800-814-0324 *E-mail:* info@cheneliere.ca *Web Site:* www.cheneliere.ca, pg 450

Lutzy, Patrick, Gaetan Morin Editeur, 5800, rue St-Denis, bureau 900, Montreal, QC H2S 3L5, Canada *Tel:* 514-273-1066 *Toll Free Tel:* 800-565-5531 *Fax:* 514-276-0324 *Toll Free Fax:* 800-814-0324 *E-mail:* info@cheneliere.ca *Web Site:* www.cheneliere.ca, pg 457

Luvaas, William, Joy Harjo Poetry Award, PO Box 2414, Durango, CO 81302 *Tel:* 970-903-7914 *E-mail:* cutthroatmag@gmail.com *Web Site:* www.cutthroatmag.com, pg 652

Lyman, Joe, Great Lakes Graphics Association, W232 N2950 Roundy Circle E, Pewaukee, WI 53072 *Tel:* 262-522-2210 *Toll Free Tel:* 855-522-2210 *Fax:* 262-522-2211 *E-mail:* admin@piw.org *Web Site:* www.piw.org, pg 566

Lynch, Catharine, GP Putnam's Sons (Hardcover), 375 Hudson St, New York, NY 10014 *Tel:* 212-366-2000 *Fax:* 212-366-2643 *E-mail:* online@penguinputnam.com *Web Site:* www.penguin.com/publishers/gpputnamssons, pg 192

Lynch, Chris, Simon & Schuster Audio, 1230 Avenue of the Americas, New York, NY 10020 *Web Site:* audio.simonandschuster.com, pg 213

Lynch, Chris, Simon & Schuster, Inc, 1230 Avenue of the Americas, New York, NY 10020 *Tel:* 212-698-7000 *Fax:* 212-698-7007 *E-mail:* firstname.lastname@simonandschuster.com *Web Site:* www.simonandschuster.com, pg 213

Lynch, Jen, Society of Environmental Toxicology & Chemistry (SETAC), 229 S Baylen St, 2nd fl, Pensacola, FL 32502 *Tel:* 850-469-1500 *Toll Free Fax:* 888-296-4136 *E-mail:* setac@setac.org; etc@setac.org (edit) *Web Site:* www.setac.org, pg 216

Lynch, John (Jack) J Jr, Houghton Mifflin Harcourt, 125 High St, Boston, MA 02110 *Tel:* 617-351-5000 *Toll Free Tel:* 855-969-4642; 800-225-5425 (K-12 educ materials); 800-323-9540 (assessment materials); 877-219-1537 (SkillsTutor); 888-242-6747 (Innovation in Educ Group); 800-225-3362 (Trade & Ref Div) *Toll Free Fax:* 800-269-5232 *E-mail:* myhmhco@hmhco.com *Web Site:* www.hmhco.com, pg 110

Lynch, John (Jack) J Jr, Houghton Mifflin Harcourt Trade & Reference Division, 125 High St, Boston, MA 02110 *Tel:* 617-351-5000 *Toll Free Tel:* 800-225-3362 *Web Site:* www.hmhco.com, pg 111

Lynch, Katy, Sourcebooks Inc, 1935 Brookdale Rd, Suite 139, Naperville, IL 60563 *Tel:* 630-961-3900 *Toll Free Tel:* 800-432-7444 *Fax:* 630-961-2168 *E-mail:* info@sourcebooks.com; customersupport@sourcebooks.com *Web Site:* www.sourcebooks.com, pg 218

Lynch, Megan, HarperCollins General Books Group, 195 Broadway, New York, NY 10007 *Tel:* 212-207-7000 *Web Site:* www.harpercollins.com, pg 101

Lynch, Patrick, Oxford University Press USA, 198 Madison Ave, New York, NY 10016 *Tel:* 212-726-6000 *Toll Free Tel:* 800-451-7556 (orders); 800-445-9714 (cust serv) *Fax:* 919-677-1303 *E-mail:* custserv.us@oup.com *Web Site:* www.oup.com/us, pg 171

Lynell, James, Multicultural Publications Inc, 1939 Manchester Rd, Akron, OH 44314 *Tel:* 330-865-9578 *Fax:* 330-865-9578 *E-mail:* multiculturalpub@prodigy.net *Web Site:* www.multiculturalpub.net, pg 155

Lynley, Cason, Duke University Press, 905 W Main St, Suite 18B, Durham, NC 27701 *Tel:* 919-688-5134 *Toll Free Tel:* 888-651-0122 (US) *Fax:* 919-688-2615 *Toll Free Fax:* 888-651-0124 *E-mail:* orders@dukeupress.edu *Web Site:* www.dukeupress.edu, pg 73

Lynn, Kira, Kane Miller Books, 4901 Morena Blvd, Suite 213, San Diego, CA 92117 *E-mail:* submissions@kanemiller.com; info@kanemiller.com *Web Site:* www.kanemiller.com, pg 124

Lyon, Kevan, Marsal Lyon Literary Agency LLC, 665 San Rodolfo Dr, Suite 124, PMB 121, Solana Beach, CA 92075 *Tel:* 760-814-8507 *Web Site:* www.marsallyonliteraryagency.com, pg 527

Lyons, Brad, Chalice Press, 483 E Lockwood Ave, Suite 100, St Louis, MO 63119 *Tel:* 314-231-8500 *Toll Free Tel:* 800-366-3383 *Fax:* 314-231-8524; 770-280-4039 (orders) *E-mail:* customerservice@chalicepress.com *Web Site:* www.chalicepress.com, pg 52

Lyons, Emilie, Greenleaf Book Group LLC, 3 Park Place, 4005 Banister Lane, Suite B, Austin, TX 78704 *Tel:* 512-891-6100 *Fax:* 512-891-6150 *E-mail:* contact@greenleafbookgroup.com *Web Site:* www.greenleafbookgroup.com, pg 96

Lyons, Jed, Rowman & Littlefield Publishers Inc, 4501 Forbes Blvd, Suite 200, Lanham, MD 20706 *Tel:* 301-459-3366 *Toll Free Tel:* 800-462-6420 (cust serv) *Fax:* 301-429-5748 *Web Site:* rowman.com, pg 202

Lyons, Jed, Scarecrow Press Inc, 4501 Forbes Blvd, Suite 200, Lanham, MD 20706 *Tel:* 301-459-3366 *Fax:* 301-429-5748 *Web Site:* www.scarecrowpress.com, pg 207

Lyons, Jonathan, Curtis Brown Ltd, 10 Astor Place, New York, NY 10003 *Tel:* 212-473-5400 *Web Site:* www.curtisbrown.com, pg 510

Lyons, Michael, Tower Publishing Co, 588 Saco Rd, Standish, ME 04084 *Tel:* 207-642-5400 *Toll Free Tel:* 800-969-8693 *Fax:* 207-264-3870 *E-mail:* info@towerpub.com *Web Site:* www.towerpub.com, pg 233

Lyons, Tony, Arcade Publishing Inc, 307 W 36 St, 11th fl, New York, NY 10018 *Tel:* 212-643-6816 *Fax:* 212-643-6819 *E-mail:* info@skyhorsepublishing.com (subs & foreign rts) *Web Site:* www.arcadepub.com, pg 20

Lypen, Krestyna, Algonquin Books, 400 Silver Cedar Ct, Suite 300, Chapel Hill, NC 27514-1585 *Tel:* 919-967-0108 *Fax:* 919-933-0272 *E-mail:* inquiry@algonquin.com *Web Site:* www.workman.com/algonquin, pg 7

Lytton, Alison, Scholastic International, 557 Broadway, New York, NY 10012 *Tel:* 212-343-6100; 646-330-5288 (intl cust serv) *Toll Free Tel:* 800-SCHOLASTIC (724-6527) *Fax:* 646-837-7878 *E-mail:* international@scholastic.com, pg 208

Ma, Amy, Immedium, 535 Rockdale Dr, San Francisco, CA 94127 *Tel:* 415-452-8546 *Fax:* 360-937-6272 *E-mail:* orders@immedium.com; sales@immedium.com *Web Site:* www.immedium.com, pg 115

Ma, Cindy, House of Anansi Press Inc, 128 Sterling Rd, Lower Level, Toronto, ON M6R 2B7, Canada *Tel:* 416-363-4343 *Fax:* 416-363-1017 *E-mail:* customerservice@houseofanansi.com *Web Site:* www.houseofanansi.com, pg 460

Maaghul, Johanna, Waterside Productions Inc, 2055 Oxford Ave, Cardiff, CA 92007 *Tel:* 760-632-9190 *Fax:* 760-632-9295 *E-mail:* admin@waterside.com *Web Site:* www.waterside.com, pg 541

Maas, John, Sterling Lord Literistic Inc, 115 Broadway, Suite 1602, New York, NY 10006 *Tel:* 212-780-6050 *Fax:* 212-780-6095 *E-mail:* info@sll.com *Web Site:* www.sll.com, pg 537

Maass, Donald, Donald Maass Literary Agency, 1000 Dean St, Suite 252, Brooklyn, NY 11238 *Tel:* 212-727-8383 *Fax:* 212-727-3271 *E-mail:* info@maassagency.com *Web Site:* www.maassagency.com, pg 526

Mabry, John R, The Apocryphile Press, 1700 Shattuck Ave, Suite 81, Berkeley, CA 94709 *Tel:* 510-290-4349 *E-mail:* apocryphile@me.com *Web Site:* www.apocryphilepress.com, pg 18

Macavage, Joe, HarperCollins General Books Group, 195 Broadway, New York, NY 10007 *Tel:* 212-207-7000 *Web Site:* www.harpercollins.com, pg 101

MacBrien, Nathan, Northwestern University Press, 629 Noyes St, Evanston, IL 60208-4210 *Tel:* 847-491-2046 *Toll Free Tel:* 800-621-2736 (orders only) *Fax:* 847-491-8150 *E-mail:* nupress@northwestern.edu *Web Site:* www.nupress.northwestern.edu, pg 164

Macca, Joe, Scholastic International, 557 Broadway, New York, NY 10012 *Tel:* 212-343-6100; 646-330-5288 (intl cust serv) *Toll Free Tel:* 800-SCHOLASTIC (724-6527) *Fax:* 646-837-7878 *E-mail:* international@scholastic.com, pg 208

Maccarone, Grace, Holiday House Inc, 425 Madison Ave, New York, NY 10017 *Tel:* 212-688-0085 *Fax:* 212-421-6134 *E-mail:* info@holidayhouse.com *Web Site:* www.holidayhouse.com, pg 109

Macchiusi, Mary, Pembroke Publishers Ltd, 538 Hood Rd, Markham, ON L3R 3K9, Canada *Tel:* 905-477-0650 *Toll Free Tel:* 800-997-9807 *Fax:* 905-477-3691 *Toll Free Fax:* 800-339-5568 *Web Site:* www.pembrokepublishers.com, pg 466

Maccoby, Gina, Gina Maccoby Literary Agency, PO Box 60, Chappaqua, NY 10514-0060 *Tel:* 914-238-5630 *E-mail:* query@maccobylit.com *Web Site:* www.publishersmarketplace.com/members/GinaMaccoby, pg 526

MacColl, Pamela, Beacon Press, 24 Farnsworth St, Boston, MA 02210-1409 *Tel:* 617-742-2110 *Fax:* 617-723-3097; 617-742-2290 *Web Site:* www.beacon.org, pg 31

MacDonald, Brian, University of Toronto Press, 10 St Mary St, Suite 700, Toronto, ON M4Y 2W8, Canada *Tel:* 416-978-2239 *Fax:* 416-978-4738 *E-mail:* info@utpress.utoronto.ca *Web Site:* www.utpress.utoronto.ca; www.utppublishing.com, pg 475

MacDonald, Brian A, National Braille Press, 88 Saint Stephen St, Boston, MA 02115-4302 *Tel:* 617-266-6160 *Toll Free Tel:* 800-548-7323 (cust serv); 888-965-8965 *Fax:* 617-437-0456 *E-mail:* orders@nbp.org; contact@nbp.org *Web Site:* www.nbp.org, pg 157

MacDonald, Dougald, The American Alpine Club Press, 710 Tenth St, Suite 100, Golden, CO 80401 *Tel:* 303-384-0110 *Fax:* 303-384-0111 *E-mail:* info@americanalpineclub.org *Web Site:* americanalpineclub.org, pg 9

Macdonald, Jane, University of Chicago Press, 1427 E 60 St, Chicago, IL 60637-2954 *Tel:* 773-702-7700; 773-702-7600 *Toll Free Tel:* 800-621-2736 (orders) *Fax:* 773-702-9756; 773-660-2235 (orders); 773-702-2708 *E-mail:* custserv@press.uchicago.edu; marketing@press.uchicago.edu *Web Site:* www.press.uchicago.edu, pg 241

MacDonald, Leo, HarperCollins Canada Ltd, 2 Bloor St E, 20th fl, Toronto, ON M4W 1A8, Canada *Tel:* 416-975-9334 *Fax:* 416-975-5223 *E-mail:* hcorder@harpercollins.com *Web Site:* www.harpercollins.ca, pg 459

MacDonald, Nora, Random House Children's Books, 1745 Broadway, 10th fl, New York, NY 10019 *Tel:* 212-782-9000 *Web Site:* www.randomhousekids.com, pg 194

MacDonald, Tim, David C Cook, 4050 Lee Vance View, Colorado Springs, CO 80918 *Tel:* 719-536-0100 *Toll Free Tel:* 800-708-5550; 800-323-7543 (orders & cust serv) *Toll Free Fax:* 800-430-0726 (cust serv) *Web Site:* www.davidccook.com, pg 60

MacDonnell, Margo, Rocky Mountain Mineral Law Foundation, 9191 Sheridan Blvd, Suite 203, Westminster, CO 80031 *Tel:* 303-321-8100 *Fax:* 303-321-7657 *E-mail:* info@rmmlf.org *Web Site:* www.rmmlf.org, pg 200

MacFarlane, Fraser, One Act Play Depot, 618 Memorial Dr, PO Box 335, Spiritwood, SK S0J 2M0, Canada *E-mail:* plays@oneactplays.net; orders@oneactplays.net *Web Site:* oneactplays.net, pg 465

MacGowan, Melissa, National Freedom of Information Coalition (NFOIC), 101C Reynolds Journalism Institute, Columbia, MO 65211 *Tel:* 573-882-4856 *Web Site:* nfoic.org, pg 572

MacGregor, Rob, Crabtree Publishing Co Ltd, 616 Welland Ave, St Catharines, ON L2M 5V6, Canada *Tel:* 905-682-5221 *Toll Free Tel:* 800-387-7650 *Fax:* 905-682-7166 *Toll Free Fax:* 800-355-7166 *E-mail:* custserv@crabtreebooks.com; sales@crabtreebooks.com; orders@crabtreebooks.com *Web Site:* www.crabtreebooks.com, pg 451

MacGregor, Robert, Crabtree Publishing Co, 350 Fifth Ave, 59th fl, PMB 59051, New York, NY 10118 *Tel:* 212-496-5040 *Toll Free Tel:* 800-387-7650 *Toll Free Fax:* 800-355-7166 *E-mail:* custserv@crabtreebooks.com *Web Site:* www.crabtreebooks.com, pg 63

Mach, Jo Meserve, Finding My Way Books, 3512 SW Huntoon St, Topeka, KS 66604 *Tel:* 785-273-6239 *E-mail:* info@findingmywaybooks.com; findingmywaybooks@gmail.com *Web Site:* www.findingmywaybooks.net, pg 84

Machado, Sierra, Perseus Books, 250 W 57 St, 15th fl, New York, NY 10107 *Tel:* 212-340-8100 *Toll Free Tel:* 800-343-4499 (cust serv) *Fax:* 212-340-8105 *Web Site:* www.perseusbooks.com, pg 180

Machat, Joshua, Yale University Press, 302 Temple St, New Haven, CT 06511-8909 *Tel:* 203-432-0960; 203-432-0966 (sales); 401-531-2800 (cust serv) *Toll Free Tel:* 800-405-1619 (cust serv) *Fax:* 203-432-0948; 203-432-8485 (sales); 401-531-2801 (cust serv) *Toll Free Fax:* 800-406-9145 (cust serv) *E-mail:* sales.press@yale.edu (sales); customer.care@triliteral.org (cust serv) *Web Site:* www.yalebooks.com; yalepress.yale.edu/yupbooks, pg 261

Machinist, Alexandra, ICM Partners, 65 E 55 St, New York, NY 10022 *Tel:* 212-556-5600 *Web Site:* www.icmtalent.com, pg 521

MacIlwaine, Paula I, American Water Works Association (AWWA), 6666 W Quincy Ave, Denver, CO 80235 *Tel:* 303-794-7711 *Toll Free Tel:* 800-926-7337 *Fax:* 303-347-0804 *E-mail:* service@awwa.org (cust serv) *Web Site:* www.awwa.org, pg 15

Macintosh, Adrienne, Harlequin Enterprises Ltd, 225 Duncan Mill Rd, Don Mills, ON M3B 3K9, Canada *Tel:* 416-445-5860 *Toll Free Tel:* 888-432-4879; 800-370-5838 (ebook inquiries) *E-mail:* customerservice@harlequin.com *Web Site:* www.harlequin.com, pg 459

MacIntyre, Mary, Canadian Bookbinders and Book Artists Guild (CBBAG), 80 Ward St, Suite 207, Toronto, ON M6H 4A6, Canada *Tel:* 416-581-1071 *E-mail:* cbbag@cbbag.ca *Web Site:* www.cbbag.ca, pg 561

Macios, Laurin, George Bogin Memorial Award, 15 Gramercy Park, New York, NY 10003 *Tel:* 212-254-9628 *Web Site:* www.poetrysociety.org, pg 633

Macios, Laurin, Alice Fay Di Castagnola Award, 15 Gramercy Park, New York, NY 10003 *Tel:* 212-254-9628 *Web Site:* www.poetrysociety.org, pg 641

Macios, Laurin, Norma Farber First Book Award, 15 Gramercy Park, New York, NY 10003 *Tel:* 212-254-9628 *Web Site:* www.poetrysociety.org, pg 645

Macios, Laurin, Cecil Hemley Memorial Award, 15 Gramercy Park, New York, NY 10003 *Tel:* 212-254-9628 *Web Site:* www.poetrysociety.org, pg 652

Macios, Laurin, Louise Louis/Emily F Bourne Student Poetry Award, 15 Gramercy Park, New York, NY 10003 *Tel:* 212-254-9628 *Web Site:* www.poetrysociety.org, pg 663

Macios, Laurin, Lyric Poetry Award, 15 Gramercy Park, New York, NY 10003 *Tel:* 212-254-9628 *Web Site:* www.poetrysociety.org, pg 664

Macios, Laurin, Lucille Medwick Memorial Award, 15 Gramercy Park, New York, NY 10003 *Tel:* 212-254-9628 *Web Site:* www.poetrysociety.org, pg 667

Macios, Laurin, Poetry Society of America (PSA), 15 Gramercy Park, New York, NY 10003 *Tel:* 212-254-9628 *Web Site:* www.poetrysociety.org, pg 575

Macios, Laurin, William Carlos Williams Award, 15 Gramercy Park, New York, NY 10003 *Tel:* 212-254-9628 *Web Site:* www.poetrysociety.org, pg 698

Macios, Laurin, The Writer Magazine/Emily Dickinson Award, 15 Gramercy Park, New York, NY 10003 *Tel:* 212-254-9628 *Web Site:* www.poetrysociety.org, pg 700

Mack, Amelia, Chronicle Books LLC, 680 Second St, San Francisco, CA 94107 *Tel:* 415-537-4200 *Toll Free Tel:* 800-759-0190 (cust serv) *Fax:* 415-537-4460 *Toll Free Fax:* 800-858-7787 (orders); 800-286-9471 (cust serv) *E-mail:* frontdesk@chroniclebooks.com *Web Site:* www.chroniclebooks.com, pg 55

Mackay, Mary, The American Library Association (ALA), 50 E Huron St, Chicago, IL 60611 *Tel:* 312-944-6780 *Toll Free Tel:* 800-545-2433 *Fax:* 312-280-5275 *E-mail:* editionsmarketing@ala.org *Web Site:* www.alastore.ala.org, pg 12

MacKeen, Alison, Sterling Lord Literistic Inc, 115 Broadway, Suite 1602, New York, NY 10006 *Tel:* 212-780-6050 *Fax:* 212-780-6095 *E-mail:* info@sll.com *Web Site:* www.sll.com, pg 537

MacKenzie, Joanna, Browne & Miller Literary Associates, 410 S Michigan Ave, Suite 460, Chicago, IL 60605 *Tel:* 312-922-3063 *E-mail:* mail@browneandmiller.com *Web Site:* www.browneandmiller.com, pg 510

Mackenzie, Leslie, Grey House Publishing Inc™, 4919 Rte 22, Amenia, NY 12501 *Tel:* 518-789-8700 *Toll Free Tel:* 800-562-2139 *Fax:* 518-789-0556 *E-mail:* books@greyhouse.com; customerservice@greyhouse.com *Web Site:* www.greyhouse.com, pg 96

Mackey, Zoe, Berrett-Koehler Publishers Inc, 1333 Broadway, Suite 1000, Oakland, CA 94612 *Tel:* 510-817-2277 *Fax:* 510-817-2278 *E-mail:* bkpub@bkpub.com *Web Site:* www.bkconnection.com, pg 34

Mackinnon, Margo, IODE Jean Throop Book Award, 9-45 Frid St, Hamilton, ON L8P 4M3, Canada *Tel:* 905-522-9537 *Fax:* 905-522-3637 *E-mail:* iodeontario@bellnet.ca *Web Site:* www.iodeontario.ca, pg 656

Mackintosh, Teresa, CCH, a Wolters Kluwer business, 2700 Lake Cook Rd, Riverwoods, IL 60015 *Tel:* 847-267-7000 *Web Site:* www.cch.com, pg 50

Macklem, Ann, University of British Columbia Press, 2029 West Mall, Vancouver, BC V6T 1Z2, Canada *Tel:* 604-822-5959 *Toll Free Tel:* 877-377-9378 *Fax:* 604-822-6083 *Toll Free Fax:* 800-668-0821 *E-mail:* frontdesk@ubcpress.ca *Web Site:* www.ubcpress.ca, pg 473

Macklem, Michael, Oberon Press, 145 Spruce St, Suite 205, Ottawa, ON K1R 6P1, Canada *Tel:* 613-238-3275 *Fax:* 613-238-3275 *E-mail:* oberon@sympatico.ca *Web Site:* www.oberonpress.ca, pg 465

Macklem, Nicholas, Oberon Press, 145 Spruce St, Suite 205, Ottawa, ON K1R 6P1, Canada *Tel:* 613-238-3275 *Fax:* 613-238-3275 *E-mail:* oberon@sympatico.ca *Web Site:* www.oberonpress.ca, pg 465

Mackwood, Robert, Seventh Avenue Literary Agency, 2052 124 St, South Surrey, BC V4A 9K3, Canada *Tel:* 604-538-7252 *Fax:* 604-538-7252 *E-mail:* info@seventhavenuelit.com *Web Site:* www.seventhavenuelit.com, pg 535

MacLachlan, Christina, Wildflower Press, c/o Oakbrook Press, 3301 S Valley Dr, Rapid City, SD 57703 *Tel:* 605-381-6385 *E-mail:* info@wildflowerpress.org *Web Site:* www.wildflowerpress.org, pg 255

MacLachlan, Sarah, Groundwood Books, 128 Sterling Rd, Lower Level, Toronto, ON M6R 2B7, Canada *Tel:* 416-363-4343 *Fax:* 416-363-1017 *E-mail:* genmail@groundwoodbooks.com *Web Site:* www.houseofanansi.com, pg 458

MacLachlan, Sarah, House of Anansi Press Inc, 128 Sterling Rd, Lower Level, Toronto, ON M6R 2B7, Canada *Tel:* 416-363-4343 *Fax:* 416-363-1017 *E-mail:* customerservice@houseofanansi.com *Web Site:* www.houseofanansi.com, pg 460

Maclagan, Maral, Scholastic Canada Ltd, 604 King St W, Toronto, ON M5V 1E1, Canada *Tel:* 905-887-7323 *Toll Free Tel:* 800-268-3860 (CN) *Toll Free Fax:* 866-387-4944 *E-mail:* custserve@scholastic.ca *Web Site:* www.scholastic.ca, pg 469

MacLeod, Lauren E, Strothman Agency LLC, 63 E Ninth St, 10X, New York, NY 10003 *E-mail:* info@strothmanagency.com *Web Site:* www.strothmanagency.com, pg 538

MacLeod, Nancy, Short Prose Competition for Developing Writers, 600-460 Richmond St W, Toronto, ON M5V 1Y1, Canada *Tel:* 416-703-8982 *Fax:* 416-504-9090 *E-mail:* info@writersunion.ca *Web Site:* www.writersunion.ca, pg 689

MacMahon, Ted, Newbury Street Press, 99-101 Newbury St, Boston, MA 02116 *Tel:* 617-536-5740 *Toll Free Tel:* 888-296-3447 (NEHGS membership) *Fax:* 617-536-7307 *E-mail:* sales@nehgs.org *Web Site:* www.americanancestors.org, pg 162

Macnair, Randal, Oolichan Books, PO Box 2278, Fernie, BC V0B 1M0, Canada *Tel:* 250-423-6113 *E-mail:* info@oolichan.com *Web Site:* www.oolichan.com, pg 465

MacNeil, Mary, The University of Virginia Press, PO Box 400318, Charlottesville, VA 22904-4318 *Tel:* 434-924-3468 (cust serv); 434-924-3469 (cust serv) *Toll Free Tel:* 800-831-3406 (orders) *Fax:* 434-982-2655 *Toll Free Fax:* 877-288-6400 *E-mail:* vapress@virginia.edu *Web Site:* www.upress.virginia.edu, pg 245

MacNevin, James, University of British Columbia Press, 2029 West Mall, Vancouver, BC V6T 1Z2, Canada *Tel:* 604-822-5959 *Toll Free Tel:* 877-377-9378 *Fax:* 604-822-6083 *Toll Free Fax:* 800-668-0821 *E-mail:* frontdesk@ubcpress.ca *Web Site:* www.ubcpress.ca, pg 473

Maco, Mary Kate, Stanford University Press, 425 Broadway St, Redwood City, CA 94063-3126 *Tel:* 650-723-9434 *Fax:* 650-725-3457 *E-mail:* info@www.sup.org; publicity@www.sup.org *Web Site:* www.sup.org, pg 220

Macris, Natalie, Solano Press Books, PO Box 773, Point Arena, CA 95468 *Tel:* 707-884-4508 *Toll Free Tel:* 800-931-9373 *Fax:* 707-884-4109 *E-mail:* spbooks@solano.com *Web Site:* www.solano.com, pg 217

MacVaugh, Kim, Just World Books LLC, PO Box 5484, Charlottesville, VA 22905 *Toll Free Tel:* 888-506-3769 *E-mail:* sales@justworldbooks.com *Web Site:* justworldbooks.com, pg 124

Madan, Ashish, Aptara Inc, 3110 Fairview Park Dr, Suite 900, Falls Church, VA 22042 *Tel:* 703-352-0001 *E-mail:* moreinfo@aptaracorp.com *Web Site:* www.aptaracorp.com, pg 488

Madan, Neeti, Sterling Lord Literistic Inc, 115 Broadway, Suite 1602, New York, NY 10006 *Tel:* 212-780-6050 *Fax:* 212-780-6095 *E-mail:* info@sll.com *Web Site:* www.sll.com, pg 537

Madara, James L MD, American Medical Association, AMA Plaza, 330 N Wabash, Suite 39300, Chicago, IL 60611-5885 *Tel:* 312-464-5000 *Toll Free Tel:* 800-621-8335 *Fax:* 312-464-4184 *Web Site:* www.ama-assn.org, pg 13, 555

Madden, Kyla, McGill-Queen's University Press, 1010 Sherbrooke W, Suite 1720, Montreal, QC H3A 2R7, Canada *Tel:* 514-398-3750 *Fax:* 514-398-4333 *E-mail:* mqup@mqup.ca *Web Site:* www.mqup.ca, pg 463

Maddex, John, Ancient Faith Publishing, 2747 Bond St, University Park, IL 60484 *Tel:* 219-728-2216 *Toll Free Tel:* 800-967-7377 *Toll Free Fax:* 866-599-5208 *E-mail:* info@ancientfaith.com; orders@ancientfaith.com *Web Site:* www.ancientfaith.com/publishing, pg 16

Madhubuti, Haki R, Third World Press, 7822 S Dobson Ave, Chicago, IL 60619 *Tel:* 773-651-0700 *Fax:* 773-651-7286 *E-mail:* twpress3@aol.com *Web Site:* www.thirdworldpressfoundation.com, pg 231

Madonia, Nena, Dupree, Miller & Associates Inc, 100 Highland Park Village, Suite 350, Dallas, TX 75205 *Tel:* 214-559-2665 *Fax:* 214-559-7243 *E-mail:* editorial@dupreemiller.com *Web Site:* www.dupreemiller.com, pg 515

Madrus, Ingel, The League of Canadian Poets, 192 Spadina Ave, Suite 312, Toronto, ON M5T 2C2, Canada *Tel:* 416-504-1657 *Fax:* 416-504-0096 *Web Site:* poets.ca, pg 568

Maeshiro, Jesse, Portfolio, 375 Hudson St, New York, NY 10014 *Web Site:* www.penguin.com/meet/publishers/portfolio, pg 186

Mafchir, James, Sherman Asher Publishing, 126 Candelario St, Santa Fe, NM 87501 *Tel:* 505-988-7214 *E-mail:* westernedge@santa-fe.net *Web Site:* www.shermanasher.com; www.westernedgepress.com, pg 211

Mafchir, James, Western Edge Press, 126 Candelario St, Santa Fe, NM 87501 *Tel:* 505-988-7214 *E-mail:* westernedge@santa-fe.net *Web Site:* www.westernedgepress.com, pg 254

Maffei, Ms Dorian, Kimberley Cameron & Associates LLC, 1550 Tiburon Blvd, Suite 704, Tiburon, CA 94920 *Tel:* 415-789-9191 *Fax:* 415-789-9177 *Web Site:* www.kimberleycameron.com, pg 511

Magallanes, Anna, Columbia Books & Information Services (CBIS), 4340 East-West Hwy, Suite 300, Bethesda, MD 20814 *Tel:* 202-464-1662 *Fax:* 301-664-9600 *E-mail:* info@columbiabooks.com *Web Site:* www.columbiabooks.com; www.lobbyists.info; www.associationexecs.com, pg 59

Magill, Dr David, John Dos Passos Prize for Literature, Dept of English & Modern Languages, 201 High St, Farmville, VA 23909 *Tel:* 434-395-2155 *Fax:* 434-395-2145 *Web Site:* www.longwood.edu/english/dos-passos-prize, pg 642

Magnus, Mary H, Health Professions Press, 409 Washington Ave, Suite 500, Towson, MD 21204 *Tel:* 410-337-9585 *Toll Free Tel:* 888-337-8808 *Fax:* 410-337-8539 *E-mail:* custserv@healthpropress.com *Web Site:* www.healthpropress.com, pg 105

Magnus, Dr Sandra, American Institute of Aeronautics & Astronautics (AIAA), 1801 Alexander Bell Dr, Suite 500, Reston, VA 20191-4344 *Tel:* 703-264-7500 *Toll Free Tel:* 800-639-AIAA (639-2422) *Fax:* 703-264-7551 *E-mail:* custserv@aiaa.org *Web Site:* www.aiaa.org, pg 12

Magoulias, Michael, University of Chicago Press, 1427 E 60 St, Chicago, IL 60637-2954 *Tel:* 773-702-7700; 773-702-7600 *Toll Free Tel:* 800-621-2736 (orders) *Fax:* 773-702-9756; 773-660-2235 (orders); 773-702-2708 *E-mail:* custserv@press.uchicago.edu; marketing@press.uchicago.edu *Web Site:* www.press.uchicago.edu, pg 241

Magowan, Mark, The Vendome Press, 244 Fifth Ave, Suite 2043, New York, NY 10001 *Tel:* 212-737-1857 *E-mail:* info@vendomepress.com *Web Site:* www.vendomepress.com, pg 250

Magruder, Munro, New World Library, 14 Pamaron Way, Novato, CA 94949 *Tel:* 415-884-2100 *Toll Free Tel:* 800-227-3900 (ext 52, retail orders); 800-972-6657 *Fax:* 415-884-2199 *E-mail:* escort@newworldlibrary.com *Web Site:* www.newworldlibrary.com, pg 161

Maguire, Julia, Random House Children's Books, 1745 Broadway, 10th fl, New York, NY 10019 *Tel:* 212-782-9000 *Web Site:* www.randomhousekids.com, pg 194

Maguire, Julia, Random House Publishing Group, 1745 Broadway, New York, NY 10019 *Toll Free Tel:* 800-200-3552 *Web Site:* atrandom.com, pg 195

Maguire, Kevin, Paulist Press, 997 Macarthur Blvd, Mahwah, NJ 07430-9990 *Tel:* 201-825-7300 *Toll Free Tel:* 800-218-1903 *Fax:* 201-825-6921 *Toll Free Fax:* 800-836-3161 *E-mail:* info@paulistpress.com; publicity@paulistpress.com *Web Site:* www.paulistpress.com, pg 175

Mahajan, Vinod, Nataraj Books, 7967 Twist Lane, Springfield, VA 22153 *Tel:* 703-455-4996 *Fax:* 703-455-4001 *E-mail:* nataraj@erols.com; orders@natarajbooks.com; natarajbooks@gmail.com *Web Site:* www.natarajbooks.com, pg 156

Mahalek, Gina M, The University of North Carolina Press, 116 S Boundary St, Chapel Hill, NC 27514-3808 *Tel:* 919-966-3561 *Fax:* 919-966-3829 *E-mail:* uncpress@unc.edu *Web Site:* www.uncpress.unc.edu, pg 243

Maharaj, Davan, Los Angeles Times Book Prizes, 202 W First St, Los Angeles, CA 90012 *Tel:* 213-237-5775 *Toll Free Tel:* 800-528-4637 (ext 75775) *Web Site:* www.latimesbookprizes.com, pg 663

Maher, Bess, Colorado Book Awards, 7935 E Prentice Ave, Suite 450, Greenwood Village, CO 80111 *Tel:* 303-894-7951 (ext 19) *Fax:* 303-864-9361 *E-mail:* info@coloradohumanities.org *Web Site:* www.coloradohumanities.org, pg 638

Mahler, Cathy, The Edna Staebler Award for Creative Non-Fiction, Office of the Dean, Faculty of Arts, 75 University Ave W, Waterloo, ON N2L 3C5, Canada *Tel:* 519-884-1970 (ext 3361) *E-mail:* staebleraward@wlu.ca *Web Site:* wlu.ca/staebleraward, pg 691

Mahoney, Ann, International City/County Management Association (ICMA), 777 N Capitol St NE, Suite 500, Washington, DC 20002-4201 *Tel:* 202-289-4262 *Toll Free Tel:* 800-745-8780 *Fax:* 202-962-3500 *E-mail:* customerservices@icma.org *Web Site:* icma.org, pg 119

Mahoney, Judy, Teach Me Tapes Inc, 10400 N Enterprise Dr, Mequon, WI 53092 *Toll Free Tel:* 800-456-4656 *E-mail:* marie@teachmetapes.com *Web Site:* www.teachmetapes.com, pg 228

Mahoney, Natasha, Management Sciences for Health, 200 Rivers Edge Dr, Medford, MA 02155 *Tel:* 617-250-9500 *Fax:* 617-250-9090 *E-mail:* bookstore@msh.org *Web Site:* www.msh.org, pg 140

Mahoney, Tyrrell, Chronicle Books LLC, 680 Second St, San Francisco, CA 94107 *Tel:* 415-537-4200 *Toll Free Tel:* 800-759-0190 (cust serv) *Fax:* 415-537-4460 *Toll Free Fax:* 800-858-7787 (orders); 800-286-9471 (cust serv) *E-mail:* frontdesk@chroniclebooks.com *Web Site:* www.chroniclebooks.com, pg 55

Mai, Phuong, Chronicle Books LLC, 680 Second St, San Francisco, CA 94107 *Tel:* 415-537-4200 *Toll Free Tel:* 800-759-0190 (cust serv) *Fax:* 415-537-4460 *Toll Free Fax:* 800-858-7787 (orders); 800-286-9471 (cust serv) *E-mail:* frontdesk@chroniclebooks.com *Web Site:* www.chroniclebooks.com, pg 55

Maille, Michel, Les Editions Fides, 7333 place des Roseraies, bureau 100, Anjou, QC H1M 2X6, Canada *Tel:* 514-745-4290 *Fax:* 514-745-4299 *E-mail:* editions@groupefides.com *Web Site:* www.editionsfides.com, pg 454

Maillet, Neal, Berrett-Koehler Publishers Inc, 1333 Broadway, Suite 1000, Oakland, CA 94612 *Tel:* 510-817-2277 *Fax:* 510-817-2278 *E-mail:* bkpub@bkpub.com *Web Site:* www.bkconnection.com, pg 34

Maines, Kevin Murphy, New Women's Voices Chapbook Competition, PO Box 1626, Georgetown, KY 40324 *Tel:* 502-603-0670 *E-mail:* finishingbooks@aol.com; flpbookstore@aol.com *Web Site:* www.finishinglinepress.com, pg 673

Maines, Kevin Murphy, Open Chapbook Competition, PO Box 1626, Georgetown, KY 40324 *Tel:* 502-603-0670 *E-mail:* finishingbooks@aol.com; flpbookstore@aol.com *Web Site:* www.finishinglinepress.com, pg 675

Maines, Leah, New Women's Voices Chapbook Competition, PO Box 1626, Georgetown, KY 40324 *Tel:* 502-603-0670 *E-mail:* finishingbooks@aol.com; flpbookstore@aol.com *Web Site:* www.finishinglinepress.com, pg 673

Maines, Leah, Open Chapbook Competition, PO Box 1626, Georgetown, KY 40324 *Tel:* 502-603-0670 *E-mail:* finishingbooks@aol.com; flpbookstore@aol.com *Web Site:* www.finishinglinepress.com, pg 675

Mainhardt, Ricia, RMA, 85 Lincoln St, 1st fl, Meriden, CT 06451 *Tel:* 718-434-1893 *Fax:* 203-440-1013 *Web Site:* www.ricia.com, pg 533

Mainville, Lara MA, University of Ottawa Press (Presses de l'Université d'Ottawa), 542 King Edward Ave, Ottawa, ON K1N 6N5, Canada *Tel:* 613-562-5246 *Fax:* 613-562-5247 *E-mail:* puo-oup@uottawa.ca *Web Site:* press.uottawa.ca, pg 474

Mairs, Jane, Merriam-Webster Inc, 47 Federal St, Springfield, MA 01102 *Tel:* 413-734-3134 *Toll Free Tel:* 800-828-1880 (orders & cust serv) *Fax:* 413-731-5979 (sales) *E-mail:* support@merriam-webster.com *Web Site:* www.merriam-webster.com, pg 149

Maitland, Arnaud, Dharma Publishing, 35788 Hauser Bridge Rd, Cazadero, CA 95421 *Tel:* 707-847-3717 *Toll Free Tel:* 800-873-4276 *Fax:* 707-847-3380 *E-mail:* contact@dharmapublishing.com; customerservice@dharmapublishing.com *Web Site:* www.dharmapublishing.com, pg 70

Majczyk, Amy, RAND Corp, 1776 Main St, Santa Monica, CA 90407-2138 *Tel:* 310-393-0411 *Fax:* 310-393-4818 *Web Site:* www.rand.org, pg 193

Majer, Carrie, Perseus Books, 250 W 57 St, 15th fl, New York, NY 10107 *Tel:* 212-340-8100 *Toll Free Tel:* 800-343-4499 (cust serv) *Fax:* 212-340-8105 *Web Site:* www.perseusbooks.com, pg 181

Majuk, Irene, AMACOM Books, 1601 Broadway, New York, NY 10019-7420 *Tel:* 212-586-8100 *Toll Free Tel:* 800-250-5308 (cust serv) *Fax:* 212-903-8083; 518-891-2372 (orders) *E-mail:* pubs_cust_serv@amanet.org *Web Site:* www.amacombooks.org, pg 8

Make, Jonathan, Warren Communications News Inc, 2115 Ward Ct NW, Washington, DC 20037 *Tel:* 202-872-9200 *Toll Free Tel:* 800-771-9202 *Fax:* 202-293-3435; 202-318-8350 *E-mail:* info@warren-news.com; newsroom@warren-news.com *Web Site:* www.warren-news.com, pg 252

Makholm, Lauren, The Art Institute of Chicago, 111 S Michigan Ave, Chicago, IL 60603-6404 *Tel:* 312-443-3600; 312-443-3540 (pubns) *Fax:* 312-443-1334 (pubns) *Web Site:* www.artic.edu; www.artinstituteshop.org, pg 21

Makin, Michael F, Naomi Berber Memorial Award, 301 Brush Creek Rd, Warrendale, PA 15086-7529 *Tel:* 412-741-6860 *Toll Free Tel:* 800-910-4283 *Fax:* 412-741-2311 *E-mail:* printingind@comm.printing.org *Web Site:* www.printing.org/berberaward, pg 631

Makin, Michael F, Education Awards of Excellence, 301 Brush Creek Rd, Warrendale, PA 15086-7529 *Tel:* 412-741-6860 *Toll Free Tel:* 800-910-4283 *Fax:* 412-741-2311 *E-mail:* printingind@comm.printing.org *Web Site:* www.printing.org/educationaward, pg 643

Makin, Michael F, InterTech™ Technology Awards, 301 Brush Creek Rd, Warrendale, PA 15086-7529 *Tel:* 412-741-6860 *Toll Free Tel:* 800-910-4283 *Fax:* 412-741-2311 *E-mail:* intertech@printing.org *Web Site:* www.printing.org/intertechawards, pg 656

Makin, Michael F, Frederick D Kagy Education Award of Excellence, 301 Brush Creek Rd, Warrendale, PA 15086-7529 *Tel:* 412-741-6860 *Toll Free Tel:* 800-910-4283 *Fax:* 412-741-2311 *E-mail:* printingind@comm.printing.org *Web Site:* www.printing.org, pg 658

Makin, Michael F, Orientation to the Graphic Arts, 301 Brush Creek Rd, Warrendale, PA 15086-7529 *Tel:* 412-741-6860 *Toll Free Tel:* 800-910-4283 *Fax:* 412-741-2311 *E-mail:* printingind@comm.printing.org *Web Site:* www.printing.org, pg 613

Makin, Michael F, Premier Print Awards, 301 Brush Creek Rd, Warrendale, PA 15086-7529 *Tel:* 412-741-6860 *Toll Free Tel:* 800-910-4283 *Fax:* 412-741-2311 *E-mail:* printingind@comm.printing.org *Web Site:* www.printing.org/premierprint, pg 682

Makin, Michael F, Printing Industries of America, 301 Brush Creek Rd, Warrendale, PA 15086-7529 *Tel:* 412-741-6860 *Toll Free Tel:* 800-910-4283 *Fax:* 412-741-2311 *E-mail:* printingind@comm.printing.org *Web Site:* www.printing.org, pg 576

Makin, Michael F, Robert F Reed Technology Medal, 301 Brush Creek Rd, Warrendale, PA 15086-7529 *Tel:* 412-741-6860 *Toll Free Tel:* 800-910-4283 *Fax:* 412-741-2311 *E-mail:* printingind@comm.printing.org *Web Site:* www.printing.org/reedaward, pg 684

Makin, Michael F, William D Schaeffer Environmental Award, 301 Brush Creek Rd, Warrendale, PA 15086-7529 *Tel:* 412-741-6860 *Toll Free Tel:* 800-910-4283 *Fax:* 412-741-2311 *E-mail:* printingind@comm.printing.org *Web Site:* www.printing.org/schaefferaward, pg 688

Makk, Catherine, HarperCollins Publishers, 195 Broadway, New York, NY 10007 *Tel:* 212-207-7000 *Fax:* 212-207-7145 *Web Site:* www.harpercollins.com, pg 101

Makras, Penny, HarperCollins General Books Group, 195 Broadway, New York, NY 10007 *Tel:* 212-207-7000 *Web Site:* www.harpercollins.com, pg 101

Malarkey, Sarah, Chronicle Books LLC, 680 Second St, San Francisco, CA 94107 *Tel:* 415-537-4200 *Toll Free Tel:* 800-759-0190 (cust serv) *Fax:* 415-537-4460 *Toll Free Fax:* 800-858-7787 (orders); 800-286-9471 (cust serv) *E-mail:* frontdesk@chroniclebooks.com *Web Site:* www.chroniclebooks.com, pg 55

Malavarca, Bernadette, Backbeat Books, 33 Plymouth St, Suite 302, Montclair, NJ 07042 *Tel:* 973-337-5034 *Toll Free Tel:* 800-637-2852 (Music Dispatch) *Fax:* 973-337-5227 *Web Site:* www.backbeatbooks.com, pg 28

Malaviya, Nihar, Random House Publishing Group, 1745 Broadway, New York, NY 10019 *Toll Free Tel:* 800-200-3552 *Web Site:* atrandom.com, pg 195

Malavolti, Angela, Jungle Wagon Press, 5116 Didier Ave, Rockford, IL 61101 *Tel:* 815-988-9048 *E-mail:* junglewagonpress@gmail.com *Web Site:* www.junglewagonpress.com, pg 124

Malcolm, Ian, Harvard University Press, 79 Garden St, Cambridge, MA 02138-1499 *Tel:* 617-495-2600; 401-531-2800 (intl orders) *Toll Free Tel:* 800-405-1619 (orders) *Fax:* 617-495-5898 (general); 617-496-4677 (edit & rts); 401-531-2801 (intl orders) *Toll Free Fax:* 800-406-9145 (orders) *E-mail:* contact_hup@harvard.edu *Web Site:* www.hup.harvard.edu, pg 103

Malcolm, Reed, University of California Press, 155 Grand Ave, Suite 400, Oakland, CA 94612-3758 *Tel:* 510-883-8232 *Fax:* 510-836-8910 *E-mail:* customerservice@ucpressjournals.com *Web Site:* www.ucpress.edu, pg 240

Malden, Cheryl, The H W Wilson Library Staff Development Grant, 50 E Huron St, Chicago, IL 60611 *Tel:* 312-280-3247 *Toll Free Tel:* 800-545-2433 (ext 3247) *Fax:* 312-944-3897; 312-440-9379 *E-mail:* awards@ala.org *Web Site:* www.ala.org, pg 698

Malden, Cheryl M, Joseph W Lippincott Award, 50 E Huron St, Chicago, IL 60611 *Tel:* 312-280-3247 *Toll Free Tel:* 800-545-2433 (ext 3247) *Fax:* 312-944-3897 *E-mail:* awards@ala.org *Web Site:* www.ala.org, pg 661

Maldonado, Ricardo, Discovery/Boston Review Poetry Contest, 1395 Lexington Ave, New York, NY 10128 *Tel:* 212-415-5760 *E-mail:* unterberg@92y.org *Web Site:* www.92y.org/discovery, pg 641

Malecha, Allison, Grove Atlantic Inc, 154 W 14 St, 12th fl, New York, NY 10011 *Tel:* 212-614-7850 *Toll Free Tel:* 800-521-0178 *Fax:* 212-614-7886 *E-mail:* info@groveatlantic.com; sales@groveatlantic.com; publicity@groveatlantic.com; rights@groveatlantic.com *Web Site:* www.groveatlantic.com, pg 97

Malek, Nancy, Fernwood Publishing, 32 Oceanvista Lane, Black Point, NS B0J 1B0, Canada *Tel:* 902-857-1388 *Fax:* 902-857-1328 *E-mail:* info@fernpub.ca; roseway@fernpub.ca *Web Site:* fernwoodpublishing.ca, pg 456

Malis, Renee, Perseus Books, 250 W 57 St, 15th fl, New York, NY 10107 *Tel:* 212-340-8100 *Toll Free Tel:* 800-343-4499 (cust serv) *Fax:* 212-340-8105 *Web Site:* www.perseusbooks.com, pg 180

Mallardi, Vincent, Printing Brokerage/Buyers Association International (PBBA), 74-5576 Pawai Place, No 599, Kailua Kona, HI 96740 *Tel:* 808-339-0880 *E-mail:* contactus@pbba.org *Web Site:* pbba.org, pg 576

Mallinson, Margot, Harlequin Enterprises Ltd, 225 Duncan Mill Rd, Don Mills, ON M3B 3K9, Canada *Tel:* 416-445-5860 *Toll Free Tel:* 888-432-4879; 800-370-5838 (ebook inquiries) *E-mail:* customerservice@harlequin.com *Web Site:* www.harlequin.com, pg 459

Mallory, Dan, HarperCollins General Books Group, 195 Broadway, New York, NY 10007 *Tel:* 212-207-7000 *Web Site:* www.harpercollins.com, pg 101

Mallory, Erin, Groundwood Books, 128 Sterling Rd, Lower Level, Toronto, ON M6R 2B7, Canada *Tel:* 416-363-4343 *Fax:* 416-363-1017 *E-mail:* genmail@groundwoodbooks.com *Web Site:* www.houseofanansi.com, pg 458

Mallory, Erin, House of Anansi Press Inc, 128 Sterling Rd, Lower Level, Toronto, ON M6R 2B7, Canada *Tel:* 416-363-4343 *Fax:* 416-363-1017 *E-mail:* customerservice@houseofanansi.com *Web Site:* www.houseofanansi.com, pg 460

Malmud, Deborah A, W W Norton & Company Inc, 500 Fifth Ave, New York, NY 10110-0017 *Tel:* 212-354-5500 *Toll Free Tel:* 800-233-4830 (orders & cust serv) *Fax:* 212-869-0856 *Toll Free Fax:* 800-458-6515 *E-mail:* orders@wwnorton.com *Web Site:* books.wwnorton.com, pg 164

Malnor, Bruce, Dawn Publications Inc, 12402 Bitney Springs Rd, Nevada City, CA 95959 *Tel:* 530-274-7775 *Toll Free Tel:* 800-545-7475 *Fax:* 530-274-7778 *E-mail:* nature@dawnpub.com; orders@dawnpub.com *Web Site:* www.dawnpub.com, pg 68

Malone, Robert Jay, Watson Davis & Helen Miles Davis Prize, 440 Geddes Hall, Notre Dame, IN 46556 *Tel:* 574-631-1194 *E-mail:* info@hssonline.org *Web Site:* www.hssonline.org, pg 640

Malone, Robert Jay, Pfizer Award, 440 Geddes Hall, Notre Dame, IN 46556 *Tel:* 574-631-1194 *E-mail:* info@hssonline.org *Web Site:* www.hssonline.org, pg 679

Malone, Robert Jay, Derek Price/Rod Webster Prize Award, 440 Geddes Hall, Notre Dame, IN 46556 *Tel:* 574-631-1194 *E-mail:* info@hssonline.org *Web Site:* www.hssonline.org, pg 682

Malone, Robert Jay, Nathan Reingold Prize, 440 Geddes Hall, Notre Dame, IN 46556 *Tel:* 574-631-1194 *E-mail:* info@hssonline.org *Web Site:* www.hssonline.org, pg 684

Malone, Robert Jay, Margaret W Rossiter History of Women in Science Prize, 440 Geddes Hall, Notre Dame, IN 46556 *Tel:* 574-631-1194 *E-mail:* info@hssonline.org *Web Site:* www.hssonline.org, pg 685

Maloney, Casey, Avery, 375 Hudson St, New York, NY 10014 *Tel:* 212-366-2000 *Fax:* 212-366-2643 *Web Site:* www.penguin.com; www.penguinrandomhouse.com, pg 27

Maloney, Dennis, White Pine Press, PO Box 236, Buffalo, NY 14201 *Tel:* 716-627-4665 *Fax:* 716-627-4665 *E-mail:* wpine@whitepine.org *Web Site:* www.whitepine.org, pg 255

Maloney, Joy, Southern Playwrights Competition, 700 Pelham Rd N, Jacksonville, AL 36265-1602 *Tel:* 256-782-5412 *Web Site:* www.jsu.edu/english/southpla.html, pg 691

Marcus, Barbara, Random House Children's Books, 1745 Broadway, 10th fl, New York, NY 10019 *Tel:* 212-782-9000 *Web Site:* www.randomhousekids.com, pg 194

Marcus, David, Oscar Williams/Gene Derwood Award, 909 Third Ave, New York, NY 10022 *Tel:* 212-686-0010 *Fax:* 212-532-8528 *E-mail:* info@nycommunitytrust.org *Web Site:* www.nycommunitytrust.org, pg 698

Marcus, James, Harper's Magazine Foundation, 666 Broadway, 11th fl, New York, NY 10012 *Tel:* 212-420-5720 *Toll Free Tel:* 800-444-4653 *Fax:* 212-228-5889 *E-mail:* harpers@harpers.org *Web Site:* www.harpers.org, pg 102

Marcus, Jim, Leadership Directories, 1407 Broadway, Suite 318, New York, NY 10018 *Tel:* 212-627-4140 *Toll Free Tel:* 800-627-0311 *Fax:* 212-645-0931 *E-mail:* info@leadershipdirectories.com *Web Site:* www.leadershipdirectories.com, pg 130

Marcus, Karyn, Simon & Schuster, 1230 Avenue of the Americas, New York, NY 10020 *Tel:* 212-698-7000 *Toll Free Tel:* 800-223-2348 (cust serv); 800-223-2336 (orders) *Toll Free Fax:* 800-943-9831 (orders) *Web Site:* www.simonandschuster.com, pg 212

Marcus, Kendra, BookStop Literary Agency LLC, 67 Meadow View Rd, Orinda, CA 94563 *E-mail:* info@bookstopliterary.com *Web Site:* www.bookstopliterary.com, pg 509

Mardak, Keith, Hal Leonard Corp, 7777 W Bluemound Rd, Milwaukee, WI 53213 *Tel:* 414-774-3630 *Fax:* 414-774-3259 *E-mail:* halinfo@halleonard.com; info@halleonard.com *Web Site:* www.halleonard.com, pg 99

Mardon, Austin, Golden Meteorite Press, 11919 82 St NW, Suite 103, Edmonton, AB T5B 2W4, Canada *Tel:* 780-378-0063 *Fax:* 780-378-0063, pg 458

Margolis, Amy, Iowa Summer Writing Festival, 250 Continuing Educ Facility, University of Iowa, Iowa City, IA 52242 *Tel:* 319-335-4160 *E-mail:* iswfestival@uiowa.edu *Web Site:* iowasummerwritingfestival.org, pg 612

Margolis, Wendy, Law School Admission Council, 662 Penn St, Newtown, PA 18940 *Tel:* 215-968-1101 *E-mail:* lsacaccounts@lsac.org *Web Site:* www.lsac.org, pg 130

Marinacci, Barbara, The Bookmill, 501 Palisades Dr, No 315, Pacific Palisades, CA 90272-2848 *Tel:* 310-459-0190 *E-mail:* thebookmill1@verizon.net *Web Site:* www.thebookmill.us, pg 490

Marinaccio, Fran, Woodbine House, 6510 Bells Mill Rd, Bethesda, MD 20817 *Tel:* 301-897-3570 *Toll Free Tel:* 800-843-7323 *Fax:* 301-897-5838 *E-mail:* info@woodbinehouse.com *Web Site:* www.woodbinehouse.com, pg 258

Marinaccio, Fran M, Woodbine House, 6510 Bells Mill Rd, Bethesda, MD 20817 *Tel:* 301-897-3570 *Toll Free Tel:* 800-843-7323 *Fax:* 301-897-5838 *E-mail:* info@woodbinehouse.com *Web Site:* www.woodbinehouse.com, pg 258

Marini, Victoria, Irene Goodman Literary Agency, 27 W 24 St, Suite 700B, New York, NY 10010 *Tel:* 212-604-0330 *E-mail:* queries@irenegoodman.com *Web Site:* www.irenegoodman.com, pg 519

Marino, Krista, Random House Children's Books, 1745 Broadway, 10th fl, New York, NY 10019 *Tel:* 212-782-9000 *Web Site:* www.randomhousekids.com, pg 194

Mark, P J, Janklow & Nesbit Associates, 285 Madison Ave, 21st fl, New York, NY 10017 *Tel:* 212-421-1700 *Fax:* 212-355-1403 *E-mail:* info@janklow.com *Web Site:* www.janklowandnesbit.com, pg 522

Markell, Rick, Gingko Press Inc, 1321 Fifth St, Berkeley, CA 94710 *Tel:* 510-898-1195 *Fax:* 510-898-1196 *E-mail:* books@gingkopress.com *Web Site:* www.gingkopress.com, pg 92

Markham, Judy, Discovery House Publishers, 3000 Kraft Ave SE, Grand Rapids, MI 49512 *Tel:* 616-942-2803 *Toll Free Tel:* 800-653-8333 (cust serv) *E-mail:* support@dhp.org *Web Site:* www.dhp.org, pg 70

Markland, Marcia, St Martin's Press, LLC, 175 Fifth Ave, New York, NY 10010 *Tel:* 646-307-5151 *Web Site:* us.macmillan.com/smp, pg 204

Markoe, Kaija, Rizzoli International Publications Inc, 300 Park Ave S, 4th fl, New York, NY 10010-5399 *Tel:* 212-387-3400 *Toll Free Tel:* 800-522-6657 (orders only) *Fax:* 212-387-3535 *E-mail:* publicity@rizzoliusa.com *Web Site:* www.rizzoliusa.com, pg 199

Markowski, Mike, Markowski International Publishers, One Oakglade Circle, Hummelstown, PA 17036-9525 *Tel:* 717-566-0468 *E-mail:* info@possibilitypress.com *Web Site:* www.possibilitypress.com; www.aeronauticalpublishers.com, pg 142

Marks, Fred, Marquis Who's Who, 100 Connell Dr, Suite 2300, Berkeley Heights, NJ 07922 *Tel:* 908-673-0100 *Toll Free Tel:* 844-394-6946 *Fax:* 908-356-0184 *E-mail:* info@marquisww.com; customerservice@marquisww.com (cust serv, sales) *Web Site:* www.marquiswhoswho.com, pg 142

Marlowe, Emily, Ransom Note Press, 143 E Ridgewood Ave, Box 419, Ridgewood, NJ 07451 *Tel:* 201-835-2790 *E-mail:* editorial@ransomnotepress.com *Web Site:* www.ransomnotepress.com, pg 478

Marmion, Kevin M, William S Hein & Co Inc, 2350 N Forest Rd, Getzville, NY 14068 *Tel:* 716-882-2600 *Toll Free Tel:* 800-828-7571 *Fax:* 716-883-8100 *E-mail:* mail@wshein.com; marketing@wshein.com *Web Site:* www.wshein.com, pg 105

Marmur, Mildred, Mildred Marmur Associates Ltd, 2005 Palmer Ave, PMB 127, Larchmont, NY 10538 *Tel:* 914-834-1170 *Fax:* 914-833-1175 *E-mail:* marmur@westnet.com, pg 527

Marohn, Stephanie, Angel Editing Services, PO Box 752, Mountain Ranch, CA 95246 *Tel:* 209-728-8364 *E-mail:* info@stephaniemarohn.com *Web Site:* www.stephaniemarohn.com, pg 488

Marohn, Stephanie, Elite Books, PO Box 442, Fulton, CA 95439 *Tel:* 707-525-9292 *Toll Free Fax:* 800-330-9798 *E-mail:* support@eftuniverse.com *Web Site:* www.elitebooksonline.com, pg 77

Marohn, Stephanie, Energy Psychology Press, 1490 Mark West Springs Rd, Santa Rosa, CA 95404 *Tel:* 707-525-9292 *Toll Free Fax:* 800-330-9798 *E-mail:* support@eftuniverse.com *Web Site:* www.energypsychologypress.com; www.elitebooksonline.com, pg 79

Marotta, Mary, DK Publishing, 345 Hudson St, 2nd fl, New York, NY 10014 *Tel:* 646-674-4000 *Toll Free Tel:* 877-342-5357 (cust serv); 800-733-3000 *Web Site:* www.dk.com; www.penguin.com, pg 71

Marotte, Liz, Chronicle Books LLC, 680 Second St, San Francisco, CA 94107 *Tel:* 415-537-4200 *Toll Free Tel:* 800-759-0190 (cust serv) *Fax:* 415-537-4460 *Toll Free Fax:* 800-858-7787 (orders); 800-286-9471 (cust serv) *E-mail:* frontdesk@chroniclebooks.com *Web Site:* www.chroniclebooks.com, pg 55

Marr, Jill, Sandra Dijkstra Literary Agency, 1155 Camino del Mar, PMB 515, Del Mar, CA 92014-2605 *E-mail:* queries@dijkstraagency.com *Web Site:* dijkstraagency.com, pg 514

Marrelli, Nancy, Vehicule Press, PO Box 42094, CP Roy, Montreal, QC H2W-2T3, Canada *Tel:* 514-844-6073 *Fax:* 514-844-7543 *E-mail:* vp@vehiculepress.com; admin@vehiculepress.com *Web Site:* www.vehiculepress.com, pg 475

Marriott, Michael, Education Writers Association (EWA), 3516 Connecticut Ave NW, Washington, DC 20008 *Tel:* 202-452-9830 *Fax:* 202-452-9837 *E-mail:* ewa@ewa.org *Web Site:* www.ewa.org, pg 565

Marriott, Michael, Education Writers Association Workshops, 3516 Connecticut Ave NW, Washington, DC 20008 *Tel:* 202-452-9830 *Fax:* 202-452-9837 *E-mail:* ewa@ewa.org *Web Site:* www.ewa.org, pg 610

Marriott, Michael, National Awards for Education Reporting, 3516 Connecticut Ave NW, Washington, DC 20008 *Tel:* 202-452-9830 *Fax:* 202-452-9837 *E-mail:* ewa@ewa.org *Web Site:* www.ewa.org, pg 670

Marrow, Linda, Random House Publishing Group, 1745 Broadway, New York, NY 10019 *Toll Free Tel:* 800-200-3552 *Web Site:* atrandom.com, pg 195

Mars, Laura, Grey House Publishing Inc™, 4919 Rte 22, Amenia, NY 12501 *Tel:* 518-789-8700 *Toll Free Tel:* 800-562-2139 *Fax:* 518-789-0556 *E-mail:* books@greyhouse.com; customerservice@greyhouse.com *Web Site:* www.greyhouse.com, pg 96

Marsal, Jill, Marsal Lyon Literary Agency LLC, 665 San Rodolfo Dr, Suite 124, PMB 121, Solana Beach, CA 92075 *Tel:* 760-814-8507 *Web Site:* www.marsallyonliteraryagency.com, pg 527

Marsh, Amy Rose, Samuel French Inc, 235 Park Ave S, 5th fl, New York, NY 10003 *Tel:* 212-206-8990 *Toll Free Tel:* 866-598-8449 *Fax:* 212-206-1429 *E-mail:* info@samuelfrench.com; publications@samuelfrench.com *Web Site:* www.samuelfrench.com, pg 88

Marsh, Amy Rose, Samuel French Inc, 235 Park Ave S, 5th fl, New York, NY 10003 *Tel:* 212-206-8990 *Toll Free Tel:* 866-598-8449 *Fax:* 212-206-1429 *E-mail:* info@samuelfrench.com *Web Site:* www.samuelfrench.com, pg 518

Marsh, Amy Rose, Annual Off Off Broadway Short Play Festival, 235 Park Ave S, 5th fl, New York, NY 10003 *Tel:* 212-206-8990 *Toll Free Tel:* 866-598-8449 *Fax:* 212-206-1429 *E-mail:* oobfestival@samuelfrench.com *Web Site:* oob.samuelfrench.com; www.samuelfrench.com, pg 675

Marsh, Carole, Gallopade International Inc, 611 Hwy 74 S, Suite 2000, Peachtree City, GA 30269 *Tel:* 770-631-4222 *Toll Free Tel:* 800-536-2GET (536-2438) *Fax:* 770-631-4810 *Toll Free Fax:* 800-871-2979 *E-mail:* customerservice@gallopade.com *Web Site:* www.gallopade.com, pg 90

Marsh, Lyn PhD, Dreaming Publications LLC, 1126 Bel Air Dr, Santa Barbara, CA 93103 *Tel:* 661-776-5152; 310-560-4732 *E-mail:* dreamingpublications@gmail.com *Web Site:* dreamingpublications.com, pg 477

Marsh, Dr Peter, The Mongolia Society Inc, Indiana University, 322 Goodbody Hall, 1011 E Third St, Bloomington, IN 47405-7005 *Tel:* 812-855-4078 *Fax:* 812-855-4078 *E-mail:* monsoc@indiana.edu *Web Site:* www.mongoliasociety.org, pg 153

Marsh, Rebecca, Penguin Books, 375 Hudson St, New York, NY 10014 *Tel:* 212-366-2000 *E-mail:* penguinpublicity@us.penguingroup.com *Web Site:* www.penguinclassics.com; www.penguin.com, pg 177

Marsh, Rebecca, Penguin Group USA, A Penguin Random House Company, 375 Hudson St, New York, NY 10014 *Tel:* 212-366-2000 *Toll Free Tel:* 800-847-5515 (inside sales); 800-631-8571 (cust serv) *Fax:* 212-366-2666; 607-775-4829 (inside sales) *E-mail:* online@us.penguingroup.com *Web Site:* www.penguin.com, pg 177

Marsh, Rebecca, Viking, 375 Hudson St, New York, NY 10014 *Tel:* 212-366-2000 *Fax:* 212-243-6002 *Web Site:* www.penguin.com/publishers/vikingbooks, pg 250

Marsh, Robert, Rowman & Littlefield Publishers Inc, 4501 Forbes Blvd, Suite 200, Lanham, MD 20706 *Tel:* 301-459-3366 *Toll Free Tel:* 800-462-6420 (cust serv) *Fax:* 301-429-5748 *Web Site:* rowman.com, pg 202

Marshall, David, Berrett-Koehler Publishers Inc, 1333 Broadway, Suite 1000, Oakland, CA 94612 *Tel:* 510-817-2277 *Fax:* 510-817-2278 *E-mail:* bkpub@bkpub.com *Web Site:* www.bkconnection.com, pg 34

Marshall, David K, Society for Industrial & Applied Mathematics, 3600 Market St, 6th fl, Philadelphia, PA 19104-2688 *Tel:* 215-382-9800 *Toll Free Tel:* 800-447-7426 *Fax:* 215-386-7999 *E-mail:* siambooks@siam.org *Web Site:* www.siam.org, pg 216

Marshall, Elyse, Penguin Young Readers Group, 345 Hudson St, New York, NY 10014 *Tel:* 212-366-2000; 212-414-3553 *Fax:* 212-414-3340 *Web Site:* www.penguin.com/children, pg 179

Marshall, Evan S, The Evan Marshall Agency, One Pacio Ct, Roseland, NJ 07068-1121 *Tel:* 973-287-6216 *Fax:* 973-488-7910 *Web Site:* www.evanmarshallagency.com, pg 528

Marshall, Jen, Aevitas Creative Management, 19 W 21 St, Suite 501, New York, NY 10010 *Tel:* 212-765-6900 *Web Site:* aevitascreative.com, pg 506

Marshall, Julie, Island Press, 2000 "M" St NW, Suite 650, Washington, DC 20036 *Tel:* 202-232-7933 *Toll Free Tel:* 800-828-1302 *Fax:* 202-234-1328 *E-mail:* info@islandpress.org *Web Site:* www.islandpress.org, pg 121

Marshall, Kate, University of California Press, 155 Grand Ave, Suite 400, Oakland, CA 94612-3758 *Tel:* 510-883-8232 *Fax:* 510-836-8910 *E-mail:* customerservice@ucpressjournals.com *Web Site:* www.ucpress.edu, pg 240

Marshall, Len, HarperCollins General Books Group, 195 Broadway, New York, NY 10007 *Tel:* 212-207-7000 *Web Site:* www.harpercollins.com, pg 101

Marshall, Thomas, Random House Children's Books, 1745 Broadway, 10th fl, New York, NY 10019 *Tel:* 212-782-9000 *Web Site:* www.randomhousekids.com, pg 194

Marshall, Tim, Thomas Nelson, 501 Nelson Place, Nashville, TN 37214 *Tel:* 615-889-9000 *Toll Free Tel:* 800-251-4000 *Fax:* 615-902-1548 *Web Site:* www.thomasnelson.com, pg 231

Marshall, Tim, Zondervan, 3900 Sparks Dr, Grand Rapids, MI 49546 *Tel:* 616-698-6900 *Toll Free Tel:* 800-226-1122; 800-727-1309 (retail orders) *Fax:* 616-698-3350 *Toll Free Fax:* 800-698-3256 (retail orders) *E-mail:* zinfo@zondervan.com *Web Site:* www.zondervan.com, pg 263

Marsham, Nachie, Disney Press, 1101 Flower St, Glendale, CA 91201 *Web Site:* books.disney.com, pg 70

Marson, Amy, C&T Publishing Inc, 1651 Challenge Dr, Concord, CA 94520-5206 *Tel:* 925-677-0377 *Toll Free Tel:* 800-284-1114 *Fax:* 925-677-0373 *E-mail:* support@ctpub.com *Web Site:* www.ctpub.com, pg 47

Martel, Manon, Les Editions Un Monde Different, 3905 Isabelle, bureau 101, Brossard, QC J4Y 2R2, Canada *Tel:* 450-656-2660 *Toll Free Tel:* 800-443-2582 *Fax:* 450-659-9328 *E-mail:* info@umd.ca *Web Site:* www.umd.ca, pg 455

Martell, Alice Fried, The Martell Agency, 1350 Avenue of the Americas, Suite 1205, New York, NY 10019 *Tel:* 212-317-2672 *Web Site:* www.themartellagency.com, pg 528

Martell, Joy, Wisconsin Department of Public Instruction, 125 S Webster St, Madison, WI 53703 *Tel:* 608-266-2188 *Toll Free Tel:* 800-441-4563 *Fax:* 608-267-9110 *Web Site:* pubsales.dpi.wi.gov, pg 257

Martens, Julie S, Human Kinetics Inc, 1607 N Market St, Champaign, IL 61820 *Tel:* 217-351-5076 *Toll Free Tel:* 800-747-4457 *Fax:* 217-351-1549 (orders/cust serv) *E-mail:* info@hkusa.com *Web Site:* www.humankinetics.com, pg 112

Martens, Patricia, Boys Town Press, 13603 Flanagan Blvd, 2nd fl, Boys Town, NE 68010 *Tel:* 402-498-1320 *Toll Free Tel:* 800-282-6657 *Fax:* 402-498-1310 *E-mail:* btpress@boystown.org *Web Site:* www.boystownpress.org, pg 41

Martens, Rainer, Human Kinetics Inc, 1607 N Market St, Champaign, IL 61820 *Tel:* 217-351-5076 *Toll Free Tel:* 800-747-4457 *Fax:* 217-351-1549 (orders/cust serv) *E-mail:* info@hkusa.com *Web Site:* www.humankinetics.com, pg 112

Martenz, Arden, MAR*CO Products Inc, PO Box 686, Hatfield, PA 19440 *Tel:* 215-956-0313 *Toll Free Tel:* 800-448-2197 *Fax:* 215-956-9041 *E-mail:* help@marcoproducts.com *Web Site:* www.marcoproducts.com, pg 141

Marthe, L, Laurier Books Ltd, PO Box 8493, Ottawa, ON K1G 3H9, Canada *Tel:* 613-738-2163 *Toll Free Fax:* 855-736-9160 *E-mail:* laurierbooks@yahoo.com, pg 462

Martin, Andrew, St Martin's Press, LLC, 175 Fifth Ave, New York, NY 10010 *Tel:* 646-307-5151 *Web Site:* us.macmillan.com/smp, pg 204

Martin, Barbara, Southern Illinois University Press, 1915 University Press Dr, SIUC Mail Code 6806, Carbondale, IL 62901-4323 *Tel:* 618-453-2281 *Fax:* 618-453-1221 *E-mail:* custserv@press.uchicago.edu; rights@siu.edu *Web Site:* www.siupress.com, pg 218

Martin, Betsy, Skinner House Books, c/o Unitarian Universalist Assn, 24 Farnsworth St, Boston, MA 02210-1409 *Tel:* 617-742-2100 *Fax:* 617-948-6466 *E-mail:* skinnerhouse@uua.org *Web Site:* www.skinnerhouse.org, pg 214

Martin, Brad, Doubleday Canada, 320 Front St W, Suite 1400, Toronto, ON M5V 3B6, Canada *Tel:* 416-364-4449 *Fax:* 416-598-7764 *Web Site:* www.penguinrandomhouse.ca, pg 452

Martin, Brad, Knopf Canada, 320 Front St W, Suite 1400, Toronto, ON M5V 3B6, Canada *Tel:* 416-364-4449 *Toll Free Tel:* 888-523-9292 *Fax:* 416-598-7764 *Web Site:* www.penguinrandomhouse.ca, pg 462

Martin, Brad, Penguin Random House Canada, 320 Front St W, Suite 1400, Toronto, ON M5V 3B6, Canada *Tel:* 416-364-4449 *Toll Free Tel:* 888-523-9292 (cust serv) *Fax:* 416-598-7764 *Web Site:* www.penguinrandomhouse.ca, pg 467

Martin, Brad, Seal Books, 320 Front St W, Suite 1400, Toronto, ON M5V 3B6, Canada *Tel:* 416-364-4449 *Toll Free Tel:* 888-523-9292 (order desk) *Fax:* 416-598-7764 *Web Site:* www.penguinrandomhouse.ca, pg 470

Martin, Cynthia Parkinson, Research Press, 2612 N Mattis Ave, Champaign, IL 61822 *Tel:* 217-352-3273 *Toll Free Tel:* 800-519-2707 *Fax:* 217-352-1221 *E-mail:* rp@researchpress.com; orders@researchpress.com *Web Site:* www.researchpress.com, pg 198

Martin, Denny, Piano Press, 1425 Ocean Ave, Suite 5, Del Mar, CA 92014 *Tel:* 619-884-1401 *Fax:* 858-755-1104 *E-mail:* pianopress@pianopress.com *Web Site:* www.pianopress.com, pg 182

Martin, Emily, Harlequin Enterprises Ltd, 225 Duncan Mill Rd, Don Mills, ON M3B 3K9, Canada *Tel:* 416-445-5860 *Toll Free Tel:* 888-432-4879; 800-370-5838 (ebook inquiries) *E-mail:* customerservice@harlequin.com *Web Site:* www.harlequin.com, pg 459

Martin, Howard, HeartMath LLC, 14700 W Park Ave, Boulder Creek, CA 95006 *Tel:* 831-338-8700 *Toll Free Tel:* 800-450-9111 *Fax:* 831-338-9861 *E-mail:* info@heartmath.com; inquiry@heartmath.com *Web Site:* www.heartmath.com, pg 105

Martin, James, Oxford University Press USA, 198 Madison Ave, New York, NY 10016 *Tel:* 212-726-6000 *Toll Free Tel:* 800-451-7556 (orders); 800-445-9714 (cust serv) *Fax:* 919-677-1303 *E-mail:* custserv.us@oup.com *Web Site:* www.oup.com/us, pg 171

Martin, Jehu, Money Market Directories, 401 E Market St, Charlottesville, VA 22902 *Tel:* 434-977-1450 *Toll Free Tel:* 800-446-2810 *Fax:* 434-979-9962 *E-mail:* mmdsales@spcapitaliq.com *Web Site:* www.mmdwebaccess.com, pg 153

Martin, Jennie Taylor, ARE Press, 215 67 St, Virginia Beach, VA 23451 *Tel:* 757-428-3588 *Toll Free Tel:* 800-333-4499 *Fax:* 757-491-0689 *Web Site:* www.edgarcayce.org, pg 20

Martin, John, Rod & Staff Publishers Inc, Hwy 172, Crockett, KY 41413 *Tel:* 606-522-4348 *Fax:* 606-522-4896 *Toll Free Fax:* 800-643-1244 (US orders), pg 200

Martin, Jynne Dilling, Riverhead Books, 375 Hudson St, New York, NY 10014 *Tel:* 212-366-2000 *Web Site:* www.penguin.com/publishers/riverhead, pg 199

Martin, Katherine, Oxford University Press USA, 198 Madison Ave, New York, NY 10016 *Tel:* 212-726-6000 *Toll Free Tel:* 800-451-7556 (orders); 800-445-9714 (cust serv) *Fax:* 919-677-1303 *E-mail:* custserv.us@oup.com *Web Site:* www.oup.com/us, pg 171

Martin, Lesley, Aperture Books, 547 W 27 St, 4th fl, New York, NY 10001 *Tel:* 212-505-5555 *Toll Free Tel:* 800-929-2323 *Fax:* 212-979-7759 *E-mail:* info@aperture.org *Web Site:* www.aperture.org, pg 18

Martin, Lisa Ann PhD, Martin-McLean Literary Associates LLC, 5023 W 120 Ave, Suite 228, Broomfield, CO 80020 *Tel:* 303-465-2056 *Fax:* 303-465-2057 *E-mail:* martinmcleanlit@aol.com *Web Site:* www.martinmcleanlit.com; www.mcleanlit.com, pg 528

Martin, Marianne K, Bywater Books, PO Box 3671, Ann Arbor, MI 48106-3671 *Tel:* 734-662-8815 *Web Site:* bywaterbooks.com, pg 46

Martin, Matthew, Penguin Random House Inc, 1745 Broadway, New York, NY 10019 *Tel:* 212-782-9000 *Toll Free Tel:* 800-726-0600 *Web Site:* www.penguinrandomhouse.com, pg 178

Martin, Dr Michael, University of Louisiana at Lafayette Press, PO Box 43558, Lafayette, LA 70504-3558 *Tel:* 337-482-6027 *Fax:* 337-482-6028 *E-mail:* ulpress@louisiana.edu *Web Site:* www.ulpress.org, pg 242

Martin, Michele, Gallery Books, 1230 Avenue of the Americas, New York, NY 10020 *Toll Free Tel:* 800-456-6798 *Fax:* 212-698-7284 *E-mail:* consumer.customerservice@simonandschuster.com *Web Site:* www.simonsays.com, pg 90

Martin, Patrick, Prometheus Books, 59 John Glenn Dr, Amherst, NY 14228-2119 *Tel:* 716-691-0133 *Fax:* 716-691-0137 *E-mail:* marketing@prometheusbooks.com; editorial@prometheusbooks.com; rights@prometheusmail.com *Web Site:* www.prometheusbooks.com, pg 190

Martin, Philip, Crickhollow Books, 3147 S Pennsylvania Ave, Milwaukee, WI 53207 *Tel:* 414-294-4319 *E-mail:* info@crickhollowbooks.com *Web Site:* www.crickhollowbooks.com, pg 64

Martin, Rux, Houghton Mifflin Harcourt Trade & Reference Division, 125 High St, Boston, MA 02110 *Tel:* 617-351-5000 *Toll Free Tel:* 800-225-3362 *Web Site:* www.hmhco.com, pg 111

Martin, Sharlene, Martin Literary Management, 15601 32 Ave SE, Mill Creek, WA 98012 *Tel:* 206-466-1773 (no queries) *Fax:* 206-466-1774 *Web Site:* www.martinliterarymanagement.com, pg 528

Martin, Wayne, North Carolina Arts Council Writers Fellowships, 109 E Jones St, Raleigh, NC 27601 *Tel:* 919-807-6500 *Fax:* 919-807-6532 *E-mail:* ncarts@ncdcr.gov *Web Site:* www.ncarts.org, pg 674

Martin-Retortillo, Teresa, McGraw-Hill Education, 2 Penn Plaza, New York, NY 10121-2298 *Tel:* 212-904-2000 *E-mail:* customer.service@mheducation.com; international_cs@mheducation.com *Web Site:* www.mheducation.com, pg 145

Martinek, Jason, William Morris Society in the United States Fellowships, PO Box 53263, Washington, DC 20009 *E-mail:* us@morrissociety.org *Web Site:* www.morrissociety.org, pg 669

Martinelli, Theresa, Wayne State University Press, Leonard N Simons Bldg, 4809 Woodward Ave, Detroit, MI 48201-1309 *Tel:* 313-577-6120 *Toll Free Tel:* 800-978-7323 *Fax:* 313-577-6131 *E-mail:* bookorders@wayne.edu *Web Site:* www.wsupress.wayne.edu, pg 253

Martinet, Caroline L, J Anthony Lukas Book Prize, 2950 Broadway, New York, NY 10027 *Tel:* 212-854-6468 *Web Site:* www.journalism.columbia.edu, pg 663

Martinet, Caroline L, J Anthony Lukas Work-in-Progress Award, 2950 Broadway, New York, NY 10027 *Tel:* 212-854-6468 *Web Site:* www.journalism.columbia.edu, pg 663

Martinet, Caroline L, Mark Lynton History Prize, 2950 Broadway, New York, NY 10027 *Tel:* 212-854-6468 *Web Site:* www.journalism.columbia.edu, pg 663

Martinez, Amanda, Book Sales, 142 W 36 St, 4th fl, New York, NY 10018 *Tel:* 212-779-4972; 212-779-4971 *Fax:* 212-779-6058 *E-mail:* booksales@quarto.com; customerservice@quarto.com *Web Site:* www.quartoknows.com, pg 40

Martinez, Claudia, Anchor Books, c/o Penguin Random House Inc, 1745 Broadway, New York, NY 10019 *Tel:* 212-572-2420 *E-mail:* vintageanchorpublicity@randomhouse.com *Web Site:* knopfdoubleday.com/imprint/anchor, pg 16

Martinez, Claudia, Vintage Books, c/o Penguin Random House Inc, 1745 Broadway, New York, NY 10019 *Tel:* 212-572-2420 *E-mail:* vintageanchorpublicity@randomhouse.com *Web Site:* knopfdoubleday.com/imprint/vintage, pg 251

Martinez, Lulu, Kensington Publishing Corp, 119 W 40 St, New York, NY 10018 *Tel:* 212-407-1500 *Toll Free Tel:* 800-221-2647 *Fax:* 212-935-0699 *Web Site:* www.kensingtonbooks.com, pg 125

Martinez, Michelle, Tiger Tales, 5 River Rd, Suite 128, Wilton, CT 06897-4069 *Tel:* 920-387-2333 *Fax:* 920-387-9994 *Web Site:* www.tigertalesbooks.com, pg 232

Martinez, Rudy, Soho Press Inc, 853 Broadway, New York, NY 10003 *Tel:* 212-260-1900 *E-mail:* soho@sohopress.com; publicity@sohopress.com; contact@sohopress.com *Web Site:* www.sohopress.com, pg 216

Martino, Alfred C, Listen & Live Audio Inc, 1700 Manhattan Ave, Union City, NJ 07087 *Tel:* 201-558-9000 *Toll Free Tel:* 800-653-9400 (orders) *Fax:* 201-558-9800 *Web Site:* www.listenandlive.com, pg 135

Martino, John B, The Catholic University of America Press, 240 Leahy Hall, 620 Michigan Ave NE, Washington, DC 20064 *Tel:* 202-319-5052 *Toll Free Tel:* 800-537-5487 (orders only) *Fax:* 202-319-4985 *E-mail:* cua-press@cua.edu *Web Site:* cuapress.cua.edu, pg 49

Martins, Tim H, Barbour Publishing Inc, 1810 Barbour Dr, Uhrichsville, OH 44683 *Tel:* 740-922-6045 *Fax:* 740-922-5948 *E-mail:* info@barbourbooks.com *Web Site:* www.barbourbooks.com, pg 29

Martone, Michael, University of Alabama Program in Creative Writing, PO Box 870244, Tuscaloosa, AL 35487-0244 *Tel:* 205-348-5065 *Fax:* 205-348-1388 *E-mail:* english@ua.edu *Web Site:* www.as.ua.edu/english, pg 622

Martone, Robert, F A Davis Co, 1915 Arch St, Philadelphia, PA 19103 *Tel:* 215-568-2270; 215-440-3001 *Toll Free Tel:* 800-523-4049 *Fax:* 215-568-5065; 215-440-3016 *E-mail:* info@fadavis.com; orders@fadavis.com *Web Site:* www.fadavis.com, pg 68

Martorelli, Nick, Penguin Random House Audio Publishing, 1745 Broadway, New York, NY 10019 *E-mail:* audio@penguinrandomhouse.com *Web Site:* www.penguinrandomhouseaudio.com, pg 178

Martynick, Christine, SLACK® Incorporated, A Wyanoke Group Company, 6900 Grove Rd, Thorofare, NJ 08086-9447 *Tel:* 856-848-1000 *Toll Free Tel:* 800-257-8290 *Fax:* 856-848-6091 *E-mail:* sales@slackinc.com; editor@slackinc.com; customerservice@slackinc.com *Web Site:* www.healio.com/books, pg 215

Marun, Serdar, Autism Asperger Publishing Co, 11209 Strang Line Rd, Lenexa, KS 66215 *Tel:* 913-897-1004 *Toll Free Tel:* 877-277-8254 *Fax:* 913-681-9473 *E-mail:* info@aapcpublishing.net *Web Site:* www.aapcpublishing.net, pg 26

Maruno, Jennifer, Canadian Society of Children's Authors, Illustrators & Performers (CANSCAIP), 720 Bathurst St, Suite 503, Toronto, ON M5S 2R4, Canada *Tel:* 416-515-1559 *E-mail:* office@canscaip.org *Web Site:* www.canscaip.org, pg 562

Marven, Shannon, Dupree, Miller & Associates Inc, 100 Highland Park Village, Suite 350, Dallas, TX 75205 *Tel:* 214-559-2665 *Fax:* 214-559-7243 *E-mail:* editorial@dupreemiller.com *Web Site:* www.dupreemiller.com, pg 515

Marvin, Sally, Random House Publishing Group, 1745 Broadway, New York, NY 10019 *Toll Free Tel:* 800-200-3552 *Web Site:* atrandom.com, pg 195

Marwell, Josh, HarperCollins Publishers, 195 Broadway, New York, NY 10007 *Tel:* 212-207-7000 *Fax:* 212-207-7145 *Web Site:* www.harpercollins.com, pg 101

Marzano, Vincent, John Wiley & Sons Inc, 111 River St, Hoboken, NJ 07030-5774 *Tel:* 201-748-6000 *Toll Free Tel:* 800-225-5945 (cust serv) *Fax:* 201-748-6088 *E-mail:* info@wiley.com *Web Site:* www.wiley.com, pg 256

Masaryk, Hanna, Sanford J Greenburger Associates Inc, 55 Fifth Ave, New York, NY 10003 *Tel:* 212-206-5600 *Fax:* 212-463-8718 *Web Site:* greenburger.com; www.sjga.com, pg 520

Maschino, Matt, Regnery Publishing, 300 New Jersey Ave NW, Washington, DC 20001 *Tel:* 202-216-0600 *Toll Free Tel:* 888-219-4747 *Fax:* 202-393-1795 *Web Site:* www.regnery.com, pg 198

Masciovecchio, Alison, Random House Publishing Group, 1745 Broadway, New York, NY 10019 *Toll Free Tel:* 800-200-3552 *Web Site:* atrandom.com, pg 195

Maselli, Elisabeth, Rutgers University Press, 106 Somerset St, 3rd fl, New Brunswick, NJ 08901 *Tel:* 848-445-7762 *Toll Free Tel:* 800-848-6224 (orders only) *Fax:* 732-745-4935 (acqs, edit, mktg, perms & prodn) *Toll Free Fax:* 800-272-6817 (fulfillment) *Web Site:* rutgerspress.rutgers.edu, pg 202

Maslin, Ella, Random House Publishing Group, 1745 Broadway, New York, NY 10019 *Toll Free Tel:* 800-200-3552 *Web Site:* atrandom.com, pg 195

Maslow, Zoe, Doubleday Canada, 320 Front St W, Suite 1400, Toronto, ON M5V 3B6, Canada *Tel:* 416-364-4449 *Fax:* 416-598-7764 *Web Site:* www.penguinrandomhouse.ca, pg 452

Masnik, Julia, Watkins/Loomis Agency Inc, PO Box 20925, New York, NY 10025 *Tel:* 212-532-0080 *Fax:* 646-383-2449 *E-mail:* assistant@watkinsloomis.com *Web Site:* www.watkinsloomis.com, pg 541

Mason, Alane, W W Norton & Company Inc, 500 Fifth Ave, New York, NY 10110-0017 *Tel:* 212-354-5500 *Toll Free Tel:* 800-233-4830 (orders & cust serv) *Fax:* 212-869-0856 *Toll Free Fax:* 800-458-6515 *E-mail:* orders@wwnorton.com *Web Site:* books.wwnorton.com, pg 164

Mason, Jonathan, Don Buchwald & Associates Inc, 10 E 44 St, New York, NY 10017 *Tel:* 212-867-1200 *Fax:* 212-867-2434 *E-mail:* info@buchwald.com *Web Site:* www.buchwald.com, pg 510

Mason, Linda, Publishers Information Bureau (PIB)®, 757 Third Ave, 11th fl, New York, NY 10017 *Tel:* 212-872-3745; 212-872-3700 (MPA) *E-mail:* infocenter@magazine.org *Web Site:* www.magazine.org, pg 577

Mason, Lizzy, Bloomsbury Publishing Inc, 1385 Broadway, 5th fl, New York, NY 10018 *Tel:* 212-419-5300 *E-mail:* marketingusa@bloomsbury.com; adultpublicityusa@bloomsbury.com; askacademic@bloomsbury.com *Web Site:* www.bloomsbury.com, pg 37

Mason, Rena, Bram Stoker Awards®, c/o Horror Writers Association, PO Box 56687, Sherman Oaks, CA 91413 *Tel:* 818-220-3965 *E-mail:* hwa@horror.org *Web Site:* horror.org/awards/stokers.htm, pg 692

Mason, Val, The BC Book Prizes, 207 W Hastings St, Suite 901, Vancouver, BC V6B 1H7, Canada *Fax:* 604-687-2435 *E-mail:* info@bcbookprizes.ca *Web Site:* www.bcbookprizes.ca, pg 630

Masquelier, Chelsea, Chronicle Books LLC, 680 Second St, San Francisco, CA 94107 *Tel:* 415-537-4200 *Toll Free Tel:* 800-759-0190 (cust serv) *Fax:* 415-537-4460 *Toll Free Fax:* 800-858-7787 (orders); 800-286-9471 (cust serv) *E-mail:* frontdesk@chroniclebooks.com *Web Site:* www.chroniclebooks.com, pg 55

Masry, Susan, Rizzoli International Publications Inc, 300 Park Ave S, 4th fl, New York, NY 10010-5399 *Tel:* 212-387-3400 *Toll Free Tel:* 800-522-6657 (orders only) *Fax:* 212-387-3535 *E-mail:* publicity@rizzoliusa.com *Web Site:* www.rizzoliusa.com, pg 199

Massey, Jeanne, Adler Publishing Inc, 46937 Monarch Dr, Parker, CO 80138 *Tel:* 303-660-2158 *Toll Free Tel:* 800-660-5107 (sales & orders) *E-mail:* customerservice@adlerpublishing.com; orders@4wdbooks.com *Web Site:* www.adlerpublishing.com, pg 4

Massey, Peter, Adler Publishing Inc, 46937 Monarch Dr, Parker, CO 80138 *Tel:* 303-660-2158 *Toll Free Tel:* 800-660-5107 (sales & orders) *E-mail:* customerservice@adlerpublishing.com; orders@4wdbooks.com *Web Site:* www.adlerpublishing.com, pg 4

Massicotte, Celine, Groupe Sogides Inc, 955 rue Amherst, Montreal, QC H2L 3K4, Canada *Tel:* 514-523-1182 *Fax:* 514-597-0370 *Web Site:* www.sogides.com, pg 458

Massoud, Alia, Perseus Books, 250 W 57 St, 15th fl, New York, NY 10107 *Tel:* 212-340-8100 *Toll Free Tel:* 800-343-4499 (cust serv) *Fax:* 212-340-8105 *Web Site:* www.perseusbooks.com, pg 181

Massov, Olga, Phaidon, 65 Bleecker St, 8th fl, New York, NY 10012 *Tel:* 212-652-5400 *Toll Free Tel:* 800-759-0190 (cust serv) *Fax:* 212-652-5410 *Toll Free Fax:* 800-286-9471 (cust serv) *E-mail:* ussales@phaidon.com *Web Site:* www.phaidon.com, pg 182

Massy, Julie, La Courte Echelle, 4388, rue Saint-Denis, Suite 315, Montreal, QC H2J 2L1, Canada *Tel:* 514-312-6950 *E-mail:* info@courteechelle.com *Web Site:* courteechelle.groupecourteechelle.com, pg 451

Mastandrea, Damon, BioTechniques Books, 52 Vanderbilt Ave, 11th fl, New York, NY 10017 *Tel:* 212-520-2777 *Fax:* 212-520-2705 *Web Site:* www.biotechniques.com, pg 35

Masterson, Amanda, Bureau of Economic Geology, University of Texas at Austin, 10100 Burnet Rd, Bldg 130, Austin, TX 78758 *Tel:* 512-471-1534 *Fax:* 512-471-0140 *E-mail:* pubsales@beg.utexas.edu *Web Site:* www.beg.utexas.edu, pg 45

Mastrolia, Barbara, Catholic Book Awards, 205 W Monroe St, Suite 470, Chicago, IL 60606 *Tel:* 312-380-6789 *Fax:* 312-361-0256 *E-mail:* cathjourn@catholicpress.org *Web Site:* www.catholicpress.org, pg 636

Mastrolia, Barbara, Catholic Press Awards, 205 W Monroe St, Suite 470, Chicago, IL 60606 *Tel:* 312-380-6789 *Fax:* 312-361-0256 *E-mail:* cathjourn@catholicpress.org *Web Site:* www.catholicpress.org, pg 636

Matarazzo, James, The H W Wilson Foundation, 420 Lexington Ave, Suite 2450, New York, NY 10170 *Tel:* 212-972-6490 *Web Site:* www.thwwf.org, pg 583

Matejovsky, Char, Polebridge Press, PO Box 346, Farmington, MN 55024 *Tel:* 651-200-2372 *E-mail:* orders@westarinstitute.org *Web Site:* www.westarinstitute.org, pg 185

Matheson, Ed, Ampersand Group, 12 Morenz Terr, Kanata, ON K2K 3G9, Canada *Tel:* 613-435-5066, pg 487

Matheson, Laurie, University of Illinois Press, 1325 S Oak St, MC-566, Champaign, IL 61820-6903 *Tel:* 217-333-0950 *Fax:* 217-244-8082 *E-mail:* uipress@uillinois.edu; journals@uillinois.edu *Web Site:* www.press.uillinois.edu, pg 241

Mathews, Lisa Vitarisi, Evan-Moor Educational Publishers, 18 Lower Ragsdale Dr, Monterey, CA 93940-5746 *Tel:* 831-649-5901 *Toll Free Tel:* 800-777-4362 (orders) *Fax:* 831-649-6256 *Toll Free Fax:* 800-777-4332 (orders) *E-mail:* sales@evan-moor.com; marketing@evan-moor.com *Web Site:* www.evan-moor.com, pg 80

Mathews, Richard, The Danahy Fiction Prize, University of Tampa Press, 401 W Kennedy Blvd, Tampa, FL 33606 *Tel:* 813-253-6266 *E-mail:* utpress@ut.edu *Web Site:* tampareview.ut.edu, pg 640

Mathews, Richard, The Tampa Review Prize for Poetry, University of Tampa Press, 401 W Kennedy Blvd, Tampa, FL 33606 *Tel:* 813-253-6266 *E-mail:* utpress@ut.edu *Web Site:* tampareview.ut.edu, pg 693

Mathieson, Tim, Faith & Fellowship Publishing, 1020 W Alcott Ave, Fergus Falls, MN 56537 *Tel:* 218-736-7357 *Toll Free Tel:* 800-332-9232 *E-mail:* clb@clba.org *Web Site:* www.clba.org, pg 82

Mathieu, James R PhD, University of Pennsylvania Museum of Archaeology & Anthropology, 3260 South St, Philadelphia, PA 19104-6324 *Tel:* 215-898-6322; 215-898-4119 *E-mail:* publications@pennmuseum.org; info@pennmuseum.org *Web Site:* www.penn.museum, pg 244

Mathis, Catherine J, McGraw-Hill Education, 2 Penn Plaza, New York, NY 10121-2298 *Tel:* 212-904-2000 *E-mail:* customer.service@mheducation.com; international_cs@mheducation.com *Web Site:* www.mheducation.com, pg 145

Mathoslah, Donna, Romance Writers of America®, 14615 Benfer Rd, Houston, TX 77069 *Tel:* 832-717-5200 *Fax:* 832-717-5201 *E-mail:* info@rwa.org *Web Site:* www.rwa.org, pg 577

Mativat, Genevieve, Les Editions Pierre Tisseyre, 155, rue Maurice, Rosemere, QC J7A 2S8, Canada *Tel:* 514-335-0777 *Fax:* 514-335-6723 *E-mail:* info@edtisseyre.ca *Web Site:* www.tisseyre.ca, pg 455

Matloff, Robert, The Guilford Press, 370 Seventh Ave, Suite 1200, New York, NY 10001-1020 *Tel:* 212-431-9800 *Toll Free Tel:* 800-365-7006 *Fax:* 212-966-6708 *E-mail:* info@guilford.com *Web Site:* www.guilford.com, pg 97

Matney, Mallory, Random House Children's Books, 1745 Broadway, 10th fl, New York, NY 10019 *Tel:* 212-782-9000 *Web Site:* www.randomhousekids.com, pg 194

Matson, Katinka, Brockman Inc, 260 Fifth Ave, 10th fl, New York, NY 10001 *Tel:* 212-935-8900 *Fax:* 212-935-5535 *E-mail:* rights@brockman.com *Web Site:* www.brockman.com, pg 510

Matson, Peter, Sterling Lord Literistic Inc, 115 Broadway, Suite 1602, New York, NY 10006 *Tel:* 212-780-6050 *Fax:* 212-780-6095 *E-mail:* info@sll.com *Web Site:* www.sll.com, pg 537

Matsuda, Hisae, Parallax Press, 2236-B Sixth St, Berkeley, CA 94710 *Tel:* 510-540-6411 *Toll Free Tel:* 800-863-5290 (orders) *Fax:* 510-981-1157 *Web Site:* www.parallax.org, pg 174

Matsui, Victory, Random House Publishing Group, 1745 Broadway, New York, NY 10019 *Toll Free Tel:* 800-200-3552 *Web Site:* atrandom.com, pg 195

Matthews, Claire, The Pacific Spirit Poetry Prize, University of British Columbia, Buch E462, 1866 Main Mall, Vancouver, BC V6T 1Z1, Canada *Tel:* 778-822-2514 *Fax:* 778-822-3616 *E-mail:* prismwritingcontest@gmail.com *Web Site:* www.prismmagazine.ca, pg 676

Matthews, Claire, PRISM international Literary Non-Fiction Contest, University of British Columbia, Buch E462, 1866 Main Mall, Vancouver, BC V6T 1Z1, Canada *Tel:* 778-822-2514 *Fax:* 778-822-3616 *E-mail:* prismwritingcontest@gmail.com *Web Site:* www.prismmagazine.ca, pg 682

Matthews, Claire, The Jacob Zilber Prize for Short Fiction, University of British Columbia, Buch E462, 1866 Main Mall, Vancouver, BC V6T 1Z1, Canada *Tel:* 778-822-2514 *Fax:* 778-822-3616 *E-mail:* prismwritingcontest@gmail.com *Web Site:* www.prismmagazine.ca, pg 701

Matthews, Darryl R Sr, National Association of Black Journalists (NABJ), 1100 Knight Hall, Suite 3100, College Park, MD 20742 *Tel:* 301-405-0248 *Fax:* 301-314-1714 *E-mail:* nabj@nabj.org *Web Site:* www.nabj.org, pg 570

Matthews, Jermey, The MIT Press, One Rogers St, Cambridge, MA 02142 *Tel:* 617-253-5255 *Toll Free Tel:* 800-207-8354 (orders) *Fax:* 617-258-6779; 617-577-1545 (orders) *Web Site:* mitpress.mit.edu, pg 152

Matthews, Joe, Chicago Review Press, 814 N Franklin St, Chicago, IL 60610 *Tel:* 312-337-0747 *Toll Free Tel:* 800-888-4741 *Fax:* 312-337-5110 *E-mail:* frontdesk@chicagoreviewpress.com *Web Site:* www.chicagoreviewpress.com, pg 54

Matthews, Katherine, Lucky Marble Books, 2671 Bristol Rd, Columbus, OH 43221 *Tel:* 614-264-5588 *E-mail:* sales@pagespringpublishing.com *Web Site:* www.luckymarblebooks.com, pg 139

Mattison, Celia, Milkweed Editions, 1011 Washington Ave S, Suite 300, Minneapolis, MN 55415-1246 *Tel:* 612-332-3192 *Toll Free Tel:* 800-520-6455 *Fax:* 612-215-2550 *Web Site:* milkweed.org, pg 151

Mattson, Stewart, Business Expert Press, 222 E 46 St, New York, NY 10017-2906 *Tel:* 630-207-5927 *E-mail:* charlene.kronstadt@businessexpertpress.com *Web Site:* www.businessexpertpress.com, pg 45

Mattura, Cat, McGraw-Hill Create, 2 Penn Plaza, New York, NY 10121 *Toll Free Tel:* 800-962-9342 *E-mail:* mhhe.create@mheducation.com *Web Site:* create.mheducation.com; shop.mheducation.com, pg 145

Matus, Robyn, Seedling Publications Inc, 520 E Bainbridge St, Elizabethtown, PA 17022 *Toll Free Tel:* 800-233-0759 *Toll Free Fax:* 888-834-1303 *E-mail:* info@continentalpress.com *Web Site:* www.continentalpress.com, pg 210

Matysik, Julie, Perseus Books, 250 W 57 St, 15th fl, New York, NY 10107 *Tel:* 212-340-8100 *Toll Free Tel:* 800-343-4499 (cust serv) *Fax:* 212-340-8105 *Web Site:* www.perseusbooks.com, pg 181

Matysko, Harriet I, Mary Ann Liebert Inc, 140 Huguenot St, 3rd fl, New Rochelle, NY 10801-5215 *Tel:* 914-740-2100 *Toll Free Tel:* 800-654-3237 *Fax:* 914-740-2101 *E-mail:* info@liebertpub.com *Web Site:* www.liebertonline.com, pg 133

Matzen, Kristin, Penguin Books, 375 Hudson St, New York, NY 10014 *Tel:* 212-366-2000 *E-mail:* penguinpublicity@us.penguingroup.com *Web Site:* www.penguinclassics.com; www.penguin.com, pg 177

Matzie, Bridget Wagner, Aevitas Creative Management, 19 W 21 St, Suite 501, New York, NY 10010 *Tel:* 212-765-6900 *Web Site:* aevitascreative.com, pg 506

Mauer, Harry, Flashlight Press, 527 Empire Blvd, Brooklyn, NY 11225 *Tel:* 718-288-8300 *Fax:* 718-972-6307 *Web Site:* www.flashlightpress.com, pg 85

Mauer, Tzvi, Urim Publications, 527 Empire Blvd, Brooklyn, NY 11225-3121 *Tel:* 718-972-5449 *Fax:* 718-972-6307 *E-mail:* publisher@urimpublications.com; editor@urimpublications.com *Web Site:* urimpublications.com, pg 249

Maurer, Rolf, New Star Books Ltd, 107-3477 Commercial St, Vancouver, BC V5N 4E8, Canada *Tel:* 604-738-9429 *E-mail:* info@newstarbooks.com *Web Site:* www.newstarbooks.com, pg 464

Mausser, Therese, AMACOM Books, 1601 Broadway, New York, NY 10019-7420 *Tel:* 212-586-8100 *Toll Free Tel:* 800-250-5308 (cust serv) *Fax:* 212-903-8083; 518-891-2372 (orders) *E-mail:* pubs_cust_serv@amanet.org *Web Site:* www.amacombooks.org, pg 8

Mautner, Stephen, National Academies Press (NAP), Lockbox 285, 500 Fifth St NW, Washington, DC 20001 *Tel:* 202-334-3313 *Fax:* 202-334-2451 (cust serv); 202-334-2793 (mktg dept) *E-mail:* customer_service@nap.edu *Web Site:* www.nap.edu, pg 156

Mavjee, Maya, Penguin Random House Inc, 1745 Broadway, New York, NY 10019 *Tel:* 212-782-9000 *Toll Free Tel:* 800-726-0600 *Web Site:* www.penguinrandomhouse.com, pg 178

Mavreshko, Lana, Business Marketing Association (BMA), 708 Third Ave, New York, NY 10017 *Tel:* 212-697-5950 *Fax:* 212-687-7310 *E-mail:* info@marketing.org *Web Site:* www.marketing.org, pg 561

Max, P J, Easy Money Press, 5419 87 St, Lubbock, TX 79424 *Tel:* 806-543-5215 *E-mail:* easymoneypress@yahoo.com, pg 75

Maxick, Jill, Prometheus Books, 59 John Glenn Dr, Amherst, NY 14228-2119 *Tel:* 716-691-0133 *Fax:* 716-691-0137 *E-mail:* marketing@prometheusbooks.com; editorial@prometheusbooks.com; rights@prometheusmail.com *Web Site:* www.prometheusbooks.com, pg 190

Maxwell, Edward, Sanford J Greenburger Associates Inc, 55 Fifth Ave, New York, NY 10003 *Tel:* 212-206-5600 *Fax:* 212-463-8718 *Web Site:* greenburger.com; www.sjga.com, pg 520

Maxwell, Mitchell, The Story Plant, PO Box 4331, Stamford, CT 06907 *Tel:* 203-722-7920 *E-mail:* thestoryplant@thestoryplant.com *Web Site:* www.thestoryplant.com, pg 223

Maxwell, Nancy, Ariel Press, 2317 Quail Cove Dr, Jasper, GA 30143 *Tel:* 770-894-4226 *E-mail:* lig201@lightariel.com *Web Site:* www.lightariel.com, pg 20

May, Brendan, Simon & Schuster Canada, 166 King St E, Suite 300, Toronto, ON M5A 1J3, Canada *Tel:* 647-427-8882 *Toll Free Tel:* 800-387-0446; 800-268-3216 (orders) *Fax:* 647-430-9446 *Toll Free Fax:* 888-849-8151 (orders) *E-mail:* info@simonandschuster.ca *Web Site:* www.simonandschuster.ca, pg 471

May, Christopher, Dufour Editions Inc, PO Box 7, Chester Springs, PA 19425 *Tel:* 610-458-5005 *Fax:* 610-458-7103 *E-mail:* info@dufoureditions.com *Web Site:* www.dufoureditions.com, pg 73

May, Duncan, Dufour Editions Inc, PO Box 7, Chester Springs, PA 19425 *Tel:* 610-458-5005 *Fax:* 610-458-7103 *E-mail:* info@dufoureditions.com *Web Site:* www.dufoureditions.com, pg 73

May, Linda, The Apex Press, 4501 Forbes Blvd, Suite 200, Lanham, MD 20706 *Tel:* 301-459-3366 *Toll Free Tel:* 800-462-6420 (orders) *Toll Free Fax:* 800-388-4450 *E-mail:* customercare@rowman.com *Web Site:* rowman.com/page/apex, pg 18

May, Linda, Scarecrow Press Inc, 4501 Forbes Blvd, Suite 200, Lanham, MD 20706 *Tel:* 301-459-3366 *Fax:* 301-429-5748 *Web Site:* www.scarecrowpress.com, pg 207

May, Louise, Lee & Low Books Inc, 95 Madison Ave, New York, NY 10016 *Tel:* 212-779-4400 *Toll Free Tel:* 888-320-3190 (ext 28, orders only) *Fax:* 212-683-1894 (orders only); 212-532-6035 *E-mail:* general@leeandlow.com *Web Site:* www.leeandlow.com, pg 131

Mayer, Christie, Dissertation.com, 23331 Water Circle, Boca Raton, FL 33486-8540 *Tel:* 561-750-4344 *Toll Free Tel:* 800-636-8329 *Fax:* 561-750-6797 *Web Site:* www.dissertation.com, pg 71

Mayer, Christie, Universal-Publishers Inc, 23331 Water Circle, Boca Raton, FL 33486-8540 *Tel:* 561-750-4344 *Toll Free Tel:* 800-636-8329 (US only) *Fax:* 561-750-6797 *Web Site:* www.universal-publishers.com, pg 239

Mayer, Dan, Prometheus Books, 59 John Glenn Dr, Amherst, NY 14228-2119 *Tel:* 716-691-0133 *Fax:* 716-691-0137 *E-mail:* marketing@prometheusbooks.com; editorial@prometheusbooks.com; rights@prometheusmail.com *Web Site:* www.prometheusbooks.com, pg 190

Mayer, Dariel, Vanderbilt University Press, 2014 Broadway, Suite 320, Nashville, TN 37203 *Tel:* 615-322-3585 *Toll Free Tel:* 800-627-7377 (orders only) *Fax:* 615-343-8823 *Toll Free Fax:* 800-735-0476 (orders only) *E-mail:* vupress@vanderbilt.edu *Web Site:* www.vanderbiltuniversitypress.com, pg 249

Mayer, Karen, Penguin Group USA, A Penguin Random House Company, 375 Hudson St, New York, NY 10014 *Tel:* 212-366-2000 *Toll Free Tel:* 800-847-5515 (inside sales); 800-631-8571 (cust serv) *Fax:* 212-366-2666; 607-775-4829 (inside sales) *E-mail:* online@us.penguingroup.com *Web Site:* www.penguin.com, pg 177

Mayer, Liese, Bloomsbury Publishing Inc, 1385 Broadway, 5th fl, New York, NY 10018 *Tel:* 212-419-5300 *E-mail:* marketingusa@bloomsbury.com; adultpublicityusa@bloomsbury.com; askacademic@bloomsbury.com *Web Site:* www.bloomsbury.com, pg 38

Mayer, Margery, Houghton Mifflin Harcourt, 125 High St, Boston, MA 02110 *Tel:* 617-351-5000 *Toll Free Tel:* 855-969-4642; 800-225-5425 (K-12 educ materials); 800-323-9540 (assessment materials); 877-

219-1537 (SkillsTutor); 888-242-6747 (Innovation in Educ Group); 800-225-3362 (Trade & Ref Div) *Toll Free Fax:* 800-269-5232 *E-mail:* myhmhco@hmhco.com *Web Site:* www.hmhco.com, pg 110

Mayer, Peter, The Overlook Press, 141 Wooster St, Suite 4-B, New York, NY 10012 *Tel:* 212-673-2210; 845-679-6838 (orders & dist) *Fax:* 212-673-2296 *E-mail:* sales@overlookny.com (orders) *Web Site:* www.overlookpress.com, pg 171

Mayer, Tom, W W Norton & Company Inc, 500 Fifth Ave, New York, NY 10110-0017 *Tel:* 212-354-5500 *Toll Free Tel:* 800-233-4830 (orders & cust serv) *Fax:* 212-869-0856 *Toll Free Fax:* 800-458-6515 *E-mail:* orders@wwnorton.com *Web Site:* books.wwnorton.com, pg 164

Mayers, Hazel-Ann, Simon & Schuster, Inc, 1230 Avenue of the Americas, New York, NY 10020 *Tel:* 212-698-7000 *Fax:* 212-698-7007 *E-mail:* firstname.lastname@simonandschuster.com *Web Site:* www.simonandschuster.com, pg 213

Mayers, Roy, Abrams Learning Trends, 16310 Bratton Lane, Suite 250, Austin, TX 78728-2403 *Toll Free Tel:* 800-227-9120 *Toll Free Fax:* 800-737-3322 *E-mail:* customerservice@abramslearningtrends.com (orders, cust serv); contactus@abramslearningtrends.com *Web Site:* www.abramslearningtrends.com (orders, cust serv), pg 3

Mayfield, Tyler, Louisville Grawemeyer Award in Religion, 1044 Alta Vista Rd, Louisville, KY 40205-1798 *Tel:* 502-895-3411 *Toll Free Tel:* 800-264-1839 *Fax:* 502-894-2286 *E-mail:* grawemeyer@lpts.edu *Web Site:* www.grawemeyer.org, pg 663

Mayhew, Alice E, Simon & Schuster, 1230 Avenue of the Americas, New York, NY 10020 *Tel:* 212-698-7000 *Toll Free Tel:* 800-223-2348 (cust serv); 800-223-2336 (orders) *Toll Free Fax:* 800-943-9831 (orders) *Web Site:* www.simonandschuster.com, pg 212

Maynard, Audrey, Tilbury House Publishers, 12 Starr St, Thomaston, ME 04861 *Tel:* 207-582-1899 *Toll Free Tel:* 800-582-1899 (orders) *Fax:* 207-582-8227 *E-mail:* tilbury@tilburyhouse.com *Web Site:* www.tilburyhouse.com, pg 232

Maynard, Gary, The Gary-Paul Agency, 1549 Main St, Stratford, CT 06615 *Tel:* 203-345-6167 *Web Site:* www.thegarypaulagency.com; www.nutmegpictures.com, pg 494

Maynard, Jim, Quicksilver Productions, PO Box 340, Ashland, OR 97520-0012 *Tel:* 541-482-5343 *Toll Free Fax:* 888-974-6462 *E-mail:* celestialcalendars@email.com *Web Site:* www.quicksilverproductions.com, pg 192

Mayotte, Alain, Prise de parole Inc, 109 Elm St, Suite 205, Sudbury, ON P3C 1T4, Canada *Tel:* 705-675-6491 *Fax:* 705-673-1817 *E-mail:* info@prisedeparole.ca *Web Site:* www.prisedeparole.ca, pg 468

Mays, Wendy, WendyLynn & Co, 504 Wilson Rd, Annapolis, MD 21401 *Tel:* 410-224-2729; 410-507-1059 *Web Site:* wendylynn.com, pg 544

Maze, Stephanie, Moonstone Press LLC, 4816 Carrington Circle, Sarasota, FL 34243 *Tel:* 301-765-1081 *Fax:* 301-765-0510 *E-mail:* mazeprod@erols.com *Web Site:* www.moonstonepress.net, pg 478

Mazer, Laura, Perseus Books, 250 W 57 St, 15th fl, New York, NY 10107 *Tel:* 212-340-8100 *Toll Free Tel:* 800-343-4499 (cust serv) *Fax:* 212-340-8105 *Web Site:* www.perseusbooks.com, pg 181

Mazes, Annie, Workman Publishing Co Inc, 225 Varick St, 9th fl, New York, NY 10014-4381 *Tel:* 212-254-5900 *Toll Free Tel:* 800-722-7202 *Fax:* 212-254-8098 *E-mail:* info@workman.com *Web Site:* www.workman.com, pg 259

Mazia, Judith, Alan Wofsy Fine Arts, 1109 Geary Blvd, San Francisco, CA 94109 *Tel:* 415-292-6500 *Toll Free Tel:* 800-660-6403 *Fax:* 415-292-6594 (off & cust serv); 510-251-1840 (acctg) *E-mail:* order@art-books.com (orders); editeur@earthlink.net (edit); beauxarts@earthlink.net (cust serv) *Web Site:* www.art-books.com, pg 258

Mazurkiewicz, Orchid, UCLA Latin American Center Publications, UCLA Latin American Institute, 10343 Bunche Hall, Los Angeles, CA 90095 *Tel:* 310-825-4571 *Fax:* 310-206-6859 *E-mail:* latinamctr@international.ucla.edu *Web Site:* www.international.ucla.edu/lai, pg 238

Mazza, Cris, University of Illinois at Chicago, Program for Writers, College of Liberal Arts & Sciences, 2027 University Hall, 601 S Morgan St, Chicago, IL 60607-7120 *Tel:* 312-413-2200 (Eng dept) *Fax:* 312-413-1005 *Web Site:* www.uic.edu, pg 623

McAdam, Elena Goranescu, McGill-Queen's University Press, 1010 Sherbrooke W, Suite 1720, Montreal, QC H3A 2R7, Canada *Tel:* 514-398-3750 *Fax:* 514-398-4333 *E-mail:* mqup@mqup.ca *Web Site:* www.mqup.ca, pg 463

McAdam, Matthew, The Johns Hopkins University Press, 2715 N Charles St, Baltimore, MD 21218-4363 *Tel:* 410-516-6900; 410-516-6987 (journal orders outside US & CN) *Toll Free Tel:* 800-537-5487 (book orders & cust serv); 800-548-1784 (journal orders) *Fax:* 410-516-6968; 410-516-3866 (journal orders) *E-mail:* hfscustserv@press.jhu.edu (cust serv); jrnlcirc@press.jhu.edu (journal orders) *Web Site:* www.press.jhu.edu; muse.jhu.edu, pg 122

McAdams, Heather, CN Times Books, 501 Fifth Ave, Suite 1708, New York, NY 10017 *Tel:* 212-867-8666 *Web Site:* cntimesbooks.com, pg 57

McAdams, Kevin, Schiavone Literary Agency Inc, 236 Trails End, West Palm Beach, FL 33413-2135 *Tel:* 561-966-9294 *Fax:* 561-966-9294 *E-mail:* profschia@aol.com *Web Site:* www.publishersmarketplace.com/members/profschia, pg 534

McAnespia, Elena, University of California Press, 155 Grand Ave, Suite 400, Oakland, CA 94612-3758 *Tel:* 510-883-8232 *Fax:* 510-836-8910 *E-mail:* customerservice@ucpressjournals.com *Web Site:* www.ucpress.edu, pg 240

McArdle, Nicole, Simon & Schuster, 1230 Avenue of the Americas, New York, NY 10020 *Tel:* 212-698-7000 *Toll Free Tel:* 800-223-2348 (cust serv); 800-223-2336 (orders) *Toll Free Fax:* 800-943-9831 (orders) *Web Site:* www.simonandschuster.com, pg 212

McAuley, Genny, Chronicle Books LLC, 680 Second St, San Francisco, CA 94107 *Tel:* 415-537-4200 *Toll Free Tel:* 800-759-0190 (cust serv) *Fax:* 415-537-4460 *Toll Free Fax:* 800-858-7787 (orders); 800-286-9471 (cust serv) *E-mail:* frontdesk@chroniclebooks.com *Web Site:* www.chroniclebooks.com, pg 55

McAuley, Scott, Angel City Press, 2118 Wilshire Blvd, Suite 880, Santa Monica, CA 90403 *Tel:* 310-395-9982 *Toll Free Tel:* 800-949-8039 *Fax:* 310-395-3353 *E-mail:* info@angelcitypress.com *Web Site:* www.angelcitypress.com, pg 17

McAvey, Gerard, Milady, Executive Woods, 5 Maxwell Dr, Clifton Park, NY 12065-2919 *Tel:* 518-348-2300 *Toll Free Tel:* 800-998-7498 *Fax:* 518-373-6309 *E-mail:* info@milady.com *Web Site:* milady.cengage.com, pg 150

McAweeney, Terry, MFA Publications, 465 Huntington Ave, Boston, MA 02115 *Tel:* 617-369-4233 *Fax:* 617-369-3459 *E-mail:* publications@mfa.org *Web Site:* www.mfa.org/publications, pg 149

McBeath, Kasey, Texas Tech University Press, 1120 Main St, 2nd fl, Lubbock, TX 79401 *Tel:* 806-742-2982 *Toll Free Tel:* 800-832-4042 *Fax:* 806-742-2979 *E-mail:* ttup@ttu.edu *Web Site:* www.ttupress.org, pg 230

McBride, David, Oxford University Press USA, 198 Madison Ave, New York, NY 10016 *Tel:* 212-726-6000 *Toll Free Tel:* 800-451-7556 (orders); 800-445-9714 (cust serv) *Fax:* 919-677-1303 *E-mail:* custserv.us@oup.com *Web Site:* www.oup.com/us, pg 171

McBride, Margret, Margret McBride Literary Agency, PO Box 9128, La Jolla, CA 92038 *Tel:* 858-454-1550 *E-mail:* staff@mcbridelit.com *Web Site:* www.mcbrideliterary.com, pg 528

McCabe, Don, AVKO Educational Research Foundation Inc, 3084 Willard Rd, Birch Run, MI 48415-9404 *Tel:* 810-686-9283 (orders & billing) *Fax:* 810-686-1101 *E-mail:* info@avko.org (gen inquiry) *Web Site:* www.avko.org; www.avko.blogspot.org, pg 27

McCabe, Robert, AVKO Educational Research Foundation Inc, 3084 Willard Rd, Birch Run, MI 48415-9404 *Tel:* 810-686-9283 (orders & billing) *Fax:* 810-686-1101 *E-mail:* info@avko.org (gen inquiry) *Web Site:* www.avko.org; www.avko.blogspot.org, pg 27

McCaffery, Greg, Bloomberg BNA Books, 1801 S Bell St, Arlington, VA 22202 *Tel:* 732-476-6397 *Toll Free Tel:* 800-960-1220 *Fax:* 732-346-1624 *E-mail:* books@bna.com *Web Site:* www.bna.com/bnabooks, pg 37

McCaffrey, Roger A, Roman Catholic Books, PO Box 2286, Fort Collins, CO 80522-2286 *Tel:* 970-490-2735 *Fax:* 904-493-8781 *Web Site:* www.booksforcatholics.com, pg 201

McCahill, Katherine, Penguin Random House Inc, 1745 Broadway, New York, NY 10019 *Tel:* 212-782-9000 *Toll Free Tel:* 800-726-0600 *Web Site:* www.penguinrandomhouse.com, pg 178

McCain, Rev Paul T, Concordia Publishing House, 3558 S Jefferson Ave, St Louis, MO 63118-3968 *Tel:* 314-268-1000; 314-268-1268 (bookshop) *Toll Free Tel:* 800-325-3040 (cust serv) *Toll Free Fax:* 800-490-9889 (cust serv) *E-mail:* order@cph.org *Web Site:* www.cph.org, pg 59

McCall, Jay, The Society of Southwestern Authors (SSA), PO Box 30355, Tucson, AZ 85751-0355 *E-mail:* info@ssa-az.org *Web Site:* www.ssa-az.org, pg 579

McCall, Jeff, Twenty-Third Publications, One Montauk Ave, Suite 200, New London, CT 06320 *Tel:* 860-437-3012 *Toll Free Tel:* 800-321-0411 (orders) *Toll Free Fax:* 800-572-0788 *E-mail:* resources@twentythirdpublications.com *Web Site:* www.twentythirdpublications.com, pg 237

McCall, Michael, Country Music Foundation Press, 222 Fifth Ave S, Nashville, TN 37203 *Tel:* 615-416-2001 *Fax:* 615-255-2245 *E-mail:* info@countrymusichalloffame.com *Web Site:* www.countrymusichalloffame.com, pg 63

McCamley, Maren, Living Language, c/o Penguin Random House Inc, 1745 Broadway, New York, NY 10019 *Tel:* 212-782-9000 *Toll Free Tel:* 800-733-3000 (orders) *Toll Free Fax:* 800-659-2436 *E-mail:* livinglanguage@randomhouse.com *Web Site:* www.livinglanguage.com, pg 136

McCann, Peg, American Society of Agricultural & Biological Engineers (ASABE), 2950 Niles Rd, St Joseph, MI 49085-9659 *Tel:* 269-429-0300 *Toll Free Tel:* 800-371-2723 *Fax:* 269-429-3852 *E-mail:* hq@asabe.org *Web Site:* www.asabe.org, pg 14

McCants, Cassidy, The Pablo Neruda Prize for Poetry, Nimrod International Journal, 800 S Tucker Dr, Tulsa, OK 74104 *Tel:* 918-631-3080 *Fax:* 918-631-3033 *E-mail:* nimrod@utulsa.edu *Web Site:* www.utulsa.edu/nimrod, pg 672

McCants, Cassidy, Katherine Anne Porter Prize for Fiction, Nimrod International Journal, 800 S Tucker Dr, Tulsa, OK 74104 *Tel:* 918-631-3080 *Fax:* 918-631-3033 *E-mail:* nimrod@utulsa.edu *Web Site:* www.utulsa.edu/nimrod, pg 681

McCarren, William, National Press Club (NPC), 529 14 St NW, 13th fl, Washington, DC 20045 *Tel:* 202-662-7500 *Fax:* 202-662-7569 *E-mail:* infocenter@npcpress.org *Web Site:* www.press.org, pg 572

McCarthy, Aja, Sophia Institute Press®, 522 Donald St, Unit 3, Bedford, NH 03110 *Tel:* 603-836-5505 *Toll Free Tel:* 800-888-9344 *Fax:* 603-641-8108 *Toll Free Fax:* 888-288-2259 *E-mail:* orders@sophiainstitute.com *Web Site:* www.sophiainstitute.com, pg 217

McCarthy, Brian, The Library of America, 14 E 60 St, New York, NY 10022-1006 *Tel:* 212-308-3360 *Fax:* 212-750-8352 *E-mail:* info@loa.org *Web Site:* www.loa.org, pg 133

McCarthy, Dan, The Taunton Press Inc, 63 S Main St, Newtown, CT 06470 *Tel:* 203-426-8171 *Toll Free Tel:* 800-477-8727 (cust serv); 800-888-8286 (orders) *Fax:* 203-426-3434 *E-mail:* booksales@taunton.com *Web Site:* www.taunton.com, pg 227

McCarthy, Donna, Houghton Mifflin Harcourt Trade & Reference Division, 125 High St, Boston, MA 02110 *Tel:* 617-351-5000 *Toll Free Tel:* 800-225-3362 *Web Site:* www.hmhco.com, pg 111

McCarthy, E J, E J McCarthy Agency, 405 Maple St, Suite A, Mill Valley, CA 94941 *Tel:* 415-383-6639 *Fax:* 415-383-6639 *E-mail:* ejmagency@gmail.com *Web Site:* www.publishersmarketplace.com/members/ejmccarthy, pg 529

McCarthy, Genevieve, BioTechniques Books, 52 Vanderbilt Ave, 11th fl, New York, NY 10017 *Tel:* 212-520-2777 *Fax:* 212-520-2705 *Web Site:* www.biotechniques.com, pg 35

McCarthy, Jim, Dystel, Goderich & Bourret LLC, One Union Sq W, Suite 904, New York, NY 10003 *Tel:* 212-627-9100 *Fax:* 212-627-9313 *Web Site:* www.dystel.com, pg 515

McCarthy, Juliana M, The Johns Hopkins University Press, 2715 N Charles St, Baltimore, MD 21218-4363 *Tel:* 410-516-6900; 410-516-6987 (journal orders outside US & CN) *Toll Free Tel:* 800-537-5487 (book orders & cust serv); 800-548-1784 (journal orders) *Fax:* 410-516-6968; 410-516-3866 (journal orders) *E-mail:* hfscustserv@press.jhu.edu (cust serv); jrnlcirc@press.jhu.edu (journal orders) *Web Site:* www.press.jhu.edu; muse.jhu.edu, pg 122

McCarthy, Nora, Penguin Books, 375 Hudson St, New York, NY 10014 *Tel:* 212-366-2000 *E-mail:* penguinpublicity@us.penguingroup.com *Web Site:* www.penguinclassics.com; www.penguin.com, pg 177

McCarthy, Pat, Cornell & McCarthy LLC, 2-D Cross Hwy, Westport, CT 06880 *Tel:* 203-454-4210 *E-mail:* contact@cmartreps.com *Web Site:* www.cmartreps.com, pg 543

McCarthy, Thomas, Wisconsin Department of Public Instruction, 125 S Webster St, Madison, WI 53703 *Tel:* 608-266-2188 *Toll Free Tel:* 800-441-4563 *Fax:* 608-267-9110 *Web Site:* pubsales.dpi.wi.gov, pg 257

McCaskey, Caitlin, Penguin Random House Speakers Bureau, A Penguin Random House Company, 1745 Broadway, Mail Drop 13-1, New York, NY 10019 *Tel:* 212-572-2013 *E-mail:* speakers@penguinrandomhouse.com *Web Site:* www.prhspeakers.com, pg 547

McCauley, Gerard, Gerard McCauley Agency Inc, PO Box 844, Katonah, NY 10536-0844 *Tel:* 914-232-5700, pg 529

McCauley, Katie, American College of Surgeons, 633 N Saint Clair St, Chicago, IL 60611-3211 *Tel:* 312-202-5000 *Fax:* 312-202-5001 *E-mail:* postmaster@facs.org *Web Site:* www.facs.org, pg 11

McCauley, Kay, Aurous Inc, PO Box 20490, New York, NY 10017 *Tel:* 212-628-9729 *Fax:* 212-535-7861, pg 507

McCauley, Kirby, Aurous Inc, PO Box 20490, New York, NY 10017 *Tel:* 212-628-9729 *Fax:* 212-535-7861, pg 507

McCaull, June, The MIT Press, One Rogers St, Cambridge, MA 02142 *Tel:* 617-253-5255 *Toll Free Tel:* 800-207-8354 (orders) *Fax:* 617-258-6779; 617-577-1545 (orders) *Web Site:* mitpress.mit.edu, pg 152

McClain, J Cameron, Cedar Grove Books, 2215 High Point Dr, Carrollton, TX 75007 *Tel:* 415-364-8292 *Fax:* 415-276-9858 *E-mail:* queries@cedargrovebooks.com *Web Site:* www.cedargrovebooks.com, pg 50

McClanahan, Pamela, Minnesota Historical Society Press, 345 Kellogg Blvd W, St Paul, MN 55102-1906 *Tel:* 651-259-3205 *Toll Free Tel:* 800-621-2736 (warehouse) *Fax:* 651-297-1345 *Toll Free Fax:* 800-621-8476 (warehouse) *E-mail:* info-mnhspress@mnhs.org *Web Site:* www.mnhs.org/mnhspress, pg 151

McClay, Ashley Pattison, GP Putnam's Sons (Hardcover), 375 Hudson St, New York, NY 10014 *Tel:* 212-366-2000 *Fax:* 212-366-2643 *E-mail:* online@penguinputnam.com *Web Site:* www.penguin.com/publishers/gpputnamssons, pg 192

McClearn, Lauren, Sourcebooks Inc, 1935 Brookdale Rd, Suite 139, Naperville, IL 60563 *Tel:* 630-961-3900 *Toll Free Tel:* 800-432-7444 *Fax:* 630-961-2168 *E-mail:* info@sourcebooks.com; customersupport@sourcebooks.com *Web Site:* www.sourcebooks.com, pg 218

McClellan, Anita, Anita D McClellan Associates, 464 Common St, Suite 142, Belmont, MA 02478-2704 *Tel:* 617-575-9203 *E-mail:* adm@anitamcclellan.com *Web Site:* www.anitamcclellan.com, pg 529

McClellan, Anita D, Anita D McClellan Associates, 464 Common St, Suite 142, Belmont, MA 02478-2704 *Tel:* 617-575-9203 *E-mail:* adm@anitamcclellan.com *Web Site:* www.anitamcclellan.com, pg 498

McClelland, Anne, Book & Periodical Council (BPC), 192 Spadina Ave, Suite 107, Toronto, ON M5T 2C2, Canada *Tel:* 416-975-9366 *Fax:* 416-975-1839 *E-mail:* info@thebpc.ca *Web Site:* www.thebpc.ca, pg 560

McClure, Cameron, Donald Maass Literary Agency, 1000 Dean St, Suite 252, Brooklyn, NY 11238 *Tel:* 212-727-8383 *Fax:* 212-727-3271 *E-mail:* info@maassagency.com *Web Site:* www.maassagency.com, pg 526

McClure, Dr Donald E, American Mathematical Society, 201 Charles St, Providence, RI 02904-2294 *Tel:* 401-455-4000 *Toll Free Tel:* 800-321-4267 *Fax:* 401-331-3842; 401-455-4046 (cust serv) *E-mail:* ams@ams.org; cust-serv@ams.org *Web Site:* www.ams.org, pg 13

McClure, John, Signalman Publishing, 3700 Commerce Blvd, Kissimmee, FL 34741 *Tel:* 407-504-4103 *Toll Free Tel:* 888-907-4423 *E-mail:* info@signalmanpublishing.com *Web Site:* www.signalmanpublishing.com, pg 212

McClure, Urmila, Signalman Publishing, 3700 Commerce Blvd, Kissimmee, FL 34741 *Tel:* 407-504-4103 *Toll Free Tel:* 888-907-4423 *E-mail:* info@signalmanpublishing.com *Web Site:* www.signalmanpublishing.com, pg 212

McCollom, Tamar, Scribner, 1230 Avenue of the Americas, New York, NY 10020, pg 209

McCollum, Lauren, Chain Store Guide (CSG), 10117 Princess Palm Ave, Suite 375, Tampa, FL 33610 *Tel:* 813-627-6957 *Toll Free Tel:* 800-927-9292 (orders) *Fax:* 813-627-6888 *E-mail:* info@csgis.com *Web Site:* www.csgis.com, pg 52

McConkey, Jill, University of Manitoba Press, University of Manitoba, 301 St Johns College, 92 Dysart Rd, Winnipeg, MB R3T 2M5, Canada *Tel:* 204-474-9495 *Fax:* 204-474-7566 *E-mail:* uofmpress@umanitoba.ca *Web Site:* uofmpress.ca, pg 474

McConnell, David B, Hillsdale Educational Publishers Inc, 39 North St, Hillsdale, MI 49242 *Tel:* 517-437-3179 *Fax:* 517-437-0531 *E-mail:* davestory@aol.com *Web Site:* www.hillsdalepublishers.com; michbooks.com, pg 107

McConnell, Ted, Advertising Research Foundation (ARF), 432 Park Ave S, 4th fl, New York, NY 10016-8013 *Tel:* 212-751-5656 *Fax:* 212-319-5265 *E-mail:* info@thearf.org; jar@thearf.org (edit) *Web Site:* www.thearf.org, pg 553

McConville, Sarah, Harvard Business Review Press, 300 N Beacon St, Watertown, MA 02472 *Tel:* 617-783-7400 *Fax:* 617-783-7489 *E-mail:* custserv@hbsp.harvard.edu *Web Site:* www.harvardbusiness.org, pg 102

McCoy, Crystal, Little Bee Books, 853 Broadway, Suite 2014, New York, NY 10003 *E-mail:* info@littlebeebooks.com *Web Site:* www.littlebeebooks.com, pg 135

McCoy, James, Iowa Poetry Prize, 119 W Park Rd, 100 Kuhl House, Iowa City, IA 52242-1000 *Tel:* 319-335-2000 *Fax:* 319-335-2055 *E-mail:* uipress@uiowa.edu *Web Site:* www.uiowapress.org, pg 656

McCoy, James, University of Iowa Press, 119 W Park Rd, 100 Kuhl House, Iowa City, IA 52242-1000 *Tel:* 319-335-2000 *Toll Free Tel:* 800-621-2736 (orders only) *Fax:* 319-335-2055 *Toll Free Fax:* 800-621-8476 (orders only) *E-mail:* uipress@uiowa.edu *Web Site:* www.uiowapress.org, pg 242

McCoy, Melody, Jhpiego, 1615 Thames St, Baltimore, MD 21231-3492 *Tel:* 410-537-1800 *Fax:* 410-537-1473 *E-mail:* info@jhpiego.net *Web Site:* www.jhpiego.org, pg 122

McCracken, Elizabeth, University of Texas at Austin, New Writers Project, Dept of English, Calhoun Hall, Rm 226, 204 W 21 St, B-5000, Austin, TX 78712 *Tel:* 512-471-5132; 512-471-4991 *Fax:* 512-471-4909 *Web Site:* newwritersproject.org, pg 623

McCrae, Fiona, Graywolf Press, 250 Third Ave N, Suite 600, Minneapolis, MN 55401 *Tel:* 651-641-0077 *Fax:* 651-641-0036 *E-mail:* wolves@graywolfpress.org (no ms queries, sample chapters or proposals) *Web Site:* www.graywolfpress.org, pg 95

McCrae, Shane, Oberlin College Press, 50 N Professor St, Oberlin, OH 44074-1091 *Tel:* 440-775-8408 *Fax:* 440-775-8124 *E-mail:* oc.press@oberlin.edu *Web Site:* www.oberlin.edu/ocpress, pg 166

McCreary, Courtney, University Press of Mississippi, 3825 Ridgewood Rd, Jackson, MS 39211-6492 *Tel:* 601-432-6205 *Toll Free Tel:* 800-737-7788 (orders & cust serv) *Fax:* 601-432-6217 *E-mail:* press@mississippi.edu *Web Site:* www.upress.state.ms.us, pg 247

McCrosky, Judy, SF Canada, c/o Judy McCrosky, Secy-Treas, 516 Ninth St E, Saskatoon, SK S7N 0B1, Canada *Web Site:* www.sfcanada.org, pg 577

McCue, Mary, Random House Children's Books, 1745 Broadway, 10th fl, New York, NY 10019 *Tel:* 212-782-9000 *Web Site:* www.randomhousekids.com, pg 194

McCullough, Mark S, Wyndham Hall Press, 5050 Kerr Rd, Lima, OH 45806 *Tel:* 419-648-9124 *Toll Free Tel:* 866-895-0977 *Fax:* 419-648-9124; 413-208-2409 *Web Site:* www.wyndhamhallpress.com, pg 260

McCullough, Michael, Duke University Press, 905 W Main St, Suite 18B, Durham, NC 27701 *Tel:* 919-688-5134 *Toll Free Tel:* 888-651-0122 (US) *Fax:* 919-688-2615 *Toll Free Fax:* 888-651-0124 *E-mail:* orders@dukeupress.edu *Web Site:* www.dukeupress.edu, pg 73

McCullough, Robert, Penguin Random House Canada, 320 Front St W, Suite 1400, Toronto, ON M5V 3B6, Canada *Tel:* 416-364-4449 *Toll Free Tel:* 888-523-9292 (cust serv) *Fax:* 416-598-7764 *Web Site:* www.penguinrandomhouse.ca, pg 467

McCune, Sara Miller, SAGE Publishing, 2455 Teller Rd, Thousand Oaks, CA 91320 *Toll Free Tel:* 800-818-7243 *Toll Free Fax:* 800-583-2665 *E-mail:* info@sagepub.com *Web Site:* www.sagepublishing.com, pg 203

McCurdy, Wendy, Kensington Publishing Corp, 119 W 40 St, New York, NY 10018 *Tel:* 212-407-1500 *Toll Free Tel:* 800-221-2647 *Fax:* 212-935-0699 *Web Site:* www.kensingtonbooks.com, pg 125

McCutcheon, Camille, Southern Books Competition, PO Box 950, Rex, GA 30273 *Tel:* 678-466-4334 *Fax:* 678-466-4349 *Web Site:* selaonline.org, pg 691

McDermott, Kathleen, Harvard University Press, 79 Garden St, Cambridge, MA 02138-1499 *Tel:* 617-495-2600; 401-531-2800 (intl orders) *Toll Free Tel:* 800-405-1619 (orders) *Fax:* 617-495-5898 (general); 617-496-4677 (edit & rts); 401-531-2801 (intl orders) *Toll Free Fax:* 800-406-9145 (orders) *E-mail:* contact_hup@harvard.edu *Web Site:* www.hup.harvard.edu, pg 103

McDevitt, Jo-Ann, AAP PreK-12 Learning Group, 455 Massachusetts Ave NW, Suite 700, Washington, DC 20001 *Tel:* 267-351-4310 *Fax:* 267-351-4317 *E-mail:* prek12learning@publishers.org *Web Site:* www.aepweb.org, pg 553

McDonald, Alison, Gagosian Gallery, 980 Madison Ave, New York, NY 10075 *Tel:* 212-744-2313 *Fax:* 212-772-7962 *E-mail:* newyork@gagosian.com *Web Site:* www.gagosian.com, pg 89

McDonald, Brandy, Ozark Mountain Publishing Inc, PO Box 754, Huntsville, AR 72740-0754 *Tel:* 479-738-2348 *Toll Free Tel:* 800-935-0045 *Fax:* 479-738-2448 *E-mail:* info@ozarkmt.com *Web Site:* www.ozarkmt.com, pg 172

McDonald, Caitlin, Donald Maass Literary Agency, 1000 Dean St, Suite 252, Brooklyn, NY 11238 *Tel:* 212-727-8383 *Fax:* 212-727-3271 *E-mail:* info@maassagency.com *Web Site:* www.maassagency.com, pg 526

McDonald, Erroll, Pantheon Books/Schocken Books, c/o Penguin Random House Inc, 1745 Broadway, New York, NY 10019 *Tel:* 212-751-2600 *Web Site:* knopfdoubleday.com/imprint/pantheon, pg 173

McDonald, Jerry N, The McDonald & Woodward Publishing Co, 695 Tall Oaks Dr, Newark, OH 43055 *Tel:* 740-641-2691 *Toll Free Tel:* 800-233-8787 *Fax:* 740-641-2692 *E-mail:* mwpubco@mwpubco.com *Web Site:* www.mwpubco.com, pg 145

McDonald, Kathy, Bisk Education, 9417 Princess Palm Ave, Suite 400, Tampa, FL 33619 *Tel:* 813-621-6200 *Toll Free Tel:* 800-280-9718 (cust serv) *E-mail:* customerservice@bisk.com *Web Site:* www.bisk.com, pg 35

McDonald, Mary, American Philosophical Society, 104 S Fifth St, Philadelphia, PA 19106 *Tel:* 215-440-3425 *Fax:* 215-440-3450 *E-mail:* orders@dianepublishing.net *Web Site:* www.amphilsoc.org, pg 13

McDonald, Nikki, Peachpit Press, 1301 Sansome St, San Francisco, CA 94111 *Toll Free Tel:* 800-283-9444 *E-mail:* info@peachpit.com; ask@peachpit.com *Web Site:* www.peachpit.com, pg 175

McDonald, Sean, Farrar, Straus & Giroux, LLC, 18 W 18 St, New York, NY 10011 *Tel:* 212-741-6900 *E-mail:* fsg.publicity@fsgbooks.com *Web Site:* us.macmillan.com/fsg.aspx, pg 82

McDonnell, Joshua, Perseus Books, 250 W 57 St, 15th fl, New York, NY 10107 *Tel:* 212-340-8100 *Toll Free Tel:* 800-343-4499 (cust serv) *Fax:* 212-340-8105 *Web Site:* www.perseusbooks.com, pg 181

McDonnell, Mark, Bloom's Literary Criticism, 132 W 31 St, 17th fl, New York, NY 10001 *Toll Free Tel:* 800-322-8755 *Toll Free Fax:* 800-678-3633 *E-mail:* custserv@factsonfile.com *Web Site:* www.infobasepublishing.com, pg 37

McDonnell, Mark, Cambridge Educational, 132 W 31 St, 17th fl, New York, NY 10001 *Toll Free Tel:* 800-322-8755 *Fax:* 609-671-0266 *Toll Free Fax:* 800-329-6687 *E-mail:* custserve@infobaselearning.com *Web Site:* www.infobasepublishing.com, pg 46

McDonnell, Mark, Chelsea House Publishers, 132 W 31 St, 17th fl, New York, NY 10001 *Tel:* 212-967-8800 *Toll Free Tel:* 800-322-8755 *Fax:* 917-339-0325 *Toll Free Fax:* 800-678-3633 *E-mail:* custserv@factsonfile.com *Web Site:* www.infobasepublishing.com; www.infobaselearning.com, pg 53

McDonnell, Mark, Facts On File, 132 W 31 St, 17th fl, New York, NY 10001 *Tel:* 212-967-8800 *Toll Free Tel:* 800-322-8755 *Toll Free Fax:* 800-678-3633 *E-mail:* custserv@factsonfile.com *Web Site:* infobasepublishing.com, pg 81

McDonnell, Mark, Ferguson Publishing, 132 W 31 St, 17th fl, New York, NY 10001 *Tel:* 212-967-8800 *Toll Free Tel:* 800-322-8755 *Fax:* 917-339-0323 *Toll Free Fax:* 800-678-3633 *E-mail:* custserv@factsonfile.com *Web Site:* infobasepublishing.com, pg 84

McDonough, Brian, Gale, 27500 Drake Rd, Farmington Hills, MI 48331-3535 *Tel:* 248-699-4253 *Toll Free Tel:* 800-877-4253 *Toll Free Fax:* 800-414-5043 (orders) *E-mail:* gale.customercare@cengage.com *Web Site:* www.gale.com, pg 89

McDonough, Brian, Macmillan Reference USA™, 27500 Drake Rd, Farmington Hills, MI 48331-3535 *Tel:* 248-699-4253 *Toll Free Tel:* 800-877-4253 *Toll Free Fax:* 877-363-4253 *E-mail:* gale.customercare@cengage.com *Web Site:* www.gale.cengage.com/macmillan, pg 140

McDonough, Liz, University of California Extension Professional Sequence in Copyediting & Courses in Publishing, 1995 University Ave, Suite 110, Berkeley, CA 94720-7000 *Tel:* 510-642-6362 *Fax:* 510-643-0216 *E-mail:* letters@unex.berkeley.edu *Web Site:* www.unex.berkeley.edu, pg 623

McDowall, Katy, Prufrock Press, PO Box 8813, Waco, TX 76714-8813 *Tel:* 254-756-3337 *Toll Free Tel:* 800-998-2208 *Fax:* 254-756-3339 *Toll Free Fax:* 800-240-0333 *E-mail:* info@prufrock.com *Web Site:* www.prufrock.com, pg 191

McDuffie, John, American Psychiatric Association Publishing, 1000 Wilson Blvd, Suite 1825, Arlington, VA 22209 *Tel:* 703-907-7322 *Toll Free Tel:* 800-368-5777 *Fax:* 703-907-1091 *E-mail:* appi@psych.org *Web Site:* www.appi.org; www.psychiatryonline.org, pg 14

McElvane, Clyde, Hurston/Wright Award for College Writers, 840 First St NE, 3rd fl, Washington, DC 20002 *Tel:* 202-248-5051 *E-mail:* info@hurstonwright.org *Web Site:* www.hurstonwright.org, pg 654

McElvane, Clyde, Hurston/Wright Legacy Awards, 840 First St NE, 3rd fl, Washington, DC 20002 *Tel:* 202-248-5051 *E-mail:* info@hurstonwright.org *Web Site:* www.hurstonwright.org, pg 654

McElvane, Clyde, Hurston/Wright Writers Week, 840 First St NE, 3rd fl, Washington, DC 20002 *Tel:* 202-248-5051 *E-mail:* info@hurstonwright.org *Web Site:* www.hurstonwright.org, pg 611

McElvane, Clyde, The Zora Neale Hurston/Richard Wright Foundation, 840 First St NE, 3rd fl, Washington, DC 20002 *Tel:* 202-248-5051 *E-mail:* info@hurstonwright.org *Web Site:* www.hurstonwright.org, pg 583

McEvoy, Nion, Chronicle Books LLC, 680 Second St, San Francisco, CA 94107 *Tel:* 415-537-4200 *Toll Free Tel:* 800-759-0190 (cust serv) *Fax:* 415-537-4460 *Toll Free Fax:* 800-858-7787 (orders); 800-286-9471 (cust serv) *E-mail:* frontdesk@chroniclebooks.com *Web Site:* www.chroniclebooks.com, pg 55

McEvoy, William, The Guilford Press, 370 Seventh Ave, Suite 1200, New York, NY 10001-1020 *Tel:* 212-431-9800 *Toll Free Tel:* 800-365-7006 *Fax:* 212-966-6708 *E-mail:* info@guilford.com *Web Site:* www.guilford.com, pg 97

McEwen, Rebecca, Fulcrum Publishing Inc, 4690 Table Mountain Dr, Suite 100, Golden, CO 80403 *Tel:* 303-277-1623 *Toll Free Tel:* 800-992-2908 *Fax:* 303-279-7111 *Toll Free Fax:* 800-726-7112 *E-mail:* info@fulcrumbooks.com; orders@fulcrumbooks.com *Web Site:* www.fulcrumbooks.com, pg 89

McFadden, Daniel, Psychological Assessment Resources Inc (PAR), 16204 N Florida Ave, Lutz, FL 33549 *Tel:* 813-968-3003; 813-449-4065 *Toll Free Tel:* 800-331-8378 *Fax:* 813-968-2598; 813-961-2196 *Toll Free Fax:* 800-727-9329 *E-mail:* custsup@parinc.com *Web Site:* www4.parinc.com, pg 191

McFadden, Trinity, Zondervan, 3900 Sparks Dr, Grand Rapids, MI 49546 *Tel:* 616-698-6900 *Toll Free Tel:* 800-226-1122; 800-727-1309 (retail orders) *Fax:* 616-698-3350 *Toll Free Fax:* 800-698-3256 (retail orders) *E-mail:* zinfo@zondervan.com *Web Site:* www.zondervan.com, pg 263

McFadden, Wendy, Brethren Press, 1451 Dundee Ave, Elgin, IL 60120 *Tel:* 847-742-5100 *Toll Free Tel:* 800-323-8039 *Toll Free Fax:* 800-667-8188 *E-mail:* brethrenpress@brethren.org *Web Site:* www.brethrenpress.com, pg 42

McFeely, W Drake, The Countryman Press, c/o W W Norton & Company Inc, 500 Fifth Ave, New York, NY 10110 *Tel:* 212-354-5500 *Fax:* 212-869-0856 *E-mail:* countrymanpress@wwnorton.com *Web Site:* www.countrymanpress.com, pg 63

McFeely, W Drake, W W Norton & Company Inc, 500 Fifth Ave, New York, NY 10110-0017 *Tel:* 212-354-5500 *Toll Free Tel:* 800-233-4830 (orders & cust serv) *Fax:* 212-869-0856 *Toll Free Fax:* 800-458-6515 *E-mail:* orders@wwnorton.com *Web Site:* books.wwnorton.com, pg 164

McGahern, Liam, ABAC/ALAC, 368 Dalhousie St, Suite 301, Ottawa, ON K1N 7G3, Canada *Tel:* 416-364-2376 *E-mail:* info@abac.org *Web Site:* www.abac.org, pg 553

McGandy, Michael J, Cornell University Press, Sage House, 512 E State St, Ithaca, NY 14850 *Tel:* 607-277-2338 *Fax:* 607-277-2374 *E-mail:* cupressinfo@cornell.edu; cupress-sales@cornell.edu *Web Site:* www.cornellpress.cornell.edu, pg 61

McGarity, Todd, Hachette Book Group, 1290 Avenue of the Americas, New York, NY 10019 *Tel:* 212-364-1100 *Toll Free Tel:* 800-759-0190 (cust serv) *Fax:* 212-364-0933 (intl orders) *Toll Free Fax:* 800-286-9471 (cust serv) *Web Site:* www.hachettebookgroup.com, pg 98

McGarvey, Joey, Milkweed Editions, 1011 Washington Ave S, Suite 300, Minneapolis, MN 55415-1246 *Tel:* 612-332-3192 *Toll Free Tel:* 800-520-6455 *Fax:* 612-215-2550 *Web Site:* milkweed.org, pg 151

McGee, Chris, Children's Literature Association Beiter Graduate Student Research Grants, 1301 W 22 St, Suite 202, Oak Brook, IL 60523 *Tel:* 630-571-4520 *Fax:* 708-876-5598 *E-mail:* info@childlitassn.org *Web Site:* www.childlitassn.org, pg 637

McGee, Colin, Jessica Kingsley Publishers Inc, 400 Market St, Suite 400, Philadelphia, PA 19106 *Tel:* 215-922-1161 *Toll Free Tel:* 866-416-1078 (cust serv) *Fax:* 215-922-1474 *E-mail:* orders@jkp.com; hello.usa@jkp.com *Web Site:* www.jkp.com, pg 126

McGee, Linda, Bearport Publishing Co Inc, 45 W 21 St, Suite 3B, New York, NY 10010 *Tel:* 212-337-8577 *Toll Free Tel:* 877-337-8577 *Fax:* 212-337-8557 *Toll Free Fax:* 866-337-8557 *E-mail:* service@bearportpublishing.com; info@bearportpublishing.com *Web Site:* www.bearportpublishing.com, pg 31

McGee, Mary, PennWell Books, 1421 S Sheridan Rd, Tulsa, OK 74112 *Tel:* 918-831-9421 *Toll Free Tel:* 800-752-9764 *Fax:* 918-831-9555 *Toll Free Fax:* 877-218-1348 *E-mail:* sales@pennwell.com *Web Site:* www.pennwellbooks.com, pg 179

McGeehon, Allison, Artisan Books, 225 Varick St, New York, NY 10014-4381 *Tel:* 212-254-5900 *Toll Free Tel:* 800-722-7202 *Fax:* 212-677-6692 *E-mail:* artisaninfo@artisanbooks.com *Web Site:* www.workman.com/artisanbooks, pg 22

McGhee, Holly M, Pippin Properties Inc, 110 W 40 St, Suite 1704, New York, NY 10018 *Tel:* 212-338-9310 *Fax:* 212-338-9579 *E-mail:* info@pippinproperties.com *Web Site:* www.pippinproperties.com; www.facebook.com/pippinproperties, pg 531

McGill, Julia Lee, Scribner, 1230 Avenue of the Americas, New York, NY 10020, pg 209

McGinley, Paul, Rodale Inc, 400 S Tenth St, Emmaus, PA 18049 *Tel:* 610-967-5171 *Toll Free Tel:* 866-387-0509 *E-mail:* bookmarketing@rodale.com; bookpublicity@rodale.com *Web Site:* www.rodale.com, pg 200

McGinn, Patrick, Clinical Laboratory & Standards Institute (CLSI), 950 W Valley Rd, Suite 2500, Wayne, PA 19087 *Tel:* 610-688-0100 *Toll Free Tel:* 877-447-1888 (orders) *Fax:* 610-688-0700 *E-mail:* customerservice@clsi.org *Web Site:* www.clsi.org, pg 57

McGinnis, Claire, Riverhead Books, 375 Hudson St, New York, NY 10014 *Tel:* 212-366-2000 *Web Site:* www.penguin.com/publishers/riverhead, pg 199

McGinnis, Meredith, W W Norton & Company Inc, 500 Fifth Ave, New York, NY 10110-0017 *Tel:* 212-354-5500 *Toll Free Tel:* 800-233-4830 (orders & cust serv) *Fax:* 212-869-0856 *Toll Free Fax:* 800-458-6515 *E-mail:* orders@wwnorton.com *Web Site:* books.wwnorton.com, pg 164

McKinney, Anne, PREP Publishing, 3528 Turnberry Circle, Fayetteville, NC 28303 *Tel:* 910-483-6611 *Toll Free Tel:* 800-533-2814 *E-mail:* preppub@aol.com *Web Site:* www.prep-pub.com, pg 187

McKinney, Betty, Alpine Publications Inc, PO Box 188, Crawford, CO 81415 *Tel:* 970-921-5005 *Toll Free Tel:* 800-777-7257 *E-mail:* alpinepublishing@aol.com; customerservice@alpinepub.com *Web Site:* www.alpinepub.com, pg 8

McKinney, Charlie, Sophia Institute Press®, 522 Donald St, Unit 3, Bedford, NH 03110 *Tel:* 603-836-5505 *Toll Free Tel:* 800-888-9344 *Fax:* 603-641-8108 *Toll Free Fax:* 888-288-2259 *E-mail:* orders@sophiainstitute.com *Web Site:* www.sophiainstitute.com, pg 217

McKinney, Joe, Horror Writers Association (HWA), c/o Horror Writers Association, PO Box 56687, Sherman Oaks, CA 91413 *E-mail:* hwa@horror.org *Web Site:* horror.org, pg 566

McKinstry, Nancy, Wolters Kluwer US Corp, 2700 Lake Cook Rd, Riverwoods, IL 60015 *Tel:* 847-267-7000 *Fax:* 847-580-5192 *E-mail:* info@wolterskluwer.com *Web Site:* www.wolterskluwer.com, pg 258

McKinzie, Akira, American Booksellers Association, 333 Westchester Ave, Suite S202, White Plains, NY 10604 *Tel:* 914-406-7500 *Toll Free Tel:* 800-637-0037 *Fax:* 914-410-6297 *E-mail:* info@bookweb.org *Web Site:* www.bookweb.org, pg 554

McKirahan, Matthew, School of Government, University of North Carolina, CB 3330, Chapel Hill, NC 27599-3330 *Tel:* 919-966-4119 *Fax:* 919-962-2709 *Web Site:* www.sog.unc.edu, pg 208

McKitterick, Christopher, John W Campbell Memorial Award, University of Kansas, Wescoe Hall, Rm 3001, Dept of English, 1445 Jayhawk Blvd, Lawrence, KS 66045 *Tel:* 785-864-2518 *Fax:* 785-864-1159 *Web Site:* www.sfcenter.ku.edu/campbell.htm, pg 635

McKitterick, Christopher, Science Fiction Writers Workshop, University of Kansas, Wescoe Hall, Rm 3001, Dept of English, 1445 Jayhawk Blvd, Lawrence, KS 66045 *Tel:* 785-864-2518 *Fax:* 785-864-1159 *Web Site:* www.sfcenter.ku.edu; www.sfcenter.ku.edu/sfworkshop; www.sfcenter.ku.edu/novel-workshop, pg 614

McLain, Casey, Annual Off Off Broadway Short Play Festival, 235 Park Ave S, 5th fl, New York, NY 10003 *Tel:* 212-206-8990 *Toll Free Tel:* 866-598-8449 *Fax:* 212-206-1429 *E-mail:* oobfestival@samuelfrench.com *Web Site:* oob.samuelfrench.com; www.samuelfrench.com, pg 675

McLain, Kevin, Perseus Books, 250 W 57 St, 15th fl, New York, NY 10107 *Tel:* 212-340-8100 *Toll Free Tel:* 800-343-4499 (cust serv) *Fax:* 212-340-8105 *Web Site:* www.perseusbooks.com, pg 180

McLaughlin, Brenna, Association of American University Presses (AAUP), 1412 Broadway, Suite 2135, New York, NY 10018 *Tel:* 212-989-1010 *Fax:* 212-989-0275 *E-mail:* info@aaupnet.org *Web Site:* www.aaupnet.org, pg 558

McLaughlin, Kellie, Aperture Books, 547 W 27 St, 4th fl, New York, NY 10001 *Tel:* 212-505-5555 *Toll Free Tel:* 800-929-2323 *Fax:* 212-979-7759 *E-mail:* info@aperture.org *Web Site:* www.aperture.org, pg 18

McLaughlin, Larin, University of Washington Press, 4333 Brooklyn Ave NE, Seattle, WA 98105-9570 *Tel:* 206-543-4050 *Toll Free Tel:* 800 537 5487 (orders) *Fax:* 206-543-3932; 410-516-6998 (orders) *E-mail:* uwapress@uw.edu *Web Site:* www.washington.edu/uwpress, pg 246

McLaughlin, Maureen, Random House Children's Books, 1745 Broadway, 10th fl, New York, NY 10019 *Tel:* 212-782-9000 *Web Site:* www.randomhousekids.com, pg 194

McLaughlin, Nancy, Solano Press Books, PO Box 773, Point Arena, CA 95468 *Tel:* 707-884-4508 *Toll Free Tel:* 800-931-9373 *Fax:* 707-884-4109 *E-mail:* spbooks@solano.com *Web Site:* www.solano.com, pg 217

McLean, Christian, Southampton Writers' Conference, 239 Montauk Hwy, Southampton, NY 11968 *Tel:* 631-632-5007 *E-mail:* southamptonwriters@notes.cc.sunysb.edu; southamptonarts@stonybrook.edu *Web Site:* www.stonybrook.edu/southampton/mfa/summer/cwl_home.html, pg 615

McLean, George F, Council for Research in Values & Philosophy (RVP), The Catholic University of America, Gibbons Hall, Rm B-12, 620 Michigan Ave NE, Washington, DC 20064 *Tel:* 202-319-6089 *Fax:* 202-319-6089 *E-mail:* cua-rvp@cua.edu *Web Site:* www.crvp.org, pg 62

McLean, Laurie, San Francisco Writers Conference, 1029 Jones St, San Francisco, CA 94109 *Tel:* 415-673-0939 *E-mail:* sfwriterscon@aol.com *Web Site:* www.sfwriters.org, pg 614

McLean, Laurie, San Francisco Writing Contest (SFWC), 1029 Jones St, San Francisco, CA 94109 *Tel:* 415-673-0939 *E-mail:* sfwriterscon@aol.com *Web Site:* www.sfwriters.org, pg 686

McLean, Tom, Simon & Schuster Audio, 1230 Avenue of the Americas, New York, NY 10020 *Web Site:* audio.simonandschuster.com, pg 213

McLendon, Brian, Grand Central Publishing, 1290 Avenue of the Americas, New York, NY 10019 *Tel:* 212-364-1100 *Web Site:* www.hachettebookgroup.com, pg 95

McLennan, David, University of Regina Press, 2 Research Dr, Suite 246, Regina, SK S4S 7H9, Canada *Tel:* 306-585-4758 *Fax:* 306-585-4699 *E-mail:* uofrpress@uregina.ca *Web Site:* uofrpress.ca, pg 474

McLindon, R Mark, FPMI Solutions Inc, 689 Discovery Dr, Suite 300, Huntsville, AL 35806 *Toll Free Tel:* 888-644-3764 *E-mail:* info@fpmi.com *Web Site:* www.fpmisolutions.com; www.fpmi.com, pg 87

McMahon, Daniel J, New York State Bar Association, One Elk St, Albany, NY 12207 *Tel:* 518-463-3200 *Toll Free Tel:* 800-582-2452 *Fax:* 518-487-5517 *E-mail:* mrc@nysba.org *Web Site:* www.nysba.org, pg 162

McMahon, Donna, SF Canada, c/o Judy McCrosky, Secy-Treas, 516 Ninth St E, Saskatoon, SK S7N 0B1, Canada *Web Site:* www.sfcanada.org, pg 577

McMahon, Hilary, Westwood Creative Artists Ltd, 138 Sussex Mews, Toronto, ON M5S-2K1, Canada *Tel:* 416-964-3302 *Fax:* 416-964-3302 *E-mail:* wca_office@wcaltd.com *Web Site:* www.wcaltd.com, pg 541

McMan, Ann, Bywater Books, PO Box 3671, Ann Arbor, MI 48106-3671 *Tel:* 734-662-8815 *Web Site:* bywaterbooks.com, pg 46

Mcmanus, Kerry, Boyds Mills Press, 815 Church St, Honesdale, PA 18431 *Tel:* 570-253-1164 *Toll Free Tel:* 800-490-5111 *Fax:* 570-253-0179 *E-mail:* contact@boydsmillspress.com *Web Site:* www.boydsmillspress.com, pg 41

McManus, Rosanne, Reader's Digest Trade Publishing, 44 S Broadway, White Plains, NY 10601 *Tel:* 914-238-1000 *Web Site:* www.rdtradepublishing.com, pg 196

McMeel, John P, Andrews McMeel Publishing LLC, 1130 Walnut St, Kansas City, MO 64106-2109 *Toll Free Tel:* 800-851-8923; 800-943-9839 (cust serv) *Toll Free Fax:* 800-943-9831 (orders) *Web Site:* www.andrewsmcmeel.com, pg 16

McMenemy, Siobhan, Wilfrid Laurier University Press, 75 University Ave W, Waterloo, ON N2L 3C5, Canada *Tel:* 519-884-0710 *Toll Free Tel:* 866-836-5551 (CN & US) *Fax:* 519-725-1399 *E-mail:* press@wlu.ca *Web Site:* www.wlupress.wlu.ca, pg 476

McMillan, Sally Hill, Sally Hill McMillan LLC, 429 E Kingston Ave, Charlotte, NC 28203 *Tel:* 704-334-0897 *E-mail:* mcmagency@aol.com, pg 529

McMillan, Stephanie, Association of American Editorial Cartoonists, PO Box 460673, Fort Lauderdale, FL 33346 *Tel:* 954-356-4945 *Web Site:* www.editorialcartoonists.com, pg 558

McMillen, Wendy, University of Notre Dame Press, 310 Flanner Hall, Notre Dame, IN 46556 *Tel:* 574-631-6346 *Fax:* 574-631-8148 *E-mail:* undpress@nd.edu *Web Site:* www.undpress.nd.edu, pg 244

McMullen, Tammy C, Global Authors Publications (GAP), 38 Bluegrass, Middleberg, FL 32068 *Tel:* 904-425-1608 *E-mail:* gapbook@yahoo.com *Web Site:* www.globalauthorspublications.com, pg 93

McMurray, Debbie, Nilgiri Press, 3600 Tomales Rd, Tomales, CA 94971 *Tel:* 707-878-2369 *E-mail:* info@easwaran.org *Web Site:* www.easwaran.org, pg 162

McMurray, Heather, SBL Press, The Luce Ctr, Suite 350, 825 Houston Mill Rd, Atlanta, GA 30329 *Tel:* 404-727-3100 *Fax:* 404-727-3101 (corp) *E-mail:* sbl@sbl-site.org *Web Site:* www.sbl-site.org, pg 207

McMurray, Mary PhD, Harry S Truman Book Award, 500 W US Hwy 24, Independence, MO 64050 *Tel:* 816-268-8245 *Toll Free Tel:* 800-833-1225 *Web Site:* trumanlibraryinstitute.org, pg 694

McMurtray, Lisa, University Press of Mississippi, 3825 Ridgewood Rd, Jackson, MS 39211-6492 *Tel:* 601-432-6205 *Toll Free Tel:* 800-737-7788 (orders & cust serv) *Fax:* 601-432-6217 *E-mail:* press@mississippi.edu *Web Site:* www.upress.state.ms.us, pg 247

McNair, Shanna, Knightville Poetry Contest, PO Box 5101, Hanover, NH 03755 *E-mail:* info@newguardreview.com *Web Site:* www.newguardreview.com, pg 659

McNair, Shanna, Machigonne Fiction Contest, PO Box 5101, Hanover, NH 03755 *E-mail:* info@newguardreview.com *Web Site:* www.newguardreview.com, pg 664

McNally, Katie, Random House Publishing Group, 1745 Broadway, New York, NY 10019 *Toll Free Tel:* 800-200-3552 *Web Site:* atrandom.com, pg 195

McNaughton, Charlotte, American Society of Civil Engineers (ASCE), 1801 Alexander Bell Dr, Reston, VA 20191-4400 *Tel:* 703-295-6300 *Toll Free Tel:* 800-548-2723 *Fax:* 703-295-6278 *E-mail:* ascelibrary@asce.org *Web Site:* www.asce.org, pg 15

McNeely, Joe, Brilliance Audio, 1704 Eaton Dr, Grand Haven, MI 49417 *Tel:* 616-846-5256 *Toll Free Tel:* 800-648-2312 (orders only) *Fax:* 616-846-0630 *E-mail:* customerservice@brillianceaudio.com *Web Site:* www.brillianceaudio.com, pg 44

McNeill, Matt, Nimbus Publishing Ltd, 3731 Mackintosh St, Halifax, NS B3K 5A5, Canada *Tel:* 902-455-4286 *Toll Free Tel:* 800-NIMBUS9 (646-2879) *Fax:* 902-455-5440 *Toll Free Fax:* 888-253-3133 *E-mail:* customerservice@nimbus.ca *Web Site:* www.nimbus.ca, pg 465

McNeill, Timothy, Wisdom Publications Inc, 199 Elm St, Somerville, MA 02144 *Tel:* 617-776-7416 *Toll Free Tel:* 800-272-4050 (orders) *Fax:* 617-776-7841 *E-mail:* info@wisdompubs.org; submission@wisdompubs.org *Web Site:* www.wisdompubs.org, pg 257

McNeillie, Carolyn, Groundwood Books, 128 Sterling Rd, Lower Level, Toronto, ON M6R 2B7, Canada *Tel:* 416-363-4343 *Fax:* 416-363-1017 *E-mail:* genmail@groundwoodbooks.com *Web Site:* www.houseofanansi.com, pg 458

McNeillie, Carolyn, House of Anansi Press Inc, 128 Sterling Rd, Lower Level, Toronto, ON M6R 2B7, Canada *Tel:* 416-363-4343 *Fax:* 416-363-1017 *E-mail:* customerservice@houseofanansi.com *Web Site:* www.houseofanansi.com, pg 460

McNicholl, Damian, The Jennifer DeChiara Literary Agency, 299 Park Ave, 6th fl, New York, NY 10171 *Tel:* 212-739-0803 *Web Site:* www.jdlit.com, pg 513

McParland, Connie, Guernica Editions Inc, 1569 Heritage Way, Oakville, ON L6M 2Z7, Canada *Tel:* 905-599-5304 *E-mail:* info@guernicaeditions.com *Web Site:* www.guernicaeditions.com, pg 459

McPartland, Pat, Albert Whitman & Co, 250 S Northwest Hwy, Suite 320, Park Ridge, IL 60068 *Tel:* 847-232-2800 *Toll Free Tel:* 800-255-7675 *Fax:* 847-581-0039 *E-mail:* mail@albertwhitman.com *Web Site:* www.albertwhitman.com, pg 6

McPartlin, Oliver, Arsenal Pulp Press, 211 E Georgia St, No 202, Vancouver, BC V6A 1Z6, Canada *Tel:* 604-687-4233 *Toll Free Tel:* 888-600-PULP (600-7857) *Fax:* 604-687-4283 *E-mail:* info@arsenalpulp.com *Web Site:* www.arsenalpulp.com, pg 445

McPherson, Bruce R, McPherson & Co, 148 Smith Ave, Kingston, NY 12401 *Tel:* 845-331-5807 *Fax:* 845-331-5807 *E-mail:* bmcphersonco@gmail.com *Web Site:* www.mcphersonco.com, pg 146

McQuagge, Cassie, ARE Press, 215 67 St, Virginia Beach, VA 23451 *Tel:* 757-428-3588 *Toll Free Tel:* 800-333-4499 *Fax:* 757-491-0689 *Web Site:* www.edgarcayce.org, pg 20

McQuilkin, Robert Rennie, Antrim House, 21 Goodrich Rd, Simsbury, CT 06070-1804 *Tel:* 860-217-0023 *E-mail:* eds@antrimhousebooks.com *Web Site:* www.antrimhousebooks.com, pg 18

McSweeney, Prof Joyelle, The Ernest Sandeen & Richard Sullivan Prizes in Fiction & Poetry, 356 O'Shaughnessy Hall, Notre Dame, IN 46556 *Tel:* 574-631-7526 *Fax:* 574-631-4795 *E-mail:* creativewriting@nd.edu *Web Site:* creativewriting.nd.edu, pg 644

McWilliams, Skip, Teacher's Discovery, 2741 Paldan Dr, Auburn Hills, MI 48326 *Toll Free Tel:* 800-832-2437 *Toll Free Fax:* 800-287-4509 *E-mail:* help@teachersdiscovery.com *Web Site:* www.teachersdiscovery.com, pg 228

Mdhlongwa, Ndaba, Out of Your Mind...and Into the Marketplace™, 13381 White Sand Dr, Tustin, CA 92780-4565 *Tel:* 714-544-0248 *Toll Free Tel:* 800-419-1513 *Fax:* 714-730-1414 *Web Site:* www.business-plan.com, pg 171

Meacham, Beth, Tom Doherty Associates, LLC, 175 Fifth Ave, 14th fl, New York, NY 10010 *Tel:* 646-307-5511 *Toll Free Tel:* 800-455-0340 *Web Site:* www.tor-forge.com, pg 71

Meader, James, Picador, 175 Fifth Ave, 19th fl, New York, NY 10010 *Tel:* 646-307-5151 *Fax:* 212-253-9627 *Web Site:* www.picadorusa.com, pg 182

Meador, Craig, American Printing House for the Blind Inc, 1839 Frankfort Ave, Louisville, KY 40206 *Tel:* 502-895-2405 *Toll Free Tel:* 800-223-1839 (cust serv) *Fax:* 502-899-2274 *E-mail:* info@aph.org *Web Site:* www.aph.org; shop.aph.org, pg 14

Meadows, Laura, Carl Vinson Institute of Government, University of Georgia, 201 N Milledge Ave, Athens, GA 30602 *Tel:* 706-542-2736 *Fax:* 706-542-9301 *Web Site:* www.cviog.uga.edu, pg 251

Meadows, Rob, Bear & Co Inc, One Park St, Rochester, VT 05767 *Tel:* 802-767-3174 *Toll Free Tel:* 800-932-3277 *Fax:* 802-767-3726 *E-mail:* customerservice@InnerTraditions.com *Web Site:* InnerTraditions.com, pg 31

Meakin, Jonathan, J M Abraham Poetry Award, 1113 Marginal Rd, Halifax, NS B3H 4P7, Canada *Tel:* 902-423-8116 *Fax:* 902-422-0881 *E-mail:* contact@writers.ns.ca *Web Site:* writers.ns.ca, pg 625

Meakin, Jonathan, Thomas Raddall Atlantic Fiction Award, 1113 Marginal Rd, Halifax, NS B3H 4P7, Canada *Tel:* 902-423-8116 *Fax:* 902-422-0881 *E-mail:* contact@writers.ns.ca *Web Site:* writers.ns.ca, pg 683

Meakin, Jonathan, Evelyn Richardson Nonfiction Award, 1113 Marginal Rd, Halifax, NS B3H 4P7, Canada *Tel:* 902-423-8116 *Fax:* 902-422-0881 *E-mail:* contact@writers.ns.ca *Web Site:* writers.ns.ca, pg 684

Meakin, Jonathan, Writers' Federation of Nova Scotia, 1113 Marginal Rd, Halifax, NS B3H 4P7, Canada *Tel:* 902-423-8116 *Fax:* 902-422-0881 *E-mail:* contact@writers.ns.ca *Web Site:* writers.ns.ca, pg 581

Means, Lindsay, Simon & Schuster, 1230 Avenue of the Americas, New York, NY 10020 *Tel:* 212-698-7000 *Toll Free Tel:* 800-223-2348 (cust serv); 800-223-2336 (orders) *Toll Free Fax:* 800-943-9831 (orders) *Web Site:* www.simonandschuster.com, pg 212

Mechanic, Joline, Black Mountain Press, PO Box 9907, Asheville, NC 28815 *Tel:* 828-273-3332 *Web Site:* www.theblackmountainpress.com, pg 36

Mecklenborg, Mark, The American Ceramic Society, 600 N Cleveland Ave, Suite 210, Westerville, OH 43082 *Tel:* 240-646-7054 *Toll Free Tel:* 866-721-3322 *Fax:* 240-396-5637 *E-mail:* customerservice@ceramics.org *Web Site:* ceramics.org, pg 10

Medaille, Jessica, International Society for Technology in Education, 1530 Wilson Blvd, Suite 730, Arlington, VA 22209 *Tel:* 503-342-2848 (intl) *Toll Free Tel:* 800-336-5191 (US & CN) *E-mail:* iste@iste.org *Web Site:* www.iste.org; www.isteconference.org, pg 120

Medeiros, Maria, Novalis Publishing, 10 Lower Spadina Ave, Suite 400, Toronto, ON M5V 2Z2, Canada *Tel:* 416-363-3303 *Toll Free Tel:* 877-702-7773 *Fax:* 416-363-9409 *Toll Free Fax:* 877-702-7775 *E-mail:* books@novalis.ca *Web Site:* www.novalis.ca, pg 465

Medeot, William, Orbis Books, Price Bldg, Box 302, Maryknoll, NY 10545-0302 *Tel:* 914-941-7636 *Toll Free Tel:* 800-258-5838 (orders) *Fax:* 914-941-7005 *E-mail:* orbisbooks@maryknoll.org *Web Site:* orbisbooks.com, pg 169

Medina, Kate, Random House Publishing Group, 1745 Broadway, New York, NY 10019 *Toll Free Tel:* 800-200-3552 *Web Site:* atrandom.com, pg 195

Medley, Mandy, Coffee House Press, 79 13 Ave NE, Suite 110, Minneapolis, MN 55413 *Tel:* 612-338-0125 *Fax:* 612-338-4004 *E-mail:* info@coffeehousepress.org *Web Site:* coffeehousepress.org, pg 58

Mednansky, Kristine, Productivity Press, 711 Third Ave, 8th fl, New York, NY 10017 *Tel:* 212-216-7800 *Toll Free Tel:* 800-634-7064 (orders); 800-797-3803 *E-mail:* orders@taylorandfrancis.com *Web Site:* www.productivitypress.com, pg 189

Meehan, Emily, Disney-Hyperion Books, 1101 Flower St, Glendale, CA 91201 *Web Site:* books.disney.com, pg 70

Meeks, Barbara, Show What You Know® Publishing, A Lorenz Company, c/o The Lorenz Corp, 501 E Third St, Dayton, OH 45402 *Tel:* 614-764-1211; 937-228-6118 *Toll Free Tel:* 877-PASSING (727-7464) *Fax:* 937-233-2042 *E-mail:* info@lorenz.com *Web Site:* www.lorenzeducationalpress.com, pg 212

Meerdink, Jan, The Russell Meerdink Co Ltd, 1555 S Park Ave, Neenah, WI 54956 *Tel:* 920-725-0955 *Toll Free Tel:* 800-635-6499 *Fax:* 920-725-0709 *E-mail:* questions@horseinfo.com *Web Site:* www.horseinfo.com, pg 148

Meere, Selina, Workman Publishing Co Inc, 225 Varick St, 9th fl, New York, NY 10014-4381 *Tel:* 212-254-5900 *Toll Free Tel:* 800-722-7202 *Fax:* 212-254-8098 *E-mail:* info@workman.com *Web Site:* www.workman.com, pg 259

Meeropol, Ellen, Chocorua Writing Workshop, PO Box 2280, Conway, NH 03818-2280 *Tel:* 603-447-2280 *E-mail:* reservations@worldfellowship.org *Web Site:* www.worldfellowship.org; www.facebook.com/World.Fellowship.Center, pg 610

Megargee, Moira, Interlink Publishing Group Inc, 46 Crosby St, Northampton, MA 01060 *Tel:* 413-582-7054 *Toll Free Tel:* 800-238-LINK (238-5465) *Fax:* 413-582-7057 *E-mail:* info@interlinkbooks.com *Web Site:* www.interlinkbooks.com, pg 118

Megged, Semadar, Philomel, 345 Hudson St, New York, NY 10014 *Tel:* 212-366-2000, pg 182

Meglio, Leila, Houghton Mifflin Harcourt, 125 High St, Boston, MA 02110 *Tel:* 617-351-5000 *Toll Free Tel:* 855-969-4642; 800-225-5425 (K-12 educ materials); 800-323-9540 (assessment materials); 877-219-1537 (SkillsTutor); 888-242-6747 (Innovation in Educ Group); 800-225-3362 (Trade & Ref Div) *Toll Free Fax:* 800-269-5232 *E-mail:* myhmhco@hmhco.com *Web Site:* www.hmhco.com, pg 110

Mehta, Sonny, Doubleday/Nan A Talese, c/o Penguin Random House Inc, 1745 Broadway, New York, NY 10019 *Tel:* 212-751-2600 *Fax:* 212-572-2662 *E-mail:* ddaypub@randomhouse.com *Web Site:* knopfdoubleday.com, pg 72

Mehta, Sonny, Alfred A Knopf/Everyman's Library, c/o Penguin Random House Inc, 1745 Broadway, New York, NY 10019 *Tel:* 212-751-2600 *Toll Free Tel:* 800-638-6460 *Fax:* 212-572-2593 *Web Site:* www.knopfdoubleday.com, pg 127

Mehta, Sonny, Penguin Random House Inc, 1745 Broadway, New York, NY 10019 *Tel:* 212-782-9000 *Toll Free Tel:* 800-726-0600 *Web Site:* www.penguinrandomhouse.com, pg 178

Meier, Anna, Houghton Mifflin Harcourt Trade & Reference Division, 125 High St, Boston, MA 02110 *Tel:* 617-351-5000 *Toll Free Tel:* 800-225-3362 *Web Site:* www.hmhco.com, pg 111

Meints, Rick, Chaosium Inc, 3450 Wooddale Ct, Ann Arbor, MI 48104 *Tel:* 734-972-9551 *E-mail:* customerservice@chaosium.com *Web Site:* www.chaosium.com, pg 52

Meissner, Bill, Mississippi River Creative Writing Workshop, 720 Fourth Ave S, B-151, Rm 100, St Cloud, MN 56301-4498 *Tel:* 320-308-4947 *Fax:* 320-308-5524 *Web Site:* www.stcloudstate.edu, pg 612

Meister, Mark, The Ambassador Richard C Holbrooke Distinguished Achievement Award, PO Box 461, Wright Brothers Branch, Dayton, OH 45409-0461 *Tel:* 937-298-5072 *E-mail:* sharon.rab@daytonliterarypeaceprize.org *Web Site:* www.daytonliterarypeaceprize.org/holbrooke.htm, pg 627

Meixelsperger, Wes, Soil Science Society of America, 5585 Guilford Rd, Madison, WI 53711-5801 *Tel:* 608-273-8080 *Web Site:* www.soils.org, pg 217

Meizlik, Shelby, HarperCollins General Books Group, 195 Broadway, New York, NY 10007 *Tel:* 212-207-7000 *Web Site:* www.harpercollins.com, pg 101

Melancon, Barry C, AICPA Professional Publications, 220 Leigh Farm Rd, Durham, NC 27707 *Tel:* 919-402-4500 *Toll Free Tel:* 888-777-7077 (memb serv ctr) *Fax:* 919-402-4505 *Toll Free Fax:* 800-362-5066 (memb serv ctr) *E-mail:* acquisitions@aicpa.org; service@aicpa.org *Web Site:* www.aicpa.org, pg 6

Melando, Edward J, John Wiley & Sons Inc, 111 River St, Hoboken, NJ 07030-5774 *Tel:* 201-748-6000 *Toll Free Tel:* 800-225-5945 (cust serv) *Fax:* 201-748-6088 *E-mail:* info@wiley.com *Web Site:* www.wiley.com, pg 256

Mell, Prof Donald C, University of Delaware Press, 200A Morris Library, 181 S College Ave, Newark, DE 19717-5267 *Tel:* 302-831-1149 *Fax:* 302-831-6549 *E-mail:* ud-press@udel.edu *Web Site:* library.udel.edu/udpress, pg 241

Mello, Felice, W W Norton & Company Inc, 500 Fifth Ave, New York, NY 10110-0017 *Tel:* 212-354-5500 *Toll Free Tel:* 800-233-4830 (orders & cust serv) *Fax:* 212-869-0856 *Toll Free Fax:* 800-458-6515 *E-mail:* orders@wwnorton.com *Web Site:* books.wwnorton.com, pg 164

Melnyk, Emma, Canadian Scholars' Press Inc, 425 Adelaide St W, Suite 200, Toronto, ON M5V 3C1, Canada *Tel:* 416-929-2774 *Toll Free Tel:* 800-463-1998 *Fax:* 416-929-1926 *E-mail:* info@cspi.org; info@canadianscholars.ca; editorial@canadianscholars.ca; orders@canadianscholars.ca *Web Site:* www.canadianscholars.ca; www.womenspress.ca, pg 449

Melnyk, Sarah, St Martin's Press, LLC, 175 Fifth Ave, New York, NY 10010 *Tel:* 646-307-5151 *Web Site:* us.macmillan.com/smp, pg 204

Meloche, Luc, LexisNexis® Canada Inc, 111 Gordon Baker Rd, Suite 900, Toronto, ON M2H 3R1, Canada *Tel:* 905-479-2665 *Toll Free Tel:* 800-668-6481; 800-387-0899 (cust care); 800-255-5174 (sales) *E-mail:* service@lexisnexis.ca (cust serv); sales@lexisnexis.ca *Web Site:* www.lexisnexis.ca, pg 462

Melton, Dianne, Summerthought Publishing, PO Box 2309, Banff, AB T1L 1C1, Canada *Tel:* 403-762-0535 *Fax:* 403-762-3095 *Toll Free Fax:* 800-762-3095 (orders) *E-mail:* info@summerthought.com; sales@summerthought.com *Web Site:* summerthought.com, pg 471

Meltzer, Kate, GP Putnam's Sons (Children's), 345 Hudson St, New York, NY 10014 *Tel:* 212-366-2000 *Fax:* 212-414-3393 *Web Site:* www.penguin.com/publishers/gpputnamssonsbooksforyoungread, pg 192

Meltzer, Lauren, The Charles Press, Publishers, 230 N 21 St, Suite 312, Philadelphia, PA 19103 *Tel:* 215-561-2786 *Fax:* 215-600-1248 *E-mail:* mail@charlespresspub.com *Web Site:* www.charlespresspub.com, pg 53

Meltzer, Steve, Celebra, 375 Hudson St, New York, NY 10014 *Tel:* 212-366-2000 *E-mail:* ecommerce@us.penguingroup.com *Web Site:* www.penguin.com, pg 50

Meltzer, Steve, Dial Books for Young Readers, 345 Hudson St, New York, NY 10014 *Tel:* 212-366-2000 *Toll Free Tel:* 800-733-3000 (orders) *Fax:* 212-414-3396 *Web Site:* www.penguin.com, pg 70

Melville, Kirsty, Andrews McMeel Publishing LLC, 1130 Walnut St, Kansas City, MO 64106-2109 *Toll Free Tel:* 800-851-8923; 800-943-9839 (cust serv) *Toll Free Fax:* 800-943-9831 (orders) *Web Site:* www.andrewsmcmeel.com, pg 17

Melvin, Annette, Random House Publishing Group, 1745 Broadway, New York, NY 10019 *Toll Free Tel:* 800-200-3552 *Web Site:* atrandom.com, pg 195

Melvin, Becky, Thomas Nelson, 501 Nelson Place, Nashville, TN 37214 *Tel:* 615-889-9000 *Toll Free Tel:* 800-251-4000 *Fax:* 615-902-1548 *Web Site:* www.thomasnelson.com, pg 231

Membrino, Anna, Random House Children's Books, 1745 Broadway, 10th fl, New York, NY 10019 *Tel:* 212-782-9000 *Web Site:* www.randomhousekids.com, pg 194

Mendel, Scott, Mendel Media Group LLC, 115 W 30 St, Suite 800, New York, NY 10001 *Tel:* 646-239-9896 *Fax:* 212-685-4717 *Web Site:* www.mendelmedia.com, pg 529

Mendelsohn, Aaron, Writers Guild of America Awards, 7000 W Third St, Los Angeles, CA 90048 *Tel:* 323-951-4000; 323-782-4569 *Fax:* 323-782-4800 *Web Site:* www.wga.org, pg 700

Mendelsohn, Aaron, Writers Guild of America, West (WGAW), 7000 W Third St, Los Angeles, CA 90048 *Tel:* 323-951-4000 *Toll Free Tel:* 800-548-4532 *Fax:* 323-782-4800 *Web Site:* www.wga.org, pg 581

Mendelson, John, Candlewick Press, 99 Dover St, Somerville, MA 02144-2825 *Tel:* 617-661-3330 *Fax:* 617-661-0565 *E-mail:* bigbear@candlewick.com; salesinfo@candlewick.com *Web Site:* www.candlewick.com, pg 46

Mendoza, Isabel, Santillana USA Publishing Co, 2023 NW 84 Ave, Doral, FL 33122 *Tel:* 305-591-9522 *Toll Free Tel:* 800-245-8584 *E-mail:* customerservice@santillanausa.com *Web Site:* www.santillanausa.com, pg 206

Mendoza, Stephanie, HarperCollins General Books Group, 195 Broadway, New York, NY 10007 *Tel:* 212-207-7000 *Web Site:* www.harpercollins.com, pg 101

Menick, Jim, Reader's Digest USA Select Editions, 44 S Broadway, 7th fl, White Plains, NY 10601 *Tel:* 914-238-1000 *Toll Free Tel:* 800-304-2807 (cust serv) *Fax:* 914-831-1560, pg 196

Menn, Don, Immedium, 535 Rockdale Dr, San Francisco, CA 94127 *Tel:* 415-452-8546 *Fax:* 360-937-6272 *E-mail:* orders@immedium.com; sales@immedium.com *Web Site:* www.immedium.com, pg 115

Mennel, Timothy, University of Chicago Press, 1427 E 60 St, Chicago, IL 60637-2954 *Tel:* 773-702-7700; 773-702-7600 *Toll Free Tel:* 800-621-2736 (orders) *Fax:* 773-702-9756; 773-660-2235 (orders); 773-702-2708 *E-mail:* custserv@press.uchicago.edu; marketing@press.uchicago.edu *Web Site:* www.press.uchicago.edu, pg 241

Mennitt, Meredith, St Martin's Press, LLC, 175 Fifth Ave, New York, NY 10010 *Tel:* 646-307-5151 *Web Site:* us.macmillan.com/smp, pg 204

Menon, Pooja, Kimberley Cameron & Associates LLC, 1550 Tiburon Blvd, Suite 704, Tiburon, CA 94920 *Tel:* 415-789-9191 *Fax:* 415-789-9177 *Web Site:* www.kimberleycameron.com, pg 511

Menzies, Tracey, HarperCollins General Books Group, 195 Broadway, New York, NY 10007 *Tel:* 212-207-7000 *Web Site:* www.harpercollins.com, pg 101

Menzies, Tracey, HarperCollins Publishers, 195 Broadway, New York, NY 10007 *Tel:* 212-207-7000 *Fax:* 212-207-7145 *Web Site:* www.harpercollins.com, pg 101

Meradji, Ahmad, BookLogix, 1264 Old Alpharetta Rd, Alpharetta, GA 30005 *Tel:* 470-239-8547 *Toll Free Fax:* 888-564-7890 *E-mail:* sales@booklogix.com *Web Site:* www.booklogix.com, pg 40

Mercandetti, Susan, Random House Publishing Group, 1745 Broadway, New York, NY 10019 *Toll Free Tel:* 800-200-3552 *Web Site:* atrandom.com, pg 195

Merchant, Ann, National Academies Press (NAP), Lockbox 285, 500 Fifth St NW, Washington, DC 20001 *Tel:* 202-334-3313 *Fax:* 202-334-2451 (cust serv); 202-334-2793 (mktg dept) *E-mail:* customer_service@nap.edu *Web Site:* www.nap.edu, pg 156

Merchant, Leigh, Random House Publishing Group, 1745 Broadway, New York, NY 10019 *Toll Free Tel:* 800-200-3552 *Web Site:* atrandom.com, pg 195

Mercy, Jon, ANR Publications University of California, 1301 S 46 St, Bldg 478 - MC 3580, Richmond, CA 94804 *Tel:* 510-665-2195 (cust serv) *Toll Free Tel:* 800-994-8849 *Fax:* 510-665-3427 *E-mail:* anrcatalog@ucdavis.edu *Web Site:* anrcatalog.ucanr.edu, pg 17

Meredith, Mimi, Society of Environmental Toxicology & Chemistry (SETAC), 229 S Baylen St, 2nd fl, Pensacola, FL 32502 *Tel:* 850-469-1500 *Toll Free Fax:* 888-296-4136 *E-mail:* setac@setac.org; etc@setac.org (edit) *Web Site:* www.setac.org, pg 216

Mergenthaler, Gretchen, Grove Atlantic Inc, 154 W 14 St, 12th fl, New York, NY 10011 *Tel:* 212-614-7850 *Toll Free Tel:* 800-521-0178 *Fax:* 212-614-7886 *E-mail:* info@groveatlantic.com; sales@groveatlantic.com; publicity@groveatlantic.com; rights@groveatlantic.com *Web Site:* www.groveatlantic.com, pg 97

Merkle, Dieter, Springer, 233 Spring St, New York, NY 10013-1578 *Tel:* 212-460-1500 *Toll Free Tel:* 800-SPRINGER (777-4643) *Fax:* 212-460-1700 *E-mail:* customerservice@springer.com *Web Site:* www.springer.com, pg 219

Merkle, Molly, AdventureKEEN, 2204 First Ave S, Suite 102, Birmingham, AL 35233 *Tel.* 763-689-9800 *Toll Free Tel:* 800-678-7006 *Fax:* 763-689-9039 *Toll Free Fax:* 877-374-9016 *E-mail:* info@adventurewithkeen.com *Web Site:* adventurewithkeen.com, pg 5

Merkle, Molly B, Menasha Ridge Press Inc, 2204 First Ave S, Suite 102, Birmingham, AL 35233 *Toll Free Tel:* 888-604-4537 *Fax:* 205-326-1012 *E-mail:* info@adventurewithkeen.com *Web Site:* www.menasharidge.com, pg 148

Merola, Marianne, Brandt & Hochman Literary Agents Inc, 1501 Broadway, Suite 2310, New York, NY 10036 *Tel:* 212-840-5760 *Fax:* 212-840-5776 *Web Site:* brandthochman.com, pg 509

Merola, Marianne, The Joy Harris Literary Agency Inc, 1501 Broadway, Suite 2310, New York, NY 10036 *Tel:* 212-924-6269 *Fax:* 212-840-5776 *E-mail:* contact@joyharrisliterary.com *Web Site:* www.joyharrisliterary.com, pg 520

Merriam, Ray, Merriam Press, 133 Elm St, Suite 3R, Bennington, VT 05201-2250 *Tel:* 802-447-0313 *Web Site:* www.merriam-press.com, pg 149

Merz, Kathleen, Wm B Eerdmans Publishing Co, 2140 Oak Industrial Dr NE, Grand Rapids, MI 49505 *Tel:* 616-459-4591 *Toll Free Tel:* 800-253-7521 *Fax:* 616-459-6540 *E-mail:* customerservice@eerdmans.com; sales@eerdmans.com *Web Site:* www.eerdmans.com, pg 76

Mesecher, Kim, M Lee Smith Publishers, 100 Winners Circle, Suite 300, Brentwood, TN 37027 *Tel:* 615-373-7517 *Toll Free Tel:* 800-274-6774; 800-727-5257 *E-mail:* custserv@mleesmith.com; service@blr.com *Web Site:* www.mleesmith.com; www.blr.com, pg 215

Messer, Miwa, Discover Great New Writers Award, 122 Fifth Ave, New York, NY 10011 *Web Site:* www.barnesandnoble.com, pg 641

Messer, Randy, Perfection Learning Corp, 1000 N Second Ave, Logan, IA 51546 *Tel:* 712-644-2831 *Toll Free Tel:* 800-831-4190 *Toll Free Fax:* 800-543-2745 *E-mail:* orders@perfectionlearning.com *Web Site:* perfectionlearning.com, pg 180

Messerli, Douglas, Green Integer, 6210 Wilshire Blvd, Suite 211, Los Angeles, CA 90048 *Tel:* 323-857-1115 *Fax:* 323-857-0143 *Web Site:* www.greeninteger.com, pg 96

Messick, Mary K, Schoolhouse Network, PO Box 1518, Northampton, MA 01061 *Tel:* 480-427-4836 *E-mail:* schoolhousenetwork@gmail.com, pg 501

Messitte, Anne, Anchor Books, c/o Penguin Random House Inc, 1745 Broadway, New York, NY 10019 *Tel:* 212-572-2420 *E-mail:* vintageanchorpublicity@randomhouse.com *Web Site:* knopfdoubleday.com/imprint/anchor, pg 16

Messitte, Anne, Alfred A Knopf/Everyman's Library, c/o Penguin Random House Inc, 1745 Broadway, New York, NY 10019 *Tel:* 212-751-2600 *Toll Free Tel:* 800-638-6460 *Fax:* 212-572-2593 *Web Site:* www.knopfdoubleday.com, pg 127

Messitte, Anne, Vintage Books, c/o Penguin Random House Inc, 1745 Broadway, New York, NY 10019 *Tel:* 212-572-2420 *E-mail:* vintageanchorpublicity@randomhouse.com *Web Site:* knopfdoubleday.com/imprint/vintage, pg 251

Meszaros, Abel, Central European University Press, 224 W 57 St, New York, NY 10019 *Web Site:* www.ceupress.com, pg 51

Meth, David L, Writers' Productions, PO Box 630, Westport, CT 06881-0630 *Tel:* 203-227-8199, pg 542

Metivier, Michael, Chelsea Green Publishing Co, 85 N Main St, Suite 120, White River Junction, VT 05001 *Tel:* 802-295-6300 *Toll Free Tel:* 800-639-4099 (cust serv, consumer & trade orders) *Fax:* 802-295-6444 *Web Site:* www.chelseagreen.com, pg 53

Metro, Judy, National Gallery of Art, Sixth & Constitution Ave NW, Washington, DC 20565 *Tel:* 202-737-4215; 202-842-6480 *Fax:* 202-842-6733 *E-mail:* casva@nga.gov *Web Site:* www.nga.gov, pg 158

Metsch, Amy, Penguin Random House Large Print, 1745 Broadway, New York, NY 10019 *Tel:* 212-782-9000 *Web Site:* www.penguinrandomhouse.com, pg 179

Metz, Mary, The Mountaineers Books, 1001 SW Klickitat Way, Suite 201, Seattle, WA 98134 *Tel:* 206-223-6303 *Toll Free Tel:* 800-553-4453 *Fax:* 206-223-6306 *Toll Free Fax:* 800-568-7604 *E-mail:* mbooks@mountaineersbooks.org; customerservice@mountaineersbooks.org *Web Site:* www.mountaineersbooks.org, pg 155

Metzger, Jennifer, Insight Editions, 800 "A" St, San Rafael, CA 94901 *Tel:* 415-526-1370 *Toll Free Tel:* 800-809-3792 *Toll Free Fax:* 866-509-0515 *E-mail:* info@insighteditions.com *Web Site:* www.insighteditions.com, pg 117

Metzner, Joerg, Rand McNally, 9855 Woods Dr, Skokie, IL 60077 *Tel:* 847-329-8100 *E-mail:* ctsales@randmcnally.com; mediarelations@randmcnally.com *Web Site:* www.randmcnally.com, pg 194

Meyer, Astrid, The Pennsylvania State University Press, University Support Bldg 1, Suite C, 820 N University Dr, University Park, PA 16802-1003 *Tel:* 814-865-

1327 *Toll Free Tel:* 800-326-9180 *Fax:* 814-863-1408 *Toll Free Fax:* 877-778-2665 *E-mail:* info@psupress.org *Web Site:* www.psupress.org, pg 179

Meyer, Caitlin, Beacon Press, 24 Farnsworth St, Boston, MA 02210-1409 *Tel:* 617-742-2110 *Fax:* 617-723-3097; 617-742-2290 *Web Site:* www.beacon.org, pg 31

Meyer, Dan, Doubleday/Nan A Talese, c/o Penguin Random House Inc, 1745 Broadway, New York, NY 10019 *Tel:* 212-751-2600 *Fax:* 212-572-2662 *E-mail:* ddaypub@randomhouse.com *Web Site:* knopfdoubleday.com, pg 72

Meyer, Kathleen, Duquesne University Press, 600 Forbes Ave, Pittsburgh, PA 15282 *Tel:* 412-396-6610 *Fax:* 412-396-5984 *E-mail:* dupress@duq.edu *Web Site:* www.dupress.duq.edu, pg 74

Meyer, Laura, Groundwood Books, 128 Sterling Rd, Lower Level, Toronto, ON M6R 2B7, Canada *Tel:* 416-363-4343 *Fax:* 416-363-1017 *E-mail:* genmail@groundwoodbooks.com *Web Site:* www.houseofanansi.com, pg 458

Meyer, Laura, House of Anansi Press Inc, 128 Sterling Rd, Lower Level, Toronto, ON M6R 2B7, Canada *Tel:* 416-363-4343 *Fax:* 416-363-1017 *E-mail:* customerservice@houseofanansi.com *Web Site:* www.houseofanansi.com, pg 460

Meyer, Steve, LAMA Books, 2381 Sleepy Hollow Ave, Hayward, CA 94545-3429 *Tel:* 510-785-1091 *Toll Free Tel:* 888-452-6244 *Fax:* 510-785-1099 *Web Site:* www.lamabooks.com, pg 129

Meyers, Amy, Yale Center for British Art, 1080 Chapel St, New Haven, CT 06510-2302 *Tel:* 203-432-2800 *Fax:* 203-432-4538 *Web Site:* britishart.yale.edu, pg 261

Meyers, Bob, National Press Foundation, 1211 Connecticut Ave NW, Suite 310, Washington, DC 20036 *Tel:* 202-663-7280 *Web Site:* nationalpress.org, pg 572

Meyers, Catharine A, New Harbinger Publications Inc, 5674 Shattuck Ave, Oakland, CA 94609 *Tel:* 510-652-0215 *Toll Free Tel:* 800-748-6273 (orders only) *Fax:* 510-652-5472 *Toll Free Fax:* 800-652-1613 *E-mail:* nhhelp@newharbinger.com; customerservice@newharbinger.com *Web Site:* www.newharbinger.com, pg 160

Meyers, Rachel, Sinauer Associates Inc, 23 Plumtree Rd, Sunderland, MA 01375 *Tel:* 413-549-4300 *Fax:* 413-549-1118 *E-mail:* publish@sinauer.com; orders@sinauer.com *Web Site:* sinauer.com, pg 214

Meyers, Tona Pearce, New World Library, 14 Pamaron Way, Novato, CA 94949 *Tel:* 415-884-2100 *Toll Free Tel:* 800-227-3900 (ext 52, retail orders); 800-972-6657 *Fax:* 415-884-2199 *E-mail:* escort@newworldlibrary.com *Web Site:* www.newworldlibrary.com, pg 161

Miceli, Jaya, Scribner, 1230 Avenue of the Americas, New York, NY 10020, pg 209

Michaels, Ken, Macmillan Learning, 41 Madison Ave, New York, NY 10010 *Tel:* 212-576-9400 *Fax:* 212-689-2383 *Web Site:* www.macmillanlearning.com, pg 140

Michaels, Samantha, Wood Lake Publishing Inc, 485 Beaver Lake Rd, Kelowna, BC V4V 1S5, Canada *Tel:* 250-766-2778 *Toll Free Tel:* 800-663-2775 (orders & cust serv) *Fax:* 250-766-2736 *Toll Free Fax:* 888-841-9991 (orders & cust serv) *E-mail:* info@woodlake.com; customerservice@woodlake.com *Web Site:* www.woodlakebooks.com, pg 476

Michailidis, Parisa, Firefly Books Ltd, 50 Staples Ave, Unit 1, Richmond Hill, ON L4B 0A7, Canada *Tel:* 416-499-8412 *Toll Free Tel:* 800-387-6192 (CN); 800-387-5085 (US) *Fax:* 416-499-8313 *Toll Free Fax:* 800-450-0391 (CN); 800-565-6034 (US) *E-mail:* info@fireflybooks.com *Web Site:* www.fireflybooks.com, pg 456

Michalicek, Steven S, Heuer Publishing LLC, PO Box 248, Cedar Rapids, IA 52406 *Tel:* 319-368-8008 *Toll Free Tel:* 800-950-7529 *Fax:* 319-368-8011 *E-mail:* editor@heuerpub.com; customerservice@heuerpub.com *Web Site:* www.hitplays.com, pg 106

Michalski, Chris, Ascension Press, PO Box 1990, West Chester, PA 19380 *Tel:* 610-696-7795; 484-875-4550 (admin) *Toll Free Tel:* 800-376-0520 (sales & cust serv) *Web Site:* ascensionpress.com, pg 22

Michaud, Jacques, Les Editions Vents d'Ouest, 109, rue Wright, bureau 202, Gatineau, QC J8X 2G7, Canada *Tel:* 819-770-6377 *E-mail:* info@ventsdouest.ca *Web Site:* www.ventsdouest.ca, pg 455

Michel, Christie, Other Press, 267 Fifth Ave, 6th fl, New York, NY 10016 *Tel:* 212-414-0054 *Toll Free Tel:* 877-843-6843 *Fax:* 212-414-0939 *E-mail:* editor@otherpress.com; marketing@otherpress.com; publicity@otherpress.com *Web Site:* www.otherpress.com, pg 170

Michels, Anna, Sourcebooks Inc, 1935 Brookdale Rd, Suite 139, Naperville, IL 60563 *Tel:* 630-961-3900 *Toll Free Tel:* 800-432-7444 *Fax:* 630-961-2168 *E-mail:* info@sourcebooks.com; customersupport@sourcebooks.com *Web Site:* www.sourcebooks.com, pg 218

Michels, Dia L, Platypus Media LLC, 725 Eighth St SE, Washington, DC 20003 *Tel:* 202-546-1674 *Toll Free Tel:* 877-PLATYPS (752-8977) *Fax:* 202-546-2356 *E-mail:* info@platypusmedia.com *Web Site:* www.platypusmedia.com, pg 183

Michels, Dia L, Science, Naturally, 725 Eighth St SE, Washington, DC 20003 *Tel:* 202-465-4798 *Toll Free Tel:* 866-724-9876 *Fax:* 202-558-2132 *E-mail:* info@sciencenaturally.com *Web Site:* www.sciencenaturally.com, pg 209

Michels, Greg, Municipal Analysis Services Inc, PO Box 13453, Austin, TX 78711-3453 *Tel:* 512-704-7194 *E-mail:* munilysis@gmail.com *Web Site:* sites.google.com/site/gregmichels/home, pg 155

Michelson, David, Artech House Inc, 685 Canton St, Norwood, MA 02062 *Tel:* 781-769-9750 *Toll Free Tel:* 800-225-9977 *Fax:* 781-769-6334 *E-mail:* artech@artechhouse.com *Web Site:* www.artechhouse.com, pg 22

Miciak, Kate, Random House Publishing Group, 1745 Broadway, New York, NY 10019 *Toll Free Tel:* 800-200-3552 *Web Site:* atrandom.com, pg 195

Mickulas, Peter, Rutgers University Press, 106 Somerset St, 3rd fl, New Brunswick, NJ 08901 *Tel:* 848-445-7762 *Toll Free Tel:* 800-848-6224 (orders only) *Fax:* 732-745-4935 (acqs, edit, mktg, perms & prodn) *Toll Free Fax:* 800-272-6817 (fulfillment) *Web Site:* rutgerspress.rutgers.edu, pg 202

Middlebrook, Ron, Centerstream Publishing LLC, PO Box 17878, Anaheim Hills, CA 92817-7878 *Tel:* 714-779-9390 *E-mail:* centerstrm@aol.com *Web Site:* www.centerstream-usa.com, pg 51

Middleton, Jean F, IndexEmpire Indexing Services, 16740 Orville Wright Dr, Riverside, CA 92518 *Tel:* 951-697-2819 *E-mail:* indexempire@gmail.com *Web Site:* www.indexempire.com, pg 496

Middleton, Kathy, Crabtree Publishing Co, 350 Fifth Ave, 59th fl, PMB 59051, New York, NY 10118 *Tel:* 212-496-5040 *Toll Free Tel:* 800-387-7650 *Toll Free Fax:* 800-355-7166 *E-mail:* custserv@crabtreebooks.com *Web Site:* www.crabtreebooks.com, pg 63

Middleton, Kathy, Crabtree Publishing Co Ltd, 616 Welland Ave, St Catharines, ON L2M 5V6, Canada *Tel:* 905-682-5221 *Toll Free Tel:* 800-387-7650 *Fax:* 905-682-7166 *Toll Free Fax:* 800-355-7166 *E-mail:* custserv@crabtreebooks.com; sales@crabtreebooks.com; orders@crabtreebooks.com *Web Site:* www.crabtreebooks.com, pg 451

Middleton, Lydia, Association for Information Science & Technology (ASIS&T), 8555 16 St, Suite 850, Silver Spring, MD 20910 *Tel:* 301-495-0900 *Fax:* 301-495-0810 *E-mail:* asist@asist.org *Web Site:* www.asist.org, pg 24, 557

Middleton, Maria, Random House Children's Books, 1745 Broadway, 10th fl, New York, NY 10019 *Tel:* 212-782-9000 *Web Site:* www.randomhousekids.com, pg 194

Middleton, Stephanie, American Law Institute, 4025 Chestnut St, Philadelphia, PA 19104-3099 *Tel:* 215-243-1600 *Toll Free Tel:* 800-253-6397 *Fax:* 215-243-1664 *Web Site:* www.ali.org, pg 12

Middleton, Stephanie, American Law Institute Continuing Legal Education (ALI CLE), 4025 Chestnut St, Philadelphia, PA 19104 *Tel:* 215-243-1600 *Toll Free Tel:* 800-CLE-NEWS (253-6397) *Fax:* 215-243-1664; 215-243-1608 *Web Site:* www.ali-cle.org, pg 12

Midgley, Peter, University of Alberta Press, Ring House 2, Edmonton, AB T6G 2E1, Canada *Tel:* 780-492-3662 *Fax:* 780-492-0719 *Web Site:* www.uap.ualberta.ca, pg 473

Miers, Charles, Rizzoli International Publications Inc, 300 Park Ave S, 4th fl, New York, NY 10010-5399 *Tel:* 212-387-3400 *Toll Free Tel:* 800-522-6657 (orders only) *Fax:* 212-387-3535 *E-mail:* publicity@rizzoliusa.com *Web Site:* www.rizzoliusa.com, pg 199

Miesionczek, Julie, Words into Print, 208 Java St, 6th fl, Brooklyn, NY 11222 *E-mail:* query@wordsintoprint.org *Web Site:* wordsintoprint.org, pg 503

Migner-Laurin, Anne, Les Editions du Remue-Menage, La Maison Parent-Roback, 110 rue Sainte-Therese, bureau 303, Montreal, QC H2Y 1E6, Canada *Tel:* 514-876-0097 *Fax:* 514-876-7951 *E-mail:* info@editions-rm.ca *Web Site:* www.editions-rm.ca, pg 453

Miholer, Sue, Oregon Christian Writers (OCW), 1075 Willow Lake Rd N, Keizer, OR 97303 *Tel:* 503-393-3356 *E-mail:* contact@oregonchristianwriters.org *Web Site:* www.oregonchristianwriters.org, pg 574

Miholer, Sue, Oregon Christian Writers Coaching Conference, 1075 Willow Lake Rd N, Keizer, OR 97303 *Tel:* 503-393-3356 *E-mail:* contact@oregonchristianwriters.org *Web Site:* www.oregonchristianwriters.org, pg 613

Miholer, Sue, Oregon Christian Writers Seminar, 1075 Willow Lake Rd N, Keizer, OR 97303 *Tel:* 503-393-3356 *E-mail:* contact@oregonchristianwriters.org *Web Site:* www.oregonchristianwriters.org, pg 613

Miklos, Lauren, Encounter Books, 900 Broadway, Suite 601, New York, NY 10003 *Tel:* 212-871-6310 *Toll Free Tel:* 800-786-3839 *Fax:* 212-871-6311 *E-mail:* publicity@encounterbooks.com *Web Site:* www.encounterbooks.com, pg 78

Mikula, Catherine, Random House Publishing Group, 1745 Broadway, New York, NY 10019 *Toll Free Tel:* 800-200-3552 *Web Site:* atrandom.com, pg 195

Milano, Patrick, McGraw-Hill Education, 2 Penn Plaza, New York, NY 10121-2298 *Tel:* 212-904-2000 *E-mail:* customer.service@mheducation.com; international_cs@mheducation.com *Web Site:* www.mheducation.com, pg 145

Milazzo, Richard, Edgewise Press Inc, 24 Fifth Ave, Suite 224, New York, NY 10011 *Tel:* 212-982-4818 *Fax:* 212-982-1364 *E-mail:* epinc@mindspring.com *Web Site:* www.edgewisepress.org, pg 75

Miles, Steve, Harlequin Enterprises Ltd, 225 Duncan Mill Rd, Don Mills, ON M3B 3K9, Canada *Tel:* 416-445-5860 *Toll Free Tel:* 888-432-4879; 800-370-5838 (ebook inquiries) *E-mail:* customerservice@harlequin.com *Web Site:* www.harlequin.com, pg 459

Miley, Daniel, Rainbow Publishers, 4733 Torrance Blvd, No 259, Torrance, CA 90503 *Tel:* 858-277-1167 *Toll Free Tel:* 800-323-7337; 800-532-4278 *Fax:* 310-353-2116 *Toll Free Fax:* 800-331-0297 *E-mail:* info@rainbowpublishers.com; editor@rainbowpublishers.com (edit dept); orders@rainbowpublishers.com *Web Site:* www.rainbowpublishers.com, pg 193

Millar, David, Simon & Schuster Canada, 166 King St E, Suite 300, Toronto, ON M5A 1J3, Canada *Tel:* 647-427-8882 *Toll Free Tel:* 800-387-0446; 800-268-3216 (orders) *Fax:* 647-430-9446 *Toll Free Fax:* 888-849-8151 (orders) *E-mail:* info@simonandschuster.ca *Web Site:* www.simonandschuster.ca, pg 471

Millard, Martha, Sterling Lord Literistic Inc, 115 Broadway, Suite 1602, New York, NY 10006 *Tel:* 212-780-6050 *Fax:* 212-780-6095 *E-mail:* info@sll.com *Web Site:* www.sll.com, pg 537

Miller, Andra, Random House Publishing Group, 1745 Broadway, New York, NY 10019 *Toll Free Tel:* 800-200-3552 *Web Site:* atrandom.com, pg 195

Miller, Andrew, Alfred A Knopf/Everyman's Library, c/o Penguin Random House Inc, 1745 Broadway, New York, NY 10019 *Tel:* 212-751-2600 *Toll Free Tel:* 800-638-6460 *Fax:* 212-572-2593 *Web Site:* www.knopfdoubleday.com, pg 127

Miller, Anelle, Society of Illustrators (SI), 128 E 63 St, New York, NY 10065 *Tel:* 212-838-2560 *Fax:* 212-838-2561 *E-mail:* info@societyillustrators.org *Web Site:* www.societyillustrators.org, pg 578

Miller, Angela, The Miller Agency Inc, 630 Ninth Ave, Suite 1102, New York, NY 10036 *Tel:* 212-206-0913 *Fax:* 212-206-1473, pg 530

Miller, Avital, Crystal Clarity Publishers, 14618 Tyler Foote Rd, Nevada City, CA 95959 *Tel:* 530-478-7600 *Toll Free Tel:* 800-424-1055 *Fax:* 530-478-7610 *E-mail:* clarity@crystalclarity.com *Web Site:* www.crystalclarity.com, pg 65

Miller, Betsy, Robert Miller Gallery, 524 W 26 St, New York, NY 10001 *Tel:* 212-366-4774 *Fax:* 212-366-4454 *E-mail:* rmg@robertmillergallery.com *Web Site:* www.robertmillergallery.com, pg 151

Miller, Bill, OptumInsight™, 13625 Technology Dr, Eden Prairie, MN 55334 *Tel:* 952-833-7100 *Toll Free Tel:* 888-445-8745; 800-765-6713 *E-mail:* info@optum.com *Web Site:* www.optum.com, pg 169

Miller, Fr Byron, Liguori Publications, One Liguori Dr, Liguori, MO 63057-1000 *Tel:* 636-464-2500 *Toll Free Tel:* 866-848-2492; 800-325-9521 *Fax:* 636-464-8449 *Toll Free Fax:* 800-325-9526 (sales) *E-mail:* liguori@liguori.org (sales & cust serv) *Web Site:* www.liguori.org/contact-us.html, pg 134

Miller, Ceci, CeciBooks Editorial & Publishing Consultation, 7057 26 Ave NW, Seattle, WA 98117 *Tel:* 206-706-9565 *E-mail:* cecibooks@gmail.com *Web Site:* www.cecibooks.com, pg 491

Miller, Connie, Standard International Media Holdings, 568 Ninth St S, Suite 201, Naples, FL 34102-7336 *Tel:* 239-248-5550 *Fax:* 239-649-5832 *Toll Free Fax:* 866-948-7883 *E-mail:* sales@standardinternationalmedia.com *Web Site:* www.standardinternationalmedia.com, pg 220

Miller, David, Evan-Moor Educational Publishers, 18 Lower Ragsdale Dr, Monterey, CA 93940-5746 *Tel:* 831-649-5901 *Toll Free Tel:* 800-777-4362 (orders) *Fax:* 831-649-6256 *Toll Free Fax:* 800-777-4332 (orders) *E-mail:* sales@evan-moor.com; marketing@evan-moor.com *Web Site:* www.evan-moor.com, pg 80

Miller, David, The Garamond Agency Inc, 12 Horton St, Newburyport, MA 01950 *E-mail:* query@garamondagency.com *Web Site:* www.garamondagency.com, pg 518

Miller, David, Island Press, 2000 "M" St NW, Suite 650, Washington, DC 20036 *Tel:* 202-232-7933 *Toll Free Tel:* 800-828-1302 *Fax:* 202-234-1328 *E-mail:* info@islandpress.org *Web Site:* www.islandpress.org, pg 121

Miller, Diana Tejerina, Pantheon Books/Schocken Books, c/o Penguin Random House Inc, 1745 Broadway, New York, NY 10019 *Tel:* 212-751-2600 *Web Site:* knopfdoubleday.com/imprint/pantheon, pg 173

Miller, Gary, Marshall & Swift, 777 S Fiqueroa St, 12th fl, Los Angeles, CA 90017 *Tel:* 213-683-9000 *Toll Free Tel:* 800-544-2678 *Fax:* 213-683-9043 *Web Site:* www.marshallswift.com, pg 143

Miller, George, Cengage Learning, 20 Channel Center St, Boston, MA 02210 *Tel:* 617-289-7700 *Toll Free Tel:* 800-354-9706 *Fax:* 617-289-7844 *Toll Free Fax:* 800-487-8488 *E-mail:* esales@cengage.com *Web Site:* www.cengage.com, pg 50

Miller, Harold, Taylor-Dth Publishing, 108 Caribe Isle, Novato, CA 94949 *Tel:* 415-299-1087 *Web Site:* www.taylor-dth.com, pg 228

Miller, Irene, The Edwin Mellen Press, 415 Ridge St, Lewiston, NY 14092 *Tel:* 716-754-2266; 716-754-1400 (mktg); 716-754-2788 (order fulfillment) *Fax:* 716-754-4056 *E-mail:* editor@mellenpress.com *Web Site:* www.mellenpress.com, pg 148

Miller, Jan, Dupree, Miller & Associates Inc, 100 Highland Park Village, Suite 350, Dallas, TX 75205 *Tel:* 214-559-2665 *Fax:* 214-559-7243 *E-mail:* editorial@dupreemiller.com *Web Site:* www.dupreemiller.com, pg 515

Miller, Jeffrey, Irwin Law Inc, 14 Duncan St, Suite 206, Toronto, ON M5H 3G8, Canada *Tel:* 416-862-7690 *Toll Free Tel:* 888-314-9014 *Fax:* 416-862-9236 *Web Site:* www.irwinlaw.com, pg 461

Miller, Kathlyn, Brilliance Audio, 1704 Eaton Dr, Grand Haven, MI 49417 *Tel:* 616-846-5256 *Toll Free Tel:* 800-648-2312 (orders only) *Fax:* 616-846-0630 *E-mail:* customerservice@brillianceaudio.com *Web Site:* www.brillianceaudio.com, pg 44

Miller, Kevin, Atlantic Center for the Arts Artists-in-Residence Program, 1414 Art Center Ave, New Smyrna Beach, FL 32168 *Tel:* 386-427-6975 *Toll Free Tel:* 800-393-6975 *Fax:* 386-427-5669 *E-mail:* program@atlanticcenterforthearts.org *Web Site:* atlanticcenterforthearts.org, pg 609

Miller, Kim, AAUP Book, Jacket & Journal Design Show, 1412 Broadway, Suite 2135, New York, NY 10018 *Tel:* 212-989-1010 *Fax:* 212-989-0275 *E-mail:* info@aaupnet.org *Web Site:* www.aaupnet.org, pg 625

Miller, Kim, Association of American University Presses (AAUP), 1412 Broadway, Suite 2135, New York, NY 10018 *Tel:* 212-989-1010 *Fax:* 212-989-0275 *E-mail:* info@aaupnet.org *Web Site:* www.aaupnet.org, pg 558

Miller, Kristen, Sarabande Books Inc, 2234 Dundee Rd, Suite 200, Louisville, KY 40205 *Tel:* 502-458-4028 *Fax:* 502-458-4065 *E-mail:* info@sarabandebooks.org *Web Site:* www.sarabandebooks.org, pg 206

Miller, Lauren, Thames & Hudson, 500 Fifth Ave, New York, NY 10110 *Tel:* 212-354-3763 *Toll Free Tel:* 800-233-4830 *Fax:* 212-398-1252 *E-mail:* bookinfo@thames.wwnorton.com *Web Site:* www.thamesandhudsonusa.com, pg 230

Miller, Lawton, M Lee Smith Publishers, 100 Winners Circle, Suite 300, Brentwood, TN 37027 *Tel:* 615-373-7517 *Toll Free Tel:* 800-274-6774; 800-727-5257 *E-mail:* custserv@mleesmith.com; service@blr.com *Web Site:* www.mleesmith.com; www.blr.com, pg 215

Miller, Matthew, The Toby Press LLC, PO Box 8531, New Milford, CT 06776-8531 *Tel:* 203-830-8508 *Fax:* 203-830-8512 *E-mail:* toby@tobypress.com; sales@korenpub.com *Web Site:* www.tobypress.com; www.korenpub.com, pg 232

Miller, Melissa, American Society of Agricultural & Biological Engineers (ASABE), 2950 Niles Rd, St Joseph, MI 49085-9659 *Tel:* 269-429-0300 *Toll Free Tel:* 800-371-2723 *Fax:* 269-429-3852 *E-mail:* hq@asabe.org *Web Site:* www.asabe.org, pg 14

Miller, Melissa, HarperCollins Children's Books, 195 Broadway, New York, NY 10007 *Tel:* 212-207-7000 *Web Site:* www.harpercollins.com/childrens, pg 101

Miller, Meredith, United Talent Agency, 9336 Civic Center Dr, Beverly Hills, CA 90210 *Tel:* 310-273-6700 *Fax:* 310-247-1111 *Web Site:* www.unitedtalent.com, pg 540

Miller, Nancy, Bloomsbury Publishing Inc, 1385 Broadway, 5th fl, New York, NY 10018 *Tel:* 212-419-5300 *E-mail:* marketingusa@bloomsbury.com; adultpublicityusa@bloomsbury.com; askacademic@bloomsbury.com *Web Site:* www.bloomsbury.com, pg 37

Miller, Nikki, Temple University Press, 1852 N Tenth St, Philadelphia, PA 19122-6099 *Tel:* 215-926-2140 *Toll Free Tel:* 800-621-2736 *Fax:* 215-926-2141 *E-mail:* tempress@temple.edu *Web Site:* www.temple.edu/tempress, pg 228

Miller, Peter, Global Lion Intellectual Property Management Inc, PO Box 669238, Pompano Beach, FL 33066 *Tel:* 754-222-6948 *Fax:* 754-222-6948 *E-mail:* queriesgloballionmgt@gmail.com *Web Site:* www.globallionmanagement.com, pg 519

Miller, Peter, The Institutes™, 720 Providence Rd, Suite 100, Malvern, PA 19355-3433 *Tel:* 610-644-2100 *Toll Free Tel:* 800-644-2101 *Fax:* 610-640-9576 *E-mail:* customerservice@theinstitutes.org *Web Site:* www.theinstitutes.org, pg 118

Miller, Richard K, Richard K Miller Associates, 4132 Atlanta Hwy, Suite 110, Loganville, GA 30052 *Toll Free Tel:* 888-928-RKMA (928-7562) *Toll Free Fax:* 877-928-7562 *Web Site:* rkma.com, pg 151

Miller, Robin, Business Forms Management Association (BFMA), 1147 Fleetwood Ave, Madison, WI 53716 *Toll Free Tel:* 888-367-3078 *E-mail:* bfma@bfma.org *Web Site:* www.bfma.org, pg 561

Miller, Sarah, Yale Series of Younger Poets, 302 Temple St, New Haven, CT 06511 *Tel:* 203-432-0960 *Fax:* 203-432-0948 *Web Site:* www.yalebooks.com, pg 701

Miller, Sarah, Yale University Press, 302 Temple St, New Haven, CT 06511-8909 *Tel:* 203-432-0960; 203-432-0966 (sales); 401-531-2800 (cust serv) *Toll Free Tel:* 800-405-1619 (cust serv) *Fax:* 203-432-0948; 203-432-8485 (sales); 401-531-2801 (cust serv) *Toll Free Fax:* 800-406-9145 (cust serv) *E-mail:* sales.press@yale.edu (sales); customer.care@triliteral.org (cust serv) *Web Site:* www.yalebooks.com; yalepress.yale.edu/yupbooks, pg 261

Miller, Scott, David C Cook, 4050 Lee Vance View, Colorado Springs, CO 80918 *Tel:* 719-536-0100 *Toll Free Tel:* 800-708-5550; 800-323-7543 (orders & cust serv) *Toll Free Fax:* 800-430-0726 (cust serv) *Web Site:* www.davidccook.com, pg 60

Miller, Scott, Trident Media Group LLC, 41 Madison Ave, 36th fl, New York, NY 10010 *Tel:* 212-333-1511 *E-mail:* info@tridentmediagroup.com; press@tridentmediagroup.com *Web Site:* www.tridentmediagroup.com, pg 540

Miller, Stephen M, Stephen M Miller Inc, 15727 S Madison Dr, Olathe, KS 66062 *Tel:* 913-768-7997 *Web Site:* www.stephenmillerbooks.com, pg 499

Miller, Sue, Boydell & Brewer Inc, 668 Mount Hope Ave, Rochester, NY 14620-2731 *Tel:* 585-275-0419 *Fax:* 585-271-8778 *E-mail:* boydell@boydellusa.net *Web Site:* www.boydellandbrewer.com, pg 41

Miller, Ted, Human Kinetics Inc, 1607 N Market St, Champaign, IL 61820 *Tel:* 217-351-5076 *Toll Free Tel:* 800-747-4457 *Fax:* 217-351-1549 (orders/cust serv) *E-mail:* info@hkusa.com *Web Site:* www.humankinetics.com, pg 112

Miller, Terri, Pentecostal Publishing House, 8855 Dunn Rd, Hazelwood, MO 63042 *Tel:* 314-837-7300 *Toll Free Tel:* 866-819-7667 *Fax:* 314-837-6574 (orders) *Web Site:* www.pentecostalpublishing.com; wordaflamepress.com, pg 180

Miller, Tom, Carol Mann Agency, 55 Fifth Ave, New York, NY 10003 *Tel:* 212-206-5635 *Fax:* 212-675-4809 *E-mail:* submissions@carolmannagency.com *Web Site:* www.carolmannagency.com, pg 527

Miller, Dr Yvette E, Latin American Literary Review Press, PO Box 7530, Pittsburgh, PA 15213 *Tel:* 412-824-7903 *E-mail:* lalrp.editor@gmail.com *Web Site:* www.lalrp.org, pg 130

Miller-Castells, Diana, Palm Springs Writers Guild, PO Box 947, Rancho Mirage, CA 92270-0947 *Web Site:* www.palmspringswritersguild.org, pg 575

Milligan, Bryce, Wings Press, 627 E Guenther, San Antonio, TX 78210-1134 *Tel:* 210-271-7805 *E-mail:* press@wingspress.com *Web Site:* www.wingspress.com, pg 257

Milliken, Jean Mellichamp, Lyric Poetry Prizes, PO Box 110, Jericho, VT 05465 *Tel:* 802-899-3993 *Fax:* 802-899-3993 *E-mail:* themuse@thelyricmagazine.com *Web Site:* thelyricmagazine.com, pg 664

Milliken, Leif, University of Nebraska Press, 1111 Lincoln Mall, Lincoln, NE 68588-0630 *Tel:* 402-472-3581; 919-966-7449 (cust serv & foreign orders) *Toll Free Tel:* 800-848-6224 (cust serv & US orders) *Fax:* 402-472-6214; 919-962-2704 (cust serv & foreign orders) *Toll Free Fax:* 800-526-2617 (cust serv & US orders) *E-mail:* pressmail@unl.edu *Web Site:* www.nebraskapress.unl.edu, pg 243

Millman, Norman N, Summit University Press, 63 Summit Way, Gardiner, MT 59030-9314 *Tel:* 406-848-9742; 406-848-9500 (retail orders) *Toll Free Tel:* 800-245-5445 (retail orders) *Fax:* 406-848-9744 *E-mail:* info@summituniversitypress.com; marketing@summituniversitypress.com; production@summituniversitypress.com; rights@summituniversitypress.com *Web Site:* www.summituniversitypress.com, pg 224

Mills, Elizabeth M, Temporal Mechanical Press, 6760 Hwy 7, Estes Park, CO 80517-6404 *Tel:* 970-586-4706 *E-mail:* info@enosmills.com *Web Site:* www.enosmills.com, pg 229

Mills, Eryn, Temporal Mechanical Press, 6760 Hwy 7, Estes Park, CO 80517-6404 *Tel:* 970-586-4706 *E-mail:* info@enosmills.com *Web Site:* www.enosmills.com, pg 229

Mills, Kathleen, Kathleen Mills Editorial Services, 327 E King St, Chardon, OH 44024 *Tel:* 440-285-4347 *E-mail:* mills_edit@yahoo.com, pg 499

Mills, Kevin, The Tuesday Agency, 132 1/2 E Washington St, Iowa City, IA 52240 *Tel:* 319-338-7080 *E-mail:* trinity@tuesdayagency.com *Web Site:* tuesdayagency.com, pg 548

Mills, Megan, Books on Tape®, 1745 Broadway, New York, NY 10019 *Toll Free Tel:* 800-733-3000 (cust serv) *Toll Free Fax:* 800-940-7046 *Web Site:* www.booksontape.com, pg 40

Mills, Nancy L, Pie in the Sky Publishing LLC, 8031 E Phillips Circle, Centennial, CO 80112 *Tel:* 303-773-0851 *Fax:* 303-773-0851 *E-mail:* pieintheskypublishing@msn.com *Web Site:* www.pieintheskypublishing.com, pg 183

Mills, Pamela, Association of Writers & Writing Programs (AWP), George Mason University, 4400 University Dr, MSN 1E3, Fairfax, VA 22030 *Tel:* 703-993-4301 *Fax:* 703-993-4302 *E-mail:* awp@awpwriter.org *Web Site:* www.awpwriter.org, pg 559

Mills, Pamela, AWP Award Series, George Mason University, 4400 University Dr, MSN 1E3, Fairfax, VA 22030 *Tel:* 703-993-4301 *Fax:* 703-993-4302 *E-mail:* awp@awpwriter.org *Web Site:* www.awpwriter.org, pg 629

Mills, Sharon, Texas A&M University Press, John H Lindsey Bldg, Lewis St, 4354 TAMU, College Station, TX 77843-4354 *Tel:* 979-845-1436 *Toll Free Tel:* 800-826-8911 (orders) *Fax:* 979-847-8752 *Toll Free Fax:* 888-617-2421 (orders) *E-mail:* bookorders@tamu.edu *Web Site:* www.tamupress.com, pg 230

Milsten, Melissa, Random House Publishing Group, 1745 Broadway, New York, NY 10019 *Toll Free Tel:* 800-200-3552 *Web Site:* atrandom.com, pg 195

Milward, Andrew, Mississippi Review/University of Southern Mississippi, Center for Writers, 118 College Dr 5144, Hattiesburg, MS 39406-0001 *Tel:* 601-266-5600 *Fax:* 601-266-5757 *Web Site:* www.usm.edu/english/c4w.html; www.usm.edu/english/mississippireview.html, pg 621

Minar, Scott, Marick Press, PO Box 36253, Grosse Pointe Farms, MI 48236 *Tel:* 313-407-9236 *E-mail:* orders@marickpress.com *Web Site:* www.marickpress.com, pg 142

Minard, Jeff, William Carey Library Publishers, 1605 E Elizabeth St, Pasadena, CA 91104 *Tel:* 626-720-8210 *Toll Free Tel:* 866-732-6657 (orders & cust serv) *E-mail:* assistant@wclbooks.com *Web Site:* www.missionbooks.org, pg 256

Minchew, Laura, Thomas Nelson, 501 Nelson Place, Nashville, TN 37214 *Tel:* 615-889-9000 *Toll Free Tel:* 800-251-4000 *Fax:* 615-902-1548 *Web Site:* www.thomasnelson.com, pg 231

Mindlin, Ivy, The Ivy League of Artists Inc, 18 Edgemere Rd, Livingston, NJ 07039 *Tel:* 973-992-4048 *Fax:* 973-992-4049 *E-mail:* ilartists2@gmail.com, pg 543

Minick, James, Sandhills Writers' Series, Dept of English & Foreign Languages, 1120 15 St, Augusta, GA 30912 *Tel:* 706-729-2417, pg 614

Minnich, Sara, GP Putnam's Sons (Hardcover), 375 Hudson St, New York, NY 10014 *Tel:* 212-366-2000 *Fax:* 212-366-2643 *E-mail:* online@penguinputnam.com *Web Site:* www.penguin.com/publishers/gpputnamssons, pg 192

Minortti, Bob, New Leaf Press, 3142 Hwy 103 N, Green Forest, AR 72638-2233 *Tel:* 870-438-5288 *Toll Free Tel:* 800-999-3777 *Fax:* 870-438-5120 *E-mail:* nlp@newleafpress.net; submissions@newleafpress.net *Web Site:* www.nlpg.com/imprint/new-leaf-press; www.nlpg.com, pg 161

Mintcheva, Svetlana, National Coalition Against Censorship (NCAC), 19 Fulton St, Suite 407, New York, NY 10038 *Tel:* 212-807-6222 *Fax:* 212-807-6245 *E-mail:* ncac@ncac.org *Web Site:* www.ncac.org, pg 571

Miracle, Tracy, Candlewick Press, 99 Dover St, Somerville, MA 02144-2825 *Tel:* 617-661-3330 *Fax:* 617-661-0565 *E-mail:* bigbear@candlewick.com; salesinfo@candlewick.com *Web Site:* www.candlewick.com, pg 46

Miranda, Joe, Fairchild Books, 1385 Broadway, 5th fl, New York, NY 10018 *Tel:* 212-419-5300 *Toll Free Tel:* 800-932-4724; 888-330-8477 (orders) *Fax:* 212-704-5975 *Web Site:* bloomsbury.com/us/academic/fairchildbooks, pg 81

Miranda, Lori, Cognizant Communication Corp, 18 Peekskill Hollow Rd, Putnam Valley, NY 10579-0037 *Tel:* 845-603-6440; 845-603-6441 (warehouse & orders) *Fax:* 845-603-6442 *E-mail:* inquiries@cognizantcommunication.com; sales@cognizantcommunication.com *Web Site:* www.cognizantcommunication.com, pg 58

Miranda, Robert N, Cognizant Communication Corp, 18 Peekskill Hollow Rd, Putnam Valley, NY 10579-0037 *Tel:* 845-603-6440; 845-603-6441 (warehouse & orders) *Fax:* 845-603-6442 *E-mail:* inquiries@cognizantcommunication.com; sales@cognizantcommunication.com *Web Site:* www.cognizantcommunication.com, pg 58

Mirolla, Michael, Guernica Editions Inc, 1569 Heritage Way, Oakville, ON L6M 2Z7, Canada *Tel:* 905-599-5304 *E-mail:* info@guernicaeditions.com *Web Site:* www.guernicaeditions.com, pg 459

Mironov, Stacey, CRC Press, 6000 Broken Sound Pkwy NW, Suite 300, Boca Raton, FL 33487 *Tel:* 561-994-0555 *Toll Free Tel:* 800-272-7737 (orders) *Toll Free Fax:* 800-643-9428 (sales); 800-374-3401 (orders) *E-mail:* orders@crcpress.com; orders@taylorandfrancis.com *Web Site:* www.crcpress.com, pg 64

Mirr, Ron, Scholastic Education, 557 Broadway, New York, NY 10012 *Tel:* 212-343-6100 *Fax:* 212-343-6189 *Web Site:* www.scholastic.com, pg 207

Mirsky, Danielle, Scholastic Education, 557 Broadway, New York, NY 10012 *Tel:* 212-343-6100 *Fax:* 212-343-6189 *Web Site:* www.scholastic.com, pg 207

Mirza, Ayesha, Houghton Mifflin Harcourt Trade & Reference Division, 125 High St, Boston, MA 02110 *Tel:* 617-351-5000 *Toll Free Tel:* 800-225-3362 *Web Site:* www.hmhco.com, pg 111

Mishra, Pradeep C, Arkansas State University Graphic Communications Program, PO Box 1930, Dept of Media, State University, AR 72467-1930 *Tel:* 870-972-3114 *Fax:* 870-972-3321 *Web Site:* www.astate.edu, pg 619

Miskin, Michael J, Tapestry Press Ltd, 19 Nashoba Rd, Littleton, MA 01460 *Tel:* 978-486-0200 *Toll Free Tel:* 800-535-2007 *Fax:* 978-486-0244 *E-mail:* publish@tapestrypress.com *Web Site:* www.tapestrypress.com, pg 227

Mitchard, Jacquelyn, F+W Media Inc, 10151 Carver Rd, Suite 200, Blue Ash, OH 45242 *Tel:* 513-531-2690 *Toll Free Tel:* 800-289-0963 (trade accts); 800-258-0929 (cust serv) *E-mail:* contact_us@fwmedia.com *Web Site:* www.fwcommunity.com, pg 82

Mitchell, Barbara J, Mitchell Lane Publishers Inc, PO Box 196, Hockessin, DE 19707 *Tel:* 302-234-9426 *Toll Free Tel:* 800-814-5484 *Fax:* 302-234-4742 *Toll Free Fax:* 866-834-4164 *E-mail:* orders@mitchelllane.com *Web Site:* www.mitchelllane.com, pg 152

Mitchell, Carine, Cambridge University Press, 1 Liberty Plaza, 20th fl, New York, NY 10006 *Tel:* 212-924-3900; 212-337-5000 *Fax:* 212-691-3239 *E-mail:* newyork@cambridge.org *Web Site:* www.cambridge.org/us, pg 46

Mitchell, Chuck, The Conference Board Inc, 845 Third Ave, New York, NY 10022-6600 *Tel:* 212-759-0900; 212-339-0345 (cust serv) *Fax:* 212-980-7014; 212-836-9740 (cust serv) *E-mail:* customer.service@conferenceboard.org; membership@conferenceboard.org *Web Site:* www.conference-board.org; www.linkedin.com/company/the-conference-board, pg 60

Mitchell, David, The Guilford Press, 370 Seventh Ave, Suite 1200, New York, NY 10001-1020 *Tel:* 212-431-9800 *Toll Free Tel:* 800-365-7006 *Fax:* 212-966-6708 *E-mail:* info@guilford.com *Web Site:* www.guilford.com, pg 97

Mitchell, Douglas C, University of Chicago Press, 1427 E 60 St, Chicago, IL 60637-2954 *Tel:* 773-702-7700; 773-702-7600 *Toll Free Tel:* 800-621-2736 (orders) *Fax:* 773-702-9756; 773-660-2235 (orders); 773-702-2708 *E-mail:* custserv@press.uchicago.edu; marketing@press.uchicago.edu *Web Site:* www.press.uchicago.edu, pg 241

Mitchell, Dr Francis, New World Publishing (Canada), PO Box 36075, Halifax, NS B3J 3S9, Canada *Tel:* 902-576-2055 (inquiries) *Toll Free Tel:* 877-211-3334 (orders) *Fax:* 902-576-2095 *Web Site:* www.newworldpublishing.com, pg 464

Mitchell, Gary, Anne & Philip Yandle Best Article Award, PO Box 5254, Sta B, Victoria, BC V8R 6N4, Canada *E-mail:* info@bchistory.ca; recognition@bchistory.ca *Web Site:* www.bchistory.ca, pg 701

Mitchell, Gwendolyn, Third World Press, 7822 S Dobson Ave, Chicago, IL 60619 *Tel:* 773-651-0700 *Fax:* 773-651-7286 *E-mail:* twpress3@aol.com *Web Site:* www.thirdworldpressfoundation.com, pg 231

Mitchell, Jack, Lumina Datamatics Inc, 4 Collins Ave, Plymouth, MA 02360 *Tel:* 508-746-0300 *Fax:* 508-746-3233 *Web Site:* luminadatamatics.com, pg 497

Mitchell, Nicole, University of Washington Press, 4333 Brooklyn Ave NE, Seattle, WA 98105-9570 *Tel:* 206-543-4050 *Toll Free Tel:* 800-537-5487 (orders) *Fax:* 206-543-3932; 410-516-6998 (orders) *E-mail:* uwapress@uw.edu *Web Site:* www.washington.edu/uwpress, pg 246

Mitchell, Patricia, The Pennsylvania State University Press, University Support Bldg 1, Suite C, 820 N University Dr, University Park, PA 16802-1003 *Tel:* 814-865-1327 *Toll Free Tel:* 800-326-9180 *Fax:* 814-863-1408 *Toll Free Fax:* 877-778-2665 *E-mail:* info@psupress.org *Web Site:* www.psupress.org, pg 179

Mitchell, Robert P, Mitchell Lane Publishers Inc, PO Box 196, Hockessin, DE 19707 *Tel:* 302-234-9426 *Toll Free Tel:* 800-814-5484 *Fax:* 302-234-4742 *Toll Free Fax:* 866-834-4164 *E-mail:* orders@mitchelllane.com *Web Site:* www.mitchelllane.com, pg 152

Mitchell, Scott, Chain Store Guide (CSG), 10117 Princess Palm Ave, Suite 375, Tampa, FL 33610 *Tel:* 813-627-6957 *Toll Free Tel:* 800-927-9292 (orders) *Fax:* 813-627-6888 *E-mail:* info@csgis.com *Web Site:* www.csgis.com, pg 52

Mitchell, Steven L, Prometheus Books, 59 John Glenn Dr, Amherst, NY 14228-2119 *Tel:* 716-691-0133 *Fax:* 716-691-0137 *E-mail:* marketing@prometheusbooks.com; editorial@prometheusbooks.com; rights@prometheusmail.com *Web Site:* www.prometheusbooks.com, pg 190

Mitchem, Gary, McFarland, 960 NC Hwy 88 W, Jefferson, NC 28640 *Tel:* 336-246-4460 *Toll Free Tel:* 800-253-2187 (orders) *Fax:* 336-246-5018; 336-246-4403 (orders) *E-mail:* info@mcfarlandpub.com *Web Site:* www.mcfarlandpub.com, pg 145

Mitchem, Terri, TotalRecall Publications Inc, 1103 Middlecreek, Friendswood, TX 77546 *Tel:* 281-992-3131 *E-mail:* sales@totalrecallpress.com *Web Site:* www.totalrecallpress.com, pg 233

Mitchner, Leslie, Rutgers University Press, 106 Somerset St, 3rd fl, New Brunswick, NJ 08901 *Tel:* 848-445-7762 *Toll Free Tel:* 800-848-6224 (orders only) *Fax:* 732-745-4935 (acqs, edit, mktg, perms & prodn) *Toll Free Fax:* 800-272-6817 (fulfillment) *Web Site:* rutgerspress.rutgers.edu, pg 202

Mitnick, Audrey, Sleeping Bear Press™, 2395 S Huron Pkwy, Suite 200, Ann Arbor, MI 48104 *Toll Free Tel:* 800-487-2323 *Fax:* 734-929-2649 *E-mail:* customerservice@sleepingbearpress.com *Web Site:* www.sleepingbearpress.com, pg 215

Mitsuda, Kristi, Perseus Books, 250 W 57 St, 15th fl, New York, NY 10107 *Tel:* 212-340-8100 *Toll Free Tel:* 800-343-4499 (cust serv) *Fax:* 212-340-8105 *Web Site:* www.perseusbooks.com, pg 180

Mixon, Jennifer, University Press of Mississippi, 3825 Ridgewood Rd, Jackson, MS 39211-6492 *Tel:* 601-432-6205 *Toll Free Tel:* 800-737-7788 (orders & cust serv) *Fax:* 601-432-6217 *E-mail:* press@mississippi.edu *Web Site:* www.upress.state.ms.us, pg 247

Moberg, David, Thomas Nelson, 501 Nelson Place, Nashville, TN 37214 *Tel:* 615-889-9000 *Toll Free Tel:* 800-251-4000 *Fax:* 615-902-1548 *Web Site:* www.thomasnelson.com, pg 231

Mobley, Jen-Scott, Jane Chambers Playwriting Award, Georgetown University, 108 David Performing Arts Ctr, Box 571063, 37 & "O" St, NW, Washington, DC 20057-1063 *Web Site:* www.athe.org/?page=Jane_Chambers, pg 636

Mock, Katie, Perseus Books, 250 W 57 St, 15th fl, New York, NY 10107 *Tel:* 212-340-8100 *Toll Free Tel:* 800-343-4499 (cust serv) *Fax:* 212-340-8105 *Web Site:* www.perseusbooks.com, pg 180

Modugno, Maria, Random House Children's Books, 1745 Broadway, 10th fl, New York, NY 10019 *Tel:* 212-782-9000 *Web Site:* www.randomhousekids.com, pg 194

Modys, Rob, Florida Outdoor Writers Association Inc, 24 NW 33 Ct, Suite A, Gainesville, FL 32607 *Tel:* 352-284-1763 *E-mail:* info@fowa.org *Web Site:* www.fowa.org, pg 565

Modzelewski, Joe, EMC Publishing LLC, 875 Montreal Way, St Paul, MN 55102 *Tel:* 651-290-2800 (corp) *Toll Free Tel:* 800-328-1452 *Toll Free Fax:* 800-328-4564 *E-mail:* educate@emcp.com *Web Site:* www.emcp.com, pg 77

Moe, Jack, Black Mountain Press, PO Box 9907, Asheville, NC 28815 *Tel:* 828-273-3332 *Web Site:* www.theblackmountainpress.com, pg 36

Moe, Madeleine, Chronicle Books LLC, 680 Second St, San Francisco, CA 94107 *Tel:* 415-537-4200 *Toll Free Tel:* 800-759-0190 (cust serv) *Fax:* 415-537-4460 *Toll Free Fax:* 800-858-7787 (orders); 800-286-9471 (cust serv) *E-mail:* frontdesk@chroniclebooks.com *Web Site:* www.chroniclebooks.com, pg 55

Moeckel, Prof Thorpe, Hollins University-Jackson Center for Creative Writing, PO Box 9677, Roanoke, VA 24020 *Tel:* 540-362-6317 *Fax:* 540-362-6097 *E-mail:* creative.writing@hollins.edu *Web Site:* www.hollins.edu, pg 620

Moen, Jeff, University of Minnesota Press, 111 Third Ave S, Suite 290, Minneapolis, MN 55401-2520 *Tel:* 612-301-1990 *Fax:* 612-301-1980 *E-mail:* ump@umn.edu *Web Site:* www.upress.umn.edu, pg 242

Moench, Dan, Gibbs Smith Publisher, 1877 E Gentile St, Layton, UT 84041 *Tel:* 801-544-9800 *Toll Free Tel:* 800-748-5439; 800-835-4993 (orders) *Fax:* 801-544-5582 *Toll Free Fax:* 800-213-3023 (orders only) *E-mail:* info@gibbs-smith.com; tradeorders@gibbs-smith.com *Web Site:* www.gibbs-smith.com, pg 92

Moench, David, Random House Publishing Group, 1745 Broadway, New York, NY 10019 *Toll Free Tel:* 800-200-3552 *Web Site:* atrandom.com, pg 195

Moggy, Dianne, Harlequin Enterprises Ltd, 225 Duncan Mill Rd, Don Mills, ON M3B 3K9, Canada *Tel:* 416-445-5860 *Toll Free Tel:* 888-432-4879; 800-370-5838 (ebook inquiries) *E-mail:* customerservice@harlequin.com *Web Site:* www.harlequin.com, pg 459

Moghari, Francesca, National Academies Press (NAP), Lockbox 285, 500 Fifth St NW, Washington, DC 20001 *Tel:* 202-334-3313 *Fax:* 202-334-2451 (cust serv); 202-334-2793 (mktg dept) *E-mail:* customer_service@nap.edu *Web Site:* www.nap.edu, pg 156

Mohan, Joseph, The Art Institute of Chicago, 111 S Michigan Ave, Chicago, IL 60603-6404 *Tel:* 312-443-3600; 312-443-3540 (pubns) *Fax:* 312-443-1334 (pubns) *Web Site:* www.artic.edu; www.artinstituteshop.org, pg 21

Mohyde, Colleen, The Doe Coover Agency, PO Box 668, Winchester, MA 01890 *Tel:* 781-721-6000 *Fax:* 781-721-6727 *E-mail:* info@doecooveragency.com *Web Site:* www.doecooveragency.com, pg 512

Mojica, JoAnne, Scholastic Trade Division, 557 Broadway, New York, NY 10012 *Tel:* 212-343-6100; 212-343-4685 (export sales) *Fax:* 212-343-4714 (export sales) *Web Site:* www.scholastic.com, pg 208

Mokotoff, Gary, Avotaynu Inc, 794 Edgewood Ave, New Haven, CT 06515 *Tel:* 475-202-6575 *Toll Free Tel:* 800-AVOTAYNU (286-8296) *E-mail:* info@avotaynu.com *Web Site:* www.avotaynu.com, pg 27

Moldes Gomez, Marta, Santillana USA Publishing Co, 2023 NW 84 Ave, Doral, FL 33122 *Tel:* 305-591-9522 *Toll Free Tel:* 800-245-8584 *E-mail:* customerservice@santillanausa.com *Web Site:* www.santillanausa.com, pg 206

Moldow, Susan, Scribner, 1230 Avenue of the Americas, New York, NY 10020, pg 209

Moldow, Susan, Simon & Schuster, Inc, 1230 Avenue of the Americas, New York, NY 10020 *Tel:* 212-698-7000 *Fax:* 212-698-7007 *E-mail:* firstname.lastname@simonandschuster.com *Web Site:* www.simonandschuster.com, pg 213

Moldow, Susan, Touchstone, 1230 Avenue of the Americas, New York, NY 10020, pg 233

Mole, Alan, American Literacy Council, 1441 Mariposa Ave, Boulder, CO 80302 *Tel:* 303-440-7385 *Web Site:* www.americanliteracy.com, pg 555

Moller, Marilyn, W W Norton & Company Inc, 500 Fifth Ave, New York, NY 10110-0017 *Tel:* 212-354-5500 *Toll Free Tel:* 800-233-4830 (orders & cust serv) *Fax:* 212-869-0856 *Toll Free Fax:* 800-458-6515 *E-mail:* orders@wwnorton.com *Web Site:* books.wwnorton.com, pg 164

Molnar, Szilvia, Sterling Lord Literistic Inc, 115 Broadway, Suite 1602, New York, NY 10006 *Tel:* 212-780-6050 *Fax:* 212-780-6095 *E-mail:* info@sll.com *Web Site:* www.sll.com, pg 537

Moloney, Thomas, Harry N Abrams Inc, 195 Broadway, 9th fl, New York, NY 10007 *Tel:* 212-206-7715 *Toll Free Tel:* 800-345-1359 *Fax:* 212-519-1210 *E-mail:* abrams@abramsbooks.com *Web Site:* www.abramsbooks.com, pg 2

Moltke, Nina von, Random House Publishing Group, 1745 Broadway, New York, NY 10019 *Toll Free Tel:* 800-200-3552 *Web Site:* atrandom.com, pg 195

Molyneaux, David G, SATW Foundation Lowell Thomas Travel Journalism Competition, 306 Summer Hill Dr, Fredericksburg, TX 78654 *Tel:* 281-217-2872 *E-mail:* awards@satwf.com *Web Site:* www.satwfoundation.org, pg 687

Molyneux, Beverly, AAPG (American Association of Petroleum Geologists), 1444 S Boulder Ave, Tulsa, OK 74119 *Tel:* 918-584-2555 *Toll Free Tel:* 800-364-AAPG (364-2274) *Fax:* 918-580-2665 *E-mail:* info@aapg.org *Web Site:* www.aapg.org, pg 1

Mommer, Kerri, Open Court, 70 E Lake St, Suite 800, Chicago, IL 60601 *Tel:* 312-701-1720 *Toll Free Tel:* 800-815-2280 *Fax:* 312-701-1728 *E-mail:* opencourt@cricketmedia.com *Web Site:* www.opencourtbooks.com, pg 168

Monacelli, Gianfranco, The Monacelli Press, 236 W 27 St, 4th fl, New York, NY 10001 *Tel:* 212-229-9925 (ext 25) *E-mail:* contact@monacellipress.com *Web Site:* www.monacellipress.com, pg 152

Monaco, Lauren, Penguin Group USA, A Penguin Random House Company, 375 Hudson St, New York, NY 10014 *Tel:* 212-366-2000 *Toll Free Tel:* 800-847-5515 (inside sales); 800-631-8571 (cust serv) *Fax:* 212-366-2666; 607-775-4829 (inside sales) *E-mail:* online@us.penguingroup.com *Web Site:* www.penguin.com, pg 177

Monaghan, Katie, Scribner, 1230 Avenue of the Americas, New York, NY 10020, pg 209

Monaghan, Kelly, The Intrepid Traveler, 152 Staltonstall Pkwy (rear entrance), East Haven, CT 06512 *Tel:* 203-469-0214 *E-mail:* admin@intrepidtraveler.com *Web Site:* www.intrepidtraveler.com, pg 121

Monfried, Lucia, Dial Books for Young Readers, 345 Hudson St, New York, NY 10014 *Tel:* 212-366-2000 *Toll Free Tel:* 800-733-3000 (orders) *Fax:* 212-414-3396 *Web Site:* www.penguin.com, pg 70

Monge, Sr Marlyn Evangelina, Pauline Books & Media, 50 Saint Paul's Ave, Boston, MA 02130 *Tel:* 617-522-8911 *Toll Free Tel:* 800-876-4463 (orders); 800-836-9723 (cust serv) *Fax:* 617-541-9805 *E-mail:* editorial@paulinemedia.com (ms submissions); orderentry@pauline.org (cust serv) *Web Site:* www.pauline.org/publishing; www.pauline.org/PBMPublishing, pg 175

Monroe, Elvira, Wide World Publishing, PO Box 476, San Carlos, CA 94070-0476 *Tel:* 650-593-2839 *Fax:* 650-595-0802 *E-mail:* wwpbl@aol.com *Web Site:* wideworldpublishing.com, pg 255

Monson, Ander, Diagram Essay Contest, University of Arizona, ML-445, PO Box 210067, Tucson, AZ 85721 *E-mail:* editor@thediagram.com *Web Site:* www.thediagram.com/contest.html, pg 641

Monson, Cheryl, EMC Publishing LLC, 875 Montreal Way, St Paul, MN 55102 *Tel:* 651-290-2800 (corp) *Toll Free Tel:* 800-328-1452 *Toll Free Fax:* 800-328-4564 *E-mail:* educate@emcp.com *Web Site:* www.emcp.com, pg 77

Montagni, Patricia, International Council of Shopping Centers (ICSC), 1221 Avenue of the Americas, 41st fl, New York, NY 10020-1099 *Tel:* 646-728-3800 *Fax:* 732-694-1755 *E-mail:* icsc@icsc.org *Web Site:* www.icsc.org, pg 119

Montague, Larry N, Technical Association of the Pulp & Paper Industry (TAPPI), 15 Technology Pkwy S, Suite 115, Peachtree Corners, GA 30092 *Tel:* 770-446-1400 *Toll Free Tel:* 800-332-8686 (US); 800-446-9431 (CN) *Fax:* 770-446-6947 *E-mail:* memberconnection@tappi.org *Web Site:* www.tappi.org, pg 579

Montecel, Dr Maria "Cuca" Robledo PhD, Intercultural Development Research Association (IDRA), 5815 Callaghan Rd, Suite 101, San Antonio, TX 78228 *Tel:* 210-444-1710 *Fax:* 210-444-1714 *E-mail:* contact@idra.org *Web Site:* www.idra.org, pg 118

Monteith, Barnas, Tumblehome Learning Inc, 201 Newbury St, Suite 201, Boston, MA 02116 *E-mail:* info@tumblehomelearning.com *Web Site:* www.tumblehomelearning.com, pg 236

Montgomery, Heather, Energy Psychology Press, 1490 Mark West Springs Rd, Santa Rosa, CA 95404 *Tel:* 707-525-9292 *Toll Free Fax:* 800-330-9798 *E-mail:* support@eftuniverse.com *Web Site:* www.energypsychologypress.com; www.elitebooksonline.com, pg 79

Monti, Joe, Simon & Schuster Children's Publishing, 1230 Avenue of the Americas, New York, NY 10020 *Tel:* 212-698-7000 *Web Site:* www.simonandschuster.com/kids; www.simonandschuster.com/teen; simonandschuster.net; simonandschuster.biz, pg 213

Montoya, Martha, National Association of Hispanic Publications Inc (NAHP), 529 14 St NW, Suite 1126, Washington, DC 20045 *Tel:* 202-662-7250 *Web Site:* www.nahp.org, pg 571

Moody, Douglas, Educational Directories Inc (EDI), 1025 W Wise Rd, Suite 101, Schaumburg, IL 60193 *Tel:* 847-891-1250 *Toll Free Tel:* 800-357-6183 *Fax:* 847-891-0945 *E-mail:* info@ediusa.com *Web Site:* www.ediusa.com, pg 76

Moody, Jeanne C, Beaver Wood Associates, 655 Alstead Center Rd, Alstead, NH 03602 *Tel:* 603-835-7900 *Web Site:* www.beaverwood.com, pg 489

Moody, Jessica, Grey House Publishing Inc™, 4919 Rte 22, Amenia, NY 12501 *Tel:* 518-789-8700 *Toll Free Tel:* 800-562-2139 *Fax:* 518-789-0556 *E-mail:* books@greyhouse.com; customerservice@greyhouse.com *Web Site:* www.greyhouse.com, pg 96

Moody, Matt, Vault.com Inc, 132 W 31 St, 16th fl, New York, NY 10001 *Tel:* 212-366-4212 *Toll Free Tel:* 800-535-2074 *Fax:* 212-366-6117 (cust serv) *E-mail:* editors@vault.com; customerservice@vault.com *Web Site:* www.vault.com, pg 250

Moody, Rodger, Gerald Cable Book Award, PO Box 3541, Eugene, OR 97403 *Tel:* 541-344-5060 *E-mail:* sfrpress@earthlink.net *Web Site:* www.silverfishreviewpress.com, pg 635

Moog, Bob, BePuzzled, 2030 Harrison St, San Francisco, CA 94110 *Tel:* 415-503-1600 *Toll Free Tel:* 800-347-4818 *Fax:* 415-503-0085 *E-mail:* info@ugames.com *Web Site:* www.ugames.com, pg 33

Moon, Amanda, Farrar, Straus & Giroux, LLC, 18 W 18 St, New York, NY 10011 *Tel:* 212-741-6900 *E-mail:* fsg.publicity@fsgbooks.com *Web Site:* us.macmillan.com/fsg.aspx, pg 83

Mooney, Dr Robert, Etruscan Press, Wilkes University, 84 W South St, Wilkes-Barre, PA 18766 *Tel:* 570-408-4546 *Fax:* 570-408-3333 *E-mail:* books@etruscanpress.org *Web Site:* www.etruscanpress.org, pg 80

Moore, Allison, Bloomsbury Publishing Inc, 1385 Broadway, 5th fl, New York, NY 10018 *Tel:* 212-419-5300 *E-mail:* marketingusa@bloomsbury.com; adultpublicityusa@bloomsbury.com; askacademic@bloomsbury.com *Web Site:* www.bloomsbury.com, pg 38

Moore, Berwyn, Gannon University's High School Poetry Contest, Gannon University, 109 University Sq, Erie, PA 16541 *Tel:* 814-871-7504 *Web Site:* www.gannon.edu/departmental/english/poetry.asp, pg 648

Moore, Brian, Houghton Mifflin Harcourt Trade & Reference Division, 125 High St, Boston, MA 02110 *Tel:* 617-351-5000 *Toll Free Tel:* 800-225-3362 *Web Site:* www.hmhco.com, pg 111

Moore, Declan, National Geographic Books, 1145 17 St NW, Washington, DC 20036-4688 *Tel:* 202-857-7000 *Toll Free Tel:* 877-866-6486 *E-mail:* ngbooks@cdsfulfillment.com *Web Site:* www.nationalgeographic.com/books/; ngbooks.buysub.com, pg 158

Moore, Dinty W, Ohio University, English Department, Creative Writing Program, Ohio University, English Dept, Ellis Hall, Athens, OH 45701 *Tel:* 740-593-2838 (English Dept) *Fax:* 740-593-2832 *E-mail:* english.department@ohio.edu *Web Site:* www.ohio.edu/cas/english, pg 621

Moore, George, Cengage Learning, 20 Channel Center St, Boston, MA 02210 *Tel:* 617-289-7700 *Toll Free Tel:* 800-354-9706 *Fax:* 617-289-7844 *Toll Free Fax:* 800-487-8488 *E-mail:* esales@cengage.com *Web Site:* www.cengage.com, pg 50

Moore, Heather, Sourcebooks Inc, 1935 Brookdale Rd, Suite 139, Naperville, IL 60563 *Tel:* 630-961-3900 *Toll Free Tel:* 800-432-7444 *Fax:* 630-961-2168 *E-mail:* info@sourcebooks.com; customersupport@sourcebooks.com *Web Site:* www.sourcebooks.com, pg 218

Moore, John, BNi Building News, 990 Park Center Dr, Suite E, Vista, CA 92081-8352 *Tel:* 760-734-1113 *Toll Free Tel:* 888-BNI-BOOK (264-2665) *Web Site:* www.bnibooks.com, pg 39

Moore, Karen, Literary Management Group LLC, 521 Oakley Dr, Nashville, TN 37220 *Tel:* 615-812-4445 *Web Site:* www.literarymanagementgroup.com, pg 526

Moore, Katharine, Perseus Books, 250 W 57 St, 15th fl, New York, NY 10107 *Tel:* 212-340-8100 *Toll Free Tel:* 800-343-4499 (cust serv) *Fax:* 212-340-8105 *Web Site:* www.perseusbooks.com, pg 180

Moore, Lisa, University of Texas at Austin, New Writers Project, Dept of English, Calhoun Hall, Rm 226, 204 W 21 St, B-5000, Austin, TX 78712 *Tel:* 512-471-5132; 512-471-4991 *Fax:* 512-471-4909 *Web Site:* newwritersproject.org, pg 623

Moore, Marvin, Pacific Press Publishing Association, 1350 N Kings Rd, Nampa, ID 83687-3193 *Tel:* 208-465-2500 *Toll Free Tel:* 800-447-7377 *Fax:* 208-465-2531 *Web Site:* www.pacificpress.com, pg 172

Moore, Mary, Kimberley Cameron & Associates LLC, 1550 Tiburon Blvd, Suite 704, Tiburon, CA 94920 *Tel:* 415-789-9191 *Fax:* 415-789-9177 *Web Site:* www.kimberleycameron.com, pg 511

Moore, Mary-Alice, Boyds Mills Press, 815 Church St, Honesdale, PA 18431 *Tel:* 570-253-1164 *Toll Free Tel:* 800-490-5111 *Fax:* 570-253-0179 *E-mail:* contact@boydsmillspress.com *Web Site:* www.boydsmillspress.com, pg 41

Moore, Mary-Alice, Highlights for Children, 1800 Watermark Dr, Columbus, OH 43215 *Tel:* 614-486-0631 *Toll Free Tel:* 800-962-3661 (Highlights Club cust serv); 800-255-9517 (Highlights Magazine cust serv) *Web Site:* www.highlights.com; www.facebook.com/HighlightsforChildren, pg 107

Moore, Michael, Augsburg Fortress Publishers, Publishing House of the Evangelical Lutheran Church in America, 510 Marquette Ave S, Minneapolis, MN 55402 *Tel:* 612-330-3300 *Toll Free Tel:* 800-426-0115 (ext 639, subns); 800-328-4648 (orders) *Fax:* 612-330-3455 *E-mail:* info@augsburgfortress.org; copyright@augsburgfortress.org (reprint permission requests); customercare@augsburgfortress.org *Web Site:* www.augsburgfortress.org, pg 26

Moore, Nancy, Gerald & Cullen Rapp, 420 Lexington Ave, New York, NY 10170 *Tel:* 212-889-3337 *Fax:* 212-889-3341 *E-mail:* info@rappart.com *Web Site:* www.rappart.com, pg 544

Moore, Richard, Marshall Cavendish Corp, 99 White Plains Rd, Tarrytown, NY 10591-9001 *Tel:* 914-332-8888 *Toll Free Tel:* 800-821-9881 *Fax:* 914-332-8102 *E-mail:* mce@marshallcavendish.com *Web Site:* www.marshallcavendish.com; www.mceducation.us, pg 143

Moore, Stacey, Zeig, Tucker & Theisen Inc, 2632 E Thomas Rd, Suite 200, Phoenix, AZ 85016 *Tel:* 480-389-4342 *Fax:* 602-944-8118 *E-mail:* marketing@zeigtucker.com *Web Site:* www.zeigtucker.com, pg 262

Moore, Stephen, Paul Kohner Agency, 9300 Wilshire Blvd, Suite 555, Beverly Hills, CA 90212 *Tel:* 310-550-1060 *Fax:* 310-276-1083, pg 525

Moore, Steve, Ram Publishing Co, 1881 W State St, Garland, TX 75042 *Tel:* 972-494-6151 *Toll Free Tel:* 800-527-4011 *Fax:* 972-494-1881 *E-mail:* sales@garrett.com *Web Site:* www.garrett.com, pg 193

Moore, Susan, Oregon Book Awards, 925 SW Washington St, Portland, OR 97205 *Tel:* 503-227-2583 *Fax:* 503-241-4256 *E-mail:* la@literary-arts.org *Web Site:* www.literary-arts.org, pg 676

Moore, Tim, Baha'i Publishing, 401 Greenleaf Ave, Wilmette, IL 60091 *Tel:* 847-425-7950 *Toll Free Tel:* 800-999-9019 (orders) *Fax:* 847-425-7951 *E-mail:* bds@usbnc.org *Web Site:* books.bahai.us; www.bahaibookstore.com, pg 28

Moore-Swafford, Angela, Southern Illinois University Press, 1915 University Press Dr, SIUC Mail Code 6806, Carbondale, IL 62901-4323 *Tel:* 618-453-2281 *Fax:* 618-453-1221 *E-mail:* custserv@press.uchicago.edu; rights@siu.edu *Web Site:* www.siupress.com, pg 218

Moose, Christina, Davies Publishing Inc, 32 S Raymond Ave, Suites 4 & 5, Pasadena, CA 91105-1961 *Tel:* 626-792-3046 *Toll Free Tel:* 877-792-0005 *Fax:* 626-792-5308 *E-mail:* info@daviespublishing.com *Web Site:* daviespublishing.com, pg 68

Mooser, Stephen, The Don Freeman Memorial Grant-In-Aid, 4727 Wilshire Blvd, Suite 301, Los Angeles, CA 90010 *Tel:* 323-782-1010; 310-403-0675 (cell) *Fax:* 323-782-1892 *E-mail:* grants@scbwi.org; scbwi@scbwi.org *Web Site:* www.scbwi.org, pg 648

Mooser, Stephen, Golden Kite Awards, 4727 Wilshire Blvd, Suite 301, Los Angeles, CA 90010 *Tel:* 323-782-1010; 310-403-0675 (cell) *Fax:* 323-782-1892 *E-mail:* grants@scbwi.org; scbwi@scbwi.org *Web Site:* www.scbwi.org, pg 650

Mooser, Stephen, Magazine Merit Awards, 4727 Wilshire Blvd, Suite 301, Los Angeles, CA 90010 *Tel:* 323-782-1010; 310-403-0675 (cell) *Fax:* 323-782-1892 *E-mail:* grants@scbwi.org; scbwi@scbwi.org *Web Site:* www.scbwi.org, pg 664

Mooser, Stephen, SCBWI Work-In-Progress Grants, 4727 Wilshire Blvd, Suite 301, Los Angeles, CA 90010 *Tel:* 323-782-1010; 310-403-0675 (cell) *Fax:* 323-782-1892 *E-mail:* grants@scbwi.org; scbwi@scbwi.org *Web Site:* www.scbwi.org, pg 688

Mooser, Stephen, Society of Children's Book Writers and Illustrators (SCBWI), 4727 Wilshire Blvd, Suite 301, Los Angeles, CA 90010 *Tel:* 323-782-1010 *Fax:* 323-782-1892 *E-mail:* scbwi@scbwi.org; membership@scbwi.org *Web Site:* www.scbwi.org, pg 578

Moraleda, Lisa, Simon & Schuster Children's Publishing, 1230 Avenue of the Americas, New York, NY 10020 *Tel:* 212-698-7000 *Web Site:* www.simonandschuster.com/kids; www.simonandschuster.com/teen; simonandschuster.net; simonandschuster.biz, pg 213

Morales, Ruth, University of Puerto Rico Press, Edificio La Editorial (level 2), Carr No 1, KM 12.0, Jardin Botanico Norte, San Juan, PR 00927 *Tel:* 787-250-0435; 787-250-0550 *Toll Free Tel:* 877-338-7788 *Fax:* 787-753-9116 *E-mail:* info@laeditorialupr.com *Web Site:* www.laeditorialupr.com, pg 245

Morales-Pitts, Lisa, Holiday House Inc, 425 Madison Ave, New York, NY 10017 *Tel:* 212-688-0085 *Fax:* 212-421-6134 *E-mail:* info@holidayhouse.com *Web Site:* www.holidayhouse.com, pg 109

Moran, Bruce, TotalRecall Publications Inc, 1103 Middlecreek, Friendswood, TX 77546 *Tel:* 281-992-3131 *E-mail:* sales@totalrecallpress.com *Web Site:* www.totalrecallpress.com, pg 233

Moran, James David, Fellowships for Creative & Performing Artists & Writers, 185 Salisbury St, Worcester, MA 01609-1634 *Tel:* 508-755-5221 *Fax:* 508-753-3311 *Web Site:* www.americanantiquarian.org, pg 646

Moran, James David, Fellowships for Historical Research, 185 Salisbury St, Worcester, MA 01609-1634 *Tel:* 508-471-2131 *Fax:* 508-754-9069 *Web Site:* www.americanantiquarian.org, pg 646

Moran, Josalyn, Quarto Publishing Group USA Inc, 400 First Ave N, Suite 400, Minneapolis, MN 55401 *Tel:* 612-344-8100 *Toll Free Tel:* 800-328-0590 (sales); 800-458-0454 *Fax:* 612-344-8691 *E-mail:* sales@quartous.com *Web Site:* www.quartoknows.com, pg 192

Moran, Michael, Gem Guides Book Co, 1275 W Ninth St, Upland, CA 91786 *Tel:* 626-855-1611 *Toll Free Tel:* 800-824-5118 (orders) *Fax:* 626-855-1610 *E-mail:* info@gemguidesbooks.com *Web Site:* www.gemguidesbooks.com, pg 91

Moran, Viniita, Chronicle Books LLC, 680 Second St, San Francisco, CA 94107 *Tel:* 415-537-4200 *Toll Free Tel:* 800-759-0190 (cust serv) *Fax:* 415-537-4460 *Toll Free Fax:* 800-858-7787 (orders); 800-286-9471 (cust serv) *E-mail:* frontdesk@chroniclebooks.com *Web Site:* www.chroniclebooks.com, pg 55

Moran, Whitney, Nimbus Publishing Ltd, 3731 Mackintosh St, Halifax, NS B3K 5A5, Canada *Tel:* 902-455-4286 *Toll Free Tel:* 800-NIMBUS9 (646-2879) *Fax:* 902-455-5440 *Toll Free Fax:* 888-253-3133 *E-mail:* customerservice@nimbus.ca *Web Site:* www.nimbus.ca, pg 465

Morano, Nicole, Penguin Random House Audio Publishing, 1745 Broadway, New York, NY 10019 *E-mail:* audio@penguinrandomhouse.com *Web Site:* www.penguinrandomhouseaudio.com, pg 178

Morehouse, Jim, Paradise Cay Publications Inc, 120 Monda Way, Blue Lake, CA 95525 *Tel:* 707-822-9063 *Toll Free Tel:* 800-736-4509 *Fax:* 707-822-9163 *E-mail:* info@paracay.com *Web Site:* www.paracay.com, pg 174

Morel, Madeleine, 2M Communications Ltd, 19 W 21 St, Suite 501, New York, NY 10010 *Tel:* 212-741-1509 *Fax:* 212-691-4460 *Web Site:* www.2mcommunications.com, pg 540

Morello, Frank, Florida Outdoor Writers Association Inc, 24 NW 33 Ct, Suite A, Gainesville, FL 32607 *Tel:* 352-284-1763 *E-mail:* info@fowa.org *Web Site:* www.fowa.org, pg 565

Moreno, Jennifer, Random House Children's Books, 1745 Broadway, 10th fl, New York, NY 10019 *Tel:* 212-782-9000 *Web Site:* www.randomhousekids.com, pg 194

Moreno, Luis Alberto, Inter-American Development Bank, 1300 New York Ave NW, Washington, DC 20577 *Tel:* 202-623-1000 *Fax:* 202-623-3096 *E-mail:* pic@iadb.org *Web Site:* www.iadb.org/pub, pg 118

Morgan, Cal, Riverhead Books, 375 Hudson St, New York, NY 10014 *Tel:* 212-366-2000 *Web Site:* www.penguin.com/publishers/riverhead, pg 199

Morgan, Dr Jean, Castle Connolly Medical Ltd, 42 W 24 St, 2nd fl, New York, NY 10010 *Tel:* 212-367-8400 *Fax:* 212-367-0964 *Web Site:* www.castleconnolly.com, pg 49

Morgan, Jess, James Lorimer & Co Ltd, Publishers, 117 Peter St, Suite 304, Toronto, ON M5V 0M3, Canada *Tel:* 416-362-4762 *Fax:* 416-362-3939 *Web Site:* www.lorimer.ca, pg 462

Morgan, Jill, Purple House Press, 8100 US Hwy 62 E, Cynthiana, KY 41031 *Tel:* 859-235-9970 *Web Site:* www.purplehousepress.com, pg 191

Morgan, Kristina, Lynx House Press, 420 W 24 St, Spokane, WA 99203 *Tel:* 509-624-4894 *E-mail:* lynxhousepress@gmail.com *Web Site:* www.lynxhousepress.org, pg 139

Morgan, Lael, Epicenter Press Inc, 6524 NE 181 St, Suite 2, Kenmore, WA 98028 *Tel:* 425-485-6822 (edit, mktg, busn off) *Fax:* 425-481-8253 *E-mail:* info@epicenterpress.com *Web Site:* www.epicenterpress.com, pg 79

Morgan, Lauren, Random House Children's Books, 1745 Broadway, 10th fl, New York, NY 10019 *Tel:* 212-782-9000 *Web Site:* www.randomhousekids.com, pg 194

Morgan, Mary, Aegean Publishing Co, PO Box 6790, Santa Barbara, CA 93160 *Tel:* 805-964-6669 *Fax:* 805-683-4798 *E-mail:* info@aegeanpublishing.com *Web Site:* aegeanpublishing.com, pg 5

Morgan, Michelle, Nicholas Brealey Publishing, 53 State St, 9th fl, Boston, MA 02109 *Tel:* 617-523-3801 *E-mail:* info@nicholasbrealey.com; sales-us@nicholasbrealey.com *Web Site:* www.nicholasbrealey.com, pg 42

Morgan, Scott, Thomson Reuters Westlaw™, 610 Opperman Dr, Eagan, MN 55123 *Tel:* 651-687-7000 *Toll Free Tel:* 888-728-7677 (sales); 800-328-4880 (cust serv) *E-mail:* legalsolutions@thomsonreuters.com *Web Site:* legalsolutions.thomsonreuters.com, pg 231

Morgan, Stephen, Simon & Schuster, Inc, 1230 Avenue of the Americas, New York, NY 10020 *Tel:* 212-698-7000 *Fax:* 212-698-7007 *E-mail:* firstname.lastname@simonandschuster.com *Web Site:* www.simonandschuster.com, pg 213

Morgan, Tom, Little Bee Books, 853 Broadway, Suite 2014, New York, NY 10003 *E-mail:* info@littlebeebooks.com *Web Site:* www.littlebeebooks.com, pg 135

Morgan-Sanders, Hayley, Purple House Press, 8100 US Hwy 62 E, Cynthiana, KY 41031 *Tel:* 859-235-9970 *Web Site:* www.purplehousepress.com, pg 191

Morgen, Emmanuelle, The Stonesong Press LLC, 270 W 39 St, No 201, New York, NY 10018 *Tel:* 212-929-4600 *E-mail:* editors@stonesong.com *Web Site:* www.stonesong.com, pg 538

Morgenfeld, Michael, Perseus Books, 250 W 57 St, 15th fl, New York, NY 10107 *Tel:* 212-340-8100 *Toll Free Tel:* 800-343-4499 (cust serv) *Fax:* 212-340-8105 *Web Site:* www.perseusbooks.com, pg 181

Morgenstein, Leslie, Alloy Entertainment LLC, 1325 Avenue of the Americas, 29th fl, New York, NY 10019 *E-mail:* collaborative@alloyentertainment.com, pg 8

Morgridge, Sally, Holiday House Inc, 425 Madison Ave, New York, NY 10017 *Tel:* 212-688-0085 *Fax:* 212-421-6134 *E-mail:* info@holidayhouse.com *Web Site:* www.holidayhouse.com, pg 109

Morhaim, Howard, Howard Morhaim Literary Agency Inc, 30 Pierrepont St, Brooklyn, NY 11201-3371 *Tel:* 718-222-8400 *Fax:* 718-222-5056 *E-mail:* info@morhaimliterary.com *Web Site:* www.morhaimliterary.com, pg 530

Mori, Iris, Chronicle Books LLC, 680 Second St, San Francisco, CA 94107 *Tel:* 415-537-4200 *Toll Free Tel:* 800-759-0190 (cust serv) *Fax:* 415-537-4460 *Toll Free Fax:* 800-858-7787 (orders); 800-286-9471 (cust serv) *E-mail:* frontdesk@chroniclebooks.com *Web Site:* www.chroniclebooks.com, pg 55

Moriarty, Amy, WordCo Indexing Services Inc, 49 Church St, Norwich, CT 06360 *Tel:* 860-886-2532 *Toll Free Tel:* 877-WORDCO-3 (967-3263) *Fax:* 860-886-1155 *E-mail:* office@wordco.com *Web Site:* www.wordco.com, pg 502

Moriarty, Kerry, Twenty-Third Publications, One Montauk Ave, Suite 200, New London, CT 06320 *Tel:* 860-437-3012 *Toll Free Tel:* 800-321-0411 (orders) *Toll Free Fax:* 800-572-0788 *E-mail:* resources@twentythirdpublications.com *Web Site:* www.twentythirdpublications.com, pg 237

Morin-Spatz, Patrice, MedBooks, 101 W Buckingham Rd, Richardson, TX 75081-4802 *Tel:* 972-643-1809 *Fax:* 972-643-1859 *E-mail:* medbooks@medbooks.com *Web Site:* www.medbooks.com, pg 147

Morisset, Chantel, Les Editions Goelette Inc, 1350 Marie-Victorin, St-Bruno-de-Montarville, Quebec, QC J3V 6B9, Canada *Tel:* 450-653-1337 *Toll Free Tel:* 800-463-4961 *Fax:* 450-653-9924 *E-mail:* info@boutiquegoelette.com *Web Site:* www.boutiquegeolette.com, pg 454

Morita, Joseph, Springer Publishing Co, 11 W 42 St, 15th fl, New York, NY 10036-8002 *Tel:* 212-431-4370 *Toll Free Tel:* 877-687-7476 *Fax:* 212-941-7842 *E-mail:* marketing@springerpub.com; cs@springerpub.com (orders); editorial@springerpub.com *Web Site:* www.springerpub.com, pg 219

Morley, Jane, Quirk Books, 215 Church St, Philadelphia, PA 19106 *Tel:* 215-627-3581 *Fax:* 215-627-5220 *E-mail:* general@quirkbooks.com *Web Site:* www.quirkbooks.com, pg 193

Morley, Mike, Triumph Learning LLC, 136 Madison Ave, 7th fl, New York, NY 10016 *Tel:* 212-652-0200 *Toll Free Tel:* 800-338-6519 (cust serv) *Toll Free Fax:* 866-805-5723 *E-mail:* info@triumphlearning.com; customerservice@triumphlearning.com *Web Site:* www.triumphlearning.com, pg 235

Morneau, Claude, Ulysses Travel Guides, 4176, rue Saint-Denis, Montreal, QC H2W 2M5, Canada *Tel:* 514-843-9882 (ext 2232); 514-843-9447 (bookstore) *Toll Free Tel:* 800-748-9171 *Fax:* 514-843-9448 *E-mail:* info@ulysses.ca; st-denis@ulysses.ca *Web Site:* www.ulyssesguides.com, pg 473

Morris, Candice E, Mercer University Press, 368 Orange St, Macon, GA 31201 *Tel:* 478-301-2880 *Toll Free Tel:* 866-895-1472 *Fax:* 478-301-2585 *E-mail:* mupressorders@mercer.edu *Web Site:* www.mupress.org, pg 148

Morris, David, Zondervan, 3900 Sparks Dr, Grand Rapids, MI 49546 *Tel:* 616-698-6900 *Toll Free Tel:* 800-226-1122; 800-727-1309 (retail orders) *Fax:* 616-698-3350 *Toll Free Fax:* 800-698-3256 (retail orders) *E-mail:* zinfo@zondervan.com *Web Site:* www.zondervan.com, pg 263

Morris, Gary, David Black Agency, 335 Adams St, 27th fl, Suite 2707, Brooklyn, NY 11201 *Tel:* 718-852-5500 *Fax:* 718-852-5539 *Web Site:* www.davidblackagency.com, pg 508

Morris, Heather, Sourcebooks Inc, 1935 Brookdale Rd, Suite 139, Naperville, IL 60563 *Tel:* 630-961-3900 *Toll Free Tel:* 800-432-7444 *Fax:* 630-961-2168 *E-mail:* info@sourcebooks.com; customersupport@sourcebooks.com *Web Site:* www.sourcebooks.com, pg 218

Morris, Michael A, Cornell University Press, Sage House, 512 E State St, Ithaca, NY 14850 *Tel:* 607-277-2338 *Fax:* 607-277-2374 *E-mail:* cupressinfo@cornell.edu; cupress-sales@cornell.edu *Web Site:* www.cornellpress.cornell.edu, pg 61

Morris, Paul, The Authors Guild, 31 E 32 St, 7th fl, New York, NY 10016 *Tel:* 212-563-5904 *Fax:* 212-564-5363 *E-mail:* staff@authorsguild.org *Web Site:* www.authorsguild.org, pg 559

Morris, Paul, The PEN Award for Poetry in Translation, 588 Broadway, Suite 303, New York, NY 10012 *Tel:* 212-334-1660 *Fax:* 212-334-2181 *E-mail:* awards@pen.org *Web Site:* pen.org/press/grants-awards-database, pg 677

Morris, Paul, PEN/Bellwether Prize for Socially Engaged Fiction, 588 Broadway, Suite 303, New York, NY 10012 *Tel:* 212-334-1660 *E-mail:* awards@pen.org *Web Site:* pen.org/press/grants-awards-database, pg 677

Morris, Paul, PEN/Diamonstein-Spielvogel Award for the Art of the Essay, 588 Broadway, Suite 303, New York, NY 10012 *Tel:* 212-334-1660 *E-mail:* awards@pen.org *Web Site:* pen.org/literary-awards, pg 677

Morris, Paul, PEN/E O Wilson Literary Science Writing Award, 588 Broadway, Suite 303, New York, NY 10012 *Tel:* 212-334-1660 *E-mail:* awards@pen.org *Web Site:* pen.org/literary-awards, pg 677

Morris, Paul, PEN/ESPN Award for Literary Sports Writing, 588 Broadway, Suite 303, New York, NY 10012 *Tel:* 212-334-1660 *E-mail:* awards@pen.org *Web Site:* pen.org/literary-awards, pg 677

Morris, Paul, PEN/ESPN Lifetime Achievement Award for Literary Sports Writing, 588 Broadway, Suite 303, New York, NY 10012 *Tel:* 212-334-1660 *E-mail:* awards@pen.org *Web Site:* pen.org/literary-awards, pg 677

Morris, Paul, PEN/Fusion Emerging Writers Prize, 588 Broadway, Suite 303, New York, NY 10012 *Tel:* 212-334-1660 *E-mail:* awards@pen.org *Web Site:* pen.org/literary-awards, pg 678

Morris, Paul, PEN/Jacqueline Bograd Weld Award for Biography, 588 Broadway, Suite 303, New York, NY 10012 *Tel:* 212-334-1660 *E-mail:* awards@pen.org *Web Site:* pen.org/literary-awards, pg 678

Morris, Paul, PEN/Jean Stein Book Award, 588 Broadway, Suite 303, New York, NY 10012 *Tel:* 212-334-1660 *E-mail:* info@pen.org *Web Site:* pen.org/press/grants-awards-database, pg 678

Morris, Paul, PEN/Joyce Osterweil Award for Poetry, 588 Broadway, Suite 303, New York, NY 10012 *Tel:* 212-334-1660 *E-mail:* awards@pen.org *Web Site:* pen.org/press/grants-awards-database, pg 678

Morris, Paul, PEN/Nabokov Award for Achievement in International Literature, 588 Broadway, Suite 303, New York, NY 10012 *Tel:* 212-334-1660 *Fax:* 212-334-2181 *E-mail:* awards@pen.org *Web Site:* pen.org/literary-awards, pg 678

Morris, Paul, PEN Open Book Award, 588 Broadway, Suite 303, New York, NY 10012 *Tel:* 212-334-1660 *E-mail:* awards@pen.org *Web Site:* pen.org/literary-awards, pg 678

Morris, Paul, PEN/Phyllis Naylor Working Writer Fellowship, 588 Broadway, Suite 303, New York, NY 10012 *Tel:* 212-334-1660 *Fax:* 212-334-2181 *E-mail:* awards@pen.org *Web Site:* pen.org/press/grants-awards-database, pg 678

Morris, Paul, PEN/Ralph Manheim Medal for Translation, 588 Broadway, Suite 303, New York, NY 10012 *Tel:* 212-334-1660 *Fax:* 212-334-2181 *E-mail:* awards@pen.org *Web Site:* pen.org/press/grants-awards-database, pg 678

Morris, Paul, PEN/Robert Bingham Prize for Debut Fiction, 588 Broadway, Suite 303, New York, NY 10012 *Tel:* 212-334-1660 *Fax:* 212-334-2181 *E-mail:* awards@pen.org *Web Site:* pen.org/press/grants-awards-database, pg 678

Morris, Paul, PEN/Saul Bellow Award for Achievement in American Fiction, 588 Broadway, Suite 303, New York, NY 10012 *Tel:* 212-334-1660 *Fax:* 212-334-2181 *E-mail:* awards@pen.org *Web Site:* pen.org/press/grants-awards-database, pg 679

Morris, Paul, PEN Translation Prize, 588 Broadway, Suite 303, New York, NY 10012 *Tel:* 212-334-1660 *Fax:* 212-334-2181 *E-mail:* awards@pen.org *Web Site:* pen.org/press/grants-awards-database, pg 679

Morris, Paul, PEN/Voelcker Award, 588 Broadway, Suite 303, New York, NY 10012 *Tel:* 212-334-1660 *E-mail:* awards@pen.org *Web Site:* pen.org/literary-awards, pg 679

Morris, Paul, PEN Writers' Emergency Fund, 588 Broadway, Suite 303, New York, NY 10012 *Tel:* 212-334-1660 *Fax:* 212-334-2181 *Web Site:* pen.org/press/grants-awards-database, pg 679

Morris, Richard, Janklow & Nesbit Associates, 285 Madison Ave, 21st fl, New York, NY 10017 *Tel:* 212-421-1700 *Fax:* 212-355-1403 *E-mail:* info@janklow.com *Web Site:* www.janklowandnesbit.com, pg 522

Morris-Babb, Meredith, University Press of Florida, 15 NW 15 St, Gainesville, FL 32603-2079 *Tel:* 352-392-1351 *Toll Free Tel:* 800-226-3822 (orders only) *Fax:* 352-392-0590 *Toll Free Fax:* 800-680-1955 (orders only) *E-mail:* press@upress.ufl.edu; orders@upress.ufl.edu *Web Site:* www.upf.com, pg 246

Morrison, Bill, National Cartoonists Society (NCS), PO Box 592927, Orlando, FL 32859-2927 *Tel:* 407-994-6703 *Fax:* 407-442-0786 *E-mail:* info@reuben.org *Web Site:* www.reuben.org, pg 571

Morrison, Charles, Prometheus Awards, 650 Castro St, Suite 120-433, Mountain View, CA 94041 *Tel:* 650-968-6319 *Web Site:* www.lfs.org, pg 682

Morrison, Heath, McGraw-Hill Education, 2 Penn Plaza, New York, NY 10121-2298 *Tel:* 212-904-2000 *E-mail:* customer.service@mheducation.com; international_cs@mheducation.com *Web Site:* www.mheducation.com, pg 145

Morrison, Henry, Henry Morrison Inc, PO Box 235, Bedford Hills, NY 10507-0235 *Tel:* 914-666-3500 *Fax:* 914-241-7846 *E-mail:* hmorrison1@aol.com, pg 530

Morrison, Jeff, LexisNexis® Canada Inc, 111 Gordon Baker Rd, Suite 900, Toronto, ON M2H 3R1, Canada *Tel:* 905-479-2665 *Toll Free Tel:* 800-668-6481; 800-387-0899 (cust care); 800-255-5174 (sales) *E-mail:* service@lexisnexis.ca (cust serv); sales@lexisnexis.ca *Web Site:* www.lexisnexis.ca, pg 462

Morrison, Margaret, Harlequin Enterprises Ltd, 225 Duncan Mill Rd, Don Mills, ON M3B 3K9, Canada *Tel:* 416-445-5860 *Toll Free Tel:* 888-432-4879; 800-370-5838 (ebook inquiries) *E-mail:* customerservice@harlequin.com *Web Site:* www.harlequin.com, pg 459

Morrison, Megan, American Society of News Editors (ASNE), 209 Reynolds Journalism Institute, Missouri School of Journalism, Columbia, MO 65211 *Tel:* 573-882-2430 *Fax:* 573-884-3824 *Web Site:* asne.org, pg 556

Morrison, Michael, HarperCollins General Books Group, 195 Broadway, New York, NY 10007 *Tel:* 212-207-7000 *Web Site:* www.harpercollins.com, pg 101

Morrison, Richard, Fordham University Press, Joseph A Martino Hall, 45 Columbus Ave, New York, NY 10023 *Fax:* 347-842-3083 *Web Site:* www.fordhampress.com, pg 86

Morrison, Rusty, Omnidawn Publishing, 1632 Elm Ave, Richmond, CA 94805-1614 *Tel:* 510-237-5472 *Toll Free Tel:* 800-792-4957 *Fax:* 510-232-8525 *E-mail:* manager@omnidawn.com *Web Site:* www.omnidawn.com, pg 168

Morrison, Stephen, Picador, 175 Fifth Ave, 19th fl, New York, NY 10010 *Tel:* 646-307-5151 *Fax:* 212-253-9627 *Web Site:* www.picadorusa.com, pg 182

Morrissey, Jake, Riverhead Books, 375 Hudson St, New York, NY 10014 *Tel:* 212-366-2000 *Web Site:* www.penguin.com/publishers/riverhead, pg 199

Morrissey, Robert, Resilient Publishing, 406 S Third St, Boise, ID 83702 *Tel:* 208-258-9544 *E-mail:* submissions@resilientpublishing.com *Web Site:* www.resilientpublishing.com; www.facebook.com/ResilientPub, pg 198

Morrongiello, Brittany, Alfred A Knopf/Everyman's Library, c/o Penguin Random House Inc, 1745 Broadway, New York, NY 10019 *Tel:* 212-751-2600 *Toll Free Tel:* 800-638-6460 *Fax:* 212-572-2593 *Web Site:* www.knopfdoubleday.com, pg 127

Morrow, David, University of Chicago Press, 1427 E 60 St, Chicago, IL 60637-2954 *Tel:* 773-702-7700; 773-702-7600 *Toll Free Tel:* 800-621-2736 (orders) *Fax:* 773-702-9756; 773-660-2235 (orders); 773-702-2708 *E-mail:* custserv@press.uchicago.edu; marketing@press.uchicago.edu *Web Site:* www.press.uchicago.edu, pg 241

Morrow, Diane, The Barnabas Agency, PO Box 3113, Corsicana, TX 75151-3113 *Toll Free Tel:* 800-927-0517 *E-mail:* info@barnabasagency.com *Web Site:* www.barnabasagency.com, pg 547

Morrow, Stephen, Dutton, 375 Hudson St, New York, NY 10014 *Tel:* 212-366-2000 *Fax:* 212-366-2262 *Web Site:* www.penguin.com, pg 74

Morse, Garry Thomas, Signature Editions, PO Box 206, RPO Corydon, Winnipeg, MB R3M 3S7, Canada *Tel:* 204-779-7803 *E-mail:* submissions@signature-editions.com; orders@signature-editions.com *Web Site:* www.signature-editions.com, pg 470

Morse, John M, Merriam-Webster Inc, 47 Federal St, Springfield, MA 01102 *Tel:* 413-734-3134 *Toll Free Tel:* 800-828-1880 (orders & cust serv) *Fax:* 413-731-5979 (sales) *E-mail:* support@merriam-webster.com *Web Site:* www.merriam-webster.com, pg 149

Morse, Leah, Touchstone, 1230 Avenue of the Americas, New York, NY 10020, pg 233

Mortensen, Dee, Indiana University Press, Herman B Wells Library 350, 1320 E Tenth St, Bloomington, IN 47405-3907 *Tel:* 812-855-8817 *Toll Free Tel:* 800-842-6796 (orders only) *Fax:* 812-855-7931; 812-855-8507 *E-mail:* iupress@indiana.edu; iuporder@indiana.edu (orders) *Web Site:* www.iupress.indiana.edu, pg 116

Mortimer, Bryce, Cedar Fort Inc, 2373 W 700 S, Springville, UT 84663 *Tel:* 801-489-4084 *Toll Free Tel:* 800-SKY-BOOK (759-2665) *Fax:* 801-489-1097 *Toll Free Fax:* 800-388-3727 *Web Site:* cedarfort.com, pg 50

Mortimer, Frank, Oxford University Press USA, 198 Madison Ave, New York, NY 10016 *Tel:* 212-726-6000 *Toll Free Tel:* 800-451-7556 (orders); 800-445-9714 (cust serv) *Fax:* 919-677-1303 *E-mail:* custserv.us@oup.com *Web Site:* www.oup.com/us, pg 171

Mortimer, Michele, Darhansoff & Verrill, 133 W 72 St, Rm 304, New York, NY 10023 *Tel:* 917-305-1300 *E-mail:* permissions@dvagency.com *Web Site:* www.dvagency.com, pg 512

Mortis, Steffanie, Trinity University Press, One Trinity Place, San Antonio, TX 78212-7200 *Tel:* 210-999-8884 *Fax:* 210-999-8838 *E-mail:* books@trinity.edu *Web Site:* www.tupress.org, pg 235

Morton, David, Rizzoli International Publications Inc, 300 Park Ave S, 4th fl, New York, NY 10010-5399 *Tel:* 212-387-3400 *Toll Free Tel:* 800-522-6657 (orders only) *Fax:* 212-387-3535 *E-mail:* publicity@rizzoliusa.com *Web Site:* www.rizzoliusa.com, pg 199

Morton, Larry, Hal Leonard Corp, 7777 W Bluemound Rd, Milwaukee, WI 53213 *Tel:* 414-774-3630 *Fax:* 414-774-3259 *E-mail:* halinfo@halleonard.com; info@halleonard.com *Web Site:* www.halleonard.com, pg 99

Morton, Lisa, Horror Writers Association (HWA), c/o Horror Writers Association, PO Box 56687, Sherman Oaks, CA 91413 *E-mail:* hwa@horror.org *Web Site:* horror.org, pg 566

Mosberg, Stephen R, College Publishing, 12309 Lynwood Dr, Glen Allen, VA 23059 *Tel:* 804-364-8410 *Toll Free Tel:* 800-827-0723 *Fax:* 804-364-8408 *E-mail:* collegepub@mindspring.com *Web Site:* www.collegepublishing.us, pg 58

Mosbrook, Bill, Pathfinder Publishing Inc, 120 S Houghton Rd, Suite 138, Tucson, AZ 85748 *Tel:* 520-647-0158 *Web Site:* www.pathfinderpublishing.com, pg 175

Mosbrook, Evelyn, Pathfinder Publishing Inc, 120 S Houghton Rd, Suite 138, Tucson, AZ 85748 *Tel:* 520-647-0158 *Web Site:* www.pathfinderpublishing.com, pg 175

Moschovakis, Anna, Ugly Duckling Presse, The Old American Can Factory, 232 Third St, Suite E303, Brooklyn, NY 11215 *Tel:* 347-948-5170 *E-mail:* info@uglyducklingpresse.org *Web Site:* www.uglyducklingpresse.org, pg 238

Moscovich, Rotem, Disney-Hyperion Books, 1101 Flower St, Glendale, CA 91201 *Web Site:* books.disney.com, pg 70

Moseley, Lauren, Algonquin Books, 400 Silver Cedar Ct, Suite 300, Chapel Hill, NC 27514-1585 *Tel:* 919-967-0108 *Fax:* 919-933-0272 *E-mail:* inquiry@algonquin.com *Web Site:* www.workman.com/algonquin, pg 7

Moselle, Ben, Craftsman Book Co, 6058 Corte Del Cedro, Carlsbad, CA 92011 *Tel:* 760-438-7828 *Toll Free Tel:* 800-829-8123 *Fax:* 760-438-0398 *Web Site:* www.craftsman-book.com, pg 64

Moselle, Gary, Craftsman Book Co, 6058 Corte Del Cedro, Carlsbad, CA 92011 *Tel:* 760-438-7828 *Toll Free Tel:* 800-829-8123 *Fax:* 760-438-0398 *Web Site:* www.craftsman-book.com, pg 64

Moses, James, Primary Research Group Inc, 2753 Broadway, Suite 156, New York, NY 10025 *Tel:* 212-736-2316 *Fax:* 212-412-9097 *E-mail:* primaryresearchgroup@gmail.com *Web Site:* www.primaryresearch.com, pg 187

Mosher, Jessica, Nelson Education Ltd, 1120 Birchmount Rd, Scarborough, ON M1K 5G4, Canada *Tel:* 416-752-9100 *Toll Free Tel:* 800-268-2222 (cust serv) *Fax:* 416-752-8101 *Toll Free Fax:* 800-430-4445 *E-mail:* peopleandengagement@nelson.com *Web Site:* www.nelson.com, pg 464

Moskow, Shirley, Boston Authors Club Inc, 33 Brayton Rd, Brighton, MA 02135 *Tel:* 617-783-1357 *E-mail:* bostonauthors@aol.com *Web Site:* www.bostonauthorsclub.org, pg 561

Moskow, Shirley, Julia Ward Howe Book Awards, c/o Professor Mary Cronin, 2400 Beacon St, Unit 208, Beacon Hill, MA 02467 *Tel:* 617-783-1357 *E-mail:* bostonauthors@aol.com *Web Site:* www.bostonauthorsclub.org, pg 654

Mosley, Jody, Harry N Abrams Inc, 195 Broadway, 9th fl, New York, NY 10007 *Tel:* 212-206-7715 *Toll Free Tel:* 800-345-1359 *Fax:* 212-519-1210 *E-mail:* abrams@abramsbooks.com *Web Site:* www.abramsbooks.com, pg 3

Moss, Sr Mary Martha, Pauline Books & Media, 50 Saint Paul's Ave, Boston, MA 02130 *Tel:* 617-522-8911 *Toll Free Tel:* 800-876-4463 (orders); 800-836-9723 (cust serv) *Fax:* 617-541-9805 *E-mail:* editorial@paulinemedia.com (ms submissions); orderentry@pauline.org (cust serv) *Web Site:* www.pauline.org/publishing; www.pauline.org/PBMPublishing, pg 175

Munoz, Gabriela, Artist Research & Development Grants, 417 W Roosevelt St, Phoenix, AZ 85003-1326 *Tel:* 602-771-6501 *Fax:* 602-256-0282 *E-mail:* info@azarts.gov *Web Site:* www.azarts.gov, pg 628

Munro, Bob, Elsevier, Health Sciences Division, 1600 John F Kennedy Blvd, Suite 1800, Philadelphia, PA 19103-2899 *Tel:* 215-239-3900 *Toll Free Tel:* 800-523-1649 *Fax:* 215-239-3990 *Web Site:* www.us.elsevierhealth.com, pg 77

Munro, James, Writers House, 21 W 26 St, New York, NY 10010 *Tel:* 212-685-2400 *Fax:* 212-685-1781 *Web Site:* www.writershouse.com, pg 542

Munro, Susan, The Continuing Legal Education Society of British Columbia (CLEBC), 500-1155 W Pender St, Vancouver, BC V6E 2P4, Canada *Tel:* 604-669-3544; 604-893-2121 (cust serv) *Toll Free Tel:* 800-663-0437 (CN) *Fax:* 604-669-9260 *E-mail:* custserv@cle.bc.ca *Web Site:* www.cle.bc.ca, pg 451

Murach, Ben, Mike Murach & Associates Inc, 4340 N Knoll Ave, Fresno, CA 93722 *Tel:* 559-440-9071 *Toll Free Tel:* 800-221-5528 *Fax:* 559-440-0963 *E-mail:* murachbooks@murach.com *Web Site:* www.murach.com, pg 150

Muranaka, Royden, University of Hawaii Press, 2840 Kolowalu St, Honolulu, HI 96822 *Tel:* 808-956-8255 *Toll Free Tel:* 888-UHPRESS (847-7377) *Fax:* 808-988-6052 *Toll Free Fax:* 800-650-7811 *E-mail:* uhpbooks@hawaii.edu *Web Site:* www.uhpress.hawaii.edu, pg 241

Murari, Raj, Disney Publishing Worldwide, 1101 Flower St, Glendale, CA 91201 *Web Site:* books.disney.com, pg 71

Murello, Judy, Berkley Publishing Group, 375 Hudson St, New York, NY 10014 *Tel:* 212-366-2000 *Fax:* 212-366-2385 *Web Site:* www.penguin.com, pg 33

Murgolo, Karen, Grand Central Publishing, 1290 Avenue of the Americas, New York, NY 10019 *Tel:* 212-364-1100 *Web Site:* www.hachettebookgroup.com, pg 95

Murkette, Julie, Satya House Publications, 22 Turkey St, Hardwick, MA 01037 *Tel:* 413-477-8743 *E-mail:* info@satyahouse.com; orders@satyahouse.com *Web Site:* www.satyahouse.com, pg 206

Murphy, Bekky, William Holmes McGuffey Longevity Award, PO Box 367, Fountain City, WI 54629 *E-mail:* info@taaonline.net *Web Site:* www.taaonline.net/mcguffey-longevity-award, pg 666

Murphy, Bekky, Most Promising New Textbook Award, PO Box 367, Fountain City, WI 54629 *E-mail:* info@taaonline.net *Web Site:* www.taaonline.net/promising-new-textbook-award, pg 670

Murphy, Bekky, Ron Pynn Award, PO Box 367, Fountain City, WI 54629 *E-mail:* info@taaonline.net *Web Site:* www.taaonline.net/ron-pynn-award, pg 683

Murphy, Bekky, TAA Council of Fellows, PO Box 367, Fountain City, WI 54629 *E-mail:* info@taaonline.net *Web Site:* www.taaonline.net/council-of-fellows, pg 693

Murphy, Bekky, Textbook Excellence Award, PO Box 367, Fountain City, WI 54629 *E-mail:* info@taaonline.net *Web Site:* www.taaonline.net/textbook-excellence-award, pg 694

Murphy, Christopher, Hachette Book Group, 1290 Avenue of the Americas, New York, NY 10019 *Tel:* 212-364-1100 *Toll Free Tel:* 800-759-0190 (cust serv) *Fax:* 212-364-0933 (intl orders) *Toll Free Fax:* 800-286-9471 (cust serv) *Web Site:* www.hachettebookgroup.com, pg 98

Murphy, Colleen, Houghton Mifflin Harcourt, 125 High St, Boston, MA 02110 *Tel:* 617-351-5000 *Toll Free Tel:* 855-969-4642; 800-225-5425 (K-12 educ materials); 800-323-9540 (assessment materials); 877-219-1537 (SkillsTutor); 888-242-6747 (Innovation in Educ Group); 800-225-3362 (Trade & Ref Div) *Toll Free Fax:* 800-269-5232 *E-mail:* myhmhco@hmhco.com *Web Site:* www.hmhco.com, pg 110

Murphy, Emily, Pantheon Books/Schocken Books, c/o Penguin Random House Inc, 1745 Broadway, New York, NY 10019 *Tel:* 212-751-2600 *Web Site:* knopfdoubleday.com/imprint/pantheon, pg 173

Murphy, Jacqueline, FinePrint Literary Management, 207 W 106 St, Suite 1D, New York, NY 10025 *Tel:* 212-279-6214 *E-mail:* assist@fineprint.com *Web Site:* www.fineprintlit.com, pg 516

Murphy, John, St Martin's Press, LLC, 175 Fifth Ave, New York, NY 10010 *Tel:* 646-307-5151 *Web Site:* us.macmillan.com/smp, pg 204

Murphy, Kevin, Soho Press Inc, 853 Broadway, New York, NY 10003 *Tel:* 212-260-1900 *E-mail:* soho@sohopress.com; publicity@sohopress.com; contact@sohopress.com *Web Site:* www.sohopress.com, pg 216

Murphy, Kim, Coachlight Press LLC, 1704 Craig's Store Rd, Afton, VA 22920-2017 *Tel:* 434-823-1692 *E-mail:* sales@coachlightpress.com *Web Site:* www.coachlightpress.com, pg 58

Murphy, Laurie, Theatre Library Association (TLA), c/o The New York Public Library for the Performing Arts, 40 Lincoln Center Plaza, New York, NY 10023 *E-mail:* TheatreLibraryAssociation@gmail.com *Web Site:* www.tla-online.org/awards/bookawards, pg 580

Murphy, Megan, Canadian Energy Research Institute, 3512 33 St NW, Suite 150, Calgary, AB T2L 2A6, Canada *Tel:* 403-282-1231 *Fax:* 403-284-4181 *E-mail:* info@ceri.ca *Web Site:* www.ceri.ca, pg 448

Murphy, Michael, Jessie Bernard Award, c/o Governance Off, 1430 "K" St NW, Suite 600, Washington, DC 20005 *Tel:* 202-383-9005 *Fax:* 202-638-0882 *E-mail:* governance@asanet.org *Web Site:* www.asanet.org, pg 631

Murphy, Michael, Distinguished Scholarly Book Award, c/o Governance Off, 1430 "K" St NW, Suite 600, Washington, DC 20005 *Tel:* 202-383-9005 *Fax:* 202-638-0882 *E-mail:* governance@asanet.org *Web Site:* www.asanet.org, pg 641

Murphy, Pat, James Tiptree Jr Award, 680 66 St, Oakland, CA 94609 *Tel:* 510-658-7176 *E-mail:* info@tiptree.org *Web Site:* tiptree.org, pg 694

Murphy, Paul, RAND Corp, 1776 Main St, Santa Monica, CA 90407-2138 *Tel:* 310-393-0411 *Fax:* 310-393-4818 *Web Site:* www.rand.org, pg 193

Murphy, Richard J, BPA Worldwide, 100 Beard Sawmill Rd, 6th fl, Shelton, CT 06484 *Tel:* 203-447-2800 *Fax:* 203-447-2900 *E-mail:* info@bpaww.com *Web Site:* www.bpaww.com, pg 561

Murphy, Robert, Higginson Book Co, 10 Colonial Rd, Salem, MA 01970 *Tel:* 978-745-7170 *Fax:* 978-745-8025 *Web Site:* www.higginsonbooks.com, pg 107

Murphy, Ryan, Penguin Books, 375 Hudson St, New York, NY 10014 *Tel:* 212-366-2000 *E-mail:* penguinpublicity@us.penguingroup.com *Web Site:* www.penguinclassics.com; www.penguin.com, pg 177

Murphy, Sarah, HarperCollins General Books Group, 195 Broadway, New York, NY 10007 *Tel:* 212-207-7000 *Web Site:* www.harpercollins.com, pg 101

Murphy, Sarah, Random House Publishing Group, 1745 Broadway, New York, NY 10019 *Toll Free Tel:* 800-200-3552 *Web Site:* atrandom.com, pg 195

Murphy, Sean, Schaffner Press, PO Box 41567, Tucson, AZ 85717 *E-mail:* tim@schaffnerpress.com *Web Site:* www.schaffnerpress.com, pg 207

Murphy, Suzanne, HarperCollins Children's Books, 195 Broadway, New York, NY 10007 *Tel:* 212-207-7000 *Web Site:* www.harpercollins.com/childrens, pg 101

Murphy, Tessa, Insight Editions, 800 "A" St, San Rafael, CA 94901 *Tel:* 415-526-1370 *Toll Free Tel:* 800-809-3792 *Toll Free Fax:* 866-509-0515 *E-mail:* info@insighteditions.com *Web Site:* www.insighteditions.com, pg 117

Murphy, Trace, Paulist Press, 997 Macarthur Blvd, Mahwah, NJ 07430-9990 *Tel:* 201-825-7300 *Toll Free Tel:* 800-218-1903 *Fax:* 201-825-6921 *Toll Free Fax:* 800-836-3161 *E-mail:* info@paulistpress.com; publicity@paulistpress.com *Web Site:* www.paulistpress.com, pg 175

Murphy, Will, Random House Publishing Group, 1745 Broadway, New York, NY 10019 *Toll Free Tel:* 800-200-3552 *Web Site:* atrandom.com, pg 195

Murray, Brian, HarperCollins Publishers, 195 Broadway, New York, NY 10007 *Tel:* 212-207-7000 *Fax:* 212-207-7145 *Web Site:* www.harpercollins.com, pg 101

Murray, Cindy, Random House Publishing Group, 1745 Broadway, New York, NY 10019 *Toll Free Tel:* 800-200-3552 *Web Site:* atrandom.com, pg 195

Murray, David, Piano Press, 1425 Ocean Ave, Suite 5, Del Mar, CA 92014 *Tel:* 619-884-1401 *Fax:* 858-755-1104 *E-mail:* pianopress@pianopress.com *Web Site:* www.pianopress.com, pg 182

Murray, Michael, Cricket Cottage Publishing LLC, 1500 Beville Rd, Suite 606-346, Daytona Beach, FL 32114 *Tel:* 585-687-7291 *E-mail:* cricketcottage@att.net *Web Site:* thecricketpublishing.com, pg 64

Murray, Nancy, Artisan Books, 225 Varick St, New York, NY 10014-4381 *Tel:* 212-254-5900 *Toll Free Tel:* 800-722-7202 *Fax:* 212-677-6692 *E-mail:* artisaninfo@artisanbooks.com *Web Site:* www.workman.com/artisanbooks, pg 22

Murray, Phyllis, Nimbus Publishing Ltd, 3731 Mackintosh St, Halifax, NS B3K 5A5, Canada *Tel:* 902-455-4286 *Toll Free Tel:* 800-NIMBUS9 (646-2879) *Fax:* 902-455-5440 *Toll Free Fax:* 888-253-3133 *E-mail:* customerservice@nimbus.ca *Web Site:* www.nimbus.ca, pg 465

Muschett, Jim, Rizzoli International Publications Inc, 300 Park Ave S, 4th fl, New York, NY 10010-5399 *Tel:* 212-387-3400 *Toll Free Tel:* 800-522-6657 (orders only) *Fax:* 212-387-3535 *E-mail:* publicity@rizzoliusa.com *Web Site:* www.rizzoliusa.com, pg 199

Musgrove, Panda, McBooks Press Inc, ID Booth Bldg, 520 N Meadow St, Ithaca, NY 14850 *Tel:* 607-272-2114 *E-mail:* mcbooks@mcbooks.com *Web Site:* www.mcbooks.com, pg 144

Musser, Jacqueline, Adams Media, 57 Littlefield St, Avon, MA 02322 *Tel:* 508-427-7100 *Web Site:* www.simonandschuster.com, pg 4

Musser, Jane, Perseus Books, 250 W 57 St, 15th fl, New York, NY 10107 *Tel:* 212-340-8100 *Toll Free Tel:* 800-343-4499 (cust serv) *Fax:* 212-340-8105 *Web Site:* www.perseusbooks.com, pg 180

Musto, Ronald G, Italica Press, 595 Main St, Suite 605, New York, NY 10044 *Tel:* 917-371-0563 *E-mail:* inquiries@italicapress.com *Web Site:* www.italicapress.com, pg 121

Mutean, Eva, Ignatius Press, 1348 Tenth Ave, San Francisco, CA 94122-2304 *Toll Free Tel:* 800-651-1531 (orders); 888-615-3186 (cust serv) *E-mail:* info@ignatius.com *Web Site:* www.ignatius.com, pg 114

Mutrux, Sarah, Annual & Rolling Grants for Artists, 136 State St, Montpelier, VT 05602 *Tel:* 802-828-5425 *Fax:* 802-828-3363 *E-mail:* info@vermontartscouncil.org *Web Site:* www.vermontartscouncil.org, pg 627

Muzinic, Jason, Human Kinetics Inc, 1607 N Market St, Champaign, IL 61820 *Tel:* 217-351-5076 *Toll Free Tel:* 800-747-4457 *Fax:* 217-351-1549 (orders/cust serv) *E-mail:* info@hkusa.com *Web Site:* www.humankinetics.com, pg 112

Muzzarelli, Linda, Consumer Press, 13326 SW 28 St, Suite 102, Fort Lauderdale, FL 33330-1102 *Tel:* 954-370-9153 *Fax:* 954-472-1008 *E-mail:* info@consumerpress.com *Web Site:* www.consumerpress.com, pg 60

Myatovich, Paul, CN Times Books, 501 Fifth Ave, Suite 1708, New York, NY 10017 *Tel:* 212-867-8666 *Web Site:* cntimesbooks.com, pg 57

Myers, Chuck, University of Chicago Press, 1427 E 60 St, Chicago, IL 60637-2954 *Tel:* 773-702-7700; 773-702-7600 *Toll Free Tel:* 800-621-2736 (orders) *Fax:* 773-702-9756; 773-660-2235 (orders); 773-

Neely, Judith Illov, F A Davis Co, 1915 Arch St, Philadelphia, PA 19103 *Tel:* 215-568-2270; 215-440-3001 *Toll Free Tel:* 800-523-4049 *Fax:* 215-568-5065; 215-440-3016 *E-mail:* info@fadavis.com; orders@fadavis.com *Web Site:* www.fadavis.com, pg 68

Neesemann, Cynthia, CS International Literary Agency, 43 W 39 St, New York, NY 10018 *Tel:* 212-921-1610; 212-391-9208 *E-mail:* query@csliterary.com; csliterary08@gmail.com *Web Site:* www.csliterary.com, pg 492

Nehmer, Kathy, Educators Progress Service Inc, 214 Center St, Randolph, WI 53956 *Tel:* 920-326-3126 *Toll Free Tel:* 888-951-4469 *Fax:* 920-326-3127 *E-mail:* epsinc@centurytel.net, pg 76

Nehmetallah, Norman, Coach House Books, 80 bpNichol Lane, Toronto, ON M5S 3J4, Canada *Tel:* 416-979-2217 *Toll Free Tel:* 800-367-6360 (outside Toronto) *Fax:* 416-977-1158 *E-mail:* mail@chbooks.com *Web Site:* www.chbooks.com, pg 450

Neibauer, Nathan, Neibauer Press, 20 Industrial Dr, Warminster, PA 18974 *Tel:* 215-322-6200 *Toll Free Tel:* 800-322-6203 (orders) *Fax:* 215-322-2495 *E-mail:* info@neibauer.com *Web Site:* www.neibauer.com; www.churchsupplier.com (orders), pg 160

Neimark, Nina, Nina Neimark Editorial Services, 543 Third St, Brooklyn, NY 11215 *Tel:* 718-499-6804 *E-mail:* pneimark@hotmail.com, pg 499

Nellis, Muriel G, Literary & Creative Artists Inc, 3543 Albemarle St NW, Washington, DC 20008-4213 *Tel:* 202-362-4688 *Fax:* 202-362-8875 *E-mail:* lcadc@earthlink.net (queries, no attachments) *Web Site:* www.lcadc.com, pg 526

Nelson, Bonita K, BK Nelson Inc Lecture Bureau, 6726 Moonriver St, Mira Loma, CA 91752-3428 *Tel:* 760-902-1868 *Fax:* 760-778-6242 *E-mail:* bknelson4@cs.com, pg 547

Nelson, Bonita K, BK Nelson Inc Literary Agency, 6726 Moonriver St, Mira Loma, CA 91752-3428 *Tel:* 760-902-1868 *Fax:* 760-778-6242 *E-mail:* bknelson4@cs.com, pg 530

Nelson, Brian, Nelson Literary Agency LLC, 1732 Wazee St, Suite 207, Denver, CO 80202-1284 *Tel:* 303-292-2805 *E-mail:* query@nelsonagency.com *Web Site:* www.nelsonagency.com, pg 530

Nelson, Dan, Visual Media Alliance (VMA), 665 Third St, Suite 500, San Francisco, CA 94107-1956 *Tel:* 415-489-7601 *Toll Free Tel:* 800-659-3363 *Toll Free Fax:* 800-824-1911 *E-mail:* info@vma.bz *Web Site:* main.vma.bz, pg 580

Nelson, David, Waterside Productions Inc, 2055 Oxford Ave, Cardiff, CA 92007 *Tel:* 760-632-9190 *Fax:* 760-632-9295 *E-mail:* admin@waterside.com *Web Site:* www.waterside.com, pg 541

Nelson, Diane, DC Entertainment, 2900 Alameda, Burbank, CA 91505 *Toll Free Tel:* 800-887-6789 *E-mail:* dccomics@cambeywest.com *Web Site:* www.dcentertainment.com; www.dccomics.com; www.madmag.com, pg 69

Nelson, Eric, HarperCollins General Books Group, 195 Broadway, New York, NY 10007 *Tel:* 212-207-7000 *Web Site:* www.harpercollins.com, pg 101

Nelson, Eric, Penguin Group USA, A Penguin Random House Company, 375 Hudson St, New York, NY 10014 *Tel:* 212-366-2000 *Toll Free Tel:* 800-847-5515 (inside sales); 800-631-8571 (cust serv) *Fax:* 212-366-2666; 607-775-4829 (inside sales) *E-mail:* online@us.penguingroup.com *Web Site:* www.penguin.com, pg 177

Nelson, Kristin, Nelson Literary Agency LLC, 1732 Wazee St, Suite 207, Denver, CO 80202-1284 *Tel:* 303-292-2805 *E-mail:* query@nelsonagency.com *Web Site:* www.nelsonagency.com, pg 530

Nelson, Patricia, Marsal Lyon Literary Agency LLC, 665 San Rodolfo Dr, Suite 124, PMB 121, Solana Beach, CA 92075 *Tel:* 760-814-8507 *Web Site:* www.marsallyonliteraryagency.com, pg 527

Nelson, Priya, University of Chicago Press, 1427 E 60 St, Chicago, IL 60637-2954 *Tel:* 773-702-7700; 773-702-7600 *Toll Free Tel:* 800-621-2736 (orders) *Fax:* 773-702-9756; 773-660-2235 (orders); 773-702-2708 *E-mail:* custserv@press.uchicago.edu; marketing@press.uchicago.edu *Web Site:* www.press.uchicago.edu, pg 241

Nelson, Sara, HarperCollins General Books Group, 195 Broadway, New York, NY 10007 *Tel:* 212-207-7000 *Web Site:* www.harpercollins.com, pg 101

Nemeth, Terence, Theatre Communications Group, 520 Eighth Ave, 24th fl, New York, NY 10018-4156 *Tel:* 212-609-5900 *Fax:* 212-609-5901 *E-mail:* tcg@tcg.org *Web Site:* www.tcg.org, pg 231

Neptune, Alyssa, Alice James Books, 114 Prescott St, Farmington, ME 04938 *Tel:* 207-778-7071 *Fax:* 207-778-7766 *E-mail:* info@alicejamesbooks.org *Web Site:* alicejamesbooks.org, pg 7

Nericcio, Dr Bill, San Diego State University Press, Arts & Letters 283/MC 6020, 5500 Campanile Dr, San Diego, CA 92182-6020 *Tel:* 619-594-6220 (orders) *E-mail:* memo@sdsu.edu *Web Site:* sdsupress.sdsu.edu, pg 205

Nesbit, Lynn, Janklow & Nesbit Associates, 285 Madison Ave, 21st fl, New York, NY 10017 *Tel:* 212-421-1700 *Fax:* 212-355-1403 *E-mail:* info@janklow.com *Web Site:* www.janklowandnesbit.com, pg 522

Nesbit, Yelena Gitlin, HarperCollins General Books Group, 195 Broadway, New York, NY 10007 *Tel:* 212-207-7000 *Web Site:* www.harpercollins.com, pg 101

Nesbitt, Bruce, Cenveo Publisher Services, 555 Virginia Dr, Fort Washington, PA 19034 *Tel:* 215-591-9125 *E-mail:* info.psg@cenveo.com *Web Site:* cenveopublisherservices.com, pg 491

Nesbitt, Harry J III, Cenveo Publisher Services, 555 Virginia Dr, Fort Washington, PA 19034 *Tel:* 215-591-9125 *E-mail:* info.psg@cenveo.com *Web Site:* cenveopublisherservices.com, pg 491

Netschert, Linda, Farcountry Press, 2750 Broadwater Ave, Helena, MT 59602-9202 *Tel:* 406-422-1263 *Toll Free Tel:* 800-821-3874 (sales off) *Fax:* 406-443-5480 *E-mail:* books@farcountrypress.com; sales@farcountrypress.com *Web Site:* www.farcountrypress.com, pg 82

Nettleton, Kathleen Calhoun, Pelican Publishing Co, 1000 Burmaster St, Gretna, LA 70053-2246 *Tel:* 504-368-1175 *Toll Free Tel:* 800-843-1724 *Fax:* 504-368-1195 *E-mail:* sales@pelicanpub.com (sales); office@pelicanpub.com (permission); promo@pelicanpub.com (publicity) *Web Site:* www.pelicanpub.com, pg 176

Neubauer, Erica, Letterbox/Papyrus of London Publishers USA, 10501 Broom Hill Dr, Suite 1-F, Las Vegas, NV 89134-7339 *Tel:* 702-256-3838 *E-mail:* lb27383@cox.net, pg 132

Neubauer, Mrs H, Letterbox/Papyrus of London Publishers USA, 10501 Broom Hill Dr, Suite 1-F, Las Vegas, NV 89134-7339 *Tel:* 702-256-3838 *E-mail:* lb27383@cox.net, pg 133

Neufeld, Jacque, Safari Press, 15621 Chemical Lane, Bldg B, Huntington Beach, CA 92649 *Tel:* 714-894-9080 *Toll Free Tel:* 800-451-4788 *Fax:* 714-894-4949 *E-mail:* info@safaripress.com *Web Site:* www.safaripress.com, pg 203

Neuhaus, Dana, Concordia Publishing House, 3558 S Jefferson Ave, St Louis, MO 63118-3968 *Tel:* 314-268-1000; 314-268-1268 (bookshop) *Toll Free Tel:* 800-325-3040 (cust serv) *Toll Free Fax:* 800-490-9889 (cust serv) *E-mail:* order@cph.org *Web Site:* www.cph.org, pg 59

Neumann, Grant, Random House Publishing Group, 1745 Broadway, New York, NY 10019 *Toll Free Tel:* 800-200-3552 *Web Site:* atrandom.com, pg 195

Neumann, Rachel, Parallax Press, 2236-B Sixth St, Berkeley, CA 94710 *Tel:* 510-540-6411 *Toll Free Tel:* 800-863-5290 (orders) *Fax:* 510-981-1157 *Web Site:* www.parallax.org, pg 174

Neusner, Dena, Behrman House Inc, 11 Edison Place, Springfield, NJ 07081 *Tel:* 973-379-7200 *Toll Free Tel:* 800-221-2755 *Fax:* 973-379-7280 *E-mail:* customersupport@behrmanhouse.com *Web Site:* www.behrmanhouse.com, pg 32

Nevins, Alan, Renaissance Literary & Talent, PO Box 17379, Beverly Hills, CA 90209 *Tel:* 323-848-8305 *Fax:* 424-298-2588 *E-mail:* query@renaissancemgmt.net *Web Site:* renaissancemgmt.net, pg 532

Nevins, Larry, HarperCollins Publishers, 195 Broadway, New York, NY 10007 *Tel:* 212-207-7000 *Fax:* 212-207-7145 *Web Site:* www.harpercollins.com, pg 101

Nevins, Tyler, Disney-Hyperion Books, 1101 Flower St, Glendale, CA 91201 *Web Site:* books.disney.com, pg 70

Newberg, Esther, ICM Partners, 65 E 55 St, New York, NY 10022 *Tel:* 212-556-5600 *Web Site:* www.icmtalent.com, pg 521

Newborn, Sasha "Birdie", Bandanna Books, 1212 Punta Gorda St, No 13, Santa Barbara, CA 93103 *E-mail:* bandanna@cox.net *Web Site:* www.bandannabooks.com; www.mudbornpress.us; www.betabooks.us; www.shakespeareplaybook.com; www.bookdoc.us; catandbirdiebooks.com, pg 29

Newcomb, Doug, Special Libraries Association (SLA), 7918 Jones Branch Dr, Suite 300, McLean, VA 22102 *Tel:* 703-647-4900 *Fax:* 703-506-3266 *Web Site:* www.sla.org, pg 579

Newcomb, Trish, The McDonald & Woodward Publishing Co, 695 Tall Oaks Dr, Newark, OH 43055 *Tel:* 740-641-2691 *Toll Free Tel:* 800-233-8787 *Fax:* 740-641-2692 *E-mail:* mwpubco@mwpubco.com *Web Site:* www.mwpubco.com, pg 145

Newell, Patricia, North Country Press, 126 Main St, Unity, ME 04988 *Tel:* 207-948-2208 *Fax:* 207-948-9000 *E-mail:* info@northcountrypress.com *Web Site:* www.northcountrypress.com, pg 163

Newell, Terry, Insight Editions, 800 "A" St, San Rafael, CA 94901 *Tel:* 415-526-1370 *Toll Free Tel:* 800-809-3792 *Toll Free Fax:* 866-509-0515 *E-mail:* info@insighteditions.com *Web Site:* www.insighteditions.com, pg 117

Newell, Tricia, Soil Science Society of America, 5585 Guilford Rd, Madison, WI 53711-5801 *Tel:* 608-273-8080 *Web Site:* www.soils.org, pg 217

Newlin, Bill, Perseus Books, 250 W 57 St, 15th fl, New York, NY 10107 *Tel:* 212-340-8100 *Toll Free Tel:* 800-343-4499 (cust serv) *Fax:* 212-340-8105 *Web Site:* www.perseusbooks.com, pg 180

Newlin, Shanta, Penguin Young Readers Group, 345 Hudson St, New York, NY 10014 *Tel:* 212-366-2000; 212-414-3553 *Fax:* 212-414-3340 *Web Site:* www.penguin.com/children, pg 179

Newman, Barbara, Frederick Fell Publishers Inc, 2131 Hollywood Blvd, Suite 305, Hollywood, FL 33020 *Tel:* 954-925-5242 *E-mail:* fellpub@aol.com (admin only) *Web Site:* www.fellpub.com, pg 88

Newman, Brent, Accuity, 4709 W Golf Rd, Skokie, IL 60076 *Tel:* 847-676-9600 *Toll Free Tel:* 800-321-3373 *Fax:* 847-933-8101 *E-mail:* custserv@accuity.com; sales@accuity.com *Web Site:* www.accuity.com, pg 3

Newman, Dr Carey C, Baylor University Press, Baylor University, One Bear Place, Waco, TX 76798-7363 *Tel:* 254-710-3164 *Fax:* 254-710-3440 *Web Site:* www.baylorpress.com, pg 30

Newman, Carolyn, River City Publishing LLC, 1719 Mulberry St, Montgomery, AL 36106 *Tel:* 334-265-6753 *Fax:* 334-265-8880 *E-mail:* sales@rivercitypublishing.com *Web Site:* rivercitypublishing.com, pg 199

Newman, Eric, Fordham University Press, Joseph A Martino Hall, 45 Columbus Ave, New York, NY 10023 *Fax:* 347-842-3083 *Web Site:* www.fordhampress.com, pg 86

Newman, Jack, Shadow Mountain, PO Box 30178, Salt Lake City, UT 84130-0178 *Tel:* 801-534-1515 *Toll Free Tel:* 800-453-3876 *Fax:* 801-517-3119 *E-mail:* submissions@shadowmountain.com *Web Site:* shadowmountain.com, pg 211

Newman, Judy A, Scholastic Inc, 557 Broadway, New York, NY 10012 *Tel:* 212-343-6100 *Toll Free Tel:* 800-SCHOLASTIC (724-6527) *Web Site:* www.scholastic.com, pg 208

Newman, Megan, Avery, 375 Hudson St, New York, NY 10014 *Tel:* 212-366-2000 *Fax:* 212-366-2643 *Web Site:* www.penguin.com; www.penguinrandomhouse.com, pg 27

Newton, Kendra, HarperCollins General Books Group, 195 Broadway, New York, NY 10007 *Tel:* 212-207-7000 *Web Site:* www.harpercollins.com, pg 101

Newton, Michael, Zone Books, 633 Vanderbilt St, Brooklyn, NY 11218 *Tel:* 718-686-0048 *Toll Free Tel:* 800-405-1619 (orders & cust serv) *Fax:* 718-686-9045 *E-mail:* orders@triliteral.org *Web Site:* www.zonebooks.org, pg 263

Ney, Alison, Radcliffe Fellowship, 8 Garden St, Cambridge, MA 02138 *Tel:* 617-496-1324 (application off) *Fax:* 617-495-8136 *Web Site:* www.radcliffe.harvard.edu, pg 683

Ng, Joanna, TarcherPerigee, 375 Hudson St, New York, NY 10014 *Tel:* 212-366-2000 *Fax:* 212-366-2643 *E-mail:* customerservice@penguinrandomhouse.com (cust serv); TarcherPerigeePublicity@penguinrandomhouse.com (media queries) *Web Site:* www.tarcherbooks.com; www.facebook.com/TarcherPerigee/; www.penguin.com/publishers/tarcherperigee, pg 227

Ngo, Dung, Rizzoli International Publications Inc, 300 Park Ave S, 4th fl, New York, NY 10010-5399 *Tel:* 212-387-3400 *Toll Free Tel:* 800-522-6657 (orders only) *Fax:* 212-387-3535 *E-mail:* publicity@rizzoliusa.com *Web Site:* www.rizzoliusa.com, pg 199

Nicholas, Calliope, Residency, 454 E Hill Rd, Austerlitz, NY 12017 *Tel:* 518-392-3103; 518-392-4144 *E-mail:* apply@millaycolony.org *Web Site:* www.millaycolony.org, pg 684

Nicholas, John, St Martin's Press, LLC, 175 Fifth Ave, New York, NY 10010 *Tel:* 646-307-5151 *Web Site:* us.macmillan.com/smp, pg 204

Nicholls, Shawn, HarperCollins General Books Group, 195 Broadway, New York, NY 10007 *Tel:* 212-207-7000 *Web Site:* www.harpercollins.com, pg 101

Nichols, Bruce, Houghton Mifflin Harcourt Trade & Reference Division, 125 High St, Boston, MA 02110 *Tel:* 617-351-5000 *Toll Free Tel:* 800-225-3362 *Web Site:* www.hmhco.com, pg 111

Nichols, Hannah, Ambassador International, 411 University Ridge, Suite B14, Greenville, SC 29601 *Tel:* 864-751-4844 *E-mail:* info@emeraldhouse.com; publisher@emeraldhouse.com (ms submissions); sales@emeraldhouse.com (orders/order inquiries) *Web Site:* ambassador-international.com; www.facebook.com/AmbassadorIntl; twitter.com/ambassadorintl, pg 9

Nichols, Robby, Covenant Communications Inc, 920 E State Rd, Suite F, American Fork, UT 84003-0416 *Tel:* 801-756-1041 *E-mail:* info@covenant-lds.com *Web Site:* www.covenant-lds.com, pg 63

Nichols, Sally, University of Massachusetts Press, East Experiment Sta, 671 N Pleasant St, Amherst, MA 01003 *Tel:* 413-545-2217 *Fax:* 413-545-1226 *E-mail:* info@umpress.umass.edu *Web Site:* www.umass.edu/umpress, pg 242

Nichols, Suzanne, Russell Sage Foundation, 112 E 64 St, New York, NY 10065 *Tel:* 212-750-6000 *Toll Free Tel:* 800-524-6401 *Fax:* 212-371-4761 *E-mail:* info@rsage.org *Web Site:* www.russellsage.org, pg 202

Nicholson, Leah, Jenkins Group Inc, 1129 Woodmere Ave, Suite B, Traverse City, MI 49686 *Tel:* 231-933-0445 *Toll Free Tel:* 800-706-4636 *Fax:* 231-933-0448 *E-mail:* info@bookpublishing.com *Web Site:* www.bookpublishing.com, pg 496

Nicholson, Sam, Random House Publishing Group, 1745 Broadway, New York, NY 10019 *Toll Free Tel:* 800-200-3552 *Web Site:* atrandom.com, pg 195

Nici, Joanne, Don Buchwald & Associates Inc, 10 E 44 St, New York, NY 10017 *Tel:* 212-867-1200 *Fax:* 212-867-2434 *E-mail:* info@buchwald.com *Web Site:* www.buchwald.com, pg 510

Nicolajsen, Alex, Kensington Publishing Corp, 119 W 40 St, New York, NY 10018 *Tel:* 212-407-1500 *Toll Free Tel:* 800-221-2647 *Fax:* 212-935-0699 *Web Site:* www.kensingtonbooks.com, pg 125

Nieginski, Elizabeth, Springer Publishing Co, 11 W 42 St, 15th fl, New York, NY 10036-8002 *Tel:* 212-431-4370 *Toll Free Tel:* 877-687-7476 *Fax:* 212-941-7842 *E-mail:* marketing@springerpub.com; cs@springerpub.com (orders); editorial@springerpub.com *Web Site:* www.springerpub.com, pg 219

Nielsen, Margarete, Hay House Inc, 2776 Loker Ave W, Carlsbad, CA 92010 *Tel:* 760-431-7695 (ext 2, intl) *Toll Free Tel:* 800-654-5126 (ext 2, US) *Toll Free Fax:* 800-650-5115 *E-mail:* info@hayhouse.com; editorial@hayhouse.com *Web Site:* www.hayhouse.com, pg 103

Nieman, James, Standard Publishing, 4050 Lee Vance View, Colorado Springs, CO 80918 *Tel:* 513-931-4050 *Toll Free Tel:* 800-323-7543 *Fax:* 513-931-0950 *Toll Free Fax:* 800-323-0726 *E-mail:* customerservice@standardpub.com *Web Site:* www.standardpub.com, pg 220

Nieto, Nadxieli, The PEN Award for Poetry in Translation, 588 Broadway, Suite 303, New York, NY 10012 *Tel:* 212-334-1660 *Fax:* 212-334-2181 *E-mail:* awards@pen.org *Web Site:* pen.org/press/grants-awards-database, pg 677

Nieto, Nadxieli, PEN/Bellwether Prize for Socially Engaged Fiction, 588 Broadway, Suite 303, New York, NY 10012 *Tel:* 212-334-1660 *E-mail:* awards@pen.org *Web Site:* pen.org/press/grants-awards-database, pg 677

Nieto, Nadxieli, PEN/Diamonstein-Spielvogel Award for the Art of the Essay, 588 Broadway, Suite 303, New York, NY 10012 *Tel:* 212-334-1660 *E-mail:* awards@pen.org *Web Site:* pen.org/literary-awards, pg 677

Nieto, Nadxieli, PEN/E O Wilson Literary Science Writing Award, 588 Broadway, Suite 303, New York, NY 10012 *Tel:* 212-334-1660 *E-mail:* awards@pen.org *Web Site:* pen.org/literary-awards, pg 677

Nieto, Nadxieli, PEN/ESPN Award for Literary Sports Writing, 588 Broadway, Suite 303, New York, NY 10012 *Tel:* 212-334-1660 *E-mail:* awards@pen.org *Web Site:* pen.org/literary-awards, pg 677

Nieto, Nadxieli, PEN/ESPN Lifetime Achievement Award for Literary Sports Writing, 588 Broadway, Suite 303, New York, NY 10012 *Tel:* 212-334-1660 *E-mail:* awards@pen.org *Web Site:* pen.org/literary-awards, pg 677

Nieto, Nadxieli, PEN/Fusion Emerging Writers Prize, 588 Broadway, Suite 303, New York, NY 10012 *Tel:* 212-334-1660 *E-mail:* awards@pen.org *Web Site:* pen.org/literary-awards, pg 678

Nieto, Nadxieli, PEN/Jacqueline Bograd Weld Award for Biography, 588 Broadway, Suite 303, New York, NY 10012 *Tel:* 212-334-1660 *E-mail:* awards@pen.org *Web Site:* pen.org/literary-awards, pg 678

Nieto, Nadxieli, PEN/Jean Stein Book Award, 588 Broadway, Suite 303, New York, NY 10012 *Tel:* 212-334-1660 *E-mail:* info@pen.org *Web Site:* pen.org/press/grants-awards-database, pg 678

Nieto, Nadxieli, PEN/Joyce Osterweil Award for Poetry, 588 Broadway, Suite 303, New York, NY 10012 *Tel:* 212-334-1660 *E-mail:* awards@pen.org *Web Site:* pen.org/press/grants-awards-database, pg 678

Nieto, Nadxieli, PEN/Nabokov Award for Achievement in International Literature, 588 Broadway, Suite 303, New York, NY 10012 *Tel:* 212-334-1660 *Fax:* 212-334-2181 *E-mail:* awards@pen.org *Web Site:* pen.org/literary-awards, pg 678

Nieto, Nadxieli, PEN Open Book Award, 588 Broadway, Suite 303, New York, NY 10012 *Tel:* 212-334-1660 *E-mail:* awards@pen.org *Web Site:* pen.org/literary-awards, pg 678

Nieto, Nadxieli, PEN/Phyllis Naylor Working Writer Fellowship, 588 Broadway, Suite 303, New York, NY 10012 *Tel:* 212-334-1660 *Fax:* 212-334-2181 *E-mail:* awards@pen.org *Web Site:* pen.org/press/grants-awards-database, pg 678

Nieto, Nadxieli, PEN/Ralph Manheim Medal for Translation, 588 Broadway, Suite 303, New York, NY 10012 *Tel:* 212-334-1660 *Fax:* 212-334-2181 *E-mail:* awards@pen.org *Web Site:* pen.org/press/grants-awards-database, pg 678

Nieto, Nadxieli, PEN/Robert Bingham Prize for Debut Fiction, 588 Broadway, Suite 303, New York, NY 10012 *Tel:* 212-334-1660 *Fax:* 212-334-2181 *E-mail:* awards@pen.org *Web Site:* pen.org/press/grants-awards-database, pg 678

Nieto, Nadxieli, PEN/Saul Bellow Award for Achievement in American Fiction, 588 Broadway, Suite 303, New York, NY 10012 *Tel:* 212-334-1660 *Fax:* 212-334-2181 *E-mail:* awards@pen.org *Web Site:* pen.org/press/grants-awards-database, pg 679

Nieto, Nadxieli, PEN Translation Prize, 588 Broadway, Suite 303, New York, NY 10012 *Tel:* 212-334-1660 *Fax:* 212-334-2181 *E-mail:* awards@pen.org *Web Site:* pen.org/press/grants-awards-database, pg 679

Nieto, Nadxieli, PEN/Voelcker Award, 588 Broadway, Suite 303, New York, NY 10012 *Tel:* 212-334-1660 *E-mail:* awards@pen.org *Web Site:* pen.org/literary-awards, pg 679

Nigro, Alissa, Random House Children's Books, 1745 Broadway, 10th fl, New York, NY 10019 *Tel:* 212-782-9000 *Web Site:* www.randomhousekids.com, pg 194

Nikitina, Elena, Corwin, a Sage Co, 2455 Teller Rd, Thousand Oaks, CA 91320 *Tel:* 805-499-9734 *Toll Free Tel:* 800-233-9936 *Fax:* 805-499-5323 *Toll Free Fax:* 800-417-2466 *E-mail:* info@corwin.com; order@corwin.com *Web Site:* www.corwin.com, pg 61

Nikodym, Carolyn, Oolichan Books, PO Box 2278, Fernie, BC V0B 1M0, Canada *Tel:* 250-423-6113 *E-mail:* info@oolichan.com *Web Site:* www.oolichan.com, pg 465

Nikolic, Maja, Writers House, 21 W 26 St, New York, NY 10010 *Tel:* 212-685-2400 *Fax:* 212-685-1781 *Web Site:* www.writershouse.com, pg 542

Nintzel, Katherine, HarperCollins General Books Group, 195 Broadway, New York, NY 10007 *Tel:* 212-207-7000 *Web Site:* www.harpercollins.com, pg 101

Nisbet, Lynette, Prometheus Books, 59 John Glenn Dr, Amherst, NY 14228-2119 *Tel:* 716-691-0133 *Fax:* 716-691-0137 *E-mail:* marketing@prometheusbooks.com; editorial@prometheusbooks.com; rights@prometheusmail.com *Web Site:* www.prometheusbooks.com, pg 190

Nishan, Rachel, Twin Oaks Indexing, 138 Twin Oaks Rd, Suite W, Louisa, VA 23093 *Tel:* 540-894-5126 *Web Site:* www.twinoakscommunity.org, pg 502

Nishimoto, Kathleen, WME, 11 Madison Ave, 18th fl, New York, NY 10010 *Tel:* 212-586-5100 *Web Site:* www.wmeentertainment.com, pg 542

Nitz, Caroline, Graywolf Press, 250 Third Ave N, Suite 600, Minneapolis, MN 55401 *Tel:* 651-641-0077 *Fax:* 651-641-0036 *E-mail:* wolves@graywolfpress.org (no ms queries, sample chapters or proposals) *Web Site:* www.graywolfpress.org, pg 95

Niumata, Erin, Folio Literary Management, The Film Center Bldg, 630 Ninth Ave, Suite 1101, New York, NY 10036 *Tel:* 212-400-1494 *Fax:* 212-967-0977 *Web Site:* www.foliolit.com, pg 517

Nivens, Michele R, Beyond the Book, 222 Rosewood Dr, Danvers, MA 01923 *Tel:* 978-750-8400 (sales) *E-mail:* beyondthebook@copyright.com *Web Site:* www.copyright.com; beyondthebookcast.com, pg 610

Noakes-Fry, Kristen, Rothstein Associates Inc, 4 Arapaho Rd, Brookfield, CT 06804-3104 *Tel:* 203-740-7400 *Toll Free Tel:* 888-768-4783 *Fax:* 203-740-7401 *E-mail:* info@rothstein.com *Web Site:* www.rothstein.com; www.rothsteinpublishing.com, pg 201

Nobile, Courtney, Perseus Books, 250 W 57 St, 15th fl, New York, NY 10107 *Tel:* 212-340-8100 *Toll Free Tel:* 800-343-4499 (cust serv) *Fax:* 212-340-8105 *Web Site:* www.perseusbooks.com, pg 181

Noble, Claire, Naval Institute Press, 291 Wood Rd, Annapolis, MD 21402-5034 *Tel:* 410-268-6110 *Toll Free Tel:* 800-233-8764 *Fax:* 410-295-1084; 410-571-1703 (cust serv) *E-mail:* webmaster@navalinstitute.org; customer@navalinstitute.org (cust serv) *Web Site:* www.nip.org; www.usni.org, pg 159

Noble, Katrina, University of Washington Press, 4333 Brooklyn Ave NE, Seattle, WA 98105-9570 *Tel:* 206-543-4050 *Toll Free Tel:* 800-537-5487 (orders) *Fax:* 206-543-3932; 410-516-6998 (orders) *E-mail:* uwapress@uw.edu *Web Site:* www.washington.edu/uwpress, pg 246

Noble, Nicole, National Braille Press, 88 Saint Stephen St, Boston, MA 02115-4302 *Tel:* 617-266-6160 *Toll Free Tel:* 800-548-7323 (cust serv); 888-965-8965 *Fax:* 617-437-0456 *E-mail:* orders@nbp.org; contact@nbp.org *Web Site:* www.nbp.org, pg 157

Noble, Rick, Haights Cross Communications®, 136 Madison Ave, 8th fl, New York, NY 10016 *Tel:* 212-209-0500 *E-mail:* info@haightscross.com *Web Site:* www.haightscross.com, pg 99

Noble, Rick, Triumph Learning LLC, 136 Madison Ave, 7th fl, New York, NY 10016 *Tel:* 212-652-0200 *Toll Free Tel:* 800-338-6519 (cust serv) *Toll Free Fax:* 866-805-5723 *E-mail:* info@triumphlearning.com; customerservice@triumphlearning.com *Web Site:* www.triumphlearning.com, pg 235

Nodarse, Sarah, Perseus Books, 250 W 57 St, 15th fl, New York, NY 10107 *Tel:* 212-340-8100 *Toll Free Tel:* 800-343-4499 (cust serv) *Fax:* 212-340-8105 *Web Site:* www.perseusbooks.com, pg 181

Noelle, Ashley, Whiskey Creek Press, c/o Start Publishing LLC, 101 Hudson St, 37th fl, Suite 3705, Jersey City, NJ 07302 *Tel:* 212-431-5455 *Fax:* 917-464-6394 *E-mail:* publisher@whiskeycreekpress.com *Web Site:* whiskeycreekpress.com, pg 254

Noh, Chrissy, Simon & Schuster Children's Publishing, 1230 Avenue of the Americas, New York, NY 10020 *Tel:* 212-698-7000 *Web Site:* www.simonandschuster.com/kids; www.simonandschuster.com/teen; simonandschuster.net; simonandschuster.biz, pg 213

Nolan, Betsy, The Betsy Nolan Literary Agency, 112 E 17 St, Suite 1W, New York, NY 10003 *Tel:* 212-967-8200 *Fax:* 212-967-7292 *E-mail:* dblehr@cs.com, pg 531

Nolan, Elizabeth, The Optical Society (OSA), 2010 Massachusetts Ave NW, Washington, DC 20036-1023 *Tel:* 202-223-8130 *Toll Free Tel:* 800-766-4672 *E-mail:* custserv@osa.org *Web Site:* www.osa.org, pg 169

Nolan, Laura, Aevitas Creative Management, 19 W 21 St, Suite 501, New York, NY 10010 *Tel:* 212-765-6900 *Web Site:* aevitascreative.com, pg 506

Nolan, Patrick, Penguin Books, 375 Hudson St, New York, NY 10014 *Tel:* 212-366-2000 *E-mail:* penguinpublicity@us.penguingroup.com *Web Site:* www.penguinclassics.com; www.penguin.com, pg 177

Noland, Terrance, Nelson Algren Awards, Chicago Tribune, TT200, 435 N Michigan Ave, Chicago, IL 60611 *Toll Free Tel:* 800-874-2863 (classifieds) *Fax:* 312-222-5816 *Web Site:* www.chicagotribune.com/about; algren.submittable.com, pg 626

Nolin, Leslie, Fairwinds Press, PO Box 668, Lions Bay, BC V0N 2E0, Canada *Tel:* 604-913-0649 *E-mail:* orders@fairwinds-press.com *Web Site:* www.fairwinds-press.com, pg 456

Noll, Michael, Writers' League of Texas (WLT), 611 S Congress Ave, Suite 200 A-3, Austin, TX 78704 *Tel:* 512-499-8914 *E-mail:* wlt@writersleague.org *Web Site:* www.writersleague.org, pg 548, 581, 616

Noll, Michael, Writers' League of Texas Book Awards, 611 S Congress Ave, Suite 200 A-3, Austin, TX 78704 *Tel:* 512-499-8914 *E-mail:* wlt@writersleague.org *Web Site:* www.writersleague.org, pg 700

Nonbello, Michael, Andrews McMeel Publishing LLC, 1130 Walnut St, Kansas City, MO 64106-2109 *Toll Free Tel:* 800-851-8923; 800-943-9839 (cust serv) *Toll Free Fax:* 800-943-9831 (orders) *Web Site:* www.andrewsmcmeel.com, pg 17

Noonan, Margaret, Fordham University Press, Joseph A Martino Hall, 45 Columbus Ave, New York, NY 10023 *Fax:* 347-842-3083 *Web Site:* www.fordhampress.com, pg 86

Noonan, Robin, Naval Institute Press, 291 Wood Rd, Annapolis, MD 21402-5034 *Tel:* 410-268-6110 *Toll Free Tel:* 800-233-8764 *Fax:* 410-295-1084; 410-571-1703 (cust serv) *E-mail:* webmaster@navalinstitute.org; customer@navalinstitute.org (cust serv) *Web Site:* www.nip.org; www.usni.org, pg 159

Noorda, Rachel, ThunderStone Books, 6575 Horse Dr, Las Vegas, NV 89131 *E-mail:* info@thunderstonebooks.com *Web Site:* www.thunderstonebooks.com, pg 232

Noorda, Robert, ThunderStone Books, 6575 Horse Dr, Las Vegas, NV 89131 *E-mail:* info@thunderstonebooks.com *Web Site:* www.thunderstonebooks.com, pg 232

Nordling, Kerry, St Martin's Press, LLC, 175 Fifth Ave, New York, NY 10010 *Tel:* 646-307-5151 *Web Site:* us.macmillan.com/smp, pg 204

Nordstrom, Robyn, The Pilgrim Press/United Church Press, 700 Prospect Ave, Cleveland, OH 44115-1100 *Tel:* 216-736-2100 *Toll Free Tel:* 800-537-3394 (orders) *Fax:* 216-736-2207 (orders) *E-mail:* permissions@thepilgrimpress.com; store@ucc.org *Web Site:* www.thepilgrimpress.com; www.uccresources.com, pg 183

Noreika, Sarah, Philadelphia Museum of Art, 2525 Pennsylvania Ave, Philadelphia, PA 19130 *Tel:* 215-684-7250 *Fax:* 215-235-8715 *Web Site:* www.philamuseum.org, pg 182

Norell, Kristin, Chronicle Books LLC, 680 Second St, San Francisco, CA 94107 *Tel:* 415-537-4200 *Toll Free Tel:* 800-759-0190 (cust serv) *Fax:* 415-537-4460 *Toll Free Fax:* 800-858-7787 (orders); 800-286-9471 (cust serv) *E-mail:* frontdesk@chroniclebooks.com *Web Site:* www.chroniclebooks.com, pg 55

Nori, Don, Destiny Image Inc, 167 Walnut Bottom Rd, Shippensburg, PA 17257-0310 *Tel:* 717-532-3040 *Toll Free Tel:* 800-722-6774 (orders only) *Fax:* 717-532-9291 *Web Site:* www.destinyimage.com, pg 69

Norin, Melinda Sue, Book Publicists of Southern California, 714 Crescent Dr, Beverly Hills, CA 90210 *Tel:* 323-461-3921 *Fax:* 323-461-0917 *Web Site:* www.bookpublicists.org, pg 560

Norman, Anne Cole, Words into Print, 208 Java St, 6th fl, Brooklyn, NY 11222 *E-mail:* query@wordsintoprint.org *Web Site:* wordsintoprint.org, pg 503

Norman, Nancy Lowden, Atlantic Center for the Arts Artists-in-Residence Program, 1414 Art Center Ave, New Smyrna Beach, FL 32168 *Tel:* 386-427-6975 *Toll Free Tel:* 800-393-6975 *Fax:* 386-427-5669 *E-mail:* program@atlanticcenterforthearts.org *Web Site:* atlanticcenterforthearts.org, pg 609

Norman, Taylor, Chronicle Books LLC, 680 Second St, San Francisco, CA 94107 *Tel:* 415-537-4200 *Toll Free Tel:* 800-759-0190 (cust serv) *Fax:* 415-537-4460 *Toll Free Fax:* 800-858-7787 (orders); 800-286-9471 (cust serv) *E-mail:* frontdesk@chroniclebooks.com *Web Site:* www.chroniclebooks.com, pg 55

Norris, Fran, River City Publishing LLC, 1719 Mulberry St, Montgomery, AL 36106 *Tel:* 334-265-6753 *Fax:* 334-265-8880 *E-mail:* sales@rivercitypublishing.com *Web Site:* rivercitypublishing.com, pg 199

Norton, Debra, Alice James Books, 114 Prescott St, Farmington, ME 04938 *Tel:* 207-778-7071 *Fax:* 207-778-7766 *E-mail:* info@alicejamesbooks.org *Web Site:* alicejamesbooks.org, pg 7

Norton, Jennifer, The Pennsylvania State University Press, University Support Bldg 1, Suite C, 820 N University Dr, University Park, PA 16802-1003 *Tel:* 814-865-1327 *Toll Free Tel:* 800-326-9180 *Fax:* 814-863-1408 *Toll Free Fax:* 877-778-2665 *E-mail:* info@psupress.org *Web Site:* www.psupress.org, pg 179

Norton, Kim, Peace Hill Press, 18021 The Glebe Lane, Charles City, VA 23030 *Tel:* 804-829-5043 *Toll Free Tel:* 877-322-3445 (orders) *Fax:* 804-829-5704 *E-mail:* info@peacehillpress.com *Web Site:* www.peacehillpress.com, pg 175

Norton, Paul, AMMO Books LLC, 5022 N Eagle Rock Blvd, Los Angeles, CA 90041 *Tel:* 323-223-AMMO (223-2666) *Fax:* 323-978-4200 *E-mail:* weborders@ammobooks.com; orders@ammobooks.com *Web Site:* ammobooks.com, pg 16

Nosan, Gregory, The Art Institute of Chicago, 111 S Michigan Ave, Chicago, IL 60603-6404 *Tel:* 312-443-3600; 312-443-3540 (pubns) *Fax:* 312-443-1334 (pubns) *Web Site:* www.artic.edu; www.artinstituteshop.org, pg 21

Nossel, Suzanne, PEN American Center, 588 Broadway, Suite 303, New York, NY 10012 *Tel:* 212-334-1660 *Fax:* 212-334-2181 *E-mail:* info@pen.org *Web Site:* pen.org, pg 575

Nossel, Suzanne, The PEN Award for Poetry in Translation, 588 Broadway, Suite 303, New York, NY 10012 *Tel:* 212-334-1660 *Fax:* 212-334-2181 *E-mail:* awards@pen.org *Web Site:* pen.org/press/grants-awards-database, pg 677

Nossel, Suzanne, PEN/Phyllis Naylor Working Writer Fellowship, 588 Broadway, Suite 303, New York, NY 10012 *Tel:* 212-334-1660 *Fax:* 212-334-2181 *E-mail:* awards@pen.org *Web Site:* pen.org/press/grants-awards-database, pg 678

Nossel, Suzanne, PEN/Ralph Manheim Medal for Translation, 588 Broadway, Suite 303, New York, NY 10012 *Tel:* 212-334-1660 *Fax:* 212-334-2181 *E-mail:* awards@pen.org *Web Site:* pen.org/press/grants-awards-database, pg 678

Nossel, Suzanne, PEN/Robert Bingham Prize for Debut Fiction, 588 Broadway, Suite 303, New York, NY 10012 *Tel:* 212-334-1660 *Fax:* 212-334-2181 *E-mail:* awards@pen.org *Web Site:* pen.org/press/grants-awards-database, pg 678

Nossel, Suzanne, PEN Translation Prize, 588 Broadway, Suite 303, New York, NY 10012 *Tel:* 212-334-1660 *Fax:* 212-334-2181 *E-mail:* awards@pen.org *Web Site:* pen.org/press/grants-awards-database, pg 679

Nossel, Suzanne, PEN Writers' Emergency Fund, 588 Broadway, Suite 303, New York, NY 10012 *Tel:* 212-334-1660 *Fax:* 212-334-2181 *Web Site:* pen.org/press/grants-awards-database, pg 679

Notarantonio, Pam, Harry N Abrams Inc, 195 Broadway, 9th fl, New York, NY 10007 *Tel:* 212-206-7715 *Toll Free Tel:* 800-345-1359 *Fax:* 212-519-1210 *E-mail:* abrams@abramsbooks.com *Web Site:* www.abramsbooks.com, pg 3

Noudehou, Lisa, Barranca Press, 1450 Couse St, No 10, Taos, NM 87571 *Tel:* 575-613-1026 *E-mail:* editor@barrancapress.com *Web Site:* www.barrancapress.com, pg 29

Novack, Matt, Alan Wofsy Fine Arts, 1109 Geary Blvd, San Francisco, CA 94109 *Tel:* 415-292-6500 *Toll Free Tel:* 800-660-6403 *Fax:* 415-292-6594 (off & cust serv); 510-251-1840 (acctg) *E-mail:* order@art-books.com (orders); editeur@earthlink.net (edit); beauxarts@earthlink.net (cust serv) *Web Site:* www.art-books.com, pg 258

Novakshonoff, Vasili, Synaxis Press, 37323 Hawkins Rd, Dewdney, BC V0M 1H0, Canada *Tel:* 604-826-9336 *E-mail:* synaxis@new-ostrog.org *Web Site:* synaxispress.ca, pg 471

Novara, Stephanie, Cold Spring Harbor Laboratory Press, 500 Sunnyside Blvd, Woodbury, NY 11797-2924 *Tel:* 516-422-4100 *Toll Free Tel:* 800-843-4388 *Fax:* 516-422-4097; 516-422-4092 (submissions) *E-mail:* cshpress@cshl.edu *Web Site:* www.cshlpress.com, pg 58

O'Halloran, Paul, Scribner, 1230 Avenue of the Americas, New York, NY 10020, pg 209

O'Halloran, Paul, Touchstone, 1230 Avenue of the Americas, New York, NY 10020, pg 233

O'Hanlon, Martin, CWA/SCA Canada, 2200 Prince of Wales Dr, Suite 301, Ottawa, ON K2E 6Z9, Canada *Tel:* 613-820-9777 *Toll Free Tel:* 877-486-4292 *Fax:* 613-820-8188 *E-mail:* info@cwa-scacanada.ca *Web Site:* www.cwa-scacanada.ca, pg 564

O'Hara, Lisa, Wilkinson Studios Inc, 2955 Kelly Dr, Elgin, IL 60124-4349 *Tel:* 312-286-3683 *Web Site:* www.wilkinsonstudios.com, pg 545

O'Hara, Mary, Chronicle Books LLC, 680 Second St, San Francisco, CA 94107 *Tel:* 415-537-4200 *Toll Free Tel:* 800-759-0190 (cust serv) *Fax:* 415-537-4460 *Toll Free Fax:* 800-858-7787 (orders); 800-286-9471 (cust serv) *E-mail:* frontdesk@chroniclebooks.com *Web Site:* www.chroniclebooks.com, pg 55

O'Hara, Samantha, Simon & Schuster, 1230 Avenue of the Americas, New York, NY 10020 *Tel:* 212-698-7000 *Toll Free Tel:* 800-223-2348 (cust serv); 800-223-2336 (orders) *Toll Free Fax:* 800-943-9831 (orders) *Web Site:* www.simonandschuster.com, pg 212

O'Hare, Siobhan, Fodor's Travel Publications, 1745 Broadway, 15th fl, New York, NY 10019 *Toll Free Tel:* 800-733-3000 *E-mail:* publicity@fodors.com; editors@fodors.com *Web Site:* www.fodors.com, pg 86

O'Keefe, Carolyn, Henry Holt and Company, LLC, 175 Fifth Ave, New York, NY 10010 *Tel:* 646-307-5151 *Toll Free Tel:* 888-330-8477 (orders) *Fax:* 646-307-5285 *E-mail:* firstname.lastname@hholt.com *Web Site:* www.henryholt.com, pg 109

O'Leary, Brian, Book Industry Study Group Inc (BISG), 1412 Broadway, Suite 2119, New York, NY 10018 *Tel:* 646-336-7141 *E-mail:* info@bisg.org *Web Site:* bisg.org, pg 560

O'Malley, Janine, Farrar, Straus & Giroux Books for Young Readers, 175 Fifth Ave, 7th fl, New York, NY 10010 *Tel:* 212-741-6900 *Toll Free Tel:* 888-330-8477 (orders) *Fax:* 212-633-9385 *Web Site:* us.macmillan.com/mackids; www.mackidsbooks.com, pg 82

O'Mara, Mary, Harry N Abrams Inc, 195 Broadway, 9th fl, New York, NY 10007 *Tel:* 212-206-7715 *Toll Free Tel:* 800-345-1359 *Fax:* 212-519-1210 *E-mail:* abrams@abramsbooks.com *Web Site:* www.abramsbooks.com, pg 3

O'Mara, Paul, American Society for Quality (ASQ), 600 N Plankinton Ave, Milwaukee, WI 53203 *Tel:* 414-272-8575 *Toll Free Tel:* 800-248-1946 (US & CN); 800-514-1564 (Mexico) *Fax:* 414-272-1734 *E-mail:* help@asq.org *Web Site:* www.asq.org, pg 14

O'Moore-Klopf, Katharine, KOK Edit, 15 Hare Lane, East Setauket, NY 11733-3606 *Tel:* 631-997-8191 *Fax:* 631-474-9849 *E-mail:* editor@kokedit.com *Web Site:* www.kokedit.com; twitter.com/kokedit; www.facebook.com/K.OmooreKlopf; www.linkedin.com/in/kokedit; www.editor-mom.blogspot.com, pg 497

O'Neal, David, Shambhala Publications Inc, 4720 Walnut St, Boulder, CO 80301 *Tel:* 303-222-9598 *Toll Free Tel:* 866-424-0030 (off); 888-424-2329 (cust serv) *Fax:* 303-200-9406 *E-mail:* customercare@shambhala.com *Web Site:* www.shambhala.com, pg 211

O'Neal, Eilis, The Pablo Neruda Prize for Poetry, Nimrod International Journal, 800 S Tucker Dr, Tulsa, OK 74104 *Tel:* 918-631-3080 *Fax:* 918-631-3033 *E-mail:* nimrod@utulsa.edu *Web Site:* www.utulsa.edu/nimrod, pg 672

O'Neal, Eilis, Katherine Anne Porter Prize for Fiction, Nimrod International Journal, 800 S Tucker Dr, Tulsa, OK 74104 *Tel:* 918-631-3080 *Fax:* 918-631-3033 *E-mail:* nimrod@utulsa.edu *Web Site:* www.utulsa.edu/nimrod, pg 681

O'Neal, Jon, Turner Publishing Co, 4507 Charlotte Ave, Suite 100, Nashville, TN 37209 *Tel:* 615-255-BOOK (255-2665) *Fax:* 615-255-5081 *E-mail:* marketing@turnerpublishing.com; submissions@turnerpublishing.com *Web Site:* www.turnerpublishing.com; www.facebook.com/turner.publishing, pg 236

O'Neil, Casey, Graywolf Press, 250 Third Ave N, Suite 600, Minneapolis, MN 55401 *Tel:* 651-641-0077 *Fax:* 651-641-0036 *E-mail:* wolves@graywolfpress.org (no ms queries, sample chapters or proposals) *Web Site:* www.graywolfpress.org, pg 95

O'Neil, Joan, John Wiley & Sons Inc, 111 River St, Hoboken, NJ 07030-5774 *Tel:* 201-748-6000 *Toll Free Tel:* 800-225-5945 (cust serv) *Fax:* 201-748-6088 *E-mail:* info@wiley.com *Web Site:* www.wiley.com, pg 256

O'Neil, Michael, National Coalition Against Censorship (NCAC), 19 Fulton St, Suite 407, New York, NY 10038 *Tel:* 212-807-6222 *Fax:* 212-807-6245 *E-mail:* ncac@ncac.org *Web Site:* www.ncac.org, pg 571

O'Neill, Brendan, Adams Media, 57 Littlefield St, Avon, MA 02322 *Tel:* 508-427-7100 *Web Site:* www.simonandschuster.com, pg 4

O'Neill, Colleen, Canadian Publishers' Council (CPC), 250 Merton St, Suite 203, Toronto, ON M4S 1B1, Canada *Tel:* 416-322-7011 *Fax:* 416-322-6999 *Web Site:* www.pubcouncil.ca, pg 562

O'Neill, Mary Ellen, Workman Publishing Co Inc, 225 Varick St, 9th fl, New York, NY 10014-4381 *Tel:* 212-254-5900 *Toll Free Tel:* 800-722-7202 *Fax:* 212-254-8098 *E-mail:* info@workman.com *Web Site:* www.workman.com, pg 259

O'Neill, Michael, BMI®, 7 World Trade Ctr, 250 Greenwich St, New York, NY 10007-0030 *Tel:* 212-586-2000; 212-220-3000 *Toll Free Tel:* 888-689-5264 (sales); 800-925-8451 (cust rel) *Fax:* 212-246-2163 *E-mail:* foundation@bmi.com *Web Site:* www.bmi.com, pg 560

O'Neill, Molly, Waxman Leavell Literary Agency, 443 Park Ave S, No 1004, New York, NY 10016 *Tel:* 212-675-5556 *Fax:* 212-675-1381 *Web Site:* www.waxmanleavell.com, pg 541

O'Neill, Robert J Jr, International City/County Management Association (ICMA), 777 N Capitol St NE, Suite 500, Washington, DC 20002-4201 *Tel:* 202-289-4262 *Toll Free Tel:* 800-745-8780 *Fax:* 202-962-3500 *E-mail:* customerservices@icma.org *Web Site:* icma.org, pg 119

O'Reilly, James, Travelers' Tales, 2320 Bowdoin St, Palo Alto, CA 94306 *Tel:* 650-462-2110 *Fax:* 650-462-6305 *E-mail:* ttales@travelerstales.com *Web Site:* travelerstales.com, pg 235

O'Reilly, Sean, Travelers' Tales, 2320 Bowdoin St, Palo Alto, CA 94306 *Tel:* 650-462-2110 *Fax:* 650-462-6305 *E-mail:* ttales@travelerstales.com *Web Site:* travelerstales.com, pg 235

O'Reilly, Tim, O'Reilly Media Inc, 1005 Gravenstein Hwy N, Sebastopol, CA 95472 *Tel:* 707-827-7000; 707-827-7019 (cust support) *Toll Free Tel:* 800-998-9938; 800-889-8969 *Fax:* 707-829-0104; 707-824-8268 *E-mail:* orders@oreilly.com *Web Site:* www.oreilly.com, pg 170

O'Rourke, Jim, Bright Connections Media, A World Book Encyclopedia Company, 180 N LaSalle St, Suite 900, Chicago, IL 60601 *Tel:* 312-729-5800 *Web Site:* www.brightconnectionsmedia.com, pg 43

O'Rourke, Jim, World Book Inc, 180 N LaSalle, Suite 900, Chicago, IL 60601 *Tel:* 312-729-5800 *Toll Free Tel:* 800-967-5325 (consumer sales, US); 800-463-8845 (consumer sales, CN); 800-975-3250 (school & lib sales, US); 800-837-5365 (school & lib sales, CN); 866-866-5200 (web sales) *Fax:* 312-729-5600; 312-729-5606 *Toll Free Fax:* 800-433-9330 (school & lib sales, US); 888-690-4002 (school lib sales, CN) *E-mail:* customercare@worldbook.com *Web Site:* www.worldbook.com, pg 259

O'Rourke, T Patrick, TJ Publishers Inc, PO Box 702701, Dallas, TX 75370 *Toll Free Tel:* 800-999-1168 *Fax:* 972-416-0944 *E-mail:* TJPubinc@aol.com, pg 478

O'Shaughnessy, Caitlin, The Penguin Press, 375 Hudson St, New York, NY 10014 *Web Site:* thepenguinpress.com, pg 178

O'Shea, Patti, University of Chicago Press, 1427 E 60 St, Chicago, IL 60637-2954 *Tel:* 773-702-7700; 773-702-7600 *Toll Free Tel:* 800-621-2736 (orders) *Fax:* 773-702-9756; 773-660-2235 (orders); 773-702-2708 *E-mail:* custserv@press.uchicago.edu; marketing@press.uchicago.edu *Web Site:* www.press.uchicago.edu, pg 240

O'Sullivan, Kate, Houghton Mifflin Harcourt Trade & Reference Division, 125 High St, Boston, MA 02110 *Tel:* 617-351-5000 *Toll Free Tel:* 800-225-3362 *Web Site:* www.hmhco.com, pg 111

O'Sullivan, Melanie, Sovereign Award for Outstanding Writing, Woodbine Sales Pavilion, 555 Rexdale Blvd, Toronto, ON M9W 5L2, Canada *Tel:* 416-675-7756 *Fax:* 416-675-6378 *E-mail:* jockeyclub@bellnet.ca *Web Site:* www.jockeyclubcanada.com; www.sovereignawards.ca, pg 691

Oakes, Roger B, Adams & Ambrose Publishing, PO Box 259684, Madison, WI 53725-9684 *Tel:* 608-977-1825 *E-mail:* info@adamsambrose.com, pg 4

Oakley, Eric, Haynes Manuals Inc, 859 Lawrence Dr, Newbury Park, CA 91320-2232 *Tel:* 805-498-6703 *Toll Free Tel:* 800-4-HAYNES (442-9637) *Fax:* 805-498-2867 *E-mail:* cstn@haynes.com *Web Site:* www.haynes.com, pg 104

Oates, Steve, Bethany House Publishers, 11400 Hampshire Ave S, Bloomington, MN 55438 *Tel:* 952-829-2500 *Toll Free Tel:* 800-877-2665 (orders) *Fax:* 952-829-2568 *Toll Free Fax:* 800-398-3111 (orders) *Web Site:* www.bethanyhouse.com; www.bakerpublishinggroup.com, pg 34

Obeng, Samuel, Indiana University African Studies Program, Indiana University, 221 Woodburn Hall, Bloomington, IN 47405 *Tel:* 812-855-8284 *Fax:* 812-855-6734 *E-mail:* afrist@indiana.edu *Web Site:* www.indiana.edu/~afrist, pg 115

Oberlin, Brent, The MIT Press, One Rogers St, Cambridge, MA 02142 *Tel:* 617-253-5255 *Toll Free Tel:* 800-207-8354 (orders) *Fax:* 617-258-6779; 617-577-1545 (orders) *Web Site:* mitpress.mit.edu, pg 151

Oberrender, Maggie, Random House Publishing Group, 1745 Broadway, New York, NY 10019 *Toll Free Tel:* 800-200-3552 *Web Site:* atrandom.com, pg 195

Obry, Carrie, Midwest Independent Booksellers Association (MIBA), 2355 Louisiana Ave N, Suite A, Golden Valley, MN 55427-3646 *Tel:* 763-544-2993 *Toll Free Tel:* 800-784-7522 *Fax:* 612-354-5728 *E-mail:* info@midwestbooksellers.org *Web Site:* midwestbooksellers.org, pg 569

Ocampo, Patricia, Simon & Schuster Canada, 166 King St E, Suite 300, Toronto, ON M5A 1J3, Canada *Tel:* 647-427-8882 *Toll Free Tel:* 800-387-0446; 800-268-3216 (orders) *Fax:* 647-430-9446 *Toll Free Fax:* 888-849-8151 (orders) *E-mail:* info@simonandschuster.ca *Web Site:* www.simonandschuster.ca, pg 471

Ochsner, Daniel, University of Minnesota Press, 111 Third Ave S, Suite 290, Minneapolis, MN 55401-2520 *Tel:* 612-301-1990 *Fax:* 612-301-1980 *E-mail:* ump@umn.edu *Web Site:* www.upress.umn.edu, pg 242

Ode, Jeanne, South Dakota Historical Society Press, 900 Governors Dr, Pierre, SD 57501 *Tel:* 605-773-6009 *Fax:* 605-773-6041 *E-mail:* info@sdshspress.com; orders@sdshspress.com *Web Site:* sdshspress.com, pg 218

Oden, Kelly, Ballinger Publishing, 314 N Spring St, Suite A, Pensacola, FL 32501 *Tel:* 850-433-1166 *Fax:* 850-435-9174 *E-mail:* info@ballingerpublishing.com *Web Site:* www.ballingerpublishing.com, pg 28

Odiseos, Nikko, Shambhala Publications Inc, 4720 Walnut St, Boulder, CO 80301 *Tel:* 303-222-9598 *Toll Free Tel:* 866-424-0030 (off); 888-424-2329 (cust serv) *Fax:* 303-200-9406 *E-mail:* customercare@shambhala.com *Web Site:* www.shambhala.com, pg 211

Odom, Monica, Bradford Literary Agency, 5694 Mission Center Rd, Suite 347, San Diego, CA 92108 *Tel:* 619-521-1201 *E-mail:* queries@bradfordlit.com *Web Site:* www.bradfordlit.com, pg 509

Oerlemans, Onno, Hamilton College, English/Creative Writing, English/Creative Writing Dept, 198 College Hill Rd, Clinton, NY 13323 *Tel:* 315-859-4370 *Fax:* 315-859-4390 *Web Site:* www.hamilton.edu, pg 620

Oestreich, Julia, University of Delaware Press, 200A Morris Library, 181 S College Ave, Newark, DE 19717-5267 *Tel:* 302-831-1149 *Fax:* 302-831-6549 *E-mail:* ud-press@udel.edu *Web Site:* library.udel.edu/udpress, pg 241

Oey, Eric, Tuttle Publishing, Airport Business Park, 364 Innovation Dr, North Clarendon, VT 05759-9436 *Tel:* 802-773-8930 *Toll Free Tel:* 800-526-2778 *Fax:* 802-773-6993 *Toll Free Fax:* 800-FAX-TUTL (329-8885) *E-mail:* info@tuttlepublishing.com; orders@tuttlepublishing.com *Web Site:* www.tuttlepublishing.com, pg 237

Offit, Sidney, The Authors League Fund, 31 E 32 St, 7th fl, New York, NY 10016 *Tel:* 212-268-1208 *Fax:* 212-564-5363 *E-mail:* staff@authorsleaguefund.org *Web Site:* www.authorsleaguefund.org, pg 559

Ogden, Abe, American Diabetes Association, 1701 N Beauregard St, Alexandria, VA 22311 *Toll Free Tel:* 800-342-2383 *E-mail:* booksinfo@diabetes.org *Web Site:* www.diabetes.org, pg 11

Ogden, Page, McLemore Prize, William F Winter Archives & History Bldg, 200 North St, Jackson, MS 39201 *Tel:* 601-576-6850 *Fax:* 601-576-6975 *E-mail:* mhs@mdah.ms.gov *Web Site:* www.mdah.ms.gov, pg 667

Ogle, Jim, F+W Media Inc, 10151 Carver Rd, Suite 200, Blue Ash, OH 45242 *Tel:* 513-531-2690 *Toll Free Tel:* 800-289-0963 (trade accts); 800-258-0929 (cust serv) *E-mail:* contact_us@fwmedia.com *Web Site:* www.fwcommunity.com, pg 82

Ogle, Jim, Krause Publications Inc, 700 E State St, Iola, WI 54990 *Tel:* 715-445-2214 *Toll Free Tel:* 800-258-0929 (cust serv); 888-457-2873 (orders) *Fax:* 715-445-4087 *E-mail:* bookorders@krause.com *Web Site:* www.krausebooks.com, pg 128

Ognibene, Peter E, Breakthrough Publications Inc, 3 Iroquois St, Barn, Emmaus, PA 18049 *Toll Free Tel:* 800-824-5001 (ext 12) *Fax:* 610-928-4064 *E-mail:* dot@booksonhorses.com; ruth@booksonhorses.com *Web Site:* www.booksonhorses.com, pg 42

Ogorek, Keith, AuthorHouse, 1663 Liberty Dr, Bloomington, IN 47403 *Tel:* 812-339-6000 (outside US) *Toll Free Tel:* 888-519-5121 *E-mail:* authorsupport@authorhouse.com *Web Site:* www.authorhouse.com, pg 26

Ogorek, Keith, iUniverse, 1663 Liberty Dr, Bloomington, IN 47403 *Toll Free Tel:* 800-AUTHORS (288-4677) *Fax:* 812-355-4085 *Web Site:* www.iuniverse.com, pg 121

Ogorek, Keith, Trafford, 1663 Liberty Dr, Bloomington, IN 47403 *Toll Free Tel:* 888-232-4444 *E-mail:* customersupport@trafford.com; sales@trafford.com *Web Site:* www.trafford.com, pg 234

Ogorek, Keith, Xlibris Corp, 1663 Liberty Dr, Suite 200, Bloomington, IN 47403 *Toll Free Tel:* 888-795-4274 *Fax:* 610-915-0294 *E-mail:* info@xlibris.com *Web Site:* www.xlibris.com, pg 261

Ohl, Helaine, Macmillan, 175 Fifth Ave, New York, NY 10010 *Tel:* 646-307-5151 *E-mail:* press.inquiries@macmillan.com *Web Site:* www.macmillan.com, pg 140

Ohle, Heather, Encounter Books, 900 Broadway, Suite 601, New York, NY 10003 *Tel:* 212-871-6310 *Toll Free Tel:* 800-786-3839 *Fax:* 212-871-6311 *E-mail:* publicity@encounterbooks.com *Web Site:* www.encounterbooks.com, pg 78

Ohmart, Ben, BearManor Media, PO Box 71426, Albany, GA 31708 *Tel:* 580-252-3547 *E-mail:* orders@benohmart.com; books@benohmart.com *Web Site:* www.bearmanormedia.com, pg 31

Oishi, Marie, Chronicle Books LLC, 680 Second St, San Francisco, CA 94107 *Tel:* 415-537-4200 *Toll Free Tel:* 800-759-0190 (cust serv) *Fax:* 415-537-4460 *Toll Free Fax:* 800-858-7787 (orders); 800-286-9471 (cust serv) *E-mail:* frontdesk@chroniclebooks.com *Web Site:* www.chroniclebooks.com, pg 55

Ojakli, Sumya, Simon & Schuster Sales Division, 1230 Avenue of the Americas, New York, NY 10020 *Tel:* 212-698-7000, pg 214

Olafsson, Johann G, Edda USA, 373 Park Ave S, 6th fl, New York, NY 10016 *Tel:* 646-755-9210 *Web Site:* eddausa.com, pg 75

Olafsson, Jon Axel, Edda USA, 373 Park Ave S, 6th fl, New York, NY 10016 *Tel:* 646-755-9210 *Web Site:* eddausa.com, pg 75

Olah, Michael, Dreamscape Media LLC, 6940 Hall St, Holland, OH 43528 *Tel:* 419-867-6965 *Toll Free Tel:* 877-983-7326 *E-mail:* info@dreamscapeab.com *Web Site:* www.dreamscapeab.com, pg 73

Olander, Rebecca, Perugia Press Prize for a First or Second Book by a Woman, PO Box 60364, Florence, MA 01062 *Web Site:* www.perugiapress.com; perugiapress.org, pg 679

Olenick, Michelle, Emmaus Road Publishing Inc, 1468 Parkview Circle, Steubenville, OH 43952 *Tel:* 740-283-2880 (outside US) *Toll Free Tel:* 800-398-5470 (orders) *Fax:* 740-283-4011 (orders) *E-mail:* questions@emmausroad.org *Web Site:* www.emmausroad.org, pg 78

Oleniczak, Beth, Sourcebooks Inc, 1935 Brookdale Rd, Suite 139, Naperville, IL 60563 *Tel:* 630-961-3900 *Toll Free Tel:* 800-432-7444 *Fax:* 630-961-2168 *E-mail:* info@sourcebooks.com; customersupport@sourcebooks.com *Web Site:* www.sourcebooks.com, pg 218

Olinger, Chauncey G Jr, Metropolitan Editorial & Writing Service, 4455 Douglas Ave, Riverdale, NY 10471 *Tel:* 718-549-5518, pg 498

Oliphant, Mike, Annie Dillard Award for Creative Nonfiction, Mail Stop 9053, Western Washington University, Bellingham, WA 98225 *Tel:* 360-650-4863 *E-mail:* bhreview@wwu.edu *Web Site:* www.bhreview.org, pg 641

Oliphant, Mike, 49th Parallel Poetry Award, Mail Stop 9053, Western Washington University, Bellingham, WA 98225 *Tel:* 360-650-4863 *E-mail:* bhreview@wwu.edu *Web Site:* www.bhreview.org, pg 647

Oliphant, Mike, Tobias Wolff Award for Fiction, Mail Stop 9053, Western Washington University, Bellingham, WA 98225 *Tel:* 360-650-4863 *E-mail:* bhreview@wwu.edu *Web Site:* www.bhreview.org, pg 699

Oliver, Becka, Writers' League of Texas (WLT), 611 S Congress Ave, Suite 200 A-3, Austin, TX 78704 *Tel:* 512-499-8914 *E-mail:* wlt@writersleague.org *Web Site:* www.writersleague.org, pg 581, 616

Oliver, Lin, The Don Freeman Memorial Grant-In-Aid, 4727 Wilshire Blvd, Suite 301, Los Angeles, CA 90010 *Tel:* 323-782-1010; 310-403-0675 (cell) *Fax:* 323-782-1892 *E-mail:* grants@scbwi.org; scbwi@scbwi.org *Web Site:* www.scbwi.org, pg 648

Oliver, Lin, Golden Kite Awards, 4727 Wilshire Blvd, Suite 301, Los Angeles, CA 90010 *Tel:* 323-782-1010; 310-403-0675 (cell) *Fax:* 323-782-1892 *E-mail:* grants@scbwi.org; scbwi@scbwi.org *Web Site:* www.scbwi.org, pg 650

Oliver, Lin, Magazine Merit Awards, 4727 Wilshire Blvd, Suite 301, Los Angeles, CA 90010 *Tel:* 323-782-1010; 310-403-0675 (cell) *Fax:* 323-782-1892 *E-mail:* grants@scbwi.org; scbwi@scbwi.org *Web Site:* www.scbwi.org, pg 664

Oliver, Lin, SCBWI Work-In-Progress Grants, 4727 Wilshire Blvd, Suite 301, Los Angeles, CA 90010 *Tel:* 323-782-1010; 310-403-0675 (cell) *Fax:* 323-782-1892 *E-mail:* grants@scbwi.org; scbwi@scbwi.org *Web Site:* www.scbwi.org, pg 688

Oliver, Lin, Society of Children's Book Writers and Illustrators (SCBWI), 4727 Wilshire Blvd, Suite 301, Los Angeles, CA 90010 *Tel:* 323-782-1010 *Fax:* 323-782-1892 *E-mail:* scbwi@scbwi.org; membership@scbwi.org *Web Site:* www.scbwi.org, pg 578

Oliver, Paul, Soho Press Inc, 853 Broadway, New York, NY 10003 *Tel:* 212-260-1900 *E-mail:* soho@sohopress.com; publicity@sohopress.com; contact@sohopress.com *Web Site:* www.sohopress.com, pg 216

Oliver, Ramona, National Education Association (NEA), 1201 16 St NW, Washington, DC 20036-3290 *Tel:* 202-833-4000 *Fax:* 202-822-7974 *Web Site:* www.nea.org, pg 158

Oliver-Vallely, Nancy, Mel Bay Publications Inc, 4 Industrial Dr, Pacific, MO 63069-0066 *Tel:* 636-257-3970 *Toll Free Tel:* 800-863-5229 *Fax:* 636-257-5062 *Toll Free Fax:* 800-660-9818 *E-mail:* email@melbay.com *Web Site:* www.melbay.com, pg 148

Olivieri, John, Abbeville Publishing Group, 137 Varick St, Suite 504, New York, NY 10013-1105 *Tel:* 212-366-5585 *Toll Free Tel:* 800-ART-BOOK (278-2665) *Fax:* 212-366-6966 *E-mail:* abbeville@abbeville.com; marketing@abbeville.com; sales@abbeville.com; rights@abbeville.com *Web Site:* www.abbeville.com, pg 2

Olsen, Eric, Twilight Times Books, PO Box 3340, Kingsport, TN 37664-0340 *Tel:* 423-323-0183 *Fax:* 423-323-0183 *E-mail:* publisher@twilighttimes.com *Web Site:* www.twilighttimesbooks.com, pg 237

Olsen, Kevin, W W Norton & Company Inc, 500 Fifth Ave, New York, NY 10110-0017 *Tel:* 212-354-5500 *Toll Free Tel:* 800-233-4830 (orders & cust serv) *Fax:* 212-869-0856 *Toll Free Fax:* 800-458-6515 *E-mail:* orders@wwnorton.com *Web Site:* books.wwnorton.com, pg 164

Olsen, Lance, The FC2 Catherine Doctorow Innovative Fiction Prize, c/o Dept of English, Languages & Communincations Bldg, 255 S Central Campus Dr, Rm 3500, Salt Lake City, UT 84112-0494 *Tel:* 773-702-7000 *Web Site:* www.fc2.org/prizes.html, pg 645

Olsen, Lance, Fiction Collective Two Inc (FC2), c/o Dept of English, Languages & Communincations Bldg, 255 S Central Campus Dr, Rm 3500, Salt Lake City, UT 84112-0494 *Tel:* 773-702-7000 *E-mail:* fc2.cmu@gmail.com *Web Site:* www.fc2.org/prizes.html, pg 84

Olsen, Lance, Ronald Sukenick American Book Review Innovative Fiction Prize, c/o Dept of English, Languages & Communincations Bldg, 255 S Central Campus Dr, Rm 3500, Salt Lake City, UT 84112-0494 *Tel:* 773-702-7000 *Web Site:* www.fc2.org/prizes.html, pg 692

Olsen, Marilyn, Oak Tree Press, 1700 Dairy Ave, No 149, Corcoran, CA 93212 *Tel:* 217-824-6500 *E-mail:* publisher@oaktreebooks.com; info@oaktreebooks.com; query@oaktreebooks.com; pressdept@oaktreebooks.com; bookorders@oaktreebooks.com *Web Site:* www.oaktreebooks.com; www.otpblog.blogspot.com, pg 166

Olsen, William, The Green Rose Prize in Poetry, c/o Western Michigan University, 1903 W Michigan Ave, Kalamazoo, MI 49008-5463 *Tel:* 269-387-8185 *E-mail:* new-issues@wmich.edu *Web Site:* www.wmich.edu/newissues/sub-guide.html, pg 651

Olsen, William, New Issues Poetry & Prose, c/o Western Michigan University, 1903 W Michigan Ave, Kalamazoo, MI 49008-5463 *Tel:* 269-387-8185 *E-mail:* new-issues@wmich.edu *Web Site:* www.wmich.edu/newissues, pg 160

Olsen-Smith, Steven, The Melville Society, Johns Hopkins University Press, PO Box 19966, Baltimore, MD 21211-0966 *Web Site:* melvillesociety.org, pg 569

Olsewski, Paul, Atria Books, 1230 Avenue of the Americas, New York, NY 10020 *Tel:* 212-698-7000 *Fax:* 212-698-7007 *Web Site:* www.simonandschuster.com, pg 25

Olson, Bianca, Houghton Mifflin Harcourt, 125 High St, Boston, MA 02110 *Tel:* 617-351-5000 *Toll Free Tel:* 855-969-4642; 800-225-5425 (K-12 educ materials); 800-323-9540 (assessment materials); 877-219-1537 (SkillsTutor); 888-242-6747 (Innovation in Educ Group); 800-225-3362 (Trade & Ref Div) *Toll Free Fax:* 800-269-5232 *E-mail:* myhmhco@hmhco.com *Web Site:* www.hmhco.com, pg 110

Olson, Elke, Chronicle Books LLC, 680 Second St, San Francisco, CA 94107 *Tel:* 415-537-4200 *Toll Free Tel:* 800-759-0190 (cust serv) *Fax:* 415-537-4460 *Toll Free Fax:* 800-858-7787 (orders); 800-286-9471 (cust serv) *E-mail:* frontdesk@chroniclebooks.com *Web Site:* www.chroniclebooks.com, pg 55

Olson, Georgine, Historical Novel Society North American Conference, 400 Dark Star Ct, Fairbanks, AK 99709 *Tel:* 217-581-7538 *Fax:* 217-581-7534 *Web Site:* historicalnovelsociety.org, pg 611

Olson, Kaitlin, Touchstone, 1230 Avenue of the Americas, New York, NY 10020, pg 233

Olson, Neil, Donadio & Olson Inc, 40 W 27 St, 5th fl, New York, NY 10001 *Tel:* 212-691-8077 *Fax:* 212-633-2837 *E-mail:* mail@donadio.com *Web Site:* donadio.com, pg 514

Olstein, Lisa, University of Texas at Austin, New Writers Project, Dept of English, Calhoun Hall, Rm 226, 204 W 21 St, B-5000, Austin, TX 78712 *Tel:* 512-471-5132; 512-471-4991 *Fax:* 512-471-4909 *Web Site:* newwritersproject.org, pg 623

Oluwek, Monica, Touchstone, 1230 Avenue of the Americas, New York, NY 10020, pg 233

Onder, Catherine, Houghton Mifflin Harcourt Trade & Reference Division, 125 High St, Boston, MA 02110 *Tel:* 617-351-5000 *Toll Free Tel:* 800-225-3362 *Web Site:* www.hmhco.com, pg 111

Onken, Janice, WendyLynn & Co, 504 Wilson Rd, Annapolis, MD 21401 *Tel:* 410-224-2729; 410-507-1059 *Web Site:* wendylynn.com, pg 544

Oppel, Frank, Book Sales, 142 W 36 St, 4th fl, New York, NY 10018 *Tel:* 212-779-4972; 212-779-4971 *Fax:* 212-779-6058 *E-mail:* booksales@quarto.com; customerservice@quarto.com *Web Site:* www.quartoknows.com, pg 40

Opper, Lauren, W W Norton & Company Inc, 500 Fifth Ave, New York, NY 10110-0017 *Tel:* 212-354-5500 *Toll Free Tel:* 800-233-4830 (orders & cust serv) *Fax:* 212-869-0856 *Toll Free Fax:* 800-458-6515 *E-mail:* orders@wwnorton.com *Web Site:* books.wwnorton.com, pg 164

Opsomer, Liliane, AdventureKEEN, 2204 First Ave S, Suite 102, Birmingham, AL 35233 *Tel:* 763-689-9800 *Toll Free Tel:* 800-678-7006 *Fax:* 763-689-9039 *Toll Free Fax:* 877-374-9016 *E-mail:* info@adventurewithkeen.com *Web Site:* adventurewithkeen.com, pg 5

Oren, Tiffany, Foster City International Writers Contest, 650 Shell Blvd, Foster City, CA 94404 *Tel:* 650-286-3380 *E-mail:* fostercity_writers@yahoo.com *Web Site:* www.fostercity.org, pg 647

Oria, Mary Beth, Association of Catholic Publishers Inc, 4725 Dorsey Hall Dr, Suite A, PMB 709, Elliott City, MD 21042 *Tel:* 410-988-2926 *Fax:* 410-571-4946 *Web Site:* www.catholicsread.org; www.catholicpublishers.org; www.midatlanticcongress.org, pg 558

Orlando, Kris, Hendrickson Publishers Inc, PO Box 3473, Peabody, MA 01961-3473 *Tel:* 978-532-6546 *Toll Free Tel:* 800-358-3111 *Fax:* 978-573-8111 *E-mail:* orders@hendrickson.com *Web Site:* www.hendrickson.com, pg 106

Ornstein, Michael, IET USA Inc, 379 Thornall St, Edison, NJ 08837 *Tel:* 732-321-5575 *Fax:* 732-321-5702 *E-mail:* ietusa@theiet.org *Web Site:* www.theiet.org, pg 114

Orphee, Mr Matanya, Editions Orphee Inc, 1240 Clubview Blvd N, Columbus, OH 43235-1226 *Tel:* 614-846-9517 *Fax:* 614-846-9794 *E-mail:* sales@editionsorphee.com *Web Site:* www.editionsorphee.com, pg 75

Orr, John, Lynx House Press, 420 W 24 St, Spokane, WA 99203 *Tel:* 509-624-4894 *E-mail:* lynxhousepress@gmail.com *Web Site:* www.lynxhousepress.org, pg 139

Orr, Rachel, Prospect Agency, 285 Fifth Ave, PMB 445, Brooklyn, NY 11215 *Tel:* 718-788-3217 *Fax:* 718-360-9582 *Web Site:* www.prospectagency.com, pg 532

Ortego, Juan, McGraw-Hill International & Professional Publishing Group, 2 Penn Plaza, New York, NY 10121 *Tel:* 646-766-2000 *Web Site:* www.mheducation.com, pg 146

Ortiz, Lukas, Philip G Spitzer Literary Agency Inc, 50 Talmage Farm Lane, East Hampton, NY 11937 *Tel:* 631-329-3650 *Fax:* 631-329-3651 *Web Site:* www.spitzeragency.com, pg 537

Ortiz, Shirley, Workman Publishing Co Inc, 225 Varick St, 9th fl, New York, NY 10014-4381 *Tel:* 212-254-5900 *Toll Free Tel:* 800-722-7202 *Fax:* 212-254-8098 *E-mail:* info@workman.com *Web Site:* www.workman.com, pg 259

Ortlund, Dane, Crossway, 1300 Crescent St, Wheaton, IL 60187 *Tel:* 630-682-4300 *Toll Free Tel:* 800-635-7993 (orders); 800-543-1659 (cust serv) *Fax:* 630-682-4785 *E-mail:* info@crossway.org *Web Site:* www.crossway.org, pg 65

Ortman, Tyler, No Starch Press, 245 Eighth St, San Francisco, CA 94103 *Tel:* 415-863-9900 *Toll Free Tel:* 800-420-7240 *Fax:* 415-863-9950 *E-mail:* info@nostarch.com; sales@nostarch.com *Web Site:* www.nostarch.com, pg 162

Ortner, Renee, OPIS/STALSBY Directories & Databases, 3349 Hwy 138, Bldg D, Suite D, Wall, NJ 07719 *Tel:* 732-901-8800 *Toll Free Tel:* 800-275-0950 *Toll Free Fax:* 800-450-5864 *E-mail:* opisstalsbylistings@opisnet.com *Web Site:* www.opisnet.com, pg 168

Orton, Jeramie, Penguin Group USA, A Penguin Random House Company, 375 Hudson St, New York, NY 10014 *Tel:* 212-366-2000 *Toll Free Tel:* 800-847-5515 (inside sales); 800-631-8571 (cust serv) *Fax:* 212-366-2666; 607-775-4829 (inside sales) *E-mail:* online@us.penguingroup.com *Web Site:* www.penguin.com, pg 177

Orton, Jeramie, Viking, 375 Hudson St, New York, NY 10014 *Tel:* 212-366-2000 *Fax:* 212-243-6002 *Web Site:* www.penguin.com/publishers/vikingbooks, pg 250

Osborn, April, St Martin's Press, LLC, 175 Fifth Ave, New York, NY 10010 *Tel:* 646-307-5151 *Web Site:* us.macmillan.com/smp, pg 204

Osborne, Mary, Matt Cohen Prize: In Celebration of a Writing Life, 460 Richmond St W, Suite 600, Toronto, ON M5V 1Y1, Canada *Tel:* 416-504-8222 *Toll Free Tel:* 877-906-6548 *Fax:* 416-504-9090 *E-mail:* info@writerstrust.com *Web Site:* www.writerstrust.com, pg 666

Osborne, Mary, Dayne Ogilvie Prize, 460 Richmond St W, Suite 600, Toronto, ON M5V 1Y1, Canada *Tel:* 416-504-8222 *Toll Free Tel:* 877-906-6548 *Fax:* 416-504-9090 *E-mail:* info@writerstrust.com *Web Site:* www.writerstrust.com, pg 675

Osborne, Mary, RBC Bronwen Wallace Award for Emerging Writers, 460 Richmond St W, Suite 600, Toronto, ON M5V 1Y1, Canada *Tel:* 416-504-8222 *Toll Free Tel:* 877-906-6548 *Fax:* 416-504-9090 *E-mail:* info@writerstrust.com *Web Site:* www.writerstrust.com, pg 684

Osborne, Mary, Rogers Writers' Trust Fiction Prize, 460 Richmond St W, Suite 600, Toronto, ON M5V 1Y1, Canada *Tel:* 416-504-8222 *Toll Free Tel:* 877-906-6548 *Fax:* 416-504-9090 *E-mail:* info@writerstrust.com *Web Site:* www.writerstrust.com, pg 685

Osborne, Mary, Shaughnessy Cohen Prize for Political Writing, 460 Richmond St W, Suite 600, Toronto, ON M5V 1Y1, Canada *Tel:* 416-504-8222 *Toll Free Tel:* 877-906-6548 *Fax:* 416-504-9090 *E-mail:* info@writerstrust.com *Web Site:* www.writerstrust.com, pg 688

Osborne, Mary, Vicky Metcalf Award for Literature for Young People, 460 Richmond St W, Suite 600, Toronto, ON M5V 1Y1, Canada *Tel:* 416-504-8222 *Toll Free Tel:* 877-906-6548 *Fax:* 416-504-9090 *E-mail:* info@writerstrust.com *Web Site:* www.writerstrust.com, pg 696

Osborne, Mary, Hilary Weston Writers' Trust Prize for Nonfiction, 460 Richmond St W, Suite 600, Toronto, ON M5V 1Y1, Canada *Tel:* 416-504-8222 *Toll Free Tel:* 877-906-6548 *Fax:* 416-504-9090 *E-mail:* info@writerstrust.com *Web Site:* www.writerstrust.com, pg 697

Osborne, Mary, Writers' Trust Engel/Findley Prize, 460 Richmond St W, Suite 600, Toronto, ON M5V 1Y1, Canada *Tel:* 416-504-8222 *Toll Free Tel:* 877-906-6548 *Fax:* 416-504-9090 *E-mail:* info@writerstrust.com *Web Site:* www.writerstrust.com, pg 700

Osborne, Mary, The Writers Trust/McClelland & Stewart Journey Prize, 460 Richmond St W, Suite 600, Toronto, ON M5V 1Y1, Canada *Tel:* 416-504-8222 *Toll Free Tel:* 877-906-6548 *Fax:* 416-504-9090 *E-mail:* info@writerstrust.com *Web Site:* www.writerstrust.com, pg 700

Osteen, Eileen, Michelin Maps & Guides, One Parkway S, Greenville, SC 29615-5022 *Tel:* 864-458-5565 *Fax:* 864-458-5665 *Toll Free Fax:* 866-297-0914; 888-773-7979 *E-mail:* orders@americanmap.com (orders) *Web Site:* www.michelintravel.com; www.michelinguide.com, pg 149

Ostertag, Genny, ASCD, 1703 N Beauregard St, Alexandria, VA 22311-1714 *Tel:* 703-578-9600 *Toll Free Tel:* 800-933-2723 *Fax:* 703-575-5400 *E-mail:* member@ascd.org *Web Site:* www.ascd.org, pg 22

Ostfield, Sue, Redleaf Press, 10 Yorkton Ct, St Paul, MN 55117 *Tel:* 651-641-0508 *Toll Free Tel:* 800-423-8309 *Toll Free Fax:* 800-641-0115 *E-mail:* customerservice@redleafpress.org *Web Site:* www.redleafpress.org, pg 197

Osuszek, Alex, Harlequin Enterprises Ltd, 225 Duncan Mill Rd, Don Mills, ON M3B 3K9, Canada *Tel:* 416-445-5860 *Toll Free Tel:* 888-432-4879; 800-370-5838 (ebook inquiries) *E-mail:* customerservice@harlequin.com *Web Site:* www.harlequin.com, pg 459

Oswald, Dan, Business & Legal Resources Inc, 100 Winners Circle, Suite 300, Brentwood, TN 37027 *Tel:* 860-510-0100 *Toll Free Tel:* 800-727-5257 *E-mail:* service@blr.com *Web Site:* www.blr.com, pg 45

Oswald, Dan, M Lee Smith Publishers, 100 Winners Circle, Suite 300, Brentwood, TN 37027 *Tel:* 615-373-7517 *Toll Free Tel:* 800-274-6774; 800-727-5257 *E-mail:* custserv@mleesmith.com; service@blr.com *Web Site:* www.mleesmith.com; www.blr.com, pg 215

Oswald, Denise, HarperCollins General Books Group, 195 Broadway, New York, NY 10007 *Tel:* 212-207-7000 *Web Site:* www.harpercollins.com, pg 101

Otero, Rosa Vanessa, University of Puerto Rico Press, Edificio La Editorial (level 2), Carr No 1, KM 12.0, Jardin Botanico Norte, San Juan, PR 00927 *Tel:* 787-250-0435; 787-250-0550 *Toll Free Tel:* 877-338-7788 *Fax:* 787-753-9116 *E-mail:* info@laeditorialupr.com *Web Site:* www.laeditorialupr.com, pg 245

Ottaviano, Lia, Diversion Books, 443 Park Ave S, Suite 1008, New York, NY 10016 *Tel:* 212-961-6390 *E-mail:* info@diversionbooks.com *Web Site:* www.diversionbooks.com, pg 71

Otte, Liz, Sourcebooks Inc, 1935 Brookdale Rd, Suite 139, Naperville, IL 60563 *Tel:* 630-961-3900 *Toll Free Tel:* 800-432-7444 *Fax:* 630-961-2168 *E-mail:* info@sourcebooks.com; customersupport@sourcebooks.com *Web Site:* www.sourcebooks.com, pg 218

Otter, Samuel, The Melville Society, Johns Hopkins University Press, PO Box 19966, Baltimore, MD 21211-0966 *Web Site:* melvillesociety.org, pg 569

Ou, Michelle, Editors' Association of Canada (Association canadienne des reviseurs), 27 Carlton St, Suite 505, Toronto, ON M5B 1L2, Canada *Tel:* 416-975-1379 *Toll Free Tel:* 866-CAN-EDIT (226-3348) *Fax:* 416-975-1637 *E-mail:* info@editors.ca; info@reviseurs.ca *Web Site:* www.editors.ca; www.reviseurs.ca, pg 564

Pandya, Ruchir, HarperCollins Publishers, 195 Broadway, New York, NY 10007 *Tel:* 212-207-7000 *Fax:* 212-207-7145 *Web Site:* www.harpercollins.com, pg 102

Panec, Don, Treasure Bay Inc, PO Box 119, Novato, CA 94948 *Tel:* 415-884-2888 *Fax:* 415-884-2840 *E-mail:* webothread@comcast.net *Web Site:* www.webothread.com, pg 235

Panepinto, Lauren, Orbit, 1290 Avenue of the Americas, New York, NY 10019 *Tel:* 212-364-1100 *Toll Free Tel:* 800-759-0190 *Web Site:* www.orbitbooks.net, pg 169

Panger, Bob, American Marketing Association, 130 E Randolph St, 22nd fl, Chicago, IL 60601 *Tel:* 312-542-9000 *Toll Free Tel:* 800-AMA-1150 (262-1150) *Fax:* 312-542-9001 *E-mail:* info@ama.org *Web Site:* www.ama.org, pg 555

Paniagua, Nancy A, Cedar Grove Books, 2215 High Point Dr, Carrollton, TX 75007 *Tel:* 415-364-8292 *Fax:* 415-276-9858 *E-mail:* queries@cedargrovebooks.com *Web Site:* www.cedargrovebooks.com, pg 50

Panico, Neil, The Dawn Horse Press, 10336 Loch Lomond Rd, No 305, Middletown, CA 95461 *Tel:* 707-928-6590 *Toll Free Tel:* 877-770-0772 *Fax:* 707-928-6590 *E-mail:* dhp@adidam.org *Web Site:* www.dawnhorsepress.com, pg 68

Panikian, Katherine Allnutt Esq, Standard Publishing Corp, 10 High St, Boston, MA 02110 *Tel:* 617-457-0600 *Toll Free Tel:* 800-682-5759 *Fax:* 617-457-0608 *Web Site:* www.spcpub.com, pg 220

Panning, Jeanette, American Geophysical Union (AGU), 2000 Florida Ave NW, Washington, DC 20009 *Tel:* 202-462-6900 *Toll Free Tel:* 800-966-2481 (North America) *Fax:* 202-328-0566 *E-mail:* service@agu.org (cust serv); earthspacescience@agu.org *Web Site:* www.agu.org, pg 11

Panzer, Robert, Visual Artists & Galleries Association Inc (VAGA), 111 Broadway, Suite 1006, New York, NY 10006 *Tel:* 212-736-6666 *Fax:* 212-736-6767 *E-mail:* info@vagarights.com *Web Site:* vagarights.com, pg 580

Papademetriou, Dean, Somerset Hall Press, 416 Commonwealth Ave, Suite 612, Boston, MA 02215 *Tel:* 617-236-5126 *E-mail:* info@somersethallpress.com *Web Site:* www.somersethallpress.com, pg 217

Papadopoulos, Niki, Portfolio, 375 Hudson St, New York, NY 10014 *Web Site:* www.penguin.com/meet/publishers/portfolio, pg 186

Paparozzi, Andrew D, Epicomm, 1800 Diagonal Rd, Suite 320, Alexandria, VA 22314-2862 *Tel:* 703-836-9200 *E-mail:* webmaster@epicomm.org *Web Site:* epicomm.org, pg 565

Pape, Don, NavPress Publishing Group, 3820 N 30 St, Colorado Springs, CO 80904 *Tel:* 719-598-1212 *Toll Free Tel:* 800-323-9400; 855-277-9400 (cust serv) *Toll Free Fax:* 800-684-0247 *Web Site:* www.navpress.com, pg 159

Papin, Jessica, Dystel, Goderich & Bourret LLC, One Union Sq W, Suite 904, New York, NY 10003 *Tel:* 212-627-9100 *Fax:* 212-627-9313 *Web Site:* www.dystel.com, pg 515

Pappas, Cheryl, Harvard Art Museums, 32 Quincy St, Cambridge, MA 02138 *Tel:* 617-495-1440; 617-496-6529 (edit) *Fax:* 617-495-9985 *Web Site:* www.harvardartmuseums.org, pg 102

Pappas, Evangeline A, ASIS International, 1625 Prince St, Alexandria, VA 22314 *Tel:* 703-519-6200 *Fax:* 703-519-6299 *E-mail:* asis@asisonline.org *Web Site:* www.asisonline.org, pg 23

Pappas, Joseph J, Consumer Press, 13326 SW 28 St, Suite 102, Fort Lauderdale, FL 33330-1102 *Tel:* 954-370-9153 *Fax:* 954-472-1008 *E-mail:* info@consumerpress.com *Web Site:* www.consumerpress.com, pg 60

Pappenheimer, Andrea, HarperCollins Children's Books, 195 Broadway, New York, NY 10007 *Tel:* 212-207-7000 *Web Site:* www.harpercollins.com/childrens, pg 101

Paprocki, Karin, Simon & Schuster Children's Publishing, 1230 Avenue of the Americas, New York, NY 10020 *Tel:* 212-698-7000 *Web Site:* www.simonandschuster.com/kids; www.simonandschuster.com/teen; simonandschuster.net; simonandschuster.biz, pg 213

Paradis, Anne, Chouette Publishing, 1001 Lenoir St, Suite B-238, Montreal, QC H4C 2Z6, Canada *Tel:* 514-925-3325 *Fax:* 514-925-3323 *E-mail:* info@editions-chouette.com *Web Site:* www.chouette-publishing.com, pg 450

Paradis, Lucille, Paulines Editions, 5610 rue Beaubien est, Montreal, QC H1T 1X5, Canada *Tel:* 514-253-5610 *Fax:* 514-253-1907 *E-mail:* fsp-paulines@videotron.ca *Web Site:* www.editions.paulines.qc.ca, pg 466

Paradise, Bridgett, Houghton Mifflin Harcourt, 125 High St, Boston, MA 02110 *Tel:* 617-351-5000 *Toll Free Tel:* 855-969-4642; 800-225-5425 (K-12 educ materials); 800-323-9540 (assessment materials); 877-219-1537 (SkillsTutor); 888-242-6747 (Innovation in Educ Group); 800-225-3362 (Trade & Ref Div) *Toll Free Fax:* 800-269-5232 *E-mail:* myhmhco@hmhco.com *Web Site:* www.hmhco.com, pg 110

Paraskevopoulos, D Jane, Forward Movement, 412 Sycamore St, Cincinnati, OH 45202-4110 *Tel:* 513-721-6659 *Toll Free Tel:* 800-543-1813 *Fax:* 513-721-0729 (orders) *E-mail:* orders@forwardmovement.org (orders & cust serv) *Web Site:* www.forwardmovement.org, pg 87

Pare, Jean, Guy Saint-Jean Editeur Inc, 4490, rue Garand, Laval, QC H7L 5Z6, Canada *Tel:* 450-663-1777 *E-mail:* info@saint-jeanediteur.com *Web Site:* saint-jeanediteur.com, pg 469

Paredes, Ingrid, Penguin Random House Inc, 1745 Broadway, New York, NY 10019 *Tel:* 212-782-9000 *Toll Free Tel:* 800-726-0600 *Web Site:* www.penguinrandomhouse.com, pg 178

Paredes, Nikay, The Academy of American Poets Inc, 75 Maiden Lane, Suite 901, New York, NY 10038 *Tel:* 212-274-0343 *Fax:* 212-274-9427 *E-mail:* academy@poets.org *Web Site:* www.poets.org, pg 553

Paredes, Nikay, Raiziss/de Palchi Fellowship, 75 Maiden Lane, Suite 901, New York, NY 10038 *Tel:* 212-274-0343 *Fax:* 212-274-9427 *E-mail:* academy@poets.org *Web Site:* www.poets.org, pg 684

Paredes, Nikay, Wallace Stevens Award, 75 Maiden Lane, Suite 901, New York, NY 10038 *Tel:* 212-274-0343 *Fax:* 212-274-9427 *E-mail:* awards@poets.org *Web Site:* www.poets.org, pg 692

Paredes, Nikay, Walt Whitman Award, 75 Maiden Lane, Suite 901, New York, NY 10038 *Tel:* 212-274-0343 *Fax:* 212-274-9427 *E-mail:* academy@poets.org *Web Site:* www.poets.org, pg 697

Paredez, Deborah, University of Texas at Austin, New Writers Project, Dept of English, Calhoun Hall, Rm 226, 204 W 21 St, B-5000, Austin, TX 78712 *Tel:* 512-471-5132; 512-471-4991 *Fax:* 512-471-4909 *Web Site:* newwritersproject.org, pg 623

Parent, Gilles, Les Editions Vents d'Ouest, 109, rue Wright, bureau 202, Gatineau, QC J8X 2G7, Canada *Tel:* 819-770-6377 *E-mail:* info@ventsdouest.ca *Web Site:* www.ventsdouest.ca, pg 455

Parfrey, Adam, Feral House, 1240 W Sims Way, Suite 124, Port Townsend, WA 98368 *Tel:* 323-666-3311 *Fax:* 323-297-4331 *E-mail:* info@feralhouse.com *Web Site:* feralhouse.com, pg 84

Parikh, Dhara, Random House Publishing Group, 1745 Broadway, New York, NY 10019 *Toll Free Tel:* 800-200-3552 *Web Site:* atrandom.com, pg 195

Paris, Shirley, Carroll Publishing, 4701 Sangamore Rd, Suite S-155, Bethesda, MD 20816 *Tel:* 301-263-9800 *Toll Free Tel:* 800-336-4240 *Fax:* 301-263-9801 *E-mail:* info@carrollpub.com; customersvc@carrollpub.com *Web Site:* www.carrollpublishing.com, pg 48

Park, Ed, The Penguin Press, 375 Hudson St, New York, NY 10014 *Web Site:* thepenguinpress.com, pg 178

Park, Michael, ABAC/ALAC, 368 Dalhousie St, Suite 301, Ottawa, ON K1N 7G3, Canada *Tel:* 416-364-2376 *E-mail:* info@abac.org *Web Site:* www.abac.org, pg 553

Park, Michelle, Chronicle Books LLC, 680 Second St, San Francisco, CA 94107 *Tel:* 415-537-4200 *Toll Free Tel:* 800-759-0190 (cust serv) *Fax:* 415-537-4460 *Toll Free Fax:* 800-858-7787 (orders); 800-286-9471 (cust serv) *E-mail:* frontdesk@chroniclebooks.com *Web Site:* www.chroniclebooks.com, pg 55

Park, Rick, Newbury Street Press, 99-101 Newbury St, Boston, MA 02116 *Tel:* 617-536-5740 *Toll Free Tel:* 888-296-3447 (NEHGS membership) *Fax:* 617-536-7307 *E-mail:* sales@nehgs.org *Web Site:* www.americanancestors.org, pg 162

Parker, Harvey, Specialty Press Inc, 300 NW 70 Ave, Suite 102, Plantation, FL 33317 *Tel:* 954-792-8100 *Toll Free Tel:* 800-233-9273 *Fax:* 954-792-8545 *E-mail:* websales@addwarehouse.com *Web Site:* addwarehouse.com, pg 219

Parker, Jim, Do It Now Foundation, PO Box 27568, Tempe, AZ 85285-7568 *Tel:* 480-736-0599 *Fax:* 480-736-0771 *E-mail:* e-mail@doitnow.org; orders@doitnow.org *Web Site:* www.doitnow.org, pg 71

Parker, Mary Elizabeth, Dana Awards, Literary Competition, 200 Fosseway Dr, Greensboro, NC 27455 *Tel:* 336-644-8028 *E-mail:* danaawards@gmail.com *Web Site:* www.danaawards.com, pg 640

Parker, Miriam, HarperCollins General Books Group, 195 Broadway, New York, NY 10007 *Tel:* 212-207-7000 *Web Site:* www.harpercollins.com, pg 101

Parker, Nick, Bloomsbury Publishing Inc, 1385 Broadway, 5th fl, New York, NY 10018 *Tel:* 212-419-5300 *E-mail:* marketingusa@bloomsbury.com; adultpublicityusa@bloomsbury.com; askacademic@bloomsbury.com *Web Site:* www.bloomsbury.com, pg 38

Parkerson, Ami, New World Library, 14 Pamaron Way, Novato, CA 94949 *Tel:* 415-884-2100 *Toll Free Tel:* 800-227-3900 (ext 52, retail orders); 800-972-6657 *Fax:* 415-884-2199 *E-mail:* escort@newworldlibrary.com *Web Site:* www.newworldlibrary.com, pg 161

Parkinson, Judy, Research Press, 2612 N Mattis Ave, Champaign, IL 61822 *Tel:* 217-352-3273 *Toll Free Tel:* 800-519-2707 *Fax:* 217-352-1221 *E-mail:* rp@researchpress.com; orders@researchpress.com *Web Site:* www.researchpress.com, pg 198

Parkinson, Matt, Dark Horse Comics, 10956 SE Main St, Milwaukie, OR 97222 *Tel:* 503-652-8815 *Fax:* 503-654-9440 *E-mail:* dhcomics@darkhorse.com *Web Site:* www.darkhorse.com, pg 67

Parks, DeVonne, National Information Standards Organization (NISO), 3600 Clipper Mill Rd, Suite 302, Baltimore, MD 21211 *Tel:* 301-654-2512 *Fax:* 410-685-5278 *E-mail:* nisohq@niso.org *Web Site:* www.niso.org, pg 158, 572

Parks, Walter, UnKnownTruths.com Publishing Co, 8815 Conroy Windermere Rd, Suite 190, Orlando, FL 32835 *Tel:* 407-929-9207 *E-mail:* info@unknowntruths.com *Web Site:* unknowntruths.com, pg 248

Parliman, Emily, Books on Tape®, 1745 Broadway, New York, NY 10019 *Toll Free Tel:* 800-733-3000 (cust serv) *Toll Free Fax:* 800-940-7046 *Web Site:* www.booksontape.com, pg 40

Parms, Jericho, Vermont College of Fine Arts, MFA in Writing Program, 36 College St, Montpelier, VT 05602 *Tel:* 802-828-8840; 802-828-8839 *Toll Free Tel:* 866-934-VCFA (934-8232) *Fax:* 802-828-8649 *Web Site:* www.vcfa.edu, pg 624

Parr, Roz, Alfred A Knopf/Everyman's Library, c/o Penguin Random House Inc, 1745 Broadway, New York, NY 10019 *Tel:* 212-751-2600 *Toll Free Tel:* 800-638-6460 *Fax:* 212-572-2593 *Web Site:* www.knopfdoubleday.com, pg 127

Parrish, Jim, Bethany House Publishers, 11400 Hampshire Ave S, Bloomington, MN 55438 *Tel:* 952-829-2500 *Toll Free Tel:* 800-877-2665 (orders) *Fax:* 952-829-2568 *Toll Free Fax:* 800-398-3111 (orders) *Web Site:* www.bethanyhouse.com; www.bakerpublishinggroup.com, pg 34

Parro, Sarah, Holy Cross Orthodox Press, 50 Goddard Ave, Brookline, MA 02445 *Tel:* 617-731-3500; 617-850-1200 *Fax:* 617-850-1460 *E-mail:* info@hchc.edu *Web Site:* www.hchc.edu, pg 109

Parry, Emma, Janklow & Nesbit Associates, 285 Madison Ave, 21st fl, New York, NY 10017 *Tel:* 212-421-1700 *Fax:* 212-355-1403 *E-mail:* info@janklow.com *Web Site:* www.janklowandnesbit.com, pg 522

Parry, Katie, Dutton, 375 Hudson St, New York, NY 10014 *Tel:* 212-366-2000 *Fax:* 212-366-2262 *Web Site:* www.penguin.com, pg 74

Parry, Katie, GP Putnam's Sons (Hardcover), 375 Hudson St, New York, NY 10014 *Tel:* 212-366-2000 *Fax:* 212-366-2643 *E-mail:* online@penguinputnam.com *Web Site:* www.penguin.com/publishers/gpputnamssons, pg 192

Parsley, John, Dutton, 375 Hudson St, New York, NY 10014 *Tel:* 212-366-2000 *Fax:* 212-366-2262 *Web Site:* www.penguin.com, pg 74

Parsons, Brad, Houghton Mifflin Harcourt Trade & Reference Division, 125 High St, Boston, MA 02110 *Tel:* 617-351-5000 *Toll Free Tel:* 800-225-3362 *Web Site:* www.hmhco.com, pg 111

Parsons, Tara, Touchstone, 1230 Avenue of the Americas, New York, NY 10020, pg 233

Parsont, Meg, Phaidon, 65 Bleecker St, 8th fl, New York, NY 10012 *Tel:* 212-652-5400 *Toll Free Tel:* 800-759-0190 (cust serv) *Fax:* 212-652-5410 *Toll Free Fax:* 800-286-9471 (cust serv) *E-mail:* ussales@phaidon.com *Web Site:* www.phaidon.com, pg 182

Partland, J P, Editorial Freelancers Association (EFA), 71 W 23 St, 4th fl, New York, NY 10010-4102 *Tel:* 212-929-5400 *Toll Free Tel:* 866-929-5425 *Fax:* 212-929-5439 *Toll Free Fax:* 866-929-5439 *E-mail:* office@the-efa.org *Web Site:* www.the-efa.org, pg 564

Parvel, Andrew, eLit Awards, 1129 Woodmere Ave, Suite B, Traverse City, MI 49686 *Tel:* 231-933-0445 *Toll Free Tel:* 800-706-4636 *Fax:* 231-933-0448 *E-mail:* info@elitawards.com *Web Site:* www.elitawards.com, pg 644

Pascal, Paul, Abraham Lincoln Institute Book Award, 105 Mount Olive Lane, Ephrata, PA 17522 *E-mail:* secretary@lincoln-institute.org *Web Site:* www.lincoln-institute.org, pg 661

Paska, Lawrence, Carter G Woodson Book Awards, 8555 16 St, Suite 500, Silver Spring, MD 20910 *Tel:* 301-588-1800 *Toll Free Tel:* 800-296-7840 *Fax:* 301-588-2049 *E-mail:* excellence@ncss.org; publications@ncss.org *Web Site:* www.socialstudies.org, pg 699

Passick, Sarah, Sterling Lord Literistic Inc, 115 Broadway, Suite 1602, New York, NY 10006 *Tel:* 212-780-6050 *Fax:* 212-780-6095 *E-mail:* info@sll.com *Web Site:* www.sll.com, pg 537

Pasternack, Gail, Kay Snow Writing Contest, 5331 SW Macadam Ave, Suite 258, PMB 215, Portland, OR 97239 *Tel:* 901-200-5385 *E-mail:* wilwrite@willamettewriters.org *Web Site:* willamettewriters.org, pg 690

Pasternack, Gail, Willamette Writers, 5331 SW Macadam Ave, Suite 258, PMB 215, Portland, OR 97239 *Tel:* 901-200-5385 *E-mail:* wilwrite@willamettewriters.org *Web Site:* willamettewriters.org, pg 580

Pasternack, Gail, Willamette Writers' Conference, 5331 SW Macadam Ave, Suite 258, PMB 215, Portland, OR 97239 *Tel:* 901-200-5385 *E-mail:* wilwrite@willamettewriters.org *Web Site:* willamettewriters.org, pg 616

Pasternak, Tricia, Random House Publishing Group, 1745 Broadway, New York, NY 10019 *Toll Free Tel:* 800-200-3552 *Web Site:* atrandom.com, pg 195

Pasternak, Vicki, Scholastic Canada Ltd, 604 King St W, Toronto, ON M5V 1E1, Canada *Tel:* 905-887-7323 *Toll Free Tel:* 800-268-3860 (CN) *Toll Free Fax:* 866-387-4944 *E-mail:* custserve@scholastic.ca *Web Site:* www.scholastic.ca, pg 469

Pastor, Tony, BK Nelson Inc Lecture Bureau, 6726 Moonriver St, Mira Loma, CA 91752-3428 *Tel:* 760-902-1868 *Fax:* 760-778-6242 *E-mail:* bknelson4@cs.com, pg 547

Pastor, Tony, BK Nelson Inc Literary Agency, 6726 Moonriver St, Mira Loma, CA 91752-3428 *Tel:* 760-902-1868 *Fax:* 760-778-6242 *E-mail:* bknelson4@cs.com, pg 530

Pastore, Julia, HarperCollins General Books Group, 195 Broadway, New York, NY 10007 *Tel:* 212-207-7000 *Web Site:* www.harpercollins.com, pg 101

Pate, Ginger, Women Who Write Inc, PO Box 652, Madison, NJ 07940-0652 *E-mail:* info@womenwhowrite.org *Web Site:* womenwhowrite.org, pg 580

Patel, Punam, Harlequin Enterprises Ltd, 225 Duncan Mill Rd, Don Mills, ON M3B 3K9, Canada *Tel:* 416-445-5860 *Toll Free Tel:* 888-432-4879; 800-370-5838 (ebook inquiries) *E-mail:* customerservice@harlequin.com *Web Site:* www.harlequin.com, pg 459

Paterson, Shelagh, Ontario Library Association, 2 Toronto St, 3rd fl, Toronto, ON M5C 2B6, Canada *Tel:* 416-363-3388 *Toll Free Tel:* 866-873-9867 *Fax:* 416-941-9581 *E-mail:* info@accessola.com *Web Site:* www.accessola.com, pg 574

Patnaik, Gayatri, Beacon Press, 24 Farnsworth St, Boston, MA 02210-1409 *Tel:* 617-742-2110 *Fax:* 617-723-3097; 617-742-2290 *Web Site:* www.beacon.org, pg 31

Paton, Kathi J, Kathi J Paton Literary Agency, Box 2236, Radio City Sta, New York, NY 10101-2236 *Tel:* 212-265-6586 *E-mail:* kjplitbiz@optonline.net *Web Site:* www.patonliterary.com, pg 531

Patota, Anne, The Guilford Press, 370 Seventh Ave, Suite 1200, New York, NY 10001-1020 *Tel:* 212-431-9800 *Toll Free Tel:* 800-365-7006 *Fax:* 212-966-6708 *E-mail:* info@guilford.com *Web Site:* www.guilford.com, pg 97

Patrick, Amy, Sleeping Bear Press™, 2395 S Huron Pkwy, Suite 200, Ann Arbor, MI 48104 *Toll Free Tel:* 800-487-2323 *Fax:* 734-929-2649 *E-mail:* customerservice@sleepingbearpress.com *Web Site:* www.sleepingbearpress.com, pg 215

Patrick, Harley B, Hellgate Press, PO Box 3531, Ashland, OR 97520 *Tel:* 541-973-5154 *Toll Free Tel:* 800-795-4059 *E-mail:* sales@hellgatepress.com *Web Site:* www.hellgatepress.com, pg 105

Patrick, Julia, Chronicle Books LLC, 680 Second St, San Francisco, CA 94107 *Tel:* 415-537-4200 *Toll Free Tel:* 800-759-0190 (cust serv) *Fax:* 415-537-4460 *Toll Free Fax:* 800-858-7787 (orders); 800-286-9471 (cust serv) *E-mail:* frontdesk@chroniclebooks.com *Web Site:* www.chroniclebooks.com, pg 55

Patterson, David, Stuart Krichevsky Literary Agency Inc, 6 E 39 St, Suite 500, New York, NY 10016 *Tel:* 212-725-5288 *Fax:* 212-725-5275 *E-mail:* query@skagency.com *Web Site:* skagency.com, pg 525

Patterson, Elaine, Maryland History Press, PO Box 206, Fruitland, MD 21826-0206 *Tel:* 410-742-2682 *E-mail:* sales@marylandhistorypress.com *Web Site:* www.marylandhistorypress.com, pg 143

Patterson, Emma, Brandt & Hochman Literary Agents Inc, 1501 Broadway, Suite 2310, New York, NY 10036 *Tel:* 212-840-5760 *Fax:* 212-840-5776 *Web Site:* brandthochman.com, pg 509

Patterson, Hallie, Harry N Abrams Inc, 195 Broadway, 9th fl, New York, NY 10007 *Tel:* 212-206-7715 *Toll Free Tel:* 800-345-1359 *Fax:* 212-519-1210 *E-mail:* abrams@abramsbooks.com *Web Site:* www.abramsbooks.com, pg 3

Patterson, James, Fernwood Publishing, 32 Oceanvista Lane, Black Point, NS B0J 1B0, Canada *Tel:* 902-857-1388 *Fax:* 902-857-1328 *E-mail:* info@fernpub.ca; roseway@fernpub.ca *Web Site:* fernwoodpublishing.ca, pg 456

Patterson, Karen, Adams Media, 57 Littlefield St, Avon, MA 02322 *Tel:* 508-427-7100 *Web Site:* www.simonandschuster.com, pg 4

Patterson, Karen, F+W Media Inc, 10151 Carver Rd, Suite 200, Blue Ash, OH 45242 *Tel:* 513-531-2690 *Toll Free Tel:* 800-289-0963 (trade accts); 800 258 0929 (cust serv) *E-mail:* contact_us@fwmedia.com *Web Site:* www.fwcommunity.com, pg 82

Patterson, Marla, PennWell Books, 1421 S Sheridan Rd, Tulsa, OK 74112 *Tel:* 918-831-9421 *Toll Free Tel:* 800-752-9764 *Fax:* 918-831-9555 *Toll Free Fax:* 877-218-1348 *E-mail:* sales@pennwell.com *Web Site:* www.pennwellbooks.com, pg 179

Patterson, Monique, St Martin's Press, LLC, 175 Fifth Ave, New York, NY 10010 *Tel:* 646-307-5151 *Web Site:* us.macmillan.com/smp, pg 204

Patterson, Tracy, Stackpole Books, 5067 Ritter Rd, Mechanicsburg, PA 17055 *Tel:* 717-796-0411 *Toll Free Tel:* 800-732-3669 *Fax:* 717-796-0412 *Web Site:* www.stackpolebooks.com, pg 220

Patton, Susan, Association of American University Presses (AAUP), 1412 Broadway, Suite 2135, New York, NY 10018 *Tel:* 212-989-1010 *Fax:* 212-989-0275 *E-mail:* info@aaupnet.org *Web Site:* www.aaupnet.org, pg 558

Patukas, Jane, Fox Chapel Publishing Co Inc, 1970 Broad St, East Petersburg, PA 17520 *Tel:* 717-560-4703 *Toll Free Tel:* 800-457-9112 *Fax:* 717-560-4702 *E-mail:* customerservice@foxchapelpublishing.com *Web Site:* www.foxchapelpublishing.com, pg 87

Paul, Chris, Candlewick Press, 99 Dover St, Somerville, MA 02144-2825 *Tel:* 617-661-3330 *Fax:* 617-661-0565 *E-mail:* bigbear@candlewick.com; salesinfo@candlewick.com *Web Site:* www.candlewick.com, pg 46

Paul, Joey, Zondervan, 3900 Sparks Dr, Grand Rapids, MI 49546 *Tel:* 616-698-6900 *Toll Free Tel:* 800-226-1122; 800-727-1309 (retail orders) *Fax:* 616-698-3350 *Toll Free Fax:* 800-698-3256 (retail orders) *E-mail:* zinfo@zondervan.com *Web Site:* www.zondervan.com, pg 263

Paul, Miranda, Wisconsin Annual Fall Conference, PO Box 1463, Green Bay, WI 54305-1463 *Tel:* 323-782-1010 (corp off) *E-mail:* wisconsin@scbwi.org *Web Site:* www.scbwi.org; www.facebook.com/SCBWIWisconsin, pg 616

Paul, Nancy Gray, Woodbine House, 6510 Bells Mill Rd, Bethesda, MD 20817 *Tel:* 301-897-3570 *Toll Free Tel:* 800-843-7323 *Fax:* 301-897-5838 *E-mail:* info@woodbinehouse.com *Web Site:* www.woodbinehouse.com, pg 258

Pauley, Arron, Jackie White Memorial National Children's Playwriting Contest, 1400 Forum Blvd, 1C No 214, Columbia, MO 65203 *E-mail:* jwm@cectheatre.org *Web Site:* www.cectheatre.org, pg 657

Paulsen, Nancy, GP Putnam's Sons (Children's), 345 Hudson St, New York, NY 10014 *Tel:* 212-366-2000 *Fax:* 212-414-3393 *Web Site:* www.penguin.com/publishers/gpputnamssonsbooksforyoungread, pg 192

Paulsen, Nancy Rose, Penguin Young Readers Group, 345 Hudson St, New York, NY 10014 *Tel:* 212-366-2000; 212-414-3553 *Fax:* 212-414-3340 *Web Site:* www.penguin.com/children, pg 179

Paulson, Jamis, Turnstone Press, Artspace Bldg, 206-100 Arthur St, Winnipeg, MB R3B 1H3, Canada *Tel:* 204-947-1555 *Toll Free Tel:* 888-363-7718 *Fax:* 204-942-1556 *E-mail:* info@turnstonepress.com *Web Site:* www.turnstonepress.com, pg 473

Paulson, Tim, Augsburg Fortress Publishers, Publishing House of the Evangelical Lutheran Church in America, 510 Marquette Ave S, Minneapolis, MN 55402 *Tel:* 612-330-3300 *Toll Free Tel:* 800-426-0115 (ext 639, subns); 800-328-4648 (orders) *Fax:* 612-330-3455 *E-mail:* info@augsburgfortress.org; copyright@

augsburgfortress.org (reprint permission requests); customercare@augsburgfortress.org *Web Site:* www.augsburgfortress.org, pg 26

Pautz, Peter Dennis, World Fantasy Awards, PO Box 43, Mukilteo, WA 98275-0043 *Web Site:* www.worldfantasy.org, pg 699

Pavlin, Jordan, Alfred A Knopf/Everyman's Library, c/o Penguin Random House Inc, 1745 Broadway, New York, NY 10019 *Tel:* 212-751-2600 *Toll Free Tel:* 800-638-6460 *Fax:* 212-572-2593 *Web Site:* www.knopfdoubleday.com, pg 127

Pawlak, Kim, William Holmes McGuffey Longevity Award, PO Box 367, Fountain City, WI 54629 *E-mail:* info@taaonline.net *Web Site:* www.taaonline.net/mcguffey-longevity-award, pg 666

Pawlak, Kim, Most Promising New Textbook Award, PO Box 367, Fountain City, WI 54629 *E-mail:* info@taaonline.net *Web Site:* www.taaonline.net/promising-new-textbook-award, pg 669

Pawlak, Kim, Ron Pynn Award, PO Box 367, Fountain City, WI 54629 *E-mail:* info@taaonline.net *Web Site:* www.taaonline.net/ron-pynn-award, pg 683

Pawlak, Kim, TAA Council of Fellows, PO Box 367, Fountain City, WI 54629 *E-mail:* info@taaonline.net *Web Site:* www.taaonline.net/council-of-fellows, pg 693

Pawlak, Kim, Textbook Excellence Award, PO Box 367, Fountain City, WI 54629 *E-mail:* info@taaonline.net *Web Site:* www.taaonline.net/textbook-excellence-award, pg 694

Pawlak, Mark, Hanging Loose Press, 231 Wyckoff St, Brooklyn, NY 11217 *Tel:* 347-529-4738 *Fax:* 347-227-8215 *E-mail:* print225@aol.com *Web Site:* www.hangingloosepress.com, pg 100

Pawlitz, Mr Loren, Concordia Publishing House, 3558 S Jefferson Ave, St Louis, MO 63118-3968 *Tel:* 314-268-1000; 314-268-1268 (bookshop) *Toll Free Tel:* 800-325-3040 (cust serv) *Toll Free Fax:* 800-490-9889 (cust serv) *E-mail:* order@cph.org *Web Site:* www.cph.org, pg 59

Pawluk, Justyna, Facts On File, 132 W 31 St, 17th fl, New York, NY 10001 *Tel:* 212-967-8800 *Toll Free Tel:* 800-322-8755 *Toll Free Fax:* 800-678-3633 *E-mail:* custserv@factsonfile.com *Web Site:* infobasepublishing.com, pg 81

Pawluk, Justyna, Ferguson Publishing, 132 W 31 St, 17th fl, New York, NY 10001 *Tel:* 212-967-8800 *Toll Free Tel:* 800-322-8755 *Fax:* 917-339-0323 *Toll Free Fax:* 800-678-3633 *E-mail:* custserv@factsonfile.com *Web Site:* infobasepublishing.com, pg 84

Payette, Jacques, Les Editions Heritage Inc, 1101, ave Victoria, St-Lambert, QC J4R 1P8, Canada *Tel:* 514-875-0327, pg 454

Payette, Sylvie, Les Editions Heritage Inc, 1101, ave Victoria, St-Lambert, QC J4R 1P8, Canada *Tel:* 514-875-0327, pg 454

Payne, Maribeth, W W Norton & Company Inc, 500 Fifth Ave, New York, NY 10110-0017 *Tel:* 212-354-5500 *Toll Free Tel:* 800-233-4830 (orders & cust serv) *Fax:* 212-869-0856 *Toll Free Fax:* 800-458-6515 *E-mail:* orders@wwnorton.com *Web Site:* books.wwnorton.com, pg 164

Payton, Thomas, Trinity University Press, One Trinity Place, San Antonio, TX 78212-7200 *Tel:* 210-999-8884 *Fax:* 210-999-8838 *E-mail:* books@trinity.edu *Web Site:* www.tupress.org, pg 235

Peabody, William, GP Putnam's Sons (Hardcover), 375 Hudson St, New York, NY 10014 *Tel:* 212-366-2000 *Fax:* 212-366-2643 *E-mail:* online@penguinputnam.com *Web Site:* www.penguin.com/publishers/gpputnamssons, pg 192

Peacock, Hannah, Dorothy Canfield Fisher Book Award, 109 State St, Montpelier, VT 05609-0601 *Tel:* 802-828-2721 *Web Site:* libraries.vermont.gov, pg 642

Peacock, Kathleen, Goose Lane Editions, 500 Beaverbrook Ct, Suite 330, Fredericton, NB E3B 5X4, Canada *Tel:* 506-450-4251 *Toll Free Tel:* 888-926-8377 *Fax:* 506-459-4991 *E-mail:* info@gooselane.com; customerservice@gooselane.com *Web Site:* www.gooselane.com, pg 458

Pearce, Anne, Simon & Schuster, 1230 Avenue of the Americas, New York, NY 10020 *Tel:* 212-698-7000 *Toll Free Tel:* 800-223-2348 (cust serv); 800-223-2336 (orders) *Toll Free Fax:* 800-943-9831 (orders) *Web Site:* www.simonandschuster.com, pg 212

Pearce, Beth, The Fairmont Press Inc, 700 Indian Trail, Lilburn, GA 30047 *Tel:* 770-925-9388 *Fax:* 770-381-9865 *Web Site:* www.fairmontpress.com, pg 81

Pearce, John, Westwood Creative Artists Ltd, 138 Sussex Mews, Toronto, ON M5S-2K1, Canada *Tel:* 416-964-3302 *Fax:* 416-964-3302 *E-mail:* wca_office@wcaltd.com *Web Site:* www.wcaltd.com, pg 541

Pearce, Dr Scott, Center for East Asian Studies (CEAS), Western Washington University, 516 High St, Bellingham, WA 98225 *Tel:* 360-650-3339 *Fax:* 360-650-6110 *E-mail:* easpress@wwu.edu *Web Site:* www.wwu.edu/eas, pg 51

Pearl, Allyson, Random House Publishing Group, 1745 Broadway, New York, NY 10019 *Toll Free Tel:* 800-200-3552 *Web Site:* atrandom.com, pg 195

Pearlman, Robb, Rizzoli International Publications Inc, 300 Park Ave S, 4th fl, New York, NY 10010-5399 *Tel:* 212-387-3400 *Toll Free Tel:* 800-522-6657 (orders only) *Fax:* 212-387-3535 *E-mail:* publicity@rizzoliusa.com *Web Site:* www.rizzoliusa.com, pg 199

Pearpoint, Jack, Inclusion Press International, 47 Indian Trail, Toronto, ON M6R 1Z8, Canada *Tel:* 416-658-5363 *Fax:* 416-658-5067 *E-mail:* inclusionpress@inclusion.com *Web Site:* www.inclusion.com, pg 460

Pearson, Gina, Energy Information Administration (EIA), 1000 Independence Ave SW, Washington, DC 20585 *Tel:* 202-586-8800 *Fax:* 202-586-0727 *E-mail:* infoctr@eia.doe.gov *Web Site:* www.eia.doe.gov, pg 79

Pearson, Karen, Pacific Press Publishing Association, 1350 N Kings Rd, Nampa, ID 83687-3193 *Tel:* 208-465-2500 *Toll Free Tel:* 800-447-7377 *Fax:* 208-465-2531 *Web Site:* www.pacificpress.com, pg 172

Pearson, Lisa, Siglio, PO Box 111, Catskill, NY 12414 *Tel:* 310-857-6935 *E-mail:* publisher@sigliopress.com *Web Site:* sigliopress.com, pg 212

Pearson, Michael, The Mathematical Association of America, 1529 18 St NW, Washington, DC 20036-1358 *Tel:* 202-387-5200 *Toll Free Tel:* 800-741-9415 *Fax:* 202-265-2384 *E-mail:* maahq@maa.org; advertising@maa.org (pubns) *Web Site:* www.maa.org, pg 144

Pearson, Nancy, Scholastic Canada Ltd, 604 King St W, Toronto, ON M5V 1E1, Canada *Tel:* 905-887-7323 *Toll Free Tel:* 800-268-3860 (CN) *Toll Free Fax:* 866-387-4944 *E-mail:* custserve@scholastic.ca *Web Site:* www.scholastic.ca, pg 469

Pearson, Tawny, Michigan Municipal League, 1675 Green Rd, Ann Arbor, MI 48105 *Tel:* 734-662-3246 *Toll Free Tel:* 800-653-2483 *E-mail:* contact@mml.org *Web Site:* www.mml.org, pg 150

Pease, Pamela, Paintbox Press, 275 Madison Ave, Suite 600, New York, NY 10016 *Tel:* 212-878-6610 *E-mail:* info@paintboxpress.com *Web Site:* www.paintboxpress.com, pg 172

Pease, Roland, Steerforth Press, 45 Lyme Rd, Suite 208, Hanover, NH 03755-1222 *Tel:* 603-643-4787 *Fax:* 603-643-4788 *E-mail:* info@steerforth.com *Web Site:* www.steerforth.com, pg 221

Peattie, Gary R, DeVorss & Co, 553 Constitution Ave, Camarillo, CA 93012-8510 *Tel:* 805-322-9010 *Toll Free Tel:* 800-843-5743 *Fax:* 805-322-9011 *E-mail:* service@devorss.com *Web Site:* www.devorss.com, pg 70

Pecorale, Christina, Simon & Schuster Sales Division, 1230 Avenue of the Americas, New York, NY 10020 *Tel:* 212-698-7000, pg 214

Pedersen, Nadine, University of British Columbia Press, 2029 West Mall, Vancouver, BC V6T 1Z2, Canada *Tel:* 604-822-5959 *Toll Free Tel:* 877-377-9378 *Fax:* 604-822-6083 *Toll Free Fax:* 800-668-0821 *E-mail:* frontdesk@ubcpress.ca *Web Site:* www.ubcpress.ca, pg 473

Peed, Sarah, Penguin Random House Inc, 1745 Broadway, New York, NY 10019 *Tel:* 212-782-9000 *Toll Free Tel:* 800-726-0600 *Web Site:* www.penguinrandomhouse.com, pg 178

Peel, Tim, CCAB Inc, One Concorde Gate, Suite 800, Toronto, ON M3C 3N6, Canada *Tel:* 416-487-2418 *Fax:* 416-487-6405 *E-mail:* info@bpaww.com *Web Site:* www.bpaww.com, pg 562

Peeler, Denise, University of Illinois Press, 1325 S Oak St, MC-566, Champaign, IL 61820-6903 *Tel:* 217-333-0950 *Fax:* 217-244-8082 *E-mail:* uipress@uillinois.edu; journals@uillinois.edu *Web Site:* www.press.uillinois.edu, pg 241

Peirez, Josh, Dun & Bradstreet, 103 JFK Pkwy, Short Hills, NJ 07078 *Tel:* 973-921-5500 *Toll Free Tel:* 800-526-0651; 800-234-3867 (cust serv) *E-mail:* custserv@dnb.com *Web Site:* www.dnb.com, pg 73

Pekoll, Kristen, John Phillip Immroth Memorial Award, 50 E Huron St, Chicago, IL 60611 *Tel:* 312-280-4226 *Toll Free Tel:* 800-545-2433 *E-mail:* oif@ala.org *Web Site:* www.ala.org/ifrt, pg 655

Pekoll, Kristen, Eli M Oboler Memorial Award, 50 E Huron St, Chicago, IL 60611 *Tel:* 312-280-4226 *Toll Free Tel:* 800-545-2433 *E-mail:* oif@ala.org *Web Site:* www.ala.org/ifrt, pg 674

Pelehach, Laura, Academy of Nutrition & Dietetics, 120 S Riverside Plaza, Suite 2000, Chicago, IL 60606-6995 *Tel:* 312-899-0040 (ext 5000) *Toll Free Tel:* 800-877-1600 *E-mail:* sales@eatright.org *Web Site:* www.eatright.org, pg 3

Peller, Allan W, Educational Impressions Inc, 785 Franklin Ave, Franklin Lakes, NJ 07417 *Tel:* 201-644-0908 *Toll Free Tel:* 800-451-7450 *Fax:* 201-644-0907 *Web Site:* www.edimpressions.com; www.awpeller.com, pg 76

Peller, Neil, Educational Impressions Inc, 785 Franklin Ave, Franklin Lakes, NJ 07417 *Tel:* 201-644-0908 *Toll Free Tel:* 800-451-7450 *Fax:* 201-644-0907 *Web Site:* www.edimpressions.com; www.awpeller.com, pg 76

Pellerin, Alexandra, Les Editions de Mortagne, CP 116, Boucherville, QC J4B 5E6, Canada *Tel:* 450-641-2387 *Fax:* 450-655-6092 *E-mail:* info@editionsdemortagne.com *Web Site:* www.editionsdemortagne.com, pg 453

Pellerin, Sandy, Les Editions de Mortagne, CP 116, Boucherville, QC J4B 5E6, Canada *Tel:* 450-641-2387 *Fax:* 450-655-6092 *E-mail:* info@editionsdemortagne.com *Web Site:* www.editionsdemortagne.com, pg 453

Pelletier, James L, Marine Techniques Publishing, 311 W River Rd, Augusta, ME 04330-3991 *Tel:* 207-622-7984 *E-mail:* promariner@roadrunner.com; sales@marinetechpublishing.com; promariner@roadrunner.com *Web Site:* marinetechpublishing.com; www.groups.yahoo.com/group/marinetechniquespublishing, pg 142

Pelletier, Liz, Entangled Publishing, 2614 S Timberline Rd, Suite 109, Fort Collins, CO 80525 *Toll Free Tel:* 877-677-9451 *E-mail:* publisher@entangledpublishing.com *Web Site:* www.entangledpublishing.com, pg 79

Pelletier, Sharon, Dystel, Goderich & Bourret LLC, One Union Sq W, Suite 904, New York, NY 10003 *Tel:* 212-627-9100 *Fax:* 212-627-9313 *Web Site:* www.dystel.com, pg 515

Pellien, Jessica, Georgetown University Press, 3240 Prospect St NW, Suite 250, Washington, DC 20007 *Tel:* 202-687-5889 (busn) *Fax:* 202-687-6340 (edit) *E-mail:* gupress@georgetown.edu *Web Site:* press.georgetown.edu, pg 91

Pelton, Liz, Yale University Press, 302 Temple St, New Haven, CT 06511-8909 *Tel:* 203-432-0960; 203-432-0966 (sales); 401-531-2800 (cust serv) *Toll Free Tel:* 800-405-1619 (cust serv) *Fax:* 203-432-0948; 203-432-8485 (sales); 401-531-2801 (cust serv) *Toll*

Free Fax: 800-406-9145 (cust serv) E-mail: sales.press@yale.edu (sales); customer.care@triliteral.org (cust serv) Web Site: www.yalebooks.com; yalepress.yale.edu/yupbooks, pg 261

Peltz, Amy, The Art Institute of Chicago, 111 S Michigan Ave, Chicago, IL 60603-6404 Tel: 312-443-3600; 312-443-3540 (pubns) Fax: 312-443-1334 (pubns) Web Site: www.artic.edu; www.artinstituteshop.org, pg 21

Peltz, James, Excelsior Editions, 10 N Pearl St, 4th fl, Albany, NY 12207 Tel: 518-944-2800 Toll Free Tel: 866-430-7869 Fax: 518-320-1592 E-mail: info@sunypress.edu Web Site: www.sunypress.edu, pg 80

Peltz, James, State University of New York Press, 10 N Pearl St, 4th fl, Albany, NY 12207 Tel: 518-944-2800 Toll Free Tel: 877-204-6073 (orders) Fax: 518-320-1592 Toll Free Fax: 877-204-6074 (orders) E-mail: info@sunypress.edu (edit off); suny@presswarehouse.com (orders) Web Site: www.sunypress.edu, pg 221

Peluse, Michael, Cambridge University Press, 1 Liberty Plaza, 20th fl, New York, NY 10006 Tel: 212-924-3900; 212-337-5000 Fax: 212-691-3239 E-mail: newyork@cambridge.org Web Site: www.cambridge.org/us, pg 46

Pelz, Katherine, Berkley Publishing Group, 375 Hudson St, New York, NY 10014 Tel: 212-366-2000 Fax: 212-366-2385 Web Site: www.penguin.com, pg 33

Pelz, Sarah, Atria Books, 1230 Avenue of the Americas, New York, NY 10020 Tel: 212-698-7000 Fax: 212-698-7007 Web Site: www.simonandschuster.com, pg 25

Penick, Holly, Emond Montgomery Publications Ltd, 60 Shaftesbury Ave, Toronto, ON M4T 1A3, Canada Tel: 416-975-3925 Toll Free Tel: 888-837-0815 Fax: 416-975-3924 E-mail: orders@emp.ca Web Site: www.emp.ca, pg 456

Pennefeather, Shannon M, Minnesota Historical Society Press, 345 Kellogg Blvd W, St Paul, MN 55102-1906 Tel: 651-259-3205 Toll Free Tel: 800-621-2736 (warehouse) Fax: 651-297-1345 Toll Free Fax: 800-621-8476 (warehouse) E-mail: info-mnhspress@mnhs.org Web Site: www.mnhs.org/mnhspress, pg 151

Pennell, Kimberly, Pen-L Publishing, 12 W Dickson St, No 4455, Fayetteville, AR 72702 Web Site: www.pen-l.com, pg 177

Pennock, Laura, Candlewick Press, 99 Dover St, Somerville, MA 02144-2825 Tel: 617-661-3330 Fax: 617-661-0565 E-mail: bigbear@candlewick.com; salesinfo@candlewick.com Web Site: www.candlewick.com, pg 46

Pennoyer, Peter, Whiting Awards, 16 Court St, Suite 2308, Brooklyn, NY 11241 Tel: 718-701-5962 E-mail: info@whiting.org Web Site: www.whiting.org, pg 697

Pennoyer, Peter, Whiting Creative Nonfiction Grant, 16 Court St, Suite 2308, Brooklyn, NY 11241 Tel: 718-701-5962 E-mail: nonfiction@whiting.org; info@whiting.org Web Site: www.whiting.org, pg 697

Pennypacker, Jim, Maven House Press, 4 Snead Ct, Palmyra, VA 22963 Tel: 610-883-7988 Toll Free Fax: 888-894-3403 E-mail: info@mavenhousepress.com Web Site: mavenhousepress.com, pg 144

Pentes, Jennifer, Lonely Planet, 150 Linden St, Oakland, CA 94607 Tel: 510-893-8555; 510-250-6400 Toll Free Tel: 800-275-8555 (orders) Fax: 510-893-8572 E-mail: info@lonelyplanet.com Web Site: www.lonelyplanet.com, pg 137

Pepe, Christine, GP Putnam's Sons (Hardcover), 375 Hudson St, New York, NY 10014 Tel: 212-366-2000 Fax: 212-366-2643 E-mail: online@penguinputnam.com Web Site: www.penguin.com/publishers/gpputnamssons, pg 192

Pepe, Paolo, Random House Publishing Group, 1745 Broadway, New York, NY 10019 Toll Free Tel: 800-200-3552 Web Site: atrandom.com, pg 195

Pepper, Douglas, McClelland & Stewart Ltd, 320 Front St W, Suite 1400, Toronto, ON M5V 3B6, Canada Tel: 416-364-4449 Fax: 416-598-7764 E-mail: customerservicescanada@penguinrandomhouse.com; publicity@ca.penguingroup.com Web Site: penguinrandomhouse.ca/imprints/mcclelland-stewart, pg 463

Pepper, Eric, SPIE, 1000 20 St, Bellingham, WA 98225-6705 Tel: 360-676-3290 Toll Free Tel: 888-504-8171 (orders) Fax: 360-647-1445 E-mail: help@spie.org; customerservice@spie.org (orders) Web Site: www.spie.org, pg 219

Pepper, Lana, Saint Louis Literary Award, Pius XII Memorial Library, 3650 Lindell Blvd, St Louis, MO 63108 Tel: 314-977-3100; 314-977-3087 Fax: 314-977-3108 E-mail: slula@slu.edu Web Site: lib.slu.edu/about/associates/literary-award, pg 686

Pera, Cristobal, Penguin Random House Inc, 1745 Broadway, New York, NY 10019 Tel: 212-782-9000 Toll Free Tel: 800-726-0600 Web Site: www.penguinrandomhouse.com, pg 178

Peragine, Dan, Dan Peragine Literary Agency, 227 Beechwood Ave, Bogota, NJ 07603 Tel: 201-390-0468 Fax: 201-390-0468 E-mail: dpliterary@aol.com, pg 531

Peranteau, Paul, John Benjamins Publishing Co, 763 N 24 St, Philadelphia, PA 19130 Tel: 207-725-7250 Toll Free Tel: 800-562-5666 (orders) Fax: 207-725-7252 E-mail: service@benjamins.com Web Site: www.benjamins.com, pg 33

Perciasepe, Laura, Riverhead Books, 375 Hudson St, New York, NY 10014 Tel: 212-366-2000 Web Site: www.penguin.com/publishers/riverhead, pg 199

Perdue, Charles, McFarland, 960 NC Hwy 88 W, Jefferson, NC 28640 Tel: 336-246-4460 Toll Free Tel: 800-253-2187 (orders) Fax: 336-246-5018; 336-246-4403 (orders) E-mail: info@mcfarlandpub.com Web Site: www.mcfarlandpub.com, pg 145

Pereira, Mark, Brilliance Audio, 1704 Eaton Dr, Grand Haven, MI 49417 Tel: 616-846-5256 Toll Free Tel: 800-648-2312 (orders only) Fax: 616-846-0630 E-mail: customerservice@brillianceaudio.com Web Site: www.brillianceaudio.com, pg 44

Perel, Kim, Irene Goodman Literary Agency, 27 W 24 St, Suite 700B, New York, NY 10010 Tel: 212-604-0330 E-mail: queries@irenegoodman.com Web Site: www.irenegoodman.com, pg 519

Perez, Jeanette, HarperCollins General Books Group, 195 Broadway, New York, NY 10007 Tel: 212-207-7000 Web Site: www.harpercollins.com, pg 101

Perez, Joe, Random House Publishing Group, 1745 Broadway, New York, NY 10019 Toll Free Tel: 800-200-3552 Web Site: atrandom.com, pg 195

Perez, Ruby, McSweeney's Publishing, 849 Valencia St, San Francisco, CA 94110 Tel: 415-642-5609 (cust serv) Web Site: www.mcsweeneys.net, pg 147

Perillo, Sarah, Curtis Brown Ltd, 10 Astor Place, New York, NY 10003 Tel: 212-473-5400 Web Site: www.curtisbrown.com, pg 510

Perkins, Dorothy, Diane Publishing Co, 330 Pusey Ave, Suite 3 (rear), Collingdale, PA 19023 0617 Tel: 610 461-6200 Toll Free Tel: 800-782-3833 Fax: 610-461-6130 Web Site: www.dianepublishing.net, pg 70

Perkins, Gareth K, Berkeley Slavic Specialties, PO Box 3034, Oakland, CA 94609-0034 Tel: 510-653-8048 Fax: 510-653-6313 E-mail: 71034.456@compuserve.com Web Site: www.berkslav.com, pg 33

Perkins, Katherine, GP Putnam's Sons (Children's), 345 Hudson St, New York, NY 10014 Tel: 212-366-2000 Fax: 212-414-3393 Web Site: www.penguin.com/publishers/gpputnamssonsbooksforyoungread, pg 192

Perkins, Lori, Riverdale Avenue Books (RAB), 5676 Riverdale Ave, Bronx, NY 10471 Tel: 212-279-6418 E-mail: customerservice@riverdaleavebooks.com Web Site: www.riverdaleavebooks.com, pg 199

Perkins, Terry, Pflaum Publishing Group, 2621 Dryden Rd, Suite 300, Dayton, OH 45439 Tel: 937-293-1415 Toll Free Tel: 800-543-4383 (sales) Fax: 937-293-1310 Toll Free Fax: 800-370-4450 E-mail: service@pflaum.com Web Site: pflaum.com, pg 182

Perl, Liz, Simon & Schuster, Inc, 1230 Avenue of the Americas, New York, NY 10020 Tel: 212-698-7000 Fax: 212-698-7007 E-mail: firstname.lastname@simonandschuster.com Web Site: www.simonandschuster.com, pg 213

Perlee, Mr Christian, McGraw-Hill Contemporary Learning Series, 501 Bell St, Dubuque, IA 52001 Toll Free Tel: 800-243-6532 Web Site: www.mhcls.com, pg 145

Perlman, Jim, Holy Cow! Press, PO Box 3170, Mount Royal Sta, Duluth, MN 55803 Tel: 218-724-1653 E-mail: holycow@holycowpress.org Web Site: www.holycowpress.org, pg 109

Perlman, Michael, Simon & Schuster Sales Division, 1230 Avenue of the Americas, New York, NY 10020 Tel: 212-698-7000, pg 214

Perlstein, Jill, American Booksellers Association, 333 Westchester Ave, Suite S202, White Plains, NY 10604 Tel: 914-406-7500 Toll Free Tel: 800-637-0037 Fax: 914-410-6297 E-mail: info@bookweb.org Web Site: www.bookweb.org, pg 554

Permingeat, Max, Les Editions de Mortagne, CP 116, Boucherville, QC J4B 5E6, Canada Tel: 450-641-2387 Fax: 450-655-6092 E-mail: info@editionsdemortagne.com Web Site: www.editionsdemortagne.com, pg 453

Perreault, Diane, Beliveau Editeur, 567 rue Bienville, Boucherville, QC J4B 2Z5, Canada Tel: 450-679-1933 Web Site: www.beliveauediteur.com, pg 446

Perreault, Melanie, Les Editions Pierre Tisseyre, 155, rue Maurice, Rosemere, QC J7A 2S8, Canada Tel: 514-335-0777 Fax: 514-335-6723 E-mail: info@edtisseyre.ca Web Site: www.tisseyre.ca, pg 455

Perreault, Michel, Les Editions Fides, 7333 place des Roseraies, bureau 100, Anjou, QC H1M 2X6, Canada Tel: 514-745-4290 Fax: 514-745-4299 E-mail: editions@groupefides.com Web Site: www.editionsfides.com, pg 454

Perreault, Russell, Anchor Books, c/o Penguin Random House Inc, 1745 Broadway, New York, NY 10019 Tel: 212-572-2420 E-mail: vintageanchorpublicity@randomhouse.com Web Site: knopfdoubleday.com/imprint/anchor, pg 16

Perreault, Russell, Vintage Books, c/o Penguin Random House Inc, 1745 Broadway, New York, NY 10019 Tel: 212-572-2420 E-mail: vintageanchorpublicity@randomhouse.com Web Site: knopfdoubleday.com/imprint/vintage, pg 251

Perrin, Brian, HarperCollins General Books Group, 195 Broadway, New York, NY 10007 Tel: 212-207-7000 Web Site: www.harpercollins.com, pg 101

Perrin, Christopher, Classical Academic Press, 2151 Market St, Camp Hill, PA 17011 Tel: 717-730-0711 Fax: 717-730-0721 E-mail: office@classicalsubjects.com Web Site: classicalacademicpress.com, pg 57

Perrin, Christopher, Plum Tree Books, 2151 Market St, Camp Hill, PA 17011 Tel: 717-730-0711 Fax: 717-730-0721 E-mail: info@classicalsubjects.com Web Site: www.plumtreebooks.com, pg 184

Perrin, Dr James, American Academy of Pediatrics, 141 NW Point Blvd, Elk Grove Village, IL 60007-1098 Tel: 847-434-4000 Toll Free Tel: 888-227-1770 Fax: 847-434-8000 E-mail: pubs@aap.org Web Site: www.aap.org, pg 9

Perrone, Madeline, Literary Artists Representatives, 575 West End Ave, Suite GRC, New York, NY 10024-2711 Tel: 212-679-7788 E-mail: litartists@aol.com, pg 526

Perry, Ava, Circlet Press Inc, 39 Hurlbut St, Cambridge, MA 02138 Toll Free Tel: 800-729-6423 E-mail: circletintern@gmail.com Web Site: www.circlet.com, pg 56

Perry, Bonnie, Beacon Hill Press of Kansas City, PO Box 419527, Kansas City, MO 64141 *Tel:* 816-931-1900 *Toll Free Tel:* 800-877-0700 (cust serv) *Fax:* 816-753-4071 *Web Site:* www.nph.com, pg 30

Perry, David, Artists' Fellowships, 20 Jay St, 7th fl, Brooklyn, NY 11201 *Tel:* 212-366-6900 *Fax:* 212-366-1778 *E-mail:* info@nyfa.org *Web Site:* www.nyfa.org, pg 628

Perry, Jack, Boyds Mills Press, 815 Church St, Honesdale, PA 18431 *Tel:* 570-253-1164 *Toll Free Tel:* 800-490-5111 *Fax:* 570-253-0179 *E-mail:* contact@boydsmillspress.com *Web Site:* www.boydsmillspress.com, pg 41

Perry, Jack W, Highlights for Children, 1800 Watermark Dr, Columbus, OH 43215 *Tel:* 614-486-0631 *Toll Free Tel:* 800-962-3661 (Highlights Club cust serv); 800-255-9517 (Highlights Magazine cust serv) *Web Site:* www.highlights.com; www.facebook.com/HighlightsforChildren, pg 107

Perry, Rochon, Cedar Grove Books, 2215 High Point Dr, Carrollton, TX 75007 *Tel:* 415-364-8292 *Fax:* 415-276-9858 *E-mail:* queries@cedargrovebooks.com *Web Site:* www.cedargrovebooks.com, pg 50

Perry, Ronald, Sheron Enterprises Inc, 1035 S Carley Ct, North Bellmore, NY 11710 *Tel:* 516-783-5885 *E-mail:* sheronent1@msn.com *Web Site:* www.longislandbookpublisher.com, pg 211

Perry, Sheila M, Sophia Institute Press®, 522 Donald St, Unit 3, Bedford, NH 03110 *Tel:* 603-836-5505 *Toll Free Tel:* 800-888-9344 *Fax:* 603-641-8108 *Toll Free Fax:* 888-288-2259 *E-mail:* orders@sophiainstitute.com *Web Site:* www.sophiainstitute.com, pg 217

Perry, Sheryl, Sheron Enterprises Inc, 1035 S Carley Ct, North Bellmore, NY 11710 *Tel:* 516-783-5885 *E-mail:* sheronent1@msn.com *Web Site:* www.longislandbookpublisher.com, pg 211

Perry, Thomas, Random House Publishing Group, 1745 Broadway, New York, NY 10019 *Toll Free Tel:* 800-200-3552 *Web Site:* atrandom.com, pg 195

Pershing, John, Hackett Publishing Co Inc, 3333 Massachusetts Ave, Indianapolis, IN 46218 *Tel:* 317-635-9250 (orders & cust serv); 617-497-6303 (edit off & sales) *Fax:* 317-635-9292; 617-661-8703 (edit off) *Toll Free Fax:* 800-783-9213 *E-mail:* customer@hackettpublishing.com; editorial@hackettpublishing.com *Web Site:* www.hackettpublishing.com, pg 99

Persichetti, James, Nelson Literary Agency LLC, 1732 Wazee St, Suite 207, Denver, CO 80202-1284 *Tel:* 303-292-2805 *E-mail:* query@nelsonagency.com *Web Site:* www.nelsonagency.com, pg 530

Person, Hara, Central Conference of American Rabbis/CCAR Press, 355 Lexington Ave, 18th fl, New York, NY 10017 *Tel:* 212-972-3636 *E-mail:* info@ccarnet.org *Web Site:* www.ccarpress.org, pg 51

Pesch, Fran, Dayton Playhouse FutureFest, PO Box 3017, Dayton, OH 45401-3017 *Tel:* 937-424-8477 *Fax:* 937-424-0062 *E-mail:* futurefest@thedaytonplayhouse.com *Web Site:* wordpress.daytonplayhouse.com, pg 640

Peskin, Elizabeth, Random House Children's Books, 1745 Broadway, 10th fl, New York, NY 10019 *Tel:* 212-782-9000 *Web Site:* www.randomhousekids.com, pg 194

Peskin, Joy, Farrar, Straus & Giroux Books for Young Readers, 175 Fifth Ave, 7th fl, New York, NY 10010 *Tel:* 212-741-6900 *Toll Free Tel:* 888-330-8477 (orders) *Fax:* 212-633-9385 *Web Site:* us.macmillan.com/mackids; www.mackidsbooks.com, pg 82

Pester, John, Living Stream Ministry (LSM), 2431 W La Palma Ave, Anaheim, CA 92801 *Tel:* 714-991-4681 *Toll Free Tel:* 800-549-5164 *Fax:* 714-236-6005 *E-mail:* books@lsm.org *Web Site:* www.lsm.org, pg 136

Pestritto, Carrie, Prospect Agency, 285 Fifth Ave, PMB 445, Brooklyn, NY 11215 *Tel:* 718-788-3217 *Fax:* 718-360-9582 *Web Site:* www.prospectagency.com, pg 532

Peter, Judith, Stemmer House Publishers Inc, 4 White Brook Rd, Gilsum, NH 03448 *Tel:* 603-357-0236 *Toll Free Tel:* 800-345-6665 *Fax:* 603-965-2181 *E-mail:* pbs@pathwaybook.com *Web Site:* www.stemmer.com, pg 222

Peter, Steven, Princeton University Press, 41 William St, Princeton, NJ 08540-5237 *Tel:* 609-258-4900 *Fax:* 609-258-6305 *Web Site:* press.princeton.edu, pg 188

Peters, Barbara, Poisoned Pen Press, 6962 E First Ave, Suite 103, Scottsdale, AZ 85251 *Tel:* 480-945-3375 *Toll Free Tel:* 800-421-3976 *Fax:* 480-949-1707 *E-mail:* info@poisonedpenpress.com *Web Site:* www.poisonedpenpress.com, pg 185

Peters, Michelle, Association of Manitoba Book Publishers, 100 Arthur St, Suite 404, Winnipeg, MB R3B 1H3, Canada *Tel:* 204-947-3335 *Fax:* 204-956-4689 *E-mail:* ambp@mts.net *Web Site:* ambp.ca, pg 559

Peters, Simone, Tortuga Press, 2777 Yulupa Ave, PMB 181, Santa Rosa, CA 95405 *Tel:* 707-544-4720 *Fax:* 707-595-5331 *E-mail:* info@tortugapress.com *Web Site:* www.tortugapress.com, pg 233

Peterseil, Shlomo, The Toby Press LLC, PO Box 8531, New Milford, CT 06776-8531 *Tel:* 203-830-8508 *Fax:* 203-830-8512 *E-mail:* toby@tobypress.com; sales@korenpub.com *Web Site:* www.tobypress.com; www.korenpub.com, pg 232

Peterson, Carol, Penguin Group USA, A Penguin Random House Company, 375 Hudson St, New York, NY 10014 *Tel:* 212-366-2000 *Toll Free Tel:* 800-847-5515 (inside sales); 800-631-8571 (cust serv) *Fax:* 212-366-2666; 607-775-4829 (inside sales) *E-mail:* online@us.penguingroup.com *Web Site:* www.penguin.com, pg 177

Peterson, Gayla, Foil & Specialty Effects Association (FSEA), 2150 SW Westport Dr, Suite 101, Topeka, KS 66614 *Tel:* 785-271-5816 *Fax:* 785-271-6404 *E-mail:* info@fsea.com; fseamail@fsea.com *Web Site:* www.fsea.com, pg 566

Peterson, James, Coaches Choice, 514 Airport Way, Monterey, CA 93940 *Toll Free Tel:* 888-229-5745 *Fax:* 831-372-6075 *E-mail:* info@coacheschoice.com *Web Site:* www.coacheschoice.com, pg 57

Peterson, Jeff, Foil & Specialty Effects Association (FSEA), 2150 SW Westport Dr, Suite 101, Topeka, KS 66614 *Tel:* 785-271-5816 *Fax:* 785-271-6404 *E-mail:* info@fsea.com; fseamail@fsea.com *Web Site:* www.fsea.com, pg 566

Peterson, Jeff, Search Institute Press®, The Banks Bldg, Suite 125, 615 First Ave NE, Minneapolis, MN 55413 *Tel:* 612-376-8955; 612-692-5520 *Toll Free Tel:* 800-888-7828 *Fax:* 612-692-5553 *E-mail:* si@search-institute.org *Web Site:* www.search-institute.org, pg 210

Peterson, Kathryn, Atlantic Center for the Arts Artists-in-Residence Program, 1414 Art Center Ave, New Smyrna Beach, FL 32168 *Tel:* 386-427-6975 *Toll Free Tel:* 800-393-6975 *Fax:* 386-427-5669 *E-mail:* program@atlanticcenterforthearts.org *Web Site:* atlanticcenterforthearts.org, pg 609

Peterson, Kristina, Workman Publishing Co Inc, 225 Varick St, 9th fl, New York, NY 10014-4381 *Tel:* 212-254-5900 *Toll Free Tel:* 800-722-7202 *Fax:* 212-254-8098 *E-mail:* info@workman.com *Web Site:* www.workman.com, pg 259

Peterson, Laura Blake, Curtis Brown Ltd, 10 Astor Place, New York, NY 10003 *Tel:* 212-473-5400 *Web Site:* www.curtisbrown.com, pg 510

Peterson, Lowell, Writers Guild of America, East (WGAE), 250 Hudson St, Suite 700, New York, NY 10013 *Tel:* 212-767-7800 *Fax:* 212-582-1909 *Web Site:* www.wgaeast.org, pg 581

Peterson, Mike, The Child's World Inc, 1980 Lookout Dr, North Mankato, MN 56003-1705 *Tel:* 507-385-1044 *Toll Free Tel:* 800-599-READ (599-7323) *Toll Free Fax:* 888-320-2329 *E-mail:* sales@childsworld.com *Web Site:* childsworld.com, pg 54

Peterson, Nancy, Peachpit Press, 1301 Sansome St, San Francisco, CA 94111 *Toll Free Tel:* 800-283-9444 *E-mail:* info@peachpit.com; ask@peachpit.com *Web Site:* www.peachpit.com, pg 175

Peterson, Tami, Meadowbrook Press, 6110 Blue Circle Dr, Suite 237, Minnetonka, MN 55343 *Toll Free Tel:* 800-338-2232 *Fax:* 952-930-1940 *E-mail:* info@meadowbrookpress.com *Web Site:* www.meadowbrookpress.com, pg 147

Peterson, Tom, The Creative Co, PO Box 227, Mankato, MN 56002 *Tel:* 507-388-6273 *Toll Free Tel:* 800-445-6209 *Fax:* 507-388-2746 *E-mail:* info@thecreativecompany.us; orders@thecreativecompany.us *Web Site:* www.thecreativecompany.us, pg 64

Peterson, Tony, The Society of Professional Journalists (SPJ), Eugene S Pulliam National Journalism Ctr, 3909 N Meridian St, Indianapolis, IN 46208 *Tel:* 317-927-8000 *Fax:* 317-920-4789 *E-mail:* spj@spj.org *Web Site:* www.spj.org, pg 580

Petilos, Randolph, University of Chicago Press, 1427 E 60 St, Chicago, IL 60637-2954 *Tel:* 773-702-7700; 773-702-7600 *Toll Free Tel:* 800-621-2736 (orders) *Fax:* 773-702-9756; 773-660-2235 (orders); 773-702-2708 *E-mail:* custserv@press.uchicago.edu; marketing@press.uchicago.edu *Web Site:* www.press.uchicago.edu, pg 241

Petitt, Tracey, Rizzoli International Publications Inc, 300 Park Ave S, 4th fl, New York, NY 10010-5399 *Tel:* 212-387-3400 *Toll Free Tel:* 800-522-6657 (orders only) *Fax:* 212-387-3535 *E-mail:* publicity@rizzoliusa.com *Web Site:* www.rizzoliusa.com, pg 199

Petrick, Emily, Random House Children's Books, 1745 Broadway, 10th fl, New York, NY 10019 *Tel:* 212-782-9000 *Web Site:* www.randomhousekids.com, pg 194

Petrie, Jeremy, Willow Creek Press, 9931 Hwy 70 W, Minocqua, WI 54548 *Tel:* 715-358-7010 *Toll Free Tel:* 800-850-9453 *Fax:* 715-358-2807 *E-mail:* info@willowcreekpress.com *Web Site:* www.willowcreekpress.com, pg 256

Petrie, Tom, Willow Creek Press, 9931 Hwy 70 W, Minocqua, WI 54548 *Tel:* 715-358-7010 *Toll Free Tel:* 800-850-9453 *Fax:* 715-358-2807 *E-mail:* info@willowcreekpress.com *Web Site:* www.willowcreekpress.com, pg 256

Petrillo, Alan M, Excalibur Publications, PO Box 89667, Tucson, AZ 85752-9667 *Tel:* 520-575-9057 *E-mail:* excaliburpublications@centurylink.net, pg 80

Petrovich, Aaron, Akashic Books, 232 Third St, Suite A-115, Brooklyn, NY 11215 *Tel:* 718-643-9193 *Fax:* 718-643-9195 *E-mail:* info@akashicbooks.com *Web Site:* www.akashicbooks.com, pg 6

Pettigrew, Jean, Les Editions Alire, 120 cote du Passage, Levis, QC G6V 5S9, Canada *Tel:* 418-835-4441 *Fax:* 418-838-4443 *E-mail:* info@alire.com *Web Site:* www.alire.com, pg 452

Pettit, Kristen, HarperCollins Children's Books, 195 Broadway, New York, NY 10007 *Tel:* 212-207-7000 *Web Site:* www.harpercollins.com/childrens, pg 101

Petty, Jill, Northwestern University Press, 629 Noyes St, Evanston, IL 60208-4210 *Tel:* 847-491-2046 *Toll Free Tel:* 800-621-2736 (orders only) *Fax:* 847-491-8150 *E-mail:* nupress@northwestern.edu *Web Site:* www.nupress.northwestern.edu, pg 164

Pfaff, Eugene E Jr, Tudor Publishers Inc, 3109 Shady Lawn Dr, Greensboro, NC 27408 *Tel:* 336-288-5395 *E-mail:* tudorpublishers@triad.rr.com, pg 236

Pfeffer, Keith, Harvard Business Review Press, 300 N Beacon St, Watertown, MA 02472 *Tel:* 617-783-7400 *Fax:* 617-783-7489 *E-mail:* custserv@hbsp.harvard.edu *Web Site:* www.harvardbusiness.org, pg 102

Pfeiffer, Alice Randal, Syracuse University Press, 621 Skytop Rd, Suite 110, Syracuse, NY 13244-5290 *Tel:* 315-443-5534 *Toll Free Tel:* 800-365-8929 (cust serv) *Fax:* 315-443-5545 *E-mail:* supress@syr.edu *Web Site:* syracuseuniversitypress.syr.edu, pg 226

Pfister, Jenny, The Goddard Riverside Stephan Russo Book Prize, 593 Columbus Ave, New York, NY 10024 *Web Site:* bookprize.goddard.org, pg 650

Pfund, Niko, Oxford University Press USA, 198 Madison Ave, New York, NY 10016 Tel: 212-726-6000 Toll Free Tel: 800-451-7556 (orders); 800-445-9714 (cust serv) Fax: 919-677-1303 E-mail: custserv.us@oup.com Web Site: www.oup.com/us, pg 171

Phair, Sarah Bush, Trident Media Group LLC, 41 Madison Ave, 36th fl, New York, NY 10010 Tel: 212-333-1511 E-mail: info@tridentmediagroup.com; press@tridentmediagroup.com Web Site: www.tridentmediagroup.com, pg 540

Phelan, Shani, IACP Cookbook Awards, 45 Rockefeller Plaza, Suite 2000, New York, NY 10111 Tel: 646-358-4957 Toll Free Tel: 866-358-4951 Toll Free Fax: 866-358-2524 E-mail: info@iacp.com Web Site: www.iacp.com; www.iacp.com/award/more/cookbook, pg 654

Phelan, Sheila, DK Publishing, 345 Hudson St, 2nd fl, New York, NY 10014 Tel: 646-674-4000 Toll Free Tel: 877-342-5357 (cust serv); 800-733-3000 Web Site: www.dk.com; www.penguin.com, pg 71

Phelps, Chad, F+W Media Inc, 10151 Carver Rd, Suite 200, Blue Ash, OH 45242 Tel: 513-531-2690 Toll Free Tel: 800-289-0963 (trade accts); 800-258-0929 (cust serv) E-mail: contact_us@fwmedia.com Web Site: www.fwcommunity.com, pg 82

Phi, Bao, McKnight Artist Fellowship for Writers, Open Book, Suite 200, 1011 Washington Ave S, Minneapolis, MN 55415 Tel: 612-215-2575 Fax: 612-215-2576 E-mail: loft@loft.org Web Site: www.loft.org, pg 667

Philips, Becky, AMWA Annual Conference, 30 W Gude Dr, Suite 525, Rockville, MD 20850-4357 Tel: 240-238-0940 Fax: 301-294-9006 E-mail: amwa@amwa.org Web Site: www.amwa.org, pg 609

Philipsheck, Susan, Transaction Publishers Inc, 10 Corporate Place S, Suite 102, Piscataway, NJ 08854 Tel: 732-445-2280; 703-661-1589 (orders) Toll Free Tel: 888-999-6778 (dist ctr) Fax: 732-445-3138 E-mail: trans@transactionpub.com; orders@transactionpub.om Web Site: www.transactionpub.com, pg 234

Phillips, Andrew, AuthorHouse, 1663 Liberty Dr, Bloomington, IN 47403 Tel: 812-339-6000 (outside US) Toll Free Tel: 888-519-5121 E-mail: authorsupport@authorhouse.com Web Site: www.authorhouse.com, pg 26

Phillips, Andrew, Xlibris Corp, 1663 Liberty Dr, Suite 200, Bloomington, IN 47403 Toll Free Tel: 888-795-4274 Fax: 610-915-0294 E-mail: info@xlibris.com Web Site: www.xlibris.com, pg 261

Phillips, Andrew V, Windhaven®, 466 Rte 10, Orford, NH 03777 Tel: 603-512-9251 (cell) Web Site: www.windhavenpress.com, pg 502

Phillips, Barb, The Literary Press Group of Canada, 425 Adelaide St W, Suite 700, Toronto, ON M5V 3C1, Canada Tel: 416-483-1321 Fax: 416-483-2510 Web Site: www.lpg.ca, pg 568

Phillips, Betsy, Vanderbilt University Press, 2014 Broadway, Suite 320, Nashville, TN 37203 Tel: 615-322-3585 Toll Free Tel: 800-627-7377 (orders only) Fax: 615-343-8823 Toll Free Fax: 800-735-0476 (orders only) E-mail: vupress@vanderbilt.edu Web Site: www.vanderbiltuniversitypress.com, pg 249

Phillips, Frances, Northern California Book Awards, c/o Poetry Flash, 1450 Fourth St, Suite 4, Berkeley, CA 94710 Tel: 510-525-5476 Fax: 510-525-6752 E-mail: editor@poetryflash.org; ncbr@poetryflash.org Web Site: poetryflash.org, pg 674

Phillips, Jenna, Vanderbilt University Press, 2014 Broadway, Suite 320, Nashville, TN 37203 Tel: 615-322-3585 Toll Free Tel: 800-627-7377 (orders only) Fax: 615-343-8823 Toll Free Fax: 800-735-0476 (orders only) E-mail: vupress@vanderbilt.edu Web Site: www.vanderbiltuniversitypress.com, pg 249

Phillips, Kathleen, North American Agricultural Journalists (NAAJ), 6434 Hurta Lane, Bryan, TX 77808 Tel: 979-845-2872 Web Site: www.naaj.net, pg 573

Phillips, Kirsten, Portage & Main Press, 318 McDermot, Suite 100, Winnipeg, MB R3A 0A2, Canada Tel: 204-987-3500 Toll Free Tel: 800-667-9673 Fax: 204-947-0080 Toll Free Fax: 866-734-8477 E-mail: books@portageandmainpress.com Web Site: www.portageandmainpress.com, pg 467

Phillips, Ted, United States Holocaust Memorial Museum, 100 Raoul Wallenberg Place SW, Washington, DC 20024-2126 Tel: 202-314-7837; 202-488-6144 (orders) Toll Free Tel: 800-259-9998 (orders) Fax: 202-479-9726; 202-488-0438 (orders) E-mail: cahs_publications@ushmm.org Web Site: www.ushmm.org, pg 239

Phinn, Jessica, Nelson Education Ltd, 1120 Birchmount Rd, Scarborough, ON M1K 5G4, Canada Tel: 416-752-9100 Toll Free Tel: 800-268-2222 (cust serv) Fax: 416-752-8101 Toll Free Fax: 800-430-4445 E-mail: peopleandengagement@nelson.com Web Site: www.nelson.com, pg 464

Phua, Max, World Scientific Publishing Co Inc, 27 Warren St, Suite 401-402, Hackensack, NJ 07601 Tel: 201-487-9655 Fax: 201-487-9656 E-mail: wspc_us@wspc.com; sales@wspc.com; mkt@wspc.com; editor@wspc.com Web Site: www.worldscientific.com, pg 260

Phuna, K K, World Scientific Publishing Co Inc, 27 Warren St, Suite 401-402, Hackensack, NJ 07601 Tel: 201-487-9655 Fax: 201-487-9656 E-mail: wspc_us@wspc.com; sales@wspc.com; mkt@wspc.com; editor@wspc.com Web Site: www.worldscientific.com, pg 260

Picazio, Mr Ryan, Hackett Publishing Co Inc, 3333 Massachusetts Ave, Indianapolis, IN 46218 Tel: 317-635-9250 (orders & cust serv); 617-497-6303 (edit off & sales) Fax: 317-635-9292; 617-661-8703 (edit off) Toll Free Fax: 800-783-9213 E-mail: customer@hackettpublishing.com; editorial@hackettpublishing.com Web Site: www.hackettpublishing.com, pg 99

Pickett, Patty, Accuity, 4709 W Golf Rd, Skokie, IL 60076 Tel: 847-676-9600 Toll Free Tel: 800-321-3373 Fax: 847-933-8101 E-mail: custserv@accuity.com; sales@accuity.com Web Site: www.accuity.com, pg 3

Pientka, Cheryl, Jill Grinberg Literary Management LLC, 392 Vanderbilt Ave, Brooklyn, NY 11238 Tel: 212-620-5883 E-mail: info@jillgrinbergliterary.com Web Site: www.jillgrinbergliterary.com, pg 520

Pieper, Molly, Plume, 375 Hudson St, New York, NY 10014 Tel: 212-366-2000 Fax: 212-243-6002 Web Site: www.penguin.com/publishers/plume, pg 184

Pierce, Carol, National Federation of Press Women Inc (NFPW), PO Box 3007, Mechanicsville, VA 23116-0026 Tel: 703-237-9804 Fax: 703-237-9808 E-mail: presswomen@aol.com Web Site: www.nfpw.org, pg 572

Pierce, Gregory, ACTA Publications, 4848 N Clark St, Chicago, IL 60640 Tel: 773-271-1030 Toll Free Tel: 800-397-2282 Fax: 773-271-7399 Toll Free Fax: 800-397-0079 E-mail: info@actapublications.com Web Site: www.actapublications.com, pg 4

Pierce, Valerie, Sourcebooks Inc, 1935 Brookdale Rd, Suite 139, Naperville, IL 60563 Tel: 630-961-3900 Toll Free Tel: 800-432-7444 Fax: 630-961-2168 E-mail: info@sourcebooks.com; customersupport@sourcebooks.com Web Site: www.sourcebooks.com, pg 218

Piergies, Mary, Manning Publications Co, PO Box 761, Shelter Island, NY 11964 Tel: 203-626-1510 E-mail: sales@manning.com; support@manning.com (cust serv) Web Site: www.manning.com, pg 141

Pierpont, Amy, Grand Central Publishing, 1290 Avenue of the Americas, New York, NY 10019 Tel: 212-364-1100 Web Site: www.hachettebookgroup.com, pg 95

Piersanti, Steven, Berrett-Koehler Publishers Inc, 1333 Broadway, Suite 1000, Oakland, CA 94612 Tel: 510-817-2277 Fax: 510-817-2278 E-mail: bkpub@bkpub.com Web Site: www.bkconnection.com, pg 34

Pierson, Caryl K, Math Teachers Press Inc, 4850 Park Glen Rd, Minneapolis, MN 55416 Tel: 952-545-6535 Toll Free Tel: 800-852-2435 Fax: 952-546-7502 E-mail: info@movingwithmath.com Web Site: www.movingwithmath.com, pg 144

Pierson, Jennifer deForest, Rizzoli International Publications Inc, 300 Park Ave S, 4th fl, New York, NY 10010-5399 Tel: 212-387-3400 Toll Free Tel: 800-522-6657 (orders only) Fax: 212-387-3535 E-mail: publicity@rizzoliusa.com Web Site: www.rizzoliusa.com, pg 199

Piervincenzi, Ronald T PhD, United States Pharmacopeia, 12601 Twinbrook Pkwy, Rockville, MD 20852-1790 Tel: 301-881-0666 Toll Free Tel: 800-227-8772 Fax: 301-816-8237 (mktg) E-mail: marketing@usp.org Web Site: www.usp.org, pg 239

Pietsch, Michael, Hachette Book Group, 1290 Avenue of the Americas, New York, NY 10019 Tel: 212-364-1100 Toll Free Tel: 800-759-0190 (cust serv) Fax: 212-364-0933 (intl orders) Toll Free Fax: 800-286-9471 (cust serv) Web Site: www.hachettebookgroup.com, pg 98

Pigeon, Bob, Perseus Books, 250 W 57 St, 15th fl, New York, NY 10107 Tel: 212-340-8100 Toll Free Tel: 800-343-4499 (cust serv) Fax: 212-340-8105 Web Site: www.perseusbooks.com, pg 181

Pike, Bryan, The BC Book Prizes, 207 W Hastings St, Suite 901, Vancouver, BC V6B 1H7, Canada Fax: 604-687-2435 E-mail: info@bcbookprizes.ca Web Site: www.bcbookprizes.ca, pg 630

Pike, Nadyne, Sterling Lord Literistic Inc, 115 Broadway, Suite 1602, New York, NY 10006 Tel: 212-780-6050 Fax: 212-780-6095 E-mail: info@sll.com Web Site: www.sll.com, pg 537

Pike, Paula, Emond Montgomery Publications Ltd, 60 Shaftesbury Ave, Toronto, ON M4T 1A3, Canada Tel: 416-975-3925 Toll Free Tel: 888-837-0815 Fax: 416-975-3924 E-mail: orders@emp.ca Web Site: www.emp.ca, pg 456

Pilguy, Natalya, Workman Publishing Co Inc, 225 Varick St, 9th fl, New York, NY 10014-4381 Tel: 212-254-5900 Toll Free Tel: 800-722-7202 Fax: 212-254-8098 E-mail: info@workman.com Web Site: www.workman.com, pg 259

Pillai, Devi, Tom Doherty Associates, LLC, 175 Fifth Ave, 14th fl, New York, NY 10010 Tel: 646-307-5511 Toll Free Tel: 800-455-0340 Web Site: www.tor-forge.com, pg 71

Pilo, Nicole, Women's National Book Association Award, PO Box 237, FDR Sta, New York, NY 10150-0231 Tel: 212-208-4629 (headquarters) Toll Free Tel: 866-610-9622 Fax: 212-208-4629 Web Site: www.wnba-books.org; www.NationalReadingGroupMonth.org, pg 699

Pimentel, Sasha, University of Texas at El Paso, Department of Creative Writing, MFA/Department of Creative Writing, 901 EDUC, 500 W University Ave, El Paso, TX 79968-9991 Tel: 915-747-5713 Fax: 915-747-5523 E-mail: creativewriting@utep.edu Web Site: www.utep.edu/cw, pg 624

Pimlott, Philip, Gravure Association of the Americas Inc, 8281 Pine Lake Rd, Denver, NC 28037 Tel: 201-523-6042 Fax: 201-523-6048 E-mail: gaa@gaa.org Web Site: www.gaa.org, pg 566

Pincus, Caroline, Caroline Pincus Book Midwife, 101 Wool St, San Francisco, CA 94110 Tel: 415-516-6206 E-mail: caroline@carolinepincus.com Web Site: carolinepincus.com, pg 500

Pincus, Caroline, Sounds True Inc, 413 S Arthur Ave, Louisville, CO 80027 Tel: 303-665-3151 Toll Free Tel: 800-333-9185 E-mail: customerservice@soundstrue.com; sales@soundstrue.com Web Site: www.soundstrue.com, pg 217

Pine, Ralph, Quite Specific Media Group Ltd, 141 N Clark Dr, Unit 1, West Hollywood, CA 90048 Tel: 310-205-0665 E-mail: info@silmanjamespress.com Web Site: www.quitespecificmedia.com; www.silmanjamespress.com, pg 193

Pine, Richard S, InkWell Management, 521 Fifth Ave, 26th fl, New York, NY 10175 Tel: 212-922-3500 Fax: 212-922-0535 E-mail: info@inkwellmanagement.com Web Site: inkwellmanagement.com, pg 522

Pinkney, Andrea, Scholastic Trade Division, 557 Broadway, New York, NY 10012 *Tel:* 212-343-6100; 212-343-4685 (export sales) *Fax:* 212-343-4714 (export sales) *Web Site:* www.scholastic.com, pg 208

Pinney, Marilyn R, EDC Publishing, 10302 E 55 Place, Tulsa, OK 74146-6515 *Tel:* 918-622-4522 *Toll Free Tel:* 800-475-4522 *Fax:* 918-665-7919 *Toll Free Fax:* 800-743-5660 *E-mail:* edc@edcpub.com *Web Site:* www.edcpub.com, pg 75

Pinsker, Joanna, Hachette Books, 1290 Avenue of the Americas, New York, NY 10019 *Tel:* 212-364-1100 *Web Site:* www.hachettebookgroup.com, pg 98

Pinsky, Prof Robert, Boston University Creative Writing Program, 236 Bay State Rd, Boston, MA 02215 *Tel:* 617-353-2510 *Fax:* 617-353-3653 *E-mail:* crwr@bu.edu *Web Site:* www.bu.edu/creativewriting, pg 619

Pinson, Linda, Out of Your Mind...and Into the Marketplace™, 13381 White Sand Dr, Tustin, CA 92780-4565 *Tel:* 714-544-0248 *Toll Free Tel:* 800-419-1513 *Fax:* 714-730-1414 *Web Site:* www.business-plan.com, pg 171

Pintaudi-Jones, Rose, Oxford University Press USA, 198 Madison Ave, New York, NY 10016 *Tel:* 212-726-6000 *Toll Free Tel:* 800-451-7556 (orders); 800-445-9714 (cust serv) *Fax:* 919-677-1303 *E-mail:* custserv.us@oup.com *Web Site:* www.oup.com/us, pg 171

Pinter, Jason, Polis Books, 1201 Hudson St, No 211S, Hoboken, NJ 07030 *E-mail:* info@polisbooks.com; submissions@polisbooks.com *Web Site:* www.polisbooks.com; facebook.com/PolisBooks; twitter.com/PolisBooks, pg 185

Pinto, Matthew, Ascension Press, PO Box 1990, West Chester, PA 19380 *Tel:* 610-696-7795; 484-875-4550 (admin) *Toll Free Tel:* 800-376-0520 (sales & cust serv) *Web Site:* ascensionpress.com, pg 22

Pires, Lauren, Simon & Schuster Audio, 1230 Avenue of the Americas, New York, NY 10020 *Web Site:* audio.simonandschuster.com, pg 213

Pitaro, James, Disney Publishing Worldwide, 1101 Flower St, Glendale, CA 91201 *Web Site:* books.disney.com, pg 71

Pitoniak, Anna, Random House Publishing Group, 1745 Broadway, New York, NY 10019 *Toll Free Tel:* 800-200-3552 *Web Site:* atrandom.com, pg 195

Pittman, Judith, Books We Love Ltd, 100 Chinook Winds Place SW, Unit 4407, Airdrie, AB T4B 4B4, Canada *Tel:* 403-710-4869 *E-mail:* bookswelove@telus.net *Web Site:* bookswelove.net; www.facebook.com/Books.We.Love.Ltd, pg 447

Pitts, John, Doubleday/Nan A Talese, c/o Penguin Random House Inc, 1745 Broadway, New York, NY 10019 *Tel:* 212-751-2600 *Fax:* 212-572-2662 *E-mail:* ddaypub@randomhouse.com *Web Site:* knopfdoubleday.com, pg 72

Pitts, Kathryn D, University of Notre Dame Press, 310 Flanner Hall, Notre Dame, IN 46556 *Tel:* 574-631-6346 *Fax:* 574-631-8148 *E-mail:* undpress@nd.edu *Web Site:* www.undpress.nd.edu, pg 244

Pitts, Melissa, University of British Columbia Press, 2029 West Mall, Vancouver, BC V6T 1Z2, Canada *Tel:* 604-822-5959 *Toll Free Tel:* 877-377-9378 *Fax:* 604-822-6083 *Toll Free Fax:* 800-668-0821 *E-mail:* frontdesk@ubcpress.ca *Web Site:* www.ubcpress.ca, pg 473

Pitts, Naomi, New York State Bar Association, One Elk St, Albany, NY 12207 *Tel:* 518-463-3200 *Toll Free Tel:* 800-582-2452 *Fax:* 518-487-5517 *E-mail:* mrc@nysba.org *Web Site:* www.nysba.org, pg 162

Pitts, Stephanie, Random House Children's Books, 1745 Broadway, 10th fl, New York, NY 10019 *Tel:* 212-782-9000 *Web Site:* www.randomhousekids.com, pg 194

Pjandra, Lia, University of California Press, 155 Grand Ave, Suite 400, Oakland, CA 94612-3758 *Tel:* 510-883-8232 *Fax:* 510-836-8910 *E-mail:* customerservice@ucpressjournals.com *Web Site:* www.ucpress.edu, pg 240

Plafsky, Danielle, Alfred A Knopf/Everyman's Library, c/o Penguin Random House Inc, 1745 Broadway, New York, NY 10019 *Tel:* 212-751-2600 *Toll Free Tel:* 800-638-6460 *Fax:* 212-572-2593 *Web Site:* www.knopfdoubleday.com, pg 127

Plafsky, Danielle, Pantheon Books/Schocken Books, c/o Penguin Random House Inc, 1745 Broadway, New York, NY 10019 *Tel:* 212-751-2600 *Web Site:* knopfdoubleday.com/imprint/pantheon, pg 173

Plant, Alisa, University of Nebraska Press, 1111 Lincoln Mall, Lincoln, NE 68588-0630 *Tel:* 402-472-3581; 919-966-7449 (cust serv & foreign orders) *Toll Free Tel:* 800-848-6224 (cust serv & US orders) *Fax:* 402-472-6214; 919-962-2704 (cust serv & foreign orders) *Toll Free Fax:* 800-526-2617 (cust serv & US orders) *E-mail:* pressmail@unl.edu *Web Site:* www.nebraskapress.unl.edu, pg 243

Plantier, Paula, EditAmerica, 115 Jacobs Creek Rd, Ewing, NJ 08628 *Tel:* 609-882-5852 *Web Site:* www.editamerica.com; www.linkedin.com/in/PaulaPlantier, pg 493

Plata, Glory, Riverhead Books, 375 Hudson St, New York, NY 10014 *Tel:* 212-366-2000 *Web Site:* www.penguin.com/publishers/riverhead, pg 199

Platkin, Charles, Diversion Books, 443 Park Ave S, Suite 1008, New York, NY 10016 *Tel:* 212-961-6390 *E-mail:* info@diversionbooks.com *Web Site:* www.diversionbooks.com, pg 71

Platt, Julie M, SAS Publishing, 100 SAS Campus Dr, Cary, NC 27513-2414 *Tel:* 919-677-8000 *Toll Free Tel:* 800-727-0025 *Fax:* 919-677-4444 *E-mail:* saspress@sas.com *Web Site:* www.sas.com/publishing, pg 206

Plunkett, Jack W, Plunkett Research Ltd, PO Drawer 541737, Houston, TX 77254-1737 *Tel:* 713-932-0000 *Fax:* 713-932-7080 *E-mail:* customersupport@plunkettresearch.com *Web Site:* www.plunkettresearch.com, pg 184

Pneuman, Angela, Napa Valley Writers' Conference, 1088 College Ave, St Helena, CA 94574 *Tel:* 707-967-2900 (ext 4) *Fax:* 707-967-2909 *E-mail:* info@napawritersconference.org; media@napawritersconference.org; fiction@napawritersconference.org; poetry@napawritersconference.org *Web Site:* www.napawritersconference.org, pg 613

Pochron, J P, J P Pochron Writer for Hire, 830 Lake Orchid Circle, No 203, Vero Beach, FL 32962 *Tel:* 772-569-2967 *E-mail:* hotwriter15@hotmail.com, pg 500

Podos, Rebecca, Rees Literary Agency, 14 Beacon St, Suite 710, Boston, MA 02108 *Tel:* 617-227-9014 *Fax:* 617-227-8762 *Web Site:* www.reesagency.com, pg 532

Podrasky, Bob, Recorded Books Inc, an RBmedia company, 270 Skipjack Rd, Prince Frederick, MD 20678 *Tel:* 410-535-5590 *Toll Free Tel:* 877-732-2898 *Fax:* 410-535-5499 *E-mail:* customerservice@recordedbooks.com *Web Site:* www.recordedbooks.com, pg 196

Poelle, Barbara, Irene Goodman Literary Agency, 27 W 24 St, Suite 700B, New York, NY 10010 *Tel:* 212-604-0330 *E-mail:* queries@irenegoodman.com *Web Site:* www.irenegoodman.com, pg 519

Poettcker, Jess, Books We Love Ltd, 100 Chinook Winds Place SW, Unit 4407, Airdrie, AB T4B 4B4, Canada *Tel:* 403-710-4869 *E-mail:* bookswelove@telus.net *Web Site:* bookswelove.net; www.facebook.com/Books.We.Love.Ltd, pg 447

Poggione, Mary, Minnesota Historical Society Press, 345 Kellogg Blvd W, St Paul, MN 55102-1906 *Tel:* 651-259-3205 *Toll Free Tel:* 800-621-2736 (warehouse) *Fax:* 651-297-1345 *Toll Free Fax:* 800-621-8476 (warehouse) *E-mail:* info-mnhspress@mnhs.org *Web Site:* www.mnhs.org/mnhspress, pg 151

Pogodzinski, Mark, No Frills Buffalo, 119 Dorchester Rd, Buffalo, NY 14213 *Tel:* 716-510-0520 *E-mail:* contact@nofrillsbuffalo.com; submissions@nofrillsbuffalo.com *Web Site:* www.nofrillsbuffalo.com, pg 162

Pogorzelski, Steve, Avention Inc, 300 Baker Ave, Concord, MA 01742 *Tel:* 978-318-4300 *Toll Free Tel:* 866-354-6936 *Fax:* 978-318-4690 *E-mail:* sales@avention.com *Web Site:* www.avention.com, pg 27

Pohland, Liz, Society for Technical Communication, 9401 Lee Hwy, Suite 300, Fairfax, VA 22031 *Tel:* 703-522-4114 *Fax:* 703-522-2075 *E-mail:* stc@stc.org *Web Site:* www.stc.org, pg 578

Pohlen, Jerome, Chicago Review Press, 814 N Franklin St, Chicago, IL 60610 *Tel:* 312-337-0747 *Toll Free Tel:* 800-888-4741 *Fax:* 312-337-5110 *E-mail:* frontdesk@chicagoreviewpress.com *Web Site:* www.chicagoreviewpress.com, pg 54

Pointer, Ryan, Annual Off Off Broadway Short Play Festival, 235 Park Ave S, 5th fl, New York, NY 10003 *Tel:* 212-206-8990 *Toll Free Tel:* 866-598-8449 *Fax:* 212-206-1429 *E-mail:* oobfestival@samuelfrench.com *Web Site:* oob.samuelfrench.com; www.samuelfrench.com, pg 675

Poirier, Etienne, Ecrits des Forges, 992-A rue Royale, Trois-Rivieres, QC G9A 4H9, Canada *Tel:* 819-840-8492 *E-mail:* ecritsdesforges@gmail.com *Web Site:* www.ecritsdesforges.com, pg 452

Pola, Matthew Dela, Piano Press, 1425 Ocean Ave, Suite 5, Del Mar, CA 92014 *Tel:* 619-884-1401 *Fax:* 858-755-1104 *E-mail:* pianopress@pianopress.com *Web Site:* www.pianopress.com, pg 182

Polachek, Grant, Institute of Environmental Sciences & Technology - IEST, 2340 S Arlington Heights Rd, Suite 620, Arlington Heights, IL 60005-4510 *Tel:* 847-981-0100 *Fax:* 847-981-4130 *E-mail:* information@iest.org *Web Site:* www.iest.org, pg 118

Polansky, Debra, Penguin Young Readers Group, 345 Hudson St, New York, NY 10014 *Tel:* 212-366-2000; 212-414-3553 *Fax:* 212-414-3340 *Web Site:* www.penguin.com/children, pg 179

Polese, Richard, New Mexico Book Association (NMBA), 1219 Luisa St, Suite 1, Santa Fe, NM 87505 *Tel:* 505-660-6357 *E-mail:* admin@nmbook.org *Web Site:* www.nmbook.org, pg 573

Polese, Richard, Ocean Tree Books, 1325 Cerro Gordo Rd, Santa Fe, NM 87501 *Tel:* 505-983-1412 *Fax:* 505-983-0899 *Web Site:* www.oceantree.com, pg 166

Polin, Cathy, Manhattan Publishing Co, 670 White Plains Rd, Scarsdale, NY 10583 *Tel:* 914-472-4650 *Fax:* 914-472-4316 *E-mail:* coe@manhattanpublishing.com *Web Site:* www.manhattanpublishing.com, pg 141

Polin, Kenneth, Manhattan Publishing Co, 670 White Plains Rd, Scarsdale, NY 10583 *Tel:* 914-472-4650 *Fax:* 914-472-4316 *E-mail:* coe@manhattanpublishing.com *Web Site:* www.manhattanpublishing.com, pg 141

Poling, Jan A, American Forest & Paper Association (AF&PA), 1101 "K" St NW, Suite 700, Washington, DC 20005 *Tel:* 202-463-2700 *E-mail:* info@afandpa.org *Web Site:* www.afandpa.org, pg 555

Poling, Victoria, Copper Canyon Press, Fort Worden State Park, Bldg 313, Port Townsend, WA 98368 *Tel:* 360-385-4925 *Toll Free Tel:* 877-501-1393 (orders) *Fax:* 360-385-4985 *E-mail:* poetry@coppercanyonpress.org *Web Site:* www.coppercanyonpress.org, pg 60

Polivka, Raina, University of California Press, 155 Grand Ave, Suite 400, Oakland, CA 94612-3758 *Tel:* 510-883-8232 *Fax:* 510-836-8910 *E-mail:* customerservice@ucpressjournals.com *Web Site:* www.ucpress.edu, pg 240

Polizzotti, Mark, The Metropolitan Museum of Art, 1000 Fifth Ave, New York, NY 10028 *Tel:* 212-879-5500; 212-570-3725 (edit) *Fax:* 212-396-5062 *E-mail:* editorial@metmuseum.org *Web Site:* www.metmuseum.org, pg 149

Polkinhorn, Prof Harry, San Diego State University Press, Arts & Letters 283/MC 6020, 5500 Campanile Dr, San Diego, CA 92182-6020 *Tel:* 619-594-6220 (orders) *E-mail:* memo@sdsu.edu *Web Site:* sdsupress.sdsu.edu, pg 205

Poll, Michael R, Cornerstone Book Publishers, PO Box 24652, New Orleans, LA 70184 *E-mail:* info@cornerstonepublishers.com *Web Site:* www.cornerstonepublishers.com, pg 61

Pollert, Annette, Sourcebooks Inc, 1935 Brookdale Rd, Suite 139, Naperville, IL 60563 *Tel:* 630-961-3900 *Toll Free Tel:* 800-432-7444 *Fax:* 630-961-2168 *E-mail:* info@sourcebooks.com; customersupport@sourcebooks.com *Web Site:* www.sourcebooks.com, pg 218

Pollock, William, No Starch Press, 245 Eighth St, San Francisco, CA 94103 *Tel:* 415-863-9900 *Toll Free Tel:* 800-420-7240 *Fax:* 415-863-9950 *E-mail:* info@nostarch.com; sales@nostarch.com *Web Site:* www.nostarch.com, pg 162

Pollock-Nelson, Anna, The MIT Press, One Rogers St, Cambridge, MA 02142 *Tel:* 617-253-5255 *Toll Free Tel:* 800-207-8354 (orders) *Fax:* 617-258-6779; 617-577-1545 (orders) *Web Site:* mitpress.mit.edu, pg 152

Poloski, Rachel, Random House Children's Books, 1745 Broadway, 10th fl, New York, NY 10019 *Tel:* 212-782-9000 *Web Site:* www.randomhousekids.com, pg 194

Polster, Emilie, Little, Brown Books for Young Readers, 1290 Avenue of the Americas, New York, NY 10019 *Tel:* 212-364-1100 *Toll Free Tel:* 800-759-0190 (cust serv) *Web Site:* www.HachetteBookGroup.com, pg 136

Polvino, Lynne, Clarion Books, 3 Park Ave, New York, NY 10016 *Tel:* 212-420-5800 *Toll Free Tel:* 800-225-3362 (orders) *Fax:* 212-420-5855 *Toll Free Fax:* 800-634-7568 (orders) *Web Site:* www.hmhco.com, pg 56

Pomerance, Ruth, Folio Literary Management, The Film Center Bldg, 630 Ninth Ave, Suite 1101, New York, NY 10036 *Tel:* 212-400-1494 *Fax:* 212-967-0977 *Web Site:* www.foliolit.com, pg 517

Pomerico, David, HarperCollins General Books Group, 195 Broadway, New York, NY 10007 *Tel:* 212-207-7000 *Web Site:* www.harpercollins.com, pg 101

Pomes, Anthony, Square One Publishers Inc, 115 Herricks Rd, Garden City Park, NY 11040 *Tel:* 516-535-2010 *Toll Free Tel:* 877-900-BOOK (900-2665) *Fax:* 516-535-2014 *E-mail:* sq1publish@aol.com *Web Site:* www.squareonepublishers.com, pg 220

Pomije, Steven, Shambhala Publications Inc, 4720 Walnut St, Boulder, CO 80301 *Tel:* 303-222-9598 *Toll Free Tel:* 866-424-0030 (off); 888-424-2329 (cust serv) *Fax:* 303-200-9406 *E-mail:* customercare@shambhala.com *Web Site:* www.shambhala.com, pg 211

Pompillo, Lisa Marie, Orbit, 1290 Avenue of the Americas, New York, NY 10019 *Tel:* 212-364-1100 *Toll Free Tel:* 800-759-0190 *Web Site:* www.orbitbooks.net, pg 169

Ponturo, Kayla, Young Lions Fiction Award, 445 Fifth Ave, 4th fl, New York, NY 10016 *Tel:* 212-930-0887 *Fax:* 212-930-0983 *E-mail:* younglions@nypl.org *Web Site:* www.nypl.org, pg 701

Poole, Kristie, The BC Book Prizes, 207 W Hastings St, Suite 901, Vancouver, BC V6B 1H7, Canada *Fax:* 604-687-2435 *E-mail:* info@bcbookprizes.ca *Web Site:* www.bcbookprizes.ca, pg 630

Poor, Edith, Montemayor Press, 663 Hyland Hill Rd, Washington, VT 05675 *Tel:* 802-552-0750 *E-mail:* mail@montemayorpress.com *Web Site:* www.montemayorpress.com, pg 153

Pope, Anna, Book Publishing Co, 415 Farm Rd, Summertown, TN 38483 *Tel:* 931-964-3571 *Fax:* 931-964-3518 *E-mail:* info@bookpubco.com *Web Site:* www.bookpubco.com, pg 39

Pope, Barbara Kline, The Johns Hopkins University Press, 2715 N Charles St, Baltimore, MD 21218-4363 *Tel:* 410-516-6900; 410-516-6987 (journal orders outside US & CN) *Toll Free Tel:* 800-537-5487 (book orders & cust serv); 800-548-1784 (journal orders) *Fax:* 410-516-6968; 410-516-3866 (journal orders) *E-mail:* hfscustserv@press.jhu.edu (cust serv); jrnlcirc@press.jhu.edu (journal orders) *Web Site:* www.press.jhu.edu; muse.jhu.edu, pg 122

Popelars, Craig, Algonquin Books, 400 Silver Cedar Ct, Suite 300, Chapel Hill, NC 27514-1585 *Tel:* 919-967-0108 *Fax:* 919-933-0272 *E-mail:* inquiry@algonquin.com *Web Site:* www.workman.com/algonquin, pg 7

Poreda, Alexandra, Other Press, 267 Fifth Ave, 6th fl, New York, NY 10016 *Tel:* 212-414-0054 *Toll Free Tel:* 877-843-6843 *Fax:* 212-414-0939 *E-mail:* editor@otherpress.com; marketing@otherpress.com; publicity@otherpress.com *Web Site:* www.otherpress.com, pg 170

Porter, Carolyn, One On One Book Publishing/Film-Video Publications, 7944 Capistrano Ave, West Hills, CA 91304 *Tel:* 818-340-6620; 818-340-0175 *Fax:* 818-340-6620 *E-mail:* onebookpro@aol.com, pg 168

Porter, Neal, Holiday House Inc, 425 Madison Ave, New York, NY 10017 *Tel:* 212-688-0085 *Fax:* 212-421-6134 *E-mail:* info@holidayhouse.com *Web Site:* www.holidayhouse.com, pg 109

Porter, Susanna, Random House Publishing Group, 1745 Broadway, New York, NY 10019 *Toll Free Tel:* 800-200-3552 *Web Site:* atrandom.com, pg 195

Portwood, Nigel, Oxford University Press USA, 198 Madison Ave, New York, NY 10016 *Tel:* 212-726-6000 *Toll Free Tel:* 800-451-7556 (orders); 800-445-9714 (cust serv) *Fax:* 919-677-1303 *E-mail:* custserv.us@oup.com *Web Site:* www.oup.com/us, pg 171

Posen, Adam, Peterson Institute for International Economics (PIIE), 1750 Massachusetts Ave NW, Washington, DC 20036-1903 *Tel:* 202-328-9000 *Fax:* 202-328-5432; 202-659-3225 *E-mail:* orders@petersoninstitute.org; media@piie.com *Web Site:* www.petersoninstitute.org, pg 181

Posesorski, Alisa, Irwin Law Inc, 14 Duncan St, Suite 206, Toronto, ON M5H 3G8, Canada *Tel:* 416-862-7690 *Toll Free Tel:* 888-314-9014 *Fax:* 416-862-9236 *Web Site:* www.irwinlaw.com, pg 461

Posner, Marcy, Folio Literary Management, The Film Center Bldg, 630 Ninth Ave, Suite 1101, New York, NY 10036 *Tel:* 212-400-1494 *Fax:* 212-967-0977 *Web Site:* www.foliolit.com, pg 517

Posner-Sanchez, Andrea, Random House Children's Books, 1745 Broadway, 10th fl, New York, NY 10019 *Tel:* 212-782-9000 *Web Site:* www.randomhousekids.com, pg 194

Poss, Marielle, Columbia University Press, 61 W 62 St, New York, NY 10023 *Tel:* 212-459-0600 *Toll Free Tel:* 800-944-8648 *Fax:* 212-459-3678 *E-mail:* cup_book@columbia.edu (orders & cust serv) *Web Site:* cup.columbia.edu, pg 59

Post, Ana, Carter G Woodson Book Awards, 8555 16 St, Suite 500, Silver Spring, MD 20910 *Tel:* 301-588-1800 *Toll Free Tel:* 800-296-7840 *Fax:* 301-588-2049 *E-mail:* excellence@ncss.org; publications@ncss.org *Web Site:* www.socialstudies.org, pg 699

Post, Chad, Best Translated Book Award, c/o Open Letter, University of Rochester, Dewey Hall 1-219, Box 278968, Rochester, NY 14627 *Tel:* 585-276-5305 *E-mail:* msc@rochester.edu *Web Site:* besttranslatedbook.org, pg 631

Post, Marcie Craig, ILA Children's & Young Adults' Book Awards, PO Box 8139, Newark, DE 19714-8139 *Tel:* 302-731-1600 *Toll Free Tel:* 800-336-7323 (US & CN) *Fax:* 302-731-1057 *E-mail:* ilaawards@reading.org *Web Site:* www.literacyworldwide.org, pg 654

Post, Marcie Craig, International Literacy Association (ILA), 800 Barksdale Rd, Newark, DE 19711-3204 *Tel:* 302 731 1600 *Toll Free Tel:* 800-336-7323 (US & CN) *Fax:* 302-731-1057 *E-mail:* customerservice@reading.org *Web Site:* www.literacyworldwide.org; www.reading.org, pg 119, 567

Post, Tom, University of Tennessee Press, 110 Conference Center Bldg, 600 Henley St, Knoxville, TN 37996-4108 *Tel:* 865-974-3321 *Toll Free Tel:* 800-621-2736 (orders) *Fax:* 865-974-3724 *Toll Free Fax:* 800-621-8476 (orders) *E-mail:* custserv@utpress.org *Web Site:* www.utpress.org, pg 245

Poster, Kendra, Algonquin Books, 400 Silver Cedar Ct, Suite 300, Chapel Hill, NC 27514-1585 *Tel:* 919-967-0108 *Fax:* 919-933-0272 *E-mail:* inquiry@algonquin.com *Web Site:* www.workman.com/algonquin, pg 7

Posternak, Jeffrey, The Wylie Agency LLC, 250 W 57 St, Suite 2114, New York, NY 10107 *Tel:* 212-246-0069 *Fax:* 212-586-8953 *E-mail:* mail@wylieagency.com *Web Site:* www.wylieagency.com, pg 542

Poston, Ann, The Pilgrim Press/United Church Press, 700 Prospect Ave, Cleveland, OH 44115-1100 *Tel:* 216-736-2100 *Toll Free Tel:* 800-537-3394 (orders) *Fax:* 216-736-2207 (orders) *E-mail:* permissions@thepilgrimpress.com; store@ucc.org *Web Site:* www.thepilgrimpress.com; www.uccresources.com, pg 183

Potash, Dan, Simon & Schuster Children's Publishing, 1230 Avenue of the Americas, New York, NY 10020 *Tel:* 212-698-7000 *Web Site:* www.simonandschuster.com/kids; www.simonandschuster.com/teen; simonandschuster.net; simonandschuster.biz, pg 213

Potorti, David, North Carolina Arts Council Writers Fellowships, 109 E Jones St, Raleigh, NC 27601 *Tel:* 919-807-6500 *Fax:* 919-807-6532 *E-mail:* ncarts@ncdcr.gov *Web Site:* www.ncarts.org, pg 674

Pottebaum, Gerard A, Treehaus Communications Inc, PO Box 249, Loveland, OH 45140-0249 *Tel:* 513-683-5716 *Toll Free Tel:* 800-638-4287 (orders) *Fax:* 513-683-2882 (orders) *E-mail:* treehaus@treehaus1.com *Web Site:* www.treehaus1.com, pg 235

Potter, Donn King, Elizabeth H Backman, 86 Johnnycake Hollow Rd, Pine Plains, NY 12567 *Tel:* 518-398-9344 *Fax:* 518-398-6368 *E-mail:* bethcountry@fairpoint.net, pg 507

Potter, Dr Beverly, Ronin Publishing Inc, PO Box 3436, Oakland, CA 94609 *Tel:* 510-420-3669 *Fax:* 510-420-3672 *E-mail:* ronin@roninpub.com *Web Site:* www.roninpub.com, pg 201

Potter, Peter, Cornell University Press, Sage House, 512 E State St, Ithaca, NY 14850 *Tel:* 607-277-2338 *Fax:* 607-277-2374 *E-mail:* cupressinfo@cornell.edu; cupress-sales@cornell.edu *Web Site:* www.cornellpress.cornell.edu, pg 61

Pottetti, Kathy, Gell: A Finger Lakes Creative Retreat, 740 University Ave, Rochester, NY 14607-1259 *Tel:* 585-473-2590 *Fax:* 585-442-9333 *Web Site:* www.wab.org, pg 611

Potts, Patricia, BuilderBooks.com, 1201 15 St NW, Washington, DC 20005 *Tel:* 202-822-0200 *Toll Free Tel:* 800-223-2665 *Fax:* 202-266-8096 (edit) *E-mail:* builderbooks@nahb.com *Web Site:* www.builderbooks.com, pg 45

Poulin, Joseph R, The Scriptural Research & Publishing Co Inc, 344 E Johnson Ave, Cheshire, CT 06410 *Tel:* 203-272-1780 *Fax:* 203-272-2296 *E-mail:* src1@srpublish.org *Web Site:* www.scripturalresearch.com, pg 210

Pound, William T, National Conference of State Legislatures (NCSL), 7700 E First Place, Denver, CO 80230 *Tel:* 303-364-7700 *Fax:* 303-364-7800 *E-mail:* books@ncsl.org *Web Site:* www.ncsl.org, pg 157

Pourciau, Emily, Random House Children's Books, 1745 Broadway, 10th fl, New York, NY 10019 *Tel:* 212-782-9000 *Web Site:* www.randomhousekids.com, pg 194

Powell, Jan, Alpha II LLC, 7480 Halcyon Pointe Dr, Suite 204, Montgomery, AL 36117 *Tel:* 334-260-8150 *Toll Free Tel:* 800-825-7421 *Toll Free Fax:* 800-305-8030 *E-mail:* sales@alphaii.com *Web Site:* www.alphaii.com, pg 8

Powell, Judith, Top of the Mountain Publishing, 4837 62 St N, St Petersburg, FL 33709 *Tel:* 727-391-3958 *Web Site:* www.topofthemountain.com, pg 233

Powell, Sherri, Contemporary Publishing Co of Raleigh Inc, 5849 Lease Lane, Raleigh, NC 27617 *Tel:* 919-851-8221 *Fax:* 919-851-6666 *E-mail:* questions@contemporarypublishing.com *Web Site:* www.contemporarypublishing.com, pg 60

Powell, Tag, Top of the Mountain Publishing, 4837 62 St N, St Petersburg, FL 33709 *Tel:* 727-391-3958 *Web Site:* www.topofthemountain.com, pg 233

Power, Daniel, powerHouse Books, 37 Main St, Brooklyn, NY 11201 *Tel:* 212-604-9074 *E-mail:* info@powerhousebooks.com *Web Site:* www.powerhousebooks.com, pg 186

Power, Stephen, St Martin's Press, LLC, 175 Fifth Ave, New York, NY 10010 *Tel:* 646-307-5151 *Web Site:* us.macmillan.com/smp, pg 204

Powers, David, Pants On Fire Press, 2062 Harbor Cove Way, Winter Garden, FL 34787 *Tel:* 863-546-0760 *E-mail:* submission@pantsonfirepress.com *Web Site:* www.pantsonfirepress.com, pg 173

Powers, Joan, Candlewick Press, 99 Dover St, Somerville, MA 02144-2825 *Tel:* 617-661-3330 *Fax:* 617-661-0565 *E-mail:* bigbear@candlewick.com; salesinfo@candlewick.com *Web Site:* www.candlewick.com, pg 46

Powers, Marcia, Wilshire Book Co, 22647 Ventura Blvd, No 314, Woodland Hills, CA 91364-1416 *Tel:* 818-700-1522 *E-mail:* sales@mpowers.com *Web Site:* www.mpowers.com, pg 257

Powers, Retha, Publishing Certificate Program at City College of New York, Division of Humanities NAC 5225, City College of New York, New York, NY 10031 *Tel:* 212-650-7925 *Fax:* 212-650-7912 *E-mail:* ccnypub@aol.com *Web Site:* www.ccny.cuny.edu/publishing_certificate/index.html, pg 622

Powers, Thomas, Steerforth Press, 45 Lyme Rd, Suite 208, Hanover, NH 03755-1222 *Tel:* 603-643-4787 *Fax:* 603-643-4788 *E-mail:* info@steerforth.com *Web Site:* www.steerforth.com, pg 221

Pozier, Bernard, Ecrits des Forges, 992-A rue Royale, Trois-Rivieres, QC G9A 4H9, Canada *Tel:* 819-840-8492 *E-mail:* ecritsdesforges@gmail.com *Web Site:* www.ecritsdesforges.com, pg 452

Prabhu, Prashant, Lumina Datamatics Inc, 4 Collins Ave, Plymouth, MA 02360 *Tel:* 508-746-0300 *Fax:* 508-746-3233 *Web Site:* luminadatamatics.com, pg 497

Pracher, Richard, Henry Holt and Company, LLC, 175 Fifth Ave, New York, NY 10010 *Tel:* 646-307-5151 *Toll Free Tel:* 888-330-8477 (orders) *Fax:* 646-307-5285 *E-mail:* firstname.lastname@hholt.com *Web Site:* www.henryholt.com, pg 109

Praded, Joni, Chelsea Green Publishing Co, 85 N Main St, Suite 120, White River Junction, VT 05001 *Tel:* 802-295-6300 *Toll Free Tel:* 800-639-4099 (cust serv, consumer & trade orders) *Fax:* 802-295-6444 *Web Site:* www.chelseagreen.com, pg 53

Praeger, Marta, Robert A Freedman Dramatic Agency Inc, 1501 Broadway, Suite 2310, New York, NY 10036 *Tel:* 212-840-5760 *Fax:* 212-840-5776, pg 518

Pranzatelli, Robert, Yale University Press, 302 Temple St, New Haven, CT 06511-8909 *Tel:* 203-432-0960; 203-432-0966 (sales); 401-531-2800 (cust serv) *Toll Free Tel:* 800-405-1619 (cust serv) *Fax:* 203-432-0948; 203-432-8485 (sales); 401-531-2801 (cust serv) *Toll Free Fax:* 800-406-9145 (cust serv) *E-mail:* sales.press@yale.edu (sales); customer.care@triliteral.org (cust serv) *Web Site:* www.yalebooks.com; yalepress.yale.edu/yupbooks, pg 261

Prasher, Madhu, Perseus Books, 250 W 57 St, 15th fl, New York, NY 10107 *Tel:* 212-340-8100 *Toll Free Tel:* 800-343-4499 (cust serv) *Fax:* 212-340-8105 *Web Site:* www.perseusbooks.com, pg 180

Pratt, Darrin, University Press of Colorado, 5589 Arapahoe Ave, Suite 206-C, Boulder, CO 80303 *Tel:* 720-406-8849 *Toll Free Tel:* 800-621-2736 (orders) *Fax:* 720-406-3443 *Web Site:* www.upcolorado.com, pg 246

Pratt, Darrin, Utah State University Press, 3078 Old Main Hill, Logan, UT 84322-3078 *Tel:* 435-797-1362 *Web Site:* www.usupress.com, pg 249

Precourt, Geoffrey, Advertising Research Foundation (ARF), 432 Park Ave S, 4th fl, New York, NY 10016-8013 *Tel:* 212-751-5656 *Fax:* 212-319-5265 *E-mail:* info@thearf.org; jar@thearf.org (edit) *Web Site:* www.thearf.org, pg 553

Preeg, Jessica, St Martin's Press, LLC, 175 Fifth Ave, New York, NY 10010 *Tel:* 646-307-5151 *Web Site:* us.macmillan.com/smp, pg 204

Prellwitz, Gwendolyn, Coretta Scott King Book Awards, 50 E Huron St, Chicago, IL 60611 *Toll Free Tel:* 800-545-2433 *E-mail:* olos@ala.org *Web Site:* www.ala.org/emiert/cskbookawards, pg 658

Prentiss, Winnie, Fair Winds Press, 100 Cummings Ctr, Suite 406-L, Beverly, MA 01915 *Tel:* 978-282-9590 *Fax:* 978-282-7765 *E-mail:* sales@quarto.com *Web Site:* www.quartoknows.com, pg 81

Prentiss, Winnie, The Harvard Common Press, 100 Cummings Ctr, Suite 265-D, Beverly, MA 01915 *Tel:* 978-282-9590 *Fax:* 978-282-7765 *Web Site:* www.quartoknows.com/harvard-common-press, pg 102

Prescott, Deborah, Creative Writing Day & Workshops, PO Box 801, Abingdon, VA 24212-0801 *Tel:* 276-623-5266 *Fax:* 276-676-3076 *E-mail:* info@vahighlandsfestival.org *Web Site:* vahighlandsfestival.org, pg 610

Presley, Ali, Chronicle Books LLC, 680 Second St, San Francisco, CA 94107 *Tel:* 415-537-4200 *Toll Free Tel:* 800-759-0190 (cust serv) *Fax:* 415-537-4460 *Toll Free Fax:* 800-858-7787 (orders); 800-286-9471 (cust serv) *E-mail:* frontdesk@chroniclebooks.com *Web Site:* www.chroniclebooks.com, pg 55

Presley, Ron, Florida Outdoor Writers Association Inc, 24 NW 33 Ct, Suite A, Gainesville, FL 32607 *Tel:* 352-284-1763 *E-mail:* info@fowa.org *Web Site:* www.fowa.org, pg 565

Presley, Todd, Chronicle Books LLC, 680 Second St, San Francisco, CA 94107 *Tel:* 415-537-4200 *Toll Free Tel:* 800-759-0190 (cust serv) *Fax:* 415-537-4460 *Toll Free Fax:* 800-858-7787 (orders); 800-286-9471 (cust serv) *E-mail:* frontdesk@chroniclebooks.com *Web Site:* www.chroniclebooks.com, pg 55

Prevette, Lindsay, Viking, 375 Hudson St, New York, NY 10014 *Tel:* 212-366-2000 *Fax:* 212-243-6002 *Web Site:* www.penguin.com/publishers/vikingbooks, pg 250

Pricci, Linda, Rizzoli International Publications Inc, 300 Park Ave S, 4th fl, New York, NY 10010-5399 *Tel:* 212-387-3400 *Toll Free Tel:* 800-522-6657 (orders only) *Fax:* 212-387-3535 *E-mail:* publicity@rizzoliusa.com *Web Site:* www.rizzoliusa.com, pg 199

Price, B Byron, University of Oklahoma Press, 2800 Venture Dr, Norman, OK 73069-8216 *Tel:* 405-325-2000 *Toll Free Tel:* 800-627-7377 (orders) *Fax:* 405-364-5798 (orders) *Toll Free Fax:* 800-735-0476 (orders) *E-mail:* presscs@ou.edu *Web Site:* www.oupress.com, pg 244

Price, Bernadette B, Orbis Books, Price Bldg, Box 302, Maryknoll, NY 10545-0302 *Tel:* 914-941-7636 *Toll Free Tel:* 800-258-5838 (orders) *Fax:* 914-941-7005 *E-mail:* orbisbooks@maryknoll.org *Web Site:* orbisbooks.com, pg 169

Price, Bruce, Marathon Press, 1500 Square Turn Blvd, Norfolk, NE 68701 *Tel:* 402-371-5040 *Toll Free Tel:* 800-228-0629 *Fax:* 402-371-9382 *Web Site:* www.marathonpress.com, pg 141

Price, Jodi, Princeton University Press, 41 William St, Princeton, NJ 08540-5237 *Tel:* 609-258-4900 *Fax:* 609-258-6305 *Web Site:* press.princeton.edu, pg 188

Price, Mathew, Mathew Price International Inc, 2404 W Main St, Wailuku, HI 96793 *Tel:* 808-244-9585 *E-mail:* info@mathewprice.com *Web Site:* www.mathewprice.com, pg 187

Price, Robert, Gatekeeper Press, 3971 Hoover Rd, Suite 77, Columbus, OH 43123-2839 *Toll Free Tel:* 866-535-0913 *Fax:* 216-803-0350 *E-mail:* info@gatekeeperpress.com *Web Site:* www.gatekeeperpress.com, pg 90

Price, Robert Esq, Price World Publishing, 3971 Hoover Rd, Suite 77, Columbus, OH 43123-2839 *Toll Free Tel:* 888-234-6896 *Fax:* 216-803-0350 *E-mail:* info@priceworldpublishing.com *Web Site:* www.priceworldpublishing.com, pg 187

Price, Todd Alan, Stanley Drama Award, One Campus Rd, Staten Island, NY 10301 *Tel:* 718-390-3223 *Fax:* 718-390-3323 *Web Site:* wagner.edu/theatre/stanley-drama, pg 691

Prichard, Rob, Penguin Group (Canada), 320 Front St W, Suite 1400, Toronto, ON M5V 3B6, Canada *Tel:* 416-364-4449 *Fax:* 416-598-7764 *E-mail:* customerservicescanada@penguinrandomhouse.com; publicity@ca.penguingroup.com *Web Site:* penguinrandomhouse.ca/imprints/penguin-canada, pg 466

Priddis, Ronald L, Signature Books Publishing LLC, 564 W 400 N, Salt Lake City, UT 84116-3411 *Tel:* 801-531-1483 *Fax:* 801-531-1488 *E-mail:* people@signaturebooks.com *Web Site:* www.signaturebooks.com; www.signaturebookslibrary.org, pg 212

Priddle, Clive, Perseus Books, 250 W 57 St, 15th fl, New York, NY 10107 *Tel:* 212-340-8100 *Toll Free Tel:* 800-343-4499 (cust serv) *Fax:* 212-340-8105 *Web Site:* www.perseusbooks.com, pg 180

Priddy, Kristine, Southern Illinois University Press, 1915 University Press Dr, SIUC Mail Code 6806, Carbondale, IL 62901-4323 *Tel:* 618-453-2281 *Fax:* 618-453-1221 *E-mail:* custserv@press.uchicago.edu; rights@siu.edu *Web Site:* www.siupress.com, pg 218

Pride, Christine, Simon & Schuster, 1230 Avenue of the Americas, New York, NY 10020 *Tel:* 212-698-7000 *Toll Free Tel:* 800-223-2348 (cust serv); 800-223-2336 (orders) *Toll Free Fax:* 800-943-9831 (orders) *Web Site:* www.simonandschuster.com, pg 212

Priest, Aaron M, The Aaron M Priest Literary Agency Inc, 200 W 41 St, 21st fl, New York, NY 10036 *Tel:* 212-818-0344 *Fax:* 212-573-9417 *E-mail:* info@aaronpriest.com *Web Site:* www.aaronpriest.com, pg 532

Prieur, Richard, Association Nationale des Editeurs de Livres, 2514, blvd Rosemont, Montreal, QC H1Y 1K4, Canada *Tel:* 514-273-8130 *Toll Free Tel:* 866-900-ANEL (900-2635) *E-mail:* info@anel.qc.ca *Web Site:* www.anel.qc.ca, pg 558

Prin, Joel, New World Library, 14 Pamaron Way, Novato, CA 94949 *Tel:* 415-884-2100 *Toll Free Tel:* 800-227-3900 (ext 52, retail orders); 800-972-6657 *Fax:* 415-884-2199 *E-mail:* escort@newworldlibrary.com *Web Site:* www.newworldlibrary.com, pg 161

Prince, Danforth, Blood Moon Productions Ltd, 75 Saint Marks Place, Staten Island, NY 10301-1606 *Tel:* 718-556-9410 *E-mail:* editors@bloodmoonproductions.com *Web Site:* bloodmoonproductions.com, pg 37

Pringle, Becky, National Education Association (NEA), 1201 16 St NW, Washington, DC 20036-3290 *Tel:* 202-833-4000 *Fax:* 202-822-7974 *Web Site:* www.nea.org, pg 158, 572

Prior, Robert, The MIT Press, One Rogers St, Cambridge, MA 02142 *Tel:* 617-253-5255 *Toll Free Tel:* 800-207-8354 (orders) *Fax:* 617-258-6779; 617-577-1545 (orders) *Web Site:* mitpress.mit.edu, pg 152

Proia, Brandon, The University of North Carolina Press, 116 S Boundary St, Chapel Hill, NC 27514-3808 *Tel:* 919-966-3561 *Fax:* 919-966-3829 *E-mail:* uncpress@unc.edu *Web Site:* www.uncpress.unc.edu, pg 243

Pronk, Gord, Pronk Media Inc, PO Box 340, Beaverton, ON L0K 1A0, Canada *Tel:* 416-441-3760 *E-mail:* info@pronk.com *Web Site:* www.pronk.com, pg 500

Pronovost, Nita, Simon & Schuster Canada, 166 King St E, Suite 300, Toronto, ON M5A 1J3, Canada *Tel:* 647-427-8882 *Toll Free Tel:* 800-387-0446; 800-268-3216 (orders) *Fax:* 647-430-9446 *Toll Free Fax:* 888-849-8151 (orders) *E-mail:* info@simonandschuster.ca *Web Site:* www.simonandschuster.ca, pg 471

Propheter, Lori, Northern Illinois University Press, 2280 Bethany Rd, DeKalb, IL 60115 *Tel:* 815-753-1075 *Fax:* 815-753-1845 *Web Site:* www.niupress.niu.edu, pg 164

Proppe, Tinna, Edda USA, 373 Park Ave S, 6th fl, New York, NY 10016 *Tel:* 646-755-9210 *Web Site:* eddausa.com, pg 75

Prosser, Julia, Simon & Schuster, 1230 Avenue of the Americas, New York, NY 10020 *Tel:* 212-698-7000 *Toll Free Tel:* 800-223-2348 (cust serv); 800-223-2336 (orders) *Toll Free Fax:* 800-943-9831 (orders) *Web Site:* www.simonandschuster.com, pg 212

Prosswimmer, Kate, Sourcebooks Inc, 1935 Brookdale Rd, Suite 139, Naperville, IL 60563 *Tel:* 630-961-3900 *Toll Free Tel:* 800-432-7444 *Fax:* 630-961-2168 *E-mail:* info@sourcebooks.com; customersupport@sourcebooks.com *Web Site:* www.sourcebooks.com, pg 218

Prost, Jennifer, Joelle Delbourgo Associates Inc, 101 Park St, Montclair, NJ 07042 *Tel:* 973-773-0836 (call only during standard business hours) *Web Site:* www.delbourgo.com, pg 513

Protano, Generosa Gina, GGP Publishing Inc, 105 Calvert St, Suite 201, Harrison, NY 10528-3138 *Tel:* 914-834-8896 *Fax:* 914-834-7566 *Web Site:* www.GGPPublishing.com, pg 494, 518

Proulx, Marc, Editions FouLire, 4339, rue des Becassines, Quebec, QC G1G 1V5, Canada *Tel:* 418-628-4029 *Toll Free Tel:* 877-628-4029 (CN & US) *Fax:* 418-628-4801 *E-mail:* info@foulire.com; edition@foulire.com *Web Site:* www.foulire.com, pg 454

Provost, Cherry, Medal of Honor for Literature, 15 Gramercy Park S, New York, NY 10003 *E-mail:* literary@thenationalartsclub.org *Web Site:* www.nationalartsclub.org, pg 667

Pruett, Robert H, Brandylane Publishers Inc, 5 S First St, Richmond, VA 23219 *Tel:* 804-644-3090 *Fax:* 804-644-3092 *Web Site:* brandylanepublishers.com, pg 42

Prunty, Wyatt, Sewanee Writers' Conference, Stamler Ctr, 119 Gailor Hall, 735 University Ave, Sewanee, TN 37383 *Tel:* 931-598-1141; 931-598-1654 *E-mail:* swc@sewanee.edu *Web Site:* www.sewaneewriters.org, pg 614

Prybylowski, Doug, Comex Systems Inc, 101 Pleasant Hill Rd, Chester, NJ 07930 *Tel:* 908-881-6301 *Toll Free Tel:* 800-543-6959 *Fax:* 908-879-0070 *E-mail:* mail@comexsystems.com *Web Site:* www.comexsystems.com, pg 59

Pryor, Victoria Gould, Arcadia, 31 Lake Place N, Danbury, CT 06810 *Tel:* 203-797-0993 *E-mail:* arcadialit@sbcglobal.net, pg 507

Psaltis, Elizabeth, Gallery Books, 1230 Avenue of the Americas, New York, NY 10020 *Toll Free Tel:* 800-456-6798 *Fax:* 212-698-7284 *E-mail:* consumer.customerservice@simonandschuster.com *Web Site:* www.simonsays.com, pg 90

Pucci, Cameron, Institute of Police Technology & Management, 12000 Alumni Dr, Jacksonville, FL 32224-2678 *Tel:* 904-620-4786 *Fax:* 904-620-2453 *E-mail:* info@iptm.org *Web Site:* www.iptm.org, pg 118

Pucillo, Ann-Marie, Houghton Mifflin Harcourt Trade & Reference Division, 125 High St, Boston, MA 02110 *Tel:* 617-351-5000 *Toll Free Tel:* 800-225-3362 *Web Site:* www.hmhco.com, pg 111

Pugh, Marsha, Dog Writers' Association of America Inc (DWAA), 66 Adams St, Jamestown, NY 14701 *Tel:* 716-484-6155 *E-mail:* dogwriter@windstream.net *Web Site:* www.dwaa.org, pg 564

Pugh, Marsha, Dog Writers' Association of America Inc (DWAA) Annual Writing Competition, 2243 Kelmscott Ct, Westlake Village, CA 91361 *Tel:* 805-418-7899 *Fax:* 831-374-9231 *E-mail:* dogwriter@windstream.net *Web Site:* www.dwaa.org, pg 642

Puglisi, Jess, Fence Books, University at Albany, Science Library 320, 1400 Washington Ave, Albany, NY 12222 *Tel:* 518-591-8162 *E-mail:* fence.fencebooks@gmail.com *Web Site:* www.fenceportal.org, pg 84

Puglisi, Jess, Fence Modern Poets Series, University at Albany, Science Library 320, 1400 Washington Ave, Albany, NY 12222 *Tel:* 518-591-8162 *E-mail:* fence.fencebooks@gmail.com *Web Site:* www.fenceportal.org, pg 646

Puglisi, Jess, Ottoline Morrell Prize, University at Albany, Science Library 320, 1400 Washington Ave, Albany, NY 12222 *Tel:* 518-591-8162 *E-mail:* fence.fencebooks@gmail.com *Web Site:* www.fenceportal.org, pg 669

Puhalo, Archbishop Lazar, Synaxis Press, 37323 Hawkins Rd, Dewdney, BC V0M 1H0, Canada *Tel:* 604-826-9336 *E-mail:* synaxis@new-ostrog.org *Web Site:* synaxispress.ca, pg 471

Pulice, Mario, Little, Brown and Company, 1290 Avenue of the Americas, New York, NY 10019 *Tel:* 212-364-1100 *Fax:* 212-364-0952 *E-mail:* firstname.lastname@hbgusa.com *Web Site:* www.littlebrown.com; www.HachetteBookGroup.com, pg 135

Pullano, Michelle, The MIT Press, One Rogers St, Cambridge, MA 02142 *Tel:* 617-253-5255 *Toll Free Tel:* 800-207-8354 (orders) *Fax:* 617-258-6779; 617-577-1545 (orders) *Web Site:* mitpress.mit.edu, pg 152

Pult, Richard, University Press of New England, One Court St, Suite 250, Lebanon, NH 03766 *Tel:* 603-448-1533 *Toll Free Tel:* 800-421-1561 (orders only) *Fax:* 603-448-7006; 603-448-9429 (orders only) *E-mail:* university.press@dartmouth.edu *Web Site:* www.upne.com, pg 247

Punia, Katherine Fleming, Living Language, c/o Penguin Random House Inc, 1745 Broadway, New York, NY 10019 *Tel:* 212-782-9000 *Toll Free Tel:* 800-733-3000 (orders) *Toll Free Fax:* 800-659-2436 *E-mail:* livinglanguage@randomhouse.com *Web Site:* www.livinglanguage.com, pg 136

Punia, Katie, Penguin Random House Audio Publishing, 1745 Broadway, New York, NY 10019 *E-mail:* audio@penguinrandomhouse.com *Web Site:* www.penguinrandomhouseaudio.com, pg 178

Puopolo, Kristine, Doubleday/Nan A Talese, c/o Penguin Random House Inc, 1745 Broadway, New York, NY 10019 *Tel:* 212-751-2600 *Fax:* 212-572-2662 *E-mail:* ddaypub@randomhouse.com *Web Site:* knopfdoubleday.com, pg 72

Puppa, Brian, TCP Press, 20200 Marsh Hill Rd, Uxbridge, ON L9P 1R3, Canada *Tel:* 905-852-3777 *Toll Free Tel:* 800-772-7765 *E-mail:* tcp@tcpnow.com *Web Site:* www.tcppress.com, pg 471

Purcell, Anita, CAA Award for Canadian History, 6 West St N, Suite 203, Orillia, ON L3V 5B8, Canada *Tel:* 705-325-3926 *E-mail:* admin@canadianauthors.org *Web Site:* www.canadianauthors.org, pg 635

Purcell, Anita, CAA Award for Fiction, 6 West St N, Suite 203, Orillia, ON L3V 5B8, Canada *Tel:* 705-325-3926 *E-mail:* admin@canadianauthors.org *Web Site:* www.canadianauthors.org, pg 635

Purcell, Anita, CAA Emerging Writer Award, 6 West St N, Suite 203, Orillia, ON L3V 5B8, Canada *Tel:* 705-325-3926 *E-mail:* admin@canadianauthors.org *Web Site:* www.canadianauthors.org, pg 635

Purcell, Anita, CAA Poetry Award, 6 West St N, Suite 203, Orillia, ON L3V 5B8, Canada *Tel:* 705-325-3926 *E-mail:* admin@canadianauthors.org *Web Site:* www.canadianauthors.org, pg 635

Purcell, Anita, Canadian Authors Association (CAA), 6 West St N, Suite 203, Orillia, ON L3V 5B8, Canada *Tel:* 705-325-3926 *E-mail:* admin@canadianauthors.org *Web Site:* www.canadianauthors.org, pg 561

Purcell, Jessica, Alfred A Knopf/Everyman's Library, c/o Penguin Random House Inc, 1745 Broadway, New York, NY 10019 *Tel:* 212-751-2600 *Toll Free Tel:* 800-638-6460 *Fax:* 212-572-2593 *Web Site:* www.knopfdoubleday.com, pg 127

Purcell, Nancy, Simon & Schuster Canada, 166 King St E, Suite 300, Toronto, ON M5A 1J3, Canada *Tel:* 647-427-8882 *Toll Free Tel:* 800-387-0446; 800-268-3216 (orders) *Fax:* 647-430-9446 *Toll Free Fax:* 888-849-8151 (orders) *E-mail:* info@simonandschuster.ca *Web Site:* www.simonandschuster.ca, pg 471

Purelis, Eileen, Springer, 233 Spring St, New York, NY 10013-1578 *Tel:* 212-460-1500 *Toll Free Tel:* 800-SPRINGER (777-4643) *Fax:* 212-460-1700 *E-mail:* customerservice@springer.com *Web Site:* www.springer.com, pg 219

Purple, Katherine, Purdue University Press, Stewart Ctr 190, 504 W State St, West Lafayette, IN 47907-2058 *Tel:* 765-494-2038 *Fax:* 765-496-2442 *E-mail:* pupress@purdue.edu *Web Site:* www.thepress.purdue.edu, pg 191

Purtell, April, Hewitt Homeschooling Resources, 3140 Evergreen Way, Washougal, WA 98671 *Tel:* 360-835-8708 *Toll Free Tel:* 800-348-1750 *Fax:* 360-835-8697 *E-mail:* sales@hewitthomeschooling.com *Web Site:* hewitthomeschooling.com, pg 106

Purvis, Khelsea, Adams Media, 57 Littlefield St, Avon, MA 02322 *Tel:* 508-427-7100 *Web Site:* www.simonandschuster.com, pg 4

Pusey, Stacey, AAP PreK-12 Learning Group, 455 Massachusetts Ave NW, Suite 700, Washington, DC 20001 *Tel:* 267-351-4310 *Fax:* 267-351-4317 *E-mail:* prek12learning@publishers.org *Web Site:* www.aepweb.org, pg 553

Putman, Becca, Grove Atlantic Inc, 154 W 14 St, 12th fl, New York, NY 10011 *Tel:* 212-614-7850 *Toll Free Tel:* 800-521-0178 *Fax:* 212-614-7886 *E-mail:* info@groveatlantic.com; sales@groveatlantic.com; publicity@groveatlantic.com; rights@groveatlantic.com *Web Site:* www.groveatlantic.com, pg 97

Putnam, Richelle, MWG Writer Workshops & State Conference, 9 Janice Circle, Natchez, MS 39120 *Tel:* 601-442-0980 *E-mail:* mississippi.writersguild@outlook.com *Web Site:* www.mississippiwritersguild.com, pg 613

Puton, Chloe, Workman Publishing Co Inc, 225 Varick St, 9th fl, New York, NY 10014-4381 *Tel:* 212-254-5900 *Toll Free Tel:* 800-722-7202 *Fax:* 212-254-8098 *E-mail:* info@workman.com *Web Site:* www.workman.com, pg 259

Puyans, Tomas, Templeton Press, 300 Conshohocken State Rd, Suite 665, West Conshohocken, PA 19428 *Tel:* 484-531-8380 *Fax:* 484-531-8382 *E-mail:* tpinfo@templetonpress.org *Web Site:* www.templetonpress.org, pg 229

Pye, Michael, The Career Press Inc, 12 Parish Dr, Wayne, NJ 07470 *Tel:* 201-848-0310 *Toll Free Tel:* 800-CAREER-1 (227-3371) *Fax:* 201-848-1727 *E-mail:* sales@careerpress.com *Web Site:* www.careerpress.com, pg 47

Pyland, Mike, Recorded Books Inc, an RBmedia company, 270 Skipjack Rd, Prince Frederick, MD 20678 *Tel:* 410-535-5590 *Toll Free Tel:* 877-732-2898 *Fax:* 410-535-5499 *E-mail:* customerservice@recordedbooks.com *Web Site:* www.recordedbooks.com, pg 196

Pyle, Ellie, DC Entertainment, 2900 Alameda, Burbank, CA 91505 *Toll Free Tel:* 800-887-6789 *E-mail:* dccomics@cambeywest.com *Web Site:* www.dcentertainment.com; www.dccomics.com; www.madmag.com, pg 69

Pyster, Phil, National Cartoonists Society (NCS), PO Box 592927, Orlando, FL 32859-2927 *Tel:* 407 994 6703 *Fax:* 407-442-0786 *E-mail:* info@reuben.org *Web Site:* www.reuben.org, pg 571

Qualben, Lois, LangMarc Publishing, 7500 Shadowridge Run, No 28, Austin, TX 78749 *Tel:* 512-394-0989 *Toll Free Tel:* 800-864-1648 (orders) *Fax:* 512-394-0829 *E-mail:* langmarc@booksails.com *Web Site:* www.langmarc.com, pg 129

Quasha, George, Barrytown/Station Hill Press, 120 Station Hill Rd, Barrytown, NY 12507 *Tel:* 845-758-5293 *E-mail:* publishers@stationhill.org *Web Site:* www.stationhill.org, pg 30

Quattrocchi, John, Albert Whitman & Co, 250 S Northwest Hwy, Suite 320, Park Ridge, IL 60068 *Tel:* 847-232-2800 *Toll Free Tel:* 800-255-7675 *Fax:* 847-581-0039 *E-mail:* mail@albertwhitman.com *Web Site:* www.albertwhitman.com, pg 6

Quillen, Lida E, Twilight Times Books, PO Box 3340, Kingsport, TN 37664-0340 *Tel:* 423-323-0183 *Fax:* 423-323-0183 *E-mail:* publisher@twilighttimes.com *Web Site:* www.twilighttimesbooks.com, pg 237

Quincannon, Alan, Quincannon Publishing Group, PO Box 8100, Glen Ridge, NJ 07028-8100 *Tel:* 973-380-9942 *E-mail:* editors@quincannongroup.com *Web Site:* www.quincannongroup.com, pg 192

Quinlan, Alex, Southeast Review Narrative Nonfiction Contest, Florida State University, Dept of English, Tallahassee, FL 32306 *E-mail:* southeastreview@gmail.com *Web Site:* www.southeastreview.org, pg 691

Quinlan, Alex, Southeast Review's Gearhart Poetry Contest, Florida State University, Dept of English, Tallahassee, FL 32306 *E-mail:* southeastreview@gmail.com *Web Site:* www.southeastreview.org, pg 691

Quinlan, Alex, World's Best Short-Short Story Contest, Florida State University, Dept of English, Tallahassee, FL 32306 *E-mail:* southeastreview@gmail.com *Web Site:* www.southeastreview.org, pg 699

Quinlan, Kathleen, DK Publishing, 345 Hudson St, 2nd fl, New York, NY 10014 *Tel:* 646-674-4000 *Toll Free Tel:* 877-342-5357 (cust serv); 800-733-3000 *Web Site:* www.dk.com; www.penguin.com, pg 71

Quinn, Alice, George Bogin Memorial Award, 15 Gramercy Park, New York, NY 10003 *Tel:* 212-254-9628 *Web Site:* www.poetrysociety.org, pg 633

Quinn, Alice, Alice Fay Di Castagnola Award, 15 Gramercy Park, New York, NY 10003 *Tel:* 212-254-9628 *Web Site:* www.poetrysociety.org, pg 641

Quinn, Alice, Norma Farber First Book Award, 15 Gramercy Park, New York, NY 10003 *Tel:* 212-254-9628 *Web Site:* www.poetrysociety.org, pg 645

Quinn, Alice, Cecil Hemley Memorial Award, 15 Gramercy Park, New York, NY 10003 *Tel:* 212-254-9628 *Web Site:* www.poetrysociety.org, pg 652

Quinn, Alice, Louise Louis/Emily F Bourne Student Poetry Award, 15 Gramercy Park, New York, NY 10003 *Tel:* 212-254-9628 *Web Site:* www.poetrysociety.org, pg 663

Quinn, Alice, Lyric Poetry Award, 15 Gramercy Park, New York, NY 10003 *Tel:* 212-254-9628 *Web Site:* www.poetrysociety.org, pg 664

Quinn, Alice, Lucille Medwick Memorial Award, 15 Gramercy Park, New York, NY 10003 *Tel:* 212-254-9628 *Web Site:* www.poetrysociety.org, pg 667

Quinn, Alice, Poetry Society of America (PSA), 15 Gramercy Park, New York, NY 10003 *Tel:* 212-254-9628 *Web Site:* www.poetrysociety.org, pg 575

Quinn, Alice, William Carlos Williams Award, 15 Gramercy Park, New York, NY 10003 *Tel:* 212-254-9628 *Web Site:* www.poetrysociety.org, pg 698

Quinn, Alice, The Writer Magazine/Emily Dickinson Award, 15 Gramercy Park, New York, NY 10003 *Tel:* 212-254-9628 *Web Site:* www.poetrysociety.org, pg 700

Quinn, Ann, Firefly Books Ltd, 50 Staples Ave, Unit 1, Richmond Hill, ON L4B 0A7, Canada *Tel:* 416-499-8412 *Toll Free Tel:* 800-387-6192 (CN); 800-387-5085 (US) *Fax:* 416-499-8313 *Toll Free Fax:* 800-450-0391 (CN); 800-565-6034 (US) *E-mail:* info@fireflybooks.com *Web Site:* www.fireflybooks.com, pg 456

Quinn, Kevin, Writer's Digest University, 10151 Carver Rd, Suite 200, Blue Ash, OH 45242-4760 *Tel:* 513-531-2690 *Toll Free Tel:* 800-759-0963 *Fax:* 513-531-0798 *E-mail:* contact_us@fwmedia.com *Web Site:* www.writersonlineworkshops.com, pg 624

Quinn, Lisa, Wilfrid Laurier University Press, 75 University Ave W, Waterloo, ON N2L 3C5, Canada *Tel:* 519-884-0710 *Toll Free Tel:* 866-836-5551 (CN & US) *Fax:* 519-725-1399 *E-mail:* press@wlu.ca *Web Site:* www.wlupress.wlu.ca, pg 476

Quinn, Yelba, The Brookings Institution Press, 1775 Massachusetts Ave NW, Washington, DC 20036-2188 *Tel:* 202-536-3600 *Toll Free Tel:* 800-537-5487 *Fax:* 202-536-3623 *E-mail:* permissions@brookings.edu *Web Site:* www.brookings.edu, pg 44

Quinney, Nigel, Roaring Forties Press, 1053 Santa Fe Ave, Berkeley, CA 94706 *Tel:* 510-527-5461 *E-mail:* info@roaringfortiespress.com *Web Site:* www.roaringfortiespress.com, pg 200

Quintanilla, Joseph, National Braille Press, 88 Saint Stephen St, Boston, MA 02115-4302 *Tel:* 617-266-6160 *Toll Free Tel:* 800-548-7323 (cust serv); 888-965-8965 *Fax:* 617-437-0456 *E-mail:* orders@nbp.org; contact@nbp.org *Web Site:* www.nbp.org, pg 157

Quintin, Michel, Editions Michel Quintin, 2259 Papineau Ave, Suite 104, Montreal, QC H2K 4J5, Canada *Tel:* 514-379-3774 *E-mail:* info@editionsmichelquintin.ca *Web Site:* www.editionsmichelquintin.ca, pg 455

Quinton, Debbie, ACTA Press, 2451 Dieppe Ave SW, Bldg B1, Suite 230, Calgary, AB T3E 7K1, Canada *Tel:* 403-288-1195 *Fax:* 403-247-6851 *E-mail:* journals@actapress.com; publish@actapress.com; sales@actapress.com *Web Site:* www.actapress.com, pg 445

Quinton, Linda, Tom Doherty Associates, LLC, 175 Fifth Ave, 14th fl, New York, NY 10010 *Tel:* 646-307-5511 *Toll Free Tel:* 800-455-0340 *Web Site:* www.tor-forge.com, pg 71

Quist, Norman, University Publishing Group, 6 W Washington St, Suite 302, Hagerstown, MD 21740 *Tel:* 240-420-0036 *Fax:* 240-718-7100 *E-mail:* orders@upgbooks.com, pg 247

Quon, Felicia, Simon & Schuster Canada, 166 King St E, Suite 300, Toronto, ON M5A 1J3, Canada *Tel:* 647-427-8882 *Toll Free Tel:* 800-387-0446; 800-268-3216 (orders) *Fax:* 647-430-9446 *Toll Free Fax:* 888-849-8151 (orders) *E-mail:* info@simonandschuster.ca *Web Site:* www.simonandschuster.ca, pg 471

Raab, Jackie, Barron's Educational Series Inc, 250 Wireless Blvd, Hauppauge, NY 11788 *Tel:* 631-434-3311 *Toll Free Tel:* 800-645-3476 *Fax:* 631-434-3723 *E-mail:* barrons@barronseduc.com *Web Site:* www.barronseduc.com, pg 30

Raagas, Lorna, Financial Executives Research Foundation Inc (FERF), West Tower, 7th fl, 1250 Headquarters Plaza, Morristown, NJ 07960-6837 *Tel:* 973-765-1000 *Fax:* 973-765-1023 *Web Site:* www.financialexecutives.org, pg 84

Rab, Sharon, The Ambassador Richard C Holbrooke Distinguished Achievement Award, PO Box 461, Wright Brothers Branch, Dayton, OH 45409-0461 *Tel:* 937-298-5072 *E-mail:* sharon.rab@daytonliterarypeaceprize.org *Web Site:* www.daytonliterarypeaceprize.org/holbrooke.htm, pg 627

Rab, Sharon, Dayton Literary Peace Prize, 25 Harman Terr, Dayton, OH 45419 *Tel:* 937-298-5072 *Web Site:* daytonliterarypeaceprize.org, pg 640

Rabinovitch, Elana, Giller Prize, 543 Logan Ave, Toronto, ON M4K 3B6, Canada *Web Site:* www.scotiabankgillerprize.ca, pg 649

Raccah, Dominique, Cumberland House, 1935 Brookdale Rd, Suite 139, Naperville, IL 60563 *Tel:* 630-961-3900 *Toll Free Tel:* 800-43-BRIGHT (432-7444) *Fax:* 630-961-2168 *E-mail:* info@sourcebooks.com *Web Site:* www.sourcebooks.com, pg 66

Raccah, Dominique, Sourcebooks Inc, 1935 Brookdale Rd, Suite 139, Naperville, IL 60563 *Tel:* 630-961-3900 *Toll Free Tel:* 800-432-7444 *Fax:* 630-961-2168 *E-mail:* info@sourcebooks.com; customersupport@sourcebooks.com *Web Site:* www.sourcebooks.com, pg 217

Race, Justin, University of Nevada Press, c/o University of Nevada, Continuing Educ Bldg, MS 0166, Reno, NV 89557-0166 *Tel:* 775-784-6573 *Fax:* 775-784-6200 *Web Site:* www.unpress.nevada.edu, pg 243

Racette, Ann-Christine, Fordham University Press, Joseph A Martino Hall, 45 Columbus Ave, New York, NY 10023 *Fax:* 347-842-3083 *Web Site:* www.fordhampress.com, pg 86

Rach, Beverly, Fernwood Publishing, 32 Oceanvista Lane, Black Point, NS B0J 1B0, Canada *Tel:* 902-857-1388 *Fax:* 902-857-1328 *E-mail:* info@fernpub.ca; roseway@fernpub.ca *Web Site:* fernwoodpublishing.ca, pg 456

Rada, Monica, OCP, 5536 NE Hassalo St, Portland, OR 97213 *Tel:* 503-281-1191 *Toll Free Tel:* 800-548-8749 *Fax:* 503-282-3486 *Toll Free Fax:* 800-843-8181 *E-mail:* liturgy@ocp.org *Web Site:* www.ocp.org, pg 166

Radant, Cyndi, Carolrhoda Books, 241 First Ave N, Minneapolis, MN 55401 *Tel:* 612-332-3344 *Toll Free Tel:* 800-328-4929 *Fax:* 612-332-7615 *Toll Free Fax:* 800-332-1132 *E-mail:* info@lernerbooks.com; custserve@lernerbooks.com *Web Site:* www.lernerbooks.com; www.facebook.com/lernerbooks, pg 48

Radant, Cyndi, Carolrhoda Lab™, 241 First Ave N, Minneapolis, MN 55401 *Tel:* 612-332-3344 *Toll Free Tel:* 800-328-4929 *Fax:* 612-332-7615 *Toll Free Fax:* 800-332-1132 (US) *E-mail:* info@lernerbooks.com; custserve@lernerbooks.com *Web Site:* www.lernerbooks.com; www.facebook.com/lernerbooks, pg 48

Radant, Cyndi, ediciones Lerner, 241 First Ave N, Minneapolis, MN 55401 *Tel:* 612-332-3344 *Toll Free Tel:* 800-328-4929 *Fax:* 612-332-7615 *Toll Free Fax:* 800-332-1132 *E-mail:* info@lernerbooks.com; custserve@lernerbooks.com *Web Site:* www.lernerbooks.com; www.facebook.com/lernerbooks, pg 75

Radant, Cyndi, First Avenue Editions, 241 First Ave N, Minneapolis, MN 55401 *Tel:* 612-332-3344 *Toll Free Tel:* 800-328-4929 *Fax:* 612-332-7615 *Toll Free Fax:* 800-332-1132 *E-mail:* info@lernerbooks.com; custserve@lernerbooks.com *Web Site:* www.lernerbooks.com; www.facebook.com/lernerbooks, pg 85

Radant, Cyndi, Graphic Universe™, 241 First Ave N, Minneapolis, MN 55401 *Tel:* 612-332-3344 *Toll Free Tel:* 800-328-4929 *Fax:* 612-332-7615 *Toll Free Fax:* 800-332-1132 *E-mail:* info@lernerbooks.com; custserve@lernerbooks.com *Web Site:* www.lernerbooks.com; www.facebook.com/lernerbooks, pg 95

Radant, Cyndi, Lerner Publications, 241 First Ave N, Minneapolis, MN 55401 *Tel:* 612-332-3344 *Toll Free Tel:* 800-328-4929 *Fax:* 612-332-7615 *Toll Free Fax:* 800-332-1132 *E-mail:* info@lernerbooks.com; custserve@lernerbooks.com *Web Site:* www.lernerbooks.com; www.facebook.com/lernerbooks, pg 132

Radant, Cyndi, Lerner Publishing Group Inc, 241 First Ave N, Minneapolis, MN 55401 *Tel:* 612-332-3344 *Toll Free Tel:* 800-328-4929 *Fax:* 612-332-7615 *Toll Free Fax:* 800-332-1132 *E-mail:* info@lernerbooks.com; custserve@lernerbooks.com *Web Site:* www.lernerbooks.com; www.facebook.com/lernerbooks, pg 132

Radant, Cyndi, LernerClassroom, 241 First Ave N, Minneapolis, MN 55401 *Tel:* 612-332-3344 *Toll Free Tel:* 800-328-4929 *Fax:* 612-332-7615 *Toll Free Fax:* 800-332-1132 *E-mail:* info@lernerbooks.com; custserve@lernerbooks.com *Web Site:* www.lernerbooks.com; www.facebook.com/lernerbooks, pg 132

Radant, Cyndi, Millbrook Press, 241 First Ave N, Minneapolis, MN 55401 *Tel:* 612-332-3344 *Toll Free Tel:* 800-328-4929 (US only) *Fax:* 612-332-7615 *Toll Free Fax:* 800-332-1132 *E-mail:* info@lernerbooks.com; custserve@lernerbooks.com *Web Site:* www.lernerbooks.com; www.facebook.com/millbrookpress, pg 151

Radant, Cyndi, Twenty-First Century Books, 241 First Ave N, Minneapolis, MN 55401 *Tel:* 612-332-3344 *Toll Free Tel:* 800-328-4929 *Fax:* 612-332-7615 *Toll Free Fax:* 800-332-1132 *E-mail:* info@lernerbooks.com; custserve@lernerbooks.com *Web Site:* www.lernerbooks.com; www.facebook.com/lernerbooks, pg 237

Radcliffe, Barbara, Center for the Collaborative Classroom, 1250 53 St, Suite 3, Emeryville, CA 94608 *Tel:* 510-533-0213 *Toll Free Tel:* 800-666-7270 *Fax:* 510-464-3670 *E-mail:* info@

collaborativeclassroom.org; clientsupport@collaborativeclassroom.org *Web Site:* www.collaborativeclassroom.org, pg 51

Rade, David, Swan Isle Press, 11030 S Langley Ave, Chicago, IL 60628 *Tel:* 773-728-3780 (edit); 773-702-7000 (cust serv) *Toll Free Tel:* 800-621-2736 (cust serv) *Fax:* 773-702-7212 (cust serv) *Toll Free Fax:* 800-621-8476 (cust serv) *E-mail:* info@swanislepress.com *Web Site:* www.swanislepress.com, pg 225

Radice, Neal, Maxim Mazumdar New Play Competition, One Curtain Up Alley, Buffalo, NY 14202-1911 *Tel:* 716-852-2600 *E-mail:* publicrelations@alleyway.com *Web Site:* alleyway.com, pg 666

Radich, Anthony, Western States Arts Federation, 1743 Wazee St, Suite 300, Denver, CO 80202 *Tel:* 303-629-1166 *Toll Free Tel:* 888-562-7232 *Fax:* 303-629-9717 *E-mail:* staff@westaf.org *Web Site:* www.westaf.org, pg 583

Radke, Linda F, Dragonfly Book Awards, 4696 W Tyson St, Chandler, AZ 85226-2903 *Tel:* 480-940-8182 *Fax:* 480-940-8787 *E-mail:* info@StoryMonsters.com *Web Site:* www.DragonflyBookAwards.com, pg 642

Radke, Linda F, Story Monsters Approved! Program, 4696 W Tyson St, Chandler, AZ 85226-2903 *Tel:* 480-940-8182 *Fax:* 480-940-8787 *Web Site:* www.StoryMonstersApproved.com, pg 692

Radke, Linda F, Story Monsters LLC, 4696 W Tyson St, Chandler, AZ 85226-2903 *Tel:* 480-940-8182 *Fax:* 480-940-8787 *Web Site:* www.StoryMonsters.com; www.DragonflyBookAwards.com; www.AuthorsandExperts.com; www.SchoolBookings.com, pg 223

Radler, Kyle, W W Norton & Company Inc, 500 Fifth Ave, New York, NY 10110-0017 *Tel:* 212-354-5500 *Toll Free Tel:* 800-233-4830 (orders & cust serv) *Fax:* 212-869-0856 *Toll Free Fax:* 800-458-6515 *E-mail:* orders@wwnorton.com *Web Site:* books.wwnorton.com, pg 164

Raducanu, Teodor, Teora USA LLC, 505 Hampton Park Blvd, Unit G, Capitol Heights, MD 20743 *Tel:* 301-986-6990 *Fax:* 301-350-5480 *E-mail:* 2010@teora.com *Web Site:* www.teora.com, pg 229

Radziewicz, John, Perseus Books, 250 W 57 St, 15th fl, New York, NY 10107 *Tel:* 212-340-8100 *Toll Free Tel:* 800-343-4499 (cust serv) *Fax:* 212-340-8105 *Web Site:* www.perseusbooks.com, pg 180

Raeber, Rick, W W Norton & Company Inc, 500 Fifth Ave, New York, NY 10110-0017 *Tel:* 212-354-5500 *Toll Free Tel:* 800-233-4830 (orders & cust serv) *Fax:* 212-869-0856 *Toll Free Fax:* 800-458-6515 *E-mail:* orders@wwnorton.com *Web Site:* books.wwnorton.com, pg 164

Rafer, Suzanne, Workman Publishing Co Inc, 225 Varick St, 9th fl, New York, NY 10014-4381 *Tel:* 212-254-5900 *Toll Free Tel:* 800-722-7202 *Fax:* 212-254-8098 *E-mail:* info@workman.com *Web Site:* www.workman.com, pg 259

Raffensperger, Daniel, Seedling Publications Inc, 520 E Bainbridge St, Elizabethtown, PA 17022 *Toll Free Tel:* 800-233-0759 *Toll Free Fax:* 888-834-1303 *E-mail:* info@continentalpress.com *Web Site:* www.continentalpress.com, pg 210

Raffio, Michael, Pflaum Publishing Group, 2621 Dryden Rd, Suite 300, Dayton, OH 45439 *Tel:* 937-293-1415 *Toll Free Tel:* 800-543-4383 (sales) *Fax:* 937-293-1310 *Toll Free Fax:* 800-370-4450 *E-mail:* service@pflaum.com *Web Site:* pflaum.com, pg 182

Raft, Steven, Alfred Music Publishing, PO Box 10003, Van Nuys, CA 91410 *Tel:* 818-891-5999 (dealer sales, intl); 818-891-2452 (cust serv) *Toll Free Tel:* 800-292-6122 (dealer sales, US & CN) *Fax:* 818-893-5560 (dealer sales); 818-830-6252 (cust serv) *Toll Free Fax:* 800-632-1928 (dealer sales) *E-mail:* customerservice@alfred.com; sales@alfred.com *Web Site:* www.alfred.com, pg 7

Rafter, Katherine, Art of Living, PrimaMedia Inc, 1250 Bethlehem Pike, Suite 241, Hatfield, PA 19440 *Tel:* 215-660-5045 *E-mail:* primamedia4@yahoo.com, pg 21

Ragan, Lise B, Course Crafters Inc, PO Box 100, Amesbury, MA 01913 *Tel:* 978-372-3446 *E-mail:* info@coursecrafters.com *Web Site:* www.coursecrafters.com, pg 492

Rager, Shari, American Medical Writers Association (AMWA), 30 W Gude Dr, Suite 525, Rockville, MD 20850-4357 *Tel:* 240-238-0940 *Fax:* 301-294-9006 *E-mail:* amwa@amwa.org *Web Site:* www.amwa.org, pg 555

Ragland, Kelley, St Martin's Press, LLC, 175 Fifth Ave, New York, NY 10010 *Tel:* 646-307-5151 *Web Site:* us.macmillan.com/smp, pg 204

Rago, Martha, Random House Children's Books, 1745 Broadway, 10th fl, New York, NY 10019 *Tel:* 212-782-9000 *Web Site:* www.randomhousekids.com, pg 194

Rahaeuser, Alice, Random House Children's Books, 1745 Broadway, 10th fl, New York, NY 10019 *Tel:* 212-782-9000 *Web Site:* www.randomhousekids.com, pg 194

Rahja, John, Augsburg Fortress Publishers, Publishing House of the Evangelical Lutheran Church in America, 510 Marquette Ave S, Minneapolis, MN 55402 *Tel:* 612-330-3300 *Toll Free Tel:* 800-426-0115 (ext 639, subns); 800-328-4648 (orders) *Fax:* 612-330-3455 *E-mail:* info@augsburgfortress.org; copyright@augsburgfortress.org (reprint permission requests); customercare@augsburgfortress.org *Web Site:* www.augsburgfortress.org, pg 26

Rahm, Willi, Alan Wofsy Fine Arts, 1109 Geary Blvd, San Francisco, CA 94109 *Tel:* 415-292-6500 *Toll Free Tel:* 800-660-6403 *Fax:* 415-292-6594 (off & cust serv); 510-251-1840 (acctg) *E-mail:* order@art-books.com (orders); editeur@earthlink.net (edit); beauxarts@earthlink.net (cust serv) *Web Site:* www.art-books.com, pg 258

Raihofer, Susan, David Black Agency, 335 Adams St, 27th fl, Suite 2707, Brooklyn, NY 11201 *Tel:* 718-852-5500 *Fax:* 718-852-5539 *Web Site:* www.davidblackagency.com, pg 508

Raim, Sam, Penguin Group USA, A Penguin Random House Company, 375 Hudson St, New York, NY 10014 *Tel:* 212-366-2000 *Toll Free Tel:* 800-847-5515 (inside sales); 800-631-8571 (cust serv) *Fax:* 212-366-2666; 607-775-4829 (inside sales) *E-mail:* online@us.penguingroup.com *Web Site:* www.penguin.com, pg 177

Rainer, Thom S, B&H Publishing Group, One LifeWay Plaza, Nashville, TN 37234 *Tel:* 615-251-2520 *Fax:* 615-251-5004 *Web Site:* www.bhpublishinggroup.com, pg 29

Raines, Joan, Raines & Raines, 103 Kenyon Rd, Medusa, NY 12120 *Tel:* 518-239-8311 *Fax:* 518-239-6029, pg 532

Raissian, Katie, Grove Atlantic Inc, 154 W 14 St, 12th fl, New York, NY 10011 *Tel:* 212-614-7850 *Toll Free Tel:* 800-521-0178 *Fax:* 212-614-7886 *E-mail:* info@groveatlantic.com; sales@groveatlantic.com; publicity@groveatlantic.com; rights@groveatlantic.com *Web Site:* www.groveatlantic.com, pg 97

Rajagopalan, Pari, PEN Canada, 24 Ryerson Ave, Suite 301, Toronto, ON M5T 2P3, Canada *Tel:* 416-703-8448 *Fax:* 416-703-3870 *E-mail:* queries@pencanada.ca *Web Site:* www.pencanada.ca, pg 575

Rajamani, Madhu, LaurelTech, 4 S Market St, 4th fl, Boston, MA 02109-6201 *Tel:* 617-600-3366 *Fax:* 617-848-2938 *Web Site:* www.diacritech.com, pg 497

Rak, Brian, Focus, PO Box 44937, Indianapolis, IN 46244-0937 *Tel:* 317-635-9250 *Fax:* 317-635-9292 *E-mail:* customer@hackettpublishing.com; editorial@hackettpublishing.com *Web Site:* focusbookstore.com, pg 86

Ram, Hari, Chronicle Books LLC, 680 Second St, San Francisco, CA 94107 *Tel:* 415-537-4200 *Toll Free Tel:* 800-759-0190 (cust serv) *Fax:* 415-537-4460 *Toll Free Fax:* 800-858-7787 (orders); 800-286-9471 (cust serv) *E-mail:* frontdesk@chroniclebooks.com *Web Site:* www.chroniclebooks.com, pg 55

Rambo, Cat, Science Fiction & Fantasy Writers of America Inc (SFWA), PO Box 3238, Enfield, CT 06083-3238 *E-mail:* office@sfwa.org *Web Site:* www.sfwa.org, pg 577

Rambo, Cat, SFWA Nebula Awards, PO Box 3238, Enfield, CT 06083-3238 *E-mail:* office@sfwa.org *Web Site:* www.sfwa.org, pg 688

Ramer, Susan, Don Congdon Associates Inc, 110 William St, Suite 2202, New York, NY 10038-3914 *Tel:* 212-645-1229 *Fax:* 212-727-2688 *E-mail:* dca@doncongdon.com *Web Site:* www.doncongdon.com, pg 512

Ramin, Sue Berger, David R Godine Publisher Inc, 15 Court Sq, Suite 320, Boston, MA 02108-4715 *Tel:* 617-451-9600 *Fax:* 617-350-0250 *E-mail:* info@godine.com *Web Site:* www.godine.com, pg 93

Ramondo, Anthony, Berkley Publishing Group, 375 Hudson St, New York, NY 10014 *Tel:* 212-366-2000 *Fax:* 212-366-2385 *Web Site:* www.penguin.com, pg 33

Ramos, Luis Arturo, University of Texas at El Paso, Department of Creative Writing, MFA/Department of Creative Writing, 901 EDUC, 500 W University Ave, El Paso, TX 79968-9991 *Tel:* 915-747-5713 *Fax:* 915-747-5523 *E-mail:* creativewriting@utep.edu *Web Site:* www.utep.edu/cw, pg 624

Ramos, Mariana, Random House Children's Books, 1745 Broadway, 10th fl, New York, NY 10019 *Tel:* 212-782-9000 *Web Site:* www.randomhousekids.com, pg 194

Ramsayer, Lee, Houghton Mifflin Harcourt, 125 High St, Boston, MA 02110 *Tel:* 617-351-5000 *Toll Free Tel:* 855-969-4642; 800-225-5425 (K-12 educ materials); 800-323-9540 (assessment materials); 877-219-1537 (SkillsTutor); 888-242-6747 (Innovation in Educ Group); 800-225-3362 (Trade & Ref Div) *Toll Free Fax:* 800-269-5232 *E-mail:* myhmhco@hmhco.com *Web Site:* www.hmhco.com, pg 110

Rand Silverman, Erica, Stimola Literary Studio Inc, 308 Livingston Ct, Edgewater, NJ 07020 *Tel:* 201-945-9353 *Fax:* 201-945-9353; 201-490-5920 *E-mail:* info@stimolaliterarystudio.com *Web Site:* www.stimolaliterarystudio.com, pg 537

Randall, Deidre C, Peter E Randall Publisher, 5 Greenleaf Woods Dr, Suite 102, Portsmouth, NH 03801 *Tel:* 603-431-5667 *Fax:* 603-431-3566 *E-mail:* media@perpublisher.com *Web Site:* www.perpublisher.com, pg 194

Randall, Lee, Oceanview Publishing, CEO Center at Mediterranean Plaza, Suite 120-G, 595 Bay Isles Rd, Longboat Key, FL 34228 *Tel:* 941-387-8500 *Web Site:* oceanviewpub.com, pg 166

Randall, Michele E, Bibliographical Society of America, PO Box 1537, Lenox Hill Sta, New York, NY 10021-0043 *Tel:* 212-452-2710 *Fax:* 212-452-2710 *E-mail:* bsa@bibsocamer.org *Web Site:* www.bibsocamer.org, pg 560

Randolph, Ladette, Ploughshares, Emerson College, 120 Boylston St, Boston, MA 02116 *Tel:* 617-824-3757 *E-mail:* pshares@pshares.org *Web Site:* www.pshares.org, pg 184

Randolph, Tony, Regular Baptist Press, 3715 N Ventura Dr, Arlington Heights, IL 60004 *Tel:* 847-843-1600 *Toll Free Tel:* 800-727-4440; 800-727-4440 (cust serv) *Fax:* 847-843-3757 *E-mail:* rbp@garbc.org *Web Site:* regularbaptistpress.org, pg 198

Rankin, Charles, University of Oklahoma Press, 2800 Venture Dr, Norman, OK 73069-8216 *Tel:* 405-325-2000 *Toll Free Tel:* 800-627-7377 (orders) *Fax:* 405-364-5798 (orders) *Toll Free Fax:* 800-735-0476 (orders) *E-mail:* presscs@ou.edu *Web Site:* www.oupress.com, pg 244

Rankin, Jenni, Annual Reviews, 4139 El Camino Way, Palo Alto, CA 94306 *Tel:* 650-493-4400 *Toll Free Tel:* 800-523-8635 *Fax:* 650-424-0910; 650-855-9815 *E-mail:* service@annualreviews.org *Web Site:* www.annualreviews.org, pg 17

Rankin, Samuel M III, American Mathematical Society, 201 Charles St, Providence, RI 02904-2294 *Tel:* 401-455-4000 *Toll Free Tel:* 800-321-4267 *Fax:* 401-331-3842; 401-455-4046 (cust serv) *E-mail:* ams@ams.org; cust-serv@ams.org *Web Site:* www.ams.org, pg 13

Raoult, Marie-Madeleine, Editions de la Pleine Lune, 223 34 Ave, Lachine, QC H8T 1Z4, Canada *Tel:* 514-634-7954 *E-mail:* editpllune@videotron.ca *Web Site:* www.pleinelune.qc.ca, pg 453

Raphel, Neil, Brigantine Media, 211 North Ave, St Johnsbury, VT 05819 *Tel:* 802-751-8802 *Fax:* 802-751-8804 *Web Site:* brigantinemedia.com, pg 43

Rapp, Alan, The Monacelli Press, 236 W 27 St, 4th fl, New York, NY 10001 *Tel:* 212-229-9925 (ext 25) *E-mail:* contact@monacellipress.com *Web Site:* www.monacellipress.com, pg 153

Rapp, Daniela, St Martin's Press, LLC, 175 Fifth Ave, New York, NY 10010 *Tel:* 646-307-5151 *Web Site:* us.macmillan.com/smp, pg 204

Rarick, Ethan, Institute of Governmental Studies, 109 Moses Hall, No 2370, Berkeley, CA 94720-2370 *Tel:* 510-642-1428 *Fax:* 510-642-3020; 510-642-5537 (orders) *E-mail:* igspress@berkeley.edu *Web Site:* www.igs.berkeley.edu, pg 118

Rasanen, John P, American Geosciences Institute (AGI), 4220 King St, Alexandria, VA 22302-1502 *Tel:* 703-379-2480 (ext 246) *Fax:* 703-379-7563 *E-mail:* pubs@agiweb.org *Web Site:* www.agiweb.org, pg 12

Rasenberger, Mary, The Authors Guild, 31 E 32 St, 7th fl, New York, NY 10016 *Tel:* 212-563-5904 *Fax:* 212-564-5363 *E-mail:* staff@authorsguild.org *Web Site:* www.authorsguild.org, pg 559

Rasi, Cayla, Random House Children's Books, 1745 Broadway, 10th fl, New York, NY 10019 *Tel:* 212-782-9000 *Web Site:* www.randomhousekids.com, pg 194

Raskin, Sherman, Pace University, Master of Science in Publishing, Dept of Publishing, Rm 805-E, 551 Fifth Ave, New York, NY 10176 *Tel:* 212-346-1431 *Toll Free Tel:* 877-284-7670 *Fax:* 212-346-1165 *Web Site:* www.pace.edu/dyson/mspub, pg 621

Raskin, Sherman, Pace University Press, Dept of Publishing, Rm 805-E, 551 Fifth Ave, New York, NY 10176 *Tel:* 212-346-1417 *Fax:* 212-346-1165 *Web Site:* www.pace.edu/press, pg 172

Rasmussen, Jim, Bethlehem Books, 10194 Garfield St S, Bathgate, ND 58216 *Toll Free Tel:* 800-757-6831 *Fax:* 701-265-3716 *E-mail:* contact@bethlehembooks.com *Web Site:* www.bethlehembooks.com, pg 34

Rasset, Anne, North Star Press of Saint Cloud Inc, PO Box 451, St Cloud, MN 56302-0451 *Tel:* 320-558-9062 *E-mail:* info@northstarpress.com *Web Site:* www.northstarpress.com, pg 164

Ratliff, Therese, Twenty-Third Publications, One Montauk Ave, Suite 200, New London, CT 06320 *Tel:* 860-437-3012 *Toll Free Tel:* 800-321-0411 (orders) *Toll Free Fax:* 800-572-0788 *E-mail:* resources@twentythirdpublications.com *Web Site:* www.twentythirdpublications.com, pg 237

Ratner, Hope, Northeast-Midwest Institute, 50 "F" St NW, Suite 950, Washington, DC 20001 *Tel:* 202-544-5200 *Fax:* 202-544-0043 *E-mail:* info@nemw.org *Web Site:* www.nemw.org, pg 164

Rattray, Jessica, Coach House Books, 80 bpNichol Lane, Toronto, ON M5S 3J4, Canada *Tel:* 416-979-2217 *Toll Free Tel:* 800-367-6360 (outside Toronto) *Fax:* 416-977-1158 *E-mail:* mail@chbooks.com *Web Site:* www.chbooks.com, pg 450

Ratzlaff, Cindy, Gallery Books, 1230 Avenue of the Americas, New York, NY 10020 *Toll Free Tel:* 800-456-6798 *Fax:* 212-698-7284 *E-mail:* consumer.customerservice@simonandschuster.com *Web Site:* www.simonsays.com, pg 90

Rawa, Lisa, Premier Print Awards, 301 Brush Creek Rd, Warrendale, PA 15086-7529 *Tel:* 412-741-6860 *Toll Free Tel:* 800-910-4283 *Fax:* 412-741-2311 *E-mail:* printingind@comm.printing.org *Web Site:* www.printing.org/premierprint, pg 682

Rawa, Lisa, Printing Industries of America, 301 Brush Creek Rd, Warrendale, PA 15086-7529 *Tel:* 412-741-6860 *Toll Free Tel:* 800-910-4283 *Fax:* 412-741-2311 *E-mail:* printingind@comm.printing.org *Web Site:* www.printing.org, pg 576

Rawitch, Jeremy, RAND Corp, 1776 Main St, Santa Monica, CA 90407-2138 *Tel:* 310-393-0411 *Fax:* 310-393-4818 *Web Site:* www.rand.org, pg 193

Rawlings, Jeremy, HarperCollins Canada Ltd, 2 Bloor St E, 20th fl, Toronto, ON M4W 1A8, Canada *Tel:* 416-975-9334 *Fax:* 416-975-5223 *E-mail:* hcorder@harpercollins.com *Web Site:* www.harpercollins.ca, pg 459

Rawlings, Kelly, American Diabetes Association, 1701 N Beauregard St, Alexandria, VA 22311 *Toll Free Tel:* 800-342-2383 *E-mail:* booksinfo@diabetes.org *Web Site:* www.diabetes.org, pg 11

Rawlings, Wendy, University of Alabama Program in Creative Writing, PO Box 870244, Tuscaloosa, AL 35487-0244 *Tel:* 205-348-5065 *Fax:* 205-348-1388 *E-mail:* english@ua.edu *Web Site:* www.as.ua.edu/english, pg 622

Ray, Jo-Anne, Canadian Institute for Studies in Publishing, Simon Fraser University at Harbour Centre, 515 W Hastings St, Suite 3576, Vancouver, BC V6B 5K3, Canada *Tel:* 778-782-5242 *E-mail:* pub-info@sfu.ca *Web Site:* publishing.sfu.ca, pg 562

Ray, Terresa, Quail Ridge Press, 101 Brooks Dr, Brandon, MS 39042 *Tel:* 601-825-2063 *Toll Free Tel:* 800-343-1583 *Fax:* 601-825-3091 *Toll Free Fax:* 800-864-1082 *E-mail:* info@quailridge.com *Web Site:* quailridge.com, pg 192

Ray, Trinity, The Tuesday Agency, 132 1/2 E Washington St, Iowa City, IA 52240 *Tel:* 319-338-7080 *E-mail:* trinity@tuesdayagency.com *Web Site:* tuesdayagency.com, pg 548

Raye, Janis, Brigantine Media, 211 North Ave, St Johnsbury, VT 05819 *Tel:* 802-751-8802 *Fax:* 802-751-8804 *Web Site:* brigantinemedia.com, pg 43

Raymo, Margaret, Houghton Mifflin Harcourt Trade & Reference Division, 125 High St, Boston, MA 02110 *Tel:* 617-351-5000 *Toll Free Tel:* 800-225-3362 *Web Site:* www.hmhco.com, pg 111

Raymond, Andrea, Bear & Co Inc, One Park St, Rochester, VT 05767 *Tel:* 802-767-3174 *Toll Free Tel:* 800-932-3277 *Fax:* 802-767-3726 *E-mail:* customerservice@InnerTraditions.com *Web Site:* InnerTraditions.com, pg 31

Raymond, Andrea, Inner Traditions International Ltd, One Park St, Rochester, VT 05767 *Tel:* 802-767-3174 *Toll Free Tel:* 800-246-8648 *Fax:* 802-767-3726 *E-mail:* customerservice@InnerTraditions.com *Web Site:* www.InnerTraditions.com, pg 117

Raymond, Melissa, Perseus Books, 250 W 57 St, 15th fl, New York, NY 10107 *Tel:* 212-340-8100 *Toll Free Tel:* 800-343-4499 (cust serv) *Fax:* 212-340-8105 *Web Site:* www.perseusbooks.com, pg 181

Raymond, Midge, Ashland Creek Press, 2305 Ashland St, Suite C417, Ashland, OR 97520 *Tel:* 760-300-3620 *E-mail:* editors@ashlandcreekpress.com *Web Site:* www.ashlandcreekpress.com, pg 23

Rayner, Terry, Wimmer Cookbooks, 4650 Shelby Air Dr, Memphis, TN 38118 *Toll Free Tel:* 800-548-2537 *Fax:* 901-363-1771 *E-mail:* info@wimmerco.com *Web Site:* www.wimmerco.com, pg 257

Raynor, Bruce, Hillman Prizes for Journalism, 330 W 42 St, Suite 900, New York, NY 10036 *Tel:* 646-448-6413 *Web Site:* www.hillmanfoundation.org, pg 653

Raynor, Jacqueline Hope, The Boston Mills Press, 50 Staples Ave, Unit 1, Richmond Hill, ON L4B 0A7, Canada *Tel:* 416-499-8412 *Toll Free Tel:* 800-387-6192 *Fax:* 416-499-8313 *Toll Free Fax:* 800-450-0391 *E-mail:* service@fireflybooks.com *Web Site:* www.fireflybooks.com, pg 447

Rea, Elizabeth R, The Rea Award for the Short Story, 53 W Church Hill Rd, Washington, CT 06794 *Web Site:* reaaward.org, pg 684

Reach, Anna Duke, The Writers Workshop, Finn House, 102 W Wiggin St, Gambier, OH 43022 *Tel:* 740-427-5207 *Fax:* 740-427-5417 *E-mail:* kenyonreview@kenyon.edu *Web Site:* www.kenyonreview.org, pg 616

Read, Bridget, HarperCollins General Books Group, 195 Broadway, New York, NY 10007 *Tel:* 212-207-7000 *Web Site:* www.harpercollins.com, pg 101

Reade, Amy, Women Who Write Inc, PO Box 652, Madison, NJ 07940-0652 *E-mail:* info@womenwhowrite.org *Web Site:* womenwhowrite.org, pg 580

Ream, Robaire, Polebridge Press, PO Box 346, Farmington, MN 55024 *Tel:* 651-200-2372 *E-mail:* orders@westarinstitute.org *Web Site:* www.westarinstitute.org, pg 185

Reaman, Ms Micki, Oregon State University Press, 121 The Valley Library, Corvallis, OR 97331-4501 *Tel:* 541-737-3166 *Toll Free Tel:* 800-621-2736 (orders), pg 170

Reamer, Jodi Esq, Writers House, 21 W 26 St, New York, NY 10010 *Tel:* 212-685-2400 *Fax:* 212-685-1781 *Web Site:* www.writershouse.com, pg 542

Reardon, Lisa, Chicago Review Press, 814 N Franklin St, Chicago, IL 60610 *Tel:* 312-337-0747 *Toll Free Tel:* 800-888-4741 *Fax:* 312-337-5110 *E-mail:* frontdesk@chicagoreviewpress.com *Web Site:* www.chicagoreviewpress.com, pg 54

Reaume, Julie K, Michigan State University Press (MSU Press), Manly Miles Bldg, Suite 25, 1405 S Harrison Rd, East Lansing, MI 48823-5245 *Tel:* 517-355-9543 *Fax:* 517-432-2611 *Web Site:* msupress.org, pg 150

Reback, Erin, Simon & Schuster, 1230 Avenue of the Americas, New York, NY 10020 *Tel:* 212-698-7000 *Toll Free Tel:* 800-223-2348 (cust serv); 800-223-2336 (orders) *Toll Free Fax:* 800-943-9831 (orders) *Web Site:* www.simonandschuster.com, pg 212

Rebhun, Elliott, Scholastic Education, 557 Broadway, New York, NY 10012 *Tel:* 212-343-6100 *Fax:* 212-343-6189 *Web Site:* www.scholastic.com, pg 207

Redd, Kimberly, LITA/Christian Larew Memorial Scholarship in Library & Information Technology, c/o American Library Association, 50 E Huron St, Chicago, IL 60611-2795 *Toll Free Tel:* 800-545-2433 *E-mail:* scholarships@ala.org *Web Site:* www.ala.org/lita, pg 661

Redd, Kimberly, LITA/LSSI Minority Scholarship in Library & Information Technology, c/o American Library Association, 50 E Huron St, Chicago, IL 60611-2795 *Toll Free Tel:* 800-545-2433 *E-mail:* scholarships@ala.org *Web Site:* www.ala.org/lita, pg 661

Redd, Kimberly, LITA/OCLC Minority Scholarship in Library & Information Technology, c/o American Library Association, 50 E Huron St, Chicago, IL 60611-2795 *Toll Free Tel:* 800-545-2433 *E-mail:* scholarships@ala.org *Web Site:* www.ala.org/lita, pg 662

Redd, Kimberly L, David H Clift Scholarship, 50 E Huron St, Chicago, IL 60611 *Toll Free Tel:* 800-545-2433 (ext 4279) *Fax:* 312-280-3256 *E-mail:* scholarships@ala.org *Web Site:* www.ala.org/scholarships, pg 638

Redkin, Andy, Alan Wofsy Fine Arts, 1109 Geary Blvd, San Francisco, CA 94109 *Tel:* 415-292-6500 *Toll Free Tel:* 800-660-6403 *Fax:* 415-292-6594 (off & cust serv); 510-251-1840 (acctg) *E-mail:* order@art-books.com (orders); editeur@earthlink.net (edit); beauxarts@earthlink.net (cust serv) *Web Site:* www.art-books.com, pg 258

Redlich, Josh, Random House Children's Books, 1745 Broadway, 10th fl, New York, NY 10019 *Tel:* 212-782-9000 *Web Site:* www.randomhousekids.com, pg 194

Redmon, Hilary, Random House Publishing Group, 1745 Broadway, New York, NY 10019 *Toll Free Tel:* 800-200-3552 *Web Site:* atrandom.com, pg 195

Reilly, Colleen, Theatre Library Association (TLA), c/o The New York Public Library for the Performing Arts, 40 Lincoln Center Plaza, New York, NY 10023 *E-mail:* TheatreLibraryAssociation@gmail.com *Web Site:* www.tla-online.org/awards/bookawards, pg 580

Reilly, Edward T, American Management Association (AMA), 1601 Broadway, New York, NY 10019 *Tel:* 212-586-8100 *Toll Free Tel:* 877-566-9441 *Fax:* 212-903-8168; 518-891-0368 *E-mail:* customerservice@amanet.org *Web Site:* www.amanet.org, pg 555

Reilly, J C, International Poetry Competition, 686 Cherry St NW, Suite 333, Atlanta, GA 30332-0161 *E-mail:* atlantareview@gatech.edu *Web Site:* www.atlantareview.com, pg 656

Reilly, Michael, American Association of Collegiate Registrars & Admissions Officers (AACRAO), One Dupont Circle NW, Suite 520, Washington, DC 20036 *Tel:* 202-293-9161 *Fax:* 202-872-8857 *Web Site:* www.aacrao.org, pg 10

Reimnitz, Arlen, ASET - The Neurodiagnostic Society, 402 E Bannister Rd, Suite A, Kansas City, KS 64131-3019 *Tel:* 816-931-1120 *Fax:* 816-931-1145 *E-mail:* info@aset.org *Web Site:* www.aset.org, pg 23

Rein, Jody, Jody Rein Books Inc, 7741 S Ash Ct, Centennial, CO 80122 *Tel:* 303-694-9386 *Web Site:* www.jodyreinbooks.com, pg 523

Reina, Jeanne, HarperCollins General Books Group, 195 Broadway, New York, NY 10007 *Tel:* 212-207-7000 *Web Site:* www.harpercollins.com, pg 101

Reinertsen, Claire, W W Norton & Company Inc, 500 Fifth Ave, New York, NY 10110-0017 *Tel:* 212-354-5500 *Toll Free Tel:* 800-233-4830 (orders & cust serv) *Fax:* 212-869-0856 *Toll Free Fax:* 800-458-6515 *E-mail:* orders@wwnorton.com *Web Site:* books.wwnorton.com, pg 164

Reisdorff, James J, South Platte Press, PO Box 163, David City, NE 68632-0163 *Tel:* 402-367-3554 *E-mail:* railroads@windstream.net *Web Site:* www.southplattepress.net, pg 218

Reiser, Annie M, Morton N Cohen Award for a Distinguished Edition of Letters, 85 Broad St, Suite 500, New York, NY 10004-2434 *Tel:* 646-576-5141; 646-576-5000 *Fax:* 646-458-0030 *E-mail:* awards@mla.org *Web Site:* www.mla.org, pg 638

Reiser, Annie M, Katherine Singer Kovacs Prize, 85 Broad St, Suite 500, New York, NY 10004-2434 *Tel:* 646-576-5141; 646-576-5000 *Fax:* 646-458-0030 *E-mail:* awards@mla.org *Web Site:* www.mla.org, pg 659

Reiser, Annie M, Fenia & Yaakov Leviant Memorial Prize in Yiddish Studies, 85 Broad St, Suite 500, New York, NY 10004-2434 *Tel:* 646-576-5141; 646-576-5000 *Fax:* 646-458-0030 *E-mail:* awards@mla.org *Web Site:* www.mla.org, pg 660

Reiser, Annie M, James Russell Lowell Prize, 85 Broad St, Suite 500, New York, NY 10004-2434 *Tel:* 646-576-5141; 646-576-5000 *Fax:* 646-458-0030 *E-mail:* awards@mla.org *Web Site:* www.mla.org, pg 663

Reiser, Annie M, Howard R Marraro Prize, 85 Broad St, Suite 500, New York, NY 10004-2434 *Tel:* 646-576-5141; 646-576-5000 *Fax:* 646-458-0030 *E-mail:* awards@mla.org *Web Site:* www.mla.org, pg 666

Reiser, Annie M, Kenneth W Mildenberger Prize, 85 Broad St, Suite 500, New York, NY 10004-2434 *Tel:* 646-576-5141; 646-576-5000 *Fax:* 646-458-0030 *E-mail:* awards@mla.org *Web Site:* www.mla.org, pg 668

Reiser, Annie M, MLA Prize for a Bibliography, Archive or Digital Project, 85 Broad St, Suite 500, New York, NY 10004-2434 *Tel:* 646-576-5141; 646-576-5000 *Fax:* 646-458-0030 *E-mail:* awards@mla.org *Web Site:* www.mla.org, pg 668

Reiser, Annie M, MLA Prize for a First Book, 85 Broad St, Suite 500, New York, NY 10004-2434 *Tel:* 646-576-5141; 646-576-5000 *Fax:* 646-458-0030 *E-mail:* awards@mla.org *Web Site:* www.mla.org, pg 668

Reiser, Annie M, MLA Prize for a Scholarly Edition, 85 Broad St, Suite 500, New York, NY 10004-2434 *Tel:* 646-576-5141; 646-576-5000 *Fax:* 646-458-0030 *E-mail:* awards@mla.org *Web Site:* www.mla.org, pg 668

Reiser, Annie M, MLA Prize for Independent Scholars, 85 Broad St, Suite 500, New York, NY 10004-2434 *Tel:* 646-576-5141; 646-576-5000 *Fax:* 646-458-0030 *E-mail:* awards@mla.org *Web Site:* www.mla.org, pg 668

Reiser, Annie M, MLA Prize for Studies in Native American Literatures, Cultures & Languages, 85 Broad St, Suite 500, New York, NY 10004-2434 *Tel:* 646-576-5141; 646-576-5000 *Fax:* 646-458-0030 *E-mail:* awards@mla.org *Web Site:* www.mla.org, pg 669

Reiser, Annie M, MLA Prize in United States Latina & Latino & Chicana & Chicano Literary & Cultural Studies, 85 Broad St, Suite 500, New York, NY 10004-2434 *Tel:* 646-576-5141; 646-576-5000 *Fax:* 646-458-0030 *E-mail:* awards@mla.org *Web Site:* www.mla.org, pg 669

Reiser, Annie M, Lois Roth Award, 85 Broad St, Suite 500, New York, NY 10004-2434 *Tel:* 646-576-5141; 646-576-5000 *Fax:* 646-458-0030 *E-mail:* awards@mla.org *Web Site:* www.mla.org, pg 686

Reiser, Annie M, Aldo & Jeanne Scaglione Prize for a Translation of a Literary Work, 85 Broad St, Suite 500, New York, NY 10004-2434 *Tel:* 646-576-5141; 646-576-5000 *Fax:* 646-458-0030 *E-mail:* awards@mla.org *Web Site:* www.mla.org, pg 687

Reiser, Annie M, Aldo & Jeanne Scaglione Prize for a Translation of a Scholarly Study of Literature, 85 Broad St, Suite 500, New York, NY 10004-2434 *Tel:* 646-576-5141; 646-576-5000 *Fax:* 646-458-0030 *E-mail:* awards@mla.org *Web Site:* www.mla.org, pg 687

Reiser, Annie M, Aldo & Jeanne Scaglione Prize for Comparative Literary Studies, 85 Broad St, Suite 500, New York, NY 10004-2434 *Tel:* 646-576-5141; 646-576-5000 *Fax:* 646-458-0030 *E-mail:* awards@mla.org *Web Site:* www.mla.org, pg 687

Reiser, Annie M, Aldo & Jeanne Scaglione Prize for French & Francophone Studies, 85 Broad St, Suite 500, New York, NY 10004-2434 *Tel:* 646-576-5141; 646-576-5000 *Fax:* 646-458-0030 *E-mail:* awards@mla.org *Web Site:* www.mla.org, pg 687

Reiser, Annie M, Aldo & Jeanne Scaglione Prize for Italian Studies, 85 Broad St, Suite 500, New York, NY 10004-2434 *Tel:* 646-576-5141; 646-576-5000 *Fax:* 646-458-0030 *E-mail:* awards@mla.org *Web Site:* www.mla.org, pg 687

Reiser, Annie M, Aldo & Jeanne Scaglione Prize for Studies in Germanic Languages & Literatures, 85 Broad St, Suite 500, New York, NY 10004-2434 *Tel:* 646-576-5141; 646-576-5000 *Fax:* 646-458-0030 *E-mail:* awards@mla.org *Web Site:* www.mla.org, pg 687

Reiser, Annie M, Aldo & Jeanne Scaglione Prize for Studies in Slavic Languages & Literatures, 85 Broad St, Suite 500, New York, NY 10004-2434 *Tel:* 646-576-5141; 646-576-5000 *Fax:* 646-458-0030 *E-mail:* awards@mla.org *Web Site:* www.mla.org, pg 687

Reiser, Annie M, Aldo & Jeanne Scaglione Publication Award for a Manuscript in Italian Literary Studies, 85 Broad St, Suite 500, New York, NY 10004-2434 *Tel:* 646-576-5141; 646-576-5000 *Fax:* 646-458-0030 *E-mail:* awards@mla.org *Web Site:* www.mla.org, pg 687

Reiser, Annie M, William Sanders Scarborough Prize, 85 Broad St, Suite 500, New York, NY 10004-2434 *Tel:* 646-576-5141; 646-576-5000 *Fax:* 646-458-0030 *E-mail:* awards@mla.org *Web Site:* www.mla.org, pg 688

Reiser, Annie M, Mina P Shaughnessy Prize, 85 Broad St, Suite 500, New York, NY 10004-2434 *Tel:* 646-576-5141; 646-576-5000 *Fax:* 646-458-0030 *E-mail:* awards@mla.org *Web Site:* www.mla.org, pg 689

Reiss, Mitchell, The Colonial Williamsburg Foundation, PO Box 1776, Williamsburg, VA 23187-1776 *Tel:* 757-229-1000 *Toll Free Tel:* 800-HISTORY (447-8679) *E-mail:* geninfo@cwf.org *Web Site:* www.colonialwilliamsburg.org, pg 58

Reiss, William, John Hawkins and Associates Inc, 80 Maiden Lane, Suite 1503, New York, NY 10038 *Tel:* 212-807-7040 *E-mail:* jha@jhalit.com *Web Site:* jhalit.com, pg 521

Reiter, Jendi, Tom Howard/John H Reid Fiction & Essay Contest, 351 Pleasant St, PMB 222, Northampton, MA 01060-3961 *Tel:* 413-320-1847 *Toll Free Tel:* 866-WINWRIT (946-9748) *Fax:* 413-280-0539 *Web Site:* www.winningwriters.com, pg 653

Reiter, Jendi, Tom Howard/Margaret Reid Poetry Contest, 351 Pleasant St, PMB 222, Northampton, MA 01060-3961 *Tel:* 413-320-1847 *Toll Free Tel:* 866-WINWRIT (946-9748) *Fax:* 413-280-0539 *Web Site:* www.winningwriters.com, pg 653

Reiter, Jendi, North Street Book Prize, 351 Pleasant St, PMB 222, Northampton, MA 01060-3961 *Tel:* 413-320-1847 *Toll Free Tel:* 866-WINWRIT (946-9748) *Fax:* 413-280-0539 *Web Site:* www.winningwriters.com, pg 674

Reiter, Jendi, Wergle Flomp Humor Poetry Contest, 351 Pleasant St, PMB 222, Northampton, MA 01060-3961 *Tel:* 413-320-1847 *Toll Free Tel:* 866-WINWRIT (946-9748) *Fax:* 413-280-0539 *Web Site:* www.winningwriters.com, pg 696

Rekulak, Jason, Quirk Books, 215 Church St, Philadelphia, PA 19106 *Tel:* 215-627-3581 *Fax:* 215-627-5220 *E-mail:* general@quirkbooks.com *Web Site:* www.quirkbooks.com, pg 193

Remazeilles, Ingrid, Les Editions Goelette Inc, 1350 Marie-Victorin, St-Bruno-de-Montarville, Quebec, QC J3V 6B9, Canada *Tel:* 450-653-1337 *Toll Free Tel:* 800-463-4961 *Fax:* 450-653-9924 *E-mail:* info@boutiquegoelette.com *Web Site:* www.boutiquegeolette.com, pg 454

Remcheck, Allison, Stimola Literary Studio Inc, 308 Livingston Ct, Edgewater, NJ 07020 *Tel:* 201-945-9353 *Fax:* 201-945-9353; 201-490-5920 *E-mail:* info@stimolaliterarystudio.com *Web Site:* www.stimolaliterarystudio.com, pg 537

Renaud, Alain-Nicolas, Les Editions de l'Hexagone, 1055, blvd Rene Levesque Est, Bureau 300, Montreal, QC H2L 4S5, Canada *Tel:* 514-523-7993 *Fax:* 514-849-1388 *Web Site:* www.edhexagone.com, pg 453

Renaud, Alain-Nicolas, VLB Editeur Inc, 1055, boul Rene-Levesque Est, bureau 300, Montréal, QC H2L 4S5, Canada *Tel:* 514-849-5259 *Fax:* 514-849-1388 *Web Site:* www.edvlb.com, pg 475

Renaud, Marie-Lyne, Innis-Gerin Medal, Walter House, 282 Somerset W, Ottawa, ON K2P 0J6, Canada *Tel:* 613-991-6990 (ext 106) *Fax:* 613-991-6996 *E-mail:* nominations@rsc-src.ca *Web Site:* www.rsc-src.ca, pg 656

Renaud, Marie-Lyne, Lorne Pierce Medal, Walter House, 282 Somerset W, Ottawa, ON K2P 0J6, Canada *Tel:* 613-991-6990 (ext 106) *Fax:* 613-991-6996 *E-mail:* nominations@rsc-src.ca *Web Site:* www.rsc-src.ca, pg 679

Renaud, Michelle, Harlequin Enterprises Ltd, 225 Duncan Mill Rd, Don Mills, ON M3B 3K9, Canada *Tel:* 416-445-5860 *Toll Free Tel:* 888-432-4879; 800-370-5838 (ebook inquiries) *E-mail:* customerservice@harlequin.com *Web Site:* www.harlequin.com, pg 459

Renheim, Jessica, Dutton, 375 Hudson St, New York, NY 10014 *Tel:* 212-366-2000 *Fax:* 212-366-2262 *Web Site:* www.penguin.com, pg 74

Renker, Jason, The Century Foundation Press, One Whitehall St, 15th fl, New York, NY 10004 *Tel:* 212-452-7700 *Fax:* 212-535-7534 *E-mail:* info@tcf.org *Web Site:* www.tcf.org, pg 52

Ripianzi, David, YMAA Publication Center Inc, PO Box 480, Wolfeboro, NH 03894 *Tel:* 603-569-7988 *Toll Free Tel:* 800-669-8892 *Fax:* 603-569-1889 *E-mail:* info@ymaa.com *Web Site:* www.ymaa.com, pg 262

Riske, Douglas, Manitoba Arts Council, 525-93 Lombard Ave, Winnipeg, MB R3B 3B1, Canada *Tel:* 204-945-2237 *Toll Free Tel:* 866-994-2787 *Fax:* 204-945-5925 *E-mail:* info@artscouncil.mb.ca *Web Site:* artscouncil.mb.ca, pg 569

Riske, Kris Brandt, American Federation of Astrologers Inc, 6535 S Rural Rd, Tempe, AZ 85283-3746 *Tel:* 480-838-1751 *Toll Free Tel:* 888-301-7630 *Fax:* 480-838-8293 *Web Site:* www.astrologers.com, pg 11

Riskey, Curtis, CBA: The Association for Christian Retail, 1365 Garden of the Gods Rd, Suite 105, Colorado Springs, CO 80907 *Tel:* 719-265-9895 *Toll Free Tel:* 800-252-1950 *Fax:* 719-272-3508 *E-mail:* info@cbaonline.org *Web Site:* cbaonline.org, pg 562

Rissi, Anica, HarperCollins Children's Books, 195 Broadway, New York, NY 10007 *Tel:* 212-207-7000 *Web Site:* www.harpercollins.com/childrens, pg 101

Ristau, Todd, Southeastern Theatre Conference New Play Project, 1175 Revolution Mill Dr, Suite 14, Greensboro, NC 27405 *Tel:* 336-272-3645 *Fax:* 336-272-8810 *E-mail:* info@setc.org *Web Site:* www.setc.org, pg 691

Ritchie, Adele, Canadian Newspaper Association, 890 Yonge St, Suite 200, Toronto, ON M4W 3P4, Canada *Tel:* 416-923-3567; 416-482-1090 *Toll Free Tel:* 877-305-2262 *Fax:* 416-923-7206; 416-482-1908 *E-mail:* info@newspaperscanada.ca *Web Site:* www.newspaperscanada.ca, pg 562

Ritchken, Deborah, Marsal Lyon Literary Agency LLC, 665 San Rodolfo Dr, Suite 124, PMB 121, Solana Beach, CA 92075 *Tel:* 760-814-8507 *Web Site:* www.marsallyonliteraryagency.com, pg 527

Ritt, Judith W, Professional Resource Press, 1958 Barber Rd, Sarasota, FL 34240 *Tel:* 941-343-9601 *Toll Free Tel:* 800-443-3364 (orders & cust serv) *Fax:* 941-343-9201 *Toll Free Fax:* 866-804-4843 (orders only) *E-mail:* cs.prpress@gmail.com *Web Site:* www.prpress.com, pg 189

Rittenberg, Ann, Ann Rittenberg Literary Agency Inc, 15 Maiden Lane, Suite 206, New York, NY 10038 *Tel:* 212-684-6936 *Fax:* 212-684-6929 *E-mail:* info@rittlit.com *Web Site:* www.rittlit.com, pg 532

Ritter, Carol, Romance Writers of America®, 14615 Benfer Rd, Houston, TX 77069 *Tel:* 832-717-5200 *Fax:* 832-717-5201 *E-mail:* info@rwa.org *Web Site:* www.rwa.org, pg 577

Ritter, Carol, Romance Writers of America Awards, 14615 Benfer Rd, Houston, TX 77069 *Tel:* 832-717-5200 *Fax:* 832-717-5201 *E-mail:* info@rwa.org *Web Site:* www.rwa.org, pg 685

Ritter, Emily, Bloomsbury Publishing Inc, 1385 Broadway, 5th fl, New York, NY 10018 *Tel:* 212-419-5300 *E-mail:* marketingusa@bloomsbury.com; adultpublicityusa@bloomsbury.com; askacademic@bloomsbury.com *Web Site:* www.bloomsbury.com, pg 38

Riva, Peter, International Transactions Inc, 28 Alope Way, Gila, NM 88038 *Tel:* 845-373-9696 *Fax:* 480-393-5162 *E-mail:* info@intltrans.com *Web Site:* www.intltrans.com, pg 522

Riva, Sandra Anne, International Transactions Inc, 28 Alope Way, Gila, NM 88038 *Tel:* 845-373-9696 *Fax:* 480-393-5162 *E-mail:* info@intltrans.com *Web Site:* www.intltrans.com, pg 522

Rivas, Laura, Candlewick Press, 99 Dover St, Somerville, MA 02144-2825 *Tel:* 617-661-3330 *Fax:* 617-661-0565 *E-mail:* bigbear@candlewick.com; salesinfo@candlewick.com *Web Site:* www.candlewick.com, pg 46

Rivas-Smith, Alexandra, William H Sadlier Inc, 9 Pine St, New York, NY 10005 *Tel:* 212-227-2120 *Toll Free Tel:* 800-221-5175 (cust serv) *Fax:* 212-312-6080 *E-mail:* customerservice@sadlier.com *Web Site:* www.sadlier.com, pg 203

Riven, Judith, Judith Riven Literary Agent LLC, 250 W 16 St, Suite 4F, New York, NY 10011 *Tel:* 212-255-1009 *Fax:* 212-255-8547 *E-mail:* rivenlitqueries@gmail.com *Web Site:* rivenlit.com, pg 500, 533

Rivera, Frank, Adams Media, 57 Littlefield St, Avon, MA 02322 *Tel:* 508 427-7100 *Web Site:* www.simonandschuster.com, pg 4

Rivera, Jacqueline, Santillana USA Publishing Co, 2023 NW 84 Ave, Doral, FL 33122 *Tel:* 305-591-9522 *Toll Free Tel:* 800-245-8584 *E-mail:* customerservice@santillanausa.com *Web Site:* www.santillanausa.com, pg 206

Rizzo, Adriana, Houghton Mifflin Harcourt Trade & Reference Division, 125 High St, Boston, MA 02110 *Tel:* 617-351-5000 *Toll Free Tel:* 800-225-3362 *Web Site:* www.hmhco.com, pg 111

Roach, Brian, The Catholic University of America Press, 240 Leahy Hall, 620 Michigan Ave NE, Washington, DC 20064 *Tel:* 202-319-5052 *Toll Free Tel:* 800-537-5487 (orders only) *Fax:* 202-319-4985 *E-mail:* cua-press@cua.edu *Web Site:* cuapress.cua.edu, pg 49

Roach, Reginald, Palmetto Bug Books, 121 N Hibiscus Dr, Miami Beach, FL 33139 *Tel:* 305-531-9813 *Fax:* 305-604-1516 *E-mail:* palmettobugbooks@gmail.com, pg 173

Roane, Rick, Cherry Hill Publishing LLC, 24344 Del Amo Rd, Ramona, CA 92065 *Tel:* 858-829-5550 *Toll Free Tel:* 800-407-1072 *Fax:* 760-203-1200 *E-mail:* operations@cherryhillpublishing.com; sales@cherryhillpublishing.com *Web Site:* www.cherryhillpublishing.com, pg 54

Roane, Sharon, Cherry Hill Publishing LLC, 24344 Del Amo Rd, Ramona, CA 92065 *Tel:* 858-829-5550 *Toll Free Tel:* 800-407-1072 *Fax:* 760-203-1200 *E-mail:* operations@cherryhillpublishing.com; sales@cherryhillpublishing.com *Web Site:* www.cherryhillpublishing.com, pg 54

Robbins, Arnie, American Society of News Editors (ASNE), 209 Reynolds Journalism Institute, Missouri School of Journalism, Columbia, MO 65211 *Tel:* 573-882-2430 *Fax:* 573-884-3824 *Web Site:* asne.org, pg 556

Robbins, BJ, BJ Robbins Literary Agency, 5130 Bellaire Ave, North Hollywood, CA 91607 *E-mail:* robbinsliterary@gmail.com, pg 533

Robbins, Caroline, Trafalgar Square Books, 388 Howe Hill Rd, North Pomfret, VT 05053 *Tel:* 802-457-1911 *Toll Free Tel:* 800-423-4525 *Fax:* 802-457-1913 *E-mail:* contact@trafalgarbooks.com *Web Site:* www.trafalgarbooks.com; www.horseandriderbooks.com, pg 234

Robbins, Christopher, Familius, 1254 Commerce Way, Sanger, CA 93657 *Tel:* 559-876-2170 *Fax:* 559-876-2180 *E-mail:* orders@familius.com *Web Site:* www.familius.com, pg 82

Robbins, Fleetwood, Waxman Leavell Literary Agency, 443 Park Ave S, No 1004, New York, NY 10016 *Tel:* 212-675-5556 *Fax:* 212-675-1381 *Web Site:* www.waxmanleavell.com, pg 541

Robbins, Lara, Berkley Publishing Group, 375 Hudson St, New York, NY 10014 *Tel:* 212-366-2000 *Fax:* 212-366-2385 *Web Site:* www.penguin.com, pg 33

Robbins, Michele, Familius, 1254 Commerce Way, Sanger, CA 93657 *Tel:* 559-876-2170 *Fax:* 559-876-2180 *E-mail:* orders@familius.com *Web Site:* www.familius.com, pg 82

Robbins, Sandra, See-More's Workshop Arts & Education Workshops, 325 West End Ave, Suite 12-B, New York, NY 10023 *Tel:* 212-724-0677 *Fax:* 212-724-0767 *E-mail:* sbt@shadowboxtheatre.org *Web Site:* www.shadowboxtheatre.org, pg 614

Roberge, Amelie, Kids Can Press Ltd, 25 Dockside Dr, Toronto, ON M5A 0B5, Canada *Tel:* 416-479-7000 *Toll Free Tel:* 800-265-0884 *Fax:* 416-960-5437 *E-mail:* info@kidscan.com; customerservice@kidscan.com *Web Site:* www.kidscanpress.com; www.kidscanpress.ca, pg 461

Roberson, Nancy, AMACOM Books, 1601 Broadway, New York, NY 10019-7420 *Tel:* 212-586-8100 *Toll Free Tel:* 800-250-5308 (cust serv) *Fax:* 212-903-8083; 518-891-2372 (orders) *E-mail:* pubs_cust_serv@amanet.org *Web Site:* www.amacombooks.org, pg 8

Roberson, Rick, The Barnabas Agency, PO Box 3113, Corsicana, TX 75151-3113 *Toll Free Tel:* 800-927-0517 *E-mail:* info@barnabasagency.com *Web Site:* www.barnabasagency.com, pg 547

Robert, Katie, American Industrial Hygiene Association - AIHA, 3141 Fairview Park Dr, Suite 777, Falls Church, VA 22042 *Tel:* 703-849-8888 *Fax:* 703-207-3561 *E-mail:* infonet@aiha.org *Web Site:* www.aiha.org, pg 12

Roberts, Brian, Books We Love Ltd, 100 Chinook Winds Place SW, Unit 4407, Airdrie, AB T4B 4B4, Canada *Tel:* 403-710-4869 *E-mail:* bookswelove@telus.net *Web Site:* bookswelove.net; www.facebook.com/Books.We.Love.Ltd, pg 447

Roberts, Claire, Trident Media Group LLC, 41 Madison Ave, 36th fl, New York, NY 10010 *Tel:* 212-333-1511 *E-mail:* info@tridentmediagroup.com; press@tridentmediagroup.com *Web Site:* www.tridentmediagroup.com, pg 540

Roberts, Conrad, University Press of Kansas, 2502 Westbrooke Circle, Lawrence, KS 66045-4444 *Tel:* 785-864-4154; 785-864-4155 (orders) *Fax:* 785-864-4586 *E-mail:* upress@ku.edu; upkorders@ku.edu (orders) *Web Site:* www.kansaspress.ku.edu, pg 246

Roberts, Jane F, Literary & Creative Artists Inc, 3543 Albemarle St NW, Washington, DC 20008-4213 *Tel:* 202-362-4688 *Fax:* 202-362-8875 *E-mail:* lcadc@earthlink.net (queries, no attachments) *Web Site:* www.lcadc.com, pg 526

Roberts, Janet, Centering Corp, 7230 Maple St, Omaha, NE 68134 *Tel:* 402-553-1200 *Toll Free Tel:* 866-218-0101 *Fax:* 402-553-0507 *E-mail:* orders@centering.org *Web Site:* www.centering.org, pg 51

Roberts, Jennifer, Candlewick Press, 99 Dover St, Somerville, MA 02144-2825 *Tel:* 617-661-3330 *Fax:* 617-661-0565 *E-mail:* bigbear@candlewick.com; salesinfo@candlewick.com *Web Site:* www.candlewick.com, pg 46

Roberts, Jill, Tachyon Publications LLC, 1459 18 St, No 139, San Francisco, CA 94107 *Tel:* 415-285-5615 *E-mail:* tachyon@tachyonpublications.com *Web Site:* www.tachyonpublications.com, pg 226

Roberts, LaTisha, Texas Tech University Press, 1120 Main St, 2nd fl, Lubbock, TX 79401 *Tel:* 806-742-2982 *Toll Free Tel:* 800-832-4042 *Fax:* 806-742-2979 *E-mail:* ttup@ttu.edu *Web Site:* www.ttupress.org, pg 230

Roberts, Laura Weiss MD, American Psychiatric Association Publishing, 1000 Wilson Blvd, Suite 1825, Arlington, VA 22209 *Tel:* 703-907-7322 *Toll Free Tel:* 800-368-5777 *Fax:* 703-907-1091 *E-mail:* appi@psych.org *Web Site:* www.appi.org; www.psychiatryonline.org, pg 14

Roberts, Marc, Centering Corp, 7230 Maple St, Omaha, NE 68134 *Tel:* 402-553-1200 *Toll Free Tel:* 866-218-0101 *Fax:* 402-553-0507 *E-mail:* orders@centering.org *Web Site:* www.centering.org, pg 51

Roberts, Megan, Sewanee Writers' Conference, Stamler Ctr, 119 Gailor Hall, 735 University Ave, Sewanee, TN 37383 *Tel:* 931-598-1141; 931-598-1654 *E-mail:* swc@sewanee.edu *Web Site:* www.sewaneewriters.org, pg 614

Roberts, Michele, Liberty Fund Inc, 8335 Allison Pointe Trail, Suite 300, Indianapolis, IN 46250-1684 *Tel:* 317-842-0880 *Toll Free Tel:* 800-955-8335; 800 866 3520; 800-368-7897 ext 6069 (cust serv) *Fax:* 317-577-9067; 317-579-6060 (cust serv); 708-534-7803 *E-mail:* books@libertyfund.org; info@libertyfund.org *Web Site:* www.libertyfund.org, pg 133

Roberts, Nate, Emmaus Road Publishing Inc, 1468 Parkview Circle, Steubenville, OH 43952 *Tel:* 740-283-2880 (outside US) *Toll Free Tel:* 800-

PERSONNEL INDEX

398-5470 (orders) *Fax:* 740-283-4011 (orders) *E-mail:* questions@emmausroad.org *Web Site:* www.emmausroad.org, pg 78

Roberts, Sherry, The Roberts Group, 12803 Eastview Curve, Apple Valley, MN 55124 *Tel:* 952-322-4005 *E-mail:* info@editorialservice.com *Web Site:* www.editorialservice.com, pg 500

Roberts, Stuart, Simon & Schuster, 1230 Avenue of the Americas, New York, NY 10020 *Tel:* 212-698-7000 *Toll Free Tel:* 800-223-2348 (cust serv); 800-223-2336 (orders) *Toll Free Fax:* 800-943-9831 (orders) *Web Site:* www.simonandschuster.com, pg 212

Roberts, Tim, Counterpath Press, 613 22 St, Denver, CO 80205 *E-mail:* counterpath@counterpathpress.org; editors@counterpathpress.org *Web Site:* www.counterpathpress.org, pg 63

Roberts, Tony, The Roberts Group, 12803 Eastview Curve, Apple Valley, MN 55124 *Tel:* 952-322-4005 *E-mail:* info@editorialservice.com *Web Site:* www.editorialservice.com, pg 500

Roberts, Tony, University of Oklahoma Press, 2800 Venture Dr, Norman, OK 73069-8216 *Tel:* 405-325-2000 *Toll Free Tel:* 800-627-7377 (orders) *Fax:* 405-364-5798 (orders) *Toll Free Fax:* 800-735-0476 (orders) *E-mail:* presscs@ou.edu *Web Site:* www.oupress.com, pg 244

Roberts, U D, Brentwood Christian Press, 4000 Beallwood Ave, Columbus, GA 31904 *Toll Free Tel:* 800-334-8861 *E-mail:* brentwood@aol.com *Web Site:* www.brentwoodbooks.com, pg 42

Robertson, Jocelyn, Literature Fellowship, 2410 N Old Penitentiary Rd, Boise, ID 83712 *Tel:* 208-334-2119 *E-mail:* info@arts.idaho.gov *Web Site:* www.arts.idaho.gov, pg 662

Robertson, Jocelyn, Writer in Residence, 2410 N Old Penitentiary Rd, Boise, ID 83712 *Tel:* 208-334-2119 *E-mail:* info@arts.idaho.gov *Web Site:* www.arts.idaho.gov, pg 700

Robertson, Randy, Susquehanna University, Department of English and Creative Writing, 514 University Ave, Selinsgrove, PA 17870 *Tel:* 570-372-0101, pg 622

Robertson, Sarah, Schlager Group Inc, 325 N Saint Paul, Suite 3425, Dallas, TX 75201 *Toll Free Tel:* 888-416-5727 *Fax:* 214-347-9469 *E-mail:* info@schlagergroup.com *Web Site:* www.schlagergroup.com, pg 207

Robey, Annelise, Jane Rotrosen Agency LLC, 85 Broad St, 28th fl, New York, NY 10004 *Tel:* 212-593-4330 *Fax:* 212-935-6985 *Web Site:* janerotrosen.com, pg 533

Robinson, David, Linguistic Society of America, 522 21 St NW, Suite 120, Washington, DC 20006-5012 *Tel:* 202-835-1714 *Fax:* 202-835-1717 *E-mail:* lsa@lsadc.org *Web Site:* www.linguisticsociety.org, pg 568

Robinson, James J, The Minerals, Metals & Materials Society (TMS), 5700 Corporate Dr, Suite 750, Pittsburgh, PA 15237 *Tel:* 724-776-9000 *Toll Free Tel:* 800-759-4867 *Fax:* 724-776-3770 *E-mail:* publications@tms.org (orders) *Web Site:* www.tms.org/bookstore (orders); www.tms.org, pg 151

Robinson, Jennifer, Gallery Books, 1230 Avenue of the Americas, New York, NY 10020 *Toll Free Tel:* 800-456-6798 *Fax:* 212-698-7284 *E-mail:* consumer.customerservice@simonandschuster.com *Web Site:* www.simonsays.com, pg 90

Robinson, Jim, Harlequin Enterprises Ltd, 225 Duncan Mill Rd, Don Mills, ON M3B 3K9, Canada *Tel:* 416-445-5860 *Toll Free Tel:* 888-432-4879; 800-370-5838 (ebook inquiries) *E-mail:* customerservice@harlequin.com *Web Site:* www.harlequin.com, pg 459

Robinson, Julie, R Ross Annett Award for Children's Literature, 11759 Groat Rd, Edmonton, AB T5M 3K6, Canada *Tel:* 780-422-8174 *Toll Free Tel:* 800-665-5354 (AB only) *Fax:* 780-422-2663 (attn WGA) *E-mail:* mail@writersguild.ca *Web Site:* writersguild.ca, pg 627

Robinson, Julie, Georges Bugnet Award for Fiction, 11759 Groat Rd, Edmonton, AB T5M 3K6, Canada *Tel:* 780-422-8174 *Toll Free Tel:* 800-665-5354 (AB only) *Fax:* 780-422-2663 (attn WGA) *E-mail:* mail@writersguild.ca *Web Site:* writersguild.ca, pg 634

Robinson, Julie, The City of Calgary W O Mitchell Book Prize, 11759 Groat Rd, Edmonton, AB T5M 3K6, Canada *Tel:* 780-422-8174 *Toll Free Tel:* 800-665-5354 (AB only) *Fax:* 780-422-2663 (attn WGA) *E-mail:* mail@writersguild.ca *Web Site:* writersguild.ca, pg 637

Robinson, Julie, Wilfrid Eggleston Award for Nonfiction, 11759 Groat Rd, Edmonton, AB T5M 3K6, Canada *Tel:* 780-422-8174 *Toll Free Tel:* 800-665-5354 (AB only) *Fax:* 780-422-2663 (attn WGA) *E-mail:* mail@writersguild.ca *Web Site:* writersguild.ca, pg 644

Robinson, Julie, James H Gray Award for Short Nonfiction, 11759 Groat Rd, Edmonton, AB T5M 3K6, Canada *Tel:* 780-422-8174 *Toll Free Tel:* 800-665-5354 (AB only) *Fax:* 780-422-2663 (attn WGA) *E-mail:* mail@writersguild.ca *Web Site:* writersguild.ca, pg 650

Robinson, Julie, The Robert Kroetsch City of Edmonton Book Prize, 11759 Groat Rd, Edmonton, AB T5M 3K6, Canada *Tel:* 780-422-8174 *Toll Free Tel:* 800-665-5354 (AB only) *Fax:* 780-422-2663 (attn WGA) *E-mail:* mail@writersguild.ca *Web Site:* writersguild.ca, pg 659

Robinson, Julie, Howard O'Hagan Award for Short Story, 11759 Groat Rd, Edmonton, AB T5M 3K6, Canada *Tel:* 780-422-8174 *Toll Free Tel:* 800-665-5354 (AB only) *Fax:* 780-422-2663 (attn WGA) *E-mail:* mail@writersguild.ca *Web Site:* writersguild.ca, pg 675

Robinson, Julie, Gwen Pharis Ringwood Award for Drama, 11759 Groat Rd, Edmonton, AB T5M 3K6, Canada *Tel:* 780-422-8174 *Toll Free Tel:* 800-665-5354 (AB only) *Fax:* 780-422-2663 (attn WGA) *E-mail:* mail@writersguild.ca *Web Site:* writersguild.ca, pg 685

Robinson, Julie, Stephan G Stephansson Award for Poetry, 11759 Groat Rd, Edmonton, AB T5M 3K6, Canada *Tel:* 780-422-8174 *Toll Free Tel:* 800-665-5354 (AB only) *Fax:* 780-422-2663 (attn WGA) *E-mail:* mail@writersguild.ca *Web Site:* writersguild.ca, pg 692

Robinson, Julie, Jon Whyte Memorial Essay Prize, 11759 Groat Rd, Edmonton, AB T5M 3K6, Canada *Tel:* 780-422-8174 *Toll Free Tel:* 800-665-5354 (AB only) *Fax:* 780-422-2663 (attn WGA) *E-mail:* mail@writersguild.ca *Web Site:* writersguild.ca, pg 697

Robinson, Julie, Writers' Guild of Alberta, 11759 Groat Rd, Edmonton, AB T5M 3K6, Canada *Tel:* 780-422-8174 *Toll Free Tel:* 800-665-5354 (AB only) *Fax:* 780-422-2663 (attn WGA) *E-mail:* mail@writersguild.ca *Web Site:* writersguild.ca, pg 581

Robinson, Kelly, Milner Award, One Margaret Mitchell Sq NW, Atlanta, GA 30303 *Tel:* 404-730-1865 *E-mail:* info@themilneraward.org *Web Site:* www.themilneraward.org, pg 668

Robinson, Kim, University of California Press, 155 Grand Ave, Suite 400, Oakland, CA 94612-3758 *Tel:* 510-883-8232 *Fax:* 510-836-8910 *E-mail:* customerservice@ucpressjournals.com *Web Site:* www.ucpress.edu, pg 240

Robinson, Marian, The Guilford Press, 370 Seventh Ave, Suite 1200, New York, NY 10001-1020 *Tel:* 212-431-9800 *Toll Free Tel:* 800-365-7006 *Fax:* 212-966-6708 *E-mail:* info@guilford.com *Web Site:* www.guilford.com, pg 97

Robinson, Morris (Dino), Northwestern University Press, 629 Noyes St, Evanston, IL 60208-4210 *Tel:* 847-491-2046 *Toll Free Tel:* 800-621-2736 (orders only) *Fax:* 847-491-8150 *E-mail:* nupress@northwestern.edu *Web Site:* www.nupress.northwestern.edu, pg 164

Robinson, Richard, Scholastic Inc, 557 Broadway, New York, NY 10012 *Tel:* 212-343-6100 *Toll Free Tel:* 800-SCHOLASTIC (724-6527) *Web Site:* www.scholastic.com, pg 208

Robinson, Roxana, The Authors Guild, 31 E 32 St, 7th fl, New York, NY 10016 *Tel:* 212-563-5904 *Fax:* 212-564-5363 *E-mail:* staff@authorsguild.org *Web Site:* www.authorsguild.org, pg 559

Robinson, Terry, Gale, 27500 Drake Rd, Farmington Hills, MI 48331-3535 *Tel:* 248-699-4253 *Toll Free Tel:* 800-877-4253 *Toll Free Fax:* 800-414-5043 (orders) *E-mail:* gale.customercare@cengage.com *Web Site:* www.gale.com, pg 89

Robinson, Terry, Macmillan Reference USA™, 27500 Drake Rd, Farmington Hills, MI 48331-3535 *Tel:* 248-699-4253 *Toll Free Tel:* 800-877-4253 *Toll Free Fax:* 877-363-4253 *E-mail:* gale.customercare@cengage.com *Web Site:* www.gale.cengage.com/macmillan, pg 140

Robison, Jordan, Jessie Bernard Award, c/o Governance Off, 1430 "K" St NW, Suite 600, Washington, DC 20005 *Tel:* 202-383-9005 *Fax:* 202-638-0882 *E-mail:* governance@asanet.org *Web Site:* www.asanet.org, pg 631

Robison, Jordan, Distinguished Scholarly Book Award, c/o Governance Off, 1430 "K" St NW, Suite 600, Washington, DC 20005 *Tel:* 202-383-9005 *Fax:* 202-638-0882 *E-mail:* governance@asanet.org *Web Site:* www.asanet.org, pg 641

Robson, William B P, C D Howe Institute, 67 Yonge St, Suite 300, Toronto, ON M5E 1J8, Canada *Tel:* 416-865-1904 *Fax:* 416-865-1866 *E-mail:* cdhowe@cdhowe.org *Web Site:* www.cdhowe.org, pg 460

Robyn, Chris, China Books, 360 Swift Ave, Suite 48, South San Francisco, CA 94080 *Tel:* 650-872-7076 *Toll Free Tel:* 800-818-2017 (US only) *Fax:* 650-872-7808 *E-mail:* info@chinabooks.com *Web Site:* www.chinabooks.com, pg 54

Robyn, Chris, Long River Press, 360 Swift Ave, Suite 48, South San Francisco, CA 94080 *Tel:* 650-872-7718 (ext 312) *Fax:* 650-872-7808 *E-mail:* info@longriverpress.com *Web Site:* www.chinabooks.com, pg 137

Rocco, Renee, Kensington Publishing Corp, 119 W 40 St, New York, NY 10018 *Tel:* 212-407-1500 *Toll Free Tel:* 800-221-2647 *Fax:* 212-935-0699 *Web Site:* www.kensingtonbooks.com, pg 125

Roche, Art, Dubuque Fine Arts Players Annual One Act Play Festival, PO Box 1160, Dubuque, IA 52004-1160 *Tel:* 563-588-3438 *E-mail:* contact@dbqoneacts.org *Web Site:* www.dbqoneacts.org, pg 643

Roche, Mary Beth, Macmillan, 175 Fifth Ave, New York, NY 10010 *Tel:* 646-307-5151 *E-mail:* press.inquiries@macmillan.com *Web Site:* www.macmillan.com, pg 139

Roche, Mary Beth, Macmillan Audio, 175 Fifth Ave, New York, NY 10010 *Tel:* 646-307-5151 *Toll Free Tel:* 888-330-8477 (cust serv) *Fax:* 917-534-0980 *Web Site:* www.macmillanaudio.com, pg 140

Rockwell, Lew, Ludwig von Mises Institute, 518 W Magnolia Ave, Auburn, AL 36832 *Tel:* 334-321-2100 *Fax:* 334-321-2119 *E-mail:* info@mises.org *Web Site:* www.mises.org, pg 251

Rodale, Maria, Rodale Inc, 400 S Tenth St, Emmaus, PA 18049 *Tel:* 610-967-5171 *Toll Free Tel:* 866-387-0509 *E-mail:* bookmarketing@rodale.com; bookpublicity@rodale.com *Web Site:* www.rodale.com, pg 200

Rodenberger, Jean, F A Davis Co, 1915 Arch St, Philadelphia, PA 19103 *Tel:* 215-568-2270; 215-440-3001 *Toll Free Tel:* 800-523-4049 *Fax:* 215-568-5065; 215-440-3016 *E-mail:* info@fadavis.com; orders@fadavis.com *Web Site:* www.fadavis.com, pg 68

Rodengen, Jeffrey L, Write Stuff Enterprises LLC, 1001 S Andrews Ave, Suite 120, Fort Lauderdale, FL 33316 *Tel:* 954-462-6657 *Toll Free Tel:* 800-900-2665 *Fax:* 954-462-6023 *E-mail:* legends@writestuffbooks.com *Web Site:* www.writestuffbooks.com, pg 260

Rodgers, Emma, Second Story Press, 20 Maud St, Suite 401, Toronto, ON M5V 2M5, Canada *Tel:* 416-537-7850 *Fax:* 416-537-0588 *E-mail:* info@secondstorypress.ca *Web Site:* secondstorypress.ca, pg 470

Rodgers, Loren, National Center For Employee Ownership (NCEO), 1629 Telegraph Ave, Suite 200, Oakland, CA 94612 *Tel:* 510-208-1300 *Fax:* 510-272-9510 *E-mail:* customerservice@nceo.org *Web Site:* www.nceo.org, pg 157

Rodman, Howard, Writers Guild of America Awards, 7000 W Third St, Los Angeles, CA 90048 *Tel:* 323-951-4000; 323-782-4569 *Fax:* 323-782-4800 *Web Site:* www.wga.org, pg 700

Rodman, Howard, Writers Guild of America, West (WGAW), 7000 W Third St, Los Angeles, CA 90048 *Tel:* 323-951-4000 *Toll Free Tel:* 800-548-4532 *Fax:* 323-782-4800 *Web Site:* www.wga.org, pg 581

Rodman, Jordan, Alfred A Knopf/Everyman's Library, c/o Penguin Random House Inc, 1745 Broadway, New York, NY 10019 *Tel:* 212-751-2600 *Toll Free Tel:* 800-638-6460 *Fax:* 212-572-2593 *Web Site:* www.knopfdoubleday.com, pg 127

Rodmell, Emily, Love Inspired Books, 233 Broadway, Suite 1001, New York, NY 10279 *Tel:* 212-553-4200 *Fax:* 212-227-8969 *E-mail:* customer_service@harlequin.ca *Web Site:* www.harlequin.com, pg 138

Rodrick, Scott, National Center For Employee Ownership (NCEO), 1629 Telegraph Ave, Suite 200, Oakland, CA 94612 *Tel:* 510-208-1300 *Fax:* 510-272-9510 *E-mail:* customerservice@nceo.org *Web Site:* www.nceo.org, pg 157

Roeder, Taryn, Houghton Mifflin Harcourt Trade & Reference Division, 125 High St, Boston, MA 02110 *Tel:* 617-351-5000 *Toll Free Tel:* 800-225-3362 *Web Site:* www.hmhco.com, pg 111

Roessner, Maura, University of California Press, 155 Grand Ave, Suite 400, Oakland, CA 94612-3758 *Tel:* 510-883-8232 *Fax:* 510-836-8910 *E-mail:* customerservice@ucpressjournals.com *Web Site:* www.ucpress.edu, pg 240

Rogatz, Mitch, Triumph Books, 814 N Franklin St, Chicago, IL 60610 *Tel:* 312-337-0747 *Toll Free Tel:* 800-888-4741 (cust serv) *Fax:* 312-280-5470; 312-337-5985 *Web Site:* www.triumphbooks.com, pg 235

Rogen, Jessica, Boulevard Magazine Short Fiction Contest for Emerging Writers, 6614 Clayton Rd, PMB 325, Richmond Heights, MO 63117 *E-mail:* editors@boulevardmagazine.org *Web Site:* www.boulevardmagazine.org, pg 634

Rogers, Dr Amy, ScienceThrillers Media, PO Box 601392, Sacramento, CA 95860-1392 *Tel:* 916-712-3334 *E-mail:* query@sciencethrillersmedia.com *Web Site:* www.sciencethrillersmedia.com, pg 209

Rogers, Annette, Poisoned Pen Press, 6962 E First Ave, Suite 103, Scottsdale, AZ 85251 *Tel:* 480-945-3375 *Toll Free Tel:* 800-421-3976 *Fax:* 480-949-1707 *E-mail:* info@poisonedpenpress.com *Web Site:* www.poisonedpenpress.com, pg 185

Rogers, Christopher, Yale University Press, 302 Temple St, New Haven, CT 06511-8909 *Tel:* 203-432-0960; 203-432-0966 (sales); 401-531-2800 (cust serv) *Toll Free Tel:* 800-405-1619 (cust serv) *Fax:* 203-432-0948; 203-432-8485 (sales); 401-531-2801 (cust serv) *Toll Free Fax:* 800-406-9145 (cust serv) *E-mail:* sales.press@yale.edu (sales); customer.care@triliteral.org (cust serv) *Web Site:* www.yalebooks.com; yalepress.yale.edu/yupbooks, pg 261

Rogers, Kate, The Mountaineers Books, 1001 SW Klickitat Way, Suite 201, Seattle, WA 98134 *Tel:* 206-223-6303 *Toll Free Tel:* 800-553-4453 *Fax:* 206-223-6306 *Toll Free Fax:* 800-568-7604 *E-mail:* mbooks@mountaineersbooks.org; customerservice@mountaineersbooks.org *Web Site:* www.mountaineersbooks.org, pg 155

Rogers, Kelly, The Johns Hopkins University Press, 2715 N Charles St, Baltimore, MD 21218-4363 *Tel:* 410-516-6900; 410-516-6987 (journal orders outside US & CN) *Toll Free Tel:* 800-537-5487 (book orders & cust serv); 800-548-1784 (journal orders) *Fax:* 410-516-6968; 410-516-3866 (journal orders) *E-mail:* hfscustserv@press.jhu.edu (cust serv); jrnlcirc@press.jhu.edu (journal orders) *Web Site:* www.press.jhu.edu; muse.jhu.edu, pg 122

Rogers, Marian Hartman, Bibliogenesis, 152 Coddington Rd, Ithaca, NY 14850 *Tel:* 607-277-9660 *Web Site:* www.bibliogenesis.com, pg 489

Rogers, Tamara, Windbreak House Writing Retreat, PO Box 169, Hermosa, SD 57744-0169 *Tel:* 605-255-4064 *E-mail:* info@windbreakhouse.com *Web Site:* www.windbreakhouse.com, pg 616

Roghaar, Linda L, Linda Roghaar Literary Agency LLC, 133 High Point Dr, Amherst, MA 01002 *Tel:* 413-256-1921 *E-mail:* contact@lindaroghaar.com *Web Site:* www.lindaroghaar.com, pg 533

Roginsky, Gwen, The Metropolitan Museum of Art, 1000 Fifth Ave, New York, NY 10028 *Tel:* 212-879-5500; 212-570-3725 (edit) *Fax:* 212-396-5062 *E-mail:* editorial@metmuseum.org *Web Site:* www.metmuseum.org, pg 149

Rohrbach, Lewis Bunker, Picton Press, 814 E Elkcam Circle, Marco Island, FL 34145-2558 *Tel:* 239-970-2442 *E-mail:* sales@pictonpress.com (orders) *Web Site:* www.pictonpress.com, pg 183

Roistacher, Robert E, The Roistacher Literary Agency, 545 W 111 St, Suite 7-J, New York, NY 10025 *Tel:* 212-222-1405, pg 533

Rolfs, Erin, Louisiana State University Press, 338 Johnston Hall, Baton Rouge, LA 70803 *Tel:* 225-578-6294 *Fax:* 225-578-6461 *E-mail:* lsupress@lsu.edu *Web Site:* lsupress.org, pg 138

Rollans, Glenn, Brush Education Inc, 6531-111 St, Edmonton, AB T6H 4R5, Canada *Tel:* 780-989-0910 *Toll Free Tel:* 855-283-0900 *Fax:* 780-989-0930 *Toll Free Fax:* 855-283-6947 *E-mail:* contact@brusheducation.ca *Web Site:* www.brusheducation.ca, pg 448

Rolley, Chip, PEN American Center, 588 Broadway, Suite 303, New York, NY 10012 *Tel:* 212-334-1660 *Fax:* 212-334-2181 *E-mail:* info@pen.org *Web Site:* pen.org, pg 575

Rollins, Danielle, Random House Children's Books, 1745 Broadway, 10th fl, New York, NY 10019 *Tel:* 212-782-9000 *Web Site:* www.randomhousekids.com, pg 194

Rollins, John D, Yale University Press, 302 Temple St, New Haven, CT 06511-8909 *Tel:* 203-432-0960; 203-432-0966 (sales); 401-531-2800 (cust serv) *Toll Free Tel:* 800-405-1619 (cust serv) *Fax:* 203-432-0948; 203-432-8485 (sales); 401-531-2801 (cust serv) *Toll Free Fax:* 800-406-9145 (cust serv) *E-mail:* sales.press@yale.edu (sales); customer.care@triliteral.org (cust serv) *Web Site:* www.yalebooks.com; yalepress.yale.edu/yupbooks, pg 261

Rollins, Leslie, Getty Publications, 1200 Getty Center Dr, Suite 500, Los Angeles, CA 90049-1682 *Tel:* 310-440-7365 *Toll Free Tel:* 800-223-3431 (orders) *Fax:* 310-440-7758 *E-mail:* pubsinfo@getty.edu *Web Site:* www.getty.edu/publications, pg 92

Rollins, Onie, Winterthur Museum, Garden & Library, 5105 Kennett Pike, Winterthur, DE 19735 *Tel:* 302-888-4663 *Toll Free Tel:* 800-448-3883 *Fax:* 302-888-4950 *Web Site:* www.winterthur.org, pg 257

Romack, Conor, Glitterati Inc, 630 Ninth Ave, Suite 603, New York, NY 10036 *Tel:* 212-362-9119 *Fax:* 646-607-4433 *E-mail:* info@glitteratiincorporated.com *Web Site:* glitteratiincorporated.com, pg 93

Romano, Janet, Industrial Press Inc, 32 Haviland St, Suite 3, Norwalk, CT 06854 *Tel:* 203-956-5593 ext 0 (cust serv) *Toll Free Tel:* 888-528-7852 ext 0 (cust serv) *Fax:* 203-354-9391 (cust serv) *E-mail:* info@industrialpress.com (cust serv) *Web Site:* new.industrialpress.com, pg 116

Romano, Rich, Random House Children's Books, 1745 Broadway, 10th fl, New York, NY 10019 *Tel:* 212-782-9000 *Web Site:* www.randomhousekids.com, pg 194

Rome, Dee, Piano Press, 1425 Ocean Ave, Suite 5, Del Mar, CA 92014 *Tel:* 619-884-1401 *Fax:* 858-755-1104 *E-mail:* pianopress@pianopress.com *Web Site:* www.pianopress.com, pg 182

Romero, Anthony D, American Civil Liberties Union, 125 Broad St, 18th fl, New York, NY 10004 *Tel:* 212-549-2500 *E-mail:* media@aclu.org *Web Site:* www.aclu.org, pg 554

Romero, Emily, Penguin Young Readers Group, 345 Hudson St, New York, NY 10014 *Tel:* 212-366-2000; 212-414-3553 *Fax:* 212-414-3340 *Web Site:* www.penguin.com/children, pg 179

Romero, Kim, Chronicle Books LLC, 680 Second St, San Francisco, CA 94107 *Tel:* 415-537-4200 *Toll Free Tel:* 800-759-0190 (cust serv) *Fax:* 415-537-4460 *Toll Free Fax:* 800-858-7787 (orders); 800-286-9471 (cust serv) *E-mail:* frontdesk@chroniclebooks.com *Web Site:* www.chroniclebooks.com, pg 55

Romig, Anna, GP Putnam's Sons (Hardcover), 375 Hudson St, New York, NY 10014 *Tel:* 212-366-2000 *Fax:* 212-366-2643 *E-mail:* online@penguinputnam.com *Web Site:* www.penguin.com/publishers/gpputnamssons, pg 192

Rominger, Wray, Purple Mountain Press Ltd, 1060 Main St, Fleischmanns, NY 12430 *Tel:* 845-254-4062 *Toll Free Tel:* 800-325-2665 (orders) *Fax:* 845-254-4476 *E-mail:* purple@catskill.net *Web Site:* www.catskill.net/purple, pg 191

Rondeau, James, The Art Institute of Chicago, 111 S Michigan Ave, Chicago, IL 60603-6404 *Tel:* 312-443-3600; 312-443-3540 (pubns) *Fax:* 312-443-1334 (pubns) *Web Site:* www.artic.edu; www.artinstituteshop.org, pg 21

Ronk, Bret, Gulf Publishing Co, 2 Greenway Plaza, Suite 1020, Houston, TX 77046 *Tel:* 713-529-4301 *Fax:* 713-520-4433 *E-mail:* store@gulfpub.com; customerservice@gulfpub.com *Web Site:* www.gulfpub.com, pg 98

Ronn, Vicki, Mythopoeic Awards, Friends University, 2100 W University Ave, Wichita, KS 67213 *Tel:* 316-295-5563 *E-mail:* awards@mythsoc.org *Web Site:* www.mythsoc.org, pg 670

Ronnen, Lia, Artisan Books, 225 Varick St, New York, NY 10014-4381 *Tel:* 212-254-5900 *Toll Free Tel:* 800-722-7202 *Fax:* 212-677-6692 *E-mail:* artisaninfo@artisanbooks.com *Web Site:* www.workman.com/artisanbooks, pg 22

Roome, Hugh, Scholastic Education, 557 Broadway, New York, NY 10012 *Tel:* 212-343-6100 *Fax:* 212-343-6189 *Web Site:* www.scholastic.com, pg 207

Roome, Hugh, Scholastic Inc, 557 Broadway, New York, NY 10012 *Tel:* 212-343-6100 *Toll Free Tel:* 800-SCHOLASTIC (724-6527) *Web Site:* www.scholastic.com, pg 208

Rooney, Robert, National Association of Independent Publishers Representatives, 111 E 14 St, PMB 157, New York, NY 10003 *Tel:* 267-546-6561 *Toll Free Tel:* 888-624-7779 *Web Site:* naipr.org, pg 571

Root, William Pitt, Joy Harjo Poetry Award, PO Box 2414, Durango, CO 81302 *Tel:* 970-903-7914 *E-mail:* cutthroatmag@gmail.com *Web Site:* www.cutthroatmag.com, pg 652

Rosa-Mendoza, Gladys, me+mi publishing inc, 400 S Knoll St, Suite B, Wheaton, IL 60187 *Toll Free Tel:* 888-251-1444 *Fax:* 630-588-9804 *E-mail:* rw@rosawesley.com *Web Site:* www.memima.com, pg 147

Rosado, Darlene, BMI®, 7 World Trade Ctr, 250 Greenwich St, New York, NY 10007-0030 *Tel:* 212-586-2000; 212-220-3000 *Toll Free Tel:* 888-689-5264 (sales); 800-925-8451 (cust rel) *Fax:* 212-246-2163 *E-mail:* foundation@bmi.com *Web Site:* www.bmi.com, pg 560

Rosamilia, Michael, Kensington Publishing Corp, 119 W 40 St, New York, NY 10018 *Tel:* 212-407-1500 *Toll Free Tel:* 800-221-2647 *Fax:* 212-935-0699 *Web Site:* www.kensingtonbooks.com, pg 125

Rosati, Daniel, William S Hein & Co Inc, 2350 N Forest Rd, Getzville, NY 14068 *Tel:* 716-882-2600 *Toll Free Tel:* 800-828-7571 *Fax:* 716-883-8100 *E-mail:* mail@wshein.com; marketing@wshein.com *Web Site:* www.wshein.com, pg 105

Rose, Jean Anne, Gallery Books, 1230 Avenue of the Americas, New York, NY 10020 *Toll Free Tel:* 800-456-6798 *Fax:* 212-698-7284 *E-mail:* consumer.customerservice@simonandschuster.com *Web Site:* www.simonsays.com, pg 90

Rose, Jen, Wm B Eerdmans Publishing Co, 2140 Oak Industrial Dr NE, Grand Rapids, MI 49505 *Tel:* 616-459-4591 *Toll Free Tel:* 800-253-7521 *Fax:* 616-459-6540 *E-mail:* customerservice@eerdmans.com; sales@eerdmans.com *Web Site:* www.eerdmans.com, pg 76

Rose, Rebecca, Breakwater Books Ltd, One Stamp's Lane, St John's, NL A1C 6E6, Canada *Tel:* 709-722-6680 *Toll Free Tel:* 800-563-3333 (orders) *Fax:* 709-753-0708 *E-mail:* info@breakwaterbooks.com; orders@breakwaterbooks.com *Web Site:* www.breakwaterbooks.com, pg 447

Rose, Rie Sheridan, Zumaya Publications LLC, 3209 S IH 35, Suite 1086, Austin, TX 78741 *Tel:* 512-537-3145 *Fax:* 512-276-6745 *E-mail:* acquisitions@zumayapublications.com *Web Site:* www.zumayapublications.com, pg 263

Rose, Verena, Agatha Awards, PO Box 8007, Gaithersburg, MD 20898-8007 *E-mail:* malicedomesticpr@gmail.com *Web Site:* www.malicedomestic.org, pg 625

Roselli, Leena, Financial Executives Research Foundation Inc (FERF), West Tower, 7th fl, 1250 Headquarters Plaza, Morristown, NJ 07960-6837 *Tel:* 973-765-1000 *Fax:* 973-765-1023 *Web Site:* www.financialexecutives.org, pg 84

Rosema, Randy, HarperCollins Children's Books, 195 Broadway, New York, NY 10007 *Tel:* 212-207-7000 *Web Site:* www.harpercollins.com/childrens, pg 101

Roseman, Karl-Heinz, McFarland, 960 NC Hwy 88 W, Jefferson, NC 28640 *Tel:* 336-246-4460 *Toll Free Tel:* 800-253-2187 (orders) *Fax:* 336-246-5018; 336-246-4403 (orders) *E-mail:* info@mcfarlandpub.com *Web Site:* www.mcfarlandpub.com, pg 145

Roseman, Mike, Thieme Medical Publishers Inc, 333 Seventh Ave, 18th fl, New York, NY 10001 *Tel:* 212-760-0888 *Toll Free Tel:* 800-782-3488 *Fax:* 212-947-1112 *E-mail:* customerservice@thieme.com *Web Site:* www.thieme.com, pg 231

Rosen, Joan, Charlotte Sheedy Literary Agency Inc, 928 Broadway, Suite 901, New York, NY 10010 *Tel:* 212-780-9800 *Web Site:* www.sheedylit.com, pg 535

Rosen, Lynn, Yard Dog Press, 710 W Redbud Lane, Alma, AR 72921-7247 *Tel:* 479-632-4693 *Fax:* 479-632-4693 *Web Site:* www.yarddogpress.com, pg 261

Rosen, Roger, The Rosen Publishing Group Inc, 29 E 21 St, New York, NY 10010 *Toll Free Tel:* 800-237-9932 *Toll Free Fax:* 888-436-4643 *E-mail:* info@rosenpub.com *Web Site:* www.rosenpublishing.com, pg 201

Rosen, Sara, Glitterati Inc, 630 Ninth Ave, Suite 603, New York, NY 10036 *Tel:* 212-362-9119 *Fax:* 646-607-4433 *E-mail:* info@glitteratiincorporated.com *Web Site:* glitteratiincorporated.com, pg 93

Rosen, Selina, Yard Dog Press, 710 W Redbud Lane, Alma, AR 72921-7247 *Tel:* 479-632-4693 *Fax:* 479-632-4693 *Web Site:* www.yarddogpress.com, pg 261

Rosenbaum, David M, University of Missouri Press, 113 Heinkel Bldg, 201 S Seventh St, Columbia, MO 65211 *Tel:* 573-882-7641 *Toll Free Tel:* 800-621-2736 (orders) *Fax:* 573-884-4498 *Toll Free Fax:* 800-621-8476 (orders) *E-mail:* upress@missouri.edu *Web Site:* upress.missouri.edu; press.umsystem.edu, pg 243

Rosenberg, Barbara Collins, The Rosenberg Group, 23 Lincoln Ave, Marblehead, MA 01945 *Tel:* 781-990-1341 *Fax:* 781-990-1344 *E-mail:* rosenberglitsubmit@icloud.com *Web Site:* www.rosenberggroup.com, pg 533

Rosenberg, Dan, The Harvard Common Press, 100 Cummings Ctr, Suite 265-D, Beverly, MA 01915 *Tel:* 978-282-9590 *Fax:* 978-282-7765 *Web Site:* www.quartoknows.com/harvard-common-press, pg 102

Rosenberg, Jessica, Harlequin Enterprises Ltd, 233 Broadway, Suite 1001, New York, NY 10279 *Tel:* 212-553-4200 *Fax:* 212-227-8969 *E-mail:* customerservice@harlequin.com *Web Site:* www.harlequin.com, pg 101

Rosenberg, Julie, Disney-Hyperion Books, 1101 Flower St, Glendale, CA 91201 *Web Site:* books.disney.com, pg 70

Rosenberg, Linda, GP Putnam's Sons (Hardcover), 375 Hudson St, New York, NY 10014 *Tel:* 212-366-2000 *Fax:* 212-366-2643 *E-mail:* online@penguinputnam.com *Web Site:* www.penguin.com/publishers/gpputnamssons, pg 192

Rosenberg, Liz, Binghamton University Creative Writing Program, c/o Dept of English, PO Box 6000, Binghamton, NY 13902-6000 *Tel:* 607-777-2168 *Fax:* 607-777-2408 *E-mail:* cwpro@binghamton.edu *Web Site:* english.binghamton.edu/cwpro, pg 619

Rosenberg, Tracy, Media Alliance, 2830 20 St, Suite 102, San Francisco, CA 94110 *Tel:* 415-746-9475 *E-mail:* information@media-alliance.org *Web Site:* www.media-alliance.org, pg 569

Rosenblum, Batya, The Experiment, 220 E 23 St, Suite 301, New York, NY 10010-4674 *Tel:* 212-889-1659 *E-mail:* info@theexperimentpublishing.com *Web Site:* www.theexperimentpublishing.com, pg 81

Rosenblum, Bruce, Television Academy, 5220 Lankershim Blvd, North Hollywood, CA 91601-3109 *Tel:* 818-754-2800 *Fax:* 818-761-2827 *Web Site:* www.emmys.com, pg 579

Rosenblum, Jill, Walch Education, 40 Walch Dr, Portland, ME 04103-1286 *Tel:* 207-772-2846 *Toll Free Tel:* 800-558-2846 *Fax:* 207-772-3105 *Toll Free Fax:* 888-991-5755 *E-mail:* customerservice@walch.com *Web Site:* www.walch.com, pg 251

Rosenblum, Stefanie, Portfolio, 375 Hudson St, New York, NY 10014 *Web Site:* www.penguin.com/meet/publishers/portfolio, pg 186

Rosenbush, Ellen, Harper's Magazine Foundation, 666 Broadway, 11th fl, New York, NY 10012 *Tel:* 212-420-5720 *Toll Free Tel:* 800-444-4653 *Fax:* 212-228-5889 *E-mail:* harpers@harpers.org *Web Site:* www.harpers.org, pg 102

Rosenfeld, Dina, Hachai Publishing, 527 Empire Blvd, Brooklyn, NY 11225 *Tel:* 718-633-0100 *Fax:* 718-633-0103 *E-mail:* info@hachai.com *Web Site:* www.hachai.com, pg 98

Rosenfeld, Erv, BK Nelson Inc Lecture Bureau, 6726 Moonriver St, Mira Loma, CA 91752-3428 *Tel:* 760-902-1868 *Fax:* 760-778-6242 *E-mail:* bknelson4@cs.com, pg 547

Rosenfeld, Erv, BK Nelson Inc Literary Agency, 6726 Moonriver St, Mira Loma, CA 91752-3428 *Tel:* 760-902-1868 *Fax:* 760-778-6242 *E-mail:* bknelson4@cs.com, pg 530

Rosenfeld, Nancy, AAA Books Unlimited, 3060 Blackthorn Rd, Riverwoods, IL 60015 *Tel:* 847-444-1220 *Fax:* 847-607-8335 *Web Site:* www.aaabooksunlimited.com, pg 505

Rosenfeld, Theodore D, Taplinger Publishing Co Inc, PO Box 175, Marlboro, NJ 07746-0175 *Tel:* 305-256-7880 *Fax:* 305-256-7816 *E-mail:* taplingerpub@yahoo.com (rts & perms, edit, corp only), pg 227

Rosenfelt, Rachel, Verso, 20 Jay St, Suite 1010, Brooklyn, NY 11201 *Tel:* 718-246-8160 *Fax:* 718-246-8165 *E-mail:* verso@versobooks.com *Web Site:* www.versobooks.com, pg 250

Rosengrave, Tracey, AuthorHouse, 1663 Liberty Dr, Bloomington, IN 47403 *Tel:* 812-339-6000 (outside US) *Toll Free Tel:* 888-519-5121 *E-mail:* authorsupport@authorhouse.com *Web Site:* www.authorhouse.com, pg 26

Rosenkranz, Randi, Penguin Random House Inc, 1745 Broadway, New York, NY 10019 *Tel:* 212-782-9000 *Toll Free Tel:* 800-726-0600 *Web Site:* www.penguinrandomhouse.com, pg 178

Rosenkranz, Rita, Rita Rosenkranz Literary Agency, 440 West End Ave, Suite 15D, New York, NY 10024-5358 *Tel:* 212-873-6333 *Fax:* 212-873-5225 *Web Site:* www.ritarosenkranzliteraryagency.com, pg 533

Rosenstein, Natalee, Berkley Publishing Group, 375 Hudson St, New York, NY 10014 *Tel:* 212-366-2000 *Fax:* 212-366-2385 *Web Site:* www.penguin.com, pg 33

Rosenstreich, Lilian, Eclectic Book Press, 11 Larchdell Way, Mountain Lakes, NJ 07046 *Tel:* 862-251-2296 *E-mail:* info@eclecticbookpress.com *Web Site:* eclecticbookpress.com, pg 75

Rosenthal, Carole, Hamilton Stone Editions, PO Box 43, Maplewood, NJ 07040 *Tel:* 973-378-8361 *E-mail:* hstone@hamiltonstone.org *Web Site:* www.hamiltonstone.org, pg 99

Rosenthal, Elise, Rosenthal Represents, 23725 Hartland St, West Hills, CA 91307 *Tel:* 818-222-5445 *E-mail:* eliselicenses@earthlink.net, pg 544

Rosenthal, Maggie, Viking Children's Books, 345 Hudson St, New York, NY 10014 *Fax:* 212-414-3393 *E-mail:* youngreaderspublicity@us.penguingroup.com *Web Site:* www.penguin.com/publishers/vikingchildrensbooks, pg 251

Rosenwald, Robert, Poisoned Pen Press, 6962 E First Ave, Suite 103, Scottsdale, AZ 85251 *Tel:* 480-945-3375 *Toll Free Tel:* 800-421-3976 *Fax:* 480-949-1707 *E-mail:* info@poisonedpenpress.com *Web Site:* www.poisonedpenpress.com, pg 185

Rosenwasser, Rena, Kelsey Street Press, 2824 Kelsey St, Berkeley, CA 94705 *E-mail:* info@kelseyst.com *Web Site:* www.kelseyst.com, pg 125

Rosoff, Jodi, Grand Central Publishing, 1290 Avenue of the Americas, New York, NY 10019 *Tel:* 212-364-1100 *Web Site:* www.hachettebookgroup.com, pg 95

Rosokoff, Sylvie, Trident Media Group LLC, 41 Madison Ave, 36th fl, New York, NY 10010 *Tel:* 212-333-1511 *E-mail:* info@tridentmediagroup.com; press@tridentmediagroup.com *Web Site:* www.tridentmediagroup.com, pg 540

Ross, Andy, Andy Ross Literary Agency, 767 Santa Ray Ave, Oakland, CA 94610 *Tel:* 510-238-8965 *E-mail:* andyrossagency@hotmail.com *Web Site:* www.andyrossagency.com, pg 506

Ross, Carol, Hachette Book Group, 1290 Avenue of the Americas, New York, NY 10019 *Tel:* 212-364-1100 *Toll Free Tel:* 800-759-0190 (cust serv) *Fax:* 212-364-0933 (intl orders) *Toll Free Fax:* 800-286-9471 (cust serv) *Web Site:* www.hachettebookgroup.com, pg 98

Ross, Franz H, Ross Books, PO Box 4340, Berkeley, CA 94704-0340 *Tel:* 510-841-2474 *Fax:* 510-295-2531 *E-mail:* sales@rossbooks.com *Web Site:* www.rossbooks.com, pg 201

Ross, Marjory G, Regnery Publishing, 300 New Jersey Ave NW, Washington, DC 20001 *Tel:* 202-216-0600 *Toll Free Tel:* 888-219-4747 *Fax:* 202-393-1795 *Web Site:* www.regnery.com, pg 198

Ross, Maureen, LaurelTech, 4 S Market St, 4th fl, Boston, MA 02109-6201 *Tel:* 617-600-3366 *Fax:* 617-848-2938 *Web Site:* www.diacritech.com, pg 497

Ross, Michael, Encyclopaedia Britannica Inc, 325 N La Salle St, Chicago, IL 60654 *Tel:* 312-347-7159 (all other countries) *Toll Free Tel:* 800-323-1229 (US & CN) *Fax:* 312-294-2104 *E-mail:* contact@eb.com *Web Site:* www.eb.com; www.britannica.com, pg 78

Ross, Mimi, Henry Holt and Company, LLC, 175 Fifth Ave, New York, NY 10010 *Tel:* 646-307-5151 *Toll Free Tel:* 888-330-8477 (orders) *Fax:* 646-307-5285 *E-mail:* firstname.lastname@hholt.com *Web Site:* www.henryholt.com, pg 109

Ross, Steve, Abrams Artists Agency, 275 Seventh Ave, 26th fl, New York, NY 10001 *Tel:* 646-486-4600 *Fax:* 646-486-0100 *E-mail:* literary@abramsartny.com *Web Site:* www.abramsartists.com, pg 505

Rossi, Janet, The MIT Press, One Rogers St, Cambridge, MA 02142 *Tel:* 617-253-5255 *Toll Free Tel:* 800-207-8354 (orders) *Fax:* 617-258-6779; 617-577-1545 (orders) *Web Site:* mitpress.mit.edu, pg 152

Rossi, Janice, Kensington Publishing Corp, 119 W 40 St, New York, NY 10018 *Tel:* 212-407-1500 *Toll Free Tel:* 800-221-2647 *Fax:* 212-935-0699 *Web Site:* www.kensingtonbooks.com, pg 125

Rossi, Stefani, Janet B McCabe Poetry Prize, 1041 N Taft Hill Rd, Fort Collins, CO 80521 *Tel:* 970-449-2726 *E-mail:* editor@ruminatemagazine.org *Web Site:* www.ruminatemagazine.com, pg 666

Rossi, Stefani, William Van Dyke Short Story Prize, 1041 N Taft Hill Rd, Fort Collins, CO 80521 *Tel:* 970-449-2726 *E-mail:* editor@ruminatemagazine.org *Web Site:* www.ruminatemagazine.com, pg 695

Rossi, Stefani, VanderMey Nonfiction Prize, 1041 N Taft Hill Rd, Fort Collins, CO 80521 *Tel:* 970-449-2726 *E-mail:* editor@ruminatemagazine.org *Web Site:* www.ruminatemagazine.com, pg 695

Rossi, Tony, The Christopher Awards, 5 Hanover Sq, 22nd fl, New York, NY 10004-2751 *Tel:* 212-759-4050 *Toll Free Tel:* 888-298-4050 (orders) *Fax:* 212-838-5073 *E-mail:* mail@christophers.org *Web Site:* www.christophers.org, pg 637

Rosso, Don, Waveland Press Inc, 4180 IL Rte 83, Suite 101, Long Grove, IL 60047-9580 *Tel:* 847-634-0081 *Fax:* 847-634-9501 *E-mail:* info@waveland.com *Web Site:* www.waveland.com, pg 253

Rostan, Stephanie, Levine|Greenberg|Rostan Literary Agency, 307 Seventh Ave, Suite 2407, New York, NY 10001 *Tel:* 212-337-0934 *Fax:* 212-337-0948 *Web Site:* lgrliterary.com, pg 525

Roth, Jason, Springer Publishing Co, 11 W 42 St, 15th fl, New York, NY 10036-8002 *Tel:* 212-431-4370 *Toll Free Tel:* 877-687-7476 *Fax:* 212-941-7842 *E-mail:* marketing@springerpub.com; cs@springerpub.com (orders); editorial@springerpub.com *Web Site:* www.springerpub.com, pg 219

Roth, Jessica, Touchstone, 1230 Avenue of the Americas, New York, NY 10020, pg 233

Roth, Laurence, Susquehanna University, Department of English and Creative Writing, 514 University Ave, Selinsgrove, PA 17870 *Tel:* 570-372-0101, pg 622

Roth, Maya E, Jane Chambers Playwriting Award, Georgetown University, 108 David Performing Arts Ctr, Box 571063, 37 & "O" St, NW, Washington, DC 20057-1063 *Web Site:* www.athe.org/?page=Jane_Chambers, pg 636

Roth, Melanie, Fulcrum Publishing Inc, 4690 Table Mountain Dr, Suite 100, Golden, CO 80403 *Tel:* 303-277-1623 *Toll Free Tel:* 800-992-2908 *Fax:* 303-279-7111 *Toll Free Fax:* 800-726-7112 *E-mail:* info@fulcrumbooks.com; orders@fulcrumbooks.com *Web Site:* www.fulcrumbooks.com, pg 89

Roth, Rachel, Transcontinental Music Publications (TMP), 1375 Remington Rd, Suite M, Schaumburg, IL 60173-4844 *Tel:* 847-781-7800 *Fax:* 847-781-7801 *E-mail:* tmp@accantors.org *Web Site:* www.transcontinentalmusic.com, pg 234

Roth, Ruth Gleason, Society for Scholarly Publishing (SSP), 10200 W 44 Ave, Suite 304, Wheat Ridge, CO 80033-2840 *Tel:* 303-422-3914 *Fax:* 720-881-6101 *E-mail:* info@sspnet.org *Web Site:* www.sspnet.org, pg 578

Roth, Stefani, ASCD, 1703 N Beauregard St, Alexandria, VA 22311-1714 *Tel:* 703-578-9600 *Toll Free Tel:* 800-933-2723 *Fax:* 703-575-5400 *E-mail:* member@ascd.org *Web Site:* www.ascd.org, pg 22

Rothberg, Adam, Simon & Schuster, Inc, 1230 Avenue of the Americas, New York, NY 10020 *Tel:* 212-698-7000 *Fax:* 212-698-7007 *E-mail:* firstname.lastname@simonandschuster.com *Web Site:* www.simonandschuster.com, pg 213

Rothman, Valinda, Book Publicists of Southern California, 714 Crescent Dr, Beverly Hills, CA 90210 *Tel:* 323-461-3921 *Fax:* 323-461-0917 *Web Site:* www.bookpublicists.org, pg 560

Rothmeyer, Bob, Concordia Publishing House, 3558 S Jefferson Ave, St Louis, MO 63118-3968 *Tel:* 314-268-1000; 314-268-1268 (bookshop) *Toll Free Tel:* 800-325-3040 (cust serv) *Toll Free Fax:* 800-490-9889 (cust serv) *E-mail:* order@cph.org *Web Site:* www.cph.org, pg 59

Rothschild, Eileen, St Martin's Press, LLC, 175 Fifth Ave, New York, NY 10010 *Tel:* 646-307-5151 *Web Site:* us.macmillan.com/smp, pg 204

Rothschild, Richard, American Book Producers Association (ABPA), 31 W Eighth St, 2nd fl, New York, NY 10011 *Tel:* 212-675-1363 *Fax:* 212-675-1364 *E-mail:* office@abpaonline.org *Web Site:* www.abpaonline.org, pg 554

Rothstein, Philip Jan, Rothstein Associates Inc, 4 Arapaho Rd, Brookfield, CT 06804-3104 *Tel:* 203-740-7400 *Toll Free Tel:* 888-768-4783 *Fax:* 203-740-7401 *E-mail:* info@rothstein.com *Web Site:* www.rothstein.com; www.rothsteinpublishing.com, pg 201

Rotor, Elda, Penguin Books, 375 Hudson St, New York, NY 10014 *Tel:* 212-366-2000 *E-mail:* penguinpublicity@us.penguingroup.com *Web Site:* www.penguinclassics.com; www.penguin.com, pg 177

Rotstein, David, St Martin's Press, LLC, 175 Fifth Ave, New York, NY 10010 *Tel:* 646-307-5151 *Web Site:* us.macmillan.com/smp, pg 204

Rouleau, Lauren, F+W Media Inc, 10151 Carver Rd, Suite 200, Blue Ash, OH 45242 *Tel:* 513-531-2690 *Toll Free Tel:* 800-289-0963 (trade accts); 800-258-0929 (cust serv) *E-mail:* contact_us@fwmedia.com *Web Site:* www.fwcommunity.com, pg 82

Rounds, John, St Martin's Press, LLC, 175 Fifth Ave, New York, NY 10010 *Tel:* 646-307-5151 *Web Site:* us.macmillan.com/smp, pg 204

Rourke, Kathleen, Candlewick Press, 99 Dover St, Somerville, MA 02144-2825 *Tel:* 617-661-3330 *Fax:* 617-661-0565 *E-mail:* bigbear@candlewick.com; salesinfo@candlewick.com *Web Site:* www.candlewick.com, pg 46

Rourke, Stacey, Anchor Group Publishing, PO Box 551, Flushing, MI 48433 *E-mail:* anchorgrouppublishing@gmail.com *Web Site:* anchorgrouppublishing.com, pg 16

Rouse, William R, Capstone Publishers™, 1710 Roe Crest Dr, North Mankato, MN 56003 *Toll Free Tel:* 800-747-4992 (cust serv) *Toll Free Fax:* 888-262-0705 *Web Site:* www.capstonepress.com, pg 47

Rousseau, Christopher, Practising Law Institute, 1177 Avenue of the Americas, New York, NY 10036 *Tel:* 212-824-5700 *Toll Free Tel:* 800-260-4PLI (260-4754, cust serv) *Fax:* 212-265-4742 (intl) *Toll Free Fax:* 800-321-0093 (local) *E-mail:* info@pli.edu (cust serv) *Web Site:* www.pli.edu, pg 186

Roux, Michael, University of Illinois Press, 1325 S Oak St, MC-566, Champaign, IL 61820-6903 *Tel:* 217-333-0950 *Fax:* 217-244-8082 *E-mail:* uipress@uillinois.edu; journals@uillinois.edu *Web Site:* www.press.uillinois.edu, pg 241

Rowe, Alan, Torah Aura Productions, 4423 Fruitland Ave, Los Angeles, CA 90058 *Tel:* 323-585-7312 *Toll Free Tel:* 800-238-6724 *Fax:* 323-585-0327 *E-mail:* misrad@torahaura.com; orders@torahaura.com *Web Site:* www.torahaura.com, pg 233

Rowe, Carol, Waveland Press Inc, 4180 IL Rte 83, Suite 101, Long Grove, IL 60047-9580 *Tel:* 847-634-0081 *Fax:* 847-634-9501 *E-mail:* info@waveland.com *Web Site:* www.waveland.com, pg 253

Rowe, Jane, Canadian Institute of Resources Law (L'Institut canadien du droit des ressources), Faculty of Law, University of Calgary, 2500 University Dr NW, MFH 3353, Calgary, AB T2N 1N4, Canada *Tel:* 403-220-3200 *Fax:* 403-282-6182 *E-mail:* cirl@ucalgary.ca *Web Site:* www.cirl.ca, pg 449

Rowe, Martin, Lantern Books, 128 Second Place, Garden Suite, Brooklyn, NY 11231 *Tel:* 212-414-2275 *E-mail:* editorial@lanternbooks.com; info@lanternmedia.net *Web Site:* lanternbooks.presswarehouse.com/Home/home.aspx, pg 129

Rowe, Neil, Waveland Press Inc, 4180 IL Rte 83, Suite 101, Long Grove, IL 60047-9580 *Tel:* 847-634-0081 *Fax:* 847-634-9501 *E-mail:* info@waveland.com *Web Site:* www.waveland.com, pg 253

Rowland, Melissa, Levine|Greenberg|Rostan Literary Agency, 307 Seventh Ave, Suite 2407, New York, NY 10001 *Tel:* 212-337-0934 *Fax:* 212-337-0948 *Web Site:* lgrliterary.com, pg 525

Roy, Mary Lou, University of Alberta Press, Ring House 2, Edmonton, AB T6G 2E1, Canada *Tel:* 780-492-3662 *Fax:* 780-492-0719 *Web Site:* www.uap.ualberta.ca, pg 473

Roy, Michael, American Psychiatric Association Publishing, 1000 Wilson Blvd, Suite 1825, Arlington, VA 22209 *Tel:* 703-907-7322 *Toll Free Tel:* 800-368-5777 *Fax:* 703-907-1091 *E-mail:* appi@psych.org *Web Site:* www.appi.org; www.psychiatryonline.org, pg 14

Roy, Stephanie, Les Editions JCL, 688, rue St-Joseph, Marieville, QC J3M 1H1, Canada *Tel:* 450-460-4438 *E-mail:* info@jcl.qc.ca *Web Site:* www.jcl.qc.ca, pg 454

Royal, Jaynie, Regal House Publishing, 1723 Hickory Overlook Trail, No 110, Raleigh, NC 27607 *Tel:* 305-360-5969 *E-mail:* info@regalhousepublishing.com *Web Site:* regalhousepublishing.com, pg 198

Royall, John T, Gulf Publishing Co, 2 Greenway Plaza, Suite 1020, Houston, TX 77046 *Tel:* 713-529-4301 *Fax:* 713-520-4433 *E-mail:* store@gulfpub.com; customerservice@gulfpub.com *Web Site:* www.gulfpub.com, pg 98

Royce, Adam, Penguin Young Readers Group, 345 Hudson St, New York, NY 10014 *Tel:* 212-366-2000; 212-414-3553 *Fax:* 212-414-3340 *Web Site:* www.penguin.com/children, pg 179

Royce, Michael, Artists' Fellowships, 20 Jay St, 7th fl, Brooklyn, NY 11201 *Tel:* 212-366-6900 *Fax:* 212-366-1778 *E-mail:* info@nyfa.org *Web Site:* www.nyfa.org, pg 628

Rozansky, David A, Flying Pen Press LLC, 1416 S Newport St, Denver, CO 80224 *Tel:* 303-375-0499 *Fax:* 303-375-0499 *Web Site:* www.flyingpenpress.com, pg 86

Rozek, Jessica, Water Environment Federation, 601 Wythe St, Alexandria, VA 22314-1994 *Tel:* 703-684-2400 *Toll Free Tel:* 800-666-0206 (cust serv) *Fax:* 703-684-2492 *E-mail:* inquiry@wef.org *Web Site:* www.wef.org, pg 252

Rubenstein, Ellis, New York Academy of Sciences (NYAS), 7 World Trade, 40th fl, 250 Greenwich St, New York, NY 10007-2157 *Tel:* 212-298-8600 *Toll Free Tel:* 800-843-6927 *Fax:* 212-298-3668 *E-mail:* nyas@nyas.org; annals@nyas.org; customerservice@nyas.org *Web Site:* www.nyas.org, pg 161

Rubenstein, Kerry, Perseus Books, 250 W 57 St, 15th fl, New York, NY 10107 *Tel:* 212-340-8100 *Toll Free Tel:* 800-343-4499 (cust serv) *Fax:* 212-340-8105 *Web Site:* www.perseusbooks.com, pg 181

Rubie, Peter, FinePrint Literary Management, 207 W 106 St, Suite 1D, New York, NY 10025 *Tel:* 212-279-6214 *E-mail:* assist@fineprint.com *Web Site:* www.fineprintlit.com, pg 516

Rubin, Barry, Lederer Books, 6120 Day Long Lane, Clarksville, MD 21029 *Tel:* 410-531-6644 *Toll Free Tel:* 800-410-7367 (orders) *Fax:* 410-531-9440 *E-mail:* lederer@messianicjewish.net; customerservice@messianicjewish.net *Web Site:* www.messianicjewish.net, pg 131

Rubin, Barry, Messianic Jewish Publishers, 6120 Day Long Lane, Clarksville, MD 21029 *Tel:* 410-531-6644 *Toll Free Tel:* 800-410-7367 (orders) *Fax:* 410-531-9440; 717-761-7273 (orders) *Toll Free Fax:* 800-327-0048 (orders) *E-mail:* editor@messianicjewish.net; customerservice@messianicjewish.net; permissions@messianicjewish.net (rights & perms) *Web Site:* messianicjewish.net/publish, pg 149

Rubin, Lorna, Triad Publishing Co, PO Box 13355, Gainesville, FL 32604 *Fax:* 304-727-9345 *Toll Free Fax:* 800-854-4947 *E-mail:* orders@triadpublishing.com *Web Site:* www.triadpublishing.com, pg 235

PERSONNEL INDEX

Rubin, Reka, Harlequin Enterprises Ltd, 225 Duncan Mill Rd, Don Mills, ON M3B 3K9, Canada *Tel:* 416-445-5860 *Toll Free Tel:* 888-432-4879; 800-370-5838 (ebook inquiries) *E-mail:* customerservice@harlequin.com *Web Site:* www.harlequin.com, pg 459

Rubin, Stephen, Henry Holt and Company, LLC, 175 Fifth Ave, New York, NY 10010 *Tel:* 646-307-5151 *Toll Free Tel:* 888-330-8477 (orders) *Fax:* 646-307-5285 *E-mail:* firstname.lastname@hholt.com *Web Site:* www.henryholt.com, pg 109

Rubin, Stephen, Macmillan, 175 Fifth Ave, New York, NY 10010 *Tel:* 646-307-5151 *E-mail:* press.inquiries@macmillan.com *Web Site:* www.macmillan.com, pg 140

Rubins, Jennifer, Penguin Random House Audio Publishing, 1745 Broadway, New York, NY 10019 *E-mail:* audio@penguinrandomhouse.com *Web Site:* www.penguinrandomhouseaudio.com, pg 178

Rubinstein, Elizabeth Winick, McIntosh & Otis Inc, 353 Lexington Ave, New York, NY 10016-0900 *Tel:* 212-687-7400 *Fax:* 212-687-6894 *E-mail:* info@mcintoshandotis.com *Web Site:* www.mcintoshandotis.com, pg 529

Rubsam, Jeannie, Tiger Tales, 5 River Rd, Suite 128, Wilton, CT 06897-4069 *Tel:* 920-387-2333 *Fax:* 920-387-9994 *Web Site:* www.tigertalesbooks.com, pg 232

Ruby-Strauss, Jeremie, Gallery Books, 1230 Avenue of the Americas, New York, NY 10020 *Toll Free Tel:* 800-456-6798 *Fax:* 212-698-7284 *E-mail:* consumer.customerservice@simonandschuster.com *Web Site:* www.simonsays.com, pg 90

Rucci, Marysue, Simon & Schuster, 1230 Avenue of the Americas, New York, NY 10020 *Tel:* 212-698-7000 *Toll Free Tel:* 800-223-2348 (cust serv); 800-223-2336 (orders) *Toll Free Fax:* 800-943-9831 (orders) *Web Site:* www.simonandschuster.com, pg 212

Ruchti, Cynthia, Books & Such, 52 Mission Circle, Suite 122, PMB 170, Santa Rosa, CA 95409-5370 *Tel:* 707-538-4184 *Web Site:* booksandsuch.com, pg 509

Ruck, Holly, Macmillan, 175 Fifth Ave, New York, NY 10010 *Tel:* 646-307-5151 *E-mail:* press.inquiries@macmillan.com *Web Site:* www.macmillan.com, pg 140

Ruder, Karen, Optometric Extension Program Foundation, 2300 York Rd, Suite 113, Timonium, MD 21093 *Tel:* 410-561-3791 *E-mail:* oep@oep.org *Web Site:* www.oepf.org, pg 169

Rudick, Nicole, The Plimpton Prize, 544 W 27 St, New York, NY 10001 *Tel:* 212-343-1333 *Fax:* 212-343-1988 *E-mail:* queries@theparisreview.org *Web Site:* www.theparisreview.org, pg 680

Rudin, Max, The Library of America, 14 E 60 St, New York, NY 10022-1006 *Tel:* 212-308-3360 *Fax:* 212-750-8352 *E-mail:* info@loa.org *Web Site:* www.loa.org, pg 133

Rudman, Michael P, National Learning Corp, 212 Michael Dr, Syosset, NY 11791 *Tel:* 516-921-8888 *Toll Free Tel:* 800-632-8888 *Fax:* 516-921-8743 *E-mail:* info@passbooks.com *Web Site:* www.passbooks.com, pg 159

Rudolph, Janet, Macavity Award, 7155 Marlborough Terr, Berkeley, CA 94705 *Tel:* 510-845-3600 *Web Site:* www.mysteryreaders.org, pg 664

Rudolph, John, Dystel, Goderich & Bourret LLC, One Union Sq W, Suite 904, New York, NY 10003 *Tel:* 212-627-9100 *Fax:* 212-627-9313 *Web Site:* www.dystel.com, pg 515

Rudolph, Kelly, HarperCollins General Books Group, 195 Broadway, New York, NY 10007 *Tel:* 212-207-7000 *Web Site:* www.harpercollins.com, pg 101

Rudy, Bryan, Wolf Pirate Project Inc, 337 Lost Lake Dr, Divide, CO 80814 *Tel:* 305-333-3186 *E-mail:* contact@wolfpiratebooks.com; workshop@wolfpiratebooks.com *Web Site:* www.wolf-pirate.com, pg 502

Rudy, Caryn Karmatz, DeFiore and Company Literary Management Inc, 47 E 19 St, 3rd fl, New York, NY 10003 *Tel:* 212-925-7744 *Fax:* 212-925-9803 *E-mail:* info@defliterary.com; submissions@defliterary.com *Web Site:* www.defliterary.com, pg 513

Rudy, Catherine, Wolf Pirate Project Inc, 337 Lost Lake Dr, Divide, CO 80814 *Tel:* 305-333-3186 *E-mail:* contact@wolfpiratebooks.com; workshop@wolfpiratebooks.com *Web Site:* www.wolf-pirate.com, pg 502

Rue, Robin, Writers House, 21 W 26 St, New York, NY 10010 *Tel:* 212-685-2400 *Fax:* 212-685-1781 *Web Site:* www.writershouse.com, pg 542

Ruenzel, Nancy, Peachpit Press, 1301 Sansome St, San Francisco, CA 94111 *Toll Free Tel:* 800-283-9444 *E-mail:* info@peachpit.com; ask@peachpit.com *Web Site:* www.peachpit.com, pg 175

Ruffin, Katherine McCanless, American Printing History Association, PO Box 4519, Grand Central Sta, New York, NY 10163 *Tel:* 202-544-2422 *E-mail:* secretary@printinghistory.org *Web Site:* printinghistory.org, pg 556

Ruffin, Katherine McCanless, American Printing History Association Award, PO Box 4519, Grand Central Sta, New York, NY 10163 *Tel:* 202-544-2422 *E-mail:* secretary@printinghistory.org *Web Site:* printinghistory.org, pg 627

Ruffino, Dan, Simon & Schuster, Inc, 1230 Avenue of the Americas, New York, NY 10020 *Tel:* 212-698-7000 *Fax:* 212-698-7007 *E-mail:* firstname.lastname@simonandschuster.com *Web Site:* www.simonandschuster.com, pg 213

Ruffner, Frederick G Jr, Omnigraphics Inc, 615 Griswold, Suite 901, Detroit, MI 48226 *Tel:* 610-461-3548 *Toll Free Tel:* 800-234-1340 (cust serv) *Fax:* 610-532-9001 *Toll Free Fax:* 800-875-1340 (cust serv) *E-mail:* contact@omnigraphics.com; customerservice@omnigraphics.com *Web Site:* omnigraphics.com, pg 168

Ruffner, Peter E, Omnigraphics Inc, 615 Griswold, Suite 901, Detroit, MI 48226 *Tel:* 610-461-3548 *Toll Free Tel:* 800-234-1340 (cust serv) *Fax:* 610-532-9001 *Toll Free Fax:* 800-875-1340 (cust serv) *E-mail:* contact@omnigraphics.com; customerservice@omnigraphics.com *Web Site:* omnigraphics.com, pg 168

Ruggiero, Anthony, Pauline Books & Media, 50 Saint Paul's Ave, Boston, MA 02130 *Tel:* 617-522-8911 *Toll Free Tel:* 800-876-4463 (orders); 800-836-9723 (cust serv) *Fax:* 617-541-9805 *E-mail:* editorial@paulinemedia.com (ms submissions); orderentry@pauline.org (cust serv) *Web Site:* www.pauline.org/publishing; www.pauline.org/PBMPublishing, pg 175

Ruggiero, Greg, City Lights Publishers, 261 Columbus Ave, San Francisco, CA 94133 *Tel:* 415-362-8193 *Fax:* 415-362-4921 *E-mail:* staff@citylights.com *Web Site:* www.citylights.com, pg 56

Ruggiero, Vincenzo, Penguin Group USA, A Penguin Random House Company, 375 Hudson St, New York, NY 10014 *Tel:* 212-366-2000 *Toll Free Tel:* 800-847-5515 (inside sales); 800-631-8571 (cust serv) *Fax:* 212-366-2666; 607-775-4829 (inside sales) *E-mail:* online@us.penguingroup.com *Web Site:* www.penguin.com, pg 177

Ruhl, Peter, American Catholic Press (ACP), 16565 S State St, South Holland, IL 60473 *Tel:* 708-331-5485 *Fax:* 708-331-5484 *E-mail:* acp@acpress.org *Web Site:* www.acpress.org, pg 10

Ruhlig, Steve, Human Kinetics Inc, 1607 N Market St, Champaign, IL 61820 *Tel:* 217-351-5076 *Toll Free Tel:* 800-747-4457 *Fax:* 217-351-1549 (orders/cust serv) *E-mail:* info@hkusa.com *Web Site:* www.humankinetics.com, pg 112

Ruiz, Bea, National Catholic Educational Association, 1005 N Glebe Rd, Suite 525, Arlington, VA 22201 *Tel:* 571-257-0010 *Toll Free Tel:* 800-711-6232 *Fax:* 703-243-0025 *E-mail:* nceaadmin@ncea.org *Web Site:* www.ncea.org, pg 157

Ruiz, Jonathan, Velazquez Press, 9682 Telstar Ave, Suite 110, El Monte, CA 91731 *Tel:* 626-448-3448 *Fax:* 626-602-3817 *E-mail:* info@academiclearningcompany.com *Web Site:* www.velazquezpress.com, pg 250

Rukkila, Roy, Bagwyn Books, Lattie F Coor Hall, 4th fl, Rms 4426-4442, 975 S Myrtle Ave, Tempe, AZ 85281 *Tel:* 480-965-5900 *Fax:* 480-965-1681 *E-mail:* bagwynbooks@acmrs.org *Web Site:* acmrs.org/publications/bagwyn, pg 28

Rukkila, Roy, MRTS, PO Box 874402, Tempe, AZ 85287-4402 *Tel:* 480-727-6503 *Toll Free Tel:* 800-621-2736 (orders) *Fax:* 480-965-1681 *Toll Free Fax:* 800-621-8476 (orders) *E-mail:* mrts@asu.edu *Web Site:* acmrs.org/publications/mrts, pg 155

Ruley, Meg, Jane Rotrosen Agency LLC, 85 Broad St, 28th fl, New York, NY 10004 *Tel:* 212-593-4330 *Fax:* 212-935-6985 *Web Site:* janerotrosen.com, pg 533

Rumberger, Anne, Verso, 20 Jay St, Suite 1010, Brooklyn, NY 11201 *Tel:* 718-246-8160 *Fax:* 718-246-8165 *E-mail:* verso@versobooks.com *Web Site:* www.versobooks.com, pg 250

Rummel-Hudson, Robert, University of Texas at Arlington College of Architecture, Planning & Public Affairs, 601 S Nedderman Dr, Suite 203, Arlington, TX 76019 *Fax:* 817-272-5008 *E-mail:* cappa@uta.edu *Web Site:* www.uta.edu/cappa, pg 245

Rumsch, BreAnn, ABDO Publishing Group, 8000 W 78 St, Suite 310, Edina, MN 55439 *Tel:* 952-831-2120 *Toll Free Tel:* 800-800-1312 *Toll Free Fax:* 800-862-3480 *E-mail:* customerservice@abdopublishing.com *Web Site:* abdopublishing.com, pg 2

Rundall, Nick, Whitecap Books, 314 W Cordova St, Suite 209, Vancouver, BC V6B 1E8, Canada *Tel:* 604-681-6181 *Toll Free Tel:* 800-387-9776 *Toll Free Fax:* 800-260-9777 *Web Site:* www.whitecap.ca, pg 475

Runde, Kate, Anchor Books, c/o Penguin Random House Inc, 1745 Broadway, New York, NY 10019 *Tel:* 212-572-2420 *E-mail:* vintageanchorpublicity@randomhouse.com *Web Site:* knopfdoubleday.com/imprint/anchor, pg 16

Runde, Kate, Vintage Books, c/o Penguin Random House Inc, 1745 Broadway, New York, NY 10019 *Tel:* 212-572-2420 *E-mail:* vintageanchorpublicity@randomhouse.com *Web Site:* knopfdoubleday.com/imprint/vintage, pg 251

Rundle, Lisa, HarperCollins Canada Ltd, 2 Bloor St E, 20th fl, Toronto, ON M4W 1A8, Canada *Tel:* 416-975-9334 *Fax:* 416-975-5223 *E-mail:* hcorder@harpercollins.com *Web Site:* www.harpercollins.ca, pg 459

Rundquist, Nathan, New Rivers Press, c/o Minnesota State University Moorhead, 1104 Seventh Ave S, Moorhead, MN 56563 *Tel:* 218-477-5870 *Fax:* 218-477-2236 *E-mail:* nrp@mnstate.edu *Web Site:* www.newriverspress.com; www.mnstate.edu/newriverspress, pg 161

Runge, Gailen, C&T Publishing Inc, 1651 Challenge Dr, Concord, CA 94520-5206 *Tel:* 925-677-0377 *Toll Free Tel:* 800-284-1114 *Fax:* 925-677-0373 *E-mail:* support@ctpub.com *Web Site:* www.ctpub.com, pg 47

Runk, David, FaithWalk Publishing, 5450 N Dixie Hwy, Lima, OH 45807 *Tel:* 419-227-1818 *Toll Free Tel:* 800-537-1030 (orders: non-bookstore mkts) *Fax:* 419-224-9184 *E-mail:* orders@csspub.com *Web Site:* www.faithwalkpub.com, pg 82

Runyan, Brad, Quarto Publishing Group USA Inc, 400 First Ave N, Suite 400, Minneapolis, MN 55401 *Tel:* 612-344-8100 *Toll Free Tel:* 800-328-0590 (sales); 800-458-0454 *Fax:* 612-344-8691 *E-mail:* sales@quartous.com *Web Site:* www.quartoknows.com, pg 192

Runyon, Ashley, Indiana University Press, Herman B Wells Library 350, 1320 E Tenth St, Bloomington, IN 47405-3907 *Tel:* 812-855-8817 *Toll Free Tel:* 800-842-6796 (orders only) *Fax:* 812-855-7931; 812-855-8507 *E-mail:* iupress@indiana.edu; iuporder@indiana.edu (orders) *Web Site:* www.iupress.indiana.edu, pg 116

Runyon, Nancy, McCutchan Publishing Corp, 2694 Ohart Rd, Richmond, CA 94806 *Tel:* 510-758-5510 *Toll Free Tel:* 800-227-1540 *Fax:* 510-758-6078 *E-mail:* mccutchanpublish@sbcglobal.net *Web Site:* www.mccutchanpublishing.com, pg 145

Rupert, James, United States Institute of Peace Press, 2301 Constitution Ave NW, Washington, DC 20037 *Tel:* 202-457-1700 (edit); 703-661-1590 (cust serv) *Toll Free Tel:* 800-868-8064 (cust serv) *Fax:* 202-429-6063; 703-661-1501 (cust serv) *E-mail:* usipmail@presswarehouse.com (orders) *Web Site:* bookstore.usip.org, pg 239

Rupnow, Dr John, The Edwin Mellen Press, 415 Ridge St, Lewiston, NY 14092 *Tel:* 716-754-2266; 716-754-1400 (mktg); 716-754-2788 (order fulfillment) *Fax:* 716-754-4056 *E-mail:* editor@mellenpress.com *Web Site:* www.mellenpress.com, pg 148

Rupp, Katherine, American Quilter's Society, 5801 Kentucky Dam Rd, Paducah, KY 42003-9323 *Tel:* 270-898-7903 *Toll Free Tel:* 800-626-5420 (orders) *Fax:* 270-898-1173 *E-mail:* orders@americanquilter.com *Web Site:* www.americanquilter.com, pg 14

Ruppel, Philip, Phaidon, 65 Bleecker St, 8th fl, New York, NY 10012 *Tel:* 212-652-5400 *Toll Free Tel:* 800-759-0190 (cust serv) *Fax:* 212-652-5410 *Toll Free Fax:* 800-286-9471 (cust serv) *E-mail:* ussales@phaidon.com *Web Site:* www.phaidon.com, pg 182

Rusch, Vanessa, University of Alabama Press, 200 Hackberry Lane, 2nd fl, Tuscaloosa, AL 35487 *Tel:* 205-348-5180 *Fax:* 205-348-9201 *Web Site:* www.uapress.ua.edu, pg 239

Russ, Brice, Linguistic Society of America, 522 21 St NW, Suite 120, Washington, DC 20006-5012 *Tel:* 202-835-1714 *Fax:* 202-835-1717 *E-mail:* lsa@lsadc.org *Web Site:* www.linguisticsociety.org, pg 568

Russell, Cheryl, New Strategist Press LLC, 26 Austin Ave, Amityville, NY 11701 *Tel:* 631-608-8795 *Toll Free Tel:* 800-848-0842 *Fax:* 631-691-1770 *E-mail:* demographics@newstrategist.com; info@newstrategist.com *Web Site:* www.newstrategist.com, pg 161

Russell, Christie, Peter Lampack Agency Inc, 350 Fifth Ave, Suite 5300, New York, NY 10118 *Tel:* 212-687-9106 *Fax:* 212-687-9109 *Web Site:* www.peterlampackagency.com, pg 525

Russell, Kenn, Henry Holt and Company, LLC, 175 Fifth Ave, New York, NY 10010 *Tel:* 646-307-5151 *Toll Free Tel:* 888-330-8477 (orders) *Fax:* 646-307-5285 *E-mail:* firstname.lastname@hholt.com *Web Site:* www.henryholt.com, pg 109

Russell, Mary, New Hampshire Literary Awards, 2500 N River Rd, Manchester, NH 03106 *Tel:* 603-314-7980 *Fax:* 603-314-7981 *E-mail:* info@nhwritersproject.org; awards@nhwritersproject.org *Web Site:* www.nhwritersproject.org, pg 672

Russell, Pam, Council for Advancement & Support of Education (CASE), 1307 New York Ave NW, Suite 1000, Washington, DC 20005-4701 *Tel:* 202-328-CASE (328-2273) *Fax:* 202-387-4973 *E-mail:* membersupportcenter@case.org *Web Site:* www.case.org, pg 564

Russell, Rick, Naval Institute Press, 291 Wood Rd, Annapolis, MD 21402-5034 *Tel:* 410-268-6110 *Toll Free Tel:* 800-233-8764 *Fax:* 410-295-1084; 410-571-1703 (cust serv) *E-mail:* webmaster@navalinstitute.org; customer@navalinstitute.org (cust serv) *Web Site:* www.nip.org; www.usni.org, pg 159

Russo, Carmine, Prevention Products & Services Inc dba The Bureau for At-Risk Youth, PO Box 170, Farmingville, NY 11738 *Toll Free Tel:* 800-99YOUTH (999-6884) *Fax:* 631-389-2511 *Web Site:* www.at-risk.com, pg 187

Russo, Emmalea, Ugly Duckling Presse, The Old American Can Factory, 232 Third St, Suite E303, Brooklyn, NY 11215 *Tel:* 347-948-5170 *E-mail:* info@uglyducklingpresse.org *Web Site:* www.uglyducklingpresse.org, pg 238

Russo, Nicole, Simon & Schuster Children's Publishing, 1230 Avenue of the Americas, New York, NY 10020 *Tel:* 212-698-7000 *Web Site:* www.simonandschuster.com/kids; www.simonandschuster.com/teen; simonandschuster.net; simonandschuster.biz, pg 213

Russo, Olivia, HarperCollins Children's Books, 195 Broadway, New York, NY 10007 *Tel:* 212-207-7000 *Web Site:* www.harpercollins.com/childrens, pg 101

Russo, Richard, The Authors Guild, 31 E 32 St, 7th fl, New York, NY 10016 *Tel:* 212-563-5904 *Fax:* 212-564-5363 *E-mail:* staff@authorsguild.org *Web Site:* www.authorsguild.org, pg 559

Russo, Sarah, Oxford University Press USA, 198 Madison Ave, New York, NY 10016 *Tel:* 212-726-6000 *Toll Free Tel:* 800-451-7556 (orders); 800-445-9714 (cust serv) *Fax:* 919-677-1303 *E-mail:* custserv.us@oup.com *Web Site:* www.oup.com/us, pg 171

Russo, Mr Seth, Simon & Schuster Sales Division, 1230 Avenue of the Americas, New York, NY 10020 *Tel:* 212-698-7000, pg 214

Rust, Ned, Little, Brown and Company, 1290 Avenue of the Americas, New York, NY 10019 *Tel:* 212-364-1100 *Fax:* 212-364-0952 *E-mail:* firstname.lastname@hbgusa.com *Web Site:* www.littlebrown.com; www.HachetteBookGroup.com, pg 135

Rutenberg, Sara, Spark Award, 4727 Wilshire Blvd, Suite 301, Los Angeles, CA 90010 *Tel:* 323-782-1010 *Fax:* 323-782-1892 *E-mail:* grants@scbwi.org; scbwi@scbwi.org *Web Site:* www.scbwi.org, pg 691

Rutman, Jim, Sterling Lord Literistic Inc, 115 Broadway, Suite 1602, New York, NY 10006 *Tel:* 212-780-6050 *Fax:* 212-780-6095 *E-mail:* info@sll.com *Web Site:* www.sll.com, pg 537

Rutter, Sandy, American Society of Agricultural & Biological Engineers (ASABE), 2950 Niles Rd, St Joseph, MI 49085-9659 *Tel:* 269-429-0300 *Toll Free Tel:* 800-371-2723 *Fax:* 269-429-3852 *E-mail:* hq@asabe.org *Web Site:* www.asabe.org, pg 14

Ryan, Anthony J, Ignatius Press, 1348 Tenth Ave, San Francisco, CA 94122-2304 *Toll Free Tel:* 800-651-1531 (orders); 888-615-3186 (cust serv) *E-mail:* info@ignatius.com *Web Site:* www.ignatius.com, pg 114

Ryan, Becky, DawnSignPress, 6130 Nancy Ridge Dr, San Diego, CA 92121-3223 *Tel:* 858-625-0600 *Toll Free Tel:* 800-549-5350 *Fax:* 858-625-2336 *E-mail:* contactus@dawnsign.com *Web Site:* www.dawnsign.com, pg 68

Ryan, Becky, SDSU Writers' Conference, 5250 Campanile Dr, Rm 2503, San Diego, CA 92182-1920 *Tel:* 619-594-5821 *Fax:* 619-594-8566 *E-mail:* sdsuwritersconference@mail.sdsu.edu *Web Site:* www.neverstoplearning.net/writers, pg 614

Ryan, Dawn, Random House Children's Books, 1745 Broadway, 10th fl, New York, NY 10019 *Tel:* 212-782-9000 *Web Site:* www.randomhousekids.com, pg 194

Ryan, James, The Electrochemical Society (ECS), 65 S Main St, Bldg D, Pennington, NJ 08534-2839 *Tel:* 609-737-1902 *Fax:* 609-737-2743 *E-mail:* publications@electrochem.org; customerservice@electrochem.org *Web Site:* www.electrochem.org, pg 77

Ryan, John R, Center for Creative Leadership LLC, One Leadership Place, Greensboro, NC 27410-9427 *Tel:* 336-545-2810; 336-288-7210 *Fax:* 336-282-3284 *E-mail:* info@ccl.org *Web Site:* www.ccl.org/publications, pg 51

Ryan, Matt, Eric Hoffer Award for Short Prose, PO Box 11, Titusville, NJ 08560 *Fax:* 609-964-1718 *E-mail:* info@hofferaward.com *Web Site:* www.hofferaward.com, pg 653

Ryan, Mike, McGraw-Hill Humanities, Social Sciences, Languages, 2 Penn Plaza, 21st fl, New York, NY 10121 *Tel:* 212-904-2000 *Toll Free Tel:* 800-338-3987 (cust serv) *Fax:* 614-755-5645 (cust serv) *Web Site:* www.mhhe.com, pg 146

Ryan, Regina, Regina Ryan Books, 251 Central Park W, Suite 7-D, New York, NY 10024 *Tel:* 212-787-5589 *E-mail:* queries@reginaryanbooks.com *Web Site:* www.reginaryanbooks.com, pg 534

Ryan, Regina Sara, Hohm Press, PO Box 4410, Chino Valley, AZ 86323 *Tel:* 928-636-3331 *Toll Free Tel:* 800-381-2700 *Fax:* 928-636-7519 *E-mail:* hppublisher@cableone.net; hohmpresseditor@gmail.com *Web Site:* www.hohmpress.com, pg 108

Ryan, Sean, McGraw-Hill School Education Group, 8787 Orion Place, Columbus, OH 43240 *Tel:* 614-430-4000 *Toll Free Tel:* 800-848-1567 *Web Site:* www.mheducation.com, pg 146

Ryan, Suzanne, Oxford University Press USA, 198 Madison Ave, New York, NY 10016 *Tel:* 212-726-6000 *Toll Free Tel:* 800-451-7556 (orders); 800-445-9714 (cust serv) *Fax:* 919-677-1303 *E-mail:* custserv.us@oup.com *Web Site:* www.oup.com/us, pg 171

Ryan, Tammy, Montana Historical Society Press, Capitol Complex, 225 N Roberts St, Helena, MT 59620 *Tel:* 406-444-0090 (edit); 406-444-2890 (orders/mktg); 406-444-2694 *Toll Free Tel:* 800-243-9900 *Fax:* 406-444-2696 (orders/mktg) *Web Site:* mhs.mt.gov/pubs, pg 153

Ryce, Chris, Pacific Printing Industries Association, 6825 SW Sandburg St, Portland, OR 97223 *Tel:* 503-221-3944 *Toll Free Tel:* 877-762-7742 *Fax:* 503-221-5691 *E-mail:* info@ppiassociation.org *Web Site:* www.ppiassociation.org, pg 575

Saada, Yves, Disney Publishing Worldwide, 1101 Flower St, Glendale, CA 91201 *Web Site:* books.disney.com, pg 71

Sabia, Mary Ann, Charlesbridge Publishing Inc, 85 Main St, Watertown, MA 02472 *Tel:* 617-926-0329 *Toll Free Tel:* 800-225-3214 *Fax:* 617-926-5720 *Toll Free Fax:* 800-926-5775 *E-mail:* books@charlesbridge.com *Web Site:* www.charlesbridge.com, pg 53

Sablik, Filip, Boom! Studios, 5670 Wilshire Blvd, Suite 450, Los Angeles, CA 90036 *Web Site:* www.boom-studios.com, pg 40

Sablosky, Lindsay, Chronicle Books LLC, 680 Second St, San Francisco, CA 94107 *Tel:* 415-537-4200 *Toll Free Tel:* 800-759-0190 (cust serv) *Fax:* 415-537-4460 *Toll Free Fax:* 800-858-7787 (orders); 800-286-9471 (cust serv) *E-mail:* frontdesk@chroniclebooks.com *Web Site:* www.chroniclebooks.com, pg 55

Sacilotto, Loriana, Harlequin Enterprises Ltd, 225 Duncan Mill Rd, Don Mills, ON M3B 3K9, Canada *Tel:* 416-445-5860 *Toll Free Tel:* 888-432-4879; 800-370-5838 (ebook inquiries) *E-mail:* customerservice@harlequin.com *Web Site:* www.harlequin.com, pg 459

Sacilotto, Loriana, Love Inspired Books, 233 Broadway, Suite 1001, New York, NY 10279 *Tel:* 212-553-4200 *Fax:* 212-227-8969 *E-mail:* customer_service@harlequin.ca *Web Site:* www.harlequin.com, pg 138

Sadowski, Br Frank, St Pauls, 2187 Victory Blvd, Staten Island, NY 10314-6603 *Tel:* 718-761-0047 (edit & prodn); 718-698-2759 (mktg & billing) *Toll Free Tel:* 800-343-2522 *Fax:* 718-761-0057 *E-mail:* sales@stpauls.us; marketing@stpauls.us *Web Site:* www.stpauls.us, pg 205

Saffel, Than, West Virginia University Press, West Virginia University, PO Box 6295, Morgantown, WV 26506-6295 *Tel:* 304-293-8400 *Fax:* 304-293-6585 *Web Site:* www.wvupress.com, pg 254

Safon, Teresa, Corporation for Public Broadcasting (CPB), 401 Ninth St NW, Washington, DC 20004-2129 *Tel:* 202-879-9600 *Web Site:* www.cpb.org, pg 564

Safyan, Susan, Arsenal Pulp Press, 211 E Georgia St, No 202, Vancouver, BC V6A 1Z6, Canada *Tel:* 604-687-4233 *Toll Free Tel:* 888-600-PULP (600-7857) *Fax:* 604-687-4283 *E-mail:* info@arsenalpulp.com *Web Site:* www.arsenalpulp.com, pg 445

Sagalyn, Raphael, ICM/Sagalyn, 2 Wisconsin Circle, Suite 650, Chevy Chase, MD 20815-7045 *Tel:* 240-802-2760 *E-mail:* info@sagalyn.com *Web Site:* www.sagalyn.com, pg 521

Sagan, Kathy, Harlequin Enterprises Ltd, 233 Broadway, Suite 1001, New York, NY 10279 *Tel:* 212-553-4200 *Fax:* 212-227-8969 *E-mail:* customerservice@harlequin.com *Web Site:* www.harlequin.com, pg 100

Sagan, Raymond, William H Sadlier Inc, 9 Pine St, New York, NY 10005 *Tel:* 212-227-2120 *Toll Free Tel:* 800-221-5175 (cust serv) *Fax:* 212-312-6080 *E-mail:* customerservice@sadlier.com *Web Site:* www.sadlier.com, pg 203

Sagara, Mike, Stanford University Press, 425 Broadway St, Redwood City, CA 94063-3126 *Tel:* 650-723-9434 *Fax:* 650-725-3457 *E-mail:* info@www.sup.org; publicity@www.sup.org *Web Site:* www.sup.org, pg 220

Saikia-Wilson, Becky, Houghton Mifflin Harcourt Trade & Reference Division, 125 High St, Boston, MA 02110 *Tel:* 617-351-5000 *Toll Free Tel:* 800-225-3362 *Web Site:* www.hmhco.com, pg 111

Saint-Jean, Marie-Claire, Guy Saint-Jean Editeur Inc, 4490, rue Garand, Laval, QC H7L 5Z6, Canada *Tel:* 450-663-1777 *E-mail:* info@saint-jeanediteur.com *Web Site:* saint-jeanediteur.com, pg 469

Saint-Jean, Nicole, Guy Saint-Jean Editeur Inc, 4490, rue Garand, Laval, QC H7L 5Z6, Canada *Tel:* 450-663-1777 *E-mail:* info@saint-jeanediteur.com *Web Site:* saint-jeanediteur.com, pg 469

Sakalenka, Elvira, Mountain n' Air Books, 2947-A Honolulu Ave, La Crescenta, CA 91214 *Tel:* 818-248-9345 *Toll Free Tel:* 800-446-9696 *Toll Free Fax:* 800-303-5578 *Web Site:* www.mountain-n-air.com, pg 154

Sakamoto, Dawn, Watermark Publishing, 1000 Bishop St, Suite 806, Honolulu, HI 96813 *Tel:* 808-587-7766 *Toll Free Tel:* 866-900-BOOK (900-2665) *Fax:* 808-521-3461 *E-mail:* info@bookshawaii.net *Web Site:* www.bookshawaii.net, pg 252

Sakoian, Carol, Scholastic International, 557 Broadway, New York, NY 10012 *Tel:* 212-343-6100; 646-330-5288 (intl cust serv) *Toll Free Tel:* 800-SCHOLASTIC (724-6527) *Fax:* 646-837-7878 *E-mail:* international@scholastic.com, pg 208

Sakowski, Carolyn, John F Blair Publisher, 1406 Plaza Dr, Winston-Salem, NC 27103 *Tel:* 336-768-1374 *Toll Free Tel:* 800-222-9796 *Fax:* 336-768-9194 *Web Site:* www.blairpub.com, pg 37

Sakuda, Takashi, Kodansha USA Inc, 451 Park Ave S, 7th fl, New York, NY 10016 *Tel:* 917-322-6200 *Fax:* 212-935-6929 *E-mail:* info@kodansha-usa.com *Web Site:* www.kodanshausa.com, pg 127

Sala, Edward, Washington State University Press, Cooper Publications Bldg, Grimes Way, Pullman, WA 99164-5910 *Tel:* 509-335-3518; 509-335-7880 (order fulfillment) *Toll Free Tel:* 800-354-7360 (orders) *Fax:* 509-335-8568 *E-mail:* wsupress@wsu.edu *Web Site:* wsupress.wsu.edu, pg 252

Salane, Jeffrey, Simon & Schuster Children's Publishing, 1230 Avenue of the Americas, New York, NY 10020 *Tel:* 212-698-7000 *Web Site:* www.simonandschuster.com/kids; www.simonandschuster.com/teen; simonandschuster.net; simonandschuster.biz, pg 213

Salayi, Jill, Workman Publishing Co Inc, 225 Varick St, 9th fl, New York, NY 10014-4381 *Tel:* 212-254-5900 *Toll Free Tel:* 800-722-7202 *Fax:* 212-254-8098 *E-mail:* info@workman.com *Web Site:* www.workman.com, pg 259

Salek, Tina, Playwrights Guild of Canada, 401 Richmond St W, Suite 350, Toronto, ON M5V 3A8, Canada *Tel:* 416-703-0201 *Fax:* 416-703-0059 *E-mail:* info@playwrightsguild.ca *Web Site:* www.playwrightsguild.ca, pg 575

Salerno, Carey, Alice James Books, 114 Prescott St, Farmington, ME 04938 *Tel:* 207-778-7071 *Fax:* 207-778-7766 *E-mail:* info@alicejamesbooks.org *Web Site:* alicejamesbooks.org, pg 7

Saletan, Rebecca, Riverhead Books, 375 Hudson St, New York, NY 10014 *Tel:* 212-366-2000 *Web Site:* www.penguin.com/publishers/riverhead, pg 199

Salicup, Jim, Papercutz, 160 Broadway, E Wing, Suite 700, New York, NY 10038 *Tel:* 646-559-4681 *Toll Free Tel:* 800-886-1223 *Fax:* 212-643-1545 *E-mail:* papercutz@papercutz.com *Web Site:* www.papercutz.com, pg 173

Salinas, Simon, 4Kidz Publishing, 265 El Dorado Blvd, No 1712, Webster, TX 77598 *Tel:* 601-467-2743 *E-mail:* info@4kidzpublishing.com *Web Site:* www.facebook.com/4kidzpublishing/, pg 477

Salk, Judy, Elsevier Engineering Information (Ei), 230 Park Ave, 8th fl, New York, NY 10169-0123 *Tel:* 212-989-5800 *Fax:* 212-633-3990 *E-mail:* eicustomersupport@elsevier.com *Web Site:* www.ei.org, pg 77

Sallick, Hillary, Barbara Bradley Prize, 46 Wallace St, Somerville, MA 02144 *Tel:* 617-744-6034 *E-mail:* info@nepoetryclub.org *Web Site:* www.nepoetryclub.org, pg 634

Sallick, Hillary, Der-Hovanessian Translation Prize, 46 Wallace St, Somerville, MA 02144 *Tel:* 617-744-6034 *E-mail:* info@nepoetryclub.org *Web Site:* www.nepoetryclub.org, pg 640

Sallick, Hillary, Golden Rose Award, 46 Wallace St, Somerville, MA 02144 *Tel:* 617-744-6034 *E-mail:* info@nepoetryclub.org *Web Site:* www.nepoetryclub.org, pg 650

Sallick, Hillary, Firman Houghton Prize, 46 Wallace St, Somerville, MA 02144 *Tel:* 617-744-6034 *E-mail:* info@nepoetryclub.org *Web Site:* www.nepoetryclub.org, pg 653

Sallick, Hillary, Sheila Margaret Motton Prize, 46 Wallace St, Somerville, MA 02144 *Tel:* 617-744-6034 *E-mail:* info@nepoetryclub.org *Web Site:* www.nepoetryclub.org, pg 670

Sallick, Hillary, Erika Mumford Prize, 46 Wallace St, Somerville, MA 02144 *Tel:* 617-744-6034 *E-mail:* info@nepoetryclub.org *Web Site:* www.nepoetryclub.org, pg 670

Sallick, Hillary, May Sarton Award, 46 Wallace St, Somerville, MA 02144 *Tel:* 617-744-6034 *E-mail:* info@nepoetryclub.org *Web Site:* www.nepoetryclub.org, pg 686

Sallick, Hillary, Daniel Varoujan Award, 46 Wallace St, Somerville, MA 02144 *Tel:* 617-744-6034 *E-mail:* info@nepoetryclub.org *Web Site:* www.nepoetryclub.org, pg 695

Salo, Gay, Piano Press, 1425 Ocean Ave, Suite 5, Del Mar, CA 92014 *Tel:* 619-884-1401 *Fax:* 858-755-1104 *E-mail:* pianopress@pianopress.com *Web Site:* www.pianopress.com, pg 182

Salomon, Jake, Caribe Betania Editores, PO Box 141000, Nashville, TN 37214-1000 *Tel:* 615-902-1893 *Fax:* 615-883-9376 *Web Site:* www.caribebetania.com, pg 47

Salpeter, Steven, Curtis Brown Ltd, 10 Astor Place, New York, NY 10003 *Tel:* 212-473-5400 *Web Site:* www.curtisbrown.com, pg 510

Salser, Mark R, National Book Co, PO Box 19069, Portland, OR 97280-0069 *Tel:* 503-228-6345 *Fax:* 810-885-5811 *E-mail:* info@eralearning.com *Web Site:* www.eralearning.com, pg 157

Saltmarsh, Fiona, Chicago Women in Publishing, PO Box 268107, Chicago, IL 60626 *Tel:* 773-508-0351 *Fax:* 303-942-7164 *E-mail:* info@cwip.org *Web Site:* www.cwip.org, pg 563

Saltz, Carole, Teachers College Press, 1234 Amsterdam Ave, New York, NY 10027 *Tel:* 212-678-3929 *Toll Free Tel:* 800-575-6566 *Fax:* 212-678-4149; 802-864-7626 *E-mail:* tcpress@tc.columbia.edu; tcp.orders@aidcvt.com (orders) *Web Site:* www.teacherscollegepress.com, pg 228

Saltzman, Glenn, Georgetown University Press, 3240 Prospect St NW, Suite 250, Washington, DC 20007 *Tel:* 202-687-5889 (busn) *Fax:* 202-687-6340 (edit) *E-mail:* gupress@georgetown.edu *Web Site:* press.georgetown.edu, pg 92

Salva, Richard, Crystal Clarity Publishers, 14618 Tyler Foote Rd, Nevada City, CA 95959 *Tel:* 530-478-7600 *Toll Free Tel:* 800-424-1055 *Fax:* 530-478-7610 *E-mail:* clarity@crystalclarity.com *Web Site:* www.crystalclarity.com, pg 65

Salvador, Vanda, Paulines Editions, 5610 rue Beaubien est, Montreal, QC H1T 1X5, Canada *Tel:* 514-253-5610 *Fax:* 514-253-1907 *E-mail:* fsp-paulines@videotron.ca *Web Site:* www.editions.paulines.qc.ca, pg 466

Salvatore, Laurea, Oxford University Press USA, 198 Madison Ave, New York, NY 10016 *Tel:* 212-726-6000 *Toll Free Tel:* 800-451-7556 (orders); 800-445-9714 (cust serv) *Fax:* 919-677-1303 *E-mail:* custserv.us@oup.com *Web Site:* www.oup.com/us, pg 171

Salvatore, Ruth, Ucross Foundation Residency Program, 30 Big Red Lane, Clearmont, WY 82835 *Tel:* 307-737-2291 *Fax:* 307-737-2322 *E-mail:* info@ucross.org *Web Site:* www.ucrossfoundation.org, pg 695

Salzano, Tammi, Tiger Tales, 5 River Rd, Suite 128, Wilton, CT 06897-4069 *Tel:* 920-387-2333 *Fax:* 920-387-9994 *Web Site:* www.tigertalesbooks.com, pg 232

Salzman, Rachel, W W Norton & Company Inc, 500 Fifth Ave, New York, NY 10110-0017 *Tel:* 212-354-5500 *Toll Free Tel:* 800-233-4830 (orders & cust serv) *Fax:* 212-869-0856 *Toll Free Fax:* 800-458-6515 *E-mail:* orders@wwnorton.com *Web Site:* books.wwnorton.com, pg 164

Salzman, Richard, Salzman International, 1751 Charles Ave, Arcata, CA 95521 *Tel:* 415-285-8267 *Fax:* 707-822-5500 *Web Site:* www.salzint.com, pg 544

Salzmann, Oliver, Madison Press Books, 155 Edward St, Suite 1, Aurora, ON L4G 1W3, Canada *E-mail:* info@madisonpressbooks.com *Web Site:* www.madisonpressbooks.com, pg 462

Sammon, Patricia, H E Francis Award Short Story Competition, UAH Huntsville Dept of English, Morton Hall 222, Huntsville, AL 35899 *Web Site:* www.uah.edu/la/departments/english, pg 647

Samms, June, Kids Can Press Ltd, 25 Dockside Dr, Toronto, ON M5A 0B5, Canada *Tel:* 416-479-7000 *Toll Free Tel:* 800-265-0884 *Fax:* 416-960-5437 *E-mail:* info@kidscan.com; customerservice@kidscan.com *Web Site:* www.kidscanpress.com; www.kidscanpress.ca, pg 461

Samuel, Benjamin, National Book Awards, 90 Broad St, Suite 604, New York, NY 10004 *Tel:* 212-685-0261 *Fax:* 212-213-6570 *E-mail:* nationalbook@nationalbook.org *Web Site:* www.nationalbook.org, pg 670

Samuels, Alicia, Presbyterian Publishing Corp (PPC), 100 Witherspoon St, Louisville, KY 40202 *Tel:* 502-569-5000 *Toll Free Tel:* 800-523-1631 (US only) *Fax:* 502-569-5113 *E-mail:* ppcmail@presbypub.com *Web Site:* www.ppcbooks.com, pg 187

Samuels, Gary, Metropolitan Lithographers Association Inc, c/o Pictorial Offset, 111 Amor Ave, Carlstadt, NJ 07072 *Tel:* 201-935-7100, pg 569

Samuelson, Paul, Grand Central Publishing, 1290 Avenue of the Americas, New York, NY 10019 *Tel:* 212-364-1100 *Web Site:* www.hachettebookgroup.com, pg 95

San Filippo, Karen, Association of Manitoba Book Publishers, 100 Arthur St, Suite 404, Winnipeg, MB R3B 1H3, Canada *Tel:* 204-947-3335 *Fax:* 204-956-4689 *E-mail:* ambp@mts.net *Web Site:* ambp.ca, pg 559

Sanborn, Geoffrey, The Melville Society, Johns Hopkins University Press, PO Box 19966, Baltimore, MD 21211-0966 *Web Site:* melvillesociety.org, pg 569

Sanborn, Kat, Llewellyn Publications, 2143 Wooddale Dr, Woodbury, MN 55125 *Tel:* 651-291-1970 *Toll Free Tel:* 800-843-6666 *Fax:* 651-291-1908 *E-mail:* publicity@llewellyn.com; customerservice@llewellyn.com *Web Site:* www.llewellyn.com, pg 137

Sanchez, Irene, Liturgy Training Publications, 3949 S Racine Ave, Chicago, IL 60609-2523 *Tel:* 773-579-4900 *Toll Free Tel:* 800-933-1800 (US & CN only orders) *Fax:* 773-579-4929 *Toll Free Fax:* 800-933-7094 (US & CN only orders) *E-mail:* orders@ltp.org *Web Site:* www.ltp.org, pg 136

Sanchez, Wanda, Mary Ann Liebert Inc, 140 Huguenot St, 3rd fl, New Rochelle, NY 10801-5215 *Tel:* 914-740-2100 *Toll Free Tel:* 800-654-3237 *Fax:* 914-740-2101 *E-mail:* info@liebertpub.com *Web Site:* www.liebertonline.com, pg 133

Sand, Michael, Harry N Abrams Inc, 195 Broadway, 9th fl, New York, NY 10007 *Tel:* 212-206-7715 *Toll Free Tel:* 800-345-1359 *Fax:* 212-519-1210 *E-mail:* abrams@abramsbooks.com *Web Site:* www.abramsbooks.com, pg 3

Sand, Michael, Stewart, Tabori & Chang, 115 W 18 St, 6th fl, New York, NY 10011 *Tel:* 212-519-1200; 212-206-7715 *Fax:* 212-519-1210 *E-mail:* abrams@abramsbooks.com *Web Site:* www.abramsbooks.com/imprints/stc, pg 222

Sandberg, Rachel, Faith Childs Literary Agency Inc, 111 John St, Suite 1620, New York, NY 10038 *Tel:* 212-995-9600 *Web Site:* faithchildsliteraryagency.com, pg 511

Sanders, Bob, Mundania Press LLC, 6457 Glenway Ave, Suite 109, Cincinnati, OH 45211 *Tel:* 513-404-7357 *Fax:* 513-598-9220 *Toll Free Fax:* 888-460-4752 *E-mail:* books@mundania.com; inquiry@mundania.com *Web Site:* www.mundania.com, pg 155

Sanders, Keith P PhD, Frank Luther Mott-Kappa Tau Alpha Research Award, University of Missouri, School of Journalism, 76 Gannett Hall, Columbia, MO 65211-1200 *Tel:* 573-882-7685 *Fax:* 573-884-1720 *E-mail:* umcjourkta@missouri.edu *Web Site:* www.kappataualpha.org, pg 670

Sanders, Meredith K, Goose River Press, 3400 Friendship Rd, Waldoboro, ME 04572-6337 *Tel:* 207-832-6665 *E-mail:* gooseriverpress@roadrunner.com *Web Site:* gooseriverpress.com, pg 94

Sanders, Michael, Alpha Books, 6081 E 82 St, 4th fl, Indianapolis, IN 46250 *Tel:* 212-366-2000 *E-mail:* ecommerce@us.penguingroup.com *Web Site:* www.dk.com; www.idiotguides.com, pg 8

Sanders, Patricia, Manitoba Arts Council, 525-93 Lombard Ave, Winnipeg, MB R3B 3B1, Canada *Tel:* 204-945-2237 *Toll Free Tel:* 866-994-2787 *Fax:* 204-945-5925 *E-mail:* info@artscouncil.mb.ca *Web Site:* artscouncil.mb.ca, pg 569

Sanders, Ray, Purple House Press, 8100 US Hwy 62 E, Cynthiana, KY 41031 *Tel:* 859-235-9970 *Web Site:* www.purplehousepress.com, pg 191

Sanders, Rob, Greystone Books Ltd, 343 Railway St, Suite 201, Vancouver, BC V6A 1A4, Canada *Tel:* 604-875-1550 *Fax:* 604-875-1556 *E-mail:* info@greystonebooks.com *Web Site:* www.greystonebooks.com, pg 458

Sanders, Victoria, Victoria Sanders & Associates LLC, 241 Avenue of the Americas, Suite 11-H, New York, NY 10014 *Tel:* 212-633-8811 *Fax:* 212-633-0525 *E-mail:* queriesvsa@gmail.com *Web Site:* www.victoriasanders.com, pg 534

Sandford, Bria, Portfolio, 375 Hudson St, New York, NY 10014 *Web Site:* www.penguin.com/meet/publishers/portfolio, pg 186

Sandler, Neil, Rosenthal Represents, 23725 Hartland St, West Hills, CA 91307 *Tel:* 818-222-5445 *E-mail:* eliselicenses@earthlink.net, pg 544

Sandler, Zoe, ICM Partners, 65 E 55 St, New York, NY 10022 *Tel:* 212-556-5600 *Web Site:* www.icmtalent.com, pg 521

Sandoz, Claude, Galaxy Press, 7051 Hollywood Blvd, Suite 200, Hollywood, CA 90028 *Tel:* 323-466-7815 *Toll Free Tel:* 877-8GALAXY (842-5299) *E-mail:* info@galaxypress.com; customers@galaxypress.com *Web Site:* www.galaxypress.com, pg 89

Sands, Katharine, Sarah Jane Freymann Literary Agency LLC, 59 W 71 St, Suite 9-B, New York, NY 10023 *Tel:* 212-362-9277 *E-mail:* submissions@sarahjanefreymann.com *Web Site:* www.sarahjanefreymann.com, pg 518

Sandstrum, Anna-Lisa, Chronicle Books LLC, 680 Second St, San Francisco, CA 94107 *Tel:* 415-537-4200 *Toll Free Tel:* 800-759-0190 (cust serv) *Fax:* 415-537-4460 *Toll Free Fax:* 800-858-7787 (orders); 800-286-9471 (cust serv) *E-mail:* frontdesk@chroniclebooks.com *Web Site:* www.chroniclebooks.com, pg 55

Sanfilippo, Tony, The Ohio State University Press, 180 Pressey Hall, 1070 Carmack Rd, Columbus, OH 43210-1002 *Tel:* 614-292-6930 *Fax:* 614-292-2065 *Toll Free Fax:* 800-621-8476 *E-mail:* info@osupress.org *Web Site:* ohiostatepress.org, pg 167

Sanford, Bria, Penguin Group USA, A Penguin Random House Company, 375 Hudson St, New York, NY 10014 *Tel:* 212-366-2000 *Toll Free Tel:* 800-847-5515 (inside sales); 800-631-8571 (cust serv) *Fax:* 212-366-2666; 607-775-4829 (inside sales) *E-mail:* online@us.penguingroup.com *Web Site:* www.penguin.com, pg 177

Sankaran, Vanitha, Historical Novel Society North American Conference, 400 Dark Star Ct, Fairbanks, AK 99709 *Tel:* 217-581-7538 *Fax:* 217-581-7534 *Web Site:* historicalnovelsociety.org, pg 611

Sankel, Melanie, Bloomsbury Publishing Inc, 1385 Broadway, 5th fl, New York, NY 10018 *Tel:* 212-419-5300 *E-mail:* marketingusa@bloomsbury.com; adultpublicityusa@bloomsbury.com; askacademic@bloomsbury.com *Web Site:* www.bloomsbury.com, pg 38

Sanmartin, Cristina, The MIT Press, One Rogers St, Cambridge, MA 02142 *Tel:* 617-253-5255 *Toll Free Tel:* 800-207-8354 (orders) *Fax:* 617-258-6779; 617-577-1545 (orders) *Web Site:* mitpress.mit.edu, pg 152

Santana, Melissa, Hippocrene Books Inc, 171 Madison Ave, New York, NY 10016 *Tel:* 212-685-4373 *Fax:* 212-779-9338 *E-mail:* info@hippocrenebooks.com; orderdept@hippocrenebooks.com (orders) *Web Site:* www.hippocrenebooks.com, pg 108

Santana, Reina, Demos Medical Publishing, 11 W 42 St, 15th fl, New York, NY 10036 *Tel:* 212-683-0072 *E-mail:* info@demosmedpub.com; orderdept@demosmedical.com; editorial@demosmedical.com *Web Site:* www.demosmedical.com, pg 69

Santella, Mark, Random House Children's Books, 1745 Broadway, 10th fl, New York, NY 10019 *Tel:* 212-782-9000 *Web Site:* www.randomhousekids.com, pg 194

Santini, Robert, Pearson Humanities & Social Sciences, 225 River St, Hoboken, NJ 07030-4772 *Tel:* 201-236-7000, pg 176

Santo, Courtney Miller, The Pinch Writing Awards in Fiction, University of Memphis, English Dept, 435 Patterson Hall, Memphis, TN 38152 *Tel:* 901-678-2651 *Fax:* 901-678-2226 *E-mail:* editor@pinchjournal.com *Web Site:* www.pinchjournal.com, pg 680

Santo, Courtney Miller, The Pinch Writing Awards in Poetry, University of Memphis, English Dept, 435 Patterson Hall, Memphis, TN 38152 *Tel:* 901-678-2651 *Fax:* 901-678-2226 *E-mail:* editor@pinchjournal.com *Web Site:* www.pinchjournal.com, pg 680

Santopolo, Jill, Philomel, 345 Hudson St, New York, NY 10014 *Tel:* 212-366-2000, pg 182

Santoro, Corina, Milady, Executive Woods, 5 Maxwell Dr, Clifton Park, NY 12065-2919 *Tel:* 518-348-2300 *Toll Free Tel:* 800-998-7498 *Fax:* 518-373-6309 *E-mail:* info@milady.com *Web Site:* milady.cengage.com, pg 150

Santoro, Jamie, The American Library Association (ALA), 50 E Huron St, Chicago, IL 60611 *Tel:* 312-944-6780 *Toll Free Tel:* 800-545-2433 *Fax:* 312-280-5275 *E-mail:* editionsmarketing@ala.org *Web Site:* www.alastore.ala.org, pg 12

Santoro, Jed, Merriam-Webster Inc, 47 Federal St, Springfield, MA 01102 *Tel:* 413-734-3134 *Toll Free Tel:* 800-828-1880 (orders & cust serv) *Fax:* 413-731-5979 (sales) *E-mail:* support@merriam-webster.com *Web Site:* www.merriam-webster.com, pg 149

Santucci, Ernest, Agency Chicago, 332 S Michigan Ave, Suite 1032, No A600, Chicago, IL 60604 *E-mail:* ernsant@aol.com, pg 506

Saphire-Bernstein, Evie, Jewish Book Council, 520 Eighth Ave, 4th fl, New York, NY 10018 *Tel:* 212-201-2920 *Fax:* 212-532-4952 *E-mail:* jbc@jewishbooks.org *Web Site:* www.jewishbookcouncil.org, pg 568

Saphire-Bernstein, Evie, National Jewish Book Award-Children's Literature, 520 Eighth Ave, 4th fl, New York, NY 10018 *Tel:* 212-201-2920 *Fax:* 212-532-4952 *E-mail:* jbc@jewishbooks.org *Web Site:* www.jewishbookcouncil.org, pg 671

Saphire-Bernstein, Evie, National Jewish Book Award-Natan Book Award, 520 Eighth Ave, 4th fl, New York, NY 10018 *Tel:* 212-201-2920 *Fax:* 212-532-4952 *E-mail:* jbc@jewishbooks.org; natanbookawards@jewishbooks.org *Web Site:* www.jewishbookcouncil.org, pg 671

Saphire-Bernstein, Evie, National Jewish Book Award-Young Adult Literature, 520 Eighth Ave, 4th fl, New York, NY 10018 *Tel:* 212-201-2920 *Fax:* 212-532-4952 *E-mail:* jbc@jewishbooks.org *Web Site:* www.jewishbookcouncil.org, pg 671

Saphire-Bernstein, Evie, National Jewish Book Awards, 520 Eighth Ave, 4th fl, New York, NY 10018 *Tel:* 212-201-2920 *Fax:* 212-532-4952 *E-mail:* jbc@jewishbooks.org *Web Site:* www.jewishbookcouncil.org, pg 671

Saphire-Bernstein, Evie, Sami Rohr Prize for Jewish Literature, 520 Eighth Ave, 4th fl, New York, NY 10018 *Tel:* 212-201-2920 *Fax:* 212-532-4952 *E-mail:* jbc@jewishbooks.org *Web Site:* www.jewishbookcouncil.org, pg 685

Sapir, Marc, The Museum of Modern Art (MoMA), 11 W 53 St, New York, NY 10019 *Tel:* 212-708-9443 *Fax:* 212-333-6575 *E-mail:* moma_publications@moma.org *Web Site:* www.moma.org, pg 155

Saranson, Richard, Hebrew Union College Press, 3101 Clifton Ave, Cincinnati, OH 45220 *Tel:* 513-221-1875 *Fax:* 513-221-0321 *Web Site:* press.huc.edu, pg 105

Saraydarian, Gita, TSG Publishing Foundation Inc, 28641 N 63 Place, Cave Creek, AZ 85331 *Tel:* 480-502-1909 *Fax:* 480-502-0713 *E-mail:* info@tsgfoundation.org *Web Site:* www.tsgfoundation.org, pg 236

Sargent, Dave Jr, Ozark Publishing Inc, PO Box 228, Prairie Grove, AR 72753-0228 *Tel:* 479-595-9522 *Toll Free Tel:* 800-321-5671 *Fax:* 479-846-2843 *E-mail:* srg304@yahoo.com *Web Site:* www.ozarkpublishing.us, pg 172

Sargent, Dave, Ozark Publishing Inc, PO Box 228, Prairie Grove, AR 72753-0228 *Tel:* 479-595-9522 *Toll Free Tel:* 800-321-5671 *Fax:* 479-846-2843 *E-mail:* srg304@yahoo.com *Web Site:* www.ozarkpublishing.us, pg 172

Sargent, John, Macmillan, 175 Fifth Ave, New York, NY 10010 *Tel:* 646-307-5151 *E-mail:* press.inquiries@macmillan.com *Web Site:* www.macmillan.com, pg 139

Sargent, Kara, Little, Brown Books for Young Readers, 1290 Avenue of the Americas, New York, NY 10019 *Tel.* 212-364-1100 *Toll Free Tel:* 800-759-0190 (cust serv) *Web Site:* www.HachetteBookGroup.com, pg 136

Sargent, Michael, Tuttle Publishing, Airport Business Park, 364 Innovation Dr, North Clarendon, VT 05759-9436 *Tel:* 802-773-8930 *Toll Free Tel:* 800-526-2778 *Fax:* 802-773-6993 *Toll Free Fax:* 800-FAX-TUTL (329-8885) *E-mail:* info@tuttlepublishing.com; orders@tuttlepublishing.com *Web Site:* www.tuttlepublishing.com, pg 237

Sarlo, Susan, Vermont College of Fine Arts MFA in Writing for Children & Young Adults Program, 36 College St, Montpelier, VT 05602 *Tel:* 802-828-8637; 802-828-8696 *Toll Free Tel:* 866-934-VCFA (934-8232) *Fax:* 802-828-8649 *Web Site:* www.vcfa.edu, pg 624

Sarmiento, Jessamyn, National Endowment for the Arts, 400 Seventh St SW, Washington, DC 20506-0001 *Tel:* 202-682-5400 *Web Site:* www.arts.gov, pg 583

Sarmiento, Jessamyn, The National Medal of Arts, 400 Seventh St SW, Washington, DC 20506-0001 *Tel:* 202-682-5434 *Web Site:* www.arts.gov/honors/medals, pg 671

Sarratt, Blanche, University of Alabama Press, 200 Hackberry Lane, 2nd fl, Tuscaloosa, AL 35487 *Tel:* 205-348-5180 *Fax:* 205-348-9201 *Web Site:* www.uapress.ua.edu, pg 239

Sassa, Jackie, Houghton Mifflin Harcourt Trade & Reference Division, 125 High St, Boston, MA 02110 *Tel:* 617-351-5000 *Toll Free Tel:* 800-225-3362 *Web Site:* www.hmhco.com, pg 111

Sassi, Lynda Zuber, Chronicle Books LLC, 680 Second St, San Francisco, CA 94107 *Tel:* 415-537-4200 *Toll Free Tel:* 800-759-0190 (cust serv) *Fax:* 415-537-4460 *Toll Free Fax:* 800-858-7787 (orders); 800-286-9471 (cust serv) *E-mail:* frontdesk@chroniclebooks.com *Web Site:* www.chroniclebooks.com, pg 55

Sato, Janine, Chronicle Books LLC, 680 Second St, San Francisco, CA 94107 *Tel:* 415-537-4200 *Toll Free Tel:* 800-759-0190 (cust serv) *Fax:* 415-537-4460 *Toll Free Fax:* 800-858-7787 (orders); 800-286-9471 (cust serv) *E-mail:* frontdesk@chroniclebooks.com *Web Site:* www.chroniclebooks.com, pg 55

Satrom, Ellen, The University of Virginia Press, PO Box 400318, Charlottesville, VA 22904-4318 *Tel:* 434-924-3468 (cust serv); 434-924-3469 (cust serv) *Toll Free Tel:* 800-831-3406 (orders) *Fax:* 434-982-2655 *Toll Free Fax:* 877-288-6400 *E-mail:* vapress@virginia.edu *Web Site:* www.upress.virginia.edu, pg 245

Sattler, Maggie, University of Minnesota Press, 111 Third Ave S, Suite 290, Minneapolis, MN 55401-2520 *Tel:* 612-301-1990 *Fax:* 612-301-1980 *E-mail:* ump@umn.edu *Web Site:* www.upress.umn.edu, pg 242

Satyal, Mr Rakesh, Atria Books, 1230 Avenue of the Americas, New York, NY 10020 *Tel:* 212-698-7000 *Fax:* 212-698-7007 *Web Site:* www.simonandschuster.com, pg 25

Sauers, Sara T, American Printing History Association, PO Box 4519, Grand Central Sta, New York, NY 10163 *Tel:* 202-544-2422 *E-mail:* secretary@printinghistory.org *Web Site:* printinghistory.org, pg 556

Sauers, Sara T, American Printing History Association Award, PO Box 4519, Grand Central Sta, New York, NY 10163 *Tel:* 202-544-2422 *E-mail:* secretary@printinghistory.org *Web Site:* printinghistory.org, pg 627

Saul, John Ralston, PEN American Center, 588 Broadway, Suite 303, New York, NY 10012 *Tel:* 212-334-1660 *Fax:* 212-334-2181 *E-mail:* info@pen.org *Web Site:* pen.org, pg 575

Saul, Terri, Parallax Press, 2236-B Sixth St, Berkeley, CA 94710 *Tel:* 510-540-6411 *Toll Free Tel:* 800-863-5290 (orders) *Fax:* 510-981-1157 *Web Site:* www.parallax.org, pg 174

Saunders, Christine, Diversion Books, 443 Park Ave S, Suite 1008, New York, NY 10016 *Tel:* 212-961-6390 *E-mail:* info@diversionbooks.com *Web Site:* www.diversionbooks.com, pg 71

Saunders, David, APA Talent & Literary Agency, 405 S Beverly Dr, Beverly Hills, CA 90212 *Tel:* 310-888-4200 *Fax:* 310-888-4242 *Web Site:* www.apa-agency.com, pg 507

Saunders, Marci, Storey Publishing LLC, 210 MASS MoCA Way, North Adams, MA 01247 *Tel:* 413-346-2100 *Toll Free Tel:* 800-441-5700 (orders); 800-793-9396 (edit) *Fax:* 413-346-2199; 413-346-2196 (edit) *E-mail:* sales@storey.com *Web Site:* www.storey.com, pg 223

Saunders, Mark H, The University of Virginia Press, PO Box 400318, Charlottesville, VA 22904-4318 *Tel:* 434-924-3468 (cust serv); 434-924-3469 (cust serv) *Toll Free Tel:* 800-831-3406 (orders) *Fax:* 434-982-2655 *Toll Free Fax:* 877-288-6400 *E-mail:* vapress@virginia.edu *Web Site:* www.upress.virginia.edu, pg 245

Sauvgeau, Annie, Editions Le Dauphin Blanc Inc, 825, blvd Lebourgneuf, Suite 125, Quebec, QC G2J 0B9, Canada *Tel:* 418-845-4045 *Fax:* 418-845-1933 *E-mail:* info@dauphinblanc.com *Web Site:* www.dauphinblanc.com, pg 455

Savanh, Victoria, Penguin Books, 375 Hudson St, New York, NY 10014 *Tel:* 212-366-2000 *E-mail:* penguinpublicity@us.penguingroup.com *Web Site:* www.penguinclassics.com; www.penguin.com, pg 177

Savarese, Anne, Princeton University Press, 41 William St, Princeton, NJ 08540-5237 *Tel:* 609-258-4900 *Fax:* 609-258-6305 *Web Site:* press.princeton.edu, pg 188

Savarese, Carolyn, Kneerim & Williams Agency, 90 Canal St, Boston, MA 02114 *Tel:* 617-303-1650 *Web Site:* www.kwlit.com, pg 524

Savasta, Jenifer, Chronicle Books LLC, 680 Second St, San Francisco, CA 94107 *Tel:* 415-537-4200 *Toll Free Tel:* 800-759-0190 (cust serv) *Fax:* 415-537-4460 *Toll Free Fax:* 800-858-7787 (orders); 800-286-9471 (cust serv) *E-mail:* frontdesk@chroniclebooks.com *Web Site:* www.chroniclebooks.com, pg 55

Savo, Nancy Mellichamp, Lyric Poetry Prizes, PO Box 110, Jericho, VT 05465 *Tel:* 802-899-3993 *Fax:* 802-899-3993 *E-mail:* themuse@thelyricmagazine.com *Web Site:* thelyricmagazine.com, pg 664

Sawhney, Divya, Penguin Random House Inc, 1745 Broadway, New York, NY 10019 *Tel:* 212-782-9000 *Toll Free Tel:* 800-726-0600 *Web Site:* www.penguinrandomhouse.com, pg 178

Sawyer, Peter, Fifi Oscard Agency Inc, 1440 Broadway, 23rd fl, New York, NY 10018 *Tel:* 212-764-1100 *E-mail:* agency@fifioscard.com *Web Site:* fifioscard.com, pg 531

Saxton, Heidi Hess, Ave Maria Press, PO Box 428, Notre Dame, IN 46556 *Tel:* 574-287-2831 *Toll Free Tel:* 800-282-1865 *Fax:* 574-239-2904 *Toll Free Fax:* 800-282-5681 *E-mail:* avemariapress.1@nd.edu *Web Site:* www.avemariapress.com, pg 27

Sayar, Kevin, ProQuest LLC, 789 E Eisenhower Pkwy, Ann Arbor, MI 48108 *Tel:* 734-761-4700 *Toll Free Tel:* 800-521-0600 *Web Site:* www.proquest.com, pg 190

Sayle, Kim, Hachette Audio, 1290 Avenue of the Americas, New York, NY 10019 *Tel:* 212-364-1100 *Web Site:* www.hachetteaudio.com, pg 98

Saylor, David, Scholastic Trade Division, 557 Broadway, New York, NY 10012 *Tel:* 212-343-6100; 212-343-4685 (export sales) *Fax:* 212-343-4714 (export sales) *Web Site:* www.scholastic.com, pg 208

Scagnetti, Jack, Jack Scagnetti Talent & Literary Agency, 5136 Vineland Ave, North Hollywood, CA 91601 *Tel:* 818-762-3871 *Web Site:* www.jackscagnettiagency.com; www.facebook.com/jackscagnettiagency/, pg 534

Scalissi, Linda, 3 Seas Literary Agency, PO Box 444, Sun Prairie, WI 53590 *Tel:* 608-834-9317 *E-mail:* threeseaslit@aol.com *Web Site:* threeseasagency.com, pg 539

Scalora, Joseph, Random House Children's Books, 1745 Broadway, 10th fl, New York, NY 10019 *Tel:* 212-782-9000 *Web Site:* www.randomhousekids.com, pg 194

Scanlan, Brian, Thieme Medical Publishers Inc, 333 Seventh Ave, 18th fl, New York, NY 10001 *Tel:* 212-760-0888 *Toll Free Tel:* 800-782-3488 *Fax:* 212-947-1112 *E-mail:* customerservice@thieme.com *Web Site:* www.thieme.com, pg 231

Scanlon, Elizabeth, Honickman First Book Prize, University of the Arts (UARTS), Hamilton Hall, 320 S Broad St, Rm 313, Philadelphia, PA 19102-4901 *Tel:* 215-717-6801 *Fax:* 215-717-6805 *Web Site:* www.aprweb.org, pg 653

Scanlon, Sally, The Intrepid Traveler, 152 Staltonstall Pkwy (rear entrance), East Haven, CT 06512 *Tel:* 203-469-0214 *E-mail:* admin@intrepidtraveler.com *Web Site:* www.intrepidtraveler.com, pg 121

Scarpulla, Zina, Bloom's Literary Criticism, 132 W 31 St, 17th fl, New York, NY 10001 *Toll Free Tel:* 800-322-8755 *Toll Free Fax:* 800-678-3633 *E-mail:* custserv@factsonfile.com *Web Site:* www.infobasepublishing.com, pg 37

Scarpulla, Zina, Chelsea House Publishers, 132 W 31 St, 17th fl, New York, NY 10001 *Tel:* 212-967-8800 *Toll Free Tel:* 800-322-8755 *Fax:* 917-339-0325 *Toll Free Fax:* 800-678-3633 *E-mail:* custserv@factsonfile.com *Web Site:* www.infobasepublishing.com; www.infobaselearning.com, pg 53

Scarpulla, Zina, Facts On File, 132 W 31 St, 17th fl, New York, NY 10001 *Tel:* 212-967-8800 *Toll Free Tel:* 800-322-8755 *Toll Free Fax:* 800-678-3633 *E-mail:* custserv@factsonfile.com *Web Site:* infobasepublishing.com, pg 81

Scarpulla, Zina, Ferguson Publishing, 132 W 31 St, 17th fl, New York, NY 10001 *Tel:* 212-967-8800 *Toll Free Tel:* 800-322-8755 *Fax:* 917-339-0323 *Toll Free Fax:* 800-678-3633 *E-mail:* custserv@factsonfile.com *Web Site:* infobasepublishing.com, pg 84

Scartz-Montesano, Sara, Teton NewMedia Inc, 90 E Simpson, Suite 110, Jackson, WY 83001 *Tel:* 307-732-0028 *Toll Free Tel:* 877-306-9793 *Fax:* 307-734-0841 *E-mail:* sales@tetonnm.com *Web Site:* www.tetonnm.com, pg 230

Schademann, Beth, The Electrochemical Society (ECS), 65 S Main St, Bldg D, Pennington, NJ 08534-2839 *Tel:* 609-737-1902 *Fax:* 609-737-2743 *E-mail:* publications@electrochem.org; customerservice@electrochem.org *Web Site:* www.electrochem.org, pg 77

Schaefer, Elizabeth, Random House Publishing Group, 1745 Broadway, New York, NY 10019 *Toll Free Tel:* 800-200-3552 *Web Site:* atrandom.com, pg 195

Schaefer, Peggy, WorthyKids/Ideals, 6100 Tower Circle, Suite 210, Franklin, TN 37067 *Tel:* 615-932-7600 *E-mail:* idealsinfo@worthypublishing.com *Web Site:* www.idealsbooks.com, pg 260

Schaeffer, Dave, Simon & Schuster, Inc, 1230 Avenue of the Americas, New York, NY 10020 *Tel:* 212-698-7000 *Fax:* 212-698-7007 *E-mail:* firstname.lastname@simonandschuster.com *Web Site:* www.simonandschuster.com, pg 213

Schafer, Ben, Perseus Books, 250 W 57 St, 15th fl, New York, NY 10107 *Tel:* 212-340-8100 *Toll Free Tel:* 800-343-4499 (cust serv) *Fax:* 212-340-8105 *Web Site:* www.perseusbooks.com, pg 181

Schafer, Kate Gales, HarperCollins General Books Group, 195 Broadway, New York, NY 10007 *Tel:* 212-207-7000 *Web Site:* www.harpercollins.com, pg 101

Schaffer, Julie, Naomi Berber Memorial Award, 301 Brush Creek Rd, Warrendale, PA 15086-7529 *Tel:* 412-741-6860 *Toll Free Tel:* 800-910-4283 *Fax:* 412-741-2311 *E-mail:* printingind@comm.printing.org *Web Site:* www.printing.org/berberaward, pg 631

Schaffer, Julie, Education Awards of Excellence, 301 Brush Creek Rd, Warrendale, PA 15086-7529 *Tel:* 412-741-6860 *Toll Free Tel:* 800-910-4283 *Fax:* 412-741-2311 *E-mail:* printingind@comm.printing.org *Web Site:* www.printing.org/educationaward, pg 643

Schaffer, Julie, InterTech™ Technology Awards, 301 Brush Creek Rd, Warrendale, PA 15086-7529 *Tel:* 412-741-6860 *Toll Free Tel:* 800-910-4283 *Fax:* 412-741-2311 *E-mail:* intertech@printing.org *Web Site:* www.printing.org/intertechawards, pg 656

Schaffer, Julie, Frederick D Kagy Education Award of Excellence, 301 Brush Creek Rd, Warrendale, PA 15086-7529 *Tel:* 412-741-6860 *Toll Free Tel:* 800-910-4283 *Fax:* 412-741-2311 *E-mail:* printingind@comm.printing.org *Web Site:* www.printing.org, pg 658

Schaffer, Julie, Premier Print Awards, 301 Brush Creek Rd, Warrendale, PA 15086-7529 *Tel:* 412-741-6860 *Toll Free Tel:* 800-910-4283 *Fax:* 412-741-2311 *E-mail:* printingind@comm.printing.org *Web Site:* www.printing.org/premierprint, pg 682

Schaffer, Julie, Robert F Reed Technology Medal, 301 Brush Creek Rd, Warrendale, PA 15086-7529 *Tel:* 412-741-6860 *Toll Free Tel:* 800-910-4283 *Fax:* 412-741-2311 *E-mail:* printingind@comm.printing.org *Web Site:* www.printing.org/reedaward, pg 684

Schaffer, Julie, William D Schaeffer Environmental Award, 301 Brush Creek Rd, Warrendale, PA 15086-7529 *Tel:* 412-741-6860 *Toll Free Tel:* 800-910-4283 *Fax:* 412-741-2311 *E-mail:* printingind@comm.printing.org *Web Site:* www.printing.org/schaefferaward, pg 688

Schanck, Denise, Garland Science Publishing, 711 Third Ave, 8th fl, New York, NY 10017 *Tel:* 212-216-7800; 212-281-4487 *Fax:* 212-947-3027 *E-mail:* science@garland.com *Web Site:* www.garlandscience.com, pg 90

Schang, Scott, Environmental Law Institute, 1730 "M" St NW, Suite 700, Washington, DC 20036 *Tel:* 202-939-3800 *Toll Free Tel:* 800-433-5120 *Fax:* 202-939-3868 *E-mail:* law@eli.org *Web Site:* www.eli.org, pg 79

Schantz, Jessica, Cleveland State University Poetry Center Prizes, 2121 Euclid Ave, Cleveland, OH 44115 *Tel:* 216-687-3986 *Toll Free Tel:* 888-278-6473 *Fax:* 216-687-6943 *E-mail:* poetrycenter@csuohio.edu *Web Site:* www.csupoetrycenter.com, pg 638

Schaper, Jennifer, Duke University Press, 905 W Main St, Suite 18B, Durham, NC 27701 *Tel:* 919-688-5134 *Toll Free Tel:* 888-651-0122 (US) *Fax:* 919-688-2615 *Toll Free Fax:* 888-651-0124 *E-mail:* orders@dukeupress.edu *Web Site:* www.dukeupress.edu, pg 73

Schaps, Eric, Center for the Collaborative Classroom, 1250 53 St, Suite 3, Emeryville, CA 94608 *Tel:* 510-533-0213 *Toll Free Tel:* 800-666-7270 *Fax:* 510-464-3670 *E-mail:* info@collaborativeclassroom.org; clientsupport@collaborativeclassroom.org *Web Site:* www.collaborativeclassroom.org, pg 51

Scharfenberg, Brianna, Picador, 175 Fifth Ave, 19th fl, New York, NY 10010 *Tel:* 646-307-5151 *Fax:* 212-253-9627 *Web Site:* www.picadorusa.com, pg 182

Scharlatt, Elisabeth, Algonquin Books, 400 Silver Cedar Ct, Suite 300, Chapel Hill, NC 27514-1585 *Tel:* 919-967-0108 *Fax:* 919-933-0272 *E-mail:* inquiry@algonquin.com *Web Site:* www.workman.com/algonquin, pg 7

Schaub, Patricia, University of Texas at Austin, New Writers Project, Dept of English, Calhoun Hall, Rm 226, 204 W 21 St, B-5000, Austin, TX 78712 *Tel:* 512-471-5132; 512-471-4991 *Fax:* 512-471-4909 *Web Site:* newwritersproject.org, pg 623

Schaut, Diane, University of Notre Dame Press, 310 Flanner Hall, Notre Dame, IN 46556 *Tel:* 574-631-6346 *Fax:* 574-631-8148 *E-mail:* undpress@nd.edu *Web Site:* www.undpress.nd.edu, pg 244

Schear, Adam, DeFiore and Company Literary Management Inc, 47 E 19 St, 3rd fl, New York, NY 10003 *Tel:* 212-925-7744 *Fax:* 212-925-9803 *E-mail:* info@defliterary.com; submissions@defliterary.com *Web Site:* www.defliterary.com, pg 513

Schechter, Pamela, The Experiment, 220 E 23 St, Suite 301, New York, NY 10010-4674 *Tel:* 212-889-1659 *E-mail:* info@theexperimentpublishing.com *Web Site:* www.theexperimentpublishing.com, pg 81

Scheel, Joanne, CWA/SCA Canada, 2200 Prince of Wales Dr, Suite 301, Ottawa, ON K2E 6Z9, Canada *Tel:* 613-820-9777 *Toll Free Tel:* 877-486-4292 *Fax:* 613-820-8188 *E-mail:* info@cwa-scacanada.ca *Web Site:* www.cwa-scacanada.ca, pg 564

Scheeler, Rev Jeff OFM, Franciscan Media, 28 W Liberty St, Cincinnati, OH 45202 *Tel:* 513-241-5615 *Toll Free Tel:* 800-488-0488 *Fax:* 513-241-0399 *E-mail:* books@americancatholic.org *Web Site:* www.americancatholic.org; www.franciscanmedia.org, pg 87

Scheer, Andy, Hartline Literary Agency LLC, 123 Queenston Dr, Pittsburgh, PA 15235 *Web Site:* www.hartlineliterary.com, pg 520

Scheffers, Todd, Goodheart-Willcox Publisher, 18604 W Creek Dr, Tinley Park, IL 60477-6243 *Tel:* 708-687-5000 *Toll Free Tel:* 800-323-0440 *Fax:* 708-468-8692 *Toll Free Fax:* 888-409-3900 *E-mail:* custserv@g-w.com; orders@g-w.com *Web Site:* www.g-w.com, pg 94

Scheiner, C J, C J Scheiner Books, PO Box 96, Brooklyn, NY 11226-0096 *Tel:* 718-469-1089, pg 501

Schenck, Gina, The Career Press Inc, 12 Parish Dr, Wayne, NJ 07470 *Tel:* 201-848-0310 *Toll Free Tel:* 800-CAREER-1 (227-3371) *Fax:* 201-848-1727 *E-mail:* sales@careerpress.com *Web Site:* www.careerpress.com, pg 47

Schenck, Nancy, Central Recovery Press (CRP), 3321 N Buffalo Dr, Suite 275, Las Vegas, NV 89129 *Tel:* 702-868-5830 *Fax:* 702-868-5831 *E-mail:* info@centralrecovery.com *Web Site:* centralrecoverypress.com, pg 52

Schenck, Robert B, F A Davis Co, 1915 Arch St, Philadelphia, PA 19103 *Tel:* 215-568-2270; 215-440-3001 *Toll Free Tel:* 800-523-4049 *Fax:* 215-568-5065; 215-440-3016 *E-mail:* info@fadavis.com; orders@fadavis.com *Web Site:* www.fadavis.com, pg 68

Schenk, Pamela W, Golden Cylindar Awards, 8281 Pine Lake Rd, Denver, NC 28037 *Tel:* 201-523-6042 *Fax:* 201-523-6048 *E-mail:* gaa@gaa.org *Web Site:* www.gaa.org, pg 650

Schenk, Pamela W, Gravure Association of the Americas Inc, 8281 Pine Lake Rd, Denver, NC 28037 *Tel:* 201-523-6042 *Fax:* 201-523-6048 *E-mail:* gaa@gaa.org *Web Site:* www.gaa.org, pg 566

Scherer, Rebecca, Jane Rotrosen Agency LLC, 85 Broad St, 28th fl, New York, NY 10004 *Tel:* 212-593-4330 *Fax:* 212-935-6985 *Web Site:* janerotrosen.com, pg 534

Scherman, Nosson, Mesorah Publications Ltd, 4401 Second Ave, Brooklyn, NY 11232 *Tel:* 718-921-9000 *Toll Free Tel:* 800-637-6724 *Fax:* 718-680-1875 *E-mail:* info@artscroll.com; orders@artscroll.com *Web Site:* www.artscroll.com, pg 149

Schiavone, Dr James, Schiavone Literary Agency Inc, 236 Trails End, West Palm Beach, FL 33413-2135 *Tel:* 561-966-9294 *Fax:* 561-966-9294 *E-mail:* profschia@aol.com *Web Site:* www.publishersmarketplace.com/members/profschia, pg 534

Schiff, Robbin, Random House Publishing Group, 1745 Broadway, New York, NY 10019 *Toll Free Tel:* 800-200-3552 *Web Site:* atrandom.com, pg 195

Schiffer, Nancy, Cornell Maritime Press Inc, 4880 Lower Valley Rd, Atglen, PA 19310 *Tel:* 610-593-1777 *Fax:* 610-593-2002 *E-mail:* info@schifferbooks.com *Web Site:* www.cmptp.com, pg 61

Schiffer, Nancy, Schiffer Publishing Ltd, 4880 Lower Valley Rd, Atglen, PA 19310 *Tel:* 610-593-1777 *Fax:* 610-593-2002 *E-mail:* info@schifferbooks.com *Web Site:* www.schifferbooks.com, pg 207

Schiffer, Pete, Cornell Maritime Press Inc, 4880 Lower Valley Rd, Atglen, PA 19310 *Tel:* 610-593-1777 *Fax:* 610-593-2002 *E-mail:* info@schifferbooks.com *Web Site:* www.cmptp.com, pg 61

Schiffer, Pete, Schiffer Publishing Ltd, 4880 Lower Valley Rd, Atglen, PA 19310 *Tel:* 610-593-1777 *Fax:* 610-593-2002 *E-mail:* info@schifferbooks.com *Web Site:* www.schifferbooks.com, pg 207

Schiller, David, Workman Publishing Co Inc, 225 Varick St, 9th fl, New York, NY 10014 4381 *Tel:* 212-254-5900 *Toll Free Tel:* 800-722-7202 *Fax:* 212-254-8098 *E-mail:* info@workman.com *Web Site:* www.workman.com, pg 259

Schiller, Howard, Hollywood Film Archive, 8391 Beverly Blvd, Los Angeles, CA 90048 *Tel:* 323-655-4968 *Web Site:* hfarchive.com, pg 109

Schiller, Lawrence, Mailer Prize, 1841 Broadway, Suite 322, New York, NY 10023 *Tel:* 646-374-3940 *Web Site:* nmcenter.org, pg 665

Schilling, Tracy, Hospital & Healthcare Compensation Service, 3 Post Rd, Suite 3, Oakland, NJ 07436 *Tel:* 201-405-0075 *Fax:* 201-405-2110 *E-mail:* allinfo@hhcsinc.com *Web Site:* www.hhcsinc.com, pg 110

Schivley, Caryl, Merriam-Webster Inc, 47 Federal St, Springfield, MA 01102 *Tel:* 413-734-3134 *Toll Free Tel:* 800-828-1880 (orders & cust serv) *Fax:* 413-731-5979 (sales) *E-mail:* support@merriam-webster.com *Web Site:* www.merriam-webster.com, pg 149

Schlager, Neil, Schlager Group Inc, 325 N Saint Paul, Suite 3425, Dallas, TX 75201 *Toll Free Tel:* 888-416-5727 *Fax:* 214-347-9469 *E-mail:* info@schlagergroup.com *Web Site:* www.schlagergroup.com, pg 207

Schleifer, Lisa, SDP Publishing Solutions LLC, 36 Captain's Way, East Bridgewater, MA 02333 *Tel:* 617-775-0656 *Web Site:* www.sdppublishingsolutions.com, pg 501

Schlesinger, Edward, Gallery Books, 1230 Avenue of the Americas, New York, NY 10020 *Toll Free Tel:* 800-456-6798 *Fax:* 212-698-7284 *E-mail:* consumer.customerservice@simonandschuster.com *Web Site:* www.simonsays.com, pg 90

Schlesinger, Jeff, Barringer Publishing, 3259 Sundance Circle, Naples, FL 34109 *Tel:* 239-514-7364 *E-mail:* schlesadv@gmail.com *Web Site:* www.barringerpublishing.com, pg 30

Schley, Jim, Dorset Prize, 243 Union St, Suite 305, North Adams, MA 01247 *Tel:* 413-664-9611 *Fax:* 413-664-9711 *E-mail:* info@tupelopress.org *Web Site:* www.tupelopress.org, pg 642

Schley, Jim, Tupelo Press Berkshire Prize for a First or Second Book of Poetry, 243 Union St, Suite 305, North Adams, MA 01247 *Tel:* 413-664-9611 *Fax:* 413-664-9711 *E-mail:* info@tupelopress.org *Web Site:* www.tupelopress.org, pg 695

Schley, Jim, Tupelo Press Inc, 243 Union St, Suite 305, North Adams, MA 01247 *Tel:* 413-664-9611 *Fax:* 413-664-9711 *E-mail:* info@tupelopress.org *Web Site:* www.tupelopress.org, pg 236

Schley, Jim, Tupelo Press Snowbound Series Chapbook Award, 243 Union St, Suite 305, North Adams, MA 01247 *Tel:* 413-664-9611 *Fax:* 413-664-9711 *E-mail:* info@tupelopress.org *Web Site:* www.tupelopress.org, pg 695

Schlichte, Dave, Amicus, PO Box 1329, Mankato, MN 56002 *Tel:* 507-388-9357 *Fax:* 507-388-1779 *E-mail:* info@amicuspublishing.us; orders@amicuspublishing.us *Web Site:* www.amicuspublishing.us, pg 16

Schmalz, Wendy, Wendy Schmalz Agency, 402 Union St, Unit 831, Hudson, NY 12534 *Tel:* 518-672-7697 *E-mail:* wendy@schmalzagency.com *Web Site:* www.schmalzagency.com, pg 534

Schmidt, Alfred, Windsor Books, 260 W Main St, Suite 5, Bayshore, NY 11706 *Tel:* 631-665-6688 *Toll Free Tel:* 800-321-5934 *E-mail:* windsor.books@att.net *Web Site:* www.windsorpublishing.com, pg 257

Schmidt, Anja, Oxmoor House, 4100 Old Montgomery Hwy, Birmingham, AL 35209 *Tel:* 205-445-6000 *Toll Free Tel:* 800-366-4712; 888-891-8935 (cust serv); 800-765-6400 (orders) *Web Site:* www.oxmoorhouse.com, pg 171

Schmidt, Eric A, University of California Press, 155 Grand Ave, Suite 400, Oakland, CA 94612-3758 *Tel:* 510-883-8232 *Fax:* 510-836-8910 *E-mail:* customerservice@ucpressjournals.com *Web Site:* www.ucpress.edu, pg 240

Schmidt, Harold D, Harold Schmidt Literary Agency, 415 W 23 St, Suite 6-F, New York, NY 10011 *Tel:* 212-727-7473, pg 534

Schmidt, Helga, Steerforth Press, 45 Lyme Rd, Suite 208, Hanover, NH 03755-1222 *Tel:* 603-643-4787 *Fax:* 603-643-4788 *E-mail:* info@steerforth.com *Web Site:* www.steerforth.com, pg 221

Schmidt, Jeff, Windsor Books, 260 W Main St, Suite 5, Bayshore, NY 11706 *Tel:* 631-665-6688 *Toll Free Tel:* 800-321-5934 *E-mail:* windsor.books@att.net *Web Site:* www.windsorpublishing.com, pg 257

Schmidt, Jessica, Perseus Books, 250 W 57 St, 15th fl, New York, NY 10107 *Tel:* 212-340-8100 *Toll Free Tel:* 800-343-4499 (cust serv) *Fax:* 212-340-8105 *Web Site:* www.perseusbooks.com, pg 181

Schmidt, Jocelyn, Penguin Young Readers Group, 345 Hudson St, New York, NY 10014 *Tel:* 212-366-2000; 212-414-3553 *Fax:* 212-414-3340 *Web Site:* www.penguin.com/children, pg 179

Schmidt, Randy, University of British Columbia Press, 2029 West Mall, Vancouver, BC V6T 1Z2, Canada *Tel:* 604-822-5959 *Toll Free Tel:* 877-377-9378 *Fax:* 604-822-6083 *Toll Free Fax:* 800-668-0821 *E-mail:* frontdesk@ubcpress.ca *Web Site:* www.ubcpress.ca, pg 473

Schmierer-Lee, Melonie PhD, Gorgias Press LLC, PO Box 6939, Piscataway, NJ 08854-6939 *Tel:* 732-885-8900 *Fax:* 732-885-8908 *E-mail:* helpdesk@gorgiaspress.com *Web Site:* www.gorgiaspress.com, pg 94

Schmitz, Elisabeth, Grove Atlantic Inc, 154 W 14 St, 12th fl, New York, NY 10011 *Tel:* 212-614-7850 *Toll Free Tel:* 800-521-0178 *Fax:* 212-614-7886 *E-mail:* info@groveatlantic.com; sales@groveatlantic.com; publicity@groveatlantic.com; rights@groveatlantic.com *Web Site:* www.groveatlantic.com, pg 97

Schneider, Bill, Etruscan Press, Wilkes University, 84 W South St, Wilkes-Barre, PA 18766 *Tel:* 570-408-4546 *Fax:* 570-408-3333 *E-mail:* books@etruscanpress.org *Web Site:* www.etruscanpress.org, pg 80

Schneider, Deborah, Gelfman Schneider/ICM Partners, 850 Seventh Ave, Suite 903, New York, NY 10019 *Tel:* 212-245-1993 *Fax:* 212-245-8678 *E-mail:* mail@gelfmanschneider.com *Web Site:* gelfmanschneider.com, pg 518

Schneider, James, Princeton University Press, 41 William St, Princeton, NJ 08540-5237 *Tel:* 609-258-4900 *Fax:* 609-258-6305 *Web Site:* press.princeton.edu, pg 188

Schneider, Jennifer, National Institute for Trial Advocacy (NITA), 1685 38 St, Suite 200, Boulder, CO 80301-2735 *Tel:* 720-890-4860 *Toll Free Tel:* 877-648-2632; 800-225-6482 (orders & returns) *Fax:* 720-890-7069 *E-mail:* info@nita.org *Web Site:* www.nita.org, pg 158

Schneider, Kathy, Jane Rotrosen Agency LLC, 85 Broad St, 28th fl, New York, NY 10004 *Tel:* 212-593-4330 *Fax:* 212-935-6985 *Web Site:* janerotrosen.com, pg 533

Schneider, Naomi, University of California Press, 155 Grand Ave, Suite 400, Oakland, CA 94612-3758 *Tel:* 510-883-8232 *Fax:* 510-836-8910 *E-mail:* customerservice@ucpressjournals.com *Web Site:* www.ucpress.edu, pg 240

Schneider, Nina, American Printing History Association, PO Box 4519, Grand Central Sta, New York, NY 10163 *Tel:* 202-544-2422 *E-mail:* secretary@printinghistory.org *Web Site:* printinghistory.org, pg 556

Schneider, Nina, American Printing History Association Award, PO Box 4519, Grand Central Sta, New York, NY 10163 *Tel:* 202-544-2422 *E-mail:* secretary@printinghistory.org *Web Site:* printinghistory.org, pg 627

Schneider, Ravina, Perseus Books, 250 W 57 St, 15th fl, New York, NY 10107 *Tel:* 212-340-8100 *Toll Free Tel:* 800-343-4499 (cust serv) *Fax:* 212-340-8105 *Web Site:* www.perseusbooks.com, pg 180

Schneider, Sam, Encounter Books, 900 Broadway, Suite 601, New York, NY 10003 *Tel:* 212-871-6310 *Toll Free Tel:* 800-786-3839 *Fax:* 212-871-6311 *E-mail:* publicity@encounterbooks.com *Web Site:* www.encounterbooks.com, pg 78

Schneider, Sara, Chronicle Books LLC, 680 Second St, San Francisco, CA 94107 *Tel:* 415-537-4200 *Toll Free Tel:* 800-759-0190 (cust serv) *Fax:* 415-537-4460 *Toll Free Fax:* 800-858-7787 (orders); 800-286-9471 (cust serv) *E-mail:* frontdesk@chroniclebooks.com *Web Site:* www.chroniclebooks.com, pg 55

Schneider, Wendy Caruso, New York Academy of Sciences (NYAS), 7 World Trade, 40th fl, 250 Greenwich St, New York, NY 10007-2157 *Tel:* 212-298-8600 *Toll Free Tel:* 800-843-6927 *Fax:* 212-298-3668 *E-mail:* nyas@nyas.org; annals@nyas.org; customerservice@nyas.org *Web Site:* www.nyas.org, pg 161

Schnell, Judith, Stackpole Books, 5067 Ritter Rd, Mechanicsburg, PA 17055 *Tel:* 717-796-0411 *Toll Free Tel:* 800-732-3669 *Fax:* 717-796-0412 *Web Site:* www.stackpolebooks.com, pg 220

Schnitzler, Alex, Keller Media Inc, 578 Washington Blvd, No 745, Marina del Rey, CA 90292 *Toll Free Tel:* 800-278-8706 *E-mail:* query@kellermedia.com *Web Site:* kellermedia.com/query, pg 523

Schoder, Katie, Alfred A Knopf/Everyman's Library, c/o Penguin Random House Inc, 1745 Broadway, New York, NY 10019 *Tel:* 212-751-2600 *Toll Free Tel:* 800-638-6460 *Fax:* 212-572-2593 *Web Site:* www.knopfdoubleday.com, pg 127

Schoen, John, SLACK® Incorporated, A Wyanoke Group Company, 6900 Grove Rd, Thorofare, NJ 08086-9447 *Tel:* 856-848-1000 *Toll Free Tel:* 800-257-8290 *Fax:* 856-848-6091 *E-mail:* sales@slackinc.com; editor@slackinc.com; customerservice@slackinc.com *Web Site:* www.healio.com/books, pg 215

Schoenborn, Melina, La Courte Echelle, 4388, rue Saint-Denis, Suite 315, Montreal, QC H2J 2L1, Canada *Tel:* 514-312-6950 *E-mail:* info@courteechelle.com *Web Site:* courteechelle.groupecourteechelle.com, pg 451

Schoenwald, Mark, Thomas Nelson, 501 Nelson Place, Nashville, TN 37214 *Tel:* 615-889-9000 *Toll Free Tel:* 800-251-4000 *Fax:* 615-902-1548 *Web Site:* www.thomasnelson.com, pg 231

Schoenwald, Mark, Tommy Nelson, 501 Nelson Place, Nashville, TN 37214 *Tel:* 615-889-9000; 615-902-1485 (cust serv) *Toll Free Tel:* 800-251-4000 *Fax:* 615-391-5225 *Web Site:* www.tommynelson.com, pg 233

Schofield, Brianna, Authors Alliance, 2705 Webster St, No 5805, Berkeley, CA 94705 *E-mail:* info@authorsalliance.org *Web Site:* www.authorsalliance.org, pg 559

Schofield, William, Paul Dry Books, 1700 Sansom St, Suite 700, Philadelphia, PA 19103 *Tel:* 215-231-9939 *Fax:* 215-231-9942 *E-mail:* editor@pauldrybooks.com *Web Site:* www.pauldrybooks.com, pg 175

Scholl, Steve, White Cloud Press, 300 E Hersey St, Suite 11, Ashland, OR 97520 *Tel:* 541-488-6415 *Fax:* 541-482-7708 *E-mail:* info@whitecloudpress.com *Web Site:* www.whitecloudpress.com, pg 255

Schoo, Julie, National Press Club (NPC), 529 14 St NW, 13th fl, Washington, DC 20045 *Tel:* 202-662-7500 *Fax:* 202-662-7569 *E-mail:* infocenter@npcpress.org *Web Site:* www.press.org, pg 572

Schooler, Marta, HarperCollins General Books Group, 195 Broadway, New York, NY 10007 *Tel:* 212-207-7000 *Web Site:* www.harpercollins.com, pg 101

Schor, Lynda, Hamilton Stone Editions, PO Box 43, Maplewood, NJ 07040 *Tel:* 973-378-8361 *E-mail:* hstone@hamiltonstone.org *Web Site:* www.hamiltonstone.org, pg 99

Schorr, Sari, Levy Creative Management LLC, 425 E 58 St, Suite 37F, New York, NY 10022 *Tel:* 212-687-6463 *Fax:* 212-661-4839 *E-mail:* info@levycreative.com *Web Site:* www.levycreative.com, pg 543

Schott, Abby, Allen A Knoll Publishers, 200 W Victoria St, Santa Barbara, CA 93101-3627 *Tel:* 805-564-3377 *Toll Free Tel:* 800-777-7623 *Fax:* 805-966-6657 *E-mail:* bookinfo@knollpublishers.com *Web Site:* www.knollpublishers.com, pg 127

Schouten, Cory, Society of American Business Editors & Writers Inc (SABEW), Walter Cronkite School of Journalism & Mass Communication, Arizona State University, 555 N Central Ave, Suite 406E, Phoenix, AZ 85004-1248 *Tel:* 602-496-7862 *Fax:* 602-496-7041 *E-mail:* sabew@sabew.org *Web Site:* sabew.org, pg 578

Schrager, Marla, Society of American Travel Writers (SATW), One Parkview Plaza, Suite 800, Oakbrook Terrace, IL 60181 *Tel:* 202-591-2476 *E-mail:* info@satw.org *Web Site:* www.satw.org, pg 578

Schrank, Ben, Razorbill, 345 Hudson St, New York, NY 10014 *Tel:* 212-366-2000 *Web Site:* www.penguin.com/meet/publishers/razorbill, pg 196

Schreiber, Laura, Disney-Hyperion Books, 1101 Flower St, Glendale, CA 91201 *Web Site:* books.disney.com, pg 70

Schreiber, Sarah, Glitterati Inc, 630 Ninth Ave, Suite 603, New York, NY 10036 *Tel:* 212-362-9119 *Fax:* 646-607-4433 *E-mail:* info@glitteratiincorporated.com *Web Site:* glitteratiincorporated.com, pg 93

Schreider, Ilene, Sourcebooks Inc, 1935 Brookdale Rd, Suite 139, Naperville, IL 60563 *Tel:* 630-961-3900 *Toll Free Tel:* 800-432-7444 *Fax:* 630-961-2168 *E-mail:* info@sourcebooks.com; customersupport@sourcebooks.com *Web Site:* www.sourcebooks.com, pg 218

Schreier, Carl, Homestead Publishing, Box 193, Moose, WY 83012-0193 *Tel:* 307-733-6248 *Fax:* 307-733-6248 *E-mail:* orders@homesteadpublishing.net *Web Site:* www.homesteadpublishing.net, pg 110

Schroeder, Ben, Centering Corp, 7230 Maple St, Omaha, NE 68134 *Tel:* 402-553-1200 *Toll Free Tel:* 866-218-0101 *Fax:* 402-553-0507 *E-mail:* orders@centering.org *Web Site:* www.centering.org, pg 51

Schroeder, Dave, B&H Publishing Group, One LifeWay Plaza, Nashville, TN 37234 *Tel:* 615-251-2520 *Fax:* 615-251-5004 *Web Site:* www.bhpublishinggroup.com, pg 29

Schroeder, Meredith, American Quilter's Society, 5801 Kentucky Dam Rd, Paducah, KY 42003-9323 *Tel:* 270-898-7903 *Toll Free Tel:* 800-626-5420 (orders) *Fax:* 270-898-1173 *E-mail:* orders@americanquilter.com *Web Site:* www.americanquilter.com, pg 14

Schroeder, Sandi, Schroeder Indexing Services, 23 Camilla Pink Ct, Bluffton, SC 29909 *Tel:* 843-705-9779 *E-mail:* sanindex@schroederindexing.com *Web Site:* www.schroederindexing.com, pg 501

Schubert, Lori, Quebec Writers' Federation (QWF), 1200 Atwater Ave, Rm 3, Westmount, QC H3Z 1X4, Canada *Tel:* 514-933-0878 *E-mail:* info@qwf.org *Web Site:* www.qwf.org; www.hireawriter.ca, pg 577

Schubert, Lori, QWF Literary Awards, 1200 Atwater Ave, Rm 3, Westmount, QC H3Z 1X4, Canada *Tel:* 514-933-0878 *E-mail:* info@qwf.org *Web Site:* www.qwf.org, pg 683

Schuetz, Richard, University of New Mexico Press, One University of New Mexico, Albuquerque, NM 87131-0001 *Tel:* 505-272-7777 *Fax:* 505-277-3343; 505-272-7778 (cust serv) *Toll Free Fax:* 800-622-8667 (orders only) *E-mail:* unmpress@unm.edu; custserv@unm.edu (order dept) *Web Site:* unmpress.com, pg 243

Schulman, Susan, Susan Schulman Literary Agency LLC, 454 W 44 St, New York, NY 10036 *Tel:* 212-713-1633 *E-mail:* queries@schulmanagency.com; linda@schulmanagency.com (translation & audio rts), pg 534

Schultz, Brandon, Glitterati Inc, 630 Ninth Ave, Suite 603, New York, NY 10036 *Tel:* 212-362-9119 *Fax:* 646-607-4433 *E-mail:* info@glitteratiincorporated.com *Web Site:* glitteratiincorporated.com, pg 93

Schultz, Donna, Zaner-Bloser Inc, 1201 Dublin Rd, Columbus, OH 43215 *Tel:* 614-486-0221 *Toll Free Tel:* 800-421-3018 (cust serv) *Toll Free Fax:* 800-992-6087 (orders) *E-mail:* zbcsd@zaner-bloser.com; international@zaner-bloser.com *Web Site:* www.zaner-bloser.com, pg 262

Schultz, Jonathan D, Concordia Publishing House, 3558 S Jefferson Ave, St Louis, MO 63118-3968 *Tel:* 314-268-1000; 314-268-1268 (bookshop)

Toll Free Tel: 800-325-3040 (cust serv) *Toll Free Fax:* 800-490-9889 (cust serv) *E-mail:* order@cph.org *Web Site:* www.cph.org, pg 59

Schultz, Kristin, Random House Children's Books, 1745 Broadway, 10th fl, New York, NY 10019 *Tel:* 212-782-9000 *Web Site:* www.randomhousekids.com, pg 194

Schultz, Kyle, Incentive Publications by World Book, 180 N LaSalle St, Suite 900, Chicago, IL 60101 *Toll Free Tel:* 800-967-5325; 800-975-3250; 888-482-9764 (trade dept) *Toll Free Fax:* 888-922-3766 *E-mail:* tradeorders@worldbook.com *Web Site:* www.incentivepublications.com, pg 115

Schultz, Patricia, The Edwin Mellen Press, 415 Ridge St, Lewiston, NY 14092 *Tel:* 716-754-2266; 716-754-1400 (mktg); 716-754-2788 (order fulfillment) *Fax:* 716-754-4056 *E-mail:* editor@mellenpress.com *Web Site:* www.mellenpress.com, pg 148

Schultz, Thom, Group Publishing Inc, 1515 Cascade Ave, Loveland, CO 80538 *Tel:* 970-669-3836 *Toll Free Tel:* 800-447-1070 *E-mail:* puorgbus@group.com (submissions) *Web Site:* www.group.com, pg 97

Schulz, Andrea, Penguin Group USA, A Penguin Random House Company, 375 Hudson St, New York, NY 10014 *Tel:* 212-366-2000 *Toll Free Tel:* 800-847-5515 (inside sales); 800-631-8571 (cust serv) *Fax:* 212-366-2666; 607-775-4829 (inside sales) *E-mail:* online@us.penguingroup.com *Web Site:* www.penguin.com, pg 177

Schulz, Andrea, Viking, 375 Hudson St, New York, NY 10014 *Tel:* 212-366-2000 *Fax:* 212-243-6002 *Web Site:* www.penguin.com/publishers/vikingbooks, pg 250

Schulz, Chris, City & Regional Magazine Association, 2512 Artesia Blvd, Suite 200, Redondo Beach, CA 90278 *Tel:* 310-379-8261 *Fax:* 310-379-8283 *E-mail:* admin@citymag.org *Web Site:* www.citymag.org, pg 563

Schulze, Karin, Harry N Abrams Inc, 195 Broadway, 9th fl, New York, NY 10007 *Tel:* 212-206-7715 *Toll Free Tel:* 800-345-1359 *Fax:* 212-519-1210 *E-mail:* abrams@abramsbooks.com *Web Site:* www.abramsbooks.com, pg 3

Schumacher, George, Penguin Young Readers Group, 345 Hudson St, New York, NY 10014 *Tel:* 212-366-2000; 212-414-3553 *Fax:* 212-414-3340 *Web Site:* www.penguin.com/children, pg 179

Schumacher, Ryan R, Texas State Historical Association, 3001 Lake Austin Blvd, Suite 3.116, Austin, TX 78703 *Tel:* 512-471-2600 *Fax:* 512-473-8691 *Web Site:* www.tshaonline.org, pg 230

Schumacher, Thomas, Summit University Press, 63 Summit Way, Gardiner, MT 59030-9314 *Tel:* 406-848-9742; 406-848-9500 (retail orders) *Toll Free Tel:* 800-245-5445 (retail orders) *Fax:* 406-848-9744 *E-mail:* info@summituniversitypress.com; marketing@summituniversitypress.com; production@summituniversitypress.com; rights@summituniversitypress.com *Web Site:* www.summituniversitypress.com, pg 224

Schumer, Fran, Joelle Delbourgo Associates Inc, 101 Park St, Montclair, NJ 07042 *Tel:* 973-773-0836 (call only during standard business hours) *Web Site:* www.delbourgo.com, pg 513

Schuna, Jo Anne, The Schuna Group Inc, 1503 Briarknoll Dr, Arden Hills, MN 55112 *Tel:* 651-631-8480 *Web Site:* www.schunagroup.com, pg 544

Schutt, David L, SAE (Society of Automotive Engineers International), 400 Commonwealth Dr, Warrendale, PA 15096-0001 *Tel:* 724-776-4841; 724-776-4970 (outside US & CN) *Toll Free Tel:* 877-606-7323 (cust serv) *Fax:* 724-776-0790 (cust serv) *E-mail:* publications@sae.org; customerservice@sae.org *Web Site:* www.sae.org, pg 203

Schwab, Ann, Black Rabbit Books, 515 N Riverfront Dr, Suite 200, Mankato, MN 56001 *Tel:* 507-388-1609 *Fax:* 507-388-1364 *E-mail:* info@blackrabbitbooks.com; orders@blackrabbitbooks.com *Web Site:* www.blackrabbitbooks.com, pg 36

Schwacke, Susanna Sharp, Bottom Dog Press, 813 Seneca Ave, Huron, OH 44839 *Tel:* 419-433-3573 *Fax:* 419-616-3966 *Web Site:* smithdocs.net, pg 41

Schwaiger, Elizabeth, University of Ottawa Press (Presses de l'Université d'Ottawa), 542 King Edward Ave, Ottawa, ON K1N 6N5, Canada *Tel:* 613-562-5246 *Fax:* 613-562-5247 *E-mail:* puo-oup@uottawa.ca *Web Site:* press.uottawa.ca, pg 474

Schwalbe, Will, Macmillan, 175 Fifth Ave, New York, NY 10010 *Tel:* 646-307-5151 *E-mail:* press.inquiries@macmillan.com *Web Site:* www.macmillan.com, pg 140

Schwartz, Adam, The Career Press Inc, 12 Parish Dr, Wayne, NJ 07470 *Tel:* 201-848-0310 *Toll Free Tel:* 800-CAREER-1 (227-3371) *Fax:* 201-848-1727 *E-mail:* sales@careerpress.com *Web Site:* www.careerpress.com, pg 47

Schwartz, Anne, Random House Children's Books, 1745 Broadway, 10th fl, New York, NY 10019 *Tel:* 212-782-9000 *Web Site:* www.randomhousekids.com, pg 194

Schwartz, Barry L, Jewish Publication Society, 2100 Arch St, Philadelphia, PA 19103 *Tel:* 215-832-0600 *Toll Free Tel:* 800-234-3151 *Fax:* 215-568-2017 *Web Site:* www.jps.org, pg 122

Schwartz, Dan, Macmillan, 175 Fifth Ave, New York, NY 10010 *Tel:* 646-307-5151 *E-mail:* press.inquiries@macmillan.com *Web Site:* www.macmillan.com, pg 140

Schwartz, Eric, Columbia University Press, 61 W 62 St, New York, NY 10023 *Tel:* 212-459-0600 *Toll Free Tel:* 800-944-8648 *Fax:* 212-459-3678 *E-mail:* cup_book@columbia.edu (orders & cust serv) *Web Site:* cup.columbia.edu, pg 59

Schwartz, Hannah, Stuart Krichevsky Literary Agency Inc, 6 E 39 St, Suite 500, New York, NY 10016 *Tel:* 212-725-5288 *Fax:* 212-725-5275 *E-mail:* query@skagency.com *Web Site:* skagency.com, pg 525

Schwartz, Jenny Wesselmann, AMACOM Books, 1601 Broadway, New York, NY 10019-7420 *Tel:* 212-586-8100 *Toll Free Tel:* 800-250-5308 (cust serv) *Fax:* 212-903-8083; 518-891-2372 (orders) *E-mail:* pubs_cust_serv@amanet.org *Web Site:* www.amacombooks.org, pg 8

Schwartz, Matt, Penguin Random House Inc, 1745 Broadway, New York, NY 10019 *Tel:* 212-782-9000 *Toll Free Tel:* 800-726-0600 *Web Site:* www.penguinrandomhouse.com, pg 178

Schwartz, Matt, Random House Publishing Group, 1745 Broadway, New York, NY 10019 *Toll Free Tel:* 800-200-3552 *Web Site:* atrandom.com, pg 195

Schwartz, Rick, HarperCollins Publishers, 195 Broadway, New York, NY 10007 *Tel:* 212-207-7000 *Fax:* 212-207-7145 *Web Site:* www.harpercollins.com, pg 101

Schwartz, Steven, Sarah Jane Freymann Literary Agency LLC, 59 W 71 St, Suite 9-B, New York, NY 10023 *Tel:* 212-362-9277 *E-mail:* submissions@sarahjanefreymann.com *Web Site:* www.sarahjanefreymann.com, pg 518

Schwartz, Susan, Dutton, 375 Hudson St, New York, NY 10014 *Tel:* 212-366-2000 *Fax:* 212-366-2262 *Web Site:* www.penguin.com, pg 74

Schwartz, Susan, The Editors Circle, 462 Grove St, Montclair, NJ 07043 *Tel:* 862-596-9709 *E-mail:* query@theeditorscircle.com *Web Site:* www.theeditorscircle.com, pg 493

Schwartzman, Jill, Dutton, 375 Hudson St, New York, NY 10014 *Tel:* 212-366-2000 *Fax:* 212-366-2262 *Web Site:* www.penguin.com, pg 74

Schwarz, Benjamin, Yale University Press, 302 Temple St, New Haven, CT 06511-8909 *Tel:* 203-432-0960; 203-432-0966 (sales); 401-531-2800 (cust serv) *Toll Free Tel:* 800-405-1619 (cust serv) *Fax:* 203-432-0948; 203-432-8485 (sales); 401-531-2801 (cust serv) *Toll Free Fax:* 800-406-9145 (cust serv) *E-mail:* sales.press@yale.edu (sales); customer.care@triliteral.org (cust serv) *Web Site:* www.yalebooks.com; yalepress.yale.edu/yupbooks, pg 261

Schwarze, Diane, Book Peddlers, 18330 Minnetonka Blvd, Deephaven, MN 55391 *Tel:* 952-544-1154 *Fax:* 206-339-6913 *E-mail:* bookpeddlers@aol.com *Web Site:* www.bookpeddlers.com, pg 39

Schweitzer, Maxine, Scott Meredith Literary Agency LP, Exchange Plaza, 55 Broadway, Suite 2002, New York, NY 10006 *Tel:* 646-218-9240 *Fax:* 212-977-5997 *E-mail:* info@scottmeredith.com *Web Site:* www.scottmeredith.com, pg 529

Schwoeri, Lindsey, Penguin Books, 375 Hudson St, New York, NY 10014 *Tel:* 212-366-2000 *E-mail:* penguinpublicity@us.penguingroup.com *Web Site:* www.penguinclassics.com; www.penguin.com, pg 177

Scinta, Sam, Fulcrum Publishing Inc, 4690 Table Mountain Dr, Suite 100, Golden, CO 80403 *Tel:* 303-277-1623 *Toll Free Tel:* 800-992-2908 *Fax:* 303-279-7111 *Toll Free Fax:* 800-726-7112 *E-mail:* info@fulcrumbooks.com; orders@fulcrumbooks.com *Web Site:* www.fulcrumbooks.com, pg 89

Sciortino, Joseph, Editions Mediaspaul, 3965, blvd Henri-Bourassa E, Montreal, QC H1H 1L1, Canada *Tel:* 514-322-7341 *Fax:* 514-322-4281 *E-mail:* editeur@mediaspaul.ca *Web Site:* mediaspaul.ca, pg 455

Scivener, Brian, University of Calgary Press, 2500 University Dr NW, Calgary, AB T2N 1N4, Canada *Tel:* 403-220-7578 *Fax:* 403-282-0085 *E-mail:* ucpress@ucalgary.ca *Web Site:* press.ucalgary.ca, pg 474

Scognamiglio, John, Kensington Publishing Corp, 119 W 40 St, New York, NY 10018 *Tel:* 212-407-1500 *Toll Free Tel:* 800-221-2647 *Fax:* 212-935-0699 *Web Site:* www.kensingtonbooks.com, pg 125

Scollans, Colleen, Oxford University Press USA, 198 Madison Ave, New York, NY 10016 *Tel:* 212-726-6000 *Toll Free Tel:* 800-451-7556 (orders); 800-445-9714 (cust serv) *Fax:* 919-677-1303 *E-mail:* custserv.us@oup.com *Web Site:* www.oup.com/us, pg 171

Scordato, Ellen, The Stonesong Press LLC, 270 W 39 St, No 201, New York, NY 10018 *Tel:* 212-929-4600 *E-mail:* editors@stonesong.com *Web Site:* www.stonesong.com, pg 538

Scott, Ardy M, Twilight Times Books, PO Box 3340, Kingsport, TN 37664-0340 *Tel:* 423-323-0183 *Fax:* 423-323-0183 *E-mail:* publisher@twilighttimes.com *Web Site:* www.twilighttimesbooks.com, pg 237

Scott, Craig R, Heritage Books Inc, 5810 Ruatan St, Berwyn Heights, MD 20740 *Toll Free Tel:* 800-876-6103 *Toll Free Fax:* 800-876-6103 *E-mail:* orders@heritagebooks.com; submissions@heritagebooks.com *Web Site:* www.heritagebooks.com, pg 106

Scott, Debra Leigh, Hidden River Arts Playwriting Award, PO Box 63927, Philadelphia, PA 19147 *Tel:* 610-764-0813 *E-mail:* hiddenriverarts@gmail.com *Web Site:* www.hiddenriverarts.org; www.hiddenriverarts.com, pg 653

Scott, Debra Leigh, The William Van Wert Memorial Fiction Award, PO Box 63927, Philadelphia, PA 19147 *Tel:* 610-764-0813 *E-mail:* hiddenriverarts@gmail.com *Web Site:* www.hiddenriverarts.org; www.hiddenriverarts.com, pg 695

Scott, Katherine, Canadian Council on Social Development (Conseil canadien de developpement social), 190 O'Connor St, Suite 100, Ottawa, ON K2P 2R3, Canada *Tel:* 613-236-8977 *Fax:* 613-236-2750 *E-mail:* info@ccsd.ca *Web Site:* www.ccsd.ca, pg 448

Scott, Lisa W, Periodical & Book Association of America Inc (PBAA), 481 Eighth Ave, Suite 526, New York, NY 10001 *Tel:* 212-563-6502 *Fax:* 212-563-4098 *Web Site:* www.pbaa.net, pg 575

Scott, Marianne, The Canadian Writers' Foundation Inc (La Fondation des Ecrivains Canadiens), PO Box 13281, Kanata Sta, Ottawa, ON K2K 1X4, Canada *Tel:* 613-256-6937 *Fax:* 613-256-5457 *E-mail:* info@canadianwritersfoundation.org *Web Site:* www.canadianwritersfoundation.org, pg 583

Scott, Michael, Aptara Inc, 3110 Fairview Park Dr, Suite 900, Falls Church, VA 22042 *Tel:* 703-352-0001 *E-mail:* moreinfo@aptaracorp.com *Web Site:* www.aptaracorp.com, pg 488

Scott, Nita, Educators Award, PO Box 1589, Austin, TX 78767-1589 *Tel:* 512-478-5748 *Toll Free Tel:* 888-762-4685 *Fax:* 512-478-3961 *E-mail:* societyexec@dkg.org *Web Site:* www.dkg.org, pg 643

Scott, Richard, Dorland Health, 4 Choke Cherry Rd, 2nd fl, Rockville, MD 20850 *Tel:* 301-354-2000 *Toll Free Tel:* 855-225-5341 *Fax:* 301-287-2535 *E-mail:* customer@decisionhealth.com *Web Site:* www.dorlandhealth.com, pg 72

Scott, Tony, National Newspaper Association, 900 Community Dr, Springfield, IL 62703-5180 *Tel:* 217-241-1400 *Fax:* 217-241-1301 *E-mail:* nna@nna.org *Web Site:* nnaweb.org, pg 572

Scott, Yolanda, Charlesbridge Publishing Inc, 85 Main St, Watertown, MA 02472 *Tel:* 617-926-0329 *Toll Free Tel:* 800-225-3214 *Fax:* 617-926-5720 *Toll Free Fax:* 800-926-5775 *E-mail:* books@charlesbridge.com *Web Site:* www.charlesbridge.com, pg 53

Scriver, Julie, Goose Lane Editions, 500 Beaverbrook Ct, Suite 330, Fredericton, NB E3B 5X4, Canada *Tel:* 506-450-4251 *Toll Free Tel:* 888-926-8377 *Fax:* 506-459-4991 *E-mail:* info@gooselane.com; customerservice@gooselane.com *Web Site:* www.gooselane.com, pg 458

Scudder, Dean H, Sinauer Associates Inc, 23 Plumtree Rd, Sunderland, MA 01375 *Tel:* 413-549-4300 *Fax:* 413-549-1118 *E-mail:* publish@sinauer.com; orders@sinauer.com *Web Site:* sinauer.com, pg 214

Scudder, Dr James A, Victory in Grace Press, 60 Quentin Rd, Lake Zurich, IL 60047 *Tel:* 847-438-4494 *Toll Free Tel:* 800-78-GRACE (784-7223) *Fax:* 847-438-4232 *E-mail:* feedback@victoryingrace.org *Web Site:* www.victoryingrace.org, pg 250

Scully, Leslie, New York State Bar Association, One Elk St, Albany, NY 12207 *Tel:* 518-463-3200 *Toll Free Tel:* 800-582-2452 *Fax:* 518-487-5517 *E-mail:* mrc@nysba.org *Web Site:* www.nysba.org, pg 162

Seager, Deb, Grove Atlantic Inc, 154 W 14 St, 12th fl, New York, NY 10011 *Tel:* 212-614-7850 *Toll Free Tel:* 800-521-0178 *Fax:* 212-614-7886 *E-mail:* info@groveatlantic.com; sales@groveatlantic.com; publicity@groveatlantic.com; rights@groveatlantic.com *Web Site:* www.groveatlantic.com, pg 97

Searcy, Maggie, HarperCollins Children's Books, 195 Broadway, New York, NY 10007 *Tel:* 212-207-7000 *Web Site:* www.harpercollins.com/childrens, pg 101

Searle, Linnea, Playwrights Project, 3675 Ruffin Rd, Suite 330, San Diego, CA 92123 *Tel:* 858-384-2970 *Fax:* 858-384-2974 *E-mail:* write@playwrightsproject.org *Web Site:* www.playwrightsproject.org, pg 680

Sears, Rebecca, AIGA, the professional association for design, 233 Broadway, Suite 1740, New York, NY 10279 *Tel:* 212-807-1990 *Fax:* 212-807-1799 *E-mail:* general@aiga.org *Web Site:* www.aiga.org, pg 553

Sears, Rene, Prometheus Books, 59 John Glenn Dr, Amherst, NY 14228-2119 *Tel:* 716-691-0133 *Fax:* 716-691-0137 *E-mail:* marketing@prometheusbooks.com; editorial@prometheusbooks.com; rights@prometheusmail.com *Web Site:* www.prometheusbooks.com, pg 190

Seaton, Ann, Northern California Independent Booksellers Association (NCIBA), 651 Broadway, Sonoma, CA 95476 *Tel:* 415-561-7686 *Fax:* 415-561-7685 *E-mail:* info@nciba.com *Web Site:* www.nciba.com, pg 574

Secara, Andrea, Algora Publishing, 1732 First Ave, No 20330, New York, NY 10128 *Tel:* 212-678-0232 *Fax:* 212-666-3682 *E-mail:* editors@algora.com *Web Site:* www.algora.com, pg 7

Secara, Claudiu A, Algora Publishing, 1732 First Ave, No 20330, New York, NY 10128 *Tel:* 212-678-0232 *Fax:* 212-666-3682 *E-mail:* editors@algora.com *Web Site:* www.algora.com, pg 7

Secondari, Linda, Oxford University Press USA, 198 Madison Ave, New York, NY 10016 *Tel:* 212-726-6000 *Toll Free Tel:* 800-451-7556 (orders); 800-445-9714 (cust serv) *Fax:* 919-677-1303 *E-mail:* custserv.us@oup.com *Web Site:* www.oup.com/us, pg 171

Sedgeley, Carlton, Royce Carlton Inc, 866 United Nations Plaza, Suite 587, New York, NY 10017-1880 *Tel:* 212-355-7700 *Toll Free Tel:* 800-LECTURE (532-8873) *Fax:* 212-888-8659 *E-mail:* info@roycecarlton.com *Web Site:* www.roycecarlton.com, pg 548

Sedita, Francesco, Grosset & Dunlap, 345 Hudson St, New York, NY 10014 *Tel:* 212-366-2000 *Web Site:* www.penguinrandomhouse.com, pg 96

Sedita, Francesco, Price Stern Sloan, 345 Hudson St, New York, NY 10014 *Tel:* 212-366-2000 *E-mail:* online@penguinputnam.com *Web Site:* www.penguinrandomhouse.com; www.penguin.com/meet/publishers/grossetdunlap, pg 187

Sedliar, Renee, Perseus Books, 250 W 57 St, 15th fl, New York, NY 10107 *Tel:* 212-340-8100 *Toll Free Tel:* 800-343-4499 (cust serv) *Fax:* 212-340-8105 *Web Site:* www.perseusbooks.com, pg 181

See, Sandy, University of Oklahoma Press, 2800 Venture Dr, Norman, OK 73069-8216 *Tel:* 405-325-2000 *Toll Free Tel:* 800-627-7377 (orders) *Fax:* 405-364-5798 (orders) *Toll Free Fax:* 800-735-0476 (orders) *E-mail:* presscs@ou.edu *Web Site:* www.oupress.com, pg 244

Seelen, Michael, Unveiled Media LLC, PO Box 930463, Verona, WI 53593 *Tel:* 707-986-8345 *Web Site:* www.unveiledmedia.com, pg 248

Seeley, Wes, Princeton Architectural Press, 37 E Seventh St, New York, NY 10003 *Tel:* 212-995-9620 *Toll Free Tel:* 800-722-6657 (dist); 800-759-0190 (sales) *Fax:* 212-995-9454 *E-mail:* sales@papress.com *Web Site:* www.papress.com, pg 188

Seely, Steve, Balance Sports Publishing LLC, 195 Lucero Way, Portola Valley, CA 94028 *Tel:* 650-561-9586 *Fax:* 650-391-9850 *E-mail:* info@balancesportspublishing.com *Web Site:* www.balancesportspublishing.com, pg 28

Seepersad, Ravi, Bisk Education, 9417 Princess Palm Ave, Suite 400, Tampa, FL 33619 *Tel:* 813-621-6200 *Toll Free Tel:* 800-280-9718 (cust serv) *E-mail:* customerservice@bisk.com *Web Site:* www.bisk.com, pg 35

Segal, Jonathan, Alfred A Knopf/Everyman's Library, c/o Penguin Random House Inc, 1745 Broadway, New York, NY 10019 *Tel:* 212-751-2600 *Toll Free Tel:* 800-638-6460 *Fax:* 212-572-2593 *Web Site:* www.knopfdoubleday.com, pg 127

Segal, Joyce, Pippin Press, 229 E 85 St, New York, NY 10028 *Tel:* 212-288-4920 *Fax:* 908-237-2407, pg 183

Seger, Rebecca, Oxford University Press USA, 198 Madison Ave, New York, NY 10016 *Tel:* 212-726-6000 *Toll Free Tel:* 800-451-7556 (orders); 800-445-9714 (cust serv) *Fax:* 919-677-1303 *E-mail:* custserv.us@oup.com *Web Site:* www.oup.com/us, pg 171

Sehlinger, Robert W, AdventureKEEN, 2204 First Ave S, Suite 102, Birmingham, AL 35233 *Tel:* 763-689-9800 *Toll Free Tel:* 800-678-7006 *Fax:* 763-689-9039 *Toll Free Fax:* 877-374-9016 *E-mail:* info@adventurewithkeen.com *Web Site:* adventurewithkeen.com, pg 5

Sehlinger, Robert W, Menasha Ridge Press Inc, 2204 First Ave S, Suite 102, Birmingham, AL 35233 *Toll Free Tel:* 888-604-4537 *Fax:* 205-326-1012 *E-mail:* info@adventurewithkeen.com *Web Site:* www.menasharidge.com, pg 148

Seibold, Doug, Surrey Books, 1328 Greenleaf St, Evanston, IL 60202 *Tel:* 847-475-4457 *Toll Free Tel:* 800-326-4430 *Web Site:* agatepublishing.com/surrey, pg 225

Seidlitz, Lauri, Brush Education Inc, 6531-111 St, Edmonton, AB T6H 4R5, Canada *Tel:* 780-989-0910 *Toll Free Tel:* 855-283-0900 *Fax:* 780-989-0930 *Toll Free Fax:* 855-283-6947 *E-mail:* contact@brusheducation.ca *Web Site:* www.brusheducation.ca, pg 448

Seidman, Brian, NewSouth Books, 105 S Court St, Montgomery, AL 36104 *Tel:* 334-834-3556 *Fax:* 334-834-3557 *E-mail:* info@newsouthbooks.com *Web Site:* www.newsouthbooks.com, pg 162

Seidman, Erika, Farrar, Straus & Giroux, LLC, 18 W 18 St, New York, NY 10011 *Tel:* 212-741-6900 *E-mail:* fsg.publicity@fsgbooks.com *Web Site:* us.macmillan.com/fsg.aspx, pg 82

Seidman, Erika, Hill & Wang, 18 W 18 St, New York, NY 10011 *Tel:* 212-741-6900 *Fax:* 212-633-9385 *E-mail:* fsg.publicity@fsgbooks.com; fsg.editorial@fsgbooks.com; sales@fsgbooks.com *Web Site:* us.macmillan.com/hillandwang.aspx, pg 107

Seidman, Erika, North Point Press, 18 W 18 St, 8th fl, New York, NY 10011 *Tel:* 212-741-6900 *Toll Free Tel:* 888-330-8477 *Fax:* 212-633-9385 *Web Site:* www.fsgbooks.com, pg 163

Seidman, Yishai, Dunow, Carlson & Lerner Literary Agency Inc, 27 W 20 St, Suite 1107, New York, NY 10011 *Tel:* 212-645-7606 *E-mail:* mail@dclagency.com *Web Site:* www.dclagency.com, pg 515

Seiler, Alice, Chronicle Books LLC, 680 Second St, San Francisco, CA 94107 *Tel:* 415-537-4200 *Toll Free Tel:* 800-759-0190 (cust serv) *Fax:* 415-537-4460 *Toll Free Fax:* 800-858-7787 (orders); 800-286-9471 (cust serv) *E-mail:* frontdesk@chroniclebooks.com *Web Site:* www.chroniclebooks.com, pg 55

Seiler, Gretchen, American Association for the Advancement of Science (AAAS), 1200 New York Ave NW, Washington, DC 20005 *Tel:* 202-326-6400 *Web Site:* www.aaas.org, pg 554

Seiler, Maggie, W D Hoard & Sons Co, 28 W Milwaukee Ave, Fort Atkinson, WI 53538 *Tel:* 920-563-5551 *Fax:* 920-563-7298 *E-mail:* hdbooks@hoards.com; editors@hoards.com *Web Site:* www.hoards.com; www.hoardprinting.com, pg 108

Seitz, Don, AuthorHouse, 1663 Liberty Dr, Bloomington, IN 47403 *Tel:* 812-339-6000 (outside US) *Toll Free Tel:* 888-519-5121 *E-mail:* authorsupport@authorhouse.com *Web Site:* www.authorhouse.com, pg 26

Selah, Stephanie, HarperCollins General Books Group, 195 Broadway, New York, NY 10007 *Tel:* 212-207-7000 *Web Site:* www.harpercollins.com, pg 101

Self, Robert, Baby Tattoo Books, 6045 Longridge Ave, Van Nuys, CA 91401 *Tel:* 818-416-5314 *E-mail:* info@babytattoo.com *Web Site:* www.babytattoo.com, pg 27

Self, Ron, Brick Road Poetry Book Contest, 513 Broadway, Columbus, GA 31901-3117 *Web Site:* brickroadpoetrypress.com, pg 634

Selinsky, Page PhD, University of Pennsylvania Museum of Archaeology & Anthropology, 3260 South St, Philadelphia, PA 19104-6324 *Tel:* 215-898-6322; 215-898-4119 *E-mail:* publications@pennmuseum.org; info@pennmuseum.org *Web Site:* www.penn.museum, pg 244

Selleck, Carol, Society of Manufacturing Engineers, One SME Dr, Dearborn, MI 48121 *Tel:* 313-425-3000 *Toll Free Tel:* 800-733-4763 (cust serv) *Fax:* 313-425-3400 *E-mail:* publications@sme.org *Web Site:* www.sme.org, pg 216

Selleck, Michael, Simon & Schuster, Inc, 1230 Avenue of the Americas, New York, NY 10020 *Tel:* 212-698-7000 *Fax:* 212-698-7007 *E-mail:* firstname.lastname@simonandschuster.com *Web Site:* www.simonandschuster.com, pg 213

Selleck, Michael, Simon & Schuster Sales Division, 1230 Avenue of the Americas, New York, NY 10020 *Tel:* 212-698-7000, pg 214

Sellers, Scott, Seal Books, 320 Front St W, Suite 1400, Toronto, ON M5V 3B6, Canada *Tel:* 416-364-4449 *Toll Free Tel:* 888-523-9292 (order desk) *Fax:* 416-598-7764 *Web Site:* www.penguinrandomhouse.ca, pg 470

Sells, Dianna, Texas A&M University Press, John H Lindsey Bldg, Lewis St, 4354 TAMU, College Station, TX 77843-4354 *Tel:* 979-845-1436 *Toll Free Tel:* 800-826-8911 (orders) *Fax:* 979-847-8752 *Toll Free Fax:* 888-617-2421 (orders) *E-mail:* bookorders@tamu.edu *Web Site:* www.tamupress.com, pg 230

Selman, Edythea Ginis, Edythea Ginis Selman Literary Agency Inc, 14 Washington Place, New York, NY 10003 *Tel:* 212-473-1874 *Fax:* 212-473-1875, pg 535

Selman, Richard, Edythea Ginis Selman Literary Agency Inc, 14 Washington Place, New York, NY 10003 *Tel:* 212-473-1874 *Fax:* 212-473-1875, pg 535

Seltz, Martin, Augsburg Fortress Publishers, Publishing House of the Evangelical Lutheran Church in America, 510 Marquette Ave S, Minneapolis, MN 55402 *Tel:* 612-330-3300 *Toll Free Tel:* 800-426-0115 (ext 639, subns); 800-328-4648 (orders) *Fax:* 612-330-3455 *E-mail:* info@augsburgfortress.org; copyright@augsburgfortress.org (reprint permission requests); customercare@augsburgfortress.org *Web Site:* www.augsburgfortress.org, pg 26

Seltzer, Joyce, Harvard University Press, 79 Garden St, Cambridge, MA 02138-1499 *Tel:* 617-495-2600; 401-531-2800 (intl orders) *Toll Free Tel:* 800-405-1619 (orders) *Fax:* 617-495-5898 (general); 617-496-4677 (edit & rts); 401-531-2801 (intl orders) *Toll Free Fax:* 800-406-9145 (orders) *E-mail:* contact_hup@harvard.edu *Web Site:* www.hup.harvard.edu, pg 103

Selvaggio, Victoria, The Jennifer DeChiara Literary Agency, 299 Park Ave, 6th fl, New York, NY 10171 *Tel:* 212-739-0803 *Web Site:* www.jdlit.com, pg 513

Semel, John, John Wiley & Sons Inc, 111 River St, Hoboken, NJ 07030-5774 *Tel:* 201-748-6000 *Toll Free Tel:* 800-225-5945 (cust serv) *Fax:* 201-748-6088 *E-mail:* info@wiley.com *Web Site:* www.wiley.com, pg 256

Semens, Zak, Goodheart-Willcox Publisher, 18604 W Creek Dr, Tinley Park, IL 60477-6243 *Tel:* 708-687-5000 *Toll Free Tel:* 800-323-0440 *Fax:* 708-468-8692 *Toll Free Fax:* 888-409-3900 *E-mail:* custserv@g-w.com; orders@g-w.com *Web Site:* www.g-w.com, pg 94

Sen, Sharmila, Harvard University Press, 79 Garden St, Cambridge, MA 02138-1499 *Tel:* 617-495-2600; 401-531-2800 (intl orders) *Toll Free Tel:* 800-405-1619 (orders) *Fax:* 617-495-5898 (general); 617-496-4677 (edit & rts); 401-531-2801 (intl orders) *Toll Free Fax:* 800-406-9145 (orders) *E-mail:* contact_hup@harvard.edu *Web Site:* www.hup.harvard.edu, pg 103

Senders, Marci, Disney-Hyperion Books, 1101 Flower St, Glendale, CA 91201 *Web Site:* books.disney.com, pg 70

Senechal, David, Les Editions Fides, 7333 place des Roseraies, bureau 100, Anjou, QC H1M 2X6, Canada *Tel:* 514-745-4290 *Fax:* 514-745-4299 *E-mail:* editions@groupefides.com *Web Site:* www.editionsfides.com, pg 454

Senftleben, Peter, Kensington Publishing Corp, 119 W 40 St, New York, NY 10018 *Tel:* 212-407-1500 *Toll Free Tel:* 800-221-2647 *Fax:* 212-935-0699 *Web Site:* www.kensingtonbooks.com, pg 125

Sengthavy, Khamla, Norma Epstein Foundation Awards in Creative Writing, 15 King's College Circle, UC 165, Toronto, ON M5S 3H7, Canada *Tel:* 416-978-8083 *Fax:* 416-978-8854 *E-mail:* uc.programs@utoronto.ca *Web Site:* www.uc.utoronto.ca/writing-centre, pg 644

Sennholz, Lyn M, Center for Futures Education Inc, 345 Erie St, Grove City, PA 16127 *Tel:* 724-458-5860 *Fax:* 724-458-5962 *E-mail:* info@thectr.com *Web Site:* www.thectr.com, pg 51

Sensale, Danielle, JayJo Books LLC, One Huntington Quadrangle, Suite 1N03, Melville, NY 11747 *Tel:* 516-496-4863 *Toll Free Tel:* 800-999-6884 *Fax:* 516-496-4050 *Toll Free Fax:* 800-262-1886 *E-mail:* jayjobooks@guidance-group.com *Web Site:* www.guidance-group.com; www.jayjo.com, pg 121

Senturk, Huseyin, Tughra Books, 335 Clifton Ave, Clifton, NJ 07011 *Tel:* 973-777-2704 *Fax:* 973-457-7334 *E-mail:* info@tughrabooks.com *Web Site:* www.tughrabooks.com, pg 236

Senuta, Ann, ANR Publications University of California, 1301 S 46 St, Bldg 478 - MC 3580, Richmond, CA 94804 *Tel:* 510-665-2195 (cust serv) *Toll Free Tel:* 800-994-8849 *Fax:* 510-665-3427 *E-mail:* anrcatalog@ucdavis.edu *Web Site:* anrcatalog.ucanr.edu, pg 17

Senz, Lisa, St Martin's Press, LLC, 175 Fifth Ave, New York, NY 10010 *Tel:* 646-307-5151 *Web Site:* us.macmillan.com/smp, pg 204

Seo, Ginee, Chronicle Books LLC, 680 Second St, San Francisco, CA 94107 *Tel:* 415-537-4200 *Toll Free Tel:* 800-759-0190 (cust serv) *Fax:* 415-537-4460 *Toll Free Fax:* 800-858-7787 (orders); 800-286-9471 (cust serv) *E-mail:* frontdesk@chroniclebooks.com *Web Site:* www.chroniclebooks.com, pg 55

Seow, Jackie, Simon & Schuster, 1230 Avenue of the Americas, New York, NY 10020 *Tel:* 212-698-7000 *Toll Free Tel:* 800-223-2348 (cust serv); 800-223-2336 (orders) *Toll Free Fax:* 800-943-9831 (orders) *Web Site:* www.simonandschuster.com, pg 212

Sepehri, Amin, Mage Publishers Inc, 1408 35 St NW, Washington, DC 20007 *Tel:* 202-342-1642 *Web Site:* www.mage.com, pg 140

Seplow-Jolley, Elana, Random House Publishing Group, 1745 Broadway, New York, NY 10019 *Toll Free Tel:* 800-200-3552 *Web Site:* atrandom.com, pg 195

Serafimidis, Sarah, North Atlantic Books, 2526 Martin Luther King Jr Way, Berkeley, CA 94704 *Tel:* 510-549-4270 *Fax:* 510-549-4276 *Web Site:* www.northatlanticbooks.com, pg 163

Serafini, Julie, The Texas Bluebonnet Award, 3355 Bee Cave Rd, Suite 401, Austin, TX 78746-6763 *Tel:* 512-328-1518 *Toll Free Tel:* 800-580-2852 *Fax:* 512-328-8852 *E-mail:* tla@txla.org *Web Site:* www.txla.org, pg 693

Seraphim, Joshua, Leilah Publications, 510 E University Dr, No 3413, Tempe, AZ 85281 *Tel:* 847-275-1657 *E-mail:* leilah@leilahpublications.com *Web Site:* facebook.com/leilahpublications, pg 131

Sergel, Christopher III, Dramatic Publishing Co, 311 Washington St, Woodstock, IL 60098-3308 *Tel:* 815-338-7170 *Toll Free Tel:* 800-448-7469 *Fax:* 815-338-8981 *Toll Free Fax:* 800-334-5302 *E-mail:* plays@dramaticpublishing.com; customerservice@dpcplays.com *Web Site:* www.dramaticpublishing.com, pg 73

Sergel, Gayle, Dramatic Publishing Co, 311 Washington St, Woodstock, IL 60098-3308 *Tel:* 815-338-7170 *Toll Free Tel:* 800-448-7469 *Fax:* 815-338-8981 *Toll Free Fax:* 800-334-5302 *E-mail:* plays@dramaticpublishing.com; customerservice@dpcplays.com *Web Site:* www.dramaticpublishing.com, pg 73

Sergel, Susan, Dramatic Publishing Co, 311 Washington St, Woodstock, IL 60098-3308 *Tel:* 815-338-7170 *Toll Free Tel:* 800-448-7469 *Fax:* 815-338-8981 *Toll Free Fax:* 800-334-5302 *E-mail:* plays@dramaticpublishing.com; customerservice@dpcplays.com *Web Site:* www.dramaticpublishing.com, pg 73

Sergio, Christopher, Portfolio, 375 Hudson St, New York, NY 10014 *Web Site:* www.penguin.com/meet/publishers/portfolio, pg 186

Seroy, Jeff, Farrar, Straus & Giroux, LLC, 18 W 18 St, New York, NY 10011 *Tel:* 212-741-6900 *E-mail:* fsg.publicity@fsgbooks.com *Web Site:* us.macmillan.com/fsg.aspx, pg 82

Seroy, Jeff, Hill & Wang, 18 W 18 St, New York, NY 10011 *Tel:* 212-741-6900 *Fax:* 212-633-9385 *E-mail:* fsg.publicity@fsgbooks.com; fsg.editorial@fsgbooks.com; sales@fsgbooks.com *Web Site:* us.macmillan.com/hillandwang.aspx, pg 107

Seroy, Jeff, North Point Press, 18 W 18 St, 8th fl, New York, NY 10011 *Tel:* 212-741-6900 *Toll Free Tel:* 888-330-8477 *Fax:* 212-633-9385 *Web Site:* www.fsgbooks.com, pg 163

Servant, Sylvie, Les Presses de l'Universite Laval, 2180, Chemin Sainte-Foy, 1st fl, Quebec, QC G1V 0A6, Canada *Tel:* 418-656-2803 *Fax:* 418-656-3305 *E-mail:* presses@pul.ulaval.ca *Web Site:* www.pulaval.com, pg 468

Sery, Douglas, The MIT Press, One Rogers St, Cambridge, MA 02142 *Tel:* 617-253-5255 *Toll Free Tel:* 800-207-8354 (orders) *Fax:* 617-258-6779; 617-577-1545 (orders) *Web Site:* mitpress.mit.edu, pg 152

Seum, Rebecca, Cup of Tea Books, PO Box 21133, Columbus, OH 43221 *Tel:* 614-264-5588 *E-mail:* sales@pagespringpublishing.com *Web Site:* www.cupofteabooks.com, pg 66

Severini, Giorgia, R Ross Annett Award for Children's Literature, 11759 Groat Rd, Edmonton, AB T5M 3K6, Canada *Tel:* 780-422-8174 *Toll Free Tel:* 800-665-5354 (AB only) *Fax:* 780-422-2663 (attn WGA) *E-mail:* mail@writersguild.ca *Web Site:* writersguild.ca, pg 627

Severini, Giorgia, Georges Bugnet Award for Fiction, 11759 Groat Rd, Edmonton, AB T5M 3K6, Canada *Tel:* 780-422-8174 *Toll Free Tel:* 800-665-5354 (AB only) *Fax:* 780-422-2663 (attn WGA) *E-mail:* mail@writersguild.ca *Web Site:* writersguild.ca, pg 634

Severini, Giorgia, The City of Calgary W O Mitchell Book Prize, 11759 Groat Rd, Edmonton, AB T5M 3K6, Canada *Tel:* 780-422-8174 *Toll Free Tel:* 800-665-5354 (AB only) *Fax:* 780-422-2663 (attn WGA) *E-mail:* mail@writersguild.ca *Web Site:* writersguild.ca, pg 637

Severini, Giorgia, Wilfrid Eggleston Award for Nonfiction, 11759 Groat Rd, Edmonton, AB T5M 3K6, Canada *Tel:* 780-422-8174 *Toll Free Tel:* 800-665-5354 (AB only) *Fax:* 780-422-2663 (attn WGA) *E-mail:* mail@writersguild.ca *Web Site:* writersguild.ca, pg 644

Severini, Giorgia, James H Gray Award for Short Nonfiction, 11759 Groat Rd, Edmonton, AB T5M 3K6, Canada *Tel:* 780-422-8174 *Toll Free Tel:* 800-665-5354 (AB only) *Fax:* 780-422-2663 (attn WGA) *E-mail:* mail@writersguild.ca *Web Site:* writersguild.ca, pg 650

Severini, Giorgia, The Robert Kroetsch City of Edmonton Book Prize, 11759 Groat Rd, Edmonton, AB T5M 3K6, Canada *Tel:* 780-422-8174 *Toll Free Tel:* 800-665-5354 (AB only) *Fax:* 780-422-2663 (attn WGA) *E-mail:* mail@writersguild.ca *Web Site:* writersguild.ca, pg 659

Severini, Giorgia, Howard O'Hagan Award for Short Story, 11759 Groat Rd, Edmonton, AB T5M 3K6, Canada *Tel:* 780-422-8174 *Toll Free Tel:* 800-665-5354 (AB only) *Fax:* 780-422-2663 (attn WGA) *E-mail:* mail@writersguild.ca *Web Site:* writersguild.ca, pg 675

Severini, Giorgia, Gwen Pharis Ringwood Award for Drama, 11759 Groat Rd, Edmonton, AB T5M 3K6, Canada *Tel:* 780-422-8174 *Toll Free Tel:* 800-665-5354 (AB only) *Fax:* 780-422-2663 (attn WGA) *E-mail:* mail@writersguild.ca *Web Site:* writersguild.ca, pg 685

Severini, Giorgia, Stephan G Stephansson Award for Poetry, 11759 Groat Rd, Edmonton, AB T5M 3K6, Canada *Tel:* 780-422-8174 *Toll Free Tel:* 800-665-5354 (AB only) *Fax:* 780-422-2663 (attn WGA) *E-mail:* mail@writersguild.ca *Web Site:* writersguild.ca, pg 692

Severini, Giorgia, Jon Whyte Memorial Essay Prize, 11759 Groat Rd, Edmonton, AB T5M 3K6, Canada *Tel:* 780-422-8174 *Toll Free Tel:* 800-665-5354 (AB only) *Fax:* 780-422-2663 (attn WGA) *E-mail:* mail@writersguild.ca *Web Site:* writersguild.ca, pg 697

Severini, Giorgia, Writers' Guild of Alberta, 11759 Groat Rd, Edmonton, AB T5M 3K6, Canada *Tel:* 780-422-8174 *Toll Free Tel:* 800-665-5354 (AB only) *Fax:* 780-422-2663 (attn WGA) *E-mail:* mail@writersguild.ca *Web Site:* writersguild.ca, pg 581

Sevier, Ben, Grand Central Publishing, 1290 Avenue of the Americas, New York, NY 10019 *Tel:* 212-364-1100 *Web Site:* www.hachettebookgroup.com, pg 95

Sevier, Ben, Hachette Book Group, 1290 Avenue of the Americas, New York, NY 10019 *Tel:* 212-364-1100 *Toll Free Tel:* 800-759-0190 (cust serv) *Fax:* 212-364-0933 (intl orders) *Toll Free Fax:* 800-286-9471 (cust serv) *Web Site:* www.hachettebookgroup.com, pg 98

Sewell, Emily, Bull Publishing Co, PO Box 1377, Boulder, CO 80306 *Tel:* 303-545-6350 *Toll Free Tel:* 800-676-2855 *Fax:* 303-545-6354 *E-mail:* bullpublishing@msn.com *Web Site:* www.bullpub.com, pg 45

Sewell, Vicki, University of South Carolina Press, 1600 Hampton St, Suite 544, Columbia, SC 29208 *Tel:* 803-777-5245 *Toll Free Tel:* 800-768-2500 (orders) *Fax:* 803-777-0160 *Toll Free Fax:* 800-868-0740 (orders) *Web Site:* www.sc.edu/uscpress, pg 245

Sexton, Kim, SDP Publishing Solutions LLC, 36 Captain's Way, East Bridgewater, MA 02333 *Tel:* 617-775-0656 *Web Site:* www.sdppublishingsolutions.com, pg 501

Shabelman, Doug, Burns Entertainment & Sports Marketing, 820 Davis St, Suite 222, Evanston, IL 60201 *Tel:* 847-866-9400 *Fax:* 847-491-9778 *E-mail:* burnsl@burnsent.com *Web Site:* burnsent.com, pg 547

Shadek, Ed, Wildlife Education Ltd, 2418 Noyes St, Evanston, IL 60201 *Tel:* 859-261-2556 *Toll Free Tel:* 800-477-5034 *Fax:* 859-261-2355 *Web Site:* www.zoobooks.com; wildlife-ed.com, pg 256

Shafeyeva, Yelena, Begell House Inc Publishers, 50 North St, Danbury, CT 06810 *Tel:* 203-456-6161 *Fax:* 203-456-6167 *E-mail:* orders@begellhouse.com *Web Site:* www.begellhouse.com, pg 32

Shaffer, Bryan, Purdue University Press, Stewart Ctr 190, 504 W State St, West Lafayette, IN 47907-2058 *Tel:* 765-494-2038 *Fax:* 765-496-2442 *E-mail:* pupress@purdue.edu *Web Site:* www.thepress.purdue.edu, pg 191

Shaffer, Mike, New Readers Press, 104 Marcellus, Syracuse, NY 13204 *Tel:* 315-422-9121 *Toll Free Tel:* 800-448-8878 *Toll Free Fax:* 866-894-2100 *E-mail:* nrp@proliteracy.org *Web Site:* www.newreaderspress.com, pg 161

Shah, Monica, Harry N Abrams Inc, 195 Broadway, 9th fl, New York, NY 10007 *Tel:* 212-206-7715 *Toll Free Tel:* 800-345-1359 *Fax:* 212-519-1210 *E-mail:* abrams@abramsbooks.com *Web Site:* www.abramsbooks.com, pg 3

Shah, Vijay, University Press of Mississippi, 3825 Ridgewood Rd, Jackson, MS 39211-6492 *Tel:* 601-432-6205 *Toll Free Tel:* 800-737-7788 (orders & cust serv) *Fax:* 601-432-6217 *E-mail:* press@mississippi.edu *Web Site:* www.upress.state.ms.us, pg 247

Shaine, Ilene, Foster City International Writers Contest, 650 Shell Blvd, Foster City, CA 94404 *Tel:* 650-286-3380 *E-mail:* fostercity_writers@yahoo.com *Web Site:* www.fostercity.org, pg 647

Shallcross, Andrea, Hachette Book Group, 1290 Avenue of the Americas, New York, NY 10019 *Tel:* 212-364-1100 *Toll Free Tel:* 800-759-0190 (cust serv) *Fax:* 212-364-0933 (intl orders) *Toll Free Fax:* 800-286-9471 (cust serv) *Web Site:* www.hachettebookgroup.com, pg 98

Shaloo, Sharon, Massachusetts Book Awards, Simons College - GSLIS, 300 The Fenway, Boston, MA 02115 *Tel:* 617-521-2719 *E-mail:* bookawards@massbook.org *Web Site:* www.massbook.org, pg 666

Shalva, Sara, The Sugarman Family Award for Jewish Children's Literature, Irwin P Edlavitch Bldg, 1529 16 St NW, Washington, DC 20036 *Tel:* 202-518-9400 *Fax:* 202-518-9420 *Web Site:* www.washingtondcjcc.org, pg 692

Shamah, Lydia, Carol Mann Agency, 55 Fifth Ave, New York, NY 10003 *Tel:* 212-206-5635 *Fax:* 212-675-4809 *E-mail:* submissions@carolmannagency.com *Web Site:* www.carolmannagency.com, pg 527

Shamroe, Amy, Axiom Business Book Awards, 1129 Woodmere Ave, Suite B, Traverse City, MI 49686 *Tel:* 231-933-0445 *Toll Free Tel:* 800-706-4636 *Fax:* 231-933-0448 *E-mail:* info@axiomawards.com *Web Site:* www.axiomawards.com, pg 629

Shamroe, Amy, Illumination Book Awards, 1129 Woodmere Ave, Suite B, Traverse City, MI 49686 *Tel:* 231-933-0445 *Toll Free Tel:* 800-706-4636 *Fax:* 231-933-0448 *E-mail:* awards@bookpublishing.com *Web Site:* www.illuminationawards.com, pg 654

Shamroe, Amy, The Independent Publisher Book Awards, 1129 Woodmere Ave, Suite B, Traverse City, MI 49686 *Tel:* 231-933-0445 *Toll Free Tel:* 800-706-4636 *Fax:* 231-933-0448 *E-mail:* awards@bookpublishing.com *Web Site:* www.independentpublisher.com/ipland/ipawards.php, pg 655

Shamroe, Amy, Living Now Book Awards, 1129 Woodmere Ave, Suite B, Traverse City, MI 49686 *Tel:* 231-933-0445 *Toll Free Tel:* 800-706-4636 *Fax:* 231-933-0448 *E-mail:* awards@bookpublishing.com *Web Site:* www.livingnowawards.com, pg 662

Shamroe, Amy, Moonbeam Children's Book Awards, 1129 Woodmere Ave, Suite B, Traverse City, MI 49686 *Tel:* 231-933-0445 *Toll Free Tel:* 800-706-4636 *Fax:* 231-933-0448 *E-mail:* info@moonbeamawards.com *Web Site:* www.moonbeamawards.com, pg 669

Shanahan, Tara, Houghton Mifflin Harcourt Trade & Reference Division, 125 High St, Boston, MA 02110 *Tel:* 617-351-5000 *Toll Free Tel:* 800-225-3362 *Web Site:* www.hmhco.com, pg 111

Shandler, Geoff, HarperCollins General Books Group, 195 Broadway, New York, NY 10007 *Tel:* 212-207-7000 *Web Site:* www.harpercollins.com, pg 101

Shandler, Sara, Alloy Entertainment LLC, 1325 Avenue of the Americas, 29th fl, New York, NY 10019 *E-mail:* collaborative@alloyentertainment.com, pg 8

Shangle, Barbara, American Products Publishing Co, 8260 SW Nimbus Ave, Beaverton, OR 97008 *Tel:* 503-672-7502 *Toll Free Tel:* 800-668-8181 *Fax:* 503-672-7104 *E-mail:* info@american-products.com *Web Site:* www.american-products.com, pg 14

Shangle, Robert, American Products Publishing Co, 8260 SW Nimbus Ave, Beaverton, OR 97008 *Tel:* 503-672-7502 *Toll Free Tel:* 800-668-8181 *Fax:* 503-672-7104 *E-mail:* info@american-products.com *Web Site:* www.american-products.com, pg 14

Shank, Merna B, Christian Light Publications Inc, 1051 Mount Clinton Pike, Harrisonburg, VA 22802 *Tel:* 540-434-1003 *Toll Free Tel:* 800-776-0478 *Fax:* 540-433-8896 *E-mail:* info@clp.org; orders@clp.org *Web Site:* www.clp.org, pg 55

Shankland, Sally, McGraw-Hill Education, 2 Penn Plaza, New York, NY 10121-2298 *Tel:* 212-904-2000 *E-mail:* customer.service@mheducation.com; international_cs@mheducation.com *Web Site:* www.mheducation.com, pg 145

Shannon, Kari, Omnibus Press, 257 Park Ave S, 20th fl, New York, NY 10010 *Tel:* 212-254-2100 *Toll Free Tel:* 800-431-7187 *Fax:* 212-254-2013 *Toll Free Fax:* 800-345-6842 *E-mail:* info@omnibuspress.com *Web Site:* www.omnibuspress.com; www.musicsales.com, pg 167

Shannon, Kim, Penguin Random House Inc, 1745 Broadway, New York, NY 10019 *Tel:* 212-782-9000 *Toll Free Tel:* 800-726-0600 *Web Site:* www.penguinrandomhouse.com, pg 178

Shannon, Scott, Penguin Random House Inc, 1745 Broadway, New York, NY 10019 *Tel:* 212-782-9000 *Toll Free Tel:* 800-726-0600 *Web Site:* www.penguinrandomhouse.com, pg 178

Shannon, Scott, Random House Publishing Group, 1745 Broadway, New York, NY 10019 *Toll Free Tel:* 800-200-3552 *Web Site:* atrandom.com, pg 195

Shapiro, Anita C, Practising Law Institute, 1177 Avenue of the Americas, New York, NY 10036 *Tel:* 212-824-5700 *Toll Free Tel:* 800-260-4PLI (260-4754, cust serv) *Fax:* 212-265-4742 (intl) *Toll Free Fax:* 800-321-0093 (local) *E-mail:* info@pli.edu (cust serv) *Web Site:* www.pli.edu, pg 186

Shapiro, Howard, Animal Media Group LLC, 100 First Ave, Suite 1100, Pittsburgh, PA 15222-1519 *Tel:* 412-566-5656 *Fax:* 412-566-5656 *E-mail:* info@animalmediagroup.com *Web Site:* www.animalmediagroup.com, pg 17

Shapiro, James, The Authors Guild, 31 E 32 St, 7th fl, New York, NY 10016 *Tel:* 212-563-5904 *Fax:* 212-564-5363 *E-mail:* staff@authorsguild.org *Web Site:* www.authorsguild.org, pg 559

Shapiro, Karen, Sourcebooks Inc, 1935 Brookdale Rd, Suite 139, Naperville, IL 60563 *Tel:* 630-961-3900 *Toll Free Tel:* 800-432-7444 *Fax:* 630-961-2168 *E-mail:* info@sourcebooks.com; customersupport@sourcebooks.com *Web Site:* www.sourcebooks.com, pg 218

Shapiro, Norman, Judaica Press Inc, 123 Ditmas Ave, Brooklyn, NY 11218 *Tel:* 718-972-6200 *Toll Free Tel:* 800-972-6201 *Fax:* 718-972-6204 *E-mail:* info@judaicapress.com; orders@judaicapress.com *Web Site:* www.judaicapress.com, pg 123

Shapiro, Norman, Soncino Press Ltd, 123 Ditmas Ave, Brooklyn, NY 11218 *Tel:* 718-972-6200 *Toll Free Tel:* 800-972-6201 *Fax:* 718-972-6204 *E-mail:* info@soncino.com *Web Site:* www.soncino.com, pg 217

Shapiro, Shelly, Random House Publishing Group, 1745 Broadway, New York, NY 10019 *Toll Free Tel:* 800-200-3552 *Web Site:* atrandom.com, pg 195

Shapland, Juliette, HarperCollins Publishers, 195 Broadway, New York, NY 10007 *Tel:* 212-207-7000 *Fax:* 212-207-7145 *Web Site:* www.harpercollins.com, pg 101

Shappel, Ray, Random House Children's Books, 1745 Broadway, 10th fl, New York, NY 10019 *Tel:* 212-782-9000 *Web Site:* www.randomhousekids.com, pg 194

Share, Don, Ruth Lilly Poetry Prize, 61 W Superior St, Chicago, IL 60654 *Tel:* 312-787-7070 *Fax:* 312-787-6650 *E-mail:* editors@poetrymagazine.org *Web Site:* poetrymagazine.org, pg 661

Shareck, Michael, Macmillan, 175 Fifth Ave, New York, NY 10010 *Tel:* 646-307-5151 *E-mail:* press.inquiries@macmillan.com *Web Site:* www.macmillan.com, pg 140

Sharp, Brian, Dayton Playhouse FutureFest, PO Box 3017, Dayton, OH 45401-3017 *Tel:* 937-424-8477 *Fax:* 937-424-0062 *E-mail:* futurefest@thedaytonplayhouse.com *Web Site:* wordpress.daytonplayhouse.com, pg 640

Sharp, Lauren, Aevitas Creative Management, 19 W 21 St, Suite 501, New York, NY 10010 *Tel:* 212-765-6900 *Web Site:* aevitascreative.com, pg 506

Sharp, Sydney, Society for the History of Authorship, Reading & Publishing Inc (SHARP), c/o The Johns Hopkins University Press, Journals Publishing Div, PO Box 19966, Baltimore, MD 21211-0966 *Tel:* 410-516-6987 *Toll Free Tel:* 800-548-1784 *Fax:* 410-516-3866 *E-mail:* members@sharpweb.org *Web Site:* www.sharpweb.org, pg 578

Sharpe, Errol, Fernwood Publishing, 32 Oceanvista Lane, Black Point, NS B0J 1B0, Canada *Tel:* 902-857-1388 *Fax:* 902-857-1328 *E-mail:* info@fernpub.ca; roseway@fernpub.ca *Web Site:* fernwoodpublishing.ca, pg 456

Sharpe, Jack, Bethlehem Books, 10194 Garfield St S, Bathgate, ND 58216 *Toll Free Tel:* 800-757-6831 *Fax:* 701-265-3716 *E-mail:* contact@bethlehembooks.com *Web Site:* www.bethlehembooks.com, pg 34

Sharpton, Jeff, Resilient Publishing, 406 S Third St, Boise, ID 83702 *Tel:* 208-258-9544 *E-mail:* submissions@resilientpublishing.com *Web Site:* www.resilientpublishing.com; www.facebook.com/ResilientPub, pg 198

Sharrar, Kim, McCutchan Publishing Corp, 2694 Ohart Rd, Richmond, CA 94806 *Tel:* 510-758-5510 *Toll Free Tel:* 800-227-1540 *Fax:* 510-758-6078 *E-mail:* mccutchanpublish@sbcglobal.net *Web Site:* www.mccutchanpublishing.com, pg 145

Sharrard, Robert, City Lights Publishers, 261 Columbus Ave, San Francisco, CA 94133 *Tel:* 415-362-8193 *Fax:* 415-362-4921 *E-mail:* staff@citylights.com *Web Site:* www.citylights.com, pg 56

Shaub, Ms Bobbett, Medical Physics Publishing Corp (MPP), 4555 Helgesen Dr, Madison, WI 53718 *Tel:* 608-262-4021; 608-224-4508 *Toll Free Tel:* 800-442-5778 (cust serv) *Fax:* 608-224-5016 *E-mail:* mpp@medicalphysics.org *Web Site:* www.medicalphysics.org, pg 147

Shaughnessy, Sandy, Individual Artist Project Grant, 500 S Bronough St, Tallahassee, FL 32399-0250 *Tel:* 850-245-6470 *Fax:* 850-245-6497 *E-mail:* info@dos.myflorida.com *Web Site:* dos.myflorida.com/cultural, pg 655

Shaw, Ann Curme, Search Institute Press®, The Banks Bldg, Suite 125, 615 First Ave NE, Minneapolis, MN 55413 *Tel:* 612-376-8955; 612-692-5520 *Toll Free Tel:* 800-888-7828 *Fax:* 612-692-5553 *E-mail:* si@search-institute.org *Web Site:* www.search-institute.org, pg 210

Shaw, Connie, Sentient Publications LLC, PO Box 7204, Boulder, CO 80306 *Tel:* 303-443-2188 *Fax:* 303-381-2538 *E-mail:* contact@sentientpublications.com *Web Site:* www.sentientpublications.com, pg 210

Shaw, Jeanette, Prentice Hall Press, 375 Hudson St, New York, NY 10014 *Tel:* 212-366-2000 *Fax:* 212-366-2666, pg 187

Shaw, Joe, Cypress House, 155 Cypress St, Fort Bragg, CA 95437 *Tel:* 707-964-9520 *Toll Free Tel:* 800-773-7782 *Fax:* 707-964-7531 *E-mail:* cypresshouse@cypresshouse.com *Web Site:* www.cypresshouse.com, pg 66, 492

Shaw, Kathy Ann, Individual Artist Fellowships, 25 State House Sta, 193 State St, Augusta, ME 04333-0025 *Tel:* 207-287-2726 *Fax:* 207-287-2725 *Web Site:* mainearts.maine.gov, pg 655

Shaw, Laura, RAND Corp, 1776 Main St, Santa Monica, CA 90407-2138 *Tel:* 310-393-0411 *Fax:* 310-393-4818 *Web Site:* www.rand.org, pg 193

Shaw, Lisa, Corwin, a Sage Co, 2455 Teller Rd, Thousand Oaks, CA 91320 *Tel:* 805-499-9734 *Toll Free Tel:* 800-233-9936 *Fax:* 805-499-5323 *Toll Free Fax:* 800-417-2466 *E-mail:* info@corwin.com; order@corwin.com *Web Site:* www.corwin.com, pg 61

Shaw, Liz, Shambhala Publications Inc, 4720 Walnut St, Boulder, CO 80301 *Tel:* 303-222-9598 *Toll Free Tel:* 866-424-0030 (off); 888-424-2329 (cust serv) *Fax:* 303-200-9406 *E-mail:* customercare@shambhala.com *Web Site:* www.shambhala.com, pg 211

Shaw, Marjorie, Wildlife Education Ltd, 2418 Noyes St, Evanston, IL 60201 *Tel:* 859-261-2556 *Toll Free Tel:* 800-477-5034 *Fax:* 859-261-2355 *Web Site:* www.zoobooks.com; wildlife-ed.com, pg 256

Shay, Alison, Syracuse University Press, 621 Skytop Rd, Suite 110, Syracuse, NY 13244-5290 *Tel:* 315-443-5534 *Toll Free Tel:* 800-365-8929 (cust serv) *Fax:* 315-443-5545 *E-mail:* supress@syr.edu *Web Site:* syracuseuniversitypress.syr.edu, pg 226

Shea, Sam, Printing Industries of America, 301 Brush Creek Rd, Warrendale, PA 15086-7529 *Tel:* 412-741-6860 *Toll Free Tel:* 800-910-4283 *Fax:* 412-741-2311 *E-mail:* info@printing.org *Web Site:* www.printing.org, pg 188

Shea, Samantha, Georges Borchardt Inc, 136 E 57 St, New York, NY 10022 *Tel:* 212-753-5785 *E-mail:* georges@gbagency.com *Web Site:* www.gbagency.com, pg 509

Shea-Joyce, Tep, Appraisal Institute, 200 W Madison, Suite 1500, Chicago, IL 60606 *Tel:* 312-335-4100 *Toll Free Tel:* 888-756-4624 *Fax:* 312-335-4400 *Web Site:* www.appraisalinstitute.org, pg 19

Shealy, Dennis, Random House Children's Books, 1745 Broadway, 10th fl, New York, NY 10019 *Tel:* 212-782-9000 *Web Site:* www.randomhousekids.com, pg 194

Sheanin, Wendy, Simon & Schuster, Inc, 1230 Avenue of the Americas, New York, NY 10020 *Tel:* 212-698-7000 *Fax:* 212-698-7007 *E-mail:* firstname.lastname@simonandschuster.com *Web Site:* www.simonandschuster.com, pg 213

Shear, Donna, University of Nebraska Press, 1111 Lincoln Mall, Lincoln, NE 68588-0630 *Tel:* 402-472-3581; 919-966-7449 (cust serv & foreign orders) *Toll Free Tel:* 800-848-6224 (cust serv & US orders) *Fax:* 402-472-6214; 919-962-2704 (cust serv & foreign orders) *Toll Free Fax:* 800-526-2617 (cust serv & US orders) *E-mail:* pressmail@unl.edu *Web Site:* www.nebraskapress.unl.edu, pg 243

Shearon, Sam, Vesuvian Books, 2817 West End Ave, Nashville, TN 37203 *E-mail:* info@vesuvianmedia.com *Web Site:* www.vesuvianbooks.com, pg 250

Sheedy, Charlotte, Charlotte Sheedy Literary Agency Inc, 928 Broadway, Suite 901, New York, NY 10010 *Tel:* 212-780-9800 *Web Site:* www.sheedylit.com, pg 535

Sheehan, David P, Red Chair Press, PO Box 333, South Egremont, MA 01258-0333 *Tel:* 413-528-2398 (edit off) *Toll Free Tel:* 800-328-4929 (orders & cust serv) *Toll Free Fax:* 800-332-1132 *E-mail:* info@redchairpress.com *Web Site:* www.redchairpress.com, pg 196

Sheehan, Katie, Berrett-Koehler Publishers Inc, 1333 Broadway, Suite 1000, Oakland, CA 94612 *Tel:* 510-817-2277 *Fax:* 510-817-2278 *E-mail:* bkpub@bkpub.com *Web Site:* www.bkconnection.com, pg 34

Sheinkopf, Barry, The Writing Center, 601 E Palisade Ave, Suite 4, Englewood Cliffs, NJ 07632 *Tel:* 201-567-4017 *Fax:* 201-567-7202 *E-mail:* writingcenter@optonline.net *Web Site:* www.writingcenternj.com, pg 616

Shekari, Lauren, Other Press, 267 Fifth Ave, 6th fl, New York, NY 10016 *Tel:* 212-414-0054 *Toll Free Tel:* 877-843-6843 *Fax:* 212-414-0939 *E-mail:* editor@otherpress.com; marketing@otherpress.com; publicity@otherpress.com *Web Site:* www.otherpress.com, pg 170

Shelley, Jessica, Marshall Cavendish Corp, 99 White Plains Rd, Tarrytown, NY 10591-9001 *Tel:* 914-332-8888 *Toll Free Tel:* 800-821-9881 *Fax:* 914-332-8102 *E-mail:* mce@marshallcavendish.com *Web Site:* www.marshallcavendish.com; www.mceducation.us, pg 143

Shelton, Darryl, Christian Schools International, 3350 E Paris Ave SE, Grand Rapids, MI 49512-3054 *Tel:* 616-957-1070 *Toll Free Tel:* 800-635-8288 *Fax:* 616-957-5022 *E-mail:* info@csionline.org *Web Site:* www.csionline.org, pg 55

Shelton, Otis, American Institute of Chemical Engineers (AIChE), 120 Wall St, 23rd fl, New York, NY 10005-4020 *Tel:* 203-702-7660 *Toll Free Tel:* 800-242-4363 *Fax:* 203-775-5177 *E-mail:* customerservice@aiche.org *Web Site:* www.aiche.org, pg 12

Shepard, Aaron, Shepard Publications, PO Box 280, Friday Harbor, WA 98250 *Web Site:* www.shepardpub.com, pg 211

Shepard, Christopher, Aurous Inc, PO Box 20490, New York, NY 10017 *Tel:* 212-628-9729 *Fax:* 212-535-7861, pg 507

Shepard, Diane, Bear & Co Inc, One Park St, Rochester, VT 05767 *Tel:* 802-767-3174 *Toll Free Tel:* 800-932-3277 *Fax:* 802-767-3726 *E-mail:* customerservice@InnerTraditions.com *Web Site:* InnerTraditions.com, pg 31

Shepard, Diane, Inner Traditions International Ltd, One Park St, Rochester, VT 05767 *Tel:* 802-767-3174 *Toll Free Tel:* 800-246-8648 *Fax:* 802-767-3726 *E-mail:* customerservice@InnerTraditions.com *Web Site:* www.InnerTraditions.com, pg 117

Shepard, Judith, The Permanent Press, 4170 Noyac Rd, Sag Harbor, NY 11963 *Tel:* 631-725-1101 *E-mail:* info@thepermanentpress.com *Web Site:* www.thepermanentpress.com, pg 180

Shepard, Judith, Second Chance Press, 4170 Noyac Rd, Sag Harbor, NY 11963 *Tel:* 631-725-1101 *E-mail:* info@thepermanentpress.com *Web Site:* www.thepermanentpress.com, pg 210

Shepard, Martin, The Permanent Press, 4170 Noyac Rd, Sag Harbor, NY 11963 *Tel:* 631-725-1101 *E-mail:* info@thepermanentpress.com *Web Site:* www.thepermanentpress.com, pg 180

Shepard, Martin, Second Chance Press, 4170 Noyac Rd, Sag Harbor, NY 11963 *Tel:* 631-725-1101 *E-mail:* info@thepermanentpress.com *Web Site:* www.thepermanentpress.com, pg 210

Sheppard, Christine, Library Association of Alberta (LAA), 80 Baker Crescent NW, Calgary, AB T2L 1R4, Canada *Tel:* 403-284-5818 *Toll Free Tel:* 877-522-5550 *Fax:* 403-282-6646 *E-mail:* info@laa.ca *Web Site:* www.laa.ca, pg 568

Sheppard, Nancy, St Martin's Press, LLC, 175 Fifth Ave, New York, NY 10010 *Tel:* 646-307-5151 *Web Site:* us.macmillan.com/smp, pg 204

Sherer, John, The University of North Carolina Press, 116 S Boundary St, Chapel Hill, NC 27514-3808 *Tel:* 919-966-3561 *Fax:* 919-966-3829 *E-mail:* uncpress@unc.edu *Web Site:* www.uncpress.unc.edu, pg 243

Sheridan, Jackie, National Braille Press, 88 Saint Stephen St, Boston, MA 02115-4302 *Tel:* 617-266-6160 *Toll Free Tel:* 800-548-7323 (cust serv); 888-965-8965 *Fax:* 617-437-0456 *E-mail:* orders@nbp.org; contact@nbp.org *Web Site:* www.nbp.org, pg 157

Sherk, Mary Lou, Galen Press Ltd, PO Box 64400-WB, Tucson, AZ 85728-4400 *Tel:* 520-577-8363 *Fax:* 520-529-6459 *E-mail:* sales@galenpress.com *Web Site:* www.galenpress.com, pg 89

Sherman, Brooks, Janklow & Nesbit Associates, 285 Madison Ave, 21st fl, New York, NY 10017 *Tel:* 212-421-1700 *Fax:* 212-355-1403 *E-mail:* info@janklow.com *Web Site:* www.janklowandnesbit.com, pg 522

Sherman, James, Perseus Books, 250 W 57 St, 15th fl, New York, NY 10107 *Tel:* 212-340-8100 *Toll Free Tel:* 800-343-4499 (cust serv) *Fax:* 212-340-8105 *Web Site:* www.perseusbooks.com, pg 180

Sherman, Ken, Ken Sherman & Associates, 1275 N Hayworth, Suite 103, Los Angeles, CA 90046 *Tel:* 310-273-8840 *E-mail:* kenshermanassociates@gmail.com *Web Site:* www.kenshermanassociates.com, pg 535

Sherman, Rebecca, Writers House, 21 W 26 St, New York, NY 10010 *Tel:* 212-685-2400 *Fax:* 212-685-1781 *Web Site:* www.writershouse.com, pg 542

Sherman, Stephen, Radix Press, 11715 Bandlon Dr, Houston, TX 77072 *Tel:* 281-879-5688 *Web Site:* www.vvfh.org; www.specialforcesbooks.com, pg 193

Sherman, Susan, Charlesbridge Publishing Inc, 85 Main St, Watertown, MA 02472 *Tel:* 617-926-0329 *Toll Free Tel:* 800-225-3214 *Fax:* 617-926-5720 *Toll Free Fax:* 800-926-5775 *E-mail:* books@charlesbridge.com *Web Site:* www.charlesbridge.com, pg 53

Sherman, Wendy, Wendy Sherman Associates Inc, 27 W 24 St, Suite 700-B, New York, NY 10010 *Tel:* 212-279-9027 *E-mail:* submissions@wsherman.com *Web Site:* www.wsherman.com, pg 536

Sherr, Roger, Genealogical Publishing Co, 3600 Clipper Mill Rd, Suite 260, Baltimore, MD 21211 *Tel:* 410-837-8271 *Toll Free Tel:* 800-296-6687 *Fax:* 410-752-8492 *Toll Free Fax:* 800-599-9561 *E-mail:* info@genealogical.com; web@genealogical.com *Web Site:* www.genealogical.com, pg 91

Sherrod, Tracy, HarperCollins General Books Group, 195 Broadway, New York, NY 10007 *Tel:* 212-207-7000 *Web Site:* www.harpercollins.com, pg 101

Sherry, Cynthia, Academy Chicago, 814 N Franklin St, Chicago, IL 60610 *Tel:* 312-337-0747 *Toll Free Tel:* 800-888-4741 (orders) *Fax:* 312-337-5110 *E-mail:* frontdesk@chicagoreviewpress.com *Web Site:* www.chicagoreviewpress.com, pg 3

Sherry, Cynthia, Chicago Review Press, 814 N Franklin St, Chicago, IL 60610 *Tel:* 312-337-0747 *Toll Free Tel:* 800-888-4741 *Fax:* 312-337-5110 *E-mail:* frontdesk@chicagoreviewpress.com *Web Site:* www.chicagoreviewpress.com, pg 54

Shield, Nina, Plume, 375 Hudson St, New York, NY 10014 *Tel:* 212-366-2000 *Fax:* 212-243-6002 *Web Site:* www.penguin.com/publishers/plume, pg 184

Shurtleff, William, Soyinfo Center, PO Box 234, Lafayette, CA 94549-0234 *Tel:* 925-283-2991 *Web Site:* www.soyinfocenter.com, pg 219

Shuster, Todd, Aevitas Creative Management, 19 W 21 St, Suite 501, New York, NY 10010 *Tel:* 212-765-6900 *Web Site:* aevitascreative.com, pg 506

Sibbald, Anne, Janklow & Nesbit Associates, 285 Madison Ave, 21st fl, New York, NY 10017 *Tel:* 212-421-1700 *Fax:* 212-355-1403 *E-mail:* info@janklow.com *Web Site:* www.janklowandnesbit.com, pg 522

Sibley, Ellen, Barron's Educational Series Inc, 250 Wireless Blvd, Hauppauge, NY 11788 *Tel:* 631-434-3311 *Toll Free Tel:* 800-645-3476 *Fax:* 631-434-3723 *E-mail:* barrons@barronseduc.com *Web Site:* www.barronseduc.com, pg 30

Siciliano, John, Penguin Books, 375 Hudson St, New York, NY 10014 *Tel:* 212-366-2000 *E-mail:* penguinpublicity@us.penguingroup.com *Web Site:* www.penguinclassics.com; www.penguin.com, pg 177

Sickles, Danielle, Jane Rotrosen Agency LLC, 85 Broad St, 28th fl, New York, NY 10004 *Tel:* 212-593-4330 *Fax:* 212-935-6985 *Web Site:* janerotrosen.com, pg 534

Sicoli, Dan, Slipstream Annual Poetry Chapbook Contest, PO Box 2071, Dept W-1, Niagara Falls, NY 14301 *Web Site:* www.slipstreampress.org, pg 690

Siconolfi, Marcie, Cold Spring Harbor Laboratory Press, 500 Sunnyside Blvd, Woodbury, NY 11797-2924 *Tel:* 516-422-4100 *Toll Free Tel:* 800-843-4388 *Fax:* 516-422-4097; 516-422-4092 (submissions) *E-mail:* cshpress@cshl.edu *Web Site:* www.cshlpress.com, pg 58

Siddiqui, Leila, Dutton, 375 Hudson St, New York, NY 10014 *Tel:* 212-366-2000 *Fax:* 212-366-2262 *Web Site:* www.penguin.com, pg 74

Siddiqui, Shereen, Dissertation.com, 23331 Water Circle, Boca Raton, FL 33486-8540 *Tel:* 561-750-4344 *Toll Free Tel:* 800-636-8329 *Fax:* 561-750-6797 *Web Site:* www.dissertation.com, pg 71

Siddiqui, Shereen PhD, Universal-Publishers Inc, 23331 Water Circle, Boca Raton, FL 33486-8540 *Tel:* 561-750-4344 *Toll Free Tel:* 800-636-8329 (US only) *Fax:* 561-750-6797 *Web Site:* www.universal-publishers.com, pg 239

Siegel, Lois, National Press Club of Canada Foundation Inc, 17 York St, Suite 201, Ottawa, ON K1N 9J6, Canada *E-mail:* info@pressclubcanada.ca *Web Site:* pressclubcanada.ca, pg 572

Siegel, Mark, Roaring Brook Press, 175 Fifth Ave, New York, NY 10010 *Tel:* 646-307-5151 *Web Site:* us.macmillan.com/publishers/roaring-brook-press, pg 200

Siegel, Roz, Fine Creative Media, Inc, 322 Eighth Ave, 15th fl, New York, NY 10001 *Tel:* 212-595-3500 *Fax:* 212-595-3779, pg 85

Sieger, Daniel, Cengage Learning, 20 Channel Center St, Boston, MA 02210 *Tel:* 617 289 7700 *Toll Free Tel:* 800-354-9706 *Fax:* 617-289-7844 *Toll Free Fax:* 800-487-8488 *E-mail:* esales@cengage.com *Web Site:* www.cengage.com, pg 50

Siegfried, Carin, Soho Press Inc, 853 Broadway, New York, NY 10003 *Tel:* 212-260-1900 *E-mail:* soho@sohopress.com; publicity@sohopress.com; contact@sohopress.com *Web Site:* www.sohopress.com, pg 216

Siembieda, Kevin, Palladium Books Inc, 39074 Webb Ct, Westland, MI 48185 *Tel:* 734-721-2903 (orders) *Fax:* 734-721-1238 *Web Site:* www.palladiumbooks.com, pg 172

Sierra, Hector, National Geographic Books, 1145 17 St NW, Washington, DC 20036-4688 *Tel:* 202-857-7000 *Toll Free Tel:* 877-866-6486 *E-mail:* ngbooks@cdsfulfillment.com *Web Site:* www.nationalgeographic.com/books/; ngbooks.buysub.com, pg 158

Siess, Danielle, Random House Publishing Group, 1745 Broadway, New York, NY 10019 *Toll Free Tel:* 800-200-3552 *Web Site:* atrandom.com, pg 195

Signorino, Kathy, Individual Excellence Awards, 30 E Broad St, 33rd fl, Columbus, OH 43215 *Tel:* 614-466-2613 *Fax:* 614-466-4494 *Web Site:* www.oac.state.oh.us, pg 655

Silag, Lucy, Random House Publishing Group, 1745 Broadway, New York, NY 10019 *Toll Free Tel:* 800-200-3552 *Web Site:* atrandom.com, pg 195

Silber, Blake, Bridge Publications Inc, 5600 E Olympic Blvd, Commerce, CA 90022 *Tel:* 323-888-6200 *Toll Free Tel:* 800-722-1733 *Fax:* 323-888-6202 *E-mail:* info@bridgepub.com *Web Site:* www.bridgepub.com, pg 43

Silberer, Zsolt, American Water Works Association (AWWA), 6666 W Quincy Ave, Denver, CO 80235 *Tel:* 303-794-7711 *Toll Free Tel:* 800-926-7337 *Fax:* 303-347-0804 *E-mail:* service@awwa.org (cust serv) *Web Site:* www.awwa.org, pg 15

Silberfeld, Ms Heath Lynn, Enough Said, 3959 NW 29 Lane, Gainesville, FL 32606 *Tel:* 352-262-2971 *Fax:* 352-372-5747 (call first) *E-mail:* enoughsaid@cox.net *Web Site:* users.navi.net/~heathlynn, pg 493

Silberman, Jeff, Folio Literary Management, The Film Center Bldg, 630 Ninth Ave, Suite 1101, New York, NY 10036 *Tel:* 212-400-1494 *Fax:* 212-967-0977 *Web Site:* www.foliolit.com, pg 517

Silberman, Karen, Federal Bar Association, 1220 N Filmore St, Suite 444, Arlington, VA 22201 *Tel:* 571-481-9100 *Fax:* 571-481-9090 *E-mail:* fba@fedbar.org *Web Site:* www.fedbar.org, pg 83

Silbersack, John, Philip K Dick Award, PO Box 3447, Hoboken, NJ 07030 *Tel:* 201-876-2551 *Web Site:* www.philipkdickaward.org, pg 641

Silbersack, John, Trident Media Group LLC, 41 Madison Ave, 36th fl, New York, NY 10010 *Tel:* 212-333-1511 *E-mail:* info@tridentmediagroup.com; press@tridentmediagroup.com *Web Site:* www.tridentmediagroup.com, pg 540

Silburg, Richard, Poetry Flash Reading Series, 1450 Fourth St, Suite 4, Berkeley, CA 94710 *Tel:* 510-525-5476 *Fax:* 510-525-6752 *E-mail:* editor@poetryflash.org *Web Site:* poetryflash.org, pg 613

Sileno, Helen, LearningExpress LLC, 80 Broad St, 4th fl, New York, NY 10004 *Toll Free Tel:* 800-295-9556 (ext 2) *E-mail:* marketing@learningexpressllc.com (cust serv) *Web Site:* www.learningexpressllc.com, pg 131

Siler, Nikki V, Alpha II LLC, 7480 Halcyon Pointe Dr, Suite 204, Montgomery, AL 36117 *Tel:* 334-260-8150 *Toll Free Tel:* 800-825-7421 *Toll Free Fax:* 800-305-8030 *E-mail:* sales@alphaii.com *Web Site:* www.alphaii.com, pg 8

Silfin, Beth, HarperCollins General Books Group, 195 Broadway, New York, NY 10007 *Tel:* 212-207-7000 *Web Site:* www.harpercollins.com, pg 101

Sillah, Andrea, R S Means from The Gordian Group, 1099 Hingham St, Suite 201, Rockland, MA 02370 *Tel:* 781-422-5000 *Toll Free Tel:* 800-448-8182 *Fax:* 781-585-8814 *Toll Free Fax:* 800-632-6701 *Web Site:* www.rsmeans.com, pg 147

Silver, Carly, Harlequin Enterprises Ltd, 233 Broadway, Suite 1001, New York, NY 10279 *Tel:* 212-553-4200 *Fax:* 212-227-8969 *E-mail:* customerservice@harlequin.com *Web Site:* www.harlequin.com, pg 100

Silver, David, YMAA Publication Center Inc, PO Box 480, Wolfeboro, NH 03894 *Tel:* 603-569-7988 *Toll Free Tel:* 800-669-8892 *Fax:* 603-569-1889 *E-mail:* info@ymaa.com *Web Site:* www.ymaa.com, pg 262

Silver, Janet, Aevitas Creative Management, 19 W 21 St, Suite 501, New York, NY 10010 *Tel:* 212-765-6900 *Web Site:* aevitascreative.com, pg 506

Silver, Joanne S, Beach Lloyd Publishers LLC, 40 Cabot Dr, Wayne, PA 19087-5619 *Tel:* 610-407-9107 *Fax:* 775-254-0633 *E-mail:* beachlloyd@erols.com *Web Site:* www.beachlloyd.com, pg 30

Silver, Noel, Mazda Publishers Inc, One Park Plaza, Suite 600, Irvine, CA 92614 *Tel:* 714-751-5252 *Fax:* 714-751-4805 *E-mail:* mazdapub@aol.com *Web Site:* www.mazdapublishers.com, pg 144

Silver, Tom, Leadership Directories, 1407 Broadway, Suite 318, New York, NY 10018 *Tel:* 212-627-4140 *Toll Free Tel:* 800-627-0311 *Fax:* 212-645-0931 *E-mail:* info@leadershipdirectories.com *Web Site:* www.leadershipdirectories.com, pg 130

Silverberg, Ira, Simon & Schuster, 1230 Avenue of the Americas, New York, NY 10020 *Tel:* 212-698-7000 *Toll Free Tel:* 800-223-2348 (cust serv); 800-223-2336 (orders) *Toll Free Fax:* 800-943-9831 (orders) *Web Site:* www.simonandschuster.com, pg 212

Silverman, Leanne, Rowman & Littlefield Publishers Inc, 4501 Forbes Blvd, Suite 200, Lanham, MD 20706 *Tel:* 301-459-3366 *Toll Free Tel:* 800-462-6420 (cust serv) *Fax:* 301-429-5748 *Web Site:* rowman.com, pg 202

Silverstein, Clara, Chautauqua Writers' Workshop, One Ames Ave, Chautauqua, NY 14722 *Tel:* 716-357-6316; 716-357-6250 *Toll Free Tel:* 800-836-ARTS (836-2787) *Fax:* 716-357-9014 *Web Site:* ciweb.org, pg 610

Silvestri, Charles Anthony, Acroterion Books, 5305 Harvard Rd, Lawrence, KS 66049-4781 *Tel:* 785-917-0773 *E-mail:* info@acroterionbooks.com *Web Site:* www.acroterionbooks.com, pg 477

Silvestro, Denise, Kensington Publishing Corp, 119 W 40 St, New York, NY 10018 *Tel:* 212-407-1500 *Toll Free Tel:* 800-221-2647 *Fax:* 212-935-0699 *Web Site:* www.kensingtonbooks.com, pg 125

Silvis, Carol, Pennwriters Conference, PO Box 685, Dalton, PA 18414 *E-mail:* conferencecoordinator@pennwriters.org; info@pennwriters.org *Web Site:* pennwriters.org, pg 613

Simard, Camille, Les Editions du Remue-Menage, La Maison Parent-Roback, 110 rue Sainte-Therese, bureau 303, Montreal, QC H2Y 1E6, Canada *Tel:* 514-876-0097 *Fax:* 514-876-7951 *E-mail:* info@editions-rm.ca *Web Site:* www.editions-rm.ca, pg 454

Simkins, Noelle, Chronicle Books LLC, 680 Second St, San Francisco, CA 94107 *Tel:* 415-537-4200 *Toll Free Tel:* 800-759-0190 (cust serv) *Fax:* 415-537-4460 *Toll Free Fax:* 800-858-7787 (orders); 800-286-9471 (cust serv) *E-mail:* frontdesk@chroniclebooks.com *Web Site:* www.chroniclebooks.com, pg 55

Simmons, Ann, Pie in the Sky Publishing LLC, 8031 E Phillips Circle, Centennial, CO 80112 *Tel:* 303-773-0851 *Fax:* 303-773-0851 *E-mail:* pieintheskypublishing@msn.com *Web Site:* www.pieintheskypublishing.com, pg 183

Simmons, Carolyn, Getty Publications, 1200 Getty Center Dr, Suite 500, Los Angeles, CA 90049-1682 *Tel:* 310-440-7365 *Toll Free Tel:* 800-223-3431 (orders) *Fax:* 310-440-7758 *E-mail:* pubsinfo@getty.edu *Web Site:* www.getty.edu/publications, pg 92

Simmons, Zoe, PAGE International Screenwriting Awards, 7190 Sunset Blvd, Suite 610, Hollywood, CA 90046 *E-mail:* info@pageawards.com *Web Site:* www.pageawards.com, pg 676

Simms, Maria K, Starcrafts LLC, 334-A Calef Hwy, Epping, NH 03042 *Tel:* 603-734-4300 *Toll Free Tel:* 866-953-8458 (24/7 message ctr) *Fax:* 603-734-4311 *E-mail:* astrosales@astrocom.com *Web Site:* acspublications.com; www.starcraftseast.com; www.astrocom.com, pg 221

Simon, Daniel, Neustadt International Prize for Literature, c/o University of Oklahoma, 630 Parrington Oval, Suite 110, Norman, OK 73019-4033 *Tel:* 405-325-4531 *Web Site:* www.worldliteraturetoday.org; www.worldlit.org, pg 672

Simon, Daniel, NSK Neustadt Prize for Children's Literature, c/o University of Oklahoma, 630 Parrington Oval, Suite 110, Norman, OK 73019-4033 *Tel:* 405-325-4531 *Web Site:* www.worldliteraturetoday.org; www.worldlit.org, pg 674

Simon, Daniel, Seven Stories Press, 140 Watts St, New York, NY 10013 *Tel:* 212-226-8760 *Toll Free Tel:* 800-733-3000 (orders) *Fax:* 212-226-1411 *E-mail:* info@sevenstories.com *Web Site:* www.sevenstories.com, pg 211

Simon, Elizabeth, CSWE Press, 1701 Duke St, Suite 200, Alexandria, VA 22314-3457 *Tel:* 703-683-8080 *Fax:* 703-683-8493 *E-mail:* publications@cswe.org; info@cswe.org *Web Site:* www.cswe.org, pg 66

Simon, Peter J, W W Norton & Company Inc, 500 Fifth Ave, New York, NY 10110-0017 *Tel:* 212-354-5500 *Toll Free Tel:* 800-233-4830 (orders & cust serv) *Fax:* 212-869-0856 *Toll Free Fax:* 800-458-6515 *E-mail:* orders@wwnorton.com *Web Site:* books.wwnorton.com, pg 164

Simon, Robin, Berkley Publishing Group, 375 Hudson St, New York, NY 10014 *Tel:* 212-366-2000 *Fax:* 212-366-2385 *Web Site:* www.penguin.com, pg 33

Simon, Tami, Sounds True Inc, 413 S Arthur Ave, Louisville, CO 80027 *Tel:* 303-665-3151 *Toll Free Tel:* 800-333-9185 *E-mail:* customerservice@soundstrue.com; sales@soundstrue.com *Web Site:* www.soundstrue.com, pg 217

Simonello, Lorraine, Morehouse Publishing, 19 E 34 St, New York, NY 10016 *Tel:* 212-592-1800 *Toll Free Tel:* 800-672-1789 (retail orders only); 800-251-3320 (wholesale orders only) *Web Site:* www.morehousepublishing.com; www.churchpublishing.org, pg 154

Simonoff, Eric, WME, 11 Madison Ave, 18th fl, New York, NY 10010 *Tel:* 212-586-5100 *Web Site:* www.wmeentertainment.com, pg 542

Simonoff, Meredith Kaffel, DeFiore and Company Literary Management Inc, 47 E 19 St, 3rd fl, New York, NY 10003 *Tel:* 212-925-7744 *Fax:* 212-925-9803 *E-mail:* info@defliterary.com; submissions@defliterary.com *Web Site:* www.defliterary.com, pg 513

Simons, D Brenton, Newbury Street Press, 99-101 Newbury St, Boston, MA 02116 *Tel:* 617-536-5740 *Toll Free Tel:* 888-296-3447 (NEHGS membership) *Fax:* 617-536-7307 *E-mail:* sales@nehgs.org *Web Site:* www.americanancestors.org, pg 162

Simons, Jasper, American Psychological Association, 750 First St NE, Washington, DC 20002-4242 *Tel:* 202-336-5510 *Toll Free Tel:* 800-374-2721 *Fax:* 202-336-5502 *E-mail:* order@apa.org *Web Site:* www.apa.org/books, pg 14

Simons, Jasper, American Psychological Association, 750 First St NE, Washington, DC 20002-4242 *Tel:* 202-336-5500 *Toll Free Tel:* 800-374-2721 *E-mail:* order@apa.org *Web Site:* www.apa.org, pg 556

Simons, Natasha, Gallery Books, 1230 Avenue of the Americas, New York, NY 10020 *Toll Free Tel:* 800-456-6798 *Fax:* 212-698-7284 *E-mail:* consumer.customerservice@simonandschuster.com *Web Site:* www.simonsays.com, pg 90

Simonsen, Reka, Simon & Schuster Children's Publishing, 1230 Avenue of the Americas, New York, NY 10020 *Tel:* 212-698-7000 *Web Site:* www.simonandschuster.com/kids; www.simonandschuster.com/teen; simonandschuster.net; simonandschuster.biz, pg 213

Simpkins, Adam, The Continuing Legal Education Society of British Columbia (CLEBC), 500-1155 W Pender St, Vancouver, BC V6E 2P4, Canada *Tel:* 604-669-3544; 604-893-2121 (cust serv) *Toll Free Tel:* 800-663-0437 (CN) *Fax:* 604-669-9260 *E-mail:* custserv@cle.bc.ca *Web Site:* www.cle.bc.ca, pg 451

Simpson, Amy, University of Alaska Press, 1760 Westwood Way, Fairbanks, AK 99709 *Tel:* 907-474-5831 *Toll Free Tel:* 888-252-6657 (US only) *Fax:* 907-474-5502 *Web Site:* www.alaska.edu/uapress, pg 240

Simpson, Erin, Penguin Random House Speakers Bureau, A Penguin Random House Company, 1745 Broadway, Mail Drop 13-1, New York, NY 10019 *Tel:* 212-572-2013 *E-mail:* speakers@penguinrandomhouse.com *Web Site:* www.prhspeakers.com, pg 547

Simpson, Fiona, Simon & Schuster Children's Publishing, 1230 Avenue of the Americas, New York, NY 10020 *Tel:* 212-698-7000 *Web Site:* www.simonandschuster.com/kids; www.simonandschuster.com/teen; simonandschuster.net; simonandschuster.biz, pg 213

Simpson, Jonathan, Morgan Kaufmann, 50 Hampshire St, 5th fl, Cambridge, MA 02139 *Toll Free Tel:* 866-607-1417 *Fax:* 617-661-7061 *Web Site:* www.mkp.com; www.elsevier.com, pg 154

Simpson, Michael, Carter G Woodson Book Awards, 8555 16 St, Suite 500, Silver Spring, MD 20910 *Tel:* 301-588-1800 *Toll Free Tel:* 800-296-7840 *Fax:* 301-588-2049 *E-mail:* excellence@ncss.org; publications@ncss.org *Web Site:* www.socialstudies.org, pg 699

Simpson-Vos, Mark, The University of North Carolina Press, 116 S Boundary St, Chapel Hill, NC 27514-3808 *Tel:* 919-966-3561 *Fax:* 919-966-3829 *E-mail:* uncpress@unc.edu *Web Site:* www.uncpress.unc.edu, pg 243

Simqu, Blaise R, SAGE Publishing, 2455 Teller Rd, Thousand Oaks, CA 91320 *Toll Free Tel:* 800-818-7243 *Toll Free Fax:* 800-583-2665 *E-mail:* info@sagepub.com *Web Site:* www.sagepublishing.com, pg 203

Sims, Linsey, University of Tennessee Press, 110 Conference Center Bldg, 600 Henley St, Knoxville, TN 37996-4108 *Tel:* 865-974-3321 *Toll Free Tel:* 800-621-2736 (orders) *Fax:* 865-974-3724 *Toll Free Fax:* 800-621-8476 (orders) *E-mail:* custserv@utpress.org *Web Site:* www.utpress.org, pg 245

Sims, Michael, The MIT Press, One Rogers St, Cambridge, MA 02142 *Tel:* 617-253-5255 *Toll Free Tel:* 800-207-8354 (orders) *Fax:* 617-258-6779; 617-577-1545 (orders) *Web Site:* mitpress.mit.edu, pg 152

Sims-Nichols, Rebecca, Cedar Grove Books, 2215 High Point Dr, Carrollton, TX 75007 *Tel:* 415-364-8292 *Fax:* 415-276-9858 *E-mail:* queries@cedargrovebooks.com *Web Site:* www.cedargrovebooks.com, pg 50

Sinasac, Joseph, Novalis Publishing, 10 Lower Spadina Ave, Suite 400, Toronto, ON M5V 2Z2, Canada *Tel:* 416-363-3303 *Toll Free Tel:* 877-702-7773 *Fax:* 416-363-9409 *Toll Free Fax:* 877-702-7775 *E-mail:* books@novalis.ca *Web Site:* www.novalis.ca, pg 465

Sinauer, Andrew D, Sinauer Associates Inc, 23 Plumtree Rd, Sunderland, MA 01375 *Tel:* 413-549-4300 *Fax:* 413-549-1118 *E-mail:* publish@sinauer.com; orders@sinauer.com *Web Site:* sinauer.com, pg 214

Sinclair, Stephanie, Transatlantic Agency, 2 Bloor St E, Suite 3500, Toronto, ON M4W 1A8, Canada *Tel:* 416-488-9214 *E-mail:* info@transatlanticagency.com *Web Site:* www.transatlanticagency.com, pg 539

Sindler, Jessica, HarperCollins General Books Group, 195 Broadway, New York, NY 10007 *Tel:* 212-207-7000 *Web Site:* www.harpercollins.com, pg 101

Singer, Jeremy, The College Board, 250 Vesey St, New York, NY 10281 *Tel:* 212-713-8000 *Web Site:* www.collegeboard.com, pg 58

Singerline, Robert, Scepter Publishers, PO Box 360694, Strongsville, OH 44149 *Tel:* 212-354-0670 *Toll Free Tel:* 800-322-8773 *Fax:* 212-354-0736 *Web Site:* www.scepterpublishers.org, pg 207

Singerman, Jerome E, University of Pennsylvania Press, 3905 Spruce St, Philadelphia, PA 19104 *Tel:* 215-898-6261 *Fax:* 215-898-0404 *E-mail:* custserv@pobox.upenn.edu *Web Site:* www.pennpress.org, pg 244

Singh, Archana, John Wiley & Sons Inc, 111 River St, Hoboken, NJ 07030-5774 *Tel:* 201-748-6000 *Toll Free Tel:* 800-225-5945 (cust serv) *Fax:* 201-748-6088 *E-mail:* info@wiley.com *Web Site:* www.wiley.com, pg 256

Sinnett, William, Financial Executives Research Foundation Inc (FERF), West Tower, 7th fl, 1250 Headquarters Plaza, Morristown, NJ 07960-6837 *Tel:* 973-765-1000 *Fax:* 973-765-1023 *Web Site:* www.financialexecutives.org, pg 84

Sinocchi, Michael, Productivity Press, 711 Third Ave, 8th fl, New York, NY 10017 *Tel:* 212-216-7800 *Toll Free Tel:* 800-634-7064 (orders); 800-797-3803 *E-mail:* orders@taylorandfrancis.com *Web Site:* www.productivitypress.com, pg 189

Sinsheimer, Jessica, Sarah Jane Freymann Literary Agency LLC, 59 W 71 St, Suite 9-B, New York, NY 10023 *Tel:* 212-362-9277 *E-mail:* submissions@sarahjanefreymann.com *Web Site:* www.sarahjanefreymann.com, pg 518

Sioles, Lee, Louisiana State University Press, 338 Johnston Hall, Baton Rouge, LA 70803 *Tel:* 225-578-6294 *Fax:* 225-578-6461 *E-mail:* lsupress@lsu.edu *Web Site:* lsupress.org, pg 138

Sipala, Frank, Perseus Books, 250 W 57 St, 15th fl, New York, NY 10107 *Tel:* 212-340-8100 *Toll Free Tel:* 800-343-4499 (cust serv) *Fax:* 212-340-8105 *Web Site:* www.perseusbooks.com, pg 181

Sipe, Keith R, Carolina Academic Press, 700 Kent St, Durham, NC 27701 *Tel:* 919-489-7486 *Toll Free Tel:* 800-489-7486 *Fax:* 919-493-5668 *E-mail:* cap@cap-press.com *Web Site:* www.cap-press.com; www.caplaw.com, pg 48

Sipe, Scott, Carolina Academic Press, 700 Kent St, Durham, NC 27701 *Tel:* 919-489-7486 *Toll Free Tel:* 800-489-7486 *Fax:* 919-493-5668 *E-mail:* cap@cap-press.com *Web Site:* www.cap-press.com; www.caplaw.com, pg 48

Sippola, Carlene, Whole Person Associates Inc, 101 W Second St, Suite 203, Duluth, MN 55802 *Tel:* 218-727-0500 *Toll Free Tel:* 800-247-6789 *Fax:* 218-727-0505 *E-mail:* books@wholeperson.com *Web Site:* www.wholeperson.com, pg 255

Sirkin, Jeff, University of Texas at El Paso, Department of Creative Writing, MFA/Department of Creative Writing, 901 EDUC, 500 W University Ave, El Paso, TX 79968-9991 *Tel:* 915-747-5713 *Fax:* 915-747-5523 *E-mail:* creativewriting@utep.edu *Web Site:* www.utep.edu/cw, pg 624

Sirna-Bruder, Anet, Harry N Abrams Inc, 195 Broadway, 9th fl, New York, NY 10007 *Tel:* 212-206-7715 *Toll Free Tel:* 800-345-1359 *Fax:* 212-519-1210 *E-mail:* abrams@abramsbooks.com *Web Site:* www.abramsbooks.com, pg 3

Sirota, Mark, Trusted Media Brands Inc, 750 Third Ave, 3rd fl, New York, NY 10017 *Toll Free Tel:* 800-310-6261 (cust serv) *E-mail:* customercare@tmbi.com *Web Site:* www.tmbi.com; www.rd.com, pg 236

Siscoe, Nancy, Random House Children's Books, 1745 Broadway, 10th fl, New York, NY 10019 *Tel:* 212-782-9000 *Web Site:* www.randomhousekids.com, pg 194

Sisk, Jonathan, Rowman & Littlefield Publishers Inc, 4501 Forbes Blvd, Suite 200, Lanham, MD 20706 *Tel:* 301-459-3366 *Toll Free Tel:* 800-462-6420 (cust serv) *Fax:* 301-429-5748 *Web Site:* rowman.com, pg 202

Sisson, Walter R, American Geosciences Institute (AGI), 4220 King St, Alexandria, VA 22302-1502 *Tel:* 703-379-2480 (ext 246) *Fax:* 703-379-7563 *E-mail:* pubs@agiweb.org *Web Site:* www.agiweb.org, pg 11

Sita, Joe, Octane Press, 809 S Lamar Blvd, Suite H, Austin, TX 78704 *Tel:* 512-334-9441 *Fax:* 512-852-4737 *E-mail:* info@octanepress.com; orders@octanepress.com; sales@octanepress.com *Web Site:* octanepress.com, pg 167

Sitzes, Jason, Writers Retreat Workshop (WRW), PO Box 170657, Austin, TX 78717 *E-mail:* info@writersretreatworkshop.com *Web Site:* www.writersretreatworkshop.com, pg 616

Sivasubramaniam, Jeevan, Berrett-Koehler Publishers Inc, 1333 Broadway, Suite 1000, Oakland, CA 94612 *Tel:* 510-817-2277 *Fax:* 510-817-2278 *E-mail:* bkpub@bkpub.com *Web Site:* www.bkconnection.com, pg 34

Sizemore, Terrie, A 2 Z Press LLC, 445 Cortez Ave, Deleon Springs, FL 32130 *Tel:* 386-681-7402 *Web Site:* www.a2zpress.com; www.terriesizemorestoryteller.com, pg 1

Skaj, Paul, ABDO Publishing Group, 8000 W 78 St, Suite 310, Edina, MN 55439 *Tel:* 952-831-2120 *Toll Free Tel:* 800-800-1312 *Toll Free Fax:* 800-862-3480 *E-mail:* customerservice@abdopublishing.com *Web Site:* abdopublishing.com, pg 2

Skeehan, Mary Kate, Sanford J Greenburger Associates Inc, 55 Fifth Ave, New York, NY 10003 *Tel:* 212-206-5600 *Fax:* 212-463-8718 *Web Site:* greenburger.com; www.sjga.com, pg 520

Skeel, Joe, The Society of Professional Journalists (SPJ), Eugene S Pulliam National Journalism Ctr, 3909 N Meridian St, Indianapolis, IN 46208 *Tel:* 317-927-8000 *Fax:* 317-920-4789 *E-mail:* spj@spj.org *Web Site:* www.spj.org, pg 580

Skehan, Mary Kate, W W Norton & Company Inc, 500 Fifth Ave, New York, NY 10110-0017 *Tel:* 212-354-5500 *Toll Free Tel:* 800-233-4830 (orders & cust serv) *Fax:* 212-869-0856 *Toll Free Fax:* 800-458-6515 *E-mail:* orders@wwnorton.com *Web Site:* books.wwnorton.com, pg 164

Skewes, Eva, Yale Series of Younger Poets, 302 Temple St, New Haven, CT 06511 *Tel:* 203-432-0960 *Fax:* 203-432-0948 *Web Site:* www.yalebooks.com, pg 701

Skewes, Eva, Yale University Press, 302 Temple St, New Haven, CT 06511-8909 *Tel:* 203-432-0960; 203-432-0966 (sales); 401-531-2800 (cust serv) *Toll Free Tel:* 800-405-1619 (cust serv) *Fax:* 203-432-0948; 203-432-8485 (sales); 401-531-2801 (cust serv) *Toll Free Fax:* 800-406-9145 (cust serv) *E-mail:* sales.press@yale.edu (sales); customer.care@triliteral.org (cust serv) *Web Site:* www.yalebooks.com; yalepress.yale.edu/yupbooks, pg 261

Skinker, Will, Counterpath Press, 613 22 St, Denver, CO 80205 *E-mail:* counterpath@counterpathpress.org; editors@counterpathpress.org *Web Site:* www.counterpathpress.org, pg 63

Skinner, Heather, University of Minnesota Press, 111 Third Ave S, Suite 290, Minneapolis, MN 55401-2520 *Tel:* 612-301-1990 *Fax:* 612-301-1980 *E-mail:* ump@umn.edu *Web Site:* www.upress.umn.edu, pg 242

Sklena, Jennifer, Institute of Environmental Sciences & Technology - IEST, 2340 S Arlington Heights Rd, Suite 620, Arlington Heights, IL 60005-4510 *Tel:* 847-981-0100 *Fax:* 847-981-4130 *E-mail:* information@iest.org *Web Site:* www.iest.org, pg 118

Skokut, Joyce, Educational Book & Media Association (EBMA), 11 Main St, Suite D, Warrenton, VA 20186 *Tel:* 540-318-7770 *Fax:* 202-962-3939 *E-mail:* info@edupaperback.org *Web Site:* www.edupaperback.org, pg 565

Skolkin, David, Museum of New Mexico Press, 725 Camino Lejo, Suite C, Santa Fe, NM 87505 *Tel:* 505-476-1155; 505-272-7777 (orders); 505-277-4810 *Toll Free Tel:* 800-249-7737 (orders) *Fax:* 505-476-1156 *Toll Free Fax:* 800-622-8667 (orders) *Web Site:* www.mnmpress.org, pg 156

Skolnick, Irene, Irene Skolnick Literary Agency, 27 W 20 St, Suite 305, New York, NY 10011 *Tel:* 212-727-3648 *Fax:* 212-352-2059 *E-mail:* office@skolnickliterary.com (queries) *Web Site:* www.skolnickagency.com, pg 536

Skrabek, Alison, Living Language, c/o Penguin Random House Inc, 1745 Broadway, New York, NY 10019 *Tel:* 212-782-9000 *Toll Free Tel:* 800 733-3000 (orders) *Toll Free Fax:* 800-659-2436 *E-mail:* livinglanguage@randomhouse.com *Web Site:* www.livinglanguage.com, pg 136

Skulnik, Brian, Second Chance Press, 4170 Noyac Rd, Sag Harbor, NY 11963 *Tel:* 631-725-1101 *E-mail:* info@thepermanentpress.com *Web Site:* www.thepermanentpress.com, pg 210

Skurnick, Victoria, Levine|Greenberg|Rostan Literary Agency, 307 Seventh Ave, Suite 2407, New York, NY 10001 *Tel:* 212-337-0934 *Fax:* 212-337-0948 *Web Site:* lgrliterary.com, pg 525

Skutt, Alexander, McBooks Press Inc, ID Booth Bldg, 520 N Meadow St, Ithaca, NY 14850 *Tel:* 607-272-2114 *E-mail:* mcbooks@mcbooks.com *Web Site:* www.mcbooks.com, pg 144

Skwiot, Suzee, Rodale Inc, 400 S Tenth St, Emmaus, PA 18049 *Tel:* 610-967-5171 *Toll Free Tel:* 866-387-0509 *E-mail:* bookmarketing@rodale.com; bookpublicity@rodale.com *Web Site:* www.rodale.com, pg 201

Sky-Peck, Kathryn, Red Wheel/Weiser/Conari, 65 Parker St, Suite 7, Newburyport, MA 01950 *Tel:* 978-465-0504 *Toll Free Tel:* 800-423-7087 (orders) *Fax:* 978-465-0243 *E-mail:* info@rwwbooks.com *Web Site:* www.redwheelweiser.com, pg 197

Skyberg, Andrea, Wisconsin Annual Fall Conference, PO Box 1463, Green Bay, WI 54305-1463 *Tel:* 323-782-1010 (corp off) *E-mail:* wisconsin@scbwi.org *Web Site:* www.scbwi.org; www.facebook.com/SCBWIWisconsin, pg 616

Skyvara, Suzanne, Goodreads Choice Awards, 188 Spear St, 3rd fl, San Francisco, CA 94105 *E-mail:* press@goodreads.com *Web Site:* www.goodreads.com/award, pg 650

Slachta, Pedro, Casa Bautista de Publicaciones, 7000 Alabama Ave, El Paso, TX 79904 *Tel:* 915-566-9656 *Toll Free Tel:* 800-755-5958 (cust serv & orders) *Fax:* 915-562-6502; 915-565-9008 (orders) *E-mail:* orders@editorialmh.org *Web Site:* www.editorialmh.org, pg 48

Slager, Daniel, Milkweed Editions, 1011 Washington Ave S, Suite 300, Minneapolis, MN 55415-1246 *Tel:* 612-332-3192 *Toll Free Tel:* 800-520-6455 *Fax:* 612-215-2550 *Web Site:* milkweed.org, pg 151

Slager, Daniel, Milkweed National Fiction Prize, 1011 Washington Ave S, Suite 300, Minneapolis, MN 55415-1246 *Tel:* 612-332-3192 *Toll Free Tel:* 800-520-6455 *Fax:* 612-215-2550 *E-mail:* submissions@milkweed.org *Web Site:* www.milkweed.org, pg 668

Slater, Alex, Trident Media Group LLC, 41 Madison Ave, 36th fl, New York, NY 10010 *Tel:* 212-333-1511 *E-mail:* info@tridentmediagroup.com; press@tridentmediagroup.com *Web Site:* www.tridentmediagroup.com, pg 540

Slayton, Phillip, PEN Canada, 24 Ryerson Ave, Suite 301, Toronto, ON M5T 2P3, Canada *Tel:* 416-703-8448 *Fax:* 416-703-3870 *E-mail:* queries@pencanada.ca *Web Site:* www.pencanada.ca, pg 575

Slesin, Suzanne, Pointed Leaf Press, 136 Baxter St, New York, NY 10013 *Tel:* 212-941-1800 *Fax:* 212-941-1822 *E-mail:* info@pointedleafpress.com *Web Site:* www.pointedleafpress.com, pg 185

Sleven, Paul, Macmillan, 175 Fifth Ave, New York, NY 10010 *Tel:* 646-307-5151 *E-mail:* press.inquiries@macmillan.com *Web Site:* www.macmillan.com, pg 140

Slopen, Beverley, Beverley Slopen Literary Agency, 131 Bloor St W, Suite 711, Toronto, ON M5S 1S3, Canada *Tel:* 416-964-9598 *Fax:* 416-921-7726 *Web Site:* www.slopenagency.com, pg 536

Slovak, Paul, Penguin Books, 375 Hudson St, New York, NY 10014 *Tel:* 212-366-2000 *E-mail:* penguinpublicity@us.penguingroup.com *Web Site:* www.penguinclassics.com; www.penguin.com, pg 177

Slovak, Paul, Viking, 375 Hudson St, New York, NY 10014 *Tel:* 212-366-2000 *Fax:* 212-243-6002 *Web Site:* www.penguin.com/publishers/vikingbooks, pg 250

Slutsky, Lorie, Oscar Williams/Gene Derwood Award, 909 Third Ave, New York, NY 10022 *Tel:* 212-686-0010 *Fax:* 212-532-8528 *E-mail:* info@nycommunitytrust.org *Web Site:* www.nycommunitytrust.org, pg 698

Smagler, Alan, Scholastic Trade Division, 557 Broadway, New York, NY 10012 *Tel:* 212-343-6100; 212-343-4685 (export sales) *Fax:* 212-343-4714 (export sales) *Web Site:* www.scholastic.com, pg 208

Small, Christopher, Sinauer Associates Inc, 23 Plumtree Rd, Sunderland, MA 01375 *Tel:* 413-549-4300 *Fax:* 413 549-1118 *E-mail:* publish@sinauer.com; orders@sinauer.com *Web Site:* sinauer.com, pg 214

Small, Ellen, Publishing Synthesis Ltd, 39 Crosby St, New York, NY 10013 *Tel:* 212-219-0135 *Fax:* 212-219-0136 *E-mail:* mainmail@pubsyn.com *Web Site:* www.pubsyn.com, pg 500

Small, Nick, Grand Central Publishing, 1290 Avenue of the Americas, New York, NY 10019 *Tel:* 212-364-1100 *Web Site:* www.hachettebookgroup.com, pg 95

Small, Rachael, Europa Editions, 214 W 29 St, Suite 1003, New York, NY 10001 *Tel:* 212-868-6844 *Fax:* 212-868-6845 *E-mail:* info@europaeditions.com *Web Site:* www.europaeditions.com, pg 80

Smallfield, Edward, Apogee Press, 2308 Sixth St, Berkeley, CA 94710 *E-mail:* editors.apogee@gmail.com *Web Site:* www.apogeepress.com, pg 18

Smallwood, Wendi, Fresh Fish Award for Emerging Writers, Haymarket Sq, 223 Duckworth St, St John's, NL A1C 6N1, Canada *Tel:* 709-739-5215 *Toll Free Tel:* 866-739-5215 *E-mail:* wanl@nf.aibn.com *Web Site:* wanl.ca, pg 648

Smallwood, Wendi, Newfoundland and Labrador Book Awards, Haymarket Sq, 223 Duckworth St, St John's, NL A1C 6N1, Canada *Tel:* 709-739-5215 *Toll Free Tel:* 866-739-5215 *E-mail:* wanl@nf.aibn.com *Web Site:* wanl.ca, pg 673

Smart, Dan, Twenty-Third Publications, One Montauk Ave, Suite 200, New London, CT 06320 *Tel:* 860-437-3012 *Toll Free Tel:* 800-321-0411 (orders) *Toll Free Fax:* 800-572-0788 *E-mail:* resources@twentythirdpublications.com *Web Site:* www.twentythirdpublications.com, pg 237

Smetanka, Dan, Counterpoint Press LLC, 1919 Fifth St, Berkeley, CA 94710 *Tel:* 510-704-0230 *Fax:* 510-704-0268 *E-mail:* info@counterpointpress.com *Web Site:* counterpointpress.com; www.sierraclub.org/books; softskull.com, pg 63

Smiley, Matt, University of Minnesota Press, 111 Third Ave S, Suite 290, Minneapolis, MN 55401-2520 *Tel:* 612-301-1990 *Fax:* 612-301-1980 *E-mail:* ump@umn.edu *Web Site:* www.upress.umn.edu, pg 242

Smist, Erik, The Johns Hopkins University Press, 2715 N Charles St, Baltimore, MD 21218-4363 *Tel:* 410-516-6900; 410-516-6987 (journal orders outside US & CN) *Toll Free Tel:* 800-537-5487 (book orders & cust serv); 800-548-1784 (journal orders) *Fax:* 410-516-6968; 410-516-3866 (journal orders) *E-mail:* hfscustserv@press.jhu.edu (cust serv); jrnlcirc@press.jhu.edu (journal orders) *Web Site:* www.press.jhu.edu; muse.jhu.edu, pg 122

Smith, Allan H, Success Advertising & Publishing, 3419 Dunham Rd, Warsaw, NY 14569 *Tel:* 585-786-5663, pg 224

Smith, Andrew, Harry N Abrams Inc, 195 Broadway, 9th fl, New York, NY 10007 *Tel:* 212-206-7715 *Toll Free Tel:* 800-345-1359 *Fax:* 212-519-1210 *E-mail:* abrams@abramsbooks.com *Web Site:* www.abramsbooks.com, pg 2

Smith, Betty, International Publishers Co Inc, 235 W 23 St, New York, NY 10011 *Tel:* 212-366-9816 *Fax:* 212-366-9820 *E-mail:* service@intpubnyc.com *Web Site:* www.intpubnyc.com, pg 120

Smith, Bradford K, The Foundation Center, 32 Old Slip, 24th fl, New York, NY 10005-3500 *Tel:* 212-620-4230 *Toll Free Tel:* 800-424-9836 *Fax:* 212-807-3677 *E-mail:* customerservice@foundationcenter.org *Web Site:* foundationcenter.org, pg 87

Smith, Bridget, Dunham Literary Inc, 110 William St, Suite 2202, New York, NY 10038 *Tel:* 212-929-0994 *Web Site:* dunhamlit.com, pg 514

Smith, Chris, Penguin Books, 375 Hudson St, New York, NY 10014 *Tel:* 212-366-2000 *E-mail:* penguinpublicity@us.penguingroup.com *Web Site:* www.penguinclassics.com; www.penguin.com, pg 177

Smith, Chris, Viking, 375 Hudson St, New York, NY 10014 *Tel:* 212-366-2000 *Fax:* 212-243-6002 *Web Site:* www.penguin.com/publishers/vikingbooks, pg 250

Smith, David Cloyce, The Library of America, 14 E 60 St, New York, NY 10022-1006 *Tel:* 212-308-3360 *Fax:* 212-750-8352 *E-mail:* info@loa.org *Web Site:* www.loa.org, pg 133

Smith, Dean J, Cornell University Press, Sage House, 512 E State St, Ithaca, NY 14850 *Tel:* 607-277-2338 *Fax:* 607-277-2374 *E-mail:* cupressinfo@cornell.edu; cupress-sales@cornell.edu *Web Site:* www.cornellpress.cornell.edu, pg 61

Smith, Deborah, BelleBooks, PO Box 300921, Memphis, TN 38130 *Tel:* 901-344-9024 *Fax:* 901-344-9068 *E-mail:* bellebooks@bellebooks.com *Web Site:* www.bellebooks.com, pg 32

Smith, Diane E, Baylor University Press, Baylor University, One Bear Place, Waco, TX 76798-7363 *Tel:* 254-710-3164 *Fax:* 254-710-3440 *Web Site:* www.baylorpress.com, pg 30

Smith, Elizabeth, Chronicle Books LLC, 680 Second St, San Francisco, CA 94107 *Tel:* 415-537-4200 *Toll Free Tel:* 800-759-0190 (cust serv) *Fax:* 415-537-4460 *Toll Free Fax:* 800-858-7787 (orders); 800-286-9471 (cust serv) *E-mail:* frontdesk@chroniclebooks.com *Web Site:* www.chroniclebooks.com, pg 55

Smith, Erica, Interweave Press LLC, 201 E Fourth St, Loveland, CO 80537 *Toll Free Tel:* 800-272-2193; 800-289-0963 *Fax:* 970-613-4656 *Toll Free Fax:* 888-590-4082 *Web Site:* www.interweave.com, pg 120

Smith, Frederick B, Two Thousand Three Associates, 135 Chilean Ave, Palm Beach, FL 33480 *Tel:* 386-690-2503 *E-mail:* ttta1@att.net *Web Site:* www.twothousandthree.com, pg 237

Smith, George D, Signature Books Publishing LLC, 564 W 400 N, Salt Lake City, UT 84116-3411 *Tel:* 801-531-1483 *Fax:* 801-531-1488 *E-mail:* people@signaturebooks.com *Web Site:* www.signaturebooks.com; www.signaturebookslibrary.org, pg 212

Smith, Ginger B, Success Advertising & Publishing, 3419 Dunham Rd, Warsaw, NY 14569 *Tel:* 585-786-5663, pg 224

Smith, Gordon H, National Association of Broadcasters (NAB), 1771 "N" St NW, Washington, DC 20036 *Tel:* 202-429-5300 *E-mail:* nab@nab.org *Web Site:* www.nab.org, pg 157, 570

Smith, Icy, East West Discovery Press, PO Box 3585, Manhattan Beach, CA 90266 *Tel:* 310-545-3730 *Fax:* 310-545-3731 *E-mail:* info@eastwestdiscovery.com *Web Site:* www.eastwestdiscovery.com, pg 74

Smith, Ileene, Farrar, Straus & Giroux, LLC, 18 W 18 St, New York, NY 10011 *Tel:* 212-741-6900 *E-mail:* fsg.publicity@fsgbooks.com *Web Site:* us.macmillan.com/fsg.aspx, pg 83

Smith, James Clois Jr, Sunstone Press, PO Box 2321, Santa Fe, NM 87504-2321 *Tel:* 505-988-4418 *Toll Free Tel:* 800-243-5644 *Fax:* 505-988-1025 (orders only) *Web Site:* www.sunstonepress.com, pg 225

Smith, Jeffrey, Bridge to Asia, 1505 Juanita Way, Berkeley, CA 94702-1103 *Tel:* 510-665-3998 *E-mail:* asianet@bridge.org *Web Site:* www.bridge.org, pg 583

Smith, Jerome K, Gollehon Press Inc, 3655 Glenn Dr SE, Grand Rapids, MI 49546 *Tel:* 616-949-3515 *Fax:* 616-949-8674 *E-mail:* sales@gollehonbooks.com; editorial@gollehonbooks.com *Web Site:* www.gollehonbooks.com, pg 94

Smith, Jill, University of Denver Publishing Institute, 2000 E Asbury Ave, Denver, CO 80208 *Tel:* 303-871-2570 *Fax:* 303-871-2501 *Web Site:* www.du.edu/publishinginstitute, pg 623

Smith, Jordan, Writers' League of Texas (WLT), 611 S Congress Ave, Suite 200 A-3, Austin, TX 78704 *Tel:* 512-499-8914 *E-mail:* wlt@writersleague.org *Web Site:* www.writersleague.org, pg 581

Smith, Joseph, Bisk Education, 9417 Princess Palm Ave, Suite 400, Tampa, FL 33619 *Tel:* 813-621-6200 *Toll Free Tel:* 800-280-9718 (cust serv) *E-mail:* customerservice@bisk.com *Web Site:* www.bisk.com, pg 35

Smith, Kayleigh, Naomi Berber Memorial Award, 301 Brush Creek Rd, Warrendale, PA 15086-7529 *Tel:* 412-741-6860 *Toll Free Tel:* 800-910-4283 *Fax:* 412-741-2311 *E-mail:* printingind@comm.printing.org *Web Site:* www.printing.org/berberaward, pg 631

Smith, Kayleigh, Education Awards of Excellence, 301 Brush Creek Rd, Warrendale, PA 15086-7529 *Tel:* 412-741-6860 *Toll Free Tel:* 800-910-4283 *Fax:* 412-741-2311 *E-mail:* printingind@comm.printing.org *Web Site:* www.printing.org/educationaward, pg 643

Smith, Kayleigh, InterTech™ Technology Awards, 301 Brush Creek Rd, Warrendale, PA 15086-7529 *Tel:* 412-741-6860 *Toll Free Tel:* 800-910-4283 *Fax:* 412-741-2311 *E-mail:* intertech@printing.org *Web Site:* www.printing.org/intertechawards, pg 656

Smith, Kayleigh, Frederick D Kagy Education Award of Excellence, 301 Brush Creek Rd, Warrendale, PA 15086-7529 *Tel:* 412-741-6860 *Toll Free Tel:* 800-910-4283 *Fax:* 412-741-2311 *E-mail:* printingind@comm.printing.org *Web Site:* www.printing.org, pg 658

Smith, Kayleigh, Robert F Reed Technology Medal, 301 Brush Creek Rd, Warrendale, PA 15086-7529 *Tel:* 412-741-6860 *Toll Free Tel:* 800-910-4283 *Fax:* 412-741-2311 *E-mail:* printingind@comm.printing.org *Web Site:* www.printing.org/reedaward, pg 684

Smith, Kayleigh, William D Schaeffer Environmental Award, 301 Brush Creek Rd, Warrendale, PA 15086-7529 *Tel:* 412-741-6860 *Toll Free Tel:* 800-910-4283 *Fax:* 412-741-2311 *E-mail:* printingind@comm.printing.org *Web Site:* www.printing.org/schaefferaward, pg 688

Smith, Kelly, Bywater Books, PO Box 3671, Ann Arbor, MI 48106-3671 *Tel:* 734-662-8815 *Web Site:* bywaterbooks.com, pg 46

Smith, Kelly, Paintbox Press, 275 Madison Ave, Suite 600, New York, NY 10016 *Tel:* 212-878-6610 *E-mail:* info@paintboxpress.com *Web Site:* www.paintboxpress.com, pg 172

Smith, Kristi, Thomas Nelson, 501 Nelson Place, Nashville, TN 37214 *Tel:* 615-889-9000 *Toll Free Tel:* 800-251-4000 *Fax:* 615-902-1548 *Web Site:* www.thomasnelson.com, pg 231

Smith, Lance, The Little Entrepreneur, c/o Harper Arrington Media, 18701 Grand River, Suite 105, Detroit, MI 48223 *Toll Free Tel:* 888-435-9234 *Fax:* 248-281-0373 *E-mail:* info@harperarringtonmedia.com *Web Site:* www.thelittlee.com, pg 136

Smith, Larry, Bottom Dog Press, 813 Seneca Ave, Huron, OH 44839 *Tel:* 419-433-3573 *Fax:* 419-616-3966 *Web Site:* smithdocs.net, pg 41

Smith, Laura, Bottom Dog Press, 813 Seneca Ave, Huron, OH 44839 *Tel:* 419-433-3573 *Fax:* 419-616-3966 *Web Site:* smithdocs.net, pg 41

Smith, Mary Dupuy, Teacher Created Resources Inc, 12621 Western Ave, Garden Grove, CA 92481 *Tel:* 714-891-7895 *Toll Free Tel:* 800-662-4321; 888-343-4335 *Toll Free Fax:* 800-525-1254 *E-mail:* custserv@teachercreated.com *Web Site:* www.teachercreated.com, pg 228

Smith, Mary P, Thorndike Press, 10 Water St, Suite 310, Waterville, ME 04901 *Toll Free Tel:* 800-223-1244 (ext 4, cust serv/orders) *Toll Free Fax:* 800-558-4676 (orders) *E-mail:* gale.printorders@cengage.com; international@cengage.com (cust orders outside US & CN) *Web Site:* www.gale.com/thorndike, pg 232

Smith, Meg Z, American Booksellers Association, 333 Westchester Ave, Suite S202, White Plains, NY 10604 *Tel:* 914-406-7500 *Toll Free Tel:* 800-637-0037 *Fax:* 914-410-6297 *E-mail:* info@bookweb.org *Web Site:* www.bookweb.org, pg 554

Smith, Michael, East West Discovery Press, PO Box 3585, Manhattan Beach, CA 90266 *Tel:* 310-545-3730 *Fax:* 310-545-3731 *E-mail:* info@eastwestdiscovery.com *Web Site:* www.eastwestdiscovery.com, pg 74

Smith, Monte, Eagle's View Publishing, 6756 North Fork Rd, Liberty, UT 84310 *Tel:* 801-393-4555; 801-745-0905 (edit) *Fax:* 801-745-0903 (edit); 801-393-4647 *E-mail:* sales@eaglefeathertrading.com *Web Site:* www.eaglefeathertrading.com, pg 74

Smith, P David, Western Reflections Publishing Co, 951B N Hwy 149, Lake City, CO 81235 *Tel:* 970-944-0110 *E-mail:* publisher@westernreflectionspublishing.com *Web Site:* www.westernreflectionspublishing.com, pg 254

Smith, Paige, Anchor Books, c/o Penguin Random House Inc, 1745 Broadway, New York, NY 10019 *Tel:* 212-572-2420 *E-mail:* vintageanchorpublicity@randomhouse.com *Web Site:* knopfdoubleday.com/imprint/anchor, pg 16

Smith, Paige, Vintage Books, c/o Penguin Random House Inc, 1745 Broadway, New York, NY 10019 *Tel:* 212-572-2420 *E-mail:* vintageanchorpublicity@randomhouse.com *Web Site:* knopfdoubleday.com/imprint/vintage, pg 251

Smith, Pat, Oolichan Books, PO Box 2278, Fernie, BC V0B 1M0, Canada *Tel:* 250-423-6113 *E-mail:* info@oolichan.com *Web Site:* www.oolichan.com, pg 465

Smith, Patricia A, Texas Library Association (TLA), 3355 Bee Cave Rd, Suite 401, Austin, TX 78746-6763 *Tel:* 512-328-1518 *Toll Free Tel:* 800-580-2852 *Fax:* 512-328-8852 *E-mail:* tla@txla.org *Web Site:* www.txla.org, pg 579

Smith, Peggy Boulos, Writers House, 21 W 26 St, New York, NY 10010 *Tel:* 212-685-2400 *Fax:* 212-685-1781 *Web Site:* www.writershouse.com, pg 542

Smith, Piper, Lindgren & Smith, 888C Eighth Ave, No 329, New York, NY 10019 *Tel:* 212-397-7330 *E-mail:* info@lindgrensmith.com *Web Site:* lindgrensmith.com, pg 543

Smith, R Bob III, Psychological Assessment Resources Inc (PAR), 16204 N Florida Ave, Lutz, FL 33549 *Tel:* 813-968-3003; 813-449-4065 *Toll Free Tel:* 800-331-8378 *Fax:* 813-968-2598; 813-961-2196 *Toll Free Fax:* 800-727-9329 *E-mail:* custsup@parinc.com *Web Site:* www4.parinc.com, pg 191

Smith, R T, The James Boatwright III Prize for Poetry, Washington & Lee University, Mattingly House, 204 W Washington St, Lexington, VA 24450-2116 *Tel:* 540-458-8908 *E-mail:* shenandoah@wlu.edu *Web Site:* shenandoahliterary.org, pg 633

Smith, R T, The Carter Prize For The Essay, Washington & Lee University, Mattingly House, 204 W Washington St, Lexington, VA 24450-2116 *Tel:* 540-458-8908 *E-mail:* shenandoah@wlu.edu *Web Site:* shenandoahliterary.org, pg 636

Smith, Robert Ellis, Privacy Journal, PO Box 28577, Providence, RI 02908 *Tel:* 401-274-7861 *E-mail:* orders@privacyjournal.net *Web Site:* www.privacyjournal.net, pg 189

Smith, Ronald, Oolichan Books, PO Box 2278, Fernie, BC V0B 1M0, Canada *Tel:* 250-423-6113 *E-mail:* info@oolichan.com *Web Site:* www.oolichan.com, pg 465

Smith, Ronnie L, Writer's Relief, Inc, 207 Hackensack St, Wood-Ridge, NJ 07075 *Tel:* 201-641-3003 *Toll Free Tel:* 866-405-3003 *Fax:* 201-641-1253 *E-mail:* info@wrelief.com *Web Site:* www.WritersRelief.com, pg 503

Smith, Sandy, Chronicle Books LLC, 680 Second St, San Francisco, CA 94107 *Tel:* 415-537-4200 *Toll Free Tel:* 800-759-0190 (cust serv) *Fax:* 415-537-4460 *Toll Free Fax:* 800-858-7787 (orders); 800-286-9471 (cust serv) *E-mail:* frontdesk@chroniclebooks.com *Web Site:* www.chroniclebooks.com, pg 55

Smith, Sarah, David Black Agency, 335 Adams St, 27th fl, Suite 2707, Brooklyn, NY 11201 *Tel:* 718-852-5500 *Fax:* 718-852-5539 *Web Site:* www.davidblackagency.com, pg 508

Smith, Sarah, The Experiment, 220 E 23 St, Suite 301, New York, NY 10010-4674 *Tel:* 212-889-1659 *E-mail:* info@theexperimentpublishing.com *Web Site:* www.theexperimentpublishing.com, pg 81

Smith, Scott, R S Means from The Gordian Group, 1099 Hingham St, Suite 201, Rockland, MA 02370 *Tel:* 781-422-5000 *Toll Free Tel:* 800-448-8182 *Fax:* 781-585-8814 *Toll Free Fax:* 800-632-6701 *Web Site:* www.rsmeans.com, pg 147

Smith, Stephen R, American Institute of Chemical Engineers (AIChE), 120 Wall St, 23rd fl, New York, NY 10005-4020 *Tel:* 203-702-7660 *Toll Free Tel:* 800-242-4363 *Fax:* 203-775-5177 *E-mail:* customerservice@aiche.org *Web Site:* www.aiche.org, pg 12

Smith, Steve, Steve Smith Autosports, PO Box 11631, Santa Ana, CA 92711-1631 *Tel:* 714-639-7681 *Fax:* 714-639-9741 *Web Site:* www.stevesmithautosports.com, pg 215

Smith, Steven Rathgeb, American Political Science Association, 1527 New Hampshire Ave NW, Washington, DC 20036-1203 *Tel:* 202-483-2512 *Fax:* 202-483-2657 *E-mail:* apsa@apsanet.org *Web Site:* www.apsanet.org, pg 555

Smith, Sue, Boydell & Brewer Inc, 668 Mount Hope Ave, Rochester, NY 14620-2731 *Tel:* 585-275-0419 *Fax:* 585-271-8778 *E-mail:* boydell@boydellusa.net *Web Site:* www.boydellandbrewer.com, pg 41

Smith, Sue, CBA: The Association for Christian Retail, 1365 Garden of the Gods Rd, Suite 105, Colorado Springs, CO 80907 *Tel:* 719-265-9895 *Toll Free Tel:* 800-252-1950 *Fax:* 719-272-3508 *E-mail:* info@cbaonline.org *Web Site:* cbaonline.org, pg 562

Smith, Sue, Eagle's View Publishing, 6756 North Fork Rd, Liberty, UT 84310 *Tel:* 801-393-4555; 801-745-0905 (edit) *Fax:* 801-745-0903 (edit); 801-393-4647 *E-mail:* sales@eaglefeathertrading.com *Web Site:* www.eaglefeathertrading.com, pg 74

Smith, Sue, University of Rochester Press, 668 Mount Hope Ave, Rochester, NY 14620-2731 *Tel:* 585-275-0419 *Fax:* 585-271-8778 *E-mail:* boydell@boydellusa.net *Web Site:* www.urpress.com, pg 245

Smith, Summer, Bloomsbury Publishing Inc, 1385 Broadway, 5th fl, New York, NY 10018 *Tel:* 212-419-5300 *E-mail:* marketingusa@bloomsbury.com; adultpublicityusa@bloomsbury.com; askacademic@bloomsbury.com *Web Site:* www.bloomsbury.com, pg 37

Smith, Suzanne, Doubleday/Nan A Talese, c/o Penguin Random House Inc, 1745 Broadway, New York, NY 10019 *Tel:* 212-751-2600 *Fax:* 212-572-2662 *E-mail:* ddaypub@randomhouse.com *Web Site:* knopfdoubleday.com, pg 72

Smith, Suzanne, Alfred A Knopf/Everyman's Library, c/o Penguin Random House Inc, 1745 Broadway, New York, NY 10019 *Tel:* 212-751-2600 *Toll Free Tel:* 800-638-6460 *Fax:* 212-572-2593 *Web Site:* www.knopfdoubleday.com, pg 127

Smith, Suzanne, Pantheon Books/Schocken Books, c/o Penguin Random House Inc, 1745 Broadway, New York, NY 10019 *Tel:* 212-751-2600 *Web Site:* knopfdoubleday.com/imprint/pantheon, pg 173

Smith, Valerie, Valerie Smith, Literary Agent, 1746 Rte 44-55, Modena, NY 12548 *Tel:* 845-883-5848, pg 536

Smith, William, The MIT Press, One Rogers St, Cambridge, MA 02142 *Tel:* 617-253-5255 *Toll Free Tel:* 800-207-8354 (orders) *Fax:* 617-258-6779; 617-577-1545 (orders) *Web Site:* mitpress.mit.edu, pg 151

Smith Mandell, Barbara, T S Eliot Prize for Poetry, 100 E Normal Ave, Kirksville, MO 63501-4221 *Tel:* 660-785-7336 *Toll Free Tel:* 800-916-6802 *Fax:* 660-785-4480 *E-mail:* tsup@truman.edu *Web Site:* tsup.truman.edu, pg 644

Smith-Mandell, Barbara, Truman State University Press, 100 E Normal Ave, Kirksville, MO 63501-4221 *Tel:* 660-785-7336 *Toll Free Tel:* 800-916-6802 *Fax:* 660-785-4480 *E-mail:* tsup@truman.edu *Web Site:* tsup.truman.edu, pg 236

Smithers, Westwood Jr, Corporation for Public Broadcasting (CPB), 401 Ninth St NW, Washington, DC 20004-2129 *Tel:* 202-879-9600 *Web Site:* www.cpb.org, pg 564

Smolin, Ronald, Trans-Atlantic Publications Inc, 311 Bainbridge St, Philadelphia, PA 19147 *Tel:* 215-925-5083 *Fax:* 215-925-1912 *Web Site:* www.transatlanticpub.com; www.businesstitles.com, pg 234

Smulski, Lauren, Harlequin Enterprises Ltd, 233 Broadway, Suite 1001, New York, NY 10279 *Tel:* 212-553-4200 *Fax:* 212-227-8969 *E-mail:* customerservice@harlequin.com *Web Site:* www.harlequin.com, pg 100

Smyk, Dorothy, New Harbinger Publications Inc, 5674 Shattuck Ave, Oakland, CA 94609 *Tel:* 510-652-0215 *Toll Free Tel:* 800-748-6273 (orders only) *Fax:* 510-652-5472 *Toll Free Fax:* 800-652-1613 *E-mail:* nhhelp@newharbinger.com; customerservice@newharbinger.com *Web Site:* www.newharbinger.com, pg 160

Smyth, Anne, National Geographic Books, 1145 17 St NW, Washington, DC 20036-4688 *Tel:* 202-857-7000 *Toll Free Tel:* 877-866-6486 *E-mail:* ngbooks@cdsfulfillment.com *Web Site:* www.nationalgeographic.com/books/; ngbooks.buysub.com, pg 158

Smyth, Sam, StarGroup International Inc, 1194 Old Dixie Hwy, Suite 201, West Palm Beach, FL 33413 *Tel:* 561-547-0667 *Fax:* 561-843-8530 *E-mail:* info@stargroupinternational.com *Web Site:* stargroupinternational.com, pg 221

Snavely, Sheri, W W Norton & Company Inc, 500 Fifth Ave, New York, NY 10110-0017 *Tel:* 212-354-5500 *Toll Free Tel:* 800-233-4830 (orders & cust serv) *Fax:* 212-869-0856 *Toll Free Fax:* 800-458-6515 *E-mail:* orders@wwnorton.com *Web Site:* books.wwnorton.com, pg 164

Snead, Beth, The Flannery O'Connor Award for Short Fiction, Main Library, 3rd fl, 320 S Jackson St, Athens, GA 30602 *Fax:* 706-542-2558 *Web Site:* www.ugapress.org, pg 675

Snell, Michael, Michael Snell Literary Agency, PO Box 1206, Truro, MA 02666-1206 *Tel:* 508-349-3718 *Web Site:* www.michaelsnellagency.com, pg 536

Snell, Patricia, Michael Snell Literary Agency, PO Box 1206, Truro, MA 02666-1206 *Tel:* 508-349-3718 *Web Site:* www.michaelsnellagency.com, pg 536

Snider, Rebecca, American Printing House for the Blind Inc, 1839 Frankfort Ave, Louisville, KY 40206 *Tel:* 502-895-2405 *Toll Free Tel:* 800-223-1839 (cust serv) *Fax:* 502-899-2274 *E-mail:* info@aph.org *Web Site:* www.aph.org; shop.aph.org, pg 14

Snider, Stephen, St Martin's Press, LLC, 175 Fifth Ave, New York, NY 10010 *Tel:* 646-307-5151 *Web Site:* us.macmillan.com/smp, pg 204

Snodgrass, Kristine, Anhinga Press, PO Box 3665, Tallahassee, FL 32315 *Tel:* 850-577-0745 *E-mail:* info@anhinga.org *Web Site:* www.anhingapress.org; www.facebook.com/anhingapress, pg 17

Snodgrass, Kristine, Robert Dana-Anhinga Prize for Poetry, PO Box 3665, Tallahassee, FL 32315 *Tel:* 850-577-0745 *E-mail:* info@anhinga.org *Web Site:* www.anhingapress.org, pg 640

Snodgrass, Robert, Ascend Books LLC, 12710 Pflumm Rd, Suite 200, Olathe, KS 66062 *Tel:* 913-948-5500 *Web Site:* www.ascendbooks.com, pg 22

Snouck-Hurgronje, Jan W, The Nautical & Aviation Publishing Co of America Inc, 845-A Lowcountry Blvd, Mount Pleasant, SC 29464 *Tel:* 843-856-0561 *Fax:* 843-856-3164 *Web Site:* www.nauticalandaviation.com, pg 159

Snow, Todd, Maren Green Publishing Inc, 5630 Memorial Ave N, Suite 3, Oak Park Heights, MN 55082 *Tel:* 651-439-4500 *Toll Free Tel:* 800-287-1512 *Fax:* 651-439-4532 *E-mail:* info@marengreen.com *Web Site:* www.marengreen.com, pg 141

Snowden, Elizabeth Regina, Alan Wofsy Fine Arts, 1109 Geary Blvd, San Francisco, CA 94109 *Tel:* 415-292-6500 *Toll Free Tel:* 800-660-6403 *Fax:* 415-292-6594 (off & cust serv); 510-251-1840 (acctg) *E-mail:* order@art-books.com (orders); editeur@earthlink.net (edit); beauxarts@earthlink.net (cust serv) *Web Site:* www.art-books.com, pg 258

Snyder, Becky, ABC-CLIO, 130 Cremona Dr, Santa Barbara, CA 93117 *Tel:* 805-968-1911 *Toll Free Tel:* 800-368-6868 *Fax:* 805-685-9685 *Toll Free Fax:* 866-270-3856 *E-mail:* customerservice@abc-clio.com *Web Site:* www.abc-clio.com, pg 2

Snyder, Jake, Dalkey Archive Press, University of Houston-Victoria, 3402 N Ben Wilson, Victoria, TX 77901 *E-mail:* contact@dalkeyarchive.com *Web Site:* www.dalkeyarchive.com, pg 66

Snyder, James, Celebrity Profiles Publishing, PO Box 344, Stony Brook, NY 11790 *Tel:* 631-862-8555 *Fax:* 631-862-0139 *E-mail:* celebpro4@aol.com *Web Site:* www.richardgrudens.com; richardgrudensblog.blogspot.com, pg 50

Snyder, Ruth L, InScribe Christian Writers' Fellowship (ICWF), PO Box 6201, Wetaskiwin, AB T9A 2E9, Canada *E-mail:* inscribe.mail@gmail.com *Web Site:* inscribe.org, pg 567

Snyder, Tanya, The Literary Press Group of Canada, 425 Adelaide St W, Suite 700, Toronto, ON M5V 3C1, Canada *Tel:* 416-483-1321 *Fax:* 416-483-2510 *Web Site:* www.lpg.ca, pg 568

So, Mark, Piano Press, 1425 Ocean Ave, Suite 5, Del Mar, CA 92014 *Tel:* 619-884-1401 *Fax:* 858-755-1104 *E-mail:* pianopress@pianopress.com *Web Site:* www.pianopress.com, pg 182

Soares, Manuela, Pace University Press, Dept of Publishing, Rm 805-E, 551 Fifth Ave, New York, NY 10176 *Tel:* 212-346-1417 *Fax:* 212-346-1165 *Web Site:* www.pace.edu/press, pg 172

Sobel, Nat, Sobel Weber Associates Inc, 146 E 19 St, New York, NY 10003-2404 *Tel:* 212-420-8585 *E-mail:* info@sobelweber.com *Web Site:* www.sobelweber.com, pg 536

Sobson, Lorraine, Council for Exceptional Children (CEC), 2900 Crystal Dr, Suite 100, Arlington, VA 22202 *Toll Free Tel:* 888-232-7733; 866-915-5000 (TTY) *E-mail:* service@cec.sped.org *Web Site:* www.cec.sped.org, pg 62

Sochacki, Beth, Sourcebooks Inc, 1935 Brookdale Rd, Suite 139, Naperville, IL 60563 *Tel:* 630-961-3900 *Toll Free Tel:* 800-432-7444 *Fax:* 630-961-2168 *E-mail:* info@sourcebooks.com; customersupport@sourcebooks.com *Web Site:* www.sourcebooks.com, pg 218

Sogah, Esi, Kensington Publishing Corp, 119 W 40 St, New York, NY 10018 *Tel:* 212-407-1500 *Toll Free Tel:* 800-221-2647 *Fax:* 212-935-0699 *Web Site:* www.kensingtonbooks.com, pg 125

Soha, Yaniv, Doubleday/Nan A Talese, c/o Penguin Random House Inc, 1745 Broadway, New York, NY 10019 *Tel:* 212-751-2600 *Fax:* 212-572-2662 *E-mail:* ddaypub@randomhouse.com *Web Site:* knopfdoubleday.com, pg 72

Sokol, Dr Mick, Drury University One-Act Play Competition, 900 N Benton Ave, Springfield, MO 65802-3344 *Tel:* 417-873-6821 *Web Site:* www.drury.edu, pg 642

Sokoloski, Robin, Playwrights Guild of Canada, 401 Richmond St W, Suite 350, Toronto, ON M5V 3A8, Canada *Tel:* 416-703-0201 *Fax:* 416-703-0059 *E-mail:* info@playwrightsguild.ca *Web Site:* www.playwrightsguild.ca, pg 575

Solheim, Tara, The Summer Experience, 1831 College Ave, Suite 324, Regina, SK S4P 4V5, Canada *Tel:* 306-537-7243 *E-mail:* sage.hill@sasktel.net *Web Site:* www.sagehillwriting.ca, pg 615

Soliz, Sarah, School for Advanced Research Press, 660 Garcia St, Santa Fe, NM 87505 *Tel:* 505-954-7206 *Toll Free Tel:* 888-390-6070 *E-mail:* press@sarsf.org *Web Site:* sarweb.org, pg 208

Solomon, Andrew, PEN American Center, 588 Broadway, Suite 303, New York, NY 10012 *Tel:* 212-334-1660 *Fax:* 212-334-2181 *E-mail:* info@pen.org *Web Site:* pen.org, pg 575

Solomon, Andrew, The PEN Award for Poetry in Translation, 588 Broadway, Suite 303, New York, NY 10012 *Tel:* 212-334-1660 *Fax:* 212-334-2181 *E-mail:* awards@pen.org *Web Site:* pen.org/press/grants-awards-database, pg 677

Solomon, Andrew, PEN/Phyllis Naylor Working Writer Fellowship, 588 Broadway, Suite 303, New York, NY 10012 *Tel:* 212-334-1660 *Fax:* 212-334-2181 *E-mail:* awards@pen.org *Web Site:* pen.org/press/grants-awards-database, pg 678

Solomon, Andrew, PEN/Ralph Manheim Medal for Translation, 588 Broadway, Suite 303, New York, NY 10012 *Tel:* 212-334-1660 *Fax:* 212-334-2181 *E-mail:* awards@pen.org *Web Site:* pen.org/press/grants-awards-database, pg 678

Solomon, Andrew, PEN/Robert Bingham Prize for Debut Fiction, 588 Broadway, Suite 303, New York, NY 10012 *Tel:* 212-334-1660 *Fax:* 212-334-2181 *E-mail:* awards@pen.org *Web Site:* pen.org/press/grants-awards-database, pg 678

Solomon, Andrew, PEN Translation Prize, 588 Broadway, Suite 303, New York, NY 10012 *Tel:* 212-334-1660 *Fax:* 212-334-2181 *E-mail:* awards@pen.org *Web Site:* pen.org/press/grants-awards-database, pg 679

Solomon, Andrew, PEN Writers' Emergency Fund, 588 Broadway, Suite 303, New York, NY 10012 *Tel:* 212-334-1660 *Fax:* 212-334-2181 *Web Site:* pen.org/press/grants-awards-database, pg 679

Solomon, Jeremy, Inkwater Press, 6750 SW Franklin St, Suite A, Portland, OR 97223 *Tel:* 503-968-6777 *Fax:* 503-968-6779 *E-mail:* orders@inkwaterbooks.com *Web Site:* www.inkwater.com, pg 117

Solorzano, Elsa, Global Training Center Inc, 550 S Mesa Hills Dr, Suite E4, El Paso, TX 79912 *Tel:* 915-534-7900 *Toll Free Tel:* 800-860-5030 *Fax:* 915-534-7903 *E-mail:* contact@globaltrainingcenter.com *Web Site:* www.globaltrainingcenter.com, pg 93

Solorzano, Sarah, Workers Compensation Research Institute, 955 Massachusetts Ave, Cambridge, MA 02139 *Tel:* 617-661-9274 *Fax:* 617-661-9284 *E-mail:* wcri@wcrinet.org *Web Site:* www.wcrinet.org, pg 258

Somberg, Andrea, Harvey Klinger Inc, 300 W 55 St, Suite 11V, New York, NY 10019 *Tel:* 212-581-7068 *Fax:* 212-315-3823 *E-mail:* queries@harveyklinger.com *Web Site:* www.harveyklinger.com, pg 524

Somers, Evelyn, William Peden Prize in Fiction, 357 McReynolds Hall, Columbia, MO 65211 *Tel:* 573-882-4474 *Toll Free Tel:* 800-949-2505 *Fax:* 573-884-4671 *E-mail:* question@moreview.com *Web Site:* www.missourireview.com, pg 677

Somers, Sandi, InScribe Christian Writers' Fellowship (ICWF), PO Box 6201, Wetaskiwin, AB T9A 2E9, Canada *E-mail:* inscribe.mail@gmail.com *Web Site:* inscribe.org, pg 567

Somerset, Gary, US Government Publishing Office (GPO), Superintendent of Documents, 732 N Capitol St NW, Washington, DC 20401 *Tel:* 202-512-1800 *Toll Free Tel:* 866-512-1800 (orders) *Fax:* 202-512-2104 *E-mail:* contactcenter@gpo.gov *Web Site:* www.gpo.gov; bookstore.gpo.gov (sales), pg 249

Sommaruga, Rossana, QA International (QAI), 329 De la Commune W, 3rd fl, Montreal, QC H2Y 2E1, Canada *Tel:* 514-499-3000 *Fax:* 514-499-3010 *Web Site:* www.qa-international.com, pg 468

Sommer, John, Advance Publishing Inc, 6950 Fulton St, Houston, TX 77022 *Tel:* 713-695-0600 *Toll Free Tel:* 800-917-9630 *Fax:* 713-695-8585 *E-mail:* info@advancepublishing.com *Web Site:* www.advancepublishing.com, pg 4

Sommers, Pam, Rizzoli International Publications Inc, 300 Park Ave S, 4th fl, New York, NY 10010-5399 *Tel:* 212-387-3400 *Toll Free Tel:* 800-522-6657 (orders only) *Fax:* 212-387-3535 *E-mail:* publicity@rizzoliusa.com *Web Site:* www.rizzoliusa.com, pg 199

Song, DongWon, Howard Morhaim Literary Agency Inc, 30 Pierrepont St, Brooklyn, NY 11201-3371 *Tel:* 718-222-8400 *Fax:* 718-222-5056 *E-mail:* info@morhaimliterary.com *Web Site:* www.morhaimliterary.com, pg 530

Sonin, Tara, Houghton Mifflin Harcourt Trade & Reference Division, 125 High St, Boston, MA 02110 *Tel:* 617-351-5000 *Toll Free Tel:* 800-225-3362 *Web Site:* www.hmhco.com, pg 111

Sonnenfeld, Mark, Marymark Press, 45-08 Old Millstone Dr, East Windsor, NJ 08520 *Tel:* 609-443-0646, pg 143

Soo Ping Chow, Frances, Perseus Books, 250 W 57 St, 15th fl, New York, NY 10107 *Tel:* 212-340-8100 *Toll Free Tel:* 800-343-4499 (cust serv) *Fax:* 212-340-8105 *Web Site:* www.perseusbooks.com, pg 181

Sorensen, Eric H, National Institute for Trial Advocacy (NITA), 1685 38 St, Suite 200, Boulder, CO 80301-2735 *Tel:* 720-890-4860 *Toll Free Tel:* 877-648-2632; 800-225-6482 (orders & returns) *Fax:* 720-890-7069 *E-mail:* info@nita.org *Web Site:* www.nita.org, pg 158

Sorensen, Nan, New England Book Awards, 1955 Massachusetts Ave, Cambridge, MA 02140 *Web Site:* www.newenglandbooks.org/bookawards, pg 672

Sorensen, Nan, New England Independent Booksellers Association Inc (NEIBA), 1955 Massachusetts Ave, Cambridge, MA 02140 *Web Site:* www.newenglandbooks.org, pg 573

Soroka-Dunn, Cynthia, Ariel Starr Productions Inc, PO Box 575, Woodstock, NY 12498 *Tel:* 201-784-9148 *E-mail:* arielstarrprod@aol.com *Web Site:* arielstarrprod.wix.com/arielstarr, pg 20

Sorsky, Richard, Linden Publishing Co Inc, 2006 S Mary St, Fresno, CA 93721 *Tel:* 559-233-6633 *Toll Free Tel:* 800-345-4447 (orders) *Fax:* 559-233-6933 *Web Site:* lindenpub.com, pg 134

Sottile, Matthew, Novalis Publishing, 10 Lower Spadina Ave, Suite 400, Toronto, ON M5V 2Z2, Canada *Tel:* 416-363-3303 *Toll Free Tel:* 877-702-7773 *Fax:* 416-363-9409 *Toll Free Fax:* 877-702-7775 *E-mail:* books@novalis.ca *Web Site:* www.novalis.ca, pg 465

Souksamrane, Santhana, Random House Children's Books, 1745 Broadway, 10th fl, New York, NY 10019 *Tel:* 212-782-9000 *Web Site:* www.randomhousekids.com, pg 194

Soule, Susan, Cambridge University Press, 1 Liberty Plaza, 20th fl, New York, NY 10006 *Tel:* 212-924-3900; 212-337-5000 *Fax:* 212-691-3239 *E-mail:* newyork@cambridge.org *Web Site:* www.cambridge.org/us, pg 46

Soules, Gordon, Gordon Soules Book Publishers Ltd, 2372 Haywood Ave, West Vancouver, BC V7V 1X7, Canada *Tel:* 604-922-6588 *Fax:* 604-922-6574 *E-mail:* books@gordonsoules.com *Web Site:* www.gordonsoules.com, pg 471

Soules, Mike, Corwin, a Sage Co, 2455 Teller Rd, Thousand Oaks, CA 91320 *Tel:* 805-499-9734 *Toll Free Tel:* 800-233-9936 *Fax:* 805-499-5323 *Toll Free Fax:* 800-417-2466 *E-mail:* info@corwin.com; order@corwin.com *Web Site:* www.corwin.com, pg 61

Soussan, Lionel, Les Editions Phidal Inc, 5740 Ferrier, Montreal, QC H4P 1M7, Canada *Tel:* 514-738-0202 *Toll Free Tel:* 800-738-7349 *Fax:* 514-738-5102 *E-mail:* info@phidal.com; customer@phidal.com (sales & export) *Web Site:* www.phidal.com, pg 455

South, Mary, Lowenstein Associates Inc, 115 E 23 St, 4th fl, New York, NY 10010 *Tel:* 212-206-1630 *E-mail:* assistant@bookhaven.com (queries, no attachments) *Web Site:* www.lowensteinassociates.com, pg 526

Southard, Lauren, Workman Publishing Co Inc, 225 Varick St, 9th fl, New York, NY 10014-4381 *Tel:* 212-254-5900 *Toll Free Tel:* 800-722-7202 *Fax:* 212-254-8098 *E-mail:* info@workman.com *Web Site:* www.workman.com, pg 259

Southern, Ed, Doris Betts Fiction Prize, PO Box 21591, Winston-Salem, NC 27120-1591 *Tel:* 336-293-8844 *E-mail:* mail@ncwriters.org; nclrsubmissions@ecu.edu *Web Site:* www.ncwriters.org, pg 631

Southern, Ed, North Carolina Writers' Network, PO Box 21591, Winston-Salem, NC 27120-1591 *Tel:* 336-293-8844 *Web Site:* www.ncwriters.org, pg 574

Southern, Ed, North Carolina Writers' Network Annual Fall Conference, PO Box 21591, Winston-Salem, NC 27120-1591 *Tel:* 336-293-8844 *E-mail:* mail@ncwriters.org *Web Site:* www.ncwriters.org, pg 613

Southern, Ed, Thomas Wolfe Fiction Prize, PO Box 21591, Winston-Salem, NC 27120-1591 *E-mail:* mail@ncwriters.org *Web Site:* www.ncwriters.org, pg 699

Sova, Kathy, Theatre Communications Group, 520 Eighth Ave, 24th fl, New York, NY 10018-4156 *Tel:* 212-609-5900 *Fax:* 212-609-5901 *E-mail:* tcg@tcg.org *Web Site:* www.tcg.org, pg 231

Sowards, Anne, Berkley Publishing Group, 375 Hudson St, New York, NY 10014 *Tel:* 212-366-2000 *Fax:* 212-366-2385 *Web Site:* www.penguin.com, pg 33

Sox, Aileen Andres, Pacific Press Publishing Association, 1350 N Kings Rd, Nampa, ID 83687-3193 *Tel:* 208-465-2500 *Toll Free Tel:* 800-447-7377 *Fax:* 208-465-2531 *Web Site:* www.pacificpress.com, pg 172

Spahr, Charles, The American Ceramic Society, 600 N Cleveland Ave, Suite 210, Westerville, OH 43082 *Tel:* 240-646-7054 *Toll Free Tel:* 866-721-3322 *Fax:* 240-396-5637 *E-mail:* customerservice@ceramics.org *Web Site:* ceramics.org, pg 10

Spahr, John F, Teton NewMedia Inc, 90 E Simpson, Suite 110, Jackson, WY 83001 *Tel:* 307-732-0028 *Toll Free Tel:* 877-306-9793 *Fax:* 307-734-0841 *E-mail:* sales@tetonnm.com *Web Site:* www.tetonnm.com, pg 230

Spahr, Welmoed, Apress Media LLC, 233 Spring St, New York, NY 10013 *Tel:* 212-460-1500 *E-mail:* editorial@apress.com *Web Site:* www.apress.com, pg 19

Spain, Molly, TCU Press, 3000 Sandage Ave, Fort Worth, TX 76109 *Tel:* 817-257-7822 *Toll Free Tel:* 800-826-8911 (orders) *Fax:* 817-257-5075 *Web Site:* www.prs.tcu.edu, pg 228

Spain, Tom, Simon & Schuster Audio, 1230 Avenue of the Americas, New York, NY 10020 *Web Site:* audio.simonandschuster.com, pg 213

Spangler, Stephen, DEStech Publications Inc, 439 N Duke St, Lancaster, PA 17602-4967 *Tel:* 717-290-1660 *Toll Free Tel:* 877-500-4337 *Fax:* 717-509-6100 *E-mail:* info@destechpub.com *Web Site:* www.destechpub.com, pg 69

Sparhawk, Bud, Science Fiction & Fantasy Writers of America Inc (SFWA), PO Box 3238, Enfield, CT 06083-3238 *E-mail:* office@sfwa.org *Web Site:* www.sfwa.org, pg 577

Sparhawk, Bud, SFWA Nebula Awards, PO Box 3238, Enfield, CT 06083-3238 *E-mail:* office@sfwa.org *Web Site:* www.sfwa.org, pg 688

Sparkes, Kathy, Dumbarton Oaks, 1703 32 St NW, Washington, DC 20007 *Tel:* 202-339-6400 *Fax:* 202-339-6401; 202-298-8407 *E-mail:* doaksbooks@doaks.org *Web Site:* www.doaks.org, pg 73

Sparks, Kerry, Levine|Greenberg|Rostan Literary Agency, 307 Seventh Ave, Suite 2407, New York, NY 10001 *Tel:* 212-337-0934 *Fax:* 212-337-0948 *Web Site:* lgrliterary.com, pg 525

Sparks, Lee Ann, Trinity University Press, One Trinity Place, San Antonio, TX 78212-7200 *Tel:* 210-999-8884 *Fax:* 210-999-8838 *E-mail:* books@trinity.edu *Web Site:* www.tupress.org, pg 235

Spear, Jody, Aaron-Spear, PO Box 42, Brooksville, ME 04617 *Tel:* 207-326-8764, pg 487

Spector, Jon, The Conference Board Inc, 845 Third Ave, New York, NY 10022-6600 *Tel:* 212-759-0900; 212-339-0345 (cust serv) *Fax:* 212-980-7014; 212-836-9740 (cust serv) *E-mail:* customer.service@conferenceboard.org; membership@conferenceboard.org *Web Site:* www.conference-board.org; www.linkedin.com/company/the-conference-board, pg 60

Speer, Mark, Simon & Schuster, Inc, 1230 Avenue of the Americas, New York, NY 10020 *Tel:* 212-698-7000 *Fax:* 212-698-7007 *E-mail:* firstname.lastname@simonandschuster.com *Web Site:* www.simonandschuster.com, pg 213

Spellman-Silverman, Erica, Trident Media Group LLC, 41 Madison Ave, 36th fl, New York, NY 10010 *Tel:* 212-333-1511 *E-mail:* info@tridentmediagroup.com; press@tridentmediagroup.com *Web Site:* www.tridentmediagroup.com, pg 540

Spence, Bill, Information Today, Inc, 143 Old Marlton Pike, Medford, NJ 08055-8750 *Tel:* 609-654-6266 *Toll Free Tel:* 800-300-9868 (cust serv) *Fax:* 609-654-4309 *E-mail:* custserv@infotoday.com *Web Site:* www.infotoday.com, pg 116

Spence, Craig, Federation of BC Writers, PO Box 16028, 617 Belmont St, New Westminster, BC V3M 6W6, Canada *E-mail:* info@bcwriters.ca *Web Site:* bcwriters.ca, pg 565

Spence, Heather, AFB Press, 1401 S Clark St, Suite 730, Arlington, VA 22202 *Tel:* 304-710-3043 *Toll Free Tel:* 800-232-3044 (orders) *Fax:* 917-210-3979 (orders) *E-mail:* afbpress@afb.net *Web Site:* www.afb.org, pg 5

Spence, Katie, Spry Publishing, 315 E Eisenhower Pkwy, Suite 2, Ann Arbor, MI 48108 *Tel:* 734-531-7600 *Toll Free Tel:* 877-722-2264 *E-mail:* info@sprypub.com *Web Site:* www.sprypub.com, pg 219

Spence, Marya, Janklow & Nesbit Associates, 285 Madison Ave, 21st fl, New York, NY 10017 *Tel:* 212-421-1700 *Fax:* 212-355-1403 *E-mail:* info@janklow.com *Web Site:* www.janklowandnesbit.com, pg 522

Spencer, Denise, American Fisheries Society, 425 Barlow Place, Suite 110, Bethesda, MD 20814-2144 *Tel:* 301-897-8616; 703-661-1570 (book orders) *Fax:* 301-897-8096; 703-996-1010 (book orders) *E-mail:* main@fisheries.org *Web Site:* www.fisheries.org, pg 11

Spencer, Elaine, The Knight Agency Inc, 570 East Ave, Madison, GA 30650 *E-mail:* submissions@knightagency.net *Web Site:* www.knightagency.net, pg 524

Spencer, Rowan, The Karpfinger Agency, 357 W 20 St, New York, NY 10011-3379 *Tel:* 212-691-2690 *Fax:* 212-691-7129 *E-mail:* info@karpfinger.com (no queries or submissions) *Web Site:* karpfinger.com, pg 523

Spengler-Jaffee, Pamela, HarperCollins General Books Group, 195 Broadway, New York, NY 10007 *Tel:* 212-207-7000 *Web Site:* www.harpercollins.com, pg 101

Sperling, Ehud C, Bear & Co Inc, One Park St, Rochester, VT 05767 *Tel:* 802-767-3174 *Toll Free Tel:* 800-932-3277 *Fax:* 802-767-3726 *E-mail:* customerservice@InnerTraditions.com *Web Site:* InnerTraditions.com, pg 31

Sperling, Ehud C, Inner Traditions International Ltd, One Park St, Rochester, VT 05767 *Tel:* 802-767-3174 *Toll Free Tel:* 800-246-8648 *Fax:* 802-767-3726 *E-mail:* customerservice@InnerTraditions.com *Web Site:* www.InnerTraditions.com, pg 117

Speyer, Anne, Random House Publishing Group, 1745 Broadway, New York, NY 10019 *Toll Free Tel:* 800-200-3552 *Web Site:* atrandom.com, pg 195

Spicer, Charles, St Martin's Press, LLC, 175 Fifth Ave, New York, NY 10010 *Tel:* 646-307-5151 *Web Site:* us.macmillan.com/smp, pg 204

Spicer, Ed, The Pennsylvania State University Press, University Support Bldg 1, Suite C, 820 N University Dr, University Park, PA 16802-1003 *Tel:* 814-865-1327 *Toll Free Tel:* 800-326-9180 *Fax:* 814-863-1408 *Toll Free Fax:* 877-778-2665 *E-mail:* info@psupress.org *Web Site:* www.psupress.org, pg 179

Spiegel, Cindy, Random House Publishing Group, 1745 Broadway, New York, NY 10019 *Toll Free Tel:* 800-200-3552 *Web Site:* atrandom.com, pg 195

Spiegel, Lauren, Touchstone, 1230 Avenue of the Americas, New York, NY 10020, pg 233

Spieler, Joseph, The Spieler Agency, 27 W 20 St, Suite 302, New York, NY 10011 *Tel:* 212-757-4439 *Fax:* 212-333-2019 *E-mail:* spieleragency@spieleragency.com, pg 537

Spieller, Lauren, TriadaUS Literary Agency, PO Box 561, Sewickley, PA 15143 *Tel:* 412-401-3376 *Web Site:* www.triadaus.com, pg 540

Spinella, Michael, William Holmes McGuffey Longevity Award, PO Box 367, Fountain City, WI 54629 *E-mail:* info@taaonline.net *Web Site:* www.taaonline.net/mcguffey-longevity-award, pg 666

Spinella, Michael, Most Promising New Textbook Award, PO Box 367, Fountain City, WI 54629 *E-mail:* info@taaonline.net *Web Site:* www.taaonline.net/promising-new-textbook-award, pg 669

Spinella, Michael, Ron Pynn Award, PO Box 367, Fountain City, WI 54629 *E-mail:* info@taaonline.net *Web Site:* www.taaonline.net/ron-pynn-award, pg 683

Spinella, Michael, TAA Council of Fellows, PO Box 367, Fountain City, WI 54629 *E-mail:* info@taaonline.net *Web Site:* www.taaonline.net/council-of-fellows, pg 693

Spinella, Michael, Textbook Excellence Award, PO Box 367, Fountain City, WI 54629 *E-mail:* info@taaonline.net *Web Site:* www.taaonline.net/textbook-excellence-award, pg 694

Spinelli, Melissa, Berghahn Books, 20 Jay St, Suite 512, Brooklyn, NY 11201 *Tel:* 212-233-6004 *Fax:* 212-233-6007 *E-mail:* info@berghahnbooks.com; salesus@berghahnbooks.com; editorial@journals.berghahnbooks.com *Web Site:* www.berghahnbooks.com, pg 33

Spinner, Dianna, The PRS Group Inc, 5800 Heritage Landing Dr, Suite E, East Syracuse, NY 13057-9358 *Tel:* 315-431-0511 *Fax:* 315-431-0200 *E-mail:* custserv@prsgroup.com *Web Site:* www.prsgroup.com, pg 190

Spittal, Robin, Writers' Federation of Nova Scotia, 1113 Marginal Rd, Halifax, NS B3H 4P7, Canada *Tel:* 902-423-8116 *Fax:* 902-422-0881 *E-mail:* contact@writers.ns.ca *Web Site:* writers.ns.ca, pg 581

Spitzer, Anne-Lise, Alfred A Knopf/Everyman's Library, c/o Penguin Random House Inc, 1745 Broadway, New York, NY 10019 *Tel:* 212-751-2600 *Toll Free Tel:* 800-638-6460 *Fax:* 212-572-2593 *Web Site:* www.knopfdoubleday.com, pg 127

Spitzer, Philip, Philip G Spitzer Literary Agency Inc, 50 Talmage Farm Lane, East Hampton, NY 11937 *Tel:* 631-329-3650 *Fax:* 631-329-3651 *Web Site:* www.spitzeragency.com, pg 537

Spivey, Jim, The Vendome Press, 244 Fifth Ave, Suite 2043, New York, NY 10001 *Tel:* 212-737-1857 *E-mail:* info@vendomepress.com *Web Site:* www.vendomepress.com, pg 250

Spizzirri, Linda, Spizzirri Publishing Inc, PO Box 9397, Rapid City, SD 57709-9397 *Tel:* 605-348-2749 *Toll Free Tel:* 800-325-9819 *Fax:* 605-348-6251 *Toll Free Fax:* 800-322-9819 *E-mail:* spizzpub@aol.com *Web Site:* www.spizzirri.com, pg 219

Spooner, Andrea, Little, Brown Books for Young Readers, 1290 Avenue of the Americas, New York, NY 10019 *Tel:* 212-364-1100 *Toll Free Tel:* 800-759-0190 (cust serv) *Web Site:* www.HachetteBookGroup.com, pg 136

Spraggins, Crystal, F A Davis Co, 1915 Arch St, Philadelphia, PA 19103 *Tel:* 215-568-2270; 215-440-3001 *Toll Free Tel:* 800-523-4049 *Fax:* 215-568-5065; 215-440-3016 *E-mail:* info@fadavis.com; orders@fadavis.com *Web Site:* www.fadavis.com, pg 68

Sprague, Peter, Piano Press, 1425 Ocean Ave, Suite 5, Del Mar, CA 92014 *Tel:* 619-884-1401 *Fax:* 858-755-1104 *E-mail:* pianopress@pianopress.com *Web Site:* www.pianopress.com, pg 182

Spratt-Williams, Tonya, Agatha Awards, PO Box 8007, Gaithersburg, MD 20898-8007 *E-mail:* malicedomesticpr@gmail.com *Web Site:* www.malicedomestic.org, pg 625

Spreeuw, Remy, City & Regional Magazine Association, 2512 Artesia Blvd, Suite 200, Redondo Beach, CA 90278 *Tel:* 310-379-8261 *Fax:* 310-379-8283 *E-mail:* admin@citymag.org *Web Site:* www.citymag.org, pg 563

Spretnjak, Dr Christine, SOM Publishing, 163 Moon Valley Rd, Windyville, MO 65783 *Tel:* 417-345-8411 *Fax:* 417-345-6668 *E-mail:* som@som.org; dreams@dreamschool.org *Web Site:* www.som.org; www.dreamschool.org, pg 217

Spring, Kathleen, Spring Time Writers Creative Writing & Journaling Workshop, PO Box 512, Lyons, CO 80540-0512 *Tel:* 303-823-0997 *E-mail:* writers@springtimewriters.com *Web Site:* www.springtimewriters.com, pg 615

Springer, Danielle, GP Putnam's Sons (Hardcover), 375 Hudson St, New York, NY 10014 *Tel:* 212-366-2000 *Fax:* 212-366-2643 *E-mail:* online@penguinputnam.com *Web Site:* www.penguin.com/publishers/gpputnamssons, pg 192

Springer, Rebecca, Houghton Mifflin Harcourt Trade & Reference Division, 125 High St, Boston, MA 02110 *Tel:* 617-351-5000 *Toll Free Tel:* 800-225-3362 *Web Site:* www.hmhco.com, pg 111

Springmeyer, Kathy, Farcountry Press, 2750 Broadwater Ave, Helena, MT 59602-9202 *Tel:* 406-422-1263 *Toll Free Tel:* 800-821-3874 (sales off) *Fax:* 406-443-5480 *E-mail:* books@farcountrypress.com; sales@farcountrypress.com *Web Site:* www.farcountrypress.com, pg 82

Sproles, Cindy, Lighthouse Publishing of the Carolinas, 2333 Barton Oaks Dr, Raleigh, NC 27614-7940 *Tel:* 919-562-8439 *E-mail:* lighthousepublishingcarolinas@gmail.com *Web Site:* lighthousepublishingofthecarolinas.com, pg 134

Srivastava, Rahul, Simon & Schuster, Inc, 1230 Avenue of the Americas, New York, NY 10020 *Tel:* 212-698-7000 *Fax:* 212-698-7007 *E-mail:* firstname.lastname@simonandschuster.com *Web Site:* www.simonandschuster.com, pg 213

St John, Asia, Elderberry Press Inc, 1393 Old Homestead Dr, Oakland, OR 97462-9690 *Tel:* 541-459-6043 *Web Site:* www.elderberrypress.com, pg 76

St John, Max, Ransom Note Press, 143 E Ridgewood Ave, Box 419, Ridgewood, NJ 07451 *Tel:* 201-835-2790 *E-mail:* editorial@ransomnotepress.com *Web Site:* www.ransomnotepress.com, pg 478

St John, Valerie, Elderberry Press Inc, 1393 Old Homestead Dr, Oakland, OR 97462-9690 *Tel:* 541-459-6043 *Web Site:* www.elderberrypress.com, pg 76

St Lifer, Evan, Scholastic Education, 557 Broadway, New York, NY 10012 *Tel:* 212-343-6100 *Fax:* 212-343-6189 *Web Site:* www.scholastic.com, pg 207

St Louis, Caroline, Editions de la Pleine Lune, 223 34 Ave, Lachine, QC H8T 1Z4, Canada *Tel:* 514-634-7954 *E-mail:* editpllune@videotron.ca *Web Site:* www.pleinelune.qc.ca, pg 453

St Pierre, Louisa, Bernstein & Andriulli Inc, 190 Bowery, 3rd fl, New York, NY 10012 *Tel:* 212-682-1490 *Fax:* 212-286-1890 *E-mail:* info@ba-reps.com *Web Site:* www.ba-reps.com, pg 543

St-Hilaire, France, Institute for Research on Public Policy (IRPP), 1470 Peel St, No 200, Montreal, QC H3A 1T1, Canada *Tel:* 514-985-2461 *Fax:* 514-985-2559 *E-mail:* irpp@irpp.org *Web Site:* irpp.org, pg 460

Stackler, Ed, Stackler Editorial Agency, 200 Woodland Ave, Summit, NJ 07901 *Tel:* 510-912-9187 *E-mail:* ed.stackler@gmail.com *Web Site:* www.fictioneditor.com, pg 502

Stackpole, Kerry C, Printing & Graphics Association MidAtlantic (PGAMA), 9685 Gerwig Lane, Suite A, Columbia, MD 21046-1520 *Tel:* 410-319-0900 *Toll Free Tel:* 877-319-0906 *Fax:* 410-319-0905 *E-mail:* info@pgama.com *Web Site:* www.pgama.com, pg 576

Staff, Bruce, Blue Poppy Press, 1990 57 Ct, Unit A, Boulder, CO 80301 *Tel:* 303-447-8372 *Toll Free Tel:* 800-487-9296 *Fax:* 303-245-8362 *E-mail:* info@bluepoppy.com *Web Site:* www.bluepoppy.com, pg 38

Stafford, David, McGraw-Hill Education, 2 Penn Plaza, New York, NY 10121-2298 *Tel:* 212-904-2000 *E-mail:* customer.service@mheducation.com; international_cs@mheducation.com *Web Site:* www.mheducation.com, pg 145

Staib, Erich, Duke University Press, 905 W Main St, Suite 18B, Durham, NC 27701 *Tel:* 919-688-5134 *Toll Free Tel:* 888-651-0122 (US) *Fax:* 919-688-2615 *Toll Free Fax:* 888-651-0124 *E-mail:* orders@dukeupress.edu *Web Site:* www.dukeupress.edu, pg 73

Stakes, Robert, Texas Western Press, c/o University of Texas at El Paso, 500 W University Ave, El Paso, TX 79968-0633 *Tel:* 915-747-5688 *Toll Free Tel:* 800-488-3798 (orders only) *Fax:* 915-747-7515 *E-mail:* twpress@utep.edu *Web Site:* twp.utep.edu, pg 230

Stakes, Robert L, Carl Hertzog Award for Excellence in Book Design, c/o Dir of the Library, University of Texas at El Paso, El Paso, TX 79968-0582 *Tel:* 915-747-5683 *Fax:* 915-747-5345 *Web Site:* libraryweb.utep.edu/about/hertzog_call.php, pg 652

Stamas, Margot, Penguin Group USA, A Penguin Random House Company, 375 Hudson St, New York, NY 10014 *Tel:* 212-366-2000 *Toll Free Tel:* 800-847-5515 (inside sales); 800-631-8571 (cust serv) *Fax:* 212-366-2666; 607-775-4829 (inside sales) *E-mail:* online@us.penguingroup.com *Web Site:* www.penguin.com, pg 177

Stamathis, George S, Brookes Publishing Co Inc, PO Box 10624, Baltimore, MD 21285-0624 *Tel:* 410-337-9580 (outside US & CN) *Toll Free Tel:* 800-638-3775 (US & CN) *Fax:* 410-337-8539 *E-mail:* custserv@brookespublishing.com *Web Site:* www.brookespublishing.com, pg 44

Stamatkin, Susan, Institute of Environmental Sciences & Technology - IEST, 2340 S Arlington Heights Rd, Suite 620, Arlington Heights, IL 60005-4510 *Tel:* 847-981-0100 *Fax:* 847-981-4130 *E-mail:* information@iest.org *Web Site:* www.iest.org, pg 118

Stambaugh, Doug, Simon & Schuster, Inc, 1230 Avenue of the Americas, New York, NY 10020 *Tel:* 212-698-7000 *Fax:* 212-698-7007 *E-mail:* firstname.lastname@simonandschuster.com *Web Site:* www.simonandschuster.com, pg 213

Stamper-Halpin, Phillip, Penguin Random House Inc, 1745 Broadway, New York, NY 10019 *Tel:* 212-782-9000 *Toll Free Tel:* 800-726-0600 *Web Site:* www.penguinrandomhouse.com, pg 178

Stampfel, Peter, DAW Books Inc, 375 Hudson St, New York, NY 10014 *Tel:* 212-366-2096 *Fax:* 212-366-2090 *E-mail:* daw@penguinrandomhouse.com *Web Site:* www.dawbooks.com; www.penguin.com; www.penguinrandomhouse.com, pg 68

Stanczyk, Ms Soki, New City Press, 202 Comforter Blvd, Hyde Park, NY 12538 *Tel:* 845-229-0335 *Toll Free Tel:* 800-462-5980 (orders only) *Fax:* 845-229-0351 *E-mail:* info@newcitypress.com *Web Site:* www.newcitypress.com, pg 160

Stanford, Elisa, Edit Resource LLC, 19265 Lincoln Green Lane, Monument, CO 80132 *Tel:* 719-290-0757 *E-mail:* info@editresource.com *Web Site:* www.editresource.com, pg 493

Stanford, Eric, Edit Resource LLC, 19265 Lincoln Green Lane, Monument, CO 80132 *Tel:* 719-290-0757 *E-mail:* info@editresource.com *Web Site:* www.editresource.com, pg 493

Stanley, Erika, Manhattanville College Master of Fine Arts in Creative Writing Program, 2900 Purchase St, Purchase, NY 10577 *Tel:* 914-323-5239 *Fax:* 914-323-3122 *Web Site:* www.mville.edu/writing, pg 620

Stanley, James, Fine Arts Work Center in Provincetown, 24 Pearl St, Provincetown, MA 02657 *Tel:* 508-487-9960 *Fax:* 508-487-8873 *E-mail:* general@fawc.org *Web Site:* www.fawc.org, pg 646

Stanley, Lindsay, Cengage Learning, 20 Channel Center St, Boston, MA 02210 *Tel:* 617-289-7700 *Toll Free Tel:* 800-354-9706 *Fax:* 617-289-7844 *Toll Free Fax:* 800-487-8488 *E-mail:* esales@cengage.com *Web Site:* www.cengage.com, pg 50

Stansfield, Gwyneth, Plume, 375 Hudson St, New York, NY 10014 *Tel:* 212-366-2000 *Fax:* 212-243-6002 *Web Site:* www.penguin.com/publishers/plume, pg 184

Stanton, William, The H W Wilson Foundation, 420 Lexington Ave, Suite 2450, New York, NY 10170 *Tel:* 212-972-6490 *Web Site:* www.thwwf.org, pg 583

Stanulis, Roxanne, Delaware Division of the Arts Individual Artist Fellowships, Carvel State Off Bldg, 4th fl, 820 N French St, Wilmington, DE 19801 *Tel:* 302-577-8278 *Fax:* 302-577-6561 *E-mail:* delarts@state.de.us *Web Site:* www.artsdel.org, pg 640

Stanwood, Karen G, SLACK® Incorporated, A Wyanoke Group Company, 6900 Grove Rd, Thorofare, NJ 08086-9447 *Tel:* 856-848-1000 *Toll Free Tel:* 800-257-8290 *Fax:* 856-848-6091 *E-mail:* sales@slackinc.com; editor@slackinc.com; customerservice@slackinc.com *Web Site:* www.healio.com/books, pg 215

Staples, Debra, SynergEbooks, 948 New Hwy 7, Columbia, TN 38401 *Tel:* 931-548-2494 *E-mail:* synergebooks@aol.com *Web Site:* www.synergebooks.com, pg 226

Stapleton, Janet, Beacon Hill Press of Kansas City, PO Box 419527, Kansas City, MO 64141 *Tel:* 816-931-1900 *Toll Free Tel:* 800-877-0700 (cust serv) *Fax:* 816-753-4071 *Web Site:* www.nph.com, pg 30

Stapleton, Victoria, Little, Brown Books for Young Readers, 1290 Avenue of the Americas, New York, NY 10019 *Tel:* 212-364-1100 *Toll Free Tel:* 800-759-0190 (cust serv) *Web Site:* www.HachetteBookGroup.com, pg 136

Star, Alex, Farrar, Straus & Giroux, LLC, 18 W 18 St, New York, NY 10011 *Tel:* 212-741-6900 *E-mail:* fsg.publicity@fsgbooks.com *Web Site:* us.macmillan.com/fsg.aspx, pg 83

Star, Brenda, StarGroup International Inc, 1194 Old Dixie Hwy, Suite 201, West Palm Beach, FL 33413 *Tel:* 561-547-0667 *Fax:* 561-843-8530 *E-mail:* info@stargroupinternational.com *Web Site:* stargroupinternational.com, pg 221

Stark, Kate, Riverhead Books, 375 Hudson St, New York, NY 10014 *Tel:* 212-366-2000 *Web Site:* www.penguin.com/publishers/riverhead, pg 199

Stark, Kate, Viking, 375 Hudson St, New York, NY 10014 *Tel:* 212-366-2000 *Fax:* 212-243-6002 *Web Site:* www.penguin.com/publishers/vikingbooks, pg 250

Stark, Rachel, Sky Pony Press, 307 W 36 St, 11th fl, New York, NY 10018 *Tel:* 212-643-6816 *Fax:* 212-643-6819 *E-mail:* skypony@skyhorsepublishing.com; info@skyhorsepublishing.com; submissions@skyhorsepublishing.com *Web Site:* www.skyponypress.com, pg 214

Starke, Alexis, History Publishing Co LLC, PO Box 700, Palisades, NY 10964 *Tel:* 845-359-1765 *Fax:* 845-818-3730 (sales) *E-mail:* info@historypublishingco.com *Web Site:* www.historypublishingco.com, pg 108

Starkman, Stanley, Chestnut Publishing Group Inc, 44 Stubbs Dr, Suite 207, Toronto, ON M2L 2R3, Canada *Tel:* 416-224-5824 *Fax:* 416-224-0595 *Web Site:* www.chestnutpublishing.com, pg 450

Starmack, Sophia, Fine Arts Work Center in Provincetown, 24 Pearl St, Provincetown, MA 02657 *Tel:* 508-487-9960 *Fax:* 508-487-8873 *E-mail:* general@fawc.org *Web Site:* www.fawc.org, pg 646

Starmer, Cate, Fodor's Travel Publications, 1745 Broadway, 15th fl, New York, NY 10019 *Toll Free Tel:* 800-733-3000 *E-mail:* publicity@fodors.com; editors@fodors.com *Web Site:* www.fodors.com, pg 86

Starnino, Carmine, Vehicule Press, PO Box 42094, CP Roy, Montreal, QC H2W-2T3, Canada *Tel:* 514-844-6073 *Fax:* 514-844-7543 *E-mail:* vp@vehiculepress.com; admin@vehiculepress.com *Web Site:* www.vehiculepress.com, pg 475

Starowitz, Todd, Tyndale House Publishers Inc, 351 Executive Dr, Carol Stream, IL 60188 *Tel:* 630-668-8300 *Toll Free Tel:* 800-323-9400 *Toll Free Fax:* 800-684-0247 *Web Site:* www.tyndale.com, pg 237

Starr, Brent, Indiana University Press, Herman B Wells Library 350, 1320 E Tenth St, Bloomington, IN 47405-3907 *Tel:* 812-855-8817 *Toll Free Tel:* 800-842-6796 (orders only) *Fax:* 812-855-7931; 812-855-8507 *E-mail:* iupress@indiana.edu; iuporder@indiana.edu (orders) *Web Site:* www.iupress.indiana.edu, pg 116

Starr, Josh, Phi Delta Kappa International®, 1525 Wilson Blvd, Suite 705, Arlington, VA 22209 *Tel:* 812-339-1156 *Toll Free Tel:* 800-766-1156 *Fax:* 812-339-0018 *E-mail:* memberservices@pdkintl.org *Web Site:* www.pdkintl.org, pg 182

Starr, Lara, Chronicle Books LLC, 680 Second St, San Francisco, CA 94107 *Tel:* 415-537-4200 *Toll Free Tel:* 800-759-0190 (cust serv) *Fax:* 415-537-4460 *Toll Free Fax:* 800-858-7787 (orders); 800-286-9471 (cust serv) *E-mail:* frontdesk@chroniclebooks.com *Web Site:* www.chroniclebooks.com, pg 55

Starrett, Margaret, Branden Books, PO Box 812094, Wellesley, MA 02482-0013 *Tel:* 781-235-3347 *E-mail:* branden@brandenbooks.com *Web Site:* www.brandenbooks.com, pg 42

Staton, Cecil P Jr, Smyth & Helwys Publishing Inc, 6316 Peake Rd, Macon, GA 31210-3960 *Tel:* 478-757-0564 *Toll Free Tel:* 800-747-3016 (orders only); 800-568-1248 (orders only) *Fax:* 478-757-1305 *E-mail:* information@helwys.com *Web Site:* www.helwys.com, pg 215

Staveteig, Rev Timothy, The Pilgrim Press/United Church Press, 700 Prospect Ave, Cleveland, OH 44115-1100 *Tel:* 216-736-2100 *Toll Free Tel:* 800-537-3394 (orders) *Fax:* 216-736-2207 (orders) *E-mail:* permissions@thepilgrimpress.com; store@ucc.org *Web Site:* www.thepilgrimpress.com; www.uccresources.com, pg 183

Stebbins, Dr Chad, International Society of Weekly Newspaper Editors, Missouri Southern State University, 3950 E Newman Rd, Joplin, MO 64801-1595 *Tel:* 417-625-9736 *Fax:* 417-659-4445 *Web Site:* www.iswne.org, pg 567

Stech, Marko R, Canadian Institute of Ukrainian Studies Press, University of Toronto, 256 McCaul St, Rm 308, Toronto, ON M5T 1W5, Canada *Tel:* 416-946-7326 *Fax:* 416-978-2672 *E-mail:* cius@ualberta.ca *Web Site:* www.ciuspress.com, pg 449

Stecher, Leah, Perseus Books, 250 W 57 St, 15th fl, New York, NY 10107 *Tel:* 212-340-8100 *Toll Free Tel:* 800-343-4499 (cust serv) *Fax:* 212-340-8105 *Web Site:* www.perseusbooks.com, pg 181

Stecopoulos, Harilaos, The Iowa Review Awards, 308 EPB, Iowa City, IA 52242-1408 *E-mail:* iowa-review@uiowa.edu *Web Site:* www.iowareview.org, pg 656

Steele, Alex, Gotham Writers' Workshop, 555 Eighth Ave, Suite 1402, New York, NY 10018-4358 *Tel:* 212-974-8377 *E-mail:* contact@gothamwriters.com *Web Site:* www.gothamwriters.com, pg 611

Steele, David Ramsay, Open Court, 70 E Lake St, Suite 800, Chicago, IL 60601 *Tel:* 312-701-1720 *Toll Free Tel:* 800-815-2280 *Fax:* 312-701-1728 *E-mail:* opencourt@cricketmedia.com *Web Site:* www.opencourtbooks.com, pg 168

Steele, Samantha, Chronicle Books LLC, 680 Second St, San Francisco, CA 94107 *Tel:* 415-537-4200 *Toll Free Tel:* 800-759-0190 (cust serv) *Fax:* 415-537-4460 *Toll Free Fax:* 800-858-7787 (orders); 800-286-9471 (cust serv) *E-mail:* frontdesk@chroniclebooks.com *Web Site:* www.chroniclebooks.com, pg 55

Steelman, Cheryl, Charles C Thomas Publisher Ltd, 2600 S First St, Springfield, IL 62704 *Tel:* 217-789-8980 *Toll Free Tel:* 800-258-8980 *Fax:* 217-789-9130 *E-mail:* books@ccthomas.com *Web Site:* www.ccthomas.com, pg 231

Steffen, Zach, North Country Books Inc, 220 Lafayette St, Utica, NY 13502-4312 *Tel:* 315-735-4877 *Toll Free Tel:* 800-342-7409 (orders) *Fax:* 315-738-4342 *E-mail:* ncbooks@verizon.net *Web Site:* www.northcountrybooks.com, pg 163

Stehlik, Liate, HarperCollins General Books Group, 195 Broadway, New York, NY 10007 *Tel:* 212-207-7000 *Web Site:* www.harpercollins.com, pg 101

Steiker, Valerie, Scribner, 1230 Avenue of the Americas, New York, NY 10020, pg 209

Stein, Anna, ICM Partners, 65 E 55 St, New York, NY 10022 *Tel:* 212-556-5600 *Web Site:* www.icmtalent.com, pg 521

Stein, Anne Marie, Massachusetts College of Art & Design Writing Children's Literature, 621 Huntington Ave, Boston, MA 02115 *Tel:* 617-879-7200 *Fax:* 617-879-7171 *E-mail:* ce@massart.edu *Web Site:* www.massart.edu/ce, pg 620

Stein, Jonathan, Open Road Publishing, 32 Turkey Lane, Cold Spring Harbor, NY 11724 *Tel:* 631-692-7172 *E-mail:* jopenroad@aol.com *Web Site:* www.openroadguides.com, pg 168

Stein, Judith, The Author's Friend, 548 Ocean Blvd, No 12, Long Branch, NJ 07740 *Tel:* 732-571-8051, pg 489

Stein, Liz, Harlequin Enterprises Ltd, 233 Broadway, Suite 1001, New York, NY 10279 *Tel:* 212-553-4200 *Fax:* 212-227-8969 *E-mail:* customerservice@harlequin.com *Web Site:* www.harlequin.com, pg 100

Stein, Lonny R, Barron's Educational Series Inc, 250 Wireless Blvd, Hauppauge, NY 11788 *Tel:* 631-434-3311 *Toll Free Tel:* 800-645-3476 *Fax:* 631-434-3723 *E-mail:* barrons@barronseduc.com *Web Site:* www.barronseduc.com, pg 30

Stein, Lorin, Farrar, Straus & Giroux, LLC, 18 W 18 St, New York, NY 10011 *Tel:* 212-741-6900 *E-mail:* fsg.publicity@fsgbooks.com *Web Site:* us.macmillan.com/fsg.aspx, pg 83

Stein, Sarah, Penguin Books, 375 Hudson St, New York, NY 10014 *Tel:* 212-366-2000 *E-mail:* penguinpublicity@us.penguingroup.com *Web Site:* www.penguinclassics.com; www.penguin.com, pg 177

Steinberg, Andrew, Modern Publishing, 6198 Butler Pike, Suite 200, Blue Bell, PA 19422 *Tel:* 215-643-6385 *Fax:* 215-628-3571 *Web Site:* www.modernpublishing.com, pg 152

Steinberg, Benjamin, HarperCollins General Books Group, 195 Broadway, New York, NY 10007 *Tel:* 212-207-7000 *Web Site:* www.harpercollins.com, pg 101

Steinberg, Michael, Michael Steinberg Literary Agent, PO Box 274, Glencoe, IL 60022-0274 *Tel:* 847-626-1000 *Fax:* 847-626-1002 *E-mail:* michael14steinberg@comcast.net, pg 537

Steinbock, Steven, International Association of Crime Writers Inc, North American Branch, 243 Fifth Ave, Suite 537, New York, NY 10016 *Tel:* 212-243-8966 *Fax:* 815-361-1477 *E-mail:* info@crimewritersna.org *Web Site:* www.crimewritersna.org, pg 567

Steinecke, Anke, Penguin Random House Inc, 1745 Broadway, New York, NY 10019 *Tel:* 212-782-9000 *Toll Free Tel:* 800-726-0600 *Web Site:* www.penguinrandomhouse.com, pg 178

Steiner, Beth, Chronicle Books LLC, 680 Second St, San Francisco, CA 94107 *Tel:* 415-537-4200 *Toll Free Tel:* 800-759-0190 (cust serv) *Fax:* 415-537-4460 *Toll Free Fax:* 800-858-7787 (orders); 800-286-9471 (cust serv) *E-mail:* frontdesk@chroniclebooks.com *Web Site:* www.chroniclebooks.com, pg 55

Steiner, Karen, Research Press, 2612 N Mattis Ave, Champaign, IL 61822 *Tel:* 217-352-3273 *Toll Free Tel:* 800-519-2707 *Fax:* 217-352-1221 *E-mail:* rp@researchpress.com; orders@researchpress.com *Web Site:* www.researchpress.com, pg 198

Steinert, Frank, Penguin Random House Inc, 1745 Broadway, New York, NY 10019 *Tel:* 212-782-9000 *Toll Free Tel:* 800-726-0600 *Web Site:* www.penguinrandomhouse.com, pg 178

Steinhardt, David J, IDEAlliance®, 1800 Diagonal Rd, Suite 320, Alexandria, VA 22314-2862 *Tel:* 703-837-1070 *Fax:* 703-837-1072 *E-mail:* registrar@idealliance.org *Web Site:* www.idealliance.org, pg 567

Steinmetz, Kay, Syracuse University Press, 621 Skytop Rd, Suite 110, Syracuse, NY 13244-5290 *Tel:* 315-443-5534 *Toll Free Tel:* 800-365-8929 (cust serv) *Fax:* 315-443-5545 *E-mail:* supress@syr.edu *Web Site:* syracuseuniversitypress.syr.edu, pg 226

Stelzig, Christopher, Entomological Society of America, 3 Park Place, Suite 307, Annapolis, MD 21401-3722 *Tel:* 301-731-4535 *Fax:* 301-731-4538 *E-mail:* esa@entsoc.org *Web Site:* www.entsoc.org, pg 79

Stender, Dr Uwe, TriadaUS Literary Agency, PO Box 561, Sewickley, PA 15143 *Tel:* 412-401-3376 *Web Site:* www.triadaus.com, pg 540

Stenning, Blake, Marfield Prize, 2017 "I" St NW, Washington, DC 20006-1804 *E-mail:* award@artsclubofwashington.org *Web Site:* artsclubofwashington.org, pg 665

Stephanides, Myrsini, Carol Mann Agency, 55 Fifth Ave, New York, NY 10003 *Tel:* 212-206-5635 *Fax:* 212-675-4809 *E-mail:* submissions@carolmannagency.com *Web Site:* www.carolmannagency.com, pg 527

Stephens, Jenny, Sterling Lord Literistic Inc, 115 Broadway, Suite 1602, New York, NY 10006 *Tel:* 212-780-6050 *Fax:* 212-780-6095 *E-mail:* info@sll.com *Web Site:* www.sll.com, pg 537

Stephens, Michael, Manning Publications Co, PO Box 761, Shelter Island, NY 11964 *Tel:* 203-626-1510 *E-mail:* sales@manning.com; support@manning.com (cust serv) *Web Site:* www.manning.com, pg 141

Stephenson, Dave, National Notary Association (NNA), 9350 De Soto Ave, Chatsworth, CA 91311-4926 *Tel:* 818-739-4000 *Toll Free Tel:* 800-876-6827 *Toll Free Fax:* 800-833-1211 *E-mail:* nna@nationalnotary.org *Web Site:* www.nationalnotary.org, pg 159

Sterling, Jeremy, Spry Publishing, 315 E Eisenhower Pkwy, Suite 2, Ann Arbor, MI 48108 *Tel:* 734-531-7600 *Toll Free Tel:* 877-722-2264 *E-mail:* info@sprypub.com *Web Site:* www.sprypub.com, pg 219

Sterling, John, Macmillan, 175 Fifth Ave, New York, NY 10010 *Tel:* 646-307-5151 *E-mail:* press.inquiries@macmillan.com *Web Site:* www.macmillan.com, pg 140

Stern, Amy, Sheldon Fogelman Agency Inc, 420 E 72 St, New York, NY 10021 *Tel:* 212-532-7250 *Fax:* 212-685-8939 *E-mail:* info@sheldonfogelmanagency.com *Web Site:* sheldonfogelmanagency.com, pg 517

Stern, Chris, The Society of Southwestern Authors (SSA), PO Box 30355, Tucson, AZ 85751-0355 *E-mail:* info@ssa-az.org *Web Site:* www.ssa-az.org, pg 579

Stern, Walter B, Prayer Book Press Inc, 221 E 48 St, New York, NY 10017 *Tel:* 212-319-6666 *Fax:* 212-688-8597 *E-mail:* mediajudaica@aol.com, pg 186

Sternberg, Joan, Practising Law Institute, 1177 Avenue of the Americas, New York, NY 10036 *Tel:* 212-824-5700 *Toll Free Tel:* 800-260-4PLI (260-4754, cust serv) *Fax:* 212-265-4742 (intl) *Toll Free Fax:* 800-321-0093 (local) *E-mail:* info@pli.edu (cust serv) *Web Site:* www.pli.edu, pg 186

Sternlicht, Moshe, Moznaim Publishing Corp, 4304 12 Ave, Brooklyn, NY 11219 *Tel:* 718-438-7680 *Fax:* 718-438-1305 *E-mail:* sales@moznaim.com *Web Site:* www.moznaim.com, pg 155

Stets, Mary Anne, Mystic Seaport Museum Inc, PO Box 6000, Mystic, CT 06355-0990 *Tel:* 860-572-5302; 860-572-0711 (visitor serv) *Toll Free Tel:* 800 248-1066 (wholesale orders only); 800-331-2665 (retail orders only) *Fax:* 860-572-5321 *E-mail:* info@mysticseaport.org *Web Site:* www.mysticseaport.org, pg 156

Stetz, Jeffrey, Transaction Publishers Inc, 10 Corporate Place S, Suite 102, Piscataway, NJ 08854 *Tel:* 732-445-2280; 703-661-1589 (orders) *Toll Free Tel:* 888-999-6778 (dist ctr) *Fax:* 732-445-3138 *E-mail:* trans@transactionpub.com; orders@transactionpub.com *Web Site:* www.transactionpub.com, pg 234

Stetzinger, Nancy, Educational Book & Media Association (EBMA), 11 Main St, Suite D, Warrenton, VA 20186 *Tel:* 540-318-7770 *Fax:* 202-962-3939 *E-mail:* info@edupaperback.org *Web Site:* www.edupaperback.org, pg 565

Steve, Betsy, New York University Press, 838 Broadway, 3rd fl, New York, NY 10003-4812 *Tel:* 212-998-2575 (edit) *Toll Free Tel:* 800-996-6987 (orders) *Fax:* 212-995-4798 (orders) *E-mail:* information@nyupress.org; nyupressinfo@nyu.edu; orders@nyupress.org *Web Site:* www.nyupress.org, pg 162

Stevens, Drew, The Feminist Press at The City University of New York, 365 Fifth Ave, Suite 5406, New York, NY 10016 *Tel:* 212-817-7915 *Fax:* 212-817-1593 *E-mail:* info@feministpress.org *Web Site:* www.feministpress.org, pg 83

Stevens, Iisha, Other Press, 267 Fifth Ave, 6th fl, New York, NY 10016 *Tel:* 212-414-0054 *Toll Free Tel:* 877-843-6843 *Fax:* 212-414-0939 *E-mail:* editor@otherpress.com; marketing@otherpress.com; publicity@otherpress.com *Web Site:* www.otherpress.com, pg 170

Stevens, Jacob, Verso, 20 Jay St, Suite 1010, Brooklyn, NY 11201 *Tel:* 718-246-8160 *Fax:* 718-246-8165 *E-mail:* verso@versobooks.com *Web Site:* www.versobooks.com, pg 250

Stevens, Martin, Forum Publishing Co, 383 E Main St, Centerport, NY 11721 *Tel:* 631-754-5000 *Toll Free Tel:* 800-635-7654 *Fax:* 631-754-0630 *E-mail:* forumpublishing@aol.com *Web Site:* www.forum123.com, pg 87

Stevens, Paul, Donald Maass Literary Agency, 1000 Dean St, Suite 252, Brooklyn, NY 11238 *Tel:* 212-727-8383 *Fax:* 212-727-3271 *E-mail:* info@maassagency.com *Web Site:* www.maassagency.com, pg 526

Stevens, R Blake, Collector Grade Publications Inc, PO Box 1046, Cobourg, ON K9A 4W5, Canada *Tel:* 905-342-3434 *Fax:* 905-342-3688 *E-mail:* info@collectorgrade.com *Web Site:* www.collectorgrade.com, pg 451

Stevenson, Courtney, Pippin Properties Inc, 110 W 40 St, Suite 1704, New York, NY 10018 *Tel:* 212-338-9310 *Fax:* 212-338-9579 *E-mail:* info@pippinproperties.com *Web Site:* www.pippinproperties.com; www.facebook.com/pippinproperties, pg 531

Stevenson, Deborah, Scott O'Dell Award for Historical Fiction, c/o Horn Book Inc, 300 The Fenway, Suite P-311, Palace Road Bldg, Boston, MA 02215 *Tel:* 617-278-0225 *Toll Free Tel:* 888-628-0225 *Fax:* 617-278-6062 *Web Site:* www.scottodell.com/Pages/ScottO'DellAwardforHistoricalFiction.aspx, pg 675

Stevenson, Dinah, Clarion Books, 3 Park Ave, New York, NY 10016 *Tel:* 212-420-5800 *Toll Free Tel:* 800-225-3362 (orders) *Fax:* 212-420-5855 *Toll Free Fax:* 800-634-7568 (orders) *Web Site:* www.hmhco.com, pg 56

Stevenson, Dinah, Houghton Mifflin Harcourt Trade & Reference Division, 125 High St, Boston, MA 02110 *Tel:* 617-351-5000 *Toll Free Tel:* 800-225-3362 *Web Site:* www.hmhco.com, pg 111

Steward, Carlos, Black Mountain Press, PO Box 9907, Asheville, NC 28815 *Tel:* 828-273-3332 *Web Site:* www.theblackmountainpress.com, pg 36

Steward, Scott C, Newbury Street Press, 99-101 Newbury St, Boston, MA 02116 *Tel:* 617-536-5740 *Toll Free Tel:* 888-296-3447 (NEHGS membership) *Fax:* 617-536-7307 *E-mail:* sales@nehgs.org *Web Site:* www.americanancestors.org, pg 162

Stewart, Caitlin, Tom Fairley Award for Editorial Excellence, 27 Carlton St, Suite 505, Toronto, ON M5B 1L2, Canada *Tel:* 416-975-1379 *Toll Free Tel:* 866-CAN-EDIT (226-3348) *Fax:* 416-975-1637 *E-mail:* fairley_award@editors.ca; info@editors.ca *Web Site:* www.editors.ca; www.reviseurs.ca, pg 645

Stewart, Douglas, Sterling Lord Literistic Inc, 115 Broadway, Suite 1602, New York, NY 10006 *Tel:* 212-780-6050 *Fax:* 212-780-6095 *E-mail:* info@sll.com *Web Site:* www.sll.com, pg 537

PERSONNEL INDEX

Stewart, James B, The Authors League Fund, 31 E 32 St, 7th fl, New York, NY 10016 *Tel:* 212-268-1208 *Fax:* 212-564-5363 *E-mail:* staff@authorsleaguefund.org *Web Site:* www.authorsleaguefund.org, pg 559

Stewart, Jenna, Chelsea Green Publishing Co, 85 N Main St, Suite 120, White River Junction, VT 05001 *Tel:* 802-295-6300 *Toll Free Tel:* 800-639-4099 (cust serv, consumer & trade orders) *Fax:* 802-295-6444 *Web Site:* www.chelseagreen.com, pg 53

Stewart, Nicholas, T&T Clark International, 1385 Broadway, 5th fl, New York, NY 10018, pg 227

Stewart, Robert, BkMk Press - University of Missouri-Kansas City, University House, 5101 Rockhill Rd, Kansas City, MO 64110-2499 *Tel:* 816-235-2558 *Fax:* 816-235-2611 *E-mail:* bkmk@umkc.edu *Web Site:* www.umkc.edu/bkmk, pg 36

Stewart, Robert, G S Sharat Chandra Prize for Short Fiction, University House, 5101 Rockhill Rd, Kansas City, MO 64110-2499 *Tel:* 816-235-2558 *Fax:* 816-235-2611 *E-mail:* bkmk@umkc.edu *Web Site:* www.umkc.edu/bkmk, pg 636

Stewart, Robert, John Ciardi Prize for Poetry, University House, 5101 Rockhill Rd, Kansas City, MO 64110-2499 *Tel:* 816-235-2558 *Fax:* 816-235-2611 *E-mail:* bkmk@umkc.edu *Web Site:* www.umkc.edu/bkmk, pg 637

Stewart, Mrs Shane Gong, University Press of Mississippi, 3825 Ridgewood Rd, Jackson, MS 39211-6492 *Tel:* 601-432-6205 *Toll Free Tel:* 800-737-7788 (orders & cust serv) *Fax:* 601-432-6217 *E-mail:* press@mississippi.edu *Web Site:* www.upress.state.ms.us, pg 247

Stibel, Aaron, MDR, A D&B Co, 6 Armstrong Rd, Suite 301, Shelton, CT 06484 *Tel:* 203-926-4800 *Toll Free Tel:* 800-333-8802 *Fax:* 203-225-4603 *Toll Free Fax:* 866-532-7097 *E-mail:* mdrinfo@dnb.com *Web Site:* www.schooldata.com, pg 147

Sticco, Maria, University of Pittsburgh Press, 7500 Thomas Blvd, Pittsburgh, PA 15260 *Tel:* 412-383-2456 *Fax:* 412-383-2466 *E-mail:* info@upress.pitt.edu *Web Site:* www.upress.pitt.edu, pg 244

Stillwell, Winston, Red Deer Press Inc, 195 Allstate Pkwy, Markham, ON L3R 4T8, Canada *Tel:* 905-477-9700 *Toll Free Tel:* 800-387-9776 (orders) *E-mail:* rdp@reddeerpress.com; bookinfo@fitzhenry.ca *Web Site:* www.reddeerpress.com, pg 468

Stilson, Joyce, Maxim Mazumdar New Play Competition, One Curtain Up Alley, Buffalo, NY 14202-1911 *Tel:* 716-852-2600 *E-mail:* publicrelations@alleyway.com *Web Site:* alleyway.com, pg 666

Stilwell, Haleh Roshan, Dramatists Play Service Inc, 440 Park Ave S, New York, NY 10016 *Tel:* 212-683-8960 *Fax:* 212-213-1539 *E-mail:* postmaster@dramatists.com; orders@dramatists.com; publications@dramatists.com *Web Site:* www.dramatists.com, pg 73

Stilwell, Winston, Fitzhenry & Whiteside Limited, 195 Allstate Pkwy, Markham, ON L3R 4T8, Canada *Tel:* 905-477-9700 *Toll Free Tel:* 800-387-9776 *Fax:* 905-477-2834 *Toll Free Fax:* 800-260-9777 *E-mail:* bookinfo@fitzhenry.ca; godwit@fitzhenry.ca *Web Site:* www.fitzhenry.ca, pg 457

Stimola, Adriana, Stimola Literary Studio Inc, 308 Livingston Ct, Edgewater, NJ 07020 *Tel:* 201-945-9353 *Fax:* 201-945-9353; 201-490-5920 *E-mail:* info@stimolaliterarystudio.com *Web Site:* www.stimolaliterarystudio.com, pg 537

Stimola, Rosemary B, Stimola Literary Studio Inc, 308 Livingston Ct, Edgewater, NJ 07020 *Tel:* 201-945-9353 *Fax:* 201-945-9353; 201-490-5920 *E-mail:* info@stimolaliterarystudio.com *Web Site:* www.stimolaliterarystudio.com, pg 537

Stine, Jane, Parachute Publishing LLC, 157 Columbus Ave, Suite 518, New York, NY 10023 *Tel:* 212-691-1421 *Web Site:* www.parachutepublishing.com, pg 173

Stinnett, Barbara, Saint Johann Press, 315 Schraalenburgh Rd, Haworth, NJ 07641 *Tel:* 201-387-1529 *Fax:* 201-501-0698 *Web Site:* www.stjohannpress.com, pg 204

Stitzer, Tina, Fun in the Sun Writer's Cruise Conference, PO Box 823414, Pembroke Pines, FL 33082 *E-mail:* frwfuninthesun@yahoo.com *Web Site:* frwfuninthesunmain.blogspot.com/; www.frwriters.org, pg 610

Stobaugh, Blair, Bisk Education, 9417 Princess Palm Ave, Suite 400, Tampa, FL 33619 *Tel:* 813-621-6200 *Toll Free Tel:* 800-280-9718 (cust serv) *E-mail:* customerservice@bisk.com *Web Site:* www.bisk.com, pg 35

Stobaugh, Clay, John Wiley & Sons Inc, 111 River St, Hoboken, NJ 07030-5774 *Tel:* 201-748-6000 *Toll Free Tel:* 800-225-5945 (cust serv) *Fax:* 201-748-6088 *E-mail:* info@wiley.com *Web Site:* www.wiley.com, pg 256

Stocke, Todd, Sourcebooks Inc, 1935 Brookdale Rd, Suite 139, Naperville, IL 60563 *Tel:* 630-961-3900 *Toll Free Tel:* 800-432-7444 *Fax:* 630-961-2168 *E-mail:* info@sourcebooks.com; customersupport@sourcebooks.com *Web Site:* www.sourcebooks.com, pg 218

Stockfield, Mindy, Scholastic Trade Division, 557 Broadway, New York, NY 10012 *Tel:* 212-343-6100; 212-343-4685 (export sales) *Fax:* 212-343-4714 (export sales) *Web Site:* www.scholastic.com, pg 208

Stockland, Patricia M, Carolrhoda Books, 241 First Ave N, Minneapolis, MN 55401 *Tel:* 612-332-3344 *Toll Free Tel:* 800-328-4929 *Fax:* 612-332-7615 *Toll Free Fax:* 800-332-1132 *E-mail:* info@lernerbooks.com; custserve@lernerbooks.com *Web Site:* www.lernerbooks.com; www.facebook.com/lernerbooks, pg 48

Stockland, Patricia M, Carolrhoda Lab™, 241 First Ave N, Minneapolis, MN 55401 *Tel:* 612-332-3344 *Toll Free Tel:* 800-328-4929 *Fax:* 612-332-7615 *Toll Free Fax:* 800-332-1132 (US) *E-mail:* info@lernerbooks.com; custserve@lernerbooks.com *Web Site:* www.lernerbooks.com; www.facebook.com/lernerbooks, pg 48

Stockland, Patricia M, ediciones Lerner, 241 First Ave N, Minneapolis, MN 55401 *Tel:* 612-332-3344 *Toll Free Tel:* 800-328-4929 *Fax:* 612-332-7615 *Toll Free Fax:* 800-332-1132 *E-mail:* info@lernerbooks.com; custserve@lernerbooks.com *Web Site:* www.lernerbooks.com; www.facebook.com/lernerbooks, pg 75

Stockland, Patricia M, First Avenue Editions, 241 First Ave N, Minneapolis, MN 55401 *Tel:* 612-332-3344 *Toll Free Tel:* 800-328-4929 *Fax:* 612-332-7615 *Toll Free Fax:* 800-332-1132 *E-mail:* info@lernerbooks.com; custserve@lernerbooks.com *Web Site:* www.lernerbooks.com; www.facebook.com/lernerbooks, pg 85

Stockland, Patricia M, Graphic Universe™, 241 First Ave N, Minneapolis, MN 55401 *Tel:* 612-332-3344 *Toll Free Tel:* 800-328-4929 *Fax:* 612-332-7615 *Toll Free Fax:* 800-332-1132 *E-mail:* info@lernerbooks.com; custserve@lernerbooks.com *Web Site:* www.lernerbooks.com; www.facebook.com/lernerbooks, pg 95

Stockland, Patricia M, LernerClassroom, 241 First Ave N, Minneapolis, MN 55401 *Tel:* 612-332-3344 *Toll Free Tel:* 800-328-4929 *Fax:* 612-332-7615 *Toll Free Fax:* 800-332-1132 *E-mail:* info@lernerbooks.com; custserve@lernerbooks.com *Web Site:* www.lernerbooks.com; www.facebook.com/lernerbooks, pg 132

Stockland, Patricia M, Millbrook Press, 241 First Ave N, Minneapolis, MN 55401 *Tel:* 612-332-3344 *Toll Free Tel:* 800-328-4929 (US only) *Fax:* 612-332-7615 *Toll Free Fax:* 800-332-1132 *E-mail:* info@lernerbooks.com; custserve@lernerbooks.com *Web Site:* www.lernerbooks.com; www.facebook.com/millbrookpress, pg 151

Stockland, Patricia M, Twenty-First Century Books, 241 First Ave N, Minneapolis, MN 55401 *Tel:* 612-332-3344 *Toll Free Tel:* 800-328-4929 *Fax:* 612-332-7615 *Toll Free Fax:* 800-332-1132 *E-mail:* info@lernerbooks.com; custserve@lernerbooks.com *Web Site:* www.lernerbooks.com; www.facebook.com/lernerbooks, pg 237

Stocks, John C, National Education Association (NEA), 1201 16 St NW, Washington, DC 20036-3290 *Tel:* 202-833-4000 *Fax:* 202-822-7974 *Web Site:* www.nea.org, pg 158, 572

Stockton, Hope, MFA Publications, 465 Huntington Ave, Boston, MA 02115 *Tel:* 617-369-4233 *Fax:* 617-369-3459 *E-mail:* publications@mfa.org *Web Site:* www.mfa.org/publications, pg 149

Stockwell, Diane, Globo Libros Literary Agency, 450 E 63 St, New York, NY 10065 *Web Site:* www.globo-libros.com; www.publishersmarketplace.com/members/dstockwell, pg 519

Stockwell, Gail Provost, Writers Retreat Workshop (WRW), PO Box 170657, Austin, TX 78717 *E-mail:* info@writersretreatworkshop.com *Web Site:* www.writersretreatworkshop.com, pg 616

Stoddard, Bill, Prometheus Awards, 650 Castro St, Suite 120-433, Mountain View, CA 94041 *Tel:* 650-968-6319 *Web Site:* www.lfs.org, pg 682

Stoddard, Brooke C, Archon Editorial LLC, 815 King St, Suite 204, Alexandria, VA 22314 *Tel:* 703-838-1650 *E-mail:* stoddardbc@gmail.com *Web Site:* www.archoneditorial.com, pg 488

Stokes, Jennifer, Kids Can Press Ltd, 25 Dockside Dr, Toronto, ON M5A 0B5, Canada *Tel:* 416-479-7000 *Toll Free Tel:* 800-265-0884 *Fax:* 416-960-5437 *E-mail:* info@kidscan.com; customerservice@kidscan.com *Web Site:* www.kidscanpress.com; www.kidscanpress.ca, pg 461

Stokes, Susan S, Woodbine House, 6510 Bells Mill Rd, Bethesda, MD 20817 *Tel:* 301-897-3570 *Toll Free Tel:* 800-843-7323 *Fax:* 301-897-5838 *E-mail:* info@woodbinehouse.com *Web Site:* www.woodbinehouse.com, pg 258

Stokes-Peters, Natalie, Black Classic Press, 3921 Vero Rd, Suite F, Baltimore, MD 21203-3414 *Tel:* 410-242-6954 *Toll Free Tel:* 800-476-8870 *Fax:* 410-242-6959 *E-mail:* email@blackclassicbooks.com; blackclassicpress@yahoo.com *Web Site:* www.blackclassicbooks.com; www.bcpdigital.com, pg 36

Stolls, Amy, National Endowment for the Arts, 400 Seventh St SW, Washington, DC 20506-0001 *Tel:* 202-682-5400 *Web Site:* www.arts.gov, pg 583

Stoloff, Sam, Frances Goldin Literary Agency, Inc, 214 W 29 St, Suite 410, New York, NY 10001 *Tel:* 212-777-0047 *Fax:* 212-228-1660 *E-mail:* agency@goldinlit.com *Web Site:* www.goldinlit.com, pg 519

Stoltz, Jamison, Harry N Abrams Inc, 195 Broadway, 9th fl, New York, NY 10007 *Tel:* 212-206-7715 *Toll Free Tel:* 800-345-1359 *Fax:* 212-519-1210 *E-mail:* abrams@abramsbooks.com *Web Site:* www.abramsbooks.com, pg 3

Stoltzfus, Alison, The Princeton Review, c/o Penguin Random House Inc, 1745 Broadway, New York, NY 10019 *Toll Free Tel:* 800-273-8439 *Web Site:* www.princetonreview.com, pg 188

Stone, Annie, Harlequin Enterprises Ltd, 233 Broadway, Suite 1001, New York, NY 10279 *Tel:* 212-553-4200 *Fax:* 212-227-8969 *E-mail:* customerservice@harlequin.com *Web Site:* www.harlequin.com, pg 100

Stone, Judi, Artech House Inc, 685 Canton St, Norwood, MA 02062 *Tel:* 781-769-9750 *Toll Free Tel:* 800-225-9977 *Fax:* 781-769-6334 *E-mail:* artech@artechhouse.com *Web Site:* www.artechhouse.com, pg 21

Stone, Kevin, Cengage Learning, 20 Channel Center St, Boston, MA 02210 *Tel:* 617-289-7700 *Toll Free Tel:* 800-354-9706 *Fax:* 617-289-7844 *Toll Free Fax:* 800-487-8488 *E-mail:* esales@cengage.com *Web Site:* www.cengage.com, pg 50

Stone, Kris, Piano Press, 1425 Ocean Ave, Suite 5, Del Mar, CA 92014 *Tel:* 619-884-1401 *Fax:* 858-755-1104 *E-mail:* pianopress@pianopress.com *Web Site:* www.pianopress.com, pg 182

Stone, Madelin, Random House Children's Books, 1745 Broadway, 10th fl, New York, NY 10019 *Tel:* 212-782-9000 *Web Site:* www.randomhousekids.com, pg 194

Stone, Michelle, McClanahan Publishing House Inc, 107 W Main, Princeton, KY 42445 *Tel:* 270-963-9005 *E-mail:* books@kybooks.com *Web Site:* kybooks.com, pg 145

Stone, Patricia, Chelsea Green Publishing Co, 85 N Main St, Suite 120, White River Junction, VT 05001 *Tel:* 802-295-6300 *Toll Free Tel:* 800-639-4099 (cust serv, consumer & trade orders) *Fax:* 802-295-6444 *Web Site:* www.chelseagreen.com, pg 53

Stone, Suezen, HJ Kramer Inc, PO Box 1082, Tiburon, CA 94920 *Tel:* 415-884-2100 (ext 10) *Toll Free Tel:* 800-972-6657 *Fax:* 415-435-5364 *E-mail:* hjkramer@jps.net *Web Site:* www.hjkramer.com; www.newworldlibrary.com, pg 128

Storch, Maury, Gefen Books, c/o Storch, 255 Central Ave, B-206, Lawrence, NY 11559 *Tel:* 516-593-1234 *Toll Free Tel:* 800-477-5257 *Fax:* 516-295-2739 *E-mail:* gefenny@gefenpublishing.com; info@gefenpublishing.com *Web Site:* www.gefenpublishing.com, pg 91

Stordahl, Derek, Holiday House Inc, 425 Madison Ave, New York, NY 10017 *Tel:* 212-688-0085 *Fax:* 212-421-6134 *E-mail:* info@holidayhouse.com *Web Site:* www.holidayhouse.com, pg 109

Storm, Alison, Ambassador International, 411 University Ridge, Suite B14, Greenville, SC 29601 *Tel:* 864-751-4844 *E-mail:* info@emeraldhouse.com; publisher@emeraldhouse.com (ms submissions); sales@emeraldhouse.com (orders/order inquiries) *Web Site:* ambassador-international.com; www.facebook.com/AmbassadorIntl; twitter.com/ambassadorintl, pg 9

Storrings, Michael, St Martin's Press, LLC, 175 Fifth Ave, New York, NY 10010 *Tel:* 646-307-5151 *Web Site:* us.macmillan.com/smp, pg 204

Stoshak, Joe, Public Citizen, 1600 20 St NW, Washington, DC 20009 *Tel:* 202-588-1000 *Fax:* 202-588-7798 *E-mail:* public_citizen@citizen.org *Web Site:* www.citizen.org, pg 191

Stott, Phil, Vault.com Inc, 132 W 31 St, 16th fl, New York, NY 10001 *Tel:* 212-366-4212 *Toll Free Tel:* 800-535-2074 *Fax:* 212-366-6117 (cust serv) *E-mail:* editors@vault.com; customerservice@vault.com *Web Site:* www.vault.com, pg 250

Stouras, Tom, Macmillan, 175 Fifth Ave, New York, NY 10010 *Tel:* 646-307-5151 *E-mail:* press.inquiries@macmillan.com *Web Site:* www.macmillan.com, pg 140

Stoykova-Klemer, Katerina, Poetry Book Contest, PO Box 910456, Lexington, KY 40591-0456 *Web Site:* www.accents-publishing.com/contest.html, pg 680

Strachan, Glenn R, Jhpiego, 1615 Thames St, Baltimore, MD 21231-3492 *Tel:* 410-537-1800 *Fax:* 410-537-1473 *E-mail:* info@jhpiego.net *Web Site:* www.jhpiego.org, pg 122

Stramenga, Silvia, Seven Stories Press, 140 Watts St, New York, NY 10013 *Tel:* 212 226 8760 *Toll Free Tel:* 800-733-3000 (orders) *Fax:* 212-226-1411 *E-mail:* info@sevenstories.com *Web Site:* www.sevenstories.com, pg 211

Strand, Julie, Coffee House Press, 79 13 Ave NE, Suite 110, Minneapolis, MN 55413 *Tel:* 612-338-0125 *Fax:* 612-338-4004 *E-mail:* info@coffeehousepress.org *Web Site:* coffeehousepress.org, pg 58

Strand, Kurt, McGraw-Hill Contemporary Learning Series, 501 Bell St, Dubuque, IA 52001 *Toll Free Tel:* 800-243-6532 *Web Site:* www.mhcls.com, pg 145

Strand, Kurt, McGraw-Hill Higher Education, 1333 Burr Ridge Pkwy, Burr Ridge, IL 60527 *Tel:* 630-789-4000 *Toll Free Tel:* 800-338-3987 (cust serv) *Fax:* 614-755-5645 (cust serv) *Web Site:* www.mhhe.com, pg 146

Strand, Kurt, McGraw-Hill Humanities, Social Sciences, Languages, 2 Penn Plaza, 21st fl, New York, NY 10121 *Tel:* 212-904-2000 *Toll Free Tel:* 800-338-3987 (cust serv) *Fax:* 614-755-5645 (cust serv) *Web Site:* www.mhhe.com, pg 146

Strand, Kurt, McGraw-Hill/Irwin, 1333 Burr Ridge Pkwy, Burr Ridge, IL 60527 *Tel:* 630-789-4000 *Toll Free Tel:* 800-338-3987 (cust serv) *Fax:* 630-789-6942; 614-755-5645 (cust serv) *Web Site:* www.mhhe.com, pg 146

Strand, Kurt, McGraw-Hill Science, Engineering, Mathematics, 501 Bell St, Dubuque, IA 52001 *Tel:* 563-584-6000 *Toll Free Tel:* 800-338-3987 (cust serv) *Fax:* 614-755-5645 (cust serv) *Web Site:* www.mhhe.com, pg 146

Strang, Jenn, Naomi Berber Memorial Award, 301 Brush Creek Rd, Warrendale, PA 15086-7529 *Tel:* 412-741-6860 *Toll Free Tel:* 800-910-4283 *Fax:* 412-741-2311 *E-mail:* printingind@comm.printing.org *Web Site:* www.printing.org/berberaward, pg 631

Strang, Jenn, Education Awards of Excellence, 301 Brush Creek Rd, Warrendale, PA 15086-7529 *Tel:* 412-741-6860 *Toll Free Tel:* 800-910-4283 *Fax:* 412-741-2311 *E-mail:* printingind@comm.printing.org *Web Site:* www.printing.org/educationaward, pg 643

Strang, Jenn, InterTech™ Technology Awards, 301 Brush Creek Rd, Warrendale, PA 15086-7529 *Tel:* 412-741-6860 *Toll Free Tel:* 800-910-4283 *Fax:* 412-741-2311 *E-mail:* intertech@printing.org *Web Site:* www.printing.org/intertechawards, pg 656

Strang, Jenn, Frederick D Kagy Education Award of Excellence, 301 Brush Creek Rd, Warrendale, PA 15086-7529 *Tel:* 412-741-6860 *Toll Free Tel:* 800-910-4283 *Fax:* 412-741-2311 *E-mail:* printingind@comm.printing.org *Web Site:* www.printing.org, pg 658

Strang, Jenn, Orientation to the Graphic Arts, 301 Brush Creek Rd, Warrendale, PA 15086-7529 *Tel:* 412-741-6860 *Toll Free Tel:* 800-910-4283 *Fax:* 412-741-2311 *E-mail:* printingind@comm.printing.org *Web Site:* www.printing.org, pg 613

Strang, Jenn, Printing Industries of America, 301 Brush Creek Rd, Warrendale, PA 15086-7529 *Tel:* 412-741-6860 *Toll Free Tel:* 800-910-4283 *Fax:* 412-741-2311 *E-mail:* printingind@comm.printing.org *Web Site:* www.printing.org, pg 576

Strang, Jenn, Robert F Reed Technology Medal, 301 Brush Creek Rd, Warrendale, PA 15086-7529 *Tel:* 412-741-6860 *Toll Free Tel:* 800-910-4283 *Fax:* 412-741-2311 *E-mail:* printingind@comm.printing.org *Web Site:* www.printing.org/reedaward, pg 684

Strang, Jenn, William D Schaeffer Environmental Award, 301 Brush Creek Rd, Warrendale, PA 15086-7529 *Tel:* 412-741-6860 *Toll Free Tel:* 800-910-4283 *Fax:* 412-741-2311 *E-mail:* printingind@comm.printing.org *Web Site:* www.printing.org/schaefferaward, pg 688

Strang, Stephen, Charisma Media, 600 Rinehart Rd, Lake Mary, FL 32746 *Tel:* 407-333-0600 (all imprints) *Toll Free Tel:* 800-283-8494 (Charisma Media, Siloam Press, Creation House); 800-665-1468 *Fax:* 407-333-7100 (all imprints) *E-mail:* charisma@charismamedia.com *Web Site:* www.charismamedia.com, pg 52

Strang, Stephen, CharismaLife Publishers, 600 Rinehart Rd, Lake Mary, FL 32746 *Tel:* 407-333-0600 *Toll Free Tel:* 800-451-4598 *Fax:* 407-333-7100 *E-mail:* charismalife@charismamedia.com *Web Site:* www.charismamedia.com, pg 53

Strange, Nancy, Tudor Publishers Inc, 3109 Shady Lawn Dr, Greensboro, NC 27408 *Tel:* 336-288-5395 *E-mail:* tudorpublishers@triad.rr.com, pg 236

Strasbaugh, Joan, The Experiment, 220 E 23 St, Suite 301, New York, NY 10010-4674 *Tel:* 212-889-1659 *E-mail:* info@theexperimentpublishing.com *Web Site:* www.theexperimentpublishing.com, pg 81

Straschnov, George, Bisk Education, 9417 Princess Palm Ave, Suite 400, Tampa, FL 33619 *Tel:* 813-621-6200 *Toll Free Tel:* 800-280-9718 (cust serv) *E-mail:* customerservice@bisk.com *Web Site:* www.bisk.com, pg 35

Stratford, Madeleine, John Glassco Translation Prize, Concordia University, LB 601, 1455 De Maisonneuve W, Montreal, QC H3G 1M8, Canada *Tel:* 514-848-2424 (ext 8702) *E-mail:* info@attlc-ltac.org *Web Site:* www.attlc-ltac.org, pg 649

Stratford, Madeleine, Literary Translators' Association of Canada, Concordia University, LB 601, 1455 De Maisonneuve W, Montreal, QC H3G 1M8, Canada *Tel:* 514-848-2424 (ext 8702) *E-mail:* info@attlc-ltac.org *Web Site:* www.attlc-ltac.org, pg 568

Stratton, Penny, Newbury Street Press, 99-101 Newbury St, Boston, MA 02116 *Tel:* 617-536-5740 *Toll Free Tel:* 888-296-3447 (NEHGS membership) *Fax:* 617-536-7307 *E-mail:* sales@nehgs.org *Web Site:* www.americanancestors.org, pg 162

Stratton, W K, Carr P Collins Award, c/o 7748 Hwy 290 W, Austin, TX 78736-3202 *Tel:* 512-683-5640 *E-mail:* president@texasinstituteofletters.org *Web Site:* www.texasinstituteofletters.org, pg 638

Stratton, W K, Soeurette Diehl Fraser Translation Award, c/o 7748 Hwy 290 W, Austin, TX 78736-3202 *Tel:* 512-683-5640 *E-mail:* president@texasinstituteofletters.org *Web Site:* www.texasinstituteofletters.org, pg 647

Stratton, W K, Jesse H Jones Award, c/o 7748 Hwy 290 W, Austin, TX 78736-3202 *Tel:* 512-683-5640 *E-mail:* president@texasinstituteofletters.org *Web Site:* www.texasinstituteofletters.org, pg 657

Stratton, W K, Ramirez Family Award, c/o 7748 Hwy 290 W, Austin, TX 78736-3202 *Tel:* 512-683-5640 *E-mail:* president@texasinstituteofletters.org *Web Site:* www.texasinstituteofletters.org, pg 684

Stratton, W K, Edwin "Bud" Shrake Award for Best Short Nonfiction, c/o 7748 Hwy 290 W, Austin, TX 78736-3202 *Tel:* 512-683-5640 *E-mail:* president@texasinstituteofletters.org *Web Site:* www.texasinstituteofletters.org, pg 689

Stratton, W K, Helen C Smith Memorial Award, c/o 7748 Hwy 290 W, Austin, TX 78736-3202 *Tel:* 512-683-5640 *E-mail:* president@texasinstituteofletters.org *Web Site:* www.texasinstituteofletters.org, pg 690

Stratton, W K, Texas Institute of Letters (TIL), c/o 7748 Hwy 290 W, Austin, TX 78736-3202 *E-mail:* president@texasinstituteofletters.org; secretary@texasinstituteofletters.org *Web Site:* www.texasinstituteofletters.org, pg 579

Stratton, W K, Texas Institute of Letters Awards, c/o 7748 Hwy 290 W, Austin, TX 78736-3202 *Tel:* 512-683-5640 *E-mail:* president@texasinstituteofletters.org *Web Site:* www.texasinstituteofletters.org, pg 694

Straub, Peter, The Authors League Fund, 31 E 32 St, 7th fl, New York, NY 10016 *Tel:* 212-268-1208 *Fax:* 212-564-5363 *E-mail:* staff@authorsleaguefund.org *Web Site:* www.authorsleaguefund.org, pg 559

Straus, Jonah, Straus Literary, 319 Lafayette St, Suite 220, New York, NY 10012 *Tel:* 646-843-9950 *Fax:* 646-390-3320 *Web Site:* www.strausliterary.com, pg 538

Straus, Robin, Robin Straus Agency Inc, 229 E 79 St, Suite 5A, New York, NY 10075 *Tel:* 212-472-3282 *Fax:* 212-472-3833 *E-mail:* info@robinstrausagency.com *Web Site:* www.robinstrausagency.com, pg 538

Straus, Robin, The Wallace Literary Agency, 229 E 79 St, No 5A, New York, NY 10075 *Tel:* 212-472-3282 *Fax:* 212-472-3833 *E-mail:* info@wallaceliteraryagency.com, pg 541

Strauss, Leslie R, Housing Assistance Council, 1025 Vermont Ave NW, Suite 606, Washington, DC 20005 *Tel:* 202-842-8600 *Fax:* 202-347-3441 *E-mail:* hac@ruralhome.org *Web Site:* www.ruralhome.org, pg 112

Strauss, Rebecca, DeFiore and Company Literary Management Inc, 47 E 19 St, 3rd fl, New York, NY 10003 *Tel:* 212-925-7744 *Fax:* 212-925-9803 *E-mail:* info@defliterary.com; submissions@defliterary.com *Web Site:* www.defliterary.com, pg 513

Strauss-Gabel, Julie, Dutton, 375 Hudson St, New York, NY 10014 *Tel:* 212-366-2000 *Fax:* 212-366-2262 *Web Site:* www.penguin.com, pg 74

Strauss-Gabel, Julie, Dutton Children's Books, 345 Hudson St, New York, NY 10014 *Tel:* 212-366-2000 *Web Site:* www.penguin.com, pg 74

Streetman, Ms Burgin, Trinity University Press, One Trinity Place, San Antonio, TX 78212-7200 *Tel:* 210-999-8884 *Fax:* 210-999-8838 *E-mail:* books@trinity.edu *Web Site:* www.tupress.org, pg 235

Streitfeld, Linda Topping, National Press Foundation, 1211 Connecticut Ave NW, Suite 310, Washington, DC 20036 *Tel:* 202-663-7280 *Web Site:* nationalpress.org, pg 572

Strelecki, Heather, AIGA 50 Books|50 Covers, 233 Broadway, Suite 1740, New York, NY 10279 *Tel:* 212-807-1990 *Fax:* 212-807-1799 *E-mail:* competitions@aiga.org *Web Site:* www.aiga.org, pg 626

Strickland, Albert Lee, Pacific Publishing Services, PO Box 1150, Capitola, CA 95010-1150 *Tel:* 831-476-8284 *Fax:* 831-476-8294 *E-mail:* pacpubs@attglobal.net, pg 499

Strickland, Bill, Rodale Inc, 400 S Tenth St, Emmaus, PA 18049 *Tel:* 610-967-5171 *Toll Free Tel:* 866-387-0509 *E-mail:* bookmarketing@rodale.com; bookpublicity@rodale.com *Web Site:* www.rodale.com, pg 201

Strickland, Jonathan, Black Rabbit Books, 515 N Riverfront Dr, Suite 200, Mankato, MN 56001 *Tel:* 507-388-1609 *Fax:* 507-388-1364 *E-mail:* info@blackrabbitbooks.com; orders@blackrabbitbooks.com *Web Site:* www.blackrabbitbooks.com, pg 36

Strickland, Sherri, University Press of New England, One Court St, Suite 250, Lebanon, NH 03766 *Tel:* 603-448-1533 *Toll Free Tel:* 800-421-1561 (orders only) *Fax:* 603-448-7006; 603-448-9429 (orders only) *E-mail:* university.press@dartmouth.edu *Web Site:* www.upne.com, pg 247

Strickland, Tessa, Barefoot Books, 2067 Massachusetts Ave, 5th fl, Cambridge, MA 02140 *Tel:* 617-576-0660 *Toll Free Tel:* 866-215-1756 (cust serv); 866-417-2369 (orders) *Fax:* 617-576-0049 *E-mail:* help@barefootbooks.com *Web Site:* www.barefootbooks.com, pg 29

Stringham, Edward, American Institute for Economic Research (AIER), 250 Division St, Great Barrington, MA 01230 *Tel:* 413-528-1216 *Toll Free Tel:* 888-528-1216 (orders) *E-mail:* info@aier.org *Web Site:* www.aier.org, pg 12

Strittmatter, Aimee, ALSC Baker & Taylor Summer Reading Grant, 50 E Huron St, Chicago, IL 60611-2795 *Tel:* 312-280-2163 *Toll Free Tel:* 800-545-2433 *Fax:* 312-440-9374; 312-280-5271 *E-mail:* alsc@ala.org *Web Site:* www.ala.org/alsc, pg 627

Strittmatter, Aimee, The May Hill Arbuthnot Honor Lecture Award, 50 E Huron St, Chicago, IL 60611-2795 *Tel:* 312-280-2163 *Toll Free Tel:* 800-545-2433 *Fax:* 312-440-9374; 312-280-5271 *E-mail:* alsc@ala.org *Web Site:* www.ala.org/alsc, pg 628

Strittmatter, Aimee, The Mildred L Batchelder Award, 50 E Huron St, Chicago, IL 60611-2795 *Tel:* 312-280-2163 *Toll Free Tel:* 800-545-2433 *Fax:* 312-440-9374; 312-280-5271 *E-mail:* alsc@ala.org *Web Site:* www.ala.org/alsc, pg 630

Strittmatter, Aimee, The Pura Belpre Award, 50 E Huron St, Chicago, IL 60611-2795 *Tel:* 312-280-2163 *Toll Free Tel:* 800-545-2433 *Fax:* 312-440-9374; 312-280-5271 *E-mail:* alsc@ala.org *Web Site:* www.ala.org/alsc, pg 631

Strittmatter, Aimee, Bound to Stay Bound Books Scholarship, 50 E Huron St, Chicago, IL 60611-2795 *Tel:* 312-280-2163 *Toll Free Tel:* 800-545-2433 *Fax:* 312-440-9374; 312-280-5271 *E-mail:* alsc@ala.org *Web Site:* www.ala.org/alsc, pg 634

Strittmatter, Aimee, The Randolph Caldecott Medal, 50 E Huron St, Chicago, IL 60611-2795 *Tel:* 312-280-2163 *Toll Free Tel:* 800-545-2433 *Fax:* 312-440-9374; 312-280-5271 *E-mail:* alsc@ala.org *Web Site:* www.ala.org/alsc, pg 635

Strittmatter, Aimee, Frederic G Melcher Scholarship, 50 E Huron St, Chicago, IL 60611-2795 *Tel:* 312-280-2163 *Toll Free Tel:* 800-545-2433 *Fax:* 312-440-9374; 312-280-5271 *E-mail:* alsc@ala.org *Web Site:* www.ala.org/alsc, pg 667

Strittmatter, Aimee, John Newbery Medal, 50 E Huron St, Chicago, IL 60611-2795 *Tel:* 312-280-2163 *Toll Free Tel:* 800-545-2433 *Fax:* 312-440-9374; 312-280-5271 *E-mail:* alsc@ala.org *Web Site:* www.ala.org/alsc, pg 673

Strittmatter, Aimee, Robert F Sibert Informational Book Award, 50 E Huron St, Chicago, IL 60611-2795 *Tel:* 312-280-2163 *Toll Free Tel:* 800-545-2433 *Fax:* 312-440-9374; 312-280-5271 *E-mail:* alsc@ala.org *Web Site:* www.ala.org/alsc, pg 689

Strittmatter, Aimee, The Laura Ingalls Wilder Medal, 50 E Huron St, Chicago, IL 60611-2795 *Tel:* 312-280-2163 *Toll Free Tel:* 800-545-2433 *Fax:* 312-440-9374; 312-280-5271 *E-mail:* alsc@ala.org *Web Site:* www.ala.org/alsc, pg 698

Strohbehn, Edward, Environmental Law Institute, 1730 "M" St NW, Suite 700, Washington, DC 20036 *Tel:* 202-939-3800 *Toll Free Tel:* 800-433-5120 *Fax:* 202-939-3868 *E-mail:* law@eli.org *Web Site:* www.eli.org, pg 79

Strone, Daniel, Trident Media Group LLC, 41 Madison Ave, 36th fl, New York, NY 10010 *Tel:* 212-333-1511 *E-mail:* info@tridentmediagroup.com; press@tridentmediagroup.com *Web Site:* www.tridentmediagroup.com, pg 540

Strong, Marianne, Marianne Strong Literary Agency, 65 E 96 St, New York, NY 10128 *Tel:* 212-249-1000 *Fax:* 212-831-3241 *Web Site:* stronglit.com, pg 538

Stroschein, Steven, IBFD North America Inc (International Bureau of Fiscal Documentation), 8300 Boone Blvd, Suite 380, Vienna, VA 22182 *Tel:* 703-442-7757 *E-mail:* info@ibfd.org *Web Site:* www.ibfd.org, pg 113

Strosnider, Ashley, Prairie Schooner Annual Strousse Award, University of Nebraska, 123 Andrews Hall, 625 N 14 St, Lincoln, NE 68508 *Tel:* 402-472-0911 *Fax:* 402-472-9771 *E-mail:* prairieschooner@unl.edu *Web Site:* prairieschooner.unl.edu, pg 681

Strosnider, Ashley, Prairie Schooner Bernice Slote Award, University of Nebraska, 123 Andrews Hall, 625 N 14 St, Lincoln, NE 68508 *Tel:* 402-472-0911 *E-mail:* prairieschooner@unl.edu *Web Site:* prairieschooner.unl.edu, pg 681

Strosnider, Ashley, Prairie Schooner Book Prize Contest in Fiction, University of Nebraska, 123 Andrews Hall, 625 N 14 St, Lincoln, NE 68508 *Tel:* 402-472-0911 *Fax:* 402-472-9771 *E-mail:* psbookprize@unl.edu *Web Site:* prairieschooner.unl.edu, pg 681

Strosnider, Ashley, Prairie Schooner Book Prize Contest in Poetry, University of Nebraska, 123 Andrews Hall, 625 N 14 St, Lincoln, NE 68508 *Tel:* 402-472-0911 *Fax:* 402-472-9771 *E-mail:* psbookprize@unl.edu *Web Site:* prairieschooner.unl.edu, pg 681

Strosnider, Ashley, Prairie Schooner Edward Stanley Award, University of Nebraska, 123 Andrews Hall, 625 N 14 St, Lincoln, NE 68508 *Tel:* 402-472-0911 *Fax:* 402-472-9771 *E-mail:* prairieschooner@unl.edu *Web Site:* prairieschooner.unl.edu, pg 681

Strosnider, Ashley, Prairie Schooner Glenna Luschei Award, University of Nebraska, 123 Andrews Hall, 625 N 14 St, Lincoln, NE 68508 *Tel:* 402-472-0911 *Fax:* 402-472-9771 *E-mail:* prairieschooner@unl.edu *Web Site:* prairieschooner.unl.edu, pg 681

Strosnider, Ashley, Prairie Schooner Hugh J Luke Award, University of Nebraska, 123 Andrews Hall, 625 N 14 St, Lincoln, NE 68508 *Tel:* 402-472-0911 *Fax:* 402-472-9771 *E-mail:* prairieschooner@unl.edu *Web Site:* prairieschooner.unl.edu, pg 681

Strosnider, Ashley, Prairie Schooner Jane Geske Award, University of Nebraska, 123 Andrews Hall, 625 N 14 St, Lincoln, NE 68508 *Tel:* 402-472-0911 *Fax:* 402-472-9771 *E-mail:* prairieschooner@unl.edu *Web Site:* prairieschooner.unl.edu, pg 681

Strosnider, Ashley, Prairie Schooner Lawrence Foundation Award, University of Nebraska, 123 Andrews Hall, 625 N 14 St, Lincoln, NE 68508 *Tel:* 402-472-0911 *Fax:* 402-472-9771 *E-mail:* prairieschooner@unl.edu *Web Site:* prairieschooner.unl.edu, pg 681

Strosnider, Ashley, Prairie Schooner Virginia Faulkner Award for Excellence in Writing, University of Nebraska, 123 Andrews Hall, 625 N 14 St, Lincoln, NE 68508 *Tel:* 402-472-0911 *Fax:* 402-472-9771 *E-mail:* prairieschooner@unl.edu *Web Site:* prairieschooner.unl.edu, pg 682

Strothman, Wendy, Strothman Agency LLC, 63 E Ninth St, 10X, New York, NY 10003 *E-mail:* info@strothmanagency.com *Web Site:* www.strothmanagency.com, pg 538

Stroud, Christine, Autumn House Press, 5530 Penn Ave, Pittsburgh, PA 15206 *Tel:* 412-362-2665 *E-mail:* info@autumnhouse.org *Web Site:* www.autumnhouse.org, pg 26

Stroud, Christine, Coal Hill Review Poetry Chapbook Contest, c/o Autumn House Press, PO Box 5486, Pittsburgh, PA 15206 *E-mail:* reviewcoalhill@gmail.com *Web Site:* www.coalhillreview.com, pg 638

Stroud, Ward J, National Book Co, PO Box 19069, Portland, OR 97280-0069 *Tel:* 503-228-6345 *Fax:* 810-885-5811 *E-mail:* info@eralearning.com *Web Site:* www.eralearning.com, pg 157

Stroup-Rentier, Vera Lynne PhD, Finding My Way Books, 3512 SW Huntoon St, Topeka, KS 66604 *Tel:* 785-273-6239 *E-mail:* info@findingmywaybooks.com; findingmywaybooks@gmail.com *Web Site:* www.findingmywaybooks.net, pg 84

Struckman, Dianne, Krieger Publishing Co, 1725 Krieger Lane, Malabar, FL 32950 *Tel:* 321-724-9542 *Fax:* 321-951-3671 *E-mail:* info@krieger-publishing.com *Web Site:* www.krieger-publishing.com, pg 128

Struna, Barbara, Cape Cod Writers' Center Conference, 919 Main St, Osterville, MA 02655 *Tel:* 508-420-0200 *E-mail:* writers@capecodwriterscenter.org *Web Site:* capecodwriterscenter.org, pg 610

Struna, Barbara, Young Writers' Workshop, 919 Main St, Osterville, MA 02655 *Tel:* 508-420-0200 *E-mail:* writers@capecodwriterscenter.org *Web Site:* capecodwriterscenter.org, pg 617

Stuart, Carole, Barricade Books Inc, 2037 LeMoine Ave, Fort Lee, NJ 07024 *Tel:* 201-944-7600 *E-mail:* customerservice@barricadebooks.com *Web Site:* www.barricadebooks.com, pg 29

Stuart, Kari, ICM Partners, 65 E 55 St, New York, NY 10022 *Tel:* 212-556-5600 *Web Site:* www.icmtalent.com, pg 521

Stuart, Kathryn, Writers House, 21 W 26 St, New York, NY 10010 *Tel:* 212-685-2400 *Fax:* 212-685-1781 *Web Site:* www.writershouse.com, pg 542

Stuart, Kelly, Center for the Collaborative Classroom, 1250 53 St, Suite 3, Emeryville, CA 94608 *Tel:* 510-533-0213 *Toll Free Tel:* 800-666-7270 *Fax:* 510-464-3670 *E-mail:* info@collaborativeclassroom.org; clientsupport@collaborativeclassroom.org *Web Site:* www.collaborativeclassroom.org, pg 51

Stuart,
Nancy Rubin, Cape Cod Writers' Center Conference, 919 Main St, Osterville, MA 02655 *Tel:* 508-420-0200 *E-mail:* writers@capecodwriterscenter.org *Web Site:* capecodwriterscenter.org, pg 610

Stuart, Nancy Rubin, Young Writers' Workshop, 919 Main St, Osterville, MA 02655 *Tel:* 508-420-0200 *E-mail:* writers@capecodwriterscenter.org *Web Site:* capecodwriterscenter.org, pg 617

Stubblefield, Terri, Neustadt International Prize for Literature, c/o University of Oklahoma, 630 Parrington Oval, Suite 110, Norman, OK 73019-4033 *Tel:* 405-325-4531 *Web Site:* www.worldliteraturetoday.org; www.worldlit.org, pg 672

Stubblefield, Terri, NSK Neustadt Prize for Children's Literature, c/o University of Oklahoma, 630 Parrington Oval, Suite 110, Norman, OK 73019-4033 *Tel:* 405-325-4531 *Web Site:* www.worldliteraturetoday.org; www.worldlit.org, pg 674

Stubbs, Peter, Fitzhenry & Whiteside Limited, 195 Allstate Pkwy, Markham, ON L3R 4T8, Canada *Tel:* 905-477-9700 *Toll Free Tel:* 800-387-9776

Suzanne, Claudia, Wambtac Communications, 1512 E Santa Clara Ave, Santa Ana, CA 92705 *Tel:* 714-954-0580 *Toll Free Tel:* 800-641-3936 *E-mail:* wambtac@wambtac.com *Web Site:* www.wambtac.com; claudiasuzanne.com (prof servs), pg 502

Svehla, Gary, Midnight Marquee Press Inc, 9721 Britinay Lane, Baltimore, MD 21234 *Tel:* 410-665-1198 *E-mail:* mmarquee@aol.com *Web Site:* www.midmar.com, pg 150

Svehla, Susan, Midnight Marquee Press Inc, 9721 Britinay Lane, Baltimore, MD 21234 *Tel:* 410-665-1198 *E-mail:* mmarquee@aol.com *Web Site:* www.midmar.com, pg 150

Svetcov, Danielle, Levine|Greenberg|Rostan Literary Agency, 307 Seventh Ave, Suite 2407, New York, NY 10001 *Tel:* 212-337-0934 *Fax:* 212-337-0948 *Web Site:* lgrliterary.com, pg 525

Swaim, Dennis, Penguin Books, 375 Hudson St, New York, NY 10014 *Tel:* 212-366-2000 *E-mail:* penguinpublicity@us.penguingroup.com *Web Site:* www.penguinclassics.com; www.penguin.com, pg 177

Swaim, Dennis, Viking, 375 Hudson St, New York, NY 10014 *Tel:* 212-366-2000 *Fax:* 212-243-6002 *Web Site:* www.penguin.com/publishers/vikingbooks, pg 250

Swain, Neal, Wales Literary Agency Inc, 1508 Tenth Ave E, No 401, Seattle, WA 98102 *Tel:* 206-284-7114 *E-mail:* waleslit@waleslit.com *Web Site:* www.waleslit.com, pg 540

Swaney, Charlie, Tyndale House Publishers Inc, 351 Executive Dr, Carol Stream, IL 60188 *Tel:* 630-668-8300 *Toll Free Tel:* 800-323-9400 *Toll Free Fax:* 800-684-0247 *Web Site:* www.tyndale.com, pg 237

Swank, Linda, AAP PreK-12 Learning Group, 455 Massachusetts Ave NW, Suite 700, Washington, DC 20001 *Tel:* 267-351-4310 *Fax:* 267-351-4317 *E-mail:* prek12learning@publishers.org *Web Site:* www.aepweb.org, pg 553

Swanson, O'Ryin, Light Technology Publishing, 4030 E Huntington Dr, Flagstaff, AZ 86004 *Tel:* 928-526-1345 *Toll Free Tel:* 800-450-0985 *Fax:* 928-714-1132 *E-mail:* publishing@lighttechnology.net *Web Site:* www.lighttechnology.com, pg 134

Swanson-Davies, Linda, Glimmer Train Press Inc, PO Box 80430, Portland, OR 97280-1430 *Tel:* 503-221-0836 *Fax:* 503-221-0837 *E-mail:* editors@glimmertrain.org *Web Site:* www.glimmertrain.org, pg 93

Swauger, Amy, Teachers & Writers Collaborative, 520 Eighth Ave, Suite 2020, New York, NY 10018-4165 *Tel:* 212-691-6590 *Toll Free Tel:* 888-BOOKS-TW (266-5789) *Fax:* 212-675-0171 *E-mail:* info@twc.org *Web Site:* www.twc.org, pg 579

Swayze, Carolyn, Carolyn Swayze Literary Agency Ltd, 7360 137 St, Suite 319, Surrey, BC V3W 1A3, Canada *Tel:* 604-503-3895 *E-mail:* reception@swayzeagency.com *Web Site:* www.swayzeagency.com, pg 539

Sweany, Brian, Recorded Books Inc, an RBmedia company, 270 Skipjack Rd, Prince Frederick, MD 20678 *Tel:* 410-535-5590 *Toll Free Tel:* 877-732-2898 *Fax:* 410-535-5499 *E-mail:* customerservice@recordedbooks.com *Web Site:* www.recordedbooks.com, pg 196

Sweeney, Frances, PREP Publishing, 3528 Turnberry Circle, Fayetteville, NC 28303 *Tel:* 910-483-6611 *Toll Free Tel:* 800-533-2814 *E-mail:* preppub@aol.com *Web Site:* www.prep-pub.com, pg 187

Sweeney, Jillian, The Ned Leavitt Agency, 70 Wooster St, Suite 4-F, New York, NY 10012 *Tel:* 212-334-0999 *Web Site:* www.nedleavittagency.com, pg 525

Sweeney, Jon M, Ave Maria Press, PO Box 428, Notre Dame, IN 46556 *Tel:* 574-287-2831 *Toll Free Tel:* 800-282-1865 *Fax:* 574-239-2904 *Toll Free Fax:* 800-282-5681 *E-mail:* avemariapress.1@nd.edu *Web Site:* www.avemariapress.com, pg 27

Sweeney, Katie, Fordham University Press, Joseph A Martino Hall, 45 Columbus Ave, New York, NY 10023 *Fax:* 347-842-3083 *Web Site:* www.fordhampress.com, pg 86

Sweeney, Nick, Bloomsbury Publishing Inc, 1385 Broadway, 5th fl, New York, NY 10018 *Tel:* 212-419-5300 *E-mail:* marketingusa@bloomsbury.com; adultpublicityusa@bloomsbury.com; askacademic@bloomsbury.com *Web Site:* www.bloomsbury.com, pg 38

Sweet, Christopher, Thames & Hudson, 500 Fifth Ave, New York, NY 10110 *Tel:* 212-354-3763 *Toll Free Tel:* 800-233-4830 *Fax:* 212-398-1252 *E-mail:* bookinfo@thames.wwnorton.com *Web Site:* www.thamesandhudsonusa.com, pg 230

Swensen, Evan, Publication Consultants, 8370 Eleusis Dr, Anchorage, AK 99502 *Tel:* 907-349-2424 *Fax:* 907-349-2426 *E-mail:* books@publicationconsultants.com *Web Site:* www.publicationconsultants.com, pg 191

Swenson, Janine Y, LearningExpress LLC, 80 Broad St, 4th fl, New York, NY 10004 *Toll Free Tel:* 800-295-9556 (ext 2) *E-mail:* marketing@learningexpressllc.com (cust serv) *Web Site:* www.learningexpressllc.com, pg 131

Swerdloff, Carolyn, Simon & Schuster Children's Publishing, 1230 Avenue of the Americas, New York, NY 10020 *Tel:* 212-698-7000 *Web Site:* www.simonandschuster.com/kids; www.simonandschuster.com/teen; simonandschuster.net; simonandschuster.biz, pg 213

Sweren, Becky, Aevitas Creative Management, 19 W 21 St, Suite 501, New York, NY 10010 *Tel:* 212-765-6900 *Web Site:* aevitascreative.com, pg 506

Swetonic, Carrie, Dutton, 375 Hudson St, New York, NY 10014 *Tel:* 212-366-2000 *Fax:* 212-366-2262 *Web Site:* www.penguin.com, pg 74

Swetonic, Carrie, GP Putnam's Sons (Hardcover), 375 Hudson St, New York, NY 10014 *Tel:* 212-366-2000 *Fax:* 212-366-2643 *E-mail:* online@penguinputnam.com *Web Site:* www.penguin.com/publishers/gpputnamssons, pg 192

Swift, Eliza, Albert Whitman & Co, 250 S Northwest Hwy, Suite 320, Park Ridge, IL 60068 *Tel:* 847-232-2800 *Toll Free Tel:* 800-255-7675 *Fax:* 847-581-0039 *E-mail:* mail@albertwhitman.com *Web Site:* www.albertwhitman.com, pg 6

Swinwood, Craig, Harlequin Enterprises Ltd, 225 Duncan Mill Rd, Don Mills, ON M3B 3K9, Canada *Tel:* 416-445-5860 *Toll Free Tel:* 888-432-4879; 800-370-5838 (ebook inquiries) *E-mail:* customerservice@harlequin.com *Web Site:* www.harlequin.com, pg 459

Swinwood, Craig, Love Inspired Books, 233 Broadway, Suite 1001, New York, NY 10279 *Tel:* 212-553-4200 *Fax:* 212-227-8969 *E-mail:* customer_service@harlequin.ca *Web Site:* www.harlequin.com, pg 138

Swinwood, Susan, Harlequin Enterprises Ltd, 225 Duncan Mill Rd, Don Mills, ON M3B 3K9, Canada *Tel:* 416-445-5860 *Toll Free Tel:* 888-432-4879; 800-370-5838 (ebook inquiries) *E-mail:* customerservice@harlequin.com *Web Site:* www.harlequin.com, pg 459

Switzer, Kristi, Brewers Publications, 1372 Spruce St, Boulder, CO 80302 *Tel:* 303-447-0816 *Toll Free Tel:* 888-822-6273 (CN & US) *Fax:* 303-447-2825 *E-mail:* info@brewersassociation.org *Web Site:* www.brewersassociation.org, pg 42

Swomley, Olivia, Workman Publishing Co Inc, 225 Varick St, 9th fl, New York, NY 10014-4381 *Tel:* 212-254-5900 *Toll Free Tel:* 800-722-7202 *Fax:* 212-254-8098 *E-mail:* info@workman.com *Web Site:* www.workman.com, pg 259

Swope, Pamela K, Philosophy Documentation Center, PO Box 7147, Charlottesville, VA 22906-7147 *Tel:* 434-220-3300 *Toll Free Tel:* 800-444-2419 *Fax:* 434-220-3301 *E-mail:* order@pdcnet.org *Web Site:* www.pdcnet.org, pg 182

Sybert, Michelle, Indiana University Press, Herman B Wells Library 350, 1320 E Tenth St, Bloomington, IN 47405-3907 *Tel:* 812-855-8817 *Toll Free Tel:* 800-842-6796 (orders only) *Fax:* 812-855-7931; 812-855-8507 *E-mail:* iupress@indiana.edu; iuporder@indiana.edu (orders) *Web Site:* www.iupress.indiana.edu, pg 116

Sye, Stephen, ILA Children's & Young Adults' Book Awards, PO Box 8139, Newark, DE 19714-8139 *Tel:* 302-731-1600 *Toll Free Tel:* 800-336-7323 (US & CN) *Fax:* 302-731-1057 *E-mail:* ilaawards@reading.org *Web Site:* www.literacyworldwide.org, pg 654

Sygall, Susan, Mobility International USA, 132 E Broadway, Suite 343, Eugene, OR 97401 *Tel:* 541-343-1284 *Fax:* 541-343-6812 *E-mail:* info@miusa.org *Web Site:* www.miusa.org, pg 152

Sylbert, John, American Institute for Economic Research (AIER), 250 Division St, Great Barrington, MA 01230 *Tel:* 413-528-1216 *Toll Free Tel:* 888-528-1216 (orders) *E-mail:* info@aier.org *Web Site:* www.aier.org, pg 12

Sylvan, Tanya, Menasha Ridge Press Inc, 2204 First Ave S, Suite 102, Birmingham, AL 35233 *Toll Free Tel:* 888-604-4537 *Fax:* 205-326-1012 *E-mail:* info@adventurewithkeen.com *Web Site:* www.menasharidge.com, pg 148

Sylve, Elvira C, Clotilde's Secretarial & Management Services, PO Box 871926, New Orleans, LA 70187 *Tel:* 504-242-2912; 504-800-4853 (cell) *E-mail:* elcsy58@aol.com; elcsy58@att.net, pg 491

Symonds, Laurel, Albert Whitman & Co, 250 S Northwest Hwy, Suite 320, Park Ridge, IL 60068 *Tel:* 847-232-2800 *Toll Free Tel:* 800-255-7675 *Fax:* 847-581-0039 *E-mail:* mail@albertwhitman.com *Web Site:* www.albertwhitman.com, pg 6

Synatschk, Kathy, PRO-ED Inc, 8700 Shoal Creek Blvd, Austin, TX 78757-6897 *Tel:* 512-451-3246 *Toll Free Tel:* 800-897-3202 *Fax:* 512-451-8542 *Toll Free Fax:* 800-397-7633 *E-mail:* general@proedinc.com; info@proedinc.com *Web Site:* www.proedinc.com, pg 189

Szakonyi, Mark, The JOC Group Inc, 2 Penn Plaza E, Newark, NJ 07105 *Tel:* 973-776-8660 *Web Site:* www.joc.com, pg 122

Szczebak, Patricia, Pauline Books & Media, 50 Saint Paul's Ave, Boston, MA 02130 *Tel:* 617-522-8911 *Toll Free Tel:* 800-876-4463 (orders); 800-836-9723 (cust serv) *Fax:* 617-541-9805 *E-mail:* editorial@paulinemedia.com (ms submissions); orderentry@pauline.org (cust serv) *Web Site:* www.pauline.org/publishing; www.pauline.org/PBMPublishing, pg 175

Szekely, Peter, Deadline Club, c/o Salmagundi Club, 47 Fifth Ave, New York, NY 10003 *Tel:* 646-481-7584 *E-mail:* info@deadlineclub.org *Web Site:* www.deadlineclub.org, pg 564

Szost, Bernadette, Portfolio Solutions LLC, 136 Jameson Hill Rd, Clinton Corners, NY 12514 *Tel:* 845-266-1001 *Web Site:* www.portfoliosolutionsllc.com, pg 544

Szpyrka, Adrienne, Perseus Books, 250 W 57 St, 15th fl, New York, NY 10107 *Tel:* 212-340-8100 *Toll Free Tel:* 800-343-4499 (cust serv) *Fax:* 212-340-8105 *Web Site:* www.perseusbooks.com, pg 181

Tackett, Jessica, Bloomsbury Academic, 1385 Broadway, 5th fl, New York, NY 10018 *Tel:* 212-419-5300 *Web Site:* www.bloomsbury.com/us/academic, pg 37

Tafolla, Carmen, Carr P Collins Award, c/o 7748 Hwy 290 W, Austin, TX 78736-3202 *Tel:* 512-683-5640 *E-mail:* president@texasinstituteofletters.org *Web Site:* www.texasinstituteofletters.org, pg 638

Tafolla, Carmen, Soeurette Diehl Fraser Translation Award, c/o 7748 Hwy 290 W, Austin, TX 78736-3202 *Tel:* 512-683-5640 *E-mail:* president@texasinstituteofletters.org *Web Site:* www.texasinstituteofletters.org, pg 647

Tafolla, Carmen, Jesse H Jones Award, c/o 7748 Hwy 290 W, Austin, TX 78736-3202 *Tel:* 512-683-5640 *E-mail:* president@texasinstituteofletters.org *Web Site:* www.texasinstituteofletters.org, pg 657

Tafolla, Carmen, Ramirez Family Award, c/o 7748 Hwy 290 W, Austin, TX 78736-3202 *Tel:* 512-683-5640 *E-mail:* president@texasinstituteofletters.org *Web Site:* www.texasinstituteofletters.org, pg 684

Tavarez, Yamberlie, The Feminist Press at The City University of New York, 365 Fifth Ave, Suite 5406, New York, NY 10016 *Tel:* 212-817-7915 *Fax:* 212-817-1593 *E-mail:* info@feministpress.org *Web Site:* www.feministpress.org, pg 83

Taverna, Alison, Autumn House Press, 5530 Penn Ave, Pittsburgh, PA 15206 *Tel:* 412-362-2665 *E-mail:* info@autumnhouse.org *Web Site:* www.autumnhouse.org, pg 26

Tavolacci, Joyce, Bearport Publishing Co Inc, 45 W 21 St, Suite 3B, New York, NY 10010 *Tel:* 212-337-8577 *Toll Free Tel:* 877-337-8577 *Fax:* 212-337-8557 *Toll Free Fax:* 866-337-8557 *E-mail:* service@bearportpublishing.com; info@bearportpublishing.com *Web Site:* www.bearportpublishing.com, pg 31

Taylor, Beth, American Marketing Association, 130 E Randolph St, 22nd fl, Chicago, IL 60601 *Tel:* 312-542-9000 *Toll Free Tel:* 800-AMA-1150 (262-1150) *Fax:* 312-542-9001 *E-mail:* info@ama.org *Web Site:* www.ama.org, pg 555

Taylor, Brent, TriadaUS Literary Agency, PO Box 561, Sewickley, PA 15143 *Tel:* 412-401-3376 *Web Site:* www.triadaus.com, pg 540

Taylor, Darlene, PEN/Faulkner Award for Fiction, Folger Shakespeare Library, 201 E Capitol St SE, Washington, DC 20003 *Tel:* 202-898-9063 *Fax:* 202-675-0360 *Web Site:* www.penfaulkner.org, pg 678

Taylor, Joe, Livingston Press, University of West Alabama, Sta 22, Livingston, AL 35470 *Tel:* 205-652-3470 *Web Site:* www.livingstonpress.uwa.edu, pg 136

Taylor, John D, Bonasa Press, PO Box 340, Crosby, ND 58730 *Tel:* 701-965-3974 *E-mail:* new@bonasapress.com (inquiries) *Web Site:* www.bonasapress.com, pg 39

Taylor, Justin, Crossway, 1300 Crescent St, Wheaton, IL 60187 *Tel:* 630-682-4300 *Toll Free Tel:* 800-635-7993 (orders); 800-543-1659 (cust serv) *Fax:* 630-682-4785 *E-mail:* info@crossway.org *Web Site:* www.crossway.org, pg 65

Taylor, Keith, Page Davidson Clayton Prize for Emerging Poets, University of Michigan, 0576 Rackham Bldg, 915 E Washington St, Ann Arbor, MI 48109-1070 *Tel:* 734-764-9265 *E-mail:* mqr@umich.edu *Web Site:* www.umich.edu/~mqr, pg 637

Taylor, Keith, Laurence Goldstein Poetry Prize, University of Michigan, 0576 Rackham Bldg, 915 E Washington St, Ann Arbor, MI 48109-1070 *Tel:* 734-764-9265 *E-mail:* mqr@umich.edu *Web Site:* www.umich.edu/~mqr, pg 650

Taylor, Marci, American Press, 60 State St, Suite 700, Boston, MA 02109 *Tel:* 617-247-0022 *E-mail:* americanpress@flash.net *Web Site:* www.americanpresspublishers.com, pg 13

Taylor, Mark, Standard Publishing, 4050 Lee Vance View, Colorado Springs, CO 80918 *Tel:* 513-931-4050 *Toll Free Tel:* 800-323-7543 *Fax:* 513-931-0950 *Toll Free Fax:* 800-323-0726 *E-mail:* customerservice@standardpub.com *Web Site:* www.standardpub.com, pg 220

Taylor, Mark, Tyndale House Publishers Inc, 351 Executive Dr, Carol Stream, IL 60188 *Tel:* 630-668-8300 *Toll Free Tel:* 800-323-9400 *Toll Free Fax:* 800-684-0247 *Web Site:* www.tyndale.com, pg 237

Taylor, Meredith, Association Media & Publishing (AM&P), 529 14 St, Suite 750, Washington, DC 20045 *Tel:* 202-591-2457 *E-mail:* info@associationmediaandpublishing.org *Web Site:* associationmediaandpublishing.org, pg 558

Taylor, Meredith, EXCEL Awards, 529 14 St, Suite 750, Washington, DC 20045 *Tel:* 202-591-2457 *E-mail:* awards@associationmediaandpublishing.org; info@associationmediaandpublishing.org *Web Site:* associationmediaandpublishing.org; kellencompany.com, pg 645

Taylor, Nathan, Stephen Leacock Memorial Medal for Humour, 149 Peter St N, Orillia, ON L3V 4Z4, Canada *Tel:* 705-326-9286 *Web Site:* www.leacock.ca, pg 660

Taylor, Robert PhD, Institute of Public Administration of Canada, 1075 Bay St, Suite 401, Toronto, ON M5S 2B1, Canada *Tel:* 416-924-8787 *Fax:* 416-924-4992 *E-mail:* ntl@ipac.ca *Web Site:* www.ipac.ca, pg 461

Taylor, Sara, Dumbarton Oaks, 1703 32 St NW, Washington, DC 20007 *Tel:* 202-339-6400 *Fax:* 202-339-6401; 202-298-8407 *E-mail:* doaksbooks@doaks.org *Web Site:* www.doaks.org, pg 73

Taylor, Victor E, The Davies Group Publishers, PO Box 440140, Aurora, CO 80044-0140 *Tel:* 303-750-8374 *Fax:* 303-337-0952 *E-mail:* info@thedaviesgrouppublishers.com; daviesgroup@msn.com (orders) *Web Site:* www.thedaviesgrouppublishers.com, pg 68

Taylor, Yuval, Chicago Review Press, 814 N Franklin St, Chicago, IL 60610 *Tel:* 312-337-0747 *Toll Free Tel:* 800-888-4741 *Fax:* 312-337-5110 *E-mail:* frontdesk@chicagoreviewpress.com *Web Site:* www.chicagoreviewpress.com, pg 54

Tayman, William P Jr, Corporation for Public Broadcasting (CPB), 401 Ninth St NW, Washington, DC 20004-2129 *Tel:* 202-879-9600 *Web Site:* www.cpb.org, pg 563

Teal-Guess, Kellie, ProQuest LLC, 789 E Eisenhower Pkwy, Ann Arbor, MI 48108 *Tel:* 734-761-4700 *Toll Free Tel:* 800-521-0600 *Web Site:* www.proquest.com, pg 190

Teeple, Charlotte, Marilyn Baillie Picture Book Award, 40 Orchard View Blvd, Suite 217, Toronto, ON M4R 1B9, Canada *Tel:* 416-975-0010 *Fax:* 416-975-8970 *E-mail:* info@bookcentre.ca *Web Site:* www.bookcentre.ca, pg 629

Teeple, Charlotte, The Geoffrey Bilson Award for Historical Fiction for Young People, 40 Orchard View Blvd, Suite 217, Toronto, ON M4R 1B9, Canada *Tel:* 416-975-0010 *Fax:* 416-975-8970 *E-mail:* info@bookcentre.ca *Web Site:* www.bookcentre.ca, pg 632

Teeple, Charlotte, Canadian Children's Book Centre, 40 Orchard View Blvd, Suite 217, Toronto, ON M4R 1B9, Canada *Tel:* 416-975-0010 *Fax:* 416-975-8970 *E-mail:* info@bookcentre.ca *Web Site:* www.bookcentre.ca, pg 562

Teeple, Charlotte, Norma Fleck Award for Canadian Children's Non-Fiction, 40 Orchard View Blvd, Suite 217, Toronto, ON M4R 1B9, Canada *Tel:* 416-975-0010 *Fax:* 416-975-8970 *E-mail:* info@bookcentre.ca *Web Site:* www.bookcentre.ca, pg 646

Teeple, Charlotte, Amy Mathers Teen Book Award, 40 Orchard View Blvd, Suite 217, Toronto, ON M4R 1B9, Canada *Tel:* 416-975-0010 *Fax:* 416-975-8970 *E-mail:* info@bookcentre.ca *Web Site:* www.bookcentre.ca, pg 666

Teeple, Charlotte, John Spray Mystery Award, 40 Orchard View Blvd, Suite 217, Toronto, ON M4R 1B9, Canada *Tel:* 416-975-0010 *Fax:* 416-975-8970 *E-mail:* info@bookcentre.ca *Web Site:* www.bookcentre.ca, pg 691

Teeple, Charlotte, TD Canadian Children's Literature Award, 40 Orchard View Blvd, Suite 217, Toronto, ON M4R 1B9, Canada *Tel:* 416-975-0010 *Fax:* 416-975-8970 *E-mail:* info@bookcentre.ca *Web Site:* www.bookcentre.ca, pg 693

Teicher, Oren, American Booksellers Association, 333 Westchester Ave, Suite S202, White Plains, NY 10604 *Tel:* 914-406-7500 *Toll Free Tel:* 800-637-0037 *Fax:* 914-410-6297 *E-mail:* info@bookweb.org *Web Site:* www.bookweb.org, pg 554

Teicher, Oren, Indies Choice Book Awards, 333 Westchester Ave, Suite S202, White Plains, NY 10604 *Tel:* 914-406-7500 *Toll Free Tel:* 800-637-0037 *Fax:* 914-410-6297 *Web Site:* www.bookweb.org, pg 655

Teichgraeber, Gretchen, Leadership Directories, 1407 Broadway, Suite 318, New York, NY 10018 *Tel:* 212-627-4140 *Toll Free Tel:* 800-627-0311 *Fax:* 212-645-0931 *E-mail:* info@leadershipdirectories.com *Web Site:* www.leadershipdirectories.com, pg 130

Teigen, Rob, Bethany House Publishers, 11400 Hampshire Ave S, Bloomington, MN 55438 *Tel:* 952-829-2500 *Toll Free Tel:* 800-877-2665 (orders) *Fax:* 952-829-2568 *Toll Free Fax:* 800-398-3111 (orders) *Web Site:* www.bethanyhouse.com; www.bakerpublishinggroup.com, pg 34

Teixeira, Ian, Fine Creative Media, Inc, 322 Eighth Ave, 15th fl, New York, NY 10001 *Tel:* 212-595-3500 *Fax:* 212-595-3779, pg 85

Tell, David, Hudson Institute, 1015 15 St NW, 6th fl, Washington, DC 20005 *Tel:* 202-974-2400 *Fax:* 202-974-2410 *E-mail:* info@hudson.org *Web Site:* www.hudson.org, pg 112

Tell, Geoffery Crawford, Two Thousand Three Associates, 135 Chilean Ave, Palm Beach, FL 33480 *Tel:* 386-690-2503 *E-mail:* ttta1@att.net *Web Site:* www.twothousandthree.com, pg 237

Temena-Husemann, Cialina, Workman Publishing Co Inc, 225 Varick St, 9th fl, New York, NY 10014-4381 *Tel:* 212-254-5900 *Toll Free Tel:* 800-722-7202 *Fax:* 212-254-8098 *E-mail:* info@workman.com *Web Site:* www.workman.com, pg 259

Tempest, Nephele, The Knight Agency Inc, 570 East Ave, Madison, GA 30650 *E-mail:* submissions@knightagency.net *Web Site:* www.knightagency.net, pg 524

Tempio, Robert, Princeton University Press, 41 William St, Princeton, NJ 08540-5237 *Tel:* 609-258-4900 *Fax:* 609-258-6305 *Web Site:* press.princeton.edu, pg 188

Templar, Kate, Stanford University Press, 425 Broadway St, Redwood City, CA 94063-3126 *Tel:* 650-723-9434 *Fax:* 650-725-3457 *E-mail:* info@www.sup.org; publicity@www.sup.org *Web Site:* www.sup.org, pg 220

Temple, Jamey, Eric Hoffer Award for Short Prose, PO Box 11, Titusville, NJ 08560 *Fax:* 609-964-1718 *E-mail:* info@hofferaward.com *Web Site:* www.hofferaward.com, pg 653

Temple, John F, Guideposts Book & Inspirational Media, 16 E 34 St, 12th fl, New York, NY 10016 *Tel:* 212-251-8100 *Toll Free Tel:* 800-431-2344 (cust serv) *Fax:* 212-684-0689 *E-mail:* gpsprod@cdsfulfillment.com *Web Site:* guideposts.org, pg 97

Temple, Johnny, Akashic Books, 232 Third St, Suite A-115, Brooklyn, NY 11215 *Tel:* 718-643-9193 *Fax:* 718-643-9195 *E-mail:* info@akashicbooks.com *Web Site:* www.akashicbooks.com, pg 6

Temple, Sam, North Star Editions Inc, 2297 Waters Dr, Mendota Heights, MN 55120 *Tel:* 651-204-3515 *Toll Free Tel:* 888-417-0195 *Fax:* 952-582-1000 *E-mail:* sales@northstareditions.com *Web Site:* www.northstareditions.com, pg 164

Temple, Travis, Penguin Random House Inc, 1745 Broadway, New York, NY 10019 *Tel:* 212-782-9000 *Toll Free Tel:* 800-726-0600 *Web Site:* www.penguinrandomhouse.com, pg 178

Tenaglia, Lisa, Hachette Books, 1290 Avenue of the Americas, New York, NY 10019 *Tel:* 212-364-1100 *Web Site:* www.hachettebookgroup.com, pg 98

Tenney, Craig, Harold Ober Associates Inc, 425 Madison Ave, New York, NY 10017 *Tel:* 212-759-8600 *Fax:* 212-759-9428 *Web Site:* www.haroldober.com, pg 531

Tepper, Michael, Genealogical Publishing Co, 3600 Clipper Mill Rd, Suite 260, Baltimore, MD 21211 *Tel:* 410-837-8271 *Toll Free Tel:* 800-296-6687 *Fax:* 410-752-8492 *Toll Free Fax:* 800-599-9561 *E-mail:* info@genealogical.com; web@genealogical.com *Web Site:* www.genealogical.com, pg 91

Teresi, Christian, Association of Writers & Writing Programs (AWP), George Mason University, 4400 University Dr, MSN 1E3, Fairfax, VA 22030 *Tel:* 703-993-4301 *Fax:* 703-993-4302 *E-mail:* awp@awpwriter.org *Web Site:* www.awpwriter.org, pg 559

Teresi, Christian, AWP Award Series, George Mason University, 4400 University Dr, MSN 1E3, Fairfax, VA 22030 *Tel:* 703-993-4301 *Fax:* 703-993-4302 *E-mail:* awp@awpwriter.org *Web Site:* www.awpwriter.org, pg 629

Terfloth, Caitlin, The Summer Experience, 1831 College Ave, Suite 324, Regina, SK S4P 4V5, Canada *Tel:* 306-537-7243 *E-mail:* sage.hill@sasktel.net *Web Site:* www.sagehillwriting.ca, pg 615

Termine, Anna, Corwin, a Sage Co, 2455 Teller Rd, Thousand Oaks, CA 91320 *Tel:* 805-499-9734 *Toll Free Tel:* 800-233-9936 *Fax:* 805-499-5323 *Toll Free Fax:* 800-417-2466 *E-mail:* info@corwin.com; order@corwin.com *Web Site:* www.corwin.com, pg 61

Terraciano, Kevin, UCLA Latin American Center Publications, UCLA Latin American Institute, 10343 Bunche Hall, Los Angeles, CA 90095 *Tel:* 310-825-4571 *Fax:* 310-206-6859 *E-mail:* latinamctr@international.ucla.edu *Web Site:* www.international.ucla.edu/lai, pg 238

Terragni, Emilia, Phaidon, 65 Bleecker St, 8th fl, New York, NY 10012 *Tel:* 212-652-5400 *Toll Free Tel:* 800-759-0190 (cust serv) *Fax:* 212-652-5410 *Toll Free Fax:* 800-286-9471 (cust serv) *E-mail:* ussales@phaidon.com *Web Site:* www.phaidon.com, pg 182

Terrell, Guy, Laura Day Boggs Bolling Memorial, 900 Timber Creek Place, Virginia Beach, VA 23464 *E-mail:* poetryinva@aol.com *Web Site:* poetrysocietyofvirginia.org, pg 633

Terrell, Guy, Joe Pendleton Campbell Narrative Contest, 900 Timber Creek Place, Virginia Beach, VA 23464 *E-mail:* poetryinva@aol.com *Web Site:* poetrysocietyofvirginia.org, pg 635

Terrell, Guy, Carleton Drewry Memorial, 900 Timber Creek Place, Virginia Beach, VA 23464 *E-mail:* poetryinva@aol.com *Web Site:* poetrysocietyofvirginia.org, pg 642

Terrell, Guy, Alfred C Gary Memorial, 900 Timber Creek Place, Virginia Beach, VA 23464 *E-mail:* poetryinva@aol.com *Web Site:* poetrysocietyofvirginia.org, pg 648

Terrell, Guy, Bess Gresham Memorial, 900 Timber Creek Place, Virginia Beach, VA 23464 *E-mail:* poetryinva@aol.com *Web Site:* poetrysocietyofvirginia.org, pg 651

Terrell, Guy, Loretta Dunn Hall Memorial, 900 Timber Creek Place, Virginia Beach, VA 23464 *E-mail:* poetryinva@aol.com *Web Site:* poetrysocietyofvirginia.org, pg 651

Terrell, Guy, Handy Andy Prize, 900 Timber Creek Place, Virginia Beach, VA 23464 *E-mail:* poetryinva@aol.com *Web Site:* poetrysocietyofvirginia.org, pg 651

Terrell, Guy, Brodie Herndon Memorial, 900 Timber Creek Place, Virginia Beach, VA 23464 *E-mail:* poetryinva@aol.com *Web Site:* poetrysocietyofvirginia.org, pg 652

Terrell, Guy, Judah, Sarah, Grace & Tom Memorial, 900 Timber Creek Place, Virginia Beach, VA 23464 *E-mail:* poetryinva@aol.com; info@poetryvirginia.org *Web Site:* poetrysocietyofvirginia.org, pg 658

Terrell, Guy, Cenie H Moon Prize, 900 Timber Creek Place, Virginia Beach, VA 23464 *E-mail:* poetryinva@aol.com *Web Site:* poetrysocietyofvirginia.org, pg 669

Terrell, Guy, Edgar Allan Poe Memorial, 900 Timber Creek Place, Virginia Beach, VA 23464 *E-mail:* poetryinva@aol.com *Web Site:* poetrysocietyofvirginia.org, pg 680

Terrell, Guy, Miriam Rachimi Memorial, 900 Timber Creek Place, Virginia Beach, VA 23464 *E-mail:* poetryinva@aol.com *Web Site:* poetrysocietyofvirginia.org, pg 683

Terrell, Guy, Ada Sanderson Memorial, 900 Timber Creek Place, Virginia Beach, VA 23464 *E-mail:* poetryinva@aol.com *Web Site:* poetrysocietyofvirginia.org, pg 686

Terrell, Guy, The Robert S Sergeant Memorial, 900 Timber Creek Place, Virginia Beach, VA 23464 *E-mail:* poetryinva@aol.com *Web Site:* poetrysocietyofvirginia.org, pg 688

Terris, Sam, Random House Children's Books, 1745 Broadway, 10th fl, New York, NY 10019 *Tel:* 212-782-9000 *Web Site:* www.randomhousekids.com, pg 194

Terry, Barbara, Waldorf Publishing, 2140 Hall Johnson Rd, No 102-345, Grapevine, TX 76051 *Tel:* 972-674-3131 *E-mail:* info@waldorfpublishing.com *Web Site:* www.waldorfpublishing.com, pg 252

Terry, J P, Business Forms Management Association (BFMA), 1147 Fleetwood Ave, Madison, WI 53716 *Toll Free Tel:* 888-367-3078 *E-mail:* bfma@bfma.org *Web Site:* www.bfma.org, pg 561

Tertel, Megan, Clinical Laboratory & Standards Institute (CLSI), 950 W Valley Rd, Suite 2500, Wayne, PA 19087 *Tel:* 610-688-0100 *Toll Free Tel:* 877-447-1888 (orders) *Fax:* 610-688-0700 *E-mail:* customerservice@clsi.org *Web Site:* www.clsi.org, pg 57

Tessier, Michel, Les Editions Vents d'Ouest, 109, rue Wright, bureau 202, Gatineau, QC J8X 2G7, Canada *Tel:* 819-770-6377 *E-mail:* info@ventsdouest.ca *Web Site:* www.ventsdouest.ca, pg 455

Tessler, Michelle, Tessler Literary Agency LLC, 27 W 20 St, Suite 1003, New York, NY 10011 *Tel:* 212-242-0466 *Web Site:* www.tessleragency.com, pg 539

Tetro, Cathleen, Perseus Books, 250 W 57 St, 15th fl, New York, NY 10107 *Tel:* 212-340-8100 *Toll Free Tel:* 800-343-4499 (cust serv) *Fax:* 212-340-8105 *Web Site:* www.perseusbooks.com, pg 180

Thackara, Will, Theosophical University Press, PO Box C, Pasadena, CA 91109-7107 *Tel:* 626-798-3378 *E-mail:* tupress@theosociety.org *Web Site:* www.theosociety.org, pg 231

Thacker, Erin, Chronicle Books LLC, 680 Second St, San Francisco, CA 94107 *Tel:* 415-537-4200 *Toll Free Tel:* 800-759-0190 (cust serv) *Fax:* 415-537-4460 *Toll Free Fax:* 800-858-7787 (orders); 800-286-9471 (cust serv) *E-mail:* frontdesk@chroniclebooks.com *Web Site:* www.chroniclebooks.com, pg 55

Tharcher, Nicholas, The Original Falcon Press, 1753 E Broadway Rd, No 101-277, Tempe, AZ 85282 *Tel:* 602-708-1409 *E-mail:* info@originalfalcon.com *Web Site:* www.originalfalcon.com, pg 170

Tharp, Brent D, Atlas Publishing, 25185 Madison Ave, Suite A, Murrieta, CA 92562 *Tel:* 858-222-3747 *E-mail:* permissions@atlaspublishing.biz *Web Site:* www.atlaspublishing.biz, pg 25

Tharpe, Arthur, Business Marketing Association (BMA), 708 Third Ave, New York, NY 10017 *Tel:* 212-697-5950 *Fax:* 212-687-7310 *E-mail:* info@marketing.org *Web Site:* www.marketing.org, pg 561

Thaw, Deborah M, National Notary Association (NNA), 9350 De Soto Ave, Chatsworth, CA 91311-4926 *Tel:* 818-739-4000 *Toll Free Tel:* 800-876-6827 *Toll Free Fax:* 800-833-1211 *E-mail:* nna@nationalnotary.org *Web Site:* www.nationalnotary.org, pg 159

Thawar, Tasleem, PEN Canada, 24 Ryerson Ave, Suite 301, Toronto, ON M5T 2P3, Canada *Tel:* 416-703-8448 *Fax:* 416-703-3870 *E-mail:* queries@pencanada.ca *Web Site:* www.pencanada.ca, pg 575

Thayer, Henry, Brandt & Hochman Literary Agents Inc, 1501 Broadway, Suite 2310, New York, NY 10036 *Tel:* 212-840-5760 *Fax:* 212-840-5776 *Web Site:* brandthochman.com, pg 509

Thegeby, Sarah, Thames & Hudson, 500 Fifth Ave, New York, NY 10110 *Tel:* 212-354-3763 *Toll Free Tel:* 800-233-4830 *Fax:* 212-398-1252 *E-mail:* bookinfo@thames.wwnorton.com *Web Site:* www.thamesandhudsonusa.com, pg 230

Theophilus, Gayna, Annick Press Ltd, 15 Patricia Ave, Toronto, ON M2M 1H9, Canada *Tel:* 416-221-4802 *Fax:* 416-221-8400 *E-mail:* annickpress@annickpress.com *Web Site:* www.annickpress.com, pg 445

Theroux, David J, Independent Institute, 100 Swan Way, Suite 200, Oakland, CA 94621-1428 *Tel:* 510-632-1366 *Toll Free Tel:* 800-927-8733 *Fax:* 510 568-6040 *E-mail:* orders@independent.org *Web Site:* www.independent.org, pg 115

Thickstun, Margaret, Hamilton College, English/Creative Writing, English/Creative Writing Dept, 198 College Hill Rd, Clinton, NY 13323 *Tel:* 315-859-4370 *Fax:* 315-859-4390 *Web Site:* www.hamilton.edu, pg 620

Thies, Sue, Perfection Learning Corp, 1000 N Second Ave, Logan, IA 51546 *Tel:* 712-644-2831 *Toll Free Tel:* 800-831-4190 *Toll Free Fax:* 800-543-2745 *E-mail:* orders@perfectionlearning.com *Web Site:* perfectionlearning.com, pg 180

Thixton, Robert, Pinder Lane & Garon-Brooke Associates Ltd, 159 W 53 St, New York, NY 10019 *Tel:* 212-489-0880 *Fax:* 212-489-7104 *E-mail:* pinderlanegaronbrooke@gmail.com *Web Site:* www.pinderlaneandgaronbrooke.com, pg 531

Thoma, Geri, Writers House, 21 W 26 St, New York, NY 10010 *Tel:* 212-685-2400 *Fax:* 212-685-1781 *Web Site:* www.writershouse.com, pg 542

Thoma, Raya, Prestel Publishing, 900 Broadway, Suite 603, New York, NY 10003 *Tel:* 212-995-2720 *Fax:* 212-995-2733 *E-mail:* sales@prestel-usa.com *Web Site:* prestelpublishing.randomhouse.de, pg 187

Thomas, Alan G, University of Chicago Press, 1427 E 60 St, Chicago, IL 60637-2954 *Tel:* 773-702-7700; 773-702-7600 *Toll Free Tel:* 800-621-2736 (orders) *Fax:* 773-702-9756; 773-660-2235 (orders); 773-702-2708 *E-mail:* custserv@press.uchicago.edu; marketing@press.uchicago.edu *Web Site:* www.press.uchicago.edu, pg 241

Thomas, Christen, The Literary Press Group of Canada, 425 Adelaide St W, Suite 700, Toronto, ON M5V 3C1, Canada *Tel:* 416-483-1321 *Fax:* 416-483-2510 *Web Site:* www.lpg.ca, pg 568

Thomas, Dominike, University of Ottawa Press (Presses de l'Université d'Ottawa), 542 King Edward Ave, Ottawa, ON K1N 6N5, Canada *Tel:* 613-562-5246 *Fax:* 613-562-5247 *E-mail:* puo-oup@uottawa.ca *Web Site:* press.uottawa.ca, pg 474

Thomas, Gretta, Vanderbilt University Press, 2014 Broadway, Suite 320, Nashville, TN 37203 *Tel:* 615-322-3585 *Toll Free Tel:* 800-627-7377 (orders only) *Fax:* 615-343-8823 *Toll Free Fax:* 800-735-0476 (orders only) *E-mail:* vupress@vanderbilt.edu *Web Site:* www.vanderbiltuniversitypress.com, pg 249

Thomas, James A, ASTM International, 100 Barr Harbor Dr, West Conshohocken, PA 19428-2959 *Tel:* 610-832-9500; 610-832-9585 (intl) *Toll Free Tel:* 877-909-2786 (sales & cust support) *Fax:* 610-832-9555 *E-mail:* service@astm.org *Web Site:* www.astm.org, pg 24

Thomas, Jerry, Pacific Press Publishing Association, 1350 N Kings Rd, Nampa, ID 83687-3193 *Tel:* 208-465-2500 *Toll Free Tel:* 800-447-7377 *Fax:* 208-465-2531 *Web Site:* www.pacificpress.com, pg 172

Thomas, JoAnne C, New Horizon Press, PO Box 669, Far Hills, NJ 07931-0669 *Tel:* 908-604-6311 *E-mail:* nhp@newhorizonpressbooks.com *Web Site:* www.newhorizonpressbooks.com, pg 160

Thomas, John, The Little Entrepreneur, c/o Harper Arrington Media, 18701 Grand River, Suite 105, Detroit, MI 48223 *Toll Free Tel:* 888-435-9234 *Fax:* 248-281-0373 *E-mail:* info@harperarringtonmedia.com *Web Site:* www.thelittlee.com, pg 136

Thomas, Joy, Chartered Professional Accountants of Canada (CPA Canada), 277 Wellington St W, Toronto, ON M5V 3H2, Canada *Tel:* 416-977-3222 *Toll Free Tel:* 800-268-3793 *Fax:* 416-977-8585 *E-mail:* member.services@cpacanada.ca *Web Site:* www.cpacanada.ca; www.facebook.com/CPACanada/, pg 450

Thomas, Karen, Cleis Press, 2246 Sixth St, Berkeley, CA 94710 *Tel:* 510-845-8000 *Toll Free Tel:* 800-780-2279 (US) *Fax:* 510-845-8001 *E-mail:* orders@cleispress.com *Web Site:* www.cleispress.com; www.vivaeditions.com, pg 57

Thomas, Kelly, Society for Industrial & Applied Mathematics, 3600 Market St, 6th fl, Philadelphia, PA 19104-2688 *Tel:* 215-382-9800 *Toll Free Tel:* 800-447-7426 *Fax:* 215-386-7999 *E-mail:* siambooks@siam.org *Web Site:* www.siam.org, pg 216

Thorne, Troy, Fox Chapel Publishing Co Inc, 1970 Broad St, East Petersburg, PA 17520 *Tel:* 717-560-4703 *Toll Free Tel:* 800-457-9112 *Fax:* 717-560-4702 *E-mail:* customerservice@foxchapelpublishing.com *Web Site:* www.foxchapelpublishing.com, pg 87

Thornton, Allen, Susan Thornton, 6090 Liberty Ave, Vermilion, OH 44089 *Tel:* 440-967-1757 *E-mail:* allenthornton@earthlink.net, pg 502

Thornton, Carrie, HarperCollins General Books Group, 195 Broadway, New York, NY 10007 *Tel:* 212-207-7000 *Web Site:* www.harpercollins.com, pg 101

Thornton, Dave, David C Cook, 4050 Lee Vance View, Colorado Springs, CO 80918 *Tel:* 719-536-0100 *Toll Free Tel:* 800-708-5550; 800-323-7543 (orders & cust serv) *Toll Free Fax:* 800-430-0726 (cust serv) *Web Site:* www.davidccook.com, pg 60

Thornton, Greg, Moody Publishers, 820 N La Salle Blvd, Chicago, IL 60610 *Tel:* 312-329-4000 *Toll Free Tel:* 800-678-8812 (cust serv) *Fax:* 312-329-2019 *E-mail:* mpcustomerservice@moody.edu *Web Site:* www.moodypublishers.com, pg 153

Thornton, Kara, Hachette Books, 1290 Avenue of the Americas, New York, NY 10019 *Tel:* 212-364-1100 *Web Site:* www.hachettebookgroup.com, pg 98

Thornton, Nan, Aevitas Creative Management, 19 W 21 St, Suite 501, New York, NY 10010 *Tel:* 212-765-6900 *Web Site:* aevitascreative.com, pg 506

Thornton, Susan, Susan Thornton, 6090 Liberty Ave, Vermilion, OH 44089 *Tel:* 440-967-1757 *E-mail:* allenthornton@earthlink.net, pg 502

Thorpe, Andrea, Sarah Josepha Hale Award, 58 N Main, Newport, NH 03773 *Tel:* 603-863-3430 *E-mail:* rfl@newport.lib.nh.us *Web Site:* www.newport.lib.nh.us, pg 651

Thorpe, Catherine, Napa Valley Writers' Conference, 1088 College Ave, St Helena, CA 94574 *Tel:* 707-967-2900 (ext 4) *Fax:* 707-967-2909 *E-mail:* info@napawritersconference.org; media@napawritersconference.org; fiction@napawritersconference.org; poetry@napawritersconference.org *Web Site:* www.napawritersconference.org, pg 613

Thorpe, Wendy, Chronicle Books LLC, 680 Second St, San Francisco, CA 94107 *Tel:* 415-537-4200 *Toll Free Tel:* 800-759-0190 (cust serv) *Fax:* 415-537-4460 *Toll Free Fax:* 800-858-7787 (orders); 800-286-9471 (cust serv) *E-mail:* frontdesk@chroniclebooks.com *Web Site:* www.chroniclebooks.com, pg 55

Thrombly, J, Wittenborn Art Books, 1109 Geary Blvd, San Francisco, CA 94109 *Tel:* 415-292-6500 *Toll Free Tel:* 800-660-6403 *Fax:* 415-292-6594 *E-mail:* wittenborn@art-books.com *Web Site:* www.art-books.com, pg 258

Thwaite, Sara, St Martin's Press, LLC, 175 Fifth Ave, New York, NY 10010 *Tel:* 646-307-5151 *Web Site:* us.macmillan.com/smp, pg 204

Tiberio, Jennifer, Between the Lines, 401 Richmond St W, No 277, Toronto, ON M5V 3A8, Canada *Tel:* 416-535-9914 *Toll Free Tel:* 800-718-7201 *Fax:* 416 535 1484 *E-mail:* info@btlbooks.com *Web Site:* btlbooks.com, pg 446

Tierney, Jeff, Boys Town Press, 13603 Flanagan Blvd, 2nd fl, Boys Town, NE 68010 *Tel:* 402-498-1320 *Toll Free Tel:* 800-282-6657 *Fax:* 402-498-1310 *E-mail:* btpress@boystown.org *Web Site:* www.boystownpress.org, pg 41

Tierney, Peggy, Tanglewood Publishing, 1060 N Capitol Ave, Suite E-395, Indianapolis, IN 46204 *Tel:* 812-877-9488 *Toll Free Tel:* 800-788-3123 (orders) *E-mail:* info@tanglewoodbooks.com; orders@tanglewoodbooks.com *Web Site:* www.tanglewoodbooks.com, pg 227

Tigay, Alan M, The Harold U Ribalow Prize, 40 Wall St, 8th fl, New York, NY 10005-1387 *Tel:* 212-451-6286 *Fax:* 212-451-6257 *E-mail:* magtemp3@hadassah.org *Web Site:* www.hadassah.org/magazine, pg 684

Tigunait, Pandit Rajmani PhD, Himalayan Institute Press, 952 Bethany Tpke, Honesdale, PA 18431 *Tel:* 570-253-5551 *Toll Free Tel:* 800-822-4547 *E-mail:* info@himalayaninstitute.org *Web Site:* www.himalayaninstitute.org, pg 107

Tiletnick, Michelle, Data & Marketing Association (DMA), 1333 Broadway, Suite 301, New York, NY 10018 *Tel:* 212-768-7277 *Fax:* 212-302-6714 *E-mail:* memberservices@the-dma.org *Web Site:* thedma.org, pg 67, 564

Tiller, Jerome, ArtWrite Productions, 1555 Gardena Ave NE, Minneapolis, MN 55432-5848 *Tel:* 612-803-0436 *E-mail:* artwriteprod@gmail.com *Web Site:* artwriteproductions.com; adaptedclassics.com, pg 22

Tillman, Lillian Gail, Clotilde's Secretarial & Management Services, PO Box 871926, New Orleans, LA 70187 *Tel:* 504-242-2912; 504-800-4853 (cell) *E-mail:* elcsy58@aol.com; elcsy58@att.net, pg 491

Timmons, Barbara K, Management Sciences for Health, 200 Rivers Edge Dr, Medford, MA 02155 *Tel:* 617-250-9500 *Fax:* 617-250-9090 *E-mail:* bookstore@msh.org *Web Site:* www.msh.org, pg 140

Timmons, Kelly, Atlantic Center for the Arts Artists-in-Residence Program, 1414 Art Center Ave, New Smyrna Beach, FL 32168 *Tel:* 386-427-6975 *Toll Free Tel:* 800-393-6975 *Fax:* 386-427-5669 *E-mail:* program@atlanticcenterforthearts.org *Web Site:* atlanticcenterforthearts.org, pg 609

Tingley, Megan, Hachette Book Group, 1290 Avenue of the Americas, New York, NY 10019 *Tel:* 212-364-1100 *Toll Free Tel:* 800-759-0190 (cust serv) *Fax:* 212-364-0933 (intl orders) *Toll Free Fax:* 800-286-9471 (cust serv) *Web Site:* www.hachettebookgroup.com, pg 98

Tingley, Megan, Little, Brown Books for Young Readers, 1290 Avenue of the Americas, New York, NY 10019 *Tel:* 212-364-1100 *Toll Free Tel:* 800-759-0190 (cust serv) *Web Site:* www.HachetteBookGroup.com, pg 136

Tinker, Scott W, Bureau of Economic Geology, University of Texas at Austin, 10100 Burnet Rd, Bldg 130, Austin, TX 78758 *Tel:* 512-471-1534 *Fax:* 512-471-0140 *E-mail:* pubsales@beg.utexas.edu *Web Site:* www.beg.utexas.edu, pg 45

Tipton, Virgil III, Liguori Publications, One Liguori Dr, Liguori, MO 63057-1000 *Tel:* 636-464-2500 *Toll Free Tel:* 866-848-2492; 800-325-9521 *Fax:* 636-464-8449 *Toll Free Fax:* 800-325-9526 (sales) *E-mail:* liguori@liguori.org (sales & cust serv) *Web Site:* www.liguori.org/contact-us.html, pg 134

Tirschwell, Peter, The JOC Group Inc, 2 Penn Plaza E, Newark, NJ 07105 *Tel:* 973-776-8660 *Web Site:* www.joc.com, pg 122

Tisdel, Laura, Viking, 375 Hudson St, New York, NY 10014 *Tel:* 212-366-2000 *Fax:* 212-243-6002 *Web Site:* www.penguin.com/publishers/vikingbooks, pg 250

Tisseyre, Charles, Les Editions Pierre Tisseyre, 155, rue Maurice, Rosemere, QC J7A 2S8, Canada *Tel:* 514-335-0777 *Fax:* 514-335-6723 *E-mail:* info@edtisseyre.ca *Web Site:* www.tisseyre.ca, pg 455

Tisseyre, Michelle, Les Editions Pierre Tisseyre, 155, rue Maurice, Rosemere, QC J7A 2S8, Canada *Tel:* 514-335-0777 *Fax:* 514-335-6723 *E-mail:* info@edtisseyre.ca *Web Site:* www.tisseyre.ca, pg 455

Titen, Andrew, Bisk Education, 9417 Princess Palm Ave, Suite 400, Tampa, FL 33619 *Tel:* 813-621-6200 *Toll Free Tel:* 800-280-9718 (cust serv) *E-mail:* customerservice@bisk.com *Web Site:* www.bisk.com, pg 35

Tivnan, Maisie, Workman Publishing Co Inc, 225 Varick St, 9th fl, New York, NY 10014-4381 *Tel:* 212-254-5900 *Toll Free Tel:* 800-722-7202 *Fax:* 212-254-8098 *E-mail:* info@workman.com *Web Site:* www.workman.com, pg 259

Tobey, Mary A, Brandylane Publishers Inc, 5 S First St, Richmond, VA 23219 *Tel:* 804-644-3090 *Fax:* 804-644-3092 *Web Site:* brandylanepublishers.com, pg 42

Tobin, Helen, Alfred A Knopf/Everyman's Library, c/o Penguin Random House Inc, 1745 Broadway, New York, NY 10019 *Tel:* 212-751-2600 *Toll Free Tel:* 800-638-6460 *Fax:* 212-572-2593 *Web Site:* www.knopfdoubleday.com, pg 127

Tod, Robert, AZ Books LLC, 320 Fifth Ave, New York, NY 10001 *Toll Free Tel:* 888-945-7723 *Toll Free Fax:* 888-945-7724 *Web Site:* www.azbooksusa.com, pg 27

Todd, Ashley, Perseus Books, 250 W 57 St, 15th fl, New York, NY 10107 *Tel:* 212-340-8100 *Toll Free Tel:* 800-343-4499 (cust serv) *Fax:* 212-340-8105 *Web Site:* www.perseusbooks.com, pg 181

Todd, Traci, Harry N Abrams Inc, 195 Broadway, 9th fl, New York, NY 10007 *Tel:* 212-206-7715 *Toll Free Tel:* 800-345-1359 *Fax:* 212-519-1210 *E-mail:* abrams@abramsbooks.com *Web Site:* www.abramsbooks.com, pg 3

Todd, Trish, Touchstone, 1230 Avenue of the Americas, New York, NY 10020, pg 233

Toke, Arun N, Skipping Stones Honor Awards, 166 W 12 Ave, Eugene, OR 97401 *Tel:* 541-342-4956 *E-mail:* info@skippingstones.org *Web Site:* www.skippingstones.org, pg 689

Toke, Arun N, The Skipping Stones Youth Honor Awards, 166 W 12 Ave, Eugene, OR 97401 *Tel:* 541-342-4956 *E-mail:* info@skippingstones.org *Web Site:* www.skippingstones.org, pg 690

Tolia, Shimul, Little Bee Books, 853 Broadway, Suite 2014, New York, NY 10003 *E-mail:* info@littlebeebooks.com *Web Site:* www.littlebeebooks.com, pg 135

Tolnay, Tom, Birch Brook Press, PO Box 81, Delhi, NY 13753-0081 *Tel:* 607-746-7453 (book sales & prodn) *Fax:* 607-746-7453 *E-mail:* birchbrook@copper.net *Web Site:* www.birchbrookpress.info, pg 35

Tomaselli, Valerie, American Book Producers Association (ABPA), 31 W Eighth St, 2nd fl, New York, NY 10011 *Tel:* 212-675-1363 *Fax:* 212-675-1364 *E-mail:* office@abpaonline.org *Web Site:* www.abpaonline.org, pg 554

Tomasi, Prof Massimiliano, Center for East Asian Studies (CEAS), Western Washington University, 516 High St, Bellingham, WA 98225 *Tel:* 360-650-3339 *Fax:* 360-650-6110 *E-mail:* easpress@wwu.edu *Web Site:* www.wwu.edu/eas, pg 51

Tomasino, Christine K, The Tomasino Agency Inc, 70 Chestnut St, Dobbs Ferry, NY 10522 *Tel:* 914-674-9659 *Fax:* 914-693-0381 *E-mail:* info@tomasinoagency.com *Web Site:* www.tomasinoagency.com, pg 539

Tomassi, Noreen, The Center for Fiction, 17 E 47 St, New York, NY 10017 *Tel:* 212-755-6710 *Fax:* 212-826-0831 *E-mail:* info@centerforfiction.org *Web Site:* centerforfiction.org/awards, pg 563

Tomassi, Noreen, The Center for Fiction First Novel Prize, 17 E 47 St, New York, NY 10017 *Tel:* 212-755-6710 *Fax:* 212-826-0831 *E-mail:* info@centerforfiction.org *Web Site:* centerforfiction.org/awards, pg 636

Tombs, Greg, David C Cook, 4050 Lee Vance View, Colorado Springs, CO 80918 *Tel:* 719-536-0100 *Toll Free Tel:* 800-708-5550; 800-323-7543 (orders & cust serv) *Toll Free Fax:* 800-430-0726 (cust serv) *Web Site:* www.davidccook.com, pg 60

Tomlin, Tiffany, Penguin Random House Speakers Bureau, A Penguin Random House Company, 1745 Broadway, Mail Drop 13-1, New York, NY 10019 *Tel:* 212-572-2013 *E-mail:* speakers@penguinrandomhouse.com *Web Site:* www.prhspeakers.com, pg 547

Tompkins, Amy, Transatlantic Agency, 2 Bloor St E, Suite 3500, Toronto, ON M4W 1A8, Canada *Tel:* 416-488-9214 *E-mail:* info@transatlanticagency.com *Web Site:* www.transatlanticagency.com, pg 539

Tompkins, Bill, National Newspaper Publishers Association (NNPA), 1816 12 St NW, Washington, DC 20009 *Tel:* 202-588-8764 *Fax:* 202-588-8960 *E-mail:* info@nnpa.org *Web Site:* www.nnpa.org; www.blackpressusa.com, pg 572

Tondorf-Dick, Mary, Little, Brown and Company, 1290 Avenue of the Americas, New York, NY 10019 *Tel:* 212-364-1100 *Fax:* 212-364-0952 *E-mail:* firstname.lastname@hbgusa.com *Web Site:* www.littlebrown.com; www.HachetteBookGroup.com, pg 135

Tonegutti, Marta, University of Chicago Press, 1427 E 60 St, Chicago, IL 60637-2954 *Tel:* 773-702-7700; 773-702-7600 *Toll Free Tel:* 800-621-2736 (orders) *Fax:* 773-702-9756; 773-660-2235 (orders); 773-702-2708 *E-mail:* custserv@press.uchicago.edu; marketing@press.uchicago.edu *Web Site:* www.press.uchicago.edu, pg 241

Tong, Murray, Wilfrid Laurier University Press, 75 University Ave W, Waterloo, ON N2L 3C5, Canada *Tel:* 519-884-0710 *Toll Free Tel:* 866-836-5551 (CN & US) *Fax:* 519-725-1399 *E-mail:* press@wlu.ca *Web Site:* www.wlupress.wlu.ca, pg 476

Toole, Jenny, Mercer University Press, 368 Orange St, Macon, GA 31201 *Tel:* 478-301-2880 *Toll Free Tel:* 866-895-1472 *Fax:* 478-301-2585 *E-mail:* mupressorders@mercer.edu *Web Site:* www.mupress.org, pg 148

Toraason, John, Wildlife Education Ltd, 2418 Noyes St, Evanston, IL 60201 *Tel:* 859-261-2556 *Toll Free Tel:* 800-477-5034 *Fax:* 859-261-2355 *Web Site:* www.zoobooks.com; wildlife-ed.com, pg 256

Tortoroli, Melanie, Penguin Group USA, A Penguin Random House Company, 375 Hudson St, New York, NY 10014 *Tel:* 212-366-2000 *Toll Free Tel:* 800-847-5515 (inside sales); 800-631-8571 (cust serv) *Fax:* 212-366-2666; 607-775-4829 (inside sales) *E-mail:* online@us.penguingroup.com *Web Site:* www.penguin.com, pg 177

Tory, Caroline, Aspen Words, 110 E Hallam St, Suite 116, Aspen, CO 81611 *Tel:* 970-925-3122 *Fax:* 970-920-5700 *E-mail:* aspenwords@aspeninstitute.org *Web Site:* www.aspenwords.org, pg 557

Tory, Caroline, Aspen Words Literary Prize, 110 E Hallam St, Suite 116, Aspen, CO 81611 *Tel:* 970-925-3122 *Fax:* 970-920-5700 *E-mail:* literary.prize@aspeninstitute.org *Web Site:* www.aspenwords.org, pg 629

Tory, Caroline, Summer Words Writing Conference & Literary Festival, 110 E Hallam St, Suite 116, Aspen, CO 81611 *Tel:* 970-925-3122 *Fax:* 970-920-5700 *E-mail:* aspenwords@aspeninstitute.org *Web Site:* www.aspenwords.org, pg 615

Tory, Caroline, Winter Words Author Series, 110 E Hallam St, Suite 116, Aspen, CO 81611 *Tel:* 970-925-3122 *Fax:* 970-920-5700 *E-mail:* aspenwords@aspeninstitute.org *Web Site:* www.aspenwords.org, pg 616

Toth, AnnJanette, Tommy Nelson, 501 Nelson Place, Nashville, TN 37214 *Tel:* 615-889-9000; 615-902-1485 (cust serv) *Toll Free Tel:* 800-251-4000 *Fax:* 615-391-5225 *Web Site:* www.tommynelson.com, pg 233

Toth, Dani, Pantheon Books/Schocken Books, c/o Penguin Random House Inc, 1745 Broadway, New York, NY 10019 *Tel:* 212-751-2600 *Web Site:* knopfdoubleday.com/imprint/pantheon, pg 173

Toth, Sara, The Chautauqua Prize, One Ames Ave, Chautauqua, NY 14722 *Toll Free Tel:* 800-836-ARTS (836-2787) *Web Site:* www.ciweb.org/prize, pg 637

Toth, Sarah, Galaxy Press, 7051 Hollywood Blvd, Suite 200, Hollywood, CA 90028 *Tel:* 323-466-7815 *Toll Free Tel:* 877-8GALAXY (842-5299) *E-mail:* info@galaxypress.com; customers@galaxypress.com *Web Site:* www.galaxypress.com, pg 89

Toto, Cheryl Cramer, Houghton Mifflin Harcourt Trade & Reference Division, 125 High St, Boston, MA 02110 *Tel:* 617-351-5000 *Toll Free Tel:* 800-225-3362 *Web Site:* www.hmhco.com, pg 111

Totten, Shay, Chelsea Green Publishing Co, 85 N Main St, Suite 120, White River Junction, VT 05001 *Tel:* 802-295-6300 *Toll Free Tel:* 800-639-4099 (cust serv, consumer & trade orders) *Fax:* 802-295-6444 *Web Site:* www.chelseagreen.com, pg 53

Touchie, Rodger, Heritage House Publishing Co Ltd, 1075 Pendergast St, No 103, Victoria, BC V8V 0A1, Canada *Tel:* 250-360-0829 *Fax:* 250-386-0829 *E-mail:* heritage@heritagehouse.ca *Web Site:* www.heritagehouse.ca, pg 459

Toupin, Tom, Blue Book Publications Inc, 8009 34 Ave S, Suite 250, Minneapolis, MN 55425 *Tel:* 952-854-5229 *Toll Free Tel:* 800-877-4867 *Fax:* 952-853-1486 *E-mail:* support@bluebookinc.com *Web Site:* www.bluebookofgunvalues.com; www.bluebookofguitarvalues.com, pg 38

Tourtelot, Nicole, DeFiore and Company Literary Management Inc, 47 E 19 St, 3rd fl, New York, NY 10003 *Tel:* 212-925-7744 *Fax:* 212-925-9803 *E-mail:* info@defliterary.com; submissions@defliterary.com *Web Site:* www.defliterary.com, pg 513

Tourtlotte, Alan N, The Optical Society (OSA), 2010 Massachusetts Ave NW, Washington, DC 20036-1023 *Tel:* 202-223-8130 *Toll Free Tel:* 800-766-4672 *E-mail:* custserv@osa.org *Web Site:* www.osa.org, pg 169

Touvell, Anne, Thurber Prize for American Humor, 77 Jefferson Ave, Columbus, OH 43215 *Tel:* 614-464-1032 *Fax:* 614-280-3645 *E-mail:* thurberhouse@thurberhouse.org *Web Site:* www.thurberhouse.org, pg 694

Tov, Matti Shem, ProQuest LLC, 789 E Eisenhower Pkwy, Ann Arbor, MI 48108 *Tel:* 734-761-4700 *Toll Free Tel:* 800-521-0600 *Web Site:* www.proquest.com, pg 190

Tower, Carol, Society of Manufacturing Engineers, One SME Dr, Dearborn, MI 48121 *Tel:* 313-425-3000 *Toll Free Tel:* 800-733-4763 (cust serv) *Fax:* 313-425-3400 *E-mail:* publications@sme.org *Web Site:* www.sme.org, pg 216

Townson, Donald, Townson Publishing Co Ltd, PO Box 1404, Sta A, Vancouver, BC V6C 2P7, Canada *Tel:* 604-886-0594 *E-mail:* townsonpublishing@gmail.com *Web Site:* generalpublishing.co.uk, pg 472

Tracten, Mark, Crown House Publishing Co LLC, 81 Brook Hills Circle, White Plains, NY 10605 *Tel:* 914-946-3517 *Toll Free Tel:* 877-925-1213 (cust serv) *Fax:* 914-946-1160 *E-mail:* info@chpus.com *Web Site:* www.crownhousepublishing.com, pg 65

Tracy, Bruce, Workman Publishing Co Inc, 225 Varick St, 9th fl, New York, NY 10014-4381 *Tel:* 212-254-5900 *Toll Free Tel:* 800-722-7202 *Fax:* 212-254-8098 *E-mail:* info@workman.com *Web Site:* www.workman.com, pg 259

Tracy, Kathleen A, SDP Publishing Solutions LLC, 36 Captain's Way, East Bridgewater, MA 02333 *Tel:* 617-775-0656 *Web Site:* www.sdppublishingsolutions.com, pg 501

Tracy, Reid, Hay House Inc, 2776 Loker Ave W, Carlsbad, CA 92010 *Tel:* 760-431-7695 (ext 2, intl) *Toll Free Tel:* 800-654-5126 (ext 2, US) *Toll Free Fax:* 800-650-5115 *E-mail:* info@hayhouse.com; editorial@hayhouse.com *Web Site:* www.hayhouse.com, pg 103

Tramble, Madrid, ASM International, 9639 Kinsman Rd, Materials Park, OH 44073-0002 *Tel:* 440-338-5151 *Toll Free Tel:* 800-336-5152; 800-368-9800 (Europe) *Fax:* 440-338-4634 *E-mail:* memberservicecenter@asminternational.org *Web Site:* www.asminternational.org, pg 23

Trammel, Madison, Zondervan, 3900 Sparks Dr, Grand Rapids, MI 49546 *Tel:* 616-698-6900 *Toll Free Tel:* 800-226-1122; 800-727-1309 (retail orders) *Fax:* 616-698-3350 *Toll Free Fax:* 800-698-3256 (retail orders) *E-mail:* zinfo@zondervan.com *Web Site:* www.zondervan.com, pg 263

Trandem, Bryan, Quarto Publishing Group USA Inc, 400 First Ave N, Suite 400, Minneapolis, MN 55401 *Tel:* 612-344-8100 *Toll Free Tel:* 800-328-0590 (sales); 800-458-0454 *Fax:* 612-344-8691 *E-mail:* sales@quartous.com *Web Site:* www.quartoknows.com, pg 192

Tranfaglia, Frank, Piano Press, 1425 Ocean Ave, Suite 5, Del Mar, CA 92014 *Tel:* 619-884-1401 *Fax:* 858-755-1104 *E-mail:* pianopress@pianopress.com *Web Site:* www.pianopress.com, pg 182

Traub, Kevin, Zondervan, 3900 Sparks Dr, Grand Rapids, MI 49546 *Tel:* 616-698-6900 *Toll Free Tel:* 800-226-1122; 800-727-1309 (retail orders) *Fax:* 616-698-3350 *Toll Free Fax:* 800-698-3256 (retail orders) *E-mail:* zinfo@zondervan.com *Web Site:* www.zondervan.com, pg 263

Travers, Kate, Workman Publishing Co Inc, 225 Varick St, 9th fl, New York, NY 10014-4381 *Tel:* 212-254-5900 *Toll Free Tel:* 800-722-7202 *Fax:* 212-254-8098 *E-mail:* info@workman.com *Web Site:* www.workman.com, pg 259

Traversy, Nancy, Barefoot Books, 2067 Massachusetts Ave, 5th fl, Cambridge, MA 02140 *Tel:* 617-576-0660 *Toll Free Tel:* 866-215-1756 (cust serv); 866-417-2369 (orders) *Fax:* 617-576-0049 *E-mail:* help@barefootbooks.com *Web Site:* www.barefootbooks.com, pg 29

Travis, Abby, Milkweed Editions, 1011 Washington Ave S, Suite 300, Minneapolis, MN 55415-1246 *Tel:* 612-332-3192 *Toll Free Tel:* 800-520-6455 *Fax:* 612-215-2550 *Web Site:* milkweed.org, pg 151

Travis, Abby, Milkweed National Fiction Prize, 1011 Washington Ave S, Suite 300, Minneapolis, MN 55415-1246 *Tel:* 612-332-3192 *Toll Free Tel:* 800-520-6455 *Fax:* 612-215-2550 *E-mail:* submissions@milkweed.org *Web Site:* www.milkweed.org, pg 668

Travis, Jennifer, Storey Publishing LLC, 210 MASS MoCA Way, North Adams, MA 01247 *Tel:* 413-346-2100 *Toll Free Tel:* 800-441-5700 (orders); 800-793-9396 (edit) *Fax:* 413-346-2199; 413-346-2196 (edit) *E-mail:* sales@storey.com *Web Site:* www.storey.com, pg 223

Traynor, Karen, Tralco-Lingo Fun, PO Box 79008, RPO Garth, Hamilton, ON L9C 7N6, Canada *Tel:* 905-575-5717 *Toll Free Tel:* 888-487-2526 *E-mail:* contact_tralco@tralco.com; sales@tralco.com *Web Site:* www.tralco.com, pg 472

Treadway, Charr, Insight Editions, 800 "A" St, San Rafael, CA 94901 *Tel:* 415-526-1370 *Toll Free Tel:* 800-809-3792 *Toll Free Fax:* 866-509-0515 *E-mail:* info@insighteditions.com *Web Site:* www.insighteditions.com, pg 117

Treadwell, Priscilla, Princeton University Press, 41 William St, Princeton, NJ 08540-5237 *Tel:* 609-258-4900 *Fax:* 609-258-6305 *Web Site:* press.princeton.edu, pg 188

Treco, Stacy, Pearson Benjamin Cummings, 1301 Sansome St, San Francisco, CA 94111-1122 *Tel:* 415-402-2500 *Toll Free Tel:* 800-922-0579 (orders) *Toll Free Fax:* 800-445-6991 (orders) *E-mail:* question@aol.com *Web Site:* home.pearsonhighered.com, pg 176

Treimel, Scott, S©ott Treimel NY, 434 Lafayette St, New York, NY 10003-6943 *Tel:* 212-505-8353 *E-mail:* general@scotttreimelny.com *Web Site:* scotttreimelny.com; scotttreimelny.blogspot.com, pg 535

Treitl, Berta, Renaissance Literary & Talent, PO Box 17379, Beverly Hills, CA 90209 *Tel:* 323-848-8305 *Fax:* 424-298-2588 *E-mail:* query@renaissancemgmt.net *Web Site:* renaissancemgmt.net, pg 532

Trelstad, Julie, Writers House, 21 W 26 St, New York, NY 10010 *Tel:* 212-685-2400 *Fax:* 212-685-1781 *Web Site:* www.writershouse.com, pg 542

Tremblay, Carole, La Courte Echelle, 4388, rue Saint-Denis, Suite 315, Montreal, QC H2J 2L1, Canada *Tel:* 514-312-6950 *E-mail:* info@courteechelle.com *Web Site:* courteechelle.groupecourteechelle.com, pg 451

Tress, Neil, Recorded Books Inc, an RBmedia company, 270 Skipjack Rd, Prince Frederick, MD 20678 *Tel:* 410-535-5590 *Toll Free Tel:* 877-732-2898 *Fax:* 410-535-5499 *E-mail:* customerservice@recordedbooks.com *Web Site:* www.recordedbooks.com, pg 196

Trevorrow, Elaine, Penguin Random House Speakers Bureau, A Penguin Random House Company, 1745 Broadway, Mail Drop 13-1, New York, NY 10019 *Tel:* 212-572-2013 *E-mail:* speakers@penguinrandomhouse.com *Web Site:* www.prhspeakers.com, pg 547

Tribble, Miriam, Harry N Abrams Inc, 195 Broadway, 9th fl, New York, NY 10007 *Tel:* 212-206-7715 *Toll Free Tel:* 800-345-1359 *Fax:* 212-519-1210 *E-mail:* abrams@abramsbooks.com *Web Site:* www.abramsbooks.com, pg 3

Tribelli, Angela, HarperCollins General Books Group, 195 Broadway, New York, NY 10007 *Tel:* 212-207-7000 *Web Site:* www.harpercollins.com, pg 101

Tricarico, Joy Elton, Carol Bancroft & Friends, PO Box 2030, Danbury, CT 06813 *Tel:* 203-730-8270 *Fax:* 203-730-8275 *E-mail:* cbfriends@sbcglobal.net *Web Site:* www.carolbancroft.com, pg 543

Trimmer, Christian, Henry Holt and Company, LLC, 175 Fifth Ave, New York, NY 10010 *Tel:* 646-307-5151 *Toll Free Tel:* 888-330-8477 (orders) *Fax:* 646-307-5285 *E-mail:* firstname.lastname@hholt.com *Web Site:* www.henryholt.com, pg 109

Tripathi, Namrata, Dial Books for Young Readers, 345 Hudson St, New York, NY 10014 *Tel:* 212-366-2000 *Toll Free Tel:* 800-733-3000 (orders) *Fax:* 212-414-3396 *Web Site:* www.penguin.com, pg 70

Trippe, Bill, The MIT Press, One Rogers St, Cambridge, MA 02142 *Tel:* 617-253-5255 *Toll Free Tel:* 800-207-8354 (orders) *Fax:* 617-258-6779; 617-577-1545 (orders) *Web Site:* mitpress.mit.edu, pg 151

Triton, Jade, Teachers & Writers Collaborative, 520 Eighth Ave, Suite 2020, New York, NY 10018-4165 *Tel:* 212-691-6590 *Toll Free Tel:* 888-BOOKS-TW (266-5789) *Fax:* 212-675-0171 *E-mail:* info@twc.org *Web Site:* www.twc.org, pg 579

Tritschler, Tracy, University of Missouri Press, 113 Heinkel Bldg, 201 S Seventh St, Columbia, MO 65211 *Tel:* 573-882-7641 *Toll Free Tel:* 800-621-2736 (orders) *Fax:* 573-884-4498 *Toll Free Fax:* 800-621-8476 (orders) *E-mail:* upress@missouri.edu *Web Site:* upress.missouri.edu; press.umsystem.edu, pg 243

Troast, Bob, VanDam Inc, The VanDam Bldg, 121 W 27 St, New York, NY 10001 *Tel:* 212-929-0416 *Toll Free Tel:* 800-UNFOLDS (863-6537) *Fax:* 212-929-0426 *E-mail:* info@vandam.com *Web Site:* www.vandam.com, pg 249

Trocker, Dana, Simon & Schuster, 1230 Avenue of the Americas, New York, NY 10020 *Tel:* 212-698-7000 *Toll Free Tel:* 800-223-2348 (cust serv); 800-223-2336 (orders) *Toll Free Fax:* 800-943-9831 (orders) *Web Site:* www.simonandschuster.com, pg 212

Troha, Steve, Folio Literary Management, The Film Center Bldg, 630 Ninth Ave, Suite 1101, New York, NY 10036 *Tel:* 212-400-1494 *Fax:* 212-967-0977 *Web Site:* www.foliolit.com, pg 517

Troiano, Patty, Lynne Rienner Publishers Inc, 1800 30 St, Suite 314, Boulder, CO 80301 *Tel:* 303-444-6684 *Fax:* 303-444-0824 *E-mail:* questions@rienner.com; cservice@rienner.com *Web Site:* www.rienner.com, pg 199

Trombi, Liza Groen, Locus Awards, PO Box 13305, Oakland, CA 94661-0305 *Tel:* 510-339-9196 *Fax:* 510-339-9198 *E-mail:* locus@locusmag.com *Web Site:* www.locusmag.com, pg 662

Trombley, Dana, HarperCollins General Books Group, 195 Broadway, New York, NY 10007 *Tel:* 212-207-7000 *Web Site:* www.harpercollins.com, pg 101

Troncoso, Sergio, Carr P Collins Award, c/o 7748 Hwy 290 W, Austin, TX 78736-3202 *Tel:* 512-683-5640 *E-mail:* president@texasinstituteofletters.org *Web Site:* www.texasinstituteofletters.org, pg 638

Troncoso, Sergio, Soeurette Diehl Fraser Translation Award, c/o 7748 Hwy 290 W, Austin, TX 78736-3202 *Tel:* 512-683-5640 *E-mail:* president@texasinstituteofletters.org *Web Site:* www.texasinstituteofletters.org, pg 647

Troncoso, Sergio, Jesse H Jones Award, c/o 7748 Hwy 290 W, Austin, TX 78736-3202 *Tel:* 512-683-5640 *E-mail:* president@texasinstituteofletters.org *Web Site:* www.texasinstituteofletters.org, pg 657

Troncoso, Sergio, Ramirez Family Award, c/o 7748 Hwy 290 W, Austin, TX 78736-3202 *Tel:* 512-683-5640 *E-mail:* president@texasinstituteofletters.org *Web Site:* www.texasinstituteofletters.org, pg 684

Troncoso, Sergio, Edwin "Bud" Shrake Award for Best Short Nonfiction, c/o 7748 Hwy 290 W, Austin, TX 78736-3202 *Tel:* 512-683-5640 *E-mail:* president@texasinstituteofletters.org *Web Site:* www.texasinstituteofletters.org, pg 689

Troncoso, Sergio, Helen C Smith Memorial Award, c/o 7748 Hwy 290 W, Austin, TX 78736-3202 *Tel:* 512-683-5640 *E-mail:* president@texasinstituteofletters.org *Web Site:* www.texasinstituteofletters.org, pg 690

Troncoso, Sergio, Texas Institute of Letters (TIL), c/o 7748 Hwy 290 W, Austin, TX 78736-3202 *E-mail:* president@texasinstituteofletters.org; secretary@texasinstituteofletters.org *Web Site:* www.texasinstituteofletters.org, pg 579

Troncoso, Sergio, Texas Institute of Letters Awards, c/o 7748 Hwy 290 W, Austin, TX 78736-3202 *Tel:* 512-683-5640 *E-mail:* president@texasinstituteofletters.org *Web Site:* www.texasinstituteofletters.org, pg 694

Trotman, Krishan, Hachette Books, 1290 Avenue of the Americas, New York, NY 10019 *Tel:* 212-364-1100 *Web Site:* www.hachettebookgroup.com, pg 98

Trotti, Ricardo, Inter American Press Association (IAPA), 3511 NW 91 Ave, Miami, FL 33172 *Tel:* 305-634-2465 *Fax:* 305-635-2272 *E-mail:* info@sipiapa.org *Web Site:* www.sipiapa.org, pg 567

Troutman, Karen, Dewey Publications Inc, 1840 Wilson Blvd, Suite 203, Arlington, VA 22201 *Tel:* 703-524-1355 *Fax:* 703-524-1463 *E-mail:* deweypublications@gmail.com *Web Site:* www.deweypub.com, pg 70

Trouwborst, Leah, Portfolio, 375 Hudson St, New York, NY 10014 *Web Site:* www.penguin.com/meet/publishers/portfolio, pg 186

Truax, Denise, Prise de parole Inc, 109 Elm St, Suite 205, Sudbury, ON P3C 1T4, Canada *Tel:* 705-675-6491 *Fax:* 705-673-1817 *E-mail:* info@prisedeparole.ca *Web Site:* www.prisedeparole.ca, pg 468

True, Nathan, Greenleaf Book Group LLC, 3 Park Place, 4005 Banister Lane, Suite B, Austin, TX 78704 *Tel:* 512-891-6100 *Fax:* 512-891-6150 *E-mail:* contact@greenleafbookgroup.com *Web Site:* www.greenleafbookgroup.com, pg 96

Truitt, Sam, Barrytown/Station Hill Press, 120 Station Hill Rd, Barrytown, NY 12507 *Tel:* 845-758-5293 *E-mail:* publishers@stationhill.org *Web Site:* www.stationhill.org, pg 30

Truong, Phuong, Second Story Press, 20 Maud St, Suite 401, Toronto, ON M5V 2M5, Canada *Tel:* 416-537-7850 *Fax:* 416-537-0588 *E-mail:* info@secondstorypress.ca *Web Site:* secondstorypress.ca, pg 470

Trupin, Jim, JET Literary Associates Inc, 941 Calle Mejia, Suite 507, Santa Fe, NM 87501 *Tel:* 505-780-0721 *E-mail:* etp@jetliterary.com *Web Site:* www.jetliterary.wordpress.com, pg 523

Trupin-Pulli, Elizabeth, JET Literary Associates Inc, 941 Calle Mejia, Suite 507, Santa Fe, NM 87501 *Tel:* 505-780-0721 *E-mail:* etp@jetliterary.com *Web Site:* www.jetliterary.wordpress.com, pg 523

Tsang, Erika, HarperCollins General Books Group, 195 Broadway, New York, NY 10007 *Tel:* 212-207-7000 *Web Site:* www.harpercollins.com, pg 101

Tubach, Greg, Houghton Mifflin Harcourt Trade & Reference Division, 125 High St, Boston, MA 02110 *Tel:* 617-351-5000 *Toll Free Tel:* 800-225-3362 *Web Site:* www.hmhco.com, pg 111

Tucher, Andie, James Fenimore Cooper Prize, 2950 Broadway, New York, NY 10027 *Tel:* 212-854-6495 *E-mail:* amhistsociety@columbia.edu *Web Site:* sah.columbia.edu, pg 639

Tucher, Andie, Allan Nevins Prize, 2950 Broadway, New York, NY 10027 *Tel:* 212-854-6495 *E-mail:* amhistsociety@columbia.edu *Web Site:* sah.columbia.edu, pg 672

Tucher, Andie, Francis Parkman Prize, 2950 Broadway, New York, NY 10027 *Tel:* 212-854-6495 *E-mail:* amhistsociety@columbia.edu *Web Site:* sah.columbia.edu, pg 676

Tucker, Jennifer, Center for Women Policy Studies, 4620 N Park Ave, Suite 302W, Chevy Chase, MD 20815 *Tel:* 301-986-0795 *E-mail:* cwps@centerwomenpolicy.org *Web Site:* www.centerwomenpolicy.org, pg 51

Tudor, Jeannie, Square One Publishers Inc, 115 Herricks Rd, Garden City Park, NY 11040 *Tel:* 516-535-2010 *Toll Free Tel:* 877-900-BOOK (900-2665) *Fax:* 516-535-2014 *E-mail:* sq1publish@aol.com *Web Site:* www.squareonepublishers.com, pg 220

Tufariello, Frank, Data Trace Publishing Co (DTP), 110 West Rd, Suite 227, Towson, MD 21204-2316 *Tel:* 410-494-4994 *Toll Free Tel:* 800-342-0454 (orders only) *Fax:* 410-494-0515 *E-mail:* info@datatrace.com; salesandmarketing@datatrace.com; editorial@datatrace.com; info@datatrace.com *Web Site:* www.datatrace.com, pg 67

Tugeau, Christina, Christina A Tugeau Artist Agency LLC, 29 Newman Place, Fairfield, CT 06825 *Tel:* 917-434-3141 *E-mail:* chris@catugeau.com *Web Site:* www.catugeau.com, pg 544

Tugeau, Nicole, Tugeau 2 Inc, 2231 Grandview Ave, Cleveland Heights, OH 44106 *Tel:* 216-707-0854 *Web Site:* www.tugeau2.com, pg 544

Tully, Nola, Encounter Books, 900 Broadway, Suite 601, New York, NY 10003 *Tel:* 212-871-6310 *Toll Free Tel:* 800-786-3839 *Fax:* 212-871-6311 *E-mail:* publicity@encounterbooks.com *Web Site:* www.encounterbooks.com, pg 78

Tumambing, Ryan, Hatherleigh Press Ltd, 62545 State Hwy 10, Hobart, NY 13788 *E-mail:* info@hatherleighpress.com; publicity@hatherleighpress.com *Web Site:* www.hatherleighpress.com, pg 103

Tuminelly, Nancy, Mighty Media Press, 1201 Currie Ave, Minneapolis, MN 55403 *Tel:* 612-455-0252 *Fax:* 612-338-4817 *Web Site:* www.mightymediapress.com, pg 150

Tung, Jennifer, Random House Publishing Group, 1745 Broadway, New York, NY 10019 *Toll Free Tel:* 800-200-3552 *Web Site:* atrandom.com, pg 195

Tupholme, Iris, HarperCollins Canada Ltd, 2 Bloor St E, 20th fl, Toronto, ON M4W 1A8, Canada *Tel:* 416-975-9334 *Fax:* 416-975-5223 *E-mail:* hcorder@harpercollins.com *Web Site:* www.harpercollins.ca, pg 459

Turnau, Crystal, Perseus Books, 250 W 57 St, 15th fl, New York, NY 10107 *Tel:* 212-340-8100 *Toll Free Tel:* 800-343-4499 (cust serv) *Fax:* 212-340-8105 *Web Site:* www.perseusbooks.com, pg 180

Turner, Erin, The Globe Pequot Press, 246 Goose Lane, Guilford, CT 06437 *Tel:* 203-458-4500 *Toll Free Tel:* 800-243-0495 (orders only); 888-249-7586 (cust serv) *Fax:* 203 458-4601 *Toll Free Fax:* 800-820-2329 (orders & cust serv) *E-mail:* editorial@globepequot.com; info@rowman.com; orders@rowman.com *Web Site:* rowman.com, pg 93

Turner, Jeffrey, US Government Publishing Office (GPO), Superintendent of Documents, 732 N Capitol St NW, Washington, DC 20401 *Tel:* 202-512-1800 *Toll Free Tel:* 866-512-1800 (orders) *Fax:* 202-512-2104 *E-mail:* contactcenter@gpo.gov *Web Site:* www.gpo.gov; bookstore.gpo.gov (sales), pg 249

Turner, Monica, Printing Association of Florida Inc (PAF), 6250 Hazeltine National Dr, Suite 114, Orlando, FL 32822 *Tel:* 407-240-8009 *Toll Free Tel:* 800-331-0461 *Fax:* 407-240-8333 *Web Site:* www.flprint.org, pg 576

Turner, Paaige K PhD, National Communication Association, 1765 "N" St NW, Washington, DC 20036 *Tel:* 202-464-4622 *Fax:* 202-464-4600 *E-mail:* inbox@natcom.org *Web Site:* www.natcom.org, pg 571

Turner, Susan, Rodale Inc, 400 S Tenth St, Emmaus, PA 18049 *Tel:* 610-967-5171 *Toll Free Tel:* 866-387-0509 *E-mail:* bookmarketing@rodale.com; bookpublicity@rodale.com *Web Site:* www.rodale.com, pg 201

Turner, T J, Antioch Writers' Workshop, 300 College Park Ave, Suite 200A, Dayton, OH 45469-0001 *Tel:* 937-567-2399 *E-mail:* info@antiochwritersworkshop.com *Web Site:* www.antiochwritersworkshop.com, pg 609

Turner-Julier, Emily, W W Norton & Company Inc, 500 Fifth Ave, New York, NY 10110-0017 *Tel:* 212-354-5500 *Toll Free Tel:* 800-233-4830 (orders & cust serv) *Fax:* 212-869-0856 *Toll Free Fax:* 800-458-6515 *E-mail:* orders@wwnorton.com *Web Site:* books.wwnorton.com, pg 164

Turney, Cathy, National Society of Newspaper Columnists Annual Conference, PO Box 411532, San Francisco, CA 94141 *Tel:* 415-488-NCNC (488-6762) *Fax:* 484-297-0336 *E-mail:* director@columnists.com *Web Site:* www.columnists.com, pg 613

Turpen, Tracy, Chronicle Books LLC, 680 Second St, San Francisco, CA 94107 *Tel:* 415-537-4200 *Toll Free Tel:* 800-759-0190 (cust serv) *Fax:* 415-537-4460 *Toll Free Fax:* 800-858-7787 (orders); 800-286-9471 (cust serv) *E-mail:* frontdesk@chroniclebooks.com *Web Site:* www.chroniclebooks.com, pg 55

Turpin, Molly, Random House Publishing Group, 1745 Broadway, New York, NY 10019 *Toll Free Tel:* 800-200-3552 *Web Site:* atrandom.com, pg 195

Turriff, Tracey, Doubleday Canada, 320 Front St W, Suite 1400, Toronto, ON M5V 3B6, Canada *Tel:* 416-364-4449 *Fax:* 416-598-7764 *Web Site:* www.penguinrandomhouse.ca, pg 452

Turriff, Tracey, Knopf Canada, 320 Front St W, Suite 1400, Toronto, ON M5V 3B6, Canada *Tel:* 416-364-4449 *Toll Free Tel:* 888-523-9292 *Fax:* 416-598-7764 *Web Site:* www.penguinrandomhouse.ca, pg 462

Turriff, Tracey, Penguin Random House Canada, 320 Front St W, Suite 1400, Toronto, ON M5V 3B6, Canada *Tel:* 416-364-4449 *Toll Free Tel:* 888-523-9292 (cust serv) *Fax:* 416-598-7764 *Web Site:* www.penguinrandomhouse.ca, pg 467

Turriff, Tracey, Seal Books, 320 Front St W, Suite 1400, Toronto, ON M5V 3B6, Canada *Tel:* 416-364-4449 *Toll Free Tel:* 888-523-9292 (order desk) *Fax:* 416-598-7764 *Web Site:* www.penguinrandomhouse.ca, pg 470

Tusman, Jordana, Perseus Books, 250 W 57 St, 15th fl, New York, NY 10107 *Tel:* 212-340-8100 *Toll Free Tel:* 800-343-4499 (cust serv) *Fax:* 212-340-8105 *Web Site:* www.perseusbooks.com, pg 181

Tutela, Joy, David Black Agency, 335 Adams St, 27th fl, Suite 2707, Brooklyn, NY 11201 *Tel:* 718-852-5500 *Fax:* 718-852-5539 *Web Site:* www.davidblackagency.com, pg 508

Tuttle, Ann Leslie, Harlequin Enterprises Ltd, 233 Broadway, Suite 1001, New York, NY 10279 *Tel:* 212-553-4200 *Fax:* 212-227-8969 *E-mail:* customerservice@harlequin.com *Web Site:* www.harlequin.com, pg 100

Tweed, Charles, Jewel Box Theatre Playwriting Competition, 3700 N Walker, Oklahoma City, OK 73118-7031 *Tel:* 405-521-1786 *Web Site:* jewelboxtheatre.org, pg 657

Tweed, Thomas P, Plowshare Media, 405 Vincente Way, La Jolla, CA 92037 *E-mail:* sales@plowsharemedia.com *Web Site:* plowsharemedia.com, pg 184

Twilliger, Stephen, Rodale Inc, 400 S Tenth St, Emmaus, PA 18049 *Tel:* 610-967-5171 *Toll Free Tel:* 866-387-0509 *E-mail:* bookmarketing@rodale.com; bookpublicity@rodale.com *Web Site:* www.rodale.com, pg 200

Twitchell, Betsy, W W Norton & Company Inc, 500 Fifth Ave, New York, NY 10110-0017 *Tel:* 212-354-5500 *Toll Free Tel:* 800-233-4830 (orders & cust serv) *Fax:* 212-869-0856 *Toll Free Fax:* 800-458-6515 *E-mail:* orders@wwnorton.com *Web Site:* books.wwnorton.com, pg 164

Twomey, Anne, Grand Central Publishing, 1290 Avenue of the Americas, New York, NY 10019 *Tel:* 212-364-1100 *Web Site:* www.hachettebookgroup.com, pg 95

Twomey, Shannon, Penguin Books, 375 Hudson St, New York, NY 10014 *Tel:* 212-366-2000 *E-mail:* penguinpublicity@us.penguingroup.com *Web Site:* www.penguinclassics.com; www.penguin.com, pg 177

Twomey, Shannon, Penguin Group USA, A Penguin Random House Company, 375 Hudson St, New York, NY 10014 *Tel:* 212-366-2000 *Toll Free Tel:* 800-847-5515 (inside sales); 800-631-8571 (cust serv) *Fax:* 212-366-2666; 607-775-4829 (inside sales) *E-mail:* online@us.penguingroup.com *Web Site:* www.penguin.com, pg 177

Twomey, Shannon, Viking, 375 Hudson St, New York, NY 10014 *Tel:* 212-366-2000 *Fax:* 212-243-6002 *Web Site:* www.penguin.com/publishers/vikingbooks, pg 250

Tyler, Drew, Human Kinetics Inc, 1607 N Market St, Champaign, IL 61820 *Tel:* 217-351-5076 *Toll Free Tel:* 800-747-4457 *Fax:* 217-351-1549 (orders/cust serv) *E-mail:* info@hkusa.com *Web Site:* www.humankinetics.com, pg 112

Tyler, Hayley, Sourced Media Books, 15 Via Picato, San Clemente, CA 92673 *Tel:* 949-813-0182 *E-mail:* editor@sourcedmediabooks.com *Web Site:* sourcedmediabooks.com, pg 218

Tyler, Tracy, Random House Children's Books, 1745 Broadway, 10th fl, New York, NY 10019 *Tel:* 212-782-9000 *Web Site:* www.randomhousekids.com, pg 194

Tynes, Emily, American Civil Liberties Union, 125 Broad St, 18th fl, New York, NY 10004 *Tel:* 212-549-2500 *E-mail:* media@aclu.org *Web Site:* www.aclu.org, pg 554

Tyrrell, Bob, Orca Book Publishers, PO Box 468, Custer, WA 98240-0468 *Tel:* 250-380-1229 *Toll Free Tel:* 800-210-5277 *Fax:* 250-380-1892 *Toll Free Fax:* 877-408-1551 *E-mail:* orca@orcabook.com *Web Site:* www.orcabook.com, pg 169

Tyson, Marie, The Pilgrim Press/United Church Press, 700 Prospect Ave, Cleveland, OH 44115-1100 *Tel:* 216-736-2100 *Toll Free Tel:* 800-537-3394 (orders) *Fax:* 216-736-2207 (orders) *E-mail:* permissions@thepilgrimpress.com; store@ucc.org *Web Site:* www.thepilgrimpress.com; www.uccresources.com, pg 183

Tzetzo, Elizabeth, Perseus Books, 250 W 57 St, 15th fl, New York, NY 10107 *Tel:* 212-340-8100 *Toll Free Tel:* 800-343-4499 (cust serv) *Fax:* 212-340-8105 *Web Site:* www.perseusbooks.com, pg 180

Tzetzo, Liz, Macmillan, 175 Fifth Ave, New York, NY 10010 *Tel:* 646-307-5151 *E-mail:* press.inquiries@macmillan.com *Web Site:* www.macmillan.com, pg 140

Ucar, Yasemin, Kids Can Press Ltd, 25 Dockside Dr, Toronto, ON M5A 0B5, Canada *Tel:* 416-479-7000 *Toll Free Tel:* 800-265-0884 *Fax:* 416-960-5437 *E-mail:* info@kidscan.com; customerservice@kidscan.com *Web Site:* www.kidscanpress.com; www.kidscanpress.ca, pg 461

Ude, Wayne, Blue & Ude Writers' Services, 4249 Nuthatch Way, Clinton, WA 98236 *Tel:* 360-341-1630 *E-mail:* blueyude@whidbey.com *Web Site:* www.bluedewritersservices.com, pg 489

Ulicky, Brian, The New Press, 38 Greene St, 4th fl, New York, NY 10013 *Tel:* 212-629-8802 *Toll Free Tel:* 800-343-4489 (orders) *Fax:* 212-629-8617 *Toll Free Fax:* 800-351-5073 (orders) *E-mail:* newpress@thenewpress.com *Web Site:* www.thenewpress.com, pg 161

Ultsch, Sarah, Oxford University Press USA, 198 Madison Ave, New York, NY 10016 *Tel:* 212-726-6000 *Toll Free Tel:* 800-451-7556 (orders); 800-445-9714 (cust serv) *Fax:* 919-677-1303 *E-mail:* custserv.us@oup.com *Web Site:* www.oup.com/us, pg 171

Underwood, April, SLACK® Incorporated, A Wyanoke Group Company, 6900 Grove Rd, Thorofare, NJ 08086-9447 *Tel:* 856-848-1000 *Toll Free Tel:* 800-257-8290 *Fax:* 856-848-6091 *E-mail:* sales@slackinc.com; editor@slackinc.com; customerservice@slackinc.com *Web Site:* www.healio.com/books, pg 215

Underwood, Will, Kent State University Press, 1118 University Library Bldg, 1125 Risman Dr, Kent, OH 44242 *Tel:* 330-672-7913 *Fax:* 330-672-3104 *E-mail:* ksupress@kent.edu *Web Site:* www.kentstateuniversitypress.com, pg 126

Unferth, Deb, University of Texas at Austin, New Writers Project, Dept of English, Calhoun Hall, Rm 226, 204 W 21 St, B-5000, Austin, TX 78712 *Tel:* 512-471-5132; 512-471-4991 *Fax:* 512-471-4909 *Web Site:* newwritersproject.org, pg 623

Ungaro, Ellen, Mondo Publishing, 980 Avenue of the Americas, New York, NY 10018 *Tel:* 212-268-3560 *Toll Free Tel:* 888-88-MONDO (886-6636) *Toll Free Fax:* 888-532-4492 *E-mail:* info@mondopub.com *Web Site:* www.mondopub.com, pg 153

Unger, David, Publishing Certificate Program at City College of New York, Division of Humanities NAC 5225, City College of New York, New York, NY 10031 *Tel:* 212-650-7925 *Fax:* 212-650-7912 *E-mail:* ccnypub@aol.com *Web Site:* www.ccny.cuny.edu/publishing_certificate/index.html, pg 622

Unrad, Keren, Fine Creative Media, Inc, 322 Eighth Ave, 15th fl, New York, NY 10001 *Tel:* 212-595-3500 *Fax:* 212-595-3779, pg 85

Unruh, Leon, Alaska Native Language Center, PO Box 757680, Fairbanks, AK 99775-7680 *Fax:* 907-474-6586 *E-mail:* uaf-anlc@alaska.edu (orders) *Web Site:* www.uaf.edu/anlc, pg 6

Unwalla, Fred R, Pontifical Institute of Mediaeval Studies, Department of Publications, 59 Queen's Park Crescent E, Toronto, ON M5S 2C4, Canada *Tel:* 416-926-7142 *Fax:* 416-926-7258 *Web Site:* www.pims.ca, pg 467

Updike, David, Philadelphia Museum of Art, 2525 Pennsylvania Ave, Philadelphia, PA 19130 *Tel:* 215-684-7250 *Fax:* 215-235-8715 *Web Site:* www.philamuseum.org, pg 182

Upton, Cody, Arts & Letters Awards, 633 W 155 St, New York, NY 10032 *Tel:* 212-368-5900 *Fax:* 212-491-4615 *E-mail:* academy@artsandletters.org *Web Site:* www.artsandletters.org, pg 628

Upton, Cody, Award of Merit, 633 W 155 St, New York, NY 10032 *Tel:* 212-368-5900 *Fax:* 212-491-4615 *E-mail:* academy@artsandletters.org *Web Site:* www.artsandletters.org, pg 629

Upton, Cody, Michael Braude Award, 633 W 155 St, New York, NY 10032 *Tel:* 212-368-5900 *Fax:* 212-491-4615 *E-mail:* academy@artsandletters.org *Web Site:* www.artsandletters.org, pg 634

Upton, Cody, Benjamin H Danks Award, 633 W 155 St, New York, NY 10032 *Tel:* 212-368-5900 *Fax:* 212-491-4615 *E-mail:* academy@artsandletters.org *Web Site:* www.artsandletters.org, pg 640

Upton, Cody, Blake Dodd Prize, 633 W 155 St, New York, NY 10032 *Tel:* 212-368-5900 *Fax:* 212-491-4615 *E-mail:* academy@artsandletters.org *Web Site:* www.artsandletters.org, pg 641

Upton, Cody, E M Forster Award, 633 W 155 St, New York, NY 10032 *Tel:* 212-368-5900 *Fax:* 212-491-4615 *E-mail:* academy@artsandletters.org *Web Site:* www.artsandletters.org, pg 647

Upton, Cody, Gold Medal, 633 W 155 St, New York, NY 10032 *Tel:* 212-368-5900 *Fax:* 212-491-4615 *E-mail:* academy@artsandletters.org *Web Site:* www.artsandletters.org, pg 650

Upton, Cody, The William Dean Howells Medal, 633 W 155 St, New York, NY 10032 *Tel:* 212-368-5900 *Fax:* 212-491-4615 *E-mail:* academy@artsandletters.org *Web Site:* www.artsandletters.org, pg 654

Upton, Cody, Sue Kaufman Prize for First Fiction, 633 W 155 St, New York, NY 10032 *Tel:* 212-368-5900 *Fax:* 212-491-4615 *E-mail:* academy@artsandletters.org *Web Site:* www.artsandletters.org, pg 658

van Beek, Emily, Folio Literary Management, The Film Center Bldg, 630 Ninth Ave, Suite 1101, New York, NY 10036 *Tel:* 212-400-1494 *Fax:* 212-967-0977 *Web Site:* www.foliolit.com, pg 517

Van Beuren, Victor, American Diabetes Association, 1701 N Beauregard St, Alexandria, VA 22311 *Toll Free Tel:* 800-342-2383 *E-mail:* booksinfo@diabetes.org *Web Site:* www.diabetes.org, pg 11

Van Dam, Stephan, VanDam Inc, The VanDam Bldg, 121 W 27 St, New York, NY 10001 *Tel:* 212-929-0416 *Toll Free Tel:* 800-UNFOLDS (863-6537) *Fax:* 212-929-0426 *E-mail:* info@vandam.com *Web Site:* www.vandam.com, pg 249

van der Plas, Rob, Cycle Publishing LLC, 1282 Seventh Ave, San Francisco, CA 94122-2526 *Tel:* 415-665-8214 *Fax:* 415-753-8572 *Web Site:* www.cyclepublishing.com, pg 66

Van Derwater, Peter, Fulbright Scholar Program, 1400 "K" St NW, Washington, DC 20005 *Tel:* 202-686-4000 *E-mail:* scholars@iie.org *Web Site:* www.cies.org; www.iie.org, pg 648

Van Doren, Elizabeth, Boyds Mills Press, 815 Church St, Honesdale, PA 18431 *Tel:* 570-253-1164 *Toll Free Tel:* 800-490-5111 *Fax:* 570-253-0179 *E-mail:* contact@boydsmillspress.com *Web Site:* www.boydsmillspress.com, pg 41

Van Doren, Liz, Highlights for Children, 1800 Watermark Dr, Columbus, OH 43215 *Tel:* 614-486-0631 *Toll Free Tel:* 800-962-3661 (Highlights Club cust serv); 800-255-9517 (Highlights Magazine cust serv) *Web Site:* www.highlights.com; www.facebook.com/HighlightsforChildren, pg 107

Van Dusen, Hilary, Candlewick Press, 99 Dover St, Somerville, MA 02144-2825 *Tel:* 617-661-3330 *Fax:* 617-661-0565 *E-mail:* bigbear@candlewick.com; salesinfo@candlewick.com *Web Site:* www.candlewick.com, pg 46

Van Dyke, Brianna, Janet B McCabe Poetry Prize, 1041 N Taft Hill Rd, Fort Collins, CO 80521 *Tel:* 970-449-2726 *E-mail:* editor@ruminatemagazine.org *Web Site:* www.ruminatemagazine.com, pg 666

Van Dyke, Brianna, William Van Dyke Short Story Prize, 1041 N Taft Hill Rd, Fort Collins, CO 80521 *Tel:* 970-449-2726 *E-mail:* editor@ruminatemagazine.org *Web Site:* www.ruminatemagazine.com, pg 695

Van Dyke, Brianna, VanderMey Nonfiction Prize, 1041 N Taft Hill Rd, Fort Collins, CO 80521 *Tel:* 970-449-2726 *E-mail:* editor@ruminatemagazine.org *Web Site:* www.ruminatemagazine.com, pg 695

Van Gelder, Gordon, Philip K Dick Award, PO Box 3447, Hoboken, NJ 07030 *Tel:* 201-876-2551 *Web Site:* www.philipkdickaward.org, pg 641

Van Hoof-Haines, Kristine, Hazelden Publishing, 15251 Pleasant Valley Rd, Center City, MN 55012-0011 *Tel:* 651-213-4200 *Toll Free Tel:* 800-257-7810 *Fax:* 651-213-4590 *E-mail:* info@hazelden.org *Web Site:* www.hazelden.org, pg 104

Van Hooft, Karen, Bilingual Press/Editorial Bilingue, Arizona State Univ, Hispanic Research Ctr, Tempe, AZ 85287-2702 *Tel:* 480-965-3867 *Toll Free Tel:* 866-965-3867 *Fax:* 480-965-0315 *E-mail:* brp@asu.edu *Web Site:* www.asu.edu/brp, pg 35

Van Horn, Susan, Perseus Books, 250 W 57 St, 15th fl, New York, NY 10107 *Tel:* 212-340-8100 *Toll Free Tel:* 800-343-4499 (cust serv) *Fax:* 212-340-8105 *Web Site:* www.perseusbooks.com, pg 181

Van Huijstee, Ryan, McGill-Queen's University Press, 1010 Sherbrooke W, Suite 1720, Montreal, QC H3A 2R7, Canada *Tel:* 514-398-3750 *Fax:* 514-398-4333 *E-mail:* mqup@mqup.ca *Web Site:* www.mqup.ca, pg 463

Van Nort, Kristin E, The Association for Women in Communications, 1717 E Republic Rd, Suite A, Springfield, MO 65804 *Tel:* 417-886-8606 *Fax:* 417-886-3685 *E-mail:* info@womcom.org *Web Site:* www.womcom.org, pg 609

van Rheinberg, Brigitta, Princeton University Press, 41 William St, Princeton, NJ 08540-5237 *Tel:* 609-258-4900 *Fax:* 609-258-6305 *Web Site:* press.princeton.edu, pg 188

van Roessel, Annemarie, George Freedley Memorial Award, c/o The New York Public Library for the Performing Arts, 111 Amsterdam Ave, New York, NY 10023 *E-mail:* TLABookAwards@gmail.com; TheatreLibraryAssociation@gmail.com *Web Site:* www.tla-online.org/awards/bookawards, pg 647

van Roessel, Annemarie, Richard Wall Memorial Award, c/o The New York Public Library for the Performing Arts, 111 Amsterdam Ave, New York, NY 10023 *E-mail:* TheatreLibraryAssociation@gmail.com; TLABookAwards@gmail.com *Web Site:* www.tla-online.org/awards/bookawards, pg 696

Van Sant, Jules, Pacific Printing Industries Association, 6825 SW Sandburg St, Portland, OR 97223 *Tel:* 503-221-3944 *Toll Free Tel:* 877-762-7742 *Fax:* 503-221-5691 *E-mail:* info@ppiassociation.org *Web Site:* www.ppiassociation.org, pg 575

van Straaten, Tracy, Scholastic Trade Division, 557 Broadway, New York, NY 10012 *Tel:* 212-343-6100; 212-343-4685 (export sales) *Fax:* 212-343-4714 (export sales) *Web Site:* www.scholastic.com, pg 208

Van Wagner, CJ, Tyndale House Publishers Inc, 351 Executive Dr, Carol Stream, IL 60188 *Tel:* 630-668-8300 *Toll Free Tel:* 800-323-9400 *Toll Free Fax:* 800-684-0247 *Web Site:* www.tyndale.com, pg 237

Van Zandt, Christine, Write for Success Editing Services, PO Box 292153, Los Angeles, CA 90029-8653 *Tel:* 323-356-8833 *E-mail:* writeforsuccess@yahoo.com *Web Site:* www.write-for-success.com, pg 503

Vance, Lisa Erbach, The Aaron M Priest Literary Agency Inc, 200 W 41 St, 21st fl, New York, NY 10036 *Tel:* 212-818-0344 *Fax:* 212-573-9417 *E-mail:* info@aaronpriest.com *Web Site:* www.aaronpriest.com, pg 532

Vance, V Ellis, US Board on Books For Young People (USBBY), c/o V Ellis Vance, 5503 N El Adobe Dr, Fresno, CA 93711-2363 *Tel:* 559-351-6119 *Web Site:* www.usbby.org, pg 580

Vance-Cooks, Davita, US Government Publishing Office (GPO), Superintendent of Documents, 732 N Capitol St NW, Washington, DC 20401 *Tel:* 202-512-1800 *Toll Free Tel:* 866-512-1800 (orders) *Fax:* 202-512-2104 *E-mail:* contactcenter@gpo.gov *Web Site:* www.gpo.gov; bookstore.gpo.gov (sales), pg 249

Vandall, Jillian, Random House Children's Books, 1745 Broadway, 10th fl, New York, NY 10019 *Tel:* 212-782-9000 *Web Site:* www.randomhousekids.com, pg 194

VanDam, Arthur, Small Business Advisors Inc, 11 Franklin Ave, Hewlett, NY 11557 *Tel:* 516-374-1387 *Fax:* 516-374-1175 *Web Site:* www.smallbusinessadvice.com, pg 215

Vanderhart, Ruth, Faith Alive Christian Resources, 1700 28 St SE, Grand Rapids, MI 49508-1407 *Tel:* 616-224-0728 *Toll Free Tel:* 800-333-8300 *Toll Free Fax:* 888-642-8606 *E-mail:* info@faithaliveresources.org; sales@faithaliveresources.org; orders@faithaliveresources.org *Web Site:* www.faithaliveresources.org, pg 81

VanderKam, Claire, Wm B Eerdmans Publishing Co, 2140 Oak Industrial Dr NE, Grand Rapids, MI 49505 *Tel:* 616-459-4591 *Toll Free Tel:* 800-253-7521 *Fax:* 616-459-6540 *E-mail:* customerservice@eerdmans.com; sales@eerdmans.com *Web Site:* www.eerdmans.com, pg 76

Vanderlip, Kendra, The Pinch Writing Awards in Fiction, University of Memphis, English Dept, 435 Patterson Hall, Memphis, TN 38152 *Tel:* 901-678-2651 *Fax:* 901-678-2226 *E-mail:* editor@pinchjournal.com *Web Site:* www.pinchjournal.com, pg 680

Vanderlip, Kendra, The Pinch Writing Awards in Poetry, University of Memphis, English Dept, 435 Patterson Hall, Memphis, TN 38152 *Tel:* 901-678-2651 *Fax:* 901-678-2226 *E-mail:* editor@pinchjournal.com *Web Site:* www.pinchjournal.com, pg 680

Vandewater, Cathy, Vault.com Inc, 132 W 31 St, 16th fl, New York, NY 10001 *Tel:* 212-366-4212 *Toll Free Tel:* 800-535-2074 *Fax:* 212-366-6117 (cust serv) *E-mail:* editors@vault.com; customerservice@vault.com *Web Site:* www.vault.com, pg 250

VanHees, Robert, ProQuest LLC, 789 E Eisenhower Pkwy, Ann Arbor, MI 48108 *Tel:* 734-761-4700 *Toll Free Tel:* 800-521-0600 *Web Site:* www.proquest.com, pg 190

VanMeter, Joann, Standard Publishing, 4050 Lee Vance View, Colorado Springs, CO 80918 *Tel:* 513-931-4050 *Toll Free Tel:* 800-323-7543 *Fax:* 513-931-0950 *Toll Free Fax:* 800-323-0726 *E-mail:* customerservice@standardpub.com *Web Site:* www.standardpub.com, pg 220

Vardanian, Carissa, Academy of Nutrition & Dietetics, 120 S Riverside Plaza, Suite 2000, Chicago, IL 60606-6995 *Tel:* 312-899-0040 (ext 5000) *Toll Free Tel:* 800-877-1600 *E-mail:* sales@eatright.org *Web Site:* www.eatright.org, pg 3

Vardigan, Mary, Inter-University Consortium for Political & Social Research (ICPSR), 330 Packard St, Ann Arbor, MI 48104 *Tel:* 734-647-5000 *Fax:* 734-647-8200 *E-mail:* netmail@icpsr.umich.edu *Web Site:* www.icpsr.umich.edu, pg 118

Varga, Lisa R, Jefferson Cup Award, c/o Virginia Library Association (VLA), PO Box 56312, Virginia Beach, VA 23456 *Tel:* 757-689-0594 *Fax:* 757-447-3478 *Web Site:* www.vla.org, pg 657

Vargas, Allison Astor, Nuestras Voces National Playwriting Competition, 138 E 27 St, New York, NY 10016 *Tel:* 212-225-9950 *Fax:* 212-225-9085 *Web Site:* www.repertorio.org, pg 674

Vargo, Linda, National Association of College Stores (NACS), 500 E Lorain St, Oberlin, OH 44074 *Tel:* 440-775-7777 *Toll Free Tel:* 800-622-7498 *Fax:* 440-775-4769 *Web Site:* www.nacs.org, pg 570

Vari, Frank, Cengage Learning, 20 Channel Center St, Boston, MA 02210 *Tel:* 617-289-7700 *Toll Free Tel:* 800-354-9706 *Fax:* 617-289-7844 *Toll Free Fax:* 800-487-8488 *E-mail:* esales@cengage.com *Web Site:* www.cengage.com, pg 50

Varma, Sarita, Farrar, Straus & Giroux, LLC, 18 W 18 St, New York, NY 10011 *Tel:* 212-741-6900 *E-mail:* fsg.publicity@fsgbooks.com *Web Site:* us.macmillan.com/fsg.aspx, pg 83

Varma, Sarita, Hill & Wang, 18 W 18 St, New York, NY 10011 *Tel:* 212-741-6900 *Fax:* 212-633-9385 *E-mail:* fsg.publicity@fsgbooks.com; fsg.editorial@fsgbooks.com; sales@fsgbooks.com *Web Site:* us.macmillan.com/hillandwang.aspx, pg 107

Varma, Sarita, North Point Press, 18 W 18 St, 8th fl, New York, NY 10011 *Tel:* 212-741-6900 *Toll Free Tel:* 888-330-8477 *Fax:* 212-633-9385 *Web Site:* www.fsgbooks.com, pg 163

Varnado, Deb, Ascension Press, PO Box 1990, West Chester, PA 19380 *Tel:* 610-696-7795; 484-875-4550 (admin) *Toll Free Tel:* 800-376-0520 (sales & cust serv) *Web Site:* ascensionpress.com, pg 22

Varner, William, Stenhouse Publishers, 480 Congress St, Portland, ME 04101-3451 *Tel:* 207-253-1600 *Toll Free Tel:* 888-363-0566 *Fax:* 207-253-5121 *Toll Free Fax:* 800-833-9164 *E-mail:* customerservice@stenhouse.com *Web Site:* www.stenhouse.com, pg 222

Varrette, Dan, Insomniac Press, 520 Princess Ave, London, ON N6B 2B8, Canada *Tel:* 519-266-3556 *Web Site:* www.insomniacpress.com, pg 460

Vasquez, Cynthia, Mike Murach & Associates Inc, 4340 N Knoll Ave, Fresno, CA 93722 *Tel:* 559-440-9071 *Toll Free Tel:* 800-221-5528 *Fax:* 559-440-0963 *E-mail:* murachbooks@murach.com *Web Site:* www.murach.com, pg 150

Vasquez-Perez, Carmen, Chain Store Guide (CSG), 10117 Princess Palm Ave, Suite 375, Tampa, FL 33610 *Tel:* 813-627-6957 *Toll Free Tel:* 800-927-9292 (orders) *Fax:* 813-627-6888 *E-mail:* info@csgis.com *Web Site:* www.csgis.com, pg 52

Vaugeois, Denis, Les Editions du Septentrion, 835 Turnbull Ave, Quebec City, QC G1R 2X4, Canada *Tel:* 418-688-3556 *Fax:* 418-527-4978 *E-mail:* info@septentrion.qc.ca *Web Site:* www.septentrion.qc.ca, pg 454

Vaughan, Brendan, Random House Publishing Group, 1745 Broadway, New York, NY 10019 *Toll Free Tel:* 800-200-3552 *Web Site:* atrandom.com, pg 195

Vaughan, James M, Pennsylvania Historical & Museum Commission, Commonwealth Keystone Bldg, 400 North St, Harrisburg, PA 17120-0053 *Tel:* 717-783-8946; 717-787-5526 (orders) *E-mail:* ra-shoppaheritage@pa.gov *Web Site:* www.shoppaheritage.com; www.phmc.pa.gov, pg 179

Vaughan, Jeanne, Paladin Press, 5540 Central Ave, Suite 200, Boulder, CO 80301 *Tel:* 303-443-7250 *Toll Free Tel:* 800-392-2400 *Fax:* 303-442-8741 *E-mail:* service@paladin-press.com *Web Site:* www.paladin-press.com, pg 172

Vaughn, Lizzie, Chronicle Books LLC, 680 Second St, San Francisco, CA 94107 *Tel:* 415-537-4200 *Toll Free Tel:* 800-759-0190 (cust serv) *Fax:* 415-537-4460 *Toll Free Fax:* 800-858-7787 (orders); 800-286-9471 (cust serv) *E-mail:* frontdesk@chroniclebooks.com *Web Site:* www.chroniclebooks.com, pg 55

Vega, Javier, School of Visual Arts, 209 E 23 St, New York, NY 10010-3994 *Tel:* 212-592-2100 *Fax:* 212-592-2116 *Web Site:* www.sva.edu, pg 622

Vegso, Peter, Health Communications Inc, 3201 SW 15 St, Deerfield Beach, FL 33442 *Tel:* 954-360-0909 *Toll Free Tel:* 800-851-9100; 800-441-5569 (cust serv & orders) *Fax:* 954-360-0034 *Toll Free Fax:* 800-424-7652 (cust serv & orders) *E-mail:* customerservice2@hcibooks.com *Web Site:* www.hcibooks.com, pg 104

Veith, Richard, Cengage Learning, 20 Channel Center St, Boston, MA 02210 *Tel:* 617-289-7700 *Toll Free Tel:* 800-354-9706 *Fax:* 617-289-7844 *Toll Free Fax:* 800-487-8488 *E-mail:* esales@cengage.com *Web Site:* www.cengage.com, pg 50

Velasquez, Diana, Gallery Books, 1230 Avenue of the Americas, New York, NY 10020 *Toll Free Tel:* 800-456-6798 *Fax:* 212-698-7284 *E-mail:* consumer.customerservice@simonandschuster.com *Web Site:* www.simonsays.com, pg 90

Velella, Justin, St Martin's Press, LLC, 175 Fifth Ave, New York, NY 10010 *Tel:* 646-307-5151 *Web Site:* us.macmillan.com/smp, pg 204

Velez, Roberto, Little, Brown Books for Young Readers, 1290 Avenue of the Americas, New York, NY 10019 *Tel:* 212-364-1100 *Toll Free Tel:* 800-759-0190 (cust serv) *Web Site:* www.HachetteBookGroup.com, pg 136

Velkei, Laura, The Amy Rennert Agency Inc, 1550 Tiburon Blvd, Suite 302, Tiburon, CA 94920 *Tel:* 415-789-8955 *E-mail:* queries@amyrennert.com *Web Site:* amyrennert.com, pg 532

Veltre, J Joseph III, The Gersh Agency (TGA), 41 Madison Ave, 33rd fl, New York, NY 10010 *Tel:* 212-997-1818 *Web Site:* gershbooks.com, pg 518

Venable, Colleen, Workman Publishing Co Inc, 225 Varick St, 9th fl, New York, NY 10014-4381 *Tel:* 212-254-5900 *Toll Free Tel:* 800-722-7202 *Fax:* 212-254-8098 *E-mail:* info@workman.com *Web Site:* www.workman.com, pg 259

Venditti, Michelle, Harlequin Enterprises Ltd, 225 Duncan Mill Rd, Don Mills, ON M3B 3K9, Canada *Tel:* 416-445-5860 *Toll Free Tel:* 888-432-4879; 800-370-5838 (ebook inquiries) *E-mail:* customerservice@harlequin.com *Web Site:* www.harlequin.com, pg 459

Venezia, Angie, Anchor Books, c/o Penguin Random House Inc, 1745 Broadway, New York, NY 10019 *Tel:* 212-572-2420 *E-mail:* vintageanchorpublicity@randomhouse.com *Web Site:* knopfdoubleday.com/imprint/anchor, pg 16

Venezia, Angie, Vintage Books, c/o Penguin Random House Inc, 1745 Broadway, New York, NY 10019 *Tel:* 212-572-2420 *E-mail:* vintageanchorpublicity@randomhouse.com *Web Site:* knopfdoubleday.com/imprint/vintage, pg 251

Ventimiglia, Diana, Gallery Books, 1230 Avenue of the Americas, New York, NY 10020 *Toll Free Tel:* 800-456-6798 *Fax:* 212-698-7284 *E-mail:* consumer.customerservice@simonandschuster.com *Web Site:* www.simonsays.com, pg 90

Verburg, Bonnie, Scholastic Trade Division, 557 Broadway, New York, NY 10012 *Tel:* 212-343-6100; 212-343-4685 (export sales) *Fax:* 212-343-4714 (export sales) *Web Site:* www.scholastic.com, pg 208

Verdick, Dan, ABDO Publishing Group, 8000 W 78 St, Suite 310, Edina, MN 55439 *Tel:* 952-831-2120 *Toll Free Tel:* 800-800-1312 *Toll Free Fax:* 800-862-3480 *E-mail:* customerservice@abdopublishing.com *Web Site:* abdopublishing.com, pg 2

Vergilio, Trish, Templeton Press, 300 Conshohocken State Rd, Suite 665, West Conshohocken, PA 19428 *Tel:* 484-531-8380 *Fax:* 484-531-8382 *E-mail:* tpinfo@templetonpress.org *Web Site:* www.templetonpress.org, pg 229

Verhowsky, Victoria, Rutgers University Press, 106 Somerset St, 3rd fl, New Brunswick, NJ 08901 *Tel:* 848-445-7762 *Toll Free Tel:* 800-848-6224 (orders only) *Fax:* 732-745-4935 (acqs, edit, mktg, perms & prodn) *Toll Free Fax:* 800-272-6817 (fulfillment) *Web Site:* rutgerspress.rutgers.edu, pg 202

Verkuilen, Michelle, Liturgical Press, PO Box 7500, St John's Abbey, Collegeville, MN 56321-7500 *Tel:* 320-363-2213 *Toll Free Tel:* 800-858-5450 *Fax:* 320-363-3299 *Toll Free Fax:* 800-445-5899 *E-mail:* sales@litpress.org *Web Site:* www.litpress.org, pg 136

Verlin, Nicole Vines, Sterling Publishing Co Inc, 1166 Avenue of the Americas, 17th fl, New York, NY 10036 *Tel:* 212-532-7160 *Toll Free Tel:* 800-367-9692 *Fax:* 212-213-2495 *Web Site:* www.sterlingpublishing.com, pg 222

Verma, Monika, Levine|Greenberg|Rostan Literary Agency, 307 Seventh Ave, Suite 2407, New York, NY 10001 *Tel:* 212-337-0934 *Fax:* 212-337-0948 *Web Site:* lgrliterary.com, pg 525

Vernon, Nancy, Ozark Mountain Publishing Inc, PO Box 754, Huntsville, AR 72740-0754 *Tel:* 479-738-2348 *Toll Free Tel:* 800-935-0045 *Fax:* 479-738-2448 *E-mail:* info@ozarkmt.com *Web Site:* www.ozarkmt.com, pg 172

VernonClark, Kayla, Kane Miller Books, 4901 Morena Blvd, Suite 213, San Diego, CA 92117 *E-mail:* submissions@kanemiller.com; info@kanemiller.com *Web Site:* www.kanemiller.com, pg 124

Verrill, Chuck, Darhansoff & Verrill, 133 W 72 St, Rm 304, New York, NY 10023 *Tel:* 917-305-1300 *E-mail:* permissions@dvagency.com *Web Site:* www.dvagency.com, pg 512

Verrillo, Jillian, HarperCollins General Books Group, 195 Broadway, New York, NY 10007 *Tel:* 212-207-7000 *Web Site:* www.harpercollins.com, pg 101

Verses, Judy, John Wiley & Sons Inc, 111 River St, Hoboken, NJ 07030-5774 *Tel:* 201-748-6000 *Toll Free Tel:* 800-225-5945 (cust serv) *Fax:* 201-748-6088 *E-mail:* info@wiley.com *Web Site:* www.wiley.com, pg 256

Vestal, Rosemary, University of Nebraska Press, 1111 Lincoln Mall, Lincoln, NE 68588-0630 *Tel:* 402-472-3581; 919-966-7449 (cust serv & foreign orders) *Toll Free Tel:* 800-848-6224 (cust serv & US orders) *Fax:* 402-472-6214; 919-962-2704 (cust serv & foreign orders) *Toll Free Fax:* 800-526-2617 (cust serv & US orders) *E-mail:* pressmail@unl.edu *Web Site:* www.nebraskapress.unl.edu, pg 243

Vibbert, Brittany, Sourcebooks Inc, 1935 Brookdale Rd, Suite 139, Naperville, IL 60563 *Tel:* 630-961-3900 *Toll Free Tel:* 800-432-7444 *Fax:* 630-961-2168 *E-mail:* info@sourcebooks.com; customersupport@sourcebooks.com *Web Site:* www.sourcebooks.com, pg 218

Victor, Nomi, W W Norton & Company Inc, 500 Fifth Ave, New York, NY 10110-0017 *Tel:* 212-354-5500 *Toll Free Tel:* 800-233-4830 (orders & cust serv) *Fax:* 212-869-0856 *Toll Free Fax:* 800-458-6515 *E-mail:* orders@wwnorton.com *Web Site:* books.wwnorton.com, pg 164

Victorson, Emily, Allium Press of Chicago, 1530 Elgin Ave, Forest Park, IL 60130 *Tel:* 708-689-9323 *E-mail:* info@alliumpress.com *Web Site:* www.alliumpress.com, pg 8

Vieder, Deborah, NPES The Association for Suppliers of Printing, Publishing & Converting Technologies, 1899 Preston White Dr, Reston, VA 20191 *Tel:* 703-264-7200 *Fax:* 703-620-0994 *E-mail:* npes@npes.org *Web Site:* www.npes.org, pg 574

Viktorin, Brian, Greenleaf Book Group LLC, 3 Park Place, 4005 Banister Lane, Suite B, Austin, TX 78704 *Tel:* 512-891-6100 *Fax:* 512-891-6150 *E-mail:* contact@greenleafbookgroup.com *Web Site:* www.greenleafbookgroup.com, pg 96

Vilarello, Meredith, Touchstone, 1230 Avenue of the Americas, New York, NY 10020, pg 233

Villalonga, Lionel, Association pour l'Avancement des Sciences et des Techniques de la Documentation, 2065 rue Parthenais, Bureau 387, Montreal, QC H2K 3T1, Canada *Tel:* 514-281-5012 *Fax:* 514-281-8219 *E-mail:* info@asted.org *Web Site:* www.asted.org, pg 559, 609

Villalonga, Lionel, Editions ASTED, 2065 rue Parthenais, Bureau 387, Montreal, QC H2K 3T1, Canada *Tel:* 514-281-5012 *Fax:* 514-281-8219 *E-mail:* editions@asted.org; info@asted.org *Web Site:* www.asted.org, pg 446

Villalonga, Lionel, Prix Alvine-Belisle, 2065 rue Parthenais, Bureau 387, Montreal, QC H2K 3T1, Canada *Tel:* 514-281-5012 *Fax:* 514-281-8219 *E-mail:* info@asted.org *Web Site:* www.asted.org, pg 682

Villano, Laura, Jump!, 5357 Penn Ave, Minneapolis, MN 55419 *Toll Free Tel:* 888-799-1860 *Toll Free Fax:* 800-675-6679 *E-mail:* customercare@jumplibrary.com *Web Site:* www.jumplibrary.com, pg 123

Vinarub, Vanessa, Harvard University Press, 79 Garden St, Cambridge, MA 02138-1499 *Tel:* 617-495-2600; 401-531-2800 (intl orders) *Toll Free Tel:* 800-405-1619 (orders) *Fax:* 617-495-5898 (general); 617-496-4677 (edit & rts); 401-531-2801 (intl orders) *Toll Free Fax:* 800-406-9145 (orders) *E-mail:* contact_hup@harvard.edu *Web Site:* www.hup.harvard.edu, pg 103

Vincent, Dorothy, Trident Media Group LLC, 41 Madison Ave, 36th fl, New York, NY 10010 *Tel:* 212-333-1511 *E-mail:* info@tridentmediagroup.com; press@tridentmediagroup.com *Web Site:* www.tridentmediagroup.com, pg 540

Vincent, Heidi, National Geographic Books, 1145 17 St NW, Washington, DC 20036-4688 *Tel:* 202-857-7000 *Toll Free Tel:* 877-866-6486 *E-mail:* ngbooks@cdsfulfillment.com *Web Site:* www.nationalgeographic.com/books/; ngbooks.buysub.com, pg 158

Vineis, Mark, Mondo Publishing, 980 Avenue of the Americas, New York, NY 10018 *Tel:* 212-268-3560 *Toll Free Tel:* 888-88-MONDO (886-6636) *Toll Free Fax:* 888-532-4492 *E-mail:* info@mondopub.com *Web Site:* www.mondopub.com, pg 153

Vinton, Mary, Society of Motion Picture & Television Engineers® (SMPTE®), 3 Barker Ave, 5th fl, White Plains, NY 10601 *Tel:* 914-761-1100 *Fax:* 914-761-3115 *Web Site:* www.smpte.org, pg 578

Viola, Kieran, Disney-Hyperion Books, 1101 Flower St, Glendale, CA 91201 *Web Site:* books.disney.com, pg 70

Visconti, Max, Grand & Archer Publishing, 611 S Palm Canyon Dr, Suite 7451, Palm Springs, CA 92264 *Tel:* 323-493-2785 *E-mail:* grandandarcher@gmail.com, pg 94

Viskovic, Hilda, Lectorum Publications Inc, 205 Chubb Ave, Lyndhurst, NJ 07071 *Toll Free Tel:* 800-345-5946 *Fax:* 201-559-2201 *Toll Free Fax:* 877-532-8676 *E-mail:* lectorum@lectorum.com *Web Site:* www.lectorum.com, pg 131

Viswanath, Kaushik, Portfolio, 375 Hudson St, New York, NY 10014 *Web Site:* www.penguin.com/meet/publishers/portfolio, pg 186

Vitek, John M, Saint Mary's Press, 702 Terrace Heights, Winona, MN 55987-1318 *Tel:* 507-457-7900 *Toll Free Tel:* 800-533-8095 *Fax:* 507-457-7990 *Toll Free Fax:* 800-344-9225 *E-mail:* smpress@smp.org *Web Site:* www.smp.org, pg 205

Vogel, Chris, National Gallery of Art, Sixth & Constitution Ave NW, Washington, DC 20565 *Tel:* 202-737-4215; 202-842-6480 *Fax:* 202-842-6733 *E-mail:* casva@nga.gov *Web Site:* www.nga.gov, pg 158

Vogel, James, Angelus Press, 2915 Forest Ave, Kansas City, MO 64109 *Tel:* 816-753-3150 *Toll Free Tel:* 800-966-7337 *Fax:* 816-753-3557 *E-mail:* support@angeluspress.org *Web Site:* www.angeluspress.org, pg 17

Vogel, Rachel, Waxman Leavell Literary Agency, 443 Park Ave S, No 1004, New York, NY 10016 *Tel:* 212-675-5556 *Fax:* 212-675-1381 *Web Site:* www.waxmanleavell.com, pg 541

Voigt, Mark, American Academy of Pediatrics, 141 NW Point Blvd, Elk Grove Village, IL 60007-1098 *Tel:* 847-434-4000 *Toll Free Tel:* 888-227-1770 *Fax:* 847-434-8000 *E-mail:* pubs@aap.org *Web Site:* www.aap.org, pg 9

Volkman, Prof Victor R, Loving Healing Press Inc, 5145 Pontiac Trail, Ann Arbor, MI 48105 *Tel:* 734-417-4266 *Toll Free Tel:* 888-761-6268 (US & CN) *Fax:* 734-663-6861 *E-mail:* info@lovinghealing.com; info@lhpress.com *Web Site:* www.lovinghealing.com; www.modernhistorypress.com (imprint), pg 138

Vollmar, Robert, Neustadt International Prize for Literature, c/o University of Oklahoma, 630 Parrington Oval, Suite 110, Norman, OK 73019-4033 *Tel:* 405-325-4531 *Web Site:* www.worldliteraturetoday.org; www.worldlit.org, pg 672

Vollmar, Robert, NSK Neustadt Prize for Children's Literature, c/o University of Oklahoma, 630 Parrington Oval, Suite 110, Norman, OK 73019-4033 *Tel:* 405-325-4531 *Web Site:* www.worldliteraturetoday.org; www.worldlit.org, pg 674

Volpert, Amy, BioTechniques Books, 52 Vanderbilt Ave, 11th fl, New York, NY 10017 *Tel:* 212-520-2777 *Fax:* 212-520-2705 *Web Site:* www.biotechniques.com, pg 35

Volpi, Sara, Kentucky Writers Conference, 1906 College Heights Blvd, Suite 11067, Bowling Green, KY 42101-1067 *Tel:* 270-745-4502 *E-mail:* sokybookfest@wku.edu *Web Site:* www.sokybookfest.org, pg 612

Voltz, Gunnar, Abrams Learning Trends, 16310 Bratton Lane, Suite 250, Austin, TX 78728-2403 *Toll Free Tel:* 800-227-9120 *Toll Free Fax:* 800-737-3322 *E-mail:* customerservice@abramslearningtrends.com (orders, cust serv); contactus@abramslearningtrends.com *Web Site:* www.abramslearningtrends.com (orders, cust serv), pg 3

Von Beoczy, Stefanie, Penguin Random House Speakers Bureau, A Penguin Random House Company, 1745 Broadway, Mail Drop 13-1, New York, NY 10019 *Tel:* 212-572-2013 *E-mail:* speakers@penguinrandomhouse.com *Web Site:* www.prhspeakers.com, pg 547

von Bergen, Julie, APA Planners Press, 205 N Michigan Ave, Suite 1200, Chicago, IL 60601 *Tel:* 312-431-9100 *Fax:* 312-786-6700 *E-mail:* customerservice@planning.org *Web Site:* www.planning.org, pg 18

Von Drasek, Lisa, Ezra Jack Keats/Kerlan Memorial Fellowship, University of Minnesota, 113 Andersen Library, 222 21 Ave S, Minneapolis, MN 55455 *Tel:* 612-624-4576 *E-mail:* asc-clrc@umn.edu *Web Site:* www.lib.umn.edu/clrc, pg 658

von Grebmer, Klaus, International Food Policy Research Institute, 2033 "K" St NW, Washington, DC 20006-1002 *Tel:* 202-862-5600 *Fax:* 202-467-4439 *E-mail:* ifpri@cgiar.org *Web Site:* www.ifpri.org, pg 119

Von Hertsenberg, Kurt, Wildlife Education Ltd, 2418 Noyes St, Evanston, IL 60201 *Tel:* 859-261-2556 *Toll Free Tel:* 800-477-5034 *Fax:* 859-261-2355 *Web Site:* www.zoobooks.com; wildlife-ed.com, pg 256

Von Hoelscher, Russ, National Association of Book Entrepreneurs (NABE), PO Box 606, Cottage Grove, OR 97424 *Tel:* 541-942-7455 *E-mail:* nabe@bookmarketingprofits.com *Web Site:* www.bookmarketingprofits.com, pg 570

von Knorring, John, Stylus Publishing LLC, 22883 Quicksilver Dr, Sterling, VA 20166-2012 *Tel:* 703-661-1504 (edit & sales) *Toll Free Tel:* 800-232-0223 (orders & cust serv) *Fax:* 703-661-1547 *E-mail:* stylusmail@presswarehouse.com (orders & cust serv); stylusinfo@styluspub.com *Web Site:* www.styluspub.com, pg 224

von Mehren, Jane, Aevitas Creative Management, 19 W 21 St, Suite 501, New York, NY 10010 *Tel:* 212-765-6900 *Web Site:* aevitascreative.com, pg 506

von Moltke, Nina, Penguin Random House Inc, 1745 Broadway, New York, NY 10019 *Tel:* 212-782-9000 *Toll Free Tel:* 800-726-0600 *Web Site:* www.penguinrandomhouse.com, pg 178

von Schilling, Claire, Random House Publishing Group, 1745 Broadway, New York, NY 10019 *Toll Free Tel:* 800-200-3552 *Web Site:* atrandom.com, pg 195

Vondeling, Johanna, Berrett-Koehler Publishers Inc, 1333 Broadway, Suite 1000, Oakland, CA 94612 *Tel:* 510-817-2277 *Fax:* 510-817-2278 *E-mail:* bkpub@bkpub.com *Web Site:* www.bkconnection.com, pg 34

Vorenberg, Bonnie L, ArtAge Publications, PO Box 19955, Portland, OR 97280 *Tel:* 503-246-3000 *Toll Free Tel:* 800-858-4998 *Web Site:* www.seniortheatre.com, pg 21

Voros, Stephanie, Simon & Schuster Children's Publishing, 1230 Avenue of the Americas, New York, NY 10020 *Tel:* 212-698-7000 *Web Site:* www.simonandschuster.com/kids; www.simonandschuster.com/teen; simonandschuster.net; simonandschuster.biz, pg 213

Vosburgh, Andrew R, Graphic World Publishing Services, 11687 Adie Rd, St Louis, MO 63043 *Tel:* 314-567-9854 *Fax:* 314-567-7178 *E-mail:* quote@gwinc.com *Web Site:* www.gwinc.com, pg 495

Vrame, Dr Anton, Holy Cross Orthodox Press, 50 Goddard Ave, Brookline, MA 02445 *Tel:* 617-731-3500; 617-850-1200 *Fax:* 617-850-1460 *E-mail:* info@hchc.edu *Web Site:* www.hchc.edu, pg 109

Vreeland, Amy, Harry N Abrams Inc, 195 Broadway, 9th fl, New York, NY 10007 *Tel:* 212-206-7715 *Toll Free Tel:* 800-345-1359 *Fax:* 212-519-1210 *E-mail:* abrams@abramsbooks.com *Web Site:* www.abramsbooks.com, pg 3

Vroegop, Allison, Houghton Mifflin Harcourt Trade & Reference Division, 125 High St, Boston, MA 02110 *Tel:* 617-351-5000 *Toll Free Tel:* 800-225-3362 *Web Site:* www.hmhco.com, pg 111

Vukov-Kendes, Irena, Anchor Books, c/o Penguin Random House Inc, 1745 Broadway, New York, NY 10019 *Tel:* 212-572-2420 *E-mail:* vintageanchorpublicity@randomhouse.com *Web Site:* knopfdoubleday.com/imprint/anchor, pg 16

Vukov-Kendes, Irena, Vintage Books, c/o Penguin Random House Inc, 1745 Broadway, New York, NY 10019 *Tel:* 212-572-2420 *E-mail:* vintageanchorpublicity@randomhouse.com *Web Site:* knopfdoubleday.com/imprint/vintage, pg 251

Vunderink, Will, Georges Borchardt Inc, 136 E 57 St, New York, NY 10022 *Tel:* 212-753-5785 *E-mail:* georges@gbagency.com *Web Site:* www.gbagency.com, pg 509

Vuong, Kien, Simon & Schuster Canada, 166 King St E, Suite 300, Toronto, ON M5A 1J3, Canada *Tel:* 647-427-8882 *Toll Free Tel:* 800-387-0446; 800-268-3216 (orders) *Fax:* 647-430-9446 *Toll Free Fax:* 888-849-8151 (orders) *E-mail:* info@simonandschuster.ca *Web Site:* www.simonandschuster.ca, pg 471

Vyce, Stephanie, Harvard University Press, 79 Garden St, Cambridge, MA 02138-1499 *Tel:* 617-495-2600; 401-531-2800 (intl orders) *Toll Free Tel:* 800-405-1619 (orders) *Fax:* 617-495-5898 (general); 617-496-4677 (edit & rts); 401-531-2801 (intl orders) *Toll Free Fax:* 800-406-9145 (orders) *E-mail:* contact_hup@harvard.edu *Web Site:* www.hup.harvard.edu, pg 103

Wachs, Courtney, Educational Insights, 152 W Walnut St, Suite 201, Gardena, CA 90248 *Toll Free Tel:* 800-995-4436 *Toll Free Fax:* 888-892-8731 *E-mail:* cs@educationalinsights.com *Web Site:* www.educationalinsights.com, pg 76

Wacht, Sandra, MGI Management Institute Inc, 12 Skyline Dr, Hawthorne, NY 10532 *Tel:* 914-428-6500 *Toll Free Tel:* 800-932-0191 *Fax:* 914-428-0773 *E-mail:* mgiusa@aol.com *Web Site:* www.mgi.org, pg 149

Wachtel, Gina, Penguin Random House Inc, 1745 Broadway, New York, NY 10019 *Tel:* 212-782-9000 *Toll Free Tel:* 800-726-0600 *Web Site:* www.penguinrandomhouse.com, pg 178

Wachtel, Gina, Random House Publishing Group, 1745 Broadway, New York, NY 10019 *Toll Free Tel:* 800-200-3552 *Web Site:* atrandom.com, pg 195

Wachtell, Diane, The New Press, 38 Greene St, 4th fl, New York, NY 10013 *Tel:* 212-629-8802 *Toll Free Tel:* 800-343-4489 (orders) *Fax:* 212-629-8617 *Toll Free Fax:* 800-351-5073 (orders) *E-mail:* newpress@thenewpress.com *Web Site:* www.thenewpress.com, pg 161

Wackrow, Dan, Harvard University Press, 79 Garden St, Cambridge, MA 02138-1499 *Tel:* 617-495-2600; 401-531-2800 (intl orders) *Toll Free Tel:* 800-405-1619 (orders) *Fax:* 617-495-5898 (general); 617-496-4677 (edit & rts); 401-531-2801 (intl orders) *Toll Free Fax:* 800-406-9145 (orders) *E-mail:* contact_hup@harvard.edu *Web Site:* www.hup.harvard.edu, pg 103

Wade, Anthony, Letterbox/Papyrus of London Publishers USA, 10501 Broom Hill Dr, Suite 1-F, Las Vegas, NV 89134-7339 *Tel:* 702-256-3838 *E-mail:* lb27383@cox.net, pg 132

Wade, Lee, Random House Children's Books, 1745 Broadway, 10th fl, New York, NY 10019 *Tel:* 212-782-9000 *Web Site:* www.randomhousekids.com, pg 194

Wade, Linda, Crabtree Publishing Co, 350 Fifth Ave, 59th fl, PMB 59051, New York, NY 10118 *Tel:* 212-496-5040 *Toll Free Tel:* 800-387-7650 *Toll Free Fax:* 800-355-7166 *E-mail:* custserv@crabtreebooks.com *Web Site:* www.crabtreebooks.com, pg 63

Wade, Linda, Crabtree Publishing Co Ltd, 616 Welland Ave, St Catharines, ON L2M 5V6, Canada *Tel:* 905-682-5221 *Toll Free Tel:* 800-387-7650 *Fax:* 905-682-7166 *Toll Free Fax:* 800-355-7166 *E-mail:* custserv@crabtreebooks.com; sales@crabtreebooks.com; orders@crabtreebooks.com *Web Site:* www.crabtreebooks.com, pg 451

Wadsworth-Booth, Susan, Duquesne University Press, 600 Forbes Ave, Pittsburgh, PA 15282 *Tel:* 412-396-6610 *Fax:* 412-396-5984 *E-mail:* dupress@duq.edu *Web Site:* www.dupress.duq.edu, pg 74

Waechtler, Heidi, Association of Book Publishers of British Columbia, 600-402 W Pender St, Vancouver, BC V6B 1T6, Canada *Tel:* 604-684-0228 *Fax:* 604-684-5788 *E-mail:* admin@books.bc.ca *Web Site:* www.books.bc.ca, pg 558

Wagman, Zack, HarperCollins General Books Group, 195 Broadway, New York, NY 10007 *Tel:* 212-207-7000 *Web Site:* www.harpercollins.com, pg 101

Wagner, Amy, Abrams Artists Agency, 275 Seventh Ave, 26th fl, New York, NY 10001 *Tel:* 646-486-4600 *Fax:* 646-486-0100 *E-mail:* literary@abramsartny.com *Web Site:* www.abramsartists.com, pg 505

Wagner, Meredith, Publishers Information Bureau (PIB)®, 757 Third Ave, 11th fl, New York, NY 10017 *Tel:* 212-872-3745; 212-872-3700 (MPA) *E-mail:* infocenter@magazine.org *Web Site:* www.magazine.org, pg 577

Wallentine, Lois, Graphic Universe™, 241 First Ave N, Minneapolis, MN 55401 *Tel:* 612-332-3344 *Toll Free Tel:* 800-328-4929 *Fax:* 612-332-7615 *Toll Free Fax:* 800-332-1132 *E-mail:* info@lernerbooks.com; custserve@lernerbooks.com *Web Site:* www.lernerbooks.com; www.facebook.com/lernerbooks, pg 95

Wallentine, Lois, Lerner Publications, 241 First Ave N, Minneapolis, MN 55401 *Tel:* 612-332-3344 *Toll Free Tel:* 800-328-4929 *Fax:* 612-332-7615 *Toll Free Fax:* 800-332-1132 *E-mail:* info@lernerbooks.com; custserve@lernerbooks.com *Web Site:* www.lernerbooks.com; www.facebook.com/lernerbooks, pg 132

Wallentine, Lois, Lerner Publishing Group Inc, 241 First Ave N, Minneapolis, MN 55401 *Tel:* 612-332-3344 *Toll Free Tel:* 800-328-4929 *Fax:* 612-332-7615 *Toll Free Fax:* 800-332-1132 *E-mail:* info@lernerbooks.com; custserve@lernerbooks.com *Web Site:* www.lernerbooks.com; www.facebook.com/lernerbooks, pg 132

Wallentine, Lois, LernerClassroom, 241 First Ave N, Minneapolis, MN 55401 *Tel:* 612-332-3344 *Toll Free Tel:* 800-328-4929 *Fax:* 612-332-7615 *Toll Free Fax:* 800-332-1132 *E-mail:* info@lernerbooks.com; custserve@lernerbooks.com *Web Site:* www.lernerbooks.com; www.facebook.com/lernerbooks, pg 132

Wallentine, Lois, Millbrook Press, 241 First Ave N, Minneapolis, MN 55401 *Tel:* 612-332-3344 *Toll Free Tel:* 800-328-4929 (US only) *Fax:* 612-332-7615 *Toll Free Fax:* 800-332-1132 *E-mail:* info@lernerbooks.com; custserve@lernerbooks.com *Web Site:* www.lernerbooks.com; www.facebook.com/millbrookpress, pg 151

Wallentine, Lois, Twenty-First Century Books, 241 First Ave N, Minneapolis, MN 55401 *Tel:* 612-332-3344 *Toll Free Tel:* 800-328-4929 *Fax:* 612-332-7615 *Toll Free Fax:* 800-332-1132 *E-mail:* info@lernerbooks.com; custserve@lernerbooks.com *Web Site:* www.lernerbooks.com; www.facebook.com/lernerbooks, pg 237

Walling, Bonnie, OPIS/STALSBY Directories & Databases, 3349 Hwy 138, Bldg D, Suite D, Wall, NJ 07719 *Tel:* 732-901-8800 *Toll Free Tel:* 800-275-0950 *Toll Free Fax:* 800-450-5864 *E-mail:* opisstalsbylistings@opisnet.com *Web Site:* www.opisnet.com, pg 168

Wallman, Keith, Diversion Books, 443 Park Ave S, Suite 1008, New York, NY 10016 *Tel:* 212-961-6390 *E-mail:* info@diversionbooks.com *Web Site:* www.diversionbooks.com, pg 71

Walls, Kathleen, Global Authors Publications (GAP), 38 Bluegrass, Middleberg, FL 32068 *Tel:* 904-425-1608 *E-mail:* gapbook@yahoo.com *Web Site:* www.globalauthorspublications.com, pg 93

Walsh, Bruce, University of Regina Press, 2 Research Dr, Suite 246, Regina, SK S4S 7H9, Canada *Tel:* 306-585-4758 *Fax:* 306-585-4699 *E-mail:* uofrpress@uregina.ca *Web Site:* uofrpress.ca, pg 474

Walsh, Jennifer Rudolph, WME, 11 Madison Ave, 18th fl, New York, NY 10010 *Tel:* 212-586-5100 *Web Site:* www.wmeentertainment.com, pg 542

Walsh, Karen, Houghton Mifflin Harcourt Trade & Reference Division, 125 High St, Boston, MA 02110 *Tel:* 617-351-5000 *Toll Free Tel:* 800-225-3362 *Web Site:* www.hmhco.com, pg 111

Walsh, Mike, LexisNexis®, 230 Park Ave, Suite 7, New York, NY 10169 *Tel:* 212-309-8100 *Toll Free Fax:* 800-437-8674 *Web Site:* www.lexisnexis.com, pg 133

Walsh, Warren, Emerald Books, PO Box 55787, Seattle, WA 98155 *Tel:* 425-771-1153 *Toll Free Tel:* 800-922-2143 *Fax:* 425-775-2383 *E-mail:* books@ywampublishing.com *Web Site:* www.ywampublishing.com, pg 78

Walter, Timothy M, Catholic Book Awards, 205 W Monroe St, Suite 470, Chicago, IL 60606 *Tel:* 312-380-6789 *Fax:* 312-361-0256 *E-mail:* cathjourn@catholicpress.org *Web Site:* www.catholicpress.org, pg 636

Walter, Timothy M, Catholic Press Association of the United States & Canada, 205 W Monroe St, Suite 470, Chicago, IL 60606 *Tel:* 312-380-6789 *Fax:* 312-361-0256 *E-mail:* journalist@catholicpress.org *Web Site:* www.catholicpress.org, pg 562

Walter, Timothy M, Catholic Press Awards, 205 W Monroe St, Suite 470, Chicago, IL 60606 *Tel:* 312-380-6789 *Fax:* 312-361-0256 *E-mail:* cathjourn@catholicpress.org *Web Site:* www.catholicpress.org, pg 636

Walters, Ed, Tuttle Publishing, Airport Business Park, 364 Innovation Dr, North Clarendon, VT 05759-9436 *Tel:* 802-773-8930 *Toll Free Tel:* 800-526-2778 *Fax:* 802-773-6993 *Toll Free Fax:* 800-FAX-TUTL (329-8885) *E-mail:* info@tuttlepublishing.com; orders@tuttlepublishing.com *Web Site:* www.tuttlepublishing.com, pg 237

Walters, John P, Hudson Institute, 1015 15 St NW, 6th fl, Washington, DC 20005 *Tel:* 202-974-2400 *Fax:* 202-974-2410 *E-mail:* info@hudson.org *Web Site:* www.hudson.org, pg 112

Walters, Maureen, Curtis Brown Ltd, 10 Astor Place, New York, NY 10003 *Tel:* 212-473-5400 *Web Site:* www.curtisbrown.com, pg 510

Walters-Moore, Linda, George Orwell Award, 1111 W Kenyon Rd, Urbana, IL 61801-1096 *Tel:* 217-328-3870 *Toll Free Tel:* 877-369-6283 (cust serv) *Fax:* 217-328-0977 *E-mail:* publiclangawards@ncte.org *Web Site:* www.ncte.org, pg 676

Walther, Luann, Anchor Books, c/o Penguin Random House Inc, 1745 Broadway, New York, NY 10019 *Tel:* 212-572-2420 *E-mail:* vintageanchorpublicity@randomhouse.com *Web Site:* knopfdoubleday.com/imprint/anchor, pg 16

Walther, LuAnn, Alfred A Knopf/Everyman's Library, c/o Penguin Random House Inc, 1745 Broadway, New York, NY 10019 *Tel:* 212-751-2600 *Toll Free Tel:* 800-638-6460 *Fax:* 212-572-2593 *Web Site:* www.knopfdoubleday.com, pg 127

Walther, Luann, Vintage Books, c/o Penguin Random House Inc, 1745 Broadway, New York, NY 10019 *Tel:* 212-572-2420 *E-mail:* vintageanchorpublicity@randomhouse.com *Web Site:* knopfdoubleday.com/imprint/vintage, pg 251

Walther, Stevia, Rocky Mountain Mineral Law Foundation, 9191 Sheridan Blvd, Suite 203, Westminster, CO 80031 *Tel:* 303-321-8100 *Fax:* 303-321-7657 *E-mail:* info@rmmlf.org *Web Site:* www.rmmlf.org, pg 200

Waltman, Fran, Edward Lewis Wallant Book Award, 3 Brighton Rd, West Hartford, CT 06117 *Tel:* 860-232-1421, pg 696

Waltman, Irving, Edward Lewis Wallant Book Award, 3 Brighton Rd, West Hartford, CT 06117 *Tel:* 860-232-1421, pg 696

Walton, Kathy S, TCU Press, 3000 Sandage Ave, Fort Worth, TX 76109 *Tel:* 817-257-7822 *Toll Free Tel:* 800-826-8911 (orders) *Fax:* 817-257-5075 *Web Site:* www.prs.tcu.edu, pg 228

Wang, Xin, China Books, 360 Swift Ave, Suite 48, South San Francisco, CA 94080 *Tel:* 650-872-7076 *Toll Free Tel:* 800-818-2017 (US only) *Fax:* 650-872-7808 *E-mail:* info@chinabooks.com *Web Site:* www.chinabooks.com, pg 54

Wang-Iverson, Jeremy, Berghahn Books, 20 Jay St, Suite 512, Brooklyn, NY 11201 *Tel:* 212-233-6004 *Fax:* 212-233-6007 *E-mail:* info@berghahnbooks.com; salesus@berghahnbooks.com; editorial@journals.berghahnbooks.com *Web Site:* www.berghahnbooks.com, pg 33

Wanger, Shelley, Pantheon Books/Schocken Books, c/o Penguin Random House Inc, 1745 Broadway, New York, NY 10019 *Tel:* 212-751-2600 *Web Site:* knopfdoubleday.com/imprint/pantheon, pg 173

Wantland, Clydette, University of Illinois Press, 1325 S Oak St, MC-566, Champaign, IL 61820-6903 *Tel:* 217-333-0950 *Fax:* 217-244-8082 *E-mail:* uipress@uillinois.edu; journals@uillinois.edu *Web Site:* www.press.uillinois.edu, pg 241

Ward, Andy, Random House Publishing Group, 1745 Broadway, New York, NY 10019 *Toll Free Tel:* 800-200-3552 *Web Site:* atrandom.com, pg 195

Ward, Anne C, High Tide Press, 301 Veterans Pkwy, New Lenox, IL 60451 *Web Site:* cherryhillhightide.com/high-tide-press/, pg 107

Ward, Casey, Random House Children's Books, 1745 Broadway, 10th fl, New York, NY 10019 *Tel:* 212-782-9000 *Web Site:* www.randomhousekids.com, pg 194

Ward, Courtney, Pauline Books & Media, 50 Saint Paul's Ave, Boston, MA 02130 *Tel:* 617-522-8911 *Toll Free Tel:* 800-876-4463 (orders); 800-836-9723 (cust serv) *Fax:* 617-541-9805 *E-mail:* editorial@paulinemedia.com (ms submissions); orderentry@pauline.org (cust serv) *Web Site:* www.pauline.org/publishing; www.pauline.org/PBMPublishing, pg 175

Ward, Elizabeth, Random House Children's Books, 1745 Broadway, 10th fl, New York, NY 10019 *Tel:* 212-782-9000 *Web Site:* www.randomhousekids.com, pg 194

Ward, Lacy, Quail Ridge Press, 101 Brooks Dr, Brandon, MS 39042 *Tel:* 601-825-2063 *Toll Free Tel:* 800-343-1583 *Fax:* 601-825-3091 *Toll Free Fax:* 800-864-1082 *E-mail:* info@quailridge.com *Web Site:* quailridge.com, pg 192

Warden, Yorke, Living Stream Ministry (LSM), 2431 W La Palma Ave, Anaheim, CA 92801 *Tel:* 714-991-4681 *Toll Free Tel:* 800-549-5164 *Fax:* 714-236-6005 *E-mail:* books@lsm.org *Web Site:* www.lsm.org, pg 136

Wareing, Tracy, American Public Human Services Association, 1133 19 St NW, Suite 400, Washington, DC 20036 *Tel:* 202-682-0100 *Fax:* 202-289-6555 *Web Site:* www.aphsa.org, pg 556

Waricha, Joan, Parachute Publishing LLC, 157 Columbus Ave, Suite 518, New York, NY 10023 *Tel:* 212-691-1421 *Web Site:* www.parachutepublishing.com, pg 173

Warinner, J M, Professional Resource Press, 1958 Barber Rd, Sarasota, FL 34240 *Tel:* 941-343-9601 *Toll Free Tel:* 800-443-3364 (orders & cust serv) *Fax:* 941-343-9201 *Toll Free Fax:* 866-804-4843 (orders only) *E-mail:* cs.prpress@gmail.com *Web Site:* www.prpress.com, pg 189

Warlick, Dottie, Oxford University Press USA, 198 Madison Ave, New York, NY 10016 *Tel:* 212-726-6000 *Toll Free Tel:* 800-451-7556 (orders); 800-445-9714 (cust serv) *Fax:* 919-677-1303 *E-mail:* custserv.us@oup.com *Web Site:* www.oup.com/us, pg 171

Warner, Matt, Gem Guides Book Co, 1275 W Ninth St, Upland, CA 91786 *Tel:* 626-855-1611 *Toll Free Tel:* 800-824-5118 (orders) *Fax:* 626-855-1610 *E-mail:* info@gemguidesbooks.com *Web Site:* www.gemguidesbooks.com, pg 91

Warner, Sharon Oard, Taos Summer Writers' Conference, One University of New Mexico, Albuquerque, NM 87131-0001 *Tel:* 505-277-5572 *E-mail:* taosconf@unm.edu *Web Site:* taosconf.unm.edu, pg 615

Warnock, Colin, Fine Creative Media, Inc, 322 Eighth Ave, 15th fl, New York, NY 10001 *Tel:* 212-595-3500 *Fax:* 212-595-3779, pg 85

Warren, Bruce, Abrams Learning Trends, 16310 Bratton Lane, Suite 250, Austin, TX 78728-2403 *Toll Free Tel:* 800-227-9120 *Toll Free Fax:* 800-737-3322 *E-mail:* customerservice@abramslearningtrends.com (orders, cust serv); contactus@abramslearningtrends.com *Web Site:* www.abramslearningtrends.com (orders, cust serv), pg 3

Warren, Daniel, Warren Communications News Inc, 2115 Ward Ct NW, Washington, DC 20037 *Tel:* 202-872-9200 *Toll Free Tel:* 800-771-9202 *Fax:* 202-293-3435; 202-318-8350 *E-mail:* info@warren-news.com; newsroom@warren-news.com *Web Site:* www.warren-news.com, pg 252

Warren, Julie, RockBench Publishing Corp, 6101 Stillmeadow Dr, Nashville, TN 37211-6518 *Tel:* 615-831-2277 *Fax:* 615-831-2212 *E-mail:* info@rockbench.com, pg 200

Warren, Lissa, Perseus Books, 250 W 57 St, 15th fl, New York, NY 10107 *Tel:* 212-340-8100 *Toll Free Tel:* 800-343-4499 (cust serv) *Fax:* 212-340-8105 *Web Site:* www.perseusbooks.com, pg 180

Warren, Paul, Warren Communications News Inc, 2115 Ward Ct NW, Washington, DC 20037 *Tel:* 202-872-9200 *Toll Free Tel:* 800-771-9202 *Fax:* 202-293-3435; 202-318-8350 *E-mail:* info@warren-news.com; newsroom@warren-news.com *Web Site:* www.warren-news.com, pg 252

Warren, Wenche, YWAM Publishing, PO Box 55787, Seattle, WA 98155-0787 *Tel:* 425-771-1153 *Toll Free Tel:* 800-922-2143 *Fax:* 425-775-2383 *E-mail:* books@ywampublishing.com *Web Site:* www.ywampublishing.com, pg 262

Warren, Wenke, Emerald Books, PO Box 55787, Seattle, WA 98155 *Tel:* 425-771-1153 *Toll Free Tel:* 800-922-2143 *Fax:* 425-775-2383 *E-mail:* books@ywampublishing.com *Web Site:* www.ywampublishing.com, pg 78

Warren-Lynch, Isabel, Random House Children's Books, 1745 Broadway, 10th fl, New York, NY 10019 *Tel:* 212-782-9000 *Web Site:* www.randomhousekids.com, pg 194

Warshaw, Hallie, Zest Books, 2443 Stillman St, Suite 340, San Francisco, CA 94115 *Tel:* 415-777-8654; 510-984-0841 *Fax:* 415-777-8653 *E-mail:* info@zestbooks.net; publicity@zestbooks.net *Web Site:* zestbooks.net, pg 263

Warshenbrot, Amalia, AJL Judaica Bibliography Award, PO Box 1118, Teaneck, NJ 07666 *Tel:* 201-371-3255 *E-mail:* info@jewishlibraries.org *Web Site:* jewishlibraries.org, pg 626

Warshenbrot, Amalia, AJL Judaica Reference Award, PO Box 1118, Teaneck, NJ 07666 *Tel:* 201-371-3255 *E-mail:* info@jewishlibraries.org *Web Site:* jewishlibraries.org, pg 626

Warshenbrot, Amalia, Association of Jewish Libraries (AJL) Inc, PO Box 1118, Teaneck, NJ 07666 *Tel:* 201-371-3255 *E-mail:* info@jewishlibraries.org *Web Site:* jewishlibraries.org, pg 559

Warshenbrot, Amalia, Sydney Taylor Book Awards, PO Box 1118, Teaneck, NJ 07666 *Tel:* 201-371-3255 *E-mail:* chair@sydneytaylorbookaward.org; info@jewishlibraries.org *Web Site:* www.sydneytaylorbookaward.org, pg 693

Warwick-Smith, Simon, Warwick Associates, 18340 Sonoma Hwy, Sonoma, CA 95476 *Tel:* 707-939-9212 *Fax:* 707-938-3515 *E-mail:* warwick@vom.com *Web Site:* www.warwickassociates.com, pg 541

Wasch, Kenneth, CODiE Awards, 1090 Vermont Ave NW, 6th fl, Washington, DC 20005-4095 *E-mail:* info@siia.net *Web Site:* www.siia.net, pg 638

Wasch, Kenneth, Software & Information Industry Association (SIIA), 1090 Vermont Ave NW, 6th fl, Washington, DC 20005-4095 *Tel:* 202-289-7442 *Fax:* 202-289-7097 *Web Site:* www.siia.net, pg 579

Wasdyke, Rachel, Houghton Mifflin Harcourt Trade & Reference Division, 125 High St, Boston, MA 02110 *Tel:* 617-351-5000 *Toll Free Tel:* 800-225-3362 *Web Site:* www.hmhco.com, pg 111

Washburne, Carolyn Kott, The Wisconsin Writers Awards, c/o 450 E Beaumont Ave, No 1005, Whitefish Bay, WI 53217-4805 *E-mail:* wiswriters@gmail.com *Web Site:* wiswriters.org/awards, pg 698

Wasielewski, Leah, HarperCollins General Books Group, 195 Broadway, New York, NY 10007 *Tel:* 212-207-7000 *Web Site:* www.harpercollins.com, pg 101

Wasserman, Steve, Heyday Books, 1633 University Ave, Berkeley, CA 94703 *Tel:* 510-549-3564 *Fax:* 510-549-1889 *E-mail:* heyday@heydaybooks.com; orders@heydaybooks.com *Web Site:* heydaybooks.com, pg 106

Wasserman, Steve, Yale University Press, 302 Temple St, New Haven, CT 06511-8909 *Tel:* 203-432-0960; 203-432-0966 (sales); 401-531-2800 (cust serv) *Toll Free Tel:* 800-405-1619 (cust serv) *Fax:* 203-432-0948; 203-432-8485 (sales); 401-531-2801 (cust serv) *Toll Free Fax:* 800-406-9145 (cust serv) *E-mail:* sales.press@yale.edu (sales); customer.care@triliteral.org (cust serv) *Web Site:* www.yalebooks.com; yalepress.yale.edu/yupbooks, pg 261

Waterman, Daniel, University of Alabama Press, 200 Hackberry Lane, 2nd fl, Tuscaloosa, AL 35487 *Tel:* 205-348-5180 *Fax:* 205-348-9201 *Web Site:* www.uapress.ua.edu, pg 239

Waterman, Susan, New Mexico Book Association (NMBA), 1219 Luisa St, Suite 1, Santa Fe, NM 87505 *Tel:* 505-660-6357 *E-mail:* admin@nmbook.org *Web Site:* www.nmbook.org, pg 573

Waters, Lindsay, Harvard University Press, 79 Garden St, Cambridge, MA 02138-1499 *Tel:* 617-495-2600; 401-531-2800 (intl orders) *Toll Free Tel:* 800-405-1619 (orders) *Fax:* 617-495-5898 (general); 617-496-4677 (edit & rts); 401-531-2801 (intl orders) *Toll Free Fax:* 800-406-9145 (orders) *E-mail:* contact_hup@harvard.edu *Web Site:* www.hup.harvard.edu, pg 103

Waters, Michele, New Harbinger Publications Inc, 5674 Shattuck Ave, Oakland, CA 94609 *Tel:* 510-652-0215 *Toll Free Tel:* 800-748-6273 (orders only) *Fax:* 510-652-5472 *Toll Free Fax:* 800-652-1613 *E-mail:* nhhelp@newharbinger.com; customerservice@newharbinger.com *Web Site:* www.newharbinger.com, pg 160

Waters, Mitchell, Curtis Brown Ltd, 10 Astor Place, New York, NY 10003 *Tel:* 212-473-5400 *Web Site:* www.curtisbrown.com, pg 510

Watkins, Kelly, SLACK® Incorporated, A Wyanoke Group Company, 6900 Grove Rd, Thorofare, NJ 08086-9447 *Tel:* 856-848-1000 *Toll Free Tel:* 800-257-8290 *Fax:* 856-848-6091 *E-mail:* sales@slackinc.com; editor@slackinc.com; customerservice@slackinc.com *Web Site:* www.healio.com/books, pg 215

Watkinson, Charles, University of Michigan Press, 839 Greene St, Ann Arbor, MI 48104-3209 *Tel:* 734-764-4388 *Fax:* 734-615-1540 *E-mail:* esladmin@umich.edu *Web Site:* www.press.umich.edu, pg 242

Watson, Ben, Chelsea Green Publishing Co, 85 N Main St, Suite 120, White River Junction, VT 05001 *Tel:* 802-295-6300 *Toll Free Tel:* 800-639-4099 (cust serv, consumer & trade orders) *Fax:* 802-295-6444 *Web Site:* www.chelseagreen.com, pg 53

Watson, David R, Institute of Continuing Legal Education, 1020 Greene St, Ann Arbor, MI 48109-1444 *Tel:* 734-764-0533 *Toll Free Tel:* 877-229-4350 *Fax:* 734-763-2412 *Toll Free Fax:* 877-229-4351 *E-mail:* icle@umich.edu *Web Site:* www.icle.org, pg 117

Watson, Duane, Wm B Eerdmans Publishing Co, 2140 Oak Industrial Dr NE, Grand Rapids, MI 49505 *Tel:* 616-459-4591 *Toll Free Tel:* 800-253-7521 *Fax:* 616-459-6540 *E-mail:* customerservice@eerdmans.com; sales@eerdmans.com *Web Site:* www.eerdmans.com, pg 76

Watson, Joanne, Merriam-Webster Inc, 47 Federal St, Springfield, MA 01102 *Tel:* 413-734-3134 *Toll Free Tel:* 800-828-1880 (orders & cust serv) *Fax:* 413-731-5979 (sales) *E-mail:* support@merriam-webster.com *Web Site:* www.merriam-webster.com, pg 149

Watson, Kara, Scribner, 1230 Avenue of the Americas, New York, NY 10020, pg 209

Watson, Kate, Hackmatack Children's Choice Book Award, PO Box 1047, Ottawa, NS K1P 5V8, Canada *Tel:* 902-424-3774 *Fax:* 902-424-0613 *E-mail:* hackmatack@hackmatack.ca *Web Site:* www.hackmatack.ca, pg 651

Watson, Kent, Publishers Association of the West Inc (PubWest), 17501 Hill Way, Lake Oswego, OR 97035 *Tel:* 503-901-9865 *Web Site:* pubwest.org, pg 576

Watson, Kent, PubWest Book Design Awards, 17501 Hill Way, Lake Oswego, OR 97035 *Tel:* 503-901-9865 *Web Site:* pubwest.org, pg 683

Watson, Kent, Jack D Rittenhouse Award, 17501 Hill Way, Lake Oswego, OR 97035 *Tel:* 503-901-9865 *Web Site:* pubwest.org, pg 685

Watson, Lucia, Avery, 375 Hudson St, New York, NY 10014 *Tel:* 212-366-2000 *Fax:* 212-366-2643 *Web Site:* www.penguin.com; www.penguinrandomhouse.com, pg 27

Watson, Mackenzie Brady, Stuart Krichevsky Literary Agency Inc, 6 E 39 St, Suite 500, New York, NY 10016 *Tel:* 212-725-5288 *Fax:* 212-725-5275 *E-mail:* query@skagency.com *Web Site:* skagency.com, pg 525

Watson, Mary, Shenanigan Books, 84 River Rd, Summit, NJ 07901 *Tel:* 908-219-4275 *Fax:* 908-219-4485 *Web Site:* www.shenaniganbooks.com, pg 211

Watson, Neale W Esq, Watson Publishing International LLC, PO Box 1240, Sagamore Beach, MA 02562-1240 *Tel:* 508-888-9113 *E-mail:* orders@watsonpublishing.com; orders@shpusa.com *Web Site:* www.shpusa.com; www.watsonpublishing.com, pg 253

Watson, Renee, Books on Tape®, 1745 Broadway, New York, NY 10019 *Toll Free Tel:* 800-733-3000 (cust serv) *Toll Free Fax:* 800-940-7046 *Web Site:* www.booksontape.com, pg 40

Wattawa, Gayle, Heyday Books, 1633 University Ave, Berkeley, CA 94703 *Tel:* 510-549-3564 *Fax:* 510-549-1889 *E-mail:* heyday@heydaybooks.com; orders@heydaybooks.com *Web Site:* heydaybooks.com, pg 106

Wattendorf, Bob, Florida Outdoor Writers Association Inc, 24 NW 33 Ct, Suite A, Gainesville, FL 32607 *Tel:* 352-284-1763 *E-mail:* info@fowa.org *Web Site:* www.fowa.org, pg 565

Watters, Ron, National Outdoor Book Awards, 921 S Eighth Ave, Stop 8128, Pocatello, ID 83209-8128 *Tel:* 208-282-3912 *Fax:* 208-282-2127 *Web Site:* www.noba-web.org, pg 671

Watterson, Jessica, Sandra Dijkstra Literary Agency, 1155 Camino del Mar, PMB 515, Del Mar, CA 92014-2605 *E-mail:* queries@dijkstraagency.com *Web Site:* dijkstraagency.com, pg 514

Watts, Benjamin, Stipes Publishing LLC, 204 W University Ave, Champaign, IL 61820 *Tel:* 217-356-8391 *Fax:* 217-356-5753 *E-mail:* stipes01@sbcglobal.net *Web Site:* www.stipes.com, pg 222

Waugh, Rebecca, Books on Tape®, 1745 Broadway, New York, NY 10019 *Toll Free Tel:* 800-733-3000 (cust serv) *Toll Free Fax:* 800-940-7046 *Web Site:* www.booksontape.com, pg 40

Waxman, Scott, Diversion Books, 443 Park Ave S, Suite 1008, New York, NY 10016 *Tel:* 212-961-6390 *E-mail:* info@diversionbooks.com *Web Site:* www.diversionbooks.com, pg 71

Waxman, Scott, Waxman Leavell Literary Agency, 443 Park Ave S, No 1004, New York, NY 10016 *Tel:* 212-675-5556 *Fax:* 212-675-1381 *Web Site:* www.waxmanleavell.com, pg 541

Wayne, Alan, Imagination Publishing Group, PO Box 1304, Dunedin, FL 34697 *Toll Free Tel:* 888-701-6481 *Fax:* 727-361-0584 *E-mail:* info@imaginationpublishinggroup.com *Web Site:* www.imaginationpublishinggroup.com, pg 114

Wayne, Andrew, Canadian Scholars' Press Inc, 425 Adelaide St W, Suite 200, Toronto, ON M5V 3C1, Canada *Tel:* 416-929-2774 *Toll Free Tel:* 800-463-1998 *Fax:* 416-929-1926 *E-mail:* info@cspi.org; info@canadianscholars.ca; editorial@canadianscholars.ca; orders@canadianscholars.ca *Web Site:* www.canadianscholars.ca; www.womenspress.ca, pg 449

Weaver, Angela, Theatre Library Association (TLA), c/o The New York Public Library for the Performing Arts, 40 Lincoln Center Plaza, New York, NY 10023 *E-mail:* TheatreLibraryAssociation@gmail.com *Web Site:* www.tla-online.org/awards/bookawards, pg 580

Weaver, David E, Ohioana Book Awards, 274 E First Ave, Suite 300, Columbus, OH 43201 *Tel:* 614-466-3831 *Fax:* 614-728-6974 *E-mail:* ohioana@ohioana.org *Web Site:* www.ohioana.org, pg 675

Weaver, David E, Ohioana Walter Rumsey Marvin Grant, 274 E First Ave, Suite 300, Columbus, OH 43201 *Tel:* 614-466-3831 *Fax:* 614-728-6974 *E-mail:* ohioana@ohioana.org *Web Site:* www.ohioana.org, pg 675

Weaver, Kyle, Stackpole Books, 5067 Ritter Rd, Mechanicsburg, PA 17055 *Tel:* 717-796-0411 *Toll Free Tel:* 800-732-3669 *Fax:* 717-796-0412 *Web Site:* www.stackpolebooks.com, pg 220

Weaver, Michael, Chelsea Green Publishing Co, 85 N Main St, Suite 120, White River Junction, VT 05001 *Tel:* 802-295-6300 *Toll Free Tel:* 800-639-4099 (cust serv, consumer & trade orders) *Fax:* 802-295-6444 *Web Site:* www.chelseagreen.com, pg 53

Weaver, Muffy, Dawn Publications Inc, 12402 Bitney Springs Rd, Nevada City, CA 95959 *Tel:* 530-274-7775 *Toll Free Tel:* 800-545-7475 *Fax:* 530-274-7778 *E-mail:* nature@dawnpub.com; orders@dawnpub.com *Web Site:* www.dawnpub.com, pg 68

Weaver-Smith, Heidi, Forward Movement, 412 Sycamore St, Cincinnati, OH 45202-4110 *Tel:* 513-721-6659 *Toll Free Tel:* 800-543-1813 *Fax:* 513-721-0729 (orders) *E-mail:* orders@forwardmovement.org (orders & cust serv) *Web Site:* www.forwardmovement.org, pg 87

Webb, Dorothy, Write Now, 140 W Washington St, Indianapolis, IN 46204-3465 *Tel:* 317-635-5277 *Fax:* 317-236-0767 *E-mail:* info@writenow.co *Web Site:* www.writenow.co, pg 700

Webb, James T, Great Potential Press Inc, 1650 N Kolb Rd, Suite 200, Tucson, AZ 85715 *Tel:* 520-777-6161 *Fax:* 520-777-6217 *Web Site:* www.greatpotentialpress.com, pg 95

Webb, Janine, Boyds Mills Press, 815 Church St, Honesdale, PA 18431 *Tel:* 570-253-1164 *Toll Free Tel:* 800-490-5111 *Fax:* 570-253-0179 *E-mail:* contact@boydsmillspress.com *Web Site:* www.boydsmillspress.com, pg 41

Webb, Janine, Highlights for Children, 1800 Watermark Dr, Columbus, OH 43215 *Tel:* 614-486-0631 *Toll Free Tel:* 800-962-3661 (Highlights Club cust serv); 800-255-9517 (Highlights Magazine cust serv) *Web Site:* www.highlights.com; www.facebook.com/HighlightsforChildren, pg 107

Webb, Kerry, University of Tennessee Press, 110 Conference Center Bldg, 600 Henley St, Knoxville, TN 37996-4108 *Tel:* 865-974-3321 *Toll Free Tel:* 800-621-2736 (orders) *Fax:* 865-974-3724 *Toll Free Fax:* 800-621-8476 (orders) *E-mail:* custserv@utpress.org *Web Site:* www.utpress.org, pg 245

Webber, Jim, New City Press, 202 Comforter Blvd, Hyde Park, NY 12538 *Tel:* 845-229-0335 *Toll Free Tel:* 800-462-5980 (orders only) *Fax:* 845-229-0351 *E-mail:* info@newcitypress.com *Web Site:* www.newcitypress.com, pg 160

Weber, Andrew, Macmillan, 175 Fifth Ave, New York, NY 10010 *Tel:* 646-307-5151 *E-mail:* press.inquiries@macmillan.com *Web Site:* www.macmillan.com, pg 139

Weber, John, Welcome Rain Publishers LLC, 217 Thompson St, Suite 473, New York, NY 10012 *Tel:* 212-686-1909 *Web Site:* welcomerain.com, pg 253

Weber, Judith, Sobel Weber Associates Inc, 146 E 19 St, New York, NY 10003-2404 *Tel:* 212-420-8585 *E-mail:* info@sobelweber.com *Web Site:* www.sobelweber.com, pg 536

Weber, Lauren, Doubleday/Nan A Talese, c/o Penguin Random House Inc, 1745 Broadway, New York, NY 10019 *Tel:* 212-751-2600 *Fax:* 212-572-2662 *E-mail:* ddaypub@randomhouse.com *Web Site:* knopfdoubleday.com, pg 72

Weber, Louis, Publications International Ltd (PIL), 7373 N Cicero Ave, Lincolnwood, IL 60712 *Tel:* 847-676-3470 *Fax:* 847-676-3671 *E-mail:* customer_service@pubint.com *Web Site:* pilbooks.com, pg 191

Weber, Mark, The Noontide Press, PO Box 2719, Newport Beach, CA 92659-1319 *Tel:* 714-593-9725 *E-mail:* orders@noontidepress.com *Web Site:* www.noontidepress.com, pg 163

Weberman, Alisa, Listen & Live Audio Inc, 1700 Manhattan Ave, Union City, NJ 07087 *Tel:* 201-558-9000 *Toll Free Tel:* 800-653-9400 (orders) *Fax:* 201-558-9800 *Web Site:* www.listenandlive.com, pg 135

Webster, Bernadette, Peterson's, a Nelnet Company, 3 Columbia Circle, Suite 205, Albany, NY 12203-5158 *Tel:* 609-896-1800 (ext 53277) *Toll Free Tel:* 800-338-3282 *E-mail:* pubmarketing@petersons.com *Web Site:* www.petersonspublishing.com, pg 181

Wedge, Phil, Cottonwood Press, University of Kansas, Kansas Union, Rm 400, 1301 Jayhawk Blvd, Lawrence, KS 66045 *Tel:* 785-864-4520 *Web Site:* www.englishcw.ku.edu/cottonwood, pg 62

Weed, Susun, Ash Tree Publishing, PO Box 64, Woodstock, NY 12498 *Tel:* 845-246-8081 *Fax:* 845-246-8081 *Web Site:* www.ashtreepublishing.com, pg 23

Weeks, Robin, Dancing Dakini Press, 77 Morning Sun Dr, Sedona, AZ 86336 *Tel:* 928-852-0129 *E-mail:* editor@dancingdakinipress.com *Web Site:* www.dancingdakinipress.com, pg 66

Wegendt, Sr Christina, Pauline Books & Media, 50 Saint Paul's Ave, Boston, MA 02130 *Tel:* 617-522-8911 *Toll Free Tel:* 800-876-4463 (orders); 800-836-9723 (cust serv) *Fax:* 617-541-9805 *E-mail:* editorial@paulinemedia.com (ms submissions); orderentry@pauline.org (cust serv) *Web Site:* www.pauline.org/publishing; www.pauline.org/PBMPublishing, pg 175

Weghorst, Hank, Avention Inc, 300 Baker Ave, Concord, MA 01742 *Tel:* 978-318-4300 *Toll Free Tel:* 866-354-6936 *Fax:* 978-318-4690 *E-mail:* sales@avention.com *Web Site:* www.avention.com, pg 27

Wegner, Gregory R, GLCA New Writers Awards, 535 W William St, Suite 301, Ann Arbor, MI 48103 *Tel:* 734-661-2350 *Fax:* 734-661-2349 *Web Site:* www.glca.org, pg 649

Wehmueller, Jacqueline C, The Johns Hopkins University Press, 2715 N Charles St, Baltimore, MD 21218-4363 *Tel:* 410-516-6900; 410-516-6987 (journal orders outside US & CN) *Toll Free Tel:* 800-537-5487 (book orders & cust serv); 800-548-1784 (journal orders) *Fax:* 410-516-6968; 410-516-3866 (journal orders) *E-mail:* hfscustserv@press.jhu.edu (cust serv); jrnlcirc@press.jhu.edu (journal orders) *Web Site:* www.press.jhu.edu; muse.jhu.edu, pg 122

Wehrle, James, Workman Publishing Co Inc, 225 Varick St, 9th fl, New York, NY 10014-4381 *Tel:* 212-254-5900 *Toll Free Tel:* 800-722-7202 *Fax:* 212-254-8098 *E-mail:* info@workman.com *Web Site:* www.workman.com, pg 259

Weidemann, Jason, University of Minnesota Press, 111 Third Ave S, Suite 290, Minneapolis, MN 55401-2520 *Tel:* 612-301-1990 *Fax:* 612-301-1980 *E-mail:* ump@umn.edu *Web Site:* www.upress.umn.edu, pg 242

Weigl, Charles, AK Press Distribution, 370 Ryan Ave, Unit 100, Chico, CA 95973 *Tel:* 510-208-1700 *Fax:* 510-208-1701 *E-mail:* info@akpress.org *Web Site:* www.akpress.org, pg 6

Weigl, Linda, Weigl Educational Publishers Ltd, 6325 Tenth St SE, Calgary, AB T2H 2Z9, Canada *Tel:* 403-233-7747 *Toll Free Tel:* 800-668-0766 *Fax:* 403-233-7769 *Toll Free Fax:* 866-449-3445 *E-mail:* orders@weigl.com *Web Site:* www.weigl.ca; av2books.com, pg 475

Weikart, Jim, International Association of Crime Writers Inc, North American Branch, 243 Fifth Ave, Suite 537, New York, NY 10016 *Tel:* 212-243-8966 *Fax:* 815-361-1477 *E-mail:* info@crimewritersna.org *Web Site:* www.crimewritersna.org, pg 567

Weikersheimer, Joshua R, ASCP Press, 33 W Monroe St, Suite 1600, Chicago, IL 60603 *Tel:* 312-541-4999 *Toll Free Tel:* 800-267-2727 *Fax:* 312-541-4998 *Web Site:* www.ascp.org, pg 23

Weil, Gideon, HarperCollins General Books Group, 195 Broadway, New York, NY 10007 *Tel:* 212-207-7000 *Web Site:* www.harpercollins.com, pg 101

Weil, Joe, Binghamton University Creative Writing Program, c/o Dept of English, PO Box 6000, Binghamton, NY 13902-6000 *Tel:* 607-777-2168 *Fax:* 607-777-2408 *E-mail:* cwpro@binghamton.edu *Web Site:* english.binghamton.edu/cwpro, pg 619

Weil, Robert, W W Norton & Company Inc, 500 Fifth Ave, New York, NY 10110-0017 *Tel:* 212-354-5500 *Toll Free Tel:* 800-233-4830 (orders & cust serv) *Fax:* 212-869-0856 *Toll Free Fax:* 800-458-6515 *E-mail:* orders@wwnorton.com *Web Site:* books.wwnorton.com, pg 164

Weiland, Matt, W W Norton & Company Inc, 500 Fifth Ave, New York, NY 10110-0017 *Tel:* 212-354-5500 *Toll Free Tel:* 800-233-4830 (orders & cust serv) *Fax:* 212-869-0856 *Toll Free Fax:* 800-458-6515 *E-mail:* orders@wwnorton.com *Web Site:* books.wwnorton.com, pg 164

Weimann, Frank, Folio Literary Management, The Film Center Bldg, 630 Ninth Ave, Suite 1101, New York, NY 10036 *Tel:* 212-400-1494 *Fax:* 212-967-0977 *Web Site:* www.foliolit.com, pg 517

Wein, Lauren, Houghton Mifflin Harcourt Trade & Reference Division, 125 High St, Boston, MA 02110 *Tel:* 617-351-5000 *Toll Free Tel:* 800-225-3362 *Web Site:* www.hmhco.com, pg 111

Weinbaum, Robyn, Florida Writers Association Conference, PO Box 66069, St Pete Beach, FL 33736-6069 *Web Site:* www.floridawriters.net, pg 610

Weinbaum, Robyn, Florida Writers Association Inc, PO Box 66069, St Pete Beach, FL 33736-6069 *Web Site:* www.floridawriters.net, pg 566

Weinberg, Joy, Jewish Publication Society, 2100 Arch St, Philadelphia, PA 19103 *Tel:* 215-832-0600 *Toll Free Tel:* 800-234-3151 *Fax:* 215-568-2017 *Web Site:* www.jps.org, pg 122

Weinberg, Susan, Hachette Book Group, 1290 Avenue of the Americas, New York, NY 10019 *Tel:* 212-364-1100 *Toll Free Tel:* 800-759-0190 (cust serv) *Fax:* 212-364-0933 (intl orders) *Toll Free Fax:* 800-286-9471 (cust serv) *Web Site:* www.hachettebookgroup.com, pg 98

Weinberg, Susan, Perseus Books, 250 W 57 St, 15th fl, New York, NY 10107 *Tel:* 212-340-8100 *Toll Free Tel:* 800-343-4499 (cust serv) *Fax:* 212-340-8105 *Web Site:* www.perseusbooks.com, pg 180

Weinberger, Russell, Brockman Inc, 260 Fifth Ave, 10th fl, New York, NY 10001 *Tel:* 212-935-8900 *Fax:* 212-935-5535 *E-mail:* rights@brockman.com *Web Site:* www.brockman.com, pg 510

Weiner, Allison, Chronicle Books LLC, 680 Second St, San Francisco, CA 94107 *Tel:* 415-537-4200 *Toll Free Tel:* 800-759-0190 (cust serv) *Fax:* 415-537-4460 *Toll Free Fax:* 800-858-7787 (orders); 800-286-9471 (cust serv) *E-mail:* frontdesk@chroniclebooks.com *Web Site:* www.chroniclebooks.com, pg 55

Weiner, Cherry, Cherry Weiner Literary Agency, 925 Oak Bluff Ct, Dacula, GA 30019-6660 *Tel:* 732-446-2096 *Fax:* 732-792-0506 *E-mail:* cherry8486@aol.com, pg 541

Weiner, Ruth, Seven Stories Press, 140 Watts St, New York, NY 10013 *Tel:* 212-226-8760 *Toll Free Tel:* 800-733-3000 (orders) *Fax:* 212-226-1411 *E-mail:* info@sevenstories.com *Web Site:* www.sevenstories.com, pg 211

Weingarten, Seymour, The Guilford Press, 370 Seventh Ave, Suite 1200, New York, NY 10001-1020 *Tel:* 212-431-9800 *Toll Free Tel:* 800-365-7006 *Fax:* 212-966-6708 *E-mail:* info@guilford,com *Web Site:* www.guilford.com, pg 97

Weingarten, Simone, Harvard Square Editions, 2152 Beachwood Terr, Hollywood, CA 90068 *Tel:* 323-203-0233 *E-mail:* submissions@harvardsquareeditions.org *Web Site:* harvardsquareeditions.org, pg 102

Weingel-Fidel, Loretta, The Weingel-Fidel Agency, 310 E 46 St, Suite 21-E, New York, NY 10017 *Tel:* 212-599-2959 *Fax:* 212-286-1986 *E-mail:* queries@theweingel-fidelagency.com, pg 541

Weinreb, Jenya, Yale University Press, 302 Temple St, New Haven, CT 06511-8909 *Tel:* 203-432-0960; 203-432-0966 (sales); 401-531-2800 (cust serv) *Toll Free Tel:* 800-405-1619 (cust serv) *Fax:* 203-432-0948;

203-432-8485 (sales); 401-531-2801 (cust serv) *Toll Free Fax:* 800-406-9145 (cust serv) *E-mail:* sales.press@yale.edu (sales); customer.care@triliteral.org (cust serv) *Web Site:* www.yalebooks.com; yalepress.yale.edu/yupbooks, pg 261

Weinrich, Curtis, North Star Press of Saint Cloud Inc, PO Box 451, St Cloud, MN 56302-0451 *Tel:* 320-558-9062 *E-mail:* info@northstarpress.com *Web Site:* www.northstarpress.com, pg 164

Weinstein, Alexander, Summer Writing Seminar, 7 E Pasture Rd, Aquinnah, MA 02535 *Tel:* 954-242-2903 *Web Site:* mvicw.com, pg 615

Weinstein, Kenneth R, Hudson Institute, 1015 15 St NW, 6th fl, Washington, DC 20005 *Tel:* 202-974-2400 *Fax:* 202-974-2410 *E-mail:* info@hudson.org *Web Site:* www.hudson.org, pg 112

Weinstein, Michael, Book Industry Guild of New York, PO Box 2001, New York, NY 10113-2001 *E-mail:* admin@bookindustryguildofny.org *Web Site:* www.bookindustryguildofny.org, pg 560

Weintraub, Dori, St Martin's Press, LLC, 175 Fifth Ave, New York, NY 10010 *Tel:* 646-307-5151 *Web Site:* us.macmillan.com/smp, pg 204

Weintraub, Steve, Lawyers & Judges Publishing Co Inc, 917 N Swan Rd, Suite 300, Tucson, AZ 85711 *Tel:* 520-323-1500 *Toll Free Tel:* 800-209-7109 *Fax:* 520-323-0055 *Toll Free Fax:* 800-330-8795 *E-mail:* sales@lawyersandjudges.com *Web Site:* www.lawyersandjudges.com, pg 130

Weinzimer, Andrea, Hachette Book Group, 1290 Avenue of the Americas, New York, NY 10019 *Tel:* 212-364-1100 *Toll Free Tel:* 800-759-0190 (cust serv) *Fax:* 212-364-0933 (intl orders) *Toll Free Fax:* 800-286-9471 (cust serv) *Web Site:* www.hachettebookgroup.com, pg 98

Weis, Jennifer, St Martin's Press, LLC, 175 Fifth Ave, New York, NY 10010 *Tel:* 646-307-5151 *Web Site:* us.macmillan.com/smp, pg 204

Weisberg, Don, Macmillan, 175 Fifth Ave, New York, NY 10010 *Tel:* 646-307-5151 *E-mail:* press.inquiries@macmillan.com *Web Site:* www.macmillan.com, pg 139

Weisberg, Don, Macmillan Audio, 175 Fifth Ave, New York, NY 10010 *Tel:* 646-307-5151 *Toll Free Tel:* 888-330-8477 (cust serv) *Fax:* 917-534-0980 *Web Site:* www.macmillanaudio.com, pg 140

Weisfeld, Jarred, Objective Entertainment, 609 Greenwich St, 6th fl, New York, NY 10014 *Tel:* 212-431-5454 *Fax:* 917-464-6394 *Web Site:* www.objectiveent.com, pg 531

Weisman, Jacob, Tachyon Publications LLC, 1459 18 St, No 139, San Francisco, CA 94107 *Tel:* 415-285-5615 *E-mail:* tachyon@tachyonpublications.com *Web Site:* www.tachyonpublications.com, pg 226

Weisman, Margaux, Anchor Books, c/o Penguin Random House Inc, 1745 Broadway, New York, NY 10019 *Tel:* 212-572-2420 *E-mail:* vintageanchorpublicity@randomhouse.com *Web Site:* knopfdoubleday.com/imprint/anchor, pg 16

Weisman, Margaux, Vintage Books, c/o Penguin Random House Inc, 1745 Broadway, New York, NY 10019 *Tel:* 212-572-2420 *E-mail:* vintageanchorpublicity@randomhouse.com *Web Site:* knopfdoubleday.com/imprint/vintage, pg 251

Weisman, Steven R, Peterson Institute for International Economics (PIIE), 1750 Massachusetts Ave NW, Washington, DC 20036-1903 *Tel:* 202-328-9000 *Fax:* 202-328-5432; 202-659-3225 *E-mail:* orders@petersoninstitute.org; media@piie.com *Web Site:* www.petersoninstitute.org, pg 181

Weiss, Alexandra, The Jennifer DeChiara Literary Agency, 299 Park Ave, 6th fl, New York, NY 10171 *Tel:* 212-739-0803 *Web Site:* www.jdlit.com, pg 513

Weiss, Alison, Sky Pony Press, 307 W 36 St, 11th fl, New York, NY 10018 *Tel:* 212-643-6816 *Fax:* 212-643-6819 *E-mail:* skypony@skyhorsepublishing.com; info@skyhorsepublishing.com; submissions@skyhorsepublishing.com *Web Site:* www.skyponypress.com, pg 214

Weiss, Daniel, The Metropolitan Museum of Art, 1000 Fifth Ave, New York, NY 10028 *Tel:* 212-879-5500, 212-570-3725 (edit) *Fax:* 212-396-5062 *E-mail:* editorial@metmuseum.org *Web Site:* www.metmuseum.org, pg 149

Weiss, Deborah, Maven House Press, 4 Snead Ct, Palmyra, VA 22963 *Tel:* 610-883-7988 *Toll Free Fax:* 888-894-3403 *E-mail:* info@mavenhousepress.com *Web Site:* mavenhousepress.com, pg 144

Weiss, Denise, Cold Spring Harbor Laboratory Press, 500 Sunnyside Blvd, Woodbury, NY 11797-2924 *Tel:* 516-422-4100 *Toll Free Tel:* 800-843-4388 *Fax:* 516-422-4097; 516-422-4092 (submissions) *E-mail:* cshpress@cshl.edu *Web Site:* www.cshlpress.com, pg 58

Weiss, Dennis, CRC Press, 6000 Broken Sound Pkwy NW, Suite 300, Boca Raton, FL 33487 *Tel:* 561-994-0555 *Toll Free Tel:* 800-272-7737 (orders) *Toll Free Fax:* 800-643-9428 (sales); 800-374-3401 (orders) *E-mail:* orders@crcpress.com; orders@taylorandfrancis.com *Web Site:* www.crcpress.com, pg 64

Weiss, Dennis, Garland Science Publishing, 711 Third Ave, 8th fl, New York, NY 10017 *Tel:* 212-216-7800; 212-281-4487 *Fax:* 212-947-3027 *E-mail:* science@garland.com *Web Site:* www.garlandscience.com, pg 90

Weiss, Jodi, Workman Publishing Co Inc, 225 Varick St, 9th fl, New York, NY 10014-4381 *Tel:* 212-254-5900 *Toll Free Tel:* 800-722-7202 *Fax:* 212-254-8098 *E-mail:* info@workman.com *Web Site:* www.workman.com, pg 259

Weiss, Kate, Chelsea Green Publishing Co, 85 N Main St, Suite 120, White River Junction, VT 05001 *Tel:* 802-295-6300 *Toll Free Tel:* 800-639-4099 (cust serv, consumer & trade orders) *Fax:* 802-295-6444 *Web Site:* www.chelseagreen.com, pg 53

Weiss, Kathy, Springer Publishing Co, 11 W 42 St, 15th fl, New York, NY 10036-8002 *Tel:* 212-431-4370 *Toll Free Tel:* 877-687-7476 *Fax:* 212-941-7842 *E-mail:* marketing@springerpub.com; cs@springerpub.com (orders); editorial@springerpub.com *Web Site:* www.springerpub.com, pg 219

Weiss, Kim, Health Communications Inc, 3201 SW 15 St, Deerfield Beach, FL 33442 *Tel:* 954-360-0909 *Toll Free Tel:* 800-851-9100; 800-441-5569 (cust serv & orders) *Fax:* 954-360-0034 *Toll Free Fax:* 800-424-7652 (cust serv & orders) *E-mail:* customerservice2@hcibooks.com *Web Site:* www.hcibooks.com, pg 104

Weiss, Kim, Simcha Press, 3201 SW 15 St, Deerfield Beach, FL 33442-8190 *Tel:* 954-360-0909 ext 212 *Toll Free Tel:* 800-851-9100 ext 212 *Toll Free Fax:* 800-424-7652 *E-mail:* simchapress@hcibooks.com *Web Site:* www.hcibooks.com, pg 212

Weiss, Louise, Access Editorial Services, 1133 Broadway, Suite 528, New York, NY 10010 *Tel:* 212-255-7306 *E-mail:* wiseword@juno.com, pg 487

Weiss, Mitchel, Eclectic Book Press, 11 Larchdell Way, Mountain Lakes, NJ 07046 *Tel:* 862-251-2296 *E-mail:* info@eclecticbookpress.com *Web Site:* eclecticbookpress.com, pg 75

Weiss, Sara, Random House Publishing Group, 1745 Broadway, New York, NY 10019 *Toll Free Tel:* 800-200-3552 *Web Site:* atrandom.com, pg 195

Weisser, William, Portfolio, 375 Hudson St, New York, NY 10014 *Web Site:* www.penguin.com/meet/publishers/portfolio, pg 186

Weisskopf, Toni, Baen Publishing Enterprises, PO Box 1188, Wake Forest, NC 27588 *Tel:* 919-570-1640 *Fax:* 919-570-1644 *E-mail:* info@baen.com *Web Site:* www.baen.com, pg 28

Weissman, Dana, Writers Guild of America, East (WGAE), 250 Hudson St, Suite 700, New York, NY 10013 *Tel:* 212-767-7800 *Fax:* 212-582-1909 *Web Site:* www.wgaeast.org, pg 581

Weissman, Robert, Public Citizen, 1600 20 St NW, Washington, DC 20009 *Tel:* 202-588-1000 *Fax:* 202-588-7798 *E-mail:* public_citizen@citizen.org *Web Site:* www.citizen.org, pg 191

Welby, Alexis, GP Putnam's Sons (Hardcover), 375 Hudson St, New York, NY 10014 *Tel:* 212-366-2000 *Fax:* 212-366-2643 *E-mail:* online@penguinputnam.com *Web Site:* www.penguin.com/publishers/gpputnamssons, pg 192

Welch, Andrea, Simon & Schuster Children's Publishing, 1230 Avenue of the Americas, New York, NY 10020 *Tel:* 212-698-7000 *Web Site:* www.simonandschuster.com/kids; www.simonandschuster.com/teen; simonandschuster.net; simonandschuster.biz, pg 213

Welch, Sally, Ohio University Press, 31 S Court St, Suite 143, Athens, OH 45701-2979 *Fax:* 740-593-4536 *Web Site:* www.ohioswallow.com, pg 167

Welch, Sally R, Swallow Press, 31 S Court St, Suite 143, Athens, OH 45701 *Tel:* 740-593-1155 *Toll Free Tel:* 800-621-2736 *Fax:* 740-593-4536 *Web Site:* www.ohioswallow.com, pg 225

Welling, Brent, Center for the Collaborative Classroom, 1250 53 St, Suite 3, Emeryville, CA 94608 *Tel:* 510-533-0213 *Toll Free Tel:* 800-666-7270 *Fax:* 510-464-3670 *E-mail:* info@collaborativeclassroom.org; clientsupport@collaborativeclassroom.org *Web Site:* www.collaborativeclassroom.org, pg 51

Wellnitz, Clare, University of California Press, 155 Grand Ave, Suite 400, Oakland, CA 94612-3758 *Tel:* 510-883-8232 *Fax:* 510-836-8910 *E-mail:* customerservice@ucpressjournals.com *Web Site:* www.ucpress.edu, pg 240

Wells, Jason, Rodale Inc, 400 S Tenth St, Emmaus, PA 18049 *Tel:* 610-967-5171 *Toll Free Tel:* 866-387-0509 *E-mail:* bookmarketing@rodale.com; bookpublicity@rodale.com *Web Site:* www.rodale.com, pg 200

Wells, Jeff, Technical Association of the Pulp & Paper Industry (TAPPI), 15 Technology Pkwy S, Suite 115, Peachtree Corners, GA 30092 *Tel:* 770-446-1400 *Toll Free Tel:* 800-332-8686 (US); 800-446-9431 (CN) *Fax:* 770-446-6947 *E-mail:* memberconnection@tappi.org *Web Site:* www.tappi.org, pg 579

Wells, Katrina Altersitz, SLACK® Incorporated, A Wyanoke Group Company, 6900 Grove Rd, Thorofare, NJ 08086-9447 *Tel:* 856-848-1000 *Toll Free Tel:* 800-257-8290 *Fax:* 856-848-6091 *E-mail:* sales@slackinc.com; editor@slackinc.com; customerservice@slackinc.com *Web Site:* www.healio.com/books, pg 215

Wells, Phyllis, University of Georgia Press, Main Library, 3rd fl, 320 S Jackson St, Athens, GA 30602 *Fax:* 706-542-2558; 706-542-6770 *Web Site:* www.ugapress.org, pg 241

Wells, Roseanne, The Jennifer DeChiara Literary Agency, 299 Park Ave, 6th fl, New York, NY 10171 *Tel:* 212-739-0803 *Web Site:* www.jdlit.com, pg 513

Wells, Thomas, University of Tennessee Press, 110 Conference Center Bldg, 600 Henley St, Knoxville, TN 37996-4108 *Tel:* 865-974-3321 *Toll Free Tel:* 800-621-2736 (orders) *Fax:* 865-974-3724 *Toll Free Fax:* 800-621-8476 (orders) *E-mail:* custserv@utpress.org *Web Site:* www.utpress.org, pg 245

Wells, Vicky, The University of North Carolina Press, 116 S Boundary St, Chapel Hill, NC 27514-3808 *Tel:* 919-966-3561 *Fax:* 919-966-3829 *E-mail:* uncpress@unc.edu *Web Site:* www.uncpress.unc.edu, pg 243

Welsh, Kara, Penguin Random House Inc, 1745 Broadway, New York, NY 10019 *Tel:* 212-782-9000 *Toll Free Tel:* 800-726-0600 *Web Site:* www.penguinrandomhouse.com, pg 178

Welsh, Kara, Random House Publishing Group, 1745 Broadway, New York, NY 10019 *Toll Free Tel:* 800-200-3552 *Web Site:* atrandom.com, pg 195

Weltz, Jennifer, Jean V Naggar Literary Agency Inc (JVNLA), 216 E 75 St, Suite 1-E, New York, NY 10021 *Tel:* 212-794-1082 *E-mail:* jvnla@jvnla.com *Web Site:* www.jvnla.com, pg 530

Wendrich, Willeke, Cotsen Institute of Archaeology Press, 308 Charles E Young Dr N, Fowler A163, Box 951510, Los Angeles, CA 90095 *Tel:* 310-206-9384 *Fax:* 310-206-4723 *E-mail:* cioapress@ioa.ucla.edu *Web Site:* www.ioa.ucla.edu, pg 62

Wengerd, Marvin, Carlisle Press - Walnut Creek, 2673 Township Rd 421, Sugarcreek, OH 44681 *Tel:* 330-852-1900 *Toll Free Tel:* 800-852-4482 *Fax:* 330-852-3285, pg 47

Wentworth, Jillian, United for Libraries, 859 W Lancaster Ave, Suite 2-1, Bryn Mawr, PA 19010 *Tel:* 312-280-2161 *Toll Free Tel:* 800-545-2433 (ext 2161) *Fax:* 484-698-7868 *E-mail:* united@ala.org *Web Site:* www.ala.org/united, pg 580

Wentworth, K D, L Ron Hubbard's Writers of the Future Contest, 7501 Hollywood Blvd, Hollywood, CA 90028 *Tel:* 323-466-3310 *Toll Free Tel:* 800-624-6504 *Fax:* 323-466-6474 *E-mail:* contests@authorservicesinc.com *Web Site:* www.writersofthefuture.com, pg 654

Werksman, Deb, Sourcebooks Inc, 1935 Brookdale Rd, Suite 139, Naperville, IL 60563 *Tel:* 630-961-3900 *Toll Free Tel:* 800-432-7444 *Fax:* 630-961-2168 *E-mail:* info@sourcebooks.com; customersupport@sourcebooks.com *Web Site:* www.sourcebooks.com, pg 218

Werner, Doug, Tracks Publishing, 140 Brightwood Ave, Chula Vista, CA 91910 *Tel:* 619-476-7125 *Toll Free Tel:* 800-443-3570 *Fax:* 619-476-8173 *E-mail:* tracks@cox.net *Web Site:* www.startupsports.com, pg 233

Werts, Amanda, Texas Tech University Press, 1120 Main St, 2nd fl, Lubbock, TX 79401 *Tel:* 806-742-2982 *Toll Free Tel:* 800-832-4042 *Fax:* 806-742-2979 *E-mail:* ttup@ttu.edu *Web Site:* www.ttupress.org, pg 230

Werz, Ed, JayJo Books LLC, One Huntington Quadrangle, Suite 1N03, Melville, NY 11747 *Tel:* 516-496-4863 *Toll Free Tel:* 800-999-6884 *Fax:* 516-496-4050 *Toll Free Fax:* 800-262-1886 *E-mail:* jayjobooks@guidance-group.com *Web Site:* www.guidance-group.com; www.jayjo.com, pg 121

Wescott, T C, New York Academy of Sciences (NYAS), 7 World Trade, 40th fl, 250 Greenwich St, New York, NY 10007-2157 *Tel:* 212-298-8600 *Toll Free Tel:* 800-843-6927 *Fax:* 212-298-3668 *E-mail:* nyas@nyas.org; annals@nyas.org; customerservice@nyas.org *Web Site:* www.nyas.org, pg 161

Wesley, Mark, me+mi publishing inc, 400 S Knoll St, Suite B, Wheaton, IL 60187 *Toll Free Tel:* 888-251-1444 *Fax:* 630-588-9804 *E-mail:* rw@rosawesley.com *Web Site:* www.memima.com, pg 147

Wessels, Cindy, University of Pittsburgh Press, 7500 Thomas Blvd, Pittsburgh, PA 15260 *Tel:* 412-383-2456 *Fax:* 412-383-2466 *E-mail:* info@upress.pitt.edu *Web Site:* www.upress.pitt.edu, pg 244

West, Ann, Mazda Publishers Inc, One Park Plaza, Suite 600, Irvine, CA 92614 *Tel:* 714-751-5252 *Fax:* 714-751-4805 *E-mail:* mazdapub@aol.com *Web Site:* www.mazdapublishers.com, pg 144

West, Carrie MFA, Dreaming Publications LLC, 1126 Bel Air Dr, Santa Barbara, CA 93103 *Tel:* 661-776-5152; 310-560-4732 *E-mail:* dreamingpublications@gmail.com *Web Site:* dreamingpublications.com, pg 477

West, J C, Abaris Books, 70 New Canaan Ave, Norwalk, CT 06850 *Tel:* 203-838-8402 *Fax:* 203-857-0730 *E-mail:* abaris@abarisbooks.com *Web Site:* abarisbooks.com, pg 2

West, J C, EastBridge, 70 New Canaan Ave, Norwalk, CT 06850 *Tel:* 203-855-9125 *Fax:* 203-857-0730 *E-mail:* asia@eastbridgebooks.org; ask@eastbridgebooks.org *Web Site:* www.eastbridgebooks.org, pg 74

West, Krista, University of Alaska Press, 1760 Westwood Way, Fairbanks, AK 99709 *Tel:* 907-474-5831 *Toll Free Tel:* 888-252-6657 (US only) *Fax:* 907-474-5502 *Web Site:* www.alaska.edu/uapress, pg 240

West, Rachel, Oxmoor House, 4100 Old Montgomery Hwy, Birmingham, AL 35209 *Tel:* 205-445-6000 *Toll Free Tel:* 800-366-4712; 888-891-8935 (cust serv); 800-765-6400 (orders) *Web Site:* www.oxmoorhouse.com, pg 171

West, Salem, Bywater Books, PO Box 3671, Ann Arbor, MI 48106-3671 *Tel:* 734-662-8815 *Web Site:* bywaterbooks.com, pg 46

Westberg, Phyllis, Harold Ober Associates Inc, 425 Madison Ave, New York, NY 10017 *Tel:* 212-759-8600 *Fax:* 212-759-9428 *Web Site:* www.haroldober.com, pg 531

Westcott, Jean, Stylus Publishing LLC, 22883 Quicksilver Dr, Sterling, VA 20166-2012 *Tel:* 703-661-1504 (edit & sales) *Toll Free Tel:* 800-232-0223 (orders & cust serv) *Fax:* 703-661-1547 *E-mail:* stylusmail@presswarehouse.com (orders & cust serv); stylusinfo@styluspub.com *Web Site:* www.styluspub.com, pg 224

Westermann, Christian, Europa Editions, 214 W 29 St, Suite 1003, New York, NY 10001 *Tel:* 212-868-6844 *Fax:* 212-868-6845 *E-mail:* info@europaeditions.com *Web Site:* www.europaeditions.com, pg 80

Westfall, Holly, A 2 Z Press LLC, 445 Cortez Ave, Deleon Springs, FL 32130 *Tel:* 386-681-7402 *Web Site:* www.a2zpress.com; www.terriesizemorestoryteller.com, pg 1

Westfall, William, Barbour Publishing Inc, 1810 Barbour Dr, Uhrichsville, OH 44683 *Tel:* 740-922-6045 *Fax:* 740-922-5948 *E-mail:* info@barbourbooks.com *Web Site:* www.barbourbooks.com, pg 29

Westlund, Laura, University of Minnesota Press, 111 Third Ave S, Suite 290, Minneapolis, MN 55401-2520 *Tel:* 612-301-1990 *Fax:* 612-301-1980 *E-mail:* ump@umn.edu *Web Site:* www.upress.umn.edu, pg 242

Weston, Matt, Perseus Books, 250 W 57 St, 15th fl, New York, NY 10107 *Tel:* 212-340-8100 *Toll Free Tel:* 800-343-4499 (cust serv) *Fax:* 212-340-8105 *Web Site:* www.perseusbooks.com, pg 181

Weston, Pamela, Research & Education Association (REA), 61 Ethel Rd W, Piscataway, NJ 08854 *Tel:* 732-819-8880 *Fax:* 732-819-8808 (orders) *E-mail:* info@rea.com *Web Site:* www.rea.com, pg 198

Westwood, Bruce, Westwood Creative Artists Ltd, 138 Sussex Mews, Toronto, ON M5S-2K1, Canada *Tel:* 416-964-3302 *Fax:* 416-964-3302 *E-mail:* wca_office@wcaltd.com *Web Site:* www.wcaltd.com, pg 541

Wexler, Chuck, Police Executive Research Forum, 1120 Connecticut Ave NW, Suite 930, Washington, DC 20036 *Tel:* 202-466-7820 *Web Site:* www.policeforum.org, pg 185

Wexler, Daniella, Atria Books, 1230 Avenue of the Americas, New York, NY 10020 *Tel:* 212-698-7000 *Fax:* 212-698-7007 *Web Site:* www.simonandschuster.com, pg 25

Wexler, David, Carolrhoda Books, 241 First Ave N, Minneapolis, MN 55401 *Tel:* 612-332-3344 *Toll Free Tel:* 800-328-4929 *Fax:* 612-332-7615 *Toll Free Fax:* 800-332-1132 *E-mail:* info@lernerbooks.com; custserve@lernerbooks.com *Web Site:* www.lernerbooks.com; www.facebook.com/lernerbooks, pg 48

Wexler, David, Carolrhoda Lab™, 241 First Ave N, Minneapolis, MN 55401 *Tel:* 612-332-3344 *Toll Free Tel:* 800-328-4929 *Fax:* 612-332-7615 *Toll Free Fax:* 800-332-1132 (US) *E-mail:* info@lernerbooks.com; custserve@lernerbooks.com *Web Site:* www.lernerbooks.com; www.facebook.com/lernerbooks, pg 48

Wexler, David, ediciones Lerner, 241 First Ave N, Minneapolis, MN 55401 *Tel:* 612-332-3344 *Toll Free Tel:* 800-328-4929 *Fax:* 612-332-7615 *Toll Free Fax:* 800-332-1132 *E-mail:* info@lernerbooks.com; custserve@lernerbooks.com *Web Site:* www.lernerbooks.com; www.facebook.com/lernerbooks, pg 75

Wexler, David, First Avenue Editions, 241 First Ave N, Minneapolis, MN 55401 *Tel:* 612-332-3344 *Toll Free Tel:* 800-328-4929 *Fax:* 612-332-7615 *Toll Free Fax:* 800-332-1132 *E-mail:* info@lernerbooks.com; custserve@lernerbooks.com *Web Site:* www.lernerbooks.com; www.facebook.com/lernerbooks, pg 85

Wexler, David, Graphic Universe™, 241 First Ave N, Minneapolis, MN 55401 *Tel:* 612-332-3344 *Toll Free Tel:* 800-328-4929 *Fax:* 612-332-7615 *Toll Free Fax:* 800-332-1132 *E-mail:* info@lernerbooks.com; custserve@lernerbooks.com *Web Site:* www.lernerbooks.com; www.facebook.com/lernerbooks, pg 95

Wexler, David, Lerner Publications, 241 First Ave N, Minneapolis, MN 55401 *Tel:* 612-332-3344 *Toll Free Tel:* 800-328-4929 *Fax:* 612-332-7615 *Toll Free Fax:* 800-332-1132 *E-mail:* info@lernerbooks.com; custserve@lernerbooks.com *Web Site:* www.lernerbooks.com; www.facebook.com/lernerbooks, pg 132

Wexler, David, Lerner Publishing Group Inc, 241 First Ave N, Minneapolis, MN 55401 *Tel:* 612-332-3344 *Toll Free Tel:* 800-328-4929 *Fax:* 612-332-7615 *Toll Free Fax:* 800-332-1132 *E-mail:* info@lernerbooks.com; custserve@lernerbooks.com *Web Site:* www.lernerbooks.com; www.facebook.com/lernerbooks, pg 132

Wexler, David, LernerClassroom, 241 First Ave N, Minneapolis, MN 55401 *Tel:* 612-332-3344 *Toll Free Tel:* 800-328-4929 *Fax:* 612-332-7615 *Toll Free Fax:* 800-332-1132 *E-mail:* info@lernerbooks.com; custserve@lernerbooks.com *Web Site:* www.lernerbooks.com; www.facebook.com/lernerbooks, pg 132

Wexler, David, Millbrook Press, 241 First Ave N, Minneapolis, MN 55401 *Tel:* 612-332-3344 *Toll Free Tel:* 800-328-4929 (US only) *Fax:* 612-332-7615 *Toll Free Fax:* 800-332-1132 *E-mail:* info@lernerbooks.com; custserve@lernerbooks.com *Web Site:* www.lernerbooks.com; www.facebook.com/millbrookpress, pg 151

Wexler, David, Twenty-First Century Books, 241 First Ave N, Minneapolis, MN 55401 *Tel:* 612-332-3344 *Toll Free Tel:* 800-328-4929 *Fax:* 612-332-7615 *Toll Free Fax:* 800-332-1132 *E-mail:* info@lernerbooks.com; custserve@lernerbooks.com *Web Site:* www.lernerbooks.com; www.facebook.com/lernerbooks, pg 237

Wexler, Leslie, Centre for Reformation & Renaissance Studies (CRRS), 71 Queen's Park Crescent E, Toronto, ON M5S 1K7, Canada *Tel:* 416-585-4465 *Fax:* 416-585-4430 (attn: CRRS) *E-mail:* crrs.publications@utoronto.ca *Web Site:* crrs.ca, pg 450

Wexler, Pearl, Paul Kohner Agency, 9300 Wilshire Blvd, Suite 555, Beverly Hills, CA 90212 *Tel:* 310-550-1060 *Fax:* 310-276-1083, pg 525

Wexler, Tina, ICM Partners, 65 E 55 St, New York, NY 10022 *Tel:* 212-556-5600 *Web Site:* www.icmtalent.com, pg 521

Whalen, Jaclyn, Random House Children's Books, 1745 Broadway, 10th fl, New York, NY 10019 *Tel:* 212-782-9000 *Web Site:* www.randomhousekids.com, pg 194

Whalen, John F Jr, Cider Mill Press Book Publishers LLC, 12 Spring St, Kennebunkport, ME 04046 *Tel:* 207-967-8232 *Fax:* 207-967-8233 *Web Site:* www.cidermillpress.com, pg 56

Whalen, Lindsay, The Penguin Press, 375 Hudson St, New York, NY 10014 *Web Site:* thepenguinpress.com, pg 178

Whalen, Stasia, Penguin Random House Speakers Bureau, A Penguin Random House Company, 1745 Broadway, Mail Drop 13-1, New York, NY 10019 *Tel:* 212-572-2013 *E-mail:* speakers@penguinrandomhouse.com *Web Site:* www.prhspeakers.com, pg 547

Whalen, Will, Alexander Street, a ProQuest Company, 3212 Duke St, Alexandria, VA 22314 *Tel:* 703-212-8520 *Toll Free Tel:* 800-889-5937 *Fax:* 703-940-6584

Whitethorne, Baje Jr, Salina Bookshelf Inc, 3120 N Caden Ct, Suite 4, Flagstaff, AZ 86004 *Toll Free Tel:* 877-527-0070 *Fax:* 928-526-0386 *Web Site:* www.salinabookshelf.com, pg 205

Whiteway, Doug, Signature Editions, PO Box 206, RPO Corydon, Winnipeg, MB R3M 3S7, Canada *Tel:* 204-779-7803 *E-mail:* submissions@signature-editions.com; orders@signature-editions.com *Web Site:* www.signature-editions.com, pg 470

Whithaus, Carl, Writing Workshops, 1333 Research Park Dr, Davis, CA 95618 *Tel:* 510-642-6362 *E-mail:* extension@ucdavis.edu *Web Site:* extension.ucdavis.edu; writing.ucdavis.edu, pg 616

Whiting, Nancy E, Bonasa Press, PO Box 340, Crosby, ND 58730 *Tel:* 701-965-3974 *E-mail:* new@bonasapress.com (inquiries) *Web Site:* www.bonasapress.com, pg 39

Whitlatch, Paul, Hachette Books, 1290 Avenue of the Americas, New York, NY 10019 *Tel:* 212-364-1100 *Web Site:* www.hachettebookgroup.com, pg 98

Whitman, Mara, The Graduate Group/Booksellers, 86 Norwood Rd, West Hartford, CT 06117-2236 *Tel:* 860-233-2330 *E-mail:* graduategroup@hotmail.com *Web Site:* www.graduategroup.com, pg 94

Whitman, Robert, The Graduate Group/Booksellers, 86 Norwood Rd, West Hartford, CT 06117-2236 *Tel:* 860-233-2330 *E-mail:* graduategroup@hotmail.com *Web Site:* www.graduategroup.com, pg 94

Whitmore, Kimberly, Ericson Books, 1614 Redbud St, Nacogdoches, TX 75965-2936 *Tel:* 936-564-3625 *Fax:* 936-552-8999, pg 79

Whitney, April, Chronicle Books LLC, 680 Second St, San Francisco, CA 94107 *Tel:* 415-537-4200 *Toll Free Tel:* 800-759-0190 (cust serv) *Fax:* 415-537-4460 *Toll Free Fax:* 800-858-7787 (orders); 800-286-9471 (cust serv) *E-mail:* frontdesk@chroniclebooks.com *Web Site:* www.chroniclebooks.com, pg 55

Whitson, Skip, Sun Publishing Company, PO Box 5588, Santa Fe, NM 87502-5588 *Tel:* 505-471-5177; 505-473-4161 *Toll Free Tel:* 877-849-0051 *E-mail:* info@sunbooks.com *Web Site:* www.sunbooks.com, pg 224

Whittell, Polly, Deadline Club, c/o Salmagundi Club, 47 Fifth Ave, New York, NY 10003 *Tel:* 646-481-7584 *E-mail:* info@deadlineclub.org *Web Site:* www.deadlineclub.org, pg 564

Wichmann, Sonia, Northern California Translators Association, 2261 Market St, Suite 160, San Francisco, CA 94114-1600 *Tel:* 510-845-8712 *E-mail:* administrator@ncta.org *Web Site:* www.ncta.org, pg 574

Wickenhiser, Sr Mary Mark, Pauline Books & Media, 50 Saint Paul's Ave, Boston, MA 02130 *Tel:* 617-522-8911 *Toll Free Tel:* 800-876-4463 (orders); 800-836-9723 (cust serv) *Fax:* 617-541-9805 *E-mail:* editorial@paulinemedia.com (ms submissions); orderentry@pauline.org (cust serv) *Web Site:* www.pauline.org/publishing; www.pauline.org/PBMPublishing, pg 175

Wickham, Suzanne, HarperCollins General Books Group, 195 Broadway, New York, NY 10007 *Tel:* 212-207-7000 *Web Site:* www.harpercollins.com, pg 101

Wicks, Erin, HarperCollins General Books Group, 195 Broadway, New York, NY 10007 *Tel:* 212-207-7000 *Web Site:* www.harpercollins.com, pg 101

Widdicombe, Elizabeth, Macmillan Learning, 41 Madison Ave, New York, NY 10010 *Tel:* 212-576-9400 *Fax:* 212-689-2383 *Web Site:* www.macmillanlearning.com, pg 140

Widdicombe, Elizabeth, Worth Publishers, 41 Madison Ave, 37th fl, New York, NY 10010 *Tel:* 212-576-9400; 212-375-7000 *Fax:* 212-561-8281 *E-mail:* press.inquiries@macmillan.com *Web Site:* www.macmillanlearning.com, pg 260

Widmer, Joanne, F+W Media Inc, 10151 Carver Rd, Suite 200, Blue Ash, OH 45242 *Tel:* 513-531-2690 *Toll Free Tel:* 800-289-0963 (trade accts); 800-258-0929 (cust serv) *E-mail:* contact_us@fwmedia.com *Web Site:* www.fwcommunity.com, pg 82

Widner, Dan, Walter Foster Publishing Inc, 6 Orchard Rd, Suite 100, Lake Forest, CA 92630 *Tel:* 949-380-7510 *Toll Free Tel:* 800-426-0099; 800-759-0190 (orders) *Fax:* 949-380-7575 *E-mail:* walterfoster@quartous.com *Web Site:* www.quartous.com, pg 87

Wiebe, Jeff, Chronicle Books LLC, 680 Second St, San Francisco, CA 94107 *Tel:* 415-537-4200 *Toll Free Tel:* 800-759-0190 (cust serv) *Fax:* 415-537-4460 *Toll Free Fax:* 800-858-7787 (orders); 800-286-9471 (cust serv) *E-mail:* frontdesk@chroniclebooks.com *Web Site:* www.chroniclebooks.com, pg 55

Wieckowski, Ania, Harvard Business Review Press, 300 N Beacon St, Watertown, MA 02472 *Tel:* 617-783-7400 *Fax:* 617-783-7489 *E-mail:* custserv@hbsp.harvard.edu *Web Site:* www.harvardbusiness.org, pg 102

Wiegers, Michael, Copper Canyon Press, Fort Worden State Park, Bldg 313, Port Townsend, WA 98368 *Tel:* 360-385-4925 *Toll Free Tel:* 877-501-1393 (orders) *Fax:* 360-385-4985 *E-mail:* poetry@coppercanyonpress.org *Web Site:* www.coppercanyonpress.org, pg 60

Wiener, Jessica, Henry Holt and Company, LLC, 175 Fifth Ave, New York, NY 10010 *Tel:* 646-307-5151 *Toll Free Tel:* 888-330-8477 (orders) *Fax:* 646-307-5285 *E-mail:* firstname.lastname@hholt.com *Web Site:* www.henryholt.com, pg 109

Wiener, M Markus, Markus Wiener Publishers Inc, 231 Nassau St, Princeton, NJ 08542 *Tel:* 609-921-1141 *Fax:* 609-921-1140 *E-mail:* publisher@markuswiener.com *Web Site:* www.markuswiener.com, pg 255

Wiener, Robert K, Donald M Grant Publisher Inc, PO Box 187, Hampton Falls, NH 03844-0187 *Tel:* 603-778-7191 *Fax:* 603-778-7191 *E-mail:* office@grantbooks.com *Web Site:* secure.grantbooks.com, pg 95

Wiese, Michael, Michael Wiese Productions, 12400 Ventura Blvd, No 1111, Studio City, CA 91604 *Tel:* 818-379-8799 *Toll Free Tel:* 800-833-5738 (orders) *Fax:* 818-986-3408 *E-mail:* mwpsales@mwp.com; fulfillment@portcity.com *Web Site:* www.mwp.com, pg 255

Wiese, Nancy, Grand Central Publishing, 1290 Avenue of the Americas, New York, NY 10019 *Tel:* 212-364-1100 *Web Site:* www.hachettebookgroup.com, pg 95

Wiese, Nancy, Hachette Book Group, 1290 Avenue of the Americas, New York, NY 10019 *Tel:* 212-364-1100 *Toll Free Tel:* 800-759-0190 (cust serv) *Fax:* 212-364-0933 (intl orders) *Toll Free Fax:* 800-286-9471 (cust serv) *Web Site:* www.hachettebookgroup.com, pg 98

Wiese, Nancy, Little, Brown and Company, 1290 Avenue of the Americas, New York, NY 10019 *Tel:* 212-364-1100 *Fax:* 212-364-0952 *E-mail:* firstname.lastname@hbgusa.com *Web Site:* www.littlebrown.com; www.HachetteBookGroup.com, pg 135

Wiewora, Kristen, Perseus Books, 250 W 57 St, 15th fl, New York, NY 10107 *Tel:* 212-340-8100 *Toll Free Tel:* 800-343-4499 (cust serv) *Fax:* 212-340-8105 *Web Site:* www.perseusbooks.com, pg 181

Wiggins, Jana, Carl Vinson Institute of Government, University of Georgia, 201 N Milledge Ave, Athens, GA 30602 *Tel:* 706-542-2736 *Fax:* 706-542-9301 *Web Site:* www.cviog.uga.edu, pg 251

Wight, Katy, Edward Elgar Publishing Inc, The William Pratt House, 9 Dewey Ct, Northampton, MA 01060-3815 *Tel:* 413-584-5551 *Toll Free Tel:* 800-390-3149 (orders) *Fax:* 413-584-9933 *E-mail:* elgarinfo@e-elgar.com; elgarsales@e-elgar.com; elgarsubmissions@e-elgar.com (edit) *Web Site:* www.e-elgar.com; www.elgaronline.com (ebooks & journals), pg 77

Wilcox, Alana, Coach House Books, 80 bpNichol Lane, Toronto, ON M5S 3J4, Canada *Tel:* 416-979-2217 *Toll Free Tel:* 800-367-6360 (outside Toronto) *Fax:* 416-977-1158 *E-mail:* mail@chbooks.com *Web Site:* www.chbooks.com, pg 450

Wilcox, Diane L, Mazda Publishers Inc, One Park Plaza, Suite 600, Irvine, CA 92614 *Tel:* 714-751-5252 *Fax:* 714-751-4805 *E-mail:* mazdapub@aol.com *Web Site:* www.mazdapublishers.com, pg 144

Wilcox, Jeanne, Quincannon Publishing Group, PO Box 8100, Glen Ridge, NJ 07028-8100 *Tel:* 973-380-9942 *E-mail:* editors@quincannongroup.com *Web Site:* www.quincannongroup.com, pg 192

Wilcox, Lynn, Syracuse University Press, 621 Skytop Rd, Suite 110, Syracuse, NY 13244-5290 *Tel:* 315-443-5534 *Toll Free Tel:* 800-365-8929 (cust serv) *Fax:* 315-443-5545 *E-mail:* supress@syr.edu *Web Site:* syracuseuniversitypress.syr.edu, pg 226

Wilcox, Mary, Houghton Mifflin Harcourt Trade & Reference Division, 125 High St, Boston, MA 02110 *Tel:* 617-351-5000 *Toll Free Tel:* 800-225-3362 *Web Site:* www.hmhco.com, pg 111

Wilcoxon, Deborah, Research Press, 2612 N Mattis Ave, Champaign, IL 61822 *Tel:* 217-352-3273 *Toll Free Tel:* 800-519-2707 *Fax:* 217-352-1221 *E-mail:* rp@researchpress.com; orders@researchpress.com *Web Site:* www.researchpress.com, pg 198

Wilderson, Joe, Rocky Mountain Books Ltd (RMB), 103-1075 Pendergast St, Victoria, BC V8V 0A1, Canada *Tel:* 250-360-0829 *Fax:* 250-386-0829 *Web Site:* www.rmbooks.com, pg 469

Wildfong, Kathryn, Wayne State University Press, Leonard N Simons Bldg, 4809 Woodward Ave, Detroit, MI 48201-1309 *Tel:* 313-577-6120 *Toll Free Tel:* 800-978-7323 *Fax:* 313-577-6131 *E-mail:* bookorders@wayne.edu *Web Site:* www.wsupress.wayne.edu, pg 253

Wiley, Jesse C, John Wiley & Sons Inc, 111 River St, Hoboken, NJ 07030-5774 *Tel:* 201-748-6000 *Toll Free Tel:* 800-225-5945 (cust serv) *Fax:* 201-748-6088 *E-mail:* info@wiley.com *Web Site:* www.wiley.com, pg 256

Wilkes, Deborah, Focus, PO Box 44937, Indianapolis, IN 46244-0937 *Tel:* 317-635-9250 *Fax:* 317-635-9292 *E-mail:* customer@hackettpublishing.com; editorial@hackettpublishing.com *Web Site:* focusbookstore.com, pg 86

Wilkes, Deborah, Hackett Publishing Co Inc, 3333 Massachusetts Ave, Indianapolis, IN 46218 *Tel:* 317-635-9250 (orders & cust serv); 617-497-6303 (edit off & sales) *Fax:* 317-635-9292; 617-661-8703 (edit off) *Toll Free Fax:* 800-783-9213 *E-mail:* customer@hackettpublishing.com; editorial@hackettpublishing.com *Web Site:* www.hackettpublishing.com, pg 99

Wilkie, Craig, The University Press of Kentucky, 663 S Limestone St, Lexington, KY 40508-4008 *Tel:* 859-257-8400 *Fax:* 859-257-8481 *Web Site:* www.kentuckypress.com, pg 247

Wilkins, Timothy, Princeton University Press, 41 William St, Princeton, NJ 08540-5237 *Tel:* 609-258-4900 *Fax:* 609-258-6305 *Web Site:* press.princeton.edu, pg 188

Wilkinson, Christine, Wilkinson Studios Inc, 2955 Kelly Dr, Elgin, IL 60124-4349 *Tel:* 312-286-3683 *Web Site:* www.wilkinsonstudios.com, pg 545

Wilkinson, Jamie, F+W Media Inc, 10151 Carver Rd, Suite 200, Blue Ash, OH 45242 *Tel:* 513-531-2690 *Toll Free Tel:* 800-289-0963 (trade accts); 800-258-0929 (cust serv) *E-mail:* contact_us@fwmedia.com *Web Site:* www.fwcommunity.com, pg 82

Wilkinson, Marco, The Field Poetry Prize, 50 N Professor St, Oberlin, OH 44074-1091 *Tel:* 440-775-8408 *Fax:* 440-775-8124 *E-mail:* oc.press@oberlin.edu *Web Site:* www.oberlin.edu/ocpress; www.oberlin.edu/ocpress/prize.htm (guidelines), pg 646

Wilkinson, Marco, Oberlin College Press, 50 N Professor St, Oberlin, OH 44074-1091 *Tel:* 440-775-8408 *Fax:* 440-775-8124 *E-mail:* oc.press@oberlin.edu *Web Site:* www.oberlin.edu/ocpress, pg 166

Wilks, Rick, Annick Press Ltd, 15 Patricia Ave, Toronto, ON M2M 1H9, Canada *Tel:* 416-221-4802 *Fax:* 416-221-8400 *E-mail:* annickpress@annickpress.com *Web Site:* www.annickpress.com, pg 445

Will, Julie, HarperCollins General Books Group, 195 Broadway, New York, NY 10007 *Tel:* 212-207-7000 *Web Site:* www.harpercollins.com, pg 101

Ave, El Paso, TX 79968-9991 *Tel:* 915-747-5713 *Fax:* 915-747-5523 *E-mail:* creativewriting@utep.edu *Web Site:* www.utep.edu/cw, pg 623

Willig, Christine, Math Solutions®, One Harbor Dr, Suite 101, Sausalito, CA 94965 *Tel:* 415-332-4181 *Toll Free Tel:* 800-868-9092 *Fax:* 415-331-1931 *Toll Free Fax:* 877-942-8837 *E-mail:* info@mathsolutions.com; orders@mathsolutions.com *Web Site:* www.mathsolutions.com, pg 144

Willig, Christine, McGraw-Hill Education, 2 Penn Plaza, New York, NY 10121-2298 *Tel:* 212-904-2000 *E-mail:* customer.service@mheducation.com; international_cs@mheducation.com *Web Site:* www.mheducation.com, pg 145

Willig, Christine, McGraw-Hill School Education Group, 8787 Orion Place, Columbus, OH 43240 *Tel:* 614-430-4000 *Toll Free Tel:* 800-848-1567 *Web Site:* www.mheducation.com, pg 146

Willinger, James L, Wide World of Maps Inc, 2626 W Indian School Rd, Phoenix, AZ 85017 *Tel:* 602-279-2323 (ext 1) *Toll Free Tel:* 800-279-7654 *Fax:* 602-433-0695 *E-mail:* sales@maps4u.com *Web Site:* www.maps4u.com, pg 255

Willis, Clarissa, Ozark Creative Writers Inc Annual Conference, 512 Walnut St, Mount Vernon, IN 47620 *E-mail:* ozarkcreativewriters@ozarkcreativewriters.com *Web Site:* www.ozarkcreativewriters.com, pg 613

Willis, Meredith Sue, Hamilton Stone Editions, PO Box 43, Maplewood, NJ 07040 *Tel:* 973-378-8361 *E-mail:* hstone@hamiltonstone.org *Web Site:* www.hamiltonstone.org, pg 99

Willoughby-Harris, H Lee, Duke University Press, 905 W Main St, Suite 18B, Durham, NC 27701 *Tel:* 919-688-5134 *Toll Free Tel:* 888-651-0122 (US) *Fax:* 919-688-2615 *Toll Free Fax:* 888-651-0124 *E-mail:* orders@dukeupress.edu *Web Site:* www.dukeupress.edu, pg 73

Wills, Juliet, Galaxy Press, 7051 Hollywood Blvd, Suite 200, Hollywood, CA 90028 *Tel:* 323-466-7815 *Toll Free Tel:* 877-8GALAXY (842-5299) *E-mail:* info@galaxypress.com; customers@galaxypress.com *Web Site:* www.galaxypress.com, pg 89

Wilmot, Jodie, National Association of College Stores (NACS), 500 E Lorain St, Oberlin, OH 44074 *Tel:* 440-775-7777 *Toll Free Tel:* 800-622-7498 *Fax:* 440-775-4769 *Web Site:* www.nacs.org, pg 570

Wilmoth, Anna, Gryphon House Inc, 6848 Leon's Way, Lewisville, NC 27023 *Toll Free Tel:* 800-638-0928 *Toll Free Fax:* 877-638-7576 *E-mail:* info@ghbooks.com *Web Site:* www.gryphonhouse.com, pg 97

Wilmoth, Mark, PennWell Books, 1421 S Sheridan Rd, Tulsa, OK 74112 *Tel:* 918-831-9421 *Toll Free Tel:* 800-752-9764 *Fax:* 918-831-9555 *Toll Free Fax:* 877-218-1348 *E-mail:* sales@pennwell.com *Web Site:* www.pennwellbooks.com, pg 179

Wilson, Adam, Gallery Books, 1230 Avenue of the Americas, New York, NY 10020 *Toll Free Tel:* 800-456-6798 *Fax:* 212-698-7284 *E-mail:* consumer.customerservice@simonandschuster.com *Web Site:* www.simonsays.com, pg 90

Wilson, Bev, Information Gatekeepers Inc (IGI), 1340 Soldiers Field Rd, Suite 2, Boston, MA 02135 *Tel:* 617-782-5033 *Fax:* 617-507-8338 *E-mail:* info@igigroup.com *Web Site:* www.igigroup.com, pg 116

Wilson, Bob, Sunrise River Press, 838 Lake St S, Forrest Lake, MN 55025 *Tel:* 651-277-1400 *Toll Free Tel:* 800-895-4585 *Fax:* 651-277-1203 *E-mail:* info@sunriseriverpress.com; sales@sunriseriverpress.com *Web Site:* www.sunriseriverpress.com, pg 225

Wilson, Dr Cheryl, University of Baltimore - Yale Gordon College of Arts & Sciences, Ampersand Institute for Words & Images, 1420 N Charles St, Baltimore, MD 21201-5779 *Tel:* 410-837-6022 *Fax:* 410-837-6029 *E-mail:* scd@ubalt.edu *Web Site:* www.ubalt.edu, pg 623

Wilson, Cristina, Sourcebooks Inc, 1935 Brookdale Rd, Suite 139, Naperville, IL 60563 *Tel:* 630-961-3900 *Toll Free Tel:* 800-432-7444 *Fax:* 630-961-2168 *E-mail:* info@sourcebooks.com; customersupport@sourcebooks.com *Web Site:* www.sourcebooks.com, pg 218

Wilson, Erika, Authors Alliance, 2705 Webster St, No 5805, Berkeley, CA 94705 *E-mail:* info@authorsalliance.org *Web Site:* www.authorsalliance.org, pg 559

Wilson, Gary, Green Dragon Books, 2875 S Ocean Blvd, Suite 200, Palm Beach, FL 33480 *Tel:* 561-533-6231 *Toll Free Tel:* 800-874-8844 *Fax:* 561-533-6233 *Toll Free Fax:* 888-874-8844 *E-mail:* info@greendragonbooks.com *Web Site:* greendragonbooks.com, pg 96

Wilson, Jaclyn, Wesleyan University Press, 215 Long Lane, Middletown, CT 06459-0433 *Tel:* 860-685-7711 *Fax:* 860-685-7712 *Web Site:* www.wesleyan.edu/wespress, pg 253

Wilson, James, University of Louisiana at Lafayette Press, PO Box 43558, Lafayette, LA 70504-3558 *Tel:* 337-482-6027 *Fax:* 337-482-6028 *E-mail:* ulpress@louisiana.edu *Web Site:* www.ulpress.org, pg 242

Wilson, Jamia, The Feminist Press at The City University of New York, 365 Fifth Ave, Suite 5406, New York, NY 10016 *Tel:* 212-817-7915 *Fax:* 212-817-1593 *E-mail:* info@feministpress.org *Web Site:* www.feministpress.org, pg 83

Wilson, JD, Northwestern University Press, 629 Noyes St, Evanston, IL 60208-4210 *Tel:* 847-491-2046 *Toll Free Tel:* 800-621-2736 (orders only) *Fax:* 847-491-8150 *E-mail:* nupress@northwestern.edu *Web Site:* www.nupress.northwestern.edu, pg 164

Wilson, Jeff, Simon & Schuster, Inc, 1230 Avenue of the Americas, New York, NY 10020 *Tel:* 212-698-7000 *Fax:* 212-698-7007 *E-mail:* firstname.lastname@simonandschuster.com *Web Site:* www.simonandschuster.com, pg 213

Wilson, Jocie, Pacific Northwest Young Reader's Choice Award, Vancouver Mall Community Library, 8700 NE Vancouver Mall Dr, Suite 285, Vancouver, WA 98662 *Web Site:* www.pnla.org/yrca, pg 676

Wilson, Julie, Penguin Random House Audio Publishing, 1745 Broadway, New York, NY 10019 *E-mail:* audio@penguinrandomhouse.com *Web Site:* www.penguinrandomhouseaudio.com, pg 178

Wilson, Kell, DK Publishing, 345 Hudson St, 2nd fl, New York, NY 10014 *Tel:* 646-674-4000 *Toll Free Tel:* 877-342-5357 (cust serv); 800-733-3000 *Web Site:* www.dk.com; www.penguin.com, pg 71

Wilson, Lance, Top of the Mountain Publishing, 4837 62 St N, St Petersburg, FL 33709 *Tel:* 727-391-3958 *Web Site:* www.topofthemountain.com, pg 233

Wilson, Laura, Macmillan Audio, 175 Fifth Ave, New York, NY 10010 *Tel:* 646-307-5151 *Toll Free Tel:* 888-330-8477 (cust serv) *Fax:* 917-534-0980 *Web Site:* www.macmillanaudio.com, pg 140

Wilson, Lauren, American Diabetes Association, 1701 N Beauregard St, Alexandria, VA 22311 *Toll Free Tel:* 800-342-2383 *E-mail:* booksinfo@diabetes.org *Web Site:* www.diabetes.org, pg 11

Wilson, Leah, BenBella Books Inc, 10300 N Central Expwy, Suite 400, Dallas, TX 75231 *Tel:* 214-750-3600 *Fax:* 214-750-3645 *E-mail:* feedback@benbellabooks.com *Web Site:* www.benbellabooks.com; www.smartpopbooks.com, pg 32

Wilson, Martin, HarperCollins General Books Group, 195 Broadway, New York, NY 10007 *Tel:* 212-207-7000 *Web Site:* www.harpercollins.com, pg 101

Wilson, Mary Ellen, Quirk Books, 215 Church St, Philadelphia, PA 19106 *Tel:* 215-627-3581 *Fax:* 215-627-5220 *E-mail:* general@quirkbooks.com *Web Site:* www.quirkbooks.com, pg 193

Wilson, Megan, Houghton Mifflin Harcourt, 125 High St, Boston, MA 02110 *Tel:* 617-351-5000 *Toll Free Tel:* 855-969-4642; 800-225-5425 (K-12 educ materials); 800-323-9540 (assessment materials); 877-219-1537 (SkillsTutor); 888-242-6747 (Innovation in Educ Group); 800-225-3362 (Trade & Ref Div) *Toll Free Fax:* 800-269-5232 *E-mail:* myhmhco@hmhco.com *Web Site:* www.hmhco.com, pg 110

Wilson, Meredith, Houghton Mifflin Harcourt Trade & Reference Division, 125 High St, Boston, MA 02110 *Tel:* 617-351-5000 *Toll Free Tel:* 800-225-3362 *Web Site:* www.hmhco.com, pg 111

Wilson, Natashya, Harlequin Enterprises Ltd, 225 Duncan Mill Rd, Don Mills, ON M3B 3K9, Canada *Tel:* 416-445-5860 *Toll Free Tel:* 888-432-4879; 800-370-5838 (ebook inquiries) *E-mail:* customerservice@harlequin.com *Web Site:* www.harlequin.com, pg 459

Wilson, Olivia, Houghton Mifflin Harcourt Trade & Reference Division, 125 High St, Boston, MA 02110 *Tel:* 617-351-5000 *Toll Free Tel:* 800-225-3362 *Web Site:* www.hmhco.com, pg 111

Wilson, Pamela, University of Hawaii Press, 2840 Kolowalu St, Honolulu, HI 96822 *Tel:* 808-956-8255 *Toll Free Tel:* 888-UHPRESS (847-7377) *Fax:* 808-988-6052 *Toll Free Fax:* 800-650-7811 *E-mail:* uhpbooks@hawaii.edu *Web Site:* www.uhpress.hawaii.edu, pg 241

Wilson, Stefanya, The Jack London Award, Box 17897, Encino, CA 91416-7897 *E-mail:* cwcsfv@gmail.com, pg 662

Wilson, Stefanya, Masters Literary Awards, PO Box 17897, Encino, CA 91416-7897 *Tel:* 818-377-4006 *E-mail:* titan91416@yahoo.com, pg 666

Wilson, Steve, McFarland, 960 NC Hwy 88 W, Jefferson, NC 28640 *Tel:* 336-246-4460 *Toll Free Tel:* 800-253-2187 (orders) *Fax:* 336-246-5018; 336-246-4403 (orders) *E-mail:* info@mcfarlandpub.com *Web Site:* www.mcfarlandpub.com, pg 145

Wilson, Steven, Book Sales, 142 W 36 St, 4th fl, New York, NY 10018 *Tel:* 212-779-4972; 212-779-4971 *Fax:* 212-779-6058 *E-mail:* booksales@quarto.com; customerservice@quarto.com *Web Site:* www.quartoknows.com, pg 40

Wilson, Victoria, Alfred A Knopf/Everyman's Library, c/o Penguin Random House Inc, 1745 Broadway, New York, NY 10019 *Tel:* 212-751-2600 *Toll Free Tel:* 800-638-6460 *Fax:* 212-572-2593 *Web Site:* www.knopfdoubleday.com, pg 127

Wilson-Simmons, Renee, National Center for Children in Poverty, 215 W 125 St, 3rd fl, New York, NY 10027 *Tel:* 646-284-9600 *Fax:* 646-284-9623 *E-mail:* info@nccp.org *Web Site:* www.nccp.org, pg 157

Wiman, Mike, IHS Jane's, 110 N Royal St, Suite 200, Alexandria, VA 22314-1651 *Tel:* 703-683-3700 *Toll Free Tel:* 800-824-0768 (sales) *Fax:* 703-836-0297 *Toll Free Fax:* 800-836-0297 *E-mail:* customercare@ihsmarkit.com *Web Site:* www.ihs.com; ihsmarkit.com, pg 114

Wing, Frank, APA Talent & Literary Agency, 405 S Beverly Dr, Beverly Hills, CA 90212 *Tel:* 310-888-4200 *Fax:* 310-888-4242 *Web Site:* www.apa-agency.com, pg 507

Winick, Eugene H, McIntosh & Otis Inc, 353 Lexington Ave, New York, NY 10016-0900 *Tel:* 212-687-7400 *Fax:* 212-687-6894 *E-mail:* info@mcintoshandotis.com *Web Site:* www.mcintoshandotis.com, pg 529

Winicour, Mike, Round Table Companies, 1027 Kenton Rd, Deerfield, IL 60015 *Tel:* 949-375-1006 *Fax:* 815-346-2398 *Web Site:* www.roundtablecompanies.com, pg 201

Winnette, Andi, McSweeney's Publishing, 849 Valencia St, San Francisco, CA 94110 *Tel:* 415-642-5609 (cust serv) *Web Site:* www.mcsweeneys.net, pg 147

Winningham, Sharon, School Zone Publishing Co, 1819 Industrial Dr, Grand Haven, MI 49417 *Tel:* 616-846-5030 *Toll Free Tel:* 800-253-0564 *Fax:* 616-846-6181 *Toll Free Fax:* 800-550-4618 (orders only) *Web Site:* www.schoolzone.com, pg 209

Winns, Nadine, Abbeville Press, 116 W 23 St, 5th fl, New York, NY 10011 *Tel:* 212-366-5585 *Toll Free Tel:* 800-ART-BOOK (278-2665); 800-343-4499 (orders) *Fax:* 646-375-2359 *Toll Free Fax:* 800-351-5073 (orders) *E-mail:* abbeville@abbeville.com;

Wysong, Lara, De Gruyter Mouton, 125 Pearl St, Boston, MA 02110 *Tel:* 857-284-7073 *Fax:* 857-284-7358 *E-mail:* service@degruyter.com *Web Site:* www.degruyter.com, pg 155

Yaged, Jonathan, Macmillan, 175 Fifth Ave, New York, NY 10010 *Tel:* 646-307-5151 *E-mail:* press.inquiries@macmillan.com *Web Site:* www.macmillan.com, pg 139

Yager, Dr Jan, Hannacroix Creek Books Inc, 1127 High Ridge Rd, No 110-B, Stamford, CT 06905-1203 *Tel:* 203-968-8098 *Web Site:* www.hannacroixcreekbooks.com, pg 100

Yake, Sarah, Frances Collin Literary Agency, PO Box 33, Wayne, PA 19087 *Tel:* 610-254-0555 *E-mail:* queries@francescollin.com *Web Site:* www.francescollin.com, pg 512

Yamamoto, Ken, Scholastic Trade Division, 557 Broadway, New York, NY 10012 *Tel:* 212-343-6100; 212-343-4685 (export sales) *Fax:* 212-343-4714 (export sales) *Web Site:* www.scholastic.com, pg 208

Yamashita, Brianna, TarcherPerigee, 375 Hudson St, New York, NY 10014 *Tel:* 212-366-2000 *Fax:* 212-366-2643 *E-mail:* customerservice@penguinrandomhouse.com (cust serv); TarcherPerigeePublicity@penguinrandomhouse.com (media queries) *Web Site:* www.tarcherbooks.com; www.facebook.com/TarcherPerigee/; www.penguin.com/publishers/tarcherperigee, pg 227

Yammer, Channi, Simon & Schuster Children's Publishing, 1230 Avenue of the Americas, New York, NY 10020 *Tel:* 212-698-7000 *Web Site:* www.simonandschuster.com/kids; www.simonandschuster.com/teen; simonandschuster.net; simonandschuster.biz, pg 213

Yang, Caren, Saint Mary's Press, 702 Terrace Heights, Winona, MN 55987-1318 *Tel:* 507-457-7900 *Toll Free Tel:* 800-533-8095 *Fax:* 507-457-7990 *Toll Free Fax:* 800-344-9225 *E-mail:* smpress@smp.org *Web Site:* www.smp.org, pg 205

Yang, Grace, Chestnut Publishing Group Inc, 44 Stubbs Dr, Suite 207, Toronto, ON M2L 2R3, Canada *Tel:* 416-224-5824 *Fax:* 416-224-0595 *Web Site:* www.chestnutpublishing.com, pg 450

Yang, Tessa, Indiana Review Fiction Prize, Ballantine Hall 529, 1020 E Kirkwood Ave, Bloomington, IN 47405 *Tel:* 812-855-3439 *E-mail:* inreview@indiana.edu *Web Site:* indianareview.org, pg 655

Yankech, Andrew, Loyola Press, 3441 N Ashland Ave, Chicago, IL 60657 *Tel:* 773-281-1818 *Toll Free Tel:* 800-621-1008 *Fax:* 773-281-0555 (cust serv); 773-281-4129 (edit) *E-mail:* customerservice@loyolapress.com *Web Site:* www.loyolapress.com, pg 138

Yankelevich, Matvei, Ugly Duckling Presse, The Old American Can Factory, 232 Third St, Suite E303, Brooklyn, NY 11215 *Tel:* 347-948-5170 *E-mail:* info@uglyducklingpresse.org *Web Site:* www.uglyducklingpresse.org, pg 238

Yankelevitz, Harold, Printing Association of Florida Inc (PAF), 6250 Hazeltine National Dr, Suite 114, Orlando, FL 32822 *Tel:* 407-240-8009 *Toll Free Tel:* 800-331-0461 *Fax:* 407-240-8333 *Web Site:* www.flprint.org, pg 576

Yanosey, Robert J, Morning Sun Books Inc, 1200 County Rd 523, Flemington, NJ 08822 *Tel:* 908-806-6216 *Fax:* 908-237-2407 *E-mail:* sales.morningsunbooks@gmail.com *Web Site:* morningsunbooks.com, pg 154

Yao, Mei C, Chinese Connection Agency, 67 Banksville Rd, Armonk, NY 10504 *Tel:* 914-765-0296 *Fax:* 914-765-0297 *Web Site:* www.yaollc.com, pg 511

Yarborough, Elizabeth, Chronicle Books LLC, 680 Second St, San Francisco, CA 94107 *Tel:* 415-537-4200 *Toll Free Tel:* 800-759-0190 (cust serv) *Fax:* 415-537-4460 *Toll Free Fax:* 800-858-7787 (orders); 800-286-9471 (cust serv) *E-mail:* frontdesk@chroniclebooks.com *Web Site:* www.chroniclebooks.com, pg 55

Yarshater, Prof Ehsan, Bibliotheca Persica Press, 450 Riverside Dr, Suite 4, New York, NY 10027 *Tel:* 212-851-9150 *Fax:* 212-749-9524 *E-mail:* ey4@columbia.edu *Web Site:* www.iranicaonline.org, pg 34

Yates, Gary, The Alexander Graham Bell Association for the Deaf & Hard of Hearing, 3417 Volta Place NW, Washington, DC 20007 *Tel:* 202-337-5220 *Toll Free Tel:* 866-337-5220 (orders) *Fax:* 202-337-8314 *E-mail:* info@agbell.org; publications@agbell.org *Web Site:* www.agbell.org, pg 6

Yates, John, University of Toronto Press, 10 St Mary St, Suite 700, Toronto, ON M4Y 2W8, Canada *Tel:* 416-978-2239 *Fax:* 416-978-4738 *E-mail:* info@utpress.utoronto.ca *Web Site:* www.utpress.utoronto.ca; www.utppublishing.com, pg 475

Yates, Michael D, Monthly Review Press, 146 W 29 St, Suite 6W, New York, NY 10001 *Tel:* 212-691-2555 *Toll Free Tel:* 800-670-9499 *Fax:* 212-727-3676 *E-mail:* mreview@igc.org *Web Site:* monthlyreview.org, pg 153

Yates, Steve, University Press of Mississippi, 3825 Ridgewood Rd, Jackson, MS 39211-6492 *Tel:* 601-432-6205 *Toll Free Tel:* 800-737-7788 (orders & cust serv) *Fax:* 601-432-6217 *E-mail:* press@mississippi.edu *Web Site:* www.upress.state.ms.us, pg 247

Ye, Shawn, Homa & Sekey Books, 140 E Ridgewood Ave, Paramus, NJ 07652 *Tel:* 201-261-8810 *Toll Free Tel:* 800-870-HOMA (870-4662 orders) *Fax:* 201-261-8890 *E-mail:* info@homabooks.com *Web Site:* www.homabooks.com, pg 110

Yee, Henry, Picador, 175 Fifth Ave, 19th fl, New York, NY 10010 *Tel:* 646-307-5151 *Fax:* 212-253-9627 *Web Site:* www.picadorusa.com, pg 182

Yee, Jennifer, Book Sales, 142 W 36 St, 4th fl, New York, NY 10018 *Tel:* 212-779-4972; 212-779-4971 *Fax:* 212-779-6058 *E-mail:* booksales@quarto.com; customerservice@quarto.com *Web Site:* www.quartoknows.com, pg 40

Yee, Roger, Visual Profile Books Inc, 389 Fifth Ave, Suite 1105, New York, NY 10016 *Tel:* 212-279-7000 *Web Site:* www.visualprofilebooks.com, pg 251

Yeffeth, Glenn, BenBella Books Inc, 10300 N Central Expwy, Suite 400, Dallas, TX 75231 *Tel:* 214-750-3600 *Fax:* 214-750-3645 *E-mail:* feedback@benbellabooks.com *Web Site:* www.benbellabooks.com; www.smartpopbooks.com, pg 32

Yeh, Phoebe, Random House Children's Books, 1745 Broadway, 10th fl, New York, NY 10019 *Tel:* 212-782-9000 *Web Site:* www.randomhousekids.com, pg 194

Yelavich, John, American Society of Mechanical Engineers (ASME), 2 Park Ave, New York, NY 10016-5990 *Tel:* 212-591-7000 *Toll Free Tel:* 800-843-2763 (cust serv-US, CN & Mexico) *Fax:* 212-591-7674; 973-882-8113 (cust serv); 973-882-1717 (orders & inquiries) *E-mail:* infocentral@asme.org *Web Site:* www.asme.org, pg 15

Yentus, Helen, Riverhead Books, 375 Hudson St, New York, NY 10014 *Tel:* 212-366-2000 *Web Site:* www.penguin.com/publishers/riverhead, pg 199

Yeping, Hu, Council for Research in Values & Philosophy (RVP), The Catholic University of America, Gibbons Hall, Rm B-12, 620 Michigan Ave NE, Washington, DC 20064 *Tel:* 202-319-6089 *Fax:* 202-319-6089 *E-mail:* cua-rvp@cua.edu *Web Site:* www.crvp.org, pg 62

Yerian, Zachary, Global Lion Intellectual Property Management Inc, PO Box 669238, Pompano Beach, FL 33066 *Tel:* 754-222-6948 *Fax:* 754-222-6948 *E-mail:* queriesglobalionmgt@gmail.com *Web Site:* www.globallionmanagement.com, pg 519

Yersak, John, Information Today, Inc, 143 Old Marlton Pike, Medford, NJ 08055-8750 *Tel:* 609-654-6266 *Toll Free Tel:* 800-300-9868 (cust serv) *Fax:* 609-654-4309 *E-mail:* custserv@infotoday.com *Web Site:* www.infotoday.com, pg 116

Yess, Mary E, The Electrochemical Society (ECS), 65 S Main St, Bldg D, Pennington, NJ 08534-2839 *Tel:* 609-737-1902 *Fax:* 609-737-2743 *E-mail:* publications@electrochem.org; customerservice@electrochem.org *Web Site:* www.electrochem.org, pg 77

Yeung, Jade, Little Bee Books, 853 Broadway, Suite 2014, New York, NY 10003 *E-mail:* info@littlebeebooks.com *Web Site:* www.littlebeebooks.com, pg 135

Yip-Chuck, John, Editors' Association of Canada (Association canadienne des reviseurs), 27 Carlton St, Suite 505, Toronto, ON M5B 1L2, Canada *Tel:* 416-975-1379 *Toll Free Tel:* 866-CAN-EDIT (226-3348) *Fax:* 416-975-1637 *E-mail:* info@editors.ca; info@reviseurs.ca *Web Site:* www.editors.ca; www.reviseurs.ca, pg 564

Yip-Chuck, John, Tom Fairley Award for Editorial Excellence, 27 Carlton St, Suite 505, Toronto, ON M5B 1L2, Canada *Tel:* 416-975-1379 *Toll Free Tel:* 866-CAN-EDIT (226-3348) *Fax:* 416-975-1637 *E-mail:* fairley_award@editors.ca; info@editors.ca *Web Site:* www.editors.ca; www.reviseurs.ca, pg 645

Yocum, Richard, Venture Publishing Inc, 1999 Cato Ave, State College, PA 16801 *Tel:* 814-234-4561 *Fax:* 814-234-1651 *E-mail:* vpublish@venturepublish.com *Web Site:* www.venturepublish.com, pg 250

Yoke, Beth, Alex Awards, 50 E Huron St, Chicago, IL 60611 *Tel:* 312-280-4390 *Toll Free Tel:* 800-545-2433 *Fax:* 312-280-5276 *E-mail:* yalsa@ala.org *Web Site:* www.ala.org/yalsa/alex-awards, pg 626

Yoke, Beth, Baker & Taylor/YALSA Conference Grants, 50 E Huron St, Chicago, IL 60611 *Tel:* 312-280-4390 *Toll Free Tel:* 800-545-2433 *Fax:* 312-280-5276; 312-664-7459 *E-mail:* yalsa@ala.org *Web Site:* www.ala.org/yalsa, pg 630

Yoke, Beth, Margaret A Edwards Award, 50 E Huron St, Chicago, IL 60611 *Tel:* 312-280-4390 *Toll Free Tel:* 800-545-2433 *Fax:* 312-280-5276 *E-mail:* yalsa@ala.org *Web Site:* www.ala.org/yalsa/edwards, pg 643

Yoke, Beth, Frances Henne YALSA/VOYA Research Grant, 50 E Huron St, Chicago, IL 60611 *Tel:* 312-280-4390 *Toll Free Tel:* 800-545-2433 *Fax:* 312-280-5276 *E-mail:* yalsa@ala.org *Web Site:* www.ala.org/yalsa/awardsandgrants/franceshenne, pg 647

Yoke, Beth, Michael L Printz Award, 50 E Huron St, Chicago, IL 60611 *Tel:* 312-280-4390 *Toll Free Tel:* 800-545-2433 *Fax:* 312-280-5276 *E-mail:* yalsa@ala.org *Web Site:* www.ala.org/yalsa/printz, pg 682

Yokoi, Rosemary, Paragon House, 3600 Labore Rd, Suite 1, St Paul, MN 55110-4144 *Tel:* 651-644-3087 *Toll Free Tel:* 800-447-3709 *Fax:* 651-644-0997 *E-mail:* paragon@paragonhouse.com *Web Site:* www.paragonhouse.com, pg 174

Yoon, Janie, Groundwood Books, 128 Sterling Rd, Lower Level, Toronto, ON M6R 2B7, Canada *Tel:* 416-363-4343 *Fax:* 416-363-1017 *E-mail:* genmail@groundwoodbooks.com *Web Site:* www.houseofanansi.com, pg 458

Yoon, Janie, House of Anansi Press Inc, 128 Sterling Rd, Lower Level, Toronto, ON M6R 2B7, Canada *Tel:* 416-363-4343 *Fax:* 416-363-1017 *E-mail:* customerservice@houseofanansi.com *Web Site:* www.houseofanansi.com, pg 460

Yorke, Laura, Carol Mann Agency, 55 Fifth Ave, New York, NY 10003 *Tel:* 212-206-5635 *Fax:* 212-675-4809 *E-mail:* submissions@carolmannagency.com *Web Site:* www.carolmannagency.com, pg 527

Yother, Michele, Gallopade International Inc, 611 Hwy 74 S, Suite 2000, Peachtree City, GA 30269 *Tel:* 770-631-4222 *Toll Free Tel:* 800-536-2GET (536-2438) *Fax:* 770-631-4810 *Toll Free Fax:* 800-871-2979 *E-mail:* customerservice@gallopade.com *Web Site:* www.gallopade.com, pg 90

Younce, Virginia Smith, The Penguin Press, 375 Hudson St, New York, NY 10014 *Web Site:* thepenguinpress.com, pg 178

Young, Cheryl, MacDowell Fellowships, 100 High St, Peterborough, NH 03458 *Tel:* 603-924-3886 *Fax:* 603-924-9142 *E-mail:* info@macdowellcolony.org; admissions@macdowellcolony.org *Web Site:* www.macdowellcolony.org, pg 664

Zagat, Tim, Zagat Survey LLC, 76 Ninth Ave, 4th fl, New York, NY 10011 *Toll Free Tel:* 800-540-9609 *E-mail:* feedback@zagat.com *Web Site:* www.zagat.com, pg 262

Zajac, Elizabeth, Random House Children's Books, 1745 Broadway, 10th fl, New York, NY 10019 *Tel:* 212-782-9000 *Web Site:* www.randomhousekids.com, pg 194

Zajdel, George, ASTM International, 100 Barr Harbor Dr, West Conshohocken, PA 19428-2959 *Tel:* 610-832-9500; 610-832-9585 (intl) *Toll Free Tel:* 877-909-2786 (sales & cust support) *Fax:* 610-832-9555 *E-mail:* service@astm.org *Web Site:* www.astm.org, pg 24

Zajechowski, Sheryl, Brilliance Audio, 1704 Eaton Dr, Grand Haven, MI 49417 *Tel:* 616-846-5256 *Toll Free Tel:* 800-648-2312 (orders only) *Fax:* 616-846-0630 *E-mail:* customerservice@brillianceaudio.com *Web Site:* www.brillianceaudio.com, pg 44

Zalewski, Ellen, University of Chicago Press, 1427 E 60 St, Chicago, IL 60637-2954 *Tel:* 773-702-7700; 773-702-7600 *Toll Free Tel:* 800-621-2736 (orders) *Fax:* 773-702-9756; 773-660-2235 (orders); 773-702-2708 *E-mail:* custserv@press.uchicago.edu; marketing@press.uchicago.edu *Web Site:* www.press.uchicago.edu, pg 241

Zamajtuk, Jason, Random House Children's Books, 1745 Broadway, 10th fl, New York, NY 10019 *Tel:* 212-782-9000 *Web Site:* www.randomhousekids.com, pg 194

Zamani, Fay, Mazda Publishers Inc, One Park Plaza, Suite 600, Irvine, CA 92614 *Tel:* 714-751-5252 *Fax:* 714-751-4805 *E-mail:* mazdapub@aol.com *Web Site:* www.mazdapublishers.com, pg 144

Zancan, Caroline, Henry Holt and Company, LLC, 175 Fifth Ave, New York, NY 10010 *Tel:* 646-307-5151 *Toll Free Tel:* 888-330-8477 (orders) *Fax:* 646-307-5285 *E-mail:* firstname.lastname@hholt.com *Web Site:* www.henryholt.com, pg 109

Zanger, Susan, Aevitas Creative Management, 19 W 21 St, Suite 501, New York, NY 10010 *Tel:* 212-765-6900 *Web Site:* aevitascreative.com, pg 506

Zanoni, Michael, The Christian Science Publishing Society, 210 Massachusetts Ave, Boston, MA 02115 *Tel:* 617-450-2000 *Toll Free Tel:* 800-288-7090 *Fax:* 617-450-7334 *E-mail:* contact@csps.com *Web Site:* christianscience.com, pg 55

Zatyko, Barbara, Magazines Canada (MC), 425 Adelaide St W, Suite 700, Toronto, ON M5V 3C1, Canada *Tel:* 416-504-0274 *Fax:* 416-504-0437 *E-mail:* info@magazinescanada.ca *Web Site:* www.magazinescanada.ca/development/magnet, pg 569

Zavala, Megan Close, Keller Media Inc, 578 Washington Blvd, No 745, Marina del Rey, CA 90292 *Toll Free Tel:* 800-278-8706 *E-mail:* query@kellermedia.com *Web Site:* kellermedia.com/query, pg 523

Zaza, Denise, Harlequin Enterprises Ltd, 233 Broadway, Suite 1001, New York, NY 10279 *Tel:* 212-553-4200 *Fax:* 212-227-8969 *E-mail:* customerservice@harlequin.com *Web Site:* www.harlequin.com, pg 100

Zbornik, Angela, Graphic Arts Books, 7820 NE Holman St, Suite B-9, Portland, OR 97218 *Tel:* 503-254-5591 *Fax:* 503-254-5609 *E-mail:* info-ga@graphicartsbooks.com *Web Site:* www.graphicartsbooks.com, pg 95

Zeig, Jeffrey K PhD, Zeig, Tucker & Theisen Inc, 2632 E Thomas Rd, Suite 200, Phoenix, AZ 85016 *Tel:* 480-389-4342 *Fax:* 602-944-8118 *E-mail:* marketing@zeigtucker.com *Web Site:* www.zeigtucker.com, pg 262

Zell, Carla, Ancient Faith Publishing, 2747 Bond St, University Park, IL 60484 *Tel:* 219-728-2216 *Toll Free Tel:* 800-967-7377 *Toll Free Fax:* 866-599-5208 *E-mail:* info@ancientfaith.com; orders@ancientfaith.com *Web Site:* www.ancientfaith.com/publishing, pg 16

Zenner, Boyd, The University of Virginia Press, PO Box 400318, Charlottesville, VA 22904-4318 *Tel:* 434-924-3468 (cust serv); 434-924-3469 (cust serv) *Toll Free Tel:* 800-831-3406 (orders) *Fax:* 434-982-2655 *Toll Free Fax:* 877-288-6400 *E-mail:* vapress@virginia.edu *Web Site:* www.upress.virginia.edu, pg 245

Zentner, Alexi, Binghamton University Creative Writing Program, c/o Dept of English, PO Box 6000, Binghamton, NY 13902-6000 *Tel:* 607-777-2168 *Fax:* 607-777-2408 *E-mail:* cwpro@binghamton.edu *Web Site:* english.binghamton.edu/cwpro, pg 619

Zeolla, David, Dorrance Publishing Co Inc, 585 Alpha Dr, Suite 103, Pittsburgh, PA 15238 *Toll Free Tel:* 800-695-9599; 800-788-7654 (gen cust orders) *Fax:* 412-288-1786 *E-mail:* dorrinfo@dorrancepublishing.com; redleadbookorders@dorrancepublishing.com; bookorders@rosedogbooks.com *Web Site:* www.dorrancepublishing.com, pg 72

Zerillo, Nicole, Public Relations Society of America, 33 Maiden Lane, 11th fl, New York, NY 10038-5150 *Tel:* 212-460-1400 *Fax:* 212-995-0757 *Web Site:* www.prsa.org, pg 576

Zettersten, Rolf, Hachette Book Group, 1290 Avenue of the Americas, New York, NY 10019 *Tel:* 212-364-1100 *Toll Free Tel:* 800-759-0190 (cust serv) *Fax:* 212-364-0933 (intl orders) *Toll Free Fax:* 800-286-9471 (cust serv) *Web Site:* www.hachettebookgroup.com, pg 98

Zettersten, Rolf, Hachette Nashville, 12 Cadillac Dr, Suite 480, Brentwood, TN 37027 *Tel:* 615-221-0996 *Fax:* 615-221-0962 *Web Site:* www.hachettebookgroup.com, pg 98

Zhang, Nancy, Candied Plums, 7548 Ravenna Ave NE, Seattle, WA 98115 *E-mail:* candiedplums@gmail.com *Web Site:* www.candiedplums.com, pg 46

Zhu, George, CN Times Books, 501 Fifth Ave, Suite 1708, New York, NY 10017 *Tel:* 212-867-8666 *Web Site:* cntimesbooks.com, pg 57

Zialcita, Susana, Random House Publishing Group, 1745 Broadway, New York, NY 10019 *Toll Free Tel:* 800-200-3552 *Web Site:* atrandom.com, pg 195

Zidle, Abby, Gallery Books, 1230 Avenue of the Americas, New York, NY 10020 *Toll Free Tel:* 800-456-6798 *Fax:* 212-698-7284 *E-mail:* consumer.customerservice@simonandschuster.com *Web Site:* www.simonsays.com, pg 90

Ziefert, Harriet M, Blue Apple Books, 515 Valley St, Suite 170, Maplewood, NJ 07040 *Tel:* 973-763-8191 *Toll Free Tel:* 800-283-3572 (orders) *Fax:* 973-763-5944 *E-mail:* info@blueapplebooks.com *Web Site:* blueapplebooks.com, pg 38

Zielinski, Mark, Bloom's Literary Criticism, 132 W 31 St, 17th fl, New York, NY 10001 *Toll Free Tel:* 800-322-8755 *Toll Free Fax:* 800-678-3633 *E-mail:* custserv@factsonfile.com *Web Site:* www.infobasepublishing.com, pg 37

Zielinski, Mark, Chelsea House Publishers, 132 W 31 St, 17th fl, New York, NY 10001 *Tel:* 212-967-8800 *Toll Free Tel:* 800-322-8755 *Fax:* 917-339-0325 *Toll Free Fax:* 800-678-3633 *E-mail:* custserv@factsonfile.com *Web Site:* www.infobasepublishing.com; www.infobaselearning.com, pg 53

Zielinski, Mark, Facts On File, 132 W 31 St, 17th fl, New York, NY 10001 *Tel:* 212-967-8800 *Toll Free Tel:* 800-322-8755 *Toll Free Fax:* 800-678-3633 *E-mail:* custserv@factsonfile.com *Web Site:* infobasepublishing.com, pg 81

Zielinski, Mark, Ferguson Publishing, 132 W 31 St, 17th fl, New York, NY 10001 *Tel:* 212-967-8800 *Toll Free Tel:* 800-322-8755 *Fax:* 917-339-0323 *Toll Free Fax:* 800-678-3633 *E-mail:* custserv@factsonfile.com *Web Site:* infobasepublishing.com, pg 84

Zielke, Corinne, Krause Publications Inc, 700 E State St, Iola, WI 54990 *Tel:* 715-445-2214 *Toll Free Tel:* 800-258-0929 (cust serv); 888-457-2873 (orders) *Fax:* 715-445-4087 *E-mail:* bookorders@krause.com *Web Site:* www.krausebooks.com, pg 128

Ziff, Dorothy, Melissa Turk & the Artist Network, 9 Babbling Brook Lane, Suffern, NY 10901 *Tel:* 845-368-8606 *E-mail:* melissa@melissaturk.com *Web Site:* www.melissaturk.com, pg 544

Zimet, Kristin, The Sow's Ear Poetry Prize & The Sow's Ear Chapbook Prize, 1748 Cave Ridge Rd, Mount Jackson, VA 22842 *Tel:* 540-477-3257 *E-mail:* sepoetryreview@gmail.com *Web Site:* sowsearpoetry.org, pg 691

Zimmer, Jeremy, United Talent Agency, 9336 Civic Center Dr, Beverly Hills, CA 90210 *Tel:* 310-273-6700 *Fax:* 310-247-1111 *Web Site:* www.unitedtalent.com, pg 540

Zimmerman, Barbara, BZ/Rights & Permissions Inc, 145 W 86 St, New York, NY 10024 *Tel:* 212-924-3000 *Fax:* 212-924-2525 *E-mail:* info@bzrights.com *Web Site:* www.bzrights.com, pg 490

Zingarelli, Vito, Hedgebrook Master Class Retreat Series, PO Box 1231, Freeland, WA 98249 *Tel:* 360-321-4786 *Fax:* 360-321-2171 *E-mail:* hedgebrook@hedgebrook.org *Web Site:* www.hedgebrook.org; www.facebook.com/hedgebrook, pg 611

Zingarelli, Vito, Hedgebrook VORTEXT, PO Box 1231, Freeland, WA 98249 *Tel:* 360-321-4786 *Fax:* 360-321-2171 *E-mail:* hedgebrook@hedgebrook.org *Web Site:* www.hedgebrook.org; www.facebook.com/hedgebrook, pg 611

Zingarelli, Vito, Hedgebrook Winter Salon, PO Box 1231, Freeland, WA 98249 *Tel:* 360-321-4786 *Fax:* 360-321-2171 *E-mail:* hedgebrook@hedgebrook.org *Web Site:* www.hedgebrook.org; www.facebook.com/hedgebrook, pg 611

Zingarelli, Vito, Hedgebrook Writers in Residence Program, PO Box 1231, Freeland, WA 98249 *Tel:* 360-321-4786 *Fax:* 360-321-2171 *E-mail:* hedgebrook@hedgebrook.org *Web Site:* www.hedgebrook.org; www.facebook.com/hedgebrook, pg 611

Zink, Nicole, Mari Sandoz Award, PO Box 21756, Lincoln, NE 68542-1756 *E-mail:* nebraskalibraries@gmail.com *Web Site:* www.nebraskalibraries.org, pg 686

Zink, Seta, Perseus Books, 250 W 57 St, 15th fl, New York, NY 10107 *Tel:* 212-340-8100 *Toll Free Tel:* 800-343-4499 (cust serv) *Fax:* 212-340-8105 *Web Site:* www.perseusbooks.com, pg 181

Zinna, Diane, Association of Writers & Writing Programs (AWP), George Mason University, 4400 University Dr, MSN 1E3, Fairfax, VA 22030 *Tel:* 703-993-4301 *Fax:* 703-993-4302 *E-mail:* awp@awpwriter.org *Web Site:* www.awpwriter.org, pg 559

Zinna, Diane, AWP Award Series, George Mason University, 4400 University Dr, MSN 1E3, Fairfax, VA 22030 *Tel:* 703-993-4301 *Fax:* 703-993-4302 *E-mail:* awp@awpwriter.org *Web Site:* www.awpwriter.org, pg 629

Zinner, Eric, New York University Press, 838 Broadway, 3rd fl, New York, NY 10003-4812 *Tel:* 212-998-2575 (edit) *Toll Free Tel:* 800-996-6987 (orders) *Fax:* 212-995-4798 (orders) *E-mail:* information@nyupress.org; nyupressinfo@nyu.edu; orders@nyupress.org *Web Site:* www.nyupress.org, pg 162

Zion, Claire, Berkley Publishing Group, 375 Hudson St, New York, NY 10014 *Tel:* 212-366-2000 *Fax:* 212-366-2385 *Web Site:* www.penguin.com, pg 33

Zissimos, Mary Ann, Disney Publishing Worldwide, 1101 Flower St, Glendale, CA 91201 *Web Site:* books.disney.com, pg 71

Zitt, Dan, Penguin Random House Audio Publishing, 1745 Broadway, New York, NY 10019 *E-mail:* audio@penguinrandomhouse.com *Web Site:* www.penguinrandomhouseaudio.com, pg 178

Zitwer, Barbara J, Barbara J Zitwer Agency, 525 West End Ave, Unit 11-H, New York, NY 10024 *Tel:* 212-501-8423 *E-mail:* zitwer@gmail.com, pg 542

Zline, Patricia, Jason Aronson Inc, 4501 Forbes Blvd, Suite 200, Lanham, MD 20706 *Tel:* 301-459-3366 *Toll Free Tel:* 800-462-6420 (orders) *Fax:* 301-429-5748 *Web Site:* www.rowman.com, pg 21

Publishers Toll Free Directory

A-R Editions Inc, Middleton, WI *Toll Free Tel:* 800-736-0070 (North America book orders only), pg 1

AAPG (American Association of Petroleum Geologists), Tulsa, OK *Toll Free Tel:* 800-364-AAPG (364-2274), pg 1

Abbeville Press, New York, NY *Toll Free Tel:* 800-ART-BOOK (278-2665); 800-343-4499 (orders) *Toll Free Fax:* 800-351-5073 (orders), pg 2

Abbeville Publishing Group, New York, NY *Toll Free Tel:* 800-ART-BOOK (278-2665), pg 2

ABC-CLIO, Santa Barbara, CA *Toll Free Tel:* 800-368-6868 *Toll Free Fax:* 866-270-3856, pg 2

ABDO Publishing Group, Edina, MN *Toll Free Tel:* 800-800-1312 *Toll Free Fax:* 800-862-3480, pg 2

Abingdon Press, Nashville, TN *Toll Free Tel:* 800-251-3320 *Toll Free Fax:* 800-836-7802 (orders), pg 2

Harry N Abrams Inc, New York, NY *Toll Free Tel:* 800-345-1359, pg 2

Abrams Learning Trends, Austin, TX *Toll Free Tel:* 800-227-9120 *Toll Free Fax:* 800-737-3322, pg 3

Academy Chicago, Chicago, IL *Toll Free Tel:* 800-888-4741 (orders), pg 3

Academy of Nutrition & Dietetics, Chicago, IL *Toll Free Tel:* 800-877-1600, pg 3

Accuity, Skokie, IL *Toll Free Tel:* 800-321-3373, pg 3

Acres USA, Greenley, CO *Toll Free Tel:* 800-355-5313, pg 4

ACTA Publications, Chicago, IL *Toll Free Tel:* 800-397-2282 *Toll Free Fax:* 800-397-0079, pg 4

ACU Press, Abilene, TX *Toll Free Tel:* 877-816-4455, pg 4

Adams-Pomeroy Press, Albany, WI *Toll Free Tel:* 877-862-3645, pg 477

Adirondack Mountain Club (ADK), Lake George, NY *Toll Free Tel:* 800-395-8080, pg 4

Adler Publishing Inc, Parker, CO *Toll Free Tel:* 800-660-5107 (sales & orders), pg 4

Advance Publishing Inc, Houston, TX *Toll Free Tel:* 800-917-9630, pg 4

AdventureKEEN, Birmingham, AL *Toll Free Tel:* 800-678-7006 *Toll Free Fax:* 877-374-9016, pg 5

AFB Press, Arlington, VA *Toll Free Tel:* 800-232-3044 (orders), pg 5

AICPA Professional Publications, Durham, NC *Toll Free Tel:* 888-777-7077 (memb serv ctr) *Toll Free Fax:* 800-362-5066 (memb serv ctr), pg 6

ALA Neal-Schuman, Chicago, IL *Toll Free Tel:* 800-545-2433, pg 6

Albert Whitman & Co, Park Ridge, IL *Toll Free Tel:* 800-255-7675, pg 6

The Alexander Graham Bell Association for the Deaf & Hard of Hearing, Washington, DC *Toll Free Tel:* 866-337-5220 (orders), pg 6

Alexander Street, a ProQuest Company, Alexandria, VA *Toll Free Tel:* 800-889-5937, pg 7

Alfred Music Publishing, Van Nuys, CA *Toll Free Tel:* 800-292-6122 (dealer sales, US & CN) *Toll Free Fax:* 800-632-1928 (dealer sales), pg 7

Alpha II LLC, Montgomery, AL *Toll Free Tel:* 800-825-7421 *Toll Free Fax:* 800-305-8030, pg 8

Alpine Publications Inc, Crawford, CO *Toll Free Tel:* 800-777-7257, pg 8

AltaMira Press, Lanham, MD *Toll Free Tel:* 800-462-6420 (cust serv), pg 8

AMACOM Books, New York, NY *Toll Free Tel:* 800-250-5308 (cust serv), pg 8

Amadeus Press/Hal Leonard Performing Arts Publishing Group, Montclair, NJ *Toll Free Tel:* 800-524-4425, pg 8

Frank Amato Publications Inc, Milwaukie, OR *Toll Free Tel:* 800-541-9498, pg 9

Amber Lotus Publishing, Portland, OR *Toll Free Tel:* 800-326-2375 (orders only), pg 9

America West Publishers, Dalton Gardens, ID *Toll Free Tel:* 800-729-4131, pg 9

American Academy of Orthopaedic Surgeons (AAOS), Rosemont, IL *Toll Free Tel:* 800-346-2267, pg 9

American Academy of Pediatrics, Elk Grove Village, IL *Toll Free Tel:* 888-227-1770, pg 9

American Association of Blood Banks, Bethesda, MD *Toll Free Tel:* 866-222-2498 (sales), pg 10

American Bar Association, Chicago, IL *Toll Free Tel:* 800-285-2221 (orders), pg 10

American Bible Society, Philadelphia, PA *Toll Free Tel:* 800-322-4253 (cust serv); 888-596-6296, pg 10

American Carriage House Publishing, Grass Valley, CA *Toll Free Tel:* 866-986-2665, pg 10

The American Ceramic Society, Westerville, OH *Toll Free Tel:* 866-721-3322, pg 10

The American Chemical Society, Washington, DC *Toll Free Tel:* 800-227-5558 (US), pg 10

American College, Bryn Mawr, PA *Toll Free Tel:* 888-263-7265, pg 11

American Correctional Association, Alexandria, VA *Toll Free Tel:* 800-222-5646, pg 11

American Counseling Association, Alexandria, VA *Toll Free Tel:* 800-347-6647 (ext 222, book orders) *Toll Free Fax:* 800-473-2329, pg 11

American Diabetes Association, Alexandria, VA *Toll Free Tel:* 800-342-2383, pg 11

American Federation of Arts, New York, NY *Toll Free Tel:* 800-232-0270, pg 11

American Federation of Astrologers Inc, Tempe, AZ *Toll Free Tel:* 888-301-7630, pg 11

American Geophysical Union (AGU), Washington, DC *Toll Free Tel:* 800-966-2481 (North America), pg 11

American Girl Publishing, Middleton, WI *Toll Free Tel:* 800-233-0264; 800-360-1861; 800-845-0005 (US & CN), pg 12

American Institute for Economic Research (AIER), Great Barrington, MA *Toll Free Tel:* 888-528-1216 (orders), pg 12

American Institute of Aeronautics & Astronautics (AIAA), Reston, VA *Toll Free Tel:* 800-639-AIAA (639-2422), pg 12

American Institute of Chemical Engineers (AIChE), New York, NY *Toll Free Tel:* 800-242-4363, pg 12

American Law Institute, Philadelphia, PA *Toll Free Tel:* 800-253-6397, pg 12

American Law Institute Continuing Legal Education (ALI CLE), Philadelphia, PA *Toll Free Tel:* 800-CLE-NEWS (253-6397), pg 12

The American Library Association (ALA), Chicago, IL *Toll Free Tel:* 800-545-2433, pg 12

American Map Corp, Long Island City, NY *Toll Free Tel:* 888-774-7979, pg 13

American Mathematical Society, Providence, RI *Toll Free Tel:* 800-321-4267, pg 13

American Medical Association, Chicago, IL *Toll Free Tel:* 800-621-8335, pg 13

The American Occupational Therapy Association Inc (AOTA), Bethesda, MD *Toll Free Tel:* 800-377-8555 (TDD); 877-404-AOTA (404-2682, orders), pg 13

American Printing House for the Blind Inc, Louisville, KY *Toll Free Tel:* 800-223-1839 (cust serv), pg 13

American Products Publishing Co, Beaverton, OR *Toll Free Tel:* 800-668-8181, pg 14

American Psychiatric Association Publishing, Arlington, VA *Toll Free Tel:* 800-368-5777, pg 14

American Psychological Association, Washington, DC *Toll Free Tel:* 800-374-2721, pg 14

American Public Works Association (APWA), Kansas City, MO *Toll Free Tel:* 800-848-APWA (848-2792), pg 14

American Quilter's Society, Paducah, KY *Toll Free Tel:* 800-626-5420 (orders), pg 14

American Society for Nondestructive Testing, Columbus, OH *Toll Free Tel:* 800-222-2768, pg 14

American Society for Quality (ASQ), Milwaukee, WI *Toll Free Tel:* 800-248-1946 (US & CN); 800-514-1564 (Mexico), pg 14

American Society of Agricultural & Biological Engineers (ASABE), St Joseph, MI *Toll Free Tel:* 800-371-2723, pg 14

American Society of Civil Engineers (ASCE), Reston, VA *Toll Free Tel:* 800-548-2723, pg 15

American Society of Health-System Pharmacists (ASHP), Bethesda, MD *Toll Free Tel:* 866-279-0681 (orders), pg 15

American Society of Mechanical Engineers (ASME), New York, NY *Toll Free Tel:* 800-843-2763 (cust serv-US, CN & Mexico), pg 15

American Technical Publishers Inc, Orland Park, IL *Toll Free Tel:* 800-323-3471, pg 15

American Water Works Association (AWWA), Denver, CO *Toll Free Tel:* 800-926-7337, pg 15

Ancient Faith Publishing, University Park, IL *Toll Free Tel:* 800-967-7377 *Toll Free Fax:* 866-599-5208, pg 16

Andrews McMeel Publishing LLC, Kansas City, MO *Toll Free Tel:* 800-851-8923; 800-943-9839 (cust serv) *Toll Free Fax:* 800-943-9831 (orders), pg 16

Andrews University Press, Berrien Springs, MI *Toll Free Tel:* 800-467-6369 (Visa, MC & American Express orders only), pg 17

Angel City Press, Santa Monica, CA *Toll Free Tel:* 800-949-8039, pg 17

Angelus Press, Kansas City, MO *Toll Free Tel:* 800-966-7337, pg 17

Annual Reviews, Palo Alto, CA *Toll Free Tel:* 800-523-8635, pg 17

ANR Publications University of California, Richmond, CA *Toll Free Tel:* 800-994-8849, pg 17

Antique Collectors' Club Ltd, New York, NY *Toll Free Tel:* 800-252-5231, pg 17

Antique Trader, Iola, WI *Toll Free Tel:* 888-457-2873, pg 18

Aperture Books, New York, NY *Toll Free Tel:* 800-929-2323, pg 18

The Apex Press, Lanham, MD *Toll Free Tel:* 800-462-6420 (orders) *Toll Free Fax:* 800-388-4450, pg 18

Apollo Managed Care Inc, Orange, CA *Toll Free Tel:* 888-276-5563, pg 18

Appalachian Mountain Club Books, Boston, MA *Toll Free Tel:* 800-262-4455 (orders), pg 19

Appalachian Trail Conservancy, Harpers Ferry, WV *Toll Free Tel:* 888-287-8673 (orders only), pg 19

Applause Theatre & Cinema Books, Montclair, NJ *Toll Free Tel:* 800-637-2852, pg 19

Applewood Books Inc, Carlisle, MA *Toll Free Tel:* 800-277-5312 (orders), pg 19

Appraisal Institute, Chicago, IL *Toll Free Tel:* 888-756-4624, pg 19

APS PRESS, St Paul, MN *Toll Free Tel:* 800-328-7560, pg 19

Aquila Communications Inc, Beaconsville, QC Canada *Toll Free Tel:* 800-667-7071 *Toll Free Fax:* 866-338-1948, pg 445

Arbordale Publishing, Mount Pleasant, SC *Toll Free Tel:* 877-243-3457, pg 19

Arcadia Publishing Inc, Mount Pleasant, SC *Toll Free Tel:* 888-313-2665 (orders only), pg 20

ARE Press, Virginia Beach, VA *Toll Free Tel:* 800-333-4499, pg 20

Jason Aronson Inc, Lanham, MD *Toll Free Tel:* 800-462-6420 (orders), pg 21

Arsenal Pulp Press, Vancouver, BC Canada *Toll Free Tel:* 888-600-PULP (600-7857), pg 445

Art Image Publications, Derby Line, VT *Toll Free Tel:* 800-361-2598 *Toll Free Fax:* 800-559-2598, pg 21

ArtAge Publications, Portland, OR *Toll Free Tel:* 800-858-4998, pg 21

Arte Publico Press, Houston, TX *Toll Free Tel:* 800-633-2783, pg 21

Artech House Inc, Norwood, MA *Toll Free Tel:* 800-225-9977, pg 21

Artisan Books, New York, NY *Toll Free Tel:* 800-722-7202, pg 22

ASCD, Alexandria, VA *Toll Free Tel:* 800-933-2723, pg 22

Ascension Press, West Chester, PA *Toll Free Tel:* 800-376-0520 (sales & cust serv), pg 22

ASCP Press, Chicago, IL *Toll Free Tel:* 800-267-2727, pg 22

ASM International, Materials Park, OH *Toll Free Tel:* 800-336-5152; 800-368-9800 (Europe), pg 23

Aspatore Books, Eagan, MN *Toll Free Tel:* 866-ASPATORE (277-2867); 888-728-7677; 800-328-4880, pg 23

Association for Computing Machinery, New York, NY *Toll Free Tel:* 800-342-6626, pg 24

Association for Talent Development (ATD) Press, Alexandria, VA *Toll Free Tel:* 800-628-2783, pg 24

Association of College & Research Libraries (ACRL), Chicago, IL *Toll Free Tel:* 800-545-2433 (ext 2523), pg 24

Association of School Business Officials International, Reston, VA *Toll Free Tel:* 866-682-2729, pg 24

Asta Publications LLC, New City, NY *Toll Free Tel:* 800-482-4190, pg 24

ASTM International, West Conshohocken, PA *Toll Free Tel:* 877-909-2786 (sales & cust support), pg 24

Astragal Press, Apple Valley, MN *Toll Free Tel:* 866-543-3045 *Toll Free Fax:* 800-330-6232, pg 25

The Astronomical Society of the Pacific, San Francisco, CA *Toll Free Tel:* 800-335-2624, pg 25

Athletic Guide Publishing, Flagler Beach, FL *Toll Free Tel:* 800-255-1050, pg 25

Atlantic Law Book Co, West Hartford, CT *Toll Free Tel:* 800-259-5534, pg 25

Atlantic Publishing Group Inc, Ocala, FL *Toll Free Tel:* 800-814-1132, pg 25

Atwood Publishing, Madison, WI *Toll Free Tel:* 888-242-7101, pg 25

Augsburg Fortress Publishers, Publishing House of the Evangelical Lutheran Church in America, Minneapolis, MN *Toll Free Tel:* 800-426-0115 (ext 639, subns); 800-328-4648 (orders), pg 25

August House Inc, Atlanta, GA *Toll Free Tel:* 800-284-8784, pg 26

AuthorHouse, Bloomington, IN *Toll Free Tel:* 888-519-5121, pg 26

Autism Asperger Publishing Co, Lenexa, KS *Toll Free Tel:* 877-277-8254, pg 26

Ave Maria Press, Notre Dame, IN *Toll Free Tel:* 800-282-1865 *Toll Free Fax:* 800-282-5681, pg 26

Avention Inc, Concord, MA *Toll Free Tel:* 866-354-6936, pg 27

Avery Color Studios, Gwinn, MI *Toll Free Tel:* 800-722-9925, pg 27

Avotaynu Inc, New Haven, CT *Toll Free Tel:* 800-AVOTAYNU (286-8296), pg 27

Awe-Struck Publishing, Cincinnati, OH *Toll Free Tel:* 888-402-6657 *Toll Free Fax:* 888-460-4752, pg 27

AZ Books LLC, New York, NY *Toll Free Tel:* 888-945-7723 *Toll Free Fax:* 888-945-7724, pg 27

Babalu Inc, Santa Barbara, CA *Toll Free Tel:* 877-522-2258, pg 27

Backbeat Books, Montclair, NJ *Toll Free Tel:* 800-637-2852 (Music Dispatch), pg 28

Baha'i Publishing, Wilmette, IL *Toll Free Tel:* 800-999-9019 (orders), pg 28

Baker Books, Grand Rapids, MI *Toll Free Tel:* 800-877-2665; 800-679-1957 *Toll Free Fax:* 800-398-3111, pg 28

Banner of Truth, Carlisle, PA *Toll Free Tel:* 800-263-8085 (orders), pg 29

Barefoot Books, Cambridge, MA *Toll Free Tel:* 866-215-1756 (cust serv); 866-417-2369 (orders), pg 29

Barnhardt & Ashe Publishing Inc, Miami, FL *Toll Free Tel:* 800-283-6360 (orders), pg 29

Barron's Educational Series Inc, Hauppauge, NY *Toll Free Tel:* 800-645-3476, pg 30

Bartleby Press, Savage, MD *Toll Free Tel:* 800-953-9929, pg 30

Bay Tree Publishing LLC, Point Richmond, CA *Toll Free Fax:* 866-552-7329, pg 30

Beacon Hill Press of Kansas City, Kansas City, MO *Toll Free Tel:* 800-877-0700 (cust serv), pg 30

Bear & Co Inc, Rochester, VT *Toll Free Tel:* 800-932-3277, pg 31

Bearport Publishing Co Inc, New York, NY *Toll Free Tel:* 877-337-8577 *Toll Free Fax:* 866-337-8557, pg 31

Bedford/St Martin's, Boston, MA *Toll Free Tel:* 800-779-7440, pg 31

Behrman House Inc, Springfield, NJ *Toll Free Tel:* 800-221-2755, pg 32

Bella Books, Tallahassee, FL *Toll Free Tel:* 800-729-4992, pg 32

Bellerophon Books, Santa Barbara, CA *Toll Free Tel:* 800-253-9943, pg 32

John Benjamins Publishing Co, Philadelphia, PA *Toll Free Tel:* 800-562-5666 (orders), pg 33

Bentley Publishers, Cambridge, MA *Toll Free Tel:* 800-423-4595, pg 33

BePuzzled, San Francisco, CA *Toll Free Tel:* 800-347-4818, pg 33

Bethany House Publishers, Bloomington, MN *Toll Free Tel:* 800-877-2665 (orders) *Toll Free Fax:* 800-398-3111 (orders), pg 34

Bethlehem Books, Bathgate, ND *Toll Free Tel:* 800-757-6831, pg 34

Betterway Books, Blue Ash, OH *Toll Free Tel:* 800-666-0963 *Toll Free Fax:* 888-590-4082, pg 34

Between the Lines, Toronto, ON Canada *Toll Free Tel:* 800-718-7201, pg 446

Bhaktivedanta Book Trust (BBT), Los Angeles, CA *Toll Free Tel:* 800-927-4152, pg 34

Big Guy Books Inc, Encinitas, CA *Toll Free Tel:* 800-536-3030 (booksellers' cust serv), pg 35

Bilingual Press/Editorial Bilingue, Tempe, AZ *Toll Free Tel:* 866-965-3867, pg 35

George T Bisel Co Inc, Philadelphia, PA *Toll Free Tel:* 800-247-3526, pg 35

Bisk Education, Tampa, FL *Toll Free Tel:* 800-280-9718 (cust serv), pg 35

BJU Press, Greenville, SC *Toll Free Tel:* 800-845-5731, pg 36

Black Classic Press, Baltimore, MD *Toll Free Tel:* 800-476-8870, pg 36

Black Rose Books Ltd, Montreal, QC Canada *Toll Free Tel:* 800-565-9523 (orders) *Toll Free Fax:* 800-221-9985 (orders), pg 446

John F Blair Publisher, Winston-Salem, NC *Toll Free Tel:* 800-222-9796, pg 37

Bloomberg BNA Books, Arlington, VA *Toll Free Tel:* 800-960-1220, pg 37

Bloom's Literary Criticism, New York, NY *Toll Free Tel:* 800-322-8755 *Toll Free Fax:* 800-678-3633, pg 37

Blue Apple Books, Maplewood, NJ *Toll Free Tel:* 800-283-3572 (orders), pg 38

Blue Book Publications Inc, Minneapolis, MN *Toll Free Tel:* 800-877-4867, pg 38

Blue Mountain Arts Inc, Boulder, CO *Toll Free Tel:* 800-525-0642 *Toll Free Fax:* 800-545-8573, pg 38

Blue Note Publications Inc, *Toll Free Tel:* 800-624-0401 (orders), pg 38

Blue Poppy Press, Boulder, CO *Toll Free Tel:* 800-487-9296, pg 38

Bluestocking Press, Placerville, CA *Toll Free Tel:* 800-959-8586, pg 38

BNi Building News, Vista, CA *Toll Free Tel:* 888-BNI-BOOK (264-2665), pg 39

BoardSource, Washington, DC *Toll Free Tel:* 877-892-6273, pg 39

Bolchazy-Carducci Publishers Inc, Mundelein, IL *Toll Free Tel:* 800-392-6453, pg 39

The Book Tree, San Diego, CA *Toll Free Tel:* 800-700-8733 (orders), pg 40

BookLogix, Alpharetta, GA *Toll Free Fax:* 888-564-7890, pg 40

Books In Motion, Spokane Valley, WA *Toll Free Tel:* 800-752-3199, pg 40

Books on Tape®, New York, NY *Toll Free Tel:* 800-733-3000 (cust serv) *Toll Free Fax:* 800-940-7046, pg 40

Borealis Press Ltd, Nepean, ON Canada *Toll Free Tel:* 877-696-2585, pg 447

The Boston Mills Press, Richmond Hill, ON Canada *Toll Free Tel:* 800-387-6192 *Toll Free Fax:* 800-450-0391, pg 447

R R Bowker LLC, Ann Arbor, MI *Toll Free Tel:* 888-269-5372 (edit & cust serv, press 2 for returns) *Toll Free Fax:* 877-337-7015 (US & CN), pg 41

Boyds Mills Press, Honesdale, PA *Toll Free Tel:* 800-490-5111, pg 41

Boynton/Cook Publishers, Portsmouth, NH *Toll Free Tel:* 800-225-5800 *Toll Free Fax:* 877-231-6980, pg 41

Boys Town Press, Boys Town, NE *Toll Free Tel:* 800-282-6657, pg 41

Bradford Publishing Co, Denver, CO *Toll Free Tel:* 800-446-2831, pg 41

Brault & Bouthillier, Montreal, QC Canada *Toll Free Tel:* 800-361-0378 *Toll Free Fax:* 800-361-0378, pg 447

Breakthrough Publications Inc, Emmaus, PA *Toll Free Tel:* 800-824-5001 (ext 12), pg 42

Breakwater Books Ltd, St John's, NL Canada *Toll Free Tel:* 800-563-3333 (orders), pg 447

Brentwood Christian Press, Columbus, GA *Toll Free Tel:* 800-334-8861, pg 42

Brethren Press, Elgin, IL *Toll Free Tel:* 800-323-8039 *Toll Free Fax:* 800-667-8188, pg 42

Brewers Publications, Boulder, CO *Toll Free Tel:* 888-822-6273 (CN & US), pg 42

Bridge-Logos, Newberry, FL *Toll Free Tel:* 800-320-4108, pg 43

Bridge Publications Inc, Commerce, CA *Toll Free Tel:* 800-722-1733, pg 43

Brill Inc, Boston, MA *Toll Free Tel:* 800-962-4406, pg 43

Brilliance Audio, Grand Haven, MI *Toll Free Tel:* 800-648-2312 (orders only), pg 43

Brookes Publishing Co Inc, Baltimore, MD *Toll Free Tel:* 800-638-3775 (US & CN), pg 44

The Brookings Institution Press, Washington, DC *Toll Free Tel:* 800-537-5487, pg 44

Brookline Books, Northampton, MA *Toll Free Tel:* 800-666-2665 (orders), pg 44

Brooklyn Publishers LLC, Cedar Rapids, IA *Toll Free Tel:* 888-473-8521, pg 44

Brush Education Inc, Edmonton, AB Canada *Toll Free Tel:* 855-283-0900 *Toll Free Fax:* 855-283-6947, pg 448

BuilderBooks.com, Washington, DC *Toll Free Tel:* 800-223-2665, pg 45

Bull Publishing Co, Boulder, CO *Toll Free Tel:* 800-676-2855, pg 45

Burford Books, Ithaca, NY *Toll Free Fax:* 866-212-7750, pg 45

Business & Legal Resources Inc, Brentwood, TN *Toll Free Tel:* 800-727-5257, pg 45

Business Research Services Inc, Bethesda, MD *Toll Free Tel:* 800-845-8420 *Toll Free Fax:* 877-516-0818, pg 45

Butte Publications Inc, Hillsboro, OR *Toll Free Tel:* 866-312-8883 *Toll Free Fax:* 866-412-8883 (orders only), pg 45

Cambridge Educational, New York, NY *Toll Free Tel:* 800-322-8755 *Toll Free Fax:* 800-329-6687, pg 46

Campfield & Campfield Publishing LLC, Philadelphia, PA *Toll Free Tel:* 888-518-2440, pg 46

Canada Law Book®, Toronto, ON Canada *Toll Free Tel:* 800-387-5351 (cust rel, CN & US only); 800-347-5164 (cust rel & orders, CN & US) *Toll Free Fax:* 877-750-9041 (cust rel & orders, CN only), pg 448

Canadian Bible Society, Toronto, ON Canada *Toll Free Tel:* 800-465-2425, pg 448

Canadian Museum of History (Musee canadien de l'histoire), Gatineau, QC Canada *Toll Free Tel:* 800-555-5621 (North American orders only), pg 449

Canadian Scholars' Press Inc, Toronto, ON Canada *Toll Free Tel:* 800-463-1998, pg 449

C&T Publishing Inc, Concord, CA *Toll Free Tel:* 800-284-1114, pg 46

Capital Enquiry Inc, South Lake Tahoe, CA *Toll Free Tel:* 800-922-7486, pg 47

Capstone Publishers™, North Mankato, MN *Toll Free Tel:* 800-747-4992 (cust serv) *Toll Free Fax:* 888-262-0705, pg 47

Cardoza Publishing, Las Vegas, NV *Toll Free Tel:* 800-577-WINS (577-9467), pg 47

The Career Press Inc, Wayne, NJ *Toll Free Tel:* 800-CAREER-1 (227-3371), pg 47

Carlisle Press - Walnut Creek, Sugarcreek, OH *Toll Free Tel:* 800-852-4482, pg 47

Carolina Academic Press, Durham, NC *Toll Free Tel:* 800-489-7486, pg 48

Carolrhoda Books, Minneapolis, MN *Toll Free Tel:* 800-328-4929 *Toll Free Fax:* 800-332-1132, pg 48

Carolrhoda Lab™, Minneapolis, MN *Toll Free Tel:* 800-328-4929 *Toll Free Fax:* 800-332-1132 (US), pg 48

Carroll Publishing, Bethesda, MD *Toll Free Tel:* 800-336-4240, pg 48

Carson-Dellosa Publishing LLC, Greensboro, NC *Toll Free Tel:* 800-321-0943 *Toll Free Fax:* 800-535-2669, pg 48

Carswell, Toronto, ON Canada *Toll Free Tel:* 800-387-5164 (CN & US) *Toll Free Fax:* 877-750-9041 (CN only), pg 449

CarTech Inc, North Branch, MN *Toll Free Tel:* 800-551-4754, pg 48

Casa Bautista de Publicaciones, El Paso, TX *Toll Free Tel:* 800-755-5958 (cust serv & orders), pg 48

Cascade Pass Inc, Marina del Rey, CA *Toll Free Tel:* 888-837-0704, pg 49

Catholic Book Publishing Corp, Totowa, NJ *Toll Free Tel:* 877-228-2665, pg 49

The Catholic University of America Press, Washington, DC *Toll Free Tel:* 800-537-5487 (orders only), pg 49

Cato Institute, Washington, DC *Toll Free Tel:* 800-767-1241, pg 49

Caxton Press, Caldwell, ID *Toll Free Tel:* 800-657-6465, pg 49

Cedar Fort Inc, Springville, UT *Toll Free Tel:* 800-SKY-BOOK (759-2665) *Toll Free Fax:* 800-388-3727, pg 50

CEF Press, Warrenton, MO *Toll Free Tel:* 800-748-7710 (cust serv); 800-300-4033 (USA ministries), pg 50

Cengage Learning, Boston, MA *Toll Free Tel:* 800-354-9706 *Toll Free Fax:* 800-487-8488, pg 50

The Center for Learning, Culver City, CA *Toll Free Tel:* 800-421-4246 *Toll Free Fax:* 800-944-5432, pg 51

Center for the Collaborative Classroom, Emeryville, CA *Toll Free Tel:* 800-666-7270, pg 51

Centering Corp, Omaha, NE *Toll Free Tel:* 866-218-0101, pg 51

Centre Franco-Ontarien de Ressources en Alphabetisation (Centre FORA), Hanmer, ON Canada *Toll Free Tel:* 888-814-4422 (orders, CN only), pg 450

Chain Store Guide (CSG), Tampa, FL *Toll Free Tel:* 800-927-9292 (orders), pg 52

Chalice Press, St Louis, MO *Toll Free Tel:* 800-366-3383, pg 52

Charisma Media, Lake Mary, FL *Toll Free Tel:* 800-283-8494 (Charisma Media, Siloam Press, Creation House); 800-665-1468, pg 52

CharismaLife Publishers, Lake Mary, FL *Toll Free Tel:* 800-451-4598, pg 52

Charles River Media, Boston, MA *Toll Free Tel:* 800-354-9706 *Toll Free Fax:* 800-487-8488, pg 53

Charles Scribner's Sons®, Farmington Hills, MI *Toll Free Tel:* 800-877-4253 *Toll Free Fax:* 800-414-5043, pg 53

Charlesbridge Publishing Inc, Watertown, MA *Toll Free Tel:* 800-225-3214 *Toll Free Fax:* 800-926-5775, pg 53

The Charlton Press Corp, Kitchener, ON Canada *Toll Free Tel:* 866-663-8827, pg 450

Chartered Professional Accountants of Canada (CPA Canada), Toronto, ON Canada *Toll Free Tel:* 800-268-3793, pg 450

Chelsea Green Publishing Co, White River Junction, VT *Toll Free Tel:* 800-639-4099 (cust serv, consumer & trade orders), pg 53

Chelsea House Publishers, New York, NY *Toll Free Tel:* 800-322-8755 *Toll Free Fax:* 800-678-3633, pg 53

Cheneliere Education Inc, Montreal, QC Canada *Toll Free Tel:* 800-565-5531 *Toll Free Fax:* 800-814-0324, pg 450

Cheng & Tsui Co Inc, Boston, MA *Toll Free Tel:* 800-554-1963, pg 53

Cherry Hill Publishing LLC, Ramona, CA *Toll Free Tel:* 800-407-1072, pg 54

Chicago Review Press, Chicago, IL *Toll Free Tel:* 800-888-4741, pg 54

Child's Play®, Auburn, ME *Toll Free Tel:* 800-639-6404 *Toll Free Fax:* 800-854-6989, pg 54

The Child's World Inc, North Mankato, MN *Toll Free Tel:* 800-599-READ (599-7323) *Toll Free Fax:* 888-320-2329, pg 54

China Books, South San Francisco, CA *Toll Free Tel:* 800-818-2017 (US only), pg 54

Chosen Books, Bloomington, MN *Toll Free Tel:* 800-877-2665 (orders only) *Toll Free Fax:* 800-398-3111 (orders only), pg 54

Christian Liberty Press, Arlington Heights, IL *Toll Free Tel:* 800-832-2741 (cust serv), pg 55

Christian Light Publications Inc, Harrisonburg, VA *Toll Free Tel:* 800-776-0478, pg 55

Christian Schools International, Grand Rapids, MI *Toll Free Tel:* 800-635-8288, pg 55

The Christian Science Publishing Society, Boston, MA *Toll Free Tel:* 800-288-7090, pg 55

Chronicle Books LLC, San Francisco, CA *Toll Free Tel:* 800-759-0190 (cust serv) *Toll Free Fax:* 800-858-7787 (orders); 800-286-9471 (cust serv), pg 55

Cinco Puntos Press, El Paso, TX *Toll Free Tel:* 800-566-9072, pg 56

Circlet Press Inc, Cambridge, MA *Toll Free Tel:* 800-729-6423, pg 56

Cistercian Publications, Collegeville, MN *Toll Free Tel:* 800-436-8431 *Toll Free Fax:* 800-445-5899, pg 56

Clarion Books, New York, NY *Toll Free Tel:* 800-225-3362 (orders) *Toll Free Fax:* 800-634-7568 (orders), pg 56

Clarity Press Inc, Atlanta, GA *Toll Free Tel:* 877-613-1495 (edit) *Toll Free Fax:* 877-613-7868, pg 56

Clear Light Publishers, Santa Fe, NM *Toll Free Tel:* 800-253-2747 (orders), pg 57

Clearfield Co Inc, Baltimore, MD *Toll Free Tel:* 800-296-6687 (orders & cust serv), pg 57

Cleis Press, Berkeley, CA *Toll Free Tel:* 800-780-2279 (US), pg 57

Clerisy Press, Covington, KY *Toll Free Tel:* 888-604-4537, pg 57

Clinical Laboratory & Standards Institute (CLSI), Wayne, PA *Toll Free Tel:* 877-447-1888 (orders), pg 57

Close Up Publishing, Alexandria, VA *Toll Free Tel:* 800-CLOSE-UP (256-7387), pg 57

Coach House Books, Toronto, ON Canada *Toll Free Tel:* 800-367-6360 (outside Toronto), pg 450

Coaches Choice, Monterey, CA *Toll Free Tel:* 888-229-5745, pg 57

Cold Spring Harbor Laboratory Press, Woodbury, NY *Toll Free Tel:* 800-843-4388, pg 58

College & University Professional Association for Human Resources (CUPA-HR), Knoxville, TN *Toll Free Tel:* 877-CUPA-HR4 (287-2474), pg 58

College Publishing, Glen Allen, VA *Toll Free Tel:* 800-827-0723, pg 58

The Colonial Williamsburg Foundation, Williamsburg, VA *Toll Free Tel:* 800-HISTORY (447-8679), pg 58

Columbia University Press, New York, NY *Toll Free Tel:* 800-944-8648, pg 59

Comex Systems Inc, Chester, NJ *Toll Free Tel:* 800-543-6959, pg 59

Common Courage Press, Monroe, ME *Toll Free Tel:* 800-497-3207, pg 59

Commonwealth Editions, Carlisle, MA *Toll Free Tel:* 800-277-5312, pg 59

Company's Coming Publishing Ltd, Vancouver, BC Canada *Toll Free Tel:* 800-661-9017 (CN); 800-518-3541 (US), pg 451

Concordia Publishing House, St Louis, MO *Toll Free Tel:* 800-325-3040 (cust serv) *Toll Free Fax:* 800-490-9889 (cust serv), pg 59

The Connecticut Law Tribune, Hartford, CT *Toll Free Tel:* 877-256-2472, pg 60

The Continuing Legal Education Society of British Columbia (CLEBC), Vancouver, BC Canada *Toll Free Tel:* 800-663-0437 (CN), pg 451

David C Cook, Colorado Springs, CO *Toll Free Tel:* 800-708-5550; 800-323-7543 (orders & cust serv) *Toll Free Fax:* 800-430-0726 (cust serv), pg 60

Copley Custom Textbooks, Acton, MA *Toll Free Tel:* 800-562-2147, pg 60

Copper Canyon Press, Port Townsend, WA *Toll Free Tel:* 877-501-1393 (orders), pg 60

Cortina Institute of Languages, Wilton, CT *Toll Free Tel:* 800-245-2145, pg 61

Cortina Learning International Inc, Wilton, CT *Toll Free Tel:* 800-245-2145, pg 61

Corwin, a Sage Co, Thousand Oaks, CA *Toll Free Tel:* 800-233-9936 *Toll Free Fax:* 800-417-2466, pg 61

Coteau Books, Regina, SK Canada *Toll Free Tel:* 800-440-4471 (CN only), pg 451

Council for Exceptional Children (CEC), Arlington, VA *Toll Free Tel:* 888-232-7733; 866-915-5000 (TTY), pg 62

Council Oak Books LLC, San Francisco, CA *Toll Free Tel:* 888-275-2596, pg 62

Council of State Governments, Lexington, KY *Toll Free Tel:* 800-800-1910, pg 62

CQ Press, Washington, DC *Toll Free Tel:* 866-4CQ-PRESS (427-7737) *Toll Free Fax:* 800-380-3810, pg 63

Crabtree Publishing Co, New York, NY *Toll Free Tel:* 800-387-7650 *Toll Free Fax:* 800-355-7166, pg 63

Crabtree Publishing Co Ltd, St Catharines, ON Canada *Toll Free Tel:* 800-387-7650 *Toll Free Fax:* 800-355-7166, pg 451

Craftsman Book Co, Carlsbad, CA *Toll Free Tel:* 800-829-8123, pg 63

CRC Press, Boca Raton, FL *Toll Free Tel:* 800-272-7737 (orders) *Toll Free Fax:* 800-643-9428 (sales); 800-374-3401 (orders), pg 64

The Creative Co, Mankato, MN *Toll Free Tel:* 800-445-6209, pg 64

Creative Homeowner, East Petersburg, PA *Toll Free Tel:* 800-475-9112 *Toll Free Fax:* 888-369-2885, pg 64

The Crossroad Publishing Co, Chestnut Ridge, NY *Toll Free Tel:* 800-888-4741 (orders), pg 65

Crossway, Wheaton, IL *Toll Free Tel:* 800-635-7993 (orders); 800-543-1659 (cust serv), pg 65

Crown House Publishing Co LLC, White Plains, NY *Toll Free Tel:* 877-925-1213 (cust serv), pg 65

Crown Publishing Group, New York, NY *Toll Free Tel:* 888-264-1745, pg 65

Crystal Clarity Publishers, Nevada City, CA *Toll Free Tel:* 800-424-1055, pg 65

Crystal Productions, Carpinteria, CA *Toll Free Tel:* 800-255-8629 *Toll Free Fax:* 800-657-8149, pg 65

Cumberland House, Naperville, IL *Toll Free Tel:* 800-43-BRIGHT (432-7444), pg 66

Cypress House, Fort Bragg, CA *Toll Free Tel:* 800-773-7782, pg 66

Damron Co, San Francisco, CA *Toll Free Tel:* 800-462-6654, pg 66

John Daniel & Co, McKinleyville, CA *Toll Free Tel:* 800-662-8351, pg 67

The Dartnell Corporation, Durham, NC *Toll Free Tel:* 800-223-8720; 800-472-0148 (cust serv) *Toll Free Fax:* 800-508-2592, pg 67

Data Trace Publishing Co (DTP), Towson, MD *Toll Free Tel:* 800-342-0454 (orders only), pg 67

Davies Publishing Inc, Pasadena, CA *Toll Free Tel:* 877-792-0005, pg 68

F A Davis Co, Philadelphia, PA *Toll Free Tel:* 800-523-4049, pg 68

The Dawn Horse Press, Middletown, CA *Toll Free Tel:* 877-770-0772, pg 68

Dawn Publications Inc, Nevada City, CA *Toll Free Tel:* 800-545-7475, pg 68

DawnSignPress, San Diego, CA *Toll Free Tel:* 800-549-5350, pg 68

Day Owl Press Corp, Lantana, FL *Toll Free Tel:* 888-806-6981 *Toll Free Fax:* 866-854-4375, pg 68

dbS Productions, Charlottesville, VA *Toll Free Tel:* 800-745-1581, pg 68

DC Canada Education Publishing (DCCED), Ottawa, ON Canada *Toll Free Tel:* 888-565-0262, pg 452

DC Entertainment, Burbank, CA *Toll Free Tel:* 800-887-6789, pg 69

Deseret Book Co, Salt Lake City, UT *Toll Free Tel:* 800-453-4532 (orders); 888-846-7302 (orders), pg 69

DEStech Publications Inc, Lancaster, PA *Toll Free Tel:* 877-500-4337, pg 69

Destiny Image Inc, Shippensburg, PA *Toll Free Tel:* 800-722-6774 (orders only), pg 69

DeVorss & Co, Camarillo, CA *Toll Free Tel:* 800-843-5743, pg 70

Dharma Publishing, Cazadero, CA *Toll Free Tel:* 800-873-4276, pg 70

Dial Books for Young Readers, New York, NY *Toll Free Tel:* 800-733-3000 (orders), pg 70

Diane Publishing Co, Collingdale, PA *Toll Free Tel:* 800-782-3833, pg 70

Discovery House Publishers, Grand Rapids, MI *Toll Free Tel:* 800-653-8333 (cust serv), pg 70

Dissertation.com, Boca Raton, FL *Toll Free Tel:* 800-636-8329, pg 71

DK Publishing, New York, NY *Toll Free Tel:* 877-342-5357 (cust serv); 800-733-3000, pg 71

Dogwise Publishing, Wenatchee, WA *Toll Free Tel:* 800-776-2665, pg 71

Tom Doherty Associates, LLC, New York, NY *Toll Free Tel:* 800-455-0340, pg 71

The Donning Company Publishers, Virginia Beach, VA *Toll Free Tel:* 800-296-8572, pg 71

Dordt College Press, Sioux Center, IA *Toll Free Tel:* 800-343-6738, pg 72

Dorland Health, Rockville, MD *Toll Free Tel:* 855-225-5341, pg 72

Dorrance Publishing Co Inc, Pittsburgh, PA *Toll Free Tel:* 800-695-9599; 800-788-7654 (gen cust orders), pg 72

Douglas & McIntyre (2013) Ltd, Madeira Park, BC Canada *Toll Free Tel:* 800-667-2988, pg 452

Dover Publications Inc, Mineola, NY *Toll Free Tel:* 800-223-3130 (orders), pg 72

Down East Books, Rockport, ME *Toll Free Tel:* 800-685-7962 (US orders, cust serv); 800-766-1670, pg 72

Dragon Door Publications, Little Canada, MN *Toll Free Tel:* 800-899-5111 (orders & cust serv), pg 72

Dramatic Publishing Co, Woodstock, IL *Toll Free Tel:* 800-448-7469 *Toll Free Fax:* 800-334-5302, pg 73

Dreamscape Media LLC, Holland, OH *Toll Free Tel:* 877-983-7326, pg 73

Duke University Press, Durham, NC *Toll Free Tel:* 888-651-0122 (US) *Toll Free Fax:* 888-651-0124, pg 73

Dun & Bradstreet, Short Hills, NJ *Toll Free Tel:* 800-526-0651; 800-234-3867 (cust serv), pg 73

Eagan Press, St Paul, MN *Toll Free Tel:* 800-328-7560, pg 74

Eakin Press, Fort Worth, TX *Toll Free Tel:* 888-982-8270, pg 74

Eastland Press, Vista, CA *Toll Free Tel:* 800-453-3278 (orders) *Toll Free Fax:* 800-241-3329 (orders), pg 74

Ecopress, Apple Valley, MN *Toll Free Tel:* 800-846-7027 *Toll Free Fax:* 800-330-6232, pg 75

ECS Publishing Corp, Fenton, MO *Toll Free Tel:* 800-647-2117, pg 75

EDC Publishing, Tulsa, OK *Toll Free Tel:* 800-475-4522 *Toll Free Fax:* 800-743-5660, pg 75

ediciones Lerner, Minneapolis, MN *Toll Free Tel:* 800-328-4929 *Toll Free Fax:* 800-332-1132, pg 75

Editions FouLire, Quebec, QC Canada *Toll Free Tel:* 877-628-4029 (CN & US), pg 454

Les Editions Goelette Inc, Quebec, QC Canada *Toll Free Tel:* 800-463-4961, pg 454

Editions Hurtubise, Montreal, QC Canada *Toll Free Tel:* 800-361-1664, pg 454

Editions Marie-France, Montreal, QC Canada *Toll Free Tel:* 800-563-6644 (CN), pg 455

Editions MultiMondes, Montreal, QC Canada *Toll Free Tel:* 800-361-1664, pg 455

Les Editions Phidal Inc, Montreal, QC Canada *Toll Free Tel:* 800-738-7349, pg 455

Les Editions Un Monde Different, Brossard, QC Canada *Toll Free Tel:* 800-443-2582, pg 455

Editions Yvon Blais, Montreal, QC Canada *Toll Free Tel:* 800-363-3047, pg 456

Editorial Bautista Independiente, Sebring, FL *Toll Free Tel:* 800-398-7187 (US), pg 75

Editorial Portavoz, Grand Rapids, MI *Toll Free Tel:* 877-733-2607 (ext 206), pg 75

Educational Directories Inc (EDI), Schaumburg, IL *Toll Free Tel:* 800-357-6183, pg 76

Educational Impressions Inc, Franklin Lakes, NJ *Toll Free Tel:* 800-451-7450, pg 76

Educational Insights, Gardena, CA *Toll Free Tel:* 800-995-4436 *Toll Free Fax:* 888-892-8731, pg 76

Educators Progress Service Inc, Randolph, WI *Toll Free Tel:* 888-951-4469, pg 76

Edupress Inc, Madison, WI *Toll Free Tel:* 800-835-7978 *Toll Free Fax:* 800-558-9332, pg 76

Wm B Eerdmans Publishing Co, Grand Rapids, MI *Toll Free Tel:* 800-253-7521, pg 76

Eifrig Publishing LLC, Lemont, PA *Toll Free Tel:* 888-340-6543, pg 76

Edward Elgar Publishing Inc, Northampton, MA *Toll Free Tel:* 800-390-3149 (orders), pg 77

Elite Books, Fulton, CA *Toll Free Fax:* 800-330-9798, pg 77

Elsevier, Health Sciences Division, Philadelphia, PA *Toll Free Tel:* 800-523-1649, pg 77

Elsevier Inc, Cambridge, MA *Toll Free Tel:* 866-607-1414, pg 77

EMC Publishing LLC, St Paul, MN *Toll Free Tel:* 800-328-1452 *Toll Free Fax:* 800-328-4564, pg 77

Emerald Books, Seattle, WA *Toll Free Tel:* 800-922-2143, pg 78

Emmaus Road Publishing Inc, Steubenville, OH *Toll Free Tel:* 800-398-5470 (orders), pg 78

Emond Montgomery Publications Ltd, Toronto, ON Canada *Toll Free Tel:* 888-837-0815, pg 456

Encounter Books, New York, NY *Toll Free Tel:* 800-786-3839, pg 78

Encyclopaedia Britannica Inc, Chicago, IL *Toll Free Tel:* 800-323-1229 (US & CN), pg 78

Energy Psychology Press, Santa Rosa, CA *Toll Free Fax:* 800-330-9798, pg 79

Enslow Publishing LLC, New York, NY *Toll Free Tel:* 800-398-2504 *Toll Free Fax:* 877-980-4454, pg 79

Entangled Publishing, Fort Collins, CO *Toll Free Tel:* 877-677-9451, pg 79

Environmental Law Institute, Washington, DC *Toll Free Tel:* 800-433-5120, pg 79

EPS/School Specialty Literacy & Intervention, Cambridge, MA *Toll Free Tel:* 800-225-5750 *Toll Free Fax:* 888-440-2665, pg 79

Evan-Moor Educational Publishers, Monterey, CA *Toll Free Tel:* 800-777-4362 (orders) *Toll Free Fax:* 800-777-4332 (orders), pg 80

Excelsior Editions, Albany, NY *Toll Free Tel:* 866-430-7869, pg 80

Eye in the Ear Children's Audio, Portland, ME *Toll Free Tel:* 855-99-STORY (997-8679), pg 81

Facts On File, New York, NY *Toll Free Tel:* 800-322-8755 *Toll Free Fax:* 800-678-3633, pg 81

Fairchild Books, New York, NY *Toll Free Tel:* 800-932-4724; 888-330-8477 (orders), pg 81

Faith Alive Christian Resources, Grand Rapids, MI *Toll Free Tel:* 800-333-8300 *Toll Free Fax:* 888-642-8606, pg 81

Faith & Fellowship Publishing, Fergus Falls, MN *Toll Free Tel:* 800-332-9232, pg 82

Faith Library Publications, Tulsa, OK *Toll Free Tel:* 888-258-0999 (orders), pg 82

Faithlife Corp, Bellingham, WA *Toll Free Tel:* 800-875-6467, pg 82

FaithWalk Publishing, Lima, OH *Toll Free Tel:* 800-537-1030 (orders: non-bookstore mkts), pg 82

F+W Media Inc, Blue Ash, OH *Toll Free Tel:* 800-289-0963 (trade accts); 800-258-0929 (cust serv), pg 82

Farcountry Press, Helena, MT *Toll Free Tel:* 800-821-3874 (sales off), pg 82

Farrar, Straus & Giroux Books for Young Readers, New York, NY *Toll Free Tel:* 888-330-8477 (orders), pg 82

Father & Son Publishing Inc, Tallahassee, FL *Toll Free Tel:* 800-741-2712 (orders only), pg 83

FC&A Publishing, Peachtree City, GA *Toll Free Tel:* 800-226-8024, pg 83

Federal Street Press, Darien, CT *Toll Free Tel:* 877-886-2830, pg 83

Feldheim Publishers, Nanuet, NY *Toll Free Tel:* 800-237-7149 (orders), pg 83

Ferguson Publishing, New York, NY *Toll Free Tel:* 800-322-8755 *Toll Free Fax:* 800-678-3633, pg 84

Fifth Estate Publishing, Blounstville, AL *Toll Free Tel:* 855-299-2160, pg 84

Fifth House Publishers, Markham, ON Canada *Toll Free Tel:* 800-387-9776 *Toll Free Fax:* 800-260-9777, pg 456

Filter Press LLC, Palmer Lake, CO *Toll Free Tel:* 888-570-2663, pg 84

Finney Company Inc, Apple Valley, MN *Toll Free Tel:* 800-846-7027 *Toll Free Fax:* 800-330-6232, pg 85

Fire Engineering Books & Videos, Tulsa, OK *Toll Free Tel:* 800-752-9764, pg 85

Firefly Books Ltd, Richmond Hill, ON Canada *Toll Free Tel:* 800-387-6192 (CN); 800-387-5085 (US) *Toll Free Fax:* 800-450-0391 (CN); 800-565-6034 (US), pg 456

First Avenue Editions, Minneapolis, MN *Toll Free Tel:* 800-328-4929 *Toll Free Fax:* 800-332-1132, pg 85

Fitzhenry & Whiteside Limited, Markham, ON Canada *Toll Free Tel:* 800-387-9776 *Toll Free Fax:* 800-260-9777, pg 457

FJH Music Co Inc, Fort Lauderdale, FL *Toll Free Tel:* 800-262-8744, pg 85

Flanker Press Ltd, Paradise, NL Canada *Toll Free Tel:* 866-739-4420, pg 457

FleetSeek, Atlanta, GA *Toll Free Tel:* 888-ONLY-TTS (665-9887), pg 85

Flowerpot Press, Oakville, ON Canada *Toll Free Tel:* 866-927-5001, pg 457

Focus on the Family, Colorado Springs, CO *Toll Free Tel:* 800-A-FAMILY (232-6459), pg 86

Fodor's Travel Publications, New York, NY *Toll Free Tel:* 800-733-3000, pg 86

Forum Publishing Co, Centerport, NY *Toll Free Tel:* 800-635-7654, pg 87

Forward Movement, Cincinnati, OH *Toll Free Tel:* 800-543-1813, pg 87

Walter Foster Publishing Inc, Lake Forest, CA *Toll Free Tel:* 800-426-0099; 800-759-0190 (orders), pg 87

The Foundation Center, New York, NY *Toll Free Tel:* 800-424-9836, pg 87

Foundation Press, St Paul, MN *Toll Free Tel:* 877-888-1330, pg 87

Foundation Publications, La Habra, CA *Toll Free Tel:* 800-257-6272, pg 87

Fox Chapel Publishing Co Inc, East Petersburg, PA *Toll Free Tel:* 800-457-9112, pg 87

FPMI Solutions Inc, Huntsville, AL *Toll Free Tel:* 888-644-3764, pg 87

Franciscan Media, Cincinnati, OH *Toll Free Tel:* 800-488-0488, pg 87

Franklin, Beedle & Associates Inc, Portland, OR *Toll Free Tel:* 800-322-2665, pg 88

Free Spirit Publishing Inc, Minneapolis, MN *Toll Free Tel:* 800-735-7323 *Toll Free Fax:* 866-419-5199, pg 88

Samuel French Inc, New York, NY *Toll Free Tel:* 866-598-8449, pg 88

Fresh Air Books, Nashville, TN *Toll Free Tel:* 800-972-0433 (orders), pg 88

Fulcrum Publishing Inc, Golden, CO *Toll Free Tel:* 800-992-2908 *Toll Free Fax:* 800-726-7112, pg 89

FurnitureCore, Atlanta, GA *Toll Free Tel:* 800-826-8868, pg 89

Future Horizons Inc, Arlington, TX *Toll Free Tel:* 800-489-0727, pg 89

Gaetan Morin Editeur, Montreal, QC Canada *Toll Free Tel:* 800-565-5531 *Toll Free Fax:* 800-814-0324, pg 457

Galaxy Press, Hollywood, CA *Toll Free Tel:* 877-8GALAXY (842-5299), pg 89

Galde Press Inc, Lakeville, MN *Toll Free Tel:* 800-777-3454, pg 89

Gale, Farmington Hills, MI *Toll Free Tel:* 800-877-4253 *Toll Free Fax:* 800-414-5043 (orders), pg 89

Gallery Books, New York, NY *Toll Free Tel:* 800-456-6798, pg 90

Gallopade International Inc, Peachtree City, GA *Toll Free Tel:* 800-536-2GET (536-2438) *Toll Free Fax:* 800-871-2979, pg 90

Gareth Stevens Publishing, New York, NY *Toll Free Tel:* 800-542-2595 *Toll Free Fax:* 877-542-2596 (cust serv), pg 90

Gatekeeper Press, Columbus, OH *Toll Free Tel:* 866-535-0913, pg 90

Gateways Books & Tapes, Nevada City, CA *Toll Free Tel:* 800-869-0658, pg 90

Gefen Books, Lawrence, NY *Toll Free Tel:* 800-477-5257, pg 91

Gem Guides Book Co, Upland, CA *Toll Free Tel:* 800-824-5118 (orders), pg 91

Genealogical Publishing Co, Baltimore, MD *Toll Free Tel:* 800-296-6687 *Toll Free Fax:* 800-599-9561, pg 91

Genesis Press Inc, Columbus, MS *Toll Free Tel:* 888-463-4461 (orders only), pg 91

GeoLytics Inc, Branchburg, NJ *Toll Free Tel:* 800-577-6717, pg 91

Getty Publications, Los Angeles, CA *Toll Free Tel:* 800-223-3431 (orders), pg 92

GIA Publications Inc, Chicago, IL *Toll Free Tel:* 800-GIA-1358 (442-1358), pg 92

Gibbs Smith Publisher, Layton, UT *Toll Free Tel:* 800-748-5439; 800-835-4993 (orders) *Toll Free Fax:* 800-213-3023 (orders only), pg 92

Glenbridge Publishing Ltd, Centennial, CO *Toll Free Tel:* 800-986-4135 (orders), pg 93

Global Training Center Inc, El Paso, TX *Toll Free Tel:* 800-860-5030, pg 93

The Globe Pequot Press, Guilford, CT *Toll Free Tel:* 800-243-0495 (orders only); 888-249-7586 (cust serv) *Toll Free Fax:* 800-820-2329 (orders & cust serv), pg 93

Golden West Cookbooks, Phoenix, AZ *Toll Free Tel:* 800-521-9221, pg 94

Goodheart-Willcox Publisher, Tinley Park, IL *Toll Free Tel:* 800-323-0440 *Toll Free Fax:* 888-409-3900, pg 94

Goose Lane Editions, Fredericton, NB Canada *Toll Free Tel:* 888-926-8377, pg 458

Goosebottom Books, Foster City, CA *Toll Free Fax:* 888-407-5286, pg 94

Gospel Publishing House (GPH), Springfield, MO *Toll Free Tel:* 800-641-4310 *Toll Free Fax:* 800-328-0294, pg 94

Graphic Universe™, Minneapolis, MN *Toll Free Tel:* 800-328-4929 *Toll Free Fax:* 800-332-1132, pg 95

Gray & Company Publishers, Cleveland, OH *Toll Free Tel:* 800-915-3609, pg 95

Great Quotations Inc, Downers Grove, IL *Toll Free Tel:* 800-830-3020, pg 96

Green Dragon Books, Palm Beach, FL *Toll Free Tel:* 800-874-8844 *Toll Free Fax:* 888-874-8844, pg 96

Greenhaven Press®, New York, NY *Toll Free Tel:* 800-237-9932 *Toll Free Fax:* 888-436-4643, pg 96

Grey House Publishing Inc™, Amenia, NY *Toll Free Tel:* 800-562-2139, pg 96

Group Publishing Inc, Loveland, CO *Toll Free Tel:* 800-447-1070, pg 96

Groupe Educalivres Inc, Laval, QC Canada *Toll Free Tel:* 800-567-3671 (info serv), pg 458

Groupe Modulo, Montreal, QC Canada *Toll Free Tel:* 800-565-5531 *Toll Free Fax:* 800-814-0324, pg 458

Grove Atlantic Inc, New York, NY *Toll Free Tel:* 800-521-0178, pg 97

Gryphon Editions, Omaha, NE *Toll Free Tel:* 888-655-0134 (US & CN), pg 97

Gryphon House Inc, Lewisville, NC *Toll Free Tel:* 800-638-0928 *Toll Free Fax:* 877-638-7576, pg 97

Guideposts Book & Inspirational Media, New York, NY *Toll Free Tel:* 800-431-2344 (cust serv), pg 97

The Guilford Press, New York, NY *Toll Free Tel:* 800-365-7006, pg 97

Hachette Book Group, New York, NY *Toll Free Tel:* 800-759-0190 (cust serv) *Toll Free Fax:* 800-286-9471 (cust serv), pg 98

Hackett Publishing Co Inc, Indianapolis, IN *Toll Free Fax:* 800-783-9213, pg 98

Hagstrom Map, Wilmington, DE *Toll Free Tel:* 800-432-MAPS (432-6277) *Toll Free Fax:* 888-210-9654, pg 99

Hal Leonard Books, Montclair, NJ *Toll Free Tel:* 800-637-2852, pg 99

Hamilton Books, Lanham, MD *Toll Free Tel:* 800-462-6420 (cust serv) *Toll Free Fax:* 800-388-4550 (cust serv), pg 99

Hampton Press Inc, New York, NY *Toll Free Tel:* 800-894-8955, pg 100

Hampton Roads Publishing Co, Newburyport, MA *Toll Free Tel:* 800-423-7087 (orders) *Toll Free Fax:* 877-337-3309, pg 100

Hancock House Publishers, Blaine, WA *Toll Free Tel:* 800-938-1114 *Toll Free Fax:* 800-983-2262, pg 100

Hancock House Publishers Ltd, Surrey, BC Canada *Toll Free Tel:* 800-938-1114 *Toll Free Fax:* 800-983-2262, pg 459

Handprint Books Inc, Brooklyn, NY *Toll Free Tel:* 800-722-6657 (orders) *Toll Free Fax:* 800-858-7787 (orders), pg 100

Hanser Publications LLC, Cincinnati, OH *Toll Free Tel:* 800-950-8977; 877-751-5052 (orders), pg 100

Harbour Publishing Co Ltd, Madeira Park, BC Canada *Toll Free Tel:* 800-667-2988, pg 459

Hard Shell Word Factory, Cincinnati, OH *Toll Free Tel:* 888-232-0808 *Toll Free Fax:* 888-460-4752, pg 100

Harlequin Enterprises Ltd, Don Mills, ON Canada *Toll Free Tel:* 888-432-4879; 800-370-5838 (ebook inquiries), pg 459

Harper's Magazine Foundation, New York, NY *Toll Free Tel:* 800-444-4653, pg 102

Harrison House Publishers, Tulsa, OK *Toll Free Tel:* 800-888-4126 *Toll Free Fax:* 800-830-5688, pg 102

Hartman Publishing Inc, Albuquerque, NM *Toll Free Tel:* 800-999-9534 *Toll Free Fax:* 800-474-6106, pg 102

Harvard Education Publishing Group, Cambridge, MA *Toll Free Tel:* 800-513-0763 (subns); 888-437-1437 (orders), pg 102

Harvard University Press, Cambridge, MA *Toll Free Tel:* 800-405-1619 (orders) *Toll Free Fax:* 800-406-9145 (orders), pg 103

Harvest House Publishers Inc, Eugene, OR *Toll Free Tel:* 888-501-6991, pg 103

Hay House Inc, Carlsbad, CA *Toll Free Tel:* 800-654-5126 (ext 2, US) *Toll Free Fax:* 800-650-5115, pg 103

Haynes Manuals Inc, Newbury Park, CA *Toll Free Tel:* 800-4-HAYNES (442-9637), pg 104

Hazelden Publishing, Center City, MN *Toll Free Tel:* 800-257-7810, pg 104

HCPro Inc, Danvers, MA *Toll Free Tel:* 800-650-6787 *Toll Free Fax:* 800-785-9212, pg 104

Health Communications Inc, Deerfield Beach, FL *Toll Free Tel:* 800-851-9100; 800-441-5569 (cust serv & orders) *Toll Free Fax:* 800-424-7652 (cust serv & orders), pg 104

Health Forum Inc, Chicago, IL *Toll Free Tel:* 800-242-2626, pg 104

Health Professions Press, Towson, MD *Toll Free Tel:* 888-337-8808, pg 104

Health Research Books, Pomeroy, WA *Toll Free Tel:* 888-844-2386, pg 105

HeartMath LLC, Boulder Creek, CA *Toll Free Tel:* 800-450-9111, pg 105

Hearts 'n Tummies Cookbook Co, Wever, IA *Toll Free Tel:* 800-571-2665, pg 105

Heian, Albany, CA *Toll Free Fax:* 888-411-8527, pg 105

William S Hein & Co Inc, Getzville, NY *Toll Free Tel:* 800-828-7571, pg 105

Heinemann, Portsmouth, NH *Toll Free Tel:* 800-225-5800 (US) *Toll Free Fax:* 877-231-6980 (US), pg 105

Hellgate Press, Ashland, OR *Toll Free Tel:* 800-795-4059, pg 105

Hendrickson Publishers Inc, Peabody, MA *Toll Free Tel:* 800-358-3111, pg 106

Herald Press, Harrisonburg, VA *Toll Free Tel:* 800-245-7894 (orders) *Toll Free Fax:* 877-271-0760, pg 106

Herald Publishing House, Independence, MO *Toll Free Tel:* 800-767-8181, pg 106

Heritage Books Inc, Berwyn Heights, MD *Toll Free Tel:* 800-876-6103 *Toll Free Fax:* 800-876-6103, pg 106

The Heritage Foundation, Washington, DC *Toll Free Tel:* 800-544-4843, pg 106

Heuer Publishing LLC, Cedar Rapids, IA *Toll Free Tel:* 800-950-7529, pg 106

Hewitt Homeschooling Resources, Washougal, WA *Toll Free Tel:* 800-348-1750, pg 106

High Plains Press, Glendo, WY *Toll Free Tel:* 800-552-7819, pg 107

Highlights for Children, Columbus, OH *Toll Free Tel:* 800-962-3661 (Highlights Club cust serv); 800-255-9517 (Highlights Magazine cust serv), pg 107

Hillsdale College Press, Hillsdale, MI *Toll Free Tel:* 800-437-2268, pg 107

Himalayan Institute Press, Honesdale, PA *Toll Free Tel:* 800-822-4547, pg 107

Hobar Publications, Apple Valley, MN *Toll Free Tel:* 800-846-7027 *Toll Free Fax:* 800-330-6232, pg 108

Hogrefe Publishing Corp, Boston, MA *Toll Free Tel:* 866-823-4726, pg 108

Hohm Press, Chino Valley, AZ *Toll Free Tel:* 800-381-2700, pg 108

Henry Holt and Company, LLC, New York, NY *Toll Free Tel:* 888-330-8477 (orders), pg 109

Homa & Sekey Books, Paramus, NJ *Toll Free Tel:* 800-870-HOMA (870-4662 orders), pg 110

Hoover Institution Press, Stanford, CA *Toll Free Tel:* 800-935-2882, pg 110

Hoover's Inc, Austin, TX *Toll Free Tel:* 844-201-0407; 888-234-4567 (sales), pg 110

Hope Publishing Co, Carol Stream, IL *Toll Free Tel:* 800-323-1049, pg 110

Houghton Mifflin Harcourt, Boston, MA *Toll Free Tel:* 855-969-4642; 800-225-5425 (K-12 educ materials); 800-323-9540 (assessment materials); 877-219-1537 (SkillsTutor); 888-242-6747 (Innovation in Educ Group); 800-225-3362 (Trade & Ref Div) *Toll Free Fax:* 800-269-5232, pg 110

Houghton Mifflin Harcourt Assessments, Itasca, IL *Toll Free Tel:* 800-323-9540, pg 111

Houghton Mifflin Harcourt K-12 Publishers, Boston, MA *Toll Free Tel:* 800-225-5425 (cust serv), pg 111

Houghton Mifflin Harcourt Trade & Reference Division, Boston, MA *Toll Free Tel:* 800-225-3362, pg 111

House to House Publications, Lititz, PA *Toll Free Tel:* 800-848-5892, pg 112

HRD Press, Amherst, MA *Toll Free Tel:* 800-822-2801, pg 112

Human Kinetics Inc, Champaign, IL *Toll Free Tel:* 800-747-4457, pg 112

Humanix Books LLC, New York, NY *Toll Free Tel:* 855-371-7810, pg 113

Huntington Press Publishing, Las Vegas, NV *Toll Free Tel:* 800-244-2224, pg 113

I-5 Publishing LLC, Irvine, CA *Toll Free Tel:* 888-738-2665, pg 113

Ibex Publishers, Bethesda, MD *Toll Free Tel:* 888-718-8188, pg 113

IEEE Computer Society, Washington, DC *Toll Free Tel:* 800-272-6657 (memb info), pg 113

Ignatius Press, San Francisco, CA *Toll Free Tel:* 800-651-1531 (orders); 888-615-3186 (cust serv), pg 114

IHS Jane's, Alexandria, VA *Toll Free Tel:* 800-824-0768 (sales) *Toll Free Fax:* 800-836-0297, pg 114

IHS Press, Norfolk, VA *Toll Free Tel:* 877-447-7737 *Toll Free Fax:* 877-447-7737, pg 114

Imagination Publishing Group, Dunedin, FL *Toll Free Tel:* 888-701-6481, pg 114

ImaJinn Books, Phoenix, AZ *Toll Free Tel:* 877-625-3592 (US & CN), pg 115

Impact Publications/Development Concepts Inc, Manassas Park, VA *Toll Free Tel:* 800-361-1055 (cust serv), pg 115

Incentive Publications by World Book, Chicago, IL *Toll Free Tel:* 800-967-5325; 800-975-3250; 888-482-9764 (trade dept) *Toll Free Fax:* 888-922-3766, pg 115

Independent Institute, Oakland, CA *Toll Free Tel:* 800-927-8733, pg 115

Indiana Historical Society Press (IHS Press), Indianapolis, IN *Toll Free Tel:* 800-447-1830 (orders), pg 115

Indiana University Press, Bloomington, IN *Toll Free Tel:* 800-842-6796 (orders only), pg 116

Industrial Press Inc, Norwalk, CT *Toll Free Tel:* 888-528-7852 ext 0 (cust serv), pg 116

Information Today, Inc, Medford, NJ *Toll Free Tel:* 800-300-9868 (cust serv), pg 116

Inner Traditions International Ltd, Rochester, VT *Toll Free Tel:* 800-246-8648, pg 117

Insight Editions, San Rafael, CA *Toll Free Tel:* 800-809-3792 *Toll Free Fax:* 866-509-0515, pg 117

Institute of Continuing Legal Education, Ann Arbor, MI *Toll Free Tel:* 877-229-4350 *Toll Free Fax:* 877-229-4351, pg 117

Institute of Psychological Research, Inc., Montreal, QC Canada *Toll Free Tel:* 800-363-7800 *Toll Free Fax:* 888-382-3007, pg 460

The Institutes™, Malvern, PA *Toll Free Tel:* 800-644-2101, pg 118

Intercultural Press Inc, Boston, MA *Toll Free Tel:* 888-273-2539, pg 118

Interlink Publishing Group Inc, Northampton, MA *Toll Free Tel:* 800-238-LINK (238-5465), pg 118

International City/County Management Association (ICMA), Washington, DC *Toll Free Tel:* 800-745-8780, pg 119

International Code Council Inc, Brea, CA *Toll Free Tel:* 888-422-7233, pg 119

International Foundation of Employee Benefit Plans, Brookfield, WI *Toll Free Tel:* 888-334-3327, pg 119

International Linguistics Corp, Kansas City, MO *Toll Free Tel:* 800-237-1830 (orders), pg 119

International Literacy Association (ILA), Newark, DE *Toll Free Tel:* 800-336-7323 (US & CN), pg 119

International Society for Technology in Education, Arlington, VA *Toll Free Tel:* 800-336-5191 (US & CN), pg 120

International Wealth Success Inc, Merrick, NY *Toll Free Tel:* 800-323-0548, pg 120

InterVarsity Press, Westmont, IL *Toll Free Tel:* 800-843-9487, pg 120

Interweave Press LLC, Loveland, CO *Toll Free Tel:* 800-272-2193; 800-289-0963 *Toll Free Fax:* 888-590-4082, pg 120

Irwin Law Inc, Toronto, ON Canada *Toll Free Tel:* 888-314-9014, pg 461

ISI Books, Wilmington, DE *Toll Free Tel:* 800-526-7022, pg 121

Island Press, Washington, DC *Toll Free Tel:* 800-828-1302, pg 121

iUniverse, Bloomington, IN *Toll Free Tel:* 800-AUTHORS (288-4677), pg 121

Richard Ivey School of Business, London, ON Canada *Toll Free Tel:* 800-649-6355, pg 461

JayJo Books LLC, Melville, NY *Toll Free Tel:* 800-999-6884 *Toll Free Fax:* 800-262-1886, pg 121

Jewish Publication Society, Philadelphia, PA *Toll Free Tel:* 800-234-3151, pg 122

JIST Publishing, St Paul, MN *Toll Free Tel:* 800-328-1452 *Toll Free Fax:* 800-328-4564, pg 122

John Deere Publishing, Davenport, IA *Toll Free Tel:* 800-522-7448 (orders), pg 122

The Johns Hopkins University Press, Baltimore, MD *Toll Free Tel:* 800-537-5487 (book orders & cust serv); 800-548-1784 (journal orders), pg 122

Jones & Bartlett Learning LLC, Burlington, MA *Toll Free Tel:* 800-832-0034, pg 123

Jones McClure Publishing, Houston, TX *Toll Free Tel:* 800-626-6667, pg 123

Joy Publishing Co, Fountain Valley, CA *Toll Free Tel:* 800-454-8228 (orders), pg 123

Judaica Press Inc, Brooklyn, NY *Toll Free Tel:* 800-972-6201, pg 123

Judson Press, King of Prussia, PA *Toll Free Tel:* 800-458-3766, pg 123

Jump!, Minneapolis, MN *Toll Free Tel:* 888-799-1860 *Toll Free Fax:* 800-675-6679, pg 123

Just World Books LLC, Charlottesville, VA *Toll Free Tel:* 888-506-3769, pg 124

Kaeden Corp, Rocky River, OH *Toll Free Tel:* 800-890-7323, pg 124

Kalmbach Publishing Co, Waukesha, WI *Toll Free Tel:* 800-533-6644 (cust serv & orders); 800-558-1544, pg 124

Kar-Ben Publishing, Minneapolis, MN *Toll Free Tel:* 800-4-KARBEN (452-7236) *Toll Free Fax:* 800-332-1132, pg 124

J J Keller & Associates, Inc, Neenah, WI *Toll Free Tel:* 877-564-2333 *Toll Free Fax:* 800-727-7516, pg 125

Kendall Hunt Publishing Co, Dubuque, IA *Toll Free Tel:* 800-228-0810 (orders) *Toll Free Fax:* 800-772-9165, pg 125

Kennedy Information Inc, Keene, NH *Toll Free Tel:* 800-531-0140, pg 125

Kensington Publishing Corp, New York, NY *Toll Free Tel:* 800-221-2647, pg 125

Kids Can Press Ltd, Toronto, ON Canada *Toll Free Tel:* 800-265-0884, pg 461

Kindred Productions, Winnipeg, MB Canada *Toll Free Tel:* 800-545-7322, pg 461

Jessica Kingsley Publishers Inc, Philadelphia, PA *Toll Free Tel:* 866-416-1078 (cust serv), pg 126

Kirk House Publishers, Minneapolis, MN *Toll Free Tel:* 888-696-1828, pg 126

Kirkbride Bible Co Inc, Indianapolis, IN *Toll Free Tel:* 800-428-4385, pg 126

Wolters Kluwer Law & Business, New York, NY *Toll Free Tel:* 800-234-1660 (cust serv), pg 127

Allen A Knoll Publishers, Santa Barbara, CA *Toll Free Tel:* 800-777-7623, pg 127

Alfred A Knopf/Everyman's Library, New York, NY *Toll Free Tel:* 800-638-6460, pg 127

Knopf Canada, Toronto, ON Canada *Toll Free Tel:* 888-523-9292, pg 462

Koho Pono LLC, Clackamas, OR *Toll Free Tel:* 800-937-8000 (orders) *Toll Free Fax:* 800-876-0186 (orders), pg 127

HJ Kramer Inc, Tiburon, CA *Toll Free Tel:* 800-972-6657, pg 128

Krause Publications Inc, Iola, WI *Toll Free Tel:* 800-258-0929 (cust serv); 888-457-2873 (orders), pg 128

Kregel Publications, Grand Rapids, MI *Toll Free Tel:* 800-733-2607, pg 128

Lake Superior Port Cities Inc, Duluth, MN *Toll Free Tel:* 888-BIG-LAKE (244-5253), pg 129

LAMA Books, Hayward, CA *Toll Free Tel:* 888-452-6244, pg 129

Lanahan Publishers Inc, Baltimore, MD *Toll Free Tel:* 866-345-1949, pg 129

Landauer Corp, Urbandale, IA *Toll Free Tel:* 800-557-2144, pg 129

Peter Lang Publishing Inc, New York, NY *Toll Free Tel:* 800-770-5264 (cust serv), pg 129

LangMarc Publishing, Austin, TX *Toll Free Tel:* 800-864-1648 (orders), pg 129

Larson Publications, Burdett, NY *Toll Free Tel:* 800-828-2197, pg 129

Laughing Elephant, Seattle, WA *Toll Free Tel:* 800-354-0400, pg 130

Laurier Books Ltd, Ottawa, ON Canada *Toll Free Fax:* 855-736-9160, pg 462

The Lawbook Exchange Ltd, Clark, NJ *Toll Free Tel:* 800-422-6686, pg 130

Lawyers & Judges Publishing Co Inc, Tucson, AZ *Toll Free Tel:* 800-209-7109 *Toll Free Fax:* 800-330-8795, pg 130

Leadership Directories, New York, NY *Toll Free Tel:* 800-627-0311, pg 130

Leadership Ministries Worldwide/OBR, Chattanooga, TN *Toll Free Tel:* 800-987-8790, pg 130

THE Learning Connection®, Orlando, FL *Toll Free Tel:* 800-218-8489, pg 131

Learning Links Inc, Cranbury, NJ *Toll Free Tel:* 888-960-2508, pg 131

LearningExpress LLC, New York, NY *Toll Free Tel:* 800-295-9556 (ext 2), pg 131

Lectorum Publications Inc, Lyndhurst, NJ *Toll Free Tel:* 800-345-5946 *Toll Free Fax:* 877-532-8676, pg 131

Lederer Books, Clarksville, MD *Toll Free Tel:* 800-410-7367 (orders), pg 131

Lee & Low Books Inc, New York, NY *Toll Free Tel:* 888-320-3190 (ext 28, orders only), pg 131

Leisure Arts Inc, Maumelle, AR *Toll Free Tel:* 800-643-8030, pg 132

Lerner Publications, Minneapolis, MN *Toll Free Tel:* 800-328-4929 *Toll Free Fax:* 800-332-1132, pg 132

Lerner Publishing Group Inc, Minneapolis, MN *Toll Free Tel:* 800-328-4929 *Toll Free Fax:* 800-332-1132, pg 132

LernerClassroom, Minneapolis, MN *Toll Free Tel:* 800-328-4929 *Toll Free Fax:* 800-332-1132, pg 132

Lessiter Media, Brookfield, WI *Toll Free Tel:* 800-645-8455, pg 132

LexisNexis®, New York, NY *Toll Free Fax:* 800-437-8674, pg 133

LexisNexis® Canada Inc, Toronto, ON Canada *Toll Free Tel:* 800-668-6481; 800-387-0899 (cust care); 800-255-5174 (sales), pg 462

Liberty Fund Inc, Indianapolis, IN *Toll Free Tel:* 800-955-8335; 800-866-3520; 800-368-7897 ext 6069 (cust serv), pg 133

Libraries Unlimited, Santa Barbara, CA *Toll Free Tel:* 800-368-6868 *Toll Free Fax:* 866-270-3856, pg 133

Lidec Inc, Saint-Jean-sur-Richlieu, QC Canada *Toll Free Tel:* 800-350-5991 (CN only), pg 462

Mary Ann Liebert Inc, New Rochelle, NY *Toll Free Tel:* 800-654-3237, pg 133

Life Cycle Books, Fort Collins, CO *Toll Free Tel:* 800-214-5849 *Toll Free Fax:* 888-690-8532, pg 134

Life Cycle Books Ltd, Toronto, ON Canada *Toll Free Tel:* 866-880-5860 *Toll Free Fax:* 866-260-8172, pg 462

Light Technology Publishing, Flagstaff, AZ *Toll Free Tel:* 800-450-0985, pg 134

Liguori Publications, Liguori, MO *Toll Free Tel:* 866-848-2492; 800-325-9521 *Toll Free Fax:* 800-325-9526 (sales), pg 134

Linden Publishing Co Inc, Fresno, CA *Toll Free Tel:* 800-345-4447 (orders), pg 134

Linworth Publishing, Santa Barbara, CA *Toll Free Tel:* 800-368-6868 *Toll Free Fax:* 866-270-3856, pg 135

Lippincott Williams & Wilkins, New York, NY *Toll Free Tel:* 800-950-2035, pg 135

Listen & Live Audio Inc, Union City, NJ *Toll Free Tel:* 800-653-9400 (orders), pg 135

Little, Brown Books for Young Readers, New York, NY *Toll Free Tel:* 800-759-0190 (cust serv), pg 136

The Little Entrepreneur, Detroit, MI *Toll Free Tel:* 888-435-9234, pg 136

Liturgical Press, Collegeville, MN *Toll Free Tel:* 800-858-5450 *Toll Free Fax:* 800-445-5899, pg 136

Liturgy Training Publications, Chicago, IL *Toll Free Tel:* 800-933-1800 (US & CN only orders) *Toll Free Fax:* 800-933-7094 (US & CN only orders), pg 136

Living Language, New York, NY *Toll Free Tel:* 800-733-3000 (orders) *Toll Free Fax:* 800-659-2436, pg 136

Living Stream Ministry (LSM), Anaheim, CA *Toll Free Tel:* 800-549-5164, pg 136

Llewellyn Publications, Woodbury, MN *Toll Free Tel:* 800-843-6666, pg 137

The Local History Co, Pittsburgh, PA *Toll Free Tel:* 866-362-0789 (orders), pg 137

Lone Pine Publishing, Vancouver, BC Canada *Toll Free Tel:* 800-661-9017 *Toll Free Fax:* 800-424-7173, pg 462

Lonely Planet, Oakland, CA *Toll Free Tel:* 800-275-8555 (orders), pg 137

Looseleaf Law Publications Inc, Flushing, NY *Toll Free Tel:* 800-647-5547, pg 137

Lorenz Educational Press, Dayton, OH *Toll Free Tel:* 800-444-1144, pg 137

Lotus Press, Twin Lakes, WI *Toll Free Tel:* 800-824-6396 (orders), pg 138

Love Publishing Co, Denver, CO *Toll Free Tel:* 877-240-6396, pg 138

Loving Healing Press Inc, Ann Arbor, MI *Toll Free Tel:* 888-761-6268 (US & CN), pg 138

Loyola Press, Chicago, IL *Toll Free Tel:* 800-621-1008, pg 138

LRP Publications, Palm Beach Gardens, FL *Toll Free Tel:* 800-341-7874, pg 139

LRS, Torrance, CA *Toll Free Tel:* 800-255-5002, pg 139

Lucent Books®, New York, NY *Toll Free Tel:* 800-237-9932 *Toll Free Fax:* 888-436-4643, pg 139

Lutheran Braille Workers Inc, Yucaipa, CA *Toll Free Tel:* 800-925-6092, pg 139

Macmillan Audio, New York, NY *Toll Free Tel:* 888-330-8477 (cust serv), pg 140

Macmillan Reference USA™, Farmington Hills, MI *Toll Free Tel:* 800-877-4253 *Toll Free Fax:* 877-363-4253, pg 140

Madonna House Publications, Combermere, ON Canada *Toll Free Tel:* 888-703-7110 *Toll Free Fax:* 877-717-2888, pg 462

Maharishi University of Management Press, Fairfield, IA *Toll Free Tel:* 800-831-6523, pg 140

Mandala Earth, San Rafael, CA *Toll Free Fax:* 866-509-0515, pg 141

MAR*CO Products Inc, Hatfield, PA *Toll Free Tel:* 800-448-2197, pg 141

Marathon Press, Norfolk, NE *Toll Free Tel:* 800-228-0629, pg 141

Maren Green Publishing Inc, Oak Park Heights, MN *Toll Free Tel:* 800-287-1512, pg 141

Marion Street Press LLC, Portland, OR *Toll Free Fax:* 866-571-8359, pg 142

Marquis Who's Who, Berkeley Heights, NJ *Toll Free Tel:* 844-394-6946, pg 142

Marshall & Swift, Los Angeles, CA *Toll Free Tel:* 800-544-2678, pg 143

Marshall Cavendish Corp, Tarrytown, NY *Toll Free Tel:* 800-821-9881, pg 143

Martindale LLC, New Providence, NJ *Toll Free Tel:* 800-526-4902, pg 143

Martingale®, Bothell, WA *Toll Free Tel:* 800-426-3126, pg 143

Mason Crest Publishers, Broomall, PA *Toll Free Tel:* 866-MCP-BOOK (627-2665), pg 143

Mastery Education, Saddle Brook, NJ *Toll Free Tel:* 800-822-1080, pg 144

Math Solutions®, Sausalito, CA *Toll Free Tel:* 800-868-9092 *Toll Free Fax:* 877-942-8837, pg 144

Math Teachers Press Inc, Minneapolis, MN *Toll Free Tel:* 800-852-2435, pg 144

The Mathematical Association of America, Washington, DC *Toll Free Tel:* 800-741-9415, pg 144

Maven House Press, Palmyra, VA *Toll Free Fax:* 888-894-3403, pg 144

McCutchan Publishing Corp, Richmond, CA *Toll Free Tel:* 800-227-1540, pg 145

The McDonald & Woodward Publishing Co, Newark, OH *Toll Free Tel:* 800-233-8787, pg 145

McFarland, Jefferson, NC *Toll Free Tel:* 800-253-2187 (orders), pg 145

McGraw-Hill Career Education, Burr Ridge, IL *Toll Free Tel:* 800-338-3987 (cust serv), pg 145

McGraw-Hill Contemporary Learning Series, Dubuque, IA *Toll Free Tel:* 800-243-6532, pg 145

McGraw-Hill Create, New York, NY *Toll Free Tel:* 800-962-9342, pg 145

McGraw-Hill Higher Education, Burr Ridge, IL *Toll Free Tel:* 800-338-3987 (cust serv), pg 146

McGraw-Hill Humanities, Social Sciences, Languages, New York, NY *Toll Free Tel:* 800-338-3987 (cust serv), pg 146

McGraw-Hill/Irwin, Burr Ridge, IL *Toll Free Tel:* 800-338-3987 (cust serv), pg 146

McGraw-Hill Ryerson Limited, Whitby, ON Canada *Toll Free Tel:* 800-565-5758 (cust serv) *Toll Free Fax:* 800-463-5885, pg 463

McGraw-Hill School Education Group, Columbus, OH *Toll Free Tel:* 800-848-1567, pg 146

McGraw-Hill Science, Engineering, Mathematics, Dubuque, IA *Toll Free Tel:* 800-338-3987 (cust serv), pg 146

MDR, A D&B Co, Shelton, CT *Toll Free Tel:* 800-333-8802 *Toll Free Fax:* 866-532-7097, pg 147

Meadowbrook Press, Minnetonka, MN *Toll Free Tel:* 800-338-2232, pg 147

me+mi publishing inc, Wheaton, IL *Toll Free Tel:* 888-251-1444, pg 147

R S Means from The Gordian Group, Rockland, MA *Toll Free Tel:* 800-448-8182 *Toll Free Fax:* 800-632-6701, pg 147

Medical Group Management Association (MGMA), Englewood, CO *Toll Free Tel:* 877-275-6462, pg 147

Medical Physics Publishing Corp (MPP), Madison, WI *Toll Free Tel:* 800-442-5778 (cust serv), pg 147

MedMaster Inc, Fort Lauderdale, FL *Toll Free Tel:* 800-335-3480, pg 148

The Russell Meerdink Co Ltd, Neenah, WI *Toll Free Tel:* 800-635-6499, pg 148

Mel Bay Publications Inc, Pacific, MO *Toll Free Tel:* 800-863-5229 *Toll Free Fax:* 800-660-9818, pg 148

Menasha Ridge Press Inc, Birmingham, AL *Toll Free Tel:* 888-604-4537, pg 148

MennoMedia, Harrisonburg, VA *Toll Free Tel:* 800-245-7894 (orders & cust serv US) *Toll Free Fax:* 877-271-0760, pg 148

Mercer University Press, Macon, GA *Toll Free Tel:* 866-895-1472, pg 148

Meriwether Publishing, Englewood, CO *Toll Free Tel:* 800-333-7262, pg 149

Merriam-Webster Inc, Springfield, MA *Toll Free Tel:* 800-828-1880 (orders & cust serv), pg 149

Mesorah Publications Ltd, Brooklyn, NY *Toll Free Tel:* 800-637-6724, pg 149

Messianic Jewish Publishers, Clarksville, MD *Toll Free Tel:* 800-410-7367 (orders) *Toll Free Fax:* 800-327-0048 (orders), pg 149

MGI Management Institute Inc, Hawthorne, NY *Toll Free Tel:* 800-932-0191, pg 149

Michelin Maps & Guides, Greenville, SC *Toll Free Fax:* 866-297-0914; 888-773-7979, pg 149

Michigan Municipal League, Ann Arbor, MI *Toll Free Tel:* 800-653-2483, pg 150

Mike Murach & Associates Inc, Fresno, CA *Toll Free Tel:* 800-221-5528, pg 150

Milady, Clifton Park, NY *Toll Free Tel:* 800-998-7498, pg 150

Milkweed Editions, Minneapolis, MN *Toll Free Tel:* 800-520-6455, pg 151

Millbrook Press, Minneapolis, MN *Toll Free Tel:* 800-328-4929 (US only) *Toll Free Fax:* 800-332-1132, pg 151

Richard K Miller Associates, Loganville, GA *Toll Free Tel:* 888-928-RKMA (928-7562) *Toll Free Fax:* 877-928-7562, pg 151

Milliken Publishing Co, Dayton, OH *Toll Free Tel:* 800-444-1144, pg 151

The Minerals, Metals & Materials Society (TMS), Pittsburgh, PA *Toll Free Tel:* 800-759-4867, pg 151

Minnesota Historical Society Press, St Paul, MN *Toll Free Tel:* 800-621-2736 (warehouse) *Toll Free Fax:* 800-621-8476 (warehouse), pg 151

The MIT Press, Cambridge, MA *Toll Free Tel:* 800-207-8354 (orders), pg 151

Mitchell Lane Publishers Inc, Hockessin, DE *Toll Free Tel:* 800-814-5484 *Toll Free Fax:* 866-834-4164, pg 152

Mondo Publishing, New York, NY *Toll Free Tel:* 888-88-MONDO (886-6636) *Toll Free Fax:* 888-532-4492, pg 153

Money Market Directories, Charlottesville, VA *Toll Free Tel:* 800-446-2810, pg 153

Montana Historical Society Press, Helena, MT *Toll Free Tel:* 800-243-9900, pg 153

Monthly Review Press, New York, NY *Toll Free Tel:* 800-670-9499, pg 153

Moody Publishers, Chicago, IL *Toll Free Tel:* 800-678-8812 (cust serv), pg 153

Morehouse Publishing, New York, NY *Toll Free Tel:* 800-672-1789 (retail orders only); 800-251-3320 (wholesale orders only), pg 154

Morgan James Publishing, New York, NY *Toll Free Tel:* 800-485-4943, pg 154

Morgan Kaufmann, Cambridge, MA *Toll Free Tel:* 866-607-1417, pg 154

Morgan Reynolds Publishing, Greensboro, NC *Toll Free Tel:* 800-535-1504 *Toll Free Fax:* 800-535-5725, pg 154

Mountain n' Air Books, La Crescenta, CA *Toll Free Tel:* 800-446-9696 *Toll Free Fax:* 800-303-5578, pg 154

Mountain Press Publishing Co, Missoula, MT *Toll Free Tel:* 800-234-5308, pg 154

The Mountaineers Books, Seattle, WA *Toll Free Tel:* 800-553-4453 *Toll Free Fax:* 800-568-7604, pg 154

MRTS, Tempe, AZ *Toll Free Tel:* 800-621-2736 (orders) *Toll Free Fax:* 800-621-8476 (orders), pg 155

Multnomah, Colorado Springs, CO *Toll Free Tel:* 800-603-7051 (orders) *Toll Free Fax:* 800-294-5686 (orders), pg 155

Mundania Press LLC, Cincinnati, OH *Toll Free Fax:* 888-460-4752, pg 155

Museum of New Mexico Press, Santa Fe, NM *Toll Free Tel:* 800-249-7737 (orders) *Toll Free Fax:* 800-622-8667 (orders), pg 156

Mystic Seaport Museum Inc, Mystic, CT *Toll Free Tel:* 800-248-1066 (wholesale orders only); 800-331-2665 (retail orders only), pg 156

NACE International, Houston, TX *Toll Free Tel:* 800-797-NACE (797-6223), pg 156

The National Alliance Research Academy, Austin, TX *Toll Free Tel:* 800-633-2165, pg 157

National Association for Music Education (NAfME), Reston, VA *Toll Free Tel:* 800-462-6420 (orders & returns); 800-336-3768, pg 157

National Association of Secondary School Principals (NASSP), Reston, VA *Toll Free Tel:* 800-253-7746, pg 157

National Braille Press, Boston, MA *Toll Free Tel:* 800-548-7323 (cust serv); 888-965-8965, pg 157

National Catholic Educational Association, Arlington, VA *Toll Free Tel:* 800-711-6232, pg 157

National Council of Teachers of English (NCTE), Urbana, IL *Toll Free Tel:* 877-369-6283 (cust serv), pg 158

National Council of Teachers of Mathematics (NCTM), Reston, VA *Toll Free Tel:* 800-235-7566, pg 158

National Geographic Books, Washington, DC *Toll Free Tel:* 877-866-6486, pg 158

National Golf Foundation, Jupiter, FL *Toll Free Tel:* 888-275-4643, pg 158

National Institute for Trial Advocacy (NITA), Boulder, CO *Toll Free Tel:* 877-648-2632; 800-225-6482 (orders & returns), pg 158

National Learning Corp, Syosset, NY *Toll Free Tel:* 800-632-8888, pg 159

National Notary Association (NNA), Chatsworth, CA *Toll Free Tel:* 800-876-6827 *Toll Free Fax:* 800-833-1211, pg 159

National Resource Center for Youth Services (NRCYS), Tulsa, OK *Toll Free Tel:* 800-274-2687, pg 159

National Science Teachers Association (NSTA), Arlington, VA *Toll Free Tel:* 800-277-5300 (orders) *Toll Free Fax:* 888-433-0526 (orders), pg 159

The National Underwriter Co, Erlanger, KY *Toll Free Tel:* 800-543-0874, pg 159

Naval Institute Press, Annapolis, MD *Toll Free Tel:* 800-233-8764, pg 159

NavPress Publishing Group, Colorado Springs, CO *Toll Free Tel:* 800-323-9400; 855-277-9400 (cust serv) *Toll Free Fax:* 800-684-0247, pg 159

NBM Publishing Inc, New York, NY *Toll Free Tel:* 800-886-1223, pg 159

Neibauer Press, Warminster, PA *Toll Free Tel:* 800-322-6203 (orders), pg 160

Nelson Education Ltd, Scarborough, ON Canada *Toll Free Tel:* 800-268-2222 (cust serv) *Toll Free Fax:* 800-430-4445, pg 464

New City Press, Hyde Park, NY *Toll Free Tel:* 800-462-5980 (orders only), pg 160

New Forums Press Inc, Stillwater, OK *Toll Free Tel:* 800-606-3766, pg 160

New Harbinger Publications Inc, Oakland, CA *Toll Free Tel:* 800-748-6273 (orders only) *Toll Free Fax:* 800-652-1613, pg 160

New Leaf Press, Green Forest, AR *Toll Free Tel:* 800-999-3777, pg 160

The New Press, New York, NY *Toll Free Tel:* 800-343-4489 (orders) *Toll Free Fax:* 800-351-5073 (orders), pg 161

New Readers Press, Syracuse, NY *Toll Free Tel:* 800-448-8878 *Toll Free Fax:* 866-894-2100, pg 161

New Strategist Press LLC, Amityville, NY *Toll Free Tel:* 800-848-0842, pg 161

New World Library, Novato, CA *Toll Free Tel:* 800-227-3900 (ext 52, retail orders); 800-972-6657, pg 161

New World Publishing (Canada), Halifax, NS Canada *Toll Free Tel:* 877-211-3334 (orders), pg 464

New York Academy of Sciences (NYAS), New York, NY *Toll Free Tel:* 800-843-6927, pg 161

New York State Bar Association, Albany, NY *Toll Free Tel:* 800-582-2452, pg 162

New York University Press, New York, NY *Toll Free Tel:* 800-996-6987 (orders), pg 162

Newbury Street Press, Boston, MA *Toll Free Tel:* 888-296-3447 (NEHGS membership), pg 162

Nightingale-Conant, Wheeling, IL *Toll Free Tel:* 800-557-1660 (sales); 800-560-6081 (cust serv), pg 162

Nimbus Publishing Ltd, Halifax, NS Canada *Toll Free Tel:* 800-NIMBUS9 (646-2879) *Toll Free Fax:* 888-253-3133, pg 465

No Starch Press, San Francisco, CA *Toll Free Tel:* 800-420-7240, pg 162

North Country Books Inc, Utica, NY *Toll Free Tel:* 800-342-7409 (orders), pg 163

North Point Press, New York, NY *Toll Free Tel:* 888-330-8477, pg 163

North River Press Publishing Corp, Great Barrington, MA *Toll Free Tel:* 800-486-2665 *Toll Free Fax:* 800-BOOK-FAX (266-5329), pg 163

North Star Editions Inc, Mendota Heights, MN *Toll Free Tel:* 888-417-0195, pg 163

Northwestern University Press, Evanston, IL *Toll Free Tel:* 800-621-2736 (orders only), pg 164

W W Norton & Company Inc, New York, NY *Toll Free Tel:* 800-233-4830 (orders & cust serv) *Toll Free Fax:* 800-458-6515, pg 164

Norwood House Press, Chicago, IL *Toll Free Tel:* 866-565-2900 *Toll Free Fax:* 866-565-2901, pg 165

Novalis Publishing, Toronto, ON Canada *Toll Free Tel:* 877-702-7773 *Toll Free Fax:* 877-702-7775, pg 465

NRP Direct, New Providence, NJ *Toll Free Tel:* 844-592-4197, pg 165

Nursesbooks.org, The Publishing Program of ANA, Silver Spring, MD *Toll Free Tel:* 800-274-4262; 800-637-0323 (orders), pg 165

Nystrom Education, Culver City, CA *Toll Free Tel:* 800-421-4246 *Toll Free Fax:* 800-944-5432, pg 165

OAG Worldwide, Downers Grove, IL *Toll Free Tel:* 800-342-5624 (cust serv), pg 165

Oak Knoll Press, New Castle, DE *Toll Free Tel:* 800-996-2556, pg 166

OCP, Portland, OR *Toll Free Tel:* 800-548-8749 *Toll Free Fax:* 800-843-8181, pg 166

OECD Washington Center, Washington, DC *Toll Free Tel:* 800-456-6323 (dist ctr/pubns orders), pg 167

Ohio State University Foreign Language Publications, Columbus, OH *Toll Free Tel:* 800-678-6999, pg 167

The Ohio State University Press, Columbus, OH *Toll Free Fax:* 800-621-8476, pg 167

The Oliver Press Inc, Minneapolis, MN *Toll Free Tel:* 800-8-OLIVER (865-4837), pg 167

Omnibus Press, New York, NY *Toll Free Tel:* 800-431-7187 *Toll Free Fax:* 800-345-6842, pg 167

Omnidawn Publishing, Richmond, CA *Toll Free Tel:* 800-792-4957, pg 168

Omnigraphics Inc, Detroit, MI *Toll Free Tel:* 800-234-1340 (cust serv) *Toll Free Fax:* 800-875-1340 (cust serv), pg 168

Open Court, Chicago, IL *Toll Free Tel:* 800-815-2280, pg 168

OPIS/STALSBY Directories & Databases, Wall, NJ *Toll Free Tel:* 800-275-0950 *Toll Free Fax:* 800-450-5864, pg 168

The Optical Society (OSA), Washington, DC *Toll Free Tel:* 800-766-4672, pg 169

OptumInsight™, Eden Prairie, MN *Toll Free Tel:* 888-445-8745; 800-765-6713, pg 169

Orange Frazer Press Inc, Wilmington, OH *Toll Free Tel:* 800-852-9332 (orders), pg 169

Orbis Books, Maryknoll, NY *Toll Free Tel:* 800-258-5838 (orders), pg 169

Orbit, New York, NY *Toll Free Tel:* 800-759-0190, pg 169

Orca Book Publishers, Custer, WA *Toll Free Tel:* 800-210-5277 *Toll Free Fax:* 877-408-1551, pg 169

Oregon State University Press, Corvallis, OR *Toll Free Tel:* 800-621-2736 (orders), pg 170

O'Reilly Media Inc, Sebastopol, CA *Toll Free Tel:* 800-998-9938; 800-889-8969, pg 170

Original Publications, Old Beth Page, NY *Toll Free Tel:* 888-622-8581, pg 170

Other Press, New York, NY *Toll Free Tel:* 877-843-6843, pg 170

Our Sunday Visitor Publishing, Huntington, IN *Toll Free Tel:* 800-348-2440 (orders) *Toll Free Fax:* 800-498-6709, pg 170

Out of Your Mind...and Into the Marketplace™, Tustin, CA *Toll Free Tel:* 800-419-1513, pg 171

The Overmountain Press, Johnson City, TN *Toll Free Tel:* 800-992-2691 (orders), pg 171

Richard C Owen Publishers Inc, Katonah, NY *Toll Free Tel:* 800-336-5588, pg 171

Oxford University Press USA, New York, NY *Toll Free Tel:* 800-451-7556 (orders); 800-445-9714 (cust serv), pg 171

Oxmoor House, Birmingham, AL *Toll Free Tel:* 800-366-4712; 888-891-8935 (cust serv); 800-765-6400 (orders), pg 171

Ozark Mountain Publishing Inc, Huntsville, AR *Toll Free Tel:* 800-935-0045, pg 172

Ozark Publishing Inc, Prairie Grove, AR *Toll Free Tel:* 800-321-5671, pg 172

P & R Publishing Co, Phillipsburg, NJ *Toll Free Tel:* 800-631-0094, pg 172

Pacific Educational Press, Vancouver, BC Canada *Toll Free Tel:* 855-827-2232, pg 465

Pacific Press Publishing Association, Nampa, ID *Toll Free Tel:* 800-447-7377, pg 172

Paladin Press, Boulder, CO *Toll Free Tel:* 800-392-2400, pg 172

Papercutz, New York, NY *Toll Free Tel:* 800-886-1223, pg 173

Paraclete Press Inc, Brewster, MA *Toll Free Tel:* 800-451-5006, pg 173

Paradigm Publications, Taos, NM *Toll Free Tel:* 800-873-3946 (US); 888-873-3947 (CN), pg 173

Paradise Cay Publications Inc, Blue Lake, CA *Toll Free Tel:* 800-736-4509, pg 173

Paragon House, St Paul, MN *Toll Free Tel:* 800-447-3709, pg 174

Parallax Press, Berkeley, CA *Toll Free Tel:* 800-863-5290 (orders), pg 174

Parenting Press Inc, Seattle, WA *Toll Free Tel:* 800-99-BOOKS (992-6657), pg 174

Patria Press Inc, Carmel, IN *Toll Free Tel:* 888-859-8221, pg 175

Pauline Books & Media, Boston, MA *Toll Free Tel:* 800-876-4463 (orders); 800-836-9723 (cust serv), pg 175

Paulist Press, Mahwah, NJ *Toll Free Tel:* 800-218-1903 *Toll Free Fax:* 800-836-3161, pg 175

Peace Hill Press, Charles City, VA *Toll Free Tel:* 877-322-3445 (orders), pg 175

Peachpit Press, San Francisco, CA *Toll Free Tel:* 800-283-9444, pg 175

Peachtree Publishers, Atlanta, GA *Toll Free Tel:* 800-241-0113 *Toll Free Fax:* 800-875-8909, pg 176

Pearson, Glenview, IL *Toll Free Tel:* 800-535-4391 (Midwest), pg 176

Pearson Allyn & Bacon, Boston, MA *Toll Free Tel:* 800-428-4466, pg 176

Pearson Benjamin Cummings, San Francisco, CA *Toll Free Tel:* 800-922-0579 (orders) *Toll Free Fax:* 800-445-6991 (orders), pg 176

Pearson Career, Health, Education & Technology, Hoboken, NJ *Toll Free Tel:* 800-848-9500, pg 176

Pearson Education Canada, North York, ON Canada *Toll Free Tel:* 800-263-9965 *Toll Free Fax:* 800-263-7733; 888-465-0536, pg 466

Pearson ELT, Hoboken, NJ *Toll Free Tel:* 877-202-4572 *Toll Free Fax:* 800-445-6991, pg 176

Pearson ERPI, Montreal, QC Canada *Toll Free Tel:* 800-263-3678 *Toll Free Fax:* 800-643-4720, pg 466

Pearson Learning Solutions, Boston, MA *Toll Free Tel:* 800-428-4466 (orders); 800-635-1579, pg 176

Pearson School, Hoboken, NJ *Toll Free Tel:* 800-848-9500 (K-12 prods), pg 176

Pelican Publishing Co, Gretna, LA *Toll Free Tel:* 800-843-1724, pg 176

Pembroke Publishers Ltd, Markham, ON Canada *Toll Free Tel:* 800-997-9807 *Toll Free Fax:* 800-339-5568, pg 466

Pendragon Press, Hillsdale, NY *Toll Free Tel:* 877-656-6381 (orders), pg 177

Penfield Books, Iowa City, IA *Toll Free Tel:* 800-728-9998, pg 177

Penguin Group USA, A Penguin Random House Company, New York, NY *Toll Free Tel:* 800-847-5515 (inside sales); 800-631-8571 (cust serv), pg 177

Penguin Random House Canada, Toronto, ON Canada *Toll Free Tel:* 888-523-9292 (cust serv), pg 467

Penguin Random House Inc, New York, NY *Toll Free Tel:* 800-726-0600, pg 178

The Pennsylvania State University Press, University Park, PA *Toll Free Tel:* 800-326-9180 *Toll Free Fax:* 877-778-2665, pg 179

PennWell Books, Tulsa, OK *Toll Free Tel:* 800-752-9764 *Toll Free Fax:* 877-218-1348, pg 179

Pentecostal Publishing House, Hazelwood, MO *Toll Free Tel:* 866-819-7667, pg 180

Penton Media Inc, Overland Park, KS *Toll Free Tel:* 800-262-1954 (cust serv) *Toll Free Fax:* 800-633-6219, pg 180

Perfection Learning Corp, Logan, IA *Toll Free Tel:* 800-831-4190 *Toll Free Fax:* 800-543-2745, pg 180

Perseus Books, New York, NY *Toll Free Tel:* 800-343-4499 (cust serv), pg 180

Peterson's, a Nelnet Company, Albany, NY *Toll Free Tel:* 800-338-3282, pg 181

Petroleum Extension Service (PETEX), Austin, TX *Toll Free Tel:* 800-687-4132 *Toll Free Fax:* 800-687-7839, pg 181

Pflaum Publishing Group, Dayton, OH *Toll Free Tel:* 800-543-4383 (sales) *Toll Free Fax:* 800-370-4450, pg 181

Phaidon, New York, NY *Toll Free Tel:* 800-759-0190 (cust serv) *Toll Free Fax:* 800-286-9471 (cust serv), pg 182

Phi Delta Kappa International®, Arlington, VA *Toll Free Tel:* 800-766-1156, pg 182

Philosophy Documentation Center, Charlottesville, VA *Toll Free Tel:* 800-444-2419, pg 182

Phoenix Society for Burn Survivors, Grand Rapids, MI *Toll Free Tel:* 800-888-BURN (888-2876), pg 182

Pieces of Learning Inc, Marion, IL *Toll Free Tel:* 800-729-5137 *Toll Free Fax:* 800-844-0455, pg 183

The Pilgrim Press/United Church Press, Cleveland, OH *Toll Free Tel:* 800-537-3394 (orders), pg 183

Pineapple Press Inc, Sarasota, FL *Toll Free Tel:* 866-766-3850 (orders) *Toll Free Fax:* 800-838-1149 (orders), pg 183

Pippin Publishing, Toronto, ON Canada *Toll Free Tel:* 800-565-9523 (CN warehouse) *Toll Free Fax:* 800-221-9985 (CN warehouse), pg 467

Platypus Media LLC, Washington, DC *Toll Free Tel:* 877-PLATYPS (752-8977), pg 183

Plough Publishing House, Walden, NY *Toll Free Tel:* 800-521-8011, pg 184

Pocket Press Inc, Portland, OR *Toll Free Tel:* 888-237-2110 *Toll Free Fax:* 877-643-3732, pg 185

Poisoned Pen Press, Scottsdale, AZ *Toll Free Tel:* 800-421-3976, pg 185

Pomegranate Communications Inc, Portland, OR *Toll Free Tel:* 800-227-1428 *Toll Free Fax:* 800-848-4376, pg 185

Portage & Main Press, Winnipeg, MB Canada *Toll Free Tel:* 800-667-9673 *Toll Free Fax:* 866-734-8477, pg 467

Pottersfield Press, East Lawrencetown, NS Canada *Toll Free Tel:* 800-646-2879 (orders only) *Toll Free Fax:* 888-253-3133, pg 467

Practising Law Institute, New York, NY *Toll Free Tel:* 800-260-4PLI (260-4754, cust serv) *Toll Free Fax:* 800-321-0093 (local), pg 186

PrairieView Press Ltd, Gretna, MB Canada *Toll Free Tel:* 800-477-7377 *Toll Free Fax:* 866-480-0253, pg 467

PREP Publishing, Fayetteville, NC *Toll Free Tel:* 800-533-2814, pg 187

Presbyterian Publishing Corp (PPC), Louisville, KY *Toll Free Tel:* 800-523-1631 (US only), pg 187

Prevention Products & Services Inc dba The Bureau for At-Risk Youth, Farmingville, NY *Toll Free Tel:* 800-99YOUTH (999-6884), pg 187

Price World Publishing, Columbus, OH *Toll Free Tel:* 888-234-6896, pg 187

Princeton Architectural Press, New York, NY *Toll Free Tel:* 800-722-6657 (dist); 800-759-0190 (sales), pg 188

Princeton Book Co Publishers, Trenton, NJ *Toll Free Tel:* 800-220-7149, pg 188

The Princeton Review, New York, NY *Toll Free Tel:* 800-273-8439, pg 188

Printing Industries of America, Warrendale, PA *Toll Free Tel:* 800-910-4283, pg 188

PRO-ED Inc, Austin, TX *Toll Free Tel:* 800-897-3202 *Toll Free Fax:* 800-397-7633, pg 189

Pro Lingua Associates Inc, Brattleboro, VT *Toll Free Tel:* 800-366-4775, pg 189

Productive Publications, Toronto, ON Canada *Toll Free Tel:* 877-879-2669 (orders), pg 468

Productivity Press, New York, NY *Toll Free Tel:* 800-634-7064 (orders); 800-797-3803, pg 189

Professional Communications Inc, Caddo, OK *Toll Free Tel:* 800-337-9838, pg 189

The Professional Education Group LLC (PEG), Wayzata, MN *Toll Free Tel:* 800-229-2531, pg 189

Professional Resource Press, Sarasota, FL *Toll Free Tel:* 800-443-3364 (orders & cust serv) *Toll Free Fax:* 866-804-4843 (orders only), pg 189

ProQuest LLC, Ann Arbor, MI *Toll Free Tel:* 800-521-0600, pg 190

ProStar Publications Inc, Annapolis, MD *Toll Free Tel:* 800-481-6277 *Toll Free Fax:* 800-487-6277, pg 190

Prufrock Press, Waco, TX *Toll Free Tel:* 800-998-2208 *Toll Free Fax:* 800-240-0333, pg 191

PSMJ Resources Inc, Newton, MA *Toll Free Tel:* 800-537-7765, pg 191

Psychological Assessment Resources Inc (PAR), Lutz, FL *Toll Free Tel:* 800-331-8378 *Toll Free Fax:* 800-727-9329, pg 191

Les Publications du Quebec, Quebec, QC Canada *Toll Free Tel:* 800-463-2100 (Quebec province only) *Toll Free Fax:* 800-561-3479, pg 468

Purple Mountain Press Ltd, Fleischmanns, NY *Toll Free Tel:* 800-325-2665 (orders), pg 191

Quail Ridge Press, Brandon, MS *Toll Free Tel:* 800-343-1583 *Toll Free Fax:* 800-864-1082, pg 192

Quality Medical Publishing Inc, St Louis, MO *Toll Free Tel:* 800-348-7808, pg 192

Quarto Publishing Group USA Inc, Minneapolis, MN *Toll Free Tel:* 800-328-0590 (sales); 800-458-0454, pg 192

Quicksilver Productions, Ashland, OR *Toll Free Fax:* 888-974-6462, pg 192

Quintessence Publishing Co Inc, Hanover Park, IL *Toll Free Tel:* 800-621-0387, pg 193

Quixote Press, Wever, IA *Toll Free Tel:* 800-571-2665, pg 193

Rainbow Publishers, Torrance, CA *Toll Free Tel:* 800-323-7337; 800-532-4278 *Toll Free Fax:* 800-331-0297, pg 193

Ram Publishing Co, Garland, TX *Toll Free Tel:* 800-527-4011, pg 193

Random House Publishing Group, New York, NY *Toll Free Tel:* 800-200-3552, pg 195

Raven Publishing Inc, Norris, MT *Toll Free Tel:* 866-685-3545, pg 196

Reader's Digest Association Canada ULC (Selection du Reader's Digest Canada SRI), Montreal, QC Canada *Toll Free Tel:* 888-459-3333 (cust serv), pg 468

Reader's Digest USA Select Editions, White Plains, NY *Toll Free Tel:* 800-304-2807 (cust serv), pg 196

Recorded Books Inc, an RBmedia company, Prince Frederick, MD *Toll Free Tel:* 877-732-2898, pg 196

Red Chair Press, South Egremont, MA *Toll Free Tel:* 800-328-4929 (orders & cust serv) *Toll Free Fax:* 800-332-1132, pg 196

Red Deer Press Inc, Markham, ON Canada *Toll Free Tel:* 800-387-9776 (orders), pg 468

Red Wheel/Weiser/Conari, Newburyport, MA *Toll Free Tel:* 800-423-7087 (orders), pg 197

Redleaf Press, St Paul, MN *Toll Free Tel:* 800-423-8309 *Toll Free Fax:* 800-641-0115, pg 197

Reedswain Inc, Spring City, PA *Toll Free Tel:* 800-331-5191, pg 197

Referee Books, Racine, WI *Toll Free Tel:* 800-733-6100, pg 197

ReferencePoint Press Inc, San Diego, CA *Toll Free Tel:* 888-479-6436, pg 197

Regal Crest Enterprises, Maryville, TN *Toll Free Fax:* 866-294-9628, pg 198

Regnery Publishing, Washington, DC *Toll Free Tel:* 888-219-4747, pg 198

Regular Baptist Press, Arlington Heights, IL *Toll Free Tel:* 800-727-4440; 800-727-4440 (cust serv), pg 198

Research Press, Champaign, IL *Toll Free Tel:* 800-519-2707, pg 198

Revell, Grand Rapids, MI *Toll Free Tel:* 800-877-2665; 800-679-1957, pg 198

Review & Herald Publishing Association, Hagerstown, MD *Toll Free Tel:* 800-234-7630; 800-456-3991, pg 199

Rio Nuevo Publishers, Tucson, AZ *Toll Free Tel:* 800-969-9558 *Toll Free Fax:* 800-715-5888, pg 199

Rising Sun Publishing, Marietta, GA *Toll Free Tel:* 800-524-2813, pg 199

Rizzoli International Publications Inc, New York, NY *Toll Free Tel:* 800-522-6657 (orders only), pg 199

Rod & Staff Publishers Inc, Crockett, KY *Toll Free Fax:* 800-643-1244 (US orders), pg 200

Rodale Inc, Emmaus, PA *Toll Free Tel:* 866-387-0509, pg 200

Roncorp Music, Glenmoore, PA *Toll Free Tel:* 866-385-8446, pg 201

The Rosen Publishing Group Inc, New York, NY *Toll Free Tel:* 800-237-9932 *Toll Free Fax:* 888-436-4643, pg 201

Rothstein Associates Inc, Brookfield, CT *Toll Free Tel:* 888-768-4783, pg 201

The Rough Notes Co Inc, Carmel, IN *Toll Free Tel:* 800-428-4384 (cust serv) *Toll Free Fax:* 800-321-1909, pg 201

Routledge, New York, NY *Toll Free Tel:* 800-634-7064 (order enquiries, cust servs), pg 202

Rowman & Littlefield Publishers Inc, Lanham, MD *Toll Free Tel:* 800-462-6420 (cust serv), pg 202

Russell Sage Foundation, New York, NY *Toll Free Tel:* 800-524-6401, pg 202

Russian Information Services Inc, Montpelier, VT *Toll Free Tel:* 800-639-4301, pg 202

Rutgers University Press, New Brunswick, NJ *Toll Free Tel:* 800-848-6224 (orders only) *Toll Free Fax:* 800-272-6817 (fulfillment), pg 202

Saddleback Educational Publishing, Costa Mesa, CA *Toll Free Tel:* 888-SDLBACK (735-2225); 800-637-8715 *Toll Free Fax:* 888-734-4010, pg 203

William H Sadlier Inc, New York, NY *Toll Free Tel:* 800-221-5175 (cust serv), pg 203

SAE (Society of Automotive Engineers International), Warrendale, PA *Toll Free Tel:* 877-606-7323 (cust serv), pg 203

Safari Press, Huntington Beach, CA *Toll Free Tel:* 800-451-4788, pg 203

Sagamore Publishing LLC, Urbana, IL *Toll Free Tel:* 800-327-5557 (orders), pg 203

SAGE Publishing, Thousand Oaks, CA *Toll Free Tel:* 800-818-7243 *Toll Free Fax:* 800-583-2665, pg 203

St Andrews University Press, Laurinburg, NC *Toll Free Tel:* 800-763-0198, pg 204

St James Press®, Farmington Hills, MI *Toll Free Tel:* 800-877-4253 (orders) *Toll Free Fax:* 877-363-4253, pg 204

Saint Mary's Press, Winona, MN *Toll Free Tel:* 800-533-8095 *Toll Free Fax:* 800-344-9225, pg 205

Saint Nectarios Press, Seattle, WA *Toll Free Tel:* 800-643-4233, pg 205

St Pauls, Staten Island, NY *Toll Free Tel:* 800-343-2522, pg 205

Salem Press Inc, Hackensack, NJ *Toll Free Tel:* 800-221-1592; 800-221-1592, pg 205

Salina Bookshelf Inc, Flagstaff, AZ *Toll Free Tel:* 877-527-0070, pg 205

SAMS Technical Publishing LLC, Indianapolis, IN *Toll Free Tel:* 800-428-7267 *Toll Free Fax:* 800-552-3910, pg 205

Sandlapper Publishing Inc, Orangeburg, SC *Toll Free Tel:* 800-849-7263 (orders only) *Toll Free Fax:* 800-337-9420, pg 205

Santa Monica Press LLC, Solana Beach, CA *Toll Free Tel:* 800-784-9553, pg 205

Santillana USA Publishing Co, Doral, FL *Toll Free Tel:* 800-245-8584, pg 206

Sara Jordan Publishing, St Catharines, ON Canada *Toll Free Tel:* 800-567-7733 *Toll Free Fax:* 800-229-3855, pg 469

SAS Publishing, Cary, NC *Toll Free Tel:* 800-727-0025, pg 206

Sasquatch Books, Seattle, WA *Toll Free Tel:* 800-775-0817, pg 206

Scepter Publishers, Strongsville, OH *Toll Free Tel:* 800-322-8773, pg 207

Schlager Group Inc, Dallas, TX *Toll Free Tel:* 888-416-5727, pg 207

Scholastic Canada Ltd, Toronto, ON Canada *Toll Free Tel:* 800-268-3860 (CN) *Toll Free Fax:* 866-387-4944, pg 469

Scholastic Inc, New York, NY *Toll Free Tel:* 800-SCHOLASTIC (724-6527), pg 208

Scholastic International, New York, NY *Toll Free Tel:* 800-SCHOLASTIC (724-6527), pg 208

Schonfeld & Associates Inc, Libertyville, IL *Toll Free Tel:* 800-205-0030, pg 208

School for Advanced Research Press, Santa Fe, NM *Toll Free Tel:* 888-390-6070, pg 208

School Guide Publications, Mamaroneck, NY *Toll Free Tel:* 800-433-7771, pg 208

School Zone Publishing Co, Grand Haven, MI *Toll Free Tel:* 800-253-0564 *Toll Free Fax:* 800-550-4618 (orders only), pg 208

Schreiber Publishing, Rockville, MD *Toll Free Tel:* 800-296-1961 (sales), pg 209

Science, Naturally, Washington, DC *Toll Free Tel:* 866-724-9876, pg 209

Seal Books, Toronto, ON Canada *Toll Free Tel:* 888-523-9292 (order desk), pg 470

Search Institute Press®, Minneapolis, MN *Toll Free Tel:* 800-888-7828, pg 210

Seedling Publications Inc, Elizabethtown, PA *Toll Free Tel:* 800-233-0759 *Toll Free Fax:* 888-834-1303, pg 210

Self-Counsel Press Inc, North Vancouver, BC Canada *Toll Free Tel:* 800-663-3007, pg 470

Self-Realization Fellowship Publishers, Los Angeles, CA *Toll Free Tel:* 888-773-8680, pg 210

Seven Stories Press, New York, NY *Toll Free Tel:* 800-733-3000 (orders), pg 211

Shadow Mountain, Salt Lake City, UT *Toll Free Tel:* 800-453-3876, pg 211

Shambhala Publications Inc, Boulder, CO *Toll Free Tel:* 866-424-0030 (off); 888-424-2329 (cust serv), pg 211

Show What You Know® Publishing, A Lorenz Company, Dayton, OH *Toll Free Tel:* 877-PASSING (727-7464), pg 211

Signalman Publishing, Kissimmee, FL *Toll Free Tel:* 888-907-4423, pg 212

Simcha Press, Deerfield Beach, FL *Toll Free Tel:* 800-851-9100 ext 212 *Toll Free Fax:* 800-424-7652, pg 212

Simon & Schuster, New York, NY *Toll Free Tel:* 800-223-2348 (cust serv); 800-223-2336 (orders) *Toll Free Fax:* 800-943-9831 (orders), pg 212

Simon & Schuster Canada, Toronto, ON Canada *Toll Free Tel:* 800-387-0446; 800-268-3216 (orders) *Toll Free Fax:* 888-849-8151 (orders), pg 471

SkillPath Publications, Mission, KS *Toll Free Tel:* 800-873-7545, pg 214

SLACK® Incorporated, A Wyanoke Group Company, Thorofare, NJ *Toll Free Tel:* 800-257-8290, pg 215

Sleeping Bear Press™, Ann Arbor, MI *Toll Free Tel:* 800-487-2323, pg 215

Smith & Kraus Publishers Inc, Portland, ME *Toll Free Tel:* 877-668-8680, pg 215

M Lee Smith Publishers, Brentwood, TN *Toll Free Tel:* 800-274-6774; 800-727-5257, pg 215

Smyth & Helwys Publishing Inc, Macon, GA *Toll Free Tel:* 800-747-3016 (orders only); 800-568-1248 (orders only), pg 215

Society for Human Resource Management (SHRM), Alexandria, VA *Toll Free Tel:* 800-444-5006 (orders), pg 216

Society for Industrial & Applied Mathematics, Philadelphia, PA *Toll Free Tel:* 800-447-7426, pg 216

Society for Mining, Metallurgy & Exploration, Englewood, CO *Toll Free Tel:* 800-763-3132, pg 216

Society of American Archivists, Chicago, IL *Toll Free Tel:* 866-722-7858, pg 216

Society of Environmental Toxicology & Chemistry (SETAC), Pensacola, FL *Toll Free Fax:* 888-296-4136, pg 216

Society of Manufacturing Engineers, Dearborn, MI *Toll Free Tel:* 800-733-4763 (cust serv), pg 216

The Society of Naval Architects & Marine Engineers (SNAME), Alexandria, VA *Toll Free Tel:* 800-798-2188, pg 216

Solano Press Books, Point Arena, CA *Toll Free Tel:* 800-931-9373, pg 217

Solution Tree, Bloomington, IN *Toll Free Tel:* 800-733-6786, pg 217

Soncino Press Ltd, Brooklyn, NY *Toll Free Tel:* 800-972-6201, pg 217

Sophia Institute Press®, Bedford, NH *Toll Free Tel:* 800-888-9344 *Toll Free Fax:* 888-288-2259, pg 217

Sounds True Inc, Louisville, CO *Toll Free Tel:* 800-333-9185, pg 217

Sourcebooks Inc, Naperville, IL *Toll Free Tel:* 800-432-7444, pg 217

South Carolina Bar, Columbia, SC *Toll Free Tel:* 800-768-7787, pg 218

Southern Historical Press Inc, Greenville, SC *Toll Free Tel:* 800-233-0152, pg 218

Specialty Press Inc, Plantation, FL *Toll Free Tel:* 800-233-9273, pg 219

SPIE, Bellingham, WA *Toll Free Tel:* 888-504-8171 (orders), pg 219

Spinsters Ink, Tallahassee, FL *Toll Free Tel:* 800-729-4992, pg 219

Spizzirri Publishing Inc, Rapid City, SD *Toll Free Tel:* 800-325-9819 *Toll Free Fax:* 800-322-9819, pg 219

Springer, New York, NY *Toll Free Tel:* 800-SPRINGER (777-4643), pg 219

Springer Publishing Co, New York, NY *Toll Free Tel:* 877-687-7476, pg 219

Spry Publishing, Ann Arbor, MI *Toll Free Tel:* 877-722-2264, pg 219

Square One Publishers Inc, Garden City Park, NY *Toll Free Tel:* 877-900-BOOK (900-2665), pg 220

SSPC: The Society for Protective Coatings, Pittsburgh, PA *Toll Free Tel:* 877-281-7772 (US only), pg 220

ST Media Group Book Division, Cincinnati, OH *Toll Free Tel:* 866-265-0954, pg 220

Stackpole Books, Mechanicsburg, PA *Toll Free Tel:* 800-732-3669, pg 220

Standard International Media Holdings, Naples, FL *Toll Free Fax:* 866-948-7883, pg 220

Standard Publishing, Colorado Springs, CO *Toll Free Tel:* 800-323-7543 *Toll Free Fax:* 800-323-0726, pg 220

Standard Publishing Corp, Boston, MA *Toll Free Tel:* 800-682-5759, pg 220

Starcrafts LLC, Epping, NH *Toll Free Tel:* 866-953-8458 (24/7 message ctr), pg 221

Stargazer Publishing Co, Corona, CA *Toll Free Tel:* 800-606-7895 (orders), pg 221

State University of New York Press, Albany, NY *Toll Free Tel:* 877-204-6073 (orders) *Toll Free Fax:* 877-204-6074 (orders), pg 221

Stemmer House Publishers Inc, Gilsum, NH *Toll Free Tel:* 800-345-6665, pg 222

Stenhouse Publishers, Portland, ME *Toll Free Tel:* 888-363-0566 *Toll Free Fax:* 800-833-9164, pg 222

Sterling Publishing Co Inc, New York, NY *Toll Free Tel:* 800-367-9692, pg 222

Stoneydale Press Publishing Co, Stevensville, MT *Toll Free Tel:* 800-735-7006, pg 223

Storey Publishing LLC, North Adams, MA *Toll Free Tel:* 800-441-5700 (orders); 800-793-9396 (edit), pg 223

Stress Free Kids®, Marietta, GA *Toll Free Fax:* 866-302-2759, pg 224

Stylus Publishing LLC, Sterling, VA *Toll Free Tel:* 800-232-0223 (orders & cust serv), pg 224

Summerthought Publishing, Banff, AB Canada *Toll Free Fax:* 800-762-3095 (orders), pg 471

Summit University Press, Gardiner, MT *Toll Free Tel:* 800-245-5445 (retail orders), pg 224

Sun Publishing Company, Santa Fe, NM *Toll Free Tel:* 877-849-0051, pg 224

Sunbelt Publications Inc, El Cajon, CA *Toll Free Tel:* 800-626-6579 (cust serv), pg 225

Sundance/Newbridge Publishing, Marlborough, MA *Toll Free Tel:* 888-200-2720; 800-343-8204 (Sundance cust serv & orders); 800-867-0307 (Newbridge cust serv & orders) *Toll Free Fax:* 800-456-2419 (orders), pg 225

Sunrise River Press, Forrest Lake, MN *Toll Free Tel:* 800-895-4585, pg 225

Sunstone Press, Santa Fe, NM *Toll Free Tel:* 800-243-5644, pg 225

Surrey Books, Evanston, IL *Toll Free Tel:* 800-326-4430, pg 225

Swallow Press, Athens, OH *Toll Free Tel:* 800-621-2736, pg 225

Swan Isle Press, Chicago, IL *Toll Free Tel:* 800-621-2736 (cust serv) *Toll Free Fax:* 800-621-8476 (cust serv), pg 225

Swedenborg Foundation, West Chester, PA *Toll Free Tel:* 800-355-3222 (cust serv), pg 225

Synapse Information Resources Inc, Endicott, NY *Toll Free Tel:* 888-SYN-CHEM (796-2436), pg 226

Syracuse University Press, Syracuse, NY *Toll Free Tel:* 800-365-8929 (cust serv), pg 226

TAN Books, Charlotte, NC *Toll Free Tel:* 800-437-5876, pg 226

Tanglewood Publishing, Indianapolis, IN *Toll Free Tel:* 800-788-3123 (orders), pg 227

Tantor Media Inc, Old Saybrook, CT *Toll Free Tel:* 877-782-6867 *Toll Free Fax:* 888-782-7821, pg 227

Tapestry Press Ltd, Littleton, MA *Toll Free Tel:* 800-535-2007, pg 227

Taschen America, Los Angeles, CA *Toll Free Tel:* 888-TASCHEN (827-2436), pg 227

The Taunton Press Inc, Newtown, CT *Toll Free Tel:* 800-477-8727 (cust serv); 800-888-8286 (orders), pg 227

Taylor & Francis Inc, Philadelphia, PA *Toll Free Tel:* 800-354-1420, pg 227

TCP Press, Uxbridge, ON Canada *Toll Free Tel:* 800-772-7765, pg 471

TCU Press, Fort Worth, TX *Toll Free Tel:* 800-826-8911 (orders), pg 228

Teach Me Tapes Inc, Mequon, WI *Toll Free Tel:* 800-456-4656, pg 228

Teacher Created Resources Inc, Garden Grove, CA *Toll Free Tel:* 800-662-4321; 888-343-4335 *Toll Free Fax:* 800-525-1254, pg 228

Teachers College Press, New York, NY *Toll Free Tel:* 800-575-6566, pg 228

Teacher's Discovery, Auburn Hills, MI *Toll Free Tel:* 800-832-2437 *Toll Free Fax:* 800-287-4509, pg 228

Teaching & Learning Co, Dayton, OH *Toll Free Tel:* 800-444-1144, pg 228

Teaching Strategies LLC, Bethesda, MD *Toll Free Tel:* 800-637-3652, pg 228

Temple University Press, Philadelphia, PA *Toll Free Tel:* 800-621-2736, pg 228

Templegate Publishers, Springfield, IL *Toll Free Tel:* 800-367-4844 (orders only), pg 229

Ten Speed Press, Emeryville, CA *Toll Free Tel:* 800-841-BOOK (841-2665), pg 229

Teton NewMedia Inc, Jackson, WY *Toll Free Tel:* 877-306-9793, pg 229

Texas A&M University Press, College Station, TX *Toll Free Tel:* 800-826-8911 (orders) *Toll Free Fax:* 888-617-2421 (orders), pg 230

Texas Tech University Press, Lubbock, TX *Toll Free Tel:* 800-832-4042, pg 230

Texas Western Press, El Paso, TX *Toll Free Tel:* 800-488-3798 (orders only), pg 230

TFH Publications Inc, Neptune, NJ *Toll Free Tel:* 855-273-7527 (cust serv), pg 230

Thames & Hudson, New York, NY *Toll Free Tel:* 800-233-4830, pg 230

Thieme Medical Publishers Inc, New York, NY *Toll Free Tel:* 800-782-3488, pg 231

Charles C Thomas Publisher Ltd, Springfield, IL *Toll Free Tel:* 800-258-8980, pg 231

Thomas Nelson, Nashville, TN *Toll Free Tel:* 800-251-4000, pg 231

Thompson Educational Publishing Inc, Toronto, ON Canada *Toll Free Tel:* 877-366-2763, pg 472

Thomson Reuters Westlaw™, Eagan, MN *Toll Free Tel:* 888-728-7677 (sales); 800-328-4880 (cust serv), pg 231

Thorndike Press, Waterville, ME *Toll Free Tel:* 800-223-1244 (ext 4, cust serv/orders) *Toll Free Fax:* 800-558-4676 (orders), pg 231

Tide-mark Press, East Hartford, CT *Toll Free Tel:* 800-338-2508, pg 232

Tilbury House Publishers, Thomaston, ME *Toll Free Tel:* 800-582-1899 (orders), pg 232

Timber Press Inc, Portland, OR *Toll Free Tel:* 800-327-5680, pg 232

TJ Publishers Inc, Dallas, TX *Toll Free Tel:* 800-999-1168, pg 478

Tommy Nelson, Nashville, TN *Toll Free Tel:* 800-251-4000, pg 233

Torah Aura Productions, Los Angeles, CA *Toll Free Tel:* 800-238-6724, pg 233

Tower Publishing Co, Standish, ME *Toll Free Tel:* 800-969-8693, pg 233

Tracks Publishing, Chula Vista, CA *Toll Free Tel:* 800-443-3570, pg 233

Trafalgar Square Books, North Pomfret, VT *Toll Free Tel:* 800-423-4525, pg 234

Trafford, Bloomington, IN *Toll Free Tel:* 888-232-4444, pg 234

Tralco-Lingo Fun, Hamilton, ON Canada *Toll Free Tel:* 888-487-2526, pg 472

Transaction Publishers Inc, Piscataway, NJ *Toll Free Tel:* 888-999-6778 (dist ctr), pg 234

Treehaus Communications Inc, Loveland, OH *Toll Free Tel:* 800-638-4287 (orders), pg 235

Triad Publishing Co, Gainesville, FL *Toll Free Fax:* 800-854-4947, pg 235

TripBuilder Media Inc, Westport, CT *Toll Free Tel:* 800-525-9745, pg 235

TriQuarterly Books, Evanston, IL *Toll Free Tel:* 800-621-2736 (orders only), pg 235

TRISTAN Publishing, Minneapolis, MN *Toll Free Tel:* 866-545-1383, pg 235

Triumph Books, Chicago, IL *Toll Free Tel:* 800-888-4741 (cust serv), pg 235

Triumph Learning LLC, New York, NY *Toll Free Tel:* 800-338-6519 (cust serv) *Toll Free Fax:* 866-805-5723, pg 235

Truman State University Press, Kirksville, MO *Toll Free Tel:* 800-916-6802, pg 236

Trusted Media Brands Inc, New York, NY *Toll Free Tel:* 800-310-6261 (cust serv), pg 236

Tundra Books, Toronto, ON Canada *Toll Free Tel:* 888-523-9292 (orders); 800-588-1074 *Toll Free Fax:* 888-562-9924 (orders), pg 472

Turnstone Press, Winnipeg, MB Canada *Toll Free Tel:* 888-363-7718, pg 473

Tuttle Publishing, North Clarendon, VT *Toll Free Tel:* 800-526-2778 *Toll Free Fax:* 800-FAX-TUTL (329-8885), pg 236

Twenty-First Century Books, Minneapolis, MN *Toll Free Tel:* 800-328-4929 *Toll Free Fax:* 800-332-1132, pg 237

Twenty-Third Publications, New London, CT *Toll Free Tel:* 800-321-0411 (orders) *Toll Free Fax:* 800-572-0788, pg 237

Tyndale House Publishers Inc, Carol Stream, IL *Toll Free Tel:* 800-323-9400 *Toll Free Fax:* 800-684-0247, pg 237

Ulysses Press, Berkeley, CA *Toll Free Tel:* 800-377-2542, pg 238

Ulysses Travel Guides, Montreal, QC Canada *Toll Free Tel:* 800-748-9171, pg 473

Unarius Academy of Science Publications, El Cajon, CA *Toll Free Tel:* 800-475-7062, pg 238

Editorial Unilit, Medley, FL *Toll Free Tel:* 800-767-7726, pg 238

The United Educators Inc, Lake Bluff, IL *Toll Free Tel:* 800-323-5875, pg 238

United States Holocaust Memorial Museum, Washington, DC *Toll Free Tel:* 800-259-9998 (orders), pg 238

United States Institute of Peace Press, Washington, DC *Toll Free Tel:* 800-868-8064 (cust serv), pg 239

United States Pharmacopeia, Rockville, MD *Toll Free Tel:* 800-227-8772, pg 239

Universal-Publishers Inc, Boca Raton, FL *Toll Free Tel:* 800-636-8329 (US only), pg 239

University of Alaska Press, Fairbanks, AK *Toll Free Tel:* 888-252-6657 (US only), pg 239

The University of Arizona Press, Tucson, AZ *Toll Free Tel:* 800-426-3797 (orders) *Toll Free Fax:* 800-426-3797, pg 240

The University of Arkansas Press, Fayetteville, AR *Toll Free Tel:* 800-626-0090, pg 240

University of British Columbia Press, Vancouver, BC Canada *Toll Free Tel:* 877-377-9378 *Toll Free Fax:* 800-668-0821, pg 473

University of Chicago Press, Chicago, IL *Toll Free Tel:* 800-621-2736 (orders), pg 240

University of Hawaii Press, Honolulu, HI *Toll Free Tel:* 888-UHPRESS (847-7377) *Toll Free Fax:* 800-650-7811, pg 241

University of Iowa Press, Iowa City, IA *Toll Free Tel:* 800-621-2736 (orders only) *Toll Free Fax:* 800-621-8476 (orders only), pg 242

University of Missouri Press, Columbia, MO *Toll Free Tel:* 800-621-2736 (orders) *Toll Free Fax:* 800-621-8476 (orders), pg 242

University of Nebraska Press, Lincoln, NE *Toll Free Tel:* 800-848-6224 (cust serv & US orders) *Toll Free Fax:* 800-526-2617 (cust serv & US orders), pg 243

University of New Mexico Press, Albuquerque, NM *Toll Free Fax:* 800-622-8667 (orders only), pg 243

University of Oklahoma Press, Norman, OK *Toll Free Tel:* 800-627-7377 (orders) *Toll Free Fax:* 800-735-0476 (orders), pg 244

University of Puerto Rico Press, San Juan, PR *Toll Free Tel:* 877-338-7788, pg 244

University of South Carolina Press, Columbia, SC *Toll Free Tel:* 800-768-2500 (orders) *Toll Free Fax:* 800-868-0740 (orders), pg 245

University of Tennessee Press, Knoxville, TN *Toll Free Tel:* 800-621-2736 (orders) *Toll Free Fax:* 800-621-8476 (orders), pg 245

The University of Virginia Press, Charlottesville, VA *Toll Free Tel:* 800-831-3406 (orders) *Toll Free Fax:* 877-288-6400, pg 245

University of Washington Press, Seattle, WA *Toll Free Tel:* 800-537-5487 (orders), pg 246

University of Wisconsin Press, Madison, WI *Toll Free Tel:* 800-621-2736 (orders) *Toll Free Fax:* 800-621-2736 (orders), pg 246

University Press of America Inc, Lanham, MD *Toll Free Tel:* 800-462-6420 *Toll Free Fax:* 800-338-4550, pg 246

University Press of Colorado, Boulder, CO *Toll Free Tel:* 800-621-2736 (orders), pg 246

University Press of Florida, Gainesville, FL *Toll Free Tel:* 800-226-3822 (orders only) *Toll Free Fax:* 800-680-1955 (orders only), pg 246

University Press of Mississippi, Jackson, MS *Toll Free Tel:* 800-737-7788 (orders & cust serv), pg 247

University Press of New England, Lebanon, NH *Toll Free Tel:* 800-421-1561 (orders only), pg 247

W E Upjohn Institute for Employment Research, Kalamazoo, MI *Toll Free Tel:* 888-227-8569, pg 248

Upper Access Inc, Hinesburg, VT *Toll Free Tel:* 800-310-8320 (orders), pg 248

Upper Room Books, Nashville, TN *Toll Free Tel:* 800-972-0433, pg 248

Upstart Books™, Madison, WI *Toll Free Tel:* 800-448-4887 (orders) *Toll Free Fax:* 800-448-5828, pg 248

US Conference of Catholic Bishops, Washington, DC *Toll Free Tel:* 800-235-8722, pg 249

US Games Systems Inc, Stamford, CT *Toll Free Tel:* 800-54-GAMES (544-2637), pg 249

US Government Publishing Office (GPO), Washington, DC *Toll Free Tel:* 866-512-1800 (orders), pg 249

Utah Geological Survey, Salt Lake City, UT *Toll Free Tel:* 888-UTAH-MAP (882-4627 bookstore), pg 249

VanDam Inc, New York, NY *Toll Free Tel:* 800-UNFOLDS (863-6537), pg 249

Vandamere Press, St Petersburg, FL *Toll Free Tel:* 800-551-7776, pg 249

Vanderbilt University Press, Nashville, TN *Toll Free Tel:* 800-627-7377 (orders only) *Toll Free Fax:* 800-735-0476 (orders only), pg 249

Vault.com Inc, New York, NY *Toll Free Tel:* 800-535-2074, pg 250

Vedanta Press, Hollywood, CA *Toll Free Tel:* 800-816-2242 (catalog), pg 250

Victory in Grace Press, Lake Zurich, IL *Toll Free Tel:* 800-78-GRACE (784-7223), pg 250

Voyager Sopris Learning Inc, Dallas, TX *Toll Free Tel:* 800-547-6747 *Toll Free Fax:* 888-819-7767, pg 251

Walch Education, Portland, ME *Toll Free Tel:* 800-558-2846 *Toll Free Fax:* 888-991-5755, pg 251

Warner Press, Anderson, IN *Toll Free Tel:* 800-741-7721 (orders) *Toll Free Fax:* 800-347-6411, pg 252

Warren Communications News Inc, Washington, DC *Toll Free Tel:* 800-771-9202, pg 252

Washington State University Press, Pullman, WA *Toll Free Tel:* 800-354-7360 (orders), pg 252

Water Environment Federation, Alexandria, VA *Toll Free Tel:* 800-666-0206 (cust serv), pg 252

Water Resources Publications LLC, Highlands Ranch, CO *Toll Free Tel:* 800-736-2405 *Toll Free Fax:* 800-616-1971, pg 252

WaterBrook, Colorado Springs, CO *Toll Free Tel:* 800-603-7051 (orders) *Toll Free Fax:* 800-294-5686 (orders), pg 252

Watermark Publishing, Honolulu, HI *Toll Free Tel:* 866-900-BOOK (900-2665), pg 252

Wayne State University Press, Detroit, MI *Toll Free Tel:* 800-978-7323, pg 253

Wayside Publishing, Freeport, ME *Toll Free Tel:* 888-302-2519, pg 253

Weigl Educational Publishers Ltd, Calgary, AB Canada *Toll Free Tel:* 800-668-0766 *Toll Free Fax:* 866-449-3445, pg 475

Wesleyan Publishing House, Fishers, IN *Toll Free Tel:* 800-493-7539 *Toll Free Fax:* 800-788-3535, pg 253

West Academic Publishing, St Paul, MN *Toll Free Tel:* 877-888-1330, pg 254

Westminster John Knox Press (WJK), Louisville, KY *Toll Free Tel:* 800-523-1631 (US only) *Toll Free Fax:* 800-541-5113 (US & CN), pg 254

Whitecap Books, Vancouver, BC Canada *Toll Free Tel:* 800-387-9776 *Toll Free Fax:* 800-260-9777, pg 475

Whittier Publications Inc, Oceanside, NY *Toll Free Tel:* 800-897-TEXT (897-8398), pg 255

Whole Person Associates Inc, Duluth, MN *Toll Free Tel:* 800-247-6789, pg 255

Wide World of Maps Inc, Phoenix, AZ *Toll Free Tel:* 800-279-7654, pg 255

Michael Wiese Productions, Studio City, CA *Toll Free Tel:* 800-833-5738 (orders), pg 255

Wilderness Adventures Press Inc, Belgrade, MT *Toll Free Tel:* 866-400-2012, pg 255

Wildlife Education Ltd, Evanston, IL *Toll Free Tel:* 800-477-5034, pg 256

John Wiley & Sons Canada Ltd, Toronto, ON Canada *Toll Free Tel:* 800-225-5945 (orders only) *Toll Free Fax:* 800-565-6802 (orders), pg 476

John Wiley & Sons Inc, Hoboken, NJ *Toll Free Tel:* 800-225-5945 (cust serv), pg 256

John Wiley & Sons Inc Global Education, Hoboken, NJ *Toll Free Tel:* 800-225-5945 (cust serv), pg 256

John Wiley & Sons Inc Professional Development, Hoboken, NJ *Toll Free Tel:* 800-225-5945 (cust serv), pg 256

Wilfrid Laurier University Press, Waterloo, ON Canada *Toll Free Tel:* 866-836-5551 (CN & US), pg 476

William Carey Library Publishers, Pasadena, CA *Toll Free Tel:* 866-732-6657 (orders & cust serv), pg 256

Willow Creek Press, Minocqua, WI *Toll Free Tel:* 800-850-9453, pg 256

Wimmer Cookbooks, Memphis, TN *Toll Free Tel:* 800-548-2537, pg 257

Wind Canyon Books, Stockton, CA *Toll Free Tel:* 800-952-7007 *Toll Free Fax:* 888-289-7086, pg 257

Windsor Books, Bayshore, NY *Toll Free Tel:* 800-321-5934, pg 257

Windward Publishing, Apple Valley, MN *Toll Free Tel:* 800-846-7027 *Toll Free Fax:* 800-330-6232, pg 257

Winters Publishing, Greensburg, IN *Toll Free Tel:* 800-457-3230, pg 257

Winterthur Museum, Garden & Library, Winterthur, DE *Toll Free Tel:* 800-448-3883, pg 257

Wisconsin Department of Public Instruction, Madison, WI *Toll Free Tel:* 800-441-4563, pg 257

Wisdom Publications Inc, Somerville, MA *Toll Free Tel:* 800-272-4050 (orders), pg 257

Wittenborn Art Books, San Francisco, CA *Toll Free Tel:* 800-660-6403, pg 258

Alan Wofsy Fine Arts, San Francisco, CA *Toll Free Tel:* 800-660-6403, pg 258

Wood Lake Publishing Inc, Kelowna, BC Canada *Toll Free Tel:* 800-663-2775 (orders & cust serv) *Toll Free Fax:* 888-841-9991 (orders & cust serv), pg 476

Woodbine House, Bethesda, MD *Toll Free Tel:* 800-843-7323, pg 258

Woodland Publishing Inc, Salt Lake City, UT *Toll Free Tel:* 800-277-3243, pg 258

Workman Publishing Co Inc, New York, NY *Toll Free Tel:* 800-722-7202, pg 258

World Almanac®, New York, NY *Toll Free Tel:* 800-322-8755, pg 259

World Bank Publications, Washington, DC *Toll Free Tel:* 800-645-7247 (cust serv), pg 259

World Book Inc, Chicago, IL *Toll Free Tel:* 800-967-5325 (consumer sales, US); 800-463-8845 (consumer sales, CN); 800-975-3250 (school & lib sales, US); 800-837-5365 (school & lib sales, CN); 866-866-5200 (web sales) *Toll Free Fax:* 800-433-9330 (school & lib sales, US); 888-690-4002 (school lib sales, CN), pg 259

World Citizens, Mill Valley, CA *Toll Free Tel:* 800-247-6553 (orders only), pg 259

World Trade Press, Petaluma, CA *Toll Free Tel:* 800-833-8586, pg 260

WorldTariff, San Francisco, CA *Toll Free Tel:* 866-268-7602, pg 260

Worldwide Library, Don Mills, ON Canada *Toll Free Tel:* 888-432-4879, pg 476

Write Stuff Enterprises LLC, Fort Lauderdale, FL *Toll Free Tel:* 800-900-2665, pg 260

WriteLife LLC, Omaha, NE *Toll Free Tel:* 877-974-8354, pg 260

Writer's Digest, Blue Ash, OH *Toll Free Tel:* 800-289-0963, pg 260

Wyndham Hall Press, Lima, OH *Toll Free Tel:* 866-895-0977, pg 260

Xlibris Corp, Bloomington, IN *Toll Free Tel:* 888-795-4274, pg 261

Yale University Press, New Haven, CT *Toll Free Tel:* 800-405-1619 (cust serv) *Toll Free Fax:* 800-406-9145 (cust serv), pg 261

YMAA Publication Center Inc, Wolfeboro, NH *Toll Free Tel:* 800-669-8892, pg 262

YWAM Publishing, Seattle, WA *Toll Free Tel:* 800-922-2143, pg 262

Zagat Survey LLC, New York, NY *Toll Free Tel:* 800-540-9609, pg 262

Zaner-Bloser Inc, Columbus, OH *Toll Free Tel:* 800-421-3018 (cust serv) *Toll Free Fax:* 800-992-6087 (orders), pg 262

Zondervan, Grand Rapids, MI *Toll Free Tel:* 800-226-1122; 800-727-1309 (retail orders) *Toll Free Fax:* 800-698-3256 (retail orders), pg 263

Zone Books, Brooklyn, NY *Toll Free Tel:* 800-405-1619 (orders & cust serv), pg 263

Index to Sections

D

E

F

R

S

T

V

W

Index to Advertisers